ISSN 0360-2702

BIBLIOGRAPHIC GUIDE TO

BUSINESS AND ECONOMICS 1987

Volume 1

A—F

G.K. HALL & CO.
70 Lincoln Street, Boston, Massachusetts

Manufactured in the United States of America.
ISBN 0-8161-7086-X

PREFACE

G. K. Hall *Bibliographic Guides* are comprehensive annual subject bibliographies. They bring together publications cataloged by The Research Libraries of The New York Public Library and the Library of Congress for thorough subject coverage. Included are works in all languages and all forms—non-book materials as well as books and serials.

Bibliographic Guides provide complete LC cataloging information for each title, as well as ISBN and identification of NYPL holdings. Access is by main entry (personal author, corporate body, names of conference, etc.), added entries (co-authors, editors, compilers, etc.), titles, series titles, and subject headings. All entries are integrated into one alphabetical sequence. Full bibliographic information, including tracings, is given in the main entry, with abbreviated or condensed citations for secondary entries. Subject headings appear in capital letters in bold-face type. Cataloging follows the *Anglo-American Cataloging Rules*. Following is a sample entry with full bibliographic information:

> (a) **Rapoport, Anatol, 1911–** (b) N-person game theory; (c) concepts and applications. (d) Ann Arbor, (e) University of Michigan Press (f) (1970) (g) 331 p. (h) illus. 22cm. (i) (Ann Arbor science library) (j) Bibliography: p. 317-320. (k) ISBN 0-472-00117-5 (l) LC Card 79-83451 (m) DDC 512/.8 (n) 1. Games of strategy (Mathematics).
> (o) I. Title
> *(p) PA27O.R34 1970* (q) **NYPL (r) [JSD 72-370]**

(a) Author's name.
(b) Short, or main, title.
(c) Sub-title and/or other title page information.
(d) Place of publication.
(e) Publisher.
(f) Date of Publication.
(g) Pagination.
(h) Illustration statement.
(i) Series.
(j) Note(s).
(k) ISBN.
(l) LC Card number.
(m) DDC number.
(n) Subject heading.
(o) Added entry.
(p) LC Call number.
(q) NYPL indicator.
(r) NYPL Classmark.

G. K. Hall *Bibliographic Guides* offer easy, multiple access to a wealth of material in each subject area. They serve as authoritative reference sources for librarians and scholars, valuable technical aids for library acquisition and cataloging, and useful research tools for professionals.

Bibliographic Guides for 1987 are available in twenty fields:

- Anthropology
- Art and Architecture
- Black Studies
- Business and Economics
- Computer Science
- Conference Publications
- Dance
- Education
- Government Publications—Foreign
- Government Publications—U.S.
- Latin American Studies
- Law
- Maps and Atlases
- Microform Publications
- Music
- North American History
- Psychology
- Soviet and East European Studies
- Technology
- Theatre Arts

They include material cataloged between September 1, 1986 and August 31, 1987.

INTRODUCTION

The *Bibliographic Guide to Business and Economics* lists publications cataloged during the past year by the Library of Congress and The Research Libraries of The New York Public Library. Selection of titles from LC MARC tapes is based on the LC classification *HA* through *HJ*. Entries from NYPL are selected on the following basis: if an NYPL record contains two or more subject headings which correspond to two or more LC subject headings from MARC business and economics records, then that NYPL record is included in the *Guide*. LC subject headings from all business and economics records in the entire MARC data base are scanned to provide comprehensive selection of NYPL business and economics titles.

The following major subject areas in technology are included in this *Guide:*

Economic theory
Population
Demography
Economic history
Land, Agriculture
Industry
Labor
Transportation and communication
Commerce
Business administration
Finance
Foreign Exchange
Insurance
Revenue, Taxation
Public finance
Statistics

A. A. Co. see **Australian Agricultural Company.**

A. A. E. A. see **American Agricultural Economics Association.**

A. B. A. see **American Bankers Association; American Bar Association.**

A.B.C. de l'économie guadeloupéene / [initiative M.P.G.I.]. [Basse-Terre, Guadeloupe : s.n., 1986] 200 p., [27] leaves of plates : ill. ; 30 cm. "Ce document ... a été intégralement conçu à l'intérieur de la maison-d'arrêt de Basse-Terre"--Preface. LC Card 87-125723
1. Guadeloupe - Economic conditions. 2. Guadeloupe - Economic policy. I. M.P.G.I. (Guadeloupe). II. Title: ABC de l'économie guadeloupéenne.
HC158.5 .A52 1986

A.B.C.'s of air travel. Davidson, George, 1943- The ABC's of air travel /. Scottsdale, Ariz. , c1984. iv, 89 p. : ISBN 0-931921-00-7 (pbk.) : LC Card 84-71960 DDC 387.7/42/0973 19
HE9787.5.U5 D38 1984 ***NYPL [JLD 86-2219]***

A C R L. see **Association of College and Research Libraries.**

A. C. S. W. see **Canada. Advisory Council on the Status of Women.**

A. D. B. see **Asian Development Bank.**

A. D. C. see **CHILD WELFARE.**

A. D. F. see **African Development Fund.**

A droite en sortant de la gauche? /. Briançon, Pierre. Paris , c1986. 270 p. ; ISBN 2-246-34901-X : LC Card 86-159681
HC276.2 .B66 1986

AEI sudies. see **American Enterprise Institute for Public Policy Research. AEI studies.**

A. E. L. C. see **European Free Trade Association.**

A. E. L. E. see **European Free Trade Association.**

A. E., pseud. see **Russell, George William, 1867-1935.**

A. Hitler's "Tausend-Mark-Sperre" und die Folgen für Österreichs Fremdenverkehr (1933-1938) /. Otruba, Gustav. Linz , c1983. iii, 205 p. ; ISBN 3-85320-308-6 LC Card 84-213145
HG999 .O87 1983

A. I. C. P. A. For corporate body referred to by these initials see: **American Institute of Certified Public Accountants.**

A. I. D. see **International Development Association; United States. Agency for International Development.**

A. I. F. see **International Development Association.**

A.J. Cook /. Davies, Paul, 1951- Wolfeboro, NH , c1987. p. cm. ISBN 0-7190-2160-X LC Card 87-11114 DDC 331.88/122/0924 B 19
HD8393.C63 D38 1987

A. J. D. C. see **American Jewish Joint Distribution Committee.**

A. L. A. L. C. see **Asociación Latinoamericana de Libre Comercio.**

A. L. I. D. E. see **Asociación Latinoamericana de Instituciones Financieras de Desarrollo.**

A. L. P. A. see **Air Line Pilots Association.**

The A.L. Williams replacement empire . Belth, Joseph M. Ellettsville, IN , c1987. 64 p. : ISBN 0-941173-00-3 (pbk.) : LC Card 86-27715 DDC 368.3/2/00973 19
HG8963.A44 B44 1987

A la conquête du ciel /. Déplante, Henri, 1907- Aix-en-Provence [1985] 233 p. ; LC Card 86-159140
HD9711.F74 D374 1985

A. M. A. see **American Management Association.**

A. M. T. R. A. C. see **Amtrak.**

A metà decennio : riflessioni e dati sull'Italia dall'80 all'85. Milano, Italy : F. Angeli, c1986. 355 p. ; 24 cm. (CENSIS . 1) Includes index. LC Card 86-224676
1. Italy - Statistics. I. Series: CENSIS (Series) , 1.
HA1374 .A19 1986

A. N. A. see **Association of National Advertisers.**

A. P. A. see **American Psychological Association.**

A. P. O. see **Asia Productivity Organization; Asian Productivity Organization.**

A. P. R. I. A. For corporate body represented by these initials, see: **Association pour la promotion industrie-agriculture.**

A.P.S. who's who in Middle East banking & trade. The APS who's who in Middle East banking & trade. Nicosia, Cyprus , c1984. 2 v. : LC Card 83-149147 ***NYPL [JLF 86-983]***

A qui profite l'inflation? /. Susini, Jean-Jacques. Paris , c1985. 122 p. : ISBN 2-13-039288-1 LC Card 86-153761
HG979.5 .S87 1985

A. R. F. see **Advertising Research Foundation.**

A. S. A. see **American Statistical Association.**

A. S. C. E. see **American Society of Civil Engineers.**

A. S. M. E. see **American Society of Mechanical Engineers.**

A.S.M.E. Management Division history, 1886-1980. ASME Management Division history, 1886-1980 /. New York, N.Y. (345 E. 47th St., New York 10017) , c1984. x, 169 p. : LC Card 84-206982 DDC 658/.006/073 19
HD28.A6233 A86 1984 ***NYPL [JLF 86-1646]***

A. S. Q. C. see **American Society for Quality Control.**

A. S. T. D. see **American Society for Training and Development.**

A. T. P.: Sciences humaines. see **Actions thématiques programmées. A. T. P.: Sciences humaines.**

A.T. reader. The AT reader . London , 1985. xvii, 468 p. : ISBN 0-946688-10-9 ***NYPL [JLE 86-2305]***

The A to Z of Wall Street /. Hildreth, Sandra S. Chicago, Ill. , c1988. 299 p. : ISBN 0-88462-711-X (pbk.) : LC Card 87-22615 DDC 332.6/03/21 19
HG4513 .H56 1988

A-Z guide to money /. Kay, William. London , 1986, c1983. 281 p. : ISBN 0-09-467160-5 : LC Card 86-224824 DDC 332/.03/21 19
HG216 .K39 1986

A-Z of industrial relations practices at the workplace /. Phillip, George J. Kingston, Jamaica , 1987. xiii, 122 p. : ISBN 976-625-009-X (pbk.) LC Card 87-403438 DDC 331/.097292 19
HD6971 .P46 1987

The A-Z of UK marketing information sources /. Shaw, Christine. London , 1984. 233 p. ; ISBN 0-86338-048-4 (pbk.) : LC Card 84-217782 DDC 330.941/0858 19
HC256.6 .S47 1984 ***NYPL [JLD 86-2248]***

AAA Foundation for Traffic Safety.
Are you reading me? [motion picture] /. Falls Church, VA , 1985. 1 film reel (9 min.) : LC Card 85-702717 DDC 388.3 11
HE5614

Are you reading me? [videorecording] /. Falls Church, VA , 1985. 1 videocassette (9 min.) : LC Card 85-702718 DDC 388.3 11
HE5614

AAAS selected symposium .
(103) Technological prospects and population trends /. Boulder, Colo. , 1987. xxiii, 211 p. ; ISBN 0-8133-7470-7 : LC Card 87-50897 DDC 304.6 19
HB871 .T3 1987

AACHEN (GERMANY) - ECONOMIC CONDITIONS.
Erdmann, Claudia. Aachen im Jahre 1812 . Stuttgart , 1986. 257 p., [15] folded leaves of plates : ISBN 3-515-04634-8 LC Card 86-142584 DDC 330.943/55 19
HC289.A23 E73 1986

AACHEN (GERMANY) - INDUSTRIES - HISTORY.
Erdmann, Claudia. Aachen im Jahre 1812 . Stuttgart , 1986. 257 p., [15] folded leaves of plates : ISBN 3-515-04634-8 LC Card 86-142584 DDC 330.943/55 19
HC289.A23 E73 1986

AACHEN (GERMANY) - SOCIAL CONDITIONS.
Erdmann, Claudia. Aachen im Jahre 1812 . Stuttgart , 1986. 257 p., [15] folded leaves of plates : ISBN 3-515-04634-8 LC Card 86-142584 DDC 330.943/55 19
HC289.A23 E73 1986

Aachen im Jahre 1812 . Erdmann, Claudia. Stuttgart , 1986. 257 p., [15] folded leaves of plates : ISBN 3-515-04634-8 LC Card 86-142584 DDC 330.943/55 19
HC289.A23 E73 1986

Aachener Beiträge zur vergleichenden Soziologie und zur China-Forschung, 0178-1332 .
(Bd. 1) Wirtschaftsreformen und neue Entwicklungsstrategien in der Volksrepublik China /. Frankfurt am Main , New York , c1986. 185 p. ; ISBN 3-8204-9101-5 LC Card 86-220822
HC427.92 .W56 1986

Aachener China-Symposium (2nd : 1983)
Wirtschaftsreformen und neue Entwicklungsstrategien in der Volksrepublik China /. Frankfurt am Main , New York , c1986. 185 p. ; ISBN 3-8204-9101-5 LC Card 86-220822
HC427.92 .W56 1986

Aachener Studien Sozialwissenschaften .
(Bd. 3) Bangladesh im Schatten der Macht /. Aachen , c1986. vi, 328, 57 p. : ISBN 3-922868-31-2 LC Card 86-228249
HC440.8 .B358 1986

Aalberts, Monique M. J. Gezinsvorming door jonge migranten : verslag van de evaluatiestudie / M.M.J. Aalberts. 's-Gravenhage : Ministerie van Justitie : Staatsuitgeverij, 1985. 93 p. : ill. ; 25 cm. (WODC . 60) Bibliography: p. 59-60. ISBN 90-12-04999-7 LC Card 85-235621
1. Alien labor - Netherlands - Social conditions. 2. Family policy - Netherlands. 3. Netherlands - Emigration and immigration. I. Series: WODC (Series) , 60. II. Title.
HD8518.5.A2 A24 1985

Aarma, Kh. I. Voprosy razvitii͡a obsluzhivanii͡a naselenii͡a . Tallin , 1985. 140 p. : LC Card 85-158428
HD9986.S683 E888 1985

Aaron, Benjamin. Comparative labour law and industrial relations /. Deventer [Netherlands] , Boston , c1985. xiii, 527 p. ; ISBN 90-6544-236-7 (pbk.) LC Card 85-10000 DDC 344/.01 342.41 19
K1705.6 .C65 1985 ***NYPL [JLE 86-2420]***

Aaron, Henry J.
Economic choices 1987 /. Washington, D.C. , 1986. xii, 126 p. ; ISBN 0-8157-1040-2 LC Card 85-48278 ***NYPL [JLE 86-2737]***

Tax reform and the U. S. economy . Washington, D.C. , c1987. ix, 107 p. : ISBN 0-8157-6959-8 (pbk.) LC Card 87-70178 DDC 330.973/0927 19
HJ2381 .T387 1987

Aarrestad, Jostein. Oljen og norsk økonomi / Jostein Aarrestad. [Oslo] : NKS-forlaget, c1984. 118 p. : ill. ; 24 cm. ISBN 82-508-0285-3 LC Card 86-207964
1. Petroleum industry and trade - Norway. 2. Norway - Economic conditions - 1945-. I. Title.
HD9575.N62 A5 1984

AB 2477. California. Dept. of the California Highway Patrol. A special report to the Legislature on the 55 MPH national maximum speed limit. [Sacramento] [1986] vi, 95, [171] p. : LC Card 86-622347 DDC 388.3/144/09794 19
HE5620.S6 C25 1986

Abalkin, L. I. (Leonid Ivanovich) Kursom uskorenii͡a / L.I. Abalkin. Moskva : Izd-vo polit. lit-ry, 1986. 213 p. ; 17 cm. Includes bibliographical references. LC Card 87-123506 DDC 338.947/009/48 19
1. Soviet Union - Economic policy - 1981-. I. Title.
HC336.25 .A33 1986

ABANDONMENT (MARINE INSURANCE) see **INSURANCE, MARINE.**

ABATTOIRS. see **SLAUGHTERING AND SLAUGHTER-HOUSES.**

Abbadessa, Pietro. La Riforma della legge bancaria . Milano [1984] 283 p. ; ISBN 88-14-00126-X : LC Card 84-190853 DDC 346.45/082 344.50682 19
LAW ***NYPL [JLE 86-3654]***

Ābbāsa, Bi. Ema., 1911- The Ganges waters dispute / B.M. Abbas A.T. New Delhi : Vikas, c1982. xv, 157 p., 8 p. of plates : ill., 5 folded maps ; 23 cm. ISBN 0-7069-2080-5 : LC Card 83-900165 DDC 341.4/42 19
1. Ganges River (India and Bangladesh) - Water-rights. 2. India - Foreign relations - Bangladesh. 3. Bangladesh - Foreign relations - India. I. Title.
HD1698.G36 A23 1982

Abbau regionaler Strompreisdisparitäten. Wagner, Gerhard. Abbau regionaler Strompreisdisparitäten durch raumwirksame Massnahmen und Planungen /. Bonn , 1985. xv, 356 p. : ISBN 3-87994-415-6 LC Card 87-408008 DDC 338.4/336362/0943 19
HD9685.G3 W34 1985

Abbau regionaler Strompreisdisparitäten durch raumwirksame Massnahmen und Planungen /. Wagner, Gerhard. Bonn , 1985. xv, 356 p. : ISBN 3-87994-415-6 LC Card 87-408008 DDC 338.4/336362/0943 19
HD9685.G3 W34 1985

Abbott, John Cave, 1919- Agricultural marketing enterprises for the developing world : with case studies of indigenous private, transnational, cooperative, and parastatal enterprise / John C. Abbott. Cambridge [Cambridgeshire] ; New York : Cambridge University Press, 1987. xi, 217 p. : ill. ; 24 cm. Includes 26 case studies, some published previously, by 15 authors. Includes bibliographies and index. ISBN 0-521-32597-8 LC Card 86-24462 DDC 381/.41/091724 19
1. Farm produce - Developing countries - Marketing. 2. Farm produce - Developing countries - Marketing - Case studies. 3. Produce trade - Developing countries. 4. Produce trade - Developing countries - Case studies. I. Title.
HD9018.D44 A228 1987

Abbott, Langer & Associates.
The Accounting/financial report /. Crete, IL (548 First St., Crete 60417) , c1983. 2 v. ; LC Card 83-152793 DDC 331.2/81657/0973 19
HF5627 .A23 1983 ***NYPL [JLM 86-1500]***

Compensation and benefits in research & development /. Crete, IL , c1987. 692 p. ; ISBN 0-916506-34-7 (pbk.) LC Card 87-403067 DDC 331.2/816584/00973021 19
HD4965.5.U6 C656 1987

Compensation in the accounting/financial field /. Crete, IL , c1987. 489 p. ; ISBN 0-916506-36-3 (pbk.) LC Card 87-153325 DDC 331.12/81657/0973021 19
HF5627 .C57 1987

Abbott, Michael G.
Alternative estimates of union-nonunion and public-private wage differentials in Ontario, 1981 / Michael G. Abbott, Thanasis Stengos. Kingston, Ont., Canada : Institute for Economic Research, Queen's University, [1986] ii, 61 p. ; 28 cm. (Discussion paper, 0316-5078 . #670) "November 1986." "Presented at the 1986 European Meeting of the Econometric Society in Budapest, Hungary, September 1-5, 1986." Bibliography: p. 60-61. LC Card 87-146006 DDC 331.2/2/09713 19
1. Wages - Ontario. 2. Wages - Ontario - Econometric models. I. Stengos, Thanasis. II. Series: Discussion paper (Queen's University (Kingston, Ont.). Institute for Economic Research) , no. 670. III. Title.
HD4980.O5 A64 1986

Alternative estimates of union-nonunion and public-private wage differentials in Ontario, 1981 / Michael G. Abbott, Thanasis Stengos. Kingston, Ont., Canada : Industrial Relations Centre, Queen's University, 1987. ii, 47 p. ; 28 cm. (Queen's papers in industrial relations . 1987-4) "December 1986." "Shortened version of an earlier draft presented at the 1986 European Meeting of the Econometric Society in Budapest, Hungary, September 1-5, 1986." Bibliography: p. 46-47. ISBN 0-88886-166-4 (pbk.) LC Card 87-170767 DDC 331.2/2/09713 19
1. Wages - Ontario - Econometric models. 2. Ontario - Officials and employees - Salaries, etc. - Econometric models. 3. Trade-unions - Ontario - Econometric models. I. Stengos, Thanasis. II. Title. III. Series.
HD4980.O5 A64 1987

Male and female earnings in Canadian manufacturing, 1931 / Michael G. Abbott, M. Ruth Beck. Kingston, Ont., Canada : Institute for Economic Research, Queen's University, [1986] 82 p. ; 28 cm. (Discussion paper, 0316-5078 . #669) "November 1986." Bibliography: p. 58-60. LC Card 87-145991 DDC 331.2/87/0971 19
1. Wages - Canada - Manufactures - Econometric models. 2. Wages - Men, White - Canada - Econometric models. 3. Wages - Women - Canada - Econometric models. 4. Canada - Manufactures - Econometric models. I. Beck, M. Ruth. II. Series: Discussion paper (Queen's University (Kingston, Ont.). Institute for Economic Research) , no. 669. III. Title.
HD4979 .A22 1986

Abbrüche beruflicher Rehabilitationsmassnahmen . Tews, Hans Peter. Hamburg , 1986. 277 p. ; ISBN 3-925408-04-5 LC Card 87-127427 DDC 362/.0425 19
HD7256.G3 T48 1986

El ABC de la Bolsa. 2a ed. corr. y ampliada. Barcelona : Alba, [1983?] 93 p. : ill. ; 21 cm. On cover: Banca Mas Sardá, Servicio de Estudios. Includes bibliographical references. ISBN 84-383-0028-6 LC Card 86-139799
1. Investments. 2. Stock-exchange. 3. Money market. I. Banca Mas Sardá. Servicio de Estudios.
HG4521 .A213 1983

ABC de la economía política /. M. S. Madrid [1964] 205 p., [1] folded leaf of plates : LC Card 85-106062
HB178.5 .M25 1964

ABC de l'économie guadeloupéenne. A.B.C. de l'économie guadeloupéene /. [Basse-Terre, Guadeloupe , 1986] 200 p., [27] leaves of plates : LC Card 87-125723
HC158.5 .A52 1986

The ABC's of air travel /. Davidson, George, 1943- Scottsdale, Ariz. , c1984. iv, 89 p. : ISBN 0-931921-00-7 (pbk.) : LC Card 84-71960 DDC 387.7/42/0973 19
HE9787.5.U5 D38 1984
NYPL [JLD 86-2219]

The ABCs of international finance . Pool, John Charles. Lexington, Mass. , c1987. xii, 138 p. ; ISBN 0-669-15605-1 (alk. paper) LC Card 86-45933 DDC 332/.042 19
HG3851 .P66 1987

The ABC's of marketing a successful business . Easter, Walter Ray. [United States] , c1986. 118 p. : LC Card 86-91127 DDC 658.8 19
HF5415.122 .E27 1986

'Abd al-Laṭīf, Badawī, 1909- al-Niẓām al-mālī, fī al-Islām [ta'līf] Badawī 'Abd al-Laṭīf. [al-Qāhirah] al-Majlis al-A'lá lil-Shu'ūn al-Islāmīyah, 1962. 115 p. 26 cm. (Ta'rīf bi-al-Islām. al-kitāb 2) In Arabic. Bibliography: p. [101]-109. LC Card NE63-525
1. Finance--Islamic countries. 2. Economics - Religious aspects - Islam. I. Title.
HJ233 .A25 ***NYPL [*OGO 82-3888]***

'Abd Allāh, Ismā'īl Ṣabrī. Hall, Kenneth O. The Group of 77 . Nyon, Switzerland , 1979. 48 p. ; LC Card 86-202645
HF1413 .H27 1979

Abdallah, Anis. Djibouti, ville et pays en voie de développement . Djibouti [c1983] 2 v. : LC Card 87-131462
HC855.Z9 E443 1983

Abdel Ati, Hassan A. Lower River Atbara area (Nile Province) : final report / by Hassan A. Abdel Ati. [Khartoum] Sudan : Institute of Environmental Studies, University of Khartoum, [1985] vii, 166 p., [19] leaves of plates : ill., maps ; 30 cm. At head of title: Environmental Training & Management in Africa (ETMA), Environmental Management in the Sudan. "Prepared for the United States Agency for International Development, project no. 698-0427." "September 1985." Bibliography: p. 162-166. LC Card 86-981108 DDC 333.91/3/09625 19
1. Irrigation - Economic aspects - Atbara River Region (Ethiopia and Sudan). 2. Irrigation farming - Government policy - Sudan. 3. Atbara River Region (Ethiopia and Sudan) - Economic conditions. 4. Agricultural ecology - Atbara River Region (Ethiopia and Sudan). I. Jāmi'at al-Kharṭūm. Ma'had al-Dirāsāt al-Bī'īyah. II. Environmental Management in the Sudan (Program). III. United States. Agency for International Development. IV. Title.
HD1741.S852 A832 1985

Abdel Aziz Belal. see **Belal, Abdel Aziz.**

Abdel Haleem, M. A. English-Arabic business dictionary / M.A. Abdel Haleem and Ernest Kay. London : Graham & Trotman, 1984. xxxii, 263 p. ; 15 x 23 cm. ISBN 0-86010-448-6 : LC Card 83-228731 DDC 650/.03/21 19
1. Commerce - Dictionaries. 2. Business - Dictionaries. 3. English language - Dictionaries - Arabic. I. Kay, Ernest. II. Title.
HF1002 .A23 1984 ***NYPL [JLD 86-2048]***

Abdel-Malek, Anouar, 1924- Clés pour une stratégie nouvelle du développement /. Paris , c1984. 226 p. : ISBN 2-7082-2365-7 : LC Card 85-116966 DDC 338.9/009172/4 19
HC59.7 .C584 1984

Abdel-Rahman, Awad Ibrahim. Population, environment, and agricultural change : the example of the Rahad Scheme / by Awad Ibrahim Abdel-Rahman. [Khartoum] : Development Studies and Research Centre, Faculty of Economic & Social Studies, University of Khartoum, [1984] iii, 37 leaves : ill. ; 30 cm. (DSRC seminar . no. 42) "January 1984." Bibliography: leaves 36-37. LC Card 84-980808 DDC 338.1/8624 19
1. Rahad Agricultural Project. 2. Agricultural development projects - Sudan - Case studies. I. Title. II. Series.
HD2123.5 .A64 1984

Abdelkader, Benamara. OPEC aid and the challenge of development /. London , New York , c1987. x, 130 p. ; ISBN 0-7099-1969-7 LC Card 87-9160 DDC 338.91/09172/4 19
HC60 .O5754 1987

Abdil'din, S. A. (Serikbolsyn Abdil'daevich) Razvitie prodovol'stvennogo kompleksa Kazakhstana / S.A. Abdil'din. Alma-Ata : Izd-vo "Nauka" Kazakhskoĭ SSR, 1985. 158 p. ; 21 cm. At head of title: Akademii͡a nauk Kazakhskoĭ SSR. Institut ėkonomiki. Includes bibliographical references. LC Card 85-226938
1. Food industry and trade - Kazakh S.S.R. 2. Agricultural industries - Kazakh S.S.R. I. Title.
HD9015.S653 K393 1985

Abdrabboh, Bob A. Investment in Indonesia : diversity and dynamism / Bob A. Abdrabboh.1st ed. Dearborn, Mich., U. S.A. : International Economics & Research, c1987. ix, 124 p. : ill. ; 24 cm. Bibliography: p. [123]-124. ISBN 0-915597-19-7 LC Card 86-82681 DDC 332.6/7322598 19
1. Investments, Foreign - Indonesia. 2. Indonesia - Economic conditions - 1945-. I. Title.
HG5752 .A534 1987

Abdul Aziz, 1937- see **Aziz, Abdul, 1937-**

Abdul Ghafoor. see **Ghafoor, Abdul.**

Abdul Hameed Shoman Foundation. Agricultural policy in Jordan /. London ; Atlantic Highlands, NJ : 147 p. : ISBN 0-86372-070-6 LC Card 86-21480 DDC 338.1/85695 19
HD2059.Z8 A34 1986

Abdul Quddus, Syed. see **Quddus, Syed Abdul.**

Abdulah, Norma. The availability and utilization of skills in Guyana / by Norma Abdulah. St. Augustine, Trinidad : Institute of Social and Economic Research, University of the West Indies, [1981] xv, 105 p. ; 24 cm. (Occasional papers. Human resources . 4) "October, 1981." Bibliography: p. [90]-93. LC Card 84-146702 DDC 331.11/422 19
1. Labor supply - Guyana - Effect of education on. 2. Vocational education - Guyana. 3. Occupational training - Guyana. I. Series: Occasional papers (University of the West Indies (Saint Augustine, Trinidad and Tobago). Institute of Social and Economic Research). Human resources , 4. II. Title.
HD5759.3.A6 A24 1981
NYPL [JLE 86-4442]

Abdullaev, A. Kh. Zadacha razmeshchenii͡a sel'skokhozi͡aĭstvennogo proizvodstva v ob"edinenii khozi͡aĭstv meliorativnoĭ sistemy / A.Kh. Abdullaev, V.G. Kiselev. Moskva : Akademii͡a nauk SSSR, Vychislitel'nyĭ t͡sentr, 1985. 24, [2] p. ; 22 cm. (Soobshchenii͡a po prikladnoĭ matematike) Bibliography: p. [25] LC Card 86-162160
1. Agricultural industries - Soviet Union - Location - Mathematical models. I. Kiselev, V. G. II. Title. III. Series.
HD9015.S652 A23 1985

Abdullah, Fuad A. (Fuad Abdul-Kader), 1930- Financial management for the multinational firm / Fuad A. Abdullah. Englewood Cliffs, N.J. : Prentice-Hall, c1987. xiii, 594 p. : ill. ; 25 cm. Includes bibliographies and indexes. ISBN 0-13-316340-7 LC Card 86-25226 DDC

658.1/599 19
1. International business enterprises - Finance. 2. International business enterprises - Finance - Case studies. I. Title.
HG4027.5 .A23 1987

Abdurakhmanov, I. (Ibraim) Ėffektivnost′ kapital′nykh vlozheniĭ v promyshlennosti Kirgizii / I. Abdurakhmanov. Frunze : Izd-vo "Ilim", 1981. 174 p. ; 20 cm. At head of title: Akademiia nauk Kirgizskoĭ SSR. Institut ėkonomiki. Bibliography: p. 166-[173] LC Card 82-160618
1. Capital productivity - Kirghiz S.S.R. 2. Kirghiz S.S.R. - Industries. I. Title.
HC337.K5453 C32 1981

Abel, Charles. Dependency theory and the return of high politics /. Westport, Conn. , 1986. xii, 270 p. : ISBN 0-313-24860-5 (lib. bdg. : alk. paper) LC Card 85-17745 DDC 337 19
HF1411 .D35 1986 ***NYPL [JLE 86-2911]***

Ábel, István. A vállalatok pénzügyi szabályozása : tanfolyami jegyzet / Ábel István. Budapest : Országos Vezetőképző Központ, 1984. 32, [1] p. ; 30 cm. (Vállalatgazdaságtani ismeretek vezetők számára) Bibliography: p. [33] LC Card 85-175023
1. Business enterprises - Hungary - Finance. 2. Finance - Law and legislation - Hungary. I. Title. II. Series.
HG4149.5 .A54 1984

Abel, Wilhelm, 1904-
Theorie und Empirie in Wirtschaftspolitik und Wirtschaftsgeschichte . Göttingen , 1984. 245 p. : LC Card 85-111313
HC284 .T46 1984

Theorie und Empirie in Wirtschaftspolitik und Wirtschaftsgeschichte . Göttingen , 1984. 242 p. : ISBN 3-509-01366-2 : LC Card 85-120064
HC240 .T45 1984

ABEL, WILHELM, 1904-
Theorie und Empirie in Wirtschaftspolitik und Wirtschaftsgeschichte . Göttingen , 1984. 245 p. : LC Card 85-111313
HC284 .T46 1984

Theorie und Empirie in Wirtschaftspolitik und Wirtschaftsgeschichte . Göttingen , 1984. 242 p. : ISBN 3-509-01366-2 : LC Card 85-120064
HC240 .T45 1984

Abeles, Tom P. Morris, David J. Substituting agricultural materials for petroleum based industrial products /. Washington, D.C. , c1986. i, 33 p. ; ISBN 0-917582-46-2 (pbk.) : LC Card 86-21350 DDC 338.4/76628 19
HD9502.5.B543 U654 1986

Abel/Noser Corp. Earnings surprise report, February 1987. New York, N.Y. (90 Broad St., New York 10004) , c1987. 167 p. ; LC Card 87-401689 DDC 332.63/222/0973 19
HG4915 .E275 1987

Abelow, Daniel. Communications in the modern corporate environment / Daniel Abelow, Edwin J. Hilpert. Englewood Cliffs, NJ : Prentice-Hall, c1986. xviii, 236 p. : ill. ; 24 cm. Includes index. ISBN 0-13-153842-X LC Card 85-16942 DDC 658/.0546 19
1. Business - Data processing. 2. Management - Communication systems. I. Hilpert, Edwin J. II. Title.
HF5548.2 .A24 1986 ***NYPL [JLE 86-1992]***

Abelshauser, Werner.
Die Weimarer Republik als Wohlfahrtsstaat . Stuttgart , 1987. 337 p. ; ISBN 3-515-04738-7 LC Card 87-131861 DDC 338.943 19
HC286.3 .W3546 1987

Wirtschaftsgeschichte der Bundesrepublik Deutschland (1945-1980) / Werner Abelshauser. 1. Aufl. Frankfurt am Main : Suhrkamp, 1983. 186 p. : ill. ; 18 cm. (Neue historische Bibliothek) Edition Suhrkamp ; 1241 = n.F., Bd. 241 Bibliography: p. 179-[187] ISBN 3-518-11241-4 : LC Card 83-180531
1. Germany, West - Economic conditions - 1974-. 2. Germany, West - Economic conditions. 3. Reconstruction (1939-1951) - Germany (West). I. Title. II. Series.
HC286.7 .A26 1983

Abelson, P. W. The economic evaluation of roads in Australia / Peter Abelson. Mosman, N.S.W. : Australian Professional Publications, 1986. xi, 144 p. : ill. ; 25 cm. Bibliography: p. 136-144. ISBN 0-949416-06-1 (pbk.) : LC Card 87-142110 DDC 388.1/0994 19
1. Roads - Economic aspects - Australia. I. Title.
HE368.Z55 E33 1986

Aben, Jacques. L'Effort économique de défense . [Grenoble] , 1985. 235 p. : LC Card 86-199399
HC280.D4 E38 1985

Abendroth, Wolfgang. 40 Jahre danach . Frankfurt/Main , 1985. 96 p. ; ISBN 3-88367-060-X : LC Card 86-109007 DDC 322/.2/0943 19
HD6490.F582 G316 1985

Abercrombie, Nicholas.
Class, structure, and knowledge : problems in the sociology of knowledge / Nicholas Abercrombie. London : B. Blackwell, 1980. 196 p. ; 23 cm. Includes bibliographical references and index. ISBN 0-8147-0571-5 :
1. Sociology - Philosophy. 2. Ideology. 3. Marxian school of sociology. I. Title.
NYPL [JLD 80-2963]

Sovereign individuals of capitalism / Nicholas Abercrombie, Stephen Hill, Bryan S. Turner. London ; Boston : Allen & Unwin, 1986. 211 p. ; 23 cm. Includes index. Bibliography: p. 192-203. ISBN 0-04-301230-2 (alk. paper) LC Card 86-1122 DDC 330.12/2 19
1. Capitalism. 2. Individualism. I. Hill, Stephen. II. Turner, Bryan S. III. Title.
HB501 .A23 1986 ***NYPL [JLD 86-3686]***

Aberdeen studies in defence economics .
(no. 26) Greenwood, David. The SDI and Europe /. Aberdeen, Scotland [1985] 64 p. ; LC Card 86-150232 DDC 355/.07/094 19
U395.E85 G73 1985 ***NYPL [JFG 87-57]***

Åberg, Yngve.
The impact of working hours and other factors on production and employment / Yngve Åberg. Aldershot, Hants, England ; Brookfield, Vt., U.S.A. : Avebury, c1987. viii, 166 p. : ill. ; 23 cm. Bibliography: p. 164-166. ISBN 0-566-05480-9 : LC Card 87-8393 DDC 331.25/7/09485 19
1. Hours of labor - Sweden - Econometric models. 2. Labor supply - Sweden - Econometric models. 3. Unemployment - Sweden - Econometric models. I. Title.
HD5202 .A64 1987

Utvecklingen av produktion och produktivitet i svensk ekonomi, 1963-1981 / av Yngve Åberg. [Stockholm] : LiberFörlag, [1983] 83 p. : ill. ; 21 cm. "Ds A 1983:17." Bibliography: p. 83. ISBN 91-38-08070-2 LC Card 84-218343
1. Industrial productivity - Sweden - Econometric models. 2. Sweden - Economic conditions - 1945- - Econometric models. I. Title.
HC380.I52 A34 1983

Abertura do capital de empresas no Brasil . Casagrande Neto, Humberto. São Paulo , 1985. 143 p. ; ISBN 85-22-40100-4
NYPL [JLD 86-1080]

Abeysekera, Charles. Capital and peasant production . Colombo, Sri Lanka , 1985. xiv, 230 p. ; LC Card 86-900809 DDC 338.1/3/095493 19
HD2065.8 .C36 1985 ***NYPL [JLE 87-1667]***

Abeysekera, H. Karunaratne, S. W. Potential for foreign investment in rubber products manufacture with information on special projects and a selection of local collaborators /. [Colombo] , 1985. vii, 100 p. ; LC Card 86-902791 DDC 332.6/73/095493 19
HD9161.S752 K37 1985

Abgrenzung von Fördergebieten /. Klemmer, Paul. Bochum , 1983. 206 p. : ISBN 3-88339-298-7 LC Card 83-183564
HC286.7 .K59 1983

Abhandlungen aus dem Industrieseminar der Universität Mannheim .
(Heft 32) Internationale und nationale Problemfelder der Betriebswirtschaftslehre /. Berlin , c1984. 336 p., [1] leaf of plates : ISBN 3-428-05696-5 LC Card 85-141327
HD35 .I598 1984

Abhandlungen der Akademie der Wissenschaften der DDR .
(Jahrg. 1983, Nr. W 3) Ökonomische Strategie der 80er Jahre und Effektivität des Wirtschaftsrechts /. Berlin , 1984. 48 p. ; LC Card 84-159925
HC290.78 .O36 1984

(Jahrg. 1986, Nr. W 1) Sozialistischer Wettbewerb und umfassende Intensivierung . Berlin , 1986. 103 p. ; LC Card 86-200416
HC290.795.S6 S69 1986

Abhandlungen des Geographischen Instituts, Anthropogeographie .
(Bd. 30) Grupp, Monika. Entwicklung und sozio-ökonomische Bedeutung der holzverarbeitenden Industrien im Südosten der Vereinigten Staaten von Amerika /. Berlin , 1981, c1982. xii, 187, [30] p., [5] folded leaves of plates : ISBN 3-496-00301-4 LC Card 86-217598
HD9757.A13 G78 1982

(Bd. 32) Asche, H. (Hartmut) Mobile Lebensformgruppen Südost-Arabiens im Wandel . Berlin , 1981, c1982. xii, 344 p. : ISBN 3-496-00302-2 LC Card 86-217612
HD8039.F652 O522 1982

Abhandlungen des Wirtschaftswissenschaftlichen Seminars zu Jena ..
(21. Bd., 2 Hft) Schalldach, Elisabeth, 1904- Rationalisierungsmassnahmen der Nachinflationszeit im Urteil der deutschen freien Gewerkschaften. Jena, 1930. ix, [1], 186 p. LC Card AC34-383
HD70.G2 S26 1930

Abhandlungen zu den wirtschaftlichen Staatswissenschaften. For other vols. in this series, see Old Catalog.
(Bd. 27) Tiebel, Christoph. Überwälzte Kosten der Gesetze . Göttingen , c1986. xv, 256 p. : ISBN 3-525-11333-1 (Deut. Bibl.) LC Card 87-135628 DDC 336.2/4 19
HJ2309 .T48 1986

Abhandlungen zum Handels-, Gesellschafts- und Wirtschaftsrecht .
(Bd. 1) Werner, Horst S. Der aktienrechtliche Abhängigkeitstatbestand . Göttingen , 1979. xxxix, 214 p. ; ISBN 3-88415-560-1 : LC Card 80-452340 DDC 346.43/066
LAW ***NYPL [JLD 86-1592]***

(Bd. 1]) Werner, Horst S. Der aktienrechtliche Abhängigkeitstatbestand . Göttingen , 1979. xxxix, 214 p. ; ISBN 3-88415-560-1 : LC Card 80-452340 DDC 346.43/066
LAW ***NYPL [JLD 86-1592]***

(Bd. 11) Kroneberg, Jürgen. Die mitbestimmte selbständige Aktiengesellschaft /. Göttingen , 1982. xii, 211 p. ; ISBN 3-88415-554-7 : LC Card 83-159183 DDC 346.43/0664 344.306664 19
KK3000 .K76 1982 ***NYPL [JLD 86-1552]***

(Bd. 3) Stauf, Wolfgang. Der wichtige Grund bei der personengesellschaftlichen Auflösungs- und Ausschliessungsklage . Göttingen , 1980. xiv, 80 p. ; ISBN 3-88415-549-0 : LC Card 80-150978 DDC 346.73/07 347.3067 19
KK2435.7 .S7 1980 ***NYPL [JLD 86-1591]***

Abhandlungen zum Handels-, Gesellschafts-, Wirtschafts- und Arbeitsrecht .
(Bd. 11) Kroneberg, Jürgen. Die mitbestimmte selbständige Aktiengesellschaft /. Göttingen , 1982. xii, 211 p. ; ISBN 3-88415-554-7 : LC Card 83-159183 DDC 346.43/0664 344.306664 19
KK3000 .K76 1982 ***NYPL [JLD 86-1552]***

Abhandlungen zur Handels- und Sozialgeschichte, 0065-0358 .
(Bd. 24) Stark, Walter. Untersuchungen zum Profit beim hansischen Handelskapital in der ersten Hälfte des 15. Jahrhunderts /. Weimar , 1985. 147 p. ; LC Card 86-148303
HF458 .S73 1985

ABILITY, EXECUTIVE. see **EXECUTIVE ABILITY.**

Abitazione e periferie urbane nei paesi in via di sviluppo : area mediterranea e America Latina in una prospettiva comparata / di M.R. Amaral de Sampaio ... [et al.] ; a cura di Alberto Clementi e Ligia Ramírez. Milano, Italy : F. Angeli, c1985. 450 p. : ill. ; 22 cm. (Collana di studi e ricerche. 7) Includes bibliographical references. LC Card 86-132019
1. Urban poor - Housing - Latin America - Congresses. 2. Urban poor - Housing - Mediterranean Region - Congresses. 3. Squatter settlements - Latin America - Congresses. 4. Squatter settlements - Mediterranean Region - Congresses. 5. Land use, Urban - Latin America - Congresses. 6. Land use, Urban - Mediterranean Region - Congresses. I. Sampaio, Maria Ruth. II. Clementi, Alberto. III. Ramírez, Ligia. IV. Series: Collana di studi e ricerche (Italy. Ministero degli

affari esteri. Dipartimento per la cooperazione allo sviluppo) , 7.
HD7287.96.L29 A25 1985
NYPL [JLD 87-1173]

Abiturienten und Hochschulabsolventen beim Übergang vom Studium in den Beruf : Ergebnisse einer gemeinsamen Erhebung von IAB/BMBW / Manfred Kaiser, Manfred Otto (Herausgeber). Nürnberg : Institut für Arbeitsmarkt- und Berufsforschung der Bundesanstalt für Arbeit, 1983. 407 p. : ill. ; 30 cm. (Beiträge zur Arbeitsmarkt- und Berufsforschung, 0173-6574 . 25) Includes bibliographies. CONTENTS. - Hochschulabsolventen zwischen Flexibilität und Identität / Manfred Kaiser -- Biologen an der Berufsschwelle / Manfred Kaiser, Manfred Dietze -- Diplom Biologen "Fünf Jahre danach" / Manfred Kaiser -- Der Jurist als Allzweckwaffe? / Manfred Kaiser, Manfred Otto, Walter Piepenbring -- Sozialwissenschaftler, Ausbildungs- und Beschäftigungslage von Sozialwissenschaftlern mit einem deutsch-schweizerischen Vergleich / Manfred Kaiser -- Berufssituation von Hochschulabsolventen eines Lehramts / Manfred Kaiser, Manfred Otto -- Berufliche Situation von Jungakademikern / Manfred Kaiser -- Abiturienten des Jahrgangs 1970 in Studium und Beruf / Manfred Kaiser ... [et al.] -- Zur Entwicklung der Selbständigen unter den Hochschulabsolventen / Manfred Kaiser, Friedemann Stooss -- Abiturienten des Jahrgangs 1970 im Spannungsfeld zwischen Studienwunsch und Studienwirklichkeit / Manfred Kaiser -- Abiturienten des Jahrgangs 1970/71 beim Übergang vom Studium in den Beruf / Manfred Otto -- Fragebogen für die Erhebung der Abiturienten des Jahrgangs 1970/71. LC Card 84-140881
1. College graduates - Employment - Germany, West. 2. High school graduates - Employment - Germany (West). I. Kaiser, Manfred. II. Otto, Manfred. III. Institut für Arbeitsmarkt- und Berufsforschung. IV. Germany (West). Bundesministerium für Bildung und Wissenschaft. V. Series.
HD6278.G4 A25 1983

Abkin, M. H. Models for investment and disinvestment decision making under uncertainty [microform] /. East Lansing , 1982. 173 p. : ***NYPL [*XME-11,286]***

Abkowitz, Mark David. National Conference on Microcomputers in Urban Transportation (1985 : San Diego, Calif.) Microcomputer applications within the urban transportation environment . New York, N.Y. , c1985. 824 p. : ISBN 0-87262-508-7 (pbk.) LC Card 85-73250 DDC 388.4/028/5416 19
HE305 .N33 1985 ***NYPL [JSD 86-535]***

Abney, Glenn. The politics of state and city administration / Glenn Abney and Thomas P. Lauth. Albany, N.Y. : State University of New York Press, c1986. xvi, 260 p. ; 24 cm. (SUNY series in public administration in the 1980's) Includes index. Bibliography: p. 227-251. ISBN 0-88706-255-5 LC Card 85-14873 DDC 353.9 19
1. State governments. 2. Municipal government - United States. 3. Politics, Practical - United States. I. Lauth, Thomas P. II. Title.
JK2408 .A26 1986 ***NYPL [JLE 86-3711]***

Aboagye, A. A. Informal sector employment in Kenya : a survey of informal sector activities in Nairobi, Kisumu, and Mombasa / A.A. Aboagye. Addis Ababa : Jobs and Skills Programme for Africa ; Geneva, Switzerland : International Labour Organisation, 1986. vii, 117, [64] p. ; 30 cm. At head of title: International Labour Organisation. ISBN 92-2-105557-4 LC Card 87-980151 DDC 331.12/51381 19
1. Informal sector (Economics) - Kenya - Nairobi. 2. Informal sector (Economics) - Kenya - Kisumu. 3. Informal sector (Economics) - Kenya - Mombasa. I. International Labour Organisation. II. Title.
HD2346.K42 N353 1986

Aboriginal employment and training programs : report of the Committee of Review, August 1985. Canberra : Australian Govt. Pub. Service, 1985. ix, 453 p. ; 25 cm. Cover title: Report of the Committee of Review of Aboriginal Employment and Training Programs. ISBN 0-644-00712-5 (pbk.) LC Card 87-107756 DDC 331.25/92/089011094 19
1. Manpower policy - Australia. 2. Australia - Native races. I. Australia. Committee of Review of Aboriginal Employment and Training Programs. II. Title: Report of the Committee of Review of Aboriginal Employment and Training Programs.
HD5850.A6 A26 1985

ABORIGINES. see **ETHNOLOGY.**

ABORTION - HUNGARY - STATISTICS.
Pongrácz, Tiborné. A terhességmegszakításon átesett 18 éven aluli hajadonok társadalmi-demográfiai jellemzői /. Budapest , c1986. 115 p. ; LC Card 87-409645
HA1201 .A64 no. 62 HQ767.5.H8

ABORTION - POLITICAL ASPECTS - UNITED STATES.
Falik, Marilyn. Ideology and abortion policy politics /. New York, N.Y. , 1983. 228 p. ; ISBN 0-03-062813-X LC Card 83-2402 DDC 363.4/6 19
HQ767.5.U5 F34 1983 ***NYPL [JLE 85-1581]***

Abplanalp, Franz. Dieterle, Robert. Kostenrechnung . Bern , c1983. 258 p. : ISBN 3-258-03210-6 : LC Card 83-185404
HF5686.C8 D53 1983

Abraham, A. S. (Abraham Saktimangalam), 1944- Education and employment in agriculture, India : a case study / A.S. Abraham.1st ed. New Delhi : Intellectual Pub. House : Sole distributors, Intellectual Book Corner, 1985. vii, 111 p. ; 23 cm. Includes index. Bibliography: p. [106]-109. LC Card 85-904717 DDC 331.12/93/0954 19
1. Agricultural laborers - India - Case studies. 2. Farmers - Education - India - Case studies. 3. Agricultural laborers - Case studies. 4. Farmers - Education - Case studies. I. Title.
HD1537.I4 A587 1985
NYPL [JLD 86-2251]

Abraham a Santa Clara, 1644-1709. Handwerk um 1700 . Hürtgenwald , c1985. 245 p. : ISBN 3-87646-052-2 : LC Card 85-211788
HD2346.N4 H35 1985

ABRAHAM A SANTA CLARA, 1644-1709 - VIEWS ON ARTISANS.
Handwerk um 1700 . Hürtgenwald , c1985. 245 p. : ISBN 3-87646-052-2 : LC Card 85-211788
HD2346.N4 H35 1985

Abraham, David, 1946- The collapse of the Weimar Republic : political economy and crisis / David Abraham.2nd ed. New York : Holmes & Meier, 1986. liii, 352 p. ; 25 cm. Bibliography: p. 319-339. Includes index. ISBN 0-8419-1083-9 LC Card 86-27033 DDC 338.0943 19
1. Industry and state - Germany - History. 2. Agriculture and state - Germany - History. 3. Pressure groups - Germany - History. 4. Social conflict - Germany - History. 5. Germany - Politics and government - 1918-1933. I. Title.
HD3616.G35 A27 1986

Abraham, Kenneth S., 1946- Distributing risk : insurance, legal theory, and public policy / Kenneth S. Abraham. New Haven : Yale University Press, c1986. x, 254 p. ; 25 cm. Includes index. Bibliography: p. 221-247. ISBN 0-300-03460-1 (alk. paper) LC Card 85-22459 DDC 346.73/086 347.30686 19
1. Insurance law - United States. 2. Risk (Insurance) - United States. I. Title.
KF1164 .A72 1986 ***NYPL [JLE 86-4347]***

Abraham, S. (Sarah) Student research abstracts in population studies /. Bombay , 1986, c1985. xi, 434 p. ; LC Card 86-902278 DDC 304.6/095 19
HA4553 .S78 1986

Abramovici, G. Comptes économiques de la Réunion, série 1975-1980 : système élargi de comptabilité nationale / Gérard Abramovici, Laurent Vernière. Ste Clotilde, [Réunion] : INSEE, Service départemental de la Réunion, [1983?] 133 p. ; 30 cm. (Dossiers de l'économie réunionnaise . no 2) Chiefly tables. "Ce volume présente les comptes définitifs des années 1978 et 1979 et semi-définitif pour l'année 1980." LC Card 86-980541
1. Réunion - Economic conditions. 2. Réunion - Statistics. 3. National income - Réunion - Statistics. I. Vernière, Laurent. II. Title. III. Series.
HC598 .A37 1983

Abramowitz, Avie, 1933- Walk fast, talk fast, and see ten people everyday / by Avie Abramowitz. 1st ed. Charleston [S.C.] : Professional Research Pub. Co., c1987. p. cm. ISBN 0-931807-13-1 : LC Card 87-6978 DDC 658.8/5 19
1. Selling. I. Title.
HF5438.25 .A27 1987

Abrams, Bill. Alsop, Ronald. The Wall Street journal on marketing /. New York , 1987, c1986. p. cm. LC Card 87-11248 DDC 658.8 19
HF5415 .A45 1987

Abramson, Alan J. The nonprofit sector and the new federal budget / Alan J. Abramson, Lester M. Salamon. Washington, D.C. : Urban Institute Press, c1986. xviii, 138 p. : ill. ; 28 cm. At head of title: The Nonprofit Sector Project. Includes bibliographical references. ISBN 0-87766-401-3 (pbk.) : LC Card 87-154012 DDC 361.7/63/0973 19
1. United States - Appropriations and expenditures. 2. Corporations, Nonprofit - United States - Finance. I. Salamon, Lester M. II. Nonprofit Sector Project (Urban Institute). III. Title.
HJ2052 .A54 1986

Abramson, Mark A., 1947- Performance and credibility . Lexington, Mass. , c1986. x, 307 p. : ISBN 0-669-11037-X (alk. paper) LC Card 85-50707 DDC 658/.048 19
HD62.6 .P47 1986 ***NYPL [JLE 86-1159]***

Abramson, Pamela. Goldman, Peter Louis, 1933- The end of the world that was . New York , c1986. xiv, 129 p., [8] p. of plates : ISBN 0-525-24428-X LC Card 85-31223 DDC 920/.073 19
CT220 .G6 1986 ***NYPL [JFD 86-6015]***

Abreu, Alice R. de Paiva. O avesso da moda : trabalho a domicílio na indústria de confecção / Alice Rangel de Paiva Abreu. São Paulo : Editora Hucitec, 1986. 302 p. ; 21 cm. (Problemas contemporâneos. Série Memória feminina) Originally presented as the author's thesis (doctoral)--Universidade de São Paulo, 1980. Bibliography: p. 293-302. LC Card 87-129109 DDC 331.4/887/098153 19
1. Women clothing workers - Brazil - Rio de Janeiro. 2. Home labor - Brazil - Rio de Janeiro. 3. Home labor - History. 4. Piece-work - Brazil - Rio de Janeiro. 5. Informal sector (Economics) - Brazil - Rio de Janeiro. I. Series: Problemas contemporâneos (Editora Hucitec). II. Title.
HD6073.C62 B62 1986

Abreu, Antonio. Dependencia y brechas entre ricos y pobres / Antonio Abreu. Bogotá : Departamento de Pastoral Social, 1987. 112 p. ; 21 cm. (Documentos CELAM . no. 86) At head of title: Consejo Episcopal Latinoamericano, CELAM. Bibliography: p. 105-112. ISBN 958-625-058-X LC Card 87-403548 DDC 337.8 19
1. Latin America - Economic conditions. 2. Latin America - Dependency on foreign countries. I. Series: Documentos CELAM (Spanish ed.) , 86. II. Title.
HC125 .A23 1987

Abril-Ojeda, Galo. Política monetaria y desarrollo industrial en el Ecuador, 1970-1983 / Galo Abril Ojeda. Quito : Banco Central del Ecuador, 1985. 118 p. : ill. ; 26 cm. (Monografía / Instituto de Estudios Latinoamericanos, Estocolmo . no. 11) Bibliography: p. 115-118. ISBN 91-85894-10-9 LC Card 86-103812
1. Monetary policy - Ecuador. 2. Ecuador - Industries. 3. Industrial promotion - Ecuador. I. Title.
HG865 .A27 1985

Abrol, Prem Nath. Commercial banking / Prem Nath Abrol. 1st ed. Delhi, India : Anmol Publications : Distributed by Anupama Publisher's Distributors, 1987. viii, 224 p. ; 23 cm. Study, with reference to Jammu and Kashmir, India. Bibliography: p. [217]-224. LC Card 87-900129 DDC 332.1/2/09546 19
1. Banks and banking - India - Jammu and Kashmir. I. Title.
HG3289.J35 A37 1987

Abrue L., Luz M. Campesinas y políticos, 1986 . Santo Domingo, República Dominicana , 1986. 83 p. : LC Card 87-102259
HD6073.A292 D653 1986

Abrüstung und Wirtschaftswachstum . Kappus, Wolfgang. Frankfurt , New York , c1985. 329 p. : ISBN 3-593-33531-X LC Card 85-232235
HC110.D4 K37 1985

Abruzzese, Alberto. Comunicazione come dominio? /. Milano [1979] 147 p. ; ISBN 88-20-41548-8 : LC Card 79-395059 DDC 302.2/3
HM258 .C5896 ***NYPL [JLD 86-3359]***

Der Absatzbereich von Unternehmen . Bruse, Helmut. Bonn , 1980. xiv, 323 p. : LC Card 85-164955
HF5415 .B7713 1980

Abschied von Keynes? . Vomfelde, Werner.

Frankfurt am Main , New York , c1985. 205 p. : ISBN 3-593-33567-0 LC Card 86-159600
HB99.7 .V65 1985

Abschreibungsgesellschaften in Berlin (West) . Hecker, Christian. Köln , c1982. viii, 236, xix, 78 p. : ISBN 3-921379-96-2 LC Card 83-197457
HJ4720.B45 H43 1982

ABSENCE, LEAVE OF. see **LEAVE OF ABSENCE.**

Absentee entrepreneurship and the dynamics of the motor vehicle industry in Argentina /. Nofal, Maria Beatriz. New York , 1987. p. cm. ISBN 0-275-92607-9 (alk. paper) : LC Card 87-15159 DDC 629.2/0982 19
HD9710.A72 N64 1987

ABSENTEEISM (LABOR) - GERMANY (WEST)
Hollich, Franz. Analyse organisatorischer und personeller Einflussgrössen auf Fehlzeiten /. Karlsruhe , c1985. iii, 210 p. : ISBN 3-923485-03-4 LC Card 85-233162
HD5115.2.G4 H65 1985

ABSOLUTISM. see **DESPOTISM.**

Absorción creciente con subempleo persistente (América Latina, 1950-80) /. García, Norberto E. [Santiago, Chile] , 1982. 35 p. ; LC Card 87-403250 DDC 331.12/098 19
HD5730.5.A6 G355 1982

Die Absorptionskapazität für Kapital . Fritz-Krockow, Bernhard. Spardorf , c1986. 201 p. : ISBN 3-922919-78-2 LC Card 86-179843
HG4538 .F75 1986

ABSORPTIVE CAPACITY (ECONOMICS)
Fritz-Krockow, Bernhard. Die Absorptionskapazität für Kapital . Spardorf , c1986. 201 p. : ISBN 3-922919-78-2 LC Card 86-179843
HG4538 .F75 1986

ABSORPTIVE CAPACITY (ECONOMICS) - SAHEL.
Berg, Elliot. Absorptive capacity in the Sahel countries. [Paris] [Ouagadougou, Burkina Faso] [1983] xi, 133 p. ; LC Card 87-402541 DDC 338.91/0966 19
HC1002 .B47 1983

Absorptive capacity in the Sahel countries. Berg, Elliot. [Paris] [Ouagadougou, Burkina Faso] [1983] xi, 133 p. ; LC Card 87-402541 DDC 338.91/0966 19
HC1002 .B47 1983

Die Abstempelungen des Grossherzogtums Baden ab 1851 : neues Handbuch der Briefmarkenkunde / Arbeitsgemeinschaft Baden im Bund Deutscher Philatelisten e.V. [Soest] : Neues Handbuch der Briefmarkenkunde, c1980. 393 p. : ill. (some col.) ; 26 cm. (Baden-Handbuch . Bd. 3) Includes index. LC Card 86-152444
1. Postmarks - Germany (West) - Baden (Grand Duchy). I. Bund Deutscher Philatelisten. Arbeitsgemeinschaft Baden. II. Series.
HE6185.G32 B333 1980

Abu Gabal, Sayed Ahmed. Migration of Sudanese : causes and effects on Sudan economy / by Sayed Ahmed Abu Gabal. [Khartoum] : Faisal Islamic Bank, 1984. 18, [14] p. ; 23 cm. (Faisal Islamic Bank "Sudan" publications. English series . 4) Bibliography: p. [32]. LC Card 86-980176 DDC 331.6/2/6240174927 19
1. Alien labor, Sudanese - Arab countries. 2. Sudan - Emigration and immigration - Economic aspects. 3. Arab countries - Emigration and immigration. 4. Emigrant remittances - Sudan. 5. Sudan - Economic conditions - 1973-. I. Series: Faisal Islamic Bank "Sudan" publications. English series , 4. II. Title.
HD8766 .A65 1984

Abu Sin, M. E. (Mohad E.) Socio-economic aspects of integrated resource management, with special reference to the forest resources of Kassala Province, Eastern Region : the case of Rawashda and Wad Kabu forests / by M.E. Abu Sin, M.O. El Sammani. Khartoum : Govt. of the Democratic Republic of Sudan, 1986. vi leaves, 109 p. : maps ; 30 cm. (Field document . no. 13) At head of title: Fuelwood development for energy in Sudan. "February 1986." Bibliography: p. 86-88. "GCP/SUD/033/NET." LC Card 87-980440 DDC 333.75/09629/2 19
1. Forest policy - Economic aspects - Sudan - Kassala (Province). 2. Forest conservation - Economic aspects - Sudan - Kassala (Province). 3. Kassala (Sudan : Province) - Economic conditions. 4. Fuelwood consumption - Sudan - Kassala (Province). I. El Sammani, Mohammed Osman. II. Title. III. Series.
HD9767.S843 K3724 1986

ABŪ ẒABY (UNITED ARAB EMIRATES : EMIRATE) - COMMERCE - DIRECTORIES.
Dalīl rajul al-aʻmāl fī al-ṣināʻah wa-al-tijārah . [Abu Ẓaby] , 1984. 305 p. : LC Card 86-965166
HF5233.A56 D35 1984

ABŪ ẒABY (UNITED ARAB EMIRATES : EMIRATE) - ECONOMIC CONDITIONS.
ʻUtaybah, Mānīʻ Saʻīd, 1946- The economy of Abu Dhabi . [S.l. , 197-?] (Beirut, Lebanon : Commercial & Industrial Press) 247 p. ; LC Card 86-965159
HC415.36.Z7 A288 1970z

ABŪ ẒABY (UNITED ARAB EMIRATES : EMIRATE) - INDUSTRIES - DIRECTORIES.
Dalīl rajul al-aʻmāl fī al-ṣināʻah wa-al-tijārah . [Abu Ẓaby] , 1984. 305 p. : LC Card 86-965166
HF5233.A56 D35 1984

ABŪ ẒABY (UNITED ARAB EMIRATES : EMIRATE) - INDUSTRIES - HISTORY.
ʻUtaybah, Mānīʻ Saʻīd, 1946- The economy of Abu Dhabi . [S.l. , 197-?] (Beirut, Lebanon : Commercial & Industrial Press) 247 p. ; LC Card 86-965159
HC415.36.Z7 A288 1970z

ABŪ ẒABY (UNITED ARAB EMIRATES : EMIRATE) - MANUFACTURES - DIRECTORIES.
Dalīl rajul al-aʻmāl fī al-ṣināʻah wa-al-tijārah . [Abu Ẓaby] , 1984. 305 p. : LC Card 86-965166
HF5233.A56 D35 1984

Abulafia, David. Italy, Sicily, and the Mediterranean, 1100-1400 / David Abulafia. London : Variorum Reprints, 1987. 346 p. in various pagings : ill. ; 23 cm. (Variorum reprint. CS250) English and Italian. Includes bibliographies and index. ISBN 0-86078-198-4 : LC Card 87-157554 DDC 330.9182/2 19
1. Italy - Commerce - History. 2. Sicily - Commerce - History. 3. Mediterranean region - Commerce - History. 4. Middle Ages. I. Title.
HF3585 .A29 1987

Abusada-Salah, Roberto. La crisis del empresariado nacional / Roberto Abusada Salah, Miguel Vega Alvear. [Lima] : Intercampus, [1983] 41 p. ; 21 cm. Cover title. Papers presented at the VII Reunión Intercampus, 25 Julio 1983. LC Card 84-236119
1. Peru - Economic conditions - 1968-. 2. Peru - Commerce. I. Vega Alvear, Miguel. II. Title.
HC227 .A57 1983

ABUSE OF POWER. see **DESPOTISM.**

ABUSED WOMEN - EMPLOYMENT - UNITED STATES.
Moore, Janice D. Thorne. A step toward independence: economic self sufficiency . Washington, D.C. , c1986. iii, 117 p. : LC Card 86-209069 DDC 362.8/3 19
HD6059.6.U6 M66 1986

Abyssinia. see **Ethiopia.**

ABZs of economics. Lee, Susan, 1943- [ABZs of economics.] Susan Lee's ABZs of economics /. New York , c1987. 224 p. : ISBN 0-671-55711-4 LC Card 86-25481 DDC 330/.03 19
HB61 .L34 1987

Academia de Ciencias de la U. R. S. S. see **Akademiia nauk SSSR.**

Academia de Humanismo Cristiano (Santiago, Chile). Ruiz-Tagle P., Jaime. El sindicalismo chileno después del plan laboral /. Santiago, Chile [1985?] 211 p. ; ***NYPL [JLD 87-1182]***

Academia de Științe a U. R. S. S. see **Akademiia nauk SSSR.**

Academia Republicii Socialiste România. Comisia Revoluția Științifică și Tehnică. Modele matematice și semiotice ale dezvoltării sociale /. București , 1986. 190 p. : LC Card 86-208152
HD75.5 .M615 1986

Academia Scientiarum Hungarica. see **Magyar Tudományos Akadémia, Budapest.**

Académie des sciences de l'U. R. S. S. see **Akademiia nauk SSSR.**

Académie hongroise des sciences. see **Magyar Tudományos Akadémia, Budapest.**

Academie polonaise des sciences. see **Polska Akademia Nauk.**

Academy for Advancement of Corporate Governance. Sealy, Albert H. Macro blueprint . New York , 1986. viii, 407, 232 p. ; ISBN 0-89192-390-X LC Card 86-218989 DDC 338.973 19
HD2785 .S412 1986

Academy of Educational Planning and Management (Pakistan) Ghafoor, Abdul. Development of human resources . Islamabad [1984] v, ii leaves, 99 p., v, ii leaves ; LC Card 85-932024 DDC 331.11/09549/1 19
HD5819 .G48 1984

Academy of Sciences of the U. S. S. R. see **Akademiia nauk SSSR.**

Acaecimientos de Manuel Belgrano, fisiócrata, y su traducción de las "Máximas generales del gobierno económico de un reyno agricultor" de François Quesnay /. Lluch, Ernest, 1937- Madrid , 1984. 107 p. ; ISBN 84-7232-332-3 LC Card 85-179398
HB159 .L58 1984

Ação de desenvolvimento, 1979-1983 /. Brazil. Ministerio do Interior. [Brasília] [1983?] 89 p. : LC Card 87-404839 DDC 338.981 19
HC187 .B862 1983

Accademia polacca delle scienze. see **Polska Akademia Nauk.**

Accademia polacca di scienze e lettere. see **Polska Akademia Nauk.**

Accardi, Filippo. Vizzini, Sergio. Indagine socio-demografica sugli immigrati stranieri in Sicilia . Palermo [1983] 108 p. ; LC Card 86-131931
HB3600.M39 V58 1983

ACCELERATED EROSION. see **SOIL EROSION.**

ACCELERATED READING. see **RAPID READING.**

Accelerating food production in Sub-Saharan Africa / edited by John W. Mellor, Christopher L. Delgado, Malcolm J. Blackie. Baltimore : Published for the International Food Policy Research Institute [by] Johns Hopkins University Press, c1987. xix, 417 p. ; 24 cm. Papers and commentaries from a conference sponsored by the Dept. of Land Management of the University of Zimbabwe and the International Food Policy Research Institute, held at Victoria Falls, Zimbabwe in Aug. 1983. Includes index. Bibliography: p. 377-396. ISBN 0-8018-3390-6 (alk. paper) LC Card 86-10684 DDC 338.1/9/67 19
1. Agricultural productivity - Africa, Sub-Saharan - Congresses. 2. Food supply - Africa, Sub-Saharan - Congresses. 3. Agriculture and state - Africa, Sub-Saharan - Congresses. I. Mellor, John Williams, 1928-. II. Delgado, Christopher L. III. Blackie, M. J. IV. University of Zimbabwe. Dept. of Land Management. V. International Food Policy Research Institute.
HD2117 .A33 1987 ***NYPL [JLE 87-1366]***

ACCELERATION PRINCIPLE (ECONOMICS)
Karhu, Veli. Akseleraatioteoriaan perustuvia investointifunktiokokeiluja yritystason aineistolla /. Vaasa , 1982. 43, [1] leaves ; ISBN 951-683-160-5 LC Card 83-100841 DDC 332/.0415 19
HG4028.C4 K349 1982
NYPL [JLM 73-601 n:o 85]

Accent Québec. French.
Fortin, Pierre. [Unemployment, inflation, and economic stabilization in Quebec. French.] Chômage, inflation et régulation de la conjoncture au Québec /. Montréal, Québec [1980] viii, 144 p. : ISBN 0-88806-063-7 (pbk.) LC Card 87-673448
HC117.Q4 F63x 1980

Access planning as an essay on explorations in alternatives. Ramana, D. V. A monograph on access planning as an essay on explorations in alternatives /. Kuala Lumpur [1982] 86 p. : LC Card 84-940306 DDC 338.954 19
HD75 .R36 1982

ACCESS TO AIRPORTS.
Airport transportation . Arlington, Va. ,

Washington, D.C. [1961] vii, 289, 42 leaves : LC Card 84-132332
HE9797.4.A2 A38 1961

ACCESS TO AIRPORTS - GOVERNMENT POLICY - UNITED STATES.
Gilbert, Gorman, 1943- The management and regulation of ground transportation at U. S. airports . Washington, D.C. [1986] 153 p. : LC Card 87-600652 DDC 387.7/362 19
HE9797.4.A2 G55 1986

ACCESS TO AIRPORTS - UNITED STATES.
Gilbert, Gorman, 1943- The management and regulation of ground transportation at U. S. airports . Washington, D.C. [1986] 153 p. : LC Card 87-600652 DDC 387.7/362 19
HE9797.4.A2 G55 1986

ACCESS TO AIRPORTS - UNITED STATES - CASE STUDIES.
Airport transportation . Arlington, Va. , Washington, D.C. [1961] vii, 289, 42 leaves : LC Card 84-132332
HE9797.4.A2 A38 1961

Gilbert, Gorman, 1943- The management and regulation of ground transportation at U. S. airports . Washington, D.C. [1986] 153 p. : LC Card 87-600652 DDC 387.7/362 19
HE9797.4.A2 G55 1986

Accessing private industry council funding . Howe, Mike. [Northridge, CA] (17624 Romar St., Northridge 91325) [1987?] 24, [15] leaves ; LC Card 87-401761 DDC 362.8/5 19
HD5715.2 .H69 1987

Accident investigation and reporting : a guide to the investigation and reporting of occupational accidents with particular reference to enterprises subject to Part IV of the Canada Labour Code and the Canada occupational safety and health regulations. [Ottawa] : Labour Canada, c1986. 15, 16 p. : ill. ; 28 cm. English and French. "Occupational safety and health." Title on added t.p.: Les enquêtes et les rapports sur les accidents. ISBN 0-662-54332-7 (pbk.) LC Card 86-201756
1. Industrial accidents - Investigation. 2. Industrial accidents - Reporting - Canada. I. Canada. Labour Canada. II. Title: Enquêtes et les rapports sur les accidents.
HD7262.25 .A28 1986

ACCIDENT PREVENTION. see **ACCIDENTS - PREVENTION.**

Accidental deaths, suicides, and homicides . (pt. 3) Suicides and homicides, Oregon residents, 1979 to 1981. Portland, OR (1400 S.W. 5th Ave., Portland 97201) [1986] 39 p. : LC Card 87-620589 DDC 614.5/985844/09795 19
HB1323.S82 U57 1986

Accidental millionaire . Butcher, Lee. New York , c1988. xii, 224 p., [4] p. of plates : ISBN 0-913729-79-5 LC Card 87-9414 DDC 338.7/61004/0924 B 19
HD9696.C64 A863 1988

Les Accidents du travail dans la construction au Québec / Office de la construction du Québec, Service de la recherche. [Quebec] : L'Office, [1983] vii, 256 p. : ill. ; 28 cm. Bibliography: p. 255-256. ISBN 2-550-10554-0 LC Card 85-100967
1. Construction industry - Québec (Province) - Accidents. I. Office de la construction du Québec. Service de la recherche.
HD9715.C33 Q42 1983

Accidents du travail et les maladies professionnelles. Employment injuries and occupational illnesses . Ottawa, Ont. , c1986. 92 p. ; ISBN 0-662-54738-1 (pbk.) LC Card 87-147113 DDC 363.1/12/0971 19
HD7262.5.C3 E463 1986

ACCIDENTS - GERMANY (WEST) - STATISTICS.
Arbeitssicherheit '86 . Bonn [1986] 47, 46, 22 p. : LC Card 87-409083 DDC 363.1/12/0943 19
HD7708 .A7 1986

ACCIDENTS, INDUSTRIAL. see **INDUSTRIAL ACCIDENTS.**

ACCIDENTS - INVESTIGATION.
Hendrick, Kingsley. Investigating accidents with STEP /. New York , c1987. xviii, 454 p. : ISBN 0-8247-7510-4 LC Card 86-24165 DDC 363.1/065 19
HD7262.25 .H46 1987

ACCIDENTS, OCCUPATIONAL. see **INDUSTRIAL ACCIDENTS.**

ACCIDENTS - PREVENTION - COST EFFECTIVENESS.
Tasgian, Astrig. La valutazione economica della vita umana . Torino , 1980. 117 p. : LC Card 81-124532 DDC 331/.01/1 19
HD4904.7 .T34 1980 ***NYPL [JLE 86-1600]***

ACCIDENTS, TRAFFIC. see **TRAFFIC ACCIDENTS.**

ACCIDENTS - WASHINGTON (STATE) - STATISTICS.
Injury deaths in Washington State, 1968-1983 . Seattle, Wash. (1610 NE 150th, Seattle 98155) [1985] 49, [78] p. : LC Card 86-623057 DDC 363.1/02/09797021 19
HB1323.A22 U65 1985

ACCIÓN DEMOCRÁTICA (VENEZUELA)
López-Orihuela, Alcides, 1926- El pacto y la democracia sociales /. Caracas, Venezuela [1986] (Caracas : Editorial Greco) xvi, 129 p. ; ISBN 90-826548-5-X LC Card 87-402941 DDC 338.987 19
HC237 .L667 1986

ACCIÓN POPULAR (PERU) - PLATFORMS.
Casas Grieve, Luis Felipe de las. Economía y frustración social . Lima, Perú [1982?] 128 p. : LC Card 83-104684
HC227 .C27 1982

Accomodation and resistance . Rice-Maximin, Edward Francis, 1941- New York , 1986. xi, 175 p. ; ISBN 0-313-25355-2 (lib. bdg. : alk. paper) LC Card 86-4624 DDC 959.704/1 19
DS553.1 .R53 1986 ***NYPL [JFE 87-1024]***

Accornero, Aris. Il Futuro del sindacato /. Roma , c1986. xxvii, 347 p. ; LC Card 86-223517
HD6709 .F88 1986

An account of major activities in the Canterbury Labour and Trades Council District, 1929-1936 /. Christie, Alan R. [Wellington] , 1980. 38, [3] p. ; LC Card 81-120047
HD8930.5.Z8 C3623 1980

Accountabilities . Day, Patricia. London , New York , 1987. 259 p. : ISBN 0-422-79340-X : LC Card 87-164015 DDC 354.4109/2 19
HD4147 .D39 1987

ACCOUNTANTS.
Clark-James, Suzanne. Providing personal financial planning services in your CPA practice /. New York, NY (11 Penn Plaza, New York 10001) , 1987. 1 v. (various pagings) : LC Card 87-61984 DDC 657/.068/5 19
HG179 .C59 1987

ACCOUNTANTS - AFRICA.
Monday, H. R. Proposals for the establishment of an African Institute of Chartered Accountants. [New York?] [1984] 10 p. ; LC Card 86-122510 DDC 657/.06/06 19
HF5616.A35 M65 1984

Accountant's business manual /. Behrenfeld, William H. New York, N.Y. , c1987- 1 v. (loose-leaf) ; ISBN 0-87051-000-2 (loose-leaf) : LC Card 87-992 DDC 657 19
HF5616.U5 B38 1987

Accountant's complete model letter book /. Hakoun, Mitchell. Englewood Cliffs, N.J. , c1987. xxi, 424 p. : ISBN 0-13-001199-1 : LC Card 87-11548 DDC 657 19
HF5726 .H3257 1987

ACCOUNTANTS - LEGAL STATUS, LAWS, ETC. - WASHINGTON (STATE)
Washington (State). Legislature. Legislative Budget Committee. Program and fiscal review . Olympia (506 E. 16th Ave., Olympia 98504) [1985] v, 69 p. ; LC Card 86-621785 DDC 353.97970072/32 s 353.97970082/43 19
HJ11 .W2453 no. 85-13 KFN329.A25

ACCOUNTANTS - PROFESSIONAL ETHICS - HISTORY.
Previts, Gary John. The scope of CPA services . New York , c1985. xv, 187 p. ; ISBN 0-471-01149-5 : LC Card 85-22455 DDC 657/.09 19
HF5611 .P73 1985 ***NYPL [JLE 86-2961]***

ACCOUNTANTS - PROFESSIONAL ETHICS - UNITED STATES.
American Institute of Certified Public Accountants. Special Committee on Standards of Professional Conduct for Certified Public Accountants. Restructuring professional standards to achieve professional excellence in a changing environment . New York, N.Y. (1211 Ave. of the Americas, New York 10036-8775) , c1986. vi, 66 p. : LC Card 86-211085 DDC 657/.0218 19
HF5616.U5 A585 1986

Plan to restructure professional standards. New York, N.Y. (1211 Ave. of the Americas, New York 10036-8775) , c1987. xii, 68 p. ; LC Card 87-160205 DDC 657/.0218 19
HF5616.U5 P53 1987

ACCOUNTANTS - SALARIES, ETC. - UNITED STATES - STATISTICS.
Compensation in the accounting/financial field /. Crete, IL , c1987. 489 p. ; ISBN 0-916506-36-3 (pbk.) LC Card 87-153325 DDC 331.12/81657/0973021 19
HF5627 .C57 1987

ACCOUNTANTS - SALARIES, PENSIONS, ETC. - UNITED STATES - STATISTICS.
The Accounting/financial report /. Crete, IL (548 First St., Crete 60417) , c1983. 2 v. ; LC Card 83-152793 DDC 331.2/81657/0973 19
HF5627 .A23 1983 ***NYPL [JLM 86-1500]***

ACCOUNTANTS - SCOTLAND - BIOGRAPHY.
Stewart, James C. (James Cathcart) Pioneers of a profession . New York , 1986, c1977. xii, 181 p., [2] leaves of plates : ISBN 0-8240-7888-8 : LC Card 86-25636 DDC 657/.092/2 B 19
HF5604 .S73 1986

ACCOUNTANTS - SOUTH CAROLINA - DIRECTORIES.
South Carolina Board of Accountancy. Roster of certified public accountants, public accountants, and accounting practitioners registered with the South Carolina Board of Accountancy. Columbia, S.C. (P.O. Box 11376, Columbia 29211) [1986] 74 p. ; LC Card 87-620717 DDC 657/.025/757 19
HF5616.U6 S68 1986

ACCOUNTANTS - UNITED STATES.
McKell, Lynn J. A study of MAS practice and knowledge and bibliographic references for management advisory services . New York, N.Y. , c1987. 100, [iv], 72 p. ; ISBN 0-87051-002-9 (pbk.) : LC Card 87-19491 DDC 016.6584/6 19
HF5616.U5 M34 1987

Wagner, Nancy A. Eric Louis Kohler in the accounting profession /. Atlanta, Ga. , 1987. vi, 210 p. ; ISBN 0-88406-196-5 (pbk.) : LC Card 86-25633 DDC 657/.092/4 19
HF5604.5.K64 W34 1987

ACCOUNTANTS - UNITED STATES - BIOGRAPHY.
Previts, Gary John. John Raymond Wildman . University, Ala. , 1978. viii, 84 p. ; LC Card 86-224716
HF5604.5.W55 P74 1978

ACCOUNTANTS - UNITED STATES - RATING OF.
American Institute of Certified Public Accountants. Special Committee on Standards of Professional Conduct for Certified Public Accountants. Restructuring professional standards to achieve professional excellence in a changing environment . New York, N.Y. (1211 Ave. of the Americas, New York 10036-8775) , c1986. vi, 66 p. : LC Card 86-211085 DDC 657/.0218 19
HF5616.U5 A585 1986

ACCOUNTANTS - VENEZUELA - BIOGRAPHY.
Hacienda colonial venezolana /. Caracas , 1946. 170 p. ; LC Card 85-105445
HJ991 .H323 1946

ACCOUNTANTS - WASHINGTON (STATE)
Washington (State). Legislature. Legislative Budget Committee. Program and fiscal review . Olympia (506 E. 16th Ave., Olympia 98504) [1985] v, 69 p. ; LC Card 86-621785 DDC 353.97970072/32 s 353.97970082/43 19
HJ11 .W2453 no. 85-13 KFN329.A25

Accountant's workbook series.
Calder, Eugene B. Advising clients on real estate investments /. New York, NY (11 Penn Plaza, New York 10001) , 1987. 95 p. in various pagings : LC Card 87-61983 DDC

332.63/24 19
HD1382.5 .C34 1987

Clark-James, Suzanne. Providing personal financial planning services in your CPA practice /. New York, NY (11 Penn Plaza, New York 10001) , 1987. 1 v. (various pagings) : LC Card 87-61984 DDC 657/.068/5 19
HG179 .C59 1987

Accounting : principles and applications / K. Fred Skousen ... [et al.].3rd ed. New York, N.Y. : Worth Publishers, c1987. xxvi, 1047 p. : ill. (some col.) ; 26 cm. Rev. ed. of: Principles of accounting / K. Fred Skousen, Harold Q. Langenderfer, W. Steve Albrecht. 2nd ed. c1983. Includes index. ISBN 0-87901-338-9 LC Card 86-51180 DDC 657 19
1. Accounting. I. Skousen, K. Fred. II. Skousen, K. Fred. Principles of accounting.
HF5635 .S618 1987

ACCOUNTING - AFRICA.
Ghartey, J. B., 1944- Crisis accountability and development in the Third World . Aldershot, Hants, England , Brookfield, Vt., USA , c1987. x, 170 p. ; ISBN 0-566-05290-3 : LC Card 86-25777 DDC 338.91/096 19
HC800 .G52 1987

ACCOUNTING - ALGERIA.
Benaïssa, Younès. Technique comptable algérienne /. Alger , 1985- v. <1 > : LC Card 86-966696
HF5616.A4 B46 1985

ACCOUNTING AND BOOKKEEPING FOR BUILDING TRADES. see **CONSTRUCTION INDUSTRY - ACCOUNTING.**

ACCOUNTING AND BOOKKEEPING FOR HOTELS, RESTAURANTS, ETC. see **HOTELS, TAVERNS, ETC. - ACCOUNTING.**

Accounting and finance practice series.
Half, Robert. [Success guide for accountants.] Robert Half's success guide for accountants /. New York , c1987. x, 167 p. ; ISBN 0-07-172107-X LC Card 87-16430 DDC 657/.023/72 19
HF5657 .H34 1987

Hickman, James R. Management advisory services . Colorado Springs, Colo. , c1987. xxiv, 510 p. : ISBN 0-07-172102-9 LC Card 87-4482 DDC 657/.068/8 19
HF5657 .H53 1987

Accounting and information systems /. Page, John R., 1949- Englewood Cliffs, N.J. , c1987. xiii, 738 p. : ISBN 0-13-002361-2 LC Card 86-25429 DDC 657/.028/5 19
HF5679 .P25 1987

Accounting & management : field study perspectives / edited by William J. Bruns, Jr., Robert S. Kaplan. Boston, Mass. : Harvard Business School Press, c1987. ix, 374 p. : ill. ; 24 cm. Proceedings of a colloquium held June 16-18, 1986, at the Harvard Business School. Includes bibliographies and index. ISBN 0-87584-186-4 (alk. paper) LC Card 87-18373 DDC 658.4/038 19
1. Managerial accounting - Congresses. I. Bruns, William J. II. Kaplan, Robert S. III. Title: Accounting and management.
HF5657.4 .A25 1987

Accounting and management. Accounting & management . Boston, Mass. , c1987. ix, 374 p. : ISBN 0-87584-186-4 (alk. paper) LC Card 87-18373 DDC 658.4/038 19
HF5657.4 .A25 1987

ACCOUNTING AND PRICE FLUCTUATIONS.
Accounting for economic costs and changing prices . London , 1986. 2 v. : ISBN 0-11-560004-3 (pbk. : v. 1) : LC Card 86-216162 DDC 657/.42 19
HF5658.5 .A22 1986

Accounting and tax aspects of computer software manufacturing /. McGee, Robert W. New York , 1987. viii, 162 p. ; ISBN 0-275-92273-1 (alk. paper) : LC Card 87-15140 DDC 657/.73 19
HF5686.C54 M38 1987

ACCOUNTING - ARGENTINA - EFFECT OF INFLATION ON.
Badillo, Juan A. El registro contable en moneda constante . Capital Federal, Argentina , 1985. 249 p. ; LC Card 85-203677
HF5658.5 .B34 1985

Lazzati, Santiago. Análisis de normas sobre contabilidad e inflación . Buenos Aires [1981] 157 p. ; LC Card 82-216941
HF5658.5 .L39 1981

Troiano, Alberto C. (Alberto Carlos) Los revalúos técnicos de bienes . Buenos Aires [1982] 63, [2] p. : ISBN 950-0-37018-2 LC Card 84-237340
HF5658.5 .T76 1982

ACCOUNTING - BRAZIL - EFFECT OF INFLATION ON.
Issel, Catarina Irene. Die Geldwertberichtigung in Brasilien im Rechnungswesen der Unternehmung /. Hamburg , 1983. iii, 181 p. : LC Card 84-112596 DDC 332.6/73/098 s 657/.48 19
HG5160.5.A3 P7 Nr. 10 HF5658.5
NYPL [JLK 73-84 Nr.10]

ACCOUNTING - CASE STUDIES.
Ferris, Kenneth R. Financial accounting and corporate reporting . Plano, Tex. , 1987. xi, 422 p. : ISBN 0-256-03554-7 (pbk.) LC Card 86-71236 DDC 657/.3 19
HF5686.C7 F455 1987

Hoskin, Robert E. Financial accounting cases /. Chicago , c1988. 201 p. : ISBN 0-03-011778-X (pbk.) LC Card 87-22238 DDC 657 19
HF5635 .H817 1988

ACCOUNTING - COMPUTER-ASSISTED INSTRUCTION.
Cooper, Robin, 1951- CABIS, computer-aided bookkeeping instruction system /. Reading, Mass. , c1987. p. cm. ISBN 0-201-11307-4 (user's manual) LC Card 86-32148 DDC 657/.2/02855369 19
HF5630 .C68 1987

Accounting, costing, and cost estimation . Jones, Haydn. Cardiff , 1985. ix, 285 p. ; ISBN 0-7083-0882-1 : LC Card 85-172570 DDC 657/.09429 19
HF5616.G72 W35 1985
NYPL [JLD 86-2817]

ACCOUNTING - DATA PROCESSING.
Accounting information systems . Reading, Mass. , c1987. p. cm. ISBN 0-201-10376-1 : LC Card 87-1155 DDC 657/.028/5 19
HF5679 .A34 1987

Allen, Warren W. Advanced automated accounting for the microcomputer /. Cincinnati , c1988. viii, 200 p. : ISBN 0-538-02690-0 (pbk.) LC Card 87-61619 DDC 657/.028/55369 19
HF5679 .A567 1988

Bhaskar, Krish N. The impact of microprocessors on the small accounting practice /. Englewood Cliffs, N.J. , c1986. xvi, 167 p. ; ISBN 0-13-453291-0 (pbk.) LC Card 85-25764 DDC 657/.028/5416 19
HF5679 .B45 1986 ***NYPL [JLE 86-4067]***

Bien, Frederick A. Microcomputer applications for CPAs /. New York, NY , c1986. 8, 34, 34, 65 p. : LC Card 87-121259 DDC 657/.028/5536 19
HF5679 .B54 1986

Bodnar, George H. Accounting information systems /. Boston , c1987. xvii, 892 p. : ISBN 0-205-10308-1 LC Card 86-26505 DDC 657/.028/5 19
HF5679 .B59 1987

DiAntonio, Angelo E. Spreadsheet applications in financial accounting /. Englewood Cliffs, N.J. , c1986. xvii, 391 p. : ISBN 0-8359-6945-2 (pbk.) : LC Card 85-14303 DDC 657/.028/553 19
HF5679 .D52 1986 ***NYPL [JLE 86-3100]***

Greenfield, W. M. Accounting with 1-2-3 /. Englewood Cliffs, N.J. , 1987. p. cm. ISBN 0-13-001686-1 LC Card 87-12485 DDC 657/.028/55369 19
HF5679 .G737 1987

Hicks, Sam A. The use of microcomputers in accounting /. St. Paul , c1985. xx, 349 p. : ISBN 0-314-87064-4 (pbk.) LC Card 85-8950 DDC 657/.028/54 19
HF5679 .H535 1985 ***NYPL [JLF 86-1720]***

Jones, Graham. Information technology and the new accounting /. London , New York , c1988. p. cm. ISBN 0-07-084179-9 : LC Card 87-22579 DDC 657/.028/5 19
HF5679 .J634 1988

Martin, Dale R. Lotus 1-2-3 applications with disk /. Englewood Cliffs, N.J. , c1986. viii, 120 p. : ISBN 0-13-540717-6 (pbk.) LC Card 86-200542 DDC 657/.044/02855369 19
HF5679 .M37 1986

Moscove, Stephen A. Accounting information systems . New York , c1987. xxi, 824 p. : ISBN 0-471-84033-5 LC Card 86-32387 DDC 657/.028/5 19
HF5679 .M62 1987

Mosich, Donna M. Mastering Dac-Easy . Glenview, Ill. , c1988. p. cm. ISBN 0-673-18735-7 LC Card 87-4847 DDC 657/.028/55369 19
HF5679 .M64 1988

Page, John R., 1949- Accounting and information systems /. Englewood Cliffs, N.J. , c1987. xiii, 738 p. : ISBN 0-13-002361-2 LC Card 86-25429 DDC 657/.028/5 19
HF5679 .P25 1987

Sharifi, Mohsen. Integrated case studies in accounting and information systems /. Englewood Cliffs, N.J. , c1987. ix, 229 p. : ISBN 0-13-469016-8 (pbk.) LC Card 86-30297 DDC 657/.028/5 19
HF5679 .S4754 1987

Smith, Gaylord N. The Briton Manufacturing Company . New York , c1988. p. cm. ISBN 0-06-046318-X LC Card 87-15624 DDC 657/.028/55369 19
HD30.26 .S64 1988

Smith, Kenneth, 1932- Corporate accounting systems . Workingham, England , Reading, Mass. , c1988. p. cm. ISBN 0-201-17824-9 LC Card 87-24130 DDC 657/.028/55 19
HF5679 .S645 1988

Sozdanie avtomatizirovannoĭ sistemy upravleniia ėkonomikoĭ administrativnogo raĭona . Riga , 1980. 151 p. ; LC Card 81-215521
HF5679 .S717 1980

West, Gary, 1947- Dac-Easy accounting and payroll made easy /. Blue Ridge Summit, PA , c1987. ix, 261 p. : ISBN 0-8306-2914-9 (pbk.) : LC Card 87-10056 DDC 657/.028/55369 19
HF5679 .W47 1987

ACCOUNTING - DICTIONARIES.
Lebas, Michel. Glossary of accounting =. Paris , c1985. 124 p. ; ISBN 2-86644-065-X (pbk.) : LC Card 86-179932
HF5621 .L42 1985

ACCOUNTING - DICTIONARIES - FRENCH.
Lebas, Michel. Glossary of accounting =. Paris , c1985. 124 p. ; ISBN 2-86644-065-X (pbk.) : LC Card 86-179932
HF5621 .L42 1985

ACCOUNTING - ECUADOR.
Orozco Cadena, José. Contabilidad general . Quito, Ecuador , 1986. xii, 551, [1] p. : LC Card 86-218544 DDC 657/.09866 19
HF5616.E2 O76 1986

ACCOUNTING - EUROPEAN ECONOMIC COMMUNITY COUNTRIES.
The Fourth company accounts directive of 1978 and the accounting systems of the Federal Republic of Germany, France, Italy, the United Kingdom, the United States, and Japan. Luxembourg , Washington, DC , 1986. 164, [47] p. ; ISBN 92-825-6454-1 (pbk.) : LC Card 87-134287 DDC 657 19
HF5611 .F686 1986

ACCOUNTING - EXAMINATIONS, QUESTIONS, ETC.
Francisco, Albert K. Accounting theory and practice /. Belmont, CA , c1987. 1 v. (various pagings) : ISBN 0-932276-74-1 (pbk.) LC Card 87-62077 DDC 657/.076 19
HF5661 .F68 1987

Francisco, Albert K. CPA exam questions on accounting practice /. Belmont, CA , c1987. 1 v. (various pagings) ; ISBN 0-932276-80-6 (pbk.) LC Card 87-62331 DDC 657/.076 19
HF5661 .F67 1987

Francisco, Albert K. CPA exam questions on accounting theory /. Belmont, CA. , c1987. 1 v. (various pagings) ; ISBN 0-932276-79-2 (pbk.)

LC Card 87-62332 DDC 657/.076 19
HF5661 .F675 1987

Person, Samuel. Barron's how to prepare for the certified public accountant examination, CPA /. New York , c1987. vi, 537 p. ; ISBN 0-8120-3880-0 (pbk.) : LC Card 87-17914 DDC 657/.076 19
HF5661 .P48 1987

The Accounting/financial report / directed by Steven Langer. 4th ed. Crete, IL (548 First St., Crete 60417) : Abbott, Langer & Associates, c1983. 2 v. ; 22 x 28 cm. CONTENTS. - pt. 1. Public accounting firms -- pt. 2. Industry/government/education/non-profit. LC Card 83-152793 DDC 331.2/81657/0973 19
1. Accountants - Salaries, pensions, etc. - United States - Statistics. 2. Auditors - Salaries, pensions, etc. - United States - Statistics. I. Langer, Steven. II. Abbott, Langer & Associates.
HF5627 .A23 1983 ***NYPL [JLM 86-1500]***

ACCOUNTING FIRMS - GREAT BRITAIN - HISTORY.
A History of Cooper Brothers & Co., 1854-1954. New York , 1986, c1954. xi, 116 p., [13] leaves of plates : ISBN 0-8240-7881-0 (alk. paper) : LC Card 86-25720 DDC 338.7/61657/0941 19
HF5616.G73 C665 1986

ACCOUNTING FIRMS - MANAGEMENT.
Miller, Robert E. How to compete successfully in a public accounting practice /. Englewood Cliffs, N.J. , c1987. xx, 250 p. ; ISBN 0-13-402157-6 LC Card 87-18677 DDC 657/.068 19
HF5627 .M54 1987

ACCOUNTING FIRMS - UNITED STATES.
Emerson, James C. Careers in public accounting 1986/87- . Seattle, Wash. (2824 Sahalee Dr. E., Redmond 98053) , c1986. 261 p. ; LC Card 87-71857 DDC 338.7/61657/0973 19
HF5616.U5 E46 1986

Accounting for certain effects of the Tax Reform Act of 1986. Public record, FASB technical bulletin no. 86-1, Accounting for certain effects of the Tax Reform Act of 1986. Stamford, Conn. (P.O. Box 3821, Stamford 06905-0821) [1987] 172 p. ; LC Card 87-80349 DDC 657/.46 19
HF5681.T3 P83 1987

Accounting for data processing costs /. McGee, Robert W. New York , c1988. p. cm. ISBN 0-89930-214-9 (lib. bdg. : alk. paper) LC Card 87-24933 DDC 657/.7 19
HF5548.35 .M38 1988

Accounting for economic costs and changing prices : a report to HM Treasury / by an advisory group. London : H.M.S.O., 1986. 2 v. : ill. ; 30 cm. Bibliography: v. 2, p. 137. ISBN 0-11-560004-3 (pbk. : v. 1) : LC Card 86-216162 DDC 657/.42 19
1. Accounting and price fluctuations. 2. Current value accounting - Great Britain. 3. Government business enterprises - Great Britain - Accounting. I. Great Britain. Treasury.
HF5658.5 .A22 1986

Accounting for options / prepared by Task Force on Options, Accounting Standards Division, American Institute of Certified Public Accountants. New York, NY (1211 Ave. of the Americas, New York 10036-8775) : AICPA, [1986] 182 p., [4] p. of plates (some folded) : ill. ; 28 cm. (Issues paper) "86-2." "March 6, 1986." "File 3750." LC Card 86-221314 DDC 657/.76 19
1. Investments - Accounting - Standards - United States. 2. Hedging (Finance) - Accounting - Standards - United States. 3. Put and call transactions - Accounting - Standards - United States. I. American Institute of Certified Public Accountants. Accounting Standards Division. Task Force on Options. II. Series.
HF5686.16 A28 1986

Accounting for overseas operations /. Westwick, C. A. Aldershot, Hants, England , Brookfield, Vt. , c1986. ix, 184 p. ; ISBN 0-566-02586-8 : LC Card 85-30582 DDC 657/.95 19
HF5686.156 W47 1986 ***NYPL [JLG 86-202]***

Accounting for S corporations and noncorporate entities . Clay, John R. Fort Worth, Tex. , c1987. 1 v. (various pagings) ; LC Card 87-163295 DDC 657/.95/076 19
HF5686.C7 C58 1987

Accounting for the translation of foreign currencies . Griffin, Paul A. Stamford, Conn. , c1987. viii, 112 p. : ISBN 0-910065-22-5 (pbk.) LC Card 86-81640 DDC 657/.48 19
HG3853.7 .G75 1987

Accounting for treasury products . Tiner, John I. Cambridge, England , Wolfeboro, N.H., USA , 1988. p. cm. ISBN 0-85941-389-6 : LC Card 87-12531 DDC 657/.833 19
HG1708 .T56 1988

ACCOUNTING - FRANCE - QUALITY CONTROL - CONGRESSES.
Le Contrôle de qualité . [Paris] [1983] 297 p. : ISBN 2-900670-20-9 : LC Card 85-106388
HF5616.F7 C66 1983

Accounting fundamentals . Hoffman, Frank. New York , c1987. vi, 229 p. : ISBN 0-07-029210-8 (pbk.) : LC Card 86-27352 DDC 657 19
HF5635 .H678 1987

Accounting fundamentals /. Schick, P. Charlene, 1943- Englewood Cliffs, N.J. , c1987. xviii, 509 p. : ISBN 0-13-001918-6 LC Card 86-23732 DDC 657 19
HF5635 .S3124 1987

ACCOUNTING - GERMANY, WEST.
Hanisch, Bärbel, 1957- Die Ergebnisrechnung nach dem Bilanzrichtlinie-Gesetzentwurf im internationalen Vergleich (BRD, Japan, USA) /. Frankfurt am Main , New York , c1984. 286 p. : ISBN 3-8204-8559-7 : LC Card 85-164345
HF5616.G3 H35 1984

Möller, Hans Peter. Bilanzkennzahlen und Ertragsrisiken des Kapitalmarktes . Stuttgart , 1986. xii, 240 p. : ISBN 3-7910-0382-8 LC Card 86-149711
HF5681.C25 M64 1986

ACCOUNTING - GERMANY, WEST - HISTORY.
Eugen Schmalenbach . Stuttgart , 1984. xvii, 478 p. : ISBN 3-8202-0295-1 LC Card 84-215889
HF5616.G3 E93 1984

ACCOUNTING - GREAT BRITAIN.
The Regulatory framework of accounting /. Estover, Plymouth , 1985. [12], 391 p. : ISBN 0-7121-0491-7 ***NYPL [JLF 87-84]***

Robins, Paul. Advanced accounting practice book 1 . Wokingham, Berkshire, England , 1987. p. cm. ISBN 0-278-00014-2 : LC Card 87-13803 DDC 657/.046 19
HF5635 .R66 1987

ACCOUNTING - GREAT BRITAIN - HISTORY.
A History of Cooper Brothers & Co., 1854-1954. New York , 1986, c1954. xi, 116 p., [13] leaves of plates : ISBN 0-8240-7881-0 (alk. paper) : LC Card 86-25720 DDC 338.7/61657/0941 19
HF5616.G73 C665 1986

ACCOUNTING - GREAT BRITAIN - HISTORY - 20TH CENTURY.
Parker, R. H. (Robert Henry) The development of the accountancy profession in Britain to the early twentieth century /. [University, Ala.] , 1986. ix, 74 p. ; LC Card 86-226162 DDC 657/.09 19
HF5616.G7 P36 1986

ACCOUNTING - HANDBOOKS, MANUALS, ETC.
Handbook of accounting and auditing /. Boston , c1981. 1 v. (various pagings) ; ISBN 0-88712-221-3 (Update 1985) LC Card 80-53166 DDC 657/.02/02 19
HF5635.H22 ***NYPL [*R-Econ. 85-31]***

Woelfel, Charles J. The desktop encyclopedia of corporate finance & accounting /. Chicago, Ill. , c1987. viii, 518 p. : ISBN 0-917253-65-5 : LC Card 87-2302 DDC 658.1/5 19
HG4027.3 .W64 1987

ACCOUNTING - HISTORY.
Previts, Gary John. The scope of CPA services . New York , c1985. xv, 187 p. ; ISBN 0-471-01149-5 : LC Card 85-22455 DDC 657/.09 19
HF5611 .P73 1985 ***NYPL [JLE 86-2961]***

Selected papers from the Charles Waldo Haskins accounting history seminars /. [University, Ala.] , 1983. iv, 172 p. ; LC Card 86-224698 DDC 657/.09 19
HF5611 .S45 1983

Accounting history and the development of a profession.
Depreciation and capital maintenance /. New York , 1984. xi, 137 p. : ISBN 0-8240-6304-X (alk. paper) : LC Card 83-49437 DDC 657/.73 19
HF5681.D5 D45 1984 ***NYPL [JLE 86-1715]***

European equity markets . New York , 1984. 470 p. : ISBN 0-8240-6307-4 (alk. paper) : LC Card 83-49440 DDC 332.64/094
HG5430.5.A3 E84 1984 ***NYPL [JLE 86-4508]***

Lee, Thomas Alexander. The evolution of corporate financial reporting /. New York , 1984. x, 307 p. ; ISBN 0-8240-6332-5 (alk. paper) : LC Card 83-49431 DDC 657/.3 19
HF5686.C7 L43 1984 ***NYPL [JLD 86-2835]***

ACCOUNTING - HUNGARY.
Bánhidi, Ferenc. Könyvelésről és pénzgazdálkodásról vállalati vezetőknek . Budapest , 1986, c1985. 215 p. ; ISBN 963-221-649-0 : LC Card 87-118825
HF5655.H9 B36 1986

Accounting in life and health insurance companies /. Zucconi, Paul J. Atlanta, Ga. , c1987. xiv, 365 p. : ISBN 0-915322-85-4 LC Card 86-82715 DDC 657/.836 19
HG8848 .Z84 1987

Accounting information systems : a book of reading and cases / [edited by] James R. Davis, Barry E. Cushing. Reading, Mass. : Addison-Wesley, c1987. p. cm. ISBN 0-201-10376-1 : LC Card 87-1155 DDC 657/.028/5 19
1. Accounting - Data processing. 2. Information storage and retrieval systems - Accounting. I. Davis, James Richard, 1947-. II. Cushing, Barry E.
HF5679 .A34 1987

Accounting information systems /. Bodnar, George H. Boston , c1987. xvii, 892 p. : ISBN 0-205-10308-1 LC Card 86-26505 DDC 657/.028/5 19
HF5679 .B59 1987

Accounting information systems . Moscove, Stephen A. New York , c1987. xxi, 824 p. : ISBN 0-471-84033-5 LC Card 86-32387 DDC 657/.028/5 19
HF5679 .M62 1987

ACCOUNTING - JAPAN.
The Fourth company accounts directive of 1978 and the accounting systems of the Federal Republic of Germany, France, Italy, the United Kingdom, the United States, and Japan. Luxembourg , Washington, DC , 1986. 164, [47] p. ; ISBN 92-825-6454-1 (pbk.) : LC Card 87-134287 DDC 657 19
HF5611 .F686 1986

Hanisch, Bärbel, 1957- Die Ergebnisrechnung nach dem Bilanzrichtlinie-Gesetzentwurf im internationalen Vergleich (BRD, Japan, USA) /. Frankfurt am Main , New York , c1984. 286 p. : ISBN 3-8204-8559-7 : LC Card 85-164345
HF5616.G3 H35 1984

ACCOUNTING - LATVIA - DATA PROCESSING.
Sozdanie avtomatizirovannoĭ sistemy upravleniia ėkonomikoĭ administrativnogo raĭona . Riga , 1980. 151 p. ; LC Card 81-215521
HF5679 .S717 1980

ACCOUNTING - LAW AND LEGISLATION - ECUADOR.
Orozco Cadena, José. Contabilidad general . Quito, Ecuador , 1986. xii, 551, [1] p. : LC Card 86-218544 DDC 657/.09866 19
HF5616.E2 O76 1986

ACCOUNTING - LAW AND LEGISLATION - GERMANY, WEST.
Hanisch, Bärbel, 1957- Die Ergebnisrechnung nach dem Bilanzrichtlinie-Gesetzentwurf im internationalen Vergleich (BRD, Japan, USA) /. Frankfurt am Main , New York , c1984. 286 p. : ISBN 3-8204-8559-7 : LC Card 85-164345
HF5616.G3 H35 1984

ACCOUNTING - LAW AND LEGISLATION - JAPAN.
Hanisch, Bärbel, 1957- Die Ergebnisrechnung nach dem Bilanzrichtlinie-Gesetzentwurf im internationalen Vergleich (BRD, Japan, USA) /. Frankfurt am Main , New York , c1984. 286

p. : ISBN 3-8204-8559-7 : LC Card 85-164345
HF5616.G3 H35 1984

ACCOUNTING - LAW AND LEGISLATION - UNITED STATES.

Behrenfeld, William H. Accountant's business manual /. New York, N.Y. , c1987- 1 v. (loose-leaf) ; ISBN 0-87051-000-2 (loose-leaf) : LC Card 87-992 DDC 657 19
HF5616.U5 B38 1987

Hanisch, Bärbel, 1957- Die Ergebnisrechnung nach dem Bilanzrichtlinie-Gesetzentwurf im internationalen Vergleich (BRD, Japan, USA) /. Frankfurt am Main , New York , c1984. 286 p. : ISBN 3-8204-8559-7 : LC Card 85-164345
HF5616.G3 H35 1984

ACCOUNTING - MARKETING.

Hickman, James R. Management advisory services . Colorado Springs, Colo. , c1987. xxiv, 510 p. : ISBN 0-07-172102-9 LC Card 87-4482 DDC 657/.068/8 19
HF5657 .H53 1987

Ronald, Dana M. Successfully developing your accounting practice . New York , 1987. x, 314 p. ; ISBN 0-471-84736-4 LC Card 86-32388 DDC 657/.068/8 19
HF5657 .R644 1987

ACCOUNTING - OUTLINES, SYLLABI, ETC.

National CPE curriculum . New York, N.Y. , c1987- 1 v. (loose-leaf) : ISBN 0-87051-001-0 (loose-leaf : CIP data sheet) : LC Card 87-18832 DDC 657/.07/15 19
HF5635 .N25 1987

ACCOUNTING - PAKISTAN - CONGRESSES.

National Conference of Management Accountants (1981 : Karachi, Pakistan) National Conference of Management Accountants . [Karachi] [1981?] 141 p. in various pagings ; LC Card 82-930763 DDC 658.1/511 19
HF5603 .N34 1981 ***NYPL [JLF 87-296]***

ACCOUNTING - PORTUGAL - EFFECT OF INFLATION ON.

Pina, Amílcar. Análise de empresas em inflação . [Porto] , 1985. 142 p. : LC Card 86-174401
HF5658.5 .P56 1985

Accounting principles /. Fess, Philip E. Cincinnati , c1987. xxiii, 1291, [92] p. : ISBN 0-538-00300-6 LC Card 86-62984 DDC 657 19
HF5635 .F386 1987

Accounting principles /. Kiger, Jack E. New York , c1987. xxvii, 1092 p. : ISBN 0-394-35482-6 : LC Card 86-29791 DDC 657 19
HF5635 .K53 1987

Accounting principles /. Weygandt, Jerry J. New York , c1987. xxviii, 1167, [45] p. : ISBN 0-471-03863-6 LC Card 87-2001 DDC 657 19
HF5635 .W524 1987

Accounting principles and practices /. Neeley, L. Paden. Cincinnati , c1987. xx, 1052 p. : ISBN 0-538-01631-0 LC Card 86-63073 DDC 657 19
HF5635 .N38 1987b

Accounting principles for the autonomous corporate entity /. Hill, Henry P. New York , 1987. xii, 144 p. : ISBN 0-89930-212-2 (lib. bdg. : alk. paper) LC Card 86-25587 DDC 657/.95 19
HF5686.C7 H55 1987

ACCOUNTING - PROBLEMS, EXERCISES, ETC.

Clay, John R. Accounting for S corporations and noncorporate entities . Fort Worth, Tex. , c1987. 1 v. (various pagings) ; LC Card 87-163295 DDC 657/.95/076 19
HF5686.C7 C58 1987

Lerner, Joel J. Schaum's outline of theory and problems of bookkeeping and accounting /. New York , c1988. 311 p. : ISBN 0-07-037231-4 (pbk.) LC Card 87-3800 DDC 657/.076 19
HF5661 .L46 1988

The Accounting profession in [name of country] : professional accounting in foreign countries series. New York, N.Y. : American Institute of Certified Public Accountants, c1987- v. <1-5 > ; 23 cm. CONTENTS. - [1] Canada / prepared by Fuller Jenks Landau -- [2] Netherlands / prepared by Ernst & Whinney -- [3] Sweden / prepared by Pannell Kerr Forster -- [4] United Kingdom / prepared by Arthur Andersen & Co. -- [5] Italy / prepared by Arthur Young International. LC Card 87-150526 DDC 657 19

1. Accounting. 2. Comparative accounting. I. American Institute of Certified Public Accountants. II. Title: Professional accounting in foreign countries series.
HF5611 .A34 1987

ACCOUNTING - PSYCHOLOGICAL ASPECTS - RESEARCH.

Behavioral accounting research . Columbus, Ohio , c1988. ix, 368 p. : ISBN 0-939787-02-4 (pbk.) : LC Card 87-24980 DDC 657/.072 19
HF5630 .B43 1988

ACCOUNTING - SCOTLAND - HISTORY.

Stewart, James C. (James Cathcart) Pioneers of a profession . New York , 1986, c1977. xii, 181 p., [2] leaves of plates : ISBN 0-8240-7888-8 : LC Card 86-25636 DDC 657/.092/2 B 19
HF5604 .S73 1986

Accounting series (Matthew Bender (Firm))

Orsini, Larry L. World accounting /. New York, NY (11 Penn Plaza, New York 10001) , 1987- c1986- 2 v. (loose-leaf) ; LC Card 86-73012 DDC 657 19
HF5611 .O75 1987

ACCOUNTING - SOVIET UNION.

Ėkonomicheskiĭ analiz khozi͡aĭstvennoĭ dei͡atel′nosti predprii͡atiĭ i obʺedineniĭ /. Moskva , 1986. 406 p. : LC Card 86-227621
HC340.A8 E417 1986

ACCOUNTING - STANDARDS.

Harmonization of accounting standards . Paris , Washington, D.C. , 1986. 147 p. ; ISBN 92-64-12895-6 (pbk.) : LC Card 87-124490 DDC 657/.0218 19
HF5611 .H37 1986

ACCOUNTING - STANDARDS - CANADA.

Zeff, Stephen A. Forging accounting principles in five countries . Champaign, Ill. , 1971, c1972. xvii, 332 p. ; LC Card 86-226472
HF5605 .Z44 1972

ACCOUNTING - STANDARDS - ENGLAND.

Zeff, Stephen A. Forging accounting principles in five countries . Champaign, Ill. , 1971, c1972. xvii, 332 p. ; LC Card 86-226472
HF5605 .Z44 1972

ACCOUNTING - STANDARDS - GREAT BRITAIN.

Westwick, C. A. Accounting for overseas operations /. Aldershot, Hants, England , Brookfield, Vt. , c1986. ix, 184 p. ; ISBN 0-566-02586-8 : LC Card 85-30582 DDC 657/.95 19
HF5686.I56 W47 1986 ***NYPL [JLG 86-202]***

Accounting standards harmonization .

(no. 2) Consolidation policies in OECD countries . Paris , 1987. 60, 63 p. ; ISBN 92-64-02876-5 : LC Card 87-168671 DDC 657/.3 19
HF5681.B2 C593 1987

ACCOUNTING - STANDARDS - HUNGARY.

Gábor, István. Az iparvállalatok könyvvitele, 1986 /. Budapest , 1986. 265 p. : ISBN 963-221-902-3 : LC Card 87-408573
HF5616.H9 G33 1986

ACCOUNTING - STANDARDS - MEXICO.

Zeff, Stephen A. Forging accounting principles in five countries . Champaign, Ill. , 1971, c1972. xvii, 332 p. ; LC Card 86-226472
HF5605 .Z44 1972

ACCOUNTING - STANDARDS - SCOTLAND.

Zeff, Stephen A. Forging accounting principles in five countries . Champaign, Ill. , 1971, c1972. xvii, 332 p. ; LC Card 86-226472
HF5605 .Z44 1972

ACCOUNTING - STANDARDS - UNITED STATES.

American Institute of Certified Public Accountants. Private Companies Practice Section. Peer review manual /. New York, N.Y. (1121 Ave. of the Americas, New York 10036-8775) , 1986. 2 v. in 1 : LC Card 86-217293 DDC 657/.833 19
HF5616.U5 A585 1986a

American Institute of Certified Public Accountants. SEC Practice Section. Peer review manual . New York, NY (1211 Ave. of the Americas, New York 10036-8775) , 1986- 1 v. (loose-leaf) : LC Card 87-108519 DDC 657/.833 19
HF5616.U5 A585 1986b

American Institute of Certified Public Accountants. Special Committee on Standards of Professional Conduct for Certified Public Accountants. Restructuring professional standards to achieve professional excellence in a changing environment . New York, N.Y. (1211 Ave. of the Americas, New York 10036-8775) , c1986. vi, 66 p. : LC Card 86-211085 DDC 657/.0218 19
HF5616.U5 A585 1986

Jarnagin, Bill D. Financial accounting standards . Chicago, Ill. (4025 W. Peterson Ave., Chicago 60646) , 1986. xv, 1253 p. : LC Card 87-116311 DDC 657/.0218 19
HF5616.U5 B66 1986

Miller, Paul B. W. The FASB . Homewood, Ill. , 1986. xvi, 145 p. : ISBN 0-256-03520-2 LC Card 85-82340 ***NYPL [JLE 87-872]***

Other comprehensive bases of accounting /. New York, N.Y. (1211 Ave. of the Americas, New York 10036-8775) , c1986. vii, 52 p. ; LC Card 86-206776 DDC 657/.0218 19
HF5616.U5 O88 1986

Plan to restructure professional standards. New York, N.Y. (1211 Ave. of the Americas, New York 10036-8775) , c1987. xii, 68 p. ; LC Card 87-160205 DDC 657/.0218 19
HF5616.U5 P53 1987

Report on the activities of the Special Investigations Committee of the SEC Practice Section of the AICPA Division for CPA Firms . New York, N.Y. (1211 Ave. of the Americas, New York 10036-8775) , c1986. iii, 6 p. ; LC Card 86-209679 DDC 657/.0218 19
HF5657 .R46 1986

Zeff, Stephen A. Forging accounting principles in five countries . Champaign, Ill. , 1971, c1972. xvii, 332 p. ; LC Card 86-226472
HF5605 .Z44 1972

ACCOUNTING - STANDARDS - UNITED STATES - PUBLIC OPINION.

A Study of the attitudes toward and an assessment of the Financial Accounting Standards Board /. Stamford, CT , 1985. x, 141 p. : LC Card 86-230871 DDC 657/.0218 19
HF5616.U5 S78 1985

ACCOUNTING - STUDY AND TEACHING (CONTINUING EDUCATION) - UNITED STATES.

Plan to restructure professional standards. New York, N.Y. (1211 Ave. of the Americas, New York 10036-8775) , c1987. xii, 68 p. ; LC Card 87-160205 DDC 657/.0218 19
HF5616.U5 P53 1987

ACCOUNTING - STUDY AND TEACHING (GRADUATE) - UNITED STATES.

McGee, Robert W. A model program for schools of professional accountancy /. Lanham, MD , c1987. xiii, 192 p. ; ISBN 0-8191-6094-6 (alk. paper) : LC Card 86-28226 DDC 657/.07/1173 19
HF5630 .M39 1987

Accounting, systems and procedures : basic course / David H. Weaver ... [et al.].5th ed. New York : Gregg Division, McGraw-Hill, c1988. xv, 288 p. : col. ill. ; 24 cm. (McGraw-Hill accounting 10/12 series) Includes index. ISBN 0-07-069357-9 (pbk.) LC Card 87-21936 DDC 657 19

1. Accounting. I. Weaver, David H., 1935-. II. Series.
HF5635 .A222 1988b

Accounting, systems and procedures / David H. Weaver ... [et al.]. 5th ed. New York : Gregg Division, McGraw-Hill, c1988. p. cm. (McGraw-Hill accounting 10/12 series) ISBN 0-07-069356-0 LC Card 87-17234 DDC 657 19

1. Accounting. I. Weaver, David H., 1935-. II. Series.
HF5635 .A222 1988

ACCOUNTING - TANZANIA - EXAMINATIONS.

Bodi ya Taifa ya Wahasibu na Wakaguzi Hesabu Tanzania. The National accountancy examination scheme . Dar es Salaam [1983] xxviii leaves, 269 p. ; LC Card 87-118290
HF5616.T34 B63 1983

ACCOUNTING - TANZANIA - EXAMINATIONS - EVALUATION.

Bodi ya Taifa ya Wahasibu na Wakaguzi Hesabu Tanzania. The National accountancy examination scheme . Dar es Salaam [1985] xxiii leaves, 275 p. ; LC Card 86-980376 DDC 657/.09678 19
HF1176.T34 B64 1985

ACCOUNTING - TANZANIA - EXAMINATIONS - STATISTICS.
Bodi ya Taifa ya Wahasibu na Wakaguzi Hesabu Tanzania. The National accountancy examination scheme . Dar es Salaam , 1985. ii, 41 leaves ; LC Card 86-980364
HF5616.T34 B63 1985

Accounting, the basis for business decisions /. Meigs, Walter B. New York , c1987. xxiii, 1059, 14 p. : ISBN 0-07-041640-0 : LC Card 86-21104 DDC 657 19
HF5635 .M49 1987

Accounting theory and policy : a reader / edited by Robert Bloom, Pieter T. Elgers.2nd ed. San Diego : Harcourt Brace Jovanovich, c1987. xi, 654 p. : ill. ; 24 cm. Includes bibliographies. ISBN 0-15-500478-6 (pbk.) LC Card 86-81620 DDC 657 19
1. Accounting. I. Bloom, Robert. II. Elgers, Pieter T.
HF5629 .A26 1987

Accounting theory and practice /. Francisco, Albert K. Belmont, CA , c1987. 1 v. (various pagings) : ISBN 0-932276-74-1 (pbk.) LC Card 87-62077 DDC 657/.076 19
HF5661 .F68 1987

Accounting thought and practice through the years.
Hawawini, Gabriel A. Mandatory financial information and capital market equilibrium in Belgium /. New York , 1987. 271 p. : ISBN 0-8240-7852-7 (alk. paper) : LC Card 87-54 DDC 332.63/222/09493 19
HG5553 .H39 1987

A History of Cooper Brothers & Co., 1854-1954. New York , 1986, c1954. xi, 116 p., [13] leaves of plates : ISBN 0-8240-7881-0 (alk. paper) : LC Card 86-25720 DDC 338.7/61657/0941 19
HF5616.G73 C665 1986

Sheldahl, Terry K. Beta Alpha Psi, from Omega to Zeta Omega . New York , 19. xxiii, 851 p., [22] p. of plates : ISBN 0-8240-7855-1 (alk. paper) : LC Card 86-31800 DDC 657/.06/073 19
HF5601.B443 S54 1986

Stewart, James C. (James Cathcart) Pioneers of a profession . New York , 1986, c1977. xii, 181 p., [2] leaves of plates : ISBN 0-8240-7888-8 : LC Card 86-25636 DDC 657/.092/2 B 19
HF5604 .S73 1986

ACCOUNTING - UNITED STATES.
Behrenfeld, William H. Accountant's business manual /. New York, N.Y. , c1987- 1 v. (loose-leaf) ; ISBN 0-87051-000-2 (loose-leaf) : LC Card 87-992 DDC 657 19
HF5616.U5 B38 1987

The Fourth company accounts directive of 1978 and the accounting systems of the Federal Republic of Germany, France, Italy, the United Kingdom, the United States, and Japan. Luxembourg , Washington, DC , 1986. 164, [47] p. ; ISBN 92-825-6454-1 (pbk.) : LC Card 87-134287 DDC 657 19
HF5611 .F686 1986

Hanisch, Bärbel, 1957- Die Ergebnisrechnung nach dem Bilanzrichtlinie-Gesetzentwurf im internationalen Vergleich (BRD, Japan, USA) /. Frankfurt am Main , New York , c1984. 286 p. : ISBN 3-8204-8559-7 : LC Card 85-164345
HF5616.G3 H35 1984

McNairn, William N. The smart attorney's guide to accounting documents for discovery and evidence /. Redondo Beach, Calif. , 1987. x, 123 p. : ISBN 0-932621-02-3 (pbk.) LC Card 86-62954 DDC 657/.024344 19
HF5616.U5 M346 1987

Wagner, Nancy A. Eric Louis Kohler in the accounting profession /. Atlanta, Ga. , 1987. vi, 210 p. ; ISBN 0-88406-196-5 (pbk.) : LC Card 86-25633 DDC 657/.092/4 19
HF5604.5.K64 W34 1987

Weinstein, Grace W. The bottom line . New York , c1987. 233 p. ; ISBN 0-453-00563-2 LC Card 87-11228 DDC 657 19
HF5616.U5 W44 1987

ACCOUNTING - UNITED STATES - HISTORY.
Previts, Gary John. John Raymond Wildman . University, Ala. , 1978. viii, 84 p. ; LC Card 86-224716
HF5604.5.W55 P74 1978

ACCOUNTING - UNITED STATES - QUALITY CONTROL.
American Institute of Certified Public Accountants. Private Companies Practice Section. Peer review manual /. New York, N.Y. (1121 Ave. of the Americas, New York 10036-8775) , 1986. 2 v. in 1 : LC Card 86-217293 DDC 657/.833 19
HF5616.U5 A585 1986a

American Institute of Certified Public Accountants. SEC Practice Section. Peer review manual . New York, NY (1211 Ave. of the Americas, New York 10036-8775) , 1986- 1 v. (loose-leaf) : LC Card 87-108519 DDC 657/.833 19
HF5616.U5 A585 1986b

Report on the activities of the Special Investigations Committee of the SEC Practice Section of the AICPA Division for CPA Firms . New York, N.Y. (1211 Ave. of the Americas, New York 10036-8775) , c1986. iii, 6 p. ; LC Card 86-209679 DDC 657/.0218 19
HF5657 .R46 1986

ACCOUNTING - UNITED STATES - SOCIETIES, ETC. - HISTORY.
Sheldahl, Terry K. Beta Alpha Psi, from Omega to Zeta Omega . New York , 19. xxiii, 851 p., [22] p. of plates : ISBN 0-8240-7855-1 (alk. paper) : LC Card 86-31800 DDC 657/.06/073 19
HF5601.B443 S54 1986

ACCOUNTING - VOCATIONAL GUIDANCE.
Half, Robert. [Success guide for accountants.] Robert Half's success guide for accountants /. New York , c1987. x, 167 p. ; ISBN 0-07-172107-X LC Card 87-16430 DDC 657/.023/72 19
HF5657 .H34 1987

ACCOUNTING - WALES - HISTORY - 18TH CENTURY.
Jones, Haydn. Accounting, costing, and cost estimation . Cardiff , 1985. ix, 285 p. ; ISBN 0-7083-0882-1 : LC Card 85-172570 DDC 657/.09429 19
HF5616.G72 W35 1985
NYPL [JLD 86-2817]

ACCOUNTING - WALES - HISTORY - 19TH CENTURY.
Jones, Haydn. Accounting, costing, and cost estimation . Cardiff , 1985. ix, 285 p. ; ISBN 0-7083-0882-1 : LC Card 85-172570 DDC 657/.09429 19
HF5616.G72 W35 1985
NYPL [JLD 86-2817]

Accounting with one-two-three. Greenfield, W. M. Accounting with 1-2-3 /. Englewood Cliffs, N.J. , 1987. p. cm. ISBN 0-13-001686-1 LC Card 87-12485 DDC 657/.028/55369 19
HF5679 .G737 1987

Accounting with 1-2-3 /. Greenfield, W. M. Englewood Cliffs, N.J. , 1987. p. cm. ISBN 0-13-001686-1 LC Card 87-12485 DDC 657/.028/55369 19
HF5679 .G737 1987

ACCOUNTS, COLLECTING OF. see **COLLECTING OF ACCOUNTS.**

Accounts receivable and inventory lending . Robinson, David Alexander, 1909- Boston , 1987. xii, 299 p. : ISBN 0-87267-104-6 LC Card 86-32252 DDC 332.1/753/068 19
HG3752.3 .R63 1987

ACCOUNTS RECEIVABLE AS COLLATERAL. see **ACCOUNTS RECEIVABLE LOANS.**

ACCOUNTS RECEIVABLE FINANCING. see **ACCOUNTS RECEIVABLE LOANS.**

ACCOUNTS RECEIVABLE LENDING. see **ACCOUNTS RECEIVABLE LOANS.**

ACCOUNTS RECEIVABLE LOANS.
Robinson, David Alexander, 1909- Accounts receivable and inventory lending . Boston , 1987. xii, 299 p. : ISBN 0-87267-104-6 LC Card 86-32252 DDC 332.1/753/068 19
HG3752.3 .R63 1987

Walia, Tirlochan S. Credit policy of the firm and issues in cost of financing accounts receivable . Lake Success, N.Y. (3000 Marcus Ave., Lake Success 11042) , c1986. [16] p. : LC Card 86-212977 DDC 658.1/5244 19
HG3752.3 .W35 1986

ACCOUNTS RECEIVABLE - MANAGEMENT.
Bukics, Rosie L. The handbook of credit and accounts receivable management /. Chicago, Ill. , c1987. xi, 252 p. : ISBN 0-917253-67-1 : LC Card 87-7008 DDC 658.8/8 19
HG3751 .B85 1987

ACCUMULATION, CAPITAL. see **SAVING AND INVESTMENT.**

Accumulation, employment, and labour aristocracy . Ranadive, K. R. Bombay [1982] 55 p. ; LC Card 83-903051 DDC 305.5/62/0954 19
HD8686.5 .R325 1982 ***NYPL [JLF 87-500]***

Aceituno, Gerardo. Arroyo, Gonzalo. Agricultura y alimentos en América Latina . México, D.F. , 1985. 267 p. ; ISBN 968-8373-33-8 LC Card 86-208283
HD9014.L32 A77 1985

Acevedo Conde, María Luisa. Pobreza y riqueza en 378 municipios de México / María Luisa Acevedo. 1a ed. México, D.F. : Centro de Ecodesarrollo, 1984. 281 p. : ill., maps ; 23 cm. Bibliography: p. 277-281. LC Card 86-219445
1. Rural poor - Mexico. 2. Mexico - Rural conditions. 3. Mexico - Economic conditions - 1970- - Regional disparities. 4. Agriculture - Economic aspects - Mexico. 5. Rural development - Mexico. I. Title.
HC140.P6 A25 1984

ACH marketing handbook. [Washington, DC] (1901 L St., NW, Suite 640, Washington 20036) : National Automated Clearing House Association, [c1987] 123, [24] p. ; 28 cm. Cover title. LC Card 87-130512 DDC 332.1/028 19
1. Cash management - United States - Data processing. 2. Electronic funds transfer - United States. 3. Clearinghouse - United States - Data processing. I. National Automated Clearing House Association.
HG4028.C45 A28 1987

ACH receivers handbook. Washington, D.C. (1901 L St., N.W., Suite 640, Washington 20036) : National Automated Clearing House Association, c1986. 104 p. : ill. ; 23 cm. LC Card 87-112783 DDC 332.1/028 19
1. Clearinghouse - Data processing. 2. Electronic funds transfers. I. National Automated Clearing House Association.
HG2306 .A25 1986

Acharya, K. C. S., 1930- Food security system of India : evolution of the buffer stocking policy and its evaluation / K.C.S. Acharya. New Delhi : Concept, 1983. xviii, 285 p. : ill. ; 22 cm. Revision of the author's thesis (Ph. D.--Bhopal University, 1981) Errata slip inserted. Includes bibliographical references and index. LC Card 83-906857 DDC 338.1/9/54 19
1. Food supply - Government policy - India - Evaluation. 2. Food supply - Government policy - India - History. I. Title.
HD9016.I42 A63 1983 ***NYPL [JLD 87-652]***

Acharya, Rabi Narayan, 1960- Television in India : a sociological study of policies and perspectives / Rabi Narayan Acharya.1st ed. Delhi : Manas Publications, 1987. vi, 166 p. : map ; 23 cm. Bibliography: p. [155]-159. Includes index. ISBN 81-7049-015-4 : LC Card 87-900915 DDC 384.55/0954 19
1. Television - India. I. Title.
HE8700.9.I5 A24 1987

Acharya, Radheshyam. Malla, B. C. An evaluation of development activities within Sixth Plan period in Bajhang District /. Kathmandu , 1985 [i.e. 1986] 76, [3] p. : LC Card 86-903487 DDC 338.9549/6 19
HC425.Z7 B355 1986

Acharya, Rajeshwar. Basic needs delivery system in Birendranagar, Surkhet /. Kathmandu , 1985. 143, [23], iii p. (some folded) ; LC Card 86-903561 DDC 338.9549/6 19
HF5415.12.N35 B36 1985

Acharya, Shankar N.
Aspects of the black economy in India. Kabra, Kamal Nayan. Black money : comment on

the NIPFP report on Aspects of black economy in India / K.N. Kabra, N.S. Jagannathan. New Delhi , 1985. 47 p. ; LC Card 87-900898 DDC 381 19
HJ2348.5 .K32 1985

Achegas à história do rodoviarismo no Brasil /. Oliveira, Maria Chambarelli de. Rio de Janeiro-RJ , c1986. 137 p., [1] leaf of plates : LC Card 86-232581
HE359.B7 O45 1986

ACHIEVEMENT TESTS - TANZANIA - STATISTICS.
Bodi ya Taifa ya Wahasibu na Wakaguzi Hesabu Tanzania. The National accountancy examination scheme . Dar es Salaam [1985] xxiii leaves, 275 p. ; LC Card 86-980376 DDC 657/.09678 19
HF1176.T34 B64 1985

Achieving change . Lupton, Tom. Aldershots, Hants, England , Brookfield, Vt., U. S.A. , c1987. xv, 86 p. : ISBN 0-566-02526-4 : LC Card 87-17665 DDC 658.4/06 19
HD58.9 .L86 1987

Achieving quality in financial service organizations . Hessick, Michael H. New York , c1988. p. cm. ISBN 0-89930-231-9 (lib. bdg. : alk. paper) LC Card 87-24937 DDC 332.1/2/0688 19
HG181 .H44 1988

Achieving results from training . Brinkerhoff, Robert O. San Francisco , 1987. xx, 248 p. ; ISBN 1-555-42044-3 (alk. paper) LC Card 86-46331 DDC 658.3/12404 19
HF5549.5.T7 B65 1987

Achieving strategic goals through executive development /. Nilsson, William P. Reading, Mass. , c1987. xv, 266 p. : ISBN 0-201-12751-2 : LC Card 86-32201 DDC 658.4/012 19
HD38.2 .N54 1987

Achilli, Michele. Il Sistema dei trasporti nello sviluppo della cooperazione economica internazionale . Milano, Italy , c1985. 341 p. ; LC Card 85-218403
HE2449 .S57 1985

Achío Tacsan, Mayra. Azúcar y política en Costa Rica / Mayra Achio, Ana C. Escalante. San José : Editorial Costa Rica, c1985. 172 p. : ill. ; 21 cm. Bibliography: p. 159-166. ISBN 997-7231-67-2 LC Card 86-209103
1. Sugar trade - Costa Rica. 2. Sugar trade - Government policy - Costa Rica. I. Escalante Herrera, Ana Cecilia. II. Title.
HD9114.C82 A24 1985

Achleitner, Paul M. Sozio-politische Strategien multinationaler Unternehmungen : ein Ansatz gezielten Umweltmanagements / Paul M. Achleitner. Bern : P. Haupt, c1985. ii, 334 p. : ill. ; 23 cm. (Veröffentlichungen der Hochschule St. Gallen für Wirtschafts- und Sozialwissenschaften. Schriftenreihe Betriebswirtschaft . Bd. 13) German and English. Bibliography: p. 243-255. ISBN 3-258-03490-7 : LC Card 85-208760
1. International business enterprises - Management. 2. Environmental policy. I. Title. II. Series.
HD62.4 .A24 1985

Achminow, Herman F., 1921- Am grossen Krieg "vorbeischleichen"? : zur Friedensstrategie des Konservatismus / Herman F. Achminow. Bonn : Europrisma-Verlag, c1983. 304 p. ; 21 cm. Includes bibliographical references and index. ISBN 3-923920-00-8 LC Card 84-150915 DDC 355/.03304 19
1. World politics - 1975-1985. 2. Conservatism. 3. Europe - Defenses. I. Title.
UA646 .A38 1983 ***NYPL [JFD 87-1743]***

Achten, Udo, 1943-
Arbeitskampf um Arbeitszeit . Marburg , c1985. 218 p. : ISBN 3-921630-52-5 LC Card 86-160526
HD5378 .A73 1985

Mein Vaterland ist international . Oberhausen , 1986. 331 p. : ISBN 3-921541-62-X LC Card 86-224091
HD7791 .M45 1986

Achtzig Jahre kritischer Bürger im 20. Jahrhundert . Wittkamp, Heinrich, 1903- Mannheim , c1986. 232 p., [16] p. of plates : ISBN 3-87804-182-9 (Deut. Bibl.) LC Card 86-230657
HD6695.W58 A3 1986

Açıklamalı maliye ve vergi sözlüğü /. Akdoğan, Abdurrahman. [Ankara?] , Yenişehir, Ankara , 1986. 229 p. ; LC Card 87-968120
HJ129.T9 A43 1986

Ackerl, Isabella. Loewenfeld-Russ, Hans, 1873-1945. Im Kampf gegen den Hunger . München , 1986. xxiv, 381 p., [1] leaf of plates : ISBN 3-486-52451-8 LC Card 86-224948
HC270.F3 L64 1986

Ackerman, Susan Rose- see **Rose-Ackerman, Susan.**

Ackland, Len. Assessing the nuclear age . Chicago, Ill. , c1986. xvii, 382 p. ; ISBN 0-941682-07-2 LC Card 85-82511 DDC 355/.0217 19
U264 .A79 1986 ***NYPL [JLE 87-11]***

ACLO (Organization)
Estudio cultural y socio económico de Mojocoya--Redención Pampa. Estudio cultural socio económico, Mojocoya y Redención Pampa. Sucre, Bolivia , 1979. 266 p. : LC Card 83-204567
HC183.M65 E77 1979

Estudio de factibilidad para una cadena de silos intercomunales de papa . [Sucre, Bolivia] 1982. 178 p., [2] leaves of plates : LC Card 83-202593 DDC 338.1/6 19
HD9235.P82 B525 1982
NYPL [JLF 87-711]

"Estudio de participación campesina en la estructura y acción de ACLO" : 24 de septiembre al 6 de octubre 1979, Sucre, Potosí, Tarija / [DESAL-ACLO]. [Sucre, Bolivia] : ACLO, 1980. 94 leaves ; 29 cm. Binder's title: Participación campesina. "Bolivia-1980"--Cover. LC Card 83-203590
1. Peasantry - Bolivia - Political activity - Congresses. 2. ACLO (Organization) - Congresses. 3. Rural development - Bolivia - Congresses. I. Centro para el Desarrollo Económico y Social de América Latina. II. Title. III. Title: Participación campesina.
HD1531.B6 A24 1980

ACLO (ORGANIZATION) - CONGRESSES.
ACLO (Organization) "Estudio de participación campesina en la estructura y acción de ACLO" . [Sucre, Bolivia] , 1980. 94 leaves ; LC Card 83-203590
HD1531.B6 A24 1980

Acocella, Giovanni, 1932- Di là dalle rovine : i temi della rinascita nella cornice politica ed istituzionale del Mezzogiorno / Giovanni Acocella. Napoli : Guida, c1982. 172, [4] p. ; 23 cm. Bibliography: p. [173] ISBN 88-7042-185-6 : LC Card 82-181323 DDC 363.3/495 19
1. Disaster relief - Italy, Southern. 2. Earthquakes - Economic aspects - Italy, Southern. 3. Italy, Southern - Economic policy. 4. Italy, Southern - Social policy. I. Title.
HC307.S69 A36 1982 ***NYPL [JLD 86-485]***

Acomb, Betty L.
Below, Patrick J. The executive guide to strategic planning /. San Francisco, Calif. , c1987. xxiii, 136 p. : ISBN 1-555-42032-X (alk. paper) LC Card 86-27863 DDC 658.4/012 19
HD30.28 .B45 1987

Morrisey, George L. The executive guide to operational planning /. San Francisco , 1988. xxvii, 130 p. : ISBN 1-555-42064-8 (alk. paper) LC Card 87-45508 DDC 658.4/012 19
HD30.28 .M65 1988

Acordagoikoetxea, Jon Kepa. Cambio cultural e imagen del hombre /. Bilbao, España , c1984. 248 p. ; ISBN 84-271-1384-6 LC Card 85-234026
CB245 .C29 1984 ***NYPL [JFD 86-6394]***

Os acordos SENAI/empresa . Silva, Angela Inês Gandra e. Rio de Janeiro-RJ-Brasil , 1985. xvii, 97 p. ; LC Card 86-176735
HD5715.5.B68 S55 1985

Acosta, Antonio. Mercado, Thomas de, d. 1575. [Tratos y contratos de mercaderes. Selections.] La economia en la Andalucia del descubrimiento /. Sevilla [1985?] 276 p. ; ISBN 84-7587-047-3 LC Card 86-151225
HF1003 .M525 1985

Acosta M., Amylkar (Acosta Medina), 1950- [Selections. 1986]
Escritos, 1978-1986 / Amylkar Acosta M. 1a ed. Medellín, Colombia : Editorial Lealon, 1986. 201 p. ; 23 cm. Cover title: Escritos, 1978-1985. Bibliography: p. 149. LC Card 87-404338 DDC 330.9861/0632 19
1. Colombia - Economic conditions - 1970-. 2. Colombia - Social conditions. 3. La Guajira, Colombia (Dept.) - Economic conditions. 4. Coal trade - Colombia - Ejón Hill. I. Title. II. Title: Escritos, 1978-1985.
HC197 .A5562 1986

Acquaviva, Mike.
International trade [microform] . Frederick, MD , 1987. microfilm reel ISBN 0-89093-551-3 (microfilm) : LC Card 87-6240 DDC 382 19
HF1008

Multinational corporations, OPEC, cartels, foreign investment, and technology transfer [microform] . Frederick, MD , 1987. microfilm reel ISBN 0-89093-552-1 (microfilm) : LC Card 87-6249 DDC 338.8 19
HD2755.5

Acquiring, enhancing, replacing apparel systems : a nontechnical approach / prepared by the Management Systems Committee, American Apparel Manufacturers Association. Arlington, VA (2500 Wilson Blvd., Suite 301, Arlington 22201) : The Committee, 1986. iii, 28 p. : ill. ; 28 cm. LC Card 87-107487 DDC 687/.028/5 19
1. Clothing trade - Management - Data processing - Equipment and supplies. I. American Apparel Manufacturers Association. Management Systems Committee.
HD9940.A2 A26 1986

Acquisitions, mergers, sales, buyouts, and takeovers . Scharf, Charles A. Englewood Cliffs, N.J. , c1985. xi, 452 p. : ISBN 0-13-003120-8 LC Card 85-6566 DDC 658.1/6/0973 19
HD2741 .S35 1985 ***NYPL [JLF 86-611]***

ACREAGE ALLOTMENTS - MALAWI.
Mills, J. C. (Joseph C.) Price responses of Malawi smallholder farmers--fast, slow or none? [microform] /. [Zomba] [1975] 42, [2] p. ; LC Card 80-980238 DDC 338.1/3/096897 19
HD1476.M33 M54 1975
NYPL [*ZT-1646 no.53]

ACS research report .
(no. 53) Yager, Francis P. Financial profile of cooperatives handling grain . [Washington, D.C.] [1986] vii, 24 p. : LC Card 86-601622 DDC 334/.6831/0973021 19
HD9034 .Y34 1986

Ács, Rudolf. A komplex meliorációs beruházások történeti áttekintése és gazdasági hatásának vizsgálata különböző agroökológiai tipusu gazdaságokban / Ács Rudolf, Horváth Imre. Budapest : Agrárgazdasági Kutató Intézet, 1986. 118 p. ; 29 cm. (Agrárgazdasági Kutató Intézet, 0209-5696 . 1986/4) Bibliography: p. 97-99. ISBN 963-491-237-0 LC Card 87-137972
1. Reclamation of land - Hungary. I. Horváth, Imre. II. Series: Agrárgazdasági Kutató Intézet (Series) , 1986/4. III. Title.
HD1940.5 .A65 1986

Ács, Zoltán J. The determinants of innovation in large and small firms / Zoltán J. Ács, David B. Audretsch. Berlin : Wissenschaftszentrum Berlin für Sozialforschung, [1986] 39 p. ; 30 cm. (Discussion papers, 0722-6748 . IIM/IP 86-18) "August 1986." Bibliography: p. 38-39. LC Card 87-156684 DDC 338.6/4 19
1. Technological innovations - Economic aspects - United States - Econometric models. 2. Industries, Size of - United States - Econometric models. I. Audretsch, David B. II. Series: Discussion papers (International Institute of Management. Industrial Policy) , IIM/IP 86-18. III. Title.
HC110.T4 A59 1986

Acsádi, György. Policy relevance of findings of the world fertility survey for developing countries / Department of International Economic and Social Affairs. New York : United Nations, 1986. vi, 160 p. ; 28 cm. Prepared by George T. Acsadi and Gwendolyn Johnson-Acsadi. Bibliography: p. 145-160. "ST/ESA/SER.R/59." LC Card 85-37681 DDC 304.6/32/091724 19
1. Fertility, Human - Developing countries. 2. World Fertility Survey. 3. Birth control - Developing countries. 4. Demographic surveys - Developing countries. 5. Developing countries - Population policy. I. Johnson-Acsadi, Gwendolyn. II. United Nations. Dept. of International Economic and Social Affairs. III. Title.
HB1108 .A28 1986

Acta Regiae Societatis Scientiarum et Litterarum Gothoburgensis. Humaniora, 0072-4823 .

(24) Attman, Artur, 1910- Swedish aspirations and the Russian market during the 17th century /. Göteborg , Atlantic Highlands, N.J. , c1985. 41 p. : ISBN 91-85252-35-2 (pbk.) LC Card 86-214014 DDC 382/.09485/047 19
HF3678.S58 A88 1985

(26) Attman, Artur, 1910- American bullion in the European world trade, 1600-1800 /. Göteborg , 1986. 115 p. ; ISBN 91-85252-38-7 (pbk.) LC Card 87-147250 DDC 382/.4242/0973 19
HG285.A45 A88 1986

Acta Salmanticensia. Científicos y literarios . (61) Charro Valls, José María. Sociedades de garantía recíproca . Salamanca, España , 1985. 73 p. ; ISBN 84-7481-349-2 LC Card 87-133330
HG5634.5 .C47 1985

Acta Universitatis Stockholmiensis. Stockholm studies in economic history .
(7) Köll, Anu-Mai. Tradition och reform i västra Södermanlands jordbruk, 1810-1890 . Stockholm , 1983. 252 p. : ISBN 91-22-00633-8 LC Card 84-114628
HD2020.S63 K65 1983

Acta Universitatis Stockholmiensis. Stockholm studies in economic history, 0346-8305.
Bjessmo, Lars-Erik. Industrin i Södertälje 1920-1970 . Stockholm , 1987. 236 p. ; ISBN 91-7146-468-9 LC Card 87-151742
HC378.S7 B54 1987

Acta Universitatis Stockholmiensis. Stockholm studies in history, 0491-0842 .
(36) Horgby, Björn. Den disciplinerade arbetaren . Stockholm [1986] 322 p. : ISBN 91-22-00804-7 LC Card 87-105821
HC378.N67 H67 1986

Acta Universitatis Upsaliensis. Studia historica Upsaliensia .
(115) Kälvemark, Ann-Sofie, 1941- More children of better quality? . Uppsala , Stockholm , 1980. 160 p. : ISBN 91-554-1094-4 LC Card 81-114081
HB3617 .K34 1980

Acta Universitatis Upsaliensis. Studia oeconomica Upsaliensia, 0585-539X .
(10) Atsé, David. Commodity futures trading and international market stabilization /. Uppsala , Stockholm, Sweden , 1986. 151 p. : ISBN 91-554-1961-5 (pbk.) LC Card 87-148645 DDC 330 s 332.64/42 19
HB51 .S7 no. 10 HG6046

(9) Agell, Jonas. The effects of capital taxation . Uppsala , Stockholm, Sweden , 1986. 123 p. : ISBN 91-554-1938-0 (pbk.) LC Card 87-100538 DDC 330 s 336.2/009481 19
HB51 .S7 no. 9 HJ2838

Acta Universitatis Upsaliensis. Uppsala studies in economic history, 0346-6493 .
(25) Magnusson, Lars, 1941- Kapitalbildning i Sverige 1750-1860 . Uppsala , Stockholm , 1983. 95 p. ; ISBN 91-554-1443-5 LC Card 83-228044
HC374 .M34 1983

(26) Larsson, Mats, 1953- Arbete och lön vid Bredsjö bruk . Uppsala , Stockholm , 1986. 233 p. : ISBN 91-554-1822-8 LC Card 86-212849
HD4966.I52 S845 1986

Acta Universitatis Wratislaviensis. Prawo .
(113) Samborska-Boć, Elżbieta. Układy powiązań w kooperacji przemysłowej /. Wrocław , 1982. 103 p. ; LC Card 83-109302
HD3517.7.A4 S28 1982

Actes du Colloque Les Périphéries urbaines . Colloque Les Périphéries urbaines (1984 : Angers, France) Caen , c1985. 270 p. : ISBN 2-905461-03-9 : LC Card 86-173712
HB2263 .C65 1984

Actes du Colloque "Poitiers 1981" . Colloque "Poitiers 1981" (1981 : Université de Poitiers) Poitiers [France] [1983] 472 p. : LC Card 84-119227
HB3594.P65 C65 1981

Actes du Gerpisa .
(no 2) Travail et automatisation dans l'industrie automobile /. [France] , Grenoble , 1986. 141 p. ; ISBN 2-86561-070-5 : LC Card 87-151670
HD9710.F72 T72 1986

Action culturelle du bassin houiller lorrain (France) Glück auf! . Paris [1986] 117 p. : ISBN 2-86738-115-0 : LC Card 86-178958
HD8039.M6152 F84 1986

Action-planning workshops for development management . Silverman, Jerry M. Washington, D.C., U. S.A. , 1986. ix, 74 p. : ISBN 0-8213-0864-5 (pbk.) LC Card 86-28215 DDC 338.9/0068 19
HC59.7 .S4656 1986

Action Society Trust. Parris, Henry. Public enterprise in Western Europe /. London , Wolfeboro, N.H. , c1987. viii, 197 p. : ISBN 0-7099-0548-3 : LC Card 86-24133 DDC 338.7/4/094 19
HD4138 .P37 1987 ***NYPL [JLD 87-757]***

Action taken by Government on the recommendations contained in the sixteenth report of the Committee on Public Undertakings (Sixth Lok Sabha) on Jute Corporation of India Ltd. . India. Parliament. Committee on Public Undertakings. New Delhi , 1979. vii, 82 p. ; LC Card 79-906770
HD9156.J8 I355 1979

ACTIONS AND DEFENSES - UNITED STATES.
Kohn, Stephen M. (Stephen Martin) Protecting environmental & nuclear whistleblowers . Washington, D.C. , c1985. xiii, 346 p. : ISBN 0-9615323-0-0 (pbk.) LC Card 85-61844 DDC 342.73/0684 347.302684 19
KF5342 .K64 1985 ***NYPL [JLE 86-1787]***

Actions thématiques programmées. A. T. P.: Sciences humaines.
(no 2954) Lacour, Claude. Croissance urbaine . Paris , 1981. 219 p. : ISBN 2-222-02928-7 (pbk.) : LC Card 82-153821 DDC 388.4/068 19
HE4764 .L3 1981 ***NYPL [JLG 86-56]***

Actividad económica del hombre del suburbio /. Maldonado Calderón, Arturo. Machala, Ecuador , 1985. 168 p., [3] folded leaves of plates : LC Card 87-110202 DDC 330.9866/31 19
HC203.M33 M35 1985

Activities of the Institute and Summary of the 3rd yearbook, 1960-1961. Magyar Tudományos Akadémia. Közgazdaságtudományi Intézet. Budapest , 1962. 61 p. ; LC Card 87-146537
HB74.9.H9 M35 1962

Actuarial mathematics / by Newton L. Bowers, Jr. ... [et al.]. 1st ed. Itasca, Ill. : Society of Actuaries, 1986. xxiii, 624 p. ; 29 cm. Includes bibliographies and index. ISBN 0-938959-10-7 LC Card 86-61747 DDC 368/.01 19
1. Insurance - Mathematics. I. Bowers, Newton L., 1933-. II. Society of Actuaries.
HG8781 .A26 1986

Actuarial projections for the old-age, survivors, and disability insurance program of social security in the United States of America /. Andrews, George H., 1932- Itasca, Ill., U. S.A. , c1987. viii, 188 p. : LC Card 87-1101 DDC 368.4/301/0973 19
HC106.8 .A56 1987

ACTUARIAL SCIENCE. see **INSURANCE, LIFE; INSURANCE - MATHEMATICS; INSURANCE, LIFE - MATHEMATICS.**

Actuels (Sycomore (Firm))
Bisilliat, Jeanne. Femmes du tiers-monde . Paris , c1983. 122 p. : ISBN 2-86262-201-X ***NYPL [JLD 87-456]***

Schwab, Laurent. Le Japon . [Paris] , c1984. 115 p. : ISBN 2-86262-221-4 (pbk.) : LC Card 84-164308 DDC 330.952/048 19
HC462.9 .S338 1984 ***NYPL [JLD 86-3612]***

O açúcar num documento colonial /. Pôrto, Josè da Costa, 1909- Recife , 1984. 116 p. ; LC Card 87-102690
HD9114.B7 P448 1984

ACUERDO DE CARTAGENA.
Sirumbal, Luis Miguel. La crisis de la industria automotriz (1971-1982) /. Lima, Perú [1983] 54 p. : LC Card 84-123601 DDC 338.4/76292/0985 19
HD9710.P382 S57 1983 ***NYPL [JLD 86-365]***

El Acuerdo de Cartagena y el trato preferencial en favor de Bolivia y Ecuador. [Buenos Aires, Argentina] : Banco Interamericano de Desarrollo, Instituto para la Integración de América Latina, [1982] 148 leaves ; 29 cm. Includes bibliographical references. LC Card 86-202605 DDC 337.1/8 19
1. Andes region - Economic integration. 2. Bolivia - Commerce - Andes Region. 3. Andes Region - Commerce - Bolivia. 4. Ecuador - Commerce - Andes Region. 5. Andes Region - Commerce - Ecuador. I. Institute for Latin American Integration.
HC167.A5 A285 1982

Acuerdo de Integración Subregional. see **Acuerdo de Cartagena.**

Acuerdo Subregional Andino. see **Acuerdo de Cartagena.**

Acuerdos y documentos de la nueva política económica, 1986 / Müller & Machicado Asociados. [1a ed.]. [La Paz, Bolivia?] : Los Asociados, [1987] 134 p. ; 21 cm. (Serie Documentos) Cover title. LC Card 87-403664 DDC 338.984 19
1. Bolivia - Economic policy - Sources. 2. Bolivia - Economic conditions - 1982- - Sources. I. Muller y Machicado Asociados. II. Series: Serie Documentos (Muller y Machicado Asociados).
HC182 .A585 1987

A acumulação capitalista em Portugal . Ferreira, António Fonseca. Porto , 1977. 156 p. ; LC Card 85-194898
HF3696 .F47 1977

Acumulação capitalista, emprego e crise . Casimiro, Liana Maria Carleial de. São Paulo , 1986. 216 p. : LC Card 87-152202 DDC 331.12/0981/31 19
HD5755.F6 C37 1986

Acumulación agrícola y agroindustrial /. Molina Osegueda, Carlos Alberto. [San Salvador, El Salvador, C.A. , 1980] 187 p. : LC Card 86-174381
HD1827 .M65 1980

La acumulación originaria de capital agrario en Sonora ; Registro de los archivos del Estado de Sonora /. Radding, Cynthia. [Acumulación originaria de capital agrario en Sonora.] [Hermosillo, Sonora] , 1981. 90 p. : LC Card 82-118209
HD329.S6 R33 1981

Acumulación y crisis en la minería peruana, 1900-1977 /. Dore, Elizabeth. [Lima] [1986] 168 p. : LC Card 86-235232
HD9506.P42 D66 1986

Acuña B., Olda M. Denton L., Carlos F. Población, fecundidad y desarrollo en Costa Rica, 1950-1970 /. [Heredia, Costa Rica] , 1984. iv, 150 p. : LC Card 86-117583 DDC 304.6/097286 19
HB3531 .D44 1984 ***NYPL [JLF 87-144]***

Acuña, Miguel. Boom en el agro chileno? /. Santiago de Chile , 1985. 123 p. ; LC Card 87-401452 DDC 338.1/0983 19
HD1877 .B66 1985

Acuña Ortega, Víctor H.
El desarrollo económico y social de Costa Rica : de la colonia a la crisis de 1930 / Víctor H. Acuña Ortega, Iván Molina Jiménez.1a ed. [San José, Costa Rica] : Alma Mater, 1986. vi, 135 p. ; 17 cm. Includes bibliographical references. ISBN 997-7440-08-5 LC Card 87-100815
1. Costa Rica - Economic conditions. 2. Costa Rica - Social conditions. I. Molina Jiménez, Iván. II. Title.
HC143 .A54 1986

Los orígenes de la clase obrera en Costa Rica : las huelgas de 1920 por la jornada de ocho horas / Víctor H. Acuña Ortega. San José : Centro Nacional de Acción Pastoral : Centro de Estudios para la Acción Social, [1986] 85 p. : ill., facsims. ; 22 cm. Bibliography: p. 85. LC Card 87-402904 DDC 331/.097286 19
1. Labor and laboring classes - Costa Rica - history. 2. Strikes and lockouts - Costa Rica - History. 3. Eight-hour movement - History. I. Title.
HD8136 .A28 1986

AD VALOREM TARIFF. see **TARIFF.**

ADA (COMPUTER PROGRAM LANGUAGE)
Ada military & commercial markets. Norwalk, Conn., U. S.A. (6 Prowitt St., Norwalk 06855) , c1986. vii, 196 leaves ; LC Card 87-400056 DDC 381/.45005133/0973 19
HD9696.C63 U51123 1986

Buhr, R. J. A. System design with Ada /. Englewood Cliffs, N.J. , c1984. xv, 256 p. : ISBN 0-13-881623-9 : LC Card 83-13673

DDC 001.64/2 19
QA76.73.A35 B83 1984
NYPL [JSE 86-1253]

Freedman, Roy S. Programming with APSE software tools /. Princeton, N.J. , c1984. viii, 253 p. : ISBN 0-89433-220-1 LC Card 84-20739 DDC 001.64/24 19
QA76.73.A35 F74 1984
NYPL [JSE 86-1512]

Gehani, Narain, 1947- UNIX Ada programming /. Englewood Cliffs, NJ , c1987. xix, 310 p. : ISBN 0-13-938325-5 LC Card 86-22547 DDC 005.4/465 19
QA76.73.A35 G437 1987
NYPL [JSE 87-568]

Ada military & commercial markets. Norwalk, Conn., U. S.A. (6 Prowitt St., Norwalk 06855) : International Resource Development Inc., c1986. vii, 196 leaves ; 28 cm. (Report / International Resource Development Inc. . #719) "December 1986." LC Card 87-400056 DDC 381/.45005133/0973 19
1. Computer software industry - United States. 2. Ada (Computer program language). 3. Market surveys - United States. I. International Resource Development, inc. II. Title: Ada military and commercial markets. III. Series: Report / International Resource Development Inc. , #719.
HD9696.C63 U51123 1986

Ada military and commercial markets. Ada military & commercial markets. Norwalk, Conn., U. S.A. (6 Prowitt St., Norwalk 06855) , c1986. vii, 196 leaves ; LC Card 87-400056 DDC 381/.45005133/0973 19
HD9696.C63 U51123 1986

ADAC.
Strassenverkehr 2000 : eine Studie des ADAC über die zukünftige Entwicklung des Strassenverkehrs und seiner sozio-ökonomischen Rahmenbedingungen / [Verfasser, R. Linde, H.-J. Vorholz, G. Weich]. München : Der Automobil-Club, [1979] 24 p. : ill. ; 30 cm. Cover title. LC Card 85-147077
1. Traffic engineering - Germany, West. 2. Traffic safety - Germany, West. 3. Transportation, Automotive - Germany, West. I. Linde, R. II. Vorholz, H.-J. III. Weich, Götz. IV. Title. V. Title: Strassenverkehr zweitausend.
HE363.G3 A33 1979

ADAC.
Grosse-Berndt, Gisela. Wirksamkeitsuntersuchung zum ADAC-Motorrad-Sicherheitstraining. Köln [1983] iii, 160, ii, 112, 27 p. : LC Card 84-147564
HE5614.5.G3 G75 1983

ADAC. Abteilung Verkehrstechnik.
Analyse von Unfällen motorisierter Zweiradbenutzer . [West Germany] [1976] 32 p. : LC Card 85-135424
HE5614.5.G3 A65 1976

Untersuchung der Unfälle auf Bundesautobahnen . [München?] [1976] 84 p. : LC Card 85-135444
HE5614.5.G3 U58 1976

Adagala, Kavetsa. Self-employed women in the peri-urban setting : petty traders in Nairobi / Kavetsa Adagala, Patricia Bifani. Nairobi : Derika Associates, 1985. ii, 99 leaves : ill. ; 29 cm. Cover title. Includes bibliographical references. LC Card 85-980984 DDC 331.4/8138118/0967625 19
1. Women merchants - Kenya - Nairobi. 2. Self-employed women - Kenya - Nairobi. I. Bifani, Patricia. II. Title.
HF3893.Z9 N343 1985

Adalékok a tartósitóipar hosszútávu fejlesztésének megalapozásához /. Lányfalvi, Sándor. Budapest , 1984. 115 p. ; ISBN 963-491-199-4 LC Card 86-199120
HD9326.H82 L36 1984

Adam, Jan, 1920- Employment and wage policies in Poland, Czechoslovakia, and Hungary since 1950 / Jan Adam. New York : St. Martin's Press, 1984. xix, 251 p. ; 23 cm. Includes index. Bibliography: p. 235-243. ISBN 0-312-24457-6 : LC Card 83-40125 DDC 331.12/042/0943 19
1. Manpower policy - Poland. 2. Manpower policy - Czechoslovakia. 3. Manpower policy - Hungary. 4. Wages - Government policy - Poland. 5. Wages - Government policy - Czechoslovakia. 6. Wages - Government policy - Hungary. I. Title.
HD5797.7.A6 A3 1984
NYPL [JLD 86-4389]

Adam, Martin, 1955- Kapitalstock und Nutzungsdauer : eine methodische Betrachtung zur Schätzung des Brutto-Anlagevermögens in der Bundesrepublik Deutschland / Martin Adam. Frankfurt am Main ; New York : P. Lang, c1985. v, 151 p. : ill. ; 21 cm. (Europäische Hochschulschriften. Reihe V, Volks- und Betriebswirtschaft, 0531-7339 . Bd. 626 = vol. 626 = vol. 626) Bibliography: p. 140-151. ISBN 3-8204-8860-X LC Card 85-202132 DDC 332/.0414/0943 19
1. Capital investments - Germany, West. 2. Capital. I. Series: Europäische Hochschulschriften. Reihe V, Volks- und Betriebswirtschaft , Bd. 626. II. Title.
HG4028.C4 A24 1985

Adam Smith Institute. London Conference on Taxes and Growth (1986) London Conference on Taxes and Growth . New York, NY [1986] 61 p. ; LC Card 87-404887 DDC 339.5/25 19
HJ2279 .L655 1986

The Adam theory of markets. Wilder, J. Welles. The Adam theory of markets, or, What matters is profit /. McLeansville, N.C. (P.O. Box 128, Mcleansville 27301) , c1987. 131 p. : LC Card 87-166037 DDC 332.64/4 19
HG4523 .W54 1987

The Adam theory of markets, or, What matters is profit /. Wilder, J. Welles. McLeansville, N.C. (P.O. Box 128, Mcleansville 27301) , c1987. 131 p. : LC Card 87-166037 DDC 332.64/4 19
HG4523 .W54 1987

Adamova, L. G. Gazovyĭ most . Sverdlovsk , 1985. 206 p. : LC Card 86-186324
HD9581.S653 S54 1985

Adams, Arthur G. Baxter, Raymond J., 1928- Railroad ferries of the Hudson . Woodcliff Lake, NJ , 1987. viii, 254 p. : ISBN 0-910389-01-2 : LC Card 87-22782 DDC 386/.2234/097473 19
HE5774. B39 1987

Adams, Charles F., 1945- Cook, Robert F., 1943- Public service employment . Kalamazoo, Mich. , 1985. xiii, 131 p. ; ISBN 0-88099-031-7 (pbk.) LC Card 85-22495 DDC 331.13/77/0973 19
HD5713.6.U54 C66 1985
NYPL [JLE 86-3877]

Adams, Charles, 1930- Fight, flight, fraud : the story of taxation / Charles Adams. Curaçao : Euro-Dutch Publishers, c1982. iv, 307 p. : ill. (some col.) ; 32 cm. Includes index. Bibliography: p. 294-298. LC Card 83-80155 DDC 336.2/009 19
1. Taxation - History. 2. Taxation - United States - History. I. Title.
HJ2250 .A32 1982 ***NYPL [JLG 86-104]***

Adams, Francis Gerard, 1929- The business forecasting revolution : nation, industry, firm / F. Gerard Adams. New York : Oxford University Press, 1986. xiii, 265 p. : ill. ; 22 cm. (Wharton executive library) Includes bibliographies and index. ISBN 0-19-503700-6 LC Card 85-18943 DDC 338.5/442 19
1. Business forecasting - Data processing. 2. Economic forecasting - Data processing. I. Title. II. Series.
HD30.27 .A33 1986 ***NYPL [JLD 86-2257]***

Adams, Frank T. Putting democracy to work : a practical guide for starting worker-owned businesses / by Frank T. Adams and Gary B. Hanses. Eugene, OR : Hulogos'i, 1987. p. cm. ISBN 0-938493-03-5 : LC Card 87-4246 DDC 658.1/147 19
1. Employee ownership. 2. Cooperation. I. Hansen, Gary B. II. Title.
HD5650 .A3 1987

Adams, James L.
The care and feeding of ideas : a guide to encouraging creativity / James L. Adams. Reading, Mass. : Addison-Wesley, 1986. xv, 223 p. : ill. ; 24 cm. Includes index. Spine title: The care & feeding of ideas. Bibliography: p. 212-218. ISBN 0-201-10160-2 : LC Card 86-10895 DDC 153.3/5 19
1. Creative thinking. 2. Change (Psychology). 3. Problem solving. I. Title. II. Title: Care & feeding of ideas.
BF408 .A3 1986 ***NYPL [JFE 87-1553]***

Conceptual blockbusting : a guide to better ideas / James L. Adams.3rd ed. Reading, Mass. : Addison-Wesley, c1986. xi, 161 p. : ill. ; 24 cm. Includes index. Bibliography: p. 154-161. ISBN 0-201-10149-1 LC Card 85-28722 DDC 153.4 19
1. Problem solving. 2. Creative thinking. I. Title.
BF441 .A28 1986 ***NYPL [JFE 86-4947]***

Adams, John B. Kaplan, Howard J. Scouts on stamps of the world /. [Hicksville, N.Y.] , c1986. 1 v. (loose-leaf) : LC Card 86-224816 DDC 769.56/3 19
HE6183.B63 K36 1986

Adams, John H. (John Hamilton), 1936- An Environmental agenda for the future /. Washington, D.C. , c1985. viii, 155 p. ; ISBN 0-933280-29-7 (pbk.) : LC Card 85-19760 DDC 304.2 19
TD171 .E56 1985 ***NYPL [JLE 86-2773]***

Adams, John R. Professional project management : a practical guide / John R. Adams, M. Dean Martin. Dayton, OH (1616 Mardon Dr., Dayton 45432-2634) : Universal Technology Corp., c1987. viii, 154 p. : ill. ; 24 cm. Bibliography: p. 147-154. LC Card 86-51558 DDC 658.4/04 19
1. Industrial project management. I. Martin, M. Dean. II. Title.
HD69.P75 A33 1987

Adams, John S., 1938- Housing America in the 1980s / John S. Adams. New York : Russell Sage Foundation, c1987. p. cm. (The Population of the United States in the 1980s) "For the National Committee for Research on the 1980 Census." Bibliography: p. Includes index. ISBN 0-87154-003-7 : LC Card 86-42950 DDC 363.5/0973 19
1. Housing - United States. I. Title. II. Series.
HD7293 .A625 1987

Adams, M. G. (Mike G.) Economic development in East and South-east Asia . Canberra , 1984. x, 237 p. : ISBN 0-644-02983-8 (pbk.) LC Card 86-673760
HC460.5 .E26x 1984

Adams, Richard H. Development and social change in rural Egypt / Richard H. Adams, Jr. 1st ed. Syracuse, N.Y. : Syracuse University Press, 1986. xii, 231 p. : ill. ; 24 cm. (Contemporary issues in the Middle East) Revision of the author's thesis (Ph. D.)--University of California, Berkeley, 1981. Includes index. Bibliography: p. 213-224. ISBN 0-8156-2362-3 (alk. paper) LC Card 85-30251 DDC 307.1/4/0962 19
1. Rural development - Egypt. 2. Local government - Egypt. 3. Peasantry - Egypt. I. Title.
HN786.Z9 C63 1986 ***NYPL [JLE 86-1999]***

Adams, Steve, 1948- Using Dollars and Sense on the IBM / Steve Adams. Indianapolis, Ind. : Que Corp., c1987. xviii, 439 p. : ill. ; 24 cm. Includes index. ISBN 0-88022-287-5 (pbk.) : LC Card 86-63981 DDC 332.024/0028/55369 19
1. Finance, Personal - Data processing. 2. Dollars and Sense (Computer program). I. Title.
HG179 .A34 1987

Adams, Walter, 1922 (Aug. 27)- The bigness complex : industry, labor, and government in the American economy / Walter Adams and James W. Brock. New York : Pantheon Books, 1986. xiii, 426 p. ; 24 cm. ISBN 0-394-54721-7 : LC Card 86-42624 DDC 338.6/44/0973 19
1. Big business - United States. 2. Industrial concentration - United States. 3. Industries, Size of - United States. 4. Efficiency, Industrial - United States. 5. Competition - United States. 6. Trade regulation - United States. I. Brock, James W. II. Title.
HD2785 .A68 1986 ***NYPL [JLE 87-1432]***

Adams, William James, 1947- French industrial policy /. Washington, D.C. , c1986. xii, 228 p. : ISBN 0-8157-0098-9 : LC Card 85-48203 DDC 338.944 19
HD3616.F82 F74 1986 ***NYPL [JLE 87-211]***

ADAPSO. ADAPSO guide to market research for the computer software and services industry. Arlington, Va. (1300 N. 17th St., Suite 300, Arlington 22209) , c1985. 71 p. ; LC Card 87-402047 DDC 005/.068/8 19
HD9696.C63 U511235 1985

ADAPSO guide to market research for the computer software and services industry. Arlington, Va. (1300 N. 17th St., Suite 300, Arlington 22209) : ADAPSO, c1985. 71 p. ; 28 cm. Cover title. Includes bibliographies. LC Card 87-402047 DDC 005/.068/8 19

1. Computer software industry - United States. 2. Computer service industry - United States. 3. Marketing research - United States. I. ADAPSO. II. Title: Guide to market research for the computer software and services industry.
HD9696.C63 U511235 1985

Adaptation and survival in Australian agriculture . Higgs, Peter J. (Peter John), 1959- Melbourne , New York , 1986. xxx, 320 p. : ISBN 0-19-554749-7 LC Card 87-133685 DDC 338.1/0994 19
HD2152 .H54 1986

ADAPTATION (BIOLOGY) - CONGRESSES. Proceedings of an international conference on genetic algorithms and their applications . [S.l. , 1985] 225 p. : *NYPL [JSF 87-413]*

Adaptation structurelle de l'économie française à la limitation de la consommation d'énergie /. Offant, Pierre. Dijon , c1984. 224, iii p. : ISBN 2-85975-026-6 LC Card 85-205959
HD9502.F72 O33 1984

The Adaptation to inflation / edited by Gerald D. Feldman ... [et al.] ; with contributions by Gerold Ambrosius ... [et al.] = Die Anpassung an die Inflation / herausgegeben von Gerald D. Feldman ... [el al.] ; mit Beiträgen von Gerold Ambrosius ... [et al.]. Berlin ; New York : W. de Gruyter, 1986. xvi, 512 p. : ill. ; 25 cm. (Beiträge zu Inflation und Wiederaufbau in Deutschland und Europa 1914-1924 . Bd. 8) Veröffentlichungen der Historischen Kommission zu Berlin ; Bd. 67 Includes bibliographical references. English and German. ISBN 0-89925-287-7 (U. S.) LC Card 86-29134 DDC 338.943 19
1. Germany - Economic policy - 1888-1918. 2. Germany - Economic policy - 1918-1933. 3. Monetary policy - Germany - History - 20th century. 4. Inflation (Finance) - Germany - History - 20th century. I. Feldman, Gerald D. II. Title: Anpassung an die Inflation. III. Series. IV. Series: Veröffentlichungen der Historischen Kommission zu Berlin beim Friedrich-Meinecke-Institut der Freien Universität Berlin , Bd. 67.
HC286.2 .A62 1986

ADAPTATIONS, TELEVISION. see **TELEVISION ADAPTATIONS.**

Adapting to change : labour market adjustment in Canada / W. Craig Riddell, research coordinator. Toronto [Ont.] ; Buffalo : University of Toronto Press, c1986. xv, 221 p. ; 23 cm. (The Collected research studies, 0829-2396 . vol. 18) "Published by the University of Toronto Press in cooperation with the Royal Commission on the Economic Union and Development Prospects for Canada and the Canadian Government Publishing Centre, Supply and Services Canada." Includes bibliographies. CONTENTS. - Adapting to change / W. Craig Riddell -- Formal education and the adaptability of workers and managers to technological change / Steven Globerman -- The impact of technological change on employment, wages, and the distribution of skills / Robert C. Allen -- Alternative mechanisms for dealing with permanent layoffs, dismissals, and closings / Morley Gunderson -- Training and skill development / James B. Davies. ISBN 0-8020-7260-7 (pbk.) LC Card 86-673029 DDC 331.12/0971 19
1. Labor policy - Canada. 2. Labor supply - Canada. 3. Labor supply - Canada - Effect of technological innovations on. I. Riddell, W. Craig (William Craig), 1946-. II. Royal Commission on the Economic Union and Development Prospects for Canada.
HD5728 .A596 1986 *NYPL [JLD 87-1967]*

Adaptive Verfahren der Input-Output Analyse /. Lorenzen, Gunter. Göttingen , c1985. vii, 156 p. ; ISBN 3-525-11288-2 LC Card 85-221821
HB142 .L67 1985
NYPL [JLL 76-449 Heft 17]

Adatgyűjtemény az állami iparvállalatoknál foglalkoztatottak létszám-, bér- és kereseti arányairól / [összeállította a KSH Iparstatisztikai Főosztály Módszertani és Elemzési Osztálya]. Budapest : Központi Statisztikai Hivatal, 1986. 148 p. ; 29 cm. All tables. LC Card 87-407679
1. Labor supply - Hungary - Statistics. 2. Wages - Hungary - Statistics. I. Hungary. Központi Statisztikai Hivatal. Iparstatisztikai Főosztály. Módszertani és Elemzési Osztály.
HD5772.5.A6 A34 1986

Add-on boards & peripherals for the IBM PC & compatibles. Norwalk, Conn., U. S.A. (6 Prowitt St., Norwalk 06855) : International Resource Development, c1986. x, 320 leaves ; 28 cm. (Report / International Resource Development . #709) "September 1986. LC Card 86-235156 DDC 380.1/456213984 19
1. Computer industry. 2. Computer input-output equipment. 3. Computer storage devices. 4. IBM Personal Computer. 5. Market surveys. I. International Resource Development, inc. II. Title: Add-on boards and peripherals for the IBM PC & compatibles. III. Series: Report / International Resource Development Inc. , #709.
HD9696.C62 A34 1986

Add-on boards and peripherals for the IBM PC & compatibles. Add-on boards & peripherals for the IBM PC & compatibles. Norwalk, Conn., U. S.A. (6 Prowitt St., Norwalk 06855) , c1986. x, 320 leaves ; LC Card 86-235156 DDC 380.1/456213984 19
HD9696.C62 A34 1986

Addams, Jon, 1941- How to become a professional model / by Jon Addams. Philadelphia, PA : Selleca Pub. Co., c1987. p. cm. Bibliography: p. Includes index. ISBN 0-943331-01-3 : LC Card 87-20656 DDC 659.1/52 19
1. Models, Fashion. I. Title.
HD6073.M77 A33 1987

Added t.p. has title: Factors which help or hinder productivity improvement: country report--Japan. Hirono, Ryōkichi. Factors which hinder or help productivity improvement in the Asian region, a review and the prospect . Tokyo, Japan , c1980. v, 111 p. ; ISBN 92-833-1470-0 LC Card 81-174179 DDC 338/.06/0952 19
HD56 .H57 1980 *NYPL [JLD 86-2287]*

ADDED VALUE. see **VALUE ADDED.**

Addelton, Jonathan S. Gilani, Ijaz. Citizens slaves, guest-workers . Islamabad, Pakistan , c1985. 84 p. ; LC Card 85-931825 DDC 331.6/2/54 19
HD5856.S64 G55 1985

Adding value to product through service /. Light, Donald H. Menlo Park, CA (333 Ravenswood Ave., Menlo Park 94025) , c1986. 21 leaves : LC Card 87-149955 DDC 658.8/12 19
HF5415.5 .L54 1986

Addis Ababa University. Institute of Development Research. Habtamu Wondimu. Some factors which affect peasant motivation to work in the Ethiopian agricultural producers cooperatives /. [Addis Ababa] [1983] 60 leaves : LC Card 84-980911 DDC 334/.683/0963 19
HD1491.E83 H3 1983b *NYPL [JLG 86-163]*

Addis Abaha University. Development Research Institute of. see **Addis Ababa University. Institute of Development Research.**

Addis Anteneh. Financing livestock services in some countries of east and southern Africa / Addis Anteneh. Addis Ababa, Ethiopia : International Livestock Centre for Africa, [1985] 26 p. ; 30 cm. (LPU working paper ; no. 6) "February 1985." Bibliography: p. 24-26. LC Card 86-980745 DDC 338.1/36/0096 19
1. Animal industry - Africa - Finance - Case studies. 2. Livestock - Economic aspects - Africa - Case studies. I. Title. II. Series.
HD9427.A2 A33 1985

Addison-Wesley economics /. Hodgetts, Richard M. Menlo Park, Calif. , c1988. vi, T1-T266, 31, 548 p. : ISBN 0-201-22775-4 LC Card 87-147565 DDC 330 19
HB171.5 .H676 1988

Addison-Wesley series on managing human resources.
Arvey, Richard D. Fairness in selecting employees /. Reading, Mass. , c1988. x, 361 p. : ISBN 0-201-00078-4 (pbk.) : LC Card 87-22173 DDC 658.3/112 19
HF5549.5.S38 A78 1988

The Addison-Wesley series on organization development.
Burke, W. Warner (Wyatt Warner), 1935- Organization development . Reading, Mass. , c1987. xiv, 189 p. : ISBN 0-201-10697-3 : LC Card 86-26474 DDC 658.4/06 19
HD58.8 .B878 1987

Addison-Wesley series on organizational development.
Beckhard, Richard, 1918- Organizational transitions . Reading, Mass. , c1987. xii, 117 p. : ISBN 0-201-10887-9 (pbk.) : LC Card 86-25863 DDC 658.4/06 19
HD58.8 .B4 1987

Addison-Wesley Training Systems (Firm) The Trainer's library /. Reading, Mass. , <1987-. p. cm. ISBN 0-201-12633-8 (v. 2) : LC Card 87-11415 DDC 658.3/124 19
HF5549.5.T7 T663 1987

Adebowale, Annette, 1957- Yoruba-Märkte in Nigeria : die Veränderung unter besonderer Berücksichtigung des modernen Verkehrswesen : eine Fallstudie, Ado-Ekiti / Annette Adebowale.1. Aufl. Aachen : Edition Herodot, Rader Verlag, c1987. xxvii, 225 p. : 8 ill. ; 21 cm. (Arbeiten aus dem Institut für Völkerkunde der Georg-August-Universität Göttingen . Bd. 22) Bibliography: p. 215-225. ISBN 3-922868-64-9 LC Card 87-141899 DDC 381/.18/096692 19
1. Markets - Nigeria - Ado Ekiti. 2. Marketing - Nigeria - Ado Ekiti. 3. Yorubas - Economic conditions. 4. Yorubas - Social life and customs. I. Series: Arbeiten aus dem Institut für Völkerkunde der Universität zu Göttingen , Bd. 22. II. Title.
HF5475.N52 A362 1987

Adedeji, Adebayo.
The African development problematique : demography, drought and desertification, dependency, disequilibrium, debt, and destabilization : or the paralysis of multiple debilitating crises / by Adebayo Adedeji. Addis Ababa : United Nations Economic Commission for Africa, [1985] 33 p. ; 21 cm. "April 1985"--P. [4] of cover. Includes bibliographical references. LC Card 87-980487 DDC 338.96 19
1. Africa - Economic conditions - 1960-. I. United Nations. Economic Commission for Africa. II. Title. III. Title: Paralysis of multiple debilitating crises.
HC800 .A543 1985

Some reflections on Nigeria's economic performance since independence, and thoughts on future prospects / by Adebayo Adedeji. Addis Ababa : United Nations, Economic Commission for Africa, [1985] 57 p. ; 24 cm. "Text of the contribution to the Silver Jubilee Symposium organized by the Federal Military Government of Nigeria in commemoration of the twenty-fifth independence anniversary of the Federal Republic of Nigeria held at the National Theatre, Iganmu, Lagos on 27 September 1985." LC Card 86-980957 DDC 330.9669/05 19
1. Nigeria - Economic conditions - 1960-. I. United Nations. Economic Commission for Africa. II. Title.
HC1055 .A546 1985

ADEF (Association : France) La Propriété foncière /. Paris , c1984. vii, 252 p. : ISBN 2-7178-0783-7 LC Card 84-249621
HD643 .N49 1984

Adelman, Irma. Morris, Cynthia Taft. Comparative patterns of economic development, 1850-1914 /. Baltimore , c1988. xi, 575 p. ; ISBN 0-8018-3507-0 (alk. paper) LC Card 87-45480 DDC 338.9/009 19
HC51 .M645 1988

Adelman, Irmn. The Design of alternative development strategies /. Rohtak, India , 1986. xiv, 330 p. : LC Card 86-901301 DDC 338.9 19
HD82 .D383 1986 *NYPL [JLE 86-4232]*

Adelstein, A. M. (Abraham Manie) Marmot, M. G. Immigrant mortality in England and Wales, 1970-78 . London , 1984. xii, 144 p. : ISBN 0-11-691094-1 (pbk.) : LC Card 84-222968 DDC 614.4/242 19
HB1415 .M37 1984 *NYPL [JLG 87-55]*

Ademuni-Odeke, Dr.
Protectionism and the future of international shipping : the nature, development, and role of flag discriminations and preferences, cargo reservations and cabotage restrictions, state intervention and maritime subsidies / Dr. Ademuni-Odeke. Dordrecht ; Boston : M. Nijhoff ; xxviii, 446 p. ; 25 cm. Includes bibliographies and index. ISBN 90-247-2918-1 LC Card 83-25055 DDC 387.5/068 19
1. Merchant marine - Government policy. 2. Shipping - Government policy. I. Title.
HE736 .A34 1984 *NYPL [JLE 85-1539]*

Shipping in international trade relations / Ademuni-Odeke. Brookfield, Vt. : Gower Pub., 1988. p. cm. Bibliography: p. Includes index. ISBN

0-566-05371-3 : LC Card 87-8770 DDC 387.5 19
1. Shipping. 2. Commerce. 3. Maritime law. I. Title.
HE571 .A34 1988

Adeniran, Tunde. Onimode, Bade. MNC's in Nigeria . Ibadan , 1983. ix, 144 p. ; ISBN 978-231-800-0 (pbk.) LC Card 86-195403 DDC 338.8/88669 19
HD2928 .O55 1983

A adesão de Portugal à C.E.E. . Carvalho, José António Segueira. [Lisbon, Portugal] , 1985. 97 p. : LC Card 86-150962
HC241.25.P6 C38 1985

A adesão de Portugal à CEE . Sousa, Fernando Freire de. [Porto] [1985] 96 p. ; LC Card 86-174408
HF2236 .S68 1985

A adesão portuguesa à CEE . Reizinho, Eduardo J. Costa (Eduardo José Costa) Mem Martins, Portugal , c1985. 396 p. ; LC Card 86-205515
HC241.25.P6 R45 1985

Adewunmi, Wole. Twenty five years of merchant banking in Nigeria / by Wole Adewunmi. Akoka : Lagos University Press, 1985. xvi, 136 p. ; 23 cm. "Published to commemorate the 25th anniversary of NAL Merchant Bank Limited." Spine title: 25 years of merchant banking in Nigeria. Bibliography: p. 130-136. ISBN 978-226-475-X : LC Card 87-142907 DDC 332.66/09669 19
1. Merchant banks - Nigeria - History. 2. NAL Merchant Bank - History. I. NAL Merchant Bank. II. Title. III. Title: 25 years of merchant banking in Nigeria.
HG1971.N6 A34 1985

Adhesive revenue stamps of Hawaii . Burt, Randall E. Honolulu, Hawaii (P.O. Box 10115, Honolulu 96816-0115) , c1986. ix, 114 p. : LC Card 87-136622 DDC 769.5/7 19
HJ5346.5 .B87 1986

ADHESIVES INDUSTRY - GERMANY (WEST) - HISTORY.
Schöne, Manfred, 1935- Von der Leimabteilung zum grössten Klebstoffwerk Europas /. Düsseldorf , 1979. 68 p. : LC Card 86-216773
HD9654.9.H444 S37 1979

Adirim, I. G. (Itskhok Girshevich)
Konferentsiia molodykh uchenykh-ėkonomistov respublik Pribaltiki (1978 : Riga, Latvia) Ėkonomika razvitogo sotsializma . Riga , 1978. 110 p. ; LC Card 82-100692
HC243 .K66 1978

Stagflation in the USSR / by Isaak Adirim. Falls Church, VA (7700 Leesburg Pike, #212, Falls Church 22043) : Delphic Associates, [1983] xi, 122 leaves ; 28 cm. (Monograph series on Soviet Union) "December 1983." Bibliography: p. 121-122. LC Card 84-162596 DDC 332.4/1/0947 19
1. National income - Soviet Union. 2. Inflation (Economics) - Soviet Union. 3. Stagnation (Economics). I. Title. II. Title: Stagflation in the U. S.S.R. III. Series.
HC340.I5 A44 1983 ***NYPL [JLF 86-1839]***

The Adirondack land market . Kay, David L. Ithaca, N.Y. [1985] 53 p. : LC Card 86-621939 DDC 333.33/22/0974753 19
HD266.N72 A265 1985

Adiseshiah, Malcolm S.
Balakrishnan, C. B. Review of a mid-year review of the economy, 1984 /. New Delhi , 1984. 132 p. ; LC Card 86-903796 DDC 330.954/052 19
HC435.2 .B323 1984

Mid year review of the economy, 1986-87 / Malcolm S. Adiseshiah. 1st ed. New Delhi : Lancer International in association with India International Centre, 1987. 193 p. : ill. ; 23 cm. Spine title: Review of the economy. Includes a summary by C. Balakrishnan (p. [148]-193) of the National Seminar on the Mid-Year Review of the Economy 1986-87 organized by the Economic Affairs Group of the India International Centre. Bibliography: p. [143]-147. ISBN 81-7062-016-3 : LC Card 87-900477 DDC 330.954/052 19
1. India - Economic conditions - 1947-. 2. India - Economic policy - 1980-. I. Balakrishnan, C. B. II. National Seminar on the Mid-Year Review of the Economy 1986-87 (1986 : India International Centre). III. India International Centre. Economic Affairs Group. IV. Title. V. Title: Review of the economy.
HC435.2 .A648 1987

Role of foreign trade in Indian economy /. New Delhi , 1986. 216 p. ; ISBN 81-7062-001-5 : LC Card 86-902110 DDC 382/.0954 19
HF3782 .R65 1986

Science and technology for women /. Madras [1985] 79 p. ; LC Card 85-904932 DDC 305.4/35/0954 19
Q130 .S33 1985 ***NYPL [JLD 86-3369]***

ADIVASIS.
Bhowmik, Sharit, 1948- Class formation in the plantation system /. New Delhi , 1981. xix, 263 p. : LC Card 81-903777 DDC 305/.93633 19
HD1470.5.I42 J342 1981
NYPL [JLD 86-2612]

Adjustable rate mortgages /. Friedman, Jack P. New York , c1987. viii, 293 p. ; ISBN 0-8120-3764-2 (soft) : LC Card 86-28852 DDC 332.8/2 19
HG1634 .F75 1987

Adjusting to success . Balassa, Bela A. Washington, DC , 1987. x, 121 p. : ISBN 0-88132-061-7 (pbk.) LC Card 87-3309 DDC 382.1/7/0951 19
HG3883.H66 B34 1987

Adjustment and economic performance in industrialised countries . Renshaw, Geoffrey. Geneva , 1986. xiv, 180 p. ; ISBN 92-2-105510-8 (pbk.) : LC Card 87-123435 DDC 338.9/009172/2 19
HC286.7 .R46 1986

Adjustment crisis in the Third World / Richard E. Feinberg and Valeriana Kallab, editors. New Brunswick, USA : Transaction Books, c1984. x, 186 p. ; 24 cm. (U. S.-Third World policy perspectives / Overseas Development Council . no. 1) Includes bibliographies. ISBN 0-88738-040-9 LC Card 84-8690 DDC 337/.09172/4 19
1. International Monetary Fund - Addresses, essays, lectures. 2. International Bank for Reconstruction and Development - Addresses, essays, lectures. 3. Debts, External - Developing countries - Addresses, essays, lectures. 4. Developing countries - Economic policy - Addresses, essays, lectures. 5. Developing countries - Foreign economic relations - Addresses, essays, lectures. I. Feinberg, Richard E. II. Kallab, Valeriana. III. Series: U. S.-Third World policy perspectives , no. 1.
HC59.7 .A733 1984 ***NYPL [JLE 86-2491]***

Adjustment policies and development strategies in the Arab world / edited by Said El-Naggar. Washington, D.C. : International Monetary Fund, 1987. ix, 200 p. ; 23 cm. Papers presented at a seminar held in Abu Dhabi, United Arab Emirates, February 16-18, 1987, and organized by the International Monetary Fund and the Arab Monetary Fund. Includes bibliographical references. ISBN 0-939934-96-5 (pbk.) LC Card 87-21377 DDC 338.9/00917/4927 19
1. Arab countries - Economic policy - Congresses. 2. Arab countries - Economic conditions - Congresses. 3. Economic development - Congresses. 4. International Monetary Fund - Arab countries - Congresses. 5. World Bank - Arab countries - Congresses. I. El-Naggar, Sa'id, 1920-. II. International Monetary Fund. III. Arab Monetary Fund.
HC498 .A6395 1987

Adjustment, structural change, and economic efficiency . Brabant, Jozef M. van. Cambridge [Cambridgeshire] , New York , 1987. xviii, 480 p. ; ISBN 0-521-33455-1 LC Card 87-785 DDC 332.4/947 19
HG186.E82 B7 1987

Adler, Hans A. Economic appraisal of transport projects : a manual with casestudies / Hans A. Adler.Rev. and expanded ed. Baltimore : Published for the World Bank [by] Johns Hopkins University Press, 1987. xii, 235 p. : ill. ; 25 cm. (EDI series in economic development) Bibliography: p. 208-230. Includes index. ISBN 0-8018-3411-2 : LC Card 86-21348 DDC 380.5/068/1 19
1. Transportation - Cost effectiveness. 2. Transportation - Cost effectiveness - Case studies. I. International Bank for Reconstruction and Development. II. Title. III. Series.
HE151 .A32 1987

Adler, John R. Dynamics of MacIntosh Excel / John R. Adler. Homewood, Ill. : Dow Jones-Irwin, c1987. xii, 164 p. : ill. ; 24 cm. Includes index. ISBN 0-87094-907-1 (pbk.) LC Card 86-72565 DDC 005.36/9 19
1. Microsoft Excel (Computer program). 2. Macintosh (Computer). 3. Business - Data processing. I. Title.
HF5548.4.E93 A35 1987

Adler, Stan. The magic sell : a seven step approach for consumer electronics / Stan Adler. Costa Mesa, Calif. : HDL Pub. Co., c1986. 160 p. ; 24 cm. ISBN 0-937359-03-3 : LC Card 87-111850 DDC 683/.83/0688 19
1. Selling - Household electronics. I. Title.
HF5439.H8 A36 1986

Administering management development institutions in Africa /. Rwegasira, Kami S. P. Aldershot, England , Brookfield, Vt. , 1988. p. cm. ISBN 0-566-05501-5 : LC Card 87-17688 DDC 658.4/07124/096 19
HF5549.5.A78 R94 1988

Administração da política industrial no Brasil . Cavalcanti, Bianor Scelza. Rio de Janeiro , 1986. ii, 87, 10 p. : LC Card 87-102756 DDC 338.981 19
HD3616.B83 C28 1986

A administração do "milagre" . Vianna, Maria Lúcia Teixeira Werneck. Petrópolis , 1987. 180 p. ; LC Card 87-403982 DDC 332.4/981 19
HG835 .V527 1987

Administração governamental em 1979-82. São Paulo (Brazil : State). Governor (1982- : Montoro) O orçamento de São Paulo para 1984 /. São Paulo , 1983. 24 p. ; LC Card 87-130676 DDC 354.81/6100722 19
HJ2080.5.S3 S26 1983

Administração por objetivos . Caravantes, Geraldo R. (Geraldo Ronchetti) Porto Alegre , 1977. 191 p., [1] folded leaf of plates : LC Card 85-211209
HD30.65 .C37 1977

Administración Nacional de Electricidad. Itaipu (Power plant) see Itaipu (Power plant)

ADMINISTRATION. see MANAGEMENT; POLITICAL SCIENCE; STATE, THE; CIVIL SERVICE.

Administration and management of electricity in India /. Goel, Madan Mohan, 1930- New Delhi [1986], c1987. 280 p. ; LC Card 87-900202 DDC 621.31/068 19
HD9697.A3 I43 1987

Administration et contrôle de l'économie, 1800-1914 / Michel Bruguière ... [et al.]. Genève : Libr. Droz ; Paris : Libr. Champion, 1985. 167 p. : ill. ; 25 cm. (Hautes études médiévales et modernes. 55) Includes bibliographical references. LC Card 86-128349 DDC 338.944 19
1. Industry and state - France - History. 2. France - Economic policy. I. Bruguière, Michel. II. Series.
HD3616.F82 A66 1985

ADMINISTRATION OF CRIMINAL JUSTICE. see CRIMINAL JUSTICE, ADMINISTRATION OF.

The administration of insurance /. Crockford, Neil. Cambridge [Cambridgeshire] , Wolfeboro, N.H., USA , 1987. x, 134 p. : ISBN 0-902197-42-8 : LC Card 86-27596 DDC 368/.0068 19
HG8051 .C84 1987

Administration of land reform in Korea /. Whang, In Joung. Seoul, Korea [1982] 41 p. ; LC Card 84-148921 DDC 333.3/1/519 19
HD1333.K78 W46 1982

ADMINISTRATION, PUBLIC. see PUBLIC ADMINISTRATION.

Administrations publiques. Sources et méthodes d'élaboration des comptes nationaux. [Paris] [1983] 481 p. ; LC Card 84-161813
HC271 .A218 no. 440-441 HJ9925.F8

Administrationshistoriske studier .
(bd. 9) Eriksen, August Wiemann. Eksportrådgivning i Danmark 1910-1921 . [Copenhagen] , 1984. 198 p. : ISBN 87-7497-075-5 LC Card 84-231455
HF1561 .E75 1984

Administrationskostnader för våra skatter : rapport till expertgruppen för studier i offentlig ekonomi / Finansdepartementet. [Stockholm] : Liber, [1983] 114 p. : ill. ; 21 cm. ISBN 91-38-08027-3 LC Card 84-219428
1. Tax administration and procedure - Sweden. 2. Tax collection - Sweden. I. Sweden. Expertgruppen för studier i offentlig ekonomi. II. Sweden. Finansdepartementet.
HJ3548 .A815 1983

ADMINISTRATIVE ABILITY. see **EXECUTIVE ABILITY.**

ADMINISTRATIVE AGENCIES - AUDITING.
Guidelines for auditing governmental subdivisions /. [New York, NY] [c1987] ii, 50 p. ; LC Card 87-121255 DDC 350.72/32 19
HJ9733 .G85 1987

ADMINISTRATIVE AGENCIES - GERMANY (WEST) - PLANNING.
Rucht, Dieter. Planung und Partizipation . München , c1982. 321 p. ; ISBN 3-88073-105-5 LC Card 83-672501
JN3971.A91 R82x 1982 *NYPL [JLD 86-2900]*

ADMINISTRATIVE AGENCIES - INFORMATION SERVICES - UNITED STATES.
Bloch, Carolyn. Federal energy information sources and data bases /. Park Ridge, N.J. , 1979. x, 115 p. ; ISBN 0-8155-0764-X : LC Card 79-15543 DDC 016.33379/0973 19
HD9502.U52 B58 *NYPL [JLE 86-4259]*

ADMINISTRATIVE AGENCIES - ITALY - CONGRESSES.
La Politica di bilancio in condizioni di stress fiscale . Milano, Italy , c1986. 377 p. ; LC Card 87-134343
HJ2119 .P65 1986

ADMINISTRATIVE AGENCIES - JAPAN - REORGANIZATION.
Katō, Kan, 1926- The Japanese economy in transition /. Tokyo, Japan , c1986. viii, 160 p. : LC Card 87-163640 DDC 330.952/047 19
HC462.9 .K35367 1986

ADMINISTRATIVE AGENCIES - LOUISIANA - FINANCE.
Louisiana. Legislature. Joint Legislative Committee on Economies in State Government. Final report /. [Baton Rouge] [1986] 62, 74, 105, [40] p. ; LC Card 86-621905 DDC 353.97630072 19
HJ2053.L8 L66 1986

ADMINISTRATIVE AGENCIES - MEXICO.
Flores Domínguez, David. Queremos hechos /. México, D.F. , c1982. 154 p. ; ISBN 968-7163-01-1 LC Card 83-142817
HC135 .F54 1982

ADMINISTRATIVE AGENCIES - NIGERIA - EAST-CENTRAL STATE - CORRUPT PRACTICES.
Anambra State, Nigeria. Government white paper on the report of the Administrative Board of Inquiry on Ministry of Works /. [Enugu, Nigeria] [1976?] 100 p. ; LC Card 86-205027 DDC 354.669/4 19
HD4365.5.Z8 E373 1976

ADMINISTRATIVE AGENCIES - PERU.
Saulniers, Alfred H., 1945- Beyond management control . Austin , 1985. 22 p. : LC Card 86-622251 DDC 354.8509/2 19
HD4124 .S28 1985

ADMINISTRATIVE AGENCIES - SWEDEN - MANAGEMENT.
Andersson, Per Magnus, 1951- Internprissättning inom offentlig förvaltning . Lund [1984] xii, 357 p. ; ISBN 91-44-43971-7 : LC Card 84-210334
HD62.45 .A53 1984

ADMINISTRATIVE AGENCIES - UNITED STATES.
Multi-agency financial investigative task forces [microform] Washington, D.C. [1983] 1 v. (various pagings) : *NYPL [*ZT-1708 no.61]*

Riley, Dennis D. Controlling the federal bureaucracy /. Philadelphia , 1987. xiv, 200 ; ISBN 0-87722-455-2 (alk. paper) : LC Card 86-14469 DDC 353.07/5 19
JK421 .R52 1987 *NYPL [JLD 87-1396]*

ADMINISTRATIVE AGENCIES - UNITED STATES - ACCOUNTING.
Hay, Leon Edwards, 1923- Essentials of accounting for governmental and not-for-profit organizations /. Homewood, Ill. , 1987. x, 310 p. ; ISBN 0-256-03454-0 (pbk.) LC Card 86-82587 DDC 657/.98 19
HJ9801 .H39 1987

ADMINISTRATIVE AGENCIES - UNITED STATES - AUDITING.
Moore, Mark Harrison. Inspectors-general . New York , c1986. 120 p. ; ISBN 0-87154-605-1 : LC Card 86-6728 DDC 353.0072/32 19
HJ9801 .M66 1987 *NYPL [JLE 87-1762]*

ADMINISTRATIVE AGENCIES - UNITED STATES - DIRECTORIES.
Lesko, Matthew. Getting yours . New York, N.Y., U. S.A. , 1987. x, 368 p. ; ISBN 0-14-046760-2 (pbk.) : LC Card 86-22688 DDC 658.1/5224 19
HC110.P63 L37 1987

ADMINISTRATIVE AGENCIES - UNITED STATES - STATES - DIRECTORIES.
How to find company intelligence in state documents /. Washington, D.C. , c1986. 110 p. ; ISBN 0-934940-38-X (pbk.) LC Card 86-218108 DDC 016.3387/4/0973 19
HD2785 .H67 1986

ADMINISTRATIVE COMMUNICATION. see **COMMUNICATION IN MANAGEMENT.**

The Administrative manager . Smith, Harold T., 1932- Chicago , c1987. xii, 548 p. : ISBN 0-574-20065-7 : LC Card 86-24881 DDC 651.8 19
HF5547 .S577 1987

Administrative office management /. Kallaus, Norman Francis, 1924- Cincinnati , c1987. ix, 774 p. : ISBN 0-538-07560-0 LC Card 85-61633 DDC 651.3 19
HF5547 .K43 1987

Administrative office systems management /. Tedesco, Eleanor Hollis. New York , c1987. xii, 736 p. : ISBN 0-471-01201-7 LC Card 86-26800 DDC 651.3 19
HF5547 .T37 1987

Administrative report (United States. National Marine Fisheries Service. Southwest Region)
.
(SWR-86-7) Miller, Charlotte L. The French market for U. S. seafood products /. Terminal Island, CA , 1986. ii, 63 p. ; LC Card 86-602854 DDC 382/.4566494/0944 19
HD9462.5 .M54 1986

(SWR-86-8) Miller, Charlotte L. The market for seafood in the United Kingdom /. Terminal Island, CA , 1986. ii, 73 p. : LC Card 87-601563 DDC 382.1/4370941 19
HD9461.5 .M55 1986

ADMINISTRATIVE RESPONSIBILITY - GREAT BRITAIN.
Day, Patricia. Accountabilities . London , New York , 1987. 259 p. : ISBN 0-422-79340-X : LC Card 87-164015 DDC 354.4109/2 19
HD4147 .D39 1987

Administrative Zusammenarbeit in der Entwicklungspolitik . Protz, Michael. Speyer , 1982. ix, 382, 2 p. ; LC Card 86-218043
HC60 .P77 1982

ADOLESCENT PREGNANCY. see **PREGNANCY, ADOLESCENT.**

Adolf-Weber-Stiftung. Gaugler, Eduard. Flexibilisierung der Beschäftigungsverhältnisse /. Berlin , c1986. 85 p. ; ISBN 3-428-06070-9 LC Card 87-118519 DDC 331.25/72/0943 19
HD5109.2.G3 G38 1986

Adolfsson, Eva, 1942- Arbetets döttrar /. [Stockholm] , c1986. 2 v. ; ISBN 91-7410-337-7 : LC Card 86-216247
HD6173 .A79 1986

Adolph, Brigitte. Rationale Erwartungen, Arbeitsverträge und Wirtschaftspolitik / Brigitte Adolph. München : V. Florentz, c1986. ii, 127 p. : ill. ; 21 cm. (Volkswirtschaftliche Forschung und Entwicklung . Bd. 15) Bibliography: p. 121-125. Includes index. ISBN 3-88259-346-6 LC Card 87-104701 DDC 330/.01/9 19
1. Rational expectations (Economic theory). 2. Monetary policy - Econometric models. 3. Labor contract - Econometric models. 4. Economic policy - Econometric models. I. Title. II. Series.
HB175 .A26 1986

The adoption and diffusion of imported technology . Enos, John L. (John Lawrence), 1924- New York , c1988. 272 p. : ISBN 0-7099-2030-X LC Card 87-19894 DDC 338.9519/506 19
HC470.T4 E56 1987

Adresa svershenii̇̆ / sostavitel′ O.P. Losoto]. Moskva : Izd-vo polit. lit-ry, 1980. 271 p., [16] p. of plates : ill., ; 21 cm. LC Card 81-130832
1. Economic development projects - Soviet Union. 2. Socialist competition - Soviet Union. I. Losoto, Oleg Pavlovich.
HC336.25 .A35 1980

Adresboek "Bedrijven in Vlaams-Brabant" = Répertoire "Les entreprises du Brabant Flamand" = Directory "Companies in Flemish Brabant." Vilvoorde : Gewestelijke Ontwikkelingsmaatschappij voor Vlaams-Brabant, 1985. lxi, 186, 62, 63 p. : ill. ; 24 cm. Spine title: Bedrijven in Vlaams-Brabant. LC Card 87-111619
1. Brabant (Belgium) - Industries - Directories. 2. Corporations - Belgium - Brabant - Directories. I. Gewestelijke Ontwikkelingsmaatschappij voor Vlaams-Brabant. II. Title: Répertoire "Les entreprises du Brabant Flamand.". III. Title: Directory "Companies in Flemish Brabant.". IV. Title: Bedrijven in Vlaams-Brabant.
HC317.B7 A37 1985

Adrian, James J. Construction productivity improvement / James J. Adrian. New York : Elsevier, c1987. xiii, 303 p. : ill. ; 24 cm. Includes bibliographical references and index. ISBN 0-444-01121-8 LC Card 86-24172 DDC 624/.068/3 19
1. Construction industry - Labor productivity. 2. Construction industry - Management. I. Title.
HD9715.A2 A353 1987

ADULT CHILDREN OF ALCOHOLICS - EMPLOYMENT - UNITED STATES.
Woititz, Janet Geringer. Home away from home /. Pompano Beach, Fla. , c1987. x, 137 p. : ISBN 0-932194-38-9 LC Card 86-33478 DDC 658.3/045 19
HF5549.5.A4 W65 1987

ADULT CHILDREN OF ALCOHOLICS - UNITED STATES - PSYCHOLOGY.
Woititz, Janet Geringer. Home away from home /. Pompano Beach, Fla. , c1987. x, 137 p. : ISBN 0-932194-38-9 LC Card 86-33478 DDC 658.3/045 19
HF5549.5.A4 W65 1987

ADULT EDUCATION - GERMANY, WEST.
Osmers, Dieter. Entwicklungspolitische Erwachsenenbildung in der Bundesrepublik mit Hilfe kommunaler Konfliktfelder /. Frankfurt am Main , c1983. 161 p., [2] folded leaves of plates : ISBN 3-88129-669-7 LC Card 84-135387
HD77.5.G3 O85 1983

ADULT EDUCATION - HISTORY.
Koeder, Kurt W. Berufsbegleitendes Studium . Grafenau/Württ. , c1983. 286 p. : ISBN 3-88508-901-7 LC Card 84-185882
HD5715 .K63 1983

ADULT EDUCATION - ITALY - MILAN.
Le 150 ore e la formazione professionale in azienda . Milano, Italy , c1985. 178 p. : LC Card 86-141990
HD5716.T242 I82 1985 *NYPL [JFD 87-3739]*

ADULT EDUCATION - PERU - AYACUCHO (DEPT.)
Gianotten, Vera. Organización campesina . Amsterdam , Cinnaminson, N.J. , c1985. ix, 531 p., [4] p. of plates : ISBN 90-6765-162-1 LC Card 85-200688
HD1531.P4 G5 1985

ADULTHOOD - MICHIGAN - PSYCHOLOGICAL ASPECTS - LONGITUDINAL STUDIES.
Mortimer, Jeylan T., 1943- Work, family, and personality . Norwood, N.J. , c1986. viii, 267 p. : ISBN 0-89391-293-X LC Card 85-20951 DDC 306/.36/09774 19
HD4904.25 .M67 1986 *NYPL [JLE 87-869]*

ADULTS, EDUCATION OF. see **ADULT EDUCATION.**

Advanced accounting /. Beams, Floyd A. Englewood Cliffs, N.J. , c1988. xii, 968 p. : ISBN 0-13-010182-6 LC Card 87-26226 DDC 657/.046 19
HF5635 .B41517 1988

Advanced accounting /. Hoyle, Joe Ben. Plano, Tex. , 1987. xvii, 809 p. : ISBN 0-256-03696-9 LC Card 86-72556 DDC 657/.046 19
HF5635 .H863 1987

Advanced accounting . Pahler, Arnold J. San Diego , c1988. xxi, 1208 p. : ISBN 0-15-501827-2 LC Card 87-81162 DDC

657/.046 19
HF5635 .P215 1988

Advanced accounting practice book 1 . Robins, Paul. Wokingham, Berkshire, England , 1987. p. cm. ISBN 0-278-00014-2 : LC Card 87-13803 DDC 657/.046 19
HF5635 .R66 1987

Advanced AppleWorks /. Bolocan, David. Blue Ridge Summit, PA , c1986. x, 246 p. : ISBN 0-8306-0248-8 : LC Card 85-22296 DDC 005.265 19
QA76.8.A662 B65 1986 ***NYPL [JSE 86-1874]***

Advanced applications for PFS and the IBM assistant series /. Burton, Kevin R. Blue Ridge Summit, PA , c1985. x, 213 p. : ISBN 0-8306-0989-X : LC Card 85-9885 DDC 001.64/25 19
QA76.754 .B87 1985 ***NYPL [JSE 86-2148]***

Advanced automated accounting for the microcomputer /. Allen, Warren W. Cincinnati , c1988. viii, 200 p. : ISBN 0-538-02690-0 (pbk.) LC Card 87-61619 DDC 657/.028/55369 19
HF5679 .A567 1988

Advanced ceramics market opportunities. Norwalk, Conn., U. S.A. (6 Prowitt St., Norwalk 06855) : International Resource Development, c1986. iv, 223 leaves ; 28 cm. (Report / International Resource Development Inc. . #721) "December 1986." LC Card 87-162866 DDC 380.1/45666 19
1. Ceramic industries. 2. Market surveys. I. International Resource Development, inc. II. Series: Report / International Resource Development Inc. , #721.
HD9590.5 .A38 1986

Advanced compilation and review . Clay, John R. Fort Worth, Tex. , c1987. 1 v. (various pagings) : LC Card 87-160681 DDC 657/.3 19
HF5667.65 .M42 1986 Suppl.

Advanced compilation & review. Clay, John R. Advanced compilation and review . Fort Worth, Tex. , c1987. 1 v. (various pagings) : LC Card 87-160681 DDC 657/.3 19
HF5667.65 .M42 1986 Suppl.

Advanced composites : an evaluation of commercial prospects / Joseph Mongiello, project analyst. Stamford, Conn. : Business Communications Co., c1985. x, 206 leaves : ill. ; 29 cm. (Business opportunity report . P-023R) ISBN 0-89336-442-8 (soft) LC Card 87-166023 DDC 338.4/7620118 19
1. Composite materials industry. 2. Market surveys. I. Mongiello, Joseph. II. Business Communications Co. III. Series.
HD9999.C7152 A38 1985

Advanced Excel /. Bolocan, David. Blue Ridge Summit, PA , c1986. x, 246 p. : ISBN 0-8306-0368-9 : LC Card 86-5767 DDC 005.36/9 19
HF5548.4.E93 B65 1986 ***NYPL [JSE 87-561]***

Advanced guide to Lotus One-two-three. Baras, Edward M. The advanced guide to Lotus 1-2-3 /. Berkeley, Calif. , c1986. xiii, 234 p. : ISBN 0-07-881237-2 (pbk.) LC Card 86-215569 DDC 005.36/9 19
HF5548.4.L67 B36 1986

The advanced guide to Lotus 1-2-3 /. Baras, Edward M. Berkeley, Calif. , c1986. xiii, 234 p. : ISBN 0-07-881237-2 (pbk.) LC Card 86-215569 DDC 005.36/9 19
HF5548.4.L67 B36 1986

Advanced management skills.
AHI's complete portfolio of modern business terms. A dictionary of business terms /. New York , 1987, c1986. 438 p. ; ISBN 0-531-15518-8 LC Card 86-24560 DDC 650/.03/21 19
HF1001 .A34 1987

Rachlin, Robert, 1937- Return on investment strategies for decision-making /. New York , 1987. x, 306 p. : ISBN 0-531-15528-5 LC Card 87-10633 DDC 658.1/52 19
HG4028.C4 R255 1987

Advanced online searching series.
Popovich, Charles J. Business and economics databases online . Littleton, Colo. , 1987. xviii, 276 p. : ISBN 0-87287-454-0 (pbk. : alk. paper) : LC Card 87-2672 DDC 300/.28/5 19
HF5548.2 .P612 1987

Advanced series in management .
(v. 11) Product standardization and competitive strategy /. Amsterdam ; New York : xii, 316 p. : ISBN 0-444-70232-6(U. S.) LC Card 87-8849 DDC 338/.02 19
HD62 .P75 1987

Advanced studies in theoretical and applied econometrics .
(v. 10) Kendrick, David A. Feedback . Dordrecht , Boston , 1988. vi, 147 p. : ISBN 90-247-3593-9 LC Card 87-20990 DDC 339.5 19
HB172.5 .K45 1988

(v. 11) Econometrics of planning and efficiency /. Dordrecht , Boston , 1988. vi, 193 p., [2] p. of plates : ISBN 90-247-3602-1 LC Card 87-21305 DDC 330/.028 19
HB139 .E32 1988

(v. 5) International macroeconomic modelling for policy decisions /. Dordrecht , Boston , c1986. viii, 269 p. : ISBN 90-247-3201-8 LC Card 85-13698 DDC 337/.0724 19
HF1410.5 .I577 1986 ***NYPL [JLE 86-3469]***

(v. 8) Broer, D. P. Neoclassical theory and empirical models of aggregate firm behaviour /. Dordrecht , Boston , 1987. 343 p. : ISBN 90-247-3412-6 LC Card 86-23485 DDC 338.5 19
HD30.22 .B76 1987

Advanced Symphony . Jacobson, Jay, 1946- New York , c1985. vi, 282 p. : ISBN 0-471-82430-5 (pbk.) : LC Card 85-12202 DDC 001.64/25 19
HF5548.4.S95 J3 1985 ***NYPL [JLF 86-854]***

Advanced Symphony applications . Bolocan, David. Blue Ridge Summit, PA , c1985. x, 230 p. : ISBN 0-8306-0988-1 : LC Card 85-22303 DDC 005.36/9 19
HF5548.4.S95 B64 1985 ***NYPL [JSE 86-2156]***

Advanced word/information processing operations . Varner, Jane Terzick, 1942- Chicago , c1988. 1 v. (various pagings) : ISBN 0-574-20795-3 (pbk.) : LC Card 87-13042 DDC 652/.5 19
HF5548.115 .V36 1988

Advances in economic theory : invited papers for the Fourth World Congress of the Econometric Society at Aix-en-Provence, September 1980 / edited by Werner Hildenbrand. Cambridge [Cambridgeshire] ; New York : Cambridge University Press, 1982. x, 285 p. : ill. ; 24 cm. (Econometric Society monographs in quantitative economics . no. 1) Includes bibliographies. ISBN 0-521-24443-9 LC Card 81-38500 DDC 330/.028 19
1. Economics - Congresses. 2. Economics, Mathematical - Congresses. I. Hildenbrand, Werner, 1936-. II. Econometric Society. III. Series.
HB21 .A33 1982 ***NYPL [JLE 85-2041]***

Advances in economic theory : fifth World Congress / edited by Truman F. Bewley. Cambridge [Cambridgeshire] ; New York : Cambridge University Press, 1987. vii, 428 p. ; 25 cm. (Econometric Society monographs . no. 12) Papers presented at the Fifth World Congress of the Econometric Society in Cambridge, Mass., August 1985. ISBN 0-521-34044-6 LC Card 87-889 DDC 330.1 19
1. Economics - Congresses. 2. Economics, Mathematical - Congresses. 3. Econometrics - Congresses. I. Bewley, Truman F. (Truman Fassett), 1941-. II. Series.
HB21 .A329 1987

Advances in industrial engineering .
(7) U. S.A.-Japan Conference on Manufacturing Research (1986 : Tokyo, Japan) Manufacturing research perspectives, U. S.A.-Japan . Amsterdam , New York , 1987. viii, 198 p. : ISBN 0-444-42868-2 LC Card 87-19851 DDC 338.4/767 19
HD9725 .U17 1986

Advances in organizational psychology : an international review / editors, Bernard M. Bass, Pieter J.D. Drenth ; associate editor, Peter Weissenberg. Newbury Park : Sage Publications, c1987. 314 p. ; 23 cm. Bibliography: p. 277-314. ISBN 0-8039-2802-5 LC Card 87-9484 DDC 158.7 19
1. Psychology, Industrial. 2. Organizational behavior. I. Bass, Bernard M. II. Drenth, Pieter J. D. (Pieter Johan Diederick). III. Weissenberg, Peter.
HF5548.8 .A58 1987

Advances in psychoanalysis .
(v. 2) Fast, Irene. Gender identity . Hillsdale, N.J. , 1984. vii, 189 p. ; ISBN 0-88163-014-4 LC Card 84-6366 DDC 155.3/3 19
BF692.2 .F36 1984 ***NYPL [JFE 86-4829]***

Advances in risk analysis .
(v. 4) Society for Risk Analysis International Workshop on Uncertainty in Risk Assessment, Risk Management, and Decision Making (1984 : Knoxville, Tenn.) Uncertainty in risk assessment, risk management, and decision making /. New York , c1987. x, 538 p. : ISBN 0-306-42557-2 LC Card 87-2403 DDC 658 19
HD61 .S625 1984

(v. 5) Risk assessment and management /. New York , c1987. xii, 740 p. : ISBN 0-306-42683-8 LC Card 87-21288 DDC 658 19
HD61 .R5684 1987

ADVENTURES, JOINT. see **JOINT VENTURES.**

ADVERSTISING, NEWSPAPER - GERMANY (WEST) - LOWER SAXONY - HISTORY - 19TH CENTURY.
Werbegraphik 1830-1870, aus niedersächsischen Zeitungen /. [Hannover] , Hildesheim , 1986. xv, 280 p. : ISBN 3-7848-3875-8 LC Card 87-408153 DDC 659.13/2/094359 19
HF5996.L68 W47 1986

Advertenties en affiches . Aerts, Christel. [Wilrijk, Belgium] , 1986. 165, [7] p. : LC Card 86-222214
HF5827 .A43 1986

ADVERTISEMENT WRITING. see **ADVERTISING COPY.**

Advertising /. Cohen, Dorothy. Glenview, Ill. , c1988. 626, [28] p. : ISBN 0-673-18255-X LC Card 87-15933 DDC 659.1 19
HF5821 .C56 1988

Advertising . Patti, Charles H. Chicago , c1988. xxxi, 590 p. : ISBN 0-03-071687-X LC Card 87-6898 DDC 659.1/11 19
HF5821 .P27 1988

ADVERTISING - ACCOUNTANTS.
Ronald, Dana M. Successfully developing your accounting practice . New York , 1987. x, 314 p. ; ISBN 0-471-84736-4 LC Card 86-32388 DDC 657/.068/8 19
HF5657 .R644 1987

ADVERTISING AGENCIES.
Geo. P. Rowell & Co. Newspaper Advertising Bureau. An advertising agency . New York [1878] 23 p. ; LC Card 87-158199
HF6107 .G45 1878

Laskin, David. Getting into advertising /. New York , 1986. xiii, 272 p. : ISBN 0-345-32598-2 (pbk.) LC Card 86-90721 DDC 659.1/023/73 19
HF5828.4 .L37 1986

Poppe, Fred C. 50 rules to keep a client happy /. New York , c1987. 90 p. : ISBN 0-06-015779-8 : LC Card 87-45139 DDC 659.1/125 19
HF6178 .P66 1987

Rocha, Everardo P. Guimarães, 1951- Magia e capitalismo . São Paulo, SP , 1985. 162 p. : LC Card 85-199925
HF5827 .R58 1985

An advertising agency . Geo. P. Rowell & Co. Newspaper Advertising Bureau. New York [1878] 23 p. ; LC Card 87-158199
HF6107 .G45 1878

ADVERTISING - AGENTS. see **ADVERTISING AGENCIES.**

ADVERTISING - AIRLINES - UNITED STATES.
Michaels, Susan. Points, a guide to frequent flyer bonus programs /. New York , c1987. 161 p. : ISBN 0-87052-375-9 (pbk.) : LC Card 87-8681 DDC 387.7/1 19
HF6161.A38 M53 1987

Advertising & promotion management . Farris, Paul. Malabar, Fla. , 1987, c1983. x, 301 p. : ISBN 0-89464-261-8 (pbk.) LC Card 87-15902 DDC 659.1 19
HF5821 .F36 1987

Advertising and promotion management. Farris, Paul. Advertising & promotion management . Malabar, Fla. , 1987, c1983. x, 301 p. : ISBN 0-89464-261-8 (pbk.) LC Card 87-15902 DDC 659.1 19
HF5821 .F36 1987

Advertising and promotion management /. Rossiter, John R. New York , 1987. xix, 647 p. : ISBN 0-07-053907-3 : LC Card 86-27381 DDC 659.1 19
HF5821 .R65 1987

ADVERTISING ART. see **COMMERCIAL ART.**

ADVERTISING, ART IN. see **ART AND INDUSTRY; COMMERCIAL ART.**

ADVERTISING - AUTOMOBILES.
Hudson, Adams, 1958- How to buy or sell a car by long distance /. Osceola, Wis. , 1987. 80 p. ; ISBN 0-87938-259-7 (soft) LC Card 87-12185 DDC 629.2/222 19
HF5439.A8 H83 1987

ADVERTISING - AUTOMOBILES - UNITED STATES - PICTORIAL WORKS.
American car graffiti. English. The American automobile . San Francisco , 1988. p. cm. ISBN 0-87701-451-5 (cloth) LC Card 87-25017 DDC 659.1/9629222/0973 19
HF6161.A9 A4413 1988

ADVERTISING - BABY FOODS - DEVELOPING COUNTRIES - MORAL AND ETHICAL ASPECTS.
Chetley, Andrew. The politics of baby foods . London , 1986. xv, 189 p. ; ISBN 0-86187-293-2
NYPL [JLE 86-2969]

ADVERTISING - BANKS AND BANKING - GERMANY - HISTORY.
Emmerich, Norbert-Christian. Die deutsche Sparkassenwerbung, 1750-1981 /. Stuttgart , 1983. 344 p. : LC Card 84-119079
HF6161.B2 E64 1983

ADVERTISING - BANKS AND BANKING - GERMANY (WEST)
Gessler, Joachim. Werbung der Banken /. [S.l. , 1983] (Köln : Druck- und Verlagshaus Wienand) xxvii, 200 p. ; LC Card 83-214619
HF6161.B2 G47 1983

Wünsche, Gert. Grundlagen der Bankenwerbung aus verhaltenswissenschaftlicher Sicht /. Wiesbaden , c1982. 304 p. : ISBN 3-409-47003-4 LC Card 83-151107
HF6161.B2 W86 1982

ADVERTISING - BANKS AND BANKING - GERMANY (WEST) - HISTORY.
Emmerich, Norbert-Christian. Die deutsche Sparkassenwerbung, 1750-1981 /. Stuttgart , 1983. 344 p. : LC Card 84-119079
HF6161.B2 E64 1983

ADVERTISING - BOOKS - SOVIET UNION.
Bekleshov, Dmitriĭ. Reklama knig segodnia͡ /. Moskva , 1986. 201 p. : LC Card 87-132362 DDC 659.1/90705 19
HF6161.B37 B44 1986

ADVERTISING - BRAZIL.
Arruda, Maria Arminda do Nascimento. A embalagem do sistema . São Paulo , 1985. 203 p. : LC Card 85-211063
HF5813.B8 A77 1985

Galindo, Daniel dos Santos. Comunicação mercadológica em tempo de incertezas /. S. Paulo-SP , c1986. 167 p. : LC Card 86-224127
HF5415.12.B7 G35 1986

ADVERTISING BUSINESS. see **ADVERTISING AGENCIES.**

ADVERTISING CAMPAIGNS - EVALUATION.
Donius, James F. Marketplace measurement . New York, NY (155 E. 44th St., New York 11710) , c1986. xiii, 206 p. : LC Card 87-120244 DDC 659.1/11 19
HF5823 .D655 1986

ADVERTISING CARDS - UNITED STATES - HISTORY - 19TH CENTURY.
Jay, Robert. The trade card in nineteenth-century America /. Columbia , 1987. 112 p. : ISBN 0-8262-0619-0 (alk. paper) LC Card 86-30902 DDC 769.5 19
HF5851 .J39 1987

ADVERTISING - CASE STUDIES.
Quelch, John A. Cases in advertising and promotion management /. Plano, Tex. , 1987. xv, 759 p. : ISBN 0-256-03713-2 LC Card 86-72244 DDC 659.1 19
HF5823 .Q44 1987

ADVERTISING - CIGARETTES - ADDRESSES, ESSAYS, LECTURES.
Smoking out the barons . Chichester [West Sussex] , New York , c1986. vii, 192 p.; ISBN 0-471-90937-8 (pbk.) : LC Card 85-26414 DDC 659.1/967973/0941 19
HF6161.C35 S66 1986
NYPL [JLD 86-3620]

ADVERTISING - CIGARETTES - DEVELOPING COUNTRIES.
Nath, Uma Ram. Smoking, Third World alert /. Oxford [Oxfordshire] , New York , 1986. x, 291 p. : ISBN 0-19-261402-9 : LC Card 86-5201 DDC 363.1/9 19
HD9148.D44 N37 1986
NYPL [JLD 87-992]

ADVERTISING - CIGARETTES - GREAT BRITAIN - ADDRESSES, ESSAYS, LECTURES.
Smoking out the barons . Chichester [West Sussex] , New York , c1986. vii, 192 p.; ISBN 0-471-90937-8 (pbk.) : LC Card 85-26414 DDC 659.1/967973/0941 19
HF6161.C35 S66 1986
NYPL [JLD 86-3620]

ADVERTISING, CLASSIFIED - HANDBOOKS, MANUALS, ETC.
Wolff, Rick, 1951- The encyclopedia of pre-written employment ads . Westbury, N.Y. , c1986. vi, 196 p. ; ISBN 0-87280-142-X (loose-leaf) : LC Card 86-26526 DDC 659.1/9331128 19
HF6125 .W65 1986

ADVERTISING - COLOMBIA - HISTORY.
1880-1980, un siglo de publicidad gráfica en Colombia /. [Bogotá?] [1984] 286 p. : LC Card 84-202348 DDC 659.1/09861 19
HF5813.C63 A16 1984
NYPL [3-MDW+ 86-17]

ADVERTISING, COLOR IN. see **COLOR IN ADVERTISING.**

ADVERTISING, COMPARATIVE. see **ADVERTISING, COMPARISON.**

ADVERTISING, COMPARISON.
Mähling, Friedrich W. (Friedrich Wilhelm), 1952- Werbung, Wettbewerb und Verbraucherpolitik /. München , c1983. xii, 477 p. : ISBN 3-88259-258-3 LC Card 84-144205
HF5822 .M34 1983

Advertising, competition, and public policy . McAuliffe, Robert E. Lexington, Mass. , c1987. vi, 116 p. ; ISBN 0-669-12391-9 (alk. paper) LC Card 85-45896 DDC 659.1/0973 19
HF5813.U6 M33 1987 ***NYPL [JLE 87-1426]***

ADVERTISING, COMPETITIVE. see **ADVERTISING, COMPARISON.**

Advertising, concepts and strategies /. Berkman, Harold E. New York , c1987. xxiv, 614 p. : ISBN 0-394-36165-2 : LC Card 86-29790 DDC 659.1/11 19
HF5823 .B45 1987

ADVERTISING - CONGRESSES.
Meissner, Hans-Günther. Werbung und gesellschaftlicher Wandel über die kommunikativen Voraussetzungen technischen, ökonomischen und sozialen Fortschritts . [Berlin] , Hamburg [1979] 23, [4] leaves ; LC Card 84-119751
HF5802.5 .M45 1979

Seminar on Below-the-Line and Sponsoring (1985 : Milan, Italy) Seminar on Below-the-Line and Sponsoring . Amsterdam, Netherlands [1985] vi, 270 p. : ISBN 92-831-1107-9 (pbk.) : LC Card 86-213125 DDC 658.8/2 19
HF5438.5 .S46 1985

ADVERTISING, CONSUMER. see **ADVERTISING.**

ADVERTISING COPY.
Bacon, Mark S. Write like the pros . New York , c1988. xiv, 316 p. ; ISBN 0-471-85721-1 LC Card 87-21550 DDC 808/.06665 19
HF5718.3 .B33 1988

Bayan, Richard. Words that sell . Chicago [1987], c1984. 127 p. ; ISBN 0-8092-4799-2 (pbk.) : LC Card 86-29319 DDC 659.1/014 19
HF5825 .B35 1987

Lewis, Herschell Gordon, 1926- Herschell Gordon Lewis on the art of writing copy /. Englewood Cliffs, N.J. , c1987. p. cm. ISBN 0-13-387309-9 : LC Card 87-11489 DDC 659.13/22 19
HF5825 .L44 1987

Pāṇḍeya, Āśā. Hindī vijñāpanoṃ kī bhāshā /. Bambaī , 1986. xv, 105, [3] p. ; LC Card 87-901590
HF5827 .P36 1986

Wasserman, Dick. How to get your first copywriting job in advertising /. New York , 1987. viii, 199 p. : ISBN 0-525-48281-4 (pbk.) : LC Card 86-72833 DDC 659.13/22/02373 19
HF5825 .W29 1987

ADVERTISING - DECISION MAKING.
Patti, Charles H. Advertising . Chicago , c1988. xxxi, 590 p. : ISBN 0-03-071687-X LC Card 87-6898 DDC 659.1/11 19
HF5821 .P27 1988

ADVERTISING - DICTIONARIES.
Imber, Jane. Dictionary of advertising and direct mail terms /. New York , c1987. xi, 514 p. : ISBN 0-8120-3765-0 (pbk.) : LC Card 87-1197 DDC 659.1/03/21 19
HF5803 .I46 1987

Koschnick, Wolfgang J., 1942- Standard-Wörterbuch für Werbung, Massenmedien und Marketing, Deutsch-Englisch /. Berlin , New York , 1987. 590 p. ; ISBN 0-89925-293-1 (U. S.) : LC Card 87-19928 DDC 659.1/03/21 19
HF5803 .K67 1987

ADVERTISING, DIRECT-MAIL - DICTIONARIES.
Imber, Jane. Dictionary of advertising and direct mail terms /. New York , c1987. xi, 514 p. : ISBN 0-8120-3765-0 (pbk.) : LC Card 87-1197 DDC 659.1/03/21 19
HF5803 .I46 1987

ADVERTISING, DIRECT-MAIL - UNITED STATES.
Weintz, Walter. The solid gold mailbox . New York , c1987. xiv, 268 p. : ISBN 0-471-85026-8 LC Card 86-28267 DDC 658.8/72 19
HF5466 .W45 1987

The Wholesale-by-mail catalog, 1987 /. New York [1987] p. cm. ISBN 0-312-00205-X (pbk.) : LC Card 86-27890 DDC 381/.2/02573 19
HF5861 .W527 1987

ADVERTISING, DIRECT-MAIL - UNITED STATES - DIRECTORIES.
Lynch, Christine M. (Christine Marie), 1962- The national directory of postcard deck media /. Westbury, N.Y. , c1987. ix, 238 p. ; ISBN 0-87280-156-X (pbk.) LC Card 87-1071 DDC 659.13/3 19
HF5861 .L96 1987

ADVERTISING, DUTCH - BELGIUM.
Aerts, Christel. Advertenties en affiches . [Wilrijk, Belgium] , 1986. 165, [7] p. : LC Card 86-222214
HF5827 .A43 1986

Advertising Educational Foundation (New York, N.Y.) Jacoby, Jacob. The comprehension and miscomprehension of print communications . New York, N.Y. , Hillsdale, N.J. , c1987. xvii, 273 p. : ISBN 0-8058-0087-5 (L. Erlbaum Associates) LC Card 87-1366 DDC 659.13/2 19
HF6107 .J32 1987

Advertising financial products and services . Benn, Alec. Westport, Conn. , c1986. xii, 231 p. : ISBN 0-89930-103-7 (lib bdg. : alk. paper) LC Card 85-24406 DDC 659.1/93321 19
HG1616.M3 B43 1986 ***NYPL [JLE 86-4110]***

ADVERTISING - FINANCIAL SERVICES INDUSTRY - CONGRESSES.
Advertising Research Foundation Key Issues Workshop (1986 : Boston, Mass.) Marketing-oriented financial services advertising and research . New York, NY , c1986. 119 p. : LC Card 87-404482 DDC 659.1/93321 19
HF6161.F46 A38 1986

ADVERTISING FLIERS.
Bly, Robert W. Create the perfect sales piece . New York , c1985. xii, 242 p. : ISBN 0-471-82525-5 (pbk.) : LC Card 85-12457

DDC 659.13/2 19
HF5823 .B635 1985 ***NYPL [JLE 86-3454]***

ADVERTISING - FRANCE.
Genzel, David. De la publicité à la communication /. Paris [1984?] 271 p. : ISBN 2-86737-005-1 LC Card 84-175281
HF5813.F8 G46 1984

ADVERTISING - FRANCE - PSYCHOLOGICAL ASPECTS.
Genzel, David. De la publicité à la communication /. Paris [1984?] 271 p. : ISBN 2-86737-005-1 LC Card 84-175281
HF5813.F8 G46 1984

ADVERTISING, FRAUDULENT.
Jacoby, Jacob. The comprehension and miscomprehension of print communications . New York, N.Y. , Hillsdale, N.J. , c1987. xvii, 273 p. : ISBN 0-8058-0087-5 (L. Erlbaum Associates) LC Card 87-1366 DDC 659.13/2 19
HF6107 .J32 1987

Selling dreams . Penang, Malaysia , c1986. 149 p. : ISBN 967-99502-0-4 (pbk.) LC Card 87-940287 DDC 659.1 19
HF5823 .S46 1986

ADVERTISING - GERMANY - HISTORY - 19TH CENTURY - SOURCES.
Die Schönsten Anzeigen in den Fliegenden Blättern . Hildesheim , New York , 1982. 166 p. : ISBN 3-487-08233-0 (pbk.) LC Card 87-672236
HF5813.G3 S36x 1982

ADVERTISING - GERMANY, WEST.
Berndt, Hermann, 1956- Konsumentscheidung und Informationsüberlastung . München , c1983. 368 p. : ISBN 3-89003-002-5 LC Card 84-192993
HF5821 .B42 1983

Buschmann, Vera, 1951- Wirkungsanalyse für segmentspezifische Warentestwerbung . Frankfurt am Main , New York , c1986. xii, 270 p. : ISBN 3-8204-9275-5 LC Card 86-220570
HF5827 .B87 1986

Weis, Hans Christian. Marketingkommunikation in der Investitionsgüterindustrie . Thun , c1983. v, 319, xxxix p. : ISBN 3-87144-741-2 : LC Card 83-159201
HF5415.123 .W45 1983

ADVERTISING - GOVERNMENT POLICY - UNITED STATES.
McAuliffe, Robert E. Advertising, competition, and public policy . Lexington, Mass. , c1987. vi, 116 p. ; ISBN 0-669-12391-9 (alk. paper) LC Card 85-45896 DDC 659.1/0973 19
HF5813.U6 M33 1987 ***NYPL [JLE 87-1426]***

ADVERTISING - GREAT BRITAIN - SELF-REGULATION.
Miracle, Gordon E. Voluntary regulation of advertising . Lexington, Mass. , c1987. xxvi, 322 p. : ISBN 0-669-13135-0 (alk. paper) LC Card 86-45294 DDC 338.4/76591/0941 19
HF5834 .M57 1987

ADVERTISING - GREAT BRITAIN - STATISTICS.
ISBA area information, 1978 /. London , 1978. 147 p. : ISBN 0-906241-00-6 (pbk.) LC Card 83-225656 DDC 381/.1/0941021 19
HA1134 .I83 1978

Advertising handbook for health care services / William J. Winston, editor. New York : Haworth Press, c1986. xiv, 287 p. : ill. ; 25 cm. Includes index. ISBN 0-86656-390-3 : LC Card 85-27013 DDC 659.1/93621 19
1. Advertising - Medicine - Addresses, essays, lectures. 2. Advertising - Medicine - United States - Addresses, essays, lectures. I. Winston, William J.
HF6161.M4 A38 1986 ***NYPL [JLE 86-4539]***

ADVERTISING - HISTORY.
Medici Mario, 1924- La parola pubblicitaria . Pomezia , Venezia , 1986. 178 p., 40 p. of plates : ISBN 88-317-4902-1 : LC Card 86-219876
HF5813.I8 M43 1986

ADVERTISING - HOSPITALS.
Barnett, Ned B. The state of the art in hospital advertising, 1987 /. Alexandria, VA , c1987. iii, 56 p. ; ISBN 0-937925-33-0 (pbk.) LC Card 87-61160 DDC 659.1/93621 19
HF6161.H7 B37 1987

Advertising in the yellow pages . Wagner, W. F., 1944- Los Angeles, CA , c1986. viii, 174 p. : ISBN 0-940969-00-9 (pbk.) : LC Card 86-83085 DDC 659.13/2 19
HF6146.T4 W34 1986

ADVERTISING - ITALY - HISTORY.
Medici Mario, 1924- La parola pubblicitaria . Pomezia , Venezia , 1986. 178 p., 40 p. of plates : ISBN 88-317-4902-1 : LC Card 86-219876
HF5813.I8 M43 1986

Il Pappagallo giallo . [Pisa] , Firenze , c1986. 194 p., [1] leaf of plates : LC Card 86-212573
HD9780.I82 P37 1986

ADVERTISING - JURISPRUDENCE. see **ADVERTISING LAWS.**

ADVERTISING - LANGUAGE.
Aerts, Christel. Advertenties en affiches . [Wilrijk, Belgium] , 1986. 165, [7] p. : LC Card 86-222214
HF5827 .A43 1986

ADVERTISING - LATIN AMERICA.
Benítez, José Antonio, 1921- La dependencia, el subdesarrollo y la publicidad comercial capitalista /. La Habana, Cuba , 1986. 133 p., [2] p. of plates : LC Card 87-404231 DDC 659.1/098 19
HF5813.L29 B46 1986

ADVERTISING - LAW. see **ADVERTISING LAWS.**

ADVERTISING LAWS - GREAT BRITAIN.
Miracle, Gordon E. Voluntary regulation of advertising . Lexington, Mass. , c1987. xxvi, 322 p. : ISBN 0-669-13135-0 (alk. paper) LC Card 86-45294 DDC 338.4/76591/0941 19
HF5834 .M57 1987

ADVERTISING LAWS - MALAYSIA.
Selling dreams . Penang, Malaysia , c1986. 149 p. : ISBN 967-99502-0-4 (pbk.) LC Card 87-940287 DDC 659.1 19
HF5823 .S46 1986

ADVERTISING LAWS - UNITED STATES.
Miracle, Gordon E. Voluntary regulation of advertising . Lexington, Mass. , c1987. xxvi, 322 p. : ISBN 0-669-13135-0 (alk. paper) LC Card 86-45294 DDC 338.4/76591/0941 19
HF5834 .M57 1987

ADVERTISING, MAGAZINE.
Jacoby, Jacob. The comprehension and miscomprehension of print communications . New York, N.Y. , Hillsdale, N.J. , c1987. xvii, 273 p. : ISBN 0-8058-0087-5 (L. Erlbaum Associates) LC Card 87-1366 DDC 659.13/2 19
HF6107 .J32 1987

ADVERTISING, MAIL. see **ADVERTISING, DIRECT-MAIL.**

ADVERTISING - MATHEMATICAL MODELS.
Le Vaillant de Folleville, Patrice, 1954- Nicht-sequentielle Suche, Preiswerbung und Marktgleichgewicht /. Frankfurt am Main , New York , c1986. 198 p. : ISBN 3-8204-9058-2 LC Card 86-153194
HB221 .L42 1986

Advertising media . McGann, Anthony F. Homewood, Ill. , 1988. xii, 452 p. : ISBN 0-256-05988-8 LC Card 87-81340 DDC 659.1/11 19
HF5826.5 .M36 1988

ADVERTISING MEDIA, CHOICE OF. see **ADVERTISING MEDIA PLANNING.**

ADVERTISING MEDIA PLANNING - DICTIONARIES.
Brown, William P. The complete dictionary of media terms /. Chicago, IL , c1986. vii, 151 p. ; ISBN 0-913247-01-4 (pbk.) LC Card 86-70712 DDC 302.2/34/0321 19
HF5826.5 .B77 1986

ADVERTISING MEDIA PLANNING - MATHEMATICS.
Hall, Robert W. (Robert William), 1939- Media math . Lincolnwood, Ill., U. S.A. , c1987. v, 138 p. : ISBN 0-8442-3142-8 (pbk.) : LC Card 86-62067 DDC 659.1/01/51 19
HF5826.5 .H35 1987

ADVERTISING MEDIA PLANNING - UNITED STATES.
Selnow, Gary W. Planning, implementing, and evaluating targeted communication programs . New York , 1987. vi, 291 p. : ISBN 0-89930-208-4 (lib. bdg. : alk. paper) LC Card 86-30418 DDC 659.1 19
HD30.3 .S46 1987

ADVERTISING MEDIA PLANNING - UNITED STATES - CONGRESSES.
Advertising Research Foundation Key Issues Workshop (1985 : New York, N.Y.) Transcript proceedings . New York, NY (3 E. 54th St., New York 10022-3180) , c1985. 174 p. : LC Card 86-214476 DDC 659.14/3/0973 19
HF6146.T42 A27 1985a

Advertising Research Foundation Key Issues Workshop (1986 : New York, N.Y.) Transcript proceedings . New York, NY (3 E. 54th St., New York 10022-3180) , c1986. 268 p. : LC Card 87-149342 DDC 658.8/3 19
HF5802.5 .A3826 1986

Advertising Research Foundation Key Issues Workshop (1986 : New York, N.Y.) Transcript proceedings . New York, NY (3 E. 54th St., New York 10022-3180) , c1986. 214 p. : LC Card 87-404527 DDC 659.14/3/0973 19
HF6146.T42 A27 1986

ADVERTISING MEDIA SELECTION. see **ADVERTISING MEDIA PLANNING.**

ADVERTISING - MEDICINE - ADDRESSES, ESSAYS, LECTURES.
Advertising handbook for health care services /. New York , c1986. xiv, 287 p. : ISBN 0-86656-390-3 : LC Card 85-27013 DDC 659.1/93621 19
HF6161.M4 A38 1986 ***NYPL [JLE 86-4539]***

ADVERTISING - MEDICINE - UNITED STATES - ADDRESSES, ESSAYS, LECTURES.
Advertising handbook for health care services /. New York , c1986. xiv, 287 p. : ISBN 0-86656-390-3 : LC Card 85-27013 DDC 659.1/93621 19
HF6161.M4 A38 1986 ***NYPL [JLE 86-4539]***

ADVERTISING - MEDIUMS, OUTDOOR. see **ADVERTISING, OUTDOOR.**

ADVERTISING - NETHERLANDS.
Effectiviteit in de reclame . Alphen aan den Rijn , 1986. 125 p. : ISBN 90-14-03587-X : LC Card 86-205967
HF5813.N4 E35 1986

ADVERTISING - NETHERLANDS - AWARDS.
Effectiviteit in de reclame . Alphen aan den Rijn , 1986. 125 p. : ISBN 90-14-03587-X : LC Card 86-205967
HF5813.N4 E35 1986

ADVERTISING, NEWSPAPER.
Geo. P. Rowell & Co. Newspaper Advertising Bureau. An advertising agency . New York [1878] 23 p. ; LC Card 87-158199
HF6107 .G45 1878

ADVERTISING, NEWSPAPER - GERMANY (WEST) - BAMBERG.
Bamberg in alten Zeitungsanzeigen . Bamberg , c1981. 120 p. : ISBN 3-87052-442-1 LC Card 82-214699
HF6105.G4 B36 1981

ADVERTISING, NEWSPAPER - SWEDEN - HISTORY - 20TH CENTURY.
Jonsson, Sverker, 1941- Pressen, reklamen och konkurrensen, 1935-1978 /. Göteborg , 1982. 406 p. : ISBN 91-85196-24-X : LC Card 84-157282
HF6105.S8 J66 1982

ADVERTISING - NEWSPAPERS.
Evaluating the effectiveness of newspaper promotion /. Reston, Va. (11600 Sunrise Valley Dr., Reston 22091) , c1987. iii, 123 p. : LC Card 87-152731 DDC 659.13/2 19
HF6161.N4 E93 1987

ADVERTISING - NEWSPAPERS - UNITED STATES.
Evaluating the effectiveness of newspaper promotion /. Reston, Va. (11600 Sunrise Valley Dr., Reston 22091) , c1987. iii, 123 p. : LC Card 87-152731 DDC 659.13/2 19
HF6161.N4 E93 1987

ADVERTISING, OUTDOOR.
Sport und Werbung, Präsenz und Erinnerungswirkung ausgewählter Werbeträger an Rennstrecken . München [1986] 70, lii, [iii] p. : LC Card 87-409557 DDC 659.13/42 19
HF5843 .S69 1986

ADVERTISING, OUTDOOR - FRANCE.
Benoit, Philippe. Affiches de pub, 1983/85 /. Paris , c1986. 237 p. : ISBN 2-85108-429-1 : LC Card 86-192339
HF5843 .B44 1986

ADVERTISING, PICTORIAL. see **COMMERCIAL ART.**

ADVERTISING, POLITICAL - UNITED STATES.
Gold, Philip, 1948- Advertising, politics, and American culture . New York , c1987. xix, 217 p. ; ISBN 0-913729-35-3 LC Card 86-30291 DDC 659.1/0973 19
HF5813.U6 G58 1987

Advertising, politics, and American culture . Gold, Philip, 1948- New York , c1987. xix, 217 p. ; ISBN 0-913729-35-3 LC Card 86-30291 DDC 659.1/0973 19
HF5813.U6 G58 1987

Advertising procedure. Kleppner, Otto, 1899- [Advertising procedure.] Kleppner's advertising procedure. Englewood Cliffs, N.J. , 1987, c1988. p. cm. ISBN 0-13-516451-6 LC Card 87-19346 DDC 659.1 19
HF5823 .K45 1988

ADVERTISING - PSYCHOLOGICAL ASPECTS.
The Climate of persuasion . [Richmond, VA.] , 1959. 58 p. : ***NYPL [JLF 86-1150]***

Conen, Dieter, 1951- Wirkung von Werbesprache . München , c1985. iii, 162 p., [7] p. of plates : ISBN 3-89003-021-1 LC Card 86-159595
HF5822 .C58 1985

Frontori, Laura. Il mercato dei segni . Milano , c1986. xv, 186 p., [8] p. of plates : ISBN 88-7078-040-6 : LC Card 86-161029
HF5822 .F74 1986

Mähling, Friedrich W. (Friedrich Wilhelm), 1952- Werbung, Wettbewerb und Verbraucherpolitik /. München , c1983. xii, 477 p. : ISBN 3-88259-258-3 LC Card 84-144205
HF5822 .M34 1983

Nonverbal communication in advertising /. Lexington, Mass. , c1988. viii, 296 p. : ISBN 0-669-14172-0 (alk. paper) LC Card 87-17143 DDC 659.1/01/9 19
HF5822 .N66 1988

Selling dreams . Penang, Malaysia , c1986. 149 p. : ISBN 967-99502-0-4 (pbk.) LC Card 87-940287 DDC 659.1 19
HF5823 .S46 1986

ADVERTISING - REAL ESTATE BUSINESS.
Elkman, Richard. Building better ads . Washington, D.C. , c1987. 86 p. : ISBN 0-86718-290-3 (pbk.) LC Card 87-122135 DDC 659.1/933333 19
HF6161.R3 E439 1987

ADVERTISING RESEARCH.
Fletcher, Alan D. Fundamentals of advertising research /. Belmont, Calif. , c1988. xiii, 322 p. : ISBN 0-534-08454-0 LC Card 87-23106 DDC 659.1/072 19
HF5814 .F57 1988

Templeton, Jane Farley. Focus groups . Chicago, Ill. , c1987. xiii, 315 p. ; ISBN 0-917253-78-7 : LC Card 87-4977 DDC 658.8/3 19
HF5415.2 .T43 1987

ADVERTISING RESEARCH - CONGRESSES.
Advertising Research Foundation Qualitative Research Workshop (1985 : New York, N.Y.) Qualitative research . New York, NY (3 E. 54th St., New York 10022-3180) , c1985. 121 p. : LC Card 86-212738 DDC 659.1/072 19
HF5802.5 .A383 1985

Advertising Research Foundation.
Advertising Research Foundation Key Issues Workshop (1986 : New York, N.Y.) Transcript proceedings . New York, NY (3 E. 54th St., New York 10022-3180) , c1986. 214 p. : LC Card 87-404527 DDC 659.14/3/0973 19
HF6146.T42 A27 1986

Advertising Research Foundation Key Issues Workshop (1986 : New York, N.Y.) Transcript proceedings . New York, NY (3 E. 54th St., New York 10022-3180) , c1986. 268 p. : LC Card 87-149342 DDC 658.8/3 19
HF5802.5 .A3826 1986

Advertising Research Foundation Qualitative Research Workshop (1985 : New York, N.Y.) Qualitative research . New York, NY (3 E. 54th St., New York 10022-3180) , c1985. 121 p. : LC Card 86-212738 DDC 659.1/072 19
HF5802.5 .A383 1985

ADVERTISING RESEARCH FOUNDATION - CONGRESSES.
Advertising Research Foundation Key Issues Workshop (1986 : New York, N.Y.) Transcript proceedings . New York, NY (3 E. 54th St., New York 10022-3180) , c1986. 268 p. : LC Card 87-149342 DDC 658.8/3 19
HF5802.5 .A3826 1986

Advertising Research Foundation Key Issues Workshop (1985 : New York, N.Y.)
Transcript proceedings : electronic media and research technologies-IV, coping with the reality of today's media and measurement : an Advertising Research Foundation Key Issues Workshop, New York Marriott Marquis, December 12, 1985. New York, NY (3 E. 54th St., New York 10022-3180) : The Foundation, c1985. 174 p. : ill. ; 28 cm. Spine title: ARF electronic media and research technologies-IV Workshop. Bibliography: p. 162. LC Card 86-214476 DDC 659.14/3/0973 19
1. Television advertising - Research - United States - Technological innovations - Congresses. 2. Cable television advertising - Research - United States - Technological innovations - Congresses. 3. Advertising media planning - United States - Congresses. I. Title. II. Title: Electronic media and research technologies-IV. III. Title: ARF electronic media and research technologies-IV Workshop.
HF6146.T42 A27 1985a

Transcript proceedings : 15-second commercials, is less more? : an Advertising Research Foundation Key Issues Workshop, New York Marriott Marquis, December 13, 1985. New York, NY (3 E. 54th St., New York 10022-3180) : The Foundation, c1985. 161 p. : ill. ; 28 cm. Spine title: ARF 15-second commercials workshop. LC Card 86-211136 DDC 659.14/3/0973 19
1. Television advertising - United States - Congresses. I. Title. II. Title: ARF 15-second commercials workshop. III. Title: ARF fifteen second commercials workshop. IV. Title: 15-second commercials, is less more?. V. Title: Fifteen second commercials, is less more?.
HF6146.T42 A27 1985

Advertising Research Foundation Key Issues Workshop (1986 : Boston, Mass.)
Marketing-oriented financial services advertising and research : transcript proceedings, November 21, 1986, Copley Plaza Hotel, Boston / an ARF Key Issues Workshop. New York, NY : Advertising Research Foundation, c1986. 119 p. : ill. ; 28 cm. "A special Advertising Research Foundation workshop for all financial services marketers and researchers." Cover title. LC Card 87-404482 DDC 659.1/93321 19
1. Advertising - Financial services industry - Congresses. I. Title.
HF6161.F46 A38 1986

Advertising Research Foundation Key Issues Workshop (1986 : New York, N.Y.)
Transcript proceedings : electric media and research technologies-V, new information, new leverage? how the industry is coping : a two-day ARF Key Issues Workshop, the New York Hilton, December 10-11, 1986. New York, NY (3 E. 54th St., New York 10022-3180) : Advertising Research Foundation, c1986. 214 p. : ill. ; 28 cm. Spine title: Electronic media and research technologies-V. LC Card 87-404527 DDC 659.14/3/0973 19
1. Television advertising - Research - United States - Technological innovations - Congresses. 2. Cable television advertising - Research - United States - Technological innovations - Congresses. 3. Video tapes - United States - Congresses. 4. Advertising media planning - United States - Congresses. I. Advertising Research Foundation. II. Title. III. Title: Electronic media and research technologies-V.
HF6146.T42 A27 1986

Transcript proceedings : today's marketing research : optimizing its effectiveness in the brand/advertising process : Special ARF 50th Anniversary Key Issues Workshop, New York Grand Hyatt Hotel, July 21-22, 1986. New York, NY (3 E. 54th St., New York 10022-3180) : Advertising Research Foundation, c1986. 268 p. : ill. ; 28 cm. Spine title: Advertising Research Foundation 50th Anniversary Key Issues Workshop. LC Card 87-149342 DDC 658.8/3 19
1. Advertising - Research - United States - Technological innovations - Congresses. 2. Marketing research - United States - Technological innovations - Congresses. 3. Advertising media planning - United States - Congresses. 4. Advertising - Research - United States - Data processing - Congresses. 5. Advertising Research Foundation - Congresses. I. Advertising Research Foundation. II. Title. III. Title: Today's marketing research. IV. Title: Advertising Research Foundation 50th Anniversary Key Issues Workshop.
HF5802.5 .A3826 1986

Advertising Research Foundation Qualitative Research Workshop (1985 : New York, N. Y.) Qualitative research : the state of work, today's applications, future promise : transcript proceedings / Advertising Research Foundation Qualitative Research Workshop, the New York Hilton, November 25, 1985. New York, NY (3 E. 54th St., New York 10022-3180) : ARF, c1985. 121 p. : ill. ; 28 cm. LC Card 86-212738 DDC 659.1/072 19
1. Advertising research - Congresses. I. Advertising Research Foundation. II. Title.
HF5802.5 .A383 1985

Advertising Research Foundation 50th Anniversary Key Issues Workshop. Advertising Research Foundation Key Issues Workshop (1986 : New York, N.Y.) Transcript proceedings . New York, NY (3 E. 54th St., New York 10022-3180) , c1986. 268 p. : LC Card 87-149342 DDC 658.8/3 19
HF5802.5 .A3826 1986

ADVERTISING - RESEARCH - UNITED STATES - DATA PROCESSING - CONGRESSES.
Advertising Research Foundation Key Issues Workshop (1986 : New York, N.Y.) Transcript proceedings . New York, NY (3 E. 54th St., New York 10022-3180) , c1986. 268 p. : LC Card 87-149342 DDC 658.8/3 19
HF5802.5 .A3826 1986

ADVERTISING - RESEARCH - UNITED STATES - TECHNOLOGICAL INNOVATIONS - CONGRESSES.
Advertising Research Foundation Key Issues Workshop (1986 : New York, N.Y.) Transcript proceedings . New York, NY (3 E. 54th St., New York 10022-3180) , c1986. 268 p. : LC Card 87-149342 DDC 658.8/3 19
HF5802.5 .A3826 1986

ADVERTISING, RETAIL. see **ADVERTISING.**

ADVERTISING - RETAIL TRADE. see **ADVERTISING.**

Advertising self-regulation and outside participation . Boddewyn, J. J. (Jean J.) New York , c1988. p. cm. ISBN 0-89930-295-5 (lib. bdg. : alk. paper) LC Card 87-24939 DDC 659.1/1 19
HF5834 .B63 1988

ADVERTISING - SELF-REGULATION - CASE STUDIES.
Boddewyn, J. J. (Jean J.) Advertising self-regulation and outside participation . New York , c1988. p. cm. ISBN 0-89930-295-5 (lib. bdg. : alk. paper) LC Card 87-24939 DDC 659.1/1 19
HF5834 .B63 1988

ADVERTISING - SHOPPING CENTERS.
Wenner, S. Albert. Marketing your shopping center . New York , c1987. xi, 194 p. : ISBN 0-913598-55-0 LC Card 87-2848 DDC 658.8/7 19
HF5430 .W46 1987

ADVERTISING - SLOGANS. see **SLOGANS.**

ADVERTISING - SOCIAL ASPECTS - UNITED STATES.
Gold, Philip, 1948- Advertising, politics, and American culture . New York , c1987. xix, 217 p. ; ISBN 0-913729-35-3 LC Card 86-30291 DDC 659.1/0973 19
HF5813.U6 G58 1987

ADVERTISING - SPAIN.
Ferrer Roselló, Clemente, 1938- Los profesionales . Madrid [1984?] 643 p. : ISBN 84-256-0424-9 LC Card 86-213550
HF5813.S8 F47 1984

ADVERTISING - SPORTING GOODS - UNITED STATES - CATALOGS.
Strauss, Bob. American sporting advertising /. Jefferson, Me. (Box 1060, Jefferson 04348) , 1987- v. <1 > : LC Card 87-155421 DDC 741.67/0973/074013 19
HF6161.S65 S77 1987

ADVERTISING - SWEDEN - HISTORY - 20TH CENTURY.
Jonsson, Sverker, 1941- Pressen, reklamen och konkurrensen, 1935-1978 /. Göteborg , 1982. 406 p. : ISBN 91-85196-24-X : LC Card 84-157282
HF6105.S8 J66 1982

ADVERTISING - SWITZERLAND - CONGRESSES.
Werbung in einem mehrsprachigen Land /. Freiburg, Schweiz , c1986. 152 p. : ISBN 3-7278-0382-7 LC Card 87-409238 DDC 659.1/09494 19
HF5808.S9 W47 1986

ADVERTISING - SWITZERLAND - HISTORY.
Kutter, Markus, 1925- Werbung in der Schweiz . [Zürich] , 1983. 271 p., xvi p. of plates : ISBN 3-85859-202-1 : LC Card 84-142450
HF5813.S94 K87 1983

ADVERTISING, TELEVISION. see **TELEVISION ADVERTISING.**

ADVERTISING - TOBACCO TRADE.
Chapman, Simon. Great expectorations . London , 1986. 158 p. : ISBN 0-906890-86-1 (pbk.) : LC Card 86-204305 DDC 659.1/96797 19
HF6161.T6 C48 1986

ADVERTISING, TRANSPORTATION. see **ADVERTISING CARDS.**

ADVERTISING - UNITED STATES.
Gold, Philip, 1948- Advertising, politics, and American culture . New York , c1987. xix, 217 p. ; ISBN 0-913729-35-3 LC Card 86-30291 DDC 659.1/0973 19
HF5813.U6 G58 1987

McAuliffe, Robert E. Advertising, competition, and public policy . Lexington, Mass. , c1987. vi, 116 p. ; ISBN 0-669-12391-9 (alk. paper) LC Card 85-45896 DDC 659.1/0973 19
HF5813.U6 M33 1987 ***NYPL [JLE 87-1426]***

ADVERTISING - UNITED STATES - BIOGRAPHY.
Ogilvy, David, 1911- The unpublished David Ogilvy /. New York , c1986. 178 p., [6] p. of plates : ISBN 0-517-56609-5 : LC Card 87-13583 DDC 659.1/092/4 B 19
HF5810.O34 A3 1986

ADVERTISING - UNITED STATES - HISTORY.
Levenson, Bob. Bill Bernbach's book . New York , 1987. xvii, 219 p. : ISBN 0-394-54920-1 : LC Card 86-40103 DDC 659.1/0973 19
HF5813.U6 L48 1987

ADVERTISING - UNITED STATES - HISTORY - 20TH CENTURY - PICTORIAL WORKS.
1,001 advertising cuts from the twenties and thirties /. New York , 1987. 103 p. : ISBN 0-486-25490-9 (pbk.) LC Card 87-15546 DDC 659.13/2/0973 19
HF5813.U6 A525 1987

ADVERTISING - UNITED STATES - SELF-REGULATION.
Miracle, Gordon E. Voluntary regulation of advertising . Lexington, Mass. , c1987. xxvi, 322 p. : ISBN 0-669-13135-0 (alk. paper) LC Card 86-45294 DDC 338.4/76591/0941 19
HF5834 .M57 1987

ADVERTISING - VOCATIONAL GUIDANCE.
Laskin, David. Getting into advertising /. New York , 1986. xiii, 272 p. : ISBN 0-345-32598-2 (pbk.) LC Card 86-90721 DDC 659.1/023/73 19
HF5828.4 .L37 1986

Placier, Anne. Les métiers de la publicité /. Paris , c1984. 247 p., [15] p. of plates : ISBN 2-86745-019-5 LC Card 85-118630
HF5828.4 .P58 1984

Advice, a high profit business . Holtz, Herman. Englewood Cliffs, N.J. , c1986. xii, 242 p. : ISBN 0-13-011958-X LC Card 85-24405 DDC 658.4/6/0688 19
HD69.C6 H618 1986 ***NYPL [JLE 86-3858]***

Advies inzake het sociaal-economisch beleid op middellange termijn 1986-1990 /. Sociaal-Economische Raad. Den Haag [1986] 142, 150 p. ; ISBN 90-6587-248-5 LC Card 86-234847
HC321 .S63 1986, nr. 10 HC325

Advies minimum internationale arbeidsnormen /. Netherlands. Nationale Advies Raad voor Ontwikkelingssamenwerking. 's-Gravenhage [1984] 97 p. ; ISBN 90-12-04950-4 LC Card 86-193168
HC60 .N465 no. 84a K1705.4

Advies samenloop Wet OR en ARBO-wet : advies inzake samenloop van de Wet op de Ondernemingsraden en de Arbeidsomstandighedenwet. Den Haag : Sociaal-Economische Raad, [1986] 37 p. ; 25 cm. (Publikatie . nr. 6 (23 mei 1986)) "Uitgebracht aan de minister en de staatssecretaris van Sociale Zaken en Werkgelegenheid, mevrouw A. Kappeyne van de Coppello." By Commissie Ondernemingsraden of Sociaal-Economische Raad. Includes bibliographical references. ISBN 90-6587-243-4 LC Card 87-104667
1. Industrial safety - Law and legislation - Netherlands. 2. Industrial hygiene - Law and legislation - Netherlands. 3. Works councils - Law and legislation - Netherlands. I. Sociaal-Economische Raad. Commissie Ondernemingsraden. II. Series: Publikatie (Sociaal-Economische Raad) , 86/6.
HC321 .S63 1986, nr. 6 KKM1430

Advies vereenvoudiging Wet OR . Sociaal-Economische Raad. Commissie Ondernemingsraden. Den Haag [1986] 61 p. ; ISBN 90-6587-254-X LC Card 87-165080
HC321 .S63 1986, nr. 14 KKM1350

Advies vrouwen en ontwikkeling /. Netherlands. Nationale Advies Raad voor Ontwikkelingssamenwerking. [The Hague , 1985] 53 p. ; ISBN 90-12-04985-7 LC Card 86-198854
HC60 .N465 no. 85 HQ1240

Advies wijziging Winkelsluitingswet : advies inzake mogelijke aanpassingen van de Winkelsluitingswet. Den Haag : Sociaal-Economische Raad, [1986] 78 p. ; 25 cm. (Publikatie . nr. 11 (20 juni 1986)) "Uitgebracht aan de staatssecretaris van Economische Zaken, de heer P.H. van Zeil." Includes bibliographical references. ISBN 90-6587-250-7 LC Card 86-234857
1. Store hours - Law and legislation - Netherlands. I. Sociaal-Economische Raad. II. Series: Publikatie (Sociaal-Economische Raad) , 86/11.
HC321 .S63 1986, nr. 11 KKM3419

Advising clients on real estate investments /. Calder, Eugene B. New York, NY (11 Penn Plaza, New York 10001) , 1987. 95 p. in various pagings : LC Card 87-61983 DDC 332.63/24 19
HD1382.5 .C34 1987

ADVOCACY ADVERTISING.
Heath, Robert L. (Robert Lawrence), 1941- Issues management . Beverly Hills , c1986. 288 p. ; ISBN 0-8039-2535-2 LC Card 85-14547 DDC 659.2 19
HD59 .H33 1986 ***NYPL [JLD 87-19]***

ADVOCACY ADVERTISING - GERMANY (WEST) - COLOGNE.
Haas, Ingrid. Funktion und Wirkung von Aufklebern an Personenkraftwagen /. Köln [1983] 101, [13] p. : LC Card 84-147451
HE5614.5.G3 H28 1983

ADVOCACY ADVERTISING - UNITED STATES.
Gold, Philip, 1948- Advertising, politics, and American culture . New York , c1987. xix, 217 p. ; ISBN 0-913729-35-3 LC Card 86-30291 DDC 659.1/0973 19
HF5813.U6 G58 1987

Adzhiev, M. Ė. (Murad Ėskanderovich)
Sibir′--XX vek / Murad Adzhiev. Moskva : "Mysl′", 1983. 252 p., [24] p. of plates : ill. (some col.), ports. ; 22 cm. LC Card 83-161484
1. Siberia (R.S.F.S.R.) - Economic conditions. 2. Natural resources - Russian S.F.S.R. - Siberia. I. Title. II. Title: Sibir′--20-yĭ vek. III. Title: Sibir′--dvadtsatyĭ vek.
HC337.R852 S522 1983

A.E. ext. .
(86-3) The Farm credit crisis policy options and consequences /. Ithaca, N.Y. [1986] ii, 57 p. : LC Card 86-621935 DDC 338.1 s 332.7/1/0973 19
HD1775.N8 C6 no. 86-3 HG2051.U6

A.E. research .
(85-18) Kay, David L. The Adirondack land market . Ithaca, N.Y. [1985] 53 p. : LC Card 86-621939 DDC 333.33/22/0974753 19
HD266.N72 A265 1985

(85-7) Carraro, Kenneth C. An economic evaluation of alternative sources of funding for agricultural lending by commercial banks /. Ithaca, N.Y. [1985] 48 p. ; LC Card 86-622432 DDC 332.7/1/09747 19
HG2051.U6 N53 1985

(86-13) Stanton, B. F. (Bernard Freeland), 1925- The cereals dilemma . Ithaca, N.Y. [1986] 50 p. : LC Card 86-622419 DDC 338.1/731/094 19
HD9045.A2 S7 1986

(86-2) Stanton, B. F. (Bernard Freeland), 1925- Production costs for cereals in the European community . Ithaca, N.Y. [1986] 178 p., 2 p. of plates : LC Card 86-622607 DDC 338.1/331/094 19
HD9045.E82 S73 1986

Aeberhardt, Werner. Die Umweltpolitik im Spannungsfeld politischer und wirtschaftlicher Interessen / Werner Aeberhardt. Köln : Institut für Wirtschaftspolitik an der Universität zu Köln, 1985. 134, [9] p. : ill. ; 24 cm. (Untersuchungen zur Wirtschaftspolitik, 0175-7458 . 67) Originally presented as the author's thesis (doctoral)--Universität Bern. Bibliography: p. [5]-[9] (2nd group) ISBN 3-921471-55-9 : LC Card 86-145456
1. Environmental policy - Switzerland. 2. Environmental protection - Switzerland. 3. Environmental law - Switzerland. 4. Pressure groups - Switzerland. I. Title. II. Series.
HC400.E5 A33 1985

Aebi, Ernst. SBB im Aaretal : 125 Jahre von der Stichbahn Bern-Thun zur modernen Transitlinie : offizielles Jubiläumsbuch der Schweizerischen Bundesbahnen / Ernst Aebi, Jürg Aschlimann. Luzern : Minirex, c1984. 111 p. : ill. (some col.) ; 24 cm. Ill. on lining papers. Bibliography: p. 110. LC Card 84-234665
1. Railroads - Switzerland - Aar River Valley - History. 2. Schweizerische Bundesbahnen - History. I. Aschlimann, Jürg. II. Title.
HE3898.A37 A42 1984

AEBI, JOHANN ULRICH, 1846-1919.
Tauber, Herbert. Johann Ulrich Aebi . Zürich , c1983. 84, [2] p. : LC Card 83-192282
HC395.5.A2 S3 no. 38 HD9486.S94A36

AEBI MASCHINENFABRIK (BURGDORF, SWITZERLAND) - HISTORY.
Tauber, Herbert. Johann Ulrich Aebi . Zürich , c1983. 84, [2] p. : LC Card 83-192282
HC395.5.A2 S3 no. 38 HD9486.S94A36

Aedo, Cristián. Protección efectiva en Chile, 1974-1979 / Cristián Aedo, Luis Felipe Lagos. Santiago : Pontificia Universidad Católica de Chile, Instituto de Economía, [1984] 56 leaves ; 27 cm. (Documento de trabajo . no. 94) LC Card 85-152465
1. Tariff - Chile - Mathematical models. 2. Free trade and protection - Protection - Mathematical models. 3. Chile - Commercial policy - Mathematical models. I. Lagos, Luis Felipe. II. Series: Documento de trabajo (Universidad Católica de Chile. Instituto de Economía) , no. 94. III. Title.
HF1956 .A35 1984

The AEI economist, 0149-9785.
Ross, Murray N. Public choice . [Washington, D.C.] [c1987] 8 p. ; LC Card 87-403005 DDC 338.9 19
HB846.8 .R66 1987

AEI studies .
(440) Hicks, Donald A. Automation technology and industrial renewal . Washington, D.C. [1985], c1986. xiii, 160 p. ; ISBN 0-8447-3598-1 LC Card 85-31568 DDC 671 19
HD9506.U62 H53 1986
NYPL [JSE 86-1901]

(441) Breit, William. Antitrust penalty reform . Washington, D.C. , c1986. x, 83 p. : ISBN 0-8447-3600-7 (alk. paper) LC Card 86-3203 DDC 343.73/072/0269 347.303720269 19
KF1657.T7 B74 1986 ***NYPL [JLE 86-3948]***

(448) Steuerle, C. Eugene, 1946- Who should pay for collecting taxes? . Washington, D.C. , 1986. p. cm. ISBN 0-8447-3609-0 (pbk. : alk. paper) : LC Card 86-22345 DDC 353.0072/4 19
HJ5018 .S84 1986

(450) McLure, Charles E. The value-added tax . Washington, D.C. : Lanham, MD ; xi, 184 p. : ISBN 0-8447-3613-9 (alk. paper) LC Card 86-28905 DDC 339.5/25/0973 19
HJ5715.U6 M364 1987

(451) Exchange rate targets . Washington, D.C. , c1986. ix, 59 p. ; ISBN 0-8447-3615-5 (pbk. : alk. paper) : LC Card 86-72463 DDC 332.4/5 19
HG203 .E98 1986

(457) Arndt, Sven W. Competitiveness . Washington, D.C. , Lanham, MD , c1987. 120 p. : ISBN 0-8447-3625-2 (alk. paper) LC Card 87-1250 DDC 382/.0973 19
HF3031 .A83 1987

(459) Lynn, Leonard H. Organizing business . Washington, D.C. , c1988. xviii, 191 p. ; ISBN 0-8447-3629-5 (alk. paper) LC Card 87-17468 DDC 061/.3 19
HD2425 .L96 1988

AEI studies, 0892-3981 .
(455) Contemporary economic problems . Washington, D.C. , c1987. 332 p. : ISBN 0-8447-3621-X (alk. paper) LC Card 87-1395 DDC 330.973/0927 19
HC106.8 .C665 1987

Änderung der Beitragsfinanzierung in der Rentenversicherung? . Schmähl, Winfried. Baden-Baden , 1984. 388 p. : ISBN 3-7890-1018-9 LC Card 84-206647
HD7179 .S324 1984

AER LINGUS - HISTORY.
Share, Bernard. Flight of the Iolar . Goldenbridge, Dublin , Dallas [Texas] , c1986. xii, 306 p. : ISBN 0-7171-1457-0 LC Card 86-223299
HE9846.A47 S42 1986

AERONAUTICS AND STATE - UNITED STATES.
Morrison, Steven A., 1951- The economic effects of airline deregulation /. Washington, D.C. , c1986. xi, 84 : ISBN 0-8157-5845-6 (pbk.) : LC Card 85-48202 DDC 387.7/1 19
HE9803.A4 M67 1986 NYPL [JLE 86-3309]

AERONAUTICS, COMMERCIAL - AUSTRALIA - DEREGULATION.
Findlay, Christopher C. (Christopher Charles) The flying kangaroo, an endangered species? . Sydney , Boston , 1985. xii, 121 p. : ISBN 0-86861-406-8 (pbk.) LC Card 85-71362 DDC 387.7/065/94 19
HE9889.A4 F56 1985

AERONAUTICS, COMMERCIAL - BIOGRAPHY.
Davies, R. E. G. (Ronald Edward George) Rebels and reformers of the airways /. Washington, D.C. , c1987. xvi, 440 p. : ISBN 0-87474-354-0 (alk. paper) LC Card 86-26243 DDC 387.7/092/2 19
HE9775 .D38 1987

AERONAUTICS, COMMERCIAL - BRAZIL.
Brazil. Congresso Nacional. Câmara dos Deputados. Comissão de Esporte e Turismo. Vôos "charters" e as empresas de aviação civil . Brasília , 1986. 98 p. ; LC Card 87-405035 DDC 387.7/0981 19
HE9833.A4 B7 1986

AERONAUTICS, COMMERCIAL - CANADA.
Lin, Leesha. U. S. essential air services study /. Ottawa-Hull , c1986. viii, 118 p. : ISBN 0-662-14800-2 (pbk.) LC Card 87-102545 DDC 387.7/1 19
HE9803.A4 L55 1986

AERONAUTICS, COMMERCIAL - CHARTERING - UNITED STATES - SAFETY MEASURES.
United States. Congress. House. Committee on Armed Services. Subcommittee on Investigations. Report on the safety of aircraft under charter to the Department of Defense . Washington , 1986. iii, 17 p. ; LC Card 86-603401 DDC 363.1/24 19
HE9803.Z7 C538 1986

AERONAUTICS, COMMERCIAL - DEREGULATION.
Knieps, Günter. Deregulierung im Luftverkehr . Tübingen , c1987. 69 p. ; ISBN 3-16-345148-9 LC Card 87-121052 DDC 387.7/1 19
HE9776 .K6 1987

Pryke, Richard. Competition among international airlines /. Aldershot , Brookfield, USA , 1987. xi, 113 p. : ISBN 0-566-05333-0 : LC Card 86-31877 DDC 387.7/1 19
HE9780 .P79 1987

AERONAUTICS, COMMERCIAL - EUROPE.
Naveau, Jacques, docteur en droit. L'Europe et le transport aérien /. Bruxelles , 1983. 346 p. ; ISBN 2-8027-0304-8 LC Card 85-114595
HE9842.A4 N38 1983

AERONAUTICS, COMMERCIAL - EUROPE - DEREGULATION.
Barrett, Sean D. Flying high . Aldershot , Brookfield, USA , c1987. 96 p. ; ISBN 0-566-05541-4 (pbk.) : LC Card 87-11992 DDC 387.7/1 19
HE9783.3.E85 B37 1987

AERONAUTICS, COMMERCIAL - FARES. see **AIR LINES - RATES.**

AERONAUTICS, COMMERCIAL - FINLAND - HISTORY.
Wegg, John. Bluebirds /. [Helsinki?] , c1985. 216 p. : ISBN 951-99691-4-4 LC Card 86-223952 DDC 387.7/065/4897 19
HE9855.3.F5 W4 1985

AERONAUTICS, COMMERCIAL - FRANCE - HISTORY.
Danel, Raymond. Les lignes Latécoère . Toulouse , c1986. 208 p., [16] p. of plates : ISBN 2-7089-8611-2 : LC Card 87-165510
HE9848.C66 D36 1986 vol. 1

AERONAUTICS, COMMERCIAL - FREIGHT - DATA PROCESSING - CASE STUDIES.
Krieger, Winfried. Computergestützte Auswahl interkontinentaler Distributionsverfahren /. Berlin , c1984. 143 p. : ISBN 3-428-05617-5 LC Card 84-219069
HF5765 .K75 1984

AERONAUTICS, COMMERCIAL - GERMANY (WEST) - PASSENGER TRAFFIC.
Die Struktur des von der Bundesrepublik Deutschland ausgehenden Nordatlantik-Personen-Luftverkehrs . [Frankfurt am Main] [1963] 165 p. : LC Card 85-126310
HE9787.5.G4 S77 1963

AERONAUTICS, COMMERCIAL - GOVERNMENT POLICY.
Jönsson, Christer, 1944- International aviation and the politics of regime change /. New York , 1987. vi, 185 p. : ISBN 0-312-00463-X : LC Card 86-31328 DDC 341.7/567 19
HE9762 .J65 1987

Reason in the air . [S.l.] [1977] 31 p. : LC Card 85-149832 DDC 387.7/068 19
HE9777.7 .R43 1977

AERONAUTICS, COMMERCIAL - GOVERNMENT POLICY - EUROPE.
Naveau, Jacques, docteur en droit. L'Europe et le transport aérien /. Bruxelles , 1983. 346 p. ; ISBN 2-8027-0304-8 LC Card 85-114595
HE9842.A4 N38 1983

AERONAUTICS, COMMERCIAL - GOVERNMENT POLICY - EUROPEAN ECONOMIC COMMUNITY COUNTRIES.
EEC air transport policy . Brussels [1985] iv, 72 p., [1] leaf of plates : LC Card 86-215015 DDC 387.7/094 19
HE9842.8 .E42 1985

AERONAUTICS, COMMERCIAL - GOVERNMENT POLICY - UNITED STATES - HISTORY.
Preston, Edmund, 1941- Troubled passage . Washington, D.C. , 19. vii, 340 p. ; LC Card 87-25500 DDC 353.0087/77 19
HE9803.A35 P74 1987

AERONAUTICS, COMMERCIAL - GREAT BRITAIN - HISTORY.
Campbell-Smith, Duncan. The British Airways story . London , 1986. viii, 327 p. ; ISBN 0-340-39495-1 (pbk.) : LC Card 86-206477 DDC 387.7/065/41 19
HE9843.B7 C36 1986

AERONAUTICS, COMMERCIAL - HISTORY.
Davies, R. E. G. (Ronald Edward George) Rebels and reformers of the airways /. Washington, D.C. , c1987. xvi, 440 p. : ISBN 0-87474-354-0 (alk. paper) LC Card 86-26243 DDC 387.7/092/2 19
HE9775 .D38 1987

AERONAUTICS, COMMERCIAL - INTERNATIONAL COOPERATION.
Jönsson, Christer, 1944- International aviation and the politics of regime change /. New York , 1987. vi, 185 p. : ISBN 0-312-00463-X : LC Card 86-31328 DDC 341.7/567 19
HE9762 .J65 1987

AERONAUTICS, COMMERCIAL - IRELAND - HISTORY.
Share, Bernard. Flight of the Iolar . Goldenbridge, Dublin , Dallas [Texas] , c1986. xii, 306 p. : ISBN 0-7171-1457-0 LC Card 86-223299
HE9846.A47 S42 1986

AERONAUTICS, COMMERCIAL - LAW AND LEGISLATION - UNITED STATES.
Brown, Anthony E. The politics of airline deregulation /. Knoxville , c1987. xiii, 224 p. ; ISBN 0-87049-532-1 (alk. paper) : LC Card 86-30888 DDC 387.7/1 19
HE9803.A4 B68 1987

Lin, Leesha. U. S. essential air services study /. Ottawa-Hull , c1986. viii, 118 p. : ISBN 0-662-14800-2 (pbk.) LC Card 87-102545 DDC 387.7/1 19
HE9803.A4 L55 1986

AERONAUTICS, COMMERCIAL - MARKETING.
Shaw, Stephen, 1950- Airline marketing and management /. Malabar , 1988, c1985. 296 p. ; ISBN 0-89464-256-1 LC Card 87-22639 DDC 387.7/4/0688 19
HE9781 .S35 1987

AERONAUTICS, COMMERCIAL - NEW YORK - THROOPSVILLE - HISTORY.
Ingalls, Roger W. A scrapbook history of the Auburn Aviation Co., Inc., and the Auburn Airport at Throopsville, N.Y., 1941-1952. Auburn, N.Y. , c1986. 169 p. : LC Card 87-125962
HE9803.A97 I54 1986

AERONAUTICS, COMMERCIAL - NEW ZEALAND - FREIGHT - ENERGY CONSUMPTION - COSTS.
Copeland, M. C. (Michael Campbell) Transport energy in New Zealand's overseas trade . Auckland, N.Z. [1982] iv, 130 p. : LC Card 84-159485 DDC 387.5/1 19
HE597.N4 C63 1982
NYPL [JSK 82-15 no.80]

AERONAUTICS, COMMERCIAL - NORTH AMERICA - PASSENGER TRAFFIC - STATISTICS.
1986 air travel survey /. Princeton, N.J. (53 Bank St., Princeton 08542) , c1986. 77 leaves ; LC Card 86-225970 DDC 387.7/42/0973 19
HE9787.5.N7 A17 1986

AERONAUTICS, COMMERCIAL - PASSENGER TRAFFIC - HISTORY.
Frater, Alexander, 1937- Beyond the blue horizon . New York , 1987, c1986. xviii, 430 p. : ISBN 0-684-18837-6 LC Card 87-9426 DDC 387.7/065/73 19
HE9787 .F7 1987

AERONAUTICS, COMMERCIAL - RATES. see **AIR LINES - RATES.**

AERONAUTICS, COMMERCIAL - SWEDEN - MANAGEMENT.
Carlzon, Jan. Moments of truth /. Cambridge, Mass. , c1987. xiii, 135 p. ; ISBN 0-88730-200-9 LC Card 87-1070 DDC 387.7/065/485 19
HE9860.S28 C37 1987

Carlzon, Jan. Riv pyramiderna! . [Stockholm] , c19. 219 p. : ISBN 91-0-046844-4 LC Card 86-139896
HE9860.S28 C375 1986

AERONAUTICS, COMMERCIAL - SWITZERLAND.
Mensch und Luftfahrt . Bern [1981] 177 p. : LC Card 83-116416
HE9863.A4 M45 1981

AERONAUTICS, COMMERCIAL - TANZANIA - STATISTICS.

Mkwawa, D. A. Y. A review of aerodrome statistics in Tanzania, 1970-1982. Dar es Salaam [1984] xix, 143 p. : LC Card 87-403351 DDC 387.7/36/09678021 19
HE9797.5.T34 M58 1984

AERONAUTICS, COMMERCIAL - UNITED STATES.
Taneja, Nawal K. The international airline industry . Lexington, Mass. , c1988. xvi, 167 p. : ISBN 0-669-16167-5 (alk. paper) LC Card 87-45227 DDC 387.7 19
HE9776 .T363 1988

AERONAUTICS, COMMERCIAL - UNITED STATES - DEREGULATION.
Brown, Anthony E. The politics of airline deregulation /. Knoxville , c1987. xiii, 224 p. ; ISBN 0-87049-532-1 (alk. paper) : LC Card 86-30888 DDC 387.7/1 19
HE9803.A4 B68 1987

Deregulation . Washington, D.C. [1985] vi, 86 p. : LC Card 86-602035 DDC 387.7/1 19
HE9803.A3 D47 1985

Lin, Leesha. U. S. essential air services study /. Ottawa-Hull , c1986. viii, 118 p. : ISBN 0-662-14800-2 (pbk.) LC Card 87-102545 DDC 387.7/1 19
HE9803.A4 L55 1986

Meyer, John Robert. Deregulation and the future of intercity passenger travel /. Cambridge, Mass. , c1987. xviii, 294 p. : ISBN 0-262-13225-7 LC Card 86-27308 DDC 387.7/42/0973 19
HE9803.A35 M49 1987

AERONAUTICS, COMMERCIAL - UNITED STATES - FREIGHT.
McAlpine, Pamela J. The air freight industry . Menlo Park, CA (333 Ravenswood Ave., Menlo Park 94025) , c1986. 12 leaves ; LC Card 87-402973 DDC 387.7/44/0973 19
HE9788.5.U5 M37 1986

AERONAUTICS, COMMERCIAL - UNITED STATES - HISTORY.
Cearley, George Walker. American Airlines . Dallas, Tex. (P.O. Box 12312, Dallas, 75225) , c1987. 136 p. : LC Card 87-132433 DDC 387.7/065/73 19
HE9803.A95 C4 1987

Davies, R. E. G. (Ronald Edward George) Pan Am . New York , c1987. vi, 90 p. : ISBN 0-517-56639-7 : LC Card 87-5581 DDC 387.7/065/73 19
HE9803.P36 D38 1987

AERONAUTICS, COMMERCIAL - UNITED STATES - PASSENGER TRAFFIC - HANDBOOKS, MANUALS, ETC.
Davidson, George, 1943- The ABC's of air travel /. Scottsdale, Ariz. , c1984. iv, 89 p. : ISBN 0-931921-00-7 (pbk.) : LC Card 84-71960 DDC 387.7/42/0973 19
HE9787.5.U5 D38 1984
NYPL [JLD 86-2219]

AERONAUTICS, COMMERCIAL - VENEZUELA - HISTORY.
Pacanins A., Guillermo (Pacanins Acevedo) La aviación comercial en Venezuela, de la carreta al avión /. Caracas , 1985. 159 p. : LC Card 85-184048
HE9841.A3 P33 1985

AERONAUTICS, COMMERCIAL - VOCATIONAL GUIDANCE.
Jasinski, Irv. Airline pilot interviews . Escondido, Calif. , c1987. 144 p. : ISBN 0-942195-01-9 (pbk.) LC Card 87-70680 DDC 629.132/5240423/02373 19
HE9777 .J36 1987

AERONAUTICS - COMPANIES. see **AIR LINES.**

AERONAUTICS - GOVERNMENT POLICY.
Jönsson, Christer, 1944- International aviation and the politics of regime change /. New York , 1987. vi, 185 p. : ISBN 0-312-00463-X : LC Card 86-31328 DDC 341.7/567 19
HE9762 .J65 1987

AERONAUTICS - INTERNATIONAL COOPERATION.
Jönsson, Christer, 1944- International aviation and the politics of regime change /. New York , 1987. vi, 185 p. : ISBN 0-312-00463-X : LC Card 86-31328 DDC 341.7/567 19
HE9762 .J65 1987

AERONAUTICS - LAW AND LEGISLATION.
Jönsson, Christer, 1944- International aviation and the politics of regime change /. New York , 1987. vi, 185 p. : ISBN 0-312-00463-X : LC Card 86-31328 DDC 341.7/567 19
HE9762 .J65 1987

AERONAUTICS - UNITED STATES - HISTORY.
Francis, Devon. Power to fly . [Fallbrook, CA] , 1986. 97 p. : ISBN 0-8168-7632-0 : LC Card 85-20045 DDC 338.4/76655825/0973 19
TL521 .F63 1986 ***NYPL [JSG 86-235]***

AERONAUTS. see **AIR PILOTS.**

AEROSPACE INDUSTRIES.
Aerospace markets /. Greenwich, CT, U. S.A. (100 Northfield St., Greenwich 06830) , c1987. 1 v. (various pagings) : LC Card 87-156000 DDC 380.1/456291 19
HD9711.5.A2 A37 1987

Dubarle, Patrick. The space industry . Paris, France [Washington, D.C.] c1985. 92 p. : ISBN 92-64-12772-0 : LC Card 86-210154 DDC 338.4/76291 19
HD9711.5.A2 D83 1985

AEROSPACE INDUSTRIES - BRAZIL.
Green, Ronald D. Brazilian government support for the aerospace industry /. [Washington, D.C.?] [1987] xi, 44 p. ; LC Card 87-601479 DDC 338.4/76291/0981 19
HD9711.B72 G74 1987

AEROSPACE INDUSTRIES - STATISTICS.
Todd, Daniel. World aerospace . London , New York , c1987. 226 p. : ISBN 0-7099-4325-3 LC Card 86-29368 DDC 338.4/76291/021 19
HD9711.5.A2 T629 1987

AEROSPACE INDUSTRIES - UNITED STATES - HISTORY.
Gunston, Bill. The Grumman story /. New York , 1988, c1987. p. cm. ISBN 0-517-56796-2 : LC Card 87-21964 DDC 338.7/6291/0973 19
HD9711.5.U63 G784 1988

AEROSPACE LAW. see **AERONAUTICS - LAW AND LEGISLATION.**

Aerospace markets / project director, Thomas F. Sweeney ; contributing editors, George Balin ... [et al.]. Greenwich, CT, U. S.A. (100 Northfield St., Greenwich 06830) : Defense Marketing Services, c1987. 1 v. (various pagings) : ill. ; 30 cm. LC Card 87-156000 DDC 380.1/456291 19
1. Aerospace industries. 2. Market surveys. I. Sweeney, Thomas F. II. Balin, George. III. Defense Marketing Services, inc.
HD9711.5.A2 A37 1987

AEROSTATION. see **AERONAUTICS.**

Aerts, Christel. Advertenties en affiches : kenmerken van de Nederlandse reclametaal in België / Christel Aerts en Rina Mens. [Wilrijk, Belgium] : Universiteit Antwerpen, Universitaire Instelling Antwerpen, Departement Germaanse, Afd. Linguïstiek, 1986. 165, [7] p. : ill. ; 21 cm. (Antwerp papers in linguistics . 50) Bibliography: p. [166]-[167] LC Card 86-222214
1. Advertising - Language. 2. Advertising, Dutch - Belgium. 3. Dutch language - Usage. I. Mens, Rina. II. Title. III. Series.
HF5827 .A43 1986

AESTHETICS, MODERN - 20TH CENTURY.
Zellinger, Alfred, 1945- Die Sinnlichkeit der Theorie . Wien , c1983. 173 p. : ISBN 3-85439-005-X LC Card 84-196565
HF1040.7 .Z45 1983

Affan, Bodour O. Abu.
Industrial policies and industrialization in the Sudan / Bodour Osman Abu Affan. Khartoum, Sudan : Graduate College, University of Khartoum, 1985. 180 p. ; 22 cm. (Graduate College publications . no. 16) Bibliography: p. 174-180. ISBN 0-08-637205-44 (pbk.) LC Card 86-981076 DDC 338.9624 19
1. Sudan - Economic conditions. 2. Sudan - Industries. 3. Industry and state - Sudan. 4. Sudan - Economic policy. I. Series: Graduate College publications , monograph 16. II. Title.
HC835 .A58 1985

Traffic and public transport in metropolitan Khartoum : problems and possibilities / by Bodour O. Abu Affan. Khartoum : Economic and Social Research Council, National Council for Research, [1985] iv, 73 leaves ; 32 cm. (Research report / Economic and Social Research Council, National Council for Research . no. 19) "November 1985." Bibliography: leaves 70-73. LC Card 86-980566 DDC 388.4/1/096262 19
1. Transportation - Sudan - Khartoum Metropolitan Area. I. Series: Research report (Majlis al-Abḥāth al-Iqtiṣādiyah wa-al-Ijtimāʻiyah) , no. 19. II. Title.
HE311.S742 K472 1985

AFFECT (PSYCHOLOGY) - CONGRESSES.
The Role of affect in consumer behavior . Lexington, Mass. , c1986. ix, 196 p. : ISBN 0-669-12874-0 (alk. paper) LC Card 85-46042 DDC 658.8/342 19
HF5415.3 .R65 1986 ***NYPL [JLE 86-3376]***

Affiches de pub, 1983/85 /. Benoit, Philippe. Paris , c1986. 237 p. : ISBN 2-85108-429-1 : LC Card 86-192339
HF5843 .B44 1986

Affirmative action data : state of Maryland and Baltimore metropolitan area, 1984. Baltimore, Md. (1100 N. Eutaw St., Baltimore 21201) : State of Maryland, Dept. of Employment and Training, Research and Analysis Division, [1985] [17] leaves ; 28 cm. Cover title. "September 1985"--leaf [1] Chiefly tables. Includes bibliographical references. LC Card 86-622599 DDC 331.11/43 19
1. Labor supply - Maryland - Statistics. 2. Minorities - Employment - Maryland - Statistics. 3. Women - Employment - Maryland - Statistics. I. Maryland. Dept. of Employment and Training. Research and Analysis Division.
HD5725.M35 A68 1985

Affirmative action implementation manual / Department of the Prime Minister and Cabinet, Office of the Status of Women, Affirmative Action Resource Unit. 2nd ed. Canberra : Australian Govt. Pub. Service, 1986. 66 p. ; 25 cm. ISBN 0-644-04750-X (pbk.) LC Card 87-109354 DDC 658.3 19
1. Affirmative action programs - Australia - Handbooks, manuals, etc. 2. Women - Employment - Australia - Handbooks, manuals, etc. I. Australia. Affirmative Action Resource Unit.
HD6060.5.A8 A34 1986

AFFIRMATIVE ACTION PROGRAMS - AUSTRALIA - HANDBOOKS, MANUALS, ETC.
Affirmative action implementation manual /. Canberra , 1986. 66 p. ; ISBN 0-644-04750-X (pbk.) LC Card 87-109354 DDC 658.3 19
HD6060.5.A8 A34 1986

AFFIRMATIVE ACTION PROGRAMS - CANADA.
Coates, Mary Lou. Employment equity . Kingston, Ont., Canada , 1986. 109 p. : ISBN 0-88886-131-1 (pbk.) LC Card 86-182985 DDC 331.13/3/0971 19
HD4903.5.C2 C6 1986

AFFIRMATIVE ACTION PROGRAMS - GREAT BRITAIN.
Dex, Shirley. British and American women at work . Houndmills, Basingstoke, Hampshire , 1986. xii, 159 p. : ISBN 0-333-40219-7
NYPL [JLD 86-3608]

AFFIRMATIVE ACTION PROGRAMS - LAW AND LEGISLATION - UNITED STATES.
Cope, Thom K. Executive guide to employment practices . Lincoln, Neb. , c1984. vii, 163 p. : ISBN 0-939644-14-2 (pbk.) : LC Card 84-62043 DDC 344.73/01133 347.3041133 19
KF3464.Z9 C65 1984 ***NYPL [JLE 87-75]***

Selected affirmative action topics in employment and business set-asides . Washington, D.C. , 1985- v. <1 > : LC Card 85-603434 DDC 331.13/3/0973 19
HF5549.5.A34 S45 1985

AFFIRMATIVE ACTION PROGRAMS - UNITED STATES.
Cohen, Leah. A summary of the American experience with the Federal Contract Compliance Program . [Ottawa] , 1979. 72 leaves ; ***NYPL [JLF 86-1657]***

Dex, Shirley. British and American women at work . Houndmills, Basingstoke, Hampshire , 1986. xii, 159 p. : ISBN 0-333-40219-7
NYPL [JLD 86-3608]

Equal opportunity /. Boulder , 1988. viii, 200 p. ; ISBN 0-8133-0567-5 (pbk. : alk. paper) LC Card 87-7253 DDC 331.13/3/0973 19
HF5549.5.A34 E7 1988

Fuchs, Lawrence H. When to count by race .

New York, NY , c1986. 32 p. ; ISBN 0-87495-082-1 (pbk.) : LC Card 86-71979 DDC 658.3 19
HD4903.5.U58 F83 1986

Little, Alan. Loading the law . London , 1982. 67 p. ; ISBN 0-902355-98-8 (pbk.)
NYPL [JLD 87-1941]

Selected affirmative action topics in employment and business set-asides . Washington, D.C. , 1985- v. <1 > : LC Card 85-603434 DDC 331.13/3/0973 19
HF5549.5.A34 S45 1985

Selected affirmative action topics in employment and business set-asides . Washington, D.C. , 1985-1986. 2 v. :
NYPL [JLM 86-600]

The Affluent market. New York, N.Y. (500 5th Ave., New York 10110) : Find/SVP, [1984] 227 leaves : ill. ; 29 cm. (A Business information report) "April 1984." LC Card 86-201904 DDC 658.8/348 19
1. Consumers - United States. 2. Wealth - United States. I. Find/SVP (Firm). II. Series.
HC110.C6 A63 1984

The Affluent market fact book : the financial and investment status, behavior, and preferences of affluent consumers, 1981-1985. Tampa, Fla. : Payment Systems, c1986. 83 leaves ; 28 cm. Bibliography: p. 10. LC Card 86-235264 DDC 332.1/7 19
1. Banks and banking - United States - Customer services. 2. Bank marketing - United States. 3. Rich as consumers - United States. 4. Market surveys - United States. I. Payment Systems, Inc.
HG1616.C87 A33 1986

Affording access to quality care : strategies for state medicaid cost management / edited by Richard Curtis and Ian Hill. Washington, D.C. (444 N. Capitol St., N.W., Suite 250, Washington 20001) : National Governors' Association, Center for Policy Research, c1986. xx, 245 p. ; 28 cm. (Health policy studies) LC Card 87-127057 DDC 338.4/336210452/0973 19
1. Medicaid - Costs. 2. Medical care - United States - Finance. 3. Medical care - United States - Cost control. I. Curtis, Richard (Richard E.). II. Hill, Ian, 1958-. III. National Governors' Association. Center for Policy Research. IV. Series.
HD7102.U4 A66 1986

Les affranchis de l'an 2000 /. Duboin, Marie-Louise. Paris , c1984. 303 p. ; ISBN 2-86738-026-X : LC Card 84-203792
HD83 .D74 1984

AFFREIGHTMENT. see **FREIGHT AND FREIGHTAGE.**

Afghani, Abdus Sattar. Traffic growth in Karachi : projections 1990 : presented at XIII Conference of the Mayors of the World's Major Cities on "problems of urban circulation in the 90's", at Milan / Abdus Sattar Afghani. [Karachi] : Karachi Metropolitan Corporation, [1985] [25] leaves : ill., chart, folded map ; 28 cm. "April 1985"--Cover. LC Card 85-931413 DDC 388.4/13142/09549183 19
1. Traffic estimation - Pakistan - Karachi. I. Conference of the Mayors of the World's Major Cities (13th : 1984 : Milan, Italy). II. Title. III. Title: Problems of urban circulation in the 90's.
HE373.P183 K372 1985

Afhandling (Københavns universitet. Sociologisk institut) .
(1985, nr. 3) Gydesen, Ellen. Kvinders livsgrundlag i 80-erne /. K [i.e. Copenhagen] [1985] 202 columns : LC Card 87-168500
HD6060.65.D4 G93 1985

Afheldt, Heik, 1937- Gewerbeentwicklung und Gewerbepolitik in der Grossstadtregion /. Gerlingen , c1987. 390 p., [3] leaves of plates : ISBN 3-88350-596-X LC Card 87-146643 DDC 332.6/732243 19
HC290.5.I53 G4797 1987

AFL-CIO.
Campero, Guillermo. El sindicalismo internacional y la redemocratización de Chile /. Santiago, Chile , 1984. 77 p. ; LC Card 86-139122 DDC 331.88/0983 19
HD6617 .C357 1984

AFL-CIO. Food and Allied Service Trades Dept.
The Future is now /. [Washington, D.C.] [1985] 34, xxi, [ii], leaves ; LC Card 86-211338 DDC 331.12/51/000973 19
HD5718.S452 U535 1985

Plastics industry research manual /. [S.l.] [1985] 69 leaves ; LC Card 86-219855 DDC 338.4/7668497/0973 19
HD9661.U62 P489 1985

A Profile of the baking industry. [Washington, D.C.] [1985] 49 leaves ; LC Card 86-211982 DDC 338.4/7664752/0973 19
HD9057.U59 P76 1985

A View of unions /. [Washington? D.C.] [1985] 25 p. ; LC Card 86-211350 DDC 331.88/0973 19
HD6508 .V39 1985

AFM-Europa. Sezione Italia (Series) .
(1) L'Osservatorio provinciale sul lavoro e sulle professioni . Milano, Italy , c1984. 143 p. : LC Card 84-190423
HD5785.N86 O87 1984
NYPL [JLD 86-1275]

Afogados, até quando? . Rio Grande do Sul (Brazil). Assembléia Legislativa. Comissão Especial dos Agricultores Desalojados do Passo Real. [Porto Alegre] [1984] 99 p. : LC Card 85-150200
HD500.P39 R56 1984

Africa . Coquery-Vidrovitch, Catherine. [Afrique noire. English.] Berkeley , c1988. p. cm. ISBN 0-520-05679-5 (alk. paper) LC Card 87-15316 DDC 967 19
HC800 .C67513 1988

Africa, Black. see **Africa, Sub-Saharan.**

AFRICA - COLONIAL INFLUENCE.
Batsa, Kofi, 1931- West German neo-colonialism and Africa . Accra, Ghana [1964] 98 p. ; LC Card 87-118442 DDC 337.4306 19
HF1546.15.A35 B37 1964

Rodney, Walter. How Europe underdeveloped Africa /. Washington, D.C. , 1981, c1972. xxiv, 312 p. ; ISBN 0-88258-105-8 LC Card 87-142601
HC800 .R62 1981b

AFRICA - COMMERCE - CONGRESSES.
Conference on Africa and the Market Economy (1985 : University of London) Conference on Africa and the Market Economy. London , 1985. 1 v. (various pagings) ; LC Card 86-218280 DDC 330.96/0328 19
HC800 .C657 1985

AFRICA - DEPENDENCY ON UNITED STATES.
Die Wirtschaftliche Expansion der USA . Moskau , 1986. 175 p. ; LC Card 87-408806 DDC 337.7305 19
HF1456.5.A64 W57 1986

AFRICA - DEPENDENCY ON WEST GERMANY.
Batsa, Kofi, 1931- West German neo-colonialism and Africa . Accra, Ghana [1964] 98 p. ; LC Card 87-118442 DDC 337.4306 19
HF1546.15.A35 B37 1964

AFRICA - DESCRIPTION AND TRAVEL - 1977-
Mountjoy, Alan B. Africa, geography and development /. Totowa, NJ , 1987. p. cm. ISBN 0-389-20722-5 LC Card 87-1306 DDC 330.96/0328 19
HC800 .M68 1987

AFRICA, EAST - COMMERCE - INDIA.
Saeed, M. (Muhammad), 1950- India and East Africa . Delhi , 1986. vi, 264 p. ; LC Card 87-902493 DDC 382/.0954/0676 19
HF3788.A45 S23 1986

AFRICA - ECONOMIC CONDITIONS.
Bates, Robert H. Essays on the political economy of rural Africa /. Berkeley , 1987, c1983. p. cm. ISBN 0-520-06014-8 (pbk. : alk. paper) LC Card 86-25120 DDC 330.96/0328/091734 19
HD2117 .B37 1987

Comprendre l'économie africaine /. Paris , c1985. 566 p. : ISBN 2-85802-566-2 LC Card 86-222248
HC800 .C654 1985

Nafziger, E. Wayne. Inequality in Africa . Cambridge [Cambridgeshire] , New York , c1988. p. cm. ISBN 0-521-26881-8 LC Card 87-24263 DDC 339.2/096 19
HC800.Z9 I5136 1988

Ndeshyo Rurihose. La stratégie de l'Organisation de l'unité africaine pour le développement . [Kinshasa] , 1981. 80 p. : LC Card 83-161631
HC800 .N393 1981

Rodney, Walter. How Europe underdeveloped Africa /. Washington, D.C. , 1981, c1972. xxiv, 312 p. ; ISBN 0-88258-105-8 LC Card 87-142601
HC800 .R62 1981b

AFRICA - ECONOMIC CONDITIONS - 1918-1945.
Dia, Mamadou. [Nations africaines et solidarité mondiale. English.] The African nations and world solidarity /. Westport, Conn. , 1987, c1961. xii, 145 p. ; ISBN 0-313-24569-X (lib. bdg. : alk. paper) LC Card 86-25734 DDC 330.96/03 19
HC800 .D5213 1987

AFRICA - ECONOMIC CONDITIONS - 1960-
Adedeji, Adebayo. The African development problematique . Addis Ababa [1985] 33 p. ; LC Card 87-980487 DDC 338.96 19
HC800 .A543 1985

Economic development in Africa . London , 1987. x, 266 p. ; ISBN 0-86187-909-0 : LC Card 87-15296 DDC 338.98 19
HC800 .E275 1987

Heinecke, P. Freedom in the grave . [Zaria, Nigeria] [1985] 178 p. ; LC Card 86-153310 DDC 337.66906 19
HC1055 .H45 1985

The Informal sector in Africa. Addis Ababa [Ethiopia] , 1985. 147 p. ; ISBN 92-2-103785-1 :
NYPL [JLE 86-1454]

Marsden, Keith. Private enterprise in Africa . Washington, D.C. [1987] xiii, 66 p. ; ISBN 0-8213-0945-5 (pbk.) LC Card 87-18419 DDC 330.96/032 19
HC800 .M353 1987

Mountjoy, Alan B. Africa, geography and development /. Totowa, NJ , 1987. p. cm. ISBN 0-389-20722-5 LC Card 87-1306 DDC 330.96/0328 19
HC800 .M68 1987

United Nations transport and communications decade in Africa . [Addis Ababa?] [1985?- v. <1 > : LC Card 86-981012 DDC 385/.096 19
HE3395 .U65 1985

Vilby, Knud. [Afrika i misvækst. Swedish.] Afrika på fel spår . Uppsala , 1984. 138 p. ; ISBN 91-7106-230-0 LC Card 85-158250
HC800 .V5518 1984

Walker, Brian W. Authentic development in Africa /. New York, N.Y. , c1985. 70 p. : ISBN 0-87124-102-1 (pbk.) : LC Card 85-82567 DDC 081 s 338.96 19
E744 .H43 no. 274 HC800
NYPL [JLD 86-3400]

AFRICA - ECONOMIC CONDITIONS - 1960- - CONGRESSES.
Conference on Africa and the Market Economy (1985 : University of London) Conference on Africa and the Market Economy. London , 1985. 1 v. (various pagings) ; LC Card 86-218280 DDC 330.96/0328 19
HC800 .C657 1985

World recession and the food crisis in Africa /. London , 1986. 314 p. ; ISBN 0-85255-309-9 : LC Card 86-235333 DDC 363.8/526/096 19
HD9017.A2 W67 1986b

World recession and the food crisis in Africa /. Boulder , 1986. p. cm. ISBN 0-8133-0511-X : LC Card 86-28250 DDC 363.8/526/096 19
HD9017.A2 W67 1986

AFRICA - ECONOMIC INTEGRATION.
Ramphal, S. S. The trampling of the grass . [Addis Ababa?] [1985] 41 p. : LC Card 85-981035 DDC 338.96 19
HC800 .R36 1985

AFRICA - ECONOMIC POLICY.
Growth, equity, and self reliance . Boulder , 1987. xi, 162 p. ; ISBN 0-8133-0486-5 (pbk.) : LC Card 87-14290 DDC 338.96 19
HD3616.A36 G76 1987

Marsden, Keith. Private enterprise in Africa . Washington, D.C. [1987] xiii, 66 p. ; ISBN

0-8213-0945-5 (pbk.) LC Card 87-18419 DDC 330.96/032 19
HC800 .M353 1987

Ramphal, S. S. The trampling of the grass . [Addis Ababa?] [1985] 41 p. : LC Card 85-981035 DDC 338.96 19
HC800 .R36 1985

Walker, Brian W. Authentic development in Africa /. New York, N.Y. , c1985. 70 p. : ISBN 0-87124-102-1 (pbk.) : LC Card 85-82567 DDC 081 s 338.96 19
E744 .H43 no. 274 HC800 ***NYPL [JLD 86-3400]***

AFRICA - ECONOMIC POLICY - CASE STUDIES.
Uses of census data for demographic research and development planning in Africa . New York , 1986. iv, 24 p. ; LC Card 87-118612 DDC 304.6/096 19
HB3661 .U94 1986

AFRICA - FOREIGN ECONOMIC RELATIONS.
Dia, Mamadou. [Nations africaines et solidarité mondiale. English.] The African nations and world solidarity /. Westport, Conn. , 1987, c1961. xii, 145 p. ; ISBN 0-313-24569-X (lib. bdg. : alk. paper) LC Card 86-25734 DDC 330.96/03 19
HC800 .D5213 1987

Seidman, Ann Willcox, 1926- Money, banking, and public finance in Africa /. London , Atlantic Highlands, N.J., USA , 1986. xv, 363 p. : ISBN 0-86232-429-7 LC Card 87-111822 DDC 332.1/096 19
HG187.5.A2 S45 1986

AFRICA - FOREIGN ECONOMIC RELATIONS - BRAZIL.
Collins, Paul D. Brazil in Africa . Austin , 1986. 16 p. ; LC Card 86-622252 DDC 337.8106 19
HF1514.5.A35 C65 1986

AFRICA - FOREIGN ECONOMIC RELATIONS - CONGRESSES.
Conference on Africa and the Market Economy (1985 : University of London) Conference on Africa and the Market Economy. London , 1985. 1 v. (various pagings) ; LC Card 86-218280 DDC 330.96/0328 19
HC800 .C657 1985

AFRICA - FOREIGN ECONOMIC RELATIONS - EUROPE.
Rodney, Walter. How Europe underdeveloped Africa /. Washington, D.C. , 1981, c1972. xxiv, 312 p. ; ISBN 0-88258-105-8 LC Card 87-142601
HC800 .R62 1981b

AFRICA - FOREIGN ECONOMIC RELATIONS - GERMANY, WEST.
Batsa, Kofi, 1931- West German neo-colonialism and Africa . Accra, Ghana [1964] 98 p. ; LC Card 87-118442 DDC 337.4306 19
HF1546.15.A35 B37 1964

AFRICA - FOREIGN ECONOMIC RELATIONS - UNITED STATES.
Die Wirtschaftliche Expansion der USA . Moskau , 1986. 175 p. ; LC Card 87-408806 DDC 337.7305 19
HF1456.5.A64 W57 1986

AFRICA, FRENCH-SPEAKING EQUATORIAL - ECONOMIC CONDITIONS - HANDBOOKS, MANUALS, ETC.
Africascope . Paris [1985] 426 p. : LC Card 86-192167
HC945 .A65 1985

AFRICA, FRENCH-SPEAKING WEST - ECONOMIC CONDITIONS - HANDBOOKS, MANUALS, ETC.
Africascope . Paris [1985] 426 p. : LC Card 86-192167
HC945 .A65 1985

Africa, geography and development /. Mountjoy, Alan B. Totowa, NJ , 1987. p. cm. ISBN 0-389-20722-5 LC Card 87-1306 DDC 330.96/0328 19
HC800 .M68 1987

Africa, German Southwest. see **Namibia.**

Africa in crisis . Timberlake, Lloyd. Philadelphia , 1986. 232 p. : ISBN 0-86571-082-1
NYPL [Sc D 87-100]

Africa in figures / prepared by the Statistics and Survey Unit, Division for Industrial Studies. [Vienna] : United Nations Industrial Development Organization, [1985] iv, 153 p. ; 30 cm. Chiefly tables. English and French. Cover title. "6 February 1985." Includes bibliographical references. "UNIDO/IS.517." LC Card 87-402813 DDC 338.096/021 19
1. Africa - Manufactures - Statistics. 2. Africa - Industries - Statistics. I. United Nations Industrial Development Organization. Division for Industrial Studies. Statistics and Survey Unit.
HD9737.A2 A38 1985

AFRICA - INDUSTRIES.
Policies and measures to promote industrial co-operatives in Africa /. [New York] [1985] 23 p. ; LC Card 87-104469 DDC 334/.6/096 19
HD3247 .P65 1985

AFRICA - INDUSTRIES - STATISTICS.
Africa in figures /. [Vienna] [1985] iv, 153 p. ; LC Card 87-402813 DDC 338.096/021 19
HD9737.A2 A38 1985

AFRICA - MANUFACTURES - STATISTICS.
Africa in figures /. [Vienna] [1985] iv, 153 p. ; LC Card 87-402813 DDC 338.096/021 19
HD9737.A2 A38 1985

AFRICA - POLITICS AND GOVERNMENT - 1960-
Heinecke, P. Freedom in the grave . [Zaria, Nigeria] [1985] 178 p. ; LC Card 86-153310 DDC 337.66906 19
HC1055 .H45 1985

AFRICA - POPULATION.
Locoh, Thérèse. Comprendre les problèmes de population . Lomé, Togo , 1984. 72, [3], 3 p. : LC Card 87-131146
HB871 .L57 1984

Population distribution and urbanization [in] ECA member states. [Addis Ababa?] , 1983. ix, 81 p. : LC Card 86-980945 DDC 304.6/1 19
HB2121 .P66 1983

Sembajwe, I. S. L. (Israel Serwano Lubwama), 1947- Urban population growth rates in Africa with special reference to Lesotho /. [Roma, Lesotho] [1985] 31 leaves : LC Card 87-132328 DDC 307.2 19
HB3663.7.A3 S46 1985

AFRICA - POPULATION - ADDRESSES, ESSAYS, LECTURES.
Population and development projects in Africa /. Cambridge [Cambridgeshire] , New York , 1985. xvi, 329 p. : ISBN 0-521-30527-6 LC Card 84-29323 DDC 304.6/096 19
HB2121.A3 P67 1985 ***NYPL [JLF 86-186]***

AFRICA - POPULATION - CONGRESSES.
Expert Group Meeting on Fertility and Mortality Levels and Trends in Africa and Their Policy Implications (1979 : Monrovia, Liberia) Population dynamics . [Addis Ababa] [1981] ix, 581 p. : LC Card 82-980086 DDC 304.6/3/096 19
HB3661.A3 E9 1979 ***NYPL [JLF 83-591]***

AFRICA - POPULATION, RURAL.
Population distribution and urbanization [in] ECA member states. [Addis Ababa?] , 1983. ix, 81 p. : LC Card 86-980945 DDC 304.6/1 19
HB2121 .P66 1983

AFRICA - RURAL CONDITIONS.
Bates, Robert H. Essays on the political economy of rural Africa /. Berkeley , 1987, c1983. p. cm. ISBN 0-520-06014-8 (pbk. : alk. paper) LC Card 86-25120 DDC 330.96/0328/091734 19
HD2117 .B37 1987

Gosudarstvo i agrarnaia͡ ėvoli͡utsii͡a v razvivai͡ushchikhsi͡a stranakh Azii i Afriki /. Moskva , 1980. 227 p. ; LC Card 81-143353
HD2056 .G67 1980

Harrison, Paul. The greening of Africa . New York, N.Y., U. S.A. , 1987. 380 p. : ISBN 0-14-010192-6 (pbk.) : LC Card 87-404277 DDC 338.1/9/6 19
HD2117 .H37 1987

AFRICA - SOCIAL CONDITIONS - 1960-
Heinecke, P. Freedom in the grave . [Zaria, Nigeria] [1985] 178 p. ; LC Card 86-153310 DDC 337.66906 19
HC1055 .H45 1985

AFRICA - SOCIAL CONDITIONS - ADDRESSES, ESSAYS, LECTURES.
Struggle for the city . Beverly Hills , c1983. 319 p. : ISBN 0-8039-2067-9 LC Card 83-11196 DDC 305.5/62/096 19
HD8774 .S87 1983 ***NYPL [JLD 83-3496]***

Africa, South. see **South Africa.**

AFRICA, SOUTHERN - COMMERCE.
Hanlon, Joseph. SADCC . London, U.K. , c1984. 110 p. : LC Card 86-148391 DDC 332.6/732268 19
HC900 .H35 1984

AFRICA, SOUTHERN - COMMERCE - STATISTICS.
Consumer markets in Southern Africa. London , 1986. 173 p., [1] p. of plates : ISBN 0-86338-095-6 LC Card 87-160745 DDC 330.968/063 19
HF3900 .C66 1986

AFRICA, SOUTHERN - ECONOMIC CONDITIONS.
La Grange, A. B. DBSA in the southern African development framework /. Sandton, Republic of South Africa [1985] 36 p. : LC Card 87-150256 DDC 332.2 19
HC900 .L3 1985

Libby, Ronald T. The politics of economic power in southern Africa /. Princeton, N.J. , c1987. xxii, 361 p. : ISBN 0-691-07723-1 (alk. paper) : LC Card 87-2406 DDC 337.68 19
HF1613.3.Z4 S65 1987

Odén, Bertil, 1939- Sydafrika i södra Afrika /. Uppsala , 1985. 181 p. : ISBN 91-7106-236-X LC Card 85-221741
HC905 .O34 1985 ***NYPL [Sc E 86-483]***

AFRICA, SOUTHERN - ECONOMIC CONDITIONS, 1975-
Hanlon, Joseph. SADCC . London, U.K. , c1984. 110 p. : LC Card 86-148391 DDC 332.6/732268 19
HC900 .H35 1984

AFRICA, SOUTHERN - ECONOMIC CONDITIONS, 1975- - STATISTICS.
Consumer markets in Southern Africa. London , 1986. 173 p., [1] p. of plates : ISBN 0-86338-095-6 LC Card 87-160745 DDC 330.968/063 19
HF3900 .C66 1986

AFRICA, SOUTHERN - ECONOMIC INTEGRATION.
Hanlon, Joseph. SADCC . London, U.K. , c1984. 110 p. : LC Card 86-148391 DDC 332.6/732268 19
HC900 .H35 1984

AFRICA, SOUTHERN - ECONOMIC POLICY.
Libby, Ronald T. The politics of economic power in southern Africa /. Princeton, N.J. , c1987. xxii, 361 p. : ISBN 0-691-07723-1 (alk. paper) : LC Card 87-2406 DDC 337.68 19
HF1613.3.Z4 S65 1987

AFRICA, SOUTHERN - FOREIGN ECONOMIC RELATIONS - SOUTH AFRICA.
Libby, Ronald T. The politics of economic power in southern Africa /. Princeton, N.J. , c1987. xxii, 361 p. : ISBN 0-691-07723-1 (alk. paper) : LC Card 87-2406 DDC 337.68 19
HF1613.3.Z4 S65 1987

Africa, Southwest. see **Namibia.**

AFRICA - STATISTICAL SERVICES - DIRECTORIES.

AFRICA - STATISTICS.
Afrika v tsifrakh . Moskva , 1986. 421 p. ; LC Card 87-143124
HA4675 .A37 1986

AFRICA - STATISTICS, VITAL - CONGRESSES.
Expert Group Meeting on Fertility and Mortality Levels and Trends in Africa and Their Policy Implications (1979 : Monrovia, Liberia) Population dynamics . [Addis Ababa] [1981] ix, 581 p. : LC Card 82-980086 DDC 304.6/3/096 19
HB3661.A3 E9 1979 ***NYPL [JLF 83-591]***

AFRICA, SUB-SAHARAN - CIVILIZATION.
Diop, Cheikh Anta. [Fondements économiques et culturels d'un état fédéral d'Afrique noire. English.] Black Africa . Westport, Conn. , Trenton, N.J. , 1987. 125 p. ; ISBN 0-88208-223-X (pbk.) : LC Card 87-17704

DDC 330.967 19
HC800 .D5413 1987

AFRICA, SUB-SAHARAN - COLONIAL INFLUENCE - HISTORY.
Coquery-Vidrovitch, Catherine. [Afrique noire. English.] Africa . Berkeley , c1988. p. cm. ISBN 0-520-05679-5 (alk. paper) LC Card 87-15316 DDC 967 19
HC800 .C67513 1988

AFRICA, SUB-SAHARAN - COMMERCE - HISTORY.
Austen, Ralph A. African economic history . London , Portsmouth, NH , 1987. ix, 294 p. : ISBN 0-435-08017-2 (pbk.) LC Card 86-25639 DDC 330.967 19
HC800 .A97 1987

AFRICA, SUB-SAHARAN - DEPENDENCY ON FOREIGN COUNTRIES - HISTORY.
Austen, Ralph A. African economic history . London , Portsmouth, NH , 1987. ix, 294 p. : ISBN 0-435-08017-2 (pbk.) LC Card 86-25639 DDC 330.967 19
HC800 .A97 1987

AFRICA, SUB-SAHARAN - DEPENDENCY ON UNITED STATES.
Ozadovskiĭ, A. A. (Andreĭ Andreevich) Uoll-strit protiv Afriki /. Kiev , 1985. 228, [4] p. ; LC Card 86-219442
HF1611.Z4 U556 1985

AFRICA, SUB-SAHARAN - ECONOMIC CONDITIONS.
Austen, Ralph A. African economic history . London , Portsmouth, NH , 1987. ix, 294 p. : ISBN 0-435-08017-2 (pbk.) LC Card 86-25639 DDC 330.967 19
HC800 .A97 1987

Coquery-Vidrovitch, Catherine. [Afrique noire. English.] Africa . Berkeley , c1988. p. cm. ISBN 0-520-05679-5 (alk. paper) LC Card 87-15316 DDC 967 19
HC800 .C67513 1988

Diop, Cheikh Anta. [Fondements économiques et culturels d'un état fédéral d'Afrique noire. English.] Black Africa . Westport, Conn. , Trenton, N.J. , 1987. 125 p. ; ISBN 0-88208-223-X (pbk.) : LC Card 87-17704 DDC 330.967 19
HC800 .D5413 1987

Munro, J. Forbes. Britain in tropical Africa, 1880-1960 . London , 1984. 89 p. : ISBN 0-333-32330-0 LC Card 87-672364
HC800 .M86x 1984

AFRICA, SUB-SAHARAN - ECONOMIC CONDITIONS - 1960-
Structural distortions and adjustment programmes in the poor countries of Africa . Berlin , 1985. xxxi, 377 p. : ISBN 3-88985-042-1 LC Card 86-226845 DDC 338.967 19
HC800 .S79 1985

AFRICA, SUB-SAHARAN - ECONOMIC CONDITIONS - 1960- - CASE STUDIES.
Foreign indebtedness and basic human needs in four African countries . Washington , 1986. ii, 54 p. : LC Card 86-603396 DDC 336.3/435/0967
HC800 .F67 1986

AFRICA, SUB-SAHARAN - ECONOMIC POLICY.
Committee on African Development Strategies (U. S.) Compact for African development . Berkeley, CA (2120 Berkeley Way, Berkeley 94720) [1985] 24 p. : LC Card 86-200473 DDC 338.967 19
HC800 .C645 1985

Structural distortions and adjustment programmes in the poor countries of Africa . Berlin , 1985. xxxi, 377 p. : ISBN 3-88985-042-1 LC Card 86-226845 DDC 338.967 19
HC800 .S79 1985

AFRICA, SUB-SAHARAN - FOREIGN ECONOMIC RELATIONS.
Austen, Ralph A. African economic history . London , Portsmouth, NH , 1987. ix, 294 p. : ISBN 0-435-08017-2 (pbk.) LC Card 86-25639 DDC 330.967 19
HC800 .A97 1987

AFRICA, SUB-SAHARAN - FOREIGN ECONOMIC RELATIONS - UNITED STATES.
Ozadovskiĭ, A. A. (Andreĭ Andreevich) Uoll-strit protiv Afriki /. Kiev , 1985. 228, [4] p. ; LC Card 86-219442
HF1611.Z4 U556 1985

Africa, Sub-Saharan - Government. see **Africa, Sub-Saharan - Politics and government.**

AFRICA, SUB-SAHARAN - INDUSTRIES.
Diop, Cheikh Anta. [Fondements économiques et culturels d'un état fédéral d'Afrique noire. English.] Black Africa . Westport, Conn. , Trenton, N.J. , 1987. 125 p. ; ISBN 0-88208-223-X (pbk.) : LC Card 87-17704 DDC 330.967 19
HC800 .D5413 1987

AFRICA, SUB-SAHARAN - POLITICS AND GOVERNMENT.
Coquery-Vidrovitch, Catherine. [Afrique noire. English.] Africa . Berkeley , c1988. p. cm. ISBN 0-520-05679-5 (alk. paper) LC Card 87-15316 DDC 967 19
HC800 .C67513 1988

Diop, Cheikh Anta. [Fondements économiques et culturels d'un état fédéral d'Afrique noire. English.] Black Africa . Westport, Conn. , Trenton, N.J. , 1987. 125 p. ; ISBN 0-88208-223-X (pbk.) : LC Card 87-17704 DDC 330.967 19
HC800 .D5413 1987

AFRICA, SUB-SAHARAN - POLITICS AND GOVERNMENT - 1960-
Görgens, Egon, 1941- Entwicklungshilfe und Ordnungspolitik . Bern , c1983. 111 p. ; ISBN 3-258-03324-2 : LC Card 84-108530
HC800 .G67 1983

AFRICA, SUB-SAHARAN - POPULATION.
Locoh, Thérèse. La fécondité en Afrique noire /. Lomé [1985] 36, 22 leaves : LC Card 87-126644
HB1071 .L63 1985

AFRICA, SUB-SAHARAN - POPULATION - HISTORY.
Coquery-Vidrovitch, Catherine. [Afrique noire. English.] Africa . Berkeley , c1988. p. cm. ISBN 0-520-05679-5 (alk. paper) LC Card 87-15316 DDC 967 19
HC800 .C67513 1988

AFRICA, SUB-SAHARAN - POPULATION POLICY.
United States. Congress. House. Committee on Science and Technology. Prospects for sustainable development in Sub-Saharan Africa . Washington , 1986. vii, 88 p. ; LC Card 86-603140 DDC 338.967 19
HD2117 .U48 1986

AFRICA, SUB-SAHARAN - RURAL CONDITIONS.
Coquery-Vidrovitch, Catherine. [Afrique noire. English.] Africa . Berkeley , c1988. p. cm. ISBN 0-520-05679-5 (alk. paper) LC Card 87-15316 DDC 967 19
HC800 .C67513 1988

AFRICA, SUB-SAHARAN - SOCIAL CONDITIONS - 1960-
Görgens, Egon, 1941- Entwicklungshilfe und Ordnungspolitik . Bern , c1983. 111 p. ; ISBN 3-258-03324-2 : LC Card 84-108530
HC800 .G67 1983

AFRICA, SUB-SAHARAN - STRATEGIC ASPECTS.
Ozadovskiĭ, A. A. (Andreĭ Andreevich) Uoll-strit protiv Afriki /. Kiev , 1985. 228, [4] p. ; LC Card 86-219442
HF1611.Z4 U556 1985

AFRICA, WEST - COMMERCE - PORTUGAL - HISTORY.
Carreira, António. Os portuguêses nos rios de Guiné, 1500-1900 /. Lisboa , 1984. 205 p. : LC Card 85-149851
HF3698.A358 C37 1984

AFRICA, WEST - ECONOMIC CONDITIONS.
A Critical appraisal of the economic and social conditions in the west African subregion /. [Lagos , 1979-1980] 10 v. : LC Card 87-159535 DDC 330.966 19
HC1000 .C75 1979

AFRICA, WEST - ECONOMIC CONDITIONS - 1960-
L'Economie des pays de l'Afrique de l'Ouest. Bruxelles [1978] 1 v. (various pagings) : LC Card 86-673818
HC1000 .E36x 1978

Rimmer, Douglas. The economies of West Africa /. London , c1984. xii, 308 p. : ISBN 0-297-78095-6 LC Card 87-673367
HC1000 .R56x 1984b

AFRICA, WEST - ECONOMIC INTEGRATION.
West Africa--regional cooperation and development /. Boulder , 1988. p. cm. ISBN 0-8133-7354-9 : LC Card 87-9290 DDC 338.966 19
HC1000 .W47 1988

AFRICA, WEST - ECONOMIC INTEGRATION - CONGRESSES.
Towards an African economic community . [Ibadan, Nigeria] , 1986. 401 p. ; ISBN 978-18-1040-8 LC Card 87-143033 DDC 337.1/66 19
HC1000 .T69 1986

AFRICA, WEST - ECONOMIC INTEGRATION - HISTORY.
Economic Community of West African States. Development of the community . Lagos , 1981. 51 leaves ; LC Card 87-403455 DDC 337.1/66 19
HC1000 .E23 1981

AFRICA, WEST - ECONOMIC POLICY.
Rimmer, Douglas. The economies of West Africa /. London , c1984. xii, 308 p. : ISBN 0-297-78095-6 LC Card 87-673367
HC1000 .R56x 1984b

West Africa--regional cooperation and development /. Boulder , 1988. p. cm. ISBN 0-8133-7354-9 : LC Card 87-9290 DDC 338.966 19
HC1000 .W47 1988

Africa, West, Portuguese. see **Angola.**

AFRICA, WEST - SOCIAL CONDITIONS.
A Critical appraisal of the economic and social conditions in the west African subregion /. [Lagos , 1979-1980] 10 v. : LC Card 87-159535 DDC 330.966 19
HC1000 .C75 1979

African-American Labor Center.
African-American Labor Center, 1965-1970 [microform]. New York, N.Y. : The Center, [1970] 16 p. : ill. ; 19 x 27 cm. Cover title. Microfilm New York : New York Public Library, 1986. 1 microfilm reel ; 35 mm. (MN *ZZ-25,866)
1. African-American Labor Center. 2. Trade-unions - Africa. 3. International labor activities. I. Title.
NYPL [*ZT-1646 no.23]

AFRICAN-AMERICAN LABOR CENTER.
African-American Labor Center. African-American Labor Center, 1965-1970 [microform]. New York, N.Y. [1970] 16 p. :
NYPL [*ZT-1646 no.23]

African-American Labor Center, 1965-1970 [microform]. African-American Labor Center. New York, N.Y. [1970] 16 p. :
NYPL [*ZT-1646 no.23]

AFRICAN-AMERICANS. see **AFRO-AMERICANS.**

African and Asian Inter-regional Workshop on Strategies for Improving the Employment Conditions of Rural Women (1984 : Arusha, Tanzania) Resources, power and women : proceedings of the African and Asian Inter-regional Workshop on Strategies for Improving the Employment Conditions of Rural Women, Arusha, Tanzania, 20-25 August 1984. Geneva : International Labour Office, 1985. ix, 82 p. ; 30 cm. (A WEP study) ISBN 92-2-105009-2 (pbk.) : LC Card 86-208830 DDC 331.4/83/095 19
1. Rural women - Employment - Africa - Congresses. 2. Rural women - Employment - Asia - Congresses. 3. Women in rural development - Africa - Congresses. 4. Women in rural development - Asia - Congresses. I. Title. II. Series.
HD6207 .A78 1984

African Centre for Monetary Studies.
Association of African Central Banks. Directory of African central banks /. Dakar, Senegal [1985 or 1986] ca. 150 leaves : LC Card 87-402547 DDC 332.1/1/02567 19
HG3376 .A87 1985

National financial policies and capital formation in Africa . Dakar, Senegal [1986] iii, 205 p. ; LC Card 87-404123 DDC 332/.096 19
HG5822 .N38 1986

AFRICAN COOPERATION.
Ndeshyo Rurihose. La stratégie de

l'Organisation de l'unité africaine pour le développement . [Kinshasa] , 1981. 80 p. : LC Card 83-161631
HC800 .N393 1981

Proceedings of second (special) general conference . Accra, Ghana [1985?] 73 p. ; LC Card 86-220781 DDC 338.96 19
HC800 .P77 1985

African co-operative societies in Rhodesia. Clifton-Brown, E. Project 1.04 . Salisbury, Zimbabwe [1977] 46 leaves ; LC Card 84-256608
HD3562.3.A4 C55 1977

African Development Experts (Organization) Proceedings of second (special) general conference . Accra, Ghana [1985?] 73 p. ; LC Card 86-220781 DDC 338.96 19
HC800 .P77 1985

African Development Fund. Malawi. National rural development programme /. [Lilongwe, Malawi] , 1977. 7 v. : LC Card 85-981594
HD2133.5.Z8 M35 1977

The African development problematique . Adedeji, Adebayo. Addis Ababa [1985] 33 p. ; LC Card 87-980487 DDC 338.96 19
HC800 .A543 1985

African economic history . Austen, Ralph A. London , Portsmouth, NH , 1987. ix, 294 p. : ISBN 0-435-08017-2 (pbk.) LC Card 86-25639 DDC 330.967 19
HC800 .A97 1987

African Energy Programme (Commonwealth Science Council) Regional Workshop on Wood Energy in East Africa (1982 : Nairobi, Kenya) Proceedings of the Regional Workshop on Wood Energy in East Africa . Ottawa, Canada [1983] 241 p. : LC Card 86-185703 DDC 333.75 19
HD9769.F843 A367 1982

African environment. Occasional paper . (no. 77) Sall, Alioune. Ressources humaines pour le développement . [Dakar, Sénégal , 1984] 51 p. : LC Card 85-129264 DDC 338.91/09624 19
HC1002 .S25 1984

African environments and resources /. Lewis, Lawrence. Boston , 1987. p. cm. ISBN 0-04-916010-9 (alk. paper) LC Card 87-16751 DDC 333.7/096 19
HC800 .L48 1987

AFRICAN INSTITUTE OF CHARTERED ACCOUNTANTS.
Monday, H. R. Proposals for the establishment of an African Institute of Chartered Accountants. [New York?] [1984] 10 p. ; LC Card 86-122510 DDC 657/.06/06 19
HF5616.A35 M65 1984

The African nations and world solidarity /. Dia, Mamadou. [Nations africaines et solidarité mondiale. English.] Westport, Conn. , 1987, c1961. xii, 145 p. ; ISBN 0-313-24569-X (lib. bdg. : alk. paper) LC Card 86-25734 DDC 330.96/03 19
HC800 .D5213 1987

The African poor . Iliffe, John. Cambridge [Cambridgeshire] , New York , 1987. ix, 387 p. ; ISBN 0-521-34415-8 LC Card 87-14622 DDC 305.5/62/096 19
HC800.Z9 P625 1987

African population projection according to eight models, sex & age groups (1970-2000) /. Fahmy, H. A. [Lusaka] [198-?] 34, 9, 62 leaves, [3] leaves of plates : LC Card 85-980559 DDC 304.6/2/096894021 19
HA4703 .F34 1980z

African population projection, 1970-2000. Fahmy, H. A. African population projection according to eight models, sex & age groups (1970-2000) /. [Lusaka] [198-?] 34, 9, 62 leaves, [3] leaves of plates : LC Card 85-980559 DDC 304.6/2/096894021 19
HA4703 .F34 1980z

African population studies series.
(no. 7) Population distribution and urbanization [in] ECA member states. [Addis Ababa?] , 1983. ix, 81 p. : LC Card 86-980945 DDC 304.6/1 19
HB2121 .P66 1983

African society today.
Nafziger, E. Wayne. Inequality in Africa . Cambridge [Cambridgeshire] , New York , c1988. p. cm. ISBN 0-521-26881-8 LC Card 87-24263 DDC 339.2/096 19
HC800.Z9 I5136 1988

African studies series.
(54) Turrell, Robert Vicat. Capital and labour on the Kimberley diamond fields, 1871-1890 /. Cambridge [Cambridgeshire] , New York , 1987. xviii, 297 p. : ISBN 0-521-33354-7 LC Card 86-32740 DDC 331.7/622382/0968711 19
HD9677.S63 K567 1987

(57) MacGaffey, Janet. Entrepreneurs and parasites . Cambridge [Cambridgeshire] , New York , 1987. xiii, 241 p. : ISBN 0-521-33533-7 LC Card 87-13160 DDC 338.09675/1 19
HC955.Z7 K49956 1987

(58) Iliffe, John. The African poor . Cambridge [Cambridgeshire] , New York , 1987. ix, 387 p. ; ISBN 0-521-34415-8 LC Card 87-14622 DDC 305.5/62/096 19
HC800.Z9 P625 1987

(59) Martin, Susan M. Palm oil and protest . Cambridge , New York , 1988. xi, 209 p. : ISBN 0-521-34376-3 LC Card 87-17373 DDC 338.4/76643 19
HD9490.5.P343 N66 1988

African Trade Union Unity, Organisation of. see **Organisation of African Trade Union Unity.**

African Unity, Organization of. see **Organization of African Unity.**

An African winter /. King, Preston T., 1936- Harmondsworth, Middlesex, England , New York, N.Y., U. S.A. , 1986. 249 p. : ISBN 0-14-052365-0 (pbk.) : LC Card 87-103265 DDC 363.8/096 19
HC840.Z9 F34 1986

African worker under apartheid. Brussels : International Confederation of Free Trade Unions, [1984]. 109 p. : ill. ; 21 cm. Cover title. "Updated version" of the 1978 ed.
1. Trade-unions, Black - South Africa. 2. Trade-unions - South Africa. 3. Blacks - South Africa - Economic conditions. 4. Blacks - Employment - South Africa. 5. Investments, Foreign - South Africa.
NYPL [Sc D 86-730]

Africascope : le guide économique de la francophonie. Paris : Mermon international, [1985] 426 p. : ill. (some col.) ; 21 cm. On spine: Radio France internationale. Cover title: Africascope 85. Bibliography: p. 425-426. LC Card 86-192167
1. Africa, French-speaking Equatorial - Economic conditions - Handbooks, manuals, etc. 2. Africa, French-speaking West - Economic conditions - Handbooks, manuals, etc. I. Radio-France internationale. II. Title: Africascope 85. III. Title: Guide économique de la francophonie.
HC945 .A65 1985

Africascope 85. Africascope . Paris [1985] 426 p. : LC Card 86-192167
HC945 .A65 1985

Afrika Industrieberichte.
(16) Ulbrich, Wolfgang. Kenya . Hamburg , 1971. 308 p., [1] folded leaf of plates : LC Card 85-163190
HC865 .U43 1971

Afrika på fel spår . Vilby, Knud. [Afrika i misvækst. Swedish.] Uppsala , 1984. 138 p. ; ISBN 91-7106-230-0 LC Card 85-158250
HC800 .V5518 1984

Afrika-Studien. For other vols. in this series, see old catalogs.
(Nr. 112) Kapp, Gerald B., 1956- Agroforstliche Landnutzung in der Sahel-Sudanzone . München , c1987. xii, 397 p. : ISBN 3-8039-0347-5 LC Card 87-419915 DDC 333.76/13/0966 19
HD1010.5.Z63 K37 1987

Afrika v t͡sifrakh : statisticheskiĭ spravochnik / [otvetstvennyĭ redaktor L.V. Goncharov]. Moskva : Izd-vo "Nauka," Glav. red. vostochnoĭ lit-ry, 1986. 421 p. ; 27 cm. At head of title: Akademii͡a nauk SSSR. Institut Afriki. Statistical tables. Bibliography: p. 416-[417]. LC Card 87-143124
1. Africa - Statistics. I. Goncharov, Leongard Vasil'evich. II. Institut Afriki (Akademii͡a nauk SSSR).
HA4675 .A37 1986

L'Afrique du Sud et nous : approche des relations économiques et financières entre la Belgique et le pays de l'apartheid / Groupe liégeois d'information et d'action contre l'apar[t]heid. [Liège, Belgium] : Le Groupe, [1984] [69] p. : ill. ; 30 cm. Cover title. Includes bibliography. LC Card 86-200334
1. Belgium - Foreign economic relations - South Africa. 2. South Africa - Foreign economic relations - Belgium. I. Groupe liégeois d'information et d'action contre l'apartheid.
HF1554.5.S6 A37 1984

AFRO-AMERICAN AUTOMOBILE INDUSTRY WORKERS - BIOGRAPHY.
Denby, Charles. Indignant heart . Montréal , 1979. 295 p. : ISBN 0-919618-93-6 LC Card 87-672793
HD8039.A82 U633x 1979

AFRO-AMERICAN COAL MINERS - HISTORY.
Lewis, Ronald L., 1940- Black coal miners in America . Lexington, Ky. , c1987. xv, 239 p., [8] p. of plates : ISBN 0-8131-1610-4 : LC Card 87-2086 DDC 331.6/396073 19
HD8039.M62 U6443 1987

AFRO-AMERICAN COMMUNISTS - BIOGRAPHY.
Denby, Charles. Indignant heart . Montréal , 1979. 295 p. : ISBN 0-919618-93-6 LC Card 87-672793
HD8039.A82 U633x 1979

AFRO-AMERICAN FARMERS - UNITED STATES - STATISTICS.
Banks, Vera J. Black farmers and their farms /. Washington, D.C. , 1986. v, 27 p. : LC Card 86-602201
HD8039.F32 U616 1986

AFRO-AMERICAN IRON AND STEEL WORKERS - PENNSYLVANIA - HISTORY.
Dickerson, Dennis C., 1949- Out of the crucible . Albany , c1986. xiv, 323 p. : ISBN 0-88706-305-5 LC Card 85-30450 DDC 331.6/3/960730748 19
HD8039.I52 U535 1986
NYPL [JLE 86-4411]

AFRO-AMERICAN SUFFRAGE. see **AFRO-AMERICANS - POLITICS AND SUFFRAGE.**

AFRO-AMERICAN VOTING RIGHTS. see **AFRO-AMERICANS - POLITICS AND SUFFRAGE.**

AFRO-AMERICAN WOMEN - ATTITUDES.
Morse, Roberta. The Black female professional /. Washington, D.C. [1983] i, 48 p. ; LC Card 83-80187 DDC 305.4/8896073 19
HQ1426 .M88 1983 ***NYPL [Sc F 86-230]***

AFRO-AMERICAN WOMEN - EMPLOYMENT.
Helmbold, Lois Rita. Making choices, making do [microform] . 1982. vii, 385 leaves
NYPL [Sc Micro R-4672]

Nivens, Beatryce. The Black woman's career guide /. New York , 1987. xvi, 362 p. ; ISBN 0-385-24161-5 (pbk.) : LC Card 87-1193 DDC 650.1/4/088042 19
HF5382.5.U5 N5 1987

AFRO-AMERICAN WOMEN - HISTORY.
Andolsen, Barbara Hilkert. "Daughters of Jefferson, daughters of bootblacks" . Macon, GA , c1986. xiv, 130 p. ; ISBN 0-86554-204-X : LC Card 86-816 DDC 305.4/2/0973 19
HQ1426 .A6827 1986 ***NYPL [JLE 86-3359]***

Lerner, Gerda, 1920- The majority finds its past . New York , 1979. xxxii, 217 p. ; ISBN 0-19-502597-0 LC Card 79-14048 DDC 301.41/2/0973
HQ1426 .L47 ***NYPL [JLD 86-3348]***

AFRO-AMERICAN YOUTH - EMPLOYMENT.
Williams, Donald R., 1956- Labor force participation of black and white youth /. Ann Arbor, Mich. , c1987. 125 p. ; ISBN 0-8357-1804-2 (alk. paper) LC Card 87-5868 DDC 331.3/412/0973 19
HD6273 .W48 1987

AFRO-AMERICAN YOUTH - EMPLOYMENT - CONGRESSES.
The Black youth employment crisis /. Chicago , 1986. viii, 469 p. : ISBN 0-226-26164-6 LC Card 85-20989 DDC 331.3/46396073 19
HD6273 .B57 1986 ***NYPL [JLE 86-3726]***

AFRO-AMERICANS. Here are entered works on the Black people of the United States. Works on Black people outside of the United States are entered under the heading Blacks. Theoretical works discussing the Black race from an anthropological point of view are entered under the heading Black race.

AFRO-AMERICANS - ECONOMIC CONDITIONS.
Davis, Frank Green, 1913- The Black community's social security /. Washington , c1977. xiii, 189 p. : ISBN 0-8191-0282-2 LC Card 78-304298
E185.8 .D237 ***NYPL [JLD 78-1907]***

O'Hare, William P. Wealth and economic status . Washington, D.C. , 1983. vii, 33 p. : ISBN 0-941410-35-8 (pbk.) : LC Card 83-22171 DDC 339.2/2/0973 19
HC110.W4 O33 1983 ***NYPL [JLE 86-2065]***

AFRO-AMERICANS - EMPLOYMENT - GEORGIA.
Oliveira, Victor J. Distribution of rural employment growth by race . Washington, D.C. [1986] vii, 17 p. : LC Card 86-601118 DDC 331.6/09758 19
HD5725.G4 O56 1986

AFRO-AMERICANS - EMPLOYMENT - NEW YORK (N.Y.)
Stafford, Walter W. Closed labor markets . New York, N.Y. (105 E. 22nd St., New York 10010) , c1985. xvi, 203, 3, [2] p. ; LC Card 85-186853 DDC 331.12/09747/1 19
HD5726.N5 S73 1985 ***NYPL [Sc F 86-274]***

AFRO-AMERICANS - EMPLOYMENT - PENNSYLVANIA - HISTORY.
Dickerson, Dennis C., 1949- Out of the crucible . Albany , c1986. xiv, 323 p. : ISBN 0-88706-305-5 LC Card 85-30450 DDC 331.6/3/960730748 19
HD8039.I52 U535 1986
NYPL [JLE 86-4411]

AFRO-AMERICANS - EMPLOYMENT - WASHINGTON METROPOLITAN AREA.
Gale, Dennis E. Black and white urban-to-suburban outmigrants . Washington, D.C. [1986] 46 p. : LC Card 87-404424 DDC 307.2 19
HB1987.W34 G35 1986

AFRO-AMERICANS - HISTORY.
Gutman, Herbert George, 1928- Power & culture . New York, N.Y. , c1987. xi, 452 p. ; ISBN 0-394-56171-6 LC Card 87-43018 DDC 305.5/62/0973 19
HD8072 .G97 1987

AFRO-AMERICANS IN BUSINESS - ILLINOIS - CHICAGO - BIOGRAPHY.
Chavers-Wright, Madrue, 1916- The guarantee . New York , 1985. xix, 425 p. : ISBN 0-931505-02-X (pbk.) : LC Card 84-51854 DDC 338/.04/0924 B 19
HG2463.C48 C48 1985
NYPL [Sc D 86-412]

Chavers-Wright, Madrue, 1916- The guarantee . New York , 1987, c1985. xix, 427 p. : ISBN 0-931505-05-4 : LC Card 86-51447 DDC 338/.04/0924 B 19
HG2463.C48 C48 1987

AFRO-AMERICANS - OCCUPATIONS. see **AFRO-AMERICANS - EMPLOYMENT.**

AFRO-AMERICANS - PENNSYLVANIA - PHILADELPHIA.
Haley, Charles T. To do good and do well [microform] . 1980. x, 233 leaves ;
NYPL [Sc Micro R-4654]

AFRO-AMERICANS - PENNSYLVANIA - PHILADELPHIA - ECONOMIC CONDITIONS.
Haley, Charles T. To do good and do well [microform] . 1980. x, 233 leaves ;
NYPL [Sc Micro R-4654]

AFRO-AMERICANS - PENNSYLVANIA - PHILADELPHIA - SOCIAL CONDITIONS.
Haley, Charles T. To do good and do well [microform] . 1980. x, 233 leaves ;
NYPL [Sc Micro R-4654]

AFRO-AMERICANS - PENNSYLVANIA - PHILADELPHIA - SOCIAL LIFE AND CUSTOMS.
Haley, Charles T. To do good and do well [microform] . 1980. x, 233 leaves ;
NYPL [Sc Micro R-4654]

AFRO-AMERICANS - POLITICS AND SUFFRAGE.
Oettinger, Craig Milton, 1945- The politics of excluded groups . 1978. xvi, 454 leaves :
NYPL [Sc Micro R-4615]

AFRO-AMERICANS - SOCIAL CONDITIONS - 1964-1975.
Davis, Frank Green, 1913- The Black community's social security /. Washington , c1977. xiii, 189 p. : ISBN 0-8191-0282-2 LC Card 78-304298
E185.8 .D237 ***NYPL [JLD 78-1907]***

AFRO-AMERICANS - SOCIAL CONDITIONS - 1975-
Davis, Frank Green, 1913- The Black community's social security /. Washington , c1977. xiii, 189 p. : ISBN 0-8191-0282-2 LC Card 78-304298
E185.8 .D237 ***NYPL [JLD 78-1907]***

AFRO-AMERICANS - SOUTHERN STATES - ECONOMIC CONDITIONS.
Ghelfi, Linda M. Poverty among black families in the nonmetro South /. Washington, D.C. , Supt. of Docs., U. S. G.P.O. [distributor, 1986] vii, 27 p. : LC Card 86-602435 DDC 330.975/043/0899607301734 19
HC107.A13 G48 1986

AFRO-AMERICANS - SOUTHERN STATES - POPULATION - HISTORY - 19TH CENTURY.
Steckel, Richard H. (Richard Hall), 1944- The economics of U. S. slave and southern white fertility /. New York , 1985. 253 p. ; ISBN 0-8240-6662-6 (alk. paper) : LC Card 84-48314 DDC 304.6/32/08996073075 19
HB921 .S74 1985 ***NYPL [JLE 86-2085]***

AFRO-AMERICANS - UNITED STATES. see **AFRO-AMERICANS.**

AFRO-AMERICANS - YOUTH. see **AFRO-AMERICAN YOUTH.**

Afshar, Haleh, 1944- Women, work, and ideology in the Third World /. London , New York , 1985. xvii, 265 p. : ISBN 0-422-79710-3 (U. S. : pbk.) LC Card 85-17279 DDC 305.4/09172/4 19
HQ1870.9 .W657 1985
NYPL [JLD 86-2322]

After Bennett : a new politics for British Columbia / edited by Warren Magnusson ... [et al.]. Vancouver, B.C. : New Star Books, 1986. 429 p. : ill. ; 19 cm. Bibliography: p. 392-423. ISBN 0-919573-63-0 LC Card 87-110683 DDC 338.9711 19
1. British Columbia - Economic policy. 2. British Columbia - Economic conditions. 3. British Columbia - Politics and government. I. Magnusson, Warren, 1947-.
HC117.B8 A63 1986

After full employment /. Keane, John, 1949- London , Dover, N.H., USA , 1986. 198 p. ; ISBN 0-09-164091-1 (pbk.) : LC Card 86-213691 DDC 339.5/0941 19
HD5765.A6 K42 1986

After the famine . ILO Identification and Programming Mission to the Republic of the Sudan. Geneva , 1986. xi, 309 p. : ISBN 92-2-105401-2 (pbk.) LC Card 86-226792 DDC 363.8/83/09624 19
HC835.Z9 F35 1985

After the trade . Stigum, Marcia L. Homewood, Ill. , c1988. xvii, 303 p. : ISBN 0-87094-937-3 LC Card 87-50773 DDC 332.63/232/0973 19
HG4941 .S75 1988

After the trade is made. Study guide for After the trade is made . New York, NY , c1987. ix, 217 p. : ISBN 0-13-858721-3 (pbk.) : LC Card 87-14155 DDC 332.64/273 19
HG4910 .W365 1986 Suppl.

After the trade is made . Weiss, David M., 1938- New York, N.Y. , c1986. xii, 436 p. : ISBN 0-13-018581-7 : LC Card 85-30997 DDC 332.64/273 19
HG4910 .W365 1986 ***NYPL [JLE 86-4304]***

Afterman, Allan B. Compilation and review practice manual, 1987 / Allan B. Afterman. Boston : Warren, Gorham & Lamont, c1986. 1 v. (various pagings) : ill. ; 28 cm. Includes bibliographical references and index. ISBN 0-88712-706-1 (pbk.) LC Card 87-105236 DDC 657/.3 19
1. Financial statements, Unaudited. I. Title.
HF5681.B2 A5914 1986

AG SPAK Materialien .
(46) Voigt, Wolfgang. Der Eisenbahnkönig, oder, Rumänien lag in Linden . München , 1982. 142 p. : ISBN 3-923126-15-8 (pbk.) LC Card 87-672921
HD7289.5.R1 V64x 1982

A.G.A. Gas Demand Committee. The Outlook for gas demand in new markets, 1986-2010 . Arlington, Va. (1515 Wilson Blvd., Arlington 22209) , c1986. 54 p. : LC Card 87-403083 DDC 333.8/23312 19
HD9581.U5 O95 1986

Agababʹi͡an, Ė. M. (Ėdgar Mikhaĭlovich)
Intensifikat͡sii͡a ėkonomiki i narodnoe potreblenie /. Moskva , 1983. 166 p. ; LC Card 84-227789
HC340.C6 I58 1983

Kont͡septsii͡a i napravlenii͡a rat͡sionalizat͡sii narodnogo potreblenii͡a /. Moskva , 1985. 172 p. : LC Card 86-193920
HC340.C6 K573 1985

Agafonov, Nikolaĭ Timofeevich.
Nechernozemʹe . Moskva , 1977. 94 p. ; LC Card 82-107146
HB3608.N57 N43 1977

Novikov, Ė. A. (Ėnergiĭ Alekseevich) Gorod i prirodopolʹzovanie /. Leningrad , 1984. 143 p. ; LC Card 85-125032
HC333.5 .N68 1984

Against mechanism . Mirowski, Philip, 1951- Totowa, N.J. , 1987. p. cm. ISBN 0-8476-7436-3 : LC Card 87-21925 DDC 330/.09 19
HB71 .M635 1987

Against the tide . Green, Jim. Toronto , 1986. xvii, 324 p., [16] p. of plates : ISBN 0-919396-49-6 (pbk.) LC Card 87-127604 DDC 331.88/113875/0971 19
HD6528.S4 G74 1986

Agalma.
Boyer, Robert. La théorie de la régulation . Paris , 1986. 142 p. : ISBN 2-7071-1628-9 : LC Card 87-108410
HC276.3.B69 1986

Agan, Wrexie. Bereuter, Douglas K. United States and European Community development assistance to Africa . [Washington, D.C.? , 1985?] 22, [2] leaves ; LC Card 87-108848 DDC 338.91/4/06 19
HC800 .B455 1985

Aganbegi͡an, Abel Gezevich.
Metodologicheskie polozhenii͡a razrabotki krupnykh territorialʹnykh programm /. Novosibirsk , 1986. 303 p. : LC Card 86-211369
HC337.R853 D56 1986

Ozerov, V. K. (Viktor Konstantinovich) Analiz dinamiki sotsialisticheskogo rasshirennogo vosproizvodstva /. Novosibirsk , 1984. 263 p. ; LC Card 85-151291
HC340.I52 O97 1984

Upravlenie nauchno-tekhnicheskim progressom na predprii͡atii /. Novosibirsk , 1986. 222 p. ; LC Card 87-124400
HD45 .U52 1986

Agarkova, G. D. (Galina Dmitrievna)
Leningradskie farforisty / G.D. Agarkova. Moskva : "Legkai͡a i pishchevai͡a promyshl.", 1984. 61 p. : ill., ports. ; 20 cm. (Peredovye kollektivy) Includes bibliographical references. LC Card 85-111565
1. Porcelain industry - Russian S.F.S.R. - Leningrad. I. Series: Peredovye kollektivy ("Legkai͡a i pishchevai͡a promyshlennostʹ" (Firm)). II. Title.
HD9616.S653 L463 1984

Ägarna och makten i Sveriges börsföretag 1985 =. Sundqvist, Sven-Ivan, 1939- [Stockholm] [1985] 318 p. : ISBN 91-7588-085-7 : LC Card 86-105378
HG186.S85 S86 1985 ***NYPL [JLE 86-3810]***

Agarwal, A. K. (Ashok Kumar), 1949-
Problems of Indian fiscal structure / A.K. Agarwal. Delhi, India : Mittal Publications, 1987. xii, 157 p. ; 22 cm. Includes index. LC Card 86-903836 DDC 336.54 19
1. Fiscal policy - India. 2. Finance, Public - India. I.

Title.
HJ1334. A38 1987

Shukla, Surya Pal, 1939- Agriculture in north-eastern region /. New Delhi, India , 1986. xxvi, 223 p. : LC Card 86-902178 DDC 338.1/0954/1 19
HD2075.N58 S58 1986 ***NYPL [JLD 87-938]***

Agarwal, N. L. Agricultural prices and marketing in India : an analytical case study of Rajasthan / N.L. Agarwal ; foreword by S.S. Acharya. Delhi, India : Mittal Publications, 1986. xv, 243 p. ; 22 cm. Spine title: Agricultural prices & marketing in India. Abridged version of the author's thesis (Ph. D.--Sukhadia University, Udaipur, 1982) Bibliography: p. [225]-237. Includes index. LC Card 86-902258 DDC 338.1/3/09544 19
1. Agricultural prices - India - Rajasthan - Case studies. 2. Agricultural prices - India - Case studies. 3. Farm produce - India - Rajasthan - Marketing - Case studies. 4. Farm produce - India - Marketing - Case studies. I. Title. II. Title: Agricultural prices & marketing in India.
HD2075.R27 A36 1986

Agarwal, N. P. (Narain Prashad) Analysis of financial statements / N.P. Agarwal. 1st ed. New Delhi : National, 1981. xii, 363 p. : ill. ; 22 cm. Half title: A case study of aluminium industry in India. Includes index. Bibliography: [315]-355. LC Card 81-904955 DDC 657/.33 19
1. Aluminum industry and trade - India - Finance. 2. Financial statements - India. I. Title.
HD9539.A63 I522 1981
NYPL [JLD 86-2568]

Agarwala, N. L. (Natwar Lal) Commodity taxation and India's fiscal policy / N.L. Agarwala ; foreword by B.K. Barooah. New Delhi : Deep & Deep Publications, c1985. 294 p. ; 22 cm. Includes index. Bibliography: p. [284]-291. LC Card 85-904360 DDC 339.5/25/0954 19
1. Taxation of articles of consumption - India. 2. Fiscal policy - India. I. Title.
HJ5715.I4 A73 1985 ***NYPL [JLD 87-610]***

Agatsiva, J. L. Land use mapping of Kenya using remote sensing techniques / J.L. Agatsiva & H. Mwendwa. [Nairobi] : Ministry of Environment and Natural Resources, Kenya Rangeland Ecological Monitoring Unit, 1982. iv, 39 p. : ill., maps (1 col.) ; 30 cm. (K.R.E.M.U. technical report series . no. 72) "June, 1982." One map on folded leaf in pocket. Bibliography: p. 37-39. LC Card 84-980919 DDC 333.73/13/028 19
1. Land use - Kenya - Remote sensing. 2. Artificial satellites in remote sensing - Kenya. 3. Rangelands - Kenya. I. Mwendwa, H. II. Series. III. Series: Technical report (Kenya Rangeland Ecological Monitoring Unit) , no. 72. IV. Title.
HD983.Z7 A38 1982

Agazzi, Emilio. La Forma-valore . Manduria , 1984. 301 p. : LC Card 86-130626 DDC 335.4/12 19
HB206 .F67 1984

AGE AND EMPLOYMENT - AUSTRALIA.
Crompton, Cathy. Too old for a job, too young for a pension? . Canberra , 1986. x, 69 p. ; ISBN 0-644-05599-5 LC Card 87-150775 DDC 368.4/4/00880564 19
HD6283.A8 C76 1986

AGE AND EMPLOYMENT - EUROPEAN ECONOMIC COMMUNITY COUNTRIES.
Sullerot, Évelyne. L'âge de travailler /. [Paris] , c1986. 224 p. : ISBN 2-213-01597-X : LC Card 86-176051
HD6283.E86 S85 1986

AGE AND EMPLOYMENT - GERMANY (WEST) - CASE STUDIES.
Steinrücke, Margareta, 1953- Generationen im Betrieb . Frankfurt , New York , c1986. 343 p. ; ISBN 3-593-33639-1 LC Card 87-137842 DDC 331.3/0943 19
HD6283.G4 S74 1986

AGE AND EMPLOYMENT - GREAT BRITAIN - CASE STUDIES.
Lyon, Phil, 1948- Nearing retirement . Aldershot, Hants , Brookfield, Vt., USA , c1987. xix, 196 p. : ISBN 0-566-05233-4 : LC Card 86-25680 DDC 331.3/94/0941 19
HD6283.G7 L86 1987

AGE AND EMPLOYMENT - UNITED STATES.
Birsner, E. Patricia. The 40+ job-hunting guide . New York, NY , c1987. xx, 250 p. : ISBN 0-13-329152-9 (pbk.) : LC Card 87-2438 DDC 650.1/4/024658 19
HD38.25.U6 B53 1987

Brudney, Juliet F. Forced out . New York , c1987. 208 p. ; ISBN 0-671-64411-4 (pbk.) : LC Card 87-14927 DDC 650.1/4/0240564 19
HD6280 .B78 1987

Morrison, Malcolm H. The transition to retirement . Washington, D.C. (1990 M St., N.W., Washington 20036) , c1985. 85 p. : LC Card 85-169472 DDC 306/.38/0973 19
HQ1062 .M64 1985 ***NYPL [JLE 86-2236]***

Tigges, Leann M. Changing fortunes . New York , 1987. xvi, 174 p. : ISBN 0-275-92580-3 (alk. paper) : LC Card 87-2357 DDC 331.2/973 19
HD4975 .T5 1987

Work, health, and income among the elderly /. Washington, D.C. , c1987. xiii, 276 p. : ISBN 0-8157-1176-X : LC Card 86-26892 DDC 331.3/98 19
HD6280 .W68 1987 ***NYPL [JLE 87-960]***

Age, capital, and democracy . Schuller, Tom. Aldershot, Hants., England , Brookfield, Vt., U.S.A. , c1986. ix, 172 p. ; ISBN 0-566-00928-5 : LC Card 85-24950 DDC 332.6/7254 19
HD7105.4 .S38 1986 ***NYPL [JLD 86-2477]***

L'âge de travailler /. Sullerot, Évelyne. [Paris] , c1986. 224 p. : ISBN 2-213-01597-X : LC Card 86-176051
HD6283.E86 S85 1986

AGE DISCRIMINATION IN EMPLOYMENT - UNITED STATES.
Brudney, Juliet F. Forced out . New York , c1987. 208 p. ; ISBN 0-671-64411-4 (pbk.) : LC Card 87-14927 DDC 650.1/4/0240564 19
HD6280 .B78 1987

AGE DISTRIBUTION (DEMOGRAPHY)
Economics of changing age distributions in developed countries /. Oxford [Oxfordshire] , Topsfield, Mass. , 1987. p. cm. ISBN 0-19-829503-0 : LC Card 86-25098 DDC 304.6/2/091722 19
HB1531 .E28 1987

AGE DISTRIBUTION (DEMOGRAPHY) - GREAT BRITAIN.
Economics of changing age distributions in developed countries /. Oxford [Oxfordshire] , Topsfield, Mass. , 1987. p. cm. ISBN 0-19-829503-0 : LC Card 86-25098 DDC 304.6/2/091722 19
HB1531 .E28 1987

AGE DISTRIBUTION (DEMOGRAPHY) - ISRAEL.
Economics of changing age distributions in developed countries /. Oxford [Oxfordshire] , Topsfield, Mass. , 1987. p. cm. ISBN 0-19-829503-0 : LC Card 86-25098 DDC 304.6/2/091722 19
HB1531 .E28 1987

AGE DISTRIBUTION (DEMOGRAPHY) - JAPAN.
Economics of changing age distributions in developed countries /. Oxford [Oxfordshire] , Topsfield, Mass. , 1987. p. cm. ISBN 0-19-829503-0 : LC Card 86-25098 DDC 304.6/2/091722 19
HB1531 .E28 1987

AGE DISTRIBUTION (DEMOGRAPHY) - PERU - STATISTICS.
Perú . Lima, Perú , 1984. 54 p. ; LC Card 86-111841 DDC 304.6/2/0985021 19
HA1055 .P46 1984 ***NYPL [JLG 86-190]***

AGE DISTRIBUTION (DEMOGRAPHY) - QUÉBEC (PROVINCE) - MONTRÉAL REGION.
Bussière, Yves. Vieillissement de la population et demande de transport dans la région de Montréal . Montréal, Québec [1983] 83 p. : ISBN 2-89228-036-2 LC Card 84-177163
HE4509.M68 B88 1983

AGE DISTRIBUTION (DEMOGRAPHY) - SWITZERLAND - STATISTICS.
Lüthi, Ambros, 1938- Die wirtschaftliche Ungleichheit im Rentenalter in der Schweiz /. Freiburg/Schweiz , 1983. 229 p. : ISBN 3-7278-0282-0 : LC Card 83-163287
HD7105.35.S9 L87 1983

AGE DISTRIBUTION (DEMOGRAPHY) - UNITED STATES.
Economics of changing age distributions in developed countries /. Oxford [Oxfordshire] , Topsfield, Mass. , 1987. p. cm. ISBN 0-19-829503-0 : LC Card 86-25098 DDC 304.6/2/091722 19
HB1531 .E28 1987

The age of the common millionaire /. Heller, Robert, 1932- New York , c1987. p. cm. ISBN 0-525-24588-X LC Card 87-19973 DDC 305.5/234 19
HC79.W4 H45 1987

Age structure of mortality in developing countries : a data base for cross-sectional and time series research / Department of International Economic and Social Affairs. New York : United Nations, 1986. vi, 267 p. : ill. ; 28 cm. "ST/ESA/SER.R/66." Bibliography: p. 265-267. LC Card 87-401611 DDC 304.6/4 19
1. Mortality - Developing countries - Tables. I. United Nations. Dept. of International Economic and Social Affairs.
HB1528 .A36 1986

AGED AS CONSUMERS - UNITED STATES.
Gollub, James O. Business opportunities among the aging population . Menlo Park, Calif. (333 Ravenswood Ave., Menlo Park 94025-3476) , c1984. 36 p. : LC Card 86-210219 DDC 658.8/348 19
HC110.C6 G62 1984

The Maturity market . New York, N.Y. , c1985. 1 v. (various pagings) : ISBN 0-931634-47-4 (pbk.) LC Card 86-203045 DDC 658.8/348 19
HC110.C6 M33 1985

AGED - AUSTRALIA - ECONOMIC CONDITIONS.
Crompton, Cathy. Too old for a job, too young for a pension? . Canberra , 1986. x, 69 p. ; ISBN 0-644-05599-5 LC Card 87-150775 DDC 368.4/4/00880564 19
HD6283.A8 C76 1986

AGED AUTOMOBILE DRIVERS - CALIFORNIA - STATISTICS.
Huston, Ray E. Senior driver facts /. Sacramento, CA , Springfield, VA , 1986. iii, 22 p. : LC Card 86-623189 DDC 363.1/252/09794021 19
HE5614.3.C3 H87 1986

AGED - DWELLINGS.
Housing the aged . New York , c1987. xvii, 500 p. : ISBN 0-444-01012-2 LC Card 87-5253 DDC 363.5/9
HD7287.9 .H7 1987

AGED - EDUCATION - UNITED STATES.
Education and training for older persons . [Washington, D.C.?] , 1981. iii, 64 p. :
NYPL [JLF 86-1274]

AGED - EMPLOYMENT.
Fourteen steps in managing an aging work force /. Lexington, Mass. , c1988. xi, [247] p. : ISBN 0-669-13206-3 (alk. paper) LC Card 87-3322 DDC 658.3/042 19
HF5549.5.O44 F68 1988

AGED - EMPLOYMENT - GERMANY, WEST.
Genosko, Joachim. Arbeitsangebot und Alterssicherung /. Regensburg , c1985. vii, 287 p. : ISBN 3-924956-05-7 LC Card 86-230675
HD7105.35.G3 G46 1985

AGED - EMPLOYMENT - UNITED STATES.
Education and training for older persons . [Washington, D.C.?] , 1981. iii, 64 p. :
NYPL [JLF 86-1274]

Kahne, Hilda. Reconceiving part-time work . Totowa, N.J. , 1985. xv, 180 p. : ISBN 0-8476-7376-6 : LC Card 85-2386 DDC 331.3/94 19
HD5110.2.U5 K33 1985
NYPL [JLE 86-1174]

The Problem isn't age . New York , 1987. xiii, 265 p. : ISBN 0-275-92371-1 (alk. paper) : LC Card 86-30642 DDC 331.3/94/0973 19
HD6280 .P75 1987

Work, health, and income among the elderly /. Washington, D.C. , c1987. xiii, 276 p. : ISBN 0-8157-1176-X : LC Card 86-26892 DDC 331.3/98 19
HD6280 .W68 1987 ***NYPL [JLE 87-960]***

AGED - EMPLOYMENT - UNITED STATES - CASE STUDIES.
Jacobson, Beverly. Young programs for older workers . New York , 1980. xvii, 123 p. ;

ISBN 0-442-25405-9 LC Card 80-12621 DDC 658.3/042
HD6280 .J3 ***NYPL [JLE 81-438]***

AGED - EUROPE - ECONOMIC CONDITIONS.
Schmitz, Heinz. Vermeidung von Armut im Alter . München , c1983. 267 p. : ISBN 3-89019-099-5 LC Card 84-197886
HD7164 .S29 1983

AGED - GERMANY (WEST) - RUHR (REGION) - HISTORY.
Günter, Janne, 1937- Mündliche Geschichtsschreibung . Mülheim/Ruhr , 1982. 142, [1] p. : ISBN 3-923456-00-X LC Card 85-146144
HD8039.M61 G343 1982

AGED - HEALTH AND HYGIENE - UNITED STATES.
Work, health, and income among the elderly /. Washington, D.C. , c1987. xiii, 276 p. : ISBN 0-8157-1176-X : LC Card 86-26892 DDC 331.3/98 19
HD6280 .W68 1987 ***NYPL [JLE 87-960]***

AGED - HEALTH AND HYGIENE - UNITED STATES - STATISTICAL METHODS.
Health of an aging population . Hyattsville, Md. , Washington, D.C. , 1987. p. cm. ISBN 0-8406-0362-2 LC Card 86-600392 DDC 362.1/0723 s 362.1/9897/00973 19
HA37 .U1693 no. 25 RA408.A3

AGED - HEALTH AND HYGIENE - UNITED STATES - STATISTICAL SERVICES.
Health of an aging population . Hyattsville, Md. , Washington, D.C. , 1987. p. cm. ISBN 0-8406-0362-2 LC Card 86-600392 DDC 362.1/0723 s 362.1/9897/00973 19
HA37 .U1693 no. 25 RA408.A3

AGED - HOUSING - GOVERNMENT POLICY - UNITED STATES - STATES.
Tiven, Marjorie. State initiatives in elderly housing . Washington, DC , c1987. xviii, 79 p. ; LC Card 87-154352 DDC 363.5/9 19
HD7287.92.U54 T58 1987

AGED - HOUSING - UNITED STATES.
Blank, Thomas O., 1947- Older persons and their housing, today and tomorrow /. Springfield, Ill., U. S.A. , c1988. xviii, 304 p. ; ISBN 0-398-05377-4 LC Card 87-16827 DDC 363.5/9 19
HD7287.92.U54 B554 1988

Scott, Terrence J. Elderly housing options /. Chicago , c1987. 235 p. : ISBN 0-931028-87-6 LC Card 86-63411 DDC 363.5/9 19
HD7287.92.U54 S38 1987

AGED - NETHERLANDS - DWELLINGS.
Houben, Piet. Ouderenhuisvesting in 'n emancipatieperspectief /. Delft , 1985. 178 p. : ISBN 90-6275-118-0 : LC Card 86-149527
HD7287.92.N4 H683 1985
NYPL [JLE 86-3902]

AGED - TAXATION - VIRGINIA.
Virginia's income tax age credit. [Richmond, Va.] [1984] ii, 26 leaves ; LC Card 86-622458 DDC 336.24/216 19
HJ4655.V88 A828 1984

AGED - TAXATION - VIRGINIA - STATISTICS.
Virginia's income tax age credit. [Richmond, Va.] [1984] ii, 26 leaves ; LC Card 86-622458 DDC 336.24/216 19
HJ4655.V88 A828 1984

AGED - UNITED STATES - DWELLINGS.
Blank, Thomas O., 1947- Older persons and their homes, today and tomorrow . [Harrisburg] [1986] 60 leaves : LC Card 86-623023 DDC 363.5/9 19
HD7287.92.U54 B55 1986

Blank, Thomas O., 1947- Older persons and their housing, today and tomorrow /. Springfield, Ill., U. S.A. , c1988. xviii, 304 p. ; ISBN 0-398-05377-4 LC Card 87-16827 DDC 363.5/9 19
HD7287.92.U54 B554 1988

Carlin, Vivian F., 1919- Where can mom live? . Lexington, Mass. , c1987. viii, 206 p. : ISBN 0-669-13665-4 (alk. paper) LC Card 86-45526 DDC 363.5/9 19
HD7287.92.U54 C37 1987

Gold, Margaret. [Older American's guide to housing and living arrangements.] Guide to housing alternatives for older citizens /. Mount Vernon, N.Y. , c1985. ix, 170 p. : ISBN 0-89043-031-4 (pbk.) : LC Card 87-401956 DDC 646/.79 19
HD7287.92.U54 G65 1985

Horne, Jo. Homesharing and other lifestyle options /. Washington, D.C. , Glenview, Ill. , c1988. xi, 259 p. : ISBN 0-673-24886-0 (pbk.) : LC Card 87-13028 DDC 363.5/9 19
HD7287.92.U54 H65 1988

AGED - UNITED STATES - DWELLINGS - FINANCE.
Gold, Margaret. [Older American's guide to housing and living arrangements.] Guide to housing alternatives for older citizens /. Mount Vernon, N.Y. , c1985. ix, 170 p. : ISBN 0-89043-031-4 (pbk.) : LC Card 87-401956 DDC 646/.79 19
HD7287.92.U54 G65 1985

AGED - UNITED STATES - ECONOMIC CONDITIONS.
The Maturity market . New York, N.Y. , c1985. 1 v. (various pagings) : ISBN 0-931634-47-4 (pbk.) LC Card 86-203045 DDC 658.8/348 19
HC110.C6 M33 1985

AGED - UNITED STATES - FINANCE, PERSONAL.
Vicker, Ray. The Dow Jones-Irwin guide to retirement planning /. Homewood, Ill. , c1987. ix, 332 p. : ISBN 1-556-23005-2 LC Card 86-72973 DDC 332.024/01 19
HG179 .V54 1987

AGED - UNITED STATES - HOUSING - CONGRESSES.
The Future is Now: A Home Equity Conversion Conference (1985 : Washington, D.C.) Proceedings from The Future is Now, A Home Equity Conversion Conference. Washington, D.C. [1985?] ix, 76 p. ; LC Card 86-601425 DDC 332.7/22 19
HG2040.45 .F87 1985

AGED WORKERS. see **AGE AND EMPLOYMENT.**

Ageev, V. M. (Valentin Mikhaĭlovich)
Ekonomicheskie interesy i stimuly pri sotsializme / V.M. Ageev. Moskva : "Sov. Rossiia", 1984. 190 p. ; 20 cm. Includes bibliographical references. LC Card 85-108645
1. Soviet Union - Economic policy - 1981-. 2. Marxian economics. I. Title.
HC336.25 .A375 1984

Agell, Jonas. The effects of capital taxation : an equilibrium asset market approach / Jonas Agell. Uppsala : S. Academiae Ubsaliensis ; Stockholm, Sweden : Distributor, Almqvist & Wiksell International, 1986. 123 p. : ill. ; 22 cm. (Acta Universitatis Upsaliensis. Studia oeconomica Upsaliensia, 0585-539X . 9) Originally presented as the author's thesis (doctoral--Uppsala University, 1986) Bibliography: p. 117-123. ISBN 91-554-1938-0 (pbk.) LC Card 87-100538 DDC 330 s 336.2/009481 19
1. Taxation - Sweden - Mathematical models. 2. Capital levy - Sweden - Mathematical models. 3. Investments - Sweden - Mathematical models. I. Title. II. Series.
HB51 .S7 no. 9 HJ2838

Agencia para el Desarrollo Internacional. see **United States. Agency for International Development.**

Agenda for co-operation : a discussion paper on decontrol and post-control issues. [Ottawa?] : Government of Canada, [1977?] 63, 66 p. ; 27 cm. Text in English and French. Cover title. Title on added t.p.: Programme de coopération. LC Card 84-246582
1. Wage-price policy - Canada. I. Title: Agenda for cooperation. II. Title: Programme de coopération.
HC120.W24 A64 1977

Agenda for cooperation. Agenda for co-operation . [Ottawa?] [1977?] 63, 66 p. ; LC Card 84-246582
HC120.W24 A64 1977

The Agenda for economic renewal : principles and progress / Michael H. Wilson. [Ottawa] : Dept. of Finance, [1987] 25, 26 p. : ill. ; 27 cm. At head of title: Securing economic renewal; Pour assurer le renouveau économique. "February 18, 1987." English and French. Title on added t.p.: Un Programme de renouveau économique. LC Card 87-140803 DDC 338.971 19
1. Canada - Economic policy. 2. Canada - Economic conditions - 1945-. I. Wilson, Michael H. (Michael Holcombe), 1937-. II. Canada. Dept. of Finance. III. Title: Programme de renouveau économique. IV. Title: Securing economic renewal. V. Title: Pour assurer le renouveau économique.
HC115 .A624 1987

Agenda for the future. An Environmental agenda for the future /. Washington, D.C. , c1985. viii, 155 p. ; ISBN 0-933280-29-7 (pbk.) : LC Card 85-19760 DDC 304.2 19
TD171 .E56 1985 ***NYPL [JLE 86-2773]***

Les agents de l'Etat au 31 décembre 1980 /. Quarré, Dominique. Paris [1985] 305 p. ; ISBN 2-11-064767-1 : LC Card 86-162558
HD8013.F6 Q373 1985

Agervold, Mogens. Kontorarbejde : en undersøgelse af det psykiske arbejdsmiljø / Mogens Agervold ; foretaget i samarbejde med Hanne Bruhn ... [et al.]. [Copenhagen] : Akademisk forlag, c1983. 126 p. ; 22 cm. Bibliography: p. 126. ISBN 87-500-2489-2 : LC Card 84-126389
1. Office practice - Denmark - Psychological aspects. I. Bruhn, Hanne. II. Title.
HF5547.5 .A43 1983

Aggarwal, Vinod K.

Aggarwal, Yash, 1948- Raza, Moonis. Transport geography of India . New Delhi , 1986. xii, 299 p. : LC Card 86-903251 DDC 380.5/0954 19
HE3298 .R39 1986

Agglomerazione urbana, localizzazione industriale e Mezzogiorno /. Costa, Paolo. Milano , 1983. viii, 240 p. : LC Card 83-186216 DDC 307.2 19
HB2060.S68 C67 1983 ***NYPL [JLE 86-3657]***

Aggregate supply in interlink : model specification and empirical results / by John Helliwell ... [et al.]. Paris, France : OECD, c1985. 60 p. : ill ; 30 cm. (Working papers / Economics and Statistics Department . no. 26) "November 1985." Bibliography: p. 54-55. LC Card 86-205160 DDC 338.5/213 19
1. Supply and demand - Mathematical models. I. Helliwell, John E. II. Series: Working papers (Organisation for Economic Co-operation and Development. Dept. of Economics and Development) , no. 26.
HB201 .A25 1985

Aggregation und Kausalität im Modell des allgemeinen Konkurrenzgleichgewichts . Vilks, Arnis. Göttingen , c1984. 141 p. ; ISBN 3-525-11287-4 (Deut. Bibl.) LC Card 84-225754
HB842 .V55 1984

Aggressive tax avoidance for real estate investors . Reed, John T. Danville, CA , 1986. 267 p. : ISBN 0-939224-13-5 (pbk.) :
NYPL [JLF 86-1562]

Agi, Michael. Optische Beleg- und Seitenleser : Marktübersicht / Michael Agi, Adolf Breiling. Bonn : Gesellschaft für Mathematik und Datenverarbeitung : Institut für Informationssysteme, c1976. 96 p. ; 30 cm. Includes bibliographical references. LC Card 85-112068
1. Optical scanners. I. Breiling, Adolf. II. Title.
HF5548.4.O6 A34 1976

AGICULTURE - STATISTICAL METHODS.
Guidelines for the computation of selected statistical indicators /. Rome , 1986. vii, 71 p. : ISBN 92-5-102367-0 (pbk.) LC Card 87-119289 DDC 338.1/072 19
HD1425 .G85 1986

AGING PERSONS. see **AGED.**

Las agitaciones campesinas del período bolchevista, 1918-1920 /. Díaz del Moral, Juan, 1870-1948. Sevilla [1985?] 230 p. ; ISBN 84-7587-031-7 LC Card 86-181529
HD1536.S7 D48 1985

Aglietta, Michel.
Capitalismes fin de siècle /. Paris , c1986. 268 p. : ISBN 2-13-039425-6 : LC Card 86-231136
HC106.8 .C364 1986

International monetary and financial integration . Dordrecht , Boston , c1988. xii, 403 p. : ISBN 90-247-3563-7 LC Card 87-3622 DDC 332.4/94 19
HG930.5 .I586 1988

Les métamorphoses de la société salariale : la France en projet / Michel Aglietta, Anton Brender. Paris : Calmann-Lévy, c1984. 274 p. ;

21 cm. (Perspectives de l'économique. Économie contemporaine) Includes bibliographical references. ISBN 2-7021-1230-7 : LC Card 84-176554 DDC 331/.0944 19

1. Labor and laboring classes - France. 2. Industrial relations - France. 3. Labor policy - France. I. Brender, Anton. II. Title.

HD8431 .A36 1984 *NYPL [JLD 87-478]*

AGNELLI, GIOVANNI, 1921-
Camerana, Oddone. L'enigma del cavalier Agnelli e altri itinerari /. Milano , c1985. 117 p. ; LC Card 85-191746
HD9710.I82 A6615 1985 *NYPL [JLC 87-25]*

Agnew, John A. The United States in the world-economy : a regional geography / John Agnew. Cambridge ; New York : Cambridge University Press, 1987. xvii, 264 p. : ill., maps ; 24 cm. (Geography of the world-economy) Bibliography: p. 225-245. Includes index. ISBN 0-521-30410-5 LC Card 86-32743 DDC 337.73 19

1. United States - Economic conditions. 2. United States - Economic conditions - Regional disparities. 3. United States - Foreign economic relations. 4. Regional economics. I. Title. II. Series.

HC103 .A37 1987

Agnihotri, S. K. Rural development through land reforms : Assam study / S.K. Agnihotri. Delhi : Periodical Experts Book Agency, 1986. viii, 3, 206 p. ; 23 cm. Bibliography: p. [200]-206. LC Card 87-900356 DDC 333.3/1/54162 19

1. Land reform - India - Assam - Case studies. 2. Land reform - India - Case studies. 3. Land reform - Law and legislation - India - Assam - Cases. 4. Land reform - Law and legislation - India - Cases. 5. Rural development - India - Assam - Case studies. 6. Rural development - India - Case studies. I. Title.

HD1333.I42 A773 1986

Agrarberichterstattung Nordrhein-Westfalen 1981 : Betriebssysteme und Standardbetriebseinkommen sowie sozialökonomische Gliederung und Buchführung der landwirtschaftlichen Betriebe. Düsseldorf : Landesamt für Datenverarbeitung und Statistik Nordrhein-Westfalen, [1983] 131, [5] p. ; 30 cm. (Beiträge zur Statistik des Landes Nordrhein-Westfalen . Heft 489) Chiefly tables. LC Card 87-407319 DDC 943/.55 s 338.1/0943/55021 19

1. Agriculture - Economic aspects - Germany (West) - North Rhine-Westphalia - Statistics. 2. Farms - Germany (West) - North Rhine-Westphalia - Statistics. I. Landesamt für Datenverarbeitung und Statistik Nordrhein-Westfalen. II. Series.

HA1320.N6 A32 Heft 489 HD9013.7.N6

Agrarberichterstattung Nordrhein-Westfalen 1981 : Besitzverhältnisse, ausserbetriebliches Einkommen, Arbeitsverhältnisse in Betriebsformen sowie Pachtpreise der landwirtschaftlichen Betriebe. Düsseldorf : Landesamt für Datenverarbeitung und Statistik Nordrhein-Westfalen, [1983] 189 p. ; 30 cm. (Beiträge zur Statistik des Landes Nordrhein-Westfalen . Heft 490) Chiefly tables. LC Card 87-407320 DDC 943/.55 s 338.1/0943/55021 19

1. Agriculture - Economic aspects - Germany (West) - North Rhine-Westphalia - Statistics. 2. Agricultural laborers - Germany (West) - North Rhine-Westphalia - Statistics. 3. Farmers - Germany (West) - North Rhine-Westphalia - Supplementary employment - Statistics. 4. Farms - Germany (West) - North Rhine-Westphalia - Statistics. I. Landesamt für Datenverarbeitung und Statistik Nordrhein-Westfalen. II. Series.

HA1320.N6 A32 Heft 490 HD1960.N67

Agrarberichterstattung Nordrhein-Westfalen 1983 : Bodennutzung und Rechtsform der land- und forstwirtschaftlichen Betriebe. Düsseldorf : Landesamt für Datenverarbeitung und Statistik Nordrhein-Westfalen, [1984] 263 p. ; 30 cm. (Beiträge zur Statistik des Landes Nordrhein-Westfalen . Heft 532) Chiefly tables. LC Card 87-407317 DDC 943/.55 s 338.1/0943/55021 19

1. Agriculture - Economic aspects - Germany (West) - North Rhine-Westphalia - Statistics. 2. Forest products industry - Germany (West) - North Rhine-Westphalia - Statistics. 3. Land use, rural - Germany (West) - North Rhine-Westphalia - Statistics. I. Landesamt für Datenverarbeitung und Statistik Nordrhein-Westfalen. II. Series.

HA1320.N6 A32 Heft 532 HD1960.N67

Agrarberichterstattung Nordrhein-Westfalen 1983 : Viehhaltung der land- und forstwirtschaftlichen Betriebe. Düsseldorf : Landesamt für Datenverarbeitung und Statistik Nordrhein-Westfalen, [1984] 241, [5] p. ; 30 cm. (Beiträge zur Statistik des Landes Nordrhein-Westfalen . Heft 533) Chiefly tables. LC Card 87-407318 DDC 943/.55 s 338.1/76/0094355021 19

1. Animal industry - Germany (West) - North Rhine-Westphalia - Statistics. 2. Livestock - Germany (West) - North Rhine-Westphalia - Statistics. I. Landesamt für Datenverarbeitung und Statistik Nordrhein-Westfalen. II. Series.

HA1320.N6 A32 Heft 533 HD9423.7.N6

Agrarberichterstattung Nordrhein-Westfalen 1983 : Betriebsgrössenstruktur, Bodennutzung und Viehhaltung sowie sozialökonomische Betriebstypen und -systematik (Gemeindetabellen I und II, Kreistabelle I sowie Anhang mit sonstigen ausgewählten Gemeindedaten). Düsseldorf : Landesamt für Datenverarbeitung und Statistik Nordrhein-Westfalen, [1985] 191 p. ; 30 cm. (Beiträge zur Statistik des Landes Nordrhein-Westfalen . Heft 531) Chiefly tables. LC Card 87-407316 DDC 943/.55 s 338.1/0943/55021 19

1. Agriculture - Economic aspects - Germany (West) - North Rhine-Westphalia - Statistics. 2. Farms - Germany (West) - North Rhine-Westphalia - Statistics. 3. Livestock - Germany (West) - North Rhine-Westphalia - Statistics. 4. Land use, rural - Germany (West) - North Rhine-Westphalia - Statistics. I. Landesamt für Datenverarbeitung und Statistik Nordrhein-Westfalen. II. Series.

HA1320.N6 A32 Heft 531 HD1960.N67

Agrarberichterstattung 1983 : A, Gemeindeergebnisse, B, Kreisergebnisse. Hannover : Niedersächsisches Landesverwaltungsamt, Statistik, 1985. viii, 143 p., [3] p. of plates : ill. ; 30 cm. (Statistik Niedersachsen . Bd. 416) "Zugleich Statistischer Bericht C IV 9--1983." LC Card 86-222908

1. Agriculture - Economic aspects - Germany (West) - Lower Saxony - Statistics. I. Niedersächsisches Landesverwaltungsamt. Statistik. II. Series: Statistik von Niedersachsen , Bd. 416.

HD1960.L68 A38 1985

Agrárgazdaság, agrártársadalom, agrárpolitika / szerkesztette, Hegyi András ; [a tudományos tanácskozás előadói, kötetünk szerzői, Balázs György ... et al.]. Szeged : József Attila Tudományegyetem és a Tudományos Ismeretterjesztő Társulat Csongrád Megyei Szervezete, 1985. 338 p. : ill. ; 21 cm. Includes bibliographical references. ISBN 963-481-548-0 : LC Card 86-143859

1. Agriculture - Economic aspects - Hungary - History - Congresses. 2. Agriculture - Social aspects - Hungary - History - Congresses. 3. Collectivization of agriculture - Hungary - History - Congresses. 4. Agriculture and state - Hungary - History - Congresses. I. Hegyi, András. II. Balázs, György, 1932-.

HD1940.5 .A78 1985

Agrárgazdasági Kutató Intézet. (Old Catalog form: Agrárgazdasági Kutató Intézet, Budapest)
Javaslatok az élelmiszer-gazdaság fejlesztésére . Budapest , 1984. 279 p. : ISBN 963-221-500-1 LC Card 85-229874
HD9015.H82 J38 1984

Main directions of agricultural development in Hungary . Budapest , 1985. 77 p. ; LC Card 86-232881 DDC 338.1 s 338.1/09439 19
HD1407 .M3 no. 61 HD1940.5

Agrárgazdasági Kutató Intézet (Series) .
(1983/17) Orbánné Nagy, Mária. Az élelmiszerfogyasztás várható tendenciái hosszabb távon /. Budapest , 1983. 98 p. ; ISBN 963-491-166-8 LC Card 85-219700
HD9015.H82 O73 1983

(1984/11) Kovács, Kálmán. Tervezési szintek érdekeltségének összehangolása gazdaságszabályozási eszközökkel . Budapest , 1984. 50 p. : ISBN 963-491-189-7 LC Card 86-198789
HD1940.5.Z8 K68 1984

(1984/12) Összefoglalás, Szolnok megye agroökológiai potenciálja az ezredfordulón /. Budapest , 1984. 115 p. : ISBN 963-491-193-5 LC Card 86-198809
HD1940.5.Z9 S966 1984

(1984/14) Halász, Péter. Nemzedéki vonások a mezőgazdasági kistermelésben /. Budapest , 1984. 72 p. ; ISBN 963-491-192-7 LC Card 86-198744
HD1476.H8 H252 1984

(1984/15) Árva, László. Indokina gazdasági fejlődése és hazánk lehetőségei a térség országaival való együttműködés terén /. Budapest , 1984. 69 p. : ISBN 963-491-194-3 LC Card 86-199424
HC441 .A77 1984

(1984/18) Szénay, Lászlóné. A közgazdasági szabályozás és az élelmiszeripari szakágazatok gazdasági eredményeinek összefüggései és problémái az 1977-82 közötti években /. Budapest , 1984. 161 p. ; ISBN 963-491-196-X LC Card 86-199432
HD9015.H82 S935 1984

(1984/21) Lányfalvi, Sándor. Adalékok a tartósítóipar hosszútávu fejlesztésének megalapozásához /. Budapest , 1984. 115 p. ; ISBN 963-491-199-4 LC Card 86-199120
HD9326.H82 L36 1984

(1984/5) Ivanics, András. A termelőszövetkezeti termelésirányitókról . Budapest , 1984. 83 p. ; ISBN 963-491-179-X LC Card 86-198816
HD1492.H82 B675 1984

(1984/9) Kóbor, Kálmán. A hús- és a tejgazdaság jellemző vonásai Dániában /. Budapest , 1984. 111 p. : ISBN 963-491-183-8 LC Card 86-198770
HD9425.D4 K6 1984

(1985/1) Ár- és külkereskedelmi tanulmány a búzára és kukoricára, Magyarország /. Budapest , 1984. 93 p. ; ISBN 963-491-218-4 (Magy. nemz. bibl.) LC Card 86-147569
HD9049.W5 H93 1984

(1985/10) Harza, Lajos. Az EGK szőlő- és borgazdaságának szabályozórendszere /. Budapest , 1985. 70 p. : ISBN 963-491-210-9 LC Card 86-196818
HD9259.G7 E864 1985

(1985/12) Borszéki, Éva. Élelmiszergazdaságunk versenyképessége . Budapest , 1985. 147 p. ; ISBN 963-491-213-3 LC Card 86-199073
HD1940.5 .B67 1985

(1985/14) Lugossy, Györgyi. Szándékok és lehetőségek . Budapest , 1985. 85 p. : ISBN 963-491-215-X LC Card 86-199350
HD1492.H82 S665 1985

(1985/15) Csatorday, Géza. A szállítási rendszer fejlesztési lehetőségeinek vizsgálata a tejiparban /. Budapest , 1985. 94 p. : ISBN 963-491-216-8 LC Card 86-199210
HE199.5.M5 C73 1985

(1985/3) Fórizs, Józsefné. Földértékelés, termőhelyi értékelés problémái . Budapest , 1985. 211 p., [4] folded leaves of plates : ISBN 963-491-204-4 LC Card 86-196842
HD1387 .F596 1985

(1985/4) Réder, Gyula. Helyzetkép az élelmiszeripari müvezetőkről /. Budapest , 1985. 81 p. ; ISBN 963-491-205-2 LC Card 86-196825
HD9015.H82 R43 1985

(1985/5) Pilling, András. Az önelszámoló rendszer alkalmazásának, a kistermelők integrálásának és a kihelyezett részlegeknek a hatása a mezőgazdasági vállalatok szervezeti felépitésére, s annak müködésére /. Budapest , 1985. 89 p. ; ISBN 963-491-206-0 LC Card 86-196755
HD1492.H8 P55 1985

(1985/6) Mátyás, László. Idősorok és keresztmetszeti adatok együttes felhasználása az ökonometriai vizsgálatokban /. Budapest , 1985. 119 p. ; ISBN 963-491-212-5 LC Card 86-196805
HB139 .M39 1985

(1985/7) Szajkó, Pál. A nyúlhústermelés és export gazdasági problémái /. Budapest , 1985. 57 p. ; ISBN 963-491-207-9 LC Card 86-196798
HD9438.R4 H97 1985

(1985/8) A Szabolcs-Szatmár megyei télialma-termelés, -feldolgozás és -értékesités rendszerének fejlesztése /. Budapest , 1985. 144

p. : ISBN 963-491-208-7 LC Card 86-196831
HD9259.A6 H87 1985

(1986/4) Ács, Rudolf. A komplex meliorációs beruházások történeti áttekintése és gazdasági hatásának vizsgálata különböző agroökológiai tipusu gazdaságokban /. Budapest , 1986. 118 p. ; ISBN 963-491-237-0 LC Card 87-137972
HD1940.5 .A65 1986

Agrárgazdasági Kutató Intézet. Vállalati Együttműködési és Agrárszociológiai Főosztály. A Szabolcs-Szatmár megyei télialma-termelés, -feldolgozás és -értékesités rendszerének fejlesztése /. Budapest , 1985. 144 p. : ISBN 963-491-208-7 LC Card 86-196831
HD9259.A6 H87 1985

Agrárgazdasági Kutazó Intézet (Series) . (1985/2) Kartali, János. A friss és feldolgozott zöldségek, gyümölcsök bel- és külkereskedelmi forgalmazásának aktuális problémái /. Budapest , 1985. 108 p. ; ISBN 963-491-203-6 LC Card 86-195487
HD9220.H82 K37 1985

Agrárgazdaságtan / szerkesztette, Lőkös László ; [a könyv szerzői, Bíró Ferenc ... et al.]. Budapest : Mezőgazdasági Kiadó, 1984. 465 p. : ill. ; 25 cm. Bibliography: p. 457-462. ISBN 963-231-719-X : LC Card 85-229778
1. Agriculture - Economic aspects. I. Lőkös, László. II. Bíró, Ferenc, fl. 1963-.
HD1415 .A27 1984

Agrarian change in Egypt . Raḍwān, Samīr Muḥammad. London , Dover, N.H. , c1986. xii, 167 p. : ISBN 0-7099-4214-1 : LC Card 85-11356 DDC 305.5/69/0962 19
HN786.A8 R33 1985 NYPL [JLD 86-1045]

The agrarian policy of the British in Bengal . Mukhopadhyay, Subhas Chandra, 1938- Allahabad, India , 1987. xi, 195 p. ; ISBN 81-85076-11-1 : LC Card 87-900481 DDC 338.1/85414 19
HJ4392.I4 M85 1987

The agrarian question /. Kautsky, Karl, 1854-1938. [Agrarfrage. English.] London , Atlantic Highlands, N.J. , 1988- p. cm. ISBN 1-85305-024-5 (v. 2) LC Card 87-20593 DDC 338.1 19
HD1306.G3 K315 1988

AGRARIAN QUESTION. see **AGRICULTURE AND STATE; AGRICULTURE - ECONOMIC ASPECTS; LAND TENURE.**

The agrarian question and the development of capitalism in India /. Patnaik, Utsa. Delhi , New York , 1986. 45 p. ; ISBN 0-19-561954-4 : LC Card 86-900017 DDC 338.1/0954 19
HD2072 .P33 1986

AGRARIAN REFORM. see **LAND REFORM.**

Agrarian reform in India . Bergmann, Theodor. New Delhi, India , 1984. viii, 216 p. ; LC Card 84-900254 DDC 333.3/1/54 19
HD1333.I4 B46 1984 NYPL [JLD 86-3823]

Agrarian reforms and institutional changes in India /. Haque, T. (Tajamul), 1947- New Delhi , 1986, c1985. xvi, 268 p. : LC Card 86-902575 DDC 338.1/854 19
HD1333.I4 H36 1986 NYPL [JLD 87-1547]

Agrarian relations in West Bengal . Rudra, Ashok. Bombay , c1983. x, 104 p. ; LC Card 83-902673 DDC 338.1/0954/14 19
HD879.W4 R83 1983 NYPL [JLD 86-3785]

Agrarian scene in British Punjab /. Hari Singh, Master, 1902- New Delhi , 1983-c1984. 2 v. : LC Card 83-905514 DDC 338.1/0954/5 19
HD2075.P8 H37 1983 NYPL [JLK 86-113]

Agrarian struggles in India after independence / edited by A.R. Desai. Delhi : Oxford University Press, 1986. xxvi, 666 p. : maps ; 22 cm. Includes bibliographical references and index.
1. Land reform - India. 2. Peasantry - India. 3. Peasant uprisings - India - 20th century. 4. Agriculture and state - India. I. Desai, Akshayakumar Ramanlal.
NYPL [JLD 86-3896]

The agrarian system of eastern Rajasthan, c. 1650-c. 1750 /. Gupta, Satya Prakash, 1940- Delhi , 1986. xvi, 352 p. : ISBN 81-85054-11-8 : LC Card 87-900814 DDC 338.1/0954/4 19
HD2075.R27 G86 1986

Az agráripari egyesülések útkeresése /. Benet, Iván. Budapest , 1985. 197 p. : ISBN 963-221-616-4 : LC Card 86-203013
HD9015.H82 B447 1985

Agrarismo en Guatemala /. Cambranes, J. C. Guatemala , 1986. 255 p. : LC Card 87-401042 DDC 322/.2/097281 19
HD1531.G9 C36 1986

Agrarmärkte & Agrarmarketing : Strategien im grünen Markt / mit Beiträgen von Paul Beck ... [et al.] ; Vorwort von Josef Ertl ; herausgegeben zum 60. Geburtstag von Helmut Fahrnschon. Hamburg : Behr, 1983. 220 p. : ill. ; 21 cm. Includes bibliographical references. ISBN 3-922528-45-7 LC Card 84-162297
1. Agriculture - Economic aspects - Germany, West. 2. Agriculture and state - Germany, West. 3. Agriculture - Competitions - Germany (West). I. Fahrnschon, Helmut. II. Beck, Paul, Dipl.-Kfm. III. Title: Agrarmärkte und Agrarmarketing.
HD1955 .A515 1983

Agrarmärkte und Agrarmarketing. Agrarmärkte & Agrarmarketing . Hamburg , 1983. 220 p. : ISBN 3-922528-45-7 LC Card 84-162297
HD1955 .A515 1983

Agrarmarktpolitik bei Unsicherheit . Kirschke, Dieter, 1952- Berlin , c1987. 225 p. : ISBN 3-428-06111-X LC Card 87-131255 DDC 338.1/8 19
HD1920.5 .K57 1987

Agrarnaia Indiia mezhdu mirovymi voĭnami . Ul'ianovskiĭ, R. A. (Rostislav Aleksandrovich) Moskva , 1981. 342, [2] p. ; LC Card 82-102795 DDC 338.1/0954 19
HD2072 .U44 1981

Agrarnaia politika Kommunisticheskoĭ partii na ėtape stroitel'stva MTS, 1929-1939 : sbornik nauchnykh stateĭ / [red. kollegiia Korol'kov, N.V. ... i dr.]. Vladimir : Vladimirskiĭ gos. pedagog. in-t im. P.I. Lebedeva-Polianskogo, 1985. 132 p. ; 20 cm. At head of title: Ministerstvo prosveshcheniia RSFSR. Includes bibliographical references.
1. Agriculture and state - Soviet Union. 2. Collectivization of agriculture - Soviet Union. I. Korol'kov, N. V. (Nikolaĭ Vasil'evich).
*NYPL [*QIK 87-3394]*

Agrarnaia politika KPSS v deĭstvii / [redaktsionaia kollegiia, G.S. Entelis (otv. red.) ... et al.]. Kishinev : "Shtiintsa", 1983. 202 p. ; 22 cm. At head of title: Institut istorii partii pri TSK KPM--filial Instituta marksizma-leninizma pri TSK KPSS. Summary in English. Includes bibliographies. LC Card 84-235869
1. Agriculture and state - Soviet Union. I. Entelis, G. S. II. Institutul de Istorie a Partiduluĭ (Moldavian S. S. R.).
HD1993 .A38 1983

Agrarnaia politika sotsialisticheskikh stran na sovremennom ėtape / [pod obshcheĭ redaktsieĭ Dimo Vladova, Emel'ianova A.M. ; rabota podgotovlena kollektivom avtorov v sostave D. Vladov ... et al.]. Moskva : Izd-vo polit. lit-ry, 1981. 366 p. ; 21 cm. (Sotsializm--opyt, problemy, perspktivy) Includes bibliographical references. LC Card 82-109367
1. Agriculture and state - Europe, Eastern. 2. Agriculture and state - Communist countries. I. Vladov, Dimo. II. Emel'ianov, Alekseĭ Mikhaĭlovich. III. Series: Sotsializm--opyt, problemy, perspektivy (Izdaetl'stvo politicheskoĭ literatury).
HD1918 .A37 1981

Agrarnaia revoliutsiia i sotsialisticheskie preobrazovaniia v sovetskoĭ derevne : mezhvuzovskiĭ sbornik / [redaktsionnaia kollegiia V.I. Efimov ... A.V. Sedov (otv. redaktor) ... et al.]. Gor'kiĭ : Izd. GGU, 1980. 84 p. ; 22 cm. At head of title: Ministerstvo vysshego i srednego spetsial'nogo obrazovaniia RSFSR. Gor'kovskiĭ ordena Trudovogo Krasnogo Znameni gosudarstvennyĭ universitet im. N.I. Lobachevskogo. Includes bibliographical references. LC Card 82-141565
1. Agriculture and state - Russian S.F.S.R. - History. 2. Collectivization of agriculture - Russian S.F.S.R. - History. I. Efimov, V. I. II. Sedov, A. V. (Andreĭ Vasil'evich). III. Gor'kovskiĭ gosudarstvennyĭ universitet imeni N.I. Lobachevskogo.
HD1995.R8 A68 1980

Agrarno-promyshlennyĭ kompleks /. Karliuk, I. IA. (Ippolit IAkovlevich) Moskva , 1981. 93 p. : LC Card 82-148305
HD9015.S652 K37 1981

Agrarnye otnosheniia pri sotsializme. Relaciones agrarias en el socialismo. Moscú , 1986. 223 p. ; LC Card 87-126164
HD9015.S652 R45 1986

Agrarnye preobrazovaniia v stranakh Afriki na sovremennom ėtape / [redkollegiia L.V. Goncharov (otvetstvennyĭ redaktor), V.V. Krylov (rukovoditel' avtorskogo kollektiva), A.V. Nikiforov]. Moskva : Izd-vo "Nauka," Glav. red. vostochnoĭ lit-ry, 1982. 227 p. ; 22 cm. At head of title: Akademiia nauk SSSR. Institut Afriki. Includes bibliographies. LC Card 83-143645
1. Agriculture - Economic aspects - Africa. I. Goncharov, Leongard Vasil'evich. II. Krylov, V. V. III. Nikiforov, A. V. (Andreĭ Vladimirovich). IV. Institut Afriki (Akademiia nauk SSSR).
HD2117 .A347 1982

Agrarnye problemy v svete reshenii XXVII s"ezda KPSS / [otvetstvennyĭ redaktor Kopach N.L.]. Moskva : In-t ėkonomiki Akademii nauk SSSR, 1986. 185 p. ; 20 cm. Includes bibliographical references. LC Card 87-163428
1. Agriculture and state - Soviet Union. 2. Agricultural industries - Soviet Union. I. Kopach, N. L. (Nikolaĭ Leont'evich). II. Institut ėkonomiki (Akademiia nauk SSSR).
HD1992 .A645 1986

Agrarnyĭ stroĭ feodal'noĭ Korei piatnadtsatogo-shestnadtsatogo vv. Vanin, IUriĭ Vasil'evich. Agrarnyĭ stroĭ feodal'noĭ Korei XV-XVI vv. /. Moskva , 1981. 309 p. ; LC Card 83-462393
*HD1331.K6 V36 1981 NYPL [*QI 86-3898]*

Agrarnyĭ stroĭ feodal'noĭ Korei XV-XVI vv. /. Vanin, IUriĭ Vasil'evich. Moskva , 1981. 309 p. ; LC Card 83-462393
*HD1331.K6 V36 1981 NYPL [*QI 86-3898]*

Agrarnyĭ stroĭ feodal'noĭ Korei 156-16-go vv. Vanin, IUriĭ Vasil'evich. Agrarnyĭ stroĭ feodal'noĭ Korei XV-XVI vv. /. Moskva , 1981. 309 p. ; LC Card 83-462393
*HD1331.K6 V36 1981 NYPL [*QI 86-3898]*

Agrarökonomische Studien, 0721-4731 . (Bd. 11) Kühl, Rainer. Wettbewerbstheoretische Analyse des Landwarenmarktes in der Bundesrepublik Deutschland . Kiel , 1986. 77 p. : ISBN 3-922553-79-6 LC Card 86-172903
HD9013.5 .K84 1986

Agrarpolitik in der EG . Priebe, Hermann, 1907- Baden-Baden , 1984. 269 p. ; ISBN 3-7890-1060-X LC Card 85-138555 DDC 338.1/84 19
HD1920.5.Z8 P74 1984

Agrarpolitik ohne Illusionen . Ertl, Josef, 1925- Frankfurt am Main , c1985. 208 p. : ISBN 3-87795-022-1 LC Card 86-119627 DDC 338.1/84 19
HD1920.5.Z8 E78 1985

Agrarreformen in Lateinamerika zwischen Ökonomie und Ökologie . Thielen, Helmut, 1941- Frankfurt am Main , c1985. 518 p. : ISBN 3-88129-958-0 LC Card 86-153251 DDC 333.3/1/7285 19
HD1333.N5 T48 1985 NYPL [JLD 87-467]

Agrarsektorale und gesamtwirtschaftliche Integration in der Europäischen Gemeinschaft . Bösche, Bernd, 1955- Frankfurt am Main , New York , c1987. 226 p. : ISBN 3-8204-9442-1 LC Card 87-407586 DDC 338.1/81/094 19
HD1920.5 .B67 1987

Agrarsoziale Gesellschaft.
Europäische Agrarpolitik . Göttingen , 1985. 82 p. ; LC Card 86-170925
HD1920.5.Z8 E97 1985

Landwirtschaft und Umweltschutz, Sozialpflichtigkeit oder Entschädigung? /. Göttingen , 1987. 116 p. : LC Card 87-401359 DDC 363.7/056/0943 19
HD1957 .L355 1987

Schumacher, Karl-Edzard. Entwicklungsmöglichkeiten landwirtschaftlicher Übergangsbetriebe in Niedersachsen . Göttingen , 1985. 234, vi p. : LC Card 86-186858
HD9013.7.L68 S38 1985

Agrarsoziale Gesellschaft. Sekretariat. Holla, Michael. Die Belastung der Landwirtschaft durch Beiträge zur sozialen Sicherung im Vergleich zur Situation anderer sozialer Gruppen . Göttingen [1986] viii, 174

p. ; LC Card 87-407657 DDC 368.4/00943 19
HD7179 .H635 1986

Kretschmann, Rolf. Möglichkeiten des Berufswechsels von Haupterwerbslandwirten unter besonderer Berücksichtigung von Agrarstruktur und Arbeitsmarkt /. Göttingen , 1986. xi, 109 p. : LC Card 87-408871 DDC 331.25/924 19
HD1536.G3 K746 1986

Landwirtschaftliche Übergangsbetriebe in Niedersachsen . Göttingen , 1985. xiii, 105 p. ; LC Card 86-185987
HD9013.7.L68 L36 1985

Agrarstruktur und Agrarstrukturpolitik in Spanien, eine Analyse vor dem Hintergrund der Erweiterung der Europäischen Gemeinschaft /. Möller, Ferdinand, 1955- Frankfurt am Main , New York , c1986. ix, 255 p. ; ISBN 3-8204-9529-0 LC Card 87-407540 DDC 338.1/846 19
HD2023 .M65 1986

Agrawal, Binod C. SITE to INSAT . New Delhi , 1986. viii, 165 p. : LC Card 86-902956 DDC 384.55/44/0954 19
HE8700.9.I5 S57 1986

Agrawal, Deepak, 1955- Prospects of industrial estates in under-developed countries / Deepak Agrawal. Allahabad, India : Chugh Publications, 1987. 279 p. ; 22 cm. Revision of the author's thesis (Ph. D.--University of Allahabad, 1982) under the title: Industrial estates in Uttar Pradesh-their role and prospects. Study on the industrial estates in Uttar Pradesh; with reference to the development of small scale industries and rural industrialization. Bibliography: p. [265]-275. Includes index. ISBN 81-85076-13-8 : LC Card 86-903605 DDC 338.6/042/09542 19
1. Industrial districts - India - Uttar Pradesh. 2. Small business - India - Uttar Pradesh. 3. Uttar Pradesh (India) - Industries, Rural. I. Title.
HC440.D5 A37 1987

Agrawal, R. B. L. Financing of the urban poor & small borrowers by commercial banks : a study of efficacy of bank schemes / R.B.L. Agrawal ; foreword, M.D. Sharma. Baroda : Dept. of Banking & Business Finance, Faculty of Commerce, M.S. University of Baroda : Distributors, Good Companions, 1983. 108 p. ; 23 cm. Includes bibliographical references. LC Card 83-906426 DDC 332.1/753/095475 19
1. Bank loans - India - Vadodara. 2. Credit - India - Vadodara. I. Title.
HG1642.I5 A38 1983 ***NYPL [JLD 86-4318]***

AGREEMENTS. see **CONTRACTS.**

AGREEMENTS, LICENSING. see **LICENSE AGREEMENTS.**

Agregados econômicos estaduais do Rio Grande do Norte, 1970-1982 / Estado do Rio Grande do Norte. Natal : O Estado, 1985. 35 leaves : ill. ; 23 cm. Cover title: Agregados econômicos, 1970-1982. LC Card 86-158766
1. Gross national product - Brazil - Rio Grande do Norte. I. Rio Grande do Norte (Brazil). II. Title: Agregados econômicos, 1970-1982.
HC188.R38 A53 1985

Agregados econômicos, RS. Série SIAGRO-RS . (v. 1) Cunha, Rafael Alves de. Duas décadas da produção e do produto da agropecuária RS, 1964-84 /. Porto Alegre , 1986- v. <1 > : LC Card 87-404979 DDC 338.1/0981/65 19
HD9014.B83 R5416 1986

Agregados econômicos, 1970-1982. Agregados econômicos estaduais do Rio Grande do Norte, 1970-1982 /. Natal , 1985. 35 leaves : LC Card 86-158766
HC188.R38 A53 1985

AGRIBUSINESS. see **AGRICULTURE - ECONOMIC ASPECTS.**

Agribusiness and rural enterprise /. Kinsey, B. H. London , New York , c1987. 228 p. ; ISBN 0-7099-1558-6 : LC Card 87-471 DDC 338.1/09172/4 19
HD9018.D44 K55 1987

Agribusiness finance /. Devino, Gary T. Danville, Ill. , c1981. xii, 166 p. : ISBN 0-8134-2191-8 (pbk.) LC Card 81-80386 DDC 658.1/5 19
HD1437 .D48 ***NYPL [JLE 86-4573]***

Agribusiness in Africa /. Dinham, Barbara. Trenton, N.J. , 1984. 224 p. : ISBN 0-86543-003-9 : LC Card 85-672721
HD9017.A2 D56x 1984
NYPL [Sc D 86-769]

Agricide . Fox, Michael W., 1937- New York , 1986. xv, 194 p., [10] p. of plates : ISBN 0-8052-4013-6 LC Card 85-27690 DDC 338.1/6/0973 19
S441 .F69 1986 ***NYPL [JLD 86-2542]***

Agricoltura e crisi /. Bandini, Mario. Firenze , 1937. 265 p. ; LC Card 87-116637
HB3728 .B36 1937

Agricoltura e strati sociali /. Barberis, Corrado. Milano, Italy , c1986. 269 p. ; LC Card 86-214233
HD1536.I8 B328 1986

L'agricoltura italiana tra sviluppo e crisi, 1945-1985 /. Fabiani, Guido. Bologna , 1986, c1979. 411 p. ; ISBN 88-15-00984-1 : LC Card 86-181021
HD1972 .F3 1986

Agricolture a tempo parziale /. Pieroni, Osvaldo. Bologna , c1983. 220 p. : ISBN 88-15-00024-0 LC Card 85-233534
HD1970 .P54 1983

Agricultura . Leal, Luiz Octávio Pires. Rio de Janeiro , 1985. 114 p. ; LC Card 87-140475 DDC 338.1/3/0981 19
HD1872 .L4 1985

La agricultura campesina en América Latina . Astori, Danilo. Montevideo, Uruguay [1985?] 35 p. ; LC Card 86-204310 DDC 338.1/098 19
HD1790.5 .A85 1985

Agricultura, caza, silvicultura y pesca : producto bruto a precios corrientes, período 1970/1980 / preparado por Departamento de Actividad Agropecuario. [Buenos Aires] : Banco Central de la República Argentina, Gerencia de Investigaciones y Estadísticas Económicas, [1982] 57 p. : ill. ; 29 cm. (Serie de trabajos metodológicos y sectoriales . no. 22 (dic. 1982)) LC Card 87-401763 DDC 338.1/0982/021 19
1. Agriculture - Economic aspects - Argentina - Statistics. 2. Hunting - Argentina - Statistics. 3. Forest products industry - Argentina - Statistics. 4. Fish trade - Argentina - Statistics. I. Banco Central de la República Argentina. Departamento de Actividad Agropecuaria. II. Series. III. Series: Serie de trabajos metodológicos y sectoriales , no. 22.
HD1862 .A58 1982

La agricultura colombiana en la encrucijada . Robles Bohórquez, Isabel. Bogotá, Colombia [1982] 165 p. ; LC Card 83-103208
HD1883 1982 .R62

Agricultura e industria española frente a la CEE . Capdevila Batlles, José. Barcelona [1985?] 252 p. : ISBN 84-7003-282-8 LC Card 86-171577
HC385 .C358 1985

La Agricultura en la costa del Perú, 1978-1984 / D. Martínez ... [et al.]. Lima, Perú : Centro de Estudios para el Desarrollo y la Participación, 1985. ca. 150 leaves : ill. ; 29 cm. Cover title: Diagnóstico técnico-económico de la actividad agrícola de los principales valles de la costa peruana. "Foro agro costeño, problemas y alternativas, La Molina, 16 al 18 de julio, 1985"--Cover. Chiefly tables. LC Card 87-403706 DDC 338.1/0985 19
1. Agriculture - Economic aspects - Peru - Pacific Coast Region - Statistics. 2. Pacific Coast Region (Peru) - Economic conditions - Statistics. I. Martínez, Daniel. II. Centro de Estudios para el Desarrollo y la Participación. III. Title: Diagnóstico técnico-económico de la actividad agrícola de los principales valles de la costa peruana.
HD1905.P33 A38 1985

A Agricultura irrigada como estratégia de desenvolvimento regional / Ministério do Interior, Secretaria Geral, Secretaria de Planejamento-SPL, Subsecretaria de Programas Regionais-SPR. Brasília : A Subsecretaria, [198-] 56 leaves ; 30 cm. (Série Programas especiais . 37) Bibliography: leaves 55-56. LC Card 87-403682 DDC 338.1/62 19
1. Irrigation farming - Brazil, Northeast. 2. Irrigation farming - Latin America. 3. Irrigation farming. I. Brazil. Ministério do Interior. Subsecretaria de Programas Regionais. II. Series.
HD1741.B82 N614 1980z

A Agricultura portuguesa no período 1950-1980 : de suporte do crescimento industrial a travão ao desenvolvimento económico / Armando Sevinate Pinto ... [et al.] ; prefácio de Fernando Estácio. Lisboa : Impr. Nacional/Casa da Moeda : Instituto de Estudos Para o Desenvolvimento, [1984] 74 p. : ill. ; 24 cm. Bibliography: p. 71. LC Card 85-207313
1. Agriculture - Economic aspects - Portugal - History - 20th century. 2. Portugal - Economic conditions - 1918-1974. 3. Portugal - Economic conditions - 1974-. I. Pinto, Armando Sevinate.
HD2027 .A635 1984

Agricultura y alimentación : bases de un nuevo enfoque / Manuel Lajo, Rolando Ames, Carlos Samaniego, editores ; C. Amat y León ... [et al.]. [Lima] : Pontificia Universidad Católica del Perú, Fondo Editorial, 1982. 536 p. : ill. ; 21 cm. "Programa Académico de Ciencias Sociales. Auspicio: Fundación Friedrich Ebert"--T.p. Verso. Errata slip inserted. "Este libro incluye las ponencias y conclusiones del Seminario sobre Agricultura y Alimentación, desarrollado en Chaclacayo entre el 10 y el 13 de octubre de 1979"--P. [7] Includes bibliographies. LC Card 83-174688 DDC 338.1/9/85 19
1. Produce trade - Peru - Congresses. 2. Food industry and trade - Peru - Congresses. 3. Food consumption - Peru - Congresses. I. Lajo, Manuel. II. Ames, Rolando. III. Samaniego, Carlos. IV. Amat y León Ch., Carlos. V. Lima. Pontificia Universidad Católica del Perú. VI. Seminario sobre Agricultura y Alimentación (1979 : Chaclacayo, Peru).
HD9014.P52 A57 1982 ***NYPL [JLD 86-268]***

Agricultura y alimentos en América Latina . Arroyo, Gonzalo. México, D.F. , 1985. 267 p. ; ISBN 968-8373-33-8 LC Card 86-208283
HD9014.L32 A77 1985

AGRICULTURAL ACCOUNTING. see **AGRICULTURE - ACCOUNTING.**

AGRICULTURAL ADMINISTRATION - CHILE.
Mannarelli M., Virgilio B. Organización institucional del sector agrícola /. Santiago, Chile , 1985. 81, [3] p. : LC Card 86-115545 DDC 338.1/883 19
HD1878 .M35 1985

AGRICULTURAL ADMINISTRATION - INDIA - CONGRESSES.
Agriculture administration in India /. Jaipur , 1986. xviii, 286 p. ; ISBN 81-7044-038-6 : LC Card 86-903175 DDC 338.1/854 19
HD2072 .A6546 1986

AGRICULTURAL ADMINISTRATION - INDIA - RAJASTHAN - CONGRESSES.
Agriculture administration in India /. Jaipur , 1986. xviii, 286 p. ; ISBN 81-7044-038-6 : LC Card 86-903175 DDC 338.1/854 19
HD2072 .A6546 1986

AGRICULTURAL ADMINISTRATION - UNITED STATES.
Federal marketing programs in agriculture . Danville, Ill. , c1983. x, 326 p. ; ISBN 0-8134-2292-2 : LC Card 83-80130
NYPL [JLE 86-4572]

Agricultural and socioeconomic perspectives of Arkansas . Gunderson, Ralph O. Morrilton, AR , 1987. p. cm. ISBN 0-933595-13-1 : LC Card 87-24146 DDC 338.1/09767 19
HD1775.A8 G85 1987

AGRICULTURAL ASSISTANCE.
Burch, David, 1942 Jan. 16- Overseas aid and the transfer of technology . Aldershot, [Hants, England] , Brookfield [Vt.], USA , c1987. xiv, 370 p. ; ISBN 0-566-00480-1 : LC Card 87-237 DDC 338.1/81 19
HD1431 .B87 1987

AGRICULTURAL ASSISTANCE - ADDRESSES, ESSAYS, LECTURES.
George, Susan. Ill fares the land . Washington, D.C. , c1984. xviii, 102 p. ; ISBN 0-89758-039-7 (pbk.) : LC Card 84-25124 DDC 363.8 19
HD9000.5 .G385 1984
NYPL [JLD 86-3899]

AGRICULTURAL ASSISTANCE, AMERICAN - AFRICA, SUB-SAHARAN.
United States. Congress. House. Committee on Science and Technology. Prospects for sustainable development in Sub-Saharan Africa . Washington , 1986. vii, 88 p. ; LC Card 86-603140 DDC 338.967 19
HD2117 .U48 1986

AGRICULTURAL ASSISTANCE, AMERICAN - BURKINA FASO - PLANNING.
Agricultural sector assistance strategy for Upper Volta. Washington, D.C. [1982] 1 v. (various pagings) : LC Card 87-120355 DDC 338.1/8 19
HD2144 .A38 1982

AGRICULTURAL ASSISTANCE - DEVELOPING COUNTRIES.
Information note on the technical cooperation programme /. Rome [1985?] 29 p. : LC Card 87-122600 DDC 338.9/26/091724 19
HC60 .I477 1985

Tangermann, Stefan. Welternährung und die Verantwortlichkeit der Industrieländer /. Kiel , 1986. 27 p. ; ISBN 3-925357-38-6 LC Card 87-126268 DDC 338.1/9/1724 19
HD9018.D44 T36 1986

AGRICULTURAL ASSISTANCE - DEVELOPING COUNTRIES - CASE STUDIES.
Information note on the technical cooperation programme /. Rome [1985?] 29 p. : LC Card 87-122600 DDC 338.9/26/091724 19
HC60 .I477 1985

AGRICULTURAL ASSISTANCE, EUROPEAN - DEVELOPING COUNTRIES.
Pour un rôle actif de la Communauté économique européenne sur la scène agricole internationale . Paris , c1986. 184 p. ; ISBN 2-11-001582-9 : LC Card 86-174918
HD1431 .P68 1986

AGRICULTURAL ASSISTANCE, FRENCH - DEVELOPING COUNTRIES.
France. Conseil économique et social. Les surplus agricoles et la pénurie alimentaire . [Paris] [1986] 1 v. (various pagings) : LC Card 86-179100
HD1431 .F7 1986

AGRICULTURAL ASSISTANCE - GOVERNMENT POLICY.
Stevens, Charles J. Confronting the world food crisis /. Muscatine, Iowa [1981] 24 p. : LC Card 82-127279 DDC 338.1/9 19
HD9000.6 .S73 ***NYPL [JLK 75-198 no. 27]***

AGRICULTURAL ASSISTANCE - SAHEL.
Continuing the commitment . Washington, D.C. [1986] ix, 164 p. : LC Card 86-600555 DDC 338.1/8 19
HD2120.S15 C66 1986

AGRICULTURAL BANKS. see **BANKS AND BANKING; MORTGAGE BANKS; AGRICULTURAL CREDIT.**

AGRICULTURAL BIOTECHNOLOGY - UNITED STATES.
Biotechnology in agriculture . Stamford, Conn., U. S.A. , c1985. xvii, 192 leaves : ISBN 0-89336-485-1 (pbk.) LC Card 87-403883 DDC 381/.456606 19
HD9999.B443 U615 1985

AGRICULTURAL CLIMATOLOGY. see **CROPS AND CLIMATE.**

AGRICULTURAL COLONIES - ARGENTINA.
Fogel, Ramón B. Movimientos campesinos en el Paraguay /. Asunción, Paraguay , 1986. 230 p., [1] leaf of plates : LC Card 86-189517
HD1531.P3 F64 1986

AGRICULTURAL COLONIES - BRAZIL - BATAIPORÃ.
Companhia de Viação São Paulo-Mato Grosso. Ante-projeto do núcleo de colonização "Presidente Kennedy" /. Mato Grosso, Brasil , 1962. 40 p., [15] leaves of plates : LC Card 85-135105
HD1516.B8 C64 1962

AGRICULTURAL COLONIES - CANDELARIA RIVER VALLEY (GUATEMALA AND MEXICO)
López Serrano, Francisco. Del desierto a la selva /. México , 1984. 215 p. : ISBN 968-13-1608-8 LC Card 86-189936
HD1516.M5 L66 1984

AGRICULTURAL COLONIES - ECUADOR - MORONA SANTIAGO.
Salazar, Ernesto, 1946- Pioneros de la selva . Quito, Ecuador , 1986. 228 p., [11] leaves of plates : LC Card 87-400290 DDC 338.1/09866/43 19
HD1516.E25 S25 1986

AGRICULTURAL COLONIES - MEXICO - CASE STUDIES.
López Serrano, Francisco. Del desierto a la selva /. México , 1984. 215 p. : ISBN 968-13-1608-8 LC Card 86-189936
HD1516.M5 L66 1984

AGRICULTURAL COLONIES - NIGERIA.
Spiro, Heather M. The Ilora farm settlement in Nigeria /. West Hartford, Conn. , 1985. xvii, 50 p. : ISBN 0-931816-20-3 LC Card 85-5230 DDC 331.4/83/089963 19
HD6073.F3 N667 1985
NYPL [JLF 86-1629]

AGRICULTURAL COLONIES - PALESTINE.
Bericht der Exekutive der Zionistischen Organisation an den XV. Zionisten-Kongress. Jerusalem , 1927 (Jerusalem : Azriel) 110 p., [1] folded leaf of plates : LC Card 86-122608
HD1516.P18 B525 1927

AGRICULTURAL COLONIES - PARAGUAY - CAAGUAZU (DEPT.)
Fogel, Ramón B. Movimientos campesinos en el Paraguay /. Asunción, Paraguay , 1986. 230 p., [1] leaf of plates : LC Card 86-189517
HD1531.P3 F64 1986

Agricultural commercialisation and the allocation of labour time in Mpika District, northern Zambia. Mpika, Zambia : Republic of Zambia, Integrated Rural Development Project, Serenje-Mpika-Chinsali, [1986?] iii, 42 leaves : ill. ; 30 cm. (IRDP occasional paper . no. 6) Bibliography: leaf 42. LC Card 86-981249 DDC 338.1/096894 19
1. Agriculture - Economic aspects - Zambia - Mpika District. 2. Corn trade - Zambia - Mpika District. 3. Corn - Zambia - Mpika District. 4. Agricultural productivity - Zambia - Mpika District. I. Integrated Rural Development Project, Serenje-Mpika-Chinsali (Zambia). II. Series.
HD2131.5.Z9 M653 1986

AGRICULTURAL CONSERVATION - GOVERNMENT POLICY - GERMANY (WEST)
Grünen (Political party) Grüne Agrarpolitik, Bilanz und Perspektiven . Bonn [1985?] 62 p. : LC Card 86-152151
HD1957 .G79 1985

AGRICULTURAL CONSERVATION - GOVERNMENT POLICY - NEW ENGLAND.
Schnidman, Frank. Retention of land for agriculture . Boston, MA , 1988. p. cm. ISBN 0-89946-219-7 LC Card 87-5580 DDC 333.76/16/0974 19
HD266.A11 S36 1988

AGRICULTURAL CONSERVATION - GOVERNMENT POLICY - ONTARIO.
Ontario. Foodland preservation . Toronto, Ont. [1986?] 16 p. : LC Card 86-226909 DDC 333.76/16/09713 19
HD319.O5 O5 1986

AGRICULTURAL CONSERVATION - GOVERNMENT POLICY - UNITED STATES.
Agriculture and the environment in a changing world economy. Washington, D.C. , c1986. xi, 66 p. : ISBN 0-89164-099-1 (pbk.) LC Card 86-24088 DDC 338.1/873 19
HD1761 .A6228 1986

Webb, Shwu-Eng. Idling erodible cropland . Washington, D.C. [1986] iii, 31 p. : LC Card 86-601632 DDC 338.1 s 338.1/62 19
HD1751 .A91854 no. 550 HD256

AGRICULTURAL CONSERVATION - GOVERNMENT POLICY - UNITED STATES - CONGRESSES.
Agriculture and the environment /. Washington, D.C. , c1986. xvii, 298 p. : ISBN 0-915707-33-0 (pbk.) : LC Card 87-43010 DDC 363.7/31 19
HD1755 .P47 1986

AGRICULTURAL CONSERVATION - NICARAGUA.
Thielen, Helmut, 1941- Agrarreformen in Lateinamerika zwischen Ökonomie und Ökologie . Frankfurt am Main , c1985. 518 p. : ISBN 3-88129-958-0 LC Card 86-153251 DDC 333.3/1/7285 19
HD1333.N5 T48 1985 ***NYPL [JLD 87-467]***

AGRICULTURAL COOPERATIVE CREDIT ASSOCIATIONS - ABSTRACTS.
Asociaciones campesinas como receptoras y administradoras de crédito y su dinámica de grupo. [Lima] [1979] 100 leaves in various foliations : LC Card 85-185371
HG2051.L26 A83 1979

AGRICULTURAL COOPERATIVE CREDIT ASSOCIATIONS - AUSTRIA - UPPER AUSTRIA - HISTORY.
Kreinecker, Günther. Die Anfänge der Raiffeisenkassen in Oberösterreich (1889-1914) . Linz , c1982. xvi, 276 p. : ISBN 3-85320-279-9 LC Card 83-224597
HG2051.A89 U64 1982
NYPL [JLE 87-2440]

AGRICULTURAL COOPERATIVE CREDIT ASSOCIATIONS - INDIA.
Haque, T. (Tajamul), 1947- Agrarian reforms and institutional changes in India /. New Delhi , 1986, c1985. xvi, 268 p. : LC Card 86-902575 DDC 338.1/854 19
HD1333.I4 H36 1986 ***NYPL [JLD 87-1547]***

Kunwar, Upendra. Banking and agricultural growth . New Delhi , c1987. 167 p. ; LC Card 87-901193 DDC 334/.2/0954 19
HG2051.I4 K86 1987

AGRICULTURAL COOPERATIVE CREDIT ASSOCIATIONS - INDIA - ANDHRA PRADESH.
Reddy, C. R. Cooperative long term finance . Delhi, India , 1987. ix, 128 p. : LC Card 87-900729 DDC 334/.2/095484 19
HG2051.I5 A652 1987

AGRICULTURAL COOPERATIVE CREDIT ASSOCIATIONS - INDIA - ANDHRA PRADESH - CASE STUDIES.
Obul Reddy, D. (Donthi Reddy), 1946- Co-operative agricultural development banks . Delhi , New Delhi , 1986. 429 p. ; ISBN 81-7018-378-2 : LC Card 86-902655 DDC 334/.2 19
HG2051.I5 A646 1986
NYPL [JLD 87-1527]

AGRICULTURAL COOPERATIVE CREDIT ASSOCIATIONS - INDIA - CASE STUDIES.
Obul Reddy, D. (Donthi Reddy), 1946- Co-operative agricultural development banks . Delhi , New Delhi , 1986. 429 p. ; ISBN 81-7018-378-2 : LC Card 86-902655 DDC 334/.2 19
HG2051.I5 A646 1986
NYPL [JLD 87-1527]

Partap Singh, 1948- Co-operative agricultural finance . New Delhi , 1986. xiii, 188 p. : LC Card 86-903067
HG2051.I5 P376 1986

AGRICULTURAL COOPERATIVE CREDIT ASSOCIATIONS - INDIA - PATIALA DISTRICT - CASE STUDIES.
Partap Singh, 1948- Co-operative agricultural finance . New Delhi , 1986. xiii, 188 p. : LC Card 86-903067
HG2051.I5 P376 1986

AGRICULTURAL COOPERATIVE CREDIT ASSOCIATIONS - ITALY.
Santoro, Vittorio. Profili funzionali e operativi delle casse rurali e artigiane /. Milano [1984] 181 p. ; ISBN 88-14-00380-7 : LC Card 85-147834
HG2039.I8 S26 1984 ***NYPL [JLE 86-3669]***

AGRICULTURAL COOPERATIVE CREDIT ASSOCIATIONS - ITALY - EMILIA-ROMAGNA - HISTORY.
Cooperazione di credito e sviluppo sociale ed economico delle campagne in Emilia Romagna . Bologna , c1983. 173 p. : LC Card 85-156690
HG2051.I82 E433 1983

AGRICULTURAL COOPERATIVE CREDIT ASSOCIATIONS - ITALY - VENETO - HISTORY.
Un Secolo di cooperazione di credito nel Veneto . Limena, Padova , c1985. 454 p., [29] p. of plates : LC Card 86-195743
HG2039.I8 S43 1985

AGRICULTURAL COOPERATIVE CREDIT ASSOCIATIONS - LATIN AMERICA.
González Vega, Claudio. Mercados financieros rurales en América Latina /. Santo Domingo, República Dominicana , 1986. 44 p. ; LC Card 87-400002 DDC 332.7/1/098 19
HG2051.L26 G66 1986

AGRICULTURAL COOPERATIVE CREDIT ASSOCIATIONS - LATIN AMERICA - ABSTRACTS.

Asociaciones campesinas como receptoras y administradoras de crédito y su dinámica de grupo. [Lima] [1979] 100 leaves in various foliations : LC Card 85-185371
HG2051.L26 A83 1979

AGRICULTURAL COOPERATIVE CREDIT ASSOCIATIONS - TANZANIA.
A Short introduction to the co-operative savings and credit societies and Tanzania Rural Savings and Credit Scheme /. [Dar es Salaam, Tanzania] [1977] 43 p. : LC Card 77-980630 DDC 334/.2/09678 19
HG2039.T37 S56 1977

AGRICULTURAL COOPERATIVE CREDIT ASSOCIATIONS - TURKEY - ESKIŞEHIR İLI.
Ürper, Yılmaz. Türkiye'de tarımsal kooperatiflerin toplumsal değişmeye etkileri . Eskişehir , 1985. xvi, 109, xxxiii p. ; LC Card 86-161567
HG2051.T92 I48 1985

AGRICULTURAL CREDIT - ADDRESSES, ESSAYS, LECTURES.
Crop insurance for agricultural development . Baltimore , c1986. xviii, 322 p. ISBN 0-8018-2673-X (alk. paper) LC Card 85-9810 DDC 368.1/22 19
HG9968 .C76 1985 ***NYPL [JLE 86-1082]***

AGRICULTURAL CREDIT - AFRICA - CONGRESSES.
Agricultural credit and the mobilization of resources in rural areas. [Addis Ababa?] , 1986. 45 p. ; LC Card 86-981195 DDC 332.7/1/096 19
HG2051.A3 A73 1986

Agricultural credit and the mobilization of resources in rural areas. [Addis Ababa?] : Economic Commission for Africa, 1986. 45 p. ; 28 cm. At head of title: Fourth Session of the Joint Conference of African Planners, Statisticians, and Demographers, Addis Ababa, Ethiopia, 3-12 March 1986. Study commissioned by the Third Session of the Joint Conference of African Planners, Statisticians and Demographers for submission to it's 4th Sessions. "E/ECA/PSD.4/7, 19 Feb. 1986, original: English." Bibliography: p. 38-45. LC Card 86-981195 DDC 332.7/1/096 19
1. Agricultural credit corporations - Africa - Congresses. 2. Agricultural credit - Africa - Congresses. 3. Agriculture - Africa - Finance - Congresses. I. Joint Conference of African Planners, Statisticians, and Demographers (4th : 1986 : Addis Ababa, Ethiopia).
HG2051.A3 A73 1986

AGRICULTURAL CREDIT - BRAZIL.
Delgado, Guilherme Costa. Capital financeiro e agricultura no Brasil, 1965-1985 /. S[ão] Paulo, SP, Brasil , Campinas, SP , c1985. 240 p. ; LC Card 87-102748
HD1440.B8 D45 1985

Manoel, Alvaro. Política agrícola, eficiência e concentração na agricultura brasileira . São Paulo , 1986. 180 p. : LC Card 86-234338
HD1873 .M35 1986

AGRICULTURAL CREDIT - BRAZIL - MINAS GERAIS - CASE STUDIES.
Gomes, Sebastião Teixeira. Condicionantes da modernização do pequeno agricultor /. São Paulo , 1986. 181 p. : LC Card 87-153609 DDC 338.1/0981/51 19
HD1875.M5 G65 1986

AGRICULTURAL CREDIT - COLOMBIA.
Restrepo Correa, Alejandro. Manual de crédito industrial y agropecuario . [Bogotá, D.E. , 1985] 270, 30, 4 p. : LC Card 86-110073
HG3751.9.C7 R47 1985

AGRICULTURAL CREDIT CORPORATIONS - AFRICA - CONGRESSES.
Agricultural credit and the mobilization of resources in rural areas. [Addis Ababa?] , 1986. 45 p. ; LC Card 86-981195 DDC 332.7/1/096 19
HG2051.A3 A73 1986

AGRICULTURAL CREDIT CORPORATIONS - GERMANY (WEST) - LOWER SAXONY.
Landwirtschaftliche Übergangsbetriebe in Niedersachsen . Göttingen , 1985. xiii, 105 p. ; LC Card 86-185987
HD9013.7.L68 L36 1985

Schumacher, Karl-Edzard. Entwicklungsmöglichkeiten landwirtschaftlicher Übergangsbetriebe in Niedersachsen . Göttingen , 1985. 234, vi p. : LC Card 86-186858
HD9013.7.L68 S38 1985

AGRICULTURAL CREDIT CORPORATIONS - INDIA - NAINI TAL (DISTRICT)
Kumar, Kewal. Institutional financing of Indian agriculture . New Delhi , c1987. 232 p. : LC Card 87-900911 DDC 332.7/1/09542 19
HG2051.I5 N354 1987

AGRICULTURAL CREDIT CORPORATIONS - LATIN AMERICA.
González Vega, Claudio. Mercados financieros rurales en América Latina /. Santo Domingo, República Dominicana , 1986. 44 p. ; LC Card 87-400002 DDC 332.7/1/098 19
HG2051.L26 G66 1986

AGRICULTURAL CREDIT CORPORATIONS - NIGERIA - CROSS RIVER STATE.
South-Eastern State, Nigeria. Conclusions of the government on the report and recommendations of the committee set up to study and recommend ways of solving the financial and administrative problems of the Agricultural Development Corporation /. Calabar [Nigeria] [1971?] 5 p. ; LC Card 87-404113
HG2051.N62 C767 1971

AGRICULTURAL CREDIT CORPORATIONS - UNITED STATES.
Transition in agriculture . Washington, D.C. (1120 Connecticut Ave. N.W., Washington 20036) , c1986. 2 v. : LC Card 86-233848 DDC 332.7/1/0973 19
HG2051.U5 T68 1986

AGRICULTURAL CREDIT - DEVELOPING COUNTRIES.
Farm management input to rural financial systems development /. Rome , 1985. xii, 57 p. : ISBN 92-5-102191-0 (pbk.) LC Card 86-207967 DDC 332.7/1/091724 19
HD1440.D44 F37 1985

AGRICULTURAL CREDIT - DOMINICAN REPUBLIC.
Poyo, Jeffrey. Los bancos agropecuarios y la captación de depósitos /. Santo Domingo, República Dominicana , 1986. 39 p. : LC Card 87-400523 DDC 332.7/1/097293 19
HG2051.D6 P69 1986

Tejada C., Frank A. Crédito y seguro agrícola . Santo Domingo, República Dominicana , 1986. 104 p. : LC Card 87-400183 DDC 332.7/1/097293 19
HG2051.D6 T45 1986

AGRICULTURAL CREDIT - GOVERNMENT POLICY - HISTORY - 20TH CENTURY.
Berrada, Abdelkader. Le crédit agricole au Maroc, 1917-1977 /. [Rabat] , 1979. 264 p. ; LC Card 82-136521 DDC 332.7/1/0964 19
HG2051.M8 B47 1979

AGRICULTURAL CREDIT - GOVERNMENT POLICY - UNITED STATES.
Dealing with farm sector debt . Washington, D.C. (317 Massachusetts Ave., N.E., Washington 20002) , c1986. 47 p. : LC Card 86-71068 DDC 332.7/1/0973 19
HD1440.U6 D4 1986

AGRICULTURAL CREDIT - GREECE.
Programma ependyseōn se geōrgikes viomēchanies to 1986 /. Athēna , 1986. 32, 91 leaves, [1] folded leaf of plates : LC Card 86-193452
HG2051.G9 P76 1986

AGRICULTURAL CREDIT - HUNGARY.
Kis, Pál. A mezőgazdasági nagyüzemek pénz- és hitelrendszere /. Budapest , 1985. 261 p. ; ISBN 963-232-050-6 : LC Card 85-230947
HD1440.H9 K57 1985

Reke, Barnabás. Forgóeszköz-gazdálkodás a mezőgazdaságban /. Budapest , 1986. 175 p. ; ISBN 963-232-219-3 : LC Card 87-408500
HD1440.H9 R45 1986

AGRICULTURAL CREDIT - ILLINOIS.
Seger, Daniel J. Financing Illinois agricultural exports /. [Urbana?] [1985] 74 p. : LC Card 86-621070 DDC 382/.63 19
HD9007.I3 S44 1985

AGRICULTURAL CREDIT - INDIA.
Gupta, Uttam. Impact of credit on fertiliser consumption /. New Delhi [1986] 158 p. ; LC Card 87-900336 DDC 338.4/766862/0954 19
HD9483.I42 G86 1986

AGRICULTURAL CREDIT - INDIA - CASE STUDIES.
Gill, Manohar Singh, 1936- Agriculture cooperatives . New Delhi , c1983. viii, 560 p. ; ISBN 0-7069-2371-5 : LC Card 84-900335 DDC 334/.683/0954552 19
HD1491.I392 P844 1983
NYPL [JLD 86-4240]

AGRICULTURAL CREDIT - INDIA - JHABUA (DISTRICT)
Mehta, Suresh C. (Suresh Chandra), 1947- Agricultural credit mobilization and allocation . Allahabad, India , 1987. xv, 270 p. ; ISBN 81-85072-06-X : LC Card 86-903677 DDC 332.7/1/09543 19
HG2051.I5 J466 1987

AGRICULTURAL CREDIT - INDIA - ORISSA.
Pany, Raj Kishor. Institutional credit for agriculture in India /. New Delhi , 1985. xxi, 483 p. : ISBN 81-7024-009-3 : LC Card 85-904046 DDC 332.7/1/095413 19
HD2075.O7 P36 1985

AGRICULTURAL CREDIT - INDIA - PUNJAB.
Gill, Manohar Singh, 1936- Agriculture cooperatives . New Delhi , c1983. viii, 560 p. ; ISBN 0-7069-2371-5 : LC Card 84-900335 DDC 334/.683/0954552 19
HD1491.I392 P844 1983
NYPL [JLD 86-4240]

AGRICULTURAL CREDIT - INDIA - WEST BENGAL.
Rudra, Ashok. Agrarian relations in West Bengal . Bombay , c1983. x, 104 p. ; LC Card 83-902673 DDC 338.1/0954/14 19
HD879.W4 R83 1983 ***NYPL [JLD 86-3785]***

AGRICULTURAL CREDIT - INDONESIA.
Kredit pedesaan di Indonesia /. Yogyakarta , 1986. xii, 160 p. ; LC Card 86-943011
HG2051.I65 K74 1986

AGRICULTURAL CREDIT - LATIN AMERICA.
González Vega, Claudio. Mercados financieros rurales en América Latina /. Santo Domingo, República Dominicana , 1986. 44 p. ; LC Card 87-400002 DDC 332.7/1/098 19
HG2051.L26 G66 1986

La Problemática del endeudamiento externo y el financiamiento del desarrollo agropecuario latinoamericano. Lima, Perú [1985] 131 p. : LC Card 86-122361 DDC 336.3/435/098 19
HJ8514.5 .P76 1985 ***NYPL [JLD 86-3143]***

AGRICULTURAL CREDIT - LATIN AMERICA - CONGRESSES.
Financiamiento agrícola. México, D.F. , 1985. i, 156 p. ; LC Card 86-156375
HG2051.L26 F55 1985

AGRICULTURAL CREDIT - MEXICO - LAGUNA REGION.
Rello, Fernando. Estado y ejidos en México . Ginebra , 1986. xxvi, 122 p. : LC Card 86-210274
HG2051.M62 L37 1986

Agricultural credit mobilization and allocation . Mehta, Suresh C. (Suresh Chandra), 1947- Allahabad, India , 1987. xv, 270 p. ; ISBN 81-85072-06-X : LC Card 86-903677 DDC 332.7/1/09543 19
HG2051.I5 J466 1987

AGRICULTURAL CREDIT - MOROCCO - HISTORY - 20TH CENTURY.
Berrada, Abdelkader. Le crédit agricole au Maroc, 1917-1977 /. [Rabat] , 1979. 264 p. ; LC Card 82-136521 DDC 332.7/1/0964 19
HG2051.M8 B47 1979

AGRICULTURAL CREDIT - NEW YORK (STATE)
Carraro, Kenneth C. An economic evaluation of alternative sources of funding for agricultural lending by commercial banks /. Ithaca, N.Y. [1985] 48 p. ; LC Card 86-622432 DDC 332.7/1/09747 19
HG2051.U6 N53 1985

AGRICULTURAL CREDIT - ONTARIO.
Ontario. Interministerial Task Force on Agricultural Finance. Report of the Interministerial Task Force on Agricultural Finance. [Toronto, Ont. , 1986] vii, 65, [42] p. :

LC Card 87-127476 DDC 332.7/1/09713 19
HD1790.O6 O573 1986

AGRICULTURAL CREDIT - SWAZILAND.
Guma, Xolile P. Small farmer credit and small farmer attitudes towards co-operatives /. [Kwaluseni, Swaziland] [1982] 94 p. : LC Card 86-101161 DDC 332.7/1/096813 19
HD1491.S855 G85 1982
NYPL [JLG 86-262]

AGRICULTURAL CREDIT - UNITED STATES.
Carraro, Kenneth C. An economic evaluation of alternative sources of funding for agricultural lending by commercial banks /. Ithaca, N.Y. [1985] 48 p. ; LC Card 86-622432 DDC 332.7/1/09747 19
HG2051.U6 N53 1985

The Farm credit crisis . College Station, Tex. [1986] ii, 57 p. : LC Card 86-622188 DDC 332.7/1/0973 19
HG2051.U5 F26 1986

The Farm credit crisis policy options and consequences /. Ithaca, N.Y. [1986] ii, 57 p. : LC Card 86-621935 DDC 338.1 s 332.7/1/0973 19
HD1775.N8 C6 no. 86-3 HG2051.U6

The Farm financial crisis . Boulder , 1988. xvi, 205 p. : ISBN 0-8133-7186-4 (pbk. : alk. paper) : LC Card 86-32601 DDC 338.1/3/0973 19
HD1761 .F295 1988

Transition in agriculture . Washington, D.C. (1120 Connecticut Ave. N.W., Washington 20036) , c1986. 2 v. : LC Card 86-233848 DDC 332.7/1/0973 19
HG2051.U5 T68 1986

AGRICULTURAL CREDIT - UNITED STATES - HANDBOOKS, MANUALS, ETC.
FmHA guaranteed lending manual /. Washington, D.C. (1120 Connecticut Ave., N.W., Washington 20036) , c1986. xi, 88, [59] p. : LC Card 86-226067 DDC 332.1/753 19
HG2051.U5 F55 1986

AGRICULTURAL CREDIT - ZIMBABWE.
Whitsun Foundation. Project 3,04(a), Peasant sector credit plan (revised) . Salisbury, Rhodesia [1978] ii, 18 leaves ; LC Card 86-981359
HG2051.Z55 W45 1978

AGRICULTURAL CRIDIT - INDIA.
Haque, T. (Tajamul), 1947- Agrarian reforms and institutional changes in India /. New Delhi , 1986, c1985. xvi, 268 p. : LC Card 86-902575 DDC 338.1/854 19
HD1333.I4 H36 1986 NYPL [JLD 87-1547]

Agricultural development and rural poverty /.
Singh, Ajit Kumar, 1944- New Delhi , 1987. v, 368 p. : ISBN 81-7024-069-7 : LC Card 86-903483 DDC 338.1/8542 19
HD2075.U88 S55 1987

Agricultural development in Haryana /. Gupta, D. P. (Dharm Pall), 1932- New Delhi, India , 1985. xiii, 120 p. : LC Card 85-901427 DDC 338.1/854558 19
HD2075.H3 G85 1985
NYPL [JLD 86-3862]

Agricultural development in India series .
(vol. 4) Gupta, D. P. (Dharm Pall), 1932- Agricultural development in Haryana /. New Delhi, India , 1985. xiii, 120 p. : LC Card 85-901427 DDC 338.1/854558 19
HD2075.H3 G85 1985
NYPL [JLD 86-3862]

Agricultural development in the Sahel.
Continuing the commitment . Washington, D.C. [1986] ix, 164 p. : LC Card 86-600555 DDC 338.1/8 19
HD2120.S15 C66 1986

AGRICULTURAL DEVELOPMENT PROJECTS - AFRICA - MANAGEMENT.
Leonard, David K. The political realities of African management /. Binghamton, NY, USA (P.O. Box 818, Binghamton 13902) [1984] 39 p. ; LC Card 87-153761 DDC 338.1/86 19
HD2118 .L46 1984

AGRICULTURAL DEVELOPMENT PROJECTS - AMAZON RIVER REGION.
Brazil. Ministério do Interior. Subsecretaria de Programas Regionais. Programas especiais . [Brasília] [1981] 1 v. (various foliations) ; LC Card 87-403680 DDC 338.981/1 19
HD1875.A347 B7 1981

AGRICULTURAL DEVELOPMENT PROJECTS - ASIA, SOUTHEASTERN - CASE STUDIES.
Development strategies and planning for farmers' communities . College, Laguna, Philippines , 1983. vi, 242 p. : LC Card 84-102916 DDC 338.1/859 19
HD2075.8 .D48 1983

AGRICULTURAL DEVELOPMENT PROJECTS - BOTSWANA.
Fones-Sundell, Melinda. Implementing rural development in Botswana . Uppsala , 1983. 75 p. : LC Card 86-215071 DDC 338.1/86811 19
HD2133 .F66 1983

AGRICULTURAL DEVELOPMENT PROJECTS - BRAZIL - MANAUS REGION.
Brazil. Superintendência da Zona Franca de Manaus. Plano Diretor do Distrito Agropecuário /. Manaus , 1984. 86 p. : LC Card 85-209805
HD1875.M325 B73 1984

AGRICULTURAL DEVELOPMENT PROJECTS - BRAZIL, NORTHEAST.
AGRICULTURAL DEVELOPMENT PROJECTS - DEVELOPING COUNTRIES.
Uphoff, Norman Thomas. Local institutional development . West Hartford, CT , c1986. xv, 421 p. ; ISBN 0-931816-45-9 LC Card 86-15288 DDC 302.3/5 19
HC59.7 .U64 1986 NYPL [JLE 87-1200]

AGRICULTURAL DEVELOPMENT PROJECTS - DEVELOPING COUNTRIES - EVALUATION.
Guida alla valorizzazione agricola nei paesi in via di sviluppo /. Milano, Italy , c1983. 434 p. : LC Card 83-144803 DDC 338.1/09172/4 19
HD1417 .G85 1983 NYPL [JLD 86-3296]

AGRICULTURAL DEVELOPMENT PROJECTS - EVALUATION.
Casley, D. J. Project monitoring and evaluation in agriculture /. Baltimore , c1987. xiii, 159 p. : ISBN 0-8018-3616-6 (pbk.) LC Card 87-22632 DDC 351.82/33 19
HD1415 .C335 1987

AGRICULTURAL DEVELOPMENT PROJECTS - GAMBIA.
Gambia. Preparation report, rural development programme, 1980-85 /. Banjul [1979- v. <1 > : LC Card 86-203596
HD2147 .G35 1980a

AGRICULTURAL DEVELOPMENT PROJECTS - GOVERNMENT POLICY - NIGERIA - CROSS RIVER STATE.
South-Eastern State, Nigeria. Conclusions of the government on the report and recommendations of the committee set up to study and recommend ways of solving the financial and administrative problems of the Agricultural Development Corporation /. Calabar [Nigeria] [1971?] 5 p. ; LC Card 87-404113
HG2051.N62 C767 1971

AGRICULTURAL DEVELOPMENT PROJECTS - JORDAN.
Seccombe, Ian J. Manpower and migration . [Durham, England] , c1981. viii, 110 p. : LC Card 84-673623
HD5812.25.A6 S42x 1981
NYPL [JLD 86-2457]

AGRICULTURAL DEVELOPMENT PROJECTS - KENYA.
Chavangi, Noel A. Culture as the basis for implementing self-sustaining wood fuel development programmes /. Nairobi, Kenya [1985] 24 leaves ; LC Card 87-111963 DDC 333.75 19
HD9769.F843 K433 1985

AGRICULTURAL DEVELOPMENT PROJECTS - KENYA - KAKAMEGA DISTRICT.
Bradley, Phil. The district resource analysis as applied to Kakamega District /. Nairobi [1984] 11 leaves : LC Card 87-112452 DDC 333.75 19
HD9769.F843 K425 1984

Chavangi, Noel A. Cultural aspects of fuelwood procurement in Kakamega District /. Nairobi [1984] 13 leaves ; LC Card 87-112356 DDC 333.75 19
HD9769.F843 K43 1984

AGRICULTURAL DEVELOPMENT PROJECTS - KENYA - KITUI (DISTRICT) - EVALUATION.
A Base-line study of Farm Input Supply Scheme. Nairobi , 1981. 65 leaves, [1] leaf of plates : LC Card 87-980116
HD1491.K42 K583 1981

AGRICULTURAL DEVELOPMENT PROJECTS - MALAWI.
Malawi. National rural development programme /. [Lilongwe, Malawi] , 1977. 7 v. : LC Card 85-981594
HD2133.5.Z8 M35 1977

AGRICULTURAL DEVELOPMENT PROJECTS - MALAYSIA - PAHANG - EVALUATION - CASE STUDIES.
The Jengka Triangle projects in Malaysia . Washington, D.C. , c1987. ix, 105 p., [1] leaf of plates : ISBN 0-8213-0946-3 (pbk.); 0-8213-0946-6 (cover) LC Card 87-21021 DDC 338.1/85951 19
HD2080.6.Z9 P345 1987

AGRICULTURAL DEVELOPMENT PROJECTS - MANAGEMENT.
Casley, D. J. Project monitoring and evaluation in agriculture /. Baltimore , c1987. xiii, 159 p. : ISBN 0-8018-3616-6 (pbk.) LC Card 87-22632 DDC 351.82/33 19
HD1415 .C335 1987

AGRICULTURAL DEVELOPMENT PROJECTS - MANAGEMENT - POLITICAL ASPECTS - AFRICA.
Leonard, David K. The political realities of African management /. Binghamton, NY, USA (P.O. Box 818, Binghamton 13902) [1984] 39 p. ; LC Card 87-153761 DDC 338.1/86 19
HD2118 .L46 1984

AGRICULTURAL DEVELOPMENT PROJECTS - MEXICO.
Cernea, Michael M. Measuring project impact . Washington, D.C., U. S.A. , c1979. vi, 93 p. ; LC Card 81-170764
HD1792 .C43 1979

AGRICULTURAL DEVELOPMENT PROJECTS - MEXICO - PAPALOAPAN RIVER VALLEY.
Ewell, Peter T., 1947- Uxpanapa . Ithaca, N.Y. [1982] xiv, 218 p., [35] leaves of plates : LC Card 84-621492 DDC 338.1/0972/6 19
HD1795.P3 E94 1982

AGRICULTURAL DEVELOPMENT PROJECTS - SAHEL.
Continuing the commitment . Washington, D.C. [1986] ix, 164 p. : LC Card 86-600555 DDC 338.1/8 19
HD2120.S15 C66 1986

Kapp, Gerald B., 1956- Agroforstliche Landnutzung in der Sahel-Sudanzone . München , c1987. xii, 397 p. : ISBN 3-8039-0347-5 LC Card 87-419915 DDC 333.76/13/0966 19
HD1010.5.Z63 K37 1987

AGRICULTURAL DEVELOPMENT PROJECTS - SENEGAL - BIGNONA.
Dramé, Mamadou. Une expérience de grande envergure . [Dakar] , 1980-1981 [i.e., 1981] 32, [3] leaves, [1] folded leaf of plates : LC Card 85-218589
HD2144.5.Z9 B543 1981

AGRICULTURAL DEVELOPMENT PROJECTS - SIERRA LEONE.
Okai, Matthew. Rural poverty and alleviation measures in Sierra Leone /. [Rome] , 1983. 91 p. : LC Card 87-400417 DDC 338.1/8/664 19
HC1065.Z9 P66 1983

AGRICULTURAL DEVELOPMENT PROJECTS - SUDAN.
Kapp, Gerald B., 1956- Agroforstliche Landnutzung in der Sahel-Sudanzone . München , c1987. xii, 397 p. : ISBN 3-8039-0347-5 LC Card 87-419915 DDC 333.76/13/0966 19
HD1010.5.Z63 K37 1987

AGRICULTURAL DEVELOPMENT PROJECTS - SUDAN - CASE STUDIES.
Abdel-Rahman, Awad Ibrahim. Population, environment, and agricultural change . [Khartoum] [1984] iii, 37 leaves : LC Card

84-980808 DDC 338.1/8624 19
HD2123.5 .A64 1984

AGRICULTURAL DEVELOPMENT PROJECTS - ZAMBIA - EVALUATION - CONGRESSES.
National Workshop on Project Evaluation (1984 : National Institute for Public Administration, Lusaka, Zambia) Collected papers of the National Workshop on Project Evaluation, held at the National Institute for Public Administration, 10-14 December, 1984. [Lusaka] , 1985. 1 v. in various pagings ; LC Card 85-981123 DDC 338.96894/0068 19
HC915.Z9 E446 1984

AGRICULTURAL DEVELOPMENT PROJECTS - ZAMBIA - LUSAKA PROVINCE - PLANNING - CONGRESSES.
Lusaka Province (Zambia). Provincial Planning Unit. Towards self sufficiency . [Lusaka, Zambia?] [1984] 100 p., [14] leaves of plates : LC Card 86-980293 DDC 338.1/86894 19
HD2131.5 .L87 1984

AGRICULTURAL DEVELOPMENT PROJECTS - ZIMBABWE - SANYATI RIVER REGION.
Kirk, T. Project 3.05, rural workshop and machinery centre . Salisbury, Zimbabwe , 1977. 1 v. (various pagings) : LC Card 85-104610
HD2131.Z9 S265 1977

Agricultural distress in the Midwest, past & present / edited by Lawrence E. Gelfand & Robert J. Neymeyer. Iowa City : Center for the Study of the Recent History of the United States, University of Iowa, 1986. ix, 111 p. : ill. ; 23 cm. Papers presented at a conference sponsored by the Center for the Study of the Recent History of the United States and the Henry A. Wallace Center for Agricultural History and Rural Studies, Apr. 25, 1986, at Iowa State University. Includes bibliographies. ISBN 0-87414-049-8 : LC Card 86-29932 DDC 338.1/0977 19
1. Agriculture - Economic aspects - Middle West - History - Congresses. 2. Middle West - Rural conditions - Congresses. I. Gelfand, Lawrence Emerson, 1926-. II. Neymeyer, Robert J. III. Center for the Study of the Recent History of the United States (Iowa City, Iowa). IV. Henry A. Wallace Center for Agricultural History and Rural Studies.
HD1773.A3 A37 1986

AGRICULTURAL ECOLOGY - ATBARA RIVER REGION (ETHIOPIA AND SUDAN)
Abdel Ati, Hassan A. Lower River Atbara area (Nile Province) . [Khartoum] Sudan [1985] vii, 166 p., [19] leaves of plates : LC Card 86-981108 DDC 333.91/3/09625 19
HD1741.S852 A832 1985

AGRICULTURAL ECOLOGY - DEVELOPING COUNTRIES.
Arnon, Itzhak, 1909- Modernization of agriculture in developing countries . Chichester [West Sussex] , New York , c1987. xxiii, 626 p. : ISBN 0-471-91586-6 : LC Card 87-6288 DDC 338.1/09172/4 19
HD1417 .A76 1987

AGRICULTURAL ECOLOGY - GERMANY (WEST) - LOWER SAXONY.
Reessing, Ludwig. Analyse der Wettbewerbsfähigkeit von Extensivblattfrüchten in Niedersachsen unter ökonomischen und ökologischen Gesichtspunkten /. Kiel , 1986. xiv, 251 p. : ISBN 3-922553-81-8 LC Card 86-163003
HD1960.L69 R44 1986

AGRICULTURAL ECOLOGY - GOVERNMENT POLICY - GERMANY (WEST) - CONGRESSES.
Landwirtschaft und Umweltschutz, Sozialpflichtigkeit oder Entschädigung? /. Göttingen , 1987. 116 p. : LC Card 87-401359 DDC 363.7/056/0943 19
HD1957 .L355 1987

AGRICULTURAL ECOLOGY - GOVERNMENT POLICY - UNITED STATES - CONGRESSES.
Agriculture and the environment /. Washington, D.C. , c1986. xvii, 298 p. : ISBN 0-915707-33-0 (pbk.) : LC Card 87-43010 DDC 363.7/31 19
HD1755 .P47 1986

AGRICULTURAL ECOLOGY - HUNGARY - SZOLNOK MEGYE.
Összefoglalás, Szolnok megye agroökológiai potenciálja az ezredfordulón /. Budapest , 1984. 115 p. : ISBN 963-491-193-5 LC Card 86-198809
HD1940.5.Z9 S966 1984

AGRICULTURAL ECOLOGY - KENYA.
Yeager, Rodger. Wildlife, wild death . Albany, NY , c1986. xvi, 173 p. : ISBN 0-88706-168-0 LC Card 86-5791 DDC 333.95/16/09676 19
QL84.6.K4 Y43 1986 ***NYPL [JLE 86-3870]***

AGRICULTURAL ECOLOGY - TANZANIA.
Yeager, Rodger. Wildlife, wild death . Albany, NY , c1986. xvi, 173 p. : ISBN 0-88706-168-0 LC Card 86-5791 DDC 333.95/16/09676 19
QL84.6.K4 Y43 1986 ***NYPL [JLE 86-3870]***

AGRICULTURAL ECOLOGY - UNITED STATES.
Agriculture and the environment in a changing world economy. Washington, D.C. , c1986. xi, 66 p. : ISBN 0-89164-099-1 (pbk.) LC Card 86-24088 DDC 338.1/873 19
HD1761 .A6228 1986

Fox, Michael W., 1937- Agricide . New York , 1986. xv, 194 p., [10] p. of plates : ISBN 0-8052-4013-6 LC Card 85-27690 DDC 338.1/6/0973 19
S441 .F69 1986 ***NYPL [JLD 86-2542]***

Agricultural economic report .
(no. 545) Sloggett, Gordon. Energy and U. S. agriculture . Washington, D.C. , 1985] iii, 43 p. : LC Card 86-600880 DDC 338.1 s 338.1/3 19
HD1751 .A91854 no. 545 S619.E53

(no. 550) Webb, Shwu-Eng. Idling erodible cropland . Washington, D.C. [1986] iii, 31 p. : LC Card 86-601632 DDC 338.1 s 338.1/62 19
HD1751 .A91854 no. 550 HD256

(no. 555) Sloggett, Gordon. Ground-water mining in the United States /. Washington, D.C , 1986. iv, 19 p. : LC Card 86-602788 DDC 338.1 s 338.1/4 19
HD1751 .A91854 no. 555 S616.U6

(no. 556) Florida and Mexico competition for the winter fresh vegetable market /. Washington, D.C. [1986] v, 101 p. : LC Card 86-602381 DDC 338.1 s 381/.415/0973 19
HD1751 .A91854 no. 556 HD9225.U53F5

(no. 558) Somwaru, Agapi. Disaggregated farm income by type of farm, 1959-82 /. Washington, D.C. , 1986. iii, 113 p. : LC Card 86-602571 DDC 338.1 s 338.1/3/0973021 19
HD1751 .A91854 no. 558 HD1769

(no. 561) Ribaudo, Marc. Reducing soil erosion . Washington, D.C. , 1986. v, 24 p. : LC Card 86-603068 DDC 338.1 s 333.73 19
HD1751 .A91854 no. 561 S624.A1

AGRICULTURAL ECONOMICS. see **AGRICULTURE - ECONOMIC ASPECTS.**

Agricultural economics miscellaneous report (Fargo, N.D.) .
(no. 99) Coon, Randal C. North Dakota lignite industry's contribution to the state economy /. Fargo, N.D. [1986] v, 40 p. : LC Card 86-623006 DDC 338.2/722/09784 19
HD9559.L6 U5525 1986

The agricultural economy of Northumberland and Durham in the period, 1640-1750 /. Brassley, Paul, 1946- New York , 1985. iii, 224 p. : ISBN 0-8240-6676-6 : LC Card 84-45996 DDC 338.1/09428/6 19
HD1930.N67 B73 1985
NYPL [JLE 86-3924]

AGRICULTURAL EDUCATION - FARMERS' INSTITUTES AND EXTENSION WORK. see **AGRICULTURAL EXTENSION WORK.**

AGRICULTURAL EDUCATION - HONDURAS.
International Labour Organisation. Desarrollo de la formación profesional rural . Ginebra , 1982. ii, 30 p. : ISBN 92-2-303048-X LC Card 84-113985
HD5715.5.H8 I58 1982

AGRICULTURAL EDUCATION - UNITED STATES - CONGRESSES.
National Conference on Rural Development, Des Moines, 1973. Proceedings. Washington, 1974. iii, 108 p. LC Card 74-600918 DDC 309.2/63/0973
HN65 .N35 1973 ***NYPL [JLE 81-564 no.2]***

AGRICULTURAL ENGINEERING - ITALY - HISTORY - ADDRESSES, ESSAYS, LECTURES.
Le Bonifiche in Italia dal '700 a oggi /. Roma , 1984. viii, 437 p. : ISBN 88-420-2429-5 : LC Card 85-173148
HD1683.I8 B66 1984 ***NYPL [JSD 87-50]***

Agricultural exports and economic growth .
Hubbard, Michael. London , New York , 1986. xx, 284 p. : ISBN 0-7103-0121-9
NYPL [Sc D 86-967]

AGRICULTURAL EXTENSION WORK - CHILE.
Mannarelli M., Virgilio B. Organización institucional del sector agrícola /. Santiago, Chile , 1985. 81, [3] p. : LC Card 86-115545 DDC 338.1/883 19
HD1878 .M35 1985

AGRICULTURAL FINANCE CORPORATION - RHODESIA.
Whitsun Foundation. Project 3,04(a), Peasant sector credit plan (revised) . Salisbury, Rhodesia [1978] ii, 18 leaves ; LC Card 86-981359
HG2051.Z55 W45 1978

AGRICULTURAL GEOGRAPHY - BRAZIL - CEARÁ (STATE)
O Norte cearense /. Recife , 1985. 303 p. : LC Card 86-209022
HD1875.C4 N67 1985

AGRICULTURAL GEOGRAPHY - MEXICO - HISTORY - 20TH CENTURY.
Agricultural household models : extensions, applications, and policy / by Inderjit Singh, Lyn Squire, John Strauss, editors. Baltimore, Md. : Published for the World Bank [by] the Johns Hopkins University Press, 1986. xi, 335 p. : ill. ;24 cm. "A World Bank publication." Includes bibliographical references and index. ISBN 0-8018-3149-0 LC Card 85-45102 DDC 331.7/63/091724 19
1. Agricultural laborers - Developing countries - Case studies. 2. Rural families - Developing countries - Case studies. 3. Agricultural industries - Developing countries - Case studies. 4. Agricultural laborers - Government policy - Developing countries - Case studies. 5. Developing countries - Rural conditions - Case studies. I. Singh, Inderjit, 1941-. II. Squire, Lyn, 1946-. III. Strauss, John, 1951-.
HD1542 .A34 1986 ***NYPL [JLE 86-2440]***

AGRICULTURAL INDUSTRIES - ACCOUNTING.
Devino, Gary T. Agribusiness finance /. Danville, Ill. , c1981. xii, 166 p. : ISBN 0-8134-2191-8 (pbk.) LC Card 81-80386 DDC 658.1/5 19
HD1437 .D48 ***NYPL [JLE 86-4573]***

AGRICULTURAL INDUSTRIES - ANGOLA - DIRECTORIES.
Representação do produtos alimentares de Angola na IX Feira Internacional de Lisboa . Luanda [1968] 248 p. : LC Card 87-400609 DDC 338.7/6413/0025673 19
HD9017.A532 R46 1968

AGRICULTURAL INDUSTRIES - ARGENTINA.
Boneo, Horacio. Desarrollo regional, incentivos fiscales y localización industrial /. Buenos Aires, Argentina [1985] 160 p. : ISBN 950-95720-8-X ***NYPL [JLD 86-4218]***

AGRICULTURAL INDUSTRIES - ASIA, SOUTHEASTERN.
Bhattacharya, Sib Nath, 1938- Entrepreneurship development in India and the South-East Asian countries in agricultural and industrial sectors /. New Delhi , 1983. xix, 156 p. : LC Card 83-903206 DDC 338/.04/0954 19
HC440.I53 B48 1983 ***NYPL [JLD 86-3764]***

AGRICULTURAL INDUSTRIES - BRAZIL.
Amaro, Antonio Ambrosio. Questão agrária e agroindústria /. Brasília, DF [1986] 13 p. ; LC Card 87-403237 DDC 338.1/881 19
HD1873 .A49 1986

AGRICULTURAL INDUSTRIES - BULGARIA - MANAGEMENT.
Vŭlchev, Nikola. Proizvodstvenite vrŭzki v agrarno-promishlenata oblast /. Sofiia , 1986. 183 p. ; LC Card 86-195329
HD9015.B82 V84 1986

AGRICULTURAL INDUSTRIES - COLOMBIA.
Poveda Ramos, Gabriel. Nueva alternativa para

el desarrollo . Bogotá , 1974. 249 p. : LC Card 78-345029
HD1883 1974 .P68 ***NYPL [JLE 80-482]***

AGRICULTURAL INDUSTRIES - COSTA RICA.
Las Exportaciones y la incidencia del sector externo en el desarrollo económico. [San José] , 1984. 32, [8], [7], 4 leaves ; LC Card 87-115490 DDC 338.1/097286 19
HD9014.C772 E95 1984

AGRICULTURAL INDUSTRIES - DATA PROCESSING.
Woolverton, Michael W. Computer concepts for agribusiness /. Westport, Conn. , 1985. xii, 311 p. : ISBN 0-87055-510-3 : LC Card 85-23043 DDC 631 19
HD1433 .W66 1985 ***NYPL [JLE 86-1534]***

AGRICULTURAL INDUSTRIES - DEVELOPING COUNTRIES.
Kinsey, B. H. Agribusiness and rural enterprise /. London , New York , c1987. 228 p. ; ISBN 0-7099-1558-6 : LC Card 87-471 DDC 338.1/09172/4 19
HD9018.D44 K55 1987

AGRICULTURAL INDUSTRIES - DEVELOPING COUNTRIES - CASE STUDIES.
Agricultural household models . Baltimore, Md. , 1986. xi, 335 p. : ISBN 0-8018-3149-0 LC Card 85-45102 DDC 331.7/63/091724 19
HD1542 .A34 1986 ***NYPL [JLE 86-2440]***

AGRICULTURAL INDUSTRIES - ENVIRONMENTAL ASPECTS - MOLDAVIAN S.S.R.
Todyka, IUriĭ Nikolaevich. Gosudarstvennyĭ apparat i problemy okhrany prirody v usloviiakh APK /. Kishinev , 1986. 179, [5] p. ; LC Card 86-141430
HD1995.M5 T63 1986

AGRICULTURAL INDUSTRIES - FINANCE.
Devino, Gary T. Agribusiness finance /. Danville, Ill. , c1981. xii, 166 p. : ISBN 0-8134-2191-8 (pbk.) LC Card 81-80386 DDC 658.1/5 19
HD1437 .D48 ***NYPL [JLE 86-4573]***

AGRICULTURAL INDUSTRIES - FRANCE - FINANCE.
Guide pratique du financement des industries agroalimentaires /. Paris [1986] 351 p. : LC Card 86-186921
HD9012.5 .G86 1986

AGRICULTURAL INDUSTRIES - GERMANY, WEST.
Prüsse, Dieterich. Der Landwarenhandel in der Bundesrepublik Deutschland . Münster-Hiltrup , 1983. viii, 188, [9], 21 p. : ISBN 3-7843-0291-2 : LC Card 84-141310
HD9013.5 .P78 1983

AGRICULTURAL INDUSTRIES - GERMANY (WEST) - LOWER SAXONY.
Landwirtschaftliche Übergangsbetriebe in Niedersachsen . Göttingen , 1985. xiii, 105 p. ; LC Card 86-185987
HD9013.7.L68 L36 1985

Schumacher, Karl-Edzard. Entwicklungsmöglichkeiten landwirtschaftlicher Übergangsbetriebe in Niedersachsen . Göttingen , 1985. 234, vi p. : LC Card 86-186858
HD9013.7.L68 S38 1985

AGRICULTURAL INDUSTRIES - GOVERNMENT POLICY - BRAZIL, NORTHEAST.
Industrialização rural no Nordeste /. Recife , c1986. 488 p. : LC Card 87-403045 DDC 338.981/3 19
HD9014.B83 N755 1985

AGRICULTURAL INDUSTRIES - GOVERNMENT POLICY - QUÉBEC (PROVINCE)
Conseil de planification et de développement du Québec. Le réseau décisionnel en agro-alimentation au Québec . [Québec] [1979] 29 p. ; LC Card 85-102587
HD9014.C4 Q425 1979

AGRICULTURAL INDUSTRIES - GREAT BRITAIN - CONGRESSES.
The Industrialization of the countryside /. Norwich [Norfolk] , c1985. xiv, 315 p. : ISBN 0-86094-202-3 LC Card 87-141251 DDC 338.9/009173/4 19
HC256.6 .I524 1985

AGRICULTURAL INDUSTRIES - GREECE - DIRECTORIES.
Hodēgos geōrgikōn viomēchaniōn. Athēna , 1985. 510 p. : LC Card 86-193419
HD9015.G82 H58 1985

AGRICULTURAL INDUSTRIES - GREECE - FINANCE.
Programma ependyseōn se geōrgikes viomēchanies to 1986 /. Athēna , 1986. 32, 91 leaves, [1] folded leaf of plates : LC Card 86-193452
HG2051.G9 P76 1986

AGRICULTURAL INDUSTRIES - HUNGARY.
Éliás, András. Mezőgazdasági és élelmiszeripari termékeink a külpiaci versenyben /. Budapest , 1985. 197 p. ; ISBN 963-232-064-6 : LC Card 86-185883
HD9015.H82 E59 1985

Papp, Sándor. A mezőgazdasági ipar, ellenfél vagy partner? /. [Budapest] , 1985. 154 p. : ISBN 963-09-2547-8 : LC Card 85-230966
HD9015.H82 P36 1985

AGRICULTURAL INDUSTRIES - HUNGARY - CONSOLIDATION.
Benet, Iván. Az agráripari egyesülések útkeresése /. Budapest , 1985. 197 p. : ISBN 963-221-616-4 : LC Card 86-203013
HD9015.H82 B447 1985

Halmai, Péter. Integráció és tulajdon az iparosodó mezőgazdaságban /. [Budapest] , 1984. 124 p. ; ISBN 963-673-278-7 LC Card 85-126691
HD1940.5 .H35 1984

AGRICULTURAL INDUSTRIES - INDIA.
Bhattacharya, Sib Nath, 1938- Entrepreneurship development in India and the South-East Asian countries in agricultural and industrial sectors /. New Delhi , 1983. xix, 156 p. : LC Card 83-903206 DDC 338/.04/0954 19
HC440.I53 B48 1983 ***NYPL [JLD 86-3764]***

AGRICULTURAL INDUSTRIES - INDIA - ANDHRA PRADESH - CASE STUDIES.
Venkaiah, V., 1952- Impact of agro-based industries on rural economy . Bombay , 1987. xxi, 348 p. ; LC Card 86-903766 DDC 338.1/0954/84 19
HD9016.I43 A67 1987

AGRICULTURAL INDUSTRIES - INDIA - CASE STUDIES.
Venkaiah, V., 1952- Impact of agro-based industries on rural economy . Bombay , 1987. xxi, 348 p. ; LC Card 86-903766 DDC 338.1/0954/84 19
HD9016.I43 A67 1987

AGRICULTURAL INDUSTRIES - JAPAN.
Markar'ian, S. B. (Seda Bagdasarovna) Problemy agropromyshlennoĭ integratsii v IAponii /. Moskva , 1982. 286 p. ; LC Card 83-143582
HD9017.J32 M37 1982

AGRICULTURAL INDUSTRIES - KAZAKH S.S.R.
Abdil'din, S. A. (Serikbolsyn Abdil'daevich) Razvitie prodovol'stvennogo kompleksa Kazakhstana /. Alma-Ata , 1985. 158 p. ; LC Card 85-226938
HD9015.S653 K393 1985

AGRICULTURAL INDUSTRIES - KIRGHIZ S.S.R. - MANAGEMENT.
Sovershenstvovanie ėkonomicheskikh metodov upravleniia sel'skokhoziaĭstvennym proizvodstvom /. Frunze , 1982. 158 p. ; LC Card 83-196563
HD9015.S653 K577 1982

AGRICULTURAL INDUSTRIES - LATIN AMERICA.
Astori, Danilo. La agricultura campesina en América Latina . Montevideo, Uruguay [1985?] 35 p. ; LC Card 86-204310 DDC 338.1/098 19
HD1790.5 .A85 1985

Prodovol'stvennaia problema i sel'skoe khoziaĭstvo stran Latinskoĭ Ameriki /. Moskva , 1981. 311 p. ; LC Card 82-108167
HD9014.L32 P76 1981

AGRICULTURAL INDUSTRIES - LATVIA - MATHEMATICAL MODELS.
Modelirovanie razvitiia mezhotraslevyh kompleksov Latviĭskoĭ SSR . Riga , 1985. 106 p. : LC Card 86-177817
HD9015.S653 L376 1985

AGRICULTURAL INDUSTRIES - LITHUANIA.
Lietuvos TSR žemės ūkio tvarkymo sistema /. Vilnius , 1985. 453 p. ; LC Card 86-215158
HD1995.L5 L535 1985

AGRICULTURAL INDUSTRIES - MAINE.
Colgan, Charles S. The natural resource industries of Maine . [Augusta, Me.] [1986] 135 p. : LC Card 87-620550 DDC 338.09741 19
HD9007.M2 C64 1986

AGRICULTURAL INDUSTRIES - MOLDAVIAN S.S.R. - INDUSTRIAL CAPACITY.
Otsenka ėffektivnosti proizvodstva i rezervy ee rosta . Kishinev , 1982. 130 p. : LC Card 83-179279
HD9015.S653 M6454 1982

AGRICULTURAL INDUSTRIES - MOLDAVIAN S.S.R. - MANAGEMENT.
Organizatsionnye formy i metody upravleniia proizvodstvom . Kishinev , 1980. 130 p. ; LC Card 81-140768
HD9015.S653 M6453 1980

Planirovanie ėkonomiki Moldavskoĭ SSR /. Kishinev , 1986. 161 p. ; LC Card 86-203680
HD9015.S653 M6457 1986

AGRICULTURAL INDUSTRIES - MOLDAVIAN S.S.R. - PLANNING - MATHEMATICAL MODELS.
Optimal'noe planirovanie /. Kishinev , 1982. 166 p. : LC Card 83-149332
HD9015.S653 M64526 1982

AGRICULTURAL INDUSTRIES - MOZAMBIQUE.
Caballero, Lorenzo. Mozambique, food and agriculture sector /. Uppsala , 1984. 223, [30] p. : ISBN 91-576-2129-2 (pbk.) LC Card 86-218958 DDC 338.1/0967/9 19
HD9017.M86 C33 1984

AGRICULTURAL INDUSTRIES - PERU - PLANNING.
Tealdo, Armando. La planificación en empresas agropecuarias . Lima, Perú [1985], c1983. 157 p. : LC Card 85-174266 DDC 630/.68 19
HD9000.5 .T4 1985 ***NYPL [JLD 86-1283]***

AGRICULTURAL INDUSTRIES - PLANNING.
Tealdo, Armando. La planificación en empresas agropecuarias . Lima, Perú [1985], c1983. 157 p. : LC Card 85-174266 DDC 630/.68 19
HD9000.5 .T4 1985 ***NYPL [JLD 86-1283]***

AGRICULTURAL INDUSTRIES - RUSSIAN S.F.S.R. - CHUVASHSKAIA A.S.S.R.
Ėffektivnost' proizvodstva v agropromyshlennom komplekse Chuvashskoĭ ASSR /. Cheboksary , 1985. 198 p. ; LC Card 86-203897
HD9015.S653 C483 1985

AGRICULTURAL INDUSTRIES - RUSSIAN S.F.S.R. - IRKUTSKAIA OBLAST'.
Geograficheskie osobennosti formirovaniia agrarno-promyshlennykh kompleksov v Predbaĭkal'e /. Irkutsk , 1978. 145 p. : LC Card 81-162870
HD9015.S653 I74 1978

AGRICULTURAL INDUSTRIES - RUSSIAN S.F.S.R. - MANAGEMENT.
Shiriaev, A. V. (Andreĭ Vasil'evich) RAPO . Moskva , 1985. 155 p. ; LC Card 86-142380
HD9015.S653 R8775 1985

AGRICULTURAL INDUSTRIES - RUSSIAN S.F.S.R. - NON-CHERNOZEM REGION - ABSTRACTS.
Vklad severnogo krest'ianstva v material'nuiu i dukhovnuiu kul'turu i ego znachenie v reshenii problem agropromyshlennogo kompleksa nechernozemnoĭ zony RSFSR . Vologda , 1984. 93 p. ; LC Card 85-156518
HD9015.S652 V54 1984

AGRICULTURAL INDUSTRIES - RUSSIAN S.F.S.R. - SIBERIA, WESTERN - MATHEMATICAL MODELS.
Problemy formirovaniia i upravleniia agrarno-promyshlennym kompleksom . Novosibirsk , 1979. 157 p. : LC Card 81-143766
HD9015.S652 P73 1979

AGRICULTURAL INDUSTRIES - SOVIET UNION.

Agrarnye problemy v svete reshenii XXVII s"ezda KPSS /. Moskva , 1986. 185 p. ; LC Card 87-163428
HD1992 .A645 1986

Agropromyshlennyi kompleks v usloviiakh razvitogo sotsializma . Moskva , 1986. 167 p. ; LC Card 87-166350
HD9015.S652 A38 1986

Borchenko, N. (Nikolai) Sel'skoe khoziaistvo v odinnadtsatoi piatiletke . Moskva , 1981. 93 p. ; LC Card 81-188371
HD1493.R9 B5 1981, no. 5 HD9015.S65

Ėkonomicheskie problemy novogo ėtapa osushchestvleniia Leninskogo kooperativnogo plana /. Moskva , 1979. 365 p. ; LC Card 81-165451
HD1992 .E3593 1979

Karliuk, I. IA. (Ippolit IAkovlevich) Agrarno-promyshlennyi kompleks /. Moskva , 1981. 93 p. : LC Card 82-148305
HD9015.S652 K37 1981

Kuznetsova, T. E. Proizvodstvennaia sfera sovremennogo sela /. Moskva , 1986. 199 p. ; LC Card 86-164902
HD9015.S652 K89 1986

Obobshchestvlenie sel'skokhoziaistvennogo proizvodstva /. Moskva , 1986. 159 p. ; LC Card 86-177899
HD9015.S652 O26 1986

Relaciones agrarias en el socialismo. Moscú , 1986. 223 p. ; LC Card 87-126164
HD9015.S652 R45 1986

Rukosuev, P. N. (Platon Nikolaevich) Ėkonomicheskaia ėffektivnost' zhivotnovodstva v sisteme APK /. Moskva , 1985. 127 p. ; LC Card 86-133226
HD9425.S652 R86 1985

AGRICULTURAL INDUSTRIES - SOVIET UNION - ACCOUNTING.
Val'ter, S. B. (Semen Borisovich) Spravochnik po finansovo-ėkonomicheskim raschetam v sel'skokhoziaistvennykh predpriiatiiakh /. Moskva , 1982. 411 p. ; LC Card 83-160870
HF5686.A36 V35 1982

AGRICULTURAL INDUSTRIES - SOVIET UNION - LABOR PRODUCTIVITY.
Osnovnye faktory rosta proizvoditel'nosti truda v sel'skom khoziaistve /. Moskva , 1986. 158 p. ; LC Card 87-163422
HD9015.S652 O85 1986

Vorontsov, A. P. (Alekseĭ Pavlovich) Proizvoditel'nost' i oplata truda v APK /. Moskva , 1985. 191 p. ; LC Card 86-130051
HD9015.S652 V67 1985

AGRICULTURAL INDUSTRIES - SOVIET UNION - LOCATION - MATHEMATICAL MODELS.
Abdullaev, A. Kh. Zadacha razmeshcheniia sel'skokhoziaistvennogo proizvodstva v ob"edinenii khoziaistv meliorativnoi sistemy /. Moskva , 1985. 24, [2] p. ; LC Card 86-162160
HD9015.S652 A23 1985

AGRICULTURAL INDUSTRIES - SOVIET UNION - MANAGEMENT - MATHEMATICAL MODELS.
Modelirovanie i optimizatsionnye raschety . Kiev , 1986. 222, [2] p. : LC Card 86-233713
HD9015.S652 M62 1986

AGRICULTURAL INDUSTRIES - SOVIET UNION - MATHEMATICAL MODELS.
Perspektivnoe planirovanie razvitiia agrarno-promyshlennogo kompleksa /. Novosibirsk , 1979. 159 p. : LC Card 81-143730
HD9015.S652 P47 1979

Problemy formirovaniia i upravleniia agrarno-promyshlennym kompleksom . Novosibirsk , 1979. 157 p. : LC Card 81-143766
HD9015.S652 P73 1979

AGRICULTURAL INDUSTRIES - SPAIN - CONGRESSES.
La Empresa. Madrid , 1962. 348 p. : LC Card 85-108024
HD2326 .E47 1962

AGRICULTURAL INDUSTRIES - TURKMEN S.S.R.
Stanchin, I. M. (Ivan Mikhaĭlovich) Razvitie agropromyshlennogo kompleksa Turkmenskoĭ SSR /. Ashkhabad , 1985. 181, [3] p. : LC Card 85-185696
HD9015.S653 T878 1985

AGRICULTURAL INDUSTRIES - UKRAINE.
Agropromyshlennyi kompleks i problemy obespecheniia naseleniia prodovol'stviem . Kiev , 1983. 190 p. : LC Card 86-139699
HD9015.S653 U4295 1983

Material'no-tekhnichna baza ahropromyslovoho kompleksu . Kyïv , 1985. 294 p. ; LC Card 87-109155
HD9015.S653 U453 1985

AGRICULTURAL INDUSTRIES - UKRAINE - LOCATION.
Territorial'naia organizatsiia prodovol'stvennogo kompleksa . Kiev , 1985. 163 p. ; LC Card 86-175134
HD9015.S653 U4755 1985

AGRICULTURAL INDUSTRIES - UKRAINE - MANAGEMENT.
Kulish, N. E. (Nikolaĭ Efimovich) Upravlenie agropromyshlennymi ob"edineniiami v usloviiakh integrirovannoĭ ėkonomiki /. Kiev , 1985. 174 p. : LC Card 87-104750
HD9015.S653 U4425 1985 ***NYPL [*QIP 87-4125]***

AGRICULTURAL INDUSTRIES - UKRAINE - MATHEMATICAL MODELS.
Problemy optimizatsii mezhotraslevykh sviazeĭ . Kiev , 1976. 135 p. : LC Card 87-100694
HD9015.S653 U4547 1976

AGRICULTURAL INDUSTRIES - UNITED STATES.
Browne, William Paul, 1945- Private interests, public policy, and American agriculture /. Lawrence, Kan. , c1988. p. cm. ISBN 0-7006-0334-4 : LC Card 87-23131 DDC 338.1/873 19
HD1761 .B73 1988

Fox, Michael W., 1937- Agricide . New York , 1986. xv, 194 p., [10] p. of plates : ISBN 0-8052-4013-6 LC Card 85-27690 DDC 338.1/6/0973 19
S441 .F69 1986 ***NYPL [JLD 86-2542]***

AGRICULTURAL INDUSTRIES - UZBEK S.S. R. - SURKHANDAR'INSKAIA OBLAST'.
Molozhavenko, Vladimir. Zharkoe solntse Surkhana /. Moskva , 1982. 189 p., [16] p. of plates : LC Card 82-177858
HC337.U962 S975 1982

AGRICULTURAL INDUSTRIES - VENEZUELA - ADDRESSES, ESSAYS, LECTURES.
Foro . San Felipe, Venezuela , 1984. ii, 92 p. ; LC Card 85-132901 DDC 338.1/0987 19
HD1912 .F67 1984 ***NYPL [JLD 86-424]***

AGRICULTURAL INNOVATIONS - ANDES REGION - CONGRESSES.
Investigación agraria y crisis . Quito , 1986. 498 p. : LC Card 87-400125 DDC 338.1/098 19
HD1860.A53 I58 1986

AGRICULTURAL INNOVATIONS - BRAZIL - MINAS GERAIS - CASE STUDIES.
Gomes, Sebastião Teixeira. Condicionantes da modernização do pequeno agricultor /. São Paulo , 1986. 181 p. : LC Card 87-153609 DDC 338.1/0981/51 19
HD1875.M5 G65 1986

AGRICULTURAL INNOVATIONS - DEVELOPING COUNTRIES.
Jiggins, Janice. Gender-related impacts and the work of the international agricultural research centers /. Washington, D.C. , c1986. x, 95 p. ; ISBN 0-8213-0840-8 (pbk.) LC Card 86-24709 DDC 331.4/83/091724 19
HD6073.A292 D444 1986

AGRICULTURAL INNOVATIONS - DEVELOPING COUNTRIES - CONGRESSES.
Alexander von Humboldt Award Colloquium (1984) Technology, human capital, and the world food problem /. St. Paul, MN , 1986. x, 167 p. : LC Card 86-622216 DDC 338.1/9/1724 19
HD9018.D44 A44 1984

AGRICULTURAL INNOVATIONS - ECONOMIC ASPECTS - BRAZIL - SERGIPE.
Almeida, Edimilson Machado de, 1937- Tecnologia e racionalização da agropecuária, com o aproveitamento das bacias hidrográficas /. Aracaju [1971] 100 leaves : LC Card 85-203218
HD1875.S4 A65 1971

AGRICULTURAL INNOVATIONS - ENVIRONMENTAL ASPECTS - GOVERNMENT POLICY - UNITED STATES - CONGRESSES.
Agriculture and the environment /. Washington, D.C. , c1986. xvii, 298 p. : ISBN 0-915707-33-0 (pbk.) : LC Card 87-43010 DDC 363.7/31 19
HD1755 .P47 1986

AGRICULTURAL INNOVATIONS - FRANCE.
Muller, Pierre. Le technocrate et le paysan . Paris , c1984. 173 p. ; ISBN 2-7082-2347-X : LC Card 84-171796 DDC 338.1/6 19
HD1947 .M85 1984 ***NYPL [JLD 86-3738]***

AGRICULTURAL INNOVATIONS - GERMANY (WEST)
Groebel, Wilhelm. Lebensmittelüberwachung . Dortmund , 1976. 84 p. : LC Card 86-170104
HD30 .A7 Heft 167 HD9000.9

Landhandwerk und Landwirtschaft /. Göttingen , 1964. 104 p. : LC Card 87-409231 DDC 338.1/61/0943 19
HD1955 .L17 1964

AGRICULTURAL INNOVATIONS - GOVERNMENT POLICY - DEVELOPING COUNTRIES.
Lenoir, René. Le Tiers Monde peut se nourrir . [Paris] , c1984. 210 p. : ISBN 2-213-01385-3 : LC Card 84-188021 DDC 338.1/8/091724 19
HD1417 .L46 1984 ***NYPL [JLD 85-1065]***

AGRICULTURAL INNOVATIONS - GOVERNMENT POLICY - SAUDI ARABIA.
Philipp, Hans-Jürgen. Die landwirtschaftliche Modernisierung Saudi-Arabiens im 20. Jahrhundert /. Hamburg , c1984. 132 p. : LC Card 85-166668
HD2060.Z8 P48 1984

AGRICULTURAL INNOVATIONS - INDIA - ANDHRA PRADESH.
Siva Prasad, K. Technological breakthrough in agriculture /. Allahabad, India , 1987. xii, 133 p. ; ISBN 81-85076-15-4 : LC Card 86-903607 DDC 338.1/61 19
HD2075.A5 S58 1987

AGRICULTURAL INNOVATIONS - INDIA - PUNJAB.
Kahlon, A. S., 1923- Modernization of Punjab agriculture /. New Delhi , 1984. vi, 145 p. ; LC Card 84-902491 DDC 338.1/0954/5 19
S471.I32 P845 1984 ***NYPL [JLD 86-4410]***

Sain, Inder, 1944- Transformation of Punjab agriculture /. Delhi , New Delhi , 1987. xviii, 191 p. : ISBN 81-7018-451-7 : LC Card 87-900922
HD2075.P8 S35 1985

AGRICULTURAL INNOVATIONS - INDIA - TIRUCHCHIRAPPALLI (DISTRICT)
Stanislaus, M. Sebastian. New farm technology and income distribution /. New Delhi , c1984. viii, 76 p. : LC Card 84-902272 DDC 338.1/3/095482 19
HD2075.T57 S73 1984 ***NYPL [JLD 87-669]***

AGRICULTURAL INNOVATIONS - NAMIBIA.
Kirk, Michael, 1955- Ochsenanspannung in Westafrika . Göttingen , c1984. iv, 220 p. ; ISBN 3-88694-057-8 LC Card 86-202167 DDC 338.1/09688 19
HD2134 .K57 1984

AGRICULTURAL INNOVATIONS - NIGERIA - HISTORY - 20TH CENTURY.
Rural underdevelopment in Nigeria, 1900-1980. Zaria, Nigeria , 1985. iv, 102 p. ; LC Card 86-154806 DDC 338.1/8669 19
HD2145.5.Z8 R87 1985

AGRICULTURAL INNOVATIONS - PAKISTAN - PUNJAB.
Namdar, Shamim A. Employment implications of agricultural growth /. Lahore , 1980. 82 leaves : LC Card 84-930891 DDC 331.12/93/0954914 19
HD1537.P2 N36 1980 ***NYPL [JLF 86-1956]***

AGRICULTURAL INNOVATIONS - PERU.
Sotomayor, Octavio. Racionalidad campesina y cambio técnico /. Cusco , 1985. 23 p. ; LC Card 86-200944
HD1531.P4 S67 1985

AGRICULTURAL INNOVATIONS - SAUDI ARABIA.
Philipp, Hans-Jürgen. Die landwirtschaftliche Modernisierung Saudi-Arabiens im 20. Jahrhundert /. Hamburg , c1984. 132 p. : LC Card 85-166668
HD2060.Z8 P48 1984

AGRICULTURAL INNOVATIONS - SOCIAL ASPECTS - GAMBIA.
Nath, Kamla. Labor-saving techniques in food processing . Boston, MA (270 Bay State Rd., Boston 02215) , 1985. 26 leaves ; LC Card 87-155092 DDC 331.4/25 19
HD6073.A292 G256 1985

AGRICULTURAL INNOVATIONS - SOCIAL ASPECTS - INDIA - PANCHRA.
Chakrabarti, S. B., 1943- Around the plough . Calcutta , 1986. xviii, 203 p., 8 p. of plates : LC Card 86-902283
HD2075.P36 C48 1986 ***NYPL [L-10 8468 no.67]***

AGRICULTURAL INNOVATIONS - TAIWAN.
CAPD and agricultural development in the Republic of China on Taiwan . Taipei [1984] 152 p. : LC Card 87-400057 DDC 338.1/851249 19
HD2108 .C36 1984

AGRICULTURAL INNOVATIONS - UNITED STATES.
Technology, public policy, and the changing structure of American agriculture. Washington, D.C. [1986] vi, 374 p. : LC Card 85-600632 DDC 338.1/0973 19
HD1761 .T37 1986 ***NYPL [JLF 86-1376]***

Agricultural input supply in Cameroon : a report prepared for the World Bank. Alexandria, Va. : E. Berg Associates, [1983] 2 v. : ill. ; 28 cm.
"June 1983." Includes bibliographical references.
CONTENTS. - v. 1. Main report -- v. 2. Village case-studies. LC Card 87-119188 DDC 338.1/0967/11 19
1. Agriculture - Economic aspects - Cameroon. 2. Agricultural productivity - Cameroon. 3. Farm supplies - Cameroon. I. International Bank for Reconstruction and Development. II. Elliot Berg Associates.
HD2139.5 .A68 1983

Agricultural Institute of Malaysia. Seminar "Malaysian Agriculture--What Next?" (1985 : Kuala Lumpur, Malaysia) Options for Malaysian agriculture . [Kuala Lumpur] , 1986. xxiv, 203 p. : ISBN 967-99982-0-7 (pbk.) LC Card 86-943314 DDC 338.1/8595 19
HD2080.6.Z8 S45 1985

AGRICULTURAL INSURANCE. see **INSURANCE, AGRICULTURAL.**

AGRICULTURAL LABORERS - ASIA, SOUTHEASTERN - CONGRESSES.
Sub-regional Symposium on Labour Inspection in Agriculture (1982 : Denpasar, Indonesia) Labour inspection in agriculture in Southeast Asia . Bangkok , 1983. 218 p. : ISBN 92-2-103533-6 LC Card 86-915732
HD1537.A785 S8 1982

AGRICULTURAL LABORERS - ASIA, SOUTHEASTERN - SOCIAL CONDITIONS - CONGRESSES.
Sub-regional Symposium on Labour Inspection in Agriculture (1982 : Denpasar, Indonesia) Labour inspection in agriculture in Southeast Asia . Bangkok , 1983. 218 p. : ISBN 92-2-103533-6 LC Card 86-915732
HD1537.A785 S8 1982

AGRICULTURAL LABORERS - AUSTRIA - SUPPLY AND DEMAND.
Arbeitsmarktpolitik für die Landwirtschaft und den ländlichen Raum /. Graz , c1984. 138 p. : ISBN 3-900307-15-6 LC Card 85-186643
HD1536.A9 A73 1984

AGRICULTURAL LABORERS - BRAZIL - GOIÁS (STATE)
Brandão, Carlos Rodrigues. Campesinato goiano . Goiânia , 1986. 156 p. ; ISBN 85-85003-42-1 : LC Card 87-403866 DDC 305.5/63 19
HD1531.B7 B713 1986

AGRICULTURAL LABORERS - BRAZIL - PASSO REAL.
Rio Grande do Sul (Brazil). Assembléia Legislativa. Comissão Especial dos Agricultores Desalojados do Passo Real. Afogados, até quando? . [Porto Alegre] [1984] 99 p. : LC Card 85-150200
HD500.P39 R56 1984

AGRICULTURAL LABORERS - BRAZIL - SÃO PAULO (STATE)
Política agrária /. Porto Alegre-RS , 1985. 79 p. : LC Card 86-198513
HD1531.B7 P65 1985

AGRICULTURAL LABORERS - BRAZIL - SÃO PAULO (STATE) - SUPPLY AND DEMAND - HISTORY - 19TH CENTURY - CASE STUDIES.
Witter, José Sebastião. A Revolta dos Parceiros /. São Paulo, SP , 1986. 77 p. : LC Card 87-102716
HD4875.B8 W58 1986

AGRICULTURAL LABORERS - CASE STUDIES.
Abraham, A. S. (Abraham Saktimangalam), 1944- Education and employment in agriculture, India . New Delhi , 1985. vii, 111 p. ; LC Card 85-904717 DDC 331.12/93/0954 19
HD1537.I4 A587 1985 ***NYPL [JLD 86-2251]***

AGRICULTURAL LABORERS - CENTRAL AMERICA - SUPPLY AND DEMAND.
Cambio y polarización ocupacional en Centroamérica. [San José, Costa Rica?] , 1986. 202 p. : ISBN 92-2-305432-X LC Card 86-231773
HD5733.A6 C36 1986

AGRICULTURAL LABORERS - CHILE - POLITICAL ACTIVITY.
Tapia Soko, Gonzalo. El problema de la recomposición de los actores campesinos en una perspectiva de democratización /. Santiago [Chile] [1985] ii, 49, 5 leaves ; LC Card 86-159337
HD1531.C5 T36 1985

AGRICULTURAL LABORERS - CHILE - SUPPLY AND DEMAND.
Problemas metodológicos de una encuesta rural en Chile y estructura del empleo /. [Santiago, Chile] [c1983] ii, 27 leaves ; LC Card 84-225128
HD1531.C5 P76 1983

AGRICULTURAL LABORERS - COLOMBIA.
Reproducción de fuerza de trabajo, educación y migración en el sector rural colombiano /. Bogotá, Colombia , 1985. 98, [52] p. : LC Card 87-402979 DDC 331.1/09861 19
HD5757.A6 R46 1985

AGRICULTURAL LABORERS - DEVELOPING COUNTRIES.
Beckford, George L. Persistent poverty . London , Totowa, N.J. , c1983. xxv, 244 p. : ISBN 0-86232-207-3 (pbk.) LC Card 85-149825 DDC 338.1/09172/4 19
HC59.72.P6 B43 1983 ***NYPL [JLD 87-628]***

Jiggins, Janice. Gender-related impacts and the work of the international agricultural research centers /. Washington, D.C. , c1986. x, 95 p. ; ISBN 0-8213-0840-8 (pbk.) LC Card 86-24709 DDC 331.4/83/091724 19
HD6073.A292 D444 1986

AGRICULTURAL LABORERS - DEVELOPING COUNTRIES - CASE STUDIES.
Agricultural household models . Baltimore, Md. , 1986. xi, 335 p. : ISBN 0-8018-3149-0 LC Card 85-45102 DDC 331.7/63/091724 19
HD1542 .A34 1986 ***NYPL [JLE 86-2440]***

AGRICULTURAL LABORERS - DEVELOPING COUNTRIES - CONGRESSES.
Alexander von Humboldt Award Colloquium (1984) Technology, human capital, and the world food problem /. St. Paul, MN , 1986. x, 167 p. : LC Card 86-622216 DDC 338.1/9/1724 19
HD9018.D44 A44 1984

AGRICULTURAL LABORERS - ECUADOR - ESMERALDAS (PROVINCE) - CASE STUDIES.
Campesinado y organización en Esmeraldas /. [Quito, Ecuador?] [1986] 213 p. : LC Card 86-171561
HD1531.E2 C36 1986

AGRICULTURAL LABORERS - ECUADOR - POLITICAL ACTIVITY.
Dubly, Alain. La organización campesina . Quito, Ecuador , 1985. 37 p. : LC Card 87-404544 DDC 322/.2/09866 19
HD1531.E2 D83 1985

AGRICULTURAL LABORERS - EL SALVADOR - CHALATENANGO (DEPT.) - POLITICAL ACTIVITY - HISTORY.
Pearce, Jenny. Promised land . London [S.l.] , 1986. viii, 324 p. : ISBN 0-906156-21-1 (pbk.) LC Card 86-141737 DDC 322.4/4/097284 19
HD1531.S2 P4 1986 ***NYPL [JLE 87-471]***

AGRICULTURAL LABORERS - ETHIOPIA - STATISTICS.
Rural labour force survey, April 1981-April 1982 /. Addis Ababa , 1985. xii, 170 p. ; LC Card 86-981178 DDC 331.1/0963 19
HD5839.7.A6 R87 1985

AGRICULTURAL LABORERS - FRANCE.
Nicourt, Christian. Conditions de travail en agriculture . Paris , <1985-. v. <2 > : ISBN 2-85340-585-0 (v. 2) LC Card 86-218948
HD1536.F8 N53 1985

AGRICULTURAL LABORERS - GERMANY, WEST.
Landhandwerk und Landwirtschaft /. Göttingen , 1964. 104 p. : LC Card 87-409231 DDC 338.1/61/0943 19
HD1955 .L17 1964

AGRICULTURAL LABORERS - GERMANY (WEST) - NORTH RHINE-WESTPHALIA - STATISTICS.
Agrarberichterstattung Nordrhein-Westfalen 1981 . Düsseldorf [1983] 189 p. ; LC Card 87-407320 DDC 943/.55 s 338.1/0943/55021 19
HA1320.N6 A32 Heft 490 HD1960.N67

AGRICULTURAL LABORERS - GOVERNMENT POLICY - AUSTRIA.
Arbeitsmarktpolitik für die Landwirtschaft und den ländlichen Raum /. Graz , c1984. 138 p. : ISBN 3-900307-15-6 LC Card 85-186643
HD1536.A9 A73 1984

AGRICULTURAL LABORERS - GOVERNMENT POLICY - DEVELOPING COUNTRIES - CASE STUDIES.
Agricultural household models . Baltimore, Md. , 1986. xi, 335 p. : ISBN 0-8018-3149-0 LC Card 85-45102 DDC 331.7/63/091724 19
HD1542 .A34 1986 ***NYPL [JLE 86-2440]***

AGRICULTURAL LABORERS - GOVERNMENT POLICY - EUROPEAN ECONOMIC COMMUNITY COUNTRIES - CONGRESSES.
Europäische Agrarpolitik . Göttingen , 1985. 82 p. ; LC Card 86-170925
HD1920.5.Z8 E97 1985

AGRICULTURAL LABORERS - GREAT BRITAIN.
Gasson, Ruth M. Labour sharing in agriculture /. [London] [1979] 117 p. ; ISBN 0-901859-82-6 (pbk.) LC Card 83-226074 DDC 331.25/72 19
HD5119.A292 G744 1979

Great Britain. Health and Safety Commission. Proposal to review the minimum age at which children may drive or ride on agricultural machinery /. London [1982] 12 p. ; ISBN 0-11-883635-8 (pbk.) LC Card 82-214120 DDC 363.1/89 19
HD6247.A4 G74 1982

AGRICULTURAL LABORERS - GUATEMALA.
Hintermeister, Alberto. Modernización de la agricultura y pobreza rural en Guatemala /. [Santiago, Chile] , 1982. 59 leaves : LC Card 87-403247 DDC 338.1/6/097281 19
HC144.Z9 P624 1982

AGRICULTURAL LABORERS - HUNGARY.
Simó, Tibor. Metszetek az agrártársadalom struktúrájából /. Budapest , 1985. 167 p. ; ISBN 963-7700-25-0 : LC Card 86-232606
HD1536.H9 S56 1985

AGRICULTURAL LABORERS - HUNGARY - STATISTICS.
Munkaerőhelyzet és kereseti viszonyok az állami gazdaságokban, kombinátokban és a mezőgazdasági termelőszövetkezetekben, 1980-1985 /. Budapest , 1987. 45 p. ; LC Card 87-419798
HD1536.H9 M85 1987

AGRICULTURAL LABORERS - INDIA - ANDHRA PRADESH - SUPPLEMENTARY EMPLOYMENT.

Andhra Pradesh (India). Finance and Planning (Planning Wing) Dept. Evaluation Wing. Evaluation study on the working of crash scheme for rural employment. Hyderabad , 1983. 89 p. : LC Card 86-144139 DDC 331.12/042/095484 19
HD5710.85.I42 A532 1983

AGRICULTURAL LABORERS - INDIA - BENGAL - HISTORY.
Nag Chowdhury-Zilly, Aditee. The vagrant peasant . Wiesbaden , 1982. xv, 196 p. : ISBN 3-515-03855-8 (pbk.) LC Card 86-214350
HD1537.I4 N327 1982

AGRICULTURAL LABORERS - INDIA - CASE STUDIES.
Abraham, A. S. (Abraham Saktimangalam), 1944- Education and employment in agriculture, India . New Delhi , 1985. vii, 111 p. ; LC Card 85-904717 DDC 331.12/93/0954 19
HD1537.I4 A587 1985
NYPL [JLD 86-2251]

AGRICULTURAL LABORERS - INDIA - WEST BENGAL.
Rudra, Ashok. Agrarian relations in West Bengal . Bombay , c1983. x, 104 p. ; LC Card 83-902673 DDC 338.1/0954/14 19
HD879.W4 R83 1983 ***NYPL [JLD 86-3785]***

AGRICULTURAL LABORERS - INDONESIA - JAWA TENGAH.
Hart, Gillian Patricia. Power, labor, and livelihood . Berkeley , c1986. xvi, 228 p. : ISBN 0-520-05499-7 (alk. paper) LC Card 85-8435 DDC 330.9598/2 19
HD1537.I56 H37 1986
NYPL [JLE 86-3039]

AGRICULTURAL LABORERS - ITALY.
Italy. Parlamento. Giunta per la inchiesta agraria e sulle condizioni della classe agricola. Inchiesta Jacini . Sala Bolognese , 1978- <1987. v. <1-7, 9-10; v. 13, t. 1, fasc. 1-3; v. 11, t. 1-3; v. 13, t. 2, fasc. 4-5; in 18 > : LC Card 86-143133
HD1970 .I84 1978

AGRICULTURAL LABORERS - ITALY - STATISTICS.
Barberis, Corrado. Agricoltura e strati sociali /. Milano, Italy , c1986. 269 p. ; LC Card 86-214233
HD1536.I8 B328 1986

AGRICULTURAL LABORERS - KENYA.
Livingstone, Ian. Rural development, employment and incomes in Kenya /. Aldershot, Hants , Brookfield, Vermont , 1986. xx, 389 p. : ISBN 0-566-00990-0
NYPL [Sc D 86-728]

AGRICULTURAL LABORERS - KENYA - STATISTICS.
Barnes, Carolyn. Kenyan smallholdings and the division of labour /. Nairobi , 1982. 39 leaves ; LC Card 87-156293
HD1476.K4 B37 1982

AGRICULTURAL LABORERS - KIRGHIZ S.S. R.
Boldzhurova, I. S. (Ishengul′ Sadykovna) Kolkhoznoe krest′i͡anstvo Kirgizii v uslovii͡akh razvitogo sotsializma /. Frunze , 1985. 148 p. ; LC Card 86-106126
HD1995.K53 B65 1985

AGRICULTURAL LABORERS - LATIN AMERICA - CONGRESSES.
Reforma agraria como proceso social . Piura, Perú [1984] 163 p. : LC Card 84-232526 DDC 333.3/1/85 19
HD1333.P4 R44 1984 ***NYPL [JLD 86-2537]***

Taller "Perspectivas y Alternativas de la Agricultura Familiar" (1983 : Montevideo, Uruguay) Taller "Perspectivas y Alternativas de la Agricultura Familiar". Montevideo, Uruguay [1984] 1 v. (various pagings) : LC Card 85-203149 DDC 338.1/6 19
HD1476.L29 T35 1983 ***NYPL [JLF 86-884]***

AGRICULTURAL LABORERS - MEXICO.
Astorga Lira, Enrique. Mercado de trabajo rural en México . México, D.F. , 1985. 127 p. : ISBN 968-411-139-8 LC Card 86-141300 DDC 331.7/63/0972 19
HD1531.M6 A88 1985 ***NYPL [JLC 87-68]***

Fernández, Sonia. Análisis comparativo de la información sobre población ocupada . México, D.F. [1977] 28 p. ; LC Card 84-227473
HD5731.A6 F46 1977

AGRICULTURAL LABORERS - MEXICO - AGUASCALIENTES (STATE) - HISTORY - CASE STUDIES.
Gómez Serrano, Jesús. Hacendados y campesinos en Aguascalientes /. [Aguascalientes] , 1985. 221 p., [20] p. of plates : LC Card 86-217321
HD1471.M62 A384 1985

AGRICULTURAL LABORERS - NICARAGUA.
Hintermeister, Alberto. El empleo agrícola en una estructra en transformación . [Santiago, Chile] , 1982. 27 p. ; LC Card 87-403249 DDC 331.7/63/097285 19
HD1531.N5 H56 1982

AGRICULTURAL LABORERS - NORTHERN IRELAND.
O'Fee, J. H. The input of labour on farms in Northern Ireland /. Belfast , 1986. i, 41 leaves ; LC Card 86-218985 DDC 331.11/8 19
HD1535.N675 O47 1986

AGRICULTURAL LABORERS - PAKISTAN - PUNJAB.
Elahi, Mahboob. Rural labour market, with special reference to hired labour in Pakistan's Punjab /. Lahore, Pakistan [1983] ii, ix, 186 leaves ; LC Card 86-930467
HD1537.P2 E4 1983

Namdar, Shamim A. Employment implications of agricultural growth /. Lahore , 1980. 82 leaves : LC Card 84-930891 DDC 331.12/93/0954914 19
HD1537.P2 N36 1980 ***NYPL [JLF 86-1956]***

AGRICULTURAL LABORERS - PANAMA.
Gandásegui, Marco A. La fuerza de trabajo en el agro . Panamá, R.P. , c1985. 404 p. : ISBN 84-8385-002-X LC Card 86-111074 DDC 331.7/63/097287 19
HD1822 .G36 1985 ***NYPL [JLF 86-1350]***

AGRICULTURAL LABORERS - PERU.
Maletta, Héctor. Requerimientos de mano de obra en la agricultura peruana /. Lima, Perú , 1985. 184 p. ; LC Card 86-156077
HD1531.P4 M34 1985

AGRICULTURAL LABORERS - PHILIPPINES - POLITICAL ACTIVITY.
Hanisch, Rolf, 1942- Der Staat, ländliche Armutsgruppen und legale Bauernbewegung in den Philippinen /. Baden-Baden , 1983. xii, 432 p. ; ISBN 3-7890-0980-6 LC Card 84-143058
HD1537.P5 H35 1983

AGRICULTURAL LABORERS - RUSSIAN S.F. S.R. - BIOGRAPHY.
Zasluzhennyĭ rabotnik sel′skogo khozi͡aĭstva respubliki /. Moskva , 1986. 351 p. : LC Card 86-132613
HD1536.S65 Z37 1986

AGRICULTURAL LABORERS - RUSSIAN S.F. S.R. - CAUCASUS, NORTHERN.
Krivoded, V. V. KPSS i kolkhoznoe krest′i͡anstvo v 1945-1959 gg. /. Rostov-na-Donu , 1984. 190 p. ; LC Card 87-100194
HD1492.S652 C384 1984

AGRICULTURAL LABORERS - RUSSIAN S.F. S.R. - NON-CHERNOZEM REGION.
Smekalov, Pavel Vasil′evich. Sel′skie kadry nechernozem′i͡a /. Moskva , 1981. 190 p. ; LC Card 82-177714
HD1536.S65 S64 1981

Vasil′ev, Ivan Afanas′evich. Korennye i priezzhie /. Moskva , 1980. 86 p. ; LC Card 81-178115
HD1536.S65 V375 1980

AGRICULTURAL LABORERS - RUSSIAN S.F. S.R. - SOCIAL CONDITIONS.
Kolos na ladoni . Voronezh , 1985. 237 p. : LC Card 86-195464
HD1536.S65 K65 1985

AGRICULTURAL LABORERS - SOVIET UNION.
Kuznetsova, T. E. Proizvodstvennai͡a sfera sovremennogo sela /. Moskva , 1986. 199 p. ; LC Card 86-164902
HD9015.S652 K89 1986

Syrovatko, V. G. (Vitaliĭ Grigor′evich) Industrializatsii͡a i kadry sel′skogo khozi͡aĭstva /. Moskva , 1986. 191 p. ; LC Card 86-229171
HD1536.S65 S97 1986

AGRICULTURAL LABORERS - SOVIET UNION - BIOGRAPHY.
Vernulsi͡a soldat k poli͡u, 1945-1985 /. Moskva , 1985. 429, [16] p. : LC Card 85-228297
HD1536.S65 V47 1985

AGRICULTURAL LABORERS - SPAIN - CÓRDOBA (PROVINCE) - HISTORY - 20TH CENTURY.
Díaz del Moral, Juan, 1870-1948. Las agitaciones campesinas del período bolchevista, 1918-1920 /. Sevilla [1985?] 230 p. ; ISBN 84-7587-031-7 LC Card 86-181529
HD1536.S7 D48 1985

AGRICULTURAL LABORERS - TRAINING OF - GERMANY (WEST)
Kretschmann, Rolf. Möglichkeiten des Berufswechsels von Haupterwerbslandwirten unter besonderer Berücksichtigung von Agrarstruktur und Arbeitsmarkt /. Göttingen , 1986. xi, 109 p. : LC Card 87-408871 DDC 331.25/924 19
HD1536.G3 K746 1986

AGRICULTURAL LABORERS - TRAINING OF - SENEGAL.
International Labour Organisation. Formation professionnelle rurale, SEN/71/526 . Genève , 1976. ii, 69 p. : ISBN 92-2-201512-6 LC Card 84-125056
HD5716.A292 S385 1976

AGRICULTURAL LABORERS - UNITED STATES - CONGRESSES.
Farm work and fieldwork . Ithaca , 1987. 293 p. : ISBN 0-8014-9446-X (pbk. : alk. paper) LC Card 86-19960 DDC 305.5/55/0973 19
HD8039.F32 U635 1987

AGRICULTURAL LABORERS - UZBEK S.S. R.
Toshpŭlatov, Mirzapŭlat. Prevrashchenie sel′skokhozi͡aĭstvennogo truda v raznovidnost′ industrial′nogo v uslovii͡akh razvitogo sotsializma. . Tashkent , 1980. 68 p. ; LC Card 81-149078
HD1536.S65 T67 1980

AGRICULTURAL LAWS AND LEGISLATION - EUROPE, EASTERN.
Sárándi, Imre. Világgazdasági korszakváltások és a mezőgazdasági termékforgalom . [Budapest] [1985] 92 p. ; LC Card 86-218536
HD1415 .S25 1985

AGRICULTURAL LAWS AND LEGISLATION - PERU.
Hurtado Miller, Juan Carlos. Por una causa agraria . Lima, Perú , 1986. 348 p. : LC Card 87-400122 DDC 338.1/885 19
HD1903 .H87 1986

AGRICULTURAL MACHINERY - GREAT BRITAIN - SAFETY MEASURES.
Great Britain. Health and Safety Commission. Proposal to review the minimum age at which children may drive or ride on agricultural machinery /. London [1982] 12 p. ; ISBN 0-11-883635-8 (pbk.) LC Card 82-214120 DDC 363.1/89 19
HD6247.A4 G74 1982

AGRICULTURAL MACHINERY - INDIA - FUEL CONSUMPTION.
Upadhyaya, P. K. (Pratap Krishna), 1916- Distribution and consumption of diesel oil in agriculture /. Delhi, India , 1985. xii, 150 p. : LC Card 86-902439 DDC 333.79 19
HD9579.D53 I68 1985

AGRICULTURAL MACHINERY INDUSTRY - INDIA.
Tractor industry in India. New Delhi [1982?]. 3 v. ; LC Card 83-906487 DDC 338.4/7629225 19
HD9710.4.I42 T73 1982
NYPL [JLM 86-469]

AGRICULTURAL MACHINERY INDUSTRY - SOUTH DAKOTA - WINNER - HISTORY.
Nelson, Selmer, 1917- Grossenburg's fifty years with John Deere /. Freeman, S.D. , c1987. viii, 167 p. : LC Card 87-80826 DDC 338.7/681763/0978361 19
HD9486.U6 G766 1987

AGRICULTURAL MACHINERY INDUSTRY - SWITZERLAND - HISTORY.
Tauber, Herbert. Johann Ulrich Aebi . Zürich , c1983. 84, [2] p. : LC Card 83-192282
HC395.5.A2 S3 no. 38 HD9486.S94A36

AGRICULTURAL MACHINERY INDUSTRY - UNITED STATES - HISTORY.
Nelson, Selmer, 1917- Grossenburg's fifty years with John Deere /. Freeman, S.D. , c1987. viii, 167 p. : LC Card 87-80826 DDC 338.7/681763/0978361 19
HD9486.U6 G766 1987

AGRICULTURAL MACHINERY INDUSTRY - UNITED STATES - STATISTICS.
Hanthorn, Michael. Selected farm machinery statistics /. Washington, D.C. , 1986] ii, 54 p. : LC Card 86-602408 DDC 338.1/61/0973 19
HD1751 .A5 no. 743 HD9486.U4

AGRICULTURAL MACHINERY - SOVIET UNION.
Larkin, V. A. (Vladimir Alekseevich) Sotsial'no-ėkonomicheskie problemy kompleksnoĭ mekhanizatsii sel'skokhoziaĭstvennogo proizvodstva /. Moskva , 1981. 148 p. ; LC Card 82-157096
HD1992 .L375 1981

AGRICULTURAL MACHINERY - ZIMBABWE - SANYATI RIVER REGION - MAINTENANCE AND REPAIR.
Kirk, T. Project 3.05, rural workshop and machinery centre . Salisbury, Zimbabwe , 1977. 1 v. (various pagings) : LC Card 85-104610
HD2131.Z9 S265 1977

AGRICULTURAL MARKETING. see **PRODUCE TRADE; FARM PRODUCE - MARKETING.**

Agricultural marketing and economic development . Smith, Gordon Whitford, 1934- New York , 1987. iii, 417 p. ; ISBN 0-8240-1371-9 (alk. paper) : LC Card 87-11833 DDC 381/.41318/09816 19
HD9066.B84 S687 1987

Agricultural marketing enterprises for the developing world . Abbott, John Cave, 1919- Cambridge [Cambridgeshire] , New York , 1987. xi, 217 p. : ISBN 0-521-32597-8 LC Card 86-24462 DDC 381/.41/091724 19
HD9018.D44 A228 1987

Agricultural marketing handbook for Caribbean Basin products. Spanish. Manual--mercadeo de productos agrícolas de la Cuenca del Caribe / IICA-USDA. 2a ed. rev. San José, Costa Rica : Instituto Interamericano de Cooperación para la Agricultura : Departamento de Agricultura de los Estados Unidos de América : x, 434 p. : ill. ; 23 cm. (Serie Publicaciones misceláneas . no. 666) Translation of: The Agricultural marketing handbook for Caribbean Basin products. ISBN 92-9039-101-4 LC Card 86-204686
1. Produce trade - Caribbean Area. 2. Produce trade - Central America. 3. Produce trade - United States. 4. Caribbean Basin Initiative, 1983-. I. Inter-American Institute of Agricultural Sciences. II. United States. Dept. of Agriculture. III. Title. IV. Title: Mercadeo de productos agrícolas de la Cuenca del Caribe. V. Series: Série Publicações misceláneas , no. 666.
HD9014.C442 A4718 1986

Agricultural marketing strategy and pricing policy / edited by Dieter Elz. Washington, D.C. : World Bank, c1987. xiii, 132 p. : ill. ; 27 cm. (A World Bank symposium) Based on papers from a seminar held in Washington, D.C., May 6-17, 1985. Includes bibliographies. ISBN 0-8213-0830-0 (pbk.) LC Card 86-33992 DDC 380.1/41 19
1. Farm produce - Marketing - Government policy - Developing countries - Congresses. 2. Agricultural prices - Government policy - Developing countries - Congresses. I. Elz, Dieter, 1927-. II. International Bank for Reconstruction and Development. III. Series.
HD9018.D44 A365 1987

Agricultural mechanization . Binswanger, Hans P. Washington, D.C., U. S.A. , c1987. vi, 85 p. : ISBN 0-8213-0903-X (pbk.) LC Card 87-14082 DDC 338.1/61/091724 19
HD1459 .B57 1987

Agricultural options . Angell, George. New York, NY , c1986. ix, 230 p. : ISBN 0-8144-5822-X LC Card 85-48215 DDC 332.64/25 19
HG6047.G8 A54 1986 ***NYPL [JLE 86-2854]***

Agricultural policies in the European Community : their origins, nature, and effects on production and trade / [Ivan Roberts ... et al.]. Canberra : Australian Govt. Pub. Service, 1985. xii, 373 p. : ill. ; 25 cm. (Policy monograph . no. 2) At head of title: Bureau of Agricultural Economics, Canberra. Bibliography: p. 351-358. Includes index. ISBN 0-644-04293-1 (pbk.) LC Card 86-673733
1. Agriculture and state - European Economic Community countries. 2. Agriculture - Economic aspects - European Economic Community countries. I. Roberts, Ivan. II. Australia. Bureau of Agricultural Economics. III. Series.
HD1920.5.Z8 A37x 1985

AGRICULTURAL POLICY. see **AGRICULTURE AND STATE.**

Agricultural policy implementation . Staudt, Kathleen A. West Hartford, CT , c1985. xvi, 68 p. : ISBN 0-931816-18-1 (pbk.) LC Card 84-29737 DDC 338.1/86762 19
HD2126.5.Z8 S73 1985
NYPL [JLF 86-1685]

Agricultural policy in Jordan / edited by Alison Burrell ; team leader Subhi Qasem ; programme leader A.B. Zahlan. London ; Atlantic Highlands, NJ : Published for the Abdul Hameed Shoman Foundation, Amman, by Ithaca Press : 147 p. : ill. ; 25 cm. (Middle East science policy studies . no. 7) Distributor statement from label. Papers from a conference held in Amman, Jordan, 27-28 November 1984. "Part of the Abdul Hameed Shoman Foundation series entitled 'Systems analysis and agricultural policy in the Arab world'"--P. [1] Includes bibliographies. ISBN 0-86372-070-6 LC Card 86-21480 DDC 338.1/85695 19
1. Agriculture and state - Jordan - Congresses. I. Burrell, Alison. II. Abdul Hameed Shoman Foundation. III. Series.
HD2059.Z8 A34 1986

AGRICULTURAL POLLUTION.
Yates, Geoffrey. Food, need, greed & myopia . Ryton, Tyne and Wear , 1986. 96 p. : ISBN 0-907367-04-6 (pbk.) : LC Card 87-129951 DDC 338.1/9 19
HD9000.5 .Y38 1986

AGRICULTURAL POLLUTION - GOVERNMENT POLICY - GERMANY (WEST)
Grünen (Political party) Grüne Agrarpolitik, Bilanz und Perspektiven . Bonn [1985?] 62 p. : LC Card 86-152151
HD1957 .G79 1985

AGRICULTURAL POLLUTION - GOVERNMENT POLICY - UNITED STATES - CONGRESSES.
Agriculture and the environment /. Washington, D.C. , c1986. xvii, 298 p. : ISBN 0-915707-33-0 (pbk.) : LC Card 87-43010 DDC 363.7/31 19
HD1755 .P47 1986

AGRICULTURAL POLLUTION - NICARAGUA.
Thielen, Helmut, 1941- Agrarreformen in Lateinamerika zwischen Ökonomie und Ökologie . Frankfurt am Main , c1985. 518 p. : ISBN 3-88129-958-0 LC Card 86-153251 DDC 333.3/1/7285 19
HD1333.N5 T48 1985 ***NYPL [JLD 87-467]***

AGRICULTURAL POLLUTION - UNITED STATES.
Agriculture and the environment in a changing world economy. Washington, D.C. , c1986. xi, 66 p. : ISBN 0-89164-099-1 (pbk.) LC Card 86-24088 DDC 338.1/873 19
HD1761 .A6228 1986

Fox, Michael W., 1937- Agricide . New York , 1986. xv, 194 p., [10] p. of plates : ISBN 0-8052-4013-6 LC Card 85-27690 DDC 338.1/6/0973 19
S441 .F69 1986 ***NYPL [JLD 86-2542]***

Agricultural price policy and income distribution in India /. De Janvry, Alain. Delhi , New York , 1986. xi, 113 p. ; ISBN 0-19-561952-8 : LC Card 86-900015 DDC 338.1/3/0954 19
HD9016.I42 D38 1986

Agricultural price policy in India . Gulati, Ashok, 1954- New Delhi , 1987, c1985. 196 p. : LC Card 86-903595 DDC 338.1/8 19
HD2073 .G85 1987

AGRICULTURAL PRICE SUPPORTS - BRAZIL - HISTORY.
Cardoso, Eliana A. Inflation, growth and the real exchange rate . New York , 1987. 98 p. : ISBN 0-8240-1356-5 (alk. paper) : LC Card 87-8570 DDC 330.981 19
HC187 .C218 1987

AGRICULTURAL PRICE SUPPORTS - FRANCE - STATISTICS.
Savignac, Philippe. Concours publics à l'agriculture par régions ou catégories d'exploitations en 1981. Paris [1984] 81 p. : ISBN 2-11-083993-7 LC Card 85-168478
HD1947 .S29 1984

AGRICULTURAL PRICE SUPPORTS - INDIA.
De Janvry, Alain. Agricultural price policy and income distribution in India /. Delhi , New York , 1986. xi, 113 p. ; ISBN 0-19-561952-8 : LC Card 86-900015 DDC 338.1/3/0954 19
HD9016.I42 D38 1986

Gulati, Ashok, 1954- Agricultural price policy in India . New Delhi , 1987, c1985. 196 p. : LC Card 86-903595 DDC 338.1/8 19
HD2073 .G85 1987

AGRICULTURAL PRICE SUPPORTS - SWEDEN.
Översyn av vissa frågor rörande jordbruksprisregleringen /. [Stockholm] [1981] iii, 104, 13, 22, 2, 9, 14 p. : ISBN 91-38-06616-5 LC Card 83-245209
HD2018 .O94 1981

Sweden. 1983 års livsmedelskommitté. Expertgruppen för prisregleringsfrågor. Prisstöd och jordbruksprisreglering . Stockholm [1984] xvi, 260 p. ; ISBN 91-38-08461-9 LC Card 86-109988
HD9015.S86 S883 1984

AGRICULTURAL PRICE SUPPORTS - TANZANIA.
Orback, Jens. Agriculture and incentives, the Tanzanian case . Uppsala , 1985. 37, [2] leaves, [1] leaf of plates : LC Card 86-215091 DDC 338.1/8 19
HD2128.5 .O73 1985

AGRICULTURAL PRICE SUPPORTS - UNITED STATES.
Sumner, Daniel A. (Daniel Alan), 1950- Removal of price supports and supply controls for U. S. tobacco . Demoines, Iowa , Washington, D.C. , c1985. viii, 64 p. ; ISBN 0-89068-084-1 LC Card 85-63194
NYPL [JLF 86-1014]

Agricultural prices and marketing in India . Agarwal, N. L. Delhi, India , 1986. xv, 243 p. ; LC Card 86-902258 DDC 338.1/3/09544 19
HD2075.R27 A36 1986

Agricultural prices & marketing in India. Agarwal, N. L. Agricultural prices and marketing in India . Delhi, India , 1986. xv, 243 p. ; LC Card 86-902258 DDC 338.1/3/09544 19
HD2075.R27 A36 1986

AGRICULTURAL PRICES - AUSTRALIA - HISTORY - STATISTICS.
Historical trends in Australian rural production, exports, farm income, and indexes of prices received and paid by farmers, 1952-53 to 1972-73 /. Canberra , 1974. vii, 17 p. : ISBN 0-642-00746-2 (pbk.) LC Card 85-126806 DDC 338.1/0994/021 19
HD2152 .H57 1974

AGRICULTURAL PRICES - AUSTRIA - STATISTICS.
Landeswirtschaftlicher Paritätsspiegel . Wien [1982] 11 leaves ; LC Card 86-181563
HD1935 .L325 1982

AGRICULTURAL PRICES - BRAZIL.
Análise das distorções dos preços domésticos em relação aos preços de fronteira . Brasília , 1983. 125 p. : LC Card 86-200859
HD9014.B82 A66 1983

AGRICULTURAL PRICES - CHINA.
Weitz, Maria. Entwicklungen in der chinesischen Agrarpolitik seit 1978 /. Berlin , 1986. 110 p. ; ISBN 3-428-06036-9 LC Card 87-409465 DDC 338.1/851 19
HD2097 .W45 1986

AGRICULTURAL PRICES - ETHIOPIA - STATISTICS.
Average producers' prices of agricultural commodities in rural area by region, Miazia 1973-Miazia 1974, (May 1981-April 1982) /. Addis Ababa , 1985. 14 leaves ; LC Card 85-981293 DDC 338.1/3/0963021 19
HD2124.5 .A93 1985

AGRICULTURAL PRICES - EUROPEAN ECONOMIC COMMUNITY COUNTRIES.
Kirschke, Dieter, 1952- Agrarmarktpolitik bei Unsicherheit . Berlin , c1987. 225 p. : ISBN 3-428-06111-X LC Card 87-131255 DDC 338.1/8 19
HD1920.5 .K57 1987

AGRICULTURAL PRICES - EUROPEAN ECONOMIC COMMUNITY COUNTRIES - ECONOMETRIC MODELS.
Einkommenswirkungen von Getreidepreissenkungen /. Münster-Hiltrup , 1985. viii, 158 p. : ISBN 3-7843-0315-3 LC Card 87-408928 DDC 338.1/0943 s 338.1/331/094 19
HD1920.5 .E37 1985

AGRICULTURAL PRICES - EUROPEAN ECONOMIC COMMUNITY COUNTRIES - STATISTICAL METHODS.
Methodologie der EG-Agrarpreisindizes (Output und Input) =. Luxembourg , Washington, DC , 1985. 228 p. ; ISBN 92-825-5463-5 : LC Card 87-107275 DDC 338.1/3/094021 19
HD1920.5 .M47 1985

AGRICULTURAL PRICES - EUROPEAN ECONOMIC COMMUNITY COUNTRIES - STATISTICS.
Methodologie der EG-Agrarpreisindizes (Output und Input) =. Luxembourg , Washington, DC , 1985. 228 p. ; ISBN 92-825-5463-5 : LC Card 87-107275 DDC 338.1/3/094021 19
HD1920.5 .M47 1985

AGRICULTURAL PRICES - GERMANY, WEST.
Witzke, Harald von. Personelle Einkommensverteilung in der Landwirtschaft und Agrarpreise /. Berlin , 1979. 180 p. : ISBN 3-428-04303-0 LC Card 79-389988
HC290.5.I5 W57 ***NYPL [JLE 80-439]***

AGRICULTURAL PRICES - GOVERNMENT POLICY - BRAZIL.
Análise das distorções dos preços domésticos em relação aos preços de fronteira . Brasília , 1983. 125 p. : LC Card 86-200859
HD9014.B82 A66 1983

AGRICULTURAL PRICES - GOVERNMENT POLICY - DEVELOPING COUNTRIES.
Streeten, Paul. What price food? . New York , 1987. viii, 127 p. : ISBN 0-312-00739-6 : LC Card 87-9577 DDC 338.1/8 19
HD1417 .S73 1987

AGRICULTURAL PRICES - GOVERNMENT POLICY - DEVELOPING COUNTRIES - CONGRESSES.
Agricultural marketing strategy and pricing policy /. Washington, D.C. , c1987. xiii, 132 p. : ISBN 0-8213-0830-0 (pbk.) LC Card 86-33992 DDC 380.1/41 19
HD9018.D44 A365 1987

AGRICULTURAL PRICES - GOVERNMENT POLICY - PHILIPPINES.
Bautista, Romeo M., 1941- Production incentives in Philippine agriculture . Washington, D.C., USA , c1987. 78 p. : ISBN 0-89629-061-1 (pbk.) LC Card 87-3233 DDC 338.1/8 19
HD2087 .B38 1987

AGRICULTURAL PRICES - GOVERNMENT POLICY - UNITED STATES.
Timmer, C. Peter. Getting prices right . Ithaca , 1986. 160 p. : ISBN 0-8014-9441-9 (pbk. : alk. paper) LC Card 86-47649 DDC 338.1/8 19
HD9006 .T58 1986 ***NYPL [JLE 86-4488]***

AGRICULTURAL PRICES - HUNGARY.
Borszéki, Éva. Élelmiszer-gazdaságunk versenyképessége . Budapest , 1986. 284, [1] p. : ISBN 963-221-590-7 : LC Card 87-148751
HD1940.5 .B66 1986

Borszéki, Éva. Élelmiszergazdaságunk versenyképessége . Budapest , 1985. 147 p. ; ISBN 963-491-213-3 LC Card 86-199073
HD1940.5 .B67 1985

AGRICULTURAL PRICES - HUNGARY - STATISTICAL SERVICES.
A Mezőgazdasági és az erdőgazdálkodási árstatisztika módszere /. Budapest , 1986. 81 p. ; LC Card 87-408580
HD9015.H82 M486 1986

AGRICULTURAL PRICES - INDIA.
De Janvry, Alain. Agricultural price policy and income distribution in India /. Delhi , New York , 1986. xi, 113 p. ; ISBN 0-19-561952-8 : LC Card 86-900015 DDC 338.1/3/0954 19
HD9016.I42 D38 1986

Gulati, Ashok, 1954- Agricultural price policy in India . New Delhi , 1987, c1985. 196 p. : LC Card 86-903595 DDC 338.1/8 19
HD2073 .G85 1987

AGRICULTURAL PRICES - INDIA - CASE STUDIES.
Agarwal, N. L. Agricultural prices and marketing in India . Delhi, India , 1986. xv, 243 p. ; LC Card 86-902258 DDC 338.1/3/09544 19
HD2075.R27 A36 1986

AGRICULTURAL PRICES - INDIA - ORISSA.
A Report on index numbers of parity between prices received and prices paid by the farmers in the state of Orissa /. Bhubaneswar, Orissa [1985] 11 p. : LC Card 87-401032 DDC 338.1/3/095413 19
HD2075.O7 R46 1985

AGRICULTURAL PRICES - INDIA - RAJASTHAN - CASE STUDIES.
Agarwal, N. L. Agricultural prices and marketing in India . Delhi, India , 1986. xv, 243 p. ; LC Card 86-902258 DDC 338.1/3/09544 19
HD2075.R27 A36 1986

AGRICULTURAL PRICES - LOUISIANA - STATISTICS.
Fielder, Lonnie L. Agricultural statistics and prices for Louisiana, 1909-1985 /. [Baton Rouge, LA] [1986] iv, [122] p. : LC Card 87-620749 DDC 338.1/09763 s 338.1/09763/021 19
HD1775.L8 L7 no. 659

AGRICULTURAL PRICES - MATHEMATICAL MODELS.
Inter-country comparisons of agricultural production aggregates /. Rome , 1986. v, 59 p. ; ISBN 92-5-102381-6 (pbk.) LC Card 86-222114 DDC 338.1 19
HD1425 .I59 1986

AGRICULTURAL PRICES - MEXICO.
Fragoso Gutiérrez, Juan M. El mercado y los precios de los productos agropecuarios /. México , 1983. 486 p. : LC Card 84-236815
HD9014.M62 F72 1983

AGRICULTURAL PRICES - PAKISTAN.
Some aspects of agricultural price and taxation policies in Pakistan /. Islamabad, Pakistan [1985] x, 223 p. ; LC Card 86-930932 DDC 338.1/8 19
HD2075.5 .S66 1985

Agricultural prices, production, and marketing, with special reference to the hop industry .
Baker, Dennis, 1928- New York , 1985. 779 p. : ISBN 0-8240-6675-8 : LC Card 84-45995 DDC 338.1/7382 19
HD9019.H72 G67 1985 ***NYPL [JLE 87-63]***

AGRICULTURAL PRICES - RUSSIAN S.F.S.R.
I͡Ushkov, V. I. (Vasiliĭ Il'ich) Zakupochnai͡a tsena i rasshirennoe vosproizvodstvo v sel'skom khozi͡aĭstve /. Moskva , 1980. 142 p. ; LC Card 81-134864
HD1995.R8 I95 1980

AGRICULTURAL PRICES - SPAIN.
González Rodríguez, Juan Jesús. La patronal agraria . Madrid [1986?] 46 p. ; ISBN 84-7075-335-3 LC Card 87-111477
HD6976.A292 S74 1986

AGRICULTURAL PRICES - STATISTICS.
A Mezőgazdasági termelés ár- és költségviszonyai nemzetközi összehasonlításban /. Budapest , 1986. 89 p. : LC Card 87-407682
HD1447 .M49 1986

AGRICULTURAL PRICES - TANZANIA.
Orback, Jens. Agriculture and incentives, the Tanzanian case . Uppsala , 1985. 37, [2] leaves, [1] leaf of plates : LC Card 86-215091 DDC 338.1/8 19
HD2128.5 .O73 1985

Agricultural problems in Ethiopia /. Harjinder Singh. Delhi, India , c1987. viii, 254 p. : ISBN 81-212-0078-4 : LC Card 87-900338 DDC 338.1/0963 19
HD2124.5 .H37 1987

AGRICULTURAL PRODUCTIVITY - AFRICA, SUB-SAHARAN - CONGRESSES.
Accelerating food production in Sub-Saharan Africa /. Baltimore , c1987. xix, 417 p. ; ISBN 0-8018-3390-6 (alk. paper) LC Card 86-10684 DDC 338.1/9/67 19
HD2117 .A33 1987 ***NYPL [JLE 87-1366]***

AGRICULTURAL PRODUCTIVITY - CAMEROON.
Agricultural input supply in Cameroon . Alexandria, Va. [1983] 2 v. : LC Card 87-119188 DDC 338.1/0967/11 19
HD2139.5 .A68 1983

AGRICULTURAL PRODUCTIVITY - CHINA.
Liu, Yung-ch'eng. She hui chu i ching chi tse jen chih /. [Ch'ang-ch'un shih] , 1985. 5, 264 p. ; LC Card 86-179707 DDC 658/.00951 19
HD70.C5 L58 1985 <Orien China> ***NYPL [*OVY 86-4140]***

Song, Du-Yul, 1944- Sowjetunion und China . Frankfurt/Main , New York , c1984. 255 p. : ISBN 3-593-33351-1 LC Card 84-169164
HC340.L3 S66 1984

AGRICULTURAL PRODUCTIVITY - CHINA - HUNAN PROVINCE - HISTORY.
Perdue, Peter C., 1949- Exhausting the earth . Cambridge, Mass. , 1987. xvii, 331 p. : ISBN 0-674-27504-7 LC Card 87-5067 DDC 338.1/0951/215 19
HD2100.H86 P47 1987

AGRICULTURAL PRODUCTIVITY - COMMUNIST COUNTRIES.
Wong, Lung-Fai. Agricultural productivity in the Socialist countries /. Boulder, Colo. , 1986. xvii, 195 p. : ISBN 0-8133-7152-X : LC Card 86-1539 DDC 338.1/6/091717 19
HD1415 .W54 1986 ***NYPL [JLE 86-2447]***

AGRICULTURAL PRODUCTIVITY - COMMUNIST COUNTRIES - CASE STUDIES.
Wong, Lung-Fai. Agricultural productivity in the Socialist countries /. Boulder, Colo. , 1986. xvii, 195 p. : ISBN 0-8133-7152-X : LC Card 86-1539 DDC 338.1/6/091717 19
HD1415 .W54 1986 ***NYPL [JLE 86-2447]***

AGRICULTURAL PRODUCTIVITY - ETHIOPIA.
Alemneh Dejene. Peasants, agrarian socialism, and rural development in Ethiopia /. Boulder , 1987. xiii, 162 p. : ISBN 0-8133-7247-X (pbk. : alk. paper) LC Card 86-51527 DDC 338.1/0963 19
HD2124.5 .A79 1987

AGRICULTURAL PRODUCTIVITY - EUROPE - CASE STUDIES.
Agriculture in inter-system comparison . Berlin , 1985. 443 p. : ISBN 3-428-05885-2 (pbk.) LC Card 86-190956 DDC 338.1/6/094 19
HD1920.E852 A37 1985

AGRICULTURAL PRODUCTIVITY - EUROPE, EASTERN - CASE STUDIES.
Agriculture in inter-system comparison . Berlin , 1985. 443 p. : ISBN 3-428-05885-2 (pbk.) LC Card 86-190956 DDC 338.1/6/094 19
HD1920.E852 A37 1985

AGRICULTURAL PRODUCTIVITY - FRANCE.
Systèmes de production et transformations de l'agriculture /. Paris , 1985. 2 v. : ISBN 2-85340-715-2 (v. 1) LC Card 86-214407
HD1945 .S97 1985

AGRICULTURAL PRODUCTIVITY - GERMANY (WEST)
Heilig, Bernd. Die gesamtwirtschaftliche Bedeutung der Agrar- und Ernährungswirtschaft . Kiel , 1986. 171 p. : ISBN 3-922553-80-X LC Card 86-177526
HD1955 .H38 1986

AGRICULTURAL PRODUCTIVITY - GOVERNMENT POLICY - ASIA - CASE STUDIES.
The Poor in Asia . Kuala Lumpur, Malaysia , 1985- v. <1 > ; ISBN 967-99954-0-2 (v. 1) LC Card 86-944764 DDC 362.5/8/095 19
HC415.P6 P66 1985

AGRICULTURAL PRODUCTIVITY - HONDURAS - INTIBUCÁ (DEPT.)
Consejo Superior de Planificación Económica (Honduras). Secretaría Técnica. Proyecto de desarrollo local de La Paz, Intibucá /.

[Tegucigalpa, Honduras] [1984- v. <1 > : LC Card 86-213886
HC145.Z9 E443 1984

AGRICULTURAL PRODUCTIVITY - HONDURAS - LA PAZ (DEPT.)
Consejo Superior de Planificación Económica (Honduras). Secretaría Técnica. Proyecto de desarrollo local de La Paz, Intibucá /. [Tegucigalpa, Honduras] [1984- v. <1 > : LC Card 86-213886
HC145.Z9 E443 1984

AGRICULTURAL PRODUCTIVITY - HUNGARY.
Németi, László. Hatékonyság és fejlesztési lehetőségek a mai magyar mezőgazdaságban /. Budapest , 1986. 189 p. : ISBN 963-232-238-X : LC Card 87-407758
HD1940.5 .N46 1986

AGRICULTURAL PRODUCTIVITY - HUNGARY - HISTORY.
Szabó, László. Munkaszervezet és termelékenység a magyar parasztságnál a XIX-XX. században /. Szolnok , 1968 (Debrecen : Szabadság Lapnyomda) 167 p. : LC Card 86-188720
HD1536.H9 S89 1968

Agricultural productivity in the Socialist countries /. Wong, Lung-Fai. Boulder, Colo. , 1986. xvii, 195 p. : ISBN 0-8133-7152-X : LC Card 86-1539 DDC 338.1/6/091717 19
HD1415 .W54 1986 ***NYPL [JLE 86-2447]***

AGRICULTURAL PRODUCTIVITY - INDIA - KARNATAKA.
Dadibhavi, R. V. Income, productivity, and industrial structure /. Allahabad, India , 1986. xx, 295 p. ; ISBN 81-85076-02-2 : LC Card 86-902847 DDC 339.2/0954/87 19
HC437.K27 D33 1986

AGRICULTURAL PRODUCTIVITY - INDIA - PUNJAB.
Rachhpal Singh, 1944- Farm production in rainfed sub-mountainous Punjab /. Delhi , New Delhi , 1987. vi, 349 p. ; ISBN 81-7018-450-9 : LC Card 87-902161 DDC 338.1/0954/552 19
HD2075.P8 R33 1987

AGRICULTURAL PRODUCTIVITY - INDIA - VISHAKHAPATNAM DISTRICT.
Suryanarayana Raju, S. K. V. Analysis of productivity levels and economic efficiency in agriculture /. Allahabad, India , 1987 [i.e. 1986] viii, 368 p. : ISBN 81-85076-12-X : LC Card 86-903606 DDC 338.1/0954/84 19
HD2075.V58 S87 1986

AGRICULTURAL PRODUCTIVITY - ISLAMIC COUNTRIES - STATISTICS.
Quazi, Mohammed Hanif. Food insecurity in the Muslim world /. Jeddah, Saudi Arabia (P.O. Box 9833, Jeddah) , 1985. 21, [26] p. : LC Card 87-133798 DDC 338.1/9/17671 19
HD9018.I84 Q39 1985

AGRICULTURAL PRODUCTIVITY - LATVIA.
Vaikulis, J. (Jānis) Lauksaimniecības uzņēmumu saimnieciskās darbības analīze /. Riga , 1986. 185 p. ; LC Card 86-199301
HD1492.S652 L38 1986

AGRICULTURAL PRODUCTIVITY - MATHEMATICAL MODELS.
Inter-country comparisons of agricultural production aggregates /. Rome , 1986. v, 59 p. ; ISBN 92-5-102381-6 (pbk.) LC Card 86-222114 DDC 338.1 19
HD1425 .I59 1986

AGRICULTURAL PRODUCTIVITY - NEPAL.
Svejnar, Jan. Economic policies and agricultural performance . Paris , 1986. 167 p. ; LC Card 87-120115 DDC 338.1/85496 19
HD2065.9.Z8 S84 1986

AGRICULTURAL PRODUCTIVITY - NORTHERN IRELAND.
O'Fee, J. H. The input of labour on farms in Northern Ireland /. Belfast , 1986. i, 41 leaves ; LC Card 86-218985 DDC 331.11/8 19
HD1535.N675 O47 1986

AGRICULTURAL PRODUCTIVITY - PHILIPPINES.
Bautista, Romeo M., 1941- Production incentives in Philippine agriculture . Washington, D.C., USA , c1987. 78 p. : ISBN 0-89629-061-1 (pbk.) LC Card 87-3233 DDC 338.1/8 19
HD2087 .B38 1987

AGRICULTURAL PRODUCTIVITY - POLAND - REGIONAL DISPARITIES.
Dramowicz, Elżbieta. Przestrzenne zróżnicowanie państwowej gospodarki rolnej w Polsce /. Warszawa , 1986. 125 p. ; ISBN 83-01-05021-7 : LC Card 86-212594
HD1995.7 .D73 1986

Wiatrak, Andrzej Piotr. Przestrzenne zróżnicowanie gospodarki rolnej w Polsce /. Warszawa , 1986. 207 p. : ISBN 83-01-05118-3 : LC Card 86-212769
HD1995.7 .W45 1986

AGRICULTURAL PRODUCTIVITY - PORTUGAL - ECONOMETRIC MODELS.
Pereira, Mário. O método dos modelos e a análise económica da exploração agrícola /. Lisboa , 1962. 233 p. : LC Card 85-221042
HD2027 .M415 1962

AGRICULTURAL PRODUCTIVITY - PORTUGAL - STATISTICS.
Pereira, Mário. Alguns elementos para a caracterização da assimetria regional agrária portuguesa /. Oeiras [Portugal] , 1974. 59 p. : LC Card 85-133550
HD2027 .P388 1974

AGRICULTURAL PRODUCTIVITY - RUSSIAN S.F.S.R. - CHUVASHSKAÎA A. S.S.R.
Ėffektivnost′ proizvodstva v agropromyshlennom komplekse Chuvashskoĭ ASSR /. Cheboksary , 1985. 198 p. ; LC Card 86-203897
HD9015.S653 C483 1985

AGRICULTURAL PRODUCTIVITY - RUSSIAN S.F.S.R. - SAKHALINSKAÎA OBLAST′.
Potentsial ėffektivnosti /. ÎUzhno-Sakhalinsk , 1985. 67 p. ; LC Card 87-100690
HD8039.F32 S656 1985

AGRICULTURAL PRODUCTIVITY - SOUTH AFRICA - STATISTICS.
Sensus van landbou- en veeteelproduksie, 1979 =. Pretoria [1985?] xiv, 266 p. ; ISBN 0-621-09380-7 : LC Card 86-150362 DDC 338.1/0968/021 19
HD2130.5 .S48 1985

AGRICULTURAL PRODUCTIVITY - SOVIET UNION.
Ėkonomicheskie problemy novogo ėtapa osushchestvleniîa Leninskogo kooperativnogo plana /. Moskva , 1979. 365 p. ; LC Card 81-165451
HD1992 .E3593 1979

Karlîuk, I. ÎA. (Ippolit ÎAkovlevich) Agrarno-promyshlennyĭ kompleks /. Moskva , 1981. 93 p. : LC Card 82-148305
HD9015.S652 K37 1981

Larkin, V. A. (Vladimir Alekseevich) Sotsial′no-ėkonomicheskie problemy kompleksnoĭ mekhanizatsii sel′skokhozîaĭstvennogo proizvodstva /. Moskva , 1981. 148 p. ; LC Card 82-157096
HD1992 .L375 1981

Shirinskaîa, Z. G. (Zinaida Grigor′evna) Kredit i intensifikatsiîa sovkhoznogo proizvodstva /. Moskva , 1980. 142 p. ; LC Card 81-138434
HD1493.S65 S55 1980

Song, Du-Yul, 1944- Sowjetunion und China . Frankfurt/Main , New York , c1984. 255 p. : ISBN 3-593-33351-1 LC Card 84-169164
HC340.L3 S66 1984

Vozdeĭstvie khozîaĭstvennogo mekhanizma na povyshenie ėffektivnosti obshchestvennogo proizvodstva . Dnepropetrovsk , 1984. 119 p. ; LC Card 86-181397
HC340.I52 V68 1984

AGRICULTURAL PRODUCTIVITY - SOVIET UNION, NORTHWESTERN.
Ivanov, V. A. (Valentin Aleksandrovich) Ėkonomicheskoe stimulirovanie povysheniîa ėffektivnosti intensifikatsii sovkhoznogo proizvodstva /. Moskva , 1980. 248 p. ; LC Card 81-134017
HD1493.S652 N65 1980

AGRICULTURAL PRODUCTIVITY - SRI LANKA.
Capital and peasant production . Colombo, Sri Lanka , 1985. xiv, 230 p. ; LC Card 86-900809 DDC 338.1/3/095493 19
HD2065.8 .C36 1985 ***NYPL [JLE 87-1667]***

AGRICULTURAL PRODUCTIVITY - THAR DESERT (INDIA AND PAKISTAN)
Mann, H. S. (Haracharan Singh), 1922- Halting the march . [New Delhi] [1983] 35, [1] p., [4] p. of plates : LC Card 86-204352 DDC 338.1/0954/4 19
HC437.T47 M36 1983

AGRICULTURAL PRODUCTIVITY - UKRAINE.
Zakharchenko, A. G. (Alekseĭ Gavrilovich) Kollektivnyĭ podrîad v sel′skom khozîaĭstve /. Kiev , 1985. 107 p. : LC Card 86-222274
HD1492.S652 U389 1985

AGRICULTURAL PRODUCTIVITY - UNITED STATES.
A Review of U. S. competitiveness in agricultural trade. Washington, D.C. [1986] ix, 101 p. : LC Card 86-600586 DDC 382/.41/0973 19
HD1761 .R48 1986

AGRICULTURAL PRODUCTIVITY - VENEZUELA - CARACAS REGION - HISTORY - 19TH CENTURY.
Lucena Salmoral, Manuel. Vísperas de la independencia americana . Madrid , 1986. vii, 389 p. ; ISBN 84-205-1308-3 LC Card 86-205153
HF3490.C37 L83 1986

AGRICULTURAL PRODUCTIVITY - ZAMBIA - MPIKA DISTRICT.
Agricultural commercialisation and the allocation of labour time in Mpika District, northern Zambia. Mpika, Zambia [1986?] iii, 42 leaves : LC Card 86-981249 DDC 338.1/096894 19
HD2131.5.Z9 M653 1986

AGRICULTURAL PRODUCTS. see **PRODUCE TRADE.**

Agricultural review for Europe .
(no. 28, v. 1) General review /. New York , 1986. iii, 81 p. ; ISBN 92-1-116361-7 (pbk.) LC Card 87-120391 DDC 338.1/094 19
HD1917 .U5 no. 28, vol. 1

Agricultural sector assistance strategy for Upper Volta. Washington, D.C. : Development Alternatives, [1982] 1 v. (various pagings) : ill. ; 29 cm. "March 1982." Includes bibliographies. LC Card 87-120355 DDC 338.1/8 19
1. Agricultural assistance, American - Burkina Faso - Planning. 2. Agriculture - Economic aspects - Burkina Faso. 3. Agriculture - Burkina Faso. I. Development Alternatives, inc.
HD2144 .A38 1982

AGRICULTURAL STATISTICS. see **AGRICULTURE - STATISTICS.**

Agricultural statistics and prices for Louisiana, 1909-1985 /. Fielder, Lonnie L. [Baton Rouge, LA] [1986] iv, [122] p. : LC Card 87-620749 DDC 338.1/09763 s 338.1/09763/021 19
HD1775.L8 L7 no. 659

AGRICULTURAL SUBSIDIES - DEVELOPING COUNTRIES.
Repetto, Robert C. Paying the price . Washington, DC , c1985. 33 p. ; ISBN 0-915825-12-0 (pbk.) : LC Card 86-225070 DDC 338.4/366865/091724 19
HC59.72.E5 R46 1985

AGRICULTURAL SURPLUSES - CANADA.
Stanton, B. F. (Bernard Freeland), 1925- The cereals dilemma . Ithaca, N.Y. [1986] 50 p. : LC Card 86-622419 DDC 338.1/731/094 19
HD9045.A2 S7 1986

AGRICULTURAL SURPLUSES - EUROPE.
Stanton, B. F. (Bernard Freeland), 1925- The cereals dilemma . Ithaca, N.Y. [1986] 50 p. : LC Card 86-622419 DDC 338.1/731/094 19
HD9045.A2 S7 1986

AGRICULTURAL SURPLUSES - UNITED STATES.
Stanton, B. F. (Bernard Freeland), 1925- The cereals dilemma . Ithaca, N.Y. [1986] 50 p. : LC Card 86-622419 DDC 338.1/731/094 19
HD9045.A2 S7 1986

AGRICULTURAL SURVEYS - INDIA - MAHARASHTRA.
Dhongade, M. P. Farmers' attitude survey in the Mula Command Area, Maharashtra /. Rahuri, Maharashtra, India , 1986. vi, 69 p. ;

LC Card 86-903408 DDC 338.1/0954/792 19
HD8039.F32 I44 1986

AGRICULTURAL SYSTEMS - INDIA - RAJASTHAN - HISTORY.
Gupta, Satya Prakash, 1940- The agrarian system of eastern Rajasthan, c. 1650-c. 1750 /. Delhi , 1986. xvi, 352 p. : ISBN 81-85054-11-8 : LC Card 87-900814 DDC 338.1/0954/4 19
HD2075.R27 G86 1986

Agricultural taxation in India . Jha, Ganganand. Delhi , 1987. vi, 199 p. ; LC Card 87-900333 DDC 336.2/7863/095412 19
HD1443.I42 B534 1987

Agricultural taxation in J & K. Bhat, Mohd. Sultan (Mohammad Sultan) Agricultural taxation in Jammu & Kashmir /. New Delhi , 1987. vi, 192 p. ; LC Card 87-901173 DDC 336.2/7863/09546 19
HD1443.I42 J352 1987

Agricultural taxation in Jammu & Kashmir /. Bhat, Mohd. Sultan (Mohammad Sultan) New Delhi , 1987. vi, 192 p. ; LC Card 87-901173 DDC 336.2/7863/09546 19
HD1443.I42 J352 1987

Agricultural taxation in Punjab /. Arneja, Jasbir Singh. Jalandhar , 1987. xvi, 280 p. ; ISBN 81-7072-009-5 : LC Card 86-903405 DDC 336.2/7863/0954552 19
HD1443.I42 P863 1987

Agricultural trade and protection in Japan /. Hillman, Jimmye S., 1923- Aldershot, Hants, England , Brookfield, Vt. , 1988. p. cm. ISBN 0-566-05339-X : LC Card 87-15043 DDC 382.7/3/0952 19
HD9016.J42 H55 1988

Agricultural trade research and information needs : conditions and challenges : a report / prepared by the American Agricultural Economics Association, Trade Policy Task Force. [Ames, Iowa] : The Association, [1985] 32 p. : ill. ; 28 cm. (Occasional paper. no. 1) Series and date from label mounted on t.p. "November 1985." Bibliography: p. 31-32. LC Card 86-229053 DDC 380.1/41/072073 19
1. Agriculture - Economic aspects - United States - Research - United States. 2. Agriculture - Economic aspects - United States - Information services - United States. I. American Agricultural Economics Association. Trade Policy Task Force. II. Series: Occasional paper (American Agricultural Economics Association) , no. 1.
HD1410.6.U5 A39 1985

Agricultural trade with developing countries. Paris : Organisation for Economic Co-operation and Development ; [Washington, D.C. : OECD Publications and Information Center, distributor], 1984. 113 p. ; 23 cm. Bibliography: p. 111-113. ISBN 92-64-12579-5 (pbk.) LC Card 84-221780 DDC 382/.41/091724 19
1. Produce trade - Developing countries. 2. Produce trade - Government policy - Developing countries. 3. Produce trade - Government policy. I. Organization for Economic Cooperation and Development.
HD9018.D44 A37 1984
NYPL [JLE 86-3906]

Agricultural Training Board. Gasson, Ruth M. Labour sharing in agriculture /. [London] [1979] 117 p. ; ISBN 0-901859-82-6 (pbk.) LC Card 83-226074 DDC 331.25/72 19
HD5119.A292 G744 1979

AGRICULTURAL WAGES - FRANCE.
Nicourt, Christian. Conditions de travail en agriculture . Paris , <1985-. v. <2 > : ISBN 2-85340-585-0 (v. 2) LC Card 86-218948
HD1536.F8 N53 1985

AGRICULTURAL WAGES - FRANCE - STATISTICS.
Colliez, Jean-Paul. Les salariés agricoles permanents, leur rémunération en octobre 1982. Paris [1984] 62 p. : ISBN 2-11-083969-4 LC Card 85-108387
HD4966.A292 F73 1984

AGRICULTURAL WAGES - HUNGARY - STATISTICS.
Munkaerőhelyzet és kereseti viszonyok az állami gazdaságokban, kombinátokban és a mezőgazdasági termelőszövetkezetekben, 1980-1985 /. Budapest , 1987. 45 p. ; LC Card 87-419798
HD1536.H9 M85 1987

AGRICULTURAL WAGES - SOVIET UNION.
Sazonov, S. N. (Sergeĭ Nikolaevich) Oplata truda v sel′skom khoziaĭstve . Moskva , 1984. 268 p. ; LC Card 84-244595
HD4966.A292 S6574 1984

Vorontsov, A. P. (Alekseĭ Pavlovich) Proizvoditel′nost′ i oplata truda v APK /. Moskva , 1985. 191 p. ; LC Card 86-130051
HD9015.S652 V67 1985

AGRICULTURAL WAGES - SPAIN.
González Rodríguez, Juan Jesús. La patronal agraria . Madrid [1986?] 46 p. ; ISBN 84-7075-335-3 LC Card 87-111477
HD6976.A292 S74 1986

AGRICULTURAL WARRANTS. see **AGRICULTURAL CREDIT.**

AGRICULTURAL WATER-SUPPLY. see **WATER-SUPPLY, AGRICULTURAL.**

AGRICULTURALISTS - POLAND - BIOGRAPHY.
Z Husowa po berła rektorskie . Warszawa , 1986. 340 p., [25] p. of plates : ISBN 83-205-3745-2 : LC Card 85-126839
HB114.S79 Z2 1986

AGRICULTURE - ACCOUNTING.
Devino, Gary T. Agribusiness finance /. Danville, Ill. , c1981. xii, 166 p. : ISBN 0-8134-2191-8 (pbk.) LC Card 81-80386 DDC 658.1/5 19
HD1437 .D48 *NYPL [JLE 86-4573]*

Agriculture administration in India / edited by Hoshiar Singh. Jaipur : Printwell Publishers : Exclusive distributors, Rupa Books International, 1986. xviii, 286 p. ; 23 cm. Contributed papers, with special reference to Rajasthan. Includes bibliographies and index. ISBN 81-7044-038-6 : LC Card 86-903175 DDC 338.1/854 19
1. Agricultural administration - India - Congresses. 2. Agricultural administration - India - Rajasthan - Congresses. I. Singh, Hoshiar, 1943-.
HD2072 .A6546 1986

AGRICULTURE - AFRICA.
Harrison, Paul. The greening of Africa . New York, N.Y., U. S.A. , 1987. 380 p. : ISBN 0-14-010192-6 (pbk.) : LC Card 87-404277 DDC 338.1/9/6 19
HD2117 .H37 1987

AGRICULTURE - AFRICA - FINANCE - CONGRESSES.
Agricultural credit and the mobilization of resources in rural areas. [Addis Ababa?] , 1986. 45 p. ; LC Card 86-981195 DDC 332.7/1/096 19
HG2051.A3 A73 1986

AGRICULTURE - AFRICA, SUB-SAHARAN.
United States. Congress. House. Committee on Science and Technology. Prospects for sustainable development in Sub-Saharan Africa . Washington , 1986. vii, 88 p. ; LC Card 86-603140 DDC 338.967 19
HD2117 .U48 1986

AGRICULTURE AND COMMUNISM.
Socialist agriculture in transition . Boulder, Colo. , 1986. ix, 445 p. : ISBN 0-8133-7344-1 : LC Card 86-28995 DDC 338.1/0947 19
HD1917 .S62 1986

Agriculture and economic development in Nigeria . Folayan, Adekunle. New York , c1983. x, 276 p. : ISBN 0-533-05325-0 : LC Card 81-90817 DDC 338.1/09669 19
HD2145.5 .F64 1983 *NYPL [JLE 86-1080]*

Agriculture and equitable growth . Westley, John Richard, 1942- Boulder , 1986. xv, 369 p. : ISBN 0-8133-7155-4 (alk. paper) : LC Card 85-31586 DDC 338.1/85455 19
HD2075.P8 W47 1986 *NYPL [JLE 86-1877]*

Agriculture and incentives, the Tanzanian case . Orback, Jens. Uppsala , 1985. 37, [2] leaves, [1] leaf of plates : LC Card 86-215091 DDC 338.1/8 19
HD2128.5 .O73 1985

Agriculture & regional development in Iran /. Nattagh, Nima. Wisbech, Cambridgeshire, England , 1986. 105 p. : ISBN 0-906559-26-X (pbk.) : LC Card 86-230845 DDC 338.1/0955 19
HD1565.2 .N37 1986

Agriculture and regional development in Iran. Nattagh, Nima. Agriculture & regional development in Iran /. Wisbech, Cambridgeshire, England , 1986. 105 p. : ISBN 0-906559-26-X (pbk.) : LC Card 86-230845 DDC 338.1/0955 19
HD1565.2 .N37 1986

AGRICULTURE AND STATE - ADDRESSES, ESSAYS, LECTURES.
Crop insurance for agricultural development . Baltimore , c1986. xviii, 322 p. ISBN 0-8018-2673-X (alk. paper) LC Card 85-9810 DDC 368.1/22 19
HG9968 .C76 1985 *NYPL [JLE 86-1082]*

George, Susan. Ill fares the land . Washington, D.C. , c1984. xviii, 102 p. ; ISBN 0-89758-039-7 (pbk.) : LC Card 84-25124 DDC 363.8 19
HD9000.5 .G385 1984
NYPL [JLD 86-3899]

AGRICULTURE AND STATE - AFRICA.
Bates, Robert H. Essays on the political economy of rural Africa /. Berkeley , 1987, c1983. p. cm. ISBN 0-520-06014-8 (pbk. : alk. paper) LC Card 86-25120 DDC 330.96/0328/091734 19
HD2117 .B37 1987

Gosudarstvo i agrarnaia ėvoliutsiia v razvivaiushchikhsia stranakh Azii i Afriki /. Moskva , 1980. 227 p. ; LC Card 81-143353
HD2056 .G67 1980

Harrison, Paul. The greening of Africa . New York, N.Y., U. S.A. , 1987. 380 p. : ISBN 0-14-010192-6 (pbk.) : LC Card 87-404277 DDC 338.1/9/6 19
HD2117 .H37 1987

Walker, Brian W. Authentic development in Africa /. New York, N.Y. , c1985. 70 p. : ISBN 0-87124-102-1 (pbk.) : LC Card 85-82567 DDC 081 s 338.96 19
E744 .H43 no. 274 HC800
NYPL [JLD 86-3400]

AGRICULTURE AND STATE - AFRICA, EASTERN - CONGRESSES.
Proceedings of the workshop on the "Interrelationship between agricultural settlement, agricultural development, and population change" in selected Eastern Africa Countries, Ethiopia, Kenya, Sudan, and Tanzania, held at the Population Studies and Research Institute, University of Nairobi, April 13-16, 1981. Nairobi [1981] 304 p. : LC Card 85-980248 DDC 338.1/09676 19
HD982.Z63 P76 1981

AGRICULTURE AND STATE - AFRICA, SUB-SAHARAN - CONGRESSES.
Accelerating food production in Sub-Saharan Africa /. Baltimore , c1987. xix, 417 p. ; ISBN 0-8018-3390-6 (alk. paper) LC Card 86-10684 DDC 338.1/9/67 19
HD2117 .A33 1987 *NYPL [JLE 87-1366]*

AGRICULTURE AND STATE - AMAZON RIVER REGION.
Brazil. Comissão Executiva do Plano da Lavoura Cacaueira. Departamento Especial da Amazônia. Desempenho programático do DEPEA em 1984 . Belém/Pará [Brazil] , 1985. 76 p. : LC Card 87-404555 DDC 338.981/1 19
HD1875.A347 B68 1985

AGRICULTURE AND STATE - ASIA.
Gosudarstvo i agrarnaia ėvoliutsiia v razvivaiushchikhsia stranakh Azii i Afriki /. Moskva , 1980. 227 p. ; LC Card 81-143353
HD2056 .G67 1980

James, William E. Asian agriculture in transition . Manila, Philippines , c1983. v, 93 p. ; LC Card 87-105114 DDC 338.1/095 19
HD2056 .J355 1983

AGRICULTURE AND STATE - AUSTRALIA.
Hefford, Ron. Farm policy in Australia /. St. Lucia [Brisbane] , New York , c1985. xviii, 415 p. : ISBN 0-7022-1698-4 LC Card 83-23457 DDC 338.1/894 19
HD2153 .H43 1984 *NYPL [JLD 87-867]*

AGRICULTURE AND STATE - AUSTRALIA - ECONOMETRIC MODELS.
Higgs, Peter J. (Peter John), 1959- Adaptation and survival in Australian agriculture . Melbourne , New York , 1986. xxx, 320 p. : ISBN 0-19-554749-7 LC Card 87-133685 DDC 338.1/0994 19
HD2152 .H54 1986

AGRICULTURE AND STATE - AUSTRIA.
Arbeitsmarktpolitik für die Landwirtschaft und den ländlichen Raum /. Graz , c1984. 138 p. : ISBN 3-900307-15-6 LC Card 85-186643
HD1536.A9 A73 1984

AGRICULTURE AND STATE - BRAZIL.
Amaro, Antonio Ambrosio. Questão agrária e agroindústria /. Brasília, DF [1986] 13 p. ; LC Card 87-403237 DDC 338.1/881 19
HD1873 .A49 1986

Brazil. Comissão Executiva do Plano da Lavoura Cacaueira. Departamento Especial da Amazônia. Desempenho programático do DEPEA em 1984 . Belém/Pará [Brazil] , 1985. 76 p. : LC Card 87-404555 DDC 338.981/1 19
HD1875.A347 B68 1985

Cidadão, estado e políticas no Brasil contemporâneo /. Brasília-Distrito Federal , c1986. 290 p. : ISBN 85-23-00214-6 LC Card 87-405054 DDC 338.981 19
HD1873 .C53 1986

Homem de Melo, Fernando Bento, 1942- Prioridade agrícola . São Paulo , 1985. xiii, 200 p. : LC Card 86-126447 DDC 338.1/881 19
HD1872 .H66 1985 ***NYPL [JLD 86-3809]***

Lima Sobrinho, Antonio Estevam de. Fome, agricultura e política no Brasil . Petrópolis , 1981. 120 p. ; LC Card 81-185801 DDC 338.1/0981 19
HD9014.B82 L56 1981
NYPL [JLD 86-3297]

Manoel, Alvaro. Política agrícola, eficiência e concentração na agricultura brasileira . São Paulo , 1986. 180 p. : LC Card 86-234338
HD1873 .M35 1986

AGRICULTURE AND STATE - BRAZIL - ECONOMETRIC MODELS.
Santos, José Carlos de Souza. Demanda de fatores e ofertas na agricultura brasileira . Rio de Janeiro , 1983. 110 p. ; LC Card 87-403023 DDC 338.1/0981 19
HD1872 .S25 1983

AGRICULTURE AND STATE - BRAZIL - HISTORY.
Mueller, Charles Curt. Das oligarquias agrárias ao predomínio urbano-industrial . Rio de Janeiro , 1983. 363 p. ; LC Card 87-403875 DDC 305.5/232/0981 19
HC187 .M76 1983

AGRICULTURE AND STATE - BRAZIL - MANAUS REGION.
Brazil. Superintendência da Zona Franca de Manaus. Plano Diretor do Distrito Agropecuário /. Manaus , 1984. 86 p. : LC Card 85-209805
HD1875.M325 B73 1984

AGRICULTURE AND STATE - BRAZIL, NORTHEAST.
Avaliação do polonordeste e do Projeto Sertanejo. Fortaleza , 1985. 314 p. : LC Card 87-402900 DDC 338.981/3 19
HC188.N6 A94 1985

Projeto sertanejo . [Brasília] [1982?] 20 leaves, [1] leaf of plates : LC Card 87-405007
HD1875.N6 P76 1982

AGRICULTURE AND STATE - BRAZIL - PERNAMBUCO.
Andrade, Manuel Correia de Oliveira. Classes sociais e agricultura no Nordeste /. Recife , 1985. 105 p. ; ISBN 85-7019-096-4 LC Card 87-119335
HD1875.P4 A84 1985

AGRICULTURE AND STATE - BRAZIL - PIAUÍ.
Projeto sertanejo . [Brasília] [1982?] 20 leaves, [1] leaf of plates : LC Card 87-405007
HD1875.N6 P76 1982

AGRICULTURE AND STATE - BRAZIL - RONDÔNIA (STATE)
Gonçalves, Sérgio Ricardo Vieira, 1940- Rondônia--política, agrária e transformação . Porto Velho , 1982. 40 p. : LC Card 87-401465 DDC 338.981/75 19
HC188.R6 G66 1982

AGRICULTURE AND STATE - BRAZIL - SÃO PAULO (STATE)
Política agrária /. Porto Alegre-RS , 1985. 79 p. : LC Card 86-198513
HD1531.B7 P65 1985

AGRICULTURE AND STATE - BURKINA FASO.
Lecaillon, Jacques. Economic policies and agricultural performance . Paris , 1985. 158 p. ; LC Card 86-216027 DDC 338.1/86625 19
HD2144 .L42 1985

AGRICULTURE AND STATE - CHILE.
Mannarelli M., Virgilio B. Organización institucional del sector agrícola /. Santiago, Chile , 1985. 81, [3] p. : LC Card 86-115545 DDC 338.1/883 19
HD1878 .M35 1985

AGRICULTURE AND STATE - CHINA.
On rolls the green revolution /. Beijing, China [1984] 142 p., [36] p. of plates : LC Card 86-115054 DDC 338.1/0951 19
HD2097 .O5 1984 ***NYPL [JLK 83-122 no.9]***

Weitz, Maria. Entwicklungen in der chinesischen Agrarpolitik seit 1978 /. Berlin , 1986. 110 p. ; ISBN 3-428-06036-9 LC Card 87-409465 DDC 338.1/851 19
HD2097 .W45 1986

AGRICULTURE AND STATE - CHINA - HUNAN PROVINCE - HISTORY.
Perdue, Peter C., 1949- Exhausting the earth . Cambridge, Mass. , 1987. xvii, 331 p. : ISBN 0-674-27504-7 LC Card 87-5067 DDC 338.1/0951/215 19
HD2100.H86 P47 1987

AGRICULTURE AND STATE - COLOMBIA.
Poveda Ramos, Gabriel. Nueva alternativa para el desarrollo . Bogotá , 1974. 249 p. : LC Card 78-345029
HD1883 1974 .P68 ***NYPL [JLE 80-482]***

Problemas agrarios colombianos /. [Bogotá, Colombia] , México, D.F. , 1986. 467 p. : ISBN 958-606-005-5 LC Card 86-221632
HD1882 .P75 1986

Rivera Cusicanqui, Silvia. Política e ideología en el movimiento campesino colombiano . [Bogotá] [s.l.] , 1982. 188 p. ; LC Card 84-155496
HD511.5.A87 R58 1982
NYPL [JLD 86-1208]

Robles Bohórquez, Isabel. La agricultura colombiana en la encrucijada . Bogotá, Colombia [1982] 165 p. ; LC Card 83-103208
HD1883 1982 .R62

AGRICULTURE AND STATE - COLOMBIA - ADDRESSES, ESSAYS, LECTURES.
Thomas, Vinod, 1949- Linking macroeconomic and agricultural policies for adjustment with growth . Baltimore , c1985. xv, 252 p. ; ISBN 0-8018-3121-0 : LC Card 85-45105 DDC 338.9861 19
HC197 .T38 1985 ***NYPL [JLE 86-1438]***

AGRICULTURE AND STATE - COMMUNIST COUNTRIES.
Agrarnaia politika sotsialisticheskikh stran na sovremennom ėtape /. Moskva , 1981. 366 p. ; LC Card 82-109367
HD1918 .A37 1981

Socialist agriculture in transition . Boulder, Colo. , 1986. ix, 445 p. : ISBN 0-8133-7344-1 : LC Card 86-28995 DDC 338.1/0947 19
HD1917 .S62 1986

AGRICULTURE AND STATE - CONGRESSES.
United Nations University Symposium on Energy and Agriculture Futures--Policy Implications of Global Models (1982 : Paris, France) Energy and agriculture . [Chur, Switzerland , New York] , c1984. xii, 370 p. : ISBN 3-7186-0187-7 LC Card 83-18363 DDC 333.79 19
HD1405 .E53 1983 ***NYPL [JLD 86-1837]***

AGRICULTURE AND STATE - COSTA RICA.
Guadamuz López, Ernesto. La política agraria actual . San José, Costa Rica , 1986. 33 p. ; LC Card 87-402782 DDC 338.1/87286 19
HD1803 .G83 1986

AGRICULTURE AND STATE - CUBA.
Cuba's socialist economy toward the 1990s /. Boulder, Colo. , 1987. ix, 188 p. : ISBN 1-555-87080-5 (lib. bdg. : alk. paper) : LC Card 87-12867 DDC 338.97291 19
HC152.5 .C824 1987

AGRICULTURE AND STATE - CZECHOSLOVAKIA.
Kutil, Jaroslav. Czechoslovak agriculture /. Prague , 1983. 125 p., [48] p. of plates : LC Card 84-109068 DDC 338.1/09437 19
HD1940.3.Z8 K87 1983
NYPL [JLD 86-2294]

AGRICULTURE AND STATE - CZECHOSLOVAKIA - SLOVAK SOCIALIST REPUBLIC.
Bauch, Vlastislav. Sociálno-ekonomický vývoj slovenského pol'nohospodárskeho obyvatel'stva /. Bratislava , 1986. 362, [5] p. ; LC Card 87-125324
HD1940.3.Z9 S573 1986

AGRICULTURE AND STATE - DEVELOPING COUNTRIES.
Cairncross, John. Population and agriculture in the developing countries /. Rome , 1980. ii, 52 p. ; ISBN 92-5-100885-X (pbk.) LC Card 81-198370 DDC 338.1/09172/4 19
HD1417 .C34 1980 ***NYPL [JLF 86-1573]***

Food policy . Baltimore , c1987. xiv, 567 p. : ISBN 0-8018-3500-3 (pbk.) : LC Card 86-27613 DDC 363.8/56/091724 19
HD9018.D44 F665 1987

Food, the state, and international political economy . Lincoln , c1986. xxiii, 351 p. : ISBN 0-8032-4413-4 (alk. paper) LC Card 85-30893 DDC 338.1/9/1724 19
HD9018.D44 F67 1986
NYPL [JLD 86-3440]

Lenoir, René. Le Tiers Monde peut se nourrir . [Paris] , c1984. 210 p. : ISBN 2-213-01385-3 : LC Card 84-188021 DDC 338.1/8/091724 19
HD1417 .L46 1984 ***NYPL [JLD 85-1065]***

Repetto, Robert C. Paying the price . Washington, DC , c1985. 33 p. ; ISBN 0-915825-12-0 (pbk.) : LC Card 86-225070 DDC 338.4/366865/091724 19
HC59.72.E5 R46 1985

AGRICULTURE AND STATE - DEVELOPING COUNTRIES - CONGRESSES.
U. S. agriculture and Third World economic development . Washington, D.C. , c1987. xv, 103 p. : ISBN 0-89068-086-8 (pbk.): LC Card 86-62757 DDC 338.9/009172/4 19
HD1755 .U173 1987

AGRICULTURE AND STATE - DOMINICAN REPUBLIC.
Tejada C., Frank A. Crédito y seguro agrícola . Santo Domingo, República Dominicana , 1986. 104 p. : LC Card 87-400183 DDC 332.7/1/097293 19
HG2051.D6 T45 1986

AGRICULTURE AND STATE - ECUADOR.
Cosse, Gustavo. Estado y agro en el Ecuador, 1960-1980 /. Quito , 1984. 112 p. : LC Card 85-119842 DDC 338.1/8866 19
HD1888 .C67 1984 ***NYPL [JLD 86-2738]***

Tenencia de la tierra y desarrollo socio-económico del sector agrícola. [Guayaquil] [1981] xxv, 539 p., [16] leaves of plates : LC Card 87-673171
HD526 .T46x 1981

AGRICULTURE AND STATE - EGYPT.
Commander, Simon. The state and agricultural development in Egypt since 1973 /. London , Atlantic Highlands, NJ , 1988. p. cm. ISBN 0-86372-080-3 LC Card 87-3616 DDC 338.1/862 19
HD2123.Z8 C66 1988

AGRICULTURE AND STATE - EGYPT - HISTORY.
Stuchevskiĭ, I. A. (Iosif Aleksandrovich) Zemledel'tsy gosudarstvennogo khoziaĭstva drevnego Egipta ėpokhi Ramessidov /. Moskva , 1982. 254, [2] p. ; LC Card 82-186646
HD2123 .S78 1982

AGRICULTURE AND STATE - ENVIRONMENTAL ASPECTS - MOLDAVIAN S.S.R.
Todyka, IUriĭ Nikolaevich. Gosudarstvennyĭ apparat i problemy okhrany prirody v usloviiakh APK /. Kishinev , 1986. 179, [5] p. ; LC Card 86-141430
HD1995.M5 T63 1986

AGRICULTURE AND STATE - ETHIOPIA.
Alemneh Dejene. Peasants, agrarian socialism, and rural development in Ethiopia /. Boulder , 1987. xiii, 162 p. : ISBN 0-8133-7247-X (pbk. : alk. paper) LC Card 86-51527 DDC 338.1/0963 19
HD2124.5 .A79 1987

Clay, Jason W. Politics and the Ethiopian famine, 1984-1985 /. Cambridge, MA (11 Divinity Ave., Cambridge 02138) , 1985. xi, 250 p. : LC Card 86-153948 DDC 363.8/56/0963 19
HC845.Z9 F33 1985 ***NYPL [JLF 87-364]***

Harjinder Singh. Agricultural problems in Ethiopia /. Delhi, India , c1987. viii, 254 p. : ISBN 81-212-0078-4 : LC Card 87-900338 DDC 338.1/0963 19
HD2124.5 .H37 1987

AGRICULTURE AND STATE - EUROPE, EASTERN.

Agrarnaia͡ politika sotsialisticheskikh stran na sovremennom ėtape /. Moskva , 1981. 366 p. ; LC Card 82-109367
HD1918 .A37 1981

Deutsch, Robert. The food revolution in the Soviet Union and Eastern Europe /. Boulder , 1986. xxii, 256 p. : ISBN 0-8133-7161-9 (pbk.) : LC Card 85-26625 DDC 338.1/9/47 19
HD9015.S652 D47 1986 ***NYPL [JLE 86-1588]***

AGRICULTURE AND STATE - EUROPE, SOUTHERN - CONGRESSES.

Prospective evolution of EEC common agricultural policy . Lisboa , Oeiras , 1985. 122 p. : LC Card 86-221785
HD1920.5.Z8 P77 1985

AGRICULTURE AND STATE - EUROPEAN ECONOMIC COMMUNITY COUNTRIES.

Agricultural policies in the European Community . Canberra , 1985. xii, 373 p. : ISBN 0-644-04293-1 (pbk.) LC Card 86-673733
HD1920.5.Z8 A37x 1985

Ahn, Lothar. Ökonomische und ökologische Perspektiven der Agrarpolitik . Köln , 1983. 98 p. : ISBN 3-7609-5124-4 LC Card 83-155478
HD1920.5 .A627 1983

Can the CAP be reformed? /. Maastricht, The Netherlands , c1985. xii, 127 p. ; ISBN 90-6779-013-3 (pbk.) LC Card 86-214732 DDC 338.1/84 19
HD1920.5 .C36 1985

Carfantan, Jean Yves. L'Europe verte sous influence . Paris , c1985. 282 p. ; ISBN 2-02-008982-3 : LC Card 86-140900 DDC 338.1/094 19
HD1920.5 .C37 1985 ***NYPL [JLE 87-526]***

Ertl, Josef, 1925- Agrarpolitik ohne Illusionen . Frankfurt am Main , c1985. 208 p. : ISBN 3-87795-022-1 LC Card 86-119627 DDC 338.1/84 19
HD1920.5.Z8 E78 1985

Fernández Alvarez, Antonio. El impacto de la política agrícola común en la integración española /. Madrid [1986?] 48 p. ; ISBN 84-7075-333-9 LC Card 87-111468
HC241.25.S6 F47 1986

Japanese import barriers to U. S. agricultural exports and the Common agricultural policy of the European Community and implications for U. S. agricultural trade . Washington , 1986. vii, 65 p. : LC Card 87-601384 DDC 382/.5/0952 19
HF1601 .J363 1986

Kirschke, Dieter, 1952- Agrarmarktpolitik bei Unsicherheit . Berlin , c1987. 225 p. : ISBN 3-428-06111-X LC Card 87-131255 DDC 338.1/8 19
HD1920.5 .K57 1987

La Politica agraria della CEE /. Torino [1986] 330 p. : LC Card 86-212028
HD1920.5.Z8 P625 1986

Politique agricole commune . Bruxelles, Belgique , c1982. 126 p. ; ISBN 1-8004-0773-5 LC Card 87-672469
HD1803 .P64x 1982

Priebe, Hermann, 1907- Agrarpolitik in der EG . Baden-Baden , 1984. 269 p. ; ISBN 3-7890-1060-X LC Card 85-138555 DDC 338.1/84 19
HD1920.5.Z8 P74 1984

Reig Martínez, Ernest. La política agraria de la Comunidad Económica Europea . [Valencia] [1986?] 129 p. ; ISBN 84-00-06370-8 LC Card 87-125600
HD1920.5.Z8 R45 1986

AGRICULTURE AND STATE - EUROPEAN ECONOMIC COMMUNITY COUNTRIES - CONGRESSES.

The Common agricultural policy and the Third World . London , 1986. 97 p. : ISBN 0-946848-79-3 (pbk.) : LC Card 87-150069 DDC 338.1/81/094 19
HD9015.E82 C665 1986

Confrontation or negotiation . Millwood, N.Y. , 1985. xvi, 303 p. : ISBN 0-8046-9397-8 : LC Card 85-18667 DDC 382/.41/094 19
HD9015.E82 C67 1985 ***NYPL [JLE 86-4594]***

Europäische Agrarpolitik . Göttingen , 1985. 82 p. ; LC Card 86-170925
HD1920.5.Z8 E97 1985

Prospective evolution of EEC common agricultural policy . Lisboa , Oeiras , 1985. 122 p. : LC Card 86-221785
HD1920.5.Z8 P77 1985

AGRICULTURE AND STATE - FRANCE.

Muller, Pierre. Le technocrate et le paysan . Paris , c1984. 173 p. ; ISBN 2-7082-2347-X : LC Card 84-171796 DDC 338.1/6 19
HD1947 .M85 1984 ***NYPL [JLD 86-3738]***

AGRICULTURE AND STATE - FRANCE - STATISTICS.

Savignac, Philippe. Concours publics à l'agriculture par régions ou catégories d'exploitations en 1981. Paris [1984] 81 p. : ISBN 2-11-083993-7 LC Card 85-168478
HD1947 .S29 1984

AGRICULTURE AND STATE - GAMBIA.

Gambia. Preparation report, rural development programme, 1980-85 /. Banjul [1979- v. <1 > : LC Card 86-203596
HD2147 .G35 1980a

AGRICULTURE AND STATE - GERMANY, EAST.

Rudolph, Jürgen. Aktuelle Fragen der Theorie und Praxis der staatlichen Leitung der Landwirtschaft /. Potsdam-Babelsberg , 1983. 72 p. ; LC Card 83-214391
HD1960.5.Z8 R83 1983

AGRICULTURE AND STATE - GERMANY - HISTORY.

Abraham, David, 1946- The collapse of the Weimar Republic . New York , 1986. liii, 352 p. ; ISBN 0-8419-1083-9 LC Card 86-27033 DDC 338.0943 19
HD3616.G35 A27 1986

Sondermann, Klaus. Wirtschaftsentwicklung und landwirtschaftliche Verbandspolitik . Münster-Hiltrup , 1983. vi, 300 p. : ISBN 3-7843-0283-1 : LC Card 84-126226
HD1486.G3 S66 1983

AGRICULTURE AND STATE - GERMANY - HISTORY - ADDRESSES, ESSAYS, LECTURES.

Peasants and lords in modern Germany . Boston , 1986. 267 p. ; ISBN 0-04-943037-8 (alk. paper) LC Card 85-6113 DDC 305.5/63 19
HD655 .P34 1986 ***NYPL [JLE 86-1702]***

AGRICULTURE AND STATE - GERMANY, WEST.

Agrarmärkte & Agrarmarketing . Hamburg , 1983. 220 p. : ISBN 3-922528-45-7 LC Card 84-162297
HD1955 .A515 1983

Ambros, Werner. Verbraucherinteressen und Agrarpolitik /. Krefeld , 1986. x, 260 p. : ISBN 3-88358-068-6 LC Card 87-122729 DDC 338.1/843 19
HD1957 .A63 1986

Brandt, Hartmut. Projektplanung in der kleinbäuerlichen Produktion /. Berlin , 1982. xv, 208 p. : LC Card 83-193407
HD1476.G3 B73 1982 ***NYPL [JLE 87-2903]***

Germany (West). Bundesministerium für Ernährung, Landwirtschaft und Forsten. Wissenschaftlicher Beirat. Gutachten des Wissenschaftlichen Beirats beim Bundesministerium für Ernährung, Landwirtschaft und Forsten /. Hiltrup bei Münster (Westf.) [1960?] 98 p. ; LC Card 86-185959
HD1957 .G47 1960

Grünen (Political party) Grüne Agrarpolitik, Bilanz und Perspektiven . Bonn [1985?] 62 p. : LC Card 86-152151
HD1957 .G79 1985

AGRICULTURE AND STATE - GHANA.

Konings, Piet. The state and rural class formation in Ghana . London ; Boston : xvi, 391 p. : ISBN 0-7103-0117-0 LC Card 85-28109 DDC 305.5/09667 19
HN832.Z9 S65 1986 ***NYPL [Sc D 86-574]***

AGRICULTURE AND STATE - GREAT BRITAIN.

Penning-Rowsell, Edmund. Floods and drainage . London , Boston , 1986. xx, 199 p. : ISBN 0-04-627001-9 (alk. paper) : LC Card 85-13383 DDC 363.3/4936/0941 19
HD1676.G7 P46 1985 ***NYPL [JLE 86-3996]***

AGRICULTURE AND STATE - GREECE.

Dēlēs, Dēmētrēs I. Hē anaptyxē tēs hellēnikēs geōrgias . Athēna , 1985. 3 v. in 2 : LC Card 86-203175
HD2055.5 .D44 1985

AGRICULTURE AND STATE - GUINEA.

Guinea. Comité militaire de redressement national. Premières mesures de mise en application du programme du CMRN. [Conakry, R.G. , 1984] 84 p. ; LC Card 85-143345
HD2143.Z8 G85 1984

AGRICULTURE AND STATE - GUYANA.

Parris, W. H. For survival, development, and prosperity . Georgetown, Guyana [1985] 28 p. : LC Card 87-400751 DDC 338.1/8881 19
HD1895.3.Z8 P37 1985

AGRICULTURE AND STATE - HUNGARY.

Az Élelmiszer-gazdaság távlati fejlesztése /. Budapest , 1984. 163 p. ; ISBN 963-231-717-3 : LC Card 85-194280
HD1940.5.Z8 E54 1984

Javaslatok az élelmiszer-gazdaság fejlesztésére . Budapest , 1984. 279 p. : ISBN 963-221-500-1 LC Card 85-229874
HD9015.H82 J38 1984

AGRICULTURE AND STATE - HUNGARY - HISTORY.

Simon, Péter, 1926- A magyar parasztság sorsfordulója, 1946-1949 /. [Budapest] , 1984. 212 p. : ISBN 963-09-2475-7 :
HD1333.H9 S57 1984 ***NYPL [JLD 86-3163]***

Steinbach, Antal. A Magyar Dolgozók Pártja Központi Vezetősége 1953. júniusi határozatának agrárpolitikai előzményei /. [Budapest] , 1985. 104 p. ; ISBN 963-673-321-X LC Card 86-187055
HD1940.5.Z8 S74 1985

AGRICULTURE AND STATE - HUNGARY - HISTORY - CONGRESSES.

Agrárgazdaság, agrártársadalom, agrárpolitika /. Szeged , 1985. 338 p. : ISBN 963-481-548-0 : LC Card 86-143859
HD1940.5 .A78 1985

AGRICULTURE AND STATE - HUNGARY - MATHEMATICAL MODELS.

Kovács, Kálmán. Tervezési szintek érdekeltségének összehangolása gazdaságszabályozási eszközökkel . Budapest , 1984. 50 p. : ISBN 963-491-189-7 LC Card 86-198789
HD1940.5.Z8 K68 1984

AGRICULTURE AND STATE - INDIA.

Agrarian struggles in India after independence /. Delhi , 1986. xxvi, 666 p. :
NYPL [JLD 86-3896]

Govil, Rishi Kumar, 1933- Agriculture planning and social justice in India /. Allahabad , 1986. vii, 214 p. ; LC Card 86-902616 DDC 338.1/854 19
HD2073 .G68 1986

Growth of agriculture and rural development in India /. New Delhi , c1987. xx, 496 p. ; LC Card 87-900250 DDC 338.1/0954 19
HD2072 .G7 1987

Haque, T. (Tajamul), 1947- Agrarian reforms and institutional changes in India /. New Delhi , 1986, c1985. xvi, 268 p. : LC Card 86-902575 DDC 338.1/854 19
HD1333.I4 H36 1986 ***NYPL [JLD 87-1547]***

Mahajan, V. S., 1923- Growth of agriculture and industry in India /. New Delhi , c1983. 176 p. ; LC Card 83-906175 DDC 338.0954 19
HD2072 .M23 1983 ***NYPL [JLD 87-671]***

Seshadri, K. Rural unrest in India /. New Delhi , 1983. xiii, 192 p. ; LC Card 83-905323

DDC 303.6/23/0954 19
HC440.P6 S47 1983 **NYPL [JLD 86-3704]**

Tiwary, Jai Kant. Rural development administration . Allahabad, India , 1984. xi, 248 p. ; LC Card 84-900188 DDC 307.7/2/0954 19
HN690.Z9 C68286 1984
NYPL [JLD 86-4313]

AGRICULTURE AND STATE - INDIA - ADDRESSES, ESSAYS, LECTURES.
Franda, Marcus F. Voluntary associations and local development in India . New Delhi , 1983. vi, 356 p. ; LC Card 83-900993 DDC 307/.14/0954 19
HN690.Z9 C6513 1983
NYPL [JLD 86-3866]

AGRICULTURE AND STATE - INDIA - GORAKHPUR (DISTRICT)
Pai Panandiker, V. A., 1935- Development bureaucracy /. New Delhi , c1983. ix, 252 p. ; LC Card 83-902420 DDC 352.94/233/09542 19
HD2075.K359 P34 1983
NYPL [JLD 86-3762]

AGRICULTURE AND STATE - INDIA - HARYANA.
Gupta, D. P. (Dharm Pall), 1932- Agricultural development in Haryana /. New Delhi, India , 1985. xiii, 120 p. : LC Card 85-901427 DDC 338.1/854558 19
HD2075.H3 G85 1985
NYPL [JLD 86-3862]

Westley, John Richard, 1942- Agriculture and equitable growth . Boulder , 1986. xv, 369 p. : ISBN 0-8133-7155-4 (alk. paper) : LC Card 85-31586 DDC 338.1/85455 19
HD2075.P8 W47 1986 **NYPL [JLE 86-1877]**

AGRICULTURE AND STATE - INDIA - HISTORY.
Om Prakash, 1916- Economy and food in ancient India /. Delhi , 1987- v. <1- > ; ISBN 81-217-0027-2 : LC Card 87-902484 DDC 338.1/9/34 19
HC434 .O45 1987

AGRICULTURE AND STATE - INDIA - JAMMU AND KASHMIR - HISTORY.
Sharma, Dewan Chand, 1898- Kashmir agriculture & land revenue system under the Sikh rule, 1819-46 A.D. /. New Delhi, India , 1986. xiv, 160 p., [8] p. of plates : LC Card 86-900128
HD2075.J35 S43 1986 **NYPL [JLD 86-3742]**

AGRICULTURE AND STATE - INDIA - KARNAL (DISTRICT)
Pai Panandiker, V. A., 1935- Development bureaucracy /. New Delhi , c1983. ix, 252 p. ; LC Card 83-902420 DDC 352.94/233/09542 19
HD2075.K359 P34 1983
NYPL [JLD 86-3762]

AGRICULTURE AND STATE - INDIA - PUNJAB.
Sain, Inder, 1944- Transformation of Punjab agriculture /. Delhi , New Delhi , 1987. xviii, 191 p. : ISBN 81-7018-451-7 : LC Card 87-900922
HD2075.P8 S35 1985

Westley, John Richard, 1942- Agriculture and equitable growth . Boulder , 1986. xv, 369 p. : ISBN 0-8133-7155-4 (alk. paper) : LC Card 85-31586 DDC 338.1/85455 19
HD2075.P8 W47 1986 **NYPL [JLE 86-1877]**

AGRICULTURE AND STATE - INDIA - RAJASTHAN - HISTORY.
Gupta, Satya Prakash, 1940- The agrarian system of eastern Rajasthan, c. 1650-c. 1750 /. Delhi , 1986. xvi, 352 p. : ISBN 81-85054-11-8 : LC Card 87-900814 DDC 338.1/0954/4 19
HD2075.R27 G86 1986

AGRICULTURE AND STATE - INTERNATIONAL COOPERATION.
Gerken, Egbert. Auf dem Wege zu einer Theorie der internationalen Koordination der Agrarpolitik /. Kiel [1985] 29 p. : LC Card 85-203925
HD1415 .G395 1985

AGRICULTURE AND STATE - IRAN.
Nattagh, Nima. Agriculture & regional development in Iran /. Wisbech, Cambridgeshire, England , 1986. 105 p. : ISBN 0-906559-26-X (pbk.) : LC Card 86-230845 DDC 338.1/0955 19
HD1565.2 .N37 1986

AGRICULTURE AND STATE - IRAQ.
Mukhlif, Hādī Aḥmad. al-Tawzī' al-jughrāfī li-mazārī' al-dawlah fī al-'Irāq wa-atharihā fī al-tanmiyah al-iqtiṣādiyah /. [Baghdad] , 1985. 2 v. (607 p., 3 leaves of plates) : LC Card 86-963500
HD1493.I72 M85 1985

AGRICULTURE AND STATE - ITALY - CONGRESSES.
L'Imprenditore coltivatore nella società che cambia . [Italy] [1983] (Roma : Arti grafiche Jasillo) 364 p. : LC Card 86-185731
HD1972 .I44 1983

AGRICULTURE AND STATE - ITALY - HISTORY - 20TH CENTURY.
Fabiani, Guido. L'agricoltura italiana tra sviluppo e crisi, 1945-1985 /. Bologna , 1986, c1979. 411 p. ; ISBN 88-15-00984-1 : LC Card 86-181021
HD1972 .F3 1986

AGRICULTURE AND STATE - JAPAN.
Hillman, Jimmye S., 1923- Agricultural trade and protection in Japan /. Aldershot, Hants, England , Brookfield, Vt. , 1988. p. cm. ISBN 0-566-05339-X : LC Card 87-15043 DDC 382.7/3/0952 19
HD9016.J42 H55 1988

AGRICULTURE AND STATE - JAPAN - NAKADA-CHŌ (MIYAGI-KEN)
Moore, Richard H. Japanese agriculture . Boulder , 1987. p. cm. ISBN 0-8133-7406-5 LC Card 87-13553 DDC 338.1/0952/115 19
HD920.N33 M65 1987

AGRICULTURE AND STATE - JORDAN.
Shestopalova, Zoi͡a Vladimirovna. Prodovol'stvennai͡a problema i perspektivy ee reshenii͡a v arabskikh stranakh . Moskva , 1985. 151, [4] p. : LC Card 86-130508
HD9016.S92 S44 1985
NYPL [*QIP 87-3413]

AGRICULTURE AND STATE - JORDAN - CONGRESSES.
Agricultural policy in Jordan /. London ; Atlantic Highlands, NJ : 147 p. : ISBN 0-86372-070-6 LC Card 86-21480 DDC 338.1/85695 19
HD2059.Z8 A34 1986

AGRICULTURE AND STATE - KAZAKH S.S. R. - HISTORY.
Tulepbaev, B. A. [Sot͡sialisticheskie agrarnye preobrazovanii͡a v Sredneĭ Azii i Kazakhstane. English.] Socialist Agrarian reforms in Central Asia and Kazakhstan /. Moscow , 1986. 231, [1] p. ; LC Card 86-171559
HD1995.C4 T8313 1986

AGRICULTURE AND STATE - KENYA - CASE STUDIES.
Staudt, Kathleen A. Agricultural policy implementation . West Hartford, CT , c1985. xvi, 68 p. : ISBN 0-931816-18-1 (pbk.) LC Card 84-29737 DDC 338.1/86762 19
HD2126.5.Z8 S73 1985
NYPL [JLF 86-1685]

AGRICULTURE AND STATE - KENYA - HISTORY - 20TH CENTURY.
Throup, David. Economic & social origins of Mau Mau 1945-53 /. London , Athens , c1988. xvi, 304 p. : ISBN 0-8214-0883-6 LC Card 87-12387 DDC 307.3/36 19
HD2126.5 .T48 1988

AGRICULTURE AND STATE - LEBANON.
Shestopalova, Zoi͡a Vladimirovna. Prodovol'stvennai͡a problema i perspektivy ee reshenii͡a v arabskikh stranakh . Moskva , 1985. 151, [4] p. : LC Card 86-130508
HD9016.S92 S44 1985
NYPL [*QIP 87-3413]

AGRICULTURE AND STATE - MALAWI.
Malawi. National rural development programme /. [Lilongwe, Malawi] , 1977. 7 v. : LC Card 85-981594
HD2133.5.Z8 M35 1977

AGRICULTURE AND STATE - MALAYSIA - CONGRESSES.
Seminar "Malaysian Agriculture--What Next?" (1985 : Kuala Lumpur, Malaysia) Options for Malaysian agriculture . [Kuala Lumpur] , 1986. xxiv, 203 p. : ISBN 967-99982-0-7 (pbk.) LC Card 86-943314 DDC 338.1/8595 19
HD2080.6.Z8 S45 1985

AGRICULTURE AND STATE - MALI.
Lecaillon, Jacques. Economic policies and agricultural performance . Paris , 1986. 174 p. ; LC Card 87-158595 DDC 338.1/86623 19
HD2143.5.Z8 L43 1986

AGRICULTURE AND STATE - MEXICO.
Barkin, David. El fin de la autosuficiencia alimentaria /. México, D.F. , 1985. 249 p. : ISBN 968-493-091-7 LC Card 82-230750
NYPL [JLE 87-404]

Barkin, David. El fin de la autosuficiencia alimentaria /. México, D.F. , c1985. 249 p. : ISBN 968-493-091-7 LC Card 86-209699
HD1792 .B38 1985

Estructura agraria y desarrollo agrícola en México . México , 1974 (1979 printing) xvi, 1174 p. : LC Card 81-126616 DDC 338.1/0972 19
HD1792 .E85 1974 **NYPL [JLE 81-372]**

Mares, David R. Penetrating the international market . New York , 1987. xvi, 294 p. : ISBN 0-231-06346-6 (alk. paper) LC Card 87-6358 DDC 382/.415/097232 19
HD9014.M62 M38 1987

AGRICULTURE AND STATE - MEXICO - AGUASCALIENTES (STATE) - HISTORY.
Gómez Serrano, Jesús. Hacendados y campesinos en Aguascalientes /. [Aguascalientes] , 1985. 221 p., [20] p. of plates : LC Card 86-217321
HD1471.M62 A384 1985

AGRICULTURE AND STATE - MEXICO - CONGRESSES.
U. S.-Mexico relations . Stanford, Calif. , c1987. xii, 401 p. ; ISBN 0-8047-1319-7 (alk. paper) LC Card 86-23103 DDC 338.1/872 19
HD1792 .U19 1987

AGRICULTURE AND STATE - MEXICO - LAGUNA REGION.
Rello, Fernando. Estado y ejidos en México . Ginebra , 1986. xxvi, 122 p. : LC Card 86-210274
HG2051.M62 L37 1986

AGRICULTURE AND STATE - MIDDLE WEST - CONGRESSES.
Ninth Federal Reserve District Farm Forum (1965 : Minneapolis, Minn.) Farm Forum of the Ninth Federal Reserve District . Hopkins, Minn. [1965] 99 p. : LC Card 87-110732
HD9007.A14 N56 1965

AGRICULTURE AND STATE - MONGOLIA.
Graĭvoronskiĭ, Vladimir Viktorovich. Kooperirovannoe aratstvo MNR--izmenenii͡a v urovne zhizni, 1960-1980 /. Moskva , 1982. 213 p. : LC Card 82-213253
HD1491.M55 G73 1982

AGRICULTURE AND STATE - MONGOLIA - HISTORY.
Ulymzhiev, D. B. (Dashi Batuevich) Put' mongol'skogo aratstva k sotsializmu /. Novosibirsk , 1987. 283, [5] p. ; LC Card 87-159668
HD1491.M55 U49 1987

AGRICULTURE AND STATE - MOROCCO - HISTORY.
Swearingen, Will D. (Will Davis), 1946- Moroccan mirages . Princeton, N.J. , c1987. xvii, 217 p., [9] p. of plates : ISBN 0-691-05505-X (alk. paper) : LC Card 87-6981 DDC 338.1/0964 19
HD2121 .S94 1987

AGRICULTURE AND STATE - NEPAL.
Gurung, Harka B. Food systems and society in Nepal . Kathmandu, Nepal , 1981. 53, iii p. : LC Card 83-901141 DDC 338.1/9/5496 19
HD9016.N42 G87 1981 **NYPL [JLG 86-71]**

Svejnar, Jan. Economic policies and agricultural performance . Paris , 1986. 167 p. ; LC Card 87-120115 DDC 338.1/85496 19
HD2065.9.Z8 S84 1986

AGRICULTURE AND STATE - NEW JERSEY.
New Jersey. Dept. of Agriculture. Grassroots, an agriculture retention and development program for New Jersey. [Trenton, N.J.] [1980] 65 p. : LC Card 81-621630 DDC 333.76/17/09749 19
HD211.N5 N47 1980 **NYPL [JLF 86-1575]**

AGRICULTURE AND STATE - NICARAGUA.
Glembotzki, Jürgen. Landwirtschaftliche Entwicklung und Agrarreform in Nicaragua zwischen 1960 und 1982 . Hamburg , 1984. 80,

xliv p. : LC Card 84-208160 DDC 333.3/1/7285 19
HD1333.N5 G57 1984
NYPL [JLM 75-816 Nr.21]

AGRICULTURE AND STATE - NIGERIA.
Bashir, Ibrahim Lawan, 1948- Food crisis and government response in Nigeria . Boston, MA (270 Bay State Rd., Boston 02215) , 1986. 22 leaves ; LC Card 87-155111 DDC 363.8/09669 19
HD9017.N52 B37 1986

Beckman, Björn, 1938- Public investment and agrarian transformation in northern Nigeria /. [Zaria , 1983] 33 p. ; LC Card 87-402849 DDC 338.1/8669 19
HD2145.5 .B43 1983

Eweka, J. A. (Julius A.) Village development . Ibadan, Nigeria , 1979. xvi, 194 p. ; LC Card 86-172121 DDC 338.1/9/669 19
HD2145.5 .E94 1979

Folayan, Adekunle. Agriculture and economic development in Nigeria . New York , c1983. x, 276 p. : ISBN 0-533-05325-0 : LC Card 81-90817 DDC 338.1/09669 19
HD2145.5 .F64 1983 ***NYPL [JLE 86-1080]***

Mabbs-Zeno, Carl. Nigeria . Washington, D.C. [1986] vi, 54 p. : LC Card 86-601597 DDC 382/.41/09669 19
HD9017.N52 M3 1986

Oyejide, T. Ademola. The effects of trade and exchange rate policies on agriculture in Nigeria /. Washington, D.C., USA , c1986. 61 p. : ISBN 0-89629-056-5 (pbk.) LC Card 86-21309 DDC 338.1/09669 19
HD2145.5 .O94 1986

Sano, Hans-Otto. The political economy of food in Nigeria 1960-1982 . Uppsala , 1983. 108 p. : ISBN 91-7106-210-6 ***NYPL [JLD 84-860]***

State, oil, and agriculture in Nigeria /. Berkeley , c1987. xiv, 327 p. : ISBN 0-87725-166-5 (pbk.) : LC Card 87-2941 DDC 338.1/8669 19
HD2145.5 .S73 1987

AGRICULTURE AND STATE - NIGERIA - HISTORY - 20TH CENTURY.
Rural underdevelopment in Nigeria, 1900-1980. Zaria, Nigeria , 1985. iv, 102 p. ; LC Card 86-154806 DDC 338.1/8669 19
HD2145.5.Z8 R87 1985

AGRICULTURE AND STATE - PAKISTAN.
Some aspects of agricultural price and taxation policies in Pakistan /. Islamabad, Pakistan [1985] x, 223 p. ; LC Card 86-930932 DDC 338.1/8 19
HD2075.5 .S66 1985

AGRICULTURE AND STATE - PANAMA.
Panama . Washington, D.C., U. S.A. , c1985. xxv, 307 p., [8] p., [1] leaf of plates : ISBN 0-8213-0580-8 LC Card 85-12420 DDC 338.97287 19
HC147 .P43 1985 ***NYPL [JLF 86-1919]***

AGRICULTURE AND STATE - PARAGUAY.
Palau, Tomás. El cultivo del algodón y la soya en el Paraguay y sus derivaciones sociales. Santiago de Chile , 1986. 148 p. ; ISBN 92-1-321207-0 LC Card 87-400251 DDC 338.1/7351/09892 19
HD9084.P25 P35 1986

AGRICULTURE AND STATE - PARAGUAY - HISTORY.
Ayala, Eligio. Evolución de la economía agraria en el Paraguay . Asunción, Paraguay , 1986. 196 p. : LC Card 86-234615
HD1898 1986 .A92

AGRICULTURE AND STATE - PERU.
Hurtado Miller, Juan Carlos. Por una causa agraria . Lima, Perú , 1986. 348 p. : LC Card 87-400122 DDC 338.1/885 19
HD1903 .H87 1986

AGRICULTURE AND STATE - PERU - CUZCO (DEPT.)
Barrenechea Lercari, Carlos. Cusco . Cusco [Peru] 1986. 77 p. ; LC Card 87-400243 DDC 338.1/88537 19
HD1905.C87 B37 1986

AGRICULTURE AND STATE - PERU - HISTORY - 20TH CENTURY.
Kennedy, Peter, 1954- Food and agricultural policy in Peru, 1960-1977 [microform] /. Austin (Sid Richardson Hall 1.310, Austin 78712) , 1983. 22 p. ; LC Card 83-623239 DDC 338.1/885 19
HD1903 .K46 1983 ***NYPL [*ZT-1646 no.20]***

AGRICULTURE AND STATE - PHILIPPINES.
Hanisch, Rolf, 1942- Der Staat, ländliche Armutsgruppen und legale Bauernbewegung in den Philippinen /. Baden-Baden , 1983. xii, 432 p. ; ISBN 3-7890-0980-6 LC Card 84-143058
HD1537.P5 H35 1983

Hawes, Gary, 1950- The Philippine State and the Marcos regime . Ithaca , 1987. 196 p. ; ISBN 0-8014-2012-1 (alk. paper) LC Card 86-29237 DDC 382/.41/09599 19
HD9016.P52 H38 1987

Leviste, Jose P., 1945- Food for thought . Los Baños, Laguna, Philippines , c1985. 150 p. : LC Card 86-193278 DDC 338.1/8599 19
HD2088 .L48 1985

AGRICULTURE AND STATE - POLAND.
Polityka rolna PRL . Warszawa , 1977. 246, [2] p., [24] p. of plates : LC Card 81-201110
HD1995.7.Z8 P65 1977

AGRICULTURE AND STATE - POLAND - HISTORY.
Mazurkiewicz, Eugeniusz. Podstawowe problemy polityki rolnej w PRL /. Warszawa , 1979. 306 p. ; LC Card 81-172693
HD1995.7.Z8 M39 1979

AGRICULTURE AND STATE - PORTUGAL.
Portuguese agriculture in transition /. Ithaca , 1987. 283 p. : ISBN 0-8014-1954-9 (alk. paper) LC Card 86-29198 DDC 338.1/09469 19
HD2027 .P67 1987

AGRICULTURE AND STATE - QUÉBEC (PROVINCE)
Conseil de planification et de développement du Québec. Le réseau décisionnel en agro-alimentation au Québec . [Québec] [1979] 29 p. ; LC Card 85-102587
HD9014.C4 Q425 1979

AGRICULTURE AND STATE - RUSSIA.
Deutsch, Robert. The food revolution in the Soviet Union and Eastern Europe /. Boulder , 1986. xxii, 256 p. : ISBN 0-8133-7161-9 (pbk.) : LC Card 85-26625 DDC 338.1/9/47 19
HD9015.S652 D47 1986
NYPL [JLE 86-1588]

AGRICULTURE AND STATE - RUSSIAN S.F. S.R. - BURIATSKAIA A.S.S.R.
Sistema vedeniia sel'skogo khoziaistva Buriatskoĭ ASSR . Novosibirsk , 1985. 188 p. : LC Card 86-215358
HD1995.B8 S57 1985

AGRICULTURE AND STATE - RUSSIAN S.F. S.R. - CAUCASUS, NORTHERN.
Krivoded, V. V. KPSS i kolkhoznoe krest'ianstvo v 1945-1959 gg. /. Rostov-na-Donu , 1984. 190 p. ; LC Card 87-100194
HD1492.S652 C384 1984

AGRICULTURE AND STATE - RUSSIAN S.F. S.R. - HISTORY.
Agrarnaia revoliutsiia i sotsialisticheskie preobrazovaniia v sovetskoĭ derevne . Gor'kiĭ , 1980. 84 p. ; LC Card 82-141565
HD1995.R8 A68 1980

AGRICULTURE AND STATE - RUSSIAN S.F. S.R. - SIBERIA - HISTORY.
Shishkin, V. I. (Vladimir Ivanovich) Sotsialisticheskoe stroitel'stvo v sibirskoĭ derevne, noiabr' 1919-mart 1921 g. /. Novosibirsk , 1985. 316 p. ; LC Card 86-164936
HD1995.S5 S45 1985

AGRICULTURE AND STATE - SAUDI ARABIA.
Philipp, Hans-Jürgen. Die landwirtschaftliche Modernisierung Saudi-Arabiens im 20. Jahrhundert /. Hamburg , c1984. 132 p. : LC Card 85-166668
HD2060.Z8 P48 1984

AGRICULTURE AND STATE - SOMALIA - CONGRESSES.
Somalia's rural development strategy, 1981-1990. Mogadishu, Somalia [1981?] vii, 45, [49] leaves : LC Card 83-980772 DDC 338.1/86773 19
HD2125.Z8 S65 1981 ***NYPL [JLG 86-58]***

AGRICULTURE AND STATE - SOVIET CENTRAL ASIA - HISTORY.
Tulepbaev, B. A. [Sotsialisticheskie agrarnye preobrazovaniia v Sredneĭ Azii i Kazakhstane. English.] Socialist Agrarian reforms in Central Asia and Kazakhstan /. Moscow , 1986. 231, [1] p. ; LC Card 86-171559
HD1995.C4 T8313 1986

AGRICULTURE AND STATE - SOVIET UNION.
Agrarnaia politika Kommunisticheskoĭ partii na ėtape stroitel'stva MTS, 1929-1939 . Vladimir , 1985. 132 p. ; ***NYPL [*QIK 87-3394]***

Agrarnaia politika KPSS v deĭstvii /. Kishinev , 1983. 202 p. ; LC Card 84-235869
HD1993 .A38 1983

Agrarnye problemy v svete resheniĭ XXVII s"ezda KPSS /. Moskva , 1986. 185 p. ; LC Card 87-163428
HD1992 .A645 1986

Bogoliubov, Klavdiĭ Mikhaĭlovich. Vernym kursom /. Moskva , 1984. 287 p. ; LC Card 85-164820
HD1492.S65 B64 1984

Kaplan, Cynthia Sue. The party and agricultural crisis management in the USSR /. Ithaca , 1987. xvi, 203 p ; ISBN 0-8014-2021-0 (alk. paper) LC Card 86-32223 DDC 338.1/847 19
HD1993 .K36 1987

Relaciones agrarias en el socialismo. Moscú , 1986. 223 p. ; LC Card 87-126164
HD9015.S652 R45 1986

AGRICULTURE AND STATE - SOVIET UNION - HISTORIOGRAPHY.
Cox, Terry. Peasants, class, and capitalism . Oxford [Oxfordshire] ; New York : xii, 271 p. ; ISBN 0-19-878014-1 : LC Card 86-2362 DDC 305.5/63 19
HD1536.S65 C69 1986
NYPL [JLD 86-3986]

AGRICULTURE AND STATE - SOVIET UNION - HISTORY.
Medvedev, Zhores A., 1925- Soviet agriculture /. New York , c1987. xiv, 464 p. ; ISBN 0-393-02472-5 LC Card 86-31119 DDC 338.1/0947 19
HD1992 .M385 1987

AGRICULTURE AND STATE - SOVIET UNION - HISTORY - 19TH CENTURY.
Macey, David, A. J., 1942- Government and peasant in Russia, 1861-1906 . Dekalb, Ill. , 1987. xviii, 380 p. ; ISBN 0-87580-122-6 LC Card 87-7684 DDC 338.1/847 19
HD1992 .M19 1987

AGRICULTURE AND STATE - SOVIET UNION - HISTORY - 20TH CENTURY.
Harris, Lement, 1904- My tale of two worlds . New York , 1986. 289 p. : ISBN 0-7178-0645-6 : LC Card 86-10671 DDC 338.1/092/4 B 19
S417.H35 A36 1986 ***NYPL [JLD 87-1376]***

Istoriia sovetskogo krest'ianstva . Moskva , 1986- v. : ***NYPL [*QG 87-3228]***

AGRICULTURE AND STATE - SOVIET UNION - MISCELLANEA.
Prodovol'stvennaia programma SSSR . Moskva , 1986. 285 p. ; LC Card 87-110478 DDC 338.1/9/47 19
HD9015.S652 P743 1986

AGRICULTURE AND STATE - SPAIN.
González Rodríguez, Juan Jesús. La patronal agraria . Madrid [1986?] 46 p. ; ISBN 84-7075-335-3 LC Card 87-111477
HD6976.A292 S74 1986

Möller, Ferdinand, 1955- Agrarstruktur und Agrarstrukturpolitik in Spanien, eine Analyse vor dem Hintergrund der Erweiterung der Europäischen Gemeinschaft /. Frankfurt am Main , New York , c1986. ix, 255 p. ; ISBN 3-8204-9529-0 LC Card 87-407540 DDC 338.1/846 19
HD2023 .M65 1986

AGRICULTURE AND STATE - SPAIN - HISTORY.
Biglino Campos, Paloma. El socialismo español y la cuestión agraria (1890-1936) /. Madrid [1986?] 564 p. ; ISBN 84-7434-368-2 LC Card 87-136300
HD6764.A29 B54 1986

AGRICULTURE AND STATE - SUDAN.
D'Silva, Brian. Sudan's irrigated subsector . Washington, D.C. , 1986. iv, 31 p. : LC Card

86-602812 DDC 333.91/3/09624 19
HD1741.S85 D75 1986

AGRICULTURE AND STATE - SWEDEN.
Översyn av vissa frågor rörande jordbruksprisregleringen /. [Stockholm] [1981] iii, 104, 13, 22, 2, 9, 14 p. : ISBN 91-38-06616-5 LC Card 83-245209
HD2018 .O94 1981

AGRICULTURE AND STATE - SYRIA.
Shestopalova, Zoia Vladimirovna. Prodovol'stvennaia problema i perspektivy ee resheniia v arabskikh stranakh . Moskva , 1985. 151, [4] p. : LC Card 86-130508
HD9016.S92 S44 1985 *NYPL [*QIP 87-3413]*

AGRICULTURE AND STATE - TAIWAN.
CAPD and agricultural development in the Republic of China on Taiwan . Taipei [1984] 152 p. : LC Card 87-400057 DDC 338.1/851249 19
HD2108 .C36 1984

AGRICULTURE AND STATE - TANZANIA.
Bantje, Han. Mechanised food production in Tanzania . [Dar es Salaam] [1984] 3 leaves, 73 p. : LC Card 86-980118 DDC 338.1/61/09678 19
HD1471.T34 B36 1984

AGRICULTURE AND STATE - TEXAS.
Knutson, Ronald D. Cooperative involvement in issues of domestic farm policy /. College Station, Tex. , 1986. 59 p. : LC Card 86-623063 DDC 338.1/8764 19
HD1491.U6 T45 1986

AGRICULTURE AND STATE - THAILAND.
Klempin, Arno. Contribution of state-directed land settlement to agricultural development . Saarbrücken , Fort Launderdale, 1979. viii, 169 p. : ISBN 3-88156-121-8 LC Card 80-464363 DDC 333.3/1/593
HD890.55 .K57 *NYPL [JLE 80-1270]*

AGRICULTURE AND STATE - UGANDA - BUGISU (DISTRICT)
Bunker, Stephen G., 1944- Double dependency and constraints on class formation in Bugisu, Uganda /. Urbana, Ill. , 1983. v, 88 p. : LC Card 86-229748 DDC 303.3/09676/1 19
HD1538.U43 B86 1983

AGRICULTURE AND STATE - UNITED STATES.
Agriculture and the environment in a changing world economy. Washington, D.C. , c1986. xi, 66 p. : ISBN 0-89164-099-1 (pbk.) LC Card 86-24088 DDC 338.1/873 19
HD1761 .A6228 1986

Ambur, Owen D. Selling out the family farm . Washington , 1986. v, 40 p. : LC Card 87-601379 DDC 338.1/6 19
HD1476.U5 A65 1986

Browne, William Paul, 1945- Private interests, public policy, and American agriculture /. Lawrence, Kan. , c1988. p. cm. ISBN 0-7006-0334-4 : LC Card 87-23131 DDC 338.1/873 19
HD1761 .B73 1988

Debating United States agricultural policy . Kansas City, Mo. (P.O. Box 20626, Kansas City 64195) , c1986. 111 p. ; LC Card 86-224267 DDC 338.1/873 19
HD1761 .D37 1986b

Dirt rich, dirt poor . New York , 1986. xii, 188 p. ; ISBN 0-7102-0378-0 LC Card 85-8274 DDC 338.1/9/73 19
HD1761 .D55 1986 *NYPL [JLD 87-821]*

Embargoes, surplus disposal, and U. S. agriculture . Washington, D.C. , 1986. vi, 34 p. ; LC Card 86-603452 DDC 338.1/8 19
HD1761 .E45 1986

The Farm financial crisis . Boulder , 1988. xvi, 205 p. : ISBN 0-8133-7186-4 (pbk. : alk. paper) : LC Card 86-32601 DDC 338.1/3/0973 19
HD1761 .F295 1988

Financing the agricultural sector . Boulder, Colo. , 1986. xi, 256 p. : ISBN 0-8133-0055-X (pbk. : alk. paper) LC Card 86-50152 DDC 338.1/3/0973 19
HD1761 .F5 1986 *NYPL [JLE 86-2766]*

Gardner, Bruce L. The economics of agricultural policies /. New York, NY , c1987. xi, 387 p. : ISBN 0-02-947760-3 LC Card 87-20367 DDC 338.1/8 19
HD1761 .G245 1987

Gold, Kenneth A. (Kenneth Alan) United States foreign economic policy-making . New York , 1987. 349 p. ; ISBN 0-8240-8083-1 : LC Card 87-23785 DDC 382/.456413/00973 19
HD9006 .G64 1987

Hathaway, Dale E. Agriculture and the GATT . Washington, DC , c1987. xii, 157 p. : ISBN 0-88132-052-8 LC Card 87-21430 DDC 382/.41/0973 19
HD9006 .H28 1987

Is there a moral obligation to save the family farm? /. Ames , 1987. xxvii, 427 p. : ISBN 0-8138-1000-0 (pbk.) LC Card 87-13399 DDC 338.1/0973 19
HD1476.U5 I8 1987

McKinzie, Lance. A perspective on U. S. farm problems and agricultural policy /. Boulder , 1987. xvii, 189 p. : ISBN 0-8133-7376-X (pbk. : alk. paper) LC Card 86-51501 DDC 338.1/873 19
HD1470.5.U6 M35 1987

Mares, David R. Penetrating the international market . New York , 1987. xvi, 294 p. : ISBN 0-231-06346-6 (alk. paper) LC Card 87-6358 DDC 382/.415/097232 19
HD9014.M62 M38 1987

Paarlberg, Robert L. Fixing farm trade . Cambridge, Mass. , c1988. xiv, 159 p. ; ISBN 0-88730-196-7 LC Card 87-24118 DDC 382/.41/0973 19
HD9006 .P27 1988

A Review of U. S. competitiveness in agricultural trade. Washington, D.C. [1986] ix, 101 p. : LC Card 86-600586 DDC 382/.41/0973 19
HD1761 .R48 1986

Sumner, Daniel A. (Daniel Alan), 1950- Removal of price supports and supply controls for U. S. tobacco . Demoines, Iowa , Washington, D.C. , c1985. viii, 64 p. ; ISBN 0-89068-084-1 LC Card 85-63194
NYPL [JLF 86-1014]

Technology, public policy, and the changing structure of American agriculture. Washington, D.C. [1986] vi, 374 p. : LC Card 85-600632 DDC 338.1/0973 19
HD1761 .T37 1986 *NYPL [JLF 86-1376]*

U. S. agriculture & Third World development . Boulder , 1987. xi, 258 p. ; ISBN 1-555-87011-2 (lib. bdg.) : LC Card 86-29860 DDC 338.1/09172/4 19
HD1765 .U15 1987

United States. Congress. Senate. Committee on Agriculture, Nutrition, and Forestry. Review of the implementation of the Food Security Act of 1985 . Washington , 1987. iv, 180 p. : LC Card 87-601199 DDC 338.1/9/73 19
HD1761 .U515 1987

Wallace, Luther T. Agriculture's futures . New York , c1987. x, 93 p. : ISBN 0-387-96482-7 (pbk.) LC Card 86-31390 DDC 338.1/0973 19
HD1761 .W274 1987

Waterfield, Larry W. Conflict and crisis in rural America /. New York , 1986. iv, 235 p. : ISBN 0-03-006074-5 (alk. paper) : LC Card 85-19366 DDC 333.76/0973 19
HD256 .W35 1986 *NYPL [JLE 86-2792]*

Webb, Shwu-Eng. Idling erodible cropland . Washington, D.C. [1986] iii, 31 p. : LC Card 86-601632 DDC 338.1 s 338.1/62 19
HD1751 .A91854 no. 550 HD256

AGRICULTURE AND STATE - UNITED STATES - ADDRESSES, ESSAYS, LECTURES.
Lectures in agricultural economics . [Washington? , 1977] ix, 165 p. : LC Card 77-603242
HD1759 .L4 *NYPL [JLE 79-149]*

AGRICULTURE AND STATE - UNITED STATES - CONGRESSES.
Confrontation or negotiation . Millwood, N.Y. , 1985. xvi, 303 p. : ISBN 0-8046-9397-8 : LC Card 85-18667 DDC 382/.41/094 19
HD9015.E82 C67 1985
NYPL [JLE 86-4594]

Ninth Federal Reserve District Farm Forum (1965 : Minneapolis, Minn.) Farm Forum of the Ninth Federal Reserve District . Hopkins, Minn. [1965] 99 p. : LC Card 87-110732
HD9007.A14 N56 1965

U. S. agriculture and Third World economic development . Washington, D.C. , c1987. xv, 103 p. : ISBN 0-89068-086-8 (pbk.): LC Card 86-62757 DDC 338.9/009172/4 19
HD1755 .U173 1987

U. S.-Mexico relations . Stanford, Calif. , c1987. xii, 401 p. ; ISBN 0-8047-1319-7 (alk. paper) LC Card 86-23103 DDC 338.1/872 19
HD1792 .U19 1987

AGRICULTURE AND STATE - UNITED STATES - HISTORY.
Opie, John, 1934- The law of the land . Lincoln , c1987. xxi, 231 p. : ISBN 0-8032-3553-4 (alk. paper) LC Card 86-30860 DDC 338.1/873 19
HD1761 .O65 1987

AGRICULTURE AND STATE - UNITED STATES - HISTORY - 20TH CENTURY.
Harris, Lement, 1904- My tale of two worlds . New York , 1986. 289 p. : ISBN 0-7178-0645-6 : LC Card 86-10671 DDC 338.1/092/4 B 19
S417.H35 A36 1986 *NYPL [JLD 87-1376]*

AGRICULTURE AND STATE - UNITED STATES - PUBLIC OPINION.
The American farmer book . [Smithshire, Ill.] (Box 181, Smithshire 61478) [c1986] 192 p. : LC Card 86-203314 DDC 338.1/0973 19
HD8039.F32 U614 1986

AGRICULTURE AND STATE - URUGUAY - HISTORY - 20TH CENTURY - ADDRESSES, ESSAYS, LECTURES.
El Primer batllismo . Montevideo [1985] 159 p. : LC Card 85-233561 DDC 338.9895 19
HC232 .P75 1985 *NYPL [JLC 86-259]*

AGRICULTURE AND STATE - VENEZUELA.
Portocarrero de Guzmán, Blancanieve. El capitalismo dependiente y su incidencia en el problema agrario venezolano /. Valencia, Venezuela , c1985. 189 p. : LC Card 86-226697
HD1333.V4 P67 1985

AGRICULTURE AND STATE - YUGOSLAVIA.
Tomić, Danilo. Jugoslovenska agrarna teorija i politika . Bačka Topola , 1985. 211 p. : LC Card 85-195818
HD2045.5.Z8 T62 1985

AGRICULTURE AND STATE - ZAIRE.
Tshibaka, Tshikala B., 1949- The effects of trade and exchange rate policies on agriculture in Zaire /. Washington, D.C., USA , 1986. 65 p. : ISBN 0-89629-057-3 LC Card 86-27449 DDC 338.1/09675/1 19
HD2135.5 .T75 1986

AGRICULTURE AND STATE - ZAMBIA.
Chilivumbo, Alifeyo. Communal agrarian cooperative societies . Lusaka [1986] iii, 134 p. ; LC Card 86-981399 DDC 334/.683/096894 19
HD1491.Z35 C45 1986

Agriculture and the environment / Tim T. Phipps, Pierre R. Crosson, and Kent A. Price, editors. Washington, D.C. : National Center for Food and Agricultural Policy, Resources for the Future, c1986. xvii, 298 p. : ill. ; 26 cm. On cover: The National Center for Food and Agricultural Policy annual policy review, 1986. Based on papers and discussion at a Conference on Agriculture and the Environment sponsored by the National Center for Food and Agricultural Policy held in April 1986 at Resources for the Future, Washington, D.C. Includes bibliographies. ISBN 0-915707-33-0 (pbk.) : LC Card 87-43010 DDC 363.7/31 19
1. Agricultural conservation - Government policy - United States - Congresses. 2. Agricultural pollution - Government policy - United States - Congresses. 3. Agricultural ecology - Government policy - United States - Congresses. 4. Agricultural innovations - Environmental aspects - Government policy - United States - Congresses. 5. Pesticides - Environmental aspects - Government policy - United States - Congresses. 6. Food contamination - Government policy - United States - Congresses. 7. Soil conservation - Government policy - United States - Congresses. 8. Environmental policy - United States - Congresses. I. Phipps, Tim. II. Crosson, Pierre R. III. Price, Kent A. IV. National Center for Food and Agricultural Policy (U. S.). V. Conference on Agriculture and the Environment (1986 : Resources for the Future).
HD1755 .P47 1986

Agriculture and the environment in a changing world economy. Washington, D.C. : Conservation Foundation, c1986. xi, 66 p. : ill. ; 23 cm. (An Issue report) Bibliography: p. 51-66. ISBN 0-89164-099-1 (pbk.) LC Card 86-24088 DDC 338.1/873 19
1. Agriculture and state - United States. 2. Agricultural conservation - Government policy - United States. 3. Agriculture - Economic aspects - United States. 4. Agricultural ecology - United States. 5. Agricultural pollution - United States. I. Conservation Foundation. II. State of the environment. III. Series: Issue report (Conservation Foundation).
HD1761 .A6228 1986

Agriculture and the GATT . Hathaway, Dale E. Washington, DC , c1987. xii, 157 p. : ISBN 0-88132-052-8 LC Card 87-21430 DDC 382/.41/0973 19
HD9006 .H28 1987

AGRICULTURE AND WATER. see **WATER-SUPPLY, AGRICULTURAL.**

AGRICULTURE - ARCTIC REGIONS.
Sistema vedeniīa sel'skogo i promyslovogo khoziaĭstva na Eniseĭskom Severe . Novosibirsk , 1986. 211 p. ; LC Card 86-227282
HD1995.K73 S57 1986

AGRICULTURE - ARMENIAN S.S.R. - HISTORY - CONGRESSES.
Nyut'er Hayastani gyughatntesut'yan ev gyughats'iut'yan patmut'yan /. Erevan , 1964- v. <1 > : LC Card 86-225528
HD1995.A7 N98 1964

AGRICULTURE - BRAZIL - FINANCE.
Delgado, Guilherme Costa. Capital financeiro e agricultura no Brasil, 1965-1985 /. S[ão] Paulo, SP, Brasil , Campinas, SP , c1985. 240 p. ; LC Card 87-102748
HD1440.B8 D45 1985

Leal, Luiz Octávio Pires. Agricultura . Rio de Janeiro , 1985. 114 p. ; LC Card 87-140475 DDC 338.1/3/0981 19
HD1872 .L4 1985

AGRICULTURE - BRAZIL - SERGIPE.
Projeto Tabuleiros Norte de Sergipe /. Aracaju , 1977. 521 p. : LC Card 86-131158
HD1875.S4 P76 1977

AGRICULTURE - BRAZIL - STATISTICS.
Estatísticas cadastrais . Brasília , 1985- <v. 1-2; in 2 > : LC Card 87-117732
HD498 .E77 1985

AGRICULTURE - BURKINA FASO.
Agricultural sector assistance strategy for Upper Volta. Washington, D.C. [1982] 1 v. (various pagings) : LC Card 87-120355 DDC 338.1/8 19
HD2144 .A38 1982

Lecaillon, Jacques. Economic policies and agricultural performance . Paris , 1985. 158 p. ; LC Card 86-216027 DDC 338.1/86625 19
HD2144 .L42 1985

AGRICULTURE - CANADA.
Canadian farming . Toronto , 1881. 432 p., [4] folded leaves of plates : LC Card 85-666092
HD1783 .C3x 1881

AGRICULTURE - CHINA.
Chung-kuo ch'uan t'ung nung yeh yü hsien tai nungyeh /. Pei-ching , 1986. 312 p. :
NYPL [*OVL 87-1966]

AGRICULTURE - CHINA - HISTORY.
Chung-kuo ch'uan t'ung nung yeh yü hsien tai nungyeh /. Pei-ching , 1986. 312 p. :
NYPL [*OVL 87-1966]

AGRICULTURE - COLOMBIA - FINANCE.
Robles Bohórquez, Isabel. La agricultura colombiana en la encrucijada . Bogotá, Colombia [1982] 165 p. ; LC Card 83-103208
HD1883 1982 .R62

AGRICULTURE - COMPETITIONS - GERMANY (WEST)
Agrarmärkte & Agrarmarketing . Hamburg , 1983. 220 p. : ISBN 3-922528-45-7 LC Card 84-162297
HD1955 .A515 1983

AGRICULTURE - CONGRESSES.
The World Food Conference . Washington , 1974. xv, 377 p. : LC Card 74-603025
TX345 .W58 ***NYPL [JLF 78-685]***

AGRICULTURE, COOPERATIVE - AFRICA - CONGRESSES.
Cliffe, Lionel. Experiences of agricultural and rural cooperatives in socialist countries in Africa /. [S.l.] [1985?] 40 p. ; LC Card 87-104467 DDC 334/.683/096 19
HD1491.A48 C55 1985

AGRICULTURE, COOPERATIVE - ASIA.
Gaikwad, V. R., 1933- Managing paddy-rice business of small farmers . Bombay , 1986. xxiii, 239 p. : ISBN 0-86132-129-4 : LC Card 86-903247 DDC 334/.68318/0954 19
HD9066.A7 G35 1986

AGRICULTURE, COOPERATIVE - BOLIVIA - SANTA CRUZ (DEPT.)
Gill, Lesley. Peasants, entrepreneurs, and social change . Boulder , 1987. xiv, 246 p. : ISBN 0-8133-7339-5 (pbk. : alk. paper) : LC Card 86-28207 DDC 303.4/0984/3 19
HD1870.S25 G54 1987

AGRICULTURE, COOPERATIVE - BRAZIL - RIO GRANDE DO SUL.
Duarte, Laura Maria Goulart. Capitalismo & cooperativismo no R.G.S. /. Porto Alegre-RS , c1986. 96 p. : ISBN 85-25-40088-2 : LC Card 86-150404
HD1491.B82 R563 1986

AGRICULTURE, COOPERATIVE - CHINA - HISTORY - 20TH CENTURY.
La Politique agraire en Chine . Ottignies, Louvain-la-Neuve, Belgique [1981] 84 leaves ; LC Card 86-203953
HD926 .P65 1981

AGRICULTURE, COOPERATIVE - CUBA.
AGRICULTURE, COOPERATIVE - DEVELOPING COUNTRIES.
Lombeya Bosongo L. Organisation coopérative et développement rural /. [Kinshasa] , 1985. 173 p. ; LC Card 86-185252
HD1491.5 .L66 1985

AGRICULTURE, COOPERATIVE - ETHIOPIA.
Alemneh Dejene. Peasants, agrarian socialism, and rural development in Ethiopia /. Boulder , 1987. xiii, 162 p. : ISBN 0-8133-7247-X (pbk. : alk. paper) LC Card 86-51527 DDC 338.1/0963 19
HD2124.5 .A79 1987

Habtamu Wondimu. Some factors which affect peasant motivation to work in the Ethiopian agricultural producers cooperatives /. [Addis Ababa] [1983] 60 leaves : LC Card 84-980911 DDC 334/.683/0963 19
HD1491.E83 H3 1983b ***NYPL [JLG 86-163]***

Tegegne Teke. Cooperatives and national development . Addis Ababa, Ethiopia [1984] iii, 57 leaves ; LC Card 85-980411 DDC 334/.683/0963 19
HD1491.E83 T44 1984 ***NYPL [JLG 86-173]***

AGRICULTURE, COOPERATIVE - FRANCE.
Guichard-Ayoub, Éliane. Les associations syndicales de propriétaires /. Paris , 1984. 127 p. ; ISBN 2-13-038290-8 ***NYPL [JLC 87-57]***

AGRICULTURE, COOPERATIVE - GERMANY, WEST.
Prüsse, Dieterich. Der Landwarenhandel in der Bundesrepublik Deutschland . Münster-Hiltrup , 1983. viii, 188, [9], 21 p. : ISBN 3-7843-0291-2 : LC Card 84-141310
HD9013.5 .P78 1983

AGRICULTURE, COOPERATIVE - GHANA.
Dadson, J. A. Production co-operatives and rural development in Ghana /. [Addis Ababa] [1985] 53 p. ; LC Card 87-105501 DDC 334/.6/09667 19
HD3258.3.A4 D34 1985

AGRICULTURE, COOPERATIVE - GOVERNMENT POLICY - ETHIOPIA - ADDRESSES, ESSAYS, LECTURES.
Fassil G. Kiros. Mobilizing the peasantry for rural development [microform] . [Addis Ababa , 1982] 20 leaves ; LC Card 82-980723 DDC 334/.683/0963 19
HD1538.E7 F37 1982
NYPL [*Z-3952 no.39]

AGRICULTURE, COOPERATIVE - GOVERNMENT POLICY - TEXAS.
Knutson, Ronald D. Cooperative involvement in issues of domestic farm policy /. College Station, Tex. , 1986. 59 p. : LC Card 86-623063 DDC 338.1/8764 19
HD1491.U6 T45 1986

AGRICULTURE, COOPERATIVE - HUNGARY.
Erdei Ferenc agrárgazdasági és szövetkezetelméleti munkásságáról . Budapest [1986] 39 p. ; LC Card 87-408584
HD1940.5.E72 E73 1986

AGRICULTURE, COOPERATIVE - HUNGARY - CSONGRÁD MEGYE - HISTORY.
Két évtized . Szeged , 1987. 116 p., [67] p. of plates : LC Card 87-407665
HD1492.H82 C765 1987

AGRICULTURE, COOPERATIVE - HUNGARY - PEST MEGYE.
Mezőgazdasági szövetkezetek Pest megyében, 1985 . Budapest , 1985. 442 p. : ISBN 963-02-4206-0 LC Card 87-137365
HD1492.H82 P475 1985

AGRICULTURE, COOPERATIVE - HUNGARY - SZOLNOK MEGYE - HISTORY.
Urbán, László. A földmüvesszövetkezetek, fogyasztási szövetkezetek négy évtizede Szolnok megyében /. Szolnok , 1985 ([Szolnok] : Készült a Damjanich János Múzeum Rota Gépén) 435 p. ; ISBN 963-01-6642-9 LC Card 87-407748
HD3332.5.A6 S98 1985

AGRICULTURE, COOPERATIVE - INDIA.
Corporate sector and agriculture . New Delhi [1985] 88 p. ; LC Card 87-902181 DDC 338.1/0954 19
HD2072 .C65 1985

AGRICULTURE, COOPERATIVE - INDIA - CASE STUDIES.
Gill, Manohar Singh, 1936- Agriculture cooperatives . New Delhi , c1983. viii, 560 p. ; ISBN 0-7069-2371-5 : LC Card 84-900335 DDC 334/.683/0954552 19
HD1491.I392 P844 1983
NYPL [JLD 86-4240]

AGRICULTURE, COOPERATIVE - INDIA - KURNOOL (DISTRICT) - CASE STUDIES.
Wade, Robert. Village republics . Cambridge [Cambridgeshire] , New York , 1988. p. cm. ISBN 0-521-30146-7 LC Card 86-33389 DDC 334/.683/095484 19
HD1491.I392 K878 1988

AGRICULTURE, COOPERATIVE - INDIA - PUNJAB.
Gill, Manohar Singh, 1936- Agriculture cooperatives . New Delhi , c1983. viii, 560 p. ; ISBN 0-7069-2371-5 : LC Card 84-900335 DDC 334/.683/0954552 19
HD1491.I392 P844 1983
NYPL [JLD 86-4240]

AGRICULTURE, COOPERATIVE - INDONESIA - ABAISIAT.
Geinitz, Dedo. Entwicklungszusammenarbeit mit Indonesien . Bremen , 1985. viii, 72 p. : ISBN 3-88299-046-5 LC Card 86-204688
HD9161.I63 A244 1985

AGRICULTURE, COOPERATIVE - IRAN.
Rachidzadeh, Esfandiar. Le secteur rural et le développement économique . Genève , 1978. ix, 389 p. : LC Card 79-376015 DDC 338.1/0955
HD2065.2 .R3 ***NYPL [JLE 80-2370]***

AGRICULTURE, COOPERATIVE - IRELAND.
Russell, George William, 1867-1935. Co-operation and nationality . Dublin , c1982. 103 p. ; ISBN 0-7165-0335-2 (pbk.) LC Card 82-192895 DDC 334/.683/09417 19
HD1491.I6 R87 1982 ***NYPL [JLD 86-2358]***

AGRICULTURE, COOPERATIVE - KENYA - KITUI (DISTRICT) - EVALUATION.
A Base-line study of Farm Input Supply Scheme. Nairobi , 1981. 65 leaves, [1] leaf of plates : LC Card 87-980116
HD1491.K42 K583 1981

AGRICULTURE, COOPERATIVE - LATIN AMERICA - CONGRESSES.
Reforma agraria como proceso social . Piura, Perú [1984] 163 p. : LC Card 84-232526 DDC 333.3/1/85 19
HD1333.P4 R44 1984 ***NYPL [JLD 86-2537]***

AGRICULTURE, COOPERATIVE - MEXICO - JALISCO.
Cooperativas agrarias y conflictos políticos en el sur de Jalisco /. México, D.F. , 1985 [i.e. 1986]

201 p. ; ISBN 968-8401-93-5 LC Card 87-405021 DDC 334/.683/097235 19
HD1491.M42 J353 1986

AGRICULTURE, COOPERATIVE - MONGOLIA.
Graĭvoronskiĭ, Vladimir Viktorovich. Kooperirovannoe aratstvo MNR--izmenenii͡a v urovne zhizni, 1960-1980 /. Moskva , 1982. 213 p. : LC Card 82-213253
HD1491.M55 G73 1982

AGRICULTURE, COOPERATIVE - MONGOLIA - HISTORY.
Ulymzhiev, D. B. (Dashi Batuevich) Put′ mongol′skogo aratstva k sotsializmu /. Novosibirsk , 1987. 283, [5] p. ; LC Card 87-159668
HD1491.M55 U49 1987

AGRICULTURE, COOPERATIVE - PERU.
Rojas Senisse, Hugo. Azúcar . Lima [Lima?] [1984] 131 p. : LC Card 84-234204 DDC 338.1/7361/0985 19
HD9114.P52 R65 1984 ***NYPL [JLD 85-1982]***

Wester León, Humberto. Diagnóstico situacional del movimiento cooperativo peruano /. [Lima] , 1981- v. : ***NYPL [JLL 86-146]***

AGRICULTURE, COOPERATIVE - PERU - CHANCAY (PROVINCE)
Pacheco B., Gabriel (Pacheco Bustamante) Apuntes sobre el problema parcelario en la Provincia de Chancay /. Huacho, Perú , 1984. 49 p. ; LC Card 86-124478
HD1491.P42 C56 1984

AGRICULTURE, COOPERATIVE - PERU - CONGRESSES.
Taller Alternativas de Cambio de Modelo Empresarial (1985 : Cooperativa San Bartolo del Valle del Santa (Peru)) Taller Alternativas de Cambio de Modelo Empresarial, San Bartolo, Valle del Santa. Lima, Perú [1986] 40 p. : LC Card 87-136317 DDC 334/.683/0985 19
HD1491.P4 T35 1985

AGRICULTURE, COOPERATIVE - PERU - LAMBAYEQUE (DEPT.)
Simons Munaro, Yehude. Lambayeque, producción ganadera, comunidades campesinas [microform] /. Chiclayo, Perú , 1983. 45 p. ; LC Card 84-204537 DDC 338.1/76/0098514 19
HD9424.P43 L367 1983 ***NYPL [*ZT-1708 no.72]***

AGRICULTURE, COOPERATIVE - PHILIPPINES - MISCELLANEA.
Balmores, Egmidio L., 1925- Samahang nayon . Quezon City, Philippines , c1975. x, 169 p. ; LC Card 86-132779
HD1491.P5 B34 1975

AGRICULTURE, COOPERATIVE - PORTUGAL - TRÁS-OS-MONTES - CASE STUDIES.
Portela, José, 1950- Trabalho cooperativo em duas aldeias de Trás-os-Montes /. Porto , 1986. 79 p., [4] p. of plates : LC Card 87-400109 DDC 334/.683/094692 19
HD1491.P82 T736 1986

AGRICULTURE, COOPERATIVE - SPAIN - CATALONIA.
Rendé, Josep M. Pla d'organització social agrària de Catalunya /. Barcelona , 1924. 138 p., [1] folded leaf of plates : LC Card 86-202164 DDC 334/.683/09467 19
HD1491.S82 C317 1924

AGRICULTURE, COOPERATIVE - SWAZILAND.
Guma, Xolile P. Small farmer credit and small farmer attitudes towards co-operatives /. [Kwaluseni, Swaziland] [1982] 94 p. : LC Card 86-101161 DDC 332.7/1/096813 19
HD1491.S855 G85 1982 ***NYPL [JLG 86-262]***

AGRICULTURE, COOPERATIVE - SWEDEN - HISTORY - 20TH CENTURY.
Kylebäck, Hugo, 1930- Konsument- och lantbrukskooperation i Sverige . Stockholm [1984] 277 p. ; ISBN 91-85196-18-5 : LC Card 86-120646
HD3524.A1 K663 1984

AGRICULTURE, COOPERATIVE - UNITED STATES.
Cooperative League of the U. S. A. How to organize a co-op . Washington , 1969. 53 p. : ***NYPL [JLF 86-590]***

AGRICULTURE, COOPERATIVE - UNITED STATES - FINANCE - STATISTICS.
Yager, Francis P. Financial profile of cooperatives handling grain . [Washington, D.C.] [1986] vii, 24 p. : LC Card 86-601622 DDC 334/.6831/0973021 19
HD9034 .Y34 1986

AGRICULTURE, COOPERATIVE - ZAMBIA.
Chilivumbo, Alifeyo. Communal agrarian cooperative societies . Lusaka [1986] iii, 134 p. ; LC Card 86-981399 DDC 334/.683/096894 19
HD1491.Z35 C45 1986

AGRICULTURE, COOPERATIVE - ZAMBIA - CASE STUDIES.
Chilivumbo, Alifeyo. Communal agrarian cooperative societies . Lusaka [1986] iii, 134 p. ; LC Card 86-981399 DDC 334/.683/096894 19
HD1491.Z35 C45 1986

Agriculture cooperatives . Gill, Manohar Singh, 1936- New Delhi , c1983. viii, 560 p. ; ISBN 0-7069-2371-5 : LC Card 84-900335 DDC 334/.683/0954552 19
HD1491.I392 P844 1983 ***NYPL [JLD 86-4240]***

AGRICULTURE CREDIT - GOVERNMENT POLICY - UNITED STATES.
Financing the agricultural sector . Boulder, Colo. , 1986. xi, 256 p. : ISBN 0-8133-0055-X (pbk. : alk. paper) LC Card 86-50152 DDC 338.1/3/0973 19
HD1761 .F5 1986 ***NYPL [JLE 86-2766]***

AGRICULTURE CREDIT - INDIA - NAINI TAL (DISTRICT)
Kumar, Kewal. Institutional financing of Indian agriculture . New Delhi , c1987. 232 p. : LC Card 87-900911 DDC 332.7/1/09542 19
HG2051.I5 N354 1987

AGRICULTURE - CZECHOSLOVAKIA - BOHEMIA - HISTORY - 19TH CENTURY.
Jeleček, Leoš. Zemědělství a půdní fond v Čechách ve 2. polovině 19. století /. Praha , 1985. 283 p. : LC Card 86-199876
HD640.3.Z8 B634 1985

Agriculture d'aujourd'hui.
Roux, Pierre, docteur en sciences économiques. Economie agricole /. Paris , c1986- v. <1 > : ISBN 2-85206-353-0 (set) LC Card 87-106675
HD1415 .R62 1986

AGRICULTURE - DEVELOPING COUNTRIES.
Integrating nutrition into agricultural and rural development projects . Rome , 1984. ix, 132 p. : ISBN 92-5-102150-3 ***NYPL [JLG 86-181]***

U. S. agriculture & Third World development . Boulder , 1987. xi, 258 p. ; ISBN 1-555-87011-2 (lib. bdg.) : LC Card 86-29860 DDC 338.1/09172/4 19
HD1765 .U15 1987

AGRICULTURE - DEVELOPING COUNTRIES - CASE STUDIES.
Critchfield, Richard. The golden bowl be broken . Bloomington , 1988. p. cm. ISBN 0-253-32554-4 LC Card 87-3690 DDC 305.5/63 19
HD1542 .C75 1988

AGRICULTURE - DEVELOPING COUNTRIES - FINANCE.
Farm management input to rural financial systems development /. Rome , 1985. xii, 57 p. : ISBN 92-5-102191-0 (pbk.) LC Card 86-207967 DDC 332.7/1/091724 19
HD1440.D44 F37 1985

AGRICULTURE - DEVELOPING COUNTRIES - TECHNOLOGY TRANSFER.
Burch, David, 1942 Jan. 16- Overseas aid and the transfer of technology . Aldershot, [Hants, England] , Brookfield [Vt.], USA , c1987. xiv, 370 p. ; ISBN 0-566-00480-1 : LC Card 87-237 DDC 338.1/81 19
HD1431 .B87 1987

AGRICULTURE - ECOLOGY. see **AGRICULTURAL ECOLOGY.**

AGRICULTURE - ECONOMIC ASPECTS - ADDRESSES, ESSAYS, LECTURES.
Lectures in agricultural economics . [Washington? , 1977] ix, 165 p. : LC Card 77-603242
HD1759 .L4 ***NYPL [JLE 79-149]***

AGRICULTURE - ECONOMIC ASPECTS - AFRICA.
Agrarnye preobrazovanii͡a v stranakh Afriki na sovremennom ėtape /. Moskva , 1982. 227 p. ; LC Card 83-143645
HD2117 .A347 1982

Bates, Robert H. Essays on the political economy of rural Africa /. Berkeley , 1987, c1983. p. cm. ISBN 0-520-06014-8 (pbk. : alk. paper) LC Card 86-25120 DDC 330.96/0328/091734 19
HD2117 .B37 1987

Dinham, Barbara. Agribusiness in Africa /. Trenton, N.J. , 1984. 224 p. : ISBN 0-86543-003-9 : LC Card 85-672721
HD9017.A2 D56x 1984 ***NYPL [Sc D 86-769]***

Gakou, Mohamed Lamine. [Crise de l'agriculture africaine. English.] The crisis in African agriculture /. London ; Atlantic Highlands, N.J., USA : xii, 100 p. ; ISBN 0-86232-732-6 : LC Card 87-13355 DDC 338.1/096 19
HD2117 .G3513 1987

Harrison, Paul. The greening of Africa . New York, N.Y., U. S.A. , 1987. 380 p. : ISBN 0-14-010192-6 (pbk.) : LC Card 87-404277 DDC 338.1/9/6 19
HD2117 .H37 1987

Natural resources and the human environment for food and agriculture in Africa. Rome , 1986. iv, 83 p. : ISBN 92-5-102354-9 (pbk.) LC Card 86-222103 DDC 338.1/096 19
HC800 .N34 1986

AGRICULTURE - ECONOMIC ASPECTS - ALBERTA - CONGRESSES.
Second century, opportunities for agriculture . [Edmonton] [1986] viii, 289 p. : LC Card 87-100958 DDC 338.1/097123 19
HD1790.A6 S42 1986

AGRICULTURE - ECONOMIC ASPECTS - ALGERIA - CONSTANTINE (PROVINCE)
Meuleman, Johan H. Le Constantinois entre les deux guerres mondiales . Assen, Pays-Bas , 1985. 296 p., [1] folded leaf of plates : ISBN 90-232-2093-5 : LC Card 86-119662
HC815.Z7 C666 1985

AGRICULTURE - ECONOMIC ASPECTS - ANDES REGION - CONGRESSES.
Investigación agraria y crisis . Quito , 1986. 498 p. : LC Card 87-400125 DDC 338.1/098 19
HD1860.A53 I58 1986

AGRICULTURE - ECONOMIC ASPECTS - ARGENTINA - HISTORY - 20TH CENTURY - STATISTICS.
Anuario estadístico agropecuario argentino, 1930-1984 . [Buenos Aires] [1984] 2 v. (480 leaves) ; LC Card 86-177130
HD1862 .A69 1984

AGRICULTURE - ECONOMIC ASPECTS - ARGENTINA - PAMPAS.
Solé, Miguel José. Las condiciones de vida y de trabajo de los tamberos de la pampa húmeda . Stockholm , 1983. 33 p. ; LC Card 84-107283
HD1865.P35 S65 1983

AGRICULTURE - ECONOMIC ASPECTS - ARGENTINA - STATISTICS.
Agricultura, caza, silvicultura y pesca . [Buenos Aires] [1982] 57 p. : LC Card 87-401763 DDC 338.1/0982/021 19
HD1862 .A58 1982

AGRICULTURE - ECONOMIC ASPECTS - ARKANSAS.
Gunderson, Ralph O. Agricultural and socioeconomic perspectives of Arkansas . Morrilton, AR , 1987. p. cm. ISBN 0-933595-13-1 : LC Card 87-24146 DDC 338.1/09767 19
HD1775.A8 G85 1987

AGRICULTURE - ECONOMIC ASPECTS - ARMENIAN S.S.R. - HISTORY - CONGRESSES.
Nyut'er Hayastani gyughatntesut'yan ev gyughats'iut'yan patmut'yan /. Erevan , 1964- v. <1 > : LC Card 86-225528
HD1995.A7 N98 1964

AGRICULTURE - ECONOMIC ASPECTS - ASIA.

Bray, Francesca. The rice economies . Oxford [Oxfordshire] , New York , 1986. xvii, 254 p. : ISBN 0-631-14877-9 : LC Card 85-30819 DDC 338.1/7318/095 19
HD9066.A7 B73 1986 ***NYPL [JLE 87-793]***

James, William E. Asian agriculture and economic development /. Manila, Philippines , c1982. xiii, 128 p. ; LC Card 87-104389 DDC 338.1/095 19
HD2056 .J35 1982

James, William E. Asian agriculture in transition . Manila, Philippines , c1983. v, 93 p. ; LC Card 87-105114 DDC 338.1/095 19
HD2056 .J355 1983

Oshima, Harry T. (Harry Tatsumi) The transition to an industrial economy in monsoon Asia /. Manila, Philippines , c1983. 111 p. ; LC Card 87-105003 DDC 338.095 19
HC412 .O694 1983

AGRICULTURE - ECONOMIC ASPECTS - AUSTRALIA.

Economic development in East and South-east Asia . Canberra , 1984. x, 237 p. : ISBN 0-644-02983-8 (pbk.) LC Card 86-673760
HC460.5 .E26x 1984

Hefford, Ron. Farm policy in Australia /. St. Lucia [Brisbane] , New York , c1985. xviii, 415 p. : ISBN 0-7022-1698-4 LC Card 83-23457 DDC 338.1/894 19
HD2153 .H43 1984 ***NYPL [JLD 87-867]***

AGRICULTURE - ECONOMIC ASPECTS - AUSTRALIA - ECONOMETRIC MODELS.

Higgs, Peter J. (Peter John), 1959- Adaptation and survival in Australian agriculture . Melbourne , New York , 1986. xxx, 320 p. : ISBN 0-19-554749-7 LC Card 87-133685 DDC 338.1/0994 19
HD2152 .H54 1986

AGRICULTURE - ECONOMIC ASPECTS - AUSTRALIA - FORECASTING - ECONOMETRIC MODELS.

Higgs, Peter J. (Peter John), 1959- Adaptation and survival in Australian agriculture . Melbourne , New York , 1986. xxx, 320 p. : ISBN 0-19-554749-7 LC Card 87-133685 DDC 338.1/0994 19
HD2152 .H54 1986

AGRICULTURE - ECONOMIC ASPECTS - AUSTRALIA - HISTORY - STATISTICS.

Historical trends in Australian rural production, exports, farm income, and indexes of prices received and paid by farmers, 1952-53 to 1972-73 /. Canberra , 1974. vii, 17 p. : ISBN 0-642-00746-2 (pbk.) LC Card 85-126806 DDC 338.1/0994/021 19
HD2152 .H57 1974

AGRICULTURE - ECONOMIC ASPECTS - AUSTRALIA - QUEENSLAND - HISTORY - 19TH CENTURY.

Walker, Jan, 1954- Jondaryan station . St. Lucia , New York , 1988. p. cm. ISBN 0-7022-2093-0 (pbk.) LC Card 87-13816 DDC 333.3/09943 19
HD1039.Q43 W34 1988

AGRICULTURE - ECONOMIC ASPECTS - AUSTRIA.

Landwirtschaftliche Produktionsalternativen am Beispiel Ethanol, Ölsaaten und Eiweissfutterpflanzen /. Wien , 1985. 141 p. : LC Card 86-108149 DDC 338.1/09436 19
HD1935 .L33 1985

AGRICULTURE - ECONOMIC ASPECTS - BANGLADESH.

Muqtada, M. Social and economic formations in Bangladesh agriculture . Dacca, Bangladesh , 1986. 68 p. ; LC Card 86-902421 DDC 338.1/09549/2 19
HD2075.6 .M86 1986

Rahamāna, Āsahābura, 1949- Bāṅalādeśera kṛshikāṭhāmo, kṛshaka samāja, o unnaẏan /. Ḍhākā , 1986. 39, 158 p. ; LC Card 86-903304
HD2075.6 .R33 1986

AGRICULTURE - ECONOMIC ASPECTS - BENIN.

Keddeman, Willem. Emploi et revenus dans le secteur agricole traditionnel au Bénin /. Addis Abéba , 1982. 64 p. ; LC Card 87-980402
HD2141 .K43 1982

AGRICULTURE - ECONOMIC ASPECTS - BOLIVIA - HISTORY - 17TH CENTURY.

Escobari de Querejazu, Laura. Producción y comercio en el espacio sur andino en el siglo XVII . La Paz , 1985. 218 p., [12] p. of plates : LC Card 86-174929
HC167.A5 E83 1985

AGRICULTURE - ECONOMIC ASPECTS - BOLIVIA - SANTA CRUZ (DEPT.)

Gill, Lesley. Peasants, entrepreneurs, and social change . Boulder , 1987. xiv, 246 p. : ISBN 0-8133-7339-5 (pbk. : alk. paper) : LC Card 86-28207 DDC 303.4/0984/3 19
HD1870.S25 G54 1987

AGRICULTURE - ECONOMIC ASPECTS - BOLIVIA - STATISTICS.

II censo nacional agropecuario. [La Paz], República de Bolivia [1986- v. <1-3 > : LC Card 87-109107
HD1867 .A14 1986

AGRICULTURE - ECONOMIC ASPECTS - BRAZIL.

Delgado, Guilherme Costa. Capital financeiro e agricultura no Brasil, 1965-1985 /. S[ão] Paulo, SP, Brasil , Campinas, SP , c1985. 240 p. ; LC Card 87-102748
HD1440.B8 D45 1985

Homem de Melo, Fernando Bento, 1942- Prioridade agrícola . São Paulo , 1985. xiii, 200 p. : LC Card 86-126447 DDC 338.1/881 19
HD1872 .H66 1985 ***NYPL [JLD 86-3809]***

Müller, Geraldo. Alimentação e agricultura no Brasil . [São Paulo] , 1984. 64 p. : LC Card 86-132127
HD1872 .M85 1984

Vinhas, M. A terra, o homem, as reformas /. Rio de Janeiro (R. Hermenegildo de Barros, 31-A Glória, Rio de Janeiro) , 1980. xiii, 151 p. ; ***NYPL [JLD 86-783]***

AGRICULTURE - ECONOMIC ASPECTS - BRAZIL - BRASÍLIA REGION.

Franz, Paulo Renato Ferreira. Região geoeconômica de Brasília . Planaltina-DF [Brazil] , 1985. 70 p. : LC Card 87-143606 DDC 338.1/3/098174 19
HD1875.B7 F7 1985

AGRICULTURE - ECONOMIC ASPECTS - BRAZIL - CEARÁ (STATE)

Casimiro, Liana Maria Carleial de. Seca . Fortaleza-Ceará [19]84. 63 p. ; LC Card 86-130055 DDC 330.981/31063 19
HC188.C4 C29 1984

O Norte cearense /. Recife , 1985. 303 p. : LC Card 86-209022
HD1875.C4 N67 1985

AGRICULTURE - ECONOMIC ASPECTS - BRAZIL - ECONOMETRIC MODELS.

Santos, José Carlos de Souza. Demanda de fatores e ofertas na agricultura brasileira . Rio de Janeiro , 1983. 110 p. ; LC Card 87-403023 DDC 338.1/0981 19
HD1872 .S25 1983

AGRICULTURE - ECONOMIC ASPECTS - BRAZIL - MINAS GERAIS - CASE STUDIES.

Gomes, Sebastião Teixeira. Condicionantes da modernização do pequeno agricultor /. São Paulo , 1986. 181 p. : LC Card 87-153609 DDC 338.1/0981/51 19
HD1875.M5 G65 1986

AGRICULTURE - ECONOMIC ASPECTS - BRAZIL, NORTHEAST.

Andrade, Manuel Correia de Oliveira. Sertão sul /. Recife , 1984. 648, [26] p. : LC Card 87-404838 DDC 330.981/3063 19
HC188.N6 A687 1984

Melo, Mário Lacerda de. O meio-norte /. Recife , 1983. 474 p., [1] folded leaf of plates : LC Card 84-231900
HC188.N6 M45 1983

AGRICULTURE - ECONOMIC ASPECTS - BRAZIL - PARAÍBA (STATE)

Leite, José Alfredo A. A sócio-economia do semi-árido /. João Pessoa , 1985. 47 p. : LC Card 87-141315 DDC 330.981/33/063 19
HD1875.P34 L45 1985

AGRICULTURE - ECONOMIC ASPECTS - BRAZIL - PINDARÉ RIVER VALLEY.

Luna, Regina Celi Miranda Reis. A terra era liberta . São Luís, MA , 1985. xxvii, 146 p. : LC Card 87-135907 DDC 333.3/0981/21 19
HD499.P46 L86 1985

AGRICULTURE - ECONOMIC ASPECTS - BRAZIL - RIO GRANDE DO NORTE - HISTORY - 20TH CENTURY - STATISTICS.

Séries históricas da produção agrícola do Estado do Rio Grande do Norte, 1947-1982 . Natal , 1983. 159 leaves : LC Card 84-246432
HD1875.R48 S47 1983

AGRICULTURE - ECONOMIC ASPECTS - BRAZIL - RIO GRANDE DO SUL.

Cunha, Rafael Alves de. Duas décadas da produção e do produto da agropecuária RS, 1964-84 /. Porto Alegre , 1986- v. <1 > : LC Card 87-404979 DDC 338.1/0981/65 19
HD9014.B83 R5416 1986

AGRICULTURE - ECONOMIC ASPECTS - BRAZIL - SERGIPE.

Projeto Tabuleiros Norte de Sergipe /. Aracaju , 1977. 521 p. : LC Card 86-131158
HD1875.S4 P76 1977

AGRICULTURE - ECONOMIC ASPECTS - BULGARIA - STATISTICS.

A Bolgár és a magyar mezőgazdaság összehasonlítása, 1976-1984 /. Budapest , 1987. 69 p. ; ISBN 963-02-4777-1 LC Card 87-409639 DDC 338.1/09439/021 19
HD2042 .B59 1987

AGRICULTURE - ECONOMIC ASPECTS - BURKINA FASO.

Agricultural sector assistance strategy for Upper Volta. Washington, D.C. [1982] 1 v. (various pagings) : LC Card 87-120355 DDC 338.1/8 19
HD2144 .A38 1982

Lecaillon, Jacques. Economic policies and agricultural performance . Paris , 1985. 158 p. ; LC Card 86-216027 DDC 338.1/86625 19
HD2144 .L42 1985

AGRICULTURE - ECONOMIC ASPECTS - CALIFORNIA - HISTORY - 19TH CENTURY.

Breadbasket of the world . San Francisco , 1984. 10 pamphlets : LC Card 87-100963 DDC 338.1/7311/09794 19
HD9049.W5 U414 1984

AGRICULTURE - ECONOMIC ASPECTS - CAMEROON.

Agricultural input supply in Cameroon . Alexandria, Va. [1983] 2 v. : LC Card 87-119188 DDC 338.1/0967/11 19
HD2139.5 .A68 1983

AGRICULTURE - ECONOMIC ASPECTS - CENTRAL AMERICA.

Brockett, Charles D., 1946- Land, power, and poverty . Boston , c1988. p. cm. ISBN 0-04-497027-7 LC Card 87-22746 DDC 338.1/09728 19
HD1797 .B76 1988

AGRICULTURE - ECONOMIC ASPECTS - CHILE.

Boom en el agro chileno? /. Santiago de Chile , 1985. 123 p. ; LC Card 87-401452 DDC 338.1/0983 19
HD1877 .B66 1985

Mannarelli M., Virgilio B. Organización institucional del sector agrícola /. Santiago, Chile , 1985. 81, [3] p. : LC Card 86-115545 DDC 338.1/883 19
HD1878 .M35 1985

AGRICULTURE - ECONOMIC ASPECTS - CHINA.

Feeding a billion . East Lansing , 1987. 462 p., [16] p. of plates : ISBN 0-87013-246-6 (alk. paper) : LC Card 87-60024 DDC 338.1/9/51 19
HD2098 .F45 1987

On rolls the green revolution /. Beijing, China [1984] 142 p., [36] p. of plates : LC Card 86-115054 DDC 338.1/0951 19
HD2097 .O5 1984 ***NYPL [JLK 83-122 no.9]***

Weitz, Maria. Entwicklungen in der chinesischen Agrarpolitik seit 1978 /. Berlin , 1986. 110 p. ; ISBN 3-428-06036-9 LC Card 87-409465 DDC 338.1/851 19
HD2097 .W45 1986

AGRICULTURE - ECONOMIC ASPECTS - CHINA - SHENSI PROVINCE - HISTORY - 20TH CENTURY.
Vermeer, E. B. (Eduard B.) Economic development in provincial China . Cambridge [Cambridgeshire] , New York , 1988. p. cm. ISBN 0-521-34392-5 LC Card 87-22499 DDC 330.951/17058 19
HC428.S54 V47 1988

AGRICULTURE - ECONOMIC ASPECTS - COLOMBIA.
Poveda Ramos, Gabriel. Nueva alternativa para el desarrollo . Bogotá , 1974. 249 p. : LC Card 78-345029
HD1883 1974 .P68 *NYPL [JLE 80-482]*

Problemas agrarios colombianos /. [Bogotá, Colombia] , México, D.F. , 1986. 467 p. : ISBN 958-606-005-5 LC Card 86-221632
HD1882 .P75 1986

Santa María de Cárdenas, Cecilia. El seguro agrícola como factor de desarrollo económico /. Bogotá , 1978. 168, 2, [43] p. : LC Card 85-203482
HG9966 .S25 1978

AGRICULTURE - ECONOMIC ASPECTS - COLOMBIA - ADDRESSES, ESSAYS, LECTURES.
Campesinado y capitalismo en Colombia /. Bogotá, Colombia , 1981. 233 p. ; LC Card 82-141108 DDC 338.1/09861 19
HD516 .C35 1981 *NYPL [JLD 86-1342]*

AGRICULTURE - ECONOMIC ASPECTS - COMMUNIST COUNTRIES.
Socialist agriculture in transition . Boulder, Colo. , 1986. ix, 445 p. : ISBN 0-8133-7344-1 : LC Card 86-28995 DDC 338.1/0947 19
HD1917 .S62 1986

AGRICULTURE - ECONOMIC ASPECTS - COSTA RICA.
Hallauer, Robert. Export promotion policies in Costa Rica . Austin , 1985. 17 p. ; LC Card 86-622254 DDC 382/.63/097286 19
HF1487 .H35 1985

AGRICULTURE - ECONOMIC ASPECTS - CUBA.

AGRICULTURE - ECONOMIC ASPECTS - CZECHOSLOVAKIA.
Kutil, Jaroslav. Czechoslovak agriculture /. Prague , 1983. 125 p., [48] p. of plates : LC Card 84-109068 DDC 338.1/09437 19
HD1940.3.Z8 K87 1983
NYPL [JLD 86-2294]

AGRICULTURE - ECONOMIC ASPECTS - CZECHOSLOVAKIA - SLOVAK SOCIALIST REPUBLIC.
Bauch, Vlastislav. Sociálno-ekonomický vývoj slovenského pol'nohospodárskeho obyvatel'stva /. Bratislava , 1986. 362, [5] p. ; LC Card 87-125324
HD1940.3.Z9 S573 1986

AGRICULTURE - ECONOMIC ASPECTS - DATA PROCESSING.
Woolverton, Michael W. Computer concepts for agribusiness /. Westport, Conn. , 1985. xii, 311 p. : ISBN 0-87055-510-3 : LC Card 85-23043 DDC 631 19
HD1433 .W66 1985 *NYPL [JLE 86-1534]*

AGRICULTURE - ECONOMIC ASPECTS - DENMARK - HISTORY.
Noter over dansk landbrugshistorie. Greve Strand , 1982. 53 p. : ISBN 87-7470-314-5 : LC Card 83-170741
HD2002 .N67 1982

Ulrichsen, Niels. J.A.K.--en dansk krisebevægelse /. København , 1978. 202 p. ; ISBN 87-87462-13-3 LC Card 87-462108
HD2002 .U45 1978

AGRICULTURE - ECONOMIC ASPECTS - DEVELOPING COUNTRIES.
Arnon, Itzhak, 1909- Modernization of agriculture in developing countries . Chichester [West Sussex] , New York , c1987. xxiii, 626 p. : ISBN 0-471-91586-6 : LC Card 87-6288 DDC 338.1/09172/4 19
HD1417 .A76 1987

Clayton, E. (Eric) Agriculture, poverty, and freedom in developing countries /. London , 1983. x, 277 p. : ISBN 0-333-36100-8 LC Card 86-673664
HD1417 .C52x 1983

Griffin, Keith B. World hunger and the world economy . New York , 1987. xvi, 274 p. ; ISBN 0-8419-1128-2 LC Card 86-33626 DDC 330.9172/4 19
HC59.7 .G749 1987

Guida alla valorizzazione agricola nei paesi in via di sviluppo /. Milano, Italy , c1983. 434 p. : LC Card 83-144803 DDC 338.1/09172/4 19
HD1417 .G85 1983 *NYPL [JLD 86-3296]*

Warnock, John W., 1933- The politics of hunger . Toronto , New York , c1987. xv, 334 p. ; ISBN 0-458-80630-7 (pbk.) : LC Card 87-1659 DDC 363.8/09172/4 19
HD9018.D44 W37 1987

AGRICULTURE - ECONOMIC ASPECTS - DEVELOPING COUNTRIES - CONGRESSES.
Pursuing food security . Boulder , 1987. xv, 357 p. : ISBN 1-555-87032-5 (lib. bdg. : alk. paper) : LC Card 87-4524 DDC 337/.05 s 338.1/9/1724 19
HF1410 .I579 vol. 3 HD9018.D44

U. S. agriculture and Third World economic development . Washington, D.C. , c1987. xv, 103 p. : ISBN 0-89068-086-8 (pbk.): LC Card 86-62757 DDC 338.9/009172/4 19
HD1755 .U173 1987

AGRICULTURE - ECONOMIC ASPECTS - DEVELOPING COUNTRIES - HANDBOOKS, MANUALS, ETC.
Handbuch der Landwirtschaft und Ernährung in den Entwicklungsländern /. Stuttgart , c1982- v. : ISBN 3-8001-3059-9 (Bd. 1) LC Card 84-155503 DDC 338.1/09172/4 19
HD1417 .H24 1982 *NYPL [JLL 86-257]*

AGRICULTURE - ECONOMIC ASPECTS - DOMINICAN REPUBLIC.
Tejada C., Frank A. Crédito y seguro agrícola . Santo Domingo, República Dominicana , 1986. 104 p. : LC Card 87-400183 DDC 332.7/1/097293 19
HG2051.D6 T45 1986

AGRICULTURE - ECONOMIC ASPECTS - ECUADOR.
Cosse, Gustavo. Estado y agro en el Ecuador, 1960-1980 /. Quito , 1984. 112 p. : LC Card 85-119842 DDC 338.1/8866 19
HD1888 .C67 1984 *NYPL [JLD 86-2738]*

Santana, Roberto. Campesinado indígena y el desafío de la modernidad /. [Quito, Ecuador] , 1983. 209 p. : LC Card 84-156117 DDC 330.9866/074/08998 19
F3721.3.E25 S26 1983
NYPL [HBC 86-2225]

Tenencia de la tierra y desarrollo socio-económico del sector agrícola. [Guayaquil] [1981] xxv, 539 p., [16] leaves of plates : LC Card 87-673171
HD526 .T46x 1981

AGRICULTURE - ECONOMIC ASPECTS - ECUADOR - ESMERALDAS (PROVINCE) - CASE STUDIES.
Campesinado y organización en Esmeraldas /. [Quito, Ecuador?] [1986] 213 p. : LC Card 86-171561
HD1531.E2 C36 1986

AGRICULTURE - ECONOMIC ASPECTS - EGYPT.
Raḍwān, Samīr Muḥammad. Agrarian change in Egypt . London , Dover, N.H. , c1986. xii, 167 p. : ISBN 0-7099-4214-1 : LC Card 85-11356 DDC 305.5/69/0962 19
HN786.A8 R33 1985 *NYPL [JLD 86-1045]*

AGRICULTURE - ECONOMIC ASPECTS - EL SALVADOR - HISTORY.
Molina Osegueda, Carlos Alberto. Acumulación agrícola y agroindustrial /. [San Salvador, El Salvador, C.A. , 1980] 187 p. : LC Card 86-174381
HD1827 .M65 1980

AGRICULTURE - ECONOMIC ASPECTS - ENGLAND - DURHAM (COUNTY) - HISTORY.
Brassley, Paul, 1946- The agricultural economy of Northumberland and Durham in the period, 1640-1750 /. New York , 1985. iii, 224 p. : ISBN 0-8240-6676-6 : LC Card 84-45996 DDC 338.1/09428/6 19
HD1930.N67 B73 1985
NYPL [JLE 86-3924]

AGRICULTURE - ECONOMIC ASPECTS - ENGLAND - HISTORY - 19TH CENTURY.
Brown, Jonathan, 1950- Agriculture in England, 1870-1947 /. Manchester, U.K. , Wolfeboro, N.H., U. S.A. , c1987. p. cm. ISBN 0-7190-1759-9 : LC Card 87-20381 DDC 338.1/0942 19
HD1930.E5 B76 1987

AGRICULTURE - ECONOMIC ASPECTS - ENGLAND - HISTORY - 20TH CENTURY.
Brown, Jonathan, 1950- Agriculture in England, 1870-1947 /. Manchester, U.K. , Wolfeboro, N.H., U. S.A. , c1987. p. cm. ISBN 0-7190-1759-9 : LC Card 87-20381 DDC 338.1/0942 19
HD1930.E5 B76 1987

AGRICULTURE - ECONOMIC ASPECTS - ENGLAND - KENT - HISTORY.
Baker, Dennis, 1928- Agricultural prices, production, and marketing, with special reference to the hop industry . New York , 1985. 779 p. : ISBN 0-8240-6675-8 : LC Card 84-45995 DDC 338.1/7382 19
HD9019.H72 G67 1985 *NYPL [JLE 87-63]*

AGRICULTURE - ECONOMIC ASPECTS - ENGLAND - NORTHUMBERLAND - HISTORY.
Brassley, Paul, 1946- The agricultural economy of Northumberland and Durham in the period, 1640-1750 /. New York , 1985. iii, 224 p. : ISBN 0-8240-6676-6 : LC Card 84-45996 DDC 338.1/09428/6 19
HD1930.N67 B73 1985
NYPL [JLE 86-3924]

AGRICULTURE - ECONOMIC ASPECTS - ETHIOPIA.
Harjinder Singh. Agricultural problems in Ethiopia /. Delhi, India , c1987. viii, 254 p. : ISBN 81-212-0078-4 : LC Card 87-900338 DDC 338.1/0963 19
HD2124.5 .H37 1987

AGRICULTURE - ECONOMIC ASPECTS - EUROPE.
General review /. New York , 1986. iii, 81 p. ; ISBN 92-1-116361-7 (pbk.) LC Card 87-120391 DDC 338.1/094 19
HD1917 .U5 no. 28, vol. 1

AGRICULTURE - ECONOMIC ASPECTS - EUROPE, EASTERN.
Sárándi, Imre. Világgazdasági korszakváltások és a mezőgazdasági termékforgalom . [Budapest] [1985] 92 p. ; LC Card 86-218536
HD1415 .S25 1985

Socialist agriculture in transition . Boulder, Colo. , 1986. ix, 445 p. : ISBN 0-8133-7344-1 : LC Card 86-28995 DDC 338.1/0947 19
HD1917 .S62 1986

AGRICULTURE - ECONOMIC ASPECTS - EUROPE - HISTORY.
Theorie und Empirie in Wirtschaftspolitik und Wirtschaftsgeschichte . Göttingen , 1984. 242 p. : ISBN 3-509-01366-2 : LC Card 85-120064
HC240 .T45 1984

AGRICULTURE - ECONOMIC ASPECTS - EUROPE - STATISTICS.
A Magyar mezőgazdaság európai összehasonlításban /. Budapest , 1985. 207 p. : ISBN 963-02-3856-X (Magy. nemz. bibl.) LC Card 86-157394
HD1940.5 .M34 1985

AGRICULTURE - ECONOMIC ASPECTS - EUROPEAN ECONOMIC COMMUNITY COUNTRIES.
Agricultural policies in the European Community . Canberra , 1985. xii, 373 p. : ISBN 0-644-04293-1 (pbk.) LC Card 86-673733
HD1920.5.Z8 A37x 1985

Azevedo, J. Cândido de. Portugal, Europa face ao Mercado Comum . Amadora , c1978. 300 p. ; LC Card 80-121153
HC241.25.P6 A94 1978

Bösche, Bernd, 1955- Agrarsektorale und gesamtwirtschaftliche Integration in der Europäischen Gemeinschaft . Frankfurt am Main , New York , c1987. 226 p. : ISBN 3-8204-9442-1 LC Card 87-407586 DDC 338.1/81/094 19
HD1920.5 .B67 1987

Carfantan, Jean Yves. L'Europe verte sous influence . Paris , c1985. 282 p. ; ISBN 2-02-008982-3 : LC Card 86-140900 DDC 338.1/094 19
HD1920.5 .C37 1985 ***NYPL [JLE 87-526]***

Loring, Jaime. Los sectores agrarios de Andalucía ante la integración en la C.E.E. /. Madrid , 1984. 303 p. : ISBN 84-7114-149-3 LC Card 86-152628
HD2025.A5 L67 1984

Pour un rôle actif de la Communauté économique européenne sur la scène agricole internationale . Paris , c1986. 184 p. ; ISBN 2-11-001582-9 : LC Card 86-174918
HD1431 .P68 1986

AGRICULTURE - ECONOMIC ASPECTS - FRANCE.

Muller, Pierre. Le technocrate et le paysan . Paris , c1984. 173 p. ; ISBN 2-7082-2347-X : LC Card 84-171796 DDC 338.1/6 19
HD1947 .M85 1984 ***NYPL [JLD 86-3738]***

Systèmes de production et transformations de l'agriculture /. Paris , 1985. 2 v. : ISBN 2-85340-715-2 (v. 1) LC Card 86-214407
HD1945 .S97 1985

AGRICULTURE - ECONOMIC ASPECTS - FRANCE - DÔMES MOUNTAINS.

Système agraire et pratiques paysannes dans les monts Dômes /. Paris , 1983. xi, 318 p., [8] p. of plates : ISBN 2-85340-478-1 LC Card 84-216594
HD1950.D65 S97 1983

AGRICULTURE - ECONOMIC ASPECTS - FRANCE - HISTORY.

Trunskiĭ, ÍU. G. Frantsuzskaia derevnia v XIX-XX vekakh . Moskva , 1986. 283 p. ; LC Card 86-201573
HD1945 .T78 1986

AGRICULTURE - ECONOMIC ASPECTS - FRANCE - ISÈRE.

Perrin, Jacqueline. L'enquête de 1848 sur le travail en Isère /. Grenoble , 1985. 251 p., [1] leaf of plates : ISBN 2-904661-03-4 : LC Card 86-227898
HC277.I8 P47 1985

AGRICULTURE - ECONOMIC ASPECTS - FRANCE - STATISTICS.

Franciaország és Magyarország mezőgazdasága /. Budapest , 1986. 43 p. : ISBN 963-340-783-4 : LC Card 86-189634
HD1945 .F74 1986

Recettes, dépenses et revenus des exploitations agricoles en 1983 /. Paris [1986] 138 p. : LC Card 86-187878
HD1945 .R374 1986

AGRICULTURE - ECONOMIC ASPECTS - GERMANY.

Kautsky, Karl, 1854-1938. [Agrarfrage. English.] The agrarian question /. London , Atlantic Highlands, N.J. , 1988- p. cm. ISBN 1-85305-024-5 (v. 2) LC Card 87-20593 DDC 338.1 19
HD1306.G3 K315 1988

AGRICULTURE - ECONOMIC ASPECTS - GERMANY, EAST.

Rudolph, Jürgen. Aktuelle Fragen der Theorie und Praxis der staatlichen Leitung der Landwirtschaft /. Potsdam-Babelsberg , 1983. 72 p. ; LC Card 83-214391
HD1960.5.Z8 R83 1983

AGRICULTURE - ECONOMIC ASPECTS - GERMANY (EAST) - HISTORY - 20TH CENTURY - SOURCES.

Wie wir angefangen haben . Berlin , 1985. 326 p. : LC Card 85-217979
HD1333.G35 W54 1985

AGRICULTURE - ECONOMIC ASPECTS - GERMANY - SOCIETIES, ETC. - HISTORY.

Sondermann, Klaus. Wirtschaftsentwicklung und landwirtschaftliche Verbandspolitik . Münster-Hiltrup , 1983. vi, 300 p. : ISBN 3-7843-0283-1 : LC Card 84-126226
HD1486.G3 S66 1983

AGRICULTURE - ECONOMIC ASPECTS - GERMANY, WEST.

Agrarmärkte & Agrarmarketing . Hamburg , 1983. 220 p. : ISBN 3-922528-45-7 LC Card 84-162297
HD1955 .A515 1983

Bauer, Jürgen. Quantitative Entwicklungsplanung für ländliche Regionen . Bochum , 1979. 382 p. in various pagings : ISBN 3-88339-087-9 : LC Card 80-470152
HT395.G4 B39 1979 ***NYPL [JLD 86-1628]***

Holla, Michael. Die Belastung der Landwirtschaft durch Beiträge zur sozialen Sicherung im Vergleich zur Situation anderer sozialer Gruppen . Göttingen [1986] viii, 174 p. ; LC Card 87-407657 DDC 368.4/00943 19
HD7179 .H635 1986

Witzke, Harald von. Personelle Einkommensverteilung in der Landwirtschaft und Agrarpreise /. Berlin , 1979. 180 p. : ISBN 3-428-04303-0 LC Card 79-389988
HC290.5.I5 W57 ***NYPL [JLE 80-439]***

AGRICULTURE - ECONOMIC ASPECTS - GERMANY (WEST) - LOWER SAXONY.

Reessing, Ludwig. Analyse der Wettbewerbsfähigkeit von Extensivblattfrüchten in Niedersachsen unter ökonomischen und ökologischen Gesichtspunkten /. Kiel , 1986. xiv, 251 p. : ISBN 3-922553-81-8 LC Card 86-163003
HD1960.L69 R44 1986

Schumacher, Karl-Edzard. Entwicklungsmöglichkeiten landwirtschaftlicher Übergangsbetriebe in Niedersachsen . Göttingen , 1985. 234, vi p. : LC Card 86-186858
HD9013.7.L68 S38 1985

AGRICULTURE - ECONOMIC ASPECTS - GERMANY (WEST) - LOWER SAXONY - STATISTICS.

Agrarberichterstattung 1983 . Hannover , 1985. viii, 143 p., [3] p. of plates : LC Card 86-222908
HD1960.L68 A38 1985

Landwirtschaftszählung 1979, Gartenbauerhebung 1981/82 . Hannover , 1983. xv, 132 p. ; LC Card 85-117833
HD9013.7.L68 L37 1983

AGRICULTURE - ECONOMIC ASPECTS - GERMANY (WEST) - NORTH RHINE-WESTPHALIA - STATISTICS.

Agrarberichterstattung Nordrhein-Westfalen 1981 . Düsseldorf [1983] 131, [5] p. ; LC Card 87-407319 DDC 943/.55 s 338.1/0943/55021 19
HA1320.N6 A32 Heft 489 HD9013.7.N6

Agrarberichterstattung Nordrhein-Westfalen 1981 . Düsseldorf [1983] 189 p. ; LC Card 87-407320 DDC 943/.55 s 338.1/0943/55021 19
HA1320.N6 A32 Heft 490 HD1960.N67

Agrarberichterstattung Nordrhein-Westfalen 1983 . Düsseldorf [1984] 263 p. ; LC Card 87-407317 DDC 943/.55 s 338.1/0943/55021 19
HA1320.N6 A32 Heft 532 HD1960.N67

Agrarberichterstattung Nordrhein-Westfalen 1983 . Düsseldorf [1985] 191 p. ; LC Card 87-407316 DDC 943/.55 s 338.1/0943/55021 19
HA1320.N6 A32 Heft 531 HD1960.N67

AGRICULTURE - ECONOMIC ASPECTS - GERMANY (WEST) - RHINELAND.

Ebel, Friedhelm. Landwirtschaft am Niederrhein . Bonn , 1976. 223 p. : LC Card 87-408419
HD1407 .L3 Heft 33 HD1960.R48

AGRICULTURE - ECONOMIC ASPECTS - GREAT BRITAIN.

Countryside conflicts . Aldershot, Hants, England , Brookfield, Vt., U. S. A. , c1986. vi, 378 p. [4] leaves of plates : ISBN 0-566-05088-9 : LC Card 85-24603 DDC 333.76/17/0941 19
HD596 .C675 1986 ***NYPL [JLD 86-2487]***

AGRICULTURE - ECONOMIC ASPECTS - GREECE.

Delēs, Dēmētrēs I. Hē anaptyxē tēs hellēnikēs geōrgias . Athēna , 1985. 3 v. in 2 : LC Card 86-203175
HD2055.5 .D44 1985

AGRICULTURE - ECONOMIC ASPECTS - GREECE - HISTORY.

Karapostolēs, Vasilēs. Oikonomikes metamorphōseis tēs agrotikēs Helladas . Athēna , 1981. 52 [1] p. : LC Card 86-194022
HD2055.5 .K36 1981

AGRICULTURE - ECONOMIC ASPECTS - GREECE - STATISTICS.

Oikonomikē kai koinōnikē anaptyxis Anat. Makedonias kai Thrakēs . Kavalla [1973-] v. <1 > : LC Card 87-125407
HD2055.5 .O54 1973

AGRICULTURE - ECONOMIC ASPECTS - GUATEMALA.

Hintermeister, Alberto. Modernización de la agricultura y pobreza rural en Guatemala /. [Santiago, Chile] , 1982. 59 leaves : LC Card 87-403247 DDC 338.1/6/097281 19
HC144.Z9 P624 1982

AGRICULTURE - ECONOMIC ASPECTS - HAWAII - KAUAI.

Economic development on the island of Kauai . [Honolulu] [1985] xxii, 84 p. : LC Card 86-622084 DDC 338.9969/41 19
HC107.H32 K383 1985

AGRICULTURE - ECONOMIC ASPECTS - HUNGARY.

Almási, István. Négy évtizede új úton a magyar mezőgazdaság /. [Budapest] [1985] 159 p. : ISBN 963-7252-41-X LC Card 86-228893
HD1940.5 .A85 1985

Benet, Iván. Az agráripari egyesülések útkeresése /. Budapest , 1985. 197 p. : ISBN 963-221-616-4 : LC Card 86-203013
HD9015.H82 B447 1985

Borszéki, Éva. Élelmiszer-gazdaságunk versenyképessége . Budapest , 1986. 284, [1] p. : ISBN 963-221-590-7 : LC Card 87-148751
HD1940.5 .B66 1986

Borszéki, Éva. Élelmiszergazdaságunk versenyképessége . Budapest , 1985. 147 p. ; ISBN 963-491-213-3 LC Card 86-199073
HD1940.5 .B67 1985

Az Élelmiszer-gazdaság távlati fejlesztése /. Budapest , 1984. 163 p. ; ISBN 963-231-717-3 : LC Card 85-194280
HD1940.5.Z8 E54 1984

Erdei Ferenc agrárgazdasági és szövetkezetelméleti munkásságáról . Budapest [1986] 39 p. ; LC Card 87-408584
HD1940.5.E72 E73 1986

Halmai, Péter. Integráció és tulajdon az iparosodó mezőgazdaságban /. [Budapest] , 1984. 124 p. ; ISBN 963-673-278-7 LC Card 85-126691
HD1940.5 .H35 1984

Main directions of agricultural development in Hungary . Budapest , 1985. 77 p. ; LC Card 86-232881 DDC 338.1 s 338.1/09439 19
HD1407 .M3 no. 61 HD1940.5

Németi, László. Hatékonyság és fejlesztési lehetőségek a mai magyar mezőgazdaságban /. Budapest , 1986. 189 p. : ISBN 963-232-238-X : LC Card 87-407758
HD1940.5 .N46 1986

Soós, Gábor, 1922- Mit kell tudni a magyar agrártermelésről? /. [Budapest] , 1984. 218 p. ; ISBN 963-09-2474-9 : LC Card 85-154641
HD1940.5 .S66 1984

Szelényi, Iván. Socialist entrepreneurs . Madison, Wis. , 1988. p. cm. ISBN 0-299-11360-4 : LC Card 87-16085 DDC 338.1/09439 19
HD1940.5 .S94 1988

AGRICULTURE - ECONOMIC ASPECTS - HUNGARY - CONGRESSES.

Magyar-Lengyel Agrárközgazdasági Konferencia (1984 : Gödöllő, Hungary) A nagyüzemek és a kisüzemek termelésének fejlődése, kapcsolatuk az iparosodó mezőgazdaságban =. Gödöllő , 1984. 174 p. ; LC Card 86-145249
HD1995.7 .M32 1984

AGRICULTURE - ECONOMIC ASPECTS - HUNGARY - HISTORY.

Steinbach, Antal. A Magyar Dolgozók Pártja Központi Vezetősége 1953. júniusi határozatának agrárpolitikai előzményei /. [Budapest] , 1985. 104 p. ; ISBN 963-673-321-X LC Card 86-187055
HD1940.5.Z8 S74 1985

AGRICULTURE - ECONOMIC ASPECTS - HUNGARY - HISTORY - CONGRESSES.

Agrárgazdaság, agrártársadalom, agrárpolitika /. Szeged , 1985. 338 p. : ISBN 963-481-548-0 : LC Card 86-143859
HD1940.5 .A78 1985

AGRICULTURE - ECONOMIC ASPECTS - HUNGARY - STATISTICS.

A Bolgár és a magyar mezőgazdaság

összehasonlítása, 1976-1984 /. Budapest , 1987. 69 p. ; ISBN 963-02-4777-1 LC Card 87-409639 DDC 338.1/09439/021 19
HD2042 .B59 1987

Franciaország és Magyarország mezőgazdasága /. Budapest , 1986. 43 p. : ISBN 963-340-783-4 : LC Card 86-189634
HD1945 .F74 1986

A Jugoszláv és a magyar mezőgazdaság összehasonlítása a határmenti területeken /. Budapest , 1986. 37 p. ; LC Card 87-407672
HD1940.5 .J83 1986

A Magyar mezőgazdaság európai összehasonlításban /. Budapest , 1985. 207 p. : ISBN 963-02-3856-X (Magy. nemz. bibl.) LC Card 86-157394
HD1940.5 .M34 1985

Mezőgazdasági és élelmiszeripari adattár a felszabadulástól napjainkig /. Budapest , 1985. 152 p. ; ISBN 963-502-393-6 LC Card 86-202515
HD1940.5 .M497 1985

Mezőgazdasági és élelmiszeripari adattár a felszabadulástól napjainkig. English. Collection of data of agriculture and food industry from the liberation till now /. Budapest , 1985. 85 p. ; ISBN 963-502-393-6 LC Card 86-230345
HD1940.5 .M49713 1985

AGRICULTURE - ECONOMIC ASPECTS - HUNGARY - SZOLNOK MEGYE.

Összefoglalás, Szolnok megye agroökológiai potenciálja az ezredfordulón /. Budapest , 1984. 115 p. : ISBN 963-491-193-5 LC Card 86-198809
HD1940.5.Z9 S966 1984

AGRICULTURE - ECONOMIC ASPECTS - INDIA.

Bergmann, Theodor. Agrarian reform in India . New Delhi, India , 1984. viii, 216 p. ; LC Card 84-900254 DDC 333.3/1/54 19
HD1333.I4 B46 1984 ***NYPL [JLD 86-3823]***

Chakrabarti, Rajendra M. Underdevelopment and choices in agriculture . New Delhi , 1986. xv, 322 p. : LC Card 86-903184 DDC 338.1/0954 19
HC435.2 .C466 1986

Dhawan, B. D. Irrigation in India's agricultural development . New Delhi , Newbury Park [Calif.] , 1987. p. cm. ISBN 0-8039-9544-X LC Card 87-22521 DDC 338.1/62 19
HD1741.I29 D47 1987

Étienne, Gilbert. Food and poverty . New Delhi , Newbury Park, Calif. , 1987. p. cm. ISBN 0-8039-9540-7 LC Card 87-16992 DDC 338.1/0954 19
HC440.P6 E86 1987

Growth of agriculture and rural development in India /. New Delhi , c1987. xx, 496 p. ; LC Card 87-900250 DDC 338.1/0954 19
HD2072 .G7 1987

Indian agricultural development since independence . New Delhi , c1986. viii, 519 p. ; ISBN 81-204-0118-2 : LC Card 86-902551 DDC 338.1/0954 19
HD2072 .I526 1986

Mahajan, V. S., 1923- Growth of agriculture and industry in India /. New Delhi , c1983. 176 p. ; LC Card 83-906175 DDC 338.0954 19
HD2072 .M23 1983 ***NYPL [JLD 87-671]***

Patnaik, Utsa. The agrarian question and the development of capitalism in India /. Delhi , New York , 1986. 45 p. ; ISBN 0-19-561954-4 : LC Card 86-900017 DDC 338.1/0954 19
HD2072 .P33 1986

Spitz, P. (Pierre) Food systems and society in India . Geneva [1983] 2 v. (393 p.) : LC Card 87-100437
HD9016.I42 S62 1983

Ul′i͡anovskiĭ, R. A. (Rostislav Aleksandrovich) Agrarnai͡a Indii͡a mezhdu mirovymi voĭnami . Moskva , 1981. 342, [2] p. ; LC Card 82-102795 DDC 338.1/0954 19
HD2072 .U44 1981

Zarkovic, M. Issues in Indian agricultural development /. Boulder , 1987. xviii, 203 p. ; ISBN 0-8133-7451-0 (soft : alk. paper) LC Card 87-50898 DDC 338.1/0954 19
HD2072 .Z37 1987

AGRICULTURE - ECONOMIC ASPECTS - INDIA - ANDHRA PRADESH.

Krishna Rao, Y. V. Growth of capitalism in agriculture . Vijayawada , 1984. x, 62 p. ; LC Card 84-900585 DDC 338.1/3/095484 19
HD2075.A5 K75 1984 ***NYPL [JLD 86-4256]***

Siva Prasad, K. Technological breakthrough in agriculture /. Allahabad, India , 1987. xii, 133 p. ; ISBN 81-85076-15-4 : LC Card 86-903607 DDC 338.1/61 19
HD2075.A5 S58 1987

AGRICULTURE - ECONOMIC ASPECTS - INDIA - ANDHRA PRADESH - CASE STUDIES.

Venkaiah, V., 1952- Impact of agro-based industries on rural economy . Bombay , 1987. xxi, 348 p. ; LC Card 86-903766 DDC 338.1/0954/84 19
HD9016.I43 A67 1987

AGRICULTURE - ECONOMIC ASPECTS - INDIA - BAHIRI.

Majumder, Arun. Poverty, development, and exchange relations . New Delhi , 1987. xiii, 141 p. : ISBN 81-7027-108-8 : LC Card 87-900910
HC438.B24 M35 1987

AGRICULTURE - ECONOMIC ASPECTS - INDIA - BIHAR.

Poddar, B. N. Development of irrigation and Indian agriculture /. New Delhi , c1987. 331 p. ; LC Card 87-901300 DDC 338.1/62 19
HD2075.B5 P63 1967

Singh, Kanti. The great depression and agrarian economy . Delhi, India , 1987. xii, 206 p. ; LC Card 86-903533 DDC 338.1/0954/12 19
HC437.B47 S53 1987

AGRICULTURE - ECONOMIC ASPECTS - INDIA - CASE STUDIES.

Krishna Rao, Y. V. Growth of capitalism in agriculture . Vijayawada , 1984. x, 62 p. ; LC Card 84-900585 DDC 338.1/3/095484 19
HD2075.A5 K75 1984 ***NYPL [JLD 86-4256]***

Srivastava, G. C. (Gyan Chand), 1939- Urbanization, capital formation, and labour productivity in agriculture . New Delhi , 1986. xii, 205 p. : ISBN 81-7027-097-9 : LC Card 86-902590 DDC 338.1/0954 19
HD2075.R35 S75 1986

Venkaiah, V., 1952- Impact of agro-based industries on rural economy . Bombay , 1987. xxi, 348 p. ; LC Card 86-903766 DDC 338.1/0954/84 19
HD9016.I43 A67 1987

AGRICULTURE - ECONOMIC ASPECTS - INDIA - DARPASILA.

Majumder, Arun. Poverty, development, and exchange relations . New Delhi , 1987. xiii, 141 p. : ISBN 81-7027-108-8 : LC Card 87-900910
HC438.B24 M35 1987

AGRICULTURE - ECONOMIC ASPECTS - INDIA - HARYANA.

Gupta, D. P. (Dharm Pall), 1932- Agricultural development in Haryana /. New Delhi, India , 1985. xiii, 120 p. : LC Card 85-901427 DDC 338.1/854558 19
HD2075.H3 G85 1985
NYPL [JLD 86-3862]

AGRICULTURE - ECONOMIC ASPECTS - INDIA - JAMMU AND KASHMIR - HISTORY.

Sharma, Dewan Chand, 1898- Kashmir agriculture & land revenue system under the Sikh rule, 1819-46 A.D. /. New Delhi, India , 1986. xiv, 160 p., [8] p. of plates : LC Card 86-900128
HD2075.J35 S43 1986 ***NYPL [JLD 86-3742]***

AGRICULTURE - ECONOMIC ASPECTS - INDIA - MEGHALAYA.

Sukumaran Nair, M. K., 1948- Tribal economy in transition . New Delhi, India , 1987, c1986. 159 p. ; ISBN 81-210-0180-3 : LC Card 87-901406 DDC 330.954/164052 19
HC437.M4 S85 1987

AGRICULTURE - ECONOMIC ASPECTS - INDIA, NORTHEASTERN.

Shukla, Surya Pal, 1939- Agriculture in north-eastern region /. New Delhi, India , 1986. xxvi, 223 p. : LC Card 86-902178 DDC 338.1/0954/1 19
HD2075.N58 S58 1986 ***NYPL [JLD 87-938]***

AGRICULTURE - ECONOMIC ASPECTS - INDIA - PUNJAB - HISTORY.

Hari Singh, Master, 1902- Agrarian scene in British Punjab /. New Delhi , 1983-c1984. 2 v. : LC Card 83-905514 DDC 338.1/0954/5 19
HD2075.P8 H37 1983 ***NYPL [JLK 86-113]***

AGRICULTURE - ECONOMIC ASPECTS - INDIA - PUNJAB - MATHEMATICAL MODELS.

Astroth, Joseph H., 1955- Understanding peasant agriculture . Chicago, Ill. , 1987. p. cm. ISBN 0-89065-127-2 (pbk.) : LC Card 87-15099 DDC 333.76/13/0724 19
HD879.P8 A77 1987

AGRICULTURE - ECONOMIC ASPECTS - INDIA - RANCHI - CASE STUDIES.

Srivastava, G. C. (Gyan Chand), 1939- Urbanization, capital formation, and labour productivity in agriculture . New Delhi , 1986. xii, 205 p. : ISBN 81-7027-097-9 : LC Card 86-902590 DDC 338.1/0954 19
HD2075.R35 S75 1986

AGRICULTURE - ECONOMIC ASPECTS - INDIA - UTTAR PRADESH.

Singh, Ajit Kumar, 1944- Agricultural development and rural poverty /. New Delhi , 1987. v, 368 p. : ISBN 81-7024-069-7 : LC Card 86-903483 DDC 338.1/8542 19
HD2075.U88 S55 1987

AGRICULTURE - ECONOMIC ASPECTS - INDIA - VISHAKHAPATNAM DISTRICT.

Suryanarayana Raju, S. K. V. Analysis of productivity levels and economic efficiency in agriculture /. Allahabad, India , 1987 [i.e. 1986] viii, 368 p. : ISBN 81-85076-12-X : LC Card 86-903606 DDC 338.1/0954/84 19
HD2075.V58 S87 1986

AGRICULTURE - ECONOMIC ASPECTS - INDONESIA - BANTUL (KABUPATEN) - CASE STUDIES.

Maurer, Jean-Luc. Modernisation agricole, développement économique et changement social . Paris , c1986. 323 p. : ISBN 2-13-039622-4 : LC Card 86-175394
HD2085.B37 M38 1986

AGRICULTURE - ECONOMIC ASPECTS - IRAN.

Nattagh, Nima. Agriculture & regional development in Iran /. Wisbech, Cambridgeshire, England , 1986. 105 p. : ISBN 0-906559-26-X (pbk.) : LC Card 86-230845 DDC 338.1/0955 19
HD1565.2 .N37 1986

Rachidzadeh, Esfandiar. Le secteur rural et le développement économique . Genève , 1978. ix, 389 p. : LC Card 79-376015 DDC 338.1/0955
HD2065.2 .R3 ***NYPL [JLE 80-2370]***

AGRICULTURE - ECONOMIC ASPECTS - IRAQ.

Mukhlif, Hādī Aḥmad. al-Tawzīʻ al-jughrāfī li-mazāriʻ al-dawlah fī al-ʻIrāq wa-atharihā fī al-tanmiyah al-iqtiṣādīyah /. [Baghdad] , 1985. 2 v. (607 p., 3 leaves of plates) : LC Card 86-963500
HD1493.I72 M85 1985

AGRICULTURE - ECONOMIC ASPECTS - ITALY.

Italy. Parlamento. Giunta per la inchiesta agraria e sulle condizioni della classe agricola. Inchiesta Jacini . Sala Bolognese , 1978-<1987. v. <1-7, 9-10; v. 13, t. 1, fasc. 1-3; v. 11, t. 1-3; v. 13, t. 2, fasc. 4-5; in 18 > : LC Card 86-143133
HD1970 .I84 1978

AGRICULTURE - ECONOMIC ASPECTS - ITALY - COMPUTER PROGRAMS.

Istituto nazionale di economia agraria. Il programma INEA per la progettazione e le analisi statistiche di un campione rappresentativo /. Roma , 1986. 122 p. : LC Card 86-213865
HD1970 .I773 1986

AGRICULTURE - ECONOMIC ASPECTS - ITALY - CREMONA REGION - HISTORY.

Bellabarba, Marco. Seriolanti e arzenisti . Cremona , 1986- v. <1 > : LC Card 86-167180
HD1676.I82 C743 1986

AGRICULTURE - ECONOMIC ASPECTS - ITALY - MILAN REGION.

Metropoli e agricoltura /. Milano , c1982. 319 p. : LC Card 82-246692 DDC 333.76/13/094521

19
HD680.M54 M47 1982
NYPL [JLD 86-3678]

AGRICULTURE - ECONOMIC ASPECTS - ITALY - MONTEMASSI - HISTORY.
Pertempi, Silvia. Montemassi . Torino , 1986. 238 p. ; ISBN 88-7011-250-0 : LC Card 87-134525
HD9506.I83 M656 1986

AGRICULTURE - ECONOMIC ASPECTS - ITALY - PIEMONTE - HISTORY.
Rapetti, Vittorio, 1955- Uomini, collina e vigneto in Piemonte, da metà Ottocento agli anni trenta /. Alessandria , 1984. 342 p., [16] p. of plates : LC Card 86-151345
HD9385.I82 P547 1984

AGRICULTURE - ECONOMIC ASPECTS - ITALY - PO RIVER PLAIN - HISTORY.
Bellabarba, Marco. Seriolanti e arzenisti . Cremona , 1986- v. <1 > : LC Card 86-167180
HD1676.I82 C743 1986

AGRICULTURE - ECONOMIC ASPECTS - ITALY, SOUTHERN - ADDRESSES, ESSAYS, LECTURES.
Il Mezzogiorno nelle politiche nazionali e comunitarie . Milano , 1982. 379 p. ; LC Card 82-230171 DDC 338.945/7 19
HC305 .M42156 1982 ***NYPL [JLE 86-1611]***

AGRICULTURE - ECONOMIC ASPECTS - IVORY COAST.
Trueblood, Michael A. The Ivory Coast . Washington, DC , 1986. iv, 32 p. : LC Card 86-602806 DDC 338.1 s 382/.41/096668 19
HD1411 .F59 no. 223 HD9017.I912

AGRICULTURE - ECONOMIC ASPECTS - JAMAICA - HISTORY - 19TH CENTURY.
Lobdell, Richard A. Economic structure and demographic performance in Jamaica, 1891-1935 /. New York , 1987. xii, 259 p. ; ISBN 0-8240-1365-4 (alk. paper) : LC Card 87-8345 DDC 304.6/097292 19
HB3553 .L63 1987

AGRICULTURE - ECONOMIC ASPECTS - JAMAICA - HISTORY - 20TH CENTURY.
Lobdell, Richard A. Economic structure and demographic performance in Jamaica, 1891-1935 /. New York , 1987. xii, 259 p. ; ISBN 0-8240-1365-4 (alk. paper) : LC Card 87-8345 DDC 304.6/097292 19
HB3553 .L63 1987

AGRICULTURE - ECONOMIC ASPECTS - JAMAICA - STATISTICS.
Census of agriculture, 1978-1979 . [Kingston] [1983] vi, ix, 167 p. : LC Card 83-242227 DDC 338.1/097292 19
HD1847 .C46 1983 ***NYPL [JLF 86-1028]***

AGRICULTURE - ECONOMIC ASPECTS - JAPAN - HISTORY.
Lenz, Ilse. Kapitalistische Entwicklung, Subsistenzproduktion und Frauenarbeit . Frankfurt/Main , New York , c1984. 330 p. : ISBN 3-593-33407-0(pbk.)
NYPL [JLD 87-332]

AGRICULTURE - ECONOMIC ASPECTS - KIRGHIZ S.S.R.
Boldzhurova, I. S. (Ishengul′ Sadykovna) Kolkhoznoe krest′i͡anstvo Kirgizii v uslovii͡akh razvitogo sotsializma /. Frunze , 1985. 148 p. ; LC Card 86-106126
HD1995.K53 B65 1985

Sovershenstvovanie ėkonomicheskikh metodov upravlenii͡a sel′skokhozi͡aĭstvennym proizvodstvom /. Frunze , 1982. 158 p. ; LC Card 83-196563
HD9015.S653 K577 1982

AGRICULTURE - ECONOMIC ASPECTS - LATIN AMERICA.
Astori, Danilo. La agricultura campesina en América Latina . Montevideo, Uruguay [1985?] 35 p. ; LC Card 86-204310 DDC 338.1/098 19
HD1790.5 .A85 1985

Deere, Carmen Diana. The peasantry in political economy . [Amherst, MA] , 1987. 76 p. ; LC Card 87-404080 DDC 305.5/63 19
HD1531.L3 D44 1987

AGRICULTURE - ECONOMIC ASPECTS - LESOTHO - CONGRESSES.
Employment and development in Lesotho . Addis Ababa , 1983. ii, 229 p. ; ISBN 92-2-103780-0 LC Card 84-980769 DDC 331.12/09681/6 19
HD5842.7.A6 E46 1983

AGRICULTURE - ECONOMIC ASPECTS - LITHUANIA.
Lietuvos TSR žemės ūkio tvarkymo sistema /. Vilnius , 1985. 453 p. ; LC Card 86-215158
HD1995.L5 L535 1985

AGRICULTURE - ECONOMIC ASPECTS - LIVONIA (ESTONIA AND LATVIA) - SOCIETIES, ETC. - HISTORY.
Engelhardt, Hans Dieter von. Die Livländische Gemeinnützige und Ökonomische Sozietät (1792-1939) . Köln , 1983. ix, 215 p., [3] leaves of plates : ISBN 3-412-04282-X LC Card 84-117318
HD1486.S65 E54 1983

AGRICULTURE - ECONOMIC ASPECTS - LOUISIANA - STATISTICS.
Fielder, Lonnie L. Agricultural statistics and prices for Louisiana, 1909-1985 /. [Baton Rouge, LA] [1986] iv, [122] p. : LC Card 87-620749 DDC 338.1/09763 s 338.1/09763/021 19
HD1775.L8 L7 no. 659

AGRICULTURE - ECONOMIC ASPECTS - MALAWI.
Pachai, Bridglal. Land and politics in Malawi, 1875-1975 /. Kingston, Ontario, Canada , c1978. xiv, 245 p., [20] p. of plates : ISBN 0-919642-82-9 LC Card 86-673708
HD997 .P32x 1978

AGRICULTURE - ECONOMIC ASPECTS - MALAWI - CONGRESSES.
Malawi . Edinburgh , c1985. xviii, 642 p. : LC Card 86-100522 DDC 338.96897 19
HC935 .M36 1985

AGRICULTURE - ECONOMIC ASPECTS - MALAYSIA.
Environment, agriculture, and society in the Malay world /. Kyoto, Japan , 1986. ix, 177 p. : LC Card 86-201590 DDC 338.1/09595 19
HD2080.6 .E58 1986

AGRICULTURE - ECONOMIC ASPECTS - MALI.
Lecaillon, Jacques. Economic policies and agricultural performance . Paris , 1986. 174 p. ; LC Card 87-158595 DDC 338.1/86623 19
HD2143.5.Z8 L43 1986

AGRICULTURE - ECONOMIC ASPECTS - MATHEMATICAL MODELS.
Thompson, Robert L. A survey of recent U. S. developments in international agricultural trade models /. Washington, D.C. , 1981. v, 74 p. ; LC Card 81-603138 DDC 382/.41/0973 19
HD1433 .T48 ***NYPL [JLF 84-568]***

AGRICULTURE - ECONOMIC ASPECTS - MEXICO.
Acevedo Conde, María Luisa. Pobreza y riqueza en 378 municipios de México /. México, D.F. , 1984. 281 p. : LC Card 86-219445
HC140.P6 A25 1984

Astorga Lira, Enrique. Mercado de trabajo rural en México . México, D.F. , 1985. 127 p. : ISBN 968-411-139-8 LC Card 86-141300 DDC 331.7/63/0972 19
HD1531.M6 A88 1985 ***NYPL [JLC 87-68]***

Barkin, David. El fin de la autosuficiencia alimentaria /. México, D.F. , 1985. 249 p. : ISBN 968-493-091-7 LC Card 82-230750
NYPL [JLE 87-404]

Barkin, David. El fin de la autosuficiencia alimentaria /. México, D.F. , c1985. 249 p. : ISBN 968-493-091-7 LC Card 86-209699
HD1792 .B38 1985

Estructura agraria y desarrollo agrícola en México . México , 1974 (1979 printing) xvi, 1174 p. : LC Card 81-126616 DDC 338.1/0972 19
HD1792 .E85 1974 ***NYPL [JLE 81-372]***

Salinas de Gortari, Carlos. Producción y participación política en el campo /. México , 1980. 320 p. : ISBN 968-582-934-9 LC Card 82-199421 DDC 338.1/0972 19
HD1792 .S287 1980 ***NYPL [JLD 86-2602]***

AGRICULTURE - ECONOMIC ASPECTS - MEXICO - CHIAPAS.
Thompson G., Roberto. Problemática agraria y política petrolera en Chiapas /. Tuxtla Gutiérrez, Chiapas , 1983. 37 p., [1] leaf of plates : LC Card 84-243074
HD9574.M63 C457 1983

AGRICULTURE - ECONOMIC ASPECTS - MEXICO - CHILCHOTA REGION.
Ramírez C., Luis Alfonso. Chilchota, un pueblo al pie de la sierra . Zamora, Mich. [i.e. Michoacán] [Morelia, Mexico] , 1986. 306 p. : ISBN 968-7230-23-1 LC Card 87-401034 DDC 330.972/37 19
HC138.C45 R36 1986

AGRICULTURE - ECONOMIC ASPECTS - MEXICO - CONGRESSES.
U. S.-Mexico relations . Stanford, Calif. , c1987. xii, 401 p. ; ISBN 0-8047-1319-7 (alk. paper) LC Card 86-23103 DDC 338.1/872 19
HD1792 .U19 1987

AGRICULTURE - ECONOMIC ASPECTS - MEXICO - FUERTE RIVER VALLEY - HISTORY.
Gill, Mario. La conquista del Valle del Fuerte /. Culiacán, Rosales, Sinaloa, México , c1983. 273 p., [4] folded leaves of plates : LC Card 86-121747
HC137.F84 G54 1983

AGRICULTURE - ECONOMIC ASPECTS - MEXICO - HISTORY - 20TH CENTURY.

AGRICULTURE - ECONOMIC ASPECTS - MEXICO - NAHUATZEN REGION.
García López, Lucía. Nahuatzen, agricultura y comercio en una comunidad serrana /. Zamora, Mich. , México, D.F. , c1984. 115 p. : ISBN 968-7230-03-7 LC Card 85-154045 DDC 338.1/0972/37 19
HD1795.N34 G37 1984 ***NYPL [JLD 87-16]***

AGRICULTURE - ECONOMIC ASPECTS - MIDDLE WEST - HISTORY - 19TH CENTURY.
Fite, Gilbert Courtland, 1918- The farmers' frontier, 1865-1900 /. Norman [1987], c1966. xiv, 272 p. : ISBN 0-8061-2063-0 (pbk.) LC Card 86-40534 DDC 338.1/0977 19
HD8039.F3 U643 1987

AGRICULTURE - ECONOMIC ASPECTS - MIDDLE WEST - HISTORY - CONGRESSES.
Agricultural distress in the Midwest, past & present /. Iowa City , 1986. ix, 111 p. : ISBN 0-87414-049-8 : LC Card 86-29932 DDC 338.1/0977 19
HD1773.A3 A37 1986

AGRICULTURE - ECONOMIC ASPECTS - MOROCCO - HISTORY.
Swearingen, Will D. (Will Davis), 1946- Moroccan mirages . Princeton, N.J. , c1987. xvii, 217 p., [9] p. of plates : ISBN 0-691-05505-X (alk. paper) : LC Card 87-6981 DDC 338.1/0964 19
HD2121 .S94 1987

AGRICULTURE - ECONOMIC ASPECTS - MOROCCO - MARRAKESH REGION - HISTORY.
Pascon, Paul. [Haouz de Marrakech. English.] Capitalism and agriculture in the Haouz of Marrakesh /. London ; New York : 248 p. : ISBN 0-7103-0189-8 LC Card 87-100309 DDC 338.1/0964/6 19
HD2121.Z9 M37613 1986

AGRICULTURE - ECONOMIC ASPECTS - MOZAMBIQUE.
Caballero, Lorenzo. Mozambique, food and agriculture sector /. Uppsala , 1984. 223, [30] p. : ISBN 91-576-2129-2 (pbk.) LC Card 86-218958 DDC 338.1/0967/9 19
HD9017.M86 C33 1984

Wuyts, Marc. Camponeses e economia rural em Moçambique [microform] /. Maputo , 1978. 31, A1-A6 p. ; LC Card 80-980386 DDC 338.1/0967/9 19
HD2129 .W89 1978
NYPL [*ZT-1564 no.14]

Wuyts, Marc. On the question of mechanisation of Mozambican agriculture today . [Maputo, Mozambique] , 1979. 22 p. : LC Card 83-207389
HD2129 .W893 1979

AGRICULTURE - ECONOMIC ASPECTS - NAMIBIA.
Kirk, Michael, 1955- Ochsenanspannung in Westafrika . Göttingen , c1984. iv, 220 p. ; ISBN 3-88694-057-8 LC Card 86-202167 DDC 338.1/09688 19
HD2134 .K57 1984

AGRICULTURE - ECONOMIC ASPECTS - NEPAL.
Gurung, Harka B. Food systems and society in Nepal . Kathmandu, Nepal , 1981. 53, iii p. : LC Card 83-901141 DDC 338.1/9/5496 19
HD9016.N42 G87 1981 ***NYPL [JLG 86-71]***

AGRICULTURE - ECONOMIC ASPECTS - NEPAL - STATISTICS.
A Study on the improvement of the national sample censuses of agriculture in Nepal. Kathmandu , 1986. 67 p. : LC Card 87-900372 DDC 338.1/09549/6 19
HD2065.9 .S78 1986

AGRICULTURE - ECONOMIC ASPECTS - NETHERLANDS - HISTORY.
Huizinga, W. Two lectures on the historical development of Dutch agriculture, 1600-1985 /. Den Haag [1986] 31 p. : LC Card 86-233719
HD1987 .H85 1986

AGRICULTURE - ECONOMIC ASPECTS - NICARAGUA.
Colburn, Forrest D. Post-revolutionary Nicaragua . Berkeley , c1986. xi, 145 p. : ISBN 0-520-05524-1 LC Card 85-5798 DDC 338.1/097285 19
HD1817 .C63 1986 ***NYPL [JLD 86-2414]***

Thielen, Helmut, 1941- Agrarreformen in Lateinamerika zwischen Ökonomie und Ökologie . Frankfurt am Main , c1985. 518 p. : ISBN 3-88129-958-0 LC Card 86-153251 DDC 333.3/1/7285 19
HD1333.N5 T48 1985 ***NYPL [JLD 87-467]***

Wheelock, Jaime. Entre la crisis y la agresión . Managua, Nicaragua [1985] 148 p. : LC Card 85-241401 DDC 333.3/1/7285 19
HD1333.N5 W48 1985 ***NYPL [JLC 86-312]***

AGRICULTURE - ECONOMIC ASPECTS - NIGERIA.
Eweka, J. A. (Julius A.) Village development . Ibadan, Nigeria , 1979. xvi, 194 p. ; LC Card 86-172121 DDC 338.1/9/669 19
HD2145.5 .E94 1979

Folayan, Adekunle. Agriculture and economic development in Nigeria . New York , c1983. x, 276 p. : ISBN 0-533-05325-0 : LC Card 81-90817 DDC 338.1/09669 19
HD2145.5 .F64 1983 ***NYPL [JLE 86-1080]***

Mabbs-Zeno, Carl. Nigeria . Washington, D.C. [1986] vi, 54 p. : LC Card 86-601597 DDC 382/.41/09669 19
HD9017.N52 M3 1986

Sano, Hans-Otto. The political economy of food in Nigeria 1960-1982 . Uppsala , 1983. 108 p. : ISBN 91-7106-210-6 ***NYPL [JLD 84-860]***

State, oil, and agriculture in Nigeria /. Berkeley , c1987. xiv, 327 p. : ISBN 0-87725-166-5 (pbk.) : LC Card 87-2941 DDC 338.1/8669 19
HD2145.5 .S73 1987

AGRICULTURE - ECONOMIC ASPECTS - NIGERIA - ADDRESSES, ESSAYS, LECTURES.
Nigerian small farmers . Benin-City, Bendel State, Nigeria , 1980. xv, 315 p. ; LC Card 82-206979 DDC 338.1/6 19
HD1339.N5 N54 1980 ***NYPL [Sc D 86-883]***

AGRICULTURE - ECONOMIC ASPECTS - NIGERIA - BENUE STATE.
Industrial and agricultural potentials in Benue State. Makurdi , 1986. 36 p. : LC Card 87-102274 DDC 338.09669/5 19
HC1055.Z7 B455 1986

AGRICULTURE - ECONOMIC ASPECTS - NIGERIA - CONGRESSES.
National Workshop on Self Reliance and Self Sufficiency in the Nigerian Economy (1978 : University of Ibadan) Self-reliance and self-sufficiency . [Ibadan, Nigeria] , 1979. 156 p. : LC Card 87-402546 DDC 338.9669 19
HC1055 .N386 1978

AGRICULTURE - ECONOMIC ASPECTS - NIGERIA - HISTORY - 20TH CENTURY.
Rural underdevelopment in Nigeria, 1900-1980. Zaria, Nigeria , 1985. iv, 102 p. ; LC Card 86-154806 DDC 338.1/8669 19
HD2145.5.Z8 R87 1985

AGRICULTURE - ECONOMIC ASPECTS - NORWAY.
Hegrenes, Agnar. Mekaniseringsøkonomi på enkeltbruk /. Oslo , 1985. 175 p. : ISBN 82-7077-028-0 LC Card 86-180961
HD2012 .H44 1985

Knapskog, Kåre. Økonomiske forhold ved generasjonsskifte i landbruket =. Oslo , 1986. 95 p. : ISBN 82-7077-032-9 LC Card 86-231818
HD2012 .K6 1986

AGRICULTURE - ECONOMIC ASPECTS - PAKISTAN.
Morozova, M. I͡U. (Marina I͡Ur'evna) Sovremennai͡a pakistanskai͡a derevni͡a . Moskva , 1986. 172 p. ; LC Card 86-174352
HD2075.5 .M67 1986

AGRICULTURE - ECONOMIC ASPECTS - PALOUSE RIVER VALLEY (IDAHO AND WASH.) - HISTORY - 19TH CENTURY.
Prevost, Nancy M., 1953- Paradise in the Palouse . Fairfield, Wash. , c1985. 35 p. : ISBN 0-87770-365-5 (pbk.) LC Card 85-17842 DDC 338.1/09797/39 19
HD1775.W2 P74 1985 ***NYPL [JFF 86-559]***

AGRICULTURE - ECONOMIC ASPECTS - PANAMA.
Gandásegui, Marco A. La fuerza de trabajo en el agro . Panamá, R.P. , c1985. 404 p. : ISBN 84-8385-002-X LC Card 86-111074 DDC 331.7/63/097287 19
HD1822 .G36 1985 ***NYPL [JLF 86-1350]***

AGRICULTURE - ECONOMIC ASPECTS - PARAGUAY - HISTORY.
Ayala, Eligio. Evolución de la economía agraria en el Paraguay . Asunción, Paraguay , 1986. 196 p. : LC Card 86-234615
HD1898 1986 .A92

Herken Krauer, Juan Carlos, 1953- El Paraguay rural entre 1869 y 1913 . Asunción, Paraguay , 1984. 224 p., [10] p. of plates : LC Card 84-237050
HC222 .H47 1984

AGRICULTURE - ECONOMIC ASPECTS - PARAGUAY - PARAGUARI (DEPT.)
Campos, Luis A. (Luis Alberto), 1949- Pequeños campesinos y su incertidumbre . Asunción, Paraguay [1986] 224 p. : LC Card 87-400281 DDC 305.5/63 19
HD1531.P3 C36 1986

AGRICULTURE - ECONOMIC ASPECTS - PERU.
Maletta, Héctor. Requerimientos de mano de obra en la agricultura peruana /. Lima, Perú , 1985. 184 p. ; LC Card 86-156077
HD1531.P4 M34 1985

AGRICULTURE - ECONOMIC ASPECTS - PERU - HISTORY.
Burga, Manuel. La historia agraria /. Chiclayo, Perú , 1986. 196 p. ; ***NYPL [JLD 87-1524]***

Ríos Burga, Jaime R. Ciclos productivos en el espacio peruano colonial, siglos XVI-XIX . Lima, Perú , 1986. 70 p. : LC Card 87-401070 DDC 338.5/42/0983 19
HC227 .R456 1986

AGRICULTURE - ECONOMIC ASPECTS - PERU - HISTORY - 17TH CENTURY.
Escobari de Querejazu, Laura. Producción y comercio en el espacio sur andino en el siglo XVII . La Paz , 1985. 218 p., [12] p. of plates : LC Card 86-174929
HC167.A5 E83 1985

AGRICULTURE - ECONOMIC ASPECTS - PERU - ORIENTE.
Peru, Kolonisation und Abhängigkeit . Saarbrücken , Fort Lauderdale , 1981. 192 p. : ISBN 3-88156-165-X : LC Card 82-104103
HD1905.O75 P47 1981

AGRICULTURE - ECONOMIC ASPECTS - PERU - PACIFIC COAST REGION - STATISTICS.
La Agricultura en la costa del Perú, 1978-1984 /. Lima, Perú , 1985. ca. 150 leaves : LC Card 87-403706 DDC 338.1/0985 19
HD1905.P33 A38 1985

AGRICULTURE - ECONOMIC ASPECTS - PERU - PIURA (DEPT.) - HISTORY.
Espinoza Claudio, César. Terratenientes y campesinos en Piura, ss. XVI-XIX . Lima, Perú , 1981. xxviii, 123 p., [6] leaves of plates : LC Card 82-146131
HD559.P5 E87 1981

AGRICULTURE - ECONOMIC ASPECTS - POLAND.
Wiatrak, Andrzej Piotr. Przestrzenne zróżnicowanie gospodarki rolnej w Polsce /. Warszawa , 1986. 207 p. : ISBN 83-01-05118-3 : LC Card 86-212769
HD1995.7 .W45 1986

AGRICULTURE - ECONOMIC ASPECTS - POLAND - CONGRESSES.
Magyar-Lengyel Agrárközgazdasági Konferencia (1984 : Gödöllő, Hungary) A nagyüzemek és a kisüzemek termelésének fejlődése, kapcsolatuk az iparosodó mezőgazdaságban =. Gödöllő , 1984. 174 p. ; LC Card 86-145249
HD1995.7 .M32 1984

AGRICULTURE - ECONOMIC ASPECTS - POLAND - HISTORY.
Inglot, Stefan. Z dziejów wsi polskiej i rolnictwa /. Warszawa , 1986. 448 p. : ISBN 83-205-3734-7 : LC Card 85-126716
HD1995.7 .I54 1986

AGRICULTURE - ECONOMIC ASPECTS - PORTUGAL.
Azevedo, J. Cândido de. Portugal, Europa face ao Mercado Comum . Amadora , c1978. 300 p. ; LC Card 80-121153
HC241.25.P6 A94 1978

Portuguese agriculture in transition /. Ithaca , 1987. 283 p. : ISBN 0-8014-1954-9 (alk. paper) LC Card 86-29198 DDC 338.1/09469 19
HD2027 .P67 1987

Rau, Virginia. Sesmarias medievais portuguesas /. Lisboa [1982] 288 p. : LC Card 87-673341
HD784 .R3x 1982

AGRICULTURE - ECONOMIC ASPECTS - PORTUGAL - HISTORY - 20TH CENTURY.
A Agricultura portuguesa no período 1950-1980 . Lisboa [1984] 74 p. : LC Card 85-207313
HD2027 .A635 1984

AGRICULTURE - ECONOMIC ASPECTS - ROMANIA - OLTENIA - HISTORY - 19TH CENTURY.
Pătroiu, Ion. La cumpăna a două epoci, 1849-1877 /. Craiova , 1983. 316 p. ; LC Card 84-234959
HD1333.R62 O475 1983

AGRICULTURE - ECONOMIC ASPECTS - RUSSIAN S.F.S.R.
I͡Ushkov, V. I. (Vasiliĭ Il'ich) Zakupochnai͡a tsena i rasshirennoe vosproizvodstvo v sel'skom khozi͡aĭstve /. Moskva , 1980. 142 p. ; LC Card 81-134864
HD1995.R8 I95 1980

AGRICULTURE - ECONOMIC ASPECTS - RUSSIAN S.F.S.R. - BASHKIRSKAIA A.S.S.R. - HISTORY - 19TH CENTURY.
Usmanov, Kh. F. Razvitie kapitalizma v sel'skom khozi͡aĭstve Bashkirii v poreformennyĭ period, 60-90-e gody XIX v. /. Moskva , 1981. 368 p. ; LC Card 82-118144
HD1995.B38 U86 1981

AGRICULTURE - ECONOMIC ASPECTS - RUSSIAN S.F.S.R. - BURIATSKAIA A.S.S.R.
Sistema vedenii͡a sel'skogo khozi͡aĭstva Buri͡atskoĭ ASSR . Novosibirsk , 1985. 188 p. : LC Card 86-215358
HD1995.B8 S57 1985

AGRICULTURE - ECONOMIC ASPECTS - RUSSIAN S.F.S.R. - HISTORY.
Iz istorii krest'i͡anstva Evropeĭskogo Severa, Verkhnego Povolzh'i͡a i Urala v period Velikoĭ Okti͡abr'skoĭ sotsialisticheskoĭ revoli͡utsii i pobedy sotsializma v SSSR, 1917-1937 gg. /. Kirov , 1979. 170 p. ; LC Card 82-103738
HD1492.S652 R8755 1979

Seleznev, V. A. (Valeriĭ Aleksandrovich) Pervye shagi sotsialisticheskikh preobrazovaniĭ v sel'skom khozi͡aĭstve Severo-Zapada RSFSR, 1917-1929 gg. . Leningrad , 1983. 198 p. ; LC Card 83-197523
HD1492.S652 R877 1983 ***NYPL [*QIP 87-1327]***

AGRICULTURE - ECONOMIC ASPECTS - RUSSIAN S.F.S.R. - KRASNOIARSKII KRAĬ.
Sistema vedenii͡a sel'skogo i promyslovogo khozi͡aĭstva na Eniseĭskom Severe . Novosibirsk , 1986. 211 p. ; LC Card 86-227282
HD1995.K73 S57 1986

AGRICULTURE - ECONOMIC ASPECTS - RUSSIAN S.F.S.R. - NON-CHERNOZEM REGION.
Krasnenkov, Vladimir. Ne pole pereĭti-- /. Moskva , 1986. 174 p. ; LC Card 86-132520
HD1995.N515 K73 1986

AGRICULTURE - ECONOMIC ASPECTS - SENEGAL - BIGNONA.
Dramé, Mamadou. Une expérience de grande envergure . [Dakar] , 1980-1981 [i.e., 1981] 32, [3] leaves, [1] folded leaf of plates : LC Card 85-218589
HD2144.5.Z9 B543 1981

AGRICULTURE - ECONOMIC ASPECTS - SIERRA LEONE.
Büscher, Ludger. Integrated rural development . Hamburg , 1984. xx, 238 p. : ISBN 3-87895-261-9 (pbk.) LC Card 86-672442
HD2146.5 .B87x 1984 ***NYPL [JLD 86-2789]***

Kireta-Katewu, Patrick R., 1953- Economic analyses of the farmer cropping system under risks and uncertainties in Sierra Leone /. Hamburg , 1985. xviii, 245 p. : ISBN 3-87895-266-X (pbk.) LC Card 87-103068 DDC 338.1/62 19
HD2146.5 .K57 1985

AGRICULTURE - ECONOMIC ASPECTS - SOMALIA.
Somalia, productive sectors of the economy /. Paris , 1985. 115 leaves : ISBN 2-905760-00-1 (pbk.) LC Card 87-124493 DDC 338.967/73 19
HC850 .S658 1985

AGRICULTURE - ECONOMIC ASPECTS - SOUTH ASIA.
Binswanger, Hans P. The economics of tractors in South Asia . New York , Hyderabad, India , 1978. 96 p. ; LC Card 81-908104
HD2065.3 .B56 1978

AGRICULTURE - ECONOMIC ASPECTS - SOUTH CAROLINA.
Lyson, Thomas A. The changing structure of South Carolina agriculture since 1959 /. Clemson, S.C. [1986] 29 p. : LC Card 87-620716 DDC 338.1/09757 19
HD1775.S6 L97 1986

AGRICULTURE - ECONOMIC ASPECTS - SOUTHERN CONE OF SOUTH AMERICA.
Estudios sobre integración económica y cooperación regional en el Cono Sur . Santiago de Chile , c1985. 283 p. ; LC Card 86-174604
HC167.S67 E78 1985

AGRICULTURE - ECONOMIC ASPECTS - SOUTHERN STATES.
Healy, Robert G. Competition for land in the American South . Washington, D.C. , c1985. xxxii, 333 p. : ISBN 0-89164-094-0 (pbk.) LC Card 85-25459 DDC 333.76/13/0975 19
HD266.A13 H43 1985 ***NYPL [JLE 86-2724]***

AGRICULTURE - ECONOMIC ASPECTS - SOVIET UNION.
Borchenko, N. (Nikolaĭ) Sel'skoe khoziaĭstvo v odinnadtsatoĭ piatiletke . Moskva , 1981. 93 p. ; LC Card 81-188371
HD1493.R9 B5 1981, no. 5 HD9015.S65

Ėkonomicheskie problemy novogo ėtapa osushchestvleniia Leninskogo kooperativnogo plana /. Moskva , 1979. 365 p. ; LC Card 81-165451
HD1992 .E3593 1979

Kaplan, Cynthia Sue. The party and agricultural crisis management in the USSR /. Ithaca , 1987. xvi, 203 p ; ISBN 0-8014-2021-0 (alk. paper) LC Card 86-32223 DDC 338.1/847 19
HD1993 .K36 1987

Perspektivnoe planirovanie razvitiia agrarno-promyshlennogo kompleksa /. Novosibirsk , 1979. 159 p. : LC Card 81-143730
HD9015.S652 P47 1979

Shinn, William T., 1936- The decline of the Russian peasant household /. New York , 1987. xvii, 122 p. ; ISBN 0-275-92767-9 (alk. paper) LC Card 87-2554 DDC 338.1/0947 19
HD1992 .S4735 1987

AGRICULTURE - ECONOMIC ASPECTS - SOVIET UNION - HISTORY.
Medvedev, Zhores A., 1925- Soviet agriculture /. New York , c1987. xiv, 464 p. ; ISBN 0-393-02472-5 LC Card 86-31119 DDC 338.1/0947 19
HD1992 .M385 1987

AGRICULTURE - ECONOMIC ASPECTS - SOVIET UNION - HISTORY - 19TH CENTURY.
Macey, David, A. J., 1942- Government and peasant in Russia, 1861-1906 . Dekalb, Ill. , 1987. xviii, 380 p. ; ISBN 0-87580-122-6 LC Card 87-7684 DDC 338.1/847 19
HD1992 .M19 1987

AGRICULTURE - ECONOMIC ASPECTS - SOVIET UNION, NORTHERN.
Mal'tsev, V. I. (Valer'ian Ivanovich) Ėkonomicheskie osnovy industrializatsii sel'skogo khoziaĭstva Severa /. Moskva , 1985. 142 p. ; LC Card 86-165352
HD1995.N55 M34 1985

AGRICULTURE - ECONOMIC ASPECTS - SPAIN.
Capdevila Batlles, José. Agricultura e industria española frente a la CEE . Barcelona [1985?] 252 p. : ISBN 84-7003-282-8 LC Card 86-171577
HC385 .C358 1985

La Agricultura y la pesca españolas en 1981. Madrid [1982?] 299 p. : ISBN 84-7479-164-2 : LC Card 83-125330 DDC 338.1/0946 19
HD2022 .A657 1982 ***NYPL [JLF 87-236]***

Loring, Jaime. Los sectores agrarios de Andalucía ante la integración en la C.E.E. /. Madrid , 1984. 303 p. : ISBN 84-7114-149-3 LC Card 86-152628
HD2025.A5 L67 1984

Möller, Ferdinand, 1955- Agrarstruktur und Agrarstrukturpolitik in Spanien, eine Analyse vor dem Hintergrund der Erweiterung der Europäischen Gemeinschaft /. Frankfurt am Main , New York , c1986. ix, 255 p. ; ISBN 3-8204-9529-0 LC Card 87-407540 DDC 338.1/846 19
HD2023 .M65 1986

AGRICULTURE - ECONOMIC ASPECTS - SPAIN - AMPURDÁN (REGION)
El Baix Empordà . Barcelona , c1984. xii, 303 p. : ISBN 84-505-0289-6 LC Card 85-186183
HC387.A636 B35 1984

AGRICULTURE - ECONOMIC ASPECTS - SPAIN - ANDALUSIA.
Loring, Jaime. Los sectores agrarios de Andalucía ante la integración en la C.E.E. /. Madrid , 1984. 303 p. : ISBN 84-7114-149-3 LC Card 86-152628
HD2025.A5 L67 1984

AGRICULTURE - ECONOMIC ASPECTS - SPAIN - CATALONIA - HISTORY.
Terra, treball i propietat . Barcelona , c1986. 346 p. ; ISBN 84-7423-287-2 LC Card 86-216973
HD2025.C35 T47 1986

AGRICULTURE - ECONOMIC ASPECTS - SPAIN - CIUDAD REAL (PROVINCE) - HISTORY - 18TH CENTURY - CASE STUDIES.
Gascón Bueno, Francisco. El Valle de Alcudia . Bilbao , 1978. xvi, 609 p., [10] folded leaves of plates : ISBN 84-400-5486-6 LC Card 85-227628
HD2025.C54 G37 1978

AGRICULTURE - ECONOMIC ASPECTS - SPAIN - CUENCA.
Consejo Económico Sindical Provincial (Cuenca, Spain) IV pleno del Consejo Económico Sindical de Cuenca . [Cuenca] , 1965. 128 p. : LC Card 85-105812
HD2025.C84 C65 1965

AGRICULTURE - ECONOMIC ASPECTS - SPAIN - DATA PROCESSING.
Censo agrario 1982 . Madrid , 1983. 104, 8 p. : ISBN 84-260-0803-8 LC Card 84-134551
HD2022 .C45 1983

AGRICULTURE - ECONOMIC ASPECTS - SPAIN - GARROTXA REGION.
La Garrotxa . [Barcelona , c1983. xv, 323 p. : ISBN 84-7231-912-1 LC Card 85-184803
HC387.G34 G37 1983

AGRICULTURE - ECONOMIC ASPECTS - SPAIN - HISTORY - 18TH CENTURY.
Lluch, Ernest, 1937- Agronomía y fisiocracia en España, 1750-1820 /. Valencia [1985?] lxi, 215 p. ; ISBN 84-00-05965-4 LC Card 85-240630
HD2022 .L58 1985

AGRICULTURE - ECONOMIC ASPECTS - SPAIN - HISTORY - 19TH CENTURY.
Lluch, Ernest, 1937- Agronomía y fisiocracia en España, 1750-1820 /. Valencia [1985?] lxi, 215 p. ; ISBN 84-00-05965-4 LC Card 85-240630
HD2022 .L58 1985

AGRICULTURE - ECONOMIC ASPECTS - SPAIN - HISTORY - 20TH CENTURY.
Moreno Torregrosa, Pasqual. El Mercado Común frente a la agricultura española /. Madrid [1986?] 127 p. ; ISBN 84-86293-27-8 LC Card 86-202333
HD2022 .M67 1986

AGRICULTURE - ECONOMIC ASPECTS - SPAIN - JAÉN (PROVINCE) - HISTORY - 18TH CENTURY.
Herr, Richard. Rural change and royal finances in Spain at the end of the old regime /. Berkeley , c1987. p. cm. ISBN 0-520-05948-4 (alk. paper) LC Card 86-25027 DDC 333.3/0946/25 19
HD779.J34 H47 1987

AGRICULTURE - ECONOMIC ASPECTS - SPAIN - PUENTE-GENIL REGION.
Jurado Carmona, María Isabel. Propiedad y explotación agrarias en Puente Genil /. Córdoba , 1984. 229 p. : ISBN 84-505-0063-X LC Card 85-139166 DDC 338.1/0946/84 19
HD2025.P84 J87 1984 ***NYPL [JLD 86-2522]***

AGRICULTURE - ECONOMIC ASPECTS - SPAIN - SALAMANCA (PROVINCE) - HISTORY - 18TH CENTURY.
Herr, Richard. Rural change and royal finances in Spain at the end of the old regime /. Berkeley , c1987. p. cm. ISBN 0-520-05948-4 (alk. paper) LC Card 86-25027 DDC 333.3/0946/25 19
HD779.J34 H47 1987

AGRICULTURE - ECONOMIC ASPECTS - SPAIN - SEGURA MOUNTAINS REGION.
Ruiz Avilés, Pedro. Estudio integral de la Sierra de Segura . [Jaén] [1985] 130 leaves : ISBN 84-505-1249-2 LC Card 86-187282
HC387.S438 R85 1985

AGRICULTURE - ECONOMIC ASPECTS - SPAIN - STATISTICS.
Selected agricultural statistics on Spain, 1970-82 /. Washington, D.C. (1301 New York Ave., N.W., Washington 20005-4788) , 1986. x, 142 p. : LC Card 86-602416 DDC 338.1/0973 s 338.1/0946/021 19
HD1751 .A5 no. 742 HD2022

AGRICULTURE - ECONOMIC ASPECTS - SRI LANKA.
Capital and peasant production . Colombo, Sri Lanka , 1985. xiv, 230 p. ; LC Card 86-900809 DDC 338.1/3/095493 19
HD2065.8 .C36 1985 ***NYPL [JLE 87-1667]***

AGRICULTURE - ECONOMIC ASPECTS - STATISTICS - COMPARATIVE METHOD.
Szász, Kálmán. A mezőgazdaság nemzetközi összehasonlításának módszerei . Budapest , 1986. 96 p. ; ISBN 963-02-4381-4 LC Card 87-419792
HD1425 .S95 1986

AGRICULTURE - ECONOMIC ASPECTS - SUDAN.
Kursany, Ibrahim. The dynamics and limits of capitalist development in Sudanese agriculture /. Khartoum , 1982- v. ; LC Card 83-980112 DDC 338.1/09624 19
HD2123.5 .K87 1982 ***NYPL [JLM 86-825]***

AGRICULTURE - ECONOMIC ASPECTS - SWEDEN - SÖDERMANLAND LÄN - HISTORY - 19TH CENTURY.
Köll, Anu-Mai. Tradition och reform i västra Södermanlands jordbruk, 1810-1890 . Stockholm , 1983. 252 p. : ISBN 91-22-00633-8 LC Card 84-114628
HD2020.S63 K65 1983

AGRICULTURE - ECONOMIC ASPECTS - SYRIA - HISTORY.
Khader, Bichara. La question agraire dans le monde arabe . Louvain-la-Neuve , 1984. 631 p. : LC Card 85-169871 DDC 338.1/095691 19
HD2057.5 .K45 1984 ***NYPL [JLE 86-654]***

AGRICULTURE - ECONOMIC ASPECTS - TANZANIA.
Orback, Jens. Agriculture and incentives, the Tanzanian case . Uppsala , 1985. 37, [2] leaves,

[1] leaf of plates : LC Card 86-215091 DDC 338.1/8 19
HD2128.5 .O73 1985

Tanzania . Uppsala , Stockholm, Sweden , 1986. 325 p. : ISBN 91-7106-257-2 (pbk.) LC Card 87-163353 DDC 330.9678/04 19
HD2128.5 .T36 1986

AGRICULTURE - ECONOMIC ASPECTS - TEXAS.
Economic status of Texas agriculture /. College Station, Tex. [1985] ii, 30 leaves : LC Card 87-620640 DDC 338.1/09764 19
HD1775.T4 E28 1985

Paggi, Mechel S. Impact of agricultural exports for Texas /. College Station, Tex. [1986] 20 leaves, [1] leaf of plates : LC Card 87-620821 DDC 382/.41/09764 19
HD1775.T4 P34 1986

AGRICULTURE - ECONOMIC ASPECTS - THAR DESERT (INDIA AND PAKISTAN)
Mann, H. S. (Haracharan Singh), 1922- Halting the march . [New Delhi] [1983] 35, [1] p., [4] p. of plates : LC Card 86-204352 DDC 338.1/0954/4 19
HC437.T47 M36 1983

AGRICULTURE - ECONOMIC ASPECTS - TURKEY - HISTORY.
İslamoğlu-İnan, Huri, 1947- Ottoman agriculture in 16th century Anatolia . Berlin [1982] 45, [21] p. : LC Card 86-674028
HD2056.7 .I84x 1982

AGRICULTURE - ECONOMIC ASPECTS - TURKMEN S.S.R.
Stanchin, I. M. (Ivan Mikhaĭlovich) Razvitie agropromyshlennogo kompleksa Turkmenskoĭ SSR /. Ashkhabad , 1985. 181, [3] p. : LC Card 85-185696
HD9015.S653 T878 1985

AGRICULTURE - ECONOMIC ASPECTS - UKRAINE.
Kulish, N. E. (Nikolaĭ Efimovich) Upravlenie agropromyshlennymi ob″edinenii͡ami v uslovii͡akh integrirovannoĭ ėkonomiki /. Kiev , 1985. 174 p. : LC Card 87-104750
HD9015.S653 U4425 1985
NYPL [*QIP 87-4125]

Material′no-tekhnichna baza ahropromyslovoho kompleksu . Kyïv , 1985. 294 p. ; LC Card 87-109155
HD9015.S653 U453 1985

AGRICULTURE - ECONOMIC ASPECTS - UNITED STATES.
Agriculture and the environment in a changing world economy. Washington, D.C. , c1986. xi, 66 p. : ISBN 0-89164-099-1 (pbk.) LC Card 86-24088 DDC 338.1/873 19
HD1761 .A6228 1986

Ambur, Owen D. Selling out the family farm . Washington , 1986. v, 40 p. : LC Card 87-601379 DDC 338.1/6 19
HD1476.U5 A65 1986

Coyle, Barry. Economic gains from agricultural trade . Washington, D.C. [Springfield, VA , 1986] iii, 41 p. : LC Card 86-602417 DDC 382/.41/0973 19
HD9005 .C86 1986

Embargoes, surplus disposal, and U. S. agriculture . Washington, D.C. , 1986. vi, 34 p. ; LC Card 86-603452 DDC 338.1/8 19
HD1761 .E45 1986

The Farm financial crisis . Boulder , 1988. xvi, 205 p. : ISBN 0-8133-7186-4 (pbk. : alk. paper) : LC Card 86-32601 DDC 338.1/3/0973 19
HD1761 .F295 1988

Gardner, Bruce L. The economics of agricultural policies /. New York, NY , c1987. xi, 387 p. : ISBN 0-02-947760-3 LC Card 87-20367 DDC 338.1/8 19
HD1761 .G245 1987

Goldschmidt, Yaaqov. The impact of inflation on financial activity in business, with applications to the U. S. farming sector /. Totowa, N.J. , 1986. xvi, 181 p. ; ISBN 0-8476-7427-4 : LC Card 85-14196 DDC 338.1/3/0973 19
HD1761 .G645 1986 ***NYPL [JLE 86-3484]***

Gorman, Carol. America's farm crisis /. New York , 1987. 125 p. : ISBN 0-531-10408-7 LC Card 87-2087 DDC 338.1/0973 19
HD1476.U5 G67 1987

Hope for the family farm . Newton, Kan. , c1987. viii, 231 p. : ISBN 0-87303-126-1 (pbk.) LC Card 87-81635 DDC 338.1/6 19
HD1476.U5 H67 1987

Is there a moral obligation to save the family farm? /. Ames , 1987. xxvii, 427 p. : ISBN 0-8138-1000-0 (pbk.) LC Card 87-13399 DDC 338.1/0973 19
HD1476.U5 I8 1987

National Agricultural Outlook Conference (U. S.) (1976 : Washington, D.C.) 1977 U. S. agricultural outlook . Washington , 1976. vi, 445 p. : LC Card 86-602345
HD1765 .N37 1976

Paarlberg, Robert L. Fixing farm trade . Cambridge, Mass. , c1988. xiv, 159 p. ; ISBN 0-88730-196-7 LC Card 87-24118 DDC 382/.41/0973 19
HD9006 .P27 1988

A Review of U. S. competitiveness in agricultural trade. Washington, D.C. [1986] ix, 101 p. : LC Card 86-600586 DDC 382/.41/0973 19
HD1761 .R48 1986

Technology, public policy, and the changing structure of American agriculture. Washington, D.C. [1986] vi, 374 p. : LC Card 85-600632 DDC 338.1/0973 19
HD1761 .T37 1986 ***NYPL [JLF 86-1376]***

U. S. agriculture & Third World development . Boulder , 1987. xi, 258 p. ; ISBN 1-555-87011-2 (lib. bdg.) : LC Card 86-29860 DDC 338.1/09172/4 19
HD1765 .U15 1987

United States. Congress. Senate. Committee on Agriculture, Nutrition, and Forestry. Review of the implementation of the Food Security Act of 1985 . Washington , 1987. iv, 180 p. : LC Card 87-601199 DDC 338.1/9/73 19
HD1761 .U515 1987

Wallace, Luther T. Agriculture's futures . New York , c1987. x, 93 p. : ISBN 0-387-96482-7 (pbk.) LC Card 86-31390 DDC 338.1/0973 19
HD1761 .W274 1987

Webb, Shwu-Eng. Idling erodible cropland . Washington, D.C. [1986] iii, 31 p. : LC Card 86-601632 DDC 338.1 s 338.1/62 19
HD1751 .A91854 no. 550 HD256

AGRICULTURE - ECONOMIC ASPECTS - UNITED STATES - ADDRESSES, ESSAYS, LECTURES.
Lectures in agricultural economics . [Washington? , 1977] ix, 165 p. : LC Card 77-603242
HD1759 .L4 ***NYPL [JLE 79-149]***

AGRICULTURE - ECONOMIC ASPECTS - UNITED STATES - CONGRESSES.
Economic efficiency in agricultural and food marketing /. Ames , 1987. xii, 315 p. ; ISBN 0-8138-0533-3 LC Card 87-2821 DDC 381/.41/0973 19
HD9000.5 .E26 1987

U. S. agriculture and Third World economic development . Washington, D.C. , c1987. xv, 103 p. : ISBN 0-89068-086-8 (pbk.): LC Card 86-62757 DDC 338.9/009172/4 19
HD1755 .U173 1987

U. S.-Mexico relations . Stanford, Calif. , c1987. xii, 401 p. ; ISBN 0-8047-1319-7 (alk. paper) LC Card 86-23103 DDC 338.1/872 19
HD1792 .U19 1987

AGRICULTURE - ECONOMIC ASPECTS - UNITED STATES - GOVERNMENT POLICY.
Federal marketing programs in agriculture . Danville, Ill. , c1983. x, 326 p. ; ISBN 0-8134-2292-2 : LC Card 83-80130
NYPL [JLE 86-4572]

AGRICULTURE - ECONOMIC ASPECTS - UNITED STATES - HISTORY - 19TH CENTURY.
Atack, Jeremy. To their own soil . Ames , 1987. xi, 322 p. : ISBN 0-8138-0086-2 LC Card 86-21349 DDC 338.1/0974 19
HD1773.A4 A86 1987

AGRICULTURE - ECONOMIC ASPECTS - UNITED STATES - INFORMATION SERVICES - UNITED STATES.
Agricultural trade research and information needs . [Ames, Iowa] [1985] 32 p. : LC Card 86-229053 DDC 380.1/41/072073 19
HD1410.6.U5 A39 1985

AGRICULTURE - ECONOMIC ASPECTS - UNITED STATES - PUBLIC OPINION.
The American farmer book . [Smithshire, Ill.] (Box 181, Smithshire 61478) [c1986] 192 p. : LC Card 86-203314 DDC 338.1/0973 19
HD8039.F32 U614 1986

AGRICULTURE - ECONOMIC ASPECTS - UNITED STATES - RESEARCH - UNITED STATES.
Agricultural trade research and information needs . [Ames, Iowa] [1985] 32 p. : LC Card 86-229053 DDC 380.1/41/072073 19
HD1410.6.U5 A39 1985

AGRICULTURE - ECONOMIC ASPECTS - URUGUAY.
Martorelli, Horacio. Nuevo estilo de desarrollo para Uruguay . Montevideo, Uruguay , 1982. 2 v. : LC Card 85-167867 DDC 338.1/09895 19
HD1907 .M376 1982 ***NYPL [JLF 86-935]***

AGRICULTURE - ECONOMIC ASPECTS - URUGUAY - STATISTICS.
Estadísticas agropecuarias. Montevideo, República Oriental del Uruguay , 1979. [79] p. ; LC Card 82-209370
HD9014.U82 E78 1979

AGRICULTURE - ECONOMIC ASPECTS - UZBEK S.S.R. - HISTORY.
Aminova, R. Kh. Pobeda kolkhoznogo stroi͡a v Uzbekistane . Tashkent , 1981. 289 p. ; LC Card 82-161362
HD1492.S652 U9226 1981

AGRICULTURE - ECONOMIC ASPECTS - VANUATU - LONGANA.
Rodman, Margaret, 1947- Masters of tradition . Vancouver , 1987. 198 p. : ISBN 0-7748-0234-0 LC Card 87-158135 DDC 333.3/0993/4 19
HD1125.Z9 L657 1987

AGRICULTURE - ECONOMIC ASPECTS - VENEZUELA - ADDRESSES, ESSAYS, LECTURES.
Foro . San Felipe, Venezuela , 1984. ii, 92 p. ; LC Card 85-132901 DDC 338.1/0987 19
HD1912 .F67 1984 ***NYPL [JLD 86-424]***

AGRICULTURE - ECONOMIC ASPECTS - VENEZUELA - CARACAS REGION - HISTORY - 19TH CENTURY.
Lucena Salmoral, Manuel. Vísperas de la independencia americana . Madrid , 1986. vii, 389 p. ; ISBN 84-205-1308-3 LC Card 86-205153
HF3490.C37 L83 1986

AGRICULTURE - ECONOMIC ASPECTS - VENEZUELA - CARORA - HISTORY - 20TH CENTURY.
García Ponce, Antonio, 1929- Crisis oligarquía y latifundio . Barquisimeto, Venezuela , 1986. 104 p., [1] folded leaf of plates : ISBN 980-608-701-1 : LC Card 87-134729 DDC 338.1/762/0098725 19
HF3490.C375 G37 1986

AGRICULTURE - ECONOMIC ASPECTS - VIETNAM.
Kinh t Hà N 1983. 154 p. ; LC Card 87-153552
HC444 .K56 1983

AGRICULTURE - ECONOMIC ASPECTS - WASHINGTON (STATE) - HISTORY - 19TH CENTURY.
Prevost, Nancy M., 1953- Paradise in the Palouse . Fairfield, Wash. , c1985. 35 p. : ISBN 0-87770-365-5 (pbk.) LC Card 85-17842 DDC 338.1/09797/39 19
HD1775.W2 P74 1985 ***NYPL [JFF 86-559]***

AGRICULTURE - ECONOMIC ASPECTS - WEST (U. S.) - HISTORY - 19TH CENTURY.
Fite, Gilbert Courtland, 1918- The farmers' frontier, 1865-1900 /. Norman [1987], c1966. xiv, 272 p. : ISBN 0-8061-2063-0 (pbk.) LC Card 86-40534 DDC 338.1/0977 19
HD8039.F3 U643 1987

AGRICULTURE - ECONOMIC ASPECTS - WISCONSIN.
Saupe, William E. Rural poverty in Wisconsin counties /. Madison, WI [198-] 26 p. : LC Card 86-622097
HC107.W63 P6249 1980z

AGRICULTURE - ECONOMIC ASPECTS - YUGOSLAVIA - STATISTICS.
A Jugoszláv és a magyar mezőgazdaság összehasonlítása a határmenti területeken /. Budapest , 1986. 37 p. ; LC Card 87-407672
HD1940.5 .J83 1986

AGRICULTURE - ECONOMIC ASPECTS - ZAIRE.
Tshibaka, Tshikala B., 1949- The effects of trade and exchange rate policies on agriculture in Zaire /. Washington, D.C., USA , 1986. 65 p. : ISBN 0-89629-057-3 LC Card 86-27449 DDC 338.1/09675/1 19
HD2135.5 .T75 1986

AGRICULTURE - ECONOMIC ASPECTS - ZAMBIA - CHINSALI DISTRICT.
A Survey of constraints facing small-scale farmers in Mpika and Chinsali Districts, Northern Province . [Mpika, Zambia?] [1985 or 1986] 8 p., [1] leaf of plates : LC Card 86-981416 DDC 338.1/6 19
HD1476.Z352 M657 1985

AGRICULTURE - ECONOMIC ASPECTS - ZAMBIA - LUSAKA PROVINCE - PLANNING - CONGRESSES.
Lusaka Province (Zambia). Provincial Planning Unit. Towards self sufficiency . [Lusaka, Zambia?] [1984] 100 p., [14] leaves of plates : LC Card 86-980293 DDC 338.1/86894 19
HD2131.5 .L87 1984

AGRICULTURE - ECONOMIC ASPECTS - ZAMBIA - MPIKA DISTRICT.
Agricultural commercialisation and the allocation of labour time in Mpika District, northern Zambia. Mpika, Zambia [1986?] iii, 42 leaves : LC Card 86-981249 DDC 338.1/096894 19
HD2131.5.Z9 M653 1986

A Survey of constraints facing small-scale farmers in Mpika and Chinsali Districts, Northern Province . [Mpika, Zambia?] [1985 or 1986] 8 p., [1] leaf of plates : LC Card 86-981416 DDC 338.1/6 19
HD1476.Z352 M657 1985

AGRICULTURE - ECONOMIC ASPECTS - ZIMBABWE.
Report of the Commission of Inquiry into the Agricultural Industry /. [Harare?] [1982] ix, 205 p. : LC Card 85-980325 DDC 338.1/096891 19
HD2131 .R47 1982

AGRICULTURE - ECONOMICS. see **AGRICULTURE - ECONOMIC ASPECTS.**

AGRICULTURE - ENERGY CONSUMPTION - CONGRESSES.
United Nations University Symposium on Energy and Agriculture Futures--Policy Implications of Global Models (1982 : Paris, France) Energy and agriculture . [Chur, Switzerland , New York] , c1984. xii, 370 p. : ISBN 3-7186-0187-7 LC Card 83-18363 DDC 333.79 19
HD1405 .E53 1983 ***NYPL [JLD 86-1837]***

AGRICULTURE - ENVIRONMENTAL ASPECTS.
Yates, Geoffrey. Food, need, greed & myopia . Ryton, Tyne and Wear , 1986. 96 p. : ISBN 0-907367-04-6 (pbk.) : LC Card 87-129951 DDC 338.1/9 19
HD9000.5 .Y38 1986

AGRICULTURE - ENVIRONMENTAL ASPECTS - AFRICA.
Harrison, Paul. The greening of Africa . New York, N.Y., U. S.A. , 1987. 380 p. : ISBN 0-14-010192-6 (pbk.) : LC Card 87-404277 DDC 338.1/9/6 19
HD2117 .H37 1987

AGRICULTURE - ETHIOPIA - SOCIETIES, ETC.
Tegegne Teke. Cooperatives and national development . Addis Ababa, Ethiopia [1984] iii, 57 leaves ; LC Card 85-980411 DDC 334/.683/0963 19
HD1491.E83 T44 1984 ***NYPL [JLG 86-173]***

AGRICULTURE - FINANCE.
Devino, Gary T. Agribusiness finance /. Danville, Ill. , c1981. xii, 166 p. : ISBN 0-8134-2191-8 (pbk.) LC Card 81-80386 DDC 658.1/5 19
HD1437 .D48 ***NYPL [JLE 86-4573]***

AGRICULTURE - GERMANY (WEST) - ACCOUNTING.
Ebel, Friedhelm. Was sagt mir der Buchführungsabschluss? /. Bonn , 1980. 36 p. : LC Card 84-145622
HF5686.A36 E24 1980

AGRICULTURE - GERMANY (WEST) - BAVARIA - SOCIETIES, ETC. - HISTORY.
Ratjen, Wolfgang. Die bayerischen Bauernkammern von 1920 bis 1933 /. München , 1981. vi, 204 p. ; ISBN 3-87913-108-2 : LC Card 83-194708 DDC 338.1/06/0433 19
HD1486.G3 R34 1981

AGRICULTURE - GREAT BRITAIN.
Collings, Jesse, 1831-1920. The great war, its lessons and its warnings [microform]. London [1915] 113 p. LC Card 16-1094
HC256.2 .C55 ***NYPL [*Z-4053 no.6]***

AGRICULTURE - GREECE - FINANCE.
Baltas, Nik. K. Chrēmatodotēsē ependyseōn tou agrotikou tomea . Athēna , 1984. 142 p. ; LC Card 86-201892
HD2055.5 .B35 1984

AGRICULTURE - HUNGARY.
Almási, István. Négy évtizede új úton a magyar mezőgazdaság /. [Budapest] [1985] 159 p. : ISBN 963-7252-41-X LC Card 86-228893
HD1940.5 .A85 1985

AGRICULTURE - HUNGARY - CAPITAL INVESTMENTS - STATISTICS.
Beruházások és állóeszközök a mezőgazdaságban, 1981-1985 /. Budapest , 1987. 90 p. ; ISBN 963-02-4805-0 LC Card 87-409593
HD1940.5 .B474 1987

AGRICULTURE - HUNGARY - FINANCE.
Kis, Pál. A mezőgazdasági nagyüzemek pénz- és hitelrendszere /. Budapest , 1985. 261 p. ; ISBN 963-232-050-6 : LC Card 85-230947
HD1440.H9 K57 1985

Pilling, András. Az önelszámoló rendszer alkalmazásának, a kistermelők integrálásának és a kihelyezett részlegeknek a hatása a mezőgazdasági vállalatok szervezeti felépítésére, s annak müködésére /. Budapest , 1985. 89 p. ; ISBN 963-491-206-0 LC Card 86-196755
HD1492.H8 P55 1985

Reke, Barnabás. Forgóeszköz-gazdálkodás a mezőgazdaságban /. Budapest , 1986. 175 p. ; ISBN 963-232-219-3 : LC Card 87-408500
HD1440.H9 R45 1986

AGRICULTURE - HUNGARY - FINANCE - STATISTICS.
Beruházások és állóeszközök a mezőgazdaságban, 1981-1985 /. Budapest , 1987. 90 p. ; ISBN 963-02-4805-0 LC Card 87-409593
HD1940.5 .B474 1987

A Szocialista nagyüzemek főbb ágazatainak költség- és jövedelemhelyzete 1984-ben /. Budapest , 1985. 35, [46] p. ; LC Card 85-177804
HD1492.H8 S93 1985

AGRICULTURE - HUNGARY - PUTNOK REGION.
Dobrossy, István. Termelés és életmód . Debrecen , 1983. 282 p. : ISBN 963-471-276-2 LC Card 86-100359
HD1492.H82 P873 1983

Agriculture in England, 1870-1947 /. Brown, Jonathan, 1950- Manchester, U.K. , Wolfeboro, N.H., U. S.A. , c1987. p. cm. ISBN 0-7190-1759-9 : LC Card 87-20381 DDC 338.1/0942 19
HD1930.E5 B76 1987

Agriculture in north-eastern region /. Shukla, Surya Pal, 1939- New Delhi, India , 1986. xxvi, 223 p. : LC Card 86-902178 DDC 338.1/0954/1 19
HD2075.N58 S58 1986 ***NYPL [JLD 87-938]***

Agriculture in the GATT : toward the next round of multilateral trade negotiations / prepared by the Congressional Research Service for the Committee on Agriculture, Nutrition, and Forestry, United States Senate. Washington : U. S. G.P.O., 1986. v, 47 p. ; 24 cm. (S. prt. . 99-162) At head of title: 99th Congress, 2d session. Committee print. Distributed to some depository libraries in microfiche. "June 1986." Bibliography: p. Item 1032-C, 1032-D (microfiche) LC Card 86-603393 DDC 382/.41/0973 19
1. Produce trade - Government policy - United States. 2. Tariff on farm produce. 3. General Agreement on Tariffs and Trade (Organization). I. Library of Congress. Congressional Research Service. II. United States. Congress. Senate. Committee on Agriculture, Nutrition, and Forestry. III. Series.
HD9006 .A77 1986

AGRICULTURE - INDIA.
Command Area Development programme in India . New Delhi , 1981. ii, 62 p. ; LC Card 83-907584 ***NYPL [JLF 86-818]***

AGRICULTURE - INDIA - CONGRESSES.
Indien, Probleme eines Schwellenlandes . Tübingen , c1984. 75 p. ; ISBN 3-922362-02-8 LC Card 85-157722
HC435.2 .I6235 1984

AGRICULTURE - INDIA - FINANCE - CASE STUDIES.
Partap Singh, 1948- Co-operative agricultural finance . New Delhi , 1986. xiii, 188 p. : LC Card 86-903067
HG2051.I5 P376 1986

AGRICULTURE - INDIA - MAHARASHTRA.
Desaraḍā, Eca. Ema. Śetī, udyoga, āṇi śikshaṇa . Auraṅgābāda , 1986. 18, 148 p. ; LC Card 87-900720
HC437.M32 D47 1986

AGRICULTURE - INDIA - NAINI TAL (DISTRICT) - FINANCE.
Kumar, Kewal. Institutional financing of Indian agriculture . New Delhi , c1987. 232 p. : LC Card 87-900911 DDC 332.7/1/09542 19
HG2051.I5 N354 1987

AGRICULTURE - INDIA - ORISSA - FINANCE.
Pany, Raj Kishor. Institutional credit for agriculture in India /. New Delhi , 1985. xxi, 483 p. : ISBN 81-7024-009-3 : LC Card 85-904046 DDC 332.7/1/095413 19
HD2075.O7 P36 1985

AGRICULTURE - INDIA - PATIĀLA DISTRICT - FINANCE - CASE STUDIES.
Partap Singh, 1948- Co-operative agricultural finance . New Delhi , 1986. xiii, 188 p. : LC Card 86-903067
HG2051.I5 P376 1986

AGRICULTURE - INDIA - PUNJAB.
Kahlon, A. S., 1923- Modernization of Punjab agriculture /. New Delhi , 1984. vi, 145 p. ; LC Card 84-902491 DDC 338.1/0954/5 19
S471.I32 P845 1984 ***NYPL [JLD 86-4410]***

Agriculture information bulletin .
(no. 503) Embargoes, surplus disposal, and U. S. agriculture . Washington, D.C. , 1986. vi, 34 p. ; LC Card 86-603452 DDC 338.1/8 19
HD1761 .E45 1986

AGRICULTURE - INFORMATION SERVICES - AUSTRIA - DIRECTORIES.
Gergely, Stefan M. Lebensmittel- und Agrarwissenschaften /. Wien , 1983. iii, 317 p. ; ISBN 3-205-06103-9 LC Card 87-407964 DDC 338.1/9/4360285 19
HD9015.A8 G47 1983

AGRICULTURE - ISLAMIC COUNTRIES.
Muslim world . Lanham, MD , c1987. viii, 190 p. : ISBN 0-8191-6558-1 (alk. paper) : LC Card 87-14087 DDC 330.917/671 19
HC499 .M875 1987

AGRICULTURE - ITALY - EMILIA-ROMAGNA - FINANCE - HISTORY.
Cooperazione di credito e sviluppo sociale ed economico delle campagne in Emilia Romagna . Bologna , c1983. 173 p. : LC Card 85-156690
HG2051.I82 E433 1983

AGRICULTURE - ITALY - INFORMATION SERVICES - ITALY.
Strategia dei servizi per l'agricoltura . [Roma] [1983] 158 p. : LC Card 85-155420
HD9475.I82 S77 1983

AGRICULTURE - JURISPRUDENCE. see **AGRICULTURAL LAWS AND LEGISLATION.**

AGRICULTURE - LATIN AMERICA.
A Renda da terra . [São Paulo, Brazil] , Petrópolis , c1980. 152 p. : LC Card 81-214665
HC186 .C36a no. 27 HB401

AGRICULTURE - LATIN AMERICA - FINANCE - CONGRESSES.
Financiamiento agrícola. México, D.F. , 1985. i, 156 p. ; LC Card 86-156375
HG2051.L26 F55 1985

AGRICULTURE - LAWS AND LEGISLATION. see **AGRICULTURAL LAWS AND LEGISLATION.**

AGRICULTURE - MOROCCO - MARRAKESH REGION - HISTORY.
Pascon, Paul. [Haouz de Marrakech. English.] Capitalism and agriculture in the Haouz of Marrakesh /. London ; New York : 248 p. : ISBN 0-7103-0189-8 LC Card 87-100309 DDC 338.1/0964/6 19
HD2121.Z9 M37613 1986

AGRICULTURE - NEPAL.
Maharjan, Bekha L. (Bekha Lal), 1943- Small farm development problems and strategies /. [Kathmandu] , 1984. 114 p. ; LC Card 84-901301 DDC 338.1/6 19
HD1476.N35 M33 1984
NYPL [JLD 86-4365]

AGRICULTURE - OKLAHOMA - FINANCE.
Plaxico, James Sam, 1924- Financial status of Oklahoma farmers and ranchers, 1985 . [Stillwater] [1986] 42 p. ; LC Card 86-622478 DDC 338.1/3/09766021 19
HD1775.O5 P57 1986

AGRICULTURE - ONTARIO - FINANCE.
Ontario. Interministerial Task Force on Agricultural Finance. Report of the Interministerial Task Force on Agricultural Finance. [Toronto, Ont. , 1986] vii, 65, [42] p. : LC Card 87-127476 DDC 332.7/1/09713 19
HD1790.O6 O573 1986

Agriculture planning and social justice in India /.
Govil, Rishi Kumar, 1933- Allahabad , 1986. vii, 214 p. ; LC Card 86-902616 DDC 338.1/854 19
HD2073 .G68 1986

AGRICULTURE - POLITICAL ASPECTS - EUROPEAN ECONOMIC COMMUNITY COUNTRIES.
Carfantan, Jean Yves. L'Europe verte sous influence . Paris , c1985. 282 p. ; ISBN 2-02-008982-3 : LC Card 86-140900 DDC 338.1/094 19
HD1920.5 .C37 1985 ***NYPL [JLE 87-526]***

AGRICULTURE - PORTUGAL.
Portuguese agriculture in transition /. Ithaca , 1987. 283 p. : ISBN 0-8014-1954-9 (alk. paper) LC Card 86-29198 DDC 338.1/09469 19
HD2027 .P67 1987

Agriculture, poverty, and freedom in developing countries /. Clayton, E. (Eric) London , 1983. x, 277 p. : ISBN 0-333-36100-8 LC Card 86-673664
HD1417 .C52x 1983

AGRICULTURE - RESEARCH - CHILE.
Mannarelli M., Virgilio B. Organización institucional del sector agrícola /. Santiago, Chile , 1985. 81, [3] p. : LC Card 86-115545 DDC 338.1/883 19
HD1878 .M35 1985

AGRICULTURE - RESEARCH - DEVELOPING COUNTRIES - ADDRESSES, ESSAYS, LECTURES.
George, Susan. Ill fares the land . Washington, D.C. , c1984. xviii, 102 p. ; ISBN 0-89758-039-7 (pbk.) : LC Card 84-25124 DDC 363.8 19
HD9000.5 .G385 1984
NYPL [JLD 86-3899]

AGRICULTURE - RUSSIAN S.F.S.R.
Kolos na ladoni . Voronezh , 1985. 237 p. : LC Card 86-195464
HD1536.S65 K65 1985

AGRICULTURE - RUSSIAN S.F.S.R. - KRASNOI͡ARSKIĬ KRAĬ.
Sistema vedenii͡a sel'skogo i promyslovogo khozi͡aĭstva na Eniseĭskom Severe . Novosibirsk , 1986. 211 p. ; LC Card 86-227282
HD1995.K73 S57 1986

AGRICULTURE - SENEGAL.
Agroforstliche Landnutzung im Einzugsbereich zentraler Orte im Sahel . Köln , 1983. ix, 374 p. : ISBN 3-8039-0276-2 LC Card 87-102956 DDC 333.73/13/09663 19
HD1019.Z63 A38 1983

AGRICULTURE - SOCIAL ASPECTS - BANGLADESH.
Muqtada, M. Social and economic formations in Bangladesh agriculture . Dacca, Bangladesh , 1986. 68 p. ; LC Card 86-902421 DDC 338.1/09549/2 19
HD2075.6 .M86 1986

AGRICULTURE - SOCIAL ASPECTS - HUNGARY.
Simó, Tibor. Metszetek az agrártársadalom struktúrájából /. Budapest , 1985. 167 p. ; ISBN 963-7700-25-0 : LC Card 86-232606
HD1536.H9 S56 1985

AGRICULTURE - SOCIAL ASPECTS - HUNGARY - HISTORY - CONGRESSES.
Agrárgazdaság, agrártársadalom, agrárpolitika /. Szeged , 1985. 338 p. : ISBN 963-481-548-0 : LC Card 86-143859
HD1940.5 .A78 1985

AGRICULTURE - SOCIAL ASPECTS - INDIA.
Mishra, G. P. Village industries and agriculture in changing agrarian situation /. New Delhi , c1985. 120 p. ; ISBN 81-7024-010-7 LC Card 85-904926 DDC 338.6/34/0954 19
HD2346.I5 M49 1985 ***NYPL [JLD 86-3746]***

AGRICULTURE - SOCIAL ASPECTS - INDIA - JAMMU AND KASHMIR - HISTORY.
Sharma, Dewan Chand, 1898- Kashmir agriculture & land revenue system under the Sikh rule, 1819-46 A.D. /. New Delhi, India , 1986. xiv, 160 p., [8] p. of plates : LC Card 86-900128
HD2075.J35 S43 1986 ***NYPL [JLD 86-3742]***

AGRICULTURE - SOCIAL ASPECTS - INDIA - PANCHRA.
Chakrabarti, S. B., 1943- Around the plough . Calcutta , 1986. xviii, 203 p., 8 p. of plates : LC Card 86-902283
HD2075.P36 C48 1986
NYPL [L-10 8468 no.67]

AGRICULTURE - SOCIAL ASPECTS - KENYA - HISTORY.
Leo, Christopher. Land and class in Kenya /. Toronto , Buffalo [N.Y.] , c1984. xii, 244 p. : ISBN 0-8020-2532-3 ***NYPL [JLE 86-1242]***

AGRICULTURE - SOCIAL ASPECTS - SRI LANKA.
Capital and peasant production . Colombo, Sri Lanka , 1985. xiv, 230 p. ; LC Card 86-900809 DDC 338.1/3/095493 19
HD2065.8 .C36 1985 ***NYPL [JLE 87-1667]***

AGRICULTURE - SOCIAL ASPECTS - SWEDEN - SÖDERMANLAND LÄN - HISTORY - 19TH CENTURY.
Köll, Anu-Mai. Tradition och reform i västra Södermanlands jordbruk, 1810-1890 . Stockholm , 1983. 252 p. : ISBN 91-22-00633-8 LC Card 84-114628
HD2020.S63 K65 1983

AGRICULTURE - SOCIAL ASPECTS - UNITED STATES - CONGRESSES.
Farm work and fieldwork . Ithaca , 1987. 293 p. : ISBN 0-8014-9446-X (pbk. : alk. paper) LC Card 86-19960 DDC 305.5/55/0973 19
HD8039.F32 U635 1987

AGRICULTURE - SOVIET UNION - ACCOUNTING.
Val'ter, S. B. (Semen Borisovich) Spravochnik po finansovo-ėkonomicheskim raschetam v sel'skokhozi͡aĭstvennykh predprii͡atii͡akh /. Moskva , 1982. 411 p. ; LC Card 83-160870
HF5686.A36 V35 1982

AGRICULTURE - SOVIET UNION - ACCOUNTING - DATA PROCESSING.
Vasil'ev, A. F. (Alekseĭ Fedorovich) Avtomatizirovannai͡a obrabotka uchetnoĭ informatsii v sel'skokhozi͡aĭstvennykh predprii͡atii͡akh /. Moskva , 1984. 198 p. ; LC Card 85-113739
HF5686.A36 V37 1984

AGRICULTURE - SOVIET UNION - HISTORY - 20TH CENTURY.
Harris, Lement, 1904- My tale of two worlds . New York , 1986. 289 p. : ISBN 0-7178-0645-6 : LC Card 86-10671 DDC 338.1/092/4 B 19
S417.H35 A36 1986 ***NYPL [JLD 87-1376]***

AGRICULTURE - SPAIN - CATALONIA - SOCIETIES, ETC.
Rendé, Josep M. Pla d'organització social agrària de Catalunya /. Barcelona , 1924. 138 p., [1] folded leaf of plates : LC Card 86-202164 DDC 334/.683/09467 19
HD1491.S82 C317 1924

AGRICULTURE - SPAIN - STATISTICS.
Selected agricultural statistics on Spain, 1970-82 /. Washington, D.C. (1301 New York Ave., N.W., Washington 20005-4788) , 1986. x, 142 p. : LC Card 86-602416 DDC 338.1/0973 s 338.1/0946/021 19
HD1751 .A5 no. 742 HD2022

AGRICULTURE - STATISTICS - COMPARATIVE METHOD.
Szász, Kálmán. A mezőgazdaság nemzetközi összehasonlításának módszerei . Budapest , 1986. 96 p. ; ISBN 963-02-4381-4 LC Card 87-419792
HD1425 .S95 1986

AGRICULTURE - SUDAN - DAR MASALIT.
Tully, Dennis. Culture and context in Sudan . Albany, N.Y. , c1988. p. cm. ISBN 0-88706-502-3 LC Card 86-23180 DDC 338.1/09627 19
HC835.Z7 D377 1988

AGRICULTURE - SWEDEN - CAPITAL PRODUCTIVITY - HISTORY.
Magnusson, Lars, 1941- Kapitalbildning i Sverige 1750-1860 . Uppsala , Stockholm , 1983. 95 p. ; ISBN 91-554-1443-5 LC Card 83-228044
HC374 .M34 1983

AGRICULTURE - TAXATION - DOMINICAN REPUBLIC.
Ross, Jaime. Instrumentos tributarios de financiamientos coadyuvantes a la producción agraria de alimentos /. Santo Domingo, R.D. [1983] i, 229 p. ; LC Card 84-159753
HJ4308 .R67 1983

AGRICULTURE - TAXATION - EGYPT - HISTORY.
Stuchevskiĭ, I. A. (Iosif Aleksandrovich) Zemledel'tsy gosudarstvennogo khozi͡aĭstva drevnego Egipta ėpokhi Ramessidov /. Moskva , 1982. 254, [2] p. ; LC Card 82-186646
HD2123 .S78 1982

AGRICULTURE - TAXATION - INDIA - BIHAR - CASE STUDIES.
Jha, Ganganand. Agricultural taxation in India . Delhi , 1987. vi, 199 p. ; LC Card 87-900333 DDC 336.2/7863/095412 19
HD1443.I42 B534 1987

AGRICULTURE - TAXATION - INDIA - CASE STUDIES.
Jha, Ganganand. Agricultural taxation in India . Delhi , 1987. vi, 199 p. ; LC Card 87-900333 DDC 336.2/7863/095412 19
HD1443.I42 B534 1987

AGRICULTURE - TAXATION - INDIA - JAMMU AND KASHMIR.
Bhat, Mohd. Sultan (Mohammad Sultan) Agricultural taxation in Jammu & Kashmir /. New Delhi , 1987. vi, 192 p. ; LC Card 87-901173 DDC 336.2/7863/09546 19
HD1443.I42 J352 1987

AGRICULTURE - TAXATION - INDIA - PUNJAB.
Arneja, Jasbir Singh. Agricultural taxation in Punjab /. Jalandhar , 1987. xvi, 280 p. ; ISBN 81-7072-009-5 : LC Card 86-903405 DDC 336.2/7863/0954552 19
HD1443.I42 P863 1987

AGRICULTURE - TAXATION - PAKISTAN.
Some aspects of agricultural price and taxation policies in Pakistan /. Islamabad, Pakistan [1985] x, 223 p. ; LC Card 86-930932 DDC 338.1/8 19
HD2075.5 .S66 1985

AGRICULTURE - TAXATION - SPAIN - CATALONIA.
L'IVA en els sectors agrari i pesquer catalans. [Barcelona] , 1985. 49 p. ; ISBN 84-393-0632-6 LC Card 86-165858
HJ5715.S7 L58 1985

AGRICULTURE - TROPICS.
Les Phénomènes de "frontière" dans les pays tropicaux . Paris , 1981. vii, 456 p. : LC Card 83-122397
HD1131 .P47 1981

AGRICULTURE - UGANDA - BUGISU (DISTRICT) - SOCIETIES, ETC. - POLITICAL ACTIVITY.
Bunker, Stephen G., 1944- Double dependency and constraints on class formation in Bugisu, Uganda /. Urbana, Ill. , 1983. v, 88 p. : LC Card 86-229748 DDC 303.3/09676/1 19
HD1538.U43 B86 1983

AGRICULTURE - UKRAINE - ACCOUNTING.
Murashko, V. M. (Vasiliĭ Maksimovich) Kontrol' i analiz deiatel'nosti predpriiatiĭ po zagotovkam sel'skokhoziaistvennoĭ produktsii /. Moskva , 1981. 144 p. ; LC Card 82-177216
HF5686.A36 M87 1981

AGRICULTURE - UKRAINE - AUDITING.
Murashko, V. M. (Vasiliĭ Maksimovich) Kontrol' i analiz deiatel'nosti predpriiatiĭ po zagotovkam sel'skokhoziaistvennoĭ produktsii /. Moskva , 1981. 144 p. ; LC Card 82-177216
HF5686.A36 M87 1981

AGRICULTURE - UKRAINE - CAPITAL INVESTMENTS.
IAkovlev, IU. P. (IUriĭ Prokof'evich) Ėffektivnoe ispol'zovanie kapital'nykh vlozheniĭ v sel'skom stroitel'stve /. Kiev , 1985. 104 p. : LC Card 86-214694
HD9715.S73 U383 1985

AGRICULTURE - UNITED STATES.
Fox, Michael W., 1937- Agricide . New York , 1986. xv, 194 p., [10] p. of plates : ISBN 0-8052-4013-6 LC Card 85-27690 DDC 338.1/6/0973 19
S441 .F69 1986 ***NYPL [JLD 86-2542]***

Wallace, Luther T. Agriculture's futures . New York , c1987. x, 93 p. : ISBN 0-387-96482-7 (pbk.) LC Card 86-31390 DDC 338.1/0973 19
HD1761 .W274 1987

AGRICULTURE - UNITED STATES - FINANCE.
The Farm credit crisis . College Station, Tex. [1986] ii, 57 p. : LC Card 86-622188 DDC 332.7/1/0973 19
HG2051.U5 F26 1986

The Farm credit crisis policy options and consequences /. Ithaca, N.Y. [1986] ii, 57 p. : LC Card 86-621935 DDC 338.1 s 332.7/1/0973 19
HD1775.N8 C6 no. 86-3 HG2051.U6

The Farm financial crisis . Boulder , 1988. xvi, 205 p. : ISBN 0-8133-7186-4 (pbk. : alk. paper) : LC Card 86-32601 DDC 338.1/3/0973 19
HD1761 .F295 1988

Financing the agricultural sector . Boulder, Colo. , 1986. xi, 256 p. : ISBN 0-8133-0055-X (pbk. : alk. paper) LC Card 86-50152 DDC 338.1/3/0973 19
HD1761 .F5 1986 ***NYPL [JLE 86-2766]***

McKinzie, Lance. A perspective on U. S. farm problems and agricultural policy /. Boulder , 1987. xvii, 189 p. : ISBN 0-8133-7376-X (pbk. : alk. paper) LC Card 86-51501 DDC 338.1/873 19
HD1470.5.U6 M35 1987

Transition in agriculture . Washington, D.C. (1120 Connecticut Ave. N.W., Washington 20036) , c1986. 2 v. : LC Card 86-233848 DDC 332.7/1/0973 19
HG2051.U5 T68 1986

AGRICULTURE - UNITED STATES - HISTORY - 20TH CENTURY.
Harris, Lement, 1904- My tale of two worlds . New York , 1986. 289 p. : ISBN 0-7178-0645-6 : LC Card 86-10671 DDC 338.1/092/4 B 19
S417.H35 A36 1986 ***NYPL [JLD 87-1376]***

AGRICULTURE - ZAMBIA - LUSAKA PROVINCE - PLANNING - CONGRESSES.
Lusaka Province (Zambia). Provincial Planning Unit. Towards self sufficiency . [Lusaka, Zambia?] [1984] 100 p., [14] leaves of plates : LC Card 86-980293 DDC 338.1/86894 19
HD2131.5 .L87 1984

Agriculture's futures . Wallace, Luther T. New York , c1987. x, 93 p. : ISBN 0-387-96482-7 (pbk.) LC Card 86-31390 DDC 338.1/0973 19
HD1761 .W274 1987

AGRICULTURISTS - MEXICO - POLITICAL ACTIVITY.
Cleaves, Peter S. Professions and the state . Tucson , c1987. xv, 147 p. : ISBN 0-8165-1016-4 (alk. paper) LC Card 87-5911 DDC 331.7/12/0972 19
HD8038.M6 C55 1987

Agripino, Jose. Compromisso com o povo : discurso de posse, Natal, RN, 15-03-1983 / José Agripino. [Natal, Brazil] : Assessoria de Comunicação Social do Governo do Rio Grande do Norte, [1983?] 19 p. ; 22 x 24 cm. Cover title. "1"--P. [4] of cover. LC Card 86-215313
1. Poor - Brazil - Rio Grande de Norte. 2. Brazil, Northeast - Economic conditions. I. Title.
HC188.R38 A54 1983

Agro-economics of dairy development in India /. Surendar Singh, 1946- New Delhi , 1986. xii, 188 p. ; LC Card 86-902764 DDC 338.1/77/0954 19
HD9275.I52 S87 1986

Agroforstliche Landnutzung im Einzugsbereich zentraler Orte im Sahel : Fallbeispiel Nord-Senegal / Hans-Jürgen von Maydell ... [et al.]. Köln : Weltforum, 1983. ix, 374 p. : ill. ; 21 cm. (Forschungsberichte des Bundesministeriums für Wirtschaftliche Zusammenarbeit . Bd. 47) "Diese Studie wurde als Forschungsvorhaben im Auftrag des Bundesministeriums für wirtschaftliche Zusammenarbeit von der Bundesvorschungsanstalt für Forst- und Holzwirtschaft, Hamburg, erstellt"--P. ii. Includes bibliographies. ISBN 3-8039-0276-2 LC Card 87-102956 DDC 333.73/13/09663 19
1. Land use - Senegal. 2. Agriculture - Senegal. I. Maydell, H. J. von. II. Germany (West). Bundesministerium für Wirtschaftliche Zusammenarbeit. III. Bundesforschungsanstalt für Forst- und Holzwirtschaft (Germany). IV. Series.
HD1019.Z63 A38 1983

Agroforstliche Landnutzung in der Sahel-Sudanzone . Kapp, Gerald B., 1956- München , c1987. xii, 397 p. : ISBN 3-8039-0347-5 LC Card 87-419915 DDC 333.76/13/0966 19
HD1010.5.Z63 K37 1987

Agronomía y fisiocracia en España, 1750-1820 /. Lluch, Ernest, 1937- Valencia [1985?] lxi, 215 p. ; ISBN 84-00-05965-4 LC Card 85-240630
HD2022 .L58 1985

AGRONOMY. see **AGRICULTURE.**

Agropromyshlennyĭ kompleks i problemy obespecheniia naseleniia prodovol'stviem : sbornik nauchnykh trudov / [Golovanov, A.N. (nauchnyĭ redaktor)]. Kiev : Nauchno-issl. ėkon. in-t Gosplana USSR, 1983. 190 p. : ill. ; 21 cm. At head of title: Nauchno-issledovatel'skiĭ ėkonomicheskiĭ institut Gosplana USSR. Includes bibliographies. LC Card 86-139699
1. Agricultural industries - Ukraine. 2. Food industry and trade - Ukraine. I. Golovanov, A. N. II. Naukovo-doslidnyĭ ekonomichnyĭ institut.
HD9015.S653 U4295 1983

Agropromyshlennyĭ kompleks v usloviiakh razvitogo sotsializma : sbornik obzorov / [redaktsionnaia kollegiia Arkhipov A.I., Kazakevich V.P., Tovmosian M.E. (otvetstvennyĭ redaktor)]. Moskva : INION AN SSSR, 1986. 167 p. ; 20 cm. (Seriia Aktual'nye problemy razvitogo sotsializma) At head of title: Akademiia nauk SSSR. Institut nauchnoĭ informatsii po obshchestvennym naukam. Institut ėkonomiki. Includes bibliographies. LC Card 87-166350
1. Agricultural industries - Soviet Union. 2. Food supply - Soviet Union. I. Arkhipov, Anatoliĭ Ivanovich. II. Kazakevich, V. P. III. Tovmosian, M. E. IV. Institut nauchnoĭ informatsii po obshchestvennym naukam (Akademiia nauk SSSR). V. Institut ėkonomiki (Akademiia nauk SSSR). VI. Series.
HD9015.S652 A38 1986

AGROTIKĒ TRAPEZA TĒS HELLADOS.
Baltas, N. K. Empeirikē diereunēsē tēs apotamieutikēs sympeiphoras kai tēs zētēsēs katatheseōn apo tous idiōtes /. Athēna [1979] 128 p. ; LC Card 86-203196
HG3250.5.A6 B34 1979

Agrotikē Trapeza tēs Hellados. Dieuthynsē Geōrgikōn Viomēchaniōn.
Hodēgos synetairistikōn geōrgikōn viomēchaniōn . Athēna , 1985. 102 p. : LC Card 86-194038
HD9015.G82 H59 1985

Programma ependyseōn se geōrgikes viomēchanies to 1986 /. Athēna , 1986. 32, 91 leaves, [1] folded leaf of plates : LC Card 86-193452
HG2051.G9 P76 1986

Agrotikē Trapeza tēs Hellados. Dieuthynsē Meletōn & Programmatismou.
Baltas, N. K. Empeirikē diereunēsē tēs apotamieutikēs sympeiphoras kai tēs zētēsēs katatheseōn apo tous idiōtes /. Athēna [1979] 128 p. ; LC Card 86-203196
HG3250.5.A6 B34 1979

Epistēmoniko Diēmero (1984 : Athens, Greece) Ependyseis kai trapezikes chorēgēseis se periodo krisēs . Athēna , 1984. 225 p. ; LC Card 86-193395
HG5700.5.A3 E85 1984

Hodēgos geōrgikōn viomēchaniōn. Athēna , 1985. 510 p. : LC Card 86-193419
HD9015.G82 H58 1985

Gli agrumi nella storia del Meridione . Calcaterra, Francesco. Roma , c1986. 95 p. : LC Card 87-133974
HD9259.C53 I723 1986

Agudelo, Hernando. see **Agudelo Villa, Hernando.**

Agudelo Mejía, Santiago. Lineamientos para la implantación de un servicio de certificación ocupacional / Santiago Agudelo Mejía. 1a ed. Montevideo : CINTERFOR/OIT, 1983. 67 p. : ill. ; 23 cm. (Estudios y monografías . no. 59) Bibliography: p. 55-67. LC Card 86-142627
1. Occupational training - Latin America. 2. Latin America - Occupations - Licenses. I. CINTERFOR (Organization). II. Series: Estudios y monografías (CINTERFOR (Organization)) , no. 59. III. Title.
HD5715.5.L3 A348 1983

Agudelo Villa, Hernando. (comp) La política del Ministerio de Desarrollo. Bogotá, Ministerio de Desarrollo Económico, 1972-73. 3 v. 24 cm. Vol. 3 also has title: Los fondos regionales de capitalización social. LC Card 73-208936
1. Colombia. Ministerio de Desarrollo Económico. 2. Colombia - Economic policy. I. Title.
HC197 .A63

Aguiar, César A., 1943- Escenarios políticos y sociales del desarrollo latinoamericano /. [S.l.] [Buenos Aires] , c1986. 231 p. ; ISBN 950-23-0274-5 LC Card 87-400175 DDC 338.98 19
HC125 .E82 1986

Aguiar, Leila Maria Guimarães. Substituição de óleo diesel . [Brasília, Brazil] [19]84. 84 p. : LC Card 87-404960 DDC 338.4/76553 19
HD9579.D53 B737 1984

Aguila Tello, María Luz del. Wester León, Humberto. Diagnóstico situacional del movimiento cooperativo peruano /. [Lima] , 1981- v. : ***NYPL [JLL 86-146]***

Aguilar Bolaños, Irene. Una caracterización socioeconómica del grupo ganaderoexportador (los casos de San Carlos y Guanacaste) 1960-1980 / Irene Aguilar Bolaños. San José, Costa Rica : Universidad de Costa Rica, Facultad de Ciencias Sociales, Instituto de Investigaciones Sociales, 1985. xiii, 260 p. ; 27 cm. (Serie Investigaciones. n. 5) Bibliography: p. [259]-260. LC Card 86-107500
1. Beef industry - Costa Rica - San Carlos (Canton). 2. Beef industry - Costa Rica - Guanacaste. I. Series: Serie investigaciones (Universidad de Costa Rica. Instituto de Investigaciones Sociales). II. Title.
HD9433.C83 S223 1985 ***NYPL [JLF 87-74]***

Aguilar, Francis J. (Francis Joseph) General managers in action / Francis Joseph Aguilar. New York : Oxford University Press, 1988. viii, 498 p. : ill. ; 25 cm. Includes bibliographical references and index. ISBN 0-19-504083-X (alk. paper) LC Card 87-12503 DDC 658.4 19
1. Chief executive officers - Case studies. 2. Management - Case studies. I. Title.
HD38.2 .A39 1987

Aguilar García, Javier. Los Sindicatos nacionales en el México contemporáneo /. [México, D.F.] , 1986- v. <1 > ; ISBN 968-498-020-5 (set) LC Card 87-401211 DDC 331.88/0972 19
HD6532 .S55 1986

Aguilar, Justo. Carreras, Rodrigo X. Vivienda y población en Costa Rica . Heredia, Costa Rica , 1979. 203 p. : LC Card 87-404329 DDC 363.5/097286 19
HD7308.A3 C37 1979

Aguilar, Vilma. Cobriza, Cobriza, 1971 /. [Lima? Peru] , 1981. 136 p. ; LC Card 83-106108
HD5361 .M612 1971

Aguilar Zinser, Adolfo. Aún tiembla . México , c1986. 332 p., [8] p. of plates : ISBN 968-419-620-2 LC Card 87-403523 DDC 363.3/495/097253 19
HC138.M43 A95 1986

Aguilera, Gabriel Edgardo. see **Aguilera Peralta, Gabriel Edgardo.**

Aguilera Peralta, Gabriel Edgardo. Raíces y perspectivas de la crisis económica / [Gabriel Aguilera Peralta, Edelberto Torres-Rivas]. San José, Costa Rica : Instituto Centroamericano de Documentación e Investigación Social, Proyecto de Investigación "Crisis y Alternativas en Centroamérica", 1986. 297 p. ; 21 cm. (Para entender Centroamérica . 4) Bibliography: p. 279-280. ISBN 997-7990-33-6 LC Card 87-404300 DDC 330.9728/053 19
1. Central America - Economic conditions. I. Torres-Rivas, Edelberto. II. Title. III. Series.
HC141 .A63 1986

Aguirre, Juan Antonio. Cussianovich, Pedro. Economía y energía en Costa Rica . San José, Costa Rica , 1982. viii, 71, [10] leaves : LC Card 86-179795
HD9502.C82 C87 1982

Aguirre, Luis Pérez. see **Pérez Aguirre, Luis.**

Aguirre, Mariano A. De Hiroshima a los euromisiles / Mariano Aguirre. Madrid : Tecnos, c1984. 254 p. : ill. ; 18 cm. (Colección Status quaestionis) Bibliography: p. 243-254. ISBN 84-309-1062-X LC Card 85-215587
1. Nuclear weapons. 2. Nuclear warfare. 3. Nuclear disarmament. I. Title. II. Series.
U264 .A39 1984 ***NYPL [JFC 86-1643]***

A.H. ROBINS COMPANY.
Perry, Susan. Nightmare . New York , c1985. xvii, 261 p. ; ISBN 0-02-595930-1 : LC Card 85-13710 DDC 338.7/616139435 19
HD9995.C64 A236 1985
NYPL [JLE 85-3950]

Ahad, Abdul, 1947- Kashmir to Frankfurt : a study of arts and crafts, with a chapter on the freedom struggle of Kashmir / Abdul Ahad. New Delhi, India : Rima Pub. House, 1987. xiv, 182 p., [20] p. of plates : ill. ; 29 cm. On the shawl industries in Kashmir, India. Bibliography: p. [156]-164. Includes index. LC Card 86-903828
1. Shawl industry - India - Jammu and Kashmir - History. 2. Jammu and Kashmir (India) - Industries - History. I. Title.
HD9969.S43 I425 1987

Ahde, Pasi. Karhu, Veli. Akseleraatioteoriaan perustuvia investointifunktiokokeiluja yritystason aineistolla /. Vaasa , 1982. 43, [1] leaves ; ISBN 951-683-160-5 LC Card 83-100841 DDC 332/.0415 19
HG4028.C4 K349 1982
NYPL [JLM 73-601 n:o 85]

Ahearn, Mary C. Lucier, Gary. Farm income data . Washington, DC [1986] iv, 311 p. : LC Card 86-602022 DDC 338.1/0973 s 338.1/3/0973021 19
HD1751 .A5 no. 740 HD1769

Ahiadeke, Clement. Ewusi, Kodwo. The development and resettlement of oncho-freed zones in the Volta River Basin of West Africa . [Legon, Ghana] [1985] 89 p. ; LC Card 87-127503 DDC 333.3/1/667 19
HD1022.Z8 V654 1985

Ahijado, Manuel. Piero Sraffa : notas para una biografía intelectual / por Manuel Ahijado. Madrid : Centro de Estudios Universitarios Ramón Areces, 1985. 90 p. ; 24 cm. (Cuadernos de economía aplicada) Bibliography: p. 87-90. ISBN 84-85942-31-0 LC Card 87-104173
1. Sraffa, Piero. 2. Economists - Italy - Biography. I. Title. II. Series.
HB109.S73 A35 1985

AHI's complete portfolio of modern business terms. A dictionary of business terms / Alexander Hamilton Institute. New York : F. Watts, 1987, c1986. 438 p. ; 24 cm. (Advanced management skills) Previously published as: AHI's complete portfolio of modern business terms. 1986. ISBN 0-531-15518-8 LC Card 86-24560 DDC 650/.03/21 19
1. Business - Dictionaries. 2. Finance - Dictionaries. I. Alexander Hamilton Institute (U. S.). II. Title. III. Series.
HF1001 .A34 1987

Ahlers, Theodore H. Somalia . Boston, MA [1983] vi, 164 p. : LC Card 87-108393 DDC 330.967/7305 19
HC850 .S655 1983

Ahlqvist, Berndt, 1931- I bräcklig farkost : en bok om svensk ekonomi i internationell miljö / Berndt Ahlqvist. Stockholm : Tiden, c1983. 186 p. ; 21 cm. ISBN 91-550-2917-5 : LC Card 83-230190
1. Sweden - Economic conditions - 1945-. 2. Sweden - Economic policy. I. Title.
HC375 .A63 1983

Ahmad, Nisar. Locational pattern of agricultural production/purchases : transport demand study project. Lilongwe [Malawi] : Transport Planning Unit, Economic Planning Division, Office of the President and Cabinet, 1984. ii, 33 leaves ; 29 cm. At head of cover title: Malaŵi Government. "Designed and drafted by Dr. Nisar Ahmad ... with the active assistance of Mr. L.S.C. Siwande"--Leaf 3. "October 1984." Includes bibliographical references. LC Card 86-980325 DDC 380.1/41/096897 19
1. Farm produce - Malawi - Transportation. I. Siwande, L. S. C. II. Malawi. Transport Planning Unit. III. Title.
HE199.5.F3 A38 1984

Ahmad, Qazi Kholiquzzaman, 1943- World trade in a primary commodity : the case of jute / by Qazi Kholiquzzaman Ahmad ... [et al.]. Nyon, Switzerland : Third World Forum, 1979. i, 83 p. ; 22 cm. (Third World Forum occasional paper . no. 7) "Bangladesh Institute of Development Studies." Bibliography: p. 80-83. LC Card 86-202627
1. Jute industry. I. Bangladesh Institute of Development Studies. II. Series: Occasional paper (Third World Forum) , no. 7. III. Title.
HD9156.J7 A38 1979

Ahmad, Yusuf J. Desertification : financial support for the biosphere / Yusuf J. Ahmad, Mohamed Kassas. West Hartford, CT. : Kumarian Press, 1987. xviii, 187 p. : ill. ; 24 cm. Sponsored by the United Nations Environment Programme. Includes bibliographies and index. ISBN 0-931816-99-8 (pbk.) : LC Card 87-3650 DDC 333.73 19
1. Desertification - Control - Finance. I. Kassas, Mohammed. II. Title.
HD111 .A44 1987

Ahmadu Bello University. Centre for Social and Economic Research. Ogwude, Innocent C. (Innocent Chuka) Industrial demand for freight transport in Kaduna State /. Zaria [Nigeria] [1984] 101 p. : LC Card 86-152627 DDC 380.5/24/096695 19
HE287.7.Z7 K336 1984

Ahmadu Bello University. Dept. of Political Science. Rural underdevelopment in Nigeria, 1900-1980. Zaria, Nigeria , 1985. iv, 102 p. ; LC Card 86-154806 DDC 338.1/8669 19
HD2145.5.Z8 R87 1985

Ahmed, Mahbub. Habibullah, M. Management constraints of co-operatives /. Dhaka , 1986. 92 p. ; LC Card 87-900945
HD1491.B3 H34 1986

Ahmed, Mumtaz. Project management : a management accounting perspective / by Mumtaz Ahmed and David Alderman. Hamilton, Ont. : Society of Management Accountants of Canada, [1986] xv, 254 p. : ill. ; 22 cm. "A research monograph prepared for the Research Studies Committee, the Society of Management Accountants of Canada." "December 1986"--T.p. verso. ISBN 0-920212-56-5 (pbk.) LC Card 87-158681 DDC 658.4/04 19
1. Managerial accounting. 2. Industrial project management. 3. Managerial accounting - Canada. 4. Industrial project management - Canada. I. Alderman, David. II. Society of Management Accountants of Canada. Research Studies Committee. III. Title.
HF5635 .A26 1986

Ahmed, Zia U. (Zia Uddin) Pricing policy and investment criteria in public enterprises . Ljubljana, Yugoslavia , 1982. 297 p. : ISBN 92-9038-024-1 (pbk.) LC Card 85-242542 DDC 338.7/4 19
HD3842 .P75 1985 ***NYPL [JLE 87-547]***

Ahmedabad. Sardar Patel Institute of Economic and Social Research. see **Sardar Patel Institute of Economic and Social Research.**

AHMG economic overview of fish and wildlife. Alaska habitat management guide. Juneau, Alaska , 1986- 2 v. (loose-leaf) : LC Card 86-623159 DDC 333.95/09798 19
HD9457.A4 A427 1986

Ahn, Doo-Soon. Government policy towards FDI and the reaction of foreign investors in DCs / Ahn, Doo-Soon. Bochum : Institut für Entwicklungsforschung und Entwicklungspolitik, Ruhr-Universität Bochum, [1985] 23, 33 leaves ; 30 cm. (Materialien und kleine Schriften . 103) Includes bibliographies. CONTENTS. - Interrelation between government policy and the reaction of foreign investors--the Korean case -- National treatment and safeguard of FDI in ASEAN countries. LC Card 86-219920 DDC 332.6/73225195 19
1. Investments, Foreign - Government policy - Korea (South). 2. Investments, Foreign - Government policy - Asia, Southeastern. I. Series: Materialien und kleine Schriften (Ruhr-Universität Bochum. Institut für Entwicklungsforschung und Entwicklungspolitik) , 103. II. Title.
HG5780.5.A3 A34 1985

Ahn, Lothar. Ökonomische und ökologische Perspektiven der Agrarpolitik : Situationsanalyse und Reformmöglichkeiten des europäischen Agrarmarktes / Lothar Ahn. Köln : Pahl-Rugenstein, 1983. 98 p. : ill. ; 21 cm. (Pahl-Rugenstein Hochschulschriften Gesellschafts- und Naturwissenschaften . 124) Bibliography: p. 93-98. ISBN 3-7609-5124-4 LC Card 83-155478
1. Agriculture and state - European Economic Community countries. 2. Produce trade - European Economic Community countries. I. Title. II. Series.
HD1920.5 .A627 1983

Ahonzo, Etienne. Population de la Côte d'Ivoire : analyse des donnés démographiques disponibles / Etienne Ahonzo, Bernard Barrère, Pierre Kopylov. Abidjan : République de Côte d'Ivoire, Ministère de l'économie et des finances, Direction de la statistique, 1984. ix, 324 p. : ill. ; 28 cm. Cover title. Bibliography: p. 289-296. LC Card 86-110796 DDC 304.6/09666/8 19
1. Labor supply - Ivory Coast. 2. Education - Ivory Coast. 3. Ivory Coast - Population. I. Barrère, Bernard. II. Kopylov, Pierre. III. Ivory Coast. Direction de la statistique. IV. Title.
HB3666.A3 A46 1984 ***NYPL [JLF 86-1466]***

Ahorro interno y el sistema financiero / Luis Baba Nakao ... [et al.]. 2da. ed. [Lima, Peru] : Fundación Friedrich Ebert, 1986. 70 p. : ill. ; 21 cm. (Taller de investigación) Includes bibliographies. LC Card 87-127322 DDC 332/.0985 19
1. Saving and investment - Peru. 2. Finance - Peru. I. Baba Nakao, Luis. II. Friedrich-Ebert-Stiftung. III. Series.
HC230.S3 A38 1986

El ahorro vinculado a la adquisición de viviendas . Morón Bécquer, Pedro. Madrid [1984?] 35 p. : ISBN 84-7196-476-7 : LC Card 85-201073
HG2156.S72 M67 1984

Ahrens, Gerhard, 1939-
Krisenmanagement 1857 : Staat und Kaufmannschaft in Hamburg während der ersten Weltwirtschaftskrise / Gerhard Ahrens. Hamburg : Verein für Hamburgische Geschichte, 1986. 136 p. ; 25 cm. (Veröffentlichungen des Vereins für Hamburgische Geschichte . Bd. 28) Bibliography: p. 129-134. Includes index. ISBN 3-923356-11-0 LC Card 87-127645 DDC 338.5/4 19
1. Depressions - 1857 - Germany (West) - Hamburg. 2. Hamburg (Germany) - Economic policy. 3. Hamburg (Germany) - Economic conditions. I. Title. II. Series.
HB3717 1857 .A38 1986

Staatsverschuldung ohne Ende? / Gerhard Ahrens. Bemerkungen zur "Krise der Arbeitsgesellschaft" / Bernhard Muszynski. Hamburg : Hochschule der Bundeswehr Hamburg, [1984] 37 leaves ; 30 cm. (Beiträge aus dem Fachbereich Pädagogik der Hochschule der Bundeswehr Hamburg, 0175-310X . 5/1984) Bibliography: leaves 35-36. LC Card 85-166341
1. Debts, Public - Germany - History - 19th century. 2. Deficit financing - Germany - History - 19th century. 3. Hansa towns - Economic conditions. 4. Industrial sociology - Germany, West. I. Muszynski, Bernhard. Bemerkungen zur "Krise der Arbeitsgesellschaft.". II. Title. III. Title: Bemerkungen zur "Krise der

Arbeitsgesellschaft.". IV. Series: Beiträge aus dem Fachbereich Pädagogik der Hochschule der Bundeswehr Hamburg , 1984/5.
HJ8650 .A37 1984

Ahrens, Heinz-Dietmar. Towards reducing the dependence on capital imports : a planning model for Pakistan's policy of self-reliance / by Heinz Ahrens and Wolfgang-Peter Zingel ; with a contribution by Syed Nawab Haider Naqvi. Wiesbaden : F. Steiner, 1982. xvi, 337 p. : ill. ; 24 cm. (Beiträge zur Südasienforschung. Bd. 67) Bibliography: p. 331-337. Includes index. ISBN 3-515-03853-1 (pbk.) LC Card 86-214363 DDC 338.9549/1 19
1. Pakistan - Economic conditions. 2. Pakistan - Economic policy. 3. Debts, External - Pakistan. 4. Foreign exchange problem - Pakistan. 5. Investments, Foreign - Pakistan. I. Zingel, Wolfgang-Peter. II. Title. III. Series.
HC440.5 .A726 1982

Ahrens, Philip. Rebovich, Donald. Understanding hazardous waste crime . [Trenton?] [1986] viii, 70 p. : LC Card 86-622805 DDC 364.1/42 19
HD9975.U53 A1157 1986

Ahsan, Qamar. Guru, D. D. Energy and economic development /. Delhi , c1987. xi, 257 p. : ISBN 81-85061-53-6 : LC Card 87-901433 DDC 333.79/0954 19
HD9502.I4 G87 1987

Ahuja, Dilip R. National energy data systems . New Delhi , 1984, c1983. xxvi, 511 p. ; LC Card 84-901310 DDC 333.79/09172/4 19
HD9502.D442 N37 1984
NYPL [JLD 86-4320]

Aid for just development . Hellinger, Steve. Washington, D.C. (1010 Vermont Ave., N.W., Suite 521, Washington 20005) , c1987. vii, 191 p. ; LC Card 87-404422 DDC 338.91/09172/4 19
HC60 .H38516 1987

A.I.D. program evaluation report . (no. 9) Wasserman, Gary, 1944- U. S. aid to Zimbabwe . [Washington, D.C.?] [1983] ix, 20, [71] p. ; LC Card 87-109216 DDC 338.91/73/06891 19
HC910 .W37 1983

AID (Series) .
(33) Ebel, Friedhelm. Was sagt mir der Buchführungsabschluss? /. Bonn , 1980. 36 p. : LC Card 84-145622
HF5686.A36 E24 1980

AID TO DEPENDENT CHILDREN. see **CHILD WELFARE.**

AID TO UNDERDEVELOPED AREAS. see **ECONOMIC ASSISTANCE; TECHNICAL ASSISTANCE.**

Aid to workers in declining industries /. Saunders, Ronald. [Toronto, Ont.] , c1984. 72 p. : ISBN 0-7743-9007-7 (pbk.) LC Card 84-174952 DDC 331.13/77/0971 19
HD6331.2.C2 S28 1984
NYPL [JLD 86-1287]

L'aide alimentaire, un marché de dupes /. Fryer, Jonathan. [Food for thought. French.] Genève, Suisse . 91 p. ; LC Card 86-218069
HD9018.D44 F7914 1982

L'aide britannique au développement . Biraud, Gérard. Paris , 1978. 17 leaves : LC Card 84-102197
HC60 .B52 1978

L'Aide publique au développement dans les pays membres du CILSS en 1983 = Official development assistance to CILSS member countries in 1983. Paris : Club du Sahel, OECD ; Burkina Faso : CILLS, [1984], c1985. v, 347 p. : ill. (some col.) ; 30 cm. English and French. Chiefly tables. "Sahel D(84) 250, novembre/November 84." LC Card 86-180117
1. Economic assistance - Sahel - Directories. 2. Technical assistance - Sahel - Directories. 3. Economic development projects - Sahel - Directories. I. Sahel Club. II. Permanent Inter-State Committee for Drought Control in the Sahel.
HC1000 .A64 1985

Aiginger, Karl.
Die Grösse der Kleinen : die überraschenden Erfolge kleiner und mittlerer Unternehmungen in den achtziger Jahren / von Karl Aiginger und Gunther Tichy. Wien : Signum, [between 1984 and 1987] 160, [1] p. : ill. ; 23 cm. Bibliography: p. 153-[161]. ISBN 3-85436-025-8 LC Card 87-141921 DDC 658.1/592 19
1. Small business - Austria - Finance. 2. Small business - Austria - Management. 3. Small business - Finance. 4. Small business - Management. I. Tichy, Gunther. II. Title.
HG4027.7 .A38 1984

Production and decision theory under uncertainty / Karl Aiginger. Oxford [Oxfordshire] ; New York, NY, USA : B. Blackwell, 1987. p. cm. Bibliography: p. Includes index. ISBN 0-631-14792-6 : LC Card 87-23854 DDC 338.5 19
1. Production functions (Economic theory). 2. Decision-making. 3. Uncertainty. I. Title.
HB241 .A52 1987

An ailing African economy and the IMF medicine /. Ogunba, C. K. Ile-Ife [Nigeria] [1985] 40, [1] p. ; LC Card 86-207586 DDC 332.1/52 19
HG3881.5.I58 O37 1985

Ailing steel . Goldberg, Walter, 1924- Aldershot, England , c1986. xxiv, 535 p. : ISBN 0-566-00733-9 *NYPL [JLD 87-399]*

Aĭmre, I. A. Osobennosti popolneniia osnovnykh otriadov intelligentsii /. Tallin , 1981. 131 p. : LC Card 82-125732
HD8038.S652 E775 1981

AIMS Media.
Confidential--information security [motion picture] /. Van Nuys, CA , 1986. 1 film reel (22 min.) : LC Card 87-705606 DDC 658.4 11
HD38.7

Confidential--information security [videorecording] /. Van Nuys, CA , 1986. 1 videocassette (22 min.) : LC Card 87-705607 DDC 658.4 11
HD38.7

DUII, the price is too high [motion picture] /. Van Nuys, CA , 1987. 1 film reel (23 min.) : LC Card 87-706705 DDC 363.1 11
HE5620.D7

DUII, the price is too high [videorecording] /. Van Nuys, CA , 1987. 1 videocassette (23 min.) : LC Card 87-706706 DDC 363.1 11
HE5620.D7

Seat belts are for kids, too [motion picture] /. Van Nuys, CA , 1987. 1 film reel (10 min.) : LC Card 87-706618 DDC 363.1 11
HE5614.2

Seat belts are for kids, too [videorecording] /. Van Nuys, CA , 1987. 1 videocassette (10 min.) : LC Card 87-706619 DDC 363.1 11
HE5614.2

Seat belts, the lifesaving habit [motion picture] /. Van Nuys, CA , 1986. 1 film reel (20 min.) : LC Card 87-705126 DDC 629.2 11
HE5614.2

Seat belts, the lifesaving habit [videorecording] /. Van Nuys, CA , 1986. 1 videocassette (20 min.) : LC Card 87-705127 DDC 629.2 11
HE5614.2

Aims of Industry study (Unnumbered)
Bewlay, Simon. Steel . London [1985?] 14 p. : LC Card 87-165749 DDC 338.4/7669142/0941 19
HD9521.5 .B48 1985

AIR CARGO. see **AERONAUTICS, COMMERCIAL - FREIGHT.**

AIR CHARTER CONTRACTS - GOVERNMENT POLICY - UNITED STATES.
United States. Congress. House. Committee on Armed Services. Subcommittee on Investigations. Report on the safety of aircraft under charter to the Department of Defense . Washington , 1986. iii, 17 p. ; LC Card 86-603401 DDC 363.1/24 19
HE9803.Z7 C538 1986

AIR CONDITIONING EQUIPMENT INDUSTRY - UNITED STATES.
Residential heating, ventilating & cooling systems market. New York, N.Y. , c1983. iv, 269 leaves : LC Card 87-138699 DDC 381/.45697/000973 19
HD9683.U52 R47 1983

AIR CONDITIONING INDUSTRY - MANAGEMENT.
Bak, Richard, 1954- Smart contracting . Troy, Mich. , c1987. 213 p. : ISBN 0-912524-39-1 (pbk.) : LC Card 86-28327 DDC 338.4/7697 19
HD9683.A2 B35 1987

AIR FREIGHT. see **AERONAUTICS, COMMERCIAL - FREIGHT.**

The air freight industry . McAlpine, Pamela J. Menlo Park, CA (333 Ravenswood Ave., Menlo Park 94025) , c1986. 12 leaves ; LC Card 87-402973 DDC 387.7/44/0973 19
HE9788.5.U5 M37 1986

AIR LAW. see **AERONAUTICS - LAW AND LEGISLATION.**

AIR LINE PILOTS ASSOCIATION. (Old Catalog form: Air Line Pilots Association, International)
Komons, Nick A. The third man . Washington, D.C. , 1987. iv, 162 p. : LC Card 87-21267 DDC 363.1/2475 19
HD8039.A42 U54 1987

AIR LINES - FARES. see **AIR LINES - RATES.**

AIR LINES - GOVERNMENT POLICY.
Reason in the air . [S.l.] [1977] 31 p. : LC Card 85-149832 DDC 387.7/068 19
HE9777.7 .R43 1977

AIR LINES - HISTORY.
Davies, R. E. G. (Ronald Edward George) Rebels and reformers of the airways /. Washington, D.C. , c1987. xvi, 440 p. : ISBN 0-87474-354-0 (alk. paper) LC Card 86-26243 DDC 387.7/092/2 19
HE9775 .D38 1987

AIR LINES - ICELAND - HISTORY.
Alfređ Elíasson, 1920- Alfređs saga og Loftleiđa /. Reykjavík , 1984 (1985 printing) 372 p. : LC Card 86-101929
HD9711.I22 A443 1985
NYPL [JFE 87-1455]

AIR LINES - LAW AND LEGISLATION. see **AERONAUTICS, COMMERCIAL - LAW AND LEGISLATION.**

AIR LINES - RATES.
Pryke, Richard. Competition among international airlines /. Aldershot , Brookfield, USA , 1987. xi, 113 p. : ISBN 0-566-05333-0 : LC Card 86-31877 DDC 387.7/1 19
HE9780 .P79 1987

AIR LINES - UNITED STATES.
Morrison, Steven A., 1951- The economic effects of airline deregulation /. Washington, D.C. , c1986. xi, 84 : ISBN 0-8157-5845-6 (pbk.) : LC Card 85-48202 DDC 387.7/1 19
HE9803.A4 M67 1986 NYPL [JLE 86-3309]

AIR MAIL SERVICE - HISTORY.
Jackson, Donald Dale, 1935- Flying the mail /. Alexandria, Va. , c1982. 176 p. : ISBN 0-8094-3329-X LC Card 82-2020 DDC 383/.144/09 19
HE6496 .J3 1982 NYPL [JLF 87-386]

AIR MAIL SERVICE - SEYCHELLES - HISTORY.
Seychelles . [[Newbury, Berkshire, UK] [1986] iii, 41 p. : LC Card 86-214104 DDC 383/.144/09696 19
HE7389.9.Z9 A47 1986

AIR MAIL SERVICE - UNITED STATES - HISTORY.
Jackson, Donald Dale, 1935- Flying the mail /. Alexandria, Va. , c1982. 176 p. : ISBN 0-8094-3329-X LC Card 82-2020 DDC 383/.144/09 19
HE6496 .J3 1982 NYPL [JLF 87-386]

AIR MAIL STAMPS - GERMANY - HISTORY.
Aufbruch zum Himmel . Dortmund , c1982. 99 p. : ISBN 3-88379-328-0 : LC Card 83-125566
HE6184.A4 A84 1982

AIR MAIL STAMPS - NEWFOUNDLAND.
Harmer, C. H. C. (Cyril Henry Carrington) Newfoundland air mails . Cinnaminson, N.J., U. S.A. , 1984. x, 181 p. : LC Card 87-147693 DDC 383/.144/09718 19
HE6185.C23 N475 1984

AIR NAVIGATION. see **AERONAUTICS.**

AIR PILOTS.
Jasinski, Irv. Airline pilot interviews . Escondido, Calif. , c1987. 144 p. : ISBN 0-942195-01-9 (pbk.) LC Card 87-70680 DDC

629.132/5240423/02373 19
HE9777 .J36 1987

AIR - POLLUTION - EUROPE.
Prittwitz, Volker. Umweltaussenpolitik . Frankfurt , New York , c1984. vii, 211 p. : ISBN 3-593-33369-4 LC Card 84-202897
HC240.9.A4 P75 1984

AIR - POLLUTION - LAW AND LEGISLATION.
Coal . Paris [Washington, D.C.] 1987. 108 p. ; ISBN 92-64-12909-X (pbk.) : LC Card 87-163847 DDC 363.7/31 19
HD9540.6 .C63 1987

AIR - POLLUTION - LAW AND LEGISLATION - GERMANY (WEST)
Schulz, Bernhard. Effizienzkontrolle von Umweltpolitik . Frankfurt am Main , c1983. xv, 230 p. : ISBN 3-88129-744-8 LC Card 85-103230
HC290.5.E5 S38 1983

AIR - POLLUTION - UNITED STATES.
Morandi, Larry B. Renewing resources . Denver, Colo. , 1984. vii, 133 p. ;
NYPL [JSF 86-712]

AIR QUALITY MANAGEMENT - EUROPE - INTERNATIONAL COOPERATION.
Prittwitz, Volker. Umweltaussenpolitik . Frankfurt , New York , c1984. vii, 211 p. : ISBN 3-593-33369-4 LC Card 84-202897
HC240.9.A4 P75 1984

AIR QUALITY MANAGEMENT - GERMANY (WEST)
Zimmermann, Horst, 1934- Ökonomische Anreizinstrumente in einer auflagenorientierten Umweltpolitik . Stuttgart , 1983. 59 p. ; ISBN 3-17-003279-8 : LC Card 84-148886
HC110.A4 Z55 1983

AIR QUALITY MANAGEMENT - UNITED STATES.
Zimmermann, Horst, 1934- Ökonomische Anreizinstrumente in einer auflagenorientierten Umweltpolitik . Stuttgart , 1983. 59 p. ; ISBN 3-17-003279-8 : LC Card 84-148886
HC110.A4 Z55 1983

AIR TRAFFIC RULES, INTERNATIONAL.
Mensch und Luftfahrt . Bern [1981] 177 p. : LC Card 83-116416
HE9863.A4 M45 1981

AIR TRANSPORT. see **AERONAUTICS, COMMERCIAL.**

Air Transport Association of America. 1986 air travel survey /. Princeton, N.J. (53 Bank St., Princeton 08542) , c1986. 77 leaves ; LC Card 86-225970 DDC 387.7/42/0973 19
HE9787.5.N7 A17 1986

AIR TRAVEL - HANDBOOKS, MANUALS, ETC.
Davidson, George, 1943- The ABC's of air travel /. Scottsdale, Ariz. , c1984. iv, 89 p. : ISBN 0-931921-00-7 (pbk.) : LC Card 84-71960 DDC 387.7/42/0973 19
HE9787.5.U5 D38 1984
NYPL [JLD 86-2219]

AIR TRAVEL - HISTORY.
Frater, Alexander, 1937- Beyond the blue horizon . New York , 1987, c1986. xviii, 430 p. : ISBN 0-684-18837-6 LC Card 87-9426 DDC 387.7/065/73 19
HE9787 .F7 1987

Air travel survey. 1986 air travel survey /. Princeton, N.J. (53 Bank St., Princeton 08542) , c1986. 77 leaves ; LC Card 86-225970 DDC 387.7/42/0973 19
HE9787.5.N7 A17 1986

AIR TRAVEL - UNITED STATES.
Michaels, Susan. Points, a guide to frequent flyer bonus programs /. New York , c1987. 161 p. : ISBN 0-87052-375-9 (pbk.) : LC Card 87-8681 DDC 387.7/1 19
HF6161.A38 M53 1987

Air University (U. S.). Center for Aerospace Doctrine, Research, and Education. Nuclear winter and national security . Maxwell Air Force Base, Ala. , Washington, D.C. , 1986. xiii, 76 p. ; LC Card 86-7967 DDC 355/.0217 19
U263 .N845 1986 *NYPL [JFE 87-751]*

Airbus International /. Penner, Hellmut, 1942- Stuttgart , 1986. 206 p. : ISBN 3-613-01093-3 LC Card 86-211620
HD9711.E882 P46 1986

AIRBUS (JET TRANSPORT)
Penner, Hellmut, 1942- Airbus International /. Stuttgart , 1986. 206 p. : ISBN 3-613-01093-3 LC Card 86-211620
HD9711.E882 P46 1986

AIRCRAFT INDUSTRY - BRAZIL.
Green, Ronald D. Brazilian government support for the aerospace industry /. [Washington, D.C.?] [1987] xi, 44 p. ; LC Card 87-601479 DDC 338.4/76291/0981 19
HD9711.B72 G74 1987

AIRCRAFT INDUSTRY - EUROPE.
Penner, Hellmut, 1942- Airbus International /. Stuttgart , 1986. 206 p. : ISBN 3-613-01093-3 LC Card 86-211620
HD9711.E882 P46 1986

AIRCRAFT INDUSTRY - FRANCE - HISTORY.
Déplante, Henri, 1907- A la conquête du ciel /. Aix-en-Provence [1985] 233 p. ; LC Card 86-159140
HD9711.F74 D374 1985

AIRCRAFT INDUSTRY - FRANCE - MILITARY ASPECTS - HISTORY.
Déplante, Henri, 1907- A la conquête du ciel /. Aix-en-Provence [1985] 233 p. ; LC Card 86-159140
HD9711.F74 D374 1985

AIRCRAFT INDUSTRY - GOVERNMENT OWNERSHIP - ARGENTINA - HISTORY.
Angueira, María del Carmen. Capitalismo de estado, 1927-1956 /. Buenos Aires , c1986. 116 p. : ISBN 950-25-1416-5 LC Card 87-100705
HD9711.A72 A54 1986

AIRCRAFT INDUSTRY - GOVERNMENT POLICY - BRAZIL.
Green, Ronald D. Brazilian government support for the aerospace industry /. [Washington, D.C.?] [1987] xi, 44 p. ; LC Card 87-601479 DDC 338.4/76291/0981 19
HD9711.B72 G74 1987

AIRCRAFT INDUSTRY - INTERNATIONAL COOPERATION.
Mowery, David C. Alliance politics and economics . Cambridge, Mass. , c1987. xi, 194 p. : ISBN 0-88730-213-0 LC Card 86-32178 DDC 338.8/87 19
HD9711.A2 M68 1987

AIRCRAFT INDUSTRY - SOCIAL ASPECTS - CALIFORNIA - LOS ANGELES - HISTORY.
Gluck, Sherna Berger. Rosie the Riveter revisited . Boston , c1987. xiii, 282 p. : ISBN 0-8057-9022-5 (alk. paper) LC Card 86-31852 DDC 331.4/0973 19
HD6073.A452 U64 1987

AIRCRAFT INDUSTRY - UNITED STATES.
A Competitive assessment of the U. S. general aviation aircraft industry /. Washington, D.C. , 1986. xix, 69 p. : LC Card 86-602548 DDC 338.4/762913334/0973 19
HD9711.U6 C636 1986

Green, Ronald D. Brazilian government support for the aerospace industry /. [Washington, D.C.?] [1987] xi, 44 p. ; LC Card 87-601479 DDC 338.4/76291/0981 19
HD9711.B72 G74 1987

Mowery, David C. Alliance politics and economics . Cambridge, Mass. , c1987. xi, 194 p. : ISBN 0-88730-213-0 LC Card 86-32178 DDC 338.8/87 19
HD9711.A2 M68 1987

AIRCRAFT INDUSTRY - UNITED STATES - HISTORY.
Gunston, Bill. The Grumman story /. New York , 1988, c1987. p. cm. ISBN 0-517-56796-2 : LC Card 87-21964 DDC 338.7/6291/0973 19
HD9711.5.U63 G784 1988

AIRCRAFT PRODUCTION. see **AEROSPACE INDUSTRIES.**

AIREA research series.
1986 membership profile /. Chicago, Ill. , c1986. ix, 44 p. : ISBN 0-911780-85-8 (pbk.) LC Card 87-144205 DDC 333.33/2/0973 19
HD251 .A17 1986

Airenti, Gabriella. Il Consumo dell'audiovisivo /. Milano, Italy , c1984. 173 p. : LC Card 85-178903
HE8700.66.I8 C66 1984

Airline . Smith, Jerald R. Englewood Cliffs, NJ , c1987. v, 115, [38] p. : ISBN 0-13-020801-9 (pbk.) LC Card 86-30488 DDC 387.7/068 19
HD30.28 .S57 1987

Airline crew complement controversy. Komons, Nick A. The third man . Washington, D.C. , 1987. iv, 162 p. : LC Card 87-21267 DDC 363.1/2475 19
HD8039.A42 U54 1987

Airline marketing and management /. Shaw, Stephen, 1950- Malabar , 1988, c1985. 296 p. ; ISBN 0-89464-256-1 LC Card 87-22639 DDC 387.7/4/0688 19
HE9781 .S35 1987

Airline pilot interviews . Jasinski, Irv. Escondido, Calif. , c1987. 144 p. : ISBN 0-942195-01-9 (pbk.) LC Card 87-70680 DDC 629.132/5240423/02373 19
HE9777 .J36 1987

AIRLINES.
Taneja, Nawal K. The international airline industry . Lexington, Mass. , c1988. xvi, 167 p. : ISBN 0-669-16167-5 (alk. paper) LC Card 87-45227 DDC 387.7 19
HE9776 .T363 1988

AIRLINES - AUSTRALIA.
Findlay, Christopher C. (Christopher Charles) The flying kangaroo, an endangered species? . Sydney , Boston , 1985. xii, 121 p. : ISBN 0-86861-406-8 (pbk.) LC Card 85-71362 DDC 387.7/065/94 19
HE9889.A4 F56 1985

AIRLINES - BRAZIL.
Brazil. Congresso Nacional. Câmara dos Deputados. Comissão de Esporte e Turismo. Vôos "charters" e as empresas de aviação civil . Brasília , 1986. 98 p. ; LC Card 87-405035 DDC 387.7/0981 19
HE9833.A4 B7 1986

AIRLINES - DEREGULATION.
Knieps, Günter. Deregulierung im Luftverkehr . Tübingen , c1987. 69 p. ; ISBN 3-16-345148-9 LC Card 87-121052 DDC 387.7/1 19
HE9776 .K6 1987

AIRLINES - EUROPE - RATES.
Barrett, Sean D. Flying high . Aldershot , Brookfield, USA , c1987. 96 p. ; ISBN 0-566-05541-4 (pbk.) : LC Card 87-11992 DDC 387.7/1 19
HE9783.3.E85 B37 1987

AIRLINES - GREAT BRITAIN - HISTORY.
Campbell-Smith, Duncan. The British Airways story . London , 1986. viii, 327 p. ; ISBN 0-340-39495-1 (pbk.) : LC Card 86-206477 DDC 387.7/065/41 19
HE9843.B7 C36 1986

AIRLINES - MANAGEMENT - SIMULATION METHODS.
Smith, Jerald R. Airline . Englewood Cliffs, NJ , c1987. v, 115, [38] p. : ISBN 0-13-020801-9 (pbk.) LC Card 86-30488 DDC 387.7/068 19
HD30.28 .S57 1987

AIRLINES - MARKETING.
Shaw, Stephen, 1950- Airline marketing and management /. Malabar , 1988, c1985. 296 p. ; ISBN 0-89464-256-1 LC Card 87-22639 DDC 387.7/4/0688 19
HE9781 .S35 1987

AIRLINES - RATES.
Forsyth, P. (Peter) Can international comparisons of air fares be made? /. Canberra, Australia [1985] 35 p. ; ISBN 0-949293-46-6 (pbk.) LC Card 86-212326 DDC 387.7/12 19
HE9783 .F67 1985

Martin, Bob, 1939- Fly there for less . Kissimmee, Fla. , c1988. 136 p. ; ISBN 0-937281-01-8 (pbk.) : LC Card 87-16166 DDC 387.7/12 19
HE9783.5 .M37 1988

Ross, H. Edward. Free airline tickets--worldwide!! . St. Paul, Minn., U. S.A. , c1986. 154 p. ; ISBN 0-9616129-0-8 (pbk.) LC Card 87-117304 DDC 387.7/1 19
HE9783.5 .R67 1986

AIRLINES - RESERVATIONS.
Martin, Bob, 1939- Fly there for less . Kissimmee, Fla. , c1988. 136 p. ; ISBN 0-937281-01-8 (pbk.) : LC Card 87-16166 DDC 387.7/12 19
HE9783.5 .M37 1988

AIRLINES - SWEDEN - MANAGEMENT.
Carlzon, Jan. Moments of truth /. Cambridge, Mass. , c1987. xiii, 135 p. ; ISBN 0-88730-200-9 LC Card 87-1070 DDC 387.7/065/485 19
HE9860.S28 C37 1987

Carlzon, Jan. Riv pyramiderna! . [Stockholm] , c19. 219 p. : ISBN 91-0-046844-4 LC Card 86-139896
HE9860.S28 C375 1986

AIRLINES - UNITED STATES.
Taneja, Nawal K. The international airline industry . Lexington, Mass. , c1988. xvi, 167 p. : ISBN 0-669-16167-5 (alk. paper) LC Card 87-45227 DDC 387.7 19
HE9776 .T363 1988

AIRLINES - UNITED STATES - DEREGULATION.
Brown, Anthony E. The politics of airline deregulation /. Knoxville , c1987. xiii, 224 p. ; ISBN 0-87049-532-1 (alk. paper) : LC Card 86-30888 DDC 387.7/1 19
HE9803.A4 B68 1987

Deregulation . Washington, D.C. [1985] vi, 86 p. : LC Card 86-602035 DDC 387.7/1 19
HE9803.A3 D47 1985

AIRLINES - UNITED STATES - EMPLOYEES.
Komons, Nick A. The third man . Washington, D.C. , 1987. iv, 162 p. : LC Card 87-21267 DDC 363.1/2475 19
HD8039.A42 U54 1987

AIRLINES - UNITED STATES - HISTORY.
Cearley, George Walker. American Airlines . Dallas, Tex. (P.O. Box 12312, Dallas, 75225) , c1987. 136 p. : LC Card 87-132433 DDC 387.7/065/73 19
HE9803.A95 C4 1987

Davies, R. E. G. (Ronald Edward George) Pan Am . New York , c1987. vi, 90 p. : ISBN 0-517-56639-7 : LC Card 87-5581 DDC 387.7/065/73 19
HE9803.P36 D38 1987

Lewis, W. David (Walter David), 1931- The airway to everywhere . Pittsburgh, PA [1988] p. cm. ISBN 0-8229-3579-1 LC Card 87-25176 DDC 387.7/065/73 19
HE9803.A944 L48 1988

AIRLINES - UNITED STATES - RATES.
Michaels, Susan. Points, a guide to frequent flyer bonus programs /. New York , c1987. 161 p. : ISBN 0-87052-375-9 (pbk.) : LC Card 87-8681 DDC 387.7/1 19
HF6161.A38 M53 1987

AIRPLANES - CARGO. see **AERONAUTICS, COMMERCIAL - FREIGHT.**

AIRPLANES - FREIGHT. see **AERONAUTICS, COMMERCIAL - FREIGHT.**

AIRPLANES - MARKETING.
Wells, Alexander T. General aviation marketing /. Malabar, Fla. , 1987. viii, 268 p. : ISBN 0-89874-987-5 LC Card 86-21504 DDC 629.133/340422/0688 19
HD9711.A2 W45 1987

AIRPLANES - PILOTS. see **AIR PILOTS.**

AIRPORT ACCESS. see **ACCESS TO AIRPORTS.**

AIRPORT POLICE - SALARIES, ETC. - WASHINGTON METROPOLITAN AREA.
AIRPORT POLICE - WASHINGTON METROPOLITAN AREA.

Airport transportation : a study of transportation means between airports and the metropolitan areas they serve / Peter G. Nordlie, principal investigator ; research team, Human Sciences Research, Inc., R. Popper ... [et al.] ; prepared under contract FAA/BRD-203 for Bureau of Research and Development, Federal Aviation Agency, National Aviation Facilities Experimental Center. Arlington, Va. : HSR ; Washington, D.C. : For sale by U. S. Dept. of Commerce, Business and Defense Services Administration, Office of Technical Services, [1961] vii, 289, 42 leaves : ill. ; 29 cm. "February 1961." Bibliography: leaves 1-42 (3rd group) "HSR-RR-61/5-MS." "PB 171856"--Cover. LC Card 84-132332
1. Access to airports. 2. Access to airports - United States - Case studies. I. Nordlie, Peter G. II. National Aviation Facilities Experimental Center (U. S.). III. Human Sciences Research, inc.
HE9797.4.A2 A38 1961

AIRPORTS - NEW YORK - THROOPSVILLE - HISTORY.
Ingalls, Roger W. A scrapbook history of the Auburn Aviation Co., Inc., and the Auburn Airport at Throopsville, N.Y., 1941-1952. Auburn, N.Y. , c1986. 169 p. : LC Card 87-125962
HE9803.A97 I54 1986

AIRPORTS - TANZANIA - STATISTICS.
Mkwawa, D. A. Y. A review of aerodrome statistics in Tanzania, 1970-1982. Dar es Salaam [1984] xix, 143 p. : LC Card 87-403351 DDC 387.7/36/09678021 19
HE9797.5.T34 M58 1984

The airway to everywhere . Lewis, W. David (Walter David), 1931- Pittsburgh, PA [1988] p. cm. ISBN 0-8229-3579-1 LC Card 87-25176 DDC 387.7/065/73 19
HE9803.A944 L48 1988

Aistleitner, Josef.
Aitov, Nariman Abdrakhmanovich. Rabotniki khoroshie i plokhie / N.A. Aitov. Moskva : Sov. Rossii͡a, 1983. 134 p. ; 17 cm. Includes bibliographical references. LC Card 84-178331
1. Industrial sociology - Soviet Union. 2. Employee morale - Soviet Union. I. Title.
HD6957.S65 A37 1983

Aivazi͡an, Sergeĭ Artem'evich. Programmnoe obespechenie ėkonomiko-matematicheskikh issledovaniĭ /. Moskva , 1982. 142 p. : LC Card 84-209065
HD30.25 .P76 1982

Aizawa, Minoru. Review on the development of antibiotics industry in selected countries : technical report : antibiotic industry in Japan : history and development / prepared by the United Nations Industrial Development Organization ; based on the work of Minoru Aizawa. [Vienna, Austria] : The Organization, 1985. 92 p. : ill. ; 30 cm. Cover title. "RP/INT/84/016." "UNIDO/IO.618." "2 August 1985." Bibliography: p. 82-87. LC Card 86-151674 DDC 338.4/7615329/0952 19
1. Antibiotics industry - Japan. I. United Nations. Industrial Development Organization. II. Title. III. Title: Antibiotic industry in Japan.
HD9675.A63 J33 1985

Ajaloo Instituut (Eesti NSV Teaduste Akadeemia) Osobennosti popolnenii͡a osnovnykh otri͡adov intelligentsii /. Tallin , 1981. 131 p. : LC Card 82-125732
HD8038.S652 E775 1981

Ajánlás a vállalatok stratégiai tervező munkájához /. Manczinger, Józsefné. [Budapest] [1984] 97 p. ; LC Card 86-148677
HD30.28 .M346 1984

Ajustamentos de impostos na fronteira e a alocação de receitas tributárias . Longo, Carlos Alberto. São Paulo , 1979. 208 p. ; LC Card 80-152384
HJ5715.B8 L6617 ***NYPL [JLD 86-3846]***

Ajzner, Seweryn. Związek Związków Zawodowych, 1931-1939 / Seweryn Ajzner. Wyd. 1. Warszawa : Książka i Wiedza, 1979. 458 p. ; 21 cm. Bibliography: p. 431-[436] Includes indexes. LC Card 81-172691
1. Związek Związków Zawodowych (Poland) - History. 2. Trade and professional associations - Poland - History. I. Title.
HD8537.Z873 A38 1979

Akademia Ekonomiczna im. Karola Adamieckiego w Katowicach : jej rozwój i rola w wielkoprzemysłowym regionie / opracował i zestawił Alfred Sulik. Katowice : AE, 1977. 194 p. : ports. ; 21 cm. Includes index. LC Card 82-104777
1. Akademia Ekonomiczna im. Karola Adamieckiego w Katowicach - History. 2. Economics - Study and teaching (Higher) - Poland - Katowice - History. I. Sulik, Alfred.
HB74.9.P7 A38 1977

AKADEMIA EKONOMICZNA IM. KAROLA ADAMIECKIEGO W KATOWICACH - HISTORY.
Akademia Ekonomiczna im. Karola Adamieckiego w Katowicach . Katowice , 1977. 194 p. : LC Card 82-104777
HB74.9.P7 A38 1977

Akademia Ekonomiczna w Poznaniu. Ekonomiczne i prawne problemy przedsiębiorstwa uspołecznionego /. Poznań , 1981. 137 p. ; LC Card 83-167540
HB54 .P6 nr. 101 HD4215.7

Akademia epistēmōn tēs E. S. S. D. see **Akademii͡a nauk SSSR.**

Akademia Rolnicza w Warszawie. Katedra rolnictwa światowego. Magyar-Lengyel Agrárközgazdasági Konferencia (1984 : Gödöllő, Hungary) A nagyüzemek és a kisüzemek termelésének fejlődése, kapcsolatuk az iparosodó mezőgazdaságban =. Gödöllő , 1984. 174 p. ; LC Card 86-145249
HD1995.7 .M32 1984

Akademie der Landwirtschaftswissenschaften der DDR. Institut für Agrargeschichte und Internationale Landwirtschaft. Wie wir angefangen haben . Berlin , 1985. 326 p. : LC Card 85-217979
HD1333.G35 W54 1985

Akademie der Wissenschaften der DDR. Forschungsbereich Gesellschaftswissenschaften. Soziale Aspekte der Mikroelektronik /. Berlin , 1985. 122 p. ; LC Card 87-409418 DDC 306/.46 19
HD6331 .S683 1985

Akademie der Wissenschaften der DDR. Institut für Wirtschaftsgeschichte. Proizvoditel'nye sily i monopolisticheskiĭ kapital v Rossii i Germanii v kontse XIX-nachale XX vv. /. Moskva , 1986. 223 p. ; LC Card 87-159751
HD2859 .P76 1986

Akademie der Wissenschaften der DDR. Institut für Theorie des Staates und des Rechts. Demokratie . Berlin , 1981. 188 p. ; LC Card 81-149074 DDC 320.5/315 19
HX73 .D45 1981 ***NYPL [JLD 86-3341]***

Akademie der Wissenschaften der DDR. Institute for Informatics. Large-scale modelling and interactive decision analysis . Berlin , New York , c1986. vii, 362 p. : ISBN 3-540-16785-4 : LC Card 86-20205 DDC 658.4/03 19
T57.6 .L34 1986
NYPL [JLM 72-289 v. 273]

Akademie der Wissenschaften der DDR. Rat für Staats- und Rechtswissenschaftliche Forschung. Ökonomische Strategie der 80er Jahre und Effektivität des Wirtschaftsrechts /. Berlin , 1984. 48 p. ; LC Card 84-159925
HC290.78 .O36 1984

Akademie der Wissenschaften der DDR. Wirtschaftswissenschafliche Forschung, Wissenschaftlicher Rat für die. see **Akademie der Wissenschaften der DDR. Wissenschaftlicher Rat für die Wirtschaftswissenschaftliche Forschung.**

Akademie der Wissenschaften der DDR. Wissenschaftlicher Rat für die Wirtschaftswissenschaftliche Forschung. Sozialistischer Wettbewerb und umfassende Intensivierung . Berlin , 1986. 103 p. ; LC Card 86-200416
HC290.795.S6 S69 1986

Akademie der Wissenschaften der DDR. Wissenschaftlicher Rat für Fragen des Sozialistischen Wettbewerbs. Sozialistischer Wettbewerb und umfassende Intensivierung . Berlin , 1986. 103 p. ; LC Card 86-200416
HC290.795.S6 S69 1986

Akademie der Wissenschaften der DDR. Zentralinstitut für Geschichte. Lemke, Heinz. Finanztransaktionen und Aussenpolitik . Berlin , 1985. 215 p. ; LC Card 86-196601
HG3955 .L45 1985

Akademie der Wissenschaften der DDR. Zentralinstitut für Wirtschaftswissenschaften. Forschungsgruppe "Effektivität." Effektivität und Reproduktion . Berlin , c1985. 148 p. ; LC Card 86-166628
HC290.78 .E365 1985

Akademie der Wissenschaften der Union der Sozialistischen Sowjet Republiken. see **Akademii͡a nauk SSSR.**

Akademie für Gesellschaftswissenschaften. Tetzel, Manfred. Philosophie und Ökonomie, oder, Das Exempel Bernstein /. Berlin , 1984. 187 p. : LC Card 84-166815
HB107.B52 T48 1984

Akademie für Raumforschung und Landesplanung, Hanover. Beiträge.
(Bd. 71) Arnold-Palussiére, Martine. Die grenzüberschreitende regionale Zusammenarbeit auf dem Gebiet der Raumordnung . Hannover , 1983. xvii, 393 p. ; ISBN 3-87870-869-6 : LC Card 83-239646 DDC 361.6/1/0943 19
HT395.G4 A76 1983 *NYPL [JLL 72-326 Bd. 71]*

Akademie für Gesellschaftswissenschaften beim ZK der SED.
Bonk, Heinz. Rüstungspolitik und Arbeiterklasse . Berlin , 1986. 299 p. ; LC Card 86-174039
HC79.D4 B65 1986

Ökonomische und soziale Wirksamkeit des wissenschaftlich-technischen Fortschritts /. Berlin , 1986. 314 p. ; ISBN 3-320-00713-0 LC Card 87-100866 DDC 338/.06 19
HC290.795.T4 O38 1986

Akademie für Politische Bildung (Tutzing, Germany) Renten 2000 . München , c1985. 124 p. : ISBN 3-7892-7267-1 LC Card 87-118239 DDC 331.25/2/0943 19
HD7105.35.G3 R46 1985

Akademie für Raumforschung und Landesplanung (Germany)
Angewandte Fernerkundung . Hannover , 1984. x, 285 p. : ISBN 3-87870-904-8 LC Card 85-147235
HD108.8 .A54 1984

Gestaltung künftiger Raumstrukturen durch veränderte Verkehrskonzepte . Hannover , 1986. xii, 173 p. : ISBN 3-87870-767-3 LC Card 87-401351 DDC 380.5/0943/512 19
HE249.Z7 S343 1986

Akademie für Staats- und Rechtswissenschaft der DDR. Lehrstuhl Staatliche Leitung der Volkswirtschaft. Fieber, Joachim. Die effektivere Gestaltung des Personennahverkehrs im Kreis Sondershausen . Potsdam-Babelsberg , Leipzig , 1983. 75 p. : LC Card 83-241076
HE249.5.Z7 S664 1983

Akademie für Staats- und Rechtswissenschaft der DDR. Lehrstuhl Wirtschaftsrecht. Die Sozialistische Gemeinschaftsarbeit im Territorium . Potsdam-Babelsberg , 1986. 175 p. ; LC Card 86-212526
HD3616.G48 S68 1986

Akademie für Staats- und Rechtswissenschaft der DDR. Sektion Staatliche Leitung der Volkswirtschaft. Die Verantwortung der örtlichen Staatsorgane für die planmässige Entwicklung und die effektive Inanspruchnahme von Leistungen der technischen Infrastruktur /. Potsdam-Babelsberg , 1986. 57 p. ; LC Card 87-407347 DDC 363/.09431 19
HC290.795.C3 V47 1986

Akademie van Wetenschappen, Amsterdam. Sociaal-Wetenschappelijke Raad. Handelingen.
International dimension of development problems . Amsterdam , New York , 1984. 103 p. ; ISBN 0-444-85621-8 (pbk.) LC Card 85-209291 DDC 338.9 19
HD75 .I59 1984 *NYPL [JLE 86-1391]*

International dimension of development problems . Amsterdam , New York , 1984. 103 p. ; ISBN 0-444-85621-8 (pbk.) LC Card 85-209291 DDC 338.9 19
HD75 .I59 1984 *NYPL [JLE 86-1391]*

Akademiebeiträge zur politischen Bildung .
(Bd. 14) Renten 2000 . München , c1985. 124 p. : ISBN 3-7892-7267-1 LC Card 87-118239 DDC 331.25/2/0943 19
HD7105.35.G3 R46 1985

Akademiia de Shtiintse a RSSM. Otdel filosofii i prava. see **Akademiia de Shtiintse a RSSM. Sektsiia de Filozofie shi Drept.**

Akademiia de Shtiintse a RSSM. Sektsiia de Filozofie shi Drept. Upravlenie sotsial'nymi protsessami v trudovykh kollektivakh /. Kishinev , 1983. 141 p. : LC Card 84-133794
HD6957.S65 U67 1983

Akademiia na naukite na S. S. S. R. see **Akademiia nauk SSSR.**

Akademiia narodnogo khoziaistva SSSR.
Narodnokhoziaistvennaia éffektivnost'--pokazateli, metody otsenki /. Moskva , 1984. 247 p. : LC Card 84-188306
HC336.25 .N3515 1984

Podgotovka upravlencheskikh kadrov--opyt, problemy, perspektivy (po zarubezhnym materialam) . Moskva , 1984. 188 p. ; LC Card 85-188986
HD30.4 .P6 1984

Akademiia nauk. see **Akademiia nauk SSSR.**

Akademiia nauk GDR. see **Akademie der Wissenschaften der DDR.**

Akademiia nauk SSSR. (Old Catalog form: Akademiya nauk)

Akademiia nauk SSSR. Arkheograficheskaia komissiia. Severnoe otdelenie. Vklad severnogo krest'ianstva v material'nuiu i dukhovnuiu kul'turu i ego znachenie v reshenii problem agropromyshlennogo kompleksa nechernozemnoi zony RSFSR . Vologda , 1984. 93 p. ; LC Card 85-156518
HD9015.S652 V54 1984

Akademiia nauk SSSR. Bashkirskii filial. Otdel ėkonomicheskikh issledovanii. Industrializatsiia proizvodstva i mezhkhoziaistvennoe kooperirovanie /. Ufa , 1979. 122 p. ; LC Card 82-161458
HD9425.S653 B375 1979

Puti razvitiia infrastruktury regiona /. Ufa , 1984. 117 p. : LC Card 85-199949
HE255.Z7 B377 1984

Akademiia nauk SSSR. Dagestanskii filial. Otdel ėkonomiki. Sovershenstvovanie khoziaistvennogo mekhanizma i ratsional'noe ispol'zovanie resursov . Makhachkala , 1985. 190 p. : LC Card 87-136485
HC337.D3 S655 1985

Akademiia nauk SSSR. IAkutskii filial. Otdel ėkonomiki.
Ėffektivnost' kapital'nykh vlozhenii i novoi tekhniki v narodnom khoziaistve IAkutskoi ASSR . IAkutsk , 1981. 91 p. ; LC Card 82-217455
HC337.I23 C34 1981

IUzhnaia IAkutiia, sotsial'no-ėkonomicheskii aspekt . IAkutsk , 1985. 94 p. ; LC Card 86-180767
HC337.I2 I97 1985

Mezhotraslevye sviazi v IAkutskoi ASSR . IAkutsk , 1985. 80 p. ; LC Card 86-193902
HC337.I23 I576 1985

Akademiia nauk SSSR. Institut gosudarstva i prava. (Old Catalog form: Akademiya nauk. Institut gosudarstva i prava)
Demokratie . Berlin , 1981. 188 p. ; LC Card 81-149074 DDC 320.5/315 19
HX73 .D45 1981 *NYPL [JLD 86-3341]*

Akademiia nauk SSSR. Institut vseobshchei istorii. Istoriia krest'ianstva v Evrope, Ėpokha feodalizma . Moskva , 1985- v. :
*NYPL [*QGS 86-1566]*

Akademiia nauk SSSR. Institute of State and Law. see **Akademiia nauk SSSR. Institut gosudarstva i prava.**

Akademiia nauk SSSR. Komitet po sistemnomu analizu. Stochastic optimization . Berlin , New York , c1985. x, 754 p. : ISBN 0-387-16659-9 (U. S.) LC Card 86-11865 DDC 629.8/312 19
QA402.3 .S778 1985 *NYPL [JSE 86-1596]*

Akademiia nauk SSSR. Problemnaia komissiia territorial'nogo upravleniia nauchno-tekhnicheskim progressom. Upravlenie nauchno-tekhnicheskim progressom v soiuznykh respublikakh /. Tallin , 1986. 158 p. ; LC Card 87-123175
HC340.T4 U77 1986

Akademiia nauk SSSR. Ural'skii nauchnyi tsentr. Aktual'nye problemy prirodopol'zovaniia v promyshlennom regione /. Sverdlovsk , 1985. 151 p. : LC Card 86-126638
HC337.R852 U732 1985

Ėkonomicheskaia ėffektivnost' rekonstruktsii deistvuiushchikh predpriiatii /. Sverdlovsk , 1981. 171 p. ; LC Card 83-192125
HD39.3 .E37 1981

Ėkonomicheskie problemy osvoeniia Ural'skogo Severa /. Sverdlovsk , 1982. 69 p. : LC Card 83-188353
HC336.9.N65 E37 1982

Matematicheskie metody v prilozhenii k resheniiu ėkonomicheskikh zadach /. Sverdlovsk , 1985. 116 p. : LC Card 86-135187
HC337.R852 U7355 1985

Osobennosti razvitiia i puti povysheniia ėffektivnosti proizvoditel'nykh sil regiona /. Sverdlovsk , 1984. 141 p. ; LC Card 86-135171
HC337.R852 C456 1984

Problemy osvoeniia prirodnykh resursov Ural'skogo Severa /. Sverdlovsk , 1985. 70 p. : LC Card 86-195834
HC337.R852 U7359 1985

Akademiia nauk SSSR. Vychislitel'nyi tsentr. Shakhdzhakhan, Ali. Issledovanie odnoi matematicheskoi modeli ėkonomicheskogo rosta /. Moskva , 1983. 29, [2] p. : LC Card 83-176389
HD75.5 .S52 1983

Akademiia nauk Ukraïns'koï RSR. Rada po vyvchenniu produktyvnykh syl URSR. Ėkonomika ispol'zovaniia vodnykh resursov /. Kiev , 1980. 185 p. ; LC Card 87-462040
HD1697.S653 U374 1980

Akademiia Nauk Vengerskoi Narodnoi Respubliki. see **Magyar Tudományos Akadémia, Budapest.**

Akademiia obshchestvennykh nauk (Moscow, R.S.F.S.R.)
Kardinal'nyi rost ėffektivnosti zhivogo truda--glavnyi faktor uskoreniia sotsial'no-ėkonomicheskogo razvitiia . Sverdlovsk , 1986. 2 v. ; LC Card 87-136690
HC337.R853 L35 1986

Akademiia obshchestvennykh nauk (Moscow, R.S.F.S.R.). Kafedra politicheskoi ėkonomii. Aktual'nye problemy planomernogo razvitiia narodnogo khoziaistva /. Moskva , 1980. 247 p. ; LC Card 81-131558
HC336.25 .A455 1980

Akademikertätigkeit im Wandel : auf dem Weg zum akademischen Facharbeiter / Margret Bülow (Hg.). Frankfurt [am Main] ; New York : Campus, c1984. 237 p. ; 21 cm. (Campus Forschung. Schwerpunktreihe Hochschulforschung und Hochschuldidaktik) Campus Forschung ; Bd. 383 Bibliography: p. 230-237. CONTENTS. - Der soziale Wandel in der Struktur der akademischen Berufe / M. Bülow -- Der Niederschlag des sozialen Wandels in Vorstellungswelt und Realität von Berufsanfängern / M. Bülow, K.-H. Schäfer -- Profession oder akademisch ausgebildeter Facharbeiter? / K.-H. Schäfer -- Handlungschancen und berufliches Schicksal aus eigener Sicht / M. Bülow, Elke Pieper -- Geburtswehen einer neuen Profession? / H.-G. Ottersbach -- Privilegiensicherung und Überfüllungskrise in den juristischen Berufen / G. Portele, W. Schütte -- Konkurrenzreduzierung und Monopolisierung / W. Schütte -- Ansprüche und Bewusstsein von Juraabsolventen / G. Portele. ISBN 3-593-33321-X LC Card 84-176630
1. College graduates - Employment - Germany, West. I. Bülow, Margret. II. Series.
HD6278.G4 A36 1984

Akademiya nauk. see **Akademiia nauk SSSR.**

Akakpo-Ahianyo, Anani. Contribution à l'étude des migrations au Togo / Anani Akakpo-Ahianyo. Lomé : Editafrique, 1976. 108 p., [5] p. of plates : maps ; 25 cm. At head of title: Institut national de la recherche scientifique. Includes bibliographical references. LC Card 87-150756
1. Migration, Internal - Togo. 2. Togo - Population. I. Institut national de la recherche scientifique (Togo). II. Title.
HB2125.8.A3 A38 1976

Akdoğan, Abdurrahman. Açıklamalı maliye ve vergi sözlüğü / Abdurrahman Akdoğan, Sadık Kırbaş, Saygın Eyüpgiller. 1. baskı. [Ankara?] : Birlik Yayıncılık ; Yenişehir, Ankara : Genel dağıtım, Yargı Kitabevi, 1986. 229 p. ; 20 cm. (Birlik yayınları . 3. 1) "Türkçe-İngilizce maliye terimleri": p. 217-222. "Glossary of public finance terms, English-Turkish": p. 225-229. LC Card 87-968120
1. Finance, Public - Dictionaries - Turkish. 2. Taxation - Dictionaries - Turkish. I. Kırbaş, Sadık. II. Eyüpgiller, Saygın. III. Title. IV. Title: Maliye ve vergi sözlüğü.
HJ129.T9 A43 1986

AKER (OSLO, NORWAY) - HISTORY. Winge, Harald. Føringaredskaper i Aker fogderi . Oslo , 1976. 105 p. : LC Card 86-460271
HE259.Z7 A48 1976

Akerson, Charles B. The appraiser's workbook / Charles B. Akerson. Chicago, Ill. : American Institute of Real Estate Appraisers, c1985. xv, 263 p. in various pagings : ill. ; 28 cm. Includes index. Errata slip inserted. Bibliography: p. 161. ISBN 0-911780-75-0 (pbk.) LC Card 84-3008 DDC 333.33/2/076 19
1. Real property - Valuation - Problems, exercises, etc. 2. Business mathematics - Real estate business - Problems, exercises, etc. I. Title.
HD1387 .A518 1985 ***NYPL [JLF 86-1025]***

Akhrameev, V. N. (Vasilii Nikiforovich) "IUzhdizel'mash"--podgotovka k ėkonomicheskomu ėksperimentu / V.N. Akhrameev. Moskva : "Mashinostroenie", 1984. 96 p. : ill. ; 20 cm. (Predpriiatie--samostoiatel'nost' i otvetstvennost') Includes bibliographical references. LC Card 85-144706
1. Diesel motor industry - Soviet Union - Management. 2. Industrial organization - Soviet Union. I. Title. II. Series.
HD9705.S595 A36 1984

Akhunova, M. A. Rabochiĭ klass Uzbekistana v usloviiakh nauchno-tekhnicheskoĭ revoliutsii / M.A. Akhunova, K.A. Akilov, L.G. Teteneva ; otvetstvennyĭ redaktor Ė.IU. IUsupov. Tashkent : Izd-vo "FAN" Uzbekskoĭ SSR, 1984. 181 p. ; 23 cm. At head of title: Akademiia nauk Uzbekskoĭ SSR. Institut istorii. Includes bibliographical references. LC Card 85-232015
1. Labor supply - Uzbek S.S.R. - Effect of technological innovations on. I. Akilov, K. A. II. Teteneva, L. G. (Lidiia Georgievna). III. IUsupov, Ė. IU. IV. Title.
HD6331.2.S652 U93 1984

Akilov, K. A. Akhunova, M. A. Rabochiĭ klass Uzbekistana v usloviiakh nauchno-tekhnicheskoĭ revoliutsii /. Tashkent , 1984. 181 p. ; LC Card 85-232015
HD6331.2.S652 U93 1984

Akin, Edward N. Flagler, Rockefeller partner and Florida baron / Edward N. Akin. Kent, Ohio : Kent State University Press, c1988. xiii, 305 p. : ill., map, ports. ; 24 cm. Bibliography: p. 237-292. Includes index. ISBN 0-87338-348-6 (alk. paper) LC Card 87-2070 DDC 338/.04/0924 B 19
1. Flagler, Henry Morrison, 1830-1913. 2. Businessmen - Florida - Biography. 3. Capitalists and financiers - Florida - Biography. 4. Standard Oil Company - History. 5. Florida - History - 1865-. 6. Rockefeller, John D. (John Davison), 1839-1937. I. Title.
HC102.5.F55 A75 1988

Akin Rabibhadana, M.R.
Chumchon 'ǣ'at lǣ nǣothāng kieokap kānprapprung chumchon 'ǣ'at. 1982. Salam : panhā lǣ nǣothāng kǣkhai / dōi M Krung Thēp , 2525 [1982] 16, 249 p. : LC Card 82-916400
HC445.Z7 B3678 1982

Akindele, R. A. 1939- Nigeria's external relations . Ibadan , 1986. 577 p. ; LC Card 87-132060 DDC 337.669 19
HF1616.7 .N55 1986

Akinrinade, Olusola. Economic development in Africa . London , 1987. x, 266 p. ; ISBN 0-86187-909-0 : LC Card 87-15296 DDC 338.98 19
HC800 .E275 1987

Akinyemi, A. B. Economic co-operation between Nigeria and the socialist countries of Eastern Europe /. Lagos , 1986, c1984. 210 p. : ISBN 978-13-2828-2 (pbk.) LC Card 87-155295 DDC 337.669047 19
HF1616.7.Z4 E8523 1986

Akiyama, Carol. Akiyama, Nobuo. Talking business in Japanese /. Hauppauge, N.Y. , c1987. p. cm. ISBN 0-8120-3848-7 LC Card 87-19601 DDC 650/.03/956 19
HF1002 .A34 1987

Akiyama, Nobuo. Talking business in Japanese / by Nobuo Akiyama and Carol Akiyama. Hauppauge, N.Y. : Barron's Educational Series, c1987. p. cm. ISBN 0-8120-3848-7 LC Card 87-19601 DDC 650/.03/956 19
1. Business - Dictionaries. 2. English language - Dictionaries - Japanese. 3. Business - Dictionaries - Japanese. 4. Japanese language - Dictionaries - English. I. Akiyama, Carol. II. Title.
HF1002 .A34 1987

Akiyama, T. (Takamasa), 1944- A new global tea model : specification, estimation, and simulation / Takamasa Akiyama and Pravin K. Trivedi. Washington, D.C. : World Bank, 1987. vi, 130 p. ; 29 cm. (World Bank staff commodity working papers, 0253-3537 . no. 17) Bibliography: p. 129-130. ISBN 0-8213-0868-8 LC Card 87-6238 DDC 382/.41372 19
1. Tea trade - Mathematical models. I. Trivedi, P. K. II. Series: World Bank staff commodity working paper , no. 17. III. Title.
HD9198.A2 A424 1987

Akkermans, M. J. W. M. Autonomie als arbeidssociologisch vraagstuk . Zeist , 1987. 237 p. : ISBN 90-6720-032-8 : LC Card 87-169950
HD5660.N4 A94 1987

Akopov, Mykhaĭlo Arutiunovych. Dukhovnyĭ mir sovetskogo cheloveka / M.A. Akopov. Kiev : Naukova dumka, 1985. 124, [3] p. ; 20 cm. (Voprosy ideologicheskoĭ bor'by i kontrpropagandy) Nauchno-populiarnaia literatura Bibliography: p. [126] LC Card 86-139846
1. Political socialization - Soviet Union. 2. Public opinion - Soviet Union. 3. Ideology. I. Series. II. Series: Nauchno-populiarnaia literatura (Naukova dumka (Firm)). III. Title.
JN6581 .A64 1985 ***NYPL [*QIK 87-3448]***

Akpan, Daniel U.
Importance of research and data base in economic development in Nigeria. 1975. Nigeria : economic, education, and health themes / by HEERN Consultants Inc. Hyattsville, Md. , 1975. iii, 35 p. ; LC Card 85-114200
HC1055 .N533 1975

Akpan, Paul A.
Malaria--a life-long problem. 1975. Nigeria : economic, education, and health themes / by HEERN Consultants Inc. Hyattsville, Md. , 1975. iii, 35 p. ; LC Card 85-114200
HC1055 .N533 1975

Akseleraatioteoriaan perustuvia investointifunktiokokeiluja yritystason aineistolla /. Karhu, Veli. Vaasa , 1982. 43, [1] leaves ; ISBN 951-683-160-5 LC Card 83-100841 DDC 332/.0415 19
HG4028.C4 K349 1982
NYPL [JLM 73-601 n:o 85]

Akshayakumar Ramanlal Desai. see Desai, Akshayakumar Ramanlal.

Aktienbewertung in Deutschland /. Winkelmann, Michael. Königstein/Ts. , c1984. xii, 242 p. : ISBN 3-445-02377-8 LC Card 85-103576
HG4523 .W56 1984

Aktienkurse und rationale Erwartungen . Apostolopoulos, Athanase, 1955- Frankfurt am Main , New York , c1986. 364 p. : ISBN 3-8204-9157-0 LC Card 86-220281
HG5494 .A66 1986

Aktienkursprognose auf Grundlage der Identifikation von Trend- und Saisonkomponente . Haskamp, Clemens Heinrich, 1955- Krefeld , 1985. 204 p. : ISBN 3-88358-052-1 LC Card 86-121480
HG4637 .H38 1985

Aktionsgemeinschaft Soziale Marktwirtschaft (Germany) Weissbuch Arbeitszeitverkürzung /. Stuttgart , 1983. 152 p. : ISBN 3-87959-212-8 LC Card 84-163631
HD5108.2.G47 W45 1983

Aktionskomitee gegen Berufsverbote (Berlin, Germany) Gesinnungs überprüft! . Berlin [1978] 263 p. : LC Card 84-198533
HD4903.5.G4 G47 1978

AKTIONSPROGRAMM "HUMANISIERUNG DES ARBEITSLEBENS"
Elsenau, Detlef von. Arbeitnehmerorientierte Sozialforschung . Münster [1986] ii, 233 p. ; ISBN 3-88660-246-X LC Card 86-200305
HD6957.G3 E59 1986

Aktiv butikk /. Meurling, Kim. Oslo , 1980. 186 p. : ISBN 82-7037-129-7 : LC Card 81-174134
HF5429 .M44 1980

Aktive Kolleginnen und Kollegen ziehen Bilanz : der Streik für 35 Stunden / herausgegeben von der Redaktionsgruppe Info 35.1. Aufl. Frankfurt/M. : ISP-Verlag, 1984. 100 p. : ill. ; 18 cm. (Sozialistische Gewerkschaftspolitik . 8) Cover title: Der Streik für 35 Stunden. ISBN 3-88332-092-7 : LC Card 85-233569 DDC 331.89/2 19
1. Strikes and lockouts - Germany, West. 2. Thirty-five hour week - Germany (West). I. Redaktionsgruppe Info 35 (Frankfurt am Main, Germany). II. Title: Streik für 35 Stunden. III. Title: Streik für fünfunddreissig Stunden. IV. Series: ISP Sozialistische Gewerkschaftspolitik , 8.
HD5378 .A64 1984

Aktivizirane na mladezhkoto nauchno i tekhnichesko tvorchestvo / pod obshtata redaktsiia na Doncho Denev. Sofiia : Dŭrzh. kom-t za nauka i tekhn. progres, Nauch. tsentŭr po ikonomika, organizatsiia i upr. na naukata i tekhn. progres, Klub za tekhn. i nauchno tvorchestvo na mladezhta, 1985. 135 p. : ill. ; 20 cm. Includes bibliographical references. LC Card 86-220354
1. Technological innovations - Bulgaria. 2. Youth - Government policy - Bulgaria. I. Denev, Doncho. II. Nauchen tsentŭr po ikonomika, organizatsiia i upravlenie na naukata i tekhnicheskiia progres (Bulgaria). Klub za teknichesko i nauchno tvorchestvo na mladezhta.
HC403.Z9 T419 1985

Aktivnaia sotsial'naia politika : poiski, nakhodki, resheniia / [avtorskiĭ kollektiv E.M. Kanevskiĭ ... et al.]. Moskva : "Mysl'", 1986. 156 p., [16] p. of plates : ill. ; 17 cm. Includes bibliographical references. LC Card 86-216405 DDC 354.47001/6 19
1. Industry - Social aspects - Soviet Union. 2. Quality of work life - Soviet Union. I. Kanevskiĭ, Evgeniĭ Markovich.
HD60.5.S77 A38 1986

Aktivno deĭstvovat', ne teriat' vremeni . Gorbachev, Mikhail Sergeevich, 1931- Moskva , 1985. 45 p. ; LC Card 86-181428
HC337.U53 I525 1985

Aktualni ikonomicheski problemi : uchebno posobie / [redaktsionna kolegiia Boris Dimitrov ... Petŭr Penkov (predsedatel) ... et al.]. Sofiia : Nauchnoizsledovatelski in-t po profsŭiuzni problemi "G. Dimitrov" pri TS na BPS, 1985. 227 p. ; 23 cm. Includes bibliographical references. LC Card 86-205815
1. Bulgaria - Economic policy - 1944-. 2. Labor productivity - Bulgaria. I. Dimitrov, Boris. II. Penkov, Petŭr. III. Nauchnoizsledovatelski institut po profsŭiuzni problemi Georgi Dimitrov.
HC403 .A67 1985

Aktual'nye ėkonomicheskie i sotsial'nye problemy malykh stran Severnoĭ Evropy . Babashkina, M. L. Moskva , 1986. 71 p. ; LC Card 87-166353
HC343 .B34 1986

Aktual'nye mezhdunarodnye valiutno-finansovye problemy .
(vyp. 2) Tan'kov, A. V. Mezhdunarodnyĭ valiutnyĭ fond v usloviiakh sovremennogo kapitalizma /. Moskva , 1984. 85 p. ; LC Card 87-100183
HG3881.5.I58 T35 1984

Aktual'nye problemy planomernogo razvitiia narodnogo khoziaĭstva / pod redaktsieĭ I.I. Kuz'minova, V.S. Dunaevoĭ, S.V. Rogacheva. Moskva : "Mysl'", 1980. 247 p. ; 21 cm. At head of title: Akademiia obshchestvennykh nauk pri TSK KPSS. Kafedra politicheskoĭ ėkonomii. Includes bibliographical references. LC Card 81-131558
1. Soviet Union - Economic policy - 1981-. 2. Industrial productivity - Soviet Union. 3. Central planning - Soviet Union. I. Kuz'minov, Ivan Ivanovich. II. Dunaeva, V. S. (Vera Sergeevna). III. Rogachev, S. V. (Sergeĭ Vladimirovich). IV. Akademiia obshchestvennykh nauk (Moscow, R.S.F.S.R.). Kafedra politicheskoĭ ėkonomii.
HC336.25 .A455 1980

Aktual'nye problemy prirodopol'zovaniia v promyshlennom regione / [otvetstvennye redaktory V.F. Bartov, O.V. Tiutkov]. Sverdlovsk : Akademiia nauk SSSR, Ural'skiĭ nauch. tsentr, 1985. 151 p. : ill. ; 22 cm. Includes bibliographical references. LC Card 86-126638
1. Ural Mountains Region (R.S.F.S.R.) - Industries - Environmental aspects. 2. Natural resources - Russian S.F.S.R. - Ural Mountains Region. I. Bartov, Vladimir Fotievich. II. Tiutkov, O. V. III. Akademiia nauk SSSR.

Ural'skiĭ nauchnyĭ tsentr.
HC337.R852 U732 1985

Aktual'nye problemy sotsial'no-ėkonomicheskogo razvitiia SSSR v sovremennyĭ period / [kollektiv avtorov pod rukovodstvom Chuntulova Vladimira Timofeevicha, Kokoreva Mikhaila Vladimirovicha]. Moskva : Vses. zaochnyĭ finansovo-ėkon. in-t, 1984. 153 p. ; 20 cm. (Sbornik nauchnykh trudov. vyp. 42) At head of title: Ministerstvo vysshego i srednego spetsial'nogo obrazovaniia SSSR. Vsesoiuznyĭ ordena "Znak Pocheta" zaochnyĭ finansovo-ėkonomicheskiĭ institut. Includes bibliographical references. LC Card 85-205938
1. Soviet Union - Economic conditions - 1976-. 2. Soviet Union - Social conditions - 1970-. I. Chuntulov, V. T. (Vladimir Timofeevich). II. Kokorev, Mikhail Vladimirovich. III. Series: Sbornik nauchnykh trudov (Vsesoiuznyĭ zaochnyĭ finansovo-ėkonomicheskiĭ institut (Soviet Union)) , vyp. 42.
HC336.25 .A46 1984

Aktual'nye valiutno-finansovye problemy razvivaiushchikhsia stran .
(vyp. 2) Katash, S. S. Mezhdunarodnyĭ kredit i vneshniaia zadolzhennost' razvivaiushchikhsia stran /. Moskva , 1984. 43 p. ; LC Card 87-100185
HG3877 .K37 1984

Aktuell økonomi for detaljhandelen.
Meurling, Kim. Aktiv butikk /. Oslo , 1980. 186 p. : ISBN 82-7037-129-7 : LC Card 81-174134
HF5429 .M44 1980

Aktuelle Arbeiten aus dem Gebiete der Geisteswissenschaften.
Vorträge gehalten anlässlich der Abgeordnetenversammlung vom 27. Mai 1978 =. [Bern] , 1978. 44 p. : LC Card 84-115871
HC397 .V67 1978

Aktuelle Beiträge der Staats- und Rechtswissenschaft, 0568-7551 .
(Heft 276) Rudolph, Jürgen. Aktuelle Fragen der Theorie und Praxis der staatlichen Leitung der Landwirtschaft /. Potsdam-Babelsberg , 1983. 72 p. ; LC Card 83-214391
HD1960.5.Z8 R83 1983

(Heft 280) Fieber, Joachim. Die effektivere Gestaltung des Personennahverkehrs im Kreis Sondershausen . Potsdam-Babelsberg , Leipzig , 1983. 75 p. : LC Card 83-241076
HE249.5.Z7 S664 1983

(Heft 285) Ökonomische Strategie und Vervollkommnung der staatlichen Leitung /. Potsdam-Babelsberg , 1983. 64 p. ; LC Card 84-180104
HC290.78 .O387 1983

(Heft 319) Bartsch, Heinz. Örtliche Versorgungswirtschaft . Potsdam-Babelsberg , 1985. 79 p. : LC Card 86-121253
HD2768.G4 B27 1985

(Heft 326) Die Sozialistische Gemeinschaftsarbeit im Territorium . Potsdam-Babelsberg , 1986. 175 p. ; LC Card 86-212526
HD3616.G48 S68 1986

(Heft 327) Die Verantwortung der örtlichen Staatsorgane für die planmässige Entwicklung und die effektive Inanspruchnahme von Leistungen der technischen Infrastruktur /. Potsdam-Babelsberg , 1986. 57 p. ; LC Card 87-407347 DDC 363/.09431 19
HC290.795.C3 V47 1986

Aktuelle Fragen der Energiewirtschaft.
(Bd. 29) Stromerzeugungskosten im internationalen Vergleich /. München , 1986. ca. 450 p. : ISBN 3-486-26246-7 LC Card 87-135285 DDC 338.4/336362 19
HD9685.A2 S76 1986

Aktuelle Fragen der Theorie und Praxis der staatlichen Leitung der Landwirtschaft /. Rudolph, Jürgen. Potsdam-Babelsberg , 1983. 72 p. ; LC Card 83-214391
HD1960.5.Z8 R83 1983

Aktuelle Materialien zur internationalen Politik .
(Bd. 1) Wirtschaftssanktionen im Ost-West-Verhältnis . Baden-Baden , 1983. 234 p. : ISBN 3-7890-0963-6 LC Card 84-132150
HF1413.5 .W57 1983

(Bd. 14) Wöhlcke, Manfred, 1942- Brasilien als Produzent und Exporteur von Rüstungsgütern /. Baden-Baden , 1987. 176 p. : ISBN 3-7890-1355-2 LC Card 87-135627 DDC 338.4/36234/0981 19
HD9743.B682 W64 1987

Aktuelle Probleme der Marktwirtschaft in gesamt- und einzelwirtschaftlicher Sicht : Festgabe zum 65. Geburtstag von Louis Perridon / herausgegeben von Reinhard Blum und Manfred Steiner. Berlin : Duncker & Humblot, c1984. 458 p., [1] leaf of plates : ill., port. ; 24 cm. Bibliography: p. [451]-456. Includes index. ISBN 3-428-05653-1 LC Card 85-128275
1. Capitalism. 2. Economic policy. 3. Corporations - Finance. 4. Perridon, Louis, 1918-. I. Perridon, Louis, 1918-. II. Blum, Reinhard, 1933-. III. Steiner, Manfred.
HB501 .A514 1984

Aktuelle Probleme der Wirtschaftspolitik : ökonometrische Untersuchungen anhand des F&T-Modells / von Joachim Fronia ; Wolfgang Röhling. Tübingen : Mohr, 1982. vi, 69, vii, 62 p. : ill. ; 24 cm. (Schriftenreihe / Institut für Angewandte Wirtschaftsforschung Tübingen, 0537-7838 . Bd. 39) Includes bibliographies. CONTENTS. - Auswirkungen von Umsatzsteuererhöhungen auf Preise, Produktion und Beschäftigung / von Joachim Fronia -- Der Einsatz nachfragewirksamer Staatsausgaben als konjunkturelle Steuergrösse / von Wolfgang Röhling. ISBN 3-16-344473-3 LC Card 84-125468
1. Turnover tax - Germany (West). 2. Germany (West) - Economic conditions - 1974- - Econometric models. I. Fronia, Joachim. Auswirkungen von Umsatzsteuererhöhungen auf Preise, Produktion und Beschäftigung. 1982. II. Röhling, Wolfgang. Einsatz nachfragewirksamer Staatsausgaben als konjunkturelle Steuergrösse. 1982. III. Series: Schriftenreihe (Institut für Angewandte Wirtschaftsforschung Tübingen) , Bd. 39.
HJ5715.G3 A67 1982

Aktuelle utenrikspolitiske spørsmål .
(nr. 8 (des. 1981)) Norge--EF, økonomisk samarbeid. [Oslo] [1981] 45 p. ; ISBN 82-7177-111-6 LC Card 84-167865
HC241.25.N7 N55 1981

(nr. 8) Norge--EF, økonomisk samarbeid. [Oslo] [1981] 45 p. ; ISBN 82-7177-111-6 LC Card 84-167865
HC241.25.N7 N55 1981

Akwaeze, G. C. Practical steps in raising business finance from banks / by G.C. Akwaeze. Enugu, Nigeria : Fourth Dimension Publishers, 1985. 290 p. : ill. ; 21 cm. Errata slip inserted. Bibliography: p. 290. ISBN 978-15-6214-5 (pbk.) LC Card 87-118106 DDC 658.1/5224 19
1. Commercial credit - Nigeria. 2. Banks and banking - Nigeria. I. Title. II. Title: Raising business finance from banks.
HG3754.5.N6 A38 1985

Akzeptanz von Bildschirmtext in Unternehmungen und im Markt . Schubert, Frank. Münster , c1986. xxiv, 316 p. : ISBN 3-7923-0546-1 LC Card 86-227074
HD9696.T463 G37 1986

al-Duyūn wa-al-tanmiyah . Zakī, Ramzī. al-Qāhirah , 1985. 271 p. : LC Card 86-960543
HJ8824 .Z34 1985

AL-FAYYUM, EGYPT - COMMERCE - HISTORY - SOURCES.
Rāġib, Yūsuf. Marchands d'étoffes du Fayyoum au IIIe/IXe siècle d'après leurs archives (actes et lettres) /. Le Caire , 1982- v. : LC Card 83-156837 DDC 380.1/0962/2 19
HF366 .R34 1982 ***NYPL [*OFP 86-3324]***

al-Idārah wa-al-bī'ah . 'Alāqī, Madanī 'Abd al-Qādir. [Jiddah] , 1985. 136 p. : LC Card 86-200390
HD70.S28 A422 1985

al-Markaz al-Dīmūghrāfī bi-al-Qāhirah. Seminar (13th : 1981 : Cairo, Egypt) Determinants of fertility in some African and Asian countries. Cairo , 1982. 698 p. : LC Card 84-960893 DDC 304.6/32 19
HB1071.7.A3 D48 1982
NYPL [JLL 73-297 no.10]

al-Mu'jam al-jughrāfī /. Majma' al-Lughah al-'Arabīyah, Cairo. Lajnat al-Jughrāfiyā. [al-Qāhirah] , 1974. 9,185 p. ; LC Card 77-961221
G63 .M34 1974 ***NYPL [*OEO 86-3694]***

al-Niẓām al-mālī. 'Abd al-Laṭīf, Badawī, 1909- [al-Qāhirah] 1962. 115 p. LC Card NE63-525
HJ233 .A25 ***NYPL [*OGO 82-3888]***

al-Qāmūs al-farīd fī al-māl wa-al-iqtiṣād, 'Arabī-Injilīzī /. Farīd, 'Abd Allāh Muḥammad. [S.l.] 1985 (al-Qāhirah, Miṣr : Maṭābi' al-Ahrām al-Tijārīyah) 150, 264 p. ; LC Card 86-960655
HB61 .F36 1985

al-Tawzī' al-jughrāfī li-mazāri' al-dawlah fī al-'Irāq wa-atharihā fī al-tanmiyah al-iqtiṣādīyah /. Mukhlif, Hādī Aḥmad. [Baghdad] , 1985. 2 v. (607 p., 3 leaves of plates) : LC Card 86-963500
HD1493.I72 M85 1985

A.L. WILLIAMS (FIRM)
Belth, Joseph M. The A.L. Williams replacement empire . Ellettsville, IN , c1987. 64 p. : ISBN 0-941173-00-3 (pbk.) : LC Card 86-27715 DDC 368.3/2/00973 19
HG8963.A44 B44 1987

Alabama enterprise. Flynt, J. Wayne, 1940- Mine, mill & microchip . Northridge, Calif. , 1987. 376 p. : ISBN 0-89781-215-8 LC Card 87-9192 DDC 338.09761 19
HC107.A4 F57 1987

ALABAMA - INDUSTRIES - HISTORY.
Flynt, J. Wayne, 1940- Mine, mill & microchip . Northridge, Calif. , 1987. 376 p. : ISBN 0-89781-215-8 LC Card 87-9192 DDC 338.09761 19
HC107.A4 F57 1987

ALABAMA - MANUFACTURES - HISTORY.
Flynt, J. Wayne, 1940- Mine, mill & microchip . Northridge, Calif. , 1987. 376 p. : ISBN 0-89781-215-8 LC Card 87-9192 DDC 338.09761 19
HC107.A4 F57 1987

Alabama municipal data book, 1985 /. Gilder, Gilford C. Montgomery, Ala. (State Capitol, Montgomery 36130) [1986] 97 p. : LC Card 86-622909 DDC 307.7/6/09761021 19
HA225 .G55 1986

Alabama. Office of State Planning and Federal Programs. Gilder, Gilford C. Alabama municipal data book, 1985 /. Montgomery, Ala. (State Capitol, Montgomery 36130) [1986] 97 p. : LC Card 86-622909 DDC 307.7/6/09761021 19
HA225 .G55 1986

Alabama. State Planning and Federal Programs, Office of. see **Alabama. Office of State Planning and Federal Programs.**

ALABAMA - STATISTICS.
Gilder, Gilford C. Alabama municipal data book, 1985 /. Montgomery, Ala. (State Capitol, Montgomery 36130) [1986] 97 p. : LC Card 86-622909 DDC 307.7/6/09761021 19
HA225 .G55 1986

Alaev, Ė. B. Baklanov, Petr IAkovlevich. Prostranstvennye sistemy proizvodstva . Moskva , 1986. 149 p. : LC Card 86-202803
HC340.D5 B35 1986

Alaev, L. B. Sel'skaia obshchina v Severnoĭ Indii : osnovnye ėtapy ėvoliutsii / L.B. Alaev. Moskva : Izd-vo "Nauka," Glav. red. vostochnoĭ lit-ry, 1981. 240 p. ; 22 cm. At head of title: Akademiia nauk SSSR. Ordena Trudovogo Krasnogo Znameni Institut vostokovedeniia. Bibliography: p. 220-[230] Includes indexes. LC Card 82-101919
1. Land tenure - India - History. 2. India - Rural conditions. 3. Villages - India - History. I. Title.
HD873 .A63 1981

Alagoas (Brazil)
Plano Operativo 1983, Governo Divaldo Suruagy. [Maceió] : SEPLAN/FIPLAN/AL, [1983?] 196 p. ; 22 cm. LC Card 85-200834
1. Economic development projects - Brazil - Alagoas. I. Title.
HC188.A46 A44 1983a

Alagoas (Brazil). Comissão de Controle das Entidades Estatais.
Cadastro de entidades estatais . [Maceió] , 1985. 77 p. ; LC Card 86-171884
HD4095.A4 C33 1985

Programa de dispêndios globais para 1986 : entidades estatais, Decreto 5,768 / Governo do Estado de Alagoas, Comissão de Controle das Entidades Estatais (COEST). [Maceió, Brazil] : COEST, 1985. 76 p. : ill. ; 26 cm. Cover title. LC Card 87-404783 DDC 354.81/35092 19
1. Government business enterprises - Brazil - Alagoas - Finance. I. Title. II. Title: Entidades estatais. Decreto

5,768.
HD4095.A4 A4 1985

ALAGOAS (BRAZIL) - ECONOMIC POLICY.
Suruagy, Divaldo. Diretrizes básicas do governo . Maceió, Alagoas , 1983. 84 p. ; LC Card 85-200794
HC188.A46 S87 1983

Alagoas (Brazil). Secretaria da Fazenda. Posicionamento das finanças de Alagoas na atual crise / [elaboração, equipe técnica da Secretaria da Fazenda, sob a coordenação de João Barroso Filho e orientação do titular da pasta Aloísio Barroso]. [Maceió] : Secretaria da Fazenda do Estado de Alagoas, 1983. 97 p. : ill. ; 30 cm. Cover title. LC Card 86-201070
1. Finance, Public - Brazil - Alagoas. 2. Taxation - Brazil. 3. Brazil - Economic conditions - 1964-1985. I. Barroso Filho, João. II. Barroso, Aloísio. III. Title.
HJ929.A52 A42 1983

ALAGOAS (BRAZIL) - SOCIAL POLICY.
Suruagy, Divaldo. Diretrizes básicas do governo . Maceió, Alagoas , 1983. 84 p. ; LC Card 85-200794
HC188.A46 S87 1983

ALAHUA (Association) Tierras para asentamientos populares . Quito, Ecuador , 1985. 378 p. : LC Card 87-400165 DDC 333.77/13/0986613 19
HD530.Q58 T54 1985

ALAI (Organization). Oficina Regional Andina. Luchando por nuestros derechos . Quito , 1984. 50 p. : LC Card 86-174980
HD1531.L3 L79 1984

Alaix, Ramón. Experiencias de educación y producción de fe y alegría en Oruro y Santa Cruz : estudios de caso / Ramón Alaix. La Paz, Bolivia : Centro Boliviano de Investigación y Acción Educativas, 1986. 191 p. ; 21 cm. (Serie Estudios educativos . no. 20) LC Card 86-208411 DDC 331.25/92/098413 19
1. Instituto de Aprendizaje Industrial (Oruro, Bolivia). 2. Escuela Técnica San Alonso (Santa Cruz, Bolivia). 3. Occupational training - Bolivia - Santa Cruz - Case studies. 4. Vocational education - Bolivia - Santa Cruz - Case studies. 5. Occupational training - Bolivia - Oruro - Case studies. 6. Vocational education - Bolivia - Oruro - Case studies. I. Title. II. Series.
HD5715.5.B52 S262 1986

Alalc. see **Asociación Latinoamericana de Libre Comercio.**

Alamán. López Aparicio, Alfonso. Alamán, primer economista de México /. México [1986] 118 p. ; ISBN 968-423-013-3 LC Card 87-403286 DDC 330/.092/4 B 19
HB123.M43 A435 1986

ALAMÁN, LUCAS, 1792-1853.
López Aparicio, Alfonso. Alamán, primer economista de México /. México [1986] 118 p. ; ISBN 968-423-013-3 LC Card 87-403286 DDC 330/.092/4 B 19
HB123.M43 A435 1986

Alamán, primer economista de México /. López Aparicio, Alfonso. México [1986] 118 p. ; ISBN 968-423-013-3 LC Card 87-403286 DDC 330/.092/4 B 19
HB123.M43 A435 1986

ʻAlāqī, Madanī ʻAbd al-Qādir. al-Idārah wa-al-bīʼah : dirāsah maydānīyah ʻan munaẓẓamāt al-aʻmāl al-Saʻūdīyah : baḥth maydānī / iʻdād Madanī ʻAbd al-Qādir ʻAlāqī, Ibrāhīm Fuʼād al-ʻIsawī, Ṭāhir Ḥusayn al-Dabbāgh.al-Ṭabʻah 1. [Jiddah] : Jāmiʻat al-Malik ʻAbd al-ʻAzīz, Kullīyat al-Iqtiṣād wa-al-Idārah, Markaz al-Buḥūth wa-al-Tanmiyah, 1985. 136 p. : ill. ; 24 cm. Cover title. At head of title: Barnāmaj al-baḥth al-ʻilmī. Bibliography: p. 123-124. "Baḥth raqm MQB 3/1402 H." LC Card 86-200390
1. Industrial management - Saudi Arabia. I. ʻIsawī, Ibrāhīm Fuʼād. II. Dabbāgh, Ṭāhir Ḥusayn. III. Jāmiʻat al-Malik ʻAbd al-ʻAzīz. Kullīyat al-Iqtiṣād wa-al-Idārah. Markaz al-Buḥūth wa-al-Tanmiyah. IV. Title.
HD70.S28 A422 1985

Alarco, Germán. Empleo, salarios y distribución del ingreso . [Miraflores, Lima] , 1986. 186 p. : LC Card 87-403082 DDC 331.11/0985 19
HD5761.A6 E47 1986

Alarcón Aliaga, Carlos. Privilegios y capital transnacional : el caso de Southern Peru Copper Corporation / Carlos Alarcón Aliaga. [Peru?] : Instituto José María Arguedas, [1985 or 1986] 168 p. : ill. ; 21 cm. Includes bibliographical references. LC Card 87-127159 DDC 338.8/87 19
1. Southern Peru Copper Corporation. 2. International business enterprises - Peru - Case studies. 3. Copper industry and trade - Peru - Case studies. I. Title.
HD2841.Z75 S683 1985

Alarcón, Reynaldo. Psicología, pobreza y subdesarrollo / Reynaldo Alarcón. 1a ed. Lima, Perú : Instituto Nacional de Investigación y Desarrollo de la Educación, 1986. 153 p. ; 21 cm. Bibliography: p. 145-153. LC Card 87-126266 DDC 155.9/2 19
1. Poverty - Psychological aspects. 2. Economic development - Psychological aspects. 3. Developing countries - Economic conditions. 4. Developing countries - Social conditions. 5. Dependency (Psychology). 6. Developing countries - Dependency on foreign countries. I. Title.
HC79.P6 A55 1986

Alasilta-Hagman, Lea, 1946- Työsuojelu kunnissa ja kuntainliitoissa. Swedish. Arbetarskyddet inom kommuner och kommunalförbund /. [Helsinki] [1983] 137 p. : LC Card 83-229126
HD7727.3 .T94618 1983

ALASKA - APPROPRIATIONS AND EXPENDITURES.
Goldsmith, Oliver Scott. How state spending reductions affect economic activity /. Fairbanks [1986] 40, 10 p. : LC Card 86-622972 DDC 330.9798/05 19
HJ7553 .G64 1986

Alaska. Commerce and Economic Development, Dept. of. see **Alaska. Dept. of Commerce and Economic Development.**

Alaska Commercial Fisheries Entry Commission. Focht, Rick. Employment and gross earnings of California residents in Alaska's commercial fisheries, 1977-1982 /. Juneau, AK [1984] v, 53 p. : LC Card 86-622320 DDC 331.12/5392/09798021 19
HD4966.F652 U54 1984c

Focht, Rick. Employment and gross earnings of Oregon residents in Alaska's commercial fisheries, 1977-1982 /. Juneau, AK [1984] v, 69 p. : LC Card 86-622319 DDC 331.12/5392/09798021 19
HD4966.F652 U54 1984b

Alaska. Community and Regional Affairs, Dept. of. see **Alaska. Dept. of Community and Regional Affairs.**

Alaska. Dept. of Commerce and Economic Development.
Alaska. Office of Mineral Development. Red Dog project analysis /. [Juneau?] [1984] 300 p. in various pagings : LC Card 84-622211 DDC 333.8/5/097986 19
HD9506.U63 R422 1984

Schiller, Robert, 1950- A comparison of Alaska's wholesale trade sector with other states /. [Juneau, Alaska] [1984] vi, 104 p. : LC Card 86-620623 DDC 381/.2/09798 19
HF5421 .S33 1984

Alaska. Dept. of Community and Regional Affairs. Arctic Slope Consulting Engineers. Western Arctic Coal Development Project . Anchorage, Alaska [1986] 2 v. : LC Card 87-621058 DDC 333.8/22/09798 19
HD9547.A4 A85 1986

Alaska. Dept. of Fish and Game. (Old Catalog form: Alaska. Fish and Game, Dept. of).

Alaska. Dept. of Fish and Game. Habitat Division. Alaska habitat management guide. Juneau, Alaska , 1986- 2 v. (loose-leaf) : LC Card 86-623159 DDC 333.95/09798 19
HD9457.A4 A427 1986

Alaska. Dept. of Natural Resources. Division of Oil and Gas. see **Alaska. Division of Oil and Gas.**

Alaska. Division of Oil and Gas. Historical and projected oil and gas consumption . [Juneau] [1986] 1 v. (in various pagings) : LC Card 86-622301 DDC 333.8/2313/09798 19
HD9502.U53 A4574 1986

Alaska. Economic Analysis Section. Van Patten, Jo. Alaska's commercial forest resource /. Juneau, Alaska [1986] v, 29 p. : LC Card 86-622970 DDC 333.75/09798 19
HD9757.A7 V36 1986

ALASKA - ECONOMIC CONDITIONS.
Developing America's northern frontier /. Lanham, MD , c1987. xx, 250 p. ; ISBN 0-8191-6081-4 (alk. paper) : LC Card 86-28233 DDC 338.9719 19
HC117.N48 D48 1987

Goldsmith, Oliver Scott. How state spending reductions affect economic activity /. Fairbanks [1986] 40, 10 p. : LC Card 86-622972 DDC 330.9798/05 19
HJ7553 .G64 1986

ALASKA - ECONOMIC POLICY.
Developing America's northern frontier /. Lanham, MD , c1987. xx, 250 p. ; ISBN 0-8191-6081-4 (alk. paper) : LC Card 86-28233 DDC 338.9719 19
HC117.N48 D48 1987

Alaska. Fish and Game, Dept. of. see **Alaska. Dept. of Fish and Game.**

Alaska habitat management guide. Economic overview of fish and wildlife / produced by State of Alaska Department of Fish and Game, Division of Habitat. Juneau, Alaska : The Division, 1986- 2 v. (loose-leaf) : ill. ; 30 cm. Spine title: AHMG economic overview of fish and wildlife. Updating decision: LC copy not updated. Includes bibliographies. CONTENTS. - v. 1. Commercial fishing and sportfishing -- v. 2. Hunting, trapping, nonconsumptive use, and subsistence and other local use. LC Card 86-623159 DDC 333.95/09798 19
1. Fish trade - Alaska. 2. Fishing - Alaska. 3. Fishes - Alaska - Habitat. 4. Fishery management - Alaska. 5. Fishery policy - Alaska. 6. Hunting - Government policy - Alaska. 7. Wildlife conservation - Government policy - Alaska. 8. Wildlife as food - Alaska. 9. Wildlife habitat improvement - Government policy - Alaska. I. Alaska. Dept. of Fish and Game. Habitat Division. II. Title: Economic overview of fish and wildlife. III. Title: AHMG economic overview of fish and wildlife.
HD9457.A4 A427 1986

Alaska Historical Commission studies in history . (no. 180) Bauer, Mary Cracraft. A history of coal-mining in the Sutton-Chickaloon area prior to WW II /. [Anchorage, Alaska] [1985] ii, 47 leaves : LC Card 86-620606 DDC 338.2/724/097983 19
HD9548.S87 B38 1985

Alaska. House of Representatives. see **Alaska. Legislature. House of Representatives.**

Alaska. Legislature. House of Representatives. (Old Catalog form: Alaska. House of Representatives)

Alaska. Legislature. House of Representatives. Research Agency. Pierce, Brad. The timber industry in interior Alaska . [Juneau] [1986] 65 p. ; LC Card 86-621755 DDC 338.1/7498/09798 19
HD9757.A7 P54 1986

Alaska. Legislature. Senate. (Old Catalog form: Alaska. Senate)
Rainery, Richard. Alaska's public energy resources . [Juneau?] [1985] 8, 124, 3, 7 p. : LC Card 86-622191 DDC 333.79/09798 19
HD9502.U53 A473 1985

Alaska. Legislature. Senate. Transportation Committee. RS 2477 Task Force. Roberts, Malcolm B. Senate Transportation Committee, RS 2477 Task Force report /. [Anchorage, Alaska] [1986] 121 leaves, 27 p. : LC Card 86-622718 DDC 333.78/09798 19
HE356.A4 R63 1986

Alaska Native Foundation. Arctic Slope Consulting Engineers. Western Arctic Coal Development Project . Anchorage, Alaska [1986] 2 v. : LC Card 87-621058 DDC 333.8/22/09798 19
HD9547.A4 A85 1986

Alaska occupational information / State of Alaska, Alaska Department of Labor, Administrative Services Division, Research and Analysis, Occupational Information Unit. Juneau, Alaska : Alaska Dept. of Labor, Research and Analysis Section, 1986. 126 p. : ill. ; 28 cm. "In cooperation with Alaska Occupational Information Coordinating Committee and U. S. Department of Labor, Bureau of Labor Statistics." LC Card 86-623154 DDC 331.12/09798/021 19
1. Labor supply - Alaska - Statistics. 2. Alaska - Occupations - Statistics. 3. Employment forecasting - Alaska - Statistics. I. Alaska. Occupational Information

Unit. II. Alaska Occupational Information Coordinating Committee. III. United States. Bureau of Labor Statistics.
HD5725.A4 A62 1986

Alaska Occupational Information Coordinating Committee. Alaska occupational information /. Juneau, Alaska , 1986. 126 p. : LC Card 86-623154 DDC 331.12/09798/021 19
HD5725.A4 A62 1986

Alaska. Occupational Information Unit. Alaska occupational information /. Juneau, Alaska , 1986. 126 p. : LC Card 86-623154 DDC 331.12/09798/021 19
HD5725.A4 A62 1986

ALASKA - OCCUPATIONS - STATISTICS.
Alaska occupational information /. Juneau, Alaska , 1986. 126 p. : LC Card 86-623154 DDC 331.12/09798/021 19
HD5725.A4 A62 1986

Alaska. Office of Mineral Development. Red Dog project analysis / lead agency, Office of Mineral Development, Department of Commerce and Economic Development ; contributing agencies, Department of Commerce and Economic Development ... [et al.]. [Juneau?] : The Office, [1984] 300 p. in various pagings : ill. ; 28 cm. "February 1984." Cover title: A report to the Governor, Bill Shefield. LC Card 84-622211 DDC 333.8/5/097986 19
1. Mineral industries - Alaska - Red Dog Creek Watershed. 2. Mines and mineral resources - Alaska - Red Dog Creek Watershed. I. Alaska. Dept. of Commerce and Economic Development. II. Title.
HD9506.U63 R422 1984

Alaska. Oil and Gas, Division of. see **Alaska. Division of Oil and Gas.**

ALASKA - PUBLIC LANDS - MANAGEMENT.
Skilbred, Amy. The Watt/Clark record . Washington, D.C. (1901 Pennsylvania Ave., N.W., Washington 20006) , c1984. iii, 63, [18] p. : LC Card 86-206945 DDC 363.7/009798 19
HC107.A47 E57 1984

ALASKA - PUBLIC LANDS - PLANNING.
Skilbred, Amy. The Watt/Clark record . Washington, D.C. (1901 Pennsylvania Ave., N.W., Washington 20006) , c1984. iii, 63, [18] p. : LC Card 86-206945 DDC 363.7/009798 19
HC107.A47 E57 1984

Alaska. Rural Research Agency. Rainery, Richard. Alaska's public energy resources . [Juneau?] [1985] 8, 124, 3, 7 p. : LC Card 86-622191 DDC 333.79/09798 19
HD9502.U53 A473 1985

Alaska. Senate. see **Alaska. Legislature. Senate.**

Alaska State Library historical monograph . (no. 8) Walker, David B., 1841 or 2-ca. 1906. Captain David B. Walker, journal and papers, 1864-1869 . Juneau, Alaska (Pouch G, Juneau 99811) , 1984. 60 p. : LC Card 84-622198
HD9481.U4 W359 1984

Alaska's commercial forest resource /. Van Patten, Jo. Juneau, Alaska [1986] v, 29 p. : LC Card 86-622970 DDC 333.75/09798 19
HD9757.A7 V36 1986

Alaska's public energy resources . Rainery, Richard. [Juneau?] [1985] 8, 124, 3, 7 p. : LC Card 86-622191 DDC 333.79/09798 19
HD9502.U53 A473 1985

Alasoini, Tuomo. Lakot ja yhteiskunnan muutos : tilastollisen lakkotutkimuksen kriittinen arviointi ja positiivisen tutkimusohjelman hahmottelua / Tuomo Alasoini. Helsinki : Työelämän suhteiden neuvottelukunta, [1983] ii, 132 p. : ill. ; 25 cm. (Työelämän suhteiden neuvottelukunta, 0358-7738 . 4/1983) Summary in English. Bibliography: p. 121-132. ISBN 951-46-7101-5 LC Card 84-168540
1. Strikes and lockouts. 2. Social change. 3. Strikes and lockouts - Finland. I. Series: Työelämän suhteiden neuvottelukunta (Series) , 1983/4. II. Title.
HD5306 .A42 1983

Alatri, Paolo. La Questione meridionale oggi /. Caltanissetta , 1985. 186 p. ; LC Card 86-214162
HC307.S69 Q47 1985

Albach, Horst.
Betriebswirtschaftslehre und ökonomische Krise . Wiesbaden , c1984. xxix, 412 p. : ISBN 3-409-13037-3 LC Card 85-143204
HD30.23 .B49 1984

Finanzierung mit Risikokapital / Horst Albach, Detlef Hunsdiek, Ljuba Kokalj. Stuttgart : C.E. Poeschel, c1986. 312 p. ; 24 cm. (Schriften zur Mittelstandsforschung . Nr. 15 NF) Bibliography: p. 287-305. ISBN 3-7910-5015-X LC Card 87-127700 DDC 332/.0415/0943 19
1. Venture capital - Germany (West). I. Hunsdiek, Detlef. II. Kokalj, Ljuba. III. Series. IV. Series: Schriften zur Mittelstandsforschung , n.F., Nr. 15. V. Title.
HG5492 .A797 1986

Kosten der Arbeit : Einflussfaktoren der Personalaufwendungen in Abhängigkeit von der Unternehmensgrösse / Horst Albach, Reinhard Clemens, Christina Friede. Stuttgart : C.E. Poeschel, c1985. xi, 179 p. : ill. ; 24 cm. (Schriften zur Mittelstandsforschung . Nr. 2 NF) Summary in English and German. Bibliography: p. 171-179. ISBN 3-7910-5003-6 : LC Card 86-162885 DDC 658.3/00943 19
1. Labor costs - Germany (West). 2. Small business - Germany, West. 3. Personnel management - Germany, West. I. Clemens, Reinhard. II. Friede, Christina. III. Title. IV. Series.
HD5029 .A43 1985 ***NYPL [JLL 73-505 Nr.2]***

Kritische Wachstumsschwellen in der Unternehmensentwicklung / Horst Albach, Kurt Bock, Thomas Warnke. Stuttgart : C.E. Poeschel, c1985. xxvii, 490 p. : ill. ; 24 cm. (Schriften zur Mittelstandsforschung . n.F., Nr. 7) Summary in English. Bibliography: p. 457-472. Includes index. ISBN 3-7910-5008-7 : LC Card 86-156636
1. Industrial management. 2. Economics. 3. Business forecasting. I. Bock, Kurt. II. Warnke, Thomas. III. Title. IV. Series.
HD35 .A64 1985

Neuere Entwicklungen in der Unternehmenstheorie . Wiesbaden , c1982. xiii, 290 p. : ISBN 3-409-39810-4 LC Card 87-672661
HD35 .N4814x 1982

Unternehmensführung und Logistik /. Wiesbaden , c1984. 151 p. : ISBN 3-409-13038-1 LC Card 85-126091
HD28 .Z46 nr. 84/2 HD30.28

Albagli, Claude.
Les circuits économiques en Afrique noire / Claude Albagli ; dessins de Blaise Guiratte. Abidjan : Nouvelles éditions africaines, c1983. 67 p. : ill. ; 24 cm. ISBN 2-7236-0585-X LC Card 86-179144
1. Economics - Study and teaching - Africa, Sub-Saharan - Audio-visual aids. 2. Economics - Study and teaching - Africa, Sub-Saharan. I. Title.
HB74.9.A357 A43 1983

Le rôle économique et social du paysan africain et l'autosuffisance alimentaire / Claude Albagli, Alphonse Minhoue ; dessins de Brissy. Abidjan : Nouvelles Editions africaines, c1984. 70 p. : ill. ; 24 cm. ISBN 2-7236-0648-1 LC Card 85-179020
1. Food supply - Africa, Sub-Saharan - Miscellanea. 2. Peasantry - Africa, Sub-Saharan - Miscellanea. I. Minhoue, Alphonse. II. Title.
HD9017.S82 A43 1984

ALBANIA - ECONOMIC CONDITIONS.
Fishta, Iljaz. Ekonomia e Shqipërisë në vitet e para të ndërtimit socialist, 1944-1948 /. Tiranë , 1984. 489 p. ; LC Card 85-163026
HC402 .F55 1984

ALBANIA - ECONOMIC POLICY.
Fishta, Iljaz. Ekonomia e Shqipërisë në vitet e para të ndërtimit socialist, 1944-1948 /. Tiranë , 1984. 489 p. ; LC Card 85-163026
HC402 .F55 1984

ALBANIA - STATISTICS.
40 vjet Shqipëri socialiste . Tiranë , 1984. 166 p. : LC Card 85-195974
HA1620.5 .A616 1984

Albano, Tracy. California employment and payrolls, April-June, 1985 / [prepared by Tracy Albano and Deanna Jimenez]. [Sacramento] : State of California, Health and Welfare Agency, Employment Development Dept., [1985] iii, 129 p. ; 28 cm. Cover title. LC Card 86-623197 DDC 331.12/5/09794021 19
1. Labor supply - California - Statistics. 2. Wages - California - Statistics. I. Jimenez, Deanna. II. Title.
HD5725.C2 A614 1985

Albeda, W.
Economische wetenschappen . Maastricht , Assen , 1985. 224 p. ; ISBN 90-232-2148-6 LC Card 86-111599
HB21 .E248 1985

De Verzorgingsstaat, slopen of renoveren? /. Assen , 1986. 152 p. : ISBN 90-232-2180-X : LC Card 86-186673
HC325 .V45 1986

Albeda, W., 1925- Vakbeweging in verandering . Deventer , 1986. 191 p. : ISBN 90-267-1082-8 : LC Card 86-224831
HD6727 .V29 1986

Albelda, Randy Pearl. Alternatives to economic orthodoxy . Armonk, N.Y. , c1987. 348 p. : ISBN 0-87332-409-9 : LC Card 86-33899 DDC 330 19
HB171 .A47 1987

Albentosa Puche, Luis.
El paro en España / Luis Albentosa Puche. Madrid : Instituto de Estudios Económicos, c1983. 349 p. : ill. ; 18 cm. Bibliography: p. [343]-345. ISBN 84-85719-34-4 LC Card 86-121124 DDC 331.11/0946 19
1. Labor supply - Spain. 2. Manpower policy - Spain. 3. Unemployment - Spain. I. Title.
HD5807 .A44 1983 ***NYPL [JLC 87-37]***

El sector exterior en España / Luis Albentosa Puche. Madrid : Instituto de Estudios Económicos, c1984. 343 p. : ill. ; 18 cm. Bibliography: p. [339]-340. ISBN 84-85719-40-9 LC Card 85-214668 DDC 336.3/4/0946 19
1. Balance of payments - Spain. 2. Debts, External - Spain. 3. Foreign exchange problem - Spain. 4. Spain - Economic policy. I. Title.
HG3883.S69 A45 1984 ***NYPL [JLC 86-251]***

Alber, Antone F. Videotex/teletext : principles and practices / Antone F. Alber. New York : McGraw-Hill, c1985. xiii, 498 p., [4] p. of plates : ill. (some col.) ; 24 cm. Includes bibliographies and index. ISBN 0-07-000957-0 : LC Card 84-23319 DDC 384 19
1. Videotex systems. 2. Teletext systems. I. Title.
TK5105 .A42 1985 ***NYPL [JSE 86-1907]***

Alber, Siegbert. Verbraucherpolitik in der sozialen Marktwirtschaft . Bonn , c1984. 146 p. ; ISBN 3-922335-04-7 LC Card 85-228004
HC240.9.C63 V47 1984

Albers, Willi. Renten 2000 . München , c1985. 124 p. : ISBN 3-7892-7267-1 LC Card 87-118239 DDC 331.25/2/0943 19
HD7105.35.G3 R46 1985

Albert, Cecelia A., 1954- World economic data . Santa Barbara, Calif. , c1987. x, 231 p. ; ISBN 0-87436-485-X (alk. paper) : LC Card 87-14508 DDC 330.9/04 19
HC59 .W643 1987

Albert, Hans, 1921- Ökonomisches Denken und soziale Ordnung . Tübingen , 1984. viii, 293 p. ; ISBN 3-16-344777-5 (Deut. Bibl.) LC Card 84-193300
HB175 .O46 1984

Alberta.
Position and policy statement on enhancing the Alberta capital market. [Edmonton, Alta.] : Govt. of Alberta, [1985] iii, 43 p. ; 28 cm. Cover title. "September, 1985." "Policy statement #2 in response to the white paper: An industrial and science strategy for Albertans, 1985-1990." Letter of transmittal laid into pocket. Includes bibliographical references and index. LC Card 86-137218 DDC 332.63/23 19
1. Capital market - Government policy - Alberta. I. Proposals for an industrial and science strategy for Albertans, 1985-1990. II. Title.
HG5150 .A42 1985

The Alberta advantage : Alberta profile. [Edmonton] : Alberta Economic Development and Trade, [1986] 25 p. : col. ill. ; 28 cm. Cover title. LC Card 87-167381 DDC 330.97123/03 19
1. Alberta - Economic conditions. 2. Alberta - Economic policy. 3. Alberta - Industries. I. Alberta. Alberta Economic Development and Trade.
HC117.A6 A5415 1986

Alberta. Alberta Economic Development and Trade. The Alberta advantage . [Edmonton] [1986] 25 p. : LC Card 87-167381 DDC 330.97123/03 19
HC117.A6 A5415 1986

Alberta. Alberta Municipal Affairs. McCully, Al. East Prairie Metis Settlement . [Edmonton, Alta.] [1982] iii, 99 p. :Bill. ; LC Card

82-202474 DDC 333.76/17/097123 19
HD319.A4 M52 1982

ALBERTA - ECONOMIC CONDITIONS.
The Alberta advantage . [Edmonton] [1986] 25 p. : LC Card 87-167381 DDC 330.97123/03 19
HC117.A6 A5415 1986

ALBERTA - ECONOMIC POLICY.
The Alberta advantage . [Edmonton] [1986] 25 p. : LC Card 87-167381 DDC 330.97123/03 19
HC117.A6 A5415 1986

ALBERTA - INDUSTRIES.
The Alberta advantage . [Edmonton] [1986] 25 p. : LC Card 87-167381 DDC 330.97123/03 19
HC117.A6 A5415 1986

Alberta Workers' Health, Safety and Compensation. Medical Services Branch. Butler, Elizabeth M. Alcoholism programs in industry . Edmonton, Alta. [1982] xiii, 80 p. : LC Card 86-212872 DDC 331.25/5 19
HF5549.5.A4 B88 1982

Albertini, Jean Marie. Des sous et des hommes : ce que vous n'avez jamais osé demander à un économiste / Jean-Marie Albertini. Paris : Seuil, c1985. 285 p. ; 18 cm. (Points. Virgule . v36) Includes bibliographies. ISBN 2-02-008947-5 LC Card 86-124575 DDC 330 19
1. Economics. I. Title.
HB173 .A32 1985

Albertini, Sergio. Il consolidamento strutturale dell'occupazione in specifiche aree con particolare riguardo alla provincia di Gorizia / di Sergio Albertini, Luigi Frey e Tiziana Tagliaferri ; a cura di Luigi Frey. Milano : F. Angeli, c1984. 184 p. ; 22 cm. (Quaderni di economia del lavoro. 19 [i.e. 23]) Includes bibliographical references. LC Card 84-234951 DDC 331.12/0945/392 19
1. Labor supply - Italy - Gorizia (Province). 2. Gorizia (Italy : Province) - Occupations. I. Frey, Luigi. II. Tagliaferri, Tiziana. III. Series: Quaderni di economia del lavoro (Franco Angeli editore) , 23. IV. Title.
HD5785.G67 A42 1984

Alberts, Volker. Die Bundesrepublik Deutschland und die Entwicklungspolitik der Europäischen Gemeinschaft, 1957-1983 /. Münster [1986] 111 p. ; ISBN 3-88660-214-1 LC Card 86-213020
HC241.25.G3 B87 1986

Albinski, Henry Stephen. Assessing corporate political risk . Totowa, NJ , 1986. xvii, 212 p. ; ISBN 0-86598-114-0 LC Card 85-19618 DDC 658 19
HD61 .A87 1986 ***NYPL [JLE 86-3102]***

Albon, Robert, 1951-
Rent control / Robert Albon and David C. Stafford. London ; New York : Croom Helm ; xi, 128 p. : ill. ; 23 cm. Bibliography: p. 119-123. Includes index. ISBN 0-7099-5411-5 LC Card 87-15899 DDC 363.5/6/0941 19
1. Rent control - Great Britain. 2. Rent control. I. Stafford, D. C. II. Title.
HD7288.85.G7 A4 1987

The Telecom monopoly : natural or artificial? / Robert Albon. Perth, W.A. : Australian Institute for Public Policy, 1986. 56 p. : ill. ; 21 cm. (Policy paper / Australian Institute for Public Policy, 0815-9394 . no. 5) Bibliography: p. 55-56. ISBN 0-949186-10-4 (pbk.) : LC Card 86-213521 DDC 384/.0994 19
1. Telecom Australia. 2. Telecommunication policy - Australia. 3. Telecommunication - Australia. I. Series: Policy paper (Australian Institute for Public Policy) , no. 5. II. Title.
HE8540.T44 A42 1986

Albrecht, Christoph, 1950-
Beschäftigungsentwicklung und Qualifikationsstruktur in Berlin 1977-1983 : ein Vergleich mit 11 bundesdeutschen Ballungsregionen und 20 ausgewählten Arbeitsamtsbezirken / Christoph Albrecht, Günther Schmid ; Mitarbeit, Norbert Goschin, Rolf Lambertz, Susanne Jahn ; Leitung, Günther Schmid. Berlin : Wissenschaftszentrum Berlin, [1985] 2 v. : ill. ; 30 cm. (Discussion papers / IIM/Industrial Policy, 0722-673X . IIM/LMP 85-4) Summary in English and German. Includes bibliographies. LC Card 86-204299
1. Labor supply - Berlin (Germany). 2. Employment agencies - Berlin (Germany). 3. Service industries - Berlin (Germany) - Employees. 4. Berlin (Germany) - Industries. I. Schmid, Gunther, 1942-. II. Series: Discussion paper series (International Institute of Management) , 85-4. III. Title.
HD5780.B4 A43 1985

Albrecht, Don E. A profile of 1984 Texas homebuyers / Don E. Albrecht. College Station, Tex. : Texas Real Estate Research Center, Texas A&M University, [1986] 70 p. : ill. ; 28 cm. "January 1986." "TRERC-186-1M-516." Bibliography: p. 55. LC Card 86-622194 DDC 333.33/8 19
1. Home ownership - Texas. 2. Housing surveys - Texas. 3. Housing - Texas. I. Series: Technical report / Texas Real Estate Research Center. II. Title.
HD7287.82.U62 T434 1986

Albrecht, Ernst, 1930- Knöpfel, Eckehardt. Werkbuch Jugendarbeitslosigkeit . Wuppertal , c1983. 168 p. : ISBN 3-417-12855-2 (pbk.) LC Card 87-672977
HD5779 .K59x 1983

Albrecht, James W. Job search and the transition to employment : theory / by James W. Albrecht, Bertil Holmlund, Harald Lang. Göteborg : Dept. of Economics, University of Gothenburg, [1986] 38 leaves ; 30 cm. (Memorandum . nr 100) "December 1986." Bibliography: leaf 38. LC Card 87-158051 DDC 331.12/8 19
1. Job hunting - Mathematical models. 2. Job offers - Mathematical models. 3. Markov processes. I. Holmlund, Bertil, 1947-. II. Lang, Harald. III. Series: Memorandum (Göteborgs universitet. Nationalekonomiska institutionen) , nr. 100. IV. Title.
HF5382.7 .A43 1986

Albrecht, Karl. The creative corporation / Karl Albrecht with Steven Albrecht. Homewood, Ill. : D. Jones-Irwin, c1987. x, 218 p. ; 24 cm. Bibliography: p. 209-210. Includes index. ISBN 0-87094-929-2 LC Card 86-51668 DDC 302.3/5 19
1. Creative ability in business. 2. Corporate culture. I. Albrecht, Steven. II. Title.
HD53 .A42 1987

Albrecht, Peter. Berufe der Wirtschaftsinformatik in der Schweiz /. Zürich , Stuttgart , 1986. 83 p. : ISBN 3-7281-1499-5 : LC Card 86-182797
HD8039.D372 S953 1986

Albrecht, Steven. Albrecht, Karl. The creative corporation /. Homewood, Ill. , c1987. x, 218 p. ; ISBN 0-87094-929-2 LC Card 86-51668 DDC 302.3/5 19
HD53 .A42 1987

Albright, S. Christian. Statistics for business and economics / S. Christian Albright. New York : Macmillan ; London : Collier Macmillan, c1987. xix, 1012, 5 p. : ill. (some col.) ; 25 cm. Includes bibliographies and index. ISBN 0-02-301620-5 LC Card 86-23751 DDC 519.5 19
1. Commercial statistics. 2. Statistics. I. Title.
HF1017 .A43 1987

Album der Industrie des Reichenberger Handelskammer-Bezirks. [Praha] : Národní technické muzeum v Praze, 1981. 2 v. in 1 : ill. ; 22 cm. (Bibliografie, prameny / Národní technické muzeum v Praze . 16 = 16) Original text compiled by A. Anschiringer. Reprint. Originally published: Reichenberg : F. Jannasch, 1958. With new pref. and commentary in Czech. Includes bibliographical references and index. LC Card 84-190839
1. Liberec (Czechoslovakia) - Industries - History. 2. Factory system - Czechoslovakia - Liberec - History. 3. Big business - Czechoslovakia - Liberec - History. I. Anschiringer, Anton, 1812-1873. II. Národní technické muzeum v Praze. III. Series: Bibliografie, prameny / Národní technické muzeum v Praze , 16.
HC270.292.L52 A42 1981

Albuquerque, J. A. Guilhon (José Augusto Guilhon) Serra, José. Brasil sem milagres /. São Paulo, SP , c1986. 174 p. : LC Card 87-404803 DDC 330.981/063 19
HC187 .S4153 1986

Albuquerque, Marcos Cintra Cavalcanti de.
Algumas considerações sobre a reforma agrária / Marcos Cintra Cavalcanti de Albuquerque. Brasília, DF : Instituto Tancredo Neves de Estudos Políticos e Sociais, [19]86. 23 p. ; 30 cm. (Cadernos liberais . 25/86) "Coletânea de artigos publicados na 'Folha de S. Paulo,' entre os meses de julho e agosto de 1985"--2nd prelim. leaf. LC Card 87-403236 DDC 333.3/1/81 19
1. Land reform - Brazil. I. Series: Cadernos liberais , 86/25. II. Title.
HD1333.B6 A4 1986

Riscos e perspectivas da divisão internacional do trabalho = Perspectives and risks of an international division of labour / Marcos Cintra Cavalcanti de Albuquerque. Brasília, DF : Instituto Tancredo Neves de Estudos Políticos e Sociais, [1986] 19, 17, [2] p. ; 31 cm. (Cadernos liberais . 30/86) Portuguese and English. "Texto especialmente para o Seminário 'International Trade between Liberty and Protectionism,' realizado em Hamburgo, nos dias 29 e 30 de setembro de 1986"--Prelim. p. [3]. Bibliography: p. [19], 2nd group. LC Card 87-403241 DDC 331/.01 19
1. International division of labor. 2. Comparative advantage (Commerce). I. Title. II. Title: Perspectives and risks of an international division of labour. III. Series: Cadernos liberais , 86/30.
HF1411 .A3984 1986

Alburo, Florian A.
Economic recovery and long-run growth . Makati, Metro Manila [1986- v. <1 > ; LC Card 86-232161 DDC 338.9599 19
HC453 .E27 1986

Towards recovery and sustainable growth /. [Quezon] [1985] 71 leaves ; LC Card 86-147888 DDC 338.9599 19
HC453 .T68 1985

Trade liberalization experience in the Philippines, 1960-84 / by Florian Alburo and Geoffrey Shepherd. Makati, Metro Manila : Philippine Institute for Development Studies, [1985] 159 p. : ill. ; 27 cm. (Working paper / Philippine Institute for Development Studies . no. 86-01) "December 1985." Bibliography: p. 158-159. LC Card 87-167251 DDC 382/.09599/0021 19
1. Philippines - Commercial policy. 2. Tariff - Philippines. 3. Foreign exchange - Government policy - Philippines. 4. Philippines - Commerce - Statistics. I. Shepherd, Geoffrey, 1943-. II. Series: Working paper / Philippine Institute for Development Studies , 86-01. III. Title.
HF1599 .A43 1985

Alburquerque Llorens, Francisco. La Izquierda europea . Barcelona , 1985. 282 p. ; ISBN 84-307-7438-6 LC Card 86-186087
HX238.5 .I97 1985 ***NYPL [JLD 86-4090]***

Alcabalas y protesta popular . Espinoza Claudio, César. Lima, Perú , 1981. iii, 111 p., [1] leaf of plates : LC Card 82-146025
HJ5715.P4 E86 1981

Alcalá, Graciela. Los pescadores de Tecolutla : el tiempo cotidiano y el espacio doméstico en una villa de pescadores / Graciela Alcalá.1a ed. México, D.F. : SEP Cultura, Centro de Investigaciones y Estudios Superiores en Antropología Social : Museo Nacional de Culturas Populares, 1985. 215 p. : ill. ; 23 cm. (Serie Los Pescadores de México . v. 10) Cuadernos de la Casa Chata ; 119 Originally presented as the author's thesis (maestro en antropología social--Colegio de Michoacán) under the title: El tiempo cotidiano y el espacio doméstico en una villa de pescadores, Tecolutla, Ver. Bibliography: p. [209]-215. ISBN 968-496-070-0 LC Card 86-191825
1. Fishers - Mexico - Tecolutla. 2. Tecolutla (Mexico) - Social conditions. 3. Quality of life - Mexico - Tecolutla. 4. Fishers - Housing - Mexico - Tecolutla. 5. Fishers - Mexico - Tecolutla - Dwellings. I. Title. II. Series.
HD8039.F652 M62 1985

Alcalde Cardoza, Xavier.
Fondo Monetario como actor político en la escena internacional / Javier Alcalde C. Lima, Perú : Universidad de Lima, Facultad de Economía, Centro de Investigaciones Económicas y Sociales, [1986] 54 p. ; 21 cm. (Serie Documentos. no. 3) Cover title. Includes bibliographies. LC Card 87-400166 DDC 332.1/52 19
1. International Monetary Fund. 2. International finance. I. Series: Serie Documentos (Universidad de Lima. Centro de Investigaciones Económicas y Sociales) , no. 3. II. Title.
HG3881.5.I58 A44 1986

The idea of Third World development : emerging perspectives in the United States and Britain, 1900-1950 / Javier Gonzalo Alcalde. Lanham, MD : University Press of America ; [Charlottesville, Va.] : the Miller Center, University of Virginia, c1987. xxii, 236 p. ; 23 cm. (Exxon Education Foundation series on rhetoric and political discourse . v. 8) Bibliography: p. 231-236. ISBN 0-8191-6303-1 (alk. paper) : LC Card 87-8154 DDC 338.91/009172/4 19

1. Economic assistance, American - Developing countries - History. 2. Economic assistance, British - Developing countries - History. I. White Burkett Miller Center. II. Title. III. Series.
HC60 .A4595 1987

El poder norteamericano y la renegociación de la deuda externa brasileña, 1982-1983 / Javier Alcalde Cardoza. Lima, Perú : Universidad de Lima, Facultad de Economía, Centro de Investigaciones Económicas y Sociales, 1985. 62 p. ; 30 cm. (Serie Avances de investigación . no. 9) Bibliography: p. 61-62. LC Card 86-223475
1. Debts, External - Brazil. 2. Debt relief - Brazil. 3. Loans, American - Brazil. 4. International Monetary Fund - Brazil. 5. International Monetary Fund - United States. I. Series: Avances de investigación (Universidad de Lima. Centro de Investigaciones Económicas y Sociales) , 9. II. Title.
HJ8579 .A44 1985

Alcántara, Alcides de. Métodos para la aplicación de las series metódicas ocupacionales / Alcides de Alcántara. 1a ed. Montevideo : CINTERFOR, 1978. 73 p. : ill. ; 24 cm. (Estudios y monografías . no. 37) Bibliography: p. 73. LC Card 86-142696
1. Occupational training. I. Series: Estudios y monografías (CINTERFOR (Organization)) , no. 37. II. Title.
HD5715 .A44 1978

The alchemy of finance . Soros, George. New York , c1987. 351 p. : ISBN 0-671-63455-0 LC Card 87-4745 DDC 332.6/78 19
HG4515 .S67 1987

Alcides, Otto Ohlweiler. see **Ohlweiler, Otto Alcides.**

Alcock, Peter, 1951- Poverty and state support / Peter Alcock. London ; New York : Longman, 1987. xi, 215 p. : ill. ; 20 cm. (Social policy in modern Britain) Bibliography: p. 204-212. Includes index. ISBN 0-582-29652-8 (pbk.) LC Card 86-27857 DDC 368.4/00941 19
1. Social security - Great Britain. 2. Great Britain - Social policy. I. Title. II. Series.
HD7165 .A77 1987

Alcohol and drugs . Denenberg, Tia Schneider. Washington, D.C. , c1983. xv, 201 p. : ISBN 0-87179-410-1 LC Card 83-7560 DDC 344.73/01255 347.3041255 19
KF3540 .D46 1983 ***NYPL [JLE 86-2348]***

Alcohol & drugs in the workplace : costs, controls, and controversies. Washington, D.C. : Bureau of National Affairs, c1986. iii, 136 p. ; 23 cm. (A BNA special report) Includes bibliographical references. ISBN 0-87179-905-7 (pbk.) : LC Card 87-106610 DDC 331.25/5 19
1. Alcoholism and employment - United States. 2. Drugs and employment - United States. 3. Alcoholism and employment - United States - Case studies. 4. Drugs and employment - United States - Case studies. I. Title: Alcohol and drugs in the workplace. II. Series.
HF5549.5.A4 A35 1986

Alcohol and drugs in the workplace. Alcohol & drugs in the workplace . Washington, D.C. , c1986. iii, 136 p. ; ISBN 0-87179-905-7 (pbk.) : LC Card 87-106610 DDC 331.25/5 19
HF5549.5.A4 A35 1986

ALCOHOL FUEL INDUSTRY - AUSTRIA.
Landwirtschaftliche Produktionsalternativen am Beispiel Ethanol, Ölsaaten und Eiweissfutterpflanzen /. Wien , 1985. 141 p. : LC Card 86-108149 DDC 338.1/09436 19
HD1935 .L33 1985

ALCOHOL FUEL INDUSTRY - BRAZIL.
Avaliação do Programa Nacional do Álcool /. Brasília , 1985. 175 p. : LC Card 86-146662
HD9502.5.A433 B622 1985

Pereira, A. (Armand) Ethanol, employment, and development . Geneva , 1986. xiv, 195 p. : ISBN 92-2-105380-6 (pbk.) : LC Card 87-107819 DDC 338.4/7662669 19
HD9502.5.A433 B646 1986

O Proálcool vale? /. [São Paulo-SP (Brasil)] , 1985. 52 p. : LC Card 86-220396
HD9502.5.A433 B645 1985

ALCOHOL FUEL INDUSTRY - BRAZIL - EMPLOYEES.
Pereira, A. (Armand) Ethanol, employment, and development . Geneva , 1986. xiv, 195 p. : ISBN 92-2-105380-6 (pbk.) : LC Card 87-107819 DDC 338.4/7662669 19
HD9502.5.A433 B646 1986

ALCOHOL FUEL INDUSTRY - BRAZIL - EMPLOYEES - SUPPLY AND DEMAND.
Alcool e emprego . Brasília, DF , 1983. 170 p. : LC Card 86-200307
HD5718.A4852 B63 1983

ALCOHOL FUEL INDUSTRY - BRAZIL - MINAS GERAIS.
Seminário de Energia de Biomassa (1985? : Belo Horizonte, Brazil?) Seminário de Energia de Biomassa . [Belo Horizonte?] , <[1986?-. v. <[1-2] > : LC Card 87-107998
HD9502.5.B543 B67 1985

ALCOHOL FUEL INDUSTRY - BRAZIL - SÃO PAULO (STATE)
Manoel, Alvaro. Política agrícola, eficiência e concentração na agricultura brasileira . São Paulo , 1986. 180 p. : LC Card 86-234338
HD1873 .M35 1986

ALCOHOL FUEL INDUSTRY - DEVELOPING COUNTRIES - CASE STUDIES.
Socioeconomic aspects of renewable energy technologies . New York , 1988. p. cm. ISBN 0-275-92851-9 (alk. paper) : LC Card 87-22890 DDC 333.7/09172/4 19
HD9502.D442 S63 1988

ALCOHOL FUEL INDUSTRY - DOMINICAN REPUBLIC.
Vidal, Máximo Luis. El fin de la era del petróleo y su impacto sobre la economía mundial . San Pedro de Macorís, R.D. , 1981. 103 p. : LC Card 82-202556
HD9502.5.A433 D658 1981

ALCOHOL FUEL INDUSTRY - GOVERNMENT POLICY - BRAZIL.
Dé Carli, Gileno. Desafio energético /. Recife , 1981 (Recife : Companhia Editora de Pernambuco) 309 p. ; LC Card 86-129710
HD9502.B72 D4 1981

ALCOHOL FUEL INDUSTRY - GOVERNMENT POLICY - BRAZIL, NORTHEAST.

ALCOHOL INTOXICATION. see **ALCOHOLISM.**

ALCOHOLIC BEVERAGE INDUSTRY - GOVERNMENT POLICY - NEW ZEALAND.
New Zealand. Working Party on Liquor. The sale of liquor in New Zealand . [Wellington, N.Z. , 1986] 212, [1] p. : LC Card 87-147518 DDC 338.4/76631/09931 19
HD9390.N452 N49 1986

ALCOHOLIC BEVERAGE INDUSTRY - HUNGARY - STATISTICS.
Alkoholtartalmú italok kiskereskedelmi eladási forgalmának alakulása 1960-1984 években /. Budapest , 1986. 32 p. : LC Card 86-199334
HD9365.H82 A45 1986

ALCOHOLIC BEVERAGE INDUSTRY - SOUTH AFRICA - HISTORY.
Fridjhon, Michael. Conspiracy of giants . Johannesburg , c1986. xii, 419 p. : ISBN 0-947012-34-6 LC Card 87-139111 DDC 338.4/76631/0968 19
HD9367.S7 F75 1986

ALCOHOLIC BEVERAGE INDUSTRY - SOVIET UNION.
Kochubeeva, M. T. (Mariia Tikhonovna) Ėkonomika, organizatsiia i planirovanie spirtovogo i likerno-vodochnogo proizvodstva /. Moskva , 1977. 342 p. : LC Card 82-122783
HD9365.S652 K63 1977

ALCOHOLIC BEVERAGE INDUSTRY - STATISTICS.
Korb, Penelope. U. S. and world food, beverages, and tobacco expenditures, 1970-83 /. Washington, D.C. , 1986. iv, 84 p. : LC Card 86-603160 DDC 339.4/8664/0021 19
HD9000.4 .K67 1986

ALCOHOLIC BEVERAGE INDUSTRY - UNITED STATES - STATISTICS.
Korb, Penelope. U. S. and world food, beverages, and tobacco expenditures, 1970-83 /. Washington, D.C. , 1986. iv, 84 p. : LC Card 86-603160 DDC 339.4/8664/0021 19
HD9000.4 .K67 1986

ALCOHOLICS - REHABILITATION - UNITED STATES.
Stop DWI . Lexington, Mass. , c1986. xv, 183 p. : ISBN 0-669-12157-6 (alk. paper) LC Card 85-45676 DDC 363.1/2558 19
HE5620.D7 S89 1986 ***NYPL [JLE 86-2813]***

ALCOHOLISM AND EMPLOYMENT - ALBERTA.
Butler, Elizabeth M. Alcoholism programs in industry . Edmonton, Alta. [1982] xiii, 80 p. : LC Card 86-212872 DDC 331.25/5 19
HF5549.5.A4 B88 1982

ALCOHOLISM AND EMPLOYMENT - CALIFORNIA.
Oren, Ditza L. Preventing dishonest behavior in the electronics industry . [United States , 1985] vii, 115 leaves : LC Card 86-224386 DDC 621.381/068/3 19
HD8039.E38 U65 1985

ALCOHOLISM AND EMPLOYMENT - GERMANY (WEST)
Alkohol im Betrieb und am Arbeitsplatz . Kiel , c1986. 52 p. : ISBN 3-87559-048-1 LC Card 87-409550 DDC 331.2/55 19
HF5549.5.A4 A476 1986

ALCOHOLISM AND EMPLOYMENT - GERMANY (WEST) - CONGRESSES.
Informationsseminar Alkohol am Arbeitsplatz (1985 : Obereifenberg, Schmitten, Germany) Informationsseminar Alkohol am Arbeitzplatz /. München [1985?] ii, 49 p. : LC Card 86-162315
HF5549.5.A4 I54 1985

ALCOHOLISM AND EMPLOYMENT - UNITED STATES.
Alcohol & drugs in the workplace . Washington, D.C. , c1986. iii, 136 p. ; ISBN 0-87179-905-7 (pbk.) : LC Card 87-106610 DDC 331.25/5 19
HF5549.5.A4 A35 1986

Corporate strategies for controlling substance abuse /. New York, N.Y. , c1986. xi, 50 p. ; ISBN 0-8237-0327-4 (pbk.) LC Card 86-207704 DDC 658.3/82 19
HF5549.5.E42 C66 1986

Denenberg, Tia Schneider. Alcohol and drugs . Washington, D.C. , c1983. xv, 201 p. : ISBN 0-87179-410-1 LC Card 83-7560 DDC 344.73/01255 347.3041255 19
KF3540 .D46 1983 ***NYPL [JLE 86-2348]***

Lodge, Joseph H., 1942- Drug and alcohol abuse in the workplace . New York , c1987. xi, 91 p. ; ISBN 0-8247-7769-7 LC Card 87-627 DDC 658.3/822 19
HF5549.5.D7 L63 1987

United States. Dept. of the Interior. Division of Medical and Health Services. Help for the troubled employee. Washington [1975?] 57 p. ; ***NYPL [JLF 86-1309]***

Woititz, Janet Geringer. Home away from home /. Pompano Beach, Fla. , c1987. x, 137 p. : ISBN 0-932194-38-9 LC Card 86-33478 DDC 658.3/045 19
HF5549.5.A4 W65 1987

ALCOHOLISM AND EMPLOYMENT - UNITED STATES - CASE STUDIES.
Alcohol & drugs in the workplace . Washington, D.C. , c1986. iii, 136 p. ; ISBN 0-87179-905-7 (pbk.) : LC Card 87-106610 DDC 331.25/5 19
HF5549.5.A4 A35 1986

ALCOHOLISM AND TRAFFIC ACCIDENTS. see **DRINKING AND TRAFFIC ACCIDENTS.**

Alcoholism programs in industry . Butler, Elizabeth M. Edmonton, Alta. [1982] xiii, 80 p. : LC Card 86-212872 DDC 331.25/5 19
HF5549.5.A4 B88 1982

ALCOHOLISM - TREATMENT - UNITED STATES.
The Drunk driver and jail /. [Washington, D.C.?] , 1987- v. : LC Card 87-600837 DDC 363.1/255 19
HE5620.D7 D77 1987

Schlesinger, Stephen E. Stop drinking and start living /. Blue Ridge Summit, PA , 1985. xx, 133 p. : ISBN 0-8306-1937-2 : LC Card 85-14885 DDC 362.2/92 19
HV5033 .S34 1985 ***NYPL [JLD 86-1606]***

ALCOHOLISM - UNITED STATES.
Schlesinger, Stephen E. Stop drinking and start living /. Blue Ridge Summit, PA , 1985. xx,

133 p. : ISBN 0-8306-1937-2 : LC Card 85-14885 DDC 362.2/92 19
HV5033 .S34 1985 ***NYPL [JLD 86-1606]***

Alcool e emprego : o impacto da produção de álcool de cana-de-açúar e de madeira sobre a geração de empregos / Ministério da Agricultura, COALBRA Coque e Alcool da Madeira S/A. Brasília, DF : COALBRA--Coque e Alcool da Madeira S.A., Setor de Divulgação, 1983. 170 p. : ill. ; 21 cm. (Cadernos COALBRA . 3) Summary also in English. Bibliography: p. 157-161. LC Card 86-200307
1. Alcohol fuel industry - Brazil - Employees - Supply and demand. 2. Sugarcane industry - Brazil - São Paulo (State) - Employees - Supply and demand. 3. Sugarcane industry - Brazil - Pernambuco - Employees - Supply and demand. 4. Wood-pulp industry - Brazil - Mato Grosso (State) - Employees - Supply and demand. 5. Wood-pulp industry - Brazil - Mato Grosso do Sul - Employees - Supply and demand. 6. Wood-pulp industry - Brazil - Minas Gerais - Employees - Supply and demand. I. COALBRA Coque e Alcool da Madeira (Brazil). II. Series.
HD5718.A4852 B63 1983

Alcorta, F. X. (Frank X.) Darwin Rebellion, 1911-1919 / by F.X. Alcorta. 1st ed. [Darwin, N.T.] : History Unit, Northern Territory University Planning Authority, 1984. xiv, 115 p., [8] p. of plates : ill. ; 26 cm. Includes bibliographies and index. ISBN 0-7245-0492-3 : LC Card 84-220611 DDC 331.89/294295 19
1. Strikes and lockouts - Australia - Darwin (N.T.) - History - 20th century. 2. Trade-unions - Australia - Darwin (N.T.) - History - 20th century. I. Title.
HD5450.Z9 D373 1984 ***NYPL [JLF 87-405]***

ALCOY (SPAIN) - ECONOMIC CONDITIONS.
Pérez Planelles, Francisco, fl. 1774-1807. Plan estatístico de la villa de Alcoy /. [València] [Alcoi] , 1983. xiii, 31 p. ; LC Card 86-150151
HC388.A44 P47 1983

ALCOY (SPAIN) - POPULATION - HISTORY - 18TH CENTURY.
Pérez Planelles, Francisco, fl. 1774-1807. Plan estatístico de la villa de Alcoy /. [València] [Alcoi] , 1983. xiii, 31 p. ; LC Card 86-150151
HC388.A44 P47 1983

ALCOY (SPAIN) - POPULATION - HISTORY - 19TH CENTURY.
Pérez Planelles, Francisco, fl. 1774-1807. Plan estatístico de la villa de Alcoy /. [València] [Alcoi] , 1983. xiii, 31 p. ; LC Card 86-150151
HC388.A44 P47 1983

Aldana, Ramón Losada. see **Losada Aldana, Ramón.**

Alderman, David. Ahmed, Mumtaz. Project management . Hamilton, Ont. [1986] xv, 254 p. : ISBN 0-920212-56-5 (pbk.) LC Card 87-158681 DDC 658.4/04 19
HF5635 .A26 1986

Aldred, Chris. Women at work / Chris Aldred. London : Pan Books, 1981. 173 p. : ill. ; 20 cm. (Pan trade union studies) Includes bibliographies and index. ISBN 0-330-26479-6 (pbk.) LC Card 86-673456
1. Women - Employment - Great Britain. 2. Women in trade-unions. 3. Women - Legal status, laws, etc. - Great Britain. I. Title. II. Series.
HD6135 .A79x 1981

Aldrich, Robert, 1954-
Tipton, Frank B., 1943- An economic and social history of Europe from 1939 to the present /. Baltimore, Md. , 1987. vii, 297 p. : ISBN 0-8018-3538-0 LC Card 87-3870 DDC 330.94/055 19
HC240 .T563 1987

Tipton, Frank B., 1943- An economic and social history of Europe, 1890-1939 /. Baltimore , 1987. vii, 323 p. : ISBN 0-8018-3537-2 LC Card 87-3869 DDC 330.94/028 19
HC240 .T56 1987

Aldunate B., Adolfo. Análisis tipológico del trabajador del Gran Santiago e impacto sobre el ingreso de las políticas redistributivas, 1970-1971 / Adolfo Aldunate B., Arturo León B. [Santiago, Chile?] : Programa de Intercambio CELADE-ELAS, [1972] iv, 9, [35] p. ; 28 cm. LC Card 83-169296
1. Income distribution - Chile - Santiago Metropolitan Area. 2. Santiago Metropolitan Area (Chile) - Occupations. I. León B., Arturo. II. Title.
HC193.S23 A43 1972

ALE-HOUSES. see **HOTELS, TAVERNS, ETC.**

Alegato contra el automóvil /. Sequera, Armando José, 1953- Caracas , 1985. 157 p. ; ISBN 980-222-019-1 : LC Card 87-107528 DDC 388.3/21 19
HE5613 .S46 1985

Alejandro, Carlos Federico Díaz. see **Díaz Alejandro, Carlos Federico.**

Alejo, Francisco Javier. Por una visión del desarrollo latinoamericano con autodeterminación, democracia y paz /. San Isidro, Lima, Perú [1984] 191 p. ; LC Card 86-226515
HC167.A5 P67 1984

Aleksandrov, I͡U. G. (I͡Uriĭ Georgievich) Gosudarstvo i agrarnaia ėvoliutsiia v razvivaiushchikhsia stranakh Azii i Afriki /. Moskva , 1980. 227 p. ; LC Card 81-143353
HD2056 .G67 1980

Aleksandrov, V. A. Problemy nauchno-tekhnicheskogo progressa v bratskikh sotsialisticheskikh stranakh . Moskva , 1985. 234 p. ; LC Card 86-179196
HC244.Z9 T472 1985

Aleksandrov, V. A. (Vadim Aleksandrovich)
Vlasova, I. V. (Irina Vladimirovna) Traditsii krest'ianskogo zemlepol'zovaniia v Pomor'e i Zapadnoĭ Sibiri v XVII-XVIII vv. /. Moskva , 1984. 230 p. : LC Card 85-174592
HD719.W45 V55 1984

Alekseenko, I. I. Krivoded, V. V. KPSS i kolkhoznoe krest'ianstvo v 1945-1959 gg. /. Rostov-na-Donu , 1984. 190 p. ; LC Card 87-100194
HD1492.S652 C384 1984

Alekseev, A. D. Razvitie ėnergetiki IAkutskoĭ ASSR v sviazi s sooruzheniem BAM . IAkutsk , 1985. 99, 3 p. : LC Card 86-233736
HD9502.S653 I237 1985

Alekseev, Anatoliĭ Mikhaĭlovich.
Bostandzhian, V. B. (Vardan Babkenovich) Optimizatsiia otraslevykh sistem v sostave ėkonomicheskikh programm /. Novosibirsk , 1982. 120, [1] p. : LC Card 83-107849
HC337.R852 S5234 1982

Optimizatsiia perspektivnykh planov razvitiia otraslevykh sistem . Novosibirsk , 1979. 163 p. : LC Card 81-130740
HC337.R852 S546 1979

Alekseev, V. A. Sotsial'no-ėkonomicheskie problemy ispol'zovaniia trudovykh resursov /. Cheboksary , 1986. 70 p. ; LC Card 87-137786
HD5797.C56 S68 1986

Alekseev, Veniamin Vasil'evich. Trudovye kollektivy Sibiri . Novosibirsk , 1985. 154 p. ; LC Card 86-162191
HD5797.S5 T78 1985

Alekseeva, Margarita Alekseevna. Voprosy prognozirovaniia i planirovaniia vneshneėkonomicheskikh sviazeĭ /. Moskva , 1984. 93 p. ; LC Card 86-144298
HF3626.5 .V668 1984

Aleksińska, Janina. Rozwój ludności krajów socjalistycznych . Warszawa , Moskva , 1978. 381 p. ; LC Card 81-206832
HB3608.7.A3 R69 1978

ALEMÁN, MATEO, 1547-1614?
Bleiberg, Germán, 1915- El "informe secreto" de Mateo Alemán sobre el trabajo forzoso en las minas de Almadén /. London , c1985. 150 p. ; ISBN 0-7293-0200-8 LC Card 86-178917
HD4875.S6 B58 1985

Alemneh Dejene. Peasants, agrarian socialism, and rural development in Ethiopia / Alemneh Dejene. Boulder : Westview Press, 1987. xiii, 162 p. : ill. ; 23 cm. (Westview special studies on Africa) Includes bibliographies and index. ISBN 0-8133-7247-X (pbk. : alk. paper) LC Card 86-51527 DDC 338.1/0963 19
1. Agricultural productivity - Ethiopia. 2. Agriculture, Cooperative - Ethiopia. 3. Collective farms - Ethiopia. 4. Agriculture and state - Ethiopia. 5. Socialism - Ethiopia. 6. Peasantry - Ethiopia. 7. Rural development - Ethiopia. I. Title.
HD2124.5 .A79 1987

Alessandra, Anthony J.
Non-manipulative selling / Tony Alessandra, Phil Wexler, and Rick Barrera. 2nd ed. New York : Prentice Hall Press, c1987. x, 262 p. : ill. ; 22 cm. Includes index. ISBN 0-13-623307-4 (pbk.) : LC Card 86-43174 DDC 658.8/5 19
1. Selling. I. Wexler, Phillip S. II. Barrera, Rick. III. Title.
HF5438.25 .A43 1987

Non-manipulative selling. Alessandra, Anthony J. Non-manipulative selling [sound recording] : building sales through trust / Tony Alessandra & Phil Wexler. Chicago, Ill. , p1985. 6 sound cassettes : LC Card 86-754983
HF5438.25

Non-manipulative selling [sound recording] : building sales through trust / Tony Alessandra & Phil Wexler. Chicago, Ill. : Nightingale-Conant Corp., p1985. 6 sound cassettes : analog. Title from container. Based on the book: Non-manipulative selling / Tony Alessandra, Phil Wexler, Rick Barrera. Notes inserted in container (30 cm.) Sales and communications speakers Tony Alessandra and Phil Wexler explain how to build sales through quickly establishing a bond of trust with a prospect, thus enabling a salesperson to deal from a position of mutual respect. CONTENTS. - 1-2. Removing pressure and getting the sale ; Turning tension into trust -- 3-4. The six steps of non-manipulative selling -- 5-6. Relationship selling -- 7-8. Verbal communications ; Non-verbal communications -- 9-10. The image of excellence -- 11-12. The mutual information exchange ; The mutual commitment exchange. LC Card 86-754983
1. Selling. I. Wexler, Phillip S. II. Alessandra, Anthony J. Non-manipulative selling. III. Title. IV. Title: Nonmanipulative selling.
HF5438.25

Alessandrini, Sergio.
L'Economia tedesca . Milano , c1981. 273 p. : LC Card 87-673286
HC286.7 .E29x 1981

The Unofficial economy . Aldershot, Hants, England , Brookfield, Vt., USA , c1987. 345 p. : ISBN 0-566-05131-1 : LC Card 86-25634 DDC 381 19
HD2341 .U56 1987

Alexander, Albert. The economic world of 1787 and the Constitution / by Albert Alexander and Edward C. Prehn. New York (150 Nassau St., Rm. 1625, New York 10038) : New York City Council on Economic Education, [1987] 18 p. ; 28 cm. Cover title. "In commemoration of the bicentennial of the U. S. Constitution." "March 1987." LC Card 87-403433 DDC 330.973/0318 19
1. United States - Economic conditions - To 1865. 2. United States - Constitutional history. 3. United States - History - Constitutional period, 1789-1809. I. Prehn, Edward C. II. Title.
HC105.6 .A44 1987

Alexander, Carlton. Nation building : a businessman's perspective : excerpts from selected speeches / by Carlton Alexander ; edited by George J. Phillip. Kingston, Jamaica : Grace, Kennedy, c1983. 100 p. : ill. ; 22 cm. LC Card 84-172595 DDC 338.97293 19
1. Jamaica - Economic conditions. I. Phillip, George J. II. Title.
HC154 .A79 1983

Alexander, David C., 1949- Joint Seminar on Designing Jobs for Handicapped Workers (1985 : Chicago, Ill.) Designing jobs for handicapped workers . Hot Springs, Ark. (P.O. Box 1358, Hot Spring 71902) [1986] 66 p. : LC Card 86-622317 DDC 658.3/045 19
HD7256.U5 J65 1985

Alexander, Gordon J., 1947- Portfolio analysis / Gordon J. Alexander, Jack Clark Francis. 3rd ed. Englewood Cliffs, N.J. : Prentice-Hall, c1986. xiv, 306 p. : ill. ; 24 cm. (Prentice-Hall foundations of finance series) Rev. ed. of: Portfolio analysis / Jack Clark Francis, Stephen H. Archer. 2nd ed. c1979. Includes index. Bibliography: p. 268-289. ISBN 0-13-686825-8 : LC Card 85-28317 DDC 332.6 19
1. Portfolio management - Econometric models. 2. Investment analysis - Econometric models. I. Francis, Jack Clark. Portfolio analysis. II. Title.
HG4521 .A42 1986 ***NYPL [JLE 86-4286]***

Alexander Hamilton Institute (U. S.)
AHI's complete portfolio of modern business

terms. A dictionary of business terms /. New York , 1987, c1986. 438 p. ; ISBN 0-531-15518-8 LC Card 86-24560 DDC 650/.03/21 19
HF1001 .A34 1987

Bittel, Lester R. Executive skills program. [New York, N.Y., U. S.A.] (1633 Broadway, New York 10019) [c1986] 4 v. : LC Card 86-233068 DDC 658.4/09 19
HD38.2 .B569 1986

Effective cash flow management. New York, N.Y., U. S.A. , c1985. x, 223 p. : ISBN 0-86604-176-1 (pbk.) LC Card 86-205438 DDC 658.1/5244 19
HG4028.C45 E34 1985

Kleutghen, Paul P. Profitable inventory management strategies /. New York, NY, U. S.A. , c1986. viii, 208 p. : ISBN 0-86604-233-4 (pbk.) LC Card 86-205426 DDC 658.7/87 19
HD40 .K54 1986

Sales motivation . New York, N.Y., U. S.A. , c1985. viii, 131 leaves ; ISBN 0-86604-150-8 (pbk.) LC Card 86-232974 DDC 658.3/14 19
HF5438.25 .S253 1985

Stockton, Richard B. ROI, planning for profitable growth /. New York, N.Y., U. S.A. , c1984. x, 141 leaves : ISBN 0-86604-150-8 (pbk.) LC Card 86-232254 DDC 332.63 19
HG4028.C4 S72 1984b

Structured hiring . New York, NY, U. S.A. , c1987. viii leaves, 144 p. : ISBN 0-86604-221-0 (pbk.) LC Card 87-156398 DDC 658.3/112 19
HF5549.5.R44 S83 1987

Wells, Richard C. The right choice . New York, N.Y., U. S.A. , c1985. viii, 178 p. : ISBN 0-86604-198-2 (pbk.) LC Card 86-201105 DDC 658.4/033 19
HD31 .W457 1985

Alexander, John W. (John Wesley), 1918- Economic geography. Hartshorn, Truman A. Economic geography / Truman A. Hartshorn, John W. Alexander. 3rd ed. Englewood Cliffs, N.J. , 1988. xiii, 385 p. : ISBN 0-13-225160-4 LC Card 87-17407 DDC 330.9 19
HF1025 .H296 1988

Hartshorn, Truman A. Economic geography /. Englewood Cliffs, N.J. , 1988. xiii, 385 p. : ISBN 0-13-225160-4 LC Card 87-17407 DDC 330.9 19
HF1025 .H296 1988

Alexander, Larry D. Pearce, John A. Company and industry cases in strategy and policy /. Homewood, IL , 1986. xiv, 711 p. : ISBN 0-256-03558-X : LC Card 85-82002
NYPL [JLE 87-993]

Alexander von Humboldt Award Colloquium (1984) Technology, human capital, and the world food problem / Alexander von Humboldt Award Colloquium, 1984 ; G. Edward Schuh, editor. St. Paul, MN : Institute of Agriculture, Forestry and Home Economics, Dept. of Agricultural and Applied Economics, Agricultural Experiment Station, University of Minnesota, 1986. x, 167 p. : ill. ; 28 cm. (Miscellaneous publication . 37-1986) Includes bibliographies. LC Card 86-622216 DDC 338.1/9/1724 19
1. Food supply - Developing countries - Congresses. 2. Agricultural innovations - Developing countries - Congresses. 3. Appropriate technology - Developing countries - Congresses. 4. Agricultural laborers - Developing countries - Congresses. I. Schuh, G. Edward (George Edward), 1930-. II. Series: Miscellaneous publication (University of Minnesota. Agricultural Experiment Station) , 1986-37. III. Title.
HD9018.D44 A44 1984

Alexander, William. De Old, Alan R. Transportation . Worcester, Mass. , c1986. x, 534 p. : ISBN 0-87192-126-X LC Card 86-70174 DDC 380.5 19
HE151 .D42 1986

Alexandrides, Costas G. Countertrade : practices, strategies, and tactics / Costas G. Alexandrides, Barbara L. Bowers. New York : J. Wiley, c1987. xx, 235 p. ; 24 cm. (Wiley professional banking and finance series, 0733-8945) Bibliography: p. 227-229. Includes index. ISBN 0-471-84711-9 LC Card 87-12966 DDC 382 19
1. Countertrade. I. Bowers, Barbara L. (Barbara Lynn), 1948-. II. Title. III. Series.
HF1414.3 .A44 1987

Alexandroff, Alan S. Schultz, Richard, 1945- Economic regulation and the federal system /. Toronto , Buffalo , c1985. xv, 187 p. : ISBN 0-8020-7287-9 (pbk.) LC Card 86-672574
HD3616.C23 S38x 1985
NYPL [JLD 86-2821]

Alfano, Salvatore. Work of the dividend department / Salvatore Alfano. New York, NY : New York Institute of Finance, c1987. xvi, 180 p. ; 24 cm. Includes index. ISBN 0-13-965096-2 LC Card 87-7733 DDC 332.6/068/5 19
1. Dividends. 2. Brokers. I. Title.
HG4028.D5 A43 1987

Alfaro Carvajal, Reinaldo. Matarrita Mena, José Joaquín. Areas industriales de Costa Rica /. San José, Costa Rica, América Central [1986] 151 p. : ISBN 997-7500-01-0 LC Card 87-404258 DDC 338.097286 19
HC143 .M38 1986

Alfred, Braxton M. Elements of statistics for the life and social sciences / Braxton M. Alfred. New York : Springer-Verlag, c1987. xiii, 190 p. : ill. ; 25 cm. (Springer texts in statistics) Bibliography: p. [179]-183. Includes index. ISBN 0-387-96500-9 : LC Card 87-4964 DDC 300/.1/5195 19
1. Social sciences - Statistical methods. 2. Life sciences - Statistical methods. I. Title. II. Series.
HA29 .A53 1987

Alfreð Elíasson, 1920- Alfreðs saga og Loftleiða / Jakob F. Ásgeirsson. Reykjavík : Iðunn, 1984 (1985 printing) 372 p. : ill. ; 24 cm. Includes index. LC Card 86-101929
1. Alfreð Elíasson, 1920-. 2. Loftleiðir (Airline) - History. 3. Businessmen - Iceland - Biography. 4. Air lines - Iceland - History. I. Jakob F. Ásgeirsson, 1961-. II. Title.
HD9711.I22 A443 1985
NYPL [JFE 87-1455]

ALFREÐ ELÍASSON, 1920-
Alfreð Elíasson, 1920- Alfreðs saga og Loftleiða /. Reykjavík , 1984 (1985 printing) 372 p. : LC Card 86-101929
HD9711.I22 A443 1985
NYPL [JFE 87-1455]

Alfred Higgins Productions.
What's a natural resource? [motion picture] /. Los Angeles, Calif. , 1986, c1987. 1 film reel (15 1/2 min.) : LC Card 86-708242 DDC 333.7 11
HC59

What's a natural resource? [videorecording] /. Los Angeles, Calif. , 1986, c1987. 1 videocassette (15 1/2 min.) : LC Card 86-708243 DDC 333.7 11
HC59

Alfred Kern (1850-1893), Edouard Sandoz (1853-1928) . Riedl-Ehrenberg, Renate. Zürich , c1986. 90 p. : LC Card 86-159933 DDC 338/.09494 s 338.7/66/0094943 19
HC395.5.A2 S3 no. 44 QD21

Alfred Krupp /. Blencke, Fritz. Leipzig , 1898. 127 p. : LC Card 85-665721
HD9523.9.K7 B53x 1898

Alfred Marshall, progress and politics /. Reisman, David A. New York , 1987. vii, 499 p. ; ISBN 0-312-00773-6 : LC Card 87-4811 DDC 330.15/5 19
HB98.2 .R44 1987

Alfreðs saga og Loftleiða /. Alfreð Elíasson, 1920- Reykjavík , 1984 (1985 printing) 372 p. : LC Card 86-101929
HD9711.I22 A443 1985
NYPL [JFE 87-1455]

ALGEBRA OF LOGIC. see LOGIC, SYMBOLIC AND MATHEMATICAL.

ALGEBRA - PROBLEMS, EXERCISES, ETC.
George, Thomas F. Business algebra & mathematics /. Englewood Cliffs, NJ , c1987. xiv, 634 p. : ISBN 0-13-091562-9 LC Card 86-30333 DDC 512/.1 19
HF5694 .G46 1987

Alger, Jeff. Cohen, Eli B. Business BASIC for the IBM PC with cases /. St. Louis , 1987. xxiv, 634 p. : ISBN 0-8016-1244-6 (pbk.) LC Card 86-23100 DDC 005.2/165 19
HF5548.5.B3 C64 1987

ALGERIA - ECONOMIC CONDITIONS.
Kukushkin, Vladimir IUr'evich. Neft' i razvitie, Liviia, Alzhir /. Moskva , 1985. 227 p. ; LC Card 85-180876
HD9577.L52 K85 1985
NYPL [*QIP 87-3410]

ALGERIA - RURAL CONDITIONS.
Lesbet, Djaffar. Les 1000 villages socialistes en Algérie /. Alger , Paris , c1983. 335 p. : ISBN 2-86738-008-1 : LC Card 84-156989 DDC 335/.00965 19
HX441.5.A6 L47 1983 ***NYPL [JLD 87-236]***

Algo sobre la plata en México en el siglo XVIII /. Cortina Portilla, Manuel. México , 1986. 48 p., [1] folded leaf of plates : LC Card 87-404604 DDC 332.4/042/097253 19
HG661 .C67 1986

ALGORISM. see ALGORITHMS.

ALGORITHMS - CONGRESSES.
Proceedings of an international conference on genetic algorithms and their applications . [S.l. , 1985] 225 p. : ***NYPL [JSF 87-413]***

Algumas considerações sobre a reforma agrária /. Albuquerque, Marcos Cintra Cavalcanti de. Brasília, DF [19]86. 23 p. ; LC Card 87-403236 DDC 333.3/1/81 19
HD1333.B6 A4 1986

Algunas características del inventario de vivienda . Vicario, Luis B. [Montevideo] , 1985. 42 p. : LC Card 86-152477
HD7330.M64 V53 1985

Algunas cifras sobre la fuerza de trabajo en el Uruguay /. Lombardi, Nelly Niedworok de. [Montevideo] [1979] 18 leaves : LC Card 86-164130
HD5762.A6 L66 1979

Algunas consideraciones acerca de la formación económica del Uruguay, 1726-1930 /. Jacob, Raúl, 1946- Montevideo, Uruguay [1985 or 1986] 56 p. ; LC Card 86-202376 DDC 330.9895/065 19
HC232 .J287 1985

"Algunas consideraciones sobre el tipo real de cambio en el Uruguay, período 1.78-12.82" /. Medina Spangenberg, Ernesto. Montevideo, Uruguay [1984] 39 p. : LC Card 84-253583
HG3940 .M43 1984

Algunas consideraciones sobre los efectos distributivos del proceso de liberalización comercial /. Coloma C., Fernando. Santiago , 1982. 31 leaves ; LC Card 87-102072
HF1713 .C617 1982

Algunas ideas de José Martí en relación con la clase obrera y el socialismo /. Cantón Navarro, José, 1925- La Habana , 1981, c1980. 174 p. ; LC Card 82-233789 DDC 320.5/31/097291 19
HX159 .C33 1981 ***NYPL [JLD 86-1423]***

Algunas ideas sobre tributación federal de la renta en Estados Unidos /. Zurdo y Ruiz-Ayúcar, Juan. [Madrid] [1978?] 53, [17] leaves ; LC Card 85-203311
HJ4652 .Z87 1978

Algunos antecedentes estadísticos sobre las organizaciones económicas populares /. Bustamante G., Jaime. Santiago, Chile , 1986. 23 p. ; LC Card 87-101323
HD2346.C53 B87 1986

Algunos aspectos sociográficos del área metropolitana de San José, Costa Rica / Eugenio Fonseca-Tortós ... [et al.]. [Ciudad Universitaria "Rodrigo Facio"] : Centro de Estudios Sociales y de Población, Universidad de Costa Rica, 1970. 105 p. : ill. ; 21 cm. (Proyecto estratificación social . no. 1) Includes bibliographical references. LC Card 82-196053
1. San José Metropolitan Area (Costa Rica) - Economic conditions. 2. San José Metropolitan Area (Costa Rica) - Social conditions. 3. San José Metropolitan Area (Costa Rica) - Population. I. Fonseca Tortós, Eugenio. II. Series.
HC143.Z7 S3515 1970

Alguns elementos para a caracterização da assimetria regional agrária portuguesa /. Pereira, Mário. Oeiras [Portugal] , 1974. 59 p. : LC Card 85-133550
HD2027 .P388 1974

Alguns elementos para um banco de dados económicos do ordenamento rural do Alentejo .

(no. 8) Pereira, Francisco José Piteira. A cultura da vinha na região do Redondo /. [Lisbon] , 1983. 11, 4, 30, 21 leaves, [2] leaves of plates : LC Card 84-238378
HD9259.G7 P47 1983

Alheit, Peter. Beschädigtes Leben : soziale Biographien arbeitsloser Jugendlicher : ein soziologischer Versuch über die "Entdeckung" neuer Fragestellungen / Peter Alheit, Christian Glass, unter Mitarbeit von Chr. Biesinger, B. Dausien und A. Reger. Frankfurt[/Main] ; New York : Campus, c1986. 361 p. ; 21 cm. Bibliography: p. 355-360. ISBN 3-593-33606-5 LC Card 86-148737
1. Youth - Employment - Germany, West. 2. Unemployed - Germany (West) - Interviews. I. Glass, Christian. II. Title.
HD6276.G4 A44 1986

Alho, Kari. Neuvostoliiton-kauppa Suomen kansantaloudessa /. Helsinki , 1986. 220 p. : ISBN 951-9206-18-3 LC Card 87-127628
HF3633.S65 N48 1986

Ali Akber, Md. Ali, Md. Harun, 1944- An economic study on guava cultivation in some selected areas of Bangladesh /. Mymensingh , 1986. 38 p. ; LC Card 87-902187 DDC 338.1/74421/095492 19
HD9259.G83 B353 1986

Ali, M. Hazrat. Halim, Abdul, 1945- The effects of rice based cropping system research on women in Bangladesh /. Mymensingh , 1986. 2, 30 leaves ; LC Card 86-901954 DDC 331.4/8318/095492 19
HD1537.B3 H35 1986

Ali, Md. Harun, 1944- An economic study on guava cultivation in some selected areas of Bangladesh / Md. Harun Ali, Md. Ali Akbar, Md. Abul Bashar. Mymensingh : Bureau of Socio-economic Research and Training, Bangladesh Agricultural University, 1986. 38 p. ; 25 cm. (Research report . no. 13) Bibliography: p. 38. LC Card 87-902187 DDC 338.1/74421/095492 19
1. Guava industry - Bangladesh. 2. Guava - Bangladesh. I. Ali Akber, Md. II. Bashar, Md. Abul. III. Series: Research report (Bangladesh Agricultural University. Bureau of Socio-economic Research and Training) , no. 13. IV. Title.
HD9259.G83 B353 1986

Ali, Mohammed. Regional Symposium on Water Resoures Policy in Agro-Socio-Economic Development (1985 : Dhaka, Bangladesh) Water resources policy for Asia . Rotterdam , Boston , 1987. xii, 627 p. : ISBN 90-6191-684-4 LC Card 87-170039 DDC 333.91/0095 19
HD1698.A1 R45 1985

La alianza anglo argentina . Dargoltz, Raúl E. (Raúl Eduardo) Buenos Aires [1983] 168 p. : LC Card 84-117468
HD9764.A73 S353 1983

Aliber, Robert Z.
Mayer, Thomas. Money, banking, and the economy /. New York , c1984. xiv, 574 p. : ISBN 0-393-95313-0 LC Card 83-13498 DDC 332.1/0973 19
HG540 .M39 1984 ***NYPL [JLE 86-2193]***

Mayer, Thomas, 1927- Money, banking, and the economy /. New York , c1987. xiv, 488 p. : ISBN 0-393-95557-5 LC Card 86-33160 DDC 332.1/0973 19
HG540 .M39 1987

ALIEN LABOR.
Cohen, Robin. The new helots . Aldershot, Hants, England , Brookfield, Vt., USA , c1987. xiii, 290 p. : ISBN 0-566-00932-3 : LC Card 87-19807 DDC 331.6/2 19
HD6304 .C64 1987

Sassen, Saskia. The mobility of labor and capital . Cambridge [Cambridgeshire] , New York , 1988. p. cm. ISBN 0-521-32227-8 LC Card 87-14586 DDC 331.12/791 19
HD6300 .S37 1988

ALIEN LABOR, ALGERIAN - FRANCE.
Voss, Timm. Die algerisch-französische Arbeitsmigration . Königstein/Ts. , 1981. xiii, 193 p. : ISBN 3-7756-6937-X : LC Card 81-176949 DDC 331.6/2/65044 19
HD8438.A4 V67 1981 ***NYPL [JLD 86-2466]***

ALIEN LABOR, ANTILLEAN - NETHERLANDS - STATISTICS.
Beek, P. van. De leefsituatie van Surinamers en Antillianen in Nederland, 1985 /. 's-Gravenhage , 1986- v. <1 > : ISBN 90-357-0558-0 : LC Card 87-120083
HD8518.5.S87 B44 1986

ALIEN LABOR, ASIAN - ARAB COUNTRIES.
Migration of Asian workers to the Arab world /. Tokyo, Japan , c1986. v, 358 p. ; ISBN 92-808-0555-X (pbk.) LC Card 87-131112 DDC 331.6/2/50174927 19
HD8656 .M53 1986

ALIEN LABOR, ASIAN - CALIFORNIA - HISTORY.
Muller, Thomas, 1933- The fourth wave . Washington , c1985. xvii, 217 p. ; ISBN 0-87766-349-1 LC Card 85-22646 DDC 331.6/2/720794 19
HD8081.M6 M85 1985
NYPL [JLE 86-3014]

ALIEN LABOR, AUSTRALIAN - NEW ZEALAND.
St. Hill, R. L. Labour mobility between New Zealand and Australia /. Canterbury, N.Z. [1986] ix, 68 p. : LC Card 87-109510 DDC 331.12/791 19
HD8848.5.N45 S7 1986

ALIEN LABOR - AUSTRIA.
Rainer, Norbert. Anwendung der Arbeitsmarktorientierten Input-Output-Analyse am beispiel der Gastarbeiterbeschäftigung /. Wien , 1977. 47 leaves ; LC Card 86-194737
HC270.I57 R35 1977

ALIEN LABOR - BRAZIL.
O Mercado de trabalho no Brasil . São Paulo , 1986. 263 p. : LC Card 86-221361
HD5754 .M47 1986

ALIEN LABOR - CANADA.
Ornstein, Michael D. The work experience of immigrants to Canada [microform] . Downsview, Ont. , 1983. 48 leaves ;
NYPL [*ZT-1732 no.16]

ALIEN LABOR CRIMINALS - GERMANY (WEST)
Pitsela, Angelika. Straffälligkeit und Viktimisierung ausländischer Minderheiten in der Bundesrepublik Deutschland . Freiburg [i.B.] , 1986. xxvii, 479 p. ; ISBN 3-922498-16-7 LC Card 87-131111 DDC 331.6/2/495043 19
HD8458.G7 P57 1986

ALIEN LABOR, EGYPTIAN - PERSIAN GULF REGION.
Feiler, Gil. The number of Egyptian workers in the Arab oil countries, 1974-1983 . Tel Aviv , c1986. i, 30 leaves ; LC Card 87-404430 DDC 331.6/2/620536 19
HD8662 .F45 1986

ALIEN LABOR - EUROPE.
Charbit, Yves. Enfants, familles, migrations dans le bassin méditerranéen /. [Paris] , 1985. viii, 195 p. ; ISBN 2-7332-0110-7 (pbk.)
HQ792.E8 C47 1985
NYPL [JLL 72-295 cahier no 110]

Miller, Mark J. Employer sanctions in Western Europe /. Staten Island, N.Y. , 1987. viii, 67 p. ; ISBN 0-934733-20-1 (pbk.) : LC Card 86-31739 DDC 331.6/2/094 19
HD8378.5.A2 M5395 1987

Rymarczyk, Jan. Migracja siły roboczej do krajów EWG i jej konsekwencje społeczno-gospodarcze /. [Wrocław] , 1982. 239 p., [4] folded leaves ; LC Card 83-153742
HB9 .B7522 nr. 218 HD8378.5.A2

ALIEN LABOR - FRANCE.
Raimond, Jean-Marie. Vocational training of young migrants in France /. Berlin , 1986. x, 101 p. : ISBN 92-825-6118-6
NYPL [JLG 87-134]

ALIEN LABOR - FRANCE - CONGRESSES.
Arbeiterwanderungen, Ausländerbeschäftigung und Ausländerpolitik in kapitalistischen Ländern Europas im 20. Jahrhundert. Rostock , 1981-1982. 4 v. ; LC Card 82-193086 DDC 331.6/2/094 19
HD8438.A2 A75 1982 ***NYPL [JLK 84-95]***

ALIEN LABOR - GERMANY - HISTORY.
Herbert, Ulrich, 1951- Geschichte der Ausländer, Beschäftigung in Deutschland, 1880 bis 1980 . Berlin , c1986. 272 p. : ISBN 3-8012-3019-8 LC Card 87-113703 DDC 331.6/2/0943 19
HD8458.A2 H39 1986

Herrenmensch und Arbeitsvölker . Berlin , c1986. 189 p. : ISBN 3-88022-952-X (cover); 3-88022-925-X : LC Card 87-119712 DDC 331.11/732/0943 19
HD4875.G4 H47 1986

Population, labour, and migration in 19th- and 20th-century Germany /. Leamington Spa [UK] ; New York : xii, 200 p. : ISBN 0-85496-503-3 : LC Card 86-24470 DDC 331.6/2/0943 19
HD5856.G3 P66 1987

ALIEN LABOR - GERMANY - HISTORY - 20TH CENTURY - ADDRESSES, ESSAYS, LECTURES.
Zur Haltung der herrschenden Klasse und der Arbeiterbewegung zur Beschäftigung ausländischer Arbeiter. [Rostock] , 1980. 64 p. ; LC Card 82-209919 DDC 331.6/2/0943 19
HD8458.A2 Z87 1980 ***NYPL [JLD 87-143]***

ALIEN LABOR - GERMANY, WEST.
Ausländerintegration in deutschen Industriebetrieben /. Königstein/Ts. , c1985. viii, 273 p. : ISBN 3-7756-6935-3 LC Card 85-194662 DDC 305.8/00943 19
HD8458.A2 A9265 1985
NYPL [JLD 86-2193]

Fuchs, Hans-Jürgen, 1957- Das glückliche Bewusstsein und die Krise . Frankfurt [am Main] , c1986. 133 p. ; ISBN 3-925798-25-0 LC Card 87-112965
HD8458.A2 F83 1986

Hill, Paul Bernhard, 1953- Determinanten der Eingliederung von Arbeitsmigranten /. Königstein/Ts. , c1984. 228 p. : ISBN 3-7756-6939-6 LC Card 84-219137 DDC 331.6/2/0943 19
HD8458.A2 H55 1984
NYPL [JLD 86-2467]

Koch-Arzberger, Claudia. Die schwierige Integration . Opladen , c1985. 211 p. : ISBN 3-531-11785-8 LC Card 86-101159 DDC 331.6/2/0943 19
HD8458.A2 K587 1985

Kontos, Maria. Verbandsstrategien zur Ausländerbeschäftigung in der Bundesrepublik . Königstein/Ts. , c1983. viii, 235 p. ; ISBN 3-7756-6938-8 LC Card 83-190064 DDC 331.6/2/0943 19
HD8458.A2 K598 1983
NYPL [JLD 86-2465]

Pammesberger, Hans-Peter. Ausländerbeschäftigung als dauerhafter Angebotsfaktor auf dem Arbeitsmarkt der Bundesrepublik Deutschland /. Hamburg , c1986. xii, 297 p. : ISBN 3-925630-06-6 LC Card 86-227741
HD8458.A2 P35 1986

Strukturwandel des Ausländerproblems . Bochum , c1986. 309 p. : ISBN 3-88339-529-3 LC Card 87-121913 DDC 331.6/2/0943 19
HD8458.A2 S786 1986

ALIEN LABOR - GERMANY, WEST - CONGRESSES.
Arbeiterwanderungen, Ausländerbeschäftigung und Ausländerpolitik in kapitalistischen Ländern Europas im 20. Jahrhundert. Rostock , 1981-1982. 4 v. ; LC Card 82-193086 DDC 331.6/2/094 19
HD8438.A2 A75 1982 ***NYPL [JLK 84-95]***

ALIEN LABOR - GERMANY (WEST) - MÜNSTER IN WESTFALEN - HISTORY.
Weidner, Marcus, 1964- Nur Gräber als Spuren . Münster , c1984. 134 p. : ISBN 3-924550-02-6 LC Card 86-116688 DDC 331.11/732/094355 19
HD4875.G4 W45 1984

ALIEN LABOR - GERMANY (WEST) - PSYCHOLOGICAL ASPECTS.
Görtz, Vera. Physische und psychische Erkrankungen bei Arbeitsmigranten in der BRD . Gelsenkirchen [1986?] 250 p. : ISBN 3-89049-007-7 LC Card 87-141880 DDC 331.6/2/0943 19
HD8458.A2 G67 1986

ALIEN LABOR - GERMANY (WEST) - SOCIAL CONDITIONS.
Kremer, Manfred. Assimilation ausländischer Arbeitnehmer in der Bundesrepublik

Deutschland . Königstein/Ts. , 1980. 203, 64 p. ; ISBN 3-7756-6934-5 LC Card 80-151671 DDC 303.4/8243 19
HD8458.A2 K73 1980 NYPL [JLD 86-2549]

ALIEN LABOR - GERMANY (WEST) - SOCIAL CONDITIONS - CONGRESSES.
Kongress "Ausländerpolitik und Menschenrechte" (1983 : Frankfurt am Main, Germany) Reader zum Kongress "Ausländerpolitik und Menschenrechte" /. Frankfurt , 1984. 60 p. ; LC Card 87-133583 DDC 331.6/2/0943 19
HD8458.A2 K594 1983

ALIEN LABOR - GOVERNMENT POLICY - FRANCE.
Edye, Dave, 1953- Immigrant labour and government policy . Aldershot, Hants, England , Brookfield, Vt., U. S.A. , c1987. vi, 157 p. ; ISBN 0-566-05361-6 : LC Card 86-25704 DDC 331.6/2/0943 19
HD8458.A2 E26 1987

ALIEN LABOR - GOVERNMENT POLICY - GERMANY (WEST)
Dohse, Knuth, 1948- [Ausländerpolitik und betriebeliche Ausländerdiskriminierung. English.] Foreign workers in the Federal Republic of Germany . Berlin [1982] 80 p. : LC Card 86-214190 DDC 331.6/2/0943 19
HD8458.A2 D6213 1982

Edye, Dave, 1953- Immigrant labour and government policy . Aldershot, Hants, England , Brookfield, Vt., U. S.A. , c1987. vi, 157 p. ; ISBN 0-566-05361-6 : LC Card 86-25704 DDC 331.6/2/0943 19
HD8458.A2 E26 1987

Strukturwandel des Ausländerproblems . Bochum , c1986. 309 p. : ISBN 3-88339-529-3 LC Card 87-121913 DDC 331.6/2/0943 19
HD8458.A2 S786 1986

ALIEN LABOR - GOVERNMENT POLICY - GERMANY (WEST) - CONGRESSES.
Kongress "Ausländerpolitik und Menschenrechte" (1983 : Frankfurt am Main, Germany) Reader zum Kongress "Ausländerpolitik und Menschenrechte" /. Frankfurt , 1984. 60 p. ; LC Card 87-133583 DDC 331.6/2/0943 19
HD8458.A2 K594 1983

ALIEN LABOR, GREEK - GERMANY (WEST) - SOCIAL CONDITIONS.
Pitsela, Angelika. Straffälligkeit und Viktimisierung ausländischer Minderheiten in der Bundesrepublik Deutschland . Freiburg [i.B.] , 1986. xxvii, 479 p. ; ISBN 3-922498-16-7 LC Card 87-131111 DDC 331.6/2/495043 19
HD8458.G7 P57 1986

ALIEN LABOR, HAITIAN - DOMINICAN REPUBLIC.
Báez Evertsz, Franc, 1948- Braceros haitianos en la República Dominicana /. [Santo Domingo] , c1986. 354 p. : LC Card 87-401177 DDC 331.6/2/729407293 19
HD8218.5 .B34 1986

Madruga, José Manuel. Azúcar y haitianos en la República Dominicana /. Santo Domingo , 1986. 202 p. : LC Card 87-125442 DDC 331.6/2/729407293 19
HD9114.D62 M33 1986

Plant, Roger. Sugar and modern slavery . London , Atlantic Highlands, N.J. , 1987. xiv, 177 p. : ISBN 0-86232-572-2 : LC Card 87-13315 DDC 331.7/6361/097293 19
HD8039.S86 D652 1987

ALIEN LABOR - HOUSING - GERMANY (WEST)
Koch-Arzberger, Claudia. Die schwierige Integration . Opladen , c1985. 211 p. : ISBN 3-531-11785-8 LC Card 86-101159 DDC 331.6/2/0943 19
HD8458.A2 K587 1985

ALIEN LABOR - ISRAEL.
Semyonov, Moshe. Hewers of wood and drawers of water . Ithaca, NY , c1987. xii, 152 p. : ISBN 0-87546-133-6 (pbk. : alk. paper) LC Card 87-2682 DDC 331.6/99275695 19
HD8660 .S45 1987

ALIEN LABOR, ITALIAN - GERMANY (WEST) - COLOGNE - CASE STUDIES.
Busch, Angelika. Migration und psychische Belastung . Berlin , 1983. 351 p. ; ISBN 3-496-00733-8 LC Card 83-193476
HD8458.I8 B87 1983

ALIEN LABOR, ITALIAN - MEXICO - VERACRUZ (STATE) - HISTORY.
Zilli Manica, José Benigno. Braceros italianos para México . Xalapa, México , 1986. 93 p., [6] p. of plates : ISBN 968-8340-45-6 LC Card 87-400059
HD8118.5.I83 Z55 1986

ALIEN LABOR - ITALY.
Hornziel, Ijola Maria. La condizione degli immigrati stranieri in Italia . Milano, Italy , c1986. 166 p. : LC Card 86-181215
HD8488.A2 H67 1986

ALIEN LABOR, JAMAICAN - CUBA - HISTORY.
Petras, Elizabeth McLean. Jamaican labor migration . Boulder , 1988. x, 297 p. : ISBN 0-8133-7456-1 (pbk. : alk. paper) LC Card 87-20139 DDC 331.6/2/7292072875 19
HD8178 .P47 1988

ALIEN LABOR, JAMAICAN - HISTORY.
Petras, Elizabeth McLean. Jamaican labor migration . Boulder , 1988. x, 297 p. : ISBN 0-8133-7456-1 (pbk. : alk. paper) LC Card 87-20139 DDC 331.6/2/7292072875 19
HD8178 .P47 1988

ALIEN LABOR, JAMAICAN - PANAMA - CANAL ZONE - HISTORY.
Petras, Elizabeth McLean. Jamaican labor migration . Boulder , 1988. x, 297 p. : ISBN 0-8133-7456-1 (pbk. : alk. paper) LC Card 87-20139 DDC 331.6/2/7292072875 19
HD8178 .P47 1988

ALIEN LABOR, LATIN AMERICAN - SWEDEN.
Latinamerikaner i Sverige . [Stockholm] [1984] 62 p. ; ISBN 91-38-08192-X LC Card 84-218936
HD8578.5.L37 L37 1984

ALIEN LABOR - MAURITIUS.
Ly-Tio-Fane Pineo, Huguette. Lured away . Moka, Mauritius , 1984. 261 p. :
NYPL [JLD 87-587]

ALIEN LABOR, MEXICAN - CALIFORNIA.
Calderón R., Cedric. Contrabando humano en las Californias /. [S.l. , 1978] (Guatemala : Propsa) 160 p. ; LC Card 86-218852 DDC 331.6/2/720794 19
HD8083.C2 C23 1978

ALIEN LABOR, MEXICAN - CALIFORNIA - ADDRESSES, ESSAYS, LECTURES.
Zur Haltung der herrschenden Klasse und der Arbeiterbewegung zur Beschäftigung ausländischer Arbeiter. [Rostock] , 1980. 64 p. ; LC Card 82-209919 DDC 331.6/2/0943 19
HD8458.A2 Z87 1980 NYPL [JLD 87-143]

ALIEN LABOR, MEXICAN - CALIFORNIA - HISTORY.
Muller, Thomas, 1933- The fourth wave . Washington , c1985. xvii, 217 p. ; ISBN 0-87766-349-1 LC Card 85-22646 DDC 331.6/2/720794 19
HD8081.M6 M85 1985
NYPL [JLE 86-3014]

ALIEN LABOR, MEXICAN - SOUTHWEST, NEW - HISTORY - 20TH CENTURY.
Driscoll, Bárbara A. El programa de braceros ferroviarios /. Tijuana, Baja California , 1985. 45 p. ; ISBN 968-607-501-1 LC Card 86-188661
HD8039.R432 U62 1985

ALIEN LABOR, MEXICAN - UNITED STATES.
Cockcroft, James D. Outlaws in the promised land . New York , 1986. 306 p. ; ISBN 0-394-54592-3 : LC Card 84-73206 DDC 331.6/2/72073 19
HD8081.M6 C63 1986
NYPL [JLE 86-2776]

Conover, Ted. Coyotes . New York , 1987. xix, 264 p. : ISBN 0-394-75518-9 (pbk.) : LC Card 87-6101 DDC 331.6/2/72073 19
HD8081.M6 C65 1987

ALIEN LABOR, MEXICAN - UNITED STATES - FORECASTING.
Cockcroft, James D. Outlaws in the promised land . New York , 1986. 306 p. ; ISBN 0-394-54592-3 : LC Card 84-73206 DDC 331.6/2/72073 19
HD8081.M6 C63 1986
NYPL [JLE 86-2776]

ALIEN LABOR, MOROCCAN - NETHERLANDS.
Niessen, Jan. Emancipatie in internationaal perspectief . Amsterdam , 1987. 282 p. ; ISBN 90-6256-460-7 : LC Card 87-158046
HD8518.5.M6 N54 1987

ALIEN LABOR, MOROCCAN - NETHERLANDS - SOCIAL CONDITIONS.
Bel Ghazi, Hassan. Van soek naar arbeidsmarkt . [Bussum] , 1986. 176 p. ; ISBN 90-293-0638-6 : LC Card 86-234591
HD8518.5.M6 B45 1986

ALIEN LABOR, MOROCCAN - NETHERLANDS - STATISTICS.
De Leefsituatie van Turken en Marokkanen in Nederland 1984 /. 's-Gravenhage , 1985-<1987. v. <1-3 > : ISBN 90-357-0457-6 : LC Card 86-234067
HD8518.5.T87 L44 1985

ALIEN LABOR - NETHERLANDS - SOCIAL CONDITIONS.
Aalberts, Monique M. J. Gezinsvorming door jonge migranten . 's-Gravenhage , 1985. 93 p. : ISBN 90-12-04999-7 LC Card 85-235621
HD8518.5.A2 A24 1985

Bel Ghazi, Hassan. Mythen . Amsterdam [1985] 111 p. ; ISBN 90-6617-024-7 LC Card 86-145232
HD8518.5.A2 B44 1985

ALIEN LABOR - NEW JERSEY - HISTORY - SOURCES.
Wright, Giles R. Work /. Trenton , c1987. 82 p. : ISBN 0-89743-072-7 (pbk.) LC Card 87-1573 DDC 331.6/2/09749 19
HD8083.N4 W75 1987

ALIEN LABOR, NEW ZEALAND - AUSTRALIA.
St. Hill, R. L. Labour mobility between New Zealand and Australia /. Canterbury, N.Z. [1986] ix, 68 p. : LC Card 87-109510 DDC 331.12/791 19
HD8848.5.N45 S7 1986

ALIEN LABOR, PHILIPPINE - KOREA (SOUTH) - HANDBOOKS, MANUALS, ETC.
Pinoy overseas handbook . [Manila, Philippines] , 1982. 88 p. : LC Card 83-207976
HD8656 .P56 1982

ALIEN LABOR, PHILIPPINE - NEAR EAST - HANDBOOKS, MANUALS, ETC.
Pinoy overseas handbook . [Manila, Philippines] , 1982. 88 p. : LC Card 83-207976
HD8656 .P56 1982

ALIEN LABOR, POLISH - GERMANY (WEST) - WILHELMSBURG (HAMBURG) - HISTORY - 20TH CENTURY.
Hauschildt, Elke. Polnische Arbeitsmigranten in Wilhelmsburg bei Hamburg während des Kaiserreichs und der Weimarer Republik /. Dortmund , c1986. xv, 330 p. : ISBN 3-923293-17-8 LC Card 87-127027 DDC 331.6/2/438043515 19
HD8458.P65 H38 1986

ALIEN LABOR, POLYNESIAN - AUSTRALIA - QUEENSLAND - HISTORY.
Gray, William, Rev. The kanaka, or, How the Queensland planters get and treat their-- /. Adelaide , 1895. 40 p. ; LC Card 87-123897 DDC 331.6/2/960943 19
HD8848.5.P75 G73 1895

ALIEN LABOR, PORTUGUESE - EUROPEAN ECONOMIC COMMUNITY COUNTRIES.
Ferreira, Eduardo de Sousa, 1936- Reintegração dos emigrantes portugueses . [Lisbon] , 1984. xiv, 137 p. ; LC Card 86-132652
HD8380.5 .F47 1984

ALIEN LABOR - RED SEA REGION.
Pennisi, Giuseppe. Development, manpower and migration in the Red Sea region . Hamburg , c1981. xi, 264 p. : LC Card 82-109615 DDC 331.6/2/091824 19
HD8656 .P46 1981 NYPL [JLF 86-1602]

ALIEN LABOR - RESEARCH - GERMANY (WEST) - HISTORY.
Korte, Hermann, 1937- Migration und ihre sozialen Folgen . Göttingen , c1983. 170 p. ; ISBN 3-525-85366-1 LC Card 84-150019
HD8458.A2 K65 1983

ALIEN LABOR - RHODE ISLAND - CENTRAL FALLS - HISTORY.
Lamphere, Louise. From working daughters to working mothers . Ithaca , 1987. xviii, 390 p. : ISBN 0-8014-9441-9 (pbk. : alk. paper) LC Card 86-32952 DDC 331.4/09745/1 19
HD6096.R4 L36 1987

ALIEN LABOR - SCOTLAND.
Way of life . London [1980?] 84 p. ; ISBN 0-86226-076-0 (pbk.) LC Card 82-218547 DDC 304.8 19
HD9571.7.S36 W39 1980 *NYPL [JLD 85-427]*

ALIEN LABOR, SPANISH.
Azcárate, Blanca, 1954- Ursachen, Umfang und Auswirkungen der Abwanderung im ländlichen Bereich Galiciens am Beispiel der Provinz Orense /. Frankfurt am Main , New York , c1985. 213 p. : ISBN 3-8204-8166-4 LC Card 85-190546
HD8589.O74 A92 1985

ALIEN LABOR, SUDANESE - ARAB COUNTRIES.
Abu Gabal, Sayed Ahmed. Migration of Sudanese . [Khartoum] , 1984. 18, [14] p. ; LC Card 86-980176 DDC 331.6/2/6240174927 19
HD8766 .A65 1984

Jalāl al-Dīn, Muḥammad al-'Awaḍ. Some aspects of Sudanese migration to the oil-producing Arab countries, during the 1970's /. [Khartoum] [1985] 52 p. ; LC Card 86-980666 DDC 331.6/2/62409174927 19
HD8766 .J35 1985

ALIEN LABOR, SURINAMESE - NETHERLANDS - STATISTICS.
Beek, P. van. De leefsituatie van Surinamers en Antillianen in Nederland, 1985 /. 's-Gravenhage , 1986- v. <1 > : ISBN 90-357-0558-0 : LC Card 87-120083
HD8518.5.S87 B44 1986

ALIEN LABOR, SWISS - BRAZIL - SÃO PAULO (STATE) - HISTORY - 19TH CENTURY.
Ziegler, Béatrice. Schweizer statt Sklaven . Stuttgart , c1985. 466 p., [16] p. of plates : ISBN 3-515-04174-5 : LC Card 85-133062 DDC 331.6/2/49408161 19
HD8289.S283 Z54 1985 *NYPL [JLE 87-1222]*

ALIEN LABOR - SWITZERLAND.
Fabrikbesichtigungen /. Zürich , c1986. 206 p. : ISBN 3-85791-109-3 LC Card 87-129952 DDC 305.5/62/09494 19
HD8606.5 .F33 1986

ALIEN LABOR - SWITZERLAND - CONGRESSES.
Arbeiterwanderungen, Ausländerbeschäftigung und Ausländerpolitik in kapitalistischen Ländern Europas im 20. Jahrhundert. Rostock , 1981-1982. 4 v. ; LC Card 82-193086 DDC 331.6/2/094 19
HD8438.A2 A75 1982 *NYPL [JLK 84-95]*

ALIEN LABOR, TURKISH - EUROPE.
Turkish workers in Europe . [Bloomington, Ind. (143 Goodbody Hall, Indiana University, Bloomington 47405) , c1985. 191 p. : LC Card 85-71750 DDC 331.6/2/56104 19
HD8378.5.T8 T87 1985 *NYPL [JLE 86-2980]*

ALIEN LABOR, TURKISH - GERMANY, WEST.
Arnold-Rösner, Regina. Berufliche Integration junger Türken . Hamburg , 1986. 122 p. : ISBN 3-925408-05-3 LC Card 86-223625
HD8458.T9 A76 1986

Rosen, Rita. --Muss kommen, aber nix von Herzen . Opladen , 1986. 262 p. : ISBN 3-8100-0572-X LC Card 87-112784
HD6149 .R67 1986

Turkish workers in Europe . [Bloomington, Ind. (143 Goodbody Hall, Indiana University, Bloomington 47405) , c1985. 191 p. : LC Card 85-71750 DDC 331.6/2/56104 19
HD8378.5.T8 T87 1985 *NYPL [JLE 86-2980]*

ALIEN LABOR, TURKISH - GERMANY (WEST) - CROSS-CULTURAL STUDIES.
Mihçiyazgan, Ursula. Wir haben uns vergessen . Hamburg , c1986. 428 p. ; ISBN 3-923002-30-0 : LC Card 87-104026
HD8458.T9 M54 1986

ALIEN LABOR, TURKISH - GERMANY (WEST) - DUISBURG.
Ölçen, Ali Nejat. Türken und Rückkehr . Frankfurt a.M. , 1986. 132 p. ; ISBN 3-924320-51-9 LC Card 87-138316 DDC 331.6/2/56104355 19
HD8458.T9 O43 1986

ALIEN LABOR, TURKISH - NETHERLANDS - STATISTICS.
De Leefsituatie van Turken en Marokkanen in Nederland 1984 /. 's-Gravenhage , 1985-<1987. v. <1-3 > : ISBN 90-357-0457-6 : LC Card 86-234067
HD8518.5.T87 L44 1985

ALIEN LABOR - UNITED STATES.
Bailey, Thomas Raymond. Immigrant and native workers . Boulder , 1987. xvi, 168 p. : ISBN 0-8133-7349-2 : LC Card 86-28205 DDC 331.6/2/0973 19
HD8081.A5 B35 1987

Rosenblum, Gerald. Immigrant workers; their impact on American labor radicalism. New York [1973] vi, 189 p. ISBN 0-465-03207-9 LC Card 72-89280
HD8081.A5 R67 *NYPL [JLE 73-3033]*

ALIEN LABOR - UNITED STATES - HISTORY.
Lane, A. T. Solidarity or survival? . New York , 1987. xii, 230 p. ; ISBN 0-313-25544-X (lib. bdg. : alk. paper) LC Card 86-25735 DDC 331.6/2/0973 19
HD8081.A5 L36 1987

ALIEN LABOR - UNITED STATES - HISTORY - 19TH CENTURY.
Labor migration in the Atlantic economies . Westport, Conn. , 1985. xvi, 491 p. : ISBN 0-313-24637-8 (lib. bdg. : alk. paper) LC Card 85-7975 DDC 331.12/7 19
HD8375 .L33 1985 *NYPL [JLE 86-1127]*

ALIEN LABOR, WEST INDIAN - GREAT BRITAIN - HISTORY - 20TH CENTURY.
Sherwood, Marika. Many struggles . London , 1985, c1984. 138 p. : ISBN 0-946918-00-7 (pbk.) LC Card 86-110617 DDC 305.8/00941 19
HD8398.B55 S54 1985 *NYPL [Sc D 86-815]*

ALIEN LABOR, YUGOSLAV - GERMANY, WEST.
Künne, Wilfried. Die Aussenwanderung jugoslawischer Arbeitskräfte . Königstein/Ts. , 1979. xii, 269 p. : ISBN 3-7756-6931-0 : LC Card 79-394439
HD8633.5 .K83 *NYPL [JLD 87-1148]*

ALIEN WORKERS. see **ALIEN LABOR.**

ALIENATION, SOCIAL. see **ALIENATION (SOCIAL PSYCHOLOGY)**

ALIENATION (SOCIAL PSYCHOLOGY) - FRANCE.
Neff, Werner, 1947- Entfremdung und Selbstverwaltung . Zürich , c1983. 322 p. : ISBN 3-85791-066-6 LC Card 87-672017
HD5660.F7 N43x 1983

ALIENS, ILLEGAL - CALIFORNIA.
Calderón R., Cedric. Contrabando humano en las Californias /. [S.l. , 1978] (Guatemala : Propsa) 160 p. ; LC Card 86-218852 DDC 331.6/2/720794 19
HD8083.C2 C23 1978

ALIENS, ILLEGAL - EMPLOYMENT - UNITED STATES.

ALIENS, ILLEGAL - EUROPE.
Miller, Mark J. Employer sanctions in Western Europe /. Staten Island, N.Y. , 1987. viii, 67 p. ; ISBN 0-934733-20-1 (pbk.) : LC Card 86-31739 DDC 331.6/2/094 19
HD8378.5.A2 M5395 1987

ALIENS, ILLEGAL - FLORIDA.
The Hands that feed us . Washington, D.C. , c1986. iii leaves, 150, 2 p., [3] leaves of plates : ISBN 0-86566-039-5 (pbk.) : LC Card 87-154337 DDC 331.5/44/09759 19
HD1527.F6 H36 1986

ALIENS, ILLEGAL - UNITED STATES.
Conover, Ted. Coyotes . New York , 1987. xix, 264 p. : ISBN 0-394-75518-9 (pbk.) : LC Card 87-6101 DDC 331.6/2/72073 19
HD8081.M6 C65 1987

ALIENS - ITALY - ECONOMIC CONDITIONS.
Hornziel, Ijola Maria. La condizione degli immigrati stranieri in Italia . Milano, Italy , c1986. 166 p. : LC Card 86-181215
HD8488.A2 H67 1986

ALIENS - ITALY - SOCIAL CONDITIONS.
Hornziel, Ijola Maria. La condizione degli immigrati stranieri in Italia . Milano, Italy , c1986. 166 p. : LC Card 86-181215
HD8488.A2 H67 1986

Aliev, Geĭdar Alievich. Vsi͡u organizatorskui͡u i politicheskui͡u rabotu--na vypolnenie reshenii͡ XXVI s"ezda KPSS : doklad na plenume T͡SK Kompartii Azerbaĭdzhana 15 maia͡ 1981 goda : postanovlenie plenuma T͡SK Kompartii Azerbaĭdzhana / G.A. Aliev. Baku : Azerbaĭdzhanskoe gos. izd-vo, 1981. 50 p. ; 20 cm. Title in colophon: Bütün tăshkilatchylyg ishini vă siĭasi ishi Sov. IKP XXVI gurultaĭy gărarlarynyn ĭerină ĭetirilmăsină ĭonăltmăli. LC Card 82-158175
1. Azerbaijan S.S.R. - Economic policy. 2. Azărbaĭjan Kommunist Partiĭasy - Party work. I. Title. II. Title: Bütün tăshkilatchylyg ishini vă siĭasi ishi Sov. IKP XXVI gurultaĭy gărarlarynyn ĭerină ĭetirilmăsină ĭonăltmăli.
HC337.A9 A683 1981

Aligarh Muslim University. Centre of Advanced Study in History. Gupta, Satya Prakash, 1940- The agrarian system of eastern Rajasthan, c. 1650-c. 1750 /. Delhi , 1986. xvi, 352 p. : ISBN 81-85054-11-8 : LC Card 87-900814 DDC 338.1/0954/4 19
HD2075.R27 G86 1986

Alile, H. I. The Nigerian stock market in operation / Hayford I. Alile, Richard A. Anao. [Lagos, Nigeria : s.n.], 1986 (Lagos, Nigeria : Jeromelaiho & Associates) 194, v p. : ill. ; 26 cm. "1st published 1986 for the Nigerian Stock Exchange"--T.p. verso. Includes bibliographies. LC Card 87-143647 DDC 332.64/2669 19
1. Nigerian Stock Exchange. 2. Stock-exchange - Nigeria. 3. Securities - Nigeria. I. Anao, Richard A., 1940-. II. Nigerian Stock Exchange. III. Title. IV. Title: Stock market.
HG5881.N6 A43 1986

Alimentação e agricultura no Brasil . Müller, Geraldo. [São Paulo] , 1984. 64 p. : LC Card 86-132127
HD1872 .M85 1984

ALIMENTATION. see **NUTRITION.**

Alimentos . Portilla, Belfor. México , 1983. 149, [53] p. : ISBN 968-429-384-4 LC Card 84-172348 DDC 338.1/9/1724 19
HD9018.D44 P67 1983 *NYPL [JLD 86-1520]*

ALIPHATIC COMPOUNDS.
Aliphatic solvents market. New York, N.Y. , c1983. viii, 181 leaves : LC Card 87-142189 DDC 381/.45661807 19
HD9660.S733 U525 1983

Aliphatic solvents in the U. S. Aliphatic solvents market. New York, N.Y. , c1983. viii, 181 leaves : LC Card 87-142189 DDC 381/.45661807 19
HD9660.S733 U525 1983

Aliphatic solvents market. New York, N.Y. : Frost & Sullivan, c1983. viii, 181 leaves : ill. ; 29 cm. Spine title: Aliphatic solvents in the U. S. "September 1983." "(#A1148)" LC Card 87-142189 DDC 381/.45661807 19
1. Solvents industry - United States. 2. Aliphatic compounds. 3. Market surveys - United States. I. Frost & Sullivan. II. Title: Aliphatic solvents in the U. S.
HD9660.S733 U525 1983

ALJARAFE (SPAIN) - POPULATION - HISTORY.
Herrera García, Antonio. El Aljarafe durante el antiguo régimen /. Sevilla , 1981. 147 p., [3] leaves of plates : ISBN 84-500-4850-8 LC Card 82-142028 DDC 333.3/0946/86 19
HD779.A39 H47 1981 *NYPL [JLC 86-126]*

Herrera García, Antonio. El Aljarafe sevillano durante el antiguo régimen . [Sevilla] , 1980. 517 p., [9] leaves of plates : ISBN 84-500-4373-5 LC Card 81-173649 DDC 946/.86 19
HD779.A39 H475 1980 *NYPL [JLF 86-928]*

ALJARAFE (SPAIN) - SOCIAL LIFE AND CUSTOMS.

Herrera García, Antonio. El Aljarafe durante el antiguo régimen /. Sevilla , 1981. 147 p., [3] leaves of plates : ISBN 84-500-4850-8 LC Card 82-142028 DDC 333.3/0946/86 19
HD779.A39 H47 1981 ***NYPL [JLC 86-126]***

Herrera García, Antonio. El Aljarafe sevillano durante el antiguo régimen . [Sevilla] , 1980. 517 p., [9] leaves of plates : ISBN 84-500-4373-5 LC Card 81-173649 DDC 946/.86 19
HD779.A39 H475 1980 ***NYPL [JLF 86-928]***

ALKALAI INDUSTRY AND TRADE - EARLY WORKS TO 1800.
Lavoisier, Antoine Laurent, 1743-1794. L'art de fabriquer le salin, et la potasse ... /. A Paris , 1779. [2], viij, 84 p., IV, [1] folded leaves of plates : LC Card 85-666435
HD9660.A42 L38x 1779

ALKALI INDUSTRY AND TRADE - GREAT BRITAIN - HISTORY - 19TH CENTURY.
Lischka, J. R. (Johannes Richard), 1933- Ludwig Mond and the British alkali industry /. New York , 1985. 233 p. ; ISBN 0-8240-6686-3 (alk. paper) : LC Card 84-46006 DDC 338.4/7673725/0924 19
HD9660.A43 G75 1985
NYPL [JSD 86-547]

ALKMAAR (NETHERLANDS) - ECONOMIC CONDITIONS.
Loo, L. Frank van, 1945- Armelui . Bergen (NH) , 1986. 285 p. ; ISBN 90-70805-10-3 : LC Card 86-205672
HC328.A44 L66 1986

ALKMAAR (NETHERLANDS) - SOCIAL CONDITIONS.
Loo, L. Frank van, 1945- Armelui . Bergen (NH) , 1986. 285 p. ; ISBN 90-70805-10-3 : LC Card 86-205672
HC328.A44 L66 1986

Alkohol- og narkotikarådets skriftserie, 0109-8918 .
(6) Thorsen, Thorkil. Alkoholforbrug og trafikulykker . København , 1986. 69 p. : ISBN 87-88225-38-3 LC Card 86-209934
HE5620.D7 T49 1986

Alkohol im Betrieb und am Arbeitsplatz : Bestandsaufnahme, Lösungshilfen, Rechtsfragen : ein Leitfaden für die Praxis / Bengelsdorf ... [et al.]. Kiel : Mühlau, c1986. 52 p. : ill. ; 21 cm. (Arbeitsrechtliche Schriftenreihe des Walter G. Mühlau Verlages . Heft 1) ISBN 3-87559-048-1 LC Card 87-409550 DDC 331.2/55 19
1. Alcoholism and employment - Germany (West). I. Bengelsdorf, Peter, 1938-. II. Series.
HF5549.5.A4 A476 1986

Alkoholforbrug og trafikulykker . Thorsen, Thorkil. København , 1986. 69 p. : ISBN 87-88225-38-3 LC Card 86-209934
HE5620.D7 T49 1986

Alkoholtartalmú italok kiskereskedelmi eladási forgalmának alakulása 1960-1984 években / [összeállította a KSH Kereskedelmi és Közlekedési Statisztikai Főosztály Belkereskedelmi Osztálya]. Budapest : Központi Statisztikai Hivatal, 1986. 32 p. : ill. ; 29 cm. Chiefly tables. LC Card 86-199334
1. Alcoholic beverage industry - Hungary - Statistics. I. Hungary. Központi Statisztikai Hivatal. Belkereskedelmi Osztály.
HD9365.H82 A45 1986

Alkotó teamek és alkotó módszerek : tanulmányok a csoportos alkotó munka témaköréből / szerkesztette, Magyari-Beck István. [Budapest] : Marx Károly Közgazdaságtudományi Egyetem Közgazdasági Továbbképző Intézet, 1986. 201 p. ; 20 cm. Includes bibliographies. CONTENTS. - Az alkotó teamre vonatkozó azonos és eltérő nézeteink / Magyari-Beck István -- Az alkotóképesség elmélete és alkalmazhatóságának feltételei / Mezei Árpád -- Teamek a társadalmi alakulatok káoszában / Szabó László -- Kutatóteam vagy értékközösség? / Szántó Tibor -- A team integrációja a szervezeti szociális struktúrába / Jávor István -- Nagyszámú team egyidejű alkalmazásának tapasztalatai / Mányoky István. LC Card 87-138615
1. Work groups. 2. Creative ability in business. 3. Creative ability. I. Magyari-Beck, István.
HD66 .A45 1986

All about multi-level marketing . Cunningham, Jan. Denver, CO (1020 15th St., Suite 41C, Denver 80202) , c1986. 173 p. : LC Card 86-213072 DDC 658.8/4 19
HF5415.126 .C85 1986

All about priority sector advances /. Ramachandra Rao, B. New Delhi , 1984. 350 p. : LC Card 84-901313 DDC 332.7/0954 19
HG3729.I42 R36 1984 ***NYPL [JLD 87-574]***

All about saving /. Krefetz, Gerald. New York , c1987. xvi, 224 p. : ISBN 0-471-83793-8 LC Card 86-28085 DDC 332.024/01 19
HG2491 .K74 1987

ALL AMERICAN AVIATION (FIRM) - HISTORY.
Lewis, W. David (Walter David), 1931- The airway to everywhere . Pittsburgh, PA [1988] p. cm. ISBN 0-8229-3579-1 LC Card 87-25176 DDC 387.7/065/73 19
HE9803.A944 L48 1988

ALL-AMERICAN WILDCATTERS.
Schneider, Stephen W., 1925- The big foul up awards, 1970 through 1986 . Dallas, Tex. , c1986. viii, 119 p. : LC Card 87-128382
HD9561.W53 S36 1986

"All India Seminar on National Drug Policy" (1986 : New Delhi, India) Drug industry and the Indian people : proceedings and papers presented at the "All India Seminar on National Drug Policy" held in New Delhi on 28th and 29th April 1986 / edited by Amit Sen Gupta ; foreword by P.N. Haksar.1st ed. New Delhi : Delhi Science Forum ; Patna : Federation of Medical Representatives Associations of India, 1986. 333 p. : ill. ; 24 cm. Advertising matter included in pagings. Includes bibliographies. LC Card 87-900874 DDC 338.4/76151/0954 19
1. Drug trade - India - Congresses. 2. Pharmaceutical policy - India - Congresses. I. Sen Gupta, Amit. II. Delhi Science Forum. III. Federation of Medical Representatives Association of India. IV. Title.
HD9611.I52 A44 1986

All India Seminar on Renewable Sources of Energy, Allahabad, 20th and 21st October '82 . All India Seminar on Renewable Sources of Energy (1982 : Allahabad, India) Allahabad [1982] 1 v. (various pagings) : LC Card 84-911087 ***NYPL [JSF 86-685]***

All India Seminar on Renewable Sources of Energy (1982 : Allahabad, India) All India Seminar on Renewable Sources of Energy, Allahabad, 20th and 21st October '82 : technical volume / organised by Electrical Engineering Division, Institution of Engineers' (India), Allahabad Sub-Centre. Allahabad : The Seminar, [1982] 1 v. (various pagings) : ill., maps ; 28 cm. Cover title. Advertising matter included in paging. Papers. Includes bibliographical references. LC Card 84-911087
1. Renewable energy sources - Congresses. 2. Renewable energy sources - India - Congresses. 3. Energy policy - India - Congresses. I. Title.
NYPL [JSF 86-685]

All-Industry Research Advisory Council.
Catastrophic losses . Oak Brook, Ill. (1200 Harger Rd., Suite 222, Oak Brook 60521) , c1986. vi, 73 p. : LC Card 87-106114 DDC 368.1/22014/0973 19
HG9979.3 .C38 1986

Surveys on liability insurance for government entities. Oak Brook, Ill. (1200 Harger Rd., Suite 222, Oak Brook 60521) , c1986. vi, 66 p. ; LC Card 87-110891 DDC 368.5 19
HG8207 .S87 1986

All of one company : the VOC in biographical perspective : essays in honour of prof. M.A.P. Meilink-Roelofsz, under the auspices of the Centre for the History of European Expansion, Rijksuniversiteit Leiden. Utrecht : HES Uitg., 1986. 230 p. : ill. ; 22 cm. Includes bibliographies. ISBN 90-6194-036-2 (pbk.) : LC Card 86-203885 DDC 382/.06/01 19
1. Nederlandsche Oost-Indische Compagnie - History. 2. Meilink-Roelofsz, M. A. P. (Marie Antoinette Petronella). I. Meilink-Roelofsz, M. A. P. (Marie Antoinette Petronelle). II. Rijksuniversiteit te Leiden. Werkgroep voor de Geschiedenis van de Europese Expansie.
HF483.E6 A65 1986

All organizations are public . Bozeman, Barry. San Francisco , 1987. xix, 184 p. : ISBN 1-555-42036-2 (alk. paper) LC Card 86-27699 DDC 302.3/5 19
HD58.9 .B69 1987

All-Union Communist Party. see **Kommunisticheskaia partiia Sovetskogo Soiuza.**

All you need is freedom . Katins, Sabine. Berlin [1977] 35 p. : LC Card 86-207107 DDC 968.91/05 19
HC910 .K37 1977

Allaiarova, Vera Stepanovna. Ural i problemy regional'noĭ istoriografii. Sverdlovsk , 1986. 83 p. ; LC Card 87-159699
HC337.R852 U73853 1986

Allaire, Keith D. Stanger, Robert A. How to evaluate real estate partnerships /. Shrewsbury, N.J. , c1986. xvi, 256 p. ; ISBN 0-943570-10-7 LC Card 85-90539 DDC 332.63/247 19
HD1382.55 .S73 1986

Allais, Maurice. Marchés, capital et incertitude . Paris , c1986. 265 p. : ISBN 2-7178-1002-1 : LC Card 86-160930
HB615 .M37 1986

ALLAIS, MAURICE.
Marchés, capital et incertitude . Paris , c1986. 265 p. : ISBN 2-7178-1002-1 : LC Card 86-160930
HB615 .M37 1986

Allakhverdian, D. A. (Derenik Akopovich) Sbalansirovannost' sotsialisticheskoĭ ėkonomiki i finansovo-kreditnyĭ mekhanizm /. Moskva , 1984. 108 p. ; LC Card 85-240300
HG186.S55 S27 1984

Az Állami iparvállalatoknál foglalkoztatottak létszámösszetétele bér- és kereseti viszonyai / [összeállitotta a KSH Iparstatisztikai Főosztály Módszertani és Elemzési Osztálya]. Budapest : Központi Statisztikai Hivatal, 1986. 124 p. ; 29 cm. ISBN 963-02-4488-8 LC Card 86-218968
1. Labor supply - Hungary - Statistics. 2. Wages - Hungary - Statistics. I. Hungary. Központi Statisztikai Hivatal. Iparstatisztikai Főosztály. Módszertani és Elemzési Osztály.
HD5772.5.A6 A57 1986

Az Állami vállalatok szervezete, vezetése, működése és irányítása / [szerkesztette, Szép György, Komáromi Gábor ; szerzők, Bokor János ... et al.]. Budapest : Népszava Lap- és Könyvkiadó, 1985. 262 p. ; 20 cm. "Lezárva: 1985. január 1"--T.p. verso. Includes legislation and bibliographical references. ISBN 963-322-140-4 : LC Card 86-202934
1. Government business enterprises - Hungary. 2. Government business enterprises - Law and legislation - Hungary. I. Szép, György. II. Komáromi, Gábor. III. Bokor, János.
HD4160.5 .A78 1985

Alle origini della borghesia urbana . Monti, Aldino. Bologna , c1985. 469 p. : ISBN 88-15-00833-0 : LC Card 86-110136 DDC 333.3/0945/41 19
HD680.B65 M66 1985 ***NYPL [JLD 87-481]***

Alle origini della fattoria toscana . Epstein, Stephan R., 1960- Firenze , c1986. 315 p. : LC Card 87-104355
HD1470.5.I82 S544 1986

Alle suchen nach Lösungen . Herbst, Erika. Feucht , Stuttgart , c1984. 151 p. ; ISBN 3-7724-0688-2 LC Card 85-146171
HC59 .H395 1984

Allegretti, Enzo V. Understanding and using Symphony / Enzo V. Allegretti. St. Paul, MN : West Pub. Co., c1987. xvii, 226, [31] p., [4] p. of plates : ill. ; 26 cm. (The Microcomputing series) Includes index. ISBN 0-314-34640-6 (pbk.) LC Card 87-4986 DDC 005.36/9 19
1. Symphony (Computer program). 2. Business - Data processing. I. Title. II. Series.
HF5548.4.S95 A45 1987

Allegri, Vincenzo. Credito di scopo e finanziamento bancario delle imprese / Vincenzo Allegri. Milano : Giuffrè, [1984] 166 p. ; 25 cm. (Quaderni di banca, borsa e titoli di credito . 7) Includes bibliographical references and indexes. ISBN 88-14-00299-1 : LC Card 85-187365 DDC 332.7/0945 19
1. Bank loans - Italy. 2. Credit - Italy. 3. Banks and banking - Italy. 4. Credit - Law and legislation - Italy. 5. Banking law - Italy. I. Title. II. Series.
HG1642.I8 A44 1984 ***NYPL [JLE 86-3661]***

Allegro, Jacques. Modern organiseren en menselijker werken /. 's-Gravenhage , 1985.

198 p. : ISBN 90-6095-314-2 : LC Card 85-214437
HF5548.8 .M55 1985

Allehoff, Wolfgang H., 1949- Berufswahl und berufliche Interessen / von Wolfgang H. Allehoff. Göttingen : C.J. Hogrefe, c1985. 177 p. : ill. ; 24 cm. Bibliography: p. 158-171. ISBN 3-8017-0217-0 LC Card 85-235199
1. Vocational interests - Germany, West. 2. Occupational mobility - Germany, West. I. Title.
HF5381.5 .A45 1985

Allen, Beverly A. International Law Symposium (1984 : Cambridge, Cambridgeshire) The United States, transnational business, and the law . New York , c1985. x, 132 p. ; ISBN 0-379-20783-4 LC Card 85-61594 DDC 346/.07 342.67 19
K1004.6 1984 ***NYPL [JLF 86-1046]***

Allen, Brandt R. Rotch, William. The executive's guide to management accounting and control systems /. Houston, Tex. , 1987. ix, 225 p. : ISBN 0-87393-044-4 LC Card 87-163287 DDC 658.1/511 19
HF5635 .R829 1987

Allen, Bruce T. Managerial economics / Bruce T. Allen. New York : Harper & Row, c1988. xix, 647 p. ; 26 cm. Includes indexes. ISBN 0-06-044458-4 LC Card 87-21908 DDC 338.5/024658 19
1. Managerial economics. I. Title.
HD30.22 .A4 1988

Allen, David. Funds flow management : the key to financial control in inflationary conditions / David Allen. London : Heinemann, 1980. x, 84 p. : ill. ; 21 cm. (ICMA management accounting in inflation series) Published in association with the Institute of Cost and Management Accountants. Includes index.
1. Cash management. 2. Cash flow. I. Institute of Cost and Management Accountants. II. Title. III. Series.
NYPL [JLD 86-2760]

Allen, David N. Nurturing advanced technology enterprises : emerging issues in state and local economic development policy / David N. Allen and Victor Levine. New York : Praeger, c1986. xvi, 268 p. ; 25 cm. Includes index. Bibliography: p. 239-262. ISBN 0-275-92136-0 (alk. paper) : LC Card 86-9411 DDC 338.4/762/0009748 19
1. High technology industries - Government policy - Pennsylvania. 2. Industrial promotion - Pennsylvania. 3. Industry and state - Pennsylvania. 4. Pennsylvania - Economic policy. I. Levine, Victor. II. Title.
HC107.P43 H533 1986
NYPL [JLE 86-3609]

Allen, Don C. Baehr, Melany E. Experience and background questionnaire . [Park Ridge, Ill.] (1550 Northwest Highway, Park Ridge 60068) , c1986. 20 p. ; LC Card 87-404268 DDC 658.3/1125 19
HF5381.7 .B327 1986

Allen, Frederick Lewis, 1890-1954. The lords of creation, by Frederick Lewis Allen. New York, London, Harper & Brothers, 1935. xii, 483 p. plates, ports., facsim. 23 cm. "The story of the immense financial and corporate expansion which took place in the United States between the depression of the eighteen-nineties and the crisis of the nineteen-thirties."--Pref. "First edition." Includes index. "Sources and obligations": p. 465-473. LC Card 35-20649 DDC 332.0973
1. Capitalists and financiers - United States. 2. Finance - United States - History. 3. Corporations - United States. 4. Wall Street. I. Title.
HG181 .A57 ***NYPL [JLD 86-1097]***

Allen, Kathleen E. Future perfect . Columbia, S.C. (P.O. Box 6828, Columbia 29260) , c1987. x, 104 p. : LC Card 87-143129 DDC 650.1 19
HF5549.5.C35 F87 1987

Allen, Michael Patrick. The founding fortunes : a new anatomy of the corporate-rich families in America / Michael Patrick Allen.1st ed. New York : Truman Talley Books, c1987. p. cm. Includes bibliographical references and index. LC Card 87-9912 DDC 332/.0973 19
1. Wealth - United States. 2. Millionaires - United States. I. Title.
HC110.W4 A44 1987

Allen, Robert C., 1947- Restraining the economy . Vancouver , c1986. 320 p. ; ISBN 0-919573-60-6 LC Card 87-107157 DDC 338.9711 19
HC117.B8 R475 1986

Allen, Robert E. (Robert Edward), 1946- Contemporary labor relations / Robert E. Allen, Timothy J. Keaveny. 2nd ed. Reading, Mass. : Addison-Wesley Pub. Co., c1988. xi, 724 p. : ill. ; 24 cm. Includes bibliographies and indexes. ISBN 0-201-10083-5 : LC Card 87-24128 DDC 331/.0973 19
1. Industrial relations - United States. 2. Collective bargaining - United States. 3. Labor policy - United States. I. Keaveny, Timothy J. II. Title.
HD8072.5 .A43 1988

Allen, Robert G. The challenge / Robert Allen. New York : Simon and Schuster, c1987. 301 p. ; 24 cm. ISBN 0-671-52618-9 LC Card 87-4317 DDC 650.1 19
1. Success in business - United States. I. Title.
HF5386 .A543 1987

Allen, Robert L. Blake, Robert Rogers, 1918- Spectacular teamwork . New York , c1987. viii, 219 p. : ISBN 0-471-85311-9 LC Card 86-28123 DDC 658.4/036 19
HD66 .B54 1987

Allen, Tim. Sales & distribution guide to Malaysia /. Oxford , New York , 1988. p. cm. ISBN 0-08-034987-0 (U. S.) : LC Card 87-21043 DDC 382/.61/09595 19
HG5750.6.A3 S25 1988

Allen, Warren W. Advanced automated accounting for the microcomputer / Warren W. Allen, Dale H. Klooster. Cincinnati : South-Western Pub. Co., c1988. viii, 200 p. : ill. ; 28 cm. Computer disks containing accompanying software, for Radio Shack, Apple, IBM, and Tandy 1000 microcomputers, available upon request to publisher. ISBN 0-538-02690-0 (pbk.) LC Card 87-61619 DDC 657/.028/55369 19
1. Accounting - Data processing. 2. Microcomputers. I. Klooster, Dale H. II. Title.
HF5679 .A567 1988

Allen, William Robert, 1938- Social forces and the manager . Malabar, Fla. , 1987, c1982. xiv, 502 p. : ISBN 0-89464-225-1 (pbk.) LC Card 87-3259 DDC 658.4/08/0973 19
HD60.5.U5 S635 1987

Allende und der europäische Sozialismus /. Bossle, Lothar. Würzburg [1981?] 146 p. ; ISBN 3-88567-026-7 (pbk.) LC Card 82-149701 DDC 983/.0646/0924 19
HX197.A44 B67 1981 ***NYPL [HIF 86-2151]***

Allenspach, Heinz. Bevorzugter Beamtenstatus, Möglichkeiten und Grenzen einer Reform : Referate, gehalten an einer Arbeitstagung des Redressement national vom 11. September 1986 in Zürich / Heinz Allensprach [i.e. Allenspach], Eric Honegger, Ulrich Ammann. Zürich : Redressement national, [1986] 32 p. ; 23 cm. (Zeitfragen der schweizerischen Wirtschaft und Politik = Etudes d'économie et de politique suisses . Nr. 130) Cover title. LC Card 87-407830 DDC 330.9494 s 331.7/61354494 19
1. Switzerland - Officials and employees. I. Honegger, Eric, 1946-. II. Ammann, Ulrich, 1921-. III. Redressement national (Society : Switzerland). IV. Series: Zeitfragen der schweizerischen Wirtschaft und Politik , Nr. 130. V. Title.
HC395 .Z43 Nr. 130 JN8831

ALLEPPEY (INDIA : DISTRICT) - ECONOMIC CONDITIONS.
Verghese, K. E. Socio-economic change in Kerala /. New Delhi , 1986. x, 211 p. ; ISBN 81-7024-061-1 : LC Card 86-903145 DDC 330.954/83 19
HC437.K645 V47 1986

ALLEPPEY (INDIA : DISTRICT) - SOCIAL CONDITIONS.
Verghese, K. E. Socio-economic change in Kerala /. New Delhi , 1986. x, 211 p. ; ISBN 81-7024-061-1 : LC Card 86-903145 DDC 330.954/83 19
HC437.K645 V47 1986

Allerkamp, Ferdinand. Tilgungsplanung : Analyse und Gestaltung unternehmerischer Definanzierungsentscheidungen / von Ferdinand Allerkamp. Frankfurt am Main : F. Knapp, c1983. xii, 288 p. : ill. ; 25 cm. (Band 26 der Schriftenreihe des Instituts für Kreditwesen der Westfälischen Wilhelms-Universität Münster) Originally presented as the author's thesis (doctoral)--Universität Münster. Bibliography: p. 273-288. ISBN 3-7819-0296-X LC Card 85-239167
1. Liquidation - Decision making. 2. Capital investments - Decision-making. 3. Capital budget - Decision making. I. Series: Schriftenreihe des Instituts für Kreditwesen der Westfälischen Wilhelms-Universität Münster , Bd. 26. II. Title.
HD2747 .A53 1983

Allgemeine und besondere Technologie zur Belehrung und zum Nutzen für alle Stände. Poppe, Johann Heinrich Moritz von, 1776-1854. Ausführliche Volks-Gewerbslehre, oder, Allgemeine und besondere Technologie zur Belehrung und zum Nutzen für alle Stände /. Stuttgart , Wien , 1833- v. <1 > : LC Card 87-409525 DDC 331.7/02/024042 19
HF5382.5.E84 P66 1833

Allgoo, Rajpalsingh. Le mouvement syndical à l'île Maurice / Rajpalsingh Allgoo. 1re éd. Port Louis, Ile Maurice : Artisans and General Workers' Union, 1985. 110 p., [14] leaves of plates : ill. ; 21 cm. LC Card 87-119075
1. Artisans and General Workers' Union (Mauritius) - History. 2. Trade-unions - Mauritius - History. I. Title.
HD8840.3.A5 A7825 1985

ALLIANCE FOR PROGRESS - CONGRESSES.
Mesa Redonda sobre la Carta de Punta del Este (1961 : Universidad Nacional Autónoma de México) Memoria del ciclo de conferencias de Mesa Redonda sobre la Carta de Punta del Este /. México , 1962. 224 p. : LC Card 85-105213
HC125 .M48 1961

Alliance of American Insurers. Regulation of insurance : a position paper / prepared by the Alliance of American Insurers. Chicago, Ill. : The Alliance, 1977. 68 p. ; 23 cm. "Dec. 1, 1977."
1. Insurance law - United States. 2. Insurance - United States - State supervision. I. Title.
NYPL [JLE 86-1584]

The alliance of iron and wheat in the Third French Republic, 1860-1914 . Lebovics, Herman. Baton Rouge , c1988. p. cm. ISBN 0-8071-1350-6 LC Card 87-21386 DDC 338.944 19
HC276 .L354 1988

Alliance politics and economics . Mowery, David C. Cambridge, Mass. , c1987. xi, 194 p. : ISBN 0-88730-213-0 LC Card 86-32178 DDC 338.8/87 19
HD9711.A2 M68 1987

ALLIER RIVER (FRANCE) - NAVIGATION - HISTORY.
Histoire de la navigation sur l'Allier en Bourbonnais /. Clermont-Ferrand [France] , 1983. 61 p. : LC Card 84-150630
HE668.Z7 A454 1983

Allison, Frances, 1940- James, Simon R. The comprehensibility of taxation . Aldershot, Hants, England , Brookfield, Vt., USA , c1987. xiii, 314 p. : ISBN 0-566-05348-9 : LC Card 86-25690 DDC 336.2/00941 19
HJ2619 .J36 1987

Allison, John Robert, 1948- Howell, Rate A. The legal environment of business /. Chicago , c1987. xiv, 783 p. : ISBN 0-03-008369-9 LC Card 86-4503 DDC 346.73/07 347.3067 19
KF1600 .H68 1987 ***NYPL [JLE 87-911]***

The allocation of bank credit and the efficiency of investment /. Nowak, Felicitas. Göttingen, Rep. Fed. de Alemania [1986] 23 p. : LC Card 87-121215 DDC 332.7/0724 19
HG1641 .N68 1986

Allocation of state spending by county : FY 1985-86. Lansing, MI (P.O. Box 30036, Lansing 48909) : State Fiscal Agency, [1986] 124 p. : ill. ; 28 cm. Cover title. "September 1986." LC Card 87-620967 DDC 336.3/9/09774 19
1. Michigan - Appropriations and expenditures - Statistics. I. Michigan. Legislature. Senate. Fiscal Agency.
HJ2053.M5 A554 1986

All'origine della borghesia lecchese . Sala, Edmondo. Lecco [1983] 83 p. : LC Card 85-190056
HD9765.I72 L437 1983

Allstate Insurance Group. Corporate Communications Division. Insurance handbook for reporters /. Northbrook, Ill. , 1985. 304 p. ; LC Card 87-110782 DDC 368/.002/02 19
HG8061 .I57 1985

Allvine, Fred C. Marketing principles and practices / Fred C. Allvine. San Diego :

Harcourt Brace Jovanovich, c1987. xxix, 829, 38 p. : ill. (some col.) ; 25 cm. Includes bibliographies and indexes. ISBN 0-15-555101-9 LC Card 85-82622 DDC 658.8 19
1. Marketing. I. Title.
HF5415 .A436 1987

Ally versus ally . Blinken, Antony J. New York , 1987. ix, 193 p. : ISBN 0-275-92410-6 (alk. paper) : LC Card 86-25222 DDC 388.5 19
HD9581.S652 B58 1987

ALM on micros : asset/liability management on microcomputers : a selection of articles published during 1983-86 / edited by Jera L. Thompson. York, PA (P.O. Box 1508, York 17405) : Microbanker, c1986. 86 p. : ill. ; 28 cm. LC Card 87-108676 DDC 332.1/028/5416 19
1. Asset-liability management (Banking) - Data processing. I. Thompson, Jera L.
HG1615.25 .A46 1986

The almanac of American employers . Plunkett, Jack W. Chicago , 1985. 340 p. ; ISBN 0-8092-5407-7 LC Card 85-14908 DDC 331.2/0973 19
HF5549.5.C67 P58 1985
NYPL [*R-Econ. 85-3166]

Almási, István. Négy évtizede új úton a magyar mezőgazdaság / Almási István. [Budapest] : Hungexpo, [1985] 159 p. : col. ill. ; 21 cm. ISBN 963-7252-41-X LC Card 86-228893
1. Agriculture - Economic aspects - Hungary. 2. Agriculture - Hungary. I. Title. II. Title: 4 évtizede új úton a magyar mezőgazdaság.
HD1940.5 .A85 1985

Almásy, György. Postai szakkifejezések ötnyelvű szótára . Budapest , 1978. 349 p. ; LC Card 84-248004
HE6035 .P67 1978

Almdal, Preben. Aspects of European integration : a view of the European Community and the Nordic countries / Preben Almdal. Odense C, Denmark : Odense University Press, 1986. 108 p. ; 22 cm. Includes bibliographies. ISBN 87-7492-578-4 : LC Card 87-114176 DDC 337.1/42 19
1. European Economic Community. 2. Europe - Economic integration. 3. Scandinavia - Economic integration. 4. Scandinavian cooperation. I. Title.
HC241.2 .A7344 1986

Almeida, Edimilson Machado de, 1937-
Tecnologia e racionalização da agropecuária, com o aproveitamento das bacias hidrográficas / Edimilson Machado de Almeida. Aracaju : Associação dos Diplomados da Escola Superior de Guerra, Delegacia de Alagôas e Sergipe, [1971] 100 leaves : ill. ; 22 cm. Cover title: Tecnologia e racionalização da agro-pecuária, com o apoveitamento [i.e. aproveitamento] das bacias hidrográficas sergipanas. "1o. ciclo de estudos sôbre segurança nacional e desenvolvimento"--Cover. List of author's works: leaves 8-9. Bibliography: leaves 99-100. LC Card 85-203218
1. Agricultural innovations - Economic aspects - Brazil - Sergipe. 2. Watersheds - Economic aspects - Brazil - Sergipe. I. Title. II. Title: Tecnologia e racionalização da agro-pecuária, com o aproveitamento das bacias hidrográficas sergipanas.
HD1875.S4 A65 1971

Almeida, João António R. Simões de.
Financiamento do desenvolvimento económico : o II Plano de fomento / João António R. Simões de Almeida. Lisboa : Gabinete de Investigações Económicas do Instituto Superior de Ciências Económicas e Financeiras, 1961. 60 p. ; 26 cm. LC Card 85-220891
1. Portugal - Economic policy. I. Title.
HC392 .A466 1961

Almeida, João Carreira. Fabricação de materiais de barro para construção : elementos para a definição de uma política de financiamento das produções de telha e tijolo cerâmicos e de materiais concorrentes / João Carreira Almeida. Lisboa : Banco de Fomento Nacional, 1978. 186 p., [3] leaves of plates (one folded) : ill. (some col.) ; 24 cm. (Estudos . 13) Bibliography: p. 185. LC Card 82-112167 DDC 338.4/36914/09469 19
1. Clay industries - Portugal - Finance. 2. Building materials industry - Portugal - Finance. 3. Building fittings industry - Portugal - Finance. I. Banco de Fomento Nacional. II. Series: Estudos (Banco de Fomento Nacional) , 13. III. Title.
HD9596.P82 A85 1978

Almeida, João Ferreira de. Classes sociais nos campos : camponeses parciais numa região do Noroeste / João Ferreira de Almeida. Lisboa : Instituto de Ciências Sociais da Universidade de Lisboa, [1986] 544 p. : ill. ; 22 cm. (Colecção Teses e teorias . 2) Bibliography: p. [529]-544. LC Card 87-400121 DDC 305.5/63 19
1. Peasantry - Portugal. 2. Farm tenancy - Portugal. 3. Métayer system - Portugal. 4. Portugal - Rural conditions. I. Title. II. Series.
HD1536.P77 A44 1986

Almeida Magalhães, João Paulo de. see **Magalhães, João Paulo de Almeida.**

Almeida, Pedro Fernando de. A indústria gaúcha de bens de capital na dinâmica da economia brasileira : avanços e constrangimentos / Pedro Fernando de Almeida, Roberto Silveira Marcantonio, Rubens Soares de Lima. Porto Alegre, RS : Secretaria de Coordenação e Planejamento, Fundação de Economia e Estatística, 1986. 257 p. ; 23 cm. "Convênio: FEE/CODESUL-Conselho de Desenvolvimento do Extremo Sul." Bibliography: p. [219]-221. LC Card 87-403616 DDC 338.4/76218/0981 19
1. Industrial equipment industry - Brazil - Rio Grande do Sul. 2. Brazil - Economic conditions - 1918-. I. Marcantonio, Roberto Silveira. II. Lima, Rubens Soares de. III. Title.
HD9705.B73 R562 1986

ALMOND INDUSTRY - UNITED STATES.
Noga, George. The outlook for almonds, 1986 /. Altamonte Springs, FL (1180 Spring Centre S. Blvd., Altamonte Springs 32714) [c1986] 36 p. : LC Card 86-220553 DDC 338.1/7455/0973 19
HD9259.A47 U56 1986

ALMS AND ALMSGIVING. see **CHARITY.**

Aloi, Felice. Il budget con il personal computer : con un'esemplificazione completa elaborata con Olivetti M 24 / Felice Aloi. Milano, Italy : F. Angeli, c1984. 226 p. : ill. ; 22 cm. (Azienda moderna. 181) Includes bibliographical references. LC Card 84-250395 DDC 658.1/54/02854165 19
1. Budget in business - Data processing. 2. Olivetti M-24 (Computer) - Programming. I. Title.
HG4028.B8 A46 1984

Alonso, José Antonio.
Efectos de la adhesión de España a la CEE sobre las exportaciones de Iberoamérica / José A. Alonso, Vicente Donoso. Madrid : Ediciones Cultura Hispánica del Instituto de Cooperación Iberoaméricana, 1983. 316 p. : ill. ; 24 cm. Bibliography: p. 305-310. ISBN 84-7232-299-8 LC Card 87-116624
1. Spain - Commerce - Latin America. 2. Latin America - Commerce - Spain. 3. European Economic Community - Spain. I. Donoso, Vicente. II. Title.
HF3688.L3 A45 1983

La empresa exportadora española frente a Iberoamérica y la CEE / José Antonio Alonso, Vicente Donoso. Madrid : Ediciones Cultura Hispánica del Instituto de Cooperación Iberoamericana, 1985. xiii, 263 p. ; 24 cm. Bibliography: p. 193-199. ISBN 84-7232-380-3 LC Card 86-199177
1. Export marketing - Spain. 2. Spain - Commerce - Latin America. 3. Latin America - Commerce - Spain. 4. Spain - Commerce - European Economic Community countries. 5. European Economic Community countries - Commerce - Spain. I. Donoso, Vicente. II. Title.
HF3688.L3 A46 1985 ***NYPL [JLE 87-56]***

Alonso, José Antonio Fialho. Areas estatísticamente comparáveis do Rio Grande do Sul, 1940-80 . Porto Alegre, RS , 1986. 186 p. : LC Card 87-403481 DDC 339.381/65 19
HC188.R4 A73 1986

Alonso, Marcelo. The Nuclear connection . New York , 1985. 295 p. : ISBN 0-88702-204-9 : LC Card 84-26786 DDC 333.79/24 19
HD9698.A2 N77 1985 ***NYPL [JLE 86-1546]***

Alpert, Stanley L. Lindsell, Sheryl L. CPS®--Certified Professional Secretary® examination /. New York, N.Y. , c1987. xxx, 286 p. : ISBN 0-13-122805-6 (pbk.) : LC Card 87-11381 DDC 651.3/741/076 19
HF5547.5 .L554 1987

An Alphabetical guide to Office of Revenue Sharing account numbers / Department of the Treasury, Office of Revenue Sharing. Washington, D.C. : The Office, 1981. iii, 187 p. ; 28 cm. Title from cover.
1. Intergovernmental fiscal relations - United States. 2. Revenue sharing - United States. I. United States. Office of Revenue Sharing. ***NYPL [JLF 87-470]***

Alpine Areas Workshop, May 13-17, 1974 /. Alpine Areas Workshop (1974 : Schloss Laxenburg) Laxenburg [1974] 80 p. : LC Card 82-212849
HC268.O25 A46 1974

Alpine Areas Workshop (1974 : Schloss Laxenburg) Alpine Areas Workshop, May 13-17, 1974 / sponsored by Austrian Man and Biosphere High Mountain Program (MAB 6) and the International Institute for Applied Systems Analysis ; coordinators, H. Franz, C.S. Holling. Laxenburg : International Institute for Applied Systems Analysis, [1974] 80 p. : ill. ; 24 cm. (Conference proceedings / International Institute for Applied Systems Analysis . CP 74-2) LC Card 82-212849
1. Obergurgl (Austria) - Economic conditions - Mathematical models. 2. Land use - Environmental aspects - Austria - Obergurgl - Mathematical models. 3. Alpine regions - Mathematical models. 4. Human ecology - Austria - Obergurgl - Mathematical models. I. Franz, Herbert, 1908-. II. Holling, C. S. III. Österreichisches MaB-Hochgebirgsprogramm. IV. International Institute for Applied Systems Analysis. V. Series: Conference proceedings / International Institute for Applied Systems Analysis , CP 74-2. VI. Title.
HC268.O25 A46 1974

Alpine Historical Society (Sutton, Alaska) Bauer, Mary Cracraft. A history of coal-mining in the Sutton-Chickaloon area prior to WW II /. [Anchorage, Alaska] [1985] ii, 47 leaves : LC Card 86-620606 DDC 338.2/724/097983 19
HD9548.S87 B38 1985

ALPINE REGIONS - ECONOMIC ASPECTS.
Festschrift für Univ.-Prof. Dr. Georg Zwanowetz anlässlich der Vollendung des 65. Lebensjahres /. [Innsbruck] , c1984. 332 p. : LC Card 84-183487
HC244 .F48 1984

ALPINE REGIONS - MATHEMATICAL MODELS.
Alpine Areas Workshop (1974 : Schloss Laxenburg) Alpine Areas Workshop, May 13-17, 1974 /. Laxenburg [1974] 80 p. : LC Card 82-212849
HC268.O25 A46 1974

Alptraum Auto . Bode, Peter M. München , 1986. 237 p. : ISBN 3-922696-46-5 LC Card 87-107197 DDC 303.4/832 19
HE5613 .B63 1986

ALPUJARRAS REGION (SPAIN) - POPULATION.
Luna, Paco. Demografía de la Alpujarra . [Granada] [1984] 301 p., [3] leaves of plates : ISBN 84-338-0205-4 LC Card 85-221373
HB3620.A45 L85 1984

Alreck, Pamela L. Settle, Robert B. Why they buy . New York , c1986. xvi, 351 p. ; ISBN 0-471-84457-8 : LC Card 86-13303 DDC 658.8/343/0973 19
HC110.C6 S48 1986 ***NYPL [JLE 86-4432]***

Alred, Gerald J. Brusaw, Charles T. The business writer's handbook /. New York , c1987. xxviii, 764 p. : ISBN 0-312-00571-7 : LC Card 87-4361 DDC 651.7/5 19
HF5726 .B874 1987

Als deutscher Kaufmann in Fernost . Barth, Johannes, 1891- Berlin , c1984. 206 p. : ISBN 3-503-02366-6 LC Card 84-143117
HC289.B7 B373 1984

ALSANDS PROJECT.
Eglington, Peter. An economic analysis of oilsands policy in Canada . Ottawa, Ont. [1984] 1 v. (various pagings) : LC Card 84-213823 DDC 333.8/232 19
HD9574.C23 W654 1984

Alschuler, Lawrence R., 1941- Multinationals and maldevelopment : alternative development strategies in Argentina, the Ivory Coast, and Korea / Lawrence R. Alschuler. New York : St. Martin's, 1988. xii, 218 p. : ill. ; 23 cm. Bibliography: p. 201-208. Includes index. ISBN 0-312-00531-8 : LC Card 87-4307 DDC 338.9 19
1. Economic development - Case studies. 2. International business enterprises - Case studies. 3. Argentina - Economic policy. 4. Ivory Coast - Economic policy. 5. Korea (South) - Economic policy -

1960-. I. Title.
HD82 .A5493 1988

Alsop, Ronald. The Wall Street journal on marketing / Ronald Alsop, Bill Abrams. New York : New American Library, 1987, c1986. p. cm. "A Plume book." LC Card 87-11248 DDC 658.8 19
1. Marketing. I. Abrams, Bill. II. Title.
HF5415 .A45 1987

Alston, Julian M. Sumner, Daniel A. (Daniel Alan), 1950- Removal of price supports and supply controls for U. S. tobacco . Demoines, Iowa , Washington, D.C. , c1985. viii, 64 p. ; ISBN 0-89068-084-1 LC Card 85-63194
NYPL [JLF 86-1014]

Alston, Vetoria S. Langford, Jay. Economic trends in metropolitan Washington, 1980-1985 ; [author, Jay Langford, Vetoria S. Alston]. Washington, D.C. (1875 Eye St., NW., Suite 200, Washington 20006) , c1986. viii, 68 p. : LC Card 87-105032 DDC 330.9753/04 19
HC108.W3 L36 1986

Altenburg, Lutz, 1943- Zur Einbeziehung öffentlicher Zwischenprodukte in Mehrsektorenmodelle / Lutz Altenburg. Frankfurt am Main ; New York : P. Lang, c1985. 315 p. : ill. ; 21 cm. (Europäische Hochschulschriften. Reihe V, Volks- und Betriebswirtschaft, 0531-7339 . Bd. 647 = vol. 647 = vol. 647) Originally presented as the author's thesis (doctoral--Georg-August-Universität Göttingen, 1984) Bibliography: p. 311-316. ISBN 3-8204-9046-9 LC Card 85-231430 DDC 338.4/3363/0724 19
1. Public goods - Mathematical models. 2. Expenditures, Public - Mathematical models. I. Series: Europäische Hochschulschriften. Reihe V, Volks- und Betriebswirtschaft , Bd. 647. II. Title.
HB846.5 .A47 1985

ALTENKIRCHEN/WESTERWALD (GERMANY : LANDKREIS) - ECONOMIC CONDITIONS.
Spilker, Ernst Moritz. Der Wirtschaftsraum zwischen den Wirtschaftsräumen . Köln , 1986. 223 p. : LC Card 87-408201 DDC 330.943/55 19
HC288.W46 S67 1986

Alter Kapitalismus, "neue Armut" /. Grasnick, Georg, 1927- Berlin , 1985. 78 p. : LC Card 86-132510 DDC 330.12/2 19
HB501 .G64 1985

Alternate Resource Center (Davao City, Philippines) Socio economic factbook of Mindanao. Davao City, Philippines [1985] 568 p. ; LC Card 85-234433
HA4617.M56 S63 1985

La alternativa de la izquierda . Malpica Silva Santisteban, Carlos. [Lima, Peru] [1985] 91 p. : LC Card 87-403544 DDC 338.985 19
HJ2090 .M35 1985

Alternativa ferro-hidro-rodoviária para o transporte de derivados claros de petróleo para o abastecimento das regiões oeste do Estado do Paraná e sul do Estado de Mato Grosso do Sul / Serviço Público Federal, Ministério dos Transportes, Superintendência Nacional da Marinha Mercante. [Rio de Janeiro] : MT, Superintendência Nacional da Marinha Mercante, Diretoria de Navegação Interior, Divisão de Navegação Fluvial e Lacustre, Seção de Desenvolvimento, 1984. 41 leaves : ill., maps ; 30 cm. LC Card 87-403934 DDC 380.5/24 19
1. Petroleum products - Brazil - Paraná (State) - Transportation. 2. Petroleum products - Brazil - Matto Grosso do Sul - Transportation. I. Brazil. Superintendência Nacional da Marinha Mercante.
HE199.5.P4 A48 1984

Alternativa rodo-ferro-hidroviária para o abastecimento de gás liquefeito de petróleo-GLP às regiões oeste do Estado de Mato Grosso e leste do Estado de Rondônia / Serviço Público Federal, Ministerio dos Transportes, Superintendência Nacional da Marinha Mercante. [Rio de Janeiro] : M.T., Superintendência Nacional da Marinha Mercante, Diretoria de Navegação Interior, Divisão de Navegação Fluvial e Lacustre, Seção de Desenvolvimento, [19]84. 41 leaves : ill. ; 30 cm. LC Card 87-403939 DDC 338.4/7665773 19
1. Liquefied petroleum gas - Transportation. 2. Liquefied petroleum gas industry - Brazil - Mato Grosso (State). 3. Liquefied petroleum gas industry - Brazil - Rondônia (State). I. Brazil. Superintendência Nacional da Marinha Mercante. II. Brazil. Divisão de Navegação Fluvial e Lacustre. Seção de Desenvolvimento.
HE199.5.L43 A44 1984

Alternativa rodo-ferro-hidroviária para o abastecimento de gás liquefeito de petróleo-GLP às regiões oeste do Estado de Mato Grosso e leste do Estado de Rondônia /. Brazil. Superintendência Nacional da Marinha Mercante. [Rio de Janeiro] [1984] 41 leaves : LC Card 85-197972
HE199.5.L43 B73 1984

Alternativa rodo-hidro-ferroviária para o transporte de parte da safra de soja paraguaia destinada à exportação. [Rio de Janeiro] : MT, Superintendência Nacional da Marinha Mercante, Diretoria de Navegação Interior, Divisão de Navegação Fluvial e Lacustre, Seção de Desenvolvimento, [19]84. 65 leaves : ill. ; 30 cm. LC Card 85-187436
1. Soybean - Brazil - Transportation. 2. Transportation and state - Brazil. 3. Soybean industry - Paraguay. 4. Brazil - Commerce - Paraguay. 5. Paraguay - Commerce - Brazil. I. Brazil. Divisão de Navegação Fluvial e Lacustre. Seção de Desenvolvimento.
HE199.5.S66 A47 1984

Alternativas para el desarrollo /. Solís M., Leopoldo. México, D.F. , 1985, c1980. 155 p. ; ISBN 968-270-487-1 LC Card 86-222497
HC135 .S636 1985

Alternative Betriebe . Voigt-Weber, Lore. Frankfurt am Main , c1984. 154 p. ; ISBN 3-88129-811-8 LC Card 85-139278
HD2326 .V65 1984

Alternative energy sources and technology. IASTED Symposia on Modelling, Policy and Economics of Energy and Power Systems, and Alternative Energy Sources and Technology (1981 : San Francisco, Calif.) Proceedings of the IASTED Energy Symposia : Modelling, Policy and Economics of Energy and Power Systems [and] Alternative Energy Sources and Technology, May 20-22, 1981, San Francisco, U. S.A. /. Anaheim, Calif. [1981?] 209 p. : ISBN 0-88986-027-0 ***NYPL [JSF 86-1103]***

Alternative environmental conflict management approaches : a citizens' manual / edited by Patricia Bidol, Lisa Bardwell, Nancy Manring. [Ann Arbor, MI] (Dana Bldg., Ann Arbor 48109-1115) : Environmental Conflict Project, School of Natural Resources, University of Michigan, [1986] 252 p. : ill. ; 28 cm. Includes bibliographies. LC Card 86-225219 DDC 363.7/058/0973 19
1. Environmental policy - United States - Citizen participation. 2. Conflict management - United States. I. Bidol, Patricia A. II. Bardwell, Lisa. III. Manring, Nancy. IV. University of Michigan. Environmental Conflict Project.
HC110.E5 A643 1986

Alternative estimates of union-nonunion and public-private wage differentials in Ontario, 1981 /. Abbott, Michael G. Kingston, Ont., Canada [1986] ii, 61 p. ; LC Card 87-146006 DDC 331.2/2/09713 19
HD4980.O5 A64 1986

Alternative estimates of union-nonunion and public-private wage differentials in Ontario, 1981 /. Abbott, Michael G. Kingston, Ont., Canada , 1987. ii, 47 p. ; ISBN 0-88886-166-4 (pbk.) LC Card 87-170767 DDC 331.2/2/09713 19
HD4980.O5 A64 1987

Alternative export strategies and U. S. agricultural policies for grains and oilseeds, 1950-83 /. Grigsby, S. Elaine. [Washington, D.C.] , 1986. v., 37 p. : LC Card 86-602816 DDC 382/.4131/0973 19
HD9036 .G83 1986

Alternative export strategies and US agricultural policies for grains and oilseeds, 1950-83. Grigsby, S. Elaine. Alternative export strategies and U. S. agricultural policies for grains and oilseeds, 1950-83 /. [Washington, D.C.] , 1986. v., 37 p. : LC Card 86-602816 DDC 382/.4131/0973 19
HD9036 .G83 1986

Alternative Hafen- und Küstenkonferenz (1985 : Hamburg, Germany) Alternative Hafen- und Küstenpolitik /. Hamburg , 1985. 260 p. : ISBN 3-88876-034-8 LC Card 87-133678 DDC 387.1/094 19
HE557.G3 A55 1985

Alternative Hafen- und Küstenpolitik / Herausgeber, GAL Hamburg ... [et al.]. 2. Aufl. (überarbeitet). Hamburg : P. Riekmann : Bestellungen an Förderverein Umweltschutz Unterelbe, 1985. 260 p. : ill. ; 21 cm. "Dieses Buch entstand im Zusammenhang mit der Alternativen Hafen- und Küstenkonferenz (Internationales Forum der Grünen) veranstaltet am 4./5. Mai 1985 in Hamburg"--P. 1. Includes bibliographies. ISBN 3-88876-034-8 LC Card 87-133678 DDC 387.1/094 19
1. Harbors - Germany, West. 2. Harbors - Europe. 3. Harbors - Developing countries. 4. Coastal zone management - Germany (West). 5. Coastal zone management - Europe. 6. Coastal zone management - Developing countries. I. Grün-Alternative Liste (Political party). Hamburg. II. Alternative Hafen- und Küstenkonferenz (1985 : Hamburg, Germany).
HE557.G3 A55 1985

Alternative investments /. Epstein, Rachel S. New York , c1988. 47 p. : ISBN 1-555-46633-8 LC Card 87-21766 DDC 332.6/78 19
HG4521 .E685 1988

Alternative Konzepte .
(48) Mehr Technik, weniger Arbeit? . Karlsruhe , c1984. 228 p. : ISBN 3-7880-9697-7 LC Card 85-108996
HD6331 .M384 1984

Alternative Ökonomie? / Anton Rauscher (Hrsg.). Köln : J.P. Bachem, 1982. 244 p. ; 19 cm. (Mönchengladbacher Gespräche . 4) Papers and summary of the discussions of a meeting sponsored by Katholische Sozialwissenschaftliche Zentralstelle, May 13-15, 1982, in Mönchengladbach. Includes bibliographical references. CONTENTS. - Die alternative Bewegung / Ortwin Renn -- Plädoyer für eine alternative Wirtschaftsordnung / Rudolf Hickel -- Ökonomie der "Alternativen"--eine Alternative? / Christian Watrin -- Die Sozialethik vor den Herausforderungen heute--was kann sie, was kann sie nicht leisten? / Rudolf Henning -- Alternative Ökonomie : Anmerkungen eines Wirtschaftspolitikers / Anton Jaumann -- Wachstum oder Konsumaskese? : aus der Sicht der Sozialanthropologie / Wilhelm Korff -- Wachstum oder Konsumaskese? : alternative Ökonomie aus der Sicht der Wirtschaftspsychologie / Burkhard Strümpel -- Aus der Diskussion / Josef Oelinger. ISBN 3-7616-0671-0 (pbk.) LC Card 84-109717 DDC 338.9 19
1. Economic development - Social aspects - Congresses. 2. Economic development - Moral and ethical aspects - Congresses. 3. Economic development - Environmental aspects - Congresses. I. Rauscher, Anton. II. Katholische Sozialwissenschaftliche Zentralstelle, Mönchen-Gladbach, Ger. III. Series.
HD88 .A48 1982 ***NYPL [JLC 86-230]***

Alternative policies for America.
Dirt rich, dirt poor . New York , 1986. xii, 188 p. ; ISBN 0-7102-0378-0 LC Card 85-8274 DDC 338.1/9/73 19
HD1761 .D55 1986 ***NYPL [JLD 87-821]***

Alternative systems of business organization and of worker's remuneration /. Meade, James Edward, 1907- London , Boston , 1986. x, 144 p. : ISBN 0-04-331112-1 (alk. paper) LC Card 85-26734 DDC 330/.1 19
HB238 .M4 1986 ***NYPL [JLD 86-2943]***

Alternative Wirtschaftspolitik .
(4) Staatsgrenzen . Berlin , c1982. 183 p. ; ISBN 3-88619-089-7 LC Card 84-142799
HB90 .S75 1982

Alternativen der Arbeitsgestaltung und ihre Bewertung . Schmied, Volker. Wiesbaden , c1982. 423 p. : ISBN 3-409-38642-4 LC Card 83-187066
HD6955 .S345 1982

Alternatives for the 1980's .
(no. 19) Dealing with farm sector debt . Washington, D.C. (317 Massachusetts Ave., N.E., Washington 20002) , c1986. 47 p. : LC Card 86-71068 DDC 332.7/1/0973 19
HD1440.U6 D4 1986

Alternatives to arbitration / edited by Richard Blandy, and John Niland. Sydney ; Boston : Allen & Unwin, 1986. x, 468 p. ; 22 cm. "Industrial Relations Research Centre; National Institute of Labour Studies." Bibliography: p. 431-452. Includes index. ISBN 0-86861-857-8 (pbk.) LC Card 85-81482 DDC 331/.0994 19
1. Arbitration, Industrial - Australia. 2. Industrial

relations - Australia. 3. Arbitration, Industrial. 4. Industrial relations. I. Blandy, Richard, 1938-. II. Niland, John R.
HD5630.A6 A47 1986

Alternatives to economic orthodoxy : a reader in political economy / edited by Randy Albelda, Christopher Gunn, and William Waller. Armonk, N.Y. : M.E. Sharpe, c1987. 348 p. : ill. ; 24 cm. Includes bibliographies. ISBN 0-87332-409-9 : LC Card 86-33899 DDC 330 19
1. Economics. I. Albelda, Randy Pearl. II. Gunn, Christopher Eaton. III. Waller, William, 1956-.
HB171 .A47 1987

Alternatives to unemployment and underemployment . Hopkins, Mike. Boulder , 1985. xiv, 129 p. : ISBN 0-8133-0200-5 (pbk.) LC Card 85-45007 DDC 331.13/79861 19
HD5757.A6 H67 1985 *NYPL [JLD 86-2149]*

Alternativní strategie rozvoje rozvojových zemí /. Kuře, Miroslav. Praha , 1986. 94 p. ; LC Card 86-227984
HC59.7 .K866 1986

Altersvorsorge, Kapitalschwemme oder Kapitalmangel? . Oberhänsli, Urs. Bern , c1986. xii, 222 p. : ISBN 3-258-03578-4 : LC Card 86-149614
HD7105.35.S9 O24 1986

Altieri, Giovanna. La Vertenza sul costo del lavoro e le relazioni industriali /. Milano, Italy , c1984. 243 p. : LC Card 84-144150 DDC 338.5/1/0945 19
HD5034 .V47 1984 *NYPL [JLD 86-2858]*

Altman, Richard M. Creating investor demand for company stock : a guide for financial managers / Richard M. Altman. New York : Quorum Books, c1988. p. cm. Bibliography: p. Includes index. ISBN 0-89930-173-8 (lib. bdg. : alk. paper) LC Card 86-25566 DDC 332.6/42 19
1. Stocks - Marketing. 2. Going public (Securities). 3. Corporations - Investor relations. I. Title.
HG4661 .A57 1988

Altmann, Franz-Lothar.
Tschechoslowakei 1984/85 : aussenwirtschaftliche Anpassungsprobleme bei zufriedenstellendem gesamtwirtschaftlichem Wachstum / von Franz-Lothar Altmann. München : Osteuropa-Institut München, 1985. 31 leaves ; 30 cm. (Arbeiten aus dem Osteuropa-Institut München . Nr. 105 =) Includes bibliographical references. LC Card 85-179408
1. Czechoslovakia - Economic conditions - 1945-. 2. Czechoslovakia - Economic policy - 1965-. 3. Czechoslovakia - Commerce. 4. Czechoslovakia - Industries. I. Series: Arbeiten aus dem Osteuropa-Institut München , Nr. 105. II. Title.
HC270.28 .A415 1985

Die tschechoslowakische Volkswirtschaft und der Rat für gegenseitige Wirtschaftshilfe (RGW) / Franz-Lothar Altmann. München : Osteuropa-Institut München, [1986] 31 leaves ; 29 cm. (Arbeiten aus dem Osteuropa-Institut München . Nr. 115 (Feb. 1986) =) Bibliography: leaf 31. LC Card 86-203484
1. Czechoslovakia - Commerce - Europe, Eastern. 2. Europe, Eastern - Commerce - Czechoslovakia. 3. Council for Mutual Economic Assistance. I. Series: Arbeiten aus dem Osteuropa-Institut München , Nr. 115. II. Title.
HF3550.3.Z7 E8523 1986

Altongy, Janine. Richards, Eugene. Below the line . Mount Vernon, N.Y. , c1987. 218 p. : ISBN 0-89043-062-4 LC Card 86-70834 DDC 305.5/69/0973 19
HC110.P6 R52 1987

L'Altra metà dell'economia : la ricerca internazionale sull'economia informale / a cura di Arnaldo Bagnasco.1a ed. italiana. Napoli : Liguori, 1986. 345 p. : ill. ; 22 cm. (Studi sulla modernizzazione e lo sviluppo . 2) Biblioteca Includes bibliographies. ISBN 88-20-71420-5 : LC Card 86-214178
1. Informal sector (Economics) - Case studies. I. Series.
HD2341 .A68 1986

Altrichter, Helmut, 1945- Die Bauern von Tver : vom Leben auf dem russischen Dorfe zwischen Revolution und Kollektivierung / von Helmut Altrichter. München : Oldenbourg, 1984. 373 p. : ill. ; 22 cm. The author's Habilitationsschrift--Universität Erlangen-Nürnberg. Bibliography: p. 351-369. Includes index. ISBN 3-486-52071-7 LC Card 84-162284
1. Peasantry - Russian S.F.S.R. - Kalinin Region - History - 20th century. 2. Kalinin Region (R.S.F.R.) - Rural conditions. 3. Soviet Union - History - 1917-1936. 4. Collectivization of agriculture - Russian S.F.S.R. - Kalinin Region - History - 20th century. 5. Villages - Russian S.F.S.R. - Kalinin Region - History - 20th century. I. Title.
HD1536.S65 A47 1984

ALTRUISM.
Garczyński, Stefan. O dawaniu /. Warszawa , 1985. 172 p. ; ISBN 83-10-08676-8
*NYPL [*QO 87-1235]*

ALTRUISM - ECONOMIC ASPECTS.
Kolm, Serge Christophe. La bonne économie . Paris , 1984. 472 p. : ISBN 2-13-038695-4 : LC Card 84-254896 DDC 330 19
HB173 .K64 1984

Altschuler, David M.
New York nonprofit organizations : the challenge of retrenchment / David M. Altschuler, Lester M. Salamon, Carol J. De Vita. Washington, D.C. (2100 M St., N.W., Washington 20037) : Urban Institute, c1987. vii, 43 p. : ill. ; 28 cm. (An Urban Institute research report) "Prepared under the Urban Institute Nonprofit Sector Project." Includes bibliographical references. LC Card 87-159600 DDC 658.1/5 19
1. Corporations, Nonprofit - New York (State) - Finance. 2. Social service - New York (State) - Finance. 3. New York (State) - Appropriations and expenditures. 4. Fiscal policy - New York (State). I. Salamon, Lester M. II. De Vita, Carol J. III. Nonprofit Sector Project (Urban Institute). IV. Title. V. Series.
HD2769.2.U6 A48 1987

Salamon, Lester M. San Francisco Bay Area nonprofit organizations . Washington, D.C. (2100 M St., N.W., Washington 20037) , c1987. vi, 26 p. : LC Card 87-403000 DDC 338.7/4/0979461 19
HJ9205.S3 S34 1987

Altvater, Elmar.
Arbeit 2000 . Hamburg , 1985. 236 p. : ISBN 3-87975-314-8 LC Card 86-143070
HD4813 .A68 1985

Staatsgrenzen . Berlin , c1982. 183 p. ; ISBN 3-88619-089-7 LC Card 84-142799
HB90 .S75 1982

Altvater, Elmer. Tre incognite per lo sviluppo . Milano, Italy , c1986. 383 p. : LC Card 86-198933
HC310.I53 T74 1986

Aluminio primário no Brasil . Machado, R. C. (Raimundo de Campos), 1913- [Ouro Preto, Brasil] 1983. 216 p. : LC Card 84-256552
HD9539.A3 B66 1983

Aluminiumipari Tervező és Kutató Intézet (Budapest, Hungary) A Világ aluminiumipara . Budapest , 1985. 2 v. : LC Card 86-157446
HD9539.A62 V54 1985

ALUMINUM COMPANY OF AMERICA - HISTORY.
Lamur, Carlo. The American takeover . Dordrecht, Holland , Cinnaminson, N.J., U. S.A. , 1985. vi, 209 p., [6] p. of plates : ISBN 90-6765-078-1 (pbk.) : LC Card 86-181373 DDC 338.8/87 19
HD9539.A63 G886 1985

ALUMINUM COMPANY OF CANADA, LTD.
Shahabuddeen, M., 1931- Nationalisation of Guyana's bauxite . Georgetown, Guyana , 1981. xvii, 306 p. ; LC Card 82-145233 DDC 338.2/74926 19
HD9539.A63 G888 1981 *NYPL [Sc E 86-189]*

ALUMINUM HYDROXIDE.
Infrastructural survey report for the development of the alumina resources in Rennell Island, Solomon Islands. [S.l.] [1976] xv, 321 p. : LC Card 84-230135
HC684.Z7 R455 1976

ALUMINUM INDUSTRY AND STATE - UNITED STATES.
Aluminum mill products . Washington, D.C. [1986] xvi, 111 p. : LC Card 86-602432 DDC 382/.45673722/0973 19
HD9539.A63 U5126 1986

ALUMINUM INDUSTRY AND TRADE.
Aluminum mill products . Washington, D.C. [1986] xvi, 111 p. : LC Card 86-602432 DDC 382/.45673722/0973 19
HD9539.A63 U5126 1986

Holloway, Steven Kendall, 1951- The aluminum multinationals and the bauxite cartel /. New York , 1988. vii, 93 p. : ISBN 0-312-00939-9 : LC Card 87-12991 DDC 338.8/87 19
HD9539.A62 H64 1988

A Világ aluminiumipara . Budapest , 1985. 2 v. : LC Card 86-157446
HD9539.A62 V54 1985

ALUMINUM INDUSTRY AND TRADE - AFRICA - CONGRESSES.
Regional Workshop on the Role and Prospects of Copper and Aluminium in African Development (1985 : Lusaka, Zambia) Final report /. [Addis Ababa] , 1985. 9 p. ; LC Card 86-980966 DDC 338.2/743/096 19
HD9539.C7 A427 1985

ALUMINUM INDUSTRY AND TRADE - BRAZIL - COLLECTED WORKS.
Machado, R. C. (Raimundo de Campos), 1913- Aluminio primário no Brasil . [Ouro Preto, Brasil] 1983. 216 p. : LC Card 84-256552
HD9539.A3 B66 1983

ALUMINUM INDUSTRY AND TRADE - DIRECTORIES.
A Világ aluminiumipara . Budapest , 1985. 2 v. : LC Card 86-157446
HD9539.A62 V54 1985

ALUMINUM INDUSTRY AND TRADE - GHANA.
Essays from the Ghana-Valco renegotiations, 1982-85 /. [Accra, Ghana] 1986 (Accra : Printed by the Ghana Pub. Corp.) viii, 163 p. ; ISBN 996-490-120-8 (pbk.) LC Card 87-127499 DDC 338.8/87 19
HD9539.A63 G44 1986

ALUMINUM INDUSTRY AND TRADE - GOVERNMENT OWNERSHIP - GUYANA.
Shahabuddeen, M., 1931- Nationalisation of Guyana's bauxite . Georgetown, Guyana , 1981. xvii, 306 p. ; LC Card 82-145233 DDC 338.2/74926 19
HD9539.A63 G888 1981 *NYPL [Sc E 86-189]*

ALUMINUM INDUSTRY AND TRADE - GUYANA - HISTORY.
Lamur, Carlo. The American takeover . Dordrecht, Holland , Cinnaminson, N.J., U. S.A. , 1985. vi, 209 p., [6] p. of plates : ISBN 90-6765-078-1 (pbk.) : LC Card 86-181373 DDC 338.8/87 19
HD9539.A63 G886 1985

ALUMINUM INDUSTRY AND TRADE - GUYANA - MACKENZIE - EMPLOYEES.
Quamina, Odida T. Mineworkers of Guyana . London , Atlantic Highlands, N.J., USA , 1987. xv, 118 p., [7] p. of plates : ISBN 0-86232-308-8 : LC Card 87-14719 DDC 305/.9622/098814 19
HD8039.A492 G9558 1987

ALUMINUM INDUSTRY AND TRADE - HUNGARY - HISTORY.
Szűcs, Lajos. A Magyaróvári Timföld és Műkorundgyár története, 1934-1984. [Mosonmagyaróvár , 1984] 320 p. : ISBN 963-02-3415-7 LC Card 86-127345
HD9539.A63 H858 1984

ALUMINUM INDUSTRY AND TRADE - INDIA - FINANCE.
Agarwal, N. P. (Narain Prashad) Analysis of financial statements /. New Delhi , 1981. xii, 363 p. : LC Card 81-904955 DDC 657/.33 19
HD9539.A63 I522 1981 *NYPL [JLD 86-2568]*

ALUMINUM INDUSTRY AND TRADE - SURINAM - HISTORY.
Lamur, Carlo. The American takeover . Dordrecht, Holland , Cinnaminson, N.J., U. S.A. , 1985. vi, 209 p., [6] p. of plates : ISBN 90-6765-078-1 (pbk.) : LC Card 86-181373 DDC 338.8/87 19
HD9539.A63 G886 1985

ALUMINUM INDUSTRY AND TRADE - YUGOSLAVIA.
Yugoslav aluminum and aluminium products =.

Beograd , 1986. 83 p. : LC Card 87-108615
HD9539.A63 Y89 1986

Aluminum mill products : import problem/export potential / prepared by the Nonferrous Metals Division, Office of Metals, Minerals and Commodities, Basic Industries Sector. Washington, D.C. : U. S. Dept. of Commerce, International Trade Administration : For sale by the Supt. of Docs., U. S. G.P.O., [1986] xvi, 111 p. : ill. ; 28 cm. Shipping list no.: 86-685-P. "July 1986." Includes bibliographical references. S/N 003-009-00482-9 Item 231-B-1 LC Card 86-602432 DDC 382/.45673722/0973 19
1. Aluminum industry and state - United States. 2. Aluminum industry and trade. I. United States. International Trade Administration. Nonferrous Metals Division.
HD9539.A63 U5126 1986

ALUMINUM MINES AND MINING - GUYANA - MACKENZIE.
Quamina, Odida T. Mineworkers of Guyana . London , Atlantic Highlands, N.J., USA , 1987. xv, 118 p., [7] p. of plates : ISBN 0-86232-308-8 : LC Card 87-14719 DDC 305/.9622/098814 19
HD8039.A492 G9558 1987

The aluminum multinationals and the bauxite cartel /. Holloway, Steven Kendall, 1951- New York , 1988. vii, 93 p. : ISBN 0-312-00939-9 : LC Card 87-12991 DDC 338.8/87 19
HD9539.A62 H64 1988

Alva Castro, Luis. Deuda o desarrollo : hacia la emancipación de América Latina / Luis Alva Castro. Lima, Perú : Editorial Etcetera, 1987. 127 p. : ports. ; 21 cm. CONTENTS. - Introducción -- Deuda o desarrollo -- Estancamiento y descapitalización en América Latina -- El peso de la deuda -- Ajuste o reform del sistema monetario internacional -- El camino peruano -- La capacidad de pago, un enfoque alternativo. LC Card 87-403115 DDC 336.3/4/0985 19
1. Debts, External - Peru. 2. Peru - Economic policy. I. Title.
HJ8604 .A75 1987

Alvarado Corrales, Eduardo J. Extremadura : la necesidad de una reforma agraria / autores, Eduardo J. Alvarado Corrales, José Luis Gurría Gascón, Manuel Rodríguez Cancho. Cáceres : Servicio de Publicaciones de la Universidad de Extremadura, [1984?] 101 p. : ill. ; 19 cm. (Biblioteca de bolsillo) Includes bibliographical references. ISBN 84-600-3663-4 LC Card 86-165503
1. Land reform - Spain - Estremadura. 2. Land tenure - Spain - Estremadura. I. Gurría Gascón, José Luis. II. Rodríguez Cancho, Manuel. III. Series: Biblioteca de bolsillo (Cáceres, Spain). IV. Title.
HD1333.S712 E783 1984

Alvarado Gómez, Armando. Principales productos del comercio exterior mexicano del siglo XIX / Armando Alvarado Gómez, Inés Herrera Canales. 1a ed. México, D.F. : Dirección de Estudios Históricos, Instituto Nacional de Antropología e Historia, 1985. v. <1 > ; 28 cm. (Cuaderno de trabajo . 47) Recopilación de estadísticas económicas del siglo XIX en México ; v. 1 Chiefly tables. Bibliography: p. 10-11. LC Card 87-401206 DDC 382/.0972 19
1. Mexico - Commmerce - History - History - 19th century. 2. Commercial products - Mexico - History - 19th century. I. Herrera Canales, Inés. II. Series: Cuaderno de trabajo (Instituto Nacional de Antropología e Historia (Mexico). Dirección de Estudios Históricos) , 47. III. Title.
HF3236 .A5 1985

Alvarado, Ivonne. Estaba, Rosa M. Geografía de los paisajes urbanos e industriales de Venezuela /. Caracas , c1985. 291 p., [4] folded leaves : ISBN 980-271-006-7 LC Card 86-148810 DDC 307.7/6/0987 19
HC237 .E766 1985 ***NYPL [JLD 86-2340]***

Alvarado U., Hernán (Alvarado Ugarte) Crisis económica mundial, 1974-1975 : (rasgos generales) / Hernán Alvarado Ugarte. Heredia, Costa Rica : Departamento de Publicaciones, Universidad Nacional, 1980. 62 p. ; 21 cm. At head of title: Universidad Nacional "Campus Omar Dengo," Facultad de Ciencias Sociales, Unidad Coordinadora de Investigación y Documentación. Bibliography: p. 53-55. LC Card 87-402100 DDC 330.9/047 19
1. Economic history - 1971-. I. Title.
HC59 .A765 1980

Álvares, Pedro. Portugal na CEE : a indústria, a agricultura, a pesca, os trabalhadores, os investimentos, os fundos, o presente e o futuro / Pedro Alvares ; edição realizada com a colaboração da Secretaria de Estado da Integração Europeia e do Banco Português de Investimento. [Lisbon] : Publicações Europa-América, 1986. 543 p. ; 21 cm. (Estudos e documentos. 222) Includes bibliographical references. LC Card 87-403268 DDC 341.24/22 19
1. European Economic Community - Portugal. I. Portugal. Secretaria de Estado da Integração Europeia. II. Banco Português de Investimento. III. Title.
HC241.25.P6 A48 1986

Alvarez España, Waldo. Memorias del primer ministro obrero : historia del movimiento sindical y político boliviano, 1916-1952 / Waldo Alvarez España.1a ed. La Paz, Bolivia : s.n., 1986. 300 p., [6] leaves of plates : ill. ; 22 cm. LC Card 87-403477 DDC 331.88/0984 19
1. Alvarez España, Waldo. 2. Trade-unions - Bolivia - Officials and employees - Biography. 3. Trade-unions - Bolivia - History. 4. Labor policy - Bolivia - History. I. Title.
HD6608.5.A55 A3 1986

ALVAREZ ESPAÑA, WALDO.
Alvarez España, Waldo. Memorias del primer ministro obrero . La Paz, Bolivia , 1986. 300 p., [6] leaves of plates : LC Card 87-403477 DDC 331.88/0984 19
HD6608.5.A55 A3 1986

Alvarez Noguera, José Rogelio. Diversos documentos y datos relativos al proyectado ferrocarril de Chamela a Aguascalientes /. Guadalajara, México , 1982. 24, iii, 98 p. : LC Card 86-115748 DDC 385/.0972 19
HE2818 .D58 1982

Alvarez Valdés, Ariel. Breve historia del pensamiento administrativo / Ariel Alvarez Valdés. [Santiago del Estero, Argentina] : Universidad Nacional de Santiago del Estero, Facultad de Humanidades, [1985] 129 p. : ill., ports. ; 22 cm. Bibliography: p. 123-125. LC Card 86-180293
1. Management - History. I. Title.
HD30.5 .A44 1985

Alvarez Vázquez, J. A. (José Antonio) Los diezmos en Zamora (1500-1840) / José Antonio Alvarez Vázquez. Salamanca, España : Ediciones Universidad de Salamanca ; [Zamora] : Colegio Universitario de Zamora, 1984. ii, 318 p. ; 24 cm. (Universidad de Salamanca, Colegio Universitario . 3) Includes bibliographical references. ISBN 84-7481-296-8 LC Card 85-123559
1. Tithes - Spain - Zamora (Province) - History - Statistics. I. Series: Universidad de Salamanca, Colegio Universitario de Zamora (Series) , 3. II. Title.
HJ2287.S74 A58 1984

Alvarez Vázquez, Luisa. La fecundidad en Cuba / Luisa Alvarez Vázquez. La Habana : Editorial de Ciencias Sociales, 1985. ix, 182 p. : ill. ; 21 cm. (Demografía / Editorial de Ciencias Sociales) "Esta edición ha sido tomado de La tendencia de la fecundidad en Cuba, Instituto de Desarrollo de la Salud, Ministerio de Salud Pública, La Habana, 1982"--Verso t.p. Includes bibliographical references. LC Card 87-401045 DDC 304.6/32/097291 19
1. Fertility, Human - Cuba. I. Series: Demografía / Editorial de Ciencias Sociales. II. Title.
HB959 .A44 1985

Alvarez, Waldo. see **Alvarez España, Waldo.**

ALVAREZ Y MENDIZÁBAL, JUAN, 1790?-1853.
Rueda Hernanz, Germán. La desamortización de Mendizábal y Espartero en España /. Madrid , c1986. 200 p. ; ISBN 84-376-0592-X LC Card 86-216590
HD774 .R84 1986

Alves, Denise. O desencontro marcado : a velha-mulher-nova e o machão-moderno / Denise Alves. Petrópolis : Vozes, 1985. 169 p. ; 21 cm. Originally presented as the author's thesis (mestrado)--Universidade de Brasília, 1983. Bibliography: p. 165-169. LC Card 85-226159
1. Sex role. 2. Interpersonal communication. I. Title.
HQ1075 .A44 1985 ***NYPL [JFD 86-7232]***

Alves, Isabel. Sousa, Fernando Freire de. A adesão de Portugal à CEE . [Porto] [1985] 96 p. ; LC Card 86-174408
HF2236 .S68 1985

Alvesson, Mats, 1956-
Consensus, control, and critique : three paradigms of work organization research / Mats Alvesson. Aldershot, Hants, England ; Brookfield, Vt., USA : Avebury, c1987. viii, 162 p. : ill. ; 23 cm. Bibliography: p. 151-162. ISBN 0-566-05285-7 : LC Card 87-8427 DDC 306/.36 19
1. Industrial sociology. 2. Industrial organization. 3. Work design. 4. Work groups. 5. Paradigms (Social sciences). I. Title.
HD6955 .A442 1987

[Organisationsteori och teknokratiskt medvetande. English]
Organization theory and technocratic consciousness : rationality, ideology, and quality of work / Mats Alvesson. Berlin ; New York : W. De Gruyter, 1987. ix, 286 p. : ill. ; 24 cm. (De Gruyter studies in organization . 8) Translation of: Organisationsteori och teknokratiskt medvetande. Bibliography: p. [263]-276. Includes index. ISBN 0-89925-165-X : LC Card 86-24057 DDC 306/.36 19
1. Industrial sociology. 2. Industrial organization. 3. Work - Psychological aspects. 4. Criticism (Philosophy). I. Title. II. Series.
HD6955 .A44313 1987

Alvey, Wendy. Workshop on Exact Matching Methodologies (May 9-10, 1985 : Arlington, Va.) Record linkage techniques--1985 . [Washington, D.C.] , 1985. vii, 397 p. :
NYPL [JLF 86-1723]

Alviar Ramírez, Oscar, d. 1984. Elementos de finanzas públicas en Colombia / Oscar Alviar Ramírez, Fernando Rojas Hurtado. Bogotá, Colombia : Editorial Temis Librería, 1985. xx, 584 p. ; 24 cm. Bibliography: p. [547]-560. Includes indexes. ISBN 958-604-045-3 (pbk.) LC Card 86-129809 DDC 336.861 19
1. Finance, Public - Colombia. I. Rojas H., Fernando. II. Title.
HJ945 .A48 1985

Aly, Götz, 1947- Die restlose Erfassung : Volkszählen, Identifizieren, Aussondern im Nationalsozialismus / Götz Aly, Karl Heinz Roth. Berlin : Rotbuch Verlag, c1984. 157 p. : ill. ; 20 cm. (Rotbuch. 282) Includes bibliographical references. ISBN 3-88022-282-7 : LC Card 84-206488
1. Germany - Statistical services - History - 20th century. 2. Germany - Census, 1939. I. Roth, Karl Heinz. II. Title.
HA37.G3 A49 1984

Alymov, Aleksandr Nikolaevich.
Sbalansirovannost′ narodnokhoz͡iaĭstvennogo razvit͡iia : regional′nye i otraslevye problemy / A.N. Alymov, F.D. Zastavnyĭ, D.K. Preĭger. Kiev : Nauk. dumka, 1986. 221, [3] p. ; 21 cm. (Ėkonomika razvitogo sot͡sializma) On page preceding t.p.: Akademii͡a nauk Ukrainskoĭ SSR. Sovet po izuchenii͡u proizvodstvennykh sil USSR. Bibliography: p. 218-[222] LC Card 86-214583
1. Ukraine - Economic conditions - 1945-. 2. Input-output analysis - Ukraine. I. Zastavnyĭ, F. D. (Fedor Dmitrievich). II. Preĭger, D. K. (Davyd Kasparovich). III. Title. IV. Series.
HC337.U5 A793 1986

A.M. Best Company.
Underwriting-Loss Control Dept. Best's municipal underwriting guide : the public official's guide to local government insurance risks. Oldwick, N.J. (Ambest Rd., Oldwick 08858) , c1986. 1 v. (various pagings) : LC Card 86-230785 DDC 368 19
HG8210 .B47 1986

Am grossen Krieg "vorbeischleichen"? .
Achminow, Herman F., 1921- Bonn , c1983. 304 p. ; ISBN 3-923920-00-8 LC Card 84-150915 DDC 355/.03304 19
UA646 .A38 1983 ***NYPL [JFD 87-1743]***

AMA briefings & surveys.
Close to the customer . New York, N.Y. , c1987. 96 p. ; ISBN 0-8144-3513-0 (pbk.) : LC Card 87-12558 DDC 658.8/12 19
HF5415.5 .C57 1987

The AMA handbook of key management forms / edited by David M. Brownstone, Irene M. Franck. New York, NY : AMACOM, c1987. 732 p. : chiefly forms ; 30 cm. Includes index. "1844-9." ISBN 0-8144-1144-4 LC Card 86-25955 DDC 651/.29 19
1. Management - Forms. I. Brownstone, David M. II.

Franck, Irene M. III. American Management Association.
HD38 .A44 1987

AMA management handbook. 2nd ed. What every manager needs to know about manufacturing /. New York, NY [1987], c1983. 181 p. : ISBN 0-8144-7686-4 (pbk.) LC Card 87-47714 DDC 658 19
HD9720.5 .W38 1987

AMA report on information centers. The 1986 AMA report on information centers . New York, N.Y. , c1986. viii, 92, [28] p. : ISBN 0-8144-3154-2 NYPL [JLF 86-1835]

AMA survey of hiring costs and strategies. Hiring costs and strategies . New York , c1986. v, 82 p. : ISBN 0-8144-3153-4 NYPL [JLF 86-960]

AMA Winter Educators' Conference (1987 : San Antonio, Tex.) 1987 AMA Winter Educators' Conference : marketing theory / edited by Russel W. Belk ... [et al.]. Chicago, Ill. : American Marketing Association, c1987. viii, 411 p. : ill. ; 28 cm. Includes bibliographies and index. ISBN 0-87757-185-6 (pbk.) LC Card 87-944 DDC 658.8/001 19
1. Marketing - Congresses. 2. Marketing research - Congresses. I. Belk, Russell W. II. American Marketing Association. III. Title. IV. Title: Marketing theory. V. Series: Proceedings series - American Marketing Association.
HF5411 .A53 1987

AMACOM briefings & surveys.
Hiring costs and strategies . New York, N.Y. , c1986. v, 82 p. : ISBN 0-8144-3153-4 (pbk.) LC Card 86-209862 DDC 658.4/07111/0973 19
HD38.25.U6 H57 1986

Hiring costs and strategies . New York , c1986. v, 82 p. : ISBN 0-8144-3153-4 NYPL [JLF 86-960]

The 1986 AMA report on information centers . New York, N.Y. , c1986. viii, 92, [28] p. : ISBN 0-8144-3154-2 NYPL [JLF 86-1835]

The 1986 AMA report on information centers . New York, N.Y. , c1986. viii, 92, [28] p. : ISBN 0-8144-3154-2 NYPL [JLF 86-1835]

Amalgamated Engineering Union. Delegation to the U. S.S.R. Report of the Union Delegation to the U. S.S.R. . London [1946?] iii, 40 p. : LC Card 87-100506
HD8526.5 .R46 1946

AMALGAMATION OF CORPORATIONS. see **CONSOLIDATION AND MERGER OF CORPORATIONS.**

Amanshauser, Wilfried.
Jugendarbeitsmarktförderung in Österreich / Wilfried Amanshauser. Wien : Institut für Höhere Studien, [1985] ii, 71, 3 p. ; 30 cm. (Forschungsbericht = Research memorandum . no. 210) Summary in German and English. Bibliography: p. 69-71. LC Card 86-165982
1. Youth - Employment - Austria. 2. Unemployment - Austria. 3. Occupational training - Austria. I. Series: Research memorandum (Institut für Höhere Studien, Wien) , no. 210. II. Title.
HD6276.A9 A43 1985

AMAPÁ (BRAZIL : TERRITORY) - ECONOMIC POLICY.
Platon, Clarck. Amapá, fundamento de minha luta . Brasília , 1983. 155 p. : LC Card 86-127813
HC188.A48 P53 1983

AMAPÁ (BRAZIL : TERRITORY) - POLITICS AND GOVERNMENT.
Platon, Clarck. Amapá, fundamento de minha luta . Brasília , 1983. 155 p. : LC Card 86-127813
HC188.A48 P53 1983

Amapá, fundamento de minha luta . Platon, Clarck. Brasília , 1983. 155 p. : LC Card 86-127813
HC188.A48 P53 1983

Amaro, Antonio Ambrosio. Questão agrária e agroindústria / Antonio Ambrósio Amaro. Brasília, DF : Instituto Tancredo Neves de Estudos Políticos e Sociais, [1986] 13 p. ; 30 cm. (Cadernos liberais . 26/86) Bibliography: p. 13. LC Card 87-403237 DDC 338.1/881 19
1. Agriculture and state - Brazil. 2. Agricultural industries - Brazil. I. Series: Cadernos liberais , 86/26. II. Title.
HD1873 .A49 1986

L'"Amaro della feudalità" . Rao, Anna Maria, 1949- Napoli , c1984. 382 p. ; ISBN 88-7042-265-8 : LC Card 85-200705
HD1333.I82 N367 1984

AMARU IV Cooperative. Evaluating electrification experience . Washington, D.C. , 1982- v. <1 > : LC Card 86-176385 DDC 333.91/4 19
HD9688.D44 E9 1982

Amat, Carlos. see **Amat y León Ch., Carlos.**

Amat y León Ch., Carlos. Agricultura y alimentación . [Lima] , 1982. 536 p. : LC Card 83-174688 DDC 338.1/9/85 19
HD9014.P52 A57 1982 NYPL [JLD 86-268]

Amaya, Luis Esteban. Proyecto Paraná Medio . Buenos Aires , 1985. 44 leaves : LC Card 86-218225
HD8039.F66 A746 1985

Amazing investigations . Drobot, Eve. New York , 1988. p. cm. ISBN 0-13-023714-0 LC Card 87-18661 DDC 332.4/9 19
HG173.8 .D76 1988

The amazing Pennsylvania canals /. Shank, William H. York, Pa. [1986], c1981. 128 p. : ISBN 0-933788-37-1 (pbk.) LC Card 87-400232 DDC 386/.48/09748 19
HE395.P47 S5 1986

AMAZON RIVER REGION - ECONOMIC CONDITIONS.
Miranda Neto, Manoel José de. O dilema da Amazônia /. Belém, Pará [1986] 154 p. ; LC Card 87-119394 DDC 330.981/1063 19
HC188.A5 M57 1986

Penner, Maria Eunice Soares. A dialética da atividade pesqueira no nordeste amazônico /. Belém , 1984. 158 p. : ISBN 85-24-70006-8 LC Card 86-158128
HD9464.B73 N676 1984

AMAZON RIVER REGION - ECONOMIC CONDITIONS - CONGRESSES.
Land, people, and planning in contemporary Amazonia /. [Cambridge, Cambridgeshire] , 1980. xvi, 313 p. : LC Card 87-672189
HC167.A42 L36x 1980

AMAZON RIVER REGION - ECONOMIC POLICY - CONGRESSES.
Land, people, and planning in contemporary Amazonia /. [Cambridge, Cambridgeshire] , 1980. xvi, 313 p. : LC Card 87-672189
HC167.A42 L36x 1980

AMAZON RIVER REGION - POPULATION.
Silva, Maria José Oliveira e. A sociedade amazônica e o problema social da desocupação e subocupação /. Belém , 1974. 42 p., 53 leaves : LC Card 86-183026
HB3564.A73 S55 1974

AMAZON RIVER REGION - POPULATION DENSITY.
Fearnside, Philip M. (Philip Martin) Human carrying capacity of the Brazilian rain-forest /. New York , 1986. xii, 293 p. : ISBN 0-231-06104-8 (alk. paper) LC Card 85-6643 DDC 330.981/1063 19
HC188.A5 F42 1986 NYPL [JLE 86-4554]

AMAZON RIVER REGION - SOCIAL CONDITIONS.
Silva, Maria José Oliveira e. A sociedade amazônica e o problema social da desocupação e subocupação /. Belém , 1974. 42 p., 53 leaves : LC Card 86-183026
HB3564.A73 S55 1974

AMAZONAS (BRAZIL) - POPULATION - STATISTICS.
Projeção da população do Estado do Amazonas e seus municípios /. Manaus, Amazonas , 1984. 37 leaves ; LC Card 87-402133 DDC 304.6/0981/13021 19
HA988.A5 P76 1984

Amazônia Mineração S.A. Report to the World Bank, Amazônia Mineração S.A. . London [1979?] v, 57, [31] leaves : LC Card 85-154695
HD9524.B8 R46 1979

Amazônia--o que fazer? /. Meirelles Filho, João Carlos, 1960- São Paulo , 1986. 85 p., [1] folded leaf of plates : LC Card 86-233275
HC187.5 .M45 1986

Amazônia--o que fazer por ela? Meirelles Filho, João Carlos, 1960- Amazônia--o que fazer? /. São Paulo , 1986. 85 p., [1] folded leaf of plates : LC Card 86-233275
HC187.5 .M45 1986

Ambekar Institute for Labour Studies. Tea plantation workers in the eastern Himalayas . Delhi , 1986. xxxi, 255 p. : ISBN 81-7043-055-0 : LC Card 86-903466
HD8039.T182 I48 1986

Ambirajan, S. Political economy and monetary management : India, 1766-1914 / S. Ambirajan. Madras : Affiliated East-West Press, c1984. viii, 203 p. ; 22 cm. Bibliography: p. [184]-196. Includes index. LC Card 87-900241 DDC 332.4/954 19
1. India - Economic policy. 2. Monetary policy - India - History. I. Title.
HC433 .A42 1984

Amble, Joan Lordi. A guide to implementation of Statement 87 on employer's accounting for pensions : questions and answers / Joan Lordi Amble, Jules M. Cassel. Stamford, Conn. (High Ridge Park, P.O. Box 3821, Stamford 06905-0821) : Financial Accounting Standards Board of the Financial Accounting Foundation, c1986. vii, 106 p. : ill. (some col.) ; 23 cm. (Special report / Financial Accounting Standards Board) Includes bibliographical references and index. LC Card 87-133173 DDC 657/.75
1. Old age pensions - Accounting. I. Cassel, Jules M. II. Financial Accounting Standards Board. III. Series: Special report / Financial Accounting Standards Board. IV. Title.
HF5686.O5 A56 1986

Ambros, Werner. Verbraucherinteressen und Agrarpolitik / Werner Ambros. Krefeld : Marchal und Matzenbacher Wissenschaftsverlag, 1986. x, 260 p. : 7 ill. ; 21 cm. Bibliography: p. 249-260. ISBN 3-88358-068-6 LC Card 87-122729 DDC 338.1/843 19
1. Agriculture and state - Germany, West. 2. Consumer protection - Germany, West. I. Title.
HD1957 .A63 1986

Ambrose, Peter J. Whatever happened to planning? / Peter Ambrose. London ; New York : Methuen, 1986. xiv, 288 p. : ill. ; 23 cm. Includes index. Bibliography: p. [275]-282. ISBN 0-416-37100-0 LC Card 86-12415 DDC 333.73/17/0941 19
1. Land use - Government policy - Great Britain. 2. Real estate development - Government policy - Great Britain. 3. Regional planning - Great Britain. I. Title.
HD596 .A43 1986 NYPL [JLD 87-1402]

Ambrosi, Klaus. Zur Anwendung multivariater Methoden in der Marktforschung / von Klaus Ambrosi. Augsburg : Institut für Statistik und Mathematische Wirtschaftstheorie der Universität Augsburg, 1985. 25 leaves ; 30 cm. (Arbeitspapiere zur mathematischen Wirtschaftsforschung . Heft 77) Bibliography: leaves 20-25. LC Card 87-101945
1. Marketing research. 2. Multivariate analysis. I. Title.
HF5415.2 .A344 1985

Ambrosius, Gerold. Die öffentliche Wirtschaft in der Weimarer Republik : kommunale Versorgungsunternehmen als Instrumente der Wirtschaftspolitik / Gerold Ambrosius.1. Aufl. Baden-Baden : Nomos Verlagsgesellschaft, 1984. 306 p. ; 23 cm. (Schriften zur öffentlichen Verwaltung und öffentlichen Wirtschaft. Bd. 78) A revision of the author's Habilitationsschrift--Freie Universität Berlin, 1982. Bibliography: p. 270-301. Includes index. ISBN 3-7890-0912-1 LC Card 84-230508
1. Government ownership - Germany - History - 20th century. 2. Germany - Economic policy - 1918-1933. 3. Germany - Economic conditions - 1918-1945. 4. Municipal services - Germany - History - 20th century. I. Title.
HD4175 .A626 1984

AMBULATORY MEDICAL CARE - UTILIZATION - REPORTING - UNITED STATES.
Statistical aspects of physician payment systems . Hyattsville, Md. [1987] vii, 33 p. : ISBN 0-8406-0357-6 LC Card 86-600375 DDC 362.1/0723 s 362.1/72 19
HA37 .U1693 no. 24 RA408.5

Ambur, Owen D. Selling out the family farm : a classic case of good intentions gone awry : a report / prepared for the use of the Subcommittee on Agriculture and Transportation of the Joint Economic Committee, Congress of the United States by the Republican staff. Washington : U. S.

G.P.O. : For sale by the Supt. of Docs., Congressional Sales Office, U. S. G.P.O., 1986. v, 40 p. : ill. ; 23 cm. (S. prt. . 99-208) At head of title: 99th Cogngress, 2d session. Joint committee print. Distributed to some depository libraries in microfiche. Shipping list no.: 87-28-P. "November 24, 1986." Item 1000-B, 1000-C (microfiche) LC Card 87-601379 DDC 338.1/6 19
1. Family farms - United States. 2. Agriculture and state - United States. 3. Agriculture - Economic aspects - United States. I. United States. Congress. Joint Economic Committee. Subcommittee on Agriculture and Transportation. II. Title. III. Series.
HD1476.U5 A65 1986

Aménagement du territoire et utilisation du sol . Rumley, Pierre-Alain. Zürich , c1984. x, 176 p. : LC Card 85-104773
HD796 .R86 1984

Amendola, Mario. The innovative choice : an economic analysis of the dynamics of technology / Mario Amendola and Jean-Luc Gaffard. Oxford [Oxfordshire] ; New York, NY, USA : B. Blackwell, 1988. p. cm. Bibliography: p. Includes index. ISBN 0-631-15791-3 : LC Card 87-25004 DDC 338/.06 19
1. Technological innovations - Economic aspects. 2. Economic development. I. Gaffard, Jean Luc. II. Title.
HC79.T4 A46 1988

Amerasinghe, Chittharanjan Felix, 1933- Index to decisions of the World Bank Administrative Tribunal / C.F. Amerasinghe, D. Bellinger. 2nd ed. [Washington, D.C.] : World Bank Administrative Tribunal, Office of the Executive Secretary, [c1985] vii, 32 leaves ; 28 cm. "Covers the decisions handed down from June 1, 1981 to December 31, 1985"--Introd. "May be used also in conjunction with the publication, Main points in the decisions of the World Bank Administrative Tribunal"--Introd. "December 1985." LC Card 86-172153 DDC 354.1/8252 19
1. International Bank for Reconstruction and Development. Administrative Tribunal - Indexes. I. Bellinger, D. II. International Bank for Reconstruction and Development. Administrative Tribunal. Office of the Executive Secretary. III. Title.
HG3881.5.W57 A44 1985

America and the reconstruction of Italy, 1945-1948 /. Harper, John Lamberton. Cambridge [Cambridgeshire] , New York , 1986. x, 213 p. ; ISBN 0-521-32518-8 LC Card 85-30915 DDC 338.91/73/045 19
HC305 .H36 1986 ***NYPL [JLE 86-3600]***

AMERICA - COMMERCE - EUROPE - HISTORY.
Attman, Artur, 1910- American bullion in the European world trade, 1600-1800 /. Göteborg , 1986. 115 p. ; ISBN 91-85252-38-7 (pbk.) LC Card 87-147250 DDC 382/.4242/0973 19
HG285.A45 A88 1986

AMERICA - COMMERCE - SPAIN - CATALONIA - HISTORY.
El Comerç entre Catalunya i Amèrica (segles XVIII i XIX) /. Barcelona , 1986. 173 p. : ISBN 84-85905-24-5 LC Card 86-204187
HF3689.C3 C39 1986

AMERICA - ECONOMIC CONDITIONS.
Astesano, Eduardo. [Historia socialista de América.] Historia social de América /. Buenos Aires, Argentina [1982] 177 p. : ISBN 950-0-17004-3 LC Card 83-165516
HC94 .A83 1982

Costa Rica colonial . [San José, Costa Rica , 1984] 83 p. ; LC Card 86-173945
HC389 .C67 1984

AMERICA - EMIGRATION AND IMMIGRATION - HISTORY - CONGRESSES.
Colonialism and migration . Dordrecht , Higham, MA, USA , 1986. vi, 303 p. : ISBN 90-247-3253-0 LC Card 85-21809 DDC 331.11/73 19
HD4875.A837 C65 1986
NYPL [JLE 86-3920]

America in decline . Lotta, Raymond. Chicago , c1984- v. : ISBN 0-916650-12-X (v. 1) : LC Card 83-22294 DDC 330.973/0927 19
HC54 .L63 1984 ***NYPL [JLL 87-106]***

America in transition . EBRI-ERF Policy Forum (1986 : Washington, D.C.) Washington, D.C. , c1987. xix, 269 p. : ISBN 0-86643-057-1 (hard) : LC Card 87-13421 DDC 331.25/5/0973 19
HD4928.N62 U628 1987

América Latina, desarrollo e integracíon /. Herrera, Felipe, 1922- [Santiago, Chile] [1986] 302 p., [11] p. of plates : LC Card 87-115159 DDC 337.1/8 19
HC125 .H466 1986

América Latina, Estados Unidos : evolución de las relaciones económicas (1984-1985) / por SELA (Sistema Económico Latinoamericano).1a ed. México : Siglo Veintiuno Editores, 1986. 223 p. : ill. ; 21 cm. (Economía y demografía) "XI Reunión Ordinaria del Consejo Latinoamericano, Caracas, 17 al 19 de septiembre de 1985." Includes bibliographical references. ISBN 968-231-378-3 LC Card 87-128005 DDC 337.7308 19
1. United States - Foreign economic relations - Latin America. 2. Latin America - Foreign economic realtions - United States. 3. United States - Foreign economic relations. 4. United States - Economic policy - 1981-. I. Sistema Económico Latinoamericano. II. Series: Economía y demografía (Mexico City, Mexico).
HF1456.5.L3 A44 1986

América Latina, estudios de científicos soviéticos .
(<25- >) Kontseptsii obshchestvennogo razvitiia. Spanish. Concepciones del desarrollo social. Moscú , <1984-. v. <2 > ; LC Card 87-124757
HC125 .K65517 1984

América Latina y el Caribe . Calderón González, Arnoldo. México, D.F. , 1985. 51, [25] leaves ; LC Card 87-121714 DDC 332.4/98 19
HG660.5 .C35 1985

América Latina y el sistema monetario internacional /. Glower, Carlos J., 1952- [Mexico City, Mexico] [1986] iv, 28 leaves : LC Card 87-400944 DDC 332.4/56098 29
HG3881 .G577 1986

América Latina y la concentración del poder en la arena política. Fuenzalida Faivovich, Edmundo. [América Latina y la concentración del poder en la arena política.] América Latina y la concentración del poder en la arena política ; El impacto social del cambio tecnológico actual en los países menos desarrollados /. [Santiago de Chile] [between 1974 and 1979] 24, 25 leaves ; LC Card 82-180082
HD2810.5 .F84 1974

América Latina y la economía mundial del algodón. 1a ed. Santiago de Chile : Naciones Unidas, 1985. 128 p. : ill. ; 23 cm. (Estudios e informes de la CEPAL, 0256-9795 . 50) "Este trabajo fue preparado por la División de Comercio Internacional y Desarrollo de la CEPAL"--T.p. verso. "LC/G.1353, julio de 1985"--T.p. verso. Includes bibliographical references. ISBN 92-1-321189-9 LC Card 85-230001 DDC 338.1/7351/098 19
1. Cotton trade - Argentine Republic. 2. Cotton trade - Paraguay. 3. Cotton trade - Mexico. 4. Cotton trade - Guatemala. 5. Cotton trade - Nicaragua. I. United Nations. Economic Commission for Latin America. International Trade and Development Division. II. Series.
HD9884.L3 A46 1985 ***NYPL [JLE 86-3341]***

AMERICA - POPULATION - HISTORY - CONGRESSES.
Colonialism and migration . Dordrecht , Higham, MA, USA , 1986. vi, 303 p. : ISBN 90-247-3253-0 LC Card 85-21809 DDC 331.11/73 19
HD4875.A837 C65 1986
NYPL [JLE 86-3920]

AMERICA - SOCIAL CONDITIONS.
Astesano, Eduardo. [Historia socialista de América.] Historia social de América /. Buenos Aires, Argentina [1982] 177 p. : ISBN 950-0-17004-3 LC Card 83-165516
HC94 .A83 1982

AMERICAN ABORIGINES. see **INDIANS OF NORTH AMERICA; INDIANS OF SOUTH AMERICA.**

AMERICAN AGRICULTURAL ASSISTANCE. see **AGRICULTURAL ASSISTANCE, AMERICAN.**

American Agricultural Economics Association. Proceedings of a symposium on competitiveness of U. S. grains in international markets /. Fargo, N.D. [1986] ii leaves, 67 p. : LC Card 86-622839 DDC 382/.4131/0973 19
HD9035 .P76 1986

American Agricultural Economics Association. Task Force on Dairy Marketing Orders. Federal milk marketing orders . [Ames, Iowa] [1986] 50 p. : LC Card 86-229061 DDC 338.1/771/0973 19
HD9282.U4 F43 1986

American Agricultural Economics Association. Trade Policy Task Force. Agricultural trade research and information needs . [Ames, Iowa] [1985] 32 p. : LC Card 86-229053 DDC 380.1/41/072073 19
HD1410.6.U5 A39 1985

American Air Mail Society.
Kronstein, Max. Rocket mail flights of the world to 1986 /. Cinnaminson, N.J. , 1986. 191 p. : LC Card 87-400297 DDC 383/.144 19
HE6239.R6 K76 1986

Short, Simine, 1944- Glider mail . Cinnaminson, NJ , 1987. 261 p. : ISBN 0-939429-00-4 : LC Card 86-72751 DDC 383/.144 19
HE6239.G54 S56 1987

American Airlines . Cearley, George Walker. Dallas, Tex. (P.O. Box 12312, Dallas, 75225) , c1987. 136 p. : LC Card 87-132433 DDC 387.7/065/73 19
HE9803.A95 C4 1987

AMERICAN AIRLINES, INC. - HISTORY.
Cearley, George Walker. American Airlines . Dallas, Tex. (P.O. Box 12312, Dallas, 75225) , c1987. 136 p. : LC Card 87-132433 DDC 387.7/065/73 19
HE9803.A95 C4 1987

American Apparel Manufacturers Association. Management Systems Committee. Acquiring, enhancing, replacing apparel systems . Arlington, VA (2500 Wilson Blvd., Suite 301, Arlington 22201) , 1986. iii, 28 p. : LC Card 87-107487 DDC 687/.028/5 19
HD9940.A2 A26 1986

American Apparel Manufacturers Association. Technical Advisory Committee. Planning & implementing an apparel sourcing strategy . Arlington, Va. (2500 Wilson Blvd., Suite 301, Arlington 22209) , c1986. 41 p. : LC Card 87-107327 DDC 687/.068/7 19
HD9940.U4 P52 1986

American artists' materials suppliers directory . Katlan, Alexander W. Park Ridge, N.J. , c1987. xvi, 460 p. : ISBN 0-8155-5064-2 : LC Card 87-12283 DDC 338.7/617028 19
HD9791.U52 K37 1987

American Association of Community and Junior Colleges. Waymon, Lynne. Starting and managing a business from your home /. Washington, D.C. , 1986. vi, 48 p. ; LC Card 86-602842 DDC 658/.041 19
HD62.5 .W395 1986

American Association of Equipment Lessors. Haley, Stephen W. Effective credit management in the equipment leasing and finance industry /. Arlington, VA , c1986. ix, 121 p. : ISBN 0-912413-01-8 (pbk.) LC Card 87-105306 DDC 658.1/5242 19
HD39.4 .H35 1986

American Association of Individual Investors. Nicholson, Norm. The individual investor's microcomputer resource guide /. Chicago , c1986. viii, 216 p. ; ISBN 0-930369-17-3 (pbk.) LC Card 86-204335 DDC 332.6/028/553 19
HG4515.5 .N53 1986

American Association of Motor Vehicle Administrators.
Pease, Allen. Report on the feasibility of implementing the International Registration Plan in the State of Maine . [Augusta, Me.] [1985] ii, 24 leaves ; LC Card 85-622840 DDC 388.3/24 19
HE5633.M2 P4 1985

AMERICAN ASSOCIATION OF MOTOR VEHICLE ADMINISTRATORS. INTERNATIONAL REGISTRATION PLAN.
Pease, Allen. Appendix for the feasibility report of implementing the International Registration Plan in the State of Maine . [Augusta, Me.] [1985] 39 leaves : LC Card 85-622841 DDC

388.3/24 19
HE5633.M2 P39 1985

Pease, Allen. Report on the feasibility of implementing the International Registration Plan in the State of Maine . [Augusta, Me.] [1985] ii, 24 leaves ; LC Card 85-622840 DDC 388.3/24 19
HE5633.M2 P4 1985

American Association of State Colleges and Universities. Business and economics funding guide /. Washington, D.C. , c1987. 122 p. ; ISBN 0-88044-087-2 (alk. paper) : LC Card 87-17436 DDC 001.4/4 19
HF1131 .B78 1987

American Association of State Highway and Transportation Officials. French, Alexander. Traffic data collection and analysis . Washington, D.C. [1986] 58 p. : ISBN 0-309-04406-5 (pbk.) : LC Card 86-51174 DDC 388.3/14/072 19
HE369 .F68 1986

The American automobile . American car graffiti. English. San Francisco , 1988. p. cm. ISBN 0-87701-451-5 (cloth) LC Card 87-25017 DDC 659.1/9629222/0973 19
HF6161.A9 A4413 1988

American automobile workers, 1900-1933 /. Peterson, Joyce Shaw, 1939- Albany , c1987. xiv, 231 p. ; ISBN 0-88706-573-2 LC Card 87-1942 DDC 331.7/6292/0973 19
HD8039.A82 U66 1987

American banker.
American banker 150th 1836-1986 anniversary . [New York, N.Y.] (1 State Street Plaza, New York 10004) [c1986] 192 p. : LC Card 87-115948 DDC 332.1/0973 19
HG1501 .A65 1986

AMERICAN BANKER - HISTORY.
American banker 150th 1836-1986 anniversary . [New York, N.Y.] (1 State Street Plaza, New York 10004) [c1986] 192 p. : LC Card 87-115948 DDC 332.1/0973 19
HG1501 .A65 1986

American banker 150th 1836-1986 anniversary : banking's past, financial services' future. A Commemorative ed. [New York, N.Y.] (1 State Street Plaza, New York 10004) : American Banker, [c1986] 192 p. : ill. (some col.) ; 43 cm. Cover title. LC Card 87-115948 DDC 332.1/0973 19
1. American banker - History. I. American banker.
HG1501 .A65 1986

American Bankers Association. American Institute of Banking. see **American Institute of Banking.**

American Bankers Association. Education Policy and Development Group. Beares, Paul. Consumer lending /. Washington, D.C. (1120 Connecticut Ave., N.W., Washington 20036) , c1987. xi, 335 p. : LC Card 87-410019 DDC 332.1/753/0685 19
HG3755 .B39 1987

American Bankers Association. Retail Payments Task Force. Ad Hoc Committee.
Implementation guidelines for online debit card systems at the point of sale / American Bankers Association, Payment Systems Policy Board, Retail Payments Task Force, Ad Hoc Committee. [Washington, D.C.] : The Association, c1986. 1 v. (various pagings) : ill. ; 28 cm. Cover title. "Draft." "July 9, 1986." LC Card 86-224882 DDC 332.1/028 19
1. Debit cards - United States. 2. Point-of-sale systems - United States. 3. Electronic funds transfers - United States. I. Title.
HG1710.5 .A47 1986

American Bankers Division. FmHA guaranteed lending manual /. Washington, D.C. (1120 Connecticut Ave., N.W., Washington 20036) , c1986. xi, 88, [59] p. : LC Card 86-226067 DDC 332.1/753 19
HG2051.U5 F55 1986

AMERICAN BANKS AND BANKING. see **BANKS AND BANKING, AMERICAN.**

American Bar Association. Section of International Law and Practice. International Trade Committee. International trade in textiles & apparel . [Washington, D.C.] , c1987. 1 v. (various foliations) : LC Card 87-404516 DDC 382/.45677/00973 19
HD9850.5 .I43 1987

American bullion in the European world trade, 1600-1800 /. Attman, Artur, 1910- Göteborg , 1986. 115 p. ; ISBN 91-85252-38-7 (pbk.) LC Card 87-147250 DDC 382/.4242/0973 19
HG285.A45 A88 1986

American business . Boe, Jonathan E. (Jonathan Evers) New York , 1987. p. cm. ISBN 0-8240-8075-0 LC Card 87-23693 DDC 337.73047 337.4 19
HF1456.5.S624 B64 1987

American business, a two-minute warning . Grayson, C. Jackson (Charles Jackson), 1923- New York , London , c1988. xvii, 368 p. : ISBN 0-02-912680-0 LC Card 87-19391 DDC 658/.00973 19
HD70.U5 G69 1988

American business and foreign policy . Short, Joseph N. New York , 1987. 340 p. : ISBN 0-8240-8093-9 (alk. paper) : LC Card 87-23792 DDC 382/.41373/0973 19
HD9199.U48 S46 1987

The American business community and the European Recovery Program, 1947-1952 /. Sanford, William F. New York , 1987. xiv, 366 p. ; ISBN 0-8240-8091-2 (alk. paper) LC Card 87-23765 DDC 338.91/73/04 19
HC240 .S259 1987

American business history.
Bunting, David G. The rise of large American corporations, 1889-1919 /. New York , 1986, c1987. 224 p. ; ISBN 0-8240-8353-9 (alk. paper) : LC Card 86-29527 DDC 338.6/44 19
HD2785 .B76 1987

American car graffiti. English. The American automobile : advertising from the antique and classic eras / compiled by Yasutoshi Ikuta ; translated by Barbara Rich. San Francisco : Chronicle Books, 1988. p. cm. Translation of: American car graffiti. ISBN 0-87701-451-5 (cloth) LC Card 87-25017 DDC 659.1/9629222/0973 19
1. Advertising - Automobiles - United States - Pictorial works. I. Ikuta, Yasutoshi. II. Title.
HF6161.A9 A4413 1988

American Chamber of Commerce of Mexico. Business Mexico /. México, D.F. , 1978. 343 p. : LC Card 87-405299 DDC 332.1/732272 19
HF3237 .B87 1978

AMERICAN CIVIL WAR. see **UNITED STATES - HISTORY - CIVIL WAR, 1861-1865.**

American Council for Capital Formation. Center for Policy Research. The Consumption tax . Cambridge, Mass. , c1987. xviii, 382 p. : ISBN 0-88730-159-2 LC Card 87-17838 DDC 336.2/71/0973 19
HJ5715.U6 C658 1987

American depositary receipts . Skully, Michael T. [Melbourne] [1986] 44 leaves : LC Card 86-229206 DDC 332.6/7373/094 19
HG5892 .S58 1986

AMERICAN DOLLAR. see **DOLLAR, AMERICAN.**

The American dream : a national survey / by the Wall Street Journal. [New York] : The Journal, c1987. 103 p. : ill. ; 28 cm. "Conducted for the Wall Street Journal by the Roper Organization, Inc." "February 1987." LC Card 87-404096 DDC 330.973/0927 19
1. United States - Economic conditions - 1981- - Public opinion. 2. Public opinion - United States. I. Wall Street Journal (Firm). II. Roper Organization.
HC106.8 .A437 1987

The American dream and the impact of class . Van Sickle, Larry. New York, N.Y. , c1985. 389 p. ; ISBN 0-8290-1382-2 (pbk.) LC Card 83-12613 DDC 331.3/4/0973 19
HD6273 .V36 1985 ***NYPL [JLD 86-1637]***

American Dry Milk Institute. Census of 1985 dry milk distribution & production trends /. Chicago, Ill. (130 N. Franklin St., Chicago 60606) , c1986. 13 p. ; LC Card 86-208490 DDC 338.1/77143/0973021 19
HD9282.U4 C463 1986

American Economic Association. Meeting (95th : 1982 : New York, N.Y.) Macroeconomic conflict and social institutions /. Cambridge, Mass. , c1985. xi, 249 p. : ISBN 0-88730-034-0 LC Card 84-24376 DDC 339.2 19
HC79.I5 M225 1985 ***NYPL [JLE 86-2562]***

American economic history /. Puth, Robert Christian, 1936- Chicago , c1988. xv, 640 p. : ISBN 0-03-011892-1 LC Card 87-6782 DDC 330.973 19
HC103 .P9 1988

American economic history (Garland Publishing, Inc.)
Steckel, Richard H. (Richard Hall), 1944- The economics of U. S. slave and southern white fertility /. New York , 1985. 253 p. ; ISBN 0-8240-6662-6 (alk. paper) : LC Card 84-48314 DDC 304.6/32/08996073075 19
HB921 .S74 1985 ***NYPL [JLE 86-2085]***

The American economy poster and fact book /. Rose, Stephen J., (Stephen Jay), 1947- New York , c1987. vi, 56 p. : ISBN 0-394-74390-3 (pbk.) : LC Card 86-43119 DDC 338.973 19
HC106.8 .R658 1987

American Enterprise Institute for Public Policy Research.
AEI studies. Formed by the union of its Evaluative studies; Domestic affairs studies; Foreign affairs studies; and National energy study.
(434) Futures markets . Washington, D.C. , c1985. xiii, 325 p. : ISBN 0-8447-3592-2 LC Card 85-26705 DDC 332.64/4 19
HG6049 .F86 1985 ***NYPL [JLE 86-1532]***

(440) Hicks, Donald A. Automation technology and industrial renewal . Washington, D.C. [1985], c1986. xiii, 160 p. ; ISBN 0-8447-3598-1 LC Card 85-31568 DDC 671 19
HD9506.U62 H53 1986
NYPL [JSE 86-1901]

(441) Breit, William. Antitrust penalty reform . Washington, D.C. , c1986. x, 83 p. : ISBN 0-8447-3600-7 (alk. paper) LC Card 86-3203 DDC 343.73/072/0269 347.303720269 19
KF1657.T7 B74 1986 ***NYPL [JLE 86-3948]***

Exchange rate targets . Washington, D.C. , c1986. ix, 59 p. ; ISBN 0-8447-3615-5 (pbk. : alk. paper) : LC Card 86-72463 DDC 332.4/5 19
HG203 .E98 1986

Mowery, David C. Alliance politics and economics . Cambridge, Mass. , c1987. xi, 194 p. : ISBN 0-88730-213-0 LC Card 86-32178 DDC 338.8/87 19
HD9711.A2 M68 1987

Ross, Murray N. Public choice . [Washington, D.C.] [c1987] 8 p. ; LC Card 87-403005 DDC 338.9 19
HB846.8 .R66 1987

The American farmer book : stop the heart and the body dies / by 501 farmers & friends. [Smithshire, Ill.] (Box 181, Smithshire 61478) : [F. Thompson, c1986] 192 p. : ill. ; 21 cm. Cover title. Edited by Frank Thompson. LC Card 86-203314 DDC 338.1/0973 19
1. Farmers - United States - Attitudes. 2. Agriculture - Economic aspects - United States - Public opinion. 3. Agriculture and state - United States - Public opinion. 4. Public opinion - United States. I. Thompson, Frank.
HD8039.F32 U614 1986

American Farmland Trust. Planning and zoning for farmland protection . East Lansing, MI , c1987. 58 p. : LC Card 87-119320 DDC 333.76/17/0973 19
HD256 .P57 1987

American Free Trade Association. see **Asociación Latinoamericana de Libre Comercio.**

American Friends Service Committee.
Automating apartheid . Philadelphia , c19. ix, 107 p. : ISBN 0-910082-00-6 (pbk.) : LC Card 86-201384 DDC 382/.45004/0968 19
HD9696.C63 S62 1984

American Gas Association. Planning and Analysis Group. The Outlook for gas demand in new markets, 1986-2010 . Arlington, Va. (1515 Wilson Blvd., Arlington 22209) , c1986. 54 p. : LC Card 87-403083 DDC 333.8/23312 19
HD9581.U5 O95 1986

American Gas Association. Rate Committee. Gas rate fundamentals. Arlington, VA (1515 Wilson Blvd., Arlington 22209) , 1987. xxi, 311, [118]

p. : LC Card 87-404451 DDC 353.0087/23044 19
HD9581.U5 G266 1987

The American heritage Larousse Spanish dictionary : Spanish/English, English/Spanish. Boston : Houghton Mifflin, c1986. xxx, 532, xviii, 572 p. ; 24 cm. ISBN 0-395-32429-7 : LC Card 86-7202 DDC 463/.21 19
1. Spanish language - Dictionaries - English. 2. English language - Dictionaries - Spanish. I. Title: Larousse Spanish dictionary.
PC4640 .A54 1986
NYPL [*R-RGK 86-5942]

American Hotel & Motel Association. Uniform system of accounts for hotels. New York, N.Y. (40 W. 38th St., New York 10018) , 1986. x, 139 p. : LC Card 86-220845 DDC 657/.837 19
HF5686.H75 U55 1986

AMERICAN INDIANS. see **INDIANS OF NORTH AMERICA; INDIANS OF SOUTH AMERICA.**

American industry . Caves, Richard E. Englewood Cliffs, N.J. , c1987. x, 124 p. : ISBN 0-13-027665-0 (pbk.) : LC Card 86-22706 DDC 338.0973 19
HC106.5 .C34 1987

American industry: structure, conduct, performance. Caves, Richard E. Englewood Cliffs, N.J. [c1972] vii, 117 p. ISBN 0-13-027573-5 LC Card 72-170034 DDC 338/.0973
HC106.5 .C34 1972

American Institute for Property and Liability Underwriters. Commercial liability risk management and insurance /. Malvern, Pa. , 1986. 2 v. : ISBN 0-89463-049-0 (set) LC Card 86-72708 DDC 368.8/1 19
HG8059 .C64 1986

American Institute of Accountants. see **American Institute of Certified Public Accountants.**

American Institute of Banking. Understanding the language of banking. Washington, D.C. (1120 Connecticut Ave., N.W., Washington 20036) , c1986. v, 258 p. : LC Card 87-111196 DDC 332.1/014 19
HG151 .U53 1986

American Institute of CPAs. see **American Institute of Certified Public Accountants.**

American Institute of Certified Public Accountants. Accounting Standards Division. Savings and loan associations . New York, N.Y. (1211 Avenue of the Americas, New York 10036) , 1987. vii, 212 p. ; LC Card 87-161844 DDC 657/.833 19
HF5686.B8 S27 1987

American Institute of Certified Public Accountants. Accounting Standards Division. Task Force on Options. Accounting for options /. New York, NY (1211 Ave. of the Americas, New York 10036-8775) [1986] 182 p., [4] p. of plates (some folded) : LC Card 86-221314 DDC 657/.76 19
HF5686.I6 A28 1986

American Institute of Certified Public Accountants. Continuing Professional Education Division. National CPE curriculum . New York, N.Y. , c1987- 1 v. (loose-leaf) : ISBN 0-87051-001-0 (loose-leaf : CIP data sheet) : LC Card 87-18832 DDC 657/.07/15 19
HF5635 .N25 1987

American Institute of Certified Public Accountants. Oil and Gas Committee. Audits of entities with oil and gas producing activities . New York, NY (1211 Ave. of the Americas, New York 10036-8775) , c1986. x, 133 p. ; LC Card 86-209769 DDC 657/.862 19
HF5686.P3 A93 1986

American Institute of Certified Public Accountants. Personal Financial Planning Division. Personal financial planning manual . New York, NY , c1987. 1 v. (loose-leaf) : LC Card 87-404512 DDC 332.024 19
HG179 .P3865 1987

American Institute of Certified Public Accountants. Private Companies Practice Section. Peer review manual / Division for CPA Firms, Private Companies Practice Section. Rev. ed., 4th ed. New York, N.Y. (1121 Ave. of the Americas, New York 10036-8775) : American Institute of Certified Public Accountants, 1986. 2 v. in 1 : forms ; 23-30 cm. Rev. ed. of: Peer review manual / Division for CPA Firms, SEC Practice Section. Rev. ed., 2nd ed. 1979. CONTENTS. - [1] Organizational document with membership requirements, standards for peer reviews, administrative and other peer review procedures -- [2] Instructions and checklists. LC Card 86-217293 DDC 657/.833 19
1. Accounting - United States - Quality control. 2. Accounting - Standards - United States. 3. Peer review - United States. I. American Institute of Certified Public Accountaints. SEC Practice Section. Peer review manual. II. Title.
HF5616.U5 A585 1986a

American Institute of Certified Public Accountants. SEC Practice Section. Peer review manual : instructions and checklists / American Institute of Certified Public Accountants, Division for CPA Firms, SEC Practice Section.Rev. ed., 5th ed. New York, NY (1211 Ave. of the Americas, New York 10036-8775) : The Institute, 1986- 1 v. (loose-leaf) : ill. ; 30 cm. + SECPS manual (224 p. in various pagings ; 23 cm.) Includes bibliographical references and index. LC Card 87-108519 DDC 657/.833 19
1. Accounting - United States - Quality control. 2. Accounting - Standards - United States. 3. Peer review - United States. I. Title.
HF5616.U5 A585 1986b

Peer review manual. American Institute of Certified Public Accountants. Private Companies Practice Section. Peer review manual / Division for CPA Firms, Private Companies Practice Section. Rev. ed., 4th ed. New York, N.Y. (1121 Ave. of the Americas, New York 10036-8775) , 1986. 2 v. in 1 : LC Card 86-217293 DDC 657/.833 19
HF5616.U5 A585 1986a

American Institute of Certified Public Accountants. SEC Practice Section. Special Investigations Committee. Report on the activities of the Special Investigations Committee of the SEC Practice Section of the AICPA Division for CPA Firms . New York, N.Y. (1211 Ave. of the Americas, New York 10036-8775) , c1986. iii, 6 p. ; LC Card 86-209679 DDC 657/.0218 19
HF5657 .R46 1986

AMERICAN INSTITUTE OF CERTIFIED PUBLIC ACCOUNTANTS. SEC PRACTICE SECTION. SPECIAL INVESTIGATIONS COMMITTEE. Report on the activities of the Special Investigations Committee of the SEC Practice Section of the AICPA Division for CPA Firms . New York, N.Y. (1211 Ave. of the Americas, New York 10036-8775) , c1986. iii, 6 p. ; LC Card 86-209679 DDC 657/.0218 19
HF5657 .R46 1986

American Institute of Certified Public Accountants. Special Committee on Standards of Professional Conduct for Certified Public Accountants. Restructuring professional standards to achieve professional excellence in a changing environment : report of the Special Committee on Standards of Professional Conduct for Certified Public Accountants. New York, N.Y. (1211 Ave. of the Americas, New York 10036-8775) : American Institute of Certified Public Accountants, c1986. vi, 66 p. : ill. ; 23 cm. LC Card 86-211085 DDC 657/.0218 19
1. Accountants - Professional ethics - United States. 2. Accountants - United States - Rating of. 3. Accounting - Standards - United States. I. Title.
HF5616.U5 A585 1986

American Institute of Certified Public Accountants. Special Task Force on Audits of Repurchase Securities Transactions. Special report. 1987. Savings and loan associations : an AICPA audit and accounting guide / prepared by the Committee on Savings and Loan Associations ; including statements of position issued by the Accounting Standards Division and special report prepared by the Special Task Force on Audits of Repurchase Securities Transactions.4th rev. ed. New York, N.Y. (1211 Avenue of the Americas, New York 10036) , 1987. vii, 212 p. ; LC Card 87-161844 DDC 657/.833 19
HF5686.B8 S27 1987

American Institute of Certified Public Accounts. Committee on Savings and Loan Associations. Savings and loan associations . New York, N.Y. (1211 Avenue of the Americas, New York 10036) , 1987. vii, 212 p. ; LC Card 87-161844 DDC 657/.833 19
HF5686.B8 S27 1987

AMERICAN INSTITUTE OF REAL ESTATE APPRAISERS - MEMBERSHIP - STATISTICS.
1986 membership profile /. Chicago, Ill. , c1986. ix, 44 p. : ISBN 0-911780-85-8 (pbk.) LC Card 87-144205 DDC 333.33/2/0973 19
HD251 .A17 1986

American Institute of Real Estate Appraisers. Research Dept. 1986 membership profile /. Chicago, Ill. , c1986. ix, 44 p. : ISBN 0-911780-85-8 (pbk.) LC Card 87-144205 DDC 333.33/2/0973 19
HD251 .A17 1986

American international oil policy . Bull-Berg, Hans Jacob. New York , 1987. xvi, 209 p. : ISBN 0-312-00465-6 : LC Card 86-31583 DDC 333.8/232/0973 19
HD9566 .B87 1987

American Jewish Joint Distribution Committee. [Choroba głodowa. English]
Hunger disease : studies / by the Jewish physicians in the Warsaw ghetto ; edited by Myron Winick ; translated from the Polish by Martha Osnos. New York : Wiley, c1979. xiv, 261 p. : ill. ; 24 cm. (Current concepts in nutrition . v. 7) Translation of: Choroba głodowa. "A Wiley-Interscience publication." Includes index. ISBN 0-471-05003-2 LC Card 78-26397 DDC 616.3/9
1. Malnutrition. 2. Jews - Poland - Warsaw - Persecutions. 3. Holocaust, Jewish (1939-1945) - Poland - Warsaw. 4. Starvation. 5. Hunger. I. Winick, Myron. II. Title. III. Series.
RC627.S7 A43 1979
NYPL [*PXV (Warsaw) 86-3505]

American Joint Distribution Committee. see **American Jewish Joint Distribution Committee.**

American legal and constitutional history. Townsend, John Clendenin, 1939- Running the gauntlet . New York , 1986. 341 p. ; ISBN 0-8240-8298-2 (alk. paper) : LC Card 86-25632 DDC 331.88/6 19
HD8055.I56 T68 1986

American Library Association. Association of College and Reference Libraries. see **Association of College and Research Libraries.**

American Library Association. Association of College and Research Libraries. see **Association of College and Research Libraries.**

American Library Association. College and Reference Section. see **Association of College and Research Libraries.**

American Management Association. AMA Membership Publications Division.
Drug abuse . New York, N.Y. , c1987. 132 p. : ISBN 0-8144-3511-4 (pbk.) LC Card 86-32254 DDC 658.3/822 19
HF5549.5.D7 D7 1987

Hiring costs and strategies . New York , c1986. v, 82 p. : ISBN 0-8144-3153-4
NYPL [JLF 86-960]

American Marketing Association.
AMA Winter Educators' Conference (1987 : San Antonio, Tex.) 1987 AMA Winter Educators' Conference . Chicago, Ill. , c1987. viii, 411 p. : ISBN 0-87757-185-6 (pbk.) LC Card 87-944 DDC 658.8/001 19
HF5411 .A53 1987

Creativity in services marketing . Chicago, IL , 1986. 175 p. : ISBN 0-87757-179-1 (pbk.) LC Card 85-26785 DDC 658.8 19
HD9980.5 .C74 1986 ***NYPL [JLF 86-1783]***

The Services challenge . Chicago, Ill. , 1987. vi, 108 p. : ISBN 0-87757-188-0 (pbk.) LC Card 87-12543 DDC 658.8 19
HD9980.5 .S4255 1987

1987 AMA educators' proceedings /. Chicago, Ill. , 1987. xiv, 287 p. ; ISBN 0-87757-182-1 LC Card 87-18680 DDC 658.8 19
HF5411 .A156 1987

American Marketing Association. Agricultural Chemical Marketing Research Section.
World Chemical Congress of Marketing and Business Research (1986 : Newport Beach, Calif.) The chemical industry . [Staten Island, N.Y.] , c1986. 435 p. : LC Card 86-72599 DDC 338.4/766 19
HD9650 .W67 1986

The American monetary system . Degen, Robert A. Lexington, Mass. , c1987. x, 242 p. ; ISBN 0-669-15827-5 (alk. paper) LC Card 86-46363 DDC 332.4/973 19
HG501 .D44 1987

American money and the Weimar Republic . McNeil, William C. New York , 1986. x, 352 p. : ISBN 0-231-06236-2 LC Card 85-29962 DDC 336.3/4/0943 19
HG3949 .M38 1986 ***NYPL [JLE 86-3268]***

AMERICAN NATIONAL CHARACTERISTICS. see **NATIONAL CHARACTERISTICS, AMERICAN.**

American Oriental series. For additional listing of contents, see Old Catalog.
(v. 68) Labor in the ancient Near East /. New Haven, Conn. , 1987. xiv, 289 p. : ISBN 0-940490-68-4 LC Card 86-32227 DDC 305.5/62/09394 19
HD8656 .L33 1987 ***NYPL [*OAC (American Oriental series)]***

American Payroll Association. Risteau, Delores. The American Payroll Association's basic guide to payroll /. Paramus, N.J. , c1986. iv, 251 p. : ISBN 0-13-028242-1 (pbk.) LC Card 87-153688 DDC 658.3/21 19
HG4028.P5 R57 1986

The American Payroll Association's basic guide to payroll /. Risteau, Delores. Paramus, N.J. , c1986. iv, 251 p. : ISBN 0-13-028242-1 (pbk.) LC Card 87-153688 DDC 658.3/21 19
HG4028.P5 R57 1986

American Philosophical Society, Philadelphia. Memoirs. For additional listing of vols., see Old Catalog.
(v. 160. 160) Russell, Josiah Cox, 1900- The control of late ancient and medieval population /. Philadelphia , 1985. xv, 272 p. ; ISBN 0-87169-160-4 LC Card 83-71298
NYPL [JLF 85-844]

American Planning Association. The State and local industrial policy /. Chicago, Ill. , c1987. x, 195 p. : ISBN 0-918286-46-8 (pbk.) LC Card 86-72373 DDC 338.973 19
HD3616.U47 S68 1987

The American political economy . Hibbs, Douglas A., 1944- Cambridge, Mass. , 1987. xiii, 404 p. : ISBN 0-674-02735-3 (alk. paper) LC Card 87-155 DDC 338.973 19
HB3743 .H52 1987

The American President Lines and its forebears, 1848-1984 . Niven, John. Newark , c1987. 327 p. : ISBN 0-87413-299-1 (alk. paper) LC Card 85-40660 DDC 387.5/06573 19
HE753.A465 N58 1987

AMERICAN PRESIDENT LINES, LTD. - HISTORY.
Niven, John. The American President Lines and its forebears, 1848-1984 . Newark , c1987. 327 p. : ISBN 0-87413-299-1 (alk. paper) LC Card 85-40660 DDC 387.5/06573 19
HE753.A465 N58 1987

American Psychological Association. Division of Consumer Psychology. Nonverbal communication in advertising /. Lexington, Mass. , c1988. viii, 296 p. : ISBN 0-669-14172-0 (alk. paper) LC Card 87-17143 DDC 659.1/01/9 19
HF5822 .N66 1988

AMERICAN REPUBLICS. see **AMERICA.**

American Retail Education Foundation. Federal tax reform and the states . Washington, D.C. (1616 H St., N.W., Suite 600, Washington 20006) , c1987. 84 p. ; LC Card 87-404532 DDC 336.2/05/0973 19
HJ2381 .F37 1987

AMERICAN RUSSIAN COMMERCIAL COMPANY - HISTORY - SOURCES.
Walker, David B., 1841 or 2-ca. 1906. Captain David B. Walker, journal and papers, 1864-1869 . Juneau, Alaska (Pouch G, Juneau 99811) , 1984. 60 p. : LC Card 84-622198
HD9481.U4 W359 1984

American Society for Quality Control. Human Resources Division. Human resources management /. New York , Milwaukee, Wis. , c1987. xiv, 276 p. : ISBN 0-8247-7716-6 LC Card 86-29321 DDC 658.3 19
HF5549 .H8727 1987

American Society for Training and Development. Sredl, Henry J., 1935- The ASTD reference guide to professional training roles & competencies /. New York , c1987. 2 v. : ISBN 0-394-55915-0 (v. 1) LC Card 86-26006 DDC 658.3/124 19
HF5549.5.T7 S657 1987

Training and development handbook . New York , c1987. xiv, 878 p. : ISBN 0-07-013353-0 : LC Card 87-2629 DDC 658.3/124 19
HF5549.5.T7 T6648 1987

American Society of Civil Engineers and Architects. see **American Society of Civil Engineers.**

American Society of Civil Engineers. Committee on Community Development. Facility location and land use . New York, N.Y. , c1986. vii, 40 p. : ISBN 0-87262-574-5 (pbk.) LC Card 86-25926 DDC 338.6/042 19
HD171.A15 F33 1986

American Society of Civil Engineers. Construction Division.
Specialty Conference on Engineering and Construction Projects (1982 : New Orleans, La.) Proceedings of the Specialty Conference on Engineering and Construction Projects . New York, N.Y. , c1982. vi, 329 p. : ISBN 0-87262-299-1 (pbk.) LC Card 82-70492 DDC 658.5 19
TA190 .S67 1982 ***NYPL [JLD 86-1905]***

Transition in the nuclear industry . New York, N.Y. , c1985. iii, 233 p. : ISBN 0-87262-443-9 (pbk.) LC Card 85-70499 DDC 338.4/762148/0973 19
HD9698.U52 T73 1985 ***NYPL [JSD 86-173]***

American Society of Civil Engineers. Energy Division. Transition in the nuclear industry . New York, N.Y. , c1985. iii, 233 p. : ISBN 0-87262-443-9 (pbk.) LC Card 85-70499 DDC 338.4/762148/0973 19
HD9698.U52 T73 1985 ***NYPL [JSD 86-173]***

American Society of Civil Engineers. Task Committee on Federal Policies in Water Resources Planning. Federal policies in water resources planning / prepared by the Task Committee on Federal Policies in Water Resources Planning of the Water Resources Planning and Management Division of the American Society of Civil Engineers. New York, N.Y. : The Society, c1985. 61 p. : ill. ; 22 cm. Bibliography: p. 58-60. ISBN 0-87262-465-X (pbk.) LC Card 85-71265 DDC 333.91/15/0973 19
1. Water resources development - Government policy - United States. 2. Water resources development - United States - Planning. I. Title.
HD1694.A5 A67 1985
NYPL [JLD 86-4066]

American Society of Civil Engineers. Urban Planning and Development Division. Land Use Committee. Facility location and land use . New York, N.Y. , c1986. vii, 40 p. : ISBN 0-87262-574-5 (pbk.) LC Card 86-25926 DDC 338.6/042 19
HD171.A15 F33 1986

American Society of Civil Engineers. Urban Transportation Division. National Conference on Microcomputers in Urban Transportation (1985 : San Diego, Calif.) Microcomputer applications within the urban transportation environment . New York, N.Y. , c1985. 824 p. : ISBN 0-87262-508-7 (pbk.) LC Card 85-73250 DDC 388.4/028/5416 19
HE305 .N33 1985 ***NYPL [JSD 86-535]***

American Society of Internal Medicine. The American Society of Internal Medicine's carrier accountability monitoring project . Washington, DC [1986] 8 p. ; LC Card 86-219845 DDC 368.4/26/0068 19
HD7102.U4 A753 1986

The American Society of Internal Medicine's carrier accountability monitoring project : 1986 report on Medicare carrier performance. Washington, DC : (1101 Vermont Ave., NW, Suite 500, Washington 20005) : ASIM, [1986] 8 p. ; 28 cm. LC Card 86-219845 DDC 368.4/26/0068 19
1. Medicare - Claims administration. I. American Society of Internal Medicine. II. Title: Carrier accountability monitoring project.
HD7102.U4 A753 1986

American Society of Mechanical Engineers. Management Division.
ASME Management Division history, 1886-1980 /. New York, N.Y. (345 E. 47th St., New York 10017) , c1984. x, 169 p. : LC Card 84-206982 DDC 658/.006/073 19
HD28.A6233 A86 1984
NYPL [JLF 86-1646]

AMERICAN SOCIETY OF MECHANICAL ENGINEERS. MANAGEMENT DIVISION - HISTORY.
ASME Management Division history, 1886-1980 /. New York, N.Y. (345 E. 47th St., New York 10017) , c1984. x, 169 p. : LC Card 84-206982 DDC 658/.006/073 19
HD28.A6233 A86 1984
NYPL [JLF 86-1646]

American Sociological Association. Meeting (79th : 1984 : San Antonio, Tex.) The Social fabric . Beverly Hills, Calif. , c1986. 366 p. ; ISBN 0-8039-2788-6 LC Card 86-1191 DDC 301 19
HM13 .S524 1986 ***NYPL [JLE 86-3755]***

American sociological Association. Political Economy of the World System, Section on. see **American Sociological Association. Section on Political Economy of the World System.**

American Sociological Association presidential series.
The Social fabric . Beverly Hills, Calif. , c1986. 366 p. ; ISBN 0-8039-2788-6 LC Card 86-1191 DDC 301 19
HM13 .S524 1986 ***NYPL [JLE 86-3755]***

American Sociological Association. Section on Political Economy of the World System. Rethinking the nineteenth century . New York , c1988. p. cm. ISBN 0-313-25997-6 (lib. bdg. : alk. paper) LC Card 87-17791 DDC 330.9/034 19
HC53 .R48 1988

American sporting advertising /. Strauss, Bob. Jefferson, Me. (Box 1060, Jefferson 04348) , 1987- v. <1 > : LC Card 87-155421 DDC 741.67/0973/074013 19
HF6161.S65 S77 1987

American states of mind . Reinarman, Craig. New Haven , c1987. x, 262 p. ; ISBN 0-300-03817-8 (alk. paper) LC Card 86-26752 DDC 330.12/2/0973 19
HD3616.U47 R1464 1987

American Statistical Association. Meeting (144th : 1984 : Philadelphia, Pa.) Survey of income and program participation and related longitudinal surveys, 1984 . [Washington, D.C.] , 1985. ix, 201 p. : LC Card 85-601676 DDC 339.2/3/0973 19
HC110.I5 S89 1985 ***NYPL [JLF 86-1641]***

American Supply & Machinery Manufacturers' Association. An evaluation of industrial purchasing and distribution trends . Cleveland, Ohio (1230 Keith Bldg., Cleveland 44115) , c1985. 173 p. : LC Card 86-219582 DDC 658.7 19
HD39.5 .E93 1985

The American takeover . Lamur, Carlo. Dordrecht, Holland , Cinnaminson, N.J., U. S.A. , 1985. vi, 209 p., [6] p. of plates : ISBN 90-6765-078-1 (pbk.) : LC Card 86-181373 DDC 338.8/87 19
HD9539.A63 G886 1985

American technology and the British vehicle industry /. Lewchuk, Wayne. Cambridge [Cambridgeshire] , New York , 1987. viii, 304 p. : ISBN 0-521-30269-2 LC Card 86-30994 DDC 338.4/56292/0941 19
HD9710.G72 L48 1987

The American telegrapher . Gabler, Edwin, 1949- New Brunswick, NJ , c1988. p. cm. ISBN 0-8135-1284-0 : LC Card 87-19878 DDC

331.89/2813841/0973 19
HD5325 .T252 1883

American Telephone and Telegraph Company. Chronicles of corporate change . Lexington, Mass. , c1987. xiv, 254 p. : ISBN 0-669-13685-9 (alk. paper) LC Card 86-45555 DDC 384.6/065/73 19
HE8846.A55 C47 1987

Gehani, Narain, 1947- UNIX Ada programming /. Englewood Cliffs, NJ , c1987. xix, 310 p. : ISBN 0-13-938325-5 LC Card 86-22547 DDC 005.4/465 19
QA76.73.A35 G437 1987
NYPL [JSE 87-568]

AMERICAN TELEPHONE AND TELEGRAPH COMPANY.
Customer premises telecom equipment & the regional Bell companies. Norwalk, Conn., U. S.A. (6 Prowitt St., Norwalk 06855) , c1987. ix, 193 leaves ; LC Card 87-403216 DDC 381/.45621385 19
HD9697.T453 U5245 1987

American Telephone and Telegraph Company. Learning and Development Organization. The Trainer's library /. Reading, Mass. , <1987-. p. cm. ISBN 0-201-12633-8 (v. 2) : LC Card 87-11415 DDC 658.3/124 19
HF5549.5.T7 T663 1987

AMERICAN TELEPHONE AND TELEGRAPH COMPANY - REORGANIZATION.
Chronicles of corporate change . Lexington, Mass. , c1987. xiv, 254 p. : ISBN 0-669-13685-9 (alk. paper) LC Card 86-45555 DDC 384.6/065/73 19
HE8846.A55 C47 1987

Faulhaber, Gerald R. Telecommunications in turmoil . Cambridge, Mass. , c1987. xviii, 186 p. ; ISBN 0-88730-157-6 LC Card 87-1377 DDC 384/.068 19
HE8846.A55 F38 1987

New RHC strategies /. Boston, MA (200 Portland St., Boston 02114) , c1987. iii, 117 p. ; LC Card 87-147694 DDC 384.6/065/73 19
HE8846.A55 N497 1987

AMERICAN TELEPHONE AND TELEGRAPH COMPANY - REORGANIZATION - HISTORY.
Coll, Steve. The deal of the century . New York , 1988, c1986. xv, 400 p. : ISBN 0-671-64592-7 (pbk.) : LC Card 87-23410 DDC 384.6/065/73 19
HE8846.A55 C58 1988

Kahaner, Larry. On the line . New York, NY , 1987, c1986. 344 p., [8] p. of plates : ISBN 0-446-38550-6 (pbk.) LC Card 87-10561 DDC 384.6/065/73 19
HE8846.M375 K34 1987

Temin, Peter. The fall of the Bell system . Cambridge , New York , 1987. xviii, 378 p. : ISBN 0-521-34557-X LC Card 87-10293 DDC 384.6/065/73 19
HE8846.A55 T44 1987

Weinhaus, Carol L. Behind the telephone debates /. Norwood, N.J. , 1987. p. cm. ISBN 0-89391-452-5 LC Card 87-19459 DDC 384.6/0973 19
HE8815 .W45 1987

American trade politics . Destler, I. M. Washington, DC , New York, NY , 1986. xiii, 366 p. : ISBN 0-88132-058-7 : LC Card 86-27168 DDC 380.1/3/0973 19
HF1455 .D48 1986

American Vocational Association. Howe, Mike. Accessing private industry council funding . [Northridge, CA] (17624 Romar St., Northridge 91325) [1987?] 24, [15] leaves ; LC Card 87-401761 DDC 362.8/5 19
HD5715.2 .H69 1987

American Water Works Association. Management Division. AWWA Seminar on the Rate Making Process: Going Beyond the Cost of Service (1986 : Denver, Colo.) Proceedings /. Denver, CO , c1986. vi, 58 p. ; ISBN 0-89867-368-2 (pbk.) LC Card 87-107641 DDC 338.4/336361/0973 19
HD4461 .A915 1986

American women and political participation . Beckwith, Karen, 1950- New York , 1986. xiv, 185 p. ; ISBN 0-313-24507-X
NYPL [JLD 87-36]

The Americanisation of West German industry, 1945-1973 /. Berghahn, Volker Rolf. [Unternehmer und Politik in der Bundesrepublik. English.] Leamington Spa , New York , c1986. viii, 344 p. : ISBN 0-907582-55-9 : LC Card 86-222514
HC286.5 .B37x 1986b

AMERICANS - EMPLOYMENT - FOREIGN COUNTRIES.
Cantrell, Will. 101 ways to find an overseas job /. [Merrifield, VA.] [c1987] 1 v. (various pagings) ; ISBN 0-941541-00-2 (pbk.) LC Card 86-73093 DDC 650.1/4 19
HF5549.5.E45 C33 1987

AMERICANS - EMPLOYMENT - FOREIGN COUNTRIES - HANDBOOKS, MANUALS, ETC.
Win, David. International careers . Charlotte, Vt. , c1987. 222 p. ; ISBN 0-913589-28-4 (pbk.) : LC Card 86-32547 DDC 650.1/4 19
HF5549.5.E45 W525 1987

AMERICANS - EMPLOYMENT - FOREIGN COUNTRIES - PROTECTION.
Scotti, Anthony J. Executive safety and international terrorism . Englewood Cliffs, N.J. , c1986. xv, 220 p. ; ISBN 0-13-294380-8 : LC Card 86-15079 DDC 658.4/73 19
HF5549.5.E45 S36 1986
NYPL [JLE 87-393]

America's changing role in the world-system / edited by Terry Boswell and Albert Bergesen. New York : Praeger, 1987. xi, 300 p. : ill. ; 25 cm. Includes bibliographies and index. ISBN 0-275-92417-3 (alk. paper) : LC Card 86-25245 DDC 337.73 19
1. United States - Economic policy - 1981-. 2. United States - Foreign economic relations. 3. Economic history - 1945-. 4. Depressions. 5. International relations. I. Boswell, Terry. II. Bergesen, Albert.
HC106.8 .A455 1987

America's farm crisis /. Gorman, Carol. New York , 1987. 125 p. : ISBN 0-531-10408-7 LC Card 87-2087 DDC 338.1/0973 19
HD1476.U5 G67 1987

America's habit . United States. President's Commission on Organized Crime. Washington, D.C. , 1986. 486, [312] p. ;
NYPL [JLE 86-3348]

America's new competitors : the challenge of the newly industrializing countries / edited by Thornton F. Bradshaw ... [et al.]. Cambridge, Mass. : Ballinger Pub. Co., c1988. xiv, 290 p. ; 24 cm. "Economic Policy Council of the UNA-USA"--Facing t.p. Includes bibliographies and index. ISBN 0-88730-135-5 LC Card 87-19295 DDC 337.730172/4 19
1. United States - Foreign economic relations - Developing countries. 2. Developing countries - Foreign economic relations - United States. 3. Competition, International. I. Bradshaw, Thornton F. II. United Nations Association of the United States of America. Economic Policy Council.
HF1456.5.D44 A44 1988

America's uninsured and underinsured : a nation at risk of inadequate health care and catastrophic costs : a report / presented by the chairman of the Select Committee on Aging, House of Representatives, Ninety-ninth Congress, second session. Washington : U. S. G.P.O. : For sale by the Supt. of Docs., Congressional Sales Office, U. S. G.P.O., 1986. vi, 13 p. ; 24 cm. At head of title: Committee print. Distributed to some depository libraries in microfiche. Shipping list no.: 86-780-P. "September 1986." "Comm. pub. no. 99-583." Item 1009-B-2, 1009-C-2 (microfiche) LC Card 86-603377 DDC 368.3/8/00973 19
1. Insurance, Health - United States. 2. Medical care, Cost of - United States. I. United States. Congress. House. Select Committee on Aging.
HD7102.U4 A755 1986

Amerika shingo jiten = The Kenkyūsha dictionary of new English /. Takabe, Yoshinobu, 1907- Tokyo , 1978. 717 p. ;
NYPL [*OSG 87-2157]

Amerikai Egyesült Allamok. see **United States.**

Amerikanische Wirtschaftspolitik in Österreich, 1945-1949 /. Einwitschläger, Arno. Wien , 1986. 206 p. : ISBN 3-205-08814-X LC Card 87-112406
HF1456.5.A9 E39 1986

Amerikanisches Geschäftsleben /. Cassel, H. (Hjalmar), b. 1868. Berlin , 1908. vi, 110 p. ; LC Card 85-666349
HC106 .C37x 1908

Amerikas sozialistu partija. see **Socialist Party (U. S.)**

Amérique latine--pays ibériques.
Trabis, Roland. Industrie et politique à la frontière Mexique-U. S.A. . Paris , c1985. 241 p., [1] p. of plates : ISBN 2-222-03772-7 : LC Card 86-175728
HC138.N84 T73 1985

Amerongen, Otto Wolff von. see **Wolff von Amerongen, Otto, 1918-**

Amershi, Amin H. Economic analysis of information and contracts . Boston , c1988. p. cm. ISBN 0-89838-252-1 : LC Card 87-22508 DDC 657 19
HF5625 .E28 1988

Ames, Rolando. Agricultura y alimentación . [Lima] , 1982. 536 p. : LC Card 83-174688 DDC 338.1/9/85 19
HD9014.P52 A57 1982 ***NYPL [JLD 86-268]***

Ames, Samuel, 1806-1865. (joint author) Angell, Joseph Kinnicut, 1794-1857. Treatise on the law of private corporations aggregate [microform] /. Boston , 1855. lv, 939 p. ;
NYPL [*ZT-1731]

Amherst H. Wilder Foundation. Barry, Bryan W. Strategic planning workbook for nonprofit organizations /. St. Paul, MN , c1986. 72 p., [8] leaves of plates : ISBN 0-940069-00-8 (pbk.) LC Card 87-153976 DDC 658.4/012 19
HD62.6 .B37 1986

Amin, Galal A., 1935- Tanmiyah al-ʻArabīyah wa-al-ʻalāqāt al-dawlīyah /. al-Kuwayt , 1983. 230, 96 p. ; LC Card 86-964623
HC498 .T349 1983

Amin, Nasr El Din Osman. Nomadism versus sedenterization : an environmental choice in western Sudan : (the case of Gerih el Sarha) / by Nasr El Din Osman Amin. [Khartoum?] Sudan : Institute of Environmental Studies, University of Khartoum, 1986. 105 leaves : ill., maps ; 30 cm. (Environmental monograph series. no. 5) Bibliography: leaves 85-88. LC Card 86-981112
1. Land settlement - Sudan - Case studies. 2. Nomads - Sudan - Case studies. 3. Nomads - Sudan - Sedentarisation - Case studies. I. Series: Environmental monograph series (Jāmiʻat al-Kharṭūm. Maʻhad al-Dirāsāt al-Biʼīyah) , no. 5. II. Title.
HD977 .A65 1986

Amin, S. H. (Sayed Hessan) Islamic banking and finance : the experience of Iran / by S.H. Amin. Tehran : Vahid Publications, 1986. 72 p. : ill., ports. ; 22 cm. Bibliography: p. 71-72. ISBN 0-946706-30-1 (pbk.) LC Card 86-209623 DDC 332.1/0955 19
1. Banks and banking - Iran. 2. Banks and banking - Islamic countries. 3. Banks and banking - Religious aspects - Islam. 4. Banking law - Iran. I. Title.
HG3270.2.A6 A45 1986

Amin, Samir. La déconnexion, pour sortir du système mondial / Samir Amin. Paris : La Découverte, 1986, c1985. 333 p. : ill. ; 22 cm. (Cahiers libres. 413) Includes bibliographical references. ISBN 2-7071-1588-6 : LC Card 86-219988
1. Developing countries - Dependency on foreign countries. 2. International economic relations. 3. Income distribution. 4. Capitalism. 5. Socialism. I. Title.
HF1413 .A45 1986

Aminova, R. Kh.
Kolkhoznoe krestʹianstvo Uzbekistana na puti k razvitomu sotsializmu / R.Kh. Aminova. Tashkent : "Uzbekistan", 1983. 358 p. ; 21 cm. Bibliography: p. 341-[349] Includes indexes. LC Card 84-192680
1. Collective farms - Uzbek S.S.R. 2. Collective farms - Uzbek S.S.R. - Personnel management. I. Title.
HD1492.S652 U922 1983

Pobeda kolkhoznogo stroia v Uzbekistane : 1933-1941 gg. / R.Kh. Aminova. Tashkent : Izd-vo "Fan" Uzbekskoĭ SSR, 1981. 289 p. ; 22 cm. At head of title: Akademiia nauk Uzbekskoĭ SSR. Institut istorii. Includes bibliographical references. LC Card 82-161362
1. Collectivization of agriculture - Uzbek S.S.R. - History. 2. Agriculture - Economic aspects - Uzbek S.S.R. - History. I. Title.
HD1492.S652 U9226 1981

Amler, Robert W. Analyse und Gestaltung strategischer Informationssysteme der Unternehmung : Ansätze zu einer Neuorientierung der Methodenkritik / Robert W. Amler. Göttingen : Vandenhoeck & Ruprecht, c1983. xx, 279 p. : ill. ; 24 cm. (Innovative Unternehmensführung. Bd. 8) Bibliography: p. [245]-279. ISBN 3-525-12556-9 LC Card 83-198652
1. Strategic planning. 2. Decision-making. 3. Communication in management. I. Title.
HD30.28 .A45 1983

Ammann, Ulrich, 1921- Allenspach, Heinz. Bevorzugter Beamtenstatus, Möglichkeiten und Grenzen einer Reform . Zürich [1986] 32 p. ; LC Card 87-407830 DDC 330.9494 s 331.7/61354494 19
HC395 .Z43 Nr. 130 JN8831

Ammannati, S. (Sergio) Disoccupazione e nuove forme di accesso al lavoro nel mondo bancario /. Milano, Italy , c1986. 186 p. ; LC Card 87-150276
HD5718.B262 I83 1986

Ammassari, Gloria Pirzio. see **Pirzio Ammassari, Gloria.**

AMMONIA INDUSTRY - GREAT BRITAIN - EMPLOYEES - CASE STUDIES.
Harris, Rosemary. Power and powerlessness in industry . London , New York , 1987. viii, 245 p. : ISBN 0-422-60920-X LC Card 86-14420 DDC 338.4/766134/0941 19
HD6956.A497 H37 1986
NYPL [JLD 87-825]

'Amnūai Wirawan. Tokyo Trade Symposium (1985) Trade routes to sustained economic growth . New York , 1987. lii, 178 p. ; ISBN 0-312-01263-2 : LC Card 87-3494 DDC 382 19
HF1411 .T577 1985

Among the livewires . Kramer, Arthur, 1908- [Edmonds, Wash. , c1986] 141 p. : ISBN 0-939116-14-6 (pbk.) LC Card 86-91152 DDC 338.7/6136362/09797 19
HD9685.U7 P925 1986

Amort, Jiří. Dynamika národohospodářských struktur a mezinárodních ekonomických vztahů v podmínkách SEI / Jiří Amort. Praha : Ekonomický ústav ČSAV, 1986. 211 p. ; 20 cm. (Výzkum. publ. VP . č. 235) Summary in Russian. Bibliography: p. 172-175. LC Card 86-206744
1. Europe, Eastern - Economic integration. 2. Europe, Eastern - Economic conditions - 1945-. I. Series: Výzk. publ. (Ekonomicko-matematická laboratoř (Ekonomický ústav ČSAV)) , č. 235. II. Title.
HC244 .A626 1986

La amortización de deudas en Colombia . Castillo, Julián. Bogotá, Colombia , 1985. 162 leaves ; LC Card 86-204058 DDC 332.7/09861 19
HG4028.A5 C37 1985

AMORTIZATION - COLOMBIA.
Castillo, Julián. La amortización de deudas en Colombia . Bogotá, Colombia , 1985. 162 leaves ; LC Card 86-204058 DDC 332.7/09861 19
HG4028.A5 C37 1985

Amos, Orley M., 1954-
Economics : concepts, analysis, and applications / Orley M. Amos, Jr. Belmont, Calif. : Wadsworth Pub. Co., c1987. xxiv, 786 p. : ill. ; 24 cm. Includes index. ISBN 0-534-06948-7 : LC Card 86-24569 DDC 330 19
1. Economics. I. Title.
HB171.5 .A48 1987

Microeconomics : concepts, analysis, and applications / Orley M. Amos, Jr. Belmont, Calif. : Wadsworth Pub. Co., c1987. xxi, 768 p. : ill. (some col.) ; 24 cm. Includes index. ISBN 0-534-06951-7 (pbk.) LC Card 87-110402 DDC 338.5 19
1. Microeconomics. I. Title.
HB172 .A64 1987

Amosha, Aleksandr Ivanovich. Usloviia truda v regione /. Kiev , 1985. 252 p. : LC Card 86-105167
HD7726.U39 U85 1985
*NYPL [*QGA 87-3379]*

AMPURDÁN (SPAIN : REGION) - ECONOMIC CONDITIONS.
El Baix Empordà . Barcelona , c1984. xii, 303 p. : ISBN 84-505-0289-6 LC Card 85-186183
HC387.A636 B35 1984

AMPURDÁN (SPAIN : REGION) - POPULATION.
El Baix Empordà . Barcelona , c1984. xii, 303 p. : ISBN 84-505-0289-6 LC Card 85-186183
HC387.A636 B35 1984

AMSTERDAM (NETHERLANDS) - ECONOMIC CONDITIONS - 1945-
Om het behoud van een explosieve stad . Muiderberg , 1986. 298 p. : ISBN 90-6283-661-5 : LC Card 86-205071
HC328.A5 O4 1986

AMSTERDAM (NETHERLANDS) - INDUSTRIES.
Om het behoud van een explosieve stad . Muiderberg , 1986. 298 p. : ISBN 90-6283-661-5 : LC Card 86-205071
HC328.A5 O4 1986

Amt der OÖ. Landesregierung. Beiträge zur Geschichte des Eisenwesens in Oberösterreich. Linz , 1949- v. <1 > : LC Card 87-117640
HD9525.A83 U663 1949

Amtliche Statistik in marktwirtschaftlich organisierten Industriegesellschaften . Litz, Hans Peter. Frankfurt , New York , c1986. xii, 312 p. : ISBN 3-593-33752-5 LC Card 87-108767 DDC 350.81/9 19
HA37.G3 L58 1986

AMTRAK - APPROPRIATIONS AND EXPENDITURES.
Ferris, Sally A. Federal subsidies to rail passenger service . Washington, D.C. , Congress of the United States, Congressional Budget Office [1982] xxiii, 85, [1] p. : LC Card 82-602556 DDC 385/.1 19
HE1061 .F47 1982 *NYPL [JLF 86-1384]*

AMTRAK - FINANCE.
Ferris, Sally A. Federal subsidies to rail passenger service . Washington, D.C. , Congress of the United States, Congressional Budget Office [1982] xxiii, 85, [1] p. : LC Card 82-602556 DDC 385/.1 19
HE1061 .F47 1982 *NYPL [JLF 86-1384]*

Amzalak, Moses Bensabat, 1892-
D. Alvaro Pais e o pensamento económico em Portugal na Idade Média / por Moses Bensabat Amzalak. Lisboa : Academia das Ciências de Lisboa, 1954. 71 p. : ill. ; 20 cm. (Biblioteca de altos estudos) História das doutrinas económicas em Portugal Bibliography: p. 69-70. LC Card 84-213332
1. Pelagius, Alvarus, 1280?-1353 - Views on economics. 2. Economics. I. Title. II. Title: Dom Alvaro Pais e o pensamento económico em Portugal na Idade Média. III. Series. IV. Series: Amzalak, Moses Bensabat, 1892- História das doutrinas económicas em Portugal.
HB79.P45 A49 1954

História das doutrinas económicas em Portugal.
Amzalak, Moses Bensabat, 1892- D. Alvaro Pais e o pensamento económico em Portugal na Idade Média /. Lisboa , 1954. 71 p. : LC Card 84-213332
HB79.P45 A49 1954

Pinto, Isaac de, 1715-1787. [Selections. 1960.] O economista Isaac de Pinto, o seu "Tratado da circulação e do crédito," e outros escritos económicos /. Lisboa , 1960. 247 p. : LC Card 85-125396
HJ150 .P552 1960

Anadolu Üniversitesi yayınları. İktisadi ve İdari Bilimler Fakültesi yayınları .
(24) Ürper, Yılmaz. Türkiye'de tarımsal kooperatiflerin toplumsal değişmeye etkileri . Eskişehir , 1985. xvi, 109, xxxiii p. ; LC Card 86-161567
HG2051.T92 I48 1985

Anais /. Encontro Estadual de Cooperativismo (1979 : Curitiba, Brazil) [Curitiba] [1979] 41 leaves : LC Card 84-223142
HD3475.A3 P364 1979

Anais /. Seminário Nacional de Abastecimento Alimentar em Grandes Cidades--a Experiência de São Paulo (1984 : São Paulo, Brazil) São Paulo, São Paulo, Brasil , 1984. xii, 421 p. : LC Card 87-404933 DDC 363.8/0981/61 19
HD9014.B83 S447 1984

Anais--1981 /. Seminário Permanente de Habitação Popular (1981 : Recife, Brazil) Recife [19]82. 178 p. ; LC Card 84-256147
HD7323.P37 S46 1981

Analisa perkembangan perdagangan luar negeri. Jakarta, Indonesia : Biro Pusat Statistik, [1985] iv, 80, 44 leaves : ill. ; 28 cm. Bibliography: leaf 80. LC Card 85-942679
1. Indonesia - Commerce. I. Indonesia. Biro Pusat Statistik.
HF3806.5 .A6 1985

Análise da citricultura na Bahia : perspectivas de desenvolvimento / Secretaria do Planjamento, Ciência e Tecnologia, Centro de Projetos e Estudos-CENPES. Salvador : CENPES, 1986. 88 p. : ill., maps ; 22 cm. Bibliography: p. 87-88. LC Card 86-221439
1. Citrus fruit industry - Brazil - Bahia (State). I. Centro de Projetos e Estudos (Bahia, Brazil).
HD9259.C53 B63 1986

Análise da idade média ao casamento, 1930-1978 /. Carrilho, Maria José. Lisboa, Portugal , 1984. 27 p. : LC Card 85-124431
HB1241 .C37 1984

Análise das distorções dos preços domésticos em relação aos preços de fronteira : um estudo preliminar / Ministério da Agricultura, Companhia de Financiamento da Produção. Brasília : CFP, 1983. 125 p. : ill. ; 25 cm. (Projeto de pesquisa--política de preços para a agricultura . v. especial 5) Coleção Análise e pesquisa ; vol. 30 LC Card 86-200859
1. Agricultural prices - Brazil. 2. Agricultural prices - Government policy - Brazil. I. Companhia de Financiamento da Produção (Brazil). II. Series. III. Series: Coleção Análise e pesquisa , v. 30.
HD9014.B82 A66 1983

Análise de empresas em inflação . Pina, Amílcar. [Porto] , 1985. 142 p. : LC Card 86-174401
HF5658.5 .P56 1985

Análise de sistemas de controle operacional de ônibus urbano /. Antônio, Ricardo Augusto Braga. Brasília, DF , 1985. 92 p. : LC Card 87-113222 DDC 388.4/1322/068 19
HE5613 .A775 1985

Uma análise econômica do problema do cheque sem fundos no Brasil /. Iorio de Souza, Ubiratan Jorge, 1946- Rio de Janeiro [Brasília] , 1985. 204 p. : LC Card 87-141390 DDC 332.7/6 19
HG1691 .I58 1985

Análise econômico-financeira da indústria de mineração, 1978-1982 / [supervisão, Divisão de Economia Mineral--DNPM ; coordenação, Carlos Augusto Ramos Neves, Carlos Affonso Braga ; equipe executora, DECON/CPRM, José Guedes de Andrade ... et al.]. Brasília : República Federativa do Brasil, Ministério das Minas e Energia, Departamento Nacional da Produção Mineral, 1984. viii, 105 p. : ill. ; 30 cm. Bibliography: p. [48] At head of title: Projeto perfil empresarial. LC Card 86-146667
1. Mineral industries - Brazil. I. Brazil. Departamento Nacional da Produção Mineral. II. Title: Projeto perfil empresarial.
HD9506.B72 A65 1984

Analisi microeconomica della produzione /. Tani, Piero. Roma , 1986. viii, 351 p. : LC Card 86-169971
HB241 .T36 1986

Análisis comparativo de la información sobre población ocupada . Fernández, Sonia. México, D.F. [1977] 28 p. ; LC Card 84-227473
HD5731.A6 F46 1977

Análisis de indicadores socioeconómicos, Subregión Limón : jornada de planificación para sentar las bases del plan operativo / Ministerio de la Presidencia, Oficina de Planificación Nacional y Política Económica. [San José] : La Oficina, [1981] 26 p. ; 27 cm. On cover: División de Planificación y Coordinación Regional. "Marzo 1981." Includes bibliographical references. LC Card 83-240958
1. Limón (Costa Rica : Province) - Economic conditions. 2. Limón (Costa Rica : Province) - Social conditions. I. Costa Rica. Oficina de Planificación Nacional y Política Económica. II. Costa Rica. División de Planificación y Coordinación Regional.
HC143.Z7 L554 1981

Análisis de la economía dominicana / Carlos Massad ... [et al.]. Santo Domingo, República Dominicana : Banco Central de la República Dominicana, 1985. 73 p. ; 28 cm. Spanish and English. CONTENTS. - Política cambiaria en República Dominicana / por Carlos Massad -- Options for exchange rate policy in the Dominican Republic ;

Opciones para la política cambiaria en la República Dominicana / por John Williamson -- Adjustment with Development Institute ; Ajuste con Desarrollo / por Tony Killick -- Aspectos legales de la reestructuración de la deuda externa / por Roger W. Thomas y Linda B. Klein. LC Card 86-186259
1. Foreign exchange administration - Dominican Republic. 2. Dominican Republic - Economic policy. I. Massad A., Carlos. II. Banco Central de la República Dominicana.
HG3926.5 .A53 1985

Análisis de la encuesta a líderes nacionales / Asociación Hondureña de Planificación de Familia. Tegucigalpa, D.C. : La Asociación, 1983. 49, [12] leaves ; 28 cm. Cover title. LC Card 85-203745
1. Honduras - Population policy - Public opinion. 2. Birth control - Honduras - Public opinion. 3. Asociación Hondureña de Planificación de Familia - Public opinion. 4. Public opinion - Honduras. I. Asociación Hondureña de Planificación de Familia.
HB3540.A3 A52 1983

Análisis de la encuesta sobre cambio técnico en la industria del cuero en Uruguay /. Teja, Ana María. Montevideo, Uruguay [1980] 56 p., [60] leaves ; LC Card 86-157655
HD9780.U82 T45 1980

Análisis de la previsión en Chile / editor, Sergio Baeza ; José Pablo Arellano ... [et al.]. Santiago, Chile : Centro de Estudios Públicos, [1986] 309 p. : ill. ; 23 cm. Includes bibliographical references. LC Card 87-115194
1. Social security - Chile. 2. Privitization - Chile. I. Baeza V., Sergio. II. Arellano, José Pablo.
HD7156 .A78 1986

Análisis de la problemática actual y perspectivas futuras de las industrias vinícola y conservera hortofrutícola en La Rioja. [La Rioja, Argentina] : Diputación Provincial de La Rioja, Gabinete de Estudios Económicos y Territoriales, 1981. 97 p., [3] p. of plates : maps (some col.) ; 25 cm. Includes bibliographical references. ISBN 84-7359-144-5 LC Card 86-146432
1. Wine industry - Argentina - La Rioja (Province). 2. Vegetables - Argentina - La Rioja (Province) - Preservation. I. La Rioja (Argentina : Province). Gabinete de Estudios Económicos y Territoriales.
HD9384.A8 L323 1981

Un análisis de la rentabilidad accionaria de la Bolsa de Valores de Lima, 1980-1983 /. Rocha C., Julio César de la (Rocha Corzo) Lima, Perú , 1984. ii, 56 p. ; LC Card 86-154699
HG5392 .R66 1984

Análisis de la situación económica de Guatemala, 1965-1984 /. Vides de Orive, Enna. Guatemala, Guatemala , 1985. ii leaves, 118 p. : LC Card 86-205265 DDC 330.97281/053 19
HC144 .V53 1985

Análisis de las condiciones de vivienda de los hogares colombianos, a partir de los resultados de la encuesta nacional de hogares, etapa 33, 1981 /. Jaramillo, Samuel. Bogotá, Colombia , 1985. ii, 166 p. ; LC Card 87-403605 DDC 363.5/1/09861 19
HD7325.A3 J37 1985

Análisis de las cooperativas de trabajo asociado en Madrid /. Vara Miranda, Ma. Jesús (María Jesús) [Madrid] , c1985. 463 p. : ISBN 84-7434-332-1 LC Card 87-109103 DDC 334/.6/094643 19
HD3218.M38 V37 1985

Análisis de normas sobre contabilidad e inflación . Lazzati, Santiago. Buenos Aires [1981] 157 p. ; LC Card 82-216941
HF5658.5 .L39 1981

Análisis del cambio en la concentración a través del coeficiente de Gini /. Cortés, Fernando, 1941- México, D.F. [1982] 55 leaves : LC Card 83-111847
HB523 .C67 1982

Análisis del presupuesto general del estado de 1986. [Quito, Ecuador] : Corporación de Estudios para el Desarrollo, [1986] ii, 2, 26, 8 p. ; 29 cm. (Serie Documentos de trabajo . no. 1) LC Card 87-115859
1. Budget - Ecuador. 2. Ecuador - Appropriations and expenditures. I. Corporación de Estudios para el Desarrollo (Ecuador). II. Series: Serie Documentos de trabajo (Corporación de Estudios para el Desarrollo (Ecuador)) , no. 1.
HJ955 .A523 1986

Análisis descriptivo de las exportaciones colombianas, 1950-1980 /. Rodríguez, Luis Hernando. Bogotá, Colombia , 1985. 3, 169 p. : LC Card 87-402978 DDC 382/.6/09861 19
HF3426.5 .R63 1985

Análisis económico social de las comunidades pesqueras del Estado Sucre /. Lárez, Ronald. [Carúpano, Venezuela] , 1983. 217, 19, 8 p. : LC Card 87-115222 DDC 338.3/72/098753 19
HD8039.F652 V45 1983

Análisis microeconómico de los factores que determinan el valor de mercado de las empresas industriales mexicanas y su tasa de expansión /. Mántey de Anguiano, M. G. [Mexico City] [1986] iv, 63 leaves : LC Card 87-400949 DDC 658.1/5/0972 19
HG4092 .M36 1986

Análisis tipológico del trabajador del Gran Santiago e impacto sobre el ingreso de las políticas redistributivas, 1970-1971 /. Aldunate B., Adolfo. [Santiago, Chile?] [1972] iv, 9, [35] p. ; LC Card 83-169296
HC193.S23 A43 1972

Análisis y diagnóstico de la empresa . López Navarrete, Gregorio. Barcelona [1983?] 377 p. : ISBN 84-300-9587-X LC Card 87-113212
HG5634.5 .L67 1983

Analiz dinamiki sot͡sialisticheskogo rasshirennogo vosproizvodstva /. Ozerov, V. K. (Viktor Konstantinovich) Novosibirsk , 1984. 263 p. ; LC Card 85-151291
HC340.I52 O97 1984

Analiz i sintez v sistemakh otraslevogo upravlenii͡a /. Lagosha, Boris Aleksandrovich. Moskva , 1978. 262 p., [1] folded leaf of plates : LC Card 81-167577
HD30.25 .L335 1978

Analiz khozi͡aĭstvennoĭ dei͡atel′nosti kooperativnykh organizat͡siĭ /. Kudri͡avt͡sev, A. A. (Alekseĭ Andreevich) Moskva , 1977. 262 p. ; LC Card 82-124930
HD3515 .K78 1977

Analiz khozi͡aĭstvennoĭ dei͡atel′nosti sel′skokhozi͡aĭstvennykh predprii͡atiĭ. Vaikulis, J. (Jānis) Lauksaimniecības uzņēmumu saimnieciskās darbības analīze /. Rīga , 1986. 185 p. ; LC Card 86-199301
HD1492.S652 L38 1986

Analiza ekonomiczna przedsiębiorstw przemysłowych /. Buk, Halina. Katowice , 1977. 285 p. ; LC Card 82-102080
HD36 .B775 1977

Analysa hasil survey pengupahan dan draft pedoman kebijaksanaan penetapan upah minimum, tahun 1977/1978 /. Proyek Pengaturan Pengupahan Daerah Sumatera Selatan (Indonesia) [S.l.] [1978?] 21, [2], 3 leaves ; LC Card 80-941072
HD4922.I5 P75 1978

Die Analyse . Berg, Hermann von, 1933- Köln , c1985. 240 p. : ISBN 3-7663-0942-0 LC Card 86-122582 DDC 341.24/22 19
HC241 .B47 1985

Analyse bancaire de la P.M.E. /. Guilhot, Bernard-Henri. Paris , c1985. 306 p. : ISBN 2-86325-035-3 : LC Card 86-152256
HG4027.7 .G85 1985

Analyse de l'évolution des principaux indicateurs économiques au Québec, en Ontario, au Canada et aux Etats-Unis . Morin, André, analyste en rémunération. [Québec] [1982] 209 p. ; ISBN 2-551-04641-6 LC Card 83-103355
HC117.Q4 M66 1982

Analyse der Ansiedlung von Einkaufszentren und Verbrauchermärkten in Nordrhein-Westfalen /. Döhne, Ulrich. Dortmund , Essen , 1977. 39 p. : LC Card 86-181973
HF5429.6.G42 D64 1977

Analyse der Arbeitslosigkeit in den Regionen Nordrhein-Westfalens . Bremicker, Burckhardt. Bochum , 1984. xx, 381 p. : ISBN 3-88339-362-2 LC Card 84-196621 DDC 331.13/794355 19
HD5780.N6 B74 1984 ***NYPL [JLD 86-2367]***

Analyse der strikturellen Entwicklung der deutschen Wirtschaft. Wechselwirkungen von Geldpolitik, Inflation und Strukturwandel . Hamburg , 1984. 179 p. : ISBN 3-87895-243-0 LC Card 84-221405
HB235.G3 W42 1984

Analyse der strukturellen Entwicklung der deutschen Wirtschaft. Zwischenbericht, Analyse der strukturellen Entwicklung der deutschen Wirtschaft . Hamburg , 1979. viii, 142, 49 leaves : LC Card 83-132166
HC286.7 .Z88 1979

Analyse der Wettbewerbsfähigkeit von Extensivblattfrüchten in Niedersachsen unter ökonomischen und ökologischen Gesichtspunkten /. Reessing, Ludwig. Kiel , 1986. xiv, 251 p. : ISBN 3-922553-81-8 LC Card 86-163003
HD1960.L69 R44 1986

Analyse der Wirksamkeit der Beschäftigungszulage : [Paragraph] 4b Inv. Zul. G / Bearbeiter, Shalom Apeloig ... [et al.]. München : Ifo-Institut für Wirtschaftsforschung, 1984. vii, 172 p. : 13 ill. ; 21 cm. (Ifo Studien zur Finanzpolitik, 0081-7279 . 32) Includes bibliographical references. LC Card 85-230164
1. Investment tax credit - Germany (West). 2. Capital investments - Germany, West. 3. Tax incentives - Germany (West). 4. Investment tax credit - Law and legislation - Germany (West). I. Apeloig, Shalom. II. Series.
HJ4720.A45 A53 1984

Analyse économique et gestion de l'entreprise /. Roux, Dominique. Paris , c1986- v. <1 > : ISBN 2-04-016455-3 LC Card 87-114498
HD33 .R647 1986

Analyse, épistémologie, histoire économiques. Le Bas, Christian. Histoire sociale des faits économiques . Lyon , c1984. 242 p. : ISBN 2-7297-0221-0 : LC Card 85-152656
HC275 .L45 1984

L'analyse non linéaire et ses motivations économiques /. Aubin, Jean-Pierre. Paris , New York , 1984. x, 214 p. : ISBN 2-225-79541-X : LC Card 86-135801
HB135 .A86 1984

Analyse organisatorischer und personeller Einflussgrössen auf Fehlzeiten /. Hollich, Franz. Karlsruhe , c1985. iii, 210 p. : ISBN 3-923485-03-4 LC Card 85-233162
HD5115.2.G4 H65 1985

Analyse socio-économique comparée des coopératives d'habitation en France et au Québec : rapport de recherche / Claude Vienney ... [et al.]. [Chicoutimi] : Groupe de recherche et d'intervention régionales (GRIR), Université du Québec à Chicoutimi, [1985] xvi, 391 p. : ill. ; 24 cm. (Travaux du GRIR . 5) Includes bibliographies. CONTENTS. - Les générations de formules de coopératives d'habitation en France (1850-1980) / Claud- Vienney -- Les générations de formules de coopératives d'habitation au Québec, 1938-1980 / Roland Charbonneau et Jean-Pierre Deslauriers -- Quelques leçons de la comparaison / Claude Vienney -- Prise en charge par les habitants de la gestion des habitations coopératives terminées / Alain Pringent [i.e., Prigent] -- Rapports entre professionnels de la promotion immobilière et utilisateurs des habitations / Roland Charbonneau et Jean-Pierre Deslauriers -- Bouclage des circuits de financement et coexistence de formules adaptées des catégories sociales diversifiées / Claude Vienney. ISBN 2-920730-04-5 LC Card 86-181851
1. Housing, Cooperative - France. 2. Housing, Cooperative - Québec (Province). I. Vienney, Claudde. II. Université du Québec à Chicoutimi. Groupe de recherche et d'intervention régionales. III. Series.
HD7287.72.F8 A53 1985

Analyse strategischer Faktoren . Grimm, Ulrich. Wiesbaden , c1983. 294 p. : ISBN 3-409-18720-0 LC Card 84-173895
HD30.28 .G76 1983

Analyse und Bewertung ausgewählter sozialwissenschaftlichen Forschungen /. Ochs, Peter. Dortmund , Bremerhaven , 1983. 102 p. ; ISBN 3-88314-245-X LC Card 83-207278
HD7708 .O28 1983

Analyse und Gestaltung strategischer Informationssysteme der Unternehmung . Amler, Robert W. Göttingen , c1983. xx, 279 p. : ISBN 3-525-12556-9 LC Card 83-198652
HD30.28 .A45 1983

Analyse und Planung des Erfolgs und der Überschussverwendung einer Krankenversicherungsaktiengesellschaft /. Henrich, Rudolf. Karlsruhe , c1983. xxi, 498

p. : ISBN 3-88487-053-X LC Card 85-131706
HG9399.G32 H46 1983

Analyse von Unfällen motorisierter Zweiradbenutzer : Entwicklung im Bundesgebiet, 1969-1976 : Sonderuntersuchung Bayern 1976 / [bearbeitet, ADAC-Zentrale, Abteilung Verkehrstechnik, Hans-Joachim Vorholz, Wolfgang Schön]. [West Germany] : ADAC Verkehrstechnik, [1976] 32 p. : ill. ; 30 cm. (Verkehrsunfälle . 3) Cover title. LC Card 85-135424
1. Bicycles - Germany (West) - Bavaria - Accidents. 2. Traffic accidents - Germany (West) - Bavaria - Accidents. I. Vorholz, Hans-Joachim. II. Schön, Wolfgang. III. ADAC. Abteilung Verkehrstechnik. IV. Series.
HE5614.5.G3 A65 1976

Analyseinstrumente für die strategische Marketingplanung /. Schadenhofer, Leopold. Wien , 1982. 222 p. : ISBN 3-85369-497-7 : LC Card 82-237712
HF5415 .S29 1982

Analysen aus der Abteilung Entwicklungsländerforschung .
(Nr. 92/93) Probleme der Rohstoffsicherung =. Bonn [1981] 215 p. : LC Card 85-206699
HF1051 .P76 1980

Analysen aus der Abteilung Entwicklungsländerforschung, 0174-5190 .
(Nr. 111/112) Mexiko . Bonn [1983?] 127, [2] p. ; LC Card 85-206583
HC135 .M585 1983

(Nr. 122) Nuscheler, Franz. Die Entwicklungspolitik der Regierung Thatcher . [Bonn] [1986] 93 p. : LC Card 86-186261
HC60 .N87 1986

Analyses of statistical data .
(4) LaLonde, Robert John. The manpower report of KEPE . Athens, Greece , c1986. 122 p. ; LC Card 86-205504 DDC 331.1/09495 19
HD5811.83.A6 L3 1986

Analysing conflict and its resolution : some mathematical contributions : based on the proceedings of a conference organized by the Institute of Mathematics and Its Applications on the mathematics of conflict and its resolution, held at Churchill College, Cambridge in December 1984 / edited by P.G. Bennett. Oxford [Oxfordshire] : Clarendon Press ; New York : Oxford University Press, 1987. xvi, 349 p. : ill. ; 24 cm. (The Institute of Mathematics and Its Applications conference series . new ser., 8) Includes bibliographies. ISBN 0-19-853611-9 : LC Card 86-31108 DDC 658.4 19
1. Conflict management - Mathematical models. I. Bennett, P. G. (Peter G.). II. Institute of Mathematics and Its Applications. III. Title: Analyzing conflict and its resolution. IV. Series.
HD42 .A52 1987

ANALYSIS, JOB. see **JOB ANALYSIS.**

Analysis of accounts of parastatals, 1966-1977. Dar Es Salaam : United Republic of Tanzania, Bureau of Statistics, Ministry of Finance and Planning, [1979] 43 p. ; 33 cm. Chiefly tables. "October 1979." LC Card 81-142522 DDC 354.67809/2 19
1. Government business enterprises - Tanzania - Statistics. I. Tanzania. Bureau of Statistics.
HD4348.5 .A52 1979

Analysis of commodity markets for policy purposes /. Harris, Stuart. London , 1978. ix, 81 p. ; ISBN 0-900842-42-3 (pbk.) LC Card 85-111455 DDC 332.64/4 19
HG6046 .H367 1978

The analysis of credit . Bathory, Alexander. London , New York , c1987. xiii, 385 p. ; ISBN 0-07-084938-2 : LC Card 87-2060 DDC 658.8/8 19
HG3751 .B385 1987

ANALYSIS OF ENVIRONMENT IMPACT. see **ENVIRONMENTAL IMPACT ANALYSIS.**

Analysis of financial statements /. Agarwal, N. P. (Narain Prashad) New Delhi , 1981. xii, 363 p. : LC Card 81-904955 DDC 657/.33 19
HD9539.A63 I522 1981
NYPL [JLD 86-2568]

ANALYSIS OF FOOD. see **FOOD ADULTERATION AND INSPECTION.**

An analysis of grain elevator bankruptcies in Louisiana /. Traylor, Harlon D. [Baton Rouge?] [1986] iii, 77 p. ; LC Card 87-620885 DDC 338.1/09763 s 338.1/6 19
HD1775.L8 L7 no. 661 HD9037.L6

Analysis of national and regional travel trends /. Lau, Lorrie A. Y. Washington, D.C. , 1986. iii, 78, 32 p. : LC Card 87-601033 DDC 388.3/14/0973 19
HE370.T74 L38 1986

Analysis of productivity levels and economic efficiency in agriculture /. Suryanarayana Raju, S. K. V. Allahabad, India , 1987 [i.e. 1986] viii, 368 p. : ISBN 81-85076-12-X : LC Card 86-903606 DDC 338.1/0954/84 19
HD2075.V58 S87 1986

Analysis of quoted companies JSE industrial sectional averages. Ontleding van genoteerde maatskappye JEB industriële afdelingsgemiddeldes . Pretoria , 1984. iv, 163 p. ; ISBN 0-86979-588-0 LC Card 85-156278
HD2922 .O57 1984

Analysis of rice export flows from southern states /. Wharton, Robert B. [Baton Rouge?] [1986] iii, 44 p. ; LC Card 87-620886 DDC 338.1/09763 s 382/.41318/0975021 19
HD1775.L8 L7 no. 662 HD9066.U46A13

An analysis of some aspects of employment and unemployment in the African townships of Umlazi and Lamontville . Padayachee, Vishnu. Durban [South Africa] [1985] iii, 49 p. ; ISBN 0-949947-75-X (pbk.) LC Card 87-404149 DDC 331.12/5/0968455 19
HD5842.D87 P33 1985

An analysis of the causes of savings and loan association failures /. Benston, George J. New York, N.Y. (90 Trinity Place, New York 10006) [1985] 182 p. : LC Card 86-209942 DDC 332.3/2/0973 19
HG2151 .B46 1985

Analysis of the federal residential energy tax credits [microform] : final report : prepared for U. S. Dept. of Energy / by Charles River Associates Incorporated. Boston, Mass. : The Associates, 1982. v, 102 p. : ill. ; 28 cm. "April 1982." "DE82 013841." Bibliography: p. 101-102. Microfiche. Springfield, Va. : NTIS, 1982. 1 microfiche : negative ; 11 x 15 cm. (DOE/PE/70013--T1)
1. Energy tax credits - United States. 2. Energy policy - United States. I. Charles River Associates.
NYPL [*XME-11,559]

Analysis of the 1987-88 tax expenditure budget. Sacramento, Calif. (925 L St., Suite 650, Sacramento 95814) : Office of the Legislative Analyst, [1987] 2 v. ; 28 cm. "January 1987." CONTENTS. - v. 1. Overview and analysis of selected individual programs -- v. 2. Detailed compendium of individual tax expenditure programs. LC Card 87-621598 DDC 353.97940072/4 19
1. Tax expenditures - California. I. California. Legislature. Joint Legislative Budget Committee. Legislative Analyst.
HJ4655.C23 A53 1987

ANALYSIS OF TIME SERIES. see **TIME-SERIES ANALYSIS.**

Analysis of variance /. Iversen, Gudmund R. Newbury Park , c1987. 94 p. : ISBN 0-8039-3001-1 (pbk.) LC Card 87-61276 DDC 519.5/35 19
HA31.35 .I85 1987

Analytical instrumentation market in Europe. Analytical instruments markets in Europe. New York, N.Y. , c1983. xii, 253 p. ; LC Card 87-141819 DDC 380.1/45681754 19
HD9706.65.C573 E82 1983

Analytical instruments markets in Europe. New York, N.Y. : Frost & Sullivan, c1983. xii, 253 p. ; 29 cm. Spine title: Analytical instrumentation market in Europe. "February 1983." "#E606." LC Card 87-141819 DDC 380.1/45681754 19
1. Chromatographic analysis equipment industry - Europe. 2. Market surveys - Europe. I. Frost & Sullivan. II. Title: Analytical instrumentation market in Europe.
HD9706.65.C573 E82 1983

Analytical Marxism / edited by John Roemer. Cambridge, CB ; New York : Cambridge University Press ; viii, 313 p. : ill. ; 24 cm. (Studies in Marxism and social theory) Bibliography: p. 304-313. ISBN 0-521-30025-8 LC Card 85-11697 DDC 335.4 19
1. Marxian economics - Addresses, essays, lectures. 2. Communism - Addresses, essays, lectures. I. Roemer, John E. II. Series.
HB97.5 .A487 1986 ***NYPL [JLE 86-1742]***

Analytical study for the market of white meat and eggs / Kingdom of Saudi Arabia, Jeddah Chamber of Commerce and Industry, Research Centre. Jeddah : The Centre, [1985?] 159 p. : ill. (some col.) ; 24 cm. (Researches of the Jeddah Chamber of Commerce and Industry . research no. 3) LC Card 85-964046 DDC 381/.4566493/09538 19
1. Poultry industry - Saudi Arabia. 2. Fish trade - Saudi Arabia. 3. Egg trade - Saudi Arabia. 4. Market surveys - Saudi Arabia. I. Ghurfah al-Tijārīyah al-Ṣināʻīyah bi-Jiddah. Markaz al-Buḥūth. II. Series.
HD9437.S332 A53 1985

Analyzing conflict and its resolution. Analysing conflict and its resolution . Oxford [Oxfordshire] , New York , 1987. xvi, 349 p. : ISBN 0-19-853611-9 : LC Card 86-31108 DDC 658.4 19
HD42 .A52 1987

Analyzing redistribution policies . Kakwani, Nanak. Cambridge [Cambridgeshire] , New York , 1986. ix, 293 p. : ISBN 0-521-30838-0 LC Card 85-31342 DDC 339.5/2 19
HC610.I5 K35 1986 ***NYPL [JLE 86-3491]***

Anambra State, Nigeria.
Government white paper on the Report of the Administrative Board of Inquiry into the Enugu Market Authority / Anambra/Imo States of Nigeria. Enugu : Printed by the Govt. Printer, 1976. 25 p. ; 25 cm. Cover title. LC Card 86-204970
1. East-Central State (Nigeria). Enugu Market Authority. 2. Markets - Government policy - Nigeria - East-Central State. 3. Governmental investigations - Nigeria - East-Central State. I. East-Central State (Nigeria). Administrative Board of Inquiry into the Enugu Market Authority. II. Imo State Nigeria. III. Title.
HF5475.N52 E373 1976

Government white paper on the report of the Administrative Board of Inquiry on Ministry of Works / Anambra/Imo States of Nigeria. [Enugu, Nigeria] : The States, [1976?] 100 p. ; 25 cm. Cover title. LC Card 86-205027 DDC 354.669/4 19
1. East-Central State (Nigeria). Ministry of Works and Housing. 2. Administrative agencies - Nigeria - East-Central State - Corrupt practices. 3. Corruption (in politics) - Nigeria - East-Central State. I. Imo State Nigeria. II. East-Central State (Nigeria). Administrative Board of Inquiry on Ministry of Works. III. Title.
HD4365.5.Z8 E373 1976

Anamesa se dyo exegerseis . Vrachniarēs, Chrēstos. Athēna , 1985. 139, [5] p. ; LC Card 86-206897
HD1536.G7 V73 1985

Ananta, Aris. Perilaku fertilitas di beberapa daerah di Jawa / oleh Aris Ananta, Sri Harijati Hatmadji. Jakarta : Kerjasama Kantor Menteri Negara Kependudukan dan Lingkungan Hidup dengan Lembaga Demografi, Fakultas Ekonomi, Universitas Indonesia, 1986. vi, 56, 26 p. ; 22 cm. Bibliography: p. 55-56. LC Card 86-946460
1. Fertility, Human - Indonesia - Java. I. Hatmadji, Sri Harijati. II. Indonesia. Kantor Menteri Negara Kependudukan dan Lingkungan Hidup. III. Universitas Indonesia. Lembaga Demografi. IV. Title.
HB1058.J38 A52 1986

Anao, Richard A., 1940- Alile, H. I. The Nigerian stock market in operation /. [Lagos, Nigeria] 1986 (Lagos, Nigeria : Jeromelaiho & Associates) 194, v p. : LC Card 87-143647 DDC 332.64/2669 19
HG5881.N6 A43 1986

Hē anaptyxē tēs hellēnikēs geōrgias . Delēs, Dēmētrēs I. Athēna , 1985. 3 v. in 2 : LC Card 86-203175
HD2055.5 .D44 1985

Anaptyxē tēs Hellēnikēs viomēchanias /. Kintis, Andreas A. Athēna [1982] 180 p. ; LC Card 84-132514
HC295 .K515 1982

ANARCHISM.
Vasco, Neno. Concepção anarquista do sindicalismo /. Porto , 1984. 209 p. ; LC Card 84-256086 DDC 320.5/7 19
HX833 .V37 1984 ***NYPL [JLD 86-2525]***

ANARCHISM - SPAIN - CATALONIA - HISTORY - 20TH CENTURY.
Sabater, Jordi, 1958- Anarquisme i catalanisme . Barcelona , 1986. 231 p. ; ISBN 84-297-2490-7 LC Card 87-108668
HD8582.C583 S24 1986

Anarquisme i catalanisme . Sabater, Jordi, 1958- Barcelona , 1986. 231 p. ; ISBN 84-297-2490-7 LC Card 87-108668
HD8582.C583 S24 1986

ANASAZI CULTURE. see **PUEBLO INDIANS.**

Anastassopoulos, J. P.
[Multinationales publiques. English]
State-owned multinationals / Jean-Pierre Anastassopoulos, Georges Blanc, and Pierre Dussauge ; preface by Eneko Landaburu ; translated by Valerie Katzaros. Chichester [England] ; New York : Wiley, c1987. xii, 200 p. : ill. ; 24 cm. (Wiley/IRM series on multinationals) Translation of: Les multinationales publiques. Bibliography: p. [185]-193. Includes indexes. ISBN 0-471-91502-5 : LC Card 87-2033 DDC 338.8/8 19
1. International business enterprises. 2. Government business enterprises. I. Blanc, Georges. II. Dussauge, Pierre. III. Title. IV. Series.
HD2755.5 .A613 1987

Anatomia tēs Hellēnikēs oikonomias apo to 1953 mechri sēmera /. Kamouzēs, Kōn/nos Ch. (Kōnstantinos Ch.), 1946- Thessalonikē , 1981. 197 p. : LC Card 84-140694
HC295 .K28 1981

Anatomia tēs Hellēnikēs oikonomias (1953-1980) Kamouzēs, Kōn/nos Ch. (Kōnstantinos Ch.), 1946- Anatomia tēs Hellēnikēs oikonomias apo to 1953 mechri sēmera /. Thessalonikē , 1981. 197 p. : LC Card 84-140694
HC295 .K28 1981

The anatomy of major projects . Morris, Peter W. G. Chichester , New York , c1987. p. cm. ISBN 0-471-91551-3 : LC Card 87-8176 DDC 658.4/04 19
HD69.P75 M674 1987

Anatomy of the economic crisis /. Marcy, Sam, 1911- Atlanta , c1982. viii, 120 p. : ISBN 0-89567-077-1 (pbk.) ***NYPL [JLD 86-1329]***

Anatomy of the economic crisis /. Marcy, Sam, 1911- Atlanta , 1982. viii, 120 p. ; ISBN 0-89567-077-1 (pbk.) LC Card 87-132534 DDC 330.9/048 19
HC59 .M258 1982

Anatomy of the wine trade . Loftus, Simon. New York , c1985. 179 p. ; ISBN 0-06-015785-2 : LC Card 87-45066 DDC 380.1/456632 19
HD9370.5 .L64 1985

Anaya, Ricardo. Espinoza C., Jorge. Reforma agraria en Bolivia /. Cochabamba, Bolivia , 1984. 78 p. ; LC Card 86-166584
HD1333.B5 E87 1984

Ancey, Gérard. Evaluation du développement rural /. [Paris] , c1982. 201 p. : ISBN 2-11-084484-1 LC Card 84-134740
HC59.72.E44 E93 1982

--Anche l'uomo doveva essere di ferro : classe e movimento operaio a Trieste nel secondo dopoguerra / O. Colummi ... [et al.] ; a cura di Luigi Ganapini. Milano, Italy : F. Angeli, c1986. 441 p. : ill. ; 22 cm. At head of title: Istituto regionale per la storia del movimento di liberazione nel Friuli-Venezia Giulia. On spine: 2000.294. Includes bibliographical references and index. LC Card 86-213675
1. Labor and laboring classes - Italy - Trieste Region - History - 20th century. 2. Trade-unions - Italy - Trieste Region - History - 20th century. 3. Reconstruction (1939-1951) - Italy - Trieste Region. I. Colummi, Cristiana. II. Ganapini, Luigi. III. Istituto regionale per la storia del movimento di liberazione nel Friuli-Venezia Giulia.
HD8490.T742 A53 1986

Ancona, Hedy d'. Vrouwen en economische zelfstandigheid /. Amsterdam , c1986. 199 p. : ISBN 90-6222-139-4 : LC Card 86-182832
HD6162 .V74 1986

And the wolf finally came . Hoerr, John P., 1930- Pittsburgh, PA , 1988. p. cm. ISBN 0-8229-3572-4 LC Card 87-24932 DDC 338.4/7669142/097488 19
HD9517.M85 H64 1988

ANDALUSIA (SPAIN : REGION) - COMMERCE - HISTORY.
Mercado, Thomas de, d. 1575. [Tratos y contratos de mercaderes. Selections.] La economia en la Andalucia del descubrimiento /. Sevilla [1985?] 276 p. ; ISBN 84-7587-047-3 LC Card 86-151225
HF1003 .M525 1985

ANDALUSIA (SPAIN) - ECONOMIC CONDITIONS.
Comín, Alfonso C. Noticia de Andalucía /. Sevilla [1985] 338 p. ; ISBN 84-7587-037-6 LC Card 86-219377
HC387.A64 C62 1985

González do Molina Navarro, Manuel. Desamortización, deuda pública y crecimiento económico, Andalucía, 1820/1823 /. Granada , Córdoba :bFundación Paco Natera [1985?] 443 p. : ISBN 84-505-1053-8 LC Card 86-210676
HD779.A4 G66 1985

Iniciación a la economía andaluza /. [Seville, Spain] [1986] 196, [4] p. : ISBN 84-7405-343-9 LC Card 87-152155
HC387.A64 I54 1986

ANDALUSIA (SPAIN) - ECONOMIC POLICY.
Iniciación a la economía andaluza /. [Seville, Spain] [1986] 196, [4] p. : ISBN 84-7405-343-9 LC Card 87-152155
HC387.A64 I54 1986

Junta de Andalucía. Grupo de Trabajo 14, Planificación Económica de las Corporaciones Locales y Comarcalización. Plan económico de Andalucía, 1984-1986 /. [Andalucía] , 1983. 133 p. ; ISBN 84-505-1243-3 LC Card 86-223752
HJ1249.A4 J86 1983

ANDALUSIA (SPAIN) - POPULATION.
Jordá Borrell, Rosa Ma. (Rosa Maria) Dinámica y distribución recientes de la población andaluza /. [Sevilla] [1985?] 80 p. : ISBN 84-600-3827-0 LC Card 87-124031
HB3620.A5 J67 1985

ANDALUSIA (SPAIN) - RURAL CONDITIONS.
Comín, Alfonso C. Noticia de Andalucía /. Sevilla [1985] 338 p. ; ISBN 84-7587-037-6 LC Card 86-219377
HC387.A64 C62 1985

ANDALUSIA (SPAIN) - SOCIAL CONDITIONS.
Comín, Alfonso C. Noticia de Andalucía /. Sevilla [1985] 338 p. ; ISBN 84-7587-037-6 LC Card 86-219377
HC387.A64 C62 1985

Andean Regional Agreement. see **Acuerdo de Cartagena.**

Andere Bibliothek. Special number. Ermittlungen gegen die Dresdner Bank, 1946 /. Nördlingen , 1986. cxxxiv, 353 p., [8] p. of plates : ISBN 3-89190-297-2 : LC Card 87-121689
HG3058.D7 E76 1986

Der andere Fortschritt . Lafontaine, Oskar, 1943- Hamburg , c1985. 222 p. ; ISBN 3-455-08248-3 LC Card 85-146223
HC286.7 .L33 1985

Anderla, Georges. Computer strategies, 1990-9 : technologies, costs, markets / Georges Anderla and Anthony Dunning. Chichester [West Sussex] ; New York : Wiley, c1987. xxi, 299 p. : ill. ; 24 cm. Includes index. ISBN 0-471-91585-8 : LC Card 87-8173 DDC 338.4/7004 19
1. Computer industry - Forecasting. 2. Computer industry - Planning. I. Dunning, Anthony. II. Title.
HD9696.C62 A53 1987

Anderlini, Fausto. Operai e scelte politiche . Milano, Italy , c1986. 267 p., 45 p. of plates : LC Card 86-169148
HD8439.V462 O64 1986

Anders leben : Geschichte und Zukunft der Genossenschaftskultur : Beispiele aus Nordrhein-Westfalen / Hrsg., Klaus Novy ... [et al.]. Berlin : Dietz, 1985. 231 p. : ill. ; 22 x 24 cm. Bibliography: p. 229-230. ISBN 3-8012-0107-4 LC Card 85-189669
1. Housing, Cooperative - Germany (West) - North Rhine-Westphalia. 2. Community organization - Germany (West) - North Rhine-Westphalia. I. Novy, Klaus.
HD7287.72.G32 N6725 1985

Anders, Maria, Dr. sc. phil. Die Übergangsperiode . [Leipzig] , 1986. 80 p. ; LC Card 87-407523 DDC 338.9/009171/7 19
HC704 .U24 1986

Anders, Roger M. Holl, Jack M. United States civilian nuclear power policy, 1954-1984 . Washington, D.C. , Springfield, Va. [1986] 46 p., [1] leaf of plates : LC Card 86-601137 DDC 333.79/24 19
HD9698.U52 H65 1986

Andersen, Erling B. Statistics for economics, business administration, and the social sciences / Erling B. Andersen, Niels-Erik Jensen, Nils Kousgaard. Berlin ; New York : Springer-Verlag, c1987. xi, 439 p. : ill. ; 25 cm. Includes indexes. ISBN 0-387-17720-5 (pbk. : U. S.) LC Card 87-9423 DDC 519.5 19
1. Economics - Statistical methods. 2. Commercial statistics. 3. Social sciences - Statistical methods. I. Jensen, Niels-Erik, 1939-. II. Kousgaard, Nils. III. Title.
HB137 .A525 1987

Andersen, Kirsten Gøgsig. Det skal stampes halv stamp presses og klædeskæres : farververfagets historie i Danmark 1560-1914 / udarbejdet af Kirsten Gøgsig Andersen. København : Københavns universitets Institut for kultursociologi, [1984] 179 columns : ill. ; 21 x 30 cm. (Repro-serie . 1984, nr. 7) "Magisterkonferens i kultursociologi, august 1984." Bibliography: columns 164-175. LC Card 85-242146
1. Dye industry - Denmark - History. 2. Denmark - Industries. I. Series: Repro-serie (Københavns universitet. Institut for kultursociologi) , 1984, nr. 7. II. Title.
HD9999.C483 D43 1984

Andersen, Niels Bjørn- see **Bjørn-Andersen, Niels.**

Andersen, René, 1936- Personaleadministration / René Andersen, Carsten Skovbro. 4. udg. Köbenhavn : Udgivervirksomheden, Foreningen til unge handelsmænds uddannelse, 1983. 476 p. : ill. ; 22 cm. Bibliography: p. 461-466. Includes index. ISBN 87-7040-278-7 : LC Card 84-104119
1. Personnel management - Denmark. I. Skovbro, Carsten. II. Title.
HF5549.2.D45 A53 1983

Andersen, Torben Juul. Currency and interest rate hedging : a user's guide to options, futures, swaps, and forward contracts / Torben Juul Andersen. New York, N.Y. : New York Institute of Finance, c1987. viii, 272 p. : ill. ; 24 cm. Bibliography: p. 255-263. Includes index. ISBN 0-13-195645-0 LC Card 87-7758 DDC 332.64/5 19
1. Forward exchange. 2. Hedging (Finance). 3. Financial futures. 4. Interest rate futures. 5. Option (Contract). I. Title.
HG3853 .A53 1987

Anderson, Carolyn S. Human resource management in high-technology firms /. Lexington, Mass. , 1986, c1987. x, 243 p. : ISBN 0-669-13686-7 (alk. paper) LC Card 86-45556 DDC 658.3 19
HF5549 .H875 1987 ***NYPL [JLE 87-1100]***

Anderson, David Ray, 1941- Statistics for business and economics / David R. Anderson, Dennis J. Sweeney, Thomas A. Williams. 3rd ed. St. Paul, MN : West Pub. Co., c1987. xxviii, 792 p. : ill. ; 27 cm. Includes index. ISBN 0-314-25873-6 : LC Card 86-24613 DDC 519.5 19
1. Commercial statistics. 2. Economics - Statistical methods. 3. Statistics. I. Sweeney, Dennis J. II. Williams, Thomas Arthur, 1944-. III. Title.
HF1017 .A6 1987

Anderson, Dennis, 1937- Economic growth and the returns to investment / Dennis Anderson. Washington, D.C. : World Bank, [1987] 93 p. : ill. ; 28 cm. (World Bank discussion papers, 0259-210X . 12) Bibliography: p. 88-93. ISBN 0-8213-0918-8 (pbk.) LC Card 87-14178 DDC 338.9 19
1. Economic development. 2. Economic policy. 3. Investments. 4. Rate of return. I. Title. II. Series.
HD75 .A53 1987

Anderson, F. J. Selected readings in mineral economics /. New York , c1987. ix, 399 p. : ISBN 0-08-035864-0 : LC Card 87-8237 DDC 338.2/0971 19
HD9506.C22 S44 1987

Anderson, Georgia. Equity sharing / Georgia Anderson and Sandra Lamb. Chicago :

Contemporary Books, c1986. xiv, 136 p. : ill. ; 21 cm. Includes index. ISBN 0-8092-4836-0 (pbk.) : LC Card 86-24083 DDC 332.63/24 19
1. Real estate investment. 2. Partnership. 3. House buying. 4. House selling. I. Lamb, Sandra. II. Title.
HD1382.5 .A54 1986

Anderson, Henry R., 1939- Needles, Belverd E. Principles of accounting /. Boston, MA , c1987. xx, 1100, [38] p. : ISBN 0-395-35702-0 LC Card 86-80401 DDC 657 19
HF5635 .N35 1987

Anderson, Hugold. Government without taxation / by Hugold Anderson. 4th rev. ed. Warwick, R.I. : H. Anderson, c1987. 52 p. ; 20 cm. LC Card 87-133116 DDC 336.2/00973 19
1. Taxation - United States. 2. Fiscal policy - United States. 3. Banks and banking, Central - United States. 4. Monetary policy - United States. I. Title.
HJ2381 .A76 1987

Anderson, Ina C. Forests in demand . Boston, Mass. , c1982. xv, 265 p. : ISBN 0-86569-106-1 : LC Card 81-12881 DDC 333.75/0973 19
SD565 .F58 ***NYPL [JLE 86-4465]***

Anderson, James. The Rise of the modern state /. Brighton, Sussex , 1986. viii, 255 p. ; ISBN 0-7450-0059-2 ***NYPL [JLD 86-2353]***

Anderson, Kym.
Australian protectionism : extent, causes, and effects / Kym Anderson, Ross Garnaut. Sydney ; Boston : Allen & Unwin, 1987. xii, 160 p. : ill. ; 22 cm. Bibliography: p. 130-156. Includes index. ISBN 0-04-330383-8 (pbk.) LC Card 86-47990 DDC 382.7/3/0994 19
1. Australia - Commercial policy. 2. Trade adjustment assistance - Australia. 3. Free trade and protection - Protection. I. Garnaut, Ross. II. Title.
HF1625 .A53 1987

Australia's trade growth with developing countries / Kym Anderson and Ross Garnaut. And, Intensity of trade between Pacific Basin countries / Kym Anderson. Canberra, Australia : Research School of Pacific Studies, Australian National Unversity, 1983. iv, 55 p. ; 25 cm. (Pacific economic papers) Research paper / Australia-Japan Research Centre ; no. 102 Includes bibliographies. ISBN 0-86413-001-5 (pbk.) LC Card 86-673748
1. Australia - Commerce - Developing countries. 2. Developing countries - Commerce - Australia. 3. Pacific area - Commerce. I. Garnaut, Ross. II. Anderson, Kym. Intensity of trade between Pacific Basin countries. 1983. III. Series. IV. Series: Research paper (Australia-Japan Research Centre) , no. 102. V. Title.
HF3948.D44 A52x 1983

Intensity of trade between Pacific Basin countries. 1983. Anderson, Kym. Australia's trade growth with developing countries / Kym Anderson and Ross Garnaut. And, Intensity of trade between Pacific Basin countries / Kym Anderson. Canberra, Australia , 1983. iv, 55 p. ; ISBN 0-86413-001-5 (pbk.) LC Card 86-673748
HF3948.D44 A52x 1983

Anderson, Martin, 1936- An economic bill of rights / Martin Anderson. Stanford, Calif. : Hoover Institution, Stanford University, 1984. 22 p. ; 23 cm. Cover title. Bibliography: p. 21-22. ISBN 0-8179-5122-9 (pbk.) LC Card 86-21394 DDC 338.973 19
1. United States - Economic policy - 1981-.
HC106.8 .A55 1984

Anderson, Neal B. McColly, Robert A. Availability of federally owned minerals for exploration and development in western states . [Avondale, Md.] , Washington, DC [1987] iv, 27 p. : LC Card 87-600086 DDC 333.8/5/09791 19
HD243.A7 M36 1987

ANDERSON, ROBERT O., 1917-
Harris, Kenneth, 1919- The wildcatter . New York , c1987. x, 180 p., [8] p. of plates : ISBN 1-555-84048-5 LC Card 87-8183 DDC 338.7/622338/0924 B 19
HD9570.A53 H37 1987

Anderson, Ronald W., 1946- The Industrial organization of futures markets /. Lexington, Mass. , c1984. vii, 312 p. : ISBN 0-669-06836-5 LC Card 83-48029 DDC 332.64/4 19
HG6024.A3 I52 1984 ***NYPL [JLE 86-4471]***

Anderson, Roy Claude. History of Royal Blue Express Services / R.C. Anderson and G.G.A. Frankis. 2nd ed. Newton Abbot ; North Pomfret, Vt. : David & Charles, 1985. 216 p. : ill. ; 22 cm. Includes index. ISBN 0-7153-8654-9 : LC Card 86-136155 DDC 388.3/22/09423 19
1. Royal Blue Express Services - History. 2. Bus lines - England - History. I. Frankis, G. II. Title.
HE5664.Z7 R63 1985

Anderson, S. D. (Stuart D.) Project manpower management : decision-making processes in construction practice / S.D. Anderson, R.W. Woodhead. New York : Wiley, c1987. ix, 509 p. : ill. ; 29 cm. "A Wiley-Interscience publication." Bibliography: p. 489-495. Includes index. ISBN 0-471-86189-8 LC Card 86-26728 DDC 624/.068 19
1. Construction industry - Personnel management. 2. Industrial project management. I. Woodhead, Ronald W. II. Title.
HD9715.A2 A515 1987

Andersson, Dan, 1948- Vad gör kapitalisterna? : en läsebok om ägandet i Sverige / Dan Andersson. Stockholm : Tiden, c1983. 167 p. : ill. ; 21 cm. Includes bibliographical references. ISBN 91-550-2919-1 : LC Card 84-143408
1. Capitalists and financiers - Sweden. 2. Sweden - Economic conditions - 1945-. I. Title.
HG186.S85 A53 1983

Andersson, Göran, 1944- Industrihotell och industribyar : kartläggning och fallstudier / av Göran Andersson. Stockholm : Liber : Statens industriverk, [1984] 150 p. : ill. ; 25 cm. (Kommunal näringspolitik) SIND, 0346-5748 ; 1984:5 Bibliography: p. 70-72. ISBN 91-38-08268-3 LC Card 85-106828
1. Sweden - Industries. 2. Industrial promotion - Sweden. 3. Regional planning - Sweden. I. Title. II. Series.
HC375 .A72 1984

Andersson, Ingvar. Workshop on the Institutionalization of the Shallow Wells Programme under Tanzanian Administration (1981 : University of Dar es Salaam) Proceedings of the Workshop on the Institutionalization of the Shallow Wells Programme under Tanzanian Administration /. [Dar es Salaam?] , 1981. 3, 16, 12 p. ; LC Card 85-980881 DDC 333.7/09678 s 333.91/22/09678 19
HD107 .D36 no. 71 HD1699.T33

Andersson, Krister. Comparative tax systems . Arlington, Va. , 1987. xiv, 447 p. : ISBN 0-918255-05-8 (pbk.) : LC Card 87-50143 DDC 336.2 19
HJ2599.5 .C65 1987

Andersson-Palmqvist, Lena. Decentraliserad textilindustri : förlagssystemets utveckling i Marks härad under senare delen av 1800-talet / Lena Andersson-Palmqvist. Stockholm : Konsthögskolans Arkitekturskola, 1979/80 [i.e. 1980] 68 p. : ill., map ; 25 cm. Bibliography: p. 66-68. ISBN 91-86016-06-7 LC Card 81-138133
1. Textile industry - Sweden - Marks härad - History - 19th century. 2. Cottage industries - Sweden - Marks härad - History - 19th century. I. Title.
HD9865.S87 M373 1980

Andersson, Per Magnus, 1951- Internprissättning inom offentlig förvaltning : en studie av internprissättning mellan myndigheter i svensk statsförvaltning / Per Magnus Andersson, Lennart Hansson. Lund : Studentlitteratur i samarbete med Stiftelsen för information om ekonomisk forskning, [1984] xii, 357 p. ; 22 cm. Summary in English. Bibliography: p. 346-357. ISBN 91-44-43971-7 : LC Card 84-210334
1. Transfer pricing. 2. Administrative agencies - Sweden - Management. I. Hansson, Lennart. II. Title.
HD62.45 .A53 1984

Andersson, Tommy D., 1947- Profit in small firms : a model based on case-studies from the informal sector in a developing country / Tommy D. Andersson. Aldershot, Hants, England ; Brookfield, Vt., USA : Avebury, c1987. 407 p. : ill. ; 23 cm. Bibliography: p. 381-396. Includes indexes. ISBN 0-566-05468-X : LC Card 87-21321 DDC 338.6/42/091724 19
1. Small business - Developing countries. 2. Informal sector (Economics) - Developing countries. I. Title.
HD2346.5 .A53 1987

ANDES REGION - COMMERCE - ARGENTINA.
Comercio de granos entre la Argentina y los países del Grupo Andino. [Buenos Aires, Argentina] , 1983. ii, 154 p. : LC Card 86-201891
HD9044.A8 C65 1983

ANDES REGION - COMMERCE - BOLIVIA.
El Acuerdo de Cartagena y el trato preferencial en favor de Bolivia y Ecuador. [Buenos Aires, Argentina] [1982] 148 leaves ; LC Card 86-202605 DDC 337.1/8 19
HC167.A5 A285 1982

ANDES REGION - COMMERCE - ECUADOR.
El Acuerdo de Cartagena y el trato preferencial en favor de Bolivia y Ecuador. [Buenos Aires, Argentina] [1982] 148 leaves ; LC Card 86-202605 DDC 337.1/8 19
HC167.A5 A285 1982

ANDES REGION - COMMERCE - HISTORY - 19TH CENTURY.
Mitre, Antonio. El monedero de los Andes . La Paz , 1986. 134 p. ; LC Card 87-403038 DDC 332.4/98 19
HG803 .M57 1986

ANDES REGION - ECONOMIC CONDITIONS.
Escobari de Querejazu, Laura. Producción y comercio en el espacio sur andino en el siglo XVII . La Paz , 1985. 218 p., [12] p. of plates : LC Card 86-174929
HC167.A5 E83 1985

Estrategias para el desarrollo de la Sierra /. Cusco , c1986. 418 p. : LC Card 86-199393
HC228.A54 E87 1986

Sánchez Enríquez, Rodrigo. Organización andina, drama y posibilidad /. Huancayo, Perú [1987] xxii, 219 p. : LC Card 87-404025 DDC 330.98/0038 19
HC167.A5 S26 1987

ANDES REGION - ECONOMIC INTEGRATION.
El Acuerdo de Cartagena y el trato preferencial en favor de Bolivia y Ecuador. [Buenos Aires, Argentina] [1982] 148 leaves ; LC Card 86-202605 DDC 337.1/8 19
HC167.A5 A285 1982

Dávila Andrade, Oswaldo. El Grupo Andino . [Lima? , 1985] ([Lima?] : Oficina de Publicaciones) 110 p. ; LC Card 86-158814
HC167.A5 D38 1985

Ecuador, política económica--teoría y realidad. [Guayaquil] [1986- v. <1-3 > ; LC Card 87-105005
HF1519 .E3 1986

Wong, John, 1939- Regional industrial co-operation . Vienna , 1986. xi, 102 p. : ISBN 92-1-106204-7 (pbk.) LC Card 86-214910 DDC 337.1/5 19
HC441 .W66 1986

ANDES REGION - ECONOMIC INTEGRATION - CONGRESSES.
Estrategias de desarrollo e integración en el Grupo Andino . Lima, Perú , 1985. 414 p. : LC Card 87-125026 DDC 337.1/8 19
HC167.A5 E87 1985

Por una visión del desarrollo latinoamericano con autodeterminación, democracia y paz /. San Isidro, Lima, Perú [1984] 191 p. ; LC Card 86-226515
HC167.A5 P67 1984

ANDES REGION - ECONOMIC POLICY.
Estrategias para el desarrollo de la Sierra /. Cusco , c1986. 418 p. : LC Card 86-199393
HC228.A54 E87 1986

Universidad de los Andes (Mérida, Venezuela). Instituto de Investigaciones Económicas. Plan de desarrollo regional /. Mérida , 1973- v. <1-5 > : LC Card 86-202604
HC238.A683 U55 1973

ANDES REGION - ECONOMIC POLICY - CONGRESSES.
Estrategias de desarrollo e integración en el Grupo Andino . Lima, Perú , 1985. 414 p. : LC Card 87-125026 DDC 337.1/8 19
HC167.A5 E87 1985

ANDES REGION - RURAL CONDITIONS - CONGRESSES.
Investigación agraria y crisis . Quito , 1986. 498 p. : LC Card 87-400125 DDC 338.1/098 19
HD1860.A53 I58 1986

ANDES REGION - SOCIAL CONDITIONS. Sánchez Enríquez, Rodrigo. Organización andina, drama y posibilidad /. Huancayo, Perú [1987] xxii, 219 p. : LC Card 87-404025 DDC 330.98/0038 19
HC167.A5 S26 1987

ANDHRA PRADESH (INDIA) - CENSUS, 1981. Census of India, 1981. Delhi , <1984-1986. v. in : LC Card 87-915009 DDC 304.6/0954/84021 19
HA4587.A52 C46 1984

Andhra Pradesh (India). Finance and Planning (Planning Wing) Dept. Evaluation Wing. Evaluation study on the working of crash scheme for rural employment. Hyderabad : Evaluation Wing of Finance and Planning (Planning Wing) Dept., Government of Andhra Pradesh, 1983. 89 p. : ill. ; 26 cm. (Evaluation study . no. 59) LC Card 86-144139 DDC 331.12/042/095484 19
1. Rural poor - Employment - India - Andhra Pradesh. 2. Agricultural laborers - India - Andhra Pradesh - Supplementary employment. 3. Road construction workers - India - Andhra Pradesh. I. Series: Evaluation study (Andhra Pradesh (India). Finance and Planning (Planning Wing) Dept. Evaluation Wing) , no. 59. II. Title.
HD5710.85.I42 A532 1983

ANDHRA PRADESH STATE ROAD TRANSPORT CORPORATION. Subrahmanyam, P., 1934- Organizational set-up of road transport . Delhi , New Delhi , 1987. xi, 233 [i.e. 333] p. : ISBN 81-7018-398-7 : LC Card 86-903830 DDC 354.54/8400878/09 19
HE365.I42 S83 1987

Andolsen, Barbara Hilkert. "Daughters of Jefferson, daughters of bootblacks" : racism and American feminism / by Barbara Hilkert Andolsen. Macon, GA : Mercer University Press, c1986. xiv, 130 p. ; 24 cm. Includes bibliographical references and index. ISBN 0-86554-204-X : LC Card 86-816 DDC 305.4/2/0973 19
1. Feminism - United States - History. 2. Women - Suffrage - United States - History. 3. Afro-American women - History. 4. Racism - United States - History. 5. United States - Race relations - History. I. Title.
HQ1426 .A6827 1986 ***NYPL [JLE 86-3359]***

Andorka, Rudolf. Economy and society in Hungary /. Budapest , 1986. 331 p. : LC Card 87-147704 DDC 330.9439/053 19
HC300.28 .E36 1986

ANDORRA - ECONOMIC CONDITIONS. Reichert, Thomas. Andorra, eine Landeskunde . Nürnberg , 1986. xviii, 320 p. : LC Card 87-131037 DDC 330.946/79083 19
HC390.5 .R45 1986

Andorra, eine Landeskunde . Reichert, Thomas. Nürnberg , 1986. xviii, 320 p. : LC Card 87-131037 DDC 330.946/79083 19
HC390.5 .R45 1986

Andover, James J. Credit and collections problem solver : effective strategies and controls / by James J. Andover. New York, NY, U. S.A. : Alexander Hamiton Institute, c1987. x, 175 p. : ill. ; 28 cm. (Modern business reports) ISBN 0-86604-219-9 (pbk.) LC Card 87-156416 DDC 658.8/8 19
1. Credit management. 2. Collecting of accounts. I. Title. II. Series.
HG3751 .A53 1987

Andrada, René. Reforma estructural de nuestra economía / René Andrada. [Asunción : s.n., 1986] (Asunción, Paraguay : Ediciones y Arte) 150 p. : ill. ; 20 cm. LC Card 86-227031
1. Monetary policy - Paraguay. 2. Paraguay - Economic policy. I. Title.
HG885 .A85 1986

Andrade, Luis F. The labor climate in Brazil / by Luis F. Andrade. Philadelphia, Pa. : Industrial Research Unit, Wharton School, University of Pennsylvania, c1985. viii, 133 p. ; 28 cm. (Multinational industrial relations series. No. 4, Latin American studies . 4a--Brazil) Rev. ed. of: The political, economic, and labor climate in Brazil / by James L. Schlagheck. c1977. Includes bibliographies. ISBN 0-89546-057-2 (pbk.) LC Card 85-81947 DDC 331/.0981 19
1. Labor policy - Brazil. 2. Trade-unions - Brazil. 3. Brazil - Economic conditions - 1964-1985. 4. Brazil - Politics and government - 1964-1985. I. Schlagheck, James L. Political, economic, and labor climate in Brazil. II. Title.
HD8286.5 .A67 1985 ***NYPL [JLF 86-1201]***

Andrade, Manuel Correia de Oliveira. Classes sociais e agricultura no Nordeste / Manuel Correia de Andrade. Recife : Fundação Joaquim Nabuco, Editora Massangana, 1985. 105 p. ; 21 cm. (Série Estudos e pesquisas. 39) Bibliography: p. 101-105. ISBN 85-7019-096-4 LC Card 87-119335
1. Agriculture and state - Brazil - Pernambuco. 2. Social classes - Brazil - Pernambuco. I. Series: Série Estudos e pesquisas (Fundação Joaquim Nabuco) , 39. II. Title.
HD1875.P4 A84 1985

Sertão sul / Manuel Correia de Andrade. Recife : Ministério do Interior, Superintendência do Desenvolvimento do Nordeste, Superintendência Adjunta de Planejamento, Coordenação de Planejamento Regional, Divisão de Política Espacial, 1984. 648, [26] p. : ill., maps ; 24 cm. (Série Estudos regionais . 11) Bibliography: p. 645-648. "CDU 913:631/636(812/814-071)." LC Card 87-404838 DDC 330.981/3063 19
1. Brazil, Northeast - Economic conditions. 2. Brazil, Northeast - Rural conditions. 3. Agriculture - Economic aspects - Brazil, Northeast. I. Title. II. Series.
HC188.N6 A687 1984

André Bergeron, une force ouvrière /. Validire, Jean-Louis. Paris , c1984. 244 p. ; ISBN 2-259-01206-X : LC Card 85-105625 DDC 331.88/0944 19
HD6684 .V35 1984

André, J. L. da Costa. Portugal na Associação Europeia de Comércio Livre / J.L. da Costa André. Lisboa : Gabinete de Investigações Económicas do Instituto Superior de Ciências Económicas e Financeiras, 1960. 98 p. ; 25 cm. Previously published in revista "Brotéria", 1960. Includes bibliographical references. LC Card 85-216282
1. European Free Trade Association - Portugal. 2. Europe - Commerce - Statistics. I. Title.
HC241.4 .A56 1960

André, Marc. La Verrerie champenoise, Charbonneaux-B.S.N. Reims, de 1870 à nos jours /. Die , c1984. 279 p. : ISBN 2-904638-12-1 : LC Card 84-247744
HD9623.F8 V47 1984

André, Robert, 1925- La population de la Wallonie dans la dualité démographique de la Belgique / Robert André ; préface de Stéphane Brabant ; message de Jacques Hoyaux. Bruxelles : Fondation Charles Plisnier ; Charleroi : Institut Jules Destrée, 1983. 192 p. : ill. ; 21 cm. Bibliography: p. 183-188. LC Card 85-175936
1. Wallonia, Belgium - Population. I. Title.
HB3604.W34 A53 1983

Andreadēs, Andreas Michaēl, 1876-1935. Historia tōn ethnikōn daneiōn / hypo Andr. Mich. Andreadou. Epanekdosē me euretērio. Athēna : Vivliopōleio D.N. Karavia, 1986- v. <1 > ; 25 cm. (Vivliothēkē historikōn meletōn . 202) Reprint. Originally published : En Ayhenais : Typogr. Hestia, 1904. Bibliography: v. 1, p. [9]-[15] (1st group) Includes index. CONTENTS. - meros 1. Ta daneia tēs Anexartēsias, 1824-1825 -- To dēmosion chreos epi tēs Vauarikēs Dynasteias. LC Card 87-112859
1. Debts, Public - Greece - History - 19th century. I. Title. II. Series.
HJ8672 .A53 1986

Andreae, Clemens August. Vom Boss zum Partner / Clemens-August Andreae. Zürich : Edition Interfrom, c1983. 90 p. ; 20 cm. (Texte + Thesen. 154) ISBN 3-7201-5154-9 LC Card 83-168802
1. Entrepreneur. 2. Executives. 3. Businessmen. I. Title.
HB615 .A69 1983

Andreasen, Alan R., 1934- Kotler, Philip. Strategic marketing for nonprofit organizations /. Englewood Cliffs, N.J. , c1987. xvi, 670 p. : LC Card 86-25538 DDC 658.8 19
HF5415 .K6312 1987

Andreasen, Helge. Buschaufførers arbejdsmiljø . København , c1982. 188 p. in various pagings : ISBN 87-7359-039-8 LC Card 83-111384
HD7269.M82 D44 1982

Andreasson, Arne. Caballero, Lorenzo. Mozambique, food and agriculture sector /. Uppsala , 1984. 223, [30] p. : ISBN 91-576-2129-2 (pbk.) LC Card 86-218958 DDC 338.1/0967/9 19
HD9017.M86 C33 1984

Andreev, L. G. (Leonid Grigor′evich) Sotsial′no-ėkonomicheskaia̅ sushchnost′ obshchenarodnogo khozia̅ĭstvennogo mekhanizma /. Kiev , 1985. 342 p. ; LC Card 86-197710
HC336.25 .S668 1985

Andreev, Stoi̅an. Profsu̅iu̅zno stroitelstvo . Sofii̅a , 1985. 310 p. : LC Card 86-209854
HD6782 .P78 1985

Andreoni, Diego. The cost of occupational accidents and diseases / Diego Andreoni. Geneva : International Labour Office, c1986. viii, 142 p. : ill. ; 24 cm. (Occupational safety and health series, 0078-3129 . no. 54) Bibliography: p. 135-142. ISBN 92-2-103758-4 (pbk.) : LC Card 87-119442 DDC 338.4/336311 19
1. Industrial accidents - Costs. I. Series: Occupational safety and health series , 54. II. Title.
HD7262 .A73 1986

Andres, Tomas Quintin D., 1942- Human resource training & development / Tomas D. Andres. Quezon City : New Day Publishers, c1980. viii, 134 p. : ill. ; 22 cm. Bibliography: p. 129-133. LC Card 82-102431 DDC 658.3/12404/09599 19
1. Employees, Training of - Philippines. 2. Manpower planning - Philippines. I. Title. II. Title: Human resource training and development.
HF5549.5.T7 A64 1980 ***NYPL [JLD 87-935]***

Andres, Willy. Finanzbuchhaltung / Willy Andres, Rolf Uhlmann. 1. Aufl. Zürich : Verlag des Schweizerischen Kaufmännischen Verbandes, 1983. 179 p. : ill. ; 24 cm. Bibliography: p. 179. ISBN 3-286-50261-8 LC Card 83-225439
1. Accounting. I. Uhlmann, Rolf. II. Title.
HF5645 .A64 1983

Andrews, Deborah C. Business communication / Deborah C. Andrews, William D. Andrews. New York : Macmillan ; London : Collier Macmillan, c1988. xxvi, 623 p. : ill. ; 24 cm. Bibliography: p. 611-614. Includes index. ISBN 0-02-303510-2 LC Card 87-5526 DDC 808/.06665 19
1. Communication in management. 2. Business writing. I. Andrews, William D. (William David), 1945-. II. Title.
HF5718 .A743 1988

Andrews, Emily S. The changing profile of pensions in America / by Emily S. Andrews. Washington, DC : Employee Benefit Research Institute, c1985. xxvii, 234 p. ; 23 cm. (An EBRI-ERF policy study) Includes index. Bibliography: p. 217-226. ISBN 0-86643-038-5 (pbk.) LC Card 85-25296 DDC 332.6/7254 19
1. Pension trusts - United States. 2. Retirement income - United States. 3. Retirement - Economic aspects - United States. I. Title. II. Series.
HD7105.45.U6 A53 1985 ***NYPL [JLE 87-62]***

Andrews, Frank M. Research on the quality of life /. Ann Arbor, Mich. , 1986. xiv, 365 p. ; ISBN 0-87944-308-1 : LC Card 86-15179 DDC 305/.0973 19
HN60 .R47 1986 ***NYPL [JLE 86-3621]***

Andrews, George H., 1932- Actuarial projections for the old-age, survivors, and disability insurance program of social security in the United States of America / George H. Andrews, John A. Beekman. Itasca, Ill., U. S.A. : Actuarial Education and Research Fund, c1987. viii, 188 p. : ill. ; 24 cm. Includes bibliographical references and index. LC Card 87-1101 DDC 368.4/301/0973 19
1. United States - Economic conditions - 1981-. 2. Economic forecasting - United States. 3. Old age pensions - United States - Forecasting. 4. Insurance, Disability - United States - Forecasting. 5. Social security - United States - Forecasting. I. Beekman, John A. II. Title.
HC106.8 .A56 1987

Andrews, John. Solar jobs in Victoria : the economic impact of the solar industry : executive summary / John Andrews, Environmentalists for Full Employment (Vic.). [Victoria] : Victorian Solar Energy Council, [1982] xxxix p. : ill. ; 30 cm. "September 1982." LC Card 87-160366
1. Solar energy industries - Australia - Victoria. 2. Solar

energy industries - Australia - Victoria - Employees - Supply and demand. I. Environmentalists for Full Employment (Australia). II. Title.
HD9681.A83 V5326 1982

Andrews, Wesley T. Auditing . Houston, TX , 1986. xvii, 919 p. : ISBN 0-87393-016-9 LC Card 86-127902 DDC 657/.45 19
HF5667 .A832 1986

Andrews, William D. (William David), 1945- Andrews, Deborah C. Business communication /. New York , London , c1988. xxvi, 623 p. : ISBN 0-02-303510-2 LC Card 87-5526 DDC 808/.06665 19
HF5718 .A743 1988

Andrianarivelo Rafrezy, Vincent. Population de Madagascar : situation actuelle et perspectives d'avenir / par Andrianarivelo Rafrezy Vincent, Randretsa Iarivony. [Antananarivo] : République démocratique malgache, Ministère de la recherche scientifique et technologique pour le développement, [1985] 154 p. : ill. ; 22 cm. "Janvier 1985." Summary in English. Bibliography: p. 149-150. LC Card 86-981367
1. Madagascar - Population - Statistics. 2. Population forecasting - Madagascar - Statistics. I. Randretsa, Iarivony. II. Title.
HA4699 .A84 1985

Andrianov, V. V. Za slovom--delo / V.V. Andrianov, A.A. Leonov, V.G. Nesterov. Moskva : Izd-vo polit. lit-ry, 1985. 124 p. ; 17 cm. Includes bibliographical references. LC Card 85-213388
1. Sverdlovsk (R.S.F.S.R.) - Economic policy. I. Leonov, A. A. (Aleksandr Alekseevich). II. Nesterov, V. G. (Vladimir Gavrilovich). III. Title.
HC338.S87 A53 1985

Andriello, Vincenzo. Terremoto e crisi urbana . Napoli , 1981. 207 p. ; ***NYPL [JLE 86-4532]***

Andriĭko, O. F. (Ol'ga Fedorovna) Pravovye problemy RASU /. Kiev , 1985. 303 p. : LC Card 86-139849
HC337.U5 P65 1985

Andrión Alabarca, Aurelio, 1924- Sobre el surco reviven las esperanzas / Aurelio Andrión Alabarca. Panamá, R. de P. : Instituto Nacional de Cultura, [1978] 84 p. : ill. ; 20 cm. (Colección múltiple . no. 19.) LC Card 82-100242
1. Peasantry - Panama. 2. Peasantry - Government policy - Panama. I. Series: Colección múltiple , no. 19. II. Title.
HD1531.P2 A53 1978

Andrlić, Vlasta. Rječnik terminologije jugoslavenskog političko-ekonomskog sistema : englesko-hrvatskosrpski = Dictionary of Yugoslav political and economic terminology : English-Croato-Serbian / Vlasta Andrlić, Ljiljana Jovković. Zagreb : Informator, 1985. viii, 135 p. ; 21 cm. (Informatorovi rječnici) English and Serbo-Croatian (roman). LC Card 86-182784
1. Economics - Dictionaries. 2. Political science - Dictionaries. 3. Economics - Dictionaries - Serbo-Croatian. 4. Political science - Dictionaries - Serbo-Croatian. 5. English language - Dictionaries - Serbo-Croatian. 6. Serbo-Croatian language - Dictionaries - English. I. Jovković, Ljiljana. II. Title. III. Title: Dictionary of Yugoslav political and economic terminology. IV. Series.
HB61 .A55 1985 ***NYPL [*QKK 87-1803]***

ANDROCRACY. see **PATRIARCHY.**

ANDROS ISLAND (GREECE) - ECONOMIC CONDITIONS.
Moustakas, Dion. E. Hai ploutoparagōgikai dynameis tēs nēsou Androu /. En Athēnais , 1924. 25 p. : LC Card 87-100195
HC297.A53 M68 1924

Androsch, Hannes. Wagner, Adolph, 1835-1917. Die Ordnung des österreichischen Staatshaushaltes--1863 /. Wien , c1984. 308 p. ; ISBN 3-85447-086-X LC Card 85-223615
HJ1065 .W34 1984

Androsov, V. I. (Vasiliĭ Ivanovich) Ėffektivnost' kapital'nogo stroitel'stva v torgovle / V.I. Androsov, P.V. Mel'nik, M.A. Ogorodnik. Moskva : Ėkonomika, 1980. 213 p. ; 20 cm. Includes bibliographical references. LC Card 81-132839
1. Capital productivity - Soviet Union. 2. Capital investments - Soviet Union. I. Mel'nik, P. V. (Pavel Vasil'evich). II. Ogorodnik, M. A. (Mikhail Antonovich). III. Title.
HC340.C3 A65 1980

Andrunas, E. Ch. (Elena Cheslavovna) Biznes i propaganda : sistema kontroli͡a krupnogo kapitala SShA nad sredstvami massovoĭ informatsii / E.Ch. Andrunas ; pod redaktsieĭ I͡A.N. Zasurskogo. Moskva : Izd-vo Moskovskogo universiteta, 1986. 223 p. : ill. ; 20 cm. Includes bibliographical references. LC Card 87-152425
1. Mass media and business - United States. 2. Big business - United States. I. Zasurskiĭ, I͡Asen Nikolaevich. II. Title.
HD59.6.U6 A53 1986

ANESTHESIOLOGY EQUIPMENT INDUSTRY.
Anesthesiology products and marketplace. Tustin, CA, U. S.A. (17722 Irvine Blvd., Tustin 92680) , c1987. 1 v. (various foliations) : LC Card 87-142979 DDC 381/.45681761 19
HD9995.A532 A54 1987

Anesthesiology products. Anesthesiology products and marketplace. Tustin, CA, U. S.A. (17722 Irvine Blvd., Tustin 92680) , c1987. 1 v. (various foliations) : LC Card 87-142979 DDC 381/.45681761 19
HD9995.A532 A54 1987

Anfossi, Anna. Teoria dell'organizzazione e realtà italiana . Milano [1980] 225 p. ; ISBN 88-20-41736-7 : LC Card 80-511472 DDC 302.3/5 19
HM131 .T4 ***NYPL [JLD 81-599]***

Angebotsentwicklung und Preisbildung natürlicher Ressourcen / Horst Siebert (Hrsg.) ; mit Beiträgen von H. Herz ... [et al.]. München : R. Oldenbourg, 1986. vii, 148, 10 p. : ill. ; 21 cm. (Schriftenreihe des Energiewirtschaftlichen Instituts . Bd. 30) Includes bibliographies. CONTENTS. - Ricardo- und Hotelling-Paradigmen für die Preisbildung natürlicher Ressourcen / Horst Siebert -- Die Schätzung langfristiger Angebotskurven für Kohle / Walter Schulz -- Zur Erstellung eines Angebotsmodells für Natururan / Siegfried von Wahl -- Energieumwandlung und die ökonomische Bewertung ... / Hermann Herz, Eberhard Jochem, Michael Schön -- Gesamtwirtschaftlich optimale Ressourcenausbeutung und Theorie ... / Karl-Wilhelm Müller, Wolfgang Ströbele. ISBN 3-486-26171-1 LC Card 86-182074
1. Nonrenewable natural resources - Mathematical models. 2. Price policy - Mathematical models. I. Siebert, Horst, 1938-. II. Herz, H. (Hermann). III. Series.
HC59 .A794 1986

Angebotsplanung. Barrmeyer, Martin-Christian. Die Angebotsplanung bei Submission /. Münster [1982?] xii, 198 p. : ISBN 3-88660-081-5 : LC Card 83-227153
HD2365 .B36 1982

Die Angebotsplanung bei Submission /. Barrmeyer, Martin-Christian. Münster [1982?] xii, 198 p. : ISBN 3-88660-081-5 : LC Card 83-227153
HD2365 .B36 1982

Angelier, Jean Pierre. Rente et structures des industries de l'énergie /. [Saint-Martin-d'Hères] , 1983. 268 p. : ISBN 2-7061-0217-9 : LC Card 84-173320
HD9502.A2 R45 1983 ***NYPL [JLE 87-1263]***

Angell, George.
Agricultural options : trading puts and calls in the new grain and livestock futures markets / George Angell. New York, NY : American Management Association, c1986. ix, 230 p. : ill. ; 24 cm. Includes index. ISBN 0-8144-5822-X LC Card 85-48215 DDC 332.64/25 19
1. Grain trade - United States. 2. Cattle trade - United States. 3. Put and call transactions - United States. 4. Option (Contract) - United States. I. Title.
HG6047.G8 A54 1986 ***NYPL [JLE 86-2854]***

West of Wall Street / George Angell, Barry Haigh. [Chicago] : Longman Financial Services Pub., [1987], c1988. xxiv, 215 p. ; 24 cm. Includes index. ISBN 0-88462-623-7 LC Card 87-3003 DDC 332.63/222 19
1. Stock index futures. I. Haigh, Barry. II. Title.
HG6043 .A55 1988

Angell, Joseph Kinnicut, 1794-1857. Treatise on the law of private corporations aggregate [microform] / by Joseph K. Angell and Samuel Ames. 5th ed., rev., cor., and enl. Boston : Little, Brown, 1855. lv, 939 p. ; 25 cm. Includes bibliographical references and index. Microfilm. New York : New York Public Library, 1982. 1 microfilm reel ; 35 mm. (MN *ZZ-19433)
1. Corporation law - United States. 2. Corporations - United States. I. Ames, Samuel, 1806-1865, joint author. II. Title. ***NYPL [*ZT-1731]***

Angermaier, Max. Ausstieg? . Hamburg , 1985. 159 p. : ISBN 3-87975-289-3 LC Card 85-219857 DDC 331/.0943 19
HD6694 .A97 1985 ***NYPL [JLD 87-710]***

Angestelltenversicherungsgesetz mit Sozialgesetzbuch . Germany (West) [Angestelltenversicherungsgesetz.] Berlin [1985] 788 p. : LC Card 86-145477
HD7116.M42 G4334 Nr. 18, 1985 KK3270.5

Angestelltenversicherungsgesetz mit Sozialgesetzbuch . Germany (West) [Angestelltenversicherungsgesetz.] Berlin [1986] 792 p. ; LC Card 86-229132
HD7116.M42 G4334 Nr. 18, 1986 KK3270.5

Angewandte Fernerkundung : Methoden und Beispiele / bearbeitet von Sigfrid Schneider ; Akademie für Raumforschung und Landesplanung. Hannover : C.R. Vincentz, 1984. x, 285 p. : chiefly ill. (some col.), maps (some col.) ; 30 cm. Summary in English and French. Texts by various contributors. Col. map on folded leaf in pocket. Bibliography: p. 264-266. Includes index. ISBN 3-87870-904-8 LC Card 85-147235
1. Land use - Remote sensing. 2. Regional planning - Remote sensing. 3. Land use - Germany (West) - Remote sensing. 4. Regional planning - Germany (West) - Remote sensing. 5. Remote sensing. I. Schneider, Sigfrid, 1915-. II. Akademie für Raumforschung und Landesplanung (Germany).
HD108.8 .A54 1984

Anggaran dasar dan anggaran rumah tangga . Asosiasi Pengusaha Indonesia. Jakarta [1985] 19, 14 p. ; LC Card 86-942640
HD6948.I5 A76 1985

Angheben, Leosergio. Carvão mineral /. [Porto Alegre] [19]84. 56 p. ; LC Card 86-163115
HD9554.B83 S683 1984

Anghel, Gheorghe. Pagini din gîndirea economică militară românească /. București , 1983. 219 p. ; LC Card 84-116220
HC405.Z9 D443 1983

Anglade, Georges. Eloge de la pauvreté / par Georges Anglade. Montréal, Québec, Canada : ERCE, c1983. 63 p. ; 17 cm. ISBN 2-920418-04-1 LC Card 84-140110
1. Poor - Haiti. 2. Poverty. I. Title.
HC153.Z9 P612 1983

Angliĭsko-nemsko-frensko-rusko-bŭlgarski rechnik po upravlenie i ikonomika na promishlenostta, stroitelstvoto i transporta / Ilii͡a S. Boi͡adzhiev ... [et al.]. 1. izd. Sofii͡a : Dŭrzh. izd-vo "Tekhnika", 1982. 764 p. ; 21 cm. Includes indexes in German, French, Russian and Bulgarian. LC Card 83-128751
1. Management - Dictionaries - Polyglot. 2. Economics - Dictionaries - Polyglot. I. Boi͡adzhiev, Ilii͡a S. (Ilii͡a Stanislavov).
HD30.15 .A43 1982 ***NYPL [*QAD 86-4204]***

ANGLING. see **FISHING.**

Anglo-American innovation /. Clark, Peter A. Berlin , New York , 1987. ix, 404 p. : ISBN 0-89925-164-1 (U. S.) : LC Card 87-22221 DDC 338/.06 19
HD45 .C52 1987

ANGLO-FRENCH WAR, 1755-1763 - ECONOMIC ASPECTS - FRANCE.
Riley, James C. The Seven Years War and the old regime in France . Princeton, N.J. , 1986. xxii, 256 p. : ISBN 0-691-05488-6 (alk. paper) : LC Card 86-42847 DDC 330.944/034 19
HC275 .R54 1986 ***NYPL [JLE 87-932]***

Anglo-Portuguese Foundation. Portugal, 1386-1986 . London [c1987] 156 p. : ISBN 0-947991-01-8 (pbk.) LC Card 87-404164 DDC 382/.09469/04 19
HF3698.E8 P67 1987

ANGOLA - ECONOMIC CONDITIONS - 1975-
Fituni, L. L. (Leonid Leonidovich) Ravitie ėkonomiki nezavisimoĭ Angoly /. Moskva , 1981. 171, [3] p. ; LC Card 82-115411
HC950 .F57 1981

ANGOLA - FOREIGN ECONOMIC RELATIONS.
Fituni, L. L. (Leonid Leonidovich) Ravitie ėkonomiki nezavisimoĭ Angoly /. Moskva ,

1981. 171, [3] p. ; LC Card 82-115411
HC950 .F57 1981

Angsturlaub statt Bildungsurlaub : Dokumentation zum Verhalten von Unternehmern / [Herausgeber, Vorstand des Hessischen Jugendringes]. Frankfurt am Main : Jugend & Politik, c1979. 179 p. : ill. ; 24 cm. ISBN 3-88203-044-5 LC Card 85-167471
1. Educational leave - Germany, West. 2. Continuing education - Germany, West. 3. Industry and education - Germany, West. I. Hessischer Jugendring. Vorstand.
HD5257.2.G3 A54 1979

Angueira, María del Carmen. Capitalismo de estado, 1927-1956 / María del Carmen Angueira, Alicia del Carmen Tonini. Buenos Aires : Centro Editor de América Latina, c1986. 116 p. : ill. ; 18 cm. (Biblioteca Política argentina . 155) Bibliography: p. 114-116. ISBN 950-25-1416-5 LC Card 87-100705
1. Aircraft industry - Government ownership - Argentina - History. 2. Fábrica Militar de Aviones - History. 3. Industrias Aeronáuticas y Mecánicas del Estado (Argentina) - History. 4. Government business enterprises - Argentina - History. I. Tonini, Alicia del Carmen. II. Title. III. Series.
HD9711.A72 A54 1986

ANGUILLA - ECONOMIC CONDITIONS.
Caribbean Development Bank. Economics and Programming Dept. Economic memorandum on Anguilla. [Kingston, Jamaica] [1985] 2, 55 p. : LC Card 86-204700 DDC 330.97297/3 19
HC156.Z7 A483 1985

Der Anhang als dritter Teil des Jahresabschlusses . Russ, Wolfgang, 1955- Bergisch Gladbach , 1984. xi, 332 p. : ISBN 3-89012-013-X : LC Card 85-195717
HF5681.B2 R817 1984

Anikin, Andreĭ Vladimirovich.
SSSR, SShA i Kanada . Moskva , 1987. 325 p. ; LC Card 86-205359
HF3628.U5 S77 1987

Uil'i͡am Petti / A.V. Anikin, V.A. Anikin. Moskva : Ėkonomika, 1986. 92, [3] p. ; 21 cm. Bibliography: p. 92-[93] LC Card 86-206468 DDC 330.15/3 19
1. Petty, William, Sir, 1623-1687. 2. Economists - Great Britain - Biography. I. Anikin, V. A. (Vladimir Andreevich). II. Title.
HB103.P5 A83 1986

Anikin, V. A. (Vladimir Andreevich) Anikin, Andreĭ Vladimirovich. Uil'i͡am Petti /. Moskva , 1986. 92, [3] p. ; LC Card 86-206468 DDC 330.15/3 19
HB103.P5 A83 1986

ANIMAL HUSBANDRY. see **LIVESTOCK.**

ANIMAL INDUSTRY - AFRICA - FINANCE - CASE STUDIES.
Addis Anteneh. Financing livestock services in some countries of east and southern Africa /. Addis Ababa, Ethiopia [1985] 26 p. ; LC Card 86-980745 DDC 338.1/36/0096 19
HD9427.A2 A33 1985

ANIMAL INDUSTRY - BOLIVIA - CAQUIAVIRI.
Birbuet D., Gustavo. Tierra y ganado en Pacajes . La Paz, Bolivia , 1986. 86 p. : LC Card 87-403087 DDC 333.3/0984/12 19
HD490.C34 B57 1986

ANIMAL INDUSTRY - BOLIVIA - COMANCHE.
Birbuet D., Gustavo. Tierra y ganado en Pacajes . La Paz, Bolivia , 1986. 86 p. : LC Card 87-403087 DDC 333.3/0984/12 19
HD490.C34 B57 1986

ANIMAL INDUSTRY - BRAZIL - GOIÁS (STATE) - STATISTICS.
Insumos estatísticos para o diagnóstico da pecuária no Estado de Goiás /. [Goiânia-Goiás] [19]84. 156 leaves : LC Card 86-178269
HD9424.B73 G655 1984

ANIMAL INDUSTRY - BULGARIA.
Pospelowa, Galina. Schlachttier- und Fleischproduktion in Osteuropa . Giessen , Berlin , 1981. 144 p. ; ISBN 3-428-04944-6 LC Card 82-167577
HD9425.B92 P67 1981

ANIMAL INDUSTRY - CHINA.
China, the livestock sector. Washington, D.C., U. S.A. , 1987. vii, 195 p. ; ISBN 0-8213-0940-4 (pbk.) LC Card 87-16089 DDC 338.1/76/00951 19
HD9426.C62 C475 1987

ANIMAL INDUSTRY - DEVELOPING COUNTRIES - FORECASTING.
Sarma, J. S. Cereal feed use in the Third World . Washington, D.C. , c1986. 68 p. : ISBN 0-89629-058-1 (pbk.) LC Card 86-27355 DDC 338.1/7325/091724 19
HD9052.D44 S27 1986

ANIMAL INDUSTRY - GERMANY (WEST) - NORTH RHINE-WESTPHALIA - STATISTICS.
Agrarberichterstattung Nordrhein-Westfalen 1983 . Düsseldorf [1984] 241, [5] p. ; LC Card 87-407318 DDC 943/.55 s 338.1/76/0094355021 19
HA1320.N6 A32 Heft 533 HD9423.7.N6

ANIMAL INDUSTRY - IOWA - STATISTICS.
Otto, Daniel. Economic contribution and impacts of changes in Iowa's livestock and meat processing industries /. Oakdale, Iowa [1984] xi, 95 p. : LC Card 85-621899 DDC 338.1/76/009777021 19
HD9417.I8 O88 1984 ***NYPL [JLF 86-592]***

ANIMAL INDUSTRY - ITALY - PRATO REGION - HISTORY.
Nigro, Giampiero. Gli uomini dell'irco . Firenze , 1983. xxii, 184 p. : ISBN 88-00-86022-2 : LC Card 84-238769
HD9425.I83 P76 1983 ***NYPL [JLE 86-2127]***

ANIMAL INDUSTRY - PERU - LAMBAYEQUE (DEPT.)
Simons Munaro, Yehude. Lambayeque, producción ganadera, comunidades campesinas [microform] /. Chiclayo, Perú , 1983. 45 p. ; LC Card 84-204537 DDC 338.1/76/0098514 19
HD9424.P43 L367 1983
NYPL [*ZT-1708 no.72]

ANIMAL INDUSTRY - RUSSIAN S.F.S.R. - BASHKIRSKAI͡A A.S.S.R.
Industrializat͡sii͡a proizvodstva i mezhkhozi͡aĭstvennoe kooperirovanie /. Ufa , 1979. 122 p. ; LC Card 82-161458
HD9425.S653 B375 1979

ANIMAL INDUSTRY - SOUTH AFRICA - STATISTICS.
Sensus van landbou- en veeteelproduksie, 1979 =. Pretoria [1985?] xiv, 266 p. ; ISBN 0-621-09380-7 : LC Card 86-150362 DDC 338.1/0968/021 19
HD2130.5 .S48 1985

ANIMAL INDUSTRY - SOVIET UNION.
Rukosuev, P. N. (Platon Nikolaevich) Ėkonomicheskai͡a ėffektivnost' zhivotnovodstva v sisteme APK /. Moskva , 1985. 127 p. ; LC Card 86-133226
HD9425.S652 R86 1985

ANIMAL INDUSTRY - SUDAN - JONGLEI.
Payne, W. J. A. (William John Arthur) A preliminary report on the livestock industry in the Jonglei area /. [Khartoum?] , 1977. 1 v. (various foliations) : LC Card 81-980100
HD9427.S83 J6664 1977

ANIMAL INDUSTRY - UNITED STATES - STATISTICS.
Otto, Daniel. Economic contribution and impacts of changes in Iowa's livestock and meat processing industries /. Oakdale, Iowa [1984] xi, 95 p. : LC Card 85-621899 DDC 338.1/76/009777021 19
HD9417.I8 O88 1984 ***NYPL [JLF 86-592]***

ANIMAL INDUSTRY - URUGUAY.
Uruguay, producción y comercialización de ganado y carnes. [Montevideo, Uruguay] , 1985. 90 p. : LC Card 87-403154 DDC 338.1/760883/09895 19
HD9424.U8 U783 1985

Aninat, Eduardo. Foxley, Alejandro. Las desigualdades económicas y la acción del estado . México , 1980. 271 p. ; ISBN 968-16-0365-6 LC Card 82-215955 DDC 339.2/098 19
HC130.I5 F69 1980 ***NYPL [JLD 86-2631]***

ANJOU (FRANCE) - ECONOMIC CONDITIONS.
Le Mené, Michel. Les campagnes angevines à la fin du Moyen Age . Nantes , c1982. 534 p., [1] folded leaf of plates : LC Card 87-672705
HC277.A55 L45x 1982

ANJOU (FRANCE) - RURAL CONDITIONS.
Le Mené, Michel. Les campagnes angevines à la fin du Moyen Age . Nantes , c1982. 534 p., [1] folded leaf of plates : LC Card 87-672705
HC277.A55 L45x 1982

Anker, Richard, 1943- Working women in socialist countries . Geneva , 1985. xvi, 234 p. : ISBN 92-2-103910-2 (pbk.) : LC Card 85-181464 DDC 304.6/32/091717 19
HB901 .W657 1985 ***NYPL [JLE 86-1433]***

Annales de fiscalité . Cozian, Maurice. Paris , 1981. 127 p. ; ISBN 2-7111-0289-0 : LC Card 81-150065
HJ2659 .C65 1981

Annales du Centre régional de documentation pédagogique de Clermont-Ferrand. Collection Documents régionaux.
Histoire de la navigation sur l'Allier en Bourbonnais /. Clermont-Ferrand [France] , 1983. 61 p. : LC Card 84-150630
HE668.Z7 A454 1983

Annales Universitatis Saraviensis. Rechts- und Wirtschaftswissenschaftliche Abteilung .
(Bd. 108) Naust, Hermann. Direkte Steuern und intertemporale Allokation . Köln , c1983. xiv, 374 p. : ISBN 3-452-19402-7 : LC Card 83-163600 DDC 336.2 19
HJ3851 .N38 1983

Annali dell'Istituto sperimentale per la nutrizione delle piante. Supplement.
Produttività potenziale e classificazione dei terreni. Roma , 1985- v. <1 > in <5 > : LC Card 87-105342
HD679.L39 P76 1985

ANNALS. see **HISTORY.**

The annals of labor and industry in Illinois 1890 for January, February and March; <July, August, September > 1890. Illinois Writers' Project. Chicago, Ill., 1939-<1941 > v. <1, 3 > LC Card 42-43915 DDC 331/.09773 19
HD8083.I3 I44 1939

Annaratone, Marco. Digital CMOS circuit design / by Marco Annaratone. Boston : Kluwer Academic Publishers, c1986. xv, 344 p. : ill. ; 25 cm. (The Kluwer international series in engineering and computer science. VLSI, computer architecture, and digital signal processing) Includes bibliographies and index. ISBN 0-89838-224-6 LC Card 86-10646 DDC 621.395 19
1. Metal oxide semiconductors, Complementary. 2. Integrated circuits - Very large scale integration. I. Title. II. Title: Digital C.M.O.S. circuit design. III. Series.
TK7871.99.M44 A56 1986
NYPL [JSE 87-634]

Anni d'America /. Ortona, Egidio. Bologna , c1984- v. ; ISBN 88-15-00531-5 (v. 1) : LC Card 84-240652 DDC 338.91/73/045 19
HC305 .O78 1984 ***NYPL [JLL 86-503]***

An annotated catalog of microcomputer software in economics /. Walstad, William B. New York, NY (2 Park Ave., New York 10016) , c1986. viii, 160 p. ; LC Card 86-210285 DDC 330/.028/5536 19
HB74.8 .W34 1986

Annuaire rétrospectif des statistiques du commerce extérieur du Togo, 1968-1978 / document élaboré par la Division Documentation et publications. Lomé : République togolaise, Ministère du plan et de la réforme administrative, Direction de la statistique, [1982] 37 leaves, [3] leaves of plates : ill. ; 30 cm. "Novembre 1982." Errata slip inserted. LC Card 86-130147 DDC 382/.096681/0021 19
1. Togo - Commerce - Statistics. I. Togo. Direction de la statistique. Division Documentation et publications. II. Togo. Direction de la statistique.
HF3923.A45 A56 1982

ANNUAL IMPROVEMENT FACTOR. see **WAGES AND LABOR PRODUCTIVITY.**

ANNUAL INCOME GUARANTEE. see **GUARANTEED ANNUAL INCOME; INCOME MAINTENANCE PROGRAMS.**

ANNUAL REPORTS, CORPORATE. see **CORPORATION REPORTS.**

ANNUALS. see **CALENDARS.**

ANNUITIES.
Crowe, Robert M. Time and money .

Homewood, Ill. , c1987. 1 v. (various pagings) : ISBN 1-556-23051-6 (pbk.) LC Card 87-70621 DDC 332.024 19
HG1621 .C76 1987

Annullamenti del Trentino-Alto Adige, 1850-1883 =. Sottoriva, Fabio. Rovereto , c1981. 184 p., [8] p. of plates : LC Card 86-178380
HE6185.I72 T747 1981

Anomalies in stock returns on a thin security market /. Berglund, Tom. Helsingfors , 1986. vi, 191 p. : ISBN 951-555-239-7 (pbk.) LC Card 86-224629 DDC 332.63/222 19
HG4636 .B47 1986

Anonymous struggles : democratic rights of unorganised labour in India. New Delhi : People's Union for Democratic Rights, 1983. 24 p. ; 23 cm. LC Card 83-904576 DDC 344.54/01 345.4041 19
1. Labor laws and legislation - India. 2. Right to labor - India. 3. Trade-unions - India. I. People's Union for Democratic Rights (India).
LAW ***NYPL [JLD 86-3877]***

Anpassung an die Inflation. The Adaptation to inflation /. Berlin , New York , 1986. xvi, 512 p. : ISBN 0-89925-287-7 (U. S.) LC Card 86-29134 DDC 338.943 19
HC286.2 .A62 1986

Anreizmechanismen zur Regulierung der Elektrizitätswirtschaft . Vogelsang, Ingo. Tübingen , 1982. xii, 173 p. : ISBN 3-16-344549-7 : LC Card 83-153444
HD9685.G3 V64 1982

Ansätze eines Konzepts zur Erfassung regionaler Lebensbedingungen in der Raumordnungspolitik /. Wilamowitz-Moellendorff, Ulrich von. Bonn , 1986. iv, 205 p. ; ISBN 3-88488-275-9 LC Card 87-407818 DDC 330.943/0878 19
HC286.7 .W54 1986

Ansari, Saiyad Hasan, 1952- Evolution and spatial organization of clan settlements : a case study of middle Ganga Valley / Saiyad Hasan Ansari. New Delhi : Concept Pub. Co., 1986. 212 p., [8] p. of plates : ill., folded geneal. tables, plans ; 22 cm. Includes index. Bibliography: p. [197]-208. LC Card 86-900654
1. Land settlement - India - Ghazipur - Case studies. 2. Human settlements - India - Ghazipur - Case studies. 3. Land settlement - India - Case studies. 4. Human settlements - India - Case studies. I. Title.
HD879.G45 A57 1986
NYPL [JLD 86-3220]

Ansary, Adel I. Stern, Louis W., 1935- Marketing channels /. Englewood Cliffs, N.J. , c1988. xiv, 609 p. : ISBN 0-13-557158-8 : LC Card 87-17396 DDC 658.8/4 19
HF5415.129 .S75 1988

Ansbacher, Max G. The new options market / Max G. Ansbacher. Rev. ed., 1st paperback ed. New York : Walker, c1987. xvii, 280 p. : ill. ; 23 cm. Includes index. ISBN 0-8027-7308-7 (pbk.) : LC Card 87-18892 DDC 332.64/52 19
1. Put and call transactions. I. Title.
HG6042 .A57 1987

Anschiringer, Anton, 1812-1873. Album der Industrie des Reichenberger Handelskammer-Bezirks. [Praha] , 1981. 2 v. in 1 : LC Card 84-190839
HC270.292.L52 A42 1981

ANSELLS BREWERY STRIKE, BIRMINGHAM, ENGLAND, 1981.
Waddington, David P. Trouble brewing . Aldershot , Brookfield, U. S.A. , c1987. x, 164 p. : ISBN 0-566-05374-8 : LC Card 86-31849 DDC 331.89/28633/0942496 19
HD5366.L62 1981 .B578 1987

Ansett, Bob, 1933- Bob Ansett, an autobiography / with Robert Pullan. Hartwell, Vic. : J. Kerr, 1986. 221 p., [16] p. of plates : ill. ; 25 cm. Includes index. ISBN 0-9588161-0-7 LC Card 86-228002 DDC 338.7/4/0924 B 19
1. Ansett, Bob, 1933-. 2. Businessmen - Australia - Biography. I. Pullan, Robert. II. Title.
HC602.5.A57 A33 1986

ANSETT. BOB, 1933-
Ansett, Bob, 1933- Bob Ansett, an autobiography /. Hartwell, Vic. , 1986. 221 p., [16] p. of plates : ISBN 0-9588161-0-7 LC Card 86-228002 DDC 338.7/4/0924 B 19
HC602.5.A57 A33 1986

Ansoff, H. Igor.
Corporate strategy. Ansoff, H. Igor. The new corporate strategy / H. Igor Ansoff assisted by Edward J. McDonnell. New York , 1988. xviii, 258 p. : ISBN 0-471-62950-2 LC Card 87-23266 DDC 658.4/012 19
HD30.28 .A535 1988

The new corporate strategy / H. Igor Ansoff assisted by Edward J. McDonnell. New York : Wiley, 1988. xviii, 258 p. : ill. ; 24 cm. Rev. ed. of: Corporate strategy. 1965. Bibliography: p. 243-245. Includes indexes. ISBN 0-471-62950-2 LC Card 87-23266 DDC 658.4/012 19
1. Strategic planning. I. McDonnell, Edward J. II. Ansoff, H. Igor. Corporate strategy. III. Title.
HD30.28 .A535 1988

Ansprüche an die Arbeit : Umfragedaten und Interpretationen / Hans-Joachim Hoffmann-Nowotny, Friedhelm Gehrmann (Hg.). Frankfurt [am Main] ; New York : Campus, c1984. 298 p. : ill. ; 21 cm. (Soziale Indikatoren . 11) Contributions originally presented at a meeting organized by the Werner-Reimers-Stiftung, held June 1983 in Bad Homburg. Bibliography: p. 281-296. CONTENTS. - Das "Tonio-Kröger-Syndrom" / Randolph Vollmer -- Berufliche Wertorientierung und Wohlfahrtserträge / Roland Habich -- Zwischen Anpassung und Widerstand / Wolfgang Bonss -- Berufsgruppenspezifische Ansprüche an die Arbeit und Arbeitsbedingungen / Peter Pawlowsky -- "Selbstverwirklichung" / Johann Behrens -- Krise und kompensatorische Politik / Heinz Renn und Volker Mariak -- Interdependenzen zwischen amtlicher Arbeitszeitstatistik, Sozialbilanzen und neuen betrieblichen Informationssystemen / Eberhard Seifert -- Von den Lücken zu den Grenzen des Wohlfahrtsstaates / Franz Pavelka -- Die betriebliche Sozialpolitik ... / Edmund Hemmer -- Postmaterialismus, Arbeitslosigkeit und Arbeitszeitverkürzung / Thomas Aschatz und Franz Haslinger -- Regionale Beschäftigungspolitik und veränderte Rahmenbedingungen / Klaus Müller -- Beschäftigung und Arbeitsmarkt in Österreich / Josef Christl und Peter Mitter. ISBN 3-593-33390-2 LC Card 85-103333
1. Psychology, Industrial - Germany (West). 2. Work ethic - Germany (West). 3. Job satisfaction - Germany, West. I. Hoffmann-Nowotny, Hans-Joachim. II. Gehrmann, Friedhelm. III. Werner-Reimers-Stiftung. IV. Series.
HF5548.8 .A683 1984

Ansquer, Vincent. Colloque d'étude des politiques économiques Récession et relance (1984 : Paris, France) Récession et relance /. Paris , 1984. 218 p. : ISBN 2-7178-0690-3 : LC Card 85-158199 DDC 338.5/42 19
HB3711 .C59 1984

The answer book . Dorrell, Jean, 1926- Los Angeles, CA , c1987. ix, 358 p. : ISBN 0-935732-12-8 (pbk.) : LC Card 87-23408 DDC 651 19
HF5547.5 .D63 1987

Antal, Iván. Vállalatok környezete, céljai, szervezete / Antal Iván. Budapest : Közgazdasági és Jogi Könyvkiadó, 1986. 270 p. : ill. ; 21 cm. ISBN 963-221-567-2 : LC Card 87-149512
1. Industrial management - Hungary. 2. Industrial organization - Hungary. 3. Organizational change - Hungary. 4. Business enterprises - Hungary. I. Title.
HD70.H8 A536 1986

Antanaĭtis, ÎU. A. (ÎUstinas Antanovich) Sotsialisticheskoe sorevnovanie i intensifikatsiia proizvodstva / ÎU.A. Antanaĭtis ; pod redaktsieĭ P.V. Grechishnikova. Moskva : Profizdat, 1987. 157 p. : ill. ; 21 cm. Includes bibliographical references. LC Card 87-103350
1. Socialist competition - Lithuania. 2. Industrial productivity - Lithuania. I. Grechishnikov, P. V. (Petr Vladimirovich). II. Title.
HC337.L53 S63 1987

Antanavičius, K. (Kazimieras) Kompleksinis subalansuotas statybos planavimas /. Vilnius , 1983. 115 p. : LC Card 83-187666
HD9715.S72 K66 1983

ANTARCTIC EXPEDITIONS. see **ANTARCTIC REGIONS.**

Antarctic regions - Description and travel. see **Antarctic regions.**

ANTARCTIC REGIONS - INTERNATIONAL STATUS.
Mitchell, Barbara. Frozen stakes . London , Washington, D.C. , c1983. iii, 135 p. : ISBN 0-905347-45-5 (pbk.) : LC Card 84-173206 DDC 333.8/5/09989 19
HD9506.A585 M57 1983
NYPL [JLD 86-3548]

Antecedentes estadísticos de la distribución del ingreso. Colombia, 1951-1982. 1a ed. Santiago de Chile : Naciones Unidas, 1986. 49 p. ; 25 cm. (Serie Distribución del ingreso . 1) "Este estudio fue preparado por la División de Estadísticas y Análisis Cuantitativo de la Comisión para América Latina y el Caribe (CEPAL)"--T.p. verso. "LC/G.1385, enero de 1986"--T.p. verso. Bibliography: p. 49. LC Card 87-115916 DDC 339.2/09861 19
1. Income distribution - Colombia - History - Statistics. I. United Nations. Economic Commission for Latin America and the Caribbean. División de Estadísticas y Análisis Cuantitativo. II. Series.
HC200.I5 A58 1986

Antecedentes estadísticos de la distribución del ingreso. Brasil, 1960-1983. 1a ed. Santiago de Chile : Naciones Unidas, 1986. 50 p. ; 26 cm. (Serie Distribución del ingreso . 2) "Este trabajo fue preparado por la División de Estadísticas y Análisis Cuantitativo de la Comisión Económica para América Latina y el Caribe (CEPAL)"--T.p. verso. "LC/G.1387, septiembre de 1986"--T.p. verso. Bibliography: p. 49-50. LC Card 87-115965 DDC 339.2/0981 19
1. Income distribution - Brazil - History - 20th century - Sources. I. United Nations. Economic Commission for Latin America and the Caribbean. División de Estadísticos y Análisis Cuantitativo. II. Series.
HC190.I5 A57 1986

Ante-projeto do núcleo de colonização "Presidente Kennedy" /. Companhia de Viação São Paulo-Mato Grosso. Mato Grosso, Brasil , 1962. 40 p., [15] leaves of plates : LC Card 85-135105
HD1516.B8 C64 1962

Antezana Ergueta, Luis. Evaluación económico-política de la reforma agraria / Luis Antezana Ergueta. La Paz, Bolivia : Librería Editorial "Juventud", 1986. 113 p. : ill. ; 22 cm. Bibliography: p. 63-64. LC Card 87-400948 DDC 333.3/1/84 19
1. Land reform - Bolivia. I. Title.
HD1333.B5 A56 1986

Antezana J., Luis H. Bolivia, hoy /. México, D.F. , 1983. 240 p. ; LC Card 84-148626 DDC 330.984/05 19
HC182 .B565 1983 ***NYPL [JLD 86-2825]***

Anthony, Robert Newton, 1916-
Essentials of accounting / Robert N. Anthony. 4th ed. Reading, Mass. : Addison-Wesley, 1988. p. cm. ISBN 0-201-00017-2 : LC Card 87-21944 DDC 657/.07/7 19
1. Accounting. I. Title.
HF5635 .A6879 1988

Essentials of accounting. Anthony, Robert Newton, 1916- A review of Essentials of accounting, 4th edition / Robert N. Anthony. Reading, Mass. , 1988. p. cm. ISBN 0-201-05905-3 : LC Card 87-21949 DDC 657 19
HF5635 .A69143 1988

A review of Essentials of accounting, 4th edition / Robert N. Anthony. Reading, Mass. : Addison-Wesley, 1988. p. cm. ISBN 0-201-05905-3 : LC Card 87-21949 DDC 657 19
1. Accounting. I. Anthony, Robert Newton, 1916- Essentials of accounting. II. Title.
HF5635 .A69143 1988

Anthony, William P. Envisionary management : a guide for human resources professionals in management training and development / William P. Anthony, E. Nick Maddox, and Walter Wheatley, Jr. New York : Quorum Books, c1988. p. cm. Bibliography: p. Includes index. ISBN 0-89930-257-2 (lib. bdg. : alk. paper) LC Card 87-7373 DDC 658.3 19
1. Management. 2. Imagery (Psychology). I. Maddox, E. Nick. II. Wheatley, Walter. III. Title.
HD38 .A6256 1988

Anthracite coal /. Haine, Edgar A., 1908- Chicago, Ill. , c1987. 214 p., ca. 250 p. of plates : ISBN 0-9617434-0-9 LC Card 86-90990 DDC 338.2/725/09748 19
HD9547.P4 H35 1987

ANTHRACITE COAL INDUSTRY - PENNSYLVANIA - HISTORY.

Haine, Edgar A., 1908- Anthracite coal /. Chicago, Ill. , c1987. 214 p., ca. 250 p. of plates : ISBN 0-9617434-0-9 LC Card 86-90990 DDC 338.2/725/09748 19
HD9547.P4 H35 1987

ANTHRACITE COAL INDUSTRY - PENNSYLVANIA - SCRANTON REGION - HISTORY - ADDRESSES, ESSAYS, LECTURES.
Hard coal, hard times . Scranton , 1984, c1983. xv, 193 p. ; ISBN 0-917445-00-7 LC Card 85-156422 DDC 331.7/622335/0974837
HD8039.M62 U633 1984 *NYPL [JLE 87-1218]*

ANTHROPO-GEOGRAPHY - ADDRESSES, ESSAYS, LECTURES.
Santos, Milton. Espaço e sociedade . Petrópolis [Brazil] , 1979. 152 p. : LC Card 80-109991
HT151 .S238 *NYPL [JLD 81-405]*

World patterns of modern urban change . Chicago , 1986. x, 479 p. : ISBN 0-89065-122-1 : LC Card 85-23231 DDC 910 s 307.7/6 19
H31 .C514 no.217-218
NYPL [JFM 72-132 no.217-218]

ANTHROPO-GEOGRAPHY - AFGHANISTAN - SAR-E POL.
Jebens, Albrecht. Wirtschafts- und sozialgeographische Untersuchung über das Heimgewerbe in Nordafghanistan unter besonderer Berücksichtigung der Mittelstadt Sar-e-Pul . Tübingen , 1983. xii, 415 p., [2] folded leaves of plates : LC Card 86-128235
HD2346.A52 S275 1983

ANTHROPO-GEOGRAPHY - DEVELOPING COUNTRIES.
Forbes, Dean K. The geography of underdevelopment . London , 1986. 214 p. ; ISBN 0-7099-1012-6 *NYPL [JLD 86-1233]*

ANTHROPO-GEOGRAPHY - INDIA - CHOTA NAGPUR.
Prasad, Maheshwari, 1944- Social aspects of mining towns of the tribal region /. New Delhi , 1986- v. <1- > ; LC Card 86-902979 DDC 307.7/66/095412 19
HD9506.I43 C486 1986

ANTHROPO-GEOGRAPHY - UNITED STATES.
Cutter, Susan L. Rating places . Washington, D.C. , c1985. viii, 76 p. : ISBN 0-89291-191-3 (pbk.) : LC Card 85-13469 DDC 307/.0973 19
GF503 .C87 1985 *NYPL [JLD 86-2715]*

ANTHROPOLOGY, ECONOMIC. see **ECONOMIC ANTHROPOLOGY.**

Anthropology of contemporary issues .
(8) Zavella, Patricia, 1949- Women's work and Chicano families . Ithaca , 1987. xviii, 191 p. ; ISBN 0-8014-1730-9 (pbk. : alk. paper) LC Card 87-5245 DDC 305.4/3664 19
HD6073.C272 U596 1987

Farm work and fieldwork . Ithaca , 1987. 293 p. : ISBN 0-8014-9446-X (pbk. : alk. paper) LC Card 86-19960 DDC 305.5/55/0973 19
HD8039.F32 U635 1987

Lamphere, Louise. From working daughters to working mothers . Ithaca , 1987. xviii, 390 p. : ISBN 0-8014-9441-9 (pbk. : alk. paper) LC Card 86-32952 DDC 331.4/09745/1 19
HD6096.R4 L36 1987

El anti imperialismo del APRA y los contratos petroleros /. Malpica Silva Santisteban, Carlos. [Lima, Peru] [1986 or 1987] 398 p. : LC Card 87-402097 DDC 338.2/7282/0985 19
HD9574.P52 M37 1986

Antía, Fernando. Quijano, José Manuel. Finanzas, desarrollo económico y penetración extranjera /. Puebla, Pue. , 1985. 395 p. : LC Card 86-112589 DDC 332/.0972 19
HG185.M6 Q55 1985 *NYPL [JLD 86-2195]*

Anti-Apartheid Movement.
Shell out of Namibia and South Africa . London [1986] 19 . : LC Card 87-138719 DDC 338.8/87 19
HD9571.9.S45 S54 1986

UK companies and their subsidiary or related companies in South Africa and Namibia. London [1986] [18] p. ; LC Card 87-138700 DDC 338./8941/068 19
HG5851.A3 U39 1986

Antibiotic industry in Japan. Aizawa, Minoru. Review on the development of antibiotics industry in selected countries . [Vienna, Austria] , 1985. 92 p. : LC Card 86-151674 DDC 338.4/7615329/0952 19
HD9675.A63 J33 1985

ANTIBIOTICS INDUSTRY - JAPAN.
Aizawa, Minoru. Review on the development of antibiotics industry in selected countries . [Vienna, Austria] , 1985. 92 p. : LC Card 86-151674 DDC 338.4/7615329/0952 19
HD9675.A63 J33 1985

L'antic Gremi d'Escultors de Barcelona /. Martinell, César, 1888-1973. Valls , 1956. 68 p. ; LC Card 86-180958
HD6473.S73 B356 1956

Anticipating urban growth in Africa . Van den Berg, L. M. Lusaka, Zambia , 1984. viii, 167 p., [4] p. of plates : LC Card 86-980297 DDC 307.7/6/096894 19
HD993.Z9 L88 1984

ANTI-COLONIALISM. see **COLONIES.**

ANTI-DISCRIMINATION LAWS. see **RACE DISCRIMINATION; SEX DISCRIMINATION - LAW AND LEGISLATION.**

Anti-inflation Board. see **Canada. Anti-inflation Board.**

ANTILLES, LESSER - ECONOMIC CONDITIONS.
Chemin Dupontès, P. Les Petites Antilles . [Fort-de-France] [Paris] [1979] x, 318 p., [10] p. of plates : ISBN 2-85275-105-4 LC Card 84-164674
HC151 .C49 1979

ANTIMILITARISM. see **MILITARISM.**

ANTI-NAZI MOVEMENT - GERMANY (WEST) - PENZBERG.
Tenfelde, Klaus. Proletarische Provinz . München , 1982. xvii, 409 p. : ISBN 3-486-50701-X : LC Card 83-124119
HD8460.P452 T46 1982

Antinori, Pietro. Guida alla valorizzazione agricola nei paesi in via di sviluppo /. Milano, Italy , c1983. 434 p. : LC Card 83-144803 DDC 338.1/09172/4 19
HD1417 .G85 1983 *NYPL [JLD 86-3296]*

ANTINUCLEAR MOVEMENT.
Atomkraft am Ende? /. Göttingen , 1986. 191 p. ; ISBN 3-923478-16-X LC Card 86-228667
HD9698.A2 A795 1986

Cook, Alice. Greenham women everywhere . Boston, Mass. , 1984, c1983. 127, [1] p. : ISBN 0-89608-199-0 *NYPL [JLD 87-215]*

Fehér, Ferenc, 1933- Doomsday or deterrence? . Armonk, N.Y. , c1986. 154 p. ; ISBN 0-87332-368-8 : LC Card 86-10074 DDC 327.1/74 19
JX1974.7 .F38 1986 *NYPL [JLE 86-4319]*

Gruhl, Herbert, 1921- Der atomare Selbstmord /. München , c1986. 190 p. : ISBN 3-7766-1448-X LC Card 86-226120
HD9698.A2 G74 1986

Maier-Leibnitz, Heinz. Lernschock Tschernobyl /. Zürich , c1986. 137 p. ; ISBN 3-7201-5191-3 : LC Card 87-120438
HD9698.S653 C485 1986

Wer steuert die "Anti-Kernkraft-Bewegung"-- und mit welchem Ziel? /. Wiesbaden [1977] 38 p. : LC Card 86-140106 DDC 333.79/24 19
HD9698.A2 W44 1977

ANTINUCLEAR MOVEMENT - AUSTRALIA - BROKEN HILL (N.S.W.)
Honeymoon uranium mine occupation [sound recording]. Los Angeles, Calif. , p1983. 1 sound cassette (53 min.) : LC Card 87-752867
HD9539.U72

ANTINUCLEAR MOVEMENT - GERMANY (WEST)
Tschernobyl hat unser Leben verändert . Reinbek bei Hamburg , 1986. 203 p. : ISBN 3-499-15922-8 : LC Card 87-123041 DDC 363.1/79 19
HD9698.G42 T73 1986

Wer WAA sät wird Widerstand ernten! /. Hamburg [1979] 31 p. : LC Card 85-171252
HD9698.G42 W47 1979

Der Widerstand geht weiter . Freiburg i. Br. , 1982. 261 p. : ISBN 3-921472-30-X LC Card 82-192690
HD9698.G43 W937 1982

ANTINUCLEAR MOVEMENT - GERMANY (WEST) - WACKERSDORF.
Wackersdorf . Passau , 1986. 75 p. : ISBN 3-88849-021-9 LC Card 86-183781
HD9698.G43 W338 1986

ANTINUCLEAR MOVEMENT - GERMANY (WEST) - WYHL.
Der Widerstand geht weiter . Freiburg i. Br. , 1982. 261 p. : ISBN 3-921472-30-X LC Card 82-192690
HD9698.G43 W937 1982

ANTINUCLEAR MOVEMENT - GREAT BRITAIN.
Cook, Alice. Greenham women everywhere . Boston, Mass. , 1984, c1983. 127, [1] p. : ISBN 0-89608-199-0 *NYPL [JLD 87-215]*

Towle, Philip, 1945- Protest and perish . London , 1982. 121 p. ; ISBN 0-907967-02-7 (pbk.) : LC Card 83-198296 DDC 355/.0217/0941 19
UA647 .T69 1982 *NYPL [JLD 86-1904]*

ANTINUCLEAR MOVEMENT - IRELAND.
Closing the door on a nuclear future . [Harbour View, Bantry, Co. Cork , 1986] [7] leaves : LC Card 87-111333 DDC 333.79/27/0941 19
HD9698.G72 C56 1986

ANTINUCLEAR MOVEMENT - UNITED STATES.
Garfinkle, Adam M., 1951- The politics of the nuclear freeze /. Philadelphia, Pa. , 1984. xviii, 258 p. ; ISBN 0-910191-08-5 : LC Card 84-6030 DDC 327.1/74 19
JX1974.7 .G34 1984 *NYPL [JLE 86-710]*

Loeb, Paul Rogat, 1952- Hope in hard times . Lexington, Mass. , c1987. ix, 322 p. : ISBN 0-669-12929-1 LC Card 85-46044 DDC 327.1/74 19
JX1974.7 .L63 1986 *NYPL [JLE 86-4051]*

Antioquia (Colombia : Dept.). Asamblea Departamental. Foro El Suroeste de Antioquia y el Chocó Norte (1984 : Urrao, Colombia) Foro El Suroeste de Antioquia y el Chocó Norte . [Medellín] [1985] 65 p. : LC Card 87-400457 DDC 338.9861/2 19
HC198.A5 F595 1984

ANTIOQUIA, COLOMBIA (DEPT.) - ECONOMIC CONDITIONS.
Giraldo Zuluaga, Luisa Fernanda, 1957- La colonización antioqueña y la fundación de Manizales /. Manizales, Colombia [1983] 217 p. : LC Card 84-107745
HD519.C35 G57 1983

ANTIOQUIA, COLOMBIA (DEPT.) - HISTORY.
Giraldo Zuluaga, Luisa Fernanda, 1957- La colonización antioqueña y la fundación de Manizales /. Manizales, Colombia [1983] 217 p. : LC Card 84-107745
HD519.C35 G57 1983

ANTIOQUIA, COLOMBIA (DEPT.) - INDUSTRIES.
Vellinga, Menno. Industrialization and regional development in Colombia /. Amsterdam, The Netherlands , 1983. 183 p. : ISBN 90-70280-80-9 LC Card 83-209247 DDC 338.09861/26 19
HC198.C296 V45 1983

Anti-parliamentary communism . Shipway, Mark. New York , 1988. p. cm. ISBN 0-312-01265-9 : LC Card 87-23083 DDC 338.6 19
HD5660.G7 S48 1988

ANTI-POVERTY PROGRAM (UNITED STATES) see **ECONOMIC ASSISTANCE, DOMESTIC - UNITED STATES.**

Anti-protection . Destler, I. M. Washington, DC , c1987. xii, 204 p. ; ISBN 0-88132-065-X (pbk.) LC Card 87-22545 DDC 382/.3/0973 19
HF1455 .D482 1987

Antiqua. Ministry of Finance. Statistics Division. National accounts statistics, 1977-1984. St. John's Antigua [1985] 44 leaves : LC Card 86-221979 DDC 339.37297/4 19
HC155.5.Z7 A576 1985

ANTIQUE COLLECTING. see **ANTIQUES.**

ANTIQUE DEALERS - GREAT BRITAIN.
Manston, Peter B., 1951- [Flea markets, antique fairs, and auctions of Britain.] Manston's flea

markets, antique fairs, and auctions of Britain . Sacramento, Calif., U. S.A. , New York, N.Y. , c1987. 277 p. : ISBN 0-931367-10-7 (pbk. : alk. paper) : LC Card 87-16221 DDC 381/.1 19
HF5482 .M3125 1987

ANTIQUE DEALERS - JAPAN - DIRECTORIES.
Nedlog, D'Lanor. Insider's guide to antique bazaars in Japan /. Tokyo, Japan , c1986. 124 p. : ISBN 4-906231-00-4 LC Card 87-123282 DDC 381/.18 19
HF5475.J3 N43 1986

Antique shows. Manston, Peter B., 1951- [Flea markets, antique fairs, and auctions of Germany.] Manston's flea markets, antique fairs, and auctions of Germany . Sacramento, Calif., U. S.A. , New York, N.Y. , c1987. 297 p. : ISBN 0-931367-08-5 (pbk.) : LC Card 86-30908 DDC 381/.1 19
HF5482 .M3135 1987

Antique shows. Manston, Peter B., 1951- [Flea markets, antique shows, and auctions of France.] Manston's flea markets, antique shows, and auctions of France . Sacramento, Calif., U. S.A. , New York, N.Y. , c1987. 195 p. : ISBN 0-931367-06-9 (pbk.) : LC Card 86-30909 DDC 381/.1 19
HF5482 .M313 1987

ANTIQUES - FRANCE - EXHIBITIONS.
Manston, Peter B., 1951- [Flea markets, antique shows, and auctions of France.] Manston's flea markets, antique shows, and auctions of France . Sacramento, Calif., U. S.A. , New York, N.Y. , c1987. 195 p. : ISBN 0-931367-06-9 (pbk.) : LC Card 86-30909 DDC 381/.1 19
HF5482 .M313 1987

ANTIQUES - GERMANY (WEST) - EXHIBITIONS.
Manston, Peter B., 1951- [Flea markets, antique fairs, and auctions of Germany.] Manston's flea markets, antique fairs, and auctions of Germany . Sacramento, Calif., U. S.A. , New York, N.Y. , c1987. 297 p. : ISBN 0-931367-08-5 (pbk.) : LC Card 86-30908 DDC 381/.1 19
HF5482 .M3135 1987

Antitakeover charter amendments . Rosenbaum, Virginia K. Washington, D.C. , 1986. 100 p. : ISBN 0-931035-07-4 ***NYPL [JLF 86-1964]***

Antitrust economics /. Blair, Roger D. Homewood, Ill. , 1985. xvii, 483 p. : ISBN 0-256-02807-9 LC Card 84-82009 DDC 343.73/072 347.30372 19
KF1649 .B54 1985 ***NYPL [JLE 86-3453]***

Antitrust economics . Williamson, Oliver E. Oxford, OX, UK , New York, NY, USA , 1987. viii, 363 p. : ISBN 0-631-15363-2 : LC Card 87-5153 DDC 338.8 19
HD2326 .W49 1987

ANTITRUST LAW - ECONOMIC ASPECTS.
Williamson, Oliver E. Antitrust economics . Oxford, OX, UK , New York, NY, USA , 1987. viii, 363 p. : ISBN 0-631-15363-2 : LC Card 87-5153 DDC 338.8 19
HD2326 .W49 1987

ANTITRUST LAW - ECONOMIC ASPECTS - UNITED STATES.
Asch, Peter. Economic theory and the antitrust dilemma /. Malabar, Fla. , 1984, c1970. x, 414 p. : ISBN 0-89874-699-X LC Card 83-19947 DDC 338.8/0973 19
HD2785 .A78 1984 ***NYPL [JLE 86-4132]***

Blair, Roger D. Antitrust economics /. Homewood, Ill. , 1985. xvii, 483 p. : ISBN 0-256-02807-9 LC Card 84-82009 DDC 343.73/072 347.30372 19
KF1649 .B54 1985 ***NYPL [JLE 86-3453]***

Breit, William. Antitrust penalty reform . Washington, D.C. , c1986. x, 83 p. : ISBN 0-8447-3600-7 (alk. paper) LC Card 86-3203 DDC 343.73/072/0269 347.303720269 19
KF1657.T7 B74 1986 ***NYPL [JLE 86-3948]***

Hovenkamp, Herbert, 1948- Economics and federal antitrust law /. St. Paul, Minn. , 1985. xxvii, 414 p. : ISBN 0-314-86196-3 LC Card 84-25783 DDC 343.73/072 347.30372 19
KF1649 .H67 1985 ***NYPL [JLF 86-1373]***

Issues after a century of federal competition policy /. Lexington, Mass. , c1987. vii, 387 p. ; ISBN 0-669-13320-5 (alk. paper) LC Card 86-45377 DDC 338.6/048/0973 19
HD3616.U47 I77 1987

Singleton, Ross C. Industrial organization and antitrust . Columbus, Ohio , c1986. ix, 102 p. ; ISBN 0-942280-15-6 : LC Card 85-19318 DDC 338.8/0973 19
HD70.U5 S54 1986 ***NYPL [JLD 86-3251]***

ANTITRUST LAW - EUROPEAN ECONOMIC COMMUNITY COUNTRIES - CONGRESSES.
Neuorientierung des Wettbewerbsschutzes . Köln , 1986. viii, 231 p. ; ISBN 3-452-20666-1 : LC Card 87-138003
HB41 .F22 Heft 120 KK6456

ANTITRUST LAW - GERMANY, WEST.
Maxeiner, James. Policy and methods in German and American antitrust law . New York , 1986. xiii, 174 p. ; ISBN 0-275-92113-1 (alk. paper) : LC Card 86-8108 DDC 343/.072 342.372 19
K3856 .M38 1986 ***NYPL [JLE 86-4413]***

Wettbewerbsbeschränkung in der Nachfrage. Köln , 1985. vii, 145 p. ; ISBN 3-452-20479-0 ***NYPL [JLE 86-2774]***

ANTITRUST LAW - GERMANY (WEST) - CONGRESSES.
Neuorientierung des Wettbewerbsschutzes . Köln , 1986. viii, 231 p. ; ISBN 3-452-20666-1 : LC Card 87-138003
HB41 .F22 Heft 120 KK6456

ANTITRUST LAW - UNITED STATES.
Blair, Roger D. Antitrust economics /. Homewood, Ill. , 1985. xvii, 483 p. : ISBN 0-256-02807-9 LC Card 84-82009 DDC 343.73/072 347.30372 19
KF1649 .B54 1985 ***NYPL [JLE 86-3453]***

Breit, William. Antitrust penalty reform . Washington, D.C. , c1986. x, 83 p. : ISBN 0-8447-3600-7 (alk. paper) LC Card 86-3203 DDC 343.73/072/0269 347.303720269 19
KF1657.T7 B74 1986 ***NYPL [JLE 86-3948]***

Dunfee, Thomas W. Legal aspects of government regulation of business /. New York , c1984. viii, 335 p. ; ISBN 0-471-87029-3 (pbk.) : LC Card 83-21879 DDC 346.73/07 347.3067 19
KF1600 .D86 1984 ***NYPL [JLE 86-3511]***

Hovenkamp, Herbert, 1948- Economics and federal antitrust law /. St. Paul, Minn. , 1985. xxvii, 414 p. : ISBN 0-314-86196-3 LC Card 84-25783 DDC 343.73/072 347.30372 19
KF1649 .H67 1985 ***NYPL [JLF 86-1373]***

Huber, Peter W. (Peter William), 1952- The geodesic network . Washington, D.C. , 1987. 1 v. (various pagings) : LC Card 87-601031 DDC 384/.041 19
HE8819 .H76 1987

Maxeiner, James. Policy and methods in German and American antitrust law . New York , 1986. xiii, 174 p. ; ISBN 0-275-92113-1 (alk. paper) : LC Card 86-8108 DDC 343/.072 342.372 19
K3856 .M38 1986 ***NYPL [JLE 86-4413]***

ANTITRUST LAW - UNITED STATES - HISTORY.
Sklar, Martin J., 1935- The corporate reconstruction of American capitalism, 1890-1916 . Cambridge [Cambridgeshire] , New York , 1987. p. cm. ISBN 0-521-30921-2 LC Card 87-9408 DDC 338.8/0973 19
HC110.C3 S58 1987

Antitrust penalty reform . Breit, William. Washington, D.C. , c1986. x, 83 p. : ISBN 0-8447-3600-7 (alk. paper) LC Card 86-3203 DDC 343.73/072/0269 347.303720269 19
KF1657.T7 B74 1986 ***NYPL [JLE 86-3948]***

Antler, Joyce. The educated woman and professionalization : the struggle for a new feminine identity, 1890-1920 / Joyce Antler. New York : Garland, 1987. x, 448 p. ; 23 cm. (Educated women) Thesis (Ph. D.)--State University of New York at Stony Brook, 1977. Bibliography: p. 431-448. ISBN 0-8240-6839-4 (alk. paper) : LC Card 87-17604 DDC 331.4/11423 19
1. Women in the professions - United States. 2. Women college graduates - United States. 3. Sex discrimination against women - United States. I. Title. II. Series.
HD6054.2.U6 A57 1987

Antología del pensamiento económico y social de América Latina .
(v. 4, t. 1) García, Antonio, 1912- [Bases de la economía contemporánea.] Bases de economía política /. [Bogotá] , 1981. 283 p. ; LC Card 82-138900 DDC 330/.098 19
HB122 .G37 1981 ***NYPL [JLD 87-868]***

Anton Rupert . Esterhuyse, W. P. Cape Town , c1986. 150 p. ; ISBN 0-624-02429-6 LC Card 87-122279 DDC 361.7/4/0924 B 19
HC905.R87 E88 1986

Antoncich, Ricardo.
[Cristianos ante la injusticia. English]
Christians in the face of injustice : a Latin American reading of Catholic social teaching / Ricardo Antoncich ; translated from the Spanish by Matthew J. O'Connell. Maryknoll, N.Y. : Orbis Books, c1987. xvi, 181 p. ; 24 cm. Translation of: Los cristianos ante la injusticia. Includes bibliographical references. ISBN 0-88344-413-5 (pbk.) LC Card 86-23529 DDC 261.8 19
1. Catholic Church - Latin America. 2. Sociology, Christian (Catholic). 3. Christianity and justice - Latin America. 4. Church and social problems - Latin America. 5. Latin America - Church history. I. Title.
BX1753 .A5813 1987 ***NYPL [JLE 87-1051]***

Antonelli, Gilberto. Risorse umane e redditi da lavoro : analisi economica dell'offerta di lavoro eterogeneo in Italia / Gilberto Antonelli. Milano : F. Angeli, c1985. 256 p. : ill. ; 22 cm. (Collana di economia; sezione 4. 22) Bibliography: p. [235]-238. Includes indexes. LC Card 85-191554
1. Income distribution - Italy. 2. Income - Italy. 3. Wages - Italy. 4. Labor supply - Italy. 5. Italy - Economic conditions - 1976- - Regional disparities. I. Title.
HC310.I5 A66 1985

Antoniak, Peter. Lunsford, E. Michael. Power user's guide to 1-2-3 /. San Francisco , c1988. xx, 367 p. : ISBN 0-89588-421-6 (pbk.) LC Card 87-61528 DDC 005.36/9 19
HF5548.4.L67 L87 1988

Antônio, Ricardo Augusto Braga. Análise de sistemas de controle operacional de ônibus urbano / Ricardo Augusto Braga Antônio. Brasília, DF : EBTU, 1985. 92 p. : ill. ; 28 cm. (Série Teses. 4) Summary in English. Originally presented as the author's thesis (mestrado)--Instituto Militar de Engenharia do Rio de Janeiro, 1981. Bibliography: p. 89-92. LC Card 87-113222 DDC 388.4/1322/068 19
1. Bus lines - Management. 2. Bus lines - Brazil - Management. I. Series: Série Teses / Empresa Brasileira dos Transportes Urbanos , 4. II. Title.
HE5613 .A775 1985

Antropologia ed economia dell'artigianato artistico . Pavanello, Mariano, 1944- Milano, Italy , c1984. 183 p. : LC Card 84-147193
HD2346.I82 T676 1984

Antropologische studies VU .
(5) Bavinck, Maarten, 1954- Small fry . Amsterdam , 1984. xii, 151 p. ; ISBN 90-6256-374-0 (pbk.) LC Card 84-187330 DDC 338.3/72709549/3 19
HD9466.S723 K343 1984 ***NYPL [JLD 86-2668]***

Antwerp papers in linguistics .
(50) Aerts, Christel. Advertenties en affiches . [Wilrijk, Belgium] , 1986. 165, [7] p. : LC Card 86-222214
HF5827 .A43 1986

Anuario estadístico agropecuario argentino, 1930-1984 : producción, comercio, precios, insumos. [Buenos Aires] : Centro de Estudios de Comercialización Agropecuaria y Agroindustrial, [1984] 2 v. (480 leaves) ; 30 cm. LC Card 86-177130
1. Agriculture - Economic aspects - Argentina - History - 20th century - Statistics. I. Centro de Estudios de Comercialización Agropecuaria y Agroindustrial (Argentina).
HD1862 .A69 1984

Anufriev, Evgeniĭ Aleksandrovich. Povyshenie trudovoĭ i obshchestvenno-politicheskoĭ aktivnosti mass kak reshaiushchiĭ faktor uskoreniia sotsial'no-ėkonomicheskogo progressa sotsialisticheskogo obshchestva . Kaliningrad , 1986. 382 p. ; LC Card 87-136621
HD8526.5 .P62 1986

Användarfrämjande åtgärder på dataområdet .

Sweden. Statens industriverk. PU-byrån. Stockholm , 1975. 97 leaves ; ISBN 91-7318-026-2 LC Card 84-105630
HF5548.2 .S8822 1975

Anwendung der Arbeitsmarktorientierten Input-Output-Analyse am beispiel der Gastarbeiterbeschäftigung /. Rainer, Norbert. Wien , 1977. 47 leaves ; LC Card 86-194737
HC270.I57 R35 1977

Anwendungen der Variationsrechnung auf makroökonomische Modelle /. Pimentão, Luís Nuno de Matos. Berlin , New York , c1986. xii, 220 p. : ISBN 0-387-16484-7 (U. S.) LC Card 86-209488
HB141 .P55 1986

Anyansi-Archibong, Chi. B., 1949- Strategy and structure of enterprise in a developing country / Chi. B. Anysnsi-Archibong. Aldershots, Hants, England ; Brookfield, Vt., USA : Avebury, c1988. xvii, 274 p. : ill. ; 23 cm. Bibliography: p. 255-263. Includes index. ISBN 0-566-05471-X : LC Card 87-12020 DDC 658/.009669 19
1. Industrial management - Nigeria. 2. Industrial management - Social aspects - Nigeria. 3. Nigeria - Colonial influence. 4. Industry and state - Nigeria. I. Title.
HD70.N43 A59 1988

Anzaldúa Montoya, Ricardo.
Government and private sector in contemporary Mexico /. [La Jolla, Calif.] , 1987. iv, 146 p. ; LC Card 87-622060 DDC 338.972 19
HD3616.M43 G68 1987

The Mexican Left, the popular movements, and the politics of austerity /. La Jolla, Calif. , 1986. vi, 96 p. ; LC Card 87-621353 DDC 322/.2/0972 19
HC135 .M525535 1986

ANZIO (ITALY) - HARBOR.
Blasi, Benedetto. Della strada ferrata Pia-Cassia da citta della Pieve a Civitavecchia e del ristauro del Porto Neroniano in Anzio . Roma , 1846. 56 p., [3] folded leaves of plates : LC Card 85-665949
HE3098 .B51x 1846

Ao apito do trem . Trevisan, Edilberto. [Curitiba] , 1985-1986 [i.e. 1986] 123 p. : LC Card 87-121016 DDC 385/.0981/62 19
HE2930.P34 T74 1986

Aoiz Iriarte, María Rosario. Técnicas psicosociales en la administración pública : su aplicación a la selección de personal / Ma. Rosario Aoiz Iriarte. Alcalá de Henares, Madrid, España : Instituto Nacional de Administración Pública, [1984] 238 p. : ill. ; 19 cm. (Colección Biblioteca básica de administración pública. Serie especial) Bibliography: p. 213-215. ISBN 84-7351-179-4 LC Card 85-189583
1. Employee selection. 2. Employee selection - Spain - Case studies. 3. Civil service recruiting. 4. Spain - Officials and employees - Selection and appointment - Case studies. I. Title. II. Series.
HF5549.5.S38 A57 1984

Aoyagi, Akiko, 1950- Shurtleff, William, 1941- Tofutti® & other soy ice creams . Lafayette, CA , c1985. 2 v. : ISBN 0-933332-19-X (v. 1) : LC Card 85-10829 DDC 381/.4174 19
HD9330.B323 U 1985 ***NYPL [JLF 86-1035]***

Apananskiĭ, L.
Issledovaniia Instituta ėkonomiki Akademii nauk Ėstonskoĭ SSR v X piatiletke . Tallin , 1983. 233 p. ; LC Card 86-181279
HB74.9.S65 I86 1983

Izuchenie problem narodonaseleniia v Institute ėkonomiki AN Ėstonskoĭ SSR . Tallin , 1979. 78 p. ; LC Card 81-198604
HB850.5.S65 I97 1979

Uspekhi ėkonomicheskogo i kul′turnogo razvitiia Ėstonskoĭ SSR za gody sovetskoĭ vlasti . Tallin , 1980. 222 p. ; LC Card 81-198881
HC337.E7 U86 1980

The apartheid crisis . Williams, Oliver F. San Francisco , 1986. xiv, 124 p. : ISBN 0-06-250951-9 (pbk.) : LC Card 85-45726 DDC 332.6/7373/068 19
HG5851.A3 W55 1986
NYPL [JLD 86-4023]

APARTHEID - SOUTH AFRICA.
Automating apartheid . Philadelphia , c19. ix, 107 p. : ISBN 0-910082-00-6 (pbk.) : LC Card 86-201384 DDC 382/.45004/0968 19
HD9696.C63 S62 1984

Mathabane, Mark. Kaffir boy . New York , c1986. xii, 354 p., [8] p. of plates : ISBN 0-02-581800-7 : LC Card 86-53 DDC 968/.00496024 B 19
DT779.95.M38 A34 1986
NYPL [Sc E 86-240]

Shell out of Namibia and South Africa . London [1986] 19 . : LC Card 87-138719 DDC 338.8/87 19
HD9571.9.S45 S54 1986

South Africa, the UC connection /. Berkeley, Calif. , 1985. 39 p. : LC Card 86-201134 DDC 332.6/73794/068 19
HG5851.A3 S63 1985

The South African quagmire . Cambridge, Mass. , c1987. xvi, 444 p. ; ISBN 0-88730-191-6 LC Card 86-28754 DDC 320.5/6 19
HF1613.4.Z4 U67 1987

United States Catholic Conference. Administrative Board. Divestment, disinvestment, and South Africa . Washington, D.C. , c1986. 36 p. ; ISBN 1-555-86137-7 (pbk.) LC Card 87-136857 DDC 332.6/7373/068 19
HG5851.A3 U55 1986

Wellings, Paul. Industrial decentralisation under apartheid . Durban , 1984. 48, xxxii p. : ISBN 0-86980-455-3 (pbk.) LC Card 87-127005 DDC 338.968 19
HC905.Z9 D59 1984

Williams, Oliver F. The apartheid crisis . San Francisco , 1986. xiv, 124 p. : ISBN 0-06-250951-9 (pbk.) : LC Card 85-45726 DDC 332.6/7373/068 19
HG5851.A3 W55 1986
NYPL [JLD 86-4023]

APARTMENT HOUSES.
Earle, Gary. How to sell apartment buildings . [Chicago] [1987], c1988. xiv, 183 p. : ISBN 0-88462-716-0 LC Card 87-13964 DDC 333.33/8 19
HD1394 .E24 1988

APARTMENT HOUSES - BRAZIL.
Peruzzo, Dilvo, 1941- Habitação . São Paulo-SP [1984] 133 p. ; LC Card 84-242125 DDC 363.5/0981 19
HD7287.6.B7 P47 1984
NYPL [JLD 86-2535]

APARTMENT HOUSES - BRAZIL - VITÓRIA (ESPÍRITO SANTO)
Peruzzo, Dilvo, 1941- Habitação . São Paulo-SP [1984] 133 p. ; LC Card 84-242125 DDC 363.5/0981 19
HD7287.6.B7 P47 1984
NYPL [JLD 86-2535]

APARTMENT HOUSES, COOPERATIVE.
Bloch, H. I. Sonny. Inside real estate . New York , c1987. xx, 375 p. ; ISBN 1-555-84030-2 LC Card 86-28303 DDC 333.33/8 19
HD1379 .B515 1987

Kennedy, David W. The condominium and cooperative apartment buyer's and seller's guide /. New York , c1987. viii, 312 p. : ISBN 0-471-62732-1 (pbk.) LC Card 87-21548 DDC 333.33/8 19
HD1390.5 .K46 1987

APD bulletin, 0228-5304 .
(28) Biophysical resources of the Slocan Valley /. Victoria, B.C. , 1982. ix, 102 p. : ISBN 0-7718-8310-2 (pbk.) LC Card 84-117204 DDC 333.7/09711/43 19
HC117.B8 B46 1982

Apeldoorn, G. Jan van. Senaoana, M. P. Research on rural-non farm employment in Lesotho . Roma, Lesotho [1984] 88 leaves : LC Card 86-214032 DDC 331.12/5/096816 19
HD5842.7.A6 S46 1984

Apeloig, Shalom. Analyse der Wirksamkeit der Beschäftigungszulage . München , 1984. vii, 172 p. : LC Card 85-230164
HJ4720.A45 A53 1984

Aperçu de la situation économique au Québec en 1980 / Direction de l'analyse et de la prévision économiques, Direction générale de la recherche et de la planification. Québec : Industrie, commerce et tourisme, [1980] 42 leaves : ill. ; 28 cm. On cover: Aperçu de la situation économique au Québec. 1980. "Décembre 1980." LC Card 83-150001
1. Quebec (Province) - Economic conditions. I. Québec (Province). Ministère de l'industrie, du commerce et du tourisme. Direction de l'analyse et de la prévision économiques.
HC117.Q4 A794 1980

Aperçu des résultats d'ensemble du recensement général de la population et de l'habitat au Togo de novembre 1981 : caractéristiques de la population / République togolaise, Ministère du plan et de l'industrie, Direction de la statistique, Bureau central du recensement. [Lomé] : Le Bureau, [1986] 70 p. : ill. ; 30 cm. "Février 1986." LC Card 87-126698 DDC 304.6/0966/81021 19
1. Togo - Census, 1981. 2. Togo - Population - Statistics. I. Togo. Direction de la statistique. Bureau central du recensement.
HA4723 .A4 1981

Apezechea, Héctor J., 1937- Tasas de participación y relaciobes multivariadas a partir e la información de la encuesta de hogares del segundo semestre de 1978 : informe preliminar / Héctor J. Apezechea. [Montevideo, Uruguay] : Centro de Informaciones y Estudios del Uruguay, 1980. 12, [44] leaves ; 28 cm. (Serie Documentos de trabajo . 23/80) Includes bibliographical references. LC Card 86-157658
1. Labor supply - Uruguay - Statistics. 2. Household surveys - Uruguay. I. Series: Serie Documentos de trabajo (Centro de Informaciones y Estudios del Uruguay) , 80/23. II. Title.
HD5762.A6 A64 1980

Aphichat Chamratrithirong, 1948-
Hogan, Dennis P. Cultural and economic factors in the fertility of Thai women /. Honolulu, HI [1987] p. cm. ISBN 0-86638-103-1 : LC Card 87-21459 DDC 304.6/32/09593 19
HB1054.55.A3 H64 1987

Knodel, John E. Thailand's reproductive revolution . Madison, Wis. , c1987. xiii, 251 p. : ISBN 0-299-11050-8 LC Card 87-8172 DDC 304.6/32/09593 19
HB1054.55.A3 K576 1987

Aplícano, Rodolfo. Suazo, Margarita. Problación y desarrollo socioeconómico en Honduras /. Chicago, Ill., USA (1313 E. 60th St., Chicago 60637) , c1984. 90 p., [2] leaves of plates : LC Card 85-203746
HB3540.A3 S82 1984

Apoio ao setor informal da economia de Pernambuco : atividades produtivas municipais / Governo do Estado de Pernambuco, Secretaria do Planejamento--SEPLAN, Instituto de Desenvolvimento de Pernambuco--CONDEPE. Recife : CONDEPE, 1985. 135 p. : maps ; 25 cm. Prepared by Ana Maria Collier Matos and others. Bibliography: p. 135. LC Card 87-403615 DDC 381 19
1. Informal sector (Economics) - Brazil - Pernambuco - Case studies. I. Matos, Ana Maria Collier. II. Instituto de Desenvolvimento de Pernambuco.
HD2346.B72 P473 1985

Un aporte para la liberación /. Urien, Julio César. Buenos Aires, Argentina , c1985. 51 p. ; ISBN 950-9235-13-X LC Card 85-201095
HC125 .U75 1985

Apostagmata mias zōēs /. Drakos, Geōrgios P. Athēna , c1985. 194 p. ; LC Card 86-175014
HC295 .D7 1985

Apostol, Gheorge. Capitalismul contemporan și teoria [microform] . București , 1965. 440 p. ; LC Card 77-452767
HB179.R6 C34 ***NYPL [*ZT-1732 no.2]***

Apostolopoulos, Athanase, 1955- Aktienkurse und rationale Erwartungen : eine makroökonometrische Untersuchung der Informationseffizienz des deutschen Aktienmarktes, 1965-1982 / Athanase Apostolopoulos. Frankfurt am Main ; New York : P. Lang, c1986. 364 p. : ill. ; 21 cm. (Europäische Hochschulschriften. Reihe V, Volks- und Betriebswirtschaft, 0531-7339 . Bd. 729 = vol. 729 = vol. 729) Bibliography: p. 351-364. ISBN 3-8204-9157-0 LC Card 86-220281
1. Stocks - Prices - Germany (West) - Econometric models. 2. Rational expectations (Economic theory). I. Series: Europäische Hochschulschriften. Reihe V, Volks- und Betriebswirtschaft , Bd. 729. II. Title.
HG5494 .A66 1986

Apostolou, Nicholas G. Handbook of governmental accounting and finance /. New York , c1988. 1 v. (various pagings) ; ISBN 0-471-84741-0 LC Card 87-23092 DDC 350.72/31 19
HJ9801 .H36 1988

Apparel manufacturing management systems . McPherson, Edwin M. Park Ridge, N.J., U. S.A. , c1987. xiv, 392 p. : ISBN 0-8155-1141-8 : LC Card 87-12239 DDC 687/.068 19
HD9940.A2 M42 1987

L'appel de la J.O.C., 1926-1928 /. Debès, Joseph. Paris , 1986. 292 p. : ISBN 2-204-02529-1 : LC Card 86-189508
HD8430 .D37 1986

Appelbaum, Richard P. Gilderbloom, John Ingram. Rethinking rental housing /. Philadelphia , 1987. p. cm. ISBN 0-87722-498-6 (alk. paper) LC Card 87-1958 DDC 363.5/8 19
HD7288.85.U6 G55 1987

Appendix for the feasibility report of implementing the International Registration Plan in the State of Maine . Pease, Allen. [Augusta, Me.] [1985] 39 leaves : LC Card 85-622841 DDC 388.3/24 19
HE5633.M2 P39 1985

APPLE COMPUTER, INC.
Sculley, John. Odyssey . New York , c1987. xiv, 450 p., [16] p. of plates : ISBN 0-06-015780-1 : LC Card 87-45142 DDC 331.7/61004165/0924 B 19
HD9696.C62 S38 1987

APPLE COMPUTER, INC. - HISTORY.
Butcher, Lee. Accidental millionaire . New York , c1988. xii, 224 p., [4] p. of plates : ISBN 0-913729-79-5 LC Card 87-9414 DDC 338.7/61004/0924 B 19
HD9696.C64 A863 1988

APPLE COMPUTER - PROGRAMMING.
McKelvey, James. The debugger's handbook . Belmont, Calif. , c1986. xvi, 138 p. : ISBN 0-534-06432-9 LC Card 85-22628 DDC 005.13/3 19
QA76.73.U25 M34 1986 ***NYPL [JSE 87-65]***

Mar, Jerry. The Apple WordStar book /. Glenview, Ill. , c1984. 277 p. : ISBN 0-673-15992-2 (pbk.) : LC Card 84-5400 DDC 652 19
Z52.5.W67 M37 1984 ***NYPL [JSE 86-2106]***

APPLE II (COMPUTER) - PROGRAMMING.
Bolocan, David. Advanced AppleWorks /. Blue Ridge Summit, PA , c1986. x, 246 p. : ISBN 0-8306-0248-8 : LC Card 85-22296 DDC 005.265 19
QA76.8.A662 B65 1986 ***NYPL [JSE 86-1874]***

Simpson, Henry. Serious programming for your Apple II/IIe/IIc /. Blue Ridge Summit, PA , 1985. x, 180 p. : ISBN 0-8306-0960-1 : LC Card 85-17320 DDC 005.265 19
QA76.8.A662 S57 1985 ***NYPL [JSE 86-801]***

Tice, Robert L. Hi-res graphics for the Apple II/IIe/IIc /. Blue Ridge Summit, Pa. , 1985. vii, 197 p. : ISBN 0-8306-0849-4 : LC Card 84-23954 DDC 001.64/43 19
T385 .T52 1985 ***NYPL [JSE 86-805]***

Tymes, Elna. Mastering AppleWorks /. San Francisco , c1987. xxii, 479 p. : ISBN 0-89588-398-8 (pbk.) : LC Card 87-60799 DDC 650/.028/55369 19
HF5548.4.A68 T95 1987

APPLE II PLUS (COMPUTER) - PROGRAMMING.
Wolff, Bruno B. Modular programming routines for the Apple II+/IIe/IIc /. Blue Ridge Summit, PA , 1985. x, 243 p. : ISBN 0-8306-0732-3 : LC Card 85-17331 DDC 005.265 19
QA76.8.A66 W65 1985 ***NYPL [JSE 86-1017]***

Apple IIc and IIe assembly language /. Gilder, Jules H., 1947- New York , 1986. 178 p. : ISBN 0-412-01121-2 (pbk.) : LC Card 86-2592 DDC 005.265 19
QA76.8.A66225 G55 1986 ***NYPL [JSE 87-575]***

APPLE IIC (COMPUTER) - PROGRAMMING.
Gilder, Jules H., 1947- Apple IIc and IIe assembly language /. New York , 1986. 178 p. : ISBN 0-412-01121-2 (pbk.) : LC Card 86-2592 DDC 005.265 19
QA76.8.A66225 G55 1986 ***NYPL [JSE 87-575]***

Matthews, Carole Boggs. AppleWorks made easy /. Berkeley, Calif. , c1987. xiii, 398 p. : ISBN 0-07-881260-7 (pbk.) : LC Card 87-149217 DDC 005.36/9
HF5548.4.A68 M37 1987

Simpson, Henry. Serious programming for your Apple II/IIe/IIc /. Blue Ridge Summit, PA , 1985. x, 180 p. : ISBN 0-8306-0960-1 : LC Card 85-17320 DDC 005.265 19
QA76.8.A662 S57 1985 ***NYPL [JSE 86-801]***

Tice, Robert L. Hi-res graphics for the Apple II/IIe/IIc /. Blue Ridge Summit, Pa. , 1985. vii, 197 p. : ISBN 0-8306-0849-4 : LC Card 84-23954 DDC 001.64/43 19
T385 .T52 1985 ***NYPL [JSE 86-805]***

Wolff, Bruno B. Modular programming routines for the Apple II+/IIe/IIc /. Blue Ridge Summit, PA , 1985. x, 243 p. : ISBN 0-8306-0732-3 : LC Card 85-17331 DDC 005.265 19
QA76.8.A66 W65 1985 ***NYPL [JSE 86-1017]***

APPLE IIE (COMPUTER) - PROGRAMMING.
Gilder, Jules H., 1947- Apple IIc and IIe assembly language /. New York , 1986. 178 p. : ISBN 0-412-01121-2 (pbk.) : LC Card 86-2592 DDC 005.265 19
QA76.8.A66225 G55 1986 ***NYPL [JSE 87-575]***

Matthews, Carole Boggs. AppleWorks made easy /. Berkeley, Calif. , c1987. xiii, 398 p. : ISBN 0-07-881260-7 (pbk.) : LC Card 87-149217 DDC 005.36/9
HF5548.4.A68 M37 1987

Simpson, Henry. Serious programming for your Apple II/IIe/IIc /. Blue Ridge Summit, PA , 1985. x, 180 p. : ISBN 0-8306-0960-1 : LC Card 85-17320 DDC 005.265 19
QA76.8.A662 S57 1985 ***NYPL [JSE 86-801]***

Tice, Robert L. Hi-res graphics for the Apple II/IIe/IIc /. Blue Ridge Summit, Pa. , 1985. vii, 197 p. : ISBN 0-8306-0849-4 : LC Card 84-23954 DDC 001.64/43 19
T385 .T52 1985 ***NYPL [JSE 86-805]***

Wolff, Bruno B. Modular programming routines for the Apple II+/IIe/IIc /. Blue Ridge Summit, PA , 1985. x, 243 p. : ISBN 0-8306-0732-3 : LC Card 85-17331 DDC 005.265 19
QA76.8.A66 W65 1985 ***NYPL [JSE 86-1017]***

APPLE IIGS (COMPUTER) - PROGRAMMING.
Matthews, Carole Boggs. AppleWorks made easy /. Berkeley, Calif. , c1987. xiii, 398 p. : ISBN 0-07-881260-7 (pbk.) : LC Card 87-149217 DDC 005.36/9
HF5548.4.A68 M37 1987

APPLE INDUSTRY - HUNGARY - SZABOLCS-SZATMÁR MEGYE.
A Szabolcs-Szatmár megyei télialma-termelés, -feldolgozás és -értékesités rendszerének fejlesztése /. Budapest , 1985. 144 p. : ISBN 963-491-208-7 LC Card 86-196831
HD9259.A6 H87 1985

Apple two c and two e assembly language. Gilder, Jules H., 1947- Apple IIc and IIe assembly language /. New York , 1986. 178 p. : ISBN 0-412-01121-2 (pbk.) : LC Card 86-2592 DDC 005.265 19
QA76.8.A66225 G55 1986 ***NYPL [JSE 87-575]***

The Apple WordStar book /. Mar, Jerry. Glenview, Ill. , c1984. 277 p. : ISBN 0-673-15992-2 (pbk.) : LC Card 84-5400 DDC 652 19
Z52.5.W67 M37 1984 ***NYPL [JSE 86-2106]***

Apple 2c and 2e assembly language. Gilder, Jules H., 1947- Apple IIc and IIe assembly language /. New York , 1986. 178 p. : ISBN 0-412-01121-2 (pbk.) : LC Card 86-2592 DDC 005.265 19
QA76.8.A66225 G55 1986 ***NYPL [JSE 87-575]***

Applebaum, Herbert A. Work in market and industrial societies /. Albany , c1984. viii, 316 p. ; ISBN 0-87395-810-1 LC Card 83-9267 DDC 306/.36 19
HD4901 .A659 1984 ***NYPL [JLE 86-4483]***

AppleWorks . Rubin, Charles, 1953- Redmond, Wash. [New York, N.Y.] , c1987. xv, 299 p. : ISBN 1-556-15114-4 (pbk.) : LC Card 87-20338 DDC 650/.028/55369 19
HF5548.4.A68 R83 1987

AppleWorks . Sloan, Michael L., 1944- Glenview, Ill. , c1988. vi, 312 p. : ISBN 0-673-18937-6 (pbk.) : LC Card 87-9775 DDC 650/.028/55369 19
HF5548.4.A68 S58 1988

APPLEWORKS (COMPUTER PROGRAM)
Aron, Arthur. Using AppleWorks /. Indianapolis, Ind. , c1987. xviii, 458 p. : ISBN 0-88022-280-8 (pbk.) LC Card 86-63838 DDC 005.36/9 19
HF5548.4.A68 A76 1987

Bolocan, David. Advanced AppleWorks /. Blue Ridge Summit, PA , c1986. x, 246 p. : ISBN 0-8306-0248-8 : LC Card 85-22296 DDC 005.265 19
QA76.8.A662 B65 1986 ***NYPL [JSE 86-1874]***

Matthews, Carole Boggs. AppleWorks made easy /. Berkeley, Calif. , c1987. xiii, 398 p. : ISBN 0-07-881260-7 (pbk.) : LC Card 87-149217 DDC 005.36/9
HF5548.4.A68 M37 1987

Rubin, Charles, 1953- AppleWorks . Redmond, Wash. [New York, N.Y.] , c1987. xv, 299 p. : ISBN 1-556-15114-4 (pbk.) : LC Card 87-20338 DDC 650/.028/55369 19
HF5548.4.A68 R83 1987

Sloan, Michael L., 1944- AppleWorks . Glenview, Ill. , c1988. vi, 312 p. : ISBN 0-673-18937-6 (pbk.) : LC Card 87-9775 DDC 650/.028/55369 19
HF5548.4.A68 S58 1988

Tymes, Elna. Mastering AppleWorks /. San Francisco , c1987. xxii, 479 p. : ISBN 0-89588-398-8 (pbk.) : LC Card 87-60799 DDC 650/.028/55369 19
HF5548.4.A68 T95 1987

Varnon, M. S. Developing and using office applications with AppleWorks . St. Paul , c1987. xi, 366 p. : ISBN 0-314-34129-3 (pbk.) : LC Card 86-24696 DDC 651.8/5369 19
HF5548.4.A68 V37 1987

Witkin, Ruth K. Personal money management with AppleWorks /. Hasbrouck Heights, N.J. [New York] , c1986. 418 p. : ISBN 0-471-62575-2 (Wiley : pbk.) : LC Card 87-110545 DDC 332.024/0028/55369 19
HG179 .W554 1986

Witkin, Ruth K. Personal money mangement with AppleWorks /. New York , c1987. p. cm. ISBN 0-471-62575-2 : LC Card 87-6294 DDC 332.024/0028/55369 19
HG179 .W554 1987

APPLEWORKS (COMPUTER PROGRAM) - JUVENILE LITERATURE.
Luehrmann, Arthur. AppleWorks data bases . Gilroy, Calif. , c1987. viii, 159 p. : ISBN 0-941681-03-3 (pbk.) : LC Card 87-11734 DDC 005.36/9 19
HF5548.4.A68 L838 1987

Luehrmann, Arthur. AppleWorks spreadsheets . Gilroy, Calif. , c1987. viii, 152 p. ; ISBN 0-941681-05-X (pbk.) : LC Card 87-11745 DDC 005.36/9 19
HF5548.4.A68 L847 1987

AppleWorks data bases . Luehrmann, Arthur. Gilroy, Calif. , c1987. viii, 159 p. : ISBN 0-941681-03-3 (pbk.) : LC Card 87-11734 DDC 005.36/9 19
HF5548.4.A68 L838 1987

AppleWorks made easy /. Matthews, Carole Boggs. Berkeley, Calif. , c1987. xiii, 398 p. : ISBN 0-07-881260-7 (pbk.) : LC Card 87-149217 DDC 005.36/9
HF5548.4.A68 M37 1987

AppleWorks spreadsheets . Luehrmann, Arthur. Gilroy, Calif. , c1987. viii, 152 p. ; ISBN 0-941681-05-X (pbk.) : LC Card 87-11745

DDC 005.36/9 19
HF5548.4.A68 L847 1987

Application of computer technology for development. Hungarian. A számítástechnika felhasználása a fejlődés előmozdítására : az Egyesült Nemzetek, New York, The application of computer technology for development c. kiadványának magyar nyelvű fordítása : kézirat gyanánt. [Budapest] : Központi Statisztikai Hivatal, [1971] 95 p. : ill. ; 29 cm. "1971. június." Includes bibliographical references. LC Card 85-178670
1. Economic development - Data processing. I. United Nations. Dept. of Economic and Social Affairs. II. Hungary. Központi Statisztikai Hivatal. III. Title.
HD85.H88 A6615 1971

The application of social systems thinking to organizational consulting /. Czander, William M. Lanham , c1986. 243 p. ; ISBN 0-8191-5183-1 (alk. paper) : LC Card 85-29508 DDC 658.4/6 19
HD69.C6 C9 1986 ***NYPL [JLE 86-3269]***

APPLICATIONS FOR POSITIONS.
Brennan, Lawrence D. (Lawrence David), 1915- Resumes for better jobs /. New York, NY , c1987. 202 p. ; ISBN 0-13-329152-9 : LC Card 87-2383 DDC 650.1/4 19
HF5383 .B68 1987

Jasinski, Irv. Airline pilot interviews . Escondido, Calif. , c1987. 144 p. : ISBN 0-942195-01-9 (pbk.) LC Card 87-70680 DDC 629.132/5240423/02373 19
HE9777 .J36 1987

Payne, Richard A. How to get a better job quicker /. New York , 1987. x, 242 p. ; ISBN 0-8008-3965-X : LC Card 86-23101 DDC 650.1/4 19
HF5383 .P36 1987

APPLICATIONS FOR POSITIONS - EVALUATION.
Baehr, Melany E. Experience and background inventory . [Park Ridge, Ill.] (1550 Northwest Highway, Park Ridge 60068) [c1986] 48 p. ; LC Card 87-404267 DDC 658.3/112 19
HF5549.5.S38 B34 1986

Le applicazioni dei metodi statistici alle analisi di mercato /. De Luca, Amedeo, 1945- Milano, Italy , c1984. 341 p. : LC Card 85-185924 DDC 380.1/01/5195 19
HF1017 .D4 1984

APPLIED ANTHROPOLOGY.
Baba, Marietta L. Business and industrial anthropology . Washington, D.C. , c1986. vii, 48 p. ; ISBN 0-913167-16-9 (pbk.) : LC Card 86-26602 DDC 302.3/5 19
HD58.7 .B33 1986

Applied behavioral science for plant managers / C.D. Gaddy ... [et al.]. Columbia, Md. : GP Courseware, c1987. vii, 102 p. : ill. ; 23 cm. Bibliography: p. [96]-98. ISBN 0-87683-830-1 (pbk.) LC Card 86-31926 DDC 658.3 19
1. Psychology, Industrial. 2. Communication in management. 3. Motivation. 4. Human engineering. I. Gaddy, C. D.
HF5548.8 .A715 1987

Applied demand analysis . Theil, Henri. Cambridge, Mass. , 1987. xxi, 279 p. : ISBN 0-88730-217-3 LC Card 86-32230 DDC 338.5/212 19
HB801 .T489 1987

Applied Econometric Association. International macroeconomic modelling for policy decisions /. Dordrecht , Boston , c1986. viii, 269 p. : ISBN 90-247-3201-8 LC Card 85-13698 DDC 337/.0724 19
HF1410.5 .I577 1986 ***NYPL [JLE 86-3469]***

Applied economics and Australian business /. Bennett, Raymond. Sydney , c1987. xiv, 464 p. : ISBN 0-9588541-0-6 LC Card 87-141905 DDC 330.994/063 19
HB171.5 .B454 1987

Applied empirical research on nonprofit organization management . Brown, Kathleen M. San Francisco, CA , c1986. 38 p. ; LC Card 86-207093 DDC 658/.048 19
HD62.6 .B76 1986

Applied human relations . Halloran, Jack, 1931- Englewood Cliffs, N.J. , c1987. xvi, 528 p. : ISBN 0-13-040742-9 LC Card 86-25336 DDC 658.3 19
HD58.7 .H34 1987

Applied Management Sciences, inc. Langwell, Kathryn M. A synthesis of research on competition in the financing and delivery of health services /. Hyattsville, MD. , Springfield, VA , 1982. 85 p. ; LC Card 82-600612 DDC 338.4/73621/0973 19
RA410.53 .L36 1982 ***NYPL [JLF 86-422]***

Applied marketing and social research / edited by Ute Bradley ; foreword by John Downham. 2nd ed. Chichester ; New York : J. Wiley, c1987. xvii, 488 p. : ill. ; 24 cm. Includes bibliographies. ISBN 0-471-91356-1 : LC Card 86-32447 DDC 658.8/3 19
1. Marketing research - Case studies. 2. Marketing research - Great Britain - Case studies. I. Bradley, Ute.
HF5415.2 .A654 1987

Applied mathematics for economics /. Sengupta, Jatikumar. Dordrecht ; Boston : ix, 250 p. ; ISBN 90-277-2588-8 LC Card 87-20544 DDC 330/.028 19
HB71 .S398 1987

Applied one-two-three. Nguyen, Tim K. Applied 1-2-3 . New York, N.Y. , c1987. p. cm. ISBN 0-13-729542-1 : LC Card 87-11390 DDC 005.36/9 19
HF5548.4.L67 N48 1987

Applied production analysis /. Chambers, Robert G. Cambridge [Cambridgeshire] , New York , 1988. p. cm. ISBN 0-521-30699-X LC Card 87-12511 DDC 338.5 19
HB241 .C452 1988

Applied psychology in personnel management /. Cascio, Wayne F. Englewood Cliffs, NJ , c1987. xv, 510 p. : ISBN 0-13-041427-1 : LC Card 86-25253 DDC 658.3/001/9 19
HF5549 .C297 1987

The Applied psychology of work behavior : a book of readings / Dennis W. Organ.3rd ed. Plano, Tex. : Business Publications, 1987. ix, 501 p. : ill. ; 23 cm. Includes bibliographies. ISBN 0-256-03431-1 (pbk.) LC Card 86-72246 DDC 158.7 19
1. Psychology, Industrial. 2. Organizational behavior. I. Organ, Dennis W.
HF5548.8 .A72 1987

APPLIED SCIENCE. see **TECHNOLOGY.**

Applied statistics for public administration /. Meier, Kenneth J., 1950- Monterey, Calif. , c1987. xix, 460 p. ; LC Card 87-10342 DDC 350/.0001/5195 19
HA29 .M46 1987

Applied 1-2-3 . Nguyen, Tim K. New York, N.Y. , c1987. p. cm. ISBN 0-13-729542-1 : LC Card 87-11390 DDC 005.36/9 19
HF5548.4.L67 N48 1987

Applying expert systems in business /. Chorafas, Dimitris N. New York , c1987. xii, 232 p. : ISBN 0-07-010880-3 : LC Card 86-2794 DDC 658/.05633 19
HD30.2 .C475 1987 ***NYPL [JLE 86-3893]***

Appraisal of credit facilities provided by banking institutions in rural development /. Mishra, M. N. (Maha Narain), 1945- Meerut, U.P., India [1987?] x, 251, ii p. ; LC Card 87-900918 DDC 332.2 19
HG3284 .M49 1987

An Appraisal of minerals availability for 34 commodities / compiled by staff, Bureau of Mines. [Pittsburgh, Pa.] : U. S. Dept. of the Interior, Bureau of Mines : for sale by the Supt. of Docs., U. S. G.P.O., 1987. iii, 300 p. : ill. ; 29 cm. (Bulletin . 692) Includes bibliographies. LC Card 87-600244 DDC 333.8/5 19
1. Nonfuel minerals industry. 2. Mines and mineral resources. 3. Nonfuel minerals industry - United States. 4. Mines and mineral resources - United States. I. United States. Bureau of Mines. II. Series: Bulletin (United States. Bureau of Mines) , 692.
HD9506.A2 A72 1987

The Appraisal of real estate. 9th ed. Chicago, Ill. : American Institute of Real Estate Appraisers, c1987. viii, 756 p. : ill. ; 25 cm. Bibliography: p. 725-734. Includes index. ISBN 0-911780-87-4 LC Card 87-17423 DDC 333.33/2 19
1. Real property - Valuation. I. American Institute of Real Estate Appraisers.
HD1387 .A663 1987

Appraisal of tobacco schemes in Zambia. A Report on the resources, activities, and constraints in tobacco schemes . Lusaka , 1985. iii, 37 p. ; LC Card 85-981599 DDC 338.1/7371/096894 19
HD9147.Z34 R46 1985

The appraiser's workbook /. Akerson, Charles B. Chicago, Ill. , c1985. xv, 263 p. in various pagings : ISBN 0-911780-75-0 (pbk.) LC Card 84-3008 DDC 333.33/2/076 19
HD1387 .A518 1985 ***NYPL [JLF 86-1025]***

Appraising and exploring organizations / edited by S. Tyson ... [et al.]. London ; New York : Croom Helm, c1988. p. cm. Includes index. ISBN 0-7099-4340-7 : LC Card 87-20063 DDC 658.3/14 19
1. Employee attitude surveys. I. Tyson, S. (Shaun).
HF5549.5.A83 A66 1988

APPRENTICES - CHILE - SANTIAGO.
Corvalán Vásquez, Oscar E., 1947- Empleo y capacitación en los talleres informales de Santiago /. Montevideo , 1984. 150 p. ; LC Card 86-127324
HD2346.C54 S263 1984

APPRENTICES - EUROPE - HISTORY.
Schulz, Knut. Handwerksgesellen und Lohnarbeiter . Sigmaringen , 1985. vii, 477 p., [20] p. of plates : ISBN 3-7995-7026-8 LC Card 85-149930
HD4885.E8 S38 1985 ***NYPL [JLE 86-1598]***

APPRENTICES - GERMANY, WEST.
Behnken, Imbke, 1941- Jugendbiografie und Handlungsforschung /. Frankfurt [am Main] , c1984. xi, 239 p. ; ISBN 3-88704-402-9 LC Card 84-174719 DDC 331.3/425922/0943 19
HD4885.G3 B425 1984
NYPL [JLD 86-1892]

Maier, Hans E. Das Handwerk und die Berufseingliederung Jugendlicher in der Bundesrepublik Deutschland /. Berlin [1986] 68 p. : LC Card 86-230660
HD5715.5.G4 M35 1986

APPRENTICES - GREAT BRITAIN - HISTORY.
Strange, K. H. (Kathleen H.), 1904- Climbing boys . London ; New York : xiv, 146 p. : ISBN 0-85031-431-3 : LC Card 83-143704 DDC 331.5/5 19
HD8039.C482 G77 1982
NYPL [JLD 85-681]

APPRENTICES - TEXAS.
Mercer, Kent. Directory of licensed occupations and apprenticeship programs in Texas. [Austin, Tex.] [1985] iv, 102 p. ; LC Card 86-622006 DDC 331.7/02/09764 19
HF5382.5.U6 T45 1985

Approche ethnique des phénomènes démographiques . Sala-Diakanda, Mpembele. Louvain-la-Neuve , 1980. 433 p. : LC Card 84-118066
HB3664.5.A3 S23 1980

Appropriate business skills for Third World women.
Doing a feasibility study . Washington, D.C. , c1987. 173 p. : ISBN 0-912917-07-5 (pbk.) : LC Card 86-61951 DDC 658/.022/091724 19
HD62.5 .D63 1987

Appropriate forest industries : selected papers of an Expert Consultation held in Jakarta, Indonesia, 30 September-6 October 1985. Rome : Food and Agriculture Organization of the United Nations, 1986. vii, 426 p. ; 30 cm. (FAO forestry paper. 68) Papers from the FAO/Finland Expert Consultation on Appropriate Forest Industries, sponsored by FINNIDA and the Food and Agriculture Organization of the United Nations. Includes bibliographies. ISBN 92-5-102389-1 (pbk.) LC Card 86-214549 DDC 338.1/7498/091724 19
1. Forest products industry - Developing countries - Congresses. 2. Appropriate technology - Developing countries - Congresses. I. FAO/Finland Expert Consultation on Appropriate Forest Industries (1985 : Jakarta, Indonesia). II. Finland. Ulkoasiainministeriö. Kehityhteistyöosasto. III. Food and Agriculture Organization of the United Nations.
HD9768.D44 A66 1986

Appropriate mechanization for small farmers in developing countries /. Tschiersch, Joachim E. Saarbrücken , 1978. iii, 106 p. ; ISBN 3-88156-112-9 LC Card 80-472522 DDC

338.1/61/091724
S675 .T72 *NYPL [JLE 80-1482]*

Appropriate technologies for development. Landrum, Roger L. The role of the Peace Corps in education in developing countries . Washington, D.C. [1984] iv, 258 p. ; LC Card 86-601664 DDC 371.2/07 19
HC60.5 .L27 1984

APPROPRIATE TECHNOLOGY - BRAZIL.
Economia informal, tecnologia apropriada e associativismo /. São Paulo , 1986. 176 p. : LC Card 86-233370
HC190.P6 E34 1986

APPROPRIATE TECHNOLOGY - DEVELOPING COUNTRIES.
The AT reader . London , 1985. xvii, 468 p. : ISBN 0-946688-10-9 *NYPL [JLE 86-2305]*

Lambert, Denis Clair. Le mimétisme technologique des Tiers-Mondes . Paris , 1983. 223 p. : ISBN 2-7178-0597-4 : LC Card 83-233513
HC59.72.T4 L35 1983

Marsh, Lawrence. Employment and technological choice of multinational enterprises in developing countries . Geneva , 1983. iii, 37 p. ; ISBN 92-2-103353-8 (pbk.) : LC Card 86-213692 DDC 338.8/8854 19
HD2932 .M35 1983

Pernoud, Régine, 1909- Le Moyen Age pour quoi faire? /. [Paris] , c1986. 315 p. : ISBN 2-234-01940-0 : LC Card 86-189820
HC41 .P46 1986

APPROPRIATE TECHNOLOGY - DEVELOPING COUNTRIES - CONGRESSES.
Alexander von Humboldt Award Colloquium (1984) Technology, human capital, and the world food problem /. St. Paul, MN , 1986. x, 167 p. : LC Card 86-622216 DDC 338.1/9/1724 19
HD9018.D44 A44 1984

Appropriate forest industries . Rome , 1986. vii, 426 p. ; ISBN 92-5-102389-1 (pbk.) LC Card 86-214549 DDC 338.1/7498/091724 19
HD9768.D44 A66 1986

APPROPRIATE TECHNOLOGY - NIGERIA.
Fadahunsi, Akin. The development process and technology . Uppsala , 1986. 41 p. ; ISBN 91-7106-257-2 (pbk.) LC Card 87-119156 DDC 338.9669/07 19
HC1055.Z9 T43 1986

L'appropriation de l'espace à Alger après 1962 /. Benatia, Farouk. Alger , c1978. 189 p. : LC Card 81-143253
HD7372.4.A4 B45 1978

APPROPRIATIONS AND EXPENDITURES. see **EXPENDITURES, PUBLIC.**

Appropriations and revenues, fiscal year 1985-86 . Nebraska. Legislature. [Lincoln] [1985] i, 49 leaves ; LC Card 85-623111 DDC 336.782 19
HJ2053.N34 A66 1985

Appuhn, Klaus D. Wohlfeil und köstlich : Märkte, Läden und Händler in aller Welt / Klaus D. Appuhn ; mit einem Nachwort von Ruprecht Skasa-Weiss. Dortmund : Harenberg, c1982. 148 p. : chiefly col. ill. ; 18 cm. (Die Bibliophilen Taschenbücher . Nr. 336) ISBN 3-88379-336-1 (pbk.) LC Card 87-672473
1. Markets - Pictorial works. I. Title. II. Series.
HF5470 .A66x 1982

Aprile-Gniset, Jacques. Mosquera Torres, Gilma. Clases, segregación y barrios /. Cali, Colombia , 1984. 126 p. : LC Card 86-218143
HD7325.V35 M67 1984

Aprovechamiento y dominio de las tierras en 1950-51 /. Tosco, Manuel. Tegucigalpa, D.C., Honduras [1952] 33 p. ; LC Card 85-197157
HD366 .T66 1952

Aproximación a la estructura económica de la provincia de Teruel /. Infante Díaz, Jorge. [Teruel] , 1986. 59 p. : ISBN 84-505-3546-8 LC Card 87-105066
HC387.T4 I53 1986

A.P.S. (Press and Enterprises) Ltd. The APS who's who in Middle East banking & trade. Nicosia, Cyprus , c1984. 2 v. : LC Card 83-149147 *NYPL [JLF 86-983]*

The APS who's who in Middle East banking & trade. 2nd ed., 1984-1985. Nicosia, Cyprus : APS (Press and Enterprises) Ltd, c1984. 2 v. : ill. (some col.) ; 29 cm. CONTENTS. - v. 1. The banks & the bankers -- v. 2. The trade companies & the traders. LC Card 83-149147
1. Financial institutions - Arab countries - Directories. 2. Capitalists and financiers - Arab countries - Directories. 3. Banks and banking - Arab countries - Directories. 4. Bankers - Arab countries - Biography. I. A.P.S. (Press and Enterprises) Ltd. II. Title: APS who's who in Middle East banking and trade. III. Title: A.P.S. who's who in Middle East banking & trade. IV. Title: Who's who in Middle East banking & trade.
NYPL [JLF 86-983]

APS who's who in Middle East banking and trade. The APS who's who in Middle East banking & trade. Nicosia, Cyprus , c1984. 2 v. : LC Card 83-149147 *NYPL [JLF 86-983]*

Apter, David Ernest, 1924- Rethinking development : modernization, dependency, and postmodern politics / David E. Apter. Newbury Park, Calif. : Sage Publications, c1987. 326 p. : ill. ; 23 cm. Includes bibliographies. ISBN 0-8039-2971-4 LC Card 86-29642 DDC 338.9 19
1. Economic development. 2. Dependency. 3. Developing countries - Politics and government. I. Title.
HD82 .A657 1987

APTP employer directory. McLean, Va. (7655 Old Springhouse Road, McLean 22102) : Association of Part-time Professionals, c1986. iii, 47 p. ; 28 cm. Includes index. LC Card 86-213174 DDC 338.7/61/00025753 19
1. Professional employees - Washington Metropolitan Area - Directories. 2. Part-time employment - Washington Metropolitan Area - Directories. I. Association of Part-time Professionals (U. S.).
HD8038.U52 W323 1986

Apunte técnico .
(no. 5) Coyuntura económica ecuatoriana, 1985-1986. [Quito, Ecuador] [1986] i, 39 p. ; LC Card 86-217289
HC202 .C73 1986

Apuntes sobre el capital financiero en Estados Unidos . Fernández Tabío, Luis René. La Habana , 1981 [i.e. 1982] ii, 74 p. : LC Card 87-401153
HG5851.A3 F47 1982

Apuntes sobre el problema parcelario en la Provincia de Chancay /. Pacheco B., Gabriel (Pacheco Bustamante) Huacho, Perú , 1984. 49 p. ; LC Card 86-124478
HD1491.P42 C56 1984

Aquafood Business Associates (Charleston, S.C.) Marine shrimp farming . Charleston, S.C., USA (P.O. Box 16190, Charleston 29412) , c1987. vi, 90 leaves : LC Card 87-404668 DDC 338.3/71543 19
HD9472.S62 M375 1987

Aquino, Antonio, 1946- Dinamica dei prezzi relativi nell'economia internazionale : lineamenti teorici ed esperienze dei paesi industriali / Antonio Aquino. Bologna : Il Mulino, c1986. 225 p. : ill. ; 22 cm. (Studi e ricerche. 207) Bibliography: p. 199-219. ISBN 88-15-00970-1 : LC Card 86-182318
1. Prices. 2. International economic relations. I. Title.
HB221 .A65 1986

Aquino, Cléber Pinheiro de. História empresarial vivida /. São Paulo , 1986-<1987. v. <1-3 > ; LC Card 86-226035
HD70.B7 H57 1986

AQUITAINE (FRANCE) - ECONOMIC POLICY.
Savary, Gilles. Naissance d'une région, rue Esprit-des-lois . [Bordeaux] [1986] 274 p. : ISBN 2-904506-06-5 : LC Card 86-165118
HC277.A6 S28 1986

Ár- és külkereskedelmi tanulmány a buzára és kukoricára, Magyarország / Varga Gyula ... [et al.]. Budapest : Agrárgazdasági Kutató Intézet, 1984. 93 p. ; 28 cm. (Agrárgazdasági Kutató Intézet, 0209-5696 . 1985/1) Bibliography: p. 71-72. ISBN 963-491-218-4 (Magy. nemz. bibl.) LC Card 86-147569
1. Wheat trade - Hungary. 2. Corn industry - Hungary. 3. Wheat - Prices - Hungary. 4. Corn - Prices - Hungary. I. Varga, Gyula, 1938-. II. Series: Agrárgazdasági Kutató Intézet (Series) , 1985/1.
HD9049.W5 H93 1984

Arab-British Chamber of Commerce. Focus on the Gulf Co-operation Council (GCC) . London , c1984. 48 p. : LC Card 85-211534 DDC 337.53/6/041 19
HF1584.5 .F63 1984

ARAB COUNTRIES - ECONOMIC CONDITIONS.
"Problema neftedollarov" . Moskva , 1984. 231 p. ; LC Card 85-189000
HC498 .P75 1984

Silsilat dalīl al-mustathmir fī al-aqṭār al-ʻArabīyah /. al-Kuwayt , <[1985]-. v. <2, 4-5, 7 > : LC Card 86-205217
HG5816.A3 S55 1985

Zakī, Ramzī. al-Duyūn wa-al-tanmiyah . al-Qāhirah , 1985. 271 p. : LC Card 86-960543
HJ8824 .Z34 1985

ARAB COUNTRIES - ECONOMIC CONDITIONS - CONGRESSES.
Adjustment policies and development strategies in the Arab world /. Washington, D.C. , 1987. ix, 200 p. ; ISBN 0-939934-96-5 (pbk.) LC Card 87-21377 DDC 338.9/00917/4927 19
HC498 .A6395 1987

ARAB COUNTRIES - ECONOMIC POLICY.
"Problema neftedollarov" . Moskva , 1984. 231 p. ; LC Card 85-189000
HC498 .P75 1984

ARAB COUNTRIES - ECONOMIC POLICY - CONGRESSES.
Adjustment policies and development strategies in the Arab world /. Washington, D.C. , 1987. ix, 200 p. ; ISBN 0-939934-96-5 (pbk.) LC Card 87-21377 DDC 338.9/00917/4927 19
HC498 .A6395 1987

Tanmiyah al-ʻArabīyah wa-al-ʻalāqāt al-dawlīyah /. al-Kuwayt , 1983. 230, 96 p. ; LC Card 86-964623
HC498 .T349 1983

ARAB COUNTRIES - EMIGRATION AND IMMIGRATION.
Abu Gabal, Sayed Ahmed. Migration of Sudanese . [Khartoum] , 1984. 18, [14] p. ; LC Card 86-980176 DDC 331.6/2/6240174927 19
HD8766 .A65 1984

ARAB COUNTRIES - FOREIGN ECONOMIC RELATIONS - CONGRESSES.
Tanmiyah al-ʻArabīyah wa-al-ʻalāqāt al-dawlīyah /. al-Kuwayt , 1983. 230, 96 p. ; LC Card 86-964623
HC498 .T349 1983

ARAB COUNTRIES - FOREIGN ECONOMIC RELATIONS - EUROPEAN ECONOMIC COMMUNITY COUNTRIES.
Lerche, Dietrich, 1943- Grundlagen und Perspektiven des Euro-Arabischen Dialogs /. Berlin , 1977. iii, 78 p. : LC Card 85-129693
HF1532.5.Z4 A735 1977

ARAB COUNTRIES - FOREIGN ECONOMIC RELATIONS - ISRAEL.
Sarna, A. J. Boycott and blacklist . Totowa, N.J. , 1986. xiv, 270 p. : ISBN 0-8476-7489-4 : LC Card 86-1891 DDC 337.5694/0174927 19
HF1610.Z4 I87 1986
*NYPL [*PXLB 86-6444]*

ARAB COUNTRIES - FOREIGN ECONOMIC RELATIONS - SOVIET UNION - HISTORY.
Makeev, D. A. Vneshnetorgovye svi͡azi SSSR so stranami Arabskogo Vostoka v 1922-1939 gg. /. Moskva , 1983. 112 p. ; LC Card 84-189987
HF1558.15.A65 M34 1983

Arab Empire. see **Islamic Empire.**

Arab Fund for Economic and Social Development. Arab Fund for Economic and Social Development, 1985. Kuwait, State of Kuwait : The Fund, [1986?] 15 p. : col. ill. ; 21 cm. Cover title. LC Card 87-128750 DDC 332.1/53 19
1. Arab Fund for Economic and Social Development. 2. Economic development projects - Arab countries - Finance. I. Title.
HG3881.5.A74 A73 1986

ARAB FUND FOR ECONOMIC AND SOCIAL DEVELOPMENT.
Arab Fund for Economic and Social Development. Arab Fund for Economic and Social Development, 1985. Kuwait, State of Kuwait [1986?] 15 p. : LC Card 87-128750

DDC 332.1/53 19
HG3881.5.A74 A73 1986

Arab Fund for Economic and Social Development, 1985. Arab Fund for Economic and Social Development. Kuwait, State of Kuwait [1986?] 15 p. : LC Card 87-128750 DDC 332.1/53 19
HG3881.5.A74 A73 1986

The Arab Gulf States and Japan . Joint Symposium on the Energy Industries: Prospects of Co-operation Between Arab Gulf States and Japan (1984 : Tokyo, Japan) London , Dover, N.H. , c1986. xiv, 216 p. : ISBN 0-7099-3393-2 : LC Card 85-12819 DDC 338.2/728/0952 19
HD9576.P52 J65 1984
NYPL [JLD 86-1669]

ARAB-JEWISH RELATIONS. see **JEWISH-ARAB RELATIONS.**

Arab Monetary Fund. Adjustment policies and development strategies in the Arab world /. Washington, D.C. , 1987. ix, 200 p. ; ISBN 0-939934-96-5 (pbk.) LC Card 87-21377 DDC 338.9/00917/4927 19
HC498 .A6395 1987

Arab Organization for Social Defense against Crime. Tazwīr al-mustanadāt wa-tazyīf al-ʻumlāt wa-al-asālīb al-ʻilmīyah lil-kashf ʻanhā. [Cairo] [1978] 296 p., [1] leaf of plates : ISBN 977-7049-73-0 LC Card 79-961630
HG335 .T3 1978

Arab Planning Institute.
Nadwat Tanmiyat al-Mawārid al-Basharīyah fī al-Khalīj al-ʻArabī (1975 : Bahrain) Nadwat Tanmiyat al-Mawārid al-Basharīyah fī al-Khalīj al-ʻArabī . al-Kuwayt [1975?] 361, 404 p. : LC Card 86-964662
HD5715.5.P39 N33 1975

Seminar on Investment Policies of Arab Oil Producing Countries (1974 : Kuwait, Kuwait) Seminar on Investment Policies of Arab Oil Producing Countries, 18-20 February 1974, Kuwait /. [Kuwait] [1974?] 216 p. ; LC Card 87-400750 DDC 332.6/7353 19
HG5816.A3 S46 1974

Tanmiyah al-ʻArabīyah wa-al-ʻalāqāt al-dawlīyah /. al-Kuwayt , 1983. 230, 96 p. ; LC Card 86-964623
HC498 .T349 1983

Arab Republic of Egypt. see **Egypt.**

ARABIAN AMERICAN OIL COMPANY - HISTORY.
Casillas, Rex J. Oil and diplomacy . New York , 1987. p. cm. ISBN 0-8240-8078-5 : LC Card 87-23769 DDC 337.730538 19
HF1456.5.S33 C37 1987

Arabian gulf studies / Schriftleitung, Wigand Ritter. Nürnberg : Im Selbstverlag des Wirtschafts- und Sozialgeographischen Instituts der Friedrich-Alexander-Universität, 1985- v. <1 > : ill., maps ; 21 cm. (Nürnberger wirtschafts- und sozialgeographischen Arbeiten, 0546-9112 . Bd. 37-) Includes bibliographies. LC Card 86-205380 DDC 330.953/053 19
1. Arabian Peninsula - Economic conditions. 2. Arabian Peninsula - Industries. 3. Industry and state - Arabian Peninsula. I. Ritter, Wigand. II. Series: Nürnberger wirtschafts- und sozialgeographische Arbeiten, Bd. 37, etc.
HC415.3 .A7 1985

ARABIAN PENINSULA - ECONOMIC CONDITIONS.
Arabian gulf studies /. Nürnberg , 1985- v. <1 > : LC Card 86-205380 DDC 330.953/053 19
HC415.3 .A7 1985

Osama, Abdul Rahman, 1942- The dilemma of development in the Arabian Peninsula /. London , c1987. 203 p. ; ISBN 0-7099-4240-0 : LC Card 86-29149 DDC 338.953 19
HC415.3 .O83 1987

Rumayḥī, Muḥammad Ghānim. [Khalīj laysa nafṭ. English.] Beyond oil . London , 1986. 156 p. : ISBN 0-86356-120-9 : LC Card 86-200063 DDC 330.953/053 19
HC415.3 .R8613 1986

Susanīān, K. G. (Karen Gevorkovich) Araviĭskie gosudarstva i vneshneėkonomicheskaīa strategiīa SShA /. Moskva , 1986. 229, [3] p. : LC Card 86-231698 DDC 337.73053 19
HF1456.5.A625 S87 1986

ARABIAN PENINSULA - ECONOMIC POLICY.
Osama, Abdul Rahman, 1942- The dilemma of development in the Arabian Peninsula /. London , c1987. 203 p. ; ISBN 0-7099-4240-0 : LC Card 86-29149 DDC 338.953 19
HC415.3 .O83 1987

ARABIAN PENINSULA - FOREIGN ECONOMIC RELATIONS - UNITED STATES.
Susanīān, K. G. (Karen Gevorkovich) Araviĭskie gosudarstva i vneshneėkonomicheskaīa strategiīa SShA /. Moskva , 1986. 229, [3] p. : LC Card 86-231698 DDC 337.73053 19
HF1456.5.A625 S87 1986

ARABIAN PENINSULA - INDUSTRIES.
Arabian gulf studies /. Nürnberg , 1985- v. <1 > : LC Card 86-205380 DDC 330.953/053 19
HC415.3 .A7 1985

ARABIAN PENINSULA - POLITICS AND GOVERNMENT.
Osama, Abdul Rahman, 1942- The dilemma of development in the Arabian Peninsula /. London , c1987. 203 p. ; ISBN 0-7099-4240-0 : LC Card 86-29149 DDC 338.953 19
HC415.3 .O83 1987

ARABIAN PENINSULA - SOCIAL CONDITIONS.
Field, Michael, 1949- The merchants . London , 1984. xii, 371 p., [16] p. of plates : ISBN 0-7195-4104-2 LC Card 87-672963
HC415.3 .F54x 1984

Osama, Abdul Rahman, 1942- The dilemma of development in the Arabian Peninsula /. London , c1987. 203 p. ; ISBN 0-7099-4240-0 : LC Card 86-29149 DDC 338.953 19
HC415.3 .O83 1987

Rumayḥī, Muḥammad Ghānim. [Khalīj laysa nafṭ. English.] Beyond oil . London , 1986. 156 p. : ISBN 0-86356-120-9 : LC Card 86-200063 DDC 330.953/053 19
HC415.3 .R8613 1986

ARABIC LANGUAGE - DICTIONARIES - ENGLISH.
Farīd, ʻAbd Allāh Muḥammad. al-Qāmūs al-farīd fī al-māl wa-al-iqtiṣād, ʻArabī-Injilīzī /. [S.l.] 1985 (al-Qāhirah, Miṣr : Maṭābiʻ al-Ahrām al-Tijārīyah) 150, 264 p. ; LC Card 86-960655
HB61 .F36 1985

Majmaʻ al-Lughah al-ʻArabīyah, Cairo. Lajnat al-Jughrāfiyā. al-Muʻjam al-jughrāfī /. [al-Qāhirah] , 1974. 9,185 p. ; LC Card 77-961221
G63 .M34 1974 ***NYPL [*OEO 86-3694]***

Watt, Alec. Illustrated dictionary of geology . Beirut [Harlow, Essex] , 1982. 329 p. :
NYPL [*OG 85-2903]

ARABS - HISTORY - 622-1517. see **ISLAMIC EMPIRE.**

ARABS IN PALESTINE. see **PALESTINIAN ARABS.**

Aragão, José María.
La Asociación Latinoamericana de Libre Comercio (ALALC) y la Asociación Latinoamericana de Integración (ALADI) : trabajo / elaborado por el consultor José María Aragão y supervisado por el Sector Esquemas de Integración. Buenos Aires, Argentina : Banco Interamericano de Desarrollo, Instituto para la Integración de America Latina, [1984] xiii, 172 p. ; 28 cm. Includes bibliographical references. LC Card 86-201881
1. Asociación Latinoamericana de Libre Comercio. 2. Asociación Latinoamericana de Integración. 3. Latin America - Economic integration. 4. Customs unions - Latin America. I. Institute for Latin American Integration. Sector Esquemas de Integración. II. Title.
HC125 .A69 1984

Exenciones arancelarias e integración /. [Buenos Aires] , 1986. 273 p. ; LC Card 87-400577 DDC 382.7/1/098 19
HF1733.L29 E96 1986

ARAGON (KINGDOM) - ECONOMIC CONDITIONS.
Küchler, Winfried, d. 1975. Die Finanzen der Krone Aragon während des 15. Jahrhunderts (Alfons V. und Johann II.) /. Münster, Westfalen , c1983. ix, 318 p. ; ISBN 3-402-05823-5 LC Card 85-113533
HJ1249.A7 K83 1983

ARAGON (SPAIN) - ECONOMIC CONDITIONS.
Biescas, José Antonio, 1946- El proceso de industrialización en la región aragonesa en el período 1900-1920 /. Zaragoza , 1985. 335 p. : ISBN 84-00-06130-6 LC Card 87-111810
HC387.A68 B536 1985

ARAGON (SPAIN) - INDUSTRIES - HISTORY - 20TH CENTURY.
Biescas, José Antonio, 1946- El proceso de industrialización en la región aragonesa en el período 1900-1920 /. Zaragoza , 1985. 335 p. : ISBN 84-00-06130-6 LC Card 87-111810
HC387.A68 B536 1985

ARAGUAÍNA REGION (BRAZIL) - ECONOMIC POLICY.
Projeto de Desenvolvimento Integrado da Bacia do Araguaia-Tocantins. Plano de desenvolvimento das áreas-programa de Araguaína e Tocantinópolis /. Brasília , 1985. 95 p., [8] leaves of plates : LC Card 86-200369
HC189.A67 P76 1985

ARAGUAÍNA REGION (BRAZIL) - SOCIAL POLICY.
Projeto de Desenvolvimento Integrado da Bacia do Araguaia-Tocantins. Plano de desenvolvimento das áreas-programa de Araguaína e Tocantinópolis /. Brasília , 1985. 95 p., [8] leaves of plates : LC Card 86-200369
HC189.A67 P76 1985

Arakelov, S. N. (Suren Nersesovich) Armeniīa v filatelii / S.N. Arakelov. Erevan : Izd-vo "Sovetakan grokh", 1980. 175 p., [24] p. of plates : ill. (some col.), facsims. ; 21 cm. Titles on added t.p.: Armenia in philately; Hayastanĕ filateliayum. Bibliography: p. 174. LC Card 82-105026
1. Postage-stamps - Topics - Armenia - Catalogs. 2. Postage-stamps - Soviet Union - Catalogs. I. Title. II. Title: Armenia in philately. III. Title: Hayastanĕ filateliayum.
HE6183.A69 A72 1980

Aram, John D., 1942-
Managing business and public policy : concepts, issues, & cases / John D. Aram.2nd ed. Marshfield, Mass. : Pitman, c1986. xv, 736 p. : ill. ; 25 cm. Includes bibliographical references and indexes. ISBN 0-582-98830-6 LC Card 85-16955 DDC 338.973 19
1. Industry and state - United States - Case studies. 2. Business and politics - United States - Case studies. I. Title.
HD3616.U47 A73 1985
NYPL [JLE 86-2593]

Westin, Alan F. Managerial dilemmas . Cambridge, Mass. , 1988. p. cm. ISBN 0-88730-181-9 (pbk.) LC Card 87-22476 DDC 658.4/03 19
HD30.23 .W47 1988

Aramco. see **Arabian American Oil Company.**

Arampatzēs, E. Hē mesogeiakē politikē tēs EOK : politikes, nomikes kai oikonomikes apopseis / E. Arampatzēs, A. Kotios, G. Papastamkos. Thessalonikē : Ekdoseis Aphōn Kyriakidē, 1983. 268 p. ; 21 cm. Bibliography: p. [249]-268. LC Card 84-185339
1. European Economic Community - Mediterranean region. I. Kotios, A. II. Papastamkos, G. (Geōrgios). III. Title.
HC241.25.M4 A73 1983

Aranda, Sergio. La economía venezolana : una interpretación de su modo de funcionamiento : con un resumen del período 1975-1984 / Sergio Aranda.Nueva ed. actualizada. Caracas, Venezuela : Editorial Pomaire, c1984. 328 p. ; 21 cm. Includes bibliographies. LC Card 87-400622 DDC 330.987/0633 19
1. Venezuela - Economic conditions - 1918-1958. 2. Venezuela - Economic conditions - 1958-. I. Title.
HC237 .A68 1984

ARAPIRACA REGION (BRAZIL) - ECONOMIC CONDITIONS.
Estudo especial . Maceió, AL. , 1983. 174 leaves : LC Card 86-167829
HC189.A69 E88 1983

Arasaratnam, Sinnappah. Merchants, companies, and commerce on the Coromandel Coast, 1650-1740 / Sinnappah Arasaratnam. Delhi ; New York : Oxford University Press, 1986. x, 407 p. : maps ; 22 cm. Bibliography: p. [395]-401.

Includes index. ISBN 0-19-561873-4 : LC Card 86-900014 DDC 380.1/0954 19
1. Coromandel Coast (India) - Commerce - History. I. Title.
HF3789.C67 A73 1986

Araújo Filho, Acúcio Alencar. Avaliação do polonordeste e do Projeto Sertanejo. Fortaleza , 1985. 314 p. : LC Card 87-402900 DDC 338.981/3 19
HC188.N6 A94 1985

Araujo Júnior, José Tavares de. Tecnologia, concorrência e mudança estrutural : a experiência brasileira recente / José Tavares de Araújo Jr. Rio de Janeiro : IPEA/INPES, 1985. 64 p. ; 21 cm. (Série PNPE . 11) Bibliography: p. 61-64. LC Card 87-120280 DDC 338/.06 19
1. Industrial organization - Brazil. 2. Technology and state - Brazil. I. Title. II. Series.
HD70.B7 A7 1985

Araújo, Luiz Fernando Correia de. Industrialização rural no Nordeste /. Recife , c1986. 488 p. : LC Card 87-403045 DDC 338.981/3 19
HD9014.B83 N755 1985

Araújo, Sergio. Informática : passaporte para o ano 2000 / Sergio Araújo. [Brazil? : s.n., 1986?] (Guarulhos [Brazil] : Artes Gráficas Guaru) 184 p. : ill. ; 20 cm. Cover title. LC Card 87-154279 DDC 338.4/7004 19
1. Information technology - Economic aspects. 2. Information technology - Social aspects. I. Title.
HC79.I55 A7 1986

Araúz, Eladio. Pacheco D., Rubén. Industria de la construcción . [Panamá] , 1974. 17, [1] leaves, [4] leaves of plates : LC Card 87-400643
HD9715.P223 P367 1974

Araviĭskie gosudarstva i vneshneėkonomicheskaia strategiia SShA /. Susanian, K. G. (Karen Gevorkovich) Moskva , 1986. 229, [3] p. : LC Card 86-231698 DDC 337.73053 19
HF1456.5.A625 S87 1986

Arbatov, A. A. (Aleksandr Arkad'evich) Kompleksnye problemy obespecheniia ėkonomiki mineral'nym syr'em /. Moskva , 1984. 115 p. : LC Card 85-192528
HF1051 .K64 1984

Arbeid i 80-åra.
Den Norske kvinnerevolusjonen . Oslo , c1986. 166 p. : ISBN 82-00-18318-1 LC Card 87-155462
HD6170 .N68 1986

Arbeid og samfunn . Luihn, Hans. [Oslo] , c1986. 372 p. : ISBN 82-508-0574-7 : LC Card 87-157793
HD5800.A6 L85 1986

Arbeid, plicht en vrijheid /. Santen, J. van. Nijmegen , c1985. 160 p. ; ISBN 90-6168-247-9 : LC Card 86-117515
HD4905 .S26 1985

Arbeiderbevegelsens historie i Norge / redaktører, Edvard Bull, Arne Kokkvoll, Jakob Sverdrup ; bilderedaktør, Lill-Ann Jensen. 1. oppl. Oslo : Tiden, 1985-<1987 > v. <1, 5 > : ill. ; 25 cm. Includes bibliographies and indexes. CONTENTS. - 1. Arbeiderklassen blir til, 1850-1900 / Edvard Bull -- 5. Storhetstid, 1945-1965 / Trond Bergh. ISBN 82-10-02750-6 : LC Card 87-116315
1. Trade-unions - Norway - History - 19th century. 2. Trade-unions - Norway - History - 20th century. 3. Labor and laboring classes - Norway - History - 19th century. 4. Labor and laboring classes - Norway - History - 20th century. I. Bull, Edvard, 1914-.
HD6752 .A74 1985

Arbeidsmarkt op drift : de mogelijke rol van de overheid, werkgevers en vakbonden op de arbeidsmarkt / N. Barendregt ... [et al.] ; met een voorwoord van W.F. Duisenberg. [Amsterdam] : Industriebond FNV : Raamgracht, 1986. 190 p. : ill. ; 22 cm. Includes bibliographical references. ISBN 90-6287-549-1 : LC Card 86-154853
1. Labor supply - Netherlands. 2. Manpower policy - Netherlands. 3. Trade-unions - Netherlands. I. Barendregt, N.
HD5792 .A72 1986 ***NYPL [JLD 86-4417]***

Arbeidsmarktgedrag ten tijde van massale werkloosheid . Vissers, A. M. C. 's-Gravenhage , 1986. 106 p. : ISBN 90-12-05302-1 LC Card 87-108930
HD5717.5.N45 V57 1986

Arbeidsverhoudinge in Suid-Afrika /. Gouws, P. A. (Pieter Andries), 1949- Pretoria , 1986. 127 p. ; ISBN 0-627-01492-5 : LC Card 87-127172
HD8801 .G66 1986

Arbeit, Arbeit über alles? : Arbeit und Freizeit im Umbruch / Hrsg., Günter Myrell.1. Aufl. Köln : VGS, 1985. 160 p. : ill. ; 21 cm. Eleven programs originally broadcast by the Zweites Deutsches Fernsehen. Includes bibliographies. CONTENTS. - Dimensionen der modernen Krise oder das Unzeitgemässe des gewohnten Starrsinns / Günter Myrell -- Der Arbeitstag war grenzenlos / Bernd Wiegmann -- Immer was zu tun / Margaret Ruthmann -- Arbeit ist mehr als das Geld, das man damit verdient / Hella André -- Das ist auch kein Spass mehr, denn jeder hat Angst / Hella André -- Geschichtliches, Erlebtes / Hella André -- Mit der Arbeit fertig werden / Margaret Ruthmann - Freizeit, Freizeit über alles oder ein Dilemma jagt das andere / Ulli Rothaus -- Es geht auch anders, aber wie? / Ulli Rothaus -- Mehr Zeit zur Lust / Herbert Hackl -- Vom Phänomen der freien Zeit / Manuel Esser. ISBN 3-8025-2167-6 LC Card 86-148728
1. Labor and laboring classes. 2. Right to labor. 3. Leisure. I. Myrell, Günter, 1952-. II. Zweites Deutsches Fernsehen.
HD4854 .A725 1985

Arbeit, Bildung, Gesellschaft .
(Bd. 3) Tews, Hans Peter. Abbrüche beruflicher Rehabilitationsmassnahmen . Hamburg , 1986. 277 p. ; ISBN 3-925408-04-5 LC Card 87-127427 DDC 362/.0425 19
HD7256.G3 T48 1986

Arbeit, Entropie, Apokalypse : Reagans gesammelte Alpträume : entropologische Jahrbücher 1982, letzte Ausgabe / [Herausgebergruppe der Entropologischen Jahrbücher]. Zürich : Vertrieb, Paranoia City Buchhandlung, 1982. 134 p. : ill. ; 21 cm. Includes bibliographical references. LC Card 83-128724
1. United States - Economic policy - 1981-. I. Herausgebergruppe der Entropologischen Jahrbücher (Zurich, Switzerland). II. Title: Reagans gesammelte Alpträume. III. Title: Entropologische Jahrbücher 1982.
HC106.8 .A73 1982

Die Arbeit geht weiter . Blüm, Norbert, 1935- München , 1983. 128 p. ; ISBN 3-492-00627-2 : LC Card 84-136559
HD4904 .B563 1983

Arbeit, Konsum, Akkumulation . Zinn, Karl Georg. Hamburg , 1986. 243 p. : ISBN 3-87975-347-4 LC Card 86-230933
HB103.K47 Z56 1986

Arbeit, mehr als Kapital : über die Mitbestimmung hinaus / herausgegeben von Dieter Grohmann und Harald Pawlowski. Wuppertal : P. Hammer, c1983. 191 p. ; 19 cm. (Publik-Forum-Buch im Peter Hammer Verlag) Includes bibliographical references. ISBN 3-87294-224-7 LC Card 84-182379
1. Catholic Church. Pope (1978- : John Paul II) Laborem exercens. 2. Church and labor. 3. Socialism, Christian. I. Grohmann, Dieter. II. Pawlowski, Harald.
HD6338 .A69 1983

Die Arbeit mit dem Prämienfonds /. Rogge, Werner. Berlin , c1984. 70 p. ; LC Card 86-100311 DDC 331.2/164 19
HD4928.B62 G357 1984

Arbeit und Arbeitserfahrung in der Geschichte / mit Beiträgen von Detlev J.K. Peukert ... [et al.] ; herausgegeben von Klaus Tenfelde. Göttingen : Vandenhoeck & Ruprecht, 1986. 128 p. ; 19 cm. (Kleine Vandenhoeck-Reihe. 1514) Bibliography: p. 120-126. ISBN 3-525-33516-4
1. Work - History. 2. Labor and laboring classes - History. I. Peukert, Detlev. II. Tenfelde, Klaus.
NYPL [JLC 87-12]

Arbeit und Arbeitserfahrung in der Geschichte / mit Beiträgen von Detlev J.K. Peukert ... [et al.] ; herausgegeben von Klaus Tenfelde. Göttingen : Vandenhoeck & Ruprecht, c1986. 128 p. ; 19 cm. (Kleine Vandenhoeck-Reihe. 1514) Includes bibliographical references. ISBN 3-525-33516-4 LC Card 86-226588
1. Work. 2. Labor and laboring classes - Germany (West) - Ruhr (Region) - History. I. Peukert, Detlev. II. Tenfelde, Klaus.
HD4904 .A6644 1986

Arbeit und Beruf (North Rhine-Westphalia (Germany). Ministerium für Arbeit, Gesundheit und Soziales) .
(20) Jansen, Paul Günter. Arbeitsmarktatlas . [Düsseldorf] [1977] 206, A19 p. : LC Card 85-173256
HD5780.A76 J36 1977

Arbeit und Freizeit . Bamberg, Eva, 1951- Weinheim , 1986. xiv, 306 p. ; ISBN 3-407-58288-9 LC Card 87-103692 DDC 158.7 19
HF5548.85 .B36 1986

Arbeit und Gesellschaft im Umbruch . Dachrodt, Heinz-G., 1944- Köln [1987], c1986. 128 p. : ISBN 3-7663-0961-7 LC Card 87-139264 DDC 331.12/0943 19
HD6331.2.G28 D33 1987

Arbeit zweitausend. Arbeit 2000 . Hamburg , 1985. 236 p. : ISBN 3-87975-314-8 LC Card 86-143070
HD4813 .A68 1985

Arbeit 2000 : über die Zukunft der Arbeitsgesellschaft / Elmar Altvater, Martin Baethge u.a. ; mit Beiträgen von Elmar Altvater ... [et al.]. Hamburg : VSA-Verlag, 1985. 236 p. : ill. ; 24 cm. Includes bibliographies. CONTENTS. - Wirtschaftspolitische Optionen zur Überwindung der Arbeitslosigkeit / Fritz W. Scharpf -- Das Jahr 2000, der Weltmarkt und Fidel Castro / Elmar Altvater -- Entwicklungstendenzen der Arbeit im Produktionsbereich / Michael Schumann, Klaus Peter Wittemann -- Zur Entwicklung von Arbeit und Beschäftigung im Dienstleistungssektor / Martin Baethge, Herbert Oberbeck -- Die sogenannte Informationsgesellschaft / Herbert Kubicek -- Perspektiven der Sozialpolitik / Gerhard Bäcker, Hagen Kühn -- Karriere, wie hoch ist der Preis? / Elisabeth Beck-Gernsheim -- Die neue Freizeitarbeitsethik / Horst W. Opaschowski -- Die Zukunft der Arbeit / Iring Fetscher -- Von der kapitalistischen Industriegesellschaft zur postindustriellen Dienstleistungsgesellschaft? / Joachim Bischoff, Sebastian Herkommer -- Tarifpolitik und gesellschaftliche Strukturreform / Hans Janssen, Klaus Lang -- Arbeit 2000 / Franz Steinkühler. ISBN 3-87975-314-8 LC Card 86-143070
1. Labor and laboring classes - Forecasting - Congresses. I. Altvater, Elmar. II. Baethge, Martin. III. Title: Arbeit zweitausend.
HD4813 .A68 1985

Arbeiten aus dem Institut für Afrika-Kunde .
(Heft 6) Bolz, Reinhardt. Tunesien . Hamburg , 1976. xxiii, 471 p. : LC Card 86-177615
HC820 .B66 1976

(44) Burchards, Eckehard. Strukturen und Funktionen des informellen Sektors in Ghana . Hamburg , 1983. vii, 138 p. : ISBN 3-923519-54-0 LC Card 83-214699 DDC 381 19
HD2346.G42 A243 1983

(46) Jakobeit, Cord. Die sozio-ökonomische Entwicklung der Elfenbeinküste seit der Unabhängigkeit . Hamburg , 1984. viii, 132 p. : ISBN 3-923519-57-5 LC Card 84-222859
HC1025 .J35 1984

Arbeiten aus dem Institut für Völkerkunde der Universität zu Göttingen .
(Bd. 22) Adebowale, Annette, 1957- Yoruba-Märkte in Nigeria . Aachen , c1987. xxvii, 225 p. : ISBN 3-922868-64-9 LC Card 87-141899 DDC 381/.18/096692 19
HF5475.N52 A362 1987

Arbeiten ohne Angst . Briam, Karl-Heinz. Düsseldorf , 1986. 200 p. ; ISBN 3-430-11560-4 LC Card 86-159578
HF5549.2.G3 B75 1986

Arbeiter in Hamburg : Unterschichten, Arbeiter und Arbeiterbewegung seit dem ausgehenden 18. Jahrhundert / herausgegeben von Arno Herzig, Dieter Langewiesche und Arnold Sywottek. Hamburg : Verlag Erziehung und Wissenschaft, c1983. 606 p. : ill. ; 24 cm. Includes bibliographical references. ISBN 3-8103-0807-2 LC Card 86-174037
1. Labor and laboring classes - Germany (West) - Hamburg - History. 2. Hamburg (Germany) - Economic conditions. I. Herzig, Arno. II. Langewiesche, Dieter. III. Sywottek, Arnold, 1942-.
HD8460.H36 A73 1983

Arbeiter und Bürger im neunzehnten Jahrhundert. Arbeiter und Bürger im 19. Jahrhundert . München , 1986. xiv, 342 p. ; ISBN 3-486-52871-8 LC Card 86-212379
HD8376 .A72 1986

Arbeiter und Bürger im 19. Jahrhundert : Varianten ihres Verhältnisses im europäischen

Vergleich / herausgegeben von Jürgen Kocka unter Mitarbeit von Elisabeth Müller-Luckner. München : R. Oldenbourg, 1986. xiv, 342 p. ; 24 cm. (Schriften des Historischen Kollegs. Kolloquien . 7) Papers presented at a meeting organized by the Historisches Kolleg and held in Munich, June 28-29, 1984. Contributions chiefly in German; three contributions in English and one in French. Includes bibliographical references and index. ISBN 3-486-52871-8 LC Card 86-212379
1. Labor and laboring classes - Europe - History - 19th century - Congresses. 2. Middle classes - Europe - History - 19th century - Congresses. 3. Social classes - Europe - History - 19th century - Congresses. I. Kocka, Jürgen. II. Müller-Luckner, Elisabeth. III. Stiftung Historisches Kolleg (Munich, Germany). IV. Title: Arbeiter und Bürger im neunzehnten Jahrhundert. V. Series.
HD8376 .A72 1986

Arbeiterbewegung in den Rheinlanden .
Die Arbeiterbewegung in den Rheinlanden. (Nr. 17) Der I. Kongress der Revolutionären Gewerkschafts-Opposition (RGO) im Bezirk Mittelrhein (Raum Aachen-Köln-Koblenz) im Jahre 1930 /. Reinbek , c1982. 136 p. : ISBN 3-88756-024-8 : LC Card 84-135308
HD6699.R47 I18 1982

(17) Der I. Kongress der Revolutionären Gewerkschafts-Opposition (RGO) im Bezirk Mittelrhein (Raum Aachen-Köln-Koblenz) im Jahre 1930 /. Reinbek , c1982. 136 p. : ISBN 3-88756-024-8 : LC Card 84-135308
HD6699.R47 I18 1982

Arbeiterbewegung in der Zusammenbruchsgesellschaft . Reese, Hartmut. Münster [1984?] 209 p. ; ISBN 3-88660-133-1 LC Card 85-128699
HD6694 .R35 1984

Arbeiterklasse, gibt's die noch? / Peter Fleissner, Frank Deppe (Hg.). Wien : Verlag für Gesellschaftskritik, c1985. 246 p. : ill. ; 20 cm. Includes bibliographies. CONTENTS. - Automaten statt Menschen? / Peter Fleissner -- Kapitalistische Zentren, Krisenzentren? / Jörg Goldberg -- Klasse? Schicht? Mittelstand? / Josef Ehmer -- Arbeiterklasse, gibt's die noch? / Heinz Jung -- Aussteigen aus dem "gemeinsamen Boot" / Frank Deppe -- Alternativen und dritte Wege / Ernst Wimmer -- Anpassung, Resignation, Widerstand / Julius Mende. ISBN 3-900351-46-5 LC Card 86-123225
1. Labor and laboring classes - Germany, West. 2. Labor supply - Germany (West) - Effect of automation on. I. Fleissner, Peter K. II. Deppe, Frank.
HD8451 .A836 1985

[Arbeiterkultur .
(Bd. 13]) Reese, Hartmut. Arbeiterbewegung in der Zusammenbruchsgesellschaft . Münster [1984?] 209 p. ; ISBN 3-88660-133-1 LC Card 85-128699
HD6694 .R35 1984

Die arbeiterselbstverwaltete Firma bei Unsicherheit und asymmetrischer Information . Meran, Georg. München , c1986. ii, 134 p. : ISBN 3-88259-403-9 LC Card 87-121443 DDC 658.3/152 19
HD5650 .M397 1986

Arbeitersiedlungen im neunzehnten Jahrhunderts. Arbeitersiedlungen im 19. Jahrhundert . Bochum , c1985. 189 p. : ISBN 3-88339-427-0 LC Card 85-164690
HD7289.5.A3 G42 1985

Arbeitersiedlungen im 19. Jahrhundert : historische Entwicklung, Bedeutung und aktuelles Erhaltungsinteresse / mit Beiträgen von Walter Buschmann ... [et al.] ; herausgegeben von Johannes Biecker und Walter Buschmann. Bochum : N. Brockmeyer, c1985. 189 p. : 71 ill. ; 23 cm. Papers presented at a symposium held Oct. 13-14, 1983 at the Universität Essen, sponsored by the Fachbereich Architektur, Bio- und Geowissenschaft of the Universität GHS Essen, the Rheinisches Amt für Denkmalpflege, and the ITZ (Innovationsförderungs- und Technologietransfer-Zentrum der Hochschulen des Ruhrgebietes) Includes bibliographical references. CONTENTS. - Zum Verhältnis von Arbeitersiedlungen, Stadtplanung und Stadtentwicklung im Ruhrgebiet / Renate Kastorff-Viehmann -- Architektonische und städtebauliche Formen im Arbeitersiedlungsbau des 19. Jahrhunderts in Deutschland / Walter Buschmann -- Die Formenwelt des Arbeitersiedlungsbaues / Hermann Sturm -- Arbeitersiedlungen als Dokumente spezifischen Nachbarschafts- und Gemeinschaftsverhaltens / Roland Günter -- Arbeitersiedlungen als Sozialform / Daniel Stemmrich -- Zum Quellenwert von Arbeitersiedlungen / Eduard Führ -- Denkmalschutz für Arbeitersiedlungen / Walter Buschmann. ISBN 3-88339-427-0 LC Card 85-164690
1. Industrial housing - Germany - History - 19th century - Congresses. 2. Labor and laboring classes - Dwellings - Germany - History - 19th century - Congresses. I. Buschmann, Walter. II. Biecker, Johannes. III. Universität Essen. Fachbereich Architektur, Bio- und Geowissenschaften. IV. Rheinisches Amt für Denkmalpflege. V. Innovationsförderungs- und Technologietransfer-Zentrum der Hochschulen des Ruhrgebiets. VI. Title: Arbeitersiedlungen im neunzehnten Jahrhunderts.
HD7289.5.A3 G42 1985

Arbeiterwanderungen, Ausländerbeschäftigung und Ausländerpolitik in kapitalistischen Ländern Europas im 20. Jahrhundert. Rostock : Wilhelm-Pieck-Universität Rostock, Sektion Geschichte, 1981-1982. 4 v. ; 21 cm. (Fremdarbeiterpolitik des Imperialismus, 0138-3396 . Heft 10-13) Proceedings of a colloquium held in Rostock, Apr. 21-22, 1981. Includes bibliographical references. LC Card 82-193086 DDC 331.6/2/094 19
1. Alien labor - France - Congresses. 2. Alien labor - Germany, West - Congresses. 3. Alien labor - Switzerland - Congresses. I. Wilhelm-Pieck-Universität Rostock. Sektion Geschichte. II. Series.
HD8438.A2 A75 1982 ***NYPL [JLK 84-95]***

Arbeitgeberkreis Gesamttextil (Germany) Die Textilindustrie im Ostblock . Frankfurt/Main , 1967. 88, 17 p., [3] leaves of plates : LC Card 85-116763
HD9865.E79 T49 1967

Arbeitnehmerbeteiligung bei Personengesellschaften . List, Stephan, 1959- Spardorf , c1985. v, 167 p. ; ISBN 3-922919-50-2 LC Card 86-141876
HD5660.G4 L55 1985

Arbeitnehmerfonds in Schweden, der dritte Weg? . Trautwein, Hans-Michael, 1957- Frankfurt am Main , New York , c1986. 353, 39, [116] p. : ISBN 3-8204-9336-0 LC Card 86-203867
HD4928.G342 S88 1986

Arbeitnehmerorientierte Sozialforschung . Elsenau, Detlef von. Münster [1986] ii, 233 p. ; ISBN 3-88660-246-X LC Card 86-200305
HD6957.G3 E59 1986

Arbeits- und Freizeitpädagogik . Neven, Peter, 1953- Düsseldorf [1982?] 424 p. ; ISBN 3-87864-087-0 LC Card 84-119072
HD4901 .N47 1982

Arbeits- und Organisationsgestaltung in einer post-industriellen Gesellschaft /. Peters, Nikolaus A. Bern , c1981. xi, 351 p. : ISBN 3-258-03066-9 LC Card 87-672718
HD2326 .P47x 1981

Arbeitsangebot und Alterssicherung /. Genosko, Joachim. Regensburg , c1985. vii, 287 p. : ISBN 3-924956-05-7 LC Card 86-230675
HD7105.35.G3 G46 1985

Arbeitsbedingungen in der Schweizer Hotellerie . Diedrich, Wolfgang. Bern , c1984. 185 p. : ISBN 3-258-03437-0 : LC Card 85-113566
HD5718.H82 S953 1984

Arbeitsberichte des Ibero-Amerika-Instituts für Wirtschaftsforschung der Universität Göttingen .
(Heft 21) Mohs, Ralf-Matthias. Exporte, komparative Vorteile und wirtschaftliche Entwicklung in den Schwellenländern . Göttingen [1983] 236 p. : ISBN 3-509-01345-X LC Card 84-126961
HF4055 .M64 1983

Arbeitsberichte des Wissenschaftszentrums Berlin, Internationales Institut für Management und Verwaltung/Arbeitsmarktpolitik.
Regionalisierte Arbeitsmarkt- und Beschäftigungspolitik /. Frankfurt/Main , New York , c1983. 322 p. : ISBN 3-593-33241-8 LC Card 84-106151
HC286.7 .R44 1983

Spahn, Heinz-Peter. Stagnation in der Geldwirtschaft . Frankfurt , New York , c1986. 304 p. : ISBN 3-593-33691-X LC Card 86-225253
HD5710 .S68 1986

Arbeitsberichte des Wissenschaftszentrums Berlin, Internationales Institut für Umwelt und Gesellschaft.
Knödgen, Gabriele, 1949- Umweltschutz und industrielle Standortentscheidung /. Frankfurt/Main , New York , c1982. 219 p. : ISBN 3-593-33158-6 LC Card 83-110653
HC59.72.P55 K58 1982

Prittwitz, Volker. Umweltaussenpolitik . Frankfurt , New York , c1984. vii, 211 p. : ISBN 3-593-33369-4 LC Card 84-202897
HC240.9.A4 P75 1984

Arbeitsberichte und Ergebnisse zur wirtschafts- und sozialgeographischen Regionalforschung .
(Heft 12) Pohle, Michael. Industriebrachen und extensiv genutzte Flächen in innenstadtnahen Gewerbegebieten . Paderborn , 1985. viii, 121 p. : ISBN 3-506-73577-2 : LC Card 86-183775
HC289.H2 P64 1985

Arbeitsbewertung bei flexiblem Personaleinsatz . Brumlop, Eva. Frankfurt , New York , c1986. 229 p. : ISBN 3-593-32744-9 LC Card 86-196323
HD5109.2.G3 B76 1986

Arbeitsbewertung und Disziplinierung . Heinrich, Herbert, 1938- Spardorf , c1985. v, 281 p. ; ISBN 3-922919-67-7 LC Card 86-162759
HF5549.5.J62 H36 1985

Arbeitsbuch zur Mikroökonomie /. Böhm, Volker. Berlin , New York , 1984. vi, 246 p. : ISBN 0-387-13541-3 (U. S.) LC Card 85-139852
HB172 .B544 1984

Arbeitsdirektors im Spannungsfeld von Recht und Praxis. Spie, Ulrich. Der Personalmanager im Vorstand . Stuttgart , 1985. ix, 354 p. : ISBN 3-8202-0313-3 LC Card 86-131051
HF5549.2.G3 S67 1985

Arbeitsgemeinschaft der Bitumen-Industrie (Germany) Strassenbau und Mineralölindustrie im Spiegel der Statistik . Hamburg , 1976. [48] p. : LC Card 83-126399
HD9582.A7 G37 1976

Arbeitsgemeinschaft der Industrie- und Handelskammern in Baden-Württemberg (Germany) IHK-Atlas Industrie-Ansiedlung . Stuttgart [1982?] 145 p. : LC Card 86-213370
HC287.B23 I38 1982

Arbeitsgemeinschaft Deutsche Lateinamerika-Forschung. Fachtagung "Bevölkerungsentwicklung, Bevölkerungswanderung und Urbanisierung in Lateinamerika" (1984 : Eichstätt, Germany) Desarrollo demográfico, migraciones y urbanización en América Latina . Regensburg , c1986. 432 p. : LC Card 86-181152
HB3530.5.A3 F33 1984

Arbeitsgemeinschaft Deutscher Berufsförderungswerke. Tews, Hans Peter. Abbrüche beruflicher Rehabilitationsmassnahmen . Hamburg , 1986. 277 p. ; ISBN 3-925408-04-5 LC Card 87-127427 DDC 362/.0425 19
HD7256.G3 T48 1986

Arbeitsgemeinschaft für Rationalisierung des Landes Nordrhein-Westfalen. Arbeitsgruppe Forschung und Technik. Schmidt-Tiedemann, K. J. Planung und Nutzung des technischen Fortschritts /. [Dortmund?] , 1976. 37 p. : LC Card 86-123518
HD30 .A7 Heft 173 T177.G4

Arbeitsgemeinschaft für Rationalisierung des Landes Nordrhein-Westfalen. Arbeitsgruppe Rationalisierung und Gesetzgebung. Rembser, Josef. Die Förderung des wirtschaftlichen und sozialen Wandels durch die Forschungs- und Entwicklungspolitik als präventive Strukturpolitik /. Dortmund , 1977. 100 p. : LC Card 84-130876
HD30 .A7 Heft 184 HD6331.2.G28

Arbeitsgemeinschaft für Rationalisierung des Landes Nordrhein-Westfalen. Arbeitsgruppe Vereinheitlichung.
Hens, Albert T. Einige Aspekte moderner Normung unter Berücksichtigung der Produktnormung /. Dortmund , 1977. 38 p. ; LC Card 84-121721
HD30 .A7 Heft 183 HD62

Lauer, Karl Friedrich. Das Referenzbüro der Gemeinschaften /. [Dortmund?] , 1976. 76 p. ; LC Card 85-241026
HD30 .A7 Heft 171 T59.A1

Normungsprobleme der Dritten Welt /. Dortmund , 1979. 98 p. ; LC Card 85-239680
HD30 .A7 Heft 201 T59.A1

Arbeitsgemeinschaft für Rationalisierung des Landes Nordrhein-Westfalen. Arbeitsgruppe Wissenschaftliche Unternehmungsführung. Stand und Entwicklung des Vorschlagswesens in Wirtschaft und Verwaltung /. Dortmund , 1978. 108 p. : ISBN 3-922104-00-2 LC Card 85-124069
HD30 .A7 Heft 193 HF5549.5.S8

Arbeitsgemeinschaft für Rationalisierung des Landes Nordrhein-Westfalen (Series) .
(167) Groebel, Wilhelm. Lebensmittelüberwachung . Dortmund , 1976. 84 p. : LC Card 86-170104
HD30 .A7 Heft 167 HD9000.9

(171) Lauer, Karl Friedrich. Das Referenzbüro der Gemeinschaften /. [Dortmund?] , 1976. 76 p. ; LC Card 85-241026
HD30 .A7 Heft 171 T59.A1

(173) Schmidt-Tiedemann, K. J. Planung und Nutzung des technischen Fortschritts /. [Dortmund?] , 1976. 37 p. : LC Card 86-123518
HD30 .A7 Heft 173 T177.G4

(183) Hens, Albert T. Einige Aspekte moderner Normung unter Berücksichtigung der Produktnormung /. Dortmund , 1977. 38 p. ; LC Card 84-121721
HD30 .A7 Heft 183 HD62

(184) Rembser, Josef. Die Förderung des wirtschaftlichen und sozialen Wandels durch die Forschungs- und Entwicklungspolitik als präventive Strukturpolitik /. Dortmund , 1977. 100 p. : LC Card 84-130876
HD30 .A7 Heft 184 HD6331.2.G28

(193) Stand und Entwicklung des Vorschlagswesens in Wirtschaft und Verwaltung /. Dortmund , 1978. 108 p. : ISBN 3-922104-00-2 LC Card 85-124069
HD30 .A7 Heft 193 HF5549.5.S8

(201) Normungsprobleme der Dritten Welt /. Dortmund , 1979. 98 p. ; LC Card 85-239680
HD30 .A7 Heft 201 T59.A1

Arbeitsgestaltung in der Serienfertigung : Erfahrungen zur Organisationsentwicklung aus einem Humanisierungsprojekt / Bosch-Siemens Hausgeräte GmbH (Projektleiter, Ludwig Wexlberger) ; in Zusammenarbeit mit TU Berlin, Institut für Arbeitswissenschaft (Leiter, Bernd Schulte), Friedrich Fürstenberg ; Universität Karlsruhe, Institut für Soziologie (Leiter, Hans Linde). Frankfurt [am Main] ; New York : Campus, c1984. 315 p. : 56 ill. ; 21 cm. (Schriftenreihe "Humanisierung des Arbeitslebens" . Bd. 53) Includes bibliographical references. ISBN 3-593-32733-3 LC Card 84-230390
1. Organizational change - Germany (West). 2. Corporate culture - Germany (West). 3. Personnel management - Germany, West. 4. Bosch-Siemens Hausgeräte GmbH. I. Fürstenberg, Friedrich. II. Bosch-Siemens Hausgeräte GmbH. III. Technische Universität Berlin. Institut für Arbeitswissenschaft. IV. Universität Karlsruhe. Institut für Soziologie. V. Series.
HD58.8 .A73 1984

Arbeitsgruppe Alternative Wirtschaftspolitik. Memorandum '84 . Köln , c1984. 475 p. : ISBN 3-7609-0883-7 : LC Card 85-128558
HC286.7 .M465 1984

Arbeitsgruppe Budgetpolitik (Beirat für Wirtschafts- und Sozialfragen) Budgetvorschau 1986-1990. Wien , 1986. 45 p. : LC Card 86-227246
HJ2101 .B83 1986

Arbeitshefte Ruhrgebiet. Nahwanderungen im Ruhrgebiet, 1976-1984 /. Essen , c1986. 61 p. : ISBN 3-923494-67-X LC Card 87-408772 DDC 330.943/55 19
HC288.R8 N34 1986

Noll, Wulf. Lokales Informationssystem Arbeitsmarkt (LISA) /. Essen , 1986. 262 p. ; ISBN 3-923494-64-5 LC Card 87-409105 DDC 331.12/5/094355 19
HD5780.R82 N65 1986

Arbeitshefte zur Denkmalpflege in Hamburg . (Nr. 8) Stadt und Hafen . Hamburg , 1986. 209 p. : ISBN 3-7672-0951-9 LC Card 87-130912 DDC 387.1/0943/515 19
HE558.H3 S7 1986

Arbeitshefte zur Führungspsychologie . (Heft 15) Berkel, Karl. Konflikttraining /. Heidelberg , c1985. 82 p. : ISBN 3-7938-7735-3 LC Card 85-188803
HD42 .B47 1985

Arbeitskammer des Saarlandes. Recktenwald, Werner. Wie errechne ich meinen Nettolohn? . Saarbrücken [1985?] 112 p. ; ISBN 3-88968-029-1 LC Card 85-171297 DDC 343.4305/242 344.3035242 19
HJ4720.A7 R42 1985

Arbeitskammer des Saarlandes. Referat Presse und Information. Kratz, Hans-Jürgen. Arbeitslosengeld /. Saarbrücken [1983] 176 p. ; ISBN 3-88968-006-2 LC Card 83-215450
HD7096.G32 S335 1983

Arbeitskampf um Arbeitszeit : Perspektiven gewerkschaftlicher Zukunft in flexibler Arbeitswelt / mit Beiträgen von Udo Achten ... [et al.]. Marburg : Verlag Arbeiterbewegung und Gesellschaftswissenschaft, c1985. 218 p. : ill. ; 21 cm. (Schriftenreihe der Studiengesellschaft für Sozialgeschichte und Arbeiterbewegung . Bd. 50) Includes bibliographical references. ISBN 3-921630-52-5 LC Card 86-160526
1. Labor disputes - Germany, West. 2. Hours of labor, Flexible - Germany (West). 3. Thirty-five hour week - Germany (West). I. Achten, Udo, 1943-. II. Series.
HD5378 .A73 1985

Arbeitskommunikation, Kommunikationsarbeit . Haag, Ingeborg. Berlin , 1986. viii, 258 p. ; ISBN 3-923024-08-8 LC Card 86-226373
HD6957.G35 H33 1986

Arbeitskreis Deutscher Marktforschungsinstitute. Schaefer, Felix, 1950- Muster-Stichproben-Pläne für Bevölkerungs-Stichproben in der Bundesrepublik Deutschland und West-Berlin /. München , c1979. 160 p. : ISBN 3-478-39760-X; 3-478-39760-1 LC Card 84-135457
HB3595 .S29 1979

Arbeitskreis Politische Ökonomie (Germany) Die Gegenwärtige Wachstumskrise . Regensburg , c1985. viii, 262 p. : ISBN 3-924956-08-1 LC Card 86-122363 DDC 338.9 19
HD73 .G43 1985

Arbeitslos : Betroffene erzählen / [herausgegeben von] Christiane Rumpeltes.Originalausg. Reinbek bei Hamburg : Rowohlt, 1982. 170 p. : ill. ; 19 cm. (Rororo aktuell) Bibliography: p. 169-170. ISBN 3-499-15024-7 (pbk.) LC Card 87-672730
1. Unemployed - Germany (West) - Interviews. I. Rumpeltes, Christiane, 1951-.
HD5779 .A6x 1982

Arbeitslosengeld /. Kratz, Hans-Jürgen. Saarbrücken [1983] 176 p. ; ISBN 3-88968-006-2 LC Card 83-215450
HD7096.G32 S335 1983

Arbeitslosigkeit in der Arbeitsgesellschaft / herausgegeben von Wolfgang Bonss und Rolf G. Heinze. 1. Aufl. Frankfurt am Main : Suhrkamp, 1984. 350 p. ; 18 cm. (Edition Suhrkamp. 1212 = n.F., Bd. 212) Includes bibliographies. ISBN 3-518-11212-0 : LC Card 84-192978
1. Unemployment - Psychological aspects. 2. Unemployment - Germany (West) - Psychological aspects. 3. Unemployment - France - Psychological aspects. I. Bonss, Wolfgang. II. Heinze, Rolf G., 1951-.
HD5708 .A72 1984

Arbeitslosigkeit und Neue Armut . (Bd. 1) Arbeitslosigkeit und Neue Armut in Düsseldorf . Bochum , c1986. 65 p. : ISBN 3-925222-03-0 LC Card 87-409036 DDC 331.13/794355 19
HD5780.D85 A73 1986

Arbeitslosigkeit und Neue Armut in Düsseldorf : ein Bericht über Ursachen, Ausmass und Folgen des sozialen Elends sowie Vorschläge für Gegenmassnahmen / Achim Trube ... [et al.] ; Projektgruppe Arbeitslosigkeit und Neue Armut (Hrsg.). Bochum : U. Schallwig, c1986. 65 p. : ill. ; 21 cm. (Arbeitslosigkeit und Neue Armut . Bd. 1) Includes bibliographies. ISBN 3-925222-03-0 LC Card 87-409036 DDC 331.13/794355 19
1. Unemployment - Germany (West) - Düsseldorf - Psychological aspects. 2. Poor - Germany (West) - Düsseldorf. 3. Düsseldorf (Germany) - Economic conditions. I. Trube, Achim. II. Projektgruppe Arbeitslosigkeit und Neue Armut (Germany). III. Series.
HD5780.D85 A73 1986

Arbeitslosigkeit und psychische Gesundheit . Schumacher, Egbert, 1960- München , c1986. 231 p. ; ISBN 3-89019-161-4 LC Card 87-108049 DDC 331.13/7/019 19
HD5708 .S38 1986

Arbeitsmarktatlas . Jansen, Paul Günter. [Düsseldorf] [1977] 206, A19 p. : LC Card 85-173256
HD5780.A76 J36 1977

Arbeitsmarkterfahrungen und Berufsorientierungen Jugendlicher : Beiträge zu einem Workshop der Sozialforschungsstelle Dortmund / Wilfried Kruse, Gertrud Kühnlein, Ursula Müller (Hrsg.). München : DJI, Deutsches Jugendinstitut, c1983. 177 p. : ill. ; 21 cm. (DJI Forschungsbericht) Revised papers originally presented at the workshop, held Dec. 16-17, 1982 in Dortmund. Includes bibliographies. CONTENTS. - Jugendliche und die Ausbildung für einen Arbeiterberuf / Heinz Stegmann -- Betriebliche Ausbildung als Erfahrungsprozess / Gertrud Kühnlein -- Betriebliche Personalpolitik und Reproduktionsinteressen junger Facharbeiter / Lothar Lappe -- Labilisierungstendenzen von Facharbeit in der Instandhaltung / J. Fischer, Th. Malsch, H.-J. Weissbach -- Zur Entstehung von Berufsbiographien / G. König ... [et al.] -- Lehrjahre und Berufskarriere / P. Wahler ... [et al.] -- Zukunftsentwürfe von Arbeitereltern für ihre Kinder / Norbert Schreiber -- Berufsträume und Traumberufe / Reinhard Peukert -- Anpassungsbereitschaft und Entäuschungsfestigkeit / Erich Wachtweitl, Andreas Witzl. ISBN 3-87966-202-9 LC Card 84-170074
1. Youth - Employment - Germany, West - Congresses. 2. Youth - Germany (West) - Attitudes - Congresses. 3. Education - Germany (West) - Congresses. I. Kruse, Wilfried, 1947-. II. Kühnlein, Gertrud. III. Müller, Ursula, 1949-. IV. Sozialforschungsstelle Dortmund. V. Series.
HD6276.G4 A73 1983

Arbeitsmarktpolitik für die Landwirtschaft und den ländlichen Raum / mit Beiträgen von Otto Lackinger, Karl Pelz, Manfred Sinz ; [Herausgeber, Hans Bach]. Graz : Kommissionsverlag, L. Stocker, c1984. 138 p. : ill. ; 21 cm. (Schriftenreihe für Agrarpolitik und Agrarsoziologie. Bd. 37) CONTENTS. - Zur Beschäftigungsproblematik in Oberösterreich / Otto Lackinger -- Arbeitsplatzpolitik für die Landwirtschaft / Karl Pelz -- Konsequenzen der Arbeitsmarktentwicklung und des technischen Fortschritts für die Entwicklung des ländlichen Raumes / Manfred Sinz. ISBN 3-900307-15-6 LC Card 85-186643
1. Agricultural laborers - Government policy - Austria. 2. Agriculture and state - Austria. 3. Rural development - Government policy - Austria. 4. Austria - Full employment policies. 5. Agricultural laborers - Austria - Supply and demand. I. Bach, Hans. II. Lackinger, Otto. Zur Beschäftigungsproblematik in Oberösterreich. 1984. III. Pelz, Karl. Arbeitsplatzpolitik für die Landwirtschaft. 1984. IV. Sinz, Manfred. Konsequenzen der Arbeitsmarktentwicklung und des technischen Fortschritts für die Entwicklung des ländlichen Raumes. 1984. V. Series.
HD1536.A9 A73 1984

Arbeitsmarktstrukturen im Wandel /. Hof, Bernd. Köln , c1985. 56 p. : ISBN 3-602-24737-6 LC Card 86-119065 DDC 331.12/5/0943 19
HD5779 .H638 1985

Arbeitsmarktstrukturen und Beschäftigungsprobleme im internationalen Vergleich . Hardes, Heinz-Dieter. Tübingen , 1981. xv, 484 p. : ISBN 3-16-344468-7 : LC Card 81-196609 DDC 331.13/7 19
HD5707.5 .H37 1981 ***NYPL [JLE 86-2544]***

Arbeitsmoral und Technikfeindlichkeit : über demoskopische Fehlschlüsse / Friedhelm Gehrmann (Hg.). Frankfurt ; New York : Campus, c1986. 274 p. : ill. ; 21 cm. (Soziale Indikatoren . 13) Papers presented at a meeting organized by the Studiengruppe "Soziale Indikatoren" of the Deutsche Gesellschaft für Soziologie and held at the Werner-Reimers-Stiftung, Feb. 28-Mar. 1, 1985. Bibliography: p. 263-272. CONTENTS. - Arbeitseintellungen im Spiegel der Demoskopie / Burkhard Strümpel -- Technikfeindlichkeit? / Bernhard von Rosenbladt -- Arbeitsmoral in der Freizeitgesellschaft / Randolph Vollmer -- Arbeitswerte / Peter Pawlowsky -- Was tut man nicht als Arbeitnehmer und wie schlimm es ist, wenn man es trotzdem tut? / Henry Puhe -- Verbesserte Arbeitsbedingungen bei gleichzeitiger Abnahme der Arbeitszufriedenheit? / Reinhard Rudat -- Die Relativität der Messinstrumente zur Bestimmung des

Wertwandels / Gerhard Schmidtchen -- Eine deutsche Sondersituation und keine gute / Elisabeth Noelle-Neumann -- Warum man "oben" nicht versteht, was die da "unten" bewegt / Michael von Klipstein -- Das Unbehagen um die Technik / Meinolf Dierkes -- Werteorientierte Personalpolitik, eine Antwort? / Artur Wollert -- Bedingungen einer positiven Bewertung beruflichen Aufstiegs, oder, Wer hat noch Lust auf Karriere? / Lutz von Rosenstiel und Friedemann W. Nerdinger. ISBN 3-593-33757-6 LC Card 86-212283
1. Work ethic - Germany (West) - Congresses. 2. Labor supply - Germany (West) - Effect of technological innovations on - Congresses. 3. Youth - Employment - Germany, West - Congresses. 4. Human capital - Germany (West) - Congresses. I. Gehrmann, Friedhelm, 1939-. II. Deutsche Gesellschaft für Soziologie. Sektion Soziale Indikatoren. III. Series.
HD8444 .A73 1986

Arbeitspapiere (Universität Innsbruck. Institut für Betriebswirtschaftslehre und Unternehmenspolitik) .
(Heft 14) Marzen, Walter. Ist die 35-Stunden-Woche ein Mittel zur Beseitigung der Arbeitslosigkeit? . Innsbruck , 1980. 29 leaves ; LC Card 85-170048
HD5108.2.A9 M37 1980

Arbeitspapiere zur Internationalen Politik, 0344-9815 .
(18) Machowski, Heinrich. RGW-Staaten und Dritte Welt . Bonn , 1981. iii, 84 p. ; ISBN 3-7713-0167-X LC Card 85-224767
HF1532.15.D44 M33 1981

(26) De Menil, George, 1940- Weltwirtschaftsgipfel /. Bonn [1983] iv, 130 p. ; ISBN 3-7713-0203-X LC Card 85-224780
HF1411 .D345 1983

(30) Marwege, Ulf, 1954- Neuorientierung im Westhandel der DDR? . Bonn , c1984. iv, 122 p. : ISBN 3-7713-0221-8 : LC Card 84-196602
HF3570.5.Z7 G75 1984

Arbeitsplätze morgen / herausgegeben von Werner Remmele, Manfred Sommer. Stuttgart : B.G. Teubner, c1986. 431 p. : ill. ; 24 cm. (Berichte des German Chapter of the ACM, 0724-9764 . Bd. 27) Papers presented at the 2nd Tagung of the Association for Computing Machinery, German Chapter, held in Marburg, March 10-14, 1986. Includes some summaries in English. Includes bibliographies. ISBN 3-519-02446-2 LC Card 86-171663
1. Labor supply - Effect of automation on - Congresses. 2. Labor supply - Effect of technological innovations on - Congresses. 3. Microelectronics - Social aspects - Congresses. I. Remmele, Werner. II. Sommer, Manfred. III. Series.
HD6331 .A695 1986

Arbeitsproduktivität und Beschäftigung . Pusse, Leo. Freiburg im Breisgau , c1984. viii, 311 p. : ISBN 3-448-01512-1 LC Card 85-138794
HC290.5.L3 P87 1984

Arbeitsrechtliche Schriftenreihe des Walter G. Mühlau Verlages .
(Heft 1) Alkohol im Betrieb und am Arbeitsplatz . Kiel , c1986. 52 p. : ISBN 3-87559-048-1 LC Card 87-409550 DDC 331.2/55 19
HF5549.5.A4 A476 1986

Der Arbeitsschutzbeauftragte . Peter, Gerd, 1941- Frankfurt , New York , c1986. 344 p. : ISBN 3-593-33633-2 LC Card 86-160932
HD6490.S52 G365 1986

Arbeitssicherheit sechsundachtzig.
Arbeitssicherheit '86 . Bonn [1986] 47, 46, 22 p. : LC Card 87-409083 DDC 363.1/12/0943 19
HD7708 .A7 1986

Arbeitssicherheit '86 : Unfallverhütungsbericht : Bericht dr Bundesregierung über den Stand der Unfallverhütung und das Unfallgeschehen in der Bundesrepublik Deutschland im Jahre 1985. Bonn : Der Bundesminister für Arbeit und Sozialordnung, Referat Öffentlichkeitsarbeit, [1986] 47, 46, 22 p. : ill. (some col.) ; 30 cm. (Reihe Berichte und Dokumentationen, 0172-7575) "Dezember 1986"--T.p. verso. LC Card 87-409083 DDC 363.1/12/0943 19
1. Industrial safety - Germany (West) - Statistics. 2. Accidents - Germany (West) - Statistics. 3. Children's accidents - Germany (West) - Statistics. I. Germany (West). Bundesministerium für Arbeit und Sozialordnung. II. Title: Arbeitssicherheit sechsundachtzig. III. Series: Reihe Berichte und Dokumentationen (Bonn, Germany).
HD7708 .A7 1986

Arbeitstagung Regionalpolitik und Politische Dezentralisierung in Südeuropa. Ungleiche Entwicklung und Regionalpolitik in Südeuropa . Bochum , 1985. 282 p. : ISBN 3-88339-441-6 : LC Card 85-205651
HC244.5 .U48 1985

Arbeitsunterlagen und Diskussionsbeiträge .
(Nr. 19 =) Calcagnotto, Gilberto. Brasilien 1974-1981 . Hamburg [1983] xi, 78 p. : LC Card 83-222930
HC187 .C143 1983

(Nr. 19) Calcagnotto, Gilberto. Brasilien 1974-1981 . Hamburg [1983] xi, 78 p. : LC Card 83-222930
HC187 .C143 1983

Die Arbeitsverhältnisse in deutschen Konsumgenossenschaften . Stuchlik, Karl-Heinz. Berlin , c1983. 533 p. : ISBN 3-428-05355-9 LC Card 83-191612
HD3338 .S88 1983

Arbeitswelt. Vilmar, Fritz, 1929- Arbeitswelt, Grundriss einer kritischen Soziologie der Arbeit /. Opladen , c1982. 256 p. : ISBN 3-8100-0400-6 (pbk.) LC Card 87-672408
HD6971 .V534x 1982

Arbeitswelt an der Wasserkante . Grüttner, Michael. Göttingen , 1984. 331 p. ; ISBN 3-525-35722-2 (Deut. Bibl.) LC Card 86-139479
HD8039.L82 G4335 1984

Arbeitswelt, Grundriss einer kritischen Soziologie der Arbeit /. Vilmar, Fritz, 1929- Opladen , c1982. 256 p. : ISBN 3-8100-0400-6 (pbk.) LC Card 87-672408
HD6971 .V534x 1982

Arbeitszeit im Wandel . Glaubrecht, Helmut. Freiburg im Breisgau , 1985. 273 p. : ISBN 3-448-01509-1 LC Card 85-216364 DDC 331.25/72 19
HD5109 .G55 1985

Arbeitszeitentwicklung und Arbeitszeitpolitik / Beirat für Wirtschafts- und Sozialfragen. Wien : Kommissionsverlag, C. Ueberreuter, 1984. 164 p. ; 24 cm. LC Card 85-137865
1. Hours of labor - Austria. 2. Hours of labor, Flexible - Austria. I. Beirat für Wirtschafts- und Sozialfragen.
HD5170 .A72 1984

Arbeitszeitverkürzung und sozialer Wandel . Steinisch, Irmgard. Berlin , New York , 1986. xiv, 640 p. : ISBN 3-11-010483-0 LC Card 87-110005 DDC 331.25/7/0973 19
HD5119.I52 U67 1986

Arbejderbevægelsens forhistorie . Christiansen, Niels Finn. [Copenhagen] , 1986. 188 p. : ISBN 87-87739-21-6 : LC Card 87-145749
HD6742 .C495 1986

Arbejdere og socialdemokrater i Faaborg omkring 1900 /. Venge, Mikael. [Fåborg] , 1986. 72 p. : ISBN 87-88421-01-5 LC Card 87-144687
HD6745.F33 V46 1986

Arbejdet . Weinreich, Torben. [Copenhagen] , c1984. 64 p. : ISBN 87-591-0003-6 : LC Card 84-197811
HD6250.D42 W45 1984

Arbejdsløshed og beskæftigelse : bevægelser på det danske arbejdsmarked / af H. Bunzel ... [et al.]. Aarhus : Økonomisk institut, Aarhus universitet ; [Copenhagen] : Økonomisk institut, Københavns universitet, [1983] 34 p. ; 21 cm. (Studies in labor market dynamics, 0108-2469 ; arbejdspapir. 83-4) "Juni 1983." Cover title. Bibliography: p. 34. LC Card 84-125513
1. Labor supply - Mathematical models. 2. Unemployment - Mathematical models. 3. Labor supply - Denmark - Mathematical models. 4. Unemployment - Denmark - Mathematical models. I. Bunzel, H. II. Series.
HD5701.6 .A73 1983

Arbejdsmarkedets kønsopdeling . Borchorst, Anette. Aalborg , 1984. 162 p. : ISBN 87-7307-252-4 LC Card 85-106008
HD6060.65.D4 B67 1984
NYPL [JFK 82-214 nr.15]

Arbejdsmarkedsnævn i arbejdsmarkedspolitikken /. Jørgensen, Henning, 1949- [Aalborg] [1985?]-<[1986]. v. <1-2 > : ISBN 87-88706-12-5 LC Card 87-104729
HD5799.A6 J64 1985

Arbejdspapir (Københavns universitet. Institut for samfundsfag og forvaltning) .
(1986/1) Petersen, Ib Damgaard. The political economy of long waves . København, Denmark [1986] 10, [1] p. : ISBN 87-7393-042-3 (pbk.) LC Card 86-214084 DDC 338.9 19
HB3729 .P47 1986

Arbetarskyddet inom kommuner och kommunalförbund /. Työsuojelu kunnissa ja kuntainliitoissa. Swedish. [Helsinki] [1983] 137 p. : LC Card 83-229126
HD7727.3 .T94618 1983

Arbete och arbetsformernas utveckling /. Cornell, Lasse. Göteborg , 1986. 161 p. : ISBN 91-85196-27-4 LC Card 86-212110
HD4851 .C67 1986

Arbete och lön vid Bredsjö bruk . Larsson, Mats, 1953- Uppsala , Stockholm , 1986. 233 p. : ISBN 91-554-1822-8 LC Card 86-212849
HD4966.I52 S845 1986

Arbetets döttrar / Eva Adolfsson ... [et al.]. [Stockholm] : Akademilitteratur, c1986. 2 v. ; 19 cm. (Kvinnor forskar) Includes bibliographies. CONTENTS. - 1. Litteratur- och idéhistoriska synpunkter -- 2. Sociologiska och historiska synpunkter. ISBN 91-7410-337-7 : LC Card 86-216247
1. Women - Employment - Sweden - History. I. Adolfsson, Eva, 1942-. II. Series.
HD6173 .A79 1986

Arbetsanpassning . Sweden. Samverkanskommittén. [Stockholm] [1984] 231 p. ; ISBN 91-38-08108-3 LC Card 84-193689
HD7256.S9 S945 1984

Arbetsförmedlingskontrakt . Sweden. Rekryteringsutredningen. [Stockholm] [1983] 195, 9, 2 p. ; ISBN 91-38-07728-0 LC Card 84-218571
HD4875.S8 S94 1983

Arbetslivscentrum (Stockholm, Sweden)
Ekonomisk demokrati . Stockholm [1984] ii, 169 p. : LC Card 85-108590
HD5660.S9 E38 1984

Arbetslöshetens offer. Stockholm : Statistiska centralbyrån : Liber, 1983. 56 p. : ill. ; 25 cm. (Levnadsförhållanden, 0347-7193 . rapport nr. 36) Sveriges officiella statistik Title on added t.p.: The victims of unemployment. Bibliography: p. 55-56. ISBN 91-38-07637-3 LC Card 83-181664
1. Unemployment - Sweden. 2. Unemployment - Sweden - Statistics. 3. Unemployed - Sweden. 4. Unemployed - Sweden - Statistics. I. Sweden. Statistiska centralbyrån. II. Series.
HD5803 .A72 1983

Arbetsrapport (Sveriges lantbruksuniversitet. U-landsavdelningen) .
(15) Fones-Sundell, Melinda. Implementing rural development in Botswana . Uppsala , 1983. 75 p. : LC Card 86-215071 DDC 338.1/86811 19
HD2133 .F66 1983

(32) Orback, Jens. Agriculture and incentives, the Tanzanian case . Uppsala , 1985. 37, [2] leaves, [1] leaf of plates : LC Card 86-215091 DDC 338.1/8 19
HD2128.5 .O73 1985

Arbetsskadeförsäkringens tillämpning . Hetzler, Antoinette, 1943- Lund [1984] 176 p. : ISBN 91-970351-3-0 : LC Card 84-159654
HD7103.65.S8 H48 1984

ARBITRAGE.
Harrington, Diana R., 1940- Modern portfolio theory, the capital asset pricing model, and arbitrage pricing theory . Englewood Cliffs, N.J. , c1987. x, 229 p. : ISBN 0-13-597261-2 (pbk.) LC Card 86-22693 DDC 332.6 19
HG4637 .H37 1987

ARBITRAGE - MATHEMATICAL MODELS.
Müller, Sigrid, 1953- Arbitrage pricing of contingent claims /. Berlin , New York , 1985. viii, 151 p. ; ISBN 0-387-15973-8 (U. S.) LC Card 85-22170 DDC 332.6/0724 19
HG4515.2 .M85 1985
NYPL [JLM 72-289 no.254]

Winkelmann, Michael. Aktienbewertung in Deutschland /. Königstein/Ts. , c1984. xii, 242 p. : ISBN 3-445-02377-8 LC Card 85-103576
HG4523 .W56 1984

Arbitrage pricing of contingent claims /. Müller, Sigrid, 1953- Berlin , New York , 1985. viii, 151 p. ; ISBN 0-387-15973-8 (U. S.) LC Card

85-22170 DDC 332.6/0724 19
HG4515.2 .M85 1985
NYPL [JLM 72-289 no.254]

ARBITRATION AND CONCILIATION, INDUSTRIAL. see **ARBITRATION, INDUSTRIAL.**

ARBITRATION, INDUSTRIAL.
Alternatives to arbitration /. Sydney , Boston , 1986. x, 468 p. ; ISBN 0-86861-857-8 (pbk.) LC Card 85-81482 DDC 331/.0994 19
HD5630.A6 A47 1986

ARBITRATION, INDUSTRIAL - AUSTRALIA.
Alternatives to arbitration /. Sydney , Boston , 1986. x, 468 p. ; ISBN 0-86861-857-8 (pbk.) LC Card 85-81482 DDC 331/.0994 19
HD5630.A6 A47 1986

ARBITRATION, INDUSTRIAL - GERMANY (WEST) - ADDRESSES, ESSAYS, LECTURES.
Aussperrung und Streik . Mainz , 1981, c1980. 173 p. ; ISBN 3-7867-0854-1 LC Card 81-101514 DDC 331.89/2943 19
HD5378 .A97 1981 *NYPL [JLD 86-2787]*

ARBITRATION, INDUSTRIAL - INDIA.
Kher, Manik. Conciliation and adjudication today /. Pune , c1985. 99 : LC Card 85-903388 DDC 344.54/0189143 345.404189143 19
LAW *NYPL [JLE 86-1567]*

The archaeology of economic ideas . Lowry, S. Todd. Durham , 1987. xviii, 366 p. ; ISBN 0-8223-0774-X LC Card 87-15507 DDC 330/.0938 19
HB108.A2 L68 1987

The archaeology of the Roman economy /. Greene, Kevin. London , 1986. 192 p. : ISBN 0-7134-4593-9 : LC Card 86-226151 DDC 330.937/06 19
HC39 .G72 1986

Hoi archaioi Hellēnes syngrapheis sto "Kephalaio" tou Marx /. Pappa, Hellē. Athēna , 1983. 112 p. ; LC Card 84-128852
HB501 .P24 1983

Archambault, Alberte. Garon-Audy, Muriel. Mobilités professionnelles et géographiques au Québec, 1954-64-74 /. Montréal , 1980. 61 p. ; LC Card 81-105620 DDC 331.12/7971 19
HD5717.5.C22 Q44 1980
NYPL [JLM 79-970 no.22]

Archambault, E. Les Economies non officielles /. Paris , 1984. 247 p. : ISBN 2-7071-1441-3 : LC Card 86-460169
HD2341 .E26 1984

Archeion Michaēl Iatrou, 1802-1893 /. Spēliōtakēs, K. K. Athēna , 1983. 189 p., [4] folded leaves of plates : LC Card 85-134031
HF3750.5.S64 A3 1983
NYPL [JFE 86-4131]

Archéologie. see **Besançon, France. Université. Annales littéraires.**

Archeologie van de economie . Klever, W. N. A. Nijmegen , 1986. 157 p. : ISBN 90-6772-005-4 : LC Card 86-165833
HB77 .K54 1986

Archier, Georges.
[Entreprise du 3e type. English]
The type 3 company / Georges Archier and Hervé Sérieyx ; translated by Michael Johnson. New York : Nichols Pub., 1987. xiv, 123 p. : ill. ; 22 cm. Translation of: L'entreprise du 3e type. Includes index. ISBN 0-89397-282-7 : LC Card 87-11203 DDC 658/.00973 19
1. Organizational effectiveness - Case studies. 2. Organizational change - Case studies. I. Serieyx, Hervé. II. Title. III. Title: Type three company.
HD58.9 .A7313 1987

ARCHITECTURAL ENGINEERING. see **BUILDING.**

ARCHITECTURE, DOMESTIC - GREAT BRITAIN - HISTORY.
Gaskell, S. Martin. Model housing from the great exhibition to the festival of Britain /. London , New York , 1986. x, 180 p. : ISBN 0-7201-1834-4 : LC Card 86-23775 DDC 363.5/0941 19
HD7333.A3 G37 1986

ARCHITECTURE, DOMESTIC - NEW YORK - ITHACA.
Sisler, Carol U., 1929- Enterprising families, Ithaca, New York . Ithaca, N.Y. (5 Cornell Walk, Ithaca 14850) , 1986. 159 p. : LC Card 86-81672 DDC 338/.092/2 B 19
HC102.5.A2 S55 1986

ARCHITECTURE, MODERN - 20TH CENTURY - UNITED STATES.
Hess, Alan. Googie . San Francisco, CA [1986]. 144 p. : ISBN 0-87701-334-9 (pbk.) : LC Card 85-17089 DDC 725/.71/0973 19
NA7856 .H47 1986
NYPL [3-MQWO 86-2210]

ARCHITECTURE, RURAL. see **ARCHITECTURE, DOMESTIC; COUNTRY HOMES.**

Archiv (Villigen, Switzerland) .
(Nr. 45) Basler Verkehrs-Betriebe (BVB) . Villigen AG, Schweiz , c1984. 56 p., [188] p. of plates, xv p. : ISBN 3-85649-045-0 : LC Card 84-160209
HE4919.B37 B37 1984

Archives & documents (Institut national de la statistique et des études économiques (France)) .
(no 100) Kerromes, Armelle. Tableaux normalisés simplifiés par région et département . Paris [1984] 273 p. ; ISBN 2-11-064692-6 : LC Card 86-176720
HA1214 1982p

(no 127) Quarré, Dominique. Les agents de l'Etat au 31 décembre 1980 /. Paris [1985] 305 p. ; ISBN 2-11-064767-1 : LC Card 86-162558
HD8013.F6 Q373 1985

(no 147) Cauwet, Martine. Images économiques des entreprises . Paris [1986] 41 p. ; ISBN 2-11-064902-X : LC Card 86-229455
HD9502.F72 C38 1986

(no 84) Huet, Maryse. La concentration des emplois féminins . Paris [1983] 138 p. : ISBN 2-11-064535-0 : LC Card 85-176290 DDC 331.4/12/0944 19
HD6145 .H79 1983

(no. 144) Statistique du mouvement de la population dans les D.O.M. . Paris [1985] 104 p. : ISBN 2-11-064898-8 : LC Card 86-216599
HB1003 .S73 1985

Archives départementales de l'Allier. Service éducatif. Histoire de la navigation sur l'Allier en Bourbonnais /. Clermont-Ferrand [France] , 1983. 61 p. : LC Card 84-150630
HE668.Z7 A454 1983

Archives départementales du Rhône. Service éducatif. Transports et échanges . [Lyon] , 1979. 64 p. ; LC Card 80-125866
HE192.F8 T73 1979

Archives du Lyonnais.
Lyon, l'argent, le commerce et la soie /. Lyon , c1986. 138 p. : ISBN 2-904638-63-6 : LC Card 86-184131
HC278.L9 L96 1986

ARCHIVES - MEXICO - SONORA (STATE) - CATALOGS.
Radding, Cynthia. [Acumulación originaria de capital agrario en Sonora.] La acumulación originaria de capital agrario en Sonora ; Registro de los archivos del Estado de Sonora /. [Hermosillo, Sonora] , 1981. 90 p. : LC Card 82-118209
HD329.S6 R33 1981

Archivio di Stato di Lecce. La Questione demaniale in Terra d'Otranto nel XIX secolo . [Roma] [Lecce] [1985?] 183 p., [6] leaves of plates : LC Card 86-180857
HD680.O87 Q47 1985

Archivio storico dell'industria italiana. Fonti.
Atti del Comitato dell'inchiesta industriale (1870-1874) . [Bologna?] [1984- v. <1-3 > ; LC Card 87-123944
HC304 .A87 1984

Le Condizioni industriali della provincia di Bergamo, 1891 . Bologna [1983] 130 p., [1] leaf of plates : LC Card 85-235349
HC307.B5 C59 1983

Arcila Farías, Eduardo, 1913- Fundamentos económicos del Imperio Español en América / Eduardo Arcila Farías. Caracas : Fondo Editorial de Humanidades y Educación, Universidad Central de Venezuela, 1985. 133 p. : ill. ; 22 cm. (Colección Estudio) Bibliography: p. 133. LC Card 85-242008
1. Spain - Colonies - America - Economic conditions. 2. Spain - Colonies - America - Economic policy. I. Series: Colección Estudio (Universidad Central de Venezuela. Fondo Editorial de Humanidades y Educación). II. Title.
HC389 .A73 1985

Arco civil service test tutor.
Czukor, John C. Beginning office worker /. New York , c1988. 291 p. ; ISBN 0-13-072018-6 (pbk.) : LC Card 87-20740 DDC 651.3/7/076 19
HF5547.5 .B414 1988

Arco's beginning office worker. Czukor, John C. Beginning office worker /. New York , c1988. 291 p. ; ISBN 0-13-072018-6 (pbk.) : LC Card 87-20740 DDC 651.3/7/076 19
HF5547.5 .B414 1988

Arco's Certified Professional Secretary® (CPS®) examination. Lindsell, Sheryl L. CPS®--Certified Professional Secretary® examination /. New York, N.Y. , c1987. xxx, 286 p. : ISBN 0-13-122805-6 (pbk.) : LC Card 87-11381 DDC 651.3/741/076 19
HF5547.5 .L554 1987

Arcq, Etienne. La C.S.C. et le programme gouvernemental de mars 1984 / par Etienne Arcq. Bruxelles : Centre de recherche et d'information socio-politiques, [1984] 23 leaves ; 30 cm. (Courrier hebdomadaire du CRISP, 0008-9664 . no 1032) Caption title. "Le 30 mars 1984." Includes bibliographical references and appendices. LC Card 84-171486
1. Confédération des syndicats chrétiens (Belgium). 2. Belgium - Politics and government - 1951-. 3. Trade-unions - Belgium. I. Title. II. Title: CSC et le programme gouvernemental de mars 1984. III. Series.
HD8502.C62 A73 1984

Arctic Slope Consulting Engineers. Western Arctic Coal Development Project : phase II final report / prepared by Arctic Slope Consulting Engineers ; [Kent M. Grinage, project manager]. Anchorage, Alaska : ASCE (313 E St., Suite 3, Anchorage, 99501), [1986] 2 v. : ill. (some col.) ; 29 cm. "Prepared for State of Alaska, Department of Community and Regional Affairs, and Alaska Native Foundation." "June 1986." Includes bibliographies. LC Card 87-621058 DDC 333.8/22/09798 19
1. Coal trade - Alaska. 2. Coal mines and mining - Alaska. 3. Coal - Alaska. I. Grinage, Kent M. II. Western Arctic Coal Development Project. III. Alaska. Dept. of Community and Regional Affairs. IV. Alaska Native Foundation. V. Title.
HD9547.A4 A85 1986

Ardill, John. The Tunnel . Chichester , New York , 1987. xxxi, 334 p. : ISBN 0-7458-0277-X : LC Card 87-17025 DDC 385/.312/0916336 19
HE380.G73 E547 1987

Arditi, Claude. Nourrir les villes en Afrique sub-saharienne /. Paris , c1985. 421 p. : ISBN 2-85802-562-X LC Card 86-222243
HD9017.S82 N68 1985

Are we on the road to a balanced budget? . Manchester, Paul B. Washington , 1986. v, 18 p. : LC Card 86-603373 DDC 353.0072/2 19
HJ2052 .M365 1986

Are you reading me? [motion picture] / HPS Productions. Falls Church, VA : AAA Foundation for Traffic Safety, 1985. 1 film reel (9 min.) : sd., col. ; 16 mm. Title from data sheet. Ages 16 through adult. Issued also as videorecording. Teaches the meanings of highway signs and designations. LC Card 85-702717 DDC 388.3 11
1. Traffic safety. 2. Traffic signs and signals. I. HPS Productions. II. AAA Foundation for Traffic Safety.
HE5614

Are you reading me? [videorecording] / HPS Productions. Falls Church, VA : AAA Foundation for Traffic Safety, 1985. 1 videocassette (9 min.) : sd., col. Title from data sheet. Ages 16 through adult. Issued as U-matic 3/4 in. or Beta 1/2 in. or VHS 1/2 in. Issued also as motion picture. Teaches the meanings of highway signs and designations. LC Card 85-702718 DDC 388.3 11
1. Traffic safety. 2. Traffic signs and signals. I. HPS Productions. II. AAA Foundation for Traffic Safety.
HE5614

Area planning and rural development /. Nanjundappa, D. M., 1930- New Delhi , c1981. viii, 52 p. ; LC Card 81-903723 DDC

307/.12/0954 19
HN690.Z9 C6649 1981 *NYPL [JLD 86-2687]*

Areas estatísticamente comparáveis do Rio Grande do Sul, 1940-80 : renda interna / equipe técnica, José Antônio Fialho Alonso ... [et al.]. Porto Alegre, RS : Secretaria de Coordenação e Planejamento, Fundação de Economia e Estatística, 1986. 186 p. : map ; 23 cm. Chiefly tables. Bibliography: p. [61]. LC Card 87-403481 DDC 339.381/65 19
1. National income - Brazil - Rio Grande do Sul - Accounting - Statistics. 2. Rio Grande do Sul (Brazil) - Economic condtions - Statistics. I. Alonso, José Antonio Fialho. II. Rio Grande do Sul (Brazil). Fundação de Economia e Estatística.
HC188.R4 A73 1986

Areas industriales de Costa Rica /. Matarrita Mena, José Joaquín. San José, Costa Rica, América Central [1986] 151 p. : ISBN 997-7500-01-0 LC Card 87-404258 DDC 338.097286 19
HC143 .M38 1986

Arellano, José Pablo.
Análisis de la previsión en Chile /. Santiago, Chile [1986] 309 p. : LC Card 87-115194
HD7156 .A78 1986

Foxley, Alejandro. Las desigualdades económicas y la acción del estado . México , 1980. 271 p. ; ISBN 968-16-0365-6 LC Card 82-215955 DDC 339.2/098 19
HC130.I5 F69 1980 *NYPL [JLD 86-2631]*

Modelo económico chileno . Santiago, Chile [1982] 606 p. ; LC Card 83-201307
HC192 .M63 1982

Políticas macro-económicas . Santiago de Chile [1986] 409 p. : LC Card 87-403669 DDC 338.98 19
HC125 .P657 1986

Arenal, Sandra.
Barroterán! : crónica de una tragedia / Sandra Arenal. [Mexico City?] : Editorial Macehual, c1984. 116 p. ; 17 cm. (Colección El Overol azul) ISBN 968-495-016-0 LC Card 85-195552
1. Coal miners - Mexico - Barroterán. 2. Mine accidents - Mexico - Barroterán. 3. Quality of work life - Mexico - Barroterán. I. Title. II. Series.
HD8039.M62 M63 1984

Sangre joven : las maquiladoras por dentro / Sandra Arenal.1a ed. México, D.F. : Editorial Nuestro Tiempo, 1986. 130 p., [2] p. of plates : ill. ; 19 cm. (Colección Charlas con trabajadores) ISBN 968-427-128-X LC Card 87-139058 DDC 331.4/87/0972 19
1. Women offshore assembly industry workers - Mexico - Interviews. 2. Offshore assembly industry - Employees - Health and hygiene - Mexico. I. Title. II. Series.
HD6073.O332 M4953 1986

Arend, Brigitte, 1953- Vom Lohnarbeiter zum Klienten : die Interessenkollision zwischen staatlicher Verwaltung und Arbeitslosen / Brigitte Arend, Gunter Hesse. Frankfurt am Main : A. Hain, c1986. 206 p. ; 21 cm. (Hochschulschriften: Sozialwissenschaften. 24) Bibliography: p. 195-206. ISBN 3-445-02490-1 LC Card 86-231993
1. Unemployment - Germany (West) - Psychological aspects. 2. Germany, West - Social policy. I. Hesse, Gunter, 1949-. II. Title.
HD5708 .A74 1986

Arens, Alvin A. Auditing, an integrated approach / Alvin A. Arens, James K. Loebbecke. 4th ed. Englewood Cliffs, N.J. : Prentice Hall, c1988. p. cm. (Prentice-Hall series in accounting) Includes index. ISBN 0-13-051814-X LC Card 87-26359 DDC 657/.45 19
1. Auditing. I. Loebbecke, James K. II. Title. III. Series.
HF5667 .A69 1988

Areshchenko, V. D. (Vladimir Denisovich) Ekonomika trudovykh resursov /. Minsk , 1985. 159 p. ; LC Card 87-156829
HD5796 .E35 1985

Arestis, Philip, 1941- Post Keynesian economic theory . Sussex , Armonk, N.Y. , 1985. xii, 235 p. ; ISBN 0-87332-318-1 LC Card 84-23615 DDC 330/.09/04 19
HB87 .P62 1985 *NYPL [JLD 87-1155]*

ARF electronic media and research technologies-IV Workshop. Advertising Research Foundation Key Issues Workshop (1985 : New York, N.Y.) Transcript proceedings . New York, NY (3 E. 54th St., New York 10022-3180) , c1985. 174 p. : LC Card 86-214476 DDC 659.14/3/0973 19
HF6146.T42 A27 1985a

ARF fifteen second commercials workshop. Advertising Research Foundation Key Issues Workshop (1985 : New York, N.Y.) Transcript proceedings . New York, NY (3 E. 54th St., New York 10022-3180) , c1985. 161 p. : LC Card 86-211136 DDC 659.14/3/0973 19
HF6146.T42 A27 1985

ARF 15-second commercials workshop. Advertising Research Foundation Key Issues Workshop (1985 : New York, N.Y.) Transcript proceedings . New York, NY (3 E. 54th St., New York 10022-3180) , c1985. 161 p. : LC Card 86-211136 DDC 659.14/3/0973 19
HF6146.T42 A27 1985

Argany Comas, Isabel. La segona residència a Catalunya : dades estadístiques i localització geogràfica / Isabel Argany Comas.[1a ed.]. [Barcelona] : Generalitat de Catalunya, Departament de Política Territorial i Obres Públiques, Direcció General d'Arquitectura i Habitatge : Cambra Oficial de la Propietat Urbana de Barcelona, [1984] 71 p. ; 25 cm. "2"--Spine. Includes bibliographical references. LC Card 86-160322
1. Second Homes - Spain - Catalonia. I. Title.
HD7289.3.S72 C383 1984

Argelia. see **Algeria.**

Argemí i d'Abadal, Lluís, 1945- Lluch, Ernest, 1937- Agronomía y fisiocracia en España, 1750-1820 /. Valencia [1985?] lxi, 215 p. ; ISBN 84-00-05965-4 LC Card 85-240630
HD2022 .L58 1985

Argenti, Gisela. Cambio técnico, trabajo y educación : notas preliminares sobre el caso uruguayo / Gisela Argenti, Carlos Filgueira. Montevideo : Centro de Informaciones y Estudios del Uruguay, 1985. 91, 70 leaves : ill. ; 29 cm. (Serie Informes . 28/85) Includes bibliographies. LC Card 87-124118
1. Technological innovations - Economic aspects - Uruguay. 2. Labor supply - Uruguay. 3. Education - Uruguay. I. Filgueira, Carlos H. II. Series: Serie Informes (Centro de Informaciones y Estudios del Uruguay) , 85/28. III. Title.
HC235.T4 A74 1985

Argentina . Panettieri, José. [Buenos Aires] , c1986. 219 p. ; ISBN 950-25-1317-7 LC Card 86-226796
HC175 .P334 1986

Argentina.
Cimillo, Elsa. La terciarización del empleo en la Argentina. [Buenos Aires] [1985] 23, [41], 3 p. ; LC Card 87-123708 DDC 381/.1/0982 19
HF5429.6.A7 C56 1985

ARGENTINA - APPROPRIATIONS AND EXPENDITURES - STATISTICS - HISTORY.
Argentina. Dirección Nacional de Programación Presupuestaria. Presupuesto de la administración nacional, 1961-1979. [Buenos Aires] [1982] 79 leaves : LC Card 82-199149
HJ2076 .A74 1982

ARGENTINA - CENSUS, 1960.
Chackiel, Juan. La fuerza de trabajo en los países de la Cuenca del Plata según los censos de 1960 /. San José, Costa Rica , 1976. iv, 81 p. : LC Card 83-169596
HD5746.A6 C42 1976

ARGENTINA - CENSUS, 1969.
Pantelides, Edith A. El hogar como unidad de análisis de los datos censales . Santiago de Chile , 1972. ii, 48 p. : LC Card 83-169482
HA755 .U53 no. 147 HB849.49

Argentina. Comisión Nacional de Rehabilitación del Lisiado. Comisión Nacional de Rehabilitación del Lisiado. [Buenos Aires] : La Comisión, 1965. [24] leaves ; 28 cm. Cover title. At head of title: Ministerio de Asistencia Social y Salud Pública. LC Card 85-110867
1. Comisión Nacional de Rehabilitación del Lisiado. 2. Rehabilitation - Argentina. I. Title.
HD7256.A7 A74 1965

ARGENTINA - COMMERCE.
Exportaciones industriales . Buenos Aires, República Argentina [1987] 231 p. ; LC Card 87-405033 DDC 338.4/767/0982 19
HD9734.A7 E96 1987

ARGENTINA - COMMERCE - ANDES REGION.
Comercio de granos entre la Argentina y los países del Grupo Andino. [Buenos Aires, Argentina] , 1983. ii, 154 p. : LC Card 86-201891
HD9044.A8 C65 1983

ARGENTINA - COMMERCE - CHILE.
Argerich, Federico Raúl. Posibilidades de intercambio compensado entre Argentina y Chile y exportaciones graníferas al area del Pacífico, ambos por el paso de San Francisco /. Córdoba , 1985. 35 p. ; LC Card 87-402749 DDC 382/.0983/082 19
HF3418.A7 A8 1985

ARGENTINA - DEPENDENCY ON FOREIGN COUNTRIES.
Knapp, Johannes, 1953- Argentinien und Australien . Heidelberg , c1983. 151 p. : ISBN 3-88326-129-7 LC Card 83-240132
HC175 .K58 1983

Perdía, Roberto Cirilo. Existe otra Argentina posible /. Buenos Aires , 1986. 276 p. : ISBN 950-97640-0-0 LC Card 87-139879 DDC 336.3/4/0982 19
HG3881.5.I58 P47 1986

La Argentina descentralizada /. Quadri Castillo, Mario. [Buenos Aires] , c1986. 236 p. : ISBN 950-23-0322-9 LC Card 87-402244 DDC 330.982/064 19
HC175 .Q33 1986

Argentina. Dirección Nacional de Programación Presupuestaria. Presupuesto de la administración nacional, 1961-1979. [Buenos Aires] : Ministerio de Economía, Hacienda y Finanzas, Subsecretaría de Hacienda, Dirección Nacional de Programación Presupuestaria, [1982] 79 leaves : ill. ; 30 cm. Chiefly tables. LC Card 82-199149
1. Budget - Argentina - Statistics - History. 2. Argentina - Appropriations and expenditures - Statistics - History. I. Title.
HJ2076 .A74 1982

ARGENTINA - ECONOMIC CONDITIONS - 1945-
Daneri, Oscar. El atípico caso argentino . Buenos Aires , 1986. 412 p. : ISBN 950-43-0291-4 LC Card 87-400194 DDC 338.982 19
HC175 .D26 1986

ARGENTINA - ECONOMIC CONDITIONS - 1945-1983.
Boneo, Horacio. Desarrollo regional, incentivos fiscales y localización industrial /. Buenos Aires, Argentina [1985] 160 p. : ISBN 950-95720-8-X *NYPL [JLD 86-4218]*

Cafasso, José. Ficción y realidad de la economía argentina (1976-1983) /. [Bahía Blanca, Argentina] [1983] 61 p. ; LC Card 87-400128 DDC 330.982/064 19
HC175 .C15 1983

Canitrot, Adolfo. Orden social y monetarismo /. Buenos Aires, Argentina [1982 or 1983] 50 p. ; LC Card 83-213595
HC173 .C35 1982

García, Valeriano F. A critical inquiry into Argentine economic history, 1946-1970 /. New York , 1987. vi, 127 p. : ISBN 0-8240-1361-1 (alk. paper) : LC Card 87-7620 DDC 330.982/062 19
HG815 .G27 1987

Knapp, Johannes, 1953- Argentinien und Australien . Heidelberg , c1983. 151 p. : ISBN 3-88326-129-7 LC Card 83-240132
HC175 .K58 1983

The Political economy of Argentina, 1946-83 /. Pittsburgh, Pa. , 1988. p. cm. ISBN 0-8229-1148-5 LC Card 87-24412 DDC 338.982 19
HC175 .P623 1988

ARGENTINA - ECONOMIC CONDITIONS - 1983-
Argentina 1984 . [Buenos Aires?] [1984] 95 p. ; LC Card 85-132860
HJ8569 .A75 1984

Nassif, Luís. O cruzado . São Paulo/SP , 1986.

255 p. : LC Card 86-224110
HG835 .N37 1986

Rubinstein, Juan Carlos, 1928- Estructura social, estado democrático y cambio político /. [Buenos Aires] , c1986. 159 p. : ISBN 950-23-0292-3 LC Card 87-114981 DDC 330.982/064 19
HC175 .R783 1986

ARGENTINA - ECONOMIC CONDITIONS - REGIONAL DISPARITIES - HISTORY.
Quadri Castillo, Mario. La Argentina descentralizada /. [Buenos Aires] , c1986. 236 p. : ISBN 950-23-0322-9 LC Card 87-402244 DDC 330.982/064 19
HC175 .Q33 1986

ARGENTINA - ECONOMIC POLICY.
Alschuler, Lawrence R., 1941- Multinationals and maldevelopment . New York , 1988. xii, 218 p. : ISBN 0-312-00531-8 : LC Card 87-4307 DDC 338.9 19
HD82 .A5493 1988

Argentina 1984 . [Buenos Aires?] [1984] 95 p. ; LC Card 85-132860
HJ8569 .A75 1984

Cafasso, José. Ficción y realidad de la economía argentina (1976-1983) /. [Bahía Blanca, Argentina] [1983] 61 p. ; LC Card 87-400128 DDC 330.982/064 19
HC175 .C15 1983

Canitrot, Adolfo. Orden social y monetarismo /. Buenos Aires, Argentina [1982 or 1983] 50 p. ; LC Card 83-213595
HC173 .C35 1982

Conesa, Eduardo R. Bases y puntos de partida para la recuperación de la economía argentina . Buenos Aires, Argentina , c1986. 178 p. : ISBN 950-53-7109-8 LC Card 87-400257 DDC 338.982 19
HC175 .C6145 1986

Conesa, Eduardo R. Fuga de capitales . Buenos Aires , 1986. 78 p. : LC Card 87-400256 DDC 332.4/5 19
HG3931 .C66 1986

Daneri, Oscar. El atípico caso argentino . Buenos Aires , 1986. 412 p. : ISBN 950-43-0291-4 LC Card 87-400194 DDC 338.982 19
HC175 .D26 1986

Feldman, Ernesto V. (Ernesto Víctor) Crisis financiera y endeudamiento externo en la Argentina /. [Buenos Aires] , c1986. 184 p. ; ISBN 950-25-1313-4 LC Card 86-182663
HG185.A7 F45 1986

Fundación de Investigaciones Económicas Latinoamericanas (Buenos Aires, Argentina) Gasto público . [Buenos Aires] , 1986. 6 v. in 8 : LC Card 87-403573 DDC 354.820072/252 19
HJ2075 .F86 1986

García, Valeriano F. A critical inquiry into Argentine economic history, 1946-1970 /. New York , 1987. vi, 127 p. : ISBN 0-8240-1361-1 (alk. paper) : LC Card 87-7620 DDC 330.982/062 19
HG815 .G27 1987

Gómez de Reyes, María Teresa. Experiencias de políticas de estabilización . México, D.F. , 1985. iv, 66 leaves ; LC Card 87-122042 DDC 338.982 19
HC125 .G57 1985

Lindenboim, Javier. Monetarismo y mercado de trabajo . Buenos Aires, Argentina , c1985. x, 471 p. : ISBN 950-9370-05-3 LC Card 87-122243 DDC 331.12/0982/73 19
HD5750.R56 L56 1985

Nassif, Luís. O cruzado . São Paulo/SP , 1986. 255 p. : LC Card 86-224110
HG835 .N37 1986

Panettieri, José. Argentina . [Buenos Aires] , c1986. 219 p. ; ISBN 950-25-1317-7 LC Card 86-226796
HC175 .P334 1986

Peláez, Carlos Manuel. O cruzado e o austral . São Paulo , 1986. 174 p. : ISBN 85-22-40173-X LC Card 87-102770 DDC 332.4/981 19
HG835 .P43 1986

Perdía, Roberto Cirilo. Existe otra Argentina posible /. Buenos Aires , 1986. 276 p. : ISBN 950-97640-0-0 LC Card 87-139879 DDC 336.3/4/0982 19
HG3881.5.I58 P47 1986

The Political economy of Argentina, 1946-83 /. Pittsburgh, Pa. , 1988. p. cm. ISBN 0-8229-1148-5 LC Card 87-24412 DDC 338.982 19
HC175 .P623 1988

Prebisch, Raúl. La crisis del desarrollo argentino . Buenos Aires , c1986. 195 p. ; ISBN 950-0-26293-2 LC Card 86-229773
HC180.S3 P74 1986

Rosales Díaz, Ramón. Programas de reactivación económica y sistemas financieros . [Lima] , 1986. 68 p. : LC Card 87-400247 DDC 332.4/982 19
HG815 .R67 1986

ARGENTINA - FOREIGN ECONOMIC RELATIONS.
Prebisch, Raúl. La crisis del desarrollo argentino . Buenos Aires , c1986. 195 p. ; ISBN 950-0-26293-2 LC Card 86-229773
HC180.S3 P74 1986

ARGENTINA - INDUSTRIES.
Resultados de la encuesta sobre expectativas de producción e inversión de las empresas industriales /. Buenos Aires , 1965. 81 leaves : LC Card 85-114982
HC180.I52 R47 1965

ARGENTINA - MANUFACTURES.
Exportaciones industriales . Buenos Aires, República Argentina [1987] 231 p. ; LC Card 87-405033 DDC 338.4/767/0982 19
HD9734.A7 E96 1987

ARGENTINA - MANUFACTURES - STATISTICS.
Evolución de la industria manufacturera, 1982-1984. Buenos Aires, República Argentina [1986] 115 p. : LC Card 86-226786
HD4999 .E95 1986

Argentina. Ministerio de Trabajo y Seguridad Social.
Informe del gobierno argentino sobre asuntos laborales /. Buenos Aires, República Argentina , 1965. 115 leaves ; LC Card 85-115096
HD8266.5 .I53 1965

Szretter, Héctor. La terciarización del empleo en la Argentina. Buenos Aires , 1985. iv, 82, 3 p. ; LC Card 87-122558 DDC 331.7/6164046/0982 19
HD8039.D52 A657 1985

Argentina, país productor de capitales /. Podestá, Ricardo Augusto. Mendoza , 1976. 11 p. ; LC Card 84-196569
HC180.C3 P62 1976

ARGENTINA - POLITICS AND GOVERNMENT - 1860-1910.
Panettieri, José. Argentina . [Buenos Aires] , c1986. 219 p. ; ISBN 950-25-1317-7 LC Card 86-226796
HC175 .P334 1986

ARGENTINA - POLITICS AND GOVERNMENT - 1910-1943.
Panettieri, José. Argentina . [Buenos Aires] , c1986. 219 p. ; ISBN 950-25-1317-7 LC Card 86-226796
HC175 .P334 1986

ARGENTINA - POLITICS AND GOVERNMENT - 1983-
Figuerola, Francisco José. Teoría de la democracia social . Buenos Aires , 1986. xxv, 492 p. ; ISBN 950-43-0832-5 LC Card 86-184525
HD2081 .F54 1986

Perdía, Roberto Cirilo. Existe otra Argentina posible /. Buenos Aires , 1986. 276 p. : ISBN 950-97640-0-0 LC Card 87-139879 DDC 336.3/4/0982 19
HG3881.5.I58 P47 1986

Rubinstein, Juan Carlos, 1928- Estructura social, estado democrático y cambio político /. [Buenos Aires] , c1986. 159 p. : ISBN 950-23-0292-3 LC Card 87-114981 DDC 330.982/064 19
HC175 .R783 1986

Argentina. Secretaría de Energía. El Gas y su contribución al desarrollo económico nacional. [Buenos Aires] [1983 or 1984] 316 p. : LC Card 84-222069
HD9581.A72 G37 1983

Argentina. Secretaría de Planificación. Szretter, Héctor. La terciarización del empleo en la Argentina. Buenos Aires , 1985. iv, 82, 3 p. ; LC Card 87-122558 DDC 331.7/6164046/0982 19
HD8039.D52 A657 1985

ARGENTINA - SOCIAL CONDITIONS.
Panettieri, José. Argentina . [Buenos Aires] , c1986. 219 p. ; ISBN 950-25-1317-7 LC Card 86-226796
HC175 .P334 1986

ARGENTINA - SOCIAL CONDITIONS - 1983-
Rubinstein, Juan Carlos, 1928- Estructura social, estado democrático y cambio político /. [Buenos Aires] , c1986. 159 p. : ISBN 950-23-0292-3 LC Card 87-114981 DDC 330.982/064 19
HC175 .R783 1986

Argentina 1984 : el Partido Radical, el acuerdo con el F.M.I. y la deuda externa. [Buenos Aires?] : Instituto de Estudios Latinoamericanos, [1984] 95 p. ; 22 cm. LC Card 85-132860
1. Debts, External - Argentina. 2. Argentina - Economic policy. 3. Monetary policy - Argentina. 4. Argentina - Economic conditions - 1983-. 5. International Monetary Fund - Argentina. I. Instituto de Estudios Latinoamericanos (Buenos Aires, Argentina).
HJ8569 .A75 1984

Argentine Republic. Ministerio de Economía. Instituto Nacional de Planification Económica. see Instituto Nacional de Planificación Económica.

Argentinien und Australien . Knapp, Johannes, 1953- Heidelberg , c1983. 151 p. : ISBN 3-88326-129-7 LC Card 83-240132
HC175 .K58 1983

Argenziano, R. (Riccardo) Strategie industriali e prospettive di sviluppo nel settore automobilistico /. Milano [1985] 235 p. : ISBN 88-14-00541-9 (pbk.) : LC Card 85-183335 DDC 338.4/76292/0945 19
HD9710.A2 S86 1985 ***NYPL [JLE 87-493]***

Argenziano, Riccardo. Sviluppo della finanza internazionale e interdipendenza dei sistemi finanziari . [Italy] [1984] iv, 204 p. : ISBN 88-14-00203-7 : LC Card 84-238589 DDC 332/.042 19
HG205.S85 S85 1984 ***NYPL [JLE 86-482]***

ARGENZIANO, RICCARDO.
Sviluppo della finanza internazionale e interdipendenza dei sistemi finanziari . [Italy] [1984] iv, 204 p. : ISBN 88-14-00203-7 : LC Card 84-238589 DDC 332/.042 19
HG205.S85 S85 1984 ***NYPL [JLE 86-482]***

Argerich, Federico Raúl. Posibilidades de intercambio compensado entre Argentina y Chile y exportaciones graníferas al area del Pacífico, ambos por el paso de San Francisco / por Federico Raúl Argerich. Córdoba : Gobierno de Córdoba, 1985. 35 p. ; 30 cm. Cover title. On cover: III Seminario Geoeconómico de Integración del Cono Sur. LC Card 87-402749 DDC 382/.0983/082 19
1. Chile - Commerce - Argentina. 2. Argentina - Commerce - Chile. 3. Grain - Chile - Transportation. 4. Grain - Argentina - Transportation. 5. San Francisco Pass (Argentina and Chile). I. Title.
HF3418.A7 A8 1985

Argos Villar, José Carlos. El movimiento obrero en Cantabria (1955-1977) / José Carlos Argos Villar, José Emilio Gómez Díaz ; prólogo de J.R. Saiz Viadero. [Santander?] : J.E. Gómez Díaz, [1982?] 227 p. ; 19 cm. (Puntal libros) ISBN 84-300-6979-8 LC Card 86-203186
1. Labor and laboring classes - Spain - Cantabria - History - 20th century. 2. Trade-unions - Spain - Cantabria - History - 20th century. 3. Strikes and lockouts - Spain - Cantabria - History - 20th century. I. Gómez Díaz, José Emilio. II. Title.
HD8589.C3 A74 1982

Argüelles, Alfonso. Los Oscos y la Cuenca del Eo : situación y perspectivas / [textos, Alfonso Argüelles, Rosa María González-Corugedo, Arturo Martín]. [Asturias] : Servicio de Publicaciones, Comunidad Autónoma del Principado de Asturias, Consejería de Agricultura y Pesca, [1984?] ix, 317 p. : ill. (some col.), maps ; 25 cm. ISBN 84-505-0237-3 LC Card 86-174593

1. Asturias (Spain) - Industries. 2. Asturias (Spain) - Population. 3. Housing - Spain - Asturias. 4. Public utilities - Spain - Asturias. 5. Communication and traffic - Spain - Asturias. 6. Asturias - Politics and government - Public opinion. 7. Public opinion - Spain - Asturias. I. González Corugedo, Rosa. II. Martín, Arturo. III. Consejería de Agricultura y Pesca del Principado de Asturias. IV. Title.
HC387.A7 A74 1984

Argueta, Mario. Historia laboral de Honduras : de la conquista al siglo XIX / Mario Argueta.1a ed. [Tegucigalpa] : Secretaría de Cultura y Turismo, Dirección General de Cultura, Departamento de Publicaciones, con el patrocinio de la Organización de Estados Americanos, 1985. 204 p. ; 19 cm. "Premio de ensayo "Rafael Heliodoro Valle, 1983." Includes bibliographical references. LC Card 85-199862
1. Labor and laboring classes - Honduras - History. I. Title.
HD8155 .A74 1985

Argument Studienhefte .
(SH 59) Wegner, Gerhard, 1953- Bauern, Kapital und Staat in Kenia . Berlin , c1983. 94 p. : ISBN 3-88619-038-2 : LC Card 85-171380
HD1538.K4 W44 1983

ARGUMENTATION. see **DEBATES AND DEBATING.**

Arguments for socialism.
Sutcliffe, Robert B. Hard times . London , 1983. 118 p. ; ISBN 0-86104-505-X (pbk.) : LC Card 83-126438 DDC 330.9/04 19
HC59 .S8873 1983 **NYPL [JLD 86-4088]**

Argyris, Chris, 1923-
Personality and organization : the conflict between system and the individual / Chris Argyris. New York : Garland, 1987, c1957. xiii, 291 p. ; 23 cm. (Continuity in administrative science) Reprint. Originally published: New York : Harper, 1957. Bibliography: p. 251-284. Includes index. ISBN 0-8240-8200-1 (alk. paper) : LC Card 86-27054 DDC 658.4 19
1. Organizational behavior. 2. Interorganizational relations. 3. Personnel management. I. Title. II. Series.
HD58.7 .A75 1987

Social science approaches to business behavior /. New York , 1987. vii, 183 p. : ISBN 0-8240-8201-X (alk. paper) : LC Card 86-25802 DDC 658.4 19
HD58.7 .S66 1987

Arhin, Kwame. The expansion of cocoa production in Ghana : the working conditions of migrant cocoa farmers in the central and western regions / Kwame Arhin. [Ghana] : K. Arhin, [1985] xiii, 137 p., [5] p. of plates : ill., maps ; 25 cm. Bibliography: p. 136-137. LC Card 86-222543 DDC 338.1/7374/09667 19
1. Cocoa farmers - Ghana. 2. Migration, Internal - Ghana. I. Title.
HD8039.C6362 G42 1985

Arias Abellán, Jesús. Propiedad y usos de la tierra en el Marquesado del Cenete / Jesús Arias Abellán. [Granada] : Universidad de Granada, 1984. iv, 439 p. : ill. ; 21 cm. (Colección monográfica. 85) Bibliography: p. [427]-434. ISBN 84-338-0229-1 LC Card 86-214060
1. Land tenure - Spain - Cenete - History. 2. Land use - Spain - Cenete - History. I. Series: Colección monográfica. Universidad de Granada, 85. II. Title.
HD779.C4 A75 1984

Arias, Oscar. see **Arias Sánchez, Oscar.**

Arias, Patricia. Guadalajara, la gran ciudad de la pequeña industria /. Zamora, Mich. , c1985. 301 p. : ISBN 968-7230-12-6 LC Card 86-191608
HD2346.M42 G824 1985

Arias Sánchez, Oscar. Democracia, independencia y sociedad latinoamericana / Oscar Arias Sánchez. 2a ed. San José, Costa Rica : Editorial CEDAL, 1985. 100 p. ; 18 cm. (Colección Cuadernos CEDAL . 7) ISBN 997-7956-09-X LC Card 87-400690 DDC 320.97286 19
1. Costa Rica - Economic conditions - 1948-. 2. Costa Rica - Politics and government - 1948-. 3. Socialism - Costa Rica. 4. Socialism - Latin America. I. Title. II. Series.
HC143 .A773 1985

Arid and Semi Arid Lands Development Project (Kenya) Nilsson, Roy. Kitui water resources development study . Nairobi, Kenya [1982] 13, [31] leaves : LC Card 85-980998 DDC 333.91/009676/24 19
HD1699.K42 K586 1982

ARID REGIONS AGRICULTURE - BRAZIL - CEARÁ (STATE)
Casimiro, Liana Maria Carleial de. Seca . Fortaleza-Ceará [19]84. 63 p. ; LC Card 86-130055 DDC 330.981/31063 19
HC188.C4 C29 1984

ARID REGIONS AGRICULTURE - BRAZIL, NORTHEAST.
Guerra, Paulo de Brito, 1914- A civilização da seca . Fortaleza , 1981. 324 p. : LC Card 82-231215 DDC 361.6/0981/3 19
HT395.B72 N63 1981 **NYPL [JLD 86-2873]**

ARID REGIONS AGRICULTURE - GOVERNMENT POLICY - BRAZIL, NORTHEAST.
Avaliação do polonordeste e do Projeto Sertanejo. Fortaleza , 1985. 314 p. : LC Card 87-402900 DDC 338.981/3 19
HC188.N6 A94 1985

Arief, Melanie Sritua. The Malaysian economy and politics, 1963-1983 : a bibliography / Melanie Sritua Arief. East Balmain, N.S.W., Australia : Published by ROSECONS for the Southeast Asia Research and Development Institute, c1984. iv, 364 p. ; 21 cm. Includes indexes. LC Card 85-942460 DDC 016.3309595/053 19
1. Malaysia - Economic conditions - Bibliography. 2. Malaysia - Politics and government - Bibliography. I. Title.
HC445.5 .A84 1984

Ariel economía. Serie Ciencias empresariales.
Cuervo García, Alvaro. Manual de sistema financiero . Barcelona , 1987. 427 p. : ISBN 84-344-2013-9 LC Card 87-135198
HG186.S6 C84 1987

La aristocracia del dinero en Venezuela actual, 1945-1985 /. Brito Figueroa, Federico. Barquisimeto, Venezuela , 1986- v. <1 > ; ISBN 980-608-700-3 (v. 1) : LC Card 87-404343 DDC 305.5/234/0987 19
HG185.V4 B75 1986

Aristopoiēsis paragōgēs Krētēs eis to plaision tēs Eurōpaikēs Oik. Koinotētos /. Kalitsounakēs, Dēmētrios E. Hērakleion Krētēs , 1963. p. 167-173 ; LC Card 86-235201
HE595.F3 K35 1963

The Aristotelian analysis of usury /. Langholm, Odd Inge, 1928- Bergen [Norway] , New York, NY , c1984. 153 p. ; ISBN 82-00-07290-8 LC Card 85-167906 DDC 332.8/3/09 19
HB551 .L36 1984 **NYPL [JLD 86-2545]**

ARISTOTLE - INFLUENCE.
Pappa, Hellē. Hoi archaioi Hellēnes syngrapheis sto "Kephalaio" tou Marx /. Athēna , 1983. 112 p. ; LC Card 84-128852
HB501 .P24 1983

ARITHMETIC, COMMERCIAL. see **BUSINESS MATHEMATICS.**

Arizona. Dept. of Commerce. Arizona 1986 economic profile. Phoenix, AZ (1700 W. Washington, Phoenix 85007) [1986] 28 p. : LC Card 86-622323 DDC 330.9791/053 19
HC107.A6 A763 1986

ARIZONA - ECONOMIC CONDITIONS.
Arizona 1986 economic profile. Phoenix, AZ (1700 W. Washington, Phoenix 85007) [1986] 28 p. : LC Card 86-622323 DDC 330.9791/053 19
HC107.A6 A763 1986

ARIZONA - PUBLIC LANDS.
McColly, Robert A. Availability of federally owned minerals for exploration and development in western states . [Avondale, Md.] , Washington, DC [1987] iv, 27 p. : LC Card 87-600086 DDC 333.8/5/09791 19
HD243.A7 M36 1987

Arizona 1986 economic profile. Phoenix, AZ (1700 W. Washington, Phoenix 85007) : Arizona Dept. of Commerce, [1986] 28 p. : ill. (some col.), maps ; 28 cm. Cover title. LC Card 86-622323 DDC 330.9791/053 19
1. Arizona - Economic conditions. 2. Industrial promotion - Arizona. I. Arizona. Dept. of Commerce.
HC107.A6 A763 1986

Arkansas. Employment Security Division. Research and Analysis Section.
Occupational employment statistics program . [Little Rock, Ark.] (P.O. Box 2981, Little Rock 72203) [1986] v leaves, 223 p. ; LC Card 87-620868 DDC 331.12/51/0009767021 19
HD5725.A8 O264 1986

Occupational trends, 1982-1995. Little Rock, AR (P.O. Box 2981, Little Rock, AR 72203) [1986]- v. ; **NYPL [JLM 87-353]**

ARKANSAS - MANUFACTURES - EMPLOYEES - STATISTICS.
Staffing patterns for manufacturing industries and hospitals /. Little Rock, Ark. [1983?] vi leaves, 249 p. ; LC Card 86-623216 DDC 331.12/57/09767 19
HD5725.A8 S79 1983

ARKANSAS - OCCUPATIONS.
Occupational trends, 1982-1995. Little Rock, AR (P.O. Box 2981, Little Rock, AR 72203) [1986]- v. ; **NYPL [JLM 87-353]**

ARKANSAS - OCCUPATIONS - STATISTICS.
Occupational employment statistics program . [Little Rock, Ark.] (P.O. Box 2981, Little Rock 72203) [1986] v leaves, 223 p. ; LC Card 87-620868 DDC 331.12/51/0009767021 19
HD5725.A8 O264 1986

Staffing patterns for manufacturing industries and hospitals /. Little Rock, Ark. [1983?] vi leaves, 249 p. ; LC Card 86-623216 DDC 331.12/57/09767 19
HD5725.A8 S79 1983

Arkansas Research and Training Center in Vocational Rehabilitation. Greenwood, Reed. Employer concerns regarding workers with disabilities /. Hot Springs, Ark. [1985] xii, 170 p. ; LC Card 87-620863 DDC 658.3/045 19
HD7256.U5 G74 1985

ARKHANGELSKAIA OBLAST′ (R.S.F.S.R.) - ECONOMIC CONDITIONS.
Ovchinnikov, V. P. (Veniamin Petrovich) Arkhangel′skiĭ avtograf /. Arkhangel′sk , 1983. 94 p. : LC Card 84-173501
HC337.R852 A746 1983

Arkhangel′skiĭ avtograf /. Ovchinnikov, V. P. (Veniamin Petrovich) Arkhangel′sk , 1983. 94 p. : LC Card 84-173501
HC337.R852 A746 1983

Arkhipov, Anatoliĭ Ivanovich. Agropromyshlennyĭ kompleks v usloviiakh razvitogo sotsializma . Moskva , 1986. 167 p. ; LC Card 87-166350
HD9015.S652 A38 1986

Arkhiva Chentrale de Stat a RSS Moldovenesht′.
Rabochee dvizhenie v Moldavii, 1895-fevral′ 1917 g. . Kishinev , 1985. 322 p. ; LC Card 86-100092
HD8529.M57 R32 1985

Arkin, V. I. (Vadim Iosifovich), 1937- Stochastic optimization . Berlin , New York , c1985. x, 754 p. : ISBN 0-387-16659-9 (U. S.) LC Card 86-11865 DDC 629.8/312 19
QA402.3 .S778 1985 **NYPL [JSE 86-1596]**

Armadas da carreira da India de 1560 a 1590 .
Solis, Duarte Gomes. Lisboa , 1938. xvi, 20 p. : LC Card 86-140347
HF3698.I4 S65 1938

ARMAMENTS - ECONOMIC ASPECTS.
Bonk, Heinz. Rüstungspolitik und Arbeiterklasse . Berlin , 1986. 299 p. ; LC Card 86-174039
HC79.D4 B65 1986

Entwicklung und Rüstung . Baden-Baden , 1984. 303 p. ; ISBN 3-7890-1068-5 LC Card 85-175510
HC79.D4 E58 1984

Gleditsch, Nils Petter, 1942- Economic incentives to arm? . Oslo [1986] 72 p. : ISBN 82-7288-134-9 LC Card 87-163647 DDC 338.4/36234 19
HC79.D4 G54 1986

Held, Karl, 1944- Krieg und Frieden . Frankfurt am Main , c1983. 324 p. ; ISBN 3-518-11149-3 : LC Card 83-228517
HC79.D4 H45 1983

Die Rolle der Rüstung in der Wirtschaft des heutigen Kapitalismus /. Berlin [1984] 127 p. ; LC Card 85-135711
HC281 .B39 1984 Heft 4 HC79.D4

Überlebenslesebuch . Reinbek bei Hamburg [1984], c1983. 316 p. : ISBN 3-499-17672-6 : LC Card 85-168871
HC79.D4 U24 1984

ARMAMENTS - ECONOMIC ASPECTS - CONGRESSES.
The Economics of military expenditures . New York , 1987. xxiii, 391 p. : ISBN 0-312-00421-4 : LC Card 86-27886 DDC 338.4/7355 19
HC79.D4 E27 1987

Peace, defence, and economic analysis . New York , 1987. xxxiii, 450 p. : ISBN 0-312-01321-3 : LC Card 87-19708 DDC 338.4/7355 19
HC79.D4 P43 1987

ARMAMENTS - ECONOMIC ASPECTS - GERMANY (WEST)
Die Rolle der Rüstung in der Wirtschaft des heutigen Kapitalismus /. Berlin [1984] 127 p. ; LC Card 85-135711
HC281 .B39 1984 Heft 4 HC79.D4

ARMAMENTS - ECONOMIC ASPECTS - GERMANY (WEST) - HUNSRÜCK (REGION)
Stange, Sabine. Kriegsvorbereitung im Hunsrück . Essen , 1985. 157, [35] p., [4] folded leaves of plates : ISBN 3-88474-409-7 : LC Card 86-148061
HC290.5.D4 S84 1985

ARMAMENTS - ECONOMIC ASPECTS - ROMANIA.
Pagini din gîndirea economică militară românească /. Bucureşti , 1983. 219 p. ; LC Card 84-116220
HC405.Z9 D443 1983

ARMAMENTS - ECONOMIC ASPECTS - SWITZERLAND - ECONOMETRIC MODELS.
Karas, Thomas H. Die Nachfrage nach Ausrüstungsinvestitionen in der Schweiz 1963-1980 . Frankfurt am Main , c1984. v, 91 p. : ISBN 3-88129-798-7 : LC Card 84-208150
HC400.D4 K37 1984

ARMAMENTS - ECONOMIC ASPECTS - SWITZERLAND - HISTORY - 20TH CENTURY.
Tanner, Jakob. Bundeshaushalt, Währung und Kriegswirtschaft . Zürich , c1986. 438 p. : ISBN 3-85791-100-X : LC Card 86-199729
HJ1258 .T35 1986

ARMAMENTS - ECONOMIC ASPECTS - UNITED STATES.
Braun, Axel. Rüstungskonversionsbemühungen in den USA in den 70iger Jahren . Frankfurt am Main , c1984. x, 379 p. : ISBN 3-88129-856-8 LC Card 85-154003
HC110.D4 B72 1984

DiFilippo, Anthony, 1950- Military spending and industrial decline . Westport, Conn. , c1986. x, 199 p. ; ISBN 0-313-25179-7 (lib bdg. : alk. paper) LC Card 85-27144 DDC 338.4/7621902/0973 19
HD9703.U5 D54 1986 ***NYPL [JLD 86-2930]***

Kappus, Wolfgang. Abrüstung und Wirtschaftswachstum . Frankfurt , New York , c1985. 329 p. : ISBN 3-593-33531-X LC Card 85-232235
HC110.D4 K37 1985

Müller, Erwin, 1947- Rüstungspolitik und Rüstungsdynamik . Baden-Baden , 1985. 378 p. ; ISBN 3-7890-1076-6 LC Card 85-154502
HC110.D4 M85 1985

Die Rolle der Rüstung in der Wirtschaft des heutigen Kapitalismus /. Berlin [1984] 127 p. ; LC Card 85-135711
HC281 .B39 1984 Heft 4 HC79.D4

ARMAMENTS - SOCIAL ASPECTS - GERMANY (WEST) - HUNSRÜCK (REGION)
Stange, Sabine. Kriegsvorbereitung im Hunsrück . Essen , 1985. 157, [35] p., [4] folded leaves of plates : ISBN 3-88474-409-7 : LC Card 86-148061
HC290.5.D4 S84 1985

Armand, Marcel. Histoire de la Bourse du travail de Romans et de ceux qui l'ont faite : un militant parle / Marcel Armand ; préface de Pierre Masseboeuf. [Romans-sur-Isère : Union locale C.G.T., 1982] 80 p. ; 23 cm. Cover title. LC Card 83-143101
1. Employment agencies - France - Romans-sur-Isère - History. I. Title.
HD5926.R66 A76 1982

Armandi, Barry R. Ford, Robert Clayton, 1945- Organization theory . New York , c1988. xxii, 482 p. : ISBN 0-06-042124-X LC Card 87-23796 DDC 302.3/5 19
HD31 .F5726 1988

Armbruster, Walter J.
Economic efficiency in agricultural and food marketing /. Ames , 1987. xii, 315 p. ; ISBN 0-8138-0533-3 LC Card 87-2821 DDC 381/.41/0973 19
HD9000.5 .E26 1987

Federal marketing programs in agriculture . Danville, Ill. , c1983. x, 326 p. ; ISBN 0-8134-2292-2 : LC Card 83-80130
NYPL [JLE 86-4572]

ARMED FORCES - ADDRESSES, ESSAYS, LECTURES.
The Second cold war /. New Delhi , 1983. vi, 215 p. ; LC Card 84-900004 DDC 355/.033/0047 19
UA10 .S38 1983 ***NYPL [JFD 87-1657]***

ARMED FORCES - APPROPRIATIONS AND EXPENDITURES.
United Nations. Secretary-General. [Economic and social consequences of the arms race and of military expenditures. French.] Conséquences économiques et sociales de la course aux armements /. Paris , 1983. 121 p. : ISBN 2-7178-0645-8 : LC Card 84-136625
HC79.D4 U52 1983

ARMED FORCES - APPROPRIATIONS AND EXPENDITURES - CONGRESSES.
Disarmament and world development /. Oxford, England , New York , 1986. xiii, 306 p. ; ISBN 0-08-031309-4 : LC Card 85-19231 DDC 338.4/7355 19
JX1974 .D515 1985 ***NYPL [JLE 86-3211]***

Armed forces guide to personal financial planning . Pillsbury, Hobart B. Harrisburg, PA , c1987. p. cm. ISBN 0-8117-2123-X LC Card 86-30201 DDC 332.024/355 19
HG179 .P55 1987

ARMED SERVICES. see **ARMED FORCES.**

Armelui . Loo, L. Frank van, 1945- Bergen (NH) , 1986. 285 p. ; ISBN 90-70805-10-3 : LC Card 86-205672
HC328.A44 L66 1986

Armenia in philately. Arakelov, S. N. (Suren Nersesovich) Armeniia v filatelii /. Erevan , 1980. 175 p., [24] p. of plates : LC Card 82-105026
HE6183.A69 A72 1980

ARMENIAN S.S.R. - POPULATION.
Karapetian, S. A. Regional'nye osobennosti sotsial'no-demograficheskogo razvitiia Armianskoĭ SSR /. Erevan , 1986. 215 p. ; LC Card 87-118556
HB3608.A75 K37 1986

Armeniia v filatelii /. Arakelov, S. N. (Suren Nersesovich) Erevan , 1980. 175 p., [24] p. of plates : LC Card 82-105026
HE6183.A69 A72 1980

Armet, Lluís. El Finançament autonòmic . Barcelona , 1985. 157 p. ; ISBN 84-297-2364-1 LC Card 86-145741
HJ1249.A1 F56 1985

ARMIES - ROME - HISTORY.
Brunt, P. A. Italian manpower, 225 B.C.-A.D. 14 /. Oxford [Oxfordshire] , 1987, c1971. xxi, 762 p. ; ISBN 0-19-814283-8 : LC Card 87-1644 DDC 304.6/0945 19
HB3599 .B77 1987

Armour, Hazel. New technology in the office environment / Hazel Armour. Aldershot, Hampshire, England ; Brookfield, Vt., USA : Gower, c1986. viii, 138 p. : ill. ; 23 cm. Bibliography: p. 128-138. ISBN 0-566-05031-5 LC Card 86-215701 DDC 338.4/561651 19
1. Office practice - Automation. 2. Labor supply - Effect of technological innovations on. 3. Sexual division of labor - Great Britain. 4. Sexual division of labor - United States. 5. Sexual division of labor - Japan. I. Title.
HF5547.5 .A786 1986

Arms and hunger /. Brandt, Willy, 1913- [Organisierte Wahnsinn. English.] Cambridge, Mass. , 1987, c1986. 208 p. ; ISBN 0-262-52127-X (pbk.) LC Card 87-4057 DDC 330.9172/4 19
HC59.7 .B67713 1987

ARMS CONTROL.
Poklad, B. I. (Boris Iosifovich) Real'nosti sovremennogo mira i politika konfrontatsii /. Moskva , 1985. 157 p. ; LC Card 85-170137
JX1974.7 .P585 1985 ***NYPL [*QIK 87-1550]***

Arms makers of Philadelphia /. Whisker, James B., 1939- [Morgantown, W. Va.?] [1987?] 32 p., [1] leaf of plates : LC Card 87-124428 DDC 338.7/623422/02574811 19
HD9743.U7 P48 1987

ARMS RACE - ECONOMIC ASPECTS.
Vlas'evich, IU. E. (IUriĭ Evlampievich) Ekonomicheskoe bremia militarizma /. Moskva , 1980. 181 p. ; LC Card 81-134793
HC79.D4 V58 1980

ARMS RACE - HISTORY - 20TH CENTURY.
Assessing the nuclear age . Chicago, Ill. , c1986. xvii, 382 p. ; ISBN 0-941682-07-2 LC Card 85-82511 DDC 355/.0217 19
U264 .A79 1986 ***NYPL [JLE 87-11]***

Jaipal, Rikhi, 1916- Nuclear arms and the human race . New Delhi , 1986. xix, 306 p. ; ISBN 81-7023-074-8 : LC Card 86-901813 DDC 355/.0217 19
U263 .J35 1986 ***NYPL [JLD 87-960]***

ARMS RACE - HISTORY - 20TH CENTURY - ADDRESSES, ESSAYS, LECTURES.
The Second cold war /. New Delhi , 1983. vi, 215 p. ; LC Card 84-900004 DDC 355/.033/0047 19
UA10 .S38 1983 ***NYPL [JFD 87-1657]***

Arms transfers to the Third World, 1971-85 /. Brzoska, Michael. Oxford , New York , 1987. xv, 383 p. : ISBN 0-19-829116-7 : LC Card 87-5579 DDC 382/.456234/091724 19
HD9743.D442 B79 1987

Armstrong, A. M. Land ownership and land use in the Scottish Highlands / by A.M. Armstrong and A.S. Mather. [Aberdeen, Grampian] : Dept. of Geography, University of Aberdeen, 1983. vii, 150 p. : ill., maps ; 30 cm. (O'Dell memorial monograph, 0141-1454 . no. 13) Includes bibliographies. LC Card 83-209521 DDC 333.3/09411/5 19
1. Land tenure - Scotland. 2. Land use, Rural - Scotland. I. Mather, Alexander Smith. II. Title. III. Series.
HD616 .A76 1983 ***NYPL [JLF 86-457]***

Armstrong, David L. Williams, Cecil L., 1930- The negotiable environment . Ann Arbor, Mich. , c1985. v, 82 p. : ISBN 0-936658-20-7 (pbk.) : LC Card 85-10305 DDC 658.3/82 19
HF5547.2 .W55 1985 ***NYPL [JLF 86-1138]***

Armstrong, Hugh, 1943- Armstrong, Pat, 1945- A working majority . Ottawa, Ont. , c1983. v, 280 p. : ISBN 0-660-11314-7 (pbk.) : LC Card 83-158188 DDC 331.4/0971 19
HD6067.2.C2 A75 1983
NYPL [JLD 86-1585]

Armstrong, John, 1944- Business documents : their origins, sources, and uses in historical research / John Armstrong and Stephanie Jones. London ; New York : Mansell Pub., 1987. xiv, 251 p. : facsims. ; 24 cm. Bibliography: p. 231-235. Includes index. ISBN 0-7201-1846-8 : LC Card 86-28451 DDC 651.5 19
1. Business records - Great Britain - Handbooks, manuals, etc. 2. Business enterprises - Great Britain - Archival resources - Handbooks, manuals, etc. 3. Business records - Handbooks, manuals, etc. 4. Business enterprises - Archival resources - Handbooks, manuals, etc. I. Jones, Stephanie (Stephanie Karen). II. Title.
HF5349.G7 A76 1987

Armstrong, Martin A. The greatest bull market in history : will it happen again? / by Martin A. Armstrong. [Princeton?] : Princeton Economics, <c1986- > v. <2 > : ill. ; 29 cm. "A Classical study of economics, commodity, equity, financial, and foreign exchange price movements, including government intervention covering U. S., Europe, and Japan, between 1919 and 1985"--V. 2. LC Card 87-138809 DDC 332.64 19
1. Investments - History. 2. Capital market - History. 3. Stocks - Prices - History. I. Title.
HG4516 .A75 1986

Armstrong, P. J. (Peter J.) White collar workers, trade unions, and class /. London , Dover, N.H. , c1986. 215 p. : ISBN 0-7099-0571-8 : LC Card 85-28806 DDC 331.88/041 19
HD8039.M39 W45 1986
NYPL [JLD 86-1602]

Armstrong, Pat, 1945- A working majority : what women must do for pay / Pat Armstrong and Hugh Armstrong ; with assistance from Sonja Greckol ... [et al.]. Ottawa, Ont. : Canadian Advisory Council on the Status of Women, c1983. v, 280 p. : ill. ; 23 cm. "February 1983." Bibliography: p. 276-280. ISBN 0-660-11314-7 (pbk.) : LC Card 83-158188 DDC 331.4/0971 19
1. Women - Employment - Canada. 2. Sex role in the work environment - Canada. 3. Work environment - Canada. I. Armstrong, Hugh, 1943-. II. Greckol, Sonja Ruth, 1946-. III. Canada. Advisory Council on the Status of Women. IV. Title.
HD6067.2.C2 A75 1983 ***NYPL [JLD 86-1585]***

Armstrong-Wright, Alan, 1929- Bus services : reducing costs, raising standards / Alan Armstrong-Wright and Sebastien Thiriez. Washington, D.C. : World Bank, 1987. x, 97 p. ; 28 cm. (World Bank technical paper, 0253-7494 . no. 68) Urban transport series Bibliography: p. 97. ISBN 0-8213-0943-9 (pbk.) LC Card 87-17183 DDC 388.4/1322/091724 19
1. Bus lines - Developing countries. 2. Transportation and state - Developing countries. I. Thiriez, Sebastien, 1958-. II. Title. III. Series.
HE5725 .A76 1987

Armut in Österreich : Dritte Welt in der Ersten Welt / [Herausgeber, Junge Generation der SPÖ Steiermark ; Erklärung von Graz für Solidarische Entwicklung (EVG)]. Graz : Leykam-Verlag, c1977. 168 p. : ill. ; 19 cm. Includes bibliographies. CONTENTS. - Internationalisierung von Kapital und Arbeit / Folker Fröbel ... [et al.] -- Istder Kapitalismus tot? / Arno Tausch -- Zur Arbeits- und Lebenssituation der Bauern in Österreich / Josef Krammer, Günther Scheer -- Vergessene Österreicher, die Bergbauern / Walter Tausch. ISBN 3-7011-7080-0 LC Card 86-176543
1. Poor - Austria. 2. Austria - Economic conditions - 1945-. 3. Capitalism - Austria. I. Junge Generation der SPÖ Steiermark. II. Erklärung von Graz für Solidarische Entwicklung (Association).
HC270.P6 A75 1977

Armut und Reichtum : der lange Marsch durchs Nadelöhr / [Herausgeber, Evangelisches Missionswerk im Bereich der Bundesrepublik Deutschland und Berlin (West) e.V.]. Hamburg : Missionshilfe Verlag ; Göttingen : Vandenhoeck & Ruprecht, 1981. 80 p. : ill. (some col.) ; 30 cm. Cover title. Includes bibliographical references. ISBN 3-921620-14-7 LC Card 81-159683 DDC 305.5/6 19
1. Poor - Addresses, essays, lectures. 2. Poverty - Addresses, essays, lectures. 3. Poor - Developing countries - Addresses, essays, lectures. I. Evangelisches Missionswerk im Bereich der Bundesrepublik Deutschland und Berlin West.
HC79.P6 A75 ***NYPL [JLG 85-309]***

The Army and industrial manpower /. Fairchild, Byron. Westport, Conn. , 1987. xiv, 291 p. : ISBN 0-313-25480-X (lib. bdg. : alk. paper) LC Card 86-25738 DDC 331.11/0973 19
HD5724 .F25 1987

Arn, Joseph V., 1943- Office automation : an information systems approach / Joseph V. Arn, Beverly J. Oswalt. Boston, MA : Boyd & Fraser Pub. Co., c1988. xxvii, 402 p., [8] p. of plates : ill. (some col.) ; 24 cm. Bibliography: p. [387]-389. Includes index. ISBN 0-87835-232-5 LC Card 86-28359 DDC 651.8 19
1. Office practice - Automation. 2. Information storage and retrieval systems - Business. 3. Office management. 4. Management information systems. I. Oswalt, Beverly J., 1948-. II. Title.
HF5547.5 .A79 1988

Arnáiz Burne, Stella Maris. Dachary, Alfredo César. El Caribe mexicano . México, D.F. , 1985. 110 p. : ISBN 968-496-069-7 LC Card 86-118335 DDC 338.3/7270972 19
HD8039.F66 M426 1985 ***NYPL [JLD 87-1321]***

Arnavutluk. see **Albania.**

Arndt, H. W. (Heinz Wolfgang), 1915- Economic development : the history of an idea / H.W. Arndt. Chicago : University of Chicago Press, 1987. viii, 217 p. ; 23 cm. Bibliography: p. 179-212. Includes index. ISBN 0-226-02720-1 : LC Card 86-25108 DDC 338.9 19
1. Economic development. 2. Developing countries - Economic policy. I. Title.
HD82 .A66 1987

Arndt, Hans-Jochen. Handelshäfen im Ostseeraum /. [Lübeck] [1983] 232 p. : LC Card 84-192969
HE557.A3 H36 1983

Arndt, Helmut, 1911-
Leistungswettbewerb und ruinöse Konkurrenz in ihrem Einfluss auf Wohlfahrt und Beschäftigung : von der Gleichgewichts- zur Prozessanalyse / von Helmut Arndt. Berlin : Duncker & Humblot, c1986. 147 p. ; 23 cm. Bibliography: p. [135]-140. Includes indexes. ISBN 3-428-06078-4 LC Card 87-112253 DDC 338.9 19
1. Competition. 2. Industry and state. 3. Public welfare. 4. Employment (Economic theory). I. Title.
HD41 .A755 1986

Vollbeschäftigung : Einführung in Theorie und Politik der Beschäftigung / von Helmut Arndt. Berlin : Duncker & Humblot, c1984. 196 p. : ill. ; 24 cm. Includes bibliographical references and indexes. ISBN 3-428-05602-7 LC Card 84-209024
1. Full employment policies. 2. Unemployment. 3. Economic policy. 4. Keynes, John Maynard, 1883-1946. I. Title.
HD5706 .A855 1984

Arndt, Johan. Ledning, produktion & marknadsföring av tjänster . Malmö , c1981. 318 p. : ISBN 91-40-54058-8 : LC Card 81-174255
HD9986.S82 L43 1981

Arndt, Sven W.
Competitiveness : the United States in world trade / Sven W. Arndt and Lawrence Bouton. Washington, D.C. : American Enterprise Institute for Public Policy Research ; Lanham, MD : Distributed by arrangement with UPA, Inc., c1987. 120 p. : charts ; 24 cm. (AEI studies . 457) Includes bibliographies. ISBN 0-8447-3625-2 (alk. paper) LC Card 87-1250 DDC 382/.0973 19
1. United States - Commerce. 2. Foreign exchange problem - United States. 3. United States - Economic policy - 1981-. 4. Competition, International. 5. Competition, Unfair. I. Bouton, Lawrence. II. Title. III. Series.
HF3031 .A83 1987

Exchange rates, trade, and the U. S. economy /. Cambridge, Mass. , c1985. xxi, 296 p. : ISBN 0-88410-948-8 LC Card 84-28328 DDC 332.4/560973 19
HG3851 .E94 1985 ***NYPL [JLE 85-2269]***

Real-financial linkages among open economies /. Cambridge, Mass. , c1987. x, 215 p. : ISBN 0-262-01096-8 LC Card 87-15153 DDC 337 19
HF1411 .R4135 1987

Arneja, Jasbir Singh. Agricultural taxation in Punjab / Jasbir Singh Arneja. 1st ed. Jalandhar : ABS Publications, 1987. xvi, 280 p. ; 22 cm. Bibliography: p. [262]-275. Includes index. ISBN 81-7072-009-5 : LC Card 86-903405 DDC 336.2/7863/0954552 19
1. Agriculture - Taxation - India - Punjab. I. Title.
HD1443.I42 P863 1987

Arnell, J. C. Steam and the North Atlantic mails : the impact of the Cunard Line and subsequent steamship companies on the carriage of transatlantic mails / J.C. Arnell. Toronto, Ont. : Unitrade Press, c1986. x, 295 p. : ill. ; 24 cm. Bibliography: p. 288. Includes indexes. ISBN 0-919801-36-6 : LC Card 87-127353 DDC 383/.142/091631 19
1. Mail steamers - North Atlantic Region - History. 2. Cunard Steamship Company, ltd. - History. I. Title.
HE6233 .A76 1986

Arnesen, Peter Judd, 1947- The Japanese competition . Ann Arbor, MI , 1987. xii, 124 p. ; ISBN 0-939512-30-0 LC Card 86-31756 DDC 338.4/76292/0952 19
HD9710.J32 J374 1987 ***NYPL [JFL 81-188 no.15]***

Arnold, Alix, 1956- Kaputt und auch noch selber schuld : Gesundheitsschutz am Arbeitsplatz / Alix Arnold, Rolf Satzer.Originalausg. Reinbek bei Hamburg : Rowohlt, c1986. 179, [1] p. : ill. ; 20 cm. (Rororo aktuell) Bibliography: p. 179-[180] ISBN 3-499-15908-2 : LC Card 86-226114
1. Industrial safety - Germany, West. 2. Industrial accidents - Germany, West. I. Satzer, Rolf, 1958-. II. Title.
HD7708 .A75 1986

Arnold, Alvin L. Real estate investor's deskbook / Alvin L. Arnold. Boston : Warren, Gorham & Lamont, c1982. 1 v. (various pagings) : ill. ; 26 cm. Kept up to date by supplements by various authors. Includes index. ISBN 0-88262-732-5 LC Card 82-70717 DDC 346.7304/3 347.30643 19
1. Real estate investment - Law and legislation - United States. 2. Real estate investment - Taxation - Law and legislation - United States. 3. Real property - United States. 4. Vendors and purchasers - United States. I. Title.
KF665 .A8 1982 ***NYPL [JLF 86-907]***

Arnold-Bergstraesser-Institut für kulturwissenschaftliche Forschung, Freiburg i. B. see **Freiburg i. B. Arnold-Bergstraesser-Institut für kulturwissenschaftliche Forschung.**

Arnold, Danny R., 1948- Smith, Garry D., 1948- Business strategy and policy /. Boston , c1988. xviii, 1006 p. : ISBN 0-395-36946-0 LC Card 87-80879 DDC 658.4/012 19
HD30.28 .S56 1988

Arnold, Fred. Luther, Norman Y., 1936- Consistent correction of census and vital registration data for Thailand, 1960-80 /. Honolulu, Hawaii [1986] vii, 39 p. ; ISBN 0-86638-089-2 (pbk.) : LC Card 86-32807 DDC 304.6/0723 19
HA39.T4 L87 1986

Arnold-Palussiére, Martine. Die grenzüberschreitende regionale Zusammenarbeit auf dem Gebiet der Raumordnung : Fallstudie für das Rheintal, Elsass, Pfalz, Baden, Nordwestschweiz / Martine Arnold-Palussiére. Hannover : Vincentz, 1983. xvii, 393 p. ; 30 cm. (Beiträge / Akademie für Raumforschung und Landesplanung, 0587-2642 . Bd. 71) Bibliography: p. 379-393. ISBN 3-87870-869-6 : LC Card 83-239646 DDC 361.6/1/0943 19
1. Regional planning - Germany, West. 2. Regional planning - Switzerland. 3. Regional planning - Rhine Valley. I. Series: Akademie für Raumforschung und Landesplanung, Hanover. Beiträge, Bd. 71. II. Title.
HT395.G4 A76 1983 ***NYPL [JLL 72-326 Bd. 71]***

Arnold, Ron. Ecology wars : environmentalism as if people mattered / by Ron Arnold.1st ed. Bellevue, Wash. : Free Enterprise Press : Distributed by Merril Press, c1987. 182 p. ; 23 cm. "A Free Enterprise battle book." Bibliography: p. 165-172. Includes index. ISBN 0-939571-00-5 LC Card 87-17 DDC 363.7/00973 19
1. Environmental policy - United States. 2. Capitalism - United States. I. Title.
HC110.E5 A77 1987

Arnold-Rösner, Regina. Berufliche Integration junger Türken : Chancen und Realitäten in der aktuellen Beschäftigungskrise / Regina Arnold-Rösner.1. Aufl. Hamburg : Hamburger Buchwerkstatt, 1986. 122 p. : ill. ; 21 cm. (Erziehungswissenschaft aktuell . Bd. 2) Bibliography: p. 115-122. ISBN 3-925408-05-3 LC Card 86-223625
1. Alien labor, Turkish - Germany, West. 2. Children of alien laborers - Vocational education - Germany (West). 3. Social integration - Germany (West). I. Title. II. Series.
HD8458.T9 A76 1986

Arnon, Itzhak, 1909- Modernization of agriculture in developing countries : resources, potentials, and problems / Isaac Arnon.2nd ed. Chichester [West Sussex] ; New York : Wiley, c1987. xxiii, 626 p. : ill. ; 24 cm. (Environmental monographs & symposia) "A Wiley-Interscience publication." Includes bibliographies and indexes. ISBN 0-471-91586-6 : LC Card 87-6288 DDC 338.1/09172/4 19
1. Agriculture - Economic aspects - Developing countries. 2. Agricultural ecology - Developing countries. I. Series: Environmental monographs and symposia. II. Title.
HD1417 .A76 1987

Arnould, Michel. Les termes pétroliers : dictionnaire anglais-français / Michel Arnould, Fabio Zubini, avec la participation de J.-J. Chartrou, J. Bordan, G. Terrier ; sous la direction de André Combaz ; préface de François de Wissocq. Paris : Total : Dunod, c1981. xii, 267 p. ; 25 cm. (Dunod technique. Chimie, métallurgie, pétrologie) ISBN 2-04-011414-9 LC Card 82-167169 DDC 665.5/03/21 19
1. Petroleum - Dictionaries. 2. English language -

Dictionaries - French. I. Zubini, Fabio. II. Title.
TN865 .A66 1981 ***NYPL [JSE 84-171]***

Aron, Arthur. Using AppleWorks / Arthur and Elaine Aron. 2nd ed. Indianapolis, Ind. : Que Corp., c1987. xviii, 458 p. : ill. ; 24 cm. Includes index. ISBN 0-88022-280-8 (pbk.) LC Card 86-63838 DDC 005.36/9 19
1. AppleWorks (Computer program). 2. Business - Data processing. I. Aron, Elaine. II. Title.
HF5548.4.A68 A76 1987

Aron, Elaine. Aron, Arthur. Using AppleWorks /. Indianapolis, Ind. , c1987. xviii, 458 p. : ISBN 0-88022-280-8 (pbk.) LC Card 86-63838 DDC 005.36/9 19
HF5548.4.A68 A76 1987

Aroni, Samuel. How successful was Section 8 in Los Angeles? : a case-study of a housing subsidy program / Samuel Aroni, Frederick A. Lazin. Berkeley : Institute of Governmental Studies, University of California, Berkeley, 1986. 18 p. ; 28 cm. (Institute of Governmental Studies research report . 86-2) Bibliography: p. 14-18. ISBN 0-87772-311-7 (pbk.) LC Card 86-27180 DDC 363.5/8 19
1. Rent subsidies - California - Los Angeles. 2. Housing subsidies - California - Los Angeles. I. Lazin, Frederick A., 1943-. II. Title. III. Title: How successful was Section Eight in Los Angeles?. IV. Series.
HD7288.85.U62 L73 1986

Aronoff, Craig E. The Future of private enterprise /. Atlanta, Ga. , 1984-1986. 3 v. ; ISBN 0-88406-164-7 (pbk. : v. 1) LC Card 83-25386 DDC 338.6/1 19
HB501 .F83 1984 ***NYPL [JLK 87-49]***

Aronson, J. Richard (Jay Richard), 1937- Management policies in local government finance /. Washington, D.C. , c1987. 449 p. : ISBN 0-87326-075-9 : LC Card 87-2658 DDC 352.1 19
HJ9105 .M3 1987

Aronson, Jay Richard. Forging new relationships among business, labor, and government /. Greenwich, Conn. , c1986. xiii, 210 p. ; ISBN 0-89232-656-5 : LC Card 86-2839 DDC 338.973 19
HD3616.U47 F583 1986
NYPL [JLE 86-3452]

Aronson, Jodi C. O'Reilly, James T., 1947- Unions' rights to company information /. Philadelphia, Pa. , c1987. xiii, 312 p. ; ISBN 0-89546-060-2 LC Card 85-82257
NYPL [JLL 74-174 no.21]

Around the plough . Chakrabarti, S. B., 1943- Calcutta , 1986. xviii, 203 p., 8 p. of plates : LC Card 86-902283
HD2075.P36 C48 1986
NYPL [L-10 8468 no.67]

ARPLA series .
(no. 16) Sub-regional Symposium on Labour Inspection in Agriculture (1982 : Denpasar, Indonesia) Labour inspection in agriculture in Southeast Asia . Bangkok , 1983. 218 p. : ISBN 92-2-103533-6 LC Card 86-915732
HD1537.A785 S8 1982

Arredondo Ramírez, Pablo. Comunicación social, poder y democracia en México / Pablo Arredondo Ramírez, Enrique E. Sánchez Ruiz. 1a ed. Guadalajara, Jalisco, México : Universidad de Guadalajara, c1986. 214 p. : ill. ; 21 cm. (Difusión científica) Bibliography: p. 203-214. LC Card 86-227944
1. Radio broadcasting - Mexico. 2. Television broadcasting - Mexico. 3. Mass media - Mexico. I. Sánchez Ruiz, Enrique E. II. Title. III. Series.
HE8689.9.M6 A77 1986

O arrendamento capitalista na agricultura . Beskow, Paulo Roberto. São Paulo , Brasília , 1986. 219 p. : LC Card 86-229665
HD9066.B83 R463 1986

Arretx, Carmen. Cuatro lecciones de William Brass : CELADE-Santiago, 2 al 5 de septiembre de 1975. Santiago de Chile : Centro Latinoamericano de Demografía, 1977. 88 p. : ill. ; 27 cm. (Serie D . no. 91) "Notas de las clases ... elaborada por Carmen Arretx"--Presentación. Includes bibliographies. LC Card 83-169600
1. Brass, William. 2. Mortality - Mathematical models. I. Brass, William. II. Series: Serie D (CELADE (Organization)) , no. 91. III. Title.
HB1321.B73 A77 1977

Arriaga, M. de la Luz (María de la Luz) El Proceso de trabajo en México /. [Iztapalapa, Mexico] [1983 or 1984] 227 p. : LC Card 87-401038 DDC 331/.0972 19
HD8116.5 .P76 1983

Arrighetti, A. (Alessandro), 1953- Scelte strategiche e riorganizzazione aziendale . Milano, Italy , c1985. 312 p. ; LC Card 86-146459
HD2864 .S36 1985 ***NYPL [JLD 87-1549]***

Arroba, Tanya. Pressure at work : a survival guide / Tanya Arroba, Kim James. London ; New York : McGraw-Hill Bk. Co. (UK), c1987. xvi, 192 p. : ill. ; 25 cm. Bibliography: p. 189. Includes index. ISBN 0-07-084931-5 (pbk.) : LC Card 87-3925 DDC 658.4/095 19
1. Job stress. 2. Executives. I. James, Kim. II. Title.
HF5548.85 .A77 1987

Arroio dos Ratos. Sulzbach, Ervino Lothar. Arroio dos Ratos, berço da indústria carbonífera nacional . [Rio Grande do Sul] c1985 (Rio Grande do Sul : Flores Linotipia) 163 p. : LC Card 86-150014
HD9554.B83 A777 1985

Arroio dos Ratos, berço da indústria carbonífera nacional . Sulzbach, Ervino Lothar. [Rio Grande do Sul] c1985 (Rio Grande do Sul : Flores Linotipia) 163 p. : LC Card 86-150014
HD9554.B83 A777 1985

ARROIO DOS RATOS (BRAZIL) - ECONOMIC CONDITIONS.
Sulzbach, Ervino Lothar. Arroio dos Ratos, berço da indústria carbonífera nacional . [Rio Grande do Sul] c1985 (Rio Grande do Sul : Flores Linotipia) 163 p. : LC Card 86-150014
HD9554.B83 A777 1985

ARROIO DOS RATOS (BRAZIL) - HISTORY.
Sulzbach, Ervino Lothar. Arroio dos Ratos, berço da indústria carbonífera nacional . [Rio Grande do Sul] c1985 (Rio Grande do Sul : Flores Linotipia) 163 p. : LC Card 86-150014
HD9554.B83 A777 1985

ARROIO DOS RATOS (BRAZIL) - SOCIAL CONDITIONS.
Sulzbach, Ervino Lothar. Arroio dos Ratos, berço da indústria carbonífera nacional . [Rio Grande do Sul] c1985 (Rio Grande do Sul : Flores Linotipia) 163 p. : LC Card 86-150014
HD9554.B83 A777 1985

Arroteia, Jorge Carvalho, 1947- A evolução demográfica portuguesa : reflexos e perspectivas / Jorge Carvalho Arroteia.1a. ed. Lisboa : Instituto de Cultura e Língua Portuguesa, Ministério da Educação ; Amadora, Portugal : Distribuição comercial, Livraria Bertrand, 1984 [i.e. 1985] 119 p. : ill., maps ; 20 cm. (Biblioteca breve. v. 93.) Bibliography: p. 105-107. LC Card 86-125507 DDC 304.6/09469 19
1. Portugal - Population. 2. Portugal - Population density. I. Series: Biblioteca breve (Instituto de Cultura e Língua Portuguesa (Portugal)) , v. 93. II. Title.
HB3621 .A77 1985

Arrow, Kenneth Joseph, 1921-
Social choice and multicriterion decision-making / Kenneth J. Arrow and Hervé Raynaud. Cambridge, Mass. : MIT Press, c1986. vii, 127 p. : ill. ; 22 cm. Includes index. Bibliography: p. [119]-123. ISBN 0-262-01087-9 LC Card 85-19913 DDC 302/.13 19
1. Social choice - Mathematical models. 2. Decision-making - Mathematical models. I. Raynaud, Hervé. II. Title.
HM271 .A73 1986 ***NYPL [JLD 86-3628]***

Social choice and public decision making /. Cambridge [Cambridgeshire] , New York , 1986. xix, 215 p. : ISBN 0-521-30454-7 LC Card 86-8580 DDC 339 19
HB846.8 .S59 1986 ***NYPL [JLE 86-4189]***

ARROW, KENNETH JOSEPH, 1921-
Social choice and public decision making /. Cambridge [Cambridgeshire] , New York , 1986. xix, 215 p. : ISBN 0-521-30454-7 LC Card 86-8580 DDC 339 19
HB846.8 .S59 1986 ***NYPL [JLE 86-4189]***

Arroyo, Gonzalo. Agricultura y alimentos en América Latina : el poder de las transnacionales / por Gonzalo Arroyo, Ruth Rama, Fernando Rello con la colaboración de Gerardo Aceituno ... [et al.].1a ed. México, D.F. : Universidad Nacional Autónoma de México, Instituto de Cooperación Iberoamericana, Coordinación de la Investigación Científica, Programa Universitario de Alimentos, 1985. 267 p. ; 22 cm. Includes bibliographical references. ISBN 968-8373-33-8 LC Card 86-208283
1. Produce trade - Latin America. 2. International business enterprises - Latin America. I. Rama, Ruth. II. Rello, Fernando. III. Aceituno, Gerardo. IV. Title.
HD9014.L32 A77 1985

Arruda, Maria Arminda do Nascimento. A embalagem do sistema : a publicidade no capitalismo brasileiro / Maria Arminda do Nascimento Arruda. São Paulo : Livraria Duas Cidades, 1985. 203 p. : ill. ; 21 cm. (Coleção História e sociedade) Bibliography: p. 191-200. LC Card 85-211063
1. Advertising - Brazil. I. Title.
HF5813.B8 A77 1985

Arsac, Pierre. La vente des biens de la Grande Chartreuse sous la Révolution / Pierre Arsac. Grenoble : Centre de recherche d'histoire économique, sociale et institutionnelle, 1984. 104 p. : ill. ; 24 cm. Bibliography: p. 101-104. ISBN 2-904661-02-6 LC Card 86-118639
1. Confiscations - France - History - 18th century. 2. Grande Chartreuse - History - 18th century. 3. Church lands - France - History - 18th century. 4. Church property - France - History - 18th century. 5. France - History - Revolution, 1789-1799 - Economic aspects. 6. France - History - Revolution, 1789-1799 - Confiscations and contributions. I. Title.
HD643 .A77 1984

Arsen′ev, S. P. (Sergeĭ Pavlovich) Ėkonomicheskie problemy transporta SSSR /. Moskva , 1985. 181, [3] p. ; LC Card 86-100790
HE255.A2 E38 1985

ART AND BUSINESS. see **ART AND INDUSTRY.**

ART AND INDUSTRY.
Zellinger, Alfred, 1945- Die Sinnlichkeit der Theorie . Wien , c1983. 173 p. : ISBN 3-85439-005-X LC Card 84-196565
HF1040.7 .Z45 1983

The Art and science of business management .
(v. 3) Leadership /. New York, N.Y. , c1987. xi, 368 p. : ISBN 0-8160-1462-0 : LC Card 86-24167 DDC 658.4/092 19
HD57.7 .L43 1987

(v. 4) Creativity /. New York, N.Y. , c1987. xvi, 383 p. : ISBN 0-8160-1463-9 : LC Card 86-29320 DDC 650.1 19
HD53 .C745 1987

ART AS AN INVESTMENT - JUVENILE LITERATURE.
Epstein, Rachel S. Alternative investments /. New York , c1988. 47 p. : ISBN 1-555-46633-8 LC Card 87-21766 DDC 332.6/78 19
HG4521 .E685 1988

ART, COMMERCIAL. see **COMMERCIAL ART.**

L'art de fabriquer le salin, et la potasse ... /. Lavoisier, Antoine Laurent, 1743-1794. A Paris , 1779. [2], viij, 84 p., IV, [1] folded leaves of plates : LC Card 85-666435
HD9660.A42 L38x 1779

ART IN ADVERTISING. see **COMMERCIAL ART.**

Art of conciliation and industrial unrest /. Sharma, B. D. (Banarsi Das), 1921- Bombay , 1985. xvi, 366 p. ; LC Card 87-902679 DDC 331.89/14/0954 19
HD5998.A3 S48 1985

The Art of managing human resources / edited by Edgar H. Schein. New York : Oxford University Press, 1987. xii, 307 p. : ill. ; 24 cm. (The Executive bookshelf) Bibliography: p. 279-295. Includes index. ISBN 0-19-504882-2 (alk. paper) LC Card 86-31107 DDC 658.3/01 19
1. Manpower planning. 2. Organizational effectiveness. I. Schein, Edgar H. II. Series.
HF5549.5.M3 A78 1987

The art of managing technical projects /. Silverman, Melvin. Englewood Cliffs, N.J. , c1987. xx, 346 p. : ISBN 0-13-047010-4 LC Card 87-1750 DDC 658.4/04 19
HD69.P75 S54 1987

The art of tendering /. Marsh, P. D. V. Aldershot, Hants, England , Brookfield, Vt. , c1987. ix, 171 p. ; ISBN 0-291-39736-0 : LC Card 87-7429 DDC 658.7/23 19
HD2365 .M37 1987

Arte dei brentatori a Modena /. Bergonzini, Renato. Modena , 1983. 74 p., [5] p. of plates : LC Card 85-140349
HD8039.L72 I83 1983

Artemov, ÎU. M. (ÎUriĭ Mikhaĭlovich) Finansovye metody material'nogo stimulirovaniia proizvodstva / ÎU.M. Artemov, V.T. Parasochka, F.P. Safonov. Moskva : Finansy i statistika, 1983. 126 p. ; 20 cm. Includes bibliographical references. LC Card 84-118738
1. Incentives in industry - Soviet Union. 2. Labor productivity - Soviet Union. I. Parasochka, V. T. (Valentin Timofeevich). II. Safonov, F. P. (Fedor Pavlovich). III. Title.
HF5549.5.I5 A69 1983

La Artesanía de tejidos en la ciudad de La Paz / Centro de Promoción Popular. La Paz, Bolivia : El Centro, 1986. 74, [6] p. : ill. ; 22 cm. Bibliography: p. [76]. LC Card 87-101929
1. Weavers - Bolivia - La Paz. I. Centro de Promoción Popular (La Paz, Bolivia).
HD8039.T42 B525 1986

La artesanía del queso larense /. Naranjo M., José R. Caracas , 1985. 202 p., [16] p. of plates : ISBN 980-265-223-7 LC Card 87-403552 DDC 338.1/773/098725 19
HD9280.V43 L376 1985

Artesanos de la regata del Bidasoa . Garmendia Larrañaga, Juan. San Sebastián [1983] 123 p. : ISBN 84-7148-115-4 LC Card 84-140784 DDC 331.7/94 19
HD2346.S72 B534 1983
NYPL [3-MNE 86-3657]

Artesãos e operários . Mónica, Maria Filomena, 1943- Lisboa [1986] 228 p., [24] p. of plates : LC Card 86-229921
HD8596 .M65 1986

Arthur Andersen & Co. Ausländische Investitionen in U. S.-Grundvermögen /. Herne , 1984, c1983. 86 p. ; ISBN 3-482-69041-3 LC Card 84-203818 DDC 346.43/07 344.3067 19
K3830.4 .A97 1984 ***NYPL [JLD 86-2326]***

Arthur, Diane. Managing human resources in small and mid-sized companies / Diane Arthur. New York, NY : American Management Association, c1987. x, 278 p. ; 26 cm. Bibliography: p. 271-274. Includes index. ISBN 0-8144-5884-X LC Card 87-47716 DDC 658.3 19
1. Personnel management. 2. Small business - Personnel management. I. Title.
HF5549 .A955 1987

The Arthur M. Okun memorial lectures. Kaldor, Nicholas, 1908-1986. Economics without equilibrium /. Cardiff, U.K. , 1985. 79 p. ; ISBN 0-906449-87-1 LC Card 86-673866
HB71 .K273x 1985b

Arthur, W. Brian. Economics of changing age distributions in developed countries /. Oxford [Oxfordshire] , Topsfield, Mass. , 1987. p. cm. ISBN 0-19-829503-0 : LC Card 86-25098 DDC 304.6/2/091722 19
HB1531 .E28 1987

Arthur Young and Company. see **Young (Arthur) and Company.**

The Arthur Young business plan guide /. Siegel, Eric S. New York , c1987. xii, 184 p. ; ISBN 0-471-85885-4 LC Card 86-32622 DDC 658.4/012 19
HD62.5 .S556 1987

Arthur Young guide to financing for growth . Owen, Robert R. (Robert Randolph) New York , c1986. xiv, 298 p. ; ISBN 0-471-81946-8 : LC Card 86-1612 DDC 658.1/522 19
HG4027.7 .O94 1986 ***NYPL [JLE 86-2667]***

Artificial intelligence & statistics. Artificial intelligence and statistics /. Reading, Mass. , c1986. xiv, 418 p. : ISBN 0-201-11568-9 : LC Card 85-28631 DDC 006.3 19
Q334 .A764 1986 ***NYPL [JSE 87-399]***

Artificial intelligence and statistics / edited by William A. Gale. Reading, Mass. : Addison-Wesley Pub. Co., c1986. xiv, 418 p. : ill. ; 24 cm. Papers prepared for the Workshop on Artificial Intelligence and Statistics, held in April 1985, in Princeton, N.J., and sponsored by AT&T Bell Laboratories. Spine title: Artificial intelligence & statistics. Includes bibliographies and index. ISBN 0-201-11568-9 : LC Card 85-28631 DDC 006.3 19
1. Artificial intelligence - Congresses. 2. Statistics - Congresses. 3. Expert systems (Computer science) - Congresses. I. Gale, William A. II. AT & T Bell Laboratories. III. Workshop on Artificial Intelligence and Statistics (1985 : Princeton, N.J.). IV. Title: Artificial intelligence & statistics.
Q334 .A764 1986 ***NYPL [JSE 87-399]***

An artificial intelligence approach to VLSI design /. Kowalski, Thaddeus J. Boston , c1985. x, 226 p. : ISBN 0-89838-169-X LC Card 85-7581 DDC 621.3819/5835 19
TK7874 .K675 1985 ***NYPL [JSE 86-1182]***

ARTIFICIAL INTELLIGENCE - CONGRESSES.
Artificial intelligence and statistics /. Reading, Mass. , c1986. xiv, 418 p. : ISBN 0-201-11568-9 : LC Card 85-28631 DDC 006.3 19
Q334 .A764 1986 ***NYPL [JSE 87-399]***

Artificial intelligence in economics and management /. Amsterdam ; New York : xv, 292 p. : ISBN 0-444-87961-7 LC Card 85-31139 DDC 330/.028/563 19
HB143.5 .A78 1986 ***NYPL [JLE 86-3612]***

NATO Advanced Study Institute on Intelligent Decision Support in Process Environments (1985 : San Miniato, Italy) Intelligent decision support in process environments /. Berlin , New York , c1986. xv, 524 p. : ISBN 0-387-13922-2 (U. S.) LC Card 86-6742 DDC 658.4/03 19
T57.95 .N37 1985 ***NYPL [JFE 86-4847]***

Proceedings of an international conference on genetic algorithms and their applications . [S.l. , 1985] 225 p. : ***NYPL [JSF 87-413]***

ARTIFICIAL INTELLIGENCE - DATA PROCESSING - CONGRESSES.
IFAC/IFORS/IFIP/IASC/AFCET Conference on Economics and Artificial Intelligence (1986 : Aix-en-Provence, France) Economics and artificial intelligence . Oxford [Oxfordshire] , New York , 1987. xiii, 194 p. : ISBN 0-08-034350-3 (U. S.) : LC Card 87-6943 DDC 330/.028/563 19
HB143.5 .I44 1986

Artificial intelligence in economics and management / edited by L.F. Pau. Amsterdam ; New York : North-Holland ; xv, 292 p. : ill. ; 25 cm. A collection of some of the papers written after the International Workshop on Artificial Intelligence in Economics and Management, held Mar. 12-14, 1985 in Zurich, Switzerland, whose main sponsor was IFAC. Includes bibliographies and index. ISBN 0-444-87961-7 LC Card 85-31139 DDC 330/.028/563 19
1. Economics - Data processing - Congresses. 2. Management - Data processing - Congresses. 3. Artificial intelligence - Congresses. 4. Expert systems (Computer science) - Congresses. I. Pau, L.-F. (Louis-François), 1948-. II. International Workshop on Artificial Intelligence in Economics and Management (1985 : Zurich, Switzerland).
HB143.5 .A78 1986 ***NYPL [JLE 86-3612]***

Artificial intelligence markets. Norwalk, Conn., U. S.A. (6 Prowitt St., Norwalk 06855) : International Resource Development Inc., c1986. vii, 215 leaves ; 28 cm. (Report / International Resource Development Inc. . #701) "July 1986." LC Card 86-227054 DDC 380.1/450063 19
1. Computer industry - United States. 2. Market surveys - United States. 3. Artificial intelligence. I. International Resource Development, inc. II. Series: Report / International Resource Development Inc. , #701.
HD9696.C63 U5118 1986

ARTIFICIAL SATELLITES IN REMOTE SENSING - KENYA.
Agatsiva, J. L. Land use mapping of Kenya using remote sensing techniques /. [Nairobi] , 1982. iv, 39 p. : LC Card 84-980919 DDC 333.73/13/028 19
HD983.Z7 A38 1982

ARTIFICIAL SATELLITES IN REMOTE SENSING - UNITED STATES.
Commercial newsgathering from space. Washington, DC [1987] ix, 51 p. : LC Card 87-619818 DDC 070.4/3 19
HE9721.U5 C65 1987

ARTIFICIAL SATELLITES IN TELECOMMUNICATION - EUROPE.
Howard-Healy, Marion. Aspects of the new media in Europe /. Menlo Park, CA (333 Ravenswood Ave., Menlo Park 94025) , c1986. 22 leaves : LC Card 86-220771 DDC 384/.094 19
HE8700.72.E85 H69 1986

ARTIFICIAL SATELLITES IN TELECOMMUNICATION - UNITED STATES.
Commercial newsgathering from space. Washington, DC [1987] ix, 51 p. : LC Card 87-619818 DDC 070.4/3 19
HE9721.U5 C65 1987

Transponder supply & demand forecast. Bethesda, MD, U. S.A. , c1987. v, 150 p. : LC Card 87-403373 DDC 384.4/1 19
HE9721.U5 T73 1987

ARTIFICIAL THINKING. see **ARTIFICIAL INTELLIGENCE.**

Artikler fra Statistisk sentralbyrå, 0085-431X . (147) Jensen, An-Magritt. Flere i yrke--færre barn? . Oslo , 1983. 59 p. : ISBN 82-537-2007-6 : LC Card 84-163552
HA1503 .A45 nr. 147 HQ762.N8

ARTISANS AND GENERAL WORKERS' UNION (MAURITIUS) - HISTORY.
Allgoo, Rajpalsingh. Le mouvement syndical à l'île Maurice /. Port Louis, Ile Maurice , 1985. 110 p., [14] leaves of plates : LC Card 87-119075
HD8840.3.A5 A7825 1985

ARTISANS - BIDASOA RIVER VALLEY (SPAIN AND FRANCE)
Garmendia Larrañaga, Juan. Artesanos de la regata del Bidasoa . San Sebastián [1983] 123 p. : ISBN 84-7148-115-4 LC Card 84-140784 DDC 331.7/94 19
HD2346.S72 B534 1983
NYPL [3-MNE 86-3657]

ARTISANS - BRAZIL - CAMPINAS (SÃO PAULO)
A Feira hippie de Campinas . Campinas, SP, Brasil , São Paulo, SP , 1986. 73 p. ; LC Card 87-404187 DDC 381/.18/098161 19
HF5473.B72 C364 1986

ARTISANS - BRAZIL - CEARA (STATE)
Estudos fundamentais . Fortaleza , 1986. 120 p. : LC Card 87-120224
HD2346.B72 C44 1986

ARTISANS - BRAZIL - MARANHÃO - POLITICAL ACTIVITY - HISTORY.
Corrêa, Rossini. Mudança social no Nordeste . São Luís , 1986. 176 p., [6] p. of plates : LC Card 87-152221 DDC 322/.2/098121 19
HD8289.M37 C67 1986

ARTISANS - BURKINA FASO.
Structure et perspectives de l'artisanat et de la petite industrie du sud-ouest de la Haute-Volta . Berlin (West) [1978] xxvi, 253 p. : LC Card 85-118488
HD2346.B82 S77 1978

ARTISANS - BURUNDI.
Etude sur la petite et moyenne industrie et l'artisanat /. [Bujumbara] [1984] 7 v. in 6 : LC Card 86-980948
HD2346.B94 E78 1984

ARTISANS - CALIFORNIA - HISTORY - 18TH CENTURY.
Velázquez, María del Carmen. Notas sobre sirvientes de las Californias y proyecto de obraje en Nuevo México /. México, D.F. [1985], c1984. 246 p. ; ISBN 968-12-0298-8 LC Card 85-243085
HD2346.U52 C294 1985

ARTISANS - ECUADOR.
Sandoval H., Orlando. Comercialización de artesanías /. [Quito, Ecuador] , 1985. 231 p. : LC Card 87-400169 DDC 331.7/94 19
HD2346.E2 S26 1985

ARTISANS - EUROPE - HISTORY.
John, Peter, 1946- Handwerkskammern im Zwielicht . Köln , 1983. 304 p. ; ISBN 3-7663-0597-2 LC Card 83-127836 DDC 338.6/425/0943 19
HD2346.E9 J63 1983 ***NYPL [JLD 87-1038]***

ARTISANS - FRANCE - PARIS - EXHIBITIONS.
Atget, Géniaux, Vert . Paris [1984] 63, [1] p. :

ISBN 2-901414-09-5 : LC Card 86-137985
HF5459.F8 A87 1984 NYPL [MFW 87-159]

ARTISANS - GERMANY - HISTORY - 18TH CENTURY.
Handwerk um 1700 . Hürtgenwald , c1985. 245 p. : ISBN 3-87646-052-2 : LC Card 85-211788
HD2346.N4 H35 1985

ARTISANS - GERMANY - POLITICAL ACTIVITY - HISTORY - 19TH CENTURY.
Simon, Manfred. Handwerk in Krise und Umbruch . Köln , 1983. xvii, 652 p. : ISBN 3-412-02983-1 : LC Card 83-221725 DDC 322/.2/0943 19
HD2346.G3 S47 1983

ARTISANS - GERMANY (WEST) - DÜSSELDORF - HISTORY - 19TH CENTURY.
Lenger, Friedrich. Zwischen Kleinbürgertum und Proletariat . Göttingen , c1986. 332 p. ; ISBN 3-525-35731-1 LC Card 87-134322 DDC 331/.0943/55 19
HD8460.D872 L46 1986

ARTISANS - GERMANY (WEST) - ECONOMIC CONDITIONS.
Der Goldene Boden . Stuttgart , c1987. 359 p. ; ISBN 3-421-02885-0 LC Card 87-139261 DDC 331.7/94 19
HD2346.G3 G55 1987

ARTISANS - GERMANY (WEST) - HAMBURG - STATISTICS.
Das Handwerk in Hamburg . Hamburg [1979] 140 p. ; LC Card 86-133694
HA1282 .A Heft 128 HD2346.G32H3

ARTISANS - GERMANY (WEST) - HISTORY.
Der Dressierte Arbeiter . München , c1984. 211 p. : ISBN 3-406-09286-1 LC Card 84-181068 DDC 331.25 19
HD6331.2.G28 D74 1984

Der Goldene Boden . Stuttgart , c1987. 359 p. ; ISBN 3-421-02885-0 LC Card 87-139261 DDC 331.7/94 19
HD2346.G3 G55 1987

ARTISANS - GERMANY (WEST) - KONSTANZ.
Beck, Thomas, 1950- Handwerk in Staat und Gesellschaft . München , c1987. xvii, 319 p. : ISBN 3-88259-415-2 LC Card 87-152203 DDC 331.7/94 19
HD2346.G32 K663 1987

ARTISANS - GERMANY (WEST) - POLITICAL ACTIVITY.
Wünsche und Forderungen des Handwerks an Parteien, X. Deutschen Bundestag und Bundesregierung. Bonn [1983] 80 p. ; LC Card 83-220138
HD2346.G3 W86 1983

ARTISANS - GREAT BRITAIN - HISTORY.
Haydu, Jeffrey. Between craft and class . Berkeley , c1988. p. cm. ISBN 0-520-06060-1 (alk. paper) LC Card 87-22169 DDC 322/.2/0941 19
HD8076 .H39 1988

ARTISANS - GUATEMALA - DIRECTORIES.
Directorio artesanal, 1978 /. Guatemala , 1981. 6 v. ; LC Card 87-403025
HD2346.G8 D57 1981

ARTISANS - GUATEMALA - STATISTICS.
Principales indicadores económicos . Guatemala , 1982. 487 p. ; LC Card 87-403026 DDC 331.7/94 19
HD2346.G8 P75 1982

ARTISANS - ITALY - EMILIA-ROMAGNA - PICTORIAL WORKS.
Manutenzione e sostituzione . Bologna [1983] xviii, 227 p. : LC Card 84-142790
HD2346.I82 E45 1983

ARTISANS - ITALY - NUORO (SARDINIA : PROVINCE)
L'Osservatorio provinciale sul lavoro e sulle professioni . Milano, Italy , c1984. 143 p. : LC Card 84-190423
HD5785.N86 O87 1984
NYPL [JLD 86-1275]

ARTISANS - ITALY - PESARO REGION.
Favaretto, Ilario, 1945- L'impresa artigiana tra economia e territorio . Milano, Italy , c1986. 212 p. : LC Card 86-193238
HD2346.I82 P464 1986

ARTISANS - ITALY - TORRE DEL GRECO.
Pavanello, Mariano, 1944- Antropologia ed economia dell'artigianato artistico . Milano, Italy , c1984. 183 p. : LC Card 84-147193
HD2346.I82 T676 1984

ARTISANS - JAPAN.
Nakae, Katsumi, 1935- Edo no shokunin . Tōkyō , 1986. 229 p. : ISBN 4-88470-522-X : LC Card 86-184888
HD2346.J3 N26 1986 <Orien Japan>
*NYPL [*OSM 87-1217]*

ARTISANS - MEXICO - BAJA CALIFORNIA NORTE - HISTORY - 18TH CENTURY.
Velázquez, María del Carmen. Notas sobre sirvientes de las Californias y proyecto de obraje en Nuevo México /. México, D.F. [1985], c1984. 246 p. ; ISBN 968-12-0298-8 LC Card 85-243085
HD2346.U52 C294 1985

ARTISANS - MEXICO - BAJA CALIFORNIA SUR - HISTORY - 18TH CENTURY.
Velázquez, María del Carmen. Notas sobre sirvientes de las Californias y proyecto de obraje en Nuevo México /. México, D.F. [1985], c1984. 246 p. ; ISBN 968-12-0298-8 LC Card 85-243085
HD2346.U52 C294 1985

ARTISANS - MEXICO - CHILCHOTA REGION.
Ramírez C., Luis Alfonso. Chilchota, un pueblo al pie de la sierra . Zamora, Mich. [i.e. Michoacán] [Morelia, Mexico] , 1986. 306 p. : ISBN 968-7230-23-1 LC Card 87-401034 DDC 330.972/37 19
HC138.C45 R36 1986

ARTISANS - MEXICO - GUADALAJARA.
Guadalajara, la gran ciudad de la pequeña industria /. Zamora, Mich. , c1985. 301 p. : ISBN 968-7230-12-6 LC Card 86-191608
HD2346.M42 G824 1985

ARTISANS - MEXICO - MEXICO CITY - HISTORY.
Castro Gutiérrez, Felipe. La extinción de la artesanía gremial /. México , 1986. 188 p. ; ISBN 968-8374-01-6 LC Card 87-104891
HD6473.M64 M483 1986

ARTISANS - NETHERLANDS - HISTORY - 18TH CENTURY.
Handwerk um 1700 . Hürtgenwald , c1985. 245 p. : ISBN 3-87646-052-2 : LC Card 85-211788
HD2346.N4 H35 1985

ARTISANS - NEW SPAIN - HISTORY.
Castro Gutiérrez, Felipe. La extinción de la artesanía gremial /. México , 1986. 188 p. ; ISBN 968-8374-01-6 LC Card 87-104891
HD6473.M64 M483 1986

ARTISANS - PAPUA NEW GUINEA.
Philp, Norman E. The cash incentive . Canberra , 1986. xii, 135 p. : ISBN 0-86784-984-3 (pbk.) LC Card 87-150813
HD2346.P37 P46 1986

ARTISANS - SPAIN - HISTORY - 16TH CENTURY.
Guerrina Soderini, Alfonso. El drama quijotesco de los oficios en la época cervantina /. Montevideo, Uruguay , 1980 (Montevideo : Talleres Don Bosco) 209 p., [7] : LC Card 84-132190
HD2346.S7 G84 1980

ARTISANS - SPAIN - HISTORY - 17TH CENTURY.
Guerrina Soderini, Alfonso. El drama quijotesco de los oficios en la época cervantina /. Montevideo, Uruguay , 1980 (Montevideo : Talleres Don Bosco) 209 p., [7] : LC Card 84-132190
HD2346.S7 G84 1980

ARTISANS - SPAIN - SEVILLE - HISTORY - 16TH CENTURY.
Morell Peguero, Blanca. Mercaderes y artesanos en la Sevilla del descubrimiento /. Sevilla , 1986. 222 p. ; ISBN 84-505-2883-6 LC Card 86-199625
HD2346.S72 S465 1986

ARTISANS - SWITZERLAND - ZÜRICH (CANTON) - HISTORY - 18TH CENTURY.
Meier, Thomas. Handwerk, Hauswerk, Heimarbeit . Zürich , c1986. 435 p., [44] p. of plates : ISBN 3-905278-07-3 LC Card 86-227651
HD2346.S92 Z875 1986

ARTISANS - UNITED STATES - HISTORY.
Haydu, Jeffrey. Between craft and class . Berkeley , c1988. p. cm. ISBN 0-520-06060-1 (alk. paper) LC Card 87-22169 DDC 322/.2/0941 19
HD8076 .H39 1988

ARTISTIC PHOTOGRAPHY. see **PHOTOGRAPHY, ARTISTIC.**

ARTISTS - ITALY - TORRE DEL GRECO.
Pavanello, Mariano, 1944- Antropologia ed economia dell'artigianato artistico . Milano, Italy , c1984. 183 p. : LC Card 84-147193
HD2346.I82 T676 1984

ARTISTS' MATERIALS INDUSTRY - UNITED STATES - DIRECTORIES.
Katlan, Alexander W. American artists' materials suppliers directory . Park Ridge, N.J. , c1987. xvi, 460 p. : ISBN 0-8155-5064-2 : LC Card 87-12283 DDC 338.7/617028 19
HD9791.U52 K37 1987

ARTS AND BUSINESS. see **ART AND INDUSTRY.**

ARTS, BACHELOR OF. see **BACHELOR OF ARTS DEGREE.**

ARTS, MASTER OF. see **MASTER OF ARTS DEGREE.**

ARTS, USEFUL. see **TECHNOLOGY.**

Artus, Patrick.
International macroeconomic modelling for policy decisions /. Dordrecht , Boston , c1986. viii, 269 p. : ISBN 90-247-3201-8 LC Card 85-13698 DDC 337/.0724 19
HF1410.5 .I577 1986 NYPL [JLE 86-3469]

Investissement et emploi / Patrick Artus, Pierre-Alain Muet. Paris : Economica, c1986. 260 p. : ill. ; 24 cm. Includes bibliographies. ISBN 2-7178-1196-6 : LC Card 87-125878
1. Capital investments - France - Mathematical models. 2. Production functions (Economic theory). I. Muet, Pierre-Alain. II. Title.
HG4028.C4 A74 1986

Artynov, Aleksandr Petrovich.
Avtomatizatsiia upravleniia transportnymi sistemami /. Moskva , 1984. 271 p. : LC Card 84-195421
HE255 .A93 1984

Prigorodnye passazhirskie perevozki / A.P. Artynov, N.U. Dmitriev. Izd. 2-e, perer. i dop. Moskva : "Transport", 1985. 160 p. : ill. ; 22 cm. Bibliography: p. 159. LC Card 86-208093
1. Local transit - Soviet Union. I. Dmitriev, N. U. (Nikolaĭ Ustinovich). II. Title.
HE4834 .A78 1985

Az áru mint történelmi kategória /. Bató, Sándor. [Budapest] , 1985. 104 p. ; ISBN 963-673-332-5 LC Card 86-228016
HB97.5 .B3245 1985

Árucsere és migráció : a Tokajban 1985. október 28-29-én megrendezett tanácskozás anyaga : [a 75 éves Gunda Béla professzor tiszteletére / szerkesztette, Szabadfalvi József és Viga Gyula]. Miskolc : Herman Ottó Múzeum, 1986. 237 p. : ill., maps ; 24 cm. (A Miskolci Herman Ottó Múzeum néprajzi kiadványai, 0544-4233 . 18) Summaries in German. Includes bibliographies. ISBN 963-01-6995-9 : LC Card 87-409685
1. Migrant labor - Hungary - Congresses. 2. Migration, Internal - Hungary - Congresses. 3. Gunda, Béla. I. Gunda, Béla. II. Szabadfalvi, József. III. Viga, Gyula. IV. Series.
HD5856.H9 A78 1986

ARUNACHAL PRADESH (INDIA) - CENSUS, 1981.
Census of India, 1981. Delhi , <1984-1986. v. in : LC Card 87-915032 DDC 304.6/0954/163021 19
HA4587.A78 C47 1984

ARUNĀCHAL PRADESH, INDIA - ECONOMIC CONDITIONS.
Jha, S. D. (Satya Dev), 1949- Arunachal Pradesh, rich land and poor people /. New Delhi , Guwahati, Assam , 1986. viii, 228 p. ; LC Card 86-902898 DDC 306/.0954/163 19
HC437.A77 J45 1986

ARUNĀCHAL PRADESH, INDIA - SOCIAL CONDITIONS.
Jha, S. D. (Satya Dev), 1949- Arunachal

Pradesh, rich land and poor people /. New Delhi , Guwahati, Assam , 1986. viii, 228 p. ; LC Card 86-902898 DDC 306/.0954/163 19
HC437.A77 J45 1986

ARUNACHAL PRADESH, INDIA - SOCIAL LIFE AND CUSTOMS.
Jha, S. D. (Satya Dev), 1949- Arunachal Pradesh, rich land and poor people /. New Delhi , Guwahati, Assam , 1986. viii, 228 p. ; LC Card 86-902898 DDC 306/.0954/163 19
HC437.A77 J45 1986

Arunachal Pradesh, rich land and poor people /. Jha, S. D. (Satya Dev), 1949- New Delhi , Guwahati, Assam , 1986. viii, 228 p. ; LC Card 86-902898 DDC 306/.0954/163 19
HC437.A77 J45 1986

Arunima. Mahajan, Amarjit. Problems of the aged in unorganised sector /. Delhi, India , 1987. viii, 106 p. ; LC Card 87-901315 DDC 362.6/042 19
HD7105.35.I5 M34 1987

Árva, László. Indokina gazdasági fejlődése és hazánk lehetőségei a térşég országaival való együttműködés terén / Árva László. Budapest : Agrárgazdasági Kutató Intézet, 1984. 69 p. : map ; 29 cm. (Agrárgazdasági Kutató Intézet, 0209-5696 . 1984/15) Bibliography: p. 67-69. ISBN 963-491-194-3 LC Card 86-199424
1. Indochina - Economic conditions. 2. Indochina - Foreign economic relations - Hungary. 3. Hungary - Foreign economic relaions - Indochina. I. Series: Agrárgazdasági Kutató Intézet (Series) , 1984/15. II. Title.
HC441 .A77 1984

Arvey, Richard D. Fairness in selecting employees / Richard D. Arvey, Robert H. Faley. 2nd ed. Reading, Mass. : Addison-Wesley, c1988. x, 361 p. : ill. ; 21 cm. (Addison-Wesley series on managing human resources) Includes bibliographies and indexes. ISBN 0-201-00078-4 (pbk.) : LC Card 87-22173 DDC 658.3/112 19
1. Employee selection - United States. 2. Discrimination in employment - United States. 3. Employee selection - Law and legislation - United States. 4. Discrimination in employment - Law and legislation - United States. I. Faley, Robert H. II. Title. III. Series.
HF5549.5.S38 A78 1988

Arxius dels serveis tècnics d'agricultura . (fasc. 3) Rendé, Josep M. Pla d'organització social agrària de Catalunya /. Barcelona , 1924. 138 p., [1] folded leaf of plates : LC Card 86-202164 DDC 334/.683/09467 19
HD1491.S82 C317 1924

Arya, Dwarika Prasas, 1922- Swastika removes India's poverty and problems within 100 days : the wonder solutions proposed by the Swastika Party / by Dwarka Prasad Arya, known as Acharya Kautilya.1st ed. Calcutta, West Bengal : Swastika Prakashan, 1982. vi, 153 p. ; 23 cm. "English version of this work has been prepared by Km. Jaya Agnihotri, M.A. on the basis of the original Hindi text"--Verso t.p. LC Card 82-904556 DDC 338.954 19
1. India - Economic policy - 1980-. 2. India - Economic conditions - 1980-. 3. Poor - India. 4. Swastika Party. I. Swastika Party. II. Title.
HC435.2 .A887 1982

As greves de 1917 em São Paulo e o processo de organização proletária /. Khoury, Yara Aun. São Paulo , 1981. 221 p. ; LC Card 81-210934 DDC 331.2/98161 19
HD5355.S26 K48 1981 ***NYPL [JLD 86-3514]***

As vítimas do capital . Costa, Marcia Regina da. Rio de Janeiro , 1981. 117 p. ; LC Card 82-149102
HD7262.5.B7 C67 1981 ***NYPL [JLD 86-2852]***

ASA Conference, Migrants, Workers, and the Social Order (1986 : University of Kent) Migrants, workers, and the social order / edited by Jeremy Eades. London ; New York : Tavistock, 1987. p. cm. (ASA monographs . 26) "Based on papers presented at the 1986 ASA Conference, Migrants, Workers, and the Social Order"--P. [4] of cover. Includes bibliographies and index. ISBN 0-422-61680-X (pbk.) LC Card 87-10253
1. Migrant labor - Developing countries - Congresses. 2. Rural-urban migration - Developing countries - Congresses. 3. Migration, Internal - Developing countries - Congresses. 4. Economic anthropology - Congresses. I. Eades, J. S. (Jeremy Seymour), 1945-. II. Series: A.S.A. monographs , 26. III. Title.
HD5856.D44 A72 1986

ASA Education Foundation. Pfeiffer, Paul L. Counter merchandising . Chicago, Ill. (Suite 2260, 20 N. Wacker Dr., Chicago 60606) , c1986. 84 p., [1] leaf of plates : LC Card 87-404047 DDC 658.8/5 19
HF5438.25 .P49 1986

A.S.A. monographs .
(26) ASA Conference, Migrants, Workers, and the Social Order (1986 : University of Kent) Migrants, workers, and the social order /. London , New York , 1987. p. cm. ISBN 0-422-61680-X (pbk.) LC Card 87-10253
HD5856.D44 A72 1986

ASA Studien, 0176-8433 .
(2) Mayer, Hans, 1951- Energie für die Armen? . Saarbrücken , Fort Lauderdale , 1984. 195 p. : ISBN 3-88156-288-5 : LC Card 85-199309
HD9502.I42 M38 1984

(6) Lateinamerikanische Gewerkschaften zwischen staatlicher Gängelung und Autonomie . Saarbrücken , Fort Lauderdale , 1985. 306 p. ; ISBN 3-88156-315-6 LC Card 87-135045 DDC 331.88/098 19
HD6571 .L38 1985

(7) Die Verplante Wohnmisere . Saarbrücken , Fort Lauderdale , 1986. 334 p. : ISBN 3-88156-329-6 LC Card 87-408292 DDC 363.5/1/096 19
HD7287.96.A4 V47 1986

ASA/census working paper .
(2 2) Forecasting interstate migration with limited data . Iowa City , 1982. 37 p. : ***NYPL [*ZT-1564 no.33]***

(5 5) Rogerson, Peter. Job turnover and interregional migration [microform] /. Iowa City , 1981. 25 p. : ***NYPL [*ZT-1564 no.31]***

(6 6) Beaumont, Paul (Paul M.) Regional wage rates [microform] . Iowa City , 1982. 22 p. : ***NYPL [*ZT-1564 no.29]***

Asalariados y clases populares en Lima /. Galin, Pedro. Lima [1986] 127 p. ; LC Card 87-400199 DDC 331/.0985/25 19
HD8350.L562 G35 1986

Asamoah, Ernest. Golden jubilee, July 1935-1985 /. Accra [Ghana] [1985] 64 p. : LC Card 86-155961 DDC 384.54/06/0667 19
HE8689.9.G45 G65 1985

ASBESTOS INDUSTRY - EMPLOYEES - DISEASES AND HYGIENE.
Catrina, Werner. Der Eternit-Report . Zürich , c1985. 244 p. : ISBN 3-280-01615-0 LC Card 85-225903
HD7269.A552 S93 1985 ***NYPL [JLD 87-38]***

ASBESTOS INDUSTRY - EMPLOYEES - DISEASES AND HYGIENE - SWITZERLAND.
Catrina, Werner. Der Eternit-Report . Zürich , c1985. 244 p. : ISBN 3-280-01615-0 LC Card 85-225903
HD7269.A552 S93 1985 ***NYPL [JLD 87-38]***

ASBESTOS INDUSTRY - HYGIENIC ASPECTS.
Catrina, Werner. Der Eternit-Report . Zürich , c1985. 244 p. : ISBN 3-280-01615-0 LC Card 85-225903
HD7269.A552 S93 1985 ***NYPL [JLD 87-38]***

ASBESTOS INDUSTRY - HYGIENIC ASPECTS - SWITZERLAND.
Catrina, Werner. Der Eternit-Report . Zürich , c1985. 244 p. : ISBN 3-280-01615-0 LC Card 85-225903
HD7269.A552 S93 1985 ***NYPL [JLD 87-38]***

Ascari, Sergio. Il metano in Italia : mercato, prezzi e sistema distributivo / Sergio Ascari ; introduzione di Fernando Amman. Milano, Italy : F. Angeli, c1985. 292 p. : ill. ; 22 cm. (Collana di economia e politica dell'energia . 22) Includes bibliographical references. LC Card 86-135353
1. Methane industry - Italy. I. Title. II. Series.
HD9579.M43 I82 1985

ASCC mémoire au gouvernement du Canada. Canadian Railway Labour Association. CRLA submission to the government of Canada /. Ottawa [1977] 28, 31 p. ; LC Card 84-256714
HE2807 .C33 1977

ASCE National Convention (1985 : Denver, Colo.) Transition in the nuclear industry . New York, N.Y. , c1985. iii, 233 p. : ISBN 0-87262-443-9 (pbk.) LC Card 85-70499 DDC 338.4/762148/0973 19
HD9698.U52 T73 1985 ***NYPL [JSD 86-173]***

ASCE National Convention (1986 : Boston, Mass.) Facility location and land use . New York, N.Y. , c1986. vii, 40 p. : ISBN 0-87262-574-5 (pbk.) LC Card 86-25926 DDC 338.6/042 19
HD171.A15 F33 1986

Asch, Peter. Economic theory and the antitrust dilemma / Peter Asch. Malabar, Fla. : R.E. Krieger Pub. Co., 1984, c1970. x, 414 p. : ill. ; 24 cm. Includes bibliographical references and index. Reprint. Originally published: New York : Wiley, 1970. ISBN 0-89874-699-X LC Card 83-19947 DDC 338.8/0973 19
1. Trusts, Industrial - United States. 2. Monopolies - United States. 3. Competition - United States. 4. Antitrust law - Economic aspects - United States. I. Title.
HD2785 .A78 1984 ***NYPL [JLE 86-4132]***

Asche, H. (Hartmut) Mobile Lebensformgruppen Südost-Arabiens im Wandel : die Küstenprovinz Al Bāṭinah im erdölfördernden Sultanat Oman / Hartmut Asche. Berlin : D. Reimer, 1981, c1982. xii, 344 p. : ill., 36 maps ; 30 cm. (Abhandlungen des Geographischen Instituts, Anthropogeographie . Bd. 32) Originally presented as the author's thesis (doctoral)--Universität Göttingen, 1980. Bibliography: p. 284-310. ISBN 3-496-00302-2 LC Card 86-217612
1. Fishers - Oman - Bāṭinah. 2. Bāṭinah (Oman) - Economic conditions. 3. Bāṭinah (Oman) - Social conditions. 4. Social mobility - Oman - Bāṭinah. I. Title. II. Series.
HD8039.F652 O522 1982

Aschentrupp Toledo, Hermann. La dimensión política de la crisis y renegociación de la deuda externa mexicana / Hermann Aschentrupp Toledo. México, D.F. : Centro de Investigación y Docencia Económicas, [1985] 229 p. ; 22 cm. (Documento de trabajo . núm. 3.) Cover title: La dimensión política de la crisis y renegociación de la deuda externa mexicana (1982-1984). Includes bibliographies. LC Card 87-401754 DDC 336.3/4/0972 19
1. Debt relief - Mexico. 2. Debts, External - Mexico. 3. Mexico - Foreign economic relations. I. Series: Documento de trabajo (Centro de Investigación y Docencia Económicas) núm. 3. II. Title.
HJ8519 .A8 1985

Aschhoff, Gunther, 1934- Das deutsche Genossenschaftswesen : Entwicklung, Struktur, wirtschaftliches Potential / Gunther Aschhoff, Eckart Henningsen.1. Aufl. Frankfurt am Main : Knapp, 1985. 167 p. : ill. ; 25 cm. (Veröffentlichungen der DG Bank, Deutsche Genossenschaftsbank . Bd. 15) Bibliography: p. 151-156. Includes indexes. ISBN 3-7819-0345-1 LC Card 86-145522
1. Cooperation - Germany (West) - History. 2. Banks and banking, Cooperative - Germany (West) - History. 3. Consumer cooperatives - Germany (West) - History. I. Henningsen, Eckart. II. Title. III. Series.
HD3038 .A77 1985

Aschlimann, Jürg. Aebi, Ernst. SBB im Aaretal . Luzern , c1984. 111 p. : LC Card 84-234665
HE3898.A37 A42 1984

Asdhir, Vijay, 1947- Industrial relations in India : settlement of industrial disputes / Vijay Asdhir ; foreword by Nitish De. New Delhi : Deep & Deep Publications, c1987. 376 p. ; 22 cm. Study, in the context of textile industry in Punjab. Bibliography: p. [369]-374. Includes index. LC Card 86-903540 DDC 331.89/2877/00954552 19
1. Industrial relations - India. 2. Labor disputes - India. 3. Industrial relations - India - Punjab. 4. Labor disputes - India - Punjab. 5. Textile industry - India - Punjab. 6. Collective labor agreements - Textile industry - India - Punjab. I. Title.
HD8686.5 .A85 1987

ASEAN.
The Minerals industries of ASEAN and Australia . Sydney , Boston , 1988. p. cm. ISBN 0-04-301284-1 LC Card 87-18339 DDC 338.2/0959 19
HD9506.A6592 M56 1988

ASEAN.
Denis, Pierre. L'ASEAN (Association des pays

de l'Asie et du Sud-Est) . Ottignies, Louvain-la-Neuve [1981] 61 p., [3] leaves of plates : LC Card 86-204495
HC441 .D45 1981

K. A. Mohamed Ariff, 1940- Malaysia and ASEAN economic cooperation /. Singapore , 1980, cover 1981. 177 p. ; ISBN 997-19-0207-9 LC Card 82-940035
HC441 .K18 1981

Kraft, Alfred. Aspekte der Regionalen wirtschaftlichen Integration zwischen Entwicklungsländern . Wiesbaden , 1982. x, 298 p. : ISBN 3-515-03801-9 LC Card 85-136228
HC441 .K69 1982

L'ASEAN (Association des pays de l'Asie et du Sud-Est) . Denis, Pierre. Ottignies, Louvain-la-Neuve [1981] 61 p., [3] leaves of plates : LC Card 86-204495
HC441 .D45 1981

Asean-Australia trade in manufactures / edited by David Lim. Melbourne, Australia : Longman Cheshire, c1985. xiii, 263 p. ; 22 cm. Includes bibliographical references and index. ISBN 0-582-71147-9 (pbk.) LC Card 86-228309 DDC 382/.4567/0994 19
1. Australia - Manufactures. 2. Asia, Southeastern - Manufactures. 3. Australia - Commerce - Asia, Southeastern. 4. Asia, Southeastern - Commerce - Australia. I. Lim, David.
HD9738.A82 A83 1985

ASEAN - CONGRESSES.
The ASEAN success story . Honolulu, Hawaii , 1987. xviii, 253 p. : ISBN 0-8248-1107-0 (pbk.) : LC Card 86-29373 DDC 337.1/59 19
HC441 .A864 1987

ASEAN-U. S. economic relations . Singapore , c1986. x, 54 p. : ISBN 997-19-8842-9 (pbk.) LC Card 87-940002 DDC 337.59073 19
HF1456.5.A7 A84 1986

The ASEAN success story : social, economic, and political dimensions : based on the East-West Center's 25th Anniversary Conference on ASEAN and the Pacific Basin, held in Honolulu, Hawaii from 29 October to 1 November 1985 / edited by Linda G. Martin. Honolulu, Hawaii : The Center : Distributed by the University of Hawaii Press, 1987. xviii, 253 p. : ill. ; 23 cm. Includes bibliographies and index. ISBN 0-8248-1107-0 (pbk.) : LC Card 86-29373 DDC 337.1/59 19
1. ASEAN - Congresses. 2. Asia, Southeastern - Economic integration - Congresses. 3. Asia, Southeastern - Economic conditions - Congresses. 4. Asia, Southeastern - Social conditions - Congresses. 5. Asia, Southeastern - Politics and government - Congresses. I. Martin, Linda G., 1947-. II. East-West Center. III. East-West Center's 25th Anniversary Conference on ASEAN and the Pacific Basin (1985 : Honolulu, Hawaii).
HC441 .A864 1987

ASEAN-U. S. economic relations : an overview / edited by Agustin Kintanar, Jr. and Tan Loong-Hoe. Singapore : ASEAN Economic Research Unit, Institute of Southeast Asian Studies, c1986. x, 54 p. : ill. ; 24 cm. Summaries of 8 papers presented at a workshop organized by the Institute of Southeast Asian Studies, ASEAN Economic Research Unit, Singapore, 22-24 Apr., 1985. Includes bibliographies. ISBN 997-19-8842-9 (pbk.) LC Card 87-940002 DDC 337.59073 19
1. United States - Foreign economic relations - Asia, Southeastern - Congresses. 2. Asia, Southeastern - Foreign economic relations - United States - Congresses. 3. ASEAN - Congresses. I. Kintanar, Agustin. II. Tan, Loong-Hoe. III. Institute of Southeast Asian Studies. ASEAN Economic Research Unit.
HF1456.5.A7 A84 1986

Asebrook, Richard J. Backer, Morton. Financial accounting . San Diego , c1988. xvi, 685 p. : ISBN 0-15-527371-X LC Card 87-81140 DDC 657 19
HF5635 .B139 1988

Aseptic food processing and packaging . Gipson, Beckilynn. Stamford, Conn., U. S.A. , c1986. xiii, 164 leaves ; ISBN 0-89336-471-1 (pbk.) LC Card 87-405014 DDC 381/.45664028 19
HD9999.C743 U629 1986

Asesores para el Desarrollo (Tegucigalpa, Honduras) Estudio de diagnóstico de la población de los barrios--Chamelecón, Suyapa, Fe y Esperanza, San Antonio, San José y San Miguel /. Tegucigalpa, D.C. [1984] 1 v. (various foliations) : LC Card 85-205996
HC145.Z7 T434 1984

ASG-Materialsammlung, 0344-5712 .
(Nr. 171) Schumacher, Karl-Edzard. Entwicklungsmöglichkeiten landwirtschaftlicher Übergangsbetriebe in Niedersachsen . Göttingen , 1985. 234, vi p. : LC Card 86-186858
HD9013.7.L68 S38 1985

(Nr. 172) Landwirtschaftliche Übergangsbetriebe in Niedersachsen . Göttingen , 1985. xiii, 105 p. ; LC Card 86-185987
HD9013.7.L68 L36 1985

(Nr. 174) Holla, Michael. Die Belastung der Landwirtschaft durch Beiträge zur sozialen Sicherung im Vergleich zur Situation anderer sozialer Gruppen . Göttingen [1986] viii, 174 p. ; LC Card 87-407657 DDC 368.4/00943 19
HD7179 .H635 1986

(Nr. 175) Kretschmann, Rolf. Möglichkeiten des Berufswechsels von Haupterwerbslandwirten unter besonderer Berücksichtigung von Agrarstruktur und Arbeitsmarkt /. Göttingen , 1986. xi, 109 p. : LC Card 87-408871 DDC 331.25/924 19
HD1536.G3 K746 1986

Ash, Russell. Dear cats . London , 1986. 128 p. : LC Card 87-126969 DDC 628.9/693 19
HE6939.S42 D42 1986

Ashauer, Günter.
Öffentliche Finanzen, Kredit und Kapital . Berlin , c1985. xvi, 618 p., [1] leaf of plates : ISBN 3-428-05737-6 LC Card 85-164173
HJ161 .O33 1985

Standortbestimmung . Stuttgart , c1984. 447 p. ; ISBN 3-09-311000-9 LC Card 85-150165
HG1939.G3 S73 1984

Asher, Robert.
Connecticut workers and technological change : Connecticut workers and a Half Century of Technological Change, 1930-1980, Project / Robert Asher. Storrs : Center for Oral History, University of Connecticut, c1983. 100 p. : ill. ; 23 cm. Interpretive booklet for the microfiche set: The Worker and technological change, 1930-1980. Bibliography: p. 96-98. LC Card 83-62409 DDC 306/.3/09746 19
1. Labor and laboring classes - Connecticut. 2. Technological innovations - Social aspects - Connecticut. I. Title.
HD8083.C7 A83 1983 ***NYPL [JLE 86-1507]***

Life and labor . Albany , c1986. x, 343 p. ; ISBN 0-88706-173-7 LC Card 86-14362 DDC 305.5/62/0973 19
HD8066 .L54 1986 ***NYPL [JLE 86-4350]***

Ashley, W. J. (William James), Sir, 1860-1927. Mill, John Stuart, 1806-1873. Principles of political economy . Fairfield, NJ , 1987. liii, 1013 p. ; ISBN 0-678-00073-5 LC Card 86-21290 DDC 330 19
HB161 .M6 1987

Ashmore, M. Catherine. Risks & rewards of entrepreneurship /. Saint Paul, Minn. , c1988. 123 p. : ISBN 0-8219-0323-3 (pbk.) LC Card 87-21787 DDC 338/.04 19
HB615 .R56 1988

Ashmore, Richard D. The Social psychology of female-male relations . Orlando , 1986. xvi, 351 p. ; ISBN 0-12-065280-3 (alk. paper) LC Card 85-9138 DDC 305.3 19
HM132 .S569 1986 ***NYPL [JLE 86-1746]***

Ashok Rudra. see **Rudra, Ashok.**

Ashraf, Shahid, 1959- Indian industry : restructuring and growth / Shahid Ashraf. Delhi, India : Mittal Publications, 1986. 100 p. ; 22 cm. Originally presented as the author's thesis (M. Phil.--Jawaharlal Nehru University) Bibliography: p. [94]-97. Includes index. LC Card 86-903305 DDC 338.0954 19
1. India - Industries. 2. India - Economic conditions - 1947-. I. Title.
HC435.2 .A889 1986

Ashton, D. N. Unemployment under capitalism : the sociology of British and American labour markets / David N. Ashton. Brighton, Sussex : Wheatsheaf Books : Distributd by Harvester Press, 1986. xiv, 225 p. : ill. ; 23 cm. Includes indexes. Bibliography: p. 200-218. ISBN 0-7108-0163-7
1. Unemployment - Great Britain. 2. Unemployment - United States. 3. Industrial sociology - Great Britain. 4. Industrial sociology - United States. I. Title.
NYPL [JLD 86-1049]

Ashton, Paul. Minford, Patrick. Unemployment . Oxford, UK , New York, NY, USA , 1985. x, 214 p. : ISBN 0-631-14506-0 : LC Card 85-13511 DDC 331.13/7941 19
HD5765.A6 M55 1985
NYPL [JLE 86-2297]

Ashtor, Eliyahu, 1914- East-West trade in the medieval Mediterranean / Eliyahu Ashtor ; edited by Benjamin Z. Kedar. London : Variorum Reprints, 1986. [344] p. ; 24 cm. (Variorum reprint. CS245) English, French, and Italian. Includes bibliographical references and index. ISBN 0-86078-193-3 LC Card 87-134358 DDC 382/.094/056 19
1. Middle East - Commerce - Europe - History. 2. Europe - Commerce - Middle East - History. 3. Middle East - Foreign economic relations - Europe. 4. Europe - Foreign economic relations - Middle East. I. Kedar, B. Z. II. Title.
HF3756.Z7 E92 1986

Ashurst, W. H. (William Henry), 1792-1855. Pearson, Charles, 1794-1862. Central city terminus . [S.l.] 1845 (London : Richard and John E. Taylor) 20 p. ; LC Card 85-666155
HE3019.L8 P42x 1845

Ashwood, Thomas M. Terror in the skies / Thomas M. Ashwood. New York : Stein and Day, 1987. p. cm. ISBN 0-8128-3125-X : LC Card 86-42779 DDC 363.2/876 19
1. Hijacking of aircraft - Prevention. I. Title.
HE9779 .A74 1987

Así aprendemos : al estar organizadas hemos podido trabajar y proponer una alternativa / investigación realizada por el Taller de Lavandería Santa María y el Taller de Acción Cultural. Santiago de Chile : TAC, [1986] 126 p. : ill. ; 16 x 21 cm. Bibliography: p. 125-126. LC Card 87-404640 DDC 330/.07/15 19
1. Economics - Study and teaching (Continuing education) - Chile. I. Taller de Lavandería Santa María. II. Taller de Acción Cultural (Santiago, Chile).
HB74.9.C5 A85 1986

Así cambiará España . Gómez Fuentes, Angel, 1950- Esplugues de Llobregat, Barcelona , 1986. 333 p. ; ISBN 84-01-33317-2 LC Card 87-100798
HC241.25.S6 G65 1986

Asia and World Institute. Sea lane security studies . Taipei, Taiwan, Republic of China , 1986. 100 p. ; LC Card 87-133640 DDC 359/.03 19
HE327 .S435 1986

Asia and world monograph series .
(no. 39) Sea lane security studies . Taipei, Taiwan, Republic of China , 1986. 100 p. ; LC Card 87-133640 DDC 359/.03 19
HE327 .S435 1986

ASIA - COMMERCE - UNITED STATES - CONGRESSES.
Vision of the future . Washington, D.C. , 1986. x, 189 p. : LC Card 87-125235 DDC 382/.0973/05 19
HF3118 .V57 1986

ASIA - COMMERCE - UNITED STATES - STATISTICS.
U. S. trade relations with Asia . Washington , 1987. vii, 85 p. ; LC Card 87-601359 DDC 382/.0973/05 19
HF3118 .U15 1987

ASIA - DEPENDENCY ON UNITED STATES.
Die Wirtschaftliche Expansion der USA . Moskau , 1986. 175 p. ; LC Card 87-408806 DDC 337.7305 19
HF1456.5.A64 W57 1986

ASIA - ECONOMIC CONDITIONS.
Jones, E. L. (Eric Lionel) The European miracle . Cambridge , New York , 1987. xxxiii, 279 p., [1] leaf of plates : ISBN 0-521-33449-7 LC Card 87-8092 DDC 330.94/02 19
HC240 .J57 1987

Zarubezhnyĭ Vostok . Moskva , 1986. 126 p. ; LC Card 87-126378
HC412 .Z38 1986

ASIA - ECONOMIC CONDITIONS - 1945-
Asia-Pacific report . Honolulu, Hawaii , 1986. x, 104 p. : ISBN 0-86638-071-X (pbk.) LC Card

85-27538 DDC 909/.09823/0828 19
HC412 .A7242 1986 ***NYPL [JLF 87-143]***

Asia-Pacific report, 1987-88 . Honolulu, Hawaii , 1987. p. cm. ISBN 0-86638-098-1 : LC Card 87-20074 DDC 909/.098230828 19
HC412 .A72415 1987

Asian economic handbook. London , 1987, c1986. 272 p. : ISBN 0-86338-141-3 : LC Card 87-133198 DDC 330.95/042 19
HC412 .A748 1987

Bray, Francesca. The rice economies . Oxford [Oxfordshire] , New York , 1986. xvii, 254 p. : ISBN 0-631-14877-9 : LC Card 85-30819 DDC 338.1/7318/095 19
HD9066.A7 B73 1986 ***NYPL [JLE 87-793]***

Das Dreieck Europa-Amerika-Asien /. [Diessenhofen] , 1986. 154 p. : ISBN 3-7253-0272-3 LC Card 86-231548
HC412 .D7 1986

James, William E. Asian agriculture and economic development /. Manila, Philippines , c1982. xiii, 128 p. ; LC Card 87-104389 DDC 338.1/095 19
HD2056 .J35 1982

Opyt stroitel′stva sot͡sialisticheskoĭ ėkonomiki v stranakh Azii /. Moskva , 1986. 290 p. ; LC Card 87-126301
HC412 .O675 1986

Trudovye resursy Vostoka . Moskva , 1987. 319 p. ; LC Card 87-142995
HD5811.85.A6 T78 1987

Woodward, Maria Lourdes. Business issues for the Asia-Pacific region /. Menlo Park, CA (333 Ravenswood Ave., Menlo Park 94025) , c1986. 14 p. ; LC Card 86-220779 DDC 330.95/0428
HC413.A78 W66 1986

ASIA - ECONOMIC CONDITIONS - CONGRESSES.
Europe and the rise of capitalism /. Oxford [Oxfordshire] , New York, NY, USA , 1987. p. cm. ISBN 0-631-15006-4 : LC Card 87-12293 DDC 330.94 19
HC240.9.C3 E97 1987

ASIA - ECONOMIC POLICY.
Lewis, John Prior. Asian development . Lanham, MD , New York , c1987. 49 p. ; ISBN 0-8191-6590-5 (pbk.) : LC Card 87-21599 DDC 338.91/095 19
HC412 .L45 1987

ASIA - FOREIGN ECONOMIC RELATIONS - DEVELOPING COUNTRIES.
South-South economic cooperation . New Delhi , 1987. xii, 262 p. ; ISBN 81-7027-102-9 : LC Card 86-903797 DDC 337/.09172/4 19
HF1413 .S617 1987

ASIA - FOREIGN ECONOMIC RELATIONS - EUROPE.
Das Dreieck Europa-Amerika-Asien /. [Diessenhofen] , 1986. 154 p. : ISBN 3-7253-0272-3 LC Card 86-231548
HC412 .D7 1986

ASIA - FOREIGN ECONOMIC RELATIONS - UNITED STATES.
Das Dreieck Europa-Amerika-Asien /. [Diessenhofen] , 1986. 154 p. : ISBN 3-7253-0272-3 LC Card 86-231548
HC412 .D7 1986

U. S. trade relations with Asia . Washington , 1987. vii, 85 p. ; LC Card 87-601359 DDC 382/.0973/05 19
HF3118 .U15 1987

Die Wirtschaftliche Expansion der USA . Moskau , 1986. 175 p. ; LC Card 87-408806 DDC 337.7305 19
HF1456.5.A64 W57 1986

ASIA - FOREIGN ECONOMIC RELATIONS - UNITED STATES - CONGRESSES.
Vision of the future . Washington, D.C. , 1986. x, 189 p. : LC Card 87-125235 DDC 382/.0973/05 19
HF3118 .V57 1986

ASIA - FOREIGN RELATIONS.
Asia-Pacific report, 1987-88 . Honolulu, Hawaii , 1987. p. cm. ISBN 0-86638-098-1 : LC Card 87-20074 DDC 909/.098230828 19
HC412 .A72415 1987

Asia - Government. see Asia - Politics and government.

ASIA - INDUSTRIES.
Oshima, Harry T. (Harry Tatsumi) The transition to an industrial economy in monsoon Asia /. Manila, Philippines , c1983. 111 p. ; LC Card 87-105003 DDC 338.095 19
HC412 .O694 1983

ASIA - MANUFACTURES.
Oshima, Harry T. (Harry Tatsumi) The transition to an industrial economy in monsoon Asia /. Manila, Philippines , c1983. 111 p. ; LC Card 87-105003 DDC 338.095 19
HC412 .O694 1983

Asia Pacific Centre. Chen, Edward K. Y. The markets of Asia/Pacific--People's Republic of China /. London , Aldershot, Hants, England , c1984. 124 p., [1] leaf of plates : ISBN 0-566-02316-4 LC Card 87-672541
HC427.92 .C353x 1984b

Asia-Pacific report : trends, issues, challenges. Honolulu, Hawaii : East-West Center, 1986. x, 104 p. : ill. (some col.), maps ; 29 cm. Spine title: Asia-Pacific report, 1986. Errata slip inserted. ISBN 0-86638-071-X (pbk.) LC Card 85-27538 DDC 909/.09823/0828 19
1. Natural resources - Asia. 2. Natural resources - Pacific Area. 3. Asia - Economic conditions - 1945-. 4. Pacific area - Economic conditions. 5. Pacific area - Politics and government. 6. Asia - Population. 7. Pacific Area - Population. I. Title: Asia-Pacific report, 1986.
HC412 .A7242 1986 ***NYPL [JLF 87-143]***

Asia-Pacific report, 1986. Asia-Pacific report . Honolulu, Hawaii , 1986. x, 104 p. : ISBN 0-86638-071-X (pbk.) LC Card 85-27538 DDC 909/.09823/0828 19
HC412 .A7242 1986 ***NYPL [JLF 87-143]***

Asia-Pacific report, 1987-88 : trends, issues, challenges / edited by Charles E. Morrison. Honolulu, Hawaii : East-West Center, 1987. p. cm. ISBN 0-86638-098-1 : LC Card 87-20074 DDC 909/.098230828 19
1. Asia - Economic conditions - 1945-. 2. Pacific area - Economic conditions. 3. Asia - Politics and government. 4. Pacific area - Politics and government. 5. Asia - Foreign relations. 6. Pacific area - Foreign relations. I. Morrison, Charles Edward, 1944-. II. East-West Center.
HC412 .A72415 1987

ASIA - POLITICS AND GOVERNMENT - 1945-
Woodward, Maria Lourdes. Business issues for the Asia-Pacific region /. Menlo Park, CA (333 Ravenswood Ave., Menlo Park 94025) , c1986. 14 p. ; LC Card 86-220779 DDC 330.95/0428
HC413.A78 W66 1986

ASIA - POPULATION.
Asia-Pacific report . Honolulu, Hawaii , 1986. x, 104 p. : ISBN 0-86638-071-X (pbk.) LC Card 85-27538 DDC 909/.09823/0828 19
HC412 .A7242 1986 ***NYPL [JLF 87-143]***

ASIA - POPULATION - ABSTRACTS.
Student research abstracts in population studies /. Bombay , 1986, c1985. xi, 434 p. ; LC Card 86-902278 DDC 304.6/095 19
HA4553 .S78 1986

ASIA - POPULATION - CONGRESSES.
An Integrated approach to population, food, and nutrition policies and programmes for national development . Bangkok, Thailand [1979 or 1980] 39 p. ; LC Card 82-169080
HA4553 .I58 1979

ASIA - POPULATION - ECONOMIC ASPECTS.
Trudovye resursy Vostoka . Moskva , 1987. 319 p. ; LC Card 87-142995
HD5811.85.A6 T78 1987

Asia Productivity Organization. Symposium on Linkage Between Large and Small Industries (1985 : Kuala Lumpur, Malaysia) Linkage effects and small industry development . Tokyo , 1986. iv, 191 p. : ISBN 92-833-2037-3 LC Card 87-137082 DDC 338.6/42/09595 19
HD2341 .S96 1985

ASIA - RURAL CONDITIONS.
Gosudarstvo i agrarnai͡a ėvoli͡utsii͡a v razvivai͡ushchikhsi͡a stranakh Azii i Afriki /. Moskva , 1980. 227 p. ; LC Card 81-143353
HD2056 .G67 1980

ASIA - SOCIAL CONDITIONS - CONGRESSES.
Movement for a no poverty society . Calcutta , 1980. 78 p. ; LC Card 81-902107
HC415.P6 M68 1980

Peasants and politics . Melbourne , c1978. 218 p. : ISBN 0-7267-2027-5
NYPL [JLE 81-1456]

ASIA, SOUTHEASTERN - COMMERCE.
K. A. Mohamed Ariff, 1940- Malaysia and ASEAN economic cooperation /. Singapore , 1980, cover 1981. 177 p. ; ISBN 997-19-0207-9 LC Card 82-940035
HC441 .K18 1981

ASIA, SOUTHEASTERN - COMMERCE - AUSTRALIA.
Asean-Australia trade in manufactures /. Melbourne, Australia , c1985. xiii, 263 p. ; ISBN 0-582-71147-9 (pbk.) LC Card 86-228309 DDC 382/.4567/0994 19
HD9738.A82 A83 1985

ASIA, SOUTHEASTERN - COMMERCE - CHINA.
Manezhev, S. A. (Sergeĭ Aleksandrovich) Ėkonomicheskie otnoshenii͡a KNR so stranami I͡Ugo-Vostochnoĭ Azii /. Moskva , 1980. 191 p. ; LC Card 81-130904
HF1604.Z4 A7856 1980

ASIA, SOUTHEASTERN - COMMERCE - CONGRESSES.
Wachstumsmarkt Südostasien . München , c1984. x, 807 p. : ISBN 3-8039-0292-4 : LC Card 84-249861
HF3790.8.Z5 W33 1984

ASIA, SOUTHEASTERN - COMMERCE - INDIA, SOUTH - HISTORY.
Sarkar, Himansu Bhusan. Trade and commercial activities of southern India in the Malayo-Indonesian world, up to A.D. 1511 /. Calcutta , 1986- v. <1- > : LC Card 87-900744 DDC 382/.09548/059 19
HF3788.A78 S25 1986

ASIA, SOUTHEASTERN - COMMERCIAL POLICY.
Kraus, Willy. The economic development of the Pacific Basin . New York , London , 1986. x, 180 p., [1] leaf of plates : ISBN 0-312-00452-4 (alk. paper) : LC Card 86-26292 DDC 338.95 19
HF1591 .K73 1986

ASIA, SOUTHEASTERN - ECONOMIC CONDITIONS.
Economic development in East and South-east Asia . Canberra , 1984. x, 237 p. : ISBN 0-644-02983-8 (pbk.) LC Card 86-673760
HC460.5 .E26x 1984

ASIA, SOUTHEASTERN - ECONOMIC CONDITIONS - CASE STUDIES.
Southeast Asia in the 1980s . Sydney , Boston , 1987. p. cm. ISBN 0-04-301289-2 LC Card 87-19550 DDC 338.959 19
HC441 .S69 1987

ASIA, SOUTHEASTERN - ECONOMIC CONDITIONS - CONGRESSES.
The ASEAN success story . Honolulu, Hawaii , 1987. xviii, 253 p. : ISBN 0-8248-1107-0 (pbk.) : LC Card 86-29373 DDC 337.1/59 19
HC441 .A864 1987

ASIA, SOUTHEASTERN - ECONOMIC INTEGRATION - CONGRESSES.
The ASEAN success story . Honolulu, Hawaii , 1987. xviii, 253 p. : ISBN 0-8248-1107-0 (pbk.) : LC Card 86-29373 DDC 337.1/59 19
HC441 .A864 1987

ASIA, SOUTHEASTERN - ECONOMIC POLICY.
Preston, P. W. (Peter Wallace), 1949- Rethinking development . London , New York , 1987. xv, 261 p. ; ISBN 0-7102-1263-1 LC Card 87-4905 DDC 338.959 19
HC441 .P75 1987

ASIA, SOUTHEASTERN - ECONOMIC POLICY - CASE STUDIES.
Southeast Asia in the 1980s . Sydney , Boston , 1987. p. cm. ISBN 0-04-301289-2 LC Card 87-19550 DDC 338.959 19
HC441 .S69 1987

Asia, Southeastern - Economic union. see Asia, Southeastern - Economic integration.

ASIA, SOUTHEASTERN - FOREIGN ECONOMIC RELATIONS.
Denis, Pierre. L'ASEAN (Association des pays de l'Asie et du Sud-Est) . Ottignies,

Louvain-la-Neuve [1981] 61 p., [3] leaves of plates : LC Card 86-204495
HC441 .D45 1981

ASIA, SOUTHEASTERN - FOREIGN ECONOMIC RELATIONS - CHINA.
Manezhev, S. A. (Sergeĭ Aleksandrovich) Ėkonomicheskie otnoshenii͡a KNR so stranami IUgo-Vostochnoĭ Azii /. Moskva , 1980. 191 p. ; LC Card 81-130904
HF1604.Z4 A7856 1980

ASIA, SOUTHEASTERN - FOREIGN ECONOMIC RELATIONS - EUROPEAN ECONOMIC COMMUNITY COUNTRIES.
Relations between the European Community and the member states of the Association of South-East Asian Nations /. Brussels [1986] 55 p. : LC Card 87-135576 DDC 337.4059 19
HF1532.5 .R46 1986

ASIA, SOUTHEASTERN - FOREIGN ECONOMIC RELATIONS - UNITED STATES - CONGRESSES.
ASEAN-U. S. economic relations . Singapore , c1986. x, 54 p. : ISBN 997-19-8842-9 (pbk.) LC Card 87-940002 DDC 337.59073 19
HF1456.5.A7 A84 1986

U. S. ASEAN relations . Washington, D.C. , 1987. xxii, 222 p. ; ISBN 0-943057-00-0 (pbk.) LC Card 87-50526 DDC 337.59073 19
HF1456.5.A7 U72 1987

ASIA, SOUTHEASTERN - FOREIGN RELATIONS - UNITED STATES - CONGRESSES.
U. S. ASEAN relations . Washington, D.C. , 1987. xxii, 222 p. ; ISBN 0-943057-00-0 (pbk.) LC Card 87-50526 DDC 337.59073 19
HF1456.5.A7 U72 1987

Asia, Southeastern - Government. see **Asia, Southeastern - Politics and government.**

ASIA, SOUTHEASTERN - INDUSTRIES.
K. A. Mohamed Ariff, 1940- Malaysia and ASEAN economic cooperation /. Singapore , 1980, cover 1981. 177 p. ; ISBN 997-19-0207-9 LC Card 82-940035
HC441 .K18 1981

The Pacific challenge in international business /. Ann Arbor, Mich. , 1987. viii, 342 p. ; ISBN 0-8357-1620-1 (alk. paper) LC Card 87-5008 DDC 338.09182/3 19
HC460.5 .P32 1987

Asia, Southeastern - Integration of economies. see **Asia, Southeastern - Economic integration.**

Asia, Southeastern - International economic integration. see **Asia, Southeastern - Economic integration.**

ASIA, SOUTHEASTERN - MANUFACTURES.
Asean-Australia trade in manufactures /. Melbourne, Australia , c1985. xiii, 263 p. ; ISBN 0-582-71147-9 (pbk.) LC Card 86-228309 DDC 382/.4567/0994 19
HD9738.A82 A83 1985

The Pacific challenge in international business /. Ann Arbor, Mich. , 1987. viii, 342 p. ; ISBN 0-8357-1620-1 (alk. paper) LC Card 87-5008 DDC 338.09182/3 19
HC460.5 .P32 1987

ASIA, SOUTHEASTERN - POLITICS AND GOVERNMENT - CONGRESSES.
The ASEAN success story . Honolulu, Hawaii , 1987. xviii, 253 p. : ISBN 0-8248-1107-0 (pbk.) : LC Card 86-29373 DDC 337.1/59 19
HC441 .A864 1987

ASIA, SOUTHEASTERN - POPULATION POLICY - CONGRESSES.
IGCC Workshop on Linkages Between University Based Population Activities and National Population/Family Planning Programmes (1978 : Bangkok, Thailand) IGCC Workshop on Linkages Between University Based Population Activities and National Population/Family Planning Programmes . Kuala Lumpur, Selangor [1978?] 111 p. : LC Card 81-941403
HB3641 .I35 1978

Seminar on the Effect of Internal Migration, Urbanization, and Resettlement in the IGCC Region on its Population/Family Planning Programmes (1980 : Jakarta, Indonesia) Seminar on the Effect of Internal Migration, Urbanization, and Resettlement in the IGCC Region on its Population/Family Planning Programmes . Kuala Lumpur, Malaysia [1980?] 131 p. : LC Card 81-941408
HB2101 .S45 1980

ASIA, SOUTHEASTERN - SOCIAL CONDITIONS - CONGRESSES.
The ASEAN success story . Honolulu, Hawaii , 1987. xviii, 253 p. : ISBN 0-8248-1107-0 (pbk.) : LC Card 86-29373 DDC 337.1/59 19
HC441 .A864 1987

ASIA, SOUTHEASTERN - SOCIAL POLICY.
Preston, P. W. (Peter Wallace), 1949- Rethinking development . London , New York , 1987. xv, 261 p. ; ISBN 0-7102-1263-1 LC Card 87-4905 DDC 338.959 19
HC441 .P75 1987

Asian agenda report .
(11) Lardy, Nicholas R. China's entry into the world economy . Lanham, MD , New York, N.Y. , c1987. xviii, 57 p. : ISBN 0-8191-6371-6 (alk. paper) : LC Card 87-10625 DDC 382/.0951 19
HF3820.5 .L37 1987

(7) Lewis, John Prior. Asian development . Lanham, MD , New York , c1987. 49 p. ; ISBN 0-8191-6590-5 (pbk.) : LC Card 87-21599 DDC 338.91/095 19
HC412 .L45 1987

Asian agriculture and economic development /. James, William E. Manila, Philippines , c1982. xiii, 128 p. ; LC Card 87-104389 DDC 338.1/095 19
HD2056 .J35 1982

Asian agriculture in transition . James, William E. Manila, Philippines , c1983. v, 93 p. ; LC Card 87-105114 DDC 338.1/095 19
HD2056 .J355 1983

Asian and Pacific Council. Food & Fertilizer Technology Center. International Seminar on Recent Improvements in Goat Production in Asia (1984 : Los Baños, Laguna, Philippines) Goat production in Asia . Los Baños, Laguna, Philippines , Taipei, Taiwan, Republic of China , 1985. viii, 186 p. : LC Card 86-200478
HD9438.G632 A785 1984

Asian and Pacific Development Centre. Ramana, D. V. A monograph on access planning as an essay on explorations in alternatives /. Kuala Lumpur [1982] 86 p. : LC Card 84-940306 DDC 338.954 19
HD75 .R36 1982

Asian and Pacific Skill Development Programme. New approach to vocational training /. Islamabad, Pakistan , 1985-1986. 2 v. : ISBN 92-2-105078-5 (pbk. : v. 1) LC Card 86-221389 DDC 331.25/92/0952 19
HD5715.5.J3 N48 1985

Asian development . Lewis, John Prior. Lanham, MD , New York , c1987. 49 p. ; ISBN 0-8191-6590-5 (pbk.) : LC Card 87-21599 DDC 338.91/095 19
HC412 .L45 1987

Asian Development Bank.
Asian energy problems . New York, N.Y., U. S.A. , Singapore , 1982. xxxviii, 363 p. : ISBN 0-03-061566-6 (pbk.) LC Card 81-84610
HD9502.A782 A84x 1982

Huh, Ko Kwang. Economic survey on Western Samoa. [Manila, Philippines] [1984] vii, 44 p. : LC Card 87-403365 DDC 330.996/14 19
HC687.5 .H84 1984

James, William E. Asian agriculture and economic development /. Manila, Philippines , c1982. xiii, 128 p. ; LC Card 87-104389 DDC 338.1/095 19
HD2056 .J35 1982

Oshima, Harry T. (Harry Tatsumi) The transition to an industrial economy in monsoon Asia /. Manila, Philippines , c1983. 111 p. ; LC Card 87-105003 DDC 338.095 19
HC412 .O694 1983

ASIAN DEVELOPMENT BANK.
RP-Japan relations and ADB . Metro Manila, Philippines , 1986. x, 137 p. : ISBN 971-08-3156-9 (pbk.) LC Card 86-211088 DDC 337.520599 19
HF1600.15.J3 R68 1986

Asian Development Bank economic staff paper .
(no. 18) Rana, Pradumna Bickram, 1947- The impact of the current exchange rate system on trade and inflation of selected developing member countries /. Manila, Philippines , c1983. iv, 78 p. : LC Card 87-105105 DDC 332.4/56 19
HG3877 .R36 1983

(no. 19) James, William E. Asian agriculture in transition . Manila, Philippines , c1983. v, 93 p. ; LC Card 87-105114 DDC 338.1/095 19
HD2056 .J355 1983

(no. 20) Oshima, Harry T. (Harry Tatsumi) The transition to an industrial economy in monsoon Asia /. Manila, Philippines , c1983. 111 p. ; LC Card 87-105003 DDC 338.095 19
HC412 .O694 1983

(no. 5) James, William E. Asian agriculture and economic development /. Manila, Philippines , c1982. xiii, 128 p. ; LC Card 87-104389 DDC 338.1/095 19
HD2056 .J35 1982

Asian Development Bank. Economics Office. Improving domestic resource mobilization through financial development . Manila, Philippines , c1985. vii, 51 p. : LC Card 87-101640 DDC 332.6/72/091724 19
HC415.S3 I45 1985

The Asian dream . MacKay, Donald, 1925- Vancouver , c1986. 223 p. : ISBN 0-88894-501-9 LC Card 86-225670 DDC 385/.0971 19
HE2810.C14 M33 1986

Asian economic handbook. 1st ed. London : Euromonitor Publications, 1987, c1986. 272 p. : ill. ; 25 cm. Principal contributor, John Wong. Includes index. ISBN 0-86338-141-3 : LC Card 87-133198 DDC 330.95/042 19
1. Asia - Economic conditions - 1945-. I. Wong, John, 1939-.
HC412 .A748 1987

Asian energy problems : an Asian Development Bank survey. New York, N.Y., U. S.A. : Praeger ; Singapore : [distributed by] Federal Publications, 1982. xxxviii, 363 p. : ill. ; 22 cm. Includes bibliographical references. ISBN 0-03-061566-6 (pbk.) LC Card 81-84610
1. Power resources - Asia - Statistics. 2. Energy development - Asia - Statistics. I. Asian Development Bank.
HD9502.A782 A84x 1982

Asian population studies series .
(no. 45) An Integrated approach to population, food, and nutrition policies and programmes for national development . Bangkok, Thailand [1979 or 1980] 39 p. ; LC Card 82-169080
HA4553 .I58 1979

Asian Productivity Organization.
Energy conservation in the Asian region . Tokyo, Japan [Honolulu, Hawaii] , 1986. vi, 173 p. : ISBN 92-833-2038-1 LC Card 87-122915 DDC 333.79/16/095 19
HD9502.A782 E53 1986

Mundel, Marvin Everett, 1916- Measuring total productivity in manufacturing organizations . Tokyo, Japan , c1986. iv [i.e. vi], 155 p. ; ISBN 92-833-1090-4 LC Card 86-211930 DDC 658.3/14 19
HD56.25 .M87 1986

Productivity and role of top management. Tokyo , 1986. x, 94 p. : ISBN 92-833-2041-1 (pbk.) LC Card 87-146526 DDC 658.3/14/0952 19
HC465.I52 P76 1986

Quality control circle . Tokyo , 1986. x, 170 p. : ISBN 92-833-2040-3 LC Card 87-133710 DDC 658.5/62 19
HD9987.A7852 Q35 1986

Asian stockmarkets . Rowley, Anthony, 1939- Homewood, Ill. , 1987. 290 p. : ISBN 962-7010-29-4; 0-87094-987-X (jacket) LC Card 87-137156 DDC 332.64/25 19
HG5702 .R69 1987

ASIATIC MODE OF PRODUCTION.
Pirec, Dušan. Iskušenja marksizma . Beograd , 1985. 461 p. : LC Card 86-128661
HB97.5 .P498 1985

Aşıkoğlu, Rıza. Sermaye piyasası aracı olarak enflasyon ortamında tahvilleri değerleme / Rıza Aşıkoğlu. [Eskişehir, Turkey] : Anadolu Üniversitesi, 1983. xii, 155 p. : ill. ; 24 cm. (T.C. Anadolu Üniversitesi yayınları . no. 35. no. 13) Bibliography: p. 143-155. Thesis (Ph. D.)--Anadolu

Üniversitesi, 1983. LC Card 85-221546
1. Capital market - Turkey. 2. Inflation (Finance) - Turkey. I. Series: T.C. Anadolu Üniversitesi yayınları. İktisadi ve İdari Bilimler Fakültesi yayınları , no. 13. II. Title.
HG5706.5.A3 A85 1983

Asimakopulos, A., 1930- Theories of income distribution /. Boston , c1988. x, 255 p. : ISBN 0-89838-232-7 LC Card 87-3248 DDC 339.2 19
HB523 .T44 1988

ASME Management Division history, 1886-1980 / editor, Charles M. Merrick ; sponsored by the Management Division, ASME. New York, N.Y. (345 E. 47th St., New York 10017) : American Society of Mechanical Engineers, c1984. x, 169 p. : ill. ; 28 cm. Spine title: Management Division history. Includes bibliographies. LC Card 84-206982 DDC 658/.006/073 19
1. American Society of Mechanical Engineers. Management Division - History. 2. Management - United States - History. 3. Industrial management - United States - History. I. Merrick, Charles M. II. American Society of Mechanical Engineers. Management Division. III. Title: A.S.M.E. Management Division history, 1886-1980. IV. Title: Management Division history.
HD28.A6233 A86 1984 *NYPL [JLF 86-1646]*

Asociación Aurora Vivar. Hernández, Zoila. El coraje de las mineras . Lima, Perú , 1986. 184 p. : LC Card 86-232046
HD5361.Z9 C35 1986

Asociación de Defensa y Capacitación Legal (Peru) Mujer, trabajo y empleo /. Lima, Perú [1985] 294 p. ; LC Card 86-121871 DDC 331.4/0985 19
HD6131 .M85 1985 *NYPL [JLD 87-492]*

Asociación de Libre Comercio. see **Asociación Latinoamericana de Libre Comercio.**

Asociación de Promotores Constructores de Edificios de Barcelona (Spain) El Libro blanco de la promoción-construcción. [Barcelona] , 1985. 141 p. : LC Card 86-188032
HD7351.A3 L53 1985

Asociación de Trabajadores del Campo (Nicaragua) Revolución y mujeres del campo . Managua [1985] 46 p. : LC Card 86-231936
HD1333.N5 R48 1985

Asociación de Transporte Aéro Internacional. see **International Air Transport Association.**

Asociación Demográfica Costarricense. Departamento de Investigaciones Sociodemográficas. Avance de resultados, encuesta de fecundidad y salud /. [San José] Costa Rica , 1986. [32] leaves : LC Card 87-400666 DDC 304.6/32/097286 19
HB947 .A96 1986

Asociación Europea de Libre Comercio. see **European Free Trade Association.**

Asociación Hondureña de Planificación de Familia.
Análisis de la encuesta a líderes nacionales /. Tegucigalpa, D.C. , 1983. 49, [12] leaves ; LC Card 85-203745
HB3540.A3 A52 1983

ASOCIACIÓN HONDUREÑA DE PLANIFICACIÓN DE FAMILIA - PUBLIC OPINION.
Análisis de la encuesta a líderes nacionales /. Tegucigalpa, D.C. , 1983. 49, [12] leaves ; LC Card 85-203745
HB3540.A3 A52 1983

Asociación Internacional de Fomento. see **International Development Association.**

Asociación internacional de la seguridad social. see **International Social Security Association.**

Asociación Latinoamericana de Industriales y Cámaras de la Alimentación. El Mercado regional de frutas . [Montevideo] , 1983. 63 p. ; LC Card 86-171763
HD9259.T753 L295 1983

Asociación Latinoamericana de Instituciones Financieras de Desarrollo. Servicio de Consultas. Asociaciones campesinas como receptoras y administradoras de crédito y su dinámica de grupo. [Lima] [1979] 100 leaves in various foliations : LC Card 85-185371
HG2051.L26 A83 1979

ASOCIACIÓN LATINOAMERICANA DE INTEGRACIÓN.
Aragão, José María. La Asociación Latinoamericana de Libre Comercio (ALALC) y la Asociación Latinoamericana de Integración (ALADI) . Buenos Aires, Argentina [1984] xiii, 172 p. ; LC Card 86-201881
HC125 .A69 1984

Asociación Latinoamericana de Integración. Unidad de Promoción, Complementación y Cooperación. El Mercado regional de frutas . [Montevideo] , 1983. 63 p. ; LC Card 86-171763
HD9259.T753 L295 1983

La Asociación Latinoamericana de Libre Comercio (ALALC) y la Asociación Latinoamericana de Integración (ALADI) . Aragão, José María. Buenos Aires, Argentina [1984] xiii, 172 p. ; LC Card 86-201881
HC125 .A69 1984

ASOCIACIÓN LATINOAMERICANA DE LIBRE COMERCIO - CONGRESSES.
La Industria colombiana y la "ALALC.". [Medellín] [1964] 112 p. ; LC Card 85-111774
HC197 .I36 1964

Asociación Mexicana de Investigadores de la Comunicación. Medios de comunicación, hegemonía y proyectos de desarrollo. [Mexico City] [between 1982 and 1987] 179 p. ; LC Card 87-127821 DDC 338.9/007/1 19
HD77 .M43 1982

Asociación Multidisciplinaria de Investigación y Docencia en Población (Peru) Problemas poblacionales peruanos II /. Lima , c1986. 402 p. : LC Card 86-228816
HB3575 .P763 1986

Asociación Nacional de Jovenes Empresarios (Dominican Republic) Influencia del sector privado sobre la realidad nacional. [Santo Domingo] [1986] 180 p., [1] leaf of plates : LC Card 86-190331
HC153.5 .I53 1986

ASOCIACIÓN NACIONAL DE USUARIOS CAMPESINOS (COLOMBIA)
Rivera Cusicanqui, Silvia. Política e ideología en el movimiento campesino colombiano . [Bogotá] [s.l.] , 1982. 188 p. ; LC Card 84-155496
HD511.5.A87 R58 1982 *NYPL [JLD 86-1208]*

Asociaciones campesinas como receptoras y administradoras de crédito y su dinámica de grupo. [Lima] : ALIDE, [1979] 100 leaves in various foliations : ill. ; 30 cm. "La presente consulta ha sido elaborada a solicitud del Banco Agrario de [la] República Dominicana por el Servicio de Consultas de la Red de Información de ALIDE"--P. [3] Bibliography: leaves [4]-[6] LC Card 85-185371
1. Agricultural cooperative credit associations - Latin America - Abstracts. 2. Agricultural cooperative credit associations - Abstracts. I. Asociación Latinoamericana de Instituciones Financieras de Desarrollo. Servicio de Consultas. II. Banco Agrario de la República Dominicana.
HG2051.L26 A83 1979

Asoción Amauta (Cuzco, Peru) Región sur, problemática y perspectivas /. Arequipa [1986?] 164 p. ; LC Card 87-404224 DDC 330.984/052 19
HC182 .R39 1986

Asokan, S. R. Gurdev Singh. Resin systems in India . Bombay , 1986. xiii, 100 p. ; ISBN 0-86132-128-6 : LC Card 86-903469 DDC 338.4/766837/0954 19
HD9660.R43 I44 1986

Asosiasi Pengusaha Indonesia.
Anggaran dasar dan anggaran rumah tangga : keputusan Munas II 1985 di Surabaya. Jakarta : Asosiasi Pengusaha Indonesia, [1985] 19, 14 p. ; 21 cm. Cover title. LC Card 86-942640
1. Asosiasi Pengusaha Indonesia - Constitution. I. Title.
HD6948.I5 A76 1985

ASOSIASI PENGUSAHA INDONESIA - CONSTITUTION.
Asosiasi Pengusaha Indonesia. Anggaran dasar dan anggaran rumah tangga . Jakarta [1985] 19, 14 p. ; LC Card 86-942640
HD6948.I5 A76 1985

ASPA Foundation. Lorber, Lawrence Z. Sex and salary . Alexandria, Va. , 1985. v, 61 p. ;
NYPL [JLF 86-417]

Aspectos agroeconômicos da soja /. Desgualdo Netto, Domingos. São Paulo , 1985. 139 p. ; LC Card 86-158570
HD9235.S62 B74 1985

Aspectos analíticos da distribuição da massa salarial no período de 1972 a 1983 /. Ribeiro, Maria Eduarda. Lisboa , 1985. 58 p. : LC Card 86-132683
HC394.5.I5 R52 1985

Aspectos de transporte urbano na modificação dos horários de trabalho /. Fernandes, Fátima Sobral. Brasília, DF , 1985. 105 p. : LC Card 87-404953 DDC 331.25/72 19
HD5108.2.B6 F47 1985

Aspectos demográficos regionais / Governo do Estado da Bahia, Secretaria do Planejamento, Ciência e Tecnologia, Centro de Estatística e Informações. Salvador : O Centro, 1984- <v. 1, pt. 1; in 1 > : ill. ; 21 cm. Bibliography: v. 1, pt. 1, p. 53. CONTENTS. - v. 1, t. 1. VII Região de Planejamento, Sobradinho. LC Card 84-235259
1. Bahia, Brazil (State) - Population. I. Bahia (Brazil : State). Centro de Estatística e Informações.
HB3564.B3 A87 1984

Aspectos económicos de la industria petrolera. Capital Federal : Shell Compañía Argentina de Petróleo, Departamento de Asuntos Públicos, [1985 or 1986] 28 p. : col. ill. ; 30 cm. (Problemática energética . 4) LC Card 87-120726
1. Petroleum products - Prices - Government policy - Argentina. 2. Petroleum industry and trade - Government policy - Argentina. I. Shell Compañía Argentina de Petróleo. Departamento de Asuntos Públicos. II. Series.
HD9574.A72 A84 1985

Aspectos econômicos, jurídicos e sociais da Reforma Agrária / Antônio de Pádua Ferraz Nogueira ... [et al.]. São Paulo-SP Brasil : Sopral, [1985] 75 p. ; 22 cm. (Coleção Sopral . 8) Cover title. CONTENTS. - Objetivos econômicos da reforma agrária / Ruy Miller Paiva -- Os pressupostos da reforma agrária / Miguel Reale -- A reforma agrária da nova república e sua inviabilidade sócio-econômica e jurídica / Antonio de Pádua Ferraz Nogueira -- Formas de participação do trabalhador rural na reforma agrária / Ney Bittencourt de Araújo. LC Card 86-220237
1. Land reform - Brazil. 2. Land reform - Law and legislation - Brazil. I. Nogueira, Antonio de Pádua Ferraz, 1933-. II. Series.
HD1333.B6 A85 1985

Aspectos financieros y monetarios de la integración española en la Comunidad Económica Europea /. Gil, Gonzalo. [Madrid] [1985] 187 p. : ISBN 84-505-2233-1 LC Card 87-101729
HC241.25.S6 G55 1985

Aspectos gerais da economia e da sociedade do Nordeste. Recife : Secretaria de Planejamento da Presidência da República, Instituto de Planejamento Econômico e Social : Ministério do Interior, Superintendência do Desenvolvimento do Nordeste, Banco do Nordeste do Brasil, 1984. 318 p. : ill. ; 23 cm. (Série Projeto Nordeste . v. 2) Bibliography: p. 315. LC Card 86-159446
1. Brazil, Northeast - Economic conditions. 2. Saving and investment - Brazil, Northeast. 3. Brazil, Northeast - Population. 4. Brazil, Northeast - Social conditions. 5. Community development - Brazil, Northeast. I. Instituto de Planejamento Econômico e Social. II. Banco do Nordeste do Brasil. III. Series: Série Projecto Nordeste , vol. 2.
HC188.N6 A75 1984

Aspectos industriais da política de desenvolvimento do Nordeste . Tavares, José Reinaldo Carneiro. Recife , 1985. 24 leaves ; LC Card 87-102054 DDC 338.981/3 19
HD3616.B84 N678 1985

Aspects of European integration . Almdal, Preben. Odense C, Denmark , 1986. 108 p. ; ISBN 87-7492-578-4 : LC Card 87-114176 DDC 337.1/42 19
HC241.2 .A7344 1986

Aspects of revenue administration in Assam, 1826-1874 /. Goswami, Shrutidev, 1947- Delhi, India , 1987. xii, 184 p. ; LC Card 87-900200 DDC 336.02/54162 19
HJ2939.A87 G67 1987

Aspects of social and economic development in southern Kura District before the implementation of the Kano River Project irrigation scheme /. Dottridge, M. B. Zaria, Nigeria , 1980. v, 47 p., [1] p. of plates : LC Card 84-256142
HC1055.Z7 K873 1980

Aspects of social & economic development in southern Kura District before the implementation of the Kano River Project irrigation scheme. Dottridge, M. B. Aspects of social and economic development in southern Kura District before the implementation of the Kano River Project irrigation scheme /. Zaria, Nigeria , 1980. v, 47 p., [1] p. of plates : LC Card 84-256142
HC1055.Z7 K873 1980

Aspects of the informal economic sector of Juba, southern Sudan /. Jenkins, S. J. (Susan J.) [Jūbā, Sudan] [1981?] xiii, 217 p., [4] leaves of plates : LC Card 86-980565
HD2346.S82 J85 1981

Aspects of the new media in Europe /. Howard-Healy, Marion. Menlo Park, CA (333 Ravenswood Ave., Menlo Park 94025) , c1986. 22 leaves : LC Card 86-220771 DDC 384/.094 19
HE8700.72.E85 H69 1986

Aspek-aspek proteksi dalam industri dan perdagangan /. Ibrahim, Saaduddin. Jakarta , 1987. 251 p. : LC Card 87-941314
HD4304 .I27 1987

Aspekte der libyischen Ausseninvestitionspolitik, 1972-1985 /. Mattes, Hanspeter. Hamburg , c1985. iv, 169 p. : ISBN 3-89173-001-2 LC Card 86-173976
HG4538 .M376 1985

Aspekte der Regionalen wirtschaftlichen Integration zwischen Entwicklungsländern . Kraft, Alfred. Wiesbaden , 1982. x, 298 p. : ISBN 3-515-03801-9 LC Card 85-136228
HC441 .K69 1982

Aspekte zur G.K.V.-Strukturreform. Aspekte zur GKV-Strukturreform /. Stuttgart , New York , 1984. x, 102 p. ; ISBN 3-437-10918-9 LC Card 84-187001
HD7102.G3 A87 1984

Aspekte zur GKV-Strukturreform / W. Hamm ... [et al.] ; herausgegeben von der Medizinisch Pharmazeutischen Studiengesellschaft e.V. Stuttgart ; New York : G. Fischer, 1984. x, 102 p. ; 23 cm. Includes bibliographical references. ISBN 3-437-10918-9 LC Card 84-187001
1. Insurance, Health - Germany, West. 2. Insurance, Health - Law and legislation - Germany (West). I. Hamm, Walter. II. Medizinisch Pharmazeutische Studiengesellschaft (Germany). III. Title: Aspekte zur G.K.V.-Strukturreform.
HD7102.G3 A87 1984

ASPHALT CONCRETE - ADDITIVES.
Button, Joe W. Synthetic fibers in asphalt paving mixtures /. College Station, Tex. [1984] vi, 153 p. : LC Card 86-620835 DDC 380.5 s 625.8/5 19
HE203 .T43 no. 319-1F TA443.A7

ASPHALT CONCRETE PAVEMENTS. see **PAVEMENTS, ASPHALT CONCRETE.**

ASPHALT CONCRETE - TESTING.
Benson, Fred C. Hot-mix pavement stability performance versus laboratory test results /. College Station, Tex. [1985] xi, 225 p. : LC Card 86-620969 DDC 380.5 s 625.8/5 19
HE203 .T43 no. 285-1 TE200

ASPHALT INDUSTRY - GERMANY (WEST) - STATISTICS.
Strassenbau und Mineralölindustrie im Spiegel der Statistik . Hamburg , 1976. [48] p. : LC Card 83-126399
HD9582.A7 G37 1976

ASPIRATIONS, OCCUPATIONAL. see **VOCATIONAL INTERESTS.**

ASPIRATIONS, VOCATIONAL. see **VOCATIONAL INTERESTS.**

Aspler, I. Seḳer melai ha-hon ha-ḳavu'a be-ta'aśiyah, 1.1.1982 / Y. Aspler. Yerushalayim : ha-Lishkah ha-merkazit li-sṭaṭisṭiḳah, 1986. 80, xvii p. ; 29 cm. (Sidrat pirsumim meyuḥadim, 0333-984X . mis. 785) English and Hebrew. Title on added t.p.: Survey of fixed capital stock in industry, 1.1.1982. "ha-Netunim ha-kaspiyim mutsagim bi-sheḳalim yeshanim." Chiefly tables. LC Card 87-128243
1. Capital investments - Israel - Statistics. 2. Israel - Industries - Statistics. I. Title. II. Title: Survey of fixed capital stock in industry, 1.1.1982. III. Series: Special series (Israel. Lishkah ha-merkazit li-sṭaṭisṭikah , no. 785.
HA1931 .A354 no. 785 HC415.25.Z9C3

Asplund, Rita. Short-run tax-push inflation in Finland / Rita Asplund. Helsinki : Economic Planning Centre : Available from Govt. Print. Centre, 1986. 65 p. : ill. ; 30 cm. Bibliography: p. 63-65. ISBN 951-46-9876-2 (pbk.) LC Card 87-163994 DDC 332.4/1/094897 19
1. Income tax - Finland. 2. Taxation - Finland - Effect of inflation on. 3. Inflation (Finance) - Finland. I. Taloudellinen suunnittelukeskus (Finland). II. Title.
HJ4738.3 .A86 1986

Assael, Henry. Consumer behavior and marketing action / Henry Assael. 3rd ed. Boston, Mass. : Kent Pub. Co., c1987. xix, 700 p., [8] p. of plates : ill. (some col.) ; 25 cm. Includes bibliographies and indexes. ISBN 0-534-07530-4 : LC Card 86-21336 DDC 658.8/342 19
1. Consumers. 2. Motivation research (Marketing). I. Title.
HF5415.3 .A83 1987

ASSAM CO-OPERATIVE APEX BANK.
Bhorali, Devadas. Co-operative banking and economic development /. New Delhi , c1987. 424 p. : LC Card 87-900825 DDC 334/.2/0954162 19
HG2039.I4 B47 1987

ASSAM (INDIA) - ECONOMIC CONDITIONS.
Bhorali, Devadas. Co-operative banking and economic development /. New Delhi , c1987. 424 p. : LC Card 87-900825 DDC 334/.2/0954162 19
HG2039.I4 B47 1987

ASSAM (INDIA) - HISTORY.
Goswami, Surendra Kumar, 1929-1985. A history of revenue administration in Assam, 1228-1826 A.D. . Delhi , 1986. xii, 321 p. : LC Card 86-903188 DDC 354.54/16200726/09 19
HJ2939.Z9 A874 1986

ASSEMBLY-LINE METHODS.
Montags biste sowieso geschafft . Hamburg , 1982. 167 p. : ISBN 3-88506-118-X (pbk.) LC Card 87-673006
HD6068.2.G3 M66x 1982

Assenteismo e presenteismo . Carmignani, Fabrizo. Milano, Italy , c1984. 211 p. ; LC Card 84-175594 DDC 658.3/14 19
HD5115 .C37 1984 ***NYPL [JLD 86-3383]***

Asser, Mohamud Ibrahim. Report of the joint Somali government and World Bank study of agricultural incentives and grain marketing in Somalia /. [Alexandria, Va. , 1984] xviii, 170, 2 p. : LC Card 87-404086 DDC 338.1/8 19
HD9047.S582 R47 1984

Assertive management. Taetzsch, Lyn. Taking charge on the job . New York , c1978. 144 p. ; ISBN 0-917386-22-1 : LC Card 78-111025 DDC 658.4
HD38 .T17 ***NYPL [JLE 80-1910]***

ASSERTIVENESS (PSYCHOLOGY)
Dayhoff, Signe A. Create your own career opportunities /. Andover, Mass. , c1987. x, 111 p. : ISBN 0-931790-75-1 : LC Card 86-26332 DDC 650.1/4 19
HF5549.5.C35 D38 1987

Taetzsch, Lyn. Taking charge on the job . New York , c1978. 144 p. ; ISBN 0-917386-22-1 : LC Card 78-111025 DDC 658.4
HD38 .T17 ***NYPL [JLE 80-1910]***

Assessing corporate political risk : a guide for international businessmen / [edited by] David M. Raddock ; with contributions by Henry Albinski ... [et al.]. Totowa, NJ : Rowman & Littlefield, 1986. xvii, 212 p. ; 25 cm. Includes bibliographies and index. ISBN 0-86598-114-0 LC Card 85-19618 DDC 658 19
1. Risk management. 2. Risk management - Case studies. I. Raddock, David M. II. Albinski, Henry Stephen.
HD61 .A87 1986 ***NYPL [JLE 86-3102]***

Assessing Illinois' strengths and weaknesses in a changing national economy / prepared for the Illinois Department of Commerce and Community Affairs ; submitted by the Fantus Company. Chicago, IL : The Company, [1986] 117 p. : ill. ; 28 cm. "January 1986." LC Card 87-620507 DDC 330.9773/043 19
1. Illinois - Economic conditions. 2. Illinois - Industries. I. Illinois. Dept. of Commerce and Community Affairs. II. Fantus Company.
HC107.I3 A75 1986

Assessing the nuclear age : selections from the Bulletin of the atomic scientists / edited by Len Ackland and Steven McGuire. Chicago, Ill. : Educational Foundation for Nuclear Science : Distributed by the University of Chicago Press, Marketing Dept., c1986. xvii, 382 p. ; 24 cm. Includes index. Bibliography: p. 369-378. ISBN 0-941682-07-2 LC Card 85-82511 DDC 355/.0217 19
1. Nuclear weapons. 2. Nuclear warfare. 3. Nuclear energy. 4. Nuclear disarmament. 5. Arms race - History - 20th century. 6. United States - Military policy. I. Ackland, Len. II. McGuire, Steven. III. Bulletin of the Atomic Scientists.
U264 .A79 1986 ***NYPL [JLE 87-11]***

ASSESSMENT - CALIFORNIA.
Assessment practices survey. [Sacramento, Calif.] , 1987- v. ; LC Card 87-167612 DDC 332.22/2 19
HJ4191 .A74 1987

ASSESSMENT CENTERS (PERSONNEL MANAGEMENT PROCEDURE)
Goldstein, Irwin L., 1937- Training in organizations . Monterey, Calif. , c1986. xv, 315 p. : ISBN 0-534-05604-0 : LC Card 85-21348 DDC 658.3/12404 19
HF5549.5.T7 G543 1985 ***NYPL [JLE 86-1519]***

Gruère, Jean-Pierre. Optimiser les ressources humaines dans l'entreprise . Paris , c1984. 69, 42 p. : ISBN 2-7101-0462-8 : LC Card 84-217427
HF5549.5.A78 G78 1984

Rwegasira, Kami S. P. Administering management development institutions in Africa /. Aldershot, England , Brookfield, Vt. , 1988. p. cm. ISBN 0-566-05501-5 : LC Card 87-17688 DDC 658.4/07124/096 19
HF5549.5.A78 R94 1988

Assessment jurisdictions and agency resources in the United States . Langhoff, Gary M., 1952- Chicago, Ill. , 1987. p. cm. ISBN 0-88329-061-8 : LC Card 87-4101 DDC 336.22/2 19
HJ3241 .L36 1987

ASSESSMENT - MISSOURI - RATES AND TABLES.
Kelly, Margaret. Review of 1985 property tax rates /. Jefferson City [1986] i, 6 leaves, 109, 2 p. ; LC Card 87-620606 DDC 336.22/2 19
HJ4121.M82 K45 1986

ASSESSMENT - NEW YORK (STATE)
Understanding the equalization rate /. Albany, N.Y. (Governor Nelson A. Rockefeller Empire State Plaza, Albany 12223) [1986] 28 p. : LC Card 87-620729 DDC 336.22/2 19
HJ4249 .U53 1986

ASSESSMENT OF TECHNOLOGY. see **TECHNOLOGY ASSESSMENT.**

An assessment of the effectiveness of the Bureau of Community Services, Michigan Economic and Social Opportunity Commission, and community action agencies /. Michigan. Dept. of Labor. [Lansing, Mich.] [1986] 56 p. : LC Card 87-620767 DDC 362/.9774 19
HC107.M53 P6333 1986

Assessment of the employment effects of economic development projects funded under the Urban Programme / Department of the Environment. London : H.M.S.O, 1986. vi, 52 p. : ill. ; 30 cm. ISBN 0-11-751859-X (pbk.) : LC Card 86-197217 DDC 331.12/0941 19
1. Labor supply - Great Britain. 2. Urban Programme (Great Britain). 3. Economic development projects - Great Britain. I. Urban Programme (Great Britain). II. Great Britain. Dept. of the Environment.
HD5765.A6 A87 1986

An Assessment of the surface water resources of Zimbabwe and guidelines for development planning. Harare, Zimbabwe : Ministry of Water Resources and Development, [1984?] 23 p., [3] folded leaves of plates : col. maps ; 30 cm. Cover title. Bibliography: p. 11. LC Card 86-980548 DDC 333.91/02/096891 19
1. Water resources development - Zimbabwe. I.

Zimbabwe. Ministry of Water Resources and Development.
HD1699.Z55 A84 1984

Assessment practices survey. [Sacramento, Calif.] : Assessment Standards Division, Property Taxes Dept., California State Board of Equalization, 1987- v. ; 28 cm. "A Survey conducted under the direction of section 12540 of the Government code"--Cover. Consists of a report for each county of the state, arranged alphabetically. LC Card 87-167612 DDC 332.22/2 19
1. Real property tax - California. 2. Assessment - California. I. California. Assessment Standards Division.
HJ4191 .A74 1987

ASSESSMENT - UNITED STATES.
Langhoff, Gary M., 1952- Assessment jurisdictions and agency resources in the United States . Chicago, Ill. , 1987. p. cm. ISBN 0-88329-061-8 : LC Card 87-4101 DDC 336.22/2 19
HJ3241 .L36 1987

ASSESSMENT - UNITED STATES - STATES.
Clatanoff, Robert M. Patterns of property tax administration in the United States /. Chicago, Ill. , 1986. x, 178 p. : ISBN 0-88329-145-2 (pbk.) LC Card 86-7240 DDC 353.9/37242 19
HJ4120 .C528 1986 ***NYPL [JLF 87-464]***

ASSET-LIABILITY MANAGEMENT (BANKING)
Community bank guide to asset/liability management policies /. Washington, D.C. (1120 Connecticut Ave., N.W., Washington 20036) , c1987. v, 241 p. : LC Card 87-167068 DDC 332.1/2/0681 19
HG1615.25 .C65 1987

Gardner, Mona J. Managing financial institutions . Chicago , c1988. xii, 795 p. : ISBN 0-03-005479-6 LC Card 86-32805 DDC 332.1/068/1 19
HG1615.25 .G37 1988

ASSET-LIABILITY MANAGEMENT (BANKING) - COMPUTER PROGRAMS - DIRECTORIES.
A Guide for selecting ALM microcomputer models . Washington, D.C. (1120 Connecticut Ave., N.W., Washington 20036) , c1987. iv, 147 p. : LC Card 87-159971 DDC 332.1/028/5416 19
HG1615.25 .G85 1987

ASSET-LIABILITY MANAGEMENT (BANKING) - DATA PROCESSING.
ALM on micros . York, PA (P.O. Box 1508, York 17405) , c1986. 86 p. : LC Card 87-108676 DDC 332.1/028/5416 19
HG1615.25 .A46 1986

ASSET-LIABILITY MANAGEMENT (BANKING) - UNITED STATES.
Bank investments and funds management. Washington, D.C. (1120 Connecticut Ave., N.W., Washington 20036) , c1987. vii, 357 p. : LC Card 87-405100 DDC 332.1/068/1 19
HG1615.25 .B36 1987

ASSETS (ACCOUNTING)
Chastain, Clark E. Corporate asset management . New York , 1987. xxiii, 345 p. : ISBN 0-89930-237-8 (lib. bdg. : alk. paper) LC Card 87-2493 DDC 658.1/5244 19
HG4026 .C458 1987

L'assicurazione internazionale . Padoa, Fabio. Milano , c1983. 140 p. : ISBN 88-20-31384-7 LC Card 85-189997
HG8059 .P33 1983

ASSIGNATS.
Muszynski, Maurice. Les assignats de la Révolution française /. Bruyères-le-Châtel , c1981. 163 p. : LC Card 87-672912
HG978 .M87x 1981

Les assignats de la Révolution française /. Muszynski, Maurice. Bruyères-le-Châtel , c1981. 163 p. : LC Card 87-672912
HG978 .M87x 1981

ASSIGNMENT SPECIFICATION. see **JOB DESCRIPTIONS.**

Assimilation ausländischer Arbeitnehmer in der Bundesrepublik Deutschland . Kremer, Manfred. Königstein/Ts. , 1980. 203, 64 p. ; ISBN 3-7756-6934-5 LC Card 80-151671 DDC 303.4/8243 19
HD8458.A2 K73 1980 ***NYPL [JLD 86-2549]***

Os Assinantes da praça 1834-1984. Rio de Janeiro : Xerox, 1984. 72 p. ; 27 cm. (Biblioteca reprográfica Xerox . 20) "Edição comemorativa do sesquicentenário da Associação Comercial do Rio de Janeiro." Bibliography: p. 69-72. LC Card 85-160423
1. Associação Comercial do Rio de Janeiro - History. 2. Rio de Janeiro (Brazil) - Commerce - History. I. Series.
HF300.B66 A78 1984

Assis, José Carlos de. A sombra do cruzado : o impacto da reforma monetária sobre o sistema bancário / J. Carlos de Assis. Rio de Janeiro : Paz e Terra, 1986. 137 p. : ill. ; 21 cm. (Coleção Economia. vol. 17) LC Card 87-128261 DDC 332.4/981 19
1. Monetary policy - Brazil. 2. Banks and banking - Brazil. I. Title.
HG835 .A88 1986

Assmann, U. Soziale Aspekte der Mikroelektronik /. Berlin , 1985. 122 p. ; LC Card 87-409418 DDC 306/.46 19
HD6331 .S683 1985

Assocham Trade Mission to UK, 1984. Opportunities for Indo-British economic cooperation : report of Assocham Trade Mission to UK, November 11-24, 1984. New Delhi : Associated Chambers of Commerce & Industry of India, [1985] 43, xiii p., [4] p. of plates : ill. ; 26 cm. LC Card 87-902558 DDC 337.54041 19
1. India - Commerce - Great. Britain. 2. Great Britain - Commerce - India. 3. India - Foreign economic relations - Great Britain. 4. Great Britain - Foreign economic relations - India. I. Title.
HF3788.G7 A87 1985

A associação . Goodolphim, Costa, 1842-1910. Lisboa, Portugal , 1974. 206 p. ; LC Card 87-401116 DDC 334/.09494 19
HD3529.A4 G66 1974

Associação Brasileira das Empresas Comerciais Exportadoras. As "Trading companies" no comércio exterior brasileiro. Rio de Janeiro-RJ , 1984. 148 p. : LC Card 85-208188
HF1009.7.B8 T73 1984

Associação Brasileira de Geologia de Engenharia. Mineração meio-ambiente e o planejamento municipal. São Paulo [1982] 24 leaves : LC Card 85-210329
HD9506.B73 S3664 1982

ASSOCIAÇÃO COMERCIAL DO RIO DE JANEIRO - HISTORY.
Os Assinantes da praça 1834-1984. Rio de Janeiro , 1984. 72 p. ; LC Card 85-160423
HF300.B66 A78 1984

Associação Industrial de Angola. Representação do produtos alimentares de Angola na IX Feira Internacional de Lisboa . Luanda [1968] 248 p. : LC Card 87-400609 DDC 338.7/6413/0025673 19
HD9017.A532 R46 1968

Associação Latino-Americana de Livre Comércio. see **Asociación Latinoamericana de Libre Comercio.**

Associação Nacional das Instituições do Mercado Aberto (Brazil) Setor público, reordenamento e privatização /. [Rio de Janeiro, RJ , 1986] 47 p. : LC Card 87-403308 DDC 338.981 19
HC187 .S436 1986

Associação Portuguesa para o Estudo das Relações Internacionais. Custos certos, benefícios incertos . [Lisboa] [1986] 307 p. : LC Card 87-127179 DDC 341.24/22 19
HC241.25.P6 C87 1986

Associated Chambers of Commerce & Industry of India.
Corporate sector and agriculture . New Delhi [1985] 88 p. ; LC Card 87-902181 DDC 338.1/0954 19
HD2072 .C65 1985

Inflation and personal taxation. New Delhi [1981] 21 p. ; LC Card 82-907052 DDC 336.24/2/0954 19
HJ4766.Z7 A85 1981 ***NYPL [JLF 86-236]***

Integrated fiscal policy . New Delhi [1985] viii, 101 p. : LC Card 87-902182 DDC 339.5/2/0954 19
HJ1331 .I58 1985

Resource mobilisation, medium and long-term issues . New Delhi [1986] viii, 98 p. ; LC Card 87-902180 DDC 338.954 19
HC435.2 .R46 1986

Seminar on Role of Board of Directors in Corporate Governance (1984 : Bombay, India) Seminar on Role of Board of Directors in Corporate Governance . New Delhi [1984] vii, 140 p., [6] p. of plates : LC Card 87-902533 DDC 658.4/22/0954 19
HD2745 .S45 1984

Workshop on Impact of Regulatory Mechanism on Corporate Sector (1984 : Bangalore, India) Workshop on Impact of Regulatory Mechanism on Corporate Sector . New Delhi [1985] 104 p. : LC Card 87-902536 DDC 338.954 19
HC435.2 .W67 1984

ASSOCIATION. see **SOCIAL GROUPS.**

Association des âges. Economie sociale et cycle de vie des institutions /. Paris , 1983. 162 p. : ISBN 2-7178-0631-8 : LC Card 83-174618 DDC 334/.0944 19
HD3494 .E26 1983 ***NYPL [JLE 86-537]***

Association des instituts européens de conjoncture économique. La Conjoncture économique en Europe . Lisboa, Portugal [1982] 78 p. : LC Card 83-181663
HC240 .C588 1982

L'Association des travailleurs aux choix technologiques : la contribution des actions de sensibilisation : rapport final / par ISRIL, Istituto di studi sulle relazioni industriali e di lavoro, G. Bianchi. Luxembourg : Office des publications officielles des communautés européennes ; Washington, D.C. : European Community Information Service, 1986. 45 p. : ill. ; 30 cm. French and English. ISBN 92-825-5880-0 : LC Card 86-179382
1. Labor supply - European Economic Community countries - Effect of technological innovations on. 2. Occupational retraining - European Economic Community countries. 3. Trade-unions - European Economic Community countries. I. Bianchi, Giovanni. II. Istituto di studi sulle relazioni industriali e di lavoro (Rome, Italy).
HD6331.2.E86 A88 1986

Association du transport aérien international. see **International Air Transport Association.**

Association européenne de libre échange. see **European Free Trade Association.**

Association européenne pour les études d'opinion et de marketing. see **Esomar.**

ASSOCIATION FOOTBALL. see **SOCCER.**

Association for Public Transportation. Car-free in Boston . Cambridge, MA (P.O. Box 192, Cambridge 02238) , c1986. 160 p. : LC Card 86-231024 DDC 388.4/09744 19
HE4491.B8 C37 1986

Association for Symbolic Logic. Symposium on Logic in Computer Science (1986 : Cambridge, Mass.) Proceedings, Symposium on Logic in Computer Science, Cambridge, Massachusetts, June 16-18, 1986 /. Washington, D.C. , Los Angeles, CA , 1986. xi, 383 p. : ISBN 0-8186-0720-3 (pbk.) LC Card 86-81090 DDC 004 19
QA75.5 .S9813 1986 ***NYPL [JSF 86-1041]***

Association for the Reconstruction of the Cuban Economy. Barro y Segura, Antonio. Rebuttal and commentaries to the third report on the progress of land reform in Cuba as rendered by the United Nations in 1962. Miami, Fla. , 1963. 17 p. ; LC Card 86-181697
HD1333.C9 B37 1963

Association for Union Democracy. Benson, Herman W., 1910 (ca.)- How to get an honest union election /. Brooklyn, N.Y. [c1987] 65 p. : ISBN 0-9602244-4-0 (pbk.) LC Card 86-73217 DDC 331.87/4/0973 19
HD6490.E42 U62 1987

Association française des collectionneurs de timbres fiscaux. Catalogue des timbres fiscaux et sociaux de France /. Le Havre , 1982. 135 p. : LC Card 86-159729
HJ5412 .C37 1982

Association française pour la cybernétique économique et technique.
IFAC/IFORS/IFIP/IASC/AFCET Conference on Economics and Artificial Intelligence (1986 : Aix-en-Provence, France) Economics and artificial intelligence . Oxford [Oxfordshire] , New York , 1987. xiii, 194 p. : ISBN 0-08-034350-3 (U. S.) : LC Card 87-6943

DDC 330/.028/563 19
HB143.5 .I44 1986

Association internationale de la sécurité sociale. see **International Social Security Association.**

Association internationale de sociologie. see **International Sociological Association.**

Association internationale pour le developpement. see **International Development Association.**

Association of African Central Banks. Directory of African central banks / Association of African Central Banks, African Centre for Monetary Studies. 2nd ed. Dakar, Senegal : The Centre, [1985 or 1986] ca. 150 leaves : col. map ; 28 cm. Cover title. LC Card 87-402547 DDC 332.1/1/02567 19
1. Banks and banking, Central - Africa - Directories. I. African Centre for Monetary Studies. II. Title.
HG3376 .A87 1985

Association of College and Research Libraries. Golden, Gary. Survey research methods /. Chicago, IL , c1982. 69 leaves : ISBN 0-8389-6753-1 (pbk.) LC Card 87-107560 DDC 300/.723 19
HA31.2 .G65 1982

Association of Indian Automobile Manufacturers. Documentation and Reference Centre. The Automobile industry . Bombay , 1985. x, 290 p. : LC Card 86-903383 DDC 338.4/76292/0954021 19
HD9710.I42 A974 1985

Association of National Advertisers. Donius, James F. Marketplace measurement . New York, NY (155 E. 44th St., New York 11710) , c1986. xiii, 206 p. : LC Card 87-120244 DDC 659.1/11 19
HF5823 .D655 1986

Association of Oregon Counties. Making the right turn . [Salem? Or.] [1986] iv, 39 p. : LC Card 87-621891 DDC 388.1/14/09795 19
HE356.O7 M35 1986

Association of Part-time Professionals (U. S.) APTP employer directory. McLean, Va. (7655 Old Springhouse Road, McLean 22102) , c1986. iii, 47 p. ; LC Card 86-213174 DDC 338.7/61/00025753 19
HD8038.U52 W323 1986

Association of Private Enterprise Education (U. S.) The Future of private enterprise /. Atlanta, Ga. , 1984-1986. 3 v. ; ISBN 0-88406-164-7 (pbk. : v. 1) LC Card 83-25386 DDC 338.6/1 19
HB501 .F83 1984 ***NYPL [JLK 87-49]***

Association of Schools of Public Health. Proposed national strategies for the prevention of leading work-related diseases and injuries. [Washington, D.C.] , 1986- v. <1 > ; LC Card 87-111984 DDC 363.1/17/0973 19
HD7262.5.U6 P75 1986

Association of State Colleges and Universities. see **American Association of State Colleges and Universities.**

Association pour la promotion industrie-agriculture. Les Protéines françaises, un enjeu économique . Paris [1984] 6, xiii, 258 p. : LC Card 86-187038
HD9019.P753 F76 1984

Association pour l'étude de l'histoire de la sécurité sociale. Colloque sur l'histoire de la sécurité sociale (1980 : Caen, France) Colloque sur l'histoire de la sécurité sociale . Paris , 1981. 263 p. ; LC Card 81-201274
HD7175 .C58 1980

ASSOCIATIONS, INSTITUTIONS, ETC. - ADDRESSES, ESSAYS, LECTURES.
The Private exercise of public functions /. Port Washington, N.Y. , 1985. 251 p. ; ISBN 0-8046-9368-4 LC Card 84-9254 DDC 361.6/1 19
H97 .P76 1985 ***NYPL [JLE 86-2611]***

ASSOCIATIONS, INSTITUTIONS, ETC. - CHILE.
Mannarelli M., Virgilio B. Organización institucional del sector agrícola /. Santiago, Chile , 1985. 81, [3] p. : LC Card 86-115545 DDC 338.1/883 19
HD1878 .M35 1985

ASSOCIATIONS, INSTITUTIONS, ETC. - GERMANY - HISTORY.
Vereinswesen und bürgerliche Gesellschaft in Deutschland /. München , 1984. 180 p. ; ISBN 3-486-52081-4 LC Card 84-205111
HD2429.G3 V46 1984

ASSOCIATIONS, INSTITUTIONS, ETC. - PORTUGAL - HISTORY.
Goodolphim, Costa, 1842-1910. A associação . Lisboa, Portugal , 1974. 206 p. ; LC Card 87-401116 DDC 334/.09494 19
HD3529.A4 G66 1974

ASSOCIATIONS (LAW) see **CORPORATIONS, NONPROFIT.**

Associazione conciatori. Il Pappagallo giallo . [Pisa] , Firenze , c1986. 194 p., [1] leaf of plates : LC Card 86-212573
HD9780.I82 P37 1986

Associazione italiana per l'informatica e il calcolo automatico. IFIP TC 8/WG 8.4 Working Conference on Methods and Tools for Office Systems (1986 : Pisa, Italy) Office systems . Amsterdam ; New York : xi, 347 p. : ISBN 0-444-70241-5 (U. S.) LC Card 87-8916 DDC 651.8 19
HF5548.2 .I285 1986

Associazione per lo sviluppo dell'industria nel Mezzogiorno.
Il Mezzogiorno nelle politiche nazionali e comunitarie . Milano , 1982. 379 p. ; LC Card 82-230171 DDC 338.945/7 19
HC305 .M42156 1982 ***NYPL [JLE 86-1611]***

Associazione per lo sviluppo dell'industria nel Mezzogiorno. Centro per gli studi sullo sviluppo economico.
Collana di "Monografie."
(49) Costa, Paolo. Agglomerazione urbana, localizzazione industriale e Mezzogiorno /. Milano , 1983. viii, 240 p. : LC Card 83-186216 DDC 307.2 19
HB2060.S68 C67 1983 ***NYPL [JLE 86-3657]***

ASSURANCE (INSURANCE) see **INSURANCE.**

Astaf'ev, Vladimir Egorovich. Ėkonomicheskiĭ ėksperiment v ėlektrotekhnicheskoĭ promyshlennosti / V.E. Astaf'ev. Moskva : Ėnergoatomizdat, 1984. 108, [3] p. ; 23 cm. (Predprii͡atie--samostoi͡atel'nost' i otvetstvennost') Bibliography: p. [110] LC Card 85-125403
1. Electric industries - Soviet Union - Management. I. Title. II. Series.
HD9697.A3 A77 1984

Astakhov, A. S. Narodnokhozi͡aĭstvenn͡aia ėffektivnost'--pokazateli, metody otsenki /. Moskva , 1984. 247 p. : LC Card 84-188306
HC336.25 .N3515 1984

Astakhov, A. S. (Aleksandr Semenovich) Mineral'noe syr'e i ėkonomii͡a material'nykh i ėnergeticheskikh resursov /. Moskva , 1986. 333, [3] p. : LC Card 87-119481
HD9502.S652 M56 1986

Astapovich, A. Z. (Aleksandr Zakharovich) SSSR, SShA i Kanada . Moskva , 1987. 325 p. ; LC Card 86-205359
HF3628.U5 S77 1987

ASTD reference guide. Sredl, Henry J., 1935- The ASTD reference guide to professional training roles & competencies /. New York , c1987. 2 v. : ISBN 0-394-55915-0 (v. 1) LC Card 86-26006 DDC 658.3/124 19
HF5549.5.T7 S657 1987

The ASTD reference guide to professional training roles & competencies /. Sredl, Henry J., 1935- New York , c1987. 2 v. : ISBN 0-394-55915-0 (v. 1) LC Card 86-26006 DDC 658.3/124 19
HF5549.5.T7 S657 1987

Aste Daffos, Juan. Minería peruana : empresas estatales y generación de divisas, 1970-1984 / Juan Aste Daffos. Lima : Fundación Friedrich Ebert, 1986. 102 p. ; 20 cm. (Diagnóstico y debate . 22) Bibliography: p. 100-102. LC Card 87-143088 DDC 338.2/0985 19
1. Mineral industries - Government ownership - Peru. I. Title. II. Series.
HD9506.P42 A827 1986

Astesano, Eduardo.
[Historia socialista de América]
Historia social de América / Eduardo B. Astesano. Buenos Aires, Argentina : Peña Lillo, [1982] 177 p. : ill., maps ; 18 cm. Reprint. Originally published: Historia socialista de América. Buenos Aires : Editorial Relevo, 1973. With a new introd. ISBN 950-0-17004-3 LC Card 83-165516
1. America - Economic conditions. 2. America - Social conditions. 3. Socialism - America - History. I. Title.
HC94 .A83 1982

Astoreca, Marcelo. La Opción preferencial por los pobres . [Santiago] [1987] 360 p. : LC Card 87-403060 DDC 362.5/098 19
HC130.P6 O63 1987

Astorga, Enrique [i. e. Enrique Astorga Lira] see **Astorga Lira, Enrique.**

Astorga Lira, Enrique. Mercado de trabajo rural en México : la mercancía humana / Enrique Astorga Lira.1a ed. México, D.F. : Ediciones Era, 1985. 127 p. : ill. ; 20 cm. (Colección Problemas de México) Bibliography: p. 123-127. ISBN 968-411-139-8 LC Card 86-141300 DDC 331.7/63/0972 19
1. Agricultural laborers - Mexico. 2. Agriculture - Economic aspects - Mexico. I. Series: Colección Problemas de México (Ediciones Era). II. Title.
HD1531.M6 A88 1985 ***NYPL [JLC 87-68]***

Astori, Danilo. La agricultura campesina en América Latina : sus relaciones con el crecimiento urbano y la disponibilidad alimentaria / Danilo Astori. Montevideo, Uruguay : Centro Interdisciplinario de Estudios sobre el Desarrollo, Uruguay, [1985?] 35 p. ; 28 cm. (Serie Documentos de trabajo . no. 7) "Trabajo presentado a la 'Consulta de Expertos sobre urbanización intensiva y sus repercusiones alimentarias y nutricionales en América Latina.' Organizada por FAO, Bogotá, Colombia, 9 al 13 de mayo de 1983." Bibliography: p. 32-35. LC Card 86-204310 DDC 338.1/098 19
1. Agriculture - Economic aspects - Latin America. 2. Peasantry - Latin America. 3. Agricultural industries - Latin America. 4. Rural-urban migration - Latin America. I. Series: Serie Documentos de trabajo (Centro Interdisciplinario de Estudios sobre el Desarrollo Uruguay) , no. 7. II. Title.
HD1790.5 .A85 1985

Astrachan, Anthony. How men feel : their response to women's demands for equality, and power / Anthony Astrachan.1st ed. Garden City, N.Y. : Anchor Press/Doubleday, 1986. x, 444 p. ; 24 cm. Includes bibliographic notes and index. ISBN 0-385-23333-7 : LC Card 85-22944 DDC 305.3/1 19
1. Men - United States - Attitudes. 2. Sex role - United States. 3. Feminism - United States. I. Title.
HQ1090.3 .A88 1986 ***NYPL [JLE 86-3421]***

Astroth, Joseph H., 1955- Understanding peasant agriculture : an integrated land-use model for the Punjab / by Joseph H. Astroth, Jr. Chicago, Ill. : University of Chicago, Committee on Geographical Studies, 1987. p. cm. (Research paper . no. 223) Bibliography: p. ISBN 0-89065-127-2 (pbk.) : LC Card 87-15099 DDC 333.76/13/0724 19
1. Land use, Rural - India - Punjab - Mathematical models. 2. Agriculture - Economic aspects - India - Punjab - Mathematical models. I. Series: Research paper (University of Chicago. Committee on Geographical Studies) , no. 223. II. Title.
HD879.P8 A77 1987

Asturias Montenegro, G. Ayau, Manuel F. Cómo mejorar el nivel de vida /. [Guatemala , 1982] (Guatemala : Editorial Piedra Santa) 91 p. : LC Card 86-174413
HB178.5 .A93 1982

ASTURIAS - POLITICS AND GOVERNMENT - PUBLIC OPINION.
Argüelles, Alfonso. Los Oscos y la Cuenca del Eo . [Asturias] [1984?] ix, 317 p. : ISBN 84-505-0237-3 LC Card 86-174593
HC387.A7 A74 1984

ASTURIAS (SPAIN) - ECONOMIC CONDITIONS.
Martín Alonso, Arturo. Invertir en Asturias /. [Spain] [1984?] 72 p. : ISBN 84-398-1662-6 LC Card 85-217277
HC387.A7 M37 1984

ASTURIAS (SPAIN) - INDUSTRIES.
Argüelles, Alfonso. Los Oscos y la Cuenca del Eo . [Asturias] [1984?] ix, 317 p. : ISBN 84-505-0237-3 LC Card 86-174593
HC387.A7 A74 1984

ASTURIAS (SPAIN) - POPULATION.
Argüelles, Alfonso. Los Oscos y la Cuenca del Eo . [Asturias] [1984?] ix, 317 p. : ISBN

84-505-0237-3 LC Card 86-174593
HC387.A7 A74 1984

Asuminen Helsingissä 1950-1983 =. Lankinen, Leila. Helsinki , 1985. 80 p. : LC Card 86-148571
HD7345.3.H5 L35 1985

Asuncion. Centro Paraguayo de Estudios Sociologicos. see **Centro Paraguayo de Estudios Sociológicos.**

Asymmetries in Japanese-American trade . Krasner, Stephen D., 1942- Berkeley , c1987. vii, 80 p. ; ISBN 0-87725-532-6 (pbk.) : LC Card 87-81842 DDC 382/.0973/052 19
HF3127 .K73 1987

AT & T Bell Laboratories. Artificial intelligence and statistics /. Reading, Mass. , c1986. xiv, 418 p. : ISBN 0-201-11568-9 : LC Card 85-28631 DDC 006.3 19
Q334 .A764 1986 *NYPL [JSE 87-399]*

The AT reader : theory and practice in appropriate technology / edited by Marilyn Carr, with an introduction by Frances Stewart. London : Intermediate Technology Publications, 1985. xvii, 468 p. : ill. ; 23 cm. Includes bibliographical references to original works from which extracts were taken. ISBN 0-946688-10-9
1. Appropriate technology - Developing countries. 2. Technology - Social aspects - Developing countries. I. Carr, Marilyn. II. Title: A.T. reader.
NYPL [JLE 86-2305]

ATA handbook .
(no. 110) Rothenberg, Bertram. U. S. Postal Service bicentennial postmarks, 1972-1984 /. Johnstown, PA, USA , c1986. 42 p. : ISBN 0-935991-01-8 (pbk.): LC Card 86-224991 DDC 769.56/7/0973 19
HE6187 .A635 no. 110 HE6183.A45

(106-1) Ridgely, Beverly S. Supplement to Birds of the world in philately /. Johnstown, PA , c1986. 62 p., [3] p. of plates : ISBN 0-935991-00-X (pbk.): LC Card 86-217462 DDC 769.56/4/075 769.56/432 19
HE6187 .A635 no. 106-1 HE6183.B53

(110) Rothenberg, Bertram. U. S. Postal Service bicentennial postmarks, 1972-1984 /. Johnstown, PA, USA , c1986. 42 p. : ISBN 0-935991-01-8 (pbk.): LC Card 86-224991 DDC 769.56/7/0973 19
HE6187 .A635 no. 110 HE6183.A45

ATA-projektet (Aalborg universitetscenter) Jørgensen, Henning, 1949- Arbejdsmarkedsnævn i arbejdsmarkedspolitikken /. [Aalborg] [1985?]-<[1986]. v. <1-2 > : ISBN 87-88706-12-5 LC Card 87-104729
HD5799.A6 J64 1985

Ataç, Beyhan. Kuramda ve Türkiye'de istikrar politikası açısından parasal ve mali işlemler / Beyhan Ataç. Eskişehir : Eskişehir İktisadi ve Ticari İlimler Akademisi, [1979?] iv, 173 p. ; 24 cm. (Eskişehir İktisadi ve Ticari İlimler Akademisi yayınları . no. 131/153) Bibliography: p. [145]-173. LC Card 82-245649
1. Monetary policy - Turkey. 2. Fiscal policy - Turkey. I. Title. II. Series.
HG1206.5 .A79 1979

Atack, Jeremy. To their own soil : agriculture in the Antebellum North / Jeremy Atack, Fred Bateman.1st ed. Ames : Iowa State University Press, 1987. xi, 322 p. : ill. ; 24 cm. (The Henry A. Wallace series on agricultural history and rural studies) Bibliography: p. 299-312. Includes index. ISBN 0-8138-0086-2 LC Card 86-21349 DDC 338.1/0974 19
1. Agriculture - Economic aspects - United States - History - 19th century. 2. United States - Rural conditions. I. Bateman, Fred, 1937-. II. Title. III. Series.
HD1773.A4 A86 1987

Ataev, M. (Murruk) Gosudarstvennoe upravlenie ispol'zovaniem i okhranoĭ vod / M. Ataev ; otvetstvennyĭ redaktor ÎU.M. Kozlov. Ashkhabad : Ylym, 1982. 175 p. ; 20 cm. At head of title: Akademiia nauk Turkmenskoĭ SSR. Otdel filosofii i prava. Includes bibliographical references. LC Card 82-244366
1. Water resources development - Turkmen S.S.R. 2. Water quality management - Turkmen S.S.R. I. Kozlov, ÎUriĭ Markovich. II. Title.
HD1697.S653 T873 1982

Atanasov, Mikhail, k.i.n. Vŭshnotŭrgovski aspekti na selskostopanskite i khranitelno-vkusovite stoki i problemi pred bŭlgarskiia iznos / Mikhail Atanasov. Sofiia : [s.n.], 1984. 118 p. ; 21 cm. (Biblioteka / Bŭlgarska tŭrgovsko-promishlena palata . no. 193) Bibliography: p. 113-116. LC Card 85-163481
1. Food industry and trade - Bulgaria. 2. Produce trade - Bulgaria. 3. Export marketing - Bulgaria. 4. Foreign trade promotion - Bulgaria. I. Series: Biblioteka / Bŭlgarska tŭrgovsko-promishlena palata , kn. 193. II. Title.
HD9015.B82 A86 1984

Atanasov, Velko. Po visochinite na sŭrtseto . Sofiia , 1986. 75 p., [16] p. of plates : LC Card 87-101682
HD8039.C62 B97 1986

Atarov, N. Z. Regional'nyĭ aspekt mezhotraslevykh proizvodstv : na primere mashinostroeniia / N.Z. Atarov. Moskva : Izd-vo "Nauka", 1980. 173 p. : ill. ; 20 cm. (Problemy sovetskoĭ ėkonomiki) At head of title: Akademiia nauk SSSR. Dal'nevostochnyĭ nauchnyĭ tsentr. Institut ėkonomicheskikh issledovaniĭ. Includes bibliographical references. LC Card 81-132091
1. Machinery industry - Soviet Union. 2. Input-output analysis - Soviet Union. I. Title.
HD9705.S595 A73 1980

ATBARA RIVER REGION (ETHIOPIA AND SUDAN) - ECONOMIC CONDITIONS.
Abdel Ati, Hassan A. Lower River Atbara area (Nile Province) . [Khartoum] Sudan [1985] vii, 166 p., [19] leaves of plates : LC Card 86-981108 DDC 333.91/3/09625 19
HD1741.S852 A832 1985

Atchison, Michael D. New financial instruments : a descriptive guide / by Michael D. Atchison, Richard F. DeMong, John L. Kling. Charlottesville, Va. (P.O. Box 3665, Charlottesville 22903) : Financial Analysts Research Foundation, c1985. viii, 108 p. ; 23 cm. (Monograph . 21) LC Card 85-195578 DDC 332.63 19
1. Financial futures - United States. 2. Option (Contract) - United States. I. DeMong, Richard F. II. Kling, John L. III. Series: Monograph (Financial Analysts Research Foundation) , no. 21. IV. Title.
HG6024.3 .A83 1985
NYPL [JLL 81-133 no.21]

Atchison, Thomas J. Belcher, David W. Compensation administration /. Englewood Cliffs, N.J. , c1987. xv, 464 p. : ISBN 0-13-154790-9 : LC Card 86-25494 DDC 658.3/2 19
HF5549.5.C67 B45 1987

Atehortúa, Adolfo. Café, bonanza y realidades / Adolfo Atehortúa. Edición "Escuela Nacional Sindical". [Bogotá, Colombia] : SINTRAFEC, [1986] 118 p. : ill. ; 24 cm. Bibliography: p. 115-118. LC Card 87-402940 DDC 338.1/7373/09861 19
1. Coffee trade - Colombia. I. Title.
HD9199.C62 A74 1986

Atendimento ao mercado de energia elétrica do Nordeste /. Lopes, Marcos José. Recife, PE [1984] 2 v. in 4 : LC Card 86-166126
HD9685.B83 N675 1984

Atget, Géniaux, Vert : petits métiers et types parisiens vers 1900 : [exposition] : Musée Carnavalet, 6 novembre 1984-13 janvier 1985 / organisé par Paris Audiovisuel. Paris : Le Musée, [1984] 63, [1] p. : ill. ; 24 cm. Cover title: Petits métiers et types parisiens vers 1900. Spine title: Petits métiers. "Catalogue rédigé par Sophie Grossiord et Françoise Reynaud"--Colophon. Bibliography: p. [64] ISBN 2-901414-09-5 : LC Card 86-137985
1. Peddlers and peddling - France - Paris - Exhibitions. 2. Artisans - France - Paris - Exhibitions. 3. Photography, Artistic - Exhibitions. I. Grossiord, Sophie. II. Reynaud, Françoise. III. Musée Carnavalet. IV. Paris audiovisuel (Firm). V. Title: Petits métiers et types parisiens vers 1900. VI. Title: Petits métiers.
HF5459.F8 A87 1984 *NYPL [MFW 87-159]*

Athbhreithniú ar Chuideachta Forbartha Aerfort Neamhchustam na Sionna Teoranta. Ireland. Oireachtas. Dáil. Committee on Public Expenditure. Review of Shannon Free Airport Development Company Limited . Dublin [1983?] 79 p. : LC Card 87-146082 DDC 387.7/36/094193 19
HE9797.5.I72 S54 1983

Athens. Agrotikē Trapeza tēs Hellados. see **Agrotikē Trapeza tēs Hellados.**

Athens. Center of Planning and Economic Research. see **Kentron Programmatismou kai Oikonomikōn Ereunōn.**

ATHENS (GREECE) - HISTORY - 1821-
Maroudēs, Giōrgos. To hēmerologio tēs peinas /. [Athens] , 1976. 99 p., [6] leaves of plates ; LC Card 84-107778
HC300.F3 M37 1976

Athens. Kentron Programmatismou kai Oikonomikōn Ereunōn. see **Kentron Programmatismou kai Oikonomikōn Ereunōn.**

ATHENS. MOUSEION BENAKĒ.
Spēliōtakēs, K. K. Archeion Michaēl Iatrou, 1802-1893 /. Athēna , 1983. 189 p., [4] folded leaves of plates : LC Card 85-134031
HF3750.5.S64 A3 1983
NYPL [JFE 86-4131]

Athukoralge, Premachandra. Export instability and growth : problems and prospects for the developing economies / Premachandra Athukorala and Frank Cong Hiep Huynh. London ; Wolfeboro, N.H. : Croom Helm, c1987. 244 p. : ill. ; 23 cm. Bibliography: p. 221-237. Includes indexes. ISBN 0-7099-3739-3 : LC Card 86-32833 DDC 382/.6/095493 19
1. Export marketing - Sri Lanka - Mathematical models. 2. Sri Lanka - Commerce - Mathematical models. 3. Sri Lanka - Economic conditions - Mathematical models. 4. Prices - Sri Lanka - Mathematical models. I. Huynh, Frank C. H. II. Title.
HF3770.8.Z5 A84 1987

Atif A. Rahman Saghayroun. see **Saghayroun, Atif A. Rahman.**

El atípico caso argentino . Daneri, Oscar. Buenos Aires , 1986. 412 p. : ISBN 950-43-0291-4 LC Card 87-400194 DDC 338.982 19
HC175 .D26 1986

Atkinson, Paul. The formulation of monetary policy : a reassessment in the light of recent experience / by Paul Atkinson and Jean-Claude Chouraqui. [Paris, France] : OECD, [1986, c1985] 41 p. : ill. ; 30 cm. (Working papers / OECD, Department of Economics and Statistics . no. 32) Summary in French. "March 1986." Bibliography: p. 39-41. LC Card 86-212837 DDC 332.4/6 19
1. Monetary policy. 2. Money supply. I. Chouraqui, Jean Claude. II. Series: Working papers (Organisation for Economic Co-operation and Development. Dept. of Economics and Statistics) , no. 32. III. Title.
HG230.3 .A75 1986

Atkinson, Ray N. Guy F. Atkinson Company of California : a free enterprise success story / Ray N. Atkinson. New York : Newcomen Society of the United States, 1985, c1986. 24 p. : ill. ; 23 cm. (Newcomen publication. no. 1266) LC Card 86-61271 DDC 338.7/624/0973 19
1. Guy F. Atkinson Company of California - History. 2. Construction industry - California - History. 3. California - Public works - History. 4. Construction industry - West (U. S.) - History. 5. West (U. S.) - Public works - History. I. Title.
HD9715.U54 G882 1986

ATLANTA SAW COMPANY - HISTORY - 20TH CENTURY.
Brown, Edmund D. 1594 Evans Drive, S.W. . Atlanta, Ga. (1594 Evans Dr., S.W., Atlanta 30310) , c1983. 213 p. : LC Card 82-62570 DDC 338.7/62193 19
HD9529.S294 A842 1983
NYPL [JLF 86-1803]

Atlantic Alliance. see **North Atlantic Treaty Organization.**

Atlantic Institute for International Affairs.
Henning, C. Randall. Macroeconomic diplomacy in the 1980s . London , New York , c1987. x, 76 p. ; ISBN 0-7099-3794-6 (pbk.) LC Card 87-20041 DDC 337/.09171/3 19
HF1455 .H46 1987

Kakabadse, Mario A. International trade in services . London , New York , c1987. 90 p. ; ISBN 0-7099-3130-1 (pbk.) LC Card 87-8951 DDC 382/.45/0009049 19
HD9980.5 .K35 1987

Atlantic paper .
(no. 65) Henning, C. Randall. Macroeconomic diplomacy in the 1980s . London , New York , c1987. x, 76 p. ; ISBN 0-7099-3794-6 (pbk.) LC Card 87-20041 DDC 337/.09171/3 19
HF1455 .H46 1987

Atlantic papers (Paris, France) . (no. 64) Kakabadse, Mario A. International trade in services . London , New York , c1987. 90 p. ; ISBN 0-7099-3130-1 (pbk.) LC Card 87-8951 DDC 382/.45/0009049 19
HD9980.5 .K35 1987

ATLANTIC RICHFIELD CO. - HISTORY. Harris, Kenneth, 1919- The wildcatter . New York , c1987. x, 180 p., [8] p. of plates : ISBN 1-555-84048-5 LC Card 87-8183 DDC 338.7/622338/0924 B 19
HD9570.A53 H37 1987

Atlas de cobertura 1985/86. [Rio de Janeiro] : Central Globo de Comercialização, [1985?] ca. 100 p. : ill. ; 22 x 35 cm. Cover title. "Elaborado pelo Departamento de Serviços de Marketing/Divisão de Marketing"--P. [4] of cover. LC Card 86-201241
1. Television audiences - Brazil - Statistics. 2. Television broadcasting - Brazil - Statistics. I. Central Globo de Comercialização. Divisão de Marketing.
HE8700.66.B7 A74 1985

Atlas des Français /. Savy, Michel. Paris , c1985. 331 p. : ISBN 2-01-011512-0 LC Card 86-178635
HC276.2 .S325 1985

Atlas, M. S. Rol′ finansovo-kreditnogo mekhanizma v povyshenii ėffektivnosti obshchestvennykh zatrat . Moskva , 1984. 153 p. ; LC Card 86-113408
HG186.S55 R64 1984

ATOM BOMB. see **ATOMIC BOMB.**

Der atomare Selbstmord /. Gruhl, Herbert, 1921- München , c1986. 190 p. : ISBN 3-7766-1448-X LC Card 86-226120
HD9698.A2 G74 1986

ATOMIC BOMB AND DISARMAMENT. see **ATOMIC WEAPONS AND DISARMAMENT.**

ATOMIC BOMB - JAPAN. Goldman, Peter Louis, 1933- The end of the world that was . New York , c1986. xiv, 129 p., [8] p. of plates : ISBN 0-525-24428-X LC Card 85-31223 DDC 920/.073 19
CT220 .G6 1986 ***NYPL [JFD 86-6015]***

ATOMIC POWER ENGINEERING. see **NUCLEAR ENGINEERING.**

ATOMIC WEAPONS AND DISARMAMENT. Garfinkle, Adam M., 1951- The politics of the nuclear freeze /. Philadelphia, Pa. , 1984. xviii, 258 p. ; ISBN 0-910191-08-5 : LC Card 84-6030 DDC 327.1/74 19
JX1974.7 .G34 1984 ***NYPL [JLE 86-710]***

Towle, Philip, 1945- Protest and perish . London , 1982. 121 p. ; ISBN 0-907967-02-7 (pbk.) : LC Card 83-198296 DDC 355/.0217/0941 19
UA647 .T69 1982 ***NYPL [JLD 86-1904]***

Atomkraft am Ende? / mit Beiträgen von Jens Scheer ... [et al.]. 3., erw. Aufl. Göttingen : Verlag Die Werkstatt, 1986. 191 p. ; 21 cm. Bibliography: p. 190-191. CONTENTS. - "Tschernobyl" / Helmut Hirsch -- "Es war einmal in Amerika" / Michael Pelster -- "Die Bäume wachsen nicht in den Himmel" / Jens Scheer, Reimar Paul, Mycle Schneider -- "Risse im Gebälk" / Reimar Paul, Bernd Weidmann -- "Wie Energiepolitik gemacht wird" / Michael Pelster -- "Wie warscheinlich ist ein Unfall?" / Manfred Wallenschus -- Die Grenzen der Sicherheit" / Jens Scheer, Reimar Paul -- "Die unsichtbare Gefahr" / Jens Scheer -- "Die strahlende Fracht" / Reimar Paul -- "Und am Ende türmt sich der Müll" / Helmut Hirsch. ISBN 3-923478-16-X LC Card 86-228667
1. Nuclear power plants - Government policy. 2. Nuclear power plants - Environmental aspects. 3. Antinuclear movement. I. Scheer, Jens.
HD9698.A2 A795 1986

Atria B., Raúl. Estructura política y políticas de población /. [Santiago, Chile] [1977] 442 p. ; LC Card 83-168971
HB3530.5 .E88 1977

Atria, Raúl [i. e. Raúl Atria B.] see **Atria B., Raúl.**

Atsé, David. Commodity futures trading and international market stabilization / David Atsé. Uppsala : Universitatis Upsaliensis ; Stockholm, Sweden : Distributor, Almqvist & Wiksell International, 1986. 151 p. : ill. ; 22 cm. (Acta Universitatis Upsaliensis. Studia oeconomica Upsaliensia, 0585-539X . 10) Thesis (doctoral)--Uppsala University, 1986. Bibliography: p. 144-151. ISBN 91-554-1961-5 (pbk.) LC Card 87-148645 DDC 330 s 332.64/42 19
1. Commodity exchanges. 2. Economic stabilization. 3. Produce trade. 4. Price maintenance. 5. Commodity control. I. Title. II. Series.
HB51 .S7 no. 10 HG6046

Atsitiktinių procesų savybių pasikeitimo suradimas. Obnaruzhenie izmeneniĭ svoĭstv sluchaĭnykh protsessov . Vil′nius , 1984. 243 p. : LC Card 84-168819
HD38 .S715 vyp. 65 QA274.A1

Atsitiktinių procesų su kintama tikimybinių pasiskirstymų struktūra atpažinimas. Kligene, Nerute. Raspoznavanie sluchaĭnykh protsessov s peremennoĭ strukturoĭ veroiatnostnykh raspredeleniĭ . Vil′nius , 1986. 136 p. : LC Card 87-146330
HD38 .S715 vyp.76 QA274

Atstiktinių procesų savybių pasikeitimo seminaras (1st : 1984 : Palanga, Lithuania) Obnaruzhenie izmeneniĭ svoĭstv sluchaĭnykh protsessov . Vil′nius , 1984. 243 p. : LC Card 84-168819
HD38 .S715 vyp. 65 QA274.A1

Att bevara företagsarkiv . Sweden. Riksarkivet. [Stockholm] [1984] 119 p. ; ISBN 91-38-08403-1 LC Card 84-239019
HC375 .S965 1984

Atta el Moula, Mutasim el Amin. On the problem of resource management in the Sudan / by Mutasim El Amin Atta El Moula. [Khartoum] : Institute of Environmental Studies, University of Khartoum, 1985. 131 leaves : ill., maps ; 30 cm. (Environmental monograph series. no. 4) Bibliography: leaves 126-130. LC Card 86-980662 DDC 333.7/09624 19
1. Natural resources - Sudan - Management. 2. Environmental policy - Sudan. I. Series: Environmental monograph series (Jāmi'at al-Kharṭūm. Ma'had al-Dirāsāt al-Bī'iyah) , no. 4. II. Title.
HC835 .A85 1985

Attali, Jacques.
[Homme d'influence. English]
A man of influence : Sir Siegmund Warburg, 1902-82 / Jacques Attali ; translated by Barbara Ellis. London : Weidenfeld and Nicolson, 1986. 346 p. ; 24 cm. Translation of: Un homme d'influence. Includes index. Bibliography: p. 317-323. ISBN 0-297-78978-3
1. Warburg, Siegmund, Sir, 1902-1982. 2. Jewish bankers - Biography. 3. Bankers - Great Britain - Biography. I. Carmell, Pamela. II. Title.
NYPL [JFE 87-583]

A man of influence : the extraordinary career of S.G. Warburg / Jacques Attali ; translated by Barbara Ellis.1st U. S. ed. Bethesda, Md. : Adler & Adler, 1987, c1985. xvii, 380 p. ; 24 cm. Translation of: Un homme d'influence. Bibliography: p. 350-356. Includes index. ISBN 0-917561-36-8 : LC Card 86-28735 DDC 332.1/092/4 B 19
1. Warburg, Siegmund, Sir, 1902-1982. 2. Jewish bankers - Biography. 3. Bankers - Great Britain - Biography. I. Title.
HG1552.W37 A8713 1987

Atterbury, Paul. English rivers and canals / Paul Atterbury. London : Weidenfeld and Nicolson, 1984. 152 p. : ill. ; 28 cm. Includes index. ISBN 0-297-78318-1
1. Rivers - England. 2. Canals - England. 3. Inland navigation - England. 4. England - Description and travel - Guide-books. I. Title.
NYPL [JFF 87-598]

Atti /. Conferenza economica dell'area pisana (1984 : Pisa, Italy) Pisa [1985-1986], c1985. 2 v. : LC Card 86-223161
HC308.P58 C66 1984

Atti del Comitato dell'inchiesta industriale (1870-1874) : deposizioni scritte. [Bologna?] : Analisi, [1984- v. <1-3 > ; 25 cm. (Archivio storico dell'industria italiana. Le Fonti) Reprint. Originally published in parts: Roma : Stamperia reale, 1872-1874. Includes bibliographical references. LC Card 87-123944
1. Italy - Industries. I. Italy. Parlamento. Comitato dell'inchiesta industriale (1870-1874). II. Series: Archivio storico dell'industria italiana. Fonti.
HC304 .A87 1984

Atti del Convegno nazionale "Qualche idea sui fiumi," Jesi, aprile 1983. Convegno nazionale "Qualche idea sui fiumi" (1983 : Iesi, Italy) Ancona , c1983-c1984. 2 v. ; ISBN 88-7663-030-9 (v. 1) : LC Card 84-119835
HD1697.I8 C62 1983 ***NYPL [JLK 87-40]***

Attidues to Norwegian development assistance, 1974. Oslo : Statistisk sentralbyrå, 1975. 57 p. ; 29 cm. (Rapport fra Underavdeligen for intervjuundersøkelser . nr. 34) LC Card 86-460167
1. Economic assistance, Norwegian - Developing countries - Public opinion. 2. Public opinion - Norway. I. Norway. Statistisk sentralbyrå. II. Series.
HA1503 .A18 nr. 34 HC60

ATTITUDE (PSYCHOLOGY) Cornyn-Selby, Alyce, 1946- Take your hands off my attitude! . Portland, Or. , 1987. p. cm. ISBN 0-941383-02-4 : LC Card 87-15074 DDC 158.7 19
HD58.9 .C67 1987

Attitudes to the distribution of incomes. Henriksen, Ingrid. Holdninger til den økonomiske fordeling =. København , 1985. 349 p. : ISBN 87-7487-265-6 : LC Card 85-186400
HC360.I5 S25 1985 vol. 1
NYPL [JLD 86-2002]

Attitudes toward vended coffee / prepared for the Office Coffee Development Group by Social Research, Inc. ; project staff, Sidney J. Levy, Albert G. Robles. [Chicago? : s.n., 1983] 1 v. (various pagings) : ill. ; 28 cm. "April 1983." "Study: #623/01." LC Card 86-235525 DDC 381/.4566393 19
1. Coffee trade - United States. 2. Coffee - United States. 3. Vending machines - United States. 4. Consumers' preferences - United States. 5. Consumers - United States - Attitudes. 6. Market surveys - United States. I. Levy, Sidney J., 1921-. II. Robles, Albert G. III. Office Coffee Development Group. IV. Social Research, Inc.
HD9199.U48 A88 1983

Attityder till kommunal service /. Sannerstedt, Anders, 1945- [Stockholm] [1981] vi, 166 p. : ISBN 91-38-06586-X LC Card 82-244101
HD4485.S8 S26 1981

L'Attività commerciale e industriale nello spazio : programmi futuri ed esigenze assicurative = Commercial and industrial activities in space : future programmes and insurance requirements :3o convegno internazionale, Roma, 26-27 settembre 1985. [Trieste] : Assicurazioni generali, [1986] 192 p. : ill. (some col.) ; 29 cm. English and Italian. LC Card 86-215438
1. Space industrialization - Congresses. 2. Insurance, Business - Congresses. I. Title: Commercial and industrial activities in space.
HD9711.75.A2 A77 1986

Attman, Artur, 1910-
American bullion in the European world trade, 1600-1800 / by Artur Attman ; [translated by Eva and Allan Green]. Göteborg : Kungl. Vetenskaps- och Vitterhets Samhället, 1986. 115 p. ; 22 cm. (Acta Regiae Societatis Scientiarum et Litterarum Gothoburgensis. Humaniora, 0072-4823 . 26) Bibliography: p. 107-115. ISBN 91-85252-38-7 (pbk.) LC Card 87-147250 DDC 382/.4242/0973 19
1. Precious metals - America - History. 2. Precious metals - Europe - History. 3. America - Commerce - Europe - History. 4. Europe - Commerce - America - History. 5. Balance of payments - Europe - History. I. Title. II. Series.
HG285.A45 A88 1986

Swedish aspirations and the Russian market during the 17th century / by Artur Attman ; [translated by Eva and Allan Green]. Göteborg : Kungl. Vetenskaps- och Vitterhets-Samhället ; Atlantic Highlands, N.J. : Distributed in the U. S.A. and Canada by Humanities Press, c1985. 41 p. : map ; 23 cm. (Acta Regiae Societatis Scientiarum et Litterarum Gothoburgensis. Humaniora, 0072-4823 . 24) Distributor from label on t.p. Bibliography: p. 38-40. ISBN 91-85252-35-2 (pbk.) LC Card 86-214014 DDC 382/.09485/047 19
1. Sweden - Commerce - Soviet Union - History - 17th century. 2. Soviet Union - Commerce - Sweden - History - 17th century. 3. Sweden - Foreign relations - 1523-1718. I. Title. II. Series.
HF3678.S58 A88 1985

Attner, Raymond F. Straub, Joseph T. Introduction to business /. Boston, Mass. , 1988. xxi, 639, [66] p., [12] p. of plates : ISBN 0-534-87156-9 : LC Card 87-23276 DDC 658

19
HD31 .S6965 1988

Attraktivitätsanalyse von Dienstleistungen . Schertler, Walter. München , c1983. 183 p. : ISBN 3-597-10420-7 LC Card 83-140207
HD9984.5 .S25 1983

Attwood, Donald W. Power and poverty . Boulder , 1988. v, 186 p. ; ISBN 0-8133-7351-4 (pbk. : alk. paper) : LC Card 86-32578 DDC 338.9/009172/4 19
HC59.72.E44 P68 1988

Atuação dos programas especiais no Estado do Piauí / Ministério do Interior, Secretaria Geral, Secretaria de Planejamento-SPL, Subsecretaria de Programas Regionais-SPR. [Brasília] : A Subsecretaria, [1980] [29] leaves : ill. ; 30 cm. (Série Programas especiais . 6) LC Card 87-403685 DDC 333.91/0098122 19
1. Water resources development - Brazil - Piauí. 2. Rural development - Brazil - Piauí. I. Brazil. Ministério do Interior. Subsecretaria de Programas Regionais. II. Series.
HD1696.B83 P523 1980

Atwater Institute. Martin, James, 1933- The wired world . Carnforth, Lancashire, England , 1986. xiii, 140 p. : ISBN 0-906774-49-7 (pbk.) LC Card 87-157689 DDC 384 19
HE7631 .M373 1986

Au, Norman. Selected implications for businessmen of social responsibility in South Africa : a technical report / by Norman Au. [Cape Town] : Graduate School of Business, University of Cape Town, [1977] ix, 141 leaves ; 30 cm. (MBA research paper) Thesis (M.B.A.)--University of Cape Town, 1977. "November 1977." Bibliography: leaves 139-141. LC Card 81-155073
1. Industry - Social aspects - South Africa. I. Title. II. Series.
HD60.5.S7 A92 1977

Auberger, Bernard. Pour un rôle actif de la Communauté économique européenne sur la scène agricole internationale . Paris , c1986. 184 p. ; ISBN 2-11-001582-9 : LC Card 86-174918
HD1431 .P68 1986

Aubert, Didier. Systèmes de production et transformations de l'agriculture /. Paris , 1985. 2 v. : ISBN 2-85340-715-2 (v. 1) LC Card 86-214407
HD1945 .S97 1985

Aubin, Jean-Pierre. L'analyse non linéaire et ses motivations économiques / Jean-Pierre Aubin. Paris ; New York : Masson, 1984. x, 214 p. : ill. ; 24 cm. (Collection Mathématiques appliquées pour la maîtrise) Bibliography: p. 208-209. Includes index. ISBN 2-225-79541-X : LC Card 86-135801
1. Economics, Mathematical. 2. Game theory. 3. Nonlinear theories. 4. Equilibrium (Economics). I. Title. II. Series.
HB135 .A86 1984

AUBURN AIRPORT - HISTORY.
Ingalls, Roger W. A scrapbook history of the Auburn Aviation Co., Inc., and the Auburn Airport at Throopsville, N.Y., 1941-1952. Auburn, N.Y. , c1986. 169 p. : LC Card 87-125962
HE9803.A97 I54 1986

AUBURN AVIATION CO. - HISTORY.
Ingalls, Roger W. A scrapbook history of the Auburn Aviation Co., Inc., and the Auburn Airport at Throopsville, N.Y., 1941-1952. Auburn, N.Y. , c1986. 169 p. : LC Card 87-125962
HE9803.A97 I54 1986

Auction quotas and United States trade policy / C. Fred Bergsten ... [et al.]. Washington, DC : Institute for International Economics, c1987. xiii, 241 p. : ill. ; 23 cm. (Policy analyses in international economics . 19) "September 1987." Bibliography: p. 235-241. ISBN 0-88132-050-1 (pbk.) LC Card 87-12948 DDC 382/.52/0973 19
1. United States - Commercial policy. 2. Import quotas - United States. I. Bergsten, C. Fred, 1941-. II. Institute for International Economics (U. S.). III. Series.
HF1455 .A83 1987

Auctioneering . Engelmeier, Philip. San Francisco, CA , 1980. iii, 39 p. : ISBN 0-9605002-0-0 (pbk.) LC Card 86-213457
HF5476 .E55 1980

AUCTIONS - FRANCE.
Manston, Peter B., 1951- [Flea markets, antique shows, and auctions of France.] Manston's flea markets, antique shows, and auctions of France . Sacramento, Calif., U. S.A. , New York, N.Y. , c1987. 195 p. : ISBN 0-931367-06-9 (pbk.) : LC Card 86-30909 DDC 381/.1 19
HF5482 .M313 1987

AUCTIONS - GERMANY, WEST.
Manston, Peter B., 1951- [Flea markets, antique fairs, and auctions of Germany.] Manston's flea markets, antique fairs, and auctions of Germany . Sacramento, Calif., U. S.A. , New York, N.Y. , c1987. 297 p. : ISBN 0-931367-08-5 (pbk.) : LC Card 86-30908 DDC 381/.1 19
HF5482 .M3135 1987

AUCTIONS - GREAT BRITAIN.
Manston, Peter B., 1951- [Flea markets, antique fairs, and auctions of Britain.] Manston's flea markets, antique fairs, and auctions of Britain . Sacramento, Calif., U. S.A. , New York, N.Y. , c1987. 277 p. : ISBN 0-931367-10-7 (pbk. : alk. paper) : LC Card 87-16221 DDC 381/.1 19
HF5482 .M3125 1987

AUCTIONS - HANDBOOKS, MANUALS, ETC.
Engelmeier, Philip. Auctioneering . San Francisco, CA , 1980. iii, 39 p. : ISBN 0-9605002-0-0 (pbk.) LC Card 86-213457
HF5476 .E55 1980

AUCTIONS - UNITED STATES.
Hartung, Hans. Verfahren zur Nutzung erschöpfbarer Ressourcen . Tübingen , 1986. ix, 172 p. : ISBN 3-16-345126-8 (Deut. Bibl. : pbk.) LC Card 86-233079
HD9565 .H36 1986

Audenino, Patrizia. La Cassetta degli strumenti . Milano, Italy , c1986. 305 p. : LC Card 86-160695
HC304 .C37 1986

Audience ratings . Beville, Hugh Malcolm. Hillsdale, N.J. , 1987. p. cm. ISBN 0-8058-0175-8 LC Card 87-21001 DDC 384.54/3 19
HE8697.A8 B46 1987

AUDIENCES, TELEVISION. see **TELEVISION AUDIENCES.**

AUDIO-VISUAL EQUIPMENT INDUSTRY.
International trade in services. Paris , Washington, D.C. , 1986. 46 p. ; ISBN 92-64-12860-3 (pbk.) : LC Card 87-122911 DDC 382/.45621380282 19
HD9697.A842 I58 1986

AUDIO-VISUAL MATERIALS INDUSTRY. see **INSTRUCTIONAL MATERIALS INDUSTRY.**

Audit and accounting guide.
Savings and loan associations . New York, N.Y. (1211 Avenue of the Americas, New York 10036) , 1987. vii, 212 p. ; LC Card 87-161844 DDC 657/.833 19
HF5686.B8 S27 1987

Audit Commission for LocalAuthorities in England and Wales. Performance review in local government . [London , 1986] 1 v. (various pagings) : ISBN 0-11-701302-1 (loose-leaf : set) : LC Card 87-144582 DDC 352.1/72/0942 19
HJ9779.G7 P47 1986

Auditing : concepts, standards, procedures / edited by Thomas D. Hubbard, Johnny R. Johnson, & Ann B. Pushkin ; contributing authors, Wesley T. Andrews ... [et al.].Rev. ed. Houston, TX : Dame Publications, 1986. xvii, 919 p. : ill. ; 25 cm. Includes bibliographical references and index. ISBN 0-87393-016-9 LC Card 86-127902 DDC 657/.45 19
1. Auditing - United States. 2. Auditing - Standards - United States. I. Hubbard, Thomas D., 1933-. II. Johnson, Johnny R. III. Pushkin, Ann B. IV. Andrews, Wesley T.
HF5667 .A832 1986

Auditing /. Francisco, Albert K. Belmont, CA , c1987. 1 v. (various pagings) : ISBN 0-932276-76-8 (pbk.) LC Card 87-62076 DDC 657/.45/076 19
HF5667 .F68 1987

Auditing. Montgomery, Robert Hiester, 1872-1953. [Auditing.] Montgomery's Auditing. New York , c1987. xxv, 896 p. : ISBN 0-471-85423-9 LC Card 86-28938 DDC 657/.45 19
HF5667 .M7 1987

AUDITING.
Arens, Alvin A. Auditing, an integrated approach /. Englewood Cliffs, N.J. , c1988. p. cm. ISBN 0-13-051814-X LC Card 87-26359 DDC 657/.45 19
HF5667 .A69 1988

Kowalczyk, David S., 1946- Cadmus' operational auditing /. New York , c1987. x, 422 p. ; ISBN 0-471-82660-X LC Card 87-23267 DDC 657/.458 19
HF5668.25 .K696 1987

Kropatkin, Philip. Management and the audit network . New York , 1987. xii, 188 p. : ISBN 0-471-83286-3 LC Card 86-33983 DDC 657/.45 19
HF5667 .K74 1987

Lee, Thomas Alexander. Company auditing /. Wokingham, Berkshire, England , 1986. x, 197 p. ; ISBN 0-85258-243-9 (pbk.) LC Card 85-22537 DDC 657/.45 19
HF5667 .L387 1986 ***NYPL [JLD 86-3477]***

Montgomery, Robert Hiester, 1872-1953. [Auditing.] Montgomery's Auditing. New York , c1987. xxv, 896 p. : ISBN 0-471-85423-9 LC Card 86-28938 DDC 657/.45 19
HF5667 .M7 1987

Principles of auditing /. Homewood, Ill. , 1987. xv, 724 p. : ISBN 0-256-03580-6 LC Card 86-82588 DDC 657/.45 19
HF5667 .P73 1987

Sougue, Matthieu Kounabé. La pratique de l'audit financier dans les entreprises au Sénégal, à travers le cabinet Helios . [Dakar] [1983?] 194, [18] leaves : LC Card 85-121418
HF5686.C7 S67 1984

Auditing, an integrated approach /. Arens, Alvin A. Englewood Cliffs, N.J. , c1988. p. cm. ISBN 0-13-051814-X LC Card 87-26359 DDC 657/.45 19
HF5667 .A69 1988

AUDITING - CARIBBEAN AREA - CASE STUDIES.
Mendes, Margaret. Caribbean cases in auditing /. Kingston, Jamaica , c1986. 58 p. : ISBN 976-8053-00-3 (pbk.) LC Card 87-403426 DDC 657/.45 19
HF5667 .M456 1986

AUDITING - EXAMINATIONS, QUESTIONS, ETC.
The Complete CPA examination review, auduiing, 1986-1987 /. Boston , c1986. 42, 237, 177, 12 p. : ISBN 0-395-41132-7 (pbk.) LC Card 86-80561 DDC 657/.45/076 19
HF5667 .C5852 1986

Francisco, Albert K. Auditing /. Belmont, CA , c1987. 1 v. (various pagings) : ISBN 0-932276-76-8 (pbk.) LC Card 87-62076 DDC 657/.45/076 19
HF5667 .F68 1987

AUDITING - FRANCE - HISTORY - 20TH CENTURY.
Chadeau, Emmanuel, 1956- Les inspecteurs des finances au XIXe siècle (1850-1914) . Paris , c1986. iii, 184 p. : ISBN 2-7178-1175-3 : LC Card 87-131650
HJ9925.F8 C42 1986

AUDITING - GERMANY (WEST) - DATA PROCESSING.
Rausch, Helmar. Grundsätze ordnungsmässiger EDV-Dokumentation . Schwarzenbek , 1985. vii, 323 p. : ISBN 3-921757-21-5 LC Card 86-227042
HF5667 .R335 1985

AUDITING - HANDBOOKS, MANUALS, ETC.
Handbook of accounting and auditing /. Boston , c1981. 1 v. (various pagings) ; ISBN 0-88712-221-3 (Update 1985) LC Card 80-53166 DDC 657/.02/02 19
HF5635.H22 ***NYPL [*R-Econ. 85-31]***

Perry, Larry L. Small business audit manual /. Englewood Cliffs, N.J. , c1987- 1 v. (loose-leaf) : ISBN 0-13-813155-4 (loose-leaf) LC Card 86-63242 DDC 657/.45 19
HF5667 .P416 1987

AUDITING, INTERNAL.
The Institute of Internal Auditors reports on fraud . Altamonte Springs, Fla. , c1987. xv, 74 p. : ISBN 0-89413-164-8 (pbk.) LC Card 87-401942 DDC 657/.3 19
HF5686.C7 I53 1987

Kofler, Herbert. Die Prüfung der Geschäftsführung . Wien , 1985. 196 p. ; ISBN 3-85122-183-4 : LC Card 86-203497
HF5668.25 .K68 1985

Kowalczyk, David S., 1946- Cadmus' operational auditing /. New York , c1987. x, 422 p. ; ISBN 0-471-82660-X LC Card 87-23267 DDC 657/.458 19
HF5668.25 .K696 1987

Lubos, Günter, 1958- Die Berichterstattung der internen Revision im Grossbetrieb /. München , c1986. xxvii, 207 p. ; ISBN 3-88259-421-7 LC Card 87-121827 DDC 657/.458 19
HF5668.25 .L82 1986

Sawyer, Lawrence B. The practice of modern internal auditing /. Altamonte Springs, Fla. , 1981. xiv, 882 p. : ISBN 0-89413-092-7 LC Card 87-462054 DDC 657/.458 19
HF5668.25 .S28 1981

AUDITING, INTERNAL - PSYCHOLOGICAL ASPECTS.
Wilson, James A., 1928- Managing the behavioral dynamics of internal auditing /. Altamonte Springs, Fla. [1985] xii, 112 p. : ISBN 0-89413-130-3 (pbk.) LC Card 85-169744 DDC 657/.458/019 19
HF5668.25 .W53 1985 ***NYPL [JLE 86-4318]***

AUDITING, INTERNAL - STATISTICAL METHODS.
Pöhlmann, Helmut. Jahresabschlussprüfung auf Stichprobenbasis . Pfaffenweiler , 1987. xii, 187 p. ; ISBN 3-89085-142-8 LC Card 87-133413 DDC 657/.458 19
HF5668.25 .P64 1987

AUDITING, INTERNAL - STATISTICAL METHODS - DATA PROCESSING.
Stringer, Kenneth W. Statistical techniques for analytical review in auditing /. New York , c1986. xii, 301 p. : ISBN 0-471-86076-X : LC Card 85-17874 DDC 657/.45/0285536 19
HF5667 .S85 1986 ***NYPL [JLE 86-2704]***

Auditing procedure study.
Auditing the allowance for credit losses of banks. New York, N.Y. (1211 Ave. of the Americas, New York 10036-8775) , c1986. vii, 40 p. : LC Card 86-234688 DDC 657/.833 19
HG1707.5 .A927 1986

AUDITING - STANDARDS - UNITED STATES.
Auditing . Houston, TX , 1986. xvii, 919 p. : ISBN 0-87393-016-9 LC Card 86-127902 DDC 657/.45 19
HF5667 .A832 1986

AUDITING - STATISTICAL METHODS - DATA PROCESSING.
Stringer, Kenneth W. Statistical techniques for analytical review in auditing /. New York , c1986. xii, 301 p. : ISBN 0-471-86076-X : LC Card 85-17874 DDC 657/.45/0285536 19
HF5667 .S85 1986 ***NYPL [JLE 86-2704]***

Auditing the allowance for credit losses of banks. New York, N.Y. (1211 Ave. of the Americas, New York 10036-8775) : American Institute of Certified Public Accountants, c1986. vii, 40 p. : ill. ; 23 cm. (Auditing procedure study) Bibliography: p. 33-40. LC Card 86-234688 DDC 657/.833 19
1. Bank examination - United States. 2. Bank loans - United States. I. American Institute of Certified Public Accountants. II. Series.
HG1707.5 .A927 1986

AUDITING - UNITED STATES.
Auditing . Houston, TX , 1986. xvii, 919 p. : ISBN 0-87393-016-9 LC Card 86-127902 DDC 657/.45 19
HF5667 .A832 1986

AUDITORS - FRANCE - HISTORY - 19TH CENTURY.
Chadeau, Emmanuel, 1956- Les inspecteurs des finances au XIXe siècle (1850-1914) . Paris , c1986. iii, 184 p. : ISBN 2-7178-1175-3 : LC Card 87-131650
HJ9925.F8 C42 1986

AUDITORS - GERMANY (WEST) - PROFESSIONAL ETHICS.
Binz, Hans-Bert, 1954- Kritik an deutschen Wirtschaftsprüfern, ein Glaubwürdigkeitsproblem? . Bergisch Gladbach , 1984. ix, 325 p. : ISBN 3-89012-004-0 : LC Card 84-174776
HF5627 .B55 1984

AUDITORS - PSYCHOLOGY.
Wilson, James A., 1928- Managing the behavioral dynamics of internal auditing /. Altamonte Springs, Fla. [1985] xii, 112 p. : ISBN 0-89413-130-3 (pbk.) LC Card 85-169744 DDC 657/.458/019 19
HF5668.25 .W53 1985 ***NYPL [JLE 86-4318]***

AUDITORS' REPORTS - UNITED STATES.
Mangold, Nancy R. (Nancy Rueyhwa), 1949- Changing auditors and the effect on earnings, auditors' opinions, and stock prices /. Ann Arbor, Mich. , c1987. viii, 165 p. ; ISBN 0-8357-1786-0 (alk. paper) LC Card 87-19128 DDC 338.7/4/0973 19
HF5686.C7 M3295 1987

AUDITORS - SALARIES, ETC. - UNITED STATES - STATISTICS.
Compensation in the accounting/financial field /. Crete, IL , c1987. 489 p. ; ISBN 0-916506-36-3 (pbk.) LC Card 87-153325 DDC 331.12/81657/0973021 19
HF5627 .C57 1987

AUDITORS - SALARIES, PENSIONS, ETC. - UNITED STATES - STATISTICS.
The Accounting/financial report /. Crete, IL (548 First St., Crete 60417) , c1983. 2 v. ; LC Card 83-152793 DDC 331.2/81657/0973 19
HF5627 .A23 1983 ***NYPL [JLM 86-1500]***

Audits of entities with oil and gas producing activities : [audit and accounting guide] / prepared by the Oil and Gas Committee. New York, NY (1211 Ave. of the Americas, New York 10036-8775) : American Institute of Certified Public Accountants, c1986. x, 133 p. ; 23 cm. Bibliography: p. 129-133. LC Card 86-209769 DDC 657/.862 19
1. Petroleum industry and trade - Accounting. I. American Institute of Certified Public Accountants. Oil and Gas Committee.
HF5686.P3 A93 1986

Audits of local governments. Carmichael, D. R. Douglas R.), 1941- Guide to audits of local governments /. Fort Worth, Tex. , 1986- 2 v. (loose-leaf) : LC Card 86-206730 DDC 657/.835045 19
HJ9777.A3 C37 1986

Audretsch, David B.
Ács, Zoltán J. The determinants of innovation in large and small firms /. Berlin [1986] 39 p. ; LC Card 87-156684 DDC 338.6/4 19
HC110.T4 A59 1986

Industrial policy, R&D, and U. S.-Japanese trade / David B. Audretsch, Hideki Yamawaki. Berlin : Wissenschaftszentrum Berlin für Sozialforschung, [1986] 39 p. ; 30 cm. (Discussion papers, 0722-6748 . IIM/IP 86-13) "April 1986." Bibliography: p. 34-36. LC Card 87-156721 DDC 382/.0952/073 19
1. United States - Commerce - Japan - Econometric models. 2. Japan - Commerce - United States - Econometric models. 3. Industry and state - Japan - Econometric models. 4. Research, Industrial - Economic aspects - Japan - Econometric models. I. Yamawaki, Hideki. II. Series: Discussion papers (International Institute of Management. Industrial Policy) , IIM/IP 86-13. III. Title.
HF3127 .A93 1986

Auer, Peter. Industrial relations, work organisation and new technology : the VOLVO case / Peter Auer. Berlin : Wissenschaftszentrum Berlin, [1985] 17, [6] p. ; 30 cm. (Discussion papers / IIMV Arbeitsmarktpolitik, 0722-673X = IIM Labour Market Policy . IIM/LMP 85-10) "September 1985." Bibliography: p. [4-5] (2nd sequence) LC Card 86-205891 DDC 331/.04292/09481 19
1. Volvo, Aktiebolaget. 2. Automobile industry and trade - Sweden - Case studies. 3. Industrial relations - Sweden - Case studies. 4. Industrial organization - Sweden - Case studies. I. Series: Discussion papers (International Institute of Management. Labour Market Policy) , IIM/LMP 85-10. II. Title.
HD9710.S84 V6413 1985

Auerbach, Alan J.
Dynamic fiscal policy / Alan J. Auerbach and Laurence J. Kotlikoff. Cambridge [Cambridgeshire] ; New York : Cambridge University Press, 1987. xv, 196 p. : ill. ; 24 cm. Bibliography: p. 183-189. Includes index. ISBN 0-521-30041-X LC Card 86-24447 DDC 339.5/2 19
1. Fiscal policy - Mathematical models. 2. Finance, Public - Mathematical models. 3. Equilibrium (Economics) - Mathematical models. 4. Macroeconomics - Mathematical models. I. Kotlikoff, Laurence J. II. Title.
HJ131 .A94 1987

Mergers and acquisitions /. Chicago , 1988. xi, 108 p. : ISBN 0-226-03209-4 LC Card 87-19035 DDC 658.1/6 19
HD2746.5 .M45 1988

Auerbach, Joseph, 1916- Investment banking and diligence : what price deregulation? / Joseph Auerbach and Samuel L. Hayes, III. Boston, Mass. : Harvard Business School Press, c1986. x, 274 p. : ill. ; 25 cm. Includes bibliographies and index. ISBN 0-87584-171-6 (alk. paper) LC Card 86-319 DDC 332.66/0973 19
1. Investment banking - United States. 2. Securities - United States. I. Hayes, Samuel L. II. Title.
HG4910 .A94 1986 ***NYPL [JLE 86-3128]***

Auerbach, Robert D. Money, banking, and financial markets / Robert D. Auerbach. 3rd ed. New York : Macmillan ; London : Collier Macmillan, c1988. p. cm. Includes bibliographies and index. ISBN 0-02-305040-3 LC Card 87-11173 DDC 332.1 19
1. Money. 2. Banks and banking. 3. Finance. I. Title.
HG221 .A914 1988

Auerswald, R. (Rolf) Wissenschaftliche Tagung "Nutzung Ökonomisch-Mathematischer Methoden und der Elektronischen Rechentechnik zur Erhöhung der Reaktionsfähigkeit der Industriekombinate gegenüber der Bedarfsdynamik" (1983 : Technische Hochschule Karl-Marx Stadt) Wissenschaftliche Tagung "Nutzung Ökonomisch-Mathematischer Methoden und der Elektronischen Rechentechnik zur Erhöhung der Reaktionsfähigkeit der Industriekombinate gegenüber der Bedarfsdynamik," 8. Juni 1983 . Karl-Marx-Stadt [1983] iii, 56 p. ; LC Card 84-117572
HD30.25 .W56 1983

Auf dem Weg in die Freiheit : Anstösse zu einer steirischen Zeitgeschichte / R. Hinteregger, K. Müller, E. Staudinger (Hrsg.). Graz : Kuratorium der Wanderausstellung "Für Freiheit, Arbeit und Recht," 1984. 356 p. : ill. ; 24 cm. Includes bibliographies. LC Card 87-672377
1. Labor and laboring classes - Austria - Styria - History - 19th century. 2. Labor and laboring classes - Austria - Styria - History - 20th century. I. Hinteregger, R. (Robert), 1947-. II. Müller, K. (Karl), 1953-. III. Staudinger, E. (Eduard), 1952-.
HD8419.S82 A93x 1984

Auf dem Weg zu einer neuen Weltwirtschaftsordnung? : Bedingungen und Grenzen für eine eigenständige Entwicklung / Hans-Dieter Evers, Dieter Senghaas, Huberta Wienholtz (Hrsg.).1. Aufl. Baden-Baden : Nomos Verlagsgesellschaft, 1983. 478 p. ; 23 cm. (Veröffentlichungen der DGFK) Includes bibliographies. ISBN 3-7890-0919-9 LC Card 84-113581
1. International economic relations. 2. Economic development. I. Evers, Hans-Dieter. II. Senghaas, Dieter, 1940-. III. Wienholtz, Huberta. IV. Series.
HF1411 .A92 1983

Auf dem Weg zu einer neuen Weltwirtschaftsordnung? : Bedingungen und Grenzen für eine eigenständige Entwicklung / Hans-Dieter Evers, Dieter Senghaas, Huberta Wienholtz, Hrsg.1. Aufl. Baden-Baden : Nomos, 1983. 478 p. ; 23 cm. (Veröffentlichungen der DGFK) Includes bibliographical references. ISBN 3-7890-0919-9
1. Economic assistance - Developing countries. 2. Developing countries - Economic conditions. I. Evers, Hans-Dieter. II. Senghaas, Dieter, 1940-. III. Wienholtz, Huberta. IV. Deutsche Gesellschaft für Friedens- und Konfliktforschung. V. Series.
NYPL [JLD 87-919]

Auf dem Wege zu einer Theorie der internationalen Koordination der Agrarpolitik /. Gerken, Egbert. Kiel [1985] 29 p. : LC Card 85-203925
HD1415 .G395 1985

Auf sicherem Kurs : Arbeitsmaterial zum Fünfjahrplan für die Entwicklung der Volkswirtschaft der DDR in den Jahren 1976-1980 / herausgegeben von der Parteihochschule "Karl Marx" beim ZK der SED ; [Autorenkollektiv, Harry Milke (Leiter) ... et al.]. [Berlin] : Die Hochschule, [1976] 80 leaves (some folded) : ill. ; 28 cm. LC Card 85-190579
1. Germany, East - Economic policy. 2. Germany, East - Industries. 3. Socialism - Germany (East). I. Milke, Harry. II. Parteihochschule "Karl Marx" (Berlin, Germany).
HC290.78 .A84 1976

Aufbau eines Controllingsystems für Consulting-Unternehmen /. Melcher, Horst. Darmstadt , c1982. 276 p. : ISBN 3-87820-052-8 LC Card 83-110639
HD69.C6 M45 1982

Aufbau und Ergebnisse einer Gesamtrechnung für das land- und forstwirtschaftliche Bodenvermögen in der Bundesrepublik Deutschland /. Filter, Wolfgang, 1952- Frankfurt am Main , New York , c1984. xiii, 288 p. : ISBN 3-8204-5290-7 LC Card 85-198973
HD658 .F55 1984

Aufbau und Gewinnung Shephardscher Produktionsfunktionen unter Berücksichtigung empirischer Aspekte /. Teusch, Wolfgang. Königstein/Ts. , c1983. vi, 296 p. : ISBN 3-445-02274-7 LC Card 83-195883
HB241 .T48 1983

Aufbereitung von Ergebnissen der Stadtverkehrsforschung : Sachgebiet Verkehrs- und Betriebssteuerung / herausgegeben vom Bundesminister für Verkehr ; [Bearbeiter, Peter Mott, Jens Seute, Gerhard Schenk ; Projektträger, Forschungsgesellschaft für Strassen- und Verkehrswesen, Köln]. Hof/Saale : Hoermann, 1986. 2 v. : ill. ; 24 cm. (Forschung Stadtverkehr. Reihe Auswertungen . Heft A2) "Forschungsauftrag Nr. 70 129/84"--T.p. verso. Includes bibliographies. CONTENTS. - T. A. Öffentlicher Personenverkehr -- T. B. Individualverkehr. LC Card 87-408335 DDC 388.4/0943 19
1. Local transit - Germany, West. I. Mott, Peter. II. Seute, Jens. III. Schenk, Gerhard. IV. Germany (West). Bundesministerium für Verkehr. V. Forschungsgesellschaft für Strassen- und Verkehrswesen. VI. Series.
HE4774 .A94 1986

Aufbruch zum Himmel : alte Flugmarken / herausgegeben von Lotte Maier ; Nachwort von Werner Utter. Dortmund : Harenberg, c1982. 99 p. : col. ill. ; 18 cm. (Die Bibliophilen Taschenbücher . Nr. 328) ISBN 3-88379-328-0 : LC Card 83-125566
1. Air mail stamps - Germany - History. I. Maier, Lotte. II. Utter, Werner. III. Series.
HE6184.A4 A84 1982

AUFFAY (FRANCE) - OCCUPATIONS - HISTORY.
Gullickson, Gay L. Spinners and weavers of Auffay . Cambridge [Cambridgeshire] , New York , 1986. x, 256 p. : ISBN 0-521-32280-4 LC Card 86-6808 DDC 331.4/877/02822094425 19
HD8039.T42 F834 1986 ***NYPL [JLE 87-1054]***

Aufgaben der Finanz- und Steuerpolitik in dieser Legislaturperiode. Zahn, Joachim, Professor Dr. Eine Finanzpolitik des langen Atems erforderlich /. Bonn [1984] 31 leaves ; LC Card 86-198580
HJ1120 .B65 Nr. 234

Aufgaben und Erfolge der Arbeitsgemeinschaft Industrieller Forschungsvereinigungen. Rembser, Josef. Die Förderung des wirtschaftlichen und sozialen Wandels durch die Forschungs- und Entwicklungspolitik als präventive Strukturpolitik /. Dortmund , 1977. 100 p. : LC Card 84-130876
HD30 .A7 Heft 184 HD6331.2.G28

Aufgaben und Wirkungen der Reichsbank in der Zeit des Dawes-Planes /. Flaskamp, Jürgen, 1958- Bergisch Gladbach , c1986. 210 p. : ISBN 3-89012-060-1 LC Card 87-108166 DDC 332.1/1/0943 19
HG3054 .F58 1986

Die Auflagenpolitik des Internationalen Währungsfonds . Engshuber, Wolfgang. [München] [1985?] 32 leaves ; LC Card 85-166626
HG3881.5.I58 E54 1985

Auflagenpolitik und Politik-Dialog in der entwicklungspolitischen Zusammenarbeit /. Radke, Detlef. Berlin , 1985. xiii, 91 p. : ISBN 3-88985-036-7 LC Card 85-134788
HC60 .R183 1985

Aufrisse-Buch .
(4) Czasny, Karl. Lehrjahre bei Bau-Holz . Wien , c1985. ix, 148 p. ; ISBN 3-900351-34-1 LC Card 86-227367 DDC 331.88/174/09436 19
HD6678.W62 G493 1985

Aufstieg zur Macht . Hauff, Hanns Joachim Paul. München , c1983. 85 p. : ISBN 3-597-10422-3 LC Card 83-136638
HD38.2 .H38 1983

El auge del café y la apertura de la economía costarricense /. Daremblum, Jaime. San José, Costa Rica , 1980. 62 p. ; LC Card 84-247131
HF3255 .D37 1980

Augel, Johannes. Die Verplante Wohnmisere . Saarbrücken , Fort Lauderdale , 1986. 334 p. : ISBN 3-88156-329-6 LC Card 87-408292 DDC 363.5/1/096 19
HD7287.96.A4 V47 1986

Augenti, Antonio. Verso un sistema di orientamento . Rimini , c1984. 290 p. : LC Card 85-119196 DDC 370.11/3/094 19
LC5056.I8 V47 1984 ***NYPL [JLE 86-1555]***

Augros, Jean-Claude. Finance : options et obligations convertibles / Jean-Claude Augros. Paris : Economica, c1985. 320 p. : ill. ; 24 cm. (Collection Gestion. Série Politique générale, finance et marketing) Bibliography: p. [315]-317. ISBN 2-7178-0911-2 : LC Card 85-219227 DDC 332.64/52/0944 19
1. Put and call transactions - France. 2. Convertible bonds - France. I. Series: Collection Gestion (Economica (Firm)). Série Politique générale, finance et marketing. II. Title.
HG6042 .A94 1985 ***NYPL [JLE 87-295]***

Augsburg (Germany). Amt für Wirtschaftsförderung. Gestaltungsspielräume der Arbeitsmarktpolitik auf regionalen Arbeitsmärkten . Berlin , c1984. 180 p. : ISBN 3-428-05614-0 LC Card 84-218530
HD8444 .G47 1984

Augsburger Schriften zur Wirtschaftssoziologie.
Neun, Hansjörg, 1953- Projektübergabe bei der technischen Zusammenarbeit mit Entwicklungsländer /. Augsburg [1985] viii, 315 p. : ISBN 3-87512-135-X : LC Card 86-228570
HD84 .N43 1985

August, Jochen. Herrenmensch und Arbeitsvölker . Berlin , c1986. 189 p. : ISBN 3-88022-952-X (cover); 3-88022-925-X : LC Card 87-119712 DDC 331.11/732/0943 19
HD4875.G4 H47 1986

Auld, Douglas Allen Lauriston. The Determinants of negotiated wage settlements in Canada (1966-1975) . [Ottawa] , Hull, Quebec , c1979. x, 256 p. : ISBN 0-660-10162-9 : LC Card 79-313202 DDC 331.2/971
HD4979 .D44 ***NYPL [JLE 80-447]***

Auletta, Ken.
Greed and glory on Wall Street : the fall of the house of Lehman / Ken Auletta.1st ed. New York : Random House, c1986. xiii, 253 p., [16] p. of plates : ill. ; 24 cm. Includes index. ISBN 0-394-54410-2 : LC Card 85-10700 DDC 332.66/09747/1 19
1. Lehman Brothers. 2. Wall Street. 3. Brokers - United States. I. Title.
HG5129.N5 A8 1986 ***NYPL [JLE 86-856]***

Greed and glory on Wall Street : the fall of the house of Lehman / Ken Auletta.Large print. Boston, Mass. : G.K. Hall, 1987, c1986. xii, 423 p. (large print) ; 25 cm. (G.K. Hall large print book series) ISBN 0-8161-4189-4 (lg. print) : LC Card 86-26968 DDC 332.66/09747/1 19
1. Lehman Brothers. 2. Wall Street. 3. Brokers - United States. I. Lehman Brothers. II. Title.
HG5129.N5 A8 1987b

Greed and glory on Wall Street : the fall of the house of Lehman / Ken Auletta. New York, N.Y. : Warner Books, [1987], c1986. xi, 260 p., [16] p. of plates : ill., ports. ; 23 cm. Reprint. Originally published: New York : Random House, 1986. Includes index. ISBN 0-446-38406-2 (pbk.) LC Card 86-23416 DDC 332.66/09747/1 19
1. Lehman Brothers. 2. Wall Street. 3. Brokers - United States. I. Title.
HG5129.N5 A8 1987

Aumento del ingreso y mejoramiento de las condiciones de trabajo del sector informal urbano en sietes ciudades del Perú / autores, Castiglia Miguel Angel ... [et al.]. [Lima, Perú?] : IDESI : BONIFICA, 1986. ii, 69, [25] leaves : ill. (some col.) ; 30 cm. At head of title: Presidencia de la República, Instituto Nacional de Planificación. LC Card 87-106249
1. Informal sector (Economics) - Peru - Case studies. 2. Technical assistance, Italian - Peru. 3. IDESI (Organization : Peru). I. Castiglia, Miguel Angel. II. Instituto Nacional de Planificación (Peru).
HD2346.P4 A85 1986

Aún tiembla : sociedad política y cambio social : el terremoto del 19 de septiembre de 1985 / Adolfo Aguilar Zinzer [sic], Cesáreo Morales y Rodolfo Peña, eds.1a ed. México : Grijalbo, c1986. 332 p., [8] p. of plates : ill. ; 19 cm. Includes bibliographical references. ISBN 968-419-620-2 LC Card 87-403523 DDC 363.3/495/097253 19
1. Earthquakes - Economic aspects - Mexico - Mexico City Region. 2. Earthquakes - Social aspects - Mexico - Mexico City Region. I. Aguilar Zinser, Adolfo. II. Morales, Cesáreo. III. Peña, Rodolfo F.
HC138.M43 A95 1986

Aus der Geschichte lernen.
Säumt keine Minute! . Mannheim , c1986. xiii, 683 p. : ISBN 3-923003-36-6 LC Card 87-115249 DDC 331/.0943/46 19
HD8460.M35 S28 1986

Aus eigner Kraft . Weihe, Carl, b. 1872. Leipzig , 1918. 139 p., X [i.e. 5] p. of plates : LC Card 85-666353
HC283 .W45x 1918

Der Ausbau von Fernwärmenetzen und seine Wirkungen auf Arbeitsmarkt und Beschäftigung, dargestellt am Beispiel der Freien und Hansestadt Hamburg : Endbericht eines Forschungsvorhaben im Auftrag des Bundesministers für Arbeit und Sozialordnung / GEWOS, Institut für Stadt-, Regional- und Wohnforschung GmbH ; [Projektbearbeitung, Gerald Westphalen ... et al.]. Bonn : Der Bundesminister, [1983] xiv, 172 p. : ill. ; 30 cm. (Forschungsbericht / Der Bundesminister für Arbeit und Sozialordnung, 0174-4992 . 101.) Bibliography: p. 160-162. LC Card 85-107700
1. Labor supply - Germany (West) - Hamburg. 2. Heating from central stations - Economic aspects - Germany (West) - Hamburg. I. Westphalen, Gerald. II. Germany (West). Bundesministerium für Arbeit und Sozialordnung. III. Institut für Stadt-, Regional- und Wohnforschung (Hamburg, Germany). IV. Series: Forschungsbericht (Germany (West). Bundesministerium für Arbeit und Sozialordnung) , 101.
HD5780.H34 A87 1983

Ausführliche Abhandlung von denen Steuern und Abgaben /. Justi, Johann Heinrich Gottlob von, d. 1771. Wiesbaden , 1977. 202 p., [4] p. of plates : ISBN 3-409-50171-1 LC Card 84-235228
HJ2300 .J87 1977

Ausführliche Volks-Gewerbslehre. Poppe, Johann Heinrich Moritz von, 1776-1854. Ausführliche Volks-Gewerbslehre, oder, Allgemeine und besondere Technologie zur Belehrung und zum Nutzen für alle Stände /. Stuttgart , Wien , 1833- v. <1 > : LC Card 87-409525 DDC 331.7/02/024042 19
HF5382.5.E84 P66 1833

Ausführliche Volks-Gewerbslehre, oder, Allgemeine und besondere Technologie zur Belehrung und zum Nutzen für alle Stände /. Poppe, Johann Heinrich Moritz von, 1776-1854. Stuttgart , Wien , 1833- v. <1 > : LC Card 87-409525 DDC 331.7/02/024042 19
HF5382.5.E84 P66 1833

Ausführliche Volksgewerbslehre. Poppe, Johann Heinrich Moritz von, 1776-1854. Ausführliche Volks-Gewerbslehre, oder, Allgemeine und besondere Technologie zur Belehrung und zum Nutzen für alle Stände /. Stuttgart , Wien , 1833- v. <1 > : LC Card 87-409525 DDC 331.7/02/024042 19
HF5382.5.E84 P66 1833

Ausgabeneffekte kommunaler Funktionalreformen . Rosenfeld, Martin. Baden-Baden , 1985. 395 p. : ISBN

3-7890-1077-4 LC Card 86-156503
HJ9493.5.L6 R67 1985

Ausgabenkürzungen im öffentlichen Sektor /. Boss, Alfred. Tübingen , c1987. xiii, 220 p. : ISBN 3-16-345212-4 LC Card 87-408337 DDC 336.43 19
HJ2109 .B67 1987

Ausgewählte Aufsätze zur Wirtschaftstheorie /. Merk, Gerhard, 1931- Zürich , 1986. 138 p. ; ISBN 3-9999462-1-1 LC Card 87-409558 DDC 330.9494/073 19
HB118.A2 M47 1986

Ausgewählte makroökonomische Modelle offener Volkswirtschaften /. Frenkel, Michael. St. Gallen , 1982. 183 p. : LC Card 83-112497
HG3823 .F74 1982

Ausgewählte Quellen zur deutschen Geschichte der Neuzeit, 0571-9178 . (Bd. 37) Quellen zur deutschen Wirtschafts- und Sozialgeschichte von der Reichsgründung bis zum ersten Weltkrieg /. Darmstadt , 1985. xviii, 553 p. : ISBN 3-534-07561-7 LC Card 85-229315
HC285 .Q45 1985

Ausgewählte Sendungen von Radio Tirana (Vienna, Austria) . (17) Marxismus-Leninismus, eine immer junge und wissenschaftliche Lehre (Radio Program). Selections. Neue Phänomene der kapitalistischen Gesellschaft ändern nichts an ihrem Wesen . Wien , 1976. 35 p. : LC Card 85-144894
HB501 .M338 1976

Der Ausgleich funktionaler Defizite des wirtschaftlichen Systems durch die Unternehmensberatung . Eschbach, Thomas H., 1954- Frankfurt am Main , New York , c1984. 152 p. ; ISBN 3-8204-5127-7 LC Card 85-191647
HD69.C6 E76 1984

Ausgliederung des Zahlungsverkehrs aus dem Universalbankbereich /. Vajc, Klaus, 1958- Frankfurt am Main , New York , c1986. viii, 238 p. : ISBN 3-8204-8825-1 LC Card 86-220359
HG1692 .V34 1986

Ausländerbeschäftigung als dauerhafter Angebotsfaktor auf dem Arbeitsmarkt der Bundesrepublik Deutschland /. Pammesberger, Hans-Peter. Hamburg , c1986. xii, 297 p. : ISBN 3-925630-06-6 LC Card 86-227741
HD8458.A2 P35 1986

Ausländerintegration in deutschen Industriebetrieben / von Eduard Gaugler ... [et al.]. Königstein/Ts. : Hanstein, c1985. viii, 273 p. : ill. ; 21 cm. (Materialien zur Arbeitsmigration und Ausländerbeschäftigung . Bd. 6) Includes index. Bibliography: p. 230-232. ISBN 3-7756-6935-3 LC Card 85-194662 DDC 305.8/00943 19
1. Alien labor - Germany, West. 2. Minorities - Germany, West. 3. Social integration - Germany (West). 4. Social accounting - Germany (West). 5. Industry - Social aspects - Germany, West. I. Gaugler, Eduard. II. Series.
HD8458.A2 A9265 1985 ***NYPL [JLD 86-2193]***

Ausländische Investitionen in U. S.-Grundvermögen / Herausgeber, Arthur Andersen & Co., S.C. Herne : Verlag Neue Wirtschafts-Briefe, 1984, c1983. 86 p. ; 21 cm. (NWB-Schriften für die internationale Steuerpraxis) Includes bibliographical references and index. ISBN 3-482-69041-3 LC Card 84-203818 DDC 346.43/07 344.3067 19
1. Investments, Foreign - Law and legislation - United States. 2. Real property - United States. 3. Taxation, Double - Germany, West. I. Arthur Andersen & Co. II. Title: Ausländische Investitionen in US-Grundvermögen. III. Series.
K3830.4 .A97 1984 ***NYPL [JLD 86-2326]***

Ausländische Investitionen in US-Grundvermögen. Ausländische Investitionen in U. S.-Grundvermögen /. Herne , 1984, c1983. 86 p. ; ISBN 3-482-69041-3 LC Card 84-203818 DDC 346.43/07 344.3067 19
K3830.4 .A97 1984 ***NYPL [JLD 86-2326]***

Auslandsinvestitionen kleiner und mittlerer Unternehmen . Berger, Manfred, Dipl. econ. Berlin , c1985. 164 p. : ISBN 3-428-05775-9 LC Card 85-161656
HG4538 .B4538 1985

Aussagefähigkeit von Einkommensverteilungsrechnungen für die Bundesrepublik Deutschland : Gutachten im Auftrag des Bundesministers für Wirtschaft / herausgegeben von Helmut Lindner ; mit Beiträgen von W. Kitterer, H. Enke, H. Lindner, unter Mitarbeit von B. Freitag. Tübingen : Institut für Angewandte Wirtschaftsforschung Tübingen, 1986. xxiv, 436 p. : ill. ; 21 cm. (Forschungsberichte / Institut für Angewandte Wirtschaftsforschung Tübingen. Serie A . Nr. 43) Includes bibliographies. ISBN 3-88573-027-8 LC Card 87-407588 DDC 339.2/0943 19
1. Income distribution - Germany, West. 2. Income distribution - Germany (West) - Econometric models. I. Lindner, Helmut. II. Kitterer, Wolfgang. III. Germany (West). Bundesministerium für Wirtschaft. IV. Series: Forschungsberichte / Institut für Angewandte Wirtschaftsforschung Tübingen. Serie A , Nr. 43.
HC290.5.I5 A93 1986

Ausschreibung Bundeswettbewerb 1983-1984. Bürger, es geht um Deine Gemeinde . [S.l. , 1983] ([Bonn] : Bundesdruckerei) 7 p. ; LC Card 84-198296
HD7339.A3 B97 1983

Ausschuss für Wirtschaftliche Verwaltung in Wirtschaft und Öffentlicher Hand. Bendeich, E. (Eugen), 1945- Wirtschaftliche Datenerfassung in Klein- und Mittelbetrieben . München , c1979. 211 p. : ISBN 3-478-41740-6 LC Card 85-171162
HD62.7 .B4 1979

Aussendienststeuerung im Investitionsgütermarketing . Rudolphi, Michael, 1948- Frankfurt am Main , c1981. xi, 445 p. : ISBN 3-8204-6125-6 : LC Card 81-111119
HF5439.I4 R83 1981

Aussenhandel mit Entwicklungsländern . Beyfuss, Jörg. Köln , c1978. 55 p. : ISBN 3-88054-145-0 LC Card 85-242489
HF3568.D44 B49 1978

Aussenwirtschaft /. Siebert, Horst, 1938- Stuttgart , c1984. xi, 303 p. : ISBN 3-437-40149-1 (pbk.) LC Card 87-672497
HF1007 .S49x 1984

Aussenwirtschaft der DDR und innerdeutsche Wirtschaftsbeziehungen : rechtliche und ökonomische Probleme / herausgegeben von Gernot Gutmann, Gottfried Zieger. Berlin : Duncker & Humblot, c1986. 98 p. ; 24 cm. (Schriftenreihe der Gesellschaft für Deutschlandforschung . Bd. 16) Proceedings of a symposium sponsored by the Fachgruppen Wirtschafts- und Rechtswissenschaften of the Gesellschaft für Deutschlandforschung, and held in Berlin, Sept. 14-15, 1983. Includes bibliographical references. CONTENTS. - Aussenwirtschaft als Bestimmungsfaktor von Wirtschaftspolitik und Wirtschaftsentwicklung in der DDR / Karl C. Thalheim -- Vergleich des Aussenhandelsrechts der DDR mit dem Aussenwirtschaftsrecht der Bundesrepublik Deutschland / Gottfried Zieger -- Die Einkaufs- und Lieferbedingungen im Aussenhandel der DDR / Erika Lieser-Triebnigg -- Systemspezifische Probleme des DDR-Technologietransfers / Siegfried G. Schoppe -- Neue Entwicklungen der Abstimmung der Aussenhandelsbeziehungen im RGW und ihre Auswirkungen auf die DDR / Wolfgang Seiffert -- Ost-West-Schiedsgerichtsbarkeit / Jan Peter Waehler -- Aussenwirtschaft der DDR und innerdeutsche Wirtschaftsbeziehungen / Franz Rösch. ISBN 3-428-06121-7 LC Card 87-137949 DDC 382/.0943/0431 19
1. Germany (East) - Commerce - Germany (West) - Congresses. 2. Germany (West) - Commerce - Germany (East) - Congresses. 3. Germany (East) - Commerce - Congresses. I. Gutmann, Gernot. II. Zieger, Gottfried. III. Series: Schriftenreihe der Gesellschaft für Deutschlandforschung e.V. , Bd. 16.
HF3570.5.Z7 G352 1986

Aussenwirtschafts-Alphabet : Ratgeber für das Auslandsgeschäft / [Projektleitung, Zentrale Internationale Abteilung]. Frankfurt am Main : Deutsche Bank AG, c1986. 396 p. ; 21 cm. "Abgeschlossen: Januar 1986"--Verso t.p. LC Card 87-401369 DDC 382/.03/31 19
1. Commerce - Dictionaries - German. 2. International economic relations - Dictionaries - German. 3. International finance - Dictionaries - German. I. Deutsche Bank (1957-). Zentrale Internationale Abteilung.
HF1001 .A86 1986

Aussperrung und Streik : ungleiche Mittel / hrsg. von Friedhelm Hengsbach. Mainz : Matthias-Grünewald-Verlag, 1981, c1980. 173 p. ; 20 cm. (Reihe Arbeiterbewegung und Kirche . Nr. 1) Includes bibliographical references. ISBN 3-7867-0854-1 LC Card 81-101514 DDC 331.89/2943 19
1. Strikes and lockouts - Germany (West) - Addresses, essays, lectures. 2. Church and labor - Germany (West) - Addresses, essays, lectures. 3. Arbitration, Industrial - Germany (West) - Addresses, essays, lectures. I. Hengsbach, Friedhelm. II. Series.
HD5378 .A97 1981 ***NYPL [JLD 86-2787]***

Ausstieg? : gewerkschaftliche Reformpolitik in der Industriegesellschaft / Siegfried Bleicher (Hrsg.) ; mit Beiträgen von Max Angermaier ... [et al.]. Hamburg : VSA-Verlag, 1985. 159 p. : ill. ; 21 cm. Includes bibliographical references. ISBN 3-87975-289-3 LC Card 85-219857 DDC 331/.0943 19
1. Trade-unions - Germany, West - Addresses, essays, lectures. 2. Industrial relations - Germany, West - Addresses, essays, lectures. 3. Labor supply - Germany (West) - Effect of technological innovations on - Addresses, essays, lectures. I. Bleicher, Siegfried. II. Angermaier, Max.
HD6694 .A97 1985 ***NYPL [JLD 87-710]***

Austen, Ralph A. African economic history : internal development and external dependency / Ralph A. Austen. London : J. Currey ; Portsmouth, NH : Heinemann, 1987. ix, 294 p. : ill., maps ; 23 cm. Includes bibliographies and index. ISBN 0-435-08017-2 (pbk.) LC Card 86-25639 DDC 330.967 19
1. Africa, Sub-Saharan - Economic conditions. 2. Africa, Sub-Saharan - Commerce - History. 3. Africa, Sub-Saharan - Foreign economic relations. 4. Africa, Sub-Saharan - Dependency on foreign countries - History. I. Title.
HC800 .A97 1987

Austerman, Wayne R. (Wayne Randolph), 1948- Sharps rifles and Spanish mules : the San Antonio--El Paso mail, 1851-1881 / by Wayne R. Austerman.1st ed. College Station : Texas A&M University Press, c1985. x, 367 p., [8] p. of plates : ill., maps, ports. ; 24 cm. Includes index. Bibliography: p. [325]-355. ISBN 0-89096-220-0 : LC Card 84-40557 DDC 383/.49764 19
1. Postal service - Texas - History - 19th century. 2. Coaching - Texas - History - 19th century. 3. San Antonio (Tex.) - History. 4. El Paso, Tex. - History. I. Title.
HE6376.A1 T417 1985 ***NYPL [JLE 85-3346]***

Austin, Dennis, 1922- The Third world, premises of U. S. policy /. San Francisco , c1978. xv, 332 p. : ISBN 0-917616-30-8 : LC Card 78-67593 DDC 309.1/172/4
HC59.7 .T456 ***NYPL [JLD 81-653]***

Austin, Douglas V. Modern banking : a practical guide to managing deregulated financial institutions / Douglas V. Austin, Donald R. Hakala, Thomas J. Scampini. Boston : Bankers Pub. Co., c1985. x, 406 p. : ill. ; 25 cm. (Bankers management series) Includes bibliographies and index. ISBN 0-87267-053-8 LC Card 84-21754 DDC 332.1/068 19
1. Bank management - United States. 2. Financial institutions - United States - Management. I. Hakala, Donald R. II. Scampini, Thomas J. III. Title.
HG1615 .A98 1985 ***NYPL [JLE 85-3956]***

AUSTIN, HERBERT, BARON AUSTIN OF LONGBRIDGE, 1866-1941. Church, Roy A. Herbert Austin . London , c1979. lii, 233 p., [3] leaves of plates : ISBN 0-905118-29-4 : LC Card 79-317202 DDC 338.7/62/920924 B
HD9710.G72 A93 ***NYPL [JFD 86-9452]***

Austin, Michael J. Pecora, Peter J. Managing human services personnel /. Newbury Park, Calif. , c1987. 176 p. : ISBN 0-8039-2685-5 (pbk.) LC Card 86-27995 DDC 658.3 19
HF5549 .P36 1987

AUSTIN ROVER GROUP. Williams, Karel. The breakdown of Austin Rover . Leamington Spa, UK ; New York : v, 150 p. : ISBN 0-85496-515-7 : LC Card 86-24449 DDC 338.7/6292222 19
HD9710.G74 A868 1987

Austin, Ruben Vargas, 1915- The development of economic policy in Mexico with special reference to economic doctrines, 1600-1958 /

Ruben Vargas Austin. New York : Garland Pub., 1987. 336 p. ; 24 cm. (South American and Latin American economic history) Thesis (Ph. D.)--State University of Iowa, 1958. Bibliography: p. 314-336. ISBN 0-8240-1354-9 (alk. paper) : LC Card 87-8569 DDC 338.972 19
1. Mexico - Economic policy. 2. New Spain - Economic policy. 3. Economics - Mexico - History. I. Title. II. Series.
HC135 .A84 1987

Austin, Tex. Lyndon Baines Johnson Library. see **Lyndon Baines Johnson Library.**

Australia. Affirmative Action Resource Unit.
Affirmative action implementation manual /. Canberra , 1986. 66 p. ; ISBN 0-644-04750-X (pbk.) LC Card 87-109354 DDC 658.3 19
HD6060.5.A8 A34 1986

Australia. Agricultural Economics, Bureau of. see **Australia. Bureau of Agricultural Economics.**

AUSTRALIA - APPROPRIATIONS AND EXPENDITURES - STATISTICS - HISTORY.
Barnard, A. (Alan) Some government financial data, 1850 to 1982 /. Canberra, Australia [1986] 47, 2 p. ; ISBN 0-86784-850-2 (pbk.) LC Card 86-211320 DDC 336.94 19
HJ2193.Z7 B37 1986

AUSTRALIA - ARMED FORCES - POSTAL SERVICE - HISTORY.
Emery, R. C. The postal history of the Australian Imperial Forces during World War One, 1914-1918 /. Worthing, West Sussex, England [1984] viii, 343 p. : LC Card 85-123155 DDC 355.3/41 19
HE7395 .E47 1984 ***NYPL [JLF 86-1054]***

Australia. Bureau of Agricultural Economics.
(Old Catalog form: Australia. Agricultural Economics Bureau)
Agricultural policies in the European Community . Canberra , 1985. xii, 373 p. : ISBN 0-644-04293-1 (pbk.) LC Card 86-673733
HD1920.5.Z8 A37x 1985

Economic development in East and South-east Asia . Canberra , 1984. x, 237 p. : ISBN 0-644-02983-8 (pbk.) LC Card 86-673760
HC460.5 .E26x 1984

Historical trends in Australian rural production, exports, farm income, and indexes of prices received and paid by farmers, 1952-53 to 1972-73 /. Canberra , 1974. vii, 17 p. : ISBN 0-642-00746-2 (pbk.) LC Card 85-126806 DDC 338.1/0994/021 19
HD2152 .H57 1974

Australia. Bureau of Labour Market Research.
Wooden, Mark. The effects of redundancy . [Bedford Park, S. Aust.] [1987] 52 p. : LC Card 87-170621 DDC 331.13/7994 19
HD5708.55.A8 W66 1987

AUSTRALIA - COMMERCE.
Callaghan, Bede, Sir, 1912- The investment theme in Australia's approach to international trade /. [Newcastle, N.S.W.] , 1979. 16 leaves ; ISBN 0-7259-0361-9 (pbk.) LC Card 82-133660
HG5892 .C35 1979

Lougheed, A. L. Trends in international trade and Australia's performance /. Canberra, Australia , 1986. 16, [4] p. : ISBN 0-909992-18-5 (pbk.) LC Card 87-107912 DDC 382/.0994 19
HF3946.5 .L68 1986

AUSTRALIA - COMMERCE - ASIA, SOUTHEASTERN.
Asean-Australia trade in manufactures /. Melbourne, Australia , c1985. xiii, 263 p. ; ISBN 0-582-71147-9 (pbk.) LC Card 86-228309 DDC 382/.4567/0994 19
HD9738.A82 A83 1985

AUSTRALIA - COMMERCE - DEVELOPING COUNTRIES.
Anderson, Kym. Australia's trade growth with developing countries /. Canberra, Australia , 1983. iv, 55 p. ; ISBN 0-86413-001-5 (pbk.) LC Card 86-673748
HF3948.D44 A52x 1983

AUSTRALIA - COMMERCE - SOUTH AFRICA - STATISTICS.
Kopras, Andrew. Trading with South Africa /. [Canberra] , 1986. 14 p. ; LC Card 87-164241 DDC 382/.0968/094021 19
HF3901.A45 K66 1986

AUSTRALIA - COMMERCE - STATISTICS.
Australian resources in a world context . Canberra , 1982. iv, 87 p. : ISBN 0-642-05273-5 (pbk.) LC Card 86-673749
HF3941.5 .A97x 1982

Lougheed, A. L. Trends in international trade and Australia's performance /. Canberra, Australia , 1986. 16, [4] p. : ISBN 0-909992-18-5 (pbk.) LC Card 87-107912 DDC 382/.0994 19
HF3946.5 .L68 1986

AUSTRALIA - COMMERCIAL POLICY.
Anderson, Kym. Australian protectionism . Sydney , Boston , 1987. xii, 160 p. : ISBN 0-04-330383-8 (pbk.) LC Card 86-47990 DDC 382.7/3/0994 19
HF1625 .A53 1987

Rattigan, G. A. (Godfrey Alfred), 1911- Industry assistance . Carlton, Vic. , Beaverton, Or. , 1986. viii, 289 p., [4] p. of plates : ISBN 0-522-84313-1 LC Card 86-202866 DDC 338.994 19
HF2483 .R38 1986

Australia. Committee of Review of Aboriginal Employment and Training Programs.
Aboriginal employment and training programs . Canberra , 1985. ix, 453 p. ; ISBN 0-644-00712-5 (pbk.) LC Card 87-107756 DDC 331.25/92/089011094 19
HD5850.A6 A26 1985

Australia. Dept. of Commerce and Agriculture. Bureau of Agricultural Economics. see **Australia. Bureau of Agricultural Economics.**

Australia. Dept. of Social Security. Research and Statistics Branch. Retirement income provisions overseas. [Canberra] [1984] 162 p. ; ISBN 0-642-51580-8 (pbk.) LC Card 84-252861 DDC 331.25/22 19
HD7105.3 .R46 1984

Australia. Dept. of Trade and Resources.
Australian resources in a world context . Canberra , 1982. iv, 87 p. : ISBN 0-642-05273-5 (pbk.) LC Card 86-673749
HF3941.5 .A97x 1982

AUSTRALIA - DEPENDENCY ON FOREIGN COUNTRIES.
Gannicott, K. G. (Ken G.) Australia's dependence on foreign technology /. [Canberra, Australia] [1982] 38 p. ; LC Card 84-197120 DDC 338.994/06 19
HC610.T4 G36 1982

Knapp, Johannes, 1953- Argentinien und Australien . Heidelberg , c1983. 151 p. : ISBN 3-88326-129-7 LC Card 83-240132
HC175 .K58 1983

AUSTRALIA - ECONOMIC CONDITIONS - 1918- - MAPS.
Camm, J. C. R. (Jack Charles Robert) Hardtimes--a cartographic and graphic representation of selected aspects of the depression years, 1925-1935, in Australia /. [Newcastle, N.S.W.] , 1985. 59, iii p. : ISBN 0-7259-0542-5 (pbk.) : LC Card 86-222404 DDC 330.994/042 19
HC603 .C36 1985

AUSTRALIA - ECONOMIC CONDITIONS - 1945-
The Australian economy in the long run /. Cambridge [Cambridgeshire] , New York , 1987. xi, 372 p. : ISBN 0-521-32674-5 LC Card 86-26345 DDC 330.994 19
HC605 .A7767 1987

Bennett, Raymond. Applied economics and Australian business /. Sydney , c1987. xiv, 464 p. : ISBN 0-9588541-0-6 LC Card 87-141905 DDC 330.994/063 19
HB171.5 .B454 1987

Gruen, F. H. (Fred Henry), 1921- How bad is Australia's economic performance and why? . Canberra, Australia [1985] 61 p. ; ISBN 0-949293-38-5 (pbk.) LC Card 86-228640 DDC 338.994 19
HC605 .G78 1985

Hollingworth, Peter John, 1935- Australians in poverty /. Melbourne, Vic. , 1985. x, 166 p. : ISBN 0-17-006741-6 (pbk.) : LC Card 87-108662 DDC 305.5/69/0994 19
HC610.P6 H62 1985

Knapp, Johannes, 1953- Argentinien und Australien . Heidelberg , c1983. 151 p. : ISBN 3-88326-129-7 LC Card 83-240132
HC175 .K58 1983

AUSTRALIA - ECONOMIC CONDITIONS - 1945- - ECONOMETRIC MODELS.
Brain, Peter J. The microeconomic structure of the Australian economy /. Melbourne, Australia , 1986. xxiv, 448 p. : ISBN 0-582-71502-4 (pbk.) LC Card 87-100715 DDC 330.994/063 19
HC603 .B73 1986

AUSTRALIA - ECONOMIC CONDITIONS - 1945 - STATISTICS.
Norton, W. E. Australian economic statistics, 1949-50 to 1984-85 /. [Sydney] [1985] 2 v. : ISBN 0-642-09904-9 (pbk. : v. 1) LC Card 86-222671 DDC 330.994/05/021 19
HC605 .N6326 1985

AUSTRALIA - ECONOMIC POLICY.
Gruen, F. H. (Fred Henry), 1921- How bad is Australia's economic performance and why? . Canberra, Australia [1985] 61 p. ; ISBN 0-949293-38-5 (pbk.) LC Card 86-228640 DDC 338.994 19
HC605 .G78 1985

AUSTRALIA - FOREIGN ECONOMIC RELATIONS - PACIFIC AREA.
McLean, Robert J. Exploiting opportunities in the Pacific Basin . [Melbourne] [1986] 56 p. : ISBN 0-85801-162-X (pbk.) LC Card 86-203142 DDC 337.9409 19
HF1626.5.P33 M35 1986

Australia. Industries Assistance Commission.
Interim report : fabrics for use as bed sheeting, pillow casing, or bolster casing / Industries Assistance Commission. Canberra : Australian Govt. Pub. Service, 1976. 36 p. ; 25 cm. "27 August 1976." ISBN 0-642-02317-4 (pbk.) LC Card 85-132707
1. Bedding industry - Australia. 2. Tariff on bedding industry - Australia. I. Title. II. Title: Fabrics for use as bed sheeting, pillow casing, or bolster casing.
HD9969.B433 A83 1976

AUSTRALIA. INDUSTRIES ASSISTANCE COMMISSION.
Rattigan, G. A. (Godfrey Alfred), 1911- Industry assistance . Carlton, Vic. , Beaverton, Or. , 1986. viii, 289 p., [4] p. of plates : ISBN 0-522-84313-1 LC Card 86-202866 DDC 338.994 19
HF2483 .R38 1986

AUSTRALIA - INDUSTRIES - LOCATION.
Rich, D. C. The industrial geography of Australia /. London , Wolfeboro, N.H. , c1987. xvi, 384 p. : ISBN 0-7099-2214-0 : LC Card 86-29383 DDC 338.0994 19
HC610.D5 R53 1987

Australia-Japan Research Centre. Japanese and Australian labour markets . Canberra [c1983] xx, 610 p. : ISBN 0-86413-004-X (pbk.) : LC Card 84-220557 DDC 331.12/0952 19
HD5850.A6 J36 1983 ***NYPL [JLE 86-630]***

AUSTRALIA - MANUFACTURES.
Asean-Australia trade in manufactures /. Melbourne, Australia , c1985. xiii, 263 p. ; ISBN 0-582-71147-9 (pbk.) LC Card 86-228309 DDC 382/.4567/0994 19
HD9738.A82 A83 1985

Ewer, Peter. Unions and the future of Australian manufacturing /. Sydney , Boston , 1987. xi, 189 p. : ISBN 0-04-330382-X (pbk.) LC Card 87-164410 DDC 338.4/767/0994 19
HD9738.A82 E93 1987

AUSTRALIA - NATIVE RACES.
Aboriginal employment and training programs . Canberra , 1985. ix, 453 p. ; ISBN 0-644-00712-5 (pbk.) LC Card 87-107756 DDC 331.25/92/089011094 19
HD5850.A6 A26 1985

AUSTRALIA. OVERSEAS TELECOMMUNICATIONS COMMISSION. COAST RADIO SERVICE - HISTORY.
Durrant, Lawrence L. The seawatchers . North Ryde, NSW, Australia , 1986. xii, 248 p. : ISBN 0-207-15198-9 LC Card 86-228332 DDC 384.5/3 19
HE8683.A8 D87 1986

Australia. Parliament. Joint Committee of Public Accounts.
Income maintenance programs : response to

report 213 / the Parliament of the Commonwealth of Australia, Joint Committee of Public Accounts. Canberra : Australian Govt. Pub. Service, 1986. viii, 49 p. ; 25 cm. (Report / Joint Committee of Public Accounts . 246) Bibliography: p. 47-49. ISBN 0-644-04993-6 (pbk.) LC Card 86-234535 DDC 362.5/82 19
1. Income maintenance programs - Australia. I. Series: Report (Australia. Parliament. Joint Committee of Public Accounts) , 246. II. Title.
HC610.I5 A95 1986

Proposed computer acquisition by the Australian Audit Office / the Parliament of the Commonwealth of Australia, Joint Committee of Public Accounts. Canberra : Australian Govt. Pub. Service, 1986. xiii, 256 p. : ill. ; 25 cm. (Report / the Parliament of the Commonwealth of Australia, Joint Committee of Public Accounts . 253) ISBN 0-644-05079-9 (pbk.) LC Card 86-234536 DDC 354.940072/32 19
1. Australian Audit Office. 2. Finance, Public - Australia - Accounting - Data processing. I. Series: Report (Australia. Parliament. Joint Committee of Public Accounts) , 253. II. Title.
HJ9931 .A875 1986

AUSTRALIA - POPULATION.
Hugo, Graeme. Australia's changing population . Melbourne , New York , 1986. x, 354 p. : ISBN 0-19-554680-6 LC Card 87-107294 DDC 304.6/0994 19
HB3675 .H84 1986

AUSTRALIA - POPULATION POLICY.
Hugo, Graeme. Australia's changing population . Melbourne , New York , 1986. x, 354 p. : ISBN 0-19-554680-6 LC Card 87-107294 DDC 304.6/0994 19
HB3675 .H84 1986

AUSTRALIA. PRICES SURVEILLANCE AUTHORITY.
Hall, Richard, 1937- The Prices Surveillance Authority /. Melbourne [1987] 24 p. ; ISBN 0-85801-167-0 (pbk.) LC Card 87-156317 DDC 338.5/26/0994 19
HB236.A8 H35 1987

AUSTRALIA - SOCIAL CONDITIONS.
Kakwani, Nanak. Analyzing redistribution policies . Cambridge [Cambridgeshire] , New York , 1986. ix, 293 p. : ISBN 0-521-30838-0 LC Card 85-31342 DDC 339.5/2 19
HC610.I5 K35 1986 ***NYPL [JLE 86-3491]***

AUSTRALIA. TARIFF BOARD.
Rattigan, G. A. (Godfrey Alfred), 1911- Industry assistance . Carlton, Vic. , Beaverton, Or. , 1986. viii, 289 p., [4] p. of plates : ISBN 0-522-84313-1 LC Card 86-202866 DDC 338.994 19
HF2483 .R38 1986

Australia. Trade and Resources, Dept. of. see **Australia. Dept. of Trade and Resources.**

Australian Academy of Science. Science and Industry Forum. An Industrial research and development and marketing package for Australia . [Canberra?] [1984] 48, 4 leaves : LC Card 87-153477 DDC 338/.06 19
HC610.T4 I53 1984

Australian Agricultural Company.
Pemberton, P. A. Pure merinos and others . Canberra , c1986. 125 p. : ISBN 0-86784-796-4 (pbk.) LC Card 87-164515 DDC 382/.41636/0994 19
HE565.G7 P46 1986

AUSTRALIAN AGRICULTURAL COMPANY - HISTORY.
Pemberton, P. A. Pure merinos and others . Canberra , c1986. 125 p. : ISBN 0-86784-796-4 (pbk.) LC Card 87-164515 DDC 382/.41636/0994 19
HE565.G7 P46 1986

AUSTRALIAN AGRICULTURAL COMPANY - HISTORY - SOURCES.
Pemberton, P. A. Pure merinos and others . Canberra , c1986. 125 p. : ISBN 0-86784-796-4 (pbk.) LC Card 87-164515 DDC 382/.41636/0994 19
HE565.G7 P46 1986

AUSTRALIAN AUDIT OFFICE.
Australia. Parliament. Joint Committee of Public Accounts. Proposed computer acquisition by the Australian Audit Office /. Canberra , 1986. xiii, 256 p. : ISBN 0-644-05079-9 (pbk.) LC Card 86-234536 DDC 354.940072/32 19
HJ9931 .A875 1986

Australian Bureau of Statistics. Industry concentration statistics . Canberra [1974] 194 p. ; LC Card 82-132323
HD2930 .I53 1974

Australian economic statistics, 1949-50 to 1984-85 /. Norton, W. E. [Sydney] [1985] 2 v. : ISBN 0-642-09904-9 (pbk. : v. 1) LC Card 86-222671 DDC 330.994/05/021 19
HC605 .N6326 1985

The Australian economy in the long run / edited by Rodney Maddock and Ian W. McLean. Cambridge [Cambridgeshire] ; New York : Cambridge University Press, 1987. xi, 372 p. : ill. ; 24 cm. Includes bibliographies and index. ISBN 0-521-32674-5 LC Card 86-26345 DDC 330.994 19
1. Australia - Economic conditions - 1945-. I. Maddock, Rodney. II. McLean, Ian W.
HC605 .A7767 1987

Australian grain marketing . Hussey, Denis D. Perth, W.A. , 1986. 72 p. : ISBN 0-949186-11-2 (pbk.) : LC Card 86-213695 DDC 338.1/731/0994 19
HD9048.A82 H87 1986

Australian industrial relations : summary of papers presented at a one-day conference / organised by Jean Hartley and Stephen Frenkel in conjunction with the Australian Studies Centre, University of London. London : Australian Studies Centre, Institute of Commonwealth Studies, University of London, [1986] 24 p. ; 30 cm. (Conference papers) "June 1986." Bibliography: p. 22. CONTENTS. - Pay bargaining behind the veil of compulsory arbitration / William Brown -- Corporatist industrial relations and structural change in Australia / Vic Taylor -- Management strategy and new technology in retail distribution / Greg J. Bamber and Russell D. Lansbury -- Management and workplace industrial relations in the recession / Stephen Frenkel -- Approaches to industrial democracy in Australia and Britain / Margaret Kiloh. ISBN 0-902499-56-4 (pbk.) : LC Card 86-233230 DDC 331/.0994 19
1. Industrial relations - Australia. I. Hartley, Jean, 1953-. II. Frenkel, Stephen. III. University of London. Australian Studies Centre. IV. Series: Conference papers (University of London. Australian Studies Centre).
HD8846.5 .A96 1986

Australian marketing casebook /. Gilmour, Peter, 1942- St. Lucia , c1988. p. cm. ISBN 0-7022-2091-4 (pbk.) LC Card 87-16220 DDC 658.8/00994 19
HF5415.12.A9 G54 1988

The Australian monetary system, 1851 to 1914 /. Butlin, S. J. (Sydney James), d. 1977. [s.l] , 1986. 404 p. : ISBN 1-86252-307-X (pbk.) LC Card 87-154610 DDC 332.4/994 19
HG1394 .B87 1986

Pacific research monograph. see **Pacific research monograph.**

Australian National University, Canberra. Centre for Research on Federal Financial Relations. Research monograph.
(no. 36. 36) Yonehara, Junshichirō. Local public finance in Japan /. Canberra , Miami, Fla., USA , 1981. xi, 112 p. : ISBN 0-908160-89-5 : LC Card 80-68801 DDC 352.1/0952 19
HJ9585 .Y663 1981
NYPL [JLM 75-1302 no. 36]

Australian Productivity Council. Structured chaos . Melbourne , New York , 1985. viii, 111 p. : ISBN 0-19-554687-3 LC Card 86-222312 DDC 338/.06/0994 19
HC610.I52 S77 1985

Australian protectionism . Anderson, Kym. Sydney , Boston , 1987. xii, 160 p. : ISBN 0-04-330383-8 (pbk.) LC Card 86-47990 DDC 382.7/3/0994 19
HF1625 .A53 1987

Australian resources in a world context : facts and figures / Australian Department of Trade and Resources. Canberra : Australian Govt. Pub. Service, 1982. iv, 87 p. : ill. ; 25 cm. Includes bibliographical references. ISBN 0-642-05273-5 (pbk.) LC Card 86-673749
1. Australia - Commerce - Statistics. 2. Natural resources - Australia - Statistics. I. Australia. Dept. of Trade and Resources.
HF3941.5 .A97x 1982

Studies in historical archaeology. see **Studies in historical archaeology.**

Australian trade unionism in documents /. Hagan, Jim. Melbourne, Australia , 1986. xvi, 289 p. ; ISBN 0-582-71146-0 (pbk.) LC Card 86-223615 DDC 331.88/0994 19
HD6892 .H34 1986

Australian unions, 1984 /. Rawson, Donald William. Sydney , c1985. 123 p. ; ISBN 0-949614-13-0 LC Card 85-169297 DDC 331.88/025/94 19
HD6891 .R35 1985 ***NYPL [JLD 86-1566]***

Australian Water Resources Council. National Workshop on Urban Water Demand Management (1986 : Alexander Library, Perth Cultural Centre) Working papers for the National Workshop on Urban Water Demand Management . Leederville, WA [1986] xii, 657 p. : LC Card 87-119946 DDC 333.91/2/0994 19
HD4465.A8 N37 1986

AUSTRALIAN WORKERS' UNION - HISTORY.
Merritt, John. The making of the AWU /. Melbourne , New York , 1986. x, 432 p., [16] p. of plates : ISBN 0-19-554667-9 LC Card 86-207509 DDC 331.88/13630833/0994 19
HD8842.A874 M47 1986

Australians in poverty /. Hollingworth, Peter John, 1935- Melbourne, Vic. , 1985. x, 166 p. : ISBN 0-17-006741-6 (pbk.) : LC Card 87-108662 DDC 305.5/69/0994 19
HC610.P6 H62 1985

Australia's changing population . Hugo, Graeme. Melbourne , New York , 1986. x, 354 p. : ISBN 0-19-554680-6 LC Card 87-107294 DDC 304.6/0994 19
HB3675 .H84 1986

Australia's dependence on foreign technology /. Gannicott, K. G. (Ken G.) [Canberra, Australia] [1982] 38 p. ; LC Card 84-197120 DDC 338.994/06 19
HC610.T4 G36 1982

Australia's trade growth with developing countries /. Anderson, Kym. Canberra, Australia , 1983. iv, 55 p. ; ISBN 0-86413-001-5 (pbk.) LC Card 86-673748
HF3948.D44 A52x 1983

AUSTRIA - APPROPRIATIONS AND EXPENDITURE.
Budgetvorschau 1984-1988 /. Wien , 1984. 55 p. ; LC Card 84-223024
HJ2101 .B828 1984

AUSTRIA - APPROPRIATIONS AND EXPENDITURES - FORECASTING.
Budgetvorschau 1986-1990. Wien , 1986. 45 p. : LC Card 86-227246
HJ2101 .B83 1986

Austria. Bundesministerium für Bauten und Technik. Bundesstrassenverwaltung.
Strassenverkehrszählung 1980 auf Bundesstrassen im gesamten Bundesgebiet der Republik Österreich /. Wien , 1985. 288 p. : LC Card 86-170848
HA1173 .A27 Heft 750 HE363.A93T7

AUSTRIA - CENSUS, 1981.
Clement, Werner. Einkommensverteilung und Qualifikation . Wien , 1984. vi, 201 p. : ISBN 3-85436-020-7 LC Card 84-191161
HC270.I5 C56 1984

AUSTRIA - COMMERCE.
Hutter, Monika, 1950- Die Warenstruktur des Aussenhandels . Frankfurt am Main , New York , c1987. 216 p. ; ISBN 3-8204-8810-3 LC Card 87-407938 DDC 382/.09436 19
HF3546.5 .H87 1987

AUSTRIA - COMMERCE - CENTRAL EUROPE - HISTORY - 18TH CENTURY - SOURCES.
Prokopp, Ludwig Ferdinand. Europäische Commerzreisen um die Mitte des 18. Jahrhunderts /. Linz , c1982. xiii, 446 p., [1] folded leaf of plates : ISBN 3-85320-296-1 LC Card 83-150921
HF3548.C36 P76 1982

AUSTRIA - COMMERCE - GERMANY (EAST)
Marwege, Ulf, 1954- Neuorientierung im

Westhandel der DDR? . Bonn , c1984. iv, 122 p. : ISBN 3-7713-0221-8 : LC Card 84-196602
HF3570.5.Z7 G75 1984

AUSTRIA - COMMERCE - STATISTICS.
Handel, Lagerung 1983 /. Wien , 1986- v. <1-> ; LC Card 87-408429 DDC 314.36 s 380.1/09436/021 19
HA1173 .A27 Heft 793 HF3541.5

Rau, Heinrich. Vergleichende Statistik des Handels der deutschen Staaten /. Wien , 1863. vii, 183 p. ; LC Card 85-217948
HF3561.5 .R38 1863

AUSTRIA - ECONOMIC CONDITIONS - 1918-1945.
Wirtschaftskarten von Österreich /. Berlin , 1938. 38 p. : LC Card 86-179061
HC265 .W554 1938

AUSTRIA - ECONOMIC CONDITIONS - 1918-1945 - MAPS.
Wirtschaftskarten von Österreich /. Berlin , 1938. 38 p. : LC Card 86-179061
HC265 .W554 1938

AUSTRIA - ECONOMIC CONDITIONS - 1945-
Armut in Österreich . Graz , c1977. 168 p. : ISBN 3-7011-7080-0 LC Card 86-176543
HC270.P6 A75 1977

Richter, Josef. Energiekosten und Anpassungsverhalten der Wirtschaft /. Wien , 1985. iv, 184 p. : ISBN 3-85436-031-2 LC Card 86-154099
HD9502.A92 R53 1985

Stahl und Eisen bricht . Wien [1986] xi, 202 p. : ISBN 3-900351-62-7 LC Card 87-140293 DDC 330.9436/053 19
HC265 .S736 1986

AUSTRIA - ECONOMIC CONDITIONS - 1945- - CONGRESSES.
Methoden der Politikberatung im wirtschaftspolitischen Bereich /. Wien , 1984. 116 p. ; LC Card 84-222756
HC265 .M39 1984

Vom Nachzügler zum Vorbild(?) . Stuttgart , c1985. 183 p. : ISBN 3-437-50303-0 LC Card 86-200243
HC265 .V65 1985

AUSTRIA - ECONOMIC CONDITIONS - 1945- - STATISTICS.
Die Österreichische Gemeinwirtschaft im Jahre 1976 . Wien , 1980. 102 p. ; LC Card 85-208409
HA1173 .A27 Heft 563 HC265

AUSTRIA - ECONOMIC POLICY - 1945-
Vodopivec, Alexander. 40 Jahre Wirtschaftsbund . Wien [1985?] 107 p. ; LC Card 86-169299
HC265 .V589 1985

AUSTRIA - ECONOMIC POLICY - 1945- - CONGRESSES.
Methoden der Politikberatung im wirtschaftspolitischen Bereich /. Wien , 1984. 116 p. ; LC Card 84-222756
HC265 .M39 1984

Vom Nachzügler zum Vorbild(?) . Stuttgart , c1985. 183 p. : ISBN 3-437-50303-0 LC Card 86-200243
HC265 .V65 1985

AUSTRIA - ECONOMIC POLICY - CONGRESSES.
Staatsfinanzierung und Notenbank . Wien [1984?] 211 p. : LC Card 85-198128
HG1811 .S78 1984

AUSTRIA - FOREIGN ECONOMIC RELATIONS - GERMANY.
Otruba, Gustav. A. Hitler's "Tausend-Mark-Sperre" und die Folgen für Österreichs Fremdenverkehr (1933-1938) /. Linz , c1983. iii, 205 p. ; ISBN 3-85320-308-6 LC Card 84-213145
HG999 .O87 1983

AUSTRIA - FOREIGN ECONOMIC RELATIONS - UNITED STATES.
Einwitschläger, Arno. Amerikanische Wirtschaftspolitik in Österreich, 1945-1949 /. Wien , 1986. 206 p. : ISBN 3-205-08814-X LC Card 87-112406
HF1456.5.A9 E39 1986

AUSTRIA - FULL EMPLOYMENT POLICIES.
Arbeitsmarktpolitik für die Landwirtschaft und den ländlichen Raum /. Graz , c1984. 138 p. : ISBN 3-900307-15-6 LC Card 85-186643
HD1536.A9 A73 1984

Marzen, Walter. Ist die 35-Stunden-Woche ein Mittel zur Beseitigung der Arbeitslosigkeit? . Innsbruck , 1980. 29 leaves ; LC Card 85-170048
HD5108.2.A9 M37 1980

AUSTRIA - INDUSTRIES.
Stahl und Eisen bricht . Wien [1986] xi, 202 p. : ISBN 3-900351-62-7 LC Card 87-140293 DDC 330.9436/053 19
HC265 .S736 1986

AUSTRIA - INDUSTRIES - ENERGY CONSUMPTION - COSTS.
Richter, Josef. Energiekosten und Anpassungsverhalten der Wirtschaft /. Wien , 1985. iv, 184 p. : ISBN 3-85436-031-2 LC Card 86-154099
HD9502.A92 R53 1985

AUSTRIA - INDUSTRIES - STATISTICS.
Ergebnisse der nichtlandwirtschaftlichen Betriebszählung vom 1. September 1954 /. Wien , 1958. 84 p. ; LC Card 84-252994
HD5779 .E74 1958

Die Österreichische Gemeinwirtschaft im Jahre 1976 . Wien , 1980. 102 p. ; LC Card 85-208409
HA1173 .A27 Heft 563 HC265

Statistik der gewerblichen Wirtschaft . Wien , 1986. 2 v. ; LC Card 87-409345 DDC 314.36 s 338.09436/021 19
HA1173 .A27 Heft 790 HC265

AUSTRIA - MANUFACTURES.
Serres, Marcel de, 1783-1862. Essai sur les arts at les manufactures de l'empire d'Autriche /. Paris , 1814-1815. 3 v. : LC Card 85-666370
HC263 .S47x 1814

AUSTRIA - POLITICS AND GOVERNMENT - 1740-1780.
Dickson, P. G. M. (Peter George Muir) Finance and government under Maria Theresia, 1740-1780 /. Oxford [Oxfordshire] , New York , 1987. 2 v. : ISBN 0-19-822570-9 (v. 1) : LC Card 87-1614 DDC 336.436 19
HJ1059 .D52 1987

AUSTRIA - POLITICS AND GOVERNMENT - 1945-
Vodopivec, Alexander. 40 Jahre Wirtschaftsbund . Wien [1985?] 107 p. ; LC Card 86-169299
HC265 .V589 1985

AUSTRIA - POPULATION.
Schettkat, Ronald. Bevölkerungs- und Erwerbsverhaltensentwicklung in Österreich, Schweden und der Bundesrepublik Deutschland /. Berlin [1984] 48 p. ; LC Card 85-198691
HD5771 .S34 1984

AUSTRIA - SOCIAL CONDITIONS.
Garamvölgyi, Judit. Betriebsräte und sozialer Wandel in Österreich 1919/1920 . München , c1983. 296 p. ; ISBN 3-486-51721-X LC Card 83-240283
HD5660.A8 G37 1983

Riesenfellner, Stefan. Der Sozialreporter . Wien , c1987. vi, 278 p. ; ISBN 3-900351-67-8 LC Card 87-137993 DDC 305.5/62/09436 19
HD8410 .R54 1987

Austrian National Bank. see **Österreichische Nationalbank.**

AUSTRIAN SCHOOL OF ECONOMISTS.
Boos, Margarete. Die Wissenschaftstheorie Carl Mengers . Wien , 1986. xiii, 252 p. ; ISBN 3-205-05044-4 LC Card 86-209140
HB101.M5 B6 1986

Hicks, John Richard, Sir, 1904- Capital and time . Oxford [Oxfordshire] , New York , 1987. p. cm. ISBN 0-19-877286-6 : LC Card 87-20233 DDC 332/.041 19
HB501 .H48 1987

Reiss, Winfried, 1941- Umwegproduktion und Positivität des Zinses . Berlin , c1981. 152 p. : ISBN 3-428-05009-6 LC Card 82-146836 DDC 332.8/2/0724 19
HB539 .R423 1981 ***NYPL [JLE 86-2623]***

Studies in Austrian capital theory, investment, and time /. Berlin , New York , c1986. vi, 316 p. : ISBN 0-387-16804-4 (U. S. : pbk.) LC Card 86-223780 DDC 330.15/7 19
HB98 .S83 1986

AUSTRIAN SCHOOL OF ECONOMISTS - ADDRESSES, ESSAYS, LECTURES.
Subjectivism, intelligibility, and economic understanding . Basingstoke, Hampshire , 1986. xi, 319 p. : ISBN 0-333-41788-7
NYPL [JLD 86-2215]

Austvik, Ole Gunnar. Søkelys på mekanismene i oljemarkedet / Ole Gunnar Austvik. Oslo : Norsk utenrikspolitisk institutt, [1986?] 66 p. : ill. ; 30 cm. (NUPI rapport, 0800-000X . nr. 97 (mars 1986)) Summary in English. Bibliography: p. 57-60. Includes index. LC Card 86-197742
1. Petroleum industry and trade. 2. Petroleum industry and trade - Norway. I. Series: NUPI rapport , nr. 97. II. Title.
HD9560.5 .A75 1986

Ausweg aus der Weltkrise . Lindner, Eberhard. Karlsruhe , 1984. 319 p. : ISBN 3-921653-15-0 LC Card 85-104217 DDC 363.7 19
HD75.6 .L56 1984 ***NYPL [JLD 87-484]***

Die Auswirkungen eines Geburten- und Bevölkerungsrückgangs auf Entwicklung und Ausgestaltung von gesetzlicher Alterssicherung und Familienlastenausgleich /. Dinkel, Reiner. Berlin , c1984. 344 p. : ISBN 3-428-05546-2 LC Card 84-186733
HD7179 .D65 1984

Auswirkungen industrieller Exportproduktion im Rahmen der internationalen Arbeitsteilung auf die Einkommensverteilung von Entwicklungsländern /. Hermann, Christian, 1954- Frankfurt am Main , New York , c1984. viii, 393 p. ; ISBN 3-8204-7456-0 LC Card 85-191626
HF4055 .H47 1984

Die Auswirkungen kreditfinanzierter Staatsausgaben auf das Volkseinkommen . Meyer-Cording, Claus, 1953- Frankfurt am Main , New York , c1986. v, 256 p. : ISBN 3-8204-9634-3 LC Card 86-204989
HB141.5 .M49 1986

Auswirkungen von Computeranwendungen auf die Leistungsstruktur von Unternehmensorganisationen /. Molitor, Monika. Frankfurt am Main , c1984. 278 p. : ISBN 3-88129-808-8 : LC Card 85-140214
HD70.G23 M64 1984

Auswirkungen von nicht kostenniveauneutralen Lohnänderungen auf Beschäftigung und Preisniveau . Beck, Horst. Krefeld , 1983. iii, 227 p. : ISBN 3-88358-033-3 LC Card 83-202725
HD4911 .B4 1983

Auswirkungen von Streckenstillegungen, dargestellt am Beispiel von Nebenbahnen in Bayern /. Marcinowski, Bernhard. Nürnberg , 1983. xviii, 260 p. : LC Card 84-162065
HE3079.B5 M28 1983

AUTARCHY.
Van der Ryn, Sim. Sustainable communities . San Francisco [1986] xvii, 238 p. : ISBN 0-87156-800-4 LC Card 83-4676 DDC 307/.14 19
HN90.C6 V36 1986 ***NYPL [JLF 86-1241]***

Authentic development in Africa /. Walker, Brian W. New York, N.Y. , c1985. 70 p. : ISBN 0-87124-102-1 (pbk.) : LC Card 85-82567 DDC 081 s 338.96 19
E744 .H43 no. 274 HC800
NYPL [JLD 86-3400]

AUTHORITARIANISM.
Soler, Sebastián. Temas antiliberales, marxistas y autoritarios /. Buenos Aires , 1977. 179 p. ; LC Card 80-469614
JC571 .S7173 ***NYPL [JLC 80-]***

AUTHORITARIANISM - CHILE.
Lechner, Norbert, 1939- La conflictiva y nunca acabada construcción del orden deseado /. [Santiago, Chile] [1984] 204 p. ; ISBN 84-89401-05-5 LC Card 84-227472 DDC 320.982 19
JL2624 .L43 1984 ***NYPL [JLE 87-2137]***

AUTHORITIES, PUBLIC. see **CORPORATIONS, GOVERNMENT.**

AUTHORITY, DELEGATION OF. see **DELEGATION OF AUTHORITY.**

Auto économie . Bentabet, Mohamed. Casablanca [1985] 106 p. ; LC Card 86-198953
HC59.72.T4 B46 1985

Auto outlook four. Auto outlook IV /. [New

York] , c1986. 60 leaves ; LC Card 86-231268 DDC 381/.456292/0973 19
HD9710.U52 A76 1986

Auto outlook IV / New York Times, Marketing Research Department. [New York] : The Dept., c1986. 60 leaves ; 29 cm. LC Card 86-231268 DDC 381/.456292/0973 19
1. Automobile industry and trade - United States - Statistics. 2. Consumers - United States - Attitudes - Statistics. 3. Consumer satisfaction - United States - Statistics. I. New York Times (Firm). Marketing Research Dept. II. Title: Auto outlook four.
HD9710.U52 A76 1986

AUTO WORKERS. see **AUTOMOBILE INDUSTRY WORKERS.**

Autoafirmación colectiva : una estrategia alternativa de desarrollo / selección de Enrique Oteiza ; con la colaboración de Ann Zammit y Catherine Kenrick.1a ed. México : Fondo de Cultura Económica, 1983. 327 p. ; 21 cm. (Trimestre económico. Lecturas . 49) Includes bibliographical references. ISBN 968-16-1335-X LC Card 86-159023
1. Developing countries - Economic policy. 2. Developing countries - Foreign economic relations. I. Oteiza, Enrique. II. Zammit, Ann. III. Kenrick, Catherine. IV. Series.
HC59.7 .A92 1983

La autoconstrucción de vivienda en México . Legorreta, Jorge. [México, D.F.] [1984] 204 p. : LC Card 86-232442
HD7306.A3 L44 1984

Autocracy, capitalism, and the revolution in Russia /. McDaniel, Tim. Berkeley , c1987. p. cm. ISBN 0-520-05532-2 (alk. paper) LC Card 86-30790 DDC 322.4/2/0947 19
HD8526 .M385 1987

L'autocritica del keynesiano /. Duso, Anna, 1952- Bari , c1985. 99 p. ; ISBN 88-22-03812-6 : LC Card 86-130684
HB99.7 .D87 1985

AUTOGENOUS WELDING. see **WELDING.**

AUTOMATED INFORMATION NETWORKS. see **INFORMATION NETWORKS.**

The automated office . Saffady, William, 1944- Silver Spring, Md. , c1981. viii, 241 p. : ISBN 0-89258-072-0 LC Card 81-208697 DDC 651.8/4 19
HF5548.2 .S165 ***NYPL [JLE 86-3919]***

Eine automatentheoretische Baumkonstruktion zur Simulation hierarchischer Management-Strukturen /. Niemeyer, Gerhard. [Regensburg] [1984] 64 p. : LC Card 84-181485
HD38 .N513 1984

AUTOMATIC BANKING EQUIPMENT INDUSTRY - UNITED STATES.
Consumer financial services . Boston, MA (200 Portland St., Boston 02114) , 1986. xvi, 83 p. : LC Card 86-230330 DDC 332.1/028 19
HD9696.B363 U543 1986

AUTOMATIC COMPUTERS. see **COMPUTERS.**

AUTOMATIC CONTROL EQUIPMENT INDUSTRY - UNITED STATES.
Delson, Erwin B. The factory automation industry /. New York, N.Y. , c1985. 1 v. (various pagings) : ISBN 0-931634-16-4 (pbk.) LC Card 86-203033 DDC 338.4/76298/0973 19
HD9696.A963 U635 1985

The Process control equipment market (1982-1992). New York, N.Y. , c1983. vii, 241 leaves : LC Card 87-142195 DDC 380.1/456817 19
HD9696.A963 U66 1983

AUTOMATIC DATA PROCESSING. see **ELECTRONIC DATA PROCESSING.**

AUTOMATIC DATA PROCESSORS. see **COMPUTERS.**

AUTOMATIC DATA STORAGE. see **INFORMATION STORAGE AND RETRIEVAL SYSTEMS.**

AUTOMATIC DIGITAL COMPUTERS. see **ELECTRONIC DIGITAL COMPUTERS.**

AUTOMATIC FACTORIES. see **AUTOMATION.**

AUTOMATIC INFORMATION RETRIEVAL. see **INFORMATION STORAGE AND RETRIEVAL SYSTEMS.**

AUTOMATIC PRODUCTION. see **AUTOMATION.**

AUTOMATIC SPEECH RECOGNITION - CONGRESSES.
Pervichnoe opisanie signalov rechi . Vil'nius , 1980. 67 p. : LC Card 82-107723
HD38 .S715 vyp. 42 TK7882.S65

Automating apartheid : U. S. computer exports to South Africa and the arms embargo. Philadelphia : NARMIC/America Friends Service Committee, c1982 ix, 107 p. : ill. ; 22 cm. Bibliography: p. [78]-88. ISBN 0-910082-00-6 (pbk.) : LC Card 86-201384 DDC 382/.45004/0968 19
1. Computer industry - South Africa. 2. Computer industry - United States. 3. Munitions - South Africa. 4. Munitions - United States. 5. Economic sanctions, American - South Africa. 6. Apartheid - South Africa. I. National Action/Research on the Military-Industrial Complex. II. American Friends Service Committee.
HD9696.C63 S62 1984

AUTOMATION.
Di Bernardo, Barbara. Transizione tecnologica e strategie evolutive . Padova , 1985. xiii, 432 p. : LC Card 86-214184
HD45 .D47 1985

Kofler, Leo. Beherrscht uns die Technik? . Hamburg , 1983. 160 p. ; ISBN 3-87975-249-4 LC Card 84-181044
HD6331 .K685 1983

Ravaioli, Carla. Tempo da vendere, tempo da usare . Milano, Italy , c1986. 142 p. ; LC Card 86-182560
HD5106 .R357 1986

AUTOMATION - ADDRESSES, ESSAYS, LECTURES.
Microprocessors, manpower, and society . Aldershot, Hants., England , c1984. xi, 367 p. : ISBN 0-566-00631-6 ***NYPL [JLD 86-1098]***

Automation and industrial workers : a fifteen nation study / edited by Jan Forslin, Adam Sarapata, and Arthur M. Whitehill, in collaboration with Frank Adler and Stephen Mills.1st ed. Oxford [Oxfordshire] ; New York : Pergamon Press, 1979- v. : ill. ; 26 cm. On cover, v. 1: European Coordination Centre for Research and Documentation in Social Sciences. Vol. 2 has subtitle: A cross-national comparison of fifteen countries. Editors vary. Includes bibliographical references. ISBN 0-08-023339-2 (v. 1, pt. 1) : LC Card 79-40811 DDC 331
1. Automation - Social aspects - Case studies. 2. Machinery in industry - Case studies. 3. Industrial sociology - Case studies. 4. Labor and laboring classes - Case studies. I. Forslin, Jan, 1939-. II. Sarapata, Adam. III. Whitehill, Arthur M. IV. European Centre for the Co-ordination of Research and Documentation in Social Sciences.
HD6331 .A93 1979 ***NYPL [JLM 82-242]***

AUTOMATION - ECONOMIC ASPECTS - CANADA - STATISTICS.
Betcherman, Gordon. Working with technology . [Ottawa] , 1986. 43 p. : ISBN 0-660-12174-3 (pbk.) : LC Card 86-224095 DDC 338/.06 19
HC120.A9 B47 1986

AUTOMATION - ECONOMIC ASPECTS - FRANCE.
Pastré, Olivier. L'informatisation et l'emploi /. Paris , 1983. 127 p. : ISBN 2-7071-1387-5 LC Card 83-161919 DDC 331.12/0944 19
HD6331.2.F8 P37 1983

AUTOMATION - ECONOMIC ASPECTS - GERMANY (EAST)
Technisch rationell, sozial effektiv . Berlin , 1986. 168 p. ; ISBN 3-320-00706-8 LC Card 87-144339 DDC 338/.06 19
HC290.795.A9 T43 1986

AUTOMATION - ECONOMIC ASPECTS - GERMANY, WEST.
Frauen und Beruf, zwischen Wunsch und Realität . Bonn , Bad Honnef , 1986. 142 p. ; ISBN 3-87066-629-3 : LC Card 87-409372 DDC 331.4/0943 19
HD6149 .F719 1986

AUTOMATION - FRANCE.
Knetsch, Werner. Die industrielle Anwendung der Mikroelektronik in der Bundesrepublik Deutschland, Frankreich, Grossbritannien . Haar bei München , c1985. 142 p. : ISBN 3-89090-121-2 : LC Card 86-106735
HC290.5.A9 K5 1985

Knetsch, Werner. Die industrielle Mikroelektronik-Anwendung im verarbeitenden Gewerbe der Bundesrepublik Deutschland . Haar bei München , c1986. 223 p. : ISBN 3-89090-131-X LC Card 87-132995 DDC 338/.06 19
HC290.5.A9 K524 1986

AUTOMATION - GERMANY (WEST)
Knetsch, Werner. Die industrielle Anwendung der Mikroelektronik in der Bundesrepublik Deutschland, Frankreich, Grossbritannien . Haar bei München , c1985. 142 p. : ISBN 3-89090-121-2 : LC Card 86-106735
HC290.5.A9 K5 1985

Knetsch, Werner. Die industrielle Mikroelektronik-Anwendung im verarbeitenden Gewerbe der Bundesrepublik Deutschland . Haar bei München , c1986. 223 p. : ISBN 3-89090-131-X LC Card 87-132995 DDC 338/.06 19
HC290.5.A9 K524 1986

AUTOMATION - GERMANY (WEST) - HISTORY.
Der Dressierte Arbeiter . München , c1984. 211 p. : ISBN 3-406-09286-1 LC Card 84-181068 DDC 331.25 19
HD6331.2.G28 D74 1984

AUTOMATION - GREAT BRITAIN.
Knetsch, Werner. Die industrielle Anwendung der Mikroelektronik in der Bundesrepublik Deutschland, Frankreich, Grossbritannien . Haar bei München , c1985. 142 p. : ISBN 3-89090-121-2 : LC Card 86-106735
HC290.5.A9 K5 1985

Knetsch, Werner. Die industrielle Mikroelektronik-Anwendung im verarbeitenden Gewerbe der Bundesrepublik Deutschland . Haar bei München , c1986. 223 p. : ISBN 3-89090-131-X LC Card 87-132995 DDC 338/.06 19
HC290.5.A9 K524 1986

AUTOMATION IN DOCUMENTATION. see **INFORMATION STORAGE AND RETRIEVAL SYSTEMS.**

AUTOMATION - MANAGEMENT.
Völlmar, H. De organisatie-aspecten van de automatisering /. Leiden , 1985. xiv, 316 p. : ISBN 90-207-1347-7 : LC Card 85-220224
HD45.2 .V65 1985

AUTOMATION - NETHERLANDS - MANAGEMENT.
Völlmar, H. De organisatie-aspecten van de automatisering /. Leiden , 1985. xiv, 316 p. : ISBN 90-207-1347-7 : LC Card 85-220224
HD45.2 .V65 1985

AUTOMATION - SOCIAL ASPECTS.
Dostal, Werner. Bildung und Beschäftigung im technischen Wandel . Nürnberg , 1982. viii, 380, 6 p. : LC Card 82-205035 DDC 306/.46 19
HD6331 .D53 1982 ***NYPL [JLD 86-3011]***

Soziale Aspekte der Mikroelektronik /. Berlin , 1985. 122 p. ; LC Card 87-409418 DDC 306/.46 19
HD6331 .S683 1985

AUTOMATION - SOCIAL ASPECTS - ADDRESSES, ESSAYS, LECTURES.
Heyel, Carl, 1908- John Diebold on management. Englewood Cliffs, N.J. [1972] ix, 282 p. ISBN 0-13-510214-6 LC Card 75-170643 DDC 658
HD45 .H42 ***NYPL [JLF 73-1242]***

AUTOMATION - SOCIAL ASPECTS - CASE STUDIES.
Automation and industrial workers . Oxford [Oxfordshire] , New York , 1979- v. : ISBN 0-08-023339-2 (v. 1, pt. 1) : LC Card 79-40811 DDC 331
HD6331 .A93 1979 ***NYPL [JLM 82-242]***

AUTOMATION - SOCIAL ASPECTS - FRANCE.
Pastré, Olivier. L'informatisation et l'emploi /. Paris , 1983. 127 p. : ISBN 2-7071-1387-5 LC Card 83-161919 DDC 331.12/0944 19
HD6331.2.F8 P37 1983

AUTOMATION - SOCIAL ASPECTS - GERMANY (EAST)
Technisch rationell, sozial effektiv . Berlin ,

1986. 168 p. ; ISBN 3-320-00706-8 LC Card 87-144339 DDC 338/.06 19
HC290.795.A9 T43 1986

AUTOMATION - SOCIAL ASPECTS - GERMANY, WEST.
Frauen und neue Technologien /. Hannover , 1986. 112 p. ; LC Card 87-407392 DDC 331.4/0943 19
HD6059.G3 F74 1986

AUTOMATION - SOCIAL ASPECTS - UNITED STATES.
EAPs and the information revolution . New York , c1987. 106 p. ; ISBN 0-86656-606-6 LC Card 86-33519 DDC 331.25 19
HF5549.5.E42 E37 1987

Rochell, Carlton C. Dreams betrayed . Lexington, Mass. , c1987. 138 p. ; ISBN 0-669-11105-8 (alk. paper) LC Card 85-45019 DDC 331.25 19
HD6331.2.U5 R63 1987

AUTOMATION - SOUTH AFRICA.
Mansfield, W. R. (Willard Ridgway) A management crisis in Natal . [Durban, South Africa] [1985 or 1986] 26 p. ; LC Card 87-400770 DDC 338.0968 19
HC905.Z9 I526 1985

Automation technology and industrial renewal . Hicks, Donald A. Washington, D.C. [1985], c1986. xiii, 160 p. ; ISBN 0-8447-3598-1 LC Card 85-31568 DDC 671 19
HD9506.U62 H53 1986
NYPL [JSE 86-1901]

Automatisierte Verwaltung : eine empirische Untersuchung über die Rationalisierung der Steuerverwaltung / Hans Brinckmann ... [et al.]. Frankfurt ; New York : Campus, c1981. 135 p. : ill. ; 21 cm. (Campus Forschung. Bd. 219) Includes bibliographical references. ISBN 3-593-32944-1 : LC Card 81-146994
1. Tax administration and procedure - Germany (West) - Data processing. I. Brinckmann, Hans, 1934-.
HJ3484.A4 A95 1981

Automazione d'ufficio : tecnologia, organizzazione, professionalità e formazione : studio di casi nell'area parmense / di M. Carcano ... [et al.]. Roma : Istituto per lo sviluppo della formazione professionale dei lavoratori, [1985] 248 p. : ill. ; 24 cm. (Quaderni di formazione ISFOL, 0390-3532 . n. 4/85 (luglio ag. 1985)) Bibliography: p. 229-230. LC Card 86-213829
1. Business education - Italy - Parma Region - Case studies. 2. Office practice - Automation. I. Carcano, M. (Marco). II. Series: Quaderni di formazione ISFOL , n. 85/4.
HF1152.P28 A95 1985

Automobile. Knepp, Jay. Tax[s]aver. Menlo Park, Calif. , c1987. 143 p. : ISBN 0-376-07015-3 (pbk.) : LC Card 86-80874 DDC 343.7305/23 347.303523 19
HJ4653.D4 K56 1987

AUTOMOBILE ACCIDENTS. see **TRAFFIC ACCIDENTS.**

AUTOMOBILE CONSTRUCTION WORKERS. see **AUTOMOBILE INDUSTRY WORKERS.**

AUTOMOBILE DRIVER EDUCATION - GERMANY (WEST) - COLOGNE REGION.
Echterhoff, Wilfried. Einfluss von Verkehrssicherheitsinformationen auf unfallbeteiligte Kraftfahrer /. Köln [1983], c1981. 112 p. : LC Card 84-147580
HE5614.5.G3 E34 1983

AUTOMOBILE DRIVERS' LICENSES - AUSTRIA - STATISTICS.
Lenkerberechtigungen im Jahre 1977 /. Wien , 1978. 69 p. ; LC Card 86-196229
HA1173 .A27 Heft 490 HE5667.A6

AUTOMOBILE DRIVERS' LICENSES - UNITED STATES.
Reducing highway crashes through administrative license revocation. [Washington, D.C.?] , 1986. 89 p. : *NYPL [JLF 86-1382]*

AUTOMOBILE DRIVING - STUDY AND TEACHING - CENTRAL AFRICAN REPUBLIC - BANGUI.
International Labour Organisation. Organisation de l'Institut national de formation et de perfectionnement professionnels de Bangui (INFPP) . Genève , 1980. 14 p. ; ISBN 92-2-202448-6 LC Card 82-214934
HD5716.M342 C335 1980

AUTOMOBILE ENGINES. see **AUTOMOBILES - MOTORS.**

The Automobile industry : statistical profile, 1985. Bombay : Documentation and Reference Centre, Association of Indian Automobile Manufacturers, 1985. x, 290 p. : col. ill. ; 29 cm. "AIAM silver jubilee, 1960-85." Accompanied by "Half yearly review, 1985-1984" (12 p.) LC Card 86-903383 DDC 338.4/76292/0954021 19
1. Automobile industry and trade - India - Statistics. I. Association of Indian Automobile Manufacturers. Documentation and Reference Centre.
HD9710.I42 A974 1985

The Automobile industry and its workers : between Fordism and flexibility / edited by Steven Tolliday and Jonathan Zeitlin. New York : St. Martin's Press, 1987. viii, 335 p. : ill. ; 24 cm. Includes bibliographies and index. ISBN 0-312-00553-9 : LC Card 86-29815 DDC 331/.04292 19
1. Automobile industry and trade. 2. Automobile industry workers. 3. Trade-unions - Automobile industry workers. 4. Industrial relations. I. Tolliday, Steven. II. Zeitlin, Jonathan.
HD9710.A2 A865 1987

AUTOMOBILE INDUSTRY AND TRADE - ANDES REGION.
Sirumbal, Luis Miguel. La crisis de la industria automotriz (1971-1982) /. Lima, Perú [1983] 54 p. : LC Card 84-123601 DDC 338.4/76292/0985 19
HD9710.P382 S57 1983
NYPL [JLD 86-365]

AUTOMOBILE INDUSTRY AND TRADE - ARGENTINA.
Nofal, Maria Beatriz. Absentee entrepreneurship and the dynamics of the motor vehicle industry in Argentina /. New York , 1987. p. cm. ISBN 0-275-92607-9 (alk. paper) : LC Card 87-15159 DDC 629.2/0982 19
HD9710.A72 N64 1987

AUTOMOBILE INDUSTRY AND TRADE - ASIA.
The Motor vehicle industry in Asia . [Singapore] [1983] xxv, 419 p. : ISBN 997-16-9057-8 LC Card 83-941793 DDC 338.4/76292/095 19
HD9710.3.A78 M67 1983
NYPL [JLE 85-1592]

AUTOMOBILE INDUSTRY AND TRADE - CANADA.
Canada. Task Force on the Canadian Motor Vehicle and Automotive Parts Industries. An automotive strategy for Canada . [Ottawa] , 1983. xv, 193 p. : ISBN 0-662-12626-2
NYPL [JLF 86-648]

AUTOMOBILE INDUSTRY AND TRADE - CONGRESSES.
Strategie industriali e prospettive di sviluppo nel settore automobilistico /. Milano [1985] 235 p. : ISBN 88-14-00541-9 (pbk.) : LC Card 85-183335 DDC 338.4/76292/0945 19
HD9710.A2 S86 1985 NYPL [JLE 87-493]

AUTOMOBILE INDUSTRY AND TRADE - ENGLAND - OXFORD - HISTORY.
Making cars . London , Boston , c1985. ix, 131 p. : ISBN 0-7102-0272-5 : LC Card 84-13398 DDC 338.4/76292/0942574 19
HD8039.A82 G75 1984
NYPL [JLE 86-2303]

AUTOMOBILE INDUSTRY AND TRADE - ENVIRONMENTAL ASPECTS - SPAIN - ZARAGOZA.
Todo para la G.M. . Madrid [1981?] 174 p. : ISBN 84-85639-19-7 LC Card 82-134601 DDC 338.8/87 19
HD9710.S754 G467 1981
NYPL [JLC 86-300]

AUTOMOBILE INDUSTRY AND TRADE - EUROPE - CONGRESSES.
Strukturpolitische Probleme der Automobil-Industrie unter dem Aspekt des Wettbewerbs /. Berlin , c1985. 247 p. : ISBN 3-428-05924-7 LC Card 86-165212 DDC 338.4/76292/094 19
HD9710.E82 S77 1985

AUTOMOBILE INDUSTRY AND TRADE - FRANCE - TECHNOLOGICAL INNOVATIONS.
Travail et automatisation dans l'industrie automobile /. [France] , Grenoble , 1986. 141 p. ; ISBN 2-86561-070-5 : LC Card 87-151670
HD9710.F72 T72 1986

AUTOMOBILE INDUSTRY AND TRADE - GERMANY, WEST.
Kiffe, Ulrich. Die Klassifizierung in der Bundesrepublik Deutschland angebotener Personenkraftwagen mit multivariaten Analysemethoden /. Münster , 1984. xx, 24, 340 p. : ISBN 3-88660-148-8 LC Card 84-208133
HD9710.G42 K48 1984

Osswald, Richard, 1917- Lebendige Arbeitswelt . Stuttgart , c1986. 394 p. : ISBN 3-421-06309-5 LC Card 86-148169
HD9710.G44 D385 1986

AUTOMOBILE INDUSTRY AND TRADE - GERMANY (WEST) - FORECASTING.
Schülen, Heinrich, 1957- Langfristige Automobilmarktprognosen . Idstein , 1985. 221 p. : ISBN 3-925196-14-5 LC Card 86-120500 DDC 338.4/76292/0943 19
HD9710.G42 S32 1985

AUTOMOBILE INDUSTRY AND TRADE - GERMANY (WEST) - MANAGEMENT - EMPLOYEE PARTICIPATION.
Streeck, Wolfgang, 1946- Industrial relations in West Germany . London , 1984. 178 p. ; ISBN 0-435-83839-3 LC Card 87-673421
HD6698.A8 S77x 1984b

AUTOMOBILE INDUSTRY AND TRADE - GERMANY (WEST) - MANAGEMENT - EMPLOYEE PARTICIPATION - CASE STUDIES.
Mitbestimmung, Norm und Wirklichkeit . Frankfurt , New York , c1984. 369 p. ; ISBN 3-593-33325-2 LC Card 85-128882
HD5658.A82 G35 1984

AUTOMOBILE INDUSTRY AND TRADE - GERMANY (WEST) - MATHEMATICAL MODELS.
Schülen, Heinrich, 1957- Langfristige Automobilmarktprognosen . Idstein , 1985. 221 p. : ISBN 3-925196-14-5 LC Card 86-120500 DDC 338.4/76292/0943 19
HD9710.G42 S32 1985

AUTOMOBILE INDUSTRY AND TRADE - GOVERNMENT POLICY - CANADA.
Canada. Task Force on the Canadian Motor Vehicle and Automotive Parts Industries. An automotive strategy for Canada . [Ottawa] , 1983. xv, 193 p. : ISBN 0-662-12626-2
NYPL [JLF 86-648]

AUTOMOBILE INDUSTRY AND TRADE - GOVERNMENT POLICY - GREAT BRITAIN.
Edwardes, Michael, 1930- Back from the brink . London , 1983. 301 p. : ISBN 0-00-217098-1; 0-00-217089-1 LC Card 83-127870 DDC 338.7/6292/0941 19
HD9710.G74 B573 1983
NYPL [JLD 86-3553]

AUTOMOBILE INDUSTRY AND TRADE - GOVERNMENT POLICY - PERU.
Sirumbal, Luis Miguel. La crisis de la industria automotriz (1971-1982) /. Lima, Perú [1983] 54 p. : LC Card 84-123601 DDC 338.4/76292/0985 19
HD9710.P382 S57 1983
NYPL [JLD 86-365]

AUTOMOBILE INDUSTRY AND TRADE - GOVERNMENT POLICY - UNITED STATES.
Winston, Clifford, 1952- Blind intersection? . Washington, D.C. , c1987. xii, 108 p. : ISBN 0-8157-9466-5 : LC Card 87-806 DDC 338.4/76292/0973 19
HD9710.U52 W55 1987

AUTOMOBILE INDUSTRY AND TRADE - GREAT BRITAIN.
Quinn, Dennis Patrick, 1955- Restructuring the automobile industry . New York , 1988. p. cm. ISBN 0-231-06524-8 LC Card 87-15919 DDC 338.4/76292/0941 19
HD9710.U52 Q56 1988

Williams, Karel. The breakdown of Austin Rover . Leamington Spa, UK ; New York : v, 150 p. : ISBN 0-85496-515-7 : LC Card 86-24449 DDC 338.7/6292222 19
HD9710.G74 A868 1987

AUTOMOBILE INDUSTRY AND TRADE - GREAT BRITAIN - HISTORY.
Church, Roy A. Herbert Austin . London , c1979. lii, 233 p., [3] leaves of plates : ISBN 0-905118-29-4 : LC Card 79-317202 DDC 338.7/62/920924 B
HD9710.G72 A93 ***NYPL [JFD 86-9452]***

Lewchuk, Wayne. American technology and the British vehicle industry /. Cambridge [Cambridgeshire] , New York , 1987. viii, 304 p. : ISBN 0-521-30269-2 LC Card 86-30994 DDC 338.4/56292/0941 19
HD9710.G72 L48 1987

Whyte, Andrew (Andrew John Appleton) Jaguar, the history of a great British car /. Wellingborough [Northants] , New York, N.Y. , 1985. 252 p. : ISBN 0-85059-746-3 : LC Card 85-670203 DDC 338.7/6292222/0941 19
HD9710.G74 J338 1985
NYPL [JLE 87-451]

AUTOMOBILE INDUSTRY AND TRADE - GREAT BRITAIN - MANAGEMENT.
The Car industry . London , New York , 1985. viii, 210 p. : ISBN 0-422-79550-X LC Card 85-14742 DDC 331/.04292/0941 19
HD6976.A82 G72 1985
NYPL [JLD 87-403]

Edwardes, Michael, 1930- Back from the brink . London , 1983. 301 p. : ISBN 0-00-217098-1; 0-00-217089-1 LC Card 83-127870 DDC 338.7/6292/0941 19
HD9710.G74 B573 1983
NYPL [JLD 86-3553]

AUTOMOBILE INDUSTRY AND TRADE - GREAT BRITAIN - MANAGEMENT - CASE STUDIES.
Willman, Paul. Innovation and management control . Cambridge [Cambridgeshire] , New York , 1985. viii, 215 p. ; ISBN 0-521-26802-8 LC Card 84-17481 DDC 331/.04292/0941 19
HD8039.A82 G79 1985
NYPL [JLD 85-3102]

AUTOMOBILE INDUSTRY AND TRADE - INDIA - STATISTICS.
The Automobile industry . Bombay , 1985. x, 290 p. : LC Card 86-903383 DDC 338.4/76292/0954021 19
HD9710.I42 A974 1985

AUTOMOBILE INDUSTRY AND TRADE - ITALY - CONGRESSES.
Strategie industriali e prospettive di sviluppo nel settore automobilistico /. Milano [1985] 235 p. : ISBN 88-14-00541-9 (pbk.) : LC Card 85-183335 DDC 338.4/76292/0945 19
HD9710.A2 S86 1985 ***NYPL [JLE 87-493]***

AUTOMOBILE INDUSTRY AND TRADE - ITALY - HISTORY.
Camerana, Oddone. L'enigma del cavalier Agnelli e altri itinerari /. Milano , c1985. 117 p. ; LC Card 85-191746
HD9710.I82 A6615 1985
NYPL [JLC 87-25]

AUTOMOBILE INDUSTRY AND TRADE - JAPAN - AUTOMATION.
Chacko, George Kuttickal, 1930- Robotics/artificial intelligence/productivity . Princeton, N.J. , c1986. 2 v. in 1 (xvii, 335 p.) : ISBN 0-89433-228-7 LC Card 86-12177 DDC 658.5/14 19
HD9725 .C48 1986 ***NYPL [JLE 87-1001]***

AUTOMOBILE INDUSTRY AND TRADE - JAPAN - CONGRESSES.
The Japanese competition . Ann Arbor, MI , 1987. xii, 124 p. ; ISBN 0-939512-30-0 LC Card 86-31756 DDC 338.4/76292/0952 19
HD9710.J32 J374 1987
NYPL [JFL 81-188 no.15]

AUTOMOBILE INDUSTRY AND TRADE - LAW AND LEGISLATION - PERU.
Sirumbal, Luis Miguel. La crisis de la industria automotriz (1971-1982) /. Lima, Perú [1983] 54 p. : LC Card 84-123601 DDC 338.4/76292/0985 19
HD9710.P382 S57 1983
NYPL [JLD 86-365]

AUTOMOBILE INDUSTRY AND TRADE - MANAGEMENT - DATA PROCESSING.
Dergachev, A. F. Raschet zatrat i opredelenie ėkonomicheskoĭ ėffektivnosti avtomatizirovannykh sistem operativno-proizvodstvennogo planirovaniia na avtoremontnykh predpriiatiiakh . Moskva , 1978. 35 p. ; LC Card 81-173259
HD9710.A2 D47 1978

AUTOMOBILE INDUSTRY AND TRADE - MICHIGAN - CASE STUDIES.
Jones, Bryan D. The sustaining hand . Lawrence, Kan. , c1986. xii, 247 p. : ISBN 0-7006-0278-X : LC Card 85-24631 DDC 338.4/76292/09774 19
HD9710.U53 M433 1986
NYPL [JLE 86-2386]

AUTOMOBILE INDUSTRY AND TRADE - MICHIGAN - DETROIT - HISTORY.
Bolan, Nelson. How Detroit changed history /. Lawrenceville, Va. , c1987. v, 246 p. : ISBN 1-556-18018-7 (pbk.) : LC Card 87-70325 DDC 338.4/76292/0973 19
HD9710.U52 B55 1987

AUTOMOBILE INDUSTRY AND TRADE - MICHIGAN - FLINT.
Edsforth, Ronald, 1948- Class conflict and cultural consensus . New Brunswick, N.J. , c1987. xvi, 294 p. ; ISBN 0-8135-1184-4 LC Card 86-7955 DDC 330.9774/37 19
HC108.F55 E37 1987 ***NYPL [JLE 87-978]***

AUTOMOBILE INDUSTRY AND TRADE - PERU.
Sirumbal, Luis Miguel. La crisis de la industria automotriz (1971-1982) /. Lima, Perú [1983] 54 p. : LC Card 84-123601 DDC 338.4/76292/0985 19
HD9710.P382 S57 1983
NYPL [JLD 86-365]

AUTOMOBILE INDUSTRY AND TRADE - PERU - FINANCE - CASE STUDIES.
Beltrán Alejos, Hugo. La situación del sector metal-mecánico en el Perú . Lima, Perú , 1985. 93, [77] p. : LC Card 86-218266
HD9506.P42 B45 1985

AUTOMOBILE INDUSTRY AND TRADE - SOUTH AFRICA - STATISTICS.
Sensus van motorhandel en hersteldienste, 1977 =. Pretoria [1982?] xiv, 166 p. : ISBN 0-621-07034-3 : LC Card 82-240419
HD9710.S72 S46 1982

AUTOMOBILE INDUSTRY AND TRADE - SWEDEN - CASE STUDIES.
Auer, Peter. Industrial relations, work organisation and new technology . Berlin [1985] 17, [6] p. ; LC Card 86-205891 DDC 331/.04292/09481 19
HD9710.S84 V6413 1985

AUTOMOBILE INDUSTRY AND TRADE - TECHNOLOGICAL INNOVATIONS.
Microelectronics, automation, and employment in the automobile industry /. Chichester [West Sussex] , New York , c1987. xix, 203 p. : ISBN 0-471-91484-3 : LC Card 86-32532 DDC 331.7/6292 19
HD8039.A8 M52 1987

AUTOMOBILE INDUSTRY AND TRADE - UNITED STATES.
The Changing passenger car markets . Stamford, Conn., U. S.A. , c1985. viii, 227 leaves : ISBN 0-89336-479-7 (pbk.) LC Card 87-404429 DDC 381/.4566849 19
HD9710.U52 C385 1985

Dyer, Davis. Changing alliances /. Boston, Mass. , c1987. xvi, 333 p. ; ISBN 0-87584-175-9 LC Card 86-33619 DDC 338.4/76292/0973 19
HD9710.U52 D94 1987

Halberstam, David. The reckoning /. New York , c1986. 752 p. ; ISBN 0-688-04838-2 LC Card 86-16427 DDC 338.4/76292/0973 19
HD9710.U52 H28 1986
NYPL [JLE 86-4151]

Iacocca, Lee A. The Iacocca tapes [sound recording] . Chicago, Ill. , c1985. 6 sound cassettes : LC Card 87-750990
HD9710.U I

Quinn, Dennis Patrick, 1955- Restructuring the automobile industry . New York , 1988. p. cm. ISBN 0-231-06524-8 LC Card 87-15919 DDC 338.4/76292/0941 19
HD9710.U52 Q56 1988

AUTOMOBILE INDUSTRY AND TRADE - UNITED STATES - AUTOMATION.
Chacko, George Kuttickal, 1930- Robotics/artificial intelligence/productivity . Princeton, N.J. , c1986. 2 v. in 1 (xvii, 335 p.) : ISBN 0-89433-228-7 LC Card 86-12177 DDC 658.5/14 19
HD9725 .C48 1986 ***NYPL [JLE 87-1001]***

AUTOMOBILE INDUSTRY AND TRADE - UNITED STATES - CONGRESSES.
The Japanese competition . Ann Arbor, MI , 1987. xii, 124 p. ; ISBN 0-939512-30-0 LC Card 86-31756 DDC 338.4/76292/0952 19
HD9710.J32 J374 1987
NYPL [JFL 81-188 no.15]

AUTOMOBILE INDUSTRY AND TRADE - UNITED STATES - HISTORY.
Bolan, Nelson. How Detroit changed history /. Lawrenceville, Va. , c1987. v, 246 p. : ISBN 1-556-18018-7 (pbk.) : LC Card 87-70325 DDC 338.4/76292/0973 19
HD9710.U52 B55 1987

Lewchuk, Wayne. American technology and the British vehicle industry /. Cambridge [Cambridgeshire] , New York , 1987. viii, 304 p. : ISBN 0-521-30269-2 LC Card 86-30994 DDC 338.4/56292/0941 19
HD9710.G72 L48 1987

Wyden, Peter. The unknown Iacocca /. New York , c1987. 416 p. : ISBN 0-688-06616-X LC Card 87-15240 DDC 338.7/6292/0924 B 19
HD9710.U52 I28 1987

AUTOMOBILE INDUSTRY AND TRADE - UNITED STATES - HISTORY - 20TH CENTURY.
St. Clair, David James, 1950- The motorization of American cities /. New York , 1986. xi, 192 p. ; ISBN 0-275-92126-3 (alk. paper) : LC Card 86-523 DDC 388.4/1321/0973 19
HE5623 .S617 1986 ***NYPL [JLE 86-3608]***

AUTOMOBILE INDUSTRY AND TRADE - UNITED STATES - JUVENILE LITERATURE.
Haddock, Patricia. Standing up for America . Minneapolis, Minn. , c1987. 111 p. : ISBN 0-87518-362-X : LC Card 86-32965 DDC 338.7/6292/0924 B 92 19
HD9710.U52 I246 1987

AUTOMOBILE INDUSTRY AND TRADE - UNITED STATES - MANAGEMENT - CASE STUDIES.
Roadmap for change. Chicago, Ill. , 1987. 1 film reel (28 min.) : LC Card 87-705133 DDC 658 11
HD9710

AUTOMOBILE INDUSTRY AND TRADE - UNITED STATES - STATISTICS.
Auto outlook IV /. [New York] , c1986. 60 leaves ; LC Card 86-231268 DDC 381/.456292/0973 19
HD9710.U52 A76 1986

1986 buyers of new cars . New York, N.Y. (444 Madison Ave., New York 10022) , c1986. 2 v. : LC Card 86-229142 DDC 381/.456292/0973021 19
HD9710.U52 A17 1986

AUTOMOBILE INDUSTRY - GERMANY - MILITARY ASPECTS - HISTORY - 20TH CENTURY.
Siegfried, Klaus-Jörg, 1940- Rüstungsproduktion und Zwangsarbeit im Volkswagenwerk, 1939-1945 . Frankfurt , New York , c1986. 239 p. : ISBN 3-593-33765-7 LC Card 87-133375 DDC 338.4/76234/0943 19
HD9743.G48 S56 1986

AUTOMOBILE INDUSTRY WORKERS.
The Automobile industry and its workers . New York , 1987. viii, 335 p. : ISBN 0-312-00553-9 : LC Card 86-29815 DDC 331/.04292 19
HD9710.A2 A865 1987

AUTOMOBILE INDUSTRY WORKERS - EFFECT OF TECHNOLOGICAL INNOVATIONS ON.
Microelectronics, automation, and employment in the automobile industry /. Chichester [West Sussex] , New York , c1987. xix, 203 p. : ISBN 0-471-91484-3 : LC Card 86-32532 DDC 331.7/6292 19
HD8039.A8 M52 1987

AUTOMOBILE INDUSTRY WORKERS - ENGLAND - OXFORD - HISTORY.
Making cars . London , Boston , c1985. ix, 131 p. : ISBN 0-7102-0272-5 : LC Card 84-13398

DDC 338.4/76292/0942574 19
HD8039.A82 G75 1984
NYPL [JLE 86-2303]

AUTOMOBILE INDUSTRY WORKERS - FRANCE - EFFECT OF TECHNOLOGICAL INNOVATIONS ON.
Travail et automatisation dans l'industrie automobile /. [France] , Grenoble , 1986. 141 p. ; ISBN 2-86561-070-5 : LC Card 87-151670
HD9710.F72 T72 1986

AUTOMOBILE INDUSTRY WORKERS - GERMANY (WEST) - EFFECT OF TECHNOLOGICAL INNOVATIONS ON - CASE STUDIES.
Industrial relations and technical change in the British, Italian, and German automobile industry . Berlin [1985] 1 v. (various pagings) : LC Card 86-206613 DDC 338/.04292/094 19
HD6976.A82 G75 1985

AUTOMOBILE INDUSTRY WORKERS - GREAT BRITAIN.
Willman, Paul. Innovation and management control . Cambridge [Cambridgeshire] , New York , 1985. viii, 215 p. ; ISBN 0-521-26802-8 LC Card 84-17481 DDC 331/.04292/0941 19
HD8039.A82 G79 1985
NYPL [JLD 85-3102]

AUTOMOBILE INDUSTRY WORKERS - GREAT BRITAIN - EFFECT OF TECHNOLOGICAL INNOVATIONS ON - CASE STUDIES.
Industrial relations and technical change in the British, Italian, and German automobile industry . Berlin [1985] 1 v. (various pagings) : LC Card 86-206613 DDC 338/.04292/094 19
HD6976.A82 G75 1985

AUTOMOBILE INDUSTRY WORKERS - ITALY - EFFECT OF TECHNOLOGICAL INNOVATIONS ON - CASE STUDIES.
Industrial relations and technical change in the British, Italian, and German automobile industry . Berlin [1985] 1 v. (various pagings) : LC Card 86-206613 DDC 338/.04292/094 19
HD6976.A82 G75 1985

AUTOMOBILE INDUSTRY WORKERS - MICHIGAN - FLINT.
Edsforth, Ronald, 1948- Class conflict and cultural consensus . New Brunswick, N.J. , c1987. xvi, 294 p. ; ISBN 0-8135-1184-4 LC Card 86-7955 DDC 330.9774/37 19
HC108.F55 E37 1987 ***NYPL [JLE 87-978]***

AUTOMOBILE INSURANCE. see **INSURANCE, AUTOMOBILE.**

AUTOMOBILE MECHANICS - TRAINING OF - CENTRAL AFRICAN REPUBLIC - BANGUI.
International Labour Organisation. Organisation de l'Institut national de formation et de perfectionnement professionnels de Bangui (INFPP) . Genève , 1980. 14 p. ; ISBN 92-2-202448-6 LC Card 82-214934
HD5716.M342 C335 1980

AUTOMOBILE OPERATION. see **AUTOMOBILE DRIVING.**

AUTOMOBILE PARKING - DENMARK.
Larsen, Flemming. Parkeringsbehov i ældre tætte bydele . København , 1985. 250 p. : LC Card 86-165642
HE336.P37 L37 1985

AUTOMOBILE PARKING - GERMANY (WEST) - NORTH RHINE-WESTPHALIA.
Ruhender Verkehr in Wohngebieten /. Dortmund , c1983, [1982] 121 p. : LC Card 83-236251
HE363.G32 P377 1983

AUTOMOBILE SUPPLIES INDUSTRY - ASIA.
The Motor vehicle industry in Asia . [Singapore] [1983] xxv, 419 p. : ISBN 997-16-9057-8 LC Card 83-941793 DDC 338.4/76292/095 19
HD9710.3.A78 M67 1983
NYPL [JLE 85-1592]

AUTOMOBILE SUPPLIES INDUSTRY - BRAZIL.
Industria dei pezzi per autoveicoli /. [São Paulo] , 1973. 1 v. (various pagings), [12] leaves of plates : LC Card 86-146007
HD9710.3.B72 I53 1973

AUTOMOBILE SUPPLIES INDUSTRY - BRAZIL - ADDRESSES, ESSAYS, LECTURES.
Pequena empresa . São Paulo-Brasil [Brasília] , 1985. 2 v. : LC Card 85-180776 DDC 338.6/42/0981 19
HD9710.3.B72 P46 1985
NYPL [JLD 86-1588]

AUTOMOBILE SUPPLIES INDUSTRY - GOVERNMENT POLICY - MEXICO.
Bennett, Mark. Public policy and industrial development . Boulder, Colo. , 1986. xii, 134 p. : ISBN 0-86531-821-2 : LC Card 83-23456 DDC 338.4/76292/0972 19
HD9710.3.M42 B46 1986
NYPL [JLE 86-2581]

AUTOMOBILE SUPPLIES INDUSTRY - SOUTH AFRICA - STATISTICS.
Sensus van motorhandel en hersteldienste, 1977 =. Pretoria [1982?] xiv, 166 p. : ISBN 0-621-07034-3 : LC Card 82-240419
HD9710.S72 S46 1982

AUTOMOBILE SUPPLIES INDUSTRY - UNITED STATES.
Automotive aftermarket in the U. S. New York, N.Y. , c1983. 2 v. (xiii, 435 p.) ; LC Card 87-144460
HD9710.3.U52 A93 1983

The Automotive electronics market in the U. S. New York, N.Y. , c1983. vi, 262 p. : LC Card 87-142223 DDC 381/.456292549/0973 19
HD9710.3.U52 A943 1983

AUTOMOBILE THEFT - UNITED STATES - STATISTICS.
Highway Loss Data Institute insurance theft report . Washington, D.C. (Watergate 600, Washington 20037) , c1986. 44 p. ; LC Card 87-107648 DDC 368.2/32/00973021 19
HG9970.3 .H538 1986

AUTOMOBILE WORKERS - UNITED STATES - HISTORY.
Peterson, Joyce Shaw, 1939- American automobile workers, 1900-1933 /. Albany , c1987. xiv, 231 p. ; ISBN 0-88706-573-2 LC Card 87-1942 DDC 331.7/6292/0973 19
HD8039.A82 U66 1987

AUTOMOBILES - ACCIDENTS. see **TRAFFIC ACCIDENTS.**

AUTOMOBILES, COMPANY - GREAT BRITAIN.
Tack Management Consultants. Salesmen's cars, expenses, and allowances, 1963 /. London [1963?] 163 p. ; LC Card 86-173421
HF5439.7 .T33 1963

AUTOMOBILES - DRIVING. see **AUTOMOBILE DRIVING.**

AUTOMOBILES, FOREIGN - UNITED STATES - STATISTICS.
1986 buyers of new cars . New York, N.Y. (444 Madison Ave., New York 10022) , c1986. 2 v. : LC Card 86-229142 DDC 381/.456292/0973021 19
HD9710.U52 A17 1986

AUTOMOBILES - FUEL CONSUMPTION - LAW AND LEGISLATION - UNITED STATES - COST EFFETIVENESS.
Regulating the automobile /. Washington, D.C. , c1986. xiii, 202 p. ; ISBN 0-8157-1594-3 : LC Card 85-48171 DDC 343.73/078629222 347.30378629222 19
HD9710.U52 R39 1986
NYPL [JLE 86-3240]

AUTOMOBILES, GASOLINE. see **AUTOMOBILES.**

AUTOMOBILES - GERMANY (WEST) - FUEL CONSUMPTION.
Kortzfleisch, Gert von. Energie für den Verkehr . Frankfurt am Main , c1984. 115 p. : LC Card 84-192683
HD9710.G4 V4 Nr. 42 HE5620.E53

AUTOMOBILES - GERMANY (WEST) - SPECIFICATIONS.
Kiffe, Ulrich. Die Klassifizierung in der Bundesrepublik Deutschland angebotener Personenkraftwagen mit multivariaten Analysemethoden /. Münster , 1984. xx, 24, 340 p. : ISBN 3-88660-148-8 LC Card 84-208133
HD9710.G42 K48 1984

AUTOMOBILES - GREAT BRITAIN - TECHNOLOGICAL INNOVATIONS - HISTORY.
Lewchuk, Wayne. American technology and the British vehicle industry /. Cambridge [Cambridgeshire] , New York , 1987. viii, 304 p. : ISBN 0-521-30269-2 LC Card 86-30994 DDC 338.4/56292/0941 19
HD9710.G72 L48 1987

AUTOMOBILES - HISTORY.
Bolan, Nelson. How Detroit changed history /. Lawrenceville, Va. , c1987. v, 246 p. : ISBN 1-556-18018-7 (pbk.) : LC Card 87-70325 DDC 338.4/76292/0973 19
HD9710.U52 B55 1987

AUTOMOBILES - INSURANCE. see **INSURANCE, AUTOMOBILE.**

AUTOMOBILES - MARYLAND - SOCIETIES, ETC. - DIRECTORIES.
Directory of licensed insurers, licensed motor clubs, licensed health maintenance organizations, licensed rating organizations, registered advisory organizations . [Baltimore, Md.] (501 St. Paul Pl., Baltimore 21202) [1985] viii, 150 p. ; LC Card 86-621407 DDC 368/.0025/752 19
HG8526.M3 D59 1985

AUTOMOBILES - MOTORS - EXHAUST GAS - LAW AND LEGISLATION - COST EFFECTIVENESS.
Regulating the automobile /. Washington, D.C. , c1986. xiii, 202 p. ; ISBN 0-8157-1594-3 : LC Card 85-48171 DDC 343.73/078629222 347.30378629222 19
HD9710.U52 R39 1986
NYPL [JLE 86-3240]

AUTOMOBILES - MOTORS - EXHAUST GAS - LAW AND LEGISLATION - GERMANY (WEST)
Schulz, Bernhard. Effizienzkontrolle von Umweltpolitik . Frankfurt am Main , c1983. xv, 230 p. : ISBN 3-88129-744-8 LC Card 85-103230
HC290.5.E5 S38 1983

AUTOMOBILES-PARKING. see **AUTOMOBILE PARKING.**

AUTOMOBILES PEUGEOT (FIRM) - EMPLOYEES - ATTITUDES.
Legay, Marie-Agnès. Réduction de la durée du travail et changement des modes de vie . Aix-en-Provence [1984] ix, 366 p. : LC Card 86-185902
HD6066.F8 L44 1984

AUTOMOBILES - PURCHASING.
Hudson, Adams, 1958- How to buy or sell a car by long distance /. Osceola, Wis. , 1987. 80 p. ; ISBN 0-87938-259-7 (soft) LC Card 87-12185 DDC 629.2/222 19
HF5439.A8 H83 1987

AUTOMOBILES, RENTAL - MARYLAND.
Stellman, Caroline B. Consumer automobile leasing study /. Baltimore, Md. (7 N. Calvert St., Baltimore 21202) , 1986. ii, 59 p. ; LC Card 87-620899 DDC 388.3/2 19
HE5633.M3 S74 1986

AUTOMOBILES - SAFETY REGULATIONS - UNITED STATES - COST EFFECTIVENESS.
Regulating the automobile /. Washington, D.C. , c1986. xiii, 202 p. ; ISBN 0-8157-1594-3 : LC Card 85-48171 DDC 343.73/078629222 347.30378629222 19
HD9710.U52 R39 1986
NYPL [JLE 86-3240]

AUTOMOBILES - SEAT BELTS - GOVERNMENT POLICY - NEW JERSEY.
Highway Loss Data Institute insurance special report . Washington, D.C. (Watergate 600, Washington 20037) , c1986. 11 p. ; LC Card 86-211182 DDC 368.5/72016/09747 19
HG9970.35.N7 H55 1986

AUTOMOBILES - SEAT BELTS - GOVERNMENT POLICY - NEW YORK (STATE)
Highway Loss Data Institute insurance special report . Washington, D.C. (Watergate 600, Washington 20037) , c1986. 11 p. ; LC Card 86-211182 DDC 368.5/72016/09747 19
HG9970.35.N7 H55 1986

AUTOMOBILES - SEAT BELTS - LAW AND LEGISLATION.
Marburger, Ernst-Albrecht. Internationale Erfahrungen mit der Gurtanlegepflicht =.

Köln , 1982. 29, 29 p. : LC Card 83-200842
HE5614 .M288 1982

AUTOMOBILES - SEAT BELTS - LAW AND LEGISLATION - UNITED STATES.
Campbell, Bob J. Early results of seat belt legislation in the United States of America /. Chapel Hill, N.C. [1986] 25 p. : LC Card 86-622836 DDC 363.1/2572/0973 19
HE5614.2 .C35 1986

AUTOMOBILES - SOCIAL ASPECTS - GERMANY, WEST.
Bode, Peter M. Alptraum Auto . München , 1986. 237 p. : ISBN 3-922696-46-5 LC Card 87-107197 DDC 303.4/832 19
HE5613 .B63 1986

AUTOMOBILES - SOCIAL ASPECTS - UNITED STATES - HISTORY.
Bayley, Stephen. Sex, drink, and fast cars . London , Boston , 1986. 112 p. ; ISBN 0-571-14526-4 (pbk.) : LC Card 87-672358
HD9710.U52 B34 1986

AUTOMOBILES - SPECIFICATIONS.
Kiffe, Ulrich. Die Klassifizierung in der Bundesrepublik Deutschland angebotener Personenkraftwagen mit multivariaten Analysemethoden /. Münster , 1984. xx, 24, 340 p. : ISBN 3-88660-148-8 LC Card 84-208133
HD9710.G42 K48 1984

AUTOMOBILES - TAXATION - UNITED STATES.
Knepp, Jay. Tax[s]aver. Menlo Park, Calif. , c1987. 143 p. : ISBN 0-376-07015-3 (pbk.) : LC Card 86-80874 DDC 343.7305/23 347.303523 19
HJ4653.D4 K56 1987

AUTOMOBILES - TECHNOLOGICAL INNOVATIONS - HISTORY.
Bayley, Stephen. Sex, drink, and fast cars . London , Boston , 1986. 112 p. ; ISBN 0-571-14526-4 (pbk.) : LC Card 87-672358
HD9710.U52 B34 1986

AUTOMOBILES - TESTING.
(1985) Maxeiner, Dirk, 1953- Testfahrer und Autospione . Stuttgart , 1985. 214 p. : ISBN 3-613-01022-4 : LC Card 85-170273
HD9710.A2 M385 1985

AUTOMOBILES - TRADE AND STATISTICS. see **AUTOMOBILE INDUSTRY AND TRADE.**

AUTOMOBILES - UNITED STATES - CHILD RESTRAINT SYSTEMS.
Seat belts, the lifesaving habit [motion picture] /. Van Nuys, CA , 1986. 1 film reel (20 min.) : LC Card 87-705126 DDC 629.2 11
HE5614.2

Seat belts, the lifesaving habit [videorecording] /. Van Nuys, CA , 1986. 1 videocassette (20 min.) : LC Card 87-705127 DDC 629.2 11
HE5614.2

AUTOMOBILES - UNITED STATES - CHILD RESTRAINT SYSTEMS - JUVENILE FILMS.
Seat belts are for kids, too [motion picture] /. Van Nuys, CA , 1987. 1 film reel (10 min.) : LC Card 87-706618 DDC 363.1 11
HE5614.2

Seat belts are for kids, too [videorecording] /. Van Nuys, CA , 1987. 1 videocassette (10 min.) : LC Card 87-706619 DDC 363.1 11
HE5614.2

AUTOMOBILES - UNITED STATES - DESIGN AND CONSTRUCTION - HISTORY.
Bayley, Stephen. Sex, drink, and fast cars . London , Boston , 1986. 112 p. ; ISBN 0-571-14526-4 (pbk.) : LC Card 87-672358
HD9710.U52 B34 1986

AUTOMOBILES - UNITED STATES - ELECTRONIC EQUIPMENT.
The Automotive electronics market in the U. S. New York, N.Y. , c1983. vi, 262 p. : LC Card 87-142223 DDC 381/.456292549/0973 19
HD9710.3.U52 A943 1983

AUTOMOBILES - UNITED STATES - FUEL CONSUMPTION.
Halberstam, David. The reckoning /. New York , c1986. 752 p. ; ISBN 0-688-04838-2 LC Card 86-16427 DDC 338.4/76292/0973 19
HD9710.U52 H28 1986
NYPL [JLE 86-4151]

AUTOMOBILES - UNITED STATES - SEAT BELTS.
Campbell, Bob J. Early results of seat belt legislation in the United States of America /. Chapel Hill, N.C. [1986] 25 p. : LC Card 86-622836 DDC 363.1/2572/0973 19
HE5614.2 .C35 1986

Seat belts, the lifesaving habit [motion picture] /. Van Nuys, CA , 1986. 1 film reel (20 min.) : LC Card 87-705126 DDC 629.2 11
HE5614.2

Seat belts, the lifesaving habit [videorecording] /. Van Nuys, CA , 1986. 1 videocassette (20 min.) : LC Card 87-705127 DDC 629.2 11
HE5614.2

AUTOMOBILES - UNITED STATES - STATISTICS.
1986 buyers of new cars . New York, N.Y. (444 Madison Ave., New York 10022) , c1986. 2 v. : LC Card 86-229142 DDC 381/.456292/0973021 19
HD9710.U52 A17 1986

AUTOMOBILES - UNITED STATES - TECHNOLOGICAL INNOVATIONS - HISTORY.
Lewchuk, Wayne. American technology and the British vehicle industry /. Cambridge [Cambridgeshire] , New York , 1987. viii, 304 p. : ISBN 0-521-30269-2 LC Card 86-30994 DDC 338.4/56292/0941 19
HD9710.G72 L48 1987

AUTOMOBILING. see **AUTOMOBILES.**

Automotive aftermarket in the U. S. New York, N.Y. : Frost & Sullivan, c1983. 2 v. (xiii, 435 p.) ; 29 cm. "January 1983." "A915." LC Card 87-144460
1. Automobile supplies industry - United States. 2. Market surveys - United States. I. Frost & Sullivan.
HD9710.3.U52 A93 1983

The Automotive electronics market in the U. S. New York, N.Y. : Frost & Sullivan, c1983. vi, 262 p. : ill. ; 29 cm. Spine title: Non entertainment automotive electronics. "September 1983." "#A1250." LC Card 87-142223 DDC 381/.456292549/0973 19
1. Automobile supplies industry - United States. 2. Automobiles - United States - Electronic equipment. 3. Market surveys - United States. I. Frost & Sullivan. II. Title: Non entertainment automotive electronics.
HD9710.3.U52 A943 1983

AUTOMOTIVE FUELS. see **MOTOR FUELS.**

An automotive strategy for Canada . Canada. Task Force on the Canadian Motor Vehicle and Automotive Parts Industries. [Ottawa] , 1983. xv, 193 p. : ISBN 0-662-12626-2
NYPL [JLF 86-648]

AUTOMOTIVE TRANSPORTATION. see **TRANSPORTATION, AUTOMOTIVE.**

AUTOMÓVEL CLUB DO BRASIL - HISTORY.
Oliveira, Maria Chambarelli de. Achegas à história do rodoviarismo no Brasil /. Rio de Janeiro-RJ , c1986. 137 p., [1] leaf of plates : LC Card 86-232581
HE359.B7 O45 1986

Az autonómia kérdése az olasz szakszervezeti egységért folytatott küzdelemben /. Keszthelyi, Csaba. [Budapest] , 1985. 75 p. ; ISBN 963-673-322-8 LC Card 86-185901
HD6680.5.Z65 K47 1985

Autonomie als arbeidssociologisch vraagstuk : bundel aangeboden aan Prof. dr. J.A.P. van Hoof ter gelegenheid van zijn afscheid als hoogleraar in de Sociologie van Arbeid en Bedrijf aan de Katholieke Universiteit Nijmegen / onder redactie van M.J.W.M. Akkermans, H. Doorewaard, F. Huijgen. Zeist : Kerckebosch, 1987. 237 p. : ill. ; 22 cm. (Carolingia impressa . 8) Includes bibliographies. ISBN 90-6720-032-8 : LC Card 87-169950
1. Management - Netherlands - Employee participation. 2. Industrial sociology - Netherlands. 3. Autonomy. 4. Hoof, J. A. P. van. I. Akkermans, M. J. W. M. II. Doorewaard, H. (Hans). III. Huijgen, F. IV. Hoof, J. A. P. van. V. Series.
HD5660.N4 A94 1987

Autorität und Revolte . Steffens, Horst. Weingarten , c1987. 419 p. : ISBN 3-924027-47-1 LC Card 87-141439 DDC 331/.0422334/094342 19
HD8039.M61 G383 1987

Aux origines du mouvement ouvrier français . Moss, Bernard H. [Origins of the French labor movement, 1830-1914. French.] Paris , 1985. xi, 236 p. ; ISBN 2-251-60326-3
NYPL [M-10 6410 n.326]

The availability and utilization of skills in Guyana /. Abdulah, Norma. St. Augustine, Trinidad [1981] xv, 105 p. ; LC Card 84-146702 DDC 331.11/422 19
HD5759.3.A6 A24 1981
NYPL [JLE 86-4442]

Availability of federally owned minerals for exploration and development in western states . McColly, Robert A. [Avondale, Md.] , Washington, DC [1987] iv, 27 p. : LC Card 87-600086 DDC 333.8/5/09791 19
HD243.A7 M36 1987

Availability of land for mineral exploration and development in northern Alaska, 1986 /. Maas, Kenneth M. [Washington, D.C.] [1987] iv, 34 p. : LC Card 86-607920 DDC 333.73 19
HD243.A3 M32 1987

Avak'īan, Suren Adibekovich. Sovety i rukovodstvo ėkonomikoĭ : posobie dlīa slushateleĭ narodnykh universitetov / S.A. Avak'īan. Moskva : Izd-vo "Znanie", 1985. 110 p. ; 20 cm. (Narodnyĭ universitet. Fakul'tet pravovykh znaniĭ) Includes bibliographical references. LC Card 87-118114
1. Soviet Union - Economic policy - 1981-. 2. Intergovernmental fiscal relations - Soviet Union. 3. Local government - Soviet Union. I. Title. II. Series.
HC336.25 .A87 1985

Avaliação da política industrial do Ceará . Casimiro, Liana Maria Carleial de. Fortaleza , 1983. 58 p. ; LC Card 86-129541
HD3616.B84 C422 1983

Avaliação do desempenho de transporte coletivo por ônibus /. Daibert, José Ricardo Motta. Brasília, DF , 1985. 73 p. : LC Card 87-113224 DDC 388.4/1322/0981 19
HE5653.A6 D35 1985

Avaliação do polonordeste e do Projeto Sertanejo. Fortaleza : Secretaria de Planejamento da Presidência da República, Instituto de Planejamento Econômico e Social, Ministério do Interior, Superintendência do Desenvolvimento do Nordeste, Banco do Nordeste do Brasil, 1985. 314 p. : ill. ; 23 cm. (Série Projeto Nordeste . v. 15) Edited by Acúcio Alencar Araújo Filho and Antônio Enock de Vasconcelos. Includes bibliographies. LC Card 87-402900 DDC 338.981/3 19
1. Brazil, Northeast - Economic policy. 2. Brazil, Northeast - Social policy. 3. Agriculture and state - Brazil, Northeast. 4. Arid regions agriculture - Government policy - Brazil, Northeast. 5. Seca. 6. Rural development - Brazil, Northeast. I. Araújo Filho, Acúcio Alencar. II. Vasconcelos, Antônio Enock de.
HC188.N6 A94 1985

Avaliação do programa de ação, 1984/85 / Serviço Público Federal, M.T., Superintendência Nacional da Marinha Mercante. [Brasília] : Diretoria de Navegação Interior, 1985. 90 leaves : ill. ; 30 cm. LC Card 87-403938 DDC 354.810087/6/06 19
1. Brazil. Directoria de Navegação Interior. 2. Inland water transportation - Brazil. I. Brazil. Diretoria de Navegação Interior.
HE653 .A93 1985

Avaliação do Programa Nacional do Álcool / Ministério da Indústria e do Comércio, Secretaria de Tecnologia Industrial. Brasília : MIC/STI, 1985. 175 p. : ill. ; 30 cm. (Serie Documentos. 17) Includes bibliographical references. LC Card 86-146662
1. Alcohol fuel industry - Brazil. I. Brazil. Secretaria de Tecnologia Industrial. II. Series: Série Documentos (Brazil. Secretaria de Tecnologia Industrial) , 17.
HD9502.5.A433 B622 1985

Avaliação global do programa de nutrição Brasil-BIRD : terceiro relatório. [São Paulo, SP] : Instituto de Pesquisas Econômicas ; [Brasília] : Instituto Nacional de Alimentação e Nutrição, 1981- v. <1 > : ill. ; 33 cm. Includes bibliographical references. LC Card 87-123819 DDC 363.8/56/0981 19
1. Food supply - Government policy - Brazil. 2. Nutrition policy - Brazil. I. Universidad de São Paulo.

Instituto de Pesquisas Econômicas. II. INAN (Institute : Brazil).
HD9014.B82 A82 1981

Avance de investigación .
(no. 56) Propuesta para el desarrollo de un programa de investigación sobre propiedad social con énfasis en cooperativismo /. San José, Costa Rica , 1986. ii, 70 p. : LC Card 87-125056 DDC 334/.097286 19
HD3454.A4 P76 1986

Avance de resultados, encuesta de fecundidad y salud / Associación Demográfica Costarricense, Departamento de Investigaciones Sociodemográficas. [San José] Costa Rica : El Departamento, 1986. [32] leaves : ill. (some col.) ; 28 cm. One col. chart laid in. "EFES-86." LC Card 87-400666 DDC 304.6/32/097286 19
1. Fertility, Human - Costa Rica. 2. Public health - Costa Rica. I. Asociación Demográfica Costarricense. Departamento de Investigaciones Sociodemográficas. II. Title: Encuesta de fecundidad y salud.
HB947 .A96 1986

Avances de de investigación (Universidad de Lima. Centro de Investigaciones Económicas y Sociales) .
(5) Rocha C., Julio César de la (Rocha Corzo) Un análisis de la rentabilidad accionaria de la Bolsa de Valores de Lima, 1980-1983 /. Lima, Perú , 1984. ii, 56 p. ; LC Card 86-154699
HG5392 .R66 1984

Avances de investigación (Havana, Cuba) .
(no. 11) Fernández Tabío, Luis René. Apuntes sobre el capital financiero en Estados Unidos . La Habana , 1981 [i.e. 1982] ii, 74 p. : LC Card 87-401153
HG5851.A3 F47 1982

(no. 13) Notas críticas sobre el plan Reagan para la cuenca del Caribe /. La Habana , 1982. 84 p. ; LC Card 87-400638 DDC 337.729073 19
HF1456.5.C27 N67 1982

(no. 14) Fernández Tabío, Luis René. Los intereses económicos en la producción militar de los Estados Unidos /. La Habana , 1982. ii, 87 p. : LC Card 87-400639 DDC 338.4/76234/0973 19
HD9743.U6 F46 1982

(no. 17) Hernández, Rafael. Estados Unidos y América Latina . La Habana , 1982. 209 p. : LC Card 87-403785 DDC 333.8/232/0973 19
HD9574.L3 H47 1982

Avances de investigación (Universidad de Lima. Centro de Investigaciones Económicas y Sociales) .
(6) Beltrán Alejos, Hugo. La situación del sector metal-mecánico en el Perú . Lima, Perú , 1985. 93, [77] p. : LC Card 86-218266
HD9506.P42 B45 1985

(7) Hinojosa Tapia, Juan. La problemática de los almacenes generales de depósito como instituciones financieras no bancarias en el Perú (1970-1983) /. Lima, Perú , 1985. iii, 29, [43] p. : LC Card 86-218257
HG3751.9.P4 H56 1985

(8) Ycaza Clerc, Mónica de. Política de endeudamiento público interno en el Perú . Lima, Perú , 1985. ii, 23, [39] p. : LC Card 86-223472
HJ8604 .Y33 1985

(9) Alcalde Cardoza, Xavier. El poder norteamericano y la renegociación de la deuda externa brasileña, 1982-1983 /. Lima, Perú , 1985. 62 p. ; LC Card 86-223475
HJ8579 .A44 1985

Avdem, Anna Jorunn, 1952- Oppe først og sist i seng : husarbeid i Norge fra 1850 til i dag / Anna Jorunn Avdem og Kari Melby.2. oppl. Oslo : Universitetsforlaget, 1985. 190 p. : ill. ; 27 cm. Bibliography: p. 186-189. ISBN 82-00-07512-5 LC Card 86-175305
1. Housewives - Norway. 2. Women - Norway - Social conditions. I. Melby, Kari. II. Title.
HD8039.H842 N82 1985

Avena Filho, Armando. Nordeste e Bahia : os caminhos do desenvolvimento / Armando Avena Filho. Salvador : Universidade Católica do Salvador, 1986. 196 p. ; 22 cm. Essays and articles previously published in various journals including A Tarde and Gazeta mercantil, 1983-1986. Cover title: Nordeste/Bahia. Includes bibliographical references. LC Card 87-403867 DDC 338.981/42 19
1. Bahia, Brazil (State) - Economic policy. 2. Brazil, Northeast - Economic policy. I. Title. II. Title: Nordeste/Bahia.
HC188.B3 A94 1986

L'Avenir économique de la Belgique : un rapport à la Fondation Roi Baudouin. [Bruxelles : La Fondation, 1981] 155 p. ; 24 cm. Report prepared by the Commission "Avenir économique de la Belgique." Includes bibliographical references. LC Card 87-672443
1. Belgium - Economic conditions - 1945-. 2. Economic forecasting - Belgium. I. Commission "Avenir économique de la Belgique.". II. Fondation Roi Baudouin.
HC315 .A93x 1981

L'Avenir national des capteurs à fibres optiques / CIAME, Commission industrie-administration pour la mesure. Paris : Documentation française, c1984. 42 p. : ill. ; 30 cm. ISBN 2-11-001350-8 LC Card 85-232999
1. Fiber optics industry - France. I. France. Commission industrie-administration pour la mesure.
HD9696.F523 F82 1984

Average producers' prices of agricultural commodities in rural area by region, Miazia 1973-Miazia 1974, (May 1981-April 1982) / the Provisional Military Government of Socialist Ethiopia, Office of the National Committee for Central Planning, Central Statistical Office. Addis Ababa : The Office, 1985. 14 leaves ; 29 cm. (Statistical bulletin . 44) "May 1985." Chiefly tables. LC Card 85-981293 DDC 338.1/3/0963021 19
1. Agricultural prices - Ethiopia - Statistics. I. Ethiopia. Central Statistical Office. II. Series: Statistical bulletin (Ethiopia. Central Statistical Office) , 44.
HD2124.5 .A93 1985

Averchev, V. P. Upravlencheskie novovvedeniia v SShA . Moskva , 1986. 244, [3] p. : LC Card 86-231514
HD70.U5 U67 1986

O avesso da moda . Abreu, Alice R. de Paiva. São Paulo , 1986. 302 p. ; LC Card 87-129109 DDC 331.4/887/098153 19
HD6073.C62 B62 1986

AVG/SGB. Germany (West) [Angestelltenversicherungsgesetz.] Angestelltenversicherungsgesetz mit Sozialgesetzbuch . Berlin [1986] 792 p. ; LC Card 86-229132
HD7116.M42 G4334 Nr. 18, 1986 KK3270.5

Āvhāna āṇi āvāhana /. Pāṭila, Narendra. Mumbaī , 1986. 110 p., [13] p. of plates : LC Card 87-900853
HC437.M32 P38 1986

La aviación comercial en Venezuela, de la carreta al avión /. Pacanins A., Guillermo (Pacanins Acevedo) Caracas , 1985. 159 p. : LC Card 85-184048
HE9841.A3 P33 1985

AVIATION. see **AERONAUTICS.**

AVIATION INDUSTRY. see **AIR LINES.**

Aviation insurance /. Rollo, Vera A. Foster. Lanham, Md. , 1987. x, 438 p. : ISBN 0-917882-22-9 LC Card 86-62107 DDC 368/.093/0973 19
HG9972.3 .R65 1987

AVIATION LAW. see **AERONAUTICS - LAW AND LEGISLATION.**

AVIATION REGULATION. see **AERONAUTICS - LAW AND LEGISLATION.**

AVIATORS. see **AIR PILOTS.**

Avila, Luiz Gonçalves. Desenvolvimento industrial e rendimento da terra : um estudo de caso / Luiz Gonçalves Avila.1a. ed. Rio de Janeiro, RJ : FGV-Instituto de Documentação, Editora da Fundação Getúlio Vargas, 1985. 111 p. : ill. ; 21 cm. (Série Teses. no. 11) Originally presented as the author's thesis (doctoral)--Escola de Pós-Graduação em Economia. Bibliography: p. 101-106. Includes index. LC Card 86-233493
1. Farm income - Brazil - Santa Catarina (State). 2. Farm income - Brazil - Paraná (State). 3. Santa Catarina, Brazil (State) - Industries. 4. Paraná, Brazil (State) - Industries. 5. Corn industry - Brazil - Sanata Catarina (State). 6. Corn industry - Brazil - Paraná (State). I. Series: Série Teses (Escola de Pós-Graduação em Economia) , no. 11. II. Title.
HD1875.S26 A95 1985

AVIONS MARCEL DASSAULT BREGUET AVIATION - HISTORY.
Déplante, Henri, 1907- A la conquête du ciel /. Aix-en-Provence [1985] 233 p. ; LC Card 86-159140
HD9711.F74 D374 1985

Avis et recommandations au Premier ministre et au Ministre de l'agriculture et de l'alimentation. Conseil de planification et de développement du Québec. Le réseau décisionnel en agro-alimentation au Québec . [Québec] [1979] 29 p. ; LC Card 85-102587
HD9014.C4 Q425 1979

AVIS-RENT-A-CAR SYSTEM.
Avis, Warren E. Take a chance to be first . New York , 1987, c1986. xii, 222 p. ; ISBN 0-07-002547-9 (pbk.) : LC Card 87-13236 DDC 650.1 19
HF5386 .A94 1987

Avis, Warren E. Take a chance to be first : the secrets of entrepreneurial success / Warren Avis.1st McGraw-Hill paperback ed. New York : McGraw-Hill, 1987, c1986. xii, 222 p. ; 21 cm. Includes index. ISBN 0-07-002547-9 (pbk.) : LC Card 87-13236 DDC 650.1 19
1. Success in business. 2. Avis-Rent-A-Car System. I. Title.
HF5386 .A94 1987

Avolio, Giuseppe. L'Imprenditore coltivatore nella società che cambia . [Italy] [1983] (Roma : Arti grafiche Jasillo) 364 p. : LC Card 86-185731
HD1972 .I44 1983

Avrekh, G. L. (Gennadiĭ Lipanovich) Ėkonomika na urovne molekul / G.L. Avrekh, E.B. T͡Syrkin, E.P. Shchukin. Moskva : "Khimii͡a", 1986. 141 p. : ill. ; 20 cm. LC Card 86-179247
1. Chemical industry - Soviet Union. 2. Petroleum chemicals industry - Soviet Union. I. T͡Syrkin, E. B. (Efim Borisovich). II. Shchukin, E. P. (Evgeniĭ Petrovich). III. Title.
HD9656.S55 A95 1986

Avtomatizat͡sii͡a upravlenii͡a transportnymi sistemami / otvetstvennyĭ redaktor A.A. Voronov ; [Aleksandr Petrovich Artynov ... et al.]. Moskva : Izd-vo "Nauka", 1984. 271 p. : ill. ; 23 cm. At head of title: Akademii͡a nauk SSSR. Dal′nevostochnyĭ nauchnyĭ t͡sentr. Institut avtomatiki i prot͡sessov upravlenii͡a s vychislitel′nym t͡sentrom. Bibliography: p. 256-[267] LC Card 84-195421
1. Transportation - Soviet Union - Management - Mathematical models. I. Voronov, A. A. II. Artynov, Aleksandr Petrovich. III. Institut avtomatiki i prot͡sessov upravlenii͡a s vychislitel′nym t͡sentrom (Akademii͡a nauk SSSR).
HE255 .A93 1984

Avtomatizirovannai͡a obrabotka uchetnoĭ informat͡sii v sel′skokhozi͡aĭstvennykh predprii͡atii͡akh /. Vasil′ev, A. F. (Alekseĭ Fedorovich) Moskva , 1984. 198 p. ; LC Card 85-113739
HF5686.A36 V37 1984

AWV-Schrift .
(Nr. 252) Bendeich, E. (Eugen), 1945- Wirtschaftliche Datenerfassung in Klein- und Mittelbetrieben . München , c1979. 211 p. : ISBN 3-478-41740-6 LC Card 85-171162
HD62.7 .B4 1979

AWWA Seminar on the Rate Making Process: Going Beyond the Cost of Service (1986 : Denver, Colo.) Proceedings / AWWA Seminar on the Rate Making Process: Going Beyond the Cost of Service, Annual Conference, Denver, CO, June 22, 1986 ; sponsored by the Management Division, American Water Works Association. Denver, CO : AWWA, c1986. vi, 58 p. ; 23 cm. (AWWA seminar proceedings) Cover title: The rate making process : going beyond the cost of service. Includes index. ISBN 0-89867-368-2 (pbk.) LC Card 87-107641 DDC 338.4/336361/0973 19
1. Municipal water supply - United States - Rates - Congresses. 2. Municipal water supply - United States - Congresses. I. American Water Works Association. Management Division. II. Title. III. Title: Rate making process : going beyond the cost of service. IV. Series.
HD4461 .A915 1986

AWWA seminar proceedings.
AWWA Seminar on the Rate Making Process: Going Beyond the Cost of Service (1986 : Denver, Colo.) Proceedings /. Denver, CO , c1986. vi, 58 p. ; ISBN 0-89867-368-2 (pbk.) LC

Card 87-107641 DDC 338.4/336361/0973 19
HD4461 .A915 1986

Axe économique au Ier siècle avant J.-C. Roman, Yves. De Narbonne à Bordeaux . Lyon , c1983. 333 p. : ISBN 2-7297-0200-8 : LC Card 84-179554
HF377 .R65 1983

Axe économique au premier siècle avant J.-C. Roman, Yves. De Narbonne à Bordeaux . Lyon , c1983. 333 p. : ISBN 2-7297-0200-8 : LC Card 84-179554
HF377 .R65 1983

Axe économique au 1er siècle avant J.-C. Roman, Yves. De Narbonne à Bordeaux . Lyon , c1983. 333 p. : ISBN 2-7297-0200-8 : LC Card 84-179554
HF377 .R65 1983

Axel, Helen. Corporate strategies for controlling substance abuse /. New York, N.Y. , c1986. xi, 50 p. ; ISBN 0-8237-0327-4 (pbk.) LC Card 86-207704 DDC 658.3/82 19
HF5549.5.E42 C66 1986

AXIOLOGY. see **VALUES.**

Ayacucho . Díaz Martínez, Antonio, 1933- Lima , 1985. xvi, 224 p. ; LC Card 86-134530
HC228.A9 D5 1985

AYACUCHO, PERU (DEPT.) - ECONOMIC CONDITIONS.
Díaz Martínez, Antonio, 1933- Ayacucho . Lima , 1985. xvi, 224 p. ; LC Card 86-134530
HC228.A9 D5 1985

AYACUCHO, PERU (DEPT.) - SOCIAL CONDITIONS.
Díaz Martínez, Antonio, 1933- Ayacucho . Lima , 1985. xvi, 224 p. ; LC Card 86-134530
HC228.A9 D5 1985

Ayala, Eligio. Evolución de la economía agraria en el Paraguay : ensayo escrito en Berna, Suiza, de junio a julio de 1915 / Eligio Ayala. Asunción, Paraguay : Editorial Histórica : Fundacíon Friedrich Naumann, 1986. 196 p. : ill. ; 20 cm. Bibliography: p. [187]-188. LC Card 86-234615
1. Agriculture and state - Paraguay - History. 2. Agriculture - Economic aspects - Paraguay - History. I. Title.
HD1898 1986 .A92

Ayau, Manuel F. Cómo mejorar el nivel de vida / Manuel F. Ayau C., Gonzalo Asturias Montenegro. 1a ed. [Guatemala : s.n., 1982] (Guatemala : Editorial Piedra Santa) 91 p. : ill. (some col.) ; 16 x 22 cm. LC Card 86-174413
1. Economics. 2. Economic development. I. Asturias Montenegro, G. II. Title.
HB178.5 .A93 1982

Aymans, Gerhard. Beiträge zur empirischen Wirtschaftsgeographie /. Bonn , c1986. 238 p. : ISBN 3-427-74191-5 LC Card 87-104279 DDC 330.9 19
HF1025 .B3495 1986

Ayoub, Éliane Guichard- see **Guichard-Ayoub, Éliane.**

Az Alapszervezeti munka gyakorlata, 0231-2786. Várkonyi, Margit. A vezetők véleményezése /. Budapest , 1984. 66 p. : ISBN 963-322-189-7 : LC Card 85-176949
HD70.H8 V38 1984

AZ of UK marketing information sources. Shaw, Christine. The A-Z of UK marketing information sources /. London , 1984. 233 p. ; ISBN 0-86338-048-4 (pbk.) : LC Card 84-217782 DDC 330.941/0858 19
HC256.6 .S47 1984 ***NYPL [JLD 86-2248]***

Az OKBT Tudományos Kutatási Szakbizottság kezdeményezése, illetve megbízása alapján készült kutatások, 1973-1983 / [kidolgozta, Csúcs Andrásné]. [Budapest] : OKBT Titkársága, 1983. 124 p. : ill. ; 20 cm. (Tudomány és közlekedés . 8) Summaries in English, German, Hungarian and Russian. ISBN 963-02-3169-7 (Magy. nemz. bibl.) LC Card 85-126922
1. Traffic safety - Hungary. 2. Traffic safety - Research - Hungary. I. Csúcs, Andrásné. II. OKBT Tudományos Kutatási Szakbizottság (Hungary). III. Series.
HE5614.5.H8 O38 1983
NYPL [JLD 87-1181]

AZĂRBAĬJAN KOMMUNIST PARTIIASY - PARTY WORK.
Aliev, Geĭdar Alievich. Vsiu organizatorskuiu i politicheskuiu rabotu--na vypolnenie resheniĭ XXVI s"ezda KPSS . Baku , 1981. 50 p. ; LC Card 82-158175
HC337.A9 A683 1981

AZARBĀYJĀN-I BĀKHTARĪ (IRAN) - ECONOMIC CONDITIONS.
Sāzmān-i Barnāmah (Iran) Feeder Road Programme . Tehran [1961?] ii, 117, 9 leaves, [59] leaves of plates (some folded) : LC Card 85-211363
HE365.I73 R857 1961

AZARBĀYJĀN-I BĀKHTARĪ (IRAN) - POPULATION.
Sāzmān-i Barnāmah (Iran) Feeder Road Programme . Tehran [1961?] ii, 117, 9 leaves, [59] leaves of plates (some folded) : LC Card 85-211363
HE365.I73 R857 1961

AZARBĀYJĀN-I KHĀVARĪ (IRAN) - ECONOMIC CONDITIONS.
Sāzmān-i Barnāmah (Iran) Feeder Road Programme . Tehran [1961?] ii, 117, 9 leaves, [59] leaves of plates (some folded) : LC Card 85-211363
HE365.I73 R857 1961

AZARBĀYJĀN-I KHĀVARĪ (IRAN) - POPULATION.
Sāzmān-i Barnāmah (Iran) Feeder Road Programme . Tehran [1961?] ii, 117, 9 leaves, [59] leaves of plates (some folded) : LC Card 85-211363
HE365.I73 R857 1961

Azbel', B. M. (Boris Moiseevich) Taganskiĭ, B. M. (Boris Mikhaĭlovich) Ėkonomicheskiĭ analiz v stroitel'stve /. Moskva , 1986. 148, [4] p. : LC Card 86-227177
HD9715.S72 T35 1986

Azbuka ėkonomicheskoĭ nauki. Majandusteaduse ABC . Tallinn , 1985. 511 p. : LC Card 85-195109
HB61 .M225 1985

Azcárate, Blanca, 1954- Ursachen, Umfang und Auswirkungen der Abwanderung im ländlichen Bereich Galiciens am Beispiel der Provinz Orense / Blanca Azcárate. Frankfurt am Main ; New York : Lang, c1985. 213 p. : ill. ; 21 cm. (Europäische Hochschulschriften. Reihe IV, Geographie und Heimatkunde, 0721-331X . Bd. 8 = vol. 8 = vol. 8) Bibliography: p. 190-213. ISBN 3-8204-8166-4 LC Card 85-190546
1. Labor and laboring classes - Spain - Orense. 2. Alien labor, Spanish. 3. Orense (Spain : Province) - Emigration and immigration. 4. Orense (Spain : Province) - Population, Rural. I. Title.
HD8589.O74 A92 1985

AZERBAIJAN S.S.R. - ECONOMIC CONDITIONS.
Ismailov, Makhmud. Sotsial'no-ėkonomicheskaia struktura Azerbaĭdzhana v ėpokhu imperializma /. Baku , 1982. 163 p. ; LC Card 83-189608
HC337.A9 I85 1982

Sămădzadă, Z. (Ziiad) Onunju beshillikdă Sovet Azărbaĭjanynyn igtisadi vă sosial inkishafy /. Baky , 1981. 237 p. ; LC Card 82-153126
HC337.A9 S32 1981

AZERBAIJAN S.S.R. - ECONOMIC POLICY.
Aliev, Geĭdar Alievich. Vsiu organizatorskuiu i politicheskuiu rabotu--na vypolnenie resheniĭ XXVI s"ezda KPSS . Baku , 1981. 50 p. ; LC Card 82-158175
HC337.A9 A683 1981

AZERBAIJAN S.S.R. - INDUSTRIES - HISTORY.
Ismailov, Makhmud. Sotsial'no-ėkonomicheskaia struktura Azerbaĭdzhana v ėpokhu imperializma /. Baku , 1982. 163 p. ; LC Card 83-189608
HC337.A9 I85 1982

AZERBAIJAN S.S.R. - SOCIAL CONDITIONS.
Sămădzadă, Z. (Ziiad) Onunju beshillikdă Sovet Azărbaĭjanynyn igtisadi vă sosial inkishafy /. Baky , 1981. 237 p. ; LC Card 82-153126
HC337.A9 S32 1981

AZERBAIJANI LANGUAGE - TEXTS.
Lenin, Vladimir Il'ich, 1870-1924. [Imperializm kak Vysshaia stadiia kapitalizma. Azerbaijani.] Imperijalizm kapitalizmin ăn jeni devri gibi [microform] /. Baqï , 1927. 99 p. ;
NYPL [*ZO-247 no. 1]

Azevedo, Beatriz Regina Zago de. O Emprego no Rio Grande do Sul . Porto Alegre , 1985. 163 p. : LC Card 85-207909
HD5755.R54 E46 1985

Azevedo, Edilza Araújo. Causas de evasão. [Campina Grande, Brasil] : SENAI, Departamento Regional da Paraíba, Divisão de Planejamento e Avaliação, 1984. 104 leaves : ill. ; 31 cm. Cover title. LC Card 85-203901
1. Occupational training - Brazil - Paraíba (State). 2. School attendance - Brazil - Paraíba (State). I. Brazil. Serviço Nacional de Aprendizagem Industrial. Departamento Regional da Paraíba. Divisão de Planejamento e Avaliação. II. Title.
HD5715.5.B69 P335 1984

Azevedo, J. Cândido de. Portugal, Europa face ao Mercado Comum : dossier da adesão de Portugal à CEE / J. Cândido de Azevedo. Amadora : Livraria Bertrand, c1978. 300 p. ; 21 cm. (Documentos de todos os tempos) Appendix (p. [215]-300) includes parliamentary debates, etc. Bibliography: p. [208]-211. LC Card 80-121153
1. European Economic Community - Portugal. 2. Agriculture - Economic aspects - Portugal. 3. Agriculture - Economic aspects - European Economic Community countries. 4. Socialism - Portugal. 5. Socialism - Europe. I. Title.
HC241.25.P6 A94 1978

Azfar, Jawaid, 1939-1983. Employment, distribution, and basic needs in Pakistan . Lahore , 1986. xxxiv, 408 p., [1] leaf of plates : LC Card 86-930280 DDC 330.9549/1 19
HD5820.5.A6 E47 1986

AZFAR, JAWAID, 1939-1983.
Employment, distribution, and basic needs in Pakistan . Lahore , 1986. xxxiv, 408 p., [1] leaf of plates : LC Card 86-930280 DDC 330.9549/1 19
HD5820.5.A6 E47 1986

Le aziende di credito . Franchini, Augusto. Bologna , <1986-. v. <2 > ; LC Card 87-170318
HG3751 .F73 1986

Aziz, Abdul, 1937-
Labour problems of a developing economy / Abdul Aziz. New Delhi : Ashish Pub. House, c1984. viii, 157 p. ; 22 cm. Includes bibliographical references and index. LC Card 84-901201 DDC 331/.0954 19
1. Labor and laboring classes - India - Addresses, essays, lectures. 2. Labor policy - India - Addresses, essays, lectures. I. Title.
HD8686.5 .A95 1984 ***NYPL [JLD 86-4216]***

The rural poor : problems and prospects / by Abdul Aziz. New Delhi : Ashish Pub. House, 1983. 92 p. ; 22 cm. Includes bibliographical references and index. LC Card 83-906454 DDC 330.954/052/08806942 19
1. Rural poor - India. 2. Rural development - India. I. Title.
HC440.P6 A98 1983 ***NYPL [JLD 87-544]***

Thimmaiah, G. The political economy of land reforms /. New Delhi [1983?] xiii, 94 p. ; LC Card 84-900237 DDC 333.3/1/5487 19
HD1333.I42 K3778 1983
NYPL [JLD 87-752]

Azizur Rahman Khan. see **Khan, Azizur Rahman.**

AZORES - ECONOMIC POLICY.
Casaca, José Paulo Martins. O papel do sector leiteiro no desenvolvimento económico dos Açores . Ponta Delgada , 1985. 260, [16] p., [1] leaf of plates : LC Card 86-167454
HD9282.A962 C37 1985

Azouaou, Alain. La Silicon Valley, un marché aux puces / Alain Azouaou, Robert Magnaval. Paris : Ramsay, c1986. 237 p. : ill. ; 22 cm. Bibliography: p. 229-[232]. ISBN 2-85956-494-2 : LC Card 86-217069
1. Microelectronics industry - California - Santa Clara County. 2. Santa Clara County (Calif.) - Economic conditions. I. Magnaval, Robert. II. Title.
HD9696.A3 U516 1986

Azouvi, A. Pour un rôle actif de la Communauté économique européenne sur la scène agricole internationale . Paris , c1986. 184 p. ; ISBN 2-11-001582-9 : LC Card 86-174918
HD1431 .P68 1986

Azqueta Oyarzun, Diego.
Teoría de los precios sociales / Diego Azqueta Oyarzun. Alcala de Henares-Madrid, España : Instituto Nacional de Administración Pública, [1985?] 250 p. : ill. ; 19 cm. (Colección Biblioteca

básica de administración pública. Serie especial) Bibliography: p. 241-245. ISBN 84-7351-181-6 : LC Card 87-105447
1. Externalities (Economics). I. Title. II. Series.
HB846.3 .A97 1985

Teoría económica de la acumulación socialista : análisis de dos experiencias históricas, URSS (1927-32) y China (1949-62) / Diego Azqueta Oyarzun ; prólogo de Julio Segura.1a ed. Madrid : H. Blume, 1983. 224 p. ; 22 cm. (Economía) Bibliography: p. [218]-224. ISBN 84-7214-279-5 LC Card 84-140278 DDC 332/.0415/091717 19
1. Saving and investment - Communist countries - Case studies. 2. Saving and investment - Russia. 3. Saving and investment - China. 4. Russia - Economic policy. 5. China - Economic policy. I. Series: Economía (H. Blume Ediciones). II. Title.
HC710.S3 A97 1983 ***NYPL [JLD 86-1859]***

Azúcar . Rojas Senisse, Hugo. Lima [Lima?] [1984] 131 p. : LC Card 84-234204 DDC 338.1/7361/0985 19
HD9114.P52 R65 1984
NYPL [JLD 85-1982]

Azúcar y haitianos en la República Dominicana /. Madruga, José Manuel. Santo Domingo , 1986. 202 p. : LC Card 87-125442 DDC 331.6/2/729407293 19
HD9114.D62 M33 1986

Azúcar y política en Costa Rica /. Achío Tacsan, Mayra. San José , c1985. 172 p. : ISBN 997-7231-67-2 LC Card 86-209103
HD9114.C82 A24 1985

Azykova, É. K. Sipozium "Geografiia v Kirgizii" (1980 : Frunze, Kirghiz S.S.R.) Sovremennye problemy geografii Kirgizii . Frunze , 1980. 167 p. : LC Card 82-121674
HC337.K545 S56 1980

Azzarini, Alvaro. Producción y comercialización porcina en Uruguay . Montevideo , 1986. 91 p. : LC Card 87-401290 DDC 338.1/764/009895 19
HD9435.U82 P76 1986

Azzolini, Riccardo. Politica monetaria e debito pubblico . Milano, Italy , c1984. 209 p. : LC Card 85-111306 DDC 332.4/945 19
HJ8678 .P65 1984 ***NYPL [JLD 86-1207]***

Azzoni, Carlos Roberto. Indústria e reversão da polarização no Brasil / Carlos Roberto Azzoni. São Paulo : Instituto de Pesquisas Econômicas, 1986. 176 p. : ill. ; 22 cm. (Série Ensaios econômicos . no. 58) Bibliography: p. 167-176. LC Card 87-138915 DDC 338.6/042/0981 19
1. Brazil - Industries - Location. 2. Brazil - Economic conditions - 1918- - Regional disparities. I. Series: Ensaios econômicos (Universidade de São Paulo. Instituto de Pesquisas Econômicas) , 58. II. Title.
HC190.D5 A99 1986

B. B. C. see **British Broadcasting Corporation.**

B.B.P. safety management handbook. The BBP safety management handbook. Waterford, CT , c1986. 1 v. (various pagings) : ISBN 0-87622-050-2 LC Card 87-119198 DDC 658.3/82 19
HD7262 .B38 1986

B. D. I. see **Bundesverband der Deutschen Industrie.**

B. I. R. D. see **International Bank for Reconstruction and Development.**

B. L. M. C. see **British Leyland Motor Corporation.**

B. N. H. see **Banco Nacional da Habitação.**

B-P RDP (Project : Sierra Leone) Yearwood, John. Storage facilities in the chiefdoms of Bo and Pujehun District /. Bo [1983] vi, 31 leaves : LC Card 87-110214 DDC 338.1/6 19
HD9017.S53 B599 1983

BRDE. see **Banco Regional de Desenvolvimento do Extremo sul.**

B. U. L. O. G. see **Indonesia. Badan Urusan Logistik.**

Baade, Fritz, 1893-
[Wettlauf zum Jahre 2000. English]
The race to the year 2000, our future: a paradise or the suicide of mankind. Translated from the German by Ernst Pawel. With a foreword by James P. Warburg.[1st ed. in the U. S.A.] Garden City, N.Y., Doubleday, 1962. xix, 246 p. illus. 22 cm. Includes bibliography. LC Card 62-7600 DDC 330.9/04 19
1. Economic history - 1945-. 2. Economic forecasting. 3. Population. 4. Population forecasting. 5. Twentieth century - Forecasts. 6. Economic development. 7. World politics - 1945-. I. Title.
HC59 .B2513 1962

Baba, Marietta L. Business and industrial anthropology : an overview / Marietta L. Baba. Washington, D.C. : National Association for the Practice of Anthropology, American Anthropological Association, c1986. vii, 48 p. ; 23 cm. (NAPA bulletin . 2) Bibliography: p. 38-45. ISBN 0-913167-16-9 (pbk.) : LC Card 86-26602 DDC 302.3/5 19
1. Corporate culture. 2. Applied anthropology. I. National Association for the Practice of Anthropology (U. S.). II. Title. III. Series.
HD58.7 .B33 1986

Baba Nakao, Luis. Ahorro interno y el sistema financiero /. [Lima, Peru] , 1986. 70 p. : LC Card 87-127322 DDC 332/.0985 19
HC230.S3 A38 1986

Babaev, Akmyrat. Sovkhozyn̄g shu gúni ve geljegi / Akmyrat Babaev. Ashgabat : "Tùrkmenistan" neshiriaty, 1982. 55 p. : ill. ; 17 cm. In Turkmen. Title in colophon: Nastoiashchee i budushchee sovkhoza. LC Card 84-126905
1. State farms - Turkmen S.S.R. I. Title. II. Title: Nastoiashchee i budushchee sovkhoza.
HD1493.S652 T873 1982

Babakov, V. M. (Viktor Mikhaĭlovich) Protsent sverkh plana / V.M. Babakov. Volgograd : Nizhne-Volzhskoe knizhnoe izd-vo, 1986. 45 p. : ill. ; 17 cm. Includes bibliographical references. LC Card 86-220320
1. Socialist competition - Soviet Union. 2. Labor productivity - Soviet Union. I. Title.
HC340.S6 B23 1986

Babashkina, M. L. Aktual'nye ėkonomicheskie i sotsial'nye problemy malykh stran Severnoĭ Evropy : nauchno-analiticheskiĭ obzor / [obzor podgotovlen Otdelom kapitalisticheskikh stran Evropy i Severnŏi Ameriki ; avtor obzora M.L. Babashkina ; otvetstvennyĭ redaktor É.K. Khizhnyĭ]. Moskva : Akademiia nauk SSSR, In-t nauch. informatsii po obshchestvennym naukam, 1986. 71 p. ; 20 cm. (Seriia Sotsial'no-ėkonomicheskie problemy razvitykh kapitalisticheskikh stran) Bibliography: p. 67-71. LC Card 87-166353
1. Scandinavia - Economic conditions. 2. Scandinavia - Industries. 3. Scandinavia - Social conditions. I. Khizhnyĭ, É. K. II. Institut nauchnoĭ informatsii po obshchestvennym naukam (Akademiia nauk SSSR). Otdel kapitalisticheskikh stran Evropy i Severnoĭ Ameriki. III. Title. IV. Series.
HC343 .B34 1986

Baber, Colin. Modern South Wales . Cardiff , Atlantic Highlands, N.J. , 1986. ix, 324 p. : ISBN 0-7083-0943-7 LC Card 86-226166 DDC 330.9429/4085 19
HC257.W3 M63 1986

Babić, Bogdan. Statistički informacioni sistem SR Srbije u društvenom sistemu informisanja republike : razvoj, sadašnje stanje, i perspektive od 1985. do 1990. godine / [Bogdan Babić]. Beograd : Socijalistička Republika Srbija, Republički zavod za statistiku, 1986- v. <1 > ; 23 cm. In Serbo-Croatian (roman). Bibliography: v. 1, p. 137-138. CONTENTS. - 1. Opšti deo. LC Card 87-168381
1. Serbia - Statistical services. 2. Yugoslavia - Statistical services. 3. Serbia - Statistical services - Law and legislation. 4. Yugoslavia - Statistical services - Law and legislation. I. Republički zavod za statistiku SR Srbije. II. Title.
HA37.Y83 S43 1986

Babić, Ljubo. Review of exporters and importers of Yugoslavia . Zagreb , 1965. ca. 650 p. : LC Card 84-149403
HF3732.3 .R46 1965

Babkin, S. K. Gazovyĭ most . Sverdlovsk , 1985. 206 p. : LC Card 86-186324
HD9581.S653 S54 1985

Babosov, Evgeniĭ Mikhaĭlovich. XXVII s"ezd KPSS o strategii uskoreniia sotsial'no-ėkonomicheskogo razvitiia strany / E.M. Babosov. Minsk : "Nauka i tekhnika", 1987. 124 p. ; 20 cm. At head of title: Akademiia nauk Belorusskoĭ SSR. Institut filosofii i prava. Includes bibliographical references. LC Card 87-166221
1. Byelorussian S.S.R. - Economic policy. 2. Soviet Union - Economic policy - 1981-. 3. Industrial productivity - Byelorussian S.S.R. 4. Industrial productivity - Soviet Union. I. Title.
HC337.B93 B33 1987

Babson-United Investment Advisors. Successful investing . New York , 1987. 529 p. : ISBN 0-671-64762-8 (pbk.) : LC Card 87-19736 DDC 332.6/78 19
HG4521 .S823 1987

BABY BOOM GENERATION - UNITED STATES.
Delli Carpini, Michael X., 1953- Stability and change in American politics . New York , 1986. xxv, 374 p. ; ISBN 0-8147-1780-2 (alk. paper) : LC Card 85-15348 DDC 323/.042/0973 19
JK1764 .D45 1986 ***NYPL [JLE 86-2183]***

Lewis, William, 1946- Fast-track careers . New York , c1987. x, 212 p. ; ISBN 0-471-83801-2 (pbk.) : LC Card 87-10045 DDC 331.7/02/0973 19
HF5382.5.U5 L45 1987

BABY FOODS INDUSTRY - POLITICAL ASPECTS.
Chetley, Andrew. The politics of baby foods . London , 1986. xv, 189 p. ; ISBN 0-86187-293-2
NYPL [JLE 86-2969]

Bacaria, Jordi. Clavera, Joan. La viticultura catalana davant la integració a la Comunitat Europea /. [Barcelona] [1986] 124 p. : ISBN 6-476-84021-8 LC Card 86-200618
HD9259.G7 S693 1986

Bacellar, Nely Robles Reis. Marsiglia, Cecília. S/A Central Elétrica Rio Claro /. São Paulo , 1986. 105 p. : LC Card 87-404945 DDC 363.6/2/098161 19
HD9685.B83 C4886 1986

Bach, George Leland, 1915-
Economics : analysis, decision making, and policy / George Leland Bach ; with Robert Flanagan ... [et al.].11th ed. Englewood Cliffs, N.J. : Prentice-Hall, c1987. xv, 752 p. : col. ill. ; 24 cm. Includes bibliographies and index. ISBN 0-13-227240-7 LC Card 86-25576 DDC 330.1 19
1. Economics. 2. Economic policy. I. Title.
HB171.5 .B13 1987

[Economics. Selections]
Macroeconomics : analysis, decision making, and policy / George Leland Bach with Robert Flanagan ... [et al.].11th ed. Englewood Cliffs, N.J. : Prentice-Hall, c1987. xiii, 458 p. : ill. (some col.) ; 24 cm. Includes bibliographical references and indexes. Selections from the author's Economics, 11th ed., 1987. ISBN 0-13-542887-4 (pbk.) LC Card 86-30264 DDC 339 19
1. Macroeconomics. I. Flanagan, Robert J. II. Title.
HB172.5 .B33 1987

Microeconomics : analysis, decision making, and policy / George Leland Bach ; with Robert Flanagan ... [et al.].11th ed. Englewood Cliffs, N.J. : Prentice-Hall, c1987. p. cm. Selections from: Economics. 11th ed. c1987. Includes bibliographies and index. ISBN 0-13-580408-6 LC Card 86-25577 DDC 338.5 19
1. Microeconomics. I. Title.
HB172 .B2325 1987

Bach, Hans. Arbeitsmarktpolitik für die Landwirtschaft und den ländlichen Raum /. Graz , c1984. 138 p. : ISBN 3-900307-15-6 LC Card 85-186643
HD1536.A9 A73 1984

Bach, Quintin. Soviet economic assistance to the less developed countries : a statistical analysis / Quintin Bach. Oxford [Oxfordshire] : Clarendon Press ; New York : Oxford University Press, 1987. p. cm. Bibliography: p. Includes index. ISBN 0-19-828572-8 : LC Card 87-20349 DDC 338.91/47/01724 19
1. Economic assistance, Russian - Developing countries - Statistics. I. Title.
HC60 .B23 1987

Bacha, Edmar Lisboa.
El milagro y la crisis : economía brasileña y latinoamericana : ensayos de Edmar L. Bacha. 1a ed. México : Fondo de Cultura Económica, 1986. 468 p. : ill. ; 21 cm. (Lecturas. 57) Includes bibliographies. ISBN 968-16-2152-2 LC Card

87-400019 DDC 338.981 19
1. Brazil - Economic policy. 2. Latin America - Economic policy. 3. Income distribution. 4. Debts, External. 5. Inflation (Finance). 6. Monetary policy. 7. Developing countries - Economic policy. I. Series: Trimestre económico. 57. II. Title.
HC187 .B128 1986

A Transição incompleta . Rio de Janeiro-RJ , 1986. 2 v. ; LC Card 86-224684
HC187 .T72 1986

Bachelor, Lynn W., 1947- Jones, Bryan D. The sustaining hand . Lawrence, Kan. , c1986. xii, 247 p. : ISBN 0-7006-0278-X : LC Card 85-24631 DDC 338.4/76292/09774 19
HD9710.U53 M433 1986
NYPL [JLE 86-2386]

BACHELOR OF ARTS DEGREE.
Salzman, Marian L. Wanted, liberal arts graduates . New York , 1987. xvi, 341 p. ; ISBN 0-385-24008-2 (pbk.) : LC Card 87-8846 DDC 650.1/4 19
HF5382.75.U6 S27 1987

Bachmann, Gerhard, 1935- Praxisbezug im wirtschaftswissenschaftlichen Studium : das Beispiel der Höheren Wirtschaftsfachschule / Gerhard Bachmann. Frankfurt am Main ; New York : P. Lang, c1986. 277 p. : ill. ; 22 cm. (Europäische Hochschulschriften. Reihe V, Volks- und Betriebswirtschaft, 0531-7339 . Bd. 678 = vol. 678) Bibliography: p. 257-277. ISBN 3-8204-9052-3 LC Card 86-147278
1. Economics - Study and teaching (Secondary) - Germany, West. I. Series: Europäische Hochschulschriften. Reihe V, Volks- und Betriebswirtschaft , Bd. 678. II. Title.
HB74.9.G3 B33 1986

Bachmayer, Hans Matthäus. Der Wert, die Zeichen, die Maschine : über ökonomisch-philosophische Denkformen, Triebe und Mechanismen / Hans Matthäus Bachmayer. Frankfurt/Main ; New York : Campus Verlag, c1982. 370 p. : ill. ; 21 cm. (Campus Forschung. Bd. 260) Bibliography: p. 357-370. ISBN 3-593-33014-8 : LC Card 82-241803
1. Machinery in industry. 2. Man-machine systems. 3. Technology and civilization. I. Title.
HD6331 .B23 1982

Bachollet, Raymond. Kollar, François, 1904- La France travaille /. Paris , c1986. 238 p. : ISBN 2-85108-435-6 LC Card 87-108516
HD8430 .K65 1986

Back from the brink . Edwardes, Michael, 1930- London , 1983. 301 p. : ISBN 0-00-217098-1; 0-00-217089-1 LC Card 83-127870 DDC 338.7/6292/0941 19
HD9710.G74 B573 1983
NYPL [JLD 86-3553]

Bäck, Kalle, 1949- Bondeopposition och bondeinflytande under frihetstiden : centralmakten och östgötaböndernas reaktioner i näringspolitiska frågor / Kalle Bäck. Stockholm : LT, c1984. 326 p. : ill. ; 22 cm. Thesis (doctoral)--Stockholms universitet, 1984. Summary in English. Bibliography: p. 314-319. Includes indexes. ISBN 91-36-02263-2 : LC Card 84-252422
1. Peasantry - Sweden - Östergotlands län - History - 18th century. 2. Östergotlands län (Sweden) - Rural conditions. 3. Sweden - Economic policy. 4. Sweden - Politics and government - 1718-1772. I. Title.
HD1536.S8 B33 1984

Back-offices and San Francisco's office development growth cap /. Dowall, David E. [Berkeley] [1986] 23 p. : LC Card 86-622513 DDC 333.77/17/0979461 19
HD268.S4 D68 1986

Backer, Morton. Financial accounting : concepts and practices / Morton Backer, Pieter T. Elgers, Richard J. Asebrook. San Diego : Harcourt Brace Jovanovich, c1988. xvi, 685 p. : ill. ; 25 cm. Includes bibliographical references and index. ISBN 0-15-527371-X LC Card 87-81140 DDC 657 19
1. Accounting. I. Elgers, Pieter T. II. Asebrook, Richard J. III. Title.
HF5635 .B139 1988

Background study (Canada. Commission of Inquiry on the Pharmaceutical Industry)
Maule, Christopher J., 1934- A survey of the economics of the retail pharmacy sector in Canada /. [Toronto, Ont.] , c1986. 42 p. ; ISBN 0-662-14496-1 (pbk.) LC Card 86-206188 DDC 338.4/76151/0971 19
HD9670.C22 M38 1986

Background study of Maine coastal life .
Rubertone, Patricia E. [Providence, R.I.?] , 1983. iii, 99 leaves : LC Card 86-601627 DDC 304.6/09741/45 19
HB3525.M2 R82 1983

Background/discussion paper .
(no. 12) Frey, Dianne. Survey of sole parent pensioners' workforce barriers /. Woden, ACT [1986] 40 p. : ISBN 0-642-51708-8 LC Card 87-154429 DDC 331.4/4 19
HD6220 .F74 1986

Backhaus, Jürgen, 1942- Studien zur Entwicklung der ökonomischen Theorie /. Berlin , c1981- v. ; ISBN 3-428-04862-8 (v. 1) : LC Card 81-154218 DDC 330/.09 19
HB75 .S787 1981
NYPL [JLL 73-186 Bd.115]

Backwardness and welfare of scheduled castes and scheduled tribes in India /. Hanumantha Rayappa, P. (Pullikunta), 1938- New Delhi , 1986. xi, 121 p. ; ISBN 81-7024-059-X : LC Card 86-902970
HC437.K27 H36 1986

Bacon, Jeremy. Board committees in European companies / by Jeremy Bacon. New York, N.Y. : Conference Board, c1986. vii, 16 p. ; 28 cm. (Conference Board report. no. 886) Includes bibliographical references. ISBN 0-8237-0325-8 (pbk.) LC Card 86-207711 DDC 658.4/22/094 19
1. Directors of corporations - Europe. 2. Committees. I. Title.
HD2745 .B14 1986

Bacon, Mark S. Write like the pros : using the secrets of ad writers and journalists in business / Mark S. Bacon. New York : Wiley, c1988. xiv, 316 p. ; 24 cm. Includes bibliographies and index. ISBN 0-471-85721-1 LC Card 87-21550 DDC 808/.06665 19
1. Business writing. 2. Advertising copy. 3. English language - Business English. 4. Authorship. I. Title.
HF5718.3 .B33 1988

Bacon, Nicolas, 1710-1779.
Réflexions sur l'état présent du commerce, fabriques et manufactures des Païs-Bas autrichiens. 1978. Hasquin, Hervé, 1942- Les Réflexions sur l'état présent du commerce, fabriques et manufactures des Païs-Bas autrichiens (1765) du négociant bruxellois, Nicolas Bacon (1710-1779), conseiller député aux affaires du commerce / par Hervé Hasquin. Bruxelles , 1978. vi, 190 p. ; LC Card 87-672234
HF3595 .H37x 1978

BACON, NICOLAS, 1710-1779.
Hasquin, Hervé, 1942- Les Réflexions sur l'état présent du commerce, fabriques et manufactures des Païs-Bas autrichiens (1765) du négociant bruxellois, Nicolas Bacon (1710-1779), conseiller député aux affaires du commerce /. Bruxelles , 1978. vi, 190 p. ; LC Card 87-672234
HF3595 .H37x 1978

Bácskai, Tamás. Management of public budgetary institutions /. Budapest , 1986. 37 p. ; ISBN 963-03-2343-5 (pbk.) : LC Card 86-230773 DDC 336.439 19
HJ2103 .M33 1986

BADAJOZ (SPAIN : PROVINCE) - ECONOMIC CONDITIONS.
Bohoyo Velázquez, Isidoro Francisco. Situación socio-económica y condiciones de vida en la Provincia de Badajoz, 1880-1902 /. Badajoz [1984?] 149 p., [3] p. of plates : ISBN 84-309-1055-7 LC Card 86-151914
HC387.B14 B64 1984

BADAJOZ (SPAIN : PROVINCE) - SOCIAL CONDITIONS.
Bohoyo Velázquez, Isidoro Francisco. Situación socio-económica y condiciones de vida en la Provincia de Badajoz, 1880-1902 /. Badajoz [1984?] 149 p., [3] p. of plates : ISBN 84-309-1055-7 LC Card 86-151914
HC387.B14 B64 1984

Badaloni, Nicola. Forme della politica e teorie del cambiamento : scritti e polemiche, 1962-1981 / Nicola Badaloni. Pisa : ETS, c1983. xxii, 264 p. ; 21 cm. (Filosofia e ... . 5) Cover title: Forme della politica e teoria del cambiamento. Includes bibliographical references. LC Card 85-163265 DDC 306/.2 19
1. Political sociology. 2. Marxian school of sociology. I. Title. II. Title: Forme della politica e teoria del cambiamento.
JA76 .B23 1983 ***NYPL [JLD 86-3306]***

Bade, Klaus J. Population, labour, and migration in 19th- and 20th-century Germany /. Leamington Spa [UK] ; New York : xii, 200 p. : ISBN 0-85496-503-3 : LC Card 86-24470 DDC 331.6/2/0943 19
HD5856.G3 P66 1987

Baden Fuller, Charles, 1948- Firms and markets . London , c1986. xiii, 271 p. : ISBN 0-7099-2446-1 ***NYPL [JLD 86-2134]***

Baden-Handbuch .
(Bd. 3) Die Abstempelungen des Grossherzogtums Baden ab 1851 . [Soest] , c1980. 393 p. : LC Card 86-152444
HE6185.G32 B333 1980

BADEN-WÜRTTEMBERG (GERMANY) - COMMERCE - DEVELOPING COUNTRIES.
Moosmann, Bernfried, 1957- Mittelbetriebe und Entwicklungsländer . Frankfurt am Main , New York , c1986. x, 290 p. ; ISBN 3-8204-9518-5 LC Card 86-232976
HF3569.B2 M66 1986

BADEN-WÜRTTEMBERG (GERMANY) - ECONOMIC CONDITIONS.
Boelcke, Willi A. Wirtschaftsgeschichte Baden-Württembergs . Stuttgart , c1987. 725 p., [80] p. of plates : ISBN 3-8062-0423-3 LC Card 87-152351 DDC 330.943/46 19
HC287.B23 B63 1987

Gensewich, Irmtraud. Die Tabakarbeiterin in Baden, 1870-1914 /. Mannheim , 1986. 496 p. : ISBN 3-87804-183-7 LC Card 87-121532 DDC 331.4/8797/094346 19
HD6073.T62 G34 1986

IHK-Atlas Industrie-Ansiedlung . Stuttgart [1982?] 145 p. : LC Card 86-213370
HC287.B23 I38 1982

BADEN-WÜRTTEMBERG (GERMANY) - ECONOMIC POLICY.
Boelcke, Willi A. Wirtschaftsgeschichte Baden-Württembergs . Stuttgart , c1987. 725 p., [80] p. of plates : ISBN 3-8062-0423-3 LC Card 87-152351 DDC 330.943/46 19
HC287.B23 B63 1987

BADEN-WÜRTTEMBERG (GERMANY) - INDUSTRIES.
IHK-Atlas Industrie-Ansiedlung . Stuttgart [1982?] 145 p. : LC Card 86-213370
HC287.B23 I38 1982

BADEN-WÜRTTEMBERG (GERMANY) - INDUSTRIES - HISTORY.
Boelcke, Willi A. Wirtschaftsgeschichte Baden-Württembergs . Stuttgart , c1987. 725 p., [80] p. of plates : ISBN 3-8062-0423-3 LC Card 87-152351 DDC 330.943/46 19
HC287.B23 B63 1987

Baden-Württemberg (Germany). Innenministerium. Landkreis Waiblingen /. [Stuttgart] [1965?] 25 p. : LC Card 85-230943
HC288.W34 L36 1965

BADEN-WÜRTTEMBERG (GERMANY). LANDTAG - ELECTIONS, 1976.
Gemeindestatistik 1976. Stuttgart , <1976-. v. <2 > : LC Card 86-222059
HA1320.B2 A32 Bd. 230, etc. JN4939.A15

Baden-Württemberg (Germany). Ministerium für Kultus und Sport. Zarth, Michael. Wirtschaftsunterricht an allgemeinbildenden Schulen in Baden-Württemberg . Tübingen , 1987. x, 241 p. ; ISBN 3-88573-028-6 : LC Card 87-419933 DDC 330/.07/104346 19
HB74.9.G3 Z36 1987

Baden-Württemberg (Germany). Wirtschaftsministerium. Landkreis Waiblingen /. [Stuttgart] [1965?] 25 p. : LC Card 85-230943
HC288.W34 L36 1965

Bader, U. (Udo) Haas, Hans-Dieter. Karibische Klein- und Mikrostaaten . Tübingen , 1985. xvi, 200 p. : ISBN 3-921552-62-1 LC Card 86-155952
HC141 .H25 1985

Badgett, Tom. The insider's guide to Lotus 1-2-3 : tips you won't find in the manual / Tom Badgett, Corey Sandler. Glenview, Ill. : Scott, Foresman, c1987. xix, 266 p. : ill. ; 24 cm.

Includes index. ISBN 0-673-18718-7 (pbk.) : LC Card 87-4864 DDC 005.36/9 19
1. Lotus 1-2-3 (Computer program). 2. Business - Data processing. I. Sandler, Corey, 1950-. II. Title.
HF5548.4.L67 B33 1987

Badillo, Emilce del Carmen. Badillo, Juan A. El registro contable en moneda constante . Capital Federal, Argentina , 1985. 249 p. ; LC Card 85-203677
HF5658.5 .B34 1985

Badillo, Juan A. El registro contable en moneda constante : procesamiento contable directo en el ejercicio y su articulación a los ejercicios siguientes / Juan A. Badillo, Emilce del Carmen Badillo. Capital Federal, Argentina : Sainte Claire Editora, 1985. 249 p. ; 26 cm. LC Card 85-203677
1. Accounting - Argentina - Effect of inflation on. 2. Accounting - Effect of inflation on. 3. Indexation (Economics) - Argentina. I. Badillo, Emilce del Carmen. II. Title.
HF5658.5 .B34 1985

Badisch-Elsässische Bürgerinitiativen. Der Widerstand geht weiter . Freiburg i. Br. , 1982. 261 p. : ISBN 3-921472-30-X LC Card 82-192690
HD9698.G43 W937 1982

BADISCHE ANILIN- & SODA-FABRIK - HISTORY.
Heintzeler, Wolfgang. Der rote Faden . Stuttgart , c1983. 292 p. ; ISBN 3-512-00664-7 LC Card 83-183709
HD9654.9.B27 H45 1983

Badura, Bernhard, 1943- Die Zweite Stadt . Opladen , c1986. 407 p. : ISBN 3-531-11764-5 LC Card 87-497505 DDC 331.11/0943 19
HD8451 .Z94 1986

Baechler, Jean. Europe and the rise of capitalism /. Oxford [Oxfordshire] , New York, NY, USA , 1987. p. cm. ISBN 0-631-15006-4 : LC Card 87-12293 DDC 330.94 19
HC240.9.C3 E97 1987

Baehr, Melany E.
Experience and background inventory : interpretation and research manual / developed by Melany E. Baehr and Ernest C. Froemel. [Park Ridge, Ill.] (1550 Northwest Highway, Park Ridge 60068) : London House, [c1986] 48 p. ; 28 cm. (University series) Cover title. "UP-101-2." LC Card 87-404267 DDC 658.3/112 19
1. Employee selection. 2. Vocational qualifications - Evaluation. 3. Applications for positions - Evaluation. I. Froemel, Ernest C. II. London House (Firm : Park Ridge, Ill.). III. Series: University series (Park Ridge, Ill.). IV. Title.
HF5549.5.S38 B34 1986

Experience and background questionnaire : interpretation and research manual / developed by Melany E. Baehr. [Park Ridge, Ill.] (1550 Northwest Highway, Park Ridge 60068) : London House, c1986. 20 p. ; 28 cm. (University series) Cover title. Prepared by Melany E. Baehr and Don C. Allen. "UP-102-2." LC Card 87-404268 DDC 658.3/1125 19
1. Occupational aptitude tests. 2. Vocational qualifications - Evaluation. 3. Employee selections. I. Allen, Don C. II. Series: University series (Park Ridge, Ill.). III. Title.
HF5381.7 .B327 1986

Bänsch, Axel.
Operationalisierung des Unternehmenszieles Mitgliederförderung / Axel Bänsch. Göttingen : Vandenhoeck & Ruprecht, c1983. xv, 245 p. ; 24 cm. (Hamburger Schriften zum Genossenschaftswesen . Bd. 1) The author's Habilitationsschrift, Universität Hamburg, 1982. Bibliography: p. [228]-245. ISBN 3-525-12750-2 LC Card 83-199427
1. Cooperative societies - Germany, West. I. Title. II. Series.
HD3498 .B35 1983

Operationalisierung des Unternehmenszieles, Mitgliederförderung / Axel Bänsch. Göttingen : Vandenhoeck & Ruprecht, 1983. xv, 245 p. ; 23cm. (Hamburger Schriften zum Genossenschaftswesen . Bd.1) Bibliography: p. [228]-245. ISBN 3-525-12750-2
1. Management by objectives. 2. Corporations - Investor relations. I. Title. II. Series.
NYPL [JLE 86-1770]

Baer, Mônica.
A internacionalização financeira no Brasil / Mônica Baer. Petrópolis : Vozes, 1986. 159 p. ; 21 cm. "O presente estudo foi realizado no marco do Programa de Pesquisas do Centro de Economía Transnacional (CET)"--P. 7. Includes bibliographical references. LC Card 86-200812
1. Finance - Brazil. 2. Banks and banking, Brazilian. 3. Debts, External - Brazil. 4. Banks and banking, Foreign - Brazil. 5. Investments, Foreign - Brazil. I. Title.
HG185.B7 B28 1986

Lichtensztejn, Samuel, 1934- Fondo Monetario Internacional y Banco Mundial . San José, Costa Rica , Buenos Aires, Argentina , 1986. 215 p. : LC Card 86-233561
HG3881.5.I58 L527 1986

Baer, Werner, 1931- Brazil and the Ivory Coast . Greenwich, Conn. , c1987. p. cm. ISBN 0-89232-819-3 : LC Card 87-3667 DDC 332/.042/0981 19
HG3891.5 .B72 1987

Baetge, Jörg. Kybernetik und Management . Berlin , c1983. viii, 131 p. : ISBN 3-428-05448-2 LC Card 84-109870
HD29 .K92 1983

Baethge, Martin.
Arbeit 2000 . Hamburg , 1985. 236 p. : ISBN 3-87975-314-8 LC Card 86-143070
HD4813 .A68 1985

Zukunft der Angestellten : neue Technologien und berufliche Perspektiven in Büro und Verwaltung / Martin Baethge, Herbert Oberbeck. Frankfurt ; New York : Campus, c1986. 460 p. : ill. ; 23 cm. Includes bibliographical references. ISBN 3-593-33368-6 (pbk.) LC Card 87-673317
1. Employment forecasting. 2. Office practice - Automation. 3. Clerks - Effect of automation on. I. Oberbeck, Herbert. II. Title.
HD5707 .B28x 1986

Báez Evertsz, Franc, 1948- Braceros haitianos en la República Dominicana / Franc Báez Evertsz. 2a ed. [Santo Domingo] : Instituto Dominicano de Investigaciones Sociales, c1986. 354 p. : ill. ; 23 cm. Includes bibliographical references and index. LC Card 87-401177 DDC 331.6/2/729407293 19
1. Alien labor, Haitian - Dominican Republic. I. Title.
HD8218.5 .B34 1986

BÁEZ, MAURICIO, 1910-1950.
Orbe, Justino José del. Mauricio Báez y la clase obrera /. Santo Domingo, República Dominicana , 1981. 158 p. : LC Card 82-138627 DDC 331.88/092/4 B 19
HD6584.Z55 B346 1981
NYPL [JLE 86-3246]

Baez, René. Ciencia y transformación social : visión latinoamericana / René Báez. Quito, Ecuador : Editorial Tercer Mundo : CIPAD, 1986. 141 p. ; 22 cm. (Colección Pensamiento social) Includes bibliographical references. LC Card 86-214736 DDC 330.9/0038 19
1. Latin America - Economic conditions - 1945-. 2. Economics - Latin America. 3. Ecuador - Economic conditions - 1972-. 4. Economics - Ecuador. I. Series: Colección Pensamiento social (Quito, Ecuador). II. Title.
HC125 .B195 1986

Baeza V., Sergio. Análisis de la previsión en Chile /. Santiago, Chile [1986] 309 p. : LC Card 87-115194
HD7156 .A78 1986

BAGASSE INDUSTRY - CUBA - EQUIPMENT AND SUPPLIES.
Correa, Jorge Lois. Sistemas y equipos de desmedulado en la industria del bagazo de la caña de azúcar /. Ciudad de La Habana , c1982. 77 p. : LC Card 85-198777
HD9119.B4 C83 1982

Bagby, Wesley Marvin, 1922- Introduction to social science / Wesley M. Bagby. Chicago : Nelson-Hall, c1987. xv, 427 p. : ill., maps ; 24 cm. Includes bibliographies and index. ISBN 0-8304-1146-1 LC Card 86-23487 DDC 306/.0973 19
1. United States - Economic conditions - 1981-. 2. United States - Politics and government - 1981-. 3. United States - Social conditions - 1980-. 4. United States - Foreign relations - 1981-. 5. Social sciences - United States. I. Title. II. Title: Social science.
HC106.8 .B34 1987

BAGEHOT, WALTER, 1826-1877.
St. John-Stevas, Norman. The omnipresence of Walter Bagehot /. Oxford [Oxfordshire] , New York , 1987. p. cm. ISBN 0-19-951554-9 (pbk.) : LC Card 87-13923 DDC 330/.092/4 19
HB103.B2 S29 1987

Bagella, Michele. Gli istituti di credito speciale e il mercato finanziario, 1947-1962 / Michele Bagella ; introduzione di Carlo Pace. Milano, Italy : F. Angeli, c1986. 289 p. ; 23 cm. (Efibanca/studi creditizi . 2) Bibliography: p. [283]-289. LC Card 86-232526
1. Credit - Italy. 2. Financial institutions - Italy. 3. Commercial finance companies - Italy. 4. Money market - Italy. I. Title. II. Series.
HG3729.I7 B34 1986

Baglioni, Guido. L'Europa sindacale agli inizi degli anni '80 . Bologna , c1982. 385 p. : LC Card 84-140478 DDC 331.88/094 19
HD6657 .E89 1982

Bagó, Eszter. Diverzifikáció az iparban / Bagó Eszter. Budapest : Közgazdasági és Jogi Könyvkiadó, 1985. 251, [1] p. : ill. ; 19 cm. (Időszerű közgazdasági kérdések, 0324-3214) Bibliography: p. 241-[252] ISBN 963-221-544-3 : LC Card 86-186848
1. Diversification in industry. 2. Diversification in industry - Hungary. I. Title. II. Series.
HD2755.8 .B34 1985

Bagota, Béla.
Mit kell tudni a hetedik ötéves tervről? / írta, Bagota Béla, Garam József. [Budapest] : Kossuth, 1986. 238 p. ; 19 cm. (Mit kell tudni, 0324-7813) ISBN 963-09-2815-9 : LC Card 86-210804
1. Hungary - Economic policy - 1968-. I. Garam, József. II. Title. III. Title: Mit kell tudni a 7. ötéves tervről?. IV. Series.
HC300.28 .B319 1986

Mit kell tudni az 1987. évi népgazdasági tervről? / írta, Bagota Béla, Garam József. [Budapest] : Kossuth, 1987. 239 p. ; 19 cm. (Mit kell tudni, 0324-7813) "A gazdasági szabályozás 1987. évi jogszabály-módosításai": p. 216-[217]. ISBN 963-09-3110-9 : LC Card 87-151787
1. Hungary - Economic policy - 1968-. I. Garam, József. II. Title. III. Series.
HC300.28 .B329 1987

Bagozzi, Richard P. Philosophical and radical thought in marketing /. Lexington, Mass. , c1987. xxi, 392 p. : ISBN 0-669-14301-4 (alk. paper) LC Card 86-45791 DDC 658.8 19
HF5415 .P485 1987

BAHAMAS - ECONOMIC CONDITIONS.
A General information guide on the economy of the Bahamas /. Nassau, Bahamas [1986] x, 60 p. ; LC Card 87-400226 DDC 330.97296 19
HC152 .G46 1986

Bahan instruksional pendidikan kependudukan untuk peserta diklat Departemen P.U. Ed. 1. Jakarta : Pusat Pendidikan dan Latihan Tenaga Kerja, Departemen Pekerjaan Umum : Badan Koordinasi Keluarga Berencana Nasional, 1982. v, 90 p. ; 29 cm. Bibliography: p. 90. LC Card 83-941464
1. Population - Study and teaching - Indonesia. I. Pusat Pendidikan dan Latihan Tenaga Kerja (Indonesia). II. Indonesia. Badan Koordinasi Keluarga Berencana Nasional. III. Title: Pendidikan kependudukan untuk peserta diklat Departemen P.U.
HB850.5.I5 B34 1982

Baher, Milany E. see **Baehr, Melany E.**

Bahia-Alcool Empreendimentos Energéticos e Agroindustriais S.A. Borracha natural na Bahia . [Salvador] [1982] 130 p. : LC Card 87-403935 DDC 338.4/76782/098142 19
HD9161.B82 B186 1982

Bahia (Brazil : State). Centro de Estatística e Informações. Aspectos demográficos regionais /. Salvador , 1984- <v. 1, pt. 1; in 1 > : LC Card 84-235259
HB3564.B3 A87 1984

Bahia (Brazil : State). Escola de Administração Fazendária.
Ciclo Integrado sobre Administração Financeira (1983 : Escola de Administração Fazendária) Ciclo Integrado sobre Administração Financeira /. Salvador, BA [1984] 53 p. : LC Card 86-157989
HG185.B7 C52 1983

Bahia (Brazil : State). Escola de Administração Fazendária. Coordenadoria de Programas Especiais. Catálogo de informações sócio-econômicas dos municípios, Bahia /. Salvador, BA [1984] 354 p. ; LC Card 86-210868
HA988.B3 C38 1984

BAHIA (BRAZIL : STATE) - MANUFACTURES.
A Evolução dos setores secundário e terciário da economia baiana na década de 70 /. Salvador , 1985. 80 p. : LC Card 87-124067 DDC 338.4/7/00098142 19
HD9734.B73 B334 1985

BAHIA (BRAZIL : STATE) - RACE RELATIONS.
Schwartz, Stuart B. Sugar plantations in the formation of Brazilian society . Cambridge [Cambridgeshire] , New York , 1985. xxiii, 616 p. : ISBN 0-521-30934-4 LC Card 85-6716 DDC 306/.0981/42 19
HD9114.B7 B347 1985
NYPL [JLE 86-2276]

BAHIA (BRAZIL : STATE) - STATISTICS.
Catálogo de informações sócio-econômicas dos municípios, Bahia /. Salvador, BA [1984] 354 p. ; LC Card 86-210868
HA988.B3 C38 1984

Bahia, Brazil (State). Dept. of Industry and Commerce, State. see Bahia, Brazil (State). Secretaria da Indústria e Comércio.

BAHIA, BRAZIL (STATE) - ECONOMIC CONDITIONS.
Schwartz, Stuart B. Sugar plantations in the formation of Brazilian society . Cambridge [Cambridgeshire] , New York , 1985. xxiii, 616 p. : ISBN 0-521-30934-4 LC Card 85-6716 DDC 306/.0981/42 19
HD9114.B7 B347 1985
NYPL [JLE 86-2276]

BAHIA, BRAZIL (STATE) - ECONOMIC POLICY.
Avena Filho, Armando. Nordeste e Bahia . Salvador , 1986. 196 p. ; LC Card 87-403867 DDC 338.981/42 19
HC188.B3 A94 1986

Bahia, Brazil (State) Secretaria do Planejamento, Ciência e Tecnologia. Planejamento, ciência e tecnologia . [Salvador , 1983?] 93 p. : LC Card 85-136375
HC188.B3 B334 1983

Bahia, Brazil (State). Indústria e Comércio, Secretaria da. see Bahia, Brazil (State). Secretaria da Indústria e Comércio.

Bahia, Brazil (State). Planejamento, Ciência e Tecnologia, Secretaria do. see Bahia, Brazil (State) Secretaria do Planejamento, Ciência e Tecnologia.

BAHIA, BRAZIL (STATE) - POPULATION.
Aspectos demográficos regionais /. Salvador , 1984- <v. 1, pt. 1; in 1 > : LC Card 84-235259
HB3564.B3 A87 1984

Bahia, Brazil (State). Secretaria da Indústria e Comércio. O gigante invisível . [Salvador] [1983] 105 p. : LC Card 84-181184
HD2346.B72 S25 1983

Bahia, Brazil (State). Secretaria de Indústria e Comércio. see Bahia, Brazil (State). Secretaria da Indústria e Comércio.

Bahia, Brazil (State) Secretaria do Planejamento, Ciência e Tecnologia. Planejamento, ciência e tecnologia : 4 anos do Governo Antônio Carlos Magalhães, 1979-1983. [Salvador : Secretaria do Planejamento, Ciência e Tecnologia, 1983?] 93 p. : ill. ; 30 cm. LC Card 85-136375
1. Bahia, Brazil (State) - Economic policy. 2. Technology and state - Brazil - Bahia (State). 3. Science and state - Brazil - Bahia (State). 4. Public institutions - Brazil - Bahia (State). I. Title.
HC188.B3 B334 1983

BAHIA, BRAZIL (STATE) - SOCIAL CONDITIONS.
Schwartz, Stuart B. Sugar plantations in the formation of Brazilian society . Cambridge [Cambridgeshire] , New York , 1985. xxiii, 616 p. : ISBN 0-521-30934-4 LC Card 85-6716 DDC 306/.0981/42 19
HD9114.B7 B347 1985
NYPL [JLE 86-2276]

Bahia, Brazil (State). State Dept. of Industry and Commerce. see Bahia, Brazil (State). Secretaria da Indústria e Comércio.

Bahia, catálogo de informações sócio-econômicas dos municípios. Catálogo de informações sócio-econômicas dos municípios, Bahia /. Salvador, BA [1984] 354 p. ; LC Card 86-210868
HA988.B3 C38 1984

BAHIRI (INDIA) - ECONOMIC CONDITIONS.
Majumder, Arun. Poverty, development, and exchange relations . New Delhi , 1987. xiii, 141 p. : ISBN 81-7027-108-8 : LC Card 87-900910
HC438.B24 M35 1987

Bahizi, Joseph. Monographie d'unités domestiques. Commune de Mugina, province de Cibitoke / rapporteurs, Bahizi Joseph, Hakizimana Déo, Bwimba Ntaganda. [Bujumbura] : F.S.E.A., Section Economie rurale, [1985] 41 leaves ; 30 cm. (Travaux d'étudiants / CURDES . no 1) Cover title. "Novembre 1985." LC Card 86-980542
1. Mugina (Burundi : Commune) - Economic conditions. 2. Mugina (Burundi : Commune) - Social conditions. 3. Rural development - Burundi - Mugina (Commune). 4. Households - Burundi - Mugina (Commune). I. Hakizimana, Déo. II. Bwimba Ntaganda. III. Series: Travaux d'étudiants , no 1. IV. Title.
HC880.Z7 M843 1985

Bahne, Charles. Car-free in Boston . Cambridge, MA (P.O. Box 192, Cambridge 02238) , c1986. 160 p. : LC Card 86-231024 DDC 388.4/09744 19
HE4491.B8 C37 1986

Bahrami, Homa. Leavitt, Harold J. Managerial psychology . Chicago , 1988. x, 353 p. : ISBN 0-226-46973-5 : LC Card 87-16820 DDC 158.7 19
HF5548.8 .L35 1988

Bahry, Donna. Outside Moscow : power, politics, and budgetary policy in the Soviet republics / Donna Bahry. New York : Columbia University Press, 1987. 236 p. : ill. ; 24 cm. Bibliography: p. [205]-230. Includes index. ISBN 0-231-06290-7 LC Card 87-8020 DDC 336.47 19
1. Budget - Soviet Union - Republics. 2. Intergovernmental fiscal relations - Soviet Union. I. Title.
HJ2130 .B35 1987

Bai͡anskiĭ, T. Ė. (Timur Ėmirovich) Kozlov, P. T. (Petr Tikhonovich) Sovershenstvovanie khozi͡aĭstvennogo mekhanizma v neft͡anoĭ i gazovoĭ promyshlennosti /. Alma-Ata , 1983. 134 p. : LC Card 83-194289
HD9575.S652 K69 1983

Baĭbakov, Nikolaĭ Konstantinovich. O Gosudarstvennom plane ėkonomicheskogo i sot͡sial'nogo razvitii͡a SSSR na 1981-1985 gody ... : doklad ... / N.K. Baĭbakov. Moskva : Izd-vo polit. lit-ry, 1981. 44 p. ; 20 cm. PARTIAL CONTENTS. - Zakon Soi͡uza Sovetskikh Sot͡sialisticheskikh Respublik o Gosudarstvennom plane ėkonomicheskogo i sot͡sial'nogo razvitii͡a SSSR na 1981-1985 gody -- Zakon Soi͡uza Sovetskikh Sot͡sialisticheskikh Respublik o Gosudarstvennom plane ėkonomicheskogo razvitii͡a SSSR na 1982 god -- Postanovlenie Verkhovnogo Soveta SSSR o khode vypolnenii͡a Gosudarstvennogo plana ėkonomicheskogo i sot͡sial'nogo razvitii͡a SSSR na 1981 god. LC Card 82-200045
1. Soviet Union - Economic policy - 1981-. I. Title.
HC336.25 .B33945 1981

Baier, Mark. Miegel, Meinhard. Die verkannte Revolution /. Stuttgart , 1983- v. : ISBN 3-87959-196-2 (Bd. 1) LC Card 83-206487 DDC 330.943/087 19
HC286.7 .M53 1983 ***NYPL [JLK 86-154]***

Baig, Nafees, 1941- Government controls and industrial expansion in India / by Nafees Baig. Aligarh : Printwell Publications, 1983. viii, 223 p. ; 23 cm. Revision of the author's thesis (D. Litt. -- Aligarh University, 1978) under title: Impact of government regulations and controls on industrial expansion in India since 1951. Includes index. Bibliography: p. [217]-220. LC Card 83-907504 DDC 338.954 19
1. Industry and state - India. 2. Industrial promotion - India. 3. Industrial laws and legislation - India. I. Title.
HD3616.I43 B35 1983
NYPL [JLD 86-4330]

Bailey, Elizabeth E. Public regulation . Cambridge, Mass. , c1987. xiv, 404 p. ; ISBN 0-262-02258-3 LC Card 86-21302 DDC 338.973 19
HD3616.U47 P83 1987

Bailey, Norman A. The Mexican time bomb / Norman A. Bailey and Richard Cohen. New York : Priority Press Publications, 1987. vi, 61 p. ; 23 cm. "A Twentieth Century Fund paper." Bibliography: p. 53-61. ISBN 0-87078-209-6 (pbk.) : LC Card 87-400092 DDC 336.3/4/0972 19
1. Debts, External - Mexico. 2. Loans, Foreign - Mexico. I. Cohen, Richard, 1946-. II. Title.
HJ8519 .B26 1987

Bailey, Thomas Raymond. Immigrant and native workers : contrasts and competition / Thomas R. Bailey. Boulder : Westview Press, 1987. xvi, 168 p. : ill. ; 24 cm. (Conservation of Human Resources studies in the new economy) Includes bibliographies and index. ISBN 0-8133-7349-2 : LC Card 86-28205 DDC 331.6/2/0973 19
1. Alien labor - United States. 2. Minorities - Employment - United States. I. Title. II. Series.
HD8081.A5 B35 1987

Baillie, John. Systems of profit measurement / John Baillie. New York : Gee & Co., 1985. viii, 112 p. ; 23 cm. "Published for the Institute of Chartered Accountants of Scotland." Includes bibliographies and index. ISBN 0-85258-234-X (pbk.) LC Card 84-21578 DDC 657/.48 19
1. Income accounting. 2. Corporations - Accounting. I. Title.
HF5681.I48 B34 1985

Bails, Dale. Peppers, Larry C. Managerial economics . Englewood Cliffs, N.J. , c1987. xxii, 679 p. : ISBN 0-13-550055-9 LC Card 86-25278 DDC 338.5/024658 19
HD30.22 .P43 1987

Baily, Peter J. H.
Purchasing and supply management / P.J.H. Baily. 5th ed. London ; New York : Chapman and Hall, 1987. viii, 296 p. : ill. ; 24 cm. Bibliography: p. [292]-293. Includes index. ISBN 0-412-28940-7 (pbk.) LC Card 87-11760 DDC 658.7 19
1. Industrial procurement - Management. I. Title.
HD39.5 .B335 1987

Purchasing principles and management / Peter Baily, David Farmer. 5th ed. London ; Marshfield, Mass. : Pitman, 1985. 324 p. : ill. ; 23 cm. Includes bibliographies and index. ISBN 0-273-02242-3 LC Card 85-16704 DDC 658.7/2 19
1. Purchasing - Management. 2. Industrial procurement - Management. I. Farmer, David H. II. Title.
HF5437 .B3415 1985 ***NYPL [JLE 86-3321]***

Bain, D., 1944- Management Training Seminar (1982 : Joint Research Centre, Ispra, Italy) National energy planning and management in developing countries . Dordrecht, Holland , Hingham, MA , c1983. xiii, 442 p. ; ISBN 90-277-1589-0 LC Card 83-4407 DDC 333.79/09172/4 19
HD9502.A2 M343 1982
NYPL [JLE 87-302]

Bain, Joe Staten, 1912- Industrial organization : a treatise / by Joe S. Bain, P. David Qualls. Greenwich, Conn. : JAI Press, c1987. 2 v. ; 24 cm. (Monographs in organizational behavior and industrial relations . v. 6) Includes bibliographies and index. ISBN 0-89232-702-2 (set) LC Card 87-2618 DDC 338.6 19
1. Industrial organization (Economic theory). 2. Industrial organization - United States. 3. Industrial concentration - United States. 4. Trade regulation - United States. I. Qualls, P. David. II. Title. III. Series.
HD2326 .B34 1987

Baĭramov, Dzhuma. Egengel'dyev, Ė. (Ėsengel'dy) Teoreticheskie issledovanii͡a regional'nykh faktorov razmeshchenii͡a khozi͡aĭstva /. Ashkabad , 1985. 227 p. : LC Card 86-172008
HC337.T853 D53 1985

Baird, Floyd M. Kyle, Robert C. Property management /. Chicago, IL , c1988. x, 422 p. : ISBN 0-88462-669-5 (pbk.) LC Card 87-17906 DDC 332.63/24/068 19
HD1394 .K94 1988

Baird, Lloyd. The Performance management sourcebook /. Amherst, Mass. [1987] 393 p. :

ISBN 0-87425-074-9 (pbk.) LC Card 87-153991 DDC 658.3/125 19
HF5549.5.R3 P4755 1987

Baĭriev, B. S. Optimizatsii͡a struktur upravlenii͡a / B.S. Baĭriev, B.A. Lagosha ; pod redaktsieĭ B.B. Ovezova. Ashkhabad : Ylym, 1985. 169, [23] p. : ill. ; 20 cm. At head of title: Akademii͡a nauk Turkmenskoĭ SSR. Institut ėkonomiki. Bibliography: p. 159-[170] LC Card 86-196466
1. Territorial production complexes - Tajik S.S.R. - Mathematical models. 2. Tajik S.S.R. - Economic policy - Mathematical models. 3. Industrial organization - Tajik S.S.R. - Mathematical models. I. Lagosha, Boris Aleksandrovich. II. Ovezov, Batyr Balyshevich. III. Title.
HC337.T23 B35 1985

El Baix Camp . Calleja Xifré, Carlos. Barcelona [1986] xv, 367 p. : ISBN 84-505-3567-9 LC Card 86-205881
HC388.R482 C35 1986

El Baix Empordà : recursos i estructura econòmica / [realitzat per Joan Cals i Güell (director) ... [et al.]]. Barcelona : Caixa d'Estalvis de Catalunya, c1984. xii, 303 p. : ill. (some col.) ; 24 cm. (Col·lecció Catalunya comarcal) Bibliography: p. 287-291. ISBN 84-505-0289-6 LC Card 85-186183
1. Ampurdán (Spain : Region) - Economic conditions. 2. Agriculture - Economic aspects - Spain - Ampurdán (Region). 3. Land tenure - Spain - Ampurdán (Region). 4. Ampurdán (Spain : Region) - Population. 5. Tourist trade - Spain - Ampurdán (Region). 6. Finance, Public - Spain - Ampurdán (Region). I. Cals, Joan. II. Series.
HC387.A636 B35 1984

BAIXO ALENTEJO (PORTUGAL) - ECONOMIC CONDITIONS - CASE STUDIES.
Barros, Afonso de. Do latifundismo à reforma agrária . Oeiras [Portugal] , 1986. 636 p. : LC Card 87-404938 DDC 333.3/1/46955 19
HD1333.P82 B353 1986

BAIXO ALENTEJO (PORTUGAL) - RURAL CONDITIONS - CASE STUDIES.
Barros, Afonso de. Do latifundismo à reforma agrária . Oeiras [Portugal] , 1986. 636 p. : LC Card 87-404938 DDC 333.3/1/46955 19
HD1333.P82 B353 1986

Baíz, José. Pacheco D., Rubén. Industria de la construcción . [Panamá] , 1974. 17, [1] leaves, [4] leaves of plates : LC Card 87-400643
HD9715.P223 P367 1974

BAJA CALIFORNIA NORTE (MEXICO) - CENSUS, 1980 - EVALUATION.
Corona V., Rodolfo. Evaluación de los datos censales de 1980 . Tijuana, Baja California , 1986. 172 p. : ISBN 968-607-510-0 LC Card 87-117630 DDC 304.6/0723 19
HA767.B34 C67 1986

BAJA CALIFORNIA SUR (MEXICO) - CENSUS, 1980 - EVALUATION.
Corona V., Rodolfo. Evaluación de los datos censales de 1980 . Tijuana, Baja California , 1986. 172 p. : ISBN 968-607-510-0 LC Card 87-117630 DDC 304.6/0723 19
HA767.B34 C67 1986

BAJHANG (NEPAL : DISTRICT) - ECONOMIC POLICY - EVALUATION.
Malla, B. C. An evaluation of development activities within Sixth Plan period in Bajhang District /. Kathmandu , 1985 [i.e. 1986] 76, [3] p. : LC Card 86-903487 DDC 338.9549/6 19
HC425.Z7 B355 1986

Bajpai, Brijesh K. Mishra, G. P. Village industries and agriculture in changing agrarian situation /. New Delhi , c1985. 120 p. ; ISBN 81-7024-010-7 LC Card 85-904926 DDC 338.6/34/0954 19
HD2346.I5 M49 1985 ***NYPL [JLD 86-3746]***

Bak, Richard, 1954- Smart contracting : dollar and sense strategies for HVAC/R contractors / Richard Bak. Troy, Mich. : Business News Pub. Co., c1987. 213 p. : ill. ; 21 cm. Includes index. ISBN 0-912524-39-1 (pbk.) : LC Card 86-28327 DDC 338.4/7697 19
1. Heating and ventilating industry - Management. 2. Air conditioning industry - Management. I. Title.
HD9683.A2 B35 1987

Bakaev, Aleksandr Aleksandrovich. Problemy modelirovanii͡a makroėkonomicheskikh sistem . Kiev , 1982. 100 p. ; LC Card 83-144893
HB139 .P755 1982

Bakalov, Nikola. Kotsev, Tsvetan. Formirane i izpolzvane na parichnite fondove v stopanskite organizatsii /. Varna , 1985. 117 p. ; LC Card 85-213610
HC403.Z9 C347 1985

Bakanov, K. P. (Konstantin Pavlovich)
Sovershenstvovanie organizatsii truda na predprii͡atii͡akh chernoĭ metallurgii / K.P. Bakanov, L.A. Konovalov, L.E. Strovskiĭ. Moskva : "Metallurgii͡a", 1981. 47 p. ; 22 cm. (Ėkonomika metallurgicheskogo proizvodstva) LC Card 82-104389
1. Iron industry and trade - Soviet Union - Personnel management. I. Konovalov, L. A. (Leopol′d Anatol′evich). II. Strovskiĭ, L. E. (Leonid Evgen′evich). III. Title. IV. Series.
HD9525.S652 B355 1981

BAKARIĆ, VLADIMIR.
Društvena reprodukcija u djelu Vladimira Bakarića /. Zagreb , 1985 printing. 204 p. ; LC Card 86-233326
HD5650 .D68 1985

Bakatin, V. V. Stroim Kuzbass /. Kemerovo , 1984. 417 p., [56] p. of plates : LC Card 84-103662
HC337.R852 K8975 1984

BAKED PRODUCTS.
A Profile of the baking industry. [Washington, D.C.] [1985] 49 leaves ; LC Card 86-211982 DDC 338.4/7664752/0973 19
HD9057.U59 P76 1985

Bakeman, Roger. Observing interaction : an introduction to sequential analysis / Roger Bakeman and John M. Gottman. Cambridge [Cambridgeshire] ; New York : Cambridge University Press, 1986. ix, 221 p. : ill. ; 22 cm. Includes index. Bibliography: p. 212-218. ISBN 0-521-25632-1 LC Card 85-22362 DDC 300/.1/51954 19
1. Social sciences - Statistical methods. 2. Sequential analysis. 3. Social interaction - Statistical methods. I. Gottman, John Mordechai. II. Title.
H62 .B284 1986 ***NYPL [JLD 86-3069]***

Baker & Hostetler. Highlights of the Tax Reform Act of 1986 /. Boston [1986] xi, 94 p. ;
NYPL [JLE 87-761]

Baker, Dennis, 1928- Agricultural prices, production, and marketing, with special reference to the hop industry : north-east Kent, 1680-1760 / Dennis Baker. New York : Garland Pub., 1985. 779 p. : ill. ; 24 cm. (British economic history) Bibliography: p. 762-779. ISBN 0-8240-6675-8 : LC Card 84-45995 DDC 338.1/7382 19
1. Hops industry - England - Kent - History. 2. Agriculture - Economic aspects - England - Kent - History. I. Title. II. Series.
HD9019.H72 G67 1985 ***NYPL [JLE 87-63]***

Baker, Keith, 1938- Public budgeting with Lotus 1-2-3 / Keith Baker. Portland, Or. : Management Information Source, 1988. p. cm. Includes index. ISBN 0-943518-46-6 : LC Card 87-24020 DDC 350.72/2/02855369 19
1. Budget - Data processing. 2. Lotus 1-2-3 (Computer program). I. Title.
HJ2009 .B34 1988

Baker Library. Coin and conscience . [Boston, Mass.] , 1986. [28] p. : LC Card 86-203197 DDC 332.4/94 19
HG925 .C65 1986

Baker, Richard H.
Framework applications / Richard H. Baker. 1st ed. Blue Ridge Summit, PA : Tab Books, c1985. x, 259 p. : ill. ; 25 cm. Includes index. On t.p. the registered trademark symbol "TM" is superscript following "framework" in the title. ISBN 0-8306-0908-3 : LC Card 85-9826 DDC 650/.028/5425 19
1. Framework (Computer program). 2. Business - Data processing. I. Title.
HF5548.4.F7 B35 1985 ***NYPL [JSE 86-803]***

Framework applications. Baker, Richard H. Framework II applications / Richard H. Baker. 2nd ed. Blue Ridge Summit, PA , c1987. xi, 320 p. ; ISBN 0-8306-2198-9 : LC Card 86-23104 DDC 650/.028/55369 19
HF5548.4.F7 B35 1987

Framework II applications / Richard H. Baker. 2nd ed. Blue Ridge Summit, PA : Tab Books, c1987. xi, 320 p. ; 26 cm. Rev. ed. of: Framework applications. 1st ed. c1985. Includes index. ISBN 0-8306-2198-9 : LC Card 86-23104 DDC 650/.028/55369 19
1. Framework (Computer program). 2. Business - Data processing. I. Baker, Richard H. Framework applications. II. Title. III. Title: Framework 2 applications. IV. Title: Framework two applications.
HF5548.4.F7 B35 1987

Baker, Timothy G. McKinzie, Lance. A perspective on U. S. farm problems and agricultural policy /. Boulder , 1987. xvii, 189 p. : ISBN 0-8133-7376-X (pbk. : alk. paper) LC Card 86-51501 DDC 338.1/873 19
HD1470.5.U6 M35 1987

Baker, William H., 1944- Smith, Harold T., 1932- The Administrative manager . Chicago , c1987. xii, 548 p. : ISBN 0-574-20065-7 : LC Card 86-24881 DDC 651.8 19
HF5547 .S577 1987

BAKERS AND BAKERIES - UNITED STATES.
A Profile of the baking industry. [Washington, D.C.] [1985] 49 leaves ; LC Card 86-211982 DDC 338.4/7664752/0973 19
HD9057.U59 P76 1985

BAKERY AND CONFECTIONERY WORKERS' INTERNATIONAL UNION OF AMERICA - HISTORY.
Kaufman, Stuart Bruce. A vision of unity . Kensington, Md. , c1986. ix, 182 p. : LC Card 86-225331 DDC 331.88/1 19
HD6515.B2 K38 1986

Bakhar, V. Parichno-kreditni i finansovi otnoshenii͡a v sistemata na sŭvremennii͡a dŭrzhavno-monopolisticheski kapitalizŭm /. Sofii͡a , 1985. 245 p. : LC Card 86-153156
HG3881 .P2936 1985

Bakhmetova, G. Sh. (Gi͡ul′dzhan Sharifovna)
Boi͡arskiĭ, Aron I͡Akovlevich, 1906- Praktikum po demografii /. Moskva , 1985. 141, [3] p. : LC Card 86-170070
HB3607 .B64 1985

Bakhrakh, D. N. (Dem′i͡an Nikolaevich)
Osnovnye poni͡atii͡a teorii sotsial′nogo upravlenii͡a : uchebnoe posobie po spetskursu / D.N. Bakhrakh. Perm′ : Permskiĭ gos. universitet, 1978. 100 p. ; 20 cm. At head of title: Ministerstvo vysshego i srednego spetsial′nogo obrazovanii͡a RSFSR. Permskiĭ ordena Trudovogo Krasnogo Znameni gosudarstvennyĭ universitet im. A.M. Gor′kogo. Bibliography: p. 97-[99] LC Card 81-154363
1. Management - Soviet Union. 2. Personnel management - Soviet Union. I. Title.
HD70.S63 B35 1978

BAKING.
(1985) A Profile of the baking industry. [Washington, D.C.] [1985] 49 leaves ; LC Card 86-211982 DDC 338.4/7664752/0973 19
HD9057.U59 P76 1985

Baking industry profile. A Profile of the baking industry. [Washington, D.C.] [1985] 49 leaves ; LC Card 86-211982 DDC 338.4/7664752/0973 19
HD9057.U59 P76 1985

Bakke, E. Wight (Edward Wight), 1903- Labor mobility and economic opportunity . Westport, Conn. , 1987, c1954. vii, 118 p. ; ISBN 0-313-24975-X (lib. bdg. : alk. paper) LC Card 86-25763 DDC 331.12/7973 19
HD5717.5.U6 L33 1987

Bakker, G. J. Op arbeid bezuinigd? : een verkenning van de invloed van gemeentelijke bezuinigingen op de arbeidsmarkt / G.J. Bakker, R.D.J. Nieuwenhuizen. 's-Gravenhage : Staatsuitgeverij, 1986. 116 p. ; 28 cm. (OSA-voorstudie . nr. V 13) Bibliography: p. 115-116. ISBN 90-12-05321-8 LC Card 87-108889
1. Municipal finance - Netherlands. 2. Labor supply - Netherlands. I. Nieuwenhuizen, René. II. Title.
HJ9507 .B35 1986

Baklanov, Petr I͡Akovlevich. Prostranstvennye sistemy proizvodstva : mikrostrukturnyĭ uroven′ analiza i upravlenii͡a / P.I͡A. Baklanov ; otvetstvennyĭ redaktor Ė.B. Alaev. Moskva : "Nauka", 1986. 149 p. : ill. ; 22 cm. At head of title: Akademii͡a nauk SSSR. Dal′nevostochnyĭ nauchnyĭ t͡sentr. Tikhookeanskiĭ institut geografii. Bibliography: p. 140-[148]. LC Card 86-202803
1. Soviet Union - Industries - Location. I. Alaev, Ė. B. II. Title.
HC340.D5 B35 1986

Bakonyi, Árpád. Módszerek a beruházási tevékenység kvantitatív elemzéséhez /. Budapest , 1985. 207 p. : ISBN 963-05-3607-2 : LC Card 86-100399
HG4028.C4 M57 1985

Bakonyi, Emmerich. Mitgliedererwartungen in Bankgenossenschaften : Erwartungsstrukturen und Urteile der Mitglieder (Kunden) von Genossenschaftsbanken über den Förderungsauftrag, unter besonderer Berücksichtigung der Methoden zur Erfassung der Präferenzen und zur Messung des Zufriedenheitsgrades von Individuen und Gruppen / von Emmerich Bakonyi. Stuttgart : E. Ulmer, c1983. 389 p. : 18 ill. ; 22 cm. (Hohenheimer Arbeiten. Heft 128.) Bibliography: p. [356]-359. ISBN 3-8001-8188-6 LC Card 84-106778
1. Banks and banking, Cooperative. 2. Banks and banking - Customer services. I. Series: Hohenheimer Arbeiten, Heft 128. II. Title.
HG2035 .B28 1983

Bakos, Brian D. Business communications at work / Brian D. Bakos. Englewood Cliffs, N.J. : Prentice Hall, c1988. xi, 239 p. : ill. ; 28 cm. Includes index. ISBN 0-13-091752-4 (pbk.) : LC Card 87-19690 DDC 808/.06665 19
1. Business communication. I. Title.
HF5718 .B35 1988

Balakrishnan, Anantaram. A composite algorithm for the concave-cost LTL consolidation problem / by Anantaram Balakrishnan, Stephen C. Graves. West Lafayette, Ind. : Institute for Research in the Behavioral, Economic, and Management Sciences, Krannert Graduate School of Management, Purdue University, [1985] 43, 14 p. : ill. ; 28 cm. (Paper / Institute for Research in the Behavioral, Economic, and Management Sciences, Krannert Graduate School of Management, Purdue University . no. 877) "July 1985." Bibliography: p. 42-43. LC Card 86-139493
1. Network analysis (Planning). I. Graves, Stephen C. II. Series: Paper (Krannert Graduate School of Management. Institute for Research in the Bahavioral, Economic, and Management Sciences) , no. 877. III. Title.
HD6483 .P8 no. 877 T57.85

Balakrishnan, C. B.
Adiseshiah, Malcolm S. Mid year review of the economy, 1986-87 /. New Delhi , 1987. 193 p. : ISBN 81-7062-016-3 : LC Card 87-900477 DDC 330.954/052 19
HC435.2 .A648 1987

Review of a mid-year review of the economy, 1984 / C. Balakrishnan, Malcolm S. Adiseshiah. New Delhi : India International Centre, 1984. 132 p. ; 23 cm. (IIC monograph series . no. 5) Bibliography: p. 94-98. LC Card 86-903796 DDC 330.954/052 19
1. India - Economic conditions - 1947-. I. Adiseshiah, Malcolm S. II. Title. III. Series.
HC435.2 .B323 1984

Balance de energía, 1965-1984 : Chile / Comisión Nacional de Energía. Santiago, Chile : La Comisión, [1985 or 1986] 191 p. : col. ill. ; 30 cm. Errata slip inserted. LC Card 87-401010 DDC 333.79/0983 19
1. Energy industries - Chile - Statistics. 2. Energy consumption - Chile - Statistics. I. Chile. Comisión Nacional de Energía.
HD9502.C52 B35 1985

Balance general de huelga y administración, de noviembre 1904 á abril 1906 /. Sociedad Unión Obreros Talabarteros (Argentina) Buenos Aires , 1906. 65 p. ; LC Card 85-203379
HD6604.H2 S63 1906

BALANCE OF NATURE. see **ECOLOGY.**

BALANCE OF PAYMENTS - ADDRESSES, ESSAYS, LECTURES.
Floating exchange rates and the state of world trade payments /. Cambridge, Mass. , 1984. xxvi, 309 p. ; ISBN 0-88410-998-4 (pbk.) LC Card 84-2905 DDC 332.4/562 19
HG3852 .F56 1984 ***NYPL [JLD 86-2709]***

Balance of payments adjustment, 1945 to 1986 .
De Vries, Margaret Garritsen, 1922- Washington, D.C. , 1987. xi, 336 p. ; ISBN 0-939934-93-0 (pbk.) : LC Card 87-17242 DDC 332.1/52 19
HG3890 .D4 1987

BALANCE OF PAYMENTS - AUSTRIA - STATISTICAL SERVICES.
Die Statistische Differenz in der österreichischen Zahlungsbilanz /. Wien , 1979. 68 p. : LC Card 85-179826
HG3883.A9 S73 1979

BALANCE OF PAYMENTS - BRAZIL.
Cerrado . [Rio de Janeiro] , 1984. 53 p., [2] leaves of plates : LC Card 87-132493 DDC 380.1/4131/0981 19
HD9044.B682 C47 1984

Langoni, Carlos Geraldo. A crise do desenvolvimento, uma estratégia para o futuro /. Rio de Janeiro , 1985. xix, 176 p. : ISBN 85-03-00001-6 : LC Card 85-151246 DDC 338.981 19
HG835 .L36 1985 ***NYPL [JLD 86-288]***

BALANCE OF PAYMENTS - BRAZIL - RIO GRANDE DO SUL - HISTORY - 20TH CENTURY.
Leite, Manoel Marques. Relações externas da economia do Rio Grande do Sul, 1949/79 /. [Porto Alegre] , 1985. 114 p. : ISBN 85-7025-097-5 : LC Card 87-104433 DDC 382/.098165 19
HF3409.R5 L45 1985

BALANCE OF PAYMENTS - CONGRESSES.
World monetary system in a time of change . Budapest [1987] 283 p. ; ISBN 963-01-7937-7 (pbk.) LC Card 87-169001 DDC 332.4/5 19
HG230.3 .W68 1987

BALANCE OF PAYMENTS - CUBA.
Banco Nacional de Cuba (Founded 1948) Cuba's financial crisis . Washington, D.C. (1000 Thomas Jefferson St., N.W., Suite 601, Washington 20007) , 1985. vii, 64, [19] p. : LC Card 86-105593 DDC 330.97291/064 19
HC152.5 .B36 1985 ***NYPL [JLE 86-3732]***

BALANCE OF PAYMENTS - DENMARK.
Metodologi for Danmarks betalingsbalance =. Luxembourg , Washington, D.C. , 1985. 181 p. ; ISBN 92-825-4927-5 : LC Card 86-122287
HG3883.D4 M48 1985

BALANCE OF PAYMENTS - DENMARK - STATISTICAL SERVICES.
Metodologi for Danmarks betalingsbalance =. Luxembourg , Washington, D.C. , 1985. 181 p. ; ISBN 92-825-4927-5 : LC Card 86-122287
HG3883.D4 M48 1985

BALANCE OF PAYMENTS - DEVELOPING COUNTRIES.
De Vries, Margaret Garritsen, 1922- Balance of payments adjustment, 1945 to 1986 . Washington, D.C. , 1987. xi, 336 p. ; ISBN 0-939934-93-0 (pbk.) : LC Card 87-17242 DDC 332.1/52 19
HG3890 .D4 1987

Herrmann, Roland. The compensatory financing system of the International Monetary Fund . Kiel, West-Germany , 1983. iii, 85 p. ; ISBN 3-922553-18-4 (pbk.) LC Card 83-227524 DDC 332.1/52 19
HG3881.5.I58 H47 1983 ***NYPL [JLD 97-7]***

BALANCE OF PAYMENTS - DOMINICAN REPUBLIC - CONGRESSES.
La Situación cambiaria en la República Dominicana /. Santo Domingo, República Dominicana , 1984. 252 p. : LC Card 87-401265 DDC 338.97293 19
HC153.5 .S575 1984

BALANCE OF PAYMENTS - ECONOMETRIC MODELS.
Gross, Alexander, 1953- The role of the current account in asset market models of exchange rate determination /. Berlin , New York , 1987. xiii, 391 p. : ISBN 0-89925-373-3 (U. S.) : LC Card 87-8852 DDC 332.4/56 19
HG3882 .G75 1987

BALANCE OF PAYMENTS - EUROPE, EASTERN.
Holzman, Franklyn D. The economics of Soviet bloc trade and finance /. Boulder , 1987. xi, 215 p. : ISBN 0-8133-7274-7 (alk. paper) : LC Card 86-32598 DDC 382/.0947 19
HF3496.5 .H62 1987

BALANCE OF PAYMENTS - EUROPE - HISTORY.
Attman, Artur, 1910- American bullion in the European world trade, 1600-1800 /. Göteborg , 1986. 115 p. ; ISBN 91-85252-38-7 (pbk.) LC Card 87-147250 DDC 382/.4242/0973 19
HG285.A45 A88 1986

BALANCE OF PAYMENTS - GERMANY, WEST.
Fleischer, Peter. Bestimmungsgründe von Zahlungsbilanz und Wechselkursen in der Bundesrepublik Deutschland /. Frankfurt am Main , New York , c1986. iv, 181 p. : ISBN 3-8204-9610-6 LC Card 86-232901
HG3883.G3 F57 1986

BALANCE OF PAYMENTS - GREECE.
Maroulis, Dimitris. Economic development and the structure of the balance of payments . Athens , 1986. 267 p. : LC Card 87-170680 DDC 382.1/7/09495 19
HC295 .M32 1986

BALANCE OF PAYMENTS - GREECE - STATISTICAL METHODS.
Methodologia tou isozygiou plērōmōn tēs Helladas =. Luxembourg , 1986, c1985. 155 p. ; ISBN 92-825-5642-5 : LC Card 86-176326
HG3883.G6 S72 1986

BALANCE OF PAYMENTS - HONG KONG.
Balassa, Bela A. Adjusting to success . Washington, DC , 1987. x, 121 p. : ISBN 0-88132-061-7 (pbk.) LC Card 87-3309 DDC 382.1/7/0951 19
HG3883.H66 B34 1987

BALANCE OF PAYMENTS - INDIA - HISTORY.
Goswami, Prodyot Kumar, 1940- Indian currency and exchange, 1835-1940 /. New Delhi , 1983. viii, 134 p. ; LC Card 83-903565 DDC 332.4/560954 19
HG1234 .G67 1983 ***NYPL [JLD 87-673]***

BALANCE OF PAYMENTS - IVORY COAST.
Kouassi, Jean-Claude. Transports maritimes et balance des paiements en Côte d'Ivoire /. [Abidjan] [1982?] 23, xii leaves ; LC Card 86-111436 DDC 387.5/1 19
HE597.I9 K68 1982 ***NYPL [JLF 86-1485]***

BALANCE OF PAYMENTS - KOREA (SOUTH)
Balassa, Bela A. Adjusting to success . Washington, DC , 1987. x, 121 p. : ISBN 0-88132-061-7 (pbk.) LC Card 87-3309 DDC 382.1/7/0951 19
HG3883.H66 B34 1987

BALANCE OF PAYMENTS - MATHEMATICAL MODELS.
Grössl, Ingrid. Der Zusammenhang von finanz- und realwirtschaftlichem Sektor einer offenen, stationären Volkswirtschaft . Berlin , c1986. 162 p. ; ISBN 3-428-05986-7 LC Card 86-206327
HG3882 .G76 1986

Balance of payments methodology of Denmark.
Metodologi for Danmarks betalingsbalance =. Luxembourg , Washington, D.C. , 1985. 181 p. ; ISBN 92-825-4927-5 : LC Card 86-122287
HG3883.D4 M48 1985

Balance of payments methodology of Greece.
Methodologia tou isozygiou plērōmōn tēs Helladas =. Luxembourg , 1986, c1985. 155 p. ; ISBN 92-825-5642-5 : LC Card 86-176326
HG3883.G6 S72 1986

BALANCE OF PAYMENTS - MOROCCO.
Benazzou, Chaouki, 1936- Le Maroc face à l'endettement extérieur . [Rabat] 1986 ([Rabat] : Imprimé aux Editions maghrébines) 151 p. : LC Card 87-967050
HG3883.M8 B46 1986

BALANCE OF PAYMENTS - PERU.
Scheetz, Thomas Edward. Peru and the International Monetary Fund /. Pittsburgh, PA , c1986. xi, 257 p. : ISBN 0-8229-3816-2 LC Card 85-40855 DDC 332.1/52 19
HG3881.5.I58 S34 1986
NYPL [JLD 86-2893]

BALANCE OF PAYMENTS - PORTUGAL - MATHEMATICAL MODELS.
Barbosa, Manuel P. (Manuel Pinto), 1944- Growth, migration, and the balance of payments in a small open economy, Portugal /. New York , 1984. xv, 212 p. : ISBN 0-8240-4169-0 : LC Card 79-53646 DDC 382.1/7/0724 19
HD5809.A6 B37 1984 ***NYPL [JLE 86-4171]***

BALANCE OF PAYMENTS - SINGAPORE.
Balassa, Bela A. Adjusting to success . Washington, DC , 1987. x, 121 p. : ISBN 0-88132-061-7 (pbk.) LC Card 87-3309 DDC

382.1/7/0951 19
HG3883.H66 B34 1987

BALANCE OF PAYMENTS - SOVIET UNION.
Neu, C. R. (Carl Richard), 1949- Toward a profile of Soviet behavior in international financial markets /. Santa Monica, CA [1987] xv, 58 p. : ISBN 0-8330-0865-X (pbk.) LC Card 87-13084 DDC 332/.042/0947 19
HG3955 .N48 1987

BALANCE OF PAYMENTS - SPAIN.
Albentosa Puche, Luis. El sector exterior en España /. Madrid , c1984. 343 p. : ISBN 84-85719-40-9 LC Card 85-214668 DDC 336.3/4/0946 19
HG3883.S69 A45 1984 ***NYPL [JLC 86-251]***

Requeijo, Jaime. Introducción a la balanza de pagos de España /. Madrid , 1985. 174 p. : ISBN 84-309-1221-5 LC Card 86-150983
HG3883.S69 R46 1985

BALANCE OF PAYMENTS - STATISTICS.
Oechsler, Ronald G. Statistical abstract of East-West trade and finance . Washington, D.C. [1986]. vi, 43 p. : LC Card 86-601999 DDC 382/.091713/01717021 19
HF1411 .O3455 1986

BALANCE OF PAYMENTS - TAIWAN.
Balassa, Bela A. Adjusting to success . Washington, DC , 1987. x, 121 p. : ISBN 0-88132-061-7 (pbk.) LC Card 87-3309 DDC 382.1/7/0951 19
HG3883.H66 B34 1987

BALANCE OF PAYMENTS - UNITED STATES.
Danielian, Ronald L. The forgotten deficit . Boulder , 1987. xii, 84 p. ; ISBN 0-8133-7450-2 (pbk. : alk. paper) LC Card 87-50654 DDC 332.6/7373 19
HG3883.U7 D36 1987

Thomsen, Stephen E. International capital flows and the United States . Washington, D.C. (1400 Eye St., N.W., Suite 510, Washington 20005) [1985] vi, 62 p. : LC Card 87-108428 DDC 332/.042/0973 19
HG4910 .T47 1985

The U. S. international payments crisis . Washington, D.C. (1400 Eye St., N.W., Suite 510, Washington 20005) [1986] 31 p. : LC Card 87-108567 DDC 382.1/7/0973 19
HG3883.U7 U18 1986

BALANCE OF PAYMENTS - UNITED STATES - HISTORY - 20TH CENTURY.
Hawley, James P., 1944- Dollars & borders . Armonk, N.Y. , c1987. xi, 204 p. ; ISBN 0-87332-386-6 : LC Card 86-31395 DDC 332/.041 19
HG3891 .H38 1987

BALANCE OF PAYMENTS - VENEZUELA.
Echevarría Salvat, Oscar A., 1935- Deuda--crisis cambiaria . Caracas , 1986. xx, 248 p. : ISBN 980-265-224-5 LC Card 87-400245 DDC 336.3/4/0987 19
HG3883.V4 E28 1986

BALANCE OF PAYMENTS - YUGOSLAVIA.
Yagci, Fahrettin, 1944- Macroeconomic policies and adjustment in Yugoslavia . Washington, D.C. [1987] 29 p. ; ISBN 0-8213-0938-2 (pbk.) LC Card 87-16064 DDC 339.5/09497 19
HC407.Y6 Y34 1987

BALANCE OF TRADE.
Raffer, Kunibert, 1951- Unequal exchange and the evolution of the world system . New York , 1987. ix, 301 p. ; ISBN 0-312-00440-0 : LC Card 86-31306 DDC 337 19
HF1411 .R26 1987

BALANCE OF TRADE - BRAZIL - RIO GRANDE DO SUL - HISTORY - 20TH CENTURY.
Leite, Manoel Marques. Relações externas da economia do Rio Grande do Sul, 1949/79 /. [Porto Alegre] , 1985. 114 p. : ISBN 85-7025-097-5 : LC Card 87-104433 DDC 382/.098165 19
HF3409.R5 L45 1985

BALANCE OF TRADE - CANADA.
Technology and commodity trade [microform] /. Ottawa , c1984. 40 p. : ISBN 0-660-11447-X (pbk.) : LC Card 85-132672 DDC 382/.4562/000971 19
HC120.T4 T43 1984
NYPL [*ZT-1745 no.16]

BALANCE OF TRADE - FRANCE.
Chatelain, Jacky. Les trous du commerce extérieur /. Paris , c1984. 170 p. : ISBN 2-86738-031-1 : LC Card 84-241861
HF3556.5 .C42 1984

BALANCE OF TRADE - ITALY.
Tasgian, Astrig. L'imposta e il deposito previo sugli acquisti di valuta e la crisi della lira del 1976 . Milano , c1983. 139 p. : LC Card 83-187693 DDC 332.4/945 19
HG1029.5 .T37 1983 ***NYPL [JLD 87-813]***

BALANCE OF TRADE - JAPAN - CONGRESSES.
Bergsten, C. Fred, 1941- The United States-Japan economic problem /. Washington, D.C. , c1985. x, 164 p. : ISBN 0-262-52108-3 LC Card 85-18106 DDC 382/.0973/052 19
HF3127 .B47 1985 ***NYPL [JLE 87-19]***

BALANCE OF TRADE - MATHEMATICAL MODELS.
Cuddington, John T. Budget deficits and the current account in the presence of classical unemployment /. [Madrid] [1984] 47 p. : ISBN 84-505-0847-9 (pbk.) LC Card 86-215031 DDC 339.5/23/0724 19
HJ2005 .C83 1984

BALANCE OF TRADE - SPAIN.
Requeijo, Jaime. Introducción a la balanza de pagos de España /. Madrid , 1985. 174 p. : ISBN 84-309-1221-5 LC Card 86-150983
HG3883.S69 R46 1985

BALANCE OF TRADE - UNITED STATES.
Carvounis, Chris C. The United States trade deficit of the 1980s . New York , 1987. vi, 190 p. ; ISBN 0-89930-219-X (lib. bdg. : alk. paper) LC Card 87-2561 DDC 382.1/7/0973 19
HF3031 .C37 1987

Contemporary economic problems . Washington, D.C. , c1987. 332 p. : ISBN 0-8447-3621-X (alk. paper) LC Card 87-1395 DDC 330.973/0927 19
HC106.8 .C665 1987

Economic competitiveness promoting America's living standard /] Washington , 1986 [i.e. 1987] vii, 34 p. : LC Card 87-601340 DDC 338.973 19
HC106.8 .E2745 1987

Solomon, Anthony M. The dollar, debt, and the trade deficit /. New York , 1987. 55 p. ; ISBN 0-8147-7863-1 : LC Card 86-23651 DDC 382.1/7/0973 19
HF3031 .S65 1987

The Trade deficit in manufactured goods . [Washington] , Washington, D.C. [1986] vi, 79 p. : LC Card 86-601142 DDC 382/.4567/0973 19
HD9725 .T73 1986

The Trade gap . Dayton, Ohio (100 Commons Rd., Dayton 45459-2777) , c1987. 35 p. : LC Card 87-71294 DDC 382.1/7/0973 19
HF3031 .T7 1987

Trade in services . Washington, D.C. [1986] viii, 102 p. : LC Card 86-600576 DDC 382/.45/000973 19
HD9981.5 .T7 1986

The U. S. international payments crisis . Washington, D.C. (1400 Eye St., N.W., Suite 510, Washington 20005) [1986] 31 p. : LC Card 87-108567 DDC 382.1/7/0973 19
HG3883.U7 U18 1986

BALANCE OF TRADE - UNITED STATES - CONGRESSES.
Bergsten, C. Fred, 1941- The United States-Japan economic problem /. Washington, D.C. , c1985. x, 164 p. : ISBN 0-262-52108-3 LC Card 85-18106 DDC 382/.0973/052 19
HF3127 .B47 1985 ***NYPL [JLE 87-19]***

Balance sheet management . Nunes, Morris A., 1949- New York , c1987. xvi, 288 p. : ISBN 0-471-62956-1 (pbk.) LC Card 87-23093 DDC 658.1/51 19
HF5681.B2 N86 1987

BALANCE SHEETS. see **FINANCIAL STATEMENTS.**

Balanced budgets and American politics /. Savage, James D., 1951- Ithaca, N.Y. , c1988. p. cm. ISBN 0-8014-2047-4 LC Card 87-25061 DDC 339.5/23/0973 19
HJ2050 .S28 1988

Balances energéticos del Ecuador . Kublank, Peter. Quito, Ecuador , 1983. 1 v. (various foliations) : LC Card 86-153116
HD9502.E22 K82 1983

Balancing the national interest . Committee on Science, Engineering, and Public Policy (U. S.). Panel on the Impact of National Security Controls on International Technology Transfer. Washington, D.C. , 1987. xiii, 321 p. : ISBN 0-309-03738-7 LC Card 87-60020 DDC 337.73 19
HF1456 .C65 1987

Balanço e disponibilidade interna de gêneros alimentícios de origem vegetal 1975 a 1980 / Fundação Getúlio Vargas, Instituto Brasileiro de Economia, Divisão de Estatística e Econometria, Centro de Estudos Agrícolas. Rio de Janeiro, RJ, Brasil : Centro de Estudos Agrícolas, 1983. 72 p. ; 30 cm.
1. Produce trade - Brazil - Statistics. 2. Food supply - Brazil - Statistics. I. Instituto Brasileiro de Economia. Centro de Estudos Agrícolas. ***NYPL [JLG 85-94]***

Balanço e disponibilidade interna de gêneros alimentícios de origem vegetal, 1979 a 1983 / Fundação Getúlio Vargas, Instituto Brasileiro de Economia, Divisão de Estatística e Econometria, Centro de Estudos Agrícolas. Rio de Janeiro, Brasil : CEA, 1985. 67 p. ; 31 cm. Chiefly tables. LC Card 87-404963 DDC 339.4/86413/00981021 19
1. Produce trade - Brazil - Statistics. 2. Food consumption - Brazil - Statistics. I. Centro de Estudos Agrícolas (Instituto Brasileiro de Economia).
HD9014.B82 B345 1985

Balandier, Georges. Sociologie des Brazzavilles noires / Georges Balandier. 2. éd. augm. / accompagnée d'un texte et de bibliographies de Jean Copans. Paris : Presses de la Fondation nationale des sciences politiques, c1985. xviii, 306 p., [2] leaves of plates : ill. ; 20 cm. (Références . 15) Bibliography: p. 297-306. ISBN 2-7246-0524-1 : LC Card 86-138199
1. Rural-urban migration - Congo (Brazzaville) - Brazzaville. 2. Brazzaville, Congo - Social conditions. I. Copans, Jean. II. Series: Références (Presses de la Fondation nationale des sciences politiques) , 15. III. Title.
HB2125.B73 B34 1985

Balashova, N. I. Gosplan RSFSR. Metodicheskie ukazaniia k razrabotke planov ėkonomicheskogo i sotsial'nogo razvitiia RSFSR /. Moskva , 1985. 462 p. ; LC Card 85-232541
HC337.R85 G67 1985

Balasko, Yves. Foundations of the theory of general equilibrium / Yves Balasko. Orlando, Fla. : Academic Press, c1988. p. cm. (Economic theory, econometrics, and mathematical economics) Bibliography: p. Includes index. ISBN 0-12-076975-1 (alk. paper) LC Card 87-68 DDC 339.5 19
1. Equilibrium (Economics). I. Title.
HB145 .B32 1988

Balassa, Ákos. Gazdaságirányítás, 1985 /. Budapest , 1984. 175 p. ; ISBN 963-221-540-0 : LC Card 85-229856
HC300.28 .G338 1984

Balassa, Bela A.
Adjusting to success : balance of payments policy in the East Asian NICs / Bela Balassa, John Williamson. Washington, DC : Institute for International Economics, 1987. x, 121 p. : ill. ; 22 cm. (Policy analyses in international economics . 17) "June 1987." Bibliography: p. 119-121. ISBN 0-88132-061-7 (pbk.) LC Card 87-3309 DDC 382.1/7/0951 19
1. Balance of payments - Hong Kong. 2. Balance of payments - Korea (South). 3. Balance of payments - Singapore. 4. Balance of payments - Taiwan. I. Williamson, John, 1937-. II. Title. III. Series.
HG3883.H66 B34 1987

Economic incentives . London , 1986. xiii, 497 p. ; ISBN 0-333-40473-4 ***NYPL [JLD 87-367]***

Balázs, György, 1932- Agrárgazdaság, agrártársadalom, agrárpolitika /. Szeged , 1985. 338 p. : ISBN 963-481-548-0 : LC Card 86-143859
HD1940.5 .A78 1985

Balázsy, Sándor. Iparunk 40 éve /. [Budapest] , 1985. 58, [37] p. : ISBN 963-382-009-X LC Card 85-228898
HC300.28 .I64 1985

Balbis, Jorge. El Primer batllismo . Montevideo [1985] 159 p. : LC Card 85-233561 DDC 338.9895 19
HC232 .P75 1985 *NYPL [JLC 86-259]*

Balcão de projetos.
Industria dei pezzi per autoveicoli /. [São Paulo] , 1973. 1 v. (various pagings), [12] leaves of plates : LC Card 86-146007
HD9710.3.B72 I53 1973

Industria petrolchimica /. [São Paulo] , 1973. 1 v. (various pagings), [22] leaves of plates : LC Card 86-146014
HD9579.C33 B7417 1973

Balcerowicz, Leszek. Zur Interdependenz von Unternehmens- und Wirtschaftsordnung /. Stuttgart , New York , 1986. x, 280 p. ; ISBN 3-437-50296-4 LC Card 87-134241 DDC 338.9 19
HB95 .Z87 1986

Balcet, G. (Giovanni) Italia multinazionale . Milano , 1986. 2 v. : LC Card 87-158571
HD2864 .I82 1986

Balderjahn, Ingo. Das umweltbewusste Konsumentenverhalten : eine empirische Studie / von Ingo Balderjahn. Berlin : Duncker & Humblot, c1986. ix, 277 p. ; 24 cm. (Betriebswirtschaftliche Schriften. Heft 123) Bibliography: p. 257-277. ISBN 3-428-06107-1 LC Card 87-113640 DDC 658.8/34/0724 19
1. Consumers - Mathematical models. I. Title.
HF5415.3 .B316 1986

Bâldescu, Emil. Din istoria legăturilor revoluționare româno-bulgare (1909-1916) [microform]. [București] Editura Științifică [1966] 181 p. 20 cm. Summary in Bulgarian, English and Russian. Includes bibliographical references. Microfilm. New York : New York Public Library, 1986. 1 microfilm reel ; 35 mm. (MN *ZZ-26,610) LC Card 81-475045
1. Labor and laboring classes - Romania. 2. Labor and laboring classes - Bulgaria. 3. Socialism in Romania. 4. Socialism in Bulgaria. 5. Romania - Relations (general) with Bulgaria. 6. Bulgaria - Relations (general) with Romania. I. Title.
HD8646 .B34 *NYPL [*ZT-1732 no.1]*

Baldridge, Donald C. (Donald Carl) Mexican petroleum and United States-Mexican relations, 1919-1923 / Donald C. Baldridge. New York : Garland, 1987. 255 p. ; 23 cm. (Foreign economic policy of the United States) Bibliography: p. 242-255. ISBN 0-8240-8070-X (alk. paper) LC Card 87-23817 DDC 338.2/7282/0972 19
1. Petroleum industry and trade - Mexico - History - 20th century. 2. Petroleum industry and trade - United States - History - 20th century. 3. United States - Foreign economic relations - Mexico. 4. Mexico - Foreign economic relations - United States. I. Title. II. Series.
HD9574.M6 B324 1987

Balducci, Cataldo. Il sindacato / Cataldo Balducci, Umberto Carabelli. Torino : UTET, c1984. 2 v. ; 25 cm. (Dottrina e giurisprudenza di diritto del lavoro. Diritto sindacale) Includes bibliographies and index. ISBN 88-02-03818-X (set) : LC Card 85-158972 DDC 344.45/0188 344.504188 19
1. Trade-unions - Law and legislation - Italy. 2. Collective labor agreements - Italy. 3. Labor laws and legislation - Italy. I. Carabelli, Umberto. II. Title. III. Series.
LAW *NYPL [JLE 86-3250]*

Balducci, Renato, 1947- Contrattazione salariale e ciclo economico : modalità ed effetti della lotta di classe in un modello non lineare del ciclo / REnato Balducci, Guido Candela. Roma : Nuova Italia scientifica, 1982. 174 p. : ill. ; 22 cm. (Studi NIS economia . 2) Includes index. Bibliography: p. [163]-167.
1. Wages - Mathematical models. 2. Business cycles - Mathematical models. I. Candela, Guido, 1943-. II. Title. III. Series. *NYPL [JLD 86-2868]*

Baldwin, Leo. Horne, Jo. Homesharing and other lifestyle options /. Washington, D.C. , Glenview, Ill. , c1988. xi, 259 p. : ISBN 0-673-24886-0 (pbk.) : LC Card 87-13028 DDC 363.5/9 19
HD7287.92.U54 H65 1988

Baldwin, Robert E. Current U. S. trade policy . Cambridge, Mass. (1050 Massachusetts Ave., Cambridge 02138) , 1986. iii, 128 p. ; LC Card 86-201110 DDC 382/.3/0973 19
HF1455 .C87 1986

Baldwin, Robert H. Pillsbury, Hobart B. Armed forces guide to personal financial planning . Harrisburg, PA , c1987. p. cm. ISBN 0-8117-2123-X LC Card 86-30201 DDC 332.024/355 19
HG179 .P55 1987

Baldwin, Thomas F. Cable communication / Thomas F. Baldwin, D. Stevens McVoy. Englewood Cliffs, N.J. : Prentice Hall, c1988. p. cm. Includes bibliographical references and index. ISBN 0-13-110263-X : LC Card 87-16109 DDC 384.55/56 19
1. Cable television. I. McVoy, D. Stevens. II. Title.
HE8700.7 .B35 1988

Baldwin, William L., 1928- Market structure and technological change / William L. Baldwin and John T. Scott. Chur, Switzerland ; New York : Harwood Academic Publishers, c1987. viii, 170 p. ; 29 cm. (Fundamentals of pure and applied economics . v. 17.) Bibliography: p. 147-163. Includes index. ISBN 3-7186-0375-6 (pbk.) LC Card 86-25780 DDC 338/.06 19
1. Industrial organization (Economic theory). 2. Technological innovations - Economic aspects. I. Scott, John T., 1947-. II. Series. III. Series: Fundamentals of pure and applied economics , v. 17. IV. Title.
HD2326 .B35 1987

Baletić, Zvonimir. Osnove dugoročnog razvoja SR Hrvatske--svodna studija /. Zagreb , 1984. 437 p. ; LC Card 87-151188
HC407.Z7 C7647 1984

Balevski, Dano. Nauchno-prakticheska konferentsiia "Prebroiavane na naselenieto i zhilishtniia fond--teoriia i praktika" (1986 : Slŭnchev briag, Bulgaria) Nauchno-prakticheska konferentsiia "Prebroiavane na naselenieto i zhilishtniia fond--teoriia i praktika," 9-11 oktomvri 1986 g., Slŭnchev briag /. Sofiia , 1986- v. <1 > : LC Card 87-156528
HA1621.5 1985

Balfet, Michel. Les 50 mots clefs de la consommation / Michel Balfet, Hubert Droit, Michel Truchon. Toulouse : Privat, c1985. 310 p. : ill. ; 21 cm. (Les Cinquante mots clefs) Includes bibliographies. ISBN 2-7089-1969-5 : LC Card 86-140639 DDC 339.4/7 19
1. Consumption (Economics). 2. Consumers. I. Droit, Hubert. II. Truchon, Michel. III. Title: Cinquante mots clefs de la consommation. IV. Title: Consommation.
HB801 .B276 1985

Balfour, Alan. Union-management relations in a changing economy / Alan Balfour. Englewood Cliffs, N.J. : Prentice-Hall, c1987. xiv, 482 p. : ill. ; 25 cm. Includes bibliographies and index. ISBN 0-13-938804-4 LC Card 86-30495 DDC 331/.0973 19
1. Industrial relations - United States - History. 2. Collective bargaining - United States - History. 3. Trade-unions - United States - History. I. Title.
HD8066 .B34 1987

BALI (INDONESIA : PROVINCE) - POPULATION.
Streatfield, K. Fertility decline in a traditional society . [Canberra, ACT] , 1986. xvii, 177 p. : ISBN 0-86784-711-5 (pbk.) LC Card 86-213262 DDC 304.6/32/095986 19
HB1058.B34 S87 1986

Balin, George. Aerospace markets /. Greenwich, CT, U. S.A. (100 Northfield St., Greenwich 06830) , c1987. 1 v. (various pagings) : LC Card 87-156000 DDC 380.1/456291 19
HD9711.5.A2 A37 1987

BALKAN PENINSULA - COMMERCE - GREAT BRITAIN - HISTORY - 19TH CENTURY.
Cernovodeanu, Paul. Relațiile comerciale româno-engleze în contextul politicii orientale a Marii Britanii . Cluj-Napoca , 1986. 404 p. ; LC Card 87-143711
HF3508.R6 C47 1986

Balkin, David B., 1948- New perspectives on compensation /. Englewood Cliffs, N.J. , c1987. xviii, 363 p. : ISBN 0-13-615212-0 (pbk.) LC Card 86-25534 DDC 658.3/2 19
HF5549.5.C67 N49 1987

Ball, David. The Changing labor market . Lexington, Mass. , c1986. x, 166 p. : ISBN 0-669-11943-1 (alk. paper) LC Card 85-45710 DDC 331.12/0973 19
HD6331.2.U5 C47 1986 *NYPL [JLE 86-1069]*

Ball, Helmut. Zukunftsvorsorge und ökonomische Entwicklung : Entscheidungen über Kapitalbildung, Versicherung, Ausbildung, Arbeit und Generationenvertrag aus einzel- und gesamtwirtschaftlicher Sicht / Helmut Ball. Frankfurt [am Main] ; New York : Campus, c1984. 263 p. : ill. ; 21 cm. Bibliography: p. 254-263. ISBN 3-593-33318-X LC Card 84-175872
1. Economic development - Mathematical models. 2. Uncertainty - Mathematical models. I. Title.
HD75.5 .B35 1984

Ballance, Robert H. International industry and business : structural change, industrial policy and industry strategies / Robert H. Ballance. London ; Boston : Allen & Unwin, 1987. xxi, 357 p. ; 23 cm. Bibliography: p. 330-347. Includes indexes. ISBN 0-04-339037-4 (alk. paper) LC Card 86-28793 DDC 338/.09/04048 19
1. Economic history - 1945-. 2. Industry - History. 3. Competition, International. 4. Strategic planning. 5. International economic relations. I. Title.
HC59 .B3537 1987

Ballarín, Eduard. Commercial banks amid the financial revolution : a study in competitive strategy / by Eduard Ballarín. Cambridge, Mass. : Ballinger Pub. Co., 1986. xvi, 248 p. : ill. ; 24 cm. Includes index. Bibliography: p. [241]-242. ISBN 0-88730-081-2 LC Card 85-23299 DDC 332.1/2/0973 19
1. Banks and banking - United States - Customer services. 2. Banks and banking - United States - State supervision. I. Title.
HG1616.C87 B35 1986 *NYPL [JLE 86-2810]*

Balliet, Lee.
Survey of labor relations / Lee Balliet. Washington, D.C. : Bureau of National Affairs, c1981. ix, 198 p. : ill. ; 24 cm. Includes index. Bibliography: p. 185-187. ISBN 0-87179-347-4 LC Card 80-26863 DDC 331/.0973
1. Industrial relations - United States. 2. Trade-unions - United States. 3. Collective bargaining - United States. I. Title.
HD8072.5 .B34 *NYPL [JLE 86-4719]*

Survey of labor relations / Lee Balliet. 2nd ed. Washington, D.C. : Bureau of National Affairs, c1987. xi, 212 p. : ill. ; 23 cm. Bibliography: p. 197-201. Includes index. ISBN 0-87179-544-2 (pbk.) LC Card 87-864 DDC 331/.0973 19
1. Industrial relations - United States. 2. Trade-unions - United States. 3. Collective bargaining - United States. I. Title.
HD8072.5 .B34 1987

Ballinger series in business in a global environment.
Business environment and business ethics . Cambridge, Mass. , c1987. xi, 151 p. ; ISBN 0-88730-204-1 LC Card 87-3573 DDC 174/.4 19
HF5387 .B867 1987

Comparative management . Cambridge, Mass. , c1988. xv, 321 p. : ISBN 0-88730-136-3 LC Card 87-17459 DDC 658 19
HD30.55 .C656 1988

Shapiro, H. Jack (Harris Jack) Reviving industry in America . Cambridge, Mass. , c1987. xii, 204 p. : ISBN 0-88730-118-5 LC Card 87-17585 DDC 338.4/767/0973 19
HD9725 .S46 1987

Shrivastava, Paul. Bhopal . Cambridge, Mass. , c1987. xvi, 184 p. : ISBN 0-88730-084-7 LC Card 86-26575 DDC 363.1/79 19
HD7269.C452 I5268 1987

The South African quagmire . Cambridge, Mass. , c1987. xvi, 444 p. ; ISBN 0-88730-191-6 LC Card 86-28754 DDC 320.5/6 19
HF1613.4.Z4 U67 1987

Steidlmeier, Paul, 1942- The paradox of poverty . Cambridge, Mass. , c1987. xx, 318 p. : ISBN 0-88730-184-3 LC Card 86-26589 DDC 338.9 19
HD75 .S75 1987

Ballinger series on innovation and organizational change.
The Competitive challenge . Cambridge, Mass. , c1987. xii, 256 p. : ISBN 0-88730-178-9 LC Card 87-1190 DDC 658.4/06 19
HD70.U5 C58 1987

Ballinger series on the management of innovation and change.
New technology as organizational innovation . Cambridge, Mass. , c1987. xvi, 308 p. : ISBN 0-88730-186-X LC Card 86-32110 DDC 658.5/14 19
HD45 .N43 1987

Ballivián Calderón, René. Economía de mercado y economía dirigida : aspectos de su teoría, historia y realizaciones / René Ballivián Calderón. La Paz : Editorial Los Amigos del Libro, 1979. xxii, 608 p. : ill. ; 20 cm. Limited ed. of 500 copies. Includes bibliographies. LC Card 83-167133
1. Economics - History. I. Title.
HB75 .B144 1979

Ballivián, René. see **Ballivián Calderón, René.**

Ballon, Robert J. Salary administration in Japan : "regular" workforce / by Robert J. Ballon. Tokyo : Sophia University, 1985. 44 p. ; 28 cm. (Institute of Comparative Culture business series bulletin . no. 100) Includes bibliographical references. ISBN 4-88168-100-1 LC Card 86-115944 DDC 331.2/952 19
1. Wages - Japan - Planning. 2. Compensation management - Japan. I. Title. II. Series.
HD5077 .B3454 1985

Ballot, Michael. Decision-making models in production & operations management / Michael Ballot. Malabar, Fla. : R.E. Krieger, 1986. xi, 295 p. : ill. ; 26 cm. "Original edition 1986"--verso t.p. Includes bibliographical references. ISBN 0-89874-825-9 LC Card 84-29740 DDC 658.5/036 19
1. Production management - Mathematical models. 2. Decision-making - Mathematical models. I. Title. II. Title: Decision-making models in production and operations management.
TS155 .B2435 1984 ***NYPL [JLF 86-1851]***

Ballou, Ronald H., 1937- Basic business logistics : transportation, materials management, physical distribution / Ronald H. Ballou.2nd ed. Englewood Cliffs, N.J. : Prentice-Hall, c1987. x, 438 p. : ill. ; 25 cm. Includes bibliographies and indexes. ISBN 0-13-057464-3 LC Card 86-22691 DDC 658.7/88 19
1. Physical distribution of goods - Management. 2. Materials handling. 3. Shipment of goods. I. Title.
HF5415.7 .B338 1987

Ballvé, Faustino. Fundamentos de la ciencia económica / Faustino Ballvé. 3a ed. Guatemala, Guatemala : Centro de Estudios Económico-Sociales, 1984. xii, 95 p. : port. ; 20 cm. LC Card 86-124459
1. Economics. I. Title.
HB178.5 .B325 1984

Balmores, Egmidio L., 1925- Samahang nayon : mga tanong at sagot / ni Egmidio L. Balmores. Quezon City, Philippines : New Day Publishers, c1975. x, 169 p. ; 18 cm. In Tagalog. Includes index. LC Card 86-132779
1. Agriculture, Cooperative - Philippines - Miscellanea. I. Title.
HD1491.P5 B34 1975

Balog, István. A Szakszervezetek kulturális, agitációs és propagandamunkájának kézikönyve /. [Budapest] , 1986. 246 p. : ISBN 963-322-335-0 : LC Card 87-409655
HD6680.5 .S874 1986

Balogh, Bálint. A Gazdaságirányitási rendszer továbbfejlesztése /. Budapest , 1984. 171 p. ; LC Card 86-145153
HC300.28 .G339 1984

Balogh, Sándor, Dr. Összefoglalás, Szolnok megye agroökológiai potenciálja az ezredfordulón /. Budapest , 1984. 115 p. : ISBN 963-491-193-5 LC Card 86-198809
HD1940.5.Z9 S966 1984

Balsen, Werner, 1953- Ohne Arbeit geh'ste kaputt . Köln , c1983. 183 p. : ISBN 3-7609-0798-9 LC Card 84-176249
HD5779 .O355 1983

Balser, Diane. Sisterhood & solidarity : feminism and labor in modern times / by Diane Balser.1st ed. Boston, MA : South End Press, c1987. vii, 247 p. ; 22 cm. Bibliography: p. 233-239. Includes index. ISBN 0-89608-278-4 : LC Card 87-4733 DDC 331.4 19
1. Women in trade-unions - United States - History. 2. Feminism - United States - History. I. Title.
HD6079.2.U5 B34 1987

Baltas, N. K. Empeirikē diereunēsē tēs apotamieutikēs sympериphoras kai tēs zētēsēs katatheseōn apo tous idiōtes / N.K. Baltas, V.T. Drounkas. Athēna : Agrotikē Trapeza tēs Hellados, Dieuthynsē Meletōn kai Programmatismou, [1979] 128 p. ; 24 cm. (Meletes gia tēn agrotikē oikonomia . 9) Bibliography: p. [125]-128. LC Card 86-203196
1. Bank deposits - Greece. 2. Savings accounts - Greece. 3. Saving and investment - Greece. 4. Agrotikē Trapeza tēs Hellados. I. Drounkas, V. T. II. Agrotikē Trapeza tēs Hellados. Dieuthynsē Meletōn & Programmatismou. III. Title. IV. Series.
HG3250.5.A6 B34 1979

Baltas, Nik. K. Chrēmatodotēsē ependyseōn tou agrotikou tomea : hena oikonometriko hypodeigma tēs chrēmatodotēsēs kai tōn idiōtikōn ependyseōn stēn hellēnikē geōrgia / Nik.K. Balta. Athēna : Agrotikē Trapeza tēs Hellados, Dieuthynsē Meletōn kai programmatismou, 1984. 142 p. ; 25 cm. (Meletes gia tēn agrotikē oikonomia . 15) Bibliography: p. 137-142. LC Card 86-201892
1. Agriculture - Greece - Finance. 2. Produce trade - Greece - Finance. 3. Investments - Greece. I. Title. II. Series.
HD2055.5 .B35 1984

Baltensperger, Ernst. Geldmengenpolitik und Inflationskontrolle : Möglichkeiten, Kosten, flankierende Massnahmen : Studie, erstellt im Auftrag der Kommission für Konjunkturfragen / Ernst Baltensperger und Peter Böhm. Diessenhofen : Rüegger, c1984. 132 p. : ill. ; 21 cm. (Schweizerisches Institut für Aussenwirtschafts-, Struktur- und Regionalforschung an der Hochschule St. Gallen . Bd. 6) Bibliography: p. 127-132. ISBN 3-7253-0224-3 : LC Card 84-178054 DDC 332.4/9494 19
1. Monetary policy - Switzerland. 2. Money supply - Switzerland. 3. Inflation (Finance) - Switzerland. I. Böhm, Peter. II. Kommission für Konjunkturfragen (Switzerland). III. Series: Schweizerisches Institut für Aussenwirtschafts-, Struktur- und Regionalforschung an der Hochschule St. Gallen (Series) , Bd. 6. IV. Title.
HG1155 .B345 1984 ***NYPL [JLD 87-168]***

BALTIC STATES - ECONOMIC CONDITIONS.
Feodālisms Baltijas reģionā . Rīga , 1985. 147 p. : LC Card 86-177836
HC243 .F46 1985

BALTIC STATES - ECONOMIC CONDITIONS - ABSTRACTS.
Konferentsiia molodykh uchenykh-ėkonomistov respublik Pribaltiki (1978 : Riga, Latvia) Ėkonomika razvitogo sotsializma . Riga , 1978. 110 p. ; LC Card 82-100692
HC243 .K66 1978

BALTIC STATES - ECONOMIC CONDITIONS - CONGRESSES.
Konferentsiia molodykh uchenykh-ėkonomistov respublik Pribaltiki (1978 : Riga, Latvia) Ėkonomika razvitogo sotsializma . Riga , 1978. 110 p. ; LC Card 82-100692
HC243 .K66 1978

BALTIC STATES - ECONOMIC INTEGRATION.
Druzhba i sotrudnichestvo /. Tallin , 1985. 85 p. : LC Card 86-108625
HC243.Z9 S63 1985

BALTIC STATES - ECONOMIC POLICY - ABSTRACTS.
Konferentsiia molodykh uchenykh-ėkonomistov respublik Pribaltiki (1978 : Riga, Latvia) Ėkonomika razvitogo sotsializma . Riga , 1978. 110 p. ; LC Card 82-100692
HC243 .K66 1978

BALTIC STATES - ECONOMIC POLICY - CONGRESSES.
Konferentsiia molodykh uchenykh-ėkonomistov respublik Pribaltiki (1978 : Riga, Latvia) Ėkonomika razvitogo sotsializma . Riga , 1978. 110 p. ; LC Card 82-100692
HC243 .K66 1978

BALTIC STATES - HISTORY.
Feodālisms Baltijas reģionā . Rīga , 1985. 147 p. : LC Card 86-177836
HC243 .F46 1985

Baltic states revenues /. Hall, Andrew. York, England , c1983. 40 p. : ISBN 0-906845-14-9 (pbk.) LC Card 87-100278 DDC 769.5/7 19
HJ5429.B34 H34 1983

BALTIMORE - ECONOMIC CONDITIONS - ECONOMETRIC MODELS.
Drennan, Matthew P., 1937- Modeling metropolitan economies for forecasting and policy analysis /. New York , 1985. x, 242 p. ; ISBN 0-8147-1781-0 (alk. paper) : LC Card 85-13784 DDC 330.9173/2 19
HT321 .D74 1985 ***NYPL [JLE 86-1102]***

BALTIMORE (MD.) - ECONOMIC CONDITIONS.
Szanton, Peter L. Baltimore 2000 . [Baltimore, Md.] , c1986. v, 51 p. : LC Card 87-125975 DDC 330.9752/71043 19
HC108.B2 S9 1986

BALTIMORE METROPOLITAN AREA - CENSUS.
Census '80 . Baltimore, Md. (2225 N. Charles St., Baltimore 21218) [1983] xv, 106 leaves : LC Card 83-622347 DDC 339.2/2/097526 19
HC108.B2 C46 1983 ***NYPL [JLF 86-1594]***

Baltimore two thousand. Szanton, Peter L. Baltimore 2000 . [Baltimore, Md.] , c1986. v, 51 p. : LC Card 87-125975 DDC 330.9752/71043 19
HC108.B2 S9 1986

Baltimore 2000 . Szanton, Peter L. [Baltimore, Md.] , c1986. v, 51 p. : LC Card 87-125975 DDC 330.9752/71043 19
HC108.B2 S9 1986

Baltische Getreidehandel im siebzehnten Jahrhundert. Soom, Arnold. Der baltische Getreidehandel im 17. Jahrhundert /. Stockholm , 1961. 350 p. ; LC Card 85-122593 DDC 380.1/4131/09474 19
HD9045.S63 B37 1961

Der baltische Getreidehandel im 17. Jahrhundert /. Soom, Arnold. Stockholm , 1961. 350 p. ; LC Card 85-122593 DDC 380.1/4131/09474 19
HD9045.S63 B37 1961

Balvé, Beatriz S. Balvé, Beba. De protesta a rebelión--la "subversión" (Rosario, mayo 1969) /. Buenos Aires, Argentina [1985] xvii, 123 p. ; LC Card 86-162379
HD5350.R67 B35 1985

Balvé, Beba. De protesta a rebelión--la "subversión" (Rosario, mayo 1969) / Beba C. Balvé, Beatriz S. Balvé. Buenos Aires, Argentina : CICSO, [1985] xvii, 123 p. ; 29 cm. (Cuadernos de CICSO) Serie Estudios ; no. 45 Includes bibliographical references. LC Card 86-162379
1. General Strike, Rosario, Argentina, 1969. 2. Trade-unions - Argentina - Rosario (Santa Fe). 3. Students - Argentina - Rosario (Santa Fe) - Political activity. I. Balvé, Beatriz S. II. Series: Serie Estudios (Centro de Investigaciones en Ciencias Sociales) , no. 45. III. Title.
HD5350.R67 B35 1985

Balzani, A. (Alberto) L'Imprenditore coltivatore nella società che cambia . [Italy] [1983] (Roma : Arti grafiche Jasillo) 364 p. : LC Card 86-185731
HD1972 .I44 1983

Balzereit, Heinz. Leben mit Gneisenau, hundert Jahre-- . Dortmund , Essen [1986?] 317 p. : ISBN 3-88474-323-6 LC Card 87-408388 DDC 331.7/622334/094355 19
HD8039.M62 G335 1986

Bamako Workshop on Training and Animation of Rural Women (1983) Women farmers in Africa . Syracuse, N.Y. , 1986. xvi, 212 p. : ISBN 0-8156-2358-5 (alk. paper) LC Card 85-27771 DDC 331.4/83/096 19
HD6073.A292 A358 1986
NYPL [JLE 86-2556]

Bambawale, Usha. Ramanamma, A., 1936- Women in Indian industry /. Delhi, India , 1987. 232 p. ; LC Card 87-901258 DDC 331.4/821381/0954 19
HD6189 .R347 1987

Bamberg, Eva, 1951- Arbeit und Freizeit : eine empirische Untersuchung zum Zusammenhang zwischen Stress am Arbeitsplatz, Freizeit und Familie / Eva Bamberg. Weinheim : Beltz, 1986. xiv, 306 p. ; 21 cm. (Beltz Forschungsberichte) Bibliography: p. 254-278. ISBN 3-407-58288-9 LC Card 87-103692 DDC 158.7 19
1. Job stress. 2. Work and family. 3. Leisure. I. Title.
HF5548.85 .B36 1986

Bamberg, Günter, 1940-
Capital market equilibria /. Berlin , New York , c1986. x, 228 p. : ISBN 0-387-16248-8 (U. S.)
LC Card 86-10104 DDC 332.6/0724 19
HG4523 .C33 1986 ***NYPL [JLE 86-4309]***

Decision-theoretic analysis of envisaged income tax reforms for FRG and U. S. / G. Bamberg, W.F. Richter. [Augsburg] : Institut für Statistik und Mathematische Wirtschaftstheorie der Universität Augsburg, [1986] 11 leaves : ill. ; 30 cm. (Arbeitspapiere zur mathematischen Wirtschaftsforschung . Heft 80/1986) Bibliography: leaf 11. LC Card 87-101962 DDC 336.24/0724 19
1. Income tax - Germany, West - Mathematical models. 2. Income tax - United States - Mathematical models. 3. Risk - Germany (West) - Mathematical models. 4. Risk - United States - Mathematical models. I. Richter, W. F. II. Series: Arbeitspapiere zur mathematischen Wirtschaftsforschung , Heft 80. III. Title.
HJ4719 .B35 1986

Bamberg in alten Zeitungsanzeigen : jeder Herr hat auf allen Plätzen eine Dame frei / Gerhard C. Krischker. Bamberg : Bayerische Verlagsanstalt, c1981. 120 p. : ill. ; 21 cm.
ISBN 3-87052-442-1 LC Card 82-214699
1. Advertising, Newspaper - Germany (West) - Bamberg. I. Krischker, Gerhard C.
HF6105.G4 B36 1981

BAMILEKE (AFRICAN PEOPLE)
Barbier, J. C. Migrations et développement . Paris , 1983, c1984. 372 p. : ISBN 2-7099-0711-7
NYPL [M-11 4991 no.170]

Bāmlādeśa. see **Bangladesh.**

Bāṃlādeśera unnaẏana samasyā . Islam, Nazrul. Ḍhākā , 1987. 315 p. (some folded) ; LC Card 87-902504
HC440.8 .I727 1987

Bāṃlāra ārthika itihāsa, ashṭādaśa śatābdī /. Mukhopadhyay, Subodh Kumar, 1942- Kalakātā , 1985. 214 p. ; LC Card 85-903918
HC437.B43 M85 1985

Bāṅalādeśera kr̥shikāṭhāmo, kr̥shaka samāja, o unnaẏan /. Rahamāna, Āsahābura, 1949- Ḍhākā , 1986. 39, 158 p. ; LC Card 86-903304
HD2075.6 .R33 1986

BANANA TRADE.
The World banana economy, 1970-1984 . Rome , 1986. vi, 83 p. ; ISBN 92-5-102376-X (pbk.) LC Card 86-217497 DDC 382/.414772 19
HD9259.B2 W66 1986

BANANA TRADE - CENTRAL AMERICA.
López, José Roberto. La economía del banano en Centroamérica /. San José, Costa Rica , c1986. 236 p. : ISBN 997-7904-31-6 LC Card 87-404078 DDC 338.1/74772/09728 19
HD9259.B3 C4554 1986

BANANA TRADE - COLOMBIA.
Colombia. Congreso. Cámara de Representantes. Comisión Nombrada para Estudiar el Conflicto Surgido entre la United Fruit Company y la Cooperativa Bananera Colombiana. Informe de la Comisión Nombrada para Estudiar el Conflicto Surgido entre la United Fruit Company y la Cooperativa Bananera Colombiana. Bogotá , 1930. 32 p. ; LC Card 83-189629
HD9259.B3 C728 1930

BANANA TRADE - ECUADOR - ESMERALDAS (PROVINCE) - CASE STUDIES.
Campesinado y organización en Esmeraldas /. [Quito, Ecuador?] [1986] 213 p. : LC Card 86-171561
HD1531.E2 C36 1986

BANANA TRADE - GOVERNMENT POLICY - JAMAICA.
Jamaica. Commission of Enquiry into the Banana Industry of Jamaica. Report of the Commission of Enquiry into the Banana Industry of Jamaica. Kingston , 1959- v. <1 > ; LC Card 86-221011
HD9259.B3 J346 1959

Banas, Geraldo. Os donos do Brasil : múltis, estatais e nacionais / Geraldo Banas. São Paulo : Editora Banas, 1984. 330 p. ; 23 cm. "Um estudo sobre o internacionalização e estatizaçaõ da economia brasileira. A polarização se processa através de múltis, grandes empresas nacionais e governamentais." Includes index. LC Card 87-673258
1. Corporations - Brazil. 2. Brazil - Economic conditions - 1964-1985. 3. International business enterprises - Brazil. I. Title.
HD2834 .B34 1984

Banca Catalana. Noticiari econòmic internacional, 1980 /. [Barcelona] [1981?] 116 p. : LC Card 82-144538
HF1411 .N6745 1981

BANCA D'ITALIA - BIOGRAPHY.
Bonelli, Franco. Bonaldo Stringher . [Udine] [c1985] 169 p. : LC Card 85-220896
HJ1156.S77 B66 1985

BANCA D'ITALIA - HISTORY.
Bonelli, Franco. Bonaldo Stringher . [Udine] [c1985] 169 p. : LC Card 85-220896
HJ1156.S77 B66 1985

Banca Internațională pentru Reconstrucție și Dezvoltare. see **International Bank for Reconstruction and Development.**

Banca Mas Sardá. Servicio de Estudios. El ABC de la Bolsa. Barcelona [1983?] 93 p. : ISBN 84-383-0028-6 LC Card 86-139799
HG4521 .A213 1983

La banca mexicana . Márquez, Javier, 1909- [Mexico City, Mexico] , 1987. xi, 299 p., [3] folded leaves of plates : ISBN 968-615-402-7 LC Card 87-404865 DDC 332.1/0972 19
HG2714 .M27 1987

Banca nacional /. Zúñiga A., Remigio. Chimbote, Perú , c1986. 478 p. ; LC Card 87-403541 DDC 332.1/0985 19
HG2944 .Z86 1986

Banca ricostruzione e sviluppo. see **International Bank for Reconstruction and Development.**

Banco Agrario de la República Dominicana.
Asociaciones campesinas como receptoras y administradoras de crédito y su dinámica de grupo. [Lima] [1979] 100 leaves in various foliations : LC Card 85-185371
HG2051.L26 A83 1979

Banco Central da República do Brasil. see **Banco Central do Brasil.**

Banco Central de Chile. Dirección de Estudios.
Características de los instrumentos de ahorro. Santiago, Chile , 1986. 115 p. ; LC Card 87-403226 DDC 332.63/2/0983 19
HG5342 .C37 1986

Indicadores económicos y sociales, 1960-1985 /. Santiago, Chile , c1986. xvi, 415 p. : LC Card 87-120338
HC192 .I52 1986

Banco Central de Chile, Santiago. Dirección de Política Financiera. Características de los instrumentos de ahorro. Santiago, Chile , 1983. 91 p. ; LC Card 84-119555 DDC 332.63/2/0983 19
HG5342 .C37 1983 ***NYPL [JLF 86-620]***

Banco Central de Costa Rica. Departamento de Estudios Económicos. Costa Rica--respuesta al cuestionario del Banco Interamericano de Desarrollo /. [San José] [1962] 69 leaves (some folded) ; LC Card 85-117361
HC143 .C685 1962

Banco Central de Costa Rica. División Económica. Estadísticas, 1950-1985. San José, Costa Rica , 1986. 221 p. ; LC Card 87-404209 DDC 332/.097286/021 19
HG185.C7 E84 1986

Banco Central de la República Argentina. Departamento de Actividad Agropecuaria. Agricultura, caza, silvicultura y pesca . [Buenos Aires] [1982] 57 p. : LC Card 87-401763 DDC 338.1/0982/021 19
HD1862 .A58 1982

Banco Central de la República Argentina. Departamento de Actividad Industrial. Energía eléctrica /. [Buenos Aires] [1981] 27 p., [6] leaves of plates : LC Card 87-401272 DDC 333.79/3212/0982 19
HD9685.A72 E54 1981

Banco Central de la República Argentina. Departamento de Cuentas Nacionales. Oferta y demanda global a precios corrientes /. [Buenos Aires, Argentina] , 1982. 115 leaves ; LC Card 87-402103 DDC 339.382 19
HC180.I5 O38 1982

Banco Central de la República Dominicana.
Análisis de la economía dominicana /. Santo Domingo, República Dominicana , 1985. 73 p. ; LC Card 86-186259
HG3926.5 .A53 1985

Renegociación de la deuda externa, 1985 /. Santo Domingo, República Dominicana , 1985. iv, 168 p. ; LC Card 86-186407
HJ8548 .R46 1985

Banco Central de Reserva del Perú. Gerencia de Investigación Económica. Subgerencia de Investigación y Análisis Global. Glosario de términos económicos. Lima, Perú , 1985. 129 p. ; LC Card 86-221450
HB61 .G498 1985

Banco Central del Ecuador. Seminario de Operaciones Internacionales (1981 : Quito, Ecuador) Memorias del Seminario de Operaciones Internacionales /. Quito, Ecuador , 1981. 156 p., [2] p. of plates : LC Card 86-174597
HF1519 .S46 1981

Banco Central do Brasil.
Lemgruber, Antonio Carlos. O controle da base monetária e as flutuações dos multiplicadores monetários e creditícios /. [Brasília] [1981?] 118 p. : LC Card 85-154853
HG835 .L35 1981

A Verdade sobre o "Caso Coroa-Brastel.". Brasília, DF , 1984. 156 p. ; LC Card 85-207657
HG4109 .V47 1984

BANCO CENTRAL DO BRASIL.
A Verdade sobre o "Caso Coroa-Brastel.". Brasília, DF , 1984. 156 p. ; LC Card 85-207657
HG4109 .V47 1984

El Banco Central Latinoamericano . Coers, Hermann Max. México , 1972. xv, 78 p. ; LC Card 87-401518 DDC 332.1/1/098 19
HG2710.5.A7 C6 1972

BANCO DE COLOMBIA.
Donadío, Alberto, 1953- Por qué cayó Jaime Michelsen? /. Bogotá , c1984. 142 p. : ISBN 84-89209-42-1 LC Card 85-122262
HG2908.C65 D66 1984

Banco de Crédito del Perú. Panorama del Departamento ... /. [Lima?] , 1984-<1987. v. <1-8 > : LC Card 86-202585
HC227 .P354 1984

Banco de Desenvolvimento de Minas Gerais.
Perspectivas para a ação do BDMG no período 1983-85. Belo Horizonte, MG, Brasil : Banco de Desenvolvimento de Minas Gerais, [1983] 67 p. : ill. ; 26 cm. Cover title. LC Card 83-207712
1. Banco de Desenvolvimento de Minas Gerais. 2. Minas Gerais, Brazil - Economic policy. I. Title.
HG2889.M55 B37 1983

BANCO DE DESENVOLVIMENTO DE MINAS GERAIS.
Banco de Desenvolvimento de Minas Gerais. Perspectivas para a ação do BDMG no período 1983-85. Belo Horizonte, MG, Brasil [1983] 67 p. : LC Card 83-207712
HG2889.M55 B37 1983

Banco de Desenvolvimento de Minas Gerais. Area de Coordenação e Planejamento. Ribeiro, Lêda Cristina de O. Santana Cançado. Considerações sobre o mercado das indústrias de confecções brasileiras. Belo Horizonte [Brazil] , 1985. 66 leaves : LC Card 87-404932 DDC 338.4/7687/0981 19
HD9940.B82 R53 1985

Banco de Desenvolvimento de Minas Gerais. Assessoria de Comunicação Social. Programa de modernização e expansão da indústria de cal em Minas Gerais. Belo Horizonte , 1977. 57 leaves, [8] leaves of plates : LC Card 79-123546
HD9585.L52 B77 1977

Banco de Desenvolvimento do Estado da Bahia.
A Indústria de confecções na Bahia. [Salvador] [1981] 40 p. ; LC Card 87-400671
HD9940.B83 B345 1981

Banco de Desenvolvimento do Estado de São Paulo. Criação de empresas de alta tecnologia . São Paulo . 192, [1] p. ; LC Card 87-403991 DDC 338.4/362/000981 19
HC190.H53 C75 1987

Banco de España. Cuentas financieras de la economía española, 1972-1982 /. [Madrid] , 1984. 157 p. ; ISBN 84-500-9729-0 LC Card

86-205358
HC390.F55 C84 1984

Banco de Fomento Nacional. (Old Cat. form: Banco de Fomento Nacional (Portugal)) Almeida, João Carreira. Fabricação de materiais de barro para construção . Lisboa , 1978. 186 p., [3] leaves of plates (one folded) : LC Card 82-112167 DDC 338.4/36914/09469 19
HD9596.P82 A85 1978

Banco de Fomento Nacional (Portugal) see **Banco de Fomento Nacional.**

BANCO DE LA NACIÓN (PERU)
Callegari Ramírez, Carlos. Historia del Banco de la Nación. Lima, Perú , 1986. 223 p. : LC Card 87-400236 DDC 332.1/1/0985 19
HG2946 .C35 1986

Banco de la Provincia de Buenos Aires. Reseña histórico-económica de los partidos de la provincia de Buenos Aires. [Buenos Aires] [1981- v. <1-2 > : LC Card 87-114686 DDC 330.982/12/064 19
HC177.B8 R47 1981

Banco de la República (Colombia). Departamento de Investigaciones Económicas. Colombia . Bogotá, Colombia , c1985. 109 p. : ISBN 958-9028-00-4 LC Card 86-179279
HC197 .C627 1985

Banco de México (1925-). Subdirección de Investigación Económica. Producto interno bruto y gasto, cuaderno 1970-1979. [Mexico City] [1980] 123 p. ; LC Card 82-197714
HC140.I5 P76 1980

Banco de Portugal. O Papel-moeda em Portugal. [Lisbon] [1985?] 502 p. : LC Card 86-226586
HG1147 .P36 1985

Il banco di pegni di Cava dei Tirreni del 1495 /. Patroni Griffi, Filena. Cava dei Tirreni , c1985. 149 p., [8] p. of plates : LC Card 86-195753
HG2106.I83 C386 1985

Banco do Brasil. Carteira de Comércio Exterior. Estrutura e funcionamento do comércio exterior brasileiro /. Rio de Janeiro, RJ , 1980. v, 98 p. : LC Card 84-121064
HF1513 .E85 1980

Banco do Brasil (1905-). Museu, Arquivo Histórico e Biblioteca. Cédulas brasileiras da República . Rio de Janeiro , 1965. 111 p. : LC Card 85-119119
HG837 .C43 1965

BANCO DO ESTADO DO RIO GRANDE DO NORTE (BRAZIL)
Escóssia Neto, Lauro da. O sistema financeiro nacional . [Natal] , 1985. 46, [1] p. : LC Card 86-158741
HG185.B7 E83 1985

Banco do Nordeste do Brasil.
Aspectos gerais da economia e da sociedade do Nordeste. Recife , 1984. 318 p. : LC Card 86-159446
HC188.N6 A75 1984

Incentivos fiscais e financeiros para investimentos no Nordeste do Brasil /. Recife , 1985. 92 p. ; LC Card 87-404837 DDC 332.6/7322813 19
HJ2529.N6 I53 1985

Perfil de empresas. Fortaleza-CE [1984] 248 p. ; LC Card 85-191373
HG4111.5.N67 P47 1984

Banco do Nordeste do Brasil. Escritório Técnico de Estudos Econômicos do Nordeste. Nordeste, estatísticas. [S.l.] [195-] iv, 50 leaves : LC Card 85-127235
HC188.N6 N69 1950z

Banco do Nordeste do Brasil S.A. . (4) Nordeste, estatísticas. [S.l.] [195-] iv, 50 leaves : LC Card 85-127235
HC188.N6 N69 1950z

Banco Exterior de España. Servicio de Estudios Económicos.
La Economía china de la revolución a las cuatro modernizaciones /. Madrid [1986?] 181 p. : LC Card 86-229994
HC427.9 .E319 1986

El Tráfico de perfeccionamiento . Madrid, España , 1983. 96 p. : ISBN 84-500-9221-3 LC Card 85-193715
HF1717.S7 T73 1983

Banco Hispano Americano (Madrid, Spain) Reproducciones de billetes y cheques de viaje extranjeros /. [Madrid] [1972?] 140 p. : LC Card 85-140130
HG353 .R44 1972

Banco Industrial de Catalunya. Noticiari econòmic internacional, 1980 /. [Barcelona] [1981?] 116 p. : LC Card 82-144538
HF1411 .N6745 1981

Banco interamericano de desarrollo. see **Inter-American Development Bank.**

Banco Internacional de Reconstrucción y Fomento. see **International Bank for Reconstruction and Development.**

Banco Mundial. see **International Bank for Reconstruction and Development.**

BANCO NACIONAL DA HABITAÇÃO.
A Brazilian solution to Brazilian problems. Rio de Janeiro , 1974. 32 p. ; LC Card 86-673453
HD7323.A4 B72x 1974

Banco Nacional da Habitação. Secretaria de Divulgação. A Brazilian solution to Brazilian problems. Rio de Janeiro , 1974. 32 p. ; LC Card 86-673453
HD7323.A4 B72x 1974

Banco Nacional de Cuba (Founded 1948) Cuba's financial crisis : the secret report from Banco Nacional de Cuba, February 1985. Washington, D.C. (1000 Thomas Jefferson St., N.W., Suite 601, Washington 20007) : Cuban American National Foundation, 1985. vii, 64, [19] p. : ill. ; 23 cm. (Cuban-American National Foundation Inc. . 12) LC Card 86-105593 DDC 330.97291/064 19
1. Balance of payments - Cuba. 2. Debts, External - Cuba. 3. Foreign trade promotion - Cuba. 4. Cuba - Economic conditions - 1959-. I. Title. II. Series.
HC152.5 .B36 1985 **NYPL [JLE 86-3732]**

Banco Nacional de Desenvolvimento Econômico e Social (Brazil). Departamento de Planejamento. Cenários para a economia brasileira, 1984-1990. [Rio de Janeiro] , 1984. 81 p. : LC Card 85-209337
HC187 .C28 1984

Banco Nacional de Panamá.
Informes de los gerentes generales, 1969-84. Panamá, República de Panamá : Banco Nacional de Panamá, 1984. 126 p. : col. ill. ; 28 cm. LC Card 85-124892
1. Banco Nacional de Panamá - History. 2. Banks and banking, Central - Panama - History. 3. Bankers - Panama - Biography. I. Title.
HG2773 .B35 1984

BANCO NACIONAL DE PANAMÁ.
Conte Porras, J. El crédito, la banca y la moneda panameña /. Panamá, Panamá , 1983. 204 p. : **NYPL [JLE 86-3126]**

BANCO NACIONAL DE PANAMÁ - HISTORY.
Banco Nacional de Panamá. Informes de los gerentes generales, 1969-84. Panamá, República de Panamá , 1984. 126 p. : LC Card 85-124892
HG2773 .B35 1984

Banco Português de Investimento. Álvares, Pedro. Portugal na CEE . [Lisbon] , 1986. 543 p. ; LC Card 87-403268 DDC 341.24/22 19
HC241.25.P6 A48 1986

Banco Português do Atlântico. Central de Balanços. Indicadores económicos e financeiros da Central de Balanços (1978-1980). [Porto] [1982] 204 p. : LC Card 85-166692
HC394.5.C7 I53 1982

Banco Português do Atlântico. Direcção de Estudos Económicos e de Marketing. Pina, Amílcar. Análise de empresas em inflação . [Porto] , 1985. 142 p. : LC Card 86-174401
HF5658.5 .P56 1985

Banco Regional de Desenvolvimento do Extremo sul.
BRDE : gestão 1981/1984 / [Banco Regional de Desenvolvimento do Extremo Sul]. [Curitiba] : BRDE, 1984. 95 p., [8] : ill. ; 22 cm. Bibliography: p. [101]-[103] LC Card 86-143911
1. Banco Regional de Desenvolvimento do Extremo sul. 2. Development banks - Brazil, South. 3. Brazil, South - Economic policy. I. Title.
HG2889.S6 B36 1984

Campos, José Hypólito Machado de. BRDE, a ação governamental na promoção do desenvolvimento econômico e social da Região Sul /. Porto Alegre [between 1983 and 1985] 51 p. ; LC Card 86-143903
HG2889.S6 C36 1983

Carvão mineral /. [Porto Alegre] [19]84. 56 p. ; LC Card 86-163115
HD9554.B83 S683 1984

O planejamento e os pré-investimentos / equipe técnica, Paulo de Borba Vieira ... [et al.]. [Porto Alegre?] : Banco Regional de Desenvolvimento do Extremo Sul, [19]85. 71, [6], p. 21 leaves ; 22 cm. Cover title: O planejamento e os pré-investimentos na Região Sul. Bibliography: p. [73]-[75] LC Card 86-201808
1. Brazil, South - Economic conditions. 2. Regional planning - Brazil, South. I. Vieira, Paulo de Borba. II. Title. III. Title: Planejamento e os pré-investimentos na Região Sul.
HC188.S68 B35 1985

BANCO REGIONAL DE DESENVOLVIMENTO DO EXTREMO SUL.
Banco Regional de Desenvolvimento do Extremo sul. BRDE . [Curitiba] , 1984. 95 p., [8] : LC Card 86-143911
HG2889.S6 B36 1984

Campos, José Hypólito Machado de. BRDE, a ação governamental na promoção do desenvolvimento econômico e social da Região Sul /. Porto Alegre [between 1983 and 1985] 51 p. ; LC Card 86-143903
HG2889.S6 C36 1983

Banco Regional de Desenvolvimento do Extremo Sul. Agência de Porto Alegre. Gerência de Planejamento. Proposta de consolidação do Pólo Petroquímico do Sul . [Porto Alegre] [19]86. 17, [5], 9 p. : LC Card 87-404792 DDC 338.7/661804/098165 19
HD9579.C33 B785 1986

Banco Roberts. Historia del papel moneda argentino /. Buenos Aires, Argentina , c1984. 47, [1] p. : LC Card 86-180304
HG817 .H57 1984

"Banco, Species und Courant" . Schneider, Konrad. Koblenz , c1986. 136 p. : ISBN 3-923708-03-3 LC Card 87-134369 DDC 332.1/0943/515 19
HG1010.H24 S36 1986

Los bancos agropecuarios y la captación de depósitos /. Poyo, Jeffrey. Santo Domingo, República Dominicana , 1986. 39 p. : LC Card 87-400523 DDC 332.7/1/097293 19
HG2051.D6 P69 1986

Band, Richard E. Contrary investing : the insider's guide to buying low & selling high / Richard E. Band. New York : McGraw-Hill, c1985. viii, 197 p. : ill. ; 24 cm. Includes index. Bibliography: p. 179-181. ISBN 0-07-003604-7 : LC Card 85-99 DDC 332.6/78 19
1. Investments - Handbooks, manuals, etc. 2. Speculation - Handbooks, manuals, etc. I. Title.
HG4527 .B233 1985 **NYPL [JLE 86-1234]**

Banda, Abedanigo K. A Study into the evolution and performance of the transport sector in Zambia with particular reference to the operations of the ZIMCO group of transport companies /. [Lusaka?] [1980?] 89 p. : LC Card 86-981420
HE284.6 .S78 1980

Bande B., Jorge. Chile y CIPEC ante la crisis del cobre /. Santiago de Chile , 1985. 74 p. ; LC Card 86-144485
HD9539.C7 C526 1985 **NYPL [JLD 87-363]**

Bandini, Mario. Agricoltura e crisi / Mario Bandini. Firenze : G. Barbèra, 1937. 265 p. ; 26 cm. (Biblioteca di coltura per i rurali . vol. 5) Summaries in English and German. Includes bibliographical references and index. LC Card 87-116637
1. Agriculture - Economic aspects. 2. Business cycles. I. Title. II. Series.
HB3728 .B36 1937

Bándli, Imre. Működési forma, belső mechanizmus . Budapest , 1985. 208 p. : LC Card 87-408582
HD3332.5.A4 M85 1985

Bandman, Mark Konstantinovich.
Mezhregional'nye mezhotraslevye balansy /. Novosibirsk , 1983. 220 p. : LC Card 84-172934
HF3626.5 .M49 1983

Territorial'no-proizvodstvennye kompleksy . Novosibirsk , 1986. 263 p. ; LC Card 86-231926
HC336.25 .T467 1986

Territorial'no-proizvodstvennye kompleksy--voprosy struktury i razvitiia . Novosibirsk , 1981. 152 p. ; LC Card 82-160051
HC337.R852 S5276 1981

Bandō, Satoshi, 1931- Sengo rōdō kumiai undōshi : Nihongata rōdō kumiai no seitai to mondai / Bandō Satoshi. Tokyo : Tabata Shoten, 1975. 278 p. ; 20 cm. In Japanese. Includes bibliographical references. LC Card 75-804891
1. Trade-unions - Japan. 2. Industry and state - Japan. I. Title.
HD6832 B36 ***NYPL [*OSM 86-2348]***

Bandow, Doug. Protecting the environment . Washington, D.C. , c1986. iii, 88 p. ; ISBN 0-89195-040-0 (pbk.) : LC Card 86-82962 DDC 363.7/056/0973 19
HC110.E5 P77 1986

Bandy de Nalèche, Louis. Les Maçons de la Creuse / par Louis Bandy de Nalèche. Limoges : R. Dessagne, 1984. 99 p., [16] p. of plates : ill. ; 24 cm. Reprint. Originally published: Paris : E. Dentu, 1859. ISBN 2-85521-059-3 : LC Card 85-169794 DDC 331.7/69321/094468 19
1. Creuse (France) - Population - History. 2. Creuse (France) - Economic conditions. 3. Bricklayers - France - Creuse - History. 4. Stonemasons - France - Creuse - History. I. Title.
HB2054.C74 B36 1984

Banegas Banegas, Benito. El control de gestión en la empresa moderna / Benito Banegas Banegas. Madrid : Ibérico Europea de Ediciones, c1985. 127 p. : ill. ; 21 cm. (Colección La Empresa moderna) Bibliography: p. 127. ISBN 84-256-0432-X LC Card 86-194934
1. Management. I. Title.
HD37.S66 B36 1985

Banerjee, B. N. (Biswa Nath), 1945- Identification & economic analysis of small farmers / B.N. Banerjee. Delhi, India : Mittal Publications, 1986. viii, 127 p. : ill. ; 22 cm. Spine title: Identification and economic analysis of small farmers. Originally presented as the author's thesis (Ph. D.--Indian Agricultural Research Institute, 1974) Study based on data collected from selected farmers in Varanasi District, Uttar Pradesh, for the agricultural year 1971-72. Bibliography: p. [96]-99. Includes index. LC Card 86-903139 DDC 338.1/6 19
1. Farms, Small - India - Vārānasi District. 2. Farmers - India - Vārānasi District. I. Title. II. Title: Identification and economic analysis of small farmers.
HD1476.I42 V373 1986

Banerjee, Deb Kumar. The goldsmiths : a study of an occupational group in Calcutta / Deb Kumar Banerjee. Calcutta : Calcutta University Press, 1983. ii, 56 p., [3] leaves of plates : ill. ; 25 cm. Bibliography: p. [55]-56. LC Card 85-903366 DDC 331.7/67322/095414 19
1. Goldsmiths - India - Calcutta. 2. Goldwork - India - Calcutta. I. Title.
HD8039.G72 I53 1983
NYPL [JLE 86-2038]

Banerjee, Diptendra, 1933- Marxian theory and the third world /. New Delhi , Beverly Hills , 1985. 325 p. ; ISBN 0-8039-9489-3 LC Card 85-1863 DDC 335.43/09172/4 19
HX517.8 .M37 1985 ***NYPL [JLE 86-3088]***

BANGKOK BANK LIMITED. (Old Catalog form: Thanākhar Krungdēp Chākat)
New era of professional banking . [Bangkok] , 1986. 51 p. : LC Card 86-200653 DDC 332.1/025/593 19
HG3300.55.A8 B366 1986

BANGKOK BANK LIMITED - DIRECTORIES.
New era of professional banking . [Bangkok] , 1986. 51 p. : LC Card 86-200653 DDC 332.1/025/593 19
HG3300.55.A8 B366 1986

BANGKOK METROPOLITAN AREA (THAILAND) - POPULATION.
Charoon Vitiprod. Rapid population growth, living conditions, and fertility reduction implication (Bangkok metropolis) /. [Singapore] 1979. ii, 41 leaves : LC Card 82-940038
HB3644.55.B36 C48 1979

Bangla Desh. see **Bangladesh.**

Bangladesh : country study and Norwegian aid review. Fantoft, Norway : Chr. Michelsen Institute, Dept. of Social Science and Development, DERAP-Development Research and Action Programme, 1986. xxxiii, 353 p. : map ; 22 cm. Study commissioned by the Norwegian Ministry of Development and Cooperation. Bibliography: p. 213-235. ISBN 82-905840-8-3 (pbk.) LC Card 87-128545 DDC 330.9549/205 19
1. Bangladesh - Economic conditions. 2. Economic assistance - Bangladesh. 3. Economic assistance, Norwegian - Bangladesh. I. Chr. Michelsens institutt. Forsknings- og aksjonsprogrammet for utviklingsland. II. Norway. Departementet for utviklingshjelp.
HC440.8 .B352 1986

Bangladesh : promoting higher growth and human development. Washington, D.C., U. S.A. : World Bank, c1987. xli, 279 p., [1] leaf of plates : ill., col. map ; 27 cm. (A World Bank country study) Includes bibliographical references. ISBN 0-8213-0963-3 (pbk.) LC Card 87-22920 DDC 338.9549/2 19
1. Bangladesh - Economic policy. 2. Bangladesh - Economic conditions. 3. Bangladesh - Social policy. 4. Bangladesh - Social conditions. I. International Bank for Reconstruction and Development. II. Series.
HC440.8 .B362 1987

BANGLADESH - CENSUS, 1981.
Bangladesh population census, 1981. Dhaka, Bangladesh , 1985- <v. 1-18; in 27 > ; LC Card 86-902743 DDC 304.6/09549/2021 19
HA4590.6 .A4 1981c

BANGLADESH - ECONOMIC CONDITIONS.
Bangladesh . Fantoft, Norway , 1986. xxxiii, 353 p. : ISBN 82-905840-8-3 (pbk.) LC Card 87-128545 DDC 330.9549/205 19
HC440.8 .B352 1986

Bangladesh . Washington, D.C., U. S.A. , c1987. xli, 279 p., [1] leaf of plates : ISBN 0-8213-0963-3 (pbk.) LC Card 87-22920 DDC 338.9549/2 19
HC440.8 .B362 1987

Bangladesh im Schatten der Macht /. Aachen , c1986. vi, 328, 57 p. : ISBN 3-922868-31-2 LC Card 86-228249
HC440.8 .B358 1986

Holzhausen, Walter, 1929- Vision creates hope . Dhaka, Bangladesh , 1986. viii, 118 p. ; LC Card 87-901565 DDC 330.9172/4 19
HC59.7 .H624 1986

BANGLADESH - ECONOMIC POLICY.
Bangladesh . Washington, D.C., U. S.A. , c1987. xli, 279 p., [1] leaf of plates : ISBN 0-8213-0963-3 (pbk.) LC Card 87-22920 DDC 338.9549/2 19
HC440.8 .B362 1987

Islam, Nazrul. Bāmlādeśera unnayana samasyā . Ḍhākā , 1987. 315 p. (some folded) ; LC Card 87-902504
HC440.8 .I727 1987

BANGLADESH - FOREIGN RELATIONS - INDIA.
Ābbāsa, Bi. Ema., 1911- The Ganges waters dispute /. New Delhi , c1982. xv, 157 p., 8 p. of plates : ISBN 0-7069-2080-5 : LC Card 83-900165 DDC 341.4/42 19
HD1698.G36 A23 1982

Bangladesh - Government. see **Bangladesh - Politics and government.**

Bangladesh household expenditure survey, 1981-82. Dhaka, Bangladesh : Bangladesh Bureau of Statistics, Statistics Division, Ministry of Planning, Govt. of the People's Republic of Bangladesh, 1986. 160 p., [13] leaves of plates : ill. (some col.) ; 29 cm. Cover title: Report of the Bangladesh household expenditure survey, 1981-82. LC Card 86-902560 DDC 339.4/1/095492021 19
1. Cost and standard of living - Bangladesh - Statistics. 2. Budgets, Personal - Bangladesh - Statistics. I. Bangladesh. Parisaṃkyāna Byuro. II. Title: Report of the Bangladesh household expenditure survey, 1981-82.
HD7051.6 .B36 1986

Bangladesh im Schatten der Macht / mit Beiträgen von W. Böttcher ... [et al.] ; Redaktion, Michael Nebelung. 1. Aufl. Aachen : RaderVerlag, c1986. vi, 328, 57 p. : ill. ; 21 cm. (Aachener Studien Sozialwissenschaften . Bd. 3) Bibliography: p. 317-328. ISBN 3-922868-31-2 LC Card 86-228249
1. Bangladesh - Economic conditions. 2. Bangladesh - Politics and government - 1971-. 3. Bangladesh - Social conditions. I. Böttcher, Winfried. II. Nebelung, Michael, 1958-. III. Series.
HC440.8 .B358 1986

BANGLADESH - MANUFACTURES.
Rahman, Alimur. Capacity utilisation in the large-scale manufacturing industry in Bangladesh /. [Dhaka] [1983] 123 p. ; LC Card 83-903801 DDC 338.6/44/095492 19
HD69.C3 R34 1983 ***NYPL [JLE 86-4622]***

Bangladesh. Parikalpanā Kamiśana. List of aid worth projects, 1984. [Dhaka] [1984] 431 p. ; LC Card 85-904102 DDC 338.9549/2 19
HC440.8.Z9 E445 1984

Bangladesh. Parisaṃkhyāna Bibhāga.
Bangladesh population census, 1981. Dhaka, Bangladesh , 1985- <v. 1-18; in 27 > ; LC Card 86-902743 DDC 304.6/09549/2021 19
HA4590.6 .A4 1981c

Thana statistics. [Dacca] , 1981- v. ; LC Card 82-903357 DDC 333.73/13/095492021 19
HD880.6.Z63 T46 1981
NYPL [JLM 87-178]

Bangladesh. Parisaṃkyāna Byuro. Bangladesh household expenditure survey, 1981-82. Dhaka, Bangladesh , 1986. 160 p., [13] leaves of plates : LC Card 86-902560 DDC 339.4/1/095492021 19
HD7051.6 .B36 1986

BANGLADESH - POLITICS AND GOVERNMENT - 1971-
Bangladesh im Schatten der Macht /. Aachen , c1986. vi, 328, 57 p. : ISBN 3-922868-31-2 LC Card 86-228249
HC440.8 .B358 1986

Bangladesh population census, 1981. Community tables of all thanas of [name of] District. Dhaka, Bangladesh : Bangladesh Bureau of Statistics, Statistics Division, Ministry of Planning, Govt. of the People's Republic of Bangladesh, 1985- <v. 1-18; in 27 > ; 29 cm. Prefatory matter in Bengali and English. "Thana series"--Cover. Statistical tables. CONTENTS. - [1] Barisal -- [2] Bogra -- [3] Chittagong -- [4] Comilla. v. <1 > -- [5] Dhaka. v. <1, 3 > -- [6] Dinajpur. v. <1-2 > -- [7] Faridpur. v. <1-2 > -- [8] Jessore -- [9] Khulna -- [10] Kushtia -- [11] Mimensingh. v. <1-2 > -- [12] Noakhali -- [13] Pabna -- [14] Patuakhali -- [15] Rajshahi. v. <1-2 > -- [16] Rangpur. 2 v. -- [17] Sylhet. 4 v. -- [18] Tangail. LC Card 86-902743 DDC 304.6/09549/2021 19
1. Bangladesh - Population - Statistics. 2. Bangladesh - Census, 1981. I. Bangladesh. Parisaṃkhyāna Bibhāga.
HA4590.6 .A4 1981c

BANGLADESH - POPULATION POLICY.
Noman, Ayesha. Status of women and fertility in Bangladesh /. Dhaka, Bangladesh , c1983. xv, 91 p. ; LC Card 83-905271 DDC 305.4/2/095492 19
HB1050.6.A3 N65 1983
NYPL [JLD 86-2056]

BANGLADESH - POPULATION - STATISTICS.
Bangladesh population census, 1981. Dhaka, Bangladesh , 1985- <v. 1-18; in 27 > ; LC Card 86-902743 DDC 304.6/09549/2021 19
HA4590.6 .A4 1981c

Bangladesh Public Administration Training Centre. Career planning in Bangladesh . Dhaka , c1986. 159 p. ; LC Card 86-903477 DDC 331.7/02/095492 19
HF5382.5.B27 C37 1986

Bangladesh. Śilpa Bibhāga. Industrial investment schedule for small industry, 1982-85. Dhaka , 1982. v, 283 p. ; LC Card 84-900851 DDC 338.6/42/095492 19
HD2346.B27 I53 1982 ***NYPL [JLF 87-269]***

Bangladesh Small & Cottage Industries Corporation. Counselling & Industrial Studies Dept. Industrial investment schedule for small industry, 1982-85. Dhaka , 1982. v, 283 p. ; LC Card 84-900851 DDC 338.6/42/095492 19
HD2346.B27 I53 1982 ***NYPL [JLF 87-269]***

BANGLADESH - SOCIAL CONDITIONS.
Bangladesh . Washington, D.C., U. S.A. , c1987. xli, 279 p., [1] leaf of plates : ISBN 0-8213-0963-3 (pbk.) LC Card 87-22920 DDC

338.9549/2 19
HC440.8 .B362 1987

Bangladesh im Schatten der Macht /. Aachen , c1986. vi, 328, 57 p. : ISBN 3-922868-31-2 LC Card 86-228249
HC440.8 .B358 1986

BANGLADESH - SOCIAL POLICY.
Bangladesh . Washington, D.C., U. S.A. , c1987. xli, 279 p., [1] leaf of plates : ISBN 0-8213-0963-3 (pbk.) LC Card 87-22920 DDC 338.9549/2 19
HC440.8 .B362 1987

BANGLADESH - STATISTICS, VITAL - CASE STUDIES.
D'Souza, S. M. (Stanislaus Michael) Mortality case study, Matlab, Bangladesh /. Dhaka, Bangladesh , 1985. 80 p. : LC Card 86-902788 DDC 304.6/4/0954923 19
HB1470.6.M37 D76 1985

Bangladesz. see **Bangladesh.**

Bangs, David H.
Business planning guide. Business planning guide : a handbook to help you design, write, and use a business plan and a financing proposal tailored to your specific business needs : includes detachable worksheets. Dover, N.H. (50 Mill St., Dover 03820) , c1985. vii, 115 p. : LC Card 86-622397 DDC 658.4/01 19
HD30.28 .B85 1985

Bánhidi, Ferenc. Könyvelésről és pénzgazdálkodásról vállalati vezetőknek : dinamikus szemlélet a könyvvitelben / Bánhidi Ferenc. Budapest : Közgazdasági és Jogi Könyvkiadó, 1986, c1985. 215 p. ; 20 cm. ISBN 963-221-649-0 : LC Card 87-118825
1. Accounting. 2. Accounting - Hungary. 3. Business enterprises - Finance. 4. Business enterprises - Hungary - Finance. I. Title.
HF5655.H9 B36 1986

Banis, William J. Krannich, Ronald L. High impact resumes and letters /. Manassas, Va. , c1987. viii, 136 p. : ISBN 0-942710-12-6 (pbk.) : LC Card 86-83117 DDC 650.1/4 19
HF5383 .K7 1987

Banister, Judith, 1943- China's changing population / Judith Banister. Stanford, Calif. : Stanford University Press, 1987. xiii, 488 p. : ill. ; 24 cm. Bibliography: p. [449]-471. Includes index. ISBN 0-8047-1155-0 (alk. paper) : LC Card 82-60105 DDC 304.6/0951 19
1. China - Population. 2. China - Population policy. 3. Birth control - Government policy - China. I. Title.
HB3654.A3 B36 1987

Bank- en effectenbedrijf. see **Serie Bank- en effectenbedrijf.**

BANK ACCOUNTING. see **BANKS AND BANKING - ACCOUNTING.**

BANK ACCOUNTS - UNITED STATES.
Passell, Peter. Where to put your money, 1987 /. New York, NY , c1987. 82 p. ; ISBN 0-446-38497-6 (pbk.) : LC Card 86-28917 DDC 332.6/78 19
HG179 .P27 1987

Bank al-Markazī al-Miṣrī. National financial policies and capital formation in Africa . Dakar, Senegal [1986] iii, 205 p. ; LC Card 87-404123 DDC 332/.096 19
HG5822 .N38 1986

BANK AND BANKING, COOPERATIVE - GERMANY (WEST)
Krauss, Hans-Ulrich. Erfolgsindikatoren und Betriebsvergleich bei Kreditgenossenschaften /. Gelsenkirchen , 1983. 217 p. : ISBN 3-88485-471-2 LC Card 84-153354
HG2039.G4 K73 1983

The bank book . Hoffman, Naphtali. San Diego , 1986. xiii, 222 p. ; ISBN 0-15-610676-0 (pbk.) : LC Card 85-27271 DDC 332.1/7/0973 19
HG1616.C87 H64 1986
NYPL [JLE 86-3189]

Bank costs, structure, and performance /. Kolari, James W. Lexington, Mass. , c1987. x, 240 p. : ISBN 0-669-11282-8 (alk. paper) LC Card 85-45295 DDC 332.1/068/1 19
HG1616.C6 K65 1987

BANK CREDIT CARDS - GERMANY (WEST)
Beck, Peter. Einwendungen bei Eurocheque und Kreditkarte /. [S.l. , 1986] (Köln : Druck und Verarbeitung, Druck- + Verlagshaus Wienand) xv, 146, 31 p. ; LC Card 86-233484
HG3756.G3 B43 1986

BANK CREDIT CARDS - UNITED STATES.
Krumme, Dwane. Banking and the plastic card /. Washington, D.C. (1120 Connecticut Ave., N.W., Washington 20036) , c1987. xi, 263 p. : LC Card 87-159373 DDC 332.7/6 19
HG1643 .K79 1987

BANK DEPOSITS - DOMINICAN REPUBLIC.
Poyo, Jeffrey. Los bancos agropecuarios y la captación de depósitos /. Santo Domingo, República Dominicana , 1986. 39 p. : LC Card 87-400523 DDC 332.7/1/097293 19
HG2051.D6 P69 1986

BANK DEPOSITS - GREECE.
Baltas, N. K. Empeirikē diereunēsē tēs apotamieutikēs symperiphoras kai tēs zētēsēs katatheseōn apo tous idiōtes /. Athēna [1979] 128 p. ; LC Card 86-203196
HG3250.5.A6 B34 1979

BANK DEPOSITS - UNITED STATES.
De Murguía, Valdemar. Capital flight and economic crisis . La Jolla, Calif. , 1986. 27 p. ; LC Card 87-621351 DDC 332/.042 19
HG3916 .D4 1986

The Bank director's handbook / Edwin B. Cox ... [et al.]. 2nd ed. Dover, Mass. : Auburn House Pub. Co., c1986. xxiii, 294 p. : ill. ; 25 cm. Includes index. ISBN 0-86569-145-2 : LC Card 86-3592 DDC 332.1/068 19
1. Bank management - Handbooks, manuals, etc. 2. Banks and banking - United States - Handbooks, manuals, etc. I. Cox, Edwin Burk, 1950-.
HG1615 .B34 1986 ***NYPL [JLE 86-4332]***

BANK DIRECTORS - INDIA - BIOGRAPHY.
Kamath, M. V., 1921- The innovative banker, T.A. Pai, his life and times /. Manipal , Bombay , 1983. x, 247 p., [9] p. of plates : LC Card 83-904531 DDC 332.1/2/0924 B 19
HG1552.P4 K36 1983 ***NYPL [JFE 87-879]***

BANK EMPLOYEES - EFFECT OF TECHNOLOGICAL INNOVATIONS ON.
Bankmitarbeiter und die neuen Informationstechniken . Frankfurt am Main , c1986. 240 p. ; ISBN 3-7819-0341-9 LC Card 86-228992
HG1709 .B355 1986

BANK EMPLOYEES - GERMANY (WEST) - MUNICH.
Möglichkeiten und Probleme der Realisierung flexibler Arbeitszeitstrukturen in Filialen der Bayerischen Vereinsbank München /. München , 1985. 67 p. : LC Card 87-401387 DDC 331.25/72 19
HD5109.2.G32 M866 1985

BANK EMPLOYEES - ITALY - SUPPLY AND DEMAND - CONGRESSES.
Disoccupazione e nuove forme di accesso al lavoro nel mondo bancario /. Milano, Italy , c1986. 186 p. ; LC Card 87-150276
HD5718.B262 I83 1986

BANK EMPLOYEES - KENTUCKY - SUPPLY AND DEMAND - STATISTICS.
Kentucky occupational profiles, finance, insurance, and real estate /. [Frankfort, Ky.] [1985] v, 33 p. : LC Card 85-622996 DDC 331.12/51/0009769 19
HD5718.B262 U66 1985

BANK EMPLOYEES - NORTH DAKOTA - STATISTICS.
Finance, insurance, and real estate . Bismarck, N.D. (1000 E. Divide, Bismarck 58502) [1986] 55 p. : LC Card 86-623003 DDC 332.12/51/0009784 19
HD5718.B262 U64 1986

BANK EMPLOYEES - UNITED STATES - SUPPLY AND DEMAND - FORECASTING.
Roessner, J. David. The Impact of office automation on clerical employment, 1985-2000 . Westport, Conn. , 1985. xii, 297 p. : ISBN 0-89930-119-3 (lib. bdg. : alk. paper) LC Card 85-6523 DDC 331.12/9165137 19
HD8039.B27 U548 1986
NYPL [JLE 86-1424]

BANK EXAMINATION - ITALY.
Spedale, Domenico L. L'affidamento bancario . Milano , 1985. 204 p. :
NYPL [JLD 86-3241]

BANK EXAMINATION - UNITED STATES.
Auditing the allowance for credit losses of banks. New York, N.Y. (1211 Ave. of the Americas, New York 10036-8775) , c1986. vii, 40 p. : LC Card 86-234688 DDC 657/.833 19
HG1707.5 .A927 1986

BANK FAILURES - CANADA.
Estey, Willard Z. Report of the inquiry into the collapse of the CCB and Northland Bank /. Ottawa, Canada , c1986. xiii, 641 p. : ISBN 0-660-12171-9 (pbk.) : LC Card 87-134617 DDC 332.1/2/0971 19
HG2708.C36 E89 1986

BANK FAILURES - CASE STUDIES.
Le Crisi finanziarie /. Bologna , c1985. 348 p. : ISBN 88-15-00807-1 : LC Card 85-201934 DDC 332.1 19
HG1591 .C75 1985

BANK FAILURES - GREAT BRITAIN - HISTORY - CONGRESSES.
Financial crises and the world banking system /. London , c1986. x, 270 p. : ISBN 0-333-35129-0 ***NYPL [JLD 86-2132]***

BANK FAILURES - HISTORY - CONGRESSES.
Financial crises and the world banking system /. London , c1986. x, 270 p. : ISBN 0-333-35129-0 ***NYPL [JLD 86-2132]***

BANK FAILURES - ILLINOIS - CHICAGO.
McCollom, James P. The Continental affair . New York , c1987. xv, 393 p. ; ISBN 0-396-08809-0 : LC Card 87-21471 DDC 332.1/223/0977311 19
HG2613.C44 C686 1987

BANK FAILURES - UNITED STATES.
Perspectives on safe & sound banking . Cambridge, Mass. , 1986. xxi, 358 p. ; ISBN 0-262-02246-X LC Card 85-23882 DDC 332.1/0973 19
HG2481 .P47 1986 ***NYPL [JLE 86-2960]***

Ross, Walter Sanford, 1916- People's banker . New Canaan, Conn. , c1987. viii, 288 p. ; ISBN 0-87983-429-3 LC Card 87-4066 DDC 332.1/223/0924 B 19
HG2463.R68 R67 1987

Bank Fayṣal al-Islāmī al-Sūdānī. Ṣiddīqī, Muḥammad Nejātullah, 1931- Banking and monetary polic[i]es in Islamic economics /. Khartoum [between 1983 and 1986] 40 p. ; LC Card 86-980021 DDC 332.1/0917/671 19
HG3368.A6 S53 1986

Bank finance and rural development / edited by G. Saibaba. Tirupati : Sri Venkateswara University, [1986] vi, 222 p. ; 23 cm. Papers presented at the Regional Conference on Bank Finance and Rural Development organized under the auspices of the Department of Economics, Sri Venkateswara University Postgraduate Centre, Kavali, 1980. Includes bibliographies and index. LC Card 86-903530 DDC 332.2 19
1. Development banks - India - Congresses. 2. Rural development - India - Finance - Congresses.
HG3284 .B265 1986

Bank for International Settlements. Monetary and Economic Dept. The Nationality structure of the international banking market and the role of interbank operations. Basle [1985] 12 leaves ; LC Card 86-139771 DDC 332.1/5 19
HG3881 .N33 1985

BANK HOLDING COMPANIES - BRAZIL - CASE STUDIES.
Suplicy, Eduardo Matarazzo, 1941- Investigando o Caso Coroa-Brastel . Brasília , 1984. 215 p. ; LC Card 86-200269
HG4109 .S85 1984

A Verdade sobre o "Caso Coroa-Brastel.". Brasília, DF , 1984. 156 p. ; LC Card 85-207657
HG4109 .V47 1984

BANK HOLDING COMPANIES - KENTUCKY.
Hultman, Charles W. An examination of issues related to multibank holding companies /. [Frankfort, Ky. , 1983] [8], 56 leaves ; LC Card 86-620545 DDC 332.1/6 19
HG2567 .H85 1983

BANK HOLDING COMPANIES - SPAIN.
Ekaizer, Ernesto, 1949- José María Ruiz

Mateos, el ultimo magnate /. Esplugues de Llobregat, Barcelona , 1985. 833 p., [16] p. of plates : ISBN 84-01-33291-5 LC Card 86-122394 DDC 332.1/6 B 19
HG4216.R85 E38 1985 ***NYPL [JFD 86-6856]***

BANK HOLDING COMPANIES - UNITED STATES.
Hultman, Charles W. An examination of issues related to multibank holding companies /. [Frankfort, Ky. , 1983] [8], 56 leaves ; LC Card 86-620545 DDC 332.1/6 19
HG2567 .H85 1983

BANK HOLDING COMPANIES - UNITED STATES - DEREGULATION.
Futures and options trading for commercial banks . Chicago, Ill. (30 S. Wacker Dr., Chicago 60606) , c1986. 14 p. : LC Card 87-131777 DDC 332.1/754 19
HG2491 .F87 1986

Bank investments and funds management.
Washington, D.C. (1120 Connecticut Ave., N.W., Washington 20036) : American Bankers Association, c1987. vii, 357 p. : ill. ; 25 cm. (Education policy & development) Includes bibliographical references and index. LC Card 87-405100 DDC 332.1/068/1 19
1. Asset-liability management (Banking) - United States. 2. Bank investments - United States. I. American Bankers Association. II. Series.
HG1615.25 .B36 1987

BANK INVESTMENTS - CASE STUDIES.
Le Crisi finanziarie /. Bologna , c1985. 348 p. : ISBN 88-15-00807-1 : LC Card 85-201934 DDC 332.1 19
HG1591 .C75 1985

BANK INVESTMENTS - GOVERNMENT POLICY - UNITED STATES.
Futures and options trading for commercial banks . Chicago, Ill. (30 S. Wacker Dr., Chicago 60606) , c1986. 14 p. : LC Card 87-131777 DDC 332.1/754 19
HG2491 .F87 1986

BANK INVESTMENTS - ITALY.
Fabrizi, Pier Luigi. La politica degli investimenti in titoli nelle banche di deposito /. [Milano] , 1982. xii, 138 p. ; LC Card 82-165568
HG1616.I5 F33 1982

BANK INVESTMENTS - SOUTH AFRICA.
U. S. investments and bank loans in South Africa (supplemental material to the hearings and markups of January 31 and February 7, 1984, serial no. 98-14, on District of Columbia South Africa divestment) . Washington , 1985. vi, 24 p.: LC Card 85-602615 DDC 332.6/7373/068 19
HG5851.A3 U17 1985

BANK INVESTMENTS - UNITED STATES.
Bank investments and funds management. Washington, D.C. (1120 Connecticut Ave., N.W., Washington 20036) , c1987. vii, 357 p. : LC Card 87-405100 DDC 332.1/068/1 19
HG1615.25 .B36 1987

Equity performance 1977-1986 . Washington, D.C. , c1987. 28, [A-Q] p. : LC Card 87-159010 DDC 332.1/754/0973 19
HG1616.I5 E68 1987

Giesen, David. Contemporary business planning . Chicago, IL (111 E. Wacker Dr., Chicago 60601) , c1987. 128 p. : LC Card 87-401916 DDC 332.3/2/068 19
HG1897 .G54 1987

Trading in banking . [New York?] , c1986. iv ; LC Card 87-128754 DDC 332.1/0973 19
HG2491 .T7 1986

Trading in banking . New York , c1987. x, 137 p. ; ISBN 0-939853-00-0 (pbk.) LC Card 87-404278 DDC 332.1/0973 19
HG2491 .T697 1987

U. S. investments and bank loans in South Africa (supplemental material to the hearings and markups of January 31 and February 7, 1984, serial no. 98-14, on District of Columbia South Africa divestment) . Washington , 1985. vi, 24 p.: LC Card 85-602615 DDC 332.6/7373/068 19
HG5851.A3 U17 1985

Bank letter writing handbook . Seglin, Jeffrey L., 1956- Boston , c1987. xii, 434 p. ; ISBN 0-87267-103-8 LC Card 87-965 DDC 651.7/5/024332 19
HG1616.R4 S43 1987

BANK LOANS.
Clarke, Peter S., 1941- Complete guide to loan documentation /. Englewood Cliffs, N.J. , c1986. xvii, 494 p. : ISBN 0-13-160615-8 : LC Card 85-3519 DDC 332.1/753 19
HG1641 .C55 1986 ***NYPL [JLF 86-1464]***

Credit analysis . Philadelphia, Pa. , c1987. 146 p. : ISBN 0-936742-38-0 (pbk.) : LC Card 86-28628 DDC 332.1/753/0685 19
HG1641 .C66 1987

Donaldson, T. H. (Thomas Hay), 1936- Lending in international commercial banking /. New York , c1987. p. cm. ISBN 0-471-63597-9 LC Card 87-19841 DDC 332.1/5 19
HG3891.5 .D65 1987

Milling, Bryan E. Banking strategies for businesses . Radnor, PA , c1987. viii, 231 p. : ISBN 0-8019-7651-0 (pbk.) : LC Card 86-47959 DDC 658.1/592 19
HG4027.7 .M55 1987

Wiegel, Klaus Dieter. Rentabilität und Risiko im Kreditgeschäft der Banken . Köln , c1985. 342 p. : ISBN 3-87951-125-X LC Card 87-140074 DDC 332.1/753 19
HG1641 .W54 1985

BANK LOANS - FORMS.
Clarke, Peter S., 1941- Complete guide to loan documentation /. Englewood Cliffs, N.J. , c1986. xvii, 494 p. : ISBN 0-13-160615-8 : LC Card 85-3519 DDC 332.1/753 19
HG1641 .C55 1986 ***NYPL [JLF 86-1464]***

BANK LOANS - FRANCE.
Bizot, Alain. La pratique bancaire française en matière de financement sur le marché intérieur /. Paris , c1985. 238 p. : ISBN 2-86325-033-7 : LC Card 86-159009
HG1642.F8 B59 1985

Ohinata, Yo. The lending procedures of commercial banks in the United States, the United Kingdom, Japan, Germany and France /. [Manchester] [1983] 138 p. ; ISBN 0-903808-34-X (pbk.) LC Card 86-132282 DDC 332.1/753 19
HG1642.U5 O35 1983

BANK LOANS - GERMANY (WEST)
Ohinata, Yo. The lending procedures of commercial banks in the United States, the United Kingdom, Japan, Germany and France /. [Manchester] [1983] 138 p. ; ISBN 0-903808-34-X (pbk.) LC Card 86-132282 DDC 332.1/753 19
HG1642.U5 O35 1983

Zessin, Axel, 1953- Unternehmungsbewertung von Kreditinstituten /. Göttingen , 1982. 296 p. : ISBN 3-509-01313-1 LC Card 84-109138
HG4028.V3 Z47 1982

BANK LOANS - GREAT BRITAIN.
Ohinata, Yo. The lending procedures of commercial banks in the United States, the United Kingdom, Japan, Germany and France /. [Manchester] [1983] 138 p. ; ISBN 0-903808-34-X (pbk.) LC Card 86-132282 DDC 332.1/753 19
HG1642.U5 O35 1983

BANK LOANS - GREECE - CONGRESSES.
Epistēmoniko Diēmero (1984 : Athens, Greece) Ependyseis kai trapezikes chorēgēseis se periodo krisēs . Athēna , 1984. 225 p. ; LC Card 86-193395
HG5700.5.A3 E85 1984

BANK LOANS - HANDBOOKS, MANUALS, ETC.
Disbursement handbook. Washington, D.C., U. S.A. , c1986. iv, 58 p. : ISBN 0-8213-0746-0 (pbk.) LC Card 86-210947 DDC 332.1/532/0685 19
HG3881.5.W57 D57 1986

BANK LOANS - INDIA - VADODARA.
Agrawal, R. B. L. Financing of the urban poor & small borrowers by commercial banks . Baroda , 1983. 108 p. ; LC Card 83-906426 DDC 332.1/753/095475 19
HG1642.I5 A38 1983 ***NYPL [JLD 86-4318]***

BANK LOANS - ITALY.
Allegri, Vincenzo. Credito di scopo e finanziamento bancario delle imprese /. Milano [1984] 166 p. ; ISBN 88-14-00299-1 : LC Card 85-187365 DDC 332.7/0945 19
HG1642.I8 A44 1984 ***NYPL [JLE 86-3661]***

BANK LOANS - JAPAN.
Ohinata, Yo. The lending procedures of commercial banks in the United States, the United Kingdom, Japan, Germany and France /. [Manchester] [1983] 138 p. ; ISBN 0-903808-34-X (pbk.) LC Card 86-132282 DDC 332.1/753 19
HG1642.U5 O35 1983

BANK LOANS - MATHEMATICAL MODELS.
Nowak, Felicitas. The allocation of bank credit and the efficiency of investment /. Göttingen, Rep. Fed. de Alemania [1986] 23 p. : LC Card 87-121215 DDC 332.7/0724 19
HG1641 .N68 1986

BANK LOANS - SOUTH AFRICA.
U. S. investments and bank loans in South Africa (supplemental material to the hearings and markups of January 31 and February 7, 1984, serial no. 98-14, on District of Columbia South Africa divestment) . Washington , 1985. vi, 24 p.: LC Card 85-602615 DDC 332.6/7373/068 19
HG5851.A3 U17 1985

BANK LOANS - STUDY AND TEACHING - UNITED STATES.
Pace, Edmond E. Developing a basic loan training program /. Philadelphia, Pa. , c1987. 108 p. ; ISBN 0-936742-41-0 (pbk.) : LC Card 87-7936 DDC 332.1/753/0683 19
HG1642.U5 P33 1987

BANK LOANS - SWITZERLAND.
Zellweger, Bruno. Ueberwachung kommerzieller Bankkredite /. Bern , c1983. xx, 330 p. : ISBN 3-258-03246-7 : LC Card 83-214274
HG1526 .B27 Bd. 77 HG1642.S95

BANK LOANS - UNITED STATES.
Auditing the allowance for credit losses of banks. New York, N.Y. (1211 Ave. of the Americas, New York 10036-8775) , c1986. vii, 40 p. : LC Card 86-234688 DDC 657/.833 19
HG1707.5 .A927 1986

Beares, Paul. Consumer lending /. Washington, D.C. (1120 Connecticut Ave., N.W., Washington 20036) , c1987. xi, 335 p. : LC Card 87-410019 DDC 332.1/753/0685 19
HG3755 .B39 1987

Cranfill, Steven L. Small business banking . Washington, D.C. (1120 Connecticut Ave. N.W., Washington, D.C.) , c1987. ix, 78 p. : LC Card 87-135069 DDC 332.1/753 19
HG4027.7 .C7 1987

Davis, John A., 1947- A look at the credit approval process /. Philadelphia, Pa. , c1987. 55 p. : ISBN 0-936742-36-4 (pbk.) LC Card 86-23855 DDC 332.7 19
HG1642.U5 D38 1987

Dickerson, Charles S. Current approaches to grading commercial loans /. Philadelphia, Pa. , c1987. 42 p. ; ISBN 0-936742-43-7 (pbk.) LC Card 87-18458 DDC 332.1/753/0685 19
HG1642.U5 D53 1987

Ohinata, Yo. The lending procedures of commercial banks in the United States, the United Kingdom, Japan, Germany and France /. [Manchester] [1983] 138 p. ; ISBN 0-903808-34-X (pbk.) LC Card 86-132282 DDC 332.1/753 19
HG1642.U5 O35 1983

Pricing consumer credit . Washington, D.C. (1120 Connecticut Ave., N.W., Washington 20036) , c1986. 136 p. : LC Card 86-209981 DDC 332.1/753 19
HG1642.U5 P75 1986

U. S. investments and bank loans in South Africa (supplemental material to the hearings and markups of January 31 and February 7, 1984, serial no. 98-14, on District of Columbia South Africa divestment) . Washington , 1985. vi, 24 p.: LC Card 85-602615 DDC 332.6/7373/068 19
HG5851.A3 U17 1985

Bank management /. Koch, Timothy W. Chicago [1987], c1988. xviii, 717 p. : ISBN 0-03-004773-0 LC Card 87-6761 DDC 332.1/068 19
HG1615 .K625 1988

BANK MANAGEMENT - BANGLADESH.
Taheruddin, M. Essays on banking and development /. Dhaka , 1986. 145 p. ; LC Card

87-900643 DDC 332.1/09549/2 19
HG3290.6.A6 T35 1986

BANK MANAGEMENT - DATA PROCESSING.
Kiczek, Paul. Decision making for bankers . Washington, D.C. (1120 Connecticut Ave., NW, Washington 20036) , c1986. 89 p. : LC Card 87-115307 DDC 332.1/2/02855369 19
HG1709 .K53 1986

Walker, John R. (John Rex), 1922- Reporting systems for bank management . Boston , c1987. xii, 292 p. : ISBN 0-87267-106-2 LC Card 87-17424 DDC 332.1/068 19
HG1615 .W35 1987

BANK MANAGEMENT - GERMANY (WEST)
Reuschenbach, Ruth. Ziele, Instrumente und Bedingungen der Geschäftsstellenorganisation im filialisierten Universalbankbetrieb /. Köln , c1984. 385 p. ; ISBN 3-87951-122-5 LC Card 85-131689
HG1616.B7 R48 1984

BANK MANAGEMENT - GERMANY (WEST) - CONGRESSES.
Tagung Strategische Bankplanung (1982 : Bonn, Germany) Strategische Bankplanung . Frankfurt am Main , c1983. 345 p. : ISBN 3-7819-0293-5 LC Card 83-233043
HG1615 .T34 1982

BANK MANAGEMENT - GREAT BRITAIN.
Morris, Timothy, 1953- Innovations in banking . London , Wolfeboro, N.H. , c1986. 137 p. : ISBN 0-7099-4607-4 : LC Card 86-13400 DDC 332.1/068/3 19
HG2988 .M675 1986 NYPL [JLD 87-81]

BANK MANAGEMENT - HANDBOOKS, MANUALS, ETC.
The Bank director's handbook /. Dover, Mass. , c1986. xxiii, 294 p. : ISBN 0-86569-145-2 : LC Card 86-3592 DDC 332.1/068 19
HG1615 .B34 1986 NYPL [JLE 86-4332]

BANK MANAGEMENT - INDIA.
Banking in India in the eighties . New Delhi , 1986. 533 p. in various pagings ; LC Card 86-903123 DDC 332.1/068 19
HG3284 .B267 1986

BANK MANAGEMENT - SWITZERLAND.
Bolliger, Peter. Die optimale Organisationsstruktur eines mittleren Bankbetriebes . Bern , c1984. xiii, 234 p. : ISBN 3-258-03358-7 : LC Card 84-174443
HG1526 .B27 Bd. 86 HG1616.B7

BANK MANAGEMENT - UNITED STATES.
Austin, Douglas V. Modern banking . Boston , c1985. x, 406 p. : ISBN 0-87267-053-8 LC Card 84-21754 DDC 332.1/068 19
HG1615 .A98 1985 NYPL [JLE 85-3956]

Compton, Eric N., 1925- The new world of commercial banking /. Lexington, Mass. , c1987. xvi, 316 p. : ISBN 0-669-14017-1 (alk. paper) LC Card 86-45002 DDC 332.1/2/068 19
HG2491 .C646 1987

Pricing consumer credit . Washington, D.C. (1120 Connecticut Ave., N.W., Washington 20036) , c1986. 136 p. : LC Card 86-209981 DDC 332.1/753 19
HG1642.U5 P75 1986

The bank manager's handbook . Elliott, P. A. (Peter A.), 1923- Cambridge, England , Wolfeboro, NH , 1987. p. cm. ISBN 0-85941-330-6 : LC Card 86-28293 DDC 332.1/6 19
HG1616.B7 E45 1987

BANK MARKETING.
Benn, Alec. Advertising financial products and services . Westport, Conn. , c1986. xii, 231 p. : ISBN 0-89930-103-7 (lib bdg. : alk. paper) LC Card 85-24406 DDC 659.1/93321 19
HG1616.M3 B43 1986 NYPL [JLE 86-4110]

Budde, Ramona. Marktinnovationen von Universalbanken . Berlin , c1983. xvi, 347 p. : ISBN 3-503-02192-2 LC Card 83-186914
HG1709 .B78 1983

Burns, Thomas J., 1942- Effective communications and advertising for financial institutions /. Englewood Cliffs, N.J. , c1986. xvi, 299 p. : ISBN 0-8359-1556-5 LC Card 85-25641 DDC 659.1/93321 19
HG1616.M3 B87 1986 NYPL [JLE 86-1689]

Caselli, Mario, 1944- La gestione marketing nella banca . Milano [1977] 332 p. : LC Card 77-553379
HG1616.M3 C37 NYPL [JLD 80-3228]

Moran, Justin L., 1932- Marketing strategies for community banks /. Boston [c1987] xiii, 199 p. ; ISBN 0-87267-105-4 LC Card 87-19280 DDC 332.1/068/8 19
HG1616.M3 M67 1987

BANK MARKETING - FRANCE.
Zollinger, Monique. Marketing bancaire . [Paris] , c1985. viii, 238 p. : ISBN 2-04-016433-2 : LC Card 86-152950 DDC 332.1/068/8 19
HG1616.M3 Z65 1985

BANK MARKETING - GERMANY (WEST)
Budde, Ramona. Marktinnovationen von Universalbanken . Berlin , c1983. xvi, 347 p. : ISBN 3-503-02192-2 LC Card 83-186914
HG1709 .B78 1983

Lubitz, Karl-Joachim. Bankmarketing gegenüber mittelständischen Betrieben /. Frankfurt am Main , c1984. 299 p. ; ISBN 3-7819-3012-2 LC Card 85-153969
HG4027.7 .L83 1984

Pott, Philipp. Marktpolitik von Privatbankiers . Frankfurt , c1983. 66 p. ; ISBN 3-88323-443-5 LC Card 84-154560
HG2021.G4 P67 1983

BANK MARKETING - UNITED STATES.
The Affluent market fact book . Tampa, Fla. , c1986. 83 leaves ; LC Card 86-235264 DDC 332.1/7 19
HG1616.C87 A33 1986

BANK NOTES - ARGENTINA - HISTORY.
Historia del papel moneda argentino /. Buenos Aires, Argentina , c1984. 47, [1] p. : LC Card 86-180304
HG817 .H57 1984

BANK NOTES - FRANCE - CATALOGS.
Muszynski, Maurice. Les billets de la Banque de France ; Les émissions du Trésor /. Bruyères-le-Châtel , 1985. 160 p. : LC Card 83-132282
HG985 .M88 1985

BANK NOTES - PORTUGAL - HISTORY.
O Papel-moeda em Portugal. [Lisbon] [1985?] 502 p. : LC Card 86-226586
HG1147 .P36 1985

BANK NOTES - SOUTH AFRICA - CATALOGS.
Hern, Brian. South African paper money trends . Braamfontein, Republic of South Africa , 1986. 172 p. : LC Card 86-201066 DDC 769.5/5968/0750968 19
HG1351.Z8 H47 1986

BANK-NOTES - SPAIN - CATALOGS.
Cayón, Juan Ramón. Billetes españoles, 1783-1983 . Madrid, España [1983?] 82 p. : ISBN 88-300-9799-6 LC Card 85-232320
HG1137 .C38 1983

Bank of Canada.
Technical reports .
(27) Freedman, Charles. Monetary aggregates as targets . [Ottawa] , 1981. vii, 49 p. ; LC Card 81-198954 DDC 332.4/6/0724 19
HG230.3 .F74 1981
NYPL [JLM 75-1420 no.27]

WEEKLY FINANCIAL STATISTICS.
Martin, Peter, 1942- Inside the Bank of Canada's Weekly financial statistics . Vancouver, B. C. , 1985. xix, 201 p. : ISBN 0-88975-082-3 *NYPL [JLF 87-456]*

BANK OF CANADA - HISTORY.
Fullerton, Douglas H. Graham Towers and his times . Toronto, Ont. , c1986. 348 p., [16] p. of plates : ISBN 0-7710-3218-8 : LC Card 86-231010 DDC 332.1/1/092 B 19
HG1552.T68 F85 1986

Bank of Zambia. Republic of Zambia, economic memorandum /. [Lusaka?] [1983?] 28 p. : LC Card 86-980289 DDC 330.96894/04 19
HC915 .R46 1983

Bank pricing and valuation /. Miller, William D. (William Dennis), 1953- New York, N.Y. , c1988. xiv, 279 p. : ISBN 0-88057-806-8 (pbk.) LC Card 87-81070 DDC 332.1/068/1 19
HG1708 .M55 1988

Bank profitability : financial statements of banks with methodological country notes, 1980-1984. Paris : Organisation for Economic Co-operation and Development ; Washington, D.C. : OECD Publications and Information Centre [distributor], 1987. 235 p. ; 27 cm. Prepared with the assistance of the OECD Group of Financial Statisticians. ISBN 92-64-12915-4 (pbk.) : LC Card 87-164235 DDC 332.1/021 19
1. Banks and banking - Accounting - Statistics. 2. Banks and banking - Accounting. I. OECD Group of Financial Statisticians. II. Organisation for Economic Co-operation and Development.
HG1708 .B29 1987

BANK RESERVES - SWITZERLAND.
Stuber, Barbara. Saisonschwankungen der Bankreserven und Ultimooperationen der Schweizerischen Nationalbank /. Bern , c1986. 173 p. : ISBN 3-258-03653-5 : LC Card 87-130160 DDC 332.1/12/09494 19
HG1656.S9 S77 1986

Bank services and fees. Chicago, IL (676 North St., Clair St., Chicago 60611) : Financial Services Group, Market Facts, Inc., 1987. 60, 8 p. ; 28 cm. Cover title: Bank services & fees. LC Card 87-400773 DDC 332.1/7/0973 19
1. Banks and banking - United States - Customer services. 2. Banks and banking - United States - Service charges. 3. Market surveys - United States. I. Market Facts, Inc. Financial Services Group. II. Title: Bank services & fees.
HG1616.C87 B36 1987

Bank services & fees. Bank services and fees. Chicago, IL (676 North St., Clair St., Chicago 60611) , 1987. 60, 8 p. ; LC Card 87-400773 DDC 332.1/7/0973 19
HG1616.C87 B36 1987

BANK STATEMENTS. see **BANKS AND BANKING - ACCOUNTING.**

Bankaufsicht, Bankbilanz und Bankprüfung. Beiträge zur Bankaufsicht, Bankbilanz und Bankprüfung . Düsseldorf , 1985. 226 p. : ISBN 3-8021-0267-3 LC Card 85-208772
HG1605 .B44 1985

Bankbetriebliches Zinsspannen-Management . Ippisch, Wolfgang. Wien , c1984. xxiii, 365 p. : ISBN 3-85428-022-X : LC Card 84-174308
HG1621 .I66 1984

Bankbetriebliches Zinsspannenmanagement. Ippisch, Wolfgang. Bankbetriebliches Zinsspannen-Management . Wien , c1984. xxiii, 365 p. : ISBN 3-85428-022-X : LC Card 84-174308
HG1621 .I66 1984

Die Bankbilanz als finanzielles Führungsinstrument . Meyer, Conrad. Bern , c1986. x, 655 p. : ISBN 3-258-03587-3 LC Card 86-199541
HG1526 .B27 Bd. 96 HG1778.S9

Banken : Erfahrungen und Lehren aus einem Vierteljahrhundert, 1958-1983 / [Herausgeber, Landesbank Rheinland-Pfalz, Girozentrale, Mainz]. Frankfurt am Main : Knapp, c1983. 216 p. ; 25 cm. One article in English. Includes bibliographical references and indexes. ISBN 3-7819-0297-8 : LC Card 83-217788
1. Banks and banking - Germany, West. 2. Banks and banking, International. 3. Finance - Germany, West. 4. International finance. 5. Landesbank Rheinland-Pfalz Girozentrale. I. Landesbank Rheinland-Pfalz Girozentrale.
HG3048 .B27 1983

Banker to the Third World . Stallings, Barbara. Berkeley , c1987. xvii, 434 p. : ISBN 0-520-05726-0 (alk. paper) LC Card 86-24988 DDC 332.6/7373/08 19
HG5160.5.A3 S73 1987

Banker to the 3rd World. Stallings, Barbara. Banker to the Third World . Berkeley , c1987. xvii, 434 p. : ISBN 0-520-05726-0 (alk. paper) LC Card 86-24988 DDC 332.6/7373/08 19
HG5160.5.A3 S73 1987

BANKERS - ARAB COUNTRIES - BIOGRAPHY.
The APS who's who in Middle East banking & trade. Nicosia, Cyprus , c1984. 2 v. : LC Card 83-149147 *NYPL [JLF 86-983]*

BANKERS - AUSTRIA - BIOGRAPHY.
Spitzmüller, Alexander, 1862-1953. Memoirs of Alexander Spitzmüller, Freiherr von Harmersbach (1862-1953) . Boulder , New

York , 1987. xi, 327 p., [5] p. of plates : ISBN 0-88033-124-0 LC Card 87-80511 DDC 332.3/2/0924 B 19
HG1552.S65 A3 1987

BANKERS - CANADA - BIOGRAPHY.
Fullerton, Douglas H. Graham Towers and his times . Toronto, Ont. , c1986. 348 p., [16] p. of plates : ISBN 0-7710-3218-8 : LC Card 86-231010 DDC 332.1/1/092 B 19
HG1552.T68 F85 1986

BANKERS - FRANCE - BIOGRAPHY.
Morin, Jean, 1875-1969. Souvenirs d'un banquier français . Paris , c1983. 326 p., [8] p. of plates : ISBN 2-207-22988-2 : LC Card 84-172168
HG1552.M67 A3 1983

Muhlstein, Anka. James de Rothschild . [Paris] , c1981. 242 p., [16] p. of plates : LC Card 82-149581 DDC 332.1/092/4 B 19
HG1552.R816 M84 1981
NYPL [*PWZ (Rothschild, J.) 86-6471]

BANKERS - GERMANY - CORRESPONDENCE.
Raiffeisen, F. W. (Friedrich Wilhelm), 1818-1888. [Correspondence.] Briefe . Wien , 1986. 207 p. : ISBN 0-370-40867-2 LC Card 87-139235 DDC 332.1/092/4 B 19
HG1552.R35 A4 1986

BANKERS - GREAT BRITAIN - BIOGRAPHY.
Attali, Jacques. [Homme d'influence. English.] A man of influence . London , 1986. 346 p. ; ISBN 0-297-78978-3 ***NYPL [JFE 87-583]***

Attali, Jacques. [Homme d'influence. English.] A man of influence . Bethesda, Md. , 1987, c1985. xvii, 380 p. ; ISBN 0-917561-36-8 : LC Card 86-28735 DDC 332.1/092/4 B 19
HG1552.W37 A8713 1987

BANKERS - ILLINOIS - CHICAGO - BIOGRAPHY.
Chavers-Wright, Madrue, 1916- The guarantee . New York , 1985. xix, 425 p. : ISBN 0-931505-02-X (pbk.) : LC Card 84-51854 DDC 338/.04/0924 B 19
HG2463.C48 C48 1985
NYPL [Sc D 86-412]

Chavers-Wright, Madrue, 1916- The guarantee . New York , 1987, c1985. xix, 427 p. : ISBN 0-931505-05-4 : LC Card 86-51447 DDC 338/.04/0924 B 19
HG2463.C48 C48 1987

BANKERS - ITALY - BIOGRAPHY.
Bonelli, Franco. Bonaldo Stringher . [Udine] [c1985] 169 p. : LC Card 85-220896
HJ1156.S77 B66 1985

The banker's life /. Moore, George S. (George Stevens), 1905- New York , c1987. 328 p., [20] p. of plates : ISBN 0-393-02458-X LC Card 86-31123 DDC 332.1/092/4 B 19
HG2463.M59 A3 1987

BANKERS - NEW YORK (N.Y.) - BIOGRAPHY.
Moore, George S. (George Stevens), 1905- The banker's life /. New York , c1987. 328 p., [20] p. of plates : ISBN 0-393-02458-X LC Card 86-31123 DDC 332.1/092/4 B 19
HG2463.M59 A3 1987

BANKERS - OKLAHOMA - BIOGRAPHY.
McGuire, Paul F., 1907- Genesis of Oklahoma oil banking /. Muskogee, Okla. , c1986. 160 p. : ISBN 0-86546-068-X (pbk.) LC Card 87-118559 DDC 332.1/223/0924 B 19
HG2463.M36 A3 1986

BANKERS - PANAMA - BIOGRAPHY.
Banco Nacional de Panamá. Informes de los gerentes generales, 1969-84. Panamá, República de Panamá , 1984. 126 p. : LC Card 85-124892
HG2773 .B35 1984

BANKERS - SRI LANKA - BIOGRAPHY.
Subasiṃha, Vinsant. Sandalaṅkā sanda /. [Pannipitiya?] , 1986. viii, 269 p., [6] leaves of plates : LC Card 86-903022
HG1552.S83 A3 1986

BANKERS - SWITZERLAND - BIOGRAPHY.
Somary, Felix, 1881-1956. [Erinnerungen aus meinem Leben. English.] The raven of Zürich . London , New York , c1986. xii, 310 p. : ISBN 0-312-66407-9 LC Card 86-6662 DDC 330/.092/4 B 19
HB101.S6 A313 1986 ***NYPL [JFE 87-54]***

BANKERS - SWITZERLAND - INTERVIEWS.
Weck, Philippe de, 1919- Un banquier suisse parle . Fribourg , c1983. 159 p. ; LC Card 84-119161
HG1552.W43 A3 1983

BANKERS - UNITED STATES - ATTITUDES.
Trading in banking . [New York?] , c1986. iv ; LC Card 87-128754 DDC 332.1/0973 19
HG2491 .T7 1986

BANKERS - UNITED STATES - BIOGRAPHY.
Frantz, Douglas. Levine & Co. . New York , c1987. x, 370 p. : ISBN 0-8050-0457-2 LC Card 87-8521 DDC 364.1/68 19
HG2463.L48 F72 1987

Hickman, Martin Berkeley, 1925- David Matthew Kennedy . Salt Lake City, Utah , c1987. xi, 403 p. : ISBN 0-87579-093-3 : LC Card 87-19898 DDC 332.1/092/4 B 19
HG2463.K46 H53 1987

Ross, Walter Sanford, 1916- People's banker . New Canaan, Conn. , c1987. viii, 288 p. ; ISBN 0-87983-429-3 LC Card 87-4066 DDC 332.1/223/0924 B 19
HG2463.R68 R67 1987

Banki, Ivan S. Dictionary of administration and management : authoritative, comphrehensive / Ivan S. Banki. Los Angeles, Calif., USA : Systems Research Institute, c1986. iv, 1369 p. ; 24 cm. Bibliography: p. 1223-1369. ISBN 0-912352-08-6 LC Card 85-63870 DDC 650/.03/21 19
1. Management - Dictionaries. 2. Organization - Dictionaries. I. Title.
HD30.15 .B36 1986

BANKING. see **BANKS AND BANKING.**

Banking and agricultural growth . Kunwar, Upendra. New Delhi , c1987. 167 p. ; LC Card 87-901193 DDC 334/.2/0954 19
HG2051.I4 K86 1987

Banking and development in Bangladesh. Taheruddin, M. Essays on banking and development /. Dhaka , 1986. 145 p. ; LC Card 87-900643 DDC 332.1/09549/2 19
HG3290.6.A6 T35 1986

Banking and economic growth. Nigam, Brij Mohan Lall, 1935- Bombay [1967] xii, 207 p. LC Card SA68-4077 DDC 332.1/0954
HG3284 .N5 ***NYPL [JLD 74-2222]***

Banking and financial services reports, 0264-200X.
Ohinata, Yo. The lending procedures of commercial banks in the United States, the United Kingdom, Japan, Germany and France /. [Manchester] [1983] 138 p. ; ISBN 0-903808-34-X (pbk.) LC Card 86-132282 DDC 332.1/753 19
HG1642.U5 O35 1983

The banking and financial system of Sri Lanka /. Karunatilake, H. N. S. Colombo , 1986. 320 p. ; LC Card 87-902032 DDC 332.1/09549/3 19
HG3270.8.A6 K37 1986

Banking and monetary polic[i]es in Islamic economics /. Ṣiddīqī, Muḥammad Nejātullah, 1931- Khartoum [between 1983 and 1986] 40 p. ; LC Card 86-980021 DDC 332.1/0917/671 19
HG3368.A6 S53 1986

Banking and the plastic card /. Krumme, Dwane. Washington, D.C. (1120 Connecticut Ave., N.W., Washington 20036) , c1987. xi, 263 p. : LC Card 87-159373 DDC 332.7/6 19
HG1643 .K79 1987

Banking & the plastic card. Krumme, Dwane. Banking and the plastic card /. Washington, D.C. (1120 Connecticut Ave., N.W., Washington 20036) , c1987. xi, 263 p. : LC Card 87-159373 DDC 332.7/6 19
HG1643 .K79 1987

Banking in India in the eighties : a comprehensive reference volume on policy & personnel matters relating to nationalised and other banks in India / [edited] by Raj K. Nigam ; foreword by M.N. Goiporia. New Delhi : Documentation Centre for Corporate & Business Policy Research, 1986. 533 p. in various pagings ; 26 cm. LC Card 86-903123 DDC 332.1/068 19
1. Banks and banking - India. 2. Bank management - India. 3. Banks and banking - India - Personnel management. I. Nigam, Raj Kumar, 1923-. II. Documentation Centre for Corporate & Business Policy Research (India).
HG3284 .B267 1986

Banking in nineteenth-century Ireland . Ollerenshaw, Philip, 1953- Manchester, UK , Wolfeboro, NH, USA , c1987. 263 p. : ISBN 0-7190-2276-2 : LC Card 87-11113 DDC 332.1/09416/7 19
HG950.B45 O55 1987

Banking in North Carolina . Gatton, T. Harry (Thomas Harry) Raleigh , 1987. xi, 155 p. : ISBN 0-9617806-0-6 LC Card 86-63397 DDC 332.1/09756 19
HG2611.N8 G38 1987

Banking in the American South from the age of Jackson to Reconstruction /. Schweikart, Larry. Baton Rouge , c1987. xiv, 367 p. : ISBN 0-8071-1403-0 LC Card 87-12784 DDC 332.1/0975 19
HG2604 .S39 1987

Banking in the United Kingdom. 4th ed. London : Peat, Marwick, Mitchell & Co., c1984. 215 p. ; 21 cm. ISBN 1-85061-020-7
1. Banks and banking - Great Britain. 2. Banks and banking, Foreign - Great Britain. 3. Banking law - Great Britain. I. Peat, Marwick, Mitchell and Company.
NYPL [JLD 86-2506]

Banking in 19th century Ireland. Ollerenshaw, Philip, 1953- Banking in nineteenth-century Ireland . Manchester, UK , Wolfeboro, NH, USA , c1987. 263 p. : ISBN 0-7190-2276-2 : LC Card 87-11113 DDC 332.1/09416/7 19
HG950.B45 O55 1987

BANKING LAW - GERMANY, WEST.
Holterhus, Gerhard. Früherkennung von Bankkrisen bei der Abschlussprüfung /. Frankfurt am Main , c1985. xvi, 360 p. : ISBN 3-7819-0348-6 LC Card 86-164226
HG1768.G3 H64 1985

Seifert, Ekkehard. Privilegierung und Regulierung im Bankwesen . Baden-Baden , 1984. 332 p. ; ISBN 3-7890-0861-3 LC Card 84-186059
HG3054 .S42 1984

Werner, Horst S. Der aktienrechtliche Abhängigkeitstatbestand . Göttingen , 1979. xxxix, 214 p. ; ISBN 3-88415-560-1 : LC Card 80-452340 DDC 346.43/066
LAW ***NYPL [JLD 86-1592]***

BANKING LAW - GREAT BRITAIN.
Banking in the United Kingdom. London , c1984. 215 p. ; ISBN 1-85061-020-7
NYPL [JLD 86-2506]

BANKING LAW - HUNGARY.
Körösényi, András. A takarékszövetkezetek banki reformjának alternativai /. Budapest [1985] 43 p. ; LC Card 87-408585
HG1939.H82 K67 1985

BANKING LAW - IRAN.
Amin, S. H. (Sayed Hessan) Islamic banking and finance . Tehran , 1986. 72 p. : ISBN 0-946706-30-1 (pbk.) LC Card 86-209623 DDC 332.1/0955 19
HG3270.2.A6 A45 1986

BANKING LAW (ISLAMIC LAW)
Iqbal, Zubair. Islamic banking /. Washington, D.C. , 1987. v, 62 p. ; ISBN 0-939934-82-5 (pbk.) : LC Card 87-4166 DDC 332.1/0917/671 19
HG3270.2.A6 I67 1987

Saleh, Nabil A. Unlawful gain and legitimate profit in Islamic law . Cambridge [Cambridgeshire] , New York , 1986. xii, 130 p. ; ISBN 0-521-32298-7 LC Card 85-25547 DDC 297/.14 19
LAW ***NYPL [JLE 86-2377]***

BANKING LAW - ITALY.
Allegri, Vincenzo. Credito di scopo e finanziamento bancario delle imprese /. Milano [1984] 166 p. ; ISBN 88-14-00299-1 : LC Card 85-187365 DDC 332.7/0945 19
HG1642.I8 A44 1984 ***NYPL [JLE 86-3661]***

Fabrizi, Pier Luigi. La politica degli investimenti in titoli nelle banche di deposito /. [Milano] , 1982. xii, 138 p. ; LC Card 82-165568
HG1616.I5 F33 1982

La Riforma della legge bancaria . Milano [1984] 283 p. ; ISBN 88-14-00126-X : LC Card

84-190853 DDC 346.45/082 344.50682 19
LAW ***NYPL [JLE 86-3654]***

Spedale, Domenico L. L'affidamento bancario . Milano , 1985. 204 p. : ***NYPL [JLD 86-3241]***

Banking on the world . Frieden, Jeffry A. New York , c1987. 264 p. ; ISBN 0-06-015822-0 : LC Card 87-45136 DDC 332.1/5/0973 19
HG3881 .F735 1987

Banking policy and the price level . Robertson, Dennis Holme, Sir, 1890-1963. New York , 1988. p. cm. ISBN 0-678-00675-X LC Card 87-7140 DDC 338.5/42 19
HB3725 .R63 1988

Banking strategies for businesses . Milling, Bryan E. Radnor, PA , c1987. viii, 231 p. : ISBN 0-8019-7651-0 (pbk.) : LC Card 86-47959 DDC 658.1/592 19
HG4027.7 .M55 1987

Banking without interest /. Ṣiddīqī, Muḥammad Nejātullah, 1931- Leicester, UK , c1983. 192 p. ; ISBN 0-86037-119-0 LC Card 86-673953
HG1588 .S52x 1983

Bankinnovationen : Chancen und Risiken der neuen Bankgeschäfte / herausgegeben von Rosemarie Kolbeck ; mit Beiträgen von Helmut Geiger ... [et al.]. Frankfurt am Main : F. Knapp, c1986. 131 p. ; 24 cm. Papers presented at the Bankwirtschaftliches Kolloquium held at the Universität Frankfurt am Main during the winter semester, 1985-1986. Includes bibliographical references. CONTENTS. - Finanzinnovationen als Chancen der deutschen Banken in nationalen und internationalen Wettbewerben / von Wolfgang Röller -- Risikopotentiale durch Finanzinnovationen als bankaufsichtsrechtliches Problem / von Wolfgang Kuntze -- Die neuen Banktechnologien unter Marketingaspekten / von Ulrich Weiss -- Personalpolitik in Banken unter Einfluss der neuen Technologien / von Raban von Spiegel -- Auswirkungen von Innovationen auf die Wettbewerbssituation der Genossenschaftsbanken / von Karl-Herbert Schneider-Gädicke -- Auswirkungen von Innovationen auf die Wettbewerbssituation der Sparkassen und Girozentralen / von Helmut Geiger -- Innovationen im Bankgeschäft als geld- und währungspolitisches Problem / von Claus Köhler. ISBN 3-7819-0363-X LC Card 87-120955 DDC 332.1/0943 19
1. Banks and banking - Germany, West. 2. Banks and banking - Germany (West) - Technological innovations. I. Kolbeck, Rosemarie. II. Geiger, Helmut, 1928-. III. Bankwirtschaftliches Kolloquium (1985-1986 : Universität Frankfurt am Main).
HG3048 .B287 1986

Bankmarketing gegenüber mittelständischen Betrieben /. Lubitz, Karl-Joachim. Frankfurt am Main , c1984. 299 p. ; ISBN 3-7819-3012-2 LC Card 85-153969
HG4027.7 .L83 1984

Bankmitarbeiter und die neuen Informationstechniken : Chancen und Aspekte / herausgegeben von Heribert Schneider und Peter Muthesius ; mit Beiträgen von Karl Heinz Beckurts ... [et al.]. Frankfurt am Main : F. Knapp, c1986. 240 p. ; 24 cm. Includes bibliographical references. ISBN 3-7819-0341-9 LC Card 86-228992
1. Banks and banking - Automation. 2. Bank employees - Effect of technological innovations on. I. Schneider, Heribert M. II. Muthesius, Peter, 1930-. III. Beckurts, K. H. (Karl Heinrich).
HG1709 .B355 1986

Bankrechtliche Sonderveröffentlichungen des Instituts für Bankwirtschaft und Bankrecht an der Universität zu Köln .
(30. Bd) Gessler, Joachim. Werbung der Banken /. [S.l. , 1983] (Köln : Druck- und Verlagshaus Wienand) xxvii, 200 p. ; LC Card 83-214619
HF6161.B2 G47 1983

(38. Bd) Beck, Peter. Einwendungen bei Eurocheque und Kreditkarte /. [S.l. , 1986] (Köln : Druck und Verarbeitung, Druck- + Verlagshaus Wienand) xv, 146, 31 p. ; LC Card 86-233484
HG3756.G3 B43 1986

BANKRUPTCY - ENGLAND - HISTORY - 18TH CENTURY.
Hoppit, Julian. Risk and failure in English business, 1700-1800 /. Cambridge [Cambridgeshire] , New York , 1987. vii, 228 p. : ISBN 0-521-32624-9 LC Card 87-743 DDC 332.7/5/0942 19
HG3769.G73 E54 1987

BANKRUPTCY - FORECASTING - STATISTICAL METHODS.
Bleier, Ernst. Insolvenzfrüherkennung mittels praktischer Anwendung der Diskriminanzanalyse /. Wien , c1985. 216 p. : ISBN 3-85428-043-2 : LC Card 85-201068
HG3761 .B54 1985

BANKRUPTCY - GERMANY, WEST.
Drukarczyk, Jochen. Credit contracts, collateral-based security agreements, and bankruptcy /. Regensburg [1983?] 25 leaves ; LC Card 84-181506 DDC 332.7/5/0943 19
HG3769.G34 D78 1983

Duttle, Josef. Ökonomische Analyse dinglicher Sicherheiten . Krefeld , 1986. xvii, 417 p. : ISBN 3-88358-062-7 LC Card 87-104300
HG3711.G3 D87 1986

Esser, Carsten, 1960- Das Fremdkapital im Unternehmen als Insolvenzursache und die Möglichkeiten rechtlicher Steuerung der Finanzierungsgrundlagen /. Frankfurt am Main , New York , c1986. xvi, 131 p. (1 folded) ; ISBN 3-8204-9398-0 LC Card 86-229108
HG5501 .E85 1986

Veit, Klaus-Rüdiger. Die Konkursrechnungslegung . Köln , c1982. xiv, 221 p. ; ISBN 3-452-19273-3 LC Card 83-130656 DDC 346.43/078 344.30678 19
KK4290 .V44 1982 ***NYPL [JLE 87-1129]***

BANKRUPTCY - GERMANY (WEST) - ECONOMETRIC MODELS.
Christians, Uwe, 1957- Entwicklung und empirische Überprüfung eines konjunkturgerechten Erfolgsprognosemodells zur Unterstützung der Kreditwürdigkeitsprüfung . München , c1986. xiv, 412 p. : ISBN 3-88259-430-6 (Deut. Bibl.) LC Card 87-409324 DDC 332.7/0943 19
HG3754.5.G3 C48 1986

BANKRUPTCY - GREAT BRITAIN.
Hilliard, Francis, 1808?-1878. A treatise on the law of bankruptcy and insolvency [microform] /. Philadelphia , London , 1872. xxxiii, 564, 84, xxiii p. ; ***NYPL [*ZT-1689]***

BANKRUPTCY - HUNGARY.
Veress, József, Dr. A veszélyhelyzetbe került vállalatok és a gazdaságirányítás /. Budapest , 1986. 207, [1] p. ; ISBN 963-221-778-0 : LC Card 87-136695
HG3769.H94 V47 1986

BANKRUPTCY - LOUISIANA.
Traylor, Harlon D. An analysis of grain elevator bankruptcies in Louisiana /. [Baton Rouge?] [1986] iii, 77 p. ; LC Card 87-620885 DDC 338.1/09763 s 338.1/6 19
HD1775.L8 L7 no. 661 HD9037.L6

BANKRUPTCY - MATHEMATICAL MODELS.
Drukarczyk, Jochen. Zum Problem der Auslösung insolvenzrechtlicher Verfahren /. [Regensburg] [198-?] 30, iv leaves : LC Card 84-181525
HG3761 .D79 1980z

BANKRUPTCY - PSYCHOLOGICAL ASPECTS.
Neill, Robert Hitt. How to lose your farm in ten easy lessons and cope with it /. Leland, Miss. , c1987. xi, 138 p. ; ISBN 0-9617591-1-9 (pbk.) : LC Card 87-14176 DDC 338.1/3/097624 19
HD1476.U6 A156 1987

BANKRUPTCY - STATISTICAL METHODS.
Bleier, Ernst. Insolvenzfrüherkennung mittels praktischer Anwendung der Diskriminanzanalyse /. Wien , c1985. 216 p. : ISBN 3-85428-043-2 : LC Card 85-201068
HG3761 .B54 1985

BANKRUPTCY - TEXAS - PSYCHOLOGICAL ASPECTS - CONGRESSES.
Farm Crisis Workers Conference (1986 : Arlington, Tex.) Farm Crisis Workers Conference . [Austin? , 1986] 136 p. ; LC Card 87-620630 DDC 338.1/3/09764 19
HD1476.U6 T44 1986

BANKRUPTCY - UNITED STATES.
Hilliard, Francis, 1808?-1878. A treatise on the law of bankruptcy and insolvency [microform] /. Philadelphia , London , 1872. xxxiii, 564, 84, xxiii p. ; ***NYPL [*ZT-1689]***

BANKS. see **BANKS AND BANKING.**

BANKS AND BANKING - ACCOUNTING.
Bank profitability . Paris , Washington, D.C. , 1987. 235 p. ; ISBN 92-64-12915-4 (pbk.) : LC Card 87-164235 DDC 332.1/021 19
HG1708 .B29 1987

Beiträge zur Bankaufsicht, Bankbilanz und Bankprüfung . Düsseldorf , 1985. 226 p. : ISBN 3-8021-0267-3 LC Card 85-208772
HG1605 .B44 1985

BANKS AND BANKING - ACCOUNTING - STATISTICS.
Bank profitability . Paris , Washington, D.C. , 1987. 235 p. ; ISBN 92-64-12915-4 (pbk.) : LC Card 87-164235 DDC 332.1/021 19
HG1708 .B29 1987

BANKS AND BANKING - ADVERTISING. see **ADVERTISING - BANKS AND BANKING.**

BANKS AND BANKING - AFRICA.
Seidman, Ann Willcox, 1926- Money, banking, and public finance in Africa /. London , Atlantic Highlands, N.J., USA , 1986. xv, 363 p. : ISBN 0-86232-429-7 LC Card 87-111822 DDC 332.1/096 19
HG187.5.A2 S45 1986

BANKS AND BANKING, AMERICAN.
Frieden, Jeffry A. Banking on the world . New York , c1987. 264 p. ; ISBN 0-06-015822-0 : LC Card 87-45136 DDC 332.1/5/0973 19
HG3881 .F735 1987

Gwynne, S. C. (Samuel C.), 1953- Selling money /. New York , 1987, c1986. 182 p. ; ISBN 0-14-010282-5 (pbk.) LC Card 87-6969 DDC 336.3/435 19
HG3891.5 .G98 1987

BANKS AND BANKING, AMERICAN - HISTORY - 20TH CENTURY.
Mayer, Robert Stanley. The influence of Frank A. Vanderlip and the National City Bank on American commerce and foreign policy, 1910-1920 /. New York , 1987. viii, 221 p. ; ISBN 0-8240-8087-4 : LC Card 87-23793 DDC 332.1/5/097471 19
HG2613.N54 N3555 1987

BANKS AND BANKING, AMERICAN - LATIN AMERICA.
US economic expansion . Moscow , 1986. 216 p. ; LC Card 87-112029 DDC 337.7308 19
HF1456.5.L3 U8 1986

BANKS AND BANKING, AMERICAN - SOUTH AFRICA - DIRECTORIES.
Bowers, Cathy. U. S. and Canadian investment in South Africa and Namibia . Washington, D.C. , c1986. xiii, 238 p. ; ISBN 0-931035-10-4 (pbk.) LC Card 86-209149 DDC 338.8/8973/068025 19
HG5851.A3 B69 1986

Newman, Anne, 1951- Foreign investment in South Africa and Namibia . Washington, D.C. [1984] ii, 279 p. ; ISBN 0-931035-00-7 (pbk.) LC Card 85-130985 DDC 332.6/73/0968 19
HG5851.A3 N49 1984 ***NYPL [Sc F 85-173]***

BANKS AND BANKING - ARAB COUNTRIES - DIRECTORIES.
The APS who's who in Middle East banking & trade. Nicosia, Cyprus , c1984. 2 v. : LC Card 83-149147 ***NYPL [JLF 86-983]***

BANKS AND BANKING - AUSTRALIA - HISTORY.
Butlin, S. J. (Sydney James), d. 1977. The Australian monetary system, 1851 to 1914 /. [s.l] , 1986. 404 p. : ISBN 1-86252-307-X (pbk.) LC Card 87-154610 DDC 332.4/994 19
HG1394 .B87 1986

BANKS AND BANKING - AUSTRIA.
Ḍiwok, Fritz. Struktur des Bankwesens in Österreich /. Frankfurt am Main , c1982. 142 p. ; ISBN 3-7819-2771-7 LC Card 83-190921 DDC 332.1/09436 19
HG3008 .D59 1982

Morawetz, Inge, 1955- Die verborgene Macht . Frankfurt , New York , c1986. 200 p. : ISBN 3-593-33662-6 LC Card 86-223864
HG3008 .M67 1986

BANKS AND BANKING - AUSTRIA - BRANCH BANKS.

Gach, Christian. Wirtschaftlichkeitsanalyse von Banken . Wien , c1983. iv, 75, iii, 89 p. ; ISBN 3-85428-017-3 : LC Card 84-118578
HG3008 .G28 1983

BANKS AND BANKING - AUTOMATION.
Bankmitarbeiter und die neuen Informationstechniken . Frankfurt am Main , c1986. 240 p. ; ISBN 3-7819-0341-9 LC Card 86-228992
HG1709 .B355 1986

Budde, Ramona. Marktinnovationen von Universalbanken . Berlin , c1983. xvi, 347 p. : ISBN 3-503-02192-2 LC Card 83-186914
HG1709 .B78 1983

Tüchter, Ulrich. Cash Management . Köln , c1985. 122 p. : ISBN 3-87951-126-8 LC Card 87-152212 DDC 332.1/2/0681 19
HG4028.C45 T83 1985

BANKS AND BANKING - BANGLADESH.
Rahamāna, Matiura, 1946- Dhanikagoshṭhīra luṭapāṭera kāhinī /. Ḍhākā , 1987. 136 p. : LC Card 87-902373
HG3290.6.A6 R35 1987

Taheruddin, M. Essays on banking and development /. Dhaka , 1986. 145 p. ; LC Card 87-900643 DDC 332.1/09549/2 19
HG3290.6.A6 T35 1986

BANKS AND BANKING - BANGLADESH - CORRUPT PRACTICES.
Rahamāna, Matiura, 1946- Dhanikagoshṭhīra luṭapāṭera kāhinī /. Ḍhākā , 1987. 136 p. : LC Card 87-902373
HG3290.6.A6 R35 1987

BANKS AND BANKING - BRANCH BANKS.
Elliott, P. A. (Peter A.), 1923- The bank manager's handbook . Cambridge, England , Wolfeboro, NH , 1987. p. cm. ISBN 0-85941-330-6 : LC Card 86-28293 DDC 332.1/6 19
HG1616.B7 E45 1987

BANKS AND BANKING - BRAZIL.
Assis, José Carlos de. A sombra do cruzado . Rio de Janeiro , 1986. 137 p. : LC Card 87-128261 DDC 332.4/981 19
HG835 .A88 1986

Galvêas, Ernane. Sistema financeiro e mercado de capitais /. Rio de Janeiro , 1985. 171 p. : LC Card 85-208367
HG185.B7 G35 1985

Loureiro, Orozimbo Roxo. Garimpando reminiscências /. São Paulo , 1976 (São Paulo : Grafikor) 317 p. ; LC Card 85-225740
HG5332 .L68 1976

BANKS AND BANKING - BRAZIL - AUTOMATION.
Relatório da Comissão Especial de Automação Bancária. Brasília , 1985. 304 p. : LC Card 86-230558
HG1709 .R35 1985

BANKS AND BANKING - BRAZIL - DATA PROCESSING.
Relatório da Comissão Especial de Automação Bancária. Brasília , 1985. 304 p. : LC Card 86-230558
HG1709 .R35 1985

BANKS AND BANKING - BRAZIL - SÃO PAULO (STATE) - HISTORY.
Saes, Flávio Azevedo Marques de, 1948- Crédito e bancos no desenvolvimento da economia paulista, 1850-1930 /. São Paulo , 1986. 238 p. : LC Card 87-144659 DDC 332.1/0981/61 19
HG2889.S25 S24 1986

BANKS AND BANKING, BRAZILIAN.
Baer, Mônica. A internacionalização financeira no Brasil /. Petrópolis , 1986. 159 p. ; LC Card 86-200812
HG185.B7 B28 1986

BANKS AND BANKING, BRITISH - IRAN.
Jones, Geoffrey. The history of the British Bank of the Middle East /. Cambridge [Cambridgeshire] , New York , 1986- v. : ISBN 0-521-32322-3 (v. 1) LC Card 85-31359 DDC 332.1/5/0955 19
HG3270.2.A8 B755 1986 ***NYPL [JLL 87-87]***

BANKS AND BANKING, BRITISH - MIDDLE EAST.
Jones, Geoffrey. The history of the British Bank of the Middle East /. Cambridge [Cambridgeshire] , New York , 1986- v. : ISBN 0-521-32322-3 (v. 1) LC Card 85-31359 DDC 332.1/5/0955 19
HG3270.2.A8 B755 1986 ***NYPL [JLL 87-87]***

BANKS AND BANKING - CANADA.
Johnson, Arthur, 1951- Breaking the banks /. Toronto, Canada , c1986. xi, 256 p. ; ISBN 0-88619-072-X LC Card 87-120151 DDC 332.1/2/0971 19
HG2708.C36 J64 1986

BANKS AND BANKING - CANADA - STATE SUPERVISION.
Estey, Willard Z. Report of the inquiry into the collapse of the CCB and Northland Bank /. Ottawa, Canada , c1986. xiii, 641 p. : ISBN 0-660-12171-9 (pbk.) : LC Card 87-134617 DDC 332.1/2/0971 19
HG2708.C36 E89 1986

BANKS AND BANKING, CANADIAN.
Moreau, François. Le développement international des banques canadiennes . Montréal, Québec , c1985. 159 p. ; ISBN 2-89035-120-3 LC Card 86-186883
HG2704 .M67 1985

BANKS AND BANKING - CASE STUDIES.
Le Crisi finanziarie /. Bologna , c1985. 348 p. : ISBN 88-15-00807-1 : LC Card 85-201934 DDC 332.1 19
HG1591 .C75 1985

BANKS AND BANKING, CENTRAL - AFRICA - DIRECTORIES.
Association of African Central Banks. Directory of African central banks /. Dakar, Senegal [1985 or 1986] ca. 150 leaves : LC Card 87-402547 DDC 332.1/1/02567 19
HG3376 .A87 1985

BANKS AND BANKING, CENTRAL - AUSTRIA - CONGRESSES.
Staatsfinanzierung und Notenbank . Wien [1984?] 211 p. : LC Card 85-198128
HG1811 .S78 1984

BANKS AND BANKING, CENTRAL - BRAZIL.
Galvêas, Ernane. Sistema financeiro e mercado de capitais /. Rio de Janeiro , 1985. 171 p. : LC Card 85-208367
HG185.B7 G35 1985

BANKS AND BANKING, CENTRAL - CANADA.
Howitt, Peter, 1946- Monetary policy in transition . Toronto , Scarborough, Ont. [1986] viii, 140 p. : ISBN 0-88806-136-6 (pbk.) LC Card 86-229489 DDC 332.1/12/0971 19
HG655 .H69 1986

BANKS AND BANKING, CENTRAL - CONGRESSES.
Staatsfinanzierung und Notenbank . Wien [1984?] 211 p. : LC Card 85-198128
HG1811 .S78 1984

BANKS AND BANKING, CENTRAL - DECISION MAKING.
Central bankers, bureaucratic incentives, and monetary policy /. Dordrecht ; Boston : xiv, 251 p. : ISBN 90-247-3366-9 LC Card 86-12572 DDC 332.1/12/0973 19
HG2565 .C33 1986 ***NYPL [JLE 87-394]***

BANKS AND BANKING, CENTRAL - DEVELOPING COUNTRIES - CONGRESSES.
International debt and central banking in the 1980s /. New York , 1987. viii, 234 p. ; ISBN 0-312-00530-X : LC Card 87-4300 DDC 336.3/435/091724 19
HJ8899 .I574 1987

BANKS AND BANKING, CENTRAL - GERMANY (WEST) - CONGRESSES.
Staatsfinanzierung und Notenbank . Wien [1984?] 211 p. : LC Card 85-198128
HG1811 .S78 1984

BANKS AND BANKING, CENTRAL - HAITI - HISTORY.
Marcelin, Frédéric, 1848-1917. La Banque nationale d'Haïti . Port-au-Prince, Haïti , 1985. xi, 118 p. : LC Card 86-125803 DDC 332.1/1/097294 19
HG2813 .M3 1985 ***NYPL [Sc D 86-690]***

BANKS AND BANKING, CENTRAL - LATIN AMERICA.
Coers, Hermann Max. El Banco Central Latinaoamericano . México , 1972. xv, 78 p. ; LC Card 87-401518 DDC 332.1/1/098 19
HG2710.5.A7 C6 1972

Tamagna, Frank M. [Banca central en América Latina. English.] Central banking in Latin America /. México , 1965. xii, 285 p. ; LC Card 87-403322 DDC 332.1/1/098 19
HG2710.5.A7 T3513 1965

BANKS AND BANKING, CENTRAL - PANAMA.
Conte Porras, J. El crédito, la banca y la moneda panameña /. Panamá, Panamá , 1983. 204 p. : ***NYPL [JLE 86-3126]***

BANKS AND BANKING, CENTRAL - PANAMA - HISTORY.
Banco Nacional de Panamá. Informes de los gerentes generales, 1969-84. Panamá, República de Panamá , 1984. 126 p. : LC Card 85-124892
HG2773 .B35 1984

Conte Porras, J. El crédito, la banca y la moneda panameña /. Panamá, Panamá , 1983. 204 p. : ***NYPL [JLE 86-3126]***

BANKS AND BANKING, CENTRAL - PERU.
Callegari Ramírez, Carlos. Historia del Banco de la Nación. Lima, Perú , 1986. 223 p. : LC Card 87-400236 DDC 332.1/1/0985 19
HG2946 .C35 1986

BANKS AND BANKING, CENTRAL - SRI LANKA.
Central Bank of Sri Lanka . [Colombo] [1986] 238 p. : LC Card 86-903712 DDC 332.1/1/095493 19
HG3270.8.A7 C47 1986

BANKS AND BANKING, CENTRAL - UNITED STATES.
Anderson, Hugold. Government without taxation /. Warwick, R.I. , c1987. 52 p. ; LC Card 87-133116 DDC 336.2/00973 19
HJ2381 .A76 1987

BANKS AND BANKING, CENTRAL - URUGUAY.
Compra de carteras . Montevideo [1986] 188 p. : LC Card 87-403157 DDC 332.1/09895 19
HG2954 .C66 1986

BANKS AND BANKING - COLOMBIA - CORRUPT PRACTICES - CASE STUDIES.
Donadío, Alberto, 1953- Por qué cayó Jaime Michelsen? /. Bogotá , c1984. 142 p. : ISBN 84-89209-42-1 LC Card 85-122262
HG2908.C65 D66 1984

BANKS AND BANKING - COLOMBIA - STATISTICS.
Estadísticas e indicadores de los bancos y corporaciones financieras, 1970-1985 . [Bogotá, Colombia] [1986] 64 p. : LC Card 86-167798
HG2904 .E77 1986

BANKS AND BANKING, COOPERATIVE - ECUADOR.
Da Ros, Giuseppina. El cooperativismo de ahorro y crédito en el Ecuador /. Quito , 1985. 89 p. : LC Card 86-169048
HG2156.E22 D37 1985

BANKS AND BANKING, COOPERATIVE - GERMANY, WEST.
Deppenkemper, Bernhard. Mitgliederversammlungen und Willensbildung in Genossenschaften /. Gelsenkirchen , 1984. 316 p. : ISBN 3-88485-473-9 LC Card 85-114636
HG2039.G4 D45 1984

Röhm, Helmut. Der Förderungsauftrag im Zielsystem der Bankgenossenschaften . Stuttgart , c1983. 306 p. ; ISBN 3-8001-8187-8 LC Card 84-106807
HG2039.G4 R568 1983

BANKS AND BANKING, COOPERATIVE - GERMANY (WEST) - HISTORY.
Aschhoff, Gunther, 1934- Das deutsche Genossenschaftswesen . Frankfurt am Main , 1985. 167 p. : ISBN 3-7819-0345-1 LC Card 86-145522
HD3038 .A77 1985

BANKS AND BANKING, COOPERATIVE - GOVERNMENT POLICY - AFRICA - CONGRESSES.
National financial policies and capital formation in Africa . Dakar, Senegal [1986] iii, 205 p. ; LC Card 87-404123 DDC 332/.096 19
HG5822 .N38 1986

BANKS AND BANKING, COOPERATIVE - HUNGARY.
Körösényi, András. A takarékszövetkezetek banki reformjának alternativai /. Budapest [1985] 43 p. ; LC Card 87-408585
HG1939.H82 K67 1985

BANKS AND BANKING, COOPERATIVE - HUNGARY - MANAGEMENT - HANDBOOKS, MANUALS, ETC.
Galambosi, László. Takarékszövetkezeti tisztségviselők kézikönyve /. Budapest , 1986. 135 p. ; ISBN 963-7006-73-7 LC Card 87-137992
HG1939.H82 G35 1986

BANKS AND BANKING, COOPERATIVE - INDIA - ANDHRA PRADESH.
Reddy, C. R. Cooperative long term finance . Delhi, India , 1987. ix, 128 p. : LC Card 87-900729 DDC 334/.2/095484 19
HG2051.I5 A652 1987

BANKS AND BANKING, COOPERATIVE - INDIA - ASSAM.
Bhorali, Devadas. Co-operative banking and economic development /. New Delhi , c1987. 424 p. : LC Card 87-900825 DDC 334/.2/0954162 19
HG2039.I4 B47 1987

BANKS AND BANKING, COOPERATIVE - INDIA - NAINI TAL (DISTRICT)
Kumar, Kewal. Institutional financing of Indian agriculture . New Delhi , c1987. 232 p. : LC Card 87-900911 DDC 332.7/1/09542 19
HG2051.I5 N354 1987

BANKS AND BANKING, COOPERATIVE - ITALY.
Santoro, Vittorio. Profili funzionali e operativi delle casse rurali e artigiane /. Milano [1984] 181 p. ; ISBN 88-14-00380-7 : LC Card 85-147834
HG2039.I8 S26 1984 ***NYPL [JLE 86-3669]***

BANKS AND BANKING, COOPERATIVE - ITALY - VENETO - HISTORY.
Un Secolo di cooperazione di credito nel Veneto . Limena, Padova , c1985. 454 p., [29] p. of plates : LC Card 86-195743
HG2039.I8 S43 1985

BANKS AND BANKING, COOPERATIVE - LAW AND LEGISLATION - GERMANY (WEST)
Deppenkemper, Bernhard. Mitgliederversammlungen und Willensbildung in Genossenschaften /. Gelsenkirchen , 1984. 316 p. : ISBN 3-88485-473-9 LC Card 85-114636
HG2039.G4 D45 1984

BANKS AND BANKING, COOPERATIVE - MASSACHUSETTS.
Cooperative bank . [Boston] [1986] p. A-G, 99, 42 p. ; LC Card 87-620912 DDC 334/.2/025744 19
HG2038.M4 C58 1986

BANKS AND BANKING, COOPERATIVE - SRI LANKA.
In retrospect . Colombo , 1986. 149 p. ; LC Card 86-903248 DDC 334/.2/095493
HG2039.S65 I5 1986

BANKS AND BANKING, COOPERATIVE - TANZANIA.
A Short introduction to the co-operative savings and credit societies and Tanzania Rural Savings and Credit Scheme /. [Dar es Salaam, Tanzania] [1977] 43 p. : LC Card 77-980630 DDC 334/.2/09678 19
HG2039.T37 S56 1977

BANKS AND BANKING - COSTA RICA - HISTORY.
Daremblum, Jaime. Del cacao al colón . San José, Costa Rica [1977?- v. <1- > ; LC Card 87-402194 DDC 332.4/97286 19
HG682 .D37 1977

Villalobos Vega, Bernardo. La mesocracia de Costa Rica, 1821-1926 /. San José , c1986. 309 p. ; ISBN 997-7232-15-6 LC Card 86-231140
HC143.Z9 S38 1986

BANKS AND BANKING - COSTA RICA - HISTORY - 19TH CENTURY.
Gil Pacheco, Rufino. Ciento cinco años de vida bancaria en Costa Rica /. San José , 1982. 406 p. : LC Card 83-228041 DDC 332.1/097286 19
HG2734 .G55 1982 ***NYPL [JLD 86-3356]***

BANKS AND BANKING - COSTA RICA - HISTORY - 20TH CENTURY.
Gil Pacheco, Rufino. Ciento cinco años de vida bancaria en Costa Rica /. San José , 1982. 406 p. : LC Card 83-228041 DDC 332.1/097286 19
HG2734 .G55 1982 ***NYPL [JLD 86-3356]***

BANKS AND BANKING - COSTS.
Kolari, James W. Bank costs, structure, and performance /. Lexington, Mass. , c1987. x, 240 p. : ISBN 0-669-11282-8 (alk. paper) LC Card 85-45295 DDC 332.1/068/1 19
HG1616.C6 K65 1987

BANKS AND BANKING - CUSTOMER SERVICES.
Bakonyi, Emmerich. Mitgliedererwartungen in Bankgenossenschaften . Stuttgart , c1983. 389 p. : ISBN 3-8001-8188-6 LC Card 84-106778
HG2035 .B28 1983

Reidenbach, R. Eric. Developing new banking products . Englewood Cliffs, N.J. , c1987. xii, 206 p. : ISBN 0-13-204603-2 LC Card 86-22708 DDC 332.1/7/0685 19
HG1616.C87 R45 1987 ***NYPL [JLE 87-1141]***

BANKS AND BANKING - DECISION MAKING - DATA PROCESSING.
Kiczek, Paul. Decision making for bankers . Washington, D.C. (1120 Connecticut Ave., NW, Washington 20036) , c1986. 89 p. : LC Card 87-115307 DDC 332.1/2/02855369 19
HG1709 .K53 1986

BANKS AND BANKING - DEVELOPING COUNTRIES.
Wellons, Philip A. Banks and specialised financial intermediaries in development /. Paris , Washington, D.C. , 1986. 150 p. : ISBN 92-64-12867-0 (pbk.) : LC Card 87-114506 DDC 332.1/09172/4 19
HG3550 .W45 1986

BANKS AND BANKING, DEVELOPMENT. see **DEVELOPMENT BANKS.**

BANKS AND BANKING - DICTIONARIES.
Rosenberg, Jerry Martin. Dictionary of banking and financial services /. New York , c1985. xv, 708 p. ; ISBN 0-471-83088-7 LC Card 85-12461 DDC 332/.03/21 19
HG151 .R67 1985 ***NYPL [*R-Econ. 86-3275]***

Understanding the language of banking. Washington, D.C. (1120 Connecticut Ave., N.W., Washington 20036) , c1986. v, 258 p. : LC Card 87-111196 DDC 332.1/014 19
HG151 .U53 1986

BANKS AND BANKING - DOMINICAN REPUBLIC.
González Vega, Claudio. Mercados financieros y desarrollo /. Santo Domingo, República Dominicana , 1986. 73 p. : LC Card 87-102022
HG2817 .G66 1986

Poyo, Jeffrey. Los bancos agropecuarios y la captación de depósitos /. Santo Domingo, República Dominicana , 1986. 39 p. : LC Card 87-400523 DDC 332.7/1/097293 19
HG2051.D6 P69 1986

BANKS AND BANKING - DOMINICAN REPUBLIC - CONGRESSES.
La Situación y los problemas del sistema financiero nacional. Santo Domingo, República Dominicana , 1986. 152 p. ; LC Card 86-208560
HG2817 .S57 1986

BANKS AND BANKING - EAST ASIA - STATE SUPERVISION - CONGRESSES.
Financial innovation and monetary policy . [Tokyo] , c1986. ix, 339 p. : ISBN 4-13-047029-9 : LC Card 86-222823 DDC 332/.095 19
HG187.E37 F55 1986

BANKS AND BANKING - ECUADOR.
Pensamiento monetario y financiero /. Quito, Ecuador , 1986. 2 v. : LC Card 87-150740 DDC 332.4/9866 19
HG862 .P46 1986

BANKS AND BANKING - ECUADOR - CONGRESSES.
Seminario de Operaciones Internacionales (1981 : Quito, Ecuador) Memorias del Seminario de Operaciones Internacionales /. Quito, Ecuador , 1981. 156 p., [2] p. of plates : LC Card 86-174597
HF1519 .S46 1981

BANKS AND BANKING - ETHIOPIA.
Mauri, Arnaldo. Moneta e banca in Etiopia /. Milano [1986] xi, 316 p. : ISBN 88-14-00769-1 LC Card 86-182310
HG3389.A6 M38 1986 ***NYPL [JLE 87-1721]***

BANKS AND BANKING - EUROPEAN ECONOMIC COMMUNITY COUNTRIES.
Fernández Ordóñez, Francisco. España y la CEE . Madrid, España , 1985. 74 p. ; ISBN 84-505-4317-0 LC Card 86-151137
HG2980.5.A6 F47 1985

BANKS AND BANKING, EUROPEAN - SOUTHEASTERN ASIA.
Strittmatter, Gabriele. Kooperationsstrategien westeuropäischer und japanischer Banken in den ASEAN-Staaten /. Baden-Baden , 1984. 411 p. : ISBN 3-7890-1051-0 LC Card 86-134027
HG3324 .S77 1984

BANKS AND BANKING - EXAMINATIONS. see **BANK EXAMINATION.**

BANKS AND BANKING, FEDERAL RESERVE. see **FEDERAL RESERVE BANKS.**

BANKS AND BANKING, FOREIGN.
The Nationality structure of the international banking market and the role of interbank operations. Basle [1985] 12 leaves ; LC Card 86-139771 DDC 332.1/5 19
HG3881 .N33 1985

BANKS AND BANKING, FOREIGN - BRAZIL.
Baer, Mônica. A internacionalização financeira no Brasil /. Petrópolis , 1986. 159 p. ; LC Card 86-200812
HG185.B7 B28 1986

BANKS AND BANKING, FOREIGN - EGYPT.
Caselli, Clara. L'internationalisation bancaire en Egypte /. Milano [1982] 223 p. ; LC Card 83-132087 DDC 332.1/5/0962 19
HG3386.A6 C37 1982 ***NYPL [JLE 86-1969]***

BANKS AND BANKING, FOREIGN - GREAT BRITAIN.
Banking in the United Kingdom. London , c1984. 215 p. ; ISBN 1-85061-020-7
NYPL [JLD 86-2506]

BANKS AND BANKING, FOREIGN - INDIA.
Sharma, R. D. (Ramji Dass) Financial working of foreign multinational banks in India /. Delhi, India , 1987. 244 p. ; LC Card 86-903591 DDC 332.1/5 19
HG3284 .S487 1987

BANKS AND BANKING, FOREIGN - JAPAN.
Pauly, Louis W. Regulatory politics in Japan . Ithaca, N.Y. , c1987. vi, 82 p. ; ISBN 0-939657-45-7 (pbk.) LC Card 87-403245 DDC 332.1/5/0952 19
HG3324 .P38 1987

BANKS AND BANKING, FOREIGN - LATIN AMERICA.
Labarca, Guillermo. Los bancos multinacionales en América Latina y la crisis del sistema capitalista /. México, D.F. , 1979. 201 p. ; ISBN 968-429-155-8 LC Card 80-123755
HG2710.5.A6 L3 ***NYPL [JLC 81-147]***

Quijano, José Manuel. Finanzas, desarrollo económico y penetración extranjera /. Puebla, Pue. , 1985. 395 p. : LC Card 86-112589 DDC 332/.0972 19
HG185.M6 Q55 1985 ***NYPL [JLD 86-2195]***

BANKS AND BANKING, FOREIGN - LAW AND LEGISLATION - JAPAN.
Pauly, Louis W. Regulatory politics in Japan . Ithaca, N.Y. , c1987. vi, 82 p. ; ISBN 0-939657-45-7 (pbk.) LC Card 87-403245 DDC 332.1/5/0952 19
HG3324 .P38 1987

BANKS AND BANKING, FOREIGN - PERU.
Uriarte, J. Manuel. Transnational banks and the dynamics of the Peruvian foreign debt and inflation /. New York , c1986. x, 195 p. : ISBN 0-03-002599-0 (alk. paper) : LC Card 84-26307 DDC 336.3/4/0985 19
HJ8604 .U75 1985 ***NYPL [JLE 86-1384]***

BANKS AND BANKING - FRANCE.
Binst, Olivier. Banques, le grand secret /. Paris , c1987. 166 p. ; ISBN 2-234-02032-8 : LC Card 87-156884
HG3026 .B48 1987

Bizot, Alain. La pratique bancaire française en matière de financement sur le marché intérieur /. Paris , c1985. 238 p. : ISBN 2-86325-033-7 :

LC Card 86-159009
HG1642.F8 B59 1985

Pastré, Olivier. La modernisation des banques françaises . Paris [1985] 234 p. : ISBN 2-11-001537-3 : LC Card 86-179536
HG3026 .P37 1985

Zollinger, Monique. Marketing bancaire . [Paris] , c1985. viii, 238 p. : ISBN 2-04-016433-2 : LC Card 86-152950 DDC 332.1/068/8 19
HG1616.M3 Z65 1985

BANKS AND BANKING - FRANCE - EMPLOYEES - EFFECT OF TECHNOLOGICAL INNOVATION ON - CONGRESSES.
Symposium sur les conséquences des techniques nouvelles de l'informatique sur les conditions de vie, et de travail, sur l'emploi des travailleurs des banques et des assurances (1980 : Paris, France) Symposium sur les conséquences des techniques nouvelles de l'informatique sur les conditions de vie, et de travail, sur l'emploi des travailleurs des banques et des assurances /. Berlin [1983?] 96 p. : LC Card 84-185736
HD8039.B27 F77 1980

BANKS AND BANKING - FRANCE - HISTORY.
Bouchary, Jean. Les compagnies financières à Paris à la fin du XVIIIe siècle--tome II [microform] ... /. Paris , 1941. 212 p. ;
NYPL [*ZT-1711 no.28]

Morin, Jean, 1875-1969. Souvenirs d'un banquier français . Paris , c1983. 326 p., [8] p. of plates : ISBN 2-207-22988-2 : LC Card 84-172168
HG1552.M67 A3 1983

BANKS AND BANKING - FRANCE - LYON - HISTORY.
Lyon, l'argent, le commerce et la soie /. Lyon , c1986. 138 p. : ISBN 2-904638-63-6 : LC Card 86-184131
HC278.L9 L96 1986

BANKS AND BANKING, GERMAN - CANADA - HISTORY.
Meleghy, Gyula, 1955- Die Vermittlerrolle der Banken bei deutschen Investitionen in Nord- und Mittelamerika bis zum Ersten Weltkrieg /. [Köln?] 1983 (Köln : W. Kleikamp) 330 p. : LC Card 85-229675
HG3052 .M45 1983

BANKS AND BANKING, GERMAN - MEXICO - HISTORY.
Meleghy, Gyula, 1955- Die Vermittlerrolle der Banken bei deutschen Investitionen in Nord- und Mittelamerika bis zum Ersten Weltkrieg /. [Köln?] 1983 (Köln : W. Kleikamp) 330 p. : LC Card 85-229675
HG3052 .M45 1983

BANKS AND BANKING, GERMAN - SOVIET UNION - HISTORY - 20TH CENTURY.
Lemke, Heinz. Finanztransaktionen und Aussenpolitik . Berlin , 1985. 215 p. ; LC Card 86-196601
HG3955 .L45 1985

BANKS AND BANKING, GERMAN - UNITED STATES - HISTORY.
Meleghy, Gyula, 1955- Die Vermittlerrolle der Banken bei deutschen Investitionen in Nord- und Mittelamerika bis zum Ersten Weltkrieg /. [Köln?] 1983 (Köln : W. Kleikamp) 330 p. : LC Card 85-229675
HG3052 .M45 1983

BANKS AND BANKING - GERMANY - HISTORY - 20TH CENTURY.
Ermittlungen gegen die Dresdner Bank, 1946 /. Nördlingen , 1986. cxxxiv, 353 p., [8] p. of plates : ISBN 3-89190-297-2 : LC Card 87-121689
HG3058.D7 E76 1986

BANKS AND BANKING - GERMANY, WEST.
Banken . Frankfurt am Main , c1983. 216 p. ; ISBN 3-7819-0297-8 : LC Card 83-217788
HG3048 .B27 1983

Bankinnovationen . Frankfurt am Main , c1986. 131 p. ; ISBN 3-7819-0363-X LC Card 87-120955 DDC 332.1/0943 19
HG3048 .B287 1986

Glogowski, Erhard. Neue Finanzdienstleistungen . Wiesbaden , c1986. 305 p. : ISBN 3-409-14101-4 LC Card 87-131647 DDC 332.1/0943 19
HG3048 .G57 1986

Kilhey, Ulrike. Die Beurteilung des Erfolgs von Bankprodukten als Grundlage produktpolitischer Entscheidungen /. Frankfurt am Main , c1987. xiv, 289 p. : ISBN 3-7819-0374-5 LC Card 87-136157 DDC 332.1/068/5 19
HF5415.15 .K55 1987

Langmár, Andrásné. A Német Szövetségi Köztársaság bankrendszere /. Budapest [1987] 71 p. : ISBN 963-7103-59-7 LC Card 87-409642
HG3048 .L47 1987

Pott, Philipp. Marktpolitik von Privatbankiers . Frankfurt , c1983. 66 p. ; ISBN 3-88323-443-5 LC Card 84-154560
HG2021.G4 P67 1983

Seifert, Ekkehard. Privilegierung und Regulierung im Bankwesen . Baden-Baden , 1984. 332 p. ; ISBN 3-7890-0861-3 LC Card 84-186059
HG3054 .S42 1984

BANKS AND BANKING - GERMANY (WEST) - AUTOMATION.
Budde, Ramona. Marktinnovationen von Universalbanken . Berlin , c1983. xvi, 347 p. : ISBN 3-503-02192-2 LC Card 83-186914
HG1709 .B78 1983

Christians, Volker C. Neue Zahlungsverkehrsinstrumente . Frankfurt am Main , 1985. 216 p. ; ISBN 3-922182-17-8 : LC Card 86-100407
HG1710 .C48 1985

Cordewener, Karl-Friedrich, 1951- Kundenbediente Datenstationen als marktpolitische Instrumente des Bankbetriebs /. Göttingen , 1982. 268 p. : ISBN 3-509-01312-3 LC Card 84-182492
HG3048 .C67 1982

Vajc, Klaus, 1958- Ausgliederung des Zahlungsverkehrs aus dem Universalbankbereich /. Frankfurt am Main , New York , c1986. viii, 238 p. : ISBN 3-8204-8825-1 LC Card 86-220359
HG1692 .V34 1986

BANKS AND BANKING - GERMANY, WEST - BRANCH BANKS.
Reuschenbach, Ruth. Ziele, Instrumente und Bedingungen der Geschäftsstellenorganisation im filialisierten Universalbankbetrieb /. Köln , c1984. 385 p. ; ISBN 3-87951-122-5 LC Card 85-131689
HG1616.B7 R48 1984

Seifert, Ekkehard. Privilegierung und Regulierung im Bankwesen . Baden-Baden , 1984. 332 p. ; ISBN 3-7890-0861-3 LC Card 84-186059
HG3054 .S42 1984

BANKS AND BANKING - GERMANY (WEST) - BREMEN - HISTORY.
Förster, Walter, 1914- Das Haus am Wall . Bremen , c1983. 159 p. : ISBN 3-920699-45-9 LC Card 84-155521
HG1010.B7 F67 1983

BANKS AND BANKING - GERMANY (WEST) - CUSTOMER SERVICES.
Cordewener, Karl-Friedrich, 1951- Kundenbediente Datenstationen als marktpolitische Instrumente des Bankbetriebs /. Göttingen , 1982. 268 p. : ISBN 3-509-01312-3 LC Card 84-182492
HG3048 .C67 1982

Glogowski, Erhard. Neue Finanzdienstleistungen . Wiesbaden , c1986. 305 p. : ISBN 3-409-14101-4 LC Card 87-131647 DDC 332.1/0943 19
HG3048 .G57 1986

BANKS AND BANKING - GERMANY (WEST) - HAMBURG - HISTORY.
Pohl, Manfred, 1944- Hamburger Bankengeschichte /. Mainz , c1986. 264 p., [20] p. of plates : ISBN 3-7758-1136-2 LC Card 87-104548
HG3060.H22 P64 1986

BANKS AND BANKING - GERMANY (WEST) - HAMBURG - HISTORY - 17TH CENTURY.
Schneider, Konrad. "Banco, Species und Courant" . Koblenz , c1986. 136 p. : ISBN 3-923708-03-3 LC Card 87-134369 DDC 332.1/0943/515 19
HG1010.H24 S36 1986

BANKS AND BANKING - GERMANY (WEST) - HAMBURG - HISTORY - 18TH CENTURY.
Schneider, Konrad. "Banco, Species und Courant" . Koblenz , c1986. 136 p. : ISBN 3-923708-03-3 LC Card 87-134369 DDC 332.1/0943/515 19
HG1010.H24 S36 1986

BANKS AND BANKING - GERMANY (WEST) - QUALITY CONTROL.
Metz, Matthias. Kundenfreundliches Verhalten . Frankfurt am Main , c1985. xxi, 349 p. : ISBN 3-7819-0326-5 LC Card 85-202352
HG1616.P8 M47 1985

BANKS AND BANKING - GERMANY (WEST) - SAARLAND.
Landeszentralbank im Saarland. Landeszentralbank im Saarland . Saarbrücken , 1986. 45, xii p. : LC Card 86-176290
HC287.S23 L35 1986

BANKS AND BANKING - GERMANY, WEST - STATE SUPERVISION.
Holterhus, Gerhard. Früherkennung von Bankkrisen bei der Abschlussprüfung /. Frankfurt am Main , c1985. xvi, 360 p. : ISBN 3-7819-0348-6 LC Card 86-164226
HG1768.G3 H64 1985

BANKS AND BANKING - GERMANY (WEST) - TECHNOLOGICAL INNOVATIONS.
Bankinnovationen . Frankfurt am Main , c1986. 131 p. ; ISBN 3-7819-0363-X LC Card 87-120955 DDC 332.1/0943 19
HG3048 .B287 1986

Budde, Ramona. Marktinnovationen von Universalbanken . Berlin , c1983. xvi, 347 p. : ISBN 3-503-02192-2 LC Card 83-186914
HG1709 .B78 1983

BANKS AND BANKING - GOVERNMENT OWNERSHIP - BRAZIL.
Castro, J. As instituições para-estatais no estado novo /. Rio de Janeiro, Brasil , 1939 (Rio [de Janeiro] : Companhia Carioca) 225 p., [2] leaves of plates : LC Card 85-222446
HD4094 .C35 1939

BANKS AND BANKING - GOVERNMENT OWNERSHIP - INDIA.
Chopra, Kiran. Managing profits, profitability & productivity in public sector banking /. Jalandhar , 1987. 320 p. : ISBN 81-7072-012-5 : LC Card 87-901014 DDC 332.1/0954 19
HG3284 .C56 1987

Shanker Shetty, K. Welfare state and bank nationalisation in India /. Delhi , 1982. xvii, 345 p. ; ISBN 0-333-90729-9 : LC Card 83-903489 DDC 332.1/0954 19
HG3284 .S4823 1982 ***NYPL [JLD 86-4354]***

BANKS AND BANKING - GOVERNMENT OWNERSHIP - MEXICO.
Sacristán, Antonio. Disertaciones sobre economía mexicana /. México, D.F. , 1982. 39 p. ; LC Card 87-123937 DDC 332.1/0972 19
HG2714 .S23 1982

Teichman, Judith A., 1947- Policymaking in Mexico . Boston , c1988. p. cm. ISBN 0-04-445033-8 : LC Card 87-18704 DDC 338.2/7282/0972 19
HD9574.M6 T45 1988

BANKS AND BANKING - GOVERNMENT OWNERSHIP - MEXICO - HISTORY.
Márquez, Javier, 1909- La banca mexicana . [Mexico City, Mexico] , 1987. xi, 299 p., [3] folded leaves of plates : ISBN 968-615-402-7 LC Card 87-404865 DDC 332.1/0972 19
HG2714 .M27 1987

BANKS AND BANKING - GREAT BRITAIN.
Banking in the United Kingdom. London , c1984. 215 p. ; ISBN 1-85061-020-7
NYPL [JLD 86-2506]

Blake, Hubert, 1893- Currency and credit before and since 1914 [microform] /. London , 1923. viii, 91 p. ; ***NYPL [*ZT-1736 no.1]***

Frazer, P. A. T. Plastic and electronic money . Cambridge [Cambridgeshire] , Dover, NH. USA , 1985. x, 294 p. ; ISBN 0-85941-290-3 : LC Card 85-22552 DDC 332.1/028 19
HG1710 .F73 1985 ***NYPL [JLE 86-1401]***

Hall, Peter (Peter J.), 1932- Elements of banking /. London , New York , 1987. xi, 236 p. : ISBN 0-582-29728-1 (pbk.) LC Card 86-21144

DDC 332.1 19
HG1601 .H25 1987

Mullineux, A. W. U.K. banking after deregulation /. London , New York , c1987. 180 p. ; ISBN 0-7099-4689-9 LC Card 87-6742 DDC 332.1/0941 19
HG2988 .M85 1987

Ricardo, David, 1772-1823. Scritti monetari /. Roma [1985] 495 p. ; LC Card 86-207988
HG938 .R63 1985

BANKS AND BANKING - GREAT BRITAIN - ACCOUNTING.
Tiner, John I. Accounting for treasury products . Cambridge, England , Wolfeboro, N.H., USA , 1988. p. cm. ISBN 0-85941-389-6 : LC Card 87-12531 DDC 657/.833 19
HG1708 .T56 1988

BANKS AND BANKING - GREAT BRITAIN - DEREGULATION.
Mullineux, A. W. U.K. banking after deregulation /. London , New York , c1987. 180 p. ; ISBN 0-7099-4689-9 LC Card 87-6742 DDC 332.1/0941 19
HG2988 .M85 1987

BANKS AND BANKING - GREAT BRITAIN - HISTORY.
Ollerenshaw, Philip, 1953- Banking in nineteenth-century Ireland . Manchester, UK , Wolfeboro, NH, USA , c1987. 263 p. : ISBN 0-7190-2276-2 : LC Card 87-11113 DDC 332.1/09416/7 19
HG950.B45 O55 1987

BANKS AND BANKING - GREAT BRITAIN - HISTORY - CONGRESSES.
Financial crises and the world banking system /. London , c1986. x, 270 p. : ISBN 0-333-35129-0 ***NYPL [JLD 86-2132]***

BANKS AND BANKING - GREAT BRITAIN - PERSONNEL MANAGEMENT.
Morris, Timothy, 1953- Innovations in banking . London , Wolfeboro, N.H. , c1986. 137 p. : ISBN 0-7099-4607-4 : LC Card 86-13400 DDC 332.1/068/3 19
HG2988 .M675 1986 ***NYPL [JLD 87-81]***

BANKS AND BANKING - HAITI - HISTORY.
Marcelin, Frédéric, 1848-1917. La Banque nationale d'Haïti . Port-au-Prince, Haïti , 1985. xi, 118 p. : LC Card 86-125803 DDC 332.1/1/097294 19
HG2813 .M3 1985 ***NYPL [Sc D 86-690]***

BANKS AND BANKING - HISTORY.
King, Frank H. H. The history of the Hongkong and Shanghai Banking Corporation /. Cambridge [Cambridgeshire] , New York , 1987- p. cm. ISBN 0-521-32706-7 (v. 1) LC Card 86-28339 DDC 332.1/5/095125 19
HG1571 K56

BANKS AND BANKING - HISTORY - CONGRESSES.
Financial crises and the world banking system /. London , c1986. x, 270 p. : ISBN 0-333-35129-0 ***NYPL [JLD 86-2132]***

BANKS AND BANKING - INDIA.
Banking in India in the eighties . New Delhi , 1986. 533 p. in various pagings ; LC Card 86-903123 DDC 332.1/068 19
HG3284 .B267 1986

Explanatory notes on current statistics. Bombay [1978] iii, 74 p. ; LC Card 85-229381
HG187.I4 E98 1978

Keynes, John Maynard, 1883-1946. Indian currency and finance /. London , 1913 (Edinburgh : R. & R. Clark) viii, 263 p., [1] folded leaf of plates ; LC Card A13-2169 DDC 332.4/954
HG1234 .K4 ***NYPL [*KF 1913 87-34]***

Khemani, C. L., 1934- How and why of rural banking /. New Delhi , 1987. 255, [41] p. : LC Card 87-901033 DDC 332.1/0954 19
HG3288 .K44 1987

Lakshmana Rao, V., 1940- Progress of development banking in India /. Allahabad, India , 1986. xvi, 139 p. ; ISBN 81-85076-07-3 : LC Card 86-902782 DDC 332.2 19
HG3284 .L35 1986

Nigam, Brij Mohan Lall, 1935- Banking and economic growth. Bombay [1967] xii, 207 p. LC Card SA68-4077 DDC 332.1/0954
HG3284 .N5 ***NYPL [JLD 74-2222]***

Poonia, M. S. (Mohan Singh), 1955- Development banking in India /. Jaipur , 1987. 140, iii, [i] p. ; LC Card 87-901804 DDC 332.2 19
HG3284 .P66 1987

Puri, Vijay Kumar. Nabhi's manual for Indian residents abroad, 1985 /. New Delhi , 1985. xv, 352 p., [1] leaf of plate : LC Card 86-901951 DDC 346.54/07 345.4067 19
HG5732 .P83 1985

Ranade, Sudhanshu, 1952- Rural banking adrift /. Bombay , c1984. x, 126 p. ; LC Card 84-903073 DDC 332.1/0954 19
HG3284 .R325 1984 ***NYPL [JLD 87-561]***

Shanker Shetty, K. Welfare state and bank nationalisation in India /. Delhi , 1982. xvii, 345 p. ; ISBN 0-333-90729-9 : LC Card 83-903489 DDC 332.1/0954 19
HG3284 .S4823 1982 ***NYPL [JLD 86-4354]***

BANKS AND BANKING - INDIA - BIHAR.
Singh, Awadh Bihari Prasad, 1946- Lead bank scheme . Delhi , 1987. v, 223 p. ; LC Card 87-900328 DDC 332.1/0954/12 19
HG3289.B53 S57 1987

BANKS AND BANKING - INDIA - JAMMU AND KASHMIR.
Abrol, Prem Nath. Commercial banking /. Delhi, India , 1987. viii, 224 p. ; LC Card 87-900129 DDC 332.1/2/09546 19
HG3289.J35 A37 1987

BANKS AND BANKING - INDIA - JHĀBUA (DISTRICT)
Mehta, Suresh C. (Suresh Chandra), 1947- Agricultural credit mobilization and allocation . Allahabad, India , 1987. xv, 270 p. ; ISBN 81-85072-06-X : LC Card 86-903677 DDC 332.7/1/09543 19
HG2051.I5 J466 1987

BANKS AND BANKING - INDIA - PERSONNEL MANAGEMENT.
Banking in India in the eighties . New Delhi , 1986. 533 p. in various pagings ; LC Card 86-903123 DDC 332.1/068 19
HG3284 .B267 1986

BANKS AND BANKING - INSURANCE BUSINESS.
Marketing life insurance in a bank or thrift /. Boulder, Colo. , 1986. xii, 233 p. ; ISBN 0-8133-7205-4 : LC Card 86-1644 DDC 332.1/7 19
HG1616.I47 M37 1986 ***NYPL [JLD 86-3992]***

BANKS AND BANKING, INTERNATIONAL - COMMUNICATION SYSTEMS.
Loh, Wolfram W. Das S.W.I.F.T.-System . Frankfurt am Main , c1983. vii, 198 p. : ISBN 3-7819-0285-4 : LC Card 83-211180
HG1708.5 .L64 1983

BANKS AND BANKING, INTERNATIONAL - CONGRESSES.
The Developing global securities market /. London ; Boston : viii, 192 p. ; ISBN 0-86010-979-8 LC Card 87-19086 DDC 332.6/5 19
HG4508 .D48 1987

Eurodollars and international banking /. London [Miami] , 1985. xiii, 226 p. : ISBN 0-333-36553-4 ***NYPL [JLD 85-3068]***

Finanz- und bankwirtschaftliche Probleme bei internationaler Unternehmenstätigkeit /. Stuttgart , c1985. x, 267 p. : ISBN 3-7910-0394-1 LC Card 86-121195 DDC 658.1/5 19
HG4027.5 .F56 1985

International banking /. New York , 1988. p. cm. ISBN 0-312-00862-7 : LC Card 87-21276 DDC 332.1/5 19
HG3881 .I57513 1988

International banking and global financing . New York, NY , c1983. xiv, 257 p. : ISBN 0-88239-015-5 (pbk.) : LC Card 84-60076 DDC 332.1/5 19
HG205 .I54 1983

Internationalization of banking . Seoul, Korea , c1986. 300 p. : LC Card 87-114642 DDC 332.1/5 19
HG3881 .I496 1986

BANKS AND BANKING, INTERNATIONAL - DEVELOPING COUNTRIES - ADDRESSES, ESSAYS, LECTURES.
Uncertain future . New Brunswick, N.J. , c1984. x, 129 p. ; ISBN 0-88738-041-7 : LC Card 84-16240 DDC 332.1/5 19
HG3891.5 .U53 1984 ***NYPL [JLE 86-2494]***

BANKS AND BANKING, INTERNATIONAL - LOCATION.
Walter, Herbert. Standortpolitik multinationaler Banken /. Thun , c1983. viii, 255 p. : ISBN 3-87144-737-4 : LC Card 83-159195
HG3881 .W273 1983

BANKS AND BANKING - IRAN.
Amin, S. H. (Sayed Hessan) Islamic banking and finance . Tehran , 1986. 72 p. : ISBN 0-946706-30-1 (pbk.) LC Card 86-209623 DDC 332.1/0955 19
HG3270.2.A6 A45 1986

Iqbal, Zubair. Islamic banking /. Washington, D.C. , 1987. v, 62 p. ; ISBN 0-939934-82-5 (pbk.) : LC Card 87-4166 DDC 332.1/0917/671 19
HG3270.2.A6 I67 1987

BANKS AND BANKING - IRELAND - HISTORY.
Ollerenshaw, Philip, 1953- Banking in nineteenth-century Ireland . Manchester, UK , Wolfeboro, NH, USA , c1987. 263 p. : ISBN 0-7190-2276-2 : LC Card 87-11113 DDC 332.1/09416/7 19
HG950.B45 O55 1987

BANKS AND BANKING - ISLAMIC COUNTRIES.
Amin, S. H. (Sayed Hessan) Islamic banking and finance . Tehran , 1986. 72 p. : ISBN 0-946706-30-1 (pbk.) LC Card 86-209623 DDC 332.1/0955 19
HG3270.2.A6 A45 1986

Iqbal, Zubair. Islamic banking /. Washington, D.C. , 1987. v, 62 p. ; ISBN 0-939934-82-5 (pbk.) : LC Card 87-4166 DDC 332.1/0917/671 19
HG3270.2.A6 I67 1987

Khan, Muhammad Akram. Bilā sūdī bainkārī /. Lāhaur [1983] 56 p. ; LC Card 83-931274
HG3290.5.A6 K43 1983

Khan, Waqar Masood. Towards an interest-free Islamic economic system . Leicester , Islamabad , c1985. 126 p. ; ISBN 0-86037-155-7 ***NYPL [JLD 87-381]***

Ṣiddiqi, Muḥammad Iqbal. Model of an Islamic bank /. Lahore, Pakistan , 1986. 90 p. ; LC Card 87-931018 DDC 332.1/0917/671 19
HG3368.A6 S54 1986

Ṣiddīqī, Muḥammad Nejātullah, 1931- Banking and monetary polic[i]es in Islamic economics /. Khartoum [between 1983 and 1986] 40 p. ; LC Card 86-980021 DDC 332.1/0917/671 19
HG3368.A6 S53 1986

Theoretical studies in Islamic banking and finance /. Houston, Tex. , 1987. xvi, 245 p. : ISBN 0-932625-07-X : LC Card 86-83221 DDC 332.1/0917/4927 19
HG3368.A6 T47 1987

BANKS AND BANKING - ISLAMIC COUNTRIES - CASE STUDIES.
El-Ashker, Ahmed Abdel-Fattah, 1943- The Islamic business enterprise /. London , Wolfboro, N.H. , c1987. xi, 242 p. : ISBN 0-7099-0985-3 : LC Card 86-24271 DDC 332.1/0917/671 19
HG3368.A6 E4 1987

BANKS AND BANKING - ITALY.
Allegri, Vincenzo. Credito di scopo e finanziamento bancario delle imprese /. Milano [1984] 166 p. ; ISBN 88-14-00299-1 : LC Card 85-187365 DDC 332.7/0945 19
HG1642.I8 A44 1984 ***NYPL [JLE 86-3661]***

BANKS AND BANKING - ITALY - ACCOUNTING.
Spedale, Domenico L. L'affidamento bancario . Milano , 1985. 204 p. : ***NYPL [JLD 86-3241]***

BANKS AND BANKING - ITALY - CAVA DE' TERRENI - HISTORY.
Patroni Griffi, Filena. Il banco di pegni di Cava dei Tirreni del 1495 /. Cava dei Tirreni , c1985. 149 p., [8] p. of plates : LC Card 86-195753
HG2106.I83 C386 1985

BANKS AND BANKING - ITALY - EMILIA-ROMAGNA - ACCOUNTING.
I Conti finanziari dell'Emilia-Romagna /. [Bologna] , c1984. 157 p. : ISBN 88-15-00522-6 : LC Card 84-235593 DDC 332.1/0945/4 19
HG3089.E45 C66 1984
NYPL [JLE 86-3198]

BANKS AND BANKING - ITALY - HISTORY - 20TH CENTURY.
Ciocca, Pierluigi, 1941- Interesse e profitto . Bologna , c1982. 245 p. : LC Card 84-139966 DDC 332/.0945 19
HG186.I8 C56 1982

BANKS AND BANKING - ITALY - MILAN.
Sury, Paul de. Milano, centro finanziario internazionale /. [Milano] [1984] viii, 138 p. : ISBN 88-14-00312-2 : LC Card 86-114645
HG3090.M52 S87 1984

BANKS AND BANKING - ITALY - VENICE - HISTORY.
Lane Frederic Chapin, 1900- Money and banking in medieval and Renaissance Venice /. Baltimore , c1985- v. : ISBN 0-8018-3157-1 (v. 1) LC Card 84-47947 DDC 332.1/0945/31 19
HG1040.V46 L36 1985 ***NYPL [JLL 86-121]***

BANKS AND BANKING - JAPAN - ACCOUNTING.
A Guide to the spreading and analysis of Japanese bank statements. Philadelphia, PA (1616 Philadelphia National Bank Bldg. Philadelphia 19107) , c1986. 60 p. ; LC Card 86-203674 DDC 657/.833 19
HG3324 .G85 1986

BANKS AND BANKING, JAPANESE - SOUTHEASTERN ASIA.
Strittmatter, Gabriele. Kooperationsstrategien westeuropäischer und japanischer Banken in den ASEAN-Staaten /. Baden-Baden , 1984. 411 p. : ISBN 3-7890-1051-0 LC Card 86-134027
HG3324 .S77 1984

BANKS AND BANKING - JURISPRUDENCE. see **BANKING LAW.**

BANKS AND BANKING - JUVENILE LITERATURE.
Spiselman, David, 1947- A teenager's guide to money, banking, and finance /. New York , c1987. p. cm. ISBN 0-671-64345-2 LC Card 87-11059 DDC 332.024 19
HG179 .S5554 1987

BANKS AND BANKING - LABOR PRODUCTIVITY - MEASUREMENT - DATA PROCESSING.
Mundel, Marvin Everett, 1916- Measuring the productivity of commercial banks . White Plains, N.Y. , 1987. v, 101 p. ; ISBN 0-527-91641-2 (pbk.) LC Card 87-5034 DDC 332.1/0285/57565 19
HG1588 .M94 1987

BANKS AND BANKING - LAWS AND LEGISLATION. see **BANKING LAW.**

BANKS AND BANKING - MAINE.
The Status of Maine's financial institutions . [Augusta] [1985] 38 leaves ; LC Card 86-621914 DDC 332.1/09741 19
HG2611.M2 S73 1985

BANKS AND BANKING - MALAYSIA.
Lee, S. Y. (Sheng-Yi) The monetary and banking development of Singapore and Malaysia /. Singapore , 1986. 298 p. : ISBN 997-16-9098-5 (pbk.) LC Card 86-943034 DDC 332.4/9595 19
HG1250.67 .L43 1986

BANKS AND BANKING - MALAYSIA - CORRUPT PRACTICES.
Lim, Kit Siang. BMF, scandal of scandals /. Petaling Jaya [1986] ix, 68 p. : LC Card 86-943248 DDC 364.1/68/09595 19
HG3300.6.A6 L553 1986

BANKS AND BANKING - MANAGEMENT. see **BANK MANAGEMENT.**

BANKS AND BANKING - METHODS. see **BANK MANAGEMENT; BANKS AND BANKING - ACCOUNTING.**

BANKS AND BANKING - MEXICO.
Martín-Guédez, Rafael, 1942- Vigencia de la multibanca . [Caracas? , 1982 or 1983] 122 p. ; LC Card 83-201555
HG2964 .M37 1982

BANKS AND BANKING - MEXICO - HISTORY.
Márquez, Javier, 1909- La banca mexicana . [Mexico City, Mexico] , 1987. xi, 299 p., [3] folded leaves of plates : ISBN 968-615-402-7 LC Card 87-404865 DDC 332.1/0972 19
HG2714 .M27 1987

Quijano, José Manuel. Finanzas, desarrollo económico y penetración extranjera /. Puebla, Pue. , 1985. 395 p. : LC Card 86-112589 DDC 332/.0972 19
HG185.M6 Q55 1985 ***NYPL [JLD 86-2195]***

BANKS AND BANKING - MEXICO - HISTORY - 19TH CENTURY - STATISTICS.
Ramírez Bautista, Elia. Estadísticas bancarias . México, D.F. , 1985. 10, ca. 200 p. ; ISBN 968-603-813-2 LC Card 87-401719 DDC 332.1/0972/021 19
HG2714 .R36 1985

BANKS AND BANKING - MEXICO - HISTORY - 20TH CENTURY - STATISTICS.
Ramírez Bautista, Elia. Estadísticas bancarias . México, D.F. , 1985. 10, ca. 200 p. ; ISBN 968-603-813-2 LC Card 87-401719 DDC 332.1/0972/021 19
HG2714 .R36 1985

BANKS AND BANKING - MEXICO - STATISTICS.
El Sistema bancario y financiero en México, 1970-1984. México, D.F. , c1985. 260 p. ; ISBN 968-89204-0-1 LC Card 86-223773
HG2714 .S57 1985

BANKS AND BANKING - MOROCCO.
Barrādah, Muḥammad. Les techniques de banque et de crédit au Maroc /. Casablanca , 1985. 590 p. : LC Card 86-967115
HG3382.A6 B37 1985

BANKS AND BANKING - NETHERLANDS.
Zijlstra, J. Gematigd monetarisme . Leiden , 1985. ix, 330 p. : ISBN 90-207-1382-5 : LC Card 85-201189
HG1065 .Z55 1985 ***NYPL [JLE 87-379]***

BANKS AND BANKING - NETHERLANDS ANTILLES.
Beers, H. C. [Financial sector of the Netherlands Antilles. Spanish.] El sector financiero de las Antillas Neerlandesas /. [Willemstad, Curaçao] , 1980. 72 p. : LC Card 83-238068 DDC 332.1/097298/6 19
HG2847.A6 B4318 1980
NYPL [JLG 85-297]

BANKS AND BANKING - NETHERLANDS ANTILLES - DIRECTORIES.
Beers, H. C. [Financial sector of the Netherlands Antilles. Spanish.] El sector financiero de las Antillas Neerlandesas /. [Willemstad, Curaçao] , 1980. 72 p. : LC Card 83-238068 DDC 332.1/097298/6 19
HG2847.A6 B4318 1980
NYPL [JLG 85-297]

BANKS AND BANKING - NETHERLANDS - ROTTERDAM - HISTORY.
Mees en Chabot, twee kassiers te Rotterdam . Delft , c1986. 87 p. : ISBN 90-70879-40-9 : LC Card 86-205783
HG3120.R62 M44 1986

BANKS AND BANKING - NIGERIA.
Akwaeze, G. C. Practical steps in raising business finance from banks /. Enugu, Nigeria , 1985. 290 p. : ISBN 978-15-6214-5 (pbk.) LC Card 87-118106 DDC 658.1/5224 19
HG3754.5.N6 A38 1985

Osubor, John Uche. Business finance and banking in Nigeria /. Owerri, Imo State, Nigeria , 1984. vii, 209 p. : ISBN 978-235-700-13 (pbk.) LC Card 86-207599 DDC 332.1/09669 19
HG3431.A6 O85 1984

Uzoaga, William Okefie. Money and banking in Nigeria /. Enugu, Nigeria , 1981. xiv, 304 p. ; ISBN 978-15-6175-0 ***NYPL [Sc D 84-373]***

BANKS AND BANKING - NORTH CAROLINA - HISTORY.
Gatton, T. Harry (Thomas Harry) Banking in North Carolina . Raleigh , 1987. xi, 155 p. : ISBN 0-9617806-0-6 LC Card 86-63397 DDC 332.1/09756 19
HG2611.N8 G38 1987

BANKS AND BANKING - NORTHERN IRELAND - BELFAST - HISTORY.
Ollerenshaw, Philip, 1953- Banking in nineteenth-century Ireland . Manchester, UK , Wolfeboro, NH, USA , c1987. 263 p. : ISBN 0-7190-2276-2 : LC Card 87-11113 DDC 332.1/09416/7 19
HG950.B45 O55 1987

BANKS AND BANKING - OKLAHOMA.
McGuire, Paul F., 1907- Genesis of Oklahoma oil banking /. Muskogee, Okla. , c1986. 160 p. : ISBN 0-86546-068-X (pbk.) LC Card 87-118559 DDC 332.1/223/0924 B 19
HG2463.M36 A3 1986

BANKS AND BANKING - PAKISTAN.
Iqbal, Zubair. Islamic banking /. Washington, D.C. , 1987. v, 62 p. ; ISBN 0-939934-82-5 (pbk.) : LC Card 87-4166 DDC 332.1/0917/671 19
HG3270.2.A6 I67 1987

Khan, Muhammad Akram. Bilā sūdī bainkārī /. Lāhaur [1983] 56 p. ; LC Card 83-931274
HG3290.5.A6 K43 1983

BANKS AND BANKING - PAKISTAN - CONGRESSES.
Seminar on Growth of Pakistani Banking at Home & Abroad (1982 : Peshawar, Pakistan) Growth of Pakistani banking . Karachi , 1982. 26 p. ; LC Card 83-931177 DDC 332.1/09549/1 19
HG3290.5.A6 S46 1982
NYPL [JLE 86-4582]

BANKS AND BANKING, PAKISTANI - CONGRESSES.
Seminar on Growth of Pakistani Banking at Home & Abroad (1982 : Peshawar, Pakistan) Growth of Pakistani banking . Karachi , 1982. 26 p. ; LC Card 83-931177 DDC 332.1/09549/1 19
HG3290.5.A6 S46 1982
NYPL [JLE 86-4582]

BANKS AND BANKING - PERSONNEL MANAGEMENT.
Caruth, Donald L. Compensation management for banks /. Boston , c1986. viii, 312 p. : ISBN 0-87267-060-0 LC Card 86-3543 DDC 332.1/068/3 19
HG1615.7.C65 C37 1986
NYPL [JLE 87-828]

Lippold, Dirk, 1953- Individualisierung der Organisation von Banken . Spardorf , c1982. xxiii, 170 p. : ISBN 3-922919-04-9 LC Card 83-221727
HG1615.5 .L56 1982

BANKS AND BANKING - PERU.
Zúñiga A., Remigio. Banca nacional /. Chimbote, Perú , c1986. 478 p. ; LC Card 87-403541 DDC 332.1/0985 19
HG2944 .Z86 1986

BANKS AND BANKING - PERU - CONGRESSES.
Susano Lucero, Aurelio Reynaldo. Liberalización financiera [microform] . Lima , c1982. [40] p. : LC Card 84-227503 DDC 332.1/0985 19
HG2944 .S93 1982 ***NYPL [*ZT-1745 no.6]***

BANKS AND BANKING - PORTUGAL.
Cavaco Silva, Aníbal A. (Aníbal António), 1939- O mercado financeiro português em 1966 /. Lisboa , 1968. xiv, 104 p. : LC Card 85-133959
HG186.P8 C38 1968

BANKS AND BANKING - PUBLIC RELATIONS. see **PUBLIC RELATIONS - BANKS AND BANKING.**

BANKS AND BANKING - RECORDS AND CORRESPONDENCE.
Seglin, Jeffrey L., 1956- Bank letter writing handbook . Boston , c1987. xii, 434 p. ; ISBN 0-87267-103-8 LC Card 87-965 DDC 651.7/5/024332 19
HG1616.R4 S43 1987

BANKS AND BANKING - RELIGIOUS ASPECTS - ISLAM.
Amin, S. H. (Sayed Hessan) Islamic banking and finance . Tehran , 1986. 72 p. : ISBN 0-946706-30-1 (pbk.) LC Card 86-209623 DDC 332.1/0955 19
HG3270.2.A6 A45 1986

El-Ashker, Ahmed Abdel-Fattah, 1943- The

Islamic business enterprise /. London , Wolfboro, N.H. , c1987. xi, 242 p. : ISBN 0-7099-0985-3 : LC Card 86-24271 DDC 332.1/0917/671 19
HG3368.A6 E4 1987

Khan, Muhammad Akram. Bilā sūdī bainkārī /. Lāhaur [1983] 56 p. ; LC Card 83-931274
HG3290.5.A6 K43 1983

Ṣiddiqi, Muḥammad Iqbal. Model of an Islamic bank /. Lahore, Pakistan , 1986. 90 p. ; LC Card 87-931018 DDC 332.1/0917/671 19
HG3368.A6 S54 1986

Theoretical studies in Islamic banking and finance /. Houston, Tex. , 1987. xvi, 245 p. : ISBN 0-932625-07-X : LC Card 86-83221 DDC 332.1/0917/4927 19
HG3368.A6 T47 1987

BANKS AND BANKING - SERVICE CHARGES - MATHEMATICAL MODELS.
Gladen, Werner. Gebührenpolitik im Privatgiroverkehr der Kreditinstitute /. Berlin , c1985. 248 p. : ISBN 3-428-05820-8 LC Card 85-199227
HG1616.S4 G53 1985

BANKS AND BANKING - SINGAPORE.
Lee, S. Y. (Sheng-Yi) The monetary and banking development of Singapore and Malaysia /. Singapore , 1986. 298 p. : ISBN 997-16-9098-5 (pbk.) LC Card 86-943034 DDC 332.4/9595 19
HG1250.67 .L43 1986

BANKS AND BANKING - SOUTHERN STATES - HISTORY.
Schweikart, Larry. Banking in the American South from the age of Jackson to Reconstruction /. Baton Rouge , c1987. xiv, 367 p. : ISBN 0-8071-1403-0 LC Card 87-12784 DDC 332.1/0975 19
HG2604 .S39 1987

BANKS AND BANKING - SOVIET UNION.
Braginskiĭ, L. V. (Lev Vol'fovich) Ėffektivnost' kapital'nykh vlozheniĭ i bankovskaia deiatel'nost' /. Moskva , 1981. 186 p. ; LC Card 82-144216
HG186.S55 B72 1981

Denezhnoe obrashchenie i kredit SSSR /. Moskva , 1986. 374 p. : LC Card 87-157773
HG3729.S632 D46 1986

BANKS AND BANKING - SPAIN.
Cuervo García, Alvaro. Manual de sistema financiero . Barcelona , 1987. 427 p. : ISBN 84-344-2013-9 LC Card 87-135198
HG186.S6 C84 1987

Fanjul, Oscar. La eficiencia del sistema bancario español /. Madrid , c1985. 275 p. : ISBN 84-206-2439-X LC Card 87-111325
HG3184 .F36 1985

BANKS AND BANKING - SRI LANKA.
Karunatilake, H. N. S. The banking and financial system of Sri Lanka /. Colombo , 1986. 320 p. ; LC Card 87-902032 DDC 332.1/09549/3 19
HG3270.8.A6 K37 1986

BANKS AND BANKING - STATE SUPERVISION.
Beiträge zur Bankaufsicht, Bankbilanz und Bankprüfung . Düsseldorf , 1985. 226 p. : ISBN 3-8021-0267-3 LC Card 85-208772
HG1605 .B44 1985

Zeitler, Isabella, 1956- Internationales Bankgeschäft als Problem der Bankenaufsicht /. München , c1984. viii, 353 p. : LC Card 85-103322
HG3881 .Z4 1984

BANKS AND BANKING - STATE SUPERVISION - CONGRESSES.
Financial innovation and monetary policy . [Tokyo] , c1986. ix, 339 p. : ISBN 4-13-047029-9 : LC Card 86-222823 DDC 332/.095 19
HG187.E37 F55 1986

BANKS AND BANKING - SWITZERLAND.
Chambost, Édouard. Guide de la banque suisse et de ses secrets /. [Paris] , c1987. 317 p. : ISBN 2-7158-0626-4 : LC Card 87-132185
HG3204 .C43 1987

Gross, Peter, Dr. Logistik einer Grossbank . Bern , c1983. 52 p. : ISBN 3-258-03274-2 : LC Card 83-181853
HG1526 .B27 Bd. 80 HG3208.U54

Marsh, Michael G., 1935- How to invest offshore successfully /. Geneva, Switzerland , c1986. 207 p. : LC Card 86-212027 DDC 332.6/73 19
HG4538 .M3635 1986

Staehelin, Max, 1909- Schweizer Banken und Schweizer Wirtschaft im Wandel der Zeit /. Zürich , c1984. 261 p. : LC Card 84-212396
HG3204 .S77 1984

Weck, Philippe de, 1919- Un banquier suisse parle . Fribourg , c1983. 159 p. ; LC Card 84-119161
HG1552.W43 A3 1983

BANKS AND BANKING - SWITZERLAND - ACCOUNTING.
Meyer, Conrad. Die Bankbilanz als finanzielles Führungsinstrument . Bern , c1986. x, 655 p. : ISBN 3-258-03587-3 LC Card 86-199541
HG1526 .B27 Bd. 96 HG1778.S9

BANKS AND BANKING - SWITZERLAND - AUTOMATION.
Revolution des Zahlungsverkehrs durch Automation /. Frauenfeld [1984] 160 p. : ISBN 3-7193-0929-0 : LC Card 84-153299
HG1709 .R48 1984

BANKS AND BANKING - SWITZERLAND - BRANCH BANKS.
Bolliger, Peter. Die optimale Organisationsstruktur eines mittleren Bankbetriebes . Bern , c1984. xiii, 234 p. : ISBN 3-258-03358-7 : LC Card 84-174443
HG1526 .B27 Bd. 86 HG1616.B7

BANKS AND BANKING - SWITZERLAND - CONGRESSES.
Internationale Wettbewerbsfähigkeit des Finanzplatzes Schweiz /. Bern , c1987. 131 p. : ISBN 3-258-03806-6 LC Card 87-114764 DDC 332.1 s 332.1/09494 19
HG1526 .B27 Bd. 101 HG3206

BANKS AND BANKING - SWITZERLAND - SEASONAL VARIATIONS.
Stuber, Barbara. Saisonschwankungen der Bankreserven und Ultimooperationen der Schweizerischen Nationalbank /. Bern , c1986. 173 p. : ISBN 3-258-03653-5 : LC Card 87-130160 DDC 332.1/12/09494 19
HG1656.S9 S77 1986

BANKS AND BANKING - SWITZERLAND - STATE SUPERVISION.
Meyer, Conrad. Die Bankbilanz als finanzielles Führungsinstrument . Bern , c1986. x, 655 p. : ISBN 3-258-03587-3 LC Card 86-199541
HG1526 .B27 Bd. 96 HG1778.S9

BANKS AND BANKING - TABLES.
Thorndike, David, 1925- Thorndike encyclopedia of banking and financial tables /. Boston , c1987. 1737 p. in various pagings ; ISBN 0-88712-883-1 LC Card 87-50721 DDC 332.8/0212 19
HG1626 .T49 1987

BANKS AND BANKING - TAXATION - GREAT BRITAIN.
Tiner, John I. Accounting for treasury products . Cambridge, England , Wolfeboro, N.H., USA , 1988. p. cm. ISBN 0-85941-389-6 : LC Card 87-12531 DDC 657/.833 19
HG1708 .T56 1988

BANKS AND BANKING - TECHNOLOGICAL INNOVATIONS.
Budde, Ramona. Marktinnovationen von Universalbanken . Berlin , c1983. xvi, 347 p. : ISBN 3-503-02192-2 LC Card 83-186914
HG1709 .B78 1983

BANKS AND BANKING - UNITED STATES.
Compton, Eric N., 1925- The new world of commercial banking /. Lexington, Mass. , c1987. xvi, 316 p. : ISBN 0-669-14017-1 (alk. paper) LC Card 86-45002 DDC 332.1/2/068 19
HG2491 .C646 1987

Deregulating financial services . Cambridge, Mass. , 1986. xiii, 223 p. ; ISBN 0-88730-111-8 LC Card 86-3355 DDC 332.1/0973 19
HG2491 .R42 1986 ***NYPL [JLE 86-3307]***

Hutchinson, Harry D. Money, banking, and the United States economy /. Englewood Cliffs, NJ , 1988. p. cm. ISBN 0-13-600156-4 LC Card 87-19299 DDC 332.1/0973 19
HG2491 .H8 1988

Krefetz, Gerald. All about saving /. New York , c1987. xvi, 224 p. : ISBN 0-471-83793-8 LC Card 86-28085 DDC 332.024/01 19
HG2491 .K74 1987

Litan, Robert E., 1950- What should banks do? /. Washington, D.C. , c1987. xi, 207 p. : ISBN 0-8157-5270-9 : LC Card 87-18235 DDC 332.1/0973 19
HG2491 .L58 1987

Martín-Guédez, Rafael, 1942- Vigencia de la multibanca . [Caracas? , 1982 or 1983] 122 p. ; LC Card 83-201555
HG2964 .M37 1982

Mayer, Thomas. Money, banking, and the economy /. New York , c1984. xiv, 574 p. : ISBN 0-393-95313-0 LC Card 83-13498 DDC 332.1/0973 19
HG540 .M39 1984 ***NYPL [JLE 86-2193]***

Mayer, Thomas, 1927- Money, banking, and the economy /. New York , c1987. xiv, 488 p. : ISBN 0-393-95557-5 LC Card 86-33160 DDC 332.1/0973 19
HG540 .M39 1987

Nevitt, Peter K. Equipment leasing for commercial bankers /. Philadelphia, Pa. , c1987. x, 123 p. ; ISBN 0-936742-37-2 (pbk.) : LC Card 87-5532 DDC 332.1/068/5 19
HD39.4 .N485 1987

Perspectives on safe & sound banking . Cambridge, Mass. , 1986. xxi, 358 p. ; ISBN 0-262-02246-X LC Card 85-23882 DDC 332.1/0973 19
HG2481 .P47 1986 ***NYPL [JLE 86-2960]***

Small business financing . Philadelphia, Pa. , c1987. 118 p. ; ISBN 0-936742-40-2 (pbk.) : LC Card 87-5534 DDC 332.1/753/0685 19
HG3754.5.U6 S6 1987

United States. President's Commission on Organized Crime. Organized crime and money laundering . Washington, D.C. [1985]. vi, 189 p. : ***NYPL [JLE 86-1282]***

Winders, Terry J., 1942- Profitable equipment leasing . Boston , c1987. xii, 252 p. ; ISBN 0-87267-101-1 : LC Card 86-26601 DDC 332.1/068/7 19
HD39.4 .W56 1987 ***NYPL [JLE 87-1512]***

BANKS AND BANKING - UNITED STATES - ACCOUNTING.
Disclosure checklists for banks . New York, N.Y. , c1986. 64 p. ; LC Card 86-224924 DDC 657/.833 19
HG1708 .D57 1986

BANKS AND BANKING - UNITED STATES - COSTS.
Kolari, James W. Bank costs, structure, and performance /. Lexington, Mass. , c1987. x, 240 p. : ISBN 0-669-11282-8 (alk. paper) LC Card 85-45295 DDC 332.1/068/1 19
HG1616.C6 K65 1987

BANKS AND BANKING - UNITED STATES - CUSTOMER SERVICES.
The Affluent market fact book . Tampa, Fla. , c1986. 83 leaves ; LC Card 86-235264 DDC 332.1/7 19
HG1616.C87 A33 1986

Ballarín, Eduard. Commercial banks amid the financial revolution . Cambridge, Mass. , 1986. xvi, 248 p. : ISBN 0-88730-081-2 LC Card 85-23299 DDC 332.1/2/0973 19
HG1616.C87 B35 1986
NYPL [JLE 86-2810]

Bank services and fees. Chicago, IL (676 North St., Clair St., Chicago 60611) , 1987. 60, 8 p. ; LC Card 87-400773 DDC 332.1/7/0973 19
HG1616.C87 B36 1987

Cranfill, Steven L. Small business banking . Washington, D.C. (1120 Connecticut Ave. N.W., Washington, D.C.) , c1987. ix, 78 p. : LC Card 87-135069 DDC 332.1/753 19
HG4027.7 .C7 1987

Hoffman, Naphtali. The bank book . San Diego , 1986. xiii, 222 p. ; ISBN 0-15-610676-0 (pbk.) : LC Card 85-27271 DDC 332.1/7/0973 19
HG1616.C87 H64 1986
NYPL [JLE 86-3189]

BANKS AND BANKING - UNITED STATES - CUSTOMER SERVICES - HANDBOOKS, MANUALS, ETC.
Seglin, Jeffrey L., 1956- Personal financial planning in banks . Boston , c1986. xvii, 205 p. ; ISBN 0-87267-059-7 LC Card 85-28738 DDC 332.1/7 19
HG1616.C87 S44 1986 ***NYPL [JLE 87-820]***

BANKS AND BANKING - UNITED STATES - DATA PROCESSING.
Gillis, M. Arthur. In-house computer trends for community banks /. New Orleans, LA (833 Howard Ave., Suite 501, New Orleans 70113) , 1987. 40, 18, [16] leaves : LC Card 87-147932 DDC 332.1/028/5 19
HG1709 .G525 1987

A Guide for selecting ALM microcomputer models . Washington, D.C. (1120 Connecticut Ave., N.W., Washington 20036) , c1987. iv, 147 p. : LC Card 87-159971 DDC 332.1/028/5416 19
HG1615.25 .G85 1987

BANKS AND BANKING - UNITED STATES - DEREGULATION.
Futures and options trading for commercial banks . Chicago, Ill. (30 S. Wacker Dr., Chicago 60606) , c1986. 14 p. : LC Card 87-131777 DDC 332.1/754 19
HG2491 .F87 1986

Streit, Joachim. Finanzinnovationen, Deregulierung und Geldmengensteuerung in den USA /. Tübingen , c1986. xi, 188 p. : ISBN 3-16-345156-X (pbk.) LC Card 87-408200 DDC 332/.0973 19
HG181 .S825 1986

Trading in banking . [New York?] , c1986. iv ; LC Card 87-128754 DDC 332.1/0973 19
HG2491 .T7 1986

Trading in banking . New York , c1987. x, 137 p. ; ISBN 0-939853-00-0 (pbk.) LC Card 87-404278 DDC 332.1/0973 19
HG2491 .T697 1987

BANKS AND BANKING - UNITED STATES - HANDBOOKS, MANUALS, ETC.
The Bank director's handbook /. Dover, Mass. , c1986. xxiii, 294 p. : ISBN 0-86569-145-2 : LC Card 86-3592 DDC 332.1/068 19
HG1615 .B34 1986 ***NYPL [JLE 86-4332]***

BANKS AND BANKING - UNITED STATES - HISTORY.
Degen, Robert A. The American monetary system . Lexington, Mass. , c1987. x, 242 p. ; ISBN 0-669-15827-5 (alk. paper) LC Card 86-46363 DDC 332.4/973 19
HG501 .D44 1987

BANKS AND BANKING - UNITED STATES - HISTORY - 20TH CENTURY.
Greider, William. Secrets of the temple . New York , c1987. 798 p. ; ISBN 0-671-47989-X : LC Card 87-16712 DDC 332.1/1/0973 19
HG2563 .G72 1987

BANKS AND BANKING - UNITED STATES - SERVICE CHARGES.
Bank services and fees. Chicago, IL (676 North St., Clair St., Chicago 60611) , 1987. 60, 8 p. ; LC Card 87-400773 DDC 332.1/7/0973 19
HG1616.C87 B36 1987

BANKS AND BANKING - UNITED STATES - STATE SUPERVISION.
Ballarín, Eduard. Commercial banks amid the financial revolution . Cambridge, Mass. , 1986. xvi, 248 p. : ISBN 0-88730-081-2 LC Card 85-23299 DDC 332.1/2/0973 19
HG1616.C87 B35 1986
NYPL [JLE 86-2810]

Deregulating financial services . Cambridge, Mass. , 1986. xiii, 223 p. ; ISBN 0-88730-111-8 LC Card 86-3355 DDC 332.1/0973 19
HG2491 .R42 1986 ***NYPL [JLE 86-3307]***

Perspectives on safe & sound banking . Cambridge, Mass. , 1986. xxi, 358 p. ; ISBN 0-262-02246-X LC Card 85-23882 DDC 332.1/0973 19
HG2481 .P47 1986 ***NYPL [JLE 86-2960]***

BANKS AND BANKING - UNITED STATES - STATISTICS.
Statistical information on the financial services industry. Washington, D.C. (1120 Connecticut Ave., N.W., Washington 20036) , c1984. xi, 272 p. : LC Card 84-253106 DDC 332.1/0973/021 19
HG181 .S795 1984 ***NYPL [*R-Econ. 86-285]***

Statistical information on the financial services industry. Washington, D.C. (1120 Connecticut Ave., N.W., Washington 20036) , c1987. xi, 273 p. : LC Card 87-402171 DDC 332.1/0973/021 19
HG181 .S795 1987

Trading in banking . New York , c1987. x, 137 p. ; ISBN 0-939853-00-0 (pbk.) LC Card 87-404278 DDC 332.1/0973 19
HG2491 .T697 1987

BANKS AND BANKING - UNITED STATES - TECHNOLOGICAL INNOVATIONS.
Trading in banking . [New York?] , c1986. iv ; LC Card 87-128754 DDC 332.1/0973 19
HG2491 .T7 1986

Trading in banking . New York , c1987. x, 137 p. ; ISBN 0-939853-00-0 (pbk.) LC Card 87-404278 DDC 332.1/0973 19
HG2491 .T697 1987

BANKS AND BANKING - URUGUAY.
Bouzas, Carlos, 1937- Todo lo que usted quería saber sobre los bancos, pero temía preguntar /. [Montevideo, Uruguay?] , 1986. 75 p. : LC Card 87-403156 DDC 332.1/09895 19
HG2954 .B68 1986

Compra de carteras . Montevideo [1986] 188 p. : LC Card 87-403157 DDC 332.1/09895 19
HG2954 .C66 1986

Rocca, José. Excedentes financieros y sistema bancario, Uruguay, 1974-1982 /. Montevideo, Uruguay , 1985. 39 p. : LC Card 85-213768
HC235.S3 R63 1985

BANKS AND BANKING - VALUATION.
Miller, William D. (William Dennis), 1953- Bank pricing and valuation /. New York, N.Y. , c1988. xiv, 279 p. : ISBN 0-88057-806-8 (pbk.) LC Card 87-81070 DDC 332.1/068/1 19
HG1708 .M55 1988

BANKS AND BANKING - VENEZUELA.
Martín-Guédez, Rafael, 1942- Vigencia de la multibanca . [Caracas? , 1982 or 1983] 122 p. ; LC Card 83-201555
HG2964 .M37 1982

BANKS AND BANKING, WEST GERMAN - LOCATION.
Walter, Herbert. Standortpolitik multinationaler Banken /. Thun , c1983. viii, 255 p. : ISBN 3-87144-737-4 : LC Card 83-159195
HG3881 .W273 1983

BANKS AND BANKING - YUGOSLAVIA.
Vrsaljko, Krešimir. Teorija i praksa domaćih i medunarodnih plaćanja /. Zagreb , 1982. xiv, 460 p. ; LC Card 84-160248
HG2341.Y82 V77 1982

Banks and specialised financial intermediaries in development /. Wellons, Philip A. Paris , Washington, D.C. , 1986. 150 p. : ISBN 92-64-12867-0 (pbk.) : LC Card 87-114506 DDC 332.1/09172/4 19
HG3550 .W45 1986

BANKS, CENTRAL. see **BANKS AND BANKING, CENTRAL.**

Banks, Ferdinand E. The political economy of natural gas / Ferdinand E. Banks. London ; New York : Croom Helm, c1987. 200 p. ; 24 cm. (Croom Helm commodity series) Bibliography: p. 194-197. Includes index. ISBN 0-7099-3940-X : LC Card 87-14098 DDC 338.2/7285 19
1. Gas industry. 2. Gas, Natural. I. Title.
HD9581.A2 B36 1987

Banks, Gary. Economic policy and the adjustment problem / by Gary Banks and Jan Tumlir. Aldershot, Hants., England ; Brookfield, Vt. : Gower for the Trade Policy Research Centre, 1986. x, 101 p. ; 22 cm. (Thames essay . no. 45) Bibliography: p. [92]-97. ISBN 0-566-05332-2 : LC Card 86-14934 DDC 338.9 19
1. Trade adjustment assistance. 2. Free trade and protection - Protection. I. Tumlir, Jan. II. Title. III. Series.
HF1421 .B36 1987
NYPL [JLL 74-802 no.45]

BANKS, HAL, 1909-
Edwards, Peter, 1956- Waterfront warlord . Toronto, Ont., Canada , c1987. ix, 213 p. : ISBN 1-550-13013-7 : LC Card 87-150705 DDC 331.88/113875/0924 B 19
HD6525.B36 E39 1987

Banks, Vera J. Black farmers and their farms / Vera J. Banks. Washington, D.C. : U. S. Dept. of Agriculture, Economic Research Service, 1986. v, 27 p. : ill., col. maps ; 28 cm. (Rural development research report . no. 59) Cover title. Distributed to depository libraries in microfiche. "July 1986"--P. iii. G.P.O. sales statement incorrect in publication. Bibliography: p. 18. Item 18-C-2 (microfiche) LC Card 86-602201
1. Afro-American farmers - United States - Statistics. 2. Farms, Small - United States - Statistics. I. United States. Dept. of Agriculture. Economic Research Service. II. Title. III. Series.
HD8039.F32 U616 1986

Bankwirtschaftliche Forschungen.
(Bd. 101) Internationale Wettbewerbsfähigkeit des Finanzplatzes Schweiz /. Bern , c1987. 131 p. : ISBN 3-258-03806-6 LC Card 87-114764 DDC 332.1 s 332.1/09494 19
HG1526 .B27 Bd. 101 HG3206

(Bd. 77) Zellweger, Bruno. Ueberwachung kommerzieller Bankkredite /. Bern , c1983. xx, 330 p. : ISBN 3-258-03246-7 : LC Card 83-214274
HG1526 .B27 Bd. 77 HG1642.S95

(Bd. 79) Brosset, Michel. Multinationale Bankenverflechtungen . Bern , c1983. vii, 245 p. : ISBN 3-258-03275-0 : LC Card 83-178197
HG1526 .B27 Bd. 79 HG3881

(Bd. 80) Gross, Peter, Dr. Logistik einer Grossbank . Bern , c1983. 52 p. : ISBN 3-258-03274-2 : LC Card 83-181853
HG1526 .B27 Bd. 80 HG3208.U54

(Bd. 81) Heno, Rudolf. Kreditwürdigkeitsprüfung mit Hilfe von Verfahren der Mustererkennung /. Bern , c1983. vi, 317 p. : ISBN 3-258-03245-9 : LC Card 83-228668
HG1526 .B27 Bd. 81 HG3751.9.G3

(Bd. 86) Bolliger, Peter. Die optimale Organisationsstruktur eines mittleren Bankbetriebes . Bern , c1984. xiii, 234 p. : ISBN 3-258-03358-7 : LC Card 84-174443
HG1526 .B27 Bd. 86 HG1616.B7

(Bd. 96) Meyer, Conrad. Die Bankbilanz als finanzielles Führungsinstrument . Bern , c1986. x, 655 p. : ISBN 3-258-03587-3 LC Card 86-199541
HG1526 .B27 Bd. 96 HG1778.S9

(Bd. 97) Cordero, Ricardo. Der Financial Futures Markt /. Bern , c1986. xii, 200 p. : ISBN 3-258-03638-1 LC Card 87-408496 DDC 332.1 s 332.64/4 19
HG1526 .B27 Bd. 97 HG6024.3

Bankwirtschaftliches Kolloquium (1984-1985 : Johann Wolfgang Goethe-Universität Frankfurt am Main) Internationaler Kapitalverkehr und Devisenhandel /. Frankfurt am Main , c1986. 133 p. ; ISBN 3-7819-0347-8 LC Card 87-164156 DDC 332/.042 19
HG3891 .I58 1986

Bankwirtschaftliches Kolloquium (1985-1986 : Universität Frankfurt am Main)
Bankinnovationen . Frankfurt am Main , c1986. 131 p. ; ISBN 3-7819-0363-X LC Card 87-120955 DDC 332.1/0943 19
HG3048 .B287 1986

BANNED PERSONS (SOUTH AFRICA) - BIOGRAPHY.
Mandela, Winnie. Part of my soul /. Harmondsworth , 1985. 163 p., [8] p. of plates :
NYPL [Sc C 86-121]

Mandela, Winnie. Part of my soul went with him /. New York , 1985, c1984. 163 p., [8] p. of plates : ISBN 0-393-02215-3 : LC Card 85-21632 DDC 968/.00496 19
DT779.955.M36 A35 1985
NYPL [JFD 86-7717]

Banque asiatique de développement. see **Asian Development Bank.**

Banque de developpement national (Portugal) see **Banco de Fomento Nacional.**

BANQUE DE FRANCE.
Muszynski, Maurice. Les billets de la Banque de France ; Les émissions du Trésor /. Bruyères-le-Châtel , 1985. 160 p. : LC Card 83-132282
HG985 .M88 1985

Banque du Canada. see **Bank of Canada.**

Banque interamericaine de developpement. see **Inter-American Development Bank.**

Banque internationale pour la reconstruction et la développement. see **International Bank for Reconstruction and Development.**

Banque internationale pour le reconstruction et le developpement. see **International Bank for Reconstruction and Development.**

Banque marocaine pour le commerce et l'industrie. Pourquoi, où et comment investir /. Casablanca, Maroc [1985] 126 p. ; LC Card 86-198948
HG5832.A3 P68 1985

BANQUE NATIONALE D'HAÏTI - HISTORY.
Marcelin, Frédéric, 1848-1917. La Banque nationale d'Haïti . Port-au-Prince, Haïti , 1985. xi, 118 p. : LC Card 86-125803 DDC 332.1/1/097294 19
HG2813 .M3 1985 ***NYPL [Sc D 86-690]***

Banque nationale suisse. see **Schweizerische Nationalbank.**

Banque suisse. Chambost, Édouard. Guide de la banque suisse et de ses secrets /. [Paris] , c1987. 317 p. : ISBN 2-7158-0626-4 : LC Card 87-132185
HG3204 .C43 1987

Banques, le grand secret /. Binst, Olivier. Paris , c1987. 166 p. ; ISBN 2-234-02032-8 : LC Card 87-156884
HG3026 .B48 1987

Un banquier suisse parle . Weck, Philippe de, 1919- Fribourg , c1983. 159 p. ; LC Card 84-119161
HG1552.W43 A3 1983

Bantje, Han. Mechanised food production in Tanzania : a portrait of the National Agriculture and Food Corporation / by Han Bantje. [Dar es Salaam] : Institute of Resource Assessment, University of Dar es Salaam, [1984] 3 leaves, 73 p. : ill. ; 30 cm. (Research paper . no. 6) "December 1984." Bibliography: p. 52-53. LC Card 86-980118 DDC 338.1/61/09678 19
1. National Agriculture and Food Corporation. 2. Farms, Large - Tanzania. 3. Agriculture and state - Tanzania. 4. Grain trade - Tanzania. I. Series: Research paper (Chuo Kikuu cha Dar es Salaam. Institute of Resource Assessment) , 6. II. Title.
HD1471.T34 B36 1984

BÁNYAIPARI DOLGOZÓK SZAKSZERVEZETE - HISTORY.
Gergely, Ernő. A Bányaipari Dolgozók Szakszervezetének története /. [Budapest] , 1983. 218 p. ; ISBN 963-00-0667-7 (Magy. nemz. bibl.) LC Card 85-109054
HD6680.5.Z7 M6113 1983

A Bányaipari Dolgozók Szakszervezetének története /. Gergely, Ernő. [Budapest] , 1983. 218 p. ; ISBN 963-00-0667-7 (Magy. nemz. bibl.) LC Card 85-109054
HD6680.5.Z7 M6113 1983

A Bányászat műszaki, gazdasági szakembereinek II. ágazati tanácskozása : (röviditettt jegyzőkönyv) : Budapest, 1979. május 26. [Budapest : s.n., 1979] (Szolnok : NKFV Nyomda) 83 p. ; 20 cm. Organized by the Nehézipari Minisztérium. LC Card 82-205242
1. Mineral industries - Hungary - Congresses. I. Hungary. Nehézipari Minisztérium. II. Title: Bányászat műszaki, gazdasági szakembereinek 2. ágazati tanácskozása. III. Title: Bányászat műszaki, gazdasági szakembereinek második tanácskozása.
HD9506.H92 B36 1979

Bányászat műszaki, gazdasági szakembereinek második tanácskozása. A Bányászat műszaki, gazdasági szakembereinek II. ágazati tanácskozása . [Budapest , 1979] (Szolnok : NKFV Nyomda) 83 p. ; LC Card 82-205242
HD9506.H92 B36 1979

Bányászat műszaki, gazdasági szakembereinek 2. ágazati tanácskozása. A Bányászat műszaki, gazdasági szakembereinek II. ágazati tanácskozása . [Budapest , 1979] (Szolnok : NKFV Nyomda) 83 p. ; LC Card 82-205242
HD9506.H92 B36 1979

Banze, Angelika. Die deutsch-englische Wirtschaftsrivalität : ein Beitrag zur Geschichte der deutsch-englischen Beziehungen, 1897-1907 / von Angelika Banze. Vaduz : Kraus Reprint, 1965. 105 p. ; 23 cm. Reprint. Originally published: Berlin : E. Ebering, 1935. (Historische Studien ; Heft 274) Originally presented as the author's thesis (doctoral)--Universität Berlin, 1932. Bibliography: p. [103]-105. LC Card 85-243022 DDC 337.43041 19
1. Germany - Foreign economic relations - Great Britain. 2. Great Britain - Foreign economic relations - Germany. I. Series: Historische Studien (Matthiesen Verlag) , Heft 274. II. Title.
HF1546.15.G7 B36 1965

Baptista, Lourival. Reforma tributária, federalismo e desenvolvimento nacional / Lourival Baptista. Brasília : Senado Federal, Centro Gráfico, 1983. 255 p. : ill. ; 23 cm. Includes bibliographical references. LC Card 86-210783
1. Taxation - Brazil. 2. Intergovernmental fiscal relations - Brazil. 3. Brazil - Economic policy. I. Title.
HJ2525 .B36 1983

Baqai, Moin. Employment, distribution, and basic needs in Pakistan . Lahore , 1986. xxxiv, 408 p., [1] leaf of plates : LC Card 86-930280 DDC 330.9549/1 19
HD5820.5.A6 E47 1986

Baquiast, Jean-Paul. La France dans la bataille des technologies de l'intelligence / Jean-Paul Baquiast, Roger Ganne ; préface de Hubert Curien. Paris : Documentation française, c1985. 221 p. ; 24 cm. "Janvier 1984-avril 1985." Includes bibliographical references. ISBN 2-11-001440-7 : LC Card 86-126853 DDC 338.4/7004/094 19
1. Computer industry - France. 2. Computer industry - European Economic Community countries. 3. Competition, International. I. Ganne, Roger. II. Title.
HD9696.C63 F72 1985

Bar code markets : key growth areas in service industries. Norwalk, Conn., U. S.A. (6 Prowitt St., Norwalk 06855) : International Resource Development, c1987. iv, 221 leaves : ill. ; 28 cm. (Report / International Resource Development Inc. . #729) "February 1987." LC Card 87-401927 DDC 381/.45621399 19
1. Product coding verification equipment industry - United States. 2. Service industries - United States - Automation. I. International Resource Development, inc. II. Series: Report / International Resource Development Inc. , #729.
HD9801.6.P763 U624 1987

The bar coding systems industry. Delson, Erwin B. New York, N.Y. , c1986. 1 v. (various pagings) : ISBN 0-931634-64-4 (pbk.) LC Card 87-156445 DDC 380.1/45621399 19
HD9801.6.P762 D45 1986

Bar-El, Raphael.
Rural industrialization in Israel /. Boulder , 1987. xi, 193 p. ; ISBN 0-8133-7393-X (pbk. : alk. paper) : LC Card 87-2073 DDC 338.095694 19
HC415.25 .R87 1987

Schwartz, Moshe. Non-agricultural employment for moshav youth in the Galilee /. Rehovot, Israel , c1985. 36, [2] p. ; LC Card 86-115596 DDC 331.3/4/0956945 19
HD6276.I66 G347 1985

Barakonyi, Károly. Számítógépes vállalati tervezés / Barakonyi Károly. Budapest : Közgazdasági és Jogi Könyvkiadó, 1984. 320, [1] p. : ill. ; 21 cm. Bibliography: p. 309-[321] ISBN 963-221-456-0 (Magy. nemz. bibl.) : LC Card 85-174882
1. Industrial management - Data processing. 2. Corporate planning - Data processing. I. Title.
HD30.2 .B36 1984

Baranger, Dionisio. Migración y marginalidad en Posadas : análisis de algunos datos del Proyecto "Mesubs" / Dionisio Baranger. Posadas : Programa "Urbanización y Marginalidad en Misiones," Instituto de Investigación, 1982. 53 p. : map ; 29 cm. "Documento reservado para circulación interna exclusivamente." LC Card 86-205276 DDC 304.8/0982/23 19
1. Posadas (Argentina) - Population. 2. Migration, Internal - Argentina. 3. Marginality, Social - Argentina - Posadas. I. Title.
HB2020.P67 B37 1982

Baranov, A. V. (Al'bert Vasil'evich)
Sotsial'no-demograficheskoe razvitie krupnogo goroda / A.V. Baranov. Moskva : Finansy i statistika, 1981. 189 p. : ill. ; 20 cm. Includes bibliographical references. LC Card 82-114309
1. Leningrad (R.S.F.S.R.) - Population. 2. Leningrad (R.S.F.S.R.) - Social conditions. I. Title.
HB3608.L4 B37 1981

Baranov, Ė. F. Sistema modeleĭ narodnokhoziaĭstvennogo planirovaniia /. Moskva , 1982. 375 p. ; LC Card 83-172876
HC336.25 .S564 1982

Baranova, T. N. (Tat'iana Nikolaevna) Rabochiĭ klass Ispanii boretsia : rabochie komissii--klassovaia al'ternativa frankistskim profsoiuzam / T.N. Baranova, I.V. Mikhaĭlin. Moskva : Profizdat, 1978. 151 p. ; 20 cm. Includes bibliographical references. LC Card 81-147187
1. Labor and laboring classes - Spain. 2. Trade-unions - Spain. I. Mikhaĭlin, I. V. (Igor' Viktorovich). II. Title.
HD8586.5 .B37 1978

Baranovskiĭ, V. G. (Vladimir Georgievich)
Evropeĭskoe soobshchestvo v sisteme mezhdunarodnykh otnosheniĭ / V.G. Baranovskiĭ ; otvetstvennyĭ redaktor V.I. Gantman. Moskva : "Nauka", 1986. 319 p. ; 21 cm. At head of title: Akademiia nauk SSSR. Ordena Trudovogo Krasnogo Znameni Institut mirovoĭ ėkonomiki i mezhdunarodykh otnosheniĭ. Includes bibliographical references. LC Card 86-201822
1. European Economic Community countries - Foreign economic relations. 2. European Economic Community countries - Foreign relations. I. Gantman, Vladimir Izrail'evich. II. Title.
HF1532.92 .B37 1986

BARANYA MEGYE (HUNGARY) - ECONOMIC CONDITIONS - CONGRESSES.
Múlt, jelen, jövő a műszaki haladás szolgálatában . Pécs , 1985. 305 p. : LC Card 87-408539
HC300.29.B37 M86 1985

Baranyai, István. A Magyar háztartásstatisztikai megfigyelés módszertana /. Budapest , 1986. 59 p. ; LC Card 87-408579
HA37.H92 M34 1986

Baras, Edward M. The advanced guide to Lotus 1-2-3 / Edward M. Baras. Berkeley, Calif. : Osborne McGraw-Hill, c1986. xiii, 234 p. : ill. ; 24 cm. "Covers Release 2." ISBN 0-07-881237-2 (pbk.) LC Card 86-215569 DDC 005.36/9 19
1. Lotus 1-2-3 (Computer program). 2. Macroprogramming. 3. Business - Data processing. I. Title. II. Title: Advanced guide to Lotus One-two-three.
HF5548.4.L67 B36 1986

Barata, Martha Macedo de Lima. Produção agrícola brasileira . [Rio de Janeiro] , 1986. 188 p. : LC Card 87-403944 DDC 338.1/0981/021 19
HD9014.B82 P765 1986

Baratra, Michèle. Lacour, Claude. Croissance urbaine . Paris , 1981. 219 p. : ISBN 2-222-02928-7 (pbk.) : LC Card 82-153821 DDC 388.4/068 19
HE4764 .L3 1981 ***NYPL [JLG 86-56]***

BARBADOS - APPROPRIATIONS AND EXPENDITURES.
Barbados. Duffus Commission of Enquiry. Report /. [Bridgetown, Barbados] [1978] vi, 118, 270 p. : LC Card 82-243628 DDC 354.7298/10072 19
HJ2073.B37 B37 1978 ***NYPL [JLG 86-221]***

Barbados. Duffus Commission of Enquiry. Report / the Duffus Commission of Enquiry, 1977-78. [Bridgetown, Barbados] : The Commission, [1978] vi, 118, 270 p. : facsims. ; 35 cm. At head of title: Barbados. LC Card 82-243628 DDC 354.7298/10072 19
1. Investment of public funds - Barbados. 2. Finance, Public - Barbados - Accounting. 3. Governmental investigations - Barbados. 4. Barbados - Appropriations and expenditures. I. Title. II. Title: Duffus Commission of Enquiry, 1977-78, report.
HJ2073.B37 B37 1978 ***NYPL [JLG 86-221]***

Barban, Arnold M. Essentials of media planning : a marketing viewpoint / Arnold M. Barban, Steven M. Cristol, Frank J. Kopec.2nd ed. Lincolnwood, Ill., U. S.A. : NTC Business Books, c1987. xii, 160 p. : ill. ; 26 cm. Includes bibliographies and index. ISBN 0-8442-3018-9 (pbk.) : LC Card 86-51055 DDC 659.1/11 19
1. Advertising media planning. 2. Marketing. I. Cristol, Steven M. II. Kopec, Frank J. III. Title.
HF5826.5 .B37 1987

Barbara Wootton--social science and public policy : essays in her honour / edited by Philip Bean and David Whynes. London ; New York : Tavistock Publications, 1986. xi, 291 p. ; 25 cm. "Barbara Wootton, a select bibliography": p.

[282]-284. Includes bibliographies and indexes. ISBN 0-422-79690-5 LC Card 85-27650 DDC 330 19

1. Wootton, Barbara, Baroness Wootton of Abinger, 1897- - Addresses, essays, lectures. 2. Economics - Addresses, essays, lectures. 3. Social policy - Addresses, essays, lectures. 4. Welfare state - Addresses, essays, lectures. 5. Crime and criminals - Addresses, essays, lectures. I. Bean, Philip. II. Whynes, David K. III. Wootton, Barbara, Baroness of Albinger, 1897-.

HB171 .B248 1985 ***NYPL [JLE 86-1743]***

Barbaria, Janet. The growth revolt : aftershock of Proposition 13? / prepared by Office of Planning and Research ; [Janet Barbaria and Dean J. Misczynski, principal authors ; Claudia Buckner, editor]. Sacramento, Calif. : The Office, [1980] 66 p. : ill. ; 29 cm. "August 1980." LC Card 81-620644 DDC 336.794 19

1. Real property tax - California. 2. Tax and expenditure limitations - California. I. Misczynski, Dean J. II. Buckner, Claudia. III. California. Governor's Office. Office of Planning and Research. IV. Title.

HJ4191 .B37 1980 ***NYPL [JLF 86-369]***

Barbato de Silva, Celia. La ganadería vacuna uruguaya : caracterización general / Celia Barbato de Silva, Carlos Pérez Arrarte. Montevideo, Uruguay : CINVE, [1980] 77 leaves ; 28 cm. (III. Serie Estudios . no. 5) Includes bibliographical references.

1. Cattle trade - Uruguay. 2. Beef trade - Uruguay. I. Pérez Arrarte, Carlos. II. Centro de Investigaciones Económicas (Uruguay). III. Series: Estudios (Centro de Investigaciones Económicas (Uruguay)) , no. 5. IV. Title. ***NYPL [JLF 86-1101]***

Barbedette, Loïc. Sall, Alioune. Ressources humaines pour le développement . [Dakar, Sénégal , 1984] 51 p. : LC Card 85-129264 DDC 338.91/09624 19

HC1002 .S25 1984

Barber, Clarence L., 1917- Manitoba's interest in and attitude towards a proposed Canada-United States free trade area : a study prepared for Manitoba Industry, Trade and Technology / Clarence Barber. [Winnipeg : Manitoba Industry, Trade and Technology, 1985] 35 leaves : ill. ; 28 cm. (Discussion paper) "September 1985." Bibliography: leaf 35. LC Card 86-175828 DDC 382/.0971/073 19

1. Canada - Commercial policy. 2. United States - Commercial policy. 3. Free trade and protection - Free trade. 4. Economic forecasting - Manitoba. 5. Manitoba - Economic policy. I. Series: Discussion paper (Manitoba. Manitoba Industry, Trade and Technology). II. Title.

HF1479 .B37 1985

Barber, Dan. Short, Simine, 1944- Glider mail . Cinnaminson, NJ , 1987. 261 p. : ISBN 0-939429-00-4 : LC Card 86-72751 DDC 383/.144 19

HE6239.G54 S56 1987

Barber, Donald T. Filing dynamics : developments in color coding for filing systems / by Donald T. Barber and Mark Langemo. Emeryville, Calif. : Marsdale Pub. Co., 1987. 92 p. : col. ill. ; 24 cm. Bibliography: p. 85. Includes index. ISBN 0-941151-00-X LC Card 87-60316 DDC 651.5/3 19

1. Filing systems. 2. Office equipment and supplies. I. Langemo, Mark. II. Title. III. Title: Color coding for filing systems.

HF5741 .B44 1987

Barber, William J. Breaking the academic mould . Middletown, Conn. , 1988. p. cm. ISBN 0-8195-5176-7 : LC Card 87-21023 DDC 330/.07/1173 19

HB74.8 .B74 1988

Barberis, Carlo. Guida alla valorizzazione agricola nei paesi in via di sviluppo /. Milano, Italy , c1983. 434 p. : LC Card 83-144803 DDC 338.1/09172/4 19

HD1417 .G85 1983 ***NYPL [JLD 86-3296]***

Barberis, Corrado.

Agricoltura e strati sociali / Corrado Barberis, Vincenzo Siesto ; prefazione di Giuseppe Medici. Milano, Italy : F. Angeli, c1986. 269 p. ; 22 cm. (Insor . 14) Includes bibliographical references. LC Card 86-214233

1. Agricultural laborers - Italy - Statistics. 2. Peasantry - Italy - Statistics. 3. Farmers - Italy - Statistics. 4. Farmers, Part-time - Italy - Statistics. 5. Italy - Rural conditions - Statistics. 6. Italy - Population, Rural - Statistics. 7. Social classes - Italy - Statistics. I. Siesto, Vincenzo. II. Series: Collana Insor , 14. III. Title.

HD1536.I8 B328 1986

La società italiana : redditi, occupazione, imprese / Corrado Barberis.7a ed. Milano, Italy : F. Angeli, [1984?] 382 p. ; 22 cm. (La Società. 37) Includes bibliographical references. LC Card 85-201583

1. Italy - Economic conditions - 1945-. 2. Italy - Social conditions - 1945-1976. 3. Italy - Social conditions - 1976-. 4. Social classes - Italy. I. Title.

HC305 .B365 1984

Barbier, André. Guide pratique de l'analyse financière à l'usage des banquiers / par André Barbier, Jacques Proutat. 3e éd. Paris : Revue banque, c1985. viii, 313 p. : ill. ; 30 cm. (Collection Institut technique de banque, 0293-8030) ISBN 2-86325-038-8 : LC Card 86-165653

1. Corporations - Accounting. 2. Ratio analysis. 3. Financial statements. I. Proutat, Jacques. II. Title. III. Series.

HF5686.C7 B32 1985

Barbier, Hans-Dietmar. Entwicklungspolitik im Spannungsfeld von Solidarität und Eigeninteresse . Stuttgart , New York , 1986. 155 p. ; ISBN 3-437-50306-5 LC Card 87-408212 DDC 338.91/43/01724 19

HC60 .E527 1986

Barbier, J. C.

Manjo et le Mungo central. 1983. Barbier, J. C. Migrations et développement : la région du Moungo au Cameroun / J.-C. Barbier, J. Champaud, F. Gendreau. Paris , 1983, c1984. 372 p. : ISBN 2-7099-0711-7

NYPL [M-11 4991 no.170]

Migrations et développement : la région du Moungo au Cameroun / J.-C. Barbier, J. Champaud, F. Gendreau. Paris : O.R.S.T.O.M. : L'Harmattan, Diffusion, 1983, c1984. 372 p. : ill., maps; 27 cm. (Travaux et documents de l'O.R.S.T.O.M. . no 170) "Les deux premières parties de cet ouvrage ont été publiées ... sous le titre suivant: Manjo et le Mungo central ... Yaoundé, ONAREST, 1980"--Verso t.p. Distributor from label. Bibliography: p. 353-357. Library's copy lacks distributor label. ISBN 2-7099-0711-7

1. Migration, Internal - Cameroon. 2. Mungo (Cameroon). 3. Manjo (Cameroon) - Population. 4. Bamileke (African people). I. Champaud, Jacques. II. Gendreau, Francis. III. Barbier, J. C. Manjo et le Mungo central. 1983. IV. Series: France. Recherche Scientifique Outre-Mer, Office de la. Travaux et documents de l'O.R.S.T.O.M. , no. 170. V. Title.

NYPL [M-11 4991 no.170]

Barbira-Freedman, Françoise. Land, people, and planning in contemporary Amazonia /. [Cambridge, Cambridgeshire] , 1980. xvi, 313 p. : LC Card 87-672189

HC167.A42 L36x 1980

BARBOSA (ANTIOQUIA, COLOMBIA) - ECONOMIC CONDITIONS.

Informe general y proyecto de parcelación, Antioquia # 2 (Barbosa y Santo Domingo) /. Bogotá, D.E. , 1964. 2, 73, 16 leaves, [1] leaf of plates : LC Card 85-107102

HD1476.C72 B375 1964

Barbosa, Fernando de Holanda.

Microeconomia--teoria, modelos econométricos e aplicações à economia brasileira / Fernando de Holanda Barbosa. Rio de Janeiro : IPEA/INPES, 1985. 534 p. : ill. ; 24 cm. (Série PNPE . 10) Includes bibliographies. LC Card 87-118555 DDC 338.5 19

1. Microeconomics. 2. Brazil - Economic conditions - Econometric models. I. Title. II. Series.

HB179.P75 B37 1985

Barbosa, Manuel P. (Manuel Pinto), 1944-

Growth, migration, and the balance of payments in a small open economy, Portugal / Manuel P. Barbosa. New York : Garland Pub., 1984. xv, 212 p. : ill. ; 24 cm. (Outstanding dissertations in economics) Thesis (Ph. D.)--Yale University, 1977. Bibliography: p. 210-212. ISBN 0-8240-4169-0 : LC Card 79-53646 DDC 382.1/7/0724 19

1. Labor supply - Portugal - Mathematical models. 2. Balance of payments - Portugal - Mathematical models. 3. Portugal - Emigration and immigration. 4. Portugal - Economic conditions - 1974- - Mathematical models. I. Title. II. Series.

HD5809.A6 B37 1984 ***NYPL [JLE 86-4171]***

Barbosa, Túlio. Expansión del cultivo de la caña de azúcar y de la ganadería en el Nordeste del Brasil : políticas públicas y sus derivaciones económicas y sociales / [preparado por Túlio Barbosa].1a ed. Santiago de Chile : Comision Económica para América Latina y el Caribe, Naciones Unidas ; Nueva York, NY, Estados Unidos de América : [for sale by] Publicaciones de las Naciones Unidas, Sección de Ventas, 1986. 170 p. : ill. ; 23 cm. (Estudios e informes de la CEPAL, 0256-9795 . 59) Bibliography: p. 159-164. "LC/G.1425, mayo de 1986." ISBN 92-1-321209-7 LC Card 87-400309 DDC 338.1/7361/09813 19

1. Sugarcane industry - Government policy - Brazil, Northeast. 2. Cattle trade - Government policy - Brazil, Northeast. 3. Sugarcane industry - Brazil, Northeast. 4. Cattle trade - Brazil, Northeast. I. Title. II. Series.

HD9114.B7 N67943 1986

Barcelona (Spain). Ayuntamiento.

Catalunya, la fàbrica d'Espanya . [Barcelona] , 1985. 201 p. : LC Card 86-185178

HC387.C25 C336 1985

Barcelona (Spain). Ayuntamiento. Departament d'Estudis i Programació. Estat d'execució dels programes d'actuació i pressupostos d'inversió de l'Ajuntament de Barcelona durant 1982. [Barcelona] : Ajuntament de Barcelona, Gabinet Tècnic de Programació, Departament d'Estudis i Programació, [1983] 126 leaves ; 21 x 30 cm. (Informe . 2) Cover title. "Gener 1983." LC Card 84-249883

1. Public investments - Spain - Barcelona. I. Series: Informe (Barcelona (Spain). Ayuntamiento. Departament d'Estudis i Programació) , 2. II. Title.

HC388.B3 B36 1983

BARCELONA (SPAIN) - CENSUS, 1970.

Cens d'edificis, 1970 /. [Barcelona] [1979?] 5, 9 leaves ; LC Card 84-131679

HD7351.B3 C45 1979

Cens vivendas 1970 /. [Barcelona] [1979?] 4, 9 leaves ; LC Card 84-131705

HD7351.B3 C47 1979

Barcelona (Spain). Subdepartamento de Estadística.

Cens d'edificis, 1970 /. [Barcelona] [1979?] 5, 9 leaves ; LC Card 84-131679

HD7351.B3 C45 1979

Cens vivendas 1970 /. [Barcelona] [1979?] 4, 9 leaves ; LC Card 84-131705

HD7351.B3 C47 1979

Barco, Virgilio. La lucha contra la pobreza / Virgilio Barco. 1a ed. [Bogotá] : C. Valencia Editores, 1985. 193 p. ; 17 cm. "Bibliografía del autor": p. 191-193. Includes indexes. ISBN 958-9044-11-5 LC Card 85-239429

1. Colombia - Economic policy. 2. Colombia - Economic conditions - 1970-. 3. Poor - Colombia. I. Title.

HC197 .B2765 1985

Barcza, Gabriella. A Mezőgazdasági és élelmiszeripari vállalatok gazdálkodása /. Budapest , 1984. 315, [1] p. : ISBN 963-231-968-0 : LC Card 85-230887

HD1493.H8 M48 1984

Bard, Ray.

Breaking in : the guide to over 500 top corporate training programs / Ray Bard/Fran Moody. New York : Quill, 1985. 256 p. ; 28 cm. "A Stonesong Press book." Includes indexes. Bibliography: p. 247. ISBN 0-688-05893-0 (pbk.) LC Card 85-6571 DDC 331.25/92/02573 19

1. Employees, Training of - United States - Directories. 2. Corporations - United States - Directories. I. Moody, Fran. II. Title.

HF5549.5.T7 B29 1985

NYPL [*R-Econ. 86-248]

Own your own franchise : everything you need to know about the best opportunities in America / Ray Bard and Sheila Henderson. Reading, Mass. : Addison-Wesley, 1987. vii, 455 p. ; 24 cm. "A Stonesong Press book." ISBN 0-201-11439-9 (pbk.) : LC Card 87-14389 DDC 658.8/708 19

1. Franchises (Retail trade) - United States. I. Henderson, Sheila, 1950-. II. Title.

HF5429.235.U5 B37 1987

The Trainer's professional development handbook /. San Francisco , 1987. xix, 327 p. : ISBN 1-555-42067-2 (alk. paper) LC Card 87-45507 DDC 658.3/124 19

HF5549.5.T7 T6633 1987

Bardina, A. A. Opyt razrabotki i realizatsii sistemy ukrupnennykh modeleĭ perspektivnogo

planirovaniia /. Moskva , 1984. 216 p. : LC Card 85-199888
HD75.5 .O69 1984

Bardmann, Manfred. Die Preistypdebatte, ihre Grundlagen und ihr Einfluss auf die praktische Ausgestaltung des Preissystems der DDR / Manfred Bardmann. Berlin : Berlin Verlag A. Spitz, c1986. 99 p. : ill. ; 21 cm. (Staatliche Planungen. Bd. 6) Bibliography: p. 90-97. Includes index. ISBN 3-87061-300-9 LC Card 86-148984
1. Prices - Germany, East. I. Title.
HB235.G32 B37 1986

BARDOLI TALUKA (INDIA) - HISTORY.
Mehta, Shirin. The peasantry and nationalism . New Delhi , 1984. x, 215 p. : LC Card 84-901701 DDC 322.4/4/095475 19
HD1339.I4 M44 1984 ***NYPL [JLD 86-4424]***

Bardouille, R. (Raj) Women's employment patterns, discrimination, and promotion of equality in Zambia / by R. Bardouille. [Lusaka? : s.n., 1985]. ii, 160 leaves ; 30 cm. "Prepared for the International Labour Office (JASPA), Addis Ababa." "February, 1985." Bibliography: leaves 148-152. LC Card 87-980054 DDC 331.4/133/096894 19
1. Women - Employment - Zambia. 2. Sex discrimination against women - Zambia. 3. Sex discrimination in employment - Zambia. I. Jobs and Skills Programme for Africa. II. Title.
HD6212.5 .B37 1985

Bardovskiĭ, V. P. Ėkonomicheskie sviazi i sovershenstvovanie khoziaistvennogo mekhanizma . Kursk , 1985. 107 p. ; LC Card 86-235039
HC340.I57 E37 1985

Bardwell, Lisa. Alternative environmental conflict management approaches . [Ann Arbor, MI] (Dana Bldg., Ann Arbor 48109-1115) [1986] 252 p. : LC Card 86-225219 DDC 363.7/058/0973 19
HC110.E5 A643 1986

Barefoot, John. Georgia / by John Barefoot & Andrew Hall. York, England : J. Barefoot, c1983. 66 p. : ill. ; 30 cm. (European philately . 11) Bibliography: p. 66. ISBN 0-906845-19-X (pbk.) LC Card 87-100272 DDC 769.5694795 19
1. Postage-stamps - Georgian S.S.R. - Catalogs. I. Hall, Andrew. II. Title. III. Series.
HE6185.S653 G463 1983

Barendregt, J. (Jaap) Swaziland / J. Barendregt, M.A. Brouwer. Amsterdam : Koninklijk Instituut voor de Tropen ; 's-Gravenhage : Staatsuitgeverij, 1985. 43 p., [1] folded leaf of plates : ill., maps ; 24 cm. (Landendocumentatie. 1985, nr. 4) Bibliography: p. 41-42. ISBN 90-12-05175-4 LC Card 86-174569
1. Swaziland - Economic conditions. I. Brouwer, M. A. (Maarten A.). II. Title.
HC925 .B37 1985

Barendregt, N. Arbeidsmarkt op drift . [Amsterdam] , 1986. 190 p. : ISBN 90-6287-549-1 : LC Card 86-154853
HD5792 .A72 1986 ***NYPL [JLD 86-4417]***

Barfield, Claude E. Trade policy and U. S. competitiveness /. Washington, D.C. , Lanham, Md. , c1987. xvi, 144 p. ; ISBN 0-8447-3633-3 (alk. paper) LC Card 87-18831 DDC 382/.3/0973 19
HF1455 .T65 1987

BARGAINING. see **NEGOTIATION.**

Bargaining behavior / edited by Heinz Sauermann. Tübingen : Mohr, 1978. x, 383 p. : ill. ; 24 cm. (Contributions to experimental economics, 0340-6784 . 7 = 7) Papers presented at the second Conference on Experimental Economics, Winzenhohl, Germany, August 28th to September 2nd, 1977. Includes bibliographies and index. ISBN 3-16-340972-5 LC Card 86-227549 DDC 330 s 658.4 19
1. Negotiation in business - Congresses. 2. Negotiation - Congresses. I. Sauermann, Heinz. II. Conference on Experimental Economics (2nd : 1977 : Winzenhohl, Germany). III. Series: Beitrage zur experimentellen , 7. Bd.
HB41 .B29 1967 Bd. 7 HD58.6

Bargaining in the governance of Pacific coastal resources . Dorcey, Anthony H. J., 1944- Vancouver, B.C. , c1986. xvi, 219 p. : ISBN 0-920146-34-1 (pbk.) LC Card 86-222720 DDC 333.91/7/09711 19
HC117.B8 D67 1986

Barhydt, James D. The complete book of product publicity / James D. Barhydt. New York, NY : AMACOM, c1987. xi, 308 p. : ill. ; 26 cm. Includes index. ISBN 0-8144-5668-5 LC Card 86-47592 DDC 659.2 19
1. Public relations. 2. Marketing management. I. Title.
HD59 .B35 1987

Barile, Giuseppe. Lavoro femminile, sviluppo tecnologico e segregazione occupazionale /. Milano, Italy , c1984. 458 p. : LC Card 84-190076 DDC 331.4/0945 19
HD6154 .L385 1984 ***NYPL [*QO 87-1143]***

Barkenbus, Jack N. The Nuclear connection . New York , 1985. 295 p. : ISBN 0-88702-204-9 : LC Card 84-26786 DDC 333.79/24 19
HD9698.A2 N77 1985 ***NYPL [JLE 86-1546]***

Barker, Terry. The Cambridge multisectoral dynamic model of the British economy /. Cambridge [Cambridgeshire] , New York , 1988. p. cm. ISBN 0-521-33004-1 LC Card 86-33375 DDC 330.941/00724 19
HC256.6 .C29 1988

Barkin, David.
El fin de la autosuficiencia alimentaria / David Barkin y Blanca Suárez. 1a ed. México, D.F. : Centro de Ecodesarrollo : 1985. 249 p. : ill. ; 23 cm. Bibliography: p. [245]-249. ISBN 968-493-091-7 LC Card 82-230750
1. Agriculture - Economic aspects - Mexico. 2. Agriculture and state - Mexico. 3. Grain trade - Mexico. I. Suárez San Román, Blanca. II. Title.
NYPL [JLE 87-404]

El fin de la autosuficiencia alimentaria / David Barkin y Blanca Suárez. 1a ed. México, D.F. : Océano : Centro de Ecodesarrollo, c1985. 249 p. : ill. ; 23 cm. Bibliography: p. [245]-249. ISBN 968-493-091-7 LC Card 86-209699
1. Agriculture - Economic aspects - Mexico. 2. Food supply - Mexico. 3. Agriculture and state - Mexico. 4. Grain trade - Mexico. I. Suárez San Román, Blanca. II. Title.
HD1792 .B38 1985

Por una nueva política alimentaria /. [México, D.F.] , 1984. 114 p. ; LC Card 85-131176 DDC 338.1/9/72 19
HD9014.M62 P67 1984 ***NYPL [JLC 86-348]***

Barkley, Paul W. The Farm credit crisis policy options and consequences /. Ithaca, N.Y. [1986] ii, 57 p. : LC Card 86-621935 DDC 338.1 s 332.7/1/0973 19
HD1775.N8 C6 no. 86-3 HG2051.U6

Barklow, Irene. From trails to rails : the post offices, stage stops, & wagon roads of Union County, Oregon / by Irene Barklow. Enterprise, Or. : Enchantments Pub. of Oregon, c1987. ix, 300 p. : ill., ports. ; 29 cm. Bibliography: p. 276-278. Includes index. ISBN 0-9618185-2-2 : LC Card 87-15709 DDC 383/.4979571 19
1. Postal service - Oregon - Union County - History. 2. Coaching - Oregon - Union County - History. 3. Railway mail service - Oregon - Union County - History. 4. Union County (Or.) - History. I. Title.
HE6376.A1 O727 1987

Barkus, Philip. How to prepare for the U. S. Postal Service mailhandler/mail processor examination / Philip Barkus. New York : Barron's, c1987. viii, 295 p. : ill. ; 28 cm. Cover title: Barron's how to prepare for the U. S. Postal Service mailhandler/mail processor examination. ISBN 0-8120-2995-X (pbk.) : LC Card 87-14435 DDC 383/.1/076 19
1. Postal service - United States - Examinations, questions, etc. I. Title. II. Title: Barron's how to prepare for the U. S. Postal Service mailhandler/mail processor examination.
HE6499 .B296 1987

Barling, J. Kurt. Economic development in Africa . London , 1987. x, 266 p. ; ISBN 0-86187-909-0 : LC Card 87-15296 DDC 338.98 19
HC800 .E275 1987

Barling, Julian. Behaviour in organisations . Johannesburg , New York , 1986, c1983. 924 p. : ISBN 0-07-450690-0 (pbk.) : LC Card 87-113321 DDC 158.7/0968 19
HD58.7 .B426 1986

Barlow, Raymond E. The glass industry in Sandwich / Raymond E. Barlow, Joan E. Kaiser ; photographs by Forward's Color Productions, Inc., Len Lorette, Hugo G. Poisson ; edited by Lloyd C. Nickerson. 1st ed. Windham, N.H. : Barlow-Kaiser Pub. Co., c1983- v. : ill. ; 31 cm. Vol. 3 published in conjuction with Schiffer Pub., West Chester, Pa. Includes bibliographies and indexes. "Barlow-Kaiser Sandwich glass price guide for pieces in perfect condition, second edition, to be used with volumes 3 and 4 ... ": [24] p., inserted in v. 3. ISBN 0-9610166-0-4 (v. 4) LC Card 82-73582 DDC 338.4/76661/0974492 19
1. Glass trade - Massachusetts - Sandwich - History. 2. Glass manufacture - Massachusetts - Sandwich - History. 3. Glassware - Massachusetts - Sandwich - History. 4. Glassware - Massachusetts - Sandwich - Collectors and collecting. I. Kaiser, Joan E. II. Nickerson, Lloyd C. III. Forward's Color Productions. IV. Title.
HD9623.U46 S263 1983
NYPL [3-MPW+ 84-1016]

Barnard, A. (Alan) Some government financial data, 1850 to 1982 / Alan Barnard. Canberra, Australia : Australian National University, [1986] 47, 2 p. ; 30 cm. (Source papers in economic history, 0813-5398 . no. 13) ISBN 0-86784-850-2 (pbk.) LC Card 86-211320 DDC 336.94 19
1. Australia - Appropriations and expenditures - Statistics - History. 2. Revenue - Australia - Statistics - History. 3. Taxation - Australia - Statistics - History. I. Title. II. Series.
HJ2193.Z7 B37 1986

Barnes, Carolyn. Kenyan smallholdings and the division of labour / Carolyn Barnes and Linda Werner for Central Bureau of Statistics, Ministry of Economic Planning and United States Agency for International Development, Nairobi. Nairobi : Central Bureau of Statistics, Ministry of Economic Planning, Government of Kenya : United States Agency for International Development, 1982. 39 leaves ; 29 cm. Cover title. LC Card 87-156293
1. Farms, Small - Kenya - Statistics. 2. Agricultural laborers - Kenya - Statistics. 3. Sexual division of labor - Kenya - Statistics. I. Werner, Linda H. II. Kenya. Central Bureau of Statistics. III. United States. Agency for International Development. IV. Title.
HD1476.K4 B37 1982

Barnes, Ian. The European Community / Ian Barnes with Jill Preston. London ; New York : Longman, 1988. p. cm. (Key issues in economics and business) Bibliography: p. Includes index. ISBN 0-582-29716-8 LC Card 87-16765 DDC 337.1/42 19
1. European Economic Community. I. Preston, Jill. II. Title. III. Series.
HC241.2 .B293 1988

Barnes, John, 1913- How to learn basic bookkeeping in ten easy lessons / John Barnes. 1st Barnes & Noble ed. New York : Barnes & Noble Books, 1987, c1978. 168 p. : ill. ; 28 cm. Reprint. Originally published: Newly rev., updated ed. Englewood Cliffs, N.J. : Prentice-Hall, 1982, c1978. ISBN 0-06-463721-2 (pbk.) : LC Card 86-45638 DDC 657/.2 19
1. Bookkeeping. 2. Accounting. I. Title.
HF5635 .B258 1987

Barnes, Louis B. Tagiuri, Renato. Organizational climate. Boston, 1968. viii, 246 p. LC Card 68-8418 DDC 301.4
HM131 .T27 ***NYPL [JLD 86-684]***

Barnes, William R. Employment problems and America's cities / William R. Barnes and R. Leo Penne. [Washington, D.C.] : National League of Cities, 1984. xiii, 66, 33 p. ; 28 cm. On cover: "A report on a survey conducted by the National League of Cities."
1. Labor supply - United States - Statistics. 2. Unemployed - United States - Statistics. 3. Economic assistance, Domestic - United States - Statistics. I. Penne, R. Leo. II. National League of Cities. III. Title.
NYPL [JLF 86-1]

Barnett, Correlli. The pride and the fall : the dream and illusion of Britain as a great nation / Correlli Barnett.1st American ed. New York : Free Press, 1987, c1986. xii, 359 p. ; 25 cm. Bibliography: p. [343]-354. Includes index. ISBN 0-02-901851-X LC Card 86-25701 DDC 330.941/0854 19
1. World War, 1939-1945 - Economic aspects - Great Britain. 2. Great Britain - Economic conditions - 1918-1945. 3. Great Britain - Politics and government - 1936-1945. 4. Great Britain - Industries - History - 20th century. 5. Education - Great Britain - History - 20th

century. I. Title.
HC256.4 .B28 1987

Barnett, George A. Handbook of organizational communication /. Norwood, N.J. , c1988. 502 p. : ISBN 0-89391-446-0 LC Card 87-19380 DDC 658.4/5 19
HD30.3 .H357 1988

Barnett, Ned B. The state of the art in hospital advertising, 1987 / by Ned B. Barnett. Alexandria, VA : Capitol Publications, c1987. iii, 56 p. ; 26 cm. "Health care competition week." ISBN 0-937925-33-0 (pbk.) LC Card 87-61160 DDC 659.1/93621 19
1. Advertising - Hospitals. I. Title.
HF6161.H7 B37 1987

Barney, Gerald O. Global 2000 Study (United States) The global 2000 report to the President--entering the twenty-first century . Washington, D.C. , 1980-1981. 3 v. : LC Card 80-602859 DDC 333.7
HC79.E5 G59 1980b NYPL [JLF 87-206]

Barngol′ts, S. B. (Sarra Bentsionovna) Ėkonomicheskiĭ analiz khoziaĭstvennoĭ deiatel′nosti predpriiatiĭ i ob″edineniĭ /. Moskva , 1986. 406 p. : LC Card 86-227621
HC340.A8 E417 1986

Barnouin, Barbara. The European labour movement and European integration / by Barbara Barnouin. London ; Wolfeboro, N.H. : F. Pinter, 1986. viii, 172 p. ; 24 cm. "A publication of the Graduate Institute of International Studies, Geneva." Includes index. Bibliography: p. [147]-166. ISBN 0-86187-650-4 : LC Card 86-5901 DDC 331.88/091 19
1. European Trade Union Confederation - History. 2. Trade-unions - European Economic Community countries - Political activity. 3. International labor activities. 4. European integration. I. Title.
HD8372.E86 B37 1986
NYPL [JLE 86-4058]

Baró, Albert Pérez. see **Pérez Baró, Albert.**

Barone, Giuseppe, 1947- Mezzogiorno e modernizzazione : elettricità, irrigazione e bonifica nell'Italia contemporanea / Giuseppe Barone. Torino : G. Einaudi, c1986. xii, 408 p. ; 22 cm. (Biblioteca di cultura storica. 160) Includes bibliographical references and index. ISBN 88-06-59238-6 : LC Card 86-219130
1. Italy, Southern - Economic conditions - 1945-. 2. Rural electrification - Italy, Southern. 3. Irrigation - Italy, Southern. 4. Reclamation of land - Italy, Southern. I. Title.
HC307.S69 B37 1986

Barons of labor . Kazin, Michael, 1948- Urbana , c1987. xiv, 319 p., [14] p. of plates : ISBN 0-252-01345-X (alk. paper) LC Card 86-6967 DDC 331.88/124/0979461 19
HD6515.B9 S45 1987 NYPL [JLE 87-1053]

Baross, Jenő. A kereskedelmi hitel és a váltó gyakorlata / írták, Baross Jenő, Kovács Mihályné, Vízváry Tibor. Budapest : Kereskedelmi Szervezési Intézet, 1985. 123 p. ; 24 cm. "Készült a Kereskedelmi Szervezési Intézet és a STUDIUM Szervezésmódszertani Gazdasági Társaság együttműködésében." "Kézirat lezárva: 1985. július 31"--T.p. verso. "Kereskedelmi hitel és a váltó alkalmazásához kapcsolódó jogszabályok": p. 86-123. Includes index. LC Card 86-228454
1. Commercial credit - Hungary. 2. Negotiable instruments - Hungary. 3. Commercial credit. 4. Negotiable instruments. I. Kovács, Mihályné. II. Vízváry, Tibor. III. Kereskedelmi Szervezési Intézet (Budapest, Hungary). IV. STUDIUM Szervezésmódszertani Gazdasági Társaság (Budapest, Hungary). V. Title.
HG3754.5.H9 B37 1985

Baroth, Hans Dieter, 1937- Das Gras wuchs ja umsonst / Hans Dieter Baroth. Köln : Kiepenheuer & Witsch, c1983. 232 p. ; 20 cm. ISBN 3-462-01577-X LC Card 83-227195
1. Labor and laboring classes - Germany (West) - Ruhr (Region) - History - 20th century. 2. Ruhr (Germany : Region) - Economic conditions. I. Title.
HD8459.R82 B37 1983

Barr, Andrew M. How to buy real estate with other people's money and how to assemble a real estate investment portfolio : course manual & official text / A.M. Barr.Rev. [Arlington, Va.] : Barr School of Real Estate, c1978, 1984 printing. ix, 194 p. : ill. ; 23 cm. LC Card 86-224399 DDC 332.63/24 19
1. Real estate investment. I. Title.
HD1382.5 .B37 1984

Barr Films.
Customer service [motion picture] . Pasadena, CA , 1987. 1 film reel (24 min.) : LC Card 87-706736 DDC 658.8 11
HF5415.5

Customer service [videorecording] . Pasadena, CA , 1987. 1 videocassette (24 min.) : LC Card 87-706737 DDC 658.8 11
HF5415.5

Management--emphasize your strengths [motion picture] /. Pasadena, CA , 1985, c1986. 1 film reel (22 min.) : LC Card 86-707743 DDC 658.4 11
HD38.2

Management--emphasize your strengths [videorecording] /. Pasadena, CA , 1985, c1986. 1 videocassette (22 min.) : LC Card 86-707745 DDC 658.4 11
HD38.2

Barr, Lorna R. Land of the Trust islands : a review of subdivision, housing, and ownership for the major islands / prepared by Lorna R. Barr. [Victoria, B.C.] : Ministry of Municipal Affairs and Housing, [1978] 36 p. : ill. ; 29 cm. "April 1978." "Islands Trust"--Cover. LC Card 83-226106 DDC 333.3/0996/5 19
1. Land use - Pacific Islands (Trust Territory) - Statistics. 2. Housing - Pacific Islands (Trust Territory) - Statistics. 3. Home ownership - Pacific Islands (Trust Territory) - Statistics. 4. Land subdivision - Pacific Islands (Trust Territory) - Statistics. I. British Columbia. Islands Trust. II. Title.
HD1121.Z63 B37 1978

Barr, Nicholas. The economics of the welfare state / Nicholas Barr. Stanford, Calif. : Stanford University Press, 1987. xiv, 475 p. : ill. ; 24 cm. Bibliography: p. 432-459. Includes indexes. ISBN 0-8047-1427-4 LC Card 87-60997 DDC 338.941 19
1. Welfare economics. 2. Great Britain - Economic policy - 1945-. I. Title.
HB846 .B37 1987

Barrādah, Muḥammad. Les techniques de banque et de crédit au Maroc / Berrada Mohamed Azzedine. 2ème éd., ref. et mise à jour. Casablanca : Société d'édition et de composition euro-africaine, 1985. 590 p. : ill., forms ; 24 cm. Bibliography: p. 586-589. Includes index. LC Card 86-967115
1. Banks and banking - Morocco. 2. Financial institutions - Morocco. I. Title.
HG3382.A6 B37 1985

Barral, Pierre. Mélanges Robert Laurent . Montpellier , 1980. xxi, 296 p. : LC Card 83-151672
HC273 .M43 1980

Barrancabermeja . Yunis, José. Bogotá , 1986. 102 p. : ISBN 958-9096-03-4 LC Card 87-400984 DDC 331.7/6223382/0986125 19
HD8310.B372 Y86 1986

Barreiro, José Carlos. Campesinato e capitalismo / José Carlos Barreiro. Campinas-SP : Editora da UNICAMP, [1986] 128 p. ; 23 cm. (Teses) Originally presented as the author's thesis (doctoral)--Universidade Estadual de Campinas, 1980. Bibliography: p. 121-128. LC Card 86-229683
1. Peasantry - Brazil - History. 2. Capitalism - Brazil - History. 3. Coffee trade - Brazil - São Paulo (State) - History. I. Series: Teses (Editora da UNICAMP). II. Title.
HD1531.B7 B37 1986

Barrenechea, Carles. see **Barrenechea Lercari, Carlos.**

Barrenechea Lercari, Carlos. Cusco : agro, política gubernamental y alternativa campesina / Carlos Barrenechea Lercari. Cusco [Peru : s.n.], 1986. 77 p. ; 21 cm. LC Card 87-400243 DDC 338.1/88537 19
1. Agriculture and state - Peru - Cuzco (Dept.). 2. Peasantry - Peru - Cuzco (Dept.). I. Title.
HD1905.C87 B37 1986

Barrera, Manuel.
Sindicatos y estado en el Chile actual : la negociación colectiva como instrumento de participación popular / Manuel Barrera, Helia Henriquez, Teresita Selamé ; introducción de Alain Touraine. Geneva, Switzerland : United Nations Research Institute for Social Development ; Santiago, Chile : Centro de Estudios Sociales, c1985. v, 196 p. : ill. ; 21 cm. (Informe . no. 84.1) Includes bibliographical references. LC Card 87-118607
1. Trade-unions - Chile. 2. Labor policy - Chile. I. Henríquez, Helia. II. Selamé, Teresita. III. Series: Report / United Nations Research Institute for Social Development , no. 84.1. IV. Title.
HD6617 .B27 1985

Trade unions and the state in the present day Chile : collective bargaining as an instrument of popular participation / Manuel Barrera, Helia Henríquez, Teresita Selamé ; introduction by Alain Touraine. Geneva, Switzerland : United Nations Research Institute for Social Development ; Santiago, Chile : Centro de Estudios Sociales, 1986. xx, 154 p. : ill. ; 21 cm. (Report / United Nations Research Institute for Social Development . no. 84.1) Includes bibliographical references. LC Card 87-128364 DDC 331.89/0983 19
1. Collective bargaining - Chile. 2. Trade-unions - Government policy - Chile. 3. Labor policy - Chile. I. Henríquez, Helia. II. Selamé, Teresita. III. Series. IV. Series: Report / United Nations Research Institute for Social Development , no. 84.1. V. Title.
HD6617 .B273 1986

Barrera, Rick. Alessandra, Anthony J. Non-manipulative selling /. New York , c1987. x, 262 p. : ISBN 0-13-623307-4 (pbk.) : LC Card 86-43174 DDC 658.8/5 19
HF5438.25 .A43 1987

Barrère, Alain. The Foundations of Keynesian analysis . New York , 1988. xlvi, 267 p. ; ISBN 0-312-00985-2 : LC Card 87-13048 DDC 330.15/6 19
HB99.7 .F68 1988

Barrère, Bernard. Ahonzo, Etienne. Population de la Côte d'Ivoire . Abidjan , 1984. ix, 324 p. : LC Card 86-110796 DDC 304.6/09666/8 19
HB3666.A3 A46 1984 NYPL [JLF 86-1466]

Barrese, Antonio. L'Affiliazione commerciale . Milano , 1986. 100 p. : NYPL [JLD 87-531]

Barrett, C. Richard. Ethik und Wirtschaftswissenschaft /. Berlin , c1985. 276 p. : ISBN 3-428-05910-7 LC Card 86-132826
HB72 .E79 1985

Barrett, Colin.
The practical handbook of computerization for distribution managers / Colin Barrett. 1st ed. Washington : Traffic Service Corp., c1987. xvi, 317 p. ; 24 cm. Includes index. ISBN 0-87408-040-1 LC Card 86-51299 DDC 658.7/8/0285 19
1. Physical distribution of goods - Management - Data processing. 2. Freight and freightage - Management - Data processing. I. Title.
HF5415.7 .B36 1987

Practical handbook of transportation contracting and rate negotiations / Colin Barrett. 1st ed. Washington : Traffic Service Corp., c1987. ix, 269 p. ; 24 cm. Includes bibliographical references and index. ISBN 0-87408-037-1 LC Card 86-50988 DDC 380.5/24/068 19
1. Freight and freightage - United States. 2. Shipment of goods - United States. 3. Carriers - United States. I. Title.
HE199.U5 B37 1987

Barrett, Elinore M. The Mexican colonial copper industry / Elinore M. Barrett. 1st ed. Albuquerque : University of New Mexico Press, c1987. xi, 143 p. : maps ; 24 cm. Bibliography: p. 129-133. Includes index. ISBN 0-8263-0929-1 LC Card 86-24991 DDC 338.2/743/0972 19
1. Copper industry and trade - Mexico - History. 2. Copper industry and trade - New Spain - History. 3. Tin industry - Mexico - History. 4. Mexico - History - Spanish colony, 1540-1810. I. Title.
HD9539.C7 M417 1987

Barrett, G. Vincent. How to conduct and analyze real estate market and feasibility studies / G. Vincent Barrett, John P. Blair. 2nd ed. New York : Van Nostrand Reinhold, c1988. xvii, 366 p. : ill. ; 24 cm. Bibliography: p. 353-358. Includes index. ISBN 0-442-21220-8 : LC Card 87-18861 DDC 332.63/24 19
1. Real estate development. 2. Feasibility studies. I. Blair, John P., 1947-. II. Title.
HD1390 .B37 1988

Barrett, Hazel R., 1955- The marketing of foodstuffs in the Gambia, 1400-1980 : a

geographical analysis / by Hazel R. Barrett. Aldershot, Hants., England ; Brookfield, Vt., U. S.A. : Gower, 1988, c1987. p. cm. Bibliography: p. ISBN 0-566-05487-6 LC Card 87-23063 DDC 381/.41/096651 19
1. Farm produce - Gambia - Marketing - History. 2. Produce trade - Gambia - History. I. Title.
HD9017.G262 B37 1988

Barrett, John (John J.) The industrial work model : a guide for developing transitional and supported employment / by John Barrett and Don Lavin. Menomonie, Wis. : Materials Development Center, Stout Vocational Rehabilitation Institute, School of Education and Human Services, University of Wisconsin-Stout, c1987. v, 143 p. : ill. ; 28 cm. Bibliography: p. 139-143. ISBN 0-916671-73-9 (pbk.) LC Card 87-403218 DDC 362.0425 19
1. Handicapped - Employment - United States. 2. Vocational Rehabilitation - United States. 3. Handicapped - Employment - Government policy - United States. 4. n-us. I. Lavin, Don. II. Stout Vocational Rehabilitation Institute. Materials Development Center. III. Title.
HD7256.U5 B37 1987

Barrett, Sean D. Flying high : airline prices and European regulation / by Sean D. Barrett. Aldershot ; Brookfield, USA : Avebury, c1987. 96 p. ; 30 cm. "Published in association with the Adam Smith Institute." Bibliography: p. 93-96. ISBN 0-566-05541-4 (pbk.) : LC Card 87-11992 DDC 387.7/1 19
1. Airlines - Europe - Rates. 2. Aeronautics, Commercial - Europe - Deregulation. I. Title.
HE9783.3.E85 B37 1987

Barrie, Robert W. Congress and the Executive : the making of the United States foreign trade policy, 1789-1968 / Robert W. Barrie. New York : Garland, 1987. 347 p. ; 23 cm. (Foreign economic policy of the United States) Originally presented as the author's thesis (Ph. D.)--University of Minnesota, 1968. Bibliography: p. [340]-347. ISBN 0-8240-8071-8 (alk. paper) LC Card 87-23814 DDC 382/.3/0973 19
1. United States - Commercial policy - History. 2. Separation of powers - United States - History. I. Title. II. Series.
HF1455 .B317 1987

Barrière, Antoine. Michelin : vu de l'intérieur : ce que j'ai vécu de 1950 à 1961 : témoignage de vie ouvrière / Antoine Barrière.2. éd. Nonette : Editions Créer, 1983. 289 p. ; 20 cm. (Forum Massif Central, 0182-3760 . v. no 2) ISBN 2-902894-20-1
1. Pneu Michelin (Firm). 2. Tire industry workers - France - Clermont-Ferrand. 3. Labor disputes - France - Clermont-Ferrand. I. Title.
NYPL [JLD 86-4467]

BARRIERS TO ENTRY (INDUSTRIAL ORGANIZATION)
Holler, Manfred Joseph, 1946- Trading markets and entry costs /. Aarhus, Denmark [1986] 15 p. ; LC Card 86-219580 DDC 382.1 19
HD2756.5 .H64 1986

Weiss, Leonard W. The extent and permanence of market dominance /. Berlin [1984] 30, 7 p. ; LC Card 85-183107 DDC 338.8/2 19
HD2757.3 .W45 1984

Barrig, Maruja. Mujer, trabajo y empleo /. Lima, Perú [1985] 294 p. ; LC Card 86-121871 DDC 331.4/0985 19
HD6131 .M85 1985 ***NYPL [JLD 87-492]***

Barrmeyer, Martin-Christian. Die Angebotsplanung bei Submission / Martin-Christian Barrmeyer. Münster : Lit, [1982?] xii, 198 p. : 22 ill. ; 21 cm. (Betriebswirtschaftliche Schriftenreihe . Bd. 1) Title on half title: Angebotsplanung. Bibliography: p. 190-198. ISBN 3-88660-081-5 : LC Card 83-227153
1. Contracts, Letting of. 2. Contracts, Letting of - Econometric models. 3. Arbitration agreements, Commercial. I. Title. II. Title: Angebotsplanung. III. Series.
HD2365 .B36 1982

Barro, Robert J.
Macroeconomics / Robert J. Barro. 2nd ed. New York : Wiley, c1987. xiv, 608 p. : ill. (some col.) ; 25 cm. Bibliography: p. 571-582. Includes indexes. ISBN 0-471-85125-6 LC Card 86-24667 DDC 339 19
1. Macroeconomics. I. Title.
HB172.5 .B36 1987

Monetary policy and uncertainty . Baden-Baden , 1986. 262 p. : ISBN 3-7890-1257-2 (pbk.) LC Card 86-225786 DDC 332.4/0724 19
HG230.3 .M655 1986

Barro y Segura, Antonio. Rebuttal and commentaries to the third report on the progress of land reform in Cuba as rendered by the United Nations in 1962. Miami, Fla. : Association for the Reconstruction of the Cuban Economy, 1963. 17 p. ; 21 cm. Includes bibliographical references. LC Card 86-181697
1. Land reform - Cuba. I. Association for the Reconstruction of the Cuban Economy. II. Title.
HD1333.C9 B37 1963

Barrón Coral, Marcial. Perú : "historia de un saqueo" / Marcial Barrón C. [Lima? : s.n.], 1983 ([Lima] : General S.R.L.) 191 p. ; 21 cm. Bibliography: p. 189-191. LC Card 84-253120
1. Peru - Economic conditions. 2. Spain - Colonies - America - Economic conditions. 3. Investments, American - Peru - History. I. Title.
HC227 .B3365 1983

Barron, W. J. Boulware, Lemuel Richetts, 1895- What to do about communism in unions . [Schenectady, N.Y.?] [1952?] 62 p. ;
NYPL [JLD 86-247]

Barron's bilingual business guides.
Strutz, Henry. Talking business in German . Woodbury, N.Y. , c1987. iv, 256 p. : ISBN 0-8120-3747-2 (pbk.) LC Card 86-22360 DDC 650/.03/31 19
HF1002 .S79 1987

Barron's business guides.
Friedman, Jack P. Dictionary of business terms /. New York , c1987. vi, 650 p. ; ISBN 0-8120-3775-8 (pbk.) : LC Card 87-12640 DDC 650/.03/21 19
HF1001 .F78 1987

Imber, Jane. Dictionary of advertising and direct mail terms /. New York , c1987. xi, 514 p. : ISBN 0-8120-3765-0 (pbk.) : LC Card 87-1197 DDC 659.1/03/21 19
HF5803 .I46 1987

Rubin, Harvey W. Dictionary of insurance terms /. New York , c1987. ix, 371 p. ; ISBN 0-8120-3772-3 (pbk.) : LC Card 87-12549 DDC 368/.003/21 19
HG8025 .R83 1987

Barron's business review series.
Montana, Patrick J. Management /. New York , c1987. xi, 466 p. : ISBN 0-8120-3559-3 (pbk.) : LC Card 87-1376 DDC 658 19
HD31 .M618 1987

Barron's Educational Series, inc.
Downes, John. Barron's finance and investment handbook /. Woodbury, N.Y. , c1986. xiv, 994 p. : ISBN 0-8120-5729-5 : LC Card 86-10906 DDC 332.6/78 19
HG173 .D65 1986
NYPL [*R-Econ. 86-5261]

Kornbluh, Elaine H. Barron's regents exams and answers. Woodbury, N.Y. , c1987. 318 p. in various pagings ; ISBN 0-8120-3185-7 (pbk.) : LC Card 87-403397 DDC 657/2/076 19
HF5661 .N4 1987

Barron's finance and investment handbook /. Downes, John. Woodbury, N.Y. , c1986. xiv, 994 p. : ISBN 0-8120-5729-5 : LC Card 86-10906 DDC 332.6/78 19
HG173 .D65 1986
NYPL [*R-Econ. 86-5261]

Barron's financial guides.
Friedman, Jack P. Adjustable rate mortgages /. New York , c1987. viii, 293 p. ; ISBN 0-8120-3764-2 (soft) : LC Card 86-28852 DDC 332.8/2 19
HG1634 .F75 1987

Barron's financial tables for better money management.
Solomon, Stephen S. Canadian mortgage payments /. New York , c1987. 302 p. ; ISBN 0-8120-3939-4 (pbk.) LC Card 87-13073 DDC 332.8/0212 19
HG1634 .S654 1987

Barron's how to prepare for the certified public accountant examination, CPA /. Person, Samuel. New York , c1987. vi, 537 p. ; ISBN 0-8120-3880-0 (pbk.) : LC Card 87-17914 DDC 657/.076 19
HF5661 .P48 1987

Barron's how to prepare for the U. S. Postal Service mailhandler/mail processor examination. Barkus, Philip. How to prepare for the U. S. Postal Service mailhandler/mail processor examination /. New York , c1987. viii, 295 p. : ISBN 0-8120-2995-X (pbk.) : LC Card 87-14435 DDC 383/.1/076 19
HE6499 .B296 1987

Barron's regents exams and answers. Kornbluh, Elaine H. Woodbury, N.Y. , c1987. 318 p. in various pagings ; ISBN 0-8120-3185-7 (pbk.) : LC Card 87-403397 DDC 657/2/076 19
HF5661 .N4 1987

Barros, Afonso de. Do latifundismo à reforma agrária : o caso de uma freguesia do Baixo Alentejo / Afonso de Barros. Oeiras [Portugal] : Fundação Calouste Gulbenkian, Instituto Gulbenkian de Ciência, Centro de Estudos de Economia Agrária, 1986. 636 p. : ill. ; 24 cm. (Estudos / Instituto Gulbenkian de Ciência, Centro de Estudos de Economia Agraria) Includes bibliographies. LC Card 87-404938 DDC 333.3/1/46955 19
1. Land reform - Portugal - Baixo Alentejo - Case studies. 2. Latifundio - Portugal - Baixo Alentejo - Case studies. 3. Baixo Alentejo (Portugal) - Economic conditions - Case studies. 4. Baixo Alentejo (Portugal) - Rural conditions - Case studies. I. Series: Estudos / Instituto Gulbenkian de Ciência, Centro de Estudos de Economia Agraria. II. Title.
HD1333.P82 B353 1986

Barros, Carlos. Dende Galicia, Marx . Sada, A Coruña [1985?] 258 p. : ISBN 84-7492-241-0 LC Card 86-215077
HB97.5 .D413 1985

Barros, Raimundo. El Perú frente al capital extranjero . Lima, Perú [1985] xl, 399 p. : LC Card 86-109611 DDC 332.6/73/0985 19
HG5392 .P47 1985 ***NYPL [JLD 87-384]***

Barroso, Aloísio. Alagoas (Brazil). Secretaria da Fazenda. Posicionamento das finanças de Alagoas na atual crise /. [Maceió] , 1983. 97 p. : LC Card 86-201070
HJ929.A52 A42 1983

Barroso Filho, João. Alagoas (Brazil). Secretaria da Fazenda. Posicionamento das finanças de Alagoas na atual crise /. [Maceió] , 1983. 97 p. : LC Card 86-201070
HJ929.A52 A42 1983

Barroso Rodríguez, Antonio. Estudio de las comarcas Campiña Alta y Penibética de Córdoba : directrices básicas para su ordenación territorial / Antonio Barroso Rodríguez. Córdoba : Excma. Diputación Provincial de Córdoba, Servicio de Publicaciones, 1984. 268 p. : ill. (some col.) ; 23 cm. (Estudios cordobeses . 34) One folded map laid in. Bibliography: p. [263]-268. ISBN 84-505-0166-0 LC Card 85-182568
1. Córdoba (Spain : Province) - Economic conditions. I. Title. II. Series.
HC387.C58 B37 1984

Barroterán! . Arenal, Sandra. [Mexico City?] , c1984. 116 p. ; ISBN 968-495-016-0 LC Card 85-195552
HD8039.M62 M63 1984

Barrull Pelegrí, Jaume, 1947- Les comarques de Lleida durant la segona república, 1930-1936 / Jaume Barrull Pelegrí ; presentació, Emili Giralt i Raventós. 1a ed. Barcelona : L'Avenç, 1986. 503 p. : ill. ; 22 cm. (Col·lecció Clio . 5) Bibliography: p. 479-494. ISBN 84-85905-23-7 LC Card 86-203986
1. Lérida (Spain) - Economic conditions. 2. Lérida (Spain) - Politics and government. 3. Lérida (Spain) - Social conditions. I. Title. II. Series.
HC388.L4 B37 1986

Barry, Bryan W. Strategic planning workbook for nonprofit organizations / Bryan W. Barry. St. Paul, MN : Amherst H. Wilder Foundation, c1986. 72 p., [8] leaves of plates : ill. ; 28 cm. Bibliography: p. 52. ISBN 0-940069-00-8 (pbk.) LC Card 87-153976 DDC 658.4/012 19
1. Corporations, Nonprofit - Planning. 2. Strategic planning. I. Amherst H. Wilder Foundation. II. Title.
HD62.6 .B37 1986

Barry, Marion, 1936- Meyers, Edward M. Rebuilding America's cities . Cambridge, Mass. , c1986. xxi, 290 p. : ISBN 0-88730-051-0

LC Card 85-30780 DDC 307.3/4/0973 19
HT175 .U59 1986 ***NYPL [JLE 86-2874]***

Barry, Tom, 1950-
Roots of rebellion : land & hunger in Central America / Tom Barry.1st ed. Boston : South End Press, c1987. xii, 220 p. : ill. ; 23 cm. Bibliography: p. 179-199. Includes index. ISBN 0-89608-288-1 : LC Card 87-4519 DDC 338.1/9/728 19
1. Food supply - Central America. 2. Land tenure - Central America. 3. Food industry and trade - Central America. 4. Land reform - Central America. 5. Peasant uprisings - Central America. I. Title.
HD9014.C462 B37 1987

The soft war : the uses and abuses of U. S. economic aid in Central America / by Tom Barry and Deb Preusch.1st ed. New York : Grove Press, 1988. xv, 304 p. ; 22 cm. Bibliography: p. 263-288. Includes index. ISBN 0-8021-0003-1 LC Card 87-13238 DDC 338.91/73/0728 19
1. Economic assistance, American - Central America. 2. United States - Foreign relations - Central America. 3. Central America - Foreign relations - United States. I. Preusch, Deb. II. Title.
HC141 .B375 1988

BARS (DRINKING ESTABLISHMENTS) see **HOTELS, TAVERNS, ETC.**

Barschel, Uwe. Halbzeitbilanz '85 : Regierungserklärung vor dem Schleswig-Holsteinischen Landtag, 17. September 1985 / Uwe Barschel. Kiel : Presse- und Informationsstelle der Landesregierung Schleswig-Holstein, [1985] 1 v. (various pagings) : ill. ; 21 cm. LC Card 86-211699
1. Schleswig-Holstein (Germany) - Economic conditions. 2. Schleswig-Holstein (Germany) - Economic policy. I. Schleswig-Holstein (Germany). Landtag. II. Schleswig-Holstein (Germany). Presse- und Informationsstelle der Landesregierung. III. Title.
HC287.S35 B37 1985

Barta, Imre. A beruházások döntéselőkészítése / Barta Imre. Budapest : Akadémiai Kiadó, 1986. 185, [1] p. : ill. ; 24 cm. (A Szocialista vállalat . 13) Bibliography: p. 174-[186]. ISBN 963-05-4182-3 : LC Card 87-408029
1. Capital investments - Decision-making. I. Title. II. Series.
HG4028.C4 B335 1986

Bartel, Henry. Keller, Gerald. Statistics for management and economics . Belmont, Calif. , c1988. xix, 987 p. : ISBN 0-534-08622-5 LC Card 87-19845 DDC 658.4/033 19
HD30.215 .K45 1988

Bartelmus, Peter. Environment and development / Peter Bartelmus. Boston : Allen & Unwin, 1986. xxii, 96 p. ; 23 cm. Includes index. Bibliography: p. [82]-91. ISBN 0-04-333026-6 (alk. paper) LC Card 85-22838 DDC 333.7/09172/4 19
1. Environmental policy - Developing countries. 2. Developing countries - Economic policy. I. Title.
HC59.72.E5 B37 1986 ***NYPL [JLD 86-2378]***

Bartels, Christoph. Schieferdörfer : Dachschieferbergbau im Linksrheingebiet vom Ende des Feudalzeitalters bis zur Weltwirtschaftskrise (1790-1929) / Christoph Bartels. Pfaffenweiler : Centaurus-Verlagsgesellschaft, 1986. xiv, 370 p. : ill. ; 21 cm. (Reihe Geschichtswissenschaft, 0177-2767 . Bd. 7) Originally presented as the author's thesis (doctoral)--Universität Oldenburg, 1985. Bibliography: p. 353-370. ISBN 3-89085-124-X LC Card 87-134379 DDC 338.943/43 19
1. Slate industry - Germany (West) - Rhineland - History. 2. Rhineland (Germany) - Economic conditions. I. Title. II. Series.
HD9621.G33 R463 1986

Bartels, Robert, 1913- The history of marketing thought / by Robert Bartels. 3rd ed. Columbus, Ohio : Publishing Horizons, c1988. p. cm. Includes index. ISBN 0-942280-44-X : LC Card 87-20702 DDC 658.8/009 19
1. Marketing - History. I. Title.
HF5415 .B36 1988

Bartels, Sibylle, 1955- Entwicklung und Beurteilung von Aggregationsstrategien für lineare Entscheidungsmodelle / Sibylle Bartels. Frankfurt am Main ; New York : P. Lang, c1986. xv, 265 p. : ill. ; 21 cm. (Europäische Hochschulschriften. Reihe V, Volks- und Betriebswirtschaft, 0531-7339 . Bd. 686 = vol. 686 = vol. 686) Originally presented as the author's thesis (doctoral)--Technische Universität Berlin, 1985. Bibliography: p. 255-265. ISBN 3-8204-9190-2 LC Card 86-146466
1. Decision-making - Mathematical models. I. Series: Europäische Hochschulschriften. Reihe V, Volks- und Betriebswirtschaft , Bd. 686. II. Title.
HD30.25 .B365 1986

Barth, James R. International debt : conflict and resolution [microform] / James R. Barth and Joseph Pelzman. Fairfax, Va. : aDept. of Economics, George Mason University, 1984. 36 p. ; 22 cm. "... the last in series of three studies on U. S. bank lending to LDCs and Eastern bloc nations." Includes bibliographical references. Microfilm. New York : New York Public Library, 1985. 1 microfilm reel ; 35 mm. (MN *ZZ-24,952)
1. International Monetary Fund. 2. Debts, External - Developing countries. 3. Debts, External - Europe, Eastern. 4. Loans, Foreign - Developing countries. 5. Loans, Foreign - Europe, Eastern. I. Pelzman, Joseph. II. George Mason University. Dept. of Economics. III. Title. ***NYPL [*ZT-1554 no.21]***

Barth, Johannes, 1891- Als deutscher Kaufmann in Fernost : Bremen, Tsingtau, Tōkyō, 1891-1981 / von Johannes Barth. Berlin : E. Schmidt, c1984. 206 p. : 1 port. ; 23 cm. "Eine Veröffentlichung der Deutschen Gesellschaft für Natur- und Völkerkunde Ostasiens (OAG), Tōkyō"--1st. prelim. p. ISBN 3-503-02366-6 LC Card 84-143117
1. Barth, Johannes, 1981-. 2. Businessmen - Germany - Bremen - Biography. 3. Businessmen - Japan - Biography. 4. Germany - Commerce - Japan - History. 5. Japan - Commerce - Germany - History. 6. China - Social life and customs - 1912-1949. 7. Japan - Social life and customs - 1912-1945. I. Deutsche Gesellschaft für Natur- und Völkerkunde Ostasiens. II. Title.
HC289.B7 B373 1984

BARTH, JOHANNES, 1981-
Barth, Johannes, 1891- Als deutscher Kaufmann in Fernost . Berlin , c1984. 206 p. : ISBN 3-503-02366-6 LC Card 84-143117
HC289.B7 B373 1984

Barth, Kuno. Unternehmung und Steuer . Wiesbaden , c1983. 395 p. ; ISBN 3-409-50005-7 LC Card 83-161883
HD2753.G3 U57 1983

Barth, Peter S., 1937- The tragedy of black lung : federal compensation for occupational disease / Peter S. Barth. Kalamazoo, MI : W.E. Upjohn Institute for Employment Research, 1987. xi, 292 p. ; 23 cm. Includes bibliographies and index. ISBN 0-88099-044-9 (pbk.) LC Card 87-8332 DDC 368.4/1 19
1. Lungs - Dust diseases - Government policy - United States. 2. Lungs - Dust diseases - Law and legislation - United States. 3. Workers' compensation - United States. I. W.E. Upjohn Institute for Employment Research. II. Title.
HD7264 .B37 1987

Barthel, Diane L., 1949- Putting on appearances : gender and advertising / Diane Barthel. Philadelphia : Temple University Press, 1988. p. cm. (Women in the political economy) Bibliography: p. Includes index. ISBN 0-87722-528-1 (alk. paper) : LC Card 87-20010 DDC 659.1/042 19
1. Sex role in advertising - United States. 2. Visual communication - United States - Psychological aspects. 3. Imagery (Psychology). I. Title. II. Series.
HF5827 .B37 1988

Barthélemy, Denis. La Propriété foncière /. Paris , c1984. vii, 252 p. : ISBN 2-7178-0783-7 LC Card 84-249621
HD643 .N49 1984

Barthold, Wolfgang Schneider- see **Schneider-Barthold, Wolfgang.**

Bartholmai, Bernd. Gesamtwirtschaftliche und strukturelle Auswirkungen von Veränderungen der Struktur des öffentlichen Sektors . Berlin , 1984. x, 266 p. : ISBN 3-428-05739-2 LC Card 86-138980
HC281 .B33 Heft 81 HJ1120

Bartimo, Jim, 1956- Rozells, Gia L. Making dollars and cents with dollars and sense /. Greensboro, N.C. , c1987. ix, 207 p. : ISBN 0-87455-101-3 (pbk.) : LC Card 87-160661 DDC 332.024/0028/55369 19
HG179 .R74 1987

Bartlett, Hale C. Cases in strategic management for business / Hale C. Bartlett. Chicago : Dryden Press, c1988. xiii, 784 p. : ill. ; 23 cm. (The Dryden Press series in management) Includes bibliographies and indexes. ISBN 0-03-007183-6 (pbk.) LC Card 87-20208 DDC 658.4/012 19
1. Corporate planning - Case studies. 2. Strategic planning - Case studies. 3. Industrial management - Case studies. I. Title.
HD30.28 .B369 1988

Bartókné Erdődi, Ibolya. Munkaügy a belkereskedelemben /. [Budapest] , 1986. 272 p. ; ISBN 963-01-7513-4 : LC Card 87-148137
HF5549.2.H85 M86 1986

Barton /. Oxley, Alan. Glossop, Derbyshire , c1983- v. <1 > : ISBN 0-903839-64-4 (v. 1) LC Card 86-219518 DDC 388.3/22/09425 19
HE5663.Z7 B376 1983

Barton, Taylor J. The illustrated Symphony (release 1.2) book / Taylor J. Barton & Scott Tucker. Dallas : Wordware Pub., c1987. vii, 310 p. : ill. ; 24 cm. Includes index. ISBN 0-915381-88-5 (pbk.) LC Card 87-6135 DDC 005.36/9 19
1. Symphony (Computer program). 2. Business - Data processing. I. Tucker, Scott. II. Title.
HF5548.4.S95 B385 1987

Barton, Thomas Frank, 1905- Phūmisāt sētthakit kh ph [Bangkok : Thōmat Fræng Bātan], 2500 [1957] 2, 5, 392 p. : ill., maps ; 27 cm. On the economic geography of Thailand; includes statistical information on national resources, communication, trade, etc. Bibliography: p. [367]-372. LC Card 83-921251
1. Thailand - Economic conditions. I. Sawāt Sēnānarong. II. Title.
HC445 .B36 1957

BARTON, THOMAS HENRY, 1866-1946.
Oxley, Alan. Barton /. Glossop, Derbyshire , c1983- v. <1 > : ISBN 0-903839-64-4 (v. 1) LC Card 86-219518 DDC 388.3/22/09425 19
HE5663.Z7 B376 1983

BARTON TRANSPORT - HISTORY.
Oxley, Alan. Barton /. Glossop, Derbyshire , c1983- v. <1 > : ISBN 0-903839-64-4 (v. 1) LC Card 86-219518 DDC 388.3/22/09425 19
HE5663.Z7 B376 1983

Bartosik, Zygmunt. Wybrane problemy ekonomiki przemysłu /. Wrocław , 1985. 110 p. ; LC Card 86-155957
HB9 .B7522 nr. 304 HD70.P6

Bartov, Vladimir Fotievich.
Aktual'nye problemy prirodopol'zovaniia v promyshlennom regione /. Sverdlovsk , 1985. 151 p. : LC Card 86-126638
HC337.R852 U732 1985

Kontseptsii vzaimodeĭstviia ėkonomiki i prirody / V.F. Bartov. Moskva : "Mysl'", 1984. 157 p. ; 20 cm. (Sovremennye burzhuaznye ėkonomicheskie teorii) Includes bibliographical references. LC Card 84-225876
1. Environmental policy - Economic aspects. 2. Natural resources - Economic aspects. I. Sedov, V. V. (Valentin Vasil'evich). II. Title. III. Series.
HC79.E5 B369 1984

Bartsch, Heinz. Örtliche Versorgungswirtschaft : wichtiger Bereich staatlicher Leitung / Heinz Bartsch, Michael Schargott. Potsdam-Babelsberg : Akademie für Staats- und Rechtswissenschaft der DDR, 1985. 79 p. : ill. ; 21 cm. (Aktuelle Beiträge der Staats- und Rechtswissenschaft, 0568-7551 . Heft 319) Includes bibliographical references. LC Card 86-121253
1. Public utilities - Germany (East). 2. Germany, East - Politics and government. I. Schargott, Michael. II. Title. III. Series.
HD2768.G4 B27 1985

Baruzzi, Arno, 1935- Recht auf Arbeit und Beruf? : sieben philosophisch-politische Thesen / Arno Baruzzi. Freiburg : Alber, c1983. 88 p. ; 21 cm. (Fermenta philosophica) Includes bibliographical references and index. ISBN 3-495-47518-4 LC Card 83-152808
1. Right to labor. 2. Work. I. Title.
HD4903 .B37 1983

Basche, James R., 1926- Eliminating barriers to international trade and investment in services / by James R. Basche. New York, N.Y. (845 Third Ave., New York 10022) : Conference Board, c1986. 15 p. ; 28 cm. (Research bulletin / The Conference Board . no. 200) Caption title. "Economic and Policy Analysis Program." Includes bibliographical references. LC Card 87-147770 DDC 382/.45 19

1. Service industries - Government policy. 2. International business enterprises - Government policy. 3. Commercial policy. 4. Foreign trade regulation. I. Economic and Policy Analysis Program (Conference Board). II. Series: Research bulletin (Conference Board) , no. 200. III. Title.
HD9980.6 .B37 1986

Basco, Carlos A. El comercio intrarregional de alimentos básicos. [S.l.] : Banco Interamericano de Desarrollo, Instituto para la Integración de América Latina, 1986. xi, 558 p. : ill. ; 29 cm. Prepared by Carlos A. Basco with the collaboration of Gabriel Aranda and others. At head of title: Instituto para la Integración de América Latina (INTAL), Comité de Acción para la Seguridad Alimentaria Regional (CASAR). Bibliography: p. [547]-558. LC Card 87-404784 DDC 382/.41/098 19
1. Produce trade - Latin America. 2. Tariff on farm produce - Latin America. 3. Farm produce - Latin America - Transportation - Costs. I. Institute for Latin American Integration. II. Comité de Acción para la Seguridad Alimentaria Regional (Sistema Económico Latinoamericano). III. Title.
HD9014.L32 B37 1986

Basco, Juan Ignacio. Energía eléctrica /. [Buenos Aires] [1981] 27 p., [6] leaves of plates : LC Card 87-401272 DDC 333.79/3212/0982 19
HD9685.A72 E54 1981

Bascones, Javier. Todo para la G.M. . Madrid [1981?] 174 p. : ISBN 84-85639-19-7 LC Card 82-134601 DDC 338.8/87 19
HD9710.S754 G467 1981
NYPL [JLC 86-300]

Base-line study, F.I.S.S., Kitui project area. A Base-line study of Farm Input Supply Scheme. Nairobi , 1981. 65 leaves, [1] leaf of plates : LC Card 87-980116
HD1491.K42 K583 1981

A Base-line study of Farm Input Supply Scheme, phase II : Kitui District. Nairobi : Research and Evaluation Unit, Development Planning Division, Ministry of Co-operative Development, 1981. 65 leaves, [1] leaf of plates : maps ; 30 cm. (Report / Research and Evaluation Unit, Development Planning Division, Ministry of Co-operative Development, Nairobi . no. 9) Cover title: Base-line study, F.I.S.S., Kitui project area. "June 1981." Bibliography: leaf 65. LC Card 87-980116
1. Agriculture, Cooperative - Kenya - Kitui (District) - Evaluation. 2. Agricultural development projects - Kenya - Kitui (District) - Evaluation. I. Kenya. Ministry of Co-operative Development. Development Planning Division. Research & Evaluation Unit. II. Title: Base-line study, F.I.S.S., Kitui project area. III. Series: Report (Kenya. Ministry of Co-operative Development. Development Planning Division. Research & Evaluation Unit) , no. 9.
HD1491.K42 K583 1981

Das Basel der andern . Degen, Bernard, 1952- Basel , 1986. 199 p. : ISBN 3-85990-073-6 LC Card 87-137650 DDC 331.88/09494/3 19
HD6775.B29 D44 1986

BASEL-STADT (SWITZERLAND) - ECONOMIC CONDITIONS.
Vettori, Arthur. Finanzhaushalt und Wirtschaftsverwaltung Basels (1689-1798) . Basel , 1984. xv, 439 p. : ISBN 3-7190-0878-9 LC Card 85-132787
HJ1264.B3 V47 1984

BASEL (SWITZERLAND : CANTON) - ECONOMIC CONDITIONS.
Vettori, Arthur. Finanzhaushalt und Wirtschaftsverwaltung Basels (1689-1798) . Basel , 1984. xv, 439 p. : ISBN 3-7190-0878-9 LC Card 85-132787
HJ1264.B3 V47 1984

BASEL (SWITZERLAND) - BIOGRAPHY.
Loeliger, Walter. Sind Sie frei? . Basel , 1982. 99 p. : ISBN 3-85816-043-1 : LC Card 83-100470
HD8039.T162 L64 1982

BASEL (SWITZERLAND) - COMMERCE - HISTORY.
Röthlin, Niklaus. Die Basler Handelspolitik und deren Träger in der zweiten Hälfte des 17. und im 18. Jahrhundert /. Basel , 1986. 424 p., [3] folded leaves of plates : ISBN 3-7190-0920-3 LC Card 86-187799
HF3710.B3 R67 1986

BASEL (SWITZERLAND) - ECONOMIC CONDITIONS.
Röthlin, Niklaus. Die Basler Handelspolitik und deren Träger in der zweiten Hälfte des 17. und im 18. Jahrhundert /. Basel , 1986. 424 p., [3] folded leaves of plates : ISBN 3-7190-0920-3 LC Card 86-187799
HF3710.B3 R67 1986

BASEL (SWITZERLAND) - SOCIAL LIFE AND CUSTOMS.
Loeliger, Walter. Sind Sie frei? . Basel , 1982. 99 p. : ISBN 3-85816-043-1 : LC Card 83-100470
HD8039.T162 L64 1982

Bases de contabilidad nacional /. Cortés de Pinzón, Magdalena. [Bogotá, Colombia] [1982] 96 p. : LC Card 82-216044
HC79.I5 C675 1982

Bases de economía política /. García, Antonio, 1912- [Bases de la economía contemporánea.] [Bogotá] , 1981. 283 p. ; LC Card 82-138900 DDC 330/.098 19
HB122 .G37 1981 ***NYPL [JLD 87-868]***

Las bases de un desarrollo social diferente . Fortuna, Juan Carlos. Montevideo [1985] 117 p. ; LC Card 86-131906
HC232 .F76 1985

Bases y puntos de partida para la recuperación de la economía argentina . Conesa, Eduardo R. Buenos Aires, Argentina , c1986. 178 p. : ISBN 950-53-7109-8 LC Card 87-400257 DDC 338.982 19
HC175 .C6145 1986

Başgöz, M. İlhan. Turkish workers in Europe . [Bloomington, Ind. (143 Goodbody Hall, Indiana University, Bloomington 47405) , c1985. 191 p. : LC Card 85-71750 DDC 331.6/2/56104 19
HD8378.5.T8 T87 1985
NYPL [JLE 86-2980]

Bashar, Md. Abul. Ali, Md. Harun, 1944- An economic study on guava cultivation in some selected areas of Bangladesh /. Mymensingh , 1986. 38 p. ; LC Card 87-902187 DDC 338.1/74421/095492 19
HD9259.G83 B353 1986

Bashir, Ibrahim Lawan, 1948-
Food crisis and government response in Nigeria : a critique of the River Basin authorities / by Ibrahim L. Bashir. Boston, MA (270 Bay State Rd., Boston 02215) : African Studies Center, Boston University, 1986. 22 leaves ; 28 cm. (Working papers / African Studies Center, Boston University . no. 115) Bibliography: leaves 20-22. LC Card 87-155111 DDC 363.8/09669 19
1. Food supply - Nigeria. 2. Agriculture and state - Nigeria. I. Series: Working papers (Boston University. African Studies Center) , no. 115. II. Title.
HD9017.N52 B37 1986

Sources of capital formation and accumulation among Kano entrepreneurs, 1950-1980 / by Ibrahim L. Bashir. Boston, MA (270 Bay State Rd., Boston 02215) : African Studies Center, Boston University, 1986. 17 leaves ; 28 cm. (Working papers / African Studies Center, Boston University . no. 117) Bibliography: leaves 14-17. LC Card 87-156659 DDC 332/.0415/096695 19
1. Saving and investment - Nigeria - Kano State. 2. Capital - Nigeria - Kano State. 3. Kano State (Nigeria) - Industries. I. Series: Working papers (Boston University. African Studies Center) , no. 117. II. Title.
HC1055.Z9 S33 1986

BASHKIRSKAI͡A A.S.S.R. (R.S.F.S.R.) - ECONOMIC CONDITIONS - STATISTICS.
Narodnoe khoz͡iaĭstvo Bashkirskoĭ ASSR za gody odinnadtsatoĭ pi͡atiletki, 1981-1985 gg. . Ufa , 1986. 254 p. ; LC Card 87-165386
HC337.B28 N37 1986

BASHKIRSKAI͡A A.S.S.R. (R.S.F.S.R.) - STATISTICS.
Narodnoe khoz͡iaĭstvo Bashkirskoĭ ASSR za gody odinnadtsatoĭ pi͡atiletki, 1981-1985 gg. . Ufa , 1986. 254 p. ; LC Card 87-165386
HC337.B28 N37 1986

BASIC, a personal computer language for improving productivity /. Mundel, Marvin Everett, 1916- Tokyo, Japan , c1986. v, 322 p. ; ISBN 92-833-1089-0 LC Card 86-211814 DDC 005.26 19
HF5548.5.B3 M86 1986

BASIC business analysis and operations research /. Mole, R. H. (Richard H.) London , Boston , 1987. 136 p. : ISBN 0-408-01590-X (pbk.) : LC Card 86-26398 DDC 658.4/034/0285526 19
HD30.25 .M66 1987

Basic business logistics . Ballou, Ronald H., 1937- Englewood Cliffs, N.J. , c1987. x, 438 p. : ISBN 0-13-057464-3 LC Card 86-22691 DDC 658.7/88 19
HF5415.7 .B338 1987

Basic business statistics . Jarrell, Stephen B. Newton, Mass. , 1987. p. cm. ISBN 0-205-10632-3 LC Card 87-11349 DDC 519.5 19
HF1017 .J37 1987

Basic business statistics for managers /. Donnahoe, Alan S. New York , c1988. vii, 228 p. : ISBN 0-471-62940-5 (pbk.) : LC Card 87-24273 DDC 519.5/024658 19
HF1017 .D64 1988

BASIC business systems simulation /. Stratfold, Peter. London , Boston , 1987. viii, 172 p. : ISBN 0-408-01260-9 (pbk.) : LC Card 87-18795 DDC 650/.028/55133 19
HF5548.5.B3 S78 1987

Basic concepts of accounting and taxation of property/casualty insurance companies / project director, Sean Mooney ; technical editor, Larry Cohen New York, N.Y. : Insurance Information Institute, c1984. 66 p. : ill. ; 23 cm. (Monograph / Insurance Information Institute) Includes index. ISBN 0-932387-01-2 :
1. Insurance, Casualty - Accounting. 2. Insurance, Casualty - Taxation - United States. 3. Insurance, Property - Accounting. 4. Insurance, Property - Taxation - United States. I. Mooney, Sean, 1945-. II. Cohen, Larry. III. Insurance Information Institute. IV. Series: Monograph / Insurance Information Institute.
NYPL [JLE 86-2615]

Basic data on fertility in the provinces of China, 1940-82 /. Coale, Ansley J. Honolulu, HI [1987] xvii, 366 p. : ISBN 0-86638-088-4 (pbk.) : LC Card 86-32765 DDC 304.6/32/0951 19
HB1064.A3 C63 1987

Basic econometrics /. Gujarati, Damodar N. New York , c1988. xxv, 705 p. : ISBN 0-07-025188-6 : LC Card 87-9268 DDC 330/.028 19
HB139 .G84 1988

A Basic guide to exporting / prepared by the Nevada Small Business Development Center ... et al. [Reno, Nev.] : The Center, [198-] 68 leaves ; 28 cm. Cover title. Bibliography: leaves 64-68. LC Card 86-622819
1. Exports - United States - Handbooks, manuals, etc. 2. Export marketing - United States - Handbooks, manuals, etc. 3. United States - Commerce - Handbooks, manuals, etc. I. Nevada Small Business Development Center.
HF3035 .B37 1980z

A Basic guide to exporting. Washington, D.C. : U. S. Dept. of Commerce, International Trade Administration : For sale by the Supt. of Docs., U. S. G.P.O., 1981. vii, 133 p. : ill., 1 map ; 28 cm. "November 1981." Includes glossary. S/N 003-009-00349-1 Item 231-B-5 Bibliography: p. 125-129. LC Card 82-601093 DDC 658.8/48 19
1. Export marketing - United States - Handbooks, manuals, etc. 2. Export sales - United States - Handbooks, manuals, etc. I. United States. International Trade Administration.
HF1009.5 .B344 1981 ***NYPL [JLF 87-351]***

A Basic guide to exporting. Washington, D.C. : U. S. Dept. of Commerce, International Trade Administration : For sale by the Supt. of Docs., U. S. G.P.O., [1986] viii, 148 p. : ill. ; 28 cm. "September 1986." Includes glossary. "... revised and updated by TransNational, Inc. ..." Bibliography: p. 135-142.
1. Export marketing - United States - Handbooks, manuals, etc. 2. Export sales - United States - Handbooks, manuals, etc. I. United States. International Trade Administration. II. TransNational, Inc.
NYPL [*R-Econ. 87-422]

A Basic guide to exporting. Washington, D.C. : U. S. Dept. of Commerce, International Trade Administration, U. S. and Foreign Commercial Service : For sale by the Supt. of Docs., U. S. G.P.O., [1986] viii, 148 p. : ill. ; 28 cm. "Revised and updated by TransNational, Inc., of Washington, DC, under contract with the Department of Commerce." "September 1986." Bibliography: p.

135-142. Includes index. LC Card 86-603426 DDC 658.8/48 19
1. Export marketing - United States - Handbooks, manuals, etc. 2. Export sales - United States - Handbooks, manuals, etc. I. United States and Foreign Commercial Service. II. TransNational, Inc.
HF1009.6 .B38 1986

Basic guide to payroll. Risteau, Delores. The American Payroll Association's basic guide to payroll /. Paramus, N.J. , c1986. iv, 251 p. : ISBN 0-13-028242-1 (pbk.) LC Card 87-153688 DDC 658.3/21 19
HG4028.P5 R57 1986

Basic housing . Laquian, Aprodicio A. Ottawa, Canada , c1983. 163 p. : ISBN 0-88936-370-6 (pbk.) LC Card 83-231129 DDC 363.5/8/091724 19
HD7391 .L36 1983 ***NYPL [JLE 86-1376]***

The Basic investor's library.
Epstein, Rachel S. Alternative investments /. New York , c1988. 47 p. : ISBN 1-555-46633-8 LC Card 87-21766 DDC 332.6/78 19
HG4521 .E685 1988

Epstein, Rachel S. Careers in the world of investments /. New York , c1988. 47 p. : ISBN 1-555-46631-1 LC Card 87-13182 DDC 332.6/023 19
HG4528 .E67 1988

Epstein, Rachel S. Investment banking /. New York , c1988. 48 p. : ISBN 1-555-46630-3 LC Card 87-18194 DDC 332.66 19
HG4534 .E67 1988

Little, Jeffrey B. Growth stocks /. New York , c1988. p. cm. ISBN 1-555-46624-9 LC Card 87-24482 DDC 332.63/22 19
HG4661 .L57 1988

Little, Jeffrey B. Investing and trading /. New York , c1988. 47 p. : ISBN 1-555-46627-3 LC Card 87-23852 DDC 332.6/78 19
HG4553 .L58 1988

Little, Jeffrey B. Understanding a company /. New York , c1988. 47 p. : ISBN 1-555-46622-2 LC Card 87-17654 DDC 657/.33 19
HG4028.B2 L57 1988

Little, Jeffrey B. Wall Street--how it works /. New York , c1988. 47 p. : ISBN 1-555-46621-4 LC Card 87-15139 DDC 332.64/273 19
HG4921 .L625 1988

Little, Jeffrey B. What is a share of stock? /. New York , c1988. 47 p. : ISBN 1-555-46620-6 LC Card 87-13788 DDC 332.63/22 19
HG4521 .L736 1988

Basic issues in Latin American development prospects /. Urquidi, Víctor L. Coral Gables, Fla. [between 1983 and 1986] 27 p. ; LC Card 87-118247 DDC 338.98 19
HC125 .U765 1983

Basic managerial finance /. Gitman, Lawrence J. New York , c1987. xxxi, 653 p., [2] p. of plates : ISBN 0-06-042366-8 LC Card 86-25666 DDC 658.1/5 19
HG4026 .G59 1987

Basic marketing research /. Churchill, Gilbert A. Chicago [1987], c1988. xvii, 765 p. : ISBN 0-03-007278-6 LC Card 87-5288 DDC 658.8/3 19
HF5415.2 .C49 1988

BASIC NEEDS.
Penz, G. Peter. Consumer sovereignty and human interests /. Cambridge [Cambridgeshire] , New York , 1986. xiv, 242 p. ; ISBN 0-521-26571-1 LC Card 85-22407 DDC 330.15/5 19
HB846 .P46 1986 ***NYPL [JLE 86-3311]***

BASIC NEEDS - AFRICA, SUB-SAHARAN - CASE STUDIES.
Foreign indebtedness and basic human needs in four African countries . Washington , 1986. ii, 54 p. : LC Card 86-603396 DDC 336.3/435/0967
HC800 .F67 1986

BASIC NEEDS - BRAZIL, NORTHEAST.
Rönick, Volker. Regionale Entwicklungspolitik und Massenarmut im ländlichen Raum Nordost-Brasiliens . Paderborn , 1986. 136 p. : ISBN 3-506-73225-0 LC Card 87-407836 DDC 338.981/3 19
HC188.N6 R66 1986

BASIC NEEDS - BURKINA FASO - CASE STUDIES.
Schneider-Barthold, Wolfgang. Industrie und Grundbedürfnisbefriedigung in Afrika . Frankfurt/Main , New York , c1984. 264 p. ; ISBN 3-593-33350-3 LC Card 86-125217
HC1040 .S35 1984

BASIC NEEDS - CHILE - SANTIAGO.
Schkolnik, Mariana. Sobrevivir en la población José M. Caro y en Lo Hermida /. [Santiago, Chile] [1986] 150 p., [20] p. of plates : LC Card 87-400080 DDC 362.5/8/098331 19
HC193.S2 S35 1986

Basic needs delivery system in Birendranagar, Surkhet / research team, Rajeshwar Acharya ... [et al.]. Kathmandu : Centre for Economic Development and Administration, Tribhuvan University, 1985. 143, [23], iii p. (some folded) ; 30 cm. Bibliography: p. [i]-iii. LC Card 86-903561 DDC 338.9549/6 19
1. Physical distribution of goods - Nepal - Birendranagar. 2. Birendranagar (Nepal) - Economic conditions. 3. Birendranagar (Nepal) - Economic policy. I. Acharya, Rajeshwar. II. Centre for Economic Development and Administration.
HF5415.12.N35 B36 1985

BASIC NEEDS - DEVELOPING COUNTRIES.
Cooperazione italiana allo sviluppo . Roma [1984] 144 p. ; ISBN 88-7621-170-5 : LC Card 85-223760 DDC 338.91/45/01724 19
HC60 .C65757 1984

BASIC NEEDS - DEVELOPING COUNTRIES - CONGRESSES.
Grundbedürfnisse als Gegenstand der Entwicklungspolitik . Wiesbaden , 1982. viii, 220 p. : ISBN 3-515-03838-8 (Deut. Bibl.) LC Card 85-134671
HC59.72.B38 G78 1982

BASIC NEEDS - GOVERNMENT POLICY - LATIN AMERICA.
From crisis to equitable growth ; a new development agenda for Latin America /. Aldershot , Brookfield, USA , 1987. ix, 144 p. ; ISBN 0-566-05536-8 : LC Card 87-21135 DDC 338.98 19
HC130.B38 F76 1987

BASIC NEEDS - INDONESIA.
Sjahrir, 1945- [Political economy of basic needs in Indonesia. Indonesian.] Ekonomi politik kebutuhan pokok . Jakarta , 1986. xxiii, 280 p. : ISBN 979-8015-02-9 (pbk.) LC Card 86-943050
HC450.B38 S5216 1986

BASIC NEEDS - LATIN AMERICA.
Buscando la equidad. English. In search for equity . Aldershot, Hants, England , Brookfield, USA , c1987. xvi, 249 p. ; ISBN 0-566-05537-6 : LC Card 87-21225 DDC 338.98 19
HC130.B38 B8713 1987

Basic needs manual. Bicutan, Taguig, Metro Manila : National Science and Technology Authority, Science Promotion Institute, [1985] 58 p. : ill. ; 23 cm. Bibliography: p. 58. LC Card 87-118190 DDC 338.9599 19
1. Basic needs - Philippines. 2. Technological innovations - Economic aspects - Philippines. I. Science Promotion Institute (Philippines).
HC460.B38 B37 1985

BASIC NEEDS - PHILIPPINES.
Basic needs manual. Bicutan, Taguig, Metro Manila [1985] 58 p. : LC Card 87-118190 DDC 338.9599 19
HC460.B38 B37 1985

BASIC NEEDS - SOVIET UNION.
Kurochkin, I͡U. P. (I͡Uriĭ Petrovich) Sotsial'no-ėkonomicheskai͡a priroda i formy neobkhodimogo produkta pri sotsializme /. Leningrad , 1984. 135 p. ; LC Card 84-218003
HC340.B38 K87 1984

Sotsial'no-ėkonomicheskai͡a ėffektivnost' obshchestvennogo proizvodstva--sushchnost', komponenty i voprosy ikh otsenki /. Minsk , 1983. 158 p. ; LC Card 83-206045
HC340.I52 S67 1983

BASIC NEEDS - SUDAN - SOUTHERN REGION.
House, William J. Population, poverty, and basic needs in southern Sudan . [Juba, Sudan , 1985] vi, 94 leaves ; LC Card 86-981127 DDC 338.9629 19
HC835.Z7 S684 1985

The basic principles of marketing warfare /. Durö, Robert. Chichester [West Sussex] , New York , c1987. xi, 164 p. : ISBN 0-471-91545-9 : LC Card 87-8317 DDC 658.8 19
HF5415 .D87 1987

BASIC statistics, an introduction to problem solving with your personal computer /. O'Dell, Jerry W. Blue Ridge Summit, PA , c1984. vii, 452 p. : ISBN 0-8306-0759-5 : LC Card 84-8804 DDC 519.5/028/542 19
QA276.4 .O34 1984 ***NYPL [JSD 86-378]***

The basic theory of capitalism . Itō, Makoto, 1936- Totowa, N.J. , 1987. p. cm. ISBN 0-389-20729-2 LC Card 87-905 DDC 330.12/2 19
HB97.5 .I823 1987

The basis of the bargain . O'Donnell, Carol. Sydney , Boston , 1984. 186 p. ; ISBN 0-86861-497-1 LC Card 84-70146 DDC 331.4/133/0994 19
HD6060.5.A8 O36 1984
NYPL [JLD 86-2017]

Basiuk, Jerzy. Eksport warunkiem importu / Jerzy Basiuk. Wyd. 1. Warszawa : Krajowa Agencja Wydawnicza, 1978. 57 p. ; 22 cm. (ABC Gospodarki) LC Card 81-192725
1. Poland - Commercial policy. 2. Poland - Foreign economic relations. I. Title.
HF1558.7 .B32 1978

Baskin, A. I. (Arkadiĭ Isaakovich) Planirovanie potrebnosti v material'nykh resursakh na predprii͡atii / A.I. Baskin, L.Ė. Lysikova, B.P. Mel'nik. Kiev : "Tekhnika", 1983. 48 p. ; 20 cm. Bibliography: p. 48. LC Card 83-243488
1. Industrial procurement - Ukraine. I. Lysikova, L. Ė. (Li͡udmila Ėrazmovna). II. Mel'nik, B. P. (Boris Pavlovich). III. Title.
HD39.5 .B37 1983

Baslé, Maurice. Le budget de l'Etat / Maurice Baslé. Paris : La Découverte, 1985. 127 p. : ill. ; 18 cm. (Collection Repères . 33.) Bibliography: p. 125. ISBN 2-7071-1534-7 LC Card 86-161271
1. Budget - France. 2. France - Appropriations and expenditures. I. Series: Collection Repères , 33. II. Title.
HJ2106 .B37 1985

Basler Beiträge zur Geographie. For additional listing of contents, see Old Catalog.
(Heft 29) Šimko, Dušan. Strassenverkäufer und die Versorgung der Arbeiterfamilien von Kowloon (Hong Kong) im Umfeld der staatlichen Planungspolitik /. Basel , 1983. 196 p., [9] p. of plates : ISBN 3-85977-129-9 : LC Card 83-238672
HF5459.H6 S56 1983

Basler Beiträge zur Geschichtswissenschaft. For additional listing of contents, see Old Catalog.
(Bd. 147) Fink, Paul. Geschichte der Basler Bandindustrie 1550-1800 /. Basel , 1983. 216 p. : ISBN 3-7190-0836-3 LC Card 83-220231 DDC 338.4/767776 19
HD9929.R6 S94 1983 ***NYPL [JLE 86-2781]***

(Bd. 149) Vettori, Arthur. Finanzhaushalt und Wirtschaftsverwaltung Basels (1689-1798) . Basel , 1984. xv, 439 p. : ISBN 3-7190-0878-9 LC Card 85-132787
HJ1264.B3 V47 1984

(Bd. 152) Röthlin, Niklaus. Die Basler Handelspolitik und deren Träger in der zweiten Hälfte des 17. und im 18. Jahrhundert /. Basel , 1986. 424 p., [3] folded leaves of plates : ISBN 3-7190-0920-3 LC Card 86-187799
HF3710.B3 R67 1986

Basler Gewerkschaftsbund. Degen, Bernard, 1952- Das Basel der andern . Basel , 1986. 199 p. : ISBN 3-85990-073-6 LC Card 87-137650 DDC 331.88/09494/3 19
HD6775.B29 D44 1986

Die Basler Handelspolitik und deren Träger in der zweiten Hälfte des 17. und im 18. Jahrhundert /. Röthlin, Niklaus. Basel , 1986. 424 p., [3] folded leaves of plates : ISBN 3-7190-0920-3 LC Card 86-187799
HF3710.B3 R67 1986

Basler, Hans-Peter. Lohnentwicklung und Lohnpolitik als Bestimmungsgründe konjunktureller Verläufe und struktureller Verschiebungen : eine Untersuchung im Auftrage der Beteiligungsgesellschaft für Gemeinwirtschaft / Hans-Peter Basler. Berlin : Duncker & Humblot, 1981. 102 p. : ill. ; 24 cm. (Sonderheft / Deutsches Institut für

Wirtschaftsforschung . 134) Includes bibliographical references. ISBN 3-428-04970-5 LC Card 82-100546 DDC 330 s 331.2/943 19
1. Wages - Germany, West. 2. Wages - Government policy - Germany (West). 3. Germany, West - Economic policy - 1974-. I. Beteiligungsgesellschaft für Gemeinwirtschaft (Germany). II. Series: Berlin. Deutsches Institut für Wirtschaftsforschung. Sonderhefte, 134. 134. III. Title.
HB41 .B4 Nr. 134 HD5029
NYPL [JLL 73-207 Heft 134]

Basler Nachrichten. Europa im Umbruch . [Basel] , 1963. 91 p. ; LC Card 85-125335
HC241 .E772 1963

Basler Verkehrs-Betriebe (B.V.B.) Basler Verkehrs-Betriebe (BVB) . Villigen AG, Schweiz , c1984. 56 p., [188] p. of plates, xv p. : ISBN 3-85649-045-0 : LC Card 84-160209
HE4919.B37 B37 1984

Basler Verkehrs-Betriebe (BVB) : ein Fotobuch zur Modernisierung der Basler Strassenbahnen von 1945 bis 1982 = Modern tramcars of Basle (Switzerland) / [zusammengestellt von] Claude Jeanmaire. Villigen AG, Schweiz : Verlag Eisenbahn, c1984. 56 p., [188] p. of plates, xv p. : ill. (some col.) ; 24 cm. (Archiv. Nr. 45) One folded col. map inserted. ISBN 3-85649-045-0 : LC Card 84-160209
1. Street-railroads - Switzerland - Basel - History. 2. Transportation - Switzerland - Basel - History. 3. Basler Verkehrs-Betriebe (B.V.B.) - History. I. Jeanmaire, Claude. II. Title: Basler Verkehrs-Betriebe (B.V.B.). III. Title: Modern tramcars of Basle (Switzerland). IV. Series: Archiv (Villigen, Switzerland) , Nr. 45.
HE4919.B37 B37 1984

BASLER VERKEHRS-BETRIEBE (B.V.B.) - HISTORY.
Basler Verkehrs-Betriebe (BVB) . Villigen AG, Schweiz , c1984. 56 p., [188] p. of plates, xv p. : ISBN 3-85649-045-0 : LC Card 84-160209
HE4919.B37 B37 1984

Bass, Bernard M. Advances in organizational psychology . Newbury Park , c1987. 314 p. ; ISBN 0-8039-2802-5 LC Card 87-9484 DDC 158.7 19
HF5548.8 .A58 1987

Bass, Gary J. A practical and simple guide to a home mortgage / Gary J. Bass. Irving, Tex. : G&P Pub., c1987. v, 66 p. : ill. ; 19 cm. ISBN 0-944319-00-9 (pbk.) LC Card 87-82025 DDC 332.7/22/0973 19
1. Mortgage loans - United States. 2. Housing - United States - Finance. I. Title.
HG2040.5.U5 B367 1987

Bastress, Frances. The relocating spouse's guide to employment : options and strategies in the U. S. and abroad / Frances Bastress.2nd ed. Chevy Chase, Md. : Woodley Publications, c1987. xviii, 258 p. : ill. ; 23 cm. Bibliography: p. 228-246. Includes index. ISBN 0-937623-01-6 (pbk.) : LC Card 87-16045 DDC 650.1/4 19
1. Job hunting. 2. Job hunting - United States. 3. Married people - Employment. 4. Married people - Employment - United States. I. Title.
HF5382.7 .B375 1987

La basura . Restrepo, Iván. México, D.F. , 1985. 193 p. : LC Card 86-209151
HD9014.M63 M47 1985

Basurāya, Sunila. Kaẏalā śramika, jībana o saṃgrāma / Sunila Basurāẏa. Durgāpura : Saṃhati Prakāśanī ; Kalikātā : Praptisthāna, Nyāśānāla Buka Ejensi, 1986. 239 p. ; 23 cm. In Bengali. Historical account of the socioeconomic conditions of the coal miners in India and labor and trade unions involved in their welfare. LC Card 86-903821
1. Coal-miners - India. 2. Trade-unions - Coal miners - India. I. Title.
HD8039.M62 I394 1986

Basurco Valverde, Gerardo Félix.
Herrschaftsformen und Industrialisierungsprozess in Peru : eine Analyse über den Zusammenhang zwischen Entwicklungsmodell und politischem System unter besonderer Berücksichtigung der Militärherrschaft von 1968 bis 1980 / Gerardo Félix Basurco Valverde. Freiburg [Breisgau] : Hochschulverlag, c1985. xi, 420 p. : ill. ; 21 cm. (Hochschulsammlung Philosophie. Politikwissenschaft, 0720-5406 . Bd. 6) Originally presented as the author's thesis (doctoral)--Freiburg, 1984. Bibliography: p. 397-420. ISBN 3-8107-2210-3 LC Card 86-179243
1. Peru - Economic policy. 2. Peru - Economic conditions - 1968-. 3. Peru - Industries. 4. Peru - Politics and government - 1968-. I. Title. II. Series.
HC227 .B339 1985

Bata, Jan A. Companhia de Viação São Paulo-Mato Grosso. Ante-projeto do núcleo de colonização "Presidente Kennedy" /. Mato Grosso, Brasil , 1962. 40 p., [15] leaves of plates : LC Card 85-135105
HD1516.B8 C64 1962

BATAM ISLAND (INDONESIA) - ECONOMIC CONDITIONS - 1945-
A Guide for investors. [Jakarta] [1984] 112 p. : LC Card 86-942985 DDC 332.6/73225981 19
HC448.B38 G85 1984

Bate, Joseph St. John. Burgess, Ross. Office automation using the IBM personal computer systems . London , 1986. 180 p. : ISBN 0-00-383104-3 (pbk.) : LC Card 86-220136 DDC 651.8/4165 19
HF5548.2 .B783 1986

Bate, Paul. Organization of innovation . Berlin , New York , 1987. x, 238 p. : ISBN 0-89925-167-6 (U. S.) : LC Card 87-19936 DDC 658.4/06 19
HD45 .O73 1987

Batelle-Institut. Rüter, Gert. Sicherheitsorientierte Ausbildung von Berufskraftfahren /. Köln [1983] vii, 91 p. : LC Card 83-235527
HD5716.M7952 G327 1983

Batelleries et batelliers de France . Le Sueur, Bernard. Le Côteau [1985] 208 p. : ISBN 2-7171-0339-2 LC Card 87-106621
HE443 .L39 1985

Bateman, Fred, 1937- Atack, Jeremy. To their own soil . Ames , 1987. xi, 322 p. : ISBN 0-8138-0086-2 LC Card 86-21349 DDC 338.1/0974 19
HD1773.A4 A86 1987

Bates, Don. New technology and public relations . New York, NY (310 Madison Ave., New York 10017) , c1986. xviii, 170 p. : LC Card 87-105313 DDC 659.2/028/5 19
HD59 .N44 1986

Bates, Jefferson D., 1920- The portable office : take your office on the road, now and for the future / Jefferson D. Bates & Stuart Crump, Jr. ; foreword by William F. Buckley, Jr. Washington, D.C. : Acropolis Books, c1987. 262 p. : ill. ; 24 cm. Bibliography: p. 261-262. ISBN 0-87491-491-3 :; 0-87491-841-3 (jacket) LC Card 87-1773 DDC 658.4/093 19
1. Business travel. 2. Businessmen - Time management. 3. Office equipment and supplies. I. Crump, Stuart. II. Title.
HD38 .B325 1987

Bates, Robert H.
Essays on the political economy of rural Africa / Robert H. Bates. 1st pbk. ed. Berkeley : University of California Press, 1987, c1983. p. cm. (California series on social choice and political economy) Reprint. Originally published: Cambridge [Cambridgeshire] ; New York : Cambridge University Press, 1983. (African studies series ; no. 38) With new pref. Bibliography: p. Includes index. ISBN 0-520-06014-8 (pbk. : alk. paper) LC Card 86-25120 DDC 330.96/0328/091734 19
1. Agriculture - Economic aspects - Africa. 2. Agriculture and state - Africa. 3. Peasantry - Africa. 4. Africa - Economic conditions. 5. Africa - Rural conditions. I. Title. II. Series.
HD2117 .B37 1987

Toward a political economy of development . Berkeley , c1988. p. cm. ISBN 0-520-06051-2 (alk. paper) LC Card 87-10870 DDC 338.9/009172/4 19
HC59.7 .T7376 1988

BATHING BEACHES - ECONOMIC ASPECTS - FLORIDA.
Bell, Frederick W. An economic analysis of the importance of saltwater beaches in Florida /. Gainesville, FL [1986] xi, 166 p. : LC Card 86-622310 DDC 333.91/7/09759 19
HD266.F6 B45 1986

Bathory, Alexander. The analysis of credit : foundations and development of corporate credit assessment / Alexander Bathory. London ; New York : McGraw-Hill, c1987. xiii, 385 p. ; 26 cm. Bibliography: p. 357-358. Includex index. ISBN 0-07-084938-2 : LC Card 87-2060 DDC 658.8/8 19
1. Credit management. I. Title. II. Title: Corporate credit assessment.
HG3751 .B385 1987

Bâtiments préfabriqués résidentiels et industriels à ossature de bois . Duchaine, Paul. [Québec] , c1985. 36 p. : ISBN 2-550-12116-3 LC Card 86-133426
HD9715.5.C23 Q43 1985

BĀṬINAH (OMAN) - ECONOMIC CONDITIONS.
Asche, H. (Hartmut) Mobile Lebensformgruppen Südost-Arabiens im Wandel . Berlin , 1981, c1982. xii, 344 p. : ISBN 3-496-00302-2 LC Card 86-217612
HD8039.F652 O522 1982

BĀṬINAH (OMAN) - SOCIAL CONDITIONS.
Asche, H. (Hartmut) Mobile Lebensformgruppen Südost-Arabiens im Wandel . Berlin , 1981, c1982. xii, 344 p. : ISBN 3-496-00302-2 LC Card 86-217612
HD8039.F652 O522 1982

Batista Júnior, Paulo Nogueira. International financial flows to Brazil since the late 1960s : an analysis of debt expansion and payment problems / Paulo Nogueira Batista, Jr. Washington, D.C. : World Bank, 1987. 66 p. ; 28 cm. (World Bank discussion papers, 0259-210X . 7) Bibliography: p. 59-66. ISBN 0-8213-0891-2 (pbk.) LC Card 87-6065 DDC 336.3/4/0981 19
1. Debts, External - Brazil. 2. Loans, Foreign - Brazil. 3. Debt relief - Brazil. I. Title. II. Series.
HJ8579 .B369 1987

Batistoni Ferrara, F. (Franco) Economia tra teoria e politica /. Milano , c1984. 295 p. ; LC Card 84-171327 DDC 330/.09 19
HB75 .E28 1984 ***NYPL [JLD 87-819]***

BATLLE Y ORDÓNEZ, JOSÉ, PRESS URUGUAY, 1856-1929 - ADDRESSES, ESSAYS, LECTURES.
El Primer batllismo . Montevideo [1985] 159 p. : LC Card 85-233561 DDC 338.9895 19
HC232 .P75 1985 ***NYPL [JLC 86-259]***

Bató, Sándor. Az áru mint történelmi kategória / Bató Sándor. [Budapest] : Művelődési Minisztérium Marxizmus-Leninizmus Oktatási Főosztálya, 1985. 104 p. ; 24 cm. (Politikai gazdaságtan füzetek, 0324-6396 . 50) Summary in Russian. Includes bibliographical references. ISBN 963-673-332-5 LC Card 86-228016
1. Marxian economics. 2. Right of property. 3. Production (Economic theory). I. Title. II. Series.
HB97.5 .B3245 1985

Batra, Raveendra N.
The Debt crisis and financial stability . New York, NY (Attn: Comptroller, Pace Plaza, 10038) , 1985. xi, 157 p. : ISBN 0-88239-017-1 : LC Card 85-19243 DDC 336.3/435/091724 19
HG3891.5 .D4 1985 ***NYPL [JLE 86-3911]***

The great depression of 1990 / Ravi Batra. Dallas, Tex. : Venus Books, c1985. xv, 175 p. : ill. ; 23 cm. Includes index. Bibliography: p. 168-170. ISBN 0-939352-02-8 : LC Card 85-50275 DDC 338.5/42 19
1. Economic forecasting - United States. 2. Business cycles - United States. 3. United States - Economic conditions - 1981-. I. Title.
HC106.8 .B39 1985 ***NYPL [JLD 86-4007]***

The great depression of 1990 / by Ravi Batra. Rev. ed. New York : Simon & Schuster, c1987. 235 p. ; 22 cm. Bibliography: p. 217-219. Includes index. ISBN 0-671-64022-4 LC Card 87-4816 DDC 338.5/42 19
1. United States - Economic conditions - 1981-. 2. Economic forecasting - United States. 3. Business cycles - United States. 4. Depressions. I. Title.
HC106.8 .B39 1987

Batsa, Kofi, 1931- West German neo-colonialism and Africa : documentation of the neo-colonialist policy of West Germany in Africa / by Kofi Batsa. Accra, Ghana : Spark Publikations, [1964] 98 p. ; 22 cm. LC Card 87-118442 DDC 337.4306 19
1. Germany, West - Foreign economic relations - Africa. 2. Africa - Foreign economic relations - Germany, West. 3. Africa - Dependency on West Germany. 4. Africa - Colonial influence. I. Title.
HF1546.15.A35 B37 1964

Batstone, Eric.
New technology and the process of labour

regulation /. Oxford [Oxfordshire] , New York , 1987. p. cm. ISBN 0-19-827274-X : LC Card 87-11146 DDC 331/.0941 19
HD6331.2.G7 N48 1987

Unions, unemployment and innovation / Eric Batstone and Stephen Gourlay with Hugo Levie and Roy Moore. Oxford [Oxfordshire] ; New York, N.Y., USA : B. Blackwell, 1986. viii, 320 p. ; 24 cm. Includes index. Bibliography: p. [309]-313. ISBN 0-631-14961-9 : LC Card 85-30679 DDC 331.88/0941 19
1. Trade-unions - Great Britain. 2. Unemployment - Great Britain. 3. Technological innovations - Great Britain. I. Gourlay, Stephen, 1949-. II. Title.
HD6664 .B335 1986 ***NYPL [JLE 86-4031]***

Batt, Judy. Economic reform and political change in eastern Europe : a comparison of the Czechoslovak and Hungarian experiences / Judy Batt. New York : St. Martin's Press, in association with the Centre for Russian and East European Studies, University of Birmingham, 1987. p. cm. Bibliography: p. Includes index. ISBN 0-312-01196-2 : LC Card 87-24065 DDC 338.9437 19
1. Czechoslovakia - Economic policy - 1945-. 2. Czechoslovakia - Economic conditions - 1945-. 3. Czechoslovakia - Politics and government - 1945-. 4. Hungary - Economic policy - 1945-. 5. Hungary - Economic conditions - 1945-. 6. Hungary - Politics and government - 1945-. I. University of Birmingham. Centre for Russian and East European Studies. II. Title.
HC270.28 .B37 1987

Batten, R. P. Hudson, R. W. Business computer systems . London , New York , c1986. x, 163 p. : ISBN 0-07-084976-5 (pbk.) : LC Card 86-10481 DDC 650/.028/5 19
HF5548.2 .H78 1986 ***NYPL [JLE 87-1038]***

BATTERY INDUSTRY.
Stonfer, David. The storage battery market . [Washington, D.C.?] [1985] v, 52 p. ; LC Card 85-601888 DDC 382/.45621312424/0973 19
HD9697.B323 U574 1985
NYPL [JLF 87-207]

BATTERY INDUSTRY - UNITED STATES.
Stonfer, David. The storage battery market . [Washington, D.C.?] [1985] v, 52 p. ; LC Card 85-601888 DDC 382/.45621312424/0973 19
HD9697.B323 U574 1985
NYPL [JLF 87-207]

Battison, Edwin A. De-Gennin, Vil´gel´m, 1676-1750. [Opisanie ural´skikh i sibirskikh zavodov 1735. English.] Description of Ural and Siberian factories in 1735 /. [Washington, D.C.] , 1987. p. cm. LC Card 87-600052 DDC 338.0947/87 19
HC337.R852 U733613 1987

Battle, Ellen F.
Douglas, Gordon W. Energy and regional investment in Canada /. Calgary, Alta. [1983] x, 114 p. : ISBN 0-920522-28-9 (pbk.) : LC Card 83-160268 DDC 332.6/722 19
HD9502.C32 D68 1983 ***NYPL [JLD 87-996]***

Energy efficiency in Canada's pulp & paper industry / Ellen F. Battle. Calgary, Alta. : Canadian Energy Research Institute : University of Calgary Press, [1986] xviii, 131, 4 p. : ill. ; 22 cm. (Study / Canadian Energy Research Institute . no. 23 (Oct. 1986)) Bibliography: p. 129-131. ISBN 0-920522-38-6 (pbk.) : LC Card 87-124507 DDC 333.79 19
1. Paper industry - Canada - Energy conservation. 2. Wood-pulp industry - Canada - Energy conservation. I. Series: Study / Canadian Energy Research Institute , no. 23. II. Title.
HD9834.C22 B37 1986

Reinsch, Anthony Ernest. Industrial cogeneration in Canada . Calgary, Alta. [1987] xviii, 137 p. : ISBN 0-920522-41-6 (pbk.) : LC Card 87-163062 DDC 333.79/3 19
HD9685.C2 R45 1987

The battle for Britain's gold standard in 1931 /. Kunz, Diane B., 1952- London , New York , c1987. viii, 207 p. ; ISBN 0-7099-3120-4 LC Card 87-9065 DDC 332.4/222/0941 19
HG939 .K85 1987

Battle for the high street /. Kay, William. London , 1987. 194 p., [16] p. of plates : ISBN 0-86188-621-6 : LC Card 87-143764 DDC 658.8/7 19
HF5429.6.G7 K38 1987

The battle of the boycott . Lapides, Kenneth. New York, N.Y. , 1974. 22 p., [3] p. of plates : LC Card 87-125953 DDC 331.89/3 19
HD5325.C62 1972 .L36 1974

Battle, Thomas E. French, William B. Guide to real estate licensing examinations for salespersons and brokers /. New York , c1986. ix, 367 p. : ISBN 0-471-87754-9 : LC Card 83-23484 DDC 333.33/0973 19
HD1375 .F74 1984
NYPL [*R-Econ. 86-3475]

Bättre eller sämre med datorer? . De Geer, Hans, 1944- Stockholm , c1982. 112 p. ; ISBN 91-38-90157-9 : LC Card 82-187964
HF5548.2 .D378 1982

Bättre handel.
Rylander, Stig, 1928- Säljande butik /. Lund , c1984. 272 p. : ISBN 91-44-99681-0 : LC Card 84-229201
HF5429 .R94 1984

Bau-Tarifverträge.
Rahmentarifverträge, Gehaltstarifverträge, Vermögensbildungstarifverträge, Tabelle der Kündigungsfristen, Auslösungssätze für die technischen und kaufmännischen Angestellten und für die Poliere und Schachtmeister des Baugewerbes im Gebiet der Bundesrepublik Deutschland /. Düsseldorf , 1977. 102 p. ; ISBN 3-8041-1158-0 LC Card 85-166026
HD6698.R315 R34 1977

Bauch, Vlastislav. Sociálno-ekonomický vývoj slovenského pol'nohospodárskeho obyvatel'stva / Vlastislav Bauch. 1. vyd. Bratislava : Ústav marxizmu-leninizmu ÚV KSS, v nakl. Pravda, 1986. 362, [5] p. ; 21 cm. Bibliography: p. 357-[363] LC Card 87-125324
1. Agriculture - Economic aspects - Czechoslovakia - Slovak Socialist Republic. 2. Agriculture and state - Czechoslovakia - Slovak Socialist Republic. I. Title.
HD1940.3.Z9 S573 1986

Bauchet, Pierre. Le plan dans l'économie française / Pierre Bauchet. Paris : Presses de la Fondation nationale des sciences politiques : Economica, c1986. 246 p. : ill. ; 25 cm. Bibliography: p. [237]-240. Includes index. ISBN 2-7246-0532-2 : LC Card 86-223474
1. France - Economic policy - 1945-. 2. Central planning - France. I. Title.
HC276.2 .B292 1986

Bauer, Carl-Otto. Rembser, Josef. Die Förderung des wirtschaftlichen und sozialen Wandels durch die Forschungs- und Entwicklungspolitik als präventive Strukturpolitik /. Dortmund , 1977. 100 p. : LC Card 84-130876
HD30 .A7 Heft 184 HD6331.2.G28

Bauer, Fritz. Konsumenteninformation und ihre Nutzer / Fritz Bauer. Linz : R. Trauner, 1986. ii, 113 p. : ill. ; 21 cm. (Sozialwissenschaftliche Materialien . Bd. 13) Bibliography: p. 107-111. ISBN 3-85320-388-4 LC Card 87-134585 DDC 381/.3/09436 19
1. Consumers - Austria. 2. Consumer protection - Austria. I. Title. II. Series.
HC270.C6 B38 1986

Bauer, Hans H. Die Entscheidung des Handels über die Aufnahme neuer Produkte : eine verhaltenstheoretische Analyse / von Hans H. Bauer. Berlin : Duncker & Humblot, c1980. xxiii, 479 p. ; 24 cm. (Schriften zum Marketing. Bd. 10) Originally presented as the author's thesis (doctoral)--Universität Mannheim, 1979. Bibliography: p. 450-479. ISBN 3-428-04702-8 LC Card 87-408771 DDC 658.8 s 658.8/343 19
1. New products - Marketing. 2. Consumers' preferences. I. Title.
HF5415.A2 S37 Bd. 10 HF5415.153

Bauer, Helfried. Fahrradfreundliche Verkehrspolitik in Stadt und Land : Grundsätze, Massnahmen, Instrumente : Gutachten des Kommunalwissenschaftlichen Dokumentationszentrums / Bearbeitung, H. Bauer und E. Lung. Wien : Geschäftsstelle der Österreichischen Raumordnungskonferenz, 1984. 87 p. : ill. ; 27 cm. (Schriftenreihe / Österreichische Raumordnungskonferenz (ÖROK) . Nr. 38) Bibliography: p. 84-85. LC Card 85-150945
1. Bicycle commuting - Austria. 2. Cycling paths - Austria. I. Lung, E. II. Kommunalwissenschaftliches Dokumentationszentrum (Vienna, Austria). III. Series: Schriftenreihe (Österreichische Raumordnungskonferenz) , Nr. 38. IV. Title.
HE5739.A9 B38 1984

Der Bauer im Wandel der Zeit / herausgegeben von Willi Hirdt. Bonn : Bouvier, 1986. x, 340 p., [1] leaf of plates : ill. ; 23 cm. (Studium universale, 0174-7061 . Bd. 7) French and German. Papers of a conference held in Bonn on May 13-17, 1985. Includes bibliographical references. ISBN 3-416-04010-4 LC Card 86-228506
1. Peasantry - History - Congresses. 2. Economic history - Congresses. I. Hirdt, Willi. II. Series.
HD1521 .B37 1986

Bauer, Johann, Dkfm. Entwicklungsmanagement . Berlin , c1982. 192 p. : ISBN 3-428-05208-0 LC Card 83-150764 DDC 338.9/0068 19
HD84 .E56 1982 ***NYPL [JLE 87-1179]***

Bauer, Jürgen. Quantitative Entwicklungsplanung für ländliche Regionen : [e. Systemmodell für d. Landkreis Grafschaft Diepholz] / Jürgen Bauer. Bochum : Studienverlag Brockmeyer, 1979. 382 p. in various pagings : graphs ; 21 cm. (Beiträge zur Struktur- und Konjunkturforschung . Bd. 10) Originally presented as the author's thesis, Göttingen. Bibliography: p. [337]-[353] ISBN 3-88339-087-9 : LC Card 80-470152
1. Regional planning - Germany, West - Mathematical models. 2. Land use, Rural - Germany West - Mathematical models. 3. Agriculture - Economic aspects - Germany, West. 4. Regional planning - Germany, West - Grafschaft Diepholz (Landkreis) - Ca e studies. I. Title. II. Series.
HT395.G4 B39 1979 ***NYPL [JLD 86-1628]***

Bauer, K. Jack (Karl Jack), 1926- A maritime history of the United States : the role of America's seas and waterways / by K. Jack Bauer.1st ed. Columbia, S.C. : University of South Carolina Press, c1988. p. cm. (Studies in maritime history) Bibliography: p. Includes index. ISBN 0-87249-519-1 LC Card 87-19190 DDC 387.5/0973 19
1. Merchant marine - United States - History. 2. Merchant ships - United States - History. 3. Shipping - United States - History. 4. Inland water transportation - United States - History. 5. United States. Navy - History. I. Title. II. Series.
HE745 .B38 1988

Bauer, Mary Cracraft. A history of coal-mining in the Sutton-Chickaloon area prior to WW II / by Mary Cracraft Bauer ; with Victoria A. Cole ; sponsored by the Alpine Historical Society. [Anchorage, Alaska] : Alaska Historical Commission, [1985] ii, 47 leaves : ill. ; 30 cm. (Alaska Historical Commission studies in history . no. 180) "August, 1985." Bibliography: p. 43-47. LC Card 86-620606 DDC 338.2/724/097983 19
1. Coal trade - Alaska - Sutton Region - History. 2. Coal trade - Alaska - Chickaloon Region - History. 3. Coal mines and mining - Alaska - Sutton Region - History. 4. Coal mines and mining - Alaska - Chickaloon Region - History. I. Cole, Victoria A. II. Alpine Historical Society (Sutton, Alaska). III. Series.
HD9548.S87 B38 1985

Bauern in Mexiko . Bennholdt-Thomsen, Veronika. Frankfurt [am Main] , New York , c1982. 214 p. ; ISBN 3-593-33167-5 LC Card 83-139124 DDC 305.5/63 19
HD1531.M6 B46 1982

Bauern, Kapital und Staat in Kenia . Wegner, Gerhard, 1953- Berlin , c1983. 94 p. : ISBN 3-88619-038-2 : LC Card 85-171380
HD1538.K4 W44 1983

Bauern und Staat in Westafrika . Elwert, Georg. Frankfurt , New York , c1983. 383 p. : ISBN 3-593-33206-X : LC Card 84-152007
HD1538.B46 E49 1983

Die Bauern von Tver . Altrichter, Helmut, 1945- München , 1984. 373 p. : ISBN 3-486-52071-7 LC Card 84-162284
HD1536.S65 A47 1984

Bauge, Kenneth L. (Kenneth LeRoy) Voluntary export restriction as a foreign commercial policy with special reference to Japanese cotton textiles, 1930-1962 / Kenneth L. Bauge. New York : Garland, 1987. 277 p. ; 23 cm. (Foreign economic policy of the United States) Thesis (Ph. D.)--Michigan State University, 1967. Bibliography: p. 272-277. ISBN 0-8240-8072-6 LC Card 87-23717 DDC 382/.4567721/0952 19
1. Cotton textile industry - Japan - History - 20th century. 2. Cotton textile industry - United States - History - 20th century. 3. Japan - Commerce - United States - History - 20th century. 4. United States - Commerce - Japan - History - 20th century. 5. Export controls - Japan - History - 20th century. I. Title. II.

Series.
HD9886.J3 B38 1987

Baugh, James R. Neill, Robert Hitt. How to lose your farm in ten easy lessons and cope with it /. Leland, Miss. , c1987. xi, 138 p. ; ISBN 0-9617591-1-9 (pbk.) : LC Card 87-14176 DDC 338.1/3/097624 19
HD1476.U6 A156 1987

Baughman, James L., 1952- Television's guardians : the FCC and the politics of programming, 1958-1967 / James L. Baughman. Knoxville : University of Tennessee Press, c1985. xvi, 311 p. : ill. ; 23 cm. Includes index. Bibliography: p. [265]-302. ISBN 0-87049-448-1 : LC Card 84-13178 DDC 384.55/4 19
1. Television broadcasting policy - United States. 2. Television - Law and legislation - United States. I. Title.
HE8700.8 .B38 1985
NYPL [MWGT 85-1604]

Baum, Herbert, Dr. Wettbewerbspolitik auf dem Treibstoffmarkt / Herbert Baum. 1. Aufl. Baden-Baden : Nomos, c1983. 97 p. ; 23 cm. (Schriften der Volks- und Betriebswirtschaftlichen Vereinigung im Rheinisch-Westfälischen Industriegebiet. Sonderreihe . Heft 9) Includes bibliographical references. ISBN 3-7890-0881-8 LC Card 83-187053
1. Gasoline - Prices - Germany (West). 2. Gasoline industry - Germany (West). 3. Competition - Germany, West. I. Title. II. Series.
HD9573.5 .B38 1983

Baumann, Fred E. Democratic capitalism? . Charlottesville , 1986. ix, 210 p. ; ISBN 0-8139-1112-5 LC Card 86-7755 DDC 321.8 19
JC423 .D4416 1986
NYPL [(not yet cat'd 4/16/87)]

Baumann, Hans, 1931- Der deutsche Maschinenbau im Wandel der industriellen Output-Struktur : seine Produktionsaussichten bis 1985 : eine branchenwirtschaftliche Untersuchung als Grundlage der Unternehmensplanung / Hans Baumann. München : Ifo-Institut für Wirtschaftsforschung, 1978. vi, 196 p. : ill. ; 21 cm. (Ifo-Studien zur Industriewirtschaft . 16) Bibliography: p. 188-196. LC Card 84-126586
1. Machinery industry - Germany (West) - Forecasting. I. Title. II. Series.
HD9705.G4 B26 1978

Baumann Neves, Renato. Exportações e crescimento industrial no Brasil / Renato Baumann Neves. Rio de Janeiro : IPEA/INPES, 1985. 274 p. : ill. ; 21 cm. (Monografia / Instituto de Planejamento Econômico e Social. Instituto de Pesquisas . no. 33) Bibliography: p. 255-274. LC Card 86-195612
1. Foreign trade promotion - Brazil. 2. Brazil - Commerce. 3. Brazil - Commercial policy. 4. Brazil - Industries. I. Series: Monografia / Instituto de Planejamento Econômico e Social. Instituto de Pesquisas , no. 33. II. Title.
HF1513 .B38 1985

Baumaterialien und Selbsthilfe . Ziss, Roland. Saarbrücken , Fort Lauderdale, Fl. , 1986. 319 p. : ISBN 3-88156-333-4 LC Card 86-197177
HD7287.96.M6 Z57 1986

Baumback, Clifford Mason, 1915- How to organize and operate a small business / Clifford M. Baumback. 8th ed. Englewood Cliffs, NJ : Prentice Hall, c1988. xiii, 578 p. : ill. ; 25 cm. Includes index. ISBN 0-13-424987-9 LC Card 87-20455 DDC 658/.022 19
1. Small business - Management. I. Title.
HD62.7 .B39 1988

Baumgard, Gerhard, 1952- Der Beitrag des Geldes zur gesellschaftlichen Wohlfahrt : eine theoretischen Analyse der optimalen Geldmenge / Gerhard Baumgard. München : V. Florentz, c1984. 232 p. : ill. ; 21 cm. (Volkswirtschaftliche Forschung und Entwicklung . Bd. 9) Bibliography: p. 220-232. Includes index. ISBN 3-88259-304-8 LC Card 85-113519
1. Money. 2. Money supply. I. Title. II. Series.
HG221 .B348 1984

Baumgartner, Thomas (Thomas Martin)
Burns, Tom R. Man, decisions, society . New York , c1985. xiv, 342 p. : ISBN 2-88124-004-6 (France) LC Card 84-10303 DDC 301 19
HM24 .B85 1985 ***NYPL [JLE 86-2963]***

The Politics of energy forecasting . Oxford [Oxfordshire] , New York , 1987. xiii, 314 p. : ISBN 0-19-828547-7 : LC Card 86-23885 DDC 333.79 19
HD9502.A2 P66 1987

Baumgartner, Ulrich, Dr. Die Versicherungsbedingungen und wichtigsten Prämiensätze der in der Schweiz konzessionierten Lebensversicherungsgesellschaften /. Bern , 1986. 101 p. ; LC Card 87-124065 DDC 368.3/2/009494 19
HG9148 .V47 1986

Baumier, Jean. Ces patrons qui gagnent / Jean Baumier. Paris : Plon, c1986. 262 p. ; 23 cm. Bibliography: p. [257] ISBN 2-259-01532-8 : LC Card 87-106535
1. Business enterprises - France - History. 2. Business enterprises - History. 3. Corporations - France - History. 4. Corporations - History. 5. International business enterprises - History. I. Title.
HD2855 .B38 1986

Baumol, William J.
Microtheory : applications and origins / William J. Baumol. Brighton, Sussex : Wheatsheaf Books, 1986. xxvii, 286 p. : ill. ; 25 cm. Includes bibliographies and index. ISBN 0-7450-0110-6 LC Card 86-673554
1. Economics. 2. Welfare economics. I. Title.
HB171 .B326x 1986b

Microtheory : applications and origins / William J. Baumol. Brighton, Sussex : Wheatsheaf, c1986. xxvii, 286 p. : ill. ; 26 cm. Includes bibliographies and index. ISBN 0-7450-0110-6
1. Economics - Addresses, essays, lectures. 2. Welfare economics - Addresses, essays, lectures. I. Title.
NYPL [JLF 86-1374]

Superfairness : applications and theory / by William J. Baumol, with contributions by Dietrich Fischer. Cambridge, Mass. : MIT Press, c1986. xi, 266 p. : ill. ; 24 cm. Includes index. Bibliography: p. [255]-261. ISBN 0-262-02234-6 LC Card 85-15127 DDC 305 19
1. Distributive justice. 2. Social justice. I. Fischer, Dietrich. II. Title.
HB72 .B356 1986 ***NYPL [JLE 86-2402]***

The theory of environmental policy / William J. Baumol, Wallace E. Oates ; with contributions by V.S. Bawa and David F. Bradford. 2nd ed. Cambridge [Cambridgeshire] ; New York : Cambridge University Press, 1988. x, 299 p. : ill. ; 24 cm. Includes bibliographical references and index. ISBN 0-521-32224-3 LC Card 87-24975 DDC 363.7/001 19
1. Environmental policy. 2. Externalities (Economics). 3. Expenditures, Public. 4. Quality of life. I. Oates, Wallace E. II. Title.
HC79.E5 B375 1988

Der Bausparvertrag /. Zink, Achim. Wiesbaden , 1984. 110 p. : ISBN 3-409-47001-8 LC Card 84-213485
HG2156.G3 Z55 1984

Bausteine für die Planungspraxis in Nordrhein Westfalen .
(3) Ruhender Verkehr in Wohngebieten /. Dortmund , c1983, [1982] 121 p. : LC Card 83-236251
HE363.G32 P377 1983

Bausteine zur Selbsthilfe.
Versicherungen in der Altbauerneuerung /. Berlin , c1985. 83 p. ; ISBN 3-433-02219-4 LC Card 86-104351
HG9986.4.G3 V47 1985

Bautista, Romeo M., 1941- Production incentives in Philippine agriculture : effects of trade and exchange rate policies / Romeo M. Bautista. Washington, D.C., USA : International Food Policy Research Institute, c1987. 78 p. : ill. ; 26 cm. (Research report . 59) "May 1987." Bibliography: p. 76-78. ISBN 0-89629-061-1 (pbk.) LC Card 87-3233 DDC 338.1/8 19
1. Agricultural productivity - Philippines. 2. Produce trade - Government policy - Philippines. 3. Agricultural prices - Government policy - Philippines. 4. Philippines - Commercial policy. I. Series: Research report (International Food Policy Research Institute) , 59. II. Title.
HD2087 .B38 1987

Bauwens, Jan G., 1924- Industrial co-operation and investment in Yugoslavia / Jan G. Bauwens, Nicholas Bueno De Mesquita, Martin Jones ; prepared for Commission of European Communities by Cegos Management Development, London and Transtec, Brussels. Luxembourg : Office for Official Publications of the European Communities ; Washington, D.C. : European Community Information Service [distributor], 1986. viii, 161 p. : ill. ; 29 cm. Includes bibliographical references. ISBN 92-825-6410-X (pbk.) : LC Card 86-216364 DDC 332.6/73/09497 19
1. Investments, Foreign - Yugoslavia. 2. Joint ventures - Yugoslavia. I. Bueno de Mesquita, Nicholas. II. Jones, Martin. III. Commission of the European Communities. IV. Cegos Management Development (Firm : London, England). V. Transtec (Firm ; Brussels, Belgium). VI. Title.
HG5682 .B38 1986

BAUXITE - ECONOMIC ASPECTS - DEVELOPING COUNTRIES.
Holloway, Steven Kendall, 1951- The aluminum multinationals and the bauxite cartel /. New York , 1988. vii, 93 p. : ISBN 0-312-00939-9 : LC Card 87-12991 DDC 338.8/87 19
HD9539.A62 H64 1988

BAUXITE MINES AND MINING - CARIBBEAN AREA.
The Caribbean Basin and the changing world economic structure /. Groningen , c1986. 194 p. ; ISBN 90-01-18630-0 (pbk.) : LC Card 87-117415 DDC 330.9729/052 19
HC151 .C26 1986

Bavara. Landeszentrale für Politische Bildungsarbeit. see **Bayerische Landeszentrale für Politische Bildungsarbeit.**

Bavaria (Germany). Bayerisches Staatsministerium für Landesentwicklung und Umweltfragen.
Regionalbericht Region Oberfranken-West /. [München] , 1976. 83 p. : LC Card 86-231827
HC288.O16 R44 1976

Umweltpolitik in Bayern /. München [1986] 176 p. : LC Card 86-204249
HC287.B3 U48 1986

BAVARIA (GERMANY) - ECONOMIC CONDITIONS.
Hesselmann, Hans. Das Wirtschaftsbürgertum in Bayern 1890-1914 . [Stuttgart] , 1985. 419 p. : ISBN 3-515-04565-1 LC Card 86-127555
HC287.B3 H46 1985

Jüngling, Elisabeth. Streiks in Bayern (1889-1914) . München , 1986. viii, 307 p., [24] p. of plates : ISBN 3-87821-214-3 LC Card 87-408637 DDC 331.89/29433 19
HD5380.B38 J86 1986

Stationen . Darmstadt , 1984. ix, 228 p., [1] leaf of plates : ISBN 3-534-02410-9 LC Card 85-138779
HC286.5 .S825 1984

BAVARIA (GERMANY) - ECONOMIC POLICY.
Stationen . Darmstadt , 1984. ix, 228 p., [1] leaf of plates : ISBN 3-534-02410-9 LC Card 85-138779
HC286.5 .S825 1984

BAVARIA (GERMANY) - POLITICS AND GOVERNMENT.
Stationen . Darmstadt , 1984. ix, 228 p., [1] leaf of plates : ISBN 3-534-02410-9 LC Card 85-138779
HC286.5 .S825 1984

BAVARIA (GERMANY) - POLITICS AND GOVERNMENT - 1777-1918.
Hesselmann, Hans. Das Wirtschaftsbürgertum in Bayern 1890-1914 . [Stuttgart] , 1985. 419 p. : ISBN 3-515-04565-1 LC Card 86-127555
HC287.B3 H46 1985

Bavinck, Maarten, 1954- Small fry : the economy of petty fishermen in northern Sri Lanka / Maarten Bavinck. Amsterdam : VU Uitgeverij : Free University Press, 1984. xii, 151 p. ; 21 cm. (Antropologische studies VU . 5) Bibliography: p. 148-151. ISBN 90-6256-374-0 (pbk.) LC Card 84-187330 DDC 338.3/72709549/3 19
1. Fish trade - Sri Lanka - Kadalur. 2. Fishers - Sri Lanka - Kadalur. 3. Fish trade - Government policy - Sri Lanka - History. I. Title. II. Series.
HD9466.S723 K343 1984
NYPL [JLD 86-2668]

Bawcutt, P. A. (Paul A.) Captive insurance companies : establishment, operation, and management / P.A. Bawcutt.2nd ed. Cambridge [Cambridgeshire] ; Wolfeboro, N.H. : Woodhead-Faulkner, 1987. xii, 410 p. : ill. ; 24 cm. Bibliography: p. [403]-405. Includes index. ISBN 0-85941-382-9 : LC Card 86-32621 DDC 368/.0068 19
1. Insurance companies - Captive companies. I. Title.
HG8104 .B38 1987

Baxter, David, 1945- Hamilton, S. W. (Stanley William), 1939- Foundations of real estate financing . Vancouver , c1982. xv, 319 p. : ISBN 0-409-98843-X LC Card 87-143264
HF5695.5.R3 H36 1982

Baxter, Ellen. The Heights : a community housing strategy / by Ellen Baxter. New York, N.Y. : Community Service Society : Order from Office of Information, Dept. of Public Affairs, Community Service Society, [1986] 69 leaves : ill. ; 28 cm. (CSS working papers) "October 1986." LC Card 87-401534 DDC 363.5/8 19
1. Homeless persons - Housing - New York (N. Y.) - Case studies. 2. Heights, The (New York, N. Y.). 3. Manhattan (New York, N.Y.). I. Community Service Society of New York. II. Title. III. Series.
HD7287.96.U62 N683 1986

Baxter, John O., 1927- Las carneradas : sheep trade in New Mexico, 1700-1860 / John O. Baxter.1st ed. Albuquerque : University of New Mexico Press, c1987. x, 198 p., [4] p. of plates : ill., maps, ports. ; 22 cm. "Published in cooperation with the Historical Society of New Mexico." Bibliography: p. 173-183. Includes index. ISBN 0-8263-0961-5 LC Card 86-30906 DDC 381/.4163/009789 19
1. Sheep industry - New Mexico - History. 2. Sheep ranches - New Mexico - History. 3. Sheep ranchers - New Mexico - History. 4. Sheep industry - Southwest, New - History. 5. Southwest, New - History - To 1848. 6. Land settlement - New Spain - History. I. Historical Society of New Mexico. II. Title.
HD9436.U53 N63 1987

Baxter, Raymond J., 1928- Railroad ferries of the Hudson : and stories of a deckhand / by Raymond J. Baxter and Arthur G. Adams. Woodcliff Lake, NJ : Lind Publications, 1987. viii, 254 p. : ill. ; 29 cm. Bibliography: p. 229-230. Includes index. ISBN 0-910389-01-2 : LC Card 87-22782 DDC 386/.2234/097473 19
1. Ferries - Hudson River (N.Y. and N.J.) - History - 20th century. 2. Local transit - New York Region - History - 20th century. I. Adams, Arthur G. II. Title.
HE5774. B39 1987

Bayan, Richard. Words that sell : the thesaurus to help promote your products, services, and ideas / Richard Bayan. Chicago : Contemporary Books, [1987], c1984. 127 p. ; 23 cm. Reprint. Originally published: Westbury, N.Y. : Caddylak Pub., c1984. Bibliography: p. 123-124. Includes index. ISBN 0-8092-4799-2 (pbk.) : LC Card 86-29319 DDC 659.1/014 19
1. Advertising copy. 2. Vocabulary. I. Title.
HF5825 .B35 1987

Bayat, Assef. Workers and revolution in Iran : a Third World experience of workers' control / Assef Bayat. London ; Atlantic Highlands, New Jersey, USA : Zed Books, 1987. 227 p. : ill. ; 23 cm. Bibliography: p. 208-222. Includes index. ISBN 0-86232-389-4 LC Card 87-160253 DDC 322/.2/0955 19
1. Works councils - Iran. 2. Iran - Politics and government - 1941-1979. 3. Labor and laboring classes - Iran - Political activity. 4. Works councils - Iran - Management. I. Title.
HD5660.I6 B39 1987

Bayer, B. József. A kis- és középvállalatok és a gazdasági fejlődés : néhány tőkés gazdaság példája / Bayer B. József. Budapest : Közgazdasági és Jogi Könyvkiadó, 1986. 203, [1] p. : ill. ; 19 cm. (Időszerű közgazdasági kérdések sorozat, 0324-3214) Bibliography: p. 197-[204]. ISBN 963-221-914-7 : LC Card 87-138623
1. Small business. I. Series: Időszerű közgazdasági kérdések. II. Title.
HD2341 .B29 1986

Bayerische Julius-Maximilians-Universität Würzburg. Energie und Gerechtigkeit /. München , c1984. xii, 254 p. : ISBN 3-597-10259-X LC Card 84-175053
HD9502.A2 E5192 1984

Bayerische Landeszentrale für Politische Bildungsarbeit. (Old Catalog form: Bavaria. Landeszentrale für Politische Bildungsarbeit.) Randak, Harald, 1942- Die soziale Marktwirtschaft /. München , 1985. 143 p. : LC Card 85-216985
HC286.5 .R36 1985

BAYERISCHE VEREINSBANK. (Old Catalog form: Bayerische Vereinsbank, Munich.) Möglichkeiten und Probleme der Realisierung flexibler Arbeitszeitstrukturen in Filialen der Bayerischen Vereinsbank München /. München , 1985. 67 p. : LC Card 87-401387 DDC 331.25/72 19
HD5109.2.G32 M866 1985

Die bayerischen Bauernkammern von 1920 bis 1933 /. Ratjen, Wolfgang. München , 1981. vi, 204 p. ; ISBN 3-87913-108-2 : LC Card 83-194708 DDC 338.1/06/0433 19
HD1486.G3 R34 1981

Bayes, Jane H., 1939- Comparable worth, pay equity, and public policy /. New York , 1988. xi, 280 p. ; ISBN 0-313-26014-1 (lib. bdg. : alk. paper) LC Card 87-17735 DDC 331.2/1 19
HD6061.2.U6 C656 1988

Bayley, Stephen. Sex, drink, and fast cars : the creation and consumption of images / Stephen Bayley. London ; Boston : Faber and Faber, 1986. 112 p. ; 20 cm. Bibliography: p. 111-112. ISBN 0-571-14526-4 (pbk.) : LC Card 87-672358
1. Automobiles - Social aspects - United States - History. 2. Automobiles - United States - Design and construction - History. 3. Automobiles - Technological innovations - History. 4. Consumers' preferences - History. I. Title.
HD9710.U52 B34 1986

Bayliss, Brian T. The measurement of supply and demand in freight transport / B.T. Bayliss. Aldershot, Hants, England : Avebury ; Brookfield, USA : Gower Pub. Co., 1988. p. cm. Includes index. ISBN 0-566-05526-0 : LC Card 87-19817 DDC 380.5/9 19
1. Freight and freightage - Management. I. Title.
HE199.A2 B395 1988

Bayne, Nicholas, 1937- Putnam, Robert D. Hanging together . Cambridge, Mass. , 1987. x, 293 p. ; ISBN 0-674-37226-3 (pbk.) LC Card 87-23593 DDC 337 19
HF1410.5 .P87 1987

Baynes, Peter A. Distribution of local sales tax revenue : statutory framework and current trends / Peter A. Baynes. Albany, N.Y. (119 Washington Ave., Albany 12210) : New York State Conference of Mayors, [1986] 13 p. : ill. ; 28 cm. (NYCOM municipal management series . no. 4) "A project of the New York State Conference of Mayors and Other Municipal Officials." "May 1986." LC Card 87-106773 DDC 336.2/713/09747 19
1. Sales tax - New York (State). 2. Local taxation - New York (State). I. New York State Conference of Mayors and Other Municipal Officials. II. Title. III. Series.
HJ5715.U62 N72 1986

Bayo, Eliseo. Descubro y acuso / Eliseo Bayo. 3a ed. Esplugues de Llobregat, Barcelona : Plaza & Janés, 1985,c1984. 287 p. ; 22 cm. (Hombre y sociedad) Epoca ISBN 84-01-33258-3
1. Economic history - 1971-. 2. World politics - 1945-. I. Series: Hombre y sociedad (Esplugas de Llobregat, Spain). II. Title. ***NYPL [JFD 86-7111]***

BAZAARS, ORIENTAL - DIRECTORIES.
Nedlog, D'Lanor. Insider's guide to antique bazaars in Japan /. Tokyo, Japan , c1986. 124 p. : ISBN 4-906231-00-4 LC Card 87-123282 DDC 381/.18 19
HF5475.J3 N43 1986

Bazarian, Carl J. The Gulf States = Duwal al-Khalij / by Carl J. Bazarian ; Vivien E. Fauerbach, editor. New York, N.Y. : Chase World Information Corp, c1980. 577 p. : ill. ; 30 cm. (The Chase World Information series on developing business in the Middle East and North Africa) ISBN 0-916006-07-7 LC Card 80-65496
1. Persian Gulf States - Economic conditions. 2. Economic forecasting - Persian Gulf States. 3. Persian Gulf States - Economic policy. I. Fauerbach, Vivien E. II. Chase World Information Corporation. III. Title. IV. Title: Duwal al-Khalij. V. Series.
HC415.3 .B39 1980

Bazin, G. Système agraire et pratiques paysannes dans les monts Dômes /. Paris , 1983. xi, 318 p., [8] p. of plates : ISBN 2-85340-478-1 LC Card 84-216594
HD1950.D65 S97 1983

The BBC and public service broadcasting / Colin MacCabe, Olivia Stewart, editors. Manchester : Manchester University Press, c1986. viii, 116 p. ; 22 cm. (Images of Culture) CONTENTS. - Licences and liberty / Anthony Smith -- The BBC and the concept of public service broadcasting / Janet Morgan -- Centralisation and censorship / William Maley -- Public service broadcasting and the public interest / Krishan Kumar -- The economics and technology of television financing / Charles Jonscher -- Co-existence / Brenda Maddox -- An end to protection / David Elstein -- Co-production in the next decade / Margaret Matheson, Jeremy Isaacs, John Caughie -- Broadcasting / Colin MacCabe. ISBN 0-7190-1964-8 : LC Card 86-209725 DDC 384.54/4/0941 19
1. British Broadcasting Corporation. 2. Public broadcasting - Great Britain. 3. Broadcasting - Great Britain. I. MacCabe, Colin. II. Stewart, Olivia. III. Series.
HE8689.9.G7 B34 1986

BBC TV presents . Moss, Nicholas. London , 1986. 120 p. : ISBN 0-946358-29-X LC Card 87-146728 DDC 384.55/4/06041 19
HE8700.9.G7 M67 1986

The BBP safety management handbook. Waterford, CT : Bureau of Business Practice, c1986. 1 v. (various pagings) : ill. ; 30 cm. ISBN 0-87622-050-2 LC Card 87-119198 DDC 658.3/82 19
1. Industrial safety - Management. I. Bureau of Business Practice. II. Title: B.B.P. safety management handbook.
HD7262 .B38 1986

Be your own financial advisor /. Pritchard, Robert E., 1941- Englewood Cliffs, N.J. , c1988. xiv, 187 p. ; ISBN 0-13-071242-6 LC Card 87-14366 DDC 332.024 19
HG179 .P737 1988

BEACH TRANSPORTATION CO.
Smith, Steve, 1941- Second to none . Missoula, Mont. , c1986. 120 p. : ISBN 0-933126-84-0 (pbk.) LC Card 86-62692 DDC 388.3/22/09786 19
HE5633.M9 S65 1986

BEACHES - ECONOMIC ASPECTS - FLORIDA.
Bell, Frederick W. An economic analysis of the importance of saltwater beaches in Florida /. Gainesville, FL [1986] xi, 166 p. : LC Card 86-622310 DDC 333.91/7/09759 19
HD266.F6 B45 1986

Beal, Edwin Fletcher. The practice of collective bargaining / James P. Begin, Edwin F. Beal. 7th ed. Homewood, Ill. : R.D. Irwin, 1985. xvi, 560 p. : ill. ; 25 cm. (Irwin publications in economics) Includes bibliographies and index. ISBN 0-256-03214-9 LC Card 84-82023 DDC 331.89 19
1. Collective bargaining - United States. 2. Grievance arbitration - United States - Case studies. I. Begin, James P. II. Title. III. Series.
HD6508 .B375 1985
NYPL [*R-Econ. 86-3458]

Beams, Floyd A. Advanced accounting / Floyd A. Beams. 4th ed. Englewood Cliffs, N.J. : Prentice Hall, c1988. xii, 968 p. : ill. ; 25 cm. Includes bibliographies and index. ISBN 0-13-010182-6 LC Card 87-26226 DDC 657/.046 19
1. Accounting. I. Title.
HF5635 .B41517 1988

Beamtenpolitische Arbeitstagung (27th : 1986 : Bad Kissingen, Germany) Umweltschutz und Verwaltung . Bonn , c1986. 171 p. ; ISBN 3-87999-040-9 LC Card 87-136048 DDC 363.7/056/0943 19
HC290.5.E5 U645 1986

Bean, C. R. (Charles R.), 1953- The Rise in unemployment /. Oxford, UK , New York, NY, USA , 1987, c1986. 382 p. : ISBN 0-631-15419-1 (pbk.) : LC Card 87-699 DDC 331.13/7 19
HD5707.5 .R57 1987

BEAN CURD INDUSTRY - UNITED STATES.
Shurtleff, William, 1941- Tofutti® & other soy ice creams . Lafayette, CA , c1985. 2 v. : ISBN 0-933332-19-X (v. 1) : LC Card 85-10829

DDC 381/.4174 19
HD9330.B323 U 1985 ***NYPL [JLF 86-1035]***

Bean, Philip. Barbara Wootton--social science and public policy . London , New York , 1986. xi, 291 p. ; ISBN 0-422-79690-5 LC Card 85-27650 DDC 330 19
HB171 .B248 1985 ***NYPL [JLE 86-1743]***

BEANS - BRAZIL, SOUTH - MARKETING - HISTORY - 20TH CENTURY.
Smith, Gordon Whitford, 1934- Agricultural marketing and economic development . New York , 1987. iii, 417 p. ; ISBN 0-8240-1371-9 (alk. paper) : LC Card 87-11833 DDC 381/.41318/09816 19
HD9066.B84 S687 1987

Beares, Paul. Consumer lending / Paul Beares. Washington, D.C. (1120 Connecticut Ave., N.W., Washington 20036) : Education Policy & Development, American Bankers Association, c1987. xi, 335 p. : ill. ; 25 cm. Bibliography: p. 325. Includes index. "058400"--Spine. LC Card 87-410019 DDC 332.1/753/0685 19
1. Consumer credit - United States. 2. Loans, Personal - United States. 3. Bank loans - United States. I. American Bankers Association. Education Policy and Development Group. II. Title.
HG3755 .B39 1987

Beat the MBAs to the top! . Jones, Constance. Reading, Mass. , c1987. vii, 360 p. ; ISBN 0-201-11310-4 (pbk.) : LC Card 87-11363 DDC 650/.07/15 19
HF1131 .J756 1987

Beattie, Derek. Company administration handbook /. Aldershot, Hants, England , Brookfield, Vt., U. S.A. , 1988. xxiv, 737 p. : ISBN 0-566-02667-8 : LC Card 86-31876 DDC 658/.00941 19
HD70.G7 C57 1988

Beatty, Randolph. Smirlock, Michael. Taxes and mergers . New York, N.Y. (90 Trinity Place, New York 10006) [c1986] 42 p. : LC Card 86-210061 DDC 336.24/3 19
HD2746.5 .S64 1986

Beatty, Richard W.
The Performance management sourcebook /. Amherst, Mass. [1987] 393 p. : ISBN 0-87425-074-9 (pbk.) LC Card 87-153991 DDC 658.3/125 19
HF5549.5.R3 P4755 1987

The Productivity sourcebook /. Amherst, Mass. [1987] x, 467 p. : ISBN 0-87425-075-7 (pbk.) LC Card 87-404037 DDC 658.3/14 19
HD57 .P7114 1987

Beaucage, Benoît. Les Structures productives d'une région périphérique . Rimouski , c1984. xi, 718 p. : ISBN 2-920270-27-3 LC Card 85-132709 DDC 330.9714/77 19
HC117.G37 S78 1984

Beaud, Michel.
[Histoire du capitalisme, 1500-1980. English]
A history of capitalism, 1500-1980 / Michel Beaud ; translated by Tom Dickman and Anny Lefebvre. London : Macmillan, 1984. 256 p. ; 22 cm. Translation of: Histoire du capitalisme, 1500-1980. Bibliography: p. 231-248. Includes index. ISBN 0-333-35957-7 LC Card 87-673370
1. Economic history. 2. Capitalism - History. I. Title.
HC51 .B3813x 1984

Beaumont, Paul (Paul M.) Regional wage rates [microform] : an empirical study of phillips curves and wage transmission processes / Paul M. Beaumont. Iowa City : Institute of Urban and Regional Research, University of Iowa, 1982. 22 p. : ill. ; 28 cm. (ASA/census working paper . 6 6) Bibliography: p. 21-22. Microfilm. New York : New York Public Library, 1985. 1 microfilm reel ; 35 mm. (MN *ZZ-25,047)
1. Wages - Mathematical models. 2. Phillips curve. I. Iowa. University. Institute of Urban and Regional Research. II. Title. III. Series.
NYPL [*ZT-1564 no.29]

Beaune, Jean-Claude. Les Sauvages dans la cité . Seyssel , c1985. 229 p. ; ISBN 2-903528-53-5
NYPL [JLD 86-1133]

Bebel, August, 1840-1913. Sozialreform und Rhetorik =. Wiesbaden , 1984. 174 p. ; ISBN 3-515-02857-9 ***NYPL [L-11 3778 Bd. 4]***

Bebel, Ferdinand August. see **Bebel, August, 1840-1913.**

Bebyggelsen i Pargas, S:t Mårtens och Vemo socknar i egentliga Finland under senmedeltiden och på 1500-talet /. Orrman, Eljas. Helsingfors , 1986. 293 p. : ISBN 951-9254-73-0 LC Card 86-199875
HD723 .O77 1986

Becher, Ursula A. J. Evaluation der Berufsberatung der Bundesanstalt für Arbeit . Nürnberg , 1983. vii, 282 p. : LC Card 85-107586
HF5382.5.G3 E9 1983

Bechhoefer, Ina S. Guide to real estate and mortgage banking software /. Washington, D.C. , 1986. 3 v. ; ISBN 0-917935-14-4 (pbk. : set) LC Card 86-63061 DDC 333.3/028/553 19
HD1380 .G85 1986a

Bechtold, Hartmut. Die Kartellierung der deutschen Volkswirtschaft und die sozialdemokratische Theorie-Diskussion vor 1933 / Hartmut Bechtold. Frankfurt am Main : Haag + Herchen, c1986. 291 p. ; 21 cm. Bibliography: p. 263-291. ISBN 3-89228-000-2 LC Card 86-193858
1. Cartels - Germany - History. 2. Industrial concentration - Germany - History. 3. Sozialdemokratische Partei Deutschlands - History. I. Title.
HD2757.5 .B43 1986

Bechtold, Karl-Heinz. Indien, Probleme eines Schwellenlandes . Tübingen , c1984. 75 p. ; ISBN 3-922362-02-8 LC Card 85-157722
HC435.2 .I6235 1984

Beck, George C., 1947- Scharf, Charles A. Acquisitions, mergers, sales, buyouts, and takeovers . Englewood Cliffs, N.J. , c1985. xi, 452 p. : ISBN 0-13-003120-8 LC Card 85-6566 DDC 658.1/6/0973 19
HD2741 .S35 1985 ***NYPL [JLF 86-611]***

Beck, Horst. Auswirkungen von nicht kostenniveauneutralen Lohnänderungen auf Beschäftigung und Preisniveau : Darstellung und empirische Überprüfung von Hypothesen der Cost-push-Theorie und Kaufkrafttheorie des Lohnes sowie der neuen Makroökonomie / Horst Beck. Krefeld : Marchal und Matzenbacher, 1983. iii, 227 p. : ill. ; 21 cm. Bibliography: p. 221-227. ISBN 3-88358-033-3 LC Card 83-202725
1. Wages. 2. Purchasing power. 3. Macroeconomics. 4. Wages - Germany, West. 5. Purchasing power - Germany, West. I. Title.
HD4911 .B4 1983

Beck, M. Ruth. Abbott, Michael G. Male and female earnings in Canadian manufacturing, 1931 /. Kingston, Ont., Canada [1986] 82 p. ; LC Card 87-145991 DDC 331.2/87/0971 19
HD4979 .A22 1986

Beck, Martha W., 1942- Beck, Thomas D. French notables . New York , c1987. 254 p. : ISBN 0-8204-0393-8 : LC Card 87-12156 DDC 338.0944 19
HC275 .B37 1987

Beck, Paul, Dipl.-Kfm. Agrarmärkte & Agrarmarketing . Hamburg , 1983. 220 p. : ISBN 3-922528-45-7 LC Card 84-162297
HD1955 .A515 1983

Beck, Peter. Einwendungen bei Eurocheque und Kreditkarte / Peter Beck. [S.l. : s.n., 1986] (Köln : Druck und Verarbeitung, Druck- + Verlagshaus Wienand) xv, 146, 31 p. ; 21 cm. (Bankrechtliche Sonderveröffentlichungen des Instituts für Bankwirtschaft und Bankrecht an der Universität zu Köln . 38. Bd.) Bibliography: p. vi-xv. LC Card 86-233484
1. Credit cards - Germany, West. 2. Bank credit cards - Germany (West). I. Title. II. Series.
HG3756.G3 B43 1986

Beck, Robert, 1953- Der Plan Freycinet und die Provinzen : Aspekte der infrastrukturellen Entwicklung der französischen Provinzen durch die Dritte Republik / Robert Beck. Frankfurt am Main ; New York : P. Lang, c1986. 354 p. : ill. ; 21 cm. (Europäische Hochschulschriften. Reihe III, Geschichte und ihre Hilfswissenschaften, 0531-7320 . Bd. 318 = vol. 318 = vol. 318) Bibliography: p. 326-333. ISBN 3-8204-9791-9 LC Card 87-408148 DDC 385/.068 19
1. Railroads and state - France - Provinces - History - 19th century. 2. Freycinet, Charles Louis de Saulses de 1828-1923. 3. Railroads - France - Provinces - History - 19th century. I. Series: Europäische Hochschulschriften. Reihe III, Geschichte und ihre Hilfswissenschaften , Bd. 318. II. Title.
HE3067 .B43 1986

Beck, Thomas, 1950- Handwerk in Staat und Gesellschaft : Analysen, Strategien, Erfolgskontrolle : eine empirische Untersuchung am Beispiel der Handwerkskammer Konstanz / Thomas Beck. München : V. Florentz, c1987. xvii, 319 p. : ill. ; 21 cm. (Volkswirtschaftliche Forschung und Entwicklung . Bd. 30) Bibliography: p. 299-315. Includes index. ISBN 3-88259-415-2 LC Card 87-152203 DDC 331.7/94 19
1. Handwerskammer Konstanz. 2. Artisans - Germany (West) - Konstanz. I. Title. II. Series.
HD2346.G32 K663 1987

Becker, Charles M., 1954- Mills, Edwin S. Studies in Indian urban development /. New York , 1986. viii, 214 p. ; ISBN 0-19-520507-3 : LC Card 86-2489 DDC 307.1/4/0954 19
HT147.I5 M56 1986 ***NYPL [JLE 86-3750]***

Becker, David G., 1938- Postimperialism . Boulder , 1987. x, 252 p. : ISBN 1-555-87046-5 (lib. bdg. : alk. paper) : LC Card 87-4455 DDC 338.8/881724 19
HD2932 .P67 1987

Becker, Fritz, 1947- Entwicklungseffekte durch Verkehrserschliessung in der Arabischen Republik Jemen : Karten und Erläuterungen / Fritz Becker und Karlheinz Hottes, unter zeitweiliger Mitarbeit von Uwe Meyer und Gisela Pohlig. Bochum : Institut für Entwicklungsforschung und Entwicklungspolitik, Ruhr-Universität Bochum, 1984. 50 p. : maps ; 42 cm. (Materialien und kleine Schriften . 97) "Legende der Markt- und Ringstrassenkarten" (1 p.) laid in. Includes bibliographies. LC Card 84-241945
1. Transportation - Yemen. 2. Transportation - Yemen - Maps. 3. Yemen - Economic conditions. I. Hottes, Karlheinz. II. Series: Materialien und kleine Schriften (Ruhr-Universität Bochum. Institut für Entwicklungsforschung und Entwicklungspolitik) , 97. III. Title.
HE268.7 .B4 1984 ***NYPL [JLH 86-2]***

Becker, Hans, Dr. Eine Transaktionskostentheoretische Interpretation interner Arbeitsmärkte / von Hans Becker. Berlin : Duncker & Humblot, c1985. 156 p. ; 24 cm. (Volkswirtschaftliche Schriften. Heft 351) Bibliography: p. [150]-156. ISBN 3-428-05848-8 LC Card 85-218635 DDC 331.12 19
1. Labor supply. 2. Transaction costs. I. Title. II. Series.
HD5706 .B4 1985

Becker, J. W. Enige aspecten van arbeid in de toekomst . 's-Gravenhage , 1986. 178 p. : ISBN 90-12-05246-7 LC Card 87-101491
HD5792 .E47 1986

Becker, Johann Michael. Entwurff und Beschreibung von der Papiermacherey, worinnen der Ursprung des Papiermachens, der Fortgang, wie heutiges Tages das Papier gemachet wird, wie solches viele Mühe und Arbeit hat, benebst denen bey den Papiermachern befindlichen Wörtern, denen Kayserlichen Verordnungen und andern dahin einschlagenden Dingen /. [Mainz , 1962] (Darmstadt : E. Roether) 1 v. (various pagings) : LC Card 87-107659
HD9820.5 .E57 1962

Becker, Stan. Mosley, W. Henry (Wiley Henry), 1933- The dynamics of birth spacing and marital fertility in Kenya /. [Nairobi? , 1981] 63 leaves : LC Card 85-980189
HB1072.5.A3 M66 1981

Becker, Susan. Dubarle, Patrick. The space industry . Paris, France [Washington, D.C.] c1985. 92 p. : ISBN 92-64-12772-0 : LC Card 86-210154 DDC 338.4/76291 19
HD9711.5.A2 D83 1985

Beckerman, Wilfred. Wage rigidity and unemployment /. Baltimore , 1986. viii, 221 p. : ISBN 0-8018-3400-7 LC Card 86-45446 DDC 331.2/1 19
HD4909 .W26 1986 ***NYPL [JLD 86-4077]***

Beckford, George L. Persistent poverty : underdevelopment in plantation economies of the Third World / George L. Beckford. London : Zed Books ; Totowa, N.J. : U. S. distributor, Biblio Distribution Center, c1983. xxv, 244 p. : ill. ; 22 cm. (Third World studies) Includes bibliographical references and index. ISBN 0-86232-207-3 (pbk.) LC Card 85-149825

DDC 338.1/09172/4 19
1. Poor - Developing countries. 2. Agricultural laborers - Developing countries. 3. Plantations - Developing countries. I. Title. II. Series.
HC59.72.P6 B43 1983 *NYPL [JLD 87-628]*

Beckhard, Richard, 1918- Organizational transitions : managing complex change / Richard Beckhard, Reuben T. Harris.2nd ed. Reading, Mass. : Addison-Wesley Pub. Co., c1987. xii, 117 p. : ill. ; 21 cm. (Addison-Wesley OD series) Includes bibliographical references. ISBN 0-201-10887-9 (pbk.) : LC Card 86-25863 DDC 658.4/06 19
1. Organizational change. I. Harris, Reuben T. II. Series: Addison-Wesley series on organizational development. III. Title.
HD58.8 .B4 1987

Beckman, Björn, 1938- Public investment and agrarian transformation in northern Nigeria / by Björn Beckman. Rev. and expanded version. [Zaria : Centre for Social and Economic Research, Ahmadu Bello University, 1983] 33 p. ; 33 cm. (CSER reprint . no. 13) "Originally presented to the Workshop on State and Agriculture in Nigeria, University of California, Berkeley, May 7th-9th, 1982." "May 1983." Bibliography: p. 31-33. LC Card 87-402849 DDC 338.1/8669 19
1. Agriculture and state - Nigeria. 2. Public investments - Nigeria. I. Title. II. Series.
HD2145.5 .B43 1983

Beckman, Robert C. The downwave : surviving the second great depression / Robert Beckman. Portsmouth, Hants : Milestone Publications, 1983. 216 p. : ill. ; 25 cm. Includes index. Bibliography: p. [209-212]. ISBN 0-903852-38-1
1. Investments. 2. Economic history - 1971-. I. Title.
NYPL [JLE 86-3347]

Beckmann, Michael. Schneewind, Klaus A., 1939- Eltern und Kinder . Stuttgart , c1983. 229 p. : ISBN 3-17-007744-9 LC Card 83-150745 DDC 303.3/23/0943 19
HQ739 .S29 1983 *NYPL [JLE 87-1168]*

Beckouche, Pierre, 1957- Savy, Michel. Atlas des Français /. Paris , c1985. 331 p. : ISBN 2-01-011512-0 LC Card 86-178635
HC276.2 .S325 1985

Beckurts, K. H. (Karl Heinrich) Bankmitarbeiter und die neuen Informationstechniken . Frankfurt am Main , c1986. 240 p. ; ISBN 3-7819-0341-9 LC Card 86-228992
HG1709 .B355 1986

Beckwith, Karen, 1950- American women and political participation : the impacts of work, generation, and feminism / Karen Beckwith. New York : Greenwood Press, 1986. xiv, 185 p. ; 22 cm. (Contributions in women's studies. no. 68) Includes index. Bibliography: p. [169]-177. ISBN 0-313-24507-X
1. Women in politics - United States. 2. Women - United States - Political activity. 3. Feminism - United States. I. Title. *NYPL [JLD 87-36]*

Becoming clerical workers /. Valli, Linda, 1947- Boston , 1986. xv, 261 p. ; ISBN 0-7102-0336-5
NYPL [JLD 86-1147]

Bédard, Michel G. L'Homme d'affaires québécois des années 80 /. Montréal, Québec, Canada , c1983. 418 p., [14] p. of plates : ISBN 2-89045-585-8 LC Card 83-190776
HC117.Q4 H65 1983

BEDDING INDUSTRY - AUSTRALIA.
Australia. Industries Assistance Commission. Interim report . Canberra , 1976. 36 p. ; ISBN 0-642-02317-4 (pbk.) LC Card 85-132707
HD9969.B433 A83 1976

Die Bedeutung der beruflichen Mobilität als arbeitsmarktlicher Ausgleichsprozess . Leibundgut, Hansjörg, 1947- Bern , New York , c1986. ix, 235 p. : ISBN 3-261-03630-3 LC Card 87-122350 DDC 331.12/79494 19
HD5717.5.S9 L45 1986

Bedeutung der Buntmetallhütten. Jörs, Bernd. Die Bedeutung der Buntmetallhütten des mitteleuropäischen Raumes im Rahmen der Versorgung der Bundesrepublik Deutschland . Frankfurt/Main , 1983. 579 p. in various pagings : LC Card 83-226662
HD9539.Z6 C365 1983

Die Bedeutung der Buntmetallhütten des mitteleuropäischen Raumes im Rahmen der Versorgung der Bundesrepublik Deutschland . Jörs, Bernd. Frankfurt/Main , 1983. 579 p. in various pagings : LC Card 83-226662
HD9539.Z6 C365 1983

Die Bedeutung der Kapitalintensitätshypothese im neoklassischen Zwei-Sektoren-Modell und ihre empirische Überprüfung /. Wallenwein, Erich, 1951- Frankfurt am Main , New York , c1986. x, 354 p. : ISBN 3-8204-9618-1 LC Card 86-194355
HD75.5 .W33 1986

Die Bedeutung der Lohn-Leistungsrelation . Müller, Lothar. Karlsruhe , c1983. iii, 272 p. : ISBN 3-88147-014-X LC Card 84-174174
HD4945 .M84 1983

Die Bedeutung der Seehäfen für die Industrialisierung Mitteleuropas /. Seidenfus, Hellmuth Stefan. Göttingen , 1979. 20 p. ; ISBN 3-525-85769-1 LC Card 86-194319
HE131 .M84 Heft 18 HE557.A3

Die Bedeutung des Umweltschutzes für die Wirtschaft der DDR /. Ökten, Rita. Berlin , c1986. 87 p. : ISBN 3-87061-311-4 LC Card 86-194057
HC290.795.E5 O38 1986

Bedeutung, Einsatzmöglichkeiten und -probleme des kombinierten Güterverkehrs in der Ernährungswirtschaft /. Schmelzeisen, Hans-Michael. Münster [1986] xii, 350 p. : ISBN 3-88660-357-1 (Deut. Bibl.) LC Card 87-121511 DDC 380.5/24 19
HE199.5.F6 S36 1986

Die Bedeutung kleiner und mittlerer Unternehmen im Strukturwandel /. Schatz, Klaus-Werner. Kiel , 1984. 32 p. ; LC Card 85-136545
HB44 .K45 no. 103 HD2346.G3

Bedeutung und Ausstattung von Wandel- und Optionsanleihen /. Janssen, Friedrich, 1948- Göttingen , 1982. 279 p. : ISBN 3-509-01319-0 LC Card 83-240528
HG5501 .J35 1982

Bedeutung von Produktionsfunktionen für die Input-Output-Analyse. Meyer, Peter. Die Bedeutung wichtiger Typen von Produktionsfunktionen für die Input-Output-Analyse /. Frankfurt , c1983. 109 p. : ISBN 3-88323-438-9 LC Card 83-206578
HB241 .M49 1983

Die Bedeutung wichtiger Typen von Produktionsfunktionen für die Input-Output-Analyse /. Meyer, Peter. Frankfurt , c1983. 109 p. : ISBN 3-88323-438-9 LC Card 83-206578
HB241 .M49 1983

Der Bedeutungswandel der Hedschasbahn . Fiedler, Ulrich. Berlin , 1984. ix, 338 p. : ISBN 3-922968-37-6 LC Card 86-135345
HE3380.5.M53 F54 1984

Bedford Properties (Firm) Bedford Properties, Lenexa, Kansas . Washington, D.C. (1090 Vermont Ave., N.W., Washington 20005) [1986?] 37 p. : LC Card 87-141440 DDC 333.3/8/09781675 19
HD268.L46 B43 1986

BEDFORD PROPERTIES (FIRM)
Bedford Properties, Lenexa, Kansas . Washington, D.C. (1090 Vermont Ave., N.W., Washington 20005) [1986?] 37 p. : LC Card 87-141440 DDC 333.3/8/09781675 19
HD268.L46 B43 1986

Bedford Properties, Lenexa, Kansas : an evaluation of development potentials and strategies for Bedford Properties, Inc. Washington, D.C. (1090 Vermont Ave., N.W., Washington 20005) : Urban Land Institute, [1986?] 37 p. : ill. (some col.) ; 28 cm. (A Panel Advisory Service report) "September 14-19, 1986." LC Card 87-141440 DDC 333.3/8/09781675 19
1. Real estate development - Kansas - Lenexa. 2. Land use - Kansas - Lenexa. 3. Bedford Properties (Firm). I. Bedford Properties (Firm). II. Urban Land Institute. Panel Advisory Service. III. Series.
HD268.L46 B43 1986

Bedi, M. S., 1946- Dairy development, marketing, and economic growth / M.S. Bedi. New Delhi : Deep & Deep Publications, c1987. 255 p. : ill. ; 22 cm. Study of the dairy development in Punjab. Bibliography: p. [245]-252. Includes index. LC Card 87-901246 DDC 338.1/77/0954552 19
1. Dairying - Economic aspects - India - Punjab. I. Title.
HD9275.I53 P852 1987

Die Bedingungen des Wirtschaftswachstums in Vergangenheit und Zukunft : Gedenkschrift für Walther G. Hoffmann / herausgegeben von Ernst Helmstädter. Tübingen : Mohr, 1984. viii, 321 p., [1] leaf of plates : ill., port. ; 24 cm. (Schriften zur angewandten Wirtschaftsforschung, 0582-0286 . 50) Bibliography: p. [311]-318. ISBN 3-16-344727-9 LC Card 85-165269
1. Economic development. 2. Economic history. 3. Regional planning. 4. Germany, West - Economic policy. 5. Hoffman, Walther, G., 1903-. I. Hoffmann, Walther G., 1903-. II. Helmstädter, Ernst. III. Series.
HD84 .B415 1984

Bednareck, Horst. Geschichte des FDGB . Berlin , c1985. 364 p. ; LC Card 86-124681 DDC 331.88/0943 19
HD8460.5.A5 F7326 1985

A bedolgozás helye és szerepe, perspektivája a szövetkezeti iparban . Bennó, Pál. Budapest , 1985. 153 p. ; LC Card 85-226119
HD2336.H9 B46 1985

Bedrijven in Vlaams-Brabant. Adresboek "Bedrijven in Vlaams-Brabant" =. Vilvoorde , 1985. lxi, 186, 62, 63 p. : LC Card 87-111619
HC317.B7 A37 1985

Bedürfnisse und Interessen als Triebkräfte unseres Handelns / Autorenkollektiv, Lilo Steitz (Leiter) ... [et al.]. Berlin : Dietz, 1984. 155 p. ; 18 cm. (Wissenschaftlicher Kommunismus) Includes bibliographical references. LC Card 84-229147
1. Capital - Germany, East. 2. Labor productivity - Germany, East. 3. Consumption - Germany (East). I. Steitz, Lilo. II. Series.
HC290.795.C3 B43 1984

Beecham, B. Julian, 1927-
Hall, Peter (Peter J.), 1932- Elements of banking /. London , New York , 1987. xi, 236 p. : ISBN 0-582-29728-1 (pbk.) LC Card 86-21144 DDC 332.1 19
HG1601 .H25 1987

Monetary economics / B. Julian Beecham. 2nd ed. London ; New York : Longman, 1988. p. cm. (Longman exam guides) Includes index. ISBN 0-582-02042-5 LC Card 87-17142 DDC 332.4 19
1. Money. 2. Monetary policy. 3. International finance. 4. Money - Great Britain. 5. Monetary policy - Great Britain. 6. Money - Examinations, questions, etc. I. Title. II. Series.
HG221 .B424 1988

Beechey, Veronica. A matter of hours : women, part-time work, and the labour market / Veronica Beechey and Tessa Perkins. Minneapolis, MN : University of Minnesota Press, c1987. 212 p. ; 23 cm. (Feminist perspectives) Bibliography: p. [196]-202. Includes index. ISBN 0-8166-1641-8 : LC Card 87-12459 DDC 331.4/12/0942498 19
1. Women - Employment - England - Coventry (West Midlands). 2. Part-time employment - England - Coventry (West Midlands). 3. Coventry (West Midlands, England) - Economic conditions. I. Perkins, Tessa. II. Title. III. Series.
HD6136.Z6 C683 1987

BEEF CATTLE - LESOTHO - MARKETING.
Swallow, Brent M. Cattle marketing in Lesotho /. Maseru, Lesotho [1986] iv, 75 leaves : LC Card 87-132309 DDC 381/.416213/096816 19
HD9433.L452 S9 1986

BEEF INDUSTRY - AUSTRALIA - VICTORIA - LOCATION.
Victoria. Saleyard Working Party. Distribution of saleyards in Victoria . [Melbourne] , 1986. 69, 7, 7 p. : LC Card 87-159450 DDC 338.1/760831 19
HD9428.A83 V538 1986

BEEF INDUSTRY - BOTSWANA.
Hubbard, Michael. Agricultural exports and economic growth . London , New York , 1986. xx, 284 p. : ISBN 0-7103-0121-9
NYPL [Sc D 86-967]

BEEF INDUSTRY - BRAZIL - ARAGUAIA RIVER REGION.
Estudo do mercado de carne bovina /. Brasília , 1985. 89 p. : LC Card 86-197081
HD9433.B82 A74 1985

BEEF INDUSTRY - BRAZIL - TOCANTINS RIVER REGION.
Estudo do mercado de carne bovina /. Brasília , 1985. 89 p. : LC Card 86-197081
HD9433.B82 A74 1985

BEEF INDUSTRY - CENTRAL AMERICA.
Williams, Robert G. (Robert Gregory), 1948- Export agriculture and the crisis in Central America /. Chapel Hill , c1986. xvi, 257 p. : ISBN 0-8078-1693-0 LC Card 85-20978 DDC 382/.41/09728 19
HD9884.C352 W55 1986
NYPL [JLE 86-3412]

BEEF INDUSTRY - COSTA RICA - GUANACASTE.
Aguilar Bolaños, Irene. Una caracterización socioeconómica del grupo ganaderoexportador (los casos de San Carlos y Guanacaste) 1960-1980 /. San José, Costa Rica , 1985. xiii, 260 p. ; LC Card 86-107500
HD9433.C83 S223 1985 ***NYPL [JLF 87-74]***

BEEF INDUSTRY - COSTA RICA - SAN CARLOS (CANTON)
Aguilar Bolaños, Irene. Una caracterización socioeconómica del grupo ganaderoexportador (los casos de San Carlos y Guanacaste) 1960-1980 /. San José, Costa Rica , 1985. xiii, 260 p. ; LC Card 86-107500
HD9433.C83 S223 1985 ***NYPL [JLF 87-74]***

BEEF INDUSTRY - LATIN AMERICA.
Shane, Douglas R. Hoofprints on the forest . Philadelphia , c1986. xvi, 159 p. ; ISBN 0-89727-054-1 : LC Card 83-26585 DDC 338.1/76213/098 19
HD9433.L292 S53 1984
NYPL [JLD 86-2289]

BEEF - SOUTH AFRICA - TRANSKEI - MARKETING.
Tapson, D. R. Proposals for a cattle marketing strategy for Transkei /. [Fort Hare] [1982] ii, 45 leaves, 4 leaves of plates : ISBN 0-949974-68-4 LC Card 86-209520 DDC 381/.4162/00968791 19
HD9433.S643 T77 1982

BEEF TRADE - URUGUAY.
Barbato de Silva, Celia. La ganadería vacuna uruguaya . Montevideo, Uruguay [1980] 77 leaves ; ***NYPL [JLF 86-1101]***

Beek, P. van. De leefsituatie van Surinamers en Antillianen in Nederland, 1985 / Centraal Bureau voor de Statistiek, Hoofdafdeling Sociaal-Culturele Statistieken. 's-Gravenhage : Staatsuitgeverij/CBS-publikaties, 1986- v. <1 > : ill. ; 30 cm. "Samengesteld door P. van Beek en M.J. Rooduijn"--P. 3. Title on p. [4] of cover: The quality of life of the Surinamese and Antilleans in the Netherlands. CONTENTS. - d. 1. Eerste uitkomsten. ISBN 90-357-0558-0 : LC Card 87-120083
1. Alien labor, Surinamese - Netherlands - Statistics. 2. Alien labor, Antillean - Netherlands - Statistics. 3. Quality of life - Netherlands - Statistics. I. Rooduijn, M. J. II. Netherlands. Centraal Bureau voor de Statistiek. Hoofdafdeling Sociaal-Culturele Statistieken. III. Title.
HD8518.5.S87 B44 1986

Beek, W. J. De Toekomst van onze voedingsmiddelenindustrie /. Amsterdam , 1985. 156 p. : ISBN 90-10-05574-4 : LC Card 86-116607
HD9015.N42 T64 1985

Beekman, John A. Andrews, George H., 1932- Actuarial projections for the old-age, survivors, and disability insurance program of social security in the United States of America /. Itasca, Ill., U. S.A. , c1987. viii, 188 p. : LC Card 87-1101 DDC 368.4/301/0973 19
HC106.8 .A56 1987

Beekman, Robert. Person, Samuel. Barron's how to prepare for the certified public accountant examination, CPA /. New York , c1987. vi, 537 p. ; ISBN 0-8120-3880-0 (pbk.) : LC Card 87-17914 DDC 657/.076 19
HF5661 .P48 1987

Beelen, George D. Harding and Mexico : diplomacy by economic persuasion, 1920-1923 / George D. Beelen. New York : Garland, 1987. xiii, 200 p., [16] p. of plates : ill. ; 22 cm. (Foreign economic policy of the United States) Thesis (Ph. D.)--Kent State University, 1971. Bibliography: p. [173]-200. Includes index. ISBN 0-8240-8073-4 (alk. paper) LC Card 87-23724 DDC 337.72073 19
1. United States - Foreign economic relations - Mexico. 2. Mexico - Foreign economic relations - United States. 3. United States - Foreign relations - 1921-1923. I. Title. II. Series.
HF1456.5.M6 B44 1987

Beenhakker, Henri L. Rural transportation services . Boulder, Colo. , 1987. p. cm. ISBN 0-8133-0530-6 : LC Card 87-8226 DDC 388.1/09172/4 19
HE336.R85 R87 1987

Beenstock, Michael, 1946-
Insurance for unemployment / Michael Beenstock and Valerie Brasse. London ; Boston : Allen & Unwin, 1986. 106 p. ; 23 cm. Includes index. Bibliography: p. 99-101. ISBN 0-04-331113-X (alk. paper) (Great Britain) LC Card 85-30704 DDC 368.4/4/00941 19
1. Insurance, Unemployment - Great Britain - History - 19th century. 2. Insurance, Unemployment - Great Britain - History - 20th century. I. Brasse, Valerie. II. Title.
HD7096.G7 B36 1986 ***NYPL [JLD 86-3693]***

Modelling the labour market /. London , New York , 1988. p. cm. ISBN 0-412-28830-3 LC Card 87-23084 DDC 331.12/0724 19
HD5765.A6 M63 1988

Beers, H. C.
[Financial sector of the Netherlands Antilles. Spanish]
El sector financiero de las Antillas Neerlandesas / por H.C. Beers. [Willemstad, Curaçao] : Bank v/d Ned. Ant., 1980. 72 p. : ill. ; 30 cm. Translation of: The financial sector of the Netherlands Antilles. Cover title. Bibliography: p. 44. LC Card 83-238068 DDC 332.1/097298/6 19
1. Banks and banking - Netherlands Antilles. 2. Banks and banking - Netherlands Antilles - Directories. I. Title.
HG2847.A6 B4318 1980
NYPL [JLG 85-297]

Befekadu Degefe. Exchange rate policy and economic distortions : the Ethiopian experience, 1976-1983 / Befekadu Degefe. [Addis Ababa? : s.n.], 1985. 22 leaves ; 30 cm. "December 1985." Bibliography: leaves 21-22. LC Card 86-221527 DDC 332.4/560963 19
1. Foreign exchange problem - Ethiopia. I. Title.
HG3983 .B43 1985

Beffel, John Nicholas. Pesotta, Rose, 1896- Bread upon the waters /. Ithaca, N.Y. , c1987. xxiv, 435 p., [10] p. of plates : ISBN 0-87546-127-1 (pbk. : alk. paper) LC Card 87-2953 DDC 331.88/0973 19
HD8072 .P375 1987

Befolkning, bostäder och bostadsbyggande efter stordistrikt och distrikt i Helsingfors 1970-1983. Kinturi, Jorma. Väestö, asunnot ja asuntorakentaminen suur- ja peruspiireittäin Helsingissä 1970-1983 =. Helsinki , 1984. 36 p., [1] folded leaf of plates : LC Card 85-156678
HD7345.3.H5 K563 1984

Befolkningsbeskrivelse . Mørch, Henning. [Copenhagen] , Brenderup , 1982. 160 p. : ISBN 87-87601-58-1 LC Card 83-195528
HB871 .M27 1982

Befolkningstillväxt och jordbruk . Ydborn, Lars. Göteborg , c1984. 214 p. : ISBN 91-7222-705-2 LC Card 84-194466
HB2498.H35 Y38 1984

Befreiung der Arbeit : Strategien gegen Arbeitslosigkeit, Naturzerstörung und Entfremdung / Kurt van Haaren, Hans-Ulrich Klose, Michael Müller (Hg.) ; mit einem Vorwort von Willy Brandt. Bonn : Verlag Neue Gesellschaft, c1986. 197 p. : ill. ; 21 cm. (Reihe Arbeit. Sonderheft . 6) Includes bibliographical references. ISBN 3-87831-429-9 LC Card 86-194157
1. Quality of work life. 2. Work - Moral and ethical aspects. 3. Full employment policies. 4. Management - Employee participation. 5. Labor supply - Effect of technological innovations. I. Haaren, Kurt van. II. Klose, Hans-Ulrich. III. Müller, Michael, 1948-. IV. Series.
HD6955 .B389 1986

Begert, Roland. Elemente einer politischen Ökonomie im Werke Machiavellis / Roland Begert. Bern : Haupt, c1983. 224 p. : ill. ; 23 cm. (Berner Beiträge zur Nationalökonomie. Bd. 37) Bibliography: p. 201-209. ISBN 3-258-03136-3 LC Card 83-204993
1. Machiavelli, Niccolò, 1469-1527 - Contributions in economics. 2. Economics - Italy - History - 16th century. 3. Florence (Italy) - History - 1421-1737. I. Title. II. Series.
HB109.M3 B44 1983

Begin, James P. Beal, Edwin Fletcher. The practice of collective bargaining /. Homewood, Ill. , 1985. xvi, 560 p. : ISBN 0-256-03214-9 LC Card 84-82023 DDC 331.89 19
HD6508 .B375 1985
NYPL [*R-Econ. 86-3458]

The beginner's guide to real estate wealth /. Michel, Mark. Greensboro, N.C. , c1986. xiv, 177 p. : ISBN 0-939383-04-7 (pbk.) : LC Card 86-218980 DDC 332.63/24 19
HD1382.5 .M52 1986

Begroting 1986 : meerjarenramingen 1986-1990. ['s-Hertogenbosch] : Provincie Noord-Brabant, [1985] 91 p. ; 30 cm. "Nummer 61/85." LC Card 86-136324
1. North Brabant (Netherlands) - Appropriations and expenditures - Forecasting. 2. Budget - Netherlands - North Brabant - Forecasting. I. North Brabant (Netherlands).
HJ2128.5.N6 B44 1985

Beguelin, Richard H., 1937-
The secrets of syndication : how to make money with other people's money / Richard H. Beguelin.1st ed. Boston : Little, Brown, c1985. xi, 287 p. : maps ; 25 cm. Rev. ed. of: Syndication secrets. c1983. Includes index. ISBN 0-316-08783-1 : LC Card 85-5157 DDC 658/.044 19
1. Syndicates (Finance) - Handbooks, manuals, etc. 2. Venture capital - Handbooks, manuals, etc. I. Beguelin, Richard H., 1937- Syndication secrets. II. Title.
HG6021 .B4 1985 ***NYPL [JLE 85-2259]***

Syndication secrets. Beguelin, Richard H., 1937- The secrets of syndication : how to make money with other people's money / Richard H. Beguelin.1st ed. Boston , c1985. xi, 287 p. : ISBN 0-316-08783-1 : LC Card 85-5157 DDC 658/.044 19
HG6021 .B4 1985 ***NYPL [JLE 85-2259]***

Behandlingen av oljevirksomheten i byråets makroøkonomiske årsmodeller /. Bergan, Roar. Oslo , 1983. 30 p. ; ISBN 82-537-1918-3 : LC Card 83-225651
HD9575.N62 B46 1983

Behari, Bepin. Unemployment, technology & rural poverty / Bepin Behari. New Delhi : Vikas, c1983. ix, 453 p. ; 23 cm. Includes index. Bibliography: p. [446]-448. ISBN 0-7069-2337-5 : LC Card 83-906129 DDC 338/.06 19
1. Industrial productivity - India - Technological innovations. 2. Small business - India - Production standards. 3. Rural employment - Government policy - India. 4. Rural poor - India. I. Title.
HC440.I52 B43 1983 ***NYPL [JLD 87-1132]***

BEHAVIOR MODIFICATION.
Matejka, J. Kenneth. Handling human performance /. Richmond, Va. , c1982. v, 90 p. : ISBN 0-936328-20-7 (pbk.) LC Card 81-69197 DDC 658.3/14 19
HF5549.5.I5 M337 1982
NYPL [JLE 86-4361]

Winn, Denise, 1950- The manipulated mind . London , c1983. 217 p. ; ISBN 0-86304-025-X LC Card 83-184383 DDC 302.3/3 19
BF632.5 .W56 1983 ***NYPL [JFD 87-1158]***

Behavioral accounting research : a critical analysis / edited by Kenneth R. Ferris. Columbus, Ohio : Century VII Pub. Co., c1988. ix, 368 p. : ill. ; 23 cm. Includes bibliographies. ISBN 0-939787-02-4 (pbk.) : LC Card 87-24980 DDC 657/.072 19
1. Accounting - Psychological aspects - Research. I. Ferris, Kenneth R.
HF5630 .B43 1988

BEHAVIORAL ASSISTANCE PROGRAMS. see **EMPLOYEE ASSISTANCE PROGRAMS.**

Behavioral foundations of economic theory.
Rational choice : the contrast between economics and psychology / edited by Robin M. Hogarth and Melvin W. Reder. Chicago : University of Chicago Press, 1987. ix, 332 p. : ill. ; 24 cm. Previously published as: The Behavioral foundations of economic theory. 1986. Proceedings of a conference organized by the editors and held at the University of Chicago, Oct. 13-15, 1985. "The material in this volume first appeared in the supplement to the October 1986 issue of the Journal of business"--T.p.

verso. Includes bibliographies and index. ISBN 0-226-34857-1 (alk. paper) LC Card 86-27241 DDC 330/.01/9 19
1. Economics - Psychological aspects - Congresses. 2. Choice (Psychology) - Congresses. 3. Rational expectations (Economic theory) - Congresses. 4. Decision-making - Congresses. I. Hogarth, Robin M. II. Reder, Melvin Warren, 1919-. III. Title.
HB74.P8 B44 1987

Behavioral statistics . Darlington, Richard B. New York, N.Y. , London , c1987. xxiv, 628 p. : ISBN 0-02-907860-1 LC Card 87-12040 DDC 519.5 19
HA29 .D246 1987

Behaviour in organisations : South African perspectives / Julian Barling, Clive Fullagar, and Stephen Bluen (eds).2nd ed. Johannesburg ; New York : McGraw-Hill Book Company, 1986, c1983. 924 p. : ill. ; 24 cm. Includes bibliographies and index. ISBN 0-07-450690-0 (pbk.) : LC Card 87-113321 DDC 158.7/0968 19
1. Organizational behavior. 2. Psychology, Industrial - South Africa. 3. Industrial relations - South Africa. I. Barling, Julian. II. Fullagar, Clive. III. Bluen,, Stephen.
HD58.7 .B426 1986

Behaviour of share prices and investment in India /. Dixit, R. K. (Ramesh Kumar), 1946- New Delhi , c1986. 328 p. ; LC Card 86-902907 DDC 332.63/222/0954 19
HG5733 .D59 1986

Beherrscht uns die Technik? . Kofler, Leo. Hamburg , 1983. 160 p. ; ISBN 3-87975-249-4 LC Card 84-181044
HD6331 .K685 1983

Behind the poison cloud . Everest, Larry. Chicago , 1986. 192 p. : ISBN 0-916650-26-X : LC Card 85-26863 DDC 363.1/79 19
HD7269.C452 I524 1986
NYPL [JSD 86-425]

Behind the scenes in a hotel. 1987. The Consumers' League of New York . New York , 1987. 47, 47, 55 p. : ISBN 0-8240-7684-2 (alk. paper) : LC Card 87-19804 DDC 331.4/2/09747 19
HD6096.N6 C66 1987

Behind the scenes in a restaurant. 1987. The Consumers' League of New York . New York , 1987. 47, 47, 55 p. : ISBN 0-8240-7684-2 (alk. paper) : LC Card 87-19804 DDC 331.4/2/09747 19
HD6096.N6 C66 1987

Behind the scenes in canneries. 1987. The Consumers' League of New York . New York , 1987. 47, 47, 55 p. : ISBN 0-8240-7684-2 (alk. paper) : LC Card 87-19804 DDC 331.4/2/09747 19
HD6096.N6 C66 1987

Behind the telephone debates /. Weinhaus, Carol L. Norwood, N.J. , 1987. p. cm. ISBN 0-89391-452-5 LC Card 87-19459 DDC 384.6/0973 19
HE8815 .W45 1987

Behind the veil of economics . Heilbroner, Robert L. New York , 1988. p. cm. ISBN 0-393-02542-X LC Card 87-20392 DDC 330.12/2 19
HB501 .H396 1988

Behind the wheel .
(1) DUI arrest [videorecording] /. Lincoln, NE , 1983. 1 videocassette (30 min.) : LC Card 87-706343 DDC 343 11
HE5620.D7

(2) Drunk driving [videorecording] . Lincoln, NE , 1983. 1 videocassette (30 min.) : LC Card 87-706347 DDC 363.1 11
HE5620.D7

Behnke, Hartmut, 1941-
Verletzbarkeitsmanagement bei parallelen Rohstoffpreis- und Devisenkursrisiken / Hartmut Behnke. Frankfurt am Main ; New York : Lang, c1986. vi, 288 p. : ill. ; 21 cm. (Europäische Hochschulschriften. Reihe V, Volks- und Betriebswirtschaft, 0531-7339 . Bd. 709 = vol. 709 = vol. 709) Bibliography: p. 280-288. ISBN 3-8204-9365-4 LC Card 86-190114
1. Hedging (Finance). 2. Foreign exchange. 3. Raw materials - Prices. I. Series: Europäische Hochschulschriften. Reihe V, Volks- und Betriebswirtschaft , Bd. 709. II. Title.
HG3853 .B44 1986

Behnke, Roy H., 1947- Open-range management and property rights in pastoral Africa : a case of spontaneous range enclosure in South Darfur, Sudan / by Roy H. Behnke. London : Agricultural Administrative Unit, Overseas Development Institute, [1985] 29 p. : ill. ; 21 cm. (Paper / Pastoral Development Network . 20f) Cover title. "August 1985." Bibliography: p. 26-29. LC Card 86-209817 DDC 333.2 19
1. Inclosures - Sudan. 2. Range management - Sudan. 3. Land use, Rural - Sudan. I. Series: Paper (Pastoral Development Network (Overseas Development Institute)) , 20f. II. Title.
HD977.Z63 B44 1985

Behnken, Imbke, 1941- Jugendbiografie und Handlungsforschung / Imbke Behnken. Frankfurt [am Main] : Extrabuch Verlag, c1984. xi, 239 p. ; 21 cm. (Gruppendiskussion als Methode zur Rekonstruktion der Lebenswelt von Lehrlingen . Bd. 2) Veröffentlichungen des Instituts für Jugendforschung und Jugendkultur e.V. ; Bd. 2 Originally presented as the author's thesis (doctoral--Universität Frankfurt am Main, 1983. Bibliography: p. 235-239. ISBN 3-88704-402-9 LC Card 84-174719 DDC 331.3/425922/0943 19
1. Apprentices - Germany, West. 2. Youth - Employment - Germany, West. 3. Youth - Germany (West) - Attitudes. I. Title. II. Series.
HD4885.G3 B425 1984
NYPL [JLD 86-1892]

Behr, Peter. Potts, Mark. The leading edge . New York , c1987. iv, 220 p. ; ISBN 0-07-050599-3 LC Card 86-10567 DDC 658.4/06 19
HD58.8 .P68 1987 ***NYPL [JLE 87-33]***

Behrenfeld, William H. Accountant's business manual / prepared for the AICPA by William H. Behrenfeld and Andrew R. Biebl ; contributors, Cathleen L. Bang ... [et al.]. New York, N.Y. : American Institute of Certified Public Accountants, c1987- 1 v. (loose-leaf) ; 26 cm. Kept up to date by semiannual supplements. Includes bibliographies and index. ISBN 0-87051-000-2 (loose-leaf) : LC Card 87-992 DDC 657 19
1. Accounting - United States. 2. Industrial management - United States. 3. Accounting - Law and legislation - United States. I. Biebl, Andrew R., 1948-. II. American Institute of Certified Public Accountants. III. Title.
HF5616.U5 B38 1987

Behrens-Ramberg, Wolfgang. Steuerliche Anreize bei innovativen Investitionen kleiner und mittlerer Industrieunternehmen unter vergleichender Berücksichtigung nichtsteuerlicher Hilfen / Wolfgang Behrens-Ramberg. Stuttgart : Poeschel, c1985. 299 p. ; 24 cm. (Schriften zur Mittelstandsforschung . Nr. 6 NF) Originally presented as the author's thesis (doctoral)--Universität Köln. Bibliography: p. 260-288. ISBN 3-7910-5007-9 : LC Card 86-124563 DDC 336.24/316 19
1. Tax incentives - Germany (West). 2. Capital investments - Germany, West. 3. Investment tax credit - Germany (West). I. Title. II. Series.
HJ2337.G3 B44 1985
NYPL [JLL 73-505 Nr.6]

Behrman, Jack N.
Essays on ethics in business and the professions / Jack N. Behrman. Englewood Cliffs, N.J. : Prentice Hall, c1988. x, 358 p. ; 24 cm. Bibliography: p. 356-358. ISBN 0-13-283623-8 (pbk.) LC Card 87-13697 DDC 174/.4 19
1. Business ethics. 2. Professional ethics. I. Title.
HF5387 .B44 1988

The rise of the phoenix : the United States in a restructured world economy / Jack N. Behrman. Boulder : Westview Press, 1987. xiii, 104 p. ; 23 cm. (Studies in American business and the international economy) "Published in cooperation with the International Economic Policy Association"--Prelim. p. Bibliography: p. 93-95. Includes index. ISBN 0-8133-7511-8 (pbk. : alk. paper) : LC Card 87-21689 DDC 338.973 19
1. United States - Economic policy - 1981-. 2. United States - Economic conditions - 1981-. 3. Economic history - 1971-. 4. International economic relations. I. Title. II. Series.
HC106.8 .B43 1987

Beiblatt der Fliegenden Blätter. Die Schönsten Anzeigen in den Fliegenden Blättern . Hildesheim , New York , 1982. 166 p. : ISBN 3-487-08233-0 (pbk.) LC Card 87-672236
HF5813.G3 S36x 1982

Beihefte zu Kredit und Kapital .
(Heft 8) Internationales Bankgeschäft /. Berlin , c1985. 249 p. : ISBN 3-428-05790-2 LC Card 86-178830
HG3881 .I72 1985

Beije, P. R. (Paul R.), 1952- A Competitive future for Europe? . London , New York , c1987. 324 p. : ISBN 0-7099-5032-2 LC Card 87-9096 DDC 338.94 19
HD3616.E833 C66 1987

Beijer Institute. Kristoferson, Lars A. Renewable energy technologies . Oxford [Oxfordshire] , New York , 1986. xviii, 319 p. : ISBN 0-08-034061-X : LC Card 86-766 DDC 621.042 19
TJ808 .K75 1986 ***NYPL [JSG 87-45]***

Being the boss . Lineback, L. Kent, 1943- New York , c1987. xi, 177 p. ; ISBN 0-87942-212-2 LC Card 86-27751 DDC 658.3 19
HF5549 .L4945 1987

Beinin, Joel, 1948- Workers on the Nile : nationalism, communism, Islam, and the Egyptian working class, 1882-1954 / by Joel Beinin and Zachary Lockman. Princeton, N.J. : Princeton University Press, c1987. xix, 488 p. : maps ; 25 cm. (Princeton studies on the Near East) Bibliography: p. [463]-478. Includes index. ISBN 0-691-05506-8 (alk. paper) : LC Card 87-45510 DDC 305.5/62/0962 19
1. Labor and laboring classes - Egypt - History. 2. Trade-unions - Egypt - History. 3. Nationalism - Egypt - History. 4. Egypt - Politics and government - 1882-1952. 5. Egypt - History - 1919-. I. Lockman, Zachary. II. Title.
HD8786 .B45 1987

Beinum, Gerlach van. Sterkenburg, J. J. Rural housing conditions in Kisumu District, Kenya /. [Utrecht] [Nairobi] , 1982. 95 p., [6] leaves of plates : LC Card 85-981197
HD7289.K42 K67 1982

Beirat für Wirtschafts- und Sozialfragen.
Arbeitszeitentwicklung und Arbeitszeitpolitik /. Wien , 1984. 164 p. ; LC Card 85-137865
HD5170 .A72 1984

Budgetvorschau 1984-1988 /. Wien , 1984. 55 p. ; LC Card 84-223024
HJ2101 .B828 1984

Landwirtschaftliche Produktionsalternativen am Beispiel Ethanol, Ölsaaten und Eiweissfutterpflanzen /. Wien , 1985. 141 p. : LC Card 86-108149 DDC 338.1/09436 19
HD1935 .L33 1985

Methoden der Politikberatung im wirtschaftspolitischen Bereich /. Wien , 1984. 116 p. ; LC Card 84-222756
HC265 .M39 1984

Die Statistische Differenz in der österreichischen Zahlungsbilanz /. Wien , 1979. 68 p. : LC Card 85-179826
HG3883.A9 S73 1979

Unweltpolitik /. Wien , Korneuburg , 1986. 277 p. : LC Card 86-191881
HC79.E5 U57 1986

Beiträge zur Bankaufsicht, Bankbilanz und Bankprüfung : unter Berücksichtigung der Dritten KWG-Novelle : Dr. Walter Scholz zum 65. Geburtstag / herausgegeben von Karl-Heinz Forster. Düsseldorf : IDW-Verlag, 1985. 226 p. : ill. ; 24 cm. Bibliography of works by W. Scholz: p. 225-226. Includes bibliographical references. CONTENTS. - Hat die allgemeine Betriebswirtschaftslehre eine Zukunftschance? / Horst Albach -- Wirtschaftsprüfer und Bankenaufsicht / Inge Lore Bähre -- Probleme der Rechnungslegung und Prüfung von Kreditinstituten in den Stellungnahmen des Bankenfachausschusses des IDW / Karl-Heinz Forster, Gerhard Gross -- Zweifelsfragen und Auslegungsvorschläge zu [Paragraph] 10a Kreditwesengesetz / Harald von Hoch -- Einige Probleme der Konstruktion bankaufsichtlicher Risikobegrenzungsregeln / Hans J. Krümmel -- Die Beaufsichtigung der Kreditinstitute auf konsolidierter Basis nach dem Dritten KWG-Änderungsgesetz / Wolfgang Kuntze -- Zinsen und Bankbilanzierung / Heinrich Meyer -- Strukturveränderungen am Rentenmarkt in den letzten 25 Jahren / Ludwig Schork -- Auswirkungen der KWG-Novelle auf die Abschlussprüfung / Eberhard Spieth -- Zielsetzung des [Paragraphen] 18 KWG und seine Umsetzung in die Praxis / Manfred Tröller -- Zinstermingeschäfte der Kreditinstitute / Rolf Windmöller. ISBN

3-8021-0267-3 LC Card 85-208772
1. Banks and banking. 2. Bank management. 3. Banks and banking - Accounting. 4. Banks and banking - State supervision. 5. Scholz, Walter, 1920-. I. Forster, Karl Heinz. II. Scholz, Walter, 1920-. III. Title: Bankaufsicht, Bankbilanz und Bankprüfung.
HG1605 .B44 1985

Beiträge zur betriebswirtschaftlichen Forschung. For additional listing of contents, see Old Catalog.
(Bd. 55) Haumer, Heinrich. Sequentielle stochastische Investitionsplanung /. Wiesbaden , c1983. 305 p. ; ISBN 3-409-13420-4 LC Card 83-190299
HG4515.2 .H38 1983
(Bd. 56) Grimm, Ulrich. Analyse strategischer Faktoren . Wiesbaden , c1983. 294 p. : ISBN 3-409-18720-0 LC Card 84-173895
HD30.28 .G76 1983
(Bd. 57) Leichtfuss, Reinhold. Kapitalbudgetierung in divisionalisierten Unternehmen . Wiesbaden , c1984. 389 p. ; ISBN 3-409-13701-7 LC Card 85-231538
HG4028.C4 L387 1984
(Bd. 58) Kucher, Eckhard. Scannerdaten und Preissensitivität bei Konsumgütern /. Wiesbaden , c1985. 282 p. : ISBN 3-409-13608-8 LC Card 86-128961
HB801 .K789 1985
(Bd. 59) Hartmann-Wendels, Thomas. Dividendenpolitik bei asymmetrischer Informationsverteilung /. Wiesbaden , c1986. 299 p. : ISBN 3-409-13706-8 LC Card 86-165737
HG4028.D5 H33 1986
(Bd. 60) Ringbeck, Jürgen. Qualitäts- und Werbestrategien bei Qualitätsunsicherheit der Konsumenten /. Wiesbaden , c1986. 256 p. ; ISBN 3-409-13612-6 LC Card 87-111545 DDC 658.8/02 19
HF5415.135 .R56 1986
(Bd. 61) Ewert, Ralf. Rechnungslegung, Gläubigerschutz und Agency-Probleme /. Wiesbaden , c1986. 429 p. ; ISBN 3-409-13710-6 LC Card 87-134169 DDC 657/.3 19
HG4028.B2 E92 1986
(Bd. 9) Vormbaum, Herbert. Differenzierte Preise . Köln , 1960. xi, 291 p. : LC Card 86-191408
HB235.G3 V67 1960

Beiträge zur Bevölkerungsökonomie / von Herwig Birg ... [et al.] ; herausgegeben von Bernhard Felderer. Berlin : Duncker & Humblot, c1986. 238 p. : ill. ; 24 cm. (Schriften des Vereins für Socialpolitik, Gesellschaft für Wirtschafts- und Sozialwissenschaften . n.F. Bd. 153) Papers presented at a meeting organized by the Gesellschaft für Wirtschafts- und Sozialwissenschaften, Verein für Socialpolitik, held in Köln, June 29-30, 1984. Includes bibliographies. CONTENTS. - Die ökonomische Theorie der Familie / Klaus F. Zimmermann -- Demographische Variabeln in der ökonomischen Wachstumstheorie / Gerhard Schmitt-Rink -- Bevölkerungsentwicklung und technischer Fortschritt / Gunter Steinmann -- Interregionale demo-ökonomische Modelle für die Bundesrepublik Deutschland / Herwig Birk -- Konsummaximierung, Bevölkerungswachstum und Sparquote / Klaus Jaeger -- Bevölkerungsentwicklung und soziale Sicherung / Winfried Schmähl. ISBN 3-428-05969-7 LC Card 86-172600
1. Germany (West) - Population - Economic aspects - Congresses. I. Birg, Herwig. II. Felderer, B. (Bernhard). III. Gesellschaft für Wirtschafts- und Sozialwissenschaften, Verein für Socialpolitik. IV. Series.
HB3595 .B39 1986

Beiträge zur empirischen Bürostandortforschung / Heinz Heineberg ... [et al.]. Kallmünz : M. Lassleben, 1983. 167 p. : ill., maps ; 24 cm. (Münchener geographische Hefte . Nr. 50) Eight folded maps in pocket. Summaries in English. Includes bibliographies. CONTENTS. - Konzepte und Defizite der empirischen Bürostandortforschung in der Geographie / Heinz Heineberg und Günter Heinritz -- Die Dynamik der Bürostandorte / Günter Gad -- Standortverhalten ausgewählter Bürogruppen in Innenstadtgebieten westdeutscher Metropolen / Norbert de Lange -- Der Suburbanisierungsprozess unter den kleinen Bürofirmen und freien Berufen im Verdichtungsraum München / Jürgen Hartwieg. ISBN 3-7847-6050-3 : LC Card 84-176770
1. Offices - Location - Germany (West) - Congresses. 2. Regional planning - Germany, West - Congresses. 3. Offices - Location - Germany (West) - Munich - Congresses. I. Heineberg, Heinz. II. Series.
HF5547.25 .B45 1983

Beiträge zur empirischen Wirtschaftsgeographie / mit Beiträgen von Gerhard Aymans ... [et al. ; herausgegeben von Gerhard Aymans und Klaus-Achim Boesler]. Bonn : In Kommission bei F. Dümmler, c1986. 238 p. : ill., maps (2 col.) ; 23 cm. (Colloquium geographicum, 0588-3253 . Bd. 19) "Festschrift, Helmut Hahn zum 65. Geburtstag"--P. 2. Col. maps on folded leaves in pocket. "Schriften von Helmut Hahn": p. 14-16. Includes bibliographies. ISBN 3-427-74191-5 LC Card 87-104279 DDC 330.9 19
1. Geography, Economic. 2. Hahn, Helmut. I. Hahn, Helmut. II. Aymans, Gerhard. III. Boesler, Klaus-Achim. IV. Series.
HF1025 .B3495 1986

Beiträge zur experimentellen Wirtschaftsforschung. Hrsg. von Heinz Sauermann. Tübingen, Mohr <Siebeck>, 1967-<78 > v. <1-2, 4-8 > 24 cm. Vols. 7-8 in English. Vols. 2-<8 > have parallel title: Contributions to experimental economics. Summaries in English. Includes bibliographies. LC Card 68-85600 DDC 330 19
1. Oligopolies. 2. Management games. 3. Economics - Collected works. I. Sauermann, Heinz. II. Title: Contributions to experimental economics.
HB41 .B29 1967

Beiträge zur experimentellen Wirtschaftsforschung.
(8. Bd) Coalition forming behavior /. Tübingen , 1978. viii, 375 p. : ISBN 3-16-340982-2 LC Card 86-227555 DDC 330 s 658.4 19
HB41 .B29 1967 vol. 8 HD58.6

Beiträge zur Geschichte des Eisenwesens in Oberösterreich. Linz : Verlag des Amtes der O.Ö. Landesregierung, 1949- v. <1 > : ill. ; 26 cm. (Schriftenreihe des Institutes für Landeskunde von Oberösterreich . 1) "Sonderdruck aus den 'Oberösterreichischen Heimatblättern', Jahrg. 3, Heft 3"--T.p. verso. Includes bibliographical references. LC Card 87-117640
1. Iron industry and trade - Austria - Upper Austria - History. 2. Iron-works - Austria - Upper Austria - History. I. Amt der OÖ. Landesregierung. II. Series: Schriftenreihe des Institutes für Landeskunde von Oberösterreich , 1, etc.
HD9525.A83 U663 1949

Beiträge zur Kolonial- und Überseegeschichte. For other vols. in this series, see Old Catalog.
(Bd. 29) Ziegler, Béatrice. Schweizer statt Sklaven . Stuttgart , c1985. 466 p., [16] p. of plates : ISBN 3-515-04174-5 : LC Card 85-133062 DDC 331.6/2/49408161 19
HD8289.S283 Z54 1985
NYPL [JLE 87-1222]

Beiträge zur kommunalen Versorgungswirtschaft.
(Heft 63) Erklärungen zur kommunalen Versorgungswirtschaft. Köln , 1985. 146 p. ; ISBN 3-87750-141-9
NYPL [K-10 8934 Heft 63]

Beiträge zur Multiplizität wirtschaftsgeographischer Forschung : Dankschrift für Professor Dr. Josef Matznetter / Bernd Jörs (Hrsg.). Frankfurt am Main : Haag + Herchen, c1986. 151 p. : ill. ; 21 cm. Includes bibliographies. CONTENTS. - Entwicklungsphasen maritimen Denkens in der deutschen Geographie / Bernd Jörs -- Zukunftsaufgaben einer maritimen Geographie / Bernd Jörs -- Entwicklungspolitik der ostasiatischen Länder / Phulk S. Chen -- Nationaler Tourismus in Entwicklungsländern / Werner Giersch -- Die Streckennetzgestaltung im Luftverkehr / Thomas C. Heynen -- Die Gründung der "desert cities" in Ägypten / Günter Göttlich -- Uruguay, ein Land auf "verlorenem" Posten? / Almut Irion -- Methoden zur Erfassung von Wanderungsbewegungen in Industrie- und Entwicklungsländern / Bernd Jörs. ISBN 3-89228-046-0 LC Card 87-131124 DDC 330.9 19
1. Geography, Economic. 2. Economic history - 1945-. 3. Matznetter, Josef. I. Matznetter, Josef. II. Jörs, Bernd.
HC59 .B464 1986

Beiträge zur niedersächsischen Preisgeschichte des 16. bis 19. Jahrhunderts / herausgegeben von Reinhard Oberschelp. Hildesheim : A. Lax in Kommission, 1986. lxiii, 541 p. ; 23 cm. (Veröffentlichungen der Niedersächsischen Landesbibliothek Hannover) Bibliography: p. 532-535. Includes index. ISBN 3-7848-3874-X LC Card 87-407399 DDC 338.1/331/094359 19
1. Grain - Prices - Germany (West) - Lower Saxony - History - Sources. 2. Grain trade - Germany (West) - Lower Saxony - History - Sources. I. Oberschelp, Reinhard. II. Series.
HD9043.4 .B45 1986

Beiträge zur quantitativen vergleichenden Unternehmensgeschichte / Richard Tilly (Hrsg.). Stuttgart : Klett-Cotta, c1985. 206 p. : ill. ; 21 cm. (Historisch-sozialwissenschaftliche Forschungen, 0713-2153 . Bd. 19) Papers presented at a meeting held at the Universität Münster, Oct. 1983. Includes bibliographies. ISBN 3-608-91325-4 LC Card 85-233589
1. Corporations - History - Statistical methods - Study and teaching - Congresses. 2. Corporations - Germany - History - Statistical methods - Study and teaching - Congresses. 3. Economic history - 1750-1918 - Statistical methods - Study and teaching - Congresses. 4. Germany - Economic conditions - Statistical methods - Study and teaching - Congresses. I. Tilly, Richard H. II. Series.
HD2734 .B32 1985

Beiträge zur Singener Geschichte.
(Bd. 7) Gebhard, Alfred. Das Dorf Singen und seine Finanzwirtschaft . Singen , 1985. 484 p. : ISBN 3-921413-23-0 LC Card 87-133391 DDC 336.43/46 19
HJ9494.S57 G4 1985

Beiträge zur Soziologie und Sozialkunde Lateinamerikas. For additional listing of contents, see Old Catalog.
(Bd. 25) Bonetti, Mario. Staat und Gesellschaft im karibischen Raum im 16. Jahrhundert /. München , 1984. 668 p. : ISBN 3-7705-2162-5 LC Card 85-132458 DDC 330.9729/02 19
HC151 .B66 1984

Beiträge zur Stadtforschung.
(4) Gewerbeentwicklung und Gewerbepolitik in der Grossstadtregion /. Gerlingen , c1987. 390 p., [3] leaves of plates : ISBN 3-88350-596-X LC Card 87-146643 DDC 332.6/732243 19
HC290.5.I53 G4797 1987

Beiträge zur Südasienforschung.
(Bd. 67) Ahrens, Heinz-Dietmar. Towards reducing the dependence on capital imports . Wiesbaden , 1982. xvi, 337 p. : ISBN 3-515-03853-1 (pbk.) LC Card 86-214363 DDC 338.9549/1 19
HC440.5 .A726 1982
(Bd. 68) Kraft, Alfred. Aspekte der Regionalen wirtschaftlichen Integration zwischen Entwicklungsländern . Wiesbaden , 1982. x, 298 p. : ISBN 3-515-03801-9 LC Card 85-136228
HC441 .K69 1982
(Bd. 69) Maass, Citha Doris. Indien, Nepal, Sri Lanka . Wiesbaden , 1982. xxi, 380 p. ; ISBN 3-515-03802-7 LC Card 86-214318
HF1590.15.N4 M33 1982
(Bd. 70) Grundbedürfnisse als Gegenstand der Entwicklungspolitik . Wiesbaden , 1982. viii, 220 p. : ISBN 3-515-03838-8 (Deut. Bibl.) LC Card 85-134671
HC59.72.B38 G78 1982
(Bd. 71) Nag Chowdhury-Zilly, Aditee. The vagrant peasant . Wiesbaden , 1982. xv, 196 p. : ISBN 3-515-03855-8 (pbk.) LC Card 86-214350
HD1537.I4 N327 1982
(Bd. 84) Gläser, Thomas. Fischerei und Fischereiwirtschaft im nördlichen Ceylon . Wiesbaden , 1983. xv, 196 p. : ISBN 3-515-04054-4 LC Card 86-155838
HD9466.S722 G53 1983

Der Beitrag des Geldes zur gesellschaftlichen Wohlfahrt . Baumgard, Gerhard, 1952- München , c1984. 232 p. : ISBN 3-88259-304-8 LC Card 85-113519
HG221 .B348 1984

Beiträge aus dem Fachbereich Pädagogik der Hochschule der Bundeswehr Hamburg .
(1984/5) Ahrens, Gerhard, 1939- Staatsverschuldung ohne Ende? /. Hamburg [1984] 37 leaves ; LC Card 85-166341
HJ8650 .A37 1984

Beiträge aus dem Institut für Verkehrswissenschaft an der Universität Münster .
(Heft 102) Offergeld, Johannes. Spezialisierung des Verkehrsangebotes und Strukturwandel in

der verladenden Wirtschaft . Göttingen , 1984. 185 p. : ISBN 3-525-85690-3 (Deut. Bibl.) LC Card 84-197725
HE131 .M8 Heft 102 HE249

(Heft 107) Reutersberg, Bernhard. Logistik als Instrument zur Steigerung der Marktleistungsfähigkeit von Stahlhandlungen /. Göttingen , 1985. 301 p. : ISBN 3-525-85697-0 : LC Card 86-162333
HE131 .M8 Heft 107 HE199.5.M4

(Heft 109) Verkehrs- und unternehmenspolitische Anpassungsstrategien an veränderte Ressourcenbewertungen /. Göttingen , 1986. 210 p. : ISBN 3-525-85699-7 : LC Card 86-223574
HE131 .M8 Heft 109 HE249

Beiträge zu Geschichte und Gesellschaft Vorarlbergs .
(4) Im Prinzip, Hoffnung . Bregenz , c1984. 368 p. : ISBN 3-900438-07-9 LC Card 86-120542 DDC 331.88/09436/45 19
HD6679.V67 I4 1984 ***NYPL [JLD 87-1568]***

Beiträge zu Inflation und Wiederaufbau in Deutschland und Europa 1914-1924 .
(Bd. 4) Lindenlaub, Dieter. Maschinenbauunternehmen in der Deutschen Inflation 1919-1923 . Berlin , New York , 1985. xiii, 262 p. ; ISBN 3-11-009934-9 LC Card 85-214738
HG999 .L75 1985

(Bd. 8) The Adaptation to inflation /. Berlin , New York , 1986. xvi, 512 p. : ISBN 0-89925-287-7 (U. S.) LC Card 86-29134 DDC 338.943 19
HC286.2 .A62 1986

Beiträge zu wirtschaftswissenschaftlichen Problemen der Versicherung, 0522-618X .
(Bd. 20) Dimmer, Klaus. Die optimale Versicherungsentscheidung als risikopolitisches Problem . Karlsruhe , c1986. xiv, 320 p. : LC Card 87-114755 DDC 368/.0072 19
HG8054.5 .D555 1986

Beiträge zum Beschaffungsmarketing .
(Bd. 6) Mertens, Jürgen. Zur Entwicklung und zum konstellationsadäquaten Einsatz eines Beschaffungsmarketinginstrumentariums im Einzelhandel /. Köln , 1986. 379 p. : ISBN 3-922292-13-7 LC Card 87-143182 DDC 658.8/7 19
HF5429.225 .M47 1986

Beiträge zum Rechnungs-, Finanz- und Revisionswesen, 0721-3026 .
(Bd. 11) Hanisch, Bärbel, 1957- Die Ergebnisrechnung nach dem Bilanzrichtlinie-Gesetzentwurf im internationalen Vergleich (BRD, Japan, USA) /. Frankfurt am Main , New York , c1984. 286 p. : ISBN 3-8204-8559-7 : LC Card 85-164345
HF5616.G3 H35 1984

(Bd. 15) Kraus, Rudolf, 1953- Vorkalkulation bei langfristiger Einzelfertigung /. Frankfurt am Main , New York , c1986. iii, 299 p. : ISBN 3-8204-0000-1 LC Card 86-233181
HD47.3 .K73 1986

Beiträge zum Siedlungs- und Wohnungswesen und zur Raumplanung, 0723-0389 .
(Bd. 90) Burberg, Paul-Helmuth. Zielgruppenorientierte kommunale Wirtschaftsförderung . Münster , c1983. xi, 207, 16 p. : ISBN 3-88497-042-9 LC Card 84-173863
HC289.M9 B87 1983

Beiträge zum Sonderschulwesen und zur Rehabilitationspädagogik, 0138-1725 .
(Bd. 44) Rehabilitationspädagogik für Körperbehinderte /. Berlin , 1986. 132 p. ; LC Card 86-193835
HD7256.G32 R44 1986

Beiträge zur Arbeitsmarkt- und Berufsforschung, 0173-6574 .
(25) Abiturienten und Hochschulabsolventen beim Übergang vom Studium in den Beruf . Nürnberg , 1983. 407 p. : LC Card 84-140881
HD6278.G4 A25 1983

(58) Träger, Manfred Georg. Entwicklung und Funktion des britischen und deutschen Systems der Arbeitsvermittlungs- und Berufsberatungsdienste . Nürnberg , 1981. ii, 80, 48 p. ; LC Card 82-200262 DDC 331.11/0941 19
HD5765.A6 T72 1981 ***NYPL [JLD 87-905]***

(64) Kabbert, Rainer. Jugendliche zwischen Schule und Beruf . Nürnberg , 1982. 84, [1] p. : LC Card 83-169834
HF5382.5.G3 K33 1982

(65) Dostal, Werner. Bildung und Beschäftigung im technischen Wandel . Nürnberg , 1982. viii, 380, 6 p. : LC Card 82-205035 DDC 306/.46 19
HD6331 .D53 1982 ***NYPL [JLD 86-3011]***

(69) Struktur und Arbeitsweise von Arbeitsverwaltungen in EG-Ländern Frankreich, Belgien, Italien . Nürnberg , 1982. 206 p. : LC Card 83-174401
HD8431 .S77 1982

(79) Evaluation der Berufsberatung der Bundesanstalt für Arbeit . Nürnberg , 1983. vii, 282 p. : LC Card 85-107586
HF5382.5.G3 E9 1983

(88) Staat und Beschäftigung . Nürnberg , 1985. 471 p. : LC Card 86-674027
HD5713 .S72x 1985

Beiträge zur Entwicklungspädagogik .
(Bd. 2) Osmers, Dieter. Entwicklungspolitische Erwachsenenbildung in der Bundesrepublik mit Hilfe kommunaler Konfliktfelder /. Frankfurt am Main , c1983. 161 p., [2] folded leaves of plates : ISBN 3-88129-669-7 LC Card 84-135387
HD77.5.G3 O85 1983

Beitrage zur experimentellen .
(7. Bd) Bargaining behavior /. Tübingen , 1978. x, 383 p. : ISBN 3-16-340972-5 LC Card 86-227549 DDC 330 s 658.4 19
HB41 .B29 1967 Bd. 7 HD58.6

Beiträge zur Geschichte der Isergebirgler und ihrer Industrie .
(Nr. 5) John, Walter. Glasspinnerei im Isergebirge /. Schwäbisch-Gmünd , 1984, c1974. 78 p. : LC Card 85-135799
HD9623.I94 J64 1984

Beiträge zur kommunalen und regionalen Planung, 0721-2976 .
(7) Siedlungsformen und soziale Kosten . Frankfurt am Main , New York , c1984. vi, 219 p., [1] folded leaf of plates : ISBN 3-8204-5402-0 LC Card 85-190162
HD7339.A3 S59 1984

Beiträge zur Kommunikations- und Medienpolitik .
(Bd. 2) Hunziker, Peter, 1941- Lokales Bürgerfernsehen . Aarau , c1983. 192 p. ; ISBN 3-7941-2369-7 : LC Card 83-141437
HE8700.72.S95 H85 1983

Beiträge zur Mittelstandsforschung .
(Heft 56) Scheer, Christian. Verteilungswirkungen der Einkommensteuer /. Göttingen , c1982. xii, 457 p. : ISBN 3-509-01260-7 : LC Card 83-150522
HJ4719 .S34 1982

(Heft 93) Clemens, Reinhard. Standortprobleme von Industrieunternehmen in Ballungsräumen . Göttingen , c1983. xviii, 257 p. : ISBN 3-509-01330-1 LC Card 83-198706
HC289.D6 C54 1983

Beiträge zur nationalsozialistischen Gesundheits- und Sozialpolitik .
(3) Herrenmensch und Arbeitsvölker . Berlin , c1986. 189 p. : ISBN 3-88022-952-X (cover); 3-88022-925-X : LC Card 87-119712 DDC 331.11/732/0943 19
HD4875.G4 H47 1986

Beiträge zur österreichischen Statistik .
(490. Heft) Lenkerberechtigungen im Jahre 1977 /. Wien , 1978. 69 p. ; LC Card 86-196229
HA1173 .A27 Heft 490 HE5667.A6

(563. Heft) Die Österreichische Gemeinwirtschaft im Jahre 1976 . Wien , 1980. 102 p. ; LC Card 85-208409
HA1173 .A27 Heft 563 HC265

(750. Heft) Strassenverkehrszählung 1980 auf Bundesstrassen im gesamten Bundesgebiet der Republik Österreich /. Wien , 1985. 288 p. : LC Card 86-170848
HA1173 .A27 Heft 750 HE363.A93T7

(790. Heft) Statistik der gewerblichen Wirtschaft . Wien , 1986. 2 v. ; LC Card 87-409345 DDC 314.36 s 338.09436/021 19
HA1173 .A27 Heft 790 HC265

(793. Heft) Handel, Lagerung 1983 /. Wien , 1986- v. <1- > ; LC Card 87-408429 DDC 314.36 s 380.1/09436/021 19
HA1173 .A27 Heft 793 HF3541.5

(810. Heft) Der Österreichische Baupreisindex 1971-1985 /. Wien , 1986. 107 p. ; LC Card 87-409417 DDC 314.36 s 338.4/3691/09436 19
HA1173 .A27 Heft 810 HD9715.8.A92

Beiträge zur Politikwissenschaft, 0170-8384 .
(Bd. 33) Rehfeld, Dieter, 1951- Bestimmungsfaktoren der Energiepolitik in der Bundesrepublik Deutschland . Frankfurt am Main , New York , c1986. vii, 287 p. ; ISBN 3-8204-9354-9 LC Card 86-194761
HD9502.G42 R44 1986

Beiträge zur praktischen Nationalökonomie .
(Bd. 12) Jacobi, Klaus, 1929- Der induzierte Kapitalexport /. Zürich , c1959. viii, 106 p. ; LC Card 87-408198 DDC 332.4/5609494 19
HG3891 .J33 1959

Beiträge zur psychologischen Forschung .
(Bd. 9) Marstedt, Gerd. Psychische Belastungen in der Arbeitswelt . Opladen , c1986. vii, 366 p. : ISBN 3-531-11757-2 LC Card 87-135624
HF5548.8 .M373 1986

Beiträge zur Sozialökonomik der Arbeit .
(Bd. 10) Gabriel, Jürgen. Flexibilisierung der Arbeit und wirtschaftliche Instabilität . München , c1985. x, 316 p. ; ISBN 3-597-10540-8 LC Card 86-118217 DDC 331.25/72 19
HD5109 .G33 1985

Beiträge zur sozialwissenschaftlichen Forschung, 0175-615X .
(Bd. 79) Mettler-Meibom, Barbara E. Breitbandtechnologie . Opladen , c1986. xxiv, 477, [60] p. : ISBN 3-531-11782-3 LC Card 86-184911
HE8154 .M47 1986

(Bd. 80) Koch-Arzberger, Claudia. Die schwierige Integration . Opladen , c1985. 211 p. : ISBN 3-531-11785-8 LC Card 86-101159 DDC 331.6/2/0943 19
HD8458.A2 K587 1985

(Bd. 84) Bernschneider, Wolfgang. Staat, Gewerkschaft und Arbeitsprozess . Opladen , c1986. viii, 291 p. : ISBN 3-531-11797-1 LC Card 86-222066
HD5710.75.G3 B47 1986

(Bd. 89) Leonhard, Martin. Umweltverbände . Opladen , c1986. xiii, 352 p. ; ISBN 3-531-11820-X LC Card 86-192568
HC290.5.E5 L46 1986

Beiträge zur städtebaulichen Forschung .
(Bd. 1) Fuhrich, Manfred, 1950- Sicherung des Sozialmietwohnungsbestandes /. Frankfurt am Main , c1986. xxiii, 180, 16 p. : ISBN 3-88129-996-3 LC Card 86-223886
HD7288.78.G3 F84 1986

Beiträge zur Stadtforschung (Gerlingen, Baden-Württemberg, Germany) .
(4) Gewerbeentwicklung und Gewerbepolitik in der Grossstadtregion /. Gerlingen , c1987. 390 p., [3] leaves of plates : ISBN 3-88350-596-X LC Card 87-146643 DDC 332.6/732243 19
HC290.5.I53 G4797 1987

Beiträge zur Statistik des Landes Nordrhein-Westfalen .
(Heft 477) Das Textilgewerbe in Nordrhein-Westfalen 1977 bis 1980. Düsseldorf [1982] 109 p. : LC Card 87-407312 DDC 943/.55 s 338.4/7677/0094355021 19
HA1320.N6 A32 Heft 477 HD9863.7.N67

(Heft 489) Agrarberichterstattung Nordrhein-Westfalen 1981 . Düsseldorf [1983] 131, [5] p. ; LC Card 87-407319 DDC 943/.55 s 338.1/0943/55021 19
HA1320.N6 A32 Heft 489 HD9013.7.N6

(Heft 490) Agrarberichterstattung Nordrhein-Westfalen 1981 . Düsseldorf [1983] 189 p. ; LC Card 87-407320 DDC 943/.55 s 338.1/0943/55021 19
HA1320.N6 A32 Heft 490 HD1960.N67

(Heft 497) Zensus im Bergbau und verarbeitenden Gewerbe Nordrhein-Westfalen 1979 . Düsseldorf [1983] 109 p. ; LC Card 87-407314 DDC 943/.55 s 338.2/0943/55021 19
HA1320.N6 A32 Heft 497 HD9506.G23N6

(Heft 508) Die Investitionsentwicklung in Nordrhein-Westfalen 1970-1980. Düsseldorf [1984] 94 p. : LC Card 87-407315 DDC 943/.55

s 332.6/0943/55021 19
HA1320.N6 A32 Heft 508 HG5503.N67

(Heft 531) Agrarberichterstattung Nordrhein-Westfalen 1983 . Düsseldorf [1985] 191 p. ; LC Card 87-407316 DDC 943/.55 s 338.1/0943/55021 19
HA1320.N6 A32 Heft 531 HD1960.N67

(Heft 532) Agrarberichterstattung Nordrhein-Westfalen 1983 . Düsseldorf [1984] 263 p. ; LC Card 87-407317 DDC 943/.55 s 338.1/0943/55021 19
HA1320.N6 A32 Heft 532 HD1960.N67

(Heft 533) Agrarberichterstattung Nordrhein-Westfalen 1983 . Düsseldorf [1984] 241, [5] p. ; LC Card 87-407318 DDC 943/.55 s 338.1/76/0094355021 19
HA1320.N6 A32 Heft 533 HD9423.7.N6

Beiträge zur Statistik des Landes Nordrhein-Westfalen, 0720-1664 .
(Heft 500) Vorausberechnung der Bevölkerung in den kreisfreien Städten und Kreisen Nordrhein-Westfalens . Düsseldorf [1983] 103 p. : LC Card 86-202728
HA1320.N6 A32 Heft 500

Beiträge zur Statistik Hessens .
(n.F., Nr. 88) Die Kommunalwahlen am 20. März 1977 . Wiesbaden , 1978. 116 p. ; LC Card 86-102904
HA1320 .H529 n.F., Nr. 88 JS5471.H423E44

Beiträge zur Statistik Hessens, 0440-7482 .
(n.F., Nr. 152) Gehalts- und Lohnstrukturerhebung 1978 . Wiesbaden , 1983. 285, [3] p. ; LC Card 86-217477
HA1320 .H529 n.F., Nr. 152 HD5030.H47

Beiträge zur Struktur- und Konjunkturforschung .
(Bd. 10) Bauer, Jürgen. Quantitative Entwicklungsplanung für ländliche Regionen . Bochum , 1979. 382 p. in various pagings : ISBN 3-88339-087-9 : LC Card 80-470152
HT395.G4 B39 1979 ***NYPL [JLD 86-1628]***

(Bd. 17) Die Wirtschaftliche Entwicklung in den Arbeitsmarktregionen des Bergischen Landes . Bochum , 1981. 401 p. : ISBN 3-88339-217-0 LC Card 82-164818 DDC 331/.0943/55 19
HD8459.N66 W57 1981
NYPL [JLD 86-1639]

(Bd. 19) Rau, Thomas. Bodenallokation und Bodenpolitik im Ruhrgebiet . Bochum , 1982. viii, 323 p. : ISBN 3-88339-269-3 LC Card 83-130477 DDC 333.73/13/094355 19
HD659.R8 R38 1982 ***NYPL [JLD 86-1715]***

(Bd. 20) Klemmer, Paul. Abgrenzung von Fördergebieten /. Bochum , 1983. 206 p. : ISBN 3-88339-298-7 LC Card 83-183564
HC286.7 .K59 1983

(Bd. 22) Grätz, Christian. Kommunale Wirtschaftsförderung, kritische Bestandsaufnahme ihrer Funktionen und Organisation /. Bochum , 1983. xiii, 263 p. : ISBN 3-88339-340-1 : LC Card 84-138569
HC290.5.D5 G74 1983

(Bd. 24) Bremicker, Burckhardt. Analyse der Arbeitslosigkeit in den Regionen Nordrhein-Westfalens . Bochum , 1984. xx, 381 p. : ISBN 3-88339-362-2 LC Card 84-196621 DDC 331.13/794355 19
HD5780.N6 B74 1984 ***NYPL [JLD 86-2367]***

(Bd. 26) Lindmüller, Peter. Remscheid und Solingen im industriegeographischen Entwicklungsvergleich /. Bochum , 1986. 423 p. : ISBN 3-88339-544-7 LC Card 87-146590 DDC 330.943/55 19
HC289.R38 L56 1986

Beiträge zur Verwaltungswissenschaft, 0176-0890 .
(Nr. 2) Gornas, Jürgen. Zur Berücksichtigung der finanziellen Leistungsfähigkeit in kommunalen Investitions- und Finanzplanungsmodellen /. Hamburg , 1984. 40 p. ; LC Card 85-166310
HJ9473 .G67 1984

Beiträge zur Volkskultur in Nordwestdeutschland, 0724-4096 .
(Heft 41) Höher, Peter. Heimat und Fremde . Münster , 1985. viii, 414 p., [1] p. of plates : ISBN 3-88547-290-2 LC Card 85-160726 DDC 381/.0943/42 19
HF3569.S28 H64 1985

Beitragsäquivalenz oder interpersonelle Umverteilung in der gesetzlichen Rentenversicherung? . Helberger, Christof. Berlin , 1981. 96 p. ; LC Card 81-201422 DDC 331.25/2/0943 19
HD7105.35.G3 H44 1981
NYPL [JLM 81-818 v.63]

Bekaert, s. a. Travail, loisirs, culture. [Bruxelles] [Zwevegem]] 1970. ix, 163 p. LC Card 71-856101
HD4904.7 .T7 1970

Bekemans, Léonce. Social security and employment /. Assen, The Netherlands , 1983. 116 p. : ISBN 90-232-2011-0 (pbk.) : LC Card 83-216203 DDC 331.12/094 19
HD7164 .S594 1983 ***NYPL [JLE 86-1107]***

Békés, Sándor. Az első évtized : tények, adatok, események a Magyar Televízió Pécsi Körzeti Stúdiójának történetéből, 1976-1986 / Békés Sándor. Pécs : Baranya Megyei Művelődési Központ, 1986. 221 p. : ill. ; 20 cm. Includes index. LC Card 87-148227
1. Magyar Televízió. Pécsi Körzeti Stúdio - History. 2. Television broadcasting - Hungary - Pécs - History. I. Magyar Televízió. Pécsi Körzeti Stúdió. II. Title. III. Title: 1. évtized.
HE8700.9.H8 B45 1986

Bekiroglu, Haluk. Computer models for production and inventory control /. La Jolla, Calif. , c1984. ix, 148 p. : LC Card 84-189641 DDC 658.5/0028/54 19
TS157 .C63 1984 ***NYPL [JSF 86-930]***

Bekkulov, A. B. (Ablkaĭ Bekkulovich) Problemy razvitii͡a transporta Kazakhstana : o ratsionalizatsii ėkonomicheskikh svi͡azeĭ / A.B. Bekkulov. Alma-Ata : "Kazakhstan", 1984. 229 p. ; 21 cm. Bibliography: p. 219-[228] LC Card 84-226651
1. Transportation - Kazakh S.S.R. I. Title.
HE255.Z7 K393 1984

Bekleshov, Dmitriĭ. Reklama knig segodni͡a / Dmitriĭ Bekleshov. Moskva : "Kniga", 1986. 201 p. : ill. (some col.) ; 22 cm. LC Card 87-132362 DDC 659.1/90705 19
1. Advertising - Books - Soviet Union. 2. Booksellers and bookselling - Soviet Union. I. Title.
HF6161.B37 B44 1986

Bel Adell, María del Carmen. Datos básicos para el estudio de la población en la región de Murcia / Carmen Bel Adell. [Murcia] : Departamento de Geografía Humana, Universidad de Murcia, c1985. 223 p. ; 30 cm. (Documentos de trabajo . 1) ISBN 84-600-3907-2 LC Card 86-218876
1. Murcia (Spain : Region) - Population - Statistics. 2. Labor supply - Spain - Murcia (Region) - Statistics. 3. Murcia (Spain : Region) - Social conditions - Statistics. I. Series: Documentos de trabajo (Universidad de Murcia. Departamento de Geografía Humana) 1. II. Title.
HA1558.M8 B44 1985

Bel Air, Roger. Make a fortune buying discounted mortgages / Roger Bel Air. 1st ed. Garden City, N.Y. : Doubleday, 1987. 152 p. : ill. ; 22 cm. ISBN 0-385-23924-6 : LC Card 86-23949 DDC 332.63/244 19
1. Mortgages - United States. I. Title. II. Title: Discounted mortgages.
HG5095 .B38 1987

Bel Ghazi, Hassan.
Mythen : buitenlandse arbeiders tussen kulturele konfrontatie en overheidsfalen / Hassan Bel Ghazi. Amsterdam : Populier, [1985] 111 p. ; 20 cm. ISBN 90-6617-024-7 LC Card 86-145232
1. Alien labor - Netherlands - Social conditions. 2. Netherlands - Social policy. I. Title.
HD8518.5.A2 B44 1985

Van soek naar arbeidsmarkt : Marokkaanse migranten en hun kinderen in Nederland / Hassan Bel Ghazi. [Bussum] : Wereldvenster, 1986. 176 p. ; 20 cm. (Nabije-Oostenreeks) Bibliography: p. 175-176. ISBN 90-293-0638-6 : LC Card 86-234591
1. Alien labor, Moroccan - Netherlands - Social conditions. 2. Moroccans - Netherlands. 3. Morocco - Social conditions. I. Title. II. Series.
HD8518.5.M6 B45 1986

Béládi, László. Az Elmélet és a fegyverek kritikája . Budapest [1981] xxv, 509 p. ; ISBN 963-461-775-1 (Magy. nemz. bibl.) LC Card 85-139263
HC59.7 .E45 1981

Belal, Abdel Aziz. Développement et facteurs non-économiques / Abdel Aziz Belal. Rabat : Société marocaine des éditeurs réunis, 1980. 100 p. ; 24 cm. Includes bibliographical references. LC Card 82-960502
1. Economic development. 2. Developing countries - Economic conditions. 3. Developing countries - Social conditions. I. Title.
HD83 .B388 1980

Belardi C., Arturo. La industria frente a la inflación : documento central / presentado por el Comité Ejecutivo del Consejo Venezolano de la Industria a la XII Asamblea Nacional de Cámaras y Asociaciones Industriales ; preparado por Arturo Belardi C. y Arquímedes Román. Valencia [Venezuela] : El Consejo, 1981. 92 leaves : ill. ; 27 cm. Bibliography: leaves 91-92. LC Card 85-187972
1. Inflation (Finance) - Venezuela. I. Román, Arquímedes. II. Consejo Venezolano de la Industria. Comité Ejecutivo. III. Title.
HG915 .B44 1981

Die Belastung der Einkünfte aus nichtselbständiger Arbeit mit Einkommensteuern und Sozialabgaben in den EG-Ländern und in Schweden /. Parsche, Rüdiger. München , 1981. 2 v. ; LC Card 83-115269
HJ4719 .P37 1981

Die Belastung der Landwirtschaft durch Beiträge zur sozialen Sicherung im Vergleich zur Situation anderer sozialer Gruppen . Holla, Michael. Göttingen [1986] viii, 174 p. ; LC Card 87-407657 DDC 368.4/00943 19
HD7179 .H635 1986

Belastungsabbau unter Tage : zum Einfluss öffentlicher Massnahmen auf die Humanisierung der Arbeit / Volker Döhl ... [et al.] ; unter Mitarbeit von Norbert Altmann. Essen : Glückauf, 1982. 315 p. : ill. ; 21 cm. (Schriftenreihe "Humanisierung des Arbeitslebens" . Bd. 28) Bibliography: p. 310-315. ISBN 3-7739-0380-4 : LC Card 83-186893 DDC 363.1/1/0943 19
1. Work environment - Germany, West. 2. Industrial hygiene - Germany, West. I. Döhl, Volker. II. Series.
HD7708 .B45 1982

Belcher, David W. Compensation administration / David W. Belcher, Thomas J. Atchison. 2nd ed. Englewood Cliffs, N.J. : Prentice-Hall, c1987. xv, 464 p. : ill. ; 25 cm. (Prentice-Hall series in industrial relations and personnel) Includes bibliographical references and index. ISBN 0-13-154790-9 : LC Card 86-25494 DDC 658.3/2 19
1. Compensation management. 2. Wages. I. Atchison, Thomas J. II. Title. III. Series.
HF5549.5.C67 B45 1987

Belcher, John G. Productivity plus / by John G. Belcher, Jr. Houston : Gulf Pub. Co., Book Division, 1987. p. cm. Includes index. ISBN 0-87201-451-7 LC Card 87-9222 DDC 658.3/14 19
1. Industrial productivity. 2. Industrial management. I. Title.
HD56 .B45 1987

Bel'chikov, I͡A. M.
Khozi͡aĭstvennyĭ mekhanizm proizvodstva i obrashchenii͡a tovarov narodnogo potreblenii͡a /. Riga , 1985. 115 p. ; LC Card 86-177827
HF1040.9.L38 K47 1985

Prodavet͡s i Pokupatel', ili rasskaz o tom, kakimi mogli by stat'_ikh otnoshenii͡a, bud' ri͡adom Psikholog / I͡A. Bel'chikov. Riga : "Avots", 1986. 157, [3] p. : ill. ; 17 cm. Bibliography: p. [159] LC Card 87-129915
1. Selling - Psychological aspects. 2. Customer service - Soviet Union. 3. Interpersonal relations. I. Title.
HF5438.8.P75 B45 1986

Upravlenie sot͡sialisticheskoĭ torgovleĭ : aktual'nye voprosy teorii i praktiki / I͡A.M. Bel'chikov. Riga : Izd-vo "Liesma", 1978. 170, [2] p. ; 20 cm. Bibliography: p. 166-[171] LC Card 82-106625
1. Germany (East) - Commercial policy. I. Title.
HF2546.5 .B44 1978

Bel'chuk, Aleksandr Ivanovich.
SSSR--razvivai͡ushchiesi͡a strany . Moskva , 1985. 237 p. ; LC Card 86-158191
HF1558.5.D44 S77 1985

Belden, Joseph N. Dirt rich, dirt poor . New York , 1986. xii, 188 p. ; ISBN 0-7102-0378-0 LC Card 85-8274 DDC 338.1/9/73 19
HD1761 .D55 1986 ***NYPL [JLD 87-821]***

Beleggen in effecten /. Piller, L. Utrecht , 1984. 195 p. ; ISBN 90-274-6126-0 : LC Card 85-134084
HG5562 .P55 1984

Belg (small) crop season synoptic report. Addis Abeba, Ethiopia : Early Warning and Planning Services, Relief and Rehabilitation Commission, 1985. 23 leaves : maps ; 32 cm. (Early warning system report) Cover title. LC Card 86-980254 DDC 338.1/9/63 19
1. Food supply - Ethiopia - Forecasting. I. Ethiopia. Early Warning and Planning Services. II. Series.
HD9017.E82 B44 1985

Belg synoptic report [microform] : 1973 E.C. (1981) season : crop dependent food supply system. Addis Abeba, Ethiopia : Early Warning and Planning Services, Relief and Rehabilitation Commission, [1981] iv, 21 leaves : ill. ; 28 cm. Cover title. "September 1981." Microfilm. New york : New York : New York Public Library, 1986. 1 microfilm reel ; 35mm. (MN *ZZ-26,374) LC Card 82-980790 DDC 363.8/0963 19
1. Food supply - Ethiopia. 2. Food crops - Ethiopia. I. Ethiopia. Early Warning and Planning Services.
HD9017.E82 B45 1981
NYPL [*ZT-1708 no.19]

Belgiojoso, L. B. (Lodovico Barbiano), 1909- Riuso e riqualificazione edilizia negli anni '80 /. Milano [1981] 706 p. :ill. ; ISBN 88-20-42135-6 (pbk.) : LC Card 81-210070
HD7341.A3 R58 1981 ***NYPL [JSD 86-493]***

Belgium. Direction Statistiques, études, information. Service Etudes. Chômage des jeunes . Bruxelles [1984] 49 p. : LC Card 84-222918
HD6276.B42 C48 1984

BELGIUM - ECONOMIC CONDITIONS.
Luwel, A. Een economie in spanning . Leuven , 1985. 168 p. ; ISBN 90-334-1193-8 LC Card 86-123424
HB179.D8 L89 1985

BELGIUM - ECONOMIC CONDITIONS - 1945-
L'Avenir économique de la Belgique . [Bruxelles , 1981] 155 p. ; LC Card 87-672443
HC315 .A93x 1981

Schoonbroodt, Jos., 1936- Etat de besoin, besoin d'Etat . Bruxelles , c1985. 272 p. : ISBN 2-87003-196-3 LC Card 86-146944 DDC 338.9493 19
HC315 .S17 1985

BELGIUM - ECONOMIC POLICY.
Peffer, Michel, 1948- L'Etat anthropophage /. Bruxelles , c1982. 279 p. ; ISBN 2-87005-164-5 LC Card 84-139080
HJ1197 .P44 1982

Schoonbroodt, Jos., 1936- Etat de besoin, besoin d'Etat . Bruxelles , c1985. 272 p. : ISBN 2-87003-196-3 LC Card 86-146944 DDC 338.9493 19
HC315 .S17 1985

BELGIUM - ECONOMIC POLICY - CONGRESSES.
Employment and growth . Dordrecht , Boston , 1987. xii, 310 p. : ISBN 90-247-3514-9 LC Card 87-3184 DDC 331.11 19
HD73 .E46 1987

BELGIUM - FOREIGN ECONOMIC RELATIONS - SOUTH AFRICA.
L'Afrique du Sud et nous . [Liège, Belgium] [1984] [69] p. : LC Card 86-200334
HF1554.5.S6 A37 1984

Belgium - Government. see **Belgium - Politics and government.**

BELGIUM - MANUFACTURES - ECONOMETRIC MODELS.
Lambert, Jean-Paul, 1952- Disequilibrium macroeconomic models . Cambridge [Cambridgeshire] , New York , 1988. p. cm. ISBN 0-521-32209-X LC Card 86-24966 DDC 339.5/0724 19
HB145 .L36 1988

BELGIUM - POLITICS AND GOVERNMENT - 1951-
Arcq, Etienne. La C.S.C. et le programme gouvernemental de mars 1984 /. Bruxelles [1984] 23 leaves ; LC Card 84-171486
HD8502.C62 A73 1984

Beliaevskiĭ, I. K. (Igor' Konstantinovich) Naselenie i tovarooborot : tendentsii i vzaimosviazi / I.K. Beliaevskiĭ. Moskva : "Statistika", 1980. 144 p. : ill., charts, map ; 21 cm. LC Card 81-135180
1. Consumption (Economics) - Soviet Union. 2. Demand (Economic theory). I. Title.
HB801 .B377 1980

Beliakov, A. (Aleksandr) Rukopozhatie piatiletok /. Moskva , 1981. 237 p. : LC Card 82-103792
HC335 .R76 1981

Belichenko, A. N. (Al'bert Nikolaevich) Kreditnye otnosheniia mezhdu stranami-chlenami SĖV / A.N. Belichenko, G.G. Matiukhin. Moskva : "Finansy i statistika", 1983. 134 p. : ill. ; 20 cm. Includes bibliographical references. LC Card 84-171632
1. Credit - Europe, Eastern. 2. Finance - Europe, Eastern. 3. Foreign exchange problem - Europe, Eastern. 4. Council for Mutual Economic Assistance. I. Matiukhin, Georgiĭ Gavrilovich. II. Title.
HG3729.E932 B45 1983

Beliefs and ideology /. Thompson, Kenneth, 1937- Chichester, West Sussex : London ; 135 p. ; ISBN 0-85312-858-8 : LC Card 86-2984 DDC 306/.4 19
BL60 .T49 1986 ***NYPL [JLD 86-2479]***

Belize : country environmental profile, a field study / by Gary Hartshorn ... [et al.]. Belize City, Belize : R. Nicolait & Associates, 1984. xvi, 151 p. : ill., maps ; 28 cm. "April 1984." Errata sheet inserted. "USAID contract no. 505-0000-C-00-3001-00." Bibliography: p. 125-129. LC Card 86-136310 DDC 333.7/097282 19
1. Natural resources - Belize. 2. Environmental policy - Belize. 3. Environmental law - Belize. 4. Belize - Economic conditions. 5. Belize - Social conditions. I. Hartshorn, Gary S. II. Robert Nicolait & Associates.
HC142 .B447 1984 ***NYPL [JLF 87-170]***

Belize.
Belize 1980 population census : summary tables. Belmopan : Statistical Office, Central Planning Unit, [1982-<1983 > <3 v. > ; 36 cm. CONTENTS. - bull. 1. Population, race, religion, language, marital status -- bull. 2. Employment, industrial and occupational groups -- bull. 3. Housing, education and training, migration. LC Card 87-131071 DDC 304.6/097282 19
1. Belize - Census, 1980. 2. Belize - Population - Statistics. I. Belize. Ministry of Finance and Ecomonic Planning. Central Planning Unit. Statistical Office. II. Title.
HA791.5 1980

BELIZE - CENSUS, 1980.
Belize. Belize 1980 population census . Belmopan [1982-<1983. <3 v. > ; LC Card 87-131071 DDC 304.6/097282 19
HA791.5 1980

BELIZE - ECONOMIC CONDITIONS.
Belize . Belize City, Belize , 1984. xvi, 151 p. : LC Card 86-136310 DDC 333.7/097282 19
HC142 .B447 1984 ***NYPL [JLF 87-170]***

BELIZE - ECONOMIC POLICY.
Belize. Ministry of Foreign Affairs and Economic Development. Five year macro-economic plan for Belize, 1985-1989. Belmopan [1984?] 48 p. ; LC Card 87-105155 DDC 338.97282 19
HC142 .B443 1984

Belize. Ministry of Finance and Ecomonic Planning. Central Planning Unit. Statistical Office. Belize. Belize 1980 population census . Belmopan [1982-<1983. <3 v. > ; LC Card 87-131071 DDC 304.6/097282 19
HA791.5 1980

Belize. Ministry of Foreign Affairs and Economic Development. Five year macro-economic plan for Belize, 1985-1989. Belmopan : Ministry of Foreign Affairs and Economic Development, [1984?] 48 p. ; 23 cm. LC Card 87-105155 DDC 338.97282 19
1. Belize - Economic policy. I. Title.
HC142 .B443 1984

BELIZE - POPULATION - STATISTICS.
Belize. Belize 1980 population census . Belmopan [1982-<1983. <3 v. > ; LC Card 87-131071 DDC 304.6/097282 19
HA791.5 1980

BELIZE - SOCIAL CONDITIONS.
Belize . Belize City, Belize , 1984. xvi, 151 p. : LC Card 86-136310 DDC 333.7/097282 19
HC142 .B447 1984 ***NYPL [JLF 87-170]***

Belize 1980 population census . Belize. Belmopan [1982-<1983. <3 v. > ; LC Card 87-131071 DDC 304.6/097282 19
HA791.5 1980

Belk, Russell W. AMA Winter Educators' Conference (1987 : San Antonio, Tex.) 1987 AMA Winter Educators' Conference . Chicago, Ill. , c1987. viii, 411 p. : ISBN 0-87757-185-6 (pbk.) LC Card 87-944 DDC 658.8/001 19
HF5411 .A53 1987

Belkaoui, Ahmed, 1943-
Inquiry and accounting : alternate methods and research perspectives / Ahmed Belkaoui. New York : Quorum Books, 1987. xiv, 437 p. ; 24 cm. Includes bibliographies and index. ISBN 0-89930-222-X (lib. bdg. : alk. paper) LC Card 87-2496 DDC 657 19
1. Accounting. I. Title.
HF5625 .B382 1987

The new environment in international accounting : issues and practices / Ahmed Belkaoui. New York : Quorum Books, c1988. p. cm. Includes bibliographies and index. ISBN 0-89930-267-X (lib. bdg. : alk. paper) LC Card 87-7252 DDC 657/.95 19
1. International business enterprises - Accounting. 2. Comparative accounting. I. Title.
HF5686.I56 B45 1988

Belknap, John W. Saupe, William E. Rural poverty in Wisconsin counties /. Madison, WI [198-] 26 p. : LC Card 86-622097
HC107.W63 P6249 1980z

Bell, Arthur H. (Arthur Henry), 1946- Business communication : process and practice / Arthur H. Bell. Glenview, Ill. : Scott, Foresman, c1987. 601 p., [8] p. of plates : ill. (some col.) ; 24 cm. (The Scott, Foresman series in business communication) Includes index. ISBN 0-673-18326-2 : LC Card 86-24844 DDC 808/.066651 19
1. Communication in management. I. Title. II. Series.
HF5718 .B455 1987

Bell Communications Research, Inc. Technology and the transformation of white-collar work /. Hillsdale, N.J. , 1987. x, 281 p. : ISBN 0-89859-633-5 : LC Card 86-29039 DDC 331.7/92/0973 19
HD8039.M4 U577 1987

BELL, DANIEL.
Brick, Howard, 1953- Daniel Bell and the decline of intellectual radicalism . Madison, Wis. , 1986. 215-266. ISBN 0-299-10550-4 : LC Card 85-40757 DDC 300/.92/4 19
H59.B42 B75 1986 ***NYPL [JLE 86-3046]***

Bell, Frederick W. An economic analysis of the importance of saltwater beaches in Florida / Frederick W. Bell, Vernon R. Leeworthy. Gainesville, FL : Florida Sea Grant College : Available from Sea Grant Extension Program, [1986] xi, 166 p. : ill. ; 28 cm. (Report / Florida Sea Grant College . no. 82) "Sea grant project no. R/C-P-12. Grant number NA80AA-D-00038." "February 1986." Bibliography: p. 164-166. LC Card 86-622310 DDC 333.91/7/09759 19
1. Bathing beaches - Economic aspects - Florida. 2. Beaches - Economic aspects - Florida. 3. Florida - Economic conditions. I. Leeworthy, Vernon R. II. Florida Sea Grant College. III. Series: Report / Florida Sea Grant College , no. 82. IV. Title.
HD266.F6 B45 1986

Bell, G. J. (Graham J.) The business of transport / G. Bell, P. Bowen, P. Fawcett. Plymouth [Devon] : Macdonald and Evans ;, 1984. viii, 344 p. : ill. ; 22 cm. (The M & E business studies series, 0266-4917) Includes index. Bibliography: p. [327]-328. ISBN 0-7121-2406-3 (pbk.) LC Card 84-170770 DDC 380.5 19
1. Transportation. 2. Transportation - Great Britain. I. Bowen, P. J. (Peter J.). II. Fawcett, P. (Paul). III. Title. IV. Series.
HE151 .B436 1984 ***NYPL [JLD 87-86]***

Bell, Martin L.
How to prepare a results-driven marketing plan / Martin L. Bell. New York, NY : American Management Association, c1987. p. cm. Bibliography: p. Includes index. ISBN 0-8144-7690-2 LC Card 87-47717 DDC 658.8/02 19

1. Marketing. I. Title.
HF5415 .B4285 1987

Managerial marketing : strategy and cases / Martin L. Bell, Julian W. Vincze. New York : Elsevier, c1988. xviii, 708 p. : ill. ; 27 cm. Includes bibliographical references and index. ISBN 0-444-01215-X LC Card 87-22306 DDC 658.8 19
1. Marketing management. 2. Marketing - Decision making. 3. Marketing - Decision making - Case studies. I. Vincze, Julian W. II. Title.
HF5415.13 .B434 1988

Bellabarba, Marco. Seriolanti e arzenisti : governo delle acque e agricoltura a Cremona fra Cinque e Seicento / Marco Bellabarba ; presentazione di Giorgio Politi. Cremona : Biblioteca statale e libreria civica di Cremona : distribuzione, Libreria del convegno, 1986- v. <1 > : ill. (some col.) ; 24 cm. (Annali della Biblioteca statale e libreria civica di Cremona . v. 36/1-) Includes bibliographical references. LC Card 86-167180
1. Flood control - Italy - Cremona Region - History. 2. Flood control - Italy - Po River Plain - History. 3. Irrigation - Italy - Cremona Region - History. 4. Irrigation - Italy - Po River Plain - History. 5. Agriculture - Economic aspects - Italy - Cremona Region - History. 6. Agriculture - Economic aspects - Italy - Po River Plain - History. I. Series: Annali della Biblioteca statale e libreria civica di Cremona , v. 36/1, etc. II. Title.
HD1676.I82 C743 1986

Bellamy, G. Thomas. Supported employment . Baltimore , c1988. x, 287 p. : ISBN 0-933716-83-4 (pbk.) : LC Card 87-14367 DDC 362/.0425 19
HD7256.U5 S86 1988

Bellan, Ruben C., 1918- The unnecessary evil : an answer to Canada's high unemployment / Ruben Bellan. Toronto, Ont. : McClelland and Stewart, c1986. 173 p. : ill. ; 24 cm. ISBN 0-7710-1153-9 : LC Card 86-222233 DDC 331.13/7971 19
1. Unemployment - Canada. 2. Canada - Full employment policies. 3. Budget deficits - Canada. 4. Deficit financing - Canada. I. Title.
HD5728 .B43 1986

Bellardi, Marta. Villas miseria : origen, erradicación y respuestas populares / Marta Bellardi, Aldo de Paula. Buenos Aires : Centro Editor de América Latina, c1986. 157 p. : ill. ; 18 cm. (Biblioteca Política argentina . 159) Originally presented as the authors' thesis (licenciatura en sociología)--Universidad del Salvador. Bibliography: p. 134-136. ISBN 950-25-1423-8 : LC Card 87-125510 DDC 307.3/36 19
1. Squatter settlements - Argentina - Buenos Aires. 2. Squatter settlements - Government policy - Argentina - Buenos Aires. I. Paula, Aldo de. II. Title. III. Series.
HD7321.B9 B45 1986

Bellavita, Christopher. Performance and credibility . Lexington, Mass. , c1986. x, 307 p. : ISBN 0-669-11037-X (alk. paper) LC Card 85-50707 DDC 658/.048 19
HD62.6 .P47 1986 ***NYPL [JLE 86-1159]***

Bellenger, Lionel. Etre constructif dans les négociations et les discussions / Lionel Bellenger. Paris : Entreprise moderne d'édition, c1984. 182 p. ; 24 cm. Bibliography: p. 181-182. ISBN 2-7101-0477-6 : LC Card 84-255673
I. Title.
HD58.6 .B45 1984 ***NYPL [JLE 87-551]***

Bellinger, D. Amerasinghe, Chittharanjan Felix, 1933- Index to decisions of the World Bank Administrative Tribunal /. [Washington, D.C.] [c1985] vii, 32 leaves ; LC Card 86-172153 DDC 354.1/8252 19
HG3881.5.W57 A44 1985

Bellini, James. High tech holocaust / James Bellini. Newton Abbot : David & Charles, c1986. 255 p. ; 24 cm. "A Graham Tarrant book." Bibliography: p. [252]-255. ISBN 0-7153-8812-6
1. Toxicology. 2. Pollution - Environmental aspects. 3. Industry - Environmental aspects. I. Title.
NYPL [JLE 87-827]

Belliveau, John Edward, 1913- "Crackie" : the Sumner family business dynasty / by John Edward Belliveau. Hantsport, N.S. : Lancelot Press, 1986. 192 p. : ill., ports. ; 21 cm. ISBN 0-88999-315-7 (pbk.) LC Card 87-120170 DDC 338.092/2 B 19
1. Summers family. 2. Sumner, W. H. T. (William Hunt Tyler), 1821 or 2-1909. 3. Businessmen - Maritime Provinces - Biography. I. Title.
HC112.5.A2 B44 1986

Bellmann, Klaus. Kortzfleisch, Gert von. Energie für den Verkehr . Frankfurt am Main , c1984. 115 p. : LC Card 84-192683
HD9710.G4 V4 Nr. 42 HE5620.E53

Bello-Osagie, V. E.
Eweka, J. A. (Julius A.) Village development . Ibadan, Nigeria , 1979. xvi, 194 p. ; LC Card 86-172121 DDC 338.1/9/669 19
HD2145.5 .E94 1979

Nigerian small farmers . Benin-City, Bendel State, Nigeria , 1980. xv, 315 p. ; LC Card 82-206979 DDC 338.1/6 19
HD1339.N5 N54 1980 ***NYPL [Sc D 86-883]***

Belloit, Jerry D. Smith, Halbert C., 1934- Real estate appraisal /. Dayton, Ohio , Columbus, OH [c1987] xii, 341 p. ; ISBN 0-939787-01-6 (pbk.) : LC Card 86-24520 DDC 333.33/2 19
HD1387 .S5152 1987

BELLPUIG REGION (SPAIN) - STATISTICS.
Materials per a l'estudi geogràfic dels pobles de l'àrea econòmica de Bellpuig /. [Lleida , 1985. 253 p. : LC Card 87-131722
HA1559.B45 M38 1985

Beloff, Halla. Getting into life /. London , New York , c1986. xii, 157 p. ; ISBN 0-416-40850-8 LC Card 86-16186 DDC 305.2/35/0941 19
HQ799.G7 G48 1986 ***NYPL [JLD 87-892]***

Bélot, Thérèse, 1947-
Berg, Elliot. Mobilization of the private sector in Burkina Faso . [Burkina Faso? , 1985] 21 p. ; LC Card 87-116357 DDC 338.966/25 19
HC1040 .B47 1985

Marsden, Keith. Private enterprise in Africa . Washington, D.C. [1987] xiii, 66 p. ; ISBN 0-8213-0945-5 (pbk.) LC Card 87-18419 DDC 330.96/032 19
HC800 .M353 1987

Belous, A. I. (Anatoliĭ Ivanovich)
Organizatsionnye formy i metody upravleniia proizvodstvom . Kishinev , 1980. 130 p. ; LC Card 81-140768
HD9015.S653 M6453 1980

Below, Patrick J.
The executive guide to strategic planning / Patrick J. Below, George L. Morrisey, Betty L. Acomb. 1st ed. San Francisco, Calif. : Jossey-Bass, c1987. xxiii, 136 p. : ill. ; 24 cm. (The Jossey-Bass management series) Bibliography: p. 127-131. Includes index. ISBN 1-555-42032-X (alk. paper) LC Card 86-27863 DDC 658.4/012 19
1. Strategic planning. I. Morrisey, George L. II. Acomb, Betty L. III. Title. IV. Series.
HD30.28 .B45 1987

Morrisey, George L. The executive guide to operational planning /. San Francisco , 1988. xxvii, 130 p. : ISBN 1-555-42064-8 (alk. paper) LC Card 87-45508 DDC 658.4/012 19
HD30.28 .M65 1988

Below-replacement fertility in industrial societies : causes, consequences, policies / Kingsley Davis, Mikhail S. Bernstam, Rita Ricardo-Campbell, editors. Cambridge [Cambridgeshire] ; New York : Cambridge University Press, c1987. x, 360 p. : ill. ; 26 cm. "Based on papers presented at a seminar held at the Hoover Institution, Stanford University, November 1985." Originally published: New York, N.Y. : Population Council, c1987. "Population and development review, a supplement to volume 12, 1986." Includes bibliographies. ISBN 0-521-34324-0 LC Card 87-6371 DDC 304.6/32 19
1. Fertility, Human - Congresses. I. Davis, Kingsley, 1908-. II. Bernshtam, Mikhail S. III. Ricardo-Campbell, Rita. IV. Hoover Institution on War, Revolution, and Peace. V. Population and development review. Vol. 12 (Supplement).
HB901 .B45 1987b

Below-replacement fertility in industrial societies : causes, consequences, policies / Kingsley Davis, Mikhail S. Bernstam, Rita Ricardo-Campbell, editors. New York, N.Y., USA : Population Council, c1987. x, 360 p. : ill. ; 26 cm. "Based on papers presented at a seminar held at the Hoover Institution, Stanford University, November 1985." "Population and development review, a supplement to volume 12, 1986." Includes bibliographies. LC Card 87-2458 DDC 304.6/32 19
1. Fertility, Human - Congresses. I. Davis, Kingsley, 1908-. II. Bernshtam, Mikhail S. III. Ricardo-Campbell, Rita. IV. Hoover Institution on War, Revolution, and Peace. V. Population and development review. Vol. 12 (Supplement).
HB901 .B45 1987

Below the line . Richards, Eugene. Mount Vernon, N.Y. , c1987. 218 p. : ISBN 0-89043-062-4 LC Card 86-70834 DDC 305.5/69/0973 19
HC110.P6 R52 1987

Belozerova, S. M. Distsiplina truda--delo kazhdogo /. Moskva , 1982. 77 p. ; LC Card 83-126613
HF5549.5.L3 D57 1982

Belth, Joseph M. The A.L. Williams replacement empire : articles from the Insurance forum, 1981-1986 / Joseph M. Belth. Ellettsville, IN : Insurance Forum, Inc., c1987. 64 p. : port. ; 28 cm. Includes index. ISBN 0-941173-00-3 (pbk.) : LC Card 86-27715 DDC 368.3/2/00973 19
1. A.L. Williams (Firm). 2. Insurance, Life - United States. I. Insurance forum. II. Title.
HG8963.A44 B44 1987

Beltrame, G. (Gianni) Metropoli e agricoltura /. Milano , c1982. 319 p. : LC Card 82-246692 DDC 333.76/13/094521 19
HD680.M54 M47 1982
NYPL [JLD 86-3678]

Beltrán Alejos, Hugo. La situación del sector metal-mecánico en el Perú : problemática y perspectivas / Hugo Beltrán Alejos. Lima, Perú : Universidad de Lima, Facultad de Economía, Centro de Investigaciones Económicas y Sociales, 1985. 93, [77] p. : ill. ; 30 cm. (Serie Avances de investigación . no. 6) Originally presented as the author's thesis (grado de bachiller)--Universidad de Lima, 1984. Bibliography: p. [73]-[77] (2nd group) LC Card 86-218266
1. Metal-work - Peru - Finance - Case studies. 2. Automobile industry and trade - Peru - Finance - Case studies. 3. Machinery industry - Peru - Finance - Case studies. I. Series: Avances de investigación (Universidad de Lima. Centro de Investigaciones Económicas y Sociales) , 6. II. Title.
HD9506.P42 B45 1985

Beltway cordon count of vehicular and passenger volumes. 1986 Beltway cordon count of vehicular and passenger volumes. [Washington, D.C.] [1986] iv, 35 p., [109] p. : LC Card 87-119314 DDC 388.4/1314/09753021 19
HE5634.W3 A17 1986

BELTWAYS - WASHINGTON METROPOLITAN AREA - STATISTICS.
1986 Beltway cordon count of vehicular and passenger volumes. [Washington, D.C.] [1986] iv, 35 p., [109] p. : LC Card 87-119314 DDC 388.4/1314/09753021 19
HE5634.W3 A17 1986

Beluszky, Pál. Magyarország falutipusai / Beluszky Pál, Sikos T. Tamás. Budapest : Magyar Tudományos Akadémia Földrajztudományi Kutató Intézet, 1982. 167 p. : ill., 1 col. map ; 24 cm. (Elmélet, módszer, gyakorlat, 0139-2875 . 25) One col. map on folded leaf in pocket. Bibliography: p. 155-167. ISBN 963-7321-96-9 LC Card 84-159502
1. Land use, Rural - Hungary. 2. Land settlement - Hungary. 3. Villages - Hungary. I. Sikos, T. Tamás. II. Title. III. Series.
HD640.5.Z7 B44 1982

Bemerkungen zur "Krise der Arbeitsgesellschaft." Ahrens, Gerhard, 1939- Staatsverschuldung ohne Ende? /. Hamburg [1984] 37 leaves ; LC Card 85-166341
HJ8650 .A37 1984

Ben-Horim, Moshe. Essentials of corporate finance / Moshe Ben-Horim. Boston : Allyn and Bacon, c1987. xviii, 712 p. : ill. ; 25 cm. Includes bibliographies and index. ISBN 0-205-08847-3 : LC Card 86-25882 DDC 658.1/5 19
1. Corporations - Finance. I. Title.
HG4026 .B388 1987

Benaïssa, Younès. Technique comptable algérienne / Younès Benaïssa. 2e éd. Alger : Entreprise nationale du livre, 1985- v. <1 > : ill. ; 24 cm. CONTENTS. - t. 1. Les bases de la comptabilité LC Card 86-966696
1. Accounting - Algeria. I. Title.
HF5616.A4 B46 1985

Benatia, Farouk. L'appropriation de l'espace à Alger après 1962 / Farouk Benatia. Alger : Société nationale d'édition et de diffusion, c1978. 189 p. : ill. ; 25 cm. Bibliography: p. 187-189. LC Card 81-143253
1. Housing - Algeria - Algiers. I. Title.
HD7372.4.A4 B45 1978

Benazzou, Chaouki, 1936- Le Maroc face à l'endettement extérieur : balance des paiements et dette publique extérieure, 1973-1983 / Chaouki Benazzou. [Rabat : s.n.], 1986 ([Rabat] : Imprimé aux Editions maghrébines) 151 p. : ill. ; 22 cm. Bibliography: p. 142-143. LC Card 87-967050
1. Balance of payments - Morocco. 2. Debts, External - Morocco. I. Title.
HG3883.M8 B46 1986

Bencin, Richard L., 1935- Strategic telemarketing : how to fit this new medium into your marketing plans / by Richard L. Bencin. Philadelphia, Pa., USA : Swansea Press, c1987. xviii, 182 p. : forms ; 24 cm. (Cresheim management books) Includes bibliographical references. ISBN 0-915601-02-8 LC Card 86-30057 DDC 658.8/5 19
1. Telemarketing. I. Title. II. Series.
HF5415.1265 .B46 1987

Bendahmane, Diane B.
Black labor unions in South Africa . Washington, D.C. , 1987. vi, 63 p. ; LC Card 86-600599 DDC 331.6/9/968 19
HD6870.5 .B53 1987

New dimensions in foreign economic policy . Washington, DC , 1986. xiii, 118 p. ; LC Card 86-600514 DDC 337.73 19
HF1410.5 .N488 1986

Bendeich, E. (Eugen), 1945- Wirtschaftliche Datenerfassung in Klein- und Mittelbetrieben : AWV-Projektergebnis, das insbesondere mittelständischen Unternehmen bei der Lösung ihrer speziellen Probleme auf diesem Gebiet eine fundierte und neutrale Hilfestellung ermitteln soll / bearbeitet im Auftrag des AWV vom IPA-Fraunhofer-Institut für Produktionstechnik und Automatisierung, Stuttgart ; E. Bendeich, R. Dauser, R. Gentner ; AWV-Referent, B. Phillipp. München : Verlag Moderne Industrie, W. Dummer, c1979. 211 p. : ill. ; 25 cm. (AWV-Schrift . Nr. 252) Bibliography: p. 210-211. ISBN 3-478-41740-6 LC Card 85-171162
1. Small business - Management - Data processing. I. Dauser, R. II. Gentner, R. III. Ausschuss für Wirtschaftliche Verwaltung in Wirtschaft und Öffentlicher Hand. IV. Fraunhofer-Institut für Produktionstechnik und Automatisierung. V. Title. VI. Series.
HD62.7 .B4 1979

Bendell, Leonard, 1941- Payment in full : a guide to successful bill collecting / by Leonard Bendell. Gainesville, Fla. : Triad Pub. Co., c1987. 174 p. ; 24 cm. ISBN 0-937404-05-5 : LC Card 87-10769 DDC 658.8/8 19
1. Collecting of accounts. I. Title.
HG3752.5 .B45 1987

The Bendigo and Loddon-Campaspe employment and training study / Loddon-Campaspe Resources Co-ordination Committee. [Australia] : The Committee, [1982-1984] 5 v. : ill. ; 30 cm. ISBN 0-9592508-0-8 (pbk. : v. 1) LC Card 87-168391 DDC 330.9945/4 19
1. Bendigo Region (Vic.) - Economic conditions. I. Loddon-Campaspe Resources Co-ordination Committee.
HC608.B46 B46 1982

BENDIGO REGION (VIC.) - ECONOMIC CONDITIONS.
The Bendigo and Loddon-Campaspe employment and training study /. [Australia] [1982-1984] 5 v. : ISBN 0-9592508-0-8 (pbk. : v. 1) LC Card 87-168391 DDC 330.9945/4 19
HC608.B46 B46 1982

Bendiner, Burton. International labour affairs : the world trade unions and the multinational companies / Burton Bendiner. Oxford : Clarendon Press ; New York : Oxford University Press, 1987. p. cm. Includes index. ISBN 0-19-827498-8 : LC Card 87-17829 DDC 331.88/091 19
1. International labor activities. 2. Trade-unions. 3. International business enterprises. I. Title.
HD6475.A1 B4 1987

Bendixen, Ernst Otto. Landwirtschaftliche Übergangsbetriebe in Niedersachsen . Göttingen , 1985. xiii, 105 p. ; LC Card 86-185987
HD9013.7.L68 L36 1985

Benecke, Dieter W.
Fachtagung "Bevölkerungsentwicklung, Bevölkerungswanderung und Urbanisierung in Lateinamerika" (1984 : Eichstätt, Germany) Desarrollo demográfico, migraciones y urbanización en América Latina . Regensburg , c1986. 432 p. : LC Card 86-181152
HB3530.5.A3 F33 1984

Die Notwendige Hilfe . Melle [1986] 207 p. : ISBN 3-88368-111-3 : LC Card 86-197696
HC60 .N69 1986

Benedek, István Gábor. Ez az a munkásság-- /. Budapest , 1984. 225 p., [40] p. of plates : ISBN 963-322-103-X LC Card 85-184724
HD6680.5 .E95 1984

Benefit/cost analyses of laws and regulations affecting coal . Energy and Environmental Analysis, inc. Washington , 1977. ca. 750 p. : LC Card 77-603790 DDC 363.6
TD195.C58 E53 1977 ***NYPL [JLF 81-219]***

The benefits of subsidized housing programs . Hammond, Claire Holton, 1951- Cambridge [Cambridgeshire] , New York , 1987. ix, 140 p. ; ISBN 0-521-32752-0 LC Card 86-32638 DDC 363.5/8 19
HD7288.83 .H36 1987

Benefits Processing Institute (1983 : Hollywood, Fla.) Claims processing for benefit plans, 1983 : [1983 Benefits Processing Institute, sponsored by the International Foundation of Employee Benefit Plans, November 27-30, Hollywood, Florida] / edited by Mary E. Brennan. Brookfield, Wis. : International Foundation of Employee Benefit Plans, 1984. x, 82 p. : ill. ; 23 cm. Includes bibliographical references. ISBN 0-89154-220-5 (pbk.) : LC Card 84-80454 DDC 331.25/5 19
1. Insurance, Health - United States - Congresses. 2. Insurance - Adjustment of claims - Congresses. I. Brennan, Mary E. II. International Foundation of Employee Benefit Plans. III. Title.
HG9396 .B47 1984 ***NYPL [JLD 86-3940]***

BENELUX COUNTRIES - COMMERCE - HISTORY - 18TH CENTURY.
Hasquin, Hervé, 1942- Les Réflexions sur l'état présent du commerce, fabriques et manufactures des Païs-Bas autrichiens (1765) du négociant bruxellois, Nicolas Bacon (1710-1779), conseiller député aux affaires du commerce /. Bruxelles , 1978. vi, 190 p. ; LC Card 87-672234
HF3595 .H37x 1978

Benería, Lourdes. Women, households, and the economy /. New Brunswick, N.J. , c1987. p. cm. ISBN 0-8135-1263-8 : LC Card 87-4840 DDC 331.4/0973 19
HD6060.65.U5 W65 1987

Benet, Iván. Az agráripari egyesülések útkeresése / Benet Iván. Budapest : Közgazdasági és Jogi Könyvkiadó, 1985. 197 p. : ill. ; 21 cm. (Iparosodó mezőgazdaság, 0139-1836) Summary in English and Russian. Bibliography: p. 191-194. ISBN 963-221-616-4 : LC Card 86-203013
1. Agricultural industries - Hungary - Consolidation. 2. Agriculture - Economic aspects - Hungary. I. Title. II. Series.
HD9015.H82 B447 1985

Benevides Pinho, Diva. see **Pinho, Diva Benevides.**

BENEVOLENT INSTITUTIONS. see **CHARITIES.**

BENGAL (INDIA) - ECONOMIC CONDITIONS.
Mukhopadhyay, Subodh Kumar, 1942- Bāṃlāra ārthika itihāsa, ashṭādaśa śatābdī /. Kalakātā , 1985. 214 p. ; LC Card 85-903918
HC437.B43 M85 1985

Bengal (India). Land Revenue Commission.
Mookerji, Radhakumud, 1884-1964. Indian land-system . Alipore, Bengal , 1940. 112, v p. ; LC Card 87-123602
HD879.B4 M63 1940

BENGAL (INDIA) - RURAL CONDITIONS.
Nag Chowdhury-Zilly, Aditee. The vagrant peasant . Wiesbaden , 1982. xv, 196 p. : ISBN 3-515-03855-8 (pbk.) LC Card 86-214350
HD1537.I4 N327 1982

Bengelsdorf, Peter, 1938- Alkohol im Betrieb und am Arbeitsplatz . Kiel , c1986. 52 p. : ISBN 3-87559-048-1 LC Card 87-409550 DDC 331.2/55 19
HF5549.5.A4 A476 1986

Benhaïm, J.-P. (Jean-Pierre) Les radios locales privées / J.P. Benhaïm, Fl. Bonvoisin, R. Dubois. Paris : Entreprise moderne d'édition, c1985. 153 p. : ill. ; 24 cm. At head of title: Média et vie sociale. Bibliography: p. 151-153. Includes index. ISBN 2-7101-0528-4 : LC Card 85-205602
1. Pirate radio broadcasting - France. 2. Radio - Law and legislation - France. I. Bonvoisin, Fl. (Florence). II. Dubois, R. (Raphaël). III. Média et vie sociale (Association : France). IV. Title.
HE8697.P57 B45 1985

Benigni, Glauco. Do you speak televisionese? / Glauco Benigni ; disegni di Massimo Bucchi e di Mojmir Ježek. Milano : EURO TV, [1985] 141 p. : ill. ; 19 cm. In Italian. Includes index. LC Card 85-241850
1. Television - Terminology. I. Title.
HE8700.6 .B46 1985

Benin.
Emploi d'abord . Addis Abeba , 1982. xxxviii, 499 p. ; LC Card 84-983423
hD5846.3.A6 E47 1982

BENIN - ECONOMIC CONDITIONS - 1960-
Emploi d'abord . Addis Abeba , 1982. xxxviii, 499 p. ; LC Card 84-983423
hD5846.3.A6 E47 1982

Godin, Francine. Bénin, 1972-1982 . Paris , c1986. 325 p. ; ISBN 2-85802-609-X LC Card 87-112975
HC1010 .G63 1986

Benin-Owena River Basin Development Authority.
Eweka, J. A. (Julius A.) Village development . Ibadan, Nigeria , 1979. xvi, 194 p. ; LC Card 86-172121 DDC 338.1/9/669 19
HD2145.5 .E94 1979

Nigerian small farmers . Benin-City, Bendel State, Nigeria , 1980. xv, 315 p. ; LC Card 82-206979 DDC 338.1/6 19
HD1339.N5 N54 1980 ***NYPL [Sc D 86-883]***

BENIN - POLITICS AND GOVERNMENT - 1960-
Godin, Francine. Bénin, 1972-1982 . Paris , c1986. 325 p. ; ISBN 2-85802-609-X LC Card 87-112975
HC1010 .G63 1986

BENIN - RURAL CONDITIONS.
Jobs and Skills Programme for Africa. Eléments pour une stratégie d'emploi dans les zones rurales au Bénin . Addis Abeba [1980] xii, 70, 5 p. : LC Card 87-100360
HD5846.3.A6 J63 1980

Bénin, 1972-1982 . Godin, Francine. Paris , c1986. 325 p. ; ISBN 2-85802-609-X LC Card 87-112975
HC1010 .G63 1986

Benítez Bonilla, Alberto. El sector externo de la economía salvadoreña / Alberto Benítez Bonilla. [San Salvador] : Banco Central de Reserva de El Salvador, 1982. 21 p., [7] leaves (some folded) ; 21 cm. LC Card 83-154713
1. El Salvador - Foreign economic relations. I. Title.
HF1494 .B45 1982

Benítez, José Antonio, 1921- La dependencia, el subdesarrollo y la publicidad comercial capitalista / José A. Benítez. La Habana, Cuba : Editora Política, 1986. 133 p., [2] p. of plates : facsims. ; 23 cm. Includes bibliographical references. LC Card 87-404231 DDC 659.1/098 19
1. Advertising - Latin America. 2. Capitalism - Latin America. 3. Latin America - Dependency on foreign countries. I. Title.
HF5813.L29 B46 1986

Benítez, Raúl [i. e. Raúl Benítez Zenteno] see **Benítez Zenteno, Raúl.**

Benítez Zenteno, Raúl. Los Factores del cambio demográfico en México /. México, D.F. , 1984. 422 p. : ISBN 968-231-281-7 LC Card 85-231767
HB1361 .F33 1984 ***NYPL [JLE 87-753]***

Benjamin, Anne.
Mandela, Winnie. Part of my soul /. Harmondsworth , 1985. 163 p., [8] p. of plates : *NYPL [Sc C 86-121]*
Mandela, Winnie. Part of my soul went with him /. New York , 1985, c1984. 163 p., [8] p. of plates : ISBN 0-393-02215-3 : LC Card 85-21632 DDC 968/.00496 19
DT779.955.M36 A35 1985
NYPL [JFD 86-7717]

Benjamin, Bernard, 1910- Pensions . London , Boston , 1987. xvi, 249 p. : ISBN 0-04-332127-5 (alk. paper) LC Card 86-32086 DDC 331.25/2/0941 19
HD7165 .P46 1987

Benjamin, James J. Financial accounting / James J. Benjamin, Arthur J. Francia, Robert H. Strawser. 6th ed. Houston, Tex. : Dame Publications, 1986. xii, 718 p. : ill. ; 25 cm. Includes bibliographical references and index. ISBN 0-87393-039-8 LC Card 86-214139 DDC 657/.48 19
1. Accounting. I. Francia, Arthur J. II. Strawser, Robert H. III. Title.
HF5635 .B419 1986

Benjamin, Louis. The complete book of Excel macros / Louis Benjamin, Don Nicholas, and the consultants of Lighthouse Publishing Services, Ltd. Berkeley, Calif. : Osborne McGraw-Hill, c1986. xviii, 123 p. : ill. ; 24 cm. On t.p. the registered trademark symbol "TM" is superscript following "Excel" in the title. Includes index. ISBN 0-07-881214-3 (pbk.) LC Card 86-106041 DDC 650/.028/55369 19
1. Excel (Computer program). 2. Macro instructions (Electronic computers). 3. Business - Data processing. I. Nicholas, Don. II. Lighthouse Publishing. III. Title. IV. Title: Excel macros.
HF5548.4.E93 B46 1986
NYPL [JSE 87-239]

Benjamin, Roger W. The Industrial future of the Pacific basin /. Boulder , 1984. xvi, 285 p. : ISBN 0-86531-685-6 LC Card 83-51653 DDC 338.9/009182/3 19
HC681 .I53 1984 *NYPL [JLD 86-3100]*

Benjamin, Timothy. Young drivers impaired by alcohol and other drugs /. London , New York, NY , c1987. p. cm. ISBN 0-905958-48-9 (pbk) : LC Card 87-20657 DDC 363.1/251 19
HE5620.D7 Y68 1987

Benjamin/Cummings series in the life sciences.
Chiras, Daniel D. Environmental science . Menlo Park, Calif. , c1988. xxiii, 531 p., [16] p. of plates : ISBN 0-8053-2257-4 LC Card 87-13906 DDC 363.7 19
HC79.E5 C485 1988

Benke, Istvánné. A Világgazdaság fejlődésének kérdései tanulmányozásához . [Budapest] , 1981/1982. 415 p. ; LC Card 85-138909
HC59 .V489 1981

Benkenstein, Martin. F & E und Marketing : eine Untersuchung zur Leistungsfähigkeit von Koordinationskonzeptionen bei Innovationsentscheidungen / Martin Benkenstein. Wiesbaden : Gabler, c1987. xvii, 319 p. ; 24 cm. (Schriftenreihe Unternehmensführung und Marketing. Bd.20) Bibliography: p. [275]-319. ISBN 3-409-13327-5 LC Card 87-144515 DDC 658.8/3 19
1. Marketing research. 2. Marketing - Decision making. I. Title. II. Title: F und E Marketing.
HF5415.2 .B4563 1987

Benn, Alec. Advertising financial products and services : proven techniques and principles for banks, investment firms, insurance companies, and their agencies / Alec Benn. Westport, Conn. : Quorum Books, c1986. xii, 231 p. : ill. ; 24 cm. Includes index. ISBN 0-89930-103-7 (lib bdg. : alk. paper) LC Card 85-24406 DDC 659.1/93321 19
1. Bank marketing. 2. Financial institutions - Marketing. 3. Insurance companies - Marketing. I. Title.
HG1616.M3 B43 1986 NYPL [JLE 86-4110]

Benner, Ludwig. Hendrick, Kingsley. Investigating accidents with STEP /. New York , c1987. xviii, 454 p. : ISBN 0-8247-7510-4 LC Card 86-24165 DDC 363.1/065 19
HD7262.25 .H46 1987

Benner, Wolfgang, 1940- Betriebliche Finanzwirtschaft als monetäres System / von Wolfgang Benner. Göttingen : O. Schwartz, 1983. 486 p. : ill. ; 20 cm. (Göttinger Hefte zur Bankbetriebslehre und Unternehmungsfinanzierung . Heft 3) The author's Habilitationsschrift (Universität Göttingen, 1980) Bibliography: p. 439-474. Includes indexes. ISBN 3-509-01323-9 LC Card 83-240817
1. Business enterprises - Finance. 2. Corporations - Finance. 3. Finance. 4. Money. I. Title. II. Series.
HG4011 .B433 1983

Bennett, Addison C. Making innovation practical / Addison C. Bennett, Samuel J. Tibbitts. Chicago, Ill. : Pluribus Press, c1986. vi, 238 p. : ill. ; 24 cm. Includes bibliographies and index. ISBN 0-931028-79-5 LC Card 86-62191 DDC 658.4/06 19
1. Organizational change. I. Tibbitts, Samuel J. II. Title.
HD58.8 .B46 1986

Bennett, Frieda R. Warmbrod, Catharine P. Skills for the changing workplace . Columbus, Ohio (1960 Kenny Rd., Columbus 43210-1090) , 1985. ix, 93 p. ; LC Card 86-205907 DDC 651/.07/15 19
HF1106 .W36 1985

Bennett, Georgette. Crimewarps : the future of crime in America / Georgette Bennett.1st ed. Garden City, N.Y. : Anchor Books, 1987. xix, 435 p. ; 25 cm. Includes index. Bibliography: p. [419]-423. ISBN 0-385-23090-7 : LC Card 86-10885 DDC 364/.973 19
1. Crime forecasting - United States. 2. Crime and criminals - United States. 3. Twenty-first century - Forecasts. I. Title.
HV6791 .B45 1987 *NYPL [JLE 87-1261]*

Bennett, Jon. The hunger machine : the politics of food / Jon Bennett ; introduction and conclusion by Susan George. Oxford ; New York : Polity Press in association with B. Blackwell, 1987. 232 p. : ill. ; 22 cm. Bibliography: p. [217]-222. Includes index. ISBN 0-7456-0444-7 : LC Card 87-724 DDC 363.8 19
1. Food supply. 2. Food industry and trade. 3. Agriculture - Economic aspects. 4. Food supply - Government policy. 5. Food industry and trade - Government policy. 6. Agriculture and state. I. Title.
HD9000.5 .B449 1987

Bennett, Mark. Public policy and industrial development : the case of the Mexican auto parts industry / Mark Bennett. Boulder, Colo. : Westview Press, 1986. xii, 134 p. : ill. ; 23 cm. (Westview special studies in industrial policy and development) Bibliography: p. 117-134. ISBN 0-86531-821-2 : LC Card 83-23456 DDC 338.4/76292/0972 19
1. Automobile supplies industry - Government policy - Mexico. 2. Foreign exchange problem - Mexico. 3. Mexico - Economic policy 1970-. I. Title. II. Series.
HD9710.3.M42 B46 1986
NYPL [JLE 86-2581]

Bennett, Martin. Somalia, productive sectors of the economy /. Paris , 1985. 115 leaves : ISBN 2-905760-00-1 (pbk.) LC Card 87-124493 DDC 338.967/73 19
HC850 .S658 1985

Bennett, P. G. (Peter G.) Analysing conflict and its resolution . Oxford [Oxfordshire] , New York , 1987. xvi, 349 p. : ISBN 0-19-853611-9 : LC Card 86-31108 DDC 658.4 19
HD42 .A52 1987

Bennett, Peter D. Marketing / Peter D. Bennett in collaboration with Robert P. Lamm and Robert A. Fry. New York : McGraw-Hill, c1988. xxvii, 763 p. : ill. (some col.) ; 26 cm. (McGraw-Hill series in marketing) Includes bibliographies and indexes. ISBN 0-07-004721-9 : LC Card 87-17335 DDC 658.8 19
1. Marketing. I. Lamm, Robert P. II. Fry, Robert A. III. Title.
HF5415 .B4293 1988

Bennett, Raymond. Applied economics and Australian business / Raymond Bennett and contributors. 10th ed. Sydney : M.M. & B. Book Co., c1987. xiv, 464 p. : ill. ; 24 cm. Includes bibliographies and index. ISBN 0-9588541-0-6 LC Card 87-141905 DDC 330.994/063 19
1. Economics. 2. Australia - Economic conditions - 1945-. I. Title.
HB171.5 .B454 1987

Bennett, Richard E. (Richard Earl), 1940- Structural change in an urban industrial region . New York , 1987. ix, 255 p. ; ISBN 0-275-92353-3 (alk. paper) : LC Card 86-30652 DDC 330.9771/3043 19
HC107.O3 S85 1987

Bennett, Steven J. Executive chess / Steven J. Bennett and Michael Snell. New York : New American Library, c1987. xv, 256 p. ; 23 cm. Spine subtitle: Creative problem-solving by 45 of America's top business leaders and thinkers. "NAL books." Includes index. ISBN 0-453-00550-0 LC Card 87-1723 DDC 658.4/03 19
1. Problem solving. 2. Executives - Interviews. I. Snell, Michael. II. Title.
HD30.29 .B46 1987

Bennholdt-Thomsen, Veronika. Bauern in Mexiko : zwischen Subsistenz- und Warenproduktion / Veronika Bennholdt-Thomsen. Frankfurt [am Main] ; New York : Campus, c1982. 214 p. ; 21 cm. (Campus Forschung. Bd. 311) Habilitationsschrift--Universität Bielefeld. Bibliography: p. 205-214. ISBN 3-593-33167-5 LC Card 83-139124 DDC 305.5/63 19
1. Peasantry - Mexico. 2. Subsistence economy - Mexico. 3. Chiapas. Mexico - Economic conditions. 4. Sinaloa (Mexico) - Economic conditions. I. Title.
HD1531.M6 B46 1982

Bennington, Richard R. Furniture marketing : from product development to distribution / Richard R. Bennington. New York : Fairchild Publications, c1985. x, 310 p. : ill. ; 25 cm. Includes index. ISBN 0-87005-491-0 LC Card 84-81057 DDC 684.1/068/8 19
1. Furniture - United States - Marketing. 2. Furniture - Marketing. I. Title.
HD9773.U5 B46 1985 NYPL [JLE 86-1997]

Bennó, Pál. A bedolgozás helye és szerepe, perspektívája a szövetkezeti iparban : összefoglaló tanulmány / Bennó Pál. Budapest : Szövetkezeti Kutató Intézet, 1985. 153 p. ; 29 cm. (Közlemények / Szövetkezeti Kutató Intézet, 0133-4905 . 183) Includes legislation and bibliographical references. LC Card 85-226119
1. Home labor - Hungary. 2. Producer cooperatives - Hungary. I. Series: Közlemények / Szövetkezeti Kutató Intézet, 183. II. Title.
HD2336.H9 B46 1985

Benoît, Bruno. L'or de la Dombes : Trévoux et ses tireurs d'or au XVIIIe siècle / Bruno Benoît. Trévoux : Editions de Trévoux, [1983] 120 p. : ill. ; 24 cm. Based on the author's thesis (doctoral--Université de Lyon II, 1981) under the title: Trévoux et ses tireurs d'or au XVIIIe siècle. Bibliography: p. 119-120. ISBN 2-85698-025-2 LC Card 83-229770
1. Gold industry - France - Trévoux - History - 18th century. I. Title.
HD9536.F83 T743 1983

Benoit-Cattin, Michel. L'exploitation agricole familiale en Afrique soudano-sahélienne / Michel Benoit-Cattin, Jacques Faye. Paris : Presses universitaires de France, c1982. 94 p. : ill. ; 21 cm. (Techniques vivantes) Includes bibliographies. ISBN 2-85319-106-0 LC Card 86-116718
1. Family farms - Senegal - Sine-Saloum. 2. Peasantry - Senegal - Sine-Saloum. 3. Land tenure - Senegal - Sine-Saloum. I. Faye, Jacques. II. Title.
HD1476.S382 S563 1982

Benoit, Philippe. Affiches de pub, 1983/85 / Philippe Benoit, Didier Truchot. Paris : Chêne, c1986. 237 p. : col. ill. ; 29 cm. Includes index. ISBN 2-85108-429-1 : LC Card 86-192339
1. Billboards - France. 2. Advertising, Outdoor - France. I. Truchot, Didier. II. Title.
HF5843 .B44 1986

Benokraitis, Nijole V. (Nijole Vaicaitis) Modern sexism : blatant, subtle, and covert discrimination / Nijole V. Benokraitis, Joe R. Feagin. Englewood Cliffs : Prentice-Hall, c1986. xiii, 187 p. ; 23 cm. Includes bibliographies and index. ISBN 0-13-597634-0 LC Card 85-28256
1. Sex discrimination against women - United States. 2. Sexism - United States. I. Feagin, Joe R. II. Title.
HQ1426 .B428 1986 NYPL [JLE 86-4225]

Bens de produção mecânicos : sinopse estatística--Brasil--81. São Paulo, SP, Brasil : Associação Brasileira da Indústria de Máquinas e Equipamentos, Sindicato Interestadual da Indústria de Máquinas, Divisão de Economia e Estatística, 1982. 386 p. : ill. ; 22 cm. Includes bibliographical references. LC Card 86-150156
1. Machinery industry - Brazil - Statistics. I. Sindicato Interestadual da Indústria de Máquinas (Brazil). Divisão

de Economia e Estatística.
HD9705.B72 B46 1982

Bensión, Alberto. Las opciones de política económica en Uruguay / por Alberto Bensión. Montevideo, Uruguay : Asociación Cristiana de Dirigentes de Empresas, 1986. 106 p., [48] leaves ; 28 cm. LC Card 87-121223 DDC 338.9895 19
1. Uruguay - Economic policy. 2. Uruguay - Economic conditions - 1945-. I. Title.
HC232 .B44 1986

Benson, Carolyn Vogel. Outlet shopper / by Carolyn Vogel Benson. Arlington, Va. : Washington Book Trading Co., c1985. x, 172 p. ; 22 cm. "A guide to factory outlet shopping--Pennsylvania, Maryland, Virginia, and the District of Columbia"--P. [1] of cover. Includes index. ISBN 0-915168-00-6 (pbk.) LC Card 86-229410 DDC 381/.1 19
1. Outlet stores - Pennsylvania - Directories. 2. Outlet stores - Maryland - Directories. 3. Outlet stores - Virginia - Directories. 4. Outlet stores - Washington Metropolitan Area - Directories. I. Title.
HF5429.215.U6 B46 1985

Benson, Eileen. (joint author) Taetzsch, Lyn. Taking charge on the job . New York , c1978. 144 p. ; ISBN 0-917386-22-1 : LC Card 78-111025 DDC 658.4
HD38 .T17 ***NYPL [JLE 80-1910]***

Benson, Fred C. Hot-mix pavement stability performance versus laboratory test results / by Fred C. Benson, D.F. Martinez, and Deborah A. Jessup ; sponsored by Texas State Department of Highways and Public Transportation in cooperation with U. S. Department of Transportation, Federal Highway Administration. College Station, Tex. : Texas Transportation Institute, the Texas A&M University System, [1985] xi, 225 p. : ill. ; 28 cm. (Research report (Texas Transportation Institute) . 285-1) "November 1985." "Research study number 2-9-80-285." Bibliography: p. 25-26. LC Card 86-620969 DDC 380.5 s 625.8/5 19
1. Asphalt concrete - Testing. 2. Pavements, Asphalt concrete - Testing. I. Martinez, D. F. II. Jessup, Deborah A. III. Texas Transportation Institute. IV. Texas. State Dept. of Highways and Public Transportation. V. United States. Federal Highway Administration. VI. Series. VII. Series: Research report (Texas Transportation Institute) , 285-1.
HE203 .T43 no. 285-1 TE200

Benson, Herman W., 1910 (ca.)- How to get an honest union election / by Herman Benson. Brooklyn, N.Y. : Association for Union Democracy, [c1987] 65 p. : ill. ; 22 cm. Cover title. ISBN 0-9602244-4-0 (pbk.) LC Card 86-73217 DDC 331.87/4/0973 19
1. Trade-unions - United States - Elections. I. Association for Union Democracy. II. Title.
HD6490.E42 U62 1987

Benson, Joyce. Colgan, Charles S. The natural resource industries of Maine . [Augusta, Me.] [1986] 135 p. : LC Card 87-620550 DDC 338.09741 19
HD9007.M2 C64 1986

Benson, Mary.
Mandela, Winnie. Part of my soul /. Harmondsworth , 1985. 163 p., [8] p. of plates : ***NYPL [Sc C 86-121]***

Mandela, Winnie. Part of my soul went with him /. New York , 1985, c1984. 163 p., [8] p. of plates : ISBN 0-393-02215-3 : LC Card 85-21632 DDC 968/.00496 19
DT779.955.M36 A35 1985 ***NYPL [JFD 86-7717]***

Benson, P. George, 1946- McClave, James T. Statistics for business and economics /. San Francisco , c1988. xxii, 1267 p. : ISBN 0-02-379020-2 LC Card 87-20195 DDC 519.5 19
HF1017 .M36 1988

Benson, Susan Porter, 1943- Counter cultures : saleswomen, managers, and customers in American department stores, 1890-1940 / Susan Porter Benson. Urbana : University of Illinois Press, c1986. xvi, 322 p. : ill. ; 24 cm. (The Working class in American history) Includes bibliographies and index. ISBN 0-252-01252-6 (alk. paper) LC Card 85-21012 DDC 381/.1/0973 19
1. Department stores - United States - History. 2. Department stores - Employees - United States - History. 3. Women clerks (Retail trade) - United States - History. I. Title.
HF5465.U5 B45 1986 ***NYPL [JLE 87-1091]***

Benston, George J.
An analysis of the causes of savings and loan association failures / by George J. Benston. New York, N.Y. (90 Trinity Place, New York 10006) : Salomon Brothers Center for the Study of Financial Institutions, Graduate School of Business Administration, New York University, [1985] 182 p. : ill. ; 23 cm. (Monographs series in finance and economics . monograph 1985-4/5) Bibliography: p. 178-180. LC Card 86-209942 DDC 332.3/2/0973 19
1. Building and loan associations - United States. 2. Business failures - United States. I. Salomon Brothers for the Study of Financial Institutions. II. Title. III. Series.
HG2151 .B46 1985

Perspectives on safe & sound banking . Cambridge, Mass. , 1986. xxi, 358 p. ; ISBN 0-262-02246-X LC Card 85-23882 DDC 332.1/0973 19
HG2481 .P47 1986 ***NYPL [JLE 86-2960]***

Bentabet, Mohamed. Auto économie : le progrès technologique réformateur de la civilisation industrielle / Mohamed Bentabet. Casablanca : M. Bentabet, [1985] 106 p. ; 19 cm. LC Card 86-198953
1. Technological innovations - Developing countries. 2. Developing countries - Economic policy. I. Title.
HC59.72.T4 B46 1985

Benterud, Per. Japan som veiviser : ny organisasjon og ledelse : en Europamodell / Per Benterud. [Oslo] : Cappelen, c1983. 262 p. ; 22 cm. Bibliography: p. 255-258. Includes index. ISBN 82-02-09050-4 LC Card 83-195163
1. Industrial organization - Japan. 2. Industrial organization - Europe. 3. Industrial management - Japan. 4. Industrial management - Europe. I. Title.
HD70.J3 B45 1983

Bentivegna, V. (Vincenzo) La Riconversione produttiva nell'edilizia /. Milano , 1984, c1981. 319 p. : ***NYPL [JLD 86-3381]***

Benton, Douglas, 1937- Halloran, Jack, 1931- Applied human relations . Englewood Cliffs, N.J. , c1987. xvi, 528 p. : ISBN 0-13-040742-9 LC Card 86-25336 DDC 658.3 19
HD58.7 .H34 1987

Benton, J. Edwin, 1950- Intergovernmental relations and public policy /. New York , 1986. viii, 224 p. : ISBN 0-313-25443-5 (lib. bdg. : alk. paper) LC Card 86-3155 DDC 353.9/29 19
JK325 .I575 1986 ***NYPL [JLE 87-749]***

BENUE STATE (NIGERIA) - INDUSTRIES.
Industrial and agricultural potentials in Benue State. Makurdi , 1986. 36 p. : LC Card 87-102274 DDC 338.09669/5 19
HC1055.Z7 B455 1986

BENUE STATE (NIGERIA) - MANUFACTURES.
Industrial and agricultural potentials in Benue State. Makurdi , 1986. 36 p. : LC Card 87-102274 DDC 338.09669/5 19
HC1055.Z7 B455 1986

Benue State (Nigeria). Ministry of Information, Social Development, Youth, Sports, and Culture. Industrial and agricultural potentials in Benue State. Makurdi , 1986. 36 p. : LC Card 87-102274 DDC 338.09669/5 19
HC1055.Z7 B455 1986

Benvenuto, Giorgio.
La Riforma del salario /. Milano , c1984. 150 p. ; LC Card 84-251133 DDC 331.2/945 19
HD5034 .R54 1984 ***NYPL [JLD 86-1082]***

Scheggi Merlini, Lorenzo, 1944- Il ritorno del gigante /. Milano, Italy , c1985. 140 p. ; LC Card 86-137491 DDC 331.88/0945 19
HD6709 .S39 1985

Bepin Behari. see **Behari, Bepin.**

BEQUESTS. see **INHERITANCE AND SUCCESSION.**

A bér- és keresetszabályozás müködése 1983-ban /. Németh, Ernő. [Budapest] [1984] 245 p. : ISBN 963-02-3277-4 LC Card 85-231744
HD5022.5 .N46 1984

Berardi, Gigi M. World food, population, and development /. Totowa, N.J. , 1985. xvi, 346 p. : ISBN 0-8476-7455-X : LC Card 85-14398 DDC 338.1/9 19
HD9000.5 .W59 1985 ***NYPL [JLE 86-1741]***

Berberoglu, Berch. The internationalization of capital : imperialism and capitalist development on a world scale / Berch Berberoglu. New York : Praeger, 1987. xxi, 223 p. : ill. ; 25 cm. Bibliography: p. 203-216. Includes index. ISBN 0-275-92169-7 (alk. paper) : LC Card 86-25259 DDC 337 19
1. International economic relations. 2. Developing countries - Foreign economic relations. 3. Imperialism. 4. Capitalism. 5. Revolutions. I. Title.
HF1411 .B367 1987

BERCH, ANDERS, 1711-1774.
Liedman, Sven-Eric, 1939- Den synliga handen . [Stockholm] [1986] 268 p. ; ISBN 91-7014-210-6 : LC Card 86-215138
HB116.5.B47 L54 1986

Berdie, Douglas R. The Yellow Pages report : a comprehensive guide for advertisers / Doug R. Berdie, Elaine M. Hauff. St. Paul, Minn. (905 Raymond Ave., St. Paul 55114) : Consumer Review Systems, c1986. 109 p. ; 28 cm. LC Card 86-209709 DDC 659.13/2 19
1. Advertising. 2. Telephone - Directories - Yellow pages. 3. Advertising layout and typography. I. Hauff, Elaine M. II. Consumer Review Systems. III. Title.
HF6146.T4 B45 1986

Berdiev, G. Tagtabazar raĭonynyn͡g Kirov adyndaky kolkhozynyn͡g tarykhy / G. Berdiev. Ashgabat : "Ylym", 1986. 79 p. : ill., ports. ; 20 cm. In Turkmen. Title on added t.p.: Istorii͡a kolkhoza imeni Kirova Takhta-Bazarskogo raĭona. At head of title: Tůrkmenistan SSR Ylymlar akademii͡asy. Sh. Batyrov adyndaky Tarykh instituty. A.M. Gor'kiĭ adyndaky Zăkhmet Gyzyl Baĭdak ordenli Tůrkmen dovlet universiteti. Includes bibliographical references. LC Card 86-198891
1. Collective farms - Turkmen S.S.R. - History. 2. Kirov adyndaky kolkhoz (Takhta-Bazarskiĭ raĭon, Turkmen S.S.R.) - History. I. Title. II. Title: Istorii͡a kolkhoza imeni Kirova Takhta-Bazarskogo raĭona.
HD1492.S652 T873 1986

Bereciuk, Román M. Introducción en la teoría de la planificación de la economía nacional / Román M. Bereciuk. [Managua] : Universidad Nacional Autónoma de Nicaragua, 1986. 93 leaves ; 28 cm. Bibliography: leaves 92-93. LC Card 87-403888 DDC 338.97285 19
1. Nicaragua - Economic policy. 2. Central planning - Nicaragua. I. Title.
HC146 .B47 1986

Berekoven, Ludwig.
Geschichte des deutschen Einzelhandels / Ludwig Berekoven. Frankfurt am Main : Deutscher Fachverlag, c1986. 175 p. : ill. ; 25 cm. Bibliography: p. 167-172. ISBN 3-87150-246-4 LC Card 87-121881
1. Retail trade - Germany - History. 2. Retail trade - Germany (West) - History. 3. Retail trade - Germany (East) - History. I. Title.
HF5429.6.G42 B46 1986

Konsumentenpsychologie und Markenartikel /. Heidelberg , c1986. xiii, 238 p. ; ISBN 3-7908-0353-7 LC Card 87-127600 DDC 658.8/342 19
HF5415 .K598 1986

Berenbeim, Ronald. Company programs to ease the impact of shutdowns / by Ronald E. Berenbeim. New York, N.Y. : Conference Board, c1986. ix, 57 p. : ill. ; 28 cm. (Conference Board report. no. 878) Includes bibliographical references. ISBN 0-8237-0320-7 (pbk.) LC Card 86-207794 DDC 331.25 19
1. Employees, Dismissal of - United States - Case studies. 2. Plant shutdowns - United States - Case studies. I. Title.
HF5549.5.D55 B47 1986

Berend, T. Iván (Tibor Iván), 1930-
The Hungarian economy in the twentieth century / Ivan T. Berend and György Ránki. London : Croom Helm, c1985. 316 p. ; 22 cm. (Croom Helm series on the contemporary economic history of Europe) Bibliography: p. 293-300. Includes index. ISBN 0-7099-2209-4 LC Card 86-673483
1. Hungary - Economic conditions. I. Ránki, György, 1930-. II. Title. III. Title: Hungarian economy in the 20th century. IV. Series.
HC300.24 .B44 1985b

Szocializmus és reform / Berend T. Iván. Budapest : Akadémiai Kiadó, 1986. 194, [1] p. ; 17 cm. (Kérdőjel) Bibliography: p. 188-[195]. ISBN

963-05-4386-9 : LC Card 87-407684
1. Hungary - Economic conditions - 1945-. 2. Socialism - Hungary - History. I. Title.
HC300.28 .B475 1986

Tanulmányok Magyarországról, magyarokról. [Budapest] [1985] 280 p. ; ISBN 963-01-7352-2 (Magy. nemz. bibl.) LC Card 87-408505
HC300.24 .T36 1985

Berenson, Mark L. Levine, David M., 1946- Using Minitab with Basic business statistics /. Englewood Cliffs, N.J. , c1986. viii, 160 p. : ISBN 0-13-057779-0 (pbk.) LC Card 87-400304 DDC 519.5/028/55369 19
HF1017 .L425 1986

Berényi, Zsuzsanna Ágnes. A budapesti Nagyvásártelep mikrotoponímiája / Berényi Zsuzsanna Ágnes. Budapest : ELTE Magyar Nyelvészeti Tanszékcsoport Névkutató Munkaközössége, 1983. 65 p. : ill. ; 20 cm. (Magyar névtani dolgozatok, 0133-6169 . 34) ISBN 963-461-710-7 LC Card 85-167786
1. Nagyvásártelep (Budapest, Hungary) - Language. 2. Markets - Hungary - Budapest - Language. I. Title. II. Series.
HF5474.H82 B83 1983

Beretning (Rådet for trafiksikkerhedsforskning (Denmark))
Virksomheden i årene 1981-1983 . Gentofte , København , 1984. 80 p. : ISBN 87-7327-022-9 LC Card 86-100414
HE5614.5.D4 V57 1984

Bereuter, Douglas K. United States and European Community development assistance to Africa : the 25th meeting of the United States Congress and the European Parliament : June 22, 1985, West Point, New York / prepared and presented by Doug Bereuter with major assistance from Peter Schechter and Wrexie Agan. [Washington, D.C.? : D. Bereuter, 1985?] 22, [2] leaves ; 28 cm. Bibliography: leaf [24]. LC Card 87-108848 DDC 338.91/4/06 19
1. Economic assistance, American - Africa. 2. Economic assistance, European - Africa. I. Schechter, Peter. II. Agan, Wrexie. III. Title.
HC800 .B455 1985

Berey, András. Vezetés a gyakorlatban / Berey András, Dobos Irma. Budapest : Közgazdasági és Jogi Könyvkiadó, 1986. 313 p. : ill. ; 21 cm. Bibliography: p. 301-313. ISBN 963-221-903-1 : LC Card 87-138251
1. Management. I. Dobos, Irma B. II. Title.
HD37.H82 B486 1986

Berg, Elliot.
Absorptive capacity in the Sahel countries. [Paris] : Organisation for Economic Cooperation and Development, OECD ; [Ouagadougou, Burkina Faso] : Permanent Interstate Committee for Drought Control in the Sahel, CILSS, [1983] xi, 133 p. ; 30 cm. Summary and conclusions in French. Bibliography: p. 126-133. "SAHEL D(83)197, April 1983"--Cover. LC Card 87-402541 DDC 338.91/0966 19
1. Economic assistance - Sahel. 2. Technical assistance - Sahel. 3. Absorptive capacity (Economics) - Sahel. I. Organisation for Economic Co-operation and Development. II. Permanent Inter-State Commmittee for Drought Control in the Sahel. III. Title.
HC1002 .B47 1983

Divestiture in developing countries / Elliot Berg, Mary M. Shirley. Washington, D.C. : World Bank, 1987. vii, 30 p. : 1 ill. ; 28 cm. (World Bank discussion papers . 11) Includes bibliographical references. ISBN 0-8213-0917-X (pbk.) LC Card 87-14235 DDC 338.9/009172/4 19
1. Government business enterprises - Developing countries. 2. Corporate divestiture - Developing countries. 3. Privatization - Developing countries. I. Shirley, Mary M., 1945-. II. Title. III. Series.
HD4420.8 .B45 1987

Mobilization of the private sector in Burkina Faso : report / prepared for the Ministry of Plan, Government of Burkina Faso, and the Chamber of Commerce, Agriculture, and Industry, Burkina Faso, by Elliot Berg with Therese Belot. [Burkina Faso? : s.n., 1985] 21 p. ; 28 cm. "December 1985." Bibliography: p. 21. LC Card 87-116357 DDC 338.966/25 19
1. Burkina Faso - Economic conditions. 2. Capitalism - Burkina Faso. I. Bélot, Thérèse, 1947-. II. Burkina Faso. Ministry of Plan. III. Chambre de commerce, d'industrie et d'artisanat du Burkina. IV. Title.
HC1040 .B47 1985

Berg, Hartmut. Nationale Wege der Inflationsbekämpfung /. Berlin , c1986. 223 p. : ISBN 3-428-06077-6 LC Card 87-132310 DDC 332.4/1/094 19
HC240 .N315 1986

Berg, Hermann von, 1933-
Die Analyse : die Europäische Gemeinschaft, das Zukunftsmodell für Ost und West? / Hermann von Berg. Köln : Bund-Verlag, c1985. 240 p. : 2 ill. ; 21 cm. Bibliography: p. 227-231. ISBN 3-7663-0942-0 LC Card 86-122582 DDC 341.24/22 19
1. European Economic Community. 2. European Parliament. 3. European Economic Community countries - Economic conditions. I. Title.
HC241 .B47 1985

Marxismus-Leninismus : das Elend der halb deutschen, halb russischen Ideologie / Hermann von Berg. Köln : Bund-Verlag, 1986. 335 p. : ill. ; 21 cm. ISBN 3-7663-0982-X
1. Communism - History. 2. Marxian economics. 3. Communism - Philosophy. I. Title.
NYPL [JLD 86-4000]

Berg, Ivar E. Kalleberg, Arne L. Work and industry . New York , c1987. xviii, 244 p. ; ISBN 0-306-42344-8 LC Card 87-2333 DDC 306/.36 19
HD4904 .K294 1987

Berg, Lennart. Södersten, Bo. Makroekonomi och stabiliseringspolitik /. [Malmö] , c1983. 363 p. : ISBN 91-40-05037-8 : LC Card 84-166176
HB179.S8 S63 1983

Berg, Werner. Wirtschaft und Gesellschaft in Deutschland und Grossbritannien im Übergang zum "organisierten Kapitalismus" : Unternehmer, Angestellte, Arbeiter und Staat im Steinkohlenbergbau des Ruhrgebietes und von Südwales, 1850-1914 / von Werner Berg. Berlin : Duncker & Humblot, c1984. 888 p. : ill. ; 24 cm. (Volkswirtschaftliche Schriften. Heft 339) Bibliography: p. [833]-888. ISBN 3-428-05495-4 LC Card 84-222230
1. Coal mines and mining - Germany (West) - Ruhr (Region) - History. 2. Coal mines and mining - Wales, South - History. 3. Coal mines and mining - Government policy - Germany (West) - Ruhr (Region) - History. 4. Coal mines and mining - Government policy - Wales, South - History. 5. Coal miners - Germany (West) - Ruhr (Region) - History. 6. Coal miners - Wales, South - History. I. Title. II. Series.
HD9553.7.R8 B47 1984

BERGAMO (ITALY : PROVINCE) - INDUSTRIES - STATISTICS.
Le Condizioni industriali della provincia di Bergamo, 1891 . Bologna [1983] 130 p., [1] leaf of plates : LC Card 85-235349
HC307.B5 C59 1983

Bergan, Helen, 1937- Where the money is : a fund raiser's guide to the rich / by Helen Bergan. Alexandria, Va. : BioGuide Press, c1985. 101 p. : ill. ; 22 cm. Includes index. Bibliography: p. 91-97. ISBN 0-9615277-0-6 (pbk.) : LC Card 85-72141 DDC 361.7 19
1. Fund raising - Research. 2. Millionaires - Research. 3. Millionairesses - Research. 4. Biography - Research. I. Title.
HG177 .B48 1985 ***NYPL [JLD 87-844]***

Bergan, Roar.
Behandlingen av oljevirksomheten i byråets makroøkonomiske årsmodeller / av Roar Bergan. Oslo : Statistisk sentralbyrå : I kommisjon hos H. Aschehoug og Universitetsforlaget, 1983. 30 p. ; 30 cm. (Rapporter fra Statistisk sentralbyrå, 0332-8422 . 83/7) Bibliography: p. 28. ISBN 82-537-1918-3 : LC Card 83-225651
1. Petroleum industry and trade - Norway - Mathematical models. I. Title. II. Series.
HD9575.N62 B46 1983

MINK : en finansiell ettermodell til MSG : en MSG-rapport / av Roar Bergan. Oslo : Statistisk sentralbyrå : I kommisjon hos H. Aschehoug og Universitetsforlaget, 1984. 71 p. : ill. ; 30 cm. (Rapporter fra Statistisk sentralbyrå, 0332-8422 . 84/23) Bibliography: p. 70. ISBN 82-537-2138-2 : LC Card 85-178061
1. Norway - Economic conditions - 1945- - Econometric models. 2. Economic forecasting - Norway. I. Title. II. Series.
HC365 .B388 1984

Bergano Book Co. The Standard handbook of industrial distributors. Fairfield, CT, USA , c1987- v. <1-2 > ; ISBN 0-917408-02-0 (pbk. : v. 1) LC Card 86-73258 DDC 380.1/456218/025 19
HD9680.A2 S72 1987

Bergbau und Bergarbeit.
Bis vor die Stufen des Throns . München , c1986. 530 p. : ISBN 3-406-31297-7 LC Card 87-103686 DDC 331.7/622334/0943 19
HD8039.M61 G32 1986

Bergen, D. Etude socio-économique sur la culture du riz irrigué dans le périmètre de Mugerero (S.R.D. Imbo) / D. Bergen. Bujumbura : ISABU, 1985. 96 leaves : ill. ; 30 cm. (Publication / Institut des sciences agronomiques du Burundi . no 74.) Cover title. Summary in English, French, and Rundi. Bibliography: leaves 81-82. LC Card 86-980581
1. Rice trade - Burundi. 2. Rice - Burundi - Irrigation. I. Series: Publication / Institut des sciences agronomiques du Burundi , no 74. II. Title.
HD9066.B952 B47 1985

Bergen, Jan van. Honger op ons bord . Amsterdam , 1986. 164 p. : ISBN 90-70985-05-5 : LC Card 86-166714
HD9000.5 .H655 1986

Bergeot, Paul. Champagne, la coupe est pleine : les dangers de la prospérité / Paul Bergeot ; préface de Michel Debatisse. [Paris] : Perspectives 2001, c1980. 185 p. ; 22 cm. (Bibliothèque des leaders) ISBN 2-86510-001-4 : LC Card 80-120736
1. Wine industry - France - Champagne (Province) - History. 2. Wine and wine making - France - Champagne (Province) - History. I. Title. II. Series.
HD9382.7.C5 B468 1980

Berger, Alain. Les récoltants vendeurs au kilo champenois face au contrat interprofessionnel / A. Berger, I. Foulhouze avec la collaboration de M. Leger et P. Marcellin. Paris : Institut national de la recherche agronomique ; Epernay : Comité interprofessionnel du vin de Champagne, [1984] 45, 63 p. : ill. ; 30 cm. (Economie et sociologie rurales) "Janvier 1984." ISBN 2-85340-534-6 LC Card 85-111856
1. Wine industry - France - Champagne-Ardenne. 2. Viticulture - France - Champagne-Ardenne. 3. Contracts, Agricultural - France - Champagne-Ardenne. I. Foulhouze, I. II. Series: Série Economie et sociologie rurales. III. Title.
HD9382.7.C5 B47 1984

Berger, Axel. Mitgliederförderung in Strassenverkehrsgenossenschaften / von Axel Berger. Münster : Institut für Genossenschaftswesen der Westfälischen Wilhelms-Universität, 1985. 455 p. ; 24 cm. (Kooperations- und genossenschaftswissenschaftliche Beiträge . Bd. 15) Bibliography: p. 425-436. Includes indexes. ISBN 3-7923-0537-2 (Deut. Bibl.) LC Card 86-148185
1. Bundes-Zentralgenossenschaft Strassenverkehr (Germany). 2. Trade-unions - Transport workers - Germany (West). I. Title. II. Series.
HD6698.T72 B863 1985

Berger, Dieter, Dr. sc. oec. Investitionsprozess . Leipzig , c1986. 432 p. : LC Card 86-193837
HG4028.C4 I534 1986

Berger, Gilda. Women, work, and wages / Gilda Berger. New York : F. Watts, 1986. 122 p. : ill. ; 24 cm. Includes index. Examines women in the work force in the United States, with an emphasis on sex discrimination and related problems. Bibliography: p. [115]-116. ISBN 0-531-10074-X LC Card 85-15379 DDC 331.4/0973 19
1. Women - Employment - United States. 2. Equal pay for equal work - United States. 3. Sex discrimination in education - United States. 4. Sexual harassment of women - United States. I. Title.
HD6095 .B47 1986 ***NYPL [JLE 86-4592]***

Berger, Manfred, 1921- Elektrotechnische Industrie : Strukturwandlungen und Entwicklungsperspektiven / von Manfred Berger. Berlin : Duncker & Humblot, c1984. 261 p. : ill. ; 24 cm. (Struktur und Wachstum: Reihe Industrie. Heft 38) Bibliography: p. [257]-261. ISBN 3-428-05674-4 LC Card 85-137543
1. Electronic industries - Germany, West. 2. Electric industries - Germany, West. I. Title. II. Series.
HD9696.A3 G42 1984 ***NYPL [TB (Struktur und Wachstum. Reihe Industrie. Heft 38)]***

Berger, Manfred, Dipl. econ.
Auslandsinvestitionen kleiner und mittlerer Unternehmen : eine Untersuchung über das

Auslandsinvestitionspotential kleiner und mittlerer Unternehmen / von Manfred Berger, Luitpold Uhlmann. Berlin : Duncker & Humblot, c1985. 164 p. : ill. ; 24 cm. (Schriftenreihe des IFO-Instituts für Wirtschaftsforschung . Nr. 116) Bibliography: p. [163]-164. ISBN 3-428-05775-9 LC Card 85-161656
1. Investments, West German. 2. Investments, West German - Developing countries. 3. Investments, West German - Communist countries. 4. Small business - Germany, West - Finance. I. Uhlmann, Luitpold. II. Title. III. Series.
HG4538 .B4538 1985

Uhlmann, Luitpold. Instrumentelle Aspekte der Investitionsförderung . München , 1986. vii, 270 p. : ISBN 3-88512-024-0 LC Card 86-215244 DDC 332.63 19
HG4028.C4 U367 1986

Uhlmann, Luitpold. Investitionsverhalten und Unternehmensgrösse /. Berlin , c1986. 307 p. ; ISBN 3-428-06010-5 LC Card 86-216522
HG4028.C4 U37 1986

Berger, Peter L.
Capitalism and equality in America /. Lanham [New York] , c1987. ix, 306 p. : ISBN 0-8191-5572-1 (v. 1 : alk. paper) : LC Card 86-24739 DDC 330.12/2 19
HB501 .C2423 1987

Capitalism and equality in the Third World /. Lanham [New York] , c1987. 375 p. ; ISBN 0-8191-5574-8 (v. 2 : alk. paper) : LC Card 86-24749 DDC 330.12/2 19
HB501 .C24234 1987

In search of an East Asian development model /. New Brunswick, N.J., USA , c1988. xi, 243 p. ; ISBN 0-88738-686-5 (pbk.) LC Card 87-19061 DDC 338.95 19
HC460.5 .I5 1988

BERGERON, ANDRÉ, 1922-
Validire, Jean-Louis. André Bergeron, une force ouvrière /. Paris , c1984. 244 p. ; ISBN 2-259-01206-X : LC Card 85-105625 DDC 331.88/0944 19
HD6684 .V35 1984

Bergerud, Marly, 1942-
Computers for managing information / Marly Bergerud, Thomas Keller. New York : J. Wiley, c1988. xvi, 480 p., [32] p. of plates : ill. (some col.) ; 26 cm. Includes index. ISBN 0-471-84441-1 LC Card 87-20979 DDC 650/.028/5 19
1. Business - Data processing. I. Keller, Thomas, 1950-. II. Title.
HF5548.2 .B387 1988

Introduction to office systems : an abridgment of Word and information processing / Marly Bergerud, Jean Gonzalez. New York : Wiley, c1987. xvi, 440 p., [12] p. of plates : ill. (some col.) ; 26 cm. Includes index. ISBN 0-471-85532-4 (pbk.) LC Card 86-28188 DDC 652/.5 19
1. Word processing. 2. Word processing - Equipment and supplies. 3. Office practice - Automation. I. Gonzalez, Jean, 1945-. II. Bergerud, Marly, 1942- Word and information processing. III. Title.
HF5548.115 .B462 1987

Word and information processing : concepts of office automation / Marly Bergerud, Jean Gonzalez.3rd ed. New York : Wiley, c1987. xvi, 578 p. : ill. (some col.) ; 27 cm. Rev. ed. of: Word/information processing concepts of office automation. 2nd ed. c1984. Includes index. ISBN 0-471-84504-3 LC Card 86-24748 DDC 652/.5 19
1. Word processing. 2. Word processing - Equipment and supplies. 3. Office practice - Automation. I. Gonzalez, Jean, 1945-. II. Bergerud, Marly, 1942- Word/information processing concepts of office automation. III. Title.
HF5548.115 .B46 1987

Word and information processing. Bergerud, Marly, 1942- Introduction to office systems : an abridgment of Word and information processing / Marly Bergerud, Jean Gonzalez. New York , c1987. xvi, 440 p., [12] p. of plates : ISBN 0-471-85532-4 (pbk.) LC Card 86-28188 DDC 652/.5 19
HF5548.115 .B462 1987

Word processing : concepts and careers / Marly Bergerud, Jean Gonzalez.4th ed. New York : Wiley, c1988. xiv, 336 p., [12] p. of plates : ill. (some col.) ; 26 cm. Includes index. ISBN 0-471-84503-5 (pbk.) LC Card 87-8181 DDC 652/.5/02373 19
1. Word processing. 2. Word processing - Vocational guidance. 3. Word processing equipment industry - Vocational guidance. I. Gonzalez, Jean, 1945-. II. Title.
HF5548.115 .B47 1988

Word/information processing concepts of office automation. Bergerud, Marly, 1942- Word and information processing : concepts of office automation / Marly Bergerud, Jean Gonzalez.3rd ed. New York , c1987. xvi, 578 p. : ISBN 0-471-84504-3 LC Card 86-24748 DDC 652/.5 19
HF5548.115 .B46 1987

Bergesen, Albert. America's changing role in the world-system /. New York , 1987. xi, 300 p. : ISBN 0-275-92417-3 (alk. paper) : LC Card 86-25245 DDC 337.73 19
HC106.8 .A455 1987

Bergh, Trond, 1946- Vitenskap og politikk : linjer i norsk sosialøkonomi gjennom 150 år / Trond Bergh og Tore J. Hanisch. Oslo : Aschehoug, 1984. 269 p. : ill. ; 23 cm. Includes bibliographical references and index. ISBN 82-03-11342-7 : LC Card 84-184253
1. Economics - History. 2. Norway - Economic conditions. I. Hanisch, Tore Jørgen, 1945-. II. Title.
HB116.3.A2 B47 1984

Berghahn, Volker Rolf.
Industrial relations in West Germany / Volker R. Berghahn and Detlev Karsten. Leamington Spa, UK ; New York : Berg Publishers ; p. cm. Bibliography: p. Includes index. ISBN 0-907582-64-8 : LC Card 87-9359 DDC 331/.0943 19
1. Industrial relations - Germany, West. 2. Collective bargaining - Germany, West. I. Karsten, Detlev. II. Title.
HD8451 .B45 1988

Unternehmer und Politik in der Bundesrepublik / Volker Berghahn. 1. Aufl. Frankfurt am Main : Suhrkamp, 1985. 363 p. : ill. ; 18 cm. (Edition Suhrkamp. 1265 = n.F., Bd. 265) Neue historische Bibliothek Bibliography: p. 356-[359] ISBN 3-518-11265-1 LC Card 85-235608
1. Germany, West - Industries. 2. Trade-unions - Germany, West. 3. Businessmen - Germany, West. 4. Germany, West - Politics and government. I. Title.
HC286.5 .B37 1985

[Unternehmer und Politik in der Bundesrepublik. English]
The Americanisation of West German industry, 1945-1973 / Volker R. Berghahn. Leamington Spa ; New York : Berg, c1986. viii, 344 p. : ill. ; 22 cm. Extended and revised translation of: Unternehmer und Politik in der Bundesrepublik. Bibliography: p. 338-341. Includes index. ISBN 0-907582-55-9 : LC Card 86-222514
1. Germany, West - Industries. 2. Germany, West - Economic policy. 3. Germany, West - Foreign economic relations - United States. 4. United States - Foreign economic relations - Germany, West. I. Title.
HC286.5 .B37x 1986b

Bergier, J. (Joseph) Marques d'entrée maritime du XVIIIème et du XIXème siècle et études diverses s'y rapportant, dont taxes et mouvements portuaires de provenance ou à destination des principaux ports d'outremer au XVIIIe s. / J. Bergier. Nantes : Amicale philatélique "L'Ancre", [1981] 131, x p. : ill. ; 29 cm. "Déc. 1981." Bibliography: p. 1. LC Card 82-228434
1. Maritime postal hand stamps - France - Colonies - History. 2. Postmarks - France - Colonies - History. I. Title.
HE6986 .B47 1981

Bergische Forschungen, 0405-4520 .
(Bd. 17) Walz, Rainer. Stände und frühmoderner Staat . Neustadt an der Aisch , 1982. 257 p., [1] leaf of plates : ISBN 3-87707-040-9 LC Card 83-215104
HJ2675 .W35 1982

Berglund, Tom. Anomalies in stock returns on a thin security market / Tom Berglund. Helsingfors : Swedish School of Economics and Business Administration, 1986. vi, 191 p. : ill. ; 25 cm. (Ekonomi och samhälle, 0424-7256 . nr. 37) Bibliography: p. 183-191. ISBN 951-555-239-7 (pbk.) LC Card 86-224629 DDC 332.63/222 19
1. Stocks - Prices - Mathematical models. I. Title. II. Title: Thin security market. III. Series: Ekonomi och samhälle (Svenska handelshögskolan (Helsinki, Finland)) , nr. 37.
HG4636 .B47 1986

Bergman, Åke. Den nya given : artiklar och reportage om arbetet / Åke Bergman. Stockholm : Tiden, [1986] 157 p. ; 21 cm. Bibliography: p. 143-157. ISBN 91-550-3244-3 : LC Card 86-235012
1. Industrial management - Sweden. 2. Sweden - Industries. I. Title.
HD70.S8 B48 1986

Bergman, Edward M. Cooperative forms of organization in the taxicab industry [microform] : final report / Edward M. Bergman and James I. Stein, Department of City and Regional Planning, University of North Carolina at Chapel Hill. Washington, D.C. : Urban Mass Transit Administration ; Springfield, Va. : National Technical Information Service [distributor], 1984. 87 p. : ill. ; 28 cm. Distributed to depository libraries in microfiche. "June 1983." "UMTA-NC-11-0009-83-4 ; NC-11 0009." "DOT-I-84-34." Prepared for Urban Mass Transportation Administration, U. S. Dept. of Transportation. Bibliography: p. 85-87. Microfiche. Springfield, Va. : NTIS, 1984. 1 microfiche : negative ; 11 x 15 cm. (PB83-253237)
1. Taxicabs - United States. 2. Cooperative societies - United States. I. Stein, James I. II. University of North Carolina at Chapel Hill. Dept. of City and Regional Planning. III. Title. ***NYPL [*XME-11,917]***

Bergman, Lars. Energy and economic adjustment /. Stockholm , 1983. 247 p. : ISBN 91-7204-186-2 ***NYPL [JLE 86-1351]***

Bergmann, Theodor. Agrarian reform in India : with special reference to Kerala, Karnataka, Andhra Pradesh, and West Bengal / Theodor Bergmann. New Delhi, India : Agricole Pub. Academy, 1984. viii, 216 p. ; 23 cm. Includes indexes. Bibliography: p. 202-210. LC Card 84-900254 DDC 333.3/1/54 19
1. Land reform - India. 2. Agriculture - Economic aspects - India. I. Title.
HD1333.I4 B46 1984 ***NYPL [JLD 86-3823]***

Bergner, Heinz, 1924- Internationale und nationale Problemfelder der Betriebswirtschaftslehre /. Berlin , c1984. 336 p., [1] leaf of plates : ISBN 3-428-05696-5 LC Card 85-141327
HD35 .I598 1984

BERGNER, HEINZ, 1924-
Internationale und nationale Problemfelder der Betriebswirtschaftslehre /. Berlin , c1984. 336 p., [1] leaf of plates : ISBN 3-428-05696-5 LC Card 85-141327
HD35 .I598 1984

Bergonzini, Renato. Arte dei brentatori a Modena / Renato Bergonzini. Modena : Teic, 1983. 74 p., [5] p. of plates : ill. (some col.) ; 30 cm. Bibliography: p. 31-37. LC Card 85-140349
1. Vinters - Italy - Modena (Province) - History. 2. Wine industry - Italy - Modena (Province) - History. I. Title.
HD8039.L72 I83 1983

Bergquist, Charles W. Labor in Latin America : comparative essays on Chile, Argentina, Venezuela, and Colombia / Charles Bergquist. Stanford, Calif. : Stanford University Press, 1986. xiv, 397, [8] p. of plates : ill. ; 24 cm. Includes bibliographical references and index. ISBN 0-8047-1253-0 (alk. paper) : LC Card 84-51648 DDC 331/.0968 19
1. Labor and laboring classes - South America - History. 2. Trade-unions - South America - History. I. Title.
HD8256 .B47 1986 ***NYPL [JLE 86-2972]***

Bergquist, Sven, 1926- De heta åren / Sven Bergquist. [Stockholm] : Timbro, 1985. 319 p. : ill. ; 25 cm. ISBN 91-7566-089-X LC Card 85-233735
1. Sydkraft (Firm : Sweden). 2. Nuclear industry - Sweden. I. Title.
HD9698.S84 S923 1985

Bergquist, William H. Phillips, Steven R. Solutions . San Diego, Calif. , c1987. xi, 127 p. ; ISBN 0-88390-205-2 (pbk.) : LC Card 87-5894 DDC 658.4/03 19
HD30.29 .P48 1987

Bergson, Abram, 1914- Entrepreneurship . Wien , New York , 1984, c1983. 218 p. ; ISBN 0-387-81830-8 (U. S.) LC Card 84-26677 DDC 338/.04 19
HB615 .E635 1984 ***NYPL [JLE 85-1253]***

Bergsten, C. Fred, 1941-
Auction quotas and United States trade policy /. Washington, DC , c1987. xiii, 241 p. : ISBN 0-88132-050-1 (pbk.) LC Card 87-12948 DDC 382/.52/0973 19
HF1455 .A83 1987

Global economic imbalances /. Washington, DC , 1985. x, 116 p. ; ISBN 0-88132-038-2 (pbk.) LC Card 85-8279 DDC 330.9/048 19
HD73 .G56 1985 ***NYPL [JLE 87-1314]***

The United States-Japan economic problem / C. Fred Bergsten, William R. Cline. Washington, D.C. : Institute for International Economics, c1985. x, 164 p. : ill. ; 23 cm. (Policy analyses in international economics . 13) "October 1985." Bibliography: p. 161-164. ISBN 0-262-52108-3 LC Card 85-18106 DDC 382/.0973/052 19
1. Balance of trade - United States - Congresses. 2. Balance of trade - Japan - Congresses. 3. United States - Commerce - Japan - Congresses. 4. Japan - Commerce - United States - Congresses. I. Cline, William R. II. Institute for International Economics (U. S.). III. Title. IV. Series.
HF3127 .B47 1985 ***NYPL [JLE 87-19]***

Bergstrom, John C. (John Clark) Stoll, John R. Economic impact of the recreational boating industry in Texas /. College Station, TX [1985] xiv, 86 p. : LC Card 86-622008 DDC 330.9764/063 19
HD9993.B633 U58 1985

Bericht der Exekutive der Zionistischen Organisation an den XV. Zionisten-Kongress. Bericht des Departements fuer Landwirtschaftliche Kolonisation. Jerusalem : [s.n.], 1927 (Jerusalem : Azriel) 110 p., [1] folded leaf of plates : ill. ; 23 cm. Errata slip inserted. "Auszug aus 'Zustand und Methoden der zionistischen Kolonisation in Palaestina' ... von Dipl. Ing. S. Kaplansky": p. [81]-97. LC Card 86-122608
1. Agricultural colonies - Palestine. 2. Jews - Colonization - Palestine. 3. Jews - Palestine - Economic conditions. 4. Palestine Zionist Executive. Dept. of Agricultural Colonisation. I. Zionist Organisation. Executive. II. Zionist Congress (15th : 1927 : Basel, Switzerland). III. Palestine Zionist Executive. Dept. of Agricultural Colonisation. IV. Title: Bericht des Departements fuer Landwirtschaftliche Kolonisation.
HD1516.P18 B525 1927

Bericht der vereinigten Ausschüsse I und III samt Materialien zum Referate über die Steigerung der Kosten der staatlichen inneren Verwaltung in der Periode von 1890 bis 1911 und über vorläufige Reformvorschläge bezüglich der Zentralstellen und der politischen Landesbehörden. [S.l. : s.n., 1912?] 1 v. in various pagings ; 32 cm. LC Card 87-409311 DDC 336.436 19
1. Finance, Public - Austria - History - 19th century. 2. Finance, Public - Austria - History - 20th century.
HJ1062 .B47 1912

Bericht des Departements fuer Landwirtschaftliche Kolonisation. Bericht der Exekutive der Zionistischen Organisation an den XV. Zionisten-Kongress. Jerusalem , 1927 (Jerusalem : Azriel) 110 p., [1] folded leaf of plates : LC Card 86-122608
HD1516.P18 B525 1927

Bericht (Humboldt-Universität zu Berlin) .
(86-8) Zur Theorie und Praxis imperialistischer Anpassungs- und Konfrontationspolitik in der Gegenwart /. Berlin [1986] 99 p. ; LC Card 87-409046 DDC 330.12/2 19
HB501 .Z765 1986

Berichte aus dem Weltwirtschaftlichen Colloquium der Universität Bremen .
(Nr. 5) Sell, Axel. Economic structure and development of Burma /. Bremen [1985] 39 p. ; LC Card 86-228833 DDC 338.9591 19
HC422 .S45 1985

Berichte des German Chapter of the ACM, 0724-9764 .
(Bd. 27) Arbeitsplätze morgen /. Stuttgart , c1986. 431 p. : ISBN 3-519-02446-2 LC Card 86-171663
HD6331 .A695 1986

Berichte des Osteuropa-Instituts an der Freien Universität Berlin .
(Heft 135) Collier, Irwin L., 1951- Connections, effective purchasing power, and real product in the German Democratic Republic /. Berlin , 1985. ix, 216 p. : ISBN 3-921374-34-0 (pbk.) LC Card 86-229298 DDC 330 s 338.9431/00724 19
HC244.A1 B4 Nr. 44 HC290.78

(Heft 138) Klinkmüller, Erich. Über interdisziplinäre, sozialwissenschaftliche Forschung in den USA und andernorts /. Berlin , 1986. 177 p. ; ISBN 3-921374-37-5 LC Card 86-211120
HC244.A1 B4 Nr. 47 H62.5.U5

Berichte (Humboldt-Universität zu Berlin) .
(1983, 6) Innovation und internationale Monopole /. Berlin , 1983. 85 p. ; LC Card 84-104008
HD2755.5 .I534 1983

(84-11) Sozialistisches Arbeitsverhalten als Leistungsverhalten /. Berlin [1984] 77 p. ; LC Card 84-250357
HD8460.5 .S694 1984

Berichte zur Erziehungstherapie und Eingliederungshilfe .
(33) Kornblum, Hans-Joachim. Therapie in der Berufsschule? . München , c1984. x, 458 p. : ISBN 3-597-10503-3 : LC Card 85-105593
HD5715.5.G4 K67 1984

Berichte zur Orts-, Regional- und Landesplanung .
(Nr. 37a-37b) Interregionale Wanderungen in der Schweiz . Zürich , c1978. 2 v. : LC Card 85-215084
HB2083 .I57 1978

(Nr. 50) Rumley, Pierre-Alain. Aménagement du territoire et utilisation du sol . Zürich , c1984. x, 176 p. : LC Card 85-104773
HD796 .R86 1984

Berichte zur Stadtforschung .
(Heft 2) Marx, G. Die Entwicklung der Wohnungsbautätigkeit in Leverkusen /. Leverkusen [1984] 37 p., [1] folded leaf of plates : LC Card 84-183932
HD9715.G33 L575 1984

Die Berichterstattung der internen Revision im Grossbetrieb /. Lubos, Günter, 1958- München , c1986. xxvii, 207 p. ; ISBN 3-88259-421-7 LC Card 87-121827 DDC 657/.458 19
HF5668.25 .L82 1986

Berkel, Karl. Konflikttraining / von Karl Berkel. Heidelberg : I.H. Sauer, c1985. 82 p. : ill. ; 21 cm. (Arbeitshefte zur Führungspsychologie . Heft 15) Bibliography: p. 82. ISBN 3-7938-7735-3 LC Card 85-188803
1. Conflict management. I. Title. II. Series.
HD42 .B47 1985

Berkeley, Calif. University of California. see **California. University.**

Berkeley-Duke occasional papers on the second economy in the USSR .
(paper no. 7) Treml, Vladimir G. Referent USSR economic and demographic statistics for normalization of Berkeley-Duke emigre questionnaire data /. [Durham, N.C. [1986] 1 v. (various pagings) ; LC Card 86-70618 DDC 304.6/0947/021 19
HB3607 .T74 1986

Berkman, A. Ümit. Heper, Metin. Development administration in Turkey . Bebek, Istanbul [1980] vi, 116 p. ; LC Card 87-400032 DDC 338.9561 19
HC492 .H47 1980

Berkman, Harold E. Advertising, concepts and strategies / Harold W. Berkman, Christopher Gilson ; consulting editor, M. Joseph Sirgy. 2nd ed. New York : Random House, c1987. xxiv, 614 p. : ill. (some col.) ; 27 cm. Gilson's name appears first on the 1st ed. Bibliography: p. 591-596. Includes indexes. ISBN 0-394-36165-2 : LC Card 86-29790 DDC 659.1/11 19
1. Advertising. 2. Marketing. 3. Commercial art. I. Gilson, Christopher C. II. Title.
HF5823 .B45 1987

Berko, Robert L. Consumers guide to Social Security benefits : how to get everything you are entitled to under the latest laws / compiled and edited by Robert L. Berko. South Orange, N.J. : Consumer Education Research Center, 1986. p. cm. ISBN 0-934873-04-6 (pbk.) : LC Card 86-23933 DDC 344.73/023 347.30423 19
1. Social Security - United States - Handbooks, manuals, etc. I. Title.
HD7125 .B47 1986

Berkowitz, Monroe, 1919-
Measuring the efficiency of public programs . Philadelphia , 1988. p. cm. ISBN 0-87722-527-3 (alk. paper) LC Card 87-18080 DDC 362/.0425 19
HD7256.U5 M44 1988

Permanent disability benefits in workers' compensation / Monroe Berkowitz and John F. Burton, Jr. Kalamazoo, Mich. : W.E. Upjohn Institute for Employment Research, 1987. xviii, 459 p. ; 24 cm. Bibliography: p. 433-440. Includes index. ISBN 0-88099-051-1 LC Card 87-22874 DDC 368.4/1/00973 19
1. Insurance, Disability - United States. 2. Workers' compensation - United States. I. Burton, John F. II. Title.
HD7105.25.U6 B47 1987

Berkowitz, Stephen A. The investment performance of corporate pension plans : why they do not beat the market regularly / Stephen A. Berkowitz, Louis D. Finney, and Dennis E. Logue. New York : Quorum Books, 1988. xi, 132 p. ; 24 cm. Includes bibliographies and index. ISBN 0-89930-224-6 (lib. bdg. : alk. paper) LC Card 87-19030 DDC 332.6/7154 19
1. Pension trusts - United States - Investments. I. Finney, Louis D. II. Logue, Dennis E. III. Title.
HD7105.45.U6 B475 1988

Berkshire Conference on the History of Women (6th : 1984 : Smith College) "To toil the livelong day" . Ithaca, N.Y. , 1987. xi, 312 p. ; ISBN 0-8014-1847-X (alk. paper) LC Card 86-47975 DDC 331.4/0973 19
HD6095 .T6 1987

Berlīand, Efim L'vovich. Modeli i metody reshenīīa zadach vzaimodeĭstvīīa ėkonomicheskikh sistem /. Novosibirsk , 1982. 160 p. : LC Card 83-164468
HB137 .M6 1982

Berlin. Akademie der Wissenschaften der DDR. see **Akademie der Wissenschaften der DDR.**

Berlin. Akademie für Gesellschaftswissenschaften. see **Akademie für Gesellschaftswissenschaften.**

Berlin. Deutsches Institut für Urbanistik. see **Deutsches Institut für Urbanistik.**

Berlin. Deutsches Institut für Wirtschaftsforschung. (Old Catalog form: Deutsches Institut für Wirtschaftsforschung)
Sonderhefte.
(134. 134) Basler, Hans-Peter. Lohnentwicklung und Lohnpolitik als Bestimmungsgründe konjunktureller Verläufe und struktureller Verschiebungen . Berlin , 1981. 102 p. : ISBN 3-428-04970-5 LC Card 82-100546 DDC 330 s 331.2/943 19
HB41 .B4 Nr. 134 HD5029
NYPL [JLL 73-207 Heft 134]

Sonderheft .
(139) Ziesing, Hans-Joachim. Beurteilung der Wirtschaftlichkeitsschwelle und Analyse der Produktionskapazitäten bei neuen Technologien zur Energieeinsparung in mittel- bis längerfristiger Sicht . Berlin , 1983. 458 p. : ISBN 3-428-05497-0
NYPL [JLL 73-207 Bd. 139]

Berlin Forschung .
(Bd. 10) Huter, Otto, 1952- Die Berliner Eigenbetriebe als Instrumente kommunaler Politik /. Berlin , c1984. 275 p. : ISBN 3-87061-910-4 LC Card 84-231849
HD4180.B47 H87 1984

Berlin. Freie Universität. Osteuropa-Institut.
Berichte. For additional listing of contents, see Old Catalog.
(Heft 129) Breitkopf, Stephan. Die Behandlung von Immobilienrechten Deutscher mit Wohnsitz in der Bundesrepublik Deutschland und Berlin (West), in der DDR und Berlin (Ost) /. Berlin , 1983. xii, 203 p. ; ISBN 3-921374-25-1 LC Card 84-167165 DDC 330 s 346.431/55043 19
HC244.A1 B4 Heft 129 KK1315
NYPL [STN+ (Berlin. Freie Universität. Osteuropa-Institut. Berichte. Heft 129)]

Wirtschafswissenshaftliche Folge. see **Berlin. Freie Universität. Osteuropa-Institut. Berichte.**

BERLIN (GERMANY) - COMMERCE - RESEARCH - HISTORY.
Handelsforschung heute . Berlin , c1979. 230 p. : ISBN 3-428-04408-8 LC Card 87-408239 DDC 380.1 s 380.1/06/04355 19
HF345 .F66 Folge 3, Nr. 7 HF308

BERLIN (GERMANY) - ECONOMIC CONDITIONS - CONGRESSES.
DIW-Symposion (1983 : Berlin, Germany) Strategien für mehr Arbeitsplätze in Berlin . Berlin , c1984. 209 p. : ISBN 3-87061-277-0 LC Card 84-202956
HD5780.B4 D58 1983

BERLIN (GERMANY) - ECONOMIC POLICY - CASE STUDIES.
Huter, Otto, 1952- Die Berliner Eigenbetriebe als Instrumente kommunaler Politik /. Berlin , c1984. 275 p. : ISBN 3-87061-910-4 LC Card 84-231849
HD4180.B47 H87 1984

BERLIN (GERMANY) - EXHIBITION.
Mach mich nicht an . Berlin , c1986. [48] p. : ISBN 3-88114-313-0 : LC Card 87-118837 DDC 331.4/133/0943 19
HD6060.5.G3 M33 1986

BERLIN (GERMANY) - INDUSTRIES.
Albrecht, Christoph, 1950- Beschäftigungsentwicklung und Qualifikationsstruktur in Berlin 1977-1983 . Berlin [1985] 2 v. : LC Card 86-204299
HD5780.B4 A43 1985

Hornschild, Kurt. Präferenzregelung der Forschungs- und Entwicklungsförderung in Berlin /. Berlin , 1985. v, 55 p. ; ISBN 3-428-05800-3 LC Card 86-156799
HD30.42.G39 H67 1985

BERLIN (GERMANY) - OCCUPATIONS - STATISTICS.
Ergebnisse der Volks- und Berufszählung in Berlin (West) am 27. Mai 1970 . Berlin [1976] 4 v. : LC Card 85-171340
HA1330.B6 B45 Heft 254-257 HA1249.B47

BERLIN (GERMANY) - POPULATION - STATISTICS.
Ergebnisse der Volks- und Berufszählung in Berlin (West) am 27. Mai 1970 . Berlin [1976] 4 v. : LC Card 85-171340
HA1330.B6 B45 Heft 254-257 HA1249.B47

Berlin. International Institute of Management. see **International Institute of Management.**

Berlin, Ira, 1941- Gutman, Herbert George, 1928- Power & culture . New York, N.Y. , c1987. xi, 452 p. ; ISBN 0-394-56171-6 LC Card 87-43018 DDC 305.5/62/0973 19
HD8072 .G97 1987

Berlin. Parteihochschule "Karl Marx." Lehrstuhl Wissenschaftlicher Kommunismus. Zur Entwicklung der Klassen und Schichten in der DDR / [Parteihochschule "Karl Marx" beim ZK der SED, Autorenkollektiv des Lehrstuhl Wissenschaftlicher Kommunismus ; Wolfgang Schneider (Leiter) ... et al.]. Berlin : Dietz, 1977. 147 p. ; 22 cm. (Sozialismus, Erfahrungen, Probleme und Perspektiven) Includes bibliographical references. LC Card 78-358768
1. Social classes - Germany, East. 2. Labor and laboring classes - Germany, East. 3. Socialism in East Germany. I. Title.
HN460.5.Z9 S62 NYPL [JLD 79-2817]

Die Berliner Eigenbetriebe als Instrumente kommunaler Politik /. Huter, Otto, 1952- Berlin , c1984. 275 p. : ISBN 3-87061-910-4 LC Card 84-231849
HD4180.B47 H87 1984

Die "Berliner Linie" und die Hausbesetzer-Szene /. Sonnewald, Bernd, 1947- Berlin , c1983. 149 p. ; ISBN 3-87061-170-7 LC Card 83-190228
HD7287.96.G32 B477 1983

Berman, Barry. Evans, Joel R. Principles of marketing /. New York , London , c1988. xxiii, 528, 44, 22 p. : ISBN 0-02-334340-0 LC Card 87-15223 DDC 658.8 19
HF5415 .E865 1988

Berman, Ronald. Solzhenitsyn at Harvard . Washington, D. C. , 1980. xvi, 143 p. ; ISBN 0-89633-034-6 : LC Card 79-26033 DDC 909.82
CB245.S5693 S64 NYPL [JFE 81-1327]

Bermani, Cesare, 1937- Dalla grande associazione degli operai di Novara al Circolo operaio agricolo della Bicocca : un secolo e mezzo di associazionismo a Novara / Cesare Bermani. Novara : ARCI, [1983] 345 p., [31] p. of plates : ill ; 24 cm. Includes bibliographical references. LC Card 85-148843
1. Trade-unions - Italy - Novara (Province) - History. 2. Working-men's clubs - Italy - Novara (Province) - History. 3. Labor and laboring classes - Italy - Novara (Province) - Societies, etc. - History. I. Title.
HD6714.N68 B47 1983

Bermingham, Thomas. A statistical account of foreign and English railways : extracted from synopsis of German railways, and from the Statistical journal of London as referred to by able articles in the Railway times and mining journal of Saturday, May 18, 1839. London : Fores : Smith and Elder, 1839. 24 p. ; 23 cm. Author's statement appears on p. 24. LC Card 85-665741
1. Railroads - Statistics. I. Title.
HE2271 .B47x 1839

Bermuda Islands. Finance Ministry. Statistical Office. Roberts, G. W. (George W.) Provisional estimates of population movements in Bermuda to 1990 /. Hamilton, Bermuda [198-?] 12, [8] p. : LC Card 86-173218
HB3668.A3 R63 1980z

Bermuda Islands. of Finance Ministry. Statistical Office. A Review of birth statistics, Bermuda, 1971-1978 /. [Hamilton] [1980] 62 p. ; LC Card 85-189032 DDC 304.6/3/097299021 19
HB1078.A3 R48 1980 NYPL [JLF 85-3121]

BERMUDA ISLANDS - POPULATION.
Roberts, G. W. (George W.) Provisional estimates of population movements in Bermuda to 1990 /. Hamilton, Bermuda [198-?] 12, [8] p. : LC Card 86-173218
HB3668.A3 R63 1980z

Bermúdez M., Alicia. Pacheco O., Amparo. Préstamo del BID al sector pesquero . [San José] , 1984. 50 p. : LC Card 86-185463
HD9464.A2 P33 1984

Bern, Paula. How to work for a woman boss, even if you'd rather not / Paula Bern. 1st ed. New York : Dodd, Mead, c1987. ix, 207 p. ; 24 cm. Includes bibliographical references and index. ISBN 0-396-08839-2 : LC Card 86-16735 DDC 650.1/3 19
1. Managing your boss. 2. Women executives. I. Title.
HF5548.83 .B48 1987 NYPL [JLE 87-1439]

Bern (Switzerland : Canton). Amt für Statistik. Kanton Bern (n.G.), Bilanz der erwerbstätigen Pendler, nach Gemeinden (2. 12. 1980) =. Bern , 1983. 16 p. ; LC Card 83-232809 DDC 388.3/14/094945 19
HD5717.5.S92 B46 1983

Bernanke, Ben. Readings and cases in macroeconomics /. New York , c1987. x, 485 p. : ISBN 0-07-017779-1 (pbk.) : LC Card 86-27423 DDC 339 19
HB172.5 .D67 1987 Suppl.

Bernard, Bobbi.
Aseptic food packaging and processing. Gipson, Beckilynn. Aseptic food processing and packaging : a technical/economic analysis / Becki Gipson. Stamford, Conn., U. S.A. , c1986. xiii, 164 leaves ; ISBN 0-89336-471-1 (pbk.) LC Card 87-405014 DDC 381/.45664028 19
HD9999.C743 U629 1986

Bernard, Chantal.
La politique de l'emploi-formation au Maghreb, 1970-1980 / Chantal Bernard avec la participation de R. Abdelkrim ... [et al.]. Paris : Éditions du Centre national de la recherche scientifique, 1982. 472 p. ; 24 cm. (Collection "Etudes de l'Annuaire de l'Afrique du Nord") At head of title : Centre de recherches et d'études sur les sociétés méditerranéennes.
1. Labor supply - Algeria. 2. Labor supply - Morocco. 3. Labor supply - Tunisia. I. Centre de recherches et d'études sur les sociétés méditerranéennes. II. Title. III. Title: Maghreb, 1970-1980.re de l'Afrique du nord. IV. Series. NYPL [JLE 86-568]

La Politique de l'emploi-formation au Maghreb, 1970-1980 /. Paris , 1982. 472 p. : ISBN 2-222-03122-2 LC Card 84-222103 DDC 331.11/0961 19
HD5838 .P65 1982

Bernard, Françoise. Equal opportunity counsellors . Berlin , Washington, DC , 1986. 50 p. : ISBN 92-825-6559-9 : LC Card 87-136233 DDC 331.13/3/094 19
HD4903.5.E8 E79 1986

Bernard, Martine. Gizard, Xavier. Regional development and vocational training analysis and discussion of the relationship development . Berlin , Washington, DC , 1986. 49 p. ; ISBN 92-825-5911-4 (pbk.) : LC Card 87-137374 DDC 331.25/92/094 19
HD5715.5.E8 G58 1986

Bernardin, H. John. The Productivity sourcebook /. Amherst, Mass. [1987] x, 467 p. : ISBN 0-87425-075-7 (pbk.) LC Card 87-404037 DDC 658.3/14 19
HD57 .P7114 1987

Bernát, János. Illisz, László. Személyzeti munka, társadalmi környezet /. [Budapest] , 1986. 159 p. : ISBN 963-09-2778-0 : LC Card 87-408532
HF5549.2.H85 I44 1986

BERNBACH, BILL.
Levenson, Bob. Bill Bernbach's book . New York , 1987. xvii, 219 p. : ISBN 0-394-54920-1 : LC Card 86-40103 DDC 659.1/0973 19
HF5813.U6 L48 1987

Berndt, Helmut, ao. Prof. Dr. paed. habil. Rehabilitationspädagogik für Körperbehinderte /. Berlin , 1986. 132 p. ; LC Card 86-193835
HD7256.G32 R44 1986

Berndt, Hermann, 1956- Konsumentscheidung und Informationsüberlastung : der Einfluss von Quantität und Qualität der Werbeinformation auf das Konsumentenverhalten : eine empirische Untersuchung / Hermann Berndt. München : GBI, c1983. 368 p. : ill. ; 21 cm. (Betriebswirtschaftliche Forschungsbeiträge . Bd. 3) Originally presented as the author's thesis (doctoral)--Universität München, 1983. Bibliography: p. 316-334. Includes index. ISBN 3-89003-002-5 LC Card 84-192993
1. Advertising. 2. Consumers. 3. Advertising - Germany, West. 4. Consumers - Germany, West. I. Title. II. Series.
HF5821 .B42 1983

Berner, Allan H. Pennsylvania's street railways in early postcard views : a companion book to Pennsylvania's street railways by Benson W. Rohrbeck : postcards from the Allan H. Berner collection / captions by Benson W. Rohrbeck, Allan H. Berner. [S.l.] : A.H. Berner, c1986. 106 p. : chiefly ill. (some col.) ; 28 cm. LC Card 86-221349 DDC 388.4/4/09748 19
1. Street-railroads - Pennsylvania - History - Pictorial works. 2. Postal cards - Pennsylvania - History. I. Rohrbeck, Benson W. II. Title.
HE4487.P4 B47 1986

Berner Beiträge zur Nationalökonomie. For additional listing of contents, see Old Catalog.
(Bd. 37) Begert, Roland. Elemente einer politischen Ökonomie im Werke Machiavellis /. Bern , c1983. 224 p. : ISBN 3-258-03136-3 LC Card 83-204993
HB109.M3 B44 1983

(Bd. 39) Stuber, Barbara. Saisonschwankungen der Bankreserven und Ultimooperationen der Schweizerischen Nationalbank /. Bern , c1986. 173 p. : ISBN 3-258-03653-5 : LC Card 87-130160 DDC 332.1/12/09494 19
HG1656.S9 S77 1986

(Bd. 41) Zenger, Christoph. Kursschwankungen des Schweizerfrankens in ihren Auswirkungen auf Produktion, Export, Import und Fremdenverkehr . Bern , c1982. vi, 263 p. : ISBN 3-258-03172-X : LC Card 83-242397 DDC 332.4/9494 19
HG1155 .Z46 1982

(Bd. 47) Meier, Kurt, Dr. Spitzenlasttarifierung, oekonomische Effizienz und Erhaltung der Eigenwirtschaftlichkeit . Bern , c1983. viii, 202 p. : ISBN 3-258-03322-6 : LC Card 84-108545
HD9685.S92 M45 1983

(Bd. 50) Rötheli, Tobias F. Das Volkseinkommen und die internationalen Kapitalbewegungen /. Bern , c1986. 128 p. ; ISBN 3-258-03669-1 LC Card 87-110633 DDC 332.4/5/0724 19
HG3891 .R67 1986

Berner, Rudolf. Machiavelli 2000 : ich bin der Boss und will es bleiben : eine heiter-ernste Führungs- und Lebenshilfe für alternde

Manager / Rudolf Berner. Zürich : Organisator, c1985. 62 p. ; 20 cm. ISBN 3-7220-3001-3 : LC Card 86-149021
1. Management. 2. Machiavelli, Niccolò, 1469-1527. I. Title. II. Title: Machiavelli zweitausend.
HD35 .B478 1985

Bernhardt, Kenneth L., 1944- Cases in marketing management / Kenneth L. Bernhardt, Thomas C. Kinnear. 3rd ed. Plano, Tex. : Business Publications, 1985. xiii, 705 p. : ill. ; 25 cm. Includes bibliographical references and index. ISBN 0-256-03055-3 LC Card 84-70994 DDC 658.8 19
1. Marketing management - Case studies. 2. Marketing - Decision making - Case studies. I. Kinnear, Thomas C., 1943-. II. Title.
HF5415.13 .B448 1985 *NYPL [JLE 86-2513]*

Bernholz, Peter.
Die Internationale Schuldenkrise . Berlin , 1986. 179 p. : ISBN 3-428-05972-7 LC Card 86-172589
HJ8899 .I58 1986

Studies in Austrian capital theory, investment, and time /. Berlin , New York , c1986. vi, 316 p. : ISBN 0-387-16804-4 (U. S. : pbk.) LC Card 86-223780 DDC 330.15/7 19
HB98 .S83 1986

Bernick, Michael, 1953- Urban illusions : new approaches to inner city unemployment / Michael Bernick. New York : Praeger, 1987. x, 243 p. ; 22 cm. Bibliography: p. [239]-240. Includes index. ISBN 0-275-92804-7 (alk. paper) : LC Card 87-7208 DDC 331.13/7973 19
1. Unemployed - United States. 2. Urban poor - Employment - United States. I. Title.
HD5708.85.U6 B47 1987

Bernien, Maritta. Staatsmonopolistische Intensivierung und Widersprüche der Reproduktion /. Berlin [1986] 127 p. ; LC Card 87-408424 DDC 330 s 338/.06 19
HC281 .B39 1986, Heft 4 HC79.I52

Bernschneider, Wolfgang. Staat, Gewerkschaft und Arbeitsprozess : zur "Politisierung" und zum Legitimationspotential staatlichen Handelns / Wolfgang Bernschneider. Opladen : Westdeutscher Verlag, c1986. viii, 291 p. : ill. ; 23 cm. (Beiträge zur sozialwissenschaftlichen Forschung, 0175-615X . Bd. 84) Revision of thesis (doctoral)--Universität Konstanz, 1985. Bibliography: p. 274-291. ISBN 3-531-11797-1 LC Card 86-222066
1. Foreign trade and employment - Germany (West). 2. Labor policy - Germany, West. 3. Trade-unions - Germany, West - Political activity. I. Title. II. Series.
HD5710.75.G3 B47 1986

Bernshtam, Mikhail S.
Below-replacement fertility in industrial societies . Cambridge [Cambridgeshire] , New York , c1987. x, 360 p. : ISBN 0-521-34324-0 LC Card 87-6371 DDC 304.6/32 19
HB901 .B45 1987b

Below-replacement fertility in industrial societies . New York, N.Y., USA , c1987. x, 360 p. : LC Card 87-2458 DDC 304.6/32 19
HB901 .B45 1987

Bernstein, Blanche, 1912- Saving a generation / by Blanche Bernstein. New York : Priority Press Publications, 1986. vi, 63 p. ; 23 cm. "A Twentieth Century Fund paper." Bibliography: p. 49-52. ISBN 0-87078-206-1 (pbk.) : LC Card 87-102738 DDC 362.5/8/0973 19
1. Poor - United States. 2. Women heads of households - United States. 3. Public welfare - United States. I. Twentieth Century Fund. II. Title.
HC110.P6 B47 1986

Bernstein Carabantes, Enrique. Recuerdos de un diplomático / Enrique Bernstein Carabantes. Santiago de Chile : Editorial A. Bello, [1984- v. : ports. ; 23 cm. CONTENTS. - v. 1. Haciendo camino, 1933-1957 -- v. 2. El honor de representar a Chile, 1957-1965. LC Card 84-172336 DDC 327.83 19
1. Bernstein Carabantes, Enrique. 2. World politics - 1933-1945. 3. World politics - 1945-. 4. Diplomats - Chile - Biography. 5. Chile - Foreign relations. I. Title.
F3099 .B43 1984 *NYPL [JFL 84-297]*

BERNSTEIN CARABANTES, ENRIQUE.
Bernstein Carabantes, Enrique. Recuerdos de un diplomático /. Santiago de Chile [1984- v. : LC Card 84-172336 DDC 327.83 19
F3099 .B43 1984 *NYPL [JFL 84-297]*

Bernstein, Deborah. The struggle for equality : urban women workers in pre-state Israeli society / Deborah Bernstein. New York : Praeger, 1987. x, 208 p. : ill. ; 24 cm. "Praeger special studies. Praeger scientific." Includes index. Bibliography: p. 197-203. ISBN 0-275-92139-5 (alk. paper) : LC Card 86-8203 DDC 305.4/3/0095694 19
1. Women, Jewish - Palestine - Employment. 2. Sex discrimination in employment - Palestine. 3. Jews - Palestine - Economic conditions. I. Title.
HD6182.2 .B47 1986 *NYPL [JLE 87-1462]*

BERNSTEIN, EDUARD, 1850-1932.
Tetzel, Manfred. Philosophie und Ökonomie, oder, Das Exempel Bernstein /. Berlin , 1984. 187 p. : LC Card 84-166815
HB107.B52 T48 1984

Bernstein, Irving, 1916- A caring society : the New Deal, the worker and the Great Depression : a history of the American worker, 1933-1941 / Irving Bernstein. Boston : Houghton Mifflin, 1985. 338 p., [24] p. of plates : ill. ; 24 cm. Includes index. Bibliography: p. 309-326. ISBN 0-395-33116-1 : LC Card 84-25129 DDC 362.8/5/0973 19
1. Labor and laboring classes - United States - 1914-. 2. Labor policy - United States - History. 3. Unemployment - United States - History. I. Title. II. Title: History of the American worker, 1933-1941.
HD8072 .B365 1985 *NYPL [JLD 86-2102]*

Bernstein, Jacob, 1946-
Beyond the investor's quotient : the inner world of investing / Jacob Bernstein. New York : Wiley, c1986. x, 214 p. : ill. ; 24 cm. Includes index. Bibliography: p. 207-211. ISBN 0-471-82062-8 LC Card 85-12325 DDC 332.6 19
1. Investments. 2. Investments - Psychological aspects. I. Title.
HG4521 .B443 1986 *NYPL [JLE 86-2936]*

Cyclic analysis in futures trading : advanced methods and procedures / Jacob Bernstein. New York : Wiley, c1988. p. cm. Bibliography: p. Includes index. ISBN 0-471-01185-1 LC Card 87-26350 DDC 332.64/4 19
1. Commodity exchanges. I. Title.
HG6024.A3 B48 1988

Short-term trading in futures : a manual of systems, strategies, and techniques / Jacob Bernstein. Chicago, Ill. : Probus Pub. Co., c1987. vii, 320 p. : ill. ; 30 cm. ISBN 0-917253-66-3 (loose-leaf) : LC Card 87-4940 DDC 332.64/4 19
1. Financial futures. I. Title.
HG6024.3 .B477 1987

Bernstein, Joan Brodshaug, 1933- Bernstein, Merton C. Social Security . New York , c1988. xiii, 321 p. : ISBN 0-465-07916-4 : LC Card 86-47762 DDC 368.4/3/00973 19
HD7125 .B48 1988

Bernstein, Merton C. Social Security : the system that works / Merton C. Bernstein, Joan Brodshaug Bernstein. New York : Basic Books, c1988. xiii, 321 p. : ill. ; 25 cm. Bibliography: p. 295-307. Includes index. ISBN 0-465-07916-4 : LC Card 86-47762 DDC 368.4/3/00973 19
1. Social security - United States. 2. Pension trusts - United States. 3. Medicare - United States. I. Bernstein, Joan Brodshaug, 1933-. II. Title.
HD7125 .B48 1988

Bernstein, Michael A. (Michael Alan), 1954- The Great Depression : delayed recovery and economic change in America, 1929-1939 / Michael A. Bernstein. Cambridge [Cambridgeshire] ; New York : Cambridge University Press, 1987. xvii, 269 p. : ill. ; 24 cm. (Studies in economic history and policy) Bibliography: p. 225-253. Includes index. ISBN 0-521-34048-9 LC Card 87-6403 DDC 338.5/42 19
1. Depressions - 1929 - United States. 2. United States - Economic conditions - 1918-1945. I. Title. II. Series.
HB3717 1929 .B37 1987

Bernval'd, A. R. (Arngol'd Reĭngol'dovich) Regional'nye problemy tovarnogo obrashcheniia : v raĭonakh Sibiri i Dal'nego Vostoka / A.R. Bernval'd ; otvetstvennyĭ redaktor R.I. Shniper. Novosibirsk : Izd-vo "Nauka", Sibirskoe otd-nie, 1984. 207 p. ; 21 cm. At head of title: Akademiia nauk SSSR. Sibirskoe otdelenie. Institut ėkonomiki i organizatsii promyshlennogo proizvodstva. Includes bibliographical references. LC Card 85-104041
1. Physical distribution of goods - Russian S.F.S.R. - Siberia. 2. Physical distribution of goods - Russian S.F.S.R. - Soviet Far East. I. Shniper, R. I. (Ruvin Isaakovich). II. Title.
HF5415.6 .B46 1984 *NYPL [*QIP 87-2770]*

Berque, Jacques. France. Mission "Recherche, technologie et progrès en coopération." Recherche et coopération avec le Tiers Monde . Paris , c1983. 120 p. ; ISBN 2-11-001071-1 : LC Card 83-196852
HC60 .F727 1983

Berrada, Abdelkader. Le crédit agricole au Maroc, 1917-1977 / Abdelkader Berrada. [Rabat] : Edition de la Faculté des sciences juridiques, économiques et sociales de Rabat, 1979. 264 p. ; 24 cm. (Collection de la Faculté des sciences juridiques, économiques et sociales, Université Mohammed V. Série de langue française . 28) Bibliography: p. 245-257. LC Card 82-136521 DDC 332.7/1/0964 19
1. Agricultural credit - Morocco - History - 20th century. 2. Agricultural credit - Government policy - History - 20th century. I. Series: Collection de la Faculté des sciences juridiques, économiques et sociales. Série de langue française , 28. II. Title.
HG2051.M8 B47 1979

Berridge, Geoff. The politics of the South Africa run : European shipping and Pretoria / G.R. Berridge. Oxford [Oxfordshire] : Clarendon Press ; New York : Oxford University Press, 1987. x, 254 p. ; 23 cm. Bibliography: p. [243]-247. Includes index. ISBN 0-19-827484-X : LC Card 87-1600 DDC 387.5/094 19
1. Merchant marine - South Africa - History. 2. Merchant marine - Europe - History. 3. Shipping conferences - History. 4. Union-Castle Mail Steamship Company - History. I. Title.
HE903.4 .B47 1987

Berry, Albert [i. e. Albert Berry R.] see **Berry R., Albert.**

Berry, Brian Joe Lobley, 1934- Economic geography : resource use, locational choices, and regional specialization in the global economy / Brian J.L. Berry, Edgar C. Conkling, D. Michael Ray. Englewood Cliffs, N.J. : Prentice-Hall, c1987. xi, 447 p. : ill. ; 29 cm. Includes bibliographies and index. ISBN 0-13-231440-1 : LC Card 87-2250 DDC 330.9 19
1. Geography, Economic. 2. Natural resources. 3. Industry - Location. 4. Commerce. I. Conkling, Edgar C. II. Ray, D. Michael (David Michael), 1935-. III. Title.
HC59 .B52 1987

Berry, Dick. Forecasting sales with the personal computer : guidelines for marketing and sales managers / Dick Berry. New York : Quorum Books, c1988. p. cm. Bibliography: p. Includes index. ISBN 0-89930-329-3 (lib. bdg. : alk. paper) : LC Card 87-7284 DDC 658.8/18/0285416 19
1. Sales forecasting - Data processing. 2. Microcomputers - Programming. I. Title.
HF5415.2 .B458 1988

Berry, Leonard, 1930- Lewis, Lawrence. African environments and resources /. Boston , 1987. p. cm. ISBN 0-04-916010-9 (alk. paper) LC Card 87-16751 DDC 333.7/096 19
HC800 .L48 1987

Berry, Mary Frances. Why ERA failed : politics, women's rights, and the amending process of the constitution / Mary Frances Berry. Bloomington : Indiana University Press, c1986. ix, 147 p. ; 25 cm. (Everywoman) Includes index. Bibliography: p. 125-142. ISBN 0-253-36537-6 LC Card 85-45985 DDC 342.73/0878/02632 347.30287802632 19
1. Equal rights amendments - United States. 2. Women - Legal status, laws, etc. - United States. 3. Women's rights - United States. I. Title. II. Series.
KF4758 .B45 1986 *NYPL [JLE 86-3979]*

Berry R., Albert. Cortes, Mariluz. Success in small and medium-scale enterprises . New York , c1987. xiii, 289 p. ; ISBN 0-19-520593-6 : LC Card 86-46296 DDC 338.6/42/09861 19
HD2346.C7 C69 1987

Berry, William Dale. Understanding United States government growth : an empirical analysis of the postwar era / William D. Berry and David Lowery. New York : Praeger, 1987. xiv, 212 p. : ill. ; 25 cm. Bibliography: p. 191-206. Includes index. ISBN 0-275-92509-9 (alk. paper) :

LC Card 87-11818 DDC 336.73 19
1. Finance, Public - United States - 1933- - Econometric models. 2. Government spending policy - United States - Econometric models. 3. United States - Politics and government - 1945- - Econometric models. I. Lowery, David. II. Title.
HJ257.2 .B47 1987

Bers, Günter, 1940- Der I. Kongress der Revolutionären Gewerkschafts-Opposition (RGO) im Bezirk Mittelrhein (Raum Aachen-Köln-Koblenz) im Jahre 1930 /. Reinbek , c1982. 136 p. : ISBN 3-88756-024-8 : LC Card 84-135308
HD6699.R47 I18 1982

Bersutskiĭ, ĪA. G. (ĪAkov Grigor′evich) Informatsionnaia sistema upravleniia predpriiatiem / ĪA.G. Bersutskiĭ. Kiev : Nauk. dumka, 1986. 166 p. : ill. ; 20 cm. At head of title: Akademiia nauk Ukrainskoĭ SSR. Institut ėkonomiki promyshlennosti. Bibliography: p. 162-[165] LC Card 86-214727
1. Industrial management - Information services. 2. Industrial management - Data processing. I. Title.
HD30.35 .B47 1986

Bertalan, László. Economy and society in Hungary /. Budapest , 1986. 331 p. : LC Card 87-147704 DDC 330.9439/053 19
HC300.28 .E36 1986

Bertalanfy, Béla. 200 éves a borsodi szénbányászat, 1786-1986 /. [Miskolc , 1986] 223 p. : ISBN 963-02-4565-5 (Magy. nemz. bibl.) LC Card 87-150976
HD9555.H83 B6715 1986

Bertelè, Umberto. Un modello interpretativo dell'import-export italiano, 1970-1983 / di Umberto Bertelè. Bologna : Il Mulino, c1985. 172 p. : ill. ; 22 cm. (Quaderni de "L'Industria" . 25) Bibliography: p. 127-129. ISBN 88-15-00919-1 : LC Card 86-176592
1. Italy - Commerce - Econometric models. I. Series: Quaderni de L'Industria (Società editrice Il Mulino) , 25. II. Title.
HF3586.5 .B47 1985

Berthélemy, Jean-Claude. La théorie des transferts internationaux / Jean-Claude Berthélemy ; préface de Bernard Lassudrie-Duchêne. Paris : Economica, c1986. ix, 225 p. : ill. ; 24 cm. (Collection Approfondissement de la connaissance économique) Originally presented as the author's thesis (doctoral--Université de Paris I) Bibliography: p. [205]-220. ISBN 2-7178-0982-1 : LC Card 86-176393
1. Balance of payments. 2. International finance. I. Title.
HG3882 .B48 1986

Berthelin, E. (Egmont), 1807-1860. Chemin de fer de Paris à Lyon par Troyes et Dijon : lettres à M. le comte Daru, pair de France, en réponse au rapport par lui présenté au nom d'une sous-commission à la commission supérieure instituée par décision royale du 22 juin 1843, à l'effet de donner son avis sur le choix à faire entre les différents tracés pour l'établissement des grandes lignes de chemins de fer classées par la loi du 11 juin 1842 / par E. Berthelin. Troyes : Anner-André, 1843. 54, [2] p. ; 21 cm. "Appendice: le projet de passage du chemin de fer par Montbard et le Sombernon jugé par le comité de l'Yonne que préside M. le marquis de Louvois": 2 p. at end. Includes bibliographical references. LC Card 85-665948
1. Railroads - France. I. Daru, M. le comte (Napoléon), 1807-1890. II. Title.
HE3068 .B47x 1843

Berthiaume, Nicole, 1952- Rouyn-Noranda : le développement d'une agglomération minière au coeur de l'Abitibi-Témiscamingue / Nicole Berthiaume. Rouyn [Québec] : Collège du Nord-Ouest, Cahiers du Département d'histoire et de géographie, 1981. xiii, 169 p. : ill. ; 23 cm. (Cahiers du Département d'histoire et de géographie. Monographies) Bibliography: p. 161-168. ISBN 2-89073-103-0 LC Card 83-132846
1. Mineral industries - Québec (Province) - Rouyn. 2. Rouyn (Québec) - Economic conditions. I. Title. II. Series.
HD9524.C23 R683 1981

Berthomieu, Claude. Structure industrielle et sous-traitance /. Paris , c1983. 243 p. : ISBN 2-13-038182-0 : LC Card 84-128203 DDC 331/.01 19
HD2381 .S77 1983 ***NYPL [JLE 86-1624]***

Berti, Humberto Calderón. see Calderón Berti, Humberto.

Bertin, Corrado. L'Affiliazione commerciale . Milano , 1986. 100 p. : ***NYPL [JLD 87-531]***

Bertini, Vanni. Il Pappagallo giallo . [Pisa] , Firenze , c1986. 194 p., [1] leaf of plates : LC Card 86-212573
HD9780.I82 P37 1986

Bertoni, Alberto. Il Leasing e il mercato del credito in Italia /. [Milano] [1984] iv, 82 p. : ISBN 88-14-00263-0 (pbk.) : LC Card 84-250907
HD39.4 .L37 1984 ***NYPL [JLE 87-509]***

Bertot, Cathey H. The new financial planner : a guide to client service / Cathey H. Bertot. Homewood, Ill. : Dow Jones-Irwin, c1986. xvi, 266 p. : ill. ; 24 cm. Includes index. ISBN 0-87094-587-4 LC Card 85-52442 DDC 332.024/01 19
1. Finance, Personal - United States. 2. Investments - United States. I. Title.
HG179 .B458 1986 ***NYPL [JLE 87-537]***

Bertran i Roigé, Prim. Noves aportacions sobre la repoblació de Verdú en el centenari de la seva carta de Franquesa (1184-1984) / per Prim Bertran i Roigé. Lleida : Institut d'Estudis Ilerdencs, Diputació Provincial de Lleida, Cátedra de Cultura Catalana "Samuel Gili e Gaya", 1984. 23 p., [1] leaf of plates : 1 facsim. ; 24 cm. "Apendix documental" (in Catalan and Latin): p. [11]-17. Includes bibliographical references. ISBN 84-00-05783-X LC Card 86-140657
1. Land tenure - Spain - Verdú - History - Sources. 2. Verdu (Spain) - History - Sources. I. Title.
HD780.V44 B47 1984

Bertrand, Catherine. Charbit, Yves. Enfants, familles, migrations dans le bassin méditerranéen /. [Paris] , 1985. viii, 195 p. ; ISBN 2-7332-0110-7 (pbk.)
HQ792.E8 C47 1985
NYPL [JLL 72-295 cahier no 110]

Bertuglia, Cristoforo Sergio. L'Analisi degli insediamenti umani e produttivi /. Milano, Italy , c1984. 295 p. : LC Card 84-179265 DDC 330.945/0928 19
HC305 .A6618 1984 ***NYPL [JLD 86-3298]***

Berücksichtigung der zentralen Orte im kommunalen Finanzausgleich Bayern . Leibfritz, Willi. München , 1986. vi, 151 p. : ISBN 3-88512-018-6 LC Card 86-172605
HJ9493.5.B38 L45 1986

Die Berücksichtigung des Geldes und der Banken als gesellschaftliche Institutionen in der Property Rights-Theorie /. Gesswein, Joachim P., 1955- München , c1986. vi, 309 p. ; ISBN 3-88259-374-1 LC Card 86-172234
HB711 .G47 1986

Berücksichtigung von Verbraucherinteressen bei staatlichen Anbietern / Klaus Deimer ... [et al.]. Frankfurt ; New York : Campus, c1984. x, 241 p. : ill. ; 21 cm. (Campus Forschung. Bd. 363.) ISBN 3-593-33291-4 LC Card 84-147664
1. Consumer protection - Germany, West. 2. Consumers - Germany, West. I. Deimer, Klaus.
HC290.5.C63 B47 1984

Beruf + Bildung .
(Bd. 9) Koeder, Kurt W. Berufsbegleitendes Studium . Grafenau/Württ. , c1983. 286 p. : ISBN 3-88508-901-7 LC Card 84-185882
HD5715 .K63 1983

Berufe der Wirtschaftsinformatik in der Schweiz / Autoren, Peter Albrecht ... [et al.] ; Herausgeber, SVD Schweizerische Vereinigung für Datenverarbeitung, VDF Verband der Datenverarbeitungs-Fachleute. Zürich : Verlag der Fachvereine an den Schweizerischen Hochschulen u. Techniken ; Stuttgart : C.E. Poeschel, 1986. 83 p. : ill. ; 30 cm. ISBN 3-7281-1499-5 : LC Card 86-182797
1. Electronic data processing personnel - Switzerland - Job descriptions. 2. Electronic data processing personnel - Job descriptions. I. Albrecht, Peter. II. Schweizerische Vereinigung für Datenverarbeitung. III. Verband der Datenverarbeitungs-Fachleute (Switzerland).
HD8039.D372 S953 1986

Berufliche Integration junger Türken . Arnold-Rösner, Regina. Hamburg , 1986. 122 p. : ISBN 3-925408-05-3 LC Card 86-223625
HD8458.T9 A76 1986

Berufliche Motivation und berufliches Verhalten . Kraak, Bernhard. Göttingen , c1984. i, 145 p. ; ISBN 3-8017-0218-9 LC Card 85-100278
HF5549.5.M63 K73 1984

Berufliche Weiterbildung, Arbeitsmarkt und Region . Dobischat, Rolf, 1950- Frankfurt am Main , New York , c1985. 691 p. : ISBN 3-8204-5673-2 LC Card 86-158931
HD5715.5.G42 H473 1985

Berufs- und Weiterbildung 1984/85 : die Berufs- und Weiterbildungsarbeit der Industrie- und Handelskammern / [Redaktion, Joachim Häussler ... et al.]. Bonn : Deutscher Industrie- und Handelstag, 1985. 201 p. : ill. ; 21 cm. (DIHT, 0175-713X . 224) LC Card 86-171726
1. Employees, Training of - Germany, West. I. Häussler, Joachim. II. Series: DIHT (Series) , 224.
HF5549.5.T7 B488 1985

Berufsbegleitendes Studium . Koeder, Kurt W. Grafenau/Württ. , c1983. 286 p. : ISBN 3-88508-901-7 LC Card 84-185882
HD5715 .K63 1983

Berufsbiographien im Wandel / Hanns-Georg Brose (Hrsg.). Opladen : Westdeutscher Verlag, c1986. 290 p. ; 23 cm. Includes bibliographies. ISBN 3-531-11817-X LC Card 86-227301
1. Vocational guidance - Germany, West. 2. Vocational interests - Germany, West. I. Brose, Hanns-Georg, 1945-.
HF5382.5.G3 B39 1986

Berufsqualifikation und Berufschancen von Frauen in der Bundesrepublik Deutschland /. Hegelheimer, Barbara. Berlin , 1977. viii, 303 p. ; LC Card 85-142052
HD6059.6.G4 H428 1977

Berufsverläufe von Frauen . Workshop "Berufswege von Frauen" (1984 : Berlin, Germany) München , Weinheim , c1986. 291 p. : ISBN 3-87966-253-3 LC Card 87-407975 DDC 331.7/02/024042 19
HF5382.67.G3 W67 1984

Berufswahl und berufliche Interessen /. Allehoff, Wolfgang H., 1949- Göttingen , c1985. 177 p. : ISBN 3-8017-0217-0 LC Card 85-235199
HF5381.5 .A45 1985

Berufswahlfreiheit und Kultur . Mueller, H. Dieter (Heinz Dieter), 1952- München , c1986. 276, [46] p. ; ISBN 3-89019-166-5 LC Card 87-124783 DDC 331.11/72/0943 19
HD4903.5.G4 M84 1986

Beruházási árindexek, 1968-1971 / [készült a KSH Beruházási és Építőipari Statisztikai Főosztályán]. [Budapest] : Központi Statisztikai Hivatal, [1972] 56 p. ; 29 cm. (Statisztikai időszaki közlemények . 273. köt.) "1972. december 19." Chiefly tables. LC Card 86-189972
1. Prices - Hungary - Statistics. 2. Industrial equipment - Prices - Hungary - Statistics. I. Hungary. Központi Statisztikai Hivatal. Beruházási és Építőipari Statisztikai Főosztály. II. Series.
HB235.H8 B48 1972

A beruházások döntéselőkészítése /. Barta, Imre. Budapest , 1986. 185, [1] p. : ISBN 963-05-4182-3 : LC Card 87-408029
HG4028.C4 B335 1986

Beruházások és állóeszközök a mezőgazdaságban, 1981-1985 / [készült a Központi Statisztikai Hivatal Mezőgazdasági Statisztikai Főosztályának Agrárgazdasági Osztályán]. Budapest : Központi Statisztikai Hivatal, 1987. 90 p. ; 29 cm. Chiefly tables. ISBN 963-02-4805-0 LC Card 87-409593
1. Agriculture - Hungary - Capital investments - Statistics. 2. Agriculture - Hungary - Finance - Statistics. I. Hungary. Központi Statisztikai Hivatal. Agrárgazdasági Osztály.
HD1940.5 .B474 1987

Besançon, France. Université.
Annales littéraires. For additional listing of contents, see Old Catalog. // Occasional vols. numbered also in one of several subseries. Cahiers d'études Archéologie [Besanç, France]; Centre de recherches d'histoire et littérature au XVIIIe et au XIXe siècles. [Publication]; Centre de recherches de littérature française (XIXe et XXe siècles). [Publication]

(326) Moss, Bernard H. [Origins of the French labor movement, 1830-1914. French.] Aux origines du mouvement ouvrier français . Paris , 1985. xi, 236 p. ; ISBN 2-251-60326-3
NYPL [M-10 6410 n.326]

Besanko, David, 1955- Designing regulatory policy with limited information / David Besanko and David E.M. Sappington. Chur, Switzerland ; New York : Harwood Academic Publishers, c1987. viii, 80 p. : ill. ; 22 cm. (Fundamentals of pure and applied economics, 0191-1708 . v. 20.) Bibliography: p. 71-76. Includes index. ISBN 3-7186-0385-3 (pbk.) LC Card 87-277 DDC 351.82/6 19
1. Trade regulation - Economic aspects - Mathematical models. 2. Monopolies - Mathematical models. 3. Monopolies - Government policy - Mathematical models. I. Sappington, David Edward Michael. II. Series: Fundamentals of pure and applied economics , v 20. III. Title.
HD3612 .B47 1987

Beschädigtes Leben . Alheit, Peter. Frankfurt[/Main] , New York , c1986. 361 p. ; ISBN 3-593-33606-5 LC Card 86-148737
HD6276.G4 A44 1986

Beschäftigung, Verteilung und Konjunktur : zur politischen Ökonomik der modernen Gesellschaft : Festschrift für Adolph Lowe / herausgegeben von Harald Hagemann und Heinz D. Kurz. Bremen : [s.n.] : Vertrieb, Universität Bremen, Presse und Informationsamt, 1984. 276 p. : ill. ; 24 cm. German or English. Includes bibliographies. ISBN 3-88722-088-9 : LC Card 85-176579
1. Economics. 2. Economics - Methodology. 3. Economic policy. 4. Lowe, Adolph, 1893-. I. Lowe, Adolph, 1893-. II. Hagemann, Harald. III. Kurz, Heinz-Dieter.
HB175 .B49 1984

Beschäftigungsentwicklung und Qualifikationsstruktur in Berlin 1977-1983 . Albrecht, Christoph, 1950- Berlin [1985] 2 v. : LC Card 86-204299
HD5780.B4 A43 1985

Beschastnyĭ, L. K. Ėkonomizat͡sii͡a nauki . Kiev , 1986. 221 p. ; LC Card 87-102107
HC337.U53 R44 1986

Die Beschlüsse des internationalen Eisenbahn-Congresses zu St. Petersburg nach dem am 20.-31. August 1892 angenommenen französischen Texte in getreuer deutscher Uebersetzung /. Leber, Maximilien, Edler von. Wien , 1893. 25 p. ; LC Card 85-666030
HE1005.I553 L4x 1893

Beschwerdemanagement /. Riemer, Martin. Frankfurt , New York , c1986. 295 p. ; ISBN 3-593-33756-8 LC Card 87-129210 DDC 658.8/12 19
HF5415.3 .R45 1986

Beskatningen af aktieafkast i Danmark og i det øvrige Vesteuropa / Industrirådets erhvervsøkonomiske afdeling. København : Industrirådets erhvervsøkonomiske afdeling, [1986] 23 p. ; 21 cm. (Erhvervsøkonomiske rapporter . nr. 5) ISBN 87-7353-047-6 LC Card 87-144435
1. Taxation of bonds, securities, etc. - Denmark. 2. Taxation of bonds, securities, etc. - Europe. I. Industrirådet (Denmark). Erhvervsøkonomiske afdeling. II. Series.
HJ5913.D4 B47 1986

Beskow, Paulo Roberto. O arrendamento capitalista na agricultura : evolução e situação atual da economia do arroz no Rio Grande do Sul / Paulo Roberto Beskow. São Paulo : Editora HUCITEC ; Brasília : Conselho Nacional de Desenvolvimento Científico e Tecnológico, 1986. 219 p. : ill. ; 21 cm. (Estudos rurais) Bibliography: p. 179-182. LC Card 86-229665
1. Rice trade - Brazil - Rio Grande do Sul - History. 2. Farm tenancy - Brazil - Rio Grande do Sul - History. I. Title. II. Series.
HD9066.B83 R463 1986

Beskrivende økonomi / Palle Bruus ... [et al.] ; redigeret af Erik Møllmann Bøye. [Copenhagen] : Jurist- og økonomforbundet, c1985-c1986. 2 v. (810 p.) : ill. ; 24 cm. Includes bibliographies and index. ISBN 87-574-4652-0 (set) LC Card 86-159064
1. Economics. 2. Economics - Denmark. I. Bruus, Palle. II. Møllmann Boye, Erik.
HB179.D8 B47 1986

Besluitvorming : wat weten wij ervan? : opstellen / verzameld door P. Lebelle en Sj. Muller. Deventer : Kluwer, 1986. 151 p. : ill. ; 25 cm. Includes bibliographies. ISBN 90-267-1065-8 LC Card 86-201119
1. Decision-making. I. Lebelle, P. II. Muller, S.
HD30.23 .B476 1986

Best, Fred. Reducing workweeks to prevent layoffs : the economic and social impacts of unemployment insurance supported work sharing / Fred Best ; foreword by Herbert Gans. Philadelphia : Temple University Press, 1988. p. cm. (Labor and social change) Includes index. ISBN 0-87722-506-0 LC Card 87-10097 DDC 331.25/72 19
1. Work sharing. 2. Insurance, Unemployment. I. Title. II. Series.
HD5110.5 .B467 1988

The Best of Japan. 1st ed. Tokyo : Kodansha ; New York, N.Y., U. S.A. : Distributed in the U. S. by Kodansha International/USA through Harper & Row, 1987. 288, xiv p. : ill. (some col.) ; 28 cm. Includes index. ISBN 0-87011-801-3 (U. S. : pbk.) : LC Card 86-40432 DDC 338.4/7/000952 19
1. New products - Japan - Awards. 2. Design - Japan - Awards.
HF5415.153 .B47 1987

The Best of This world / edited and with an introduction by Michael A. Scully. Lanham, MD : University Press of America, c1986. x, 405 p. ; 24 cm. "Co-published by arrangement with the Institute for Educational Affairs, Inc."--Verso t.p. ISBN 0-8191-5605-1 (alk. paper) : LC Card 86-22411 DDC 261.8 19
1. Catholic Church - Doctrines. 2. Economics - Religious aspects. 3. Peace - Religious aspects - Catholic Church. 4. War - Religious aspects - Catholic Church. I. Scully, Michael A. II. Institute for Educational Affairs (New York, N.Y.). III. This world.
HB72 .B5 1987 ***NYPL [JFE 86-5571]***

Die Bestimmung des Produktionspotentials in Theorie und Empirie . Kudiss, Reinhard, 1952- Frankfurt am Main , New York , c1984. xvi, 198 p. : ISBN 3-8204-5579-5 LC Card 85-189908
HB3730 .K766 1984

Bestimmungsfaktoren der Energiepolitik in der Bundesrepublik Deutschland . Rehfeld, Dieter, 1951- Frankfurt am Main , New York , c1986. vii, 287 p. ; ISBN 3-8204-9354-9 LC Card 86-194761
HD9502.G42 R44 1986

Bestimmungsgründe industrieller Direktinvestitionen /. Krist, Herbert. Berlin , c1985. 310 p. : ISBN 3-924859-01-9 LC Card 86-225379
HG4538 .K72 1985

Bestimmungsgründe kurzfristiger Wechselkursfluktuationen . Heri, Erwin W. Hamburg , 1982. v, 312 p. : ISBN 3-87895-225-2 LC Card 83-200160 DDC 332.4/5 19
HG3852 .H47 1982

Bestimmungsgründe von Zahlungsbilanz und Wechselkursen in der Bundesrepublik Deutschland /. Fleischer, Peter. Frankfurt am Main , New York , c1986. iv, 181 p. : ISBN 3-8204-9610-6 LC Card 86-232901
HG3883.G3 F57 1986

Best's municipal underwriting guide : the public official's guide to local government insurance risks. Oldwick, N.J. (Ambest Rd., Oldwick 08858) : A.M. Best Co., c1986. 1 v. (various pagings) : ill. ; 30 cm. Prepared by the staff of the Underwriting-Loss Control Dept. LC Card 86-230785 DDC 368 19
1. Insurance, Government risks - United States. I. A.M. Best Company. Underwriting-Loss Control Dept.
HG8210 .B47 1986

Bestyrelsens idégrundlag og funktion /. Langebæk, Steen. København , 1985. 175 p. ; ISBN 87-12-01597-0 : LC Card 86-156403
HD70.D4 L36 1985

Beta Alpha Psi, from Omega to Zeta Omega . Sheldahl, Terry K. New York , 19. xxiii, 851 p., [22] p. of plates : ISBN 0-8240-7855-1 (alk. paper) : LC Card 86-31800 DDC 657/.06/073 19
HF5601.B443 S54 1986

BETA ALPHA PSI - HISTORY.
Sheldahl, Terry K. Beta Alpha Psi, from Omega to Zeta Omega . New York , 19. xxiii, 851 p., [22] p. of plates : ISBN 0-8240-7855-1 (alk. paper) : LC Card 86-31800 DDC 657/.06/073 19
HF5601.B443 S54 1986

Betænkning om et øget dansk tv-udbud. Denmark. Mediekommissionen. [København] , 1983. 168 p. : ISBN 87-503-4624-5 LC Card 85-128700
HE8700.9.D4 D45 1983

Betænkning om principperne for den danske bistand til udviklingslandene /. Denmark. Udvalget vedrørende dansk bistandspolitik. København , 1982. 224 p. ; ISBN 87-503-4037-9 LC Card 84-103068
HC60 .D435 1982

Betaling, waardepapier en documentair krediet /. Empel, G. van. Deventer , 1985. viii, 84 p. ; ISBN 90-268-1565-4 : LC Card 85-214764
HG173.6.D8 E46 1985

Betancur, Belisario, 1923- Un semáforo en rojo : palabras del presidente Betancur en la instalación del seminario internacional patrocinado por la Fundación del Tercer Mundo y la Universidad Nacional de Colombia, Cartagena, Colombia, febrero 23 de 1984. [Bogotá] : Secretaría de Información y Prensa de la Presidencia de la República, [1984] 12, 12, 12 p. ; 28 cm. English, French, and Spanish. Cover title. At head of title: El orden económico internacional. LC Card 87-125515 DDC 338.98 19
1. Latin America - Economic policy. 2. Developing countries - Economic policy. I. Colombia. Presidencia de la República. Secretaría de Información y Prensa. II. Title.
HC125 .B42 1984

Betcherman, Gordon. Working with technology : a survey of automation in Canada / Gordon Betcherman, Kathryn McMullen. [Ottawa] : Economic Council of Canada : Canadian Govt. Pub. Centre, Supply and Services Canada [distributor], 1986. 43 p. : ill. ; 17 x 25 cm. ISBN 0-660-12174-3 (pbk.) : LC Card 86-224095 DDC 338/.06 19
1. Automation - Economic aspects - Canada - Statistics. 2. Canada - Industries - Statistics. 3. Technological innovations - Economic aspects - Canada - Statistics. I. McMullen, Kathryn Elizabeth. II. Title.
HC120.A9 B47 1986

Beteiligung im Industriebetrieb . Fricke, Werner. Frankfurt/Main , New York , c1985. 291 p. ; ISBN 3-593-32735-X LC Card 85-202742
HD5660.G4 F73 1985

Beteiligungs- und Fusionsvorhaben . Hörnig, Bodo. Berlin , c1985. xvi, 357 p. : ISBN 3-428-05786-4 LC Card 85-168610
HD2746.5 .H67 1985

Beteiligungsgesellschaft für Gemeinwirtschaft (Germany) Basler, Hans-Peter. Lohnentwicklung und Lohnpolitik als Bestimmungsgründe konjunktureller Verläufe und struktureller Verschiebungen . Berlin , 1981. 102 p. : ISBN 3-428-04970-5 LC Card 82-100546 DDC 330 s 331.2/943 19
HB41 .B4 Nr. 134 HD5029
NYPL [JLL 73-207 Heft 134]

Bethge, Hans, 1951- Die betriebliche Altersversorgung als Möglichkeit zur Deckung von Versorgungslücken in der gesetzlichen Rentenversicherung unter besonderer Berücksichtigung unternehmerischer Entscheidungsgrössen / Hans Bethge. Köln : Müller Botermann, c1986. 269 p. ; 21 cm. (Reihe Personalwesen, Organisation, Unternehmungsführung . Bd. 2) Bibliography: p. 255-269. ISBN 3-924361-16-9 LC Card 86-222067
1. Pension trusts - Germany, West. 2. Pension trusts - Law and legislation - Germany (West). I. Title. II. Series.
HD7105.45.G3 B47 1986

Bethke, Klaus W. Small projects for rural development : selection and formulation guidelines / Klaus W. Bethke. [Nairobi] : Republic of Kenya, Ministry of Finance and Planning, [1983] 33, [34] leaves ; 30 cm. "Prepared within the context of ongoing activities of the Rural Planning Division of the Ministry of Finance and Planning, Kenya." "December 1983." Bibliography: leaf [34]. LC Card 86-981325 DDC 354.676/20082 19
1. Economic development projects - Kenya - Planning. 2. Economic development projects - Kenya - Evaluation. 3. Rural development projects - Kenya - Planning. 4. Rural development projects - Kenya -

Evaluation. I. Kenya. Ministry of Finance and Planning. Rural Planning Division. II. Title.
HC865 .B48 1983

BETHLEHEM STEEL CORPORATION - HISTORY.
Leary, Thomas E., 1946- From fire to rust . Buffalo, N.Y. , c1987. 134 p. : ISBN 0-939032-00-7 (pbk.) LC Card 87-692 DDC 338.7/669142/0974796 19
HD9519.L2 L43 1987

Strohmeyer, John, 1924- Crisis in Bethlehem . New York, N.Y., U. S.A. , 1987, c1986. xii, 244 p. ; ISBN 0-14-010370-8 (pbk.) LC Card 87-11835 DDC 338.7/669142/0974822 19
HD9519.B4 S87 1987

BETHLEHEM STEEL CORPORATION - PERSONNEL MANAGEMENT - CASE STUDIES.
Copeland, Vincent. The blast furnace brothers /. New York, N.Y. , 1973. iv, 33 p. : LC Card 87-125932 DDC 331.13/3 19
HD4903.3.B582 U63 1973

Bethlen, Stefan, Graf, 1946- Vollbeschäftigung, eine Utopie? /. Bern , c1986. 330 p. : ISBN 3-258-03567-9 LC Card 86-224133
HD5779 .V64 1986

Bethmann, Johann Philipp, Freiherr von, 1924- Die Zinskatastrophe : das Buch zur Krise / Johann Philipp Freiherr von Bethmann.6., erw. Aufl. Konigstein/Ts. : Athenäum, c1985. 142 p. ; 21 cm. Bibliography: verso t.p. ISBN 3-7610-8390-4 : LC Card 86-139624
1. Interest rates. 2. Monetary policy. I. Title.
HG1621 .B48 1985

Betraying the national interest /. Lappé, Frances Moore. New York , 1987, c1986. p. cm. ISBN 0-8021-0012-0 LC Card 87-12067 DDC 338.91 19
HC60 .L325 1987

Die betriebliche Altersversorgung als Möglichkeit zur Deckung von Versorgungslücken in der gesetzlichen Rentenversicherung unter besonderer Berücksichtigung unternehmerischer Entscheidungsgrössen /. Bethge, Hans, 1951- Köln , c1986. 269 p. ; ISBN 3-924361-16-9 LC Card 86-222067
HD7105.45.G3 B47 1986

Betriebliche Altersversorgung in mittelständischen Unternehmen /. Schmidt, Axel. Stuttgart , c1985. xiii, 213 p. : ISBN 3-7910-5004-4 : LC Card 86-164220
HD7105.35.G3 S35 1985
NYPL [JLL 73-505 Nr. 3]

Das betriebliche Ausbildungswesen in der Zeit der industriellen Umgestaltung Deutschlands /. Rinneberg, Karl-Jürgen. Köln , 1985. xvi, 481 p. : ISBN 3-412-02885-1 LC Card 86-121691
HF5549.5.T7 R486 1985

Betriebliche Erfahrungen mit neuen Arbeitszeitformen . Burian, Klaus. Berlin [1984] iv, 162 p. ; LC Card 84-182592
HD5110.2.G3 B87 1984

Betriebliche Finanzwirtschaft als monetäres System /. Benner, Wolfgang, 1940- Göttingen , 1983. 486 p. : ISBN 3-509-01323-9 LC Card 83-240817
HG4011 .B433 1983

Betriebliche Informations- und Kommunikationssysteme .
(Bd. 5) Knoop, Jens. Online-Kostenrechnung für die CIM-Planung . Berlin , c1986. 242 p. : ISBN 3-503-02569-3 LC Card 86-227596
HF5686.C8 K5835 1986

Betriebliche Kooperation mit Unternehmen in Entwicklungsländern .
(4) Kooperationsführer Kamerun /. Köln , 1986. 70 p. : LC Card 87-408425 DDC 330.967/1104 19
HC995 .K66 1986

Betriebs- und Wirtschaftsinformatik .
(11) Mülder, Wilhelm. Organisatorische Implementierung von computergestützten Personalinformationssystemen . Berlin , New York , 1984. xix, 257 p. : ISBN 0-387-13360-7 (U. S.) LC Card 84-238144
HF5549.5.D37 M85 1984

(19) Schumann, Matthias. Eingangspostbearbeitung in Bürokommunikationssystemen . Berlin , New York , c1987. xi, 156 p. ; ISBN 0-387-17369-2 (U. S.) LC Card 87-133887 DDC 651.7/59 19
HF5547 .S457 1987

Betriebs-Kurier. Schriftenreihe .
(56/56a) Was ist bei der Teilzeitbeschäftigung zu beachten? /. Wien , 1985. 64 p. ; LC Card 86-210129
HD5110.2.A9 W37 1985

BETRIEBSKRANKENKASSE HENKEL (DÜSSELDORF, GERMANY)
Schöne, Manfred, 1935- Ein Vierteljahrhundert Betriebskrankenkasse Henkel, Düsseldorf /. [Düsseldorf] , 1977. 60 p. : LC Card 86-216782
HG9399.G33 B477 1977

Betriebsnahe Tarifpolitik zur Stärkung der gewerkschaftlichen Basis /. Kulke, Ulrich. Berlin , 1977. 108 p. ; ISBN 3-88114-215-0 : LC Card 80-489437
HD6694 .K82 ***NYPL [JLD 81-350]***

Betriebsräte und sozialer Wandel in Österreich 1919/1920 . Garamvölgyi, Judit. München , c1983. 296 p. ; ISBN 3-486-51721-X LC Card 83-240283
HD5660.A8 G37 1983

Betriebswirtschaftliche Abhandlungen .
(n.F., Bd. 60) Döring, Ulrich. Kostensteuern, der Einfluss von Steuern auf kurzfristige Produktions- und Absatzentscheidungen /. Stuttgart , c1984. x, 228 p. ; ISBN 3-7910-0369-0 LC Card 86-134925
HD2753.G3 D73 1984

(n.F., Bd. 62) Möller, Hans Peter. Bilanzkennzahlen und Ertragsrisiken des Kapitalmarktes . Stuttgart , 1986. xii, 240 p. : ISBN 3-7910-0382-8 LC Card 86-149711
HF5681.C25 M64 1986

(n.F., Bd. 64) Haupt, Reinhard. Produktionstheorie und Ablaufmanagement . Stuttgart , c1987. xiv, 217 p. : ISBN 3-7910-0398-4 LC Card 87-134161 DDC 338.6 19
HB241 .H37 1987

Betriebswirtschaftliche Beiträge zu Energie-, Rohstoff- und Umweltfragen, 0721-2933 .
(Bd. 3) Püschel, Manfred, 1953- Die Wahl der optimalen Wärmeversorgungskonfiguration als betriebswirtschaftliches Produktions- und Investitionsproblem /. Frankfurt am Main , New York , c1984. iv, 298 p. : ISBN 3-8204-7432-3 LC Card 86-108875
HD30.25 .P87 1984

Betriebswirtschaftliche Entscheidungen bei Stagnation : Edmund Heinen zum 65. Geburtstag / herausgegeben von Ludwig Pack und Dietrich Börner, unter Mitwirkung von Dietrich Börner ... [et al.]. Wiesbaden : Gabler, c1984. xvi, 327 p. : ill. ; 25 cm. List of works by E. Heinen: p. 321-327. ISBN 3-409-13303-8 LC Card 84-197990
1. Industrial management - Decision making. 2. Heinen, Edmund. I. Heinen, Edmund. II. Pack, Ludwig. III. Börner, Dietrich.
HD30.23 .B486 1984

Betriebswirtschaftliche Ergebnisse von Gartenbaubetrieben 1984 / Land- und Forstwirtschaftliche Landes-Buchführungs-Gesellschaft m.b.H. (LBG) in Wien ; [für den Inhalt verantwortlich, Wolfgang Schosserer]. Wien : LBG, 1985. 13 p. ; 30 cm. LC Card 86-194865
1. Horticultural products industry - Austria - Statistics. I. Schosserer, Wolfgang. II. Land- und Forstwirtschaftliche Landes-Buchführungs-Gesellschaft.
HD9015.A8 B47 1985

Betriebswirtschaftliche Erkenntnisse für Regierung, Verwaltung und öffentliche Unternehmen : 25 Jahre Öffentliche Betriebswirstschaftslehre an der Universität Mannheim / Peter Eichhorn (Hrsg.).1. Aufl. Baden-Baden : Nomos, 1985. 266 p. : ill. ; 23 cm. (Schriften zur öffentlichen Verwaltung und öffentlichen Wirtschaft. Bd. 85) Papers presented at a Symposium held Nov. 17-18, 1983 at the Fakultät für Betriebswirtschaftslehre of the Universität Mannheim. Summary in English and German. Bibliography: p. 253-261. Includes indexes. ISBN 3-7890-1104-5 LC Card 85-213984
1. Finance, Public - Accounting - Congresses. 2. Business - Congresses. 3. Government business enterprises - Accounting - Congresses. I. Eichhorn, Peter, 1939-. II. Universität Mannheim. Fakultät für Betriebswirtschaftslehre.
HJ9705 .B48 1985

Betriebswirtschaftliche Forschung und Wirtschaftspraxis . Marzen, Walter. Spardorf , c1986. ix, 229 p. ; ISBN 3-922919-82-0 LC Card 87-133392 DDC 658.4 19
HD35 .M276 1986

Betriebswirtschaftliche Forschungsbeiträge .
(Bd. 12) Zeitler, Isabella, 1956- Internationales Bankgeschäft als Problem der Bankenaufsicht /. München , c1984. viii, 353 p. : LC Card 85-103322
HG3881 .Z4 1984

(Bd. 14) Sauter, Franz, 1956- Transaktionskostentheorie der Organisation /. München , c1985. iv, 187, 2 p. : ISBN 3-89003-013-0 LC Card 85-194969
HB846.3 .S28 1985

(Bd. 15) Volkmann, Helmut, 1936- Der Informationsmarkt . München , c1985. 366 p. : ISBN 3-89003-016-5 LC Card 85-195750
HD35 .V596 1985

(Bd. 16) Hilfer, Rudolf. Stochastische Modelle für die betriebliche Planung /. München , c1985. ii, 191 p. : ISBN 3-89003-015-7 LC Card 85-189343
HD30.25 .H55 1985

(Bd. 21) Conen, Dieter, 1951- Wirkung von Werbesprache . München , c1985. iii, 162 p., [7] p. of plates : ISBN 3-89003-021-1 LC Card 86-159595
HF5822 .C58 1985

(Bd. 3) Berndt, Hermann, 1956- Konsumentscheidung und Informationsüberlastung . München , c1983. 368 p. : ISBN 3-89003-002-5 LC Card 84-192993
HF5821 .B42 1983

Betriebswirtschaftliche Forschungsergebnisse (Frankfurt am Main, Germany) .
(Bd. 2) Haueisen, Peter, 1955- Unmittelbare Versorgungszusage und Direktversicherung als Gestaltungsformen der betrieblichen Altersversorgung /. Frankfurt am Main , New York , c1983. xx, 297 p. : ISBN 3-8204-7592-3 LC Card 86-107083 DDC 331.25/2/0943 19
HD7105.35.G3 H38 1983

Betriebswirtschaftliche Kennzahlen . Geiss, Wilfried. Frankfurt am Main , New York , c1986. 405 p. : ISBN 3-8204-9629-7 LC Card 87-407301 DDC 657/.42 19
HF5686.C8 G384 1986

Betriebswirtschaftliche Schriftenreihe .
(Bd. 1) Barrmeyer, Martin-Christian. Die Angebotsplanung bei Submission /. Münster [1982?] xii, 198 p. : ISBN 3-88660-081-5 : LC Card 83-227153
HD2365 .B36 1982

(Bd. 10) Schlangen, Gerhard. Die Systematik der unternehmerischen Sicherungsmassnahmen /. Münster [1984?] vii, 179 p. : ISBN 3-88660-063-7 LC Card 84-166733
HD61 .S34 1984

(Bd. 11) Galts, Helmut. Ungewissheit und Planungsmethodik . Münster [1983] vi, 234 p. : ISBN 3-88660-143-9 LC Card 84-178712
HB615 .G35 1983

(Bd. 12) Kiffe, Ulrich. Die Klassifizierung in der Bundesrepublik Deutschland angebotener Personenkraftwagen mit multivariaten Analysemethoden /. Münster , 1984. xx, 24, 340 p. : ISBN 3-88660-148-8 LC Card 84-208133
HD9710.G42 K48 1984

(Bd. 19) Busse, Dieter. Die Wirkungen von Sonderfahrstreifen für Busse auf die Fahrzeiten im Individualverkehr und öffentlichen Personenahverkehr . Münster [1985?] xii, 274 p. : ISBN 3-88660-264-8 LC Card 86-138804
HE363.G34 M933 1985

(Bd. 27) Kohrs-Barrmeyer, Andrea. Die Problematik der Informationsgewinnung und -verarbeitung bei der Bewertung von Sand- und Kiesabbaugelände /. Münster [1986] xviii, 379 p. : ISBN 3-88660-330-X LC Card 86-223939 DDC 622/.3622/068 19
HD9585.S162 K64 1986

(Bd. 28) Wöbbeking, Karlheinz. Die Planung von Liquidationsstrategien . Münster [1986] vii, 273 p. : ISBN 3-88660-328-8 LC Card

86-213801
HD2747 .W6 1986

(Bd. 31) Hergeth, Helmut H. A., 1956- Investitionsstrategien für stagnierende Branchen . Münster [1986?] xii, 261 p. : ISBN 3-88660-338-5 LC Card 87-134812 DDC 338.4/3677/00943 19
HD9863.5 .H39 1986

(Bd. 32) Schmelzeisen, Hans-Michael. Bedeutung, Einsatzmöglichkeiten und -probleme des kombinierten Güterverkehrs in der Ernährungswirtschaft /. Münster [1986] xii, 350 p. : ISBN 3-88660-357-1 (Deut. Bibl.) LC Card 87-121511 DDC 380.5/24 19
HE199.5.F6 S36 1986

(Bd. 33) Huellen, Karl Konrad. Die Motivation von Arbeitnehmern im Innen- und Aussendienst des Vertriebs . Münster [1986] iv, 245 p. : ISBN 3-88660-356-3 (Deut. Bibl.) LC Card 87-114821 DDC 658.3/14 19
HF5549.5.M63 H84 1986

(Bd. 6) Braehmer, Uwe. Nachrichtendiffusion in Grossunternehmen . Münster [1983?] 271 p. : ISBN 3-88660-090-0 LC Card 83-206152
HD30.3 .B69 1983

(Bd. 9) Hoberg, Peter. Investitionseinzelentscheidungen . Münster [1983?] xi, 244 p. : ISBN 3-88660-137-4 LC Card 84-132141
HG4515.2 .H63 1983

Betriebswirtschaftslehre des Post- und Fernmeldewesens /. Detjen, Günther, 1930- Gelsenkirchen-Buer , c1984-c1985. 2 v. : ISBN 3-87333-070-9 (Bd. 1) LC Card 87-104294 DDC 383/.4943 19
HE6995 .D37 1984

Betriebswirtschaftslehre in sozialer und ökologischer Dimension /. Pfriem, Reinhard. Frankfurt [am Main] , New York , c1983. 210 p. ; ISBN 3-593-33223-X LC Card 83-190294
HD35 .P45 1983

Betriebswirtschaftslehre und ökonomische Krise : kontroverse Beiträge zur betriebswirtschaftlichen Krisenbewältigung / herausgegeben von Wolfgang H. Staehle und Edgar Stoll ; mit inhaltlichen Beiträgen von Horst Albach ... [et al.]. Wiesbaden : Gabler, c1984. xxix, 412 p. : ill. ; 24 cm. Bibliography: p. 383-412. ISBN 3-409-13037-3 LC Card 85-143204
1. Industrial management - Decision making. 2. Business cycles. I. Staehle, Wolfgang H., 1938-. II. Stoll, Edgar, 1945-. III. Albach, Horst.
HD30.23 .B49 1984

Betriebswirtschaftstheorie /. Busse von Colbe, Walther. Berlin , New York , <c1986-. v. <3 > : ISBN 0-387-16407-3 (Bd. 3 : U. S.) LC Card 87-103759
HD35 .B88 1986

Better business guides.
Goodworth, Clive T. Effective delegation /. London , Brookfield, Vt., USA , 1985. 148 p. : ISBN 0-09-161781-2 (pbk.) : LC Card 86-204300 DDC 658.4/02 19
HD50 .G66 1985

Better, Nancy Marx. Salzman, Marian L. Wanted, liberal arts graduates . New York , 1987. xvi, 341 p. ; ISBN 0-385-24008-2 (pbk.) : LC Card 87-8846 DDC 650.1/4 19
HF5382.75.U6 S27 1987

Betteridge, Harold T. Cassell's German-English, English-German dictionary = Deutsch-englisches, englisch-deutsches Wörterbuch / completely revised by Harold T. Betteridge.Completely rev. and reset ed. New York : Macmillan, 1978. xx, 1580 p. ; 24 cm. ISBN 0-02-522920-6 (standard) LC Card 77-18452 DDC 433/.21 19
1. German language - Dictionaries - English. 2. English language - Dictionaries - German. I. Title. II. Title: Deutsch-englisches, englisch-deutsches Wörterbuch.
PF3640 .B453 1978
NYPL [*P-Desk 86-5858]

Bettio, Francesca. The sexual division of labour : the Italian case / Francesca Bettio. Oxford [Oxfordshire] : Clarendon Press ; New York : Oxford University Press, 1988. p. cm. Revision of thesis (Ph. D.)--University of Cambridge, 1984. Bibliography: p. Includes index. ISBN 0-19-828544-2 : LC Card 87-26353 DDC 305.4/3/00945 19
1. Sexual division of labor - Italy - History. 2. Sex discrimination against women - Italy - History. 3. Women - Employment - Italy - History. I. Title.
HD6060.65.I8 B47 1988

Between craft and class . Haydu, Jeffrey. Berkeley , c1988. p. cm. ISBN 0-520-06060-1 (alk. paper) LC Card 87-22169 DDC 322/.2/0941 19
HD8076 .H39 1988

Beurteilung der Wirtschaftlichkeitsschwelle und Analyse der Produktionskapazitäten bei neuen Technologien zur Energieeinsparung in mittelbis längerfristiger Sicht . Ziesing, Hans-Joachim. Berlin , 1983. 458 p. : ISBN 3-428-05497-0
NYPL [JLL 73-207 Bd. 139]

Die Beurteilung des Erfolgs von Bankprodukten als Grundlage produktpolitischer Entscheidungen /. Kilhey, Ulrike. Frankfurt am Main , c1987. xiv, 289 p. : ISBN 3-7819-0374-5 LC Card 87-136157 DDC 332.1/068/5 19
HF5415.15 .K55 1987

Beutler, Peter. Staatliche Wirtschaftsregulierung in der Krise . Opladen , c1986. 241 p. ; ISBN 3-531-11805-6 LC Card 86-228864
HD84 .S69 1986

Bevan, David. East African lessons on economic liberalization /. Aldershot, Hampshire, U.K. ; Brookfield, Vt., U. S.A. : xxi, 72 p. : ISBN 0-566-05337-3 (pbk.) : LC Card 86-29602 DDC 338.967 19
HC865 .E27 1987

BEVERAGE INDUSTRY - DIRECTORIES.
International Beverage Industry Exhibition & Congress (1986 : Dallas, Tex.) Registration list /. Washington, D.C. (1101-16th St., N.W., Washington 20036) , c1986. ca. 400 p. ; LC Card 87-107458 DDC 338.4/7663/025 19
HD9348.A2 I57 1986

BEVERAGE INDUSTRY - SEASONAL VARIATIONS - CONGRESSES.
Tripartite Technical Meeting for the Food Products and Drink Industries, 2d, Geneva, 1978. Labour and social problems arising out of seasonal fluctuations of the food products and drink industries /. Geneva , 1978. ii, 51 p. ; ISBN 92-2-101879-2 (pbk.) : LC Card 80-477150 DDC 331.2/0464
HD9000.1 .T75 1978a ***NYPL [JLE 80-1039]***

BEVERAGE INDUSTRY - SINGAPORE - HISTORY.
1883-1983, the great years. [Singapore] , 1983. 46 p. : LC Card 84-840800 DDC 338.7/663/095957 19
HD9348.S554 F715 1983

BEVERAGE INDUSTRY - STATISTICS.
Korb, Penelope. U. S. and world food, beverages, and tobacco expenditures, 1970-83 /. Washington, D.C. , 1986. iv, 84 p. : LC Card 86-603160 DDC 339.4/8664/0021 19
HD9000.4 .K67 1986

BEVERAGE INDUSTRY - SWITZERLAND.
Lebensmittel und Getränke aus der Schweiz =. Zürich , 1984. 113 p. : ISBN 0-390-92140-3
NYPL [JFE 86-3409]

BEVERAGE INDUSTRY - UNITED STATES - DIRECTORIES.
International Beverage Industry Exhibition & Congress (1986 : Dallas, Tex.) Registration list /. Washington, D.C. (1101-16th St., N.W., Washington 20036) , c1986. ca. 400 p. ; LC Card 87-107458 DDC 338.4/7663/025 19
HD9348.A2 I57 1986

BEVERAGE INDUSTRY - UNITED STATES - STATISTICS.
Korb, Penelope. U. S. and world food, beverages, and tobacco expenditures, 1970-83 /. Washington, D.C. , 1986. iv, 84 p. : LC Card 86-603160 DDC 339.4/8664/0021 19
HD9000.4 .K67 1986

BEVERAGES INDUSTRY - SOVIET UNION.
Korobkina, Z. V. (Zoi͡a Vasil'evna) Tovarovedenie vkusovykh tovarov /. Moskva , 1986. 207 p. ; LC Card 86-220308
HD9015.S652 K67 1986

A Beveridge reader /. Beveridge, William Henry Beveridge, Baron, 1879-1963. London , Boston , 1987. viii, 190 p. ; ISBN 0-04-361070-6 (alk. paper) LC Card 87-11819 DDC 338.941 19
HB103.A2 B48 1987

Beveridge, William Henry Beveridge, Baron, 1879-1963. A Beveridge reader / [compiled by] Karel Williams, John Williams. London ; Boston : Allen & Unwin, 1987. viii, 190 p. ; 23 cm. Bibliography: p. 184-185. Includes index. ISBN 0-04-361070-6 (alk. paper) LC Card 87-11819 DDC 338.941 19
1. Economics - Great Britain - History. 2. Beveridge, William Henry Beveridge, Baron, 1879-1963. 3. Great Britain - Economic policy. I. Williams, Karel. II. Williams, John (John L.). III. Title.
HB103.A2 B48 1987

BEVERIDGE, WILLIAM HENRY BEVERIDGE, BARON, 1879-1963.
Beveridge, William Henry Beveridge, Baron, 1879-1963. A Beveridge reader /. London , Boston , 1987. viii, 190 p. ; ISBN 0-04-361070-6 (alk. paper) LC Card 87-11819 DDC 338.941 19
HB103.A2 B48 1987

Beverley, Mary Frances. Cowbells and coffins : the old general store / Mary Frances Beverley ; foreword by Tumbleweed Smith.1st ed. Austin, Tex. : Eakin Press, c1987. xi, 63 p. : ill. ; 28 cm. Bibliography: p. 59. Includes index. ISBN 0-89015-593-3 (pbk.) : LC Card 87-6711 DDC 381/.1 19
1. General stores - United States - History. I. Title.
HF5429.3 .B49 1987

Bevilacqua, Piero, 1944- Le Bonifiche in Italia dal '700 a oggi /. Roma , 1984. viii, 437 p. : ISBN 88-420-2429-5 : LC Card 85-173148
HD1683.I8 B66 1984 ***NYPL [JSD 87-50]***

Die Bevölkerung der Stadt Luzern 1850-1914 . Schüpbach, Werner. Luzern , 1983. 323 p., [17] p. of plates : ISBN 3-7252-0432-2 LC Card 83-201416
HB3624.L8 S38 1983

Bevölkerung, Haushalte, Konsum . Pflaumer, Peter, 1947- Frankfurt , New York , c1986. iv, 218 p. : ISBN 3-593-33674-X LC Card 87-408990 DDC 339.4/7 19
HB849.53 .P49 1986

Bevölkerungs- und Erwerbsverhaltensentwicklung in Österreich, Schweden und der Bundesrepublik Deutschland /. Schettkat, Ronald. Berlin [1984] 48 p. ; LC Card 85-198691
HD5771 .S34 1984

Bevölkerungsentwicklung, Wirtschaftsordnung und Industrialisierungsprozess in Südosteuropa . Doh, Rainer. Neuried , c1985. [12], 486, 19 p. : ISBN 3-88893-045-6 LC Card 87-140271 DDC 304.6/09498 19
HB3631 .D64 1985

Bevölkerungsstruktur, Mobilität und Lohn . Raschke, Freddy, 1950- Frankfurt am Main , New York , c1985. vi, 194 p. : ISBN 3-8204-5697-X LC Card 85-221450
HD4911 .R37 1985

Bevölkerungswandel in der Schweiz . Höpflinger, François. Grüsch , c1986. 179 p. : ISBN 3-7253-0269-3 LC Card 86-234328
HB3623 .H66 1986

Bevölkerungswissenschaft : die "Bevölkerungslehre" von Gerhard Mackenroth 30 Jahre danach / mit Beiträgen von K.M. Bolte ... [et al.] ; Josef Schmid (Hg.). Frankfurt ; New York : Campus, c1985. 227 p. ; 21 cm. (Campus Forschung. Bd. 443) "Der Band beruht auf dem 'Mackenroth-Symposium', veranstaltet vom Lehrstuhl für Bevölkerungswissenschaft der Universität Bamberg, September 1983"--T.p. verso. German, English or French. Includes bibliographies. ISBN 3-593-33461-5 LC Card 85-178756
1. Population - Congresses. 2. Mackenroth, Gerhard. Bevölkerungslehre. I. Bolte, Karl Martin. II. Schmid, Josef, 1937-. III. Mackenroth-Symposium (1983 : Universität Bamberg). IV. Universität Bamberg. Lehrstuhl für Bevölkerungswissenschaft.
HB849 .B48 1985

Bevolkingsensus 1980, uitgesoekte statistiese streek Port Elizabeth/Uitenhage/Kirkwood = Population census 1980, selected statistical region Port Elizabeth/Uitenhage/Kirkwood. [Pretoria] : Republiek van Suid-Afrika, Sentrale Statistiekdiens : Verkrygbaar by die Staatsdrukker, [1985] xix, 317 p. : ill. ; 30 cm. (Verslag . no. 02-80-16 = no. 02-80-16) Afrikaans and English. "April 1985"--P. iv. ISBN 0-621-09480-3 : LC Card 85-241531

1. Port Elizabeth (South Africa) - Census, 1980. 2. Uitenhage (South Africa) - Census, 1980. 3. Kirkwood (South Africa) - Census, 1980. I. South Africa. Central Statistical Services. II. Title: Population census 1980, selected statistical region Port Elizabeth/Uitenhage/Kirkwood. III. Series: Verslag (South Africa. Central Statistical Services), no. 02-80-16.
HA4701.Z9 P673 1985

Bevolkingsensus 1980, uitgesoekte statistiese streek, Pretoria/Wonderboom = Population census 1980, selected statistical region, Pretoria/Wonderboom. [Pretoria] : Republic van Suid-Afrika, Sentrale Statistiekdiens : Verkrygbaar by die Staatsdrukker, [1985?] xx, 476 p. : ill. ; 30 cm. (Verslag / Republiek van Suid-Afrika, Sentrale Statistiekdiens . no. 02-80-22 = no. 02-80-22) ISBN 0-621-09483-8 : LC Card 85-238587
1. Pretoria (South Africa) - Census, 1980. 2. Wonderboom (Transvaal, South Africa) - Census, 1980. I. South Africa. Central Statistical Services. II. Title: Population census 1980, selected statistical region, Pretoria/Wonderboom. III. Series: Verslag (South Africa. Central Statistical Services), no. 02-80-22.
HA4701.Z9 P743 1985

Bevolkingsensus 1980 uitgesoekte statistiese streek Vereeniging/Vanderbijlpark/Sasolburg = Population census 1980, selected statistical region Vereeniging/Vanderbijlpark/Sasolburg. Pretoria : Republiek van Suid-Afrika, Sentrale Statistiekdiens : Verkrygbaar by die Staatsdrukker, [1985] xx, 301 p. : ill. ; 30 cm. (Verslag . no. 02-80-23 = no. 02-80-23) Afrikaans and English. "April 1985"--P. iv. ISBN 0-621-09484-6 : LC Card 85-235498
1. Vereeniging (South Africa) - Population - Statistics. 2. Vereeniging (South Africa) - Census. 3. Vanderbijlpark (South Africa) - Population - Statistics. 4. Vanderbijlpark (South Africa) - Census. 5. Sasolburg (South Africa) - Population - Statistics. 6. Sasolburg (South Africa) - Census. 7. South Africa - Census, 1980. I. South Africa. Central Statistical Services. II. Title: Population census 1980, selected statistical region Vereeniging/Vanderbijlpark/Sasolburg. III. Series: Verslag (South Africa. Central Statistical Services), no. 02-80-23.
HA4701.Z9 V474 1985

Bevorzugter Beamtenstatus, Möglichkeiten und Grenzen einer Reform . Allenspach, Heinz. Zürich [1986] 32 p. ; LC Card 87-407830 DDC 330.9494 s 331.7/61354494 19
HC395 .Z43 Nr. 130 JN8831

Die Bewertung öffentlicher Leistungen durch die Bürger . Rondorf, Dieter, 1955- Frankfurt am Main , New York , c1985. 231 p. : ISBN 3-8204-5652-X LC Card 85-229645
HB846.5 .R65 1985

Bewertung und Abgeltungskonditionen bei der Veräusserung mittelständischer Unternehmen /. Rick, Josef. Berlin , c1985. 191 p. : ISBN 3-428-05785-6 : LC Card 85-186420
HG4028.V3 R52 1985

Die Bewertung von konzerninternen Lieferungen und Leistungen in der operativen Planung /. Jäger, Hubert. Heidelberg , c1987. xii, 345 p. ; ISBN 3-7908-0367-7 LC Card 87-145912 DDC 658.1/5/0943 19
HG4156 .J336 1987

Bewlay, Simon. Steel : performance of some UK manufacturers compared / Simon Bewlay. London : Aims of Industry, [1985?] 14 p. : ill. ; 25 cm. (An Aims of Industry study) Cover title. LC Card 87-165749 DDC 338.4/7669142/0941 19
1. Steel industry and trade - Great Britain. 2. Steel industry and trade - Great Britain - Statistics. I. Series: Aims of Industry study (Unnumbered). II. Title.
HD9521.5 .B48 1985

Bewley, Truman F. (Truman Fassett), 1941- Advances in economic theory . Cambridge [Cambridgeshire] , New York , 1987. vii, 428 p. ; ISBN 0-521-34044-6 LC Card 87-889 DDC 330.1 19
HB21 .A329 1987

Bewusstsein ohne Subjekt? . Voss, G. Günter. Grosshesselohe , 1984. vi, 512 p. : ISBN 3-924346-07-0 : LC Card 85-131494
HD6957.G35 V67 1984

Beyfuss, Jörg. Aussenhandel mit Entwicklungsländern : Entwicklung und Perspektiven / Jörg Beyfuss. Köln : Deutscher Instituts-Verlag, c1978. 55 p. : ill. ; 21 cm. (Beiträge zur Wirtschafts- und Sozialpolitik . 55, 4/1978) Includes bibliographical references. ISBN 3-88054-145-0 LC Card 85-242489
1. Germany (West) - Commerce - Developing countries. 2. Developing countries - Commerce - Germany (West). I. Series: Beiträge zur Wirtschafts- und Sozialpolitik , 55. II. Title.
HF3568.D44 B49 1978

Beynon, Huw. Digging deeper . London , 1985. xiv, 252 p. : ISBN 0-86091-820-3 (pbk.) : LC Card 87-118973 DDC 331.89/2822334/0941 19
HD5365.M6152 1984 .D54 1985

Beyond broadcasting . Hollins, Timothy. London , 1984. ix, 385 p. ; ISBN 0-85170-148-5 (pbk.) LC Card 84-125713 DDC 384.55/563 19
HE8700.72.G7 H65 1984
NYPL [JLD 86-1057]

Beyond bureaucracy : strategic management of social development / editors, John C. Ickis, Edilberto de Jesus, Rushikesh Maru. West Hartford, Conn. : Kumarian Press, c1986. xii, 256 p. : ill. ; 24 cm. (Kumarian Press library of management for development) Includes bibliographies. ISBN 0-931816-44-0 LC Card 86-34420 DDC 338.9/0068 19
1. Economic development projects - Developing countries. 2. Rural development projects - Developing countries. I. Ickis, John C., 1943-. II. De Jesus, Ed. C. III. Maru, Rushikesh M. IV. Series.
HC59.72.E44 B48 1986

Beyond management control . Saulniers, Alfred H., 1945- Austin , 1985. 22 p. : LC Card 86-622251 DDC 354.8509/2 19
HD4124 .S28 1985

Beyond national borders . Ōmae, Ken'ichi, 1943- Homewood, Ill. , c1987. xi, 128 p. : ISBN 1-556-23017-6 LC Card 86-72864 DDC 337.52 19
HF1602.15.U6 O4 1987

Beyond oil . Rumayḥī, Muḥammad Ghānim. [Khalīj laysa nafṭ. English.] London , 1986. 156 p. : ISBN 0-86356-120-9 : LC Card 86-200063 DDC 330.953/053 19
HC415.3 .R8613 1986

Beyond private lines : advanced services / Communications Systems & Services. Boston, MA (200 Portland St., Boston 02114) : Yankee Group, c1987. iv, 117 p. : ill. ; 28 cm. At head of title: Communications/Information Systems. LC Card 87-144067 DDC 384.3/0973 19
1. Telecommunication - United States. 2. Telephone - United States. 3. Telephone - United States - Multiplex systems. 4. Data transmission systems. 5. Market surveys - United States. I. Communications Systems & Services. II. Yankee Group. III. Communications/Information Systems (Firm : Yankee Group).
HE7775 .B46 1987

Beyond Reagan : setting the next agenda : timely reports to keep journalists, scholars, and the public abreast of developing issues, events, and trends. Washington, D.C. : Congressional Quarterly Inc., c1987. v, 209 p. : ill. ; 23 cm. Ten reports originally published as separate issues of Editorial research reports. Includes bibliographies and index. CONTENTS. - America's service economy -- Working on welfare -- Who cares for the elderly? -- Blueprints for national service -- New deal for the family -- The Rehnquist Court -- Western water -- Dollar diplomacy -- Euromissile negotiations -- Industrial competitiveness. ISBN 0-87187-437-7 (pbk.) : LC Card 87-3057 DDC 338.973 19
1. United States - Economic policy - 1981-. 2. United States - Social policy. I. Congressional Quarterly, inc. II. Editorial research reports.
HC106.8 .B47 1987

Beyond recrimination . Wheeler, Jimmy W. Indianapolis, IN (P.O. Box 26-919, Indianapolis 46226) , c1987. xix, 218 p. : LC Card 87-165405 DDC 382/.0951249/073 19
HF1456.5.T28 W46 1987

Beyond sex roles / [edited by] Alice G. Sargent. 2nd ed. St. Paul : West Pub. Co., c1985. xxix, 563 p. : ill. ; 25 cm. Includes indexes. Bibliography: p. 541-543. ISBN 0-314-85293-X (pbk.) : LC Card 84-21950 DDC 305.3 19
1. Sex role - United States. 2. Sexism - United States. I. Sargent, Alice G., 1939-.
HQ1075.5.U6 B49 1985
NYPL [JLF 86-1144]

Beyond the blue horizon . Frater, Alexander, 1937- New York , 1987, c1986. xviii, 430 p. : ISBN 0-684-18837-6 LC Card 87-9426 DDC 387.7/065/73 19
HE9787 .F7 1987

Beyond the investor's quotient . Bernstein, Jacob, 1946- New York , c1986. x, 214 p. : ISBN 0-471-82062-8 LC Card 85-12325 DDC 332.6 19
HG4521 .B443 1986 *NYPL [JLE 86-2936]*

Beyond the plan . Vasary, Ildiko. Boulder , 1987. xvii, 308 p. : ISBN 0-8133-7412-X (soft : alk. paper) : LC Card 87-8219 DDC 307.7/2/09439 19
HD1492.H8 V35 1987

Beyrer, Klaus. Die Postkutschenreise / Klaus Beyrer. Tübingen : Tübinger Vereinigung für Volkskunde, 1985. 284 p. : ill. ; 21 cm. (Untersuchungen des Ludwig-Uhland-Instituts der Universität Tübingen . 66. Bd.) Bibliography: p. 257-272. Includes indexes. ISBN 3-925340-35-1 LC Card 86-198761
1. Postal service - Germany - History. 2. Coaching - Germany - History. I. Title. II. Series.
HE6995 .B49 1985

Bezanson, H. A. (Harold A.), 1935- How to successfully win job interviews : the complete guide to job interviewing / by H.A. Bezanson.Rev. & expanded 2nd ed. Blaine, WA : Careers Unlimited, c1986. 106 leaves : ill. ; 29 cm. Bibliography: leaf 106. ISBN 0-9691828-0-5 (pbk.) : LC Card 86-31689 DDC 650.1/4 19
1. Employment interviewing. I. Title.
HF5549.5.I6 B48 1986

Bezerra, Agostinho Fernandes. As tarifas internas na 1a. República / Agostinho Fernandes Bezerra. Brasília, DF : Ministério da Fazenda, Escola de Administração Fazendária, Assessoria de Editoração, 1986. xv, 140 p. : ill. ; 21 cm. Originally presented as the author's thesis (master's--Universidade de São Paulo). Bibliography: p. 131-137. LC Card 87-404990 DDC 381/.5/098134 19
1. Interstate commerce - Taxation - Brazil - Pernambuco - History. 2. Fiscal policy - Brazil - Pernambuco - History. 3. Pernambuco (Brazil) - Economic conditions. I. Title. II. Title: Tarifas internas na Primeira República.
HJ5101.P47 B49 1986

Bezirk Sliven '85. Slivenski okrŭg '85 =. Sofiīa , 1985. 134 p. : LC Card 86-196443
HF5221.S56 S56 1985

Het Bezit en gebruik van motorfietsen, 1984 / Centraal Bureau voor de Statistiek, Hoofdafdeling Statistieken van Verkeer en Vervoer. 's-Gravenhage : Staatsuitgeverij/CBS-publikaties, 1985. 26 p. : ill. ; 30 cm. Title on p. [4] of cover: Ownership and use of motor-cycles 1984. ISBN 90-357-0397-9 : LC Card 86-218867
1. Motorcycles - Netherlands - Statistics. 2. Motorcycling - Netherlands - Statistics. I. Netherlands. Centraal Bureau voor de Statistiek. Hoofdafdeling Statistieken van Verkeer en Vervoer. II. Title: Ownership and use of motor-cycles 1984.
HE5616.5 .B49 1985

Beznin, M. A. Vklad severnogo krest′īanstva v material′nuīu i dukhovnuīu kul′turu i ego znachenie v reshenii problem agropromyshlennogo kompleksa nechernozemnoĭ zony RSFSR . Vologda , 1984. 93 p. ; LC Card 85-156518
HD9015.S652 V54 1984

Bezopasnost′ dorozhnogo dvizheniīa /. Luk′īanov, V. V. Moskva , 1978. 244, [4] p. ; LC Card 81-166116
HE5675.A6 L84 1978

Bezrabotitsa v SShA i ee gosudarstvenno-monopolisticheskoe regulirovanie v sovremennykh usloviīakh /. Kotlīarov, Vladimir Fedorovich. Leningrad , 1977. 18 p. ; LC Card 81-166000
HD5724 .K67 1977

Bezrukov, A. I. Transnatsional′nye korporatsii v sisteme gosudarstvenno-monopolisticheskogo regulirovaniīa ėkonomiki . Moskva , 1985. 167 p. ; LC Card 86-187630
HD2755.5 .T714 1985

Bezza, Bruno.
Energia e sviluppo . Torino , c1986. xii, 346 p.,

[16] p. of plates : ISBN 88-06-59444-3 : LC Card 86-214309
HD9685.I84 S574 1986

Le lotte degli elettromeccanici / Bruno Bezza, Stefano Datola, Roberto Gallessi. Milano : F. Angeli, c1981. 179 p. : ill. ; 22 cm. (Cultura sindacale . 17) At head of title: Centro ricerche e studi sindacale. Fiom Milano. Includes bibliographical references. ISBN 88-20-42149-6 : LC Card 81-200954 DDC 331.89/282131/0945 19
1. Strikes and lockouts - Electric machinery industry - Italy. 2. Labor disputes - Italy. 3. Trade-unions - Electric industry workers - Italy. I. Datola, Stefano. II. Gallessi, Roberto. III. Fiom Milano. Centro ricerche e studi sindacali. IV. Title.
HD5384.E3 B49 1981 ***NYPL [JLD 86-2898]***

BGRS (Series) .
(no. 85-8) Oregon county finances, fiscal 1984. Eugene, OR [1985] 17, [12] p. ; LC Card 86-622281 DDC 336/.014/795 19
HJ9302 .O725 1985

Bhabatosh Datta. see **Datta, Bhabatosh, 1911-**

Bhadouria, B. P. S. Reflections on the Indian economy /. Delhi, India , 1987. xxxi, 439 p. : ISBN 81-900026-0-0 : LC Card 87-901043 DDC 338.9 19
HC435.2 .R425 1987

Bhaduri, Amit. Macroeconomics : the dynamics of commodity production / Amit Bhaduri. Houndmills, Basingstoke, Hampshire : Macmillan, 1986. xii, 278 p. : ill. ; 23 cm. (Radical economics) Bibliography: p. [259]-263. Includes indexes. ISBN 0-333-29194-8 LC Card 86-673605
1. Macroeconomics. I. Title. II. Series.
HB172.5 .B48x 1986b

Bhaerman, Robert D. Planning for adult career counseling / Robert D. Bhaerman. Columbus, Ohio (1960 Kenny Rd., Columbus 43210-1090) : National Center for Research in Vocational Education, Ohio State University, 1985. ix, 64 p. ; 28 cm. (Information series. no. 290) Includes bibliographies. LC Card 87-108253 DDC 331.12/8 19
1. Vocational guidance. I. Series: Information series (National Center for Research in Vocational Education (U. S.) , no. 290. II. Title.
HF5381 .B4225 1985

Bhagwati, Jagdish N., 1934-
Essays in development economics / Jagdish N. Bhagwati ; edited by Gene Grossman. Oxford [Oxfordshire] : B. Blackwell, 1985. 2 v. ; 24 cm. Includes bibliographical references and indexes. CONTENTS. - v. 1. Wealth and poverty -- v. 2. Dependence and interdependence. ISBN 0-631-14178-2 (v. 1)
1. Economic development - Addresses, essays, lectures. 2. Developing countries - Economic conditions - Addresses, essays, lectures. I. Grossman, Gene M. II. Title. ***NYPL [JLL 86-16]***

International trade . Cambridge, Mass. , 1987. xii, 504 p. : ISBN 0-262-02264-8 LC Card 87-2623 DDC 382 19
HF1411 .I5185 1987

Bhairav, Kalki Kaal. Populist manifesto / Kalki Kaal Bhairav. Grand Forks, ND, USA (830 S. 48th St., Grand Forks 58201) : Populist Foundation, [c1986] vii, 85 p. ; 22 cm. Errata (2 p.) inserted. LC Card 86-201038 DDC 338.954 19
1. South Asia - Economic conditions. 2. Populism - South Asia. 3. Capitalism - South Asia. I. Title.
HC430.6 .B46 1986

Bhalla, Sushil K. The effective management of technology : a challenge for corporations / Sushil K. Bhalla. Columbus [Ohio] : Battelle Press ; Reading, Mass. : Distributed by Addison-Wesley Pub. Co., c1987. xiii, 205 p. : ill. ; 24 cm. Includes bibliographies and index. ISBN 0-201-10929-8 : LC Card 86-25847 DDC 658.5 19
1. Technological innovations - Management. 2. Strategic planning. I. Title.
HD45 .B47 1987

Bhandari, Arvind D. Telecommunications opportunities for colleges and universities /. McLean, Va. (1355 Beverly Rd., Suite 100, McLean 22101) , c1986. 208 p. ; LC Card 86-231086 DDC 384.6/3 19
HD9696.T443 U572 1986

Bhanushali, S. G., 1933- Entrepreneurship development : an interdisciplinary approach / S.G. Bhanushali.1st ed. Bombay : Himalaya Pub. House, 1987. xvi, 255 p. ; 23 cm. Originally presented as the author's thesis (Ph. D.--Shivaji University, Kolhapur) Bibliography: p. [242]-255. LC Card 86-903834 DDC 338/.04 19
1. Entrepreneur. I. Title.
HB615 .B46 1987

BHARAT HEAVY ELECTRICALS LIMITED.
Kundu, Amitabh, 1948- Location of public enterprises and regional development /. New Delhi , 1986. xv, 178 p. ; LC Card 86-903373 DDC 338.954 19
HD9697.A3 I45 1986

Bhārata kī janagaṇanā, 1981. Census of India, 1981. Delhi , <[1982]-1986. v. in : LC Card 87-915022 DDC 315.4/13 19
HA4587.O74 C46 1982

Bhārata kī janagaṇanā, 1981. Census of India, 1981. Delhi , <1983-1987. v. in : LC Card 87-915011 DDC 304.6/0954/12021 19
HA4587.B53 C46 1983

Bhārata kī janagaṇanā, 1981. Census of India, 1981. Delhi , <1983-1985. v. in : LC Card 87-915010 DDC 304.6/0954/021 19
HA4581.5 1981g

Bhārata kī janagaṇanā, 1981. Census of India, 1981. Delhi , <1983-1986. v. in : LC Card 87-915012 DDC 304.6/0954/75021 19
HA4587.G84 C46 1983

Bhārata kī janagaṇanā, 1981. Census of India, 1981. Delhi , <1984-1986. v. in : LC Card 87-915009 DDC 304.6/0954/84021 19
HA4587.A52 C46 1984

Bhārata kī janagaṇanā, 1981. Śṛṅkhalā 10, Kerala. Census of India, 1981. Delhi , <1984-1987. v. in : LC Card 87-915015 DDC 304.6/0954/83021 19
HA4587.K47 C46 1984

Bhārata kī janagaṇanā, 1981. Śṛṅkhalā 11, Madhya Pradeśa. Census of India, 1981. Delhi , <[1983]-[1986]. v. in : LC Card 87-915017 DDC 304.6/0954/3021 19
HA4587.M32 C46 1983

Bhārata kī janagaṇanā, 1981. Śṛṅkhalā 23, Paścima Baṅgāla. Census of India, 1981. Delhi , <1985-[1987]. v. in : maps (some folded) ; LC Card 87-915030 DDC 304.6/0954/14021 19
HA4587.W47 C46 1985

Bhārata meṃ āvāsīya artha-vyavasthā. Dholakia, Bakul H. 1947- The economics of housing in India . Delhi , 1982. xviii, 274 p. ; LC Card 83-905798 DDC 363.5/0954 19
HD7361.A3 D47 1982
NYPL [JLD 85-2908]

Bharucha, Kerman D. dBASE II--a comprehensive user's manual / Kerman D. Bharucha. 1st ed. Blue Ridge Summit, Pa. : Tab Books, c1985. xi, 305 p. ; 24 cm. Includes index. "No. 1884." ISBN 0-8306-0884-2 : LC Card 84-23959 DDC 001.64/25 19
1. dBASE II (Computer program). 2. Business - Data processing. I. Title. II. Title: dBASE two--a comprehensive user's manual. III. Title: dBASE2-a comprehensive user's manual.
HF5548.4.D22 B43 1985 ***NYPL [JSE 87-19]***

Bhāshā-śahīda granthamālā.
Datta, Śekhara. Tebhāgā āndolana /. Ḍhākā , 1985. 103, [1] p. ; LC Card 86-902072
HD1537.I4 D34 1985

Bhaskar, Krish N. The impact of microprocessors on the small accounting practice / K.N. Bhaskar and B.C. Williams. Englewood Cliffs, N.J. : Prentice-Hall International in association with the Institute of Chartered Accountants in England and Wales, c1986. xvi, 167 p. ; 24 cm. (Research studies in accounting) Includes index. Bibliography: p. [143]-162. ISBN 0-13-453291-0 (pbk.) LC Card 85-25764 DDC 657/.028/5416 19
1. Accounting - Data processing. 2. Microcomputers - Programming. 3. Minicomputers - Programming. I. Williams, Bernard C. II. Title. III. Series.
HF5679 .B45 1986 ***NYPL [JLE 86-4067]***

Bhat, Mohd. Sultan (Mohammad Sultan)
Agricultural taxation in Jammu & Kashmir / Mohd. Sultan Bhat. New Delhi : Ariana Pub. House, 1987. vi, 192 p. ; 23 cm. Spine title: Agricultural taxation in J & K. Bibliography: p. [163]-186. Includes index. LC Card 87-901173 DDC 336.2/7863/09546 19
1. Agriculture - Taxation - India - Jammu and Kashmir. I. Title. II. Title: Agricultural taxation in J & K.
HD1443.I42 J352 1987

Bhat, Vighnesh N., 1951- Mind managers and defiled doordarshan / Vighnesh N. Bhat. 1st ed. Jalandhar : ABS Publications, 1987. 208 p. ; 22 cm. Bibliography: p. [194]-205. Includes index. ISBN 81-7072-011-7 : LC Card 87-900504 DDC 302.2/345/0954 19
1. Television - Social aspects - India. I. Title.
HE8700.9.I5 B53 1987

Bhatia, Ramesh, 1944- Socioeconomic aspects of renewable energy technologies . New York , 1988. p. cm. ISBN 0-275-92851-9 (alk. paper) : LC Card 87-22890 DDC 333.7/09172/4 19
HD9502.D442 S63 1988

Bhattacharya, Sib Nath, 1938-
Entrepreneurship development in India and the South-East Asian countries in agricultural and industrial sectors / Sib Nath Bhattacharya. 1st ed. New Delhi : Metropolitan, 1983. xix, 156 p. : 1 folded map ; 23 cm. Includes index. Bibliography: p. 148-151. LC Card 83-903206 DDC 338/.04/0954 19
1. Industrial promotion - India. 2. Industrial promotion - Asia, Southeastern. 3. Agricultural industries - India. 4. Agricultural industries - Asia, Southeastern. I. Title.
HC440.I53 B48 1983 ***NYPL [JLD 86-3764]***

India's five-year plans in theory and practice / Sib Nath Bhattacharya. 1st ed. New Delhi, India : Metropolitan Book Co., 1987. xvi, 352 p. ; 26 cm. Bibliography: p. [348]-350. Includes index. ISBN 81-200-0076-5 : LC Card 87-900413 DDC 338.954 19
1. India - Economic policy - 1947-. I. Title.
HC435.2 .B45476 1987

Bhavnagar University. Energy use in rural Gujarat /. New Delhi , c1987. iv, 186 p. : ISBN 81-204-0216-2 : LC Card 87-901949 DDC 333.79/13/095475 19
HD9502.I43 G844 1987

Bhoite, Anuradha. Women employees and rural development : problems of employed women in rural areas / Anuradha Bhoite. Delhi, India : Gian Pub. House, c1987. xiii, 135 p. ; 23 cm. Study with reference to Prabhani District, Maharashtra. Bibliography: p. [130]-135. ISBN 81-212-0085-7 : LC Card 87-900916 DDC 331.4/0954 19
1. Women - Employment - India. 2. Rural development - India. 3. Rural women - Employment - India. 4. Women - Employment - India - Prabhani (District). 5. Rural development - India - Prabhani (District). 6. Rural women - Employment - India - Prabhani (District). I. Title.
HD6189 .B56 1987

Bhopal . Shrivastava, Paul. Cambridge, Mass. , c1987. xvi, 184 p. : ISBN 0-88730-084-7 LC Card 86-26575 DDC 363.1/79 19
HD7269.C452 I5268 1987

Bhopal disaster . Shastri, Lalit. New Delhi [1985] 102 p. [32] p. of plates : LC Card 86-902662 DDC 363.1/79 19
HD7269.C452 I5267 1985

Bhopal, its setting, responsibility, and challenge /. Sufrin, Sidney C., 1910- Delhi , 1985. 98 p. ; ISBN 81-202-0135-3 : LC Card 85-903246 DDC 363.1/79 19
HD7269.C452 I527 1985
NYPL [JLD 86-1321]

BHOPAL UNION CARBIDE PLANT DISASTER, BHOPAL, INDIA, 1984.
Chishti, Anees, 1941- Dateline Bhopal . New Delhi , 1986. 160 p. ; LC Card 86-901993 DDC 363.1/79
HD7269.C452 I5225 1986
NYPL [JLD 87-1050]

Everest, Larry. Behind the poison cloud . Chicago , 1986. 192 p. : ISBN 0-916650-26-X : LC Card 85-26863 DDC 363.1/79 19
HD7269.C452 I524 1986
NYPL [JSD 86-425]

Kurzman, Dan. A killing wind . New York , c1987. xvi, 297 p., [16] p. of plates : ISBN 0-07-035687-4 LC Card 87-3398 DDC 363.1/79 19
HD7269.C452 I525 1987

Shastri, Lalit. Bhopal disaster . New Delhi [1985] 102 p. [32] p. of plates : LC Card

86-902662 DDC 363.1/79 19
HD7269.C452 I5267 1985

Shrivastava, Paul. Bhopal . Cambridge, Mass. , c1987. xvi, 184 p. : ISBN 0-88730-084-7 LC Card 86-26575 DDC 363.1/79 19
HD7269.C452 I5268 1987

Shrivastava, Paul. Managing industrial crises . New Delhi, India , 1987. 196 p. : ISBN 81-7094-000-1 : LC Card 87-902160 DDC 363.1/79 19
HD7269.C452 I5269 1987

Sufrin, Sidney C., 1910- Bhopal, its setting, responsibility, and challenge /. Delhi , 1985. 98 p. ; ISBN 81-202-0135-3 : LC Card 85-903246 DDC 363.1/79 19
HD7269.C452 I527 1985
NYPL [JLD 86-1321]

Bhorali, Devadas. Co-operative banking and economic development / Devadas Bhorali ; foreword by P.C. Goswami. New Delhi : Deep & Deep Publications, c1987. 424 p. : map ; 23 cm. Study on the Assam Co-operative Apex Bank. Bibliography: p. [410]-419. Includes index. LC Card 87-900825 DDC 334/.2/0954162 19
1. Assam Co-operative Apex Bank. 2. Banks and banking, Cooperative - India - Assam. 3. Assam (India) - Economic conditions. I. Title.
HG2039.I4 B47 1987

Bhote, Keki R., 1925- Supply management : how to make U. S. suppliers competitive / Keki R. Bhote. New York, N.Y. : AMA Membership Publications Division, American Management Association, c1987. 150 p. : ill. ; 23 cm. (AMA management briefing) ISBN 0-8144-2330-2 (pbk.) : LC Card 86-28795 DDC 658.7/2/0973 19
1. Industrial procurement - United States - Management. 2. Materials management - United States. 3. Competition - United States. I. Title.
HD39.5 .B49 1987

Bhowmik, Sharit, 1948- Class formation in the plantation system / Sharit Bhowmik ; foreword by Andre Beteille. New Delhi : People's Pub. House, 1981. xix, 263 p. : maps ; 22 cm. Includes index. Bibliography: p. [251]-256. LC Card 81-903777 DDC 305/.93633 19
1. Plantations - India - Jalpaiguri (District). 2. Tea trade - India - Jalpaiguri (District). 3. Tea plantation workers - India - Jalpaiguri (District). 4. Adivasis. 5. Social classes - India - Jalpaiguri (District). I. Title.
HD1470.5.I42 J342 1981
NYPL [JLD 86-2612]

Bhumibol Adulyadej, King of Thailand, 1927- Khrōngkān 'an n [Bangkok] [2526 i.e. 1983] 221 p. (some folded), [1] leaf of plates : LC Card 83-916454
HC445 .K53 1983

Bhūmibyabasthā, Kamgresa, o Kṛshakasabhā /. Ghosha, Madana. Bardhamāna [1986?] 100 p. ; LC Card 87-900325
HD875 .G56 1986

Biafra. see **East-Central State, Nigeria; South-Eastern State, Nigeria.**

Białecki, Klemens. Słownik handlu zagranicznego / Klemens Białecki, Andrzej Dorosz, Włodzimierz Januszkiewicz. Wyd. 1. Warszawa : Państwowe Wydawn. Ekonomiczne, 1986. 359 p. ; 21 cm. Includes indexes. ISBN 83-208-0112-5 : LC Card 86-221378
1. Commerce - Dictionaries - Polish. 2. International economic relations - Dictionaries - Polish. I. Dorosz, Andrzej. II. Januszkiewicz, Włodzimierz. III. Title.
HF1001 .B47 1986

Bialek, Jacques, 1919- Productivity improvement management : Bialek's productivity law / Jacques Bialek.[1st ed.]. San Francisco : California Management Press, [c1986] 339 p. ; 21 cm. Errata slip pasted on p. [6]. Includes index. ISBN 0-941883-01-9 (pbk.) : LC Card 87-6557 DDC 658.5 19
1. Industrial productivity - Management. I. Title.
HD56 .B49 1986

Bianchi, Antonio. Lotte sociali e dittatura in Lunigiana storica e Versilia (1919-1930) / Antonio Bianchi. [Firenze] : L.S. Olschki, 1981. xii, 309 p. ; 21 cm. Includes bibliographical references and index. ISBN 88-22-23028-0 LC Card 82-125955
1. Labor and laboring classes - Italy - Lunigiana - History - 20th century. 2. Labor and laboring classes - Italy - Versilia Plain - History - 20th century. 3. Labor and laboring classes - Italy - Lunigiana - Political activity - History - 20th century. 4. Labor and laboring classes - Italy - Versilia Plain - Political activity - History - 20th century. 5. Fascism - Italy - Lunigiana - History - 20th century. 6. Fascism - Italy - Versilia Plain - History - 20th century. 7. Socialism - Italy - Lunigiana - History - 20th century. 8. Socialism - Italy - Versilia Plain - History - 20th century. I. Title.
HD8489.L86 B5 1981

Bianchi, Carluccio. L'Insegnamento dell'economia politica nella scuola secondaria superiore . Milano, Italy , c1982. 261 p. ; LC Card 87-673404
HB74.9.I8 I57x 1982

Bianchi, Giovanni. L'Association des travailleurs aux choix technologiques . Luxembourg , Washington, D.C. , 1986. 45 p. : ISBN 92-825-5880-0 : LC Card 86-179382
HD6331.2.E86 A88 1986

Bianchi, Roberto, 1954- Le tecniche esecutive nell'edilizia residenziale degli anni '80 : dal tradizionale evoluto al cosiddetto industrializzato / Roberto Bianchi. Milano, Italy : F. Angeli, c1986. 144 p. : ill., plans ; 22 cm. (Ricerche di tecnologia dell'architettura . 22) Bibliography: [129]-137. Includes index. LC Card 87-126093
1. Modular construction industry - Italy - Lombardy. 2. Modular construction. 3. Dwellings - Italy - Lombardy - Design and construction. I. Title. II. Series.
HD9715.5.I83 L653 1986

Bianco, Christian. Postgeschichte Südtirols / Christian Bianco. [S.l. : s.n., 1981?] 207 p. : ill. ; 31 cm. Includes bibliographical references. LC Card 86-168698
1. Postal service - Italy - Trentino-Alto Adige - History. 2. Postal service - Austria - Tyrol - History. 3. Postmarks - Italy - Trentino-Alto Adige - History. I. Title.
HE7016.T74 B53 1981

Biava, Adriano Henrique Rebelo. Contribuição de melhoria : necessidade de inovação fiscal / Adriano Henrique Rebelo Biava. São Paulo-SP : Instituto de Pesquisas Econômicas da Faculdade de Economia e Administração da Universidade de São Paulo, 1987. 243 p. : ill. ; 23 cm. (Série Ensaios econômicos . no. 61) At head of title: Universidade de São Paulo, Faculdade de Economia e Administração, Departamento de Economia. Originally presented as the author's thesis (doctoral)--Universidade de São Paulo, 1983. Bibliography: p. 238-243. LC Card 87-404978 DDC 339.5/2/0981 19
1. Taxation - Brazil. 2. Fiscal policy - Brazil. I. Series: Ensaios econômicos (Universidade de São Paulo. Instituto de Pesquisas Econômicas) , 61. II. Title.
HJ2525 .B5 1987

Bibliograf, s. a. Vox new college Spanish and English dictionary . Lincolnwood, Ill., U. S.A. , c1984. xix, 1456, 60 p. : ISBN 0-8442-7998-6 (plain-edge ed.) : LC Card 84-61106 DDC 463/.21 19
PC4640 .V696 1984
*NYPL [*R-RGK 85-1500]*

Bibliographie der EG-Zeitschriften 1952-1980 : ein Bestandsverzeichnis der periodischen Veröffentlichungen von den und über die Europäischen Gemeinschaften / bearbeitet von Ekkehart Seusing. Kiel : Bibliothek des Instituts für Weltwirtschaft an der Universität Kiel, 1981. ix, 280 p. ; 24 cm. (Kieler Schrifttumskunden zu Wirtschaft und Gesellschaft. 22) Includes index. LC Card 81-122713
1. European Economic Community - Periodicals - Bibliography. I. Seusing, Ekkehart. II. Universität Kiel. Institut für Weltwirtschaft. Bibliothek. III. Series.
HB41 .K55 Bd. 22 Z7165.E8 HC241.2

Bibliographies and literature of agriculture .
(no. 21) Thompson, Robert L. A survey of recent U. S. developments in international agricultural trade models /. Washington, D.C. , 1981. v, 74 p. ; LC Card 81-603138 DDC 382/.41/0973 19
HD1433 .T48 *NYPL [JLF 84-568]*

(no. 48) Coyle, Barry. Economic gains from agricultural trade . Washington, D.C. [Springfield, VA , 1986] iii, 41 p. : LC Card 86-602417 DDC 382/.41/0973 19
HD9005 .C86 1986

BIBLIOGRAPHY - REFERENCE BOOKS. see **REFERENCE BOOKS.**

Bibliography series (International Institute for Labour Studies) .
(no. 11) Management, work, leisure . Geneva , c1986. viii, 154 p. : ISBN 92-9014-416-5 (pbk.) : LC Card 87-163300 DDC 306/.36/094 19
HD4904.6 .M35 1986

Biblioteca agrícola Aedos.
Capdevila Batlles, José. Agricultura e industria española frente a la CEE . Barcelona [1985?] 252 p. : ISBN 84-7003-282-8 LC Card 86-171577
HC385 .C358 1985

Biblioteca básica del pensamiento ecuatoriano .
(20-21) Pensamiento monetario y financiero /. Quito, Ecuador , 1986. 2 v. : LC Card 87-150740 DDC 332.4/9866 19
HG862 .P46 1986

(23) Pensamiento agrario ecuatoriano /. Quito, Ecuador , 1986. 741 p. : LC Card 87-403503 DDC 333.3/1/866 19
HD1333.E2 P46 1986

Biblioteca breve (Instituto de Cultura e Língua Portuguesa (Portugal)) .
(v. 93) Arroteia, Jorge Carvalho, 1947- A evolução demográfica portuguesa . Lisboa , Amadora, Portugal , 1984 [i.e. 1985] 119 p. : LC Card 86-125507 DDC 304.6/09469 19
HB3621 .A77 1985

Biblioteca de altos estudos.
Amzalak, Moses Bensabat, 1892- D. Alvaro Pais e o pensamento económico em Portugal na Idade Média /. Lisboa , 1954. 71 p. : LC Card 84-213332
HB79.P45 A49 1954

Biblioteca de Autores y Temas Tachirenses (Series) .
(86) Muñoz, Arturo Guillermo. El Táchira fronterizo . Caracas , 1985. 315 p. ; ISBN 980-265-178-8 LC Card 87-402928 DDC 330.987/120633 19
HC238.T3 M86 1985

Biblioteca de bolsillo (Cáceres, Spain)
Alvarado Corrales, Eduardo J. Extremadura . Cáceres [1984?] 101 p. : ISBN 84-600-3663-4 LC Card 86-165503
HD1333.S712 E783 1984

Biblioteca de ciencias económicas. Serie administración y dirección.
Settembrino, Hugo O. La función gerencial en la empresa . Buenos Aires , c1985. viii, 127 p. : ISBN 950-0-23598-6 LC Card 85-201051
HD37.S66 S47 1985

Biblioteca de ciencias sociales (Quito, Ecuador) .
(v. 1) Cosse, Gustavo. Estado y agro en el Ecuador, 1960-1980 /. Quito , 1984. 112 p. : LC Card 85-119842 DDC 338.1/8866 19
HD1888 .C67 1984 *NYPL [JLD 86-2738]*

(v. 10) Investigación agraria y crisis . Quito , 1986. 498 p. : LC Card 87-400125 DDC 338.1/098 19
HD1860.A53 I58 1986

(v. 11) El Ecuador en la encrucijada . Quito , 1986. 307 p. : LC Card 87-400394 DDC 331.12/09866 19
HD5758.A6 E28 1986

(v. 12) La Crisis de la economía ecuatoriana . Quito , 1986. 232 p. : LC Card 87-400395 DDC 330.9866/074 19
HC202 .C755 1986

Biblioteca de economía agraria del Banco de Crédito Agrícola.
Loring, Jaime. Los sectores agrarios de Andalucía ante la integración en la C.E.E. /. Madrid , 1984. 303 p. : ISBN 84-7114-149-3 LC Card 86-152628
HD2025.A5 L67 1984

Biblioteca de ensayo .
(6) González do Molina Navarro, Manuel. Desamortización, deuda pública y crecimiento económico, Andalucía, 1820/1823 /. Granada , Córdoba :bFundación Paco Natera [1985?] 443 p. : ISBN 84-505-1053-8 LC Card 86-210676
HD779.A4 G66 1985

Biblioteca de história (Edições Graal) .
(vol. no. 14) Mendonça, Sonia Regina de. Estado e economia no Brasil . Rio de Janeiro-RJ, Brasil , 1986. 106 p. ; LC Card 86-197575
HC187 .M469 1986

Biblioteca de la cultura andaluza. Ensayo.
Comín, Alfonso C. Noticia de Andalucía /. Sevilla [1985] 338 p. ; ISBN 84-7587-037-6 LC

Card 86-219377
HC387.A64 C62 1985

Biblioteca de la culura andaluza .
(23) Díaz del Moral, Juan, 1870-1948. Las agitaciones campesinas del período bolchevista, 1918-1920 /. Sevilla [1985?] 230 p. ; ISBN 84-7587-031-7 LC Card 86-181529
HD1536.S7 D48 1985

Biblioteca de la mujer.
Mack, Macarena. Los trabajos de las mujeres entre el campo y la ciudad, 1920-1982 . [Santiago, Chile] [1986] 108 p. ; LC Card 86-217673
HD6126 .M33 1986

Biblioteca del pensamiento socialista. Serie Estudios críticos.
Mandel, Ernest. "El capital" . México, D.F. , 1985. 242 p. ; ISBN 968-231-127-6 LC Card 86-158367
HB501.M37 M355 1985

Biblioteca dell'economista. Ottava serie, Sezione sesta .
(v. 1) Tarantelli, Ezio. Economia politica del lavoro /. Torino , c1986. xxiv, 549 p. : ISBN 88-02-03977-1 LC Card 86-213541
HD4901 .T368 1986

Biblioteca di coltura per i rurali .
(vol. 5) Bandini, Mario. Agricoltura e crisi /. Firenze , 1937. 265 p. ; LC Card 87-116637
HB3728 .B36 1937

Biblioteca di economia e relazioni industriali.
Fiorito, Riccardo, 1947- Mercato del lavoro e politica economica . Venezia , 1984. 247 p. : ISBN 88-317-4733-9 : LC Card 86-163951
HD5701.6 .F56 1984

Biblioteca di economia (Etas libri (Firm)) .
(8) L'Economia tedesca . Milano , c1981. 273 p. : LC Card 87-673286
HC286.7 .E29x 1981

Biblioteca di storia e cultura meridionale. Saggi .
(3) Cozzetto, Fausto. Mezzogiorno e demografia nel XV secolo /. Soveria M.lli, CZ , c1986. ix, 202 p. ; LC Card 86-213782
HB3600.N37 C69 1986

Biblioteca di storia economica e sociale. Saggi .
(2) Cavalcanti, Maria Luisa, 1943- La politica commerciale italiana, 1945-1952 . Napoli , c1984. 288 p. ; LC Card 86-121609 DDC 380.1/3/0945 19
HF1549 .C38 1984

Biblioteca ecuatoriana (Guayaquil, Ecuador) .
(27) Tenencia de la tierra y desarrollo socio-económico del sector agrícola. [Guayaquil] [1981] xxv, 539 p., [16] leaves of plates : LC Card 87-673171
HD526 .T46x 1981

Biblioteca Mercados financieros .
(1) González Vega, Claudio. Mercados financieros y desarrollo /. Santo Domingo, República Dominicana , 1986. 73 p. : LC Card 87-102022
HG2817 .G66 1986

(2) Poyo, Jeffrey. Los bancos agropecuarios y la captación de depósitos /. Santo Domingo, República Dominicana , 1986. 39 p. : LC Card 87-400523 DDC 332.7/1/097293 19
HG2051.D6 P69 1986

(3) González Vega, Claudio. Mercados financieros rurales en América Latina /. Santo Domingo, República Dominicana , 1986. 44 p. ; LC Card 87-400002 DDC 332.7/1/098 19
HG2051.L26 G66 1986

(4) Dauhajre, Andrés. Reforma financiera en pequeñas economías abiertas /. Santo Domingo, República Dominicana , 1986. 97 p. : LC Card 87-402920 DDC 332.4/56097293 19
HG3926.5 .D38 1986

Biblioteca Pioneira de ciências sociais. Economia.
Homem de Melo, Fernando Bento, 1942- Prioridade agrícola . São Paulo , 1985. xiii, 200 p. : LC Card 86-126447 DDC 338.1/881 19
HD1872 .H66 1985 ***NYPL [JLD 86-3809]***

Biblioteca Pioneira de estudos sociais. Economia.
Kirsten, José Tiacci. Custo de vida . São Paulo , 1985. xi, 158 p. : LC Card 86-143942
HB235.B8 K57 1985

Biblioteca Política argentina .
(129) Isuani, Ernesto A. (Ernesto Aldo) Los orígenes conflictivos de la seguridad social argentina /. Buenos Aires , c1985. 140 p. ; ISBN 950-25-0128-4 : LC Card 86-174656
HD7149 .I88 1985

(142, etc) Fernández, Arturo. Ideologías de los grupos dirigentes sindicales /. Buenos Aires , c1986. 2 v. ; ISBN 950-25-1403-3 (v. 1) LC Card 86-205687
HD6603.5 .F47 1986

(142, 144) Fernández, Arturo. Ideologías de los grupos dirigentes sindicales /. Buenos Aires , c1986. 2 v. ; ISBN 950-25-1403-3 (v. 1) LC Card 86-205687
HD6603.5 .F47 1986

(151) Regalsky, Andrés Martín. Las inversiones extranjeras en la Argentina, 1860-1914 /. Buenos Aires , c1986. 129 p. ; ISBN 950-25-1412-2 : LC Card 87-100719
HG5312 .R44 1986

(153) Falcón, Ricardo. El mundo del trabajo urbano, 1890-1914 /. Buenos Aires , c1986. 141 p. ; ISBN 950-25-1414-2 : LC Card 87-101423
HD8266 .F35 1986

(155) Angueira, María del Carmen. Capitalismo de estado, 1927-1956 /. Buenos Aires , c1986. 116 p. : ISBN 950-25-1416-5 LC Card 87-100705
HD9711.A72 A54 1986

(159) Bellardi, Marta. Villas miseria . Buenos Aires , c1986. 157 p. : ISBN 950-25-1423-8 : LC Card 87-125510 DDC 307.3/36 19
HD7321.B9 B45 1986

(160) El "Sindicalismo revolucionario," 1905-1945 /. Buenos Aires , c1986. 153 p. ; ISBN 950-25-1424-6 : LC Card 87-125439 DDC 335/.82/0982 19
HD6602 .S49 1986

Biblioteca popular boliviana de "Ultimo Hora"
Poppe, René. Interior mina . La Paz, Bolivia , 1986. 236 p. ; LC Card 87-400962 DDC 331.7/622/0984 19
HD8039.M61 B634 1986

Biblioteca popular extremeña .
(5) Bohoyo Velázquez, Isidoro Francisco. Situación socio-económica y condiciones de vida en la Provincia de Badajoz, 1880-1902 /. Badajoz [1984?] 149 p., [3] p. of plates : ISBN 84-309-1055-7 LC Card 86-151914
HC387.B14 B64 1984

Biblioteca reprográfica Xerox .
(20) Os Assinantes da praça 1834-1984. Rio de Janeiro , 1984. 72 p. ; LC Card 85-160423
HF300.B66 A78 1984

Biblioteca Sindical ISMAC. Serie Conferencias .
(no. 23) Marín Taborda, Iván. María Cano en el amanecer de la clase obrera /. Bogotá , 1985. 103 p. : LC Card 86-165616
HD6642 .M37 1985 ***NYPL [JLD 86-3540]***

Biblioteca Universidad Veracruzana.
Zilli Manica, José Benigno. Braceros italianos para México . Xalapa, México , 1986. 93 p., [6] p. of plates : ISBN 968-8340-45-6 LC Card 87-400059
HD8118.5.I83 Z55 1986

Biblioteca Universidade Popular .
(6) Castro, Armando. Lições de economia II . Lisboa , c1986. 223 p. ; LC Card 87-106195 DDC 330 19
HB178.5 .C37 1986

Bibliotecas universitarias. Economía.
Feldman, Ernesto V. (Ernesto Víctor) Crisis financiera y endeudamiento externo en la Argentina /. [Buenos Aires] , c1986. 184 p. ; ISBN 950-25-1313-4 LC Card 86-182663
HG185.A7 F45 1986

Bibliotecas universitarias. Historia.
Panettieri, José. Argentina . [Buenos Aires] , c1986. 219 p. ; ISBN 950-25-1317-7 LC Card 86-226796
HC175 .P334 1986

Bibliotechka Problemy mirovogo khoziaĭstva.
Ivanov, S. F. (Sergeĭ Feliksovich) Razvivaiushchiesia strany . Moskva , 1984. 63 p. : LC Card 85-125223
HB884 .I93 1984

Bibliotechka propagandista i politinformatora.
TSygankov, P. A. (Pavel Afanas'evich) V bor'be protiv vsevlastiia kapitala /. Moskva , 1986. 139 p. ; LC Card 86-132423
HB501 .T78 1986

Bibliotechka sel'skogo profsoiuznogo aktivista .
(1981, 5) Borchenko, N. (Nikolaĭ) Sel'skoe khoziaĭstvo v odinnadtsatoĭ piatiletke . Moskva , 1981. 93 p. ; LC Card 81-188371
HD1493.R9 B5 1981, no. 5 HD9015.S65

Biblioteczka Wszechnicy NSZZ Solidarność.
Samecki, Wiesław. Czego można oczekiwać od ekonomii /. Warszawa , 1981. 35 p. ; ISBN 83-202-0150-0 LC Card 86-150577
HC340.3 .S24 1981

Biblioteka "Istraživanja i rasprave"
Društvena reprodukcija u djelu Vladimira Bakarića /. Zagreb , 1985 printing. 204 p. ; LC Card 86-233326
HD5650 .D68 1985

Biblioteka kadr kierowniczych.
Sterniczuk, Henryk. Decyzje w organizacjach gospodarczych /. Warszawa , 1980. 167 p. ; ISBN 83-208-0052-8 LC Card 81-109564
HD30.23 .S726 1980

Biblioteka Naša praksa.
Mirić, Rade. Proces samoupravne integracije . Bačka Topola , 1984. 147 p. ; LC Card 85-194104
HD5660.Y8 M57 1984

Tomić, Danilo. Jugoslovenska agrarna teorija i politika . Bačka Topola , 1985. 211 p. : LC Card 85-195818
HD2045.5.Z8 T62 1985

Biblioteka pedagogiczna .
(P-37) Kowtun, Józef. Rola, funkcje i zadania mistrza w systemie dokształcania i wychowania robotników /. Warszawa , 1979. 151, [1] p. ; LC Card 81-180277
HF5549.5.T7 K687 1979

Biblioteka peredovogo opyta (Tekhnika (Firm)). Tekhnologiia proizvodstva.
IUkhimenko, V. V. (Vladimir Vasil'evich) Izuchenie i prognozirovanie sprosa na bytovye uslugi /. Kiev , 1983. 103 p. ; LC Card 83-218585
HD9986.S683 U385 1983

Biblioteka peredovogo opyta. Tekhnologiia proizvodstva.
IUkhimenko, V. V. (Vladimir Vasil'evich) Izuchenie i prognozirovanie sprosa na bytovye uslugi /. Kiev , 1983. 103 p. ; LC Card 83-218585
HD9986.S683 U385 1983

Biblioteka Publicistika.
Pavlović, Dragiša, 1943- Ko radnike povezuje lažnim koncima . Beograd , 1984. 414 p. ; LC Card 84-178578
HC407.Z9 L36 1984

Biblioteka sekretariia partorganizatsii.
Luukas, Ants. [Majandi parteigrupid. Russian.] Partiĭnye gruppy v kolkhozakh i sovkhozakh /. Tallin , 1984. 77 p., [8] p. of plates : LC Card 87-115056
HD1492.S652 E85517 1984

Biblioteka "Spraw międzynarodowych".
(nr. 67) Winiecki, Jan. Rola pomocy gospodarczej w polityce zagranicznej USA wobec krajów rozwijających się /. Warszawa , 1979. 310, [1] p. ; LC Card 81-205172
HC60 .W54 1979

Biblioteka Udžbenici .
(103) Vrsaljko, Krešimir. Teorija i praksa domaćih i medunarodnih plaćanja /. Zagreb , 1982. xiv, 460 p. ; LC Card 84-160248
HG2341.Y82 V77 1982

Biblioteka Udžbenici i skripta.
Milošević, Nikša. Sistem udruženog rada /. Beograd , 1985. 392 p. : LC Card 86-197428
HD5660.Y8 M55 1985

Bibliotheca biographica. Sezione di scienze sociali.
Ricardo, David, 1772-1823. Scritti monetari /. Roma [1985] 495 p. ; LC Card 86-207988
HG938 .R63 1985

Walras, Léon, 1834-1910. L'economia monetaria /. Roma [1985] 2 v. (949 p.) : LC Card 87-140163
HG221 .W219 1985

Bibliotheca historico-politica .
(2) Wildenberg, Ivo W. (Ivo Willibrord) Johan & Pieter de la Court, 1622-1660 & 1618-1685 . Amsterdam , 1986. xiii, 180 p., [21] p. of plates : ISBN 90-302-1162-8 : LC Card

87-141484
HC322.5.A2 W55 1986

Bibliotheek wetenschappelijk bedrijfsbeheer.
Competitief ondernemen . Antwerpen , 1983. vi, 233 p. : ISBN 90-6716-301-5 LC Card 85-177786
HD41 .C64 1983

Bibliothèque de science financière. For additional listing of contents, see Old Catalog.
(t. 19) Zemrani, Anas Bensalah. La fiscalité face au développement économique et social du Maroc /. Rabat , 1982. 395 p. ; LC Card 83-183254
HJ3032 .Z34 1982

Bibliothèque des écoles françaises d'Athènes et de Rome. For additional listing of contents, see entry in Old Catalog under: Bibliothèque des écoles françaises d'Athènes et de Rome. ser. 1.
(fasc. 262) Bresc, Henri. Un monde méditerranéen . [Roma] , 1986. 2 v. (981 p.) : ISBN 2-7283-0103-4 (set) LC Card 87-139949
HC307.S5 B74 1986

Bibliothèque des leaders.
Bergeot, Paul. Champagne, la coupe est pleine . [Paris] , c1980. 185 p. ; ISBN 2-86510-001-4 : LC Card 80-120736
HD9382.7.C5 B468 1980

Bibliothèque des matières premières.
Bra Kanon, Denis, 1936- Développement ou appauvrissement /. Paris , c1985. 188 p. : ISBN 2-7178-0962-7 : LC Card 86-177676
HF1413 .B72 1985

Chalmin, Philippe. Négociants et chargeurs . Paris , 1985. 299 p. : ISBN 2-7178-0851-5 : LC Card 85-149921 DDC 333.7 19
HF1051 .C42 1985

Bibliothèque du développement.
Comprendre l'économie africaine /. Paris , c1985. 566 p. : ISBN 2-85802-566-2 LC Card 86-222248
HC800 .C654 1985

Salahdine, Mohamed. Maroc, tribus, makhzen et colons . Paris , c1986. 337 p. : ISBN 2-85802-525-5 LC Card 86-159041
HC810 .S23 1986

Biblograf, S. A. Vox Modern Spanish and English dictionary . Lincolnwood, Ill. , c1986. xxxiv, 487, 45, 484 p. : ISBN 0-8442-7990-0 LC Card 86-61160 ***NYPL [*R-RGK 86-7059]***

Bich, M. O. Rabochee dvizhenie v Belorussii v 1861-1904 gg. / M.O. Bich ; redaktor I.M. Ignatenko. Minsk : "Nauka i tekhnika", 1983. 278 p. ; 21 cm. At head of title: Akademiia nauk Belorusskoĭ SSR. Institut istorii. Bibliography: p. 240-[259] LC Card 83-182369
1. Labor and laboring classes - Byelorussian S.S.R. - History - 19th century. 2. Socialism - Byelorussian S.S.R. - History - 19th century. I. Ignatenko, I. M., 1919-. II. Title.
HD8529.B952 B52 1983
NYPL [*QM 87-2378]

Bichara Khader. see **Khader, Bichara.**

Bichelberger, Roger.
Tiroir aux souvenirs. German & French. 1986. Glück auf! : la vie quotidienne dans le bassin houiller lorrain / une réalisation de l'Action culturelle du bassin houiller lorrain ; [recherche photographique et légendes, Michel Sirey, Philippe Krucker, Pascal Flaus]. Nouvelle de R. Bichelberger / traduction allemande de Irmengard Peller-Séguy. Paris [1986] 117 p. : ISBN 2-86738-115-0 : LC Card 86-178958
HD8039.M6152 F84 1986

The Bickerdike machine papers /. Newman, Geoffrey R. (Geoffrey Richard), 1933- Toronto , c1986. 144 p. : ISBN 0-919801-51-X (pbk.) : LC Card 87-167878 DDC 681/.7676 19
HE6237 .N48 1986

Bickerstaff, Isaac, sen., pseud. see **Defoe, Daniel, 1661?-1731.**

BICYCLE COMMUTING - AUSTRIA.
Bauer, Helfried. Fahrradfreundliche Verkehrspolitik in Stadt und Land . Wien , 1984. 87 p. : LC Card 85-150945
HE5739.A9 B38 1984

BICYCLE COMMUTING - GERMANY (WEST) - SPROCKHÖVEL.
Radverkehrskonzept Sprockhövel /. Essen , c1985. 55 p., [3] folded col. leaves of plates : ISBN 3-923494-51-3 LC Card 86-113993
HE5739.G3 R33 1985

BICYCLE COMMUTING - SCANDINAVIA.
Cykeltrafik i nordiske byer /. København , 1982. 207 p. : ISBN 87-7303-045-7 LC Card 83-242616
HE5739.S34 C94 1982

BICYCLE INDUSTRY - DEVELOPING COUNTRIES.
Bicycles and components . Geneva , 1985. x, 160 p. ; LC Card 86-219298 DDC 380./456292272/091724 19
HD9993.B543 D442 1985

Bicycles and components : a pilot survey of opportunities for trade among developing countries. Geneva : International Trade Centre UNCTAD/GATT, 1985. x, 160 p. ; 23 cm. Bibliography: p. 157-160. LC Card 86-219298 DDC 380./456292272/091724 19
1. Bicycle industry - Developing countries. 2. Market surveys - Developing countries. I. International Trade Centre UNCTAD/GATT.
HD9993.B543 D442 1985

BICYCLES - GERMANY (WEST) - BAVARIA - ACCIDENTS.
Analyse von Unfällen motorisierter Zweiradbenutzer . [West Germany] [1976] 32 p. : LC Card 85-135424
HE5614.5.G3 A65 1976

Biczo, Dezso. Hungary, pushing the limits [videorecording] /. Alexandria, VA , 1987. 1 videocassette (60 min.) : LC Card 87-707589 DDC 943.9 11
HC300.28

BIDASOA RIVER VALLEY (SPAIN AND FRANCE) - SOCIAL LIFE AND CUSTOMS.
Garmendia Larrañaga, Juan. Artesanos de la regata del Bidasoa . San Sebastián [1983] 123 p. : ISBN 84-7148-115-4 LC Card 84-140784 DDC 331.7/94 19
HD2346.S72 B534 1983
NYPL [3-MNE 86-3657]

Bidding & estimating in the building service industry. Fairfax, VA : Building Service Contractors Association International, c1983. v, 10 p. : form ; 28 cm. LC Card 87-110623 DDC 648/.068/1 19
1. Building cleaning industry. 2. Buildings - Cleaning - Contracts and specifications. 3. Buildings - Cleaning - Estimates. 4. Contracts, Letting of. I. Building Service Contractors Association International. II. Title: Bidding and estimating in the building service industry.
HD9999.B882 B53 1983

Bidding and estimating in the building service industry. Bidding & estimating in the building service industry. Fairfax, VA , c1983. v, 10 p. : LC Card 87-110623 DDC 648/.068/1 19
HD9999.B882 B53 1983

BIDDING, COMPETITIVE. see **CONTRACTS, LETTING OF.**

Bidding for projects financed by international lending agencies / edited by David Sassoon. Aldershot, Hants. : Gower, c1982. vii, 345 p. : ill. ; 31 cm. Proceedings of a conference sponsored by Gower Conferences Ltd., held in London in 1981. ISBN 0-566-03033-0 LC Card 82-210482 DDC 332.1/53 19
1. Contracts, Letting of - Congresses. 2. Economic development projects - Congresses. 3. Financial institutions, International - Congresses. I. Sassoon, David M. II. Gower Conferences Ltd.
HD2365 .B52 1982 ***NYPL [JLG 85-120]***

Bidgoli, Hossein. Working with Lotus 1-2-3 : a comprehensive manual : release 2.01 / Hossein Bidgoli. St. Paul : West Pub. Co., c1988. xxii, 397 p. : ill. ; 26 cm. Includes index. ISBN 0-314-65031-8 (pbk.) LC Card 87-25268 DDC 005.36/9 19
1. Lotus 1-2-3 (Computer program). I. Title. II. Title: Working with Lotus One-Two-Three.
HF5548.4.L67 B53 1988

Bidol, Patricia A. Alternative environmental conflict management approaches . [Ann Arbor, MI] (Dana Bldg., Ann Arbor 48109-1115) [1986] 252 p. : LC Card 86-225219 DDC 363.7/058/0973 19
HC110.E5 A643 1986

Biebel, Belle M. The small business reference guide for home-based business, small manufacturers, self-publishers, entrepreneurs, craftsmen, retailers, writers, artists / Belle M. Biebel. Stratford, Conn. : Bluechip Books, c1987. viii, 63 p. ; 22 cm. Includes indexes. ISBN 0-941825-02-7 (pbk.) LC Card 87-91148 DDC 016.658/022 19
1. Small business - Information services - United States - Directories. 2. Small business - Bibliography. I. Title.
HD2346.U5 B49 1987

Biebl, Andrew R., 1948- Behrenfeld, William H. Accountant's business manual /. New York, N.Y. , c1987- 1 v. (loose-leaf) ; ISBN 0-87051-000-2 (loose-leaf) : LC Card 87-992 DDC 657 19
HF5616.U5 B38 1987

Biecker, Johannes. Arbeitersiedlungen im 19. Jahrhundert . Bochum , c1985. 189 p. : ISBN 3-88339-427-0 LC Card 85-164690
HD7289.5.A3 G42 1985

Biedenkopf, Kurt H.
Kontinuität und Wandel in vier Jahrzehnten deutscher Wirtschaftspolitik /. Stuttgart , New York , 1986. 111 p. ; ISBN 3-437-50310-3 LC Card 87-116017 DDC 338.943 19
HC286.5 .K618 1986

Die neue Sicht der Dinge : Plädoyer für eine freiheitliche Wirtschafts- und Sozialordnung / Kurt H. Biedenkopf. München : Piper, c1985. 458 p. ; 22 cm. ISBN 3-492-02813-6 LC Card 86-105815
1. Laissez-faire. 2. Christlich-Demokratische Union Deutschlands (Germany : West) - Platforms. 3. Germany, West - Economic policy. 4. Germany, West - Social policy. I. Title.
HB95 .B53 1985

Biedermann, Flodoard, Freiherr v., b. 1858. Deutsche Industrie, deutsche Kultur /. Berlin , 1900-1902. xvi, 388 p. : LC Card 85-666344
HC283 .D48x 1900

Biegeleisen, J. I. (Jacob Israel), 1910- Make your job interview a success : a guide for the career-minded job seeker / J.I. Biegeleisen.2nd ed. New York : Distributed by Prentice Hall Trade, c1987. 222 p. : ill. ; 28 cm. "An Arco book." Bibliography: p. 203-209. Includes index. ISBN 0-13-545716-5 : LC Card 87-19294 DDC 650.1/4 19
1. Employment interviewing. I. Title.
HF5549.5.I6 B5 1987

Bieling, Thomas, 1953- Das Entwicklungsmodell der italienischen Wirtschaft : unter besonderer Berücksichtigung sektoraler, dimensionaler und territorialer Gegebenheiten / vorgelegt von Thomas Bieling. Berlin : [s.n.], 1982 (Berlin : Copy-Center in Dahlem) 372 p. ; 21 cm. Thesis (doctoral)--Freie Universität Berlin. Bibliography: p. 358-368. LC Card 87-673359
1. Italy - Economic conditions - 1945-. I. Title.
HC305 .B46x 1982

Bien, Frederick A. Microcomputer applications for CPAs / by Frederick A. Bien. New York, NY : American Institute of Certified Public Accountants, c1986. 8, 34, 34, 65 p. : ill. ; 28 cm. LC Card 87-121259 DDC 657/.028/5536 19
1. Accounting - Data processing. 2. Microcomputers. I. American Institute of Certified Public Accountants. II. Title.
HF5679 .B54 1986

Bienewald, Erwin, 1950- Offene Jugendarbeit im Arbeiterviertel . Bensheim , 1978. 229 p. : ISBN 3-921450-57-8 LC Card 84-120278
HD6276.G4 O38 1978

Bierbach, Wolf. Rundfunk zwischen Kommerz und Politik : der Westdeutsche Rundfunk in der Weimarer Zeit / Wolf Bierbach. Frankfurt am Main ; New York : P. Lang, c1986. 2 v. (595 p.) : ill. ; 21 cm. (Europäische Hochschulschriften. Reihe XL, Kommunikationswissenschaft und Publizistik, 0176-3725 . Bd. 7 = vol. 7 = vol. 7) Bibliography: p. 547-578. CONTENTS. - Bd. 1. Darstellungsteil -- Bd. 2. Anmerkungen. ISBN 3-8204-9692-0 LC Card 86-233794
1. Radio broadcasting - Germany - History. 2. Germany - Politics and government - 1918-1933. 3. Westdeutscher Rundfunk - History. I. Title.
HE8699.G3 B54 1986

Bierbaum, Heinz. Wirtschaftsdemokratie gegen Wirtschaftskrise . Hamburg , 1986. 177 p. : ISBN 3-87975-310-5 LC Card 86-193914
HD4175 .W54 1986

Bierman, Harold.
The capital budgeting decision : economic analysis of investment projects / Harold Bierman, Jr., Seymour Smidt.7th ed. New York : Macmillan ; London : Collier Macmillan, c1988. xvi, 557 p. : ill. ; 25 cm. Includes bibliographies and index. ISBN 0-02-309941-0 LC Card 87-15257 DDC 658.1/52 19
1. Capital investments - Evaluation. 2. Capital budget. I. Smidt, Seymour. II. Title.
HG4028.C4 B54 1988

Implementation of capital budgeting techniques : a survey and synthesis / Harold Bierman, Jr. Tampa, FL : Financial Management Association, c1986. i, 69 p. : ill. ; 23 cm. (The Financial management survey and synthesis series) Spine title: Capital budgeting techniques. Includes bibliographies. ISBN 0-936795-01-8 (pbk.) LC Card 86-231118 DDC 658.1/54 19
1. Capital budget. 2. Capital investments. I. Title. II. Title: Capital budgeting techniques. III. Series.
HG4028.C4 B544 1986

Biermann, Ingrid, 1955- Leben mit kurzfristigem Denken : eine Untersuchung zur Situation arbeitsloser Akademikerinnen / Ingrid Biermann, Christiane Schmerl, Lindy Ziebell. Weinheim : Beltz Verlag, 1985. 224 p. ; 21 cm. (Ergebnisse der Frauenforschung . Bd. 1) Bibliography: p. [209]-215. ISBN 3-407-58260-9 LC Card 86-106693
1. Women college graduates - Employment - Germany (West). 2. Unemployment - Germany (West) - Psychological aspects. I. Schmerl, Christiane. II. Ziebell, Lindy, 1955-. III. Title. IV. Series.
HD6053.6.G3 B54 1985 ***NYPL [JLD 86-3122]***

Biersteker, Thomas J. Multinationals, the state, and control of the Nigerian economy / Thomas J. Biersteker. Princeton, N.J. : Princeton University Press, c1987. xvii, 344 p. : ill. ; 24 cm. Bibliography: p. [327]-335. Includes index. ISBN 0-691-07728-2 (alk. paper) : LC Card 86-25214 DDC 338.8/88669 19
1. Investments, Foreign - Nigeria. 2. International business enterprises - Nigeria. 3. Nigeria - Economic policy. 4. Nigeria - Economic policy - 1970-. I. Title.
HG5881.A3 B54 1987

Bierwag, Gerald O. Duration analysis : managing interest rate risk / Gerald O. Bierwag. Cambridge, Mass. : Ballinger, c1987. xvi, 341 p. : ill. ; 24 cm. Includes bibliographies and indexes. ISBN 0-88730-116-9 LC Card 86-28745 DDC 332.8/2 19
1. Investments - Mathematics. 2. Bonds. 3. Mortgage banks. 4. Interest rates. 5. Rate of return. I. Title.
HG4515.3 .B54 1987

Biescas, José Antonio, 1946- El proceso de industrialización en la región aragonesa en el período 1900-1920 / José Antonio Biescas Ferrer. Zaragoza : Institución "Fernando el Católico", 1985. 335 p. : ill. ; 24 cm. (Tesis doctorales. 58) Publicación núm. 1036 de la Institución "Fernando el Católico" Originally presented as the author's thesis (doctoral--Universidad de Barcelona, 1975) Bibliography: p. 319-324. Includes indexes. ISBN 84-00-06130-6 LC Card 87-111810
1. Aragon (Spain) - Industries - History - 20th century. 2. Aragon (Spain) - Economic conditions. I. Series: Tesis doctorales (Institución "Fernando el Católico") , 58. II. Title.
HC387.A68 B536 1985

Bieshaar, H. Kleinknecht, A. Industriële innovatie in Nederland . Assen , 1987. viii, 140 p. ; ISBN 90-232-2261-X : LC Card 87-157579
HC329.5.T4 K58 1987

Biethahn, Jörg. Simulation als betriebliche Entscheidungshilfe . Berlin , New York , 1987. xi, 282 p. : ISBN 0-387-17353-6 LC Card 87-121884 DDC 658.4/0352 19
HD30.23 .S56 1987

Bifani, Patricia. Adagala, Kavetsa. Self-employed women in the peri-urban setting . Nairobi , 1985. ii, 99 leaves : LC Card 85-980984 DDC 331.4/8138118/0967625 19
HF3893.Z9 N343 1985

BIFOA-Monographien .
(Bd. 26) Meyer, Rolf, 1957- Integration der Informationsverarbeitung im Büro . Bergisch Gladbach , c1986. xiv, 327 p. : ISBN 3-89012-062-8 LC Card 87-104032 DDC 651.8 19
HF5547.5 .M497 1986

The big bang /. Thomas, William Arthur. Deddington, Oxford , Atlantic Highlands, N.J. , 1986. ix, 180 p. ; ISBN 0-86003-546-8 LC Card 86-226055 DDC 332.64/241 19
HG4577 .T47 1986

"Big Bill" Haywood /. Dubofsky, Melvyn, 1934- New York , 1987. viii, 184 p. ; ISBN 0-312-01272-1 : LC Card 87-17355 DDC 331.88/6 B 19
HD6509.H3 D82 1987

The big boys . Nader, Ralph. New York , c1986. xix, 571 p. ; ISBN 0-394-53338-0 : LC Card 85-25979 DDC 338.6/44/0973 19
HD2785 .N33 1986 ***NYPL [JLE 86-2421]***

BIG BUSINESS - BANGLADESH.
Rahman, Alimur. Capacity utilisation in the large-scale manufacturing industry in Bangladesh /. [Dhaka] [1983] 123 p. ; LC Card 83-903801 DDC 338.6/44/095492 19
HD69.C3 R34 1983 ***NYPL [JLE 86-4622]***

BIG BUSINESS - CZECHOSLOVAKIA - BOHEMIA - HISTORY.
Brousek, Karl M. Die Grossindustrie Böhmens, 1848-1918 /. München , 1987. 223 p., 8 leaves of plates : ISBN 3-486-51871-2 LC Card 87-142819 DDC 338.6/44/094371 19
HD2356.C96 B643 1987

BIG BUSINESS - CZECHOSLOVAKIA - LIBEREC - HISTORY.
Album der Industrie des Reichenberger Handelskammer-Bezirks. [Praha] , 1981. 2 v. in 1 : LC Card 84-190839
HC270.292.L52 A42 1981

BIG BUSINESS - GERMANY, WEST.
Wolf, Martin, 1954- Erfahrungen mit der Profit-Center-Organisation /. Frankfurt am Main , New York , c1985. viii, 285 p. : ISBN 3-8204-8746-8 LC Card 85-243838
HD2756.2.G3 W65 1985

BIG BUSINESS - JAPAN.
Futatsugi, Yūsaku, 1935- [Gendai Nihon no kigyō shūdan. English.] Japanese enterprise groups /. [Kobe] , 1986. 179 p. : LC Card 86-220427 DDC 338.8/0952 19
HD2756.2.J3 F8813 1986

BIG BUSINESS - UNITED STATES.
Adams, Walter, 1922 (Aug. 27)- The bigness complex . New York , 1986. xiii, 426 p. ; ISBN 0-394-54721-7 : LC Card 86-42624 DDC 338.6/44/0973 19
HD2785 .A68 1986 ***NYPL [JLE 87-1432]***

Andrunas, E. Ch. (Elena Cheslavovna) Biznes i propaganda . Moskva , 1986. 223 p. : LC Card 87-152425
HD59.6.U6 A53 1986

Emerson, James C. Careers in public accounting 1986/87- . Seattle, Wash. (2824 Sahalee Dr. E., Redmond 98053) , c1986. 261 p. ; LC Card 87-71857 DDC 338.7/61657/0973 19
HF5616.U5 E46 1986

Nader, Ralph. The big boys . New York , c1986. xix, 571 p. ; ISBN 0-394-53338-0 : LC Card 85-25979 DDC 338.6/44/0973 19
HD2785 .N33 1986 ***NYPL [JLE 86-2421]***

BIG BUSINESS - UNITED STATES - DIRECTORIES.
Rosenbaum, Virginia. Takeover defenses . Washington, D.C. , c1987. 227 p. ; ISBN 0-931035-13-9 (pbk.) LC Card 87-400095 DDC 338.7/4/02573 19
HD2746.5 .R67 1987

BIG BUSINESS - UNITED STATES - HISTORY.
Bunting, David G. The rise of large American corporations, 1889-1919 /. New York , 1986, c1987. 224 p. ; ISBN 0-8240-8353-9 (alk. paper) : LC Card 86-29527 DDC 338.6/44 19
HD2785 .B76 1987

BIG BUSINESS - UNITED STATES - MANAGEMENT - HISTORY.
Managing big business . Boston, Mass. , c1986. xxvii, 425 p. ; ISBN 0-87584-142-2 LC Card 86-7683 DDC 338.6/44/0973 19
HD2785 .M353 1986 ***NYPL [JLE 87-1360]***

The big foul up awards, 1970 through 1986 . Schneider, Stephen W., 1925- Dallas, Tex. , c1986. viii, 119 p. : LC Card 87-128382
HD9561.W53 S36 1986

The big store . Katz, Donald R. New York , 1987. xiv, 604 p., [16] pages of plates : ISBN 0-670-80512-2 LC Card 87-40060 DDC 381/.45/000973 19
HF5467.S4 K38 1987

Biglino Campos, Paloma. El socialismo español y la cuestión agraria (1890-1936) / Paloma Biglino Campos. Madrid : Centro de Publicaciones, Ministerio de Trabajo y Seguridad Social, [1986?] 564 p. ; 20 cm. (Colección Ediciones de la Revista de trabajo . 11) Bibliography: p. 543-564. ISBN 84-7434-368-2 LC Card 87-136300
1. Trade-unions - Agricultural laborers - Spain - History. 2. P.S.O.E. (Political party) - History. 3. Unión General de Trabajadores de España - History. 4. Agriculture and state - Spain - History. I. Title. II. Series.
HD6764.A29 B54 1986

Bigman, David. Floating exchange rates and the state of world trade payments /. Cambridge, Mass. , 1984. xxvi, 309 p. ; ISBN 0-88410-998-4 (pbk.) LC Card 84-2905 DDC 332.4/562 19
HG3852 .F56 1984 ***NYPL [JLD 86-2709]***

The bigness complex . Adams, Walter, 1922 (Aug. 27)- New York , 1986. xiii, 426 p. ; ISBN 0-394-54721-7 : LC Card 86-42624 DDC 338.6/44/0973 19
HD2785 .A68 1986 ***NYPL [JLE 87-1432]***

BIHAR (INDIA) - CENSUS, 1981.
Census of India, 1981. Delhi , <1983-1987. v. in : LC Card 87-915011 DDC 304.6/0954/12021 19
HA4587.B53 C46 1983

BIHAR (INDIA) - ECONOMIC CONDITIONS.
Singh, Kanti. The great depression and agrarian economy . Delhi, India , 1987. xii, 206 p. ; LC Card 86-903533 DDC 338.1/0954/12 19
HC437.B47 S53 1987

BIHAR (INDIA) - ECONOMIC CONDITIONS - CONGRESSES.
Bihar, stagnation or growth /. Patna , 1987. xxix, 404 p. ; LC Card 87-902676 DDC 330.954/12052 19
HC437.B47 B49 1987

Bihar (India). Rural Development Dept.
Trysem : training of rural youth for self-employment = Svagrāyupra : sva-rojagāra ke liye grāmiṇa yuvajana kā praśikshaṇa. [Paṭanā] : Bihāra Sarakāra, Grāmiṇa Vikāsa Vibhāga, 1980. 41 p. ; 23 cm. In Hindi. LC Card 80-908290
1. Rural youth - Employment - India. 2. Self-employed - India. 3. Occupational training - India. I. Title. II. Title: Svagrāyupra.
HD6276.I42 B54 1980

BIHAR, INDIA (STATE) - ECONOMIC CONDITIONS.
Roy, Ramashray. Dialogues on development . New Delhi , Beverly Hills , 1986. 245 p. ; ISBN 0-8039-9492-3 (U. S.) LC Card 85-8368 DDC 338.954/12 19
HD87 .R69 1986 ***NYPL [JLD 86-3196]***

Bihar, stagnation or growth / edited by Alakh N. Sharma, Shaibal Gupta. Patna : Spectrum Pub. House, 1987. xxix, 404 p. ; 25 cm. Papers, most presented at a seminar held at the A.N. Sinha Institute of Social Studies, Patna, 1984. Includes bibliographies. LC Card 87-902676 DDC 330.954/12052 19
1. Bihar (India) - Economic conditions - Congresses. I. Sharma, Alakh N. II. Gupta, Shaibal.
HC437.B47 B49 1987

Bikel, Ofra. Will there always be an England? [videorecording] /. Alexandria, VA , 1986. 1 videocassette (60 min.) : LC Card 86-707796 DDC 942.085 11
HC256.5

BIKES. see **BICYCLES.**

Bilā sūdī bainkārī /. Khan, Muhammad Akram. Lāhaur [1983] 56 p. ; LC Card 83-931274
HG3290.5.A6 K43 1983

Le Bilan des conférences socio-économiques : de novembre 1979 à mai 1983 : troisième bilan /

déposé par le Secrétariat permanent des Conférences socio-économiques du Québec. [Quebec] : Secrétariat permanent des Conférences socio-économiques du Québec, [1983] xi, 124 p. : ill. ; 24 cm. ISBN 2-551-05784-1 LC Card 84-134997
1. Quebec (Province) - Economic policy - Congresses. 2. Québec (Province) - Social policy - Congresses. I. Québec (Province). Secrétariat des conférences socio-économiques.
HC117.Q4 B535 1983

Bilan socio-économique de la Loire /. Comité d'expansion de la Loire. Saint Etienne [1983] 270 p., [2] leaves of plates : LC Card 85-104338
HC277.L6 C66 1983

Bilancio della socialdemocrazia : interventi sulla crisi del consenso socialdemocratico e del welfare state / V. Cattani ... [et al.] ; prefazione di Flavio Orlandi ; introduzione di Attilio Alberto Scarpellini.1a ed. Napoli : Edizioni scientifiche italiane, 1984. 156 p. ; 21 cm. (Storia delle idee politiche e sociali . 2) Collana di studi e ricerche / Fondazione Giacomo Matteotti Includes bibliographical references. LC Card 84-249837
1. Socialism - Addresses, essays, lectures. 2. Welfare state - Addresses, essays, lectures. I. Cattani, V. (Venerio). II. Series. III. Series: Collana di studi e ricerche / Fondazione Giacomo Matteotti.
HX73 .B55 1984 ***NYPL [JLD 87-1536]***

Bilanzierung von Beteiligungen an assoziierten Unternehmen nach der Equity-Methode . Schäfer, Harald. Thun , c1982. xxiii, 428 p. ; ISBN 3-87144-714-5 LC Card 83-129280
HF5686.I6 S33 1982

Bilanzkennzahlen und Ertragsrisiken des Kapitalmarktes . Möller, Hans Peter. Stuttgart , 1986. xii, 240 p. : ISBN 3-7910-0382-8 LC Card 86-149711
HF5681.C25 M64 1986

Bilanzpolitik und Publizitätsverhalten deutscher Aktiengesellschaften . Schulte, Karl-Werner. Bergisch Gladbach , c1986. xx, 553 p. : ISBN 3-89012-070-9 LC Card 87-122912 DDC 658.1/5/0943 19
HF5686.C7 S357 1986

Bilanzpolitische Forschungsprogramme . Kern, Jürgen, 1951- Frankfurt am Main , New York , c1986. ix, 456 p. : ISBN 3-8204-9363-8 LC Card 86-218816
HF5645 .K43 1986

El Bilbao de Julio Lazúrtegui . Gondra y Oraá, María Victoria de, 1929- Bilbao , 1984. 472 p. : ISBN 84-505-0689-1 LC Card 87-125134
HC382.5.L39 G66 1984

Bilbao Díez, Juan Carlos.

Bilbao, Elena. La frontera de San Ysidro : conmoción comercial y estrategias adaptivas ante la crisis mexicana / Elena Bilbao.1a ed. Tijuana, Baja California : Centro de Estudios Fronterizos del Norte de México, 1986. 27 p. ; 23 cm. (Cuadernos CEFNOMEX) ISBN 968-607-513-5 LC Card 87-125801 DDC 330.9794/98 19
1. San Diego (Calif.) - Economic conditions. 2. San Diego, Calif. - Commerce. 3. Mexican-American Border Region - Economic conditions. 4. Mexico - Economic conditions - 1970-. 5. San Ysidro (San Diego, Calif.). I. Title. II. Series.
HC108.S65 B55 1986

BILBAO (SPAIN) - COMMERCE - HISTORY.
Lafarga Lozano, Adolfo. De Bilbao y de Vizcaya sobre sus orígenes históricos y económicos /. [Bilbao? , 1976?] (Bilbao : Gráficas Loroño) 310 p. : ISBN 84-400-1414-7 LC Card 85-142805
HF3690.B5 L34 1976

BILBAO, SPAIN - HISTORY.
Lafarga Lozano, Adolfo. De Bilbao y de Vizcaya sobre sus orígenes históricos y económicos /. [Bilbao? , 1976?] (Bilbao : Gráficas Loroño) 310 p. : ISBN 84-400-1414-7 LC Card 85-142805
HF3690.B5 L34 1976

Bilbrey, Charles P. Bittel, Lester R. Business in action . New York , c1988. vii, 597 p. : ISBN 0-07-005565-3 LC Card 87-3134 DDC 658 19
HF5343 .B57 1988

Bilby, Kenneth. The general : David Sarnoff and the rise of the communications industry / Kenneth Bilby.1st ed. New York : Harper & Row, c1986. 326 p. ; 25 cm. Includes index. Bibliography: p. 317-318. ISBN 0-06-015568-X : LC Card 85-45621 DDC 384.54/092/4 B 19
1. Sarnoff, David, 1891-1971. 2. Radio Corporation of America - History. 3. Broadcasters - United States - Biography. 4. Industrialists - United States - Biography. I. Title.
HE8689.8 B55 1985
NYPL [MWES (Sarnoff, D.) 86-4682]

Bild-Zeitung. Meissner, Hans-Günther. Werbung und gesellschaftlicher Wandel über die kommunikativen Voraussetzungen technischen, ökonomischen und sozialen Fortschritts . [Berlin] , Hamburg [1979] 23, [4] leaves ; LC Card 84-119751
HF5802.5 .M45 1979

Bilderbeek, J. Ondernemingsstrategie, theorie en praktijk . Leiden , c1986. xi, 346 p. : ISBN 90-207-1424-4 : LC Card 86-199689
HD37.D8 O54 1986

BILDERBERG MEETINGS.
Scholl, Heinz. Bilderberger & Trilaterale . Euskirchen, Bundesrepublik Deutschland , c1977. 92 p. ; LC Card 85-199172
HD2785 .S396 1977

Bilderberger & Trilaterale . Scholl, Heinz. Euskirchen, Bundesrepublik Deutschland , c1977. 92 p. ; LC Card 85-199172
HD2785 .S396 1977

Bilderberger und Trilaterale. Scholl, Heinz. Bilderberger & Trilaterale . Euskirchen, Bundesrepublik Deutschland , c1977. 92 p. ; LC Card 85-199172
HD2785 .S396 1977

Bildschirmarbeit . Köchling, Annegret, 1944- Köln , c1985. 212 p. : ISBN 3-7663-0853-X
NYPL [JLD 87-392]

Bildschirmtext . Götz, Gerd, 1956- Berlin , c1985. xi, 285 p. : ISBN 3-8007-1348-9 LC Card 87-125311 DDC 384.3/5/0943 19
HD9696.T463 G346 1985

Bildschirmtext in Unternehmen . Schmidt-Prestin, Barbara, 1953- Bergisch Gladbach , c1986. xvi, 308 p. : ISBN 3-89012-064-4 LC Card 87-129114 DDC 651.8/0943 19
HD9696.T463 G365 1986

Bildung und Beschäftigung im technischen Wandel . Dostal, Werner. Nürnberg , 1982. viii, 380, 6 p. : LC Card 82-205035 DDC 306/.46 19
HD6331 .D53 1982 ***NYPL [JLD 86-3011]***

Biles, Roger, 1950- Memphis in the Great Depression / by Roger Biles. 1st ed. Knoxville : University of Tennessee Press, c1986. 174 p. : ill. ; 23 cm. Includes index. Bibliography: p. [153]-166. ISBN 0-87049-497-X (alk. paper) : LC Card 85-22575 DDC 330.9768/19 19
1. Depressions - 1929 - United States. 2. New Deal, 1933-1939. 3. Memphis (Tenn.) - Economic conditions. 4. Memphis (Tenn.) - Politics and government. I. Title.
HC108.M417 B55 1986 ***NYPL [JLD 87-34]***

Bilîarski, Dimitŭr. Logikata i ikonomiko-matematicheskoto modelirane / Dimitŭr Bilîarski. Sofiîa : Izd-vo na Bŭlgarskata akademiîa na naukite, 1985. 307 p., [1] folded leaf of plates : ill. ; 21 cm. Titles on added t.p.: Logika ėkonomiko-matematicheskogo modelirovaniîa; The logic of economic-mathematical modelling. At head of title: Bŭlgarska akademiîa na naukite. Ikonomicheski institut. Summary in English and Russian. Bibliography: p. 288-[290] LC Card 85-213972
1. Economics - Mathematical models. I. Title. II. Title: Logika ėkonomiko-matematicheskogo modelirovaniîa. III. Title: Logic of economic-mathematical modelling.
HB135 .B523 1985

Bill Bernbach's book . Levenson, Bob. New York , 1987. xvii, 219 p. : ISBN 0-394-54920-1 : LC Card 86-40103 DDC 659.1/0973 19
HF5813.U6 L48 1987

BILLBOARDS.
Sport und Werbung, Präsenz und Erinnerungswirkung ausgewählter Werbeträger an Rennstrecken . München [1986] 70, lii, [iii] p. : LC Card 87-409557 DDC 659.13/42 19
HF5843 .S69 1986

BILLBOARDS - FRANCE.
Benoit, Philippe. Affiches de pub, 1983/85 /. Paris , c1986. 237 p. : ISBN 2-85108-429-1 : LC Card 86-192339
HF5843 .B44 1986

Billetes españoles, 1783-1983 . Cayón, Juan Ramón. Madrid, España [1983?] 82 p. : ISBN 88-300-9799-6 LC Card 85-232320
HG1137 .C38 1983

Les billets de la Banque de France ; Les émissions du Trésor /. Muszynski, Maurice. Bruyères-le-Châtel , 1985. 160 p. : LC Card 83-132282
HG985 .M88 1985

Billig, Michael. Getting into life /. London , New York , c1986. xii, 157 p. ; ISBN 0-416-40850-8 LC Card 86-16186 DDC 305.2/35/0941 19
HQ799.G7 G48 1986 ***NYPL [JLD 87-892]***

BILLINGS, FREDERICK, 1823-1890.
Curtis, Jane, 1918- Frederick Billings, Vermonter, pioneer lawyer, business man, conservationist . Woodstock, VT , c1986. 135 p. : ISBN 0-930985-04-4 (pbk.) : LC Card 86-28103 DDC 385/.092/4 B 19
HE2754.B5 C87 1986

Billingsley, J. Robots and automated manufacture /. London, U.K. , c1985. xii, 233 p. : ISBN 0-86341-053-7 ***NYPL [JSK 77-191 v.28]***

Billion dollar day [videorecording] / WGBH/Boston and BBC ; producer, Robert Thirkell. Deerfield, IL : Coronet/MTI Film & Video, 1986. 1 videocassette (30 min.) : sd., col. (Enterprise) Title from data sheet. Ages 15 through adults. Issued as U-matic 3/4 in. or Beta 1/2 in. or VHS 1/2 in. Takes viewers to New York, London, and Hong Kong for a look at the currency exchange market. LC Card 86-700167 DDC 332.4 11
1. Foreign exchange brokers - New York (N.Y.). 2. Foreign exchange brokers - England - London. 3. Foreign exchange brokers - Hong Kong. I. WGBH (Television station : Boston, Mass.). II. British Broadcasting Corporation. III. Coronet/MTI Film and Video. IV. Series: Enterprise (WGBH (Television station : Boston, Mass.)).
HG3903

Billis, David. Rowbottom, Ralph William. Organisational design . Aldershot, Hants, England , Brookfield, Vt., USA , 1987. 165 p. : ISBN 0-566-05408-6 : LC Card 86-31946 DDC 658.4/02 19
HD50 .R68 1987

BILLS AND NOTES. see **NEGOTIABLE INSTRUMENTS; PROMISSORY NOTES.**

BILLS OF CREDIT. see **NEGOTIABLE INSTRUMENTS.**

BILLS OF EXCHANGE - HUNGARY.
Hardy, Ilona. Gyakorlati útmutató a kötvény és a váltó használatához /. Budapest , 1986. 62 p. ; ISBN 963-621-315-1 LC Card 87-407776
HG5470.5.A3 H37 1986

Bilten (Republički zavod za statistiku SR Srbije) .
(239) Industrija SR Srbije, 1981-1982. godina /. Beograd , 1984. 76 p. ; LC Card 86-212264
HA1651 .A334 no. 239 HA1634.S47

Bingaman, Jeff. Economic competitiveness promoting America's living standard /] Washington , 1986 [i.e. 1987] vii, 34 p. : LC Card 87-601340 DDC 338.973 19
HC106.8 .E2745 1987

Binger, Brian R. Microeconomics with calculus / Brian R. Binger, Elizabeth Hoffman. Glenview, Ill. : Scott, Foresman, c1988. 609 p. : ill. ; 24 cm. Includes bibliographical references and index. ISBN 0-673-18002-6 LC Card 87-12132 DDC 338.5/01/515 19
1. Microeconomics. 2. Economics, Mathematical. I. Hoffman, Elizabeth, 1946-. II. Title.
HB172 .B52 1988

Bingham, John E. A handbook of systems analysis / John E. Bingham and Garth W. P. Davies. 2nd ed. London : Macmillan Press, 1978. ix, 229 p. : ill. ; 24 cm. Includes index. Bibliography: p. 220-224. ISBN 0-333-24198-3 : LC Card 79-309251
1. Business - Data processing. 2. Management information systems. I. Davies, Garth W. P. II. Title.
HF5548.2 .B47 1978b ***NYPL [JLE 80-2972]***

Bingham, Julie E. HAL plain and simple : learning Lotus HAL with 1-2-3 release 2 / Julie E. Bingham, Mark S. Scapicchio. Reading, Mass. : Addison-Wesley, c1988. vii, 296 p. : ill. ; 24 cm. Title on spine: HAL plain & simple. Includes index. ISBN 0-201-08002-8 (pbk.) : LC Card 87-17524 DDC 005.36/9 19

1. Lotus HAL (Computer program). 2. Lotus 1-2-3 (Computer program). 3. Business - Data processing. I. Scapicchio, Mark. II. Title. III. Title: HAL plain & simple.
HF5548.4.L68 B56 1988

Bingham, Robert C. Economic concepts : a programmed approach / Robert C. Bingham.8th ed. / revised by William Henry Pope. New York : McGraw-Hill, c1987. xv, 444 p. ; 27 cm. ISBN 0-07-044963-5 (pbk.) LC Card 87-3351 DDC 330/.07/7 19
1. Economics - Programmed instruction. I. Pope, W. H. (William Henry), 1923-. II. Title.
HB171.5 .B52 1987

Binkley, Clark Shepard. The Global forest sector . Chichester [West Sussex] , New York , c1987. xiii, 706 p. : ISBN 0-471-91735-4 : LC Card 87-19700 DDC 338.1/749 19
HD9750.5 .G56 1987

Das Binnenschiffahrt-Verkehrssystem . Schroiff, Franz J. Hannover , 1984. ix, 267 p. : ISBN 3-87870-951-X LC Card 84-221599
HE669 .S34 1984

Binnenwirtschaftlich orientierte Hypothesen zur Aussenwirtschaftsentwicklung und ihre Gültigkeit für die Bundesrepublik Deutschland 1969-1982 /. Peters, Kathrin. Hamburg , c1986. vii, 311 p. : ISBN 3-925630-02-3 : LC Card 86-226488
HD5710.75.G3 P48 1986

Bins, Alberto, 1869-1957. Porto Alegre (Brazil). Mayor. Mensagem apresentada á Camara Municipal /. Pôrto Alegre , 1936. 686 p., [7] folded leaves of plates : LC Card 85-135614
HD4635.P6 P67 1936

Binst, Olivier. Banques, le grand secret / Olivier Binst et Georges Ramsa. Paris : Stock, c1987. 166 p. ; 23 cm. ISBN 2-234-02032-8 : LC Card 87-156884
1. Banks and banking - France. I. Ramsa, Georges. II. Title.
HG3026 .B48 1987

Binswanger, Hans Christoph.
Studien zur Entwicklung der ökonomischen Theorie /. Berlin , c1981- v. ; ISBN 3-428-04862-8 (v. 1) : LC Card 81-154218 DDC 330/.09 19
HB75 .S787 1981 ***NYPL [JLL 73-186 Bd.115]***

Symposion "Marktwirtschaft und Umwelt" (1980 : Walter Eucken Institut) Marktwirtschaft und Umwelt . Tübingen , 1981. ix, 303 p. : ISBN 3-16-343372-3 : LC Card 81-128698 DDC 363.7/0526 19
HC79.E5 S92 1980 ***NYPL [TB (Walter Eucken Institut. Wirtschaftswissenschaftliche und wirtschaftsrechtliche Untersuchungen. Bd. 17)]***

Symposium Umweltprobleme als Herausforderung der Marktwirtschaft, Neue Ideen jenseits des Dirigismus (1983 : Stuttgart, Germany) Symposium Umweltprobleme als Herausforderung der Marktwirtschaft, Neue Ideen jenseits des Dirigismus . [Köln] [Freiburg] , 1983. 300 p. ; ISBN 3-7616-0722-9 LC Card 84-152335 DDC 363.7/058 19
HC79.E5 S96 1983 ***NYPL [JLD 86-1631]***

Binswanger, Hans P.
Agricultural mechanization : issues and options. Washington, D.C., U. S.A. : World Bank, c1987. vi, 85 p. : ill. ; 28 cm. (A World Bank policy study, 0258-2120) Prepared by Hans P. Binswanger and Graeme Donovan with the assistance of Raymund Fabre and Prabhu Pingali. Bibliography: p. 81-85. ISBN 0-8213-0903-X (pbk.) LC Card 87-14082 DDC 338.1/61/091724 19
1. Farm mechanization - Economic aspects - Developing countries. I. Donovan, Graeme. II. International Bank for Reconstruction and Development. III. Title. IV. Series.
HD1459 .B57 1987

The economics of tractors in South Asia : an analytical review / by Hans P. Binswanger. New York : Agricultural Development Council ; Hyderabad, India : International Crops Research Institute for Semi-Arid Tropics, 1978. 96 p. ; 24 cm. Includes bibliographical references. LC Card 81-908104
1. Agriculture - Economic aspects - South Asia. 2. Farm tractors - Economic aspects - South Asia. 3. Farm mechanization - South Asia. I. Title.
HD2065.3 .B56 1978

Binz, Hans-Bert, 1954- Kritik an deutschen Wirtschaftsprüfern, ein Glaubwürdigkeitsproblem? : eine Profession im Spannungsfeld der Interessen / Hans-Bert Binz ; mit einem Vorwort von A. Zybon.1. Aufl. Bergisch Gladbach : J. Eul, 1984. ix, 325 p. : ill. ; 21 cm. (Reihe Steuer, Wirtschaft und Recht . Bd. 4) Originally presented as the author's thesis (doctoral--Universität zu Köln, 1983) Bibliography: p. 303-325. ISBN 3-89012-004-0 : LC Card 84-174776
1. Auditors - Germany (West) - Professional ethics. I. Title. II. Series.
HF5627 .B55 1984

Binz, Hans Werner, 1925- "Ein Chaos wollen wir nicht" . Basel , c1985. 223 p. : ISBN 3-85787-141-5 : LC Card 86-128638
HE8689.9.S95 C57 1985

BIOBÍO (CHILE) - ECONOMIC CONDITIONS.
Ramírez C., Valeria (Ramírez Ceballos) Desarrollo socio-económico de la Octava Región de Chile /. Santiago, Chile , 1985. i, 45 leaves ; LC Card 86-115542
HC193.B5 R35 1985

Bio-demographic study of Kashmiris /. Sadhu, Kanan K. (Kanan Kusum) Delhi, India , c1987. viii, 217 p. : ISBN 81-212-0072-5 : LC Card 87-900298 DDC 304.6/0954/6 19
HB3640.J36 S23 1987

BIO-GEOGRAPHY. see **ANTHROPO-GEOGRAPHY.**

Biografii͡a ot mnogo imena : sbornik s ocherťsi za pŭrventsi v truda ot Devni͡a / sŭstavil i redaktor Ivan Popivanov. Sofii͡a : Profizdat, 1983. 232 p. : ports. ; 21 cm. LC Card 84-163061
1. Labor and laboring classes - Bulgaria - Devni͡a - Biography. 2. Devni͡a (Bulgaria) - Biography. I. Popivanov, Ivan, prof.
HD8627.A1 B56 1983

Biographical directory of the U. S. Customs Service, 1771-1989. United States. Customs Service. A biographical directory of the United States Customs Service, 1771-1989 /. Washington, D.C. [1985] ca. 350 p. ; LC Card 85-603304 DDC 353.0072/46/025 19
HJ6731 .U18 1985

A biographical directory of the United States Customs Service, 1771-1989 /. United States. Customs Service. Washington, D.C. [1985] ca. 350 p. ; LC Card 85-603304 DDC 353.0072/46/025 19
HJ6731 .U18 1985

Biographische Volksbücher .
(23-27) Blencke, Fritz. Alfred Krupp /. Leipzig , 1898. 127 p. : LC Card 85-665721
HD9523.9.K7 B53x 1898

BIOGRAPHY - RESEARCH.
Bergan, Helen, 1937- Where the money is . Alexandria, Va. , c1985. 101 p. : ISBN 0-9615277-0-6 (pbk.) : LC Card 85-72141 DDC 361.7 19
HG177 .B48 1985 ***NYPL [JLD 87-844]***

BIOLOGICAL LABORATORY EQUIPMENT INDUSTRY.
Biotechnology equipment & supplies. Norwalk, Conn., U. S.A. (6 Prowitt St., Norwalk 06855) , c1986. viii, 347 p. : LC Card 87-400044 DDC 380.1/4566063 19
HD9706.65.B552 B55 1986

Poon, Raymond S. Biotechnology instrumentation . Menlo Park, Calif. (333 Ravenswood Ave., Menlo Park 94025-3476) , c1985. 32 p. : LC Card 87-160671 DDC 338.4/766063 19
HD9706.65.B552 P66 1985

Biological resource management.
Workman, John P. Range economics /. New York , London , c1986. xvi, 217 p. : ISBN 0-02-948810-9 LC Card 85-18882 DDC 333.74 19
HD1635 .W67 1986 ***NYPL [JLE 86-2382]***

BIOLOGY - ECOLOGY. see **ECOLOGY.**

BIOMASS CHEMICALS INDUSTRY - UNITED STATES.
Morris, David J. Substituting agricultural materials for petroleum based industrial products /. Washington, D.C. , c1986. i, 33 p. ; ISBN 0-917582-46-2 (pbk.) : LC Card 86-21350 DDC 338.4/76628 19
HD9502.5.B543 U654 1986

BIOMASS ENERGY - HUNGARY.
A Biomassza komplex hasznosításának lehetőségei /. Budapest , 1985. 249 p. : ISBN 963-232-215-0 : LC Card 87-115648
HD9502.5.B543 H93 1985

Láng, István, 1931- A biomassza hasznosításának távlatai . Budapest , c1986. 28 p. ; ISBN 963-05-4357-5 : LC Card 87-407709
HD9502.5.B543 H95 1986

BIOMASS ENERGY INDUSTRIES - BRAZIL - MINAS GERAIS.
Seminário de Energia de Biomassa (1985? : Belo Horizonte, Brazil?) Seminário de Energia de Biomassa . [Belo Horizonte?] , <[1986?-. v. <[1-2] > : LC Card 87-107998
HD9502.5.B543 B67 1985

BIOMASS ENERGY INDUSTRIES - HUNGARY.
A Biomassza komplex hasznosításának lehetőségei /. Budapest , 1985. 249 p. : ISBN 963-232-215-0 : LC Card 87-115648
HD9502.5.B543 H93 1985

Láng, István, 1931- A biomassza hasznosításának távlatai . Budapest , c1986. 28 p. ; ISBN 963-05-4357-5 : LC Card 87-407709
HD9502.5.B543 H95 1986

BIOMASS ENERGY INDUSTRIES - UNITED STATES.
Morris, David J. Substituting agricultural materials for petroleum based industrial products /. Washington, D.C. , c1986. i, 33 p. ; ISBN 0-917582-46-2 (pbk.) : LC Card 86-21350 DDC 338.4/76628 19
HD9502.5.B543 U654 1986

Biomass statistics for Vermont . Frieswyk, Thomas S. [Broomall, Pa.] , 1986. 105 p. : LC Card 86-602390 DDC 333.79/38 19
HD9502.5.B543 U635 1986

A biomassza hasznosításának távlatai . Láng, István, 1931- Budapest , c1986. 28 p. ; ISBN 963-05-4357-5 : LC Card 87-407709
HD9502.5.B543 H95 1986

A Biomassza komplex hasznosításának lehetőségei / [összeállította, Láng István ... et al. ; szerkesztette, Láng István]. Budapest : Mezőgazdasági Kiadó, 1985. 249 p. : ill. ; 21 cm. ISBN 963-232-215-0 : LC Card 87-115648
1. Biomass energy industries - Hungary. 2. Biomass energy - Hungary. I. Láng, István, 1931-.
HD9502.5.B543 H93 1985

Biomathematics (Springer-Verlag, New York) .
(14) Mode, Charles J., 1927- Stochastic processes in demography and their computer implementation /. Berlin , New York , c1985. xvii, 389 p. : ISBN 0-387-13622-3 (U. S.) LC Card 84-26707 DDC 304.6/028/54 19
HB849.51 .M635 1985 ***NYPL [JSE 86-1952]***

Biomedical Business International, Inc.
Alternate site clinical testing. Tustin, CA, U. S.A. (17722 Irvine Blvd., Tustin 92680) , c1987. 167 leaves in various foliations : LC Card 87-402110 DDC 381/.45681761 19
HD9995.L33 U5412 1987

Anesthesiology products and marketplace. Tustin, CA, U. S.A. (17722 Irvine Blvd., Tustin 92680) , c1987. 1 v. (various foliations) : LC Card 87-142979 DDC 381/.45681761 19
HD9995.A532 A54 1987

Cardiovascular therapy market . Tustin, CA, U. S.A. (17722 Irvine Blvd., Tustin 92680) , c1987. 1 v. (various foliations) ; LC Card 87-402037 DDC 380.1/45681761 19
HD9995.C363 U62 1987

Catheter devices for interventional cardiology, angiography, and radiology--U. S. and international. Tustin, CA, U. S.A. (17722 Irvine Blvd., Tustin 92680) , c1987. 1 v. (various foliations) : LC Card 87-168823 DDC 381/.45681761 19
HD9995.C383 U628 1987

Growth areas in dentistry . Tustin, CA (17722 Irvine Blvd., Tustin 92680) , c1986. 1 v. (various foliations) : LC Card 86-212546 DDC 381/.45681761 19
HD9995.D42 G76 1986

Marketing communications effectiveness to the dentist. Tustin, CA (17722 Irvine Blvd., Tustin 92680) , c1986. 130 leaves in various foliations : LC Card 86-231569 DDC 681/.761 19
HD9995.D43 U55 1986

Maximizing sales to hospital national accounts /. Tustin, CA, U. S.A. (17722 Irvine Blvd., Tustin 92680) , c1987. 524 p. in various pagings : LC Card 87-401688 DDC 681/.761/0688 19
HD9994.U52 M39 1987

Nerve, muscle, bone stimulation, and augmentation. Tustin, CA, U. S.A. (17722 Irvine Blvd., Tustin 92680) , c1987. iv, 8, 144, [112] p. : LC Card 87-402023 DDC 338.4/7681761 19
HD9995.E43 U56 1987

Patient monitoring disposables and equipment for critical care. Tustin, CA (17722 Irvine Blvd., Tustin 92680) , c1986. 1 v. (various foliations) : LC Card 86-203049 DDC 381/.45681761 19
HD9995.M653 U657 1986

Sales representative effectiveness to the dentist. Tustin, CA (17722 Irvine Blvd., Tustin 92680) , c1986. 113 leaves in various foliations : LC Card 86-231841 DDC 681/.761 19
HD9995.D43 U56 1986

Sensors and transducers for biomedical applications. Tustin, CA, U. S.A. (17722 Irvine Blvd., Tustin 92680) , c1987. 1 v. (various foliations) : LC Card 87-403749 DDC 381/.45681761 19
HD9995.T733 U675 1987

Specimen collection and transport market. Tustin, CA, U. S.A. (17722 Irvine Blvd., Tustin 92680) , c1987. 1 v. (various foliations) : LC Card 87-402105 DDC 380.1/45681761 19
HD9995.L32 S64 1987

Strategic marketing of hospital pharmacy products. Tustin, CA, U. S.A. (17722 Irvine Blvd., Tustin 92680) , c1986. iii leaves, 2, 12, 134, 111 p. : LC Card 87-149442 DDC 380.1/456151 19
HD9665.5 .S77 1986

Strategic marketing of oncology products /. Tustin, CA, U. S.A. (17722 Irvine Blvd., Tustin 92680) , c1987. 242 p. in various pagings : LC Card 87-402026 DDC 381/.45681761 19
HD9995.C353 U67 1987

Strategic marketing of surgical products. Tustin, CA, U. S.A. (17722 Irvine Blvd., Tustin 92680) , c1987. 1 v. (various foliations) : LC Card 87-168617 DDC 380.1/45681761 19
HD9995.S92 S77 1987

Top emerging private companies. Tustin, CA, U. S.A. (17722 Irvine Blvd., Tustin 92680) , c1987. iv, 8, 144, [112] leaves : LC Card 87-402028 DDC 681/.761/029473 19
HD9994.U52 T66 1987

U. S. clinical testing market /. Tustin, CA, U. S.A. (17722 Irvine Blvd., Tustin 92680) , c1987. 223 leaves in various foliations ; LC Card 87-402039 DDC 381/.45681761 19
HD9995.L33 U5484 1987

Urology and incontinence products /. Tustin, CA (17722 Irvine Blvd., Tustin 92680) , c1986. 1 v. (various foliations) : LC Card 86-235104
HD9995.U742 U76 1986a

BIOMEDICAL TRANSDUCER INDUSTRY - UNITED STATES.
Sensors and transducers for biomedical applications. Tustin, CA, U. S.A. (17722 Irvine Blvd., Tustin 92680) , c1987. 1 v. (various foliations) : LC Card 87-403749 DDC 381/.45681761 19
HD9995.T733 U675 1987

BIONOMICS. see **ECOLOGY.**

Biophysical resources of the Slocan Valley / Province of British Columbia, Ministry of Environment, Assessment and Planning Division, Terrestrial Studies Branch. Victoria, B.C. : The Division, 1982. ix, 102 p. : ill. ; 28 cm. (APD bulletin, 0228-5304 . 28) Bibliography: p. 81-82. ISBN 0-7718-8310-2 (pbk.) LC Card 84-117204 DDC 333.7/09711/43 19
1. Natural resources - British Columbia - Slocan River Valley. 2. Physical geography - British Columbia - Slocan River Valley. I. British Columbia. Terrestrial Studies Branch. II. Series.
HC117.B8 B46 1982

Biotechnology . Kenney, Martin. New Haven , c1986. xvi, 306 p. : ISBN 0-300-03392-3 (alk. paper) : LC Card 86-1694 DDC 338.4/7660/6 19
TP248.2 .K46 1986 ***NYPL [JSE 86-1924]***

BIOTECHNOLOGY.
Goodman, David, 1938- From farming to biotechnology . Oxford , New York, N.Y. , 1987. 214 p. : ISBN 0-631-14405-6 : LC Card 87-687 DDC 338.1/6 19
HD1433 .G66 1987

Kenney, Martin. Biotechnology . New Haven , c1986. xvi, 306 p. : ISBN 0-300-03392-3 (alk. paper) : LC Card 86-1694 DDC 338.4/7660/6 19
TP248.2 .K46 1986 ***NYPL [JSE 86-1924]***

Biotechnology equipment and supplies.
Biotechnology equipment & supplies. Norwalk, Conn., U. S.A. (6 Prowitt St., Norwalk 06855) , c1986. viii, 347 p. : LC Card 87-400044 DDC 380.1/4566063 19
HD9706.65.B552 B55 1986

BIOTECHNOLOGY - EQUIPMENT AND SUPPLIES.
Poon, Raymond S. Biotechnology instrumentation . Menlo Park, Calif. (333 Ravenswood Ave., Menlo Park 94025-3476) , c1985. 32 p. : LC Card 87-160671 DDC 338.4/766063 19
HD9706.65.B552 P66 1985

Biotechnology in agriculture : new technologies, product developments, markets / Philip Rotheim, project analyst. Stamford, Conn., U. S.A. : Business Communications Co., c1985. xvii, 192 leaves : ill. ; 29 cm. (Business opportunity report . GA-051R) "November 1985"--T.p. verso. ISBN 0-89336-485-1 (pbk.) LC Card 87-403883 DDC 381/.456606 19
1. Biotechnology industries - United States. 2. Agricultural biotechnology - United States. I. Rotheim, Philip. II. Business Communications Co. III. Series.
HD9999.B443 U615 1985

BIOTECHNOLOGY INDUSTRIES.
Kenney, Martin. Biotechnology . New Haven , c1986. xvi, 306 p. : ISBN 0-300-03392-3 (alk. paper) : LC Card 86-1694 DDC 338.4/7660/6 19
TP248.2 .K46 1986 ***NYPL [JSE 86-1924]***

New biotechnology comes to market /. Stamford, Conn., U. S.A. , c1985. viii, 205 leaves : ISBN 0-89336-436-3 (soft) LC Card 87-167067 DDC 381/.456606 19
HD9999.B442 N48 1985

BIOTECHNOLOGY INDUSTRIES - TEXAS - SAN ANTONIO - CONGRESSES.
A Transcription of key addresses at San Antonio's Bio-Medical Seminar /. San Antonio, TX (8961 Tesoro Dr., Suite 308, San Antonio 78217) , c1985. v, 104, [4] leaves of plates : LC Card 87-144092 DDC 338.4/7681761/09764351 19
HD9999.B443 U667 1985

BIOTECHNOLOGY INDUSTRIES - UNITED STATES.
Biotechnology in agriculture . Stamford, Conn., U. S.A. , c1985. xvii, 192 leaves : ISBN 0-89336-485-1 (pbk.) LC Card 87-403883 DDC 381/.456606 19
HD9999.B443 U615 1985

Biotechnology instrumentation . Poon, Raymond S. Menlo Park, Calif. (333 Ravenswood Ave., Menlo Park 94025-3476) , c1985. 32 p. : LC Card 87-160671 DDC 338.4/766063 19
HD9706.65.B552 P66 1985

Biraud, Gérard. L'aide britannique au développement : note de synthèse / réalisée par Gérard Biraud. Paris : Ministère de la coopération, Service des études économiques et des questions internationales, 1978. 17 leaves : ill. ; 29 cm. (Études et documents. no. 30) LC Card 84-102197
1. Great Britain. Ministry of Overseas Development. 2. Economic assistance, British - Developing countries. I. Series: Etudes et documents (France. Ministère de la Coopération. Service des études et des questions internationales) , no. 30. II. Title.
HC60 .B52 1978

Birbuet D., Gustavo. Tierra y ganado en Pacajes : estructura de tenencia de la tierra y tamaño del hato ganadero familiar en la economía campesina de Caquiaviri y Comanche / Gustavo Birbuet D. La Paz, Bolivia : Servicios Múltiples de Tecnologías Apropiadas : Ediciones Labor, 1986. 86 p. : maps ; 22 cm. (INV . 4) Bibliography: p. 79-84. LC Card 87-403087 DDC 333.3/0984/12 19
1. Land tenure - Bolivia - Caquiaviri. 2. Land tenure - Bolivia - Comanche. 3. Animal industry - Bolivia - Caquiaviri. 4. Animal industry - Bolivia - Comanche. 5. Peasantry - Bolivia - Caquiaviri. 6. Peasantry - Bolivia - Comanche. I. Title. II. Series.
HD490.C34 B57 1986

Birch, David L. Job creation in America : how our smallest companies put the most people to work / David L. Birch. New York : Free Press ; London : Collier Macmillan, c1987. xi, 244 p. : ill. ; 25 cm. Includes bibliographical references and index. ISBN 0-02-903610-0 LC Card 87-8523 DDC 331.12/4/0973 19
1. Small business - United States - Employees. 2. Job vacancies - United States. I. Title.
HD2346.U5 B54 1987

Bird, Christiane. Richards, Eugene. Below the line . Mount Vernon, N.Y. , c1987. 218 p. : ISBN 0-89043-062-4 LC Card 86-70834 DDC 305.5/69/0973 19
HC110.P6 R52 1987

Bird, Richard M., 1938- Federal finance in comparative perspective / Richard M. Bird. Toronto, Canada : Canadian Tax Foundation, c1986. x, 250 p. : ill. ; 23 cm. (Financing Canadian federation, 0225-5103 . 6) Includes bibliographical references and index. ISBN 0-88808-024-7 (pbk.) LC Card 86-215918 DDC 336 19
1. Finance, Public. 2. Intergovernmental fiscal relations. 3. Federal government. 4. Finance, Public - Canada. I. Title.
HJ141 .B57 1986

BIRDS - VENEZUELA - GUAYANA REGION - IDENTIFICATION - ADDRESSES, ESSAYS, LECTURES.
Exploración de la Guayana /. [Caracas] [1983] 158 p., [20] p. of plates : LC Card 85-178221 DDC 333.7/0988/1 19
HC238.G8 E98 1983 ***NYPL [JSF 86-461]***

BIRENDRANAGAR (NEPAL) - ECONOMIC CONDITIONS.
Basic needs delivery system in Birendranagar, Surkhet /. Kathmandu , 1985. 143, [23], iii p. (some folded) ; LC Card 86-903561 DDC 338.9549/6 19
HF5415.12.N35 B36 1985

BIRENDRANAGAR (NEPAL) - ECONOMIC POLICY.
Basic needs delivery system in Birendranagar, Surkhet /. Kathmandu , 1985. 143, [23], iii p. (some folded) ; LC Card 86-903561 DDC 338.9549/6 19
HF5415.12.N35 B36 1985

Birg, Herwig. Beiträge zur Bevölkerungsökonomie /. Berlin , c1986. 238 p. : ISBN 3-428-05969-7 LC Card 86-172600
HB3595 .B39 1986

Birgir Björn Sigurjónsson, 1949- Frjálshyggjan / Birgir Björn Sigurjónsson. [Reykjavík] : Svart á hvítu, 1981. 261 p. : ill. ; 22 cm. Bibliography: p. 231-237. Includes index. LC Card 84-134561
1. Laissez-faire. 2. Iceland - Economic conditions. I. Title.
HB95 .B55 1981

Birk, Michael. Politik gegen die Krise . Marburg , 1985. 157 p. : ISBN 3-924800-01-4 : LC Card 86-119259 DDC 338.9 19
HC59 .P584 1985

Birkbeck College. L'Effort économique de défense . [Grenoble] , 1985. 235 p. : LC Card 86-199399
HC280.D4 E38 1985

Birla Institute of Scientific Research. Economic Research Division. Hajra, S. (Sridhar), 1936- Capital and technological progress in the Indian economy, 1950/51-1980/81 /. New Delhi , 1985. xvi, 198 p. : LC Card 85-900681 DDC 338.954 19
HC440.S3 H35 1985 ***NYPL [JLD 87-736]***

Birmingham Transport Historical Group. Denton, A. S. Coventry transport . Birmingham [West

Midlands, England] , c1985- v. <1 > : ISBN 0-905103-05-X (pbk.) : LC Card 86-224227 DDC 388.4/09424/98 19
HE4719.C68 D46 1985

Bíró, Ferenc, fl. 1963- Agrárgazdaságtan /. Budapest , 1984. 465 p. : ISBN 963-231-719-X : LC Card 85-229778
HD1415 .A27 1984

Biró, Gerd. A kelet-nyugati kereskedelem fejlődési tendenciái a 80-as években / Biró Gerd. Budapest : Közgazdasági és Jogi Könyvkiadó, 1986. 152 p. ; 20 cm. Includes bibliographical references. ISBN 963-221-582-6 : LC Card 87-138649
1. East-West trade (1945-). I. Title.
HF4050 .B57 1986

Birsner, E. Patricia.
Job hunting for the 40+ executive. Birsner, E. Patricia. The 40+ job-hunting guide : official handbook of the 40+ club / E. Patricia Birsner. New York, NY , c1987. xx, 250 p. : ISBN 0-13-329152-9 (pbk.) : LC Card 87-2438 DDC 650.1/4/024658 19
HD38.25.U6 B53 1987

The 40+ job-hunting guide : official handbook of the 40+ club / E. Patricia Birsner. New York, NY : Prentice Hall Press, c1987. xx, 250 p. : ill. ; 24 cm. Rev. ed. of: Job hunting for the 40+ executive. c1985. "An Arco book." Includes bibliographical references and index. ISBN 0-13-329152-9 (pbk.) : LC Card 87-2438 DDC 650.1/4/024658 19
1. Executives - United States. 2. Age and employment - United States. 3. Job hunting - United States. I. Birsner, E. Patricia. Job hunting for the 40+ executive. II. Title. III. Title: Forty-plus job-hunting guide.
HD38.25.U6 B53 1987

BIRTH. see **CHILDBIRTH.**

Birth and fortune . Easterlin, Richard A., 1926- Chicago , 1987. xii, 228 p. : ISBN 0-226-18032-8 (pbk.) : LC Card 86-30724 DDC 304.6/0973 19
HB3505 .E247 1987

BIRTH CONTROL - AFRICA, SUB-SAHARAN.
Frank, Odile. The demand for fertility control in Sub-Saharan Africa /. New York, N.Y., U. S.A. (1 Dag Hammarskjold Plaza, New York 10017) [1985] 50 p. ; LC Card 86-204127 DDC 363.9/6/09624 19
HB1071.A3 F69 1985

BIRTH CONTROL - ASIA, SOUTHEASTERN - CONGRESSES.
IGCC Workshop on Linkages Between University Based Population Activities and National Population/Family Planning Programmes (1978 : Bangkok, Thailand) IGCC Workshop on Linkages Between University Based Population Activities and National Population/Family Planning Programmes . Kuala Lumpur, Selangor [1978?] 111 p. : LC Card 81-941403
HB3641 .I35 1978

Seminar on the Effect of Internal Migration, Urbanization, and Resettlement in the IGCC Region on its Population/Family Planning Programmes (1980 : Jakarta, Indonesia) Seminar on the Effect of Internal Migration, Urbanization, and Resettlement in the IGCC Region on its Population/Family Planning Programmes . Kuala Lumpur, Malaysia [1980?] 131 p. : LC Card 81-941408
HB2101 .S45 1980

BIRTH CONTROL - BOLIVIA.
Cisneros C., Antonio. La mujer trabajadora . La Paz, Bolivia [1984] 131 leaves : LC Card 85-129000 DDC 331.4/0984 19
HD6121 .C58 1984 ***NYPL [JLF 86-1704]***

BIRTH CONTROL - BRAZIL - CONGRESSES.
Política demográfica /. Salvador [1983] 82 p. : LC Card 87-138903 DDC 304.6/0981 19
HB3563 .P65 1983

BIRTH CONTROL - CHINA.
Greenhalgh, Susan. Fertility policy in China . New York, N.Y. [1986] 31 p. ; LC Card 87-154581 DDC 304.6/6/0951 19
HB1064.A3 G74 1986

BIRTH CONTROL - CONGRESSES.
International Congress on New Dimensions in Population Planning and Development (1978 : Colombo, Sri Lanka) The International Congress on New Dimensions in Population Planning and Development, Bandaranaike Memorial International Conference Hall, Colombo, 26-28 March 1978 /. Colombo, Sri Lanka , 1978. 114 p., [5] leaves of plates : LC Card 84-902651 DDC 304.6/6/095493 19
HB883.5 .I57 1978 ***NYPL [JLF 86-1970]***

BIRTH CONTROL - DEVELOPING COUNTRIES.
Acsádi, György. Policy relevance of findings of the world fertility survey for developing countries /. New York , 1986. vi, 160 p. ; LC Card 85-37681 DDC 304.6/32/091724 19
HB1108 .A28 1986

BIRTH CONTROL - DOMINICA.
Ebanks, G. E. Mortality, fertility, and family planning . Santiago, Chile [1985] 123 p. ; LC Card 87-131697 DDC 304.6/2/09729841 19
HB1376.D65 E32 1985

BIRTH CONTROL - GOVERNMENT POLICY - CHINA.
Banister, Judith, 1943- China's changing population /. Stanford, Calif. , 1987. xiii, 488 p. : ISBN 0-8047-1155-0 (alk. paper) : LC Card 82-60105 DDC 304.6/0951 19
HB3654.A3 B36 1987

BIRTH CONTROL - HONDURAS.
Suazo, Margarita. Población y desarrollo socioeconómico en Honduras /. Chicago, Ill., USA (1313 E. 60th St., Chicago 60637) , c1984. 90 p., [2] leaves of plates : LC Card 85-203746
HB3540.A3 S82 1984

BIRTH CONTROL - HONDURAS - PUBLIC OPINION.
Análisis de la encuesta a líderes nacionales /. Tegucigalpa, D.C. , 1983. 49, [12] leaves ; LC Card 85-203745
HB3540.A3 A52 1983

BIRTH CONTROL - INDONESIA - BALI (PROVINCE)
Streatfield, K. Fertility decline in a traditional society . [Canberra, ACT] , 1986. xvii, 177 p. : ISBN 0-86784-711-5 (pbk.) LC Card 86-213262 DDC 304.6/32/095986 19
HB1058.B34 S87 1986

BIRTH CONTROL - MEXICO.
Planeación familiar y cambio demográfico. México, D.F. [1983], c1982. 554 p. : ISBN 968-8241-63-6 LC Card 84-227488 DDC 304.6/0972 19
HB3531 .P57 1983 ***NYPL [JLE 86-3248]***

BIRTH CONTROL - SAINT LUCIA.
Ebanks, G. E. Mortality, fertility, and family planning . Santiago, Chile [1985] 123 p. ; LC Card 87-131697 DDC 304.6/2/09729841 19
HB1376.D65 E32 1985

BIRTH CONTROL - THAILAND.
Suchart Prasithrathsint. Ethnicity and fertility in Thailand /. Singapore , 1985. xviii, 270 p. : ISBN 997-19-8813-5 ***NYPL [JLE 86-3668]***

BIRTH CONTROL - THAILAND - BANGKOK METROPOLITAN AREA.
Charoon Vitiprod. Rapid population growth, living conditions, and fertility reduction implication (Bangkok metropolis) /. [Singapore] 1979. ii, 41 leaves : LC Card 82-940038
HB3644.55.B36 C48 1979

The birth dearth /. Wattenberg, Ben J. New York, NY , 1987. viii, 182 p. : ISBN 0-88687-304-5 : LC Card 83-63759 DDC 304.6/32 19
HB915 .W29 1987

BIRTH INTERVALS - KENYA.
Mosley, W. Henry (Wiley Henry), 1933- The dynamics of birth spacing and marital fertility in Kenya /. [Nairobi? , 1981] 63 leaves : LC Card 85-980189
HB1072.5.A3 M66 1981

Birth of a cooperative . Hartzell, Hal, 1946- Eugene, Or. , 1987. 351 p. : ISBN 0-938493-09-4 (pbk.) : LC Card 87-2656 DDC 334/.6834956/09795 19
HD9759.H64 H37 1987

BIRTH-RATE. see **POPULATION.**

BIRTHS - SPAIN - MÉRIDA - HISTORY - 17TH CENTURY - STATISTICS.
Rodríguez Grajera, Alfonso. La población de Mérida en el siglo XVII /. [Badajoz] , 1985. xv, 162 p. : ISBN 84-505-1500-9 LC Card 86-232003
HB3620.M47 R63 1985

Bis vor die Stufen des Throns : Bittschriften und Beschwerden von Bergleuten im Zeitalter der Industrialisierung / herausgegeben von Klaus Tenfelde und Helmuth Trischler. München : C.H. Beck, c1986. 530 p. : facsims. ; 23 cm. (Bergbau und Bergarbeit) Bibliography: p. [526]-528. ISBN 3-406-31297-7 LC Card 87-103686 DDC 331.7/622334/0943 19
1. Miners - Germany - History - Sources. 2. Mine accidents - Germany - History - Sources. 3. Miners - Health and hygiene - Germany - History - Sources. I. Tenfelde, Klaus. II. Trischler, Helmuth. III. Series.
HD8039.M61 G32 1986

Bisaillon, Guy. Service national du Québec : mémoire : document préparatoire à la présentation d'un projet de loi visant à établir service national au Québec / Guy Bisaillon. Québec : [s.n., 1981] 54, [4] leaves ; 28 cm. Bibliography: leaves [55]-[58] LC Card 82-212578
1. National service - Québec (Province). 2. Youth - Employment - Québec (Province). I. Title.
HD4870.C2 B57 1981

Bischofberger, Karlheinz. Theorie und Empirie flexibler Wechselkurse : alternative theoretische Erklärungsansätze und empirische Evidenz für acht westliche Industrieländer, 1973 bis 1980 / von Karlheinz Bischofberger. Berlin : Duncker & Humblot, c1986. 248 p. : ill. ; 24 cm. (Volkswirtschaftliche Schriften. Heft 363) Bibliography: p. [234]-248. ISBN 3-428-05988-3 LC Card 86-206335
1. Foreign exchange - Mathematical models. 2. Foreign exchange administration - Europe - Econometric models. 3. Foreign exchange administration - Japan - Econometric models. 4. Foreign exchange administration - United States - Econometric models. 5. Foreign exchange administration - Canada - Econometric models. I. Title. II. Series.
HG3823 .B57 1986

Bishnoi, R. N. Pai Panandiker, V. A., 1935- Development bureaucracy /. New Delhi , c1983. ix, 252 p. ; LC Card 83-902420 DDC 352.94/233/09542 19
HD2075.K359 P34 1983
NYPL [JLD 86-3762]

Bishop, Howard, 1938- Master guide to field sales management tactics and techniques / Howard S. Bishop. Englewood Cliffs, N.J. : Prentice Hall, c1987. xxii, 306 p. : ill. ; 29 cm. Includes index. ISBN 0-13-559840-0 LC Card 87-17425 DDC 658.8/1 19
1. Sales management. 2. Traveling sales personnel. I. Title.
HF5438.4 .B57 1987

Bishop, Nancy, 1949- Camden, Thomas M., 1938- How to get a job in Dallas, Fort Worth . Chicago, IL , c1987. viii, 490 p. : ISBN 0-9609516-9-5 (pbk.) : LC Card 86-30123 DDC 650.1/4/097642812 19
HF5382.75.U6 C353 1987

Bisilliat, Jeanne.
Femmes du tiers-monde : travail et quotidien / Jeanne Bisilliat, Michèle Fiéloux. Paris : Le Sycomore, c1983. 122 p. : ill. ; 21 cm. (Actuels) Bibliography: p. 113-122. ISBN 2-86262-201-X
1. Women - Employment - Developing countries. 2. Women - Developing countries - Economic conditions. I. Fiéloux, Michèle. II. Series: Actuels (Sycomore (Firm)). III. Title. ***NYPL [JLD 87-456]***

Séminaire international sur la place des femmes dans l'autosuffisance et les stratégies alimentaires (1985 : Paris, France) Femmes et politiques alimentaires . Paris , 1985. 741 p. : ISBN 2-7099-0763-1 LC Card 86-205282
HD6073.A292 D4477 1985

Biskup, Reinhold. Partnerschaft in der sozialen Marktwirtschaft . Bern , c1986. 367 p. ; ISBN 3-258-03604-7 LC Card 86-226613 DDC 330.943/087 19
HC286.7 .P37 1986

Bisping, Heinz. Zimmermann, Horst, 1934- Die Gemeindefinanzen im Ruhrgebiet . Essen , 1983. xvi, 153 p. : ISBN 3-923494-28-9 LC Card 83-228289
HJ9493.5.R8 Z76 1983

Das bisschen Fahren-- . Plänitz, Günther. Hamburg , 1983. 317 p. : ISBN 3-87975-248-6

LC Card 84-187043
HD8039.M7952 G37 1983

Bissonette, Denise. Pimentel, Richard. Job placement for the industrially injured worker /. Northridge, Calif. (17624 Romar St., Northridge 91325) , c1987. v, 93, [1] leaves : LC Card 87-401986 DDC 650.1/4/0240816 19
HD7255 .P54 1987

Biswas, Asit K.
Integrated rural energy planning /. Guildford, Surrey, England , 1985. xii, 200 p. : ISBN 0-408-22166-6 LC Card 87-160993 DDC 333.79/09172/4 19
HD9502.D442 I57 1985

Integrated rural energy planning /. Guildford , c1985. xii, 200 p. : ISBN 0-408-22166-6
NYPL [JLF 87-3]

Bisztray, Ádám. Main directions of agricultural development in Hungary . Budapest , 1985. 77 p. ; LC Card 86-232881 DDC 338.1 s 338.1/09439 19
HD1407 .M3 no. 61 HD1940.5

Bittel, Lester R.
Business in action : an introduction to business / Lester R. Bittel, Ronald S. Burke, Charles P. Bilbrey.3rd ed. New York : Gregg Division/McGraw-Hill, c1988. vii, 597 p. : col. ill. ; 26 cm. Includes bibliographical references. Includes index. ISBN 0-07-005565-3 LC Card 87-3134 DDC 658 19
1. Business enterprises - United States. 2. Industrial management - United States. I. Burke, Ronald S. II. Bilbrey, Charles P. III. Title.
HF5343 .B57 1988

Executive skills program. 2nd ed. [New York, N.Y., U. S.A.] (1633 Broadway, New York 10019) : Alexander Hamilton Institute, [c1986] 4 v. : ill. ; 28 cm. Issued in a case. Accompanied by pamphlet "How to make the most of your program" (7 p.) CONTENTS. - v. 1. What every executive should know -- v. 2. Developing your management skills -- v. 3. Forging ahead in business -- [4] Success measurement tools (portfolio) LC Card 86-233068 DDC 658.4/09 19
1. Executives. 2. Executive ability. I. Alexander Hamilton Institute (U. S.). II. Title.
HD38.2 .B569 1986

Bitter choices . Rosen, Ellen Israel. Chicago , 1987. x, 220 p. : ISBN 0-226-72644-4 LC Card 87-5867 DDC 331.4/125/0973 19
HD6095 .R74 1987

Bitter Cuban sugar . Goizueta-Mimó, Félix. [Effects of sugar monoculture upon colonial Cuba.] New York , 1987. xvii, 287 p. : ISBN 0-8240-1362-X (alk. paper) : LC Card 87-8632 DDC 338.1/7361/097291 19
HD9114.C89 G6419 1987

Bitter sugar /. Lemoine, Maurice. [Sucre amer. English.] London , 1985. 308 p., [17] p. of plates : ISBN 0-86232-445-9 LC Card 87-672356
HD4875.D44 L4513x 1985b

Bitter sugar /. Lemoine, Maurice. [Sucre amer. English.] London , c1985. 308 p., [17] p. of plates : ISBN 0-86232-445-9
NYPL [JLD 86-814]

Bittsteller oder Gegenmacht? . Schabedoth, Hans-Joachim. Marburg , 1985. 251 p. : ISBN 3-924800-32-4 : LC Card 86-115002 DDC 331.88/0943 19
HD6694 .S254 1985 ***NYPL [JLC 87-35]***

Biucchi, Basilio M. (Basilio Mario), 1908-1983. Un Paese che cambia /. Locarno , 1985. 293 p. : LC Card 85-195116 DDC 330.9494/7 19
HC398.T5 P34 1985

Bix, Herbert P. Peasant protest in Japan, 1590-1884 / Herbert P. Bix. New Haven [Conn.] : Yale University Press, c1986. xxxix, 296 p. : maps ; 25 cm. Includes index. Bibliography: p. 271-284. ISBN 0-300-03485-7 (alk. paper) LC Card 85-17889 DDC 322.4/4/0952 19
1. Peasantry - Japan - Political activity - History. 2. Peasant uprisings - Japan - History. 3. Japan - Social conditions - 1600-1868. I. Title.
HD1339.J3 B59 1986 ***NYPL [JLE 86-2541]***

Bixby, Peter. Hastings, Colin. The superteam solution . San Diego, Calif. , c1987. x, 182 p. : ISBN 0-88390-206-0 (pbk.) : LC Card 87-19185 DDC 658.4/036 19
HD66 .H38 1987

Biznes i propaganda . Andrunas, E. Ch. (Elena Cheslavovna) Moskva , 1986. 223 p. : LC Card 87-152425
HD59.6.U6 A53 1986

Bizot, Alain. La pratique bancaire française en matière de financement sur le marché intérieur / par Alain Bizot. Paris : Revue Banque, c1985. 238 p. : ill. ; 24 cm. (Collection CESB) ISBN 2-86325-033-7 : LC Card 86-159009
1. Bank loans - France. 2. Banks and banking - France. I. Series: Collection C.E.S.B. II. Title.
HG1642.F8 B59 1985

Biztonságos, jó utat! . Buga, László. [Budapest] , 1980. 95 p. : ISBN 963-316-028-6 (Magy. nemz. bibl.) LC Card 85-177784
HE5614.5.H8 B84 1980

Bizzell, Bobby G. Smith, Garry D., 1948- Business strategy and policy /. Boston , c1988. xviii, 1006 p. : ISBN 0-395-36946-0 LC Card 87-80879 DDC 658.4/012 19
HD30.28 .S56 1988

Bjerkholt, Olav, 1942-
Gleditsch, Nils Petter, 1942- Economic incentives to arm? . Oslo [1986] 72 p. : ISBN 82-7288-134-9 LC Card 87-163647 DDC 338.4/36234 19
HC79.D4 G54 1986

Macroeconomic medium-term models in the Nordic countries /. Amsterdam ; New York : x, 324 p. : ISBN 0-444-70262-8 (U. S.) LC Card 87-13422 DDC 330.948/00724 19
HC345 .M33 1987

MODIS IV : a model for economic analysis and national planning / by Olav Bjerkholt and Svein Longva = modell for økonomisk analyse og nasjonal planlegging / av Olav Bjerkholt og Svein Longva. Oslo : Statistisk Sentralbyrå, 1980. 189 p. : ill. ; 24 cm. (Samfunnsøkonomiske studier. nr. 43) Text in English; table of contents and pref. also in Norwegian. Bibliography: p. 180-186. ISBN 82-537-1014-3 (pbk.) LC Card 81-120697 DDC 330.9481/00724 19
1. Norway - Economic conditions - 1945- - Econometric models. 2. Input-Output analysis - Norway. I. Longva, Svein. II. Norway. Statistisk sentralbyrå. III. Title. IV. Series.
HC365 .B46 1980

Bjerknes, Gro. Computers and democracy . Aldershot [Hants, England] , Brookfield [Vt.], USA , c1987. x, 434 p. : ISBN 0-566-05476-0 : LC Card 87-8398 DDC 338/.06 19
HD5650 .C65 1987

Bjessmo, Lars-Erik. Industrin i Södertälje 1920-1970 : en ekonomisk-historisk studie av industriell förändring / Lars-Erik Bjessmo. Stockholm : University of Stockholm : Almqvist & Wiksell International, 1987. 236 p. ; 25 cm. (Acta Universitatis Stockholmiensis. Stockholm studies in economic history, 0346-8305) Thesis (doctoral)--University of Stockholm, 1987. Summary in English. Bibliography: p. 221-227. ISBN 91-7146-468-9 LC Card 87-151742
1. Södertälje (Sweden) - Industries - History - 20th century. 2. Södertälje (Sweden) - Economic conditions. 3. Business cycles - Sweden - Södertälje - History - 20th century. I. Title. II. Series.
HC378.S7 B54 1987

Bjørklund, Tor, 1947- Mot strømmen : kampen mot EF 1961-1972 / Tor Bjørklund ; [billedredaksjon, Tor Bjørklund, Marit Breivik, Bo Norlin]. Oslo : Universitetsforlaget, c1982. 396 p. : ill. ; 23 cm. Bibliography: p. 361-[369] ISBN 82-00-06338-0 : LC Card 83-134961
1. European Economic Community - Norway. I. Breivik, Marit. II. Norlin, Bo. III. Title.
HC241.25.N7 B56 1982

Bjørn-Andersen, Niels. Managing computer impact : an international study of management and organizations / Niels Bjørn-Andersen, Ken Eason, Daniel Robey. Norwood, N.J. : Ablex, c1986. viii, 248 p. : ill. ; 24 cm. Includes indexes. Bibliography: p. 233-239. ISBN 0-89391-358-8 LC Card 85-30754 DDC 658/.05 19
1. Management - Data processing - Addresses, essays, lectures. 2. Comparative management - Addresses, essays, lectures. I. Eason, Ken. II. Robey, Daniel. III. Title.
HD30.2 .B55 1986 ***NYPL [JLE 86-2806]***

Bjørnland, Dag, 1935- Fra dampmaskin til jetfly : en reise gjennom vår innenlandske samferdsel / Dag Bjørnland. [Oslo] : NKS, c1982. 104 p. : ill. ; 26 cm. Bibliography: p. 87-91. ISBN 82-508-0180-6 : LC Card 83-134968
1. Communication and traffic - Norway - History. 2. Transportation - Norway - History. I. Title.
HE259 .B5 1982

BL PUBLIC LIMITED COMPANY.
Edwardes, Michael, 1930- Back from the brink . London , 1983. 301 p. : ISBN 0-00-217098-1; 0-00-217089-1 LC Card 83-127870 DDC 338.7/6292/0941 19
HD9710.G74 B573 1983
NYPL [JLD 86-3553]

Black advancement in the South African economy / edited by Roy Smollan. 1st ed. Braamfontein, Johannesburg : Macmillan South Africa, 1986. 256 p. : ill. ; 26 cm. Bibliography: p. 243-250. Includes index. ISBN 0-86954-289-3 LC Card 87-119018 DDC 331.6/9968 19
1. Manpower policy - South Africa. 2. Occupational training - South Africa. 3. Blacks - South Africa - Economic conditions. I. Smollan, Roy.
HD5842.A6 B58 1986b

Black Africa . Diop, Cheikh Anta. [Fondements économiques et culturels d'un état fédéral d'Afrique noire. English.] Westport, Conn. , Trenton, N.J. , 1987. 125 p. ; ISBN 0-88208-223-X (pbk.) : LC Card 87-17704 DDC 330.967 19
HC800 .D5413 1987

Black Africa. see Africa, Sub-Saharan.

BLACK AFRICANS. see BLACKS.

BLACK AMERICANS. see AFRO-AMERICANS.

Black and white urban-to-suburban outmigrants . Gale, Dennis E. Washington, D.C. [1986] 46 p. : LC Card 87-404424 DDC 307.2 19
HB1987.W34 G35 1986

Black, Anthony. Wellings, Paul. Industrial decentralisation under apartheid . Durban , 1984. 48, xxxii p. : ISBN 0-86980-455-3 (pbk.) LC Card 87-127005 DDC 338.968 19
HC905.Z9 D59 1984

Black, Beryl. Coping with sexual harassment / by Beryl Black. 1st ed. New York : Rosen Pub. Group, 1987. 149 p. ; 23 cm. Bibliography: p. 145. Includes index. Discusses incidents of sexual harassment experienced by young people and ways of coping with this problem. ISBN 0-8239-0732-5 : LC Card 86-26245 DDC 331.13/3 19
1. Sexual harassment of women - United States - Miscellanea. 2. Sex discrimination in employment - United States - Miscellanea. 3. Sexual harassment - United States - Miscellanea. I. Title.
HD6060.3 .B55 1987

BLACK BUSINESS ENTERPRISES - SOUTH AFRICA - DURBAN.
Nattrass, Jill. Informal Black business in Durban . Pietermaritzburg, Natal, South Africa , 1986. xviii, 138 p. : ISBN 0-909232-58-X (pbk.) : LC Card 87-112836 DDC 381 19
HD2346.S632 D86 1986

Black coal miners in America . Lewis, Ronald L., 1940- Lexington, Ky. , c1987. xv, 239 p., [8] p. of plates : ISBN 0-8131-1610-4 : LC Card 87-2086 DDC 331.6/396073 19
HD8039.M62 U6443 1987

The Black community's social security /. Davis, Frank Green, 1913- Washington , c1977. xiii, 189 p. : ISBN 0-8191-0282-2 LC Card 78-304298
E185.8 .D237 ***NYPL [JLD 78-1907]***

Black consciousness in South Africa . Fatton, Robert. Albany , c1986. ix, 189 p. ; ISBN 0-88706-127-3 LC Card 85-2855 DDC 305.8/00968 19
DT763.6 .F37 1986 ***NYPL [JLE 86-2289]***

Black, Deborah G. Success and failure of futures contracts : theory and empirical evidence / by Deborah G. Black. New York, N.Y. (90 Trinity Pl., New York 10006) : Salomon Brothers Center for the Study of Financial Institutions, Graduate School of Business Administration, New York University, [c1986] 70 p. ; 23 cm. (Monograph series in finance and economics . monograph 1986-1) Bibliography: p. 65-68. LC Card 87-129777 DDC 332.64/4 19
1. Commodity exchanges. 2. Commodity exchanges - United States. I. Salomon Brothers Center for the Study of Financial Institutions. II. Title. III. Series.
HG6046 .B52 1986

The black economy in England since 1914 /.

Smithies, Edward. London , Atlantic Highlands, N.J. , 1984. 165 p. ; ISBN 0-391-03114-7 LC Card 84-6516 DDC 364.1/33 19
HF5482.65.G7 S64 1984
NYPL [JLD 86-2509]

Black farmers and their farms /. Banks, Vera J. Washington, D.C. , 1986. v, 27 p. : LC Card 86-602201
HD8039.F32 U616 1986

The Black female professional /. Morse, Roberta. Washington, D.C. [1983] i, 48 p. ; LC Card 83-80187 DDC 305.4/8896073 19
HQ1426 .M88 1983 *NYPL [Sc F 86-230]*

Black, Fischer. Business cycles and equilibrium / Fischer Black. Oxford [Oxfordshire] UK ; New York, N.Y., USA : B. Blackwell, 1987. xi, 180 p. ; 23 cm. Includes bibliographies and index. ISBN 0-631-15754-9 (U. S.) : LC Card 87-6578 DDC 338.5/42 19
1. Business cycles. 2. Equilibrium (Economics). I. Title.
HB3711 .B497 1987

Black, Kenneth. Life insurance. 11th ed. / Kenneth Black, Jr., Harold D. Skipper, Jr. Englewood Cliffs, N.J. : Prentice-Hall, c1987. xiii, 608 p. : ill. ; 25 cm. (The Prentice-Hall series in security and insurance) Rev. ed. of: Life insurance / S.S. Huebner, Kenneth Black, Jr. 10th ed. c1982. Includes bibliographies and index. ISBN 0-13-535881-7 LC Card 86-25375 DDC 368.3/2 19
1. Insurance, Life. 2. Insurance, Health. I. Skipper, Harold D., 1947-. II. Huebner, S. S. (Solomon Stephen), 1882-1964. Life insurance. III. Title. IV. Series.
HG8771 .B55 1987

Black labor unions in South Africa : report of a symposium / edited by Anthony G. Freeman and Diane B. Bendahmane ; Center for the Study of Foreign Affairs. Washington, D.C. : Foreign Service Institute, U. S. Dept. of State : For sale by the Supt. of Docs., U. S. G.P.O., 1987. vi, 63 p. ; 24 cm. Shipping list no.: 87-165-P. "Released October 1986"--T.p. verso. Bibliography: p. 59-60. S/N 044-000-02163-3 Item 872-A LC Card 86-600599 DDC 331.6/9/968 19
1. Trade-unions, Black - South Africa - Congresses. I. Freeman, Anthony G. II. Bendahmane, Diane B. III. Center for the Study of Foreign Affairs (U. S.).
HD6870.5 .B53 1987

Black managers. Mcunu, Ernest. Top level advice to aspirant black managers /. Braamfontein [1985] 48 p. ; LC Card 87-152084 DDC 658.4/09 19
HD38.2 .M395 1985

BLACK MARKET - GERMANY (WEST) - ADDRESSES, ESSAYS, LECTURES.
Wirtschaft im Untergrund /. Reinbek bei Hamburg , 1983. 188 p. : ISBN 3-499-33035-0 : LC Card 83-206566
HF5482.65.G3 W57 1983
NYPL [JLC 86-265]

BLACK MARKET - GREAT BRITAIN - HISTORY - 20TH CENTURY.
Smithies, Edward. The black economy in England since 1914 /. London , Atlantic Highlands, N.J. , 1984. 165 p. ; ISBN 0-391-03114-7 LC Card 84-6516 DDC 364.1/33 19
HF5482.65.G7 S64 1984
NYPL [JLD 86-2509]

BLACK MARKET - SOVIET UNION.
Ėvel′son, Evgeniia. Sudebnye protsessy po ėkonomicheskim delam v SSSR . London , 1986. 370 p. ; *NYPL [*QIX 87-4024]*

BLACK MARKETEERS - FRANCE - MARSEILLE - BIOGRAPHY.
Castellani, Maurice. French solo /. Paris , c1985. 262 p. ; ISBN 2-86477-063-6 : LC Card 85-205040
HF5482.65.F7 C373 1985

Black migration to the PWV complex . Kok, P. C. Pretoria , 1985. viii, 79 p. : ISBN 0-7969-0313-1 (pbk.) : LC Card 86-232836 DDC 304.8/0968 19
HB2123.4.P68 K65 1985

Black money . Kabra, Kamal Nayan. New Delhi , 1985. 47 p. ; LC Card 87-900898 DDC 381 19
HJ2348.5 .K32 1985

BLACK PEOPLE (U. S.) see AFRO-AMERICANS.

Black, Peter E. Conservation of water and related land resources / Peter E. Black. 2nd ed. Totowa, N.J. : Rowman & Littlefield, 1987. xvi, 336 p. : ill. ; 25 cm. Bibliography: p. [299]-329. Includes index. ISBN 0-8476-7567-X LC Card 87-4770 DDC 333.91/16/0973 19
1. Water conservation - Government policy - United States. 2. Land use - Government policy - United States. I. Title.
HD1694 .A5105 1987

Black South African views on disinvestment /. Voorhes, Meg. Washington, D.C. (Suite 600, 1755 Massachusetts Ave., N.W., Washington 20036) [1986] 36 p. ; LC Card 86-209279 DDC 332.6/73/0968 19
HG5851.A3 V66 1986

Black, William E. Knutson, Ronald D. Cooperative involvement in issues of domestic farm policy /. College Station, Tex. , 1986. 59 p. : LC Card 86-623063 DDC 338.1/8764 19
HD1491.U6 T45 1986

Black, William Richard, 1942- Railroads for rent : the local rail service assistance program / William R. Black. Bloomington : Indiana University Press, c1986. x, 341 p. ; 25 cm. Includes index. Bibliography: p. 325-336. ISBN 0-253-34774-2 LC Card 84-48546 DDC 385/.1 19
1. Railroads - United States - Finance. 2. Federal aid to transportation - United States. 3. Railroads - United States - Branch lines. 4. Railroads - United States - Freight. 5. Railroads and state - United States. I. Title.
HE1061 .B57 1986 *NYPL [JLE 86-3354]*

The Black woman's career guide /. Nivens, Beatryce. New York , 1987. xvi, 362 p. ; ISBN 0-385-24161-5 (pbk.) : LC Card 87-1193 DDC 650.1/4/088042 19
HF5382.5.U5 N5 1987

The Black youth employment crisis / edited by Richard B. Freeman and Harry J. Holzer. Chicago : University of Chicago Press, 1986. viii, 469 p. : ill. ; 24 cm. (A National Bureau of Economic Research project report) Includes bibliographies and indexes. ISBN 0-226-26164-6 LC Card 85-20989 DDC 331.3/46396073 19
1. Afro-American youth - Employment - Congresses. 2. Unemployment - United States - Congresses. I. Freeman, Richard Barry, 1943-. II. Holzer, Harry J. III. Series.
HD6273 .B57 1986 *NYPL [JLE 86-3726]*

Blackaby, Frank. Peace, defence, and economic analysis . New York , 1987. xxxiii, 450 p. : ISBN 0-312-01321-3 : LC Card 87-19708 DDC 338.4/7355 19
HC79.D4 P43 1987

Blacker, Terence. If I could work / written by Terence Blacker ; illustrated by Chris Winn. 1st American ed. New York : Lippincott, c1988. p. cm. A child fantasizes about the different kinds of work he would do if he weren't so young. ISBN 0-397-32245-3 : LC Card 87-3972 DDC 331.7/02 19
1. Occupations - Juvenile literature. 2. Work - Juvenile literature. I. Winn, Chris, ill. II. Title.
HF5381.2 .B55 1988

Blackford, Mansel G., 1944-
Business enterprise in American history / Mansel G. Blackford, K. Austin Kerr. Boston : Houghton Mifflin, c1986. xi, 456 p. : ill. ; 24 cm. Includes bibliographies and index. ISBN 0-395-35155-3 (pbk.) LC Card 85-60780 DDC 338.7/4/0973 19
1. Corporations - United States - History. 2. Business enterprises - United States - History. I. Kerr, Kathel Austin. II. Title.
HD2785 .B52 1986 *NYPL [JLE 86-3008]*

The rise of modern business in Great Britain, the United States, and Japan / by Mansel G. Blackford. Chapel Hill : University of North Carolina Press, c1988. xi, 176 p. : ill. ; 24 cm. Includes bibliographies and index. ISBN 0-8078-1760-0 (alk. paper) LC Card 87-10022 DDC 338.09 19
1. Great Britain - Industries - History. 2. United States - Industries - History. 3. Japan - Industries - History. I. Title.
HC255 .B59 1988

Blackie, M. J. Accelerating food production in Sub-Saharan Africa /. Baltimore , c1987. xix, 417 p. ; ISBN 0-8018-3390-6 (alk. paper) LC Card 86-10684 DDC 338.1/9/67 19
HD2117 .A33 1987 *NYPL [JLE 87-1366]*

BLACKS - COLOMBIA - CHOCÓ - ECONOMIC CONDITIONS.
Caicedo Licona, Carlos Arturo. El Chocó por dentro /. Medellín, Colombia , 1980. 118 p. : LC Card 83-105927
HC198.C48 C33 1980

BLACKS - EMPLOYMENT - BRAZIL.
Oliveira, Lúcia Elena Garcia de. O lugar do negro na força de trabalho /. Rio de Janeiro , 1983. 86 p. ; ISBN 85-24-00024-4 LC Card 86-129924
HD8288.5.B55 O45 1983

BLACKS - EMPLOYMENT - GREAT BRITAIN.
Jenkins, Richard, 1952- Racism and recruitment . Cambridge [Cambridgeshire] , New York , 1986. xi, 281 p. ; ISBN 0-521-32028-3 LC Card 85-17483 DDC 331.13/3/0941 19
HG4903.5.G7 J46 1986
NYPL [JLE 86-3305]

BLACKS - EMPLOYMENT - SOUTH AFRICA.
African worker under apartheid. Brussels [1984]. 109 p. : *NYPL [Sc D 86-730]*

Jeeves, Alan. Migrant labour in South Africa's mining economy . Kingston, Canada , 1985. xiv, 323 p. ; ISBN 0-7735-0420-6 DDC 331.7'6223422 *NYPL [JLE 85-3148]*

Mcunu, Ernest. Top level advice to aspirant black managers /. Braamfontein [1985] 48 p. ; LC Card 87-152084 DDC 658.4/09 19
HD38.2 .M395 1985

Schneier, Steffen. Occupational mobility among Blacks in South Africa /. Cape Town [1983] vi, 219 p. : ISBN 0-7992-0567-2 (pbk.) LC Card 84-197038 DDC 331.12/72/089968 19
HD8801 .S34 1983 *NYPL [JLG 86-123]*

BLACKS - EMPLOYMENT - SOUTH AFRICA - CASE STUDIES.
Charoux, J. A. E. (J. A. Eric) The integration of the Black manager into South African organizations /. Cape Town , 1986. xi, 178 p. : ISBN 0-7021-1706-4 (pbk.) LC Card 87-113544 DDC 331.6/3/968 19
HD38.25.S6 C53 1986

The Sullivan principles at Ford--audit a [microform] /. [s.l.] , 1981. 16 p. ;
*NYPL [*ZT-1745 no.32]*

BLACKS - EMPLOYMENT - SOUTH AFRICA - DURBAN.
Nattrass, Jill. Informal Black business in Durban . Pietermaritzburg, Natal, South Africa , 1986. xviii, 138 p. : ISBN 0-909232-58-X (pbk.) : LC Card 87-112836 DDC 381 19
HD2346.S632 D86 1986

BLACKS - EMPLOYMENT - SOUTH AFRICA - KIMBERLEY - HISTORY.
Turrell, Robert Vicat. Capital and labour on the Kimberley diamond fields, 1871-1890 /. Cambridge [Cambridgeshire] , New York , 1987. xviii, 297 p. : ISBN 0-521-33354-7 LC Card 86-32740 DDC 331.7/622382/0968711 19
HD9677.S63 K567 1987

BLACKS - EMPLOYMENT - SOUTH AFRICA - KIMBERLEY - HISTORY - 19TH CENTURY.
Worger, William H. South Africa's city of diamonds . New Haven , c1987. xvi, 330 p. : ISBN 0-300-03716-3 (alk. paper) LC Card 86-24724 DDC 331.7/622382/0968711 19
HD9677.S63 K568 1987

BLACKS - EMPLOYMENT - SOUTH AFRICA - KWANDEBELE.
McCaul, Colleen. Satellite in revolt . Johannesburg, South Africa , 1987. 125 p., [11] p. of plates : ISBN 0-86982-314-0 (pbk.) LC Card 87-157406 DDC 330.9682/95063 19
HC905.Z7 K785 1987

BLACKS - GREAT BRITAIN - ECONOMIC CONDITIONS.
Ramdin, Ron. The making of the Black working class in Britain /. Aldershot, Hants, England , Brookfield, Vt., USA , c1987. x, 626 p. ; ISBN 0-566-00943-9 LC Card 87-127153 DDC 305.5/62 19
HD8398.B55 R36 1987

BLACKS - GREAT BRITAIN - SEGREGATION - HISTORY - 20TH

CENTURY.
Sherwood, Marika. Many struggles . London , 1985, c1984. 138 p. : ISBN 0-946918-00-7 (pbk.) LC Card 86-110617 DDC 305.8/00941 19
HD8398.B55 S54 1985 ***NYPL [Sc D 86-815]***

BLACKS - GREAT BRITAIN - SOCIAL CONDITIONS.
Ramdin, Ron. The making of the Black working class in Britain /. Aldershot, Hants, England , Brookfield, Vt., USA , c1987. x, 626 p. ; ISBN 0-566-00943-9 LC Card 87-127153 DDC 305.5/62 19
HD8398.B55 R36 1987

BLACKS - SAINT VINCENT AND THE GRENADINES - ECONOMIC CONDITIONS - CASE STUDIES.
Rubenstein, Hymie. Coping with poverty . Boulder, Colo. , 1987. xx, 389 p. : ISBN 0-8133-7387-5 (pbk. : alk. paper) : LC Card 86-32530 DDC 972.98/4400496 19
HC156.5.Z7 S296 1987

BLACKS - SAINT VINCENT AND THE GRENADINES - SOCIAL LIFE AND CUSTOMS - CASE STUDIES.
Rubenstein, Hymie. Coping with poverty . Boulder, Colo. , 1987. xx, 389 p. : ISBN 0-8133-7387-5 (pbk. : alk. paper) : LC Card 86-32530 DDC 972.98/4400496 19
HC156.5.Z7 S296 1987

BLACKS - SOUTH AFRICA - BIOGRAPHY.
Mathabane, Mark. Kaffir boy . New York , c1986. xii, 354 p., [8] p. of plates : ISBN 0-02-581800-7 : LC Card 86-53 DDC 968/.00496024 B 19
DT779.95.M38 A34 1986
NYPL [Sc E 86-240]

BLACKS - SOUTH AFRICA - DURBAN - ECONOMIC CONDITIONS - STATISTICS.
Van Wyk, H. de J. Income and expenditure patterns of urban Black multiple households in Durban, 1985 /. Pretoria , 1986. xi, 130 p. : ISBN 0-908408-59-5 (pbk.) LC Card 87-151639 DDC 658.8/3968 s 339.4/1/0968455021 19
HC517.S7 S48 no. 130, pt. 4 HD7064.4.Z8D8

BLACKS - SOUTH AFRICA - ECONOMIC CONDITIONS.
African worker under apartheid. Brussels [1984]. 109 p. : ***NYPL [Sc D 86-730]***

Black advancement in the South African economy /. Braamfontein, Johannesburg , 1986. 256 p. : ISBN 0-86954-289-3 LC Card 87-119018 DDC 331.6/9968 19
HD5842.A6 B58 1986b

Orkin, Mark. Disinvestment, the struggle, and the future . Johannesburg , 1986. xii, 78 p. : ISBN 0-86975-305-3 (pbk.) LC Card 87-100474 DDC 332.6/73/0968 19
HG5851.A3 O47 1986

Webster, Eddie. Cast in a racial mould . Johannesburg , 1985. xv, 299 p., [8] p. of plates : ISBN 0-86975-285-5
NYPL [JLD 87-780]

BLACKS - SOUTH AFRICA - KWANDEBELE - POLITICS AND GOVERNMENT.
McCaul, Colleen. Satellite in revolt . Johannesburg, South Africa , 1987. 125 p., [11] p. of plates : ISBN 0-86982-314-0 (pbk.) LC Card 87-157406 DDC 330.9682/95063 19
HC905.Z7 K785 1987

BLACKS - SOUTH AFRICA - MIGRATIONS - STATISTICS.
Cilliers, S. P. Patterns of migration and settlement in rural South Africa /. [Stellenbosch] , 1986. 19, 13 leaves, 5 folded leaves of plates : ISBN 0-908422-81-4 (pbk.) : LC Card 87-126315 DDC 304.8/0968 19
HB2123.4.A3 C56 1986

BLACKS - SOUTH AFRICA - POLITICS AND GOVERNMENT.
Fatton, Robert. Black consciousness in South Africa . Albany , c1986. ix, 189 p. ; ISBN 0-88706-127-3 LC Card 85-2855 DDC 305.8/00968 19
DT763.6 .F37 1986 ***NYPL [JLE 86-2289]***

Mandela, Winnie. Part of my soul /. Harmondsworth , 1985. 163 p., [8] p. of plates : ***NYPL [Sc C 86-121]***

Mandela, Winnie. Part of my soul went with him /. New York , 1985, c1984. 163 p., [8] p. of plates : ISBN 0-393-02215-3 : LC Card 85-21632 DDC 968/.00496 19
DT779.955.M36 A35 1985
NYPL [JFD 86-7717]

BLACKS - SOUTH AFRICA - PRETORIA - ECONOMIC CONDITIONS.
Kok, P. C. Black migration to the PWV complex . Pretoria , 1985. viii, 79 p. : ISBN 0-7969-0313-1 (pbk.) : LC Card 86-232836 DDC 304.8/0968 19
HB2123.4.P68 K65 1985

BLACKS - SOUTH AFRICA - PRETORIA - ECONOMIC CONDITIONS - STATISTICS.
Martins, J. H. Income and expenditure patterns of urban black multiple households in Pretoria, 1985 /. Pretoria , 1986. xi, 128 p. : ISBN 0-908408-57-9 (pbk.) LC Card 86-220725 DDC 658.8/3968 s 339.4/1/0968235 19
HC517.S7 S48 no. 130, pt. 2 HD7064.4.Z8P74

BLACKS - SOUTH AFRICA - RACE IDENTITY.
Fatton, Robert. Black consciousness in South Africa . Albany , c1986. ix, 189 p. ; ISBN 0-88706-127-3 LC Card 85-2855 DDC 305.8/00968 19
DT763.6 .F37 1986 ***NYPL [JLE 86-2289]***

BLACKS - SOUTH AFRICA - SEGREGATION.
The Sullivan principles at Ford--audit a [microform] /. [s.l.] , 1981. 16 p. ;
NYPL [*ZT-1745 no.32]

BLACKS - SOUTH AFRICA - SOCIAL CONDITIONS.
Fatton, Robert. Black consciousness in South Africa . Albany , c1986. ix, 189 p. ; ISBN 0-88706-127-3 LC Card 85-2855 DDC 305.8/00968 19
DT763.6 .F37 1986 ***NYPL [JLE 86-2289]***

Mandela, Winnie. Part of my soul /. Harmondsworth , 1985. 163 p., [8] p. of plates : ***NYPL [Sc C 86-121]***

Mandela, Winnie. Part of my soul went with him /. New York , 1985, c1984. 163 p., [8] p. of plates : ISBN 0-393-02215-3 : LC Card 85-21632 DDC 968/.00496 19
DT779.955.M36 A35 1985
NYPL [JFD 86-7717]

BLACKS - SOUTH AFRICA - VEREENIGING - ECONOMIC CONDITIONS.
Kok, P. C. Black migration to the PWV complex . Pretoria , 1985. viii, 79 p. : ISBN 0-7969-0313-1 (pbk.) : LC Card 86-232836 DDC 304.8/0968 19
HB2123.4.P68 K65 1985

BLACKS - SOUTH AFRICA - WITWATERSRAND - ECONOMIC CONDITIONS.
Kok, P. C. Black migration to the PWV complex . Pretoria , 1985. viii, 79 p. : ISBN 0-7969-0313-1 (pbk.) : LC Card 86-232836 DDC 304.8/0968 19
HB2123.4.P68 K65 1985

Blackstone, L. R. (Lance R.) UK tax savings for the higher paid (1979) / by L.R. Blackstone and D.S. Franks. London : Economist Intelligence Unit, c1979. 10 p. ; 30 cm. (EIU special report. no. 71) "October 1979." LC Card 81-112830
1. Executives - Taxation - Great Britain. 2. Employee fringe benefits - Taxation - Great Britain. 3. Income tax - Great Britain - Foreign income. I. Franks, D. S. (David S.). II. Title.
HJ4708.A7 B533 1979

The Blackwell guide to Wall Street /. Putnam, Bluford H. Oxford, UK , New York, NY, USA , 1987. viii, 222 p. : ISBN 0-631-14183-9 : LC Card 87-10299 DDC 332.63/2 19
HG4910 .P87 1987

Blades, Derek W.
Brodin, Anders. The OECD Compatible Trade and Production data base, 1970-1983 /. [Paris, France] , c1986. ii, 81 p. ; LC Card 86-213116 DDC 382/.021 19
HF1016 .B68 1986

Discrepancies between imports and exports in OECD foreign trade statistics / by Derek Blades, Marina Ivanov. Paris, France : OECD, c1984. i, 42 p. ; 30 cm. (Working papers / Economics and Statistics Department . no. 25) Cover title. "September 1985." LC Card 86-205155 DDC 382/.021 19
1. Commercial statistics. 2. Exports. 3. Imports. 4. Organisation for Economic Co-operation and Development. I. Ivanov, Marina. II. Series: Working papers (Organisation for Economic Co-operation and Development. Dept. of Economics and Statistics) , no. 25. III. Title.
HF1016 .B569 1984

Blaha, Hermann. Methoden der Politikberatung im wirtschaftspolitischen Bereich /. Wien , 1984. 116 p. ; LC Card 84-222756
HC265 .M39 1984

Blair, John P., 1947- Barrett, G. Vincent. How to conduct and analyze real estate market and feasibility studies /. New York , c1988. xvii, 366 p. : ISBN 0-442-21220-8 : LC Card 87-18861 DDC 332.63/24 19
HD1390 .B37 1988

Blair, Roger D.
Antitrust economics / Roger D. Blair, David L. Kaserman. Homewood, Ill. : R.D. Irwin, 1985. xvii, 483 p. : ill. ; 25 cm. Includes bibliographies and indexes. ISBN 0-256-02807-9 LC Card 84-82009 DDC 343.73/072 347.30372 19
1. Antitrust law - United States. 2. Antitrust law - Economic aspects - United States. I. Title.
KF1649 .B54 1985 ***NYPL [JLE 86-3453]***

Microeconomics with business applications / Roger D. Blair and Lawrence W. Kenny. New York : Wiley, c1987. xvii, 514 p. : col. ill. ; 25 cm. Includes bibliographical references and indexes. ISBN 0-471-88304-2 LC Card 86-26770 DDC 338.5 19
1. Microeconomics. I. Kenny, Lawrence W. II. Title.
HB172 .B5413 1987

Blake, Hubert, 1893- Currency and credit before and since 1914 [microform] / by Hubert Blake. London : Wilson, 1923. viii, 91 p. ; 20 cm. Microfilm. New York : New York Public Library, 1986. 1 microfilm reel ; 35 mm. (MN *ZZ-26,558)
1. Monetary policy - Great Britain. 2. Credit - Great Britain. 3. Banks and banking - Great Britain. I. Title.
NYPL [*ZT-1736 no.1]

Blake, Robert Rogers, 1918- Spectacular teamwork : how to develop the leadership skills for team success / Robert R. Blake, Jane S. Mouton, Robert L. Allen. New York : Wiley, c1987. viii, 219 p. : ill. ; 22 cm. Includes index. ISBN 0-471-85311-9 LC Card 86-28123 DDC 658.4/036 19
1. Work groups. I. Mouton, Jane Srygley. II. Allen, Robert L. III. Title.
HD66 .B54 1987

Blanc, Georges. Anastassopoulos, J. P. [Multinationales publiques. English.] State-owned multinationals /. Chichester [England] , New York , c1987. xii, 200 p. : ISBN 0-471-91502-5 : LC Card 87-2033 DDC 338.8/8 19
HD2755.5 .A613 1987

Blanc, Iris. DDC spreadsheets. Teacher manual : applications and exercises, includes solutions / [New York, N.Y.] : Dictation Disc Co., [c1986] 161 p. : ill. ; 22 cm. Cover title. "An introductory spreadsheet course at either the high school or post secondary level"--P. 2. LC Card 87-159255 DDC 005.3/07/1273 19
1. Business - Data processing - Problems, exercises, etc. 2. Electronic spreadsheets. I. Vento, Cathy. II. Dictation Disc Company. III. Title.
HF5548.2 .B527 1986

Blanchard, Kenneth H.
Hersey, Paul. Management of organizational behavior . Englewood Cliffs, N.J. , 1988. p. cm. ISBN 0-13-551268-9 : LC Card 87-23064 DDC 658.3 19
HD58.7 .H47 1988

The power of ethical management / Kenneth Blanchard, Norman Vincent Peale. 1st ed. New York : W. Morrow, 1988. 139 p. ; 22 cm. ISBN 0-688-07062-0 LC Card 87-24210 DDC 174/.4 19
1. Business ethics. 2. Conduct of life. I. Peale, Norman Vincent, 1898-. II. Title.
HF5387 .B56 1988

Blanckenburg, Peter von.
Handbuch der Landwirtschaft und Ernährung in den Entwicklungsländern /. Stuttgart , c1982- v. : ISBN 3-8001-3059-9 (Bd. 1) LC Card 84-155503 DDC 338.1/09172/4 19
HD1417 .H24 1982 ***NYPL [JLL 86-257]***

Theorie und Empirie in Wirtschaftspolitik und Wirtschaftsgeschichte . Göttingen , 1984. 245 p. : LC Card 85-111313
HC284 .T46 1984

Welternährung : Gegenwartsprobleme und Strategien für die Zukunft / Peter von Blanckenburg.Originalausg. München : C.H. Beck, c1986. 347 p. : ill. ; 18 cm. (Beck'sche schwarze Reihe. Bd. 308) Bibliography: p. 328-345. Includes index. ISBN 3-406-31300-0 LC Card 86-196307
1. Food supply. 2. Food supply - Planning. I. Title.
HD9000.5 .B49 1986

Blanco Martínez, Adolfo. Dirigir con inflación : efectos, cuantificación y decisiones / Adolfo Blanco Martínez. Bilbao : Deusto, [1983?] 239 p. : ill. ; 24 cm. Bibliography: p. [237]-239. ISBN 84-234-0537-0 LC Card 85-124395
1. Industrial management - Effect of inflation on. I. Title.
HD49.5 .B48 1983

Blandy, Richard, 1938-
Alternatives to arbitration /. Sydney , Boston , 1986. x, 468 p. ; ISBN 0-86861-857-8 (pbk.) LC Card 85-81482 DDC 331/.0994 19
HD5630.A6 A47 1986

Structured chaos . Melbourne , New York , 1985. viii, 111 p. : ISBN 0-19-554687-3 LC Card 86-222312 DDC 338/.06/0994 19
HC610.I52 S77 1985

Blang, Hans-Georg, 1953- Die Variabilität relativer Preisänderungen und die Varianz monetärer Aggregate / Hans-Georg Blang. Frankfurt am Main ; New York : P. Lang, c1986. xxvii, 338 p. : ill. ; 21 cm. (Europäische Hochschulschriften. Reihe V, Volks- und Betriebswirtschaft, 0531-7339 . Bd. 685 = vol. 685 = vol. 685) Originally presented as the author's thesis (doctoral)--Universität-GH-Siegen, 1984. Bibliography: p. 326-338. ISBN 3-8204-9074-4 LC Card 86-156110
1. Money - Mathematical models. 2. Prices - Mathematical models. 3. Inflation (Finance) - Mathematical models. 4. Monetary policy - Mathematical models. I. Series: Europäische Hochschulschriften. Reihe V, Volks- und Betriebswirtschaft , Bd. 685. II. Title.
HG229 .B555 1986

Blank, Thomas O., 1947-
Older persons and their homes, today and tomorrow : a research monograph on housing / Thomas O. Blank. [Harrisburg] : Pennsylvania Dept. of Aging, [1986] 60 leaves : ill. ; 28 cm. "Prepared under contract no. 853010 from the Pennsylvania Department of Aging to Lehigh University." "June 1986." Bibliography: leaves 43-60. LC Card 86-623023 DDC 363.5/9 19
1. Aged - United States - Dwellings. I. Pennsylvania. Dept. of Aging. II. Lehigh University. III. Title.
HD7287.92.U54 B55 1986

Older persons and their housing, today and tomorrow / by Thomas O. Blank. Springfield, Ill., U. S.A. : C.C. Thomas, c1988. xviii, 304 p. ; 26 cm. Bibliography: p. 239-288. Includes indexes. ISBN 0-398-05377-4 LC Card 87-16827 DDC 363.5/9 19
1. Aged - Housing - United States. 2. Aged - United States - Dwellings. I. Title.
HD7287.92.U54 B554 1988

Blanke, Bernhard, 1941- Die Zweite Stadt . Opladen , c1986. 407 p. : ISBN 3-531-11764-5 LC Card 87-497505 DDC 331.11/0943 19
HD8451 .Z94 1986

Blanpain, R. (Roger), 1942- L'Information et la consultation des travailleurs dans les entreprises multinationales /. [Paris] [Genève?] , 1984. 290 p. ; ISBN 2-13-038651-2 (pbk.)
HD62.4 .I53 1984 ***NYPL [JLD 87-60]***

Blanpain, Roger. Comparative labour law and industrial relations /. Deventer [Netherlands] , Boston , c1985. xiii, 527 p. ; ISBN 90-6544-236-7 (pbk.) LC Card 85-10000 DDC 344/.01 342.41 19
K1705.6 .C65 1985 ***NYPL [JLE 86-2420]***

Blanpied, William A., 1933- Governing science and technology in a democracy /. Knoxville, TN , c1986. xviii, 314 p. ; ISBN 0-87049-506-2 (alk. paper) : LC Card 86-7074 DDC 338.9/26 19
Q125 .G68 1986 ***NYPL [JLD 87-462]***

Blasi, Benedetto.
Della strada ferrata Pia-Cassia da citta della Pieve a Civitavecchia e del ristauro del Porto Neroniano in Anzio : risposta di Benedetto Blasi, segretario della Camera di commercio in Civitavecchia ad un articolo del Messaggero o l'Eclettigo ed alle osservazioni del municipio di Nettuno e di Anzio. Roma : Tip. Contedini, 1846. 56 p., [3] folded leaves of plates : ill. ; 21 cm. Includes bibliographical references. LC Card 85-665949
1. Railroads - Italy. 2. Anzio (Italy) - Harbor. I. Title.
HE3098 .B51x 1846

Sulle strade ferrate nello stato pontificio : considerazioni / di Benedetto Blasi. Roma : Tip. Contedini, 1847. 32 p. ; 20 cm. LC Card 85-665950
1. Railroads - Italy. I. Title.
HE3098 .B52x 1847

Blasi, Joseph R.
Employee ownership through ESOPs : implications for the public corporation / by Joseph Raphael Blasi. New York : Pergamon Press, c1987. 126 p. ; 28 cm. (Work in America Institute studies in productivity, 0149-8703 . 48) Bibliography: p. 107-126. ISBN 0-08-029520-7 (pbk.) : LC Card 86-30281 DDC 658.3/225 19
1. Employee ownership - United States. I. Title. II. Series.
HD5660.U5 B57 1987

Quarrey, Michael. Taking stock . Cambridge, Mass. , c1986. xxii, 176 p. ; ISBN 0-88730-131-2 LC Card 86-14045 DDC 338.7/4 19
HD5660.U5 Q37 1986 ***NYPL [JLE 87-49]***

Bläsing, J. F. E. (Joachim F. E.), 1940- Op het spoor van de Körver : onstaan, groei en transformaties van de Brabantse familieonderneming Hendrix' Fabrieken 1979/1930 : bedrijfsgeschiedkundig bekeken / J.F.E. Bläsing. Leiden : M. Nijhoff, 1986. xvi, 396 p. : ill. ; 26 cm. Bibliography: p. 325-336. Includes index. ISBN 90-247-8065-9 : LC Card 86-214829
1. Hendrix' Fabrieken - History. 2. Flour and feed trade - Netherlands - History. 3. Spice trade - Netherlands - History. 4. Specerijen-Malerij "De Körver" - History. I. Title.
HD9052.N44 H453 1986

The blast furnace brothers /. Copeland, Vincent. New York, N.Y. , 1973. iv, 33 p. : LC Card 87-125932 DDC 331.13/3 19
HD4903.3.B582 U63 1973

Błaszków, Władysław. Technologia /. [Wrocław] , 1982. 188 p. : LC Card 83-176194
HB9 .B7522 nr. 191 TP185

Blatherwick, David E. S. The international politics of telecommunications / David E.S. Blatherwick. [Berkeley, Calif.] : Institute of International Studies, University of California, Berkeley, c1987. ix, 107 p. ; 24 cm. (Research series, 0068-6093 . no. 68) Bibliography: p. 91-107. ISBN 0-87725-168-1 (pbk.) : LC Card 87-3509 DDC 384/.068 19
1. Telecommunication policy. 2. Telecommunication equipment industry. 3. Information services and state. I. Series: Research series (University of California, Berkeley. Institute of International Studies) , no. 68. II. Title.
HE7645 .B57 1987

Blau, Anne Kohn. The sex of the dollar : street-smart financial planning for women / by Anne Kohn Blau, with Ellen Thro. New York : Simon and Schuster, c1988. 190 p. : forms ; 22 cm. Includes index. ISBN 0-671-60680-8 LC Card 87-23560 DDC 332.024/042 19
1. Women - United States - Finance, Personal. I. Thro, Ellen. II. Title.
HG181 .B46 1988

Blau, Francine D. The economics of women, men, and work / Francine D. Blau, Marianne A. Ferber. Englewood Cliffs, N.J. : Prentice-Hall, c1986. xiv, 365 p. : ill. ; 24 cm. Includes bibliographies and indexes. ISBN 0-13-233719-3 LC Card 85-30746 DDC 305.3/0973 19
1. Women - United States - Economic conditions. 2. Women - United States - Social conditions. 3. Women - Employment - United States. 4. Housewives - United States. 5. Sexual division of labor - United States. I. Ferber, Marianne A., 1923-. II. Title.
HQ1426 .B62 1986 ***NYPL [JLE 86-4254]***

Blau, Gerda.
Blay, Eva Alterman. Eu não tenho onde morar : vilas operárias na cidade de São Paulo / Eva Alterman Blay. São Paulo, SP : Nobel, [1985] 332 p. : ill. ; 21 cm. Bibliography: p. 325-332. ISBN 85-21-30298-3 : LC Card 85-211285
1. Labor and laboring classes - Dwellings - Brazil - São Paulo. 2. Housing - Brazil - São Paulo. I. Title.
HD7323.S28 B56 1985

Blaydon, Colin C. Drawing the line on natural gas regulation . New York , 1987. xiii, 267 p. : ISBN 0-89930-174-6 (lib. bdg. : alk. paper) LC Card 86-25769 DDC 338.2/7285/0973 19
HD9581.U5 D73 1987

Blaylock, Bruce K., 1949- Personal financial planning for local government employees /. Washington, D.C. , c1987. 203 p. : ISBN 0-87326-051-1 (pbk.) LC Card 87-2948 DDC 332.024/354 19
HG179 .P386 1987

Blayney-Dyett, Urban and Regional Planners. California affordable housing legislation . [Sacramento] [1986?] 2 v. ; LC Card 86-622916 DDC 363.5/8 19
HD7303.C2 C275 1986

Blazovich, László. A Körös-Tisza-Maros köz középkori településrendje / Blazovich László. Békéscsaba ; Szeged : Békés- és Csongrád Megye Tanácsa VB Művelődési Osztálya, 1985. 207 p., [9] folded leaves of plates : maps (some col.) ; 25 cm. (Dél-alföldi évszázadok, 0237-4587) One col. map on folded leaf in pocket. Bibliography: p. 159-165. ISBN 963-01-6828-6 LC Card 87-408571
1. Land settlement - Great Alföld - History. 2. Human settlements - Great Alföld - History. I. Title. II. Series.
HD640.5.Z8 G743 1985

The bleak midwinter, 1947 /. Robertson, Alex. Manchester, U.K. , Wolfeboro, N.H., U. S.A. , 1987. x, 207 p. : ISBN 0-7190-1902-8 : LC Card 87-11085 DDC 333.8/22/0941 19
HD9551.5 .R56 1987

Bleak mid-winter, 1947. Robertson, Alex. The bleak midwinter, 1947 /. Manchester, U.K. , Wolfeboro, N.H., U. S.A. , 1987. x, 207 p. : ISBN 0-7190-1902-8 : LC Card 87-11085 DDC 333.8/22/0941 19
HD9551.5 .R56 1987

Bleiberg, Germán, 1915- El "informe secreto" de Mateo Alemán sobre el trabajo forzoso en las minas de Almadén / Germán Bleiberg. London : Tamesis Books, c1985. 150 p. ; 25 cm. (Colección Támesis. Serie A: monografías. 107) Includes bibliographical references. ISBN 0-7293-0200-8 LC Card 86-178917
1. Forced labor - Spain - Almadén Region - History - 16th century. 2. Mercury miners - Spain - Almadén Region - History - 16th century. 3. Mercury mines and mining - Spain - Almadén Region - History - 16th century. 4. Alemán, Mateo, 1547-1614?. I. Title.
HD4875.S6 B58 1985

Bleicher, Siegfried. Ausstieg? . Hamburg , 1985. 159 p. : ISBN 3-87975-289-3 LC Card 85-219857 DDC 331/.0943 19
HD6694 .A97 1985 ***NYPL [JLD 87-710]***

Bleicker, Ulrike. Produktbeurteilung der Konsumenten : eine psychologische Theorie der Informationsverarbeitung / Ulrike Bleicker. Würzburg : Physica-Verlag, c1983. 245 p. : ill. ; 25 cm. (Konsum und Verhalten . Bd. 5) Bibliography: p. 227-245. ISBN 3-7908-0292-1 LC Card 83-191583
1. Consumers' preferences. 2. Consumers - Attitudes. 3. Human information processing. I. Title. II. Series.
HF5415.3 .B52 1983

Bleier, Ernst. Insolvenzfrüherkennung mittels praktischer Anwendung der Diskriminanzanalyse / Ernst Bleier. Wien : Service, Fachverlag an der Wirtschaftsuniversität, c1985. 216 p. : ill. ; 21 cm. Based on the author's thesis (doctoral--Wirtschaftsuniversität Wien, 1981) presented under the title: Insolvenzprognose aus den Jahresabschlüssen nicht publizitätspflichtiger Unternehmen. Bibliography: p. 209-214. ISBN 3-85428-043-2 : LC Card 85-201068
1. Bankruptcy - Statistical methods. 2. Bankruptcy - Forecasting - Statistical methods. I. Title.
HG3761 .B54 1985

Blencke, Fritz. Alfred Krupp / von Fritz Blencke, mit 27 Abbildungen. Leipzig : R. Voigtländer, 1898. 127 p. : ill., ports. ; 19 cm. (Biographische

Volksbücher . 23-27) LC Card 85-665721
1. Krupp, Alfred, 1812-1887. 2. Steel industry and trade - Germany - Biography. I. Title. II. Series.
HD9523.9.K7 B53x 1898

Blenkhorn, David L. Leenders, Michiel R. Reverse marketing . New York , London , c1988. ix, 198 p. : ISBN 0-02-918381-2 LC Card 87-15146 DDC 658.7/2 19
HD39.5 .L435 1988

Blérald, Alain Ph. Histoire économique de la Guadeloupe et de la Martinique : du XVIIe siècle à nos jours / Alain-Philippe Blérald. Paris : Karthala, c1986. 336 p. : ill. ; 24 cm. (Hommes et sociétés) Bibliography: p. [287]-315. Includes index. ISBN 2-86537-134-4 LC Card 86-159186
1. Guadeloupe - Economic conditions. 2. Martinique - Economic conditions. I. Title. II. Series.
HC158.5 .B54 1986

Blewett, Mary H. Men, women, and work : a study of class, gender, and protest in the nineteenth-century New England shoe industry / Mary H. Blewett. Urbana : University of Illinois Press, c1988. p. cm. (The Working class in American history) Bibliography: p. Includes index. ISBN 0-252-01484-7 (alk. paper) LC Card 87-19039 DDC 338.4/768531/00974 19
1. Shoe industry - New England - Employees - History - 19th century. 2. Shoe industry - New England - History - 19th century. 3. New England - Economic conditions. I. Title.
HD8039.B72 U63 1988

Blicq, Ron, 1925-
Guidelines for report writers. Blicq, Ron, 1925- Writing reports to get results : guidelines for the computer age / Ron S. Blicq. New York , c1987. x, 203 p. : ISBN 0-87942-228-9 LC Card 87-16850 DDC 808/.066651 19
HF5719 .B55 1987

Writing reports to get results : guidelines for the computer age / Ron S. Blicq. New York : IEEE Press, c1987. x, 203 p. : ill. ; 29 cm. Rev. ed. of: Guidelines for report writers. 1982. "Published under the sponsorship of the IEEE Professional Communications Society." Includes index. ISBN 0-87942-228-9 LC Card 87-16850 DDC 808/.066651 19
1. Report writing. 2. Business report writing. 3. Technical writing. I. Blicq, Ron, 1925- Guidelines for report writers. II. IEEE Professional Communications Society. III. Title.
HF5719 .B55 1987

Blinc, R. (Robert) Vloga znanosti pri oblikovanju strategije razvoja SR Slovenije /. Ljubljana , 1981. 174 p. : LC Card 82-151266
HC407.Z7 S57 1981

Blind intersection? . Winston, Clifford, 1952- Washington, D.C. , c1987. xii, 108 p. : ISBN 0-8157-9466-5 : LC Card 87-806 DDC 338.4/76292/0973 19
HD9710.U52 W55 1987

Blind victory . Howell, David, 1936- London , 1986. xiv, 191 p. ; ISBN 0-241-11743-7 : LC Card 86-223521 DDC 338.941 19
HC256.6 .H639 1986

Blinder, Alan S. Hard heads, soft hearts : tough-minded economics for a just society / Alan S. Blinder. Reading, Mass. : Addison-Wesley Pub. Co., c1987. xi, 236 p. : ill. ; 25 cm. Bibliography: p. 216-227. Includes index. ISBN 0-201-11504-2 : LC Card 87-14078 DDC 330 19
1. Economics. 2. Economic policy. I. Title.
HB171 .B535 1987

Blinken, Antony J. Ally versus ally : America, Europe, and the Siberian pipeline crisis / Antony J. Blinken. New York : Praeger, 1987. ix, 193 p. : map ; 25 cm. Bibliography: p. 159-183. Includes index. ISBN 0-275-92410-6 (alk. paper) : LC Card 86-25222 DDC 388.5 19
1. Gas industry - Political aspects - Soviet Union. 2. Gas industry - Political aspects - Europe. 3. Gas, Natural - Soviet Union - Pipe lines. 4. Gas, Natural - Europe - Pipe lines. 5. Soviet Union - Foreign economic relations - Europe. 6. Europe - Foreign economic relations - Soviet Union. 7. United States - Foreign relations - Europe. 8. Europe - Foreign relations - United States. I. Title.
HD9581.S652 B58 1987

Bliss, Michael. Northern enterprise : five centuries of Canadian business / Michael Bliss. Toronto, Ont. : McClelland and Stewart, c1987. 640 p. : ill. ; 25 cm. Bibliography: p. 585-618. Includes index. ISBN 0-7710-1577-1 : LC Card 87-151013 DDC 380.1/0971 19
1. Canada - Commerce - History. I. Title.
HF3224 .B65 1987

Blitzer, Jeremiah. Renberg, Werner. Making money with mutual funds . New York , c1988. xviii, 217 p. : ISBN 0-471-85555-3 LC Card 87-26366 DDC 332.63/27 19
HG4530 .R46 1988

Bli͡udenov, A. F. (Anatoliĭ Fedorovich) Osobennosti razvitii͡a i puti povyshenii͡a ėffektivnosti proizvoditelʹnykh sil regiona /. Sverdlovsk , 1984. 141 p. ; LC Card 86-135171
HC337.R852 C456 1984

Blizhniĭ Sever Kanady . Saltykovskai͡a, L. V. (Lilii͡a Veniaminovna) Moskva , 1983. 78, [2] p. : LC Card 83-196848
HC117.N48 S25 1983

Bliznakov, Ĭordan Petrov. Sot͡sialisticheskoto sŭrevnovanie v uslovii͡ata na intenzifikat͡sii͡ata na proizvodstvoto / Ĭordan Bliznakov, Licho Lichev. Sofii͡a : Nauchnoizsledovatelski in-t po profsŭi͡uzni problemi "G. Dimitrov" pri T͡SS na BPS, 1983. 101 p. : ill. ; 22 cm. Includes bibliographical references. LC Card 85-140845
1. Socialist competition - Bulgaria. 2. Labor productivity - Bulgaria. I. Lichev, Licho. II. Title.
HC403.Z9 S613 1983

BLMI report .
(FY1985, no. 9, etc) County profiles . Albany, N.Y. [1984-<1985. v. : LC Card 84-623501 DDC 330.9747/043 19
HC107.N7 C64 1984

Bloch, Arnold J. Interstate highway trade-in process. Vol. 1. Assessment / Polytechnic Institute of New York, Brooklyn, [Transportation Training and Research Center] ; prepared for Dept. of Transportation, [Research and Special Programs Administration]. New York : The Center, 1982. [45] p. : ill. ; 28 cm. Vol. 1: "December 1982." "Final report." Microfiche. Springfield, Va. : NTIS, 1983. 1 microfiche : negative ; 11 x 15 cm. (PB83-180570)
1. Federal aid to transportation - United States. 2. Local transit - United States - Finance. 3. Urban transportation policy - United States. I. Polytechnic Institute of New York. Transportation Training and Research Center. II. United States. Dept. of Transportation. Research and Special Programs Administration. ***NYPL [*XME-11,324]***

Bloch, Carolyn. Federal energy information sources and data bases / Carolyn C. Bloch. Park Ridge, N.J. : Noyes Data Corp., 1979. x, 115 p. ; 25 cm. Includes indexes. ISBN 0-8155-0764-X : LC Card 79-15543 DDC 016.33379/0973 19
1. Energy policy - Information services - United States. 2. Administrative agencies - Information services - United States. 3. Power resources - United States. I. Title.
HD9502.U52 B58 ***NYPL [JLE 86-4259]***

Bloch, H. I. Sonny. Inside real estate : the complete guide to buying and selling your home, co-op, or condominium / by H.I. Sonny Bloch and Grace Lichtenstein.1st ed. New York : Weidenfeld & Nicolson, c1987. xx, 375 p. ; 25 cm. ISBN 1-555-84030-2 LC Card 86-28303 DDC 333.33/8 19
1. Real estate business. 2. House buying. 3. House selling. 4. Condominiums. 5. Apartment houses, Cooperative. I. Lichtenstein, Grace. II. Title.
HD1379 .B515 1987

Bloch-Lainé, François. La France restaurée, 1944-1954 : dialogue sur les choix d'une modernisation / François Bloch-Lainé, Jean Bouvier ; prologue de Jean-Pierre Roux. Paris : Fayard, c1986. 338 p. ; 24 cm. Bibliography: p. [277]-295. Includes index. ISBN 2-213-01803-0 : LC Card 86-215777
1. France - Economic policy - 20th century. I. Bouvier, Jean, 1920-. II. Title.
HC276.2 .B58 1986

Block, Alan A. Organizing crime / Alan A. Block, William J. Chambliss. New York, N.Y. : Elsevier, c1981. 238 p. ; 24 cm. Includes bibliographical references and index. ISBN 0-444-99079-8 LC Card 80-25099 DDC 364.1/06 19
1. Organized crime - United States. 2. Crime and criminals - United States. I. Chambliss, William J., joint author. II. Title.
HV6030 .B55 ***NYPL [JLE 86-4076]***

Block, Frank E. Graham, Benjamin, 1894- [Security analysis.] Graham and Dodd's security analysis. New York , c1988. xiii, 656 p. : ISBN 0-07-013235-6 : LC Card 87-19990 DDC 332.63/2 19
HG4529 .G7 1988

Block, Fred L. The Mean season . New York, c1987. xvi, 205 p. ; ISBN 0-394-55338-1 : LC Card 86-43126 DDC 361/.973 19
HC110.P63 M42 1987

Block Grant Advisory Task Force final report to the Governor and the Legislature of the State of California /. California. Block Grant Advisory Task Force. [Sacramento?] [1984] 36, [7] leaves ; LC Card 86-622537 DDC 336.1/85 19
HJ325 .C32 1984

BLOCK GRANTS - CALIFORNIA.
California. Block Grant Advisory Task Force. Block Grant Advisory Task Force final report to the Governor and the Legislature of the State of California /. [Sacramento?] [1984] 36, [7] leaves ; LC Card 86-622537 DDC 336.1/85 19
HJ325 .C32 1984

BLOCK GRANTS - UNITED STATES.
Ferguson, Gary D. Evaluation of the small cities community development block grant program--the role of the counties [microform] /. Cambridge, Mass. , 1981. vii, vi, 186 p. ;
NYPL [*XME-11,283]

Newman & Hermanson Company. Evaluation of the small cities component of the community development block grant program [microform] . Cambridge, Mass. , 1981. viii, xvii, 147 p. ;
NYPL [*XME-11,274]

Block, Jean Libman. Minton, Michael H. What is a wife worth? . New York , 1984, c1983. 192 p. ; ISBN 0-07-042414-4 (pbk.) : LC Card 84-11221 DDC 331.4/28164/0973 19
HD4966.H842 U65 1984
NYPL [JLD 87-12]

Block, Stanley B.
Foundations of financial management. Block, Stanley B. The Tax Reform Act of 1986 : implications for financial management / Stanley B. Block. Homewood, Ill. , 1987. v, 26 p. ; ISBN 0-256-06055-X (pbk.) LC Card 87-403584 DDC 658.1/5 19
HG4026 .B589 1987 Suppl.

Personal financial management / Stanley B. Block, John W. Peavy III, John H. Thornton. New York : Harper & Row, c1988. xvii, 603 p. : ill. ; 24 cm. Includes bibliographies and index. ISBN 0-06-040789-1 LC Card 87-19088 DDC 332.024 19
1. Finance, Personal. I. Peavy, John W. II. Thornton, John H. III. Title.
HG179 .B555 1988

The Tax Reform Act of 1986 : implications for financial management / Stanley B. Block. Homewood, Ill. : Irwin, 1987. v, 26 p. ; 24 cm. "The material in this supplement is intended to replace table 2-10 on page 41 of chapter 2 and pages 379 to 390 of chapter 12 in Foundations of financial management, 4th edition, by Block & Hirt (c1987, Richard D. Irwin, Inc., Homewood, Il.)." ISBN 0-256-06055-X (pbk.) LC Card 87-403584 DDC 658.1/5 19
1. Corporations - Finance. 2. Corporations - Taxation - United States. I. Block, Stanley B. Foundations of financial management. II. Title.
HG4026 .B589 1987 Suppl.

Block, Walter, 1941- Morality of the market . Vancouver, B.C., Canada , c1985. xxv, 601 p. ; ISBN 0-88975-074-2 (pbk.) : LC Card 86-158049 DDC 174/.4 19
HB72 .M56 1985

Bloech, Jürgen, 1936- Industrielles Management . Göttingen , c1986. vi, 276 p., [1] leaf of plates : ISBN 3-525-13182-8 LC Card 87-118224 DDC 658 19
HD35 .I555 1986

Blohowiak, Donald W. No comment! : an executive's essential guide to the news media / Donald W. Blohowiak. New York : Praeger, 1987. xvi, 221 p. ; 25 cm. Bibliography: p. [213]-214. Includes index. ISBN 0-275-92820-9 (alk. paper) : LC Card 87-15831 DDC 659.2 19
1. Mass media and business. 2. Mass media and

business - United States. I. Title.
HD59 .B57 1987

Blom, Svein-Erik. Trolle, Ulf af, 1919- Markedsføring . °slo] , 1982. 496 p. : ISBN 82-00-05931-6 : LC Card 83-184229
HF5415.12.D4 T76 1982

Blomqvist, H. C. (Hans-Christer), 1947- Lönebildningsforskning i Finland / H.C. Blomqvist. [Helsinki] : Institutionen för nationalekonomi, Svenska handelshögskolan, [1984] 23 leaves : ill. ; 30 cm. (Meddelanden från Svenska handelshögskolan, 0357-4598 = Working papers / Swedish School of Economics and Business Administration . 118 (1984)) ACQ MSG: E 52-146. "Juni 1984." Bibliography: leaves 20-22. ISBN 951-555-207-9 LC Card 85-137027
1. Wages - Finland - Econometric models. 2. Finland - Economic conditions - 1945- - Econometric models. I. Series: Meddelanden fran Svenska handelshögskolan , 118. II. Title.
HD5047.3 .B57 1984

Blondel, Eaulin. Credit unions, co-operatives, trade unions, and friendly societies in Barbados : a directory / Eaulin A. Blondel. St. Augustine, Trinidad, Trinidad and Tobago : E.A. Blondel, [1986] v, 102 p. ; 28 cm. "April 1986." Includes index. LC Card 87-403330 DDC 334/.025/72981 19
1. Cooperative societies - Barbados - Directories. 2. Credit unions - Barbados - Directories. 3. Friendly societies - Barbados - Directories. 4. Trade-unions - Barbados - Directories. I. Title.
HD3464.9.A6 B353 1986

Blood in the streets . Davidson, James Dale. New York , c1987. 386 p. ; ISBN 0-671-62735-X : LC Card 87-9935 DDC 332.6 19
HG4516 .D38 1987

Bloom, Paul N. Knowledge development in marketing : the MSI experience / Paul N. Bloom. Lexington, Mass. : Lexington Books, c1987. xvi, 238 p. ; 24 cm. Bibliography: p. [211]-227. Includes index. ISBN 0-669-12581-4 (alk. paper) LC Card 85-45938 DDC 658.83 19
1. Marketing research. 2. Marketing Science Institute. I. Marketing Science Institute. II. Title.
HF5415.2 .B57 1987

Bloom, Robert. Accounting theory and policy . San Diego , c1987. xi, 654 p. : ISBN 0-15-500478-6 (pbk.) LC Card 86-81620 DDC 657 19
HF5629 .A26 1987

Bloomfield, Barbara. The Enemy within . London , New York , 1986. xxiii, 260 p. : ISBN 0-7102-0888-X (pbk.) : LC Card 86-12192 DDC 331.89/2822334/0941 19
HD5365.M6152 1984 .E54 1986

Bloomfield, Mark A.
The Consumption tax . Cambridge, Mass. , c1987. xviii, 382 p. : ISBN 0-88730-159-2 LC Card 87-17838 DDC 336.2/71/0973 19
HJ5715.U6 C658 1987

McLure, Charles E. The value-added tax . Washington, D.C. : Lanham, MD ; xi, 184 p. : ISBN 0-8447-3613-9 (alk. paper) LC Card 86-28905 DDC 339.5/25/0973 19
HJ5715.U6 M364 1987

Bloor, Ian G. Reference guide to management techniques and activities / by Ian G. Bloor. 1st ed. Oxford, England ; New York : Pergamon Press, 1987. xi, 80 p. ; 22 cm. Bibliography: p. 63-74. Includes index. ISBN 0-08-034268-X : LC Card 86-30266 DDC 658/.003/21 19
1. Management - Dictionaries. I. Title.
HD30.15 .B46 1987

Blotko, Kazimierz. Racjonalny podział przewozów ładunków między gałęzie transportu / Kazimierz Blotko. Wyd. 1. Warszawa : Wydawnictwa Komunikacji i Łączności, 1978. 126 p. ; 21 cm. Bibliography: p. 100-[103] LC Card 81-206824
1. Delivery of goods - Poland. 2. Freight and freightage - Poland. 3. Transportation - Poland. I. Title.
HF5780.P7 B57 1978

Blow your own horn . Davidson, Jeffrey P. New York, NY , c1987. xv, 271 p. : ISBN 0-8144-5908-0 LC Card 86-47809 DDC 650.1/4 19
HF5549.5.C35 D375 1987

Blowers, Andrew. Nuclear power in crisis . New York , 1987. 327 p. : ISBN 0-89397-267-3 : LC Card 86-23710 DDC 333.79/24/0941 19
HD9698.G72 N85 1987

The blue-chip graduate . Osher, Bill. Atlanta, Ga. , c1987. 238 p. : ISBN 0-934601-19-4 (pbk.) : LC Card 86-63534 DDC 650.1/4/024375 19
HF5381 .O889 1987

The blue chip investment strategy . Hardy, C. Colburn. New York , 1987. 324 p. : ISBN 0-531-15525-0 LC Card 87-14726 DDC 332.63/22 19
HG4963 .H37 1987

Blue collar, Roman collar, white collar . Sullivan, Patrick J., 1929- Lanham, MD , c1987. xii, 346 p. ; ISBN 0-8191-5704-X (alk. paper) : LC Card 86-24593 DDC 261.85 19
HD6338.2.U5 S85 1987

BLUE CROSS AND BLUE SHIELD ASSOCIATION.
Health insurance . Washington, D.C. , 1986. 53 p. ; LC Card 86-603180 DDC 368.3/82/00973 19
HG9398.B57 H4 1986

BLUE LAWS. see **SUNDAY LEGISLATION.**

BLUE SKY LAWS. see **SECURITIES.**

Bluebirds /. Wegg, John. [Helsinki?] , c1985. 216 p. : ISBN 951-99691-4-4 LC Card 86-223952 DDC 387.7/065/4897 19
HE9855.3.F5 W4 1985

A Bluechip business book.
Saperstein, Rose, 1956- Read your way to the top with the guide /. Seattle, Wash. , c1987. 83 p. : ISBN 0-930251-00-8 (pbk.) : LC Card 87-310 DDC 428.4/3 19
HF5351 .S34 1987

Blümle, Ernst-Bernd. Willy Büchi, 75 Jahre /. Freiburg, Schweiz , 1982. 105 p., [1] leaf of plates : ISBN 3-7278-0263-4 LC Card 83-184580
HB118 .W55 1982

Bluen,, Stephen. Behaviour in organisations . Johannesburg , New York , 1986, c1983. 924 p. : ISBN 0-07-450690-0 (pbk.) : LC Card 87-113321 DDC 158.7/0968 19
HD58.7 .B426 1986

Blueprint for agricultural development in Lusaka Province. Lusaka Province (Zambia). Provincial Planning Unit. Towards self sufficiency . [Lusaka, Zambia?] [1984] 100 p., [14] leaves of plates : LC Card 86-980293 DDC 338.1/86894 19
HD2131.5 .L87 1984

The blueprint for franchising a business /. Raab, Steven S., 1949- New York , c1987. ix, 244 p. : ISBN 0-471-85617-7 LC Card 87-15932 DDC 658.8/7 19
HF5429.235.U5 R32 1987

Blum, Dieter. Herdt, Hans Konradin, 1935- Bosch, 1886-1986 . [Stuttgart] [1986] 174 p., [88] p. of plates : ISBN 3-421-06324-9 LC Card 86-229723
HD9710.3.G44 R634 1986

Blum, Laurie. Free money for small businesses and entrepreneurs / Laurie Blum. New York : Wiley, c1988. ix, 229 p. ; 24 cm. ISBN 0-471-85803-X : LC Card 87-20978 DDC 658.1/5224 19
1. Small business - United States - Finance - Directories. 2. Commercial loans - United States - Directories. 3. Endowments - United States - Directories. 4. Federal aid to community development - United States - Directories. I. Title.
HG4027.7 .B58 1988

Blüm, Norbert, 1935- Die Arbeit geht weiter : zur Krise der Erwerbsgesellschaft / Norbert Blüm.Originalausg. München : Piper, 1983. 128 p. ; 19 cm. (Serie Piper. Bd. 327) ISBN 3-492-00627-2 : LC Card 84-136559
1. Work. 2. Work ethic. 3. Work and family. I. Title.
HD4904 .B563 1983

Blum, Reinhard, 1933- Aktuelle Probleme der Marktwirtschaft in gesamt- und einzelwirtschaftlicher Sicht . Berlin , c1984. 458 p., [1] leaf of plates : ISBN 3-428-05653-1 LC Card 85-128275
HB501 .A514 1984

Blum, Ulrich. Raumwirkungen des Budgets der gesetzlichen Rentenversicherung : eine theoretische und empirische Analyse räumlicher und zeitlicher Wirkungen interregionaler Finanzflüsse / Ulrich Blum. Karlsruhe : von Loeper, c1986. xii, 184, 35 p. : ill. ; 24 cm. (Karlsruher Beiträge zur Wirtschaftspolitik und Wirtschaftsforschung. Heft 13) Bibliography: p. 26-35 (3rd group). ISBN 3-88652-029-3 LC Card 87-124826 DDC 368.4/00943 19
1. Social security - Germany, West. 2. Social security - Law and legislation - Germany, West. 3. Germany (West) - Economic conditions - 1974- - Regional disparities. I. Title. II. Series.
HD7179 .B57 1986

Blumenthal, Lassor A. Successful oral and written presentations / Lassor A. Blumenthal. New York, NY : Perigee Books, c1987. 94 p. : ill. ; 28 cm. (The Practical handbook series) "The new guide to more effective presentations for all occasions"--Cover. ISBN 0-399-51330-2 (pbk.) : LC Card 87-2272 DDC 658.4/5 19
1. Communication in management. 2. Oral communication. 3. Business writing. I. Title.
HF5718 .B57 1987

Blumentrath, L. (Ludwig) Franz, Lothar. Verkehrsberuhigung in Städten und Gemeinden /. Grafenau , c1982. 134 p. : ISBN 3-88508-780-4 : LC Card 82-204794
HE311.G3 F73 1982

Bluntschli, Franz. Schweizer Aussenwirtschaft, Wohlstand und Entwicklungsländer / Franz Bluntschli. 1. Aufl. Adliswil : Institut für Sozialethik des SEK, Entwicklungsstudien, c1983. 38 p. : ill. ; 21 cm. (Entwicklungspolitische Diskussionsbeiträge . 24) Includes bibliographical references. ISBN 3-7229-4032-X : LC Card 83-226336
1. Switzerland - Foreign economic relations. 2. Switzerland - Commercial policy. I. Title. II. Series.
HF1574 .B58 1983

Bly, Amy Sprecher. Information hotline U. S.A. / by Amy Sprecher Bly and Robert W. Bly. New York : New American Library, c1987. xviii, 286 p. ; 21 cm. "A Plume book." ISBN 0-452-25921-5 (pbk.) : LC Card 87-5687 DDC 384.6/025/73 19
1. Toll-free telephone calls - United States - Directories. I. Bly, Robert W. II. Title. III. Title: Information hotline USA.
HE8811 .B49 1987

Bly, Robert W.
Bly, Amy Sprecher. Information hotline U. S.A. /. New York , c1987. xviii, 286 p. ; ISBN 0-452-25921-5 (pbk.) : LC Card 87-5687 DDC 384.6/025/73 19
HE8811 .B49 1987

Create the perfect sales piece : how to produce brochures, catalogs, fliers, and pamphlets / Robert W. Bly. New York : Wiley, c1985. xii, 242 p. : ill. ; 24 cm. Includes index. "A Wiley Press book." ISBN 0-471-82525-5 (pbk.) : LC Card 85-12457 DDC 659.13/2 19
1. Catalogs. 2. Advertising fliers. 3. Pamphlets. I. Title.
HF5823 .B635 1985 ***NYPL [JLE 86-3454]***

Direct mail profits : how to get more leads and sales by mail / by Robert W. Bly. Westbury, N.Y. : Asher-Gallant Press : Orders, Caddylak Systems, c1987. x, 206 p. : ill. ; 30 cm. ISBN 0-87280-153-5 : LC Card 87-18678 DDC 659.13/3 19
1. Mail-order business. 2. Direct marketing. I. Title.
HF5466 .B59 1987

Blyn, Martin R. (joint author) Krooss, Herman Edward, 1912-1975. A history of financial intermediaries. New York [1971] xi, 254 p. ISBN 0-394-31001-2 LC Card 78-127552 DDC 332.1/0973
HG181 .K73 ***NYPL [JLE 87-572]***

Blyskal, Jeff. PR : how the public relations industry writes the news / Jeff & Marie Blyskal.1st ed. New York : Morrow, c1985. 241 p. ; 24 cm. Includes bibliographical references and index. ISBN 0-688-04788-2 : LC Card 85-80602
1. Public relations - United States. 2. Public opinion - United States. I. Blyskal, Marie. II. Title.
NYPL [JLE 86-268]

Blyskal, Marie. Blyskal, Jeff. PR . New York , c1985. 241 p. ; ISBN 0-688-04788-2 : LC Card 85-80602 ***NYPL [JLE 86-268]***

Blythe, Ian. Forty years on : the Market Research Society : a history of achievement / Ian Blythe. Aldershot, Hants., England ; Brookfield, Vt., USA : Gower, c1987. p. cm. Bibliography: p. Includes index. ISBN 0-566-05005-6 : LC Card 87-8653 DDC 658.8/3/06041 19

1. Market Research Society - History. 2. Marketing research - Great Britain - History. 3. Marketing research - United States - History. I. Title.
HF5410 .B58 1987

The BM industrial register and its application in industrial marketing /. Nel, P. A. Pretoria , 1977. iii, 29, [34] p. ; ISBN 0-949951-74-9 (pbk.) LC Card 85-127469
HC905 .N45 1977

BMF, scandal of scandals /. Lim, Kit Siang. Petaling Jaya [1986] ix, 68 p. : LC Card 86-943248 DDC 364.1/68/09595 19
HG3300.6.A6 L553 1986

BMF, the scandal of scandals. Lim, Kit Siang. BMF, scandal of scandals /. Petaling Jaya [1986] ix, 68 p. : LC Card 86-943248 DDC 364.1/68/09595 19
HG3300.6.A6 L553 1986

BMWI Dokumentation, 0342-9288 .
(Nr. 263) Hochtechnologien und internationale Wettbewerbsfähigkeit der deutschen Wirtschaft /. Bonn [1984] 30 p. ; LC Card 85-184765
HF3564 .H63 1984

(Nr. 268) Technologische Entwicklung und Beschäftigung /. Bonn [1985] 10 p. ; LC Card 86-154491
HC290.5.T4 T44 1985

(Nr. 270) Entwicklung und Struktur der Personalnebenkosten /. Bonn [1985] 14, [9] p. : LC Card 86-154479
HD4928.N62 G34 1985

BMWI Studien-Reihe, 0170-0049 .
(37) Der Deutsche Osthandel 1982 /. Bonn [1982] 87 p. : LC Card 86-212991
HF3568.E35 D463 1982

A BNA special report.
Alcohol & drugs in the workplace . Washington, D.C. , c1986. iii, 136 p. ; ISBN 0-87179-905-7 (pbk.) : LC Card 87-106610 DDC 331.25/5 19
HF5549.5.A4 A35 1986

The Changing workplace . Washington, D.C. [Rockville, Md.] , c1986. iv, 140 p. : ISBN 0-87179-910-3 (pbk.) LC Card 86-221689 DDC 331.25/72 19
HD5124 .C46 1986

BNH, a Brazilian solution to Brazilian problems. A Brazilian solution to Brazilian problems. Rio de Janeiro , 1974. 32 p. ; LC Card 86-673453
HD7323.A4 B72x 1974

Boanas, Guy. The Enemy within . London , New York , 1986. xxiii, 260 p. : ISBN 0-7102-0888-X (pbk.) : LC Card 86-12192 DDC 331.89/2822334/0941 19
HD5365.M6152 1984 .E54 1986

Board committees in European companies /. Bacon, Jeremy. New York, N.Y. , c1986. vii, 16 p. ; ISBN 0-8237-0325-8 (pbk.) LC Card 86-207711 DDC 658.4/22/094 19
HD2745 .B14 1986

BOARD OF GOVERNORS OF THE FEDERAL RESERVE SYSTEM (U. S.)
Central bankers, bureaucratic incentives, and monetary policy /. Dordrecht ; Boston : xiv, 251 p. : ISBN 90-247-3366-9 LC Card 86-12572 DDC 332.1/12/0973 19
HG2565 .C33 1986 ***NYPL [JLE 87-394]***

Greider, William. Secrets of the temple . New York , c1987. 798 p. ; ISBN 0-671-47989-X : LC Card 87-16712 DDC 332.1/1/0973 19
HG2563 .G72 1987

BOARD OF GOVERNORS OF THE FEDERAL RESERVE SYSTEM (U. S.) - OFFICIALS AND EMPLOYEES - BIOGRAPHY.
Neikirk, William. Volcker, portrait of the money man /. New York , Chicago, Ill. , c1987. xvi, 222 p. ; ISBN 0-86553-178-1 LC Card 87-19953 DDC 332.1/1/0924 B 19
HB119.V6 N45 1987

Board of the Cartagen Agreement. Grupo de Política Tecnológica. Metodología de evaluación y programación de sistemas de producción y consumo, MEPS /. Lima, Perú [1985]- v. <1 > : LC Card 86-215609
HD75 .M48 1985

Board of the Cartagena Agreement.
Estrategias de desarrollo e integración en el Grupo Andino . Lima, Perú , 1985. 414 p. : LC Card 87-125026 DDC 337.1/8 19
HC167.A5 E87 1985

Investigación agraria y crisis . Quito , 1986. 498 p. : LC Card 87-400125 DDC 338.1/098 19
HD1860.A53 I58 1986

Programa subregional de apoyo a la pequeña y mediana industria / Junta del Acuerdo de Cartagena. [S.l.] : La Junta, [between 1983 and 1986] (Lima, Perú : Europrint) 29 p. ; 20 cm. Includes bibliographical references. LC Card 87-400442 DDC 338.6/42/098 19
1. Small business - Government policy - Andes Region. 2. Small business - Andes Region. I. Title.
HD2346.A64 B63 1983

Board of the Cartagena Agreement. Departamento de Comunicaciones e Información. Por una visión del desarrollo latinoamericano con autodeterminación, democracia y paz /. San Isidro, Lima, Perú [1984] 191 p. ; LC Card 86-226515
HC167.A5 P67 1984

Board of the Cartagena Agreement. Unidad de Informática. Indicadores de los países del Grupo Andino. [Lima] [1985] 172 p. in various pagings : LC Card 86-137319 DDC 330.98/0038 19
HC167.A5 I52 1985

BOARDING-HOUSES. see **HOTELS, TAVERNS, ETC.**

Boardman, Robert. Pesticides in world agriculture : the politics of international regulation / Robert Boardman. Houndsmills, Basingstoke, Hampshire : Macmillan Press, c1986. x, 221 p. ; 23 cm. Includes index. Bibliography: p. 189-191. ISBN 0-333-37417-7
1. Pesticide residues in food - International cooperation. 2. Pesticides - Environmental aspects. 3. Environmental policy - International cooperation. I. Title.
NYPL [JLD 86-2934]

Boardroom reports.
The Book of business knowledge /. New York, N.Y. , c1987. p. cm. ISBN 0-932648-83-5 : LC Card 86-30962 DDC 658 19
HF5356 .B72 1987

The Boss's encyclopedia /. New York, N.Y. , c1987. xxvi, 594 p. ; ISBN 0-932648-75-4 LC Card 86-30961 DDC 658 19
HF5356 .B735 1987

Business confidential. New York, N.Y. , c1987. xi, 504 p. ; ISBN 0-932648-82-7 LC Card 86-30963 DDC 650 19
HF5356 .B9259 1987

BOARDS OF DIRECTORS. see **DIRECTORS OF CORPORATIONS.**

BOARDS OF SUPERVISION (CORPORATION LAW) see **DIRECTORS OF CORPORATIONS.**

BOARDS OF TRADE - BERLIN (GERMANY) - HISTORY.
Handelsforschung heute . Berlin , c1979. 230 p. : ISBN 3-428-04408-8 LC Card 87-408239 DDC 380.1 s 380.1/06/04355 19
HF345 .F66 Folge 3, Nr. 7 HF308

BOARDS OF TRADE - DEVELOPING COUNTRIES.
Junginger-Dittel, K.-O. Marketing Boards für Agrarexportgüter in Entwicklungsländern /. [Kiel] , 1980. iii, 48 leaves ; LC Card 85-160428
HD9018.D44 J86 1980

BOARDS OF TRADE - DIRECTORIES.
Grist, John. The Grist guide . Amherst, MA, U. S.A. (P.O. Box 227, Amherst 01004) , c1984. ii, 48 p. ; LC Card 85-108426 DDC 382/.025/73 19
HF294 .G75 1984
NYPL [*R-Econ. 87-1266]

BOARDS OF TRADE - GERMANY - HISTORY - SOURCES.
Reininghaus, Wilfried. Quellen zur Geschichte des Deutschen Industrie- und Handelstages in Kammerarchiven, 1861 bis 1918 /. Bonn , 1986. 158 p. : ISBN 3-925925-01-5 LC Card 87-408272 DDC 354.430082/09 19
HF308 .R343 1986

BOARDS OF TRADE - GERMANY (WEST) - ARCHIVAL RESOURCES - GERMANY (WEST) - CONGRESSES.
Wirtschaftsarchive und Kammern--Aspekte wirtschaftlicher selbstverwaltung gestern und heute . Köln , 1982. 250 p. ; LC Card 86-198576
HC286 .W59 1982

BOARDS OF TRADE - UNITED STATES - DIRECTORIES.
Grist, John. The Grist guide . Amherst, MA, U. S.A. (P.O. Box 227, Amherst 01004) , c1984. ii, 48 p. ; LC Card 85-108426 DDC 382/.025/73 19
HF294 .G75 1984
NYPL [*R-Econ. 87-1266]

BOAT HANDLING. see **BOATS AND BOATING.**

BOATING. see **BOATS AND BOATING.**

BOATING INDUSTRY - BRITISH VIRGIN ISLANDS.
Jackson, Ivor L. Study of the pleasure boat industry in the British Virgin Islands with emphasis on charter boats /. [S.l. , 1981?] viii, 89 p. : ***NYPL [JLF 85-543]***

BOATING INDUSTRY - TEXAS.
Stoll, John R. Economic impact of the recreational boating industry in Texas /. College Station, TX [1985] xiv, 86 p. : LC Card 86-622008 DDC 330.9764/063 19
HD9993.B633 U58 1985

BOATMEN - FRANCE - HISTORY.
Le Sueur, Bernard. Batelleries et bateliers de France . Le Côteau [1985] 208 p. : ISBN 2-7171-0339-2 LC Card 87-106621
HE443 .L39 1985

BOATS. see **BOATS AND BOATING.**

BOATS AND BOATING - BANGLADESH - CONGRESSES.
Jerve, Alf Morten. From research to implementation . Fantoft-Bergen, Norway [1984] 23 leaves ; LC Card 86-228812 DDC 386/.068 19
HE691.6 .J47 1984

BOATS AND BOATING - CHARTERING - BRITISH VIRGIN ISLANDS.
Jackson, Ivor L. Study of the pleasure boat industry in the British Virgin Islands with emphasis on charter boats /. [S.l. , 1981?] viii, 89 p. : ***NYPL [JLF 85-543]***

Bob Ansett, an autobiography /. Ansett, Bob, 1933- Hartwell, Vic. , 1986. 221 p., [16] p. of plates : ISBN 0-9588161-0-7 LC Card 86-228002 DDC 338.7/4/0924 B 19
HC602.5.A57 A33 1986

Böbel, Ingo. Wettbewerb und Industriestruktur : industrial Organization-Forschung im Überblick / Ingo Böbel. Berlin ; New York : Springer-Verlag, 1984. xiv, 336 p. : ill. ; 25 cm. (Studies in contemporary economics . 6) Bibliography: p. [262]-315. Includes indexes. ISBN 0-387-13143-4 (U. S.) LC Card 85-111698
1. Industrial concentration. 2. Competition. I. Series. II. Series: Studies in contemporary economics , v. 6. III. Title.
HD2757 .B63 1984

Bober, Stanley. Modern macroeconomics : a post-Keynsian perspective / Stanley Bober. London ; New York : Croom Helm, c1988. ix, 278 p. : ill. ; 23 cm. Includes bibliographies and index. ISBN 0-7099-5080-2 LC Card 87-15190 DDC 339 19
1. Macroeconomics. 2. Keynesian economics. I. Title.
HB172.5 .B62 1988

Bobin, Christian. Faire l'histoire du monde du travail . [Seyssel] : [Le Creusot] : 52 p. : ISBN 2-903528-49-7 : LC Card 85-180268 DDC 305.5/62/072044 19
HD8428 .F35 1985 ***NYPL [JLD 87-1157]***

Boccara, Paul. Un Chemin pour sortir de la crise /. Paris , c1985. 249 p. ; ISBN 2-209-05753-1 LC Card 86-154397
HC276.2 .C517 1985

Boccella, Nicola Maria, 1952- Il Mezzogiorno sussidiato : reddito, prodotto e trasferimenti alle famiglie nei comuni meridionali / Nicola Maria Boccella. Milano, Italy : F. Angeli, c1982. 264 p. : col. maps ; 22 cm. (Collana di economia: Sezione 5. 10) Bibliography: p. [251]-259. LC Card 85-163271
1. Social security - Italy, Southern. 2. Insurance, Unemployment - Italy, Southern. 3. Income distribution - Italy, Southern. 4. Income maintenance programs - Italy, Southern. 5. Economic security - Italy, Southern. I. Title.
HD7185.S68 B62 1982

Bochkova, V. I. Vneshnîaîa torgovlîa SSSR so stranami SÉV /. Moskva , 1986. 108, [3] p. ; LC Card 86-213259
HF3628.E9 V54 1986

Bochum. Ruhr-Universität. see **Ruhr-Universität Bochum.**

Bochum, Ulrich, 1953- Industrie und Region : ökonomischer und sozialer Strukturwandel im Ruhrgebiet / Ulrich Bochum. Frankfurt am Main ; New York : P. Lang, c1984. 340, [38] p. : ill. ; 21 cm. (Europäische Hochschulschriften. Reihe XXII, Soziologie, 0721-3379 . Bd. 92 = vol. 92 = vol. 92) Bibliography: p. 323-340. ISBN 3-8204-5550-7 LC Card 85-194544
1. Ruhr (Germany : Region) - Industries - History. 2. Ruhr (Germany : Region) - Economic conditions. 3. Social structure - Germany (West) - Ruhr (Region) - History. I. Title.
HC288.R8 B57 1984

Bochum. Universität. see **Ruhr-Universität Bochum.**

Bochumer Beiträge zur Unternehmungsführung und Unternehmensforschung. For additional listing of contents, see Old Catalog.
(Bd. 24) Schmied, Volker. Alternativen der Arbeitsgestaltung und ihre Bewertung . Wiesbaden , c1982. 423 p. : ISBN 3-409-38642-4 LC Card 83-187066
HD6955 .S345 1982

(Bd. 25) Wäscher, Gerhard. Innerbetriebliche Standortplanung bei einfacher und mehrfacher Zielsetzung /. Wiesbaden , c1982. 389 p. : ISBN 3-409-34487-X LC Card 86-105991
HD58 .W29 1982

Bochumer geographische Arbeiten.
(Heft 46) Herzog, Werner. Kartographie und Bürgerbeteiligung im Rahmen der vorbereitenden Bauleitplanung . Paderborn , 1986. xi, 164 p. : ISBN 3-506-71256-X LC Card 87-401386 DDC 333.73/17/028 19
HD108.6 .H47 1986

Bochumer Materialien zur Entwicklungsforschung und Entwicklungspolitik, 0170-1916 .
(Bd. 24) Uhlig, Christian. Internationale Produktionskooperation im Vorderen Orient . Stuttgart , c1983. xvi, 338 p. : ISBN 3-522-68000-6 LC Card 83-217029
HD2891.9 .U44 1983

Bochumer Studien zur Publizistik- und Kommunikationswissenschaft .
(Bd. 37) Gebrewold, Kiflemariam. Fernsehexport der Bundesrepublik Deutschland . Bochum , 1983. xiv, 316 p. : ISBN 3-88339-317-7 LC Card 83-232957
HE8700.66.G3 G43 1983

Bocian, Andrzej. Strategy of socio-economic development . Warsaw , 1980. 122 p. : LC Card 81-107307
HD75 .S8 1980

Bock, Hartmut. Das kollektive Bausparen : eine systemorientierte Betrachtung seiner Funktionsfähigkeit in einer sich ändernden Umwelt / Hartmut Bock. Frankfurt am Main ; New York : P. Lang, c1984. 204 p. : ill. ; 21 cm. (Europäische Hochschulschriften. Reihe V, Volks- und Betriebswirtschaft, 0531-7339 . Bd. 524 = vol. 524 = vol. 524) Bibliography: p. 194-204. ISBN 3-8204-5341-5 LC Card 85-199145
1. Saving and investment - Germany (West) - Mathematical models. 2. Building and loan associations - Germany, West. I. Series: Europäische Hochschulschriften. Reihe V, Volks- und Betriebswirtschaft , Bd. 524. II. Title.
HC290.5.S3 B63 1984

Bock, Kurt. Albach, Horst. Kritische Wachstumsschwellen in der Unternehmensentwicklung /. Stuttgart , c1985. xxvii, 490 p. : ISBN 3-7910-5008-7 : LC Card 86-156636
HD35 .A64 1985

Böckel, Thomas R., 1959- Selbstregelung und Entpolitisierung der gesetzlichen Rentenversicherung : eine Analyse aus systemtheoretischer Sicht / Thomas R. Böckel. Frankfurt am Main ; New York : Lang, c1986. xvi, 305 p. ; 21 cm. (Europäische Hochschulschriften. Reihe V, Volks- und Betriebswirtschaft, 0531-7339 . Bd. 751 = vol. 751 = vol. 751) Revision of thesis (doctoral)--Friedrich Alexander-Universität Erlangen Nürnberg, 1986. Bibliography: p. 261-305. ISBN 3-8204-8847-2 LC Card 87-407917 DDC 368.4/00943 19
1. Social security - Germany, West. 2. Insurance, Health - Germany, West. I. Series: Europäische Hochschulschriften. Reihe V, Volks- und Betriebswirtschaft , Bd. 751. II. Title.
HD7179 .B59 1986

Bocker, P., 1933- NTG-Fachtagung (1986 : Nuremberg, Germany) Von der Nachrichtentechnik zur Informationstechnik . Berlin , c1986. 104 p. : ISBN 3-8007-1485-X LC Card 87-136748 DDC 384 19
HE7604 .N74 1986

Boczar, Kazimierz. Spółdzielczość : problematyka społeczna i ekonomiczna / Kazimierz Boczar.Wyd. 1. Warszawa : Państwowe Wydawn. Ekonomiczne, 1986. 398 p. ; 21 cm. One folded leaf of plates inserted. Bibliography: p. 383-[389] Includes index. ISBN 83-208-0500-7 : LC Card 86-176276
1. Cooperation - Poland. 2. Cooperation. I. Title.
HD3057.7.A4 B63 1986

Bodanskaîa, K. M. "Problema neftedollarov" . Moskva , 1984. 231 p. ; LC Card 85-189000
HC498 .P75 1984

Bodayla, Stephen D. Financial diplomacy : the United States and Mexico, 1919-1933 / Stephen D. Bodayla. New York : Garland, 1987. x, 216 p. ; 23 cm. (Foreign economic policy of the United States) Originally presented as the author's thesis (Ph. D.)--New York University, 1975. Bibliography: p. 210-216. ISBN 0-8240-8074-2 (alk. paper) LC Card 87-23790 DDC 337.73072 19
1. United States - Foreign economic relations - Mexico. 2. Mexico - Foreign economic relations - United States. 3. United States - Foreign relations - 20th century. 4. Mexico - Foreign relations - 1910-1946. I. Title. II. Series.
HF1456.5.M6 B63 1987

Boddewyn, J. J. (Jean J.) Advertising self-regulation and outside participation : a multinational comparison / J.J. Boddewyn. New York : Quorum Books, c1988. p. cm. Bibliography: p. Includes index. ISBN 0-89930-295-5 (lib. bdg. : alk. paper) LC Card 87-24939 DDC 659.1/1 19
1. Advertising - Self-regulation - Case studies. I. Title.
HF5834 .B63 1988

Bode, Kathleen, 1947- Plogstedt, Sibylle. Übergriffe . Reinbek bei Hamburg , 1984. 157 p. ; ISBN 3-499-15353-X (pbk.) LC Card 87-672604
HD6060.3 .P56x 1984

Bode, Peter M. Alptraum Auto : eine hundertjährige Erfindung und ihre Folgen / von Peter M. Bode, Sylvia Hamberger, Wolfgang Zängl ; Mitarbeit, Ossi Baumeister.2. Aufl. München : Raben Verlag, 1986. 237 p. : ill. (some col.) ; 22 x 24 cm. "Begleitbuch zur gleichnamigen Photo-Ausstellung 'Alptraum Auto' ... Vergabe der Ausstellung: Gesellschaft für Sozialwissenschaftliche und Ökologische Forschung e.V."--P. facing t.p. Includes bibliographies. ISBN 3-922696-46-5 LC Card 87-107197 DDC 303.4/832 19
1. Automobiles - Social aspects - Germany, West. 2. Transportation and state - Germany, West. I. Hamberger, Sylvia. II. Zängl, Wolfgang. III. Gesellschaft für Sozialwissenschaftliche und Ökologische Forschung (Germany). IV. Title.
HE5613 .B63 1986

Bodenallokation und Bodenpolitik im Ruhrgebiet . Rau, Thomas. Bochum , 1982. viii, 323 p. : ISBN 3-88339-269-3 LC Card 83-130477 DDC 333.73/13/094355 19
HD659.R8 R38 1982 ***NYPL [JLD 86-1715]***

Bodenrecht in Bewegung . Usteri, Martin. Zürich [1985] 27 p. ; LC Card 86-195037
HC395 .Z43 Nr. 126 KKW683

BODENREFORM. see **SINGLE TAX.**

Bodenschutz zwischen Datenschwemme und Informationsdefizit . Scholz, Bernhard, 1948- Speyer [1986] iii leaves, 385, 4 p. : LC Card 87-126271 DDC 333.73/13/094343 19
HD659.R54 S36 1986

Bodi ya Taifa ya Wahasibu na Wakaguzi Hesabu Tanzania.
The National accountancy examination scheme : examiners' report for the 17th examination session, May, 1983. Dar es Salaam : National Board of Accountants and Auditors, Tanzania, [1983] xxviii leaves, 269 p. ; 32 cm. "August 20th., 1983." LC Card 87-118290
1. Accounting - Tanzania - Examinations. I. Title.
HF5616.T34 B63 1983

The National accountancy examination scheme : examiner's report for the 20th examination session, November 1984 / (NBAA), the National Board of Accountants and Auditors, Tanzania. Dar es Salaam : NBAA, [1985] xxiii leaves, 275 p. ; 32 cm. "23rd February 1985." LC Card 86-980376 DDC 657/.09678 19
1. Accounting - Tanzania - Examinations - Evaluation. 2. Achievement tests - Tanzania - Statistics. I. Title.
HF1176.T34 B64 1985

The National accountancy examination scheme : results for the 20th examination session, November, 1984 : statistical analysis of the examination results / (NBAA) the National Board of Accountants and Auditors, Tanzania. Dar es Salaam : NBAA, 1985. ii, 41 leaves ; 32 cm. "23rd February 1985." LC Card 86-980364
1. Accounting - Tanzania - Examinations - Statistics. I. Title.
HF5616.T34 B63 1985

Bodie, Zvi. Pensions in the U. S. economy /. Chicago , 1988. ix, 200 p. : ISBN 0-226-06285-6 LC Card 87-19987 DDC 331.25/2/0973 19
HD7105.45.U6 P46 1988

Bodinat, Henri de. Gestion internationale de l'entreprise /. Paris , 1984. 393 p. : ISBN 2-247-00496-2 : LC Card 85-114907
HD62.4 .G47 1984

Bodmer, Johann Georg, (1786-1864) Lang, Norbert. Johann Georg Bodmer (1786-1864) . Zürich , c1987. 92 p. : LC Card 87-134606 DDC 338/.09494 s 620/.0092/4 B 19
HC395.5.A2 S3 no. 45 TJ140.B53

BODMER, JOHANN GEORG, (1786-1864) Lang, Norbert. Johann Georg Bodmer (1786-1864) . Zürich , c1987. 92 p. : LC Card 87-134606 DDC 338/.09494 s 620/.0092/4 B 19
HC395.5.A2 S3 no. 45 TJ140.B53

Bodnar, George H. Accounting information systems / George H. Bodnar, William S. Hopwood. 3rd ed. Boston : Allyn and Bacon, c1987. xvii, 892 p. : ill. ; 25 cm. Includes bibliographies and index. ISBN 0-205-10308-1 LC Card 86-26505 DDC 657/.028/5 19
1. Accounting - Data processing. 2. Information storage and retrieval systems - Accounting. I. Hopwood, William S. II. Title.
HF5679 .B59 1987

Bodo, C. (Carla) Il Territorio immaginario /. Milano [1980] 106 p. ; ISBN 88-20-41848-7 : LC Card 81-123209 DDC 302.2/34/0945 19
HE8700.9.I8 T47 1980
NYPL [JFD 86-8337]

Bodrova, Valentina. Working women in socialist countries . Geneva , 1985. xvi, 234 p. : ISBN 92-2-103910-2 (pbk.) : LC Card 85-181464 DDC 304.6/32/091717 19
HB901 .W657 1985 ***NYPL [JLE 86-1433]***

Bodurov, Khr. Slivenski okrŭg '85 =. Sofiîa , 1985. 134 p. : LC Card 86-196443
HF5221.S56 S56 1985

Boe, Jonathan E. (Jonathan Evers) American business : the response to the Soviet Union, 1933-1947 / Jonathan E. Boe. New York : Garland, 1987. p. cm. (Foreign economic policy of the United States) Thesis (Ph. D.)--Stanford University, 1979. Bibliography: p. ISBN 0-8240-8075-0 LC Card 87-23693 DDC 337.73047 337.4 19
1. United States - Foreign economic relations - Soviet Union. 2. Soviet Union - Foreign economic relations - United States. I. Title. II. Series.
HF1456.5.S624 B64 1987

Boeck, Klaus. Die DM als internationale Reservewährung : Bedeutung, Ursachen u. Probieme / Klaus Boeck, Dieter Gehrmann. Hamburg : Verlag Weltarchiv, 1974. 75 p. ; 24 cm. (Veröffentlichungen--HWWA-Institut für Wirtschaftsforschung-Hamburg) HWWA Institut für Wirtschaftsforschung Hambrug. HWWA Studien zur Aussenwirtschaft und Entwicklungspolitik. Bibliographical footnotes. LC Card 75-550711
1. Money - Germany (West). 2. International liquidity. I. Gehrmann, Dieter, joint author. II. Series: HWWA-Institut für Wirtschaftsforschung-Hamburg. Veröffentlichungen. III. Title.
NYPL [JLE 80-744]

Boehme, Joachim. Innovationsförderung durch Kooperation : zwischenbetriebliche Zusammenarbeit als Instrument des Innovationsmanagements in kleinen und mittleren Unternehmen bei Einführung der Mikroelektronik in Produkte und Verfahren / von Joachim Boehme. Berlin : E. Schmidt, c1986. 227 p. ; 25 cm. (Technological economics . Bd. 22) Bibliography: p. 199-223. Includes index. ISBN 3-503-02618-5 LC Card 87-133032 DDC 338.4/762 19
1. Microelectronics industry - Technological innovations. 2. Microelectronics industry - Research. 3. Microelectronics - Research. 4. Small business - Management. I. Title. II. Series.
HD9696.A2 B64 1986

Boeker, Heiner, 1955- Qualitätspolitik in der industriellen Beschaffung : dargestellt am Beispiel der Bekleidungsindustrie / Heiner Boeker. Bochum : N. Brockmeyer, 1986. ix, 296 p. ; 21 cm. (Bochumer wirtschaftswissenschaftliche Studien. Nr. 111) Bibliography: p. 267-296. ISBN 3-88339-525-0 LC Card 87-127490 DDC 687/.068/5 19
1. Clothing trade - Quality control. 2. Industrial procurement. 3. Retail trade. 4. Quality of products. I. Title.
HD9940.A2 B64 1986

Boelcke, Willi A.
Die Kosten von Hitlers Krieg : Kriegsfinanzierung und finanzielles Kriegserbe in Deutschland 1933-1948 / Willi A. Boelcke. Paderborn : Schöningh, c1985. 220 p. : ill. ; 24 cm. (Sammlung Schöningh zur Geschichte und Gegenwart) Includes bibliographical references and index. ISBN 3-506-77471-9 LC Card 86-143362
1. World War, 1939-1945 - Finance - Germany. 2. World War, 1939-1945 - Economic aspects - Germany. 3. War, Cost of. I. Title.
HJ1119 .B66 1985

Wirtschaftsgeschichte Baden-Württembergs : von den Römern bis heute / Willi A. Boelcke. Stuttgart : K. Theiss, c1987. 725 p., [80] p. of plates : ill. ; 24 cm. Bibliography: p. [691]-694. Includes indexes. ISBN 3-8062-0423-3 LC Card 87-152351 DDC 330.943/46 19
1. Baden-Württemberg (Germany) - Economic conditions. 2. Baden-Württemberg (Germany) - Economic policy. 3. Baden-Württemberg (Germany) - Industries - History. I. Title.
HC287.B23 B63 1987

Bömer, Hermann. Die drohende Katastrophe : globale Probleme der Menschheit / Hermann Bömer. Frankfurt am Main : Verlag Marxistische Blätter, 1984. 257 p. : ill. ; 19 cm. (Mak, 0173-4733 . 182) Bibliography: p. 222-229. ISBN 3-88012-708-5 : LC Card 85-128942
1. Natural resources. 2. Economic forecasting. 3. Food supply. 4. Environmental policy. 5. Imperialism. 6. Capitalism. 7. Socialism. I. Series: Marxismus aktuell , 182. II. Title.
HC59 .B5925 1984

Boende i Helsingfors 1950-1983. Lankinen, Leila. Asuminen Helsingissä 1950-1983 =. Helsinki , 1985. 80 p. : LC Card 86-148571
HD7345.3.H5 L35 1985

Böpple, Arthur. "Sozialstaat" im Abbruch : von der Wende zur Armutsgesellschaft? / Arthur Böpple. Frankfurt/Main : Nachrichten-Verlags-Gesellschaft, c1986. 277 p. : ill. ; 19 cm. Includes index. ISBN 3-88367-062-6 LC Card 87-104497
1. Social security - Germany, West. 2. Germany, West - Social policy. 3. Welfare state. 4. Public welfare - Germany, West. I. Title.
HD7179 .B624 1986

Börsengewinne dank besserer Aktienkurs-Prognose /. Schleis, Konrad, 1935- Niederglatt , c1984. 257 p. : ISBN 3-85684-030-3 : LC Card 84-119396
HG5492 .S345 1984

Bös, Dieter.
Entrepreneurship . Wien , New York , 1984, c1983. 218 p. ; ISBN 0-387-81830-8 (U. S.) LC Card 84-26677 DDC 338/.04 19
HB615 .E635 1984 ***NYPL [JLE 85-1253]***

Welfare economics of the second best /. Wien , New York , c1986. 280 p. ; ISBN 0-387-81942-8 (pbk. : U. S.) LC Card 86-31357 DDC 330.15/5 19
HB846.6 .W45 1986

Böseke, Harry. Schlüsselgewalt . Dortmund , c1981. 190 p. : ISBN 3-88142-261-7 : LC Card 81-206444
HD7339.A3 S25 1981

Boesen, Jannik. Tanzania . Uppsala , Stockholm, Sweden , 1986. 325 p. : ISBN 91-7106-257-2 (pbk.) LC Card 87-163353 DDC 330.9678/04 19
HD2128.5 .T36 1986

Boesler, Klaus-Achim. Beiträge zur empirischen Wirtschaftsgeographie /. Bonn , c1986. 238 p. : ISBN 3-427-74191-5 LC Card 87-104279 DDC 330.9 19
HF1025 .B3495 1986

Böethius, Erland, 1951- Målarettan 100 år / Erland Boëthius. [Stockholm] : Svenska målareförbundets avd. 1, c1984. 448 p. : ill. ; 25 cm. ISBN 91-7810-054-2 : LC Card 84-239262
1. Trade-unions - Painters, Industrial - Sweden - History. I. Title. II. Title: Målarettan hundra år.
HD6759.P26 B64 1984

Boettcher, Erik. Ökonomisches Denken und soziale Ordnung . Tübingen , 1984. viii, 293 p. ; ISBN 3-16-344777-5 (Deut. Bibl.) LC Card 84-193300
HB175 .O46 1984

BOETTCHER, ERIK.
Ökonomisches Denken und soziale Ordnung . Tübingen , 1984. viii, 293 p. ; ISBN 3-16-344777-5 (Deut. Bibl.) LC Card 84-193300
HB175 .O46 1984

Böttcher, Winfried. Bangladesh im Schatten der Macht /. Aachen , c1986. vi, 328, 57 p. : ISBN 3-922868-31-2 LC Card 86-228249
HC440.8 .B358 1986

Bofinger, Peter. Währungswettbewerb : eine systematische Darstellung und kritische Würdigung von Friedrich A. von Hayeks Plänen zu einer grundlegenden Neugestaltung unserer Währungsordnung / von Peter Bofinger. Köln : C. Heymann, c1985. xiv, 235 p. : ill. ; 21 cm. (Schriftenreihe Annales Universitatis Saraviensis. Rechts- und Wirtschaftswissenschaftliche Abteilung . Bd. 118) Bibliography: p. [227]-235. ISBN 3-452-20332-8 : LC Card 86-185566
1. Money. 2. Money supply. 3. Foreign exchange. 4. Hayek, Friedrich A. von (Friedrich August), 1899-. I. Title.
HG221 .B57455 1985

The BOF3 quarterly model of the Finnish economy / edited by Juha Tarkka and Alpo Willman. Helsinki : Bank of Finland, 1985. 465 p. : ill. ; 25 cm. (Publications of the Bank of Finland. Series D, 0355-6042 . 59) "Publications connected with the BOF model": p. 463-465. Includes bibliographies. ISBN 951-686-108-3 (pbk.) LC Card 86-205002 DDC 330.94897/005 s 338.5/443/094897 19
1. Economic forecasting - Finland - Econometric models. 2. Finland - Economic conditions - 1945- - Econometric models. 3. Finland - Economic policy - Econometric models. I. Tarkka, Juha, 1954-. II. Willman, Alpo.
HB30 .S95 no. 59 HC340.2

Bogadek, F. A. (Francis Aloysius), 1882- [New English-Croatian and Croatian-English dictionary]
Cassell's New English-Croatian and Croatian-English dictionary / by F.A. Bogadek. 3rd ed., enl. and corrected. New York : Macmillan, [c1985] vii, 531, 497, 46, 7 p. ; 22 cm. Title on added t.p.: Novi englesko-hrvatski i hrvatsko-engleski rječnik. Imprint date supplied on jacket. ISBN 0-02-512140-5 LC Card 85-23140 DDC 491.8/2321 19
1. English language - Dictionaries - Serbo-Croatian. 2. Serbo-Croatian language - Dictionaries - English. I. Title. II. Title: New English-Croatian and Croatian-English dictionary. III. Title: Novi englesko-hrvatski i hrvatsko-engleski rječnik.
PG1377 .B72 1985 ***NYPL [*QAD 87-600]***

Bogan, Elizabeth Chapin. Macroeconomics : theories and applications / Elizabeth Chapin Bogan, Joseph J. Kiernan. St. Paul, MN : West Pub. Co., c1987. xviii, 569 p. : ill. ; 26 cm. Includes index. ISBN 0-314-25867-1 : LC Card 86-24643 DDC 339 19
1. Macroeconomics. I. Kiernan, Joseph J. II. Title.
HB172.5 .B64 1987

Bogan, Marcos. Carreras, Rodrigo X. Vivienda y población en Costa Rica . Heredia, Costa Rica , 1979. 203 p. : LC Card 87-404329 DDC 363.5/097286 19
HD7308.A3 C37 1979

Bogatova, E. R. Sovetsko-v'etnamskiĭ simpozium na temu "Ėkonomicheskie problemy perekhoda k sotsializmu" (1984 : Moscow, R.S.F.S.R.) Ėkonomicheskie problemy perekhoda k sotsializmu stran s nerazvitoĭ ėkonomikoĭ . [Moskva , 1986. 254 p. ; LC Card 87-108102
HC444 .S69 1984

Bogdanov, Oleg Semenovich. Kratkiĭ vneshneėkonomicheskiĭ slovar' /. Moskva , 1984. 244 p. ; LC Card 85-156834
HF1001 .K7 1984 ***NYPL [*QCK 86-3635]***

Bogdanova, Ivanka. Rabotnicheskoto profsŭiuzno dvizhenie vŭv Varnenski okrŭg /. Sofiia , 1985. 348 p., [16] p. of plates : LC Card 86-111781
HD8629.V372 R37 1985

Bogenschild, Thomas E. State and society in Brazil . Boulder , 1987. x, 349 p. ; ISBN 0-8133-7401-4 (pbk. : alk. paper) : LC Card 87-2160 DDC 981/.063 19
HC187 .S78 1987

Bogert, Judith B. W., 1941- Managing business communciations : an applied process approach / Judith B.W. Bogert, Rebecca B. Worley. Englewood Cliffs, NJ : Prentice Hall, c1988. xiv, 434 p. : ill. ; 23 cm. Bibliography: p. 424-425. Includes index. ISBN 0-13-548629-7 (pbk.) : LC Card 87-3568 DDC 658.4/5 19
1. Communication in management. I. Worley, Rebecca B., 1946-. II. Title.
HF5718 .B597 1988

Bognetti, Giuseppe.
Il Finanziamento dell'innovazione nelle imprese industriali /. Milano, Italy , c1985. 271 p. : LC Card 86-157239
HC310.T4 F55 1985

La Crisi delle partecipazioni statali, motivi e prospettive /. Milano , c1981. 240 p. ; ISBN 88-20-42148-8 : LC Card 81-200055
HC310.I53 C74 1981 ***NYPL [JLD 86-3503]***

Bogoliubov, Klavdiĭ Mikhaĭlovich. Vernym kursom / K.M. Bogoliubov. Izd. 2-e, dorabotannoe i dop. Moskva : Izd-vo polit. lit-ry, 1984. 287 p. ; 21 cm. Includes bibliographical references. LC Card 85-164820
1. Collectivization of agriculture - Soviet Union. 2. Agriculture and state - Soviet Union. 3. Communism and agriculture - Soviet Union. I. Title.
HD1492.S65 B64 1984

Bogomolov, Oleg Timofeevich. Soglasovanie ėkonomicheskoĭ politiki stran SEV /. Moskva , 1986. 287 p. ; LC Card 87-120408
HC244 .S5925 1986

Bogor, Indonesia. Agricultural University. see **Institut Pertanian Bogor.**

Bogor, Indonesia. Institut Pertanian. see **Institut Pertanian Bogor.**

Bogotá (Colombia). División de Planeamiento y Análisis Financiero.
Estadística fiscal de Bogotá, D.E., 1970-1976. [Bogotá, Colombia] [1977] 100 p. : LC Card 87-128439 DDC 336.84/14 19
HJ9394.B6 E847 1977

Estadística fiscal de Bogotá, D.E., 1971-1977. [Bogotá, Colombia] [1979] 139 p. : LC Card 87-125994 DDC 336.861/4 19
HJ9394.B6 E85 1979

Boguszewski, Jan. Wachstum und Produktivität in der Industrie und ihren Hauptbereichen in der BRD, Österreich, Polen und Ungarn im Zeitraum, 1960-1972 / Jan Boguszewski. Wien : Wiener Institut für Internationale Wirtschaftsvergleiche, [1979] 71 p. : ill. ; 30 cm. (Forschungsberichte / Wiener Institut für Internationale Wirtschaftsvergleiche beim Österreichischen Institut für Wirtschaftsforschung . Nr. 53) "Mai 1979." Includes bibliographical references. LC Card 84-119739
1. Industrial productivity - Germany, West. 2. Industrial productivity - Austria. 3. Industrial productivity - Poland. 4. Industrial productivity - Hungary. I. Series: Forschungsberichte (Wiener Institut für Internationale Wirtschaftsvergleiche) , Nr. 53. II. Title.
HC290.5.I52 B64 1979

BOHEMIA (CZECHOSLOVAKIA) - INDUSTRIES - HISTORY.
Brousek, Karl M. Die Grossindustrie Böhmens, 1848-1918 /. München , 1987. 223 p., 8 leaves of plates : ISBN 3-486-51871-2 LC Card

87-142819 DDC 338.6/44/094371 19
HD2356.C96 B643 1987

BOHEMIA (CZECHOSLOVAKIA) - SOCIAL CONDITIONS.
Brousek, Karl M. Die Grossindustrie Böhmens, 1848-1918 /. München , 1987. 223 p., 8 leaves of plates : ISBN 3-486-51871-2 LC Card 87-142819 DDC 338.6/44/094371 19
HD2356.C96 B643 1987

BOHEMIAN LANGUAGE. see **CZECH LANGUAGE.**

Bohigian, Valerie. Ladybucks / Valerie Bohigian. 1st ed. New York, N.Y. : Dodd, Mead, c1987. 246 p. ; 22 cm. Includes index. ISBN 0-396-08852-X LC Card 86-29227 DDC 650.1/024042 19
1. Self-employed women - United States. 2. Women executives - United States. 3. Success in business - United States. I. Title.
HD6072.6.U5 B64 1987

Bohl, Don Lee. The 1986 AMA report on information centers . New York, N.Y. , c1986. viii, 92, [28] p. : ISBN 0-8144-3154-2
NYPL [JLF 86-1835]

Bohle, Hans-Georg. Südindische Wochenmarktsysteme : theoriegeleitete Fallstudien zur Geschichte und Struktur polarisierter Wirtschaftskreisläufe im ländlichen Raum der Dritten Welt / Hans-Georg Bohle. Stuttgart : F. Steiner Verlag Wiesbaden, 1986. 290 p. : 70 ill. ; 24 cm. (Erdkundliches Wissen. Heft 82) Summary in English. Bibliography: p. 271-283. ISBN 3-515-04601-1 LC Card 87-136147 DDC 381/.18/09548 19
1. Markets - India, South - History. 2. Produce trade - India, South - History. 3. Peddlers and peddling - India, South - History. I. Title.
HF5475.I42 S682 1986

Bohling, Wolfgang. Lexikon Wirtschaftspolitik . München , c1986. 236 p. : ISBN 3-406-31302-7 LC Card 86-221788
HG151 .L45 1986

Bőhm, Antal. Társadalmunk ingázói, az ingázók társadalma / Bőhm Antal, Pál László. [Budapest] : Kossuth, 1985. 166, [I] p. ; 20 cm. Bibliography: p. 161-[167] ISBN 963-09-2654-7 : LC Card 86-185996
1. Commuters - Hungary. I. Pál, László. II. Title.
HD5717.5.H9 B64 1985

Böhm, Edward. Wechselkurspolitik in der Planwirtschaft : Möglichkeiten und Grenzen aus der Sicht ungarischer und polnischer Erfahrungen / Edward Böhm. Hamburg : Verlag Weltarchiv, 1986. 139 p. : ill. ; 24 cm. (Veröffentlichungen des HWWA-Institut für Wirtschaftsforschung-Hamburg) Bibliography: p. 134-139. ISBN 3-87895-301-1 LC Card 86-210978
1. Foreign exchange administration - Hungary. 2. Hungary - Economic policy - 1968-. 3. Foreign exchange administration - Poland. 4. Poland - Economic policy - 1981-. I. Title.
HG3947.5 .B64 1986

Böhm, Peter. Baltensperger, Ernst. Geldmengenpolitik und Inflationskontrolle . Diessenhofen , c1984. 132 p. : ISBN 3-7253-0224-3 : LC Card 84-178054 DDC 332.4/9494 19
HG1155 .B345 1984 ***NYPL [JLD 87-168]***

Böhm, Volker. Arbeitsbuch zur Mikroökonomie / Volker Böhm. Berlin ; New York : Springer, 1984. vi, 246 p. : ill. ; 21 cm. (Heidelberger Taschenbücher. Bd. 238) ISBN 0-387-13541-3 (U. S.) LC Card 85-139852
1. Microeconomics. I. Title.
HB172 .B544 1984

Böhm, Walter. Längsschnittanalyse des österreichischen Arbeitsmarktes : ein wahrscheinlichkeitstheoretisches Modell auf der Basis von event history data / Walter Böhm. Wien : VWGÖ, 1986. 138 p. : ill. ; 21 cm. (Dissertationen der Wirtschaftsuniversität Wien, 0259-0719 . 42) Originally presented as the author's thesis (doctoral)--Wirtschaftsuniversität Wien, 1985. Bibliography: p. 134-138. ISBN 3-85369-654-6 LC Card 87-142156 DDC 331.12/5/09436 19
1. Labor supply - Austria - Econometric models. 2. Unemployment - Austria - Econometric models. 3. Markov processes. I. Title. II. Series.
HD5771 .B64 1986

Bohnet, Armin.
China im Konflikt zwischen verschiedenen Ordnungskonzeptionen /. Berlin , c1985. 157 p. : ISBN 3-428-05923-9 LC Card 86-164406
HC427.9 .C56525 1985

Wachstumsverlangsamung und Konjunkturzyklen in unterschiedlichen Wirtschaftssystemen /. Berlin , c1984. 191 p. : ISBN 3-428-05626-4
NYPL [JLL 73-186 Bd. 142]

Bohnet, Michael.
Entwicklungstheorie, Entwicklungspraxis . Berlin , c1986. 316 p. ; ISBN 3-428-05973-5 LC Card 86-233851 DDC 338.9/009172/4 19
HC59.7 .E6473 1986

Welthandel morgen . Stuttgart , 1984. 275 p. : ISBN 3-87959-225-X LC Card 85-132786
HF4055 .W45 1984

Bohoyo Velázquez, Isidoro Francisco. Situación socio-económica y condiciones de vida en la Provincia de Badajoz, 1880-1902 / Isidoro Francisco Bohoyo Velázquez. Badajoz : Universitas, [1984?] 149 p., [3] p. of plates : ill. ; 18 cm. (Biblioteca popular extremeña . 5) Bibliography: p. 146-149. ISBN 84-309-1055-7 LC Card 86-151914
1. Badajoz (Spain : Province) - Economic conditions. 2. Badajoz (Spain : Province) - Social conditions. 3. Land tenure - Spain - Badajoz (Province) - History. 4. Quality of life - Spain - Badajoz (Province) - History. I. Title. II. Series.
HC387.B14 B64 1984

Bohring, Günther. Wie Leiter den wissenschaftlich-technischen Fortschritt bewältigen / Günther Bohring, Klaus Ladensack. Berlin : Dietz, 1986. 168 p. : ill. ; 18 cm. (Schriftenreihe "Soziologie.") Includes bibliographical references. ISBN 3-320-00704-1 LC Card 87-112384 DDC 338/.06 19
1. Technological innovations. I. Ladensack, Klaus. II. Title.
HD45 .B59 1986

Böhss, Günther. Dictionary of printed circuit technology : English-German, German-English / compiled by Günther Böhss. Amsterdam ; New York : Elsevier, 1985. 187 p. ; 23 cm. "Published in coedition with VEB Verlag Technik, Berlin"--T.p. verso. ISBN 0-444-99555-2 (U. S.) : LC Card 85-12955 DDC 621.381/74/0331 19
1. Printed circuits - Dictionaries. 2. English language - Dictionaries - German. 3. Printed circuits - Dictionaries - German. 4. German language - Dictionaries - English. I. Title.
TK7868.P7 B65 1985 ***NYPL [JSD 86-621]***

Bohynia͡, D. P. Ėffektivnost′ obsh͡chestvennogo truda v uslovii͡akh razvitogo sotsializma : problemy teorii i praktiki / D.P. Bogini͡a. Kiev : "Nauk. dumka," 1982. 316 p. ; 21 cm. (Ėkonomika razvitogo sotsializma) At head of title: Akademii͡a nauk Ukrainskoĭ SSR. Institut ėkonomiki. Bibliography: p. 301-[307] Includes indexes. LC Card 82-200989
1. Labor productivity - Soviet Union. 2. Labor supply - Soviet Union. I. Title. II. Series.
HC340.L3 B56 1982

Bóia-fria. Incao, Maria da Conceição d'. A questão do bóia-fria /. São Paulo-Brasil , 1984. 93 p. : LC Card 85-187274
HD5856.B6 I53 1984

Boi͡adzhiev, Ilii͡a S. (Ilii͡a Stanislavov)
Anglīsko-nemsko-frensko-rusko-bŭlgarski rechnik po upravlenie i ikonomika na promishlenostta, stroitelstvoto i transporta /. Sofii͡a , 1982. 764 p. ; LC Card 83-128751
HD30.15 .A43 1982 ***NYPL [*QAD 86-4204]***

Boi͡arshinova, Z. I͡A. (Zoi͡a I͡Akovlevna) Voprosy istorii dorevoli͡utsionnoĭ Sibiri /. Tomsk , 1983. 177 p. ; ***NYPL [*QI 87-171]***

Boi͡arskiĭ, Aron I͡Akovlevich, 1906- Praktikum po demografii / A. I͡A. Boi͡arskiĭ, G.Sh. Bakhmetova, L.P. Kharchenko. Moskva : "Mysl′", 1985. 141, [3] p. : ill. ; 21 cm. Bibliography: p. 140-[142] LC Card 86-170070
1. Soviet Union - Population. 2. Soviet Union - Population - Statistics. I. Bakhmetova, G. Sh. (Giu͡l′dzhan Sharifovna). II. Kharchenko, L. P. (Lii͡a Petrovna). III. Title.
HB3607 .B64 1985

Boĭko, Vladimir Ivanovich. Sotsial′nye problemy truda u narodnosteĭ Severa /. Novosibirsk , 1986. 213 p. ; LC Card 87-164784
HD5797.N75 S67 1986

Boissieu, Christian de.
Formation et rôle des taux d'intérêt /. Paris , c1982. 204 p. : ISBN 2-7178-0562-1 : LC Card 83-103493
HB539 .F63 1982

International monetary and financial integration . Dordrecht , Boston , c1988. xii, 403 p. : ISBN 90-247-3563-7 LC Card 87-3622 DDC 332.4/94 19
HG930.5 .I586 1988

Boisson, Bernard. France. Conseil économique et social. Informatique et emploi . [Paris] [1984] 24, 4 p., 8 leaves, 187, 13 p. : LC Card 84-218059
HD6331.2.F8 F73 1984

Boiteux, Marcel. Marchés, capital et incertitude . Paris , c1986. 265 p. : ISBN 2-7178-1002-1 : LC Card 86-160930
HB615 .M37 1986

Boivin, Micheline, 1950- Rheault, Sylvie. Les femmes et l'emploi /. [Québec] [1983] 64 p. ; ISBN 2-550-10471-4 LC Card 85-108850 DDC 331.4/09714 19
HD6100.Q4 R44 1983

Bokalders, Varis, 1944- Kristoferson, Lars A. Renewable energy technologies . Oxford [Oxfordshire] , New York , 1986. xviii, 319 p. : ISBN 0-08-034061-X : LC Card 86-766 DDC 621.042 19
TJ808 .K75 1986 ***NYPL [JSG 87-45]***

Bökenkamp, Joachim. Methodologische Betrachtungen der Annahmen zum menschlichen Verhalten aus der Sicht der Volkswirtschaftslehre : das "Konzept alternativer Rationalitätsgrade" / Joachim Bökenkamp. Göttingen : Ernst Oberdieck Verlag, c1985. v, 446 p. ; 21 cm. Originally presented as the author's thesis (doctoral)--Georg-August-Universität in Göttingen, 1985. Bibliography: p. 399-446. ISBN 3-925391-01-0 LC Card 87-121278 DDC 330/.01/9 19
1. Economics - Psychological aspects. 2. Rational expectations (Economic theory). I. Title.
HB74.P8 B59 1985

Bokor, János. Az Állami vállalatok szervezete, vezetése, működése és irányítása /. Budapest , 1985. 262 p. ; ISBN 963-322-140-4 : LC Card 86-202934
HD4160.5 .A78 1985

BOKOV, VANCO, 1934-1984 - CONGRESSES.
Osmanistische Studien zur Wirtschafts- und Sozialgeschichte . Wiesbaden , 1986. xi, 206 p., iv p. of plates : ISBN 3-477-02652-9 (Deut. Bibl.) LC Card 86-224062
HC492 .O85 1986

Bokros, Lajos. Piac és pénz a modern gazdaságban / Bokros Lajos, Surányi György. Budapest : Közgazdasági és Jogi Könyvkiadó, 1985. 340, [1] p. ; 21 cm. Bibliography: p. 331-[341] ISBN 963-221-551-6 : LC Card 86-185991
1. Laissez-faire. 2. Money. 3. Central planning. 4. Money - Europe, Eastern. 5. Inflation (Finance) - Europe, Eastern. I. Surányi, György. II. Title.
HB95 .B65 1985

Bolan, Nelson. How Detroit changed history / Nelson Bolan. 1st original ed. Lawrenceville, Va. : Brunswick, c1987. v, 246 p. : ill. ; 28 cm. Bibliography: p. 246. ISBN 1-556-18018-7 (pbk.) : LC Card 87-70325 DDC 338.4/76292/0973 19
1. Automobile industry and trade - United States - History. 2. Automobile industry and trade - Michigan - Detroit - History. 3. Automobiles - History. I. Title.
HD9710.U52 B55 1987

Bolchini, Piero, 1935- Metropoli e agricoltura /. Milano , c1982. 319 p. : LC Card 82-246692 DDC 333.76/13/094521 19
HD680.M54 M47 1982
NYPL [JLD 86-3678]

Boldt, Günter. Wettbewerb und Preisbildung der Seehafenverkehrswirtschaft in nordwesteuropäischen Seehäfen : eine Untersuchung der Wettbewerbssituation und der Preisbildung auf den Umschlagsdienstleistungsmärkten der Seehäfen Hamburg, Bremen, Rotterdam und Antwerpen / Günter Boldt. Göttingen : Vandenhoeck & Ruprecht, 1964. 120 p. ; 24 cm. (Vorträge und Beiträge aus dem Institut für Verkehrswissenschaft an der Universität Münster . Heft 30) Bibliography: p. 119-120. LC Card 87-408787 DDC 380.5 s 387.1

19
1. Harbors - Germany (West) - Hamburg - Rates. 2. Harbors - Germany (West) - Bremen - Rates. 3. Harbors - Netherlands - Rotterdam - Rates. 4. Harbors - Belgium - Antwerp - Rates. I. Title. II. Series.
HE131 .M84 Heft 30 HE558.H3

Boldzhurova, I. S. (Ishengul′ Sadykovna) Kolkhoznoe krest′i͡anstvo Kirgizii v uslovii͡akh razvitogo sotsializma / I.S. Boldzhurova. Frunze : Izd-vo "Ilim", 1985. 148 p. ; 20 cm. At head of title: Akademii͡a nauk Kirgizskoĭ SSR. Institut istorii. Includes bibliographical references. LC Card 86-106126
1. Agriculture - Economic aspects - Kirghiz S.S.R. 2. Agricultural laborers - Kirghiz S.S.R. 3. Kirghiz S.S.R. - Rural conditions. I. Title.
HD1995.K53 B65 1985

Boléat, Mark. The mortgage market / Mark Boléat and Adrian Coles. London ; Boston : Allen & Unwin, 1987. x, 176 p. ; 22 cm. (Studies in financial institutions and markets . 3) Bibliography: p. [170]-171. Includes index. ISBN 0-04-334011-3 (alk. paper) LC Card 86-28875 DDC 332.7/22 19
1. Mortgage loans - Great Britain. 2. Housing - Great Britain - Finance. 3. Financial institutions - Great Britain. I. Coles, Adrian, 1954-. II. Title. III. Series.
HG2040.5.G7 B65 1987

Bolen, William H., 1943- Contemporary retailing / William H. Bolen. 3rd ed. Englewood Cliffs, N.J. : Prentice Hall, c1988. xviii, 622 p. : ill. ; 25 cm. Includes bibliographies and index. ISBN 0-13-170309-9 LC Card 87-17514 DDC 658.8/7 19
1. Retail trade - Management. 2. Marketing. 3. Merchandising. I. Title.
HF5429 .B595 1988

Boletim CEDEX. Estudos especiais .
(no. 3) Formas alternativas de negociação das exportações brasileiras . Belo Horizonte, MG , c1984. 122 p. ; LC Card 86-200391
HF1513 .F67 1984

Boletín cultural (Panama, Panama) .
(v. 6) Conte Porras, J. El crédito, la banca y la moneda panameña /. Panamá, Panamá , 1983. 204 p. : *NYPL [JLE 86-3126]*

Boletín especial (Instituto Nacional de Estadística (Peru). Dirección General de Demografía) .
(no. 7) Perú . Lima, Perú , 1984. 54 p. ; LC Card 86-111841 DDC 304.6/2/0985021 19
HA1055 .P46 1984 NYPL [JLG 86-190]
(no. 9) Perú, proyecciones de población por años calendarios, según departamentos, provincias y distritos . Lima , 1985. 84 p. ; LC Card 86-173351
HA1064 .P49 1985

Boletín estadístico (Uruguay. Dirección de Investigaciones Económicas Agropecuarias) .
(no. 12, 14) Encuesta pecuaria en profundidad . Montevideo, Uruguay [1977-1978] 2 v. ; LC Card 87-402173 DDC 338.1/762/009895021 19
HD9433.U82 E53 1979

Boletín mensual de estadísticas (Colombia. Departamento Administrativo de Estadísticas) Kalmanovitz, Salomón. El desarrollo de la ganadería en Colombia, 1950-1972 . [Bogotá, Colombia] [1978] p. 195-238 : LC Card 86-157918
HD9433.C62 K35 1978

A Bolgár és a magyar mezőgazdaság összehasonlítása, 1976-1984 / [készült a Központi Statisztikai Hivatal Mezőgazdasági Statisztikai Főosztályának Termelési és Mérleg Osztályán]. Budapest : Központi Statisztikai Hivatal, 1987. 69 p. ; 29 cm. Chiefly tables. ISBN 963-02-4777-1 LC Card 87-409639 DDC 338.1/09439/021 19
1. Agriculture - Economic aspects - Bulgaria - Statistics. 2. Agriculture - Economic aspects - Hungary - Statistics. I. Hungary. Központi Statisztikai Hivatal. Termelési és Mérlegosztály.
HD2042 .B59 1987

Boligstandard . Knudsen, Jon Paschen. Oslo , 1984. 66 p. : ISBN 82-537-2088-2 : LC Card 85-125379
HD7349.A3 K58 1984

BOLÍVAR, SIMÓN, 1783-1830 - VIEWS ON COLONIES.
Nweihed, Kaldone G., 1929- Bolívar y el Tercer Mundo . Caracas, Venezuela , c1984. 400 p. : ISBN 84-499-7056-3 LC Card 85-136718
F2235.3 .N98 1984 NYPL [JFE 86-1176]

Bolívar y el Tercer Mundo . Nweihed, Kaldone G., 1929- Caracas, Venezuela , c1984. 400 p. : ISBN 84-499-7056-3 LC Card 85-136718
F2235.3 .N98 1984 NYPL [JFE 86-1176]

Bolívar y Ponte, Simón. see **Bolívar, Simón, 1783-1830.**

Bolivia : estimaciones y proyecciones de población : total del país, 1950-2025, urbana y rural, 1970-2000. [La Paz, Bolivia] : Instituto Nacional de Estadística ; [Santiago, Chile] : Centro Latinoamericano de Demografía, [1985] 107 p. : ill. ; 26 cm. Chiefly tables. Errata slip inserted. "Agencia Canadiense para el Desarrollo Internacional; fascículo F/Bol. 1, marzo, 1985"--Cover. "LC/DEM/R.4, marzo de 1984"--T.p. verso. LC Card 86-160849
1. Bolivia - Population - Statistics. 2. Population forecasting - Bolivia - Statistics. I. Institución Nacional de Estadística (Bolivia). II. CELADE (Organization).
HA954 .B64 1985

BOLIVIA - CENSUS, 1960.
Chackiel, Juan. La fuerza de trabajo en los países de la Cuenca del Plata según los censos de 1960 /. San José, Costa Rica , 1976. iv, 81 p. : LC Card 83-169596
HD5746.A6 C42 1976

BOLIVIA - CENSUS, 1984.
II censo nacional agropecuario. [La Paz], República de Bolivia [1986- v. <1-3 > : LC Card 87-109107
HD1867 .A14 1986

BOLIVIA - COMMERCE - ANDES REGION.
El Acuerdo de Cartagena y el trato preferencial en favor de Bolivia y Ecuador. [Buenos Aires, Argentina] [1982] 148 leaves ; LC Card 86-202605 DDC 337.1/8 19
HC167.A5 A285 1982

BOLIVIA - COMMERCE - HISTORY - 17TH CENTURY.
Escobari de Querejazu, Laura. Producción y comercio en el espacio sur andino en el siglo XVII . La Paz , 1985. 218 p., [12] p. of plates : LC Card 86-174929
HC167.A5 E83 1985

BOLIVIA - DEPENDENCY ON THE UNITED STATES.
La Nueva política económica . La Paz, Bolivia , 1986. 57 p. : LC Card 87-403839 DDC 338.984 19
HC182 .N84 1986

Bolivia. Dirección General de Empleo. Sector formal de la ciudad de La Paz . La Paz, Bolivia , 1980. 77 leaves ; LC Card 81-212597 DDC 331.1/0984/12 19
HD5751.L36 S42 1980 NYPL [JLF 87-369]

Bolivia. Dirección General de Normas y Tecnología. Proyecto harinas compuestas . La Paz, Bolivia , 1982. 272, [2], 3 p., [9] p. of plates : LC Card 83-195592
HD9044.B52 P76 1982

BOLIVIA - ECONOMIC CONDITIONS.
Ovando, Jorge. El tributo indígena en las finanzas bolivianas del siglo XIX /. La Paz, Bolivia [1985] 565 p. : *NYPL [JLC 86-407]*

BOLIVIA - ECONOMIC CONDITIONS - 1918-1952.
Bolivia, hoy /. México, D.F. , 1983. 240 p. ; LC Card 84-148626 DDC 330.984/05 19
HC182 .B565 1983 NYPL [JLD 86-2825]
Seiferheld, Alfredo M., 1950- Economía y petróleo durante la Guerra del Chaco . Asunción , 1983. 535 p. : LC Card 84-121699 DDC 330.9892/071 19
HC222 .S36 1983 NYPL [JLD 85-1032]

BOLIVIA - ECONOMIC CONDITIONS - 1952-1982.
Bolivia, hoy /. México, D.F. , 1983. 240 p. ; LC Card 84-148626 DDC 330.984/05 19
HC182 .B565 1983 NYPL [JLD 86-2825]
Iriarte, Gregorio. Esquemas para la interpretación de la realidad /. La Paz, Bolivia , 1985. 10 v. : LC Card 87-112879
HC182 .I727 1985

BOLIVIA - ECONOMIC CONDITIONS - 1982-
Cole, Julio Harold, 1955- Latin American inflation . New York , 1987. xv, 89 p. : ISBN 0-275-92809-8 (alk. paper) : LC Card 87-15156 DDC 332.4/1/098 19
HC125 .C62 1987
Evaluación económica, 1986 . [La Paz, Bolivia] [1986] 278 p. ; LC Card 87-403510 DDC 330.884/052 19
HC182 .E95 1986
Iriarte, Gregorio. Esquemas para la interpretación de la realidad /. La Paz, Bolivia , 1985. 10 v. : LC Card 87-112879
HC182 .I727 1985
Morales, Juan Antonio. Coyuntura económica /. La Paz , 1987. 99 p. : LC Card 87-403036 DDC 330.984/052 19
HC182 .M66 1987

BOLIVIA - ECONOMIC CONDITIONS - 1982- - CONGRESSES.
Bolivia en el año 2010. [La Paz, Bolivia?] , 1986. ii, 325 p. : LC Card 87-101220
HC182 .B564 1986
Región sur, problemática y perspectivas /. Arequipa [1986?] 164 p. ; LC Card 87-404224 DDC 330.984/052 19
HC182 .R39 1986

BOLIVIA - ECONOMIC CONDITIONS - 1982- - SOURCES.
Acuerdos y documentos de la nueva política económica, 1986 /. [La Paz, Bolivia?] [1987] 134 p. ; LC Card 87-403664 DDC 338.984 19
HC182 .A585 1987

BOLIVIA - ECONOMIC POLICY.
Conferencias sobre desarrollo económico, presupuesto, estabilización y nacionalización de empresas económicas. La Paz, Bolivia , 1955. 180 p. : LC Card 86-167406
HC182 .C54 1955
Morales, Juan Antonio. Coyuntura económica /. La Paz , 1987. 99 p. : LC Card 87-403036 DDC 330.984/052 19
HC182 .M66 1987
La Nueva política económica . La Paz, Bolivia , 1986. 57 p. : LC Card 87-403839 DDC 338.984 19
HC182 .N84 1986
Tórrez G. O., José Guillermo (Torrez Gómez Ortega) Minería e integración boliviana /. La Paz, Bolivia , 1986. 181 p., [8] leaves of plates : LC Card 87-400195 DDC 338.2/0984 19
HD9506.B64 C67 1986

BOLIVIA - ECONOMIC POLICY - SOURCES.
Acuerdos y documentos de la nueva política económica, 1986 /. [La Paz, Bolivia?] [1987] 134 p. ; LC Card 87-403664 DDC 338.984 19
HC182 .A585 1987

Bolivia en el año 2010. 1a ed. [La Paz, Bolivia?] : Centro de Prospectiva y Estudios Nacionales, 1986. ii, 325 p. : ill. ; 22 cm. Papers presented at the Seminario "Bolivia en el Año 2010," La Paz, Bolivia? 1986. Includes bibliographies. LC Card 87-101220
1. Economic forecasting - Bolivia - Congresses. 2. Bolivia - Economic conditions - 1982- - Congresses. I. Centro de Prospectiva y Estudios Nacionales (Bolivia). II. Seminario "Bolivia en el Año 2010" (1986 : La Paz, Bolivia?).
HC182 .B564 1986

BOLIVIA - FOREIGN ECONOMIC RELATIONS - UNITED STATES.
La Nueva política económica . La Paz, Bolivia , 1986. 57 p. : LC Card 87-403839 DDC 338.984 19
HC182 .N84 1986

Bolivia frente a la crisis del estaño : alternativas de defensa y acción. La Paz, Bolivia : Instituto Boliviano de Estudios Empresariales, [1986] 62 p. ; 19 cm. (Documentos. 1) Papers presented at a "mesa redonda acerca de la crisis del estaño," organized by the Instituto Boliviano de Estudios Empresariales, and held in La Paz on the 7th of Nov. 1985. LC Card 86-189109
1. Tin industry - Bolivia - Congresses. 2. Tin industry - Congresses. I. Instituto Boliviano de Estudios Empresariales. II. Series: Documentos (Instituto Boliviano de Estudios Empresariales) , 1.
HD9539.T6 B646 1986 NYPL [JLC 87-146]

Bolivia - Government. see **Bolivia - Politics and government.**

Bolivia, hoy / por René Zavaleta Mercado (compilador) ; Luis H. Antezana ... [et al.]. 1a ed. México, D.F. : Siglo Veintiuno Editores, 1983. 240 p. ; 21 cm. (Historia inmediata) Includes bibliographical references. CONTENTS. - Las masas en noviembre / por René Zavaleta Mercado -- Sistema y proceso ideológicos en Bolivia, 1935-1979 / por Luis H. Antezana -- El excedente sin acumulación / por Horst Grebe López -- Luchas campesinas contemporáneas en Bolivia / por Silvia Rivera Cusicanqui -- La clase obrera después de 1952 / por Guillermo Lora -- Forma clase y forma multitud en el proletariado minero en Bolivia / por René Zavaleta Mercado. LC Card 84-148626 DDC 330.984/05 19
1. Peasantry - Bolivia - History. 2. Labor and laboring classes - Bolivia - History. 3. Bolivia - Economic conditions - 1918-1952. 4. Bolivia - Economic conditions - 1952-1982. 5. Bolivia - Politics and government - 1938-1952. 6. Bolivia - Politics and government - 1952-1982. I. Antezana J., Luis H.
HC182 .B565 1983 NYPL [JLD 86-2825]

Bolivia. Instituto Nacional de Estadística. see **Instituto Nacional de Estadística (Bolivia)**

Bolivia. Ministerio de Planeamiento y Coordinación. Diez, Rafael. Final report of the consultancy of Rafael Diez from August 3, 1982 to August 3, 1983. La Paz [1983] 1 v. (various foliations) ; LC Card 83-243264
HC182 .D49 1983

Bolivia. Ministerio de Planeamiento y Coordinación. Instituto Nacional de Estadística. see **Instituto Nacional de Estadística (Bolivia)**

Bolivia. Planeamiento y Coordinación, Ministerio de. see **Bolivia. Ministerio de Planeamiento y Coordinación.**

BOLIVIA - POLITICS AND GOVERNMENT - 1938-1952.
Bolivia, hoy /. México, D.F. , 1983. 240 p. ; LC Card 84-148626 DDC 330.984/05 19
HC182 .B565 1983 NYPL [JLD 86-2825]

BOLIVIA - POLITICS AND GOVERNMENT - 1952-1982.
Bolivia, hoy /. México, D.F. , 1983. 240 p. ; LC Card 84-148626 DDC 330.984/05 19
HC182 .B565 1983 NYPL [JLD 86-2825]

BOLIVIA - POLITICS AND GOVERNMENT - 1982-

BOLIVIA - POPULATION - STATISTICS.
Bolivia . [La Paz, Bolivia] [Santiago, Chile] [1985] 107 p. : LC Card 86-160849
HA954 .B64 1985

Estimación de la población potencialmente votante al 1o de julio de 1985 según departamentos, provincias, ciudades capital y cantones /. La Paz, Bolivia , 1985. 58 p. : LC Card 87-400543 DDC 304.6/0984/021 19
HA965 .E85 1985

BOLIVIA - SOCIAL CONDITIONS.
Iriarte, Gregorio. Esquemas para la interpretación de la realidad /. La Paz, Bolivia , 1985. 10 v. : LC Card 87-112879
HC182 .I727 1985

BOLIVIA - SOCIAL CONDITIONS - 1982-

BOLIVIA - SOCIAL CONDITIONS - 1982- - CONGRESSES.
Región sur, problemática y perspectivas /. Arequipa [1986?] 164 p. ; LC Card 87-404224 DDC 330.984/052 19
HC182 .R39 1986

BOLIVIA - SOCIAL CONDITIONS - COLLECTED WORKS.
Taboada Terán, Néstor. Historia de las luchas sociales y el movimiento obrero en Bolivia /. Cochabamba, Bolivia , 1983- v. <1-3 > : LC Card 86-203884 DDC 331.88/0984 19
HD8275 .T32 1983

Bolles, Richard Nelson. The new quick job-hunting map / Richard Nelson Bolles. Berkeley, Calif. : Ten Speed Press, c1985. 63 p. : ill. ; 23 cm. Bibliography: p. 57. ISBN 0-89815-151-1 (pbk.) : LC Card 86-220490 DDC 650.1/4
1. Job hunting. I. Title.
HF5382.7 .B63 1985

Bolliger, Peter. Die optimale Organisationsstruktur eines mittleren Bankbetriebes : theoretische Herleitung und Darstellung an einer mittleren Kantonalbank / von Peter Bolliger. Bern : P. Haupt, c1984. xiii, 234 p. : ill. ; 23 cm. (Bankwirtschaftliche Forschungen. Bd. 86) Bibliography: p. 227-234. ISBN 3-258-03358-7 : LC Card 84-174443
1. Banks and banking - Switzerland - Branch banks. 2. Bank management - Switzerland. I. Title. II. Series.
HG1526 .B27 Bd. 86 HG1616.B7

Bolocan, David.
Advanced AppleWorks / David Chung-Hua Bolocan. 1st ed. Blue Ridge Summit, PA : TAB Books, c1986. x, 246 p. : ill. ; 25 cm. Includes index. ISBN 0-8306-0248-8 : LC Card 85-22296 DDC 005.265 19
1. Apple II (Computer) - Programming. 2. AppleWorks (Computer program). I. Title.
QA76.8.A662 B65 1986 NYPL [JSE 86-1874]

Advanced Excel / David Bolocan. 1st ed. Blue Ridge Summit, PA : TAB Books, c1986. x, 246 p. : ill. ; 25 cm. On t.p. the registered trademark symbol "TM" is superscript following "Excel" in the title. Includes index. ISBN 0-8306-0368-9 : LC Card 86-5767 DDC 005.36/9 19
1. Excel (Computer program). 2. Business - Data processing. I. Title.
HF5548.4.E93 B65 1986 NYPL [JSE 87-561]

Advanced Symphony applications : an incomparable collection of problem-solving applications and programming shortcuts / David Bolocan.1st ed. Blue Ridge Summit, PA : TAB Books, c1985. x, 230 p. : ill. ; 25 cm. On t.p. the registered trademark symbol "TM" is superscript following "Symphony" in the title. "No. 1988." Includes index. ISBN 0-8306-0988-1 : LC Card 85-22303 DDC 005.36/9 19
1. Symphony (Computer program). 2. Business - Data processing. I. Title.
HF5548.4.S95 B64 1985 NYPL [JSE 86-2156]

Lotus 1-2-3 simplified / David Bolocan. 2nd ed., including version 2.0. Blue Ridge Summit, PA : Tab Books, c1986. xii, 255 p. : ill. ; 24 cm. Includes index. "No. 2748." ISBN 0-8306-0448-0 : LC Card 86-5820 DDC 005.36/9 19
1. Lotus 1-2-3 (Computer program). 2. Business - Data processing. I. Title. II. Title: Lotus one-two-three simplified.
HF5548.4.L67 B64 1986 NYPL [JSE 87-276]

BOLOGNA (ITALY : PROVINCE) - ECONOMIC POLICY.
Modello padano, localismo e modernizzazione . Bologna , c1986. 470 p. : ISBN 88-15-01220-6 : LC Card 87-103653
HC307.B57 M63 1986

BOLOGNA (ITALY : PROVINCE) - SOCIAL POLICY.
Modello padano, localismo e modernizzazione . Bologna , c1986. 470 p. : ISBN 88-15-01220-6 : LC Card 87-103653
HC307.B57 M63 1986

Bolsa de Cereales de Buenos Aires. Comercio de granos entre la Argentina y los países del Grupo Andino. [Buenos Aires, Argentina] , 1983. ii, 154 p. : LC Card 86-201891
HD9044.A8 C65 1983

Bolsa de Comercio de Buenos Aires. see **Buenos Aires. Bolsa de Comercio.**

BOLSA DE COMERCIO DE ROSARIO - HISTORY.
De Marco, Miguel Ángel. 1884-1984, los cien años de la Bolsa de Comercio de Rosario /. [S.l. , 1984?] (Rosario : Escuela de Artes Gráficas del Colegio San José de Rosario) 167 p. : LC Card 87-115398 DDC 332.64/28224 19
HG5320.R67 D4 1984

Bolsa de commodities . Pereira, Eduardo Novo da Costa. Rio de Janeiro, RJ , 1985. ix, 69 p. ; LC Card 86-129753
HG6024.B7 P47 1985

BOLSA DE VALORES DE LIMA.
Rocha C., Julio César de la (Rocha Corzo) Un análisis de la rentabilidad accionaria de la Bolsa de Valores de Lima, 1980-1983 /. Lima, Perú , 1984. ii, 56 p. ; LC Card 86-154699
HG5392 .R66 1984

Bolsa de Valores de São Paulo.
Você e as opções de compra. [São Paulo, Brazil] [19]82. [24] p. ; LC Card 86-217458
HG6042 .V63 1982

Você e as opções de venda. [São Paulo, Brazil] [19]82. [28] p. ; LC Card 86-217459
HG6042 .V64 1982

BOLSA DE VALORES DO RIO DE JANEIRO - HISTORY.
Bolsa do Rio, 140 anos. Rio de Janeiro [1985] 200 p. : LC Card 87-146604 DDC 332.64/281 19
HG5340.R5 B66 1985

Bolsa do Rio, 140 anos. Rio de Janeiro : Bloch Editores, [1985] 200 p. : ill. (some col.), ports. ; 33 cm. Portuguese and English. LC Card 87-146604 DDC 332.64/281 19
1. Bolsa de Valores do Rio de Janeiro - History. 2. Stock-exchange - Brazil - Rio de Janeiro - History.
HG5340.R5 B66 1985

Bolsas de valores en América Latina y el Caribe. Caracas, Venezuela : Instituto Interamericano de Mercados de Capital, 1985. 401 p. : ill. ; 23 cm. LC Card 86-154738
1. Stock-exchange - Latin America. 2. Stock-exchange - Caribbean Area. I. Instituto Interamericano de Mercados de Capital.
HG5160.5 .B65 1985 NYPL [JLE 87-523]

Bol'shakov, G. F. (Gennadiĭ Fedorovich) Vsesoiuznaia konferentsiia "Razvitie proizvoditel'nykh sil Sibiri i zadachi uskoreniia nauchno-tekhnicheskogo progressa" (1985 : Tomsk, R.S.F.S.R.). Sektsiia "Khimicheskaia promyshlennost'." Razvitie khimicheskoĭ promyshlennosti Sibiri . Tomsk , 1985. 177 p. : LC Card 86-176713
HD9656.S56 S538 1985

BOLSHEVISM. see **COMMUNISM.**

Bolte, Karl Martin. Bevölkerungswissenschaft . Frankfurt , New York , c1985. 227 p. ; ISBN 3-593-33461-5 LC Card 85-178756
HB849 .B48 1985

Bölter, Hendrick H., 1957- Der geschlossene Immobilienfonds : Kapitalanlage, Finanzierungsinstrument und Banktyp / Hendrick H. Bölter. Frankfurt am Main ; New York : Lang, c1986. xv, 290 p. : ill. ; 21 cm. (Europäische Hochschulschriften. Reihe V, Volks- und Betriebswirtschaft, 0531-7339 . Bd. 704 = vol. 704 = vol. 704) Bibliography: p. 267-287. ISBN 3-8204-9460-X LC Card 86-195280
1. Real estate investment trusts - Germany, West. I. Series: Europäische Hochschulschriften. Reihe V, Volks- und Betriebswirtschaft , Bd. 704. II. Title.
HG5502 .B65 1986

BOLTON GAS COMPANY (BOLTON, GREATER MANCHESTER) - HISTORY.
Clegg, James. The Bolton Gas Company, 1818-1872 . Bolton , 1872. 46 p. ; LC Card 85-666285
HD9581.G74 B64x 1872

The Bolton Gas Company, 1818-1872 . Clegg, James. Bolton , 1872. 46 p. ; LC Card 85-666285
HD9581.G74 B64x 1872

Bolz, Klaus. Die Wirtschaftliche Entwicklung in den sozialistischen Ländern Osteuropas zur Jahreswende 1985/86 /. Hamburg , 1986. 336 p. ; ISBN 3-87895-295-3 LC Card 86-185852
HC244 .W5776 1986

Bolz, Reinhardt. Tunesien : wirtschaftliche und soziale Strukturen und Entwicklung / Reinhardt Bolz. Hamburg : Institut für Afrika-Kunde, 1976. xxiii, 471 p. : ill. ; 30 cm. (Arbeiten aus dem Institut für Afrika-Kunde . Heft 6) Includes legislation. Summary in English and French. Bibliography: p. 455-471. LC Card 86-177615
1. Tunisia - Economic policy. 2. Tunisia - Economic conditions - 1956-. 3. Tunisia - Social conditions. I. Title. II. Series.
HC820 .B66 1976

Bombach, Gottfried. Technologischer Wandel, Analyse und Fakten /. Tübingen , 1986. ix, 330 p. ; ISBN 3-16-345132-2 LC Card 87-109808 DDC 338/.06 19
HC79.T4 T4355 1986

BOMBAY CHAMBER OF COMMERCE & INDUSTRY - HISTORY.
Daruwala, Rusi J. The Bombay Chamber story . Bombay , c1986. xvii, 312 p., [19] p. of plates : LC Card 86-902920 DDC 380.1/06/054792 19
HF331.I4 D37 1986

The Bombay Chamber story . Daruwala, Rusi J. Bombay , c1986. xvii, 312 p., [19] p. of plates : LC Card 86-902920 DDC 380.1/06/054792 19
HF331.I4 D37 1986

BOMBAY (INDIA) - ECONOMIC CONDITIONS.
Daruwala, Rusi J. The Bombay Chamber story . Bombay , c1986. xvii, 312 p., [19] p. of plates : LC Card 86-902920 DDC 380.1/06/054792 19
HF331.I4 D37 1986

Un bon conseil . Zémor, Pierre. Paris , c1986. 278 p. : ISBN 2-85565-300-2 : LC Card 86-174727
HD69.C6 Z4 1986

Bon, Frédéric, 1943- Résultats des élections aux conseils de prud'hommes par département : 1982 / document établi par Frédéric Bon, Bernard Bouhet, René Mouriaux. St. Martin d'Hères [France] : Banque de données socio-politiques, [1982] 303 p. ; 21 x 30 cm. (Série Elections sociales . no 2) Bibliography: p. 11. LC Card 84-152037
1. France. Conseils de prud'hommes - Elections - Statistics. I. Bouhet, Bernard. II. Mouriaux, René. III. Title. IV. Series.
HD5555 .B65 1982

Bon, Michel, 1943- Les Industries agro-alimentaires . Paris [1986], c1987. 164 p. : ISBN 2-11-001722-8 : LC Card 87-167615
HD9012.5 .I53 1987

Bonaldo Stringher . Bonelli, Franco. [Udine] [c1985] 169 p. : LC Card 85-220896
HJ1156.S77 B66 1985

Bonanno, Alessandro. Small farms : persistence with legitimation / Alessandro Bonanno. Boulder, Colo. : Westview Press, 1987. xvi, 228 p. : map ; 23 cm. (The Rural studies series of the Rural Sociological Society) Bibliography: p. 178-195. Includes index. ISBN 0-8133-7341-7 (pbk. : alk. paper) LC Card 86-51502 DDC 338.1/6 19
1. Farms, Small - Italy - Sicily. 2. Farms, Small - Italy - Calabria. 3. Farms, Small - United States. I. Title. II. Series.
HD1339.I8 B66 1987

Bond and money market investments. Stigum, Marcia L. The Dow Jones-Irwin guide to bond and money market investments /. Homewood, Ill. , c1987. xiii, 298 p. : ISBN 0-87094-892-X : LC Card 86-71921
NYPL [*R-Econ. 87-1260]

Bond, Kenneth M. Essential business statistics : a Minitab framework / Kenneth M. Bond, James P. Scott. Boston : PWS-Kent Pub. Co., c1988. xiii, 332 p. : ill. ; 25 cm. (The Duxbury series in statistics and decision sciences) Includes index. ISBN 0-534-91530-2 LC Card 87-25652 DDC 519.5/028/55369 19
1. Minitab (Computer system). 2. Commercial statistics - Data processing. 3. Statistics - Data processing. I. Scott, James P. II. Title. III. Series.
HF1017 .B63 1988

Bond, Robert J., 1934- Bowman, Arthur G. California real estate principles. Glenview, Ill. , c1987. xiv, 368 p. : ISBN 0-673-16667-8 : LC Card 86-25985 DDC 333.33/09794 19
HD266.C2 B68 1987

Bond yield analysis . Veale, Stuart R. New York, N.Y. , c1986. p. cm. ISBN 0-13-079674-3 : LC Card 87-11305 DDC 332.63/23 19
HG4963 .V43 1986

Bondar', I. K. (Interna Kas'ianovna) Resursy narodnogo khoziaistva . Kiev , 1985. 308 p. : LC Card 86-226867
HC337.U5 P5 1985 t. 2 HC337.U53I52

Bondarenko, E. L. (Evgeniia Lavrent'eva) Lichnoe potreblenie v usloviiakh ėkonomicheskoĭ integratsii stran--chlenov SĖV / E.L. Bondarenko. Moskva : Izd-vo Moskovskogo universiteta, 1984. 110 p. ; 21 cm. Includes bibliographical references. LC Card 84-222687
1. Consumption (Economics) - Europe, Eastern. 2. Europe, Eastern - Economic integration. I. Title.
HC244.Z9 C613 1984

Bondarenko, E. L. (Evgeniia Lavrent'evna) Zakonomernosti razvitiia sotsialisticheskikh mezhdunarodnykh proizvodstvennykh otnosheniĭ / E.L. Bondarenko. Moskva : "Vysshaia shkola", 1983. 127 p. ; 22 cm. Bibliography: p. 118-[119] LC Card 84-200940
1. Europe, Eastern - Economic conditions - 1945-. 2. Europe, Eastern - Economic integration. 3. Council for Mutual Economic Assistance. I. Title.
HC244 .B694 1983

Bondarenko, V. V. (Viktor Viktorovich) Ekonomiko-statystychne vyvchenniia mizhhaluzevykh narodnohospodars'kykh kompleksiv . Kyïv , 1985. 95 p. ; LC Card 86-194555
HC337.U53 I573 1985

Bondeopposition och bondeinflytande under frihetstiden . Bäck, Kalle, 1949- Stockholm , c1984. 326 p. : ISBN 91-36-02263-2 : LC Card 84-252422
HD1536.S8 B33 1984

Bönder och gårdar i stormaktspolitikens skugga . Larsson, Lars-Olof, 1934- Växjö , 1983. 260 p. : ISBN 91-7636-011-3 : LC Card 84-159659
HD763 .L37 1983

Bondonio, Pier Vincenzo, 1942- Il Consolidamento regionale della finanza locale /. Milano [1980] 332 p. : ISBN 88-20-41859-2 : LC Card 80-143023
HJ9497 .C63 ***NYPL [JLD 87-1397]***

BONDS - ADDRESSES, ESSAYS, LECTURES.
CFA readings in fixed income securities analysis /. Charlottesville, VA (P.O. Box 3668, Charlottesville, VA 22903) , c1985. v, 255 p. :
NYPL [JLF 86-1994]

BONDS - AFRICA, SOUTHERN - CATALOGS.
The Scripophilist's guide . [Johannesburg? , 1985?] 100 p. : LC Card 87-100584 DDC 769.5 19
HG5851.A3 S37 1985

BONDS - COLLECTORS AND COLLECTING.
Garrison, G. H. Haley (George H. Haley) The insider's guide to antique securities /. Williamsburg, Va. (P.O. Drawer JH, Williamsburg 23187) , c1987. 1 v. (various pagings) : LC Card 87-149140 DDC 332.63/2/0750973 19
HG4633 .G38 1987

BONDS, CONVERTIBLE. see **CONVERTIBLE BONDS.**

BONDS - HANDBOOKS, MANUALS, ETC.
Darst, David M., 1947- The handbook of the bond and money markets /. New York , c1981. xv, 461 p. : ISBN 0-07-015401-5 LC Card 80-36816 DDC 332.63/23
HG4527 .D37 ***NYPL [JLE 87-568]***

The Handbook of fixed income securities /. Homewood, Ill. , 1987. xxx, 1376 p. : ISBN 0-87094-745-1 LC Card 86-50815
NYPL [JLE 87-939]

BONDS - HUNGARY.
Hardy, Ilona. Gyakorlati útmutató a kötvény és a váltó használatához /. Budapest , 1986. 62 p. ; ISBN 963-621-315-1 LC Card 87-407776
HG5470.5.A3 H37 1986

BONDS - PERU.
Ycaza Clerc, Mónica de. Política de endeudamiento público interno en el Perú . Lima, Perú , 1985. ii, 23, [39] p. : LC Card 86-223472
HJ8604 .Y33 1985

BONDS - SOUTH AFRICA - CATALOGS.
The Scripophilist's guide . [Johannesburg? , 1985?] 100 p. : LC Card 87-100584 DDC 769.5 19
HG5851.A3 S37 1985

BONDS - UNITED STATES.
Corporate mergers and high yield (junk) bonds . Washington , 1986. vi, 57 p. ; LC Card 87-601339 DDC 332.63/22 19
HD2746.5 .C67 1986

Petersen, John E. Innovative capital financing /. Chicago, IL (1313 E. 60th St., Chicago 60637) , 1985. ii, 38 p. : LC Card 86-175368 DDC 336.73 19
HG4936 .P424 1985

Understanding the securities markets . Jersey City, NJ (75 Montgomery St., Jersey City 07302) , c1986. 36 p. ; LC Card 87-130670 DDC 332.63/2 19
HG4910 .U53 1986

Veale, Stuart R. Bond yield analysis . New York, N.Y. , c1986. p. cm. ISBN 0-13-079674-3 : LC Card 87-11305 DDC 332.63/23 19
HG4963 .V43 1986

Wilson, Richard S. Corporate senior securities . Chicago, Ill. , c1987. xiv, 459 p. : ISBN 0-917253-79-5 : LC Card 87-6980 DDC 332.63/2 19
HG4963 .W56 1987

Bondt, Frank de. Délivrez-nous des cadres / Frank de Bondt. [Paris] : J.C. Lattès, c1984. 248 p. ; 23 cm. Includes bibliographical references. LC Card 85-103087 DDC 331.7/12/0944 19
1. Professional employees - France - Anecdotes, facetiae, satire, etc. 2. White collar workers - France - Anecdotes, facetiae, satire, etc. I. Title.
HD8038.F7 B65 1984

Bonelli, Franco. Bonaldo Stringher : 1854-1930 / Franco Bonelli. [Udine] : Casamassima, [c1985] 169 p. : ill. ; 25 cm. Includes bibliographies. LC Card 85-220896
1. Stringher, Bonaldo, 1854-1930. 2. Italy. Ministero del tesoro - Biography. 3. Banca d'Italia - Biography. 4. Italy. Ministero del tesoro - History. 5. Banca d'Italia - History. 6. Cabinet officers - Italy - Biography. 7. Bankers - Italy - Biography. I. Title.
HJ1156.S77 B66 1985

Bonenberg, Wojciech. Przemysł w mieście : ekologiczna metoda modernizacji zakładów przemysłowych zlokalizowanych na obszarach intensywnie zurbanizowanych / Wojciech Bonenberg. Gliwice : Politechnika Śląska, 1985. 181 p., [8] folded leaves of plates : ill. ; 24 cm. (Zeszyty naukowe Politechniki Śląskiej . nr 850. zesz. 3) Summary in English and Russian. Bibliography: p. [169]-181. LC Card 86-219523
1. Poland - Industry - Location. 2. Urban ecology - Poland. 3. Poland - Industries - Environmental aspects. 4. Cities and towns - Poland. I. Series. II. Series: Zeszyty naukowe Politechniki Śląskiej , nr. 850. III. Title.
HC340.3.Z9 D52 1985

Boneo, Horacio.
Desarrollo regional, incentivos fiscales y localización industrial / Horacio Boneo. Buenos Aires, Argentina : Centro de Estudios de Estado y Sociedad, [1985] 160 p. : ill. ; 22 cm. (Estudios CEDES) Bibliography: p. 145-150. ISBN 950-95720-8-X
1. Industrial promotion - Argentina. 2. Regional planning - Argentina. 3. Agricultural industries - Argentina. 4. Argentina - Economic conditions - 1945-1983. I. Title. II. Series.
NYPL [JLD 86-4218]

Interlinkages, concept, characteristics, and determining factors / Horacio Boneo. Austin : Office for Public Sector Studies, Institute of Latin American Studies, University of Texas at Austin, 1986. 17 p. : ill. ; 28 cm. (Technical papers series . no. 50) Bibliography: p. 13-15. LC Card 86-622253 DDC 338.7/4/091724 19
1. Government business enterprises - Developing countries. I. Title. II. Series.
HD4420.8 .B67 1986

Boness, Arthur. Büromaschinen, Datenverarbeitungsgeräte und -einrichtungen . Berlin [1984] xxi, 400 p. : ISBN 3-428-05740-6 LC Card 86-139011
HC281 .B33 Heft 82 HD9800.G3

Bonetti, Mario. Staat und Gesellschaft im karibischen Raum im 16. Jahrhundert / von Mario Bonetti. München : W. Fink, 1984. 668 p. : ill. ; 21 cm. (Beiträge zur Soziologie und Sozialkunde Lateinamerikas. Bd. 25) Bibliography: p. 488-504. ISBN 3-7705-2162-5 LC Card 85-132458 DDC 330.9729/02 19
1. Caribbean area - Economic conditions. 2. Caribbean area - Social conditions. 3. Spain - Colonies. I. Title. II. Series.
HC151 .B66 1984

Bongaarts, John, 1945-
Greenhalgh, Susan. Fertility policy in China . New York, N.Y. [1986] 31 p. ; LC Card 87-154581 DDC 304.6/6/0951 19
HB1064.A3 G74 1986

The transition in reproductive behavior in the third world / John Bongaarts. New York, N.Y. : Population Council, [1986] 29 p. : ill ; 23 cm. (Working papers / Center for Policy Studies . no. 125 (Aug. 1986)) Cover title. "This paper was prepared for the Seventy-first American Assembly on United States International Population Policy held at Harriman, New York, 17-20 April 1986"--T.p. verso. LC Card 87-154566 DDC 304.6/32/091724 19
1. Fertility, Human - Developing countries. I. Series: Working papers (Population Council. Center for Policy Studies) , no. 125. II. Title.
HB1108 .B65 1986

Bongenaar, Karel E. M. Nos futuro . Curaçao, NA , Zutphen , c1986. 496 p. : ISBN 90-6011-512-0 : LC Card 86-220862
HC157.5 .N67 1986

Bonifert, György. A Munkavédelem agitációs és propaganda rendszere /. Budapest , 1983. 51 p. : ISBN 963-7006-04-4 LC Card 85-110318
HD7702.5 .M85 1983

Bonilla, Alexander. Situación ambiental de Costa Rica / Alexander Bonilla. [San José] : Instituto del Libro, Ministerio de Cultura, Juventud y Deportes, [1985] 271 p. : ill. ; 25 cm. Bibliography: p. 241-249. ISBN 997-7590-57-5 LC Card 86-156609
1. Environmental policy - Costa Rica. 2. Environmental protection - Costa Rica. 3. Pollution - Costa Rica. 4. Natural resources - Costa Rica. I. Title.
HC143.Z9 E52 1985

Bonilla, Heraclio. Las Crisis económicas en la historia del Perú /. [Lima, Perú] [s.l.] , 1986. 376 p. : LC Card 87-400306 DDC 330.985 19
HC227 .C744 1986

Bonitierungsanleitung. Grundsätze für die Bewertung von Kulturland bei Güterzusammenlegungen . [Bern? , 1973?] 1 v. (loose leaf) : LC Card 86-184960
HD798 .G78 1973

Bonk, Heinz. Rüstungspolitik und Arbeiterklasse : der destruktive Charakter der imperialistischen Rüstungsproduktion und seine gesellschaftlichen Folgen / Heinz Bonk, Rainer Reinecke. Berlin : Dietz, 1986. 299 p. ; 19 cm. "Akademie für Gesellschaftswissenschaften beim ZK der SED"--P. facing t.p. Includes bibliographical references. LC Card 86-174039
1. Armaments - Economic aspects. 2. Labor and laboring classes. 3. Imperialism. I. Reinecke, Rainer. II. Akademie für Gesellschaftswissenschaften beim ZK der SED. III. Title.
HC79.D4 B65 1986

La bonne économie . Kolm, Serge Christophe. Paris , 1984. 472 p. : ISBN 2-13-038695-4 : LC Card 84-254896 DDC 330 19
HB173 .K64 1984

Bonner betriebswirtschaftliche Schriften . (10) Wanik, Bernhard. Die Lohnentwicklung deutscher Industrieaktiengesellschaften /. Bonn , 1981. vii, 268 p. : LC Card 85-165602
HD5029 .W36 1981

(8) Bruse, Helmut. Der Absatzbereich von Unternehmen . Bonn , 1980. xiv, 323 p. : LC Card 85-164955
HF5415 .B7713 1980

Bonss, Wolfgang. Arbeitslosigkeit in der Arbeitsgesellschaft /. Frankfurt am Main , 1984. 350 p. ; ISBN 3-518-11212-0 : LC Card 84-192978
HD5708 .A72 1984

Bontadini, Piero. Teoria dell'organizzazione e realtà italiana . Milano [1980] 225 p. ; ISBN 88-20-41736-7 : LC Card 80-511472 DDC 302.3/5 19
HM131 .T4 ***NYPL [JLD 81-599]***

Bontó, László. Iparfejlesztés a hetedik ötéves terv időszakában / Bontó László, Csemniczky Jánosné. [Budapest] : Kossuth, 1986. 170, [4] p. : ill. ; 20 cm. (Gazdaságpolitikai füzetek, 0230-3833) Bibliography: p. [173]-[174]. ISBN 963-09-3001-3 : LC Card 87-138631
1. Hungary - Industries. 2. Hungary - Economic policy - 1968-. 3. Industry and state - Hungary. I. Csemniczky, Jánosné. II. Title. III. Title: Iparfejlesztés a 7-dik ötéves terv időszakában. IV. Series.
HC300.28 .B659 1986

Bontrup, Heinz-J. Preisbildung bei Rüstungsgütern / Heinz-J. Bontrup. Köln : Wissenschaft und Politik, c1986. 247 p. ; 21 cm. Bibliography: p. 239-247. ISBN 3-8046-8677-X LC Card 87-122749 DDC 338.4/36234 19
1. Munitions - Prices. 2. Monopsonies. I. Title.
HD9743.A2 B59 1986

Bonus, Holger. Öffentliche Güter und der Öffentlichkeitsgrad von Gütern / Holger Bonus. Konstanz : Fakultät für Wirtschaftswissenschaften und Statistik, Universität Konstanz, [1979] 39, 3 p. ; 30 cm. (Diskussionsbeiträge. Serie B, Finanzwissenschaftliche Arbeitspapiere . Nr. 8) "17. September 1979." Bibliography: p. 37-39. LC Card 85-171986
1. Public goods - Mathematical models. 2. Social groups - Mathematical models. I. Title.
HB846.5 .B66 1979

BONUS SYSTEM - EUROPE, EASTERN.
Mikheev, S. Remuneration in Eastern European countries /. Geneva , 1985. vi, 45, ix p. ; ISBN 92-9014-408-4 (pbk.) : LC Card 86-216036 DDC 331.2/947 19
HD5014 .M55 1985

BONUS SYSTEM - GERMANY, EAST.
Rogge, Werner. Die Arbeit mit dem Prämienfonds /. Berlin , c1984. 70 p. ; LC Card 86-100311 DDC 331.2/164 19
HD4928.B62 G357 1984

Bonvoisin, Fl. (Florence) Benhaïm, J.-P. (Jean-Pierre) Les radios locales privées /. Paris , c1985. 153 p. : ISBN 2-7101-0528-4 : LC Card 85-205602
HE8697.P57 B45 1985

Boogaart, E. van den. Colonialism and migration . Dordrecht , Higham, MA, USA , 1986. vi, 303 p. : ISBN 90-247-3253-0 LC Card 85-21809 DDC 331.11/73 19
HD4875.A837 C65 1986 ***NYPL [JLE 86-3920]***

Book Club of California. Breadbasket of the world . San Francisco , 1984. 10 pamphlets : LC Card 87-100963 DDC 338.1/7311/09794 19
HD9049.W5 U414 1984

Book, Jeffrey. The one minute maniac / Jeffrey Book & Garrett Soden. Kansas City, Mo. : Andrews, McMeel & Parker, c1987. 140 p. : ill. ; 21 cm. ISBN 0-8362-1260-6 (pbk.) : LC Card 87-914 DDC 658.4/093 19
1. Time management - Anecdotes, facetiae, satire, etc. I. Soden, Garrett. II. Title. III. Title: 1 minute maniac.
HD69.T54 B66 1987

Böök, O. K. (Ole K.) Edström, N. F. (Nils Fritiof), 1918- Ekonomiordbok . Stockholm , c1984. 145 p. : ISBN 91-1-847152-8 : LC Card 84-253890
HB61 .E29 1984 ***NYPL [JFD 87-1265]***

The book of business anecdotes /. Hay, Peter. New York, N.Y. , c1988. viii, 296 p. ; ISBN 0-8160-1522-8 LC Card 87-20211 DDC 650/.0207 19
HF5351 .H34 1988

The Book of business knowledge / by the editors and experts of Boardroom reports. 3rd rev. ed. New York, N.Y. : Boardroom Books, c1987. p. cm. Includes index. ISBN 0-932648-83-5 : LC Card 86-30962 DDC 658 19
1. Business - Handbooks, manuals, etc. 2. Industrial management - Handbooks, manuals, etc. 3. Business enterprises - United States - Handbooks, manuals, etc. 4. Industrial management - United States - Handbooks, manuals, etc. 5. Corporations - Taxation - United States - Handbooks, manuals, etc. I. Boardroom reports.
HF5356 .B72 1987

BOOK SALES. see **BOOKSELLERS AND BOOKSELLING.**

Book series (Philippine Council for Agriculture and Resources Research and Development) . (no. 1985/20) International Seminar on Recent Improvements in Goat Production in Asia (1984 : Los Baños, Laguna, Philippines) Goat production in Asia . Los Baños, Laguna, Philippines , Taipei, Taiwan, Republic of China , 1985. viii, 186 p. : LC Card 86-200478
HD9438.G632 A785 1984

BOOK TRADE. see **BOOKSELLERS AND BOOKSELLING.**

Booker, Jon A. Jarnagin, Bill D. Financial accounting standards . Chicago, Ill. (4025 W. Peterson Ave., Chicago 60646) , 1986. xv, 1253 p. : LC Card 87-116311 DDC 657/.0218 19
HF5616.U5 B66 1986

BOOKKEEPERS. see **ACCOUNTANTS.**

BOOKKEEPING.
Barnes, John, 1913- How to learn basic bookkeeping in ten easy lessons /. New York , 1987, c1978. 168 p. : ISBN 0-06-463721-2 (pbk.) : LC Card 86-45638 DDC 657/.2 19
HF5635 .B258 1987

Huffman, Harry. General recordkeeping /. New York , c1988. x, 564 p. : ISBN 0-07-031054-8 LC Card 87-2982 DDC 657/.2 19
HF5635 .H8834 1988

Bookkeeping-accounting. Kornbluh, Elaine H. Barron's regents exams and answers. Woodbury, N.Y. , c1987. 318 p. in various pagings ; ISBN 0-8120-3185-7 (pbk.) : LC Card 87-403397 DDC 657/2/076 19
HF5661 .N4 1987

Bookkeeping and accounting. Lerner, Joel J. Schaum's outline of theory and problems of bookkeeping and accounting /. New York , c1988. 311 p. : ISBN 0-07-037231-4 (pbk.) LC Card 87-3800 DDC 657/.076 19
HF5661 .L46 1988

BOOKKEEPING - COMPUTER-ASSISTED INSTRUCTION.
Cooper, Robin, 1951- CABIS, computer-aided bookkeeping instruction system /. Reading, Mass. , c1987. p. cm. ISBN 0-201-11307-4 (user's manual) LC Card 86-32148 DDC 657/.2/02855369 19
HF5630 .C68 1987

BOOKKEEPING - EXAMINATIONS, QUESTIONS, ETC.
Kornbluh, Elaine H. Barron's regents exams and answers. Woodbury, N.Y. , c1987. 318 p. in various pagings ; ISBN 0-8120-3185-7 (pbk.) : LC Card 87-403397 DDC 657/2/076 19
HF5661 .N4 1987

BOOKKEEPING - PROBLEMS, EXERCISES, ETC.
Lerner, Joel J. Schaum's outline of theory and problems of bookkeeping and accounting /. New York , c1988. 311 p. : ISBN 0-07-037231-4 (pbk.) LC Card 87-3800 DDC 657/.076 19
HF5661 .L46 1988

BOOKS, REFERENCE. see **REFERENCE BOOKS.**

BOOKSELLERS AND BOOK TRADE. see **BOOKSELLERS AND BOOKSELLING.**

BOOKSELLERS AND BOOKSELLING - SOVIET UNION.
Bekleshov, Dmitriĭ. Reklama knig segodnia /. Moskva , 1986. 201 p. : LC Card 87-132362 DDC 659.1/90705 19
HF6161.B37 B44 1986

Bookstaber, Richard M., 1950-
Option pricing & investment strategies / Richard M. Bookstaber. Rev. ed. Chicago, Ill. : Probus Pub. Co., c1987. x, 233 p. : ill. ; 24 cm. Rev. ed. of: Option pricing and strategies in investing. 1981. Bibliography: p. 223-224. Includes index. ISBN 0-917253-81-7 : LC Card 87-17919 DDC 332.64/52 19
1. Put and call transactions. I. Bookstaber, Richard M., 1950- Option pricing and strategies in investing. II. Title. III. Title: Option pricing and investment strategies.
HG6042 .B65 1987

Option pricing and strategies in investing. Bookstaber, Richard M., 1950- Option pricing & investment strategies / Richard M. Bookstaber. Rev. ed. Chicago, Ill. , c1987. x, 233 p. : ISBN 0-917253-81-7 : LC Card 87-17919 DDC 332.64/52 19
HG6042 .B65 1987

Boom en el agro chileno? / [Miguel Acuña et al.]. Santiago de Chile : Grupo de Investigaciones Agrarias, Academia de Humanismo Cristiano, 1985. 123 p. ; 25 cm. (Serie Agricultura y sociedad . 2/85) Errata slip inserted. Includes bibliographies. LC Card 87-401452 DDC 338.1/0983 19
1. Agriculture - Economic aspects - Chile. I. Acuña, Miguel. II. Series: Serie Agricultura y sociedad (Santiago, Chile) , 85/2.
HD1877 .B66 1985

Boom ohne Arbeitsplätze /. Welzk, Stefan. Köln , c1986. 250 p. ; ISBN 3-462-01787-X LC Card 86-230211
HD5710.75.G3 W44 1986

Boon, Gerard Karel. El mercado de tecnología : con referencia a fibras sintéticas, telas y ropa / Gerard Karel Boon.1a ed. México, D.F. : Colegio de México, Programa de Ciencia y Tecnología para el Desarrollo, 1984, c1983. 715 p. : ill. ; 21 cm. Bibliography: p. 713-715. ISBN 968-12-0252-X LC Card 85-242124
1. Man-made fibers industry. 2. Nonwoven fabrics industry. 3. Clothing trade. 4. Technology transfer. 5. Man-made fibers industry - Mexico. 6. Man-made fibers industry - Colombia. I. Title.
HD9929.2.A2 B66 1984

Boon, Irene. Mannen in een vrouwenberoep : de positieverandering van vrouwen in de openbare bibliotheek / door Irene Boon. Den Haag : Nederlands Bibliotheek en Lektuur Centrum, 1984. 139 p. : ill. ; 30 cm. Thesis (doctoral)--Erasmus Universiteit Rotterdam, 1984. Bibliography: p. 131-134. ISBN 90-6252-426-5 : LC Card 84-243593
1. Women librarians - Netherlands. 2. Sex discrimination in employment - Netherlands. 3. Women - Employment - Netherlands. 4. Employment of men - Netherlands. 5. Public libraries - Netherlands. 6. Library employees - Netherlands. I. Title.
Z682.4.W65 B66 1984 ***NYPL [JLG 87-4]***

Boone /. Pickens, T. Boone (Thomas Boone) Boston , 1987. xii, 304 p., [8] p. of plates : ISBN 0-395-41433-4 : LC Card 86-27648 DDC 338.7/6223382/0924 B 19
HD9570.P53 A3 1987

Boone, Louis E.

Contemporary marketing. Marketing. Lesson 25, The green machine [videorecording] / Fountain Valley, CA , 1985. 1 videocassette (30 min.) : LC Card 87-705967 DDC 658.8 11
HF5415

The Great writings in management and organizational behavior /. New York , c1987. p. cm. ISBN 0-394-36099-0 LC Card 86-33900 DDC 658 19
HD31 .G74 1987

Management / Louis E. Boone, David L. Kurtz. 3rd ed. New York : Random House, Business Division, c1987. xv, 677, [48] p. : ill. (some col.) ; 24 cm. Rev. ed. of: Principles of management. 2nd ed. c1984. Includes indexes. Bibliography: p. N1-N22. ISBN 0-394-36305-1 : LC Card 86-27957 DDC 658 19
1. Management. I. Kurtz, David L. II. Boone, Louis E. Principles of management. III. Title.
HD31 .B619 1987

Principles of management. Boone, Louis E. Management / Louis E. Boone, David L. Kurtz. 3rd ed. New York , c1987. xv, 677, [48] p. : ISBN 0-394-36305-1 : LC Card 86-27957 DDC 658 19
HD31 .B619 1987

Boone, Mary E. Meyer, N. Dean. The information edge /. New York , c1987. xvii, 333 p. ; ISBN 0-07-041782-2 LC Card 86-222546 DDC 651.8 19
HF5547.5 .M495 1987

Böös, Ernst Nathorst- see Nathorst-Böös, Ernst, 1918-

Boos, Margarete. Die Wissenschaftstheorie Carl Mengers : biographische und ideengeschichtliche Zusammenhänge / Margarete Boos. Wien : H. Böhlau, 1986. xiii, 252 p. ; 21 cm. (Sozialwissenschaftliches Forum. 23) Bibliography: p. 227-252. ISBN 3-205-05044-4 LC Card 86-209140
1. Menger, Carl, 1840-1921. 2. Economists - Austria - Biography. 3. Austrian school of economists. I. Series: Sozialwissenschaftliches Forum (Cologne, Germany) , 23. II. Title.
HB101.M5 B6 1986

Boose, John H. Expertise transfer for expert system design / John H. Boose. Amsterdam ; New York : Elsevier, 1986. viii, 312 p. : ill. ; 25 cm. (Advances in human factors/ergonomics . 3) Includes index. Bibliography: p. 305-308. ISBN 0-444-42634-5 LC Card 86-9044 DDC 006.3/3 19
1. Expert systems (Computer science). 2. ETS (Computer program). 3. System design. 4. Personal construct theory. I. Title.
QA76.76.E95 B66 1986
NYPL [JSE 86-1840]

Booth, Douglas E. Regional long waves, uneven growth, and the cooperative alternative / Douglas E. Booth. New York : Praeger, 1987. 121 p. ; 25 cm. Bibliography: p. 109-115. Includes index. ISBN 0-275-92567-6 (alk. paper) : LC Card 87-2348 DDC 338.973 19
1. Long waves (Economics). 2. Regional economic disparities. 3. United States - Economic conditions - Regional disparities. 4. Economic development. I. Title.
HB3729 .B66 1987

Bopp-Schmehl, Annemarie, 1946-
Schatz, Heribert. Verbraucherinteressen im politischen Entscheidungsprozess /. Frankfurt/Main , New York , c1984. 275 p. ; ISBN 3-593-33293-0 LC Card 84-212024
HC290.5.C63 S33 1984

Technische Normung und Verbraucherinteressen im gesellschaftlichen Wandel / Annemarie Bopp-Schmehl, Uwe Heibült, Ulrich Kypke. Frankfurt am Main : Haag & Herchen, c1984. iii, 269 p. ; 21 cm. Bibliography: p. 258-269. ISBN 3-88129-834-7 : LC Card 85-119483
1. Consumers - Germany, West. 2. Standardization - Germany, West. 3. Social change. I. Heibült, Uwe. II. Kypke, Ulrich. III. Title.
HC290.5.C6 B66 1984

Bora, Ajit Kumar, 1942- Pattern of land utilization in Assam / Ajit Kumar Bora. Delhi : Manas Publications, 1986. x, 203 p. ; 25 cm. Bibliography: p. [189]-198. Includes index. ISBN 81-7049-012-X : LC Card 86-902810 DDC 333.73/13/0954162 19
1. Land use - India. 2. Land use - India - Assam. 3. Land use, Rural - India. 4. Land use, Rural - India - Assam. I. Title.
HD873 .B67 1986

Boratav, Korkut. Housing yearbook / prepared by Korkut Boratav, Hasan Ersel, Yakup Kepenek on behalf of Kent-Koop ; [translated by Sevin Osmay]. Ankara, Turkey : Kent-Koop, 1985. 32, [2] p. ; 24 cm. (Occasional papers / Kent-Koop . 1) Kent-Koop publications ; 48 Bibliography: p. [34]. LC Card 87-403323 DDC 363.5/09561 19
1. Housing - Turkey. 2. Housing policy - Turkey. 3. Real estate development - Turkey - Mathematical models. 4. Construction industry - Turkey - Mathematical models. I. Ersel, Hasan. II. Kepenek, Yakup. III. Kent-Koop (Society). IV. Series: Occasional papers (Kent-Koop (Society)) , 1. V. Title.
HD7358.25.A3 B67 1985

Bor'ba Kommunisticheskoĭ partii za provedenie kul'turnoĭ revoliutsii v derevne v gody kollektivizatsii /. Veselov, A. P. (Anatoliĭ Pavlovich) Leningrad , 1978. 127 p. ; LC Card 81-166878
HD1492.S652 R878 1978

Borchenko, N. (Nikolaĭ) Sel'skoe khoziaĭstvo v odinnadtsatoĭ piatiletke : osnovnye napravleniia razvitiia / N. Borchenko. Moskva : Profizdat, 1981. 93 p. ; 20 cm. (Bibliotechka sel'skogo profsoiuznogo aktivista, 0201-7644 . 5, 1981) LC Card 81-188371
1. Agricultural industries - Soviet Union. 2. Agriculture - Economic aspects - Soviet Union. I. Series: Bibliotechka sel'skogo profsoiuznogo aktivista , 1981, 5. II. Title.
HD1493.R9 B5 1981, no. 5 HD9015.S65

Borcherdt, Christoph. Der "Landverbrauch," seine Erfassung und Bewertung : dargestellt an einem Beispiel aus dem Nordwesten des Stuttgarter Verdichtungsraumes / Christoph Borcherdt, Stefan Kuballa. Stuttgart : Geographisches Institut der Universität Stuttgart, 1985. 196 p. : ill., maps (some col.) ; 24 cm. (Stuttgarter geographische Studien, 0343-7906 . Bd. 104) Two col. maps on folded leaves in pocket. Bibliography: p. 193-196. ISBN 3-88028-104-1 LC Card 87-136211 DDC 333.77/13/094347 19
1. Land use - Germany (West) - Stuttgart - Case studies. 2. Stuttgart (Germany) - Population density - Case studies. I. Title. II. Series.
HD660.S83 B67 1985

Borchorst, Anette. Arbejdsmarkedets kønsopdeling : patriarkalsk dominans eller kvinders valg? / Anette Borchorst. Aalborg : Aalborg universitetsforlag, 1984. 162 p. : ill. ; 21 cm. (Serien om kvindeforskning . nr. 15) Bibliography: p. 153-162. ISBN 87-7307-252-4 LC Card 85-106008
1. Sexual division of labor - Denmark. 2. Women - Employment - Denmark. 3. Patriarchy - Denmark. I. Title. II. Series.
HD6060.65.D4 B67 1984
NYPL [JFK 82-214 nr.15]

Borcz, Leszek. Przewodnik metodyczny do ekonomii politycznej dla doktorantów nieekonomistów / Leszek Borcz, Bronisław Miszewski. Wyd. 3., popr. i uzup. Gliwice : Dział Wydawnictw Politechnika Śląskiej, 1979. 79 p. ; 24 cm. (Skrypty uczelniane / Politechnika Śląska im. W. Pstrowkiego . nr. 853) Includes bibliographies. LC Card 81-182800
1. Economics - Outlines, syllabi, etc. I. Miszewski, Bronisław. II. Series: Skrypty uczelniane / Politechnika Śląska im. W. Pstrowskiego , nr. 853. III. Title.
HB74.5 .B67 1979

BORDEAUX REGION (FRANCE) - ANTIQUITIES, ROMAN.
Roman, Yves. De Narbonne à Bordeaux . Lyon , c1983. 333 p. : ISBN 2-7297-0200-8 : LC Card 84-179554
HF377 .R65 1983

Bordejé y Morencos, Fernando de. La Amenaza de guerra nuclear /. Madrid , 1985. 129 p. ; ISBN 84-7477-027-0 LC Card 86-100273 DDC 355/.0217 19
U263 .A44 1985 ***NYPL [JLD 86-2519]***

BORDEN, GAIL, B. 1801 - JUVENILE LITERATURE.
Wade, Mary Dodson. Milk, meat biscuits, and the terraqueous machine . Austin, Tex. , c1987. 49 p. : ISBN 0-89015-605-0 : LC Card 87-6813 DDC 338.7/664/00924 B 92 19
HD9010.B65 W33 1987

Border radio . Fowler, Gene, 1950- Austin, Tex. , c1987. p. cm. ISBN 0-87719-066-6 : LC Card 87-17975 DDC 384.54/53/09721 19
HE8699.M4 F68 1987

BORDER TAXES. see TARIFF.

Bordering on trouble : resources and politics in Latin America / edited by Andrew Maguire and Janet Welsh Brown.1st ed. Bethesda, Md. : Adler & Adler, 1986. xii, 448 p. : ill. ; 23 cm. Includes bibliographies and index. ISBN 0-917561-25-2 (pbk.) LC Card 86-7941 DDC 338.98 19
1. Environmental policy - Latin America. 2. Conservation of natural resources - Latin America. 3. Latin America - Economic policy. 4. Latin America - Economic conditions - 1945-. 5. Latin America - Politics and government - 1948-. 6. Latin America - Population. I. Maguire, Andrew. II. Brown, Janet Welsh.
HC125 .B594 1986 ***NYPL [JLE 86-4501]***

Bordo, Michael D. The long-run behavior of the velocity of circulation : the international evidence / Michael D. Bordo, Lars Jonung. Cambridge [Cambridgeshire] ; New York : Cambridge University Press, 1987. xiv, 181 p. : ill. ; 24 cm. Bibliography: p. 168-175. Includes indexes. ISBN 0-521-32633-8 LC Card 86-32628 DDC 332.4/14 19
1. Circular velocity of money - Econometric models. 2. Demand for money - Econometric models. 3. Money supply - Econometric models. I. Jonung, Lars. II. Title.
HG226.6 .B67 1987

Bordogna, Lorenzo. Runggaldier, Ulrich. Le politiche regionali del lavoro . Milano, Italy , c1986. 160 p. ; LC Card 86-169484
HD8376.5 .R93 1986

Boreham, Paul. Clegg, Stewart. Class, politics and the economy /. London , Boston , 1986. viii, 451 p. ; ISBN 0-7102-0452-3 : LC Card 85-8369 DDC 305.5 19
HT609 .C62 1986 ***NYPL [JLD 87-459]***

Borgan, Jens-Kristian. Dødelighet i yrker og sosioøkonomiske grupper 1970-1980 / av Jens-Kristian Borgan og Lars B. Kristofersen = Mortality by occupation and socio-economic group in Norway, 1970-1980 / by Jens-Kristian Borgan og Lars B. Kristofersen. Oslo : Statistisk sentralbyrå : I kommisjon hos H. Aschehoug og Universitetsforlaget, 1986. 217 p. : ill. ; 29 cm. (Statistiske analyser, 0333-0621 . 56) Summary in English. Bibliography: p. 104-105. ISBN 82-537-2339-3 : LC Card 86-231576
1. Mortality - Norway - Statistics. 2. Occupational mortality - Norway - Statistics. 3. Norway - Statistics, Vital. I. Kristofersen, Lars. II. Title. III. Title: Mortality by occupation and socio-economic group in Norway, 1970-1980. IV. Series: Statistiske analyser , nr. 56.
HB1445 .B66 1986

Borges Coelho, Antonio. see Coelho, Antonio Borges.

Borghesi, Antonio. La gestione dei rischi di azienda : economia e organizzazione, teoria e pratica / Antonio Borghesi ; presentazione di Giovanni Panati. Padova : CEDAM, 1985. 299 p. : ill. ; 24 cm. Bibliography: p. [17]-24. LC Card 86-214201
1. Risk management. I. Title.
HD61 .B65 1985

Borgmeier, Bernd, 1955- Der Einfluss verschiedener Preisbildungsmechanismen auf die gesamtwirtschfliche Beschäftigung / Bernd Borgmeier. Frankfurt am Main ; New York : P. Lang, c1984. 362 p. : ill. ; 21 cm. (Europäische

Hochschulschriften. Reihe V, Volks- und Betriebswirtschaft, 0531-7339 . Bd. 557 = vol. 557 = vol. 557) Originally presented as the author's thesis (doctoral--Fernuniversität Hagen, 1983) Bibliography: p. 349-362. ISBN 3-8204-5601-5 : LC Card 85-198888
1. Prices - Mathematical models. 2. Employment - Mathematical models. 3. Monetary policy - Mathematical models. I. Series: Europäische Hochschulschriften. Reihe V, Volks- und Betriebswirtschaft , Bd. 557. II. Title.
HB221 .B592 1984

Borgo reference guides .
(no. 1) Burgess, Michael, 1948- The state and province vital records guide /. San Bernardino, Calif. , 1988. p. cm. ISBN 0-89370-815-1 : LC Card 87-6312 DDC 929/.1/02573 19
HA38 .B87 1988

Borgogni, Daniela, 1949- Pavanello, Mariano, 1944- Antropologia ed economia dell'artigianato artistico . Milano, Italy , c1984. 183 p. : LC Card 84-147193
HD2346.I82 T676 1984

Borins, Sandford F., 1949- Investments in failure : five government enterprises that cost the Canadian taxpayer billions / Sandford F. Borins with Lee Brown. Toronto ; New York : Methuen, c1986. x, 175 p. ; 23 cm. Includes bibliography and index. ISBN 0-458-80340-5 (pbk.) : LC Card 87-142330 DDC 354.7109/2 19
1. Government business enterprises - Canada - Case studies. 2. Government lending - Canada - Case studies. 3. Business failures - Canada - Case studies. 4. Industry and state - Canada - Case studies. I. Brown, Lee, M.B.A. II. Title.
HD4005 .B67 1986

Borisov, Chavdar. Osnovnye prichiny i uslovii͡a vozniknovenii͡a PTP s t͡i͡azhelymi posledstvii͡ami, puti i metody ikh ustranenii͡a. Bulgarian. Osnovni prichini i uslovii͡a za vŭznikvane na PTP s tezhki posledstvii͡a, pŭtishta i metodi za t͡i͡akhnoto otstrani͡avane /. Sofii͡a , 1985. 95 p. : LC Card 87-101607
HF5614.5.S62 O7516 1985

Borisov, Ilii͡a. Deĭstvena organizatorska i ideĭno-vŭzpitatelna rabota za izpŭlnenie resheniiata na Fevruarskii͡a plenum na T͡SK na BKP /. Vratsa , 1985. 56 p. : LC Card 86-172762
HC403 .D45 1985

Borisov, I͡U. D. (I͡Uriĭ Dmitrievich)
Ėkonomicheskie problemy povysheni͡ia proizvoditel'nosti truda v stroitel'stve / I͡U.D. Borisov. Moskva : Stroĭizdat, 1985. 183 p. ; 20 cm. (Proizvoditel'nost' truda--samoe vazhnoe, samoe glavnoe) Bibliography: p. 183. LC Card 86-208622
1. Construction industry - Soviet Union - Labor productivity. I. Series: Proizvoditel'nost' truda--samoe vazhnoe, samoe glavnoe (Stroĭizdat (Firm)). II. Title.
HD9715.S72 B67 1985

Borjas, George J. The economic status of male Hispanic migrants and natives in the U. S. [microform] : a human capital approach / by George J. Borjas. Santa Barbara, Calif. : Community and Organization Research Institute, University of California, 1981. vi, 95 p. ; 28 cm. "Prepared for the Employment and Training Administration, U. S. Department of Labor." Bibliography: p. 91-95. Microfiche. Springfield, Va. : NTIS, 1983. 2 microfiches : negative ; 11 x 15 cm. (PB83-157958)
1. Hispanic Americans - Employment. 2. Hispanic Americans - Economic conditions. I. Title.
*NYPL [*XME-11,311]*

Borko, I͡Uriĭ Antonovich.
Murtazina, E. N. Problemy vali͡utnoĭ integrat͡sii v Evropeĭskom soobshchestve . Moskva , 1985. 75 p. ; LC Card 85-224384
HG3942.8 .M87 1985

Oskolkova, O. B. (Ol'ga Borisovna) Mirovai͡a prodovol'stvennai͡a problema i naselenie . Moskva , 1982. 77 p. ; LC Card 82-198944
HD9000.5 .O84 1982

Bormann, Ernest G. Howell, William Smiley. The process of presentational speaking /. New York , c19. p. cm. ISBN 0-06-042929-1 LC Card 87-8673 DDC 658.4/52 19
HF5718 .H7 1988

Born, Karl Erich. Wirtschafts- und Sozialgeschichte des Deutschen Kaiserreichs (1867/71-1914) / Karl Erich Born. Stuttgart : F. Steiner Verlag Wiesbaden, 1985. 175 p. ; 23 cm. (Wissenschaftliche Paperbacks. Sozial- und Wirtschaftsgeschichte, 0170-3579 . 21) Bibliography: p. [166]-175. ISBN 3-515-02419-0 LC Card 85-168335
1. Germany - Economic conditions - 19th century. 2. Germany - Economic conditions - 1888-1918. 3. Germany - Social conditions. I. Title. II. Series.
HC285 .B66 1985

Born, Verena. Montags biste sowieso geschafft . Hamburg , 1982. 167 p. : ISBN 3-88506-118-X (pbk.) LC Card 87-673006
HD6068.2.G3 M66x 1982

Born, Waldo L.
Harris, Jack C., 1945- 1985-86 real estate review and outlook /. College Station, Tex. [1985?] 22 p. ; LC Card 86-621364 DDC 333.33/09764 19
HD266.T4 H37 1985

A synopsis of Texas savings-and-loan associations' operations / by Waldo L. Born and John A. Valenta. College Station, Tex. : Texas Real Estate Research Center, College of Agriculture, Texas A&M University, [1986?] 38 p. : ill. ; 28 cm. (Technical report / Texas Real Estate Research Center) LC Card 86-622196 DDC 332.3/2/09764 19
1. Building and loan associations - Texas. I. Valenta, John A. II. Texas Real Estate Research Center. III. Series: Technical report / Texas Real Estate Research Center. IV. Title.
HG2153.T4 B67 1986

Börner, Dietrich. Betriebswirtschaftliche Entscheidungen bei Stagnation . Wiesbaden , c1984. xvi, 327 p. : ISBN 3-409-13303-8 LC Card 84-197990
HD30.23 .B486 1984

Borner, Silvio. Einführung in die Volkswirtschaftslehre / Silvio Borner. 3. neubearbeitete Aufl. Diessenhofen : Rüegger, c1983. 105 p. : ill. ; 21 cm. Bibliography: p. 105. ISBN 3-7253-0164-6 : LC Card 83-184501
1. Economics. 2. Switzerland - Economic conditions - 1918-. I. Title.
HB175 .B7315 1983

Borodkin, Alekseĭ Sergeevich. Uchet zatrat na osvoenie novoĭ tekhniki / A.S. Borodkin. Moskva : "Finansy i statistika", 1985. 142 p. : ill. ; 20 cm. Includes bibliographical references. LC Card 86-219761
1. Technological innovations - Soviet Union - Costs - Accounting. 2. Costs, Industrial - Soviet Union - Accounting. I. Title.
HF5686.C8 B597 1985

Boroson, Warren. Sell your own home! : up-to-date money-saving strategies that work / Warren Boroson. Tucson, AZ : Knight-Ridder Press, c1987. 238 p. : ill. ; 22 cm. Includes index. ISBN 0-89586-571-8 LC Card 87-4020 DDC 333.33/8 19
1. House selling. I. Title.
HD1379 .B645 1987

Borozdin, I͡U. V. Khozi͡aĭstvennyĭ mekhanizm i t͡senoobrazovanie /. Moskva , 1983. 77 p. ; LC Card 85-180519
HB235.S73 K47 1983

Borracha natural da Bahia. Borracha natural na Bahia . [Salvador] [1982] 130 p. : LC Card 87-403935 DDC 338.4/76782/098142 19
HD9161.B82 B186 1982

Borracha natural na Bahia : situação atual e perspectivas. [Salvador] : Bahia-Alcool, [1982] 130 p. : ill. (some col.) ; 30 cm. Spine title: Borracha natural da Bahia. At head of title: Governo Antônio Carlos Magalhães, Secretaria da Indústria e Comércio, Bahia-Alcool Empreendimentos Energéticos e Agroindustriais S.A. Bibliography: p. 129-130. LC Card 87-403935 DDC 338.4/76782/098142 19
1. Rubbber industry and trade - Brazil - Bahia (State). I. Bahia-Alcool Empreendimentos Energéticos e Agroindustriais S.A. II. Title: Borracha natural da Bahia.
HD9161.B82 B186 1982

Borrini, Héctor R. El proceso de colonización en el impenetrable chaqueño / Héctor R. Borrini, Enrique C. Schaller. Corrientes : Instituto de Investigaciones Geohistóricas, CONICET, FUNDANORD, 1981. 60 leaves : ill., maps ; 28 cm. (Cuadernos de geohistoria regional, 0325-8246 . no. 5) Limited edition of 500 copies. Bibliography: leaves 58-60. LC Card 86-204205 DDC 333.3/1/8234 19
1. Land settlement - Argentina - Chaco. 2. Land tenure - Argentina - Chaco. I. Schaller, Enrique C. II. Title. III. Series.
HD479.C47 B67 1981

Borrmann, Axel. Die Wettbewerbsposition natürlicher Rohstoffe : der Einfluss von Veränderungen der Öl- und Energiepreise, dargestellt am Beispiel Naturkautschuk : Studie im Rahmen des Schwerpunktprogramms "Ökonomik der natürlichen Ressourcen" der Deutschen Forschungsgemeinschaft / Axel Borrmann, Klaus Fertig. Hamburg : Verlag Weltarchiv, 1984. 226 p. : ill. ; 24 cm. (Veröffentlichungen des HWWA-Institut für Wirtschaftsforschung-Hamburg) Includes English summary. Bibliography: p. 219-226. ISBN 3-87895-250-3 LC Card 84-222130
1. Raw materials - Prices - Germany (West) - Econometric models. 2. Petroleum products - Prices - Germany (West) - Econometric models. 3. Fuel - Prices - Germany (West) - Econometric models. 4. Rubber - Prices - Germany (West) - Econometric models. I. Fertig, Klaus. II. Deutsche Forschungsgemeinschaft. III. Title.
HF1054.G4 B67 1984

Borsodi kismonográfiák, 0324-4563 .
(19) Dobosy, László. Gömörszőlős . Miskolc , 1984. 82 p., [16] p. of plates : ISBN 963-01-5552-4 LC Card 87-408021
HC300.292.G65 D63 1984

(22) Kamody, Miklós. Észak-Magyarország hírközlésének története /. Miskolc , 1985. 153 p., [3] leaves of plates : ISBN 963-01-6902-9 : LC Card 87-408020
HE6980.5 .K36 1985

Borsodi Szénbányák. 200 éves a borsodi szénbányászat, 1786-1986 /. [Miskolc , 1986] 223 p. : ISBN 963-02-4565-5 (Magy. nemz. bibl.) LC Card 87-150976
HD9555.H83 B6715 1986

Borszéki, Éva.
Élelmiszer-gazdaságunk versenyképessége : agrártermelésünk a világpiaci árak tükrében / Borszéki Éva, Mészáros Sándor, Varga Gyula. Budapest : Közgazdasági és Jogi Könyvkiadó, 1986. 284, [1] p. : ill. ; 20 cm. (Versenyképes mezőgazdaság, 0237-5001) Bibliography: p. 281-[285]. ISBN 963-221-590-7 : LC Card 87-148751
1. Agriculture - Economic aspects - Hungary. 2. Agricultural prices - Hungary. I. Mészáros, Sándor. II. Varga, Gyula, 1938-. III. Title. IV. Series.
HD1940.5 .B66 1986

Élelmiszergazdaságunk versenyképessége : mezőgazdasági ár- és külkereskedelmi tanulmány / Borszéki Éva, Mészáros Sándor, Varga Gyula. Budapest : Agrárgazdasági Kutató Intézet, 1985. 147 p. ; 29 cm. (Agrárgazdasági Kutató Intézet, 0209-5696 . 1985/12) Bibliography: p. 109-112. ISBN 963-491-213-3 LC Card 86-199073
1. Agriculture - Economic aspects - Hungary. 2. Agricultural prices - Hungary. I. Mészáros, Sándor. II. Varga, Gyula, 1938-. III. Series: Agrárgazdasági Kutató Intézet (Series) , 1985/12. IV. Title.
HD1940.5 .B67 1985

Bortis, Heinrich. Technologischer Wandel in Wirtschaft und Gesellschaft =. Freiburg, Schweiz , 1985. 316 p., [1] leaf of plates : ISBN 3-7278-0347-9 : LC Card 86-129382
HC79.T4 T436 1985

Bortoli, Michele. Il traffico nei centri storici / Michele Bortoli. [Lucca, Italy] : M. Pacini Fazzi editore, 1986. 236 p. : ill. (some col.) ; 27 cm. Bibliography: p. 229-231. LC Card 87-151755
1. Urban transportation - Italy - Lucca - Planning. 2. Historic districts - Italy - Lucca. 3. Urban transportation - Planning. 4. Historic districts. I. Title.
HE311.I82 L843 1986

Bortolotti, F. (Fabio) Conferenza internazionale sul tema Le zone franche industriali, nuove forme di investimento, l'America latina (1985 : Milan, Italy) Le zone franche industriali nei paesi emergenti . Milano, Italy , c1986. 207 p. ; LC Card 86-223193
HF1418 .C525 1985

Bortz, Jeff.
La estructura de salarios en México / Jeff Bortz, et al. 1a ed. Azcapotzalco, México, D.F. : Universidad Autónoma Metropolitana, Unidad Azcapotzalco, División de Ciencias Sociales y Humanidades : Secretaría del Trabajo y Previsión Social, 1985. 371 p. : ill. ; 20 cm. (Serie Economía) Biblioteca de ciencias sociales y humanidades Includes bibliographical references. ISBN

968-8402-76-1 LC Card 87-104886
1. Wages - Mexico. I. Series: Serie Economía (Azcapotzalco, Mexico). II. Title.
HD4981 .B67 1985

Industrial wages in Mexico City, 1939-1975 / Jeffrey L. Bortz. New York : Garland Pub., 1987. ix, 529 p. ; 24 cm. (South American and Latin American economic history) Originally presented as the author's thesis (Ph. D.)--University of California, Los Angeles, 1984. Bibliography: p. 521-529. ISBN 0-8240-1355-7 (alk. paper) : LC Card 87-8341 DDC 331.2/97253 19
1. Wages - Mexico - Mexico City - History - 20th century. I. Title. II. Series.
HD4981.Z9 M483 1987

El salario en México / Jeffrey Bortz. 1a ed. México, D.F. : Ediciones El Caballito, 1986. 198 p. : ill. ; 21 cm. (Economía) Fragua mexicana Includes bibliographical references. ISBN 968-612-519-1 LC Card 87-404064 DDC 331.2/972 19
1. Wages - Government policy - Mexico. 2. Wages - Mexico - History. 3. Prices - Mexico - History. I. Series: Economía (Ediciones El Caballito (Mexico City, Mexico)). II. Title.
HD4981 .B677 1986

Bortz, Paul I. Great expectations : a television manager's guide to the future / prepared by Paul I. Bortz, Mark C. Wyche, and James M. Trautman. Washington, D.C. : National Association of Broadcasters : Available through NAB Services, c1986. vii, 137 p., [3] folded leaves : ill. ; 28 cm. "April 1986." Bibliography: p. 133-136. ISBN 0-89324-012-5 (pbk.) LC Card 87-401854 DDC 384.55/453/068 19
1. Television broadcasting - United States. I. Wyche, Mark C. II. Trautman, James M. III. Title.
HE8700.8 .B66 1986

Borucki, Zenon. Osobowość a przystosowanie zawodowe marynarza / Zenon Borucki. Wrocław : Zakład Narodowy im. Ossolińskich, 1986. 174 p. : ill. ; 21 cm. (Seria Monografii / Gdańskie Towarzystwo Naukowe, Wydział I Nauk Społecznych i Humanistycznych, 0433-230X . nr. 81) Summary in English. Bibliography: p. 163-171. ISBN 83-04-02007-6 : LC Card 86-221057
1. Seamen. 2. Merchant marine. 3. Sociology, Industrial. I. Series: Seria monografii - Gdańskie Towarzystwo Naukowe, Wydział I Nauk Społecznych i Humanistycznych, nr. 81. II. Title.
HD8039.S4 B67 1986

Bosch, Ellie. Marktvrouwen van Bobo : het leven en werk van handelaarsters in de stad Bobo-Dioulasso in Boven-Volta / Ellie Bosch. Leiden : Onderzoeks- en Dokumentatiecentrum Vrouwen en Ontwikkeling, Rijksuniversiteit Leiden, Instituut voor Culturele Antropologie en Sociologie der Niet-Westerse Volken, 1983. viii, 179 p., [18] p. of plates : ill. ; 21 cm. (Serie Vrouwen en ontwikkeling in Boven-Volta) LC Card 86-212595
1. Rural women - Employment - Upper Volta - Bobo-Dioulasso. 2. Women in rural development - Upper Volta - Bobo-Dioulasso. 3. Rural women - Upper Volta - Bobo-Dioulasso - Social conditions. I. Title. II. Series.
HD6217.5.Z6 B633 1983

Bosch, Juan, 1909- Capitalismo tardío en la República Dominicana / [Juan Bosch]. 1a ed. Santo Domingo, República Dominicana : Editora Alfa y Omega, 1986. 238 p. : ill. ; 21 cm. LC Card 87-401709 DDC 330.97293/054 19
1. Dominican Republic - Economic conditions. 2. Capitalism - Dominican Republic - History. I. Title.
HC153.5 .B665 1986

BOSCH, ROBERT, 1861-1942.
Herdt, Hans Konradin, 1935- Bosch, 1886-1986 . [Stuttgart] [1986] 174 p., [88] p. of plates : ISBN 3-421-06324-9 LC Card 86-229723
HD9710.3.G44 R634 1986

Bosch-Siemens Hausgeräte GmbH.
Arbeitsgestaltung in der Serienfertigung . Frankfurt [am Main] , New York , c1984. 315 p. : ISBN 3-593-32733-3 LC Card 84-230390
HD58.8 .A73 1984

BOSCH-SIEMENS HAUSGERÄTE GMBH.
Arbeitsgestaltung in der Serienfertigung . Frankfurt [am Main] , New York , c1984. 315 p. : ISBN 3-593-32733-3 LC Card 84-230390
HD58.8 .A73 1984

Bosch, 1886-1986 . Herdt, Hans Konradin, 1935- [Stuttgart] [1986] 174 p., [88] p. of plates : ISBN 3-421-06324-9 LC Card 86-229723
HD9710.3.G44 R634 1986

Bösche, Bernd, 1955- Agrarsektorale und gesamtwirtschaftliche Integration in der Europäischen Gemeinschaft : eine vergleichende Analyse / Bernd Bösche. Frankfurt am Main ; New York : Lang, c1987. 226 p. : ill. ; 21 cm. (Europäische Hochschulschriften. Reihe V, Volks- und Betriebswirtschaft, 0531-7339 . Bd. 771 = vol. 771 = vol. 771) Bibliography: p. 209-221. ISBN 3-8204-9442-1 LC Card 87-407586 DDC 338.1/81/094 19
1. Agriculture - Economic aspects - European Economic Community countries. 2. Europe - Economic integration. I. Series: Europäische Hochschulschriften. Reihe V, Volks- und Betriebswirtschaft , Bd. 771. II. Title.
HD1920.5 .B67 1987

Boschken, Herman L. Strategic design and organizational change : Pacific Rim seaports in transition / Herman L. Boschken. Tuscaloosa, Ala. : University of Alabama press, c1989. p. cm. Bibliography: p. Includes index. ISBN 0-8173-0339-1 LC Card 86-14673 DDC 387.1/0979 19
1. Harbors - Pacific Coast (U. S.). 2. Harbors - Pacific Coast (U. S.) - Management. 3. Harbors - Government policy - Pacific Coast (U. S.). 4. Organizational change. 5. Strategic planning. I. Title.
HE554.A6 B67 1989

Boscolo, Fabrizio. Un Mestiere e un paese . Venezia , 1986. 172 p. : ISBN 88-317-4893-9 LC Card 86-219883
HD8039.S252 I85 1986

Bose, Christine E.
Hidden aspects of women's work /. New York , 1987. x, 380 p. ; ISBN 0-275-92415-7 (alk. paper) : LC Card 87-2449 DDC 331.4/133/0973 19
HD6060.5.U5 H53 1987

Jobs and gender : a study of occupational prestige / by Christine E. Bose. New York : Praeger, 1985. xiv, 206 p. ; 25 cm. Includes index. Bibliography: p. 195-201. ISBN 0-03-071692-6 (alk. paper) : LC Card 85-6305 DDC 305.4/3/00973 19
1. Women - Employment - United States. 2. Occupational prestige - United States. I. Title.
HD6058 .B67 1985 ***NYPL [JLE 86-3694]***

Bose, P. K. Graduate employment and higher education in West Bengal / P.K. Bose, B.C. Sanyal, S.P. Mukherjee. Paris : Unesco Press ; New Delhi : Wiley Eastern, 1983. vi, 288, [1] p. : ill. ; 22 cm. "A research project directed by Bikas C. Sanyal at the International Institute for Educational Planning." Bibliography: p. [289] ISBN 0-85226-078-4 (pbk.) LC Card 83-163900 DDC 331.11/423 19
1. College graduates - Employment - India - West Bengal. 2. Education, Higher - India - West Bengal. 3. Industry and education - India - West Bengal. I. Sanyal, Bikas C. II. Mukherjee, Sakti Pada. III. Title.
HD6278.I52 W473 1983
NYPL [JLD 86-2269]

Boseman, F. Glenn.
Cases in strategic management / Glenn Boseman, Arvind Phatak. New York : Wiley, c1988. ix, 476 p. : ill. ; 24 cm. Includes bibliographies. ISBN 0-471-85463-8 (pbk.) LC Card 87-24261 DDC 658.4/012 19
1. Strategic planning - Case studies. I. Phatak, Arvind V. II. Title.
HD30.28 .B67 1988

Schellenberger, Robert Earl. Strategic management . New York , c1986. xiii, 808 p. : ISBN 0-471-88059-0 : LC Card 85-9553 DDC 658.4/012 19
HD30.28 .S34 1986 ***NYPL [JLE 86-1559]***

Bosísio Júnior, Arthur. O Comércio e suas profissões . Rio de Janeiro , 1983. 127, [5] p. : LC Card 84-161651
HF5459.B7 C65 1983 ***NYPL [JLF 86-1408]***

BOSJESMEN. see SAN (AFRICAN PEOPLE)

Boskin, Michael J.
Modern developments in public finance . Oxford, UK , New York, NY, USA , 1987. xii, 259 p. : ISBN 0-631-15595-3 : LC Card 87-6568 DDC 336 19
HJ141 .M59 1987

Reagan and the economy : the successes, failures, and unfinished agenda / Michael J. Boskin ; foreword by Herbert Stein. San Francisco, Calif. : ICS Press, Institute for Contemporary Studies ; New York : Distributed by Kampmann, c1987. xvi, 301 p. : ill. ; 24 cm. Bibliography: p. [287]. Includes index. ISBN 0-917616-80-4 : LC Card 87-22544 DDC 338.973 19
1. United States - Economic policy - 1981-. 2. United States - Economic conditions - 1981-. 3. Supply-side economics - United States. 4. Reagan, Ronald. I. Title.
HC106.8 .B656 1987

Too many promises : the uncertain future of social security / Michael J. Boskin. Homewood, Ill. : Dow Jones-Irwin, c1986. xiv, 196 p. : ill. ; 24 cm. (A Twentieth Century Fund report) Includes index. Bibliography: p. 183-189. ISBN 0-87094-779-6 LC Card 86-70430 DDC 368.4/3/00973 19
1. Social security - United States. 2. Social security - United States - Evaluation. I. Title. II. Series.
HD7125 .B585 1986 ***NYPL [JLE 86-2970]***

Boškov, Vančo, 1934-1984. Osmanistische Studien zur Wirtschafts- und Sozialgeschichte . Wiesbaden , 1986. xi, 206 p., iv p. of plates : ISBN 3-477-02652-9 (Deut. Bibl.) LC Card 86-224062
HC492 .O85 1986

Bosquejo de política económica española . Campomanes, Pedro Rodríguez, Conde de, 1723-1803. Madrid , c1984. 182 p. ; ISBN 84-276-0691-5 : LC Card 86-153508
HB117.A2 C34 1984

Boss, Alfred. Ausgabenkürzungen im öffentlichen Sektor / Alfred Boss, Adrian Bothe. Tübingen : J.C.B. Mohr, c1987. xiii, 220 p. : ill. ; 24 cm. (Kieler Studien, 0340-6989 . 207) Bibliography: p. 214-220. ISBN 3-16-345212-4 LC Card 87-408337 DDC 336.43 19
1. Germany, West - Appropriations and expenditures. 2. Switzerland - Appropriations and expenditures. I. Bothe, Adrian. II. Title. III. Series.
HJ2109 .B67 1987

BOSS RULE. see CORRUPTION (IN POLITICS)

Bosshart, Louis. Technologischer Wandel in Wirtschaft und Gesellschaft =. Freiburg, Schweiz , 1985. 316 p., [1] leaf of plates : ISBN 3-7278-0347-9 : LC Card 86-129382
HC79.T4 T436 1985

Bossle, Lothar.
Allende und der europäische Sozialismus / Lothar Bossle. 2. Aufl. Würzburg : Naumann, [1981?] 146 p. ; 21 cm. Includes bibliographical references and index. Reprint.Originally published: Stuttgart : Seevald, c1975. ISBN 3-88567-026-7 (pbk.) LC Card 82-149701 DDC 983/.0646/0924 19
1. Socialism - Chile. 2. Socialism - Europe. 3. Chile - Politics and government - 1970-1973. I. Title.
HX197.A44 B67 1981 ***NYPL [HIF 86-2151]***

[Ordoliberalismus und christliche Soziallehre] Ordoliberalismus und christliche Soziallehre : die Versöhnungsidee der 80er Jahre ; Die postindustrielle Gesellschaft : zwischen "zurück zur Natur" oder "zurück zur Kultur" : zwei Vorträge / Lothar Bossle. München : Nymphenburger, c1983. 63 p. ; 20 cm. "Bd. 3"--P. 1. "Positionen ; Bd. 3"--Jacket. Includes bibliographical references. ISBN 3-485-03085-6 LC Card 84-174227
1. Economic policy. 2. Social policy. I. Bossle, Lothar. Postindustrielle Gesellschaft. 1983. II. Title.
HC55 .B64 1983

Postindustrielle Gesellschaft. 1983. Bossle, Lothar. [Ordoliberalismus und christliche Soziallehre.] Ordoliberalismus und christliche Soziallehre : die Versöhnungsidee der 80er Jahre ; Die postindustrielle Gesellschaft : zwischen "zurück zur Natur" oder "zurück zur Kultur" : zwei Vorträge / Lothar Bossle. München , c1983. 63 p. ; ISBN 3-485-03085-6 LC Card 84-174227
HC55 .B64 1983

The Boss's encyclopedia / by the editors and experts of Boardroom reports. Rev. ed. New York, N.Y. : Boardroom Classics, c1987. xxvi, 594 p. ; 29 cm. Includes bibliographical references and index. ISBN 0-932648-75-4 LC Card 86-30961 DDC 658 19
1. Business - Handbooks, manuals, etc. 2. Industrial management - Handbooks, manuals, etc. 3. Business enterprises - United States - Handbooks, manuals, etc. 4. Industrial management - United States - Handbooks, manuals, etc. 5. Corporations - Taxation - United

States - Handbooks, manuals, etc. 6. Businessmen - Life skills guides. I. Boardroom reports.
HF5356 .B735 1987

Bostadsbidragen : bilagor. [Stockholm] : Bostadsdepartementet : LiberFörlag, [1982] 207 p. : ill. ; 25 cm. Reports written by and for Bostadsbidragskommittén. "Bilagedel till Bostadsbidragskommitténs betänkande"--Verso t.p. "Ds Bo 1982:3." ISBN 91-38-72586-X LC Card 83-240044
1. Housing subsidies - Sweden. 2. Family allowances - Sweden. 3. Housing policy - Sweden. I. Sweden. Bostadsbidragskommittén. II. Sweden. Bostadsbidragskommittén. Bostadsbidragen.
HD7350.A3 B697 1982

Bostandzhian, V. B. (Vardan Babkenovich) Optimizatsiia otraslevykh sistem v sostave ėkonomicheskikh programm / V.B. Bostandzhian, G.M. Mkrtchian ; otvetstvennye redaktory A.M. Alekseev, IU.I. Maksimov. Novosibirsk : Izd-vo "Nauka," Sibirskoe otd-nie, 1982. 120, [1] p. : ill. ; 22 cm. At head of title: Akademiia nauk SSSR. Sibirskoe otdelenie. Institut ėkonomiki i organizatsii promyshlennogo proizvodstva. Bibliography: p. 117-[121] LC Card 83-107849
1. Siberia (R.S.F.S.R.) - Industries - Planning. 2. Siberia (R.S.F.S.R.) - Industries - Mathematical models. I. Mkrtchian, G. M. (Gagik Mkrtichevich). II. Alekseev, Anatoliĭ Mikhaĭlovich. III. Maksimov, IUriĭ Ivanovich. IV. Title.
HC337.R852 S5234 1982

Bostock, Frances. Jones, Geoffrey. The history of the British Bank of the Middle East /. Cambridge [Cambridgeshire] , New York , 1986- v. : ISBN 0-521-32322-3 (v. 1) LC Card 85-31359 DDC 332.1/5/0955 19
HG3270.2.A8 B755 1986 ***NYPL [JLL 87-87]***

Boston Associates. Dalzell, Robert F. Enterprising elite . Cambridge, Mass. , 1987. xviii, 298 p., [11] p. of plates : ISBN 0-674-25765-0 (alk. paper) LC Card 86-33649 DDC 338.4/7677/0097444 19
HD9858.L9 D35 1987

BOSTON REGION (MASS.) - INDUSTRIES - HISTORY - 19TH CENTURY.
Dalzell, Robert F. Enterprising elite . Cambridge, Mass. , 1987. xviii, 298 p., [11] p. of plates : ISBN 0-674-25765-0 (alk. paper) LC Card 86-33649 DDC 338.4/7677/0097444 19
HD9858.L9 D35 1987

Boston University. African Studies Center.
Gershenberg, Irving. Slack in Kenya's modern manufacturing sector /. Boston, MA (270 Bay State Rd., Boston 02215) , 1985. 15 leaves ; LC Card 87-404089 DDC 338.4/767/096762 19
HD70.K4 G47 1985

Nath, Kamla. Labor-saving techniques in food processing . Boston, MA (270 Bay State Rd., Boston 02215) , 1985. 26 leaves ; LC Card 87-155092 DDC 331.4/25 19
HD6073.A292 G256 1985

Somalia . Boston, MA [1983] vi, 164 p. : LC Card 87-108393 DDC 330.967/7305 19
HC850 .S655 1983

Bostyn, Anne-Marie. Leach, Donald. Future employment & technological change /. London , 1986. 264 p. : ISBN 1-85091-017-0 (pbk.) : LC Card 86-180981 DDC 331.12/5 19
HD6331 .L34 1986

Boswell, Terry. America's changing role in the world-system /. New York , 1987. xi, 300 p. : ISBN 0-275-92417-3 (alk. paper) : LC Card 86-25245 DDC 337.73 19
HC106.8 .A455 1987

Bosworth, Barry, 1942-
The economics of federal credit programs / Barry P. Bosworth, Andrew S. Carron, Elisabeth H. Rhyne. Washington, D.C. : Brookings Institution, c1987. xii, 214 p. : ill. ; 24 cm. Includes bibliographical references and index. ISBN 0-8157-1038-0 : LC Card 85-48205 DDC 336.3/44/0973 19
1. Government lending - United States. 2. Loans - United States - Government guaranty. 3. Credit control - United States. I. Carron, Andrew S. II. Rhyne, Elisabeth. III. Title.
HJ8119 .B67 1987

The Swedish economy /. Washington, D.C. , c1987. xvi, 338 p. : ISBN 0-8157-1042-9 : LC Card 86-29920 DDC 330.9485/058 19
HC375 .S977 1987

Bosworth, Derek L. Labour utilisation in Australia : an economic analysis / by Derek Bosworth. [Bedford Park, S. Aust.] : National Institute of Labour Studies, [1986] i, 205 p. : charts ; 30 cm. (Working paper series . no. 88) "September 1986." Bibliography: p. 201-205. LC Card 86-229498 DDC 331.12/5/0994 19
1. Labor supply - Australia. 2. Unemployment - Australia. 3. Underemployment - Australia. I. Series: Working paper series (National Institute of Labour Studies (Australia)) , no. 88. II. Title.
HD5850.A6 B67 1986

Bosworth, Seymour. Computer security handbook /. New York, N.Y. , c1987. p. cm. ISBN 0-02-915300-X LC Card 87-1735 DDC 658.4/78 19
HF5548.37 .C64 1987

Botbol, Maurice.
Madagascar . Paris , 1986, c1985. 184 p. : ISBN 2-905760-02-8 LC Card 87-123718
HC895 .M34 1986

Somalia, productive sectors of the economy /. Paris , 1985. 115 leaves : ISBN 2-905760-00-1 (pbk.) LC Card 87-124493 DDC 338.967/73 19
HC850 .S658 1985

Botchie, George. Employment and multinational enterprises in export processing zones : the cases of Liberia and Ghana / by George Botchie. Geneva : International Labour Office, 1984. iv, 74 p. ; 30 cm. (Working papers / Multinational Enterprises Programme . working paper, no. 30) Includes bibliographical references. ISBN 92-2-103770-3 (pbk.) : LC Card 86-213592
1. Export processing zones - Liberia. 2. Export processing zones - Ghana. 3. International business enterprises - Liberia. 4. International business enterprises - Ghana. 5. Labor supply - Liberia. 6. Labor supply - Ghana. I. Series: Working papers / Multinational Enterprises Programme , working paper no. 30. II. Title.
HF1417 .B68 1984

Botha, Henk. How to manage strikes through strategy : a guide for South African management / by Henk Botha. Moreletapark : PractitionIR Publications, c1986. vi, 101 p. : ill. ; 20 cm. ISBN 0-620-10384-1 LC Card 87-148504 DDC 658.3/154 19
1. Strikes and lockouts - South Africa - Management. 2. Personnel management - South Africa. I. Title.
HD5442.A6 B68 1986

Bothe, Adrian. Boss, Alfred. Ausgabenkürzungen im öffentlichen Sektor /. Tübingen , c1987. xiii, 220 p. : ISBN 3-16-345212-4 LC Card 87-408337 DDC 336.43 19
HJ2109 .B67 1987

Bothmer-Plates, Arno, Graf von. Die Internationale Finanzierungskrise /. Frankfurt am Main , c1985. 153 p. ; ISBN 3-7819-2536-6 LC Card 87-146671 DDC 336.3/435 19
HG3891.5 .I587 1985

Botifoll, Luis J. How Miami's new image was created / Luis J. Botifoll. Coral Gables, Fla. : (1531 Brescia Ave., Coral Gables 33124) : Institute of Interamerican Studies, Graduate School of International Studies, University of Miami, [1985?] 16 p. ; 22 cm. (Occasional paper / Institute of Interamerican Studies, Graduate School of International Studies, University of Miami . no. 1985-1) LC Card 87-124138
1. Miami (Fla.) - Economic conditions. 2. Miami (Fla.) - Economic policy. 3. Cuban Americans - Florida - Miami. I. Series: Occasional papers (University of Miami. Institute of Interamerican Studies) , no. 1985-1. II. Title.
HC108.M5 B68 1985

Botos, Balázs. Kérdőjelek iparunk fejlesztésében / Botos Balázs, Papanek Gábor. Budapest : Közgazdasági és Jogi Könyvkiadó, 1984. 391, [1] p. ; 19 cm. (Időszerű közgazdasági kérdések, 0324-3214) Bibliography: p. 369-[392] ISBN 963-221-392-0 : LC Card 85-156613
1. Hungary - Industries. 2. Industry and state - Hungary. 3. Industrial management - Hungary. I. Papanek, Gábor. II. Title. III. Series.
HC300.28 .B69 1984

Botswana. Central Statistics Office. Guideline for designing and executing small scale surveys in Botswana. [Gaborone] : Republic of Botswana, Central Statistics Office, Ministry of Finance and Development Planning, [1982] 53 p. in various pagings : ill., map ; 30 cm. Cover title. Bibliography: p. 2-8 (last group) LC Card 83-154943 DDC 304.6/0723 19
1. Demographic surveys - Botswana. 2. Social surveys - Botswana. 3. Economic surveys - Botswana. I. Title.
HB849.49 .B68 1982 ***NYPL [JLG 86-217]***

Botswana. Economic Planning Unit. Central Statistics Office. see **Botswana. Central Statistics Office.**

Botswana. Ministry of Finance. Central Statistics Office. see **Botswana. Central Statistics Office.**

Botswana. Statistics Office. see **Botswana. Central Statistics Office.**

Botswana Transport Sector I (Road Maintenance) (633-0073). [Botswana? : s.n., 1979?] 1 v. (various pagings) : ill. ; 27 cm. Cover title. Project paper and other papers prepared by the Agency for International Development. LC Card 86-148788
1. Roads - Maintenance and repair - Botswana. I. United States. Agency for International Development. II. Title: Transport Sector I (Road Maintenance) (633-0073).
HE367.B652 B67 1979

Le Botteghe di Firenze. Firenze : Alinari, c1985. 111 p. : ill. (some col.), ports. (some col.) ; 30 cm. ISBN 88-7292-062-0 LC Card 86-183352
1. Specialty stores - Italy - Florence - Pictorial works.
HF5429.6.I8 B67 1985

Bottesi, Valentin, 1933- Kombinatsplanung und Leistungssteigerung / Valentin Bottesi, Gertraude Hummel. Berlin : Dietz, 1984. 120 p. ; 20 cm. (Schriften zur sozialistischen Wirtschaftsführung) Includes bibliographical references. LC Card 84-217968
1. Industrial productivity - Germany, East. 2. Economic policy - Germany (East). I. Hummel, Gertraude. II. Title.
HC290.795.I52 B67 1984

Böttges, Norbert. Rationalisierung im Energiebereich : ein systemanalytischer Ansatz, dargestellt am Beispiel der Glasindustrie / Norbert Böttges.1. Aufl. Essen : W. Girardet ; Bielefeld : Vertrieb, Cornelsen-Velhagen & Klasing, 1984. 159 p. : ill. ; 21 cm. (Schriftenreihe zur Energieforschung) Based on the author's thesis (doctoral)--Rheinische Friedrich-Wilhelms-Universität Bonn. Bibliography: p. 131-137. Includes index. ISBN 3-7736-0106-9 LC Card 85-130852
1. Energy conservation. 2. Energy industries. 3. Energy policy. 4. Recycling (Waste, etc.). 5. Glass industry - Energy conservation. I. Title. II. Series.
HD9502.A2 B68 1984

Bottiglieri, Bruno. Immagini di industria in Italia . Roma , c1985. [128] p. : LC Card 86-145396
HC305 .I46 1985

Bottles, Scott L. Los Angeles and the automobile : the making of the modern city / Scott L. Bottles. Berkeley : University of California Press, c1987. xiii, 301 p. : ill. ; 24 cm. Bibliography: p. 255-294. Includes index. ISBN 0-520-05795-3 (alk. paper) LC Card 86-14660 DDC 388.4/1321/0979494 19
1. Transportation, Automotive - California - Los Angeles. 2. Street-railroads - California - Los Angeles. 3. Urban transportation - California - Los Angeles. 4. City planning - California - Los Angeles. I. Title.
HE5634.L7 B68 1987

The bottom line . Weinstein, Grace W. New York , c1987. 233 p. ; ISBN 0-453-00563-2 LC Card 87-11228 DDC 657 19
HF5616.U5 W44 1987

Boubekeur, Sid, 1952- L'habitat en Algérie : stratégies d'acteurs et logiques industrielles / Sid Boubekeur. Lyon : Presses universitaires de Lyon, c1986. 256 p. : ill. ; 24 cm. (Economie des changements technologiques) Bibliography: p. [241]-250. ISBN 2-7297-0272-5 : LC Card 86-217640
1. Housing - Algeria. 2. Housing policy - Algeria. 3. Labor and laboring classes - Dwellings - Algeria. I. Title. II. Series.
HD7372.4.A3 B68 1986

Bouchard, Jean-Anne. Les Effets des conditions de travail sur la santé des travailleuses . [Montréal] [1984] 230 p., [5] p. of plates : ISBN 2-920658-00-X : LC Card 86-158040
HD6067 .E34 1984

Bouchary, Jean. Les compagnies financières à Paris à la fin du XVIIIe siècle--tome II

[microform] ... / Jean Bouchary. Paris : Librairie des sciences politiques et sociales, 1941. 212 p. ; 25 cm. (Bibliothèque d'histoire économique) Includes bibliographical references. Microfilm. New York : New York Public Library, 1986. 1 microfilm reel ; 35 mm. (MN *ZZ-26,232)
1. Banks and banking - France - History. 2. Corporations - France - History. I. Title.
NYPL [*ZT-1711 no.28]

Bouchet, Michel Henri. The political economy of international debt : what, who, how much, and why? / Michel Henri Bouchet. New York : Quorum Books, 1987. xix, 219 p. : ill. ; 25 cm. Bibliography: p. [205]-207. Includes index. ISBN 0-89930-185-1 (lib. bdg. : alk. paper) LC Card 87-2474 DDC 336.3/435 19
1. Debts, External. I. Title.
HJ8015 .B68 1987

Bouchut, Y. (Yves) Nouvelles technologies et enjeux sociaux . Lyon , c1986. 230 p. : ISBN 2-7297-0279-2 : LC Card 86-187357
HC79.T4 N68 1986

Bouhet, Bernard. Bon, Frédéric, 1943- Résultats des élections aux conseils de prud'hommes par département . St. Martin d'Hères [France] [1982] 303 p. ; LC Card 84-152037
HD5555 .B65 1982

Boukēs, Sōtos D., 1933- Manatzment, hoi leitourgies tou kai ho cheirismos tou anthrōpinou paragonta : perilēptikes seminariakes sēmeiōseis / Sōtou D. Boukē. Athēna : Organismos Proōthēseōs Exagogōn, 1985. 58 p. : ill. ; 24 cm. Cover title. LC Card 86-160168
1. Personnel management. I. Organismos Proōthēseōs Exagogōn (Greece). II. Title.
HF5549 .B7727 1985

Boulding, Kenneth Ewart, 1910- Morality of the market . Vancouver, B.C., Canada , c1985. xxv, 601 p. ; ISBN 0-88975-074-2 (pbk.) : LC Card 86-158049 DDC 174/.4 19
HB72 .M56 1985

Boulware, Lemuel Richetts, 1895- What to do about communism in unions : statements before a senate Subcommittee / by L. R. Boulware, G. H. pfeif, W. J. Barron. [Schenectady, N.Y.?] : General Electric Employee and Plant Community Relations, [1952?] 62 p. ; 22 cm. "No. 2 in the series." Cover title. Caption title: Statement before the Senate Subcommitte on Labor-Management Relations.
1. Congress of Industrial Organizations. 2. Trade-unions and communism - United States. 3. Trade-unions - United States. 4. Communism - United States - 1917-. I. Pfeif, G. H. II. Barron, W. J. III. Title. IV. Title: Communism in unions. ***NYPL [JLD 86-247]***

The Boundaries of economics / edited by Gordon C. Winston, Richard F. Teichgraeber III. Cambridge ; New York : Cambridge University Press, 1988. xi, 122 p. ; 24 cm. (Murphy Institute studies in political economy) Includes bibliographies and index. CONTENTS. - Towards a rhetoric of economics / Donald N. McCloskey -- Three problems with the treatment of time in economics / Gordon C. Winston -- Hayek, the Scottish school, and contemporary economics / John Gray -- Reuniting economics and philosophy / Michael S. McPherson -- Economic methodology and philosophy of science / Daniel M. Hausman. ISBN 0-521-34450-6 LC Card 87-17772 DDC 330 19
1. Economics. I. Winston, Gordon C. II. Teichgraeber, Richard F. III. Series.
HB33 .B68 1988

Bour, Juan Luis. La terciarización del empleo en la Argentina. El sector de servicios a las empresas / Juan Luis Bour. Buenos Aires : Proyecto Gobierno Argentino, Programa de las Naciones Unidas para el Desarrollo, Organización Internacional del Trabajo, 1985. 117 p. ; 30 cm. (Estudios y documentos de trabajo sobre empleo, remuneraciones y recursos humanos) Includes bibliographical references. LC Card 87-123717 DDC 338.4/6/0982 19
1. Service industries - Argentina. I. Title. II. Series.
HD9985.A72 B68 1985

Bourbon, Pedro Peixoto e. Pereira, Francisco José Piteira. A cultura da vinha na região do Redondo /. [Lisbon] , 1983. 11, 4, 30, 21 leaves, [2] leaves of plates : LC Card 84-238378
HD9259.G7 P47 1983

Bourg, Claude, 1935- J'ai créé mon entreprise : les aventuriers de notre temps / Claude Bourg. [Paris] : J.C. Lattès, c1986. 223 p. ; 23 cm. LC Card 86-159708
1. New business enterprises - France. 2. Entrepreneur. I. Title.
HD62.5 .B68 1986

The bourgeois opposition to export-oriented industrialization in the Philippines /. Snow, Robert T. Diliman, Quezon City, Philippines [1983] 45 p. ; LC Card 85-196519 DDC 382/.3/09599 19
HC453 .S66 1983

BOURGEOISIE. see MIDDLE CLASSES.

Bourguignon, François.

Bourguinat, Henri.
La Crise de l'endettement international . Paris , c1986. 410 p. : ISBN 2-7178-1127-3 : LC Card 86-222862
HJ8017 .C74 1986

L'entreprise française face aux variations de change : dollar contre S.M.E.? / Henri Bourguinat, Michel Cazals, Philippe Ithurbide. Paris : Economica, c1985. vi, 123 p. : ill. ; 24 cm. Bibliography: p. [117]-119. ISBN 2-7178-0899-X : LC Card 85-190582 DDC 332.4/5 19
1. Foreign exchange problem. 2. Foreign exchange problem - France. I. Cazals, Michel. II. Ithurbide, Philippe. III. Title.
HG3815 .B68 1985 ***NYPL [JLE 86-494]***

Les vertiges de la finance internationale / Henri Bourguinat. Paris : Economica, c1987. 295 p. : ill. ; 24 cm. Bibliography: p. [271]-279. Includes indexes. ISBN 2-7178-1214-8 : LC Card 87-131661
1. International finance. I. Title.
HG3881 .B629 1987

Bourjol, Maurice. Energie et décentralisation /. Paris , 1984. 297 p. : ISBN 2-7178-0782-9 : LC Card 84-249613
HD9502.F72 E5334 1984

Bourne, Miriam Anne. A day in the life of a cross-country trucker / by Mariam Anne Bourne ; photography by Gayle Jann. Mahwah, N.J. : Troll Associates, c1988. 32 p. : col. ill. ; 24 cm. Follows a truck driver through his day as he communicates with the dispatcher, inspects and loads his truck for a cross-country trip, talks on the CB radio, and makes rest stops. ISBN 0-8167-1117-8 (lib. bdg.) : LC Card 87-13582 DDC 388.3/24/02373 19
1. Truck drivers - Juvenile literature. I. Jann, Gayle, ill. II. Title. III. Title: Cross-country trucker.
HD8039.M795 B68 1988

Bournique, Raymond A. County & postmaster postmarks of Wisconsin. Rev. & enl. ed. / by Raymond A. Bournique. Madison, WI (5401 Raymond Rd., Madison 53711) : Wisconsin Postal History Society, 1985. 12 p. : ill. ; 28 cm. (Bulletin / Wisconsin Postal History Society . no. 15) "Revision of 'County and postmaster postmarks of Wisconsin,' edited by Paul H. Segnitz and Ray Van Handel, Sr., originally published in February 1947"--P. [2] of cover. Cover title. LC Card 86-174748 DDC 769.56/7/09775 19
1. Postmarks - Wisconsin - History - 19th century. 2. Cancellations (Philately) - Wisconsin - History - 19th century. I. Segnitz, Paul H. County and postmaster postmarks of Wisconsin. II. Title. III. Title: County and postmaster postmarks of Wisconsin. IV. Series: Bulletin / Wisconsin Postal History Society , no. 15.
HE6185.U7 W573 1985

BOURSE DE PARIS.
Sassier, Philippe. Les Français à la corbeille /. Paris , c1985. 268 p. ; ISBN 2-221-04729-X : LC Card 86-126750 DDC 332.64/244 19
HG4583 .S27 1985

Boursier, François, 1947- L'économie sociale, mythes et réalités / François Boursier. Lyon : Chronique sociale, [1984] 108 p. : ill. ; 22 cm. (Collection "Alternatives économiques") Includes bibliographical references. ISBN 2-85008-045-4 : LC Card 84-154709 DDC 334/.0944 19
1. Cooperation - France. 2. Mutualism - France. 3. Cooperation - France - History. 4. Mutualism - France - History. I. Series: Collection "Alternatives économiques". II. Title.
HD3494 .B63 1984 ***NYPL [JLD 87-330]***

Boutefnouchet, Mostefa. Le socialisme dans l'entreprise : évolution de la gestion socialiste des entreprises en Algérie / Mostefa Boutefnouchet. Alger : Editions En.A.P., c1978. 253 p. ; 21 cm. Bibliography: p. 241-245. LC Card 84-207677
1. Management - Algeria - Employee participation. 2. Government business enterprises - Algeria - Management. I. Title.
HD5660.A4 B68 1978

Boutin, Raymond. Petit-Canal, une commune de la Guadeloupe au XIXe siècle / Raymond Boutin. Paris : L'Harmattan, c1983. 221 p. : ill. ; 22 cm. Bibliography: p. 209-216. ISBN 2-85802-251-8 LC Card 84-164720
1. Petit-Canal (Guadeloupe) - Population - History. I. Title.
HB3557.7.P47 B68 1983

Bouton, Lawrence. Arndt, Sven W. Competitiveness . Washington, D.C. , Lanham, MD , c1987. 120 p. : ISBN 0-8447-3625-2 (alk. paper) LC Card 87-1250 DDC 382/.0973 19
HF3031 .A83 1987

Bouvier, Jean, 1920- Bloch-Lainé, François. La France restaurée, 1944-1954 . Paris , c1986. 338 p. ; ISBN 2-213-01803-0 : LC Card 86-215777
HC276.2 .B58 1986

Bouzas, Carlos, 1937- Todo lo que usted quería saber sobre los bancos, pero temía preguntar / Carlos Bouzas. [Montevideo, Uruguay?] : Monte Sexto, 1986. 75 p. : ill. ; 20 cm. (Colección Temas. 4) LC Card 87-403156 DDC 332.1/09895 19
1. Banks and banking - Uruguay. 2. Banks and banking. I. Title.
HG2954 .B68 1986

Bovenkerk, Frank. Italiaans ijs : de opmerkelijke historie van Italiaanse ijsbereiders in Nederland / Frank Bovenkerk, Anne Eijken, Wiesje Bovenkerk-Teerink. Meppel : Boom, [1983?] 203 p. : ill. ; 21 cm. Bibliography: p. 199-201. ISBN 90-6009-551-0 LC Card 83-179690
1. Ice cream industry - Netherlands. I. Eijken, Anne. II. Bovenkerk-Teerink, Wiesje, 1941-. III. Title.
HD9281.N42 B68 1983

Bovenkerk-Teerink, Wiesje, 1941- Bovenkerk, Frank. Italiaans ijs . Meppel [1983?] 203 p. : ISBN 90-6009-551-0 LC Card 83-179690
HD9281.N42 B68 1983

Bovykin, Valeriĭ Ivanovich. Proizvoditel'nye sily i monopolisticheskiĭ kapital v Rossii i Germanii v kontse XIX-nachale XX vv. /. Moskva , 1986. 223 p. ; LC Card 87-159751
HD2859 .P76 1986

Bowen, Donald D. The Great writings in management and organizational behavior /. New York , c1987. p. cm. ISBN 0-394-36099-0 LC Card 86-33900 DDC 658 19
HD31 .G74 1987

Bowen, Howard Rothmann, 1908- Freedom and control in a democratic society /. New York , c1976. 107 p. ; ***NYPL [JLD 80-3590]***

Bowen, P. J. (Peter J.) Bell, G. J. (Graham J.) The business of transport /. Plymouth [Devon] , 1984. viii, 344 p. : ISBN 0-7121-2406-3 (pbk.) LC Card 84-170770 DDC 380.5 19
HE151 .B436 1984 ***NYPL [JLD 87-86]***

Bowerman, Bruce L. Computer modeling for business and industry / Bruce L. Bowerman, Richard T. O'Connell. New York : M. Dekker, c1984. vii, 219 p. : ill. ; 24 cm. (Statistics: textbooks and monographs. v. 59) Includes bibliographies and index. ISBN 0-8247-7296-2 LC Card 84-17063 DDC 519.5/0285425 19
1. Commercial statistics - Data processing. 2. Statistics - Data processing. I. O'Connell, Richard T. II. Title.
HF1017 .B655 1984 ***NYPL [JSE 86-623]***

Bowers, Barbara L. (Barbara Lynn), 1948- Alexandrides, Costas G. Countertrade . New York , c1987. xx, 235 p. ; ISBN 0-471-84711-9 LC Card 87-12966 DDC 382 19
HF1414.3 .A44 1987

Bowers, Cathy.
Newman, Anne, 1951- Foreign investment in South Africa and Namibia . Washington, D.C. [1984] ii, 279 p. ; ISBN 0-931035-00-7 (pbk.) LC Card 85-130985 DDC 332.6/73/0968 19
HG5851.A3 N49 1984 ***NYPL [Sc F 85-173]***

U. S. and Canadian investment in South Africa and Namibia : a directory of U. S. and Canadian corporations operating in South Africa and Namibia with a survey of the 105 largest U. S. commercial bank holding companies and their practices and policies on

lending to South Africa / by Cathy Bowers and Alison Cooper. Washington, D.C. : Investor Responsibility Research Center, c1986. xiii, 238 p. ; 28 cm. "May 1986." Includes index. ISBN 0-931035-10-4 (pbk.) LC Card 86-209149 DDC 338.8/8973/068025 19
1. Investments, Foreign - South Africa - Directories. 2. Investments, Foreign - Namibia - Directories. 3. Corporations, American - South Africa - Directories. 4. Corporations, American - Namibia - Directories. 5. Corporations, Canadian - South Africa - Directories. 6. Corporations, Canadian - Namibia - Directories. 7. Banks and banking, American - South Africa - Directories. I. Cooper, Alison. II. Title.
HG5851.A3 B69 1986

Bowers, Newton L., 1933- Actuarial mathematics /. Itasca, Ill. , 1986. xxiii, 624 p. ; ISBN 0-938959-10-7 LC Card 86-61747 DDC 368/.01 19
HG8781 .A26 1986

Bowers, Thomas A. Fletcher, Alan D. Fundamentals of advertising research /. Belmont, Calif. , c1988. xiii, 322 p. : ISBN 0-534-08454-0 LC Card 87-23106 DDC 659.1/072 19
HF5814 .F57 1988

Bowes, Lee, 1951- No one need apply : getting and keeping the best workers / Lee Bowes. Boston, Mass. : Harvard Business School Press, c1987. xiv, 268 p. ; 22 cm. Includes bibliographical references and index. ISBN 0-87584-149-X (alk. paper) LC Card 86-29512 DDC 658.3/11 19
1. Recruiting of employees. 2. Employee selection. I. Title.
HF5549.5.R44 B69 1987

Bowie, Norman E., 1942- Equal opportunity /. Boulder , 1988. viii, 200 p. ; ISBN 0-8133-0567-5 (pbk. : alk. paper) LC Card 87-7253 DDC 331.13/3/0973 19
HF5549.5.A34 E7 1988

Bowker (R. R.) Company, New York. Bowker's complete sourcebook of personal computing 1985. New York , c1984. lxviii, 1050 p. ; ISBN 0-8352-1931-3 (pbk.) : LC Card 84-20460 DDC 001.64 19
QA76.5 .B669 1984 ***NYPL [JSE 86-443]***

Bowker/Bantam 1984 complete sourcebook of personal computing. Bowker's complete sourcebook of personal computing 1985. New York , c1984. lxviii, 1050 p. ; ISBN 0-8352-1931-3 (pbk.) : LC Card 84-20460 DDC 001.64 19
QA76.5 .B669 1984 ***NYPL [JSE 86-443]***

Bowker's complete sourcebook of personal computing 1985. New York : Bowker, c1984. lxviii, 1050 p. ; 23 cm. Includes index. Rev. ed. of: Bowker/Bantam 1984 complete Sourcebook of personal computing. ISBN 0-8352-1931-3 (pbk.) : LC Card 84-20460 DDC 001.64 19
1. Microcomputers - Catalogs. 2. Computer industry - Directories. I. Bowker (R. R.) Company, New York. II. Bowker/Bantam 1984 complete sourcebook of personal computing. III. Title: Complete sourcebook of personal computing 1985. IV. Title: Sourcebook of personal computing.
QA76.5 .B669 1984 ***NYPL [JSE 86-443]***

Bowler, Susan M. O'Connor, Jessie Lloyd, 1904- Harvey and Jessie . Philadelphia , 1988. p. cm. ISBN 0-87722-519-2 (alk. paper) LC Card 87-21737 DDC 322/.2/0922 B 19
HD8073.A1 O25 1988

Bowles, Samuel. Democracy and capitalism : property, community, and the contradictions of modern social thought / Samuel Bowles, Herbert Gintis. New York : Basic Books, c1986. x, 244 p. ; 25 cm. Includes bibliographical references and index. ISBN 0-465-06052-8 : LC Card 85-47991 DDC 321.8 19
1. Capitalism. 2. Marxian economics. I. Gintis, Herbert. II. Title.
JC423 .B76 1986 ***NYPL [JLE 86-2928]***

Bowling Green State University. Social Philosophy & Policy Center. Vanberg, Viktor. Morality and economics . New Brunswick [N.J.] , 1987. p. cm ISBN 0-912051-19-1 (pbk.) LC Card 87-19213 DDC 174/.26 19
HB72 .V268 1987

Bowman, Ann O'M., 1948- The resurgence of the states / Ann O'M. Bowman, Richard C. Kearney. Englewood Cliffs, N.J. : Prentice-Hall, c1986. x, 269 p. : ill., maps ; 23 cm. Includes bibliographies and indexes. ISBN 0-13-774969-4 (pbk.) LC Card 85-19213 DDC 353.9 19
1. State governments. 2. State-local relations - United States. 3. Federal government - United States. I. Kearney, Richard C. II. Title.
JK2408 .B68 1986 ***NYPL [JLE 86-4496]***

Bowman, Arthur G. California real estate principles. 4th ed. / Arthur G. Bowman, Robert J. Bond. Glenview, Ill. : Scott, Foresman, c1987. xiv, 368 p. : ill. ; 29 cm. Bond's name appears first on the earlier edition. Includes index. ISBN 0-673-16667-8 : LC Card 86-25985 DDC 333.33/09794 19
1. Real estate business - California. I. Bond, Robert J., 1934-. II. Title.
HD266.C2 B68 1987

Bowman, Joel P. Business report writing / Joel P. Bowman, Bernadine P. Branchaw. 2nd ed. Chicago : Dryden Press, c1988. xvi, 607 p. : ill. ; 24 cm. Includes index. ISBN 0-03-013244-4 LC Card 87-15438 DDC 808/.066651 19
1. Business report writing. I. Branchaw, Bernadine P. II. Title.
HF5719 .B68 1988

Bowman, Linda. Platt, Barbara. Residential real estate . Austin, Tex. , c1987. 206 p. : ISBN 0-941089-17-7 (lib. bdg.) LC Card 87-60697 DDC 332.63/243 19
HD1379 .P57 1987

Bowman, Thomas F. Finding your best place to live in America / by Thomas F. Bowman, George A. Giuliani, M. Ronald Mingé. New York : Red Lion Books, c1981. xiii, 337 p. : ill., maps ; 23 cm. Bibliography: p. 313-322. "3rd printing, March 1982." ISBN 0-940162-00-8 (pbk.) : LC Card 81-51506 DDC 973.927 19
1. Cities and towns - United States. 2. Quality of life - United States. 3. United States - Economic conditions - 1971-1981. 4. United States - Social conditions - 1960-. I. Giuliani, George A., 1938-. II. Mingé, M. Ronald. III. Title.
HT123 .B665 ***NYPL [Pub. Cat. 86-574]***

Bowring, Joseph. Competition in a dual economy / Joseph Bowring. Princeton, N.J. : Princeton University Press, c1986. vi, 208 p. ; 23 cm. Includes index. Bibliography: p. [193]-204. ISBN 0-691-04234-9 (alk. paper) : LC Card 85-43271 DDC 338.6/048/0724 19
1. Competition - Mathematical models. 2. Industrial organization (Economic theory) - Mathematical models. I. Title.
HD41 .B687 1986 ***NYPL [JLD 86-3314]***

BOXES, WOODEN - AFRICA, EASTERN - MARKETING.
Export promotion of furniture/joinery products from east/southern Africa. Addis Ababa [1983] 34 p. in various pagings : LC Card 86-981008
HD9773.A472 E96 1983

Boxhill, Walton O. 1981 Census information on place of birth, citizenship, and immigration : some facts and figures / by Walton O. Boxhill, Robert McCrea, Michael Crew = Statistiques du recensement de 1981 sur le lieu de naissance la citoyenneté et l'immigration : quelques faits et chiffres / par Walton O. Boxhill, Robert McCrea, Michael Crew. Ottawa : Minister of Supply and Services Canada, c1986. 67, [4] p. : ill. ; 28 cm. Parallel text in English and French. At head of title: Statistics Canada. Housing, Family and Social Statistics Division. "Catalogue 99-952." Bibliography: p. [69] ISBN 0-660-52864-9 (pbk.) : LC Card 86-192857
1. Canada - Census, 1981. 2. Canada - Foreign population. I. McCrea, Robert. II. Crew, Michael. III. Title. IV. Title: Statistique du recensement de 1981 sur le lieu de naissance la citoyenneté et l'immigration.
HA741.5 1981f

Boy, L. (Laurence) Sidérurgie et droit de crise /. Paris , c1983. 207 p. ; ISBN 2-13-038363-7 : LC Card 84-128216
HD9522.6 .S53 1983

Boyarski, Aron Yakovlevich. see **Boiarskiĭ, Aron IAkovlevich, 1906-**

Boycott and blacklist . Sarna, A. J. Totowa, N.J. , 1986. xiv, 270 p. : ISBN 0-8476-7489-4 : LC Card 86-1891 DDC 337.5694/0174927 19
HF1610.Z4 I87 1986
NYPL [*PXLB 86-6444]

BOYCOTTS - NEW YORK - ROCHESTER.
Lapides, Kenneth. The battle of the boycott . New York, N.Y. , 1974. 22 p., [3] p. of plates : LC Card 87-125953 DDC 331.89/3 19
HD5325.C62 1972 .L36 1974

Boyd, Elizabeth C. Cohen, Eli B. Business BASIC for the IBM PC with cases /. St. Louis , 1987. xxiv, 634 p. : ISBN 0-8016-1244-6 (pbk.) LC Card 86-23100 DDC 005.2/165 19
HF5548.5.B3 C64 1987

Boyd, Rosalind E. International labour and the Third World . Aldershot, Hants, England , c1987. xii, 283 p. ; ISBN 0-566-00971-4 : LC Card 86-31791 DDC 331/.09172/4 19
HD8943 .I55 1987

Boye, Greta R. Lord, Montague J. Market price models for Latin America's major commodity exports /. Washington, D.C. [1986] vii, 219 p. : LC Card 87-115208 DDC 338.5/2/098 19
HD9014.A2 L67 1986

Boyer, Marcel. Riscophobie et étalement à moyenne constante : analyse et applications / par Marcel Boyer, Georges Dionne. Montréal : Université de Montréal, [1982] 32 p. : ill. ; 28 cm. (Cahier / Département de sciences économiques, 0709-9231 . 8229) Publication / Centre de recherche sur les transports ; [hash mark] 257 Summary in English. Bibliography: p. 32. LC Card 85-160864
1. Risk - Mathematical models. I. Dionne, Georges. II. Series: Cahier (Université de Montréal. Département de sciences économiques) , 8229. III. Title.
HB615 .B68 1982

Boyer, Robert.
Capitalismes fin de siècle /. Paris , c1986. 268 p. : ISBN 2-13-039425-6 : LC Card 86-231136
HC106.8 .C364 1986

La Flexibilité du travail en Europe . Paris , 1986. 330 p. : ISBN 2-7071-1598-3 : LC Card 86-173845
HD8376.5 .F57 1986

La théorie de la régulation : une analyse critique / Robert Boyer. Paris : La Découverte, 1986. 142 p. : ill. ; 21 cm. (Agalma) Bibliography: p. [137]-142. ISBN 2-7071-1628-9 : LC Card 87-108410
1. France - Economic policy - 1981-. 2. Equilibrium (Economics). I. Title. II. Series.
HC276.3.B69 1986

Boykin, James H., 1936- Ventolo, William L. Fundamentals of real estate appraisal . Chicago , c1987. 75 p. : ISBN 0-88462-571-0 (pbk.) LC Card 86-29715 DDC 333.33/2 19
HD1387 .V45 1987

BOYS - EMPLOYMENT. see YOUTH - EMPLOYMENT; CHILDREN - EMPLOYMENT.

Boza Monteverde, José. Espinoza Claudio, César. Alcabalas y protesta popular . Lima, Perú , 1981. iii, 111 p., [1] leaf of plates : LC Card 82-146025
HJ5715.P4 E86 1981

Bozem, Karlheinz. Controlling in Versorgungsunternehmen / Karlheinz Bozem. München : Oldenbourg, 1986. xiv, 468, 10 p. : ill. ; 21 cm. (Schriftenreihe des Energiewirtschaftlichen Instituts . Bd. 31) Bibliography: p. 449-468. ISBN 3-486-26236-X LC Card 87-135246 DDC 363.6/2/0681 19
1. Public utilities - Finance. 2. Controllership. I. Title. II. Series.
HD2763 .B66 1986

Bozeman, Barry. All organizations are public : bridging public and private organizational theories / Barry Bozeman.1st ed. San Francisco : Jossey-Bass, 1987. xix, 184 p. : ill. ; 24 cm. (Jossey-Bass management series) Bibliography: p. 155-174. Includes index. ISBN 1-555-42036-2 (alk. paper) LC Card 86-27699 DDC 302.3/5 19
1. Organizational effectiveness. 2. Organization. 3. Public administration. 4. Industry and state. 5. Business and politics. I. Title. II. Series.
HD58.9 .B69 1987

Bozonnet, Rémy. Sainte-Foy-Tarentaise, une montagne pour des hommes / Rémy Bozonnet, Yves Bravard. [Saint-Julien-Montdenis] : R. Bozonnet et Y. Bravard, [1984] 192 p. : ill. ; 24 cm. (Trésors de la Savoie) Bibliography: p. 190-191. LC Card 85-206948
1. Sainte-Foy-Tarentaise (France) - Economic conditions. 2. Sainte-Foy-Tarentaise (France) - Industries - History. 3. Sainte-Foy-Tarentaise (France) -

History. I. Bravard, Yves. II. Title.
HC278.S34 B69 1984

BPA cadernos.
Indicadores económicos e financeiros da Central de Balanços (1978-1980). [Porto] [1982] 204 p. : LC Card 85-166692
HC394.5.C7 I53 1982

Pina, Amílcar. Análise de empresas em inflação . [Porto] , 1985. 142 p. : LC Card 86-174401
HF5658.5 .P56 1985

Sousa, Fernando Freire de. A adesão de Portugal à CEE . [Porto] [1985] 96 p. ; LC Card 86-174408
HF2236 .S68 1985

Bra affärer med datorer? : slutrapport från studier av datoranvändning i varuhandeln / Bo Hedberg ... [et al.]. [Stockholm] : LiberFörlag, 1982. 176 p. : ill. ; 21 cm. "Ds A 1982:7"--Cover. Bibliography: p. 173-176. ISBN 91-38-06989-X LC Card 83-235564
1. Retail trade - Sweden - Data processing. 2. Wholesale trade - Sweden - Data processing. I. Hedberg, Bo, 1944-.
HF5429.15 .B72 1982

Bra Kanon, Denis, 1936- Développement ou appauvrissement / Denis Bra Kanon ; préface de Félix Houphouet-Boigny ; postface de Jean-Pierre Daloz. Paris : Economica, c1985. 188 p. : ill. ; 24 cm. (Collection Bibliothèque des matières premières) Originally presented as the author's thesis (doctoral)--Aix-Marseille II, 1980? Bibliography: p. [183]-185. ISBN 2-7178-0962-7 : LC Card 86-177676
1. Developing countries - Foreign economic relations. 2. International economic relations. 3. Foreign exchange. I. Series: Bibliothèque des matières premières. II. Title.
HF1413 .B72 1985

Braakman, T. C. Sociale zekerheid in Nederland / T. Braakman, M.P.C.M. van Schendelen, R.Ph. Schotten. Utrecht : Spectrum, 1984. 199 p. : ill. ; 19 cm. (Aula pocket . 741) Includes index. Bibliography: p. 188-193. ISBN 90-274-5513-9 : LC Card 85-110890
1. Social security - Netherlands. 2. Social security - Law and legislation - Netherlands. 3. Public welfare - Netherlands. 4. Public welfare - Law and legislation - Netherlands. I. Schendelen, M. P. C. M. van, 1944-. II. Schotten, R. Ph. III. Title.
HD7192 .B73 1984 ***NYPL [JLC 86-295]***

Braat, Leon C. Economic-ecological modeling /. Amsterdam ; New York : x, 329 p. : ISBN 0-444-70298-9 LC Card 87-20048 DDC 333.7/0724 19
HC79.E5 E267 1987

Braathu, Jan. Diversification strategies and security-of-supply : Western European gas imports and Norway / Jan Braathu. Oslo : Norsk utenrikspolitisk institutt, [1984?] 74 p. ; 30 cm. (NUPI rapport, 0800-000X . nr. 88 (okt. 1984)) Cover title. Includes bibliographical references. LC Card 85-129223 DDC 382/.42285/094 19
1. Gas industry - Europe. 2. Power resources - Europe. 3. Energy policy - Europe. 4. Gas industry - Norway. I. Series: Oslo. Norsk utenrikspolitisk institutt. NUPI-rapport, nr. 88. II. Title.
HD9581.E8552 B7 1984
NYPL [JLM 78-136 no.88]

Brabant (Belgium)
L'Information financière . Bruxelles , 1983. 220 p. ; ISBN 2-8027-0298-X LC Card 84-104169
HG151.5 .I56 1983

BRABANT (BELGIUM) - INDUSTRIES - DIRECTORIES.
Adresboek "Bedrijven in Vlaams-Brabant" =. Vilvoorde , 1985. lxi, 186, 62, 63 p. : LC Card 87-111619
HC317.B7 A37 1985

Brabant, Jozef M. van.
Adjustment, structural change, and economic efficiency : aspects of monetary cooperation in Eastern Europe / Jozef M. van Brabant. Cambridge [Cambridgeshire] ; New York : Cambridge University Press, 1987. xviii, 480 p. ; 22 cm. (Soviet and East European studies) Bibliography: p. 447-468. Includes index. ISBN 0-521-33455-1 LC Card 87-785 DDC 332.4/947 19
1. Finance - Europe, Eastern. 2. Monetary policy - Europe, Eastern. 3. Investments - Europe, Eastern. 4. Europe, Eastern - Commercial policy. 5. Europe, Eastern - Economic integration. 6. Council for Mutual Economic Assistance. I. Title.
HG186.E82 B7 1987

Bracchi, G. (Giampio), 1944- IFIP TC 8/WG 8.4 Working Conference on Methods and Tools for Office Systems (1986 : Pisa, Italy) Office systems . Amsterdam ; New York : xi, 347 p. : ISBN 0-444-70241-5 (U. S.) LC Card 87-8916 DDC 651.8 19
HF5548.2 .I285 1986

Braceros haitianos en la República Dominicana /. Báez Evertsz, Franc, 1948- [Santo Domingo] , c1986. 354 p. : LC Card 87-401177 DDC 331.6/2/729407293 19
HD8218.5 .B34 1986

Braceros italianos para México . Zilli Manica, José Benigno. Xalapa, México , 1986. 93 p., [6] p. of plates : ISBN 968-8340-45-6 LC Card 87-400059
HD8118.5.I83 Z55 1986

Brach, Wolfgang. Säumt keine Minute! . Mannheim , c1986. xiii, 683 p. : ISBN 3-923003-36-6 LC Card 87-115249 DDC 331/.0943/46 19
HD8460.M35 S28 1986

Brada, Josef C., 1942- Socialist agriculture in transition . Boulder, Colo. , 1986. ix, 445 p. : ISBN 0-8133-7344-1 : LC Card 86-28995 DDC 338.1/0947 19
HD1917 .S62 1986

Bradford, David F. Issues in the measurement and interpretation of effective tax rates / David Bradford, Charles Stuart. Cambridge, MA (1050 Massachusetts Ave., Cambridge 02138) : National Bureau of Economic Research, [1986] 21 p. : ill. ; 28 cm. (Working paper series / National Bureau of Economic Research . no. 1975) Bibliography: p. 19-21. LC Card 87-108421 DDC 336.24/26 19
1. Investments - Taxation. I. Stuart, Charles. II. Series: Working paper series / National Bureau of Economic Research , no. 1975. III. Title.
HJ4631 .B73 1986

Bradford, Helen. A taste of freedom : the ICU in rural South Africa, 1924-1930 / Helen Bradford. New Haven : Yale University Press, 1987. xvi, 364 p., [2] p. of plates : ill., maps, ports. ; 25 cm. Bibliography: p. [339]-354. Includes index. ISBN 0-300-03873-9 LC Card 87-10451 DDC 331.88/0968 19
1. I.C.U. (South Africa) - History. 2. Trade-unions, Black - South Africa - History. I. Title.
HD8801.A5 I1634 1987

Bradford, W. Murray. The Prentice Hall business tax deduction master guide / W. Murray Bradford. 1987 ed. New York : Prentice Hall Press, c1987. 368 p. : ill. ; 28 cm. Includes index. ISBN 0-13-108234-5 (pbk.) : LC Card 87-2252 DDC 343.7305/23 347.303523 19
1. Income tax - United States - Deductions. I. Prentice-Hall, inc. II. Title. III. Title: Business tax deduction master guide.
HJ4653.D4 B68 1987

Bradley, Edward S. Teweles, Richard Jack, 1924- The stock market /. New York , c1987. xii, 526 p. ; ISBN 0-471-82044-X LC Card 86-33950 DDC 332.64/2 19
HG4551 .T48 1987

Bradley, James, 1942- Introduction to data base management in business / James Bradley. 2nd ed. New York : Holt, Rinehart, and Winston, c1987. xii, 669 p. : ill. ; 25 cm. Includes bibliographies and index. ISBN 0-03-011924-3 LC Card 86-22914 DDC 658/.054 19
1. Business - Data processing. 2. Data base management. I. Title. II. Title: Introduction to database management in business.
HF5548.2 .B678 1987

Bradley, Phil. The district resource analysis as applied to Kakamega District / Phil Bradley. Nairobi : Beijer Institute, [1984] 11 leaves : ill. ; 30 cm. (Working paper / Kenya Woodfuel Development Programme . no. 2) Cover title. At head of title: KWDP. "October 1984"--Cover. LC Card 87-112452 DDC 333.75 19
1. Fuelwood industry - Kenya - Kakamega District. 2. Agricultural development projects - Kenya - Kakamega District. 3. Land use - Kenya - Kakamega District. 4. Forests and forestry - Kenya - Kakamega District. I. Kenya Woodfuel Development Programme. II. Series: Working paper / Kenya Woodfuel Development Programme , no. 2. III. Title.
HD9769.F843 K425 1984

Bradley, Philip. Kaiser, Martin. The New Zealand software industry . Wellington, N.Z. , c1986. 110 p. : ISBN 0-477-06781-6 (pbk.) LC Card 86-212814 DDC 338.4/70053/09931 19
HD9696.C63 N454 1986

Bradley, Ute. Applied marketing and social research /. Chichester , New York , c1987. xvii, 488 p. : ISBN 0-471-91356-1 : LC Card 86-32447 DDC 658.8/3 19
HF5415.2 .A654 1987

Bradlow, Daniel D. International borrowing . Washington, D.C. , c1986. 499 p. : ISBN 0-935328-40-8 LC Card 86-82157 DDC 341.7/51 19
K4450 .I576 1986 ***NYPL [JLF 86-1814]***

Bradshaw, Thornton F. America's new competitors . Cambridge, Mass. , c1988. xiv, 290 p. ; ISBN 0-88730-135-5 LC Card 87-19295 DDC 337.730172/4 19
HF1456.5.D44 A44 1988

Braehmer, Uwe. Nachrichtendiffusion in Grossunternehmen : eine empirische Fallstudie zur kommunikativen Verbreitung von unternehmensinternen Nachrichten in einer industriellen Grossorganisation / Uwe Braehmer. Münster : Lit, [1983?] 271 p. : ill. ; 21 cm. (Betriebswirtschaftliche Schriftenreihe . Bd. 6) Bibliography: p. 260-271. ISBN 3-88660-090-0 LC Card 83-206152
1. Communication in management. 2. Communication in management - Case studies. I. Title. II. Series.
HD30.3 .B69 1983

Braga, Roberto Saturnino. Saturnino, o momento histórico do Congresso Nacional. Brasília : Senado Federal, Centro Gráfico, 1983. 58 p. ; 23 cm. Cover title. CONTENTS. - A rendição ao Fundo Monetário -- O momento histórico do Congresso -- Interpelando o ministro da fazenda. LC Card 83-202638
1. Brazil - Economic policy. 2. Monetary policy - Brazil. 3. International Monetary Fund - Brazil. I. Title.
HC187 .B76 1983

Bragaw, Louis K. Social forces and the manager . Malabar, Fla. , 1987, c1982. xiv, 502 p. : ISBN 0-89464-225-1 (pbk.) LC Card 87-3259 DDC 658.4/08/0973 19
HD60.5.U5 S635 1987

Braginskiĭ, L. V. (Lev Vol′fovich) Ėffektivnost′ kapital′nykh vlozheniĭ i bankovskai͡a dei͡atel′nost′ / L.V. Braginskiĭ. Moskva : Izd-vo "Nauka", 1981. 186 p. ; 20 cm. (Problemy sovetskoĭ ėkonomiki) At head of title: Akademii͡a nauk SSSR. T͡Sentral′nyĭ ėkonomiko-matematicheskiĭ institut. Includes bibliographical references. LC Card 82-144216
1. Finance - Soviet Union. 2. Credit - Soviet Union. 3. Banks and banking - Soviet Union. 4. Capital investments - Soviet Union. 5. Central planning - Soviet Union. I. Title.
HG186.S55 B72 1981

Bragulat, Jorge. La enseñanza del cooperativismo en la Universidad / Jorge Bragulat. Madrid : Oficina de Educación Iberoamericana, [1982] 119 p. : ill. ; 27 cm. (Informe de investigación) Includes bibliographies. LC Card 85-203554
1. Cooperation - Study and teaching (Higher). 2. Cooperation - Outlines, syllabi, etc. I. Series: Informe de investigación (Madrid, Spain). II. Title.
HD2955 .B72 1982

Brahm Prakash. The urban dead-end? : pattern of employment among slum-dwellers / International Council on Social Welfare, Bombay.1st ed. Bombay : Somaiya Publications, 1983. xii, 138 p., [5] p. of plates : ill., map ; 23 cm. Includes bibliographical references. Written by Brahm Prakash -- Opposit verso t.p. LC Card 84-900007 DDC 331.12/5/0954792 19
1. Labor Supply - India - Bombay. 2. Slums - India - Bombay. 3. Unemployed - India - Bombay. I. Title.
HD5820.B6 B72 1983 ***NYPL [JLD 86-3828]***

Brahmananda, P. R. The Development process of the Indian economy /. Bombay , 1987. xxxxxxviii, 1219, 78 p. : LC Card 87-901099 DDC 338.954 19
HC435.2 .D476 1987

Brahmstedt, W. T. (William T.), 1924- The courtiers of American business / by W.T. Brahmstedt. Palm Springs, Calif. : ETC Publications, c1987. 190 p. : ill. ; 22 cm. ISBN

0-88280-118-X (pbk.) : LC Card 86-29078 DDC 650.1/3 19
1. Success in business - United States. 2. Managing your boss. 3. Interpersonal relations. I. Title.
HF5386 .B777 1987

Brain Drain . Rehsche, Guntram. Adliswil , 1981. 71 p. ; ISBN 3-7229-4019-2 LC Card 81-206028 DDC 331.12/79 19
HD8038.S85 R44 1981

BRAIN DRAIN - DEVELOPING COUNTRIES.
Rehsche, Guntram. Brain Drain . Adliswil , 1981. 71 p. ; ISBN 3-7229-4019-2 LC Card 81-206028 DDC 331.12/79 19
HD8038.S85 R44 1981

BRAIN DRAIN - SWITZERLAND.
Rehsche, Guntram. Brain Drain . Adliswil , 1981. 71 p. ; ISBN 3-7229-4019-2 LC Card 81-206028 DDC 331.12/79 19
HD8038.S85 R44 1981

Brain, Peter J. The microeconomic structure of the Australian economy / Peter J. Brain ; editor, Cosima McPhee with the assistance of, P. Burgess ... [et al.]. Melbourne, Australia : Longman Cheshire, 1986. xxiv, 448 p. : ill. ; 22 cm. Bibliography: p. [432]-441. Includes index. ISBN 0-582-71502-4 (pbk.) LC Card 87-100715 DDC 330.994/063 19
1. Australia - Economic conditions - 1945- - Econometric models. I. McPhee, Cosima. II. Title.
HC603 .B73 1986

BRAIN STORMING. see **PROBLEM SOLVING, GROUP.**

Brainard, Lawrence J. Uncertain future . New Brunswick, N.J. , c1984. x, 129 p. ; ISBN 0-88738-041-7 : LC Card 84-16240 DDC 332.1/5 19
HG3891.5 .U53 1984 ***NYPL [JLE 86-2494]***

BRAINWASHING.
Huxley, Aldous, 1894-1963. [Brave new world.] Brave new world ; and, Brave new world revisited /. London , 1984. xxii, 387 p. ; ISBN 0-7011-2769-4 : LC Card 84-134715 DDC 823/.912 19
PR6015.U9 B65 1984 ***NYPL [JFE 86-4706]***

Winn, Denise, 1950- The manipulated mind . London , c1983. 217 p. ; ISBN 0-86304-025-X LC Card 83-184383 DDC 302.3/3 19
BF632.5 .W56 1983 ***NYPL [JFD 87-1158]***

Braiotta, Louis, 1943- The essential guide to effective corporate board committees / Louis Braiotta, Jr., A.A. Sommer, Jr. Englewood Cliffs, N.J. : Prentice-Hall, c1987. xiii, 178 p. ; 24 cm. Includes bibliographies and index. ISBN 0-13-286139-9 LC Card 87-2265 DDC 658.4/22 19
1. Directors of corporations. 2. Management committees. I. Sommer, A. A. (Alphonse A.), 1924-. II. Title.
HD2745 .B63 1987

Braithwaite, Jeanine. Tretyakova, Albina. Cost estimates for the Soviet gas industry, 1970 to 1990 /. Washington, D.C. [1986] vii, 116 p. ; LC Card 87-601292 DDC 338.2/3 19
HD9581.S652 T74 1986

Bramlett, N. Kent.
Evolution of the highway-user charge principle. Highway finance : two reports on highway finance / prepared by the Office of Highway Planning. [Washington] [1983] iii, 96 p. ;
NYPL [JLF 87-431]

Branch, Alan E. Economics of shipping practice and management / Alan E. Branch. 2nd ed. London ; New York : Chapman and Hall, c1988. p. cm. Bibliography: p. Includes index. ISBN 0-412-31030-9 (pbk.) LC Card 87-24233 DDC 387/.0068 19
1. Shipping. I. Title.
HE571 .B669 1988

BRANCH BANKS. see **BANKS AND BANKING - BRANCH BANKS.**

Branchaw, Bernadine P. Bowman, Joel P. Business report writing /. Chicago , c1988. xvi, 607 p. : ISBN 0-03-013244-4 LC Card 87-15438 DDC 808/.066651 19
HF5719 .B68 1988

La branche des travaux publics en France et sur les marchés extérieurs /. France. Groupe de stratégie industrielle no 8. Sous-groupe Travaux publics. Paris , c1985. 202 p. : ISBN 2-11-001524-1 : LC Card 86-183130
HD4168 .F69 1985

Branchenorientierte Bonitätsanalyse mit Früherkennungseigenschaften . Gisteren, Roland van, 1950- München , c1986. 2, xi, 393 p. : ISBN 3-88259-370-9 LC Card 86-173025
HD9715.G32 G57 1986

Branchenportfolioanalyse und Wirtschaftsförderungsstrategien . Skutlartz, Ekkehard. [Karlsruhe] [1986] a-m, 205, vi p. : LC Card 87-103969
HG4529.5 .S58 1986

Brancoli, Mario. The financial aspects of insurance against employment accidents / Mario Brancoli. Geneva : General Secretariat of the ISSA, 1974. 42 p. ; 30 cm. At head of title: International Social Security Association, XVIIIth General Assembly, Abidjan, October-November 1973. "Report XV." LC Card 84-247775
1. Industrial accidents - Congresses. 2. Occupational diseases - Congresses. 3. Insurance, Accident - Congresses. I. Title.
HD7260.5 .B73 1974

BRAND CHOICE - UNITED STATES.
Settle, Robert B. Why they buy . New York , c1986. xvi, 351 p. ; ISBN 0-471-84457-8 : LC Card 86-13303 DDC 658.8/343/0973 19
HC110.C6 S48 1986 ***NYPL [JLE 86-4432]***

BRAND LOYALTY. see **BRAND CHOICE.**

BRAND MANAGEMENT. see **PRODUCT MANAGEMENT.**

BRAND NAME PRODUCTS.
Branding . New York , 1987. xii, 192 p., [12] p. of plates : ISBN 0-07-044055-7 : LC Card 86-27797 DDC 658.8/27 19
HD69.B7 B73 1987

BRAND NAME PRODUCTS - UNITED STATES - HISTORY.
Hambleton, Ronald, 1917- The branding of America . Dublin, N.H. , c1987. 224 p. : ISBN 0-89909-101-6 : LC Card 86-80335 DDC 338/.02/0973 19
HF1040.8 .H36 1987

Brandão, Carlos. Bulhões, Octávio Gouveia de. Desdobramentos inflacionários. [Salvador] [1984] 43 p. : LC Card 86-861354 DDC 332.4/1/0981 19
HG835 .B85 1984

Brandão, Carlos Rodrigues.
Os caipiras de São Paulo / Carlos Rodrigues Brandão. São Paulo-Brasil : Editora Brasiliense, 1983. 92, [4] p. : ill. ; 16 cm. (Tudo é história . 75) Bibliography: p. [93] LC Card 84-179661
1. Peasantry - Brazil - Sao Paulo (State). I. Series. II. Series: Tudo é história (1981) , 75. III. Title.
HD1531.B7 B72 1983

Campesinato goiano : três estudos / Carlos Rodrigues Brandão, José Ricardo Ramalho. Goiânia : Editora da Universidade Federal do Goiás, 1986. 156 p. ; 22 cm. (Coleção Documentos goianos . 16) Publicação ; n. 115 Includes bibliographies. ISBN 85-85003-42-1 : LC Card 87-403866 DDC 305.5/63 19
1. Peasantry - Brazil - Goiás (State). 2. Agricultural laborers - Brazil - Goiás (State). I. Ramalho, José Ricardo Garcia Pereira. II. Series: Coleção Documentos goianos , no. 16. III. Title.
HD1531.B7 B713 1986

BRANDENBURG (ELECTORATE) - ECONOMIC CONDITIONS.
Wolffsohn, Seew, 1916- Wirtschaftliche und soziale Entwicklungen in Brandenburg, Preussen, Schlesien und Oberschlesien in den Jahren 1640-1853, Frühindustrialisierung in Oberschlesien /. Frankfurt am Main , New York , c1985. 182 p., [2] p. of folded plates : ISBN 3-8204-8197-4 LC Card 85-219539
HC288.B68 W65 1985

BRANDENBURG (ELECTORATE) - SOCIAL CONDITIONS.
Wolffsohn, Seew, 1916- Wirtschaftliche und soziale Entwicklungen in Brandenburg, Preussen, Schlesien und Oberschlesien in den Jahren 1640-1853, Frühindustrialisierung in Oberschlesien /. Frankfurt am Main , New York , c1985. 182 p., [2] p. of folded plates : ISBN 3-8204-8197-4 LC Card 85-219539
HC288.B68 W65 1985

Brandenburg, Richard G. What every manager needs to know about manufacturing /. New York, NY [1987], c1983. 181 p. : ISBN 0-8144-7686-4 (pbk.) LC Card 87-47714 DDC 658 19
HD9720.5 .W38 1987

Branding : a key marketing tool / edited by John M. Murphy. New York : McGraw-Hill, 1987. xii, 192 p., [12] p. of plates : ill. ; 25 cm. Includes bibliographies and index. ISBN 0-07-044055-7 : LC Card 86-27797 DDC 658.8/27 19
1. Brand name products. 2. Business names. 3. Marketing. I. Murphy, John M., 1944-.
HD69.B7 B73 1987

The branding of America . Hambleton, Ronald, 1917- Dublin, N.H. , c1987. 224 p. : ISBN 0-89909-101-6 : LC Card 86-80335 DDC 338/.02/0973 19
HF1040.8 .H36 1987

Brandt, Betty. Special delivery / by Betty Brandt ; illustrated by Kathy Haubrich. Minneapolis, Minn. : Carolrhoda Books, c1988. 40 p. : ill. ; 23 cm. (Carolrhoda on my own books) A history of the postal service describing ways mail has been sent over the years. ISBN 0-87614-312-5 (lib. bdg.) LC Card 87-15647 DDC 383/.4973 19
1. Postal service - United States - History - Juvenile literature. 2. Pony express - History - Juvenile literature. 3. Express service - United States - History - Juvenile literature. I. Haubrich, Kathy, ill. II. Series: Carolrhoda on my own book. III. Title.
HE6371 .B77 1988

Brandt, Ed. Fifty and fired : how to prepare for it, what to do when it happens / Ed Brandt with Leonard Corwen. Bedford, Mass. : Mills & Sanderson, c1987. xii, 242 p. ; 22 cm. Bibliography: p. 239-242. ISBN 0-938179-07-1 : LC Card 87-12150 DDC 650.1/4/0240564 19
1. Middle managers - United States - Dismissal of. 2. Employees, Dismissal of - Law and legislation - United States. I. Corwen, Leonard. II. Title.
HD38.25.U6 B7 1987

Brandt, Franz. Ursachen für die Schwierigkeiten bei der Eingliederung von Schwerbehinderten auf dem allgemeinen Arbeitsmarkt / [von Franz Brandt]. Bonn : Der Bundesminister für Arbeit und Sozialordnung, [1984] 410 p. ; 30 cm. (Forschungsbericht, 0174-4992 . 117.) Bibliography: p. 281-289. LC Card 87-408829 DDC 331.5/9/0943 19
1. Handicapped - Employment - Germany, West. 2. Unemployment - Germany (West) - Psychological aspects. I. Series: Forschungsbericht (Germany (West). Bundesministerium für Arbeit und Sozialordnung) , 117. II. Title.
HD7256.G3 B7 1984

Brandt, Hartmut.
Projektplanung in der kleinbäuerlichen Produktion / Hartmut Brandt. Berlin : Deutsches Institut für Entwicklungspolitik, 1982. xv, 208 p. : ill. ; 24 cm. (Schriften des Deutschen Instituts für Entwicklungspolitik, DIE . Bd. 70) Includes bibliographical references. LC Card 83-193407
1. Farms, Small - Germany (West). 2. Agriculture and state - Germany, West. I. Series. II. Series: Deutsches Institut für Entwicklungspolitik. Schriften, Bd. 70. III. Title.
HD1476.G3 B73 1982 ***NYPL [JLE 87-2903]***

Structural distortions and adjustment programmes in the poor countries of Africa . Berlin , 1985. xxxi, 377 p. : ISBN 3-88985-042-1 LC Card 86-226845 DDC 338.967 19
HC800 .S79 1985

Brandt, Horst. Kostensenkung und Gewinn / Horst Brandt, Siegfried Kaergel. Berlin : Dietz, 1985. 100 p. ; 19 cm. Includes bibliographical references. LC Card 87-144350 DDC 338.5/1/09431 19
1. Costs, Industrial - Germany, East. 2. Profit - Germany, East. 3. Efficiency, Industrial - Germany (East). I. Kaergel, Siegfried. II. Title.
HC290.795.C7 B7 1985

Brandt, J. (Joke) Sterkenburg, J. J. Rural housing conditions in Kisumu District, Kenya /. [Utrecht] [Nairobi] , 1982. 95 p., [6] leaves of plates : LC Card 85-981197
HD7289.K42 K67 1982

Brandt, Karl, 1923- Struktur und Dynamik der Wirtschaft . Freiburg im Breisgau , c1983. 530 p. : ISBN 3-448-01348-X : LC Card 83-184564 DDC 330 19
HB44 .S77 1983

BRANDT, KARL, 1923-
Struktur und Dynamik der Wirtschaft . Freiburg im Breisgau , c1983. 530 p. : ISBN 3-448-01348-X : LC Card 83-184564 DDC 330 19
HB44 .S77 1983

Brandt, Willy, 1913-
[Organisierte Wahnsinn. English]
Arms and hunger / Willy Brandt ; translated by Anthea Bell. 1st MIT Press English language pbk. ed. Cambridge, Mass. : MIT Press, 1987, c1986. 208 p. ; 21 cm. Translation of: Der organisierte Wahnsinn. ISBN 0-262-52127-X (pbk.) LC Card 87-4057 DDC 330.9172/4 19
1. Developing countries - Economic conditions. 2. International economic relations. 3. World politics - 1985-1995. I. Title.
HC59.7 .B67713 1987

Brasil . Tibiriçá, Luiz Caldas. São Paulo, SP , 1984. 159 p. ; LC Card 84-215785
HC187 .T5 1984 *NYPL [JLD 87-507]*

Brasil. see **Brazil.**

O Brasil do cruzado . Rossetti, José Paschoal, 1941- São Paulo-SP , 1986. 135 p. : LC Card 87-129096 DDC 338.981 19
HC187 .R673 1986

Brasil--guia dos produtores de insumos farmacêuticos / FARMEXPORT, Câmara de Produtores-Exportadores de Insumos Farmacêuticos e Afins. 3a. ed. Rio de Janeiro, Brasil : FARMEXPORT, 1983. 71 p. ; 23 cm. Spine title: Guia dos produtores de insumos farmacêuticos. "Produtos e fabricantes": p. [7]-34. LC Card 86-202196
1. Drug trade - Brazil - Directories. I. Câmara de Produtores-Exportadores de Insumos Farmacêuticos e Afins (Rio de Janeiro, Brazil). II. Title: Guia dos produtores de insumos farmacêuticos.
HD9670.B82 B7 1983

O Brasil na economia internacional. Coes, Donald V., 1943- [Salvador, Brazil] [1984?] 55 p. : LC Card 86-234065
HF1513 .C64 1984

Brasil, os anos de autoritarismo.
Singer, Paul Israel, 1932- Repartição da renda . Rio de Janeiro , 1986. 95 p. ; ISBN 85-85061-40-5 : LC Card 86-157852
HC190.I5 S56 1986

Brasil, país das oportunidades perdidas /. Rabelo, Genival. [Brazil] 1977. 112 p. ; LC Card 85-210978
HC187 .R27 1977

O Brasil que temos, o país que queremos /. Franco, Luiz L. Guarulhos, S.P. [Brazil] , c1985. 87 p. ; LC Card 86-223053
HC187 .F7315 1985

Brasil sem milagres /. Serra, José. São Paulo, SP , c1986. 174 p. : LC Card 87-404803 DDC 330.981/063 19
HC187 .S4153 1986

Brasil 82, a grande luta para manter o espaço para crescer . Delfim Netto, Antônio. Brasília , 1982. 37 p. : LC Card 84-249919
HC187 .D552 1982

O brasileiro não é viável-- . Nogueira, Mauro R. São Paulo , c1984. 253 p. : LC Card 84-256564
HC187 .N57 1984

BRASÍLIA REGION (BRAZIL) - ECONOMIC POLICY.
Distrito Federal (Brazil). Coordenação do Sistema de Planejamento. Região geo-econômica de Brasília . [Brasília] [1980?] [28] leaves : LC Card 86-204066
HC189.B7 D57 1980

Notícias publicadas, de março de 1977 a janeiro de 1979. [Brasília] [198-?] 116 leaves : LC Card 85-108219
HC189.B7 N68 1980z

Brasilien /. Müller, Jürg. Stuttgart , 1984. 278 p. : ISBN 3-12-928881-3 (pbk.) LC Card 87-673406
HC187 .M79x 1984

Brasilien als Produzent und Exporteur von Rüstungsgütern /. Wöhlcke, Manfred, 1942- Baden-Baden , 1987. 176 p. : ISBN 3-7890-1355-2 LC Card 87-135627 DDC 338.4/36234/0981 19
HD9743.B682 W64 1987

Brasilien ohne Inflation? . Fischer, Bernhard, fl. 1979- Kiel [1986] 28 p. ; LC Card 87-120443 DDC 330 s 332.4/1/0981 19
HB44 .K45 no. 124 HG835

Brasilien 1974-1981 . Calcagnotto, Gilberto. Hamburg [1983] xi, 78 p. : LC Card 83-222930
HC187 .C143 1983

Brass, William. Arretx, Carmen. Cuatro lecciones de William Brass . Santiago de Chile , 1977. 88 p. : LC Card 83-169600
HB1321.B73 A77 1977

BRASS, WILLIAM.
Arretx, Carmen. Cuatro lecciones de William Brass . Santiago de Chile , 1977. 88 p. : LC Card 83-169600
HB1321.B73 A77 1977

Brasse, Valerie. Beenstock, Michael, 1946- Insurance for unemployment /. London , Boston , 1986. 106 p. ; ISBN 0-04-331113-X (alk. paper) (Great Britain) LC Card 85-30704 DDC 368.4/4/00941 19
HD7096.G7 B36 1986 *NYPL [JLD 86-3693]*

Brassley, Paul, 1946- The agricultural economy of Northumberland and Durham in the period, 1640-1750 / Paul Brassley. New York : Garland Pub., 1985. iii, 224 p. : ill. ; 24 cm. (British economic history) Originally presented as the author's thesis (Bachelor of Letters), Oxford, 1974. Bibliography: p. 220-223. ISBN 0-8240-6676-6 : LC Card 84-45996 DDC 338.1/09428/6 19
1. Agriculture - Economic aspects - England - Northumberland - History. 2. Agriculture - Economic aspects - England - Durham (County) - History. I. Title. II. Series.
HD1930.N67 B73 1985 *NYPL [JLE 86-3924]*

Bratschitsch, Rudolf. Marzen, Walter. Betriebswirtschaftliche Forschung und Wirtschaftspraxis . Spardorf , c1986. ix, 229 p. ; ISBN 3-922919-82-0 LC Card 87-133392 DDC 658.4 19
HD35 .M276 1986

Bratt, Rachel G., 1946- Critical perspectives on housing /. Philadelphia , 1986. xxi, 686 p. : ISBN 0-87722-395-5 LC Card 85-17274 DDC 363.5/0973 19
HD7293 .C738 1986 *NYPL [JLE 86-3639]*

Bratziōtē, Lousē. Hē Hellēnikē viomēchania apo ton 19o ston 20o aiōna /. Athēna , 1985. 32 p., [22] p. of plates : LC Card 86-212947
HC295 .H373 1985

Brauchlin, Emil. Statistische Methoden . St. Gallen , 1983. iii, 195 p. : LC Card 83-240598
HA29.5.G4 S72 1983

Braudel, Fernand. La dynamique du capitalisme / Fernand Braudel. Paris : Arthaud, c1985. 120 p. ; 19 cm. "Ce petit volume reproduit le texte de trois conférences que j'ai faites à l'Université de Johns Hopkins ... en 1977"--P. 5. ISBN 2-7003-0501-9 : LC Card 86-130442
1. Economic history. 2. Capitalism. I. Title.
HC51 .B675 1985

Brauer, Karl M. Fallstudie Haiger : zum Ersatz des Strassenverkehrs durch den kombinierten Verkehr / von Karl M. Brauer und Bernd Seiffert. Berlin : Duncker & Humblot, c1983. 55 p. ; 24 cm. (Schriften zur Betriebswirtschaftslehre des Verkehrs) Bibliography: p. 53-[54] Includes index. ISBN 3-428-05403-2 LC Card 83-233201
1. Freight and freightage - Germany (West) - Haiger - Costs - Case studies. 2. Transportation - Germany (West) - Haiger - Case studies. I. Seiffert, Bernd. II. Title. III. Series.
HE199.G3 B73 1983

Brauman, Rony. Le Tiers-mondisme en question /. Paris , c1986. 225 p. ; ISBN 2-85565-299-5 : LC Card 86-185503
HC60 .T518 1986

Braun, Axel. Rüstungskonversionsbemühungen in den USA in den 70iger Jahren : Untersuchung über die Rüstungskonversionsbemühungen in den USA in den 70iger Jahren im Bereich der Luft- und Raumfahrtindustrie, der Legislativen, der Exekutiven, bei den Gewerkschaften und Bürgerinitiativprojekten / Axel Braun. Frankfurt am Main : Haag + Herchen, c1984. x, 379 p. : ill. ; 21 cm. Bibliography: p. 360-379. ISBN 3-88129-856-8 LC Card 85-154003
1. Armaments - Economic aspects - United States. 2. Munitions - Economic aspects - United States. I. Title.
HC110.D4 B72 1984

Braun, Hans-Joachim. Wirtschafts- und finanzpolitische Entscheidungsprozesse in England in der ersten Hälfte des 19. Jahrhunderts / Hans-Joachim Braun. Frankfurt am Main ; New York : Lang, c1984. 236 p. : ill. ; 21 cm. (Europäische Hochschulschriften. Reihe III, Geschichte und ihre Hilfswissenschaften, 0531-7320 . Bd. 200 = vol. 200 = vol. 200) Abridgement of the author's Habilitationsschrift--Ruhr-Universität Bochum, 1978/79. Bibliography: p. 195-236. ISBN 3-8204-7702-0 LC Card 85-191319 DDC 338.941 19
1. Great Britain - Economic policy. 2. Finance, Public - Great Britain - History - 19th century. 3. Great Britain - Commerce - History - 19th century. 4. Great Britain - Politics and government - 1800-1837. 5. Business cycles - Great Britain - History - 19th century. I. Series: Europäische Hochschulschriften. Reihe III, Geschichte und ihre Hilfswissenschaften , Bd. 200. II. Title.
HC255 .B77 1984

Braun, Wolfram. Unternehmensökonomie : eine allgemeine Theorie der Unternehmensentscheidung / von Wolfram Braun. Wiesbaden : Gabler, c1985. 246 p. : ill. ; 24 cm. Bibliography: p. 220-230. ISBN 3-409-13316-X LC Card 85-239244 DDC 330.15/5 19
1. Neoclassical school of economics. I. Title.
HB98.2 .B74 1985

BRAUNSCHWEIG (GERMANY) - INDUSTRIES.
Die Industrie-Erzeugnisse und Handelswaren des Landes Braunschweig /. Wolfenbüttel , 1921. 120 p. : LC Card 85-666348
HC289.B7 I52x 1921

Bravard, Yves. Bozonnet, Rémy. Sainte-Foy-Tarentaise, une montagne pour des hommes /. [Saint-Julien-Montdenis] [1984] 192 p. : LC Card 85-206948
HC278.S34 B69 1984

Brave new world ; and, Brave new world revisited /. Huxley, Aldous, 1894-1963. [Brave new world.] London , 1984. xxii, 387 p. ; ISBN 0-7011-2769-4 : LC Card 84-134715 DDC 823/.912 19
PR6015.U9 B65 1984 *NYPL [JFE 86-4706]*

Brave new world revisited. Huxley, Aldous, 1894-1963. [Brave new world.] Brave new world ; and, Brave new world revisited /. London , 1984. xxii, 387 p. ; ISBN 0-7011-2769-4 : LC Card 84-134715 DDC 823/.912 19
PR6015.U9 B65 1984 *NYPL [JFE 86-4706]*

Bray, Francesca. The rice economies : technology and development in Asian societies / Francesca Bray. Oxford [Oxfordshire] ; New York : Blackwell, 1986. xvii, 254 p. : ill. ; 24 cm. Includes index. Bibliography: p. [228]-247. ISBN 0-631-14877-9 : LC Card 85-30819 DDC 338.1/7318/095 19
1. Rice trade - Asia. 2. Agriculture - Economic aspects - Asia. 3. Asia - Economic conditions - 1945-. I. Title.
HD9066.A7 B73 1986 *NYPL [JLE 87-793]*

Braybon, Gail. Out of the cage : women's experiences in two world wars / Gail Braybon and Penny Summerfield. London ; New York : Pandora Press, 1987. xiii, 330 p. : ill., ports. ; 21 cm. (Pandora Press history) Bibliography: p. 313-322. Includes index. ISBN 0-86358-046-7 : LC Card 87-13510 DDC 305.4/0941 19
1. Women - Employment - Great Britain - History - 20th century. 2. Women - Great Britain - History - 20th century. 3. Women - Great Britain - Social conditions. 4. World War, 1914-1918 - Women - Great Britain. 5. World War, 1939-1945 - Women - Great Britain. I. Summerfield, Penny. II. Title. III. Series.
HD6135 .B7 1987

Brazil and Peru . Gall, Norman. Geneva , 1987. x, 123 p., [1] leaf of plates : ISBN 92-2-105506-X (pbk.) : LC Card 87-166425 DDC 338.2/7282/0981 19
HD9574.B82 G34 1987

Brazil and the Ivory Coast : the impact of international lending, investment, and aid / edited by Werner Baer, John F. Due. Greenwich, Conn. : JAI Press, c1987. p. cm. (Contemporary studies in economic and financial analysis. v. 58) Papers presented at a conference held in April 1985 organized by the Center for Latin American and Caribbean Studies of the University of

Illinois and its African Studies Program. Includes bibliographies and index. ISBN 0-89232-819-3 : LC Card 87-3667 DDC 332/.042/0981 19
1. Loans, Foreign - Brazil - Congresses. 2. Loans, Foreign - Ivory Coast - Congresses. 3. Investments, Foreign - Brazil - Congresses. 4. Investments, Foreign - Ivory Coast - Congresses. 5. International Monetary Fund - Brazil - Congresses. 6. International Monetary Fund - Ivory Coast - Congresses. I. Baer, Werner, 1931-. II. Due, John Fitzgerald. III. University of Illinois at Urbana-Champaign. Center for Latin American and Caribbean Studies. IV. University of Illinois at Urbana-Champaign. African Studies Program.
HG3891.5 .B72 1987

Brazil. Appendizagem Industrial, Servico Nacional de. see **Brazil. Servico Nacional de Aprendizagem Industrial.**

BRAZIL - APPROPRIATIONS AND EXPENDITURES.
Cotia, Raul Fontes. Comentário sôbre os balanços gerais da União de 1963 /. [Brasília] [1964] 45 p. ; LC Card 85-194302
HJ2079 .C68 1964

BRAZIL - CENSUS, 1960.
Chackiel, Juan. La fuerza de trabajo en los países de la Cuenca del Plata según los censos de 1960 /. San José, Costa Rica , 1976. iv, 81 p. : LC Card 83-169596
HD5746.A6 C42 1976

BRAZIL - CENSUS, 1980.
Inquéritos especiais /. Rio de Janeiro, Brasil , 1984. 4 v. in 5. ; ***NYPL [JLF 86-202]***

BRAZIL, CENTRAL WEST - ECONOMIC CONDITIONS.
Brazil. Superintendência do Desenvolvimento da Região Centro-Oeste. Plano de desenvolvimento regional do Centro-Oeste . Brasília , 1985. 101 p. : LC Card 86-146677
HC188.C46 B7 1985

Centro-Oeste brasileiro /. [Brasília] , 1981. 9 v. : LC Card 87-405115 DDC 330.981/7063 19
HC188.C46 C465 1981

BRAZIL, CENTRAL WEST - ECONOMIC POLICY.
Brazil. Superintendência do Desenvolvimento da Região Centro-Oeste. Plano de desenvolvimento regional do Centro-Oeste . Brasília , 1985. 101 p. : LC Card 86-146677
HC188.C46 B7 1985

Mato Grosso do Sul (Brazil). Fundação Instituto de Apoio ao Planejamento do Estado. O Centro-Oeste e a retomada do desenvolvimento nacional . [Campo Grande] , 1985. 113 p., [1] folded leaf : LC Card 87-404972 DDC 338.981/71 19
HC188.C46 M37 1985

BRAZIL, CENTRAL WEST - SOCIAL CONDITIONS.
Brazil. Superintendência do Desenvolvimento da Região Centro-Oeste. Plano de desenvolvimento regional do Centro-Oeste . Brasília , 1985. 101 p. : LC Card 86-146677
HC188.C46 B7 1985

Centro-Oeste brasileiro /. [Brasília] , 1981. 9 v. : LC Card 87-405115 DDC 330.981/7063 19
HC188.C46 C465 1981

BRAZIL, CENTRAL WEST - SOCIAL POLICY.
Brazil. Superintendência do Desenvolvimento da Região Centro-Oeste. Plano de desenvolvimento regional do Centro-Oeste . Brasília , 1985. 101 p. : LC Card 86-146677
HC188.C46 B7 1985

Brazil (City). Universidade. São Paulo, Instituto de Pesquisas Econômicas. Lima, José Luiz. Estatísticas básicas do setor agrícola no Brasil /. São Paulo , 1983- v. : LC Card 83-219032 DDC 338.1/0981 19
HD9014.B82 L55 1983 ***NYPL [JLL 86-432]***

Brazil. Comissão Executiva do Plano da Lavoura Cacaueira. Departamento Especial da Amazônia. Desempenho programático do DEPEA em 1984 : síntese das atividades desenvolvidas no período 1976-1983, atividades desenvolvidas em 1984. Belém/Pará [Brazil] : Comissão Executiva do Plano da Lavoura Cacaueira, Departamento Especial da Amazônia, 1985. 76 p. : ill. ; 22 cm. Includes bibliographies. LC Card 87-404555 DDC 338.981/1 19
1. Agriculture and state - Amazon River Region. 2. Agriculture and state - Brazil. I. Title.
HD1875.A347 B68 1985

Brazil. Comissão Executiva para Papel e Celulose. Mercado brasileiro de celulose e papel /. Brasília, D.F. , 1982. vii, 224 leaves : LC Card 84-210712
HD9660.C43 B75 1982

BRAZIL - COMMERCE.
Baumann Neves, Renato. Exportações e crescimento industrial no Brasil /. Rio de Janeiro , 1985. 274 p. : LC Card 86-195612
HF1513 .B38 1985

Pinto, Maurício Barata de Paula. O potencial das exportações brasileiras de manufaturados /. Rio de Janeiro , 1983. 46 p. ; LC Card 87-403022 DDC 382/.4567/0981 19
HD9734.B72 P56 1983

Wöhlcke, Manfred, 1942- Brasilien als Produzent und Exporteur von Rüstungsgütern /. Baden-Baden , 1987. 176 p. : ISBN 3-7890-1355-2 LC Card 87-135627 DDC 338.4/36234/0981 19
HD9743.B682 W64 1987

BRAZIL - COMMERCE - EUROPE, EASTERN.
Kállay, Georges Christophe de. L'importance des marchés de l'Europe de l'Est . Genève , 1986. 247 p. ; LC Card 86-179357
HF3408.Z7 E8525 1986

BRAZIL - COMMERCE - EUROPEAN ECONOMIC COMMUNITY COUNTRIES.
Protectionism in the European community against Brazilian exports . Brasília , 1985. 125 p. ; LC Card 86-119107 DDC 382.7/3/094 19
HF3499.5.Z7 B76 1985

BRAZIL - COMMERCE - HANDBOOKS, MANUALS ETC.
Manual básico do exportador. [São Paulo] [1985] 270 p. : LC Card 86-200367
HF3407 .M35 1985

BRAZIL - COMMERCE - PARAGUAY.
Alternativa rodo-hidro-ferroviária para o transporte de parte da safra de soja paraguaia destinada à exportação. [Rio de Janeiro] [19]84. 65 leaves : LC Card 85-187436
HE199.5.S66 A47 1984

BRAZIL - COMMERCE - STATISTICS.
As Cooperativas na balança comercial brasileira . [Brasília] [1986] 98 p. : LC Card 87-403826 DDC 334/.63/0981021 19
HF3401.5 .C66 1986

Nunnenkamp, Peter. Manufactured export performance of Brazil . Kiel [1986] v, 114 p. : LC Card 87-101193 DDC 382/.4567/0981 19
HF1513 .N86 1986

BRAZIL - COMMERCE - UNITED STATES.
Matz, Viktor, 1947- Entwicklungsländer im internationalen Konjunkturzusammenhang . Bergisch Gladbach , c1986. 199, lxxvi p. ; ISBN 3-89012-052-0 LC Card 86-227998
HF3408.U5 M37 1986

BRAZIL - COMMERCIAL POLICY.
Baumann Neves, Renato. Exportações e crescimento industrial no Brasil /. Rio de Janeiro , 1985. 274 p. : LC Card 86-195612
HF1513 .B38 1985

Protectionism in the European community against Brazilian exports . Brasília , 1985. 125 p. ; LC Card 86-119107 DDC 382.7/3/094 19
HF3499.5.Z7 B76 1985

BRAZIL - COMMERCIAL POLICY - HISTORY.
Cardoso, Eliana A. Inflation, growth and the real exchange rate . New York , 1987. 98 p. : ISBN 0-8240-1356-5 (alk. paper) : LC Card 87-8570 DDC 330.981 19
HC187 .C218 1987

Estrutura e funcionamento do comércio exterior brasileiro /. Rio de Janeiro, RJ , 1980. v, 98 p. : LC Card 84-121064
HF1513 .E85 1980

BRAZIL - COMMERCIAL POLICY - HISTORY - 20TH CENTURY.
Fritsch, Winston. External constraints on economic policy in Brazil, 1889-1930 /. Pittsburgh, PA , 1988. p. cm. ISBN 0-8229-1147-7 LC Card 87-19209 DDC 338.981 19
HC187 .F757 1988

Brazil. Congresso Nacional. Câmara dos Deputados. Centro de Documentação e Informação. Coordenação de Publicações. Henrique, Luiz. O salário perverso . Brasília , 1983. 129 p. ; LC Card 86-129394
HD5004 .H45 1983

Luca, Walmor de. Moratória com diretas já . Brasília , 1984. 69 p. ; LC Card 86-152773
HC188.S26 L83 1984

Tavares, José, 1949- Indústria bélica brasileira . Brasília , 1983. 44 p. ; LC Card 84-235004
HC187 .T2943 1983

Brazil. Congresso Nacional. Câmara dos Deputados. Comissão de Agricultura e Política Rural. Subcomissão de Pesca. Relatório final da Subcomissão de Pesca da Comissão de Agricultura e Política Rural, durante a sessão legislativa de 1984. Brasília : Centro de Documentação e Informação, Coordenação de Publicações, 1985. 66 p. ; 23 cm. LC Card 86-203945
1. Fish trade - Government policy - Brazil. 2. Fish trade - Brazil. I. Title.
HD9464.B72 B64 1985

Brazil. Congresso Nacional. Câmara dos Deputados. Comissão de Defesa do Consumidor. Neves, Tancredo, 1910- Tancredo Neves na defesa do consumidor /. Brasília , 1985. 48 p. : LC Card 86-129214
HC190.C63 N48 1985

Brazil. Congresso Nacional. Câmara dos Deputados. Comissão de Esporte e Turismo. Vôos "charters" e as empresas de aviação civil : debates / Câmara dos Deputados, Comissão de Esporte e Turismo, reuniões realizadas na Comissão de Esporte e Turismo en 5, 12 e 19 de setembro de 1985. Brasília : Centro de Documentação e Informação, Coordenação de Publicações, 1986. 98 p. ; 23 cm. LC Card 87-405035 DDC 387.7/0981 19
1. Aeronautics, Commercial - Brazil. 2. Airlines - Brazil. 3. Tourist trade - Brazil. I. Title.
HE9833.A4 B7 1986

Brazil. Congresso Nacional. Senado Federal. Comissão Parlamentar de Inquérito. Fonseca, Aloysio de Salles. Reorientação da assistência à saúde no âmbito da previdência social . [Brasília] , 1983. 67 p. ; LC Card 86-171863
HD7102.B7 F66 1983

Brazil. Coordenação de Planejamento Regional. see **Brazil. Superintendência do Desenvolvimento do Nordeste. Coordenação de Planejamento Regional.**

Brazil. Coordenadoria de Análise de Mercado de Trabalho. Cadastro geral de empregados e desempregados (Lei 4,923/65) . [Brasília, Brazil] , 1985. [61] leaves ; LC Card 86-178290
HD5754 .C26 1985

Brazil. Departamento Nacional da Produção Mineral. (Old Catalog form: Brazil. Produção mineral, Departamento nacional da) Análise econômico-financeira da indústria de mineração, 1978-1982 /. Brasília , 1984. viii, 105 p. : LC Card 86-146667
HD9506.B72 A65 1984

Brazil. Departamento Nacional de Aguas e Energia Elétrica. Pontos básicos para uma política de eletrificação rural : Portaria MME no. 1,000, de 19/07/84, Portaria DNAEE no. 127, de 22/08/84 : diagnóstico-política / Ministério das Minas e Energia, Departamento Nacional de Aguas e Energia Elétrica. Brasília, D.F. : DNAEE, 1984. 190 p. : ill., maps ; 21 cm. Cover title. Spine title: Eletrifição rural. LC Card 86-158852
1. Rural electrification - Government policy - Brazil. I. Title. II. Title: Eletrificação rural.
HD9688.B72 B73 1984

BRAZIL - DEPENDENCY ON FOREIGN COUNTRIES.
Rabelo, Genival. Brasil, país das oportunidades perdidas /. [Brazil] 1977. 112 p. ; LC Card 85-210978
HC187 .R27 1977

Brazil. Desenvolvimento do Nordeste, Superintendênciado. see **Brazil. Superintendência do Desenvolvimento do Nordeste.**

BRAZIL. DIRECTORIA DE NAVEGAÇÃO INTERIOR.
Avaliação do programa de ação, 1984/85 /. [Brasília] , 1985. 90 leaves : LC Card 87-403938 DDC 354.810087/6/06 19
HE653 .A93 1985

Brazil. Diretoria de Navegação Interior.
Avaliação do programa de ação, 1984/85 /. [Brasília] , 1985. 90 leaves : LC Card 87-403938 DDC 354.810087/6/06 19
HE653 .A93 1985

Estudo preliminar para o establecimento de prioridades no financiamento para construção de embarcações para a navegação interior /. [Rio de Janeiro] , 1985. [84] leaves : LC Card 87-403936 DDC 386/.0981 19
HE653 .E88 1985

Brazil. Divisão de Navegação Fluvial e Lacustre. Seção de Desenvolvimento.
Alternativa rodo-ferro-hidroviária para o abastecimento de gás liquefeito de petróleo-GLP às regiões oeste do Estado de Mato Grosso e leste do Estado de Rondônia /. [Rio de Janeiro] [19]84. 41 leaves : LC Card 87-403939 DDC 338.4/7665773 19
HE199.5.L43 A44 1984

Alternativa rodo-hidro-ferroviária para o transporte de parte da safra de soja paraguaia destinada à exportação. [Rio de Janeiro] [19]84. 65 leaves : LC Card 85-187436
HE199.5.S66 A47 1984

Brazil. Superintendência Nacional da Marinha Mercante. Alternativa rodo-ferro-hidroviária para o abastecimento de gás liquefeito de petróleo-GLP às regiões oeste do Estado de Mato Grosso e leste do Estado de Rondônia /. [Rio de Janeiro] [1984] 41 leaves : LC Card 85-197972
HE199.5.L43 B73 1984

BRAZIL - ECONOMIC CONDITIONS.
Capitalismo e classe operária no Brasil /. Petrópolis , 1984. 69 p. ; LC Card 86-222585
HC51 .C35 1984

Chacon, Vamireh. Kultur und Entwicklung in Brasilien . Dortmund , 1970. v, 308 p. ; LC Card 86-172094
HC187 .C44 1970

Dornas Filho, João. O ouro das Gerais e a civilização da Capitania /. São Paulo , 1957. 238 p., [8] leaves of plates : LC Card 84-215039
HC187 .D72 1957

Miranda Neto, Manoel José de. O dilema da Amazônia /. Belém, Pará [1986] 154 p. ; LC Card 87-119394 DDC 330.981/1063 19
HC188.A5 M57 1986

Ohlweiler, Otto Alcides. Evolução sócio-econômica do Brasil /. Porto Alegre-RS, Brasil [1986?] 209 p. ; LC Card 86-229515
HC187 .O43 1986

BRAZIL - ECONOMIC CONDITIONS - 19TH CENTURY.
Mueller, Charles Curt. Das oligarquias agrárias ao predomínio urbano-industrial . Rio de Janeiro , 1983. 363 p. ; LC Card 87-403875 DDC 305.5/232/0981 19
HC187 .M76 1983

BRAZIL - ECONOMIC CONDITIONS - 1918-
Almeida, Pedro Fernando de. A indústria gaúcha de bens de capital na dinâmica da economia brasileira . Porto Alegre, RS , 1986. 257 p. ; LC Card 87-403616 DDC 338.4/76218/0981 19
HD9705.B73 R562 1986

Getúlio Vargas e a economia contemporânea /. Campinas , 1986. 179 p. ; ISBN 85-26-80033-7 LC Card 87-403048 DDC 330.981/063 19
HC187 .G45 1986

Mueller, Charles Curt. Das oligarquias agrárias ao predomínio urbano-industrial . Rio de Janeiro , 1983. 363 p. ; LC Card 87-403875 DDC 305.5/232/0981 19
HC187 .M76 1983

Smith, Gordon Whitford, 1934- Agricultural marketing and economic development . New York , 1987. iii, 417 p. ; ISBN 0-8240-1371-9 (alk. paper) : LC Card 87-11833 DDC 381/.41318/09816 19
HD9066.B84 S687 1987

BRAZIL - ECONOMIC CONDITIONS - 1918- - REGIONAL DISPARITIES.
Azzoni, Carlos Roberto. Indústria e reversão da polarização no Brasil /. São Paulo , 1986. 176 p. : LC Card 87-138915 DDC 338.6/042/0981 19
HC190.D5 A99 1986

BRAZIL - ECONOMIC CONDITIONS - 1945-
Schneider, José Odelso. Realidade brasileira . Porto Alegre-RS , c1986. 438 p. : LC Card 87-119174
HC187 .S393 1986

Serra, José. Brasil sem milagres /. São Paulo, SP , c1986. 174 p. : LC Card 87-404803 DDC 330.981/063 19
HC187 .S4153 1986

State and society in Brazil . Boulder , 1987. x, 349 p. ; ISBN 0-8133-7401-4 (pbk. : alk. paper) : LC Card 87-2160 DDC 981/.063 19
HC187 .S78 1987

BRAZIL - ECONOMIC CONDITIONS - 1945-1964.
Moreira, Marcílio Marques. The Brazilian quandary /. New York , 1986. vi, 87 p. : ISBN 0-87078-171-5 (pbk.) : LC Card 86-210942 DDC 332.3/4/0981 19
HJ8579 .M66 1986

A Transição incompleta . Rio de Janeiro-RJ , 1986. 2 v. ; LC Card 86-224684
HC187 .T72 1986

BRAZIL - ECONOMIC CONDITIONS - 1964-1985.
Alagoas (Brazil). Secretaria da Fazenda. Posicionamento das finanças de Alagoas na atual crise /. [Maceió] , 1983. 97 p. : LC Card 86-201070
HJ929.A52 A42 1983

Andrade, Luis F. The labor climate in Brazil /. Philadelphia, Pa. , c1985. viii, 133 p. ; ISBN 0-89546-057-2 (pbk.) LC Card 85-81947 DDC 331/.0981 19
HD8286.5 .A67 1985 ***NYPL [JLF 86-1201]***

Banas, Geraldo. Os donos do Brasil . São Paulo , 1984. 330 p. ; LC Card 87-673258
HD2834 .B34 1984

Cenários para a economia brasileira, 1984-1990. [Rio de Janeiro] , 1984. 81 p. : LC Card 85-209337
HC187 .C28 1984

Cysne, Rubens Penha. Breve retrospecto da economia brasileira entre 1979 e 1984 /. [Rio de Janeiro] [1985] 30 leaves ; LC Card 86-176751
HC187 .C98 1985

Franco, Luiz L. O Brasil que temos, o país que queremos /. Guarulhos, S.P. [Brazil] , c1985. 87 p. ; LC Card 86-223053
HC187 .F7315 1985

Gall, Norman. Brazil and Peru . Geneva , 1987. x, 123 p., [1] leaf of plates : ISBN 92-2-105506-X (pbk.) : LC Card 87-166425 DDC 338.2/7282/0981 19
HD9574.B82 G34 1987

Os Mistérios da inflação . São Paulo , 1986. 121 p. ; LC Card 86-189815
HG835 .M57 1986

Moreira, Marcílio Marques. The Brazilian quandary /. New York , 1986. vi, 87 p. : ISBN 0-87078-171-5 (pbk.) : LC Card 86-210942 DDC 332.3/4/0981 19
HJ8579 .M66 1986

Müller, Jürg. Brasilien /. Stuttgart , 1984. 278 p. : ISBN 3-12-928881-3 (pbk.) LC Card 87-673406
HC187 .M79x 1984

Nassif, Luís. O cruzado . São Paulo/SP , 1986. 255 p. : LC Card 86-224110
HG835 .N37 1986

Nogueira, Mauro R. O brasileiro não é viável-- . São Paulo , c1984. 253 p. : LC Card 84-256564
HC187 .N57 1984

Penna, João Camilo de Oliveira. As empresas estatais na economia brasileira /. [Brasília] , 1983. 43 p. ; LC Card 86-229392
HD4093 .P46 1983

Serra, José. A crise econômica e o flagelo do desemprego /. São Paulo , 1984. 27 p. : LC Card 87-124054 DDC 331.13/704 19
HD5708.47.B6 S47 1984

Tibiriçá, Luiz Caldas. Brasil . São Paulo, SP , 1984. 159 p. ; LC Card 84-215785
HC187 .T5 1984 ***NYPL [JLD 87-507]***

A Transição incompleta . Rio de Janeiro-RJ , 1986. 2 v. ; LC Card 86-224684
HC187 .T72 1986

BRAZIL - ECONOMIC CONDITIONS - 1964-1985 - PUBLIC OPINION.
Formiga, Marcone. Personagens da crise /. Brasília , 1984. 160 p. : LC Card 86-157831
HC187 .F636 1984

BRAZIL - ECONOMIC CONDITIONS - 1985-
Cenários para a economia brasileira, 1984-1990. [Rio de Janeiro] , 1984. 81 p. : LC Card 85-209337
HC187 .C28 1984

Mendonça, Sonia Regina de. Estado e economia no Brasil . Rio de Janeiro-RJ, Brasil , 1986. 106 p. ; LC Card 86-197575
HC187 .M469 1986

Os Mistérios da inflação . São Paulo , 1986. 121 p. ; LC Card 86-189815
HG835 .M57 1986

Modiano, Eduardo Marco. Da inflação ao cruzado . Rio de Janeiro , c1986. 126 p. : ISBN 85-7001-362-0 : LC Card 87-102624
HC187 .M593 1986

Nassif, Luís. O cruzado . São Paulo/SP , 1986. 255 p. : LC Card 86-224110
HG835 .N37 1986

Plano Cruzado . Rio de Janeiro , 1987. xii, 203 p. : LC Card 87-127770 DDC 338.981 19
HC187 .P59 1987

Política econômica da Nova República /. Rio de Janeiro, RJ [1986] 275 p. : LC Card 87-102398
HC187 .P67 1986

Rossetti, José Paschoal, 1941- O Brasil do cruzado . São Paulo-SP , 1986. 135 p. : LC Card 87-129096 DDC 338.981 19
HC187 .R673 1986

BRAZIL - ECONOMIC CONDITIONS - ECONOMETRIC MODELS.
Barbosa, Fernando de Holanda. Microeconomia--teoria, modelos econométricos e aplicações à economia brasileira /. Rio de Janeiro , 1985. 534 p. : LC Card 87-118555 DDC 338.5 19
HB179.P75 B37 1985

BRAZIL - ECONOMIC POLICY.
Bacha, Edmar Lisboa. El milagro y la crisis . México , 1986. 468 p. : ISBN 968-16-2152-2 LC Card 87-400019 DDC 338.981 19
HC187 .B128 1986

Baptista, Lourival. Reforma tributária, federalismo e desenvolvimento nacional /. Brasília , 1983. 255 p. : LC Card 86-210783
HJ2525 .B36 1983

Braga, Roberto Saturnino. Saturnino, o momento histórico do Congresso Nacional. Brasília , 1983. 58 p. ; LC Card 83-202638
HC187 .B76 1983

Brazil. Ministerio do Interior. Ação de desenvolvimento, 1979-1983 /. [Brasília] [1983?] 89 p. : LC Card 87-404839 DDC 338.981 19
HC187 .B862 1983

Brazil. Ministério do Interior. Subsecretaria de Programas Regionais. Programas especiais . [Brasília] [1981] 1 v. (various foliations) ; LC Card 87-403680 DDC 338.981/1 19
HD1875.A347 B7 1981

Calcagnotto, Gilberto. Brasilien 1974-1981 . Hamburg [1983] xi, 78 p. : LC Card 83-222930
HC187 .C143 1983

Cardoso, Eliana A. Inflation, growth and the real exchange rate . New York , 1987. 98 p. : ISBN 0-8240-1356-5 (alk. paper) : LC Card 87-8570 DDC 330.981 19
HC187 .C218 1987

Cidadão, estado e políticas no Brasil contemporâneo /. Brasília-Distrito Federal , c1986. 290 p. : ISBN 85-23-00214-6 LC Card 87-405054 DDC 338.981 19
HD1873 .C53 1986

Coelho, Carlos Nayro de Azevedo. Opções de política econômica /. Brasília , 1986. 137 p. ;

I C Card 87-403318 DDC 338.981 19
HC187 .C565 1986

Coes, Donald V., 1943- O Brasil na economia internacional. [Salvador, Brazil] [1984?] 55 p. : LC Card 86-234065
HF1513 .C64 1984

Cysne, Rubens Penha. Política macroeconômica no Brasil, 1964/66 e 1980/84 /. Rio de Janeiro, RJ [1986?] 125 p. : LC Card 86-229936
HC187 .C983 1986

Delfim Netto, Antônio. Brasil 82, a grande luta para manter o espaço para crescer . Brasília , 1982. 37 p. : LC Card 84-249919
HC187 .D552 1982

Delfim Netto, Antônio. Só o político pode salvar o economista /. Rio de Janeiro , 1986. xvii, 146 p. ; LC Card 87-137681 DDC 338.981 19
HC187 .D565 1986

Esperança e mundança. [Brasília] , 1981. 95 p. ; LC Card 86-202933
HC187 .E83 1981

Fischer, Bernhard, fl. 1979- Brasilien ohne Inflation? . Kiel [1986] 28 p. ; LC Card 87-120443 DDC 330 s 332.4/1/0981 19
HB44 .K45 no. 124 HG835

Fritsch, Winston. External constraints on economic policy in Brazil, 1889-1930 /. Pittsburgh, PA , 1988. p. cm. ISBN 0-8229-1147-7 LC Card 87-19209 DDC 338.981 19
HC187 .F757 1988

Haddad, Paulo Roberto. Dimensões do planejamento estadual no Brasil . Rio de Janeiro , 1985. 188 p. : LC Card 86-195636
HC188.M6 H33 1985

Henrique, Luiz. O salário perverso . Brasília , 1983. 129 p. ; LC Card 86-129394
HD5004 .H45 1983

Luca, Walmor de. Moratória com diretas já . Brasília , 1984. 69 p. ; LC Card 86-152773
HC188.S26 L83 1984

Martins Filho, Oséas de Souza. Desenvolvimento com equilíbrio social . São Luís, Ma. , 1985 (São Luís, MA : Serviço de Impr. e Obras Gráficas do Estado) 314 p. ; LC Card 86-229862
HC187 .M33 1985

Martins, Luciano, 1934- Estado capitalista e burocracia no Brasil pós-64 /. Rio de Janeiro, RJ , 1985. 265 p. ; LC Card 85-232969 DDC 338.981 19
HC187 .M2947 1985 ***NYPL [JLD 86-1691]***

Martone, Celso L. (Celso Luiz) Macroeconomic policies, debt accumulation, and adjustment in Brazil, 1965-84 /. Washington, D.C. , 1987. vii, 43 p. ; ISBN 0-8213-0892-0 (pbk.) LC Card 86-1527 DDC 336.3/4/0981 19
HJ8579 .M37 1987

Mendonça, Sonia Regina de. Estado e economia no Brasil . Rio de Janeiro-RJ, Brasil , 1986. 106 p. ; LC Card 86-197575
HC187 .M469 1986

Milone, Paulo Cesar. População, migração e desenvolvimento econômico . São Paulo , 1986. 150 p. : LC Card 87-118486 DDC 304.6/0981 19
HB3563 .M45 1986

Modiano, Eduardo Marco. Da inflação ao cruzado . Rio de Janeiro , c1986. 126 p. : ISBN 85-7001-362-0 : LC Card 87-102624
HC187 .M593 1986

Nassif, Luís. O cruzado . São Paulo/SP , 1986. 255 p. : LC Card 86-224110
HG835 .N37 1986

Nunes, Helvídio. Reforma tributária . Brasília , 1982. 108 p. ; LC Card 86-128083
HJ2527 .N85 1982

Peláez, Carlos Manuel. O cruzado e o austral . São Paulo , 1986. 174 p. : ISBN 85-22-40173-X LC Card 87-102770 DDC 332.4/981 19
HG835 .P43 1986

Perspectivas de longo prazo da economia brasileira /. [Rio de Janeiro, RJ] , 1985. 363 p. : LC Card 86-164342
HC187 .P415 1985

Plano Cruzado . Rio de Janeiro , 1987. xii, 203 p. : LC Card 87-127770 DDC 338.981 19
HC187 .P59 1987

Política econômica da Nova República /. Rio de Janeiro, RJ [1986] 275 p. : LC Card 87-102398
HC187 .P67 1986

Rabelo, Genival. Brasil, país das oportunidades perdidas /. [Brazil] 1977. 112 p. ; LC Card 85-210978
HC187 .R27 1977

Rossetti, José Paschoal, 1941- O Brasil do cruzado . São Paulo-SP , 1986. 135 p. : LC Card 87-129096 DDC 338.981 19
HC187 .R673 1986

Setor público, reordenamento e privatização /. [Rio de Janeiro, RJ , 1986] 47 p. : LC Card 87-403308 DDC 338.981 19
HC187 .S436 1986

Singer, Paul Israel, 1932- Dominação e desigualdade . Rio de Janeiro, RJ , 1981. 185 p. ; LC Card 82-148154
HC190.I5 S55 1981 ***NYPL [JLD 86-3364]***

State and society in Brazil . Boulder , 1987. x, 349 p. ; ISBN 0-8133-7401-4 (pbk. : alk. paper) : LC Card 87-2160 DDC 981/.063 19
HC187 .S78 1987

Tavares, José, 1949- Indústria bélica brasileira . Brasília , 1983. 44 p. ; LC Card 84-235004
HC187 .T2943 1983

Topik, Steven. The political economy of the Brazilian State, 1889-1930 /. Austin , 1987. xii, 241 p. : ISBN 0-292-76500-2 LC Card 87-5835 DDC 338.981 19
HC187 .T558 1987

Topik, Steven. State and economy . Austin , 1985. 28 p. ; LC Card 86-622250 DDC 338.981 19
HC187 .T56 1985

Vianna, Maria Lúcia Teixeira Werneck. A administração do "milagre" . Petrópolis , 1987. 180 p. ; LC Card 87-403982 DDC 332.4/981 19
HG835 .V527 1987

Vianna, Pedro Jorge Ramos. Inflação vs. indexação, uma contribuição ao tema /. Fortaleza-Ceará [19]84. 121 p. : LC Card 86-130092
HG835 .V53 1984

BRAZIL - ECONOMIC POLICY - ECONOMETRIC MODELS.
Werneck, Rogério L. Furquim. Desequilíbrio externo e reorientação do crescimento e dos investimentos . Rio de Janeiro-RJ [1983?] 130 p. ; LC Card 87-403024 DDC 338.981 19
HC187 .W47 1983

BRAZIL - ECONOMIC POLICY - PUBLIC OPINION.
Formiga, Marcone. Personagens da crise /. Brasília , 1984. 160 p. : LC Card 86-157831
HC187 .F636 1984

Brazil. Empresa Brasileira de Planejamento de Transportes. see **Empresa Brasileira de Planejamento de Transportes.**

Brazil. Fazenda, Ministério da. see **Brazil. Ministério da Fazenda.**

BRAZIL - FOREIGN ECONOMIC RELATIONS.
Coes, Donald V., 1943- O Brasil na economia internacional. [Salvador, Brazil] [1984?] 55 p. : LC Card 86-234065
HF1513 .C64 1984

Simonsen, Mário Henrique. A nova ordem econômica internacional e suas consequências no Brasil . Salvador , 1983. 60 p. ; LC Card 87-144638 DDC 337.81 19
HF1513 .S55 1983

BRAZIL - FOREIGN ECONOMIC RELATIONS - AFRICA.
Collins, Paul D. Brazil in Africa . Austin , 1986. 16 p. ; LC Card 86-622252 DDC 337.8106 19
HF1514.5.A35 C65 1986

BRAZIL - FOREIGN ECONOMIC RELATIONS - PARAGUAY.
Menezes, Alfredo da Mota, 1944- A herança de Stroessner . Campinas, SP [1987] 186 p. ; LC Card 87-404011 DDC 337.810892 19
HF1524.5.B7 M46 1987

BRAZIL - FOREIGN ECONOMIC RELATIONS - UNITED STATES.
Coes, Donald V., 1943- O Brasil na economia internacional. [Salvador, Brazil] [1984?] 55 p. : LC Card 86-234065
HF1513 .C64 1984

Hirst, Mônica. As relações dos Estados Unidos com as potências médias na América Latina, México e Brasil /. [Rio de Janeiro] , 1985. 48 leaves ; LC Card 87-143873 DDC 337.73072 19
HF1456.5.M6 H57 1985

BRAZIL - FOREIGN RELATIONS.
State and society in Brazil . Boulder , 1987. x, 349 p. ; ISBN 0-8133-7401-4 (pbk. : alk. paper) : LC Card 87-2160 DDC 981/.063 19
HC187 .S78 1987

Brazil. Fundação IBGE. see **Fundação IBGE.**

Brazil. Fundação Nacional do Bem-Estar do Meror. see **Fundação Nacional do Bem-Estar do Menor.**

Brazil - Government. see **Brazil - Politics and government.**

Brazil. Grupo de Trabalho para Reformulação do Sistema Financeiro da Habitação.
Reformulação : relatório final do GTR/SFH. [Brasília] : Gráfica BNH, 1986. 94 leaves ; 30 cm. Cover title. At head of title: Presidência da República, Ministério do Desenvolvimento Urbano e Meio Ambiente. LC Card 87-144710 DDC 363.5/8 19
1. Housing policy - Brazil. 2. Housing - Brazil - Finance. I. Title. II. Title: Relatório final do GTR/SFH.
HD7323.A3 B7 1986

Brazil. Grupo Executivo de Eletrificação Rural de Cooperativas. Eletrificação rural no Brasil / [GEER, Grupo Executivo de Eletrificação Rural de Cooperativas, Ministério da Agricultura]. Brasília, DF : GEER, [1984] 93 p. : ill. ; 22 cm. LC Card 86-200328
1. Rural electrification - Brazil. I. Title.
HD9688.B72 B74 1984

BRAZIL - HISTORY - TO 1821.
Ohlweiler, Otto Alcides. Evolução sócio-econômica do Brasil /. Porto Alegre-RS, Brasil [1986?] 209 p. ; LC Card 86-229515
HC187 .O43 1986

BRAZIL - HISTORY - 1822-
Ohlweiler, Otto Alcides. Evolução sócio-econômica do Brasil /. Porto Alegre-RS, Brasil [1986?] 209 p. ; LC Card 86-229515
HC187 .O43 1986

Topik, Steven. State and economy . Austin , 1985. 28 p. ; LC Card 86-622250 DDC 338.981 19
HC187 .T56 1985

BRAZIL - HISTORY - 1889-1930.
Topik, Steven. The political economy of the Brazilian State, 1889-1930 /. Austin , 1987. xii, 241 p. : ISBN 0-292-76500-2 LC Card 87-5835 DDC 338.981 19
HC187 .T558 1987

BRAZIL - HISTORY - 1930-1954.
BRAZIL - HISTORY - 1954-
Brazil in Africa . Collins, Paul D. Austin , 1986. 16 p. ; LC Card 86-622252 DDC 337.8106 19
HF1514.5.A35 C65 1986

Brazil. Indústria e do Comércio, Ministério da. see **Brazil. Ministério da Indústria e do Comércio.**

BRAZIL - INDUSTRIES.
Baumann Neves, Renato. Exportações e crescimento industrial no Brasil /. Rio de Janeiro , 1985. 274 p. : LC Card 86-195612
HF1513 .B38 1985

Magalhães, João Paulo de Almeida. Uma política industrial para o Brasil /. [Rio de Janeiro] [between 1985 and 1987] 161 p. ; LC Card 87-403992 DDC 338.981 19
HD3616.B83 M34 1985

Tadini, Venilton. O setor de bens de capital sob encomenda . São Paulo , 1986. 142 p. : LC Card 87-154239 DDC 332/.0414/0981 19
HC190.C3 T33 1986

BRAZIL - INDUSTRIES - ENERGY CONSERVATION.
O'Keefe, Hsu Yuet Heung. A crise do petróleo e a economia brasileira /. São Paulo , 1984. 137

p. : LC Card 85-143617 DDC 338.2/3 19
HD9574.B82 O43 1984
NYPL [JLD 86-2712]

BRAZIL - INDUSTRIES - ENERGY CONSUMPTION - ECONOMETRIC MODELS.
Santos, José Carlos de Souza. Demanda de fatores, energia e substituição na indústria brasileira, 1970/79 /. São Paulo , 1986. 183 p. : LC Card 86-234783
HB241 .S26 1986

BRAZIL - INDUSTRIES - HISTORY.
Chacon, Vamireh. Kultur und Entwicklung in Brasilien . Dortmund , 1970. v, 308 p. ; LC Card 86-172094
HC187 .C44 1970

Pena, Maria Valéria Junho. Mulheres e trabalhadoras . Rio de Janeiro, RJ , 1981. iii, 227 p. ; LC Card 81-216820 DDC 331.4/0981 19
HD6124 .P46 1981 NYPL [JLD 86-1557]

Topik, Steven. The political economy of the Brazilian State, 1889-1930 /. Austin , 1987. xii, 241 p. : ISBN 0-292-76500-2 LC Card 87-5835 DDC 338.981 19
HC187 .T558 1987

BRAZIL - INDUSTRIES - LOCATION.
Azzoni, Carlos Roberto. Indústria e reversão da polarização no Brasil /. São Paulo , 1986. 176 p. : LC Card 87-138915 DDC 338.6/042/0981 19
HC190.D5 A99 1986

BRAZIL - INDUSTRIES - STATISTICS.
Indices da produção industrial . Rio de Janeiro , 1986. 178 p. : ISBN 85-24-00246-8 LC Card 87-403858 DDC 338.0981/021 19
HC187 .I534 1986

Brazil. Inspectoria Federal de Obras contra as Seccas. Relatorio dos trabalhos executados durante o anno de 1925 : apresentado ao Sr. Dr. Francisco Sá, Ministro da Viação e Obras Publicas. Rio de Janeiro : Ministerio da Viação e Obras Publicas, Inspectoria Federal de Obras contra as Seccas, 1926. xiv, 75 p. ; 27 cm. (Publicação / Inspectoria Federal de Obras contra as Seccas . n. 70, sér. 2, M) LC Card 85-186786
1. Water resource development - Brazil. 2. Drought relief - Brazil. 3. Droughts - Economic aspects - Brazil. 4. Seca. I. Series: Publicação (Brazil. Inspectoria Federal de Obras contra as Seccas) , n. 70, sér. 2, M. II. Title.
HD1696.B8 B73 1926

Brazil. Instituto de Planejamento Econômico e Social. see Instituto de Planejamento Econômico e Social.

Brazil. Instituto Nacional de Colonização e Reforma Agraria. see Instituto Nacional de Colonização e Reforma Agraria.

Brazil. Interior, Ministerio do. see Brazil. Ministerio do Interior.

Brazil. Itaipu (Power Plant) see Itaipu (Power plant)

BRAZIL - MANUFACTURES.
Pinto, Maurício Barata de Paula. O potencial das exportações brasileiras de manufaturados /. Rio de Janeiro , 1983. 46 p. ; LC Card 87-403022 DDC 382/.4567/0981 19
HD9734.B72 P56 1983

BRAZIL - MANUFACTURES - HISTORY.
Dornas Filho, João. O ouro das Gerais e a civilização da Capitania /. São Paulo , 1957. 238 p., [8] leaves of plates : LC Card 84-215039
HC187 .D72 1957

BRAZIL - MANUFACTURES - STATISTICS.
Nunnenkamp, Peter. Manufactured export performance of Brazil . Kiel [1986] v, 114 p. : LC Card 87-101193 DDC 382/.4567/0981 19
HF1513 .N86 1986

Brazil. Ministerio da Agricultura. Instituto Nacional de Colonização e Reforma Agrarie. see Instituto Nacional de Colonização e Reforma Agraria.

Brazil. Ministério da Fazenda. (Old Catalog form: Brazil. Fazenda, Ministerio da)
Cotia, Raul Fontes. Comentário sôbre os balanços gerais da União de 1963 /. [Brasília] [1964] 45 p. ; LC Card 85-194302
HJ2079 .C68 1964

Brazil. Ministério da Indústria e do Comércio. A política industrial da nova república. [Brasília, Brazil] : Ministério da Indústria e do Comércio, [1985] 44 p. ; 21 cm. LC Card 87-404994 DDC 338.981 19
1. Industry and state - Brazil. I. Title.
HD3616.B83 B66 1985

Brazil. Ministério das Minas e Energia. Departamento Nacional da Produção Mineral. see Brazil. Departamento Nacional da Produção Mineral.

Brazil. Ministerio do Interior.
Ação de desenvolvimento, 1979-1983 / Ministério do Interior. [Brasília] : Ministério do Interior, Gabinete do Ministro, Coordenadoria de Comunicação Social, [1983?] 89 p. : maps (some col.) ; 30 cm. LC Card 87-404839 DDC 338.981 19
1. Economic development projects - Brazil. 2. Brazil - Economic policy. I. Title.
HC187 .B862 1983

Programa de Irrigação do Nordeste--PROINE : (1 milhão de hectares, 1986-1990). Brasília : Coordenadoria de Comunicação Social do Ministério do Interior, 1986. 30 p. ; 21 cm. (Publicação . 1/86) "Supervisão geral, Ministério do Interior; coordenação executiva, Superintendência de Desenvolvimento do Nordeste--SUDENE; órgãos federais executores, Companhia de Desenvolvimento do Vale do São Francisco--CODEVASF, Departamento Nacional de Obras Contra as Secas--DNOCS, Departamento Nacional de Obras de Saneamento--DNOS." LC Card 87-400672 DDC 333.91/3/09813 19
1. Irrigation - Brazil, Northeast. I. Series: Publicação (Brazil. Ministério do Interior. Coordenadoria de Comunicação Social) , 86/01. II. Title.
HD1741.B82 N623 1986

Brazil. Ministério do Interior. Secretaria de Planejamento.
Programa nacional de apoio às migrações internas / Ministério do Interior, Secretaria Geral, Secretaria de Planejamento. Brasília : Ministério do Interior, Secretaria Geral, Secretaria de Planejamento, 1980. 42 p. ; 22 cm. LC Card 86-203543 DDC 362.8/5 19
1. Migration, Internal - Government policy - Brazil. 2. Social service - Brazil. 3. Migrant labor - Brazil - Services for. I. Title.
HB2023 .B73 1980

Projeto sertanejo . [Brasília] [1982?] 20 leaves, [1] leaf of plates : LC Card 87-405007
HD1875.N6 P76 1982

Brazil. Ministério do Interior. Secretaria de Programas Regionais. Projeto sertanejo . [Brasília] [1982?] 20 leaves, [1] leaf of plates : LC Card 87-405007
HD1875.N6 P76 1982

Brazil. Ministério do Interior. Subsecretaria de Programas Regionais.
A Agricultura irrigada como estratégia de desenvolvimento regional /. Brasília [198-] 56 leaves ; LC Card 87-403682 DDC 338.1/62 19
HD1741.B82 N614 1980z

Atuação dos programas especiais no Estado do Piauí /. [Brasília] [1980] [29] leaves : LC Card 87-403685 DDC 333.91/0098122 19
HD1696.B83 P523 1980

Minutas das exposições de motivos e portarias dos programas : programação para 1983--PRODOPAR, PRONOROESTE, PROMIRIM, PRODENOR / Ministério do Interior, Secretaria Geral, Secretaria de Planejamento-SPL, Subsecretaria de Programas Regionais-SPR. [Brasília] : A Subsecretaria, [1983?] [40] leaves ; 30 cm. (Série Programas especiais . 57) LC Card 87-400579 DDC 333.91/15/0981 19
1. Water resources development - Brazil - Case studies. I. Title. II. Series.
HD1696.B8 B75 1983

Programa de aproveitamento de recursos hídricos do Nordeste : programação 1980 / Ministério do Interior, Secretaria Geral, Secretaria de Planejamento-SPL, Subsecretaria de Programas Regionais-SPR. Brasília : A Subsecretaria, [1980] [73] leaves ; 30 cm. (Série Programas especiais . 10) LC Card 87-403686 DDC 333.91/00981/3 19
1. Water resources development - Government policy - Brazil, Northeast. I. Title. II. Series.
HD1696.B84 N649 1980

Programas especiais : programação 1981 : exposições de motivos / Ministério do Interior, Secretaria Geral, Secretaria de Planejamento--SPL, Subsecretaria de Programas Regionais--SPR. [Brasília] : SPR, [1981] 1 v. (various foliations) ; 30 cm. (Série Programas especiais . 34) LC Card 87-403680 DDC 338.981/1 19
1. Agricultural development projects - Amazon River Region. 2. Economic development projects - Amazon River Region. 3. Brazil - Economic policy. I. Title. II. Series.
HD1875.A347 B7 1981

Brazil. Ministério do Interior. Superintendência do Desenvolvimento do Nordste. see Brazil. Superintendência do Desenvolvimento do Nordeste.

Brazil. Ministerio do Planejamento e Coordenação Geral. Fundação IBGE. see **Fundação IBGE.**

Brazil. Ministério do Planejamento e Coordenação Geral. Instituto de Planejamento Econômico e Social. see **Instituto de Planejamento Econômico e Social.**

Brazil. Ministério do Trabalho. Macedo, Roberto Brás Matos. FGTS e a rotatividade /. São Paulo-SP , Brasília-DF , 1985. 231 p. : ISBN 85-21-30271-1 LC Card 85-187484
HD7096.B6 M33 1985

Brazil. Ministério dos Transportes.
Conferência do Ministro dos Transportes na Escola Superior de Guerra . [Brasília] [198-] [61] p. : LC Card 86-193198
HE233 .C59 1980z

Severo, Cloraldino. A política dos transportes no Brasil, 1979/85 /. [Brasília] , 1983. 91 p. : LC Card 86-153346
HE233 .S44 1983

Brazil. Ministério dos Transportes. Empresa Brasileira de Planejamento de Transportes. see **Empresa Brasileira de Planejamento de Transportes.**

Brazil. Ministério Extraordinário para a Coordenação dos Organismos Regionais. Superintendência do Desenvolvimento do Nordeste. see **Brazil. Superintendência do Desenvolvimento do Nordeste.**

Brazil-- money and credit programming in 1983 /. National Monetary Council (Brazil) Brazil [1982] 38 p. ; LC Card 87-131446
HG835 .N36 1982

Brazil. Nordeste, Superintendência do Desenvolvimento do. see Brazil. Superintendência do Desenvolvimento do Nordeste.

BRAZIL, NORTHEAST - ECONOMIC CONDITIONS.
Agripino, Jose. Compromisso com o povo . [Natal, Brazil] [1983?] 19 p. ; LC Card 86-215313
HC188.R38 A54 1983

Andrade, Manuel Correia de Oliveira. Sertão sul /. Recife , 1984. 648, [26] p. : LC Card 87-404838 DDC 330.981/3063 19
HC188.N6 A687 1984

Aspectos gerais da economia e da sociedade do Nordeste. Recife , 1984. 318 p. : LC Card 86-159446
HC188.N6 A75 1984

Guerra, Paulo de Brito, 1914- A civilização da seca . Fortaleza , 1981. 324 p. : LC Card 82-231215 DDC 361.6/0981/3 19
HT395.B72 N63 1981 NYPL [JLD 86-2873]

Magalhães, Antônio Carlos. Meu compromisso com o Nordeste . [Salvador , 1983] 302 p. ; LC Card 86-233485
HC188.B7242 M34 1983

Malvezzi, Roberto. Mil quatrocentos e sessenta dias no império do sol . São Paulo , 1985. 197 p. : ISBN 85-05-00296-2 : LC Card 85-200637
HC188.N6 M34 1985

Melo, Mário Lacerda de. O meio-norte /. Recife , 1983. 474 p., [1] folded leaf of plates : LC Card 84-231900
HC188.N6 M45 1983

Penner, Maria Eunice Soares. A dialética da atividade pesqueira no nordeste amazônico /. Belém , 1984. 158 p. : ISBN 85-24-70006-8 LC Card 86-158128
HD9464.B73 N676 1984

Rönick, Volker. Regionale Entwicklungspolitik und Massenarmut im ländlichen Raum Nordost-Brasiliens . Paderborn , 1986. 136 p. : ISBN 3-506-73225-0 LC Card 87-407836 DDC 338.981/3 19
HC188.N6 R66 1986

BRAZIL, NORTHEAST - ECONOMIC CONDITIONS - 1964-

Pessoa, Dirceu Murilo. Espace rural et pauvreté au nord-est du Brésil /. Paris , 1981. xvii, 288 leaves : LC Card 86-208627
HC188.N6 P47 1981

BRAZIL, NORTHEAST - ECONOMIC CONDITIONS - CONGRESSES.

A Questão Nordeste . Rio de Janeiro-RJ , 1984. 137 p. ; LC Card 84-191031
HC188.N6 Q47 1984

BRAZIL, NORTHEAST - ECONOMIC CONDITIONS - STATISTICS.

Nordeste, estatísticas. [S.l.] [195-] iv, 50 leaves : LC Card 85-127235
HC188.N6 N69 1950z

BRAZIL, NORTHEAST - ECONOMIC POLICY.

Avaliação do polonordeste e do Projeto Sertanejo. Fortaleza , 1985. 314 p. : LC Card 87-402900 DDC 338.981/3 19
HC188.N6 A94 1985

Avena Filho, Armando. Nordeste e Bahia . Salvador , 1986. 196 p. ; LC Card 87-403867 DDC 338.981/42 19
HC188.B3 A94 1986

Magalhães, Antônio Carlos. Meu compromisso com o Nordeste . [Salvador , 1983] 302 p. ; LC Card 86-233485
HC188.B7242 M34 1983

Nunes, Helvídio. Reforma tributária . Brasília , 1982. 108 p. ; LC Card 86-128083
HJ2527 .N85 1982

Rönick, Volker. Regionale Entwicklungspolitik und Massenarmut im ländlichen Raum Nordost-Brasiliens . Paderborn , 1986. 136 p. : ISBN 3-506-73225-0 LC Card 87-407836 DDC 338.981/3 19
HC188.N6 R66 1986

BRAZIL, NORTHEAST - ECONOMIC POLICY - CONGRESSES.

Dinâmica da economia e absorção de mão-de-obra . Recife , 1984. 79 p. ; ISBN 85-7019-063-8 LC Card 85-156612 DDC 338.981/3 19
HD5755.N63 D56 1984
NYPL [JLE 86-3545]

Brazil, Northeast - Government. see **Brazil, Northeast - Politics and government.**

BRAZIL, NORTHEAST - INDUSTRIES.

Magalhães, Antonio Rocha. Industrialização e desenvolvimento regional . Brasília , 1983. 315 p. : LC Card 84-160221 DDC 338.981/3 19
HD3616.B84 N676 1983
NYPL [JLD 86-3120]

BRAZIL, NORTHEAST - POLITICS AND GOVERNMENT - CONGRESSES.

A Questão Nordeste . Rio de Janeiro-RJ , 1984. 137 p. ; LC Card 84-191031
HC188.N6 Q47 1984

BRAZIL, NORTHEAST - POPULATION.

Aspectos gerais da economia e da sociedade do Nordeste. Recife , 1984. 318 p. : LC Card 86-159446
HC188.N6 A75 1984

Moura, Hélio A. de (Hélio Augusto) Dinâmica demográfica recente dos estados e microrregiões do Nordeste, 1960/1980 /. Recife [Brazil] , 1986. 95 p., [6] folded p. of plates : LC Card 87-131106 DDC 304.6/0981/3 19
HB3564.N66 M68 1986

BRAZIL, NORTHEAST - RURAL CONDITIONS.

Andrade, Manuel Correia de Oliveira. Sertão sul /. Recife , 1984. 648, [26] p. : LC Card 87-404838 DDC 330.981/3063 19
HC188.N6 A687 1984

Pessoa, Dirceu Murilo. Espace rural et pauvreté au nord-est du Brésil /. Paris , 1981. xvii, 288 leaves : LC Card 86-208627
HC188.N6 P47 1981

BRAZIL, NORTHEAST - SOCIAL CONDITIONS.

Aspectos gerais da economia e da sociedade do Nordeste. Recife , 1984. 318 p. : LC Card 86-159446
HC188.N6 A75 1984

Malvezzi, Roberto. Mil quatrocentos e sessenta dias no império do sol . São Paulo , 1985. 197 p. : ISBN 85-05-00296-2 : LC Card 85-200637
HC188.N6 M34 1985

Rönick, Volker. Regionale Entwicklungspolitik und Massenarmut im ländlichen Raum Nordost-Brasiliens . Paderborn , 1986. 136 p. : ISBN 3-506-73225-0 LC Card 87-407836 DDC 338.981/3 19
HC188.N6 R66 1986

BRAZIL, NORTHEAST - SOCIAL CONDITIONS - 1964-

Pessoa, Dirceu Murilo. Espace rural et pauvreté au nord-est du Brésil /. Paris , 1981. xvii, 288 leaves : LC Card 86-208627
HC188.N6 P47 1981

BRAZIL, NORTHEAST - SOCIAL CONDITIONS - CONGRESSES.

A Questão Nordeste . Rio de Janeiro-RJ , 1984. 137 p. ; LC Card 84-191031
HC188.N6 Q47 1984

BRAZIL, NORTHEAST - SOCIAL CONDITIONS - STATISTICS.

Nordeste, estatísticas. [S.l.] [195-] iv, 50 leaves : LC Card 85-127235
HC188.N6 N69 1950z

BRAZIL, NORTHEAST - SOCIAL POLICY.

Avaliação do polonordeste e do Projeto Sertanejo. Fortaleza , 1985. 314 p. : LC Card 87-402900 DDC 338.981/3 19
HC188.N6 A94 1985

Brazil. Planejamento, Secretaria de. see **Brazil. Secretaria de Planejamento.**

BRAZIL - POLITICS AND GOVERNMENT - 1822-

Hahner, June Edith, 1940- Poverty and politics . Albuquerque , 1986. xvi, 415 p. : ISBN 0-8263-0878-3 : LC Card 86-1258 DDC 305.5/69/0981 19
HC190.P6 H34 1986 *NYPL [JLE 86-4407]*

BRAZIL - POLITICS AND GOVERNMENT - 20TH CENTURY.

Getúlio Vargas e a economia contemporânea /. Campinas , 1986. 179 p. ; ISBN 85-26-80033-7 LC Card 87-403048 DDC 330.981/063 19
HC187 .G45 1986

Muszynski, Maria Judith de Brito. O impacto político das migrações internas . São Paulo , 1986. 169 p. : LC Card 86-234794
HB2023 .M87 1986

Schneider, José Odelso. Realidade brasileira . Porto Alegre-RS , c1986. 438 p. : LC Card 87-119174
HC187 .S393 1986

BRAZIL - POLITICS AND GOVERNMENT - 1964-1985.

Andrade, Luis F. The labor climate in Brazil /. Philadelphia, Pa. , c1985. viii, 133 p. ; ISBN 0-89546-057-2 (pbk.) LC Card 85-81947 DDC 331/.0981 19
HD8286.5 .A67 1985 *NYPL [JLF 86-1201]*

Nogueira, Mauro R. O brasileiro não é viável-- . São Paulo , c1984. 253 p. : LC Card 84-256564
HC187 .N57 1984

Nunes, Helvídio. Reforma tributária . Brasília , 1982. 108 p. ; LC Card 86-128083
HJ2527 .N85 1982

Pinheiro, Saramago. Reforma agrária . Brasília , 1986. 46 p. ; LC Card 86-228887
HD1333.B6 P56 1986

BRAZIL - POLITICS AND GOVERNMENT - 1965-1984.

Tibiriçá, Luiz Caldas. Brasil . São Paulo, SP , 1984. 159 p. ; LC Card 84-215785
HC187 .T5 1984 *NYPL [JLD 87-507]*

BRAZIL - POLITICS AND GOVERNMENT - 1985-

Cidadão, estado e políticas no Brasil contemporâneo /. Brasília-Distrito Federal , c1986. 290 p. : ISBN 85-23-00214-6 LC Card 87-405054 DDC 338.981 19
HD1873 .C53 1986

State and society in Brazil . Boulder , 1987. x, 349 p. ; ISBN 0-8133-7401-4 (pbk. : alk. paper) : LC Card 87-2160 DDC 981/.063 19
HC187 .S78 1987

BRAZIL - POPULATION.

Milone, Paulo Cesar. População, migração e desenvolvimento econômico . São Paulo , 1986. 150 p. : LC Card 87-118486 DDC 304.6/0981 19
HB3563 .M45 1986

Schneider, José Odelso. Realidade brasileira . Porto Alegre-RS , c1986. 438 p. : LC Card 87-119174
HC187 .S393 1986

A Transição incompleta . Rio de Janeiro-RJ , 1986. 2 v. ; LC Card 86-224684
HC187 .T72 1986

BRAZIL - POPULATION - CONGRESSES.

Política demográfica /. Salvador [1983] 82 p. : LC Card 87-138903 DDC 304.6/0981 19
HB3563 .P65 1983

BRAZIL - POPULATION POLICY - CONGRESSES.

Política demográfica /. Salvador [1983] 82 p. : LC Card 87-138903 DDC 304.6/0981 19
HB3563 .P65 1983

Brazil. Presidência. Secretaria de Planejamento. see **Brazil. Secretaria de Planejamento.**

Brazil. Produção Mineral, Departamento Nacional da. see **Brazil. Departamento Nacional da Produção Mineral.**

BRAZIL - PUBLIC LANDS.

Ferreira, Benedito, 1932- A questão fundiária /. Brasília , 1986. 171 p. ; LC Card 86-229678
HD496 .F42 1986

BRAZIL - RURAL CONDITIONS.

A Transição incompleta . Rio de Janeiro-RJ , 1986. 2 v. ; LC Card 86-224684
HC187 .T72 1986

Brazil. Secretaria de Mão-de-Obra. Subsecretaria de Estudos, Análises e Metodologia. Grupos homogêneos no mercado de trabalho assalariado . Brasília , 1985. 56 p. : LC Card 85-231654
HD5004 .G78 1985

Brazil. Secretaria de Planejamento. Delfim Netto, Antônio. Brasil 82, a grande luta para manter o espaço para crescer . Brasília , 1982. 37 p. : LC Card 84-249919
HC187 .D552 1982

Brazil. Secretaria de Tecnologia Industrial. Avaliação do Programa Nacional do Álcool /. Brasília , 1985. 175 p. : LC Card 86-146662
HD9502.5.A433 B622 1985

BRAZIL. SERVICO NACIONAL DE APRENDIZAGEM INDUSTRIAL.

Silva, Angela Inês Gandra e. Os acordos SENAI/empresa . Rio de Janeiro-RJ-Brasil , 1985. xvii, 97 p. ; LC Card 86-176735
HD5715.5.B68 S55 1985

Zingg, Rosa Lúcia. O SENAI e o mercado de trabalho industrial paulista . [São Paulo] , 1986. 37 leaves ; LC Card 87-402164 DDC 331.12/5/098161021 19
HD5755.S3 Z56 1986

Brazil. Serviço Nacional de Aprendizagem Industrial. Departamento Regional da Paraíba. Divisão de Planejamento e Avaliação. Azevedo, Edilza Araújo. Causas de evasão. [Campina Grande, Brasil] , 1984. 104 leaves : LC Card 85-203901
HD5715.5.B69 P335 1984

Brazil. Serviço Nacional de Aprendizagem Industrial. Departamento Regional de Minas Gerais. Assessoria de Comunicação. Resenha SENAI-MG, 10 anos. Belo Horizonte , 1985. 128 p. ; LC Card 86-200862
HD5715 .R46 1985

Brazil. Serviço Nacional de Aprendizagem Industrial. Departamento Regional de Minas Gerais. Resenha SENAI-MG. Resenha SENAI-MG, 10 anos. Belo Horizonte , 1985. 128 p. ; LC Card 86-200862
HD5715 .R46 1985

BRAZIL. SERVIÇO NACIONAL DE APRENDIZAGEM INDUSTRIAL. DEPARTAMENTO REGIONAL DE MINAS GERAIS. RESENHA SENAI-MG - HISTORY.

Resenha SENAI-MG, 10 anos. Belo

Horizonte , 1985. 128 p. ; LC Card 86-200862
HD5715 .R46 1985

Brazil. Serviço Nacional de Aprendizagem Industrial. Departamento Regional de São Paulo.
Silveira, Maria Luiza Faraone. Mão-de-obra de nível médio . São Paulo , 1986. 239 p. : LC Card 87-143876 DDC 331.11/422 19
HD5754 .S55 1986

Brazil. Serviço Nacional de Aprendizagem Industrial. Departamento Regional de São Paulo. Divisão de Pesquisas, Estudos e Avaliação. Zingg, Rosa Lúcia. O SENAI e o mercado de trabalho industrial paulista . [São Paulo] , 1986. 37 leaves ; LC Card 87-402164 DDC 331.12/5/098161021 19
HD5755.S3 Z56 1986

BRAZIL - SOCIAL CONDITIONS.
Getúlio Vargas e a economia contemporânea /. Campinas , 1986. 179 p. ; ISBN 85-26-80033-7 LC Card 87-403048 DDC 330.981/063 19
HC187 .G45 1986

Hahner, June Edith, 1940- Poverty and politics . Albuquerque , 1986. xvi, 415 p. : ISBN 0-8263-0878-3 : LC Card 86-1258 DDC 305.5/69/0981 19
HC190.P6 H34 1986 *NYPL [JLE 86-4407]*

BRAZIL - SOCIAL CONDITIONS - 1945-
Calcagnotto, Gilberto. Brasilien 1974-1981 . Hamburg [1983] xi, 78 p. : LC Card 83-222930
HC187 .C143 1983

BRAZIL - SOCIAL CONDITIONS - 1945-1964.
A Transição incompleta . Rio de Janeiro-RJ , 1986. 2 v. ; LC Card 86-224684
HC187 .T72 1986

BRAZIL - SOCIAL CONDITIONS - 1964-
Müller, Jürg. Brasilien /. Stuttgart , 1984. 278 p. : ISBN 3-12-928881-3 (pbk.) LC Card 87-673406
HC187 .M79x 1984

Nogueira, Mauro R. O brasileiro não é viável-- . São Paulo , c1984. 253 p. : LC Card 84-256564
HC187 .N57 1984

Schneider, José Odelso. Realidade brasileira . Porto Alegre-RS , c1986. 438 p. : LC Card 87-119174
HC187 .S393 1986

Serra, José. Brasil sem milagres /. São Paulo, SP , c1986. 174 p. : LC Card 87-404803 DDC 330.981/063 19
HC187 .S4153 1986

Tibiriçá, Luiz Caldas. Brasil . São Paulo, SP , 1984. 159 p. ; LC Card 84-215785
HC187 .T5 1984 *NYPL [JLD 87-507]*

A Transição incompleta . Rio de Janeiro-RJ , 1986. 2 v. ; LC Card 86-224684
HC187 .T72 1986

BRAZIL - SOCIAL POLICY.
Cidadão, estado e políticas no Brasil contemporâneo /. Brasília-Distrito Federal , c1986. 290 p. : ISBN 85-23-00214-6 LC Card 87-405054 DDC 338.981 19
HD1873 .C53 1986

Esperança e mundança. [Brasília] , 1981. 95 p. ; LC Card 86-202933
HC187 .E83 1981

Martins Filho, Oséas de Souza. Desenvolvimento com equilíbrio social . São Luís, Ma. , 1985 (São Luís, MA : Serviço de Impr. e Obras Gráficas do Estado) 314 p. ; LC Card 86-229862
HC187 .M33 1985

BRAZIL, SOUTH - ECONOMIC CONDITIONS.
Banco Regional de Desenvolvimento do Extremo sul. O planejamento e os pré-investimentos /. [Porto Alegre?] [19]85. 71, [6], p. 21 leaves ; LC Card 86-201808
HC188.S68 B35 1985

BRAZIL, SOUTH - ECONOMIC POLICY.
Banco Regional de Desenvolvimento do Extremo sul. BRDE . [Curitiba] , 1984. 95 p., [8] : LC Card 86-143911
HG2889.S6 B36 1984

Campos, José Hypólito Machado de. BRDE, a ação governamental na promoção do desenvolvimento econômico e social da Região Sul /. Porto Alegre [between 1983 and 1985] 51 p. ; LC Card 86-143903
HG2889.S6 C36 1983

BRAZIL, SOUTH - SOCIAL POLICY.
Campos, José Hypólito Machado de. BRDE, a ação governamental na promoção do desenvolvimento econômico e social da Região Sul /. Porto Alegre [between 1983 and 1985] 51 p. ; LC Card 86-143903
HG2889.S6 C36 1983

BRAZIL - STATISTICS.
Inquéritos especiais /. Rio de Janeiro, Brasil , 1984. 4 v. in 5. ; *NYPL [JLF 86-202]*

Brazil. Sudene. see **Brazil. Superintendência do Desenvolvimento do Nordeste.**

Brazil. Superintendência da Zona Franca de Manaus. Plano Diretor do Distrito Agropecuário / Superintendência da Zona Franca de Manaus. Manaus : SUFRAMA, 1984. 86 p. : ill., maps ; 28 cm. Cover title. LC Card 85-209805
1. Agricultural development projects - Brazil - Manaus Region. 2. Agriculture and state - Brazil - Manaus Region. I. Title.
HD1875.M325 B73 1984

Brazil. Superintendência do Desenvolvimento da Amazônia. Coordenação de Informática. Divisão de Documentação. Silva, Maria José Oliveira e. A sociedade amazônica e o problema social da desocupação e subocupação /. Belém , 1974. 42 p., 53 leaves : LC Card 86-183026
HB3564.A73 S55 1974

Brazil. Superintendência do Desenvolvimento da Região Centro-Oeste.
Centro-Oeste . [Brasília] [1983] 196 p., [3] leaves of plates : LC Card 85-208305
HC188.C46 C47 1983

Centro-Oeste brasileiro /. [Brasília] , 1981. 9 v. : LC Card 87-405115 DDC 330.981/7063 19
HC188.C46 C465 1981

Plano de desenvolvimento regional do Centro-Oeste : síntese geral e propostas preliminares / Ministério do Interior, Superintendência do Desenvolvimento da Região Centro-Oeste. Brasília : A Superintendência, 1985. 101 p. : ill., map ; 30 cm. Cover subtitle: Organização territorial e funções econômicas do Centro-Oeste. LC Card 86-146677
1. Brazil, Central West - Economic conditions. 2. Brazil, Central West - Economic policy. 3. Brazil, Central West - Social conditions. 4. Brazil, Central West - Social policy. I. Title.
HC188.C46 B7 1985

Brazil. Superintendência do Desenvolvimento do Nordeste. Coordenação de Emprego e Mão-de-Obra. Dinâmica da economia e absorção de mão-de-obra . Recife , 1984. 79 p. ; ISBN 85-7019-063-8 LC Card 85-156612 DDC 338.981/3 19
HD5755.N63 D56 1984
NYPL [JLE 86-3545]

Brazil. Superintendência do Desenvolvimento do Nordeste. Coordenação de Planejamento Regional. A Problemática e a política da terra e água do Nordeste. Recife , 1985. 296 p. : LC Card 87-124121 DDC 333.91/00981/3 19
HD1696.B84 N675 1985

Brazil. Superintendência Nacional da Marinha Mercante.
Alternativa ferro-hidro-rodoviária para o transporte de derivados claros de petróleo para o abastecimento das regiões oeste do Estado do Paraná e sul do Estado de Mato Grosso do Sul /. [Rio de Janeiro] , 1984. 41 leaves : LC Card 87-403934 DDC 380.5/24 19
HE199.5.P4 A48 1984

Alternativa rodo-ferro-hidroviária para o abastecimento de gás liquefeito de petróleo-GLP às regiões oeste do Estado de Mato Grosso e leste do Estado de Rondônia /. [Rio de Janeiro] [19]84. 41 leaves : LC Card 87-403939 DDC 338.4/7665773 19
HE199.5.L43 A44 1984

Alternativa rodo-ferro-hidroviária para o abastecimento de gás liquefeito de petróleo-GLP às regiões oeste do Estado de Mato Grosso e leste do Estado de Rondônia / Serviço Público Federal, Ministério dos Transportes, Superintendência Nacional da Marinha Mercante. [Rio de Janeiro] : Diretoria de Navegação Interior, Divisão de Navegação Fluvial e Lacustre, Seção de Desenvolvimento, [1984] 41 leaves : ill. ; 30 cm. "Abril/84." LC Card 85-197972
1. Liquefied petroleum gas - Brazil - Mato Grosso (State) - Transportation. 2. Liquefied petroleum gas - Brazil - Rondônia (State) - Transportation. I. Brazil. Divisão de Navegação Fluvial e Lacustre. Seção de Desenvolvimento. II. Title.
HE199.5.L43 B73 1984

Estudo de custos do transporte nos rios Araguaia e Tocantins /. [Rio de Janeiro] , 1985. 95 leaves : LC Card 87-403933 DDC 386/.3/098173 19
HE424.A7 E84 1985

Estudo preliminar para o establecimento de prioridades no financiamento para construção de embarcações para a navegação interior /. [Rio de Janeiro] , 1985. [84] leaves : LC Card 87-403936 DDC 386/.0981 19
HE653 .E88 1985

Brazil. Superintendency for the Development of the Northeast. see **Brazil. Superintendência do Desenvolvimento do Nordeste.**

BRAZIL - SURVEYS.
Estudos e propostas para a organização territorial e desenvolvimento urbano do Brasil. Brasilia , 1981. 126 leaves, [7] folded leaves of plates : *NYPL [JLG 86-151]*

Brazil. Tecnologia Industrial, Secretaria de. see **Brazil. Secretaria de Tecnologia Industrial.**

Brazil. Tesouro Nacional. Cédulas brasileiras da República . Rio de Janeiro , 1965. 111 p. : LC Card 85-119119
HG837 .C43 1965

Brazil. Transportes, Ministério dos. see **Brazil. Ministério dos Transportes.**

Brazilian government support for the aerospace industry /. Green, Ronald D. [Washington, D.C.?] [1987] xi, 44 p. ; LC Card 87-601479 DDC 338.4/76291/0981 19
HD9711.B72 G74 1987

Brazilian Petroleum Company. see **Petróleo Brasileiro, S. A.**

The Brazilian quandary /. Moreira, Marcílio Marques. New York , 1986. vi, 87 p. : ISBN 0-87078-171-5 (pbk.) : LC Card 86-210942 DDC 332.3/4/0981 19
HJ8579 .M66 1986

A Brazilian solution to Brazilian problems. Rio de Janeiro : Secretaria de Divulgação do BNH, 1974. 32 p. ; 21 cm. Title on cover: BNH, a Brazilian solution to Brazilian problems. LC Card 86-673453
1. Housing - Brazil - Finance. 2. Banco Nacional da Habitação. I. Banco Nacional da Habitação. Secretaria de Divulgação. II. Title: BNH, a Brazilian solution to Brazilian problems.
HD7323.A4 B72x 1974

Brazil's experience in creating a capital market /. Costa, Roberto Teixeira da. São Paulo [1985] 114 p. : LC Card 86-207924 DDC 332.6/0981 19
HG4523 .C67 1985

BRAZZAVILLE, CONGO - SOCIAL CONDITIONS.
Balandier, Georges. Sociologie des Brazzavilles noires /. Paris , c1985. xviii, 306 p., [2] leaves of plates : ISBN 2-7246-0524-1 : LC Card 86-138199
HB2125.B73 B34 1985

BRDE . Banco Regional de Desenvolvimento do Extremo sul. [Curitiba] , 1984. 95 p., [8] : LC Card 86-143911
HG2889.S6 B36 1984

BRDE, a ação governamental na promoção do desenvolvimento econômico e social da Região Sul /. Campos, José Hypólito Machado de. Porto Alegre [between 1983 and 1985] 51 p. ; LC Card 86-143903
HG2889.S6 C36 1983

Bread broken : an action report on the food crisis in Africa / edited by J.G. Donders. Eldoret, Kenya : Gaba Publications, AMECEA Pastoral Institute, [1984] vi, 56 p. : ill. ; 21 cm. (Spearhead. no. 84) "December 1984." Bibliography: p. 42. LC Card 85-980419 DDC 363.8/0967 19
1. Famines - Africa, Sub-Saharan. 2. Food supply -

Africa, Sub-Saharan. I. Donders, Joseph G. II. Series: Spearhead (Eldoret, Kenya), no. 84.
HC800.Z9 F32 1984

BREAD INDUSTRY - BOLIVIA.
Proyecto harinas compuestas . La Paz, Bolivia , 1982. 272, [2], 3 p., [9] p. of plates : LC Card 83-195592
HD9044.B52 P76 1982

BREAD INDUSTRY - DENMARK.
Rugbrødsbranchen . København , 1985. 112 p. : ISBN 87-88149-23-4 : LC Card 86-161889
HD9058.B743 D47 1985

Bread upon the waters /. Pesotta, Rose, 1896- Ithaca, N.Y. , c1987. xxiv, 435 p., [10] p. of plates : ISBN 0-87546-127-1 (pbk. : alk. paper) LC Card 87-2953 DDC 331.88/0973 19
HD8072 .P375 1987

Breadbasket of the world : California's great wheat-growing era, 1860-1890. San Francisco : Book Club of California, 1984. 10 pamphlets : ill. ; 22 x 26 cm. Cover title. CONTENTS. - 1. Introduction and table of contents / Oscar Lewis -- 2. Dr. Glenn, "wheat king" / Richard Steven Street -- 3. Planting time / Jane Wilson -- 4. The harvest / C. Danial Elliott -- 5. The journey begins / David F. Myrick -- 6. Transfer point / Richard Hilkert -- 7. Port Costa / Richard H. Dillon -- 8. The grain fleet / Gary F. Kurutz -- 9. Isaac Friedlander, wheat merchant / Albert Shumate -- 10. The octopus / James D. Hart. LC Card 87-100963 DDC 338.1/7311/09794 19
1. Wheat trade - California - History - 19th century. 2. Wheat - California - History - 19th century. 3. Agriculture - Economic aspects - California - History - 19th century. I. Book Club of California.
HD9049.W5 U414 1984

BREADSTUFFS. see **WHEAT.**

BREAK-EVEN ANALYSIS.
Büchner, Robert. Grundzüge der Finanzanalyse /. München , c1981. x, 426 p. : ISBN 3-8006-0885-5 LC Card 82-156543
HF5693.G47 B83 1981

Break, George F. State and local finance . Madison, Wis. , 1983. x, 243 p. : ISBN 0-299-09340-9 : LC Card 83-47757 DDC 336.73 19
HJ275 .S675 1983 ***NYPL [JLE 86-4001]***

The breakdown of Austin Rover . Williams, Karel. Leamington Spa, UK ; New York : v, 150 p. : ISBN 0-85496-515-7 : LC Card 86-24449 DDC 338.7/6292222 19
HD9710.G74 A868 1987

Breakfast in hell . Harris, Myles F. New York , c1987. 271 p. ; ISBN 0-671-63272-8 : LC Card 86-25504 DDC 363.8/83/0963 19
HC845.Z9 F345 1987

Breaking in . Bard, Ray. New York , 1985. 256 p. ; ISBN 0-688-05893-0 (pbk.) LC Card 85-6571 DDC 331.25/92/02573 19
HF5549.5.T7 B29 1985
NYPL [*R-Econ. 86-248]

Breaking into the boardroom . Melia, Jinx. [Why Jenny can't lead.] New York [1987] c1986. 167 p. ; ISBN 0-399-13326-7 LC Card 87-7007 DDC 658.4/09/024042 19
HD6054.3 .M45 1987

Breaking new ground .
(no. 1) Population change, natural resources, and regionalism /. Milford, Pa. , c1986. viii, 104 p. : ISBN 0-938549-00-6 (pbk.) LC Card 86-25682 DDC 304.6/0973 19
HB3505 .P62 1986

Breaking the academic mould : economists and American higher learning in the nineteenth century / edited by William J. Barber. Middletown, Conn. : Wesleyan University Press, 1988. p. cm. Includes index. ISBN 0-8195-5176-7 : LC Card 87-21023 DDC 330/.07/1173 19
1. Economics - Study and teaching (Higher) - United States - History - 19th century. 2. Economists - United States - History - 19th century. I. Barber, William J.
HB74.8 .B74 1988

Breaking the banks /. Johnson, Arthur, 1951- Toronto, Canada , c1986. xi, 256 p. ; ISBN 0-88619-072-X LC Card 87-120151 DDC 332.1/2/0971 19
HG2708.C36 J64 1986

Breaking the glass ceiling . Morrison, Ann M. Reading, Mass. , c1987. ix, 229 p. : ISBN 0-201-15787-X : LC Card 87-1853 DDC 658.4/09/024042 19
HD6054.4.U6 M67 1987

Breaking the secretary barrier . Dight, Janet. New York , c1986. xv, 303 p. ; ISBN 0-07-016905-5 LC Card 85-11360 DDC 658.4/09/024042 19
HF5547.5 .D54 1986 ***NYPL [JLE 86-1072]***

Breakthrough for disadvantaged youth. [Washington] U. S. Dept. of Labor, Manpower Administration; [for sale by the Supt. of Docs., U. S. Govt. Print. Off.] 1969. iii, 256 p. 26 cm. Includes bibliographical references. LC Card 79-604757 DDC 331.3/4/0973
1. Youth - Employment - United States. 2. Occupational training - United States. I. United States. Dept. of Labor. Manpower Administration. II. Title.
HD6273 .B7 ***NYPL [JLF 86-435]***

Breakthroughs in telemarketing. Goodman, Gary S. [Breakthroughs in telemarketing.] Gary Goodman's breakthroughs in telemarketing /. New York , c1987. ix, 148 p. ; ISBN 0-13-346891-7 (pbk.) : LC Card 86-43170 DDC 658.8/5 19
HF5415.1265 .G66 1987

Bréard, Jean-Pierre. Les contrats de souscription à forfait de valeurs mobilières / Jean-Pierre Bréard. Montréal : Wilson & Lafleur : Sorej, 1984. xv, 158 p. : forms ; 23 cm. French or English. Bibliography: p. [145]-158. ISBN 2-89266-018-1 (pbk.) :
1. Securities - Canada. 2. Securities - United States. 3. Corporations - Finance - Law and legislation - Canada. 4. Corporations - Finance - Law and legislation - United States. I. Title. ***NYPL [JLD 87-662]***

Breen, David. The Canadian prairie west and the ranching frontier, 1874-1924 / David H. Breen. Toronto ; Buffalo : University of Toronto Press, c1983. xiii, 302 p., [4] p. of plates : ill., ports. ; 24 cm. Includes index. Bibliography: p. [289]-290. ISBN 0-8020-5548-6 LC Card 83-143575 DDC 338.1/762/009712 19
1. Cattle trade - Prairie Provinces - History. 2. Land use, Rural - Prairie Provinces - History. 3. Ranchers - Prairie Provinces - Political activity - History. I. Title.
HD9433.C22 P733 1983 ***NYPL [HY 87-755]***

Breev, B. D. (Boris Dmitrievich) Petrov, V. A. (Valeriĭ Arkad′evich) Sotsial′no-demograficheskaia struktura gorodskogo naseleniia i ego zaniatost′ /. Moskva , 1981. 151 p. ; LC Card 82-145197
HB2277 .P48 1981

Breheny, M.J. (Michael J.) The Development of high technology industries . London , New York , c1987. 363 p. : ISBN 0-7099-3942-6 LC Card 87-9086 DDC 338.4/762 19
HC79.H53 D48 1987

Brehm, Henry P. Lopata, Helena Znaniecka, 1925- Widows and dependent wives . New York , 1986. xxi, 242 p. ; ISBN 0-03-046301-7 (alk. paper) : LC Card 85-16753 DDC 362.8/382 19
HV699 .L67 1985 ***NYPL [JLE 86-2182]***

Breiling, Adolf. Agi, Michael. Optische Beleg- und Seitenleser . Bonn , c1976. 96 p. ; LC Card 85-112068
HF5548.4.O6 A34 1976

Breit, Ernst.
Mitbestimmung in der Krise--Krise der Mitbestimmung? . Köln , c1984. 192 p. : ISBN 3-7663-0895-5 LC Card 85-113842
HD5660.G4 M563 1984

Weissbuch Arbeitszeitverkürzung /. Stuttgart , 1983. 152 p. : ISBN 3-87959-212-8 LC Card 84-163631
HD5108.2.G47 W45 1983

Breit, William.
Antitrust penalty reform : an economic analysis / William Breit and Kenneth G. Elzinga. Washington, D.C. : American Enterprise Institute for Public Policy Research, c1986. x, 83 p. : ill. ; 23 cm. (AEI studies . 441) Includes bibliographical references. ISBN 0-8447-3600-7 (alk. paper) LC Card 86-3203 DDC 343.73/072/0269 347.303720269 19
1. Antitrust law - United States. 2. Damages - United States. 3. Antitrust law - Economic aspects - United States. I. Elzinga, Kenneth G. II. Series. III. Series: American Enterprise Institute for Public Policy Research. AEI studies, 441. IV. Title.
KF1657.T7 B74 1986 ***NYPL [JLE 86-3948]***

Lives of the laureates . Cambridge, Mass. , c1986. xii, 135 p. : ISBN 0-262-02255-9 LC Card 86-2919 DDC 330/.092/2 B 19
HB76 .L58 1986 ***NYPL [JFD 86-9827]***

Breitbandtechnologie . Mettler-Meibom, Barbara E. Opladen , c1986. xxiv, 477, [60] p. : ISBN 3-531-11782-3 LC Card 86-184911
HE8154 .M47 1986

Breitbard, Stanley H. The Price Waterhouse book of personal financial planning / by Stanley H. Breitbard & Donna Sammons Carpenter. 1st ed. New York : H. Holt, 1988. xi, 447 p. ; 24 cm. Includes index. ISBN 0-8050-0387-8 LC Card 87-8493 DDC 332.024 19
1. Finance, Personal. 2. Investments. I. Carpenter, Donna Sammons. II. Price Waterhouse (Firm). III. Title.
HG179 .B727 1988

Breitenacher, Michael. Strukturwandlungen und Entwicklungsperspektiven im Musikinstrumentenbau, in der Spielwaren- und Sportgeräteherstellung und in der Schmuckindustrie / von Michael Breitenacher. Berlin : Duncker & Humblot, c1984. 188 p. : ill. ; 24 cm. (Struktur und Wachstum: Reihe Industrie. Heft 35) Bibliography: p. [185]-186. ISBN 3-428-05566-7 LC Card 84-186644
1. Musical instrument industry - Germany (West). 2. Toy industry - Germany, West. 3. Sporting goods industry - Germany (West). 4. Jewelry trade - Germany (West). I. Title. II. Series.
HD9999.M83 G32 1984

Breitkopf, Stephan. Die Behandlung von Immobilienrechten Deutscher mit Wohnsitz in der Bundesrepublik Deutschland und Berlin (West), in der DDR und Berlin (Ost) / Stephan Breitkopf. Berlin : Osteuropa-Institut, 1983. xii, 203 p. ; 21 cm. (Berichte des Osteuropa-Instituts an der Freien Universität Berlin, 0409-1477 . Heft 129. Nr. 31) Bibliography: p. 186-198. ISBN 3-921374-25-1 LC Card 84-167165 DDC 330 s 346.431/55043 19
1. Real property - Germany, West. 2. Real property - Berlin. 3. Real property - Germany (East). I. Series: Berlin. Freie Universität. Osteuropa-Institut. Berichte, Heft 129. II. Title.
HC244.A1 B4 Heft 129 KK1315
NYPL [STN+ (Berlin. Freie Universität. Osteuropa-Institut. Berichte. Heft 129)]

Breitsprecher, Roland. Collins English-German dictionary =. London , Stuttgart , 1986, c1983. 2 v. (xviii, 1390, xxiii, 1380 p.) ; ISBN 3-12-517131-8 (v. 1) ***NYPL [JFC 86-2613]***

Breivik, Marit. Bjørklund, Tor, 1947- Mot strømmen . Oslo , c1982. 396 p. : ISBN 82-00-06338-0 : LC Card 83-134961
HC241.25.N7 B56 1982

Breman, Jan. Control of land and labour in colonial Java : a case study of agrarian crisis and reform in the region of Cirebon during the first decades of the 20th century / Jan Breman. Dordrecht, Netherlands ; Cinnaminson, N.J., U.S.A. : Foris Publications, 1983. xi, 158 p. : ill. ; 24 cm. (Verhandelingen van het Koninklijk Instituut voor Taal-, Land- en Volkenkunde . 101) ISBN 90-6765-048-X (pbk.) LC Card 86-145678 DDC 333.3/1/5982 19
1. Land reform - Indonesia - Cirebon (Kabupaten) - History. 2. Cirebon (Indonesia : Kabupaten) - Rural conditions. I. Title. II. Series.
HD1333.I52 C573 1983

Bremen Economic Research Institute. see **Bremer Ausschuss für Wirtschaftsforschung.**

BREMEN (GERMANY) - COMMERCE.
Wachsende Städte an der Unterweser . Bremen , 1965. xii, 243 p., [7] folded leaves of plates : LC Card 85-122713
HC289.B7 W33 1965

BREMEN (GERMANY) - ECONOMIC CONDITIONS.
Wachsende Städte an der Unterweser . Bremen , 1965. xii, 243 p., [7] folded leaves of plates : LC Card 85-122713
HC289.B7 W33 1965

BREMEN (GERMANY) - ECONOMIC CONDITIONS - PICTORIAL WORKS.
Hilfe in der Not . [Bremen] [1947] 74 p. : LC Card 87-408692 DDC 338.91/73/04352 19
HC286.5 .H545 1947

BREMEN (GERMANY) - SOCIAL CONDITIONS.

Wachsende Städte an der Unterweser . Bremen , 1965. xii, 243 p., [7] folded leaves of plates : LC Card 85-122713
HC289.B7 W33 1965

Bremer Ausschuss für Wirtschaftsforschung. Wachsende Städte an der Unterweser . Bremen , 1965. xii, 243 p., [7] folded leaves of plates : LC Card 85-122713
HC289.B7 W33 1965

Bremer, Stuart A. The Globus model . Boulder , 1986. p. cm. ISBN 0-8133-0528-4 : LC Card 87-8281 DDC 338.9/00724 19
HC59 .G577 1986

BREMERHAVEN (GERMANY) - COMMERCE.
Scheidulin, Hans. Die Häfen Bremen, Bremerhaven /. Bremen , c1985. 160 p. : ISBN 3-920699-63-7 LC Card 86-124602 DDC 330.943/52 19
HC289.B72 S34 1985

Wachsende Städte an der Unterweser . Bremen , 1965. xii, 243 p., [7] folded leaves of plates : LC Card 85-122713
HC289.B7 W33 1965

BREMERHAVEN (GERMANY) - ECONOMIC CONDITIONS.
Scheidulin, Hans. Die Häfen Bremen, Bremerhaven /. Bremen , c1985. 160 p. : ISBN 3-920699-63-7 LC Card 86-124602 DDC 330.943/52 19
HC289.B72 S34 1985

Wachsende Städte an der Unterweser . Bremen , 1965. xii, 243 p., [7] folded leaves of plates : LC Card 85-122713
HC289.B7 W33 1965

BREMERHAVEN (GERMANY) - SOCIAL CONDITIONS.
Wachsende Städte an der Unterweser . Bremen , 1965. xii, 243 p., [7] folded leaves of plates : LC Card 85-122713
HC289.B7 W33 1965

Bremicker, Burckhardt. Analyse der Arbeitslosigkeit in den Regionen Nordrhein-Westfalens : Analyse der räumlichen Diversifizierung der Arbeitslosigkeit, ihrer räumlichen Entwicklung sowie ihrer möglichen Bestimmungsgründe für den Zeitraum 1962 bis 1978 / von B. Bremicker, P. Klemmer, A. Ortmeyer. Bochum : N. Brockmeyer, 1984. xx, 381 p. : ill., maps ; 21 cm. (Beiträge zur Struktur- und Konjunkturforschung . Bd. 24) Includes bibliographical references. ISBN 3-88339-362-2 LC Card 84-196621 DDC 331.13/794355 19
1. Unemployment - Germany (West) - North Rhine-Westphalia - History - 20th century. 2. Labor supply - Germany (West) - North Rhine-Westphalia - History - 20th century. I. Klemmer, Paul. II. Ortmeyer, August. III. Title. IV. Series.
HD5780.N6 B74 1984 NYPL [JLD 86-2367]

Bremicker, Burkhardt. Klemmer, Paul. Abgrenzung von Fördergebieten /. Bochum , 1983. 206 p. : ISBN 3-88339-298-7 LC Card 83-183564
HC286.7 .K59 1983

Brémond, G. Brémond, Janine. L'économie française face aux défis mondiaux . Paris , c1985. 320 p. : ISBN 2-218-07456-7 LC Card 86-168427
HC276.2 .B657 1985

Brémond, Janine. L'économie française face aux défis mondiaux : faits, chiffres, analyses / J. et G. Brémond. Paris : Hatier, c1985. 320 p. : ill. ; 19 cm. (Collection J. Brémond) Includes bibliographical references and index. ISBN 2-218-07456-7 LC Card 86-168427
1. France - Economic conditions - 1945-. 2. France - Industries. I. Brémond, G. II. Title. III. Series.
HC276.2 .B657 1985

Brems, Hans. Pioneering economic theory, 1630-1980 : a mathematical restatement / Hans Brems. Baltimore : Johns Hopkins University Press, c1986. xv, 411 p. : ill. ; 24 cm. Includes bibliographical references and indexes. ISBN 0-8018-2667-5 (alk. paper) LC Card 85-19819 DDC 330.1 19
1. Economics - History. 2. Economics - Mathematical models. 3. Equilibrium (Economics) - Mathematical models. I. Title.
HB75 .B7845 1986 NYPL [JLE 86-2408]

Brender, Anton. Aglietta, Michel. Les métamorphoses de la société salariale . Paris , c1984. 274 p. ; ISBN 2-7021-1230-7 : LC Card 84-176554 DDC 331/.0944 19
HD8431 .A36 1984 NYPL [JLD 87-478]

Brenes Castro, Abelardo. Sandoval Aguilar, Guillermo. El desarrollo costarricense y la fecundidad del hombre /. Heredia , 1985. 233 p. ; LC Card 86-117576
HB947 .S26 1985

Brennan, H. Geoffrey, 1944- Morality of the market . Vancouver, B.C., Canada , c1985. xxv, 601 p. ; ISBN 0-88975-074-2 (pbk.) : LC Card 86-158049 DDC 174/.4 19
HB72 .M56 1985

Brennan, Lawrence D. (Lawrence David), 1915- Resumes for better jobs / Lawrence D. Brennan, Stanley Strand, Edward C. Gruber. 3rd ed. New York, NY : Prentice Hall Press, c1987. 202 p. ; 28 cm. "An Arco book." Bibliography: p. 194-196. Includes index. ISBN 0-13-329152-9 : LC Card 87-2383 DDC 650.1/4 19
1. Résumés (Employment). 2. Applications for positions. I. Strand, Stanley. II. Gruber, Edward C. III. Title.
HF5383 .B68 1987

Brennan, Mary E.
Benefits Processing Institute (1983 : Hollywood, Fla.) Claims processing for benefit plans, 1983 . Brookfield, Wis. , 1984. x, 82 p. : ISBN 0-89154-220-5 (pbk.) : LC Card 84-80454 DDC 331.25/5 19
HG9396 .B47 1984 NYPL [JLD 86-3940]

Corporate Benefits Management Conferences (1986 : Phoenix, Ariz., etc.) Managing corporate benefit plans, 1986 /. Brookfield, Wis. , 1986. x, 129 p. : ISBN 0-89154-318-X (pbk.) : LC Card 87-403111 DDC 332.6/7254 19
HD7105.45.U6 C67 1986

Brennan, Michael Joseph, 1928- Preface to quantitative economics & econometrics. 4th ed. / Michael J. Brennan, Thomas M. Carroll. Cincinnati : South-Western Pub. Co., c1987. x, 580 p. : ill. ; 24 cm. First-3rd eds. published as: Preface to econometrics. Includes index. ISBN 0-538-08230-5 (pbk.) LC Card 86-60209 DDC 330/.028 19
1. Econometrics. 2. Economics, Mathematical. I. Carroll, Thomas M. II. Title. III. Title: Quantitative economics & econometrics.
HB139 .B74 1987

Brenner (Otto) Stiftung. see **Otto Brenner Stiftung.**

Brenner, Reuven. Rivalry : in business, science, among nations / Reuven Brenner. Cambridge ; New York : Cambridge University Press, 1987. xi, 244 p. ; 24 cm. Bibliography: p. 211-234. Includes indexes. ISBN 0-521-33187-0 LC Card 86-24415 DDC 338.6/048 19
1. Competition. 2. Industrial organization (Economic theory). 3. Risk. 4. Decision-making. I. Title.
HD41 .B743 1987

Brenner, Y. S. Capitalism, competition and economic crisis : structural changes in advanced industrialised countries / Y.S. Brenner. Brighton, Sussex : Wheatsheaf Books ; Washington, D.C. : Kapitan Szabo Publishers, 1984. x, 262 p. ; 23 cm. Bibliography: p. [221]-248. Includes bibliographical references and index. ISBN 0-7108-0722-8
1. Economic history - 1971-. 2. Capitalism. I. Title.
NYPL [JLD 86-2553]

Brent-Easter, Marilyn Kay. Easter, Walter Ray. The ABC's of marketing a successful business . [United States] , c1986. 118 p. : LC Card 86-91127 DDC 658.8 19
HF5415.122 .E27 1986

Brentlinger, Marilyn E., 1925- The ultimate benefit book : how to raise $50,000-plus for your organization / Marilyn E. Brentlinger, Judith M. Weiss. Cleveland, Ohio : Octavia, c1987. 231 p. : ill. ; 26 cm. Includes index. ISBN 0-940601-01-X : LC Card 87-12171 DDC 361.7/068/1 19
1. Fund raising. I. Weiss, Judith M., 1950-. II. Title.
HG177 .B74 1987

Brepoels, Jaak. Stadsboek Leuven /. Leuven , c1985. 259 p. : ISBN 90-6303-137-8 : LC Card 86-204792
HC318.L6 S73 1985

Brera, Paolo. Denaro : saggi di economia e letteratura / Paolo Brera. [Brescia] : Shakespeare & Co., [1984] 110 p. ; 20 cm. Includes bibliographies. LC Card 86-102925
1. Economics. 2. Money - Psychological aspects. 3. Economics in literature. 4. Money in literature. I. Title.
HB49 .B74 1984

Bresc, Henri. Un monde méditerranéen : économie et société en Sicile, 1300-1450 / par Henri Bresc. [Roma] : Ecole française de Rome, 1986. 2 v. (981 p.) : ill. ; 29 cm. (Bibliothèque des écoles françaises d'Athènes et de Rome. fasc. 262) Bibliography: p. 31-57. Includes indexes. ISBN 2-7283-0103-4 (set) LC Card 87-139949
1. Sicily - Economic conditions. 2. Sicily - Social conditions. I. Title. II. Series.
HC307.S5 B74 1986

Breslin, Jud. Selecting and installing software packages : new methodology for corporate implementation / Jud Breslin ; foreword by Frank A. Sola. New York : Quorum Books, 1986. xviii, 242 p. : ill. ; 25 cm. Includes index. ISBN 0-89930-158-4 (lib. bdg. : alk. paper) LC Card 86-12403 DDC 658.4/038 19
1. Computer software. 2. Business - Data processing. I. Title.
QA76.754 .B74 1986 NYPL [JLE 87-1133]

Breslin, Patrick, 1940- Development and dignity : grassroots development and the Inter-American Foundation / Patrick Breslin. Rosslyn, Va. : Inter-American Foundation, [1987] xiii, 128 p. : ill., ports. ; 24 cm. ISBN 0-8133-0632-9 (alk. paper) LC Card 87-3920 DDC 338.91/7308/0601 19
1. Inter-American Foundation - History. 2. Economic assistance, American - Latin America - History. I. Inter-American Foundation. II. Title.
HC125 .B725 1987

Bresnan, Bill, 1940- WABC Talkradio 77 AM financial expert Bill Bresnan speaks on real estate-- in words of one syllable / Bill Bresnan. Englewood Cliffs, NJ : Prentice-Hall, c1987. xx, 172 p. ; 24 cm. Bibliography: p. 157-159. Includes index. ISBN 0-13-949629-7 LC Card 87-60220 DDC 332.63/24 19
1. Real estate business. 2. Real property. I. Title. II. Title: WABC Talk radio 77 AM financial expert Bill Bresnan speaks on real estate-- in words of one syllable. III. Title: WABC Talkradio seventy-seven AM financial expert Bill Bresnan speaks on real estate-- in words of one syllable.
HD1379 .B744 1987

Bressan, E. (Edoardo) Povertà e assistenza in Lombardia nell'età napoleonica / Edoardo Bressan. [Milano] : Cariplo ; Bari : Laterza, c1985. viii, 339 p. : ill. ; 24 cm. (Economia e società in Lombardia dall'età delle riforme alla grande crisi . 2) Bibliography: p. 289-[336] ISBN 88-420-2653-0 : LC Card 86-162978
1. Economic assistance, Domestic - Italy - Lombardy - History. 2. Poor - Italy - Lombardy - History. 3. Public welfare - Italy - Lombardy - History. 4. Charities - Italy - Lombardy - History. 5. Lombardy (Italy) - Social policy. 6. Lombardy (Italy) - Napoleonic rule, 1796-1813. I. Title. II. Series.
HC307.L8 B74 1985

Bresser Pereira, Luiz Carlos. see **Pereira, Luiz Carlos Bresser.**

Brett, Charles Edward Bainbridge, 1928- Housing a divided community / C.E.B. Brett. Dublin, Ireland : Institute of Public Administration, Dublin in association with the Institute of Irish Studies, Queen's University of Belfast, 1986. xi, 171 p., [32] p. of plates : ill. ; 26 cm. Bibliography: p. [152]-153. Includes index. ISBN 0-906980-49-6 : LC Card 86-222853 DDC 363.5/09416 19
1. Housing - Northern Ireland - History. 2. Housing policy - Northern Ireland - History. I. Title.
HD7335.5.A3 B74 1986

Brett, E. A.
International money and capitalist crisis : the anatomy of global disintegration / E.A. Brett. London : Heinemann ; Boulder, Colo. : Westview Press, 1983. viii, 271 p. ; 23 cm. Includes bibliographies and index. ISBN 0-86531-575-2 (Westview) LC Card 82-51289 DDC 332/.042 19
1. International finance - History. 2. Economic history -

1945-. I. Title.
HG3881 .B6738 1983 *NYPL [JLD 87-1020]*

The world economy since the war : the politics of uneven development / E.A. Brett. Houndmills, Basingstoke, Hampshire : Macmillan, 1985. x, 318 p. : ill. ; 23 cm. Bibliography: p. [273]-297. Includes index. ISBN 0-333-37199-2 LC Card 87-673378
1. Economic history - 1945-. 2. Economic development - Political aspects. 3. International economic relations. I. Title.
HC59 .B754x 1985

Brettell, Caroline. Men who migrate, women who wait : population and history in a Portuguese parish / Caroline B. Brettell. Princeton : Princeton University Press, c1986. xv, 329 p., [8] p. of plates : ill. ; 25 cm. Includes index. Bibliography: p. [299]-319. ISBN 0-691-09424-1 (alk. paper) : LC Card 86-11270 DDC 304.6/09469/12 19
1. Fertility, Human - Portugal - Lanhezes - History. 2. Marriage - Portugal - Lanhezes - History. 3. Lanhezes (Portugal) - Population - History. 4. Portugal - Emigration and immigration - History - Case studies. I. Title.
HB2082.L36 B74 1986 *NYPL [JLE 87-1417]*

Breuilly, John, 1946- Europäische Arbeiterbewegungen im 19. Jahrhundert . Göttingen , c1983. 169 p. ; ISBN 3-525-33488-5 (pbk.) LC Card 87-672976
HD8378 .E97x 1983

Breunig, Willi. Vom Handelsplatz zur Industriestadt : Wirtschaftsentwicklung in Ludwigshafen am Rhein 1820-1920 / Willi Breunig. Ludwigshafen am Rhein : Stadtarchiv Ludwigshafen am Rhein, 1986. 151 p. : ill. ; 21 cm. (Veröffentlichungen des Stadtarchivs Ludwigshafen am Rhein . Bd. 12) Bibliography: p. 137-151. ISBN 3-924667-13-6 LC Card 87-135540 DDC 338.0943/43 19
1. Ludwigshafen am Rhein (Germany) - Economic conditions. 2. Ludwigshafen am Rhein (Germany) - Industries - History. 3. Ludwigshafen am Rhein (Germany) - Commerce - History. I. Series: Veröffentlichungen des Stadtarchivs Ludwigshafen a. Rh. , Bd. 12. II. Title.
HC289.L95 B74 1986

Breve historia de la industria orureña /. González-Aramayo Z., Vicente (González-Aramayo Zuleta) Oruro, Bolivia [1983] 199 p. ; LC Card 85-144157
HC183.O7 G66 1983

Breve historia del pensamiento administrativo /. Alvarez Valdés, Ariel. [Santiago del Estero, Argentina] [1985] 129 p. : LC Card 86-180293
HD30.5 .A44 1985

Breve reseña histórica de la formación profesional y del trabajo / Ministerio de Trabajo y Seguridad Social, Servicio Nacional de Aprendizaje-SENA, División de Relaciones Industriales, Centro Nacional de Desarrollo de Personal. Bogotá : El Centro, [1973] 29, [1] leaves ; 30 cm. Cover title. Bibliography: leaf [30] LC Card 85-208500
1. Occupational training - History. 2. Vocational education - History. 3. Vocational education - Latin America - History. I. Centro Nacional de Desarrollo de Personal (Colombia).
HD5715 .B74 1973

Breve retrospecto da economia brasileira entre 1979 e 1984 /. Cysne, Rubens Penha. [Rio de Janeiro] [1985] 30 leaves ; LC Card 86-176751
HC187 .C98 1985

BREWERIES - UNITED STATES - DIRECTORIES.
Erickson, Jack. Star Spangled beer . Reston, Va. , 1987. v, 155 p. : ISBN 0-941397-00-9 (pbk.) : LC Card 86-63993 DDC 338.7/66342/02573 19
HD9397.U52 E75 1987

BREWERIES - UNITED STATES - HISTORY.
Erickson, Jack. Star Spangled beer . Reston, Va. , 1987. v, 155 p. : ISBN 0-941397-00-9 (pbk.) : LC Card 86-63993 DDC 338.7/66342/02573 19
HD9397.U52 E75 1987

BREWERY WORKERS - GREAT BRITAIN - EFFECT OF TECHNOLOGICAL INNOVATIONS ON.
Ghobadian, Abby, 1951- The effects of new technological change on shift work in the brewing industry /. Aldershot, Hants, England , Brookfield, Vt. , c1986. xiv, 192 p. : ISBN 0-566-05132-X : LC Card 86-17536 DDC 331.25/72 19
HD8039.L62 G74 1986
NYPL [JLD 86-3864]

BREWING INDUSTRY.
Staudinger, Hans-Joachim, 1957- Die Überwachung der Geschäftsführung, eine betriebswirtschaftliche Betrachtung . München , c1986. lxxxvi, 340 p. ; ISBN 3-88259-412-8 LC Card 87-125378 DDC 663/.3/0685 19
HD35 .S6745 1986

BREWING INDUSTRY - GREAT BRITAIN - AUTOMATION.
Ghobadian, Abby, 1951- The effects of new technological change on shift work in the brewing industry /. Aldershot, Hants, England , Brookfield, Vt. , c1986. xiv, 192 p. : ISBN 0-566-05132-X : LC Card 86-17536 DDC 331.25/72 19
HD8039.L62 G74 1986
NYPL [JLD 86-3864]

BREWING INDUSTRY - STATISTICS.
Import insights . West Nyack, NY (51 Virginia Ave., West Nyack 10994) , c19. 48 p. : LC Card 86-210235 DDC 382/.4566342/0973 19
HD9397.U52 I47 1986

BREWING INDUSTRY - UNITED STATES - DIRECTORIES.
Erickson, Jack. Star Spangled beer . Reston, Va. , 1987. v, 155 p. : ISBN 0-941397-00-9 (pbk.) : LC Card 86-63993 DDC 338.7/66342/02573 19
HD9397.U52 E75 1987

BREWING INDUSTRY - UNITED STATES - HISTORY.
Erickson, Jack. Star Spangled beer . Reston, Va. , 1987. v, 155 p. : ISBN 0-941397-00-9 (pbk.) : LC Card 86-63993 DDC 338.7/66342/02573 19
HD9397.U52 E75 1987

BREWING INDUSTRY - UNITED STATES - STATISTICS.
Import insights . West Nyack, NY (51 Virginia Ave., West Nyack 10994) , c19. 48 p. : LC Card 86-210235 DDC 382/.4566342/0973 19
HD9397.U52 I47 1986

Brewster C. Denny lecture series.
Neustadt, Richard E. Richard E. Neustadt lecture, May 13, 1986. Seattle, WA [1986] 35 p. : LC Card 87-402984 DDC 339.5/2/0973 19
HJ257.2 .N48 1986

Breyer, Friedrich. Family structure and intergenerational transfers in social health insurance : a public choice model / Friedrich Breyer, J.-Matthias Graf v.d. Schulenburg. Berlin : Wissenschaftszentrum Berlin für Sozialforschung, [1986] 24 p. : ill. ; 30 cm. (Discussion papers, 0722-6748 . IIM/IP 86-11) "April 1986." Bibliography: p. 23-24. LC Card 87-156738 DDC 368.4/2016/0724 19
1. Insurance, Health - Finance - Public opinion - Mathematical models. 2. Intergenerational relations - Mathematical models. 3. Social choice - Mathematical models. I. Schulenburg, Johann-Matthias, Graf von der. II. Series: Discussion papers (International Institute of Management. Industrial Policy) , IIM/IP 86-11. III. Title.
HD7101 .B73 1986

Brezhnev, Leonid Il'ich, 1906-
TSELINA.
Prodolzhenie podviga . Moskva , 1979. 165 p., [16] p. of plates : LC Card 81-150822
HD1995.K36 B7337 1979

Briam, Karl-Heinz. Arbeiten ohne Angst : Arbeitsmanagement im technischen Wandel / Karl-Heinz Briam.1. Aufl. Düsseldorf : Econ, 1986. 200 p. ; 21 cm. ISBN 3-430-11560-4 LC Card 86-159578
1. Employee morale - Germany (West). 2. Job satisfaction - Germany, West. 3. Employee motivation - Germany, West. I. Title.
HF5549.2.G3 B75 1986

Briançon, Pierre. A droite en sortant de la gauche? / Pierre Briançon. Paris : B. Grasset, c1986. 270 p. ; 23 cm. Includes bibliographical references. ISBN 2-246-34901-X : LC Card 86-159681
1. France - Economic conditions - 1945-. 2. France - Economic policy. 3. Privatization. I. Title.
HC276.2 .B66 1986

Bricall, Josep Maria, 1936-
Estat autonòmic i finances públiques : competències i finançament del sector públic en països amb diferents nivells de govern : una perspectiva econòmica / Josep M. Bricall, Antoni Castells, Ferran Sicart.1a ed. [Barcelona] : Diputació de Barcelona, 1984. 358 p. : ill. ; 24 cm. (Col·lecció Prat de la Riba . 1) Includes bibliographies. ISBN 84-500-9868-8 LC Card 85-106586
1. Intergovernmental fiscal relations - Europe. 2. Intergovernmental fiscal relations - Canada. 3. Intergovernmental fiscal relations - United States. 4. Local finance - Europe. 5. Local finance - Canada. 6. Local finance - United States. I. Castells, Antoni, 1950-. II. Sicart, Ferran. III. Title. IV. Series.
HJ1000 .B75 1984 *NYPL [JLE 86-3989]*

Las Finanzas municipales en el estado de las autonomías . [Barcelona] , 1985. 178 p. ; ISBN 84-505-1593-9 LC Card 85-240344
HJ9525 .F55 1985

Bricas, N. (Nicolas) Nourrir les villes en Afrique sub-saharienne /. Paris , c1985. 421 p. : ISBN 2-85802-562-X LC Card 86-222243
HD9017.S82 N68 1985

Briceño, Sálvano. New ideas in environmental education /. London , New York , c1988. xiv, 219 p. ; ISBN 0-7099-5042-X LC Card 87-15696 DDC 363.7/007/1 19
HC79.E5 N45 1988

Brick, Howard, 1953- Daniel Bell and the decline of intellectual radicalism : social theory and political reconciliation in the 1940s / Howard Brick. Madison, Wis. : University of Wisconsin Press, 1986. 215-266. (The History of American thought and culture) Includes index. Bibliography: p. ISBN 0-299-10550-4 : LC Card 85-40757 DDC 300/.92/4 19
1. Bell, Daniel. 2. Conservatism - United States. 3. Liberalism - United States. I. Title. II. Series.
H59.B42 B75 1986 *NYPL [JLE 86-3046]*

BRICKLAYERS - FRANCE - CREUSE - HISTORY.
Bandy de Nalèche, Louis. Les Maçons de la Creuse /. Limoges , 1984. 99 p., [16] p. of plates : ISBN 2-85521-059-3 : LC Card 85-169794 DDC 331.7/69321/094468 19
HB2054.C74 B36 1984

BRICKMAKERS - BOLIVIA - COCHABAMBA (DEPT.)
Calderón G., Fernando. Jatun Llajta . La Paz, Bolivia , 1982. v, 448 p., [8] leaves of plates : LC Card 83-111937 DDC 381/.1 19
HF5473.B62 C623 1982
NYPL [JLF 86-1794]

BRIDGES - OREGON - FINANCE.
Making the right turn . [Salem? Or.] [1986] iv, 39 p. : LC Card 87-621891 DDC 388.1/14/09795 19
HE356.O7 M35 1986

Bridges, William, 1933- Surviving corporate transition : rational management in a world of mergers, layoffs, start-ups, takeovers, divestitures, deregulation, and new technologies / William Bridges.1st ed. New York : Doubleday, 1988. xii, 227 p. ; 24 cm. Bibliography: p. [205]-213. Includes index. ISBN 0-385-23761-8 : LC Card 87-19978 DDC 658.4/06 19
1. Industrial management. 2. Crisis management. I. Title.
HD31 .B7395 1988

Bridging the gap between rich and poor .
Godfried, Nathan. New York , 1987. xii, 225 p. ; ISBN 0-313-25648-9 (lib. bdg. : alk. paper) LC Card 87-8471 DDC 338.91/73/056 19
HC415.15 .G63 1987

Brief, Arthur P., 1946- Managing smart : a no-gimmick handbook of management techniques that work / Arthur P. Brief, Gerald Tomlinson. Lexington, Mass. : Lexington Books, c1987. x, 164 p. ; 24 cm. Bibliography: p. [153]-158. Includes index. ISBN 0-669-12654-3 (alk. paper) LC Card 85-45978 DDC 658.3 19
1. Management. 2. Organizational behavior. 3. Personnel management. I. Tomlinson, Gerald, 1933-. II. Title.
HD31 .B7396 1987

Brief business statistics / Collin J. Watson ... [et

al.]. [Newton, Mass.] : Allyn and Bacon, 1987. p. cm. Includes index. ISBN 0-205-11090-8 LC Card 87-17543 DDC 519.5 19
1. Commercial statistics. 2. Statistics. I. Watson, Collin J.
HF1017 .B675 1987

A brief history of panics and their periodical occurrence in the United States /. Juglar, Clément, 1819-1905. [Des crises commerciales. English.] New York, NY , 1988. p. cm. ISBN 0-678-00168-5 LC Card 87-17069 DDC 338.5/42 19
HB3743 .J8513 1988

A Brief history of the rural electric and telephone programs. Rev. Dec. 1985. [Washington, D.C.] : U. S. Dept. of Agriculture, Rural Electrification Administration, [1986] 61 p. : ill. ; 28 cm. Cover title. Shipping list no.: 86-141-P. Item 116 LC Card 86-602412 DDC 353.0087/22 19
1. Rural electrification - United States - History. 2. Rural telephone - United States - History. 3. United States. Rural Electrification Administration - History. I. United States. Rural Electrification Administration.
HD9688.U52 B75 1986

Brief (Institut "Finanz und Steuern" (Germany))
(Nr. 263) Piltz, Detlev Jürgen. Vorschlag zur Verbesserung der Behandlung nichtabziehbarer Ausgaben im KStG 1977 /. Bonn , 1987. 42 leaves ; LC Card 87-401366 DDC 332 s 343.4305/267 332 s 344.3035267 19
HJ1120 .B65 Nr. 263 KK7226

Brief (Institut "Finanzen und Steuern" (Germany)) .
(Nr. 236) Dornbusch, Hans-Ludwig. Entwicklung wesentlicher Daten der öffentlichen Finanzwirtschaft in der Bundesrepublik Deutschland von 1973-1983 /. Bonn , 1984. 32 leaves ; LC Card 86-186300
HJ1120 .B65 Nr. 236

(Nr. 238) Jasper, Lothar Th. Entwicklung der Realsteuerhebesätze der Gemeinden mit mehr als 50.000 Einwohnern 1984 gegenüber 1983 /. Bonn , 1984. 29 leaves ; LC Card 86-186306
HJ1120 .B65 nr. 238 HJ4125.G35

(Nr. 244) Ziele und Möglichkeiten der Privatisierung in volkswirtschaftlicher Sicht . Bonn , 1985. 83 leaves ; LC Card 86-185728
HJ1120 .B65 Nr. 244 HD4178

(Nr. 247) Entwicklung wesentlicher Daten der öffentlichen Finanzwirtschaft in der Bundesrepublik Deutschland von 1974-1984 /. Bonn , 1985. 31 leaves ; LC Card 86-186363
HJ1120 .B65 Nr. 247

(Nr. 260) Dornbusch, Hans-Ludwig. Entwicklung wesentlicher Daten der öffentlichen Finanzwirtschaft in der Bundesrepublik Deutschland von 1975-1985 /. Bonn [1986] 31 leaves ; LC Card 87-408897 DDC 332 s 336.43 19
HJ1120 .B65 Nr. 260

(Nr. 262) Die Haushalte der Flächenländer unter Konsolidierungszwang /. Bonn , 1986. 159 p. ; LC Card 87-409459 DDC 332 s 336.43 19
HJ1120 .B65 Nr. 262

(234) Zahn, Joachim, Professor Dr. Eine Finanzpolitik des langen Atems erforderlich /. Bonn [1984] 31 leaves ; LC Card 86-198580
HJ1120 .B65 Nr. 234

Brief, Richard P., 1933- Depreciation and capital maintenance /. New York , 1984. xi, 137 p. : ISBN 0-8240-6304-X (alk. paper) : LC Card 83-49437 DDC 657/.73 19
HF5681.D5 D45 1984 ***NYPL [JLE 86-1715]***

Briefcase series .
(bk. 4) Who knows about industries and markets /. Washington, D.C. , c1986. 54 p. ; ISBN 0-934940-33-9 (pbk.) LC Card 86-217691 DDC 338/.06/072073 19
HC102.2 .W48 1986

(bk. 6) How to find company intelligence in state documents /. Washington, D.C. , c1986. 110 p. ; ISBN 0-934940-38-X (pbk.) LC Card 86-218108 DDC 016.3387/4/0973 19
HD2785 .H67 1986

Briefe . Raiffeisen, F. W. (Friedrich Wilhelm), 1818-1888. [Correspondence.] Wien , 1986. 207 p. : ISBN 0-370-40867-2 LC Card 87-139235 DDC 332.1/092/4 B 19
HG1552.R35 A4 1986

Briefe aus Mittelamerika . Matz, Manfred. Hameln , c1981. 59 p. : LC Card 83-204578
HC141 .M38 1981

Die Briefmarkenausgabe vom 12. März 1984 = L'émission de timbres-poste du 12 mars 1984 = The stamp issue of 12th March 1984 / Fürstentum Liechtenstein ; [Redaktion, Hermann Hassler]. Vaduz : Amt für Briefmarkengestaltung, Postmuseum des Fürstentums Liechtenstein, [1984?] 41 p. : ill. ; 21 cm. LC Card 84-248309
1. First day covers (Philately) - Liechtenstein. I. Hassler, Hermann. II. Liechtenstein. III. Liechtenstein. Amt für Briefmarkengestaltung. IV. Title: L'émission de timbres-poste du 12 mars 1984. V. Title: Stamp issue of 12th March 1984.
HE6184.F57 B75 1984

Brierley, William, 1951- Trade unions and the economic crisis of the 1980s /. Aldershot, Hants, England , Brookfield, Vt., U. S.A. , c1987. x, 210 p. ; ISBN 0-566-05245-8 : LC Card 86-25641 DDC 331.88/094 19
HD6657 .T68 1987

Brierty, Edward G., 1925- Reeder, Robert R., 1935- Industrial marketing . Englewood Cliffs, N.J. , c1987. xviii, 654 p. : ISBN 0-13-461526-3 LC Card 86-25195 DDC 658.8 19
HF5415 .R355 1987

Brigadirski ogn′ove . Kubadinski, Pencho P. Sofiia , 1986. 119 p., [24] p. of plates : LC Card 86-235041
HD4870.B9 K83 1986

Briganti e gentiluomini della finanza italiana /. Turani, Giuseppe. [Milano] , c1987. 394 p. ; ISBN 88-20-00657-X : LC Card 87-168620
HG186.I8 T86 1987

Briggs, Asa, 1921- The franchise affair : creating fortunes and failures in independent television / Asa Briggs and Joanna Spicer. London : Century, 1986. 226 p. ; 23 cm. Includes index. ISBN 0-7126-1201-7 : LC Card 86-190561 DDC 384.55/453/0941 19
1. Television broadcasting - Great Britain. I. Spicer, Joanna. II. Title.
HE8700.9.G7 B72 1986

Briggs, Charles L., 1953- Land, water, and culture . Albuquerque , c1987. ix, 422 p. : ISBN 0-8263-0989-5 (pbk.) LC Card 87-10957 DDC 333.1/6/09788 19
HD243.N5 L36 1987

Briggs, Dwight. Journey-to-work trends : based on 1960, 1970, and 1980 decennial censuses / [prepared by Office of Highway Information Management]. Washington, D.C. : U. S. Dept. of Transportation, Federal Highway Administration ; Springfield, VA : Available through National Technical Information Service, [1986] 1 v. (various pagings) : ill. ; 28 cm. Authors: Dwight Briggs, Alan Pisarski, and James J. McDonnell. "Prepared for U. S. Department of Transportation, Federal Highway Administration." "July 1986." LC Card 86-602387 DDC 388.4/1314/0973 19
1. Commuting - United States - Statistics. 2. United States - Census. 3. Transportation, Automotive - United States - Statistics. 4. Urban transportation - United States - Statistics. 5. Choice of transportation - Statistics. I. Pisarski, Alan. II. McDonnell, James J. III. United States. Federal Highway Administration. Office of Highway Information Management. IV. United States. Federal Highway Administration. V. Title.
HE371.A3 B75 1986

Brigham, Eugene F., 1930- Financial management : theory and practice. 5th ed. / Eugene F. Brigham, Louis C. Gapenski. Chicago : Dryden Press, c1988. xx, 901 p. : ill. ; 24 cm. (The Dryden Press series in finance) Mathematical tables (4 p.) inserted. Includes bibliograpkhies and index. ISBN 0-03-012543-X LC Card 87-15616 DDC 658.1/5 19
1. Corporations - Finance. I. Gapenski, Louis C. II. Title. III. Series.
HG4026 .B669 1988

Brightman, Harvey J. Group problem solving : an improved managerial approach / Harvey J. Brightman. Atlanta, Ga. : Business Pub. Division, College of Business Administration, Georgia State University, 1987. p. cm. Includes index. ISBN 0-88406-201-5 : LC Card 87-21876 DDC 658.4/036 19
1. Problem solving, Group. 2. Decision making, Group. 3. Organizational effectiveness. I. Title.
HD30.29 .B735 1987

BRIGHTON (EAST SUSSEX) - APPROPRIATIONS AND EXPENDITURES.
Brighton on the rocks . Brighton [1983?] 192 p. : ISBN 0-904733-00-4 (pbk.) : LC Card 84-173777 DDC 336.3/9/0942256 19
HJ9438.B75 B75 1983 ***NYPL [JLD 87-104]***

Sussex European papers. see Sussex European papers.

Brighton on the rocks : monetarism and the local state / QueenSpark Rates Book Group. Brighton : QueenSpark, [1983?] 192 p. : ill. ; 22 cm. (QueenSpark new series . 1) ISBN 0-904733-00-4 (pbk.) : LC Card 84-173777 DDC 336.3/9/0942256 19
1. Chicago school of economics. 2. Government spending policy - England - Brighton (East Sussex). 3. Public welfare - England - Brighton (East Sussex). 4. Brighton (East Sussex) - Appropriations and expenditures. I. QueenSpark Rates Book Group. II. Series.
HJ9438.B75 B75 1983 ***NYPL [JLD 87-104]***

Brij Mohan Lall Nigam. see Nigam, Brij Mohan Lall, 1935-

Brill, Howard. Petras, James F., 1937- Latin America . Totowa, N.J. , 1986. xi, 187 p. ; ISBN 0-8476-7505-X : LC Card 86-1885 DDC 337.8 19
HC125 .P4643 1986 ***NYPL [JLE 86-4366]***

Brimmer, Andrew F.
Monetary policy and the international diffusion of interest rates / by Andrew F. Brimmer. Miami, Fla. : International Banking Center & Dept. of Economics, Florida International University, [1982] iii, 47 p. : ill. ; 23 cm. (Discussion papers in economics and banking . discussion paper no. 5) "May 1982"--Cover. LC Card 86-204514 DDC 332.4/973 19
1. Monetary policy - United States. 2. International finance. 3. Interest rates - United States. 4. Interest rates. I. Title. II. Series.
HG540 .B75 1982

The world banking system : outlook in a context of crisis / Andrew F. Brimmer. New York : New York University Press, 1985. 59 p. ; 22 cm. (The Joseph I. Lubin memorial lectures . no. 1) ISBN 0-8147-1068-9 : LC Card 85-5115 DDC 332.1/5 19
1. Debts, External - Developing countries. 2. Default (Finance) - Developing countries. I. Title. II. Series.
HG3881 .B677 1985 ***NYPL [JLD 86-2189]***

Brinberg, David. Perspectives on methodology in consumer research /. New York , c1986. xi, 301 p. : ISBN 0-387-96238-7 : LC Card 85-26047 DDC 658.8/34 19
HF5415.3 .P464 1986 ***NYPL [JLE 86-4371]***

Brinckmann, Hans, 1934- Automatisierte Verwaltung . Frankfurt , New York , c1981. 135 p. : ISBN 3-593-32944-1 : LC Card 81-146994
HJ3484.A4 A95 1981

Brinco, Ricardo. Transporte urbano em questão / Ricardo Brinco. Porto Alegre : Secretaria de Coordenação e Planejamento, Fundação de Economia e Estatística, 1985. 114 p. ; 23 cm. Based in part on author's thesis (doctoral--Universidade de Paris XIII-Nanterre, 1979) presented under the title: Um estudo de transporte urbanos. Bibliography: p. [103]-114. LC Card 87-404831 DDC 388.4 19
1. Urban transportation. I. Title.
HE305 .B75 1985

Bringing innovation to market . Sheth, Jagdish N. New York , c1987. xii, 247 p. : ISBN 0-471-84977-4 LC Card 87-17611 DDC 658.5/78 19
HD69.N4 S494 1987

Bringing innovations to market . McPherson, Joseph H. Menlo Park, Calif. (333 Ravenswood Ave., Menlo Park 94025-3476) , c1984. 36 p. : LC Card 87-118382 DDC 658.5/75 19
HF5415.153 .M35 1984

BRINI FAMILY.
Sala, Edmondo. All'origine della borghesia lecchese . Lecco [1983] 83 p. : LC Card 85-190056
HD9765.I72 L437 1983

Brink, Helge. Monetarisme og økonomisk politik / af Helge Brink. [Copenhagen] : Jurist- og økonomforbundet, c1984. 125 p. ; 23 cm. Bibliography: p. 120-125. ISBN 87-574-4380-7 : LC Card 84-253099
1. Monetary policy - Denmark. 2. Money supply - Denmark. 3. Denmark - Economic policy. 4. Chicago school of economics. I. Title.
HG1092 .B75 1984

Brinkerhoff, Derick W. La gestion efficace des projets de développement : un guide a l'exécution et l'évaluation / Derick W. Brinkerhoff, Janet C. Tuthill. West Hartford, Conn. : Kumarian Press, c1987. vi, 186 p. : ill. ; 28 cm. (Kumarian Press guideline series) ISBN 0-931816-06-8 (pbk.) LC Card 86-33733 DDC 338.9/0068 19
1. Economic development projects - Management. 2. Economic development projects - Evaluation. I. Tuthill, Janet C., 1949-. II. Title.
HD75.8 .B75 1987

Brinkerhoff, Robert O. Achieving results from training : how to evaluate human resource development to strengthen programs and increase impact / Robert O. Brinkerhoff.1st ed. San Francisco : Jossey-Bass Publishers, 1987. xx, 248 p. ; 24 cm. (The Jossey-Bass management series) Bibliography: p. 235-240. Includes index. ISBN 1-555-42044-3 (alk. paper) LC Card 86-46331 DDC 658.3/12404 19
1. Employees, Training of - Evaluation. I. Title. II. Series.
HF5549.5.T7 B65 1987

Brinkmann, Eberhard. Stand und Entwicklung des Vorschlagswesens in Wirtschaft und Verwaltung /. Dortmund , 1978. 108 p. : ISBN 3-922104-00-2 LC Card 85-124069
HD30 .A7 Heft 193 HF5549.5.S8

Brinson, Gary P. Ibbotson, Roger G. Investment markets . New York , c1987. ix, 294 p. : ISBN 0-07-031673-2 : LC Card 86-33740 DDC 332.6 19
HG4523 .I23 1987

BRIONNE (EURE, FRANCE) - ECONOMIC CONDITIONS.
Durix, Pierre. Les structures économiques et sociales dans le Brionnais oriental aux XVIIe et XVIIIe siècles /. Dijon [1983] xxxiii, 608 p. : LC Card 86-200732
HC277.B68 D87 1983

BRIONNE (EURE, FRANCE) - SOCIAL CONDITIONS.
Durix, Pierre. Les structures économiques et sociales dans le Brionnais oriental aux XVIIe et XVIIIe siècles /. Dijon [1983] xxxiii, 608 p. : LC Card 86-200732
HC277.B68 D87 1983

Briquets, Sergio Diaz- see **Diaz-Briquets, Sergio.**

Bristow, J. A. (John A.) Public expenditure . Dublin, Ireland , 1986. 138 p. ; ISBN 0-906980-56-9 (pbk.) : LC Card 86-143826 DDC 336.3/9 19
HJ7461 .P83 1986 ***NYPL [JLD 87-553]***

Bristow, M. R. (M. Roger) Land-use planning in Hong Kong : history, policies, and procedures / Roger Bristow. Hong Kong ; New York : Oxford University Press, 1987, c1984. xii, 328 p., [16] p. of plates : ill., maps ; 25 cm. Two maps on lining papers. Bibliography: p. [299]-317. Includes index. ISBN 0-19-581577-7 (pbk.) : LC Card 87-5524 DDC 333.73/17/095125 19
1. Land use - Hong Kong - Planning. I. Title.
HD943.2 .B75 1987

Britain and Nigeria : exploitation or development? / edited by Toyin Falola. London ; Atlantic Highlands, New Jersey : Zed Books ; vi, 250 p. ; 23 cm. Distributor from label on p. before t.p. Includes bibliographical references and index. ISBN 0-86232-303-7 : LC Card 86-232062 DDC 337.410669 19
1. Great Britain - Foreign economic relations - Nigeria. 2. Nigeria - Foreign economic relations - Great Britain. 3. Nigeria - Economic conditions - To 1960. I. Falola, Toyin.
HF1534.5.N6 B75 1987

Britain and the multinationals /. Stopford, John M. Chichester , New York , c1985. xiv, 282 p. : ISBN 0-471-90839-8 : LC Card 85-12352 DDC 338.8/8841 19
HD2845 .S76 1985 ***NYPL [JLE 86-924]***

Britain in decline . Gamble, Andrew. Basingstoke, Hampshire , 1985. xxi, 261 p. ; ISBN 0-333-39253-1 : LC Card 86-673896
HC256.6 .G35x 1985

Britain in tropical Africa, 1880-1960 . Munro, J. Forbes. London , 1984. 89 p. : ISBN 0-333-32330-0 LC Card 87-672364
HC800 .M86x 1984

Britain's economy . Jones, Aubrey, 1911- Cambridge [Cambridgeshire] , New York , 1985. x, 158 p. : ISBN 0-521-30816-X LC Card 85-9649 DDC 330.941/0858 19
HC256.6 .J64 1985 ***NYPL [JLD 86-1581]***

Britain's energy resources / [prepared by Reference Services, Publications Division, Central Office of Information, London]. London : H.M.S.O., 1981. 27 p. : ill. ; 21 cm. (Central Office of Information reference pamphlet. 166) Bibliography: p. 27-28. ISBN 0-11-701010-3 (pbk.) LC Card 81-165936 DDC 333.79/0941 19
1. Energy industries - Great Britain. 2. Power resources - Great Britain. 3. Renewable energy sources - Great Britain. 4. Petroleum industry and trade - Great Britain. 5. Gas industry - Great Britain. I. Great Britain. Central Office of Information. Reference Services.
HD9502.G72 B74 1981

Britain's industrial future : the report of the Liberial Industrial Inquiry. New York : Garland, 1985. xxiv, 503 p. ; 23 cm. (English workers and the coming of the welfare state, 1918-1945) Includes index. Reprint. Originally published: London : E. Benn, 1926. ISBN 0-8240-7605-2 (alk. paper) : LC Card 85-13042 DDC 338.941 19
1. Industry and state - Great Britain. 2. Labor policy - Great Britain. 3. Reconstruction (1914-1939) - Great Britain. 4. Great Britain - Economic policy - 1918-1945. I. Liberal Industrial Inquiry (Great Britain). II. Series.
HC256.3 .B728 1985 ***NYPL [JLD 86-3461]***

Britische Quellen zur deutschen Geschichte. see **German Historical Institute in London. Veröffentlichungen.**

BRITISH AIRWAYS - HISTORY.
Campbell-Smith, Duncan. The British Airways story . London , 1986. viii, 327 p. ; ISBN 0-340-39495-1 (pbk.) : LC Card 86-206477 DDC 387.7/065/41 19
HE9843.B7 C36 1986

The British Airways story . Campbell-Smith, Duncan. London , 1986. viii, 327 p. ; ISBN 0-340-39495-1 (pbk.) : LC Card 86-206477 DDC 387.7/065/41 19
HE9843.B7 C36 1986

British and American women at work . Dex, Shirley. Houndmills, Basingstoke, Hampshire , 1986. xii, 159 p. : ISBN 0-333-40219-7
NYPL [JLD 86-3608]

BRITISH BANK OF THE MIDDLE EAST - HISTORY.
Jones, Geoffrey. The history of the British Bank of the Middle East /. Cambridge [Cambridgeshire] , New York , 1986- v. : ISBN 0-521-32322-3 (v. 1) LC Card 85-31359 DDC 332.1/5/0955 19
HG3270.2.A8 B755 1986 ***NYPL [JLL 87-87]***

BRITISH BROADCASTING CORPORATION - FINANCE.
Two studies concerning the British Broadcasting Corporation /. London , 1979. 48 p. : ISBN 0-11-340763-7 (pbk.) LC Card 83-221765
HE8689.9.G7 T85 1979

BRITISH BROADCASTING CORPORATION - PLANNING.
Two studies concerning the British Broadcasting Corporation /. London , 1979. 48 p. : ISBN 0-11-340763-7 (pbk.) LC Card 83-221765
HE8689.9.G7 T85 1979

BRITISH BROADCASTING CORPORATION. TELEVISION SERVICE - HISTORY.
Moss, Nicholas. BBC TV presents . London , 1986. 120 p. : ISBN 0-946358-29-X LC Card 87-146728 DDC 384.55/4/06041 19
HE8700.9.G7 M67 1986

BRITISH COLUMBIA - COMMERCE - CHINA.
China economic overview . [Victoria] [1985?] 111, [2] p. : ISBN 0-7726-0465-7 (pbk.) LC Card 86-202984 DDC 330.951/058 19
HC427.92 .C68 1985

BRITISH COLUMBIA - ECONOMIC CONDITIONS.
After Bennett . Vancouver, B.C. , 1986. 429 p. : ISBN 0-919573-63-0 LC Card 87-110683 DDC 338.9711 19
HC117.B8 A63 1986

Restraining the economy . Vancouver , c1986. 320 p. ; ISBN 0-919573-60-6 LC Card 87-107157 DDC 338.9711 19
HC117.B8 R475 1986

BRITISH COLUMBIA - ECONOMIC POLICY.
After Bennett . Vancouver, B.C. , 1986. 429 p. : ISBN 0-919573-63-0 LC Card 87-110683 DDC 338.9711 19
HC117.B8 A63 1986

Restraining the economy . Vancouver , c1986. 320 p. ; ISBN 0-919573-60-6 LC Card 87-107157 DDC 338.9711 19
HC117.B8 R475 1986

British Columbia. Islands Trust. Barr, Lorna R. Land of the Trust islands . [Victoria, B.C.] [1978] 36 p. : LC Card 83-226106 DDC 333.3/0996/5 19
HD1121.Z63 B37 1978

British Columbia. Lands and Housing Regional Operations Division. Cariboo Region. Calvert Island crown land plan /. [Victoria, B.C.] , 1981. vii, 63 p. : ISBN 0-7719-8637-8 (pbk.) LC Card 82-208343 DDC 333.1/09711/3 19
HD319.B8 C34 1981

British Columbia. Ministry of International Trade and Investment. China economic overview . [Victoria] [1985?] 111, [2] p. : ISBN 0-7726-0465-7 (pbk.) LC Card 86-202984 DDC 330.951/058 19
HC427.92 .C68 1985

British Columbia. Terrestrial Studies Branch. Biophysical resources of the Slocan Valley /. Victoria, B.C. , 1982. ix, 102 p. : ISBN 0-7718-8310-2 (pbk.) LC Card 84-117204 DDC 333.7/09711/43 19
HC117.B8 B46 1982

The British computer industry . Kelly, Tim. New York, NY , c19. 267 p. : ISBN 0-7099-3123-9 : LC Card 87-569 DDC 338.4/7004/0941 19
HD9696.C63 G765 1987

British diplomacy and finance in China, 1895-1914 /. Edwards, E. W. Oxford [Oxfordshire] , New York , 1987. 212 p. : ISBN 0-19-822916-X : LC Card 86-28567 DDC 337.41051 19
HF1534.5.C5 E39 1987

British economic and social history, 1700-1950 /. Korzeniewicz, Richard. London , c1985. 261 p. : ISBN 0-7212-0711-1 : LC Card 87-144405 DDC 330.941 19
HC254.5 .K67 1985

British economic history.
Baker, Dennis, 1928- Agricultural prices, production, and marketing, with special reference to the hop industry . New York , 1985. 779 p. : ISBN 0-8240-6675-8 : LC Card 84-45995 DDC 338.1/7382 19
HD9019.H72 G67 1985 ***NYPL [JLE 87-63]***

Brassley, Paul, 1946- The agricultural economy of Northumberland and Durham in the period, 1640-1750 /. New York , 1985. iii, 224 p. : ISBN 0-8240-6676-6 : LC Card 84-45996 DDC 338.1/09428/6 19
HD1930.N67 B73 1985
NYPL [JLE 86-3924]

Fleischman, Richard K. Conditions of life among the cotton workers of southeastern Lancashire, 1780-1850 /. New York , 1985. 475 p. ; ISBN 0-8240-6681-2 (alk. paper) : LC Card 84-46001 DDC 305/.9677/094276 19
HD8039.T42 G74 1985
NYPL [JLE 86-3899]

Higgs, Edward, 1952- Domestic servants and households in Rochdale, 1851-1871 /. New York , 1986. 423 p. ; ISBN 0-8240-6682-0 : LC Card 84-46002 DDC 305.5/6 19
HD8039.D52 G7755 1986
NYPL [JLE 86-4591]

Hueckel, Glenn R. (Glenn Russell), 1945- The Napoleonic wars and their impact on factor returns and output growth in England, 1793-1815 /. New York , 1985. lvi, 212 p. ; ISBN 0-8240-6683-9 : LC Card 84-46003

DDC 330.941/073 19
HC254.5 .H78 1985 ***NYPL [JLE 86-4294]***

Kenwood, A. G. Capital formation in north east England, 1800-1913 /. New York , 1985. xv, 444 p. : ISBN 0-8240-6685-5 : LC Card 84-46005 DDC 332/.0415/09428 19
HC260.S3 K46 1985 ***NYPL [JLE 86-3900]***

Lischka, J. R. (Johannes Richard), 1933- Ludwig Mond and the British alkali industry /. New York , 1985. 233 p. ; ISBN 0-8240-6686-3 (alk. paper) : LC Card 84-46006 DDC 338.4/7673725/0924 19
HD9660.A43 G75 1985
NYPL [JSD 86-547]

Toomey, Robert R., 1949- Vivian and Sons, 1809-1924 . New York , 1985. 427 p. ; ISBN 0-8240-6692-8 (alk. paper) : LC Card 84-46012 DDC 338.7/622343/0941 19
HD9539.C7 G778 1985
NYPL [JLE 86-4440]

British Film Institute, London. Broadcasting Research Unit. Hollins, Timothy. Beyond broadcasting . London , 1984. ix, 385 p. ; ISBN 0-85170-148-5 (pbk.) LC Card 84-125713 DDC 384.55/563 19
HE8700.72.G7 H65 1984
NYPL [JLD 86-1057]

British Guiana. [British Guiana] : Govt. Information Services of British Guiana, [1962] 47 p. : ill. (some col.) ; 18 cm. Cover title. LC Card 85-215673
1. Guyana - Industries. 2. Guyana - Economic conditions. 3. Guyana - Commerce. I. British Guiana. Government Information Services.
HC207 .B75 1962

British Guiana. Government Information Services. British Guiana. [British Guiana] [1962] 47 p. : LC Card 85-215673
HC207 .B75 1962

British historical statistics /. Mitchell, B. R. (Brian R.) Cambridge [Cambridgeshire] , New York , 1988. p. cm. ISBN 0-521-33008-4 LC Card 86-24513 DDC 314.1 19
HA1134 .M58 1988

British imports of consumer goods . Morgan, Ann D. Cambridge [Cambridgeshire] , New York , 1988. xi, 129 p. ; ISBN 0-521-35349-1 LC Card 87-25662 DDC 382/.5/0941 19
HF3506.5 .M67 1988

BRITISH - INDIA - DEATH.
Mouat, Frederic J. (Frederic John), 1816-1897. The death tribute of England to India . London , 1875. 14 p. ; LC Card 87-168950
HB1469 .M67 1875

BRITISH LEYLAND MOTOR CORPORATION.
Willman, Paul. Innovation and management control . Cambridge [Cambridgeshire] , New York , 1985. viii, 215 p. ; ISBN 0-521-26802-8 LC Card 84-17481 DDC 331/.04292/0941 19
HD8039.A82 G79 1985
NYPL [JLD 85-3102]

British Medical Association. Public Affairs Division. Smoking out the barons . Chichester [West Sussex] , New York , c1986. vii, 192 p.; ISBN 0-471-90937-8 (pbk.) : LC Card 85-26414 DDC 659.1/967973/0941 19
HF6161.C35 S66 1986
NYPL [JLD 86-3620]

British Motor Holdings. see **British Leyland Motor Corporation.**

British multinationals : origins, management, and performance / edited by Geoffrey Jones. Aldershot, Hants ; Brookfield, Vt., USA : Gower, c1986. xi, 212 p. : ill. ; 24 cm. Bibliography: p. 202-204. Includes index. CONTENTS. - Origins, management, and performance / Geoffrey Jones -- The multinational expansion of Dunlop, 1890-1939 / Geoffrey Jones -- Vickers as a multinational before 1945 / R.P.T. Davenport-Hines -- Transatlantic specialty steels / Geoffrey Tweedale -- The chocolate multinationals / Geoffrey Jones -- Courtaulds in continental Europe, 1920-1945 / Geoffrey Jones -- Glaxo as a multinational before 1963 / R.P.T. Davenport-Hines -- Steel and engineering overseas / Edgar Jones -- Pilkington, the reluctant multinational / Theo Barker. ISBN 0-566-00997-8 LC Card 86-222817 DDC 338.8/8941 19
1. International business enterprises - History. 2. Corporations, British - History. I. Jones, Geoffrey.
HD2755.5 .B75 1986

BRITISH - NAMIBIA - HISTORY - 20TH CENTURY.
Phillips, John A. S. Deutsch-englische Komödie der Irrungen um Südwestafrika . Pfaffenhofen, West Germany , 1986. 184 p., [12] p. of plates : ISBN 3-87010-105-9 LC Card 87-146587 DDC 338.4/76686366/09688 19
HD9484.G9 N366 1986

British non-bank financial intermediaries /. Goacher, D. J. (David J.) London , Boston , 1987. xxiv, 460 p. : ISBN 0-04-332109-7 (alk. paper) LC Card 86-32146 DDC 332.1/0941 19
HG186.G7 B73 1987

British social reform and German precedents . Hennock, E. P., 1926- Oxford [Oxfordshire] , New York , 1987. vi, 243 p. ; ISBN 0-19-820127-3 : LC Card 87-11082 DDC 368.4/00941 19
HD7165 .H455 1987

British Sociological Association. The Changing experience of employment . Houndmills, Basingstoke, Hampshire , 1986. x, 230 p. ; ISBN 0-333-39695-2 ***NYPL [JLD 87-933]***

BRITISH STEEL CORPORATION STRIKE, 1980.
Sirs, Bill. Hard labour /. London , 1985. 151 p., [8] p. of plates : ISBN 0-283-99241-7 : LC Card 86-191030 DDC 331.88/1691/0924 B 19
HD6665.S57 A3 1985

BRITISH TELECOM.
Newman, Karin. The selling of British Telecom /. London , New York , c1986. viii, 176 p. : ISBN 0-03-910639-X ***NYPL [JLF 86-853]***

British television . Burns, R. W. London , c1986. xv, 488 p. : ISBN 0-86341-079-0 LC Card 87-160684 DDC 384.55/0941 19
HE8700.9.G7 B87 1986

British television advertising : the first 30 years / edited by Brian Henry. London : Century Benham, 1986. 528 p., xxxii p. of plates : ill. (some col.) ; 25 cm. ISBN 0-09-165800-4 : LC Card 87-120167 DDC 659.14/3/0941 19
1. Television advertising - Great Britain - History. I. Henry, Brian.
HF6146.T42 B675 1986

British trade unionism, 1750-1850 : the formative years / edited by John Rice. London ; New York : Longman, 1988. p. cm. Bibliography: p. Includes index. ISBN 0-582-49459-1 LC Card 87-22614 DDC 331.88/0941 19
1. Trade-unions - Great Britain - History - 18th century. 2. Trade-unions - Great Britain - History - 19th century. I. Rice, John, 1944-.
HD6664 .B83 1988

British Trades Union Congress. see **Trades Union Congress.**

The British transport industry and the European Community . Mackie, Peter J., 1947- Aldershot, Hampshire, England , Brookfield, Vt., U. S.A. , c1987. xvi, 184 p. : ISBN 0-566-05368-3 : LC Card 86-24186 DDC 380.5/24/0941 19
HE199.G5 M33 1987

The British travelling post office /. Johnson, Peter, 1949- London , 1985. 104 p. : ISBN 0-7110-1459-0 : LC Card 86-164160 DDC 383/.143 19
HE6939.R2 J64 1985

British workplace industrial relations, 1980-1984 . Millward, Neil. Aldershot, England , Brookfield, Vt. , c1986. xxi, 341 p. ; ISBN 0-566-05391-8 : LC Card 86-25625 DDC 331/.0941 19
HD8391 .M55 1986 ***NYPL [JLD 87-1287]***

British Works Management Association. see **Institution of Works Managers.**

Brito, Federico. see **Brito Figueroa, Federico.**

Brito Figueroa, Federico. La aristocracia del dinero en Venezuela actual, 1945-1985 / Federico Brito Figueroa. 1a ed. Barquisimeto, Venezuela : Fondo Editorial Buría, 1986- v. <1 > ; 22 cm. (Colección Folletos . 1-) Includes bibliographical references. ISBN 980-608-700-3 (v. 1) : LC Card 87-404343 DDC 305.5/234/0987 19
1. Capitalists and financiers - Venezuela - History - 20th century. 2. Businessmen - Venezuela - History - 20th century. 3. Middle classes - Venezuela - History - 20th century. I. Title.
HG185.V4 B75 1986

BRITON FERRY IRONWORKS - HISTORY.
Roberts, C. W. (Colin William), 1916- A legacy from Victorian enterprise . [Farnborough, Berkshire?] , 1983. x, 277 p. : ISBN 0-9509107-1-6 (pbk.) : LC Card 85-109000 DDC 338.7/6691/0942984 19
HD9521.9.B74 R62 1983
NYPL [JLD 86-2141]

The Briton Manufacturing Company . Smith, Gaylord N. New York , c1988. p. cm. ISBN 0-06-046318-X LC Card 87-15624 DDC 657/.028/55369 19
HD30.26 .S64 1988

BRITTANY (FRANCE) - HISTORY.
Kerhervé, Jean. L'Etat breton aux 14e et 15e siècles . Paris , c1987. 2 v. (xii, x, 1078 p.) : ISBN 2-224-01703-0 (t. 1) LC Card 87-160693
HJ1078.B75 K47 1987

Britton, Paul R., 1933- Leadership is empowering people / Paul R. Britton, John W. Stallings. Lanham, MD : University Press of America, c1986. xxviii, 346 p. ; 22 cm. Bibliography: p. 337-346. ISBN 0-8191-5409-1 (alk. paper) : LC Card 86-9193 DDC 658.3/14 19
1. Leadership. 2. Job enrichment. 3. Job satisfaction. I. Stallings, John W., 1923-. II. Title.
HD57.7 .B75 1986 ***NYPL [JLD 86-3818]***

Broad, Robin. Unequal alliance : the World Bank, the International Monetary Fund, and the Philippines / Robin Broad. Berkeley : University of California Press, c1988. p. cm. (Studies in international political economy) Bibliography: p. Includes index. ISBN 0-520-05905-0 LC Card 87-10745 DDC 332.1/52 19
1. World Bank - Philippines. 2. International Monetary Fund - Philippines. 3. Philippines - Economic policy. I. Title. II. Series.
HG3881.5.W57 B76 1988

Broadcast and cable management /. Marcus, Norman, 1934- Englewood Cliffs, N.J. , c1986. xii, 308 p. : ISBN 0-13-083577-3 LC Card 85-3565 DDC 384.54/068 19
HE8700.8 .M37 1986 ***NYPL [JLE 86-3127]***

BROADCASTERS - SWITZERLAND - INTERVIEWS.
"Ein Chaos wollen wir nicht" . Basel , c1985. 223 p. : ISBN 3-85787-141-5 : LC Card 86-128638
HE8689.9.S95 C57 1985

BROADCASTERS - UNITED STATES - BIOGRAPHY.
Bilby, Kenneth. The general . New York , c1986. 326 p. ; ISBN 0-06-015568-X : LC Card 85-45621 DDC 384.54/092/4 B 19
HE8689.8 B55 1985
NYPL [MWES (Sarnoff, D.) 86-4682]

Paper, Lewis J. Empire . New York , 1987. x, 384 p., [16] p. of plates : ISBN 0-312-00591-1 : LC Card 87-4368 DDC 384.54/092/4 B 19
HE8689.8.P34 P36 1987

Selected radio and television criticism /. Metuchen, N.J. , c1987. ix, 203 p. ; ISBN 0-8108-1942-2 LC Card 86-27891 DDC 791.44/75/0973 19
PN1990.6.U5 S4 1987
NYPL [MWGI 87-1890]

BROADCASTING - ADDRESSES, ESSAYS, LECTURES.
The Politics of broadcasting /. New York , 1985. 305 p. ; ISBN 0-312-62660-6 : LC Card 84-15996 DDC 384.54 19
HE8689.4 .P65 1985
NYPL [MWGT 86-5102]

Broadcasting and related telecommunications in New Zealand . Royal Commission on Broadcasting and Related Telecommunications in New Zealand. Wellington, N.Z. [1986] 518 p. : LC Card 87-130605 DDC 384/.068 19
HE8620.5.Z5 R69 1986

BROADCASTING - CHILE - SOCIAL ASPECTS.
Fuenzalida, Valerio. Modelos de TV y radio y su influencia en la génesis cultural /. [Santiago, Chile] , 1980. 16 leaves ; LC Card 85-209582
HE8689.9.C5 F84 1980

BROADCASTING - GERMANY (WEST) - CONGRESSES.
Schnitzler, Bert, 1933- Die Phalanx . Herford , c1986. 279 p. ; ISBN 3-512-00752-X LC Card

86-199408
HE8689.9.G4 S36 1986

BROADCASTING - GREAT BRITAIN.
The BBC and public service broadcasting /. Manchester , c1986. viii, 116 p. ; ISBN 0-7190-1964-8 : LC Card 86-209725 DDC 384.54/4/0941 19
HE8689.9.G7 B34 1986

BROADCASTING - HUNGARY - HISTORY.
Lévai, Béla. Rádió-televízió anno-- /. Budapest , 1985. 94 p. : ISBN 963-223-331-X : LC Card 86-128497
HE8689.9.H8 L49 1985

Broadcasting in India /. Chatterji, P. C. (Probhat Chandra), 1921- New Delhi , Newbury Park Calif. , 1987. 210 p. ; ISBN 0-8039-9529-6 (U. S.) LC Card 87-4336 DDC 384.54/0954 19
HE8689.9.I4 C49 1987

BROADCASTING - INDIA.
Chatterji, P. C. (Probhat Chandra), 1921- Broadcasting in India /. New Delhi , Newbury Park Calif. , 1987. 210 p. ; ISBN 0-8039-9529-6 (U. S.) LC Card 87-4336 DDC 384.54/0954 19
HE8689.9.I4 C49 1987

BROADCASTING POLICY - ADDRESSES, ESSAYS, LECTURES.
The Politics of broadcasting /. New York , 1985. 305 p. ; ISBN 0-312-62660-6 : LC Card 84-15996 DDC 384.54 19
HE8689.4 .P65 1985
NYPL [MWGT 86-5102]

BROADCASTING POLICY - DENMARK.
Denmark. Mediekommissionen. Betænkning om et øget dansk tv-udbud. [København] , 1983. 168 p. : ISBN 87-503-4624-5 LC Card 85-128700
HE8700.9.D4 D45 1983

BROADCASTING POLICY - INDIA.
Chatterji, P. C. (Probhat Chandra), 1921- Broadcasting in India /. New Delhi , Newbury Park Calif. , 1987. 210 p. ; ISBN 0-8039-9529-6 (U. S.) LC Card 87-4336 DDC 384.54/0954 19
HE8689.9.I4 C49 1987

BROADCASTING POLICY - NEW ZEALAND.
Royal Commission on Broadcasting and Related Telecommunications in New Zealand. Broadcasting and related telecommunications in New Zealand . Wellington, N.Z. [1986] 518 p. : LC Card 87-130605 DDC 384/.068 19
HE8620.5.Z5 R69 1986

BROADCASTING POLICY - SWITZERLAND.
"Ein Chaos wollen wir nicht" . Basel , c1985. 223 p. : ISBN 3-85787-141-5 : LC Card 86-128638
HE8689.9.S95 C57 1985

BROADCASTING - POLITICAL ASPECTS - ADDRESSES, ESSAYS, LECTURES.
The Politics of broadcasting /. New York , 1985. 305 p. ; ISBN 0-312-62660-6 : LC Card 84-15996 DDC 384.54 19
HE8689.4 .P65 1985
NYPL [MWGT 86-5102]

BROADCASTING - TAXATION - GREAT BRITAIN.
Review of the ITV and ILR levy structures, 1984-85 . London , c1986. 44 p. ; ISBN 0-86252-236-6 (pbk.) LC Card 86-202703 DDC 384.54/3 19
HE8689.9.G7 R48 1986

BROADCASTING - UNITED STATES.
Selected radio and television criticism /. Metuchen, N.J. , c1987. ix, 203 p. ; ISBN 0-8108-1942-2 LC Card 86-27891 DDC 791.44/75/0973 19
PN1990.6.U5 S4 1987
NYPL [MWGI 87-1890]

BROADCASTING - UNITED STATES - FINANCE.
Investing in broadcast stations . [Washington, D.C.] (1120 20th St., NW, Washington 20036) , c1987. 318 p. in various pagings : LC Card 87-115340 DDC 384.54/3/0681 19
HE8689.8 .I58 1987

BROADCASTING - UNITED STATES - HISTORY.
Paper, Lewis J. Empire . New York , 1987. x, 384 p., [16] p. of plates : ISBN 0-312-00591-1 : LC Card 87-4368 DDC 384.54/092/4 B 19
HE8689.8.P34 P36 1987

Broader perspectives on the interest of pension plan participants / edited by Richard F. DeMong, William S. Gray III, Robert D. Milne. Charlottesville, Va. (P.O. Box 3665, Charlottesville 22903) : Financial Analysts Research Foundation, c1985. vii, 43 p. : ill. ; 23 cm. (Financial Analysts Research Foundation monograph series . 22) Includes bibliographical references. LC Card 85-196669 DDC 332.6/7254 19
1. Pension trusts - United States - Addresses, essays, lectures. 2. Pension trusts - United States - Management - Addresses, essays, lectures. I. DeMong, Richard F. II. Gray, William S. III. Milne, Robert D. IV. Series: Monograph (Financial Analysts Research Foundation) , no. 22.
HD7105.45.U6 B76 1985
NYPL [JLL 81-133 no. 22]

Brobeck, Stephen. Hoffman, Naphtali. The bank book . San Diego , 1986. xiii, 222 p. ; ISBN 0-15-610676-0 (pbk.) : LC Card 85-27271 DDC 332.1/7/0973 19
HG1616.C87 H64 1986
NYPL [JLE 86-3189]

Bröchner, Jan, 1948- Swedish national and local government programs for conservation of energy in buildings /. Gävle, Sweden [1982] 187 p. : ISBN 91-540-9134-9 (pbk.) LC Card 82-208802 DDC 333.79 19
HD9502.S82 S98 1982 NYPL [JLG 86-107]

Brock, James W. Adams, Walter, 1922 (Aug. 27)- The bigness complex . New York , 1986. xiii, 426 p. ; ISBN 0-394-54721-7 : LC Card 86-42624 DDC 338.6/44/0973 19
HD2785 .A68 1986 NYPL [JLE 87-1432]

Brocker, Manfred. Kants Besitzlehre : zur Problematik einer transzendentalphilosophischen Eigentumslehre / Manfred Brocker. Würzburg : Königshausen + Neumann, 1987. 220 p. ; 21 cm. (Epistemata: Reihe Philosophie. Bd. 30) Bibliography: p. 203-217. ISBN 3-88479-278-4 LC Card 87-136989 DDC 330/.17 19
1. Property. 2. Liberty. 3. Kant, Immanuel, 1724-1804 - Views on property. I. Title.
HB701 .B78 1987

Brockett, Charles D., 1946- Land, power, and poverty : agrarian transformations and political conflict in Central America / Charles D. Brockett. Boston : Allen & Unwin, c1988. p. cm. (Thematic studies in Latin America) Bibliography: p. Includes index. ISBN 0-04-497027-7 LC Card 87-22746 DDC 338.1/09728 19
1. Agriculture - Economic aspects - Central America. 2. Land use - Central America. 3. Land tenure - Central America. 4. Land reform - Central America. 5. Elite (Social sciences) - Central America. 6. Poor - Central America. 7. Central America - Rural conditions. I. Title. II. Series.
HD1797 .B76 1988

Brodacki, Krystian. U nas dole i niedole /. Warszawa , 1978. 283 p. ; LC Card 81-208722
HD8038.P6 U25 1978

Brodie, Peter R., 1947- Dictionary of shipping terms / by Peter R. Brodie. London ; New York : Lloyd's of London Press, 1985. 155 p. ; 22 cm. ISBN 1-85044-069-7 (pbk.) : LC Card 86-164175 DDC 387.5/03/21 19
1. Shipping - Dictionaries. I. Title.
HE567 .B68 1985

Brodin, Anders. The OECD Compatible Trade and Production data base, 1970-1983 / by Anders Brodin, Derek Blades. [Paris, France] : OECD, c1986. ii, 81 p. ; 30 cm. (Working papers / OECD, Department of Economics and Statistics . no. 31) Summary in French. Chiefly tables. Bibliography: p. 15. LC Card 86-213116 DDC 382/.021 19
1. COMTAP (Information retrieval system). 2. Commerce - Statistics. 3. Industrial productivity - Statistics. I. Blades, Derek W. II. Series: Working papers (Organisation for Economic Co-operation and Development. Dept. of Economics and Statistics) , no. 31. III. Title.
HF1016 .B68 1986

Brodmeier, Beate. Entwicklungspolitische Fachausdrücke (Auswahl) : Deutsch, Englisch, Französisch, Spanisch / Beate Brodmeier.1. Aufl. Baden-Baden : Nomos Verlagsgesellschaft, 1985. 48 p. ; 23 cm. (Schriftenreihe der Deutschen Stiftung für Internationale Entwicklung. Dialog und Training) Schriftenreihe der Deutschen Stiftung für Internationale Entwicklung. Dok. ; Nr. 1289 C/a-c Includes indexes. ISBN 3-7890-1093-6 LC Card 85-186152
1. Economic development - Dictionaries - Polyglot. 2. German language - Dictionaries - Polyglot. I. Series. II. Series: Schriftenreihe der Deutschen Stiftung für Internationale Entwicklung. Dok. , Nr. 1289. III. Title.
HD84 .B765 1985

Brody, Aaron L. Sacharow, Stanley. Packaging, an introduction /. Cleveland, OH , c1986. p. cm. ISBN 0-15-004486-0 LC Card 87-8362 DDC 658.5/64 19
HF5770 .S274 1986

Brody, David. Workers in industrial America : essays on the twentieth century struggle / David Brody. New York : Oxford University Press, 1981, 1980. ix, 257 p. ; 22 cm. Includes bibliographical references. ISBN 0-19-502491-5 (pbk.) LC Card 78-27157
1. Trade-unions - United States - History. 2. Labor and laboring classes - United States - History. I. Title.
NYPL [JLD 86-3729]

Brody, David, 1930- Labor in crisis : the steel strike of 1919 / David Brody ; with a new bibliographical afterword.Illini books ed. Urbana : University of Illinois Press, 1987, c1965. 218 p. ; 22 cm. Reprint. Originally published: 1st ed. Philadelphia : Lippincott, 1965. (Critical periods of history). "An Illini book from the University of Illinois Press"--P. [4] of cover. Bibliography: p. 199-212. Includes index. ISBN 0-252-01373-5 (pbk. : alk. paper) LC Card 86-30880 DDC 331.89/269142/0973 19
1. Steel Strike, United States, 1919-1920. 2. Trade-unions - Iron and steel workers - United States - History. I. Series: Critical periods of history. II. Title.
HD5325.I5 1919 .B7 1987

Brody, E. W.
The business of public relations / E.W. Brody. New York : Praeger, 1987. xv, 327 p. ; 24 cm. Includes index. Bibliography: p. 315-319. ISBN 0-275-92333-9 (alk. paper) : LC Card 86-30552 DDC 659.2 19
I. Title.
HD59 .B757 1987 NYPL [JLE 87-1589]

Communicating for survival : coping with diminishing human resources / E.W. Brody. New York : Praeger, 1987. xi, 264 p. : ill. ; 24 cm. Bibliography: p. [249]-252. Includes index. ISBN 0-275-92652-4 (alk. paper) : LC Card 87-11774 DDC 658.3/00141 19
1. Communication in personnel management. 2. Communication in organizations. I. Title.
HF5549.5.C6 B69 1987

Broer, D. P. Neoclassical theory and empirical models of aggregate firm behaviour / by D.P. Broer. Dordrecht ; Boston : Kluwer Academic Publishers, 1987. 343 p. : ill. ; 25 cm. (Advanced studies in theoretical and applied econometrics . v. 8) Bibliography: p. 320-331. Includes index. ISBN 90-247-3412-6 LC Card 86-23485 DDC 338.5 19
1. Managerial economics - Econometric models. 2. Microeconomics. I. Title. II. Series.
HD30.22 .B76 1987

Broer, Wolfgang, 1944- Das rote Chaos : Theorie und Praxis der sozialistischen Wirtschaft / Wolfgang Broer. München : Wirtschaftsverlag Langen-Müller/Herbig, c1982. 237 p. ; 20 cm. ISBN 3-7844-7100-55 LC Card 87-672594
1. Europe, Eastern - Economic conditions - Anecdotes, facetiae, satire, etc. 2. Europe, Eastern - Politics and government - Anecdotes, facetiae, satire, etc. 3. Europe, Eastern - Social conditions - Anecdotes, facetiae, satire, etc. I. Title.
HC244 .B76x 1982

Brogowicz, Andrew A. Readings and cases in basic marketing /. Homewood, Ill. , 1987. ix, 365 p. : ISBN 0-256-05795-8 (pbk.) LC Card 86-83136 DDC 658.8 19
HF5415 .R334 1987

Broh, C. Anthony. A horse of a different color : television's treatment of Jesse Jackson's 1984 presidential campaign / C. Anthony Broh. Washington, D.C. : Joint Center for Political Studies, 1987. xiv, 93 p. : ill. ; 23 cm. Bibliography: p. 87-91. ISBN 0-941410-54-4 (pbk.) : LC Card 87-2869 DDC 324.973/0927 19
1. Television in politics - United States. 2. Presidents - United States - Election - 1984. 3. Jackson, Jesse, 1941-. I. Title.
HE8700.76.U6 B76 1987

BROKERS.
Alfano, Salvatore. Work of the dividend department /. New York, NY , c1987. xvi, 180

p. ; ISBN 0-13-965096-2 LC Card 87-7733 DDC 332.6/068/5 19
HG4028.D5 A43 1987

Gross, LeRoy. Phone power . New York, N.Y. , c1987. xiii, 208 p. : ISBN 0-13-664350-7 LC Card 87-7740 DDC 332.6/068/8 19
HG4621 .G776 1987

Loiacono, Nicholas. Work of the purchase and sales department /. New York, NY , c1987. p. cm. ISBN 0-13-965104-7 : LC Card 87-7734 DDC 332.6/068/7 19
HG4621 .L64 1987

Veale, Stuart R. Tapping the small-business market /. New York, NY , c1987. xiii, 198 p. ; ISBN 0-13-884420-8 : LC Card 87-7732 DDC 332.6/068/8 19
HG4027.7 .V4 1987

BROKERS - CANADA.
Courchene, Thomas J. Ontario's proposals for the Canadian securities industry /. Toronto , Scarborough, Ont. [1986] 39 p. : ISBN 0-88806-137-4 (pbk.) LC Card 87-133168 DDC 332.63/2 19
HG5158 .C68 1986

Brokers course textbook. Real estate appraisal, finance, investment, and business management . [Tallahassee] , c1986. ix, 441, iv, 86 p. : LC Card 87-159867 DDC 333.33 19
HD1375 .R375 1986

BROKERS - GREAT BRITAIN.
Rutterford, Janette. The securities industry . [London] [1986] 93 p. : LC Card 87-160412 DDC 332.63/2/0941 19
HG5432 .R87 1986

BROKERS - HANDBOOKS, MANUAL, ETC.
The Successful sales assistant's handbook. New York, N.Y. , c1987. xi, 268 p. : ISBN 0-13-860305-7 (pbk.) : LC Card 87-11322 DDC 332.6/2/0688 19
HG4621 .S84 1987

BROKERS - NEW YORK (N.Y.)
Stoll, Hans R. The stock exchange specialist system . New York, N.Y. (90 Trinity Place, New York 10006) [c1985] 53 p. : LC Card 86-210049 DDC 332.64/273 19
HG4572 .S856 1985

BROKERS - UNITED STATES.
Auletta, Ken. Greed and glory on Wall Street . New York , c1986. xiii, 253 p., [16] p. of plates : ISBN 0-394-54410-2 : LC Card 85-10700 DDC 332.66/09747/1 19
HG5129.N5 A8 1986 ***NYPL [JLE 86-856]***

Auletta, Ken. Greed and glory on Wall Street . Boston, Mass. , 1987, c1986. xii, 423 p. (large print) ; ISBN 0-8161-4189-4 (lg. print) : LC Card 86-26968 DDC 332.66/09747/1 19
HG5129.N5 A8 1987b

Auletta, Ken. Greed and glory on Wall Street . New York, N.Y. [1987], c1986. xi, 260 p., [16] p. of plates : ISBN 0-446-38406-2 (pbk.) LC Card 86-23416 DDC 332.66/09747/1 19
HG5129.N5 A8 1987

The financing and regulatory capital needs of the securities industry /. [Washington, D.C.] [1985?] xiv, 69, [49] p ; ***NYPL [JLF 86-863]***

The New York Institute of Finance guide to investing. New York, N.Y. , c1987. xi, 296 p. : ISBN 0-13-620436-8 (pbk.) : LC Card 87-11323 DDC 332.6/78 19
HG4921 .N53 1987

Stocks, bonds, options, futures . New York, N.Y. [Englewood Cliffs, N.J.] , c1987. 332 p. : ISBN 0-13-846718-8 : LC Card 87-11324 DDC 332.6/78 19
HG4921 .S7945 1987

Brokken, Ray F. Swallow, Brent M. Cattle marketing in Lesotho /. Maseru, Lesotho [1986] iv, 75 leaves : LC Card 87-132309 DDC 381/.416213/096816 19
HD9433.L452 S9 1986

Brolin, Åke, 1924- Säljledaren / Åke Brolin, Lars Josefsson. Uppl. 1. Malmö : LiberFörlag, c1984. 140 p. : ill. ; 25 cm. Includes index. ISBN 91-38-61223-2 : LC Card 84-188808
1. Sales management. 2. Selling. I. Josefsson, Lars. II. Title.
HF5438.4 .B76 1984

Bromley, Daniel W., 1940- Natural resource economics . Boston , c1986. xiv, 234 p. : ISBN 0-89838-203-3 LC Card 85-24215 DDC 333.7 19
HC59 .N318 1986 ***NYPL [JLE 86-3471]***

Bromley, R. J. Política x técnica no planejamento . São Paulo [Brasília] , 1982. 251 p. ; LC Card 86-150182
HD85.P65 P65 1982

Bromwich, G. R. E. Workers' compensation : what those handling insurance need to know / by G.R.E. Bromwich.Rev. Toronto, Ont. : Insurance Institute of Canada, 1986, c1981. ii, 15 p. ; 28 cm. Bibliography: p. 11. Includes index. LC Card 87-166754 DDC 368.4/1/00971 19
1. Workers' compensation - Canada. I. Title.
HD7103.65.C2 B76 1986

Bron, Jean.
Histoire du mouvement ouvrier français .
(t. 3) Bron, Jean. La lutte des classes aujourd'hui, 1950-1981 /. Paris , 1982. 318 p. ; ISBN 2-7082-0349-5
NYPL [JLD 86-1408]

La lutte des classes aujourd'hui, 1950-1981 / Jean Bron. Paris : Les Éditions ouvrières, 1982. 318 p. ; 21 cm. (Histoire du mouvement ouvrier français / Jean Bron . t. 3) Includes index. Includes bibliographical references. ISBN 2-7082-0349-5
1. Labor and laboring classes - France - History. 2. Trade-unions - France - History. I. Series: Bron, Jean. Histoire du mouvement ouvrier français , t. 3. II. Title.
NYPL [JLD 86-1408]

Brondoni, Silvio M. Politiche di mercato dei beni industriali / Silvio M. Brondoni. [Milano] : Giuffrè, [1983] ix, 279 p. : ill. ; 24 cm. (Università "L. Bocconi," Dipartimento di economia aziendale . 55. 10.7) Bibliography: p. [267]-279. LC Card 83-234353
1. Industrial equipment - Marketing. 2. Industrial equipment industry. I. Series: Università "L. Bocconi," Dipartimento di economia aziendale (Series) , 55. II. Title.
HD9680.A2 B76 1983

Bronsard, Camille. Systems of demand equations (including labour supply) for different states of the markets and for different regimes / by Camille Bronsard and Lise Salvas-Bronsard. Montréal : Départment de science économique et Centre de recherche en développement économique, Université de Montréal, [198-] 28 p. ; 28 cm. (Cahier / Département de science économique et Centre de recherche en développement économique, 0709-9231 . no. 8015) Summary in French. Bibliography: p. 26-28. LC Card 83-222220 DDC 338.5/212 19
1. Demand functions (Economic theory). 2. Equilibrium (Economics). 3. Labor supply - Mathematical models. I. Salvas-Bronsard, Lise. II. Series: Cahier (Université de Montréal. Département de sciences économiques) , 8015. III. Title.
HB801 .B77 1980z

Bronsard, Lise Salvas- see Salvas-Bronsard, Lise.

Brookings dialogues on public policy.
Building a Canadian-American free trade area /. Washington, D.C. , c1987. xii, 217 p. ; ISBN 0-8157-2973-1 (pbk.) LC Card 87-71507 DDC 382/.0971/073 19
HF1480.15.U5 B85 1987

Tax reform and the U. S. economy . Washington, D.C. , c1987. ix, 107 p. : ISBN 0-8157-6959-8 (pbk.) LC Card 87-70178 DDC 330.973/0927 19
HJ2381 .T387 1987

Brookings Institution.
Gender in the workplace /. Washington, D.C. , c1987. xiv, 316 p. ; ISBN 0-8157-1170-0 : LC Card 87-668 DDC 331.13/3 19
HD6060.5.U5 G46 1987

Schmandt, Henry J. Federal aid to St. Louis /. Washington, D.C. , c1983. xvii, 67 p. ; ISBN 0-8157-7727-2 (pbk.) LC Card 82-74100 DDC 336.1/85 19
HJ9268.S3 S352 1983 ***NYPL [JLE 87-1]***

Tax reform and the U. S. economy . Washington, D.C. , c1987. ix, 107 p. : ISBN 0-8157-6959-8 (pbk.) LC Card 87-70178 DDC 330.973/0927 19
HJ2381 .T387 1987

Winston, Clifford, 1952- Blind intersection? . Washington, D.C. , c1987. xii, 108 p. : ISBN 0-8157-9466-5 : LC Card 87-806 DDC 338.4/76292/0973 19
HD9710.U52 W55 1987

Brookings Institution, Washington, D. C. Nivola, Pietro S. The politics of energy conservation /. Washington, D.C. , c1986. x, 294 p. ; ISBN 0-8157-6088-4 : LC Card 85-48265 DDC 333.79/16/0973 19
TJ163.4.U6 N58 1986 ***NYPL [JLE 86-2515]***

Brooklyn College. Humanities Institute. Conference on Cable Television (1981 : Brooklyn College Student Union) Proceedings /. [Albany, N.Y.] (P.O. Box 167, Albany 12248) [1982] 77 p. ; LC Card 86-622177 DDC 384.55/47/09747 19
HE8700.72.U6 C66 1981

Brooklyn Union Gas . Larson, Elwin S. New York , 1987. 23 p. : LC Card 87-60614 DDC 338.7/6657/0974723 19
HD9581.U53 B765 1987

BROOKLYN UNION GAS COMPANY - HISTORY.
Larson, Elwin S. Brooklyn Union Gas . New York , 1987. 23 p. : LC Card 87-60614 DDC 338.7/6657/0974723 19
HD9581.U53 B765 1987

Brooks, Harvey. Technology and global industry . Washington, D.C. , 1987. vi, 272 p. : ISBN 0-309-03736-0 (pbk.) LC Card 87-7765 DDC 338/.06 19
HC79.T4 T438 1987

Brooks, John, 1920- The takeover game / John Brooks. 1st ed. New York : Dutton, c1987. x, 390 p. ; 23 cm. "Truman Talley books." "A Twentieth Century Fund book." Bibliography: p. 359-372. Includes index. ISBN 0-525-24586-3 : LC Card 87-5967 DDC 338.8/3/0973 19
1. Consolidation and merger of corporations - United States. I. Title.
HD2746.5 .B76 1987

Brooks, Julie K. How to write a successful business plan / Julie K. Brooks, Barry A. Stevens. New York, NY : AMACOM, c1987. vii, 231 p. : ill. ; 24 cm. Bibliography: p. 193-194. Includes index. ISBN 0-8144-5873-4 LC Card 86-22355 DDC 658.4/012 19
1. Planning. 2. Corporate planning. 3. Communication in management. I. Stevens, Barry A. II. Title.
HD30.28 .B775 1987

Brooks, Leonard J. Canadian corporate social performance : a research monograph / prepared for the Accounting Principles and Practices Committee, the Society of Management Accountants of Canada by Leonard J. Brooks, Jr. Hamilton, Ont. : Society of Management Accountants of Canada, 1986. xii, 267 p. : ill. ; 22 cm. Includes bibliographies. ISBN 0-920212-54-9 (pbk.) LC Card 87-100492 DDC 658.4/08/0971 19
1. Industry - Social aspects - Canada. I. Society of Management Accountants of Canada. Accounting Principles and Practices Committee. II. Title.
HD60.5.C2 B76 1986

Brooks, Lloyd D., 1942- Business mathematics /. New York , c1988. p. cm. ISBN 0-07-008166-2 LC Card 87-4210 DDC 513/.93 19
HF5691 .B9 1988

Brooks, R. Inflation, tax rules, and housing in New Zealand / R. Brooks. Wellington, N.Z. : Reserve Bank of New Zealand, [1986] 22, [22] p. : ill. ; 30 cm. (Discussion paper . G86/4) Bibliography: p. 22. LC Card 87-132461 DDC 363.5/8 19
1. Home ownership - New Zealand - Costs. 2. Rental housing - New Zealand - Costs. 3. Tax expenditures - New Zealand. 4. Taxation - New Zealand. I. Series: Discussion paper (Reserve Bank of New Zealand. Economic Dept.) , G86/4. II. Title.
HD7387.5.A3 B76 1986

Brooks, William T. High impact selling : power strategies for successful selling / William T. Brooks. Englewood Cliffs, N.J. : Prentice-Hall, 1988. p. cm. Includes index. ISBN 0-13-387663-2 LC Card 87-3567 DDC 658.8/5 19
1. Selling. I. Title.
HF5438.25 .B743 1988

Brose, Hanns-Georg, 1945- Berufsbiographien im Wandel /. Opladen , c1986. 290 p. ; ISBN 3-531-11817-X LC Card 86-227301
HF5382.5.G3 B39 1986

Brose, Peter. Hentze, Joachim. Unternehmungsführung und Mitbestimmung /. Würzburg , 1985. 297 p. : ISBN 3-7908-0268-9 LC Card 85-186054
HD5660.G4 H43 1985

Brosset, Michel. Multinationale Bankenverflechtungen : joint Ventures und Partnerschaften / von Michel Brosset. Bern : P. Haupt, c1983. vii, 245 p. : ill. ; 23 cm. (Bankwirtschaftliche Forschungen. Bd. 79) Bibliography: p. 238-245. ISBN 3-258-03275-0 : LC Card 83-178197
1. Banks and banking, International. 2. Joint ventures. 3. Investments. I. Title. II. Series.
HG1526 .B27 Bd. 79 HG3881

Brotchie, J. F. The Spatial impact of technological change /. Totowa, NJ , 1987. p. cm. ISBN 0-389-20753-5 LC Card 87-11460 DDC 338/.06 19
HC79.T4 S77 1987

Brotherton, Christopher J. Industrial relations . Chichester , New York , c1979. xii, 412 p. ; ISBN 0-471-99701-3 LC Card 78-18452 DDC 301.5/5
HD6971 .I547 ***NYPL [JLE 80-1770]***

Brouillette, Benoît, 1904-1979.
[Perspectives de changements dans la manutention des marchandises aux ports canadiens. English]
Prospective changes for handling of commodities in Canadian ports. Montréal, Québec, Canada : Transportation Development Agency : Available from Information Canada, [1974] iv, 93, [3] p. ; 28 cm. Translation of: Perspectives de changements dans la manutention des marchandises aux ports canadiens. "June 1975." Bibliography: p. [94]-[96] "Catalogue no. T48-8/1975"--T.p. verso. LC Card 82-219246
1. Harbors - Canada. 2. Freight and freightage - Canada. 3. Containerization - Canada. I. Canada. Transportation Development Agency. II. Title.
HE553 .B7613 1974

Brousek, Karl M. Die Grossindustrie Böhmens, 1848-1918 / von Karl M. Brousek. München : R. Oldenbourg, 1987. 223 p., 8 leaves of plates : ill. ; 24 cm. (Veröffentlichungen des Collegium Carolinum . Bd. 50) "Quellen- und Literaturverzeichnis": p. 209-215. Includes index. ISBN 3-486-51871-2 LC Card 87-142819 DDC 338.6/44/094371 19
1. Big business - Czechoslovakia - Bohemia - History. 2. Corporations - Czechoslovakia - Bohemia - History. 3. Bohemia (Czechoslovakia) - Industries - History. 4. Bohemia (Czechoslovakia) - Social conditions. I. Title. II. Series.
HD2356.C96 B643 1987

Brouwer, M. A. (Maarten A.) Barendregt, J. (Jaap) Swaziland /. Amsterdam , 's-Gravenhage , 1985. 43 p., [1] folded leaf of plates : ISBN 90-12-05175-4 LC Card 86-174569
HC925 .B37 1985

Brovedani, Bruno. Un modelo de análisis monetario y de programación financiera / Bruno Brovedani. 2a ed. rev. y actualizada. [Mexico City, Mexico] : Centro de Estudios Monetarios Latinoamericanos, 1984. ii, 203 p. : ill. ; 21 cm. (Estudios) Includes bibliographical references. LC Card 86-158393
1. Monetary policy - Latin America. 2. Finance, Public - Latin America. I. Series: Estudios (Centro de Estudios Monetarios Latinoamericanos). II. Title.
HG660.5 .B7 1984

Browder, Clifford, 1928- The money game in old New York : Daniel Drew and his times / Clifford Browder. Lexington, KY : University Press of Kentucky, c1986. viii, 319 p., [8] p. of plates : ill., port. ; c25 cm. Includes index. Bibliography: p. 293-307. ISBN 0-8131-1573-6 LC Card 85-17938 DDC 332/.092/4 B 19
1. Drew, Daniel, 1797-1879. 2. Capitalists and financiers - United States - Biography. 3. Wall Street - History. I. Title.
HG172.D74 B76 1986 ***NYPL [JFE 86-1911]***

Brower, John C. The economic impact of coal mining in Montana / John C. Brower. Missoula, Mont. : Bureau of Business and Economic Research, University of Montana, [1985] 31 p. : ill. ; 28 cm. "September 1985." Bibliography: p. 31. LC Card 87-620608 DDC 338.2/724/09786 19
1. Coal trade - Montana. 2. Montana - Economic conditions. I. Title.
HD9547.M6 B76 1985

Brown, Anthony E. The politics of airline deregulation / Anthony E. Brown. 1st ed. Knoxville : University of Tennessee Press, c1987. xiii, 224 p. ; 23 cm. Bibliography: p. [201]-214. Includes index. ISBN 0-87049-532-1 (alk. paper) : LC Card 86-30888 DDC 387.7/1 19
1. Aeronautics, Commercial - United States - Deregulation. 2. Airlines - United States - Deregulation. 3. Aeronautics, Commercial - Law and legislation - United States. I. Title.
HE9803.A4 B68 1987

Brown, Brendan, 1951-
The flight of international capital : a contemporary history / Brendan Brown. London ; New York : Croom Helm, c1987. xiv, 447 p. : ill. ; 23 cm. Bibliography: p. 421-428. Includes index. ISBN 0-7099-5036-5 : LC Card 87-8988 DDC 332.4/5 19
1. Capital movements. 2. Foreign exchange. 3. International finance. I. Title.
HG3891 .B76 1987

Monetary chaos in Europe : the end of an era / Brendan Brown. London ; New York : Croom Helm, c1987. p. cm. Bibliography: p. Includes index. ISBN 0-7099-5035-7 : LC Card 87-23059 DDC 332.4/5/094 19
1. Finance - Europe - History - 20th century. 2. Monetary policy - Europe - History - 20th century. 3. Europe - History - 20th century. I. Title.
HG186.A2 B76 1987

Brown, Carolann D. (Carolann Doherty), 1946-
The money manager / by Carolann D. Brown. Norfolk, Va. : Donning Co., c1987. p. cm. Includes index. ISBN 0-89865-531-5 : LC Card 87-5456 DDC 332.024 19
1. Investments. 2. Finance, Personal. I. Title.
HG4527 .B675 1987

Brown, Carole Ganz. National policies for developing high technology industries . Boulder, Colo. , c1986. xiv, 247 p. : ISBN 0-8133-7280-1 (soft : alk. paper) LC Card 86-50530 DDC 338.4/762 19
HC79.H53 N38 1986 ***NYPL [JLE 86-4504]***

Brown, Clair, 1946- Gender in the workplace /. Washington, D.C. , c1987. xiv, 316 p. ; ISBN 0-8157-1170-0 : LC Card 87-668 DDC 331.13/3 19
HD6060.5.U5 G46 1987

Brown, Constance C., 1952- Preparing documents with UNIX / Constance C. Brown, Jack L. Falk, Richard D. Sperline. Englewood Cliffs, N.J. : Prentice-Hall, c1986. xv, 206 p. : ill. ; 24 cm. Includes index. Bibliography: p. 189-191. ISBN 0-13-699976-X LC Card 85-17016 DDC 652/.5 19
1. Word processing. 2. UNIX (Computer operating system). I. Falk, Jack L., 1950-. II. Sperline, Richard D., 1947-. III. Title. IV. Title: Preparing documents with U.N.I.X.
Z52.5.U54 B76 1986 ***NYPL [JSE 86-1215]***

Brown, David. Design for diversification /. Canberra , Portland, OR. [1985] 57 p. : ISBN 0-909724-68-7 (pbk.) LC Card 86-222390 DDC 363.5/0994 19
HD7379.A3 D47 1985

Brown, David S. (David Springer), 1915-
Management's hidden enemy : and what can be done about it / David S. Brown. Mt. Airy, Md. : Lomond Publications, 1987. viii, 123 p. ; 27 cm. Includes bibliographies and index. ISBN 0-912338-59-8 LC Card 86-82670 DDC 658.4/5 19
1. Communication in management. 2. Communication in organizations. 3. Personnel management. I. Title.
HD30.3 .B76 1987

Brown, Donald R., 1945- Harvey, Donald F. An experiential approach to organization development /. Englewood Cliffs, N.J. , c1988. p. cm. ISBN 0-13-295122-3 LC Card 87-26207 DDC 658.4/063 19
HD58.8 .H37 1988

Brown, Edmund D. 1594 Evans Drive, S.W. : a history of Southern Saw Service, Inc., and the Atlanta Saw Company / by Edmund D. Brown. Atlanta, Ga. (1594 Evans Dr., S.W., Atlanta 30310) : Southern Saw Service, c1983. 213 p. : ill. (some col.), ports. (some col.) ; 29 cm. LC Card 82-62570 DDC 338.7/62193 19
1. Atlanta Saw Company - History - 20th century. 2. Southern Saw Service - History - 20th century. 3. Saw industry - United States - History - 20th century. 4. Saw filing industry - United States - History - 20th century. I. Title. II. Title: One thousand five hundred ninety-four Evans Drive, Southwest.
HD9529.S294 A842 1983
NYPL [JLF 86-1803]

Brown, Eric D. Writing with a word processor : communication in the computer age / Eric D. Brown. Reston, Va. : Reston Pub. Co., c1984. viii, 136 p. : ill. ; 24 cm. Includes index. ISBN 0-8359-8857-0 (pbk.) :$19.95 LC Card 84-8306 DDC 652 19
1. Word processing. 2. Business report writing. I. Title.
HF5548.115 .B76 1984
NYPL [JLE 86-1769]

Brown, F. Lee (Franklin Lee) Water and poverty in the Southwest / F. Lee Brown and Helen M. Ingram, with contributions from Gilbert Bonem ... [et al.]. Tucson : University of Arizona Press, c1987. xi, 226 p. : maps ; 23 cm. Bibliography: p. 199-217. Includes index. ISBN 0-8165-1038-5 (alk. paper) : LC Card 87-19217 DDC 333.91/00979 19
1. Water-supply, Rural - Southwestern States. 2. Rural poor - Southwestern States. I. Ingram, Helen M., 1937-. II. Title.
HD1695.A165 B76 1987

Brown, Franklin Lee. New courses for the Colorado River . Albuquerque , c1986. xx, 253 p. : ISBN 0-8263-0854-6 LC Card 85-24577 DDC 333.91/009791/3 19
HD1695.C7 N49 1986 ***NYPL [JLE 86-1736]***

Brown, Gerald F. Robek, Mary F. Information and records management /. Encino, Calif. , c1987. vi, 580 p. : ISBN 0-02-820590-1 LC Card 87-135683 DDC 651.5 19
HF5736 .R53 1987

BROWN, HARRY GUNNISON, 1880-
Ryan, Christopher K. (Christopher Keith) Harry Gunnison Brown, economist /. Boulder , 1987. xv, 179 p. ; ISBN 0-8133-7355-7 (pbk. : alk. paper) : LC Card 86-28994 DDC 330/.092/4 B 19
HB119.B65 R93 1987

Brown, J. A. C. (James Alexander Campbell), 1911-1964. The social psychology of industry : human relations in the factory / J.A.C. Brown ; with an introduction by Sir Adrian Cadbury. Harmondsworth, Middlesex, England ; New York, N.Y., U. S.A. : Penguin Books, c1986. xviii, 335 p. ; 20 cm. (Penguin business library) Reprint. Originally published: 1954. Bibliography: p. 328-329. Includes index. ISBN 0-14-009109-2 (pbk.) : LC Card 87-132408 DDC 158.7 19
1. Psychology, Industrial. I. Title. II. Series.
HF5548.8 .B7 1986

Brown, J. Gordon. Maxton / by Gordon Brown. Edinburgh : Mainstream, 1986. 336 p., [8] p. of plates : ill., ports. ; 24 cm. Includes bibliographical references and index. ISBN 1-85158-042-5
1. Maxton, James, 1885-1946. 2. Independent Labour Party (Great Britain). 3. Politicians - Great Britain - Biography. 4. Socialists - Great Britain - Biography. I. Title. ***NYPL [JFE 87-30]***

Brown, James G., 1945- The international sugar industry : developments and prospects / James G. Brown. Washington, D.C., U. S.A. : World Bank, 1987. xii, 69 p. ; 28 cm. (World Bank staff commodity working paper, 0253-3537 . no. 18) ISBN 0-8213-0884-1 (pbk.) LC Card 87-6285 DDC 338.1/736 19
1. Sugar trade. 2. Sugar trade - Government policy. I. Title. II. Series.
HD9100.5 .B76 1987

Brown, Janet Welsh. Bordering on trouble . Bethesda, Md. , 1986. xii, 448 p. : ISBN 0-917561-25-2 (pbk.) LC Card 86-7941 DDC 338.98 19
HC125 .B594 1986 ***NYPL [JLE 86-4501]***

Brown, Jonathan, 1950- Agriculture in England, 1870-1947 / Jonathan Brown. Manchester, U.K. ; Wolfeboro, N.H., U. S.A. : Manchester University Press, c1987. p. cm. Bibliography: p. Includes index. ISBN 0-7190-1759-9 : LC Card 87-20381 DDC 338.1/0942 19
1. Agriculture - Economic aspects - England - History - 19th century. 2. Agriculture - Economic aspects - England - History - 20th century. I. Title.
HD1930.E5 B76 1987

Brown, Kathleen M. Applied empirical research on nonprofit organization management : survey and recommendations / by Kathleen M. Brown. San Francisco, CA : Institute for Nonprofit Organization Management, College of Professional Studies, University of San Francisco, c1986. 38 p. ; 28 cm. (Working paper / Institute for Nonprofit Organization Management . no. 1) Bibliography: p. 31-35. LC Card 86-207093 DDC 658/.048 19
1. Corporations, Nonprofit - Management. I. Series: Working paper (University of San Francisco Institute for Nonprofit Organization Management) , no. 1. II. Title.
HD62.6 .B76 1986

Brown, Lee, M.B.A. Borins, Sandford F., 1949- Investments in failure . Toronto , New York , c1986. x, 175 p. ; ISBN 0-458-80340-5 (pbk.) : LC Card 87-142330 DDC 354.7109/2 19
HD4005 .B67 1986

Brown, Lester Russell, 1934- Our demographically divided world / Lester R. Brown, Jodi L. Jacobson. Washington, D.C. : Worldwatch Institute, c1986. 54 p. : ill. ; 22 cm. (Worldwatch paper . 74) Bibliography: p. 49-54. ISBN 0-916468-75-5 (pbk.) LC Card 86-51475 DDC 304.6 19
1. Population. 2. Demographic transition. I. Jacobson, Jodi L. II. Worldwatch Institute. III. Title. IV. Series.
HB871 .B744 1986

Brown, Malcolm C. (Malcolm Clarence), 1941- National health insurance in Canada and Australia : a comparative political economy analysis / Malcolm C. Brown. Canberra : Australian National University, Health Economics Research Unit in association with the Centre for Research on Federal Financial Relations, 1983. vii, 108 p. ; 25 cm. (Research monograph . 3) Bibliography: p. 103-108. ISBN 0-86784-281-4 (pbk.) LC Card 86-214526 DDC 368.4/2/00971 19
1. Insurance, Health - Australia. 2. Insurance, Health - Canada. I. Series: Research monograph (Australian National University. Health Economics Research Unit) , 3. II. Title.
HD7102.A8 B75 1983

Brown, Paul B. Smith, Geoffrey N. Sweat equity . New York , c1986. 254 p. : ISBN 0-671-55210-4 LC Card 86-6622 DDC 658/.022 19
HD62.5 .S625 1986 ***NYPL [JLD 86-3014]***

Brown, Perry J. Social science in natural resource management systems /. Boulder , 1987. xii, 265 p. : ISBN 0-8133-7485-5 (pbk. : alk. paper) LC Card 87-23138 DDC 333.7/0973 19
HC103.7 .S62 1987

Brown, Richard Eric, 1946- (ill) 100 words about working /. San Diego , c1988. p. cm. ISBN 0-15-200553-6 LC Card 87-8363 DDC 331.7/02 19
HF5382 .A13 1988

Brown, Roy Chamberlain, 1927- Quantity and quality in economic research /. Lanham, MD , c1985- v. : ISBN 0-8191-5112-2 (v. 1 : alk. paper) : LC Card 85-26360 DDC 330/.072 19
HB135 .Q38 1985 ***NYPL [JLL 86-232]***

Brown, Stephen J. Quantitative methods for financial analysis /. Homewood, Ill. , c1987. xv, 229 p. : ISBN 0-87094-978-0 LC Card 86-72275 DDC 332.6/01/51 19
HG4515.3 .Q36 1987

Brown University. Public Archaeology Laboratory. Rubertone, Patricia E. Background study of Maine coastal life . [Providence, R.I.?] , 1983. iii, 99 leaves : LC Card 86-601627 DDC 304.6/09741/45 19
HB3525.M2 R82 1983

Brown University studies in population and development.
Findley, Sally E. Rural development and migration . Boulder , 1987. xxiii, 308 p. : ISBN 0-8133-7326-3 (pbk. : alk. paper) : LC Card 86-33987 DDC 304.8/09599 19
HB2110.I43 F56 1987

Brown, Vicki. Fram, Eugene H. Policy vs. paper clips . Milwaukee, Wis. , 1988. p. cm. ISBN 0-87304-227-1 LC Card 87-24377 DDC 658/.048 19
HD62.6 .F73 1988

Brown, Vivienne. Managing the UK economy . Cambridge, UK , 1987. xxvii, 328 p. : ISBN 0-7456-0316-5 : LC Card 86-26860 DDC 338.941 19
HC256.5 .M392 1987

Brown, William P. The complete dictionary of media terms / William P. Brown, Kathryn Sederberg. Chicago, IL : Commerce Communications, c1986. vii, 151 p. ; 23 cm. ISBN 0-913247-01-4 (pbk.) LC Card 86-70712 DDC 302.2/34/0321 19
1. Advertising media planning - Dictionaries. 2. Mass media - Dictionaries. I. Sederberg, Kathryn. II. Title.
HF5826.5 .B77 1986

Browne, Harry, 1933- Why the best-laid investment plans usually go wrong : & how you can find safety & profit in an uncertain world / Harry Browne.1st ed. New York : Morrow, c1987. 557 p. : ill. ; 24 cm. Includes bibliographical references and index. ISBN 0-688-05995-3 LC Card 87-16593 DDC 332.024 19
1. Finance, Personal. 2. Investments. I. Title.
HG179 .B748 1987

Browne, M. Neil, 1944- Modern economics : principles, goals, and trade-offs / M. Neil Browne, Paul F. Haas. Englewood Cliffs, N.J. : Prentice-Hall, c1987. xvi, 464 p. : ill. ; 24 cm. Includes index. ISBN 0-13-587940-X (pbk.) LC Card 86-25256 DDC 330 19
1. Economics. I. Haas, Paul F., 1939-. II. Title.
HB171.5 .B724 1987

Browne, William Paul, 1945- Private interests, public policy, and American agriculture / William P. Browne. Lawrence, Kan. : University Press of Kansas, c1988. p. cm. (Studies in government and public policy) Bibliography: p. Includes index. ISBN 0-7006-0334-4 : LC Card 87-23131 DDC 338.1/873 19
1. Agriculture and state - United States. 2. Agricultural industries - United States. 3. Food industry and trade - United States. 4. Lobbying - United States. 5. Pressure groups - United States. I. Title. II. Series.
HD1761 .B73 1988

Brownlie, William D. Life insurance : its rate of return / by William D. Brownlie.1st ed. Cincinnati, Ohio : National Underwriter Co., 1983. xii, 201 p. : ill. ; 23 cm. ISBN 0-87218-033-6 (pbk.) LC Card 83-61584 DDC 368.3/2015 19
1. Insurance, Life - Rates and tables. 2. Rate of return. I. Title.
HG8853 .B87 1983
NYPL [*R-Econ. 86-3488]

Brownstone, David M.
The AMA handbook of key management forms /. New York, NY , c1987. 732 p. : ISBN 0-8144-1144-4 LC Card 86-25955 DDC 651/.29 19
HD38 .A44 1987

Franck, Irene M. Helpers and aides /. New York, N.Y. , c1987. x, 182 p. : ISBN 0-8160-1445-0 LC Card 86-24370 DDC 331.7 19
HF5381.2 .F68 1987

The IRA survival guide : how to manange your IRA for maximum benefits under the new tax law / David M. Brownstone. New York, NY : AMACOM, c1987. 168 p. ; 21 cm. Includes index. ISBN 0-8144-5861-0 (pbk.) : LC Card 86-47806 DDC 332.024/01 19
1. Individual retirement accounts - United States. I. American Management Association. II. Title.
HG1660.U5 B76 1987

The manager's advisor / David M. Brownstone, Irene M. Franck, with Rosemary Guiley. Rev. ed. New York : American Management Association, c1987. vii, 296 p. ; 23 cm. Includes index. ISBN 0-8144-7682-1 (pbk.) : LC Card 87-47712 DDC 658.4 19
1. Executives - Handbooks, manuals, etc. 2. Management - Handbooks, manuals, etc. I. Franck, Irene M. II. Guiley, Rosemary. III. Title.
HD38.2 .B75 1987

The sales professional's advisor / David M. Brownstone, Irene M. Franck. Rev. ed. New York : American Management Association, c1987. 298 p. ; 24 cm. Includes index. ISBN 0-8144-7683-X (pbk.) : LC Card 87-47713 DDC 658.8/5 19
1. Selling. I. Franck, Irene M. II. Title.
HF5438.25 .B747 1987

Bruce, Colin R. Pick, Albert. Standard catalog of world paper money /. Iola, Wis. , München , c1986. 2 v. : ISBN 0-87341-087-4 (v. 1) LC Card 86-222186 DDC 769.5/5/075 19
HG353 .P543 1986

Bruce, Robert, 1962- Keidel, Albert. China's dairy and food processing industries . Washington, D.C. , c1986. ii, 65 leaves ; LC Card 86-233105 DDC 338.1/77/0951 19
HD9275.C62 K45 1986

The Bruce Williams book . Williams, Bruce, 1932- New York , 1987. p. cm. ISBN 0-8128-3119-5 : LC Card 86-42692 DDC 658/022 19
HD62.5 .W49 1987

Bruchey, Stuart Weems. The wealth of the nation : an economic history of the United States / Stuart Bruchey.1st ed. New York : Harper & Row, c1988. ix, 259 p. ; 22 cm. Includes index. ISBN 0-06-015854-9 : LC Card 87-45602 DDC 330.973 19
1. United States - Economic conditions. I. Title.
HC103 .B78855 1988

Bruchhaus, Eva-Maria. Frauen in Entwicklungsländern : Situationsanalyse und entwicklungspolitische Ansatzpunkte unter besonderer Berücksichtigung nicht-staatlicher Organisationen / Eva-Maria Bruchhaus, Dietlinde Lessner-Abdin, Monica Wolsky. Freiburg im Breisgau : Arnold-Bergstraesser-Institut, 1979. iii, 182 p. ; 30 cm. Includes bibliographical references. LC Card 81-121677 DDC 305.4/09172/4 19
1. Women - Developing countries. 2. Women in community development. 3. Economic development - Social aspects. 4. Economic development projects - Evaluation. 5. Economic assistance, West German - Developing countries. I. Lessner-Abdin, Dietlinde. II. Wolsky, Monica. III. Freiburg i. B. Arnold-Bergstraesser-Institut für kulturwissenschaftliche Forschung. IV. Title.
HQ1870.9 .B78 1979 ***NYPL [JLG 86-106]***

Bruck, Nicholas K., 1932- Mercados de capitales bajo inflación /. New York, N.Y. , c1982. xxi, 471 p. : ISBN 0-910365-00-8 : LC Card 82-50965 DDC 332.64 19
HG4523 .M47 1982 ***NYPL [JLE 86-3568]***

Brudney, Jeffrey L. Meier, Kenneth J., 1950- Applied statistics for public administration /. Monterey, Calif. , c1987. xix, 460 p. ; LC Card 87-10342 DDC 350/.0001/5195 19
HA29 .M46 1987

Brudney, Juliet F. Forced out : when veteran employees are driven from their careers / Juliet F. Brudney and Hilda Scott. New York : Simon & Schuster, c1987. 208 p. ; 22 cm. Subtitle on cover: Why veteran employees are driven from their careers--and what they can do. "Career comebacks and employment alternatives; featuring interviews with survivors of middle-aged job loss; how public and private agencies can help; employer reforms--voluntary and mandated"--Cover. Order of authors' names reversed on cover. "A Fireside book" Bibliography: p. 200-202. Includes index. ISBN 0-671-64411-4 (pbk.) : LC Card 87-14927 DDC 650.1/4/0240564 19
1. Age and employment - United States. 2. Age discrimination in employment - United States. 3. Career changes - United States. I. Scott, Hilda, 1915-. II. Title.
HD6280 .B78 1987

Brühl, Carlrichard, 1925- Geschichte der Philatelie / Carlrichard Brühl. Hildesheim ; New York : G. Olms, 1985-1986. 2 v. : ill. (some col.) ; 27 cm. Includes bibliographical references and indexes. ISBN 3-487-07619-5 (v. 1) LC Card 86-118167 DDC 769.569 19
1. Postage-stamps - Collectors and collecting - History. 2. Postage-stamps - Dealers - History. I. Title.
HE6203 .B78 1985 ***NYPL [JFM 86-350]***

Brugsforeningsbevægelsen 1866-1920 . Just, Flemming. Esbjerg , 1984. 192 p. : ISBN 87-88521-04-4 LC Card 85-114707
HD3059.A6 R524 1984

Bruguière, Michel.
Administration et contrôle de l'économie, 1800-1914 /. Genève , Paris , 1985. 167 p. : LC Card 86-128349 DDC 338.944 19
HD3616.F82 A66 1985

Gestionnaires et profiteurs de la Révolution : l'administration des finances françaises de Louis XVI à Bonaparte / Michel Bruguière. Paris : O. Orban, c1986. 339 p. : ill. ; 21 cm. Bibliography: p. [195]-221. "Notices biographiques": p. [223]-293.

Includes indexes. ISBN 2-85565-332-0 : LC Card 87-123230
1. Finance, Public - France - History - 18th century. 2. Capitalist and financiers - France - History - 18th century. 3. Finance - France - History - 18th century. 4. Capitalists and financiers - France - Biography. I. Title.
HJ1083 .B78 1986

Bruhn, Hanne. Agervold, Mogens. Kontorarbejde . [Copenhagen] , c1983. 126 p. ; ISBN 87-500-2489-2 : LC Card 84-126389
HF5547.5 .A43 1983

Bruhn, Manfred. Konsumentenzufriedenheit und Beschwerden : Erklärungsansätze und Ergebnisse einer empirischen Untersuchung in ausgewählten Konsumbereichen / Manfred Bruhn. Frankfurt am Main ; Bern : Lang, 1982. xiv, 211 p. ; 21 cm. (Schriften zum Marketing. Bd. 4) Bibliography: p. 203-211. ISBN 3-8204-5712-7 LC Card 82-131889
1. Consumers - Germany, West. 2. Consumer satisfaction - Germany (West). I. Series: Schriften zum Marketing (Verlag Peter Lang) , Bd. 4. II. Title.
HF5415.3 .B78 1982

Brumlop, Eva. Arbeitsbewertung bei flexiblem Personaleinsatz : das Beispiel Volkswagen AG / Eva Brumlop. Frankfurt ; New York : Campus, c1986. 229 p. : ill. ; 22 cm. (Schriftenreihe "Humanisierung des Arbeitslebens" . Bd. 71) Bibliography: p. 223-229. ISBN 3-593-32744-9 LC Card 86-196323
1. Hours of labor, Flexible - Germany (West) - Case studies. 2. Volkswagenwerk - Case studies. I. Title. II. Series.
HD5109.2.G3 B76 1986

Bruneau, Thomas C. Power and poverty . Boulder , 1988. v, 186 p. ; ISBN 0-8133-7351-4 (pbk. : alk. paper) : LC Card 86-32578 DDC 338.9/009172/4 19
HC59.72.E44 P68 1988

BRUNEI - COMMERCE - DIRECTORIES. Buku panduan badan-badan perusahaan perniagaan Negara Brunei Darussalam =. Bandar Seri Begawan, Negara Brunei Darussalam [1985] vii, 89, [9] p. ; LC Card 86-945171 DDC 338.7/4/0255955 19
HF3800.68 .B84 1985

Brunei. Unit Perancang Ekonomi. Buku panduan badan-badan perusahaan perniagaan Negara Brunei Darussalam =. Bandar Seri Begawan, Negara Brunei Darussalam [1985] vii, 89, [9] p. ; LC Card 86-945171 DDC 338.7/4/0255955 19
HF3800.68 .B84 1985

Brunelle, Dorval. L'Etat solide : sociologie du fédéralisme au Canada et au Québec / Dorval Brunelle. Montréal, Québec : Sélect, 1982. 174 p. : ill. ; 23 cm. Bibliography: p. 171-174. ISBN 2-89132-677-6 (pbk.) LC Card 87-672120
1. Canada - Economic policy. 2. Canada - Economic conditions - 1945-. 3. Canada - Politics and government - 1945-. 4. Quebec (Province) - Economic conditions. 5. Quebec (Province) - Politics and government. 6. Federal government - Canada. I. Title.
HC115 .B773x 1982

Bruning, James L. Computational handbook of statistics / James L. Bruning, B.L. Kintz. 3rd ed. Glenview, Ill. : Scott, Foresman, c1987. 372 p. ; 24 cm. Bibliography: p. 361. Includes index. ISBN 0-673-18407-2 (pbk.) LC Card 86-31593 DDC 519.5 19
1. Social sciences - Statistical methods. 2. Statistics. I. Kintz, B. L. II. Title.
HA29 .B835 1987

Brunner, Karl, 1916- Geld- und Währungsordnung /. Berlin , c1983. 249 p. : ISBN 3-428-05530-6 LC Card 84-141547
HG999.5 .G4556 1983

Brunotte, Leonard. Construction profit management : the secrets of successful contracting / Leonard Brunotte. Englewood Cliffs, N.J. : Prentice-Hall, c1987. xxvii, 324 p. : ill. ; 25 cm. Includes index. ISBN 0-13-168980-0 : LC Card 87-1168 DDC 692/.8 19
1. Construction industry - Management. 2. Building - Contracts and specifications. I. Title.
HD9715.A2 B78 1987

Brunowsky, Ralf-Dieter, 1949- Der ÖKO-Plan : durch Umweltschutz zum neuen Wirtschaftswunder / Ralf-Dieter Brunowsky, Lutz Wicke. München : Piper, c1984. 236, [1] p. ; 24 cm. Bibliography: p. 234-[237] ISBN 3-492-02922-1 LC Card 84-251156
1. Environmental policy - Germany, West. 2. Environmental protection - Economic aspects - Germany (West). I. Wicke, Lutz. II. Title.
HC290.5.E5 B78 1984

Bruns, Claudia. Westeuropean direct investment in Canada : an analysis of the period 1970-1984 / von Claudia Bruns ; Hrsg. Karl-Ernst Schenk. Hamburg : Institut für Aussenhandel und Überseewirtschaft der Universität Hamburg, [1986] 18 p. : ill. ; 22 cm. (Forschungsberichte / Institut für Aussenhandel und Überseewirtschaft der Universität Hamburg . Forschungsbericht Nr. 43) Bibliography: p. 18. LC Card 86-191095
1. Investments, European - Canada. I. Schenk, Karl Ernst. II. Title. III. Title: West European direct investment in Canada. IV. Series: Forschungsberichte / Institut für Aussenhandel und Überseewirtschaft der Universität Hamburg , Forschungsbericht Nr. 43.
HG5152 .B78 1986

Bruns, Klaus Peter. Europäische Agrarpolitik . Göttingen , 1985. 82 p. ; LC Card 86-170925
HD1920.5.Z8 E97 1985

Bruns, William J. Accounting & management . Boston, Mass. , c1987. ix, 374 p. : ISBN 0-87584-186-4 (alk. paper) LC Card 87-18373 DDC 658.4/038 19
HF5657.4 .A25 1987

Brunt, P. A. Italian manpower, 225 B.C.-A.D. 14 / P.A. Brunt. Oxford [Oxfordshire] : Clarendon Press, 1987, c1971. xxi, 762 p. ; 24 cm. Reprint. Originally published: London : Oxford University Press, 1971. Includes bibliographical references and indexes. ISBN 0-19-814283-8 : LC Card 87-1644 DDC 304.6/0945 19
1. Italy - Population - History. 2. Manpower - Italy - History. 3. Italy - History, Military. 4. Armies - Rome - History. I. Title.
HB3599 .B77 1987

Brusaw, Charles T. The business writer's handbook / Charles T. Brusaw, Gerald J. Alred, and Walter E. Oliu. 3rd rev. ed. New York : St. Martin's Press, c1987. xxviii, 764 p. : ill. ; 23 cm. Includes index. ISBN 0-312-00571-7 : LC Card 87-4361 DDC 651.7/5 19
1. Commercial correspondence - Handbooks, Manuals, etc. 2. Business writing - Handbooks, manuals, etc. I. Alred, Gerald J. II. Oliu, Walter E. III. Title.
HF5726 .B874 1987

Bruse, Helmut. Der Absatzbereich von Unternehmen : Theorie, Methoden, empirische Untersuchung / Helmut Bruse. Bonn : [s.n.], 1980. xiv, 323 p. : ill. ; 21 cm. (Bonner betriebswirtschaftliche Schriften . 8) Bibliography: p. 288-323. LC Card 85-164955
1. Marketing - Mathematical models. 2. Price policy - Mathematical models. I. Title. II. Series.
HF5415 .B7713 1980

Bruskin, R. H. A market strategy study of the whole bean coffee market : prepared for the Coffee Development Group, Washington, D.C. [New Brunswick, N.J.] : R.H. Bruskin Associates, Market Research, [1985] 1 v. (various pagings) : ill. ; 28 cm. Prepared during the summer of 1985 by R.H. Bruskin. LC Card 87-100003 DDC 381/.41373/0971 19
1. Coffee trade - United States. 2. Coffee - United States - Marketing. 3. Consumers' preferences - United States. 4. Market surveys - United States. I. Coffee Development Group (U. S.). II. Title.
HD9199.U48 B84 1985

Brussels. Université libre. Institut de sociologie. (Old Catalog form: Brussels. Université libre. Institut de sociologie Solvay.)
Vega Tapia, Héctor. L'économie du populisme et le projet de passage au socialisme proposé par l'Unité populaire au Chili /. [Brussels] , 1984. 511 p. ; LC Card 85-146534 DDC 338.983 19
HC192 .V37 1984 ***NYPL [JLE 86-3663]***

Brussels. Université libre. Institut de sociologie Solvay. see **Brussels. Université libre. Institut de sociologie.**

Brussels. Université libre. Instituut voor sociologie. see **Brussels. Université libre. Institut de sociologie.**

Bruton, Michael J. Local planning in practice / Michael Bruton and David Nicholson. London : Hutchinson, 1987. 452 p. : ill. ; 24 cm. (Built environment series) Includes index. Bibliography: p. 421-440. ISBN 0-09-165381-9
1. City planning - Great Britain. 2. Regional planning - Great Britain. I. Nicholson, D. J. II. Title. III. Series.
NYPL [JLE 87-1201]

Bruun, Kirsten Marie. Ungdomsarbejdsløshed og beskæftigelsesforanstaltninger . København [1984] 100 leaves : LC Card 85-124463
HD6276.D4 U54 1984

Bruus, Palle. Beskrivende økonomi /. [Copenhagen] , c1985-c1986. 2 v. (810 p.) : ISBN 87-574-4652-0 (set) LC Card 86-159064
HB179.D8 B47 1986

Bruyn, Severyn Ten Haut, 1927- The field of social investment / Severyn T. Bruyn. Cambridge ; New York : Cambridge University Press, 1987. xi, 304 p. : ill. ; 24 cm. (The Arnold and Caroline Rose monograph series of the American Sociological Association) Bibliography: p. 287-298. Includes indexes. ISBN 0-521-33292-3 LC Card 86-26393 DDC 332.6 19
1. Investments - Social aspects - United States. 2. Investments, American - Social aspects. 3. Industry - Social aspects - United States. I. Title. II. Title: Social investment.
HG4910 .B77 1987

Bryant, Coralie.
Managing rural development. Bryant, Coralie. Managing rural development with small farmer participation / Coralie Bryant, Louise G. White. West Hartford, CT. , c1984. xiii, 79 p. : ISBN 0-931816-52-1 (pbk.) LC Card 84-4445 DDC 307.7/2 19
HD1417 .B79 1984 ***NYPL [JLE 87-1352]***

Managing rural development with small farmer participation / Coralie Bryant, Louise G. White. West Hartford, CT. : Kumarian Press, c1984. xiii, 79 p. : ill. ; 23 cm. (K.P. development monograph . no. 3) Rev. ed. of: Managing rural development. 1980. Bibliography: p. [70]-79. ISBN 0-931816-52-1 (pbk.) LC Card 84-4445 DDC 307.7/2 19
1. Rural development projects - Developing countries - Management. 2. Farms, Small - Developing countries. I. White, Louise G. II. Bryant, Coralie. Managing rural development. III. Title. IV. Series.
HD1417 .B79 1984 ***NYPL [JLE 87-1352]***

Bryant, James W., Ph. D. Financial modelling in corporate management /. Chichester [West Sussex] , New York , c1987. xv, 404 p. : ISBN 0-471-91476-2 : LC Card 86-32446 DDC 658.1/5/0724 19
HG4012 .F54 1987

Bryant, Ralph C., 1938- International financial intermediation / Ralph C. Bryant. Washington, D.C. : Brookings Institution, c1987. xi, 181 p. : ill. ; 24 cm. (Studies in international economics) Bibliography: p. 164-175. Includes index. ISBN 0-8157-1138-7 : LC Card 87-10358 DDC 332/.042 19
1. Intermediation (Finance). 2. International finance. I. Series: Studies in international economics (Washington, D.C.). II. Title.
HG3891.5 .B79 1987

Bryant, Richard W.
New specialty metals & metallurgy for high-temperature, high-strength, low-weight applications /. Norwalk, Conn., U. S.A. , c1987. 1 v. (various foliations) : ISBN 0-89336-454-1 (pbk.) LC Card 87-168123 DDC 380.1/45669/0973 19
HD9506.U62 N45 1987

The Strategic Defense Initiative, business opportunities, and technological potential / Richard W. Bryant. Norwalk, Conn., U. S.A. : Business Communications Co., c1986. 1 v. (various foliations) : ill. ; 29 cm. (Business opportunity report . GB-088) ISBN 0-89336-477-0 (pbk.) LC Card 87-168253 DDC 338.4/762/00973 19
1. High technology industries - United States - Forecasting. 2. Strategic Defense Initiative. 3. United States - Military policy - Economic aspects. I. Title. II. Series.
HC110.H53 B79 1986

Bryce, Herrington J. Financial and strategic management for nonprofit organizations / Herrington J. Bryce. Englewood Cliffs, N.J. : Prentice-Hall, c1987. xviii, 395 p. : ill. ; 24 cm. Includes bibliographies and index. ISBN 0-13-316597-3 LC Card 86-30454 DDC 658/.049 19
1. Corporations, Nonprofit - Finance. 2. Corporations,

Nonprofit - Management. 3. Strategic planning. I. Title.
HG4027.65 .B78 1987

Brzoň, František. Marie a František Kalkusovi / František Brzoň, Jiří Rychetský. Vyd. 1. České Budějovice : Jihočeské nakl., 1985. 98 p., [64] p. of plates : ill. ; 21 cm. (Postavy jihočeského dělnického hnutí) Bibliography: p. 93. Includes index. LC Card 86-161741
1. Labor and laboring classes - Czechoslovakia - Biography. 2. Kalkusová, Marie, 1893-1979. 3. Kalkus, František, 1894-1968. I. Rychetský, Jiří. II. Title.
HD8420.3.A1 B78 1985

Brzoska, Michael. Arms transfers to the Third World, 1971-85 / Michael Brzoska and Thomas Ohlson. Oxford ; New York : Oxford University Press, 1987. xv, 383 p. : ill. ; 24 cm. "Stockholm International Peace Research Institute." Bibliography: p. [370]-375. Includes index. ISBN 0-19-829116-7 : LC Card 87-5579 DDC 382/.456234/091724 19
1. Munitions - Developing countries. I. Ohlson, Thomas. II. Stockholm International Peace Research Institute. III. Title.
HD9743.D442 B79 1987

Bublot, Georges. Politique agricole commune . Bruxelles, Belgique , c1982. 126 p. ; ISBN 1-8004-0773-5 LC Card 87-672469
HD1803 .P64x 1982

Bubnov, Boris. Foreign trade with the USSR : a manager's guide to recent reforms / by Boris Bubnov ; translated by Nikolai Shartse.1st ed. Oxford ; New York : Pergamon Press, c1987. p. cm. ISBN 0-08-035844-6 : LC Card 87-7167 DDC 382/.0947 19
1. Soviet Union - Commercial policy. 2. International business enterprises - Soviet Union. 3. Joint ventures - Soviet Union. I. Title.
HF1557 .B83 1987

Bucciero, Marina. Petrillo, Giovanna, 1952- Produttività e improduttività del lavoro domestico . Bologna , 1985. 139 p. ; LC Card 86-132212
HD8039.H842 I87 1985

Buchan, Bryan, 1945- Discovering stamps / by Bryan Buchan. Richmond Hill, Ont. : Scholastic-Tab Publications ; New York : Scholastic Book Services, [1977], c1973. 91 p. : ill. ; 20 cm. Bibliography: p. 91. "INC 319"--Cover. LC Card 85-148831
1. Postage stamps - Collectors and collecting. I. Title.
HE6213 .B83 1977

BUCHANAN, WILLIAM, 1849-1923.
Mayor, Archer H. Southern timberman . Athens , c1988. p. cm. ISBN 0-8203-0999-0 (alk. paper) LC Card 87-22897 DDC 338.7/63498/0975 19
HD9760.B83 M39 1988

Büchele, Christoph. Der Widerstand geht weiter . Freiburg i. Br. , 1982. 261 p. : ISBN 3-921472-30-X LC Card 82-192690
HD9698.G43 W937 1982

Buchführungspflicht und Besteuerung der Sitzunternehmungen und Holdinggesellschaften in Liechtenstein /. Walser, Olaf. Vaduz, Fürstentum Liechtenstein [1983] 31 p. ; LC Card 85-226619
HD2753.L76 W35 1983

Buchholz, Günter, 1946- Rationalisierung im Konjunkturverlauf / Günter Buchholz. Spardorf : R. Wilfer, c1983. 207 p. ; 21 cm. Bibliography: p. 197-207. ISBN 3-922919-18-9 LC Card 84-135309
1. Management. 2. Industrial management. 3. Industrial organization. I. Title.
HD35 .B77 1983

Buchholz, Rogene A. Management response to public issues : concepts and cases in strategy formulation / Rogene A. Buchholz, William D. Evans, Robert A. Wagley. Englewood Cliffs, N.J. : Prentice-Hall, c1985. x, 389 p. : ill. ; 24 cm. Includes bibliographies and index. ISBN 0-13-549940-2 (pbk.) : LC Card 84-18355 DDC 658.4/08 19
1. Industry - Social aspects - Case studies. 2. Industry and state - Case studies. 3. Industrial management - Case studies. I. Evans, William D. II. Wagley, Robert A. III. Title.
HD60 .B83 1985 ***NYPL [JLE 85-1984]***

Buchholz, Steve. Creating the high performance team / Steve Buchholz, Thomas Roth (Wilson Learning Corporation) ; edited by Kären Hess. New York : Wiley, c1987. xiii, 202 p. : ill. ; 24 cm. Bibliography: p. 185. Includes index. ISBN 0-471-85672-X : LC Card 86-32623 DDC 658.4/02 19
1. Work groups. 2. Industrial organization. I. Roth, Thomas. II. Hess, Karen M., 1939-. III. Wilson Learning Corporation. IV. Title. V. Title: High performance team.
HD66 .B82 1987a

Büchi Buc, Hernán. Exposición sobre el estado de la hacienda pública / presentación del ministro de hacienda, Hernán Büchi Buc. [Santiago] : República de Chile, Ministerio de Hacienda, Dirección de Presupuestos, 1985. 92 p. ; 25 cm. LC Card 87-105088 DDC 338.983 19
1. Chile - Economic policy. 2. Chile - Economic conditions - 1970-. 3. Finance, Public - Chile. I. Chile. Ministerio de Hacienda. II. Title.
HC192 .B83 1985

Büchi, Willy, 1907- Willy Büchi, 75 Jahre /. Freiburg, Schweiz , 1982. 105 p., [1] leaf of plates : ISBN 3-7278-0263-4 LC Card 83-184580
HB118 .W55 1982

BÜCHI, WILLY, 1907-
Willy Büchi, 75 Jahre /. Freiburg, Schweiz , 1982. 105 p., [1] leaf of plates : ISBN 3-7278-0263-4 LC Card 83-184580
HB118 .W55 1982

Büchner, Michael.
Ökonomische und soziale Wirksamkeit des wissenschaftlich-technischen Fortschritts /. Berlin , 1986. 314 p. ; ISBN 3-320-00713-0 LC Card 87-100866 DDC 338/.06 19
HC290.795.T4 O38 1986

Okonomische und soziale Wirksamkeit des wissenschaftlich-technischen Fortschritts /. Berlin , 1986. 314 p. : ISBN 3-320-00713-0
NYPL [JLD 86-4381]

Buchreihe der Arbeits- und Forschungsgemeinschaft für Strassenverkehr und Verkehrssicherheit, Institut an der Universität zu Köln, AFO .
(Bd. 29) Die Sicherung des Fussgängerverkehrs. Köln , 1976. ii, 169 p. : LC Card 86-185084
HE5614.5.G3 A7 Bd. 29

Buchreihe des Instituts für Verkehrswissenschaft an der Universität zu Köln, 0341-5767 .
(Nr. 45) Tress, Roland. Das Güterverkehrszentrum als infrastrukturelle Schnittstelle des Güterverkehrs /. Düsseldorf , 1984. xv, 288 p. : LC Card 86-140143
HE5 .C6 Nr. 45 HE5999.Z7G2

(Nr. 47) Mester, Bernt. Marktchancen der Binnenschiffahrt im Container-Hinterlandverkehr der Häfen der Hamburg-Antwerpen-Range /. Düsseldorf , 1986. xii, 304 p. ; LC Card 87-409549
HE5 .C6 Nr. 47 HE558.H3

Buchvarov, Stoyan. Bulgaria's chemical industry / Stoyan Buchvarov. Sofia : Sofia Press, 1986. 60 p., [16] p. of plates : ill. ; 20 cm. Title in colophon: Bŭlgarskata khimiia. LC Card 87-111684 DDC 338.4/766/0094977 19
1. Chemical industry - Bulgaria. I. Title. II. Title: Bŭlgarskata khimiia.
HD9666.B92 B83 1986

Buck, Alice L. Holl, Jack M. United States civilian nuclear power policy, 1954-1984 . Washington, D.C. , Springfield, Va. [1986] 46 p., [1] leaf of plates : LC Card 86-601137 DDC 333.79/24 19
HD9698.U52 H65 1986

Buck, Eric. Leibowitz, Dennis. The cellular communications industry /. New York, N.Y. (140 Broadway, New York 10005) , c1985. ii, 67 p. : LC Card 86-201572 DDC 384.5/33/0973 19
HD9696.R363 U65 1985

Buck, Trevor. Modern Soviet economic performance / Trevor Buck and John Cole. New York, NY : B. Blackwell, 1987. viii, 192 p. ; 24 cm. Bibliography: p. [180]-187. Includes index. ISBN 0-631-14417-X : LC Card 86-24457 DDC 330.947/085 19
1. Soviet Union - Economic conditions - 1976-. I. Cole, J. P. (John Peter), 1928-. II. Title.
HC336.25 .B826 1987

BUCKET-SHOPS. see SPECULATION.

Buckland, John A. Schabeck, Timothy A. Managing microcomputer security . Port Jefferson Station, N.Y. (492 Old Town Rd., Port Jefferson Station 11776) , c1986. 1 v. (various pagings) : LC Card 86-216667 DDC 658.4/78 19
HF5548.37 .S33 1986

Buckley, Adrian. Multinational finance / Adrian Buckley. Deddington, Oxford : P. Allan ; Atlantic Highlands, N.J. : Distributed in the U. S.A. and Canada by Humanities Press, 1986. x, 398 p. : ill. ; 26 cm. Distributor from label on t.p. Includes bibliographies and index. ISBN 0-86003-542-5 LC Card 86-226038 DDC 658.1/599 19
1. International business enterprises - Finance. 2. Foreign exchange. 3. International finance. I. Title.
HG4027.5 .B83 1986

Buckley, John, 1947- Guide to world commodity markets . London , Detroit, Mich. , 1986. 465 p. : ISBN 1-85091-116-9 LC Card 87-144180 DDC 332.64/4 19
HG6046 .G84 1986

Buckley, K. D. (Kenneth D.) South Pacific focus : a record in words and photographs of Burns Philp at work / [compiled by] K. Buckley and K. Klugman. Sydney ; Boston : Allen & Unwin, 1986. 126 p. : ill. ; 24 cm. Includes bibliographical references and index. ISBN 0-04-909030-5 LC Card 86-71304 DDC 387.5/065/94 19
1. Burns, Philp & Co. - History. 2. Burns, Philp & Co. - History - Pictorial works. 3. Merchant marine - Australia - History. 4. Merchant marine - Australia - History - Pictorial works. 5. Merchant marine - Oceania - History. 6. Merchant marine - Oceania - History - Pictorial works. I. Klugman, K. II. Burns, Philp & Co. III. Title.
HE945.B87 B83 1986

Buckley, Katharine C. Florida and Mexico competition for the winter fresh vegetable market /. Washington, D.C. [1986] v, 101 p. : LC Card 86-602381 DDC 338.1 s 381/.415/0973 19
HD1751 .A91854 no. 556 HD9225.U53F5

Buckner, Claudia. Barbaria, Janet. The growth revolt . Sacramento, Calif. [1980] 66 p. : LC Card 81-620644 DDC 336.794 19
HJ4191 .B37 1980 ***NYPL [JLF 86-369]***

BUCOMCO . Melrose, John. Chicago , c1987. vii, 187 p. : ISBN 0-574-20070-3 (pbk.) : LC Card 86-31585 DDC 651.7/4 19
HF5718 .M44 1987

Buczkowski, Piotr. Teoria ekonomiczna . Poznań , 1978. 147 p. : LC Card 81-206275
HB54 .P6 nr. 76 HB179.P7

Budaev, Dmitriĭ Ivanovich. Osnovnye kategorii krest'ian v period pozdnego feodalizma, XVII--perviaia polovina XIX vv. . Smolensk , 1985. 134 p., [1] leaf of plates : LC Card 86-120158
HD1536.S65 O86 1985

Budapest és a jelentősebb városok napi munkaerővonzási körzete népességének főbb jellemzői, 1980. január 1. / [készült a Központi Statisztikai Hivatal Népesedésstatisztikai Főosztály Munkaerő- és Foglalkozásstatisztikai Osztályán ; összeállitotta, Nagy Istvánné, Lakatos Miklós]. Budapest : Központi Statisztikai Hivatal, 1986. 106 p. : col. maps ; 29 cm. ISBN 963-02-4578-7 LC Card 87-407674
1. Hungary - Population - Statistics. 2. Central places - Hungary - Statistics. 3. Labor mobility - Hungary - Statistics. I. Nagy, Istvánné. II. Lakatos, Miklós. III. Hungary. Központi Statisztikai Hivatal. Munkaerő és Foglalkozásstatisztikai Osztály.
HA1205 .B83 1986

Budapest és Pest megye népességfejlődése, az ezredfordulóig várható tendenciák /. Szukicsné Serfőző, Klára. Budapest , 1984. 88 p. : LC Card 86-157549
HA1208.B96 S98 1984

Budapest (Hungary). Fővárosi Tanács. Művelődésügyi Főosztály. Budapesti pedagógusok közlekedési oktatási és nevelési konferenciája . [Budapest , 1978] ([Budapest] :fKészült az MTI Sokszorosító Üzemében) 100 p. ; LC Card 82-204792
HE5614 .B78 1978

BUDAPEST (HUNGARY) - POPULATION - STATISTICS.
Szukicsné Serfőző, Klára. Budapest és Pest megye népességfejlődése, az ezredfordulóig

várható tendenciák /. Budapest , 1984. 88 p. : LC Card 86-157549
HA1208.B96 S98 1984

Budapest. Magyar Nemzeti Bank. see **Magyar Nemzeti Bank.**

Budapest. Magyar Tudományos Akadémia. see **Magyar Tudományos Akadémia, Budapest.**

A budapesti Nagyvásártelep mikrotoponímiája /. Berényi, Zsuzsanna Ágnes. Budapest , 1983. 65 p. : ISBN 963-461-710-7 LC Card 85-167786
HF5474.H82 B83 1983

Budapesti pedagógusok közlekedési oktatási és nevelési konferenciája : a Fővárosi Közlekedésbiztonsági Tanács és a Fővárosi Tanács VB. Művelődésügyi Főosztálya által szervezett budapesti pedagógusok közlekedési oktatási és nevelési konferenciájának rövidített jegyzőkönyve 1977. október 18. / [szerkesztette Patkoló Károly, Molnár Lászlø]. [Budapest : s.n., 1978] ([Budapest] :fKészült az MTI Sokszorosító Üzemében) 100 p. ; 20 cm. LC Card 82-204792
1. Traffic safety - Study and teaching - Hungary - Congresses. I. Patkoló, Károly. II. Molnár, László. III. Fővárosi Közlekedésbiztonsági Tanács (Budapest, Hungary). IV. Budapest (Hungary). Fővárosi Tanács. Művelődésügyi Főosztály.
HE5614 .B78 1978

Budaveĭ, Vsevolod I͡Ur'evich. Dolgosrochnye narodnokhozi͡aĭstvennye programmy : teorii͡a i metodologii͡a programmnogo podkhoda v planirovanii NTP / V.I͡U. Budaveĭ. Moskva : "Mysl'", 1980. 205 p. ; 20 cm. (Ėkonomicheskai͡a teorii͡a i khozi͡aĭstvennai͡a praktika) Includes bibliographical references. LC Card 81-143196
1. Technological innovations - Soviet Union - Management. 2. Soviet Union - Economic policy - 1981-. I. Series: Ėkonomicheskai͡a teorii͡a i khozi͡aĭstvennai͡a praktika (Moscow, R.S.F.S.R. : 1981). II. Title.
HD45 .B792 1980

Budde, Ramona. Marktinnovationen von Universalbanken : Entscheidungsvorbereitung durch das Scoringverfahren / von Ramona Budde. Berlin : E. Schmidt, c1983. xvi, 347 p. : ill. ; 21 cm. (Grundlagen und Praxis des Bank- und Börsenwesens. Bd. 17) Bibliography: p. 296-343. Includes index. ISBN 3-503-02192-2 LC Card 83-186914
1. Banks and banking - Technological innovations. 2. Banks and banking - Automation. 3. Bank marketing. 4. Banks and banking - Germany (West) - Technological innovations. 5. Banks and banking - Germany (West) - Automation. 6. Bank marketing - Germany (West). I. Title.
HG1709 .B78 1983

Budde, Reinhold. Radverkehrskonzept Sprockhövel /. Essen , c1985. 55 p., [3] folded col. leaves of plates : ISBN 3-923494-51-3 LC Card 86-113993
HE5739.G3 R33 1985

BUDDHISM - JAPAN.
What makes Japan work [motion picture] . Cos Cob, CT , 1983. 1 film reel (11 min.) : LC Card 83-700702 DDC 181 11
HD8726.5

What makes Japan work [videorecording] . Cos Cob, CT , 1983. 1 videocassette (11 min.) : LC Card 87-705342 DDC 181 11
HD8726.5

BUDGET.
Dubinin, S. K. (Sergeĭ Konstantinovich) Krizis bi͡udzhetno-finansovogo regulirovanii͡a ėkonomiki kapitalizma /. Moskva , 1984. 100 p. ; LC Card 84-222701
HJ236 .D82 1984

Forte, Francesco, 1929- Il bilancio nell'economia pubblica /. Milano [1985] 2 v. ; ISBN 88-14-00636-9 : LC Card 86-151358 DDC 350.72/2 19
HJ2005 .F67 1985 ***NYPL [JLE 86-2653]***

New directions in budget theory /. Albany, N.Y. , 1987, c1988. p. cm. ISBN 0-88706-624-0 LC Card 87-9977 DDC 350.72/2 19
HJ2005 .N48 1987

Runge, Harry. Haushaltsfinanzierung durch Notendruck /. Berlin , c1986. 69 p. ; ISBN 3-428-05984-0 ***NYPL [JLE 86-2839]***

Swain, David, 1942- Managing public money . Lanham, MD , c1987. x, 221 p. : ISBN 0-8191-6505-0 (alk. paper) : LC Card 87-14261 DDC 350.72 19
HJ141 .S93 1987

BUDGET - ARGENTINA.
Fundación de Investigaciones Económicas Latinoamericanas (Buenos Aires, Argentina) Gasto público . [Buenos Aires] , 1986. 6 v. in 8 : LC Card 87-403573 DDC 354.820072/252 19
HJ2075 .F86 1986

BUDGET - ARGENTINA - STATISTICS - HISTORY.
Argentina. Dirección Nacional de Programación Presupuestaria. Presupuesto de la administración nacional, 1961-1979. [Buenos Aires] [1982] 79 leaves : LC Card 82-199149
HJ2076 .A74 1982

BUDGET - AUSTRIA.
Budgetvorschau 1984-1988 /. Wien , 1984. 55 p. ; LC Card 84-223024
HJ2101 .B828 1984

Budgetvorschau 1986-1990. Wien , 1986. 45 p. : LC Card 86-227246
HJ2101 .B83 1986

BUDGET - BOLIVIA.
Conferencias sobre desarrollo económico, presupuesto, estabilización y nacionalización de empresas económicas. La Paz, Bolivia , 1955. 180 p. : LC Card 86-167406
HC182 .C54 1955

BUDGET - BRAZIL.
Cotia, Raul Fontes. Comentário sôbre os balanços gerais da União de 1963 /. [Brasília] [1964] 45 p. ; LC Card 85-194302
HJ2079 .C68 1964

BUDGET - BRAZIL - SÃO PAULO (STATE)
São Paulo (Brazil : State). Governor (1982- : Montoro) O orçamento de São Paulo para 1984 /. São Paulo , 1983. 24 p. ; LC Card 87-130676 DDC 354.81/6100722 19
HJ2080.5.S3 S26 1983

BUDGET - BURUNDI.
Burundi. Budgets extraordinaires et d'investissement . [Bujumbura] [1967] [19] leaves ; LC Card 82-980377
HJ2180.8 .B87 1967

BUDGET - CALIFORNIA - STATISTICS.
California. Legislature. Senate. Committee on Budget and Fiscal Review. Report on the 1986-87 Budget Act (as amended May 21, 1986) /. [Sacramento, Calif.] [1986] 3 v. (1105 leaves) ; LC Card 86-622935 DDC 336.794 19
HJ2053.C3 C36 1986

BUDGET - CANADA.
Securing economic renewal . [Ottawa] [1987] 147, 161 p. : LC Card 87-144360 DDC 336.71 19
HJ793 .S43 1987

Swankey, Ben. The Tory budget and the corporate plan to restructure Canada, and how the system really works /. Vancouver , c1985. xi, 246 p. ; ISBN 0-920879-00-4 (pbk.) LC Card 86-209703 DDC 338.971 19
HJ2055 .S9 1985

BUDGET - COLOMBIA.
Estadística fiscal del estado . [Bogotá] , 1978. 2 v. : ***NYPL [JLE 80-831]***

BUDGET - COLOMBIA - STATISTICS.
Hacienda y crédito público . [Bogotá, Colombia] [1986] 94 p. : LC Card 87-404281 DDC 336.861 19
HJ2083 .H33 1986

BUDGET, COMMERCIAL. see **BUDGET IN BUSINESS.**

Il budget con il personal computer . Aloi, Felice. Milano, Italy , c1984. 226 p. : LC Card 84-250395 DDC 658.1/54/02854165 19
HG4028.B8 A46 1984

BUDGET - CONGRESSES.
Geyer, Herbert, 1927- Budgetpolitik im Wandel /. Berlin , c1986. 111 p. : ISBN 3-428-05922-0 LC Card 86-165210
HJ113 .G49 1986

BUDGET - DATA PROCESSING.
Baker, Keith, 1938- Public budgeting with Lotus 1-2-3 /. Portland, Or. , 1988. p. cm. ISBN 0-943518-46-6 : LC Card 87-24020 DDC 350.72/2/02855369 19
HJ2009 .B34 1988

Le budget de l'Etat /. Baslé, Maurice. Paris , 1985. 127 p. : ISBN 2-7071-1534-7 LC Card 86-161271
HJ2106 .B37 1985

BUDGET DEFICITS.
Jänicke, Martin. Staatsversagen . München , c1986. 227 p. : ISBN 3-492-02984-1 LC Card 86-230931
HD84 .J36 1986

Public sector deficits in OECD countries . New York , 1987. p. cm. ISBN 0-312-00533-4 : LC Card 87-11876 DDC 339.5/23/091724 19
HJ2043 .P8 1987

Budget deficits and the current account in the presence of classical unemployment /. Cuddington, John T. [Madrid] [1984] 47 p. : ISBN 84-505-0847-9 (pbk.) LC Card 86-215031 DDC 339.5/23/0724 19
HJ2005 .C83 1984

BUDGET DEFICITS - CANADA.
Bellan, Ruben C., 1918- The unnecessary evil . Toronto, Ont. , c1986. 173 p. : ISBN 0-7710-1153-9 : LC Card 86-222233 DDC 331.13/7971 19
HD5728 .B43 1986

BUDGET DEFICITS - CONGRESSES.
Economic effects of the government budget /. Cambridge, Mass. , c1988. p. cm. ISBN 0-262-08172-5 LC Card 87-26187 DDC 338.9 19
HJ2005 .E25 1988

BUDGET DEFICITS - GERMANY (WEST)
Sherman, Heidemarie C. Der Einfluss staatlicher Budgetdefizite auf die Zinsentwicklung in der Bundesrepublik Deutschland und den Vereinigten Staaten . München , c1986. xxiii, 190 p. : ISBN 3-88512-019-4 LC Card 86-192070
HJ2110 .S53 1986

BUDGET DEFICITS - MATHEMATICAL MODELS.
Cuddington, John T. Budget deficits and the current account in the presence of classical unemployment /. [Madrid] [1984] 47 p. : ISBN 84-505-0847-9 (pbk.) LC Card 86-215031 DDC 339.5/23/0724 19
HJ2005 .C83 1984

BUDGET DEFICITS - NEW YORK (STATE)
Green, Cynthia B. Reducing New York State's deficit /. New York, N.Y. (110 E. 42nd St., New York 10017) [1986] ii leaves, 33 p. ; LC Card 87-108691 DDC 336.747 19
HJ2053.N7 G74 1986

BUDGET DEFICITS - UNITED STATES.
Cebula, Richard J. The deficit problem in perspective /. Lexington, Mass. , c1987. x, 106 p. : ISBN 0-669-14303-0 (pbk. : alk. paper) LC Card 86-45792 DDC 339.5/23/0973 19
HJ2052 .C42 1987

McLure, Charles E. The value-added tax . Washington, D.C. : Lanham, MD ; xi, 184 p. : ISBN 0-8447-3613-9 (alk. paper) LC Card 86-28905 DDC 339.5/25/0973 19
HJ5715.U6 M364 1987

Manchester, Paul B. Are we on the road to a balanced budget? . Washington , 1986. v, 18 p. : LC Card 86-603373 DDC 353.0072/2 19
HJ2052 .M365 1986

Miller, James C., III. Spending and deficits /. Washington, D.C. , c1987. 18 p. ; ISBN 0-8447-1382-1 (pbk.) LC Card 87-134671 DDC 339.5/23/0973 19
HJ2052 .M54 1987

A Nation in debt . Frederick, Md. , c1987. p. cm. ISBN 0-89093-963-2 : LC Card 86-28254 DDC 339.5/23/0973 19
HJ2052 .N36 1987

Nevaer, Louis E. V. Corporate financial planning and management in a deficit economy /. New York , 1987. 171 p. : ISBN 0-89930-202-5 (lib. bdg. : alk. paper) LC Card 86-25582 DDC 658.1/145 19
HG4063 .N48 1987

Sherman, Heidemarie C. Der Einfluss staatlicher Budgetdefizite auf die Zinsentwicklung in der Bundesrepublik Deutschland und den Vereinigten Staaten . München , c1986. xxiii, 190 p. : ISBN 3-88512-019-4 LC Card 86-192070
HJ2110 .S53 1986

Structural budget deficits in the federal government . Lanham, Md. , c1987. x, 294 p. : ISBN 0-8191-6138-1 (alk. paper) : LC Card 86-33961 DDC 339.5/23/0973 19
HJ2052 .S74 1987

BUDGET DEFICITS - UNITED STATES - HISTORY.
Savage, James D., 1951- Balanced budgets and American politics /. Ithaca, N.Y. , c1988. p. cm. ISBN 0-8014-2047-4 LC Card 87-25061 DDC 339.5/23/0973 19
HJ2050 .S28 1988

BUDGET DEFICITS - UNITED STATES - JUVENILE LITERATURE.
Davis, Bertha, 1910- The national debt /. New York , c1987. 112 p. ; ISBN 0-531-10415-X LC Card 87-10441 DDC 336.3/4/0973 19
HJ2052 .D38 1987

BUDGET - DENMARK.
Rapport om administrationsbudgettering. [Copenhagen] [1984] 85, 33 p. ; LC Card 85-129140
HJ2133 .R36 1984

BUDGET - DICTIONARIES.
Woelfel, Charles J. Budgeting, pricing, and cost controls . Chicago, Ill. , c1987. p. cm. ISBN 0-917253-91-4 : LC Card 87-17921 DDC 658.1/5/0321 19
HG151 .W63 1987

BUDGET - ECUADOR.
Análisis del presupuesto general del estado de 1986. [Quito, Ecuador] [1986] ii, 2, 26, 8 p. ; LC Card 87-115859
HJ955 .A523 1986

BUDGET - EUROPEAN ECONOMIC COMMUNITY COUNTRIES.
Forte, Francesco, 1929- Il bilancio nell'economia pubblica /. Milano [1985] 2 v. ; ISBN 88-14-00636-9 : LC Card 86-151358 DDC 350.72/2 19
HJ2005 .F67 1985 ***NYPL [JLE 86-2653]***

BUDGET - FRANCE.
Baslé, Maurice. Le budget de l'Etat /. Paris , 1985. 127 p. : ISBN 2-7071-1534-7 LC Card 86-161271
HJ2106 .B37 1985

BUDGET - GAMBIA.
Sisay, S. S. Budget speech /. [Gambia] [1986] 60 leaves ; LC Card 87-403347 DDC 354.66/510072256 19
HJ2185 .S57 1986

BUDGET - GERMANY, WEST.
Fuest, Winfried, 1946- Quantitative und qualitative Konsolidierung /. Köln , c1986. 44 p. : ISBN 3-602-24741-4 LC Card 86-214118
HJ2110 .F84 1986

Germany (West). Bundesministerium der Finanzen. Rede zur Einbringung des Bundeshaushalts 1982 . Bonn , 1982. 56 p. : LC Card 82-221425
HJ2109 .G45 1982

BUDGET - GERMANY (WEST) - DECISION MAKING.
Engelhardt, Gunther. Haushalts- und mehrjährige Finanzplanung im Planspiel . Baden-Baden , 1984. 331 p. : ISBN 3-7890-0975-X LC Card 85-140583
HJ2109 .E54 1984

BUDGET - GERMANY (WEST) - HAMBURG - DECISION MAKING.
Engelhardt, Gunther. Haushalts- und mehrjährige Finanzplanung im Planspiel . Baden-Baden , 1984. 331 p. : ISBN 3-7890-0975-X LC Card 85-140583
HJ2109 .E54 1984

BUDGET - GERMANY (WEST) - LOWER SAXONY - STATISTICS.
2. Nachtragshaushalt des Landes Niedersachsen . [West Germany , 1981?] 178 p. ; LC Card 85-123229
HJ2110.5.L68 A12 1981

BUDGET - HUNGARY.
Management of public budgetary institutions /. Budapest , 1986. 37 p. ; ISBN 963-03-2343-5 (pbk.) : LC Card 86-230773 DDC 336.439 19
HJ2103 .M33 1986

BUDGET IN BUSINESS - CASE STUDIES.
The Impact of zero base budgeting on managerial behavior /. Hempstead, N.Y. , 1986. vii, 288 p. ; LC Card 86-80005 DDC 658.1/54 19
HG4028.B8 I55 1986

BUDGET IN BUSINESS - DATA PROCESSING.
Aloi, Felice. Il budget con il personal computer . Milano, Italy , c1984. 226 p. : LC Card 84-250395 DDC 658.1/54/02854165 19
HG4028.B8 A46 1984

BUDGET - INDIA - TRAVANCORE AND COCHIN.
Travancore and Cochin (India) Five year plan . Trivandrum , 1954. iii, 45 p. ; LC Card 83-238882
HJ2158.T7 T73 1954

BUDGET - ITALY.
Forte, Francesco, 1929- Il bilancio nell'economia pubblica /. Milano [1985] 2 v. ; ISBN 88-14-00636-9 : LC Card 86-151358 DDC 350.72/2 19
HJ2005 .F67 1985 ***NYPL [JLE 86-2653]***

BUDGET - ITALY - CONGRESSES.
La Politica di bilancio in condizioni di stress fiscale . Milano, Italy , c1986. 377 p. ; LC Card 87-134343
HJ2119 .P65 1986

BUDGET - LAW AND LEGISLATION - UNITED STATES.
Cebula, Richard J. The deficit problem in perspective /. Lexington, Mass. , c1987. x, 106 p. : ISBN 0-669-14303-0 (pbk. : alk. paper) LC Card 86-45792 DDC 339.5/23/0973 19
HJ2052 .C42 1987

A Nation in debt . Frederick, Md. , c1987. p. cm. ISBN 0-89093-963-2 : LC Card 86-28254 DDC 339.5/23/0973 19
HJ2052 .N36 1987

BUDGET - MEXICO.

BUDGET - MISSOURI - STATISTICS.
Missouri. General Assembly. Senate. Appropriations Committee. FY 87 budget summary . [Jefferson City, Mo.] [1986] 66 leaves : LC Card 87-620981 DDC 353.97780072/253 19
HJ2053.M8 M57 1986

BUDGET - NETHERLANDS - FRIESLAND - STATISTICS.
Financieel meerjarenplan, 1986-1989 /. [Leeuwarden] [1985?] vii, 169 p. ; LC Card 87-111957
HJ2128.5.F75 F563 1985

BUDGET - NETHERLANDS - NORTH BRABANT - FORECASTING.
Begroting 1986 . ['s-Hertogenbosch] [1985] 91 p. ; LC Card 86-136324
HJ2128.5.N6 B44 1985

Prognose van het budget van de Provincie op middellange termijn (zgn. meerjarenramingen) behorende bij de Ontwerp-Provinciale Begroting 1982. ['s-Hertogenbosch] [1982?] 7, [52] p. ; LC Card 86-232148
HJ2128.5.N6 P76 1982

BUDGET - NORTH CAROLINA.
North Carolina. General Assembly. Fiscal Research Division. Overview, fiscal and budgetary actions . Raleigh, N.C. (Legislative Office Bldg., Raleigh 27611) [1986]. 248 p. : LC Card 87-620950 DDC 353.97560072/2 19
HJ2053.N8 N668 1986

BUDGET - PERU.
Malpica Silva Santisteban, Carlos. La alternativa de la izquierda . [Lima, Peru] [1985] 91 p. : LC Card 87-403544 DDC 338.985 19
HJ2090 .M35 1985

BUDGET - PHILIPPINES.
Philippines. Office of Budget and Management. 1984 Philippine budget . Malacañang, Manila [1984?] viii, 461 p. : LC Card 87-105421 DDC 354.5990072/2 19
HJ2167 .P46 1984

BUDGET - POLITICAL ASPECTS - UNITED STATES.
Shuman, Howard E. Politics and the budget . Englewood Cliffs, N.J. , c1988. p. cm. ISBN 0-13-684416-2 (pbk.) : LC Card 87-14521 DDC 353.0072/231 19
HJ2051 .S49 1988

BUDGET - RHODE ISLAND.
Salamon, Lester M. Rhode Island nonprofit organizations . Washington, D.C. , Providence, RI , c1987. vii, 40 p. : LC Card 87-148803 DDC 338.7/4/09745 19
HD2769.2.U6 S25 1987

BUDGET - SENEGAL.
Répertoire financier et monétaire du Sénégal, 1985. Le Vésinet, France [1985?] ii, 98 leaves ; LC Card 86-202435
HJ2184.5 .R46 1985

BUDGET - SOVIET UNION.
Dementsev, V. V. (Viktor Vladimirovich) O Gosudarstvennom bi͡udzhete SSSR na 1986 god i ob ispolnenii Gosudarstvennogo bi͡udzheta SSSR za 1984 god . Moskva , 1985. 28 p. ; LC Card 86-203425
HJ2129 .D46 1985

BUDGET - SOVIET UNION - REPUBLICS.
Bahry, Donna. Outside Moscow . New York , 1987. 236 p. : ISBN 0-231-06290-7 LC Card 87-8020 DDC 336.47 19
HJ2130 .B35 1987

BUDGET - SPAIN.
Herrero Suazo, Santiago. Técnicas presupuestarias en la administración pública /. Alcalá de Henares-Madrid, España [1984?] 382 p. : ISBN 84-7351-173-5 LC Card 85-185202
HJ1248 .H47 1984

BUDGET - SPAIN - MADRID.
Madrid (Spain). Alcaldía. Situación de crédito, hacienda y presupuesto del Municipio de Madrid en 1907 . Madrid , 1907. viii, 137 p. ; LC Card 85-131486
HJ9528.M38 M34 1907

Budget speech /. Sisay, S. S. [Gambia] [1986] 60 leaves ; LC Card 87-403347 DDC 354.66/510072256 19
HJ2185 .S57 1986

BUDGET - SWITZERLAND.
Grossen, Andreas. Bürger, Parlament und Steuern . Bern , c1986. vi, 134 p. : ISBN 3-7165-0510-2 LC Card 86-187534
HJ2145 .G76 1986

BUDGET - SWITZERLAND - HISTORY - 20TH CENTURY.
Tanner, Jakob. Bundeshaushalt, Währung und Kriegswirtschaft . Zürich , c1986. 438 p. : ISBN 3-85791-100-X : LC Card 86-199729
HJ1258 .T35 1986

BUDGET - THAILAND.
Chanthiphā Sukhumālachāt. Ngoppramān phændin phæn mai . [Bangkok?] 2521 [1978] 173 (some folded), [3] leaves : LC Card 81-917611
HJ2162.55 .C47 1978

BUDGET - UNITED STATES.
Cannon, William B., 1920- New class politics . Washington, D.C. , c1986. 137 p. ; ISBN 0-89758-042-7 (pbk.) : LC Card 86-27511 DDC 336.73 19
HJ2051 .C35 1986

Contemporary economic problems . Washington, D.C. , c1987. 332 p. : ISBN 0-8447-3621-X (alk. paper) LC Card 87-1395 DDC 330.973/0927 19
HC106.8 .C665 1987

The Economy, small business, and the federal budget . Washington , 1986. v, 20 p. : LC Card 86-603392 DDC 338.6/42/0973 19
HC106.8 .E35 1986

Nathan, Richard P. Reagan and the States /. Princeton, N.J. , c1987. xv, 375 p. : ISBN 0-691-07748-7 (alk. paper) : LC Card 87-45529 DDC 353.0072/5 19
HJ2051 .N167 1987

Neustadt, Richard E. Richard E. Neustadt lecture, May 13, 1986. Seattle, WA [1986] 35 p. : LC Card 87-402984 DDC 339.5/2/0973 19
HJ257.2 .N48 1986

Reducing the federal deficit . Washington, D.C. , 1982. 1 v. (various pagings) :
NYPL [JLF 86-1219]

Schick, Allen. The whole and the parts . Washington , 1987. vi, 65 p. ; LC Card 87-601378 DDC 353.0072/2 19
HJ2052 .S335 1987

Sequestration report for fiscal year 1986 . Washington, D.C. [1986] 20 p. ; LC Card 87-600820 DDC 353.0072/2 19
HJ2051 .S468 1986

Shuman, Howard E. Politics and the budget .

Englewood Cliffs, N.J. , c1988. p. cm. ISBN 0-13-684416-2 (pbk.) : LC Card 87-14521 DDC 353.0072/231 19
HJ2051 .S49 1988

Stockman, David Alan, 1946- The triumph of politics . New York , c1986. 422 p. : ISBN 0-06-015560-4 : LC Card 85-45541 DDC 338.973 19
HC106.8 .S75 1986 ***NYPL [JLE 86-2647]***

Stockman, David Alan, 1946- The triumph of politics . Boston, Mass. , 1987, c1986. xxxiii, 654 p. (large print) ; ISBN 0-8161-4231-9 (lg. print) : LC Card 86-22950 DDC 338.973 19
HC106.8 .S75 1986b

Swain, David, 1942- Managing public money . Lanham, MD , c1987. x, 221 p. : ISBN 0-8191-6505-0 (alk. paper) : LC Card 87-14261 DDC 350.72 19
HJ141 .S93 1987

Tax expenditures . Washington, D.C. [1983] xiv, 82 p. ; ***NYPL [JLF 84-401]***

United States. Dept. of the Treasury. Estimate of the expenditure ... of the United States, for the year 1789. New York [1789] 26, [2] p. (the last 2 pages blank) ; LC Card 87-109324 DDC n-us 19
HJ2050 .U55 1789

Verdier, James M. Tax expenditures . Washington, D.C. , 1982. xx, 102 p. ; ***NYPL [JLF 83-663]***

Weida, William J. The political economy of national defense /. Boulder , 1987. xvii, 230 p. ; ISBN 0-8133-0432-6 (alk. paper) : LC Card 86-19015 DDC 355.6/22/0973 19
UA23 .W3694 1987 ***NYPL [JLE 87-1043]***

Wildavsky, Aaron B. The new politics of the budgetary process /. Glenview, Ill. , c1988. xxiv, 468 p. : ISBN 0-673-39754-8 (pbk.) LC Card 87-23391 DDC 353.0072/2 19
HJ2051 .W483 1988

BUDGET - UNITED STATES - HISTORY.
Savage, James D., 1951- Balanced budgets and American politics /. Ithaca, N.Y. , c1988. p. cm. ISBN 0-8014-2047-4 LC Card 87-25061 DDC 339.5/23/0973 19
HJ2050 .S28 1988

The budgetary and economic effects of oil taxes. Webre, Philip. Washington, DC , 19. xvi, 55 p. ; ***NYPL [JLF 86-1354]***

Budgeting, pricing, and cost controls . Woelfel, Charles J. Chicago, Ill. , c1987. p. cm. ISBN 0-917253-91-4 : LC Card 87-17921 DDC 658.1/5/0321 19
HG151 .W63 1987

Budgetkontrolle als Instrument zur Unternehmungssteuerung /. Posselt, Siegfried G. Darmstadt , c1986. 272 p. : ISBN 3-87820-068-4 LC Card 87-113335 DDC 658.1/54 19
HG4028.B8 P67 1986

Budgetpolitik im Wandel /. Geyer, Herbert, 1927- Berlin , c1986. 111 p. : ISBN 3-428-05922-0 LC Card 86-165210
HJ113 .G49 1986

Budgets extraordinaires et d'investissement . Burundi. [Bujumbura] [1967] [19] leaves ; LC Card 82-980377
HJ2180.8 .B87 1967

BUDGETS, PERSONAL - BANGLADESH - STATISTICS.
Bangladesh household expenditure survey, 1981-82. Dhaka, Bangladesh , 1986. 160 p., [13] leaves of plates : LC Card 86-902560 DDC 339.4/1/095492021 19
HD7051.6 .B36 1986

Budgetvorschau 1984-1988 / Beirat für Wirtschafts- und Sozialfragen. Wien : Der Beirat, 1984. 55 p. ; 24 cm. LC Card 84-223024
1. Budget - Austria. 2. Austria - Appropriations and expenditure. I. Beirat für Wirtschafts- und Sozialfragen.
HJ2101 .B828 1984

Budgetvorschau 1986-1990. Wien : Beirat für Wirtschafts- und Sozialfragen : Kommissionsverlag, C. Ueberreuter, 1986. 45 p. : ill. ; 24 cm. (Publikationen des Beirates für Wirtschafts- und Sozialfragen . 53) "Die vorliegende Budgetvorschau wurde in der Arbeitsgruppe 'Budgetpolitik' ... ausgearbeitet ..."--Fwd. Includes bibliographical references. LC Card 86-227246
1. Budget - Austria. 2. Austria - Appropriations and expenditures - Forecasting. 3. Tax revenue estimating - Austria. I. Arbeitsgruppe Budgetpolitik (Beirat für Wirtschafts- und Sozialfragen). II. Series.
HJ2101 .B83 1986

Budidaya padi di Jawa / penyunting, Sajogyo dan William L. Collier ; kata pengantar, Sajogyo. Ed. 1. Jakarta : Yayasan Obor Indonesia : Gramedia, 1986. x, 339 p. : ill., maps ; 21 cm. (Seri pembangunan pedesaan) Bibliography: p. 336. Includes index. LC Card 87-941451
1. Rice trade - Indonesia - Java. I. Sajogyo. II. Collier, William L. III. Series.
HD9066.I63 J3493 1986

Büchele, Herwig, 1935- Grundeinkommen ohne Arbeit : auf dem Weg zu einer kommunikativen Gesellschaft / Herwig Büchele, Lieselotte Wohlgenannt.2. Aufl. Wien : Europaverlag, c1985. 191 p. : ill. ; 21 cm. (Soziale Brennpunkte. 11) Bibliography: p. 191. ISBN 3-203-50898-2 LC Card 85-207929
1. Guaranteed annual income. 2. Income maintenance programs. 3. Public welfare. I. Wohlgenannt, Lieselotte. II. Title.
HC79.I5 B83 1985

Büchner, Robert. Grundzüge der Finanzanalyse / von Robert Buchner. München : F. Vahlen, c1981. x, 426 p. : ill. ; 23 cm. (Vahlens Handbücher der Wirtschafts- und Sozialwissenschaften) Includes bibliographies and index. ISBN 3-8006-0885-5 LC Card 82-156543
1. Business mathematics. 2. Financial statements. 3. Break-even analysis. 4. Corporations - Valuation. 5. Investment analysis. 6. Credit bureaus. I. Title.
HF5693.G47 B83 1981

Buede, Dennis M. Watson, Stephen R. Decision synthesis . Cambridge [Cambridgeshire] , New York , 1987. xvi, 299 p. : ISBN 0-521-32569-2 LC Card 87-10270 DDC 658.4/03 19
HD30.23 .W38 1987

Buehler, Vernon M. Quality, productivity, and innovation . New York , c1987. xx, 427 p. : ISBN 0-444-01194-3 LC Card 87-6815 DDC 658.5 19
HD58.9 .Q35 1987

Buen L., Néstor de (Buen Lozano) Sindicatos, democracia y crisis / Néstor de Buen L. 1a ed. México : Editorial Porrúa, 1985. xii, 122 p. ; 21 cm. Bibliography: p. [119]-122. ISBN 968-452-054-9 LC Card 86-209080
1. Trade-unions - Mexico. 2. Mexico - Economic conditions - 1970-. 3. Latin America - Economic conditions - 1945-. 4. Democracy. I. Title.
HD6532 .B84 1985

Buenahora Febres-Cordero, Norma. Cúcuta y sus servicios públicos básicos / Norma Buenahora Febres-Cordero. Bogotá, D.E. : República de Colombia, Pontificia Universidad Javeriana, Facultad de Ciencias Jurídicas y Socioeconómicas, 1984. 136 p. ; 23 cm. Bibliography: p. 134-136. LC Card 85-205425
1. Municipal services - Colombia. 2. Municipal services - Colombia - Cúcuta. 3. Sewerage - Colombia - Cúcuta. 4. Electric utilities - Colombia - Cúcuta. I. Title.
HD4637.A5 B84 1984

Buendía, Hernando Gómez. see **Gómez Buendía, Hernando.**

Buendía, Manuel, d. 1984. Los petroleros / Manuel Buendía. 3a ed. México, D.F. : Océano : Fundación Manuel Buendía, c1985. 312 p. ; 23 cm. Articles written between 1974 and 1984. ISBN 968-493-065-8 LC Card 86-218751
1. Petroleum industry and trade - Mexico. I. Title.
HD9574.M6 B77 1985

Bueno de Mesquita, Nicholas. Bauwens, Jan G., 1924- Industrial co-operation and investment in Yugoslavia /. Luxembourg , Washington, D.C. , 1986. viii, 161 p. : ISBN 92-825-6410-X (pbk.) : LC Card 86-216364 DDC 332.6/73/09497 19
HG5682 .B38 1986

Buenos Aires (Argentina : Province). Dirección Provincial de Estadística. Provincia de Buenos Aires : plan de gobierno 1984-87. Anexo estadístico. [Buenos Aires] : Dirección Provincial de Estadística y la Dirección Provincial de Estudios Económicos, 1985. 107 p. : ill. ; 23 cm. Chiefly tables. LC Card 86-107759
1. Buenos Aires (Argentina : Province) - Statistics - Periodicals. I. Buenos Aires (Argentina : Province). Dirección Provincial de Estudios Económicos. II. Title.
HA958.B8 B85 1985

Buenos Aires (Argentina : Province). Dirección Provincial de Estudios Económicos. Buenos Aires (Argentina : Province). Dirección Provincial de Estadística. Provincia de Buenos Aires . [Buenos Aires] , 1985. 107 p. : LC Card 86-107759
HA958.B8 B85 1985

BUENOS AIRES (ARGENTINA : PROVINCE) - ECONOMIC CONDITIONS - STATISTICS.
Reseña histórico-económica de los partidos de la provincia de Buenos Aires. [Buenos Aires] [1981- v. <1-2 > : LC Card 87-114686 DDC 330.982/12/064 19
HC177.B8 R47 1981

BUENOS AIRES (ARGENTINA : PROVINCE) - SOCIAL CONDITIONS - STATISTICS.
Reseña histórico-económica de los partidos de la provincia de Buenos Aires. [Buenos Aires] [1981- v. <1-2 > : LC Card 87-114686 DDC 330.982/12/064 19
HC177.B8 R47 1981

BUENOS AIRES (ARGENTINA : PROVINCE) - STATISTICS - PERIODICALS.
Buenos Aires (Argentina : Province). Dirección Provincial de Estadística. Provincia de Buenos Aires . [Buenos Aires] , 1985. 107 p. : LC Card 86-107759
HA958.B8 B85 1985

BUENOS AIRES (ARGENTINA) - ETHNIC RELATIONS.
Buenos Aires. Bolsa de Comercio. Mercados de capitales bajo inflación /. New York, N.Y. , c1982. xxi, 471 p. : ISBN 0-910365-00-8 : LC Card 82-50965 DDC 332.64 19
HG4523 .M47 1982 ***NYPL [JLE 86-3568]***

Buenos Aires. Instituto Torcuato di Tella. see **Instituto Torcuato di Tella.**

BUENOS AIRES METROPOLITAN AREA (ARGENTINA) - POPULATION.
Lindenboim, Javier. La terciarización del empleo en la Argentina. Buenos Aires , 1985. vi, 59, 50, 3 p. ; LC Card 87-122527 DDC 381 19
HD2346.A73 L56 1985

Bürge, Alfons. Rechtsdogmatik und Wirtschaft : das richterliche Moderationsrecht beim sittenwidrigen Rechtsgeschäft im Rechtsvergleich, Bundesrepublik Deutschland, Schweiz, Österreich, Frankreich / von Alfons Bürge. Berlin : Duncker & Humblot, c1987. 280 p. ; 24 cm. (Schriften zum bürgerlichen Recht . Bd. 102) Bibliography: p. [253]-280. ISBN 3-428-06124-1 LC Card 87-134998 DDC 332.8/3/094 19
1. Usury laws - Economic aspects - Europe. 2. Exclusive contracts - Economic aspects - Europe. 3. Judgments - Economic aspects - Europe. I. Title. II. Series.
HB551 .B87 1987

Bürger, es geht um Deine Gemeinde : Bauen und Wohnen in alter Umgebung für alle Gemeinden in der Bundesrepublik Deutschland, einschliesslich des Landes Berlin / Schirmherr, der Bundespräsident ; Auslober, der Bundesminister für Raumordnung, Bauwesen und Städtebau ... [et al.] ; fachliche Mitwirkung, Institut für Städtebau, Bodenordnung und Kulturtechnik der Rheinischen Friedrich-Wilhelms-Universität Bonn ; Geschäftsführung, Deutsche Gartenbau-Gesellschaft, Bonn-Bad Godesberg. [S.l. : s.n., 1983] ([Bonn] : Bundesdruckerei) 7 p. ; 30 cm. Cover title. At head of title: Ausschreibung Bundeswettbewerb 1983-1984. LC Card 84-198296
1. Housing - Germany, West. 2. Dwellings - Germany (West) - Designs and plans. I. Germany (West). Bundesministerium für Raumordnung, Bauwesen und Städtebau. II. Deutsche Gartenbau-Gesellschaft. III. Title: Ausschreibung Bundeswettbewerb 1983-1984.
HD7339.A3 B97 1983

Bürger, Parlament und Steuern . Grossen, Andreas. Bern , c1986. vi, 134 p. : ISBN 3-7165-0510-2 LC Card 86-187534
HJ2145 .G76 1986

Bürgerbeteiligung in der Verbraucherinformationspolitik : künftige Kriterien für den Warentest / Detlef Garbe, Anja Grothe-Senf (Hg.). Frankfurt ; New

York : Campus, c1986. 241 p. : ill. ; 21 cm. (Campus Forschung. Bd. 508) Includes bibliographical references. ISBN 3-593-33681-2 LC Card 86-230016
1. Consumer protection - Germany (West) - Citizen participation. I. Garbe, Detlef, 1949-. II. Grothe-Senf, Anja.
HC290.5.C63 B87 1986

Bürokratie und Effizienz staatlichen Handelns . Thürmer, Lothar. Berlin , c1984. 177 p. : ISBN 3-428-05543-8 LC Card 84-156948
HD38.4 .T47 1984

Bürokratisierte Demokratie? /. Laufer, Heinz, 1933- Zürich , c1983. 123 p. ; ISBN 3-7201-5157-3 LC Card 83-168788
HD38.4 .L38 1983

Büromaschinen, Datenverarbeitungsgeräte und -einrichtungen : eine Branchenstudie / von Arthur Boness ... [et al.] ; Statistik und EDV, Wolfgang Härle und Ingrid Ludwig. Berlin : Duncker & Humblot, [1984] xxi, 400 p. : ill. ; 30 cm. (Beiträge zur Strukturforschung . Heft 82, 1984) Bibliography: p. 363-371. ISBN 3-428-05740-6 LC Card 86-139011
1. Office equipment and supplies industry - Germany (West). 2. Computer industry - Germany, West. I. Boness, Arthur. II. Series: Beiträge zur Strukturforschung , Heft 82.
HC281 .B33 Heft 82 HD9800.G3

Búfalo, Enzo del. El pensamiento crítico latinoamericano / Enzo del Búfalo, Edgar Paredes ; [portada, detalle, pintura Diego Rivera]. 1. ed. [México?] : Ediciones Nueva Sociología, 1979. 236 p. ; 17 cm. Bibliography: p. 225-235. LC Card 79-120323
1. Economic development - Social aspects. 2. Developing countries - Economic conditions. 3. Latin America - Economic conditions. I. Paredes, Edgar, joint author. II. Title.
HC59.7 .B84 ***NYPL [JLC 80-383]***

BUFFET, WARREN.
Train, John. The midas touch . New York , c1987. xi, 207 p. ; ISBN 0-06-015643-0 : LC Card 86-45157 DDC 332.6/092/4 B 19
HG172.B84 T72 1987

Buga, László. Biztonságos, jó utat! : Budapest balesetveszélyes útvonalai és csomópontjai / írták, Buga László és Rózsa Tamás ; fotó, Ági Lajos. [Budapest] : Idegenforgalmi Propaganda és Kiadó Vállalat, 1980. 95 p. : ill. (some col.) ; 20 cm. ISBN 963-316-028-6 (Magy. nemz. bibl.) LC Card 85-177784
1. Traffic safety - Hungary - Budapest. 2. Traffic accidents - Hungary - Budapest. I. Rózsa, Tamás. II. Title.
HE5614.5.H8 B84 1980

Bugaev, V. K. (Vladimir Konstantinovich) Territorial'naia struktura ėkonomicheskogo raĭona : teoretiko-metodologicheskie aspekty / V.K. Bugaev ; pod redaktsieĭ A.I. Chistobaeva. Leningrad : Izd-vo "Nauka," Leningradskoe otd-nie, 1986. 164, [3] p. : ill. ; 20 cm. At head of title: Akademiia nauk SSSR. Geograficheskoe obshchestvo SSSR. Bibliography: p. 157-[165] LC Card 87-120624
1. Soviet Union - Economic conditions - 1976- - Regional disparities. 2. Regional planning - Soviet Union. I. Chistobaev, A. I. (Anatoliĭ Ivanovich). II. Title.
HC336.25 .B84 1986

Buglione, Enrico, 1948- La Politica di bilancio in condizioni di stress fiscale . Milano, Italy , c1986. 377 p. ; LC Card 87-134343
HJ2119 .P65 1986

Buhbe, Matthes, 1949- Krisenverschärfung durch Angebotspolitik . Köln , c1984. 104 p. ; ISBN 3-7663-0877-7 LC Card 84-215633
HC286.7 .K75 1984

Bühler, Marcel. Geschäfte mit der Armut : Pharma-Konzerne in der Dritten Welt / Marcel Bühler.Originalausg. Frankfurt/M. : Medico International, c1982. 200 p. : ill. ; 19 cm. Bibliography: p. 186-197. ISBN 3-923363-02-8 (pbk.) LC Card 86-674004
1. Pharmaceutical industry - Developing countries. 2. Pharmaceutical industry - Developing countries - Moral and ethical aspects. 3. Medical care - Developing countries. I. Title.
HD9673.D44 B83x 1982

Buhr, R. J. A. System design with Ada / R.J.A. Buhr. Englewood Cliffs, N.J. : Prentice-Hall, c1984. xv, 256 p. : ill. ; 25 cm. (Prentice-Hall software series) Includes index. Bibliography: p. 245. ISBN 0-13-881623-9 : LC Card 83-13673 DDC 001.64/2 19
1. Ada (Computer program language). 2. System design. I. Title.
QA76.73.A35 B83 1984 ***NYPL [JSE 86-1253]***

Builder's guide to accounting /. Thomsett, Michael C. Carlsbad, CA , c1987. 302 p. : ISBN 0-934041-18-0 (pbk.) : LC Card 87-6817 DDC 657/.869 19
HF5686.B7 T47 1987

The building /. Jackson, Mason, 1926- Interlaken, N.Y. , 1987. 128 p. : ISBN 0-932334-90-3 LC Card 86-24115 DDC 974.7/89043 19
HD8039.M4 U54 1987

Building a Canadian-American free trade area / papers by Donald S. MacDonald ... [et al.]; presented at a conference at the Brookings Institution chaired by Bruce K. MacLaury on February 3, 1987 ; edited by Edward R. Fried, Frank Stone, Philip H. Trezise. Washington, D.C. : Brookings Institution, c1987. xii, 217 p. ; 26 cm. (Brookings dialogues on public policy) ISBN 0-8157-2973-1 (pbk.) LC Card 87-71507 DDC 382/.0971/073 19
1. Canada - Foreign economic relations - United States - Congresses. 2. United States - Foreign economic relations - Canada - Congresses. 3. Free trade and protection - Free trade - Congresses. I. Macdonald, Donald S. II. Fried, Edward R. III. Stone, Frank, 1923-. IV. Trezise, Philip H., 1912-. V. Series.
HF1480.15.U5 B85 1987

BUILDING - ACCOUNTING. see **CONSTRUCTION INDUSTRY - ACCOUNTING.**

Building an import/export business /. Weiss, Kenneth D. (Kenneth Duane), 1940- New York , c1987. vii, 264 p. : ISBN 0-471-84259-1 : LC Card 86-26560 DDC 658.8 19
HF1008 .W43 1987

Building an industrial structure for the 21st century : independent high technology development. Tokyo : Keizai Doyukai, 1982. ii, 58 p. ; 26 cm. LC Card 83-201472 DDC 338.4/762/000952 19
1. High technology industries - Japan. 2. High technology industries - Government policy - Japan. I. Keizai Dōyūkai.
HC465.H53 B85 1982

BUILDING AND LOAN ASSOCIATIONS - ACCOUNTING - STANDARDS - UNITED STATES.
Savings and loan associations . New York, N.Y. (1211 Avenue of the Americas, New York 10036) , 1987. vii, 212 p. ; LC Card 87-161844 DDC 657/.833 19
HF5686.B8 S27 1987

BUILDING AND LOAN ASSOCIATIONS - AUDITING - STANDARDS - UNITED STATES.
Savings and loan associations . New York, N.Y. (1211 Avenue of the Americas, New York 10036) , 1987. vii, 212 p. ; LC Card 87-161844 DDC 657/.833 19
HF5686.B8 S27 1987

BUILDING AND LOAN ASSOCIATIONS - BRAZIL - COSTS - MATHEMATICAL MODELS.
Dantas Neto, Antônio da Costa. Custos operacionais no SBPE /. Rio de Janeiro/RJ , 1983. 67 p. : LC Card 85-108995
HG2156.B8 D36 1983

BUILDING AND LOAN ASSOCIATIONS - CALIFORNIA - STATISTICS.
Savings performance report, fourth quarter, 1985 . Los Angeles, Calif. (9100 Sunset Blvd., Suite 111, Los Angeles) , c1986- v. <1 > ; LC Card 86-202354 DDC 332.3/2/09794021 19
HG2153.C3 S287 1986

Savings performance report, fourth quarter, 1985 . Los Angeles, Calif. (9100 Sunset Blvd., Suite 111, Los Angeles) , c1986. 5 v. ; LC Card 86-213300 DDC 332.3/2/09794021 19
HG2153.C3 C288 1986

Savings performance report, second quarter, 1986 . Los Angeles, Calif. (9100 Sunset Blvd., Suite 111, Los Angeles) , c1986. 5 v. (various pagings) ; LC Card 86-224944 DDC 332.3/2/09794021 19
HG2153.C3 S284 1986

BUILDING AND LOAN ASSOCIATIONS - ECUADOR.
Da Ros, Giuseppina. El cooperativismo de ahorro y crédito en el Ecuador /. Quito , 1985. 89 p. : LC Card 86-169048
HG2156.E22 D37 1985

BUILDING AND LOAN ASSOCIATIONS - GERMANY, WEST.
Bock, Hartmut. Das kollektive Bausparen . Frankfurt am Main , New York , c1984. 204 p. : ISBN 3-8204-5341-5 LC Card 85-199145
HC290.5.S3 B63 1984

Schulze, Konrad. Ein ökonometrischer Ansatz zur Erklärung des Bausparens /. Bonn , c1985. xii, 150 p. : ISBN 3-87169-319-7 LC Card 86-231621
HC290.5.S3 S38 1985

Zink, Achim. Der Bausparvertrag /. Wiesbaden , 1984. 110 p. : ISBN 3-409-47001-8 LC Card 84-213485
HG2156.G3 Z55 1984

BUILDING AND LOAN ASSOCIATIONS - GOVERNMENT POLICY - UNITED STATES.
Ford, William F. (William Frank), 1934- The public policy roots of recent thrift crises /. Washington, D.C. , c1986. 14 p. ; ISBN 0-8447-1376-7 (pbk.) LC Card 87-164463 DDC 332.3/2/0973 19
HG2152 .F67 1986

BUILDING AND LOAN ASSOCIATIONS - LAW AND LEGISLATION - GERMANY, WEST.
Zink, Achim. Der Bausparvertrag /. Wiesbaden , 1984. 110 p. : ISBN 3-409-47001-8 LC Card 84-213485
HG2156.G3 Z55 1984

BUILDING AND LOAN ASSOCIATIONS - MARYLAND.
Report on extraordinary session of the General Assembly, May 1985 . Annapolis, Md. [1985] ii, 26 leaves ; LC Card 86-622373 DDC 332.3/2/09752 19
HG2153.M3 R46 1985

BUILDING AND LOAN ASSOCIATIONS - MARYLAND - STATE SUPERVISION.
Report on extraordinary session of the General Assembly, May 1985 . Annapolis, Md. [1985] ii, 26 leaves ; LC Card 86-622373 DDC 332.3/2/09752 19
HG2153.M3 R46 1985

BUILDING AND LOAN ASSOCIATIONS - SPAIN.
Morón Bécquer, Pedro. El ahorro vinculado a la adquisición de viviendas . Madrid [1984?] 35 p. : ISBN 84-7196-476-7 : LC Card 85-201073
HG2156.S72 M67 1984

BUILDING AND LOAN ASSOCIATIONS - TEXAS.
Born, Waldo L. A synopsis of Texas savings-and-loan associations' operations /. College Station, Tex. [1986?] 38 p. : LC Card 86-622196 DDC 332.3/2/09764 19
HG2153.T4 B67 1986

BUILDING AND LOAN ASSOCIATIONS - UNITED STATES.
Benston, George J. An analysis of the causes of savings and loan association failures /. New York, N.Y. (90 Trinity Place, New York 10006) [1985] 182 p. : LC Card 86-209942 DDC 332.3/2/0973 19
HG2151 .B46 1985

Hoffman, Naphtali. The bank book . San Diego , 1986. xiii, 222 p. ; ISBN 0-15-610676-0 (pbk.) : LC Card 85-27271 DDC 332.1/7/0973 19
HG1616.C87 H64 1986 ***NYPL [JLE 86-3189]***

Olin, Harold Bennett. Realty brokerage operations by savings institutions /. Chicago, IL (111 E. Wacker Dr., Chicago 60601) , c1986. 38, [96] p. : LC Card 86-212493 DDC 332.3/2 19
HD255 .O45 1986

BUILDING AND LOAN ASSOCIATIONS - UNITED STATES - CONGRESSES.
Financial stability of the thrift industry . San Francisco, Calif. (P.O. Box 7948, San Francisco 94120) [1986?] 230 p. : LC Card 86-81012
NYPL [JLE 86-3398]

BUILDING AND LOAN ASSOCIATIONS - UNITED STATES - STATISTICS.
Savings institutions performance analysis /. [Raleigh, N.C.] , c1987. 159 p. ; LC Card 87-404475 DDC 332.2/1/0973021 19
HG1922 .S35 1987

BUILDING AND LOAN ASSOCIATIONS - VENEZUELA.
Martín-Guédez, Rafael, 1942- Sistema financiero . Caracas [1984] (Caracas : Editorial Arte) 309 p. : LC Card 85-177967
HG2156.V42 M37 1984

BUILDING - ARGENTINA.
Hacia un planeamiento de la industria de la construcción en la Argentina /. Buenos Aires , 1943. 289 p. : LC Card 85-104409
HD9715.A72 H33 1943

Building better ads . Elkman, Richard. Washington, D.C. , c1987. 86 p. : ISBN 0-86718-290-3 (pbk.) LC Card 87-122135 DDC 659.1/933333 19
HF6161.R3 E439 1987

Building blocks of human potential. Harris, Philip R. (Philip Robert), 1926- Managing cultural differences /. Houston , c1987. xiii, 609 p. : ISBN 0-87201-161-5 LC Card 86-25618 DDC 658.1/8 19
HD62.4 .H37 1987

BUILDING CLEANING INDUSTRY.
Bidding & estimating in the building service industry. Fairfax, VA , c1983. v, 10 p. : LC Card 87-110623 DDC 648/.068/1 19
HD9999.B882 B53 1983

BUILDING - CONTRACTS AND SPECIFICATIONS - SWITZERLAND.
Finsinger, Jörg. Der Submissionswettbewerb . Bern , c1986. 104 p. : ISBN 3-258-03617-9 : LC Card 86-224617
HD9715.S92 F56 1986

Building expert systems / edited by Frederick Hayes-Roth, Donald A. Waterman, Douglas B. Lenat. Reading, Mass. : Addison-Wesley Pub. Co., 1983. xvi, 444 p. : ill. ; 24 cm. (Teknowledge series in knowledge engineering . v. 1) Includes indexes. Bibliography: p. 405-420. ISBN 0-201-10686-8 LC Card 82-24511 DDC 001.64/2 19
1. Expert systems (Computer science). 2. System design. I. Hayes-Roth, Frederick. II. Waterman, D. A. (Donald Arthur), 1936-. III. Lenat, Douglas B. IV. Series.
QA76.9.E96 B84 1983 ***NYPL [JSE 87-204]***

BUILDING FITTINGS INDUSTRY - PORTUGAL - FINANCE.
Almeida, João Carreira. Fabricação de materiais de barro para construção . Lisboa , 1978. 186 p., [3] leaves of plates (one folded) : LC Card 82-112167 DDC 338.4/36914/09469 19
HD9596.P82 A85 1978

BUILDING - GREAT BRITAIN - DATA PROCESSING - CONGRESSES.
Computer technology in construction . London , 1985. 308 p. : ISBN 0-7277-0234-3 LC Card 85-670263 DDC 338.4/5624 19
HD9715.G72 C64 1985
NYPL [JLE 86-2586]

BUILDING, HOUSE. see **HOUSE CONSTRUCTION.**

BUILDING INDUSTRY. see **CONSTRUCTION INDUSTRY.**

BUILDING LAWS - UNITED STATES.
Technology, trade, and the U.S residential construction industry . Washington, D.C. , 1986. x, 91 p. : LC Card 86-600575 DDC 338.4/769083/0973 19
HD9715.U52 T43 1986

BUILDING - MANAGEMENT. see **CONSTRUCTION INDUSTRY - MANAGEMENT.**

BUILDING MATERIALS INDUSTRY - EUROPE.
Major import markets for builders' woodwork /. Geneva , 1985. xiii, 180 p. : LC Card 87-118537 DDC 381/.45674/094 19
HD9765.A2 M29 1985

BUILDING MATERIALS INDUSTRY - PORTUGAL - FINANCE.
Almeida, João Carreira. Fabricação de materiais de barro para construção . Lisboa , 1978. 186 p., [3] leaves of plates (one folded) : LC Card 82-112167 DDC 338.4/36914/09469 19
HD9596.P82 A85 1978

BUILDING MATERIALS INDUSTRY - QUÉBEC (PROVINCE)
Ristic, Veselin. Profil de l'industrie québécoise des éléments d'architecture et de structure préfabriqués en béton /. [Québec] , c1983. 168 p. : LC Card 85-100163
HD9622.C23 Q437 1983

BUILDING MATERIALS INDUSTRY - SOVIET UNION.
Razumovskiĭ, A. V. (Al'bert Vadimovich) Ėkonomika promyshlennosti stroitel'nykh materialov /. Moskva , 1986. 350 p. : LC Card 86-204591
HD9715.8.S652 R39 1986

BUILDING MATERIALS INDUSTRY - SWEDEN.
Sveriges exportråd. Svensk byggexport . [Stockholm] [1984] v, 107, [23] p. : ISBN 91-38-08107-5 LC Card 84-217971
HD9715.8.S82 S86 1984

BUILDING MATERIALS INDUSTRY - UNITED STATES.
Major import markets for builders' woodwork /. Geneva , 1985. xiii, 180 p. : LC Card 87-118537 DDC 381/.45674/094 19
HD9765.A2 M29 1985

BUILDING MATERIALS - MEXICO.
Ziss, Roland. Baumaterialien und Selbsthilfe . Saarbrücken , Fort Lauderdale, Fl. , 1986. 319 p. : ISBN 3-88156-333-4 LC Card 86-197177
HD7287.96.M6 Z57 1986

BUILDING MATERIALS - PRICES - AUSTRIA - STATISTICS.
Der Österreichische Baupreisindex 1971-1985 /. Wien , 1986. 107 p. ; LC Card 87-409417 DDC 314.36 s 338.4/3691/09436 19
HA1173 .A27 Heft 810 HD9715.8.A92

BUILDING MATERIALS - PRICES - BERLIN (GERMANY)
Ring, Peter. Regionale Besonderheiten der Preisbildung und Ansätze zur Förderung des Wettbewerbs auf dem Berliner Baustoffmarkt /. Berlin , 1986. 187 p. : ISBN 3-428-06112-8 LC Card 87-114036 DDC 330 s 338.4/3691/09431554 19
HC281 .B33 Heft 91 HD9715.G33B52

BUILDING MATERIALS - PRICES - GUATEMALA - GUATEMALA.
Revisión del índice del costo de la construcción de vivienda en la Ciudad de Guatemala, años 1975-1979. Guatemala , 1979. 35 p. : LC Card 82-182718
HD9715.G983 G827 1979

BUILDING MATERIALS - SPECIFICATIONS. see **BUILDING - CONTRACTS AND SPECIFICATIONS.**

BUILDING MATERIALS - UNITED STATES - CATALOGS.
H.W. Johns Manufacturing Co. Trade price list . New York , c1898. 15 p. ; LC Card 86-223003
HD9715.8.U52 H14 1898

BUILDING PERMITS - ARGENTINA - STATISTICS.
Edificación, 1972-1984. Buenos Aires , 1986. 36 p. : LC Card 87-404780 DDC 338.4/7624/0982021 19
HD9715.A72 E35 1986

BUILDING REPAIR. see **BUILDINGS - REPAIR AND RECONSTRUCTION.**

Building Service Contractors Association International. Bidding & estimating in the building service industry. Fairfax, VA , c1983. v, 10 p. : LC Card 87-110623 DDC 648/.068/1 19
HD9999.B882 B53 1983

BUILDING SITES - PLANNING.
Stover, Vergil G., 1933- Transportation and land development /. Englewood Cliffs, N.J. , c1988. xiii, 239 p. : ISBN 0-13-930413-4 : LC Card 87-11419 DDC 625.7/25 19
HE335 .S76 1988

BUILDING SOCIETIES. see **BUILDING AND LOAN ASSOCIATIONS.**

BUILDING - SPECIFICATIONS. see **BUILDING - CONTRACTS AND SPECIFICATIONS.**

Building the new economy . Corporation for Enterprise Development. Washington, D.C. , 1986. iv, 178 p. ; ISBN 0-9605804-2-5 (pbk.) LC Card 86-61273 DDC 338.973 19
HC110.I53 C67 1986

BUILDING TRADES - ACCOUNTING. see **CONSTRUCTION INDUSTRY - ACCOUNTING.**

BUILDING TRADES - CALIFORNIA - SAN FRANCISCO - HISTORY.
Kazin, Michael, 1948- Barons of labor . Urbana , c1987. xiv, 319 p., [14] p. of plates : ISBN 0-252-01345-X (alk. paper) LC Card 86-6967 DDC 331.88/124/0979461 19
HD6515.B9 S45 1987 ***NYPL [JLE 87-1053]***

BUILDING TRADES COUNCIL (SAN FRANCISCO, CALIF.) - HISTORY.
Kazin, Michael, 1948- Barons of labor . Urbana , c1987. xiv, 319 p., [14] p. of plates : ISBN 0-252-01345-X (alk. paper) LC Card 86-6967 DDC 331.88/124/0979461 19
HD6515.B9 S45 1987 ***NYPL [JLE 87-1053]***

BUILDING TRADES - GERMANY - NUREMBERG - HISTORY.
Gömmel, Rainer. Vorindustrielle Bauwirtschaft in der Reichsstadt Nürnberg und ihrem Umland (16.-18. Jh.) /. [Stuttgart] , 1985. xii, 300 p. : ISBN 3-515-04481-7 LC Card 86-122013
HD9715.G33 N874 1985

BUILDING TRADES - SOCIAL ASPECTS - UNITED STATES.
Silver, Marc L., 1950- Under construction . Albany , c1986. xi, 251 p. ; ISBN 0-88706-308-X LC Card 85-30447 DDC 331.7/624/0973 19
HD6956.B92 U67 1986
NYPL [JLE 86-4616]

BUILDINGS - CLEANING - CONTRACTS AND SPECIFICATIONS.
Bidding & estimating in the building service industry. Fairfax, VA , c1983. v, 10 p. : LC Card 87-110623 DDC 648/.068/1 19
HD9999.B882 B53 1983

BUILDINGS - CLEANING - ESTIMATES.
Bidding & estimating in the building service industry. Fairfax, VA , c1983. v, 10 p. : LC Card 87-110623 DDC 648/.068/1 19
HD9999.B882 B53 1983

BUILDINGS, COMMERCIAL. see **OFFICE BUILDINGS.**

BUILDINGS, DEMOUNTABLE. see **BUILDINGS, PREFABRICATED.**

BUILDINGS, INDUSTRIAL. see **INDUSTRIAL BUILDINGS.**

BUILDINGS - ITALY - CONSERVATION AND RESTORATION - ADDRESSES, ESSAYS, LECTURES.
Riuso e riqualificazione edilizia negli anni '80 /. Milano [1981] 706 p. :ill. ; ISBN 88-20-42135-6 (pbk.) : LC Card 81-210070
HD7341.A3 R58 1981 ***NYPL [JSD 86-493]***

BUILDINGS - ITALY - REMODELING FOR OTHER USE - ADDRESSES, ESSAYS, LECTURES.
Riuso e riqualificazione edilizia negli anni '80 /. Milano [1981] 706 p. :ill. ; ISBN 88-20-42135-6 (pbk.) : LC Card 81-210070
HD7341.A3 R58 1981 ***NYPL [JSD 86-493]***

BUILDINGS - ITALY, SOUTHERN - EARTHQUAKE EFFECTS.
Mezzogiorno . [S.l. , 1980?] (København : Kunstakademiets trykkeri) 78 p. : LC Card 85-128057
HC307.S6 M49 1980

BUILDINGS - MATERIALS. see **BUILDING MATERIALS.**

BUILDINGS, OFFICE. see **OFFICE BUILDINGS.**

BUILDINGS, PACKAGED. see **BUILDINGS, PREFABRICATED.**

BUILDINGS, PREFABRICATED - QUÉBEC (PROVINCE)
Duchaine, Paul. Bâtiments préfabriqués résidentiels et industriels à ossature de bois . [Québec] , c1985. 36 p. : ISBN 2-550-12116-3 LC Card 86-133426
HD9715.5.C23 Q43 1985

BUILDINGS, RECONSTRUCTION OF. see **BUILDINGS - REPAIR AND**

RECONSTRUCTION.

BUILDINGS - REMODELING FOR OTHER USE.
Small business incubators . Washington, D.C. , c1984. 32 p. : LC Card 86-233015 DDC 333.33/8 19
HD1393.25 .S63 1984

BUILDINGS - REMODELING FOR OTHER USE - ECONOMIC ASPECTS - ITALY.
La Riconversione produttiva nell'edilizia /. Milano , 1984, c1981. 319 p. :
NYPL [JLD 86-3381]

BUILDINGS - RENOVATION. see **BUILDINGS - REMODELING FOR OTHER USE.**

BUILDINGS - REPAIR AND RECONSTRUCTION.
United States. Congress. House. Committee on Banking, Currency and Housing. Subcommittee on Historic Preservation and Coinage. Preservation programs of the Federal government in the area of housing and community development /. Washington , 1976. vi, 86 p. ; LC Card 77-601749
HT175 .U583 1976 NYPL [JLE 78-1181]

BUILDINGS - REPAIR AND RECONSTRUCTION - ECONOMIC ASPECTS - ITALY.
La Riconversione produttiva nell'edilizia /. Milano , 1984, c1981. 319 p. :
NYPL [JLD 86-3381]

BUILDINGS - SPAIN - BARCELONA - STATISTICS.
Cens d'edificis, 1970 /. [Barcelona] [1979?] 5, 9 leaves ; LC Card 84-131679
HD7351.B3 C45 1979

BUILDINGS - SWEDEN - ENERGY CONSERVATION.
Energihushållning och samhällsekonomi . [Stockholm] [1980] 70, 39, 29, 58 p. : ISBN 91-38-05980-0 LC Card 84-122675
HD9502.S82 E48 1980

Built environment series.
Bruton, Michael J. Local planning in practice /. London , 1987. 452 p. : ISBN 0-09-165381-9
NYPL [JLE 87-1201]

Buiren, S. van. The quantitative and qualitative significance of the emergence of local initiatives for employment creation : programme for research and actions on the development of the labour market / by Shirley van Buiren. Luxembourg : Office for Official Publications of the European Communities ; Washington, D.C. : European Community Information Service [distributor], 1986. iii, 141, 14, [12] p. : ill. ; 29 cm. At head of title: Commission of the European Communities. Bibliography: p. [145]-[159]. ISBN 92-825-6048-1 (pbk.) : LC Card 86-222030 DDC 331.12/042/094 19
1. Manpower policy - European Economic Community countries. 2. Informal sector (Economics) - European Economic Community countries. 3. Producer cooperatives - European Economic Community countries. I. Commission of the European Communities. II. Title. III. Title: Programme for research and actions on the development of the labour market.
HD5764.5.A6 B85 1986

Buitendam, Arend. New technology as organizational innovation . Cambridge, Mass. , c1987. xvi, 308 p. : ISBN 0-88730-186-X LC Card 86-32110 DDC 658.5/14 19
HD45 .N43 1987

Bujdosó, Attila. Múlt, jelen, jövő a műszaki haladás szolgálatában . Pécs , 1985. 305 p. : LC Card 87-408539
HC300.29.B37 M86 1985

Buk, Halina. Analiza ekonomiczna przedsiębiorstw przemsłowych / Halina Buk, Magdalena Musioł, Joachim Strzoda. Wyd. 2., zmienione i rozsz. Katowice : Akademia Ekonomiczna im. Karola Adamieckiego w Katowicach, 1977. 285 p. ; 25 cm. Bibliography: p. 277-279. LC Card 82-102080
1. Industrial management. I. Musioł, Magdalena. II. Strzoda, Joachim. III. Title.
HD36 .B775 1977

Bukhval'd, E. M. Povyshenie proizvoditel'nosti truda--kliuchevaia zadacha sovetskoĭ ėkonomiki : nauchno-analiticheskiĭ obzor / [avtory obzora E.M. Bukhval'd, M.S. Toksanbaeva, T.IA. Chetvernina ; otvetstvennyĭ redaktor M.E. Tovmosian]. Moskva : Akademiia nauk SSSR, In-t nauch. informatsii po obshchestvennym naukam, 1984. 63 p. ; 20 cm. Bibliography: p. 60-63. LC Card 85-188977
1. Labor productivity - Soviet Union. 2. Soviet Union - Economic conditions - 1976-. I. Toksanbaeva, M. S. II. Chetvernina, T. IA. III. Tovmosian, M. E. IV. Institut nauchnoĭ informatsii po obshchestvennym naukam (Akademiia nauk SSSR). V. Title.
HC340.L3 B85 1984

Bukics, Rosie L. The handbook of credit and accounts receivable management / Rosie L. Bukics and Walter T. Loven. Chicago, Ill. : Probus, c1987. xi, 252 p. : ill. ; 24 cm. Bibliography: p. 243. Includes index. ISBN 0-917253-67-1 : LC Card 87-7008 DDC 658.8/8 19
1. Credit management. 2. Accounts receivable - Management. I. Loven, Walter T. II. Title.
HG3751 .B85 1987

Bukowska, Barbara. Wyższa Szkoła Handlowa, Szkoła Główna Handlowa, Miejska Szkoła Handlowa, 1906-1945 /. Warszawa , 1984. 180 p. : LC Card 85-241871
HB74.9.P7 W98 1984

Buku panduan badan-badan perusahaan perniagaan Negara Brunei Darussalam = Directory on business undertakings, Brunei Darussalam. Bandar Seri Begawan, Negara Brunei Darussalam : Unit Perancang Ekonomi, Kementerian Kewangan, [1985] vii, 89, [9] p. ; 30 cm. English and Malay. "Ogos 1985." LC Card 86-945171 DDC 338.7/4/0255955 19
1. Brunei - Commerce - Directories. 2. Business enterprises - Brunei - Directories. I. Brunei. Unit Perancang Ekonomi. II. Title: Directory of business undertakings, Brunei Darussalam.
HF3800.68 .B84 1985

BULGARIA - CENSUS, 1985 - CONGRESSES.
Nauchno-prakticheska konferentsiia "Prebroiavane na naselenieto i zhilishtniia fond--teoriia i praktika" (1986 : Slŭnchev briag, Bulgaria) Nauchno-prakticheska konferentsiia "Prebroiavane na naselenieto i zhilishtniia fond--teoriia i praktika," 9-11 oktomvri 1986 g., Slŭnchev briag /. Sofiia , 1986- v. <1 > : LC Card 87-156528
HA1621.5 1985

BULGARIA - ECONOMIC CONDITIONS.
Lampe, John R. The Bulgarian economy in the twentieth century /. London , c1986. x, 245 p. : ISBN 0-7099-1644-2 LC Card 86-673485
HC403 .L36x 1986b

BULGARIA - ECONOMIC CONDITIONS - 1944-
Manolov, Manol Dimitrov. Narodnaia Respublika Bolgariia--40 let po puti sotsialisticheskogo voskhoda /. [Bulgaria? , 1983?] [48] p. : LC Card 85-133679
HC403 .M36 1983

TSarevski, Nesho Vŭlev. The People's Republic of Bulgaria . Sofia , 1986. 102 p. ; LC Card 87-123346 DDC 337.1/4977 19
HC403 .T748 1986

BULGARIA - ECONOMIC CONDITIONS - 1944- - CONGRESSES.
Prinosŭt na dr. Todor Zhivkov za razvitieto na sotsialno-ikonomicheskata politika na BKP v etapa na izgrazhdane na razvitoto sotsialistichesko obshtestvo . Sofiia , 1983. 398 p. ; LC Card 84-103348
HC403 .P72 1983

BULGARIA - ECONOMIC CONDITIONS - 1944- - STATISTICS.
Modern Bulgaria in figures and facts . [Sofia] [1984?] 48 p. : LC Card 87-101850 DDC 314.97/7 19
HC403 .M63 1984

BULGARIA - ECONOMIC CONDITIONS - BIBLIOGRAPHY.
Krŭstiu Dobrev . Sofiia , 1987. 80 p., [16] p. of plates : LC Card 87-170598
HB108.3.D63 K78 1987

BULGARIA - ECONOMIC POLICY.
Lampe, John R. The Bulgarian economy in the twentieth century /. London , c1986. x, 245 p. : ISBN 0-7099-1644-2 LC Card 86-673485
HC403 .L36x 1986b

BULGARIA - ECONOMIC POLICY - 1944-
Aktualni ikonomicheski problemi . Sofiia , 1985. 227 p. ; LC Card 86-205815
HC403 .A67 1985

Deĭstvena organizatorska i ideĭno-vŭzpitatelna rabota za izpŭlnenie resheniiata na Fevruarskiia plenum na TSK na BKP /. Vratsa , 1985. 56 p. : LC Card 86-172762
HC403 .D45 1985

Georgiev, IAncho. Strategiia na kachestveni promeni /. Sofiia , 1986- v. <1-2 > ; LC Card 86-232319
HC403 .G465 1986

Georgiev, Slavcho. Ikonomicheski otnosheniia ikonomicheska politika . Sofiia , 1986. 114 p. ; LC Card 86-209756
HC403 .G47 1986

Ikonomika i upravlenie na kachestvoto. Svishtov , 1985. 201 p. : LC Card 86-155955
HC403.Z9 I5239 1985

Masovo-politicheskata i organizatorska rabota v usloviiata na noviia ikonomicheski mekhanizŭm. Plovdiv , 1981. 42 p. ; LC Card 82-153766
HC403 .M376 1981

Petkov, Todor (Todor Iliev) Stopanska samostoiatelnost i stopanska otgovornost /. Sofiia , 1985. 237 p. ; LC Card 85-134177
HD8626.5 .P48 1985

Sbornik ot lektsii po aktualni problemi na sotsialno-ikonomicheskata politika na partiiata. Sofiia , 1985. 203 p. ; LC Card 86-140158
HC403 .S27 1985

TSarevski, Nesho Vŭlev. The People's Republic of Bulgaria . Sofia , 1986. 102 p. ; LC Card 87-123346 DDC 337.1/4977 19
HC403 .T748 1986

Velichkov, Ivan. Partiĭno rŭkovodstvo na ikonomikata /. Sofiia , 1985. 40 p. ; LC Card 86-173901
HC403 .V45 1985

Vidinski, Lenin. Leninskite printsipi i uchastieto na trudeshtite se v upravlenieto /. Sofiia , 1982. 196 p. : LC Card 83-130010
HC403 .V495 1982

BULGARIA - ECONOMIC POLICY - 1944- - CONGRESSES.
Prinosŭt na dr. Todor Zhivkov za razvitieto na sotsialno-ikonomicheskata politika na BKP v etapa na izgrazhdane na razvitoto sotsialistichesko obshtestvo . Sofiia , 1983. 398 p. ; LC Card 84-103348
HC403 .P72 1983

BULGARIA - FOREIGN ECONOMIC RELATIONS - DEVELOPING COUNTRIES.
Kreditni otnosheniia na Narodna republika Bŭlgariia s razvivashtite se strani /. Sofiia , 1986. 78, [1] p. ; LC Card 86-152274
HF1578.15.D44 K74 1986

BULGARIA - FOREIGN ECONOMIC RELATIONS - SOVIET UNION.
Zhamin, V. A. (Vitaliĭ Alekseevich) Sotsialisticheskaia ėkonomicheskaia integratsiia--faktor povysheniia ėffektivnosti proizvodstva stran SĖV /. Moskva , Varna , 1978. 93 p. ; LC Card 81-149558
HC244 .Z46 1978

Bulgaria. Glavna direktsiia na statistikata.
Statistika na tsenite na stokite v tŭrgoviiata na edro i drebno. Statistika na tsenitie na stokitie v tŭrgoviiata na edro i drebno =. Sofiia , 1937. 117 p. ; LC Card 86-222130
HB235.B85 S7 1937

Bulgaria - Government. see **Bulgaria - Politics and government.**

BULGARIA - INDUSTRIES - AUDITING.
Problemi na stopanskata smetka /. Sofiia , 1981. 207 p. ; LC Card 82-133037
HC403.Z9 A865 1981

BULGARIA - INDUSTRIES - LOCATION - CONGRESSES.
Efektivnost ot teritorialnata organizatsiia na proizvodstvoto v usloviiata na noviia ikonomicheski mekhanizŭm . Tŭrgovishte , 1982. 215 p. ; LC Card 84-115638
HC403.Z9 D516 1982

Bulgaria. Komitet po truda i sotsialnoto delo.
Nauchno-prakticheska konferentsiia po podobriavane na kachestvoto na razrabotvaneto na chast "Bezopasnost, khigiena na truda i

pozharna bezopasnost" (BKhTPB) kŭm proektite za obektite po kapitalnoto stroitelstvo s proizvodstveno prednaznachenie (1984) Nauchno-prakticheska konferentsiia po podobriavane na kachestvoto na razrabotvaneto na chast "Bezopasnost, khigiena na truda i pozharna bezopasnost" (BKhTPB) kŭm proektite za obektite po kapitalnoto stroitelstvo s proizvodstveno prednaznachenie . [Bulgaria] [1984?] 56 p. ; LC Card 86-102624
HD7741.5 .N39 1984

BULGARIA - POLITICS AND GOVERNMENT - 1944-
Deĭstvena organizatorska i ideĭno-vŭzpitatelna rabota za izpŭlnenie resheniiata na Fevruarskiia plenum na TSK na BKP /. Vratsa , 1985. 56 p. : LC Card 86-172762
HC403 .D45 1985

BULGARIA - RELATIONS (GENERAL) WITH ROMANIA.
Bâldescu, Emil. Din istoria legăturilor revoluţionare româno-bulgare (1909-1916) [microform]. [Bucureşti, 1966] 181 p. LC Card 81-475045
HD8646 .B34 ***NYPL [*ZT-1732 no.1]***

BULGARIA - SOCIAL POLICY.
Radev, Simeon. Sotsialnata programa na partiiata-delo na trudoviia kolektiv /. Sofiia , 1984. 173 p. ; LC Card 84-172433
HD8626.5 .R32 1984

BULGARIA - STATISTICS.
Modern Bulgaria in figures and facts . [Sofia] [1984?] 48 p. : LC Card 87-101850 DDC 314.97/7 19
HC403 .M63 1984

Bulgaria. TSentralna komisiia po bezopasnostta na dvizhenieto. Osnovnye prichiny i usloviia vozniknoveniia PTP s tiazhelymi posledstviiami, puti i metody ikh ustraneniia. Bulgarian. Osnovni prichini i usloviia za vŭznikvane na PTP s tezhki posledstviia, pŭtishta i metodi za tiakhnoto otstraniavane /. Sofiia , 1985. 95 p. : LC Card 87-101607
HF5614.5.S62 O7516 1985

Bulgaria. Tsentralno statistichesko upravlenie. Nauchno-prakticheska konferentsiia "Prebroiavane na naselenieto i zhilishtniia fond--teoriia i praktika" (1986 : Slŭnchev briag, Bulgaria) Nauchno-prakticheska konferentsiia "Prebroiavane na naselenieto i zhilishtniia fond--teoriia i praktika," 9-11 oktomvri 1986 g., Slŭnchev briag /. Sofiia , 1986- v. <1 > : LC Card 87-156528
HA1621.5 1985

Bulgarian chemical industry /. Naĭdenov, Naĭden, Kh. (Naĭden Khristov) Sofia , 1985. 59 p. : LC Card 86-218952 DDC 338.7/66/00254977 19
HD9656.B82 N35 1985

Bulgarian chemical industry directory. Naĭdenov, Naĭden, Kh. (Naĭden Khristov) Bulgarian chemical industry /. Sofia , 1985. 59 p. : LC Card 86-218952 DDC 338.7/66/00254977 19
HD9656.B82 N35 1985

Bulgarian Cummunist Party. see **Bŭlgarska komunisticheska partiia.**

The Bulgarian economy in the twentieth century /. Lampe, John R. London , c1986. x, 245 p. : ISBN 0-7099-1644-2 LC Card 86-673485
HC403 .L36x 1986b

Bulgarian economy in the 20th century. Lampe, John R. The Bulgarian economy in the twentieth century /. London , c1986. x, 245 p. : ISBN 0-7099-1644-2 LC Card 86-673485
HC403 .L36x 1986b

Bulgaria's chemical industry /. Buchvarov, Stoyan. Sofia , 1986. 60 p., [16] p. of plates : LC Card 87-111684 DDC 338.4/766/0094977 19
HD9666.B92 B83 1986

Bulgarische Kommunistische Partei. see **Bŭlgarska komunisticheska partiia.**

Bŭlgarska asotsiatsiia za turizŭm i otdikh. Modern Bulgaria in figures and facts . [Sofia] [1984?] 48 p. : LC Card 87-101850 DDC 314.97/7 19
HC403 .M63 1984

Bŭlgarska komunisticheska partiia. Okrŭzhen komitet (Sliven) Ikonomicheskiiat podkhod i ikonomicheskoto vŭzpitanie na trudeshtite se. Sliven , 1984. 195 p. ; LC Card 86-102634
HB74.9.B9 I37 1984

Bŭlgarska komunisticheska partiia. Okrŭzhen komitet (Varnenski okrŭg) Nauchno-tekhnicheskiiat progress--delo na vsichki. Varna , 1985. 187 p. : LC Card 86-198872
HC403.Z9 T46 1985

Bŭlgarska komunisticheska partiia. Okrŭzhen komitet--Plovdiv. Masovo-politicheskata i organizatorska rabota v usloviiata na noviia ikonomicheski mekhanizŭm. Plovdiv , 1981. 42 p. ; LC Card 82-153766
HC403 .M376 1981

BŬLGARSKA KOMUNISTICHESKA PARTIIA - PARTY WORK.
Masovo-politicheskata i organizatorska rabota v usloviiata na noviia ikonomicheski mekhanizŭm. Plovdiv , 1981. 42 p. ; LC Card 82-153766
HC403 .M376 1981

Bŭlgarska komunisticheska partiia. Sofiĭski gradski komitet. Elitnite iadra v trudovite kolektivi . [Sofia] [1985] 105 p. ; LC Card 86-104039
HD66 .E42 1985

Bŭlgarskata khimiia. Buchvarov, Stoyan. Bulgaria's chemical industry /. Sofia , 1986. 60 p., [16] p. of plates : LC Card 87-111684 DDC 338.4/766/0094977 19
HD9666.B92 B83 1986

Bŭlgarski profesionalni sŭiuzi. Okrŭzhen sŭvet (Starozagorski okrŭg) Problemi na dŭrzhavnoto i obshtestvenoto osiguriavane na rabotnitsite i sluzhitelite. Stara Zagora , 1984. 17 p. ; LC Card 86-204115
HD7211.5 .P75 1984

Bulhões, Octávio Gouveia de. Desdobramentos inflacionários. [Salvador] : Fundação Bahiana para Estudos Econômicos e Sociais, [1984] 43 p. : ports. ; 22 cm. "Conferência do Prof. Octávio Gouveia de Bulhões, tendo como debatedores os economistas Victor Gradin e Carlos Brandão, no auditório do Desenbanco, em 3 de setembro de 1984." LC Card 86-861354 DDC 332.4/1/0981 19
1. Inflation (Finance) - Brazil. 2. Monetary policy - Brazil. I. Gradin, Victor. II. Brandão, Carlos. III. Fundação Bahiana para Estudos Econômicos e Sociais. IV. Title.
HG835 .B85 1984

Bull-Berg, Hans Jacob. American international oil policy : causal factors and effect / Hans Jacob Bull-Berg. New York : St. Martin's Press, 1987. xvi, 209 p. : ill. ; 23 cm. Bibliography: p. [191]-201. Includes index. ISBN 0-312-00465-6 : LC Card 86-31583 DDC 333.8/232/0973 19
1. Petroleum industry and trade - Government policy - United States. 2. United States - Economic policy - 1981-. 3. United States - Foreign economic relations. 4. United States - National security. I. Title.
HD9566 .B87 1987

Bull, Edvard, 1914- Arbeiderbevegelsens historie i Norge /. Oslo , 1985-<1987. v. <1, 5 > : ISBN 82-10-02750-6 : LC Card 87-116315
HD6752 .A74 1985

Bullard, Diane L. Texas public transit reference manual / by Diane L. Bullard and Lisa G. Nungesser. College Station, Tex. : Texas Transportation Institute, Texas A&M University System, [1985] xv, 279 p. : ill. ; 28 cm. (Technical report . 1082-1F) "Study 2-10-85-1082." "Sponsored by State Department of Highways and Public Transportation in cooperation with United States Department of Transportation, Urban Mass Transportation Administration." "October 1985." Includes bibliographies. LC Card 86-623065 DDC 388.4/09764 19
1. Local transit - Texas. I. Nungesser, Lisa G. II. Texas Transportation Institute. III. Series: Technical report (Texas Transportation Institute) , 1082-1F. IV. Title.
HE4426.T4 B84 1985

Bulletin (Agrágazdasági Kutató Intézet) .
(no. 61) Main directions of agricultural development in Hungary . Budapest , 1985. 77 p. ; LC Card 86-232881 DDC 338.1 s 338.1/09439 19
HD1407 .M3 no. 61 HD1940.5

Bulletin (Majlis al-Abḥāth al-Iqtiṣādīyah wa-al-Ijtimāʻīyah) .
(no. 108) Salih, Mohamed Abdel Aal. Flow of funds in the Sudan /. Khartoum, Sudan [1984] 38 leaves ; LC Card 84-980837 DDC 339.2/6/09624 19
HC835 .S25 1984

(no. 119) Gibriel, Mohamed Farah. Groundnuts production and marketing in Sudan /. Khartoum, Sudan , 1984. 24 leaves : LC Card 85-981430 DDC 338.1/73368/09624 19
HD9235.P32 S734 1984

(no. 123) Saghayroun, Atif A. Rahman. Determinants of family size in rural Sudan /. Khartoum, Sudan [1984] 36 leaves ; LC Card 87-119805 DDC 304.6/32/09624 19
HB1071.8.A3 S22 1984

Bulletin (Montana State University (Bozeman). Cooperative Extension Service) .
(1343) House, Verne W. Trends in the Montana economy and taxation /. Bozeman [1986] 19 p. : LC Card 87-620963 DDC 330.9786/033 19
HC107.M9 H68 1986

Bulletin (Nevada. Legislature. Legislative Counsel Bureau) .
(no. 87-23) Nevada. Legislature. Legislative Commission. Study of the fees and taxes which produce revenue for the construction and maintenance of the highways. [Carson City, Nev.] [1986] viii, 74 p. ; LC Card 86-623141 DDC 388.1/14/09793 19
HE356.N37 N42 1986

Bulletin of the Atomic Scientists. Assessing the nuclear age . Chicago, Ill. , c1986. xvii, 382 p. ; ISBN 0-941682-07-2 LC Card 85-82511 DDC 355/.0217 19
U264 .A79 1986 ***NYPL [JLE 87-11]***

Bulletin (Statens institut för byggnadsforskning (Sweden)) .
(M82:14) Swedish national and local government programs for conservation of energy in buildings /. Gävle, Sweden [1982] 187 p. : ISBN 91-540-9134-9 (pbk.) LC Card 82-208802 DDC 333.79 19
HD9502.S82 S98 1982 ***NYPL [JLG 86-107]***

Bulletin (Storrs Agricultural Experiment Station) .
(472) Hadden, Kenneth. Poverty in Connecticut, 1979 /. Storrs, CT [1986] 24 p. : LC Card 86-623148 DDC 362.5/09746 19
HC107.C8 H33 1986

(474 (Jan. 1987)) Groff, William H. Income variability in Connecticut, 1980 /. Storrs, CT [1987] 32 p. : LC Card 87-621355 DDC 339.2/2/09746 19
HC107.C83 I5138 1987

(474) Groff, William H. Income variability in Connecticut, 1980 /. Storrs, CT [1987] 32 p. : LC Card 87-621355 DDC 339.2/2/09746 19
HC107.C83 I5138 1987

Bulletin (United States. Bureau of Labor Statistics) .
(2246) Consumer expenditure survey . Washington, D.C. [1986] vi, 193 p. : LC Card 86-602456 DDC 339.4/1/0973 19
HC110.C6 C5647 1986

(2253) Employment projections for 1995 . Washington, D.C. , 1986. v, 131 p. : LC Card 86-602460 DDC 331.12/0723 19
HD5724 .E47 1986

(2255) Williams, Harry B. Industry wage survey . Washington, D.C. [1986] iv, 34 p. ; LC Card 86-602194 DDC 331.2/86553/0973021 19
HD4966.P52 U5556 1986

(2257) Injuries to warehouse workers. Washington, D.C. , 1986. v, 24 p. : LC Card 87-601109 DDC 363.1/19381 19
HD7269.F82 I56 1986

(2264) Occupational employment in mining, construction, finance, and services. Washington, D.C. [1986] vi, 141 p. ; LC Card 86-603149 DDC 331.12/51/000973021 19
HD9506.U62 O23 1986

(2270) Linking employment problems to economic status . Washington, D.C. [1986] vi, 56 p. ; LC Card 86-603148 DDC 331.13/7973 19
HD5724 .L425 1986

Bulletin (United States. Bureau of Mines) .
(692) An Appraisal of minerals availability for 34 commodities /. [Pittsburgh, Pa.] , 1987. iii, 300 p. : LC Card 87-600244 DDC 333.8/5 19
HD9506.A2 A72 1987

BULLION. see **PRECIOUS METALS.**

Bullock, Paul. Youth training and employment from New Deal to New Federalism / Paul Bullock. Los Angeles : Institute of Industrial Relations, University of California, c1985. xiii, 359 p. ; 22 cm. (Monograph and research series / Institute of Industrial Relations, University of California, Los Angeles . 43) On spine: Youth employment. Includes bibliographical references. ISBN 0-89215-131-1
1. Youth - Employment - United States. 2. Manpower policy - United States. 3. Minority youth - Employment - United States. I. Title. II. Title: Youth employment. III. Series: Monograph and research series (University of California, Los Angeles. Institute of Industrial Relations) , 43. ***NYPL [JLD 86-2972]***

BULLS AND BEARS. see **STOCK-EXCHANGE.**

Bullseyes and blunders . Hartley, Robert F. New York , c1987. vii, 253 p. : ISBN 0-471-84904-9 LC Card 86-23350 DDC 658 19
HD38 .H3487 1987 ***NYPL [JLE 87-1047]***

Bulmer, Simon. The Federal Republic of Germany and The European community / Simon Bulmer, William Paterson. London ; Boston : Allen & Unwin, 1987. p. cm. Bibliography: p. Includes index. ISBN 0-04-382045-X (alk. paper) LC Card 86-25909 DDC 341.24/22 19
1. European Economic Community - Germany, West. I. Paterson, William. II. Title.
HC241.25.G3 B86 1987

Bulmer-Thomas, V. The political economy of Central America since 1920 / Victor Bulmer-Thomas. Cambridge ; New York : Cambridge University Press, 1987. xxiii, 416 p. : map ; 23 cm. (Cambridge Latin American studies. 63) Bibliography: p. 387-401. Includes indexes. ISBN 0-521-34284-8 LC Card 87-11779 DDC 338.9728 19
1. Central America - Economic policy. I. Title.
HC141 .B78 1987

Bulog. see **Indonesia. Badan Urusan Logistik.**

Bülow, Margret. Akademikertätigkeit im Wandel . Frankfurt [am Main] , New York , c1984. 237 p. ; ISBN 3-593-33321-X LC Card 84-176630
HD6278.G4 A36 1984

Bulsara, Jal F. (Jal Feerose), 1899- Perspectives on social welfare in India / by Jal F. Bulsara ; ed. R.M. Varma. New Delhi : S. Chand, 1984. xvi, 226 p. ; 23 cm. Includes bibliographical references and index. LC Card 84-900869 DDC 361/.954 19
1. Social service - India. 2. Public welfare - India. I. Varma, R. M. II. Title.
HV40 .B886 1984 ***NYPL [JLD 86-4376]***

Bulusu, L. Marmot, M. G. Immigrant mortality in England and Wales, 1970-78 . London , 1984. xii, 144 p. : ISBN 0-11-691094-1 (pbk.) : LC Card 84-222968 DDC 614.4/242 19
HB1415 .M37 1984 ***NYPL [JLG 87-55]***

BUMIPUTRA MALAYSIA FINANCE.
Lim, Kit Siang. BMF, scandal of scandals /. Petaling Jaya [1986] ix, 68 p. : LC Card 86-943248 DDC 364.1/68/09595 19
HG3300.6.A6 L553 1986

Bund Deutscher Philatelisten. Arbeitsgemeinschaft Baden. Die Abstempelungen des Grossherzogtums Baden ab 1851 . [Soest] , c1980. 393 p. : LC Card 86-152444
HE6185.G32 B333 1980

Bund Schweizerischer Werbeagenturen. Werbung in einem mehrsprachigen Land /. Freiburg, Schweiz , c1986. 152 p. : ISBN 3-7278-0382-7 LC Card 87-409238 DDC 659.1/09494 19
HF5808.S9 W47 1986

Bunder, Dennis S. Owen, Robert R. (Robert Randolph) Arthur Young guide to financing for growth . New York , c1986. xiv, 298 p. ; ISBN 0-471-81946-8 : LC Card 86-1612 DDC 658.1/522 19
HG4027.7 .O94 1986 ***NYPL [JLE 86-2667]***

BUNDES-ZENTRALGENOSSENSCHAFT STRASSENVERKEHR (GERMANY)
Berger, Axel. Mitgliederförderung in Strassenverkehrsgenossenschaften /. Münster , 1985. 455 p. ; ISBN 3-7923-0537-2 (Deut. Bibl.) LC Card 86-148185
HD6698.T72 B863 1985

Bundesanstalt für Arbeit. Institut für Arbeitsmarkt- und Berufsforschung. see **Institut für Arbeitsmarkt- und Berufsforschung.**

Bundesanstalt für Arbeitsschutz und Unfallforschung. Dienststellenverzeichnis Arbeitsschutz . Dortmund , Bremerhaven , 1983. 217 p. ; ISBN 3-88314-274-3 LC Card 83-196051
HD7708 .D55 1983

Bundesanstalt für Geowissenschaften und Rohstoffe. Wagner, Hermann, Dr. Italien /. Hannover , Stuttgart , 1982. xv, 190 p., 4 folded leaves of plates : LC Card 83-235644
HD9506.I82 W34 1982

Bundesanstalt für Arbeit (Germany) Struktur und Arbeitsweise von Arbeitsverwaltungen in EG-Ländern Frankreich, Belgien, Italien . Nürnberg , 1982. 206 p. : LC Card 83-174401
HD8431 .S77 1982

BUNDESANSTALT FÜR ARBEIT (GERMANY)
Evaluation der Berufsberatung der Bundesanstalt für Arbeit . Nürnberg , 1983. vii, 282 p. : LC Card 85-107586
HF5382.5.G3 E9 1983

Bundesanstalt für Strassenwesen (Germany) Strassenverkehrszählung 1978 in der Bundesrepublik Deutschland . Köln , 1979. 96 p. : LC Card 87-408379 DDC 388/.0943 s 388.3/0943 19
HE5601 .S89 Heft 13 HE5669.A6

Bundesanstalt für Strassenwesen (Germany). Bereich Unfallforschung.
Haas, Ingrid. Funktion und Wirkung von Aufklebern an Personenkraftwagen /. Köln [1983] 101, [13] p. : LC Card 84-147451
HE5614.5.G3 H28 1983

Methoden und Kriterien zur Überprüfung des Erfolgs von Aufklärungskampagnen . Köln , 1982. 99, [93] p. : LC Card 83-178796
HE5614.5.G3 M37 1982

Rüter, Gert. Sicherheitsorientierte Ausbildung von Berufskraftfahren /. Köln [1983] vii, 91 p. : LC Card 83-235527
HD5716.M7952 G327 1983

Bundesforschungsanstalt für Landeskunde und Raumordnung. Städte in Zahlen . Hamburg , 1985. 199 p. : ISBN 3-922421-11-3 LC Card 86-212560
HB2265 .S73 1985

Bundesforschungsanstalt für Forst- und Holzwirtschaft (Germany) Agroforstliche Landnutzung im Einzugsbereich zentraler Orte im Sahel . Köln , 1983. ix, 374 p. : ISBN 3-8039-0276-2 LC Card 87-102956 DDC 333.73/13/09663 19
HD1019.Z63 A38 1983

Bundeshaushalt, Währung und Kriegswirtschaft . Tanner, Jakob. Zürich , c1986. 438 p. : ISBN 3-85791-100-X : LC Card 86-199729
HJ1258 .T35 1986

Bundesinstitut für Bevölkerungsforschung (Germany) Schweitzer, Walter. Heiratstafeln versus Familienstandstafeln . Wiesbaden , 1985. iii, 102 p. : LC Card 87-408703 DDC 306.8/1/0943021 19
HB1215 .S39 1985

Bundesinstitut zur Bevölkerungswissenschaft (Germany) Deutsch-Französisches Arbeitstreffen auf dem Gebiet der Demographie (1985 : Dijon, France) Referate zum Deutsch-Französischen Arbeitstreffen auf dem Gebiet der Demographie vom 30. September bis 3. Oktober 1985 in Dijon. Wiesbaden , 1986. 134 p. : LC Card 87-409287 DDC 304.6/0943 19
HB3595 .D45 1985

Die Bundesrepublik Deutschland und die Entwicklungspolitik der Europäischen Gemeinschaft, 1957-1983 / Volker Alberts ... [et al.]. Münster : Lit, [1986] 111 p. ; 21 cm. (Studien zur Politikwissenschaft. Bd. 9) Includes bibliographical references. ISBN 3-88660-214-1 LC Card 86-213020
1. European Economic Community - Germany, West. 2. European Economic Community countries - Foreign economic relations - Developing countries. 3. Developing countries - Foreign economic relations - European Economic Community countries. I. Alberts, Volker. II. Series: Studien zur Politikwissenschaft (Münster in Westfalen, Germany) , Bd. 9.
HC241.25.G3 B87 1986

Bundesstelle für Aussenhandelsinformation (Germany) Guinea (Revolutionäre Volksrepublik Guinea) . Köln , 1983. viii, 89 p. : LC Card 85-104313
HC1030 .G83 1983

BUNDESVERBAND DER DEUTSCHEN INDUSTRIE.
Platzer, Hans-Wolfgang. Unternehmensverbände in der EG, ihre nationale und transnationale Organisation und Politik . Kehl am Rhein , 1984. xi, 283 p. ; ISBN 3-88357-024-9 LC Card 85-131940
HD6948.G3 P58 1984

Bundesverband des Deutschen Gross- und Aussenhandels. Vorschläge und Beiträge des Bundesverbandes des Deutschen Gross- und Aussenhandels e.V. für die X. Legislaturperiode des Deutschen Bundestages. Bonn : Der Bundesverband, [1983] 56 p. ; 25 cm. LC Card 83-243234
1. Germany, West - Commercial policy. 2. Germany, West - Economic policy - 1974-. 3. Wholesale trade - Government policy - Germany (West). 4. Transportation and state - Germany, West. I. Title.
HF1545 .B83 1983

BUNDESVEREINIGUNG DER DEUTSCHEN ARBEITGEBERVERBÄNDE.
Platzer, Hans-Wolfgang. Unternehmensverbände in der EG, ihre nationale und transnationale Organisation und Politik . Kehl am Rhein , 1984. xi, 283 p. ; ISBN 3-88357-024-9 LC Card 85-131940
HD6948.G3 P58 1984

Bundesversicherungsanstalt für Angestellte. (Old Cat. form: Germany (Federal Republic, 1949-). Bundesversicherungsanstalt für Angestellte.) Die Versichertenältesten . [Berlin] [1984] 54 p. ; LC Card 85-113867
HD7116.M42 G4334 Nr. 20, 1984 HD7179

Bundesversicherungsanstalt für Angestellte. Dezernat für Presse- und Öffentlichkeitsarbeit. Germany (West) [Angestelltenversicherungsgesetz.] Angestelltenversicherungsgesetz mit Sozialgesetzbuch . Berlin [1986] 792 p. ; LC Card 86-229132
HD7116.M42 G4334 Nr. 18, 1986 KK3270.5

Bundy, Darcie. Total coverage : the complete insurance and security guide / Darcie Bundy and Stuart Day.1st ed. New York : Perennial Library, c1987. xiv, 224 p. ; 24 cm. Includes index. ISBN 0-06-055077-5 : LC Card 86-46050 DDC 368/.0029 19
1. Insurance. 2. Security systems. 3. Burglary protection. 4. Dwellings - Security measures. 5. Self-defense. I. Day, Stuart. II. Title.
HG8051 .B846 1987

Bungai, Mária.
Mezőgazdasági és élelmiszeripari adattár a felszabadulástól napjainkig /. Budapest , 1985. 152 p. ; ISBN 963-502-393-6 LC Card 86-202515
HD1940.5 .M497 1985

Mezőgazdasági és élelmiszeripari adattár a felszabadulástól napjainkig. English. Collection of data of agriculture and food industry from the liberation till now /. Budapest , 1985. 85 p. ; ISBN 963-502-393-6 LC Card 86-230345
HD1940.5 .M49713 1985

Bungard, Walter.
Qualitätszirkel als Instrument zeitgemässer Betriebsführung /. Landsberg/Lech , c1986. 328 p. : ISBN 3-478-32520-X LC Card 86-200304
HD66 .Q33 1986

Qualitätszirkel und Kleingruppenarbeit als praktische Organisationsentwicklung /. Frankfurt am Main , 1984. vii, 149 p. : ISBN 3-7824-0348-7 LC Card 85-131916
HD66 .Q332 1984

Bunich, Pavel Grigor′evich. Khoziaĭstvennyĭ mekhanizm i povyshenie effektivnosti proizvodstva /. Moskva , 1986. 252 p. ; LC Card 86-232347
HC340.I52 K49 1986

Bunker, Stephen G., 1944- Double dependency and constraints on class formation in Bugisu, Uganda / Stephen G. Bunker. Urbana, Ill. :

African Studies Program, University of Illinois at Urbana-Champaign, 1983. v, 88 p. : ill. ; 22 cm. (Occasional paper series / African Studies Program, University of Illinois at Urbana-Champaign . no. 2) Bibliography: p. 79-88. LC Card 86-229748 DDC 303.3/09676/1 19
1. Peasantry - Uganda - Bugisu (District) - Political activity. 2. Agriculture - Uganda - Bugisu (District) - Societies, etc. - Political activity. 3. Agriculture and state - Uganda - Bugisu (District). 4. Community power - Uganda - Bugisu (District). 5. Central-local government relations - Uganda. I. Series: Occasional papers series (University of Illinois at Urbana-Champaign. African Studies Program) , no. 2. II. Title.
HD1538.U43 B86 1983

Bunster, Ximena. Sellers & servants : working women in Lima, Peru / Ximena Bunster & Elsa M. Chaney ; photography by Ellan Young. New York : Praeger, 1985. x, 258 p. : ill. ; 24 cm. (Praeger special studies. Praeger scientific) Includes index. Bibliography: p. 235-246. ISBN 0-03-060543-1 (alk. paper) : LC Card 85-6259 DDC 331.4/0985/25 19
1. Women domestics - Peru - Lima. 2. Peddlers and peddling - Peru - Lima. 3. Women - Employment - Peru - Lima. 4. Poor - Peru - Lima. 5. Marginality, Social - Peru - Lima. I. Chaney, Elsa. II. Title. III. Title: Sellers and servants.
HD6072.2.P42 L563 1985 ***NYPL [JLE 86-910]***

Bunting, David G. The rise of large American corporations, 1889-1919 / David Bunting. New York : Garland, 1986, c1987. 224 p. ; 24 cm. (American business history) Bibliography: p. 120-132. ISBN 0-8240-8353-9 (alk. paper) : LC Card 86-29527 DDC 338.6/44 19
1. Big business - United States - History. 2. Corporations - United States - History. I. Title. II. Series.
HD2785 .B76 1987

Bunyan, John A.
Practical video. Bunyan, John A. Why video works : new applications for management / by John A. Bunyan. White Plains, NY , c1987. x, 203 p. : ISBN 0-86729-079-X : LC Card 86-21106 DDC 658/.0028 19
HD30.34 .B86 1987

Why video works : new applications for management / by John A. Bunyan. White Plains, NY : Knowledge Industry Publications, c1987. x, 203 p. : ill. ; 24 cm. Rev. ed. of: Practical video. c1978. Bibliography: p. 193-195. Includes index. ISBN 0-86729-079-X : LC Card 86-21106 DDC 658/.0028 19
1. Television in management. I. Bunyan, John A. Practical video. II. Title.
HD30.34 .B86 1987

Bunyard, Peter. The Green alternative . London , 1987. xv, 368 p. : ISBN 0-413-60280-X : LC Card 87-143624 DDC 333.7/2 19
HC260.E5 G736 1987

Bunzel, H. Arbejdsløshed og beskæftigelse . Aarhus [Copenhagen] [1983] 34 p. ; LC Card 84-125513
HD5701.6 .A73 1983

A Bur oak original.
Daniels, Leroy Judson, 1882- Tales of an old horsetrader . Iowa City , 1987. viii, 235 p. : ISBN 0-87745-173-7 LC Card 87-10932 DDC 338.1/761/00924 B 19
HD9434.U6 D36 1987

Bura, Fabian. Katalog specjalizowany znaków pocztowych ziem polskich 1985 /. Warszawa , 1984-1985. 4 v. : ISBN 83-03-00691-6 (cz. 1-2) : LC Card 87-120964
HE6185.P62 K28 1984

Buračas, A. (Antanas)
Metaeconomic conceptualization and social criteria of development / Antanas J. Buračas. Vilnius : Research Committee on Logic and Methodology, ISA : Lithuanian Academy of Sciences, Dept. of Social Sciences, 1987 [i.e. 1986] 60, [4] p. ; 21 cm. "VIIIth International Congress of Logic, Methodology & Philosophy of Science, 11th Section, Foundations of Social Sciences; preprint of paper to be presented at the congress, Moscow, 1987." "The preprint is published in strictly limited quantity (110 copies)"--P. [62]. Bibliography: p. 60-[61]. LC Card 87-672211
1. Economics - Methodology. I. International Congress of Logic, Methodology, and Philosophy of Science (8th : 1987 : Moscow, R.S.F.S.R.). II. Title.
HB131 .B87x 1986

Regional'noe modelirovanie obshchestvennogo vosproizvodstva . Vil'nius , 1980. 280 p. : LC Card 81-191307
HC337.L5 R44 1980

Burbano, Felipe. Foro políticas de fomento industrial en el Ecuador /. [Quito, Ecuador] [c1985] 58 p. : LC Card 86-134947 DDC 658/.009866 19
HD70.E25 F67 1985

Burberg, Paul-Helmuth. Zielgruppenorientierte kommunale Wirtschaftsförderung : Gutachten im Auftrage der Stadt Münster / Paul-Helmuth Burberg, Winfried Michels, Peter Sallandt. Münster : Selbstverlag des Instituts für Siedlungs- und Wohnungswesen und des Zentralinstituts für Raumplanung der Universität Münster, c1983. xi, 207, 16 p. : ill. ; 21 cm. (Beiträge zum Siedlungs- und Wohnungswesen und zur Raumplanung, 0723-0389 . Bd. 90) Bibliography: p. 201-206. ISBN 3-88497-042-9 LC Card 84-173863
1. Industrial promotion - Germany (West) - Münster in Westfalen. 2. Münster in Westfalen (Germany) - Economic conditions. 3. Münster in Westfalen (Germany) - Industries. I. Michels, Winfried. II. Sallandt, Peter. III. Münster in Westfalen (Germany). IV. Title. V. Series.
HC289.M9 B87 1983

Burch, David, 1942 Jan. 16- Overseas aid and the transfer of technology : the political economy of agricultural mechanisation in the Third World / David Burch. Aldershot, [Hants, England] ; Brookfield [Vt.], USA : Avebury, c1987. xiv, 370 p. ; 23 cm. Bibliography: p. 354-370. ISBN 0-566-00480-1 : LC Card 87-237 DDC 338.1/81 19
1. Agricultural assistance. 2. Agriculture - Developing countries - Technology transfer. 3. Farm mechanization - Developing countries. I. Title.
HD1431 .B87 1987

Burchards, Eckehard. Strukturen und Funktionen des informellen Sektors in Ghana : Analyse eines sozio-ökonomischen Phänomens unter besonderer Berücksichtigung der Situation in Nima/Mamobi, Accra / Eckehard Burchards. Hamburg : Institut für Afrika-Kunde im Verbund der Stiftung Deutsches Übersee-Institut, 1983. vii, 138 p. : ill. ; 21 cm. (Arbeiten aus dem Institut für Afrika-Kunde . 44) Includes questionnaire in English. Bibliography: p. 103-112. ISBN 3-923519-54-0 LC Card 83-214699 DDC 381 19
1. Informal sector (Economics) - Ghana - Accra. I. Title. II. Series.
HD2346.G42 A243 1983

Bureau de la statistique du Québec. Centre d'information et de documentation.
Destination des expéditions des manufacturiers exportateurs du Québec, 1976-1980 /. Québec, Québec [1983] ix, 249 p. : LC Card 85-115007
HF3229.Q4 D47 1983

Bureau de la statistique du Québec. Service des entreprises. Destination des expéditions des manufacturiers exportateurs du Québec, 1976-1980 /. Québec, Québec [1983] ix, 249 p. : LC Card 85-115007
HF3229.Q4 D47 1983

Bureau de zone UNICEF de Yaoundé. Eléments du rapport annuel de la zone de Yaoundé / Bureau de zone UNICEF de Yaoundé [et] UNICEF, N'Djaména. N'Djaména : UNICEF, [1984] [43] leaves : map ; 30 cm. Cover title. LC Card 86-980240
1. Chad - Economic conditions. 2. Chad - Social conditions. I. UNICEF. II. Title.
HC990 .B87 1984

Bureau International du Travail. see **International Labor Office.**

Bureau, Jean-Christophe. Politiques vivrières, dépendances alimentaires et développement /. [Paris] , c1984. iv, 129 p. : ISBN 2-86844-000-2 : LC Card 84-248912
HD9017.S152 P65 1984

Bureau of Business Practice. The BBP safety management handbook. Waterford, CT , c1986. 1 v. (various pagings) : ISBN 0-87622-050-2 LC Card 87-119198 DDC 658.3/82 19
HD7262 .B38 1986

Bureau of Economic Analysis staff paper .
(43) Carson, Carol S. The use of national income and product accounts for public policy . Washington, D.C. , 1986. 26 p. : LC Card 86-601338 DDC 339.5/0973 19
HC110.I5 C37 1986

BUREAUCRACY.
Laufer, Heinz, 1933- Bürokratisierte Demokratie? /. Zürich , c1983. 123 p. ; ISBN 3-7201-5157-3 LC Card 83-168788
HD38.4 .L38 1983

Littler, Craig R. The development of the labour process in capitalist societies . London , Exeter, N.H. , 1982. 226 p. : ISBN 0-435-82540-2 : LC Card 82-210245 DDC 306/.36 19
HD8390 .L48 1982 ***NYPL [JLD 87-1005]***

Matejko, Alexander. The self-defeating organization . New York , 1985. xxviii, 395 p. ; ISBN 0-03-005488-5 (alk. paper) : LC Card 85-9524 DDC 302.3/5 19
HD58.9 .M38 1985 ***NYPL [JLE 86-2757]***

Motta, Fernando C. Prestes. Burocracia e autogestão . São Paulo, Brasil , 1981. 170 p. ; LC Card 82-106136
HD2961 .M658 1981

A Renda da terra . [São Paulo, Brazil] , Petrópolis , c1980. 152 p. : LC Card 81-214665
HC186 .C36a no. 27 HB401

Román de Silgado, Manuel. Burocracia y cambio social /. [Lima] , 1975. 327 p. : LC Card 77-553812
JF1355 .R688 ***NYPL [JLC 77-327]***

BUREAUCRACY - BRAZIL.
Martins, Luciano, 1934- Estado capitalista e burocracia no Brasil pós-64 /. Rio de Janeiro, RJ , 1985. 265 p. ; LC Card 85-232969 DDC 338.981 19
HC187 .M2947 1985 ***NYPL [JLD 86-1691]***

BUREAUCRACY - CHINA.
Lieberthal, Kenneth. Bureaucratic politics and Chinese energy development /. [Washington, D.C.] [1986] xii, 405 p. ; LC Card 86-602422 DDC 333.79/0951 19
HD9502.C62 L54 1986

BUREAUCRACY - CONGRESSES.
Public expenditure . Dublin, Ireland , 1986. 138 p. ; ISBN 0-906980-56-9 (pbk.) : LC Card 86-143826 DDC 336.3/9 19
HJ7461 .P83 1986 ***NYPL [JLD 87-553]***

BUREAUCRACY - EUROPE.
Thürmer, Lothar. Bürokratie und Effizienz staatlichen Handelns . Berlin , c1984. 177 p. : ISBN 3-428-05543-8 LC Card 84-156948
HD38.4 .T47 1984

BUREAUCRACY - FRANCE - HISTORY.
Godfrey, John F. Capitalism at war . Leamington Spa, UK ; New York : xiv, 313 p. ; ISBN 0-85496-519-X : LC Card 86-32708 DDC 338.944 19
HD3616.F82 G63 1987

BUREAUCRACY - GERMANY, WEST.
Herrschaft, Krise, Überleben . Münster , 1986. 396 p. : ISBN 3-924550-19-0 LC Card 86-229590
HC286.7 .H48 1986

Laufer, Heinz, 1933- Bürokratisierte Demokratie? /. Zürich , c1983. 123 p. ; ISBN 3-7201-5157-3 LC Card 83-168788
HD38.4 .L38 1983

Schelsky, Helmut. Funktionäre . Stuttgart-Degerloch , c1982. 310 p. ; ISBN 3-512-00652-3 : LC Card 83-124834
HD6694 .S2566 1982

Wersebe, Hilmar von, 1943- Struktureller und funktionaler Pluralismus in der öffentlichen Verwaltung /. Frankfurt am Main , New York , c1986. 100 p. : ISBN 3-8204-9136-8 LC Card 86-229888
HD58.7 .W36 1986

BUREAUCRACY - INDIA - GORAKHPUR (DISTRICT)
Pai Panandiker, V. A., 1935- Development bureaucracy /. New Delhi , c1983. ix, 252 p. ; LC Card 83-902420 DDC 352.94/233/09542 19
HD2075.K359 P34 1983 ***NYPL [JLD 86-3762]***

BUREAUCRACY - INDIA - KARNAL (DISTRICT)
Pai Panandiker, V. A., 1935- Development bureaucracy /. New Delhi , c1983. ix, 252 p. ;

LC Card 83-902420 DDC 352.94/233/09542 19
HD2075.K359 P34 1983
NYPL [JLD 86-3762]

BUREAUCRACY - ITALY.
Intervento straordinario e amministrazione locale nel mezzogiorno /. Milano, Italy , c1985. 348 p. ; LC Card 86-144245
HC310.153 I58 1985

BUREAUCRACY - JAPAN.
Sano, Shin'ichi, 1947- Kanryō fuyu no jidai /. Tōkyō , 1985. 6, 255 p. ; ISBN 4-8334-1266-7 : LC Card 86-179753
HC462.9 .S2534 1985 <Orien Japan>
*NYPL [*OSM 87-1196]*

BUREAUCRACY - UNITED STATES.
Riley, Dennis D. Controlling the federal bureaucracy /. Philadelphia , 1987. xiv, 200 ; ISBN 0-87722-455-2 (alk. paper) : LC Card 86-14469 DDC 353.07/5 19
JK421 .R52 1987 *NYPL [JLD 87-1396]*

BUREAUCRACY - UNITED STATES - CASE STUDIES.
Egan, Gerard. Change agent skills in helping and human service settings /. Monterey, Calif. , c1985. xi, 306 p. : ISBN 0-534-03624-4 : LC Card 84-7804 DDC 361.3/07 19
HV11 .E43 1985 *NYPL [JLE 86-1963]*

Bureaucratic politics and Chinese energy development /. Lieberthal, Kenneth. [Washington, D.C.] [1986] xii, 405 p. ; LC Card 86-602422 DDC 333.79/0951 19
HD9502.C62 L54 1986

Burga Diaz, Manuel. see **Burga, Manuel.**

Burga, Manuel. La historia agraria / Manuel Burga Díaz, Manuel Glave Testino, Víctor Peralta Ruiz. Chiclayo, Perú : Centro de Estudios Sociales "solidaridad", 1986. 196 p. ; 22 cm. (Serie Avances de investigación . 1) Includes bibliographies and indexes. CONTENTS. - Rasgos fundamentales de la historia agraria peruana / Manuel Burga -- El agrarismo "suttoniano" y el conflicto de aguas de 1928-1930 en el departamento de Lambayeque / Manuel Glave Testino -- Guía bibliográfica para el estudio de la región lambayecana / Víctor Peralta Ruiz.
1. Agriculture - Economic aspects - Peru - History. 2. Land tenure - Peru - History. 3. Indians of South America - Peru - Land tenure - History. 4. Water-rights - Peru - Lambayeque (Dept.) - History. 5. Lambayeque (Peru : Dept.) - History - Bibliography. I. Glave Testino, Manuel. II. Peralta Ruiz, Víctor. III. Series: Serie Avances de investigación (Chiclayo, Peru) , 1. IV. Title. *NYPL [JLD 87-1524]*

Burgauer, James. The do-it-yourself investor / by James Burgauer. Chicago, Ill. : Probus Pub., c1987. xi, 335 p. : ill. ; 25 cm. Bibliography: p. 187-312. Includes index. ISBN 0-917253-68-X : LC Card 87-7006 DDC 332.6/78 19
1. Investments - Handbooks, manuals, etc. I. Title.
HG4527 .B689 1987

Burgdorff, Stephan, 1944- Wirtschaft im Untergrund /. Reinbek bei Hamburg , 1983. 188 p. : ISBN 3-499-33035-0 : LC Card 83-206566
HF5482.65.G3 W57 1983
NYPL [JLC 86-265]

Burgess, Mary Wickizer, 1938- Burgess, Michael, 1948- The state and province vital records guide /. San Bernardino, Calif. , 1988. p. cm. ISBN 0-89370-815-1 : LC Card 87-6312 DDC 929/.1/02573 19
HA38 .B87 1988

Burgess, Michael, 1948- The state and province vital records guide / Mike and Mary Burgess. San Bernardino, Calif. : Borgo Press, 1988. p. cm. (Borgo reference guides . no. 1) ISBN 0-89370-815-1 : LC Card 87-6312 DDC 929/.1/02573 19
1. Registers of births, etc. - United States - Directories. 2. Registers of births, etc. - Canada - Directories. 3. United States - Genealogy - Handbooks, manuals, etc. 4. Canada - Genealogy - Handbooks, manuals, etc. I. Burgess, Mary Wickizer, 1938-. II. Title. III. Series.
HA38 .B87 1988

Burgess, Paul L. An incentives approach to improving the unemployment compensation system / Paul L. Burgess and Jerry L. Kingston. Kalamazoo, Mich. : W.E. Upjohn Institute for Employment Research, 1987. xv, 273 p. : ill. ; 24 cm. (A National Chamber Foundation report) Bibliography: p. 261-273. ISBN 0-88099-048-1 (pbk.) LC Card 87-23128 DDC 368.4/4/00973 19
1. Insurance, Unemployment - United States. I. Kingston, Jerry L. II. W.E. Upjohn Institute for Employment Research. III. Title. IV. Series.
HD7096.U5 B87 1987

Burgess, Ross. Office automation using the IBM personal computer systems : including IBM compatibles / Ross Burgess and Joseph St. John Bate ; cartoons by Glenys Harley. London : Collins, 1986. 180 p. : ill. ; 25 cm. Includes index. ISBN 0-00-383104-3 (pbk.) : LC Card 86-220136 DDC 651.8/4165 19
1. Business - Data processing. 2. Office practice - Automation. 3. IBM Personal Computer - Programming. I. Bate, Joseph St. John. II. Title.
HF5548.2 .B783 1986

Burghagen Fachwörterbuch . Schramm, Herbert F. W. Hamburg , c1964. 160 p. ; LC Card 84-256680
HF5548 .S37 1964

Bürgin, Rolf, 1956- Countertrade : eine theoretische und empirische Analyse aus der Sicht einer kleinen offenen Volkswirtschaft (Schweiz) / Rolf Bürgin. Bern ; New York : P. Lang, c1986. x, 253 p. : ill. ; 21 cm. (Europäische Hochschulschriften. Reihe V, Volks- und Betriebswirtschaft . Bd. 715 = vol. 715 = vol. 715) Originally presented as the author's thesis (doctoral)--Universität Basel, 1986. Bibliography: p. 238-253. ISBN 3-261-03584-6 LC Card 86-195899
1. Countertrade - Switzerland. I. Series: Europäische Hochschulschriften. Reihe V, Volks- und Betriebswirtschaft , Bd. 715. II. Title.
HF1573 .B79 1986

BURGLARY PROTECTION.
Bundy, Darcie. Total coverage . New York , c1987. xiv, 224 p. ; ISBN 0-06-055077-5 : LC Card 86-46050 DDC 368/.0029 19
HG8051 .B846 1987

Burgmann, Verity. In our time : socialism and the rise of labor, 1885-1905 / Verity Burgmann. Sydney ; Boston : Allen & Unwin, 1985. xii, 236 p., [24] p. of plates : ill. ; 23 cm. Includes index. Bibliography: p. 213-226. ISBN 0-86861-529-3 LC Card 84-71572 DDC 335/.00994 19
1. Labor and laboring classes - Australia - History - 19th century. 2. Socialism - Australia - History - 19th century. I. Title.
HD8846 .B87 1985 *NYPL [JLD 86-2788]*

Burgos Flores, Sigfrido. Empresas del sector social de la economía / Sigfrido Burgos Flores. [1a ed.]. [S.l. : s.n.], 1986 ([S.l.] : Lithopress Industrial) 237 p. : ill. ; 22 cm. Cover subtitle: Desarrollo económico equilibrado. Bibliography: p. 236. LC Card 87-400831 DDC 334 19
1. Cooperation. I. Title.
HD2956 .B85 1986

Burgos, Rubén. Movimientos sociales en el noroeste de México /. México , 1985. 282 p. ; ISBN 968-590-072-8 LC Card 87-102068
HD1531.M6 M684 1985

Burguesía y capitalismo en Monterrey, 1850-1910 /. Cerutti, Mario. México, D.F. , 1983. 214 p. ; ISBN 968-8430-10-2 LC Card 86-221932
HC138.M6 C47 1983

BURIAL STATISTICS. see **MORTALITY.**

Burian, Klaus. Betriebliche Erfahrungen mit neuen Arbeitszeitformen : vergleichende Auswertung empirischer Untersuchung aus der Bundesrepublik Deutschland / Klaus Burian, Friedhart Hegner. Berlin : Wissenschaftszentrum Berlin, [1984] iv, 162 p. ; 30 cm. (Discussion papers / IIM, Labour Market Policy, 0722-673X . IIM/LMP 84-1) "Überarbeitete und aktualisierte Fassung des Beitrags zum Zwischenbericht für das vom BMFT geförderte Projekt 'Praktizierte flexible Arbeitszeitformen,' Berlin/München 1983 ..." "Februar 1984." Summary in English. Bibliography: p. 154-162. LC Card 84-182592
1. Job sharing - Germany (West). 2. Part-time employment - Germany, West. 3. Industrial sociology - Germany, West. I. Hegner, Friedhart. II. Series: Discussion papers (International Institute of Management. Labour Market Policy) , IIM/LMP 84-1. III. Title.
HD5110.2.G3 B87 1984

Buri͡atskai͡a A.S.S.R. (R.S.F.S.R.). Ministerstvo sel'skogo khozi͡aĭstva. Sistema vedenii͡a sel'skogo khozi͡aĭstva Buri͡atskoĭ ASSR . Novosibirsk , 1985. 188 p. : LC Card 86-215358
HD1995.B8 S57 1985

Buri͡atskiĭ nauchno-issledovatel'skiĭ institut sel'skogo khozi͡aĭstva. Sistema vedenii͡a sel'skogo khozi͡aĭstva Buri͡atskoĭ ASSR . Novosibirsk , 1985. 188 p. : LC Card 86-215358
HD1995.B8 S57 1985

Burie, J. B. Toekomstverkenning volkshuisvesting . Delft , 1985. 100 p. : ISBN 90-6275-193-8 : LC Card 86-157352
HD7288.78.N4 T64 1985

Burisch, Hans-Rainer. Städte in Zahlen . Hamburg , 1985. 199 p. : ISBN 3-922421-11-3 LC Card 86-212560
HB2265 .S73 1985

Burisch, Rainer. Nahwanderungen im Ruhrgebiet, 1976-1984 /. Essen , c1986. 61 p. : ISBN 3-923494-67-X LC Card 87-408772 DDC 330.943/55 19
HC288.R8 N34 1986

Burke, Gerald. The Future impact of technology on work and education /. London , New York , 1987. p. cm. ISBN 1-85000-083-2 : LC Card 87-13641 DDC 331.12/0994 19
HD6331.2.A8 F87 1987

Burke, Richard C. Decision making in complex times : the contribution of a social accounting information system / by Richard C. Burke ; prepared for the Accounting Principles and Practices Committee of the Society of Management Accountants of Canada. Hamilton, Ont. : Society of Management Accountants of Canada, 1984. xii, 185 p. : ill. ; 22 cm. Includes bibliographical references. ISBN 0-920212-27-1 (pbk.) LC Card 85-154342 DDC 658.4/08 19
1. Industry - Social aspects - Decision making. 2. Industry - Social aspects - Information services. 3. Social accounting - Decision making. 4. Social accounting - Information services. I. Society of Management Accountants of Canada. Accounting Principles and Practices Committee. II. Title.
HD60 .B86 1984 *NYPL [JLD 86-2720]*

Burke, Ronald S. Bittel, Lester R. Business in action . New York , c1988. vii, 597 p. : ISBN 0-07-005565-3 LC Card 87-3134 DDC 658 19
HF5343 .B57 1988

Burke, Terry, 1942- A roof over their heads : housing issues and families in Australia / Terry Burke, Linda Hancock, Peter Newton. Melbourne : Institute of Family Studies, 1984. xiv, 178 p. : ill. ; 22 cm. (Institute of Family Studies monograph . no. 4) Includes index. Bibliography: p. 165-174. ISBN 0-642-87172-8
1. Housing - Australia. 2. Family - Australia. I. Hancock, Linda. II. Newton, Peter W. III. Title. IV. Series. *NYPL [JLD 86-2639]*

Burke, W. Warner (Wyatt Warner), 1935- Organization development : a normative view / W. Warner Burke. Reading, Mass. : Addison-Wesley, c1987. xiv, 189 p. : ill. ; 21 cm. (The Addison-Wesley series on organization development) Bibliography: p. 178-189. ISBN 0-201-10697-3 : LC Card 86-26474 DDC 658.4/06 19
1. Organizational change. I. Title. II. Series.
HD58.8 .B878 1987

Burkhalter, Rudolf. Die Effizienz der Finanzierungshilfen an Klein- und Mittelbetriebe im Berggebiet / [vorgelegt von Rudolf Burkhalter]. Bern : [s.n., 1985] (Aarau : Cooperative Drucki) 216 p. : ill. ; 21 cm. "Diese Forschungsarbeit entstand im Rahmen des Forschungsprogrammes NFP "Regionalprobleme" des Schweizerischen Nationalfonds." Thesis (doctoral)--Universität Bern, 1984. Bibliography: p. 211-216. LC Card 86-115683
1. Small business - Switzerland - Finance. 2. Subsidies - Switzerland. I. Title.
HG4027.7 .B86 1985

Burki, Shaid Javed. Pakistan's development priorities . Karachi , 1984. 390 p. ; LC Card 85-930745 DDC 338.9549/1 19
HC440.5 .P3624 1984b

Burkina-Faso . Dijk, Meine Pieter van. Paris , c1986. 203 p. ; ISBN 2-85802-638-6 LC Card 86-221033
HD2346.B822 O933 1986

Burkina Faso.
Premier plan quinquennal de développement populaire, 1986-1990. [Burkina Faso : Ministère de la planification et du développement populaire?, 1986?] 2 v. : ill. ; 29 cm. CONTENTS. - v. 1. Rapport général de synthèse -- v.

2. Politiques sectorielles. LC Card 87-159604
1. Burkina Faso - Economic policy. 2. Burkina Faso - Social policy. 3. Burkina Faso - Politics and government. I. Title.
HC1040 .B87 1986

BURKINA FASO - ECONOMIC CONDITIONS.
Berg, Elliot. Mobilization of the private sector in Burkina Faso . [Burkina Faso? , 1985] 21 p. ; LC Card 87-116357 DDC 338.966/25 19
HC1040 .B47 1985

Lecaillon, Jacques. Economic policies and agricultural performance . Paris , 1985. 158 p. ; LC Card 86-216027 DDC 338.1/86625 19
HD2144 .L42 1985

BURKINA FASO - ECONOMIC CONDITIONS - CASE STUDIES.
Schneider-Barthold, Wolfgang. Industrie und Grundbedürfnisbefriedigung in Afrika . Frankfurt/Main , New York , c1984. 264 p. ; ISBN 3-593-33350-3 LC Card 86-125217
HC1040 .S35 1984

BURKINA FASO - ECONOMIC POLICY.
Burkina Faso. Premier plan quinquennal de développement populaire, 1986-1990. [Burkina Faso , 1986?] 2 v. : LC Card 87-159604
HC1040 .B87 1986

Conseil national de la révolution (Burkina Faso) Programme populaire de développement, octobre 1984 décembre 1985 /. [Ouagadougou, Burkina Faso] [1985?] 1 v. (various pagings) : LC Card 87-160992
HC1040 .C66 1985

Conseil national de la révolution (Burkina Faso) Programme populaire de développement, octobre 1984-décembre 1985 . [Ouagadougou] [1986] 2 v. : LC Card 87-158925
HC1040 .C66 1986

BURKINA FASO - INDUSTRIES - CASE STUDIES.
Schneider-Barthold, Wolfgang. Industrie und Grundbedürfnisbefriedigung in Afrika . Frankfurt/Main , New York , c1984. 264 p. ; ISBN 3-593-33350-3 LC Card 86-125217
HC1040 .S35 1984

Burkina Faso. Ministry of Plan. Berg, Elliot. Mobilization of the private sector in Burkina Faso . [Burkina Faso? , 1985] 21 p. ; LC Card 87-116357 DDC 338.966/25 19
HC1040 .B47 1985

BURKINA FASO - POLITICS AND GOVERNMENT.
Burkina Faso. Premier plan quinquennal de développement populaire, 1986-1990. [Burkina Faso , 1986?] 2 v. : LC Card 87-159604
HC1040 .B87 1986

BURKINA FASO - SOCIAL POLICY.
Burkina Faso. Premier plan quinquennal de développement populaire, 1986-1990. [Burkina Faso , 1986?] 2 v. : LC Card 87-159604
HC1040 .B87 1986

Bürkle, Roland. Das Modell der Ausgleichslösung : ein spieltheoretisch fundierter Ansatz zur Unterstützung von Unternehmungsentscheidungen bei mehrfacher Zielsetzung / Roland Bürkle. München : Florentz, c1983. 210 p. : ill. ; 21 cm. (Hochschulschriften zur Betriebswirtschaftslehre . Bd. 22) Bibliography: p. 171-210. Includes index. ISBN 3-88259-255-9 LC Card 83-222868
1. Industrial management - Decision making - Mathematical models. 2. Game theory. I. Title. II. Series.
HD30.23 .B865 1983

Burlaku, I. N. Sindikatele Moldoveĭ sovetiche yn konstruktsiia sochialistė / I.N. Burlaku ; sub redaktsiia luĭ A.V. Repida. Kishinėu : "Shtiintsa", 1980. 148 p. ; 22 cm. Title on spine: Sindikatele Moldoveĭ Sovetiche. Title from colophon: Profsoiuzy sovetskoĭ Moldavii v sotsialisticheskom stroitel'stve. At head of title: Ministerul Ynvėtsėmyntuluĭ Superior shi Mediu de Spechialitate al RSS Moldovenesht', Universitatiia de Stat "V.I. Lenin" din Kishinėu. Summary in Russian. Includes bibliographical references. LC Card 81-135331
1. Trade-unions - Moldavian S.S.R. - History. 2. Trade-unions - Bessarabia (Moldavian S.S.R. and Ukraine) - History. I. Repida, A. V. (Afanasiĭ Vasil'evich). II. Universitatiia de Stat "V.I. Lenin.". III. Title. IV. Title: Sindikatele Moldoveĭ Sovetiche. V. Title: Profsoiuzy sovetskoĭ Moldavii v sotsialisticheskom stroitel'stve.
HD6735.M56 B87 1980

Burleson, Clyde W., 1934- Interstate commerce : regional styles of doing business / Clyde W. Burleson. New York : F. Watts, 1987. viii, 230 p. ; 24 cm. Includes index. ISBN 0-531-15519-6 LC Card 86-29019 DDC 381/.5/0973 19
1. Business etiquette - United States. 2. Regionalism - United States. 3. Interstate commerce. I. Title.
HF5387 .B856 1987

BURMA - ECONOMIC CONDITIONS - 1948-
Sell, Axel. Economic structure and development of Burma /. Bremen [1985] 39 p. ; LC Card 86-228833 DDC 338.9591 19
HC422 .S45 1985

BURMA - ECONOMIC POLICY.
Sell, Axel. Economic structure and development of Burma /. Bremen [1985] 39 p. ; LC Card 86-228833 DDC 338.9591 19
HC422 .S45 1985

Burma - Government. see **Burma - Politics and government.**

BURMA - POLITICS AND GOVERNMENT - 1948-
Sell, Axel. Economic structure and development of Burma /. Bremen [1985] 39 p. ; LC Card 86-228833 DDC 338.9591 19
HC422 .S45 1985

Burmistrov, V. N. (Vladimir Nikolaevich) Narodnaia DemokraticheskaiA Respublika Ĭemen : ėkonomika i torgovo-ėkonomicheskie otnosheniia / V.N. Burmistrov. Moskva : Izd-vo "Nauka," Glav. red. vostochnoĭ lit-ry, 1981. 173, [3] p. ; 20 cm. Bibliography: p. 172-[174] LC Card 82-107303
1. Yemen (People's Democratic Republic) - Economic conditions. 2. Yemen (People's Democratic Republic) - Economic policy. 3. Yemen (People's Democratic Republic) - Foreign economic relations. I. Title.
HC415.342 .B87 1981

Burn, Janice. Information analysis / Janice Burn and Mike O'Neil. London : Paradigm, 1987. x, 260 p. : ill. ; 23 cm. (Computer studies series) Includes index. ISBN 0-948825-50-2 (pbk.) : LC Card 87-166130 DDC 658.4/038 19
1. Management Information Services. 2. Business - Information services. 3. Information resources management. 4. Decision-making - Mathematical models. I. O'Neil, Mike. II. Title. III. Series.
HD30.35 .B87 1987

Burnel, Roger. Demographic situation in the Community . Brussels , 1986. ii, 40 p. : LC Card 87-135237 DDC 304.6/094 19
HB3582.5 .D46 1986

Burns, Alvin C. Readings and cases in marketing management /. Homewood, Ill. , 1987. xv, 443 p. : ISBN 0-256-03161-4 (pbk.) LC Card 86-82585 DDC 658.8 19
HF5415.13 .R362 1987

Burns, James MacGregor. State and local politics : government by the people / James MacGregor Burns, J.W. Peltason, Thomas E. Cronin.4th ed. Englewood Cliffs, N.J. : Prentice-Hall, c1984. xi, 266 p. : ill. ; 23 cm. Includes bibliographies and index. ISBN 0-13-843524-3 (pbk.) LC Card 83-21259 DDC 320.973 19
1. State governments. 2. Local government - United States. I. Peltason, J. W. (Jack Walter), 1923-. II. Cronin, Thomas E. III. Title.
JK2408 .B87 1984 ***NYPL [JLE 87-142]***

Burns, Patrick. Democracy at work / Patrick Burns and Mel Doyle. London : Pan Books, 1981. 164 p. : ill. ; 20 cm. (Pan trade union studies) Includes index. ISBN 0-330-26478-8 (pbk.) LC Card 86-673620
1. Management - Great Britain - Employee participation. 2. Trade-unions - Great Britain. I. Doyle, Mel. II. Title. III. Series.
HD6664 .B845x 1981

Burns, Paul, 1949- Small business in Europe /. Basingstoke, Hampshire , 1986. xx, 211 p. : ISBN 0-333-38405-9 : LC Card 86-673899
HD2346.E9 S62x 1986

Burns, Philp & Co.
Buckley, K. D. (Kenneth D.) South Pacific focus . Sydney , Boston , 1986. 126 p. : ISBN 0-04-909030-5 LC Card 86-71304 DDC 387.5/065/94 19
HE945.B87 B83 1986

BURNS, PHILP & CO. - HISTORY.
Buckley, K. D. (Kenneth D.) South Pacific focus . Sydney , Boston , 1986. 126 p. : ISBN 0-04-909030-5 LC Card 86-71304 DDC 387.5/065/94 19
HE945.B87 B83 1986

BURNS, PHILP & CO. - HISTORY - PICTORIAL WORKS.
Buckley, K. D. (Kenneth D.) South Pacific focus . Sydney , Boston , 1986. 126 p. : ISBN 0-04-909030-5 LC Card 86-71304 DDC 387.5/065/94 19
HE945.B87 B83 1986

Burns, R. W. British television : the formative years / R.W. Burns. London : P. Peregrinus in association with the Science Museum, c1986. xv, 488 p. : ill. ; 24 cm. (IEE history of technology series . 7) Includes bibliographies and index. ISBN 0-86341-079-0 LC Card 87-160684 DDC 384.55/0941 19
1. Television broadcasting - Great Britain - History. 2. Television - Great Britain - History. I. Science Museum (Great Britain). II. Series: History of technology series, 7. III. Title.
HE8700.9.G7 B87 1986

Burns, Robert, 1938- Master forms & contracts from your copier : entrepreneurs, small businesses & landlords / Robert Burns & Rees Johnson. Tucson, AZ : Knight-Ridder Press, c1987. 160 p. : forms ; 28 cm. ISBN 0-89586-513-0 (pbk.) : LC Card 86-82238 DDC 651/.29 19
1. Business - Forms. 2. Contracts - United States - Forms. I. Johnson, Rees C., 1938-. II. Title. III. Title: Master forms and contracts from your copier.
HF5371 .B845 1987

Burns, Thomas J., 1942- Effective communications and advertising for financial institutions / Thomas J. Burns. Englewood Cliffs, N.J. : Prentice-Hall, c1986. xvi, 299 p. : ill. ; 25 cm. "A Reston book." Bibliography: p. Includes bibliographies and index. ISBN 0-8359-1556-5 LC Card 85-25641 DDC 659.1/93321 19
1. Bank marketing. 2. Public relations - Banks and banking. I. Title.
HG1616.M3 B87 1986 ***NYPL [JLE 86-1689]***

Burns, Tom R. Man, decisions, society : the theory of actor-system dynamics for social scientists / Tom R. Burns, Thomas Baumgartner, Philippe DeVille. New York : Gordon and Breach Science Publishers, c1985. xiv, 342 p. : ill. ; 24 cm. (Studies in cybernetics, 0275-5807 . v. 10) Includes bibliographies. ISBN 2-88124-004-6 (France) LC Card 84-10303 DDC 301 19
1. Social systems. 2. Social action. 3. Social sciences - Methodology. I. Baumgartner, Thomas (Thomas Martin). II. DeVille, Philippe, 1920-. III. Title. IV. Series.
HM24 .B85 1985 ***NYPL [JLE 86-2963]***

Burocracia e autogestão . Motta, Fernando C. Prestes. São Paulo, Brasil , 1981. 170 p. ; LC Card 82-106136
HD2961 .M658 1981

Burocracia y cambio social /. Román de Silgado, Manuel. [Lima] , 1975. 327 p. : LC Card 77-553812
JF1355 .R688 ***NYPL [JLC 77-327]***

Burova, S. E. (Stella Efimovna) Kritika burzhuaznykh vzgliadov na ėkonomicheskoe sotrudnichestvo stran SĖV / S.E. Burova, A.M. Voinov, Ė.IA. Sheĭnin ; otvetstvennyĭ redaktor IU. S. Shiriaev. Moskva : "Nauka", 1986. 154 p. ; 20 cm. At head of title: Akademiia nauk SSSR. Institut ėkonomiki mirovoĭ sotsialisticheskoĭ sistemy. Includes bibliographical references. LC Card 86-232355
1. Council for Mutual Economic Assistance. 2. Communist countries - Economic integration. I. Voinov, A. M. (Arkadiĭ Mikhaĭlovich). II. Sheĭnin, Ė. IA. (Ėduard IAkovlevich). III. Shiriaev, IUriĭ Semenovich. IV. Title.
HC243.5 .B87 1986

Buroz Castillo, Eduardo. Programa de cooperación técnica Perú-Venezuela-OEA : informe gerencial. Caracas : República de Venezuela, Comisión del Plan Nacional de Aprovechamiento de los Recursos Hidráulicos, 1976. [11], 62 p. ; 28 cm. (Divulgativa . no 22) "Autores, Ing. Eduardo Buroz C., Ing. Maritza de Caldentey"--Prelim. p. [3] Bibliography: p. 51. LC

Card 84-136478
1. Water resources development - Peru. 2. Water resources development - Venezuela. 3. Technical assistance - Peru. 4. Technical assistance - Venezuela. I. Caldentey, Maritza de. II. Venezuela. Comisión del Plan Nacional de Aprovechamiento de los Recursos Hidráulicos. III. Series: Publicación divulgativa , no. 22. IV. Title.
HD1696.P5 B87 1976

Burpee, C. Gaye. 1985 household survey of Grenada : findings and documentation of procedures / C. Gaye Burpee and James N. Morgan with Alan Dragon. Ann Arbor, Mich. : Survey Research Center, Institute for Social Research, University of Michigan, 1986. 168 p. : ill. ; 23 cm. (Research report series / Institute for Social Research, University of Michigan) "For the government of Grenada as a part of its fiscal reform project, funded by USAID." ISBN 0-87944-317-0 (pbk.) LC Card 86-217405 DDC 339.4/1/0723 19
1. Cost and standard of living - Grenada. 2. Household surveys - Grenada. I. Morgan, James N. II. Dragon, Alan. III. Series: Research report series (University of Michigan. Institute for Social Research). IV. Title.
HD7009.9.Z8 G843 1986

Burrell, Alison. Agricultural policy in Jordan /. London ; Atlantic Highlands, NJ : 147 p. : ISBN 0-86372-070-6 LC Card 86-21480 DDC 338.1/85695 19
HD2059.Z8 A34 1986

Burrows, Geoff, 1941- The canecutters / Geoff Burrows and Clive Morton. Carlton, Vic. : Melbourne University Press, 1986. xvi, 288 p. : ill. ; 25 cm. Bibliography: p. 269-280. Includes index. ISBN 0-522-84304-2 LC Card 86-215188 DDC 331.7/6361/0994 19
1. Sugar workers - Australia - History. 2. Sugarcane industry - Australia - History. 3. Sugarcane - Australia - History. I. Morton, Clive, 1931-. II. Title.
HD8039.S86 A83 1986

Burson-Marsteller (Firm) Understanding first-time recreation vehicle buyers . Reston, VA (P.O. Box 2999, Prepared for Recreation Vehicle Industry Association, c1986. xxvi, 80 p. ; LC Card 87-108982 DDC 381/45629226/0973 19
HD9710.37.U62 U53 1986

Burst, Ardis. The management game / Ardis Burst and Leonard A. Schlesinger. New York, N.Y. : Viking, 1987. 274 p. : ill. ; 24 cm. ISBN 0-670-81225-0 LC Card 86-40617 DDC 658.4/0353 19
1. Management games. I. Schlesinger, Leonard A. II. Title.
HD30.26 .B87 1987

Burt Olney Canning Company.
The Burt Olney Canning Company (factories-Oneida, Albion, and Medina, N.Y.). [Oneida, N.Y. , 1911?] (Oneida, N.Y. : Ryan & Burkhart) [63] p. : LC Card 87-115754
HD9321.9.B85 B87 1911

BURT OLNEY CANNING COMPANY - ANNIVERSARIES, ETC.
The Burt Olney Canning Company (factories-Oneida, Albion, and Medina, N.Y.). [Oneida, N.Y. , 1911?] (Oneida, N.Y. : Ryan & Burkhart) [63] p. : LC Card 87-115754
HD9321.9.B85 B87 1911

The Burt Olney Canning Company (factories-Oneida, Albion, and Medina, N.Y.). [Oneida, N.Y. : The Company, 1911?] (Oneida, N.Y. : Ryan & Burkhart) [63] p. : ill., ports. ; 24 cm. Cover title: Twenty-five years manufacturing pure foods. Chiefly speeches made at the 25th anniversary banquet of the company, held Dec. 30, 1910, in Oneida, N.Y. Some of the ports. are mounted. LC Card 87-115754
1. Burt Olney Canning Company - Anniversaries, etc. 2. Canneries - New York - History. 3. Canned foods industry - United States - History. I. Burt Olney Canning Company. II. Title: Twenty-five years manufacturing pure foods.
HD9321.9.B85 B87 1911

Burt, Randall E. Adhesive revenue stamps of Hawaii : their history and use / by Randall E. Burt. Honolulu, Hawaii (P.O. Box 10115, Honolulu 96816-0115) : Hawaiian Philatelic Society, c1986. ix, 114 p. : ill. ; 28 cm. Bibliography: p. 111-114. LC Card 87-136622 DDC 769.5/7 19
1. Revenue-stamps - Hawaii - History. I. Title.
HJ5346.5 .B87 1986

Burtless, Gary T., 1950- Work, health, and income among the elderly /. Washington, D.C. , c1987. xiii, 276 p. : ISBN 0-8157-1176-X : LC Card 86-26892 DDC 331.3/98 19
HD6280 .W68 1987 ***NYPL [JLE 87-960]***

Burton, Cynthia E. Cohen-Rosenthal, Edward. Mutual gains . New York , 1987. xv, 287 p. : ISBN 0-275-92204-9 (alk. paper) : LC Card 86-25249 DDC 331/.01/12 19
HD6490.L33 C64 1987

Burton, Daniel F. The Jobs challenge . Cambridge, Mass. , 1986. xvi, 304 p. : ISBN 0-88410-990-9 LC Card 85-7547 DDC 331.12 19
HD5707 .J63 1985 ***NYPL [JLE 86-2190]***

Burton, G. Allan, 1915- A store of memories / G. Allan Burton. Toronto, Ont. : McClelland and Stewart, c1986. 330 p., [17] p. of plates : ill. ; 24 cm. Includes index. ISBN 0-7710-1792-8 : LC Card 87-101965 DDC 381/.45/000924 B 19
1. Burton, G. Allan, 1915-. 2. Businessmen - Canada - Biography. 3. Simpsons Limited - History. I. Title.
HF5465.C32 B87 1986

BURTON, G. ALLAN, 1915-
Burton, G. Allan, 1915- A store of memories /. Toronto, Ont. , c1986. 330 p., [17] p. of plates : ISBN 0-7710-1792-8 : LC Card 87-101965 DDC 381/.45/000924 B 19
HF5465.C32 B87 1986

Burton, John C. Handbook of accounting and auditing /. Boston , c1981. 1 v. (various pagings) ; ISBN 0-88712-221-3 (Update 1985) LC Card 80-53166 DDC 657/.02/02 19
HF5635.H22 ***NYPL [*R-Econ. 85-31]***

Burton, John F. Berkowitz, Monroe, 1919- Permanent disability benefits in workers' compensation /. Kalamazoo, Mich. , 1987. xviii, 459 p. ; ISBN 0-88099-051-1 LC Card 87-22874 DDC 368.4/1/00973 19
HD7105.25.U6 B47 1987

Burton, John W. (John Wear), 1915- Resolving deep-rooted conflict : a handbook / John W. Burton. Lanham, MD : University Press of America, c1987. vii, 74 p. ; 24 cm. Bibliography: p. 73. ISBN 0-8191-6284-1 (alk. paper) : LC Card 87-6144 DDC 658.4 19
1. Conflict management. 2. Problem solving. I. Title.
HD42 .B87 1987

Burton, Kevin R. Advanced applications for PFS and the IBM assistant series / Kevin R. Burton. 1st ed. Blue Ridge Summit, PA : TAB Books, c1985. x, 213 p. : ill. ; 24 cm. Includes index. ISBN 0-8306-0989-X : LC Card 85-9885 DDC 001.64/25 19
1. Computer software. 2. IBM Assistant Series (Computer programs). I. Title.
QA76.754 .B87 1985 ***NYPL [JSE 86-2148]***

Burton, Richard M. Innovation and entrepreneurship in organizations . Amsterdam ; New York : vii, 207 p. : ISBN 0-444-42716-3 (U. S.) : LC Card 86-24207 DDC 658.4/012 19
HD41 .I56 1986

Burundi.
Budgets extraordinaires et d'investissement : exercises, 1964 à 1966 / République du Burundi, Ministère des affaires économiques et financières. [Bujumbura] : Le Ministère, [1967] [19] leaves ; 34 cm. Cover title. LC Card 82-980377
1. Budget - Burundi. I. Burundi. Ministère des affaires économiques et financières. II. Title.
HJ2180.8 .B87 1967

BURUNDI - COMMERCE - CONGRESSES.
Enclavement et sous-développement au Burundi . Bujumbura, Burundi [1983] xi, 448 p. : LC Card 85-980729 DDC 338.967/572 19
HE283.8 .E53 1983

Burundi. Direction générale des publications de la presse burundaise. Les Cultures industrielles du Burundi . Bujumbura [1985] 63 p. : LC Card 85-981329
HD9195.B942 C85 1985

BURUNDI - ECONOMIC CONDITIONS.
Les Cultures industrielles du Burundi . Bujumbura [1985] 63 p. : LC Card 85-981329
HD9195.B942 C85 1985

BURUNDI - ECONOMIC POLICY.
Burundi. Ministère à la présidence chargé du plan. IVème plan quinquennal de développement économique et social du Burundi, 1983-1987 /. [Bujumbura] [1983?-] <v. 1, pt. 1; v. 2, 4, 7 > : LC Card 86-980056
HC880 .B88 1983

Enclavement et sous-développement au Burundi . Bujumbura, Burundi [1983] xi, 448 p. : LC Card 85-980729 DDC 338.967/572 19
HE283.8 .E53 1983

BURUNDI - INDUSTRIES, RURAL.
Etude sur la petite et moyenne industrie et l'artisanat /. [Bujumbara] [1984] 7 v. in 6 : LC Card 86-980948
HD2346.B94 E78 1984

Burundi. Ministère à la présidence chargé du plan. IVème plan quinquennal de développement économique et social du Burundi, 1983-1987 / République du Burundi, Ministère à la présidence chargé du plan. [Bujumbura] : Le Ministère, [1983?-] <v. 1, pt. 1; v. 2, 4, 7 > : ill. ; 34 cm. CONTENTS. - annexe 1, v. 1. Secteur production agricole -- annexe 2. Energie, mines, industrie, artisanat, commerce, banques, tourisme -- annexe 4. Routes et aérodromes, entretien routier -- annexe 7. Répartition des investissements par secteur et par projet. LC Card 86-980056
1. Burundi - Economic policy. 2. Burundi - Social policy. I. Title. II. Title: 4e plan quinquennal de développement économique et social du Burundi, 1983-1987. III. Title: Quatrième plan quinquennal de développement économique et social du Burundi, 1983-1987.
HC880 .B88 1983

Burundi. Ministère des affaires économiques et financières. Burundi. Budgets extraordinaires et d'investissement . [Bujumbura] [1967] [19] leaves ; LC Card 82-980377
HJ2180.8 .B87 1967

Burundi. Ministère des travaux publics, de l'équipement et du logement. Groupement Berger-BCEOM. Etude de factibilité routière, Bujumbura-Cibitoke . [[Bujumbura] [1977] 162 p. : LC Card 82-980356
HE367.B872 G76 1977a

BURUNDI - POPULATION, RURAL.
Coopératives et populations rurales . [Bujumbura] [1986] ix, 64 leaves : LC Card 86-981185
HD3561.A4 C66 1986

BURUNDI - SOCIAL POLICY.
Burundi. Ministère à la présidence chargé du plan. IVème plan quinquennal de développement économique et social du Burundi, 1983-1987 /. [Bujumbura] [1983?-] <v. 1, pt. 1; v. 2, 4, 7 > : LC Card 86-980056
HC880 .B88 1983

Burwell, Brian O. Ferguson, Gary D. Evaluation of the small cities community development block grant program--the role of the counties [microform] /. Cambridge, Mass. , 1981. vii, vi, 186 p. ; ***NYPL [*XME-11,283]***

Burzhuaznai͡a nauka upravlenii͡a i neupravli͡aemai͡a ėkonomika /. Ėpshteĭn, S. I. (Samuil Isaakovich) Moskva , 1986. 76 p. ; LC Card 86-201018 DDC 658/.00973 19
HD70.U5 E6 1986

Burzhuaznoe gosudarstvo i rynok truda . Dukhovnai͡a, L. T. (Lidii͡a Timofeevna) Kiev , 1985. 155, [3] p. ; LC Card 86-150676
HD5713 .D84 1985

Burzhuaznoe gosudarstvo i vneshneėkonomicheskie svi͡azi / otvetstvennyĭ redaktor M.M. Maksimova. Moskva : "Nauka", 1986. 350 p. : ill. ; 21 cm. At head of title: Akademii͡a nauk SSSR. Ordena Trudovogo Krasnogo Znameni Institut mirovoĭ ėkonomiki i mezhdunarodnykh otnosheniĭ. Includes bibliographical references. LC Card 86-211675
1. Commercial policy. 2. International business enterprises. 3. Foreign trade regulation. I. Maksimova, M. M. (Margarita Matveevna). II. Institut mirovoĭ ėkonomiki i mezhdunarodnykh otnosheniĭ (Akademii͡a nauk SSSR).
HF1411 .B79 1986

Burzhuaznye kont͡sept͡sii narodonaselenii͡a . Korostelev, Gennadiĭ Mikhaĭlovich. Moskva , 1981. 158 p. ; LC Card 82-140945
HB851 .K65 1981

Buržoazní sociálně politické teorie úlohy vědeckotechnického rozvoje /. Formánek,

Miloslav. Praha , 1980. 350 p. ;
*NYPL [*QT 87-1720]*

Bus and coach operation /. Faulks, Rex William. London , Boston , 1987. xi, 259 p. : ISBN 0-408-02810-6 : LC Card 87-10966 DDC 388.3/22/068 19
HE5613 .F38 1987

BUS DRIVERS - DENMARK - DISEASES.
Buschaufførers arbejdsmiljø . København , c1982. 188 p. in various pagings : ISBN 87-7359-039-8 LC Card 83-111384
HD7269.M82 D44 1982

BUS INDUSTRY - GREAT BRITAIN - HISTORY.
Oxley, Alan. Barton /. Glossop, Derbyshire , c1983- v. <1 > : ISBN 0-903839-64-4 (v. 1) LC Card 86-219518 DDC 388.3/22/09425 19
HE5663.Z7 B376 1983

BUS LANES - TRINIDAD.
Joefield-Napier, Wallace. Financial integration and interest rate linkages between North Atlantic and Caribbean economies, January 1968 to December 1976 /. St. Augustine, Trinidad [1980] vii, 82 p. : LC Card 81-132125 DDC 332.8/2/0724 19
HG1623.C27 J64 1980 NYPL [Sc E 86-329]

BUS LINES.
Faulks, Rex William. Bus and coach operation /. London , Boston , 1987. xi, 259 p. : ISBN 0-408-02810-6 : LC Card 87-10966 DDC 388.3/22/068 19
HE5613 .F38 1987

BUS LINES - BRAZIL - EVALUATION.
Daibert, José Ricardo Motta. Avaliação do desempenho de transporte coletivo por ônibus /. Brasília, DF , 1985. 73 p. : LC Card 87-113224 DDC 388.4/1322/0981 19
HE5653.A6 D35 1985

BUS LINES - BRAZIL - MANAGEMENT.
Antônio, Ricardo Augusto Braga. Análise de sistemas de controle operacional de ônibus urbano /. Brasília, DF , 1985. 92 p. : LC Card 87-113222 DDC 388.4/1322/068 19
HE5613 .A775 1985

BUS LINES - BRAZIL - PLANNING.
Soares, Nilton de Brito. Determinação de itinerários de um sistema de transporte coletivo através de ônibus . Brasília, DF , 1985. 98 p. : LC Card 87-113226 DDC 388.3/22/0981 19
HE5653.A6 S63 1985

BUS LINES - BRAZIL - SÃO PAULO.
Intervenção no transporte . [São Paulo, SP, Brasil , 1985?] 31 leaves ; LC Card 86-171230
HE5653.S23 I58 1985

BUS LINES - DENMARK.
Hansen, Christian Overgård. Forbedring og rationalisering af rutebilkørsel /. Esbjerg , 1986. 259 p. : ISBN 87-88521-37-0 LC Card 86-205999
HE5677.A6 H36 1986

BUS LINES - DENMARK - COSTS.
Hansen, Christian Overgård. Forbedring og rationalisering af rutebilkørsel /. Esbjerg , 1986. 259 p. : ISBN 87-88521-37-0 LC Card 86-205999
HE5677.A6 H36 1986

BUS LINES - DEVELOPING COUNTRIES.
Armstrong-Wright, Alan, 1929- Bus services . Washington, D.C. , 1987. x, 97 p. ; ISBN 0-8213-0943-9 (pbk.) LC Card 87-17183 DDC 388.4/1322/091724 19
HE5725 .A76 1987

BUS LINES - ENGLAND - GREATER MANCHESTER.
Kirk, David, 1937- Major bus operators . Harrow Weald, Middlesex , 1985. 96 p. : ISBN 0-904711-66-8 (pbk.) : LC Card 86-214197 DDC 388.3/22/094273 19
HE5664.M34 K57 1985

BUS LINES - ENGLAND - HISTORY.
Anderson, Roy Claude. History of Royal Blue Express Services /. Newton Abbot , North Pomfret, Vt. , 1985. 216 p. : ISBN 0-7153-8654-9 : LC Card 86-136155 DDC 388.3/22/09423 19
HE5664.Z7 R63 1985

BUS LINES - ENGLAND - LONDON - EMPLOYEES - HISTORY.
Fuller, Ken. Radical aristocrats . London , Atlantic Highlands, N.J. , 1985. 256 p. : ISBN 0-85315-649-2 (pbk.) : LC Card 86-214586 DDC 331.88/1138841322/09421 19
HD8039.M82 G74 1985

BUS LINES - ENGLAND - MERSEYSIDE.
Kirk, David, 1937- Major bus operators . Harrow Weald, Middlesex , 1985. 96 p. : ISBN 0-904711-66-8 (pbk.) : LC Card 86-214197 DDC 388.3/22/094273 19
HE5664.M34 K57 1985

BUS LINES - GERMANY (WEST) - MÜNSTER IN WESTFALEN.
Busse, Dieter. Die Wirkungen von Sonderfahrstreifen für Busse auf die Fahrzeiten im Individualverkehr und öffentlichen Personenahverkehr . Münster [1985?] xii, 274 p. : ISBN 3-88660-264-8 LC Card 86-138804
HE363.G34 M933 1985

BUS LINES - GOVERNMENT POLICY - GREAT BRITAIN.
Douglas, Neil J., 1959- A welfare assessment of transport deregulation . Aldershot, Hampshire, England , Brookfield, Vt., USA , c1987. xxiv, 349 p. : ISBN 0-566-05350-0 : LC Card 86-25703 DDC 388.3/22/0941 19
HE5663.A6 D68 1987

Savage, Ian, 1960- The deregulation of bus services /. Aldershot, Hampshire, England , Brookfield, Vt., U. S.A. , c1985. xx, 267 p. : ISBN 0-566-05051-X : LC Card 85-17650 DDC 388.3/22 19
HE5663.A6 S33 1985 NYPL [JLD 87-123]

BUS LINES - GOVERNMENT POLICY - MALAWI.
Road transport passenger policy issues /. [Lilongwe, Malawi] [1984] i, 22 leaves : LC Card 86-980328 DDC 388.3/22/096897 19
HE5705.A6 R6 1984

BUS LINES - GREAT BRITAIN.
Faulks, Rex William. Bus and coach operation /. London , Boston , 1987. xi, 259 p. : ISBN 0-408-02810-6 : LC Card 87-10966 DDC 388.3/22/068 19
HE5613 .F38 1987

Savage, Ian, 1960- The deregulation of bus services /. Aldershot, Hampshire, England , Brookfield, Vt., U. S.A. , c1985. xx, 267 p. : ISBN 0-566-05051-X : LC Card 85-17650 DDC 388.3/22 19
HE5663.A6 S33 1985 NYPL [JLD 87-123]

BUS LINES - GREAT BRITAIN - HISTORY.
Oxley, Alan. Barton /. Glossop, Derbyshire , c1983- v. <1 > : ISBN 0-903839-64-4 (v. 1) LC Card 86-219518 DDC 388.3/22/09425 19
HE5663.Z7 B376 1983

BUS LINES - GREAT BRITAIN - MANAGEMENT.
Faulks, Rex William. Bus and coach operation /. London , Boston , 1987. xi, 259 p. : ISBN 0-408-02810-6 : LC Card 87-10966 DDC 388.3/22/068 19
HE5613 .F38 1987

BUS LINES - HYGIENIC ASPECTS - DENMARK.
Buschaufførers arbejdsmiljø . København , c1982. 188 p. in various pagings : ISBN 87-7359-039-8 LC Card 83-111384
HD7269.M82 D44 1982

BUS LINES - INDIA.
Patankar, P. G. Road passenger transport in India /. Pune [1985?] xi, 226 p., [4] p. of plates : LC Card 85-905215 DDC 388/.042/0954 19
HE365.I43 B86 1985 NYPL [JLE 86-4230]

BUS LINES - MANAGEMENT.
Antônio, Ricardo Augusto Braga. Análise de sistemas de controle operacional de ônibus urbano /. Brasília, DF , 1985. 92 p. : LC Card 87-113222 DDC 388.4/1322/068 19
HE5613 .A775 1985

Faulks, Rex William. Bus and coach operation /. London , Boston , 1987. xi, 259 p. : ISBN 0-408-02810-6 : LC Card 87-10966 DDC 388.3/22/068 19
HE5613 .F38 1987

BUS LINES - MONTANA.
Smith, Steve, 1941- Second to none . Missoula, Mont. , c1986. 120 p. : ISBN 0-933126-84-0 (pbk.) LC Card 86-62692 DDC 388.3/22/09786 19
HE5633.M9 S65 1986

BUS LINES - SWITZERLAND - HISTORY.
75 Jahre Postauto . Bern [1981] 104 p. : LC Card 86-221362 DDC 388.3/22/09494 19
HE5683.A6 A14 1981

Bus services . Armstrong-Wright, Alan, 1929- Washington, D.C. , 1987. x, 97 p. ; ISBN 0-8213-0943-9 (pbk.) LC Card 87-17183 DDC 388.4/1322/091724 19
HE5725 .A76 1987

Busacker, Dietrich. Energies à la mesure des villages : l'instauration d'énergies renouvables dans les villages africains / Dietrich Busacker et Georg Elwert. Bielefeld, Federal Republic of Germany : Universität Bielefeld, Fakultät für Soziologie, Forschungsschwerpunkt Entwicklungssoziologie, 1985. 21 leaves ; 30 cm. (Working paper / University of Bielefeld, Faculty of Sociology, Sociology of Development Research Centre . no. 58) Cover title. LC Card 85-160345
1. Energy policy - Africa, West. 2. Energy conservation - Africa, West. 3. Renewable energy sources - Africa, West. I. Elwert, Georg. II. Series: Working paper (Universität Bielefeld. Forschungsschwerpunkt Entwicklungssoziologie) , no. 58. III. Title.
HD9502.A4993 B87 1985

Buscando la equidad. English. In search for equity : planning for the satisfaction of basic needs in Latin America / Regional Employment Programme for Latin America and the Caribbean (PREAlC) ; [translated by David Lehmann]. Aldershot, Hants, England ; Brookfield, USA : Avebury, c1987. xvi, 249 p. ; 23 cm. Translation of: Buscando la equidad. Bibliography: p. 243-249. ISBN 0-566-05537-6 : LC Card 87-21225 DDC 338.98 19
1. Basic needs - Latin America. 2. Food supply - Latin America. 3. Housing policy - Latin America. 4. Manpower policy - Latin America. 5. Popular participation - Latin America. I. Regional Employment Program for Latin America and the Caribbean. II. Title.
HC130.B38 B8713 1987

Buscando un techo . Feijoó, María del Carmen. Buenos Aires, Argentina [1984] 90, [5] p. : LC Card 85-214586
HD7321.B9 F45 1984

Busch, Angelika. Migration und psychische Belastung : eine Studie am Beispiel von Sizilianerinnen in Köln / Angelika Busch. Berlin : D. Reimer, 1983. 351 p. ; 21 cm. (Kölner ethnologische Studien . Bd. 8) Dissertation statement inserted. Thesis (doctoral)--Universität zu Köln, 1982. Bibliography: p. 335-351. ISBN 3-496-00733-8 LC Card 83-193476
1. Alien labor, Italian - Germany (West) - Cologne - Case studies. 2. Sicily - Economic conditions - 1945-. I. Title. II. Series.
HD8458.I8 B87 1983

Busch, Axel. Soltwedel, Rüdiger. Deregulierungspotentiale in der Bundesrepublik /. Tübingen , c1986. xi, 326 p. ; ISBN 3-16-345145-4 (Deut. Bibl. : pbk.) LC Card 87-408380 DDC 338.6/048 19
HD3616.G4 S665 1986

Busch, Wilfried, 1948- Staatsausgaben, Produktion und Beschäftigung : eine makroökonomische Modellanalyse für eine geschlossene Volkswirtschaft bei Unterbeschäftigung / Wilfried Busch. Frankfurt am Main ; New York : P. Lang, c1984. viii, 304 p. : ill. ; 21 cm. (Europäische Hochschulschriften. Reihe V, Volks- und Betriebswirtschaft, 0531-7339 . Bd. 538 = vol. 538 = vol. 538) Originally presented as the author's thesis (doctoral)--Christian-Albrechts-Universität zu Kiel, 1984. Bibliography: p. 295-304. ISBN 3-8204-5352-0 LC Card 85-199154
1. Government spending policy - Germany (West) - Econometric models. 2. National income - Germany (West) - Accounting - Econometric models. 3. Underemployment - Germany (West) - Econometric models. I. Series: Europäische Hochschulschriften. Reihe V, Volks- und Betriebswirtschaft , Bd. 538. II. Title.
HJ7792 .B87 1984

Buschaufførers arbejdsmiljø : tekniske målinger / udarbejdet af Teknologisk institut ved Helge Andreasen ... [et al.].1. udg. København : Arbejdsmiljøfondet, c1982. 188 p. in various pagings : ill. ; 24 cm. (Arbejdsmiljøfondets forskningsrapporter) Includes bibliographies. ISBN 87-7359-039-8 LC Card 83-111384
1. Bus drivers - Denmark - Diseases. 2. Bus lines -

Hygienic aspects - Denmark. I. Andreasen, Helge.
HD7269.M82 D44 1982

Buscher, Herbert S. Modelle der neuen klassischen Makroökonomie : theoretische Darstellung und empirische Ergebnisse / Herbert S. Buscher. München : V. Florentz, c1986. iv, 312 p. : ill. ; 21 cm. (Volkswirtschaftliche Forschung und Entwicklung . Bd. 24) Originally presented as the author's thesis (doctoral)--Freie Universität Berlin. Bibliography: p. 288-306. Includes index. ISBN 3-88259-386-5 LC Card 86-230281
1. Econometric models. 2. Macroeconomics - Econometric models. 3. Business cycles - Germany (West) - Econometric models. I. Title. II. Series.
HB141 .B87 1986

Büscher, Ludger. Integrated rural development : the case of Sierra Leone / Ludwig Büscher. Hamburg : Verlag Weltarchiv, 1984. xx, 238 p. : ill. ; 21 cm. (Studien zur integrierten ländlichen Entwicklung, 0177-2503 . 2) Bibliography: p. 229-238. ISBN 3-87895-261-9 (pbk.) LC Card 86-672442
1. Agriculture - Economic aspects - Sierra Leone. 2. Rural development projects - Sierra Leone. 3. Sierra Leone - Economic conditions. I. Title. II. Series.
HD2146.5 .B87x 1984 ***NYPL [JLD 86-2789]***

Buschmann, Vera, 1951- Wirkungsanalyse für segmentspezifische Warentestwerbung : die Zielgruppe, sozial schwache Jugendliche / Vera Buschmann. Frankfurt am Main ; New York : P. Lang, c1986. xii, 270 p. : ill. ; 21 cm. (Europäische Hochschulschriften. Reihe V, Volks- und Betriebswirtschaft, 0531-7339 . Bd. 726 = vol. 726 = vol. 726) Bibliography: p. 222-242. ISBN 3-8204-9275-5 LC Card 86-220570
1. Youth as consumers - Germany (West). 2. Advertising - Germany, West. 3. Mass media and youth - Germany (West). I. Series: Europäische Hochschulschriften. Reihe V, Volks- und Betriebswirtschaft , Bd. 726. II. Title.
HF5827 .B87 1986

Buschmann, Walter. Arbeitersiedlungen im 19. Jahrhundert . Bochum , c1985. 189 p. : ISBN 3-88339-427-0 LC Card 85-164690
HD7289.5.A3 G42 1985

Busel, Anatoliĭ Fedorovich. Podvig na pochtovoĭ marke . Moskva , 1985. 135 p. : LC Card 86-113767
HE6183.G47 P63 1985

Buser, Marcos. Wirtschaftsverbände in der Schweiz . Grüsch , c1986. xv, 294 p. : ISBN 3-7253-0260-X : LC Card 86-136455 DDC 322/.3/09494 19
HD2429.S92 W57 1986
NYPL [JLD 86-2919]

Bush, David B. Saliba, Bonnie. Water markets in theory and practice . Boulder , 1987. viii, 273 p. : ISBN 0-8133-7465-0 (pbk. : alk. paper) : LC Card 87-21687 DDC 333.91/00979 19
HD1695.A165 S25 1987

Bush, Fredy. Your fortune in foreclosures : today's best, low-risk, high-profit real estate investment / Fredy Bush, Carl Hunter & Bruce Erb. Tucson, Ariz. : Knight-Ridder Press, c1987. ix, 221 p. : ill. ; 24 cm. Includes index. ISBN 0-89586-572-6 LC Card 86-33793 DDC 332.63/24 19
1. Real estate investment. 2. House buying. 3. Foreclosure. 4. Real property. I. Hunter, Carl. II. Erb, Bruce. III. Title.
HD1382.5 .B87 1987

Bush, Vanessa A. How to buy a house when you're cash poor : you can afford the home of your dreams / Vanessa A. Bush. Chicago : Contemporary Books, c1986. 92 p. ; 21 cm. Includes index. ISBN 0-8092-4834-4 (pbk.) : LC Card 86-24053 DDC 332.7/22 19
1. Mortgages. 2. Housing - Finance. 3. Real property and taxation. 4. Settlement costs. 5. House buying. I. Title.
HG2040.15 .B87 1986

Bushmanov, V. B. Kolos na ladoni . Voronezh , 1985. 237 p. : LC Card 86-195464
HD1536.S65 K65 1985

BUSHMEN (AFRICAN TRIBE) see **SAN (AFRICAN PEOPLE)**

Bushnell, David S. Training for new technology / by David S. Bushnell. 1st ed. New York : Pergamon Press, c1983. 41 p. ; 28 cm. (Work in America Institute studies in productivity . 27) Includes bibliographies. ISBN 0-08-029508-8 : LC Card 83-17341 DDC 658.3/124 19
1. Occupational training - United States. 2. Employees, Training of - United States. 3. High technology - Study and teaching - United States. I. Title. II. Series.
HD5715.2 .B87 1983
NYPL [JLM 83-380 no.27]

BUSINESS ADMINISTRATION. see **BUSINESS.**

Business algebra & mathematics /. George, Thomas F. Englewood Cliffs, NJ , c1987. xiv, 634 p. : ISBN 0-13-091562-9 LC Card 86-30333 DDC 512/.1 19
HF5694 .G46 1987

Business algebra and mathematics. George, Thomas F. Business algebra & mathematics /. Englewood Cliffs, NJ , c1987. xiv, 634 p. : ISBN 0-13-091562-9 LC Card 86-30333 DDC 512/.1 19
HF5694 .G46 1987

The business amazons /. Hertz, Leah. London , 1986. xviii, 264, [1] p., [1] leaf of plates : ISBN 0-233-97892-5 : LC Card 86-200078 DDC 338.6/422/088042 19
HD2346.G7 H47 1986

BUSINESS AND ART. see **ART AND INDUSTRY.**

Business and economics databases online . Popovich, Charles J. Littleton, Colo. , 1987. xviii, 276 p. : ISBN 0-87287-454-0 (pbk. : alk. paper) : LC Card 87-2672 DDC 300/.28/5 19
HF5548.2 .P612 1987

Business and economics funding guide / American Association of State Colleges and Universities. Washington, D.C. : AASCU Press, c1987. 122 p. ; 24 cm. "Prepared by Carolyn Looff of the University of Kentucky's Center for Business and Economic Research, under a summer fellowship with AASCU's Office of Federal Programs"--P. [iii]. Bibliography: p. 121-122. Includes indexes. ISBN 0-88044-087-2 (alk. paper) : LC Card 87-17436 DDC 001.4/4 19
1. Federal aid to business research - United States - Directories. 2. Business - Research grants - United States - Directories. I. Looff, Carolyn S. II. American Association of State Colleges and Universities.
HF1131 .B78 1987

Business and industrial anthropology . Baba, Marietta L. Washington, D.C. , c1986. vii, 48 p. ; ISBN 0-913167-16-9 (pbk.) : LC Card 86-26602 DDC 302.3/5 19
HD58.7 .B33 1986

BUSINESS AND MASS MEDIA. see **MASS MEDIA AND BUSINESS.**

Business and politics . Wilson, Graham K. Houndmills, Basingstoke, Hampshire , 1985. xii, 155 p. ; ISBN 0-333-34091-4 LC Card 86-673508
HD3611 .W55x 1985

BUSINESS AND POLITICS.
Bozeman, Barry. All organizations are public . San Francisco , 1987. xix, 184 p. : ISBN 1-555-42036-2 (alk. paper) LC Card 86-27699 DDC 302.3/5 19
HD58.9 .B69 1987

Wilson, Graham K. Business and politics . Houndmills, Basingstoke, Hampshire , 1985. xii, 155 p. ; ISBN 0-333-34091-4 LC Card 86-673508
HD3611 .W55x 1985

BUSINESS AND POLITICS - BOLIVIA.
Confederación de Empresarios Privados de Bolivia. Pensamiento de la empresa privada boliviana . La Paz, Bolivia [1981] 274 p. : LC Card 82-138113 DDC 322/.3/0984 19
HC181 .C6426 1981 ***NYPL [JLF 86-1617]***

BUSINESS AND POLITICS - FRANCE.
Helbert, Jean-Pierre, 1947- L'insurrection des patrons /. Châteaugiron , 1984. 165 p. ; ISBN 2-903414-33-5 LC Card 85-180275 DDC 658/.006/044 19
HD6948.F8 H45 1984 ***NYPL [JLE 86-526]***

BUSINESS AND POLITICS - GREAT BRITAIN.
Vogel, David, 1947- National styles of regulation . Ithaca, N.Y. , 1986. 325 p. ; ISBN 0-8014-1658-2 LC Card 85-21332 DDC 363.7/056/0941 19
HC260.E5 V64 1986 ***NYPL [JLE 86-2434]***

BUSINESS AND POLITICS - MEXICO.
Government and private sector in contemporary Mexico /. [La Jolla, Calif.] , 1987. iv, 146 p. ; LC Card 87-622060 DDC 338.972 19
HD3616.M43 G68 1987

BUSINESS AND POLITICS - MICHIGAN - CASE STUDIES.
Jones, Bryan D. The sustaining hand . Lawrence, Kan. , c1986. xii, 247 p. : ISBN 0-7006-0278-X : LC Card 85-24631 DDC 338.4/76292/09774 19
HD9710.U53 M433 1986
NYPL [JLE 86-2386]

BUSINESS AND POLITICS - NEW YORK (STATE)
New York (State). Legislature. Legislative Commission on Public-Private Cooperation. Legislative Commission on Public-Private Cooperation second report . [Albany] [1984] 57 p. ; LC Card 86-622576 DDC 338.9747 19
HC107.N7 N3743 1984

New York (State). Legislature. Legislative Commission on Public-Private Cooperation. Working together for New York's economy . [Albany] [1983] 57 p. ; LC Card 86-622577 DDC 338.9747 19
HC107.N7 N3743 1983

BUSINESS AND POLITICS - SWITZERLAND.
Farago, Peter. Verbände als Träger öffentlicher Politik . Grüsch , c1987. xi, 185 p. : ISBN 3-7253-0290-1 LC Card 87-140606 DDC 322/.3/09494 19
HD2429.S92 F37 1987

Wirtschaftsverbände in der Schweiz . Grüsch , c1986. xv, 294 p. : ISBN 3-7253-0260-X : LC Card 86-136455 DDC 322/.3/09494 19
HD2429.S92 W57 1986
NYPL [JLD 86-2919]

BUSINESS AND POLITICS - UNITED STATES.
Business and society . Lexington, Mass. , c1987. xv, 654 p. : ISBN 0-669-13207-1 (pbk : alk. paper) LC Card 86-45548 DDC 658.4/08/0973 19
HD60.5.U5 B853 1987

Leone, Robert A. Who profits . New York , 1986. xiii, 248 p. ; ISBN 0-465-09183-0 : LC Card 85-47992 DDC 338.973 19
HD3616.U47 L44 1986
NYPL [JLD 86-2410]

Matasar, Ann B. Corporate PACs and federal campaign financing laws . New York , 1986. x, 161 p. ; ISBN 0-89930-086-3 (lib. bdg. : alk. paper)
NYPL [JLE 86-2492]

Short, Joseph N. American business and foreign policy . New York , 1987. 340 p. : ISBN 0-8240-8093-9 (alk. paper) : LC Card 87-23792 DDC 382/.41373/0973 19
HD9199.U48 S46 1987

Vogel, David, 1947- National styles of regulation . Ithaca, N.Y. , 1986. 325 p. ; ISBN 0-8014-1658-2 LC Card 85-21332 DDC 363.7/056/0941 19
HC260.E5 V64 1986 ***NYPL [JLE 86-2434]***

BUSINESS AND POLITICS - UNITED STATES - CASE STUDIES.
Aram, John D., 1942- Managing business and public policy . Marshfield, Mass. , c1986. xv, 736 p. : ISBN 0-582-98830-6 LC Card 85-16955 DDC 338.973 19
HD3616.U47 A73 1985
NYPL [JLE 86-2593]

BUSINESS AND POLITICS - UNITED STATES - HISTORY.
Sklar, Martin J., 1935- The corporate reconstruction of American capitalism, 1890-1916 . Cambridge [Cambridgeshire] , New York , 1987. p. cm. ISBN 0-521-30921-2 LC Card 87-9408 DDC 338.8/0973 19
HC110.C3 S58 1987

Business and society : dimensions of conflict and cooperation / edited by S. Prakash Sethi, Cecilia M. Falbe. Lexington, Mass. : Lexington Books, c1987. xv, 654 p. : ill. ; 23 cm. Includes bibliographies and index. ISBN 0-669-13207-1 (pbk : alk. paper) LC Card 86-45548 DDC 658.4/08/0973 19
1. Industry - Social aspects - United States. 2. Business and politics - United States. I. Sethi, S. Prakash. II. Falbe, Cecilia M.
HD60.5.U5 B853 1987

Business and society . Frederick, William

Crittenden, 1925- New York , c1988. xxvii, 626 p. : ISBN 0-07-015561-5 : LC Card 87-21436 DDC 658.4/08 19
HD60 .F72 1988

BUSINESS - ANECDOTES, FACETIAE, SATIRE, ETC.
Hay, Peter. The book of business anecdotes /. New York, N.Y. , c1988. viii, 296 p. ; ISBN 0-8160-1522-8 LC Card 87-20211 DDC 650/.0207 19
HF5351 .H34 1988

Business applications software for the IBM PC /. Ingalsbe, Lon. Columbus , c1987. 1 v. (various pagings) : ISBN 0-675-20760-6 (pbk.) LC Card 86-63664 DDC 650/.028/55365 19
HF5548.4.I24 I54 1987

BUSINESS ARITHMETIC. see **BUSINESS MATHEMATICS.**

Business, banking, and politics . Tolliday, Steven. Cambridge, Mass. , 1987. vi, 433 p. : ISBN 0-674-08725-9 (alk. paper) LC Card 86-31944 DDC 338.4/7669142/0941 19
HD9521.5 .T64 1987

Business BASIC for the IBM PC with cases /. Cohen, Eli B. St. Louis , 1987. xxiv, 634 p. : ISBN 0-8016-1244-6 (pbk.) LC Card 86-23100 DDC 005.2/165 19
HF5548.5.B3 C64 1987

Business behaviour & management structure /. Minkes, A. L. London , c1985. 224 p. ; ISBN 0-7099-1795-3 ***NYPL [JLD 87-1113]***

Business behaviour and management structure.
Minkes, A. L. Business behaviour & management structure /. London , c1985. 224 p. ; ISBN 0-7099-1795-3 ***NYPL [JLD 87-1113]***

BUSINESS - BIBLIOGRAPHY.
Financial Sourcebooks' sources . Naperville, Ill. , c1987. 454 p. ; ISBN 0-942061-00-4 (pbk.) : LC Card 87-8793 DDC 332/.025/73 19
HG173 .F517 1987

Johnson, H. Herbert Webster, 1906- How to use the business library . Cincinnati , c1984. iv, 267 p. : ISBN 0-538-05750-5 (pbk.) LC Card 83-60484 DDC 027.6/9 19
Z675.B8 J6 1984 ***NYPL [JLE 86-3971]***

Lavin, Michael R. Business information . Phoenix, Ariz. , 1987. x, 299 p. : ISBN 0-89774-157-9 (alk. paper) : LC Card 86-42787 DDC 650/.072 19
HF5356 .L36 1987

BUSINESS BUDGETING. see **BUDGET IN BUSINESS.**

BUSINESS CARDS. see **ADVERTISING CARDS.**

BUSINESS - CASE STUDIES.
A Casebook for systems development /. London , Baltimore, Md., USA , 1986. iv, 88, [1] p. : ISBN 0-7131-3600-6 LC Card 87-114266 DDC 658 19
HD31 .C3554 1986

BUSINESS, CHOICE OF. see **VOCATIONAL GUIDANCE.**

Business communication /. Andrews, Deborah C. New York , London , c1988. xxvi, 623 p. : ISBN 0-02-303510-2 LC Card 87-5526 DDC 808/.06665 19
HF5718 .A743 1988

Business communication . Bell, Arthur H. (Arthur Henry), 1946- Glenview, Ill. , c1987. 601 p., [8] p. of plates : ISBN 0-673-18326-2 : LC Card 86-24844 DDC 808/.066651 19
HF5718 .B455 1987

Business communication . Huseman, Richard C. Chicago , c1988. xxxi, 702 p., [8] p. of plates : ISBN 0-03-012294-5 LC Card 87-438 DDC 658.4/5 19
HF5718 .H84 1988

Business communication . Ricks, Betty R. New York , c1987. xiii, 479 p. : ISBN 0-471-81824-0 LC Card 86-26747 DDC 651.7 19
HF5718 .R53 1987

Business communication . Timm, Paul R. Englewood Cliffs, N.J. , c1987. xvi, 509 p. : ISBN 0-13-091779-6 LC Card 86-30650 DDC 658.4/5 19
HF5718 .T53 1987

Business communication.
Huseman, Richard C. Business communication . Chicago , c1988. xxxi, 702 p., [8] p. of plates : ISBN 0-03-012294-5 LC Card 87-438 DDC 658.4/5 19
HF5718 .H84 1988

BUSINESS COMMUNICATION.
Bakos, Brian D. Business communications at work /. Englewood Cliffs, N.J. , c1988. xi, 239 p. : ISBN 0-13-091752-4 (pbk.) : LC Card 87-19690 DDC 808/.06665 19
HF5718 .B35 1988

Dellinger, Susan. Communicating effectively . Millwood, N.Y., 1987, c1982. p. cm. ISBN 0-916667-14-6 LC Card 87-20830 DDC 658.4/5 19
HF5718 .D44 1987

Henry, Lauchland. The professional's guide to working smarter /. Tenafly, N.J. , 1988. xv, 208 p. : ISBN 0-935310-03-7 LC Card 87-23868 DDC 650.1 19
HD8038.A1 H47 1988

Michulka, Jean H. Let's talk business /. Cincinnati, Ohio , c1988. x, 370 p. : ISBN 0-538-05920-6 (pbk.) LC Card 86-63174 DDC 658.4/52 19
HF5718 .M5 1988

Murphy, Herta A. Effective business communications /. New York , c1988. xx, 730 p. : ISBN 0-07-044094-8 LC Card 87-17330 DDC 651.7 19
HF5721 .M85 1988

Peoples, David A., 1930- Presentations plus . New York , c1988. xi, 239 p. : ISBN 0-471-63391-7 LC Card 87-21691 DDC 658.4/5 19
HF5718 .P44 1988

Scott, W. P. The skills of communicating /. Aldershot, Hampshire, England , Brookfield, Vt. , 1987, c1986. p. cm. ISBN 0-7045-0575-4 (pbk.) : LC Card 87-17106 DDC 658.4/5 19
HF5718 .S38 1987

Thomas, David Allen, 1939- Business communication today! /. Lincolnwood, Ill., U. S.A. , c1988. xi, 532 p. : ISBN 0-8442-5595-5 LC Card 87-60193 DDC 651.7 19
HF5718 .T46 1988

BUSINESS COMMUNICATION - HANDBOOKS, MANUALS, ETC.
Dorrell, Jean, 1926- The answer book . Los Angeles, CA , c1987. ix, 358 p. : ISBN 0-935732-12-8 (pbk.) : LC Card 87-23408 DDC 651 19
HF5547.5 .D63 1987

BUSINESS - COMMUNICATION SYSTEMS.
Fischer, Barbara S. Office systems integration . New York , 1987. xxi, 215 p. : ISBN 0-89930-109-6 (lib. bdg. : alk. paper) LC Card 87-2498 DDC 651.8 19
HF5547.5 .F56 1987

Gibson, Cyrus F. The information imperative . Lexington, Mass. , c1987. xxii, 160 p. : ISBN 0-669-12338-2 (alk. paper) LC Card 85-45797 DDC 658/.05 19
HF5548.2 .G496 1987

Grover, Kenneth C. Foundations of business telecommunications management /. New York , c1986. xvi, 196 p. ; ISBN 0-306-42249-2 (pbk.) LC Card 86-5063 DDC 384 19
HF5541.T4 G76 1986 ***NYPL [JLE 86-3270]***

Gunton, Tony, 1943- Business information technology . Englewood Cliffs, N.J. , 1988. p. cm. ISBN 0-13-100843-9 LC Card 87-7365 DDC 658/.05 19
HF5548.2 .G86 1988

Rowe, Stanford H. Business telecommunications /. Chicago , c1988. xx, 529 p. : ISBN 0-574-18690-5 : LC Card 87-14001 DDC 651.7 19
HE7631 .R69 1988

Using new communications technologies . Washington, D.C. , c1986. ix, 57 p. : ISBN 0-937790-30-3 (pbk.) : LC Card 85-63320 DDC 384 19
HF5541.T4 U75 1986

Vignault, Walter L. Worldwide telecommunications guide for the business manager /. New York , c1987. xvi, 417 p. : ISBN 0-471-85828-5 LC Card 87-2002 DDC 384 19
HF5541.T4 V54 1987

Business communication today! /. Thomas, David Allen, 1939- Lincolnwood, Ill., U. S.A. , c1988. xi, 532 p. : ISBN 0-8442-5595-5 LC Card 87-60193 DDC 651.7 19
HF5718 .T46 1988

Business communications /. Dumont, Raymond A. Boston , c1987. xxii, 602 p. : ISBN 0-316-19536-7 LC Card 86-21125 DDC 808/.066651 19
HF5718 .D845 1987

Business communications at work /. Bakos, Brian D. Englewood Cliffs, N.J. , c1988. xi, 239 p. : ISBN 0-13-091752-4 (pbk.) : LC Card 87-19690 DDC 808/.06665 19
HF5718 .B35 1988

Business Communications Co.
Advanced composites . Stamford, Conn. , c1985. x, 206 leaves : ISBN 0-89336-442-8 (soft) LC Card 87-166023 DDC 338.4/7620118 19
HD9999.C7152 A38 1985

Biotechnology in agriculture . Stamford, Conn., U. S.A. , c1985. xvii, 192 leaves : ISBN 0-89336-485-1 (pbk.) LC Card 87-403883 DDC 381/.456606 19
HD9999.B443 U615 1985

Castrovilla, Joseph A. The printed circuit board industry /. Stamford, Conn., U. S.A. , c1985. ix, 116 leaves : ISBN 0-89336-451-7 (soft) LC Card 87-403911 DDC 381/.4562138174/0973 19
HD9696.P743 U634 1985

The Changing passenger car markets . Stamford, Conn., U. S.A. , c1985. viii, 227 leaves : ISBN 0-89336-479-7 (pbk.) LC Card 87-404429 DDC 381/.4566849 19
HD9710.U52 C385 1985

Crull, Anna W. New trends in gas separations . Stamford, Conn., U. S.A. , c1986. xvi, 222 leaves : ISBN 0-89336-422-3 (pbk.) LC Card 87-165549 DDC 660.2/842 19
HD9660.G372 C78 1986

Diet foods . Stamford, Conn., U. S.A. , c1986. xv, 195 leaves : ISBN 0-89336-487-8 (pbk.) LC Card 87-160485 DDC 381/.4166463/0973 19
HD9005 .D53 1986

Electrochemistry . Stamford, Conn., U. S.A. , c1986. 231 leaves : ISBN 0-89336-483-5 (pbk.) LC Card 87-403910 DDC 380.1/45660297/0973 19
HD9660.E433 U544 1986

Generic drugs . Stamford, Conn., U. S.A. , c1986. xiii, 311 leaves : ISBN 0-89336-434-7 (soft) LC Card 87-167077 DDC 380.1/456151 19
HD9665.5 .G46 1986

Geotextiles, geomembranes, geomatrices . Stamford, Conn., U. S.A. , c1986. xii, 133 leaves : ISBN 0-89336-496-7 (pbk.) LC Card 87-403913 DDC 668.9 19
HD9869.I533 U64 1986

Gipson, Beckilynn. Aseptic food processing and packaging . Stamford, Conn., U. S.A. , c1986. xiii, 164 leaves ; ISBN 0-89336-471-1 (pbk.) LC Card 87-405014 DDC 381/.45664028 19
HD9999.C743 U629 1986

Holography, new commercial opportunities /. Stamford, Conn. , c1985. vii, 149 leaves : ISBN 0-89336-480-0 (soft) LC Card 87-165251 DDC 380.1/456213675 19
HD9707.5.H342 H64 1985

The Japanese challenge . Stamford, Conn., U. S.A. , c1986. xii, 108 leaves : ISBN 0-89336-489-4 (pbk.) LC Card 87-404570 DDC 338/.06 19
HC465.T4 J365 1986

Local area networks . Stamford, Conn., U. S.A. , c1986. xvi, 186 leaves : ISBN 0-89336-438-X (pbk.) LC Card 87-404428 DDC 381/.4500468/0973 19
HD9696.C63 U52253 1986

New biotechnology comes to market /. Stamford, Conn., U. S.A. , c1985. viii, 205 leaves : ISBN 0-89336-436-3 (soft) LC Card 87-167067 DDC 381/.456606 19
HD9999.B442 N48 1985

The New ethnic food market . Norwalk, Conn.,

U. S.A. , c1986. xv, 142 leaves ; ISBN 0-89336-486-X (pbk.) LC Card 87-168111 DDC 381/.45641592/00973 19
HD9333.U62 N48 1986

New specialty metals & metallurgy for high-temperature, high-strength, low-weight applications /. Norwalk, Conn., U. S.A. , c1987. 1 v. (various foliations) : ISBN 0-89336-454-1 (pbk.) LC Card 87-168123 DDC 380.1/45669/0973 19
HD9506.U62 N45 1987

New trends in food retailing /. Stamford, Conn., U. S.A. , c1985. xiii, 135 leaves : ISBN 0-89336-457-6 (soft) LC Card 87-165228 DDC 381/.45664/00973 19
HD9321.5 .N47 1985

The Online commercial database business /. Stamford, Conn., U. S.A. , c1985. xxi, 230 leaves : ISBN 0-89336-320-0 (pbk.) LC Card 87-40457 DDC 381/.4500574/0973 19
HD9696.D363 U66 1985

Packet switching equipment markets /. Stamford, Conn., U. S.A. , c1985. v, 205 leaves : ISBN 0-89336-465-7 (pbk.) LC Card 87-403884 DDC 381/.456213878 19
HD9696.T443 U556 1985

The Pet industry . Stamford, Conn., U. S.A. , c1985. xi, 140 leaves : ISBN 0-89336-439-8 (pbk.) LC Card 87-403914 DDC 381/.4568 19
HD9340.U52 P48 1985

Plastics in business machines . Stamford, Conn. , c1986. vii, 215 leaves : ISBN 0-89336-433-6 (soft) : LC Card 87-165036 DDC 380.1/456684 19
HD9801.A2 P56 1986

Voice compression technology . Stamford, Conn., U. S.A. , c1985. xii, 146 leaves ; ISBN 0-89336-430-4 (soft) LC Card 87-165256 DDC 380.1/45621389 19
HD9696.T442 V65 1985

BUSINESS - COMPUTER-ASSISTED INSTRUCTION.
Long, Larry E. Computers in business /. Englewood Cliffs, N.J. , c1987. xxv, 609 p. : ISBN 0-13-164294-4 LC Card 86-30412 DDC 650/.028/5 19
HF5548.2 .L586 1987

BUSINESS - COMPUTER PROGRAMS.
Popyk, Marilyn K., 1945- Up and running! . Reading, Mass. , c1987. xxv, 647, [28] p. : ISBN 0-201-06274-7 (pbk.) : LC Card 86-26620 DDC 650/.028/5536 19
HF5548.2 .P614 1987

Spence, J. Wayne. Microcomputers in business . St. Louis , 1987. vii, 224 p. : ISBN 0-8016-5030-5 (pbk.) LC Card 86-30013 DDC 650/.028/5536 19
HF5548.2 .S728 1987

Business computer systems . Hudson, R. W. London , New York , c1986. x, 163 p. : ISBN 0-07-084976-5 (pbk.) : LC Card 86-10481 DDC 650/.028/5 19
HF5548.2 .H78 1986 *NYPL [JLE 87-1038]*

Business computing for small contractors /. Grout, Gary. Berkeley, Calif. , c1986. xv, 314 p. : ISBN 0-07-881229-1 (pbk.) LC Card 86-206636 DDC 690/.8/0285536 19
HF5686.B7 G75 1986

Business confidential. Rev. ed. New York, N.Y. : Boardroom Classics, c1987. xi, 504 p. ; 29 cm. Includes index. ISBN 0-932648-82-7 LC Card 86-30963 DDC 650 19
1. Business - Handbooks, manuals, etc. 2. Industrial management - Handbooks, manuals, etc. 3. Business enterprises - United States - Handbooks, manuals, etc. 4. Industrial management - United States - Handbooks, manuals, etc. 5. Corporations - Taxation - United States - Handbooks, manuals, etc. I. Boardroom reports.
HF5356 .B9259 1987

BUSINESS - CONGRESSES.
Betriebswirtschaftliche Erkenntnisse für Regierung, Verwaltung und öffentliche Unternehmen . Baden-Baden , 1985. 266 p. : ISBN 3-7890-1104-5 LC Card 85-213984
HJ9705 .B48 1985

BUSINESS CONSULTANTS - CASE STUDIES.
Davis, Nancy Yaw. Research and consulting as a business /. Washington, D.C. , c1987. v, 41 p. : ISBN 0-913167-21-5 (pbk.) LC Card 87-20254 DDC 658.4/6 19
HD69.C6 D38 1987

BUSINESS CONSULTANTS - DIRECTORIES.
National emerging industries resourceguide /. Minneapolis, MN , c1986. 368, 124 p. ; ISBN 0-8144-5851-3 LC Card 85-82163 DDC 338.7/61/0002573 19
HD62.5 .N38 1986 *NYPL [JLF 86-1717]*

BUSINESS CONSULTANTS - FRANCE.
Zémor, Pierre. Un bon conseil . Paris , c1986. 278 p. : ISBN 2-85565-300-2 : LC Card 86-174727
HD69.C6 Z4 1986

BUSINESS CONSULTANTS - GERMANY (WEST)
Eschbach, Thomas H., 1954- Der Ausgleich funktionaler Defizite des wirtschaftlichen Systems durch die Unternehmensberatung . Frankfurt am Main , New York , c1984. 152 p. ; ISBN 3-8204-5127-7 LC Card 85-191647
HD69.C6 E76 1984

BUSINESS CONSULTANTS - HANDBOOKS, MANUALS, ETC.
Van Doren, Glenn H. Management advisory services manual /. Boston , c1987- 1 v. (loose-leaf) : ISBN 0-88712-505-0 (loose-leaf) LC Card 87-50240 DDC 658.4/6 19
HD69.C6 V36 1987

BUSINESS CONSULTANTS - TRAINING OF - ITALY - CASE STUDIES.
Società di terziario avanzato e professionalità . Roma [1984] 159 p. : LC Card 85-232870
HD69.C6 S66 1984

BUSINESS CONSULTANTS - UNITED STATES.
Eschbach, Thomas H., 1954- Der Ausgleich funktionaler Defizite des wirtschaftlichen Systems durch die Unternehmensberatung . Frankfurt am Main , New York , c1984. 152 p. ; ISBN 3-8204-5127-7 LC Card 85-191647
HD69.C6 E76 1984

McKell, Lynn J. A study of MAS practice and knowledge and bibliographic references for management advisory services . New York, N.Y. , c1987. 100, [iv], 72 p. ; ISBN 0-87051-002-9 (pbk.) : LC Card 87-19491 DDC 016.6584/6 19
HF5616.U5 M34 1987

Business corporation in the democratic society. Die Unternehmung in der demokratischen Gesellschaft =. Berlin , New York , 1987. xiii, 390 p. : ISBN 0-89925-295-8 (U. S.) : LC Card 86-32864 DDC 658.3/152 19
HD5650 .U67 1987

BUSINESS CORPORATIONS. see **CORPORATIONS.**

BUSINESS CORRESPONDENCE. see **COMMERCIAL CORRESPONDENCE.**

BUSINESS CREATIVITY. see **CREATIVE ABILITY IN BUSINESS.**

Business customs and protocol in the ASEAN region /. Schmidt, Klaus D. Menlo Park, Calif. [c1985- v. <1 > : LC Card 87-404513 DDC 395/.52 19
HF5387 .S36 1985

Business cycle theory . Gabisch, Günter, 1943- Berlin , New York , c1987. vii, 229 p. : ISBN 0-387-17188-6 (U. S. : pbk.) LC Card 86-31539 DDC 338.5/42/01 19
HB3711 .G19 1987

BUSINESS CYCLES - ADDRESSES, ESSAYS, LECTURES.
Wachstumsverlangsamung und Konjunkturzyklen in unterschiedlichen Wirtschaftssystemen /. Berlin , c1984. 191 p. : ISBN 3-428-05626-4
NYPL [JLL 73-186 Bd. 142]

Business cycles and equilibrium /. Black, Fischer. Oxford [Oxfordshire] UK , New York, N.Y., USA , 1987. xi, 180 p. ; ISBN 0-631-15754-9 (U. S.) : LC Card 87-6578 DDC 338.5/42 19
HB3711 .B497 1987

BUSINESS CYCLES - CANADA - ECONOMETRIC MODELS.
Kuszczak, John. A VAR analysis of economic interdependence . [Ottawa] [1987] ii, 55 p. : LC Card 87-167407 DDC 338.5/42/0971 19
HB3755 .K87 1987

BUSINESS CYCLES - CASE STUDIES.
Le Crisi finanziarie /. Bologna , c1985. 348 p. : ISBN 88-15-00807-1 : LC Card 85-201934 DDC 332.1 19
HG1591 .C75 1985

BUSINESS CYCLES - CONGRESSES.
Colloque d'étude des politiques économiques Récession et relance (1984 : Paris, France) Récession et relance /. Paris , 1984. 218 p. : ISBN 2-7178-0690-3 : LC Card 85-158199 DDC 338.5/42 19
HB3711 .C59 1984

BUSINESS CYCLES - ECONOMETRIC MODELS.
Funke, Michael, 1956- Wachstumszyklen und funktionale Einkommensverteilung /. München , c1985. iii, 244 p. : ISBN 3-88259-319-9 LC Card 85-175617
HB3711 .F896 1985

Michie, Jonathan. Wages in the business cycle . London , 1987. vii, 194 p. : ISBN 0-86187-686-5 LC Card 87-148946 DDC 331.2/1 19
HD4906 .M43 1987

BUSINESS CYCLES - ENGLAND - HISTORY - 18TH CENTURY.
Hoppit, Julian. Risk and failure in English business, 1700-1800 /. Cambridge [Cambridgeshire] , New York , 1987. vii, 228 p. : ISBN 0-521-32624-9 LC Card 87-743 DDC 332.7/5/0942 19
HG3769.G73 E54 1987

BUSINESS CYCLES - EUROPE.
Hibbs, Douglas A., 1943- The political economy of industrial democracies /. Cambridge, Mass. , 1987. viii, 327 p. : ISBN 0-674-68580-6 LC Card 86-9799 DDC 339.5/09171/3 19
HB3743 .H53 1987 *NYPL [JLE 87-1430]*

BUSINESS CYCLES - EUROPE - HISTORY - 20TH CENTURY.
Lutz, Burkart, 1925- Der kurze Traum immerwährender Prosperität . Frankfurt/Main , New York , c1984. 272 p. ; ISBN 3-593-33418-6 LC Card 85-131822
HC240 .L88 1984

BUSINESS CYCLES - GERMANY - HISTORY - 20TH CENTURY.
Feldman, Gerald D. Vom Weltkrieg zur Weltwirtschaftskrise . Göttingen , 1984. 272 p. ; ISBN 3-525-35719-2 LC Card 85-165291
HC286.2 .F45 1984

Heindl, Wolfgang, 1951- Die Haushalte von Reich, Ländern und Gemeinden in Deutschland von 1925 bis 1933 . Frankfurt am Main , New York , c1984. 419 p. : ISBN 3-8204-5474-8 LC Card 85-198505
HJ1119 .H36 1984

BUSINESS CYCLES - GERMANY (WEST)
Glismann, Hans H. Zur Natur der Wachstumsschwäche in der Bundesrepublik Deutschland . Kiel [1978] 32 p. : LC Card 85-166323
HB44 .K45 no. 55 HB3789

Hahn, Jörg. Ökonomie, Politik und Krise . Würzburg , 1984. 137 p. ; ISBN 3-88479-183-4 LC Card 85-113948
HB3732 .H34 1984

Leibinger, Hans-Bodo. Fiskalpolitik unter veränderten Rahmenbedingungen . Berlin , c1985. 256 p. : ISBN 3-428-05862-3 LC Card 85-218522
HJ1120 .L45 1985

Wirtschaftsdemokratie gegen Wirtschaftskrise . Hamburg , 1986. 177 p. : ISBN 3-87975-310-5 LC Card 86-193914
HD4175 .W54 1986

BUSINESS CYCLES - GERMANY (WEST) - ECONOMETRIC MODELS.
Buscher, Herbert S. Modelle der neuen klassischen Makroökonomie . München , c1986. iv, 312 p. : ISBN 3-88259-386-5 LC Card 86-230281
HB141 .B87 1986

Christians, Uwe, 1957- Entwicklung und empirische Überprüfung eines konjunkturgerechten Erfolgsprognosemodells zur Unterstützung der Kreditwürdigkeitsprüfung . München , c1986. xiv, 412 p. : ISBN 3-88259-430-6 (Deut. Bibl.) LC Card 87-409324 DDC 332.7/0943 19
HG3754.5.G3 C48 1986

Lehnhardt-Ritter, Gerda. Das Kapitalanlageverhalten der deutschen Lebensversicherungsunternehmen im Wandel der Konjunktur . Karlsruhe , c1984. xxiii, 444 p. : ISBN 3-88487-067-X LC Card 85-171182
HG9078 .L44 1984

BUSINESS CYCLES - GERMANY (WEST) - POLITICAL ASPECTS - LONGITUDINAL STUDIES.
Schenkluhn, Brigitte, 1951- Konjunkturpolitik und Wahlen . Bergisch Gladbach , 1985. xi, 482 p. : ISBN 3-89012-017-2 LC Card 85-153982
HB3789 .S34 1985

BUSINESS CYCLES - GREAT BRITAIN - HISTORY - 19TH CENTURY.
Braun, Hans-Joachim. Wirtschafts- und finanzpolitische Entscheidungsprozesse in England in der ersten Hälfte des 19. Jahrhunderts /. Frankfurt am Main , New York , c1984. 236 p. : ISBN 3-8204-7702-0 LC Card 85-191319 DDC 338.941 19
HC255 .B77 1984

BUSINESS CYCLES - HISTORY - 20TH CENTURY - ADDRESSES, ESSAYS, LECTURES.
Mandel, Ernest. La crise 1974-1982 . Paris , c1985. 352 p. : ISBN 2-08-081151-7
NYPL [JLC 86-204]

BUSINESS CYCLES - HUNGARY.
Soós, Károly Attila. Terv, kampány, pénz . Budapest , 1986. 532 p. : ISBN 963-221-575-3 : LC Card 87-137237
HB3787.5 .S66 1986

BUSINESS CYCLES - ITALY.
Guatri, Luigi. Crisi e risanamento delle imprese /. Milano , 1986. viii, 339 p. : ISBN 88-14-00914-7 : LC Card 86-228719
HD58.8 .G82 1986

BUSINESS CYCLES - LATIN AMERICA.
Matz, Viktor, 1947- Entwicklungsländer im internationalen Konjunkturzusammenhang . Bergisch Gladbach , c1986. 199, lxxvi p. ; ISBN 3-89012-052-0 LC Card 86-227998
HF3408.U5 M37 1986

BUSINESS CYCLES - MATHEMATICAL MODELS.
Balducci, Renato, 1947- Contrattazione salariale e ciclo economico . Roma , 1982. 174 p. :
NYPL [JLD 86-2868]

Reetz, Norbert. Konjunktur und Wachstum . St. Gallen , 1983. viii, 121 p. : LC Card 83-141234
HD75.5 .R44 1983

BUSINESS CYCLES - MATHEMATICAL MODELS - CONGRESSES.
Nonlinear economic dynamics /. Boston , c1987. xiii, 195 p. : ISBN 0-12-295140-9 (alk. paper) LC Card 86-32129 DDC 338.5/442/0151 19
HB3711 .N655 1987

BUSINESS CYCLES - PERU.
Iguíñiz, Javier. Crisis y fluctuaciones en la economía peruana, 1950-1983 . Jesús María [Peru] [1985] 245 p. : LC Card 86-116792 DDC 338.5/42/0985 19
HB3779 .I35 1985 ***NYPL [JLC 86-268]***

BUSINESS CYCLES - PERU - HISTORY.
Ríos Burga, Jaime R. Ciclos productivos en el espacio peruano colonial, siglos XVI-XIX . Lima, Perú , 1986. 70 p. : LC Card 87-401070 DDC 338.5/42/0983 19
HC227 .R456 1986

BUSINESS CYCLES - POLITICAL ASPECTS - UNITED STATES.
Hibbs, Douglas A., 1944- The American political economy . Cambridge, Mass. , 1987. xiii, 404 p. : ISBN 0-674-02735-3 (alk. paper) LC Card 87-155 DDC 338.973 19
HB3743 .H52 1987

BUSINESS CYCLES - SPAIN.
El Ciclo industrial en España . Madrid [1984?] 436 p. : ISBN 84-7474-282-X LC Card 87-113099
HC385 .C49 1984

BUSINESS CYCLES - SWEDEN - SÖDERTÄLJE - HISTORY - 20TH CENTURY.
Bjessmo, Lars-Erik. Industrin i Södertälje 1920-1970 . Stockholm , 1987. 236 p. ; ISBN 91-7146-468-9 LC Card 87-151742
HC378.S7 B54 1987

BUSINESS CYCLES - UNITED STATES.
Batra, Raveendra N. The great depression of 1990 /. Dallas, Tex. , c1985. xv, 175 p. : ISBN 0-939352-02-8 : LC Card 85-50275 DDC 338.5/42 19
HC106.8 .B39 1985 ***NYPL [JLD 86-4007]***

Batra, Raveendra N. The great depression of 1990 /. New York , c1987. 235 p. ; ISBN 0-671-64022-4 LC Card 87-4816 DDC 338.5/42 19
HC106.8 .B39 1987

Hibbs, Douglas A., 1943- The political economy of industrial democracies /. Cambridge, Mass. , 1987. viii, 327 p. : ISBN 0-674-68580-6 LC Card 86-9799 DDC 339.5/09171/3 19
HB3743 .H53 1987 ***NYPL [JLE 87-1430]***

Hunt, Lacy H. A time to be rich . New York , c1987. xvi, 282 p. : ISBN 0-89256-325-7 : LC Card 87-9431 DDC 332.6/78 19
HG4910 .H86 1987

Lehmann, Michael B. The Dow Jones-Irwin guide to using the Wall Street journal /. Homewood, Ill. , c1987. xii, 282 p. : ISBN 0-87094-923-3 LC Card 86-71441 DDC 332/.05 19
HB3743 .L44 1987

BUSINESS CYCLES - UNITED STATES - ECONOMETRIC MODELS.
Kuszczak, John. A VAR analysis of economic interdependence . [Ottawa] [1987] ii, 55 p. : LC Card 87-167407 DDC 338.5/42/0971 19
HB3755 .K87 1987

BUSINESS CYCLES - UNITED STATES - HISTORY.
Juglar, Clément, 1819-1905. [Des crises commerciales. English.] A brief history of panics and their periodical occurrence in the United States /. New York, NY , 1988. p. cm. ISBN 0-678-00168-5 LC Card 87-17069 DDC 338.5/42 19
HB3743 .J8513 1988

BUSINESS CYCLES - YUGOSLAVIA.
Soós, Károly Attila. Terv, kampány, pénz . Budapest , 1986. 532 p. : ISBN 963-221-575-3 : LC Card 87-137237
HB3787.5 .S66 1986

BUSINESS - DATA BASES.
Popovich, Charles J. Business and economics databases online . Littleton, Colo. , 1987. xviii, 276 p. : ISBN 0-87287-454-0 (pbk. : alk. paper) : LC Card 87-2672 DDC 300/.28/5 19
HF5548.2 .P612 1987

Walsh, Brendan P., 1955- On-line information . Oxford, [Oxfordshire] , New York, NY, USA , 1987. xli, 327 p. : ISBN 0-631-15543-0 : LC Card 87-13154 DDC 025/.04/02465 19
HF5548.2 .W294 1987

Wasik, John F. The electronic business information sourcebook /. New York , c1987. xvi, 208 p. ; ISBN 0-471-62464-0 : LC Card 87-8289 DDC 026/.65 19
HF5548.2 .W324 1987

BUSINESS - DATA BASES - DIRECTORIES.
Online databases in the securities and financial markets. New York, N.Y. , c1987. xxii, 322 p. ; ISBN 0-444-01276-1 (pbk.) LC Card 87-19954 DDC 025/.0633/0025 19
HG174 .O44 1987

Staud, Josef L. Online Wirtschaftsdatenbanken 1987 . Frankfurt am Main , New York , 1987. 2 v. (953 p.) : ISBN 3-8204-9457-X LC Card 87-401300 DDC 025/.0633/025 19
HF5548.2 .S7737 1987

BUSINESS - DATA PROCESSING.
Abelow, Daniel. Communications in the modern corporate environment /. Englewood Cliffs, NJ , c1986. xviii, 236 p. : ISBN 0-13-153842-X LC Card 85-16942 DDC 658/.0546 19
HF5548.2 .A24 1986 ***NYPL [JLE 86-1992]***

Adler, John R. Dynamics of MacIntosh Excel /. Homewood, Ill. , c1987. xii, 164 p. : ISBN 0-87094-907-1 (pbk.) LC Card 86-72565 DDC 005.36/9 19
HF5548.4.E93 A35 1987

Allegretti, Enzo V. Understanding and using Symphony /. St. Paul, MN , c1987. xvii, 226, [31] p., [4] p. of plates : ISBN 0-314-34640-6 (pbk.) LC Card 87-4986 DDC 005.36/9 19
HF5548.4.S95 A45 1987

Aron, Arthur. Using AppleWorks /. Indianapolis, Ind. , c1987. xviii, 458 p. : ISBN 0-88022-280-8 (pbk.) LC Card 86-63838 DDC 005.36/9 19
HF5548.4.A68 A76 1987

Badgett, Tom. The insider's guide to Lotus 1-2-3 . Glenview, Ill. , c1987. xix, 266 p. : ISBN 0-673-18718-7 (pbk.) : LC Card 87-4864 DDC 005.36/9 19
HF5548.4.L67 B33 1987

Baker, Richard H. Framework applications /. Blue Ridge Summit, PA , c1985. x, 259 p. : ISBN 0-8306-0908-3 : LC Card 85-9826 DDC 650/.028/5425 19
HF5548.4.F7 B35 1985 ***NYPL [JSE 86-803]***

Baker, Richard H. Framework II applications /. Blue Ridge Summit, PA , c1987. xi, 320 p. ; ISBN 0-8306-2198-9 : LC Card 86-23104 DDC 650/.028/55369 19
HF5548.4.F7 B35 1987

Baras, Edward M. The advanced guide to Lotus 1-2-3 /. Berkeley, Calif. , c1986. xiii, 234 p. : ISBN 0-07-881237-2 (pbk.) LC Card 86-215569 DDC 005.36/9 19
HF5548.4.L67 B36 1986

Barton, Taylor J. The illustrated Symphony (release 1.2) book /. Dallas , c1987. vii, 310 p. : ISBN 0-915381-88-5 (pbk.) LC Card 87-6135 DDC 005.36/9 19
HF5548.4.S95 B385 1987

Benjamin, Louis. The complete book of Excel macros /. Berkeley, Calif. , c1986. xviii, 123 p. : ISBN 0-07-881214-3 (pbk.) LC Card 86-106041 DDC 650/.028/55369 19
HF5548.4.E93 B46 1986
NYPL [JSE 87-239]

Bergerud, Marly, 1942- Computers for managing information /. New York , c1988. xvi, 480 p., [32] p. of plates : ISBN 0-471-84441-1 LC Card 87-20979 DDC 650/.028/5 19
HF5548.2 .B387 1988

Bharucha, Kerman D. dBASE II--a comprehensive user's manual /. Blue Ridge Summit, Pa. , c1985. xi, 305 p. ; ISBN 0-8306-0884-2 : LC Card 84-23959 DDC 001.64/25 19
HF5548.4.D22 B43 1985 ***NYPL [JSE 87-19]***

Bingham, John E. A handbook of systems analysis /. London , 1978. ix, 229 p. : ISBN 0-333-24198-3 : LC Card 79-309251
HF5548.2 .B47 1978b ***NYPL [JLE 80-2972]***

Bingham, Julie E. HAL plain and simple . Reading, Mass. , c1988. vii, 296 p. : ISBN 0-201-08002-8 (pbk.) : LC Card 87-17524 DDC 005.36/9 19
HF5548.4.L68 B56 1988

Bolocan, David. Advanced Excel /. Blue Ridge Summit, PA , c1986. x, 246 p. : ISBN 0-8306-0368-9 : LC Card 86-5767 DDC 005.36/9 19
HF5548.4.E93 B65 1986
NYPL [JSE 87-561]

Bolocan, David. Advanced Symphony applications . Blue Ridge Summit, PA , c1985. x, 230 p. : ISBN 0-8306-0988-1 : LC Card 85-22303 DDC 005.36/9 19
HF5548.4.S95 B64 1985
NYPL [JSE 86-2156]

Bolocan, David. Lotus 1-2-3 simplified /. Blue Ridge Summit, PA , c1986. xii, 255 p. : ISBN 0-8306-0448-0 : LC Card 86-5820 DDC 005.36/9 19
HF5548.4.L67 B64 1986
NYPL [JSE 87-276]

Bradley, James, 1942- Introduction to data base management in business /. New York , c1987. xii, 669 p. : ISBN 0-03-011924-3 LC Card 86-22914 DDC 658/.054 19
HF5548.2 .B678 1987

Breslin, Jud. Selecting and installing software packages . New York , 1986. xviii, 242 p. : ISBN 0-89930-158-4 (lib. bdg. : alk. paper) LC Card 86-12403 DDC 658.4/038 19
QA76.754 .B74 1986 ***NYPL [JLE 87-1133]***

Burgess, Ross. Office automation using the IBM personal computer systems . London , 1986. 180 p. : ISBN 0-00-383104-3 (pbk.) : LC Card

86-220136 DDC 651.8/4165 19
HF5548.2 .B783 1986

Campbell, Mary V. Mastering Lotus HAL /. San Francisco , c1987. xxi, 342 p. : ISBN 0-89588-422-4 (pbk.) : LC Card 87-60797 DDC 005.36/9 19
HF5548.4.L68 C35 1987

Campbell, Mary V. 1-2-3, the complete reference /. Berkeley, Calif. , c1986. xii, 892 p. : ISBN 0-07-881005-1 (pbk.) : LC Card 86-230048 DDC 005.36/9 19
HF5548.4.L67 C35 1986

Cavuoto, James. LaserWrite it! . Reading, Mass. , 1986. viii, 198 p. : ISBN 0-201-11327-9 : LC Card 86-3406 DDC 070.5/028/5 19
Z286.E43 C38 1986 ***NYPL [JSE 86-1226]***

Chorafas, Dimitris N. Applying expert systems in business /. New York , c1987. xii, 232 p. : ISBN 0-07-010880-3 : LC Card 86-2794 DDC 658/.05633 19
HD30.2 .C475 1987 ***NYPL [JLE 86-3893]***

Cohen, Eli B. Business BASIC for the IBM PC with cases /. St. Louis , 1987. xxiv, 634 p. : ISBN 0-8016-1244-6 (pbk.) LC Card 86-23100 DDC 005.2/165 19
HF5548.5.B3 C64 1987

A Competitive assessment of the United States microcomputer industry . Washington, D.C. [1986] xiv, 123 p. : ***NYPL [JLF 87-251]***

Curwin, Jon. Business studies in context . London , New York , 1987. p. cm. ISBN 0-07-707034-8 : LC Card 87-22560 DDC 658.4/0352 19
HD30.25 .C87 1987

Dayton, Doug, 1951- Computer solutions for business . Redmond, Wash. [New York] , c1987. xi, 274 p. : ISBN 0-914845-98-5 (pbk.) : LC Card 87-23957 DDC 651.8 19
HF5548.2 .D377 1987

Doyle, William J., 1946- Using SuperCalc 4 . New York , c1987. xvi, 382 p. : ISBN 0-471-85992-3 : LC Card 87-13804 DDC 005.36/9 19
HF5548.4.S87 D69 1987

Edwards, Chris, 1947- Developing microcomputer-based business systems /. Englewood Cliffs, N.J. , 1983, c1982. x, 202 p. : ISBN 0-13-204545-1 (pbk.) LC Card 83-60581 DDC 658/.054 19
HF5548.2 .E293 1983 ***NYPL [JLE 87-1181]***

Eliason, Alan L. Program analysis and design . Chicago , c1987. ix, 134 p. : ISBN 0-574-18660-3 (pbk.) LC Card 87-4521 DDC 658/.055265 19
HF5548.2 .E4275 1987

Fischer, Barbara S. Office systems integration . New York , 1987. xxi, 215 p. : ISBN 0-89930-109-6 (lib. bdg. : alk. paper) LC Card 87-2498 DDC 651.8 19
HF5547.5 .F56 1987

Fleming, Maureen. Microcomputers and productivity . White Plains, NY , c1984. iii, 125 p. ; ISBN 0-86729-109-5 (pbk.) LC Card 84-164284 DDC 650/.028/54 19
HF5548.2 .F49 1984 ***NYPL [JLf 87-8]***

Gane, Chris, 1938- Developing business systems in SQL . New York, NY , 1986. 1 v. (various pagings) : ISBN 0-914751-02-6 (pbk.) LC Card 87-107881 DDC 650/.028/557565 19
HF5548.5.S65 G36 1986

Geis, George T. Micromanaging . Englewood Cliffs, NJ , c1987. xiv, 233 p. ; ISBN 0-13-581901-6 (pbk.) LC Card 86-30470 DDC 658/.05416 19
HD30.2 .G44 1987

Gibson, Cyrus F. The information imperative . Lexington, Mass. , c1987. xxii, 160 p. : ISBN 0-669-12338-2 (alk. paper) LC Card 85-45797 DDC 658/.05 19
HF5548.2 .G496 1987

Goldfield, Randy J. Office information technology . New York , 1986. xiv, 226 p. : ISBN 0-89930-108-8 (lib. bdg. : alk. paper) LC Card 86-614 DDC 651.8 19
HF5547.5 .G65 1986 ***NYPL [JLE 87-1107]***

Gorham, Kenneth D. Personal productivity with Lotus 1-2-3 /. Dubuque, Iowa , c1987. x, 164 p. : ISBN 0-697-05227-3 (pbk.) LC Card 87-70158 DDC 005.36/9 19
HF5548.4 L67 G67 1987

Greenberg, Eric Rolfe. The 1985 AMA report on information centers /. New York, N.Y. , c1985. vi, 121 p. ; ISBN 0-8144-3151-8 LC Card 85-7552 DDC 658.4/038 19
HF5321 .G665 1985 ***NYPL [JLF 86-1167]***

Gremillion, Lee L. (Lee Louis) Computers and information systems in business . New York , c1988. xxi, 359 p., [16] p. of plates : ISBN 0-07-051007-5 (pbk.) LC Card 87-20300 DDC 650/.028/5 19
HF5548.2 .G7196 1988

Gunton, Tony, 1943- Business information technology . Englewood Cliffs, N.J. , 1988. p. cm. ISBN 0-13-100843-9 LC Card 87-7365 DDC 658/.05 19
HF5548.2 .G86 1988

Harmon, Paul. Expert systems . New York , c1988. xii, 289 p. : ISBN 0-471-83950-7 (pbk.) LC Card 87-17608 DDC 650/.028/5633 19
HF5548.2 .H367 1988

Harvey, Greg. Lotus 1-2-3 desktop companion /. San Francisco , c1987. ix, 976 p. : ISBN 0-89588-385-6 : LC Card 86-63454 DDC 005.36/9 19
HF5548.4.L67 H38 1987

Harvey, Greg. Mastering SuperCalc3 /. Berkeley, CA , c1986. xvi, 276 p. : ISBN 0-89588-312-0 (pbk.) : LC Card 87-119243 DDC 005.36/9 19
HF5548.4.S86 H37 1986

Harvey, Greg. Mastering SuperCalc4 /. San Francisco , c1987. xix, 311 p. : ISBN 0-89588-419-4 (pbk.) : LC Card 87-60636 DDC 005.36/9 19
HF5548.4.S87 H37 1987

Hergert, Douglas. Mastering Framework II /. Berkeley , c1987. xvii, 509 p. : ISBN 0-89588-390-2 (pbk.) : LC Card 86-62808 DDC 650/.028/55369 19
HF5548.4.F72 H47 1987

Hergert, Douglas. Microsoft Excel with macros . Redmond, Wash. [New York, N.Y.] , c1986. xii, 265 p. : ISBN 0-914845-76-4 (pbk.) : LC Card 86-211548 DDC 005.36/9 19
HF5548.4.E93 H474 1986

Hertz, David Bendel, 1919- The expert executive . New York , c1988. xvi, 238 p. ; ISBN 0-471-89677-2 LC Card 87-21682 DDC 658/.05633 19
HF5548.2 .H455 1988

Ho, James K. K. Linear and dynamic programming with Lotus 1-2-3, Release 2 /. Portland, Or. , c1987. xiv, 330 p. : ISBN 0-943518-72-5 (pbk.) : LC Card 87-1586 DDC 005.36/9 19
HF5548.4.L67 H6 1987

Hoenig, Alan. Framework with applications for the IBM PC /. Dubuque, Iowa , c1985. xiii, 213 p. : ISBN 0-697-00725-1 (pbk.) : LC Card 85-60013 DDC 005.3/69 19
HF5548.4.F7 H64 1985 ***NYPL [JSE 86-2110]***

Hudson, R. W. Business computer systems . London , New York , c1986. x, 163 p. : ISBN 0-07-084976-5 (pbk.) : LC Card 86-10481 DDC 650/.028/5 19
HF5548.2 .H78 1986 ***NYPL [JLE 87-1038]***

Huff, Kathryn. Developing and using microcomputer business systems /. St. Paul , c1987. xvi, 224, [29] p. : ISBN 0-314-34730-5 (pbk.) LC Card 87-2184 DDC 658/.05416 19
HF5548.2 .H785 1987

Ingalsbe, Lon. Business applications software for the IBM PC /. Columbus , c1987. 1 v. (various pagings) : ISBN 0-675-20760-6 (pbk.) LC Card 86-63664 DDC 650/.028/55365 19
HF5548.4.I24 I54 1987

Izzo, Joseph E., 1931- The embattled fortress . San Francisco , 1987. xxii, 155 p. : ISBN 1-555-42059-1 (alk. paper) LC Card 87-45429 DDC 658.4/038 19
HF5548.2 .I97 1987

Jackson, Mary, 1936- Creative modelling with Lotus 1-2-3 /. Chichester , New York , c1985. ix, 169 p. : ISBN 0-471-90796-0 (pbk.) LC Card 86-228784 DDC 005.36/9 19
HF5548.4.L67 J33 1985b

Jacobson, Jay, 1946- Advanced Symphony . New York , c1985. vi, 282 p. : ISBN 0-471-82430-5 (pbk.) : LC Card 85-12202 DDC 001.64/25 19
HF5548.4.S95 J3 1985 ***NYPL [JLF 86-854]***

Kopeck, Ronald F. Micro to mainframe links /. Berkeley, Calif. , c1986. xviii, 286 p. : ISBN 0-07-881228-3 (pbk.) LC Card 86-210460 DDC 004.6 19
HF5548.2 .K628 1986

LeBlond, Geoffrey T. Como usar Lotus 1-2-3 . Miami, Fla. , 1986- p. cm. LC Card 86-23629 DDC 005.36/9 19
HF5548.4.L67 L418 1986

Lehrman, Stevanne Ruth. Local area networking with microcomputers . New York, N.Y. , c1986. xx, 261 p. : ISBN 0-89303-640-4 (pbk.) : LC Card 86-91466 DDC 650/.028/5468 19
HF5548.2 .L392 1986 ***NYPL [JLE 87-121]***

Lewis, Colin David. Managing with micros . Oxford, England , 1984. 200 p. : LC Card 85-103102 DDC 658/.054 19
HF5548.2 .L425 1984 ***NYPL [JLE 86-2215]***

Lientz, Bennet P. Data communications for business /. St. Louis , 1987. xx, 326 p. : ISBN 0-8016-3013-4 LC Card 86-23012 DDC 650/.028/546 19
HF5548.2 .L535 1987

Loggins, Richard, 1949- The Excel advanced user's guide /. Indianapolis, Ind., USA , c1987. x, 189 p. : ISBN 0-672-46626-0 (pbk.) : LC Card 87-60109 DDC 005.36/9 19
HF5548.4.E93 L64 1987

Long, Larry E. Computers in business /. Englewood Cliffs, N.J. , c1987. xxv, 609 p. : ISBN 0-13-164294-4 LC Card 86-30412 DDC 650/.028/5 19
HF5548.2 .L586 1987

Lord, Kenniston W. Office automation systems handbook /. Blue Ridge Summit, PA. , 1988. p. cm. ISBN 0-8306-2899-1 : LC Card 87-7112 DDC 650/.028/5 19
HF5548.2 .L589 1988

The Lotus guide to learning Symphony macros . Reading, Mass. , c1986. viii, 243 p. : ISBN 0-201-16684-4 (pbk.) LC Card 86-213051 DDC 005.36/9 19
HF5549.4.S95 L67 1986

The Lotus guide to 1-2-3 advanced macro commands . Reading, Mass. [1987], c1986. x, 278 p. : ISBN 0-201-16822-7 (pbk.) : LC Card 86-32213 DDC 005.36/9 19
HF5548.4.L67 L64 1987

Lunsford, E. Michael. Macros, menus, and miracles for Lotus 1-2-3 /. New York , c1987. xix, 234 p. : ISBN 0-471-85996-6 (pbk.) : LC Card 87-14285 DDC 005.36/9 19
HF5548.4.L67 L86 1987

Lunsford, E. Michael. Power user's guide to 1-2-3 /. San Francisco , c1988. xx, 367 p. : ISBN 0-89588-421-6 (pbk.) LC Card 87-61528 DDC 005.36/9 19
HF5548.4.L67 L87 1988

Maller, Steven. Mastering Omnis 3 /. Blue Ridge Summit, PA , 1986. xi, 207 p. : ISBN 0-8306-0374-3 : LC Card 86-5758 DDC 658/.05574 19
HF5548.4.O55 M35 1986 ***NYPL [JSE 87-264]***

Mambrey, Peter. Computer und Partizipation . Opladen , c1986. xiv, 271 p. : ISBN 3-531-11851-X LC Card 87-122986 DDC 650/.028/5 19
HF5548.2 .M27 1986

El Manejo de los riesgos de la informática . Bogotá, D.E. [1984?] 61 p. : LC Card 85-183870
HF5548.2 .M2985 1984

Maney, Tracy. A management guide to artificial intelligence /. Aldershot, Hants, England , c1986. viii, 188 p. ; ***NYPL [JLD 87-862]***

Matthews, Carole Boggs. AppleWorks made easy /. Berkeley, Calif. , c1987. xiii, 398 p. : ISBN 0-07-881260-7 (pbk.) : LC Card 87-149217 DDC 005.36/9
HF5548.4.A68 M37 1987

Mazursky, Alan D., 1955- Lotus 1-2-3 .

Chicago , c1988. 480 p. : ISBN 0-574-18645-X (pbk.) : LC Card 87-4675 DDC 005.36/9 19
HF5548.4.L67 M32 1988

Metzelaar, Lawrence C. Learning to use Lotus 1-2-3 /. Menlo Park, Calif. , c1987. xi, 286 p. : ISBN 0-8053-6736-5 (pbk.) LC Card 86-214400 DDC 005.36/9 19
HF5548.4.L67 M47 1987

Meyer, Rolf, 1957- Integration der Informationsverarbeitung im Büro . Bergisch Gladbach , c1986. xiv, 327 p. : ISBN 3-89012-062-8 LC Card 87-104032 DDC 651.8 19
HF5547.5 .M497 1986

Myers, Stanley E., 1926- Structured COBOL with business applications /. Englewood Cliffs, NJ , c1988. xi, 772 p. : ISBN 0-13-854167-1 (pbk.) : LC Card 86-30646 DDC 005.13/3 19
HF5548.5.C2 M94 1988

Mylius, Ralph, 1945- The illustrated Lotus 1-2-3 . Dallas , c1987. vi, 381 p. ; ISBN 0-915381-67-2 (pbk.) LC Card 86-28217 DDC 005.36/9 19
HF5548.4.L67 M95 1987

Nevison, John M. The elements of spreadsheet style /. New York , c1987. xiv, 197 p. : ISBN 0-13-080565-3 (pbk.) : LC Card 87-6922 DDC 005.3 19
HF5548.2 .N416 1987

Nguyen, Tim K. Applied 1-2-3 . New York, N.Y. , c1987. p. cm. ISBN 0-13-729542-1 : LC Card 87-11390 DDC 005.36/9 19
HF5548.4.L67 N48 1987

Opitz, Otto. Die EDV als Wettbewerbsinstrument des Handels /. Augsburg [1986] 37 leaves : LC Card 87-407366 DDC 650/.028/5416 19
HF5548.2 .O656 1986

Perry, William E. Management workstations . Blue Ridge Summit, PA , c1987. vi, 186 p. : ISBN 0-8306-2833-9 : LC Card 87-1903 DDC 658/.05 19
HD30.2 .P47 1987

Person, Ron, 1948- [1-2-3 business formula handbook. Spanish.] 1-2-3 en el mundo de las finanzas . Miami, Fla., E.U.A. , 1988. p. cm. ISBN 0-939573-02-4 LC Card 87-20916 DDC 005.36/9 19
HF5548.4.L67 P4718 1988

Popyk, Marilyn K., 1945- Up and running! . Reading, Mass. , c1987. xxv, 647, [28] p. : ISBN 0-201-06274-7 (pbk.) : LC Card 86-26620 DDC 650/.028/5536 19
HF5548.2 .P614 1987

Postman, Andrew. Using HAL . Berkeley, Calif. , c1987. xvi, 557 p. : ISBN 0-07-881268-2 (pbk.) : LC Card 87-403738 DDC 005.36/9 19
HF5548.4.L68 P67 1987

Proektirovanie mashinnoĭ obrabotki ėkonomicheskoĭ informatsii /. Moskva , 1979. 287 p. : LC Card 81-159368
HF5548.2 .P79 1979

Rier, David C. The guide to Lotus HAL . Reading, Mass. [1987], c1988. xv, 266 p. : ISBN 0-201-16827-8 (pbk.) : LC Card 87-22885 DDC 005.36/9 19
HF5548.4.L68 R54 1988

Rosen, Arnold, 1932- Office automation and information systems /. Columbus , c1987. xvi, 363 p. : ISBN 0-675-20557-3 (pbk.) LC Card 86-62495 DDC 651.8 19
HF5548 .R67 1987

Ross, Steven C. Understanding and using Lotus 1-2-3 . St. Paul , c1987. xv, 232, [34] p. : ISBN 0-314-34741-0 (pbk.) LC Card 86-33964 DDC 650/.028/55369 19
HF5548.4.L67 R673 1987

Ross, Steven C. Understanding and using SuperCalc 3 /. St. Paul , c1987. xiii, 184, [27] p. : ISBN 0-314-30123-2 (pbk.) LC Card 86-32548 DDC 005.36/9 19
HF5548.4.S86 R67 1987

Rubin, Charles, 1953- AppleWorks . Redmond, Wash. [New York, N.Y.] , c1987. xv, 299 p. : ISBN 1-556-15114-4 (pbk.) : LC Card 87-20338 DDC 650/.028/55369 19
HF5548.4.A68 R83 1987

Saffady, William, 1944- The automated office . Silver Spring, Md. , c1981. viii, 241 p. : ISBN 0-89258-072-0 LC Card 81-208697 DDC 651.8/4 19
HF5548.2 .S165 ***NYPL [JLE 86-3919]***

Schmidt-Prestin, Barbara, 1953- Bildschirmtext in Unternehmen . Bergisch Gladbach , c1986. xvi, 308 p. : ISBN 3-89012-064-4 LC Card 87-129114 DDC 651.8/0943 19
HD9696.T463 G365 1986

Schustack, Steve, 1952- Variations in C . Bellevue, Wash. [New York] , c1985. xiii, 344 p. ; ISBN 0-914845-48-9 : LC Card 85-5033 DDC 650/.028/5425 19
HF5548.5.C12 S38 1985 ***NYPL [JSE 87-246]***

Seybold, Patricia B. Integrated desk-top environments . New York , c1985. ix, 181 p. : ISBN 0-07-056324-1 (pbk.) : LC Card 84-27841 DDC 650/.028/5425 19
HF5548.4.S95 S49 1985 ***NYPL [JSE 86-2011]***

Shaffer, Daniel N. Macro programming for 1-2-3 . Indianapolis, Ind. , c1987. xiv, 283 p. : ISBN 0-672-46573-6 (pbk.) LC Card 86-63301 DDC 005.36/9 19
HF5548.4.L67 S48 1987

Simkin, Mark G. Introduction to computer information systems for business /. Dubuque, Iowa , c1987. xxvi, 678 p. : ISBN 0-697-00125-3 LC Card 86-72218 DDC 658/.05 19
HF5548.2 .S4498 1987

Sloan, Michael L., 1944- AppleWorks . Glenview, Ill. , c1988. vi, 312 p. : ISBN 0-673-18937-6 (pbk.) : LC Card 87-9775 DDC 650/.028/55369 19
HF5548.4.A68 S58 1988

Spence, J. Wayne. Microcomputers in business . St. Louis , 1987. vii, 224 p. : ISBN 0-8016-5030-5 (pbk.) LC Card 86-30013 DDC 650/.028/5536 19
HF5548.2 .S728 1987

Stahlknecht, Peter. Einführung in die Wirtschaftsinformatik /. Berlin , New York , c1985. xiv, 396 p. : ISBN 0-387-15466-3 (U. S.) LC Card 86-219262
HF5548.2 .S7725 1985

Stark, Robin. Encyclopedia of Lotus 1-2-3 /. Blue Ridge Summit, PA , c1987. x, 484 p. : ISBN 0-8306-7891-3 : LC Card 87-19839 DDC 005.36/9 19
HF5548.4.L67 S675 1987

Stratfold, Peter. BASIC business systems simulation /. London , Boston , 1987. viii, 172 p. : ISBN 0-408-01260-9 (pbk.) : LC Card 87-18795 DDC 650/.028/55133 19
HF5548.5.B3 S78 1987

Tampoe, M. Successful business computing /. London , 1982. 124 p. : ***NYPL [JLD 86-2491]***

Tymes, Elna. Lotus 1-2-3 financial models /. Indianapolis, Ind. , c1988. vi, 307 p. ; ISBN 0-672-48410-2 (pbk.) LC Card 87-72205 DDC 005.36/9 19
HF5548.4.L67 T95 1988

Tymes, Elna. Mastering AppleWorks /. San Francisco , c1987. xxii, 479 p. : ISBN 0-89588-398-8 (pbk.) : LC Card 87-60799 DDC 650/.028/55369 19
HF5548.4.A68 T95 1987

Tymes, Elna. Mastering First Choice /. Glenview, Ill. , c1987. ix, 301 p. : ISBN 0-673-18767-5 (pbk.) : LC Card 86-26098 DDC 650/.028/55369 19
HF5548.4.F57 T96 1987

Using 1-2-3 /. Carmel, Ind. , c1987. xxviii, 905 p. : ISBN 0-88022-332-4 (pbk.) LC Card 87-61897 DDC 005.36/9 19
HF5548.4.L67 U85 1987

Vanags, I. ÎA. (Ilmar ÎAnovich) Ėffektivnoe ispol'zovanie vychislitel'noĭ tekhniki /. Moskva , 1982. 142, [2] p. : LC Card 83-165693
HF5548.2 .V345 1982

Williams, Mark M., 1948- Expert advisor, 1-2-3 . Reading, Mass. , 1988. p. cm. ISBN 0-201-18238-6 (pbk.) : LC Card 87-19286 DDC 005.36/9 19
HF5548.4.L67 W536 1988

Willis, Jerry. SuperCalc 3 . Blue Ridge Summit, Pa. , 1986. vi, 248 p. : ISBN 0-8306-0494-4 : LC Card 86-5743 DDC 005.36/9 19
HF5548.4.S86 W55 1986 ***NYPL [JSE 87-265]***

Willis, Jerry, 1942- Working with SuperCalc 4 /. Blue Ridge Summit, PA , c1987. x, 320 p. : ISBN 0-8306-0214-3 : LC Card 86-30124 DDC 005.36/9 19
HF5548.4.S87 W54 1987

Witkin, Ruth K. Managing your business with Multiplan . Redmond, Wash. , 1987. xv, 525 p. ; ISBN 0-914845-94-2 (pbk.) : LC Card 87-7773 DDC 005.36/9 19
HF5548.4.M74 W57 1987

Wolf, Douglas, 1948- Compute!'s quick & easy guide to learning Lotus 1-2-3 /. Greensboro, N.C. , c1987. vi, 139 p. : ISBN 0-87455-106-4 (pbk.) : LC Card 87-163385 DDC 005.36/9 19
HF5548.4.L67 W65 1987

Wood, Chris. The SuperCalc program made easy /. Berkeley, Calif. , c1987. xi, 384 p. : ISBN 0-07-881002-7 (pbk.) : LC Card 86-221528 DDC 005.36/9 19
HF5548.4.S85 W66 1987

Words & Figures . Monterey, CA (411 Pacific St., Monterey 93940) , c1986. 1 v. (various pagings) : LC Card 87-111370 DDC 005.36/9 19
HF5548.4.W66 W67 1986

Wortman, Leon A. C programming with business applications /. Blue Ridge Summit, PA , c1987. xii, 231 p. ; ISBN 0-8306-1457-5 : LC Card 86-23090 DDC 005.2/65 19
HF5548.5.C12 W67 1987

Wortman, Leon A. Turbo Pascal for the Mac . Blue Ridge Summit, PA , c1987. x, 274 p. : ISBN 0-8306-2927-0 (pbk.) : LC Card 87-7134 DDC 650/.028/5416 19
HF5548.5.P14 W67 1987

Zimmerman, Steven M. Understanding and using microcomputers /. St. Paul , c1988. xxvi, 371 p. : ISBN 0-314-60096-5 (pbk.) LC Card 87-19044 DDC 650/.028/5416 19
HF5548.2 .Z58 1988

The 1986 AMA report on information centers . New York, N.Y. , c1986. viii, 92, [28] p. : ISBN 0-8144-3154-2 ***NYPL [JLF 86-1835]***

BUSINESS - DATA PROCESSING - ADDRESSES, ESSAYS, LECTURES.

Heyel, Carl, 1908- John Diebold on management. Englewood Cliffs, N.J. [1972] ix, 282 p. ISBN 0-13-510214-6 LC Card 75-170643 DDC 658
HD45 .H42 ***NYPL [JLF 73-1242]***

BUSINESS - DATA PROCESSING - AUDITING.

Handbook of EDP auditing. Boston , c1986. 1 v. (various pagings) : ISBN 0-88712-597-2 (pbk.) LC Card 87-107300 DDC 657/.45/0285 19
HF5548.35 .H36 1986

BUSINESS - DATA PROCESSING - CONGRESSES.

IEEE Computer Society Office Automation Symposium (1987 : National Bureau of Standards) IEEE Computer Society Office Automation Symposium, National Bureau of Standards, Gaithersburg, MD, 27-29 April 1987. Washington, D.C. , Los Angeles, CA , c1987. xi, 319 p. : ISBN 0-8186-0770-X (pbk.) LC Card 86-83315 DDC 651.8 19
HF5548 .I44 1987

BUSINESS - DATA PROCESSING - DIRECTORIES.

Horner, Ken. Guide to computer installations in southern California . Palo Alto, Calif. , c1986. iv, 750 p. : LC Card 87-134229 DDC 004/.025/7949 19
HD9696.C63 U518343 1986

BUSINESS - DATA PROCESSING - INFORMATION SERVICES - UNITED STATES.

Perry, William E. The information center /. Englewood Cliffs, N.J. , c1987. xi, 284 p. : ISBN 0-13-464371-2 LC Card 86-25212 DDC 658.4/038 19
HF5548.2 .P47284 1987

BUSINESS - DATA PROCESSING - JUVENILE LITERATURE.

Luehrmann, Arthur. AppleWorks data bases . Gilroy, Calif. , c1987. viii, 159 p. : ISBN 0-941681-03-3 (pbk.) : LC Card 87-11734

DDC 005.36/9 19
HF5548.4.A68 L838 1987

Luehrmann, Arthur. AppleWorks spreadsheets . Gilroy, Calif. , c1987. viii, 152 p. ; ISBN 0-941681-05-X (pbk.) : LC Card 87-11745 DDC 005.36/9 19
HF5548.4.A68 L847 1987

BUSINESS - DATA PROCESSING - MANAGEMENT.
Head, Robert V. Planning and implementing information resource centers for end-user computing /. Wellesley, MA , c1985. viii, 186 p. : ISBN 0-89435-123-0 : LC Card 84-61536
NYPL [JLE 86-2117]

BUSINESS - DATA PROCESSING - PROBLEMS, EXERCISES, ETC.
Blanc, Iris. DDC spreadsheets. [New York, N.Y.] [c1986] 161 p. : LC Card 87-159255 DDC 005.3/07/1273 19
HF5548.2 .B527 1986

Business demography . Pol, Louis G. New York , c1987. p. cm. ISBN 0-89930-218-1 (lib. bdg. : alk. paper) LC Card 87-2494 DDC 304.6 19
HB849.41 .P63 1987

BUSINESS - DICTIONARIES.
Abdel Haleem, M. A. English-Arabic business dictionary /. London , 1984. xxxii, 263 p. ; ISBN 0-86010-448-6 : LC Card 83-228731 DDC 650/.03/21 19
HF1002 .A23 1984 ***NYPL [JLD 86-2048]***

AHI's complete portfolio of modern business terms. A dictionary of business terms /. New York , 1987, c1986. 438 p. ; ISBN 0-531-15518-8 LC Card 86-24560 DDC 650/.03/21 19
HF1001 .A34 1987

Akiyama, Nobuo. Talking business in Japanese /. Hauppauge, N.Y. , c1987. p. cm. ISBN 0-8120-3848-7 LC Card 87-19601 DDC 650/.03/956 19
HF1002 .A34 1987

Dietl, Clara-Erika. Commercial dictionary . Wiesbaden , c1985-c1987. 2 v. ; ISBN 3-409-19900-4 (v. 1) LC Card 86-160868
HF1002 .D493 1985
NYPL [*R-Econ. 87-1271]

The English-Arabic dictionary of professional business terms /. London , Boulder, Colo. , c1987. 210 p. ; ISBN 0-946510-33-4 : LC Card 87-163985 DDC 650/.03/21 19
HF1002 .E583 1987

Friedman, Jack P. Dictionary of business terms /. New York , c1987. vi, 650 p. ; ISBN 0-8120-3775-8 (pbk.) : LC Card 87-12640 DDC 650/.03/21 19
HF1001 .F78 1987

Johannsen, Hano. International dictionary of management /. London , c1986. 370 p. : ISBN 0-85038-970-4 ***NYPL [JLD 86-1777]***

Picchi, Fernando. Economics and business . Bologna , 1986. 1333 p. ; ISBN 88-08-04550-1 LC Card 86-201141 DDC 330/.03/51 19
HB61 .P49 1986

Strutz, Henry. Talking business in German . Woodbury, N.Y. , c1987. iv, 256 p. : ISBN 0-8120-3747-2 (pbk.) LC Card 86-22360 DDC 650/.03/31 19
HF1002 .S79 1987

BUSINESS - DICTIONARIES - GERMAN.
Dietl, Clara-Erika. Commercial dictionary . Wiesbaden , c1985-c1987. 2 v. ; ISBN 3-409-19900-4 (v. 1) LC Card 86-160868
HF1002 .D493 1985
NYPL [*R-Econ. 87-1271]

Strutz, Henry. Talking business in German . Woodbury, N.Y. , c1987. iv, 256 p. : ISBN 0-8120-3747-2 (pbk.) LC Card 86-22360 DDC 650/.03/31 19
HF1002 .S79 1987

BUSINESS - DICTIONARIES - HEBREW.
Yaḳir, E. (Eli), 1929- Milon munaḥim be-khalkalah ṿe-nihul 'asaḳim /. Tel-Aviv , 1986. 414, 38 p. : LC Card 87-162041
HB61 .Y25 1986

BUSINESS - DICTIONARIES - ITALIAN.
Picchi, Fernando. Economics and business . Bologna , 1986. 1333 p. ; ISBN 88-08-04550-1 LC Card 86-201141 DDC 330/.03/51 19
HB61 .P49 1986

BUSINESS - DICTIONARIES - JAPANESE.
Akiyama, Nobuo. Talking business in Japanese /. Hauppauge, N.Y. , c1987. p. cm. ISBN 0-8120-3848-7 LC Card 87-19601 DDC 650/.03/956 19
HF1002 .A34 1987

Business documents . Armstrong, John, 1944- London , New York , 1987. xiv, 251 p. : ISBN 0-7201-1846-8 : LC Card 86-28451 DDC 651.5 19
HF5349.G7 A76 1987

BUSINESS ECONOMICS. see **MANAGERIAL ECONOMICS.**

BUSINESS EDUCATION.
Warmbrod, Catharine P. Skills for the changing workplace . Columbus, Ohio (1960 Kenny Rd., Columbus 43210-1090) , 1985. ix, 93 p. ; LC Card 86-205907 DDC 651/.07/15 19
HF1106 .W36 1985

BUSINESS EDUCATION - BRAZIL - HISTORY.
O Comércio e suas profissões . Rio de Janeiro , 1983. 127, [5] p. : LC Card 84-161651
HF5459.B7 C65 1983 ***NYPL [JLF 86-1408]***

BUSINESS EDUCATION - INDONESIA.
Pedoman pembinaan kewiraswastaan bagi siswa. Jakarta , 1985. 1 v. (various pagings) : LC Card 86-942929
HF1171.I5 P43 1985

BUSINESS EDUCATION - ITALY - PARMA REGION - CASE STUDIES.
Automazione d'ufficio . Roma [1985] 248 p. : LC Card 86-213829
HF1152.P28 A95 1985

BUSINESS EDUCATION - UNITED STATES.
Dunfee, Thomas W. Integrating ethics into the MBA core curriculum /. [Philadelphia] , c1986. 169 leaves : LC Card 87-123702 DDC 174/.4/071173 19
HF5387 .D86 1986

Gordon, Robert Aaron. Higher education for business /. New York , 1987, c1959. xi, 491 p. ; ISBN 0-8240-8207-9 (alk. paper) : LC Card 86-25813 DDC 650/.07/1173 19
HF1131 .G6 1987

National Center for Research in Vocational Education (U. S.) A National entrepreneurship education agenda for action /. Columbus, Ohio , 1984. xiv, 114 p. : LC Card 86-201272 DDC 658.4/2 19
HF1131 .N28 1984

BUSINESS EDUCATION - UNITED STATES - CONGRESSES.
The Evolution of education in collegiate schools of business . Hempstead, N.Y. , c1987. vi, 237 p. : LC Card 87-80670 DDC 650/.07/1073 19
HF1131 .E94 1987

BUSINESS EDUCATION - UNITED STATES - CURRICULA.
National Survey of entreprenuerial [sic] education /. [Washington, D.C.?] . v. : LC Card 86-603453 DDC 658/.022/071173 19
HF1131 .N325 1986

BUSINESS EDUCATION - UNITED STATES - DIRECTORIES.
Jones, Constance. Beat the MBAs to the top! . Reading, Mass. , c1987. vii, 360 p. ; ISBN 0-201-11310-4 (pbk.) : LC Card 87-11363 DDC 650/.07/15 19
HF1131 .J756 1987

The Official guide to MBA programs /. [Los Angeles, Calif.] , Princeton, N.J. , c1986. 603 p. ; ISBN 0-446-38437-2 (pbk.) : LC Card 87-102516 DDC 658/.007/1173 19
HF1131 .O359 1986

BUSINESS ENGLISH. see **ENGLISH LANGUAGE - BUSINESS ENGLISH.**

BUSINESS ENTERPRIESES - ANGOLA - DIRECTORIES.
Representação do produtos alimentares de Angola na IX Feira Internacional de Lisboa . Luanda [1968] 248 p. : LC Card 87-400609 DDC 338.7/6413/0025673 19
HD9017.A532 R46 1968

Business enterprise in American history /. Blackford, Mansel G., 1944- Boston , c1986. xi, 456 p. : ISBN 0-395-35155-3 (pbk.) LC Card 85-60780 DDC 338.7/4/0973 19
HD2785 .B52 1986 ***NYPL [JLE 86-3008]***

BUSINESS ENTERPRISES.
In search of profitability -- agent's business plan /. Des Plaines, Ill.] , c1986. 124 p. : LC Card 87-167903 DDC 368/.0068 19
HG8877 .I49 1986

Koblencz, József. A vállalat rendszerképe /. Budapest , 1984. 179 p. : ISBN 963-512-143-1 : LC Card 86-186873
HD37.H82 K63 1984

Marzal, Antonio, 1929- Els models d'empresa . Barcelona , 1981. 241 p. : ISBN 84-7410-078-X LC Card 81-174362
HD2736.C37 M37 1981
NYPL [JLD 87-485]

A Renda da terra . [São Paulo, Brazil] , Petrópolis , c1980. 152 p. : LC Card 81-214665
HC186 .C36a no. 27 HB401

Tomer, John F. Organizational capital . New York , 1987. xvi, 188 p. : ISBN 0-275-92582-X (alk. paper) : LC Card 87-16828 DDC 338.5 19
HD31 .T635 1987

Upravlenie prot͡sessom novovvedeniĭ v kapitalisticheskoĭ firme /. Moskva , 1985. 228 p. : LC Card 86-151912
HD58.8 .U67 1985

Voigt-Weber, Lore. Alternative Betriebe . Frankfurt am Main , c1984. 154 p. ; ISBN 3-88129-811-8 LC Card 85-139278
HD2326 .V65 1984

BUSINESS ENTERPRISES - ACCOUNTING.
Oelkers, Claus, 1952- Entscheidungsorganisation . Frankfurt am Main , New York , c1986. 263 p. : ISBN 3-8204-9396-4 LC Card 86-221177
HD2326 .O35 1986

BUSINESS ENTERPRISES - ARCHIVAL RESOURCES - HANDBOOKS, MANUALS, ETC.
Armstrong, John, 1944- Business documents . London , New York , 1987. xiv, 251 p. : ISBN 0-7201-1846-8 : LC Card 86-28451 DDC 651.5 19
HF5349.G7 A76 1987

BUSINESS ENTERPRISES - ARCHIVAL RESOURCES - SWEDEN.
Sweden. Riksarkivet. Att bevara företagsarkiv . [Stockholm] [1984] 119 p. ; ISBN 91-38-08403-1 LC Card 84-239019
HC375 .S965 1984

BUSINESS ENTERPRISES - ARGENTINA.
La Cooperación empresarial argentino-brasileña . [Buenos Aires] , 1983. viii, 160 p. ; LC Card 87-125370 DDC 338.8/8/0981 19
HD2829 .C66 1983

BUSINESS ENTERPRISES - AUSTRIA - FINANCE.
Plaschka, Martina. Gründungsfinanzierung . Wien , c1986. vii, 159 p. : ISBN 3-85428-067-X LC Card 86-225844
HG4146 .P57 1986

BUSINESS ENTERPRISES - AUSTRIA - STATISTICS.
Ergebnisse der nichtlandwirtschaftlichen Betriebszählung vom 1. September 1954 /. Wien , 1958. 84 p. ; LC Card 84-252994
HD5779 .E74 1958

BUSINESS ENTERPRISES - BOLIVIA.
Confederación de Empresarios Privados de Bolivia. Pensamiento de la empresa privada boliviana . La Paz, Bolivia [1981] 274 p. : LC Card 82-138113 DDC 322/.3/0984 19
HC181 .C6426 1981 ***NYPL [JLF 86-1617]***

BUSINESS ENTERPRISES - BRAZIL.
La Cooperación empresarial argentino-brasileña . [Buenos Aires] , 1983. viii, 160 p. ; LC Card 87-125370 DDC 338.8/8/0981 19
HD2829 .C66 1983

BUSINESS ENTERPRISES - BRUNEI - DIRECTORIES.
Buku panduan badan-badan perusahaan perniagaan Negara Brunei Darussalam =. Bandar Seri Begawan, Negara Brunei Darussalam [1985] vii, 89, [9] p. ; LC Card 86-945171 DDC 338.7/4/0255955 19
HF3800.68 .B84 1985

BUSINESS ENTERPRISES - BULGARIA - FINANCE.
Kotsev, Tsvetan. Formirane i izpolzvane na parichnite fondove v stopanskite organizatsii /. Varna , 1985. 117 p. ; LC Card 85-213610
HC403.Z9 C347 1985

BUSINESS ENTERPRISES - COMMUNICATION SYSTEMS - PLANNING.
Heldman, Robert K. Telecommunications management planning . Blue Ridge Summit, PA , c1987. xviii, 734 p. : ISBN 0-8306-2864-9 : LC Card 86-30002 DDC 658.4/038 19
HD30.335 .H45 1987

BUSINESS ENTERPRISES - CZECHOSLOVAKIA - DIRECTORIES.
Your trade partners in Czechoslovakia /. Praha , 1986. 187 p. : LC Card 87-127524 DDC 382/.025/437 19
HF3550.3.A48 Y58 1986

BUSINESS ENTERPRISES - DATA PROCESSING.
Oelkers, Claus, 1952- Entscheidungsorganisation . Frankfurt am Main , New York , c1986. 263 p. : ISBN 3-8204-9396-4 LC Card 86-221177
HD2326 .O35 1986

BUSINESS ENTERPRISES - DECISION MAKING.
Oelkers, Claus, 1952- Entscheidungsorganisation . Frankfurt am Main , New York , c1986. 263 p. : ISBN 3-8204-9396-4 LC Card 86-221177
HD2326 .O35 1986

BUSINESS ENTERPRISES - DOMINICAN REPUBLIC - CONGRESSES.
Influencia del sector privado sobre la realidad nacional. [Santo Domingo] [1986] 180 p., [1] leaf of plates : LC Card 86-190331
HC153.5 .I53 1986

BUSINESS ENTERPRISES - ENGLAND - HISTORY - 18TH CENTURY.
Hoppit, Julian. Risk and failure in English business, 1700-1800 /. Cambridge [Cambridgeshire] , New York , 1987. vii, 228 p. : ISBN 0-521-32624-9 LC Card 87-743 DDC 332.7/5/0942 19
HG3769.G73 E54 1987

BUSINESS ENTERPRISES - EUROPE, EASTERN - MANAGEMENT.
Kuligin, Pavel Ivanovich. Kriterii ėffektivnosti raboty predprii͡atiĭ . Moskva , 1986. 172 p. ; LC Card 86-211780
HD70.E7 K85 1986

BUSINESS ENTERPRISES - FINANCE.
Bánhidi, Ferenc. Könyvelésről és pénzgazdálkodásról vállalati vezetőknek . Budapest , 1986, c1985. 215 p. ; ISBN 963-221-649-0 : LC Card 87-118825
HF5655.H9 B36 1986

Benner, Wolfgang, 1940- Betriebliche Finanzwirtschaft als monetäres System /. Göttingen , 1983. 486 p. : ISBN 3-509-01323-9 LC Card 83-240817
HG4011 .B433 1983

Chardonnens, Jean-Pierre. Le financement de l'entreprise en période de récession économique /. [Fribourg] , c1984. 269 p. : ISBN 2-8271-0281-1 : LC Card 84-225557 DDC 658.1/5 19
HG4026 .C457 1984

Cómo establecer el control presupuestario /. Madrid , 1983. 95 p. : ISBN 84-256-0387-0 LC Card 85-221532
HG4026 .C56 1983

Cooley, Philip L. Business financial management /. Chicago , c1988. xxv, 924, [34] p. : ISBN 0-03-009979-X LC Card 87-20079 DDC 658.1/5 19
HG4026 .C63 1988

Engel, Gábor. A kereskedelmi tevékenység komplex finanszirozása /. Budapest [1985] 68 p. ; ISBN 963-7202-58-7 LC Card 86-157419
HG4026 .E517 1985

Fossati, Giorgio. Il finanziamento delle imprese /. Milano, Italy , 1984. 270 p. : LC Card 86-141137 DDC 658.1/5 19
HG4011 .F58 1984

Gitman, Lawrence J. Basic managerial finance /. New York , c1987. xxxi, 653 p., [2] p. of plates : ISBN 0-06-042366-8 LC Card 86-25666 DDC 658.1/5 19
HG4026 .G59 1987

Glais, Michel. Le diagnostic financier de l'entreprise . Paris , 1984. 256 p. : ISBN 2-7178-0787-X : LC Card 85-105905
HG4011 .G56 1984

Gup, Benton E. Principles of financial management /. New York , c1987. xii, 672, 16 p. : ISBN 0-471-81203-X LC Card 86-28937 DDC 658.1/5 19
HG4026 .G88 1987

Jones, Seymour, 1931- The Coopers & Lybrand guide to growing your business /. New York , c1988. xiii, 477 p. ; ISBN 0-471-85941-9 LC Card 87-21688 DDC 658 19
HD31 .J627 1988

McGee, Robert W. Fundamentals of accounting and finance . Lanham, MD , c1987. p. cm. ISBN 0-8191-6289-2 (pbk. : alk. paper) LC Card 87-21581 DDC 657 19
HF5635 .M4883 1987

Moyer, R. Charles, 1945- Contemporary financial management /. St. Paul , c1988. xxiv, 793, 24 p. : ISBN 0-314-64227-7 LC Card 87-24201 DDC 658.1/5 19
HG4026 .M68 1988

O'glove, Thornton L. Quality of earnings . New York , c1987. xviii, 204 p. : ISBN 0-02-922630-9 LC Card 86-25631 DDC 657/.33 19
HG4028.B2 O35 1987

Owen, Robert R. (Robert Randolph) Arthur Young guide to financing for growth . New York , c1986. xiv, 298 p. ; ISBN 0-471-81946-8 : LC Card 86-1612 DDC 658.1/522 19
HG4027.7 .O94 1986 ***NYPL [JLE 86-2667]***

Pringle, John J. Essentials of managerial finance /. Glenview, Ill. , c1987. xxxi, 811, [98] p. : ISBN 0-673-18331-9 : LC Card 86-31333 DDC 658.1/5 19
HG4026 .P73 1987

Romero, Carlos, 1946- Introducción a la financiación empresarial y al análisis bursátil /. Madrid , c1984. 238 p. : ISBN 84-206-8080-X LC Card 85-135755
HG4011 .R57 1984

Weber, Helmut Kurt, 1933- Rentabilität, Produktivität, Liquidität der Unternehmung . Stuttgart , c1983. x, 161 p. ; ISBN 3-7910-0346-1 LC Card 83-167883
HG4026 .W4 1983

Woelfel, Charles J. The operating executive's guide to profit planning tools and techniques /. Chicago, Ill. , c1986. ix, 199 p. : ISBN 0-917253-24-8 : LC Card 86-3222 DDC 658.1/55 19
HF5635 .W848 1986 ***NYPL [JLE 86-3007]***

BUSINESS ENTERPRISES - FINANCE - CONGRESSES.
La Maîtrise de la croissance dans l'entreprise. Paris, 1973. xx, 333 p. LC Card 73-172856 DDC 658.4
HD29 .M26 ***NYPL [JLE 74-55]***

BUSINESS ENTERPRISES - FINANCE - DATA PROCESSING.
Drew, Rodney. Microcomputers for financial planning /. Aldershot, Hampshire, England , Brookfield, Vt., U. S.A. , c1987. x, 105 p. : ISBN 0-566-02579-5 (pbk.) : LC Card 87-8405 DDC 658.1/5/0285416 19
HG4012.5 .D73 1987

BUSINESS ENTERPRISES - FINANCE - HANDBOOKS, MANUALS, ETC.
Business planning guide . Dover, N.H. (50 Mill St., Dover 03820) , c1985. vii, 115 p. : LC Card 86-622397 DDC 658.4/01 19
HD30.28 .B85 1985

Colman, Robert Douglas. Modern business financing . Englewood Cliffs, N.J. , c1986. xxi, 281 p. : ISBN 0-13-589060-8 LC Card 85-20490 DDC 658.1/5 19
HG4027.3 .C64 1986 ***NYPL [JLF 86-616]***

Financial management handbook /. Aldershot, Hants, England , c1987. p. cm. ISBN 0-566-02623-6 : LC Card 87-40 DDC 658.1/5 19
HG4027.3 .F53 1987

Handbook for raising capital . Homewood, Ill. , c1987. xxiv, 666 p. : ISBN 0-87094-705-2 LC Card 86-71216 ***NYPL [*R-Econ. 87-1124]***

BUSINESS ENTERPRISES - FINANCE - JUVENILE LITERATURE.
Little, Jeffrey B. What is a share of stock? /. New York , c1988. 47 p. : ISBN 1-555-46620-6 LC Card 87-13788 DDC 332.63/22 19
HG4521 .L736 1988

BUSINESS ENTERPRISES - FINANCE - MATHEMATICAL MODELS.
Fietz, Günter. Kurzfristige Finanzplanung und Grossprojektfertigung /. Frankfurt am Main , New York , c1986. iv, 269 p. : ISBN 3-8204-9322-0 LC Card 86-156212
HG4012 .F53 1986

BUSINESS ENTERPRISES - FLORIDA - DIRECTORIES.
Fencl, George. The central Florida career guide /. Altamonte Springs, FL. , c1987. 56, 48 p. : ISBN 0-942827-00-7 (pbk.) : LC Card 87-402073 DDC 650.1/4/09759 19
HF5382.75.U62 F64 1987

BUSINESS ENTERPRISES - FOREIGN COUNTRIES.
Kennedy, Gavin. Doing business abroad /. New York , c1985. 268 p. ; ISBN 0-671-55484-0 : LC Card 85-14416 DDC 658.4 19
HD58.6 .K45 1985 ***NYPL [JLD 86-2339]***

BUSINESS ENTERPRISES - FRANCE.
Ortscheidt, Pierre. L'entreprise face au nouveau droit de travail /. Paris , c1985. 221 p. ; ISBN 2-7178-0915-5 : LC Card 85-191518
KJV3399 .O78 1985 ***NYPL [JLE 87-358]***

Tableaux de l'état physique et moral des salariés en France /. Paris , 1986. 237 p. ; ISBN 2-7071-1626-2 : LC Card 87-122301
HD8431 .T32 1986

BUSINESS ENTERPRISES - FRANCE - DIRECTORIES.
150 meilleures entreprises françaises /. Paris , c1986. 313 p. ; ISBN 2-234-01894-3 : LC Card 87-107207
HF5382.75.F8 A13 1986

BUSINESS ENTERPRISES - FRANCE - HISTORY.
Baumier, Jean. Ces patrons qui gagnent /. Paris , c1986. 262 p. ; ISBN 2-259-01532-8 : LC Card 87-106535
HD2855 .B38 1986

Vérin, Hélène, 1940- Entrepreneurs, entreprise . Paris , c1982. 262 p. ; ISBN 2-13-037449-2 (pbk.) : LC Card 82-153537 DDC 338/.04/09 19
HB615 .V44 1982 ***NYPL [JLD 86-3019]***

BUSINESS ENTERPRISES - GERMANY, EAST.
Gothe, Richard, 1928- Zusammenwirken von örtlichen Staatsorganen und Kombinaten /. Berlin , 1983. 89 p. ; LC Card 84-166789
HD3616.G48 G67 1983

BUSINESS ENTERPRISES - GERMANY, WEST.
Mahler, Karl-Werner, 1933- Der Waste Factor . München-Gräfelfing , c1983. 64 p. ; ISBN 3-8040-0321-4 LC Card 84-214297
HC290.5.W3 M34 1983

Stauf, Wolfgang. Der wichtige Grund bei der personengesellschaftlichen Auflösungs- und Ausschliessungsklage . Göttingen , 1980. xiv, 80 p. ; ISBN 3-88415-549-0 : LC Card 80-150978 DDC 346.73/07 347.3067 19
KK2435.7 .S7 1980 ***NYPL [JLD 86-1591]***

BUSINESS ENTERPRISES - GERMANY (WEST) - ACCOUNTING.
Russ, Wolfgang, 1955- Der Anhang als dritter Teil des Jahresabschlusses . Bergisch Gladbach , 1984. xi, 332 p. : ISBN 3-89012-013-X : LC Card 85-195717
HF5681.B2 R817 1984

BUSINESS ENTERPRISES - GERMANY, WEST - FINANCE.
Eschbach, Thomas H., 1954- Der Ausgleich funktionaler Defizite des wirtschaftlichen Systems durch die Unternehmensberatung . Frankfurt am Main , New York , c1984. 152 p. ; ISBN 3-8204-5127-7 LC Card 85-191647
HD69.C6 E76 1984

Mühlbayer, Michael, 1955- Prospektive Erfolgsanalyse und Unternehmensbonität /. Frankfurt am Main , New York , c1986. vii,

388 p. : ISBN 3-8204-9462-6 LC Card 86-190036
HG4156 .M84 1986

Schoppe, Siegfried, 1944- Determinanten der Eigenkapitalbildung und Konsequenzen für die Wettbewerbsfähigkeit deutscher Grossunternehmen und Mittelbetriebe /. Hamburg , 1986. 24 p. : LC Card 86-185861
HG4156 .S36 1986

Wöbbeking, Karlheinz. Die Planung von Liquidationsstrategien . Münster [1986] vii, 273 p. : ISBN 3-88660-328-8 LC Card 86-213801
HD2747 .W6 1986

BUSINESS ENTERPRISES - GERMANY (WEST) - FINANCE - MATHEMATICAL MODELS.
Prätsch, Joachim, 1951- Langfristige Finanzplanung und Simulationsmodelle . Frankfurt am Main , New York , c1986. xii, 481 p. : ISBN 3-8204-9403-0 LC Card 86-219850
HG4157 .P73 1986

BUSINESS ENTERPRISES, GOVERNMENT. see **GOVERNMENT BUSINESS ENTERPRISES.**

BUSINESS ENTERPRISES - GOVERNMENT POLICY.
Kidron, Michael. What you need to know about business, money, and power /. New York , c1987. 187 p. : ISBN 0-671-54113-7 : LC Card 86-31571 DDC 650 19
HF5351 .K473 1987

BUSINESS ENTERPRISES - GREAT BRITAIN - ARCHIVAL RESOURCES - HANDBOOKS, MANUALS, ETC.
Armstrong, John, 1944- Business documents . London , New York , 1987. xiv, 251 p. : ISBN 0-7201-1846-8 : LC Card 86-28451 DDC 651.5 19
HF5349.G7 A76 1987

BUSINESS ENTERPRISES - GREAT BRITAIN - FINANCE.
Sudarsanam, P. S. Market and industry structure and corporate cost of capital . London [1986] 33 p. ; LC Card 86-208314 DDC 338.7/4/0941 19
HG4135 .S83 1986

BUSINESS ENTERPRISES - GREAT BRITAIN - HISTORIOGRAPHY.
Orbell, John. A guide to tracing the history of a business /. Aldershot, Hants, Eng. , Brookfield, Vt., USA , c1987. p. cm. ISBN 0-566-05591-0 : LC Card 87-15505 DDC 338.7/072 19
HD2321 .O7 1987

BUSINESS ENTERPRISES - GREAT BRITAIN - HISTORY - HANDBOOKS, MANUALS, ETC.
Orbell, John. A guide to tracing the history of a business /. Aldershot, Hants, Eng. , Brookfield, Vt., USA , c1987. p. cm. ISBN 0-566-05591-0 : LC Card 87-15505 DDC 338.7/072 19
HD2321 .O7 1987

BUSINESS ENTERPRISES - HISTORIOGRAPHY.
Orbell, John. A guide to tracing the history of a business /. Aldershot, Hants, Eng. , Brookfield, Vt., USA , c1987. p. cm. ISBN 0-566-05591-0 : LC Card 87-15505 DDC 338.7/072 19
HD2321 .O7 1987

BUSINESS ENTERPRISES - HISTORY.
Baumier, Jean. Ces patrons qui gagnent /. Paris , c1986. 262 p. ; ISBN 2-259-01532-8 : LC Card 87-106535
HD2855 .B38 1986

BUSINESS ENTERPRISES - HISTORY - HANDBOOKS, MANUALS, ETC.
Orbell, John. A guide to tracing the history of a business /. Aldershot, Hants, Eng. , Brookfield, Vt., USA , c1987. p. cm. ISBN 0-566-05591-0 : LC Card 87-15505 DDC 338.7/072 19
HD2321 .O7 1987

BUSINESS ENTERPRISES - HUNGARY.
Antal, Iván. Vállalatok környezete, céljai, szervezete /. Budapest , 1986. 270 p. : ISBN 963-221-567-2 : LC Card 87-149512
HD70.H8 A536 1986

The Hungarian enterprise in the context of intra-CMEA relations /. Budapest , 1986. 93 p. ; ISBN 963-301-138-8 (pbk.) LC Card 87-101284 DDC 337.439 19
HF1542.5.H8 H85 1986

Palicz, András. Az önálló vállalattá szervezés elméleti és módszertani megalapozása /. Budapest , 1984. 81 p. : ISBN 963-02-3351-7 : LC Card 86-126838
HD70.H8 P35 1984

BUSINESS ENTERPRISES - HUNGARY - CONGRESSES.
Gazdaságpolitikánk az élenjáró vállalatok gyakorlatában . [Budapest] , 1985. 276 p. : ISBN 963-09-2769-1 : LC Card 87-407761
HD70.H8 G39 1985

BUSINESS ENTERPRISES - HUNGARY - DIRECTORIES.
Marketing . [Budapest , 1985?] 68 p. : LC Card 86-234770 DDC 338.7/4/09439 19
HC300.227 .M37 1985

BUSINESS ENTERPRISES - HUNGARY - FINANCE.
Ábel, István. A vállalatok pénzügyi szabályozása . Budapest , 1984. 32, [1] p. ; LC Card 85-175023
HG4149.5 .A54 1984

Bánhidi, Ferenc. Könyvelésről és pénzgazdálkodásról vállalati vezetőknek . Budapest , 1986, c1985. 215 p. ; ISBN 963-221-649-0 : LC Card 87-118825
HF5655.H9 B36 1986

Engel, Gábor. A kereskedelmi tevékenység komplex finanszirozása /. Budapest [1985] 68 p. ; ISBN 963-7202-58-7 LC Card 86-157419
HG4026 .E517 1985

László, Gyula, Dr. Utmutató és példatár az 1985. január 1-től érvényes jövedelem- és keresetszabályozási rendszer alkalmazásához /. Budapest , 1985. 153 p. ; ISBN 963-621-216-3 LC Card 85-138648
HJ4715 .L37 1985

BUSINESS ENTERPRISES - HUNGARY - FINANCE - CASE STUDIES.
Szalai, Erzsébet. Kiemelt vállalat, beruházás, érdek /. Budapest , 1981. 140 p. ; ISBN 963-05-2527-5 LC Card 81-170685
HG4028.C4 S96 1981

BUSINESS ENTERPRISES - HUNGARY - SZABOLCS-SZATMÁR - HISTORY.
Ipari üzemtörténet /. Nyíregyháza , 1979 ([Nyíregyháza] : Készült a Szabolcs-Szatmár Megyei Tanács Sokszorosító Költségvetési Üzemében) 228 p. : ISBN 963-01-2796-2 LC Card 81-173980
HC300.29.S92 I62 1979

BUSINESS ENTERPRISES, INTERNATIONAL. see **INTERNATIONAL BUSINESS ENTERPRISES.**

BUSINESS ENTERPRISES - ISLAMIC COUNTRIES - CASE STUDIES.
El-Ashker, Ahmed Abdel-Fattah, 1943- The Islamic business enterprise /. London , Wolfboro, N.H. , c1987. xi, 242 p. : ISBN 0-7099-0985-3 : LC Card 86-24271 DDC 332.1/0917/671 19
HG3368.A6 E4 1987

BUSINESS ENTERPRISES - JAPAN - FINANCE.
Yoshida, Satoshi, 1948- Endaka to kigyō shūeki . [Higashimurayama-shi] , Tōkyō , 1986. 137 p. : ISBN 4-315-50263-4 : LC Card 86-205176
HC462.9 .Y638 1986 <Orien Japan>
NYPL [*OSM 87-2489]

BUSINESS ENTERPRISES - MEXICO - FINANCE.
Mántey de Anguiano, M. G. Análisis microeconómico de los factores que determinan el valor de mercado de las empresas industriales mexicanas y su tasa de expansión /. [Mexico City] [1986] iv, 63 leaves : LC Card 87-400949 DDC 658.1/5/0972 19
HG4092 .M36 1986

BUSINESS ENTERPRISES, NEW. see **NEW BUSINESS ENTERPRISES.**

BUSINESS ENTERPRISES - NEW YORK (N. Y.) - DIRECTORIES.
Major employers in and around New York City. Hillsdale, N.J. (P.O. Box 294, Hillsdale 07642-0294) , c1986. iv, 112 p. ; LC Card 86-211679 DDC 338.7/4/025741 19
HF5382.75.U62 N56 1986

BUSINESS ENTERPRISES - NIGERIA - FINANCE.
Osubor, John Uche. Business finance and banking in Nigeria /. Owerri, Imo State, Nigeria , 1984. vii, 209 p. : ISBN 978-235-700-13 (pbk.) LC Card 86-207599 DDC 332.1/09669 19
HG3431.A6 O85 1984

BUSINESS ENTERPRISES - PURCHASING.
Kellogg, Douglas E. A primer for buying and selling small manufacturing companies /. New York , c1987. xiv, 225 p. : ISBN 0-471-85235-X LC Card 87-19017 DDC 658.1/6 19
HD2341 .K44 1987

BUSINESS ENTERPRISES - ROMANIA - FINANCE.
Roşca, Teodor. Creşterea eficienţei mijloacelor circulante, cerinţă actuală /. Bucureşti , 1983. 234 p. : LC Card 84-152999
HG4028.W65 R67 1983 ***NYPL [JLD 87-49]***

BUSINESS ENTERPRISES, SALE OF.
Kellogg, Douglas E. A primer for buying and selling small manufacturing companies /. New York , c1987. xiv, 225 p. : ISBN 0-471-85235-X LC Card 87-19017 DDC 658.1/6 19
HD2341 .K44 1987

Tetreault, Wilfred F., 1927- Starting right in your new business /. Reading, Mass. , c1987. ix, 226 p. ; ISBN 0-201-07795-7 (pbk.) : LC Card 87-19464 DDC 658.1/141 19
HD62.7 .T47 1987

BUSINESS ENTERPRISES, SALE OF - UNITED STATES - HANDBOOKS, MANUALS, ETC.
Scharf, Charles A. Acquisitions, mergers, sales, buyouts, and takeovers . Englewood Cliffs, N.J. , c1985. xi, 452 p. : ISBN 0-13-003120-8 LC Card 85-6566 DDC 658.1/6/0973 19
HD2741 .S35 1985 ***NYPL [JLF 86-611]***

BUSINESS ENTERPRISES - SENEGAL - AUDITING.
Sougue, Matthieu Kounabé. La pratique de l'audit financier dans les entreprises au Sénégal, à travers le cabinet Helios . [Dakar] [1983?] 194, [18] leaves : LC Card 85-121418
HF5686.C7 S67 1984

BUSINESS ENTERPRISES - SOVIET UNION.
Shusharin, A. L. (Aleksandr Leonidovich) Sootnoshenie khozraschetnoĭ ėkonomicheskoĭ ėffektivnosti sredstv proizvodstva s ikh narodno-khozi͡aĭstvennoĭ ėffektivnost'i͡u /. Tomsk , 1979. 159 p. ; LC Card 87-462036
HD70.S63 S55 1979

BUSINESS ENTERPRISES - SOVIET UNION - FINANCE.
Rasshirenie samostoi͡atel'nosti predprii͡atiĭ i nauchno-tekhnicheskoe razvitie proizvodstva /. Moskva , 1986. 205 p. ; LC Card 87-162795
HG4186 .R37 1986

Vasil'eva, E. S. (Elena Stepanovna) Planirovanie pribyli i rentabel'nosti na promyshlennom predprii͡atii . Moskva , 1985. 40 p. : LC Card 86-204680
HG4028.P7 V39 1985

BUSINESS ENTERPRISES - SOVIET UNION - MANAGEMENT.
Odint͡sova, G. S. (Galina Sergeevna) Organizatsionnoe proektirovanie i planirovanie razvitii͡a sistem upravlenii͡a /. Kiev , 1986. 158, [2] p. : LC Card 87-162923
HD2876 .O35 1986

BUSINESS ENTERPRISES - SPAIN.
Lampreave Pérez, José Luis. La empresa española ante el impuesto sobre el valor añadido, medidas de adaptación y ajuste /. Madrid, España , 1985. 493 p. : ISBN 84-7196-571-2 : LC Card 86-208329
HJ5715.S7 L36 1985

BUSINESS ENTERPRISES - SPAIN - CONGRESSES.
La Empresa. Madrid , 1962. 348 p. : LC Card 85-108024
HD2326 .E47 1962

BUSINESS ENTERPRISES - STUDY AND TEACHING - UNITED STATES.
National Survey of entreprenuerial [sic] education /. [Washington, D.C.?] . v. : LC Card 86-603453 DDC 658/.022/071173 19
HF1131 .N325 1986

BUSINESS ENTERPRISES - TAXATION - FRANCE.
Mallard, Jean-Claude, 1947- Comprendre et

gérer la fiscalité de l'entreprise /. La Tronche , Paris [1985] 255 p. : LC Card 86-166702
HD2753.F8 M34 1985

BUSINESS ENTERPRISES - TAXATION - GERMANY, WEST.
Fangl, Hans. Zum Kostencharakter von Ertragsteuern /. Berlin , c1986. 208 p. : ISBN 3-428-06032-6 LC Card 86-219710 DDC 336.24/3/0943 19
HD2753.G3 F26 1986

Fuest, Winfried, 1946- Irrtümer in der aktuellen Steuerdiskussion /. Köln , c1987. 54 p. : ISBN 3-602-24749-X LC Card 87-409547 DDC 336.2/00943 19
HJ2687 .F834 1987

List, Stephan, 1959- Arbeitnehmerbeteiligung bei Personengesellschaften . Spardorf , c1985. v, 167 p. ; ISBN 3-922919-50-2 LC Card 86-141876
HD5660.G4 L55 1985

Unternehmung und Steuer . Wiesbaden , c1983. 395 p. ; ISBN 3-409-50005-7 LC Card 83-161883
HD2753.G3 U57 1983

BUSINESS ENTERPRISES - TAXATION - HUNGARY.
László, Gyula, Dr. Utmutató és példatár az 1985. január 1-től érvényes jövedelem- és keresetszabályozási rendszer alkalmazásához /. Budapest , 1985. 153 p. ; ISBN 963-621-216-3 LC Card 85-138648
HJ4715 .L37 1985

BUSINESS ENTERPRISES - TAXATION - NEW YORK (STATE)
New York (State). Legislature. Legislative Commission on the Modernization and Simplification of Tax Administration and the Tax Law. Interstate business locational decisions and the effect of the state's tax structure on after-tax rates-of-return of manufacturing firms . [Albany] [1984] 121 p. : LC Card 86-621116 DDC 336.2/07 19
HJ4655.N54 N55 1984

BUSINESS ENTERPRISES, TRADE-UNION - GERMANY - HISTORY.
Novy, Klaus. Illustrierte Geschichte der Gemeinwirtschaft . Berlin , c1985. 239 p. : ISBN 3-8012-0111-2 LC Card 86-122604
HD3498 .N68 1985

BUSINESS ENTERPRISES, TRADE-UNION - GERMANY (WEST) - HAMBURG.
Neue Heimat . Hamburg , 1983. 231 p. : ISBN 3-87975-238-9 LC Card 83-150360
HD7339.H3 N48 1983

BUSINESS ENTERPRISES - UNITED STATES.
Bittel, Lester R. Business in action . New York , c1988. vii, 597 p. : ISBN 0-07-005565-3 LC Card 87-3134 DDC 658 19
HF5343 .B57 1988

McAdams, Tony. Law, business, and society /. Plano, Tex. , 1986. xvi, 662, 52 p. : ISBN 0-256-03070-7 LC Card 85-73323 DDC 346.73/065 347.30665 19
KF1355 .M28 1986 ***NYPL [JLE 87-891]***

BUSINESS ENTERPRISES - UNITED STATES - CASE STUDIES.
Petras, Ross. Inside track . New York , c1986. xv, 508 p. ; ISBN 0-394-74339-3 : LC Card 85-40868 DDC 650.1/4/0973 19
HF5382.U5 P44 1986
NYPL [*R-Econ. 86-3454]

BUSINESS ENTERPRISES - UNITED STATES - FINANCE.
Eschbach, Thomas H., 1954- Der Ausgleich funktionaler Defizite des wirtschaftlichen Systems durch die Unternehmensberatung . Frankfurt am Main , New York , c1984. 152 p. ; ISBN 3-8204-5127-7 LC Card 85-191647
HD69.C6 E76 1984

Hellmuth, James G. Finding money . New York, N.Y. , c1983. p. cm. ISBN 0-932648-79-7 LC Card 86-31053 DDC 658.1/5224 19
HG4027.7 .H44 1983b

BUSINESS ENTERPRISES - UNITED STATES - HANDBOOKS, MANUALS, ETC.
The Book of business knowledge /. New York, N.Y. , c1987. p. cm. ISBN 0-932648-83-5 : LC Card 86-30962 DDC 658 19
HF5356 .B72 1987

The Boss's encyclopedia /. New York, N.Y. , c1987. xxvi, 594 p. ; ISBN 0-932648-75-4 LC Card 86-30961 DDC 658 19
HF5356 .B735 1987

Business confidential. New York, N.Y. , c1987. xi, 504 p. ; ISBN 0-932648-82-7 LC Card 86-30963 DDC 650 19
HF5356 .B9259 1987

BUSINESS ENTERPRISES - UNITED STATES - HISTORY.
Blackford, Mansel G., 1944- Business enterprise in American history /. Boston , c1986. xi, 456 p. : ISBN 0-395-35155-3 (pbk.) LC Card 85-60780 DDC 338.7/4/0973 19
HD2785 .B52 1986 ***NYPL [JLE 86-3008]***

Chandler, Alfred Dupont. The coming of managerial capitalism . Homewood, Ill. , 1985. xiv, 877 p. : ISBN 0-256-03285-8 LC Card 84-82470 DDC 338.6/44/0973 19
HD2785 .C47 1985 ***NYPL [JLE 86-4418]***

DiBacco, Thomas V. Made in the U. S.A. . New York , c1987. xii, 290 p. ; ISBN 0-06-015624-4 : LC Card 86-45652 DDC 338.0973 19
HC103 .D46 1987 ***NYPL [JLD 87-1292]***

Dobson, John M. A history of American enterprise /. Englewood Cliffs, N.J. , c1988. p. cm. ISBN 0-13-389081-3 LC Card 87-18679 DDC 338.0973 19
HF3021 .D6 1988

BUSINESS ENTERPRISES - UNITED STATES - PURCHASING - HANDBOOKS, MANUALS, ETC.
Scharf, Charles A. Acquisitions, mergers, sales, buyouts, and takeovers . Englewood Cliffs, N.J. , c1985. xi, 452 p. : ISBN 0-13-003120-8 LC Card 85-6566 DDC 658.1/6/0973 19
HD2741 .S35 1985 ***NYPL [JLF 86-611]***

BUSINESS ENTERPRISES - URUGUAY.
Peirano, Ricardo. El rol del empresario privado en el desarrollo económico y social en democracia /. Montevideo, Uruguay , 1986. 79 leaves ; LC Card 87-404359 DDC 338.9895 19
HC232 .P45 1986

BUSINESS ENTERPRISES - VALUATION.
Horn, Thomas W. Business valuation manual . Lancaster, PA , 1987. 224 p. : ISBN 0-87521-015-5 (pbk.) : LC Card 87-17887 DDC 658.1/522 19
HD1393.25 .H66 1987

Martin, Thomas John, 1942- Valuation reference manual . [Hicksville, N.Y. (383 S. Broadway, Hicksville 11801) , c1986] ix, 134 leaves ; LC Card 86-233027 DDC 658.1/522 19
HG4028.V3 M33 1986

März, Thomas. Interdependenzen in einem Kennzahlensystem . München , c1983. iv, 296 p. : ISBN 3-88259-262-1 : LC Card 83-222369
HG4028.V3 M34 1983

Rick, Josef. Bewertung und Abgeltungskonditionen bei der Veräusserung mittelständischer Unternehmen /. Berlin , c1985. 191 p. : ISBN 3-428-05785-6 : LC Card 85-186420
HG4028.V3 R52 1985

Smith, Gordon V., 1937- Corporate valuation . New York , c1988. xiv, 224 p. : ISBN 0-471-85826-9 LC Card 87-23114 DDC 658.1/522 19
HG4028.V3 S58 1988

BUSINESS ENTERPRISES - VALUATION - GERMANY, WEST.
Zessin, Axel, 1953- Unternehmungsbewertung von Kreditinstituten /. Göttingen , 1982. 296 p. : ISBN 3-509-01313-1 LC Card 84-109138
HG4028.V3 Z47 1982

BUSINESS ENTERPRISES - VALUATION - ITALY.
Masciocchi, Giuseppe. Crisi di impresa . Milano , 1983. viii, 112 p. ; LC Card 84-141092 DDC 657/.73 19
HD2747 .M37 1983 ***NYPL [JLE 86-4053]***

Business entrepreneurs in the West / edited by Ted C. Hinckley. Manhattan, Kan. : Sunflower University Press, c1986. 120 p. : ill. ; 28 cm. "From the January 1986 Journal of the West, with two additional articles." Bibliography: p. 112-116. Includes index. ISBN 0-89745-088-4 (pbk.) LC Card 87-135380 DDC 338/.04/0922 B 19
1. Businessmen - West (U. S.) - Biography. 2. Entrepreneurship - West (U. S.). I. Hinckley, Ted C. II. Journal of the West.
HC102.5.A2 B78 1986

Business environment and business ethics : the social, moral, and the political dimensions of management / edited by Karen Paul. Cambridge, Mass. : Ballinger, c1987. xi, 151 p. ; 24 cm. (Ballinger series in business in a global environment) Bibliography: p. 131-140. Includes index. ISBN 0-88730-204-1 LC Card 87-3573 DDC 174/.4 19
1. Business ethics. 2. Industry - Social aspects. I. Paul, Karen, 1944-. II. Series.
HF5387 .B867 1987

Business ethics . Velasquez, Manuel G. Englewood Cliffs, N.J. , c1988. xii, 420 p. : ISBN 0-13-096017-9 (pbk.) : LC Card 87-20453 DDC 174 19
HF5387 .V44 1988

BUSINESS ETHICS - ADDRESSES, ESSAYS, LECTURES.
Corporations and the common good /. Notre Dame, Ind. [Boston] , c1986. xii, 147 p. ; ISBN 0-268-00754-3 : LC Card 85-40597 DDC 174/.4 19
HB501 .C7614 1986 ***NYPL [JLD 86-2145]***

BUSINESS ETHICS - CASE STUDIES.
Goodpaster, Kenneth E., 1944- Ethics in management /. Boston , c1984. 154 p. : ISBN 0-87584-165-1 (course module : pbk.) LC Card 84-12847 DDC 174/.4 19
HF5387 .G66 1984

Velasquez, Manuel G. Business ethics . Englewood Cliffs, N.J. , c1988. xii, 420 p. : ISBN 0-13-096017-9 (pbk.) : LC Card 87-20453 DDC 174 19
HF5387 .V44 1988

BUSINESS ETHICS - JAPAN.
De Mente, Boye. Japanese etiquette & ethics in business /. Lincolnwood, Ill. , c1987. ix, 182 p. : ISBN 0-8442-8507-2 (pbk.) : LC Card 86-60830 DDC 395/.52 19
HF5387 .D384 1987

BUSINESS ETHICS - STUDY AND TEACHING (GRADUATE) - UNITED STATES.
Dunfee, Thomas W. Integrating ethics into the MBA core curriculum /. [Philadelphia] , c1986. 169 leaves : LC Card 87-123702 DDC 174/.4/071173 19
HF5387 .D86 1986

BUSINESS ETHICS - UNITED STATES.
McAdams, Tony. Law, business, and society /. Plano, Tex. , 1986. xvi, 662, 52 p. : ISBN 0-256-03070-7 LC Card 85-73323 DDC 346.73/065 347.30665 19
KF1355 .M28 1986 ***NYPL [JLE 87-891]***

BUSINESS ETIQUETTE - ASIA, SOUTHEASTERN.
Schmidt, Klaus D. Business customs and protocol in the ASEAN region /. Menlo Park, Calif. [c1985- v. <1 > : LC Card 87-404513 DDC 395/.52 19
HF5387 .S36 1985

BUSINESS ETIQUETTE - JAPAN.
De Mente, Boye. How to do business with the Japanese . Lincolnwood, Ill., U. S.A. , c1987. vi, 269 p. ; ISBN 0-8442-8509-9 (pbk.) LC Card 86-62724 DDC 395/.52 19
HF5387 .D3835 1987

De Mente, Boye. Japanese etiquette & ethics in business /. Lincolnwood, Ill. , c1987. ix, 182 p. : ISBN 0-8442-8507-2 (pbk.) : LC Card 86-60830 DDC 395/.52 19
HF5387 .D384 1987

BUSINESS ETIQUETTE - KOREA (SOUTH)
Doing business in Korea /. London , New York , 1987. xvi, 121 p. : ISBN 0-89397-276-2 (Nichols) : LC Card 87-5665 DDC 330.9519/5043 19
HC467 .D58 1987

BUSINESS ETIQUETTE - UNITED STATES.
Burleson, Clyde W., 1934- Interstate commerce . New York , 1987. viii, 230 p. ; ISBN 0-531-15519-6 LC Card 86-29019 DDC 381/.5/0973 19
HF5387 .B856 1987

BUSINESS - EXAMINATIONS, QUESTIONS, ETC.
Jaffe, Eugene D. How to prepare for the graduate management admission test GMAT /.

New York , c1987. x, 541 p. : ISBN 0-8120-3882-7 (pbk.) LC Card 87-18619 DDC 650/.076 19
HD30.413 .J33 1987

The Official guide for GMAT review /. Princeton, N.J. , c1986. 372 p. : ISBN 0-446-38435-6 (pbk.) : LC Card 86-229958 DDC 650/.076 19
HF1118 .O33 1986

BUSINESS EXECUTIVES. see **EXECUTIVES.**

BUSINESS FAILURES.
The Performance of small firms . London , Wolfeboro, N.H. , c1987. 342 p. : ISBN 0-7099-4411-X : LC Card 86-29052 DDC 658/.022 19
HD2341 .P399 1987

BUSINESS - FAILURES AND LOSSES. see **BUSINESS LOSSES.**

BUSINESS FAILURES - AUSTRALIA - HISTORY.
Sykes, Trevor. Two centuries of panic . Sydney , Boston , 1987. p. cm. ISBN 0-04-176013-1 LC Card 87-16107 DDC 338.7/4/0994 19
HD2747 .S95 1987

BUSINESS FAILURES - CANADA - CASE STUDIES.
Borins, Sandford F., 1949- Investments in failure . Toronto , New York , c1986. x, 175 p. ; ISBN 0-458-80340-5 (pbk.) : LC Card 87-142330 DDC 354.7109/2 19
HD4005 .B67 1986

BUSINESS FAILURES - CASE STUDIES.
Hartley, Robert F. Bullseyes and blunders . New York , c1987. vii, 253 p. : ISBN 0-471-84904-9 LC Card 86-23350 DDC 658 19
HD38 .H3487 1987 ***NYPL [JLE 87-1047]***

BUSINESS FAILURES - ITALY.
Guatri, Luigi. Crisi e risanamento delle imprese /. Milano , 1986. viii, 339 p. : ISBN 88-14-00914-7 : LC Card 86-228719
HD58.8 .G82 1986

BUSINESS FAILURES - UNITED STATES.
Benston, George J. An analysis of the causes of savings and loan association failures /. New York, N.Y. (90 Trinity Place, New York 10006) [1985] 182 p. : LC Card 86-209942 DDC 332.3/2/0973 19
HG2151 .B46 1985

Business finance and banking in Nigeria /. Osubor, John Uche. Owerri, Imo State, Nigeria , 1984. vii, 209 p. : ISBN 978-235-700-13 (pbk.) LC Card 86-207599 DDC 332.1/09669 19
HG3431.A6 O85 1984

Business financial management /. Cooley, Philip L. Chicago , c1988. xxv, 924, [34] p. : ISBN 0-03-009979-X LC Card 87-20079 DDC 658.1/5 19
HG4026 .C63 1988

The Business forecaster.
Special analysis and outlook for E.I. Du Pont De Nemours & Company (Inc.), Chemicals and Pigments Department. Boston, Mass. (7 Liberty Sq., Boston 02109) [1986] 17, [6] p. : LC Card 86-205857 DDC 338.4/766/00973 19
HD9660.P253 U672 1986

BUSINESS FORECASTING - ADDRESSES, ESSAYS, LECTURES.
Plan for information society-a national goal toward year 2000. Italian. Verso una società dell'informazione . Milano , 1974. 157 p. :
NYPL [TB (Studi e ricerche di scienze sociali. v.60)]

BUSINESS FORECASTING - DATA PROCESSING.
Adams, Francis Gerard, 1929- The business forecasting revolution . New York , 1986. xiii, 265 p. : ISBN 0-19-503700-6 LC Card 85-18943 DDC 338.5/442 19
HD30.27 .A33 1986 ***NYPL [JLD 86-2257]***

Business forecasting methods /. Jarett, Jeffrey, 1940- Oxford, UK , New York, NY, USA , 1987. 346 p. : ISBN 0-631-15289-X : LC Card 87-6408 DDC 658.4/0355 19
HD30.27 .J38 1987

The business forecasting revolution . Adams, Francis Gerard, 1929- New York , 1986. xiii, 265 p. : ISBN 0-19-503700-6 LC Card 85-18943 DDC 338.5/442 19
HD30.27 .A33 1986 ***NYPL [JLD 86-2257]***

BUSINESS - FORMS.
Burns, Robert, 1938- Master forms & contracts from your copier . Tucson, AZ , c1987. 160 p. : ISBN 0-89586-513-0 (pbk.) : LC Card 86-82238 DDC 651/.29 19
HF5371 .B845 1987

Personal financial planning . New York, N.Y. (1211 Ave. of the Americas, New York 10036-8775) , c1987. viii, 131 p. ; LC Card 87-142958 DDC 332.024 19
HG179 .P387 1987

Price, Courtney H. The entrepreneur's resource handbook /. Denver, Colo. , 1987. 178 p. : ISBN 0-944303-00-5 (pbk.) LC Card 87-62190
HD62.5 .P65 1987

BUSINESS GAMES. see **MANAGEMENT GAMES.**

BUSINESS - GRAPHIC METHODS.
Lotus Freelance Plus . Cambridge, MA (55 Cambridge Pkwy., Cambridge 02142) , c1987. 3 v. : LC Card 87-404478 DDC 650/.028/566869 19
HF5548.4.L676 L68 1987

Business guide to communications systems / [edited by] Danny Green. London : Pitman, 1987. x, 230 p. : ill. ; 23 cm. An edited and updated compilation of recent articles from the magazine Communications (published by International Thomson). ISBN 0-273-02671-2 (pbk.) : LC Card 87-147021 DDC 651.7 19
1. Management - Communication systems. 2. Telecommunication systems. I. Green, Danny. II. Title: Communications systems.
HD30.335 .B85 1987

BUSINESS - HANDBOOKS, MANUALS, ETC.
The Book of business knowledge /. New York, N.Y. , c1987. p. cm. ISBN 0-932648-83-5 : LC Card 86-30962 DDC 658 19
HF5356 .B72 1987

The Boss's encyclopedia /. New York, N.Y. , c1987. xxvi, 594 p. ; ISBN 0-932648-75-4 LC Card 86-30961 DDC 658 19
HF5356 .B735 1987

Business confidential. New York, N.Y. , c1987. xi, 504 p. ; ISBN 0-932648-82-7 LC Card 86-30963 DDC 650 19
HF5356 .B9259 1987

Business planning guide . Dover, N.H. (50 Mill St., Dover 03820) , c1985. vii, 115 p. : LC Card 86-622397 DDC 658.4/01 19
HD30.28 .B85 1985

Business history review. Managing big business . Boston, Mass. , c1986. xxvii, 425 p. ; ISBN 0-87584-142-2 LC Card 86-7683 DDC 338.6/44/0973 19
HD2785 .M353 1986 ***NYPL [JLE 87-1360]***

Business history series.
The Challenge of new technology . Aldershot, Hants, England , Brookfield, Vt., U. S.A. , c1988. x, 155 p. : ISBN 0-566-05147-8 : LC Card 87-8592 DDC 338/.06 19
HC260.T4 C46 1988

Markets and bagmen . Aldershot, Hants, England , Brookfield, Vt., USA , c1986. xii, 204 p. : ISBN 0-566-05066-8 : LC Card 86-22951 DDC 380.1/0941 19
HF5415.12.G7 M37 1986

Business in action . Bittel, Lester R. New York , c1988. vii, 597 p. : ISBN 0-07-005565-3 LC Card 87-3134 DDC 658 19
HF5343 .B57 1988

Business information . Lavin, Michael R. Phoenix, Ariz. , 1987. x, 299 p. : ISBN 0-89774-157-9 (alk. paper) : LC Card 86-42787 DDC 650/.072 19
HF5356 .L36 1987

A Business information report.
The Affluent market. New York, N.Y. (500 5th Ave., New York 10110) [1984] 227 leaves : LC Card 86-201904 DDC 658.8/348 19
HC110.C6 A63 1984

Delson, Erwin B. The bar coding systems industry. New York, N.Y. , c1986. 1 v. (various pagings) : ISBN 0-931634-64-4 (pbk.) LC Card 87-156445 DDC 380.1/45621399 19
HD9801.6.P762 D45 1986

Delson, Erwin B. The factory automation industry /. New York, N.Y. , c1985. 1 v. (various pagings) : ISBN 0-931634-16-4 (pbk.) LC Card 86-203033 DDC 338.4/76298/0973 19
HD9696.A963 U635 1985

The Maturity market . New York, N.Y. , c1985. 1 v. (various pagings) : ISBN 0-931634-47-4 (pbk.) LC Card 86-203045 DDC 658.8/348 19
HC110.C6 M33 1985

The Semiconductor industry. New York, N.Y. (500 5th Ave., New York 10110) , c1984. 1 v. (various foliations) : LC Card 86-203040 DDC 338.4/762138152 19
HD9696.S42 S375 1984

Valencia, Humberto. The U. S. Hispanic market. New York, N.Y. [1984] 1 v. (various foliations) : ISBN 0-931634-48-2 (pbk.) LC Card 86-203027 DDC 658.8/348 19
HC110.C6 V35 1984

The World market for high technology industrial ceramics. New York, N.Y. [1985] 1 v. (various pagings) ; ISBN 0-931634-52-0 (pbk.) LC Card 86-201912 DDC 382/.45666 19
HD9590.5 .W67 1985

BUSINESS - INFORMATION SERVICES.
Burn, Janice. Information analysis /. London , 1987. x, 260 p. : ISBN 0-948825-50-2 (pbk.) : LC Card 87-166130 DDC 658.4/038 19
HD30.35 .B87 1987

Greenberg, Eric Rolfe. The 1985 AMA report on information centers /. New York, N.Y. , c1985. vi, 121 p. ; ISBN 0-8144-3151-8 LC Card 85-7552 DDC 658.4/038 19
HF5321 .G665 1985 ***NYPL [JLF 86-1167]***

Wasik, John F. The electronic business information sourcebook /. New York , c1987. xvi, 208 p. ; ISBN 0-471-62464-0 : LC Card 87-8289 DDC 026/.65 19
HF5548.2 .W324 1987

The 1986 AMA report on information centers . New York, N.Y. , c1986. viii, 92, [28] p. : ISBN 0-8144-3154-2 ***NYPL [JLF 86-1835]***

BUSINESS - INFORMATION SERVICES - DATA PROCESSING.
Vella, Carolyn M. Competitive intelligence in the computer age /. New York , 1987. xv, 189 p. ; ISBN 0-89930-169-X (lib. bdg. : alk. paper) LC Card 86-25565 DDC 651.8 19
HF5548.2 .V38 1987

BUSINESS - INFORMATION SERVICES. - DIRECTORIES.
Chamber of Commerce of the United States of America. Contact . Washington, D.C. , c1980. v, 129 p. : ISBN 0-89834-024-1 (pbk.) LC Card 80-80440 DDC 650/.07/073 19
HF5351 .C46 1980 ***NYPL [JLF 86-1414]***

Encyclopedia of geographic information sources, international volume . Detroit, Mich. , c1988. 479 p. ; ISBN 0-8103-0410-4 : LC Card 87-23777 DDC 016.33 19
HF5341 .E53 1988

Financial Sourcebooks' sources . Naperville, Ill. , c1987. 454 p. ; ISBN 0-942061-00-4 (pbk.) : LC Card 87-8793 DDC 332/.025/73 19
HG173 .F517 1987

The International directory of business information sources and services. London , 1986. ix, 378 p. ; ISBN 0-946653-18-6
NYPL [*R-Econ. 86-2525]

Business information technology . Gunton, Tony, 1943- Englewood Cliffs, N.J. , 1988. p. cm. ISBN 0-13-100843-9 LC Card 87-7365 DDC 658/.05 19
HF5548.2 .G86 1988

BUSINESS INSURANCE. see **INSURANCE, BUSINESS.**

The Business insurance handbook / compiled and edited by Gray Castle, Robert F. Cushman, Peter R. Kensicki. Homewood, Ill. : Dow Jones-Irwin, c1981. xvii, 753 p. : ill., forms, ports. ; 24 cm. Includes bibliographical references and index. ISBN 0-87094-237-9 LC Card 80-70437 DDC 368.8/1/00202 19
1. Insurance, Business - Handbooks, manuals, etc. 2. Risk management - Handbooks, manuals, etc. I. Castle, Gray. II. Cushman, Robert Frank, 1931-. III. Kensicki, Peter R.
HG8059 .B87 ***NYPL [*R-Econ. 86-2502]***

Business Intelligence Program (SRI International)
Carlson, Richard C. Managing the changing work force . Menlo Park, Calif. (333 Ravenswood Ave., Menlo Park 94025-3476) , c1984. 44 p. : LC Card 86-212936 DDC 658.3 19
HD5706 .C29 1984

Howard-Healy, Marion. Aspects of the new media in Europe /. Menlo Park, CA (333 Ravenswood Ave., Menlo Park 94025) , c1986. 22 leaves : LC Card 86-220771 DDC 384/.094 19
HE8700.72.E85 H69 1986

McAlpine, Pamela J. The air freight industry . Menlo Park, CA (333 Ravenswood Ave., Menlo Park 94025) , c1986. 12 leaves ; LC Card 87-402973 DDC 387.7/44/0973 19
HE9788.5.U5 M37 1986

Morse, Diane McGinty. Involving managers in competitive analysis /. Menlo Park, CA (333 Ravenswood Ave., Menlo Park 94025) , c1986. 11 leaves : LC Card 86-220559 DDC 658.4/012 19
HD38.7 .M67 1986

Shelton, Robert D. Hazardous waste management market assessment /. Menlo Park, CA (333 Ravenswood Ave., Menlo Park 94025) , c1986. 19 p. : LC Card 86-220787 DDC 338.4/7363728 19
HD9975.U52 S54 1986

Vlitos, Irene. The European potential for a venture capital industry /. Menlo Park, CA (333 Ravenswood Ave., Menlo Park 94025) , c1986. 13 leaves : LC Card 86-220533 DDC 332.6/6 19
HG5428 .V56 1986

Woodward, Maria Lourdes. Business issues for the Asia-Pacific region /. Menlo Park, CA (333 Ravenswood Ave., Menlo Park 94025) , c1986. 14 p. ; LC Card 86-220779 DDC 330.95/0428
HC413.A78 W66 1986

Business intelligence-- putting it all together /. Tyson, Kirk W. M., 1952- Lombard, Ill. , c1986. vi, 275 p. : ISBN 0-941101-00-2 : LC Card 86-27309 DDC 658.4/7 19
HD38.7 .T95 1986

Business interest calculations /. De Lisle, Christian. London , c1985. ix, 274 p. ; ISBN 0-08-039231-8 ***NYPL [JLE 87-1030]***

Business interests, organizational development, and private interest government : an international comparative study of the food processing industry / edited by Wyn Grant. Berlin ; New York : W. de Gruyter, 1987. viii, 232 p. ; 24 cm. (Series C--Political and social sciences . 8) Bibliography: p. [220]-227. Includes index. ISBN 0-89925-380-6 (U. S.) : LC Card 87-21403 DDC 338.4/7664 19
1. Food industry and trade. 2. Food industry and trade - Societies, etc. 3. Commercial associations. I. Grant, Wyn. II. Series.
HD9000.5 .B87 1987

Business International Asia/Pacific Ltd.
Toussaint, Marcel. China market atlas /. Hong Kong , c1986. ix, 222 p. : LC Card 86-218633 DDC 330.951/058 19
HC427.92 .T69 1986

Business International Corporation. Joint ventures in the People's Republic of China . Hong Kong , New York, N.Y., U. S.A. , c1985. 347 p. ; LC Card 87-404122 DDC 658.1/8 19
HD2910 .J65 1985

A Business International multiclient study.
Joint ventures in the People's Republic of China . Hong Kong , New York, N.Y., U. S.A. , c1985. 347 p. ; LC Card 87-404122 DDC 658.1/8 19
HD2910 .J65 1985

Business issues for the Asia-Pacific region /. Woodward, Maria Lourdes. Menlo Park, CA (333 Ravenswood Ave., Menlo Park 94025) , c1986. 14 p. ; LC Card 86-220779 DDC 330.95/0428
HC413.A78 W66 1986

BUSINESS JOURNALISM. see **JOURNALISM, COMMERCIAL.**

BUSINESS LAW - GERMANY (WEST) - HANDBOOKS, MANUALS, ETC.
Roessler, Helmut R. Deutsche Geschäftskorrespondenz . Lanham, MD , c1987. xii, 218 p. : ISBN 0-8191-6277-9 (alk. paper) : LC Card 87-6086 DDC 658.4/53 19
HF5728.G3 R64 1987

BUSINESS LAW - MAINE - HANDBOOKS, MANUALS, ETC.
Doing business in Maine. [Augusta, Me. , 1983] iii, 93 p. : LC Card 86-620779 DDC 346.741/07 347.41067 19
HD62.5 .D64 1983

BUSINESS LETTERS. see **COMMERCIAL CORRESPONDENCE.**

BUSINESS LIBRARIES.
Johnson, H. Herbert Webster, 1906- How to use the business library . Cincinnati , c1984. iv, 267 p. : ISBN 0-538-05750-5 (pbk.) LC Card 83-60484 DDC 027.6/9 19
Z675.B8 J6 1984 ***NYPL [JLE 86-3971]***

BUSINESS LITERATURE.
Foote, Cameron S. The fourth medium . Homewood, Ill. , c1986. xxix, 226 p. : ISBN 0-87094-913-6 LC Card 86-70966 DDC 658.8/2 19
HF5438.5 .F66 1986 ***NYPL [JLE 87-1433]***

BUSINESS LOGISTICS.
Cuomo, Gennaro. Funzioni, strutture, strategie delle imprese commerciali complesse /. Padova , 1984. 236 p. : LC Card 86-214195
HD38.5 .C86 1984

Schellenberger, Robert Earl. Strategic management . New York , c1986. xiii, 808 p. : ISBN 0-471-88059-0 : LC Card 85-9553 DDC 658.4/012 19
HD30.28 .S34 1986 ***NYPL [JLE 86-1559]***

Unternehmensführung und Logistik /. Wiesbaden , c1984. 151 p. : ISBN 3-409-13038-1 LC Card 85-126091
HD28 .Z46 nr. 84/2 HD30.28

BUSINESS LOGISTICS - CASE STUDIES.
Schellenberger, Robert Earl. Strategic management . New York , c1986. xiii, 808 p. : ISBN 0-471-88059-0 : LC Card 85-9553 DDC 658.4/012 19
HD30.28 .S34 1986 ***NYPL [JLE 86-1559]***

BUSINESS LOSSES.
Wuillemin, Lucien. Eléments d'analyse et de gestion financières de l'entreprise en déficit /. Genève , c1982. 191 p. : ISBN 2-8257-0090-8 : LC Card 82-228134 DDC 658.1/5 19
HD49 .W84 1982 ***NYPL [JLE 87-1142]***

BUSINESS MACHINES. see **OFFICE EQUIPMENT AND SUPPLIES.**

BUSINESS - MATHEMATICAL MODELS.
Curwin, Jon. Business studies in context . London , New York , 1987. p. cm. ISBN 0-07-707034-8 : LC Card 87-22560 DDC 658.4/0352 19
HD30.25 .C87 1987

Business mathematics / Lloyd D. Brooks ... [et al.]. 10th ed. New York : Gregg Division/McGraw-Hill Book Co., c1988. p. cm. Rev. ed. of: Business mathematics / R. Robert Rosenberg, Harry Lewis, Roy W. Poe. 9th ed. c1982. Includes index. ISBN 0-07-008166-2 LC Card 87-4210 DDC 513/.93 19
1. Business mathematics. I. Brooks, Lloyd D., 1942-. II. Rosenberg, R. Robert (Reuben Robert), 1900- Business mathematics.
HF5691 .B9 1988

Business mathematics . Swindle, Robert E. Boston, Mass. , c1987. xii, 577 p. : ISBN 0-534-07572-X : LC Card 86-27441 DDC 512/.1 19
HF5691 .S85 1987

BUSINESS MATHEMATICS - DATA PROCESSING.
Mundel, Marvin Everett, 1916- BASIC, a personal computer language for improving productivity /. Tokyo, Japan , c1986. v, 322 p. ; ISBN 92-833-1089-0 LC Card 86-211814 DDC 005.26 19
HF5548.5.B3 M86 1986

BUSINESS MATHEMATICS - DICTIONARIES.
Targett, David. The Pocket guide to business numeracy /. Oxford, OX ; New York, NY, USA : x, 184 p. : ISBN 0-631-15124-9 : LC Card 86-31032 DDC 513/.93/0321 19
HF5695 .T34 1987

BUSINESS MATHEMATICS - FOOD SERVICE - PROBLEMS, EXERCISES, ETC.
McDowell, M. C. (Milton C.), 1920- Math workbook for foodservice/lodging /. New York , c1988. v, 265 p. : ISBN 0-442-21872-9 (pbk.) : LC Card 87-15960 DDC 513/.93/024642 19
HF5695.5.F616 M317 1988

Business mathematics for college . McAnelly, James R. St. Paul , c1987. xx, 531, [30] p. : ISBN 0-314-26207-5 (pbk.) LC Card 86-26681 DDC 512/.1 19
HF5691 .M375 1987b

Business mathematics for college /. McAnelly, James R. St. Paul , c1987. [584] p. : ISBN 0-314-93202-X (pbk.) LC Card 86-26670 DDC 512/.1 19
HF5691 .M375 1987

BUSINESS MATHEMATICS - HOTELS, TAVERNS, ETC. - PROBLEMS, EXERCISES, ETC.
McDowell, M. C. (Milton C.), 1920- Math workbook for foodservice/lodging /. New York , c1988. v, 265 p. : ISBN 0-442-21872-9 (pbk.) : LC Card 87-15960 DDC 513/.93/024642 19
HF5695.5.F616 M317 1988

BUSINESS MATHEMATICS - MOTELS - PROBLEMS, EXERCISES, ETC.
McDowell, M. C. (Milton C.), 1920- Math workbook for foodservice/lodging /. New York , c1988. v, 265 p. : ISBN 0-442-21872-9 (pbk.) : LC Card 87-15960 DDC 513/.93/024642 19
HF5695.5.F616 M317 1988

BUSINESS MATHEMATICS - PROBLEMS, EXERCISES, ETC.
De Lisle, Christian. Business interest calculations /. London , c1985. ix, 274 p. ; ISBN 0-08-039231-8 ***NYPL [JLE 87-1030]***

George, Thomas F. Business algebra & mathematics /. Englewood Cliffs, NJ , c1987. xiv, 634 p. : ISBN 0-13-091562-9 LC Card 86-30333 DDC 512/.1 19
HF5694 .G46 1987

Slater, Jeffrey, 1947- Practical business math procedures /. Homewood, Ill. , 1987. xiv, 440 p. : ISBN 0-256-03654-3 (pbk.) LC Card 85-82557 DDC 513/.93 19
HF5694 .S57 1987

Swindle, Robert E. Business mathematics . Boston, Mass. , c1987. xii, 577 p. : ISBN 0-534-07572-X : LC Card 86-27441 DDC 512/.1 19
HF5691 .S85 1987

BUSINESS MATHEMATICS - PROBLEMS, EXERCISES, ETC. - DATA PROCESSING.
George, Thomas F. Business algebra & mathematics /. Englewood Cliffs, NJ , c1987. xiv, 634 p. : ISBN 0-13-091562-9 LC Card 86-30333 DDC 512/.1 19
HF5694 .G46 1987

BUSINESS MATHEMATICS - REAL ESTATE BUSINESS - PROBLEMS, EXERCISES, ETC.
Akerson, Charles B. The appraiser's workbook /. Chicago, Ill. , c1985. xv, 263 p. in various pagings : ISBN 0-911780-75-0 (pbk.) LC Card 84-3008 DDC 333.33/2/076 19
HD1387 .A518 1985 ***NYPL [JLF 86-1025]***

BUSINESS MEN. see **BUSINESSMEN.**

BUSINESS MERGERS. see **CONSOLIDATION AND MERGER OF CORPORATIONS.**

Business Mexico / edited by John H. Christman. 1a ed. México, D.F. : American Chamber of Commerce of Mexico, 1978. 343 p. : ill. ; 29 cm. Includes bibliographical references. LC Card 87-405299 DDC 332.1/732272 19
1. Mexico - Commerce. 2. Mexico - Economic conditions - 1970-. 3. Business. I. Christman, John H. II. American Chamber of Commerce of Mexico.
HF3237 .B87 1978

Business, money, and power. Kidron, Michael. What you need to know about business, money, and power /. New York , c1987. 187 p. : ISBN 0-671-54113-7 : LC Card 86-31571 DDC 650 19
HF5351 .K473 1987

BUSINESS MORTALITY - FORECASTING - MATHEMATICAL MODELS.

Shailer, G. E. P. Experimental failure prediction models for small companies /. [Newcastle, Australia] [1986] 52 p. ; ISBN 0-7259-0555-7 (pbk.) LC Card 87-121092 DDC 338.6/42 19
HD2747 .S42 1986

BUSINESS MORTALITY - INDIA.
Jyothi Rani, T. Sickness in small scale industrial sector /. Warangal, Andhra Pradesh , 1985. xii, 258 p. ; LC Card 86-902876 DDC 338.6/42/0954 19
HD2747 .J96 1985

BUSINESS MORTALITY - INDIA - AHMADABAD - CONGRESSES.
Industrial sickness . Ahmedabad , c1984. xv, 459 p. ; LC Card 87-902007 DDC 363.1/19677/00954 19
HD9866.I63 A385 1984

BUSINESS MORTALITY - INDIA - GUJARAT.
Dave, Nalini V. Industrial sickness and key areas of management . New Delhi , c1987. 523 p. : LC Card 87-901105 DDC 658/.00954/75 19
HD2747 .D32 1987

BUSINESS NAMES.
Branding . New York , 1987. xii, 192 p., [12] p. of plates : ISBN 0-07-044055-7 : LC Card 86-27797 DDC 658.8/27 19
HD69.B7 B73 1987

Business not as usual . Mitroff, Ian I. San Francisco , 1987. xxi, 194 p. : ISBN 1-555-42030-3 (alk. paper) LC Card 86-46333 DDC 338.9 19
HD70.U5 M52 1987

The Business of caring [videorecording] / Women's Bureau, U. S. Dept. of Labor. Washington, DC : The Bureau : Distributed by National Audiovisual Center, 1984. 1 videocassette (23 min.) : sd., col. Title from data sheet. Parents, employeers, government agencies. Issued as U-matic 3/4 in. or Beta 1/2 in. or VHS 1/2 in. Describes a number of employer-supported child care programs and services. Includes descriptions of day care centers at the work site, the voucher system, flexible personnel policies, and information and referral programs. LC Card 84-707513 DDC 362.7 11
1. Day care centers and industry - United States. 2. Child care services - United States. I. United States. Women's Bureau. II. National Audiovisual Center.
HF5549.5.D39

The business of crime . Nelli, Humbert S., 1930- New York , 1976. xiii, 314 p. : ISBN 0-19-502010-3 : LC Card 75-32350 DDC 364.1/06/073
HV6791 .N37 ***NYPL [JLD 86-3722]***

The business of public relations /. Brody, E. W. New York , 1987. xv, 327 p. ; ISBN 0-275-92333-9 (alk. paper) : LC Card 86-30552 DDC 659.2 19
HD59 .B757 1987 ***NYPL [JLE 87-1589]***

The business of the Japanese state . Samuels, Richard J. Ithaca , 1987. xii, 359 p. : ISBN 0-8014-2022-9 (alk. paper) LC Card 87-5230 DDC 338.4/7621042/0952 19
HD9502.J32 S27 1987

The business of transport /. Bell, G. J. (Graham J.) Plymouth [Devon] , 1984. viii, 344 p. : ISBN 0-7121-2406-3 (pbk.) LC Card 84-170770 DDC 380.5 19
HE151 .B436 1984 ***NYPL [JLD 87-86]***

Business of your own in Tennessee. Yates, M. M. (Maurice M.) How to start and manage a business of your own in Tennessee. Greeneville, Tenn. , c1986. ii, 66 p. : LC Card 86-209197 DDC 658.1/141/09768 19
HD62.5 .Y28 1986

Business opportunities among the aging population . Gollub, James O. Menlo Park, Calif. (333 Ravenswood Ave., Menlo Park 94025-3476) , c1984. 36 p. : LC Card 86-210219 DDC 658.8/348 19
HC110.C6 G62 1984

Business opportunities for broadcasters in MDS pay television /. Frank, Peter. Washington, DC [c1982] 29 p. ; LC Card 86-201299
HE8700.72.U6 F73 1982

Business opportunities in China : the door opens wider / China International Economic Consultants, Inc. Menlo Park, Calif. (333 Ravenswood Ave., Menlo Park 94025-3476) : SRI International, Business Intelligence Program, c1984. 32 p. : ill. (some col.) ; 28 cm. (Report / SRI International, Business Intelligence Program . no. 710 (fall 1984)) Cover title. Bibliography: p. 28. LC Card 86-210279 DDC 338.8/8851 19
1. China - Industries. 2. Joint ventures - China. 3. Investments, Foreign - China. I. Chung-kuo kuo chi ching chi tzu hsün kung ssu. II. Series: Research report (Business Intelligence Program (SRI International)) , 710.
HC427.92 .B85 1984

Business opportunity report .
(C-032R) New biotechnology comes to market /. Stamford, Conn., U. S.A. , c1985. viii, 205 leaves : ISBN 0-89336-436-3 (soft) LC Card 87-167067 DDC 381/.456606 19
HD9999.B442 N48 1985

(C-044) Electrochemistry . Stamford, Conn., U. S.A. , c1986. 231 leaves : ISBN 0-89336-483-5 (pbk.) LC Card 87-403910 DDC 380.1/45660297/0973 19
HD9660.E433 U544 1986

(C-058) Generic drugs . Stamford, Conn., U. S.A. , c1986. xiii, 311 leaves : ISBN 0-89336-434-7 (soft) LC Card 87-167077 DDC 380.1/456151 19
HD9665.5 .G46 1986

(C-062) Crull, Anna W. New trends in gas separations . Stamford, Conn., U. S.A. , c1986. xvi, 222 leaves : ISBN 0-89336-422-3 (pbk.) LC Card 87-165549 DDC 660.2/842 19
HD9660.G372 C78 1986

(C-067) Crull, Anna W. Commercial and industrial enzymes /. Stamford, Conn., U. S.A. , c1986. xiii, 160 leaves : ISBN 0-89336-492-4 (pbk.) LC Card 87-164403 DDC 380.1/4566063 19
HD9660.E582 C783 1986

(G-067R) Castrovilla, Joseph A. The printed circuit board industry /. Stamford, Conn., U. S.A. , c1985. ix, 116 leaves : ISBN 0-89336-451-7 (soft) LC Card 87-403911 DDC 381/.4562138174/0973 19
HD9696.P743 U634 1985

(G-068) The Online commercial database business /. Stamford, Conn., U. S.A. , c1985. xxi, 230 leaves : ISBN 0-89336-320-0 (pbk.) LC Card 87-40457 DDC 381/.4500574/0973 19
HD9696.D363 U66 1985

(G-074R) Local area networks . Stamford, Conn., U. S.A. , c1986. xvi, 186 leaves : ISBN 0-89336-438-X (pbk.) LC Card 87-404428 DDC 381/.4500468/0973 19
HD9696.C63 U52253 1986

(G-089) Stotter, James. Intelligent buildings . Stamford, Conn., U. S.A. , c1986. ix, 127 leaves : ISBN 0-89336-414-2 (pbk.) LC Card 87-165953 DDC 338.4/769/0973 19
HD9715.U52 S76 1986

(G-091) O'Reilly, Francis J. Computer printers . Stamford, Conn., U. S.A. , c1985. iv, 103 leaves ; ISBN 0-89336-460-6 (pbk.) LC Card 87-163961 DDC 338.4/76213987 19
HD9696.C63 U52737 1985

(G-092) Voice compression technology . Stamford, Conn., U. S.A. , c1985. xii, 146 leaves ; ISBN 0-89336-430-4 (soft) LC Card 87-165256 DDC 380.1/45621389 19
HD9696.T442 V65 1985

(G-093) Packet switching equipment markets /. Stamford, Conn., U. S.A. , c1985. v, 205 leaves : ISBN 0-89336-465-7 (pbk.) LC Card 87-403884 DDC 381/.456213878 19
HD9696.T443 U556 1985

(G-096) Converging voice/data/video technologies at the workstation /. Stamford, Conn., U. S.A. , c1986. v, 119 leaves ; ISBN 0-89336-466-5 (pbk.) LC Card 87-168057 DDC 380.1/45004 19
HD9801.A2 C66 1986

(G-100) O'Reilly, Francis J. The "smart card" . Stamford, Conn., U. S.A. [1986] xii, 106 leaves ; ISBN 0-89336-470-3 (soft) : LC Card 87-163972 DDC 380.1/4568 19
HD9696.O672 O74 1986

(GA-034N) The Pet industry . Stamford, Conn., U. S.A. , c1985. xi, 140 leaves : ISBN 0-89336-439-8 (pbk.) LC Card 87-403914 DDC 381/.4568 19
HD9340.U52 P48 1985

(GA-045R) New trends in food retailing /. Stamford, Conn., U. S.A. , c1985. xiii, 135 leaves : ISBN 0-89336-457-6 (soft) LC Card 87-165228 DDC 381/.45664/00973 19
HD9321.5 .N47 1985

(GA-050R) Gipson, Beckilynn. Aseptic food processing and packaging . Stamford, Conn., U. S.A. , c1986. xiii, 164 leaves ; ISBN 0-89336-471-1 (pbk.) LC Card 87-405014 DDC 381/.45664028 19
HD9999.C743 U629 1986

(GA-051R) Biotechnology in agriculture . Stamford, Conn., U. S.A. , c1985. xvii, 192 leaves : ISBN 0-89336-485-1 (pbk.) LC Card 87-403883 DDC 381/.456606 19
HD9999.B443 U615 1985

(GA-055) Cholmar, Sidney. New directions in microwave ovens . Stamford, Conn., U. S.A. , c1985. x, 119 leaves ; ISBN 0-89336-459-2 (pbk.) LC Card 87-163958 DDC 381/.4568388 19
HD9971.5.S763 U53 1985

(GA-057) The New ethnic food market . Norwalk, Conn., U. S.A. , c1986. xv, 142 leaves ; ISBN 0-89336-486-X (pbk.) LC Card 87-168111 DDC 381/.45641592/00973 19
HD9333.U62 N48 1986

(GA-058) Diet foods . Stamford, Conn., U. S.A. , c1986. xv, 195 leaves : ISBN 0-89336-487-8 (pbk.) LC Card 87-160485 DDC 381/.4166463/0973 19
HD9005 .D53 1986

(GB-066R) Mooney, Peter. Plastics EMI shielding . Stamford, Conn., U. S.A. , c1985. xxii, 297 leaves : ISBN 0-89336-409-6 (soft) LC Card 87-168832 DDC 338.4/76684 19
HD9661.U62 M654 1985

(GB-074) Holography, new commercial opportunities /. Stamford, Conn. , c1985. vii, 149 leaves : ISBN 0-89336-480-0 (soft) LC Card 87-165251 DDC 380.1/456213675 19
HD9707.5.H342 H64 1985

(GB-080) New materials for new semiconductors /. Stamford, Conn., U. S.A. , c1986. xii, 198 leaves : ISBN 0-89336-475-4 (soft) LC Card 87-404262 DDC 381/.4562138152/0973 19
HD9696.S43 U492 1986

(GB-085) New specialty metals & metallurgy for high-temperature, high-strength, low-weight applications /. Norwalk, Conn., U. S.A. , c1987. 1 v. (various foliations) : ISBN 0-89336-454-1 (pbk.) LC Card 87-168123 DDC 380.1/45669/0973 19
HD9506.U62 N45 1987

(GB-088) Bryant, Richard W. The Strategic Defense Initiative, business opportunities, and technological potential /. Norwalk, Conn., U. S.A. , c1986. 1 v. (various foliations) : ISBN 0-89336-477-0 (pbk.) LC Card 87-168253 DDC 338.4/762/00973 19
HC110.H53 B79 1986

(GB-089) The Japanese challenge . Stamford, Conn., U. S.A. , c1986. xii, 108 leaves : ISBN 0-89336-489-4 (pbk.) LC Card 87-404570 DDC 338/.06 19
HC465.T4 J365 1986

(P-023R) Advanced composites . Stamford, Conn. , c1985. x, 206 leaves : ISBN 0-89336-442-8 (soft) LC Card 87-166023 DDC 338.4/7620118 19
HD9999.C7152 A38 1985

(P-055R) Reinforced plastics . Stamford, Conn., U. S.A. , c1986. v, 136 leaves : ISBN 0-89336-478-9 (pbk.) LC Card 87-167989 DDC 381/.45668494/0973 19
HD9662.F523 U57 1986

(P-064R) Plastics in business machines . Stamford, Conn. , c1986. vii, 215 leaves : ISBN 0-89336-433-6 (soft) : LC Card 87-165036 DDC 380.1/456684 19
HD9801.A2 P56 1986

(P-069) The Changing passenger car markets . Stamford, Conn., U. S.A. , c1985. viii, 227 leaves : ISBN 0-89336-479-7 (pbk.) LC Card 87-404429 DDC 381/.4566849 19
HD9710.U52 C385 1985

(P-086) Geotextiles, geomembranes, geomatrices . Stamford, Conn., U. S.A. , c1986. xii, 133 leaves : ISBN 0-89336-496-7 (pbk.) LC

Card 87-403913 DDC 668.9 19
HD9869.I533 U64 1986

BUSINESS PARKS - UNITED STATES - EMPLOYEES.
Employment and parking in suburban business parks . Washington, D.C. , c1986. iv, 31 p. : ISBN 0-87420-662-6 (pbk.) LC Card 86-219885 DDC 338.6/042 19
HD255 .E45 1986

BUSINESS PARKS - UNITED STATES - PARKING FACILITIES.
Employment and parking in suburban business parks . Washington, D.C. , c1986. iv, 31 p. : ISBN 0-87420-662-6 (pbk.) LC Card 86-219885 DDC 338.6/042 19
HD255 .E45 1986

BUSINESS - PERIODICALS - BIBLIOGRAPHY.
Encyclopedia of geographic information sources, international volume . Detroit, Mich. , c1988. 479 p. ; ISBN 0-8103-0410-4 : LC Card 87-23777 DDC 016.33 19
HF5341 .E53 1988

A business plan . West, Alan, 1951- New York , 1988. xi, 196 p. : ISBN 0-89397-288-6 (pbk.) : LC Card 87-18561 DDC 658.4/012 19
HD62.7 .W47 1988

Business planning guide : a handbook to help you design, write, and use a business plan and a financing proposal tailored to your specific business needs : includes detachable worksheets. Dover, N.H. (50 Mill St., Dover 03820) : Upstart Pub. Co., c1985. vii, 115 p. : ill. ; 28 cm. Rev. ed. of: Business planning guide / David H. Bangs, Jr., William R. Osgood. Bibliography: p. 109. LC Card 86-622397 DDC 658.4/01 19
1. Corporate planning - Handbooks, manuals, etc. 2. Business - Handbooks, manuals, etc. 3. Business enterprises - Finance - Handbooks, manuals, etc. I. Bangs, David H. Business planning guide.
HD30.28 .B85 1985

Business policy : an analytical introduction / George Luffman ... [et al.]. Oxford, UK ; New York, NY, USA : Basil Blackwell, 1987. viii, 208 p. : ill. ; 24 cm. Includes bibliographies and index. ISBN 0-631-15545-7 : LC Card 87-722 DDC 658.4/012 19
1. Strategic planning. I. Luffman, George A.
HD30.28 .B86 1987

Business policy : texts and cases / C. Roland Christensen ... [et al.].6th ed. Homewood, Ill. : Irwin, 1987. xx, 940 p. : ill., ports. ; 25 cm. Includes bibliographical references and index. ISBN 0-256-03358-7 LC Card 86-82216 DDC 658.4/012 19
1. Corporations - United States - Case studies. 2. Industrial management - United States - Case studies. I. Christensen, C. Roland (Carl Roland), 1919-.
HD2785 .B78 1987

Business policy and strategic management /. Jauch, Lawrence R. New York , c1988. xix, 940 p. : ISBN 0-7032-2347-X : LC Card 87-16859 DDC 658.4/012 19
HD30.28 .J375 1988

BUSINESS PSYCHOLOGY. see **PSYCHOLOGY, INDUSTRIAL.**

BUSINESS RECORDS - GREAT BRITAIN - HANDBOOKS, MANUALS, ETC.
Armstrong, John, 1944- Business documents . London , New York , 1987. xiv, 251 p. : ISBN 0-7201-1846-8 : LC Card 86-28451 DDC 651.5 19
HF5349.G7 A76 1987

BUSINESS RECORDS - HANDBOOKS, MANUALS, ETC.
Armstrong, John, 1944- Business documents . London , New York , 1987. xiv, 251 p. : ISBN 0-7201-1846-8 : LC Card 86-28451 DDC 651.5 19
HF5349.G7 A76 1987

BUSINESS RECORDS - MANAGEMENT.
Robek, Mary F. Information and records management /. Encino, Calif. , c1987. vi, 580 p. : ISBN 0-02-820590-1 LC Card 87-135683 DDC 651.5 19
HF5736 .R53 1987

BUSINESS - RELIGIOUS ASPECTS - CHRISTIANITY.
Templeton, John, 1912- The Templeton plan . San Francisco , c1987. x, 181, [1] p. ; ISBN 0-06-250286-7 LC Card 86-43022 DDC 174/.4 19
HF5387 .T46 1987

BUSINESS - REMOVAL. see **INDUSTRIES, LOCATION OF.**

Business report writing /. Bowman, Joel P. Chicago , c1988. xvi, 607 p. : ISBN 0-03-013244-4 LC Card 87-15438 DDC 808/.066651 19
HF5719 .B68 1988

BUSINESS REPORT WRITING.
Blicq, Ron, 1925- Writing reports to get results . New York , c1987. x, 203 p. : ISBN 0-87942-228-9 LC Card 87-16850 DDC 808/.066651 19
HF5719 .B55 1987

Bowman, Joel P. Business report writing /. Chicago , c1988. xvi, 607 p. : ISBN 0-03-013244-4 LC Card 87-15438 DDC 808/.066651 19
HF5719 .B68 1988

Brown, Eric D. Writing with a word processor . Reston, Va. , c1984. viii, 136 p. : ISBN 0-8359-8857-0 (pbk.) :$19.95 LC Card 84-8306 DDC 652 19
HF5548.115 .B76 1984 ***NYPL [JLE 86-1769]***

Holcombe, Marya W., 1944- Writing for decision makers . New York , c1987. xi, 219 p. : ISBN 0-442-23268-3 (pbk.) : LC Card 86-24700 DDC 808/.066658 19
HF5719 .H64 1987

Melrose, John. BUCOMCO . Chicago , c1987. vii, 187 p. : ISBN 0-574-20070-3 (pbk.) : LC Card 86-31585 DDC 651.7/4 19
HF5718 .M44 1987

Murphy, Herta A. Effective business communications /. New York , c1988. xx, 730 p. : ISBN 0-07-044094-8 LC Card 87-17330 DDC 651.7 19
HF5721 .M85 1988

Peoples, David A., 1930- Presentations plus . New York , c1988. xi, 239 p. : ISBN 0-471-63391-7 LC Card 87-21691 DDC 658.4/5 19
HF5718 .P44 1988

Wall, William C. Prepare power-packed reports /. Huntsville, Ala. , c1987. p. cm. ISBN 0-938745-04-2 LC Card 87-13581 DDC 658.4/53 19
HF5719 .W35 1987

Wells, Walter. Communications in business /. Boston , c1988. xvi, 632 p. : ISBN 0-534-87167-4 LC Card 87-22721 DDC 651.7/4 19
HF5721 .W36 1988

Written communication of results in MAS engagements. New York, N.Y. (1211 Ave. of the Americas, New York 10036-8775) , c1987. 7 p. ; LC Card 87-159283 DDC 808/.066657 19
HF5719 .W74 1987

BUSINESS - RESEARCH.
Zikmund, William G. Business research methods /. Chicago , 1987, c1988. xvii, 715 p. : ISBN 0-03-012362-3 LC Card 87-5284 DDC 658.4/03/072 19
HD30.4 .Z54 1988

BUSINESS - RESEARCH GRANTS - UNITED STATES - DIRECTORIES.
Business and economics funding guide /. Washington, D.C. , c1987. 122 p. ; ISBN 0-88044-087-2 (alk. paper) : LC Card 87-17436 DDC 001.4/4 19
HF1131 .B78 1987

BUSINESS - RESEARCH - HANDBOOKS, MANUALS, ETC.
Lavin, Michael R. Business information . Phoenix, Ariz. , 1987. x, 299 p. : ISBN 0-89774-157-9 (alk. paper) : LC Card 86-42787 DDC 650/.072 19
HF5356 .L36 1987

BUSINESS - RESEARCH - METHODOLOGY.
Johnson, H. Herbert Webster, 1906- How to use the business library . Cincinnati , c1984. iv, 267 p. : ISBN 0-538-05750-5 (pbk.) LC Card 83-60484 DDC 027.6/9 19
Z675.B8 J6 1984 ***NYPL [JLE 86-3971]***

Business research methods /. Zikmund, William G. Chicago , 1987, c1988. xvii, 715 p. : ISBN 0-03-012362-3 LC Card 87-5284 DDC 658.4/03/072 19
HD30.4 .Z54 1988

Business rules of thumb /. Godin, Seth. New York, NY , c1987. x, 165 p. ; ISBN 0-446-37026-6 (pbk.) LC Card 87-6262 DDC 650.1 19
HF5386 .G55 1987

BUSINESS SCHOOLS - UNITED STATES - CONGRESSES.
The Evolution of education in collegiate schools of business . Hempstead, N.Y. , c1987. vi, 237 p. : LC Card 87-80670 DDC 650/.07/1073 19
HF1131 .E94 1987

BUSINESS SITES. see **INDUSTRIES, LOCATION OF.**

BUSINESS STABILIZATION. see **ECONOMIC STABILIZATION.**

Business statistics using Lotus 1-2-3 /. Kilpatrick, Michael, 1952- New York , c1987. ix, 326 p. : ISBN 0-471-84525-6 (pbk.) : LC Card 86-24737 DDC 519.5/028/55369 19
HF1017 .K55 1987

Business strategies of multinational corporations in India . Johri, Lalit M. New Delhi , 1983. v, 172 p. ; LC Card 83-906128 DDC 338.8/87 19
HD9672.I52 J63 1983 ***NYPL [JLD 86-4081]***

Business strategy and policy /. Smith, Garry D., 1948- Boston , c1988. xviii, 1006 p. : ISBN 0-395-36946-0 LC Card 87-80879 DDC 658.4/012 19
HD30.28 .S56 1988

Business strategy and the life cycle concept . Carpenter, Gregory. Cambridge, Mass. (1000 Massachusetts Ave., Cambridge 02138) [1985] [19] leaves ; LC Card 87-108925 DDC 658.5/038 19
HF5415.155 .C37 1985

Business strategy in practice /. Karlöf, Bengt, 1939- [Strategins kärnfrågor. English.] Chichester, England , New York , c1987. viii, 184 p. : ISBN 0-471-91620-X : LC Card 87-10452 DDC 658.4/012 19
HD30.28 .K3613 1987

Business studies in context . Curwin, Jon. London , New York , 1987. p. cm. ISBN 0-07-707034-8 : LC Card 87-22560 DDC 658.4/0352 19
HD30.25 .C87 1987

BUSINESS - STUDY AND TEACHING. see **BUSINESS EDUCATION.**

BUSINESS - SWEDEN - DATA PROCESSING.
Datorer och decentralisering . [Stockholm] [1983] 52 p. : ISBN 91-38-07877-5 LC Card 84-219052
HF5548.2 .D3715 1983

Industrins datorinvesteringar 1980-1982 /. [Stockholm] [1983] 61, 2 p. : ISBN 91-38-08001-X LC Card 84-218410
HF5548.2 .I4213 1983

BUSINESS - SWEDEN - DATA PROCESSING - CASE STUDIES.
De Geer, Hans, 1944- Bättre eller sämre med datorer? . Stockholm , c1982. 112 p. ; ISBN 91-38-90157-9 : LC Card 82-187964
HF5548.2 .D378 1982

BUSINESS - SWEDEN - DATA PROCESSING - FORECASTING.
Jobb i framtid? . Stockholm , c1983. 121 p. : ISBN 91-7410-270-2 : LC Card 84-103510
HC375 .J53 1983

BUSINESS - SWEDEN - DATA PROCESSING - STATISTICS.
Industrins datorinvesteringar 1980-1982 /. [Stockholm] [1983] 61, 2 p. : ISBN 91-38-08001-X LC Card 84-218410
HF5548.2 .I4213 1983

BUSINESS - SWEDEN - DIRECTORIES.
Vem gör vad i svenskt näringsliv . Stockholm [1983] 283 p. ; LC Card 83-225142
HF3673 .V46 1983

BUSINESS TAX - BERLIN (GERMANY) - STATISTICS.
Ergebnisse der Gewerbesteuerstatistik in Berlin (West) 1966 /. Berlin [1972] 51 p. ; LC Card 85-171275
HA1330.B6 B45 Heft 200 HJ5627.G2

Business tax deduction master guide. Bradford, W. Murray. The Prentice Hall business tax deduction master guide /. New York , c1987. 368 p. : ISBN 0-13-108234-5 (pbk.) : LC Card 87-2252 DDC 343.7305/23 347.303523 19
HJ4653.D4 B68 1987

BUSINESS TAX - SPAIN - ACCOUNTING.
Román Egea, Antonio. Supuestos y consultas sobre licencia fiscal . Madrid [1984?] 235 p. ; ISBN 84-7130-439-2 LC Card 86-149143 DDC 343.4606/8 344.60368 19
HJ5627.S7 R66 1984

Business telecommunications /. Rowe, Stanford H. Chicago , c1988. xx, 529 p. : ISBN 0-574-18690-5 : LC Card 87-14001 DDC 651.7 19
HE7631 .R69 1988

Business telecommunications management. Grover, Kenneth C. Foundations of business telecommunications management /. New York , c1986. xvi, 196 p. ; ISBN 0-306-42249-2 (pbk.) LC Card 86-5063 DDC 384 19
HF5541.T4 G76 1986 ***NYPL [JLE 86-3270]***

Business, time, and thought . Shackle, G. L. S. (George Lennox Sharman), 1903- [Selections. 1987.] New York , 1988. p. cm. ISBN 0-8147-2586-4 : LC Card 87-5528 DDC 330.1 19
HB72 .S462 1988

Business today /. Rachman, David J. New York , c1987. xxiii, 643 p. : ISBN 0-394-35114-2 LC Card 86-24784 DDC 658 19
HF5351 .R26 1987

BUSINESS TRAVEL.
Bates, Jefferson D., 1920- The portable office . Washington, D.C. , c1987. 262 p. : ISBN 0-87491-491-3 :; 0-87491-841-3 (jacket) LC Card 87-1773 DDC 658.4/093 19
HD38 .B325 1987

Henderson, George, 1932- International business and cultures . New York, NY , 1987. p. cm. ISBN 0-943025-03-6 : LC Card 87-24378 DDC 658/.049 19
HF1008 .H46 1987

Ross, H. Edward. Free airline tickets--worldwide!! . St. Paul, Minn., U. S.A. , c1986. 154 p. ; ISBN 0-9616129-0-8 (pbk.) LC Card 87-117304 DDC 387.7/1 19
HE9783.5 .R67 1986

BUSINESS TRAVEL - UNITED STATES - COSTS.
Day, Denis W. How to cut business travel costs /. New York , c1986. ix, 207 p. : ISBN 0-471-83633-8 : LC Card 86-9277 DDC 658.1/553 19
HD38 .D39 1986 ***NYPL [JLE 86-4235]***

BUSINESS TRAVEL - UNITED STATES - MANAGEMENT.
Day, Denis W. How to cut business travel costs /. New York , c1986. ix, 207 p. : ISBN 0-471-83633-8 : LC Card 86-9277 DDC 658.1/553 19
HD38 .D39 1986 ***NYPL [JLE 86-4235]***

BUSINESS TRIPS. see **BUSINESS TRAVEL.**

Business valuation manual . Horn, Thomas W. Lancaster, PA , 1987. 224 p. : ISBN 0-87521-015-5 (pbk.) : LC Card 87-17887 DDC 658.1/522 19
HD1393.25 .H66 1987

BUSINESS - VOCATIONAL GUIDANCE.
Nickels, William G. Understanding business /. St. Louis , 1987. xxix, 721, 115, 2 p. : ISBN 0-8016-3627-2 LC Card 86-23080 DDC 650 19
HF5351 .N53 1987

Business without economists . Hudson, William J. New York, N.Y. , c1987. 178 p. : ISBN 0-8144-5896-3 : LC Card 86-47812 DDC 658.4/0355 19
HB3730 .H83 1987

BUSINESS WOMEN. see **WOMEN IN BUSINESS.**

Business world 2 /. Gitman, Lawrence J. New York , c1987. xvii, 616, [70] p. : ISBN 0-471-80596-3 LC Card 86-23441 DDC 658 19
HF5351 .G5 1987

The business writer's handbook /. Brusaw, Charles T. New York , c1987. xxviii, 764 p. : ISBN 0-312-00571-7 : LC Card 87-4361 DDC 651.7/5 19
HF5726 .B874 1987

BUSINESS WRITING.
Andrews, Deborah C. Business communication /. New York , London , c1988. xxvi, 623 p. : ISBN 0-02-303510-2 LC Card 87-5526 DDC 808/.06665 19
HF5718 .A743 1988

Bacon, Mark S. Write like the pros . New York , c1988. xiv, 316 p. ; ISBN 0-471-85721-1 LC Card 87-21550 DDC 808/.06665 19
HF5718.3 .B33 1988

Blumenthal, Lassor A. Successful oral and written presentations /. New York, NY , c1987. 94 p. : ISBN 0-399-51330-2 (pbk.) : LC Card 87-2272 DDC 658.4/5 19
HF5718 .B57 1987

Cross, Mary. Persuasive business writing . New York, NY , c1987. x, 179 p. : ISBN 0-8144-5898-X LC Card 86-47808 DDC 808/.066651 19
HF5718.3 .C76 1987

Holtz, Herman. The business writing problem solver . Homewood, Ill. , c1987. xii, 235 p. : ISBN 0-87094-901-2 LC Card 86-72270 DDC 651.7/4 19
HF5718.3 .H65 1987

BUSINESS WRITING - HANDBOOKS, MANUALS, ETC.
Brusaw, Charles T. The business writer's handbook /. New York , c1987. xxviii, 764 p. : ISBN 0-312-00571-7 : LC Card 87-4361 DDC 651.7/5 19
HF5726 .B874 1987

The business writing problem solver . Holtz, Herman. Homewood, Ill. , c1987. xii, 235 p. : ISBN 0-87094-901-2 LC Card 86-72270 DDC 651.7/4 19
HF5718.3 .H65 1987

BUSINESSMAN - GERMANY (WEST) - BIOGRAPHY.
Heintzeler, Wolfgang. Der rote Faden . Stuttgart , c1983. 292 p. ; ISBN 3-512-00664-7 LC Card 83-183709
HD9654.9.B27 H45 1983

BUSINESSMEN.
Andreae, Clemens August. Vom Boss zum Partner /. Zürich , c1983. 90 p. ; ISBN 3-7201-5154-9 LC Card 83-168802
HB615 .A69 1983

BUSINESSMEN - ARABIAN PENINSULA.
Field, Michael, 1949- The merchants . London , 1984. xii, 371 p., [16] p. of plates : ISBN 0-7195-4104-2 LC Card 87-672963
HC415.3 .F54x 1984

BUSINESSMEN - AUSTRALIA - BIOGRAPHY.
Ansett, Bob, 1933- Bob Ansett, an autobiography /. Hartwell, Vic. , 1986. 221 p., [16] p. of plates : ISBN 0-9588161-0-7 LC Card 86-228002 DDC 338.7/4/0924 B 19
HC602.5.A57 A33 1986

Denton, Peter, 1955- Elliott . Bedford, U.K. , c1986. 266 p. : ISBN 0-949773-47-6 LC Card 87-100702 DDC 338/.04/0924 B 19
HC602.5.E45 D45 1986

BUSINESSMEN - AUSTRALIA - HISTORY.
Sykes, Trevor. Two centuries of panic . Sydney , Boston , 1987. p. cm. ISBN 0-04-176013-1 LC Card 87-16107 DDC 338.7/4/0994 19
HD2747 .S95 1987

BUSINESSMEN - AUSTRIA - ATTITUDES.
Plaschka, Martina. Gründungsfinanzierung . Wien , c1986. vii, 159 p. : ISBN 3-85428-067-X LC Card 86-225844
HG4146 .P57 1986

BUSINESSMEN - BIOGRAPHY.
Fucini, Joseph J. Experience, Inc. . New York , London , c1987. xi, 244 p. : ISBN 0-02-910971-X LC Card 87-11984 DDC 338/.04/0922 B 19
HC29 .F834 1987

Strain, Lois S. (Lois Smith) The story of Paul J. Meyer . Hollywood, Fla. , c1986. xii, 193 p. : ISBN 0-8119-0720-1 : LC Card 86-29525 DDC 338/.04/0924 B 19
HF5386 .S8832 1986

BUSINESSMEN - BRAZIL - BIOGRAPHY.
Campos Netto, José Candido de, 1880-1963. O cavvaliere Aristides Germani /. [Caxias do Sul, Brazil] [Porto Alegre] , 1978. 111 p. : LC Card 79-121861
HD9056.B62 C35 1978 ***NYPL [JLD 81-342]***

BUSINESSMEN - BRAZIL - FORTALEZA - RECREATION.
Situação de saúde e lazer do comerciário de Fortaleza /. Fortaleza-CE , 1977/1978 [i.e. 1978] 66 leaves ; LC Card 83-116799
HD5755.F6 S58 1978

BUSINESSMEN - CANADA - BIOGRAPHY.
Burton, G. Allan, 1915- A store of memories /. Toronto, Ont. , c1986. 330 p., [17] p. of plates : ISBN 0-7710-1792-8 : LC Card 87-101965 DDC 381/.45/000924 B 19
HF5465.C32 B87 1986

BUSINESSMEN - CHINA - BIOGRAPHY.
Holzberger, Peter. Recollections of an "old China hand" /. [Hongkong , c1984] 233 p. : LC Card 86-135690 DDC 338.092/2 B 19
HC282.5.H64 A3 1984

BUSINESSMEN - DENMARK - BIOGRAPHY.
Juncker, Flemming, 1904- Men morsomt har det været /. [Copenhagen] , c1983. 423 p., [8] p. of plates : ISBN 87-00-54643-7 : LC Card 84-109657
HD9765.D42 J85 1983

BUSINESSMEN - EGYPT - DIRECTORIES.
Egyptian Businessmen Association . Guiza [1986] ca. 150 p. : LC Card 86-961030 DDC 338/.0025/62 19
HC830 .E395 1986

BUSINESSMEN - FLORIDA - BIOGRAPHY.
Akin, Edward N. Flagler, Rockefeller partner and Florida baron /. Kent, Ohio , c1988. xiii, 305 p. : ISBN 0-87338-348-6 (alk. paper) LC Card 87-2070 DDC 338/.04/0924 B 19
HC102.5.F55 A75 1988

BUSINESSMEN - FRANCE - BIOGRAPHY.
Chavane, Laurence. Le phénomène Leclerc . Paris , c1986. 253 p., [16] p. of plates : ISBN 2-259-01481-X : LC Card 86-186372
HF5469.23.F72 L422 1986

Musnik, Isabelle. Tapie, les secrets de sa réussite /. Paris , c1986. 261 p. : ISBN 2-259-01546-8 : LC Card 87-167974
HC272.5.T3 M87 1986

BUSINESSMEN - GERMANY - BIOGRAPHY.
Holzberger, Peter. Recollections of an "old China hand" /. [Hongkong , c1984] 233 p. : LC Card 86-135690 DDC 338.092/2 B 19
HC282.5.H64 A3 1984

Ohlsen, Manfred. Milliarden für den Geier, oder, Der Fall des Friedrich Flick /. Berlin , 1985. 458 p. : LC Card 86-149056
HC282.5.F54 O35 1985

BUSINESSMEN - GERMANY - BREMEN - BIOGRAPHY.
Barth, Johannes, 1891- Als deutscher Kaufmann in Fernost . Berlin , c1984. 206 p. : ISBN 3-503-02366-6 LC Card 84-143117
HC289.B7 B373 1984

BUSINESSMEN - GERMANY, WEST.
Berghahn, Volker Rolf. Unternehmer und Politik in der Bundesrepublik /. Frankfurt am Main , 1985. 363 p. : ISBN 3-518-11265-1 LC Card 85-235608
HC286.5 .B37 1985

Krelle, Wilhelm. Wachstum bei Erschöpfbaren Ressourcen, gibt es das? . Münster , c1982. 59 p. : ISBN 3-402-04434-X LC Card 83-215135
HC55 .K74 1982

Otto, Werner, 1909- Die Otto-Gruppe . Düsseldorf , 1983, c1982. 319 p., [32] p. of plates : ISBN 3-430-17322-1 : LC Card 83-199344
HD2860.O77 O78 1982

BUSINESSMEN - GERMANY, WEST - BIOGRAPHY.
Feyerabend, Joachim. Die leisen Milliarden . Düsseldorf , 1984. 187 p. : ISBN 3-430-12729-7 LC Card 84-176048
HC282.5.F54 F49 1984

Kapferer, Clodwig, 1901- Ein Leben für die Information . Zürich , 1983. 116 p. ; ISBN 3-906639-00-X LC Card 83-185401
HC282.5.K36 A3 1983

BUSINESSMEN - GREAT BRITAIN.
Scase, Richard. The real world of the small business owner /. London , New York , c1987. 170 p. ; ISBN 0-7099-5416-6 (pbk.) LC Card 87-6756 DDC 338.6/42/0941 19
HD2346.G7 S28 1987

BUSINESSMEN - GREAT BRITAIN - BIOGRAPHY.
Church, Roy A. Herbert Austin . London , c1979. lii, 233 p., [3] leaves of plates : ISBN 0-905118-29-4 : LC Card 79-317202 DDC 338.7/62/920924 B
HD9710.G72 A93 ***NYPL [JFD 86-9452]***

Wansell, Geoffrey, 1945- Tycoon . New York , 1987. 396 p., [16] p. of plates : ISBN 0-689-11817-1 LC Card 87-11473 DDC 338/.04/0924 B 19
HC252.5.G64 W36 1987

BUSINESSMEN - GREAT BRITAIN - BIOGRAPHY - DICTIONARIES.
Dictionary of business biography . London , 1984. 5 v. : ISBN 0-406-27340-5 (set) LC Card 86-188034 DDC 338/.0092/2 B 19
HC252.5.A2 D53 1984 ***NYPL [JLM 86-569]***

BUSINESSMEN - HEALTH AND HYGIENE - BRAZIL - FORTALEZA.
Situação de saúde e lazer do comerciário de Fortaleza /. Fortaleza-CE , 1977/1978 [i.e. 1978] 66 leaves ; LC Card 83-116799
HD5755.F6 S58 1978

BUSINESSMEN - ICELAND - BIOGRAPHY.
Alfreð Elíasson, 1920- Alfreðs saga og Loftleiða /. Reykjavík , 1984 (1985 printing) 372 p. : LC Card 86-101929
HD9711.I22 A443 1985 ***NYPL [JFE 87-1455]***

BUSINESSMEN - INDIA - CASE STUDIES.
Nafziger, E. Wayne. Entrepreneurship, equity, and economic development /. Greenwich, Conn. , c1986. xxiii, 308 p. : ISBN 0-89232-711-1 : LC Card 86-20151 DDC 338/.04 19
HB615 .N34 1986 ***NYPL [JLE 87-1672]***

BUSINESSMEN - INDONESIA - BIOGRAPHY.
Ning, Hasjim, 1916- Pasang surut pengusaha pejuang . Jakarta , 1986. x, 392 p., [1] leaf of plates : LC Card 86-944750
HC446.5.N56 A3 1986

BUSINESSMEN - JAPAN - BIOGRAPHY.
Barth, Johannes, 1891- Als deutscher Kaufmann in Fernost . Berlin , c1984. 206 p. : ISBN 3-503-02366-6 LC Card 84-143117
HC289.B7 B373 1984

Holzberger, Peter. Recollections of an "old China hand" /. [Hongkong , c1984] 233 p. : LC Card 86-135690 DDC 338.092/2 B 19
HC282.5.H64 A3 1984

BUSINESSMEN - JAPAN - HISTORY.
Hirschmeier, Johannes. Johannes Hirschmeier, die japanische Unternehmung . Hamburg , 1986. viii, 218 p. : ISBN 3-88910-024-4 : LC Card 86-225311
HF5349.J3 H573 1986

BUSINESSMEN - LIFE SKILLS GUIDES.
The Boss's encyclopedia /. New York, N.Y. , c1987. xxvi, 594 p. ; ISBN 0-932648-75-4 LC Card 86-30961 DDC 658 19
HF5356 .B735 1987

BUSINESSMEN - MARITIME PROVINCES - BIOGRAPHY.
Belliveau, John Edward, 1913- "Crackie" . Hantsport, N.S. , 1986. 192 p. : ISBN 0-88999-315-7 (pbk.) LC Card 87-120170 DDC 338.092/2 B 19
HC112.5.A2 B44 1986

BUSINESSMEN - MEXICO.
Government and private sector in contemporary Mexico /. [La Jolla, Calif.] , 1987. iv, 146 p. ; LC Card 87-622060 DDC 338.972 19
HD3616.M43 G68 1987

BUSINESSMEN - MEXICO - BIOGRAPHY.
Quien es quien en la empresa mexicana. México , 1985. 381 p. ; LC Card 86-190341
HF3234.5 .Q54 1985

BUSINESSMEN - MEXICO - MEXICO CITY - HISTORY.
Kicza, John E., 1947- Colonial entrepreneurs, families and business in Bourbon Mexico City /. Albuquerque , c1983. 1 v. : ISBN 0-8263-0655-1 (v. 1) LC Card 82-21962 DDC 305.5/54/097253 19
HF3240.M5 K52 1983 ***NYPL [JLL 83-164]***

BUSINESSMEN - NEW YORK - ITHACA - BIOGRAPHY.
Sisler, Carol U., 1929- Enterprising families, Ithaca, New York . Ithaca, N.Y. (5 Cornell Walk, Ithaca 14850) , 1986. 159 p. : LC Card 86-81672 DDC 338/.092/2 B 19
HC102.5.A2 S55 1986

BUSINESSMEN - NEW YORK - ITHACA - HOMES AND HAUNTS.
Sisler, Carol U., 1929- Enterprising families, Ithaca, New York . Ithaca, N.Y. (5 Cornell Walk, Ithaca 14850) , 1986. 159 p. : LC Card 86-81672 DDC 338/.092/2 B 19
HC102.5.A2 S55 1986

BUSINESSMEN - NIGERIA - CASE STUDIES.
Nafziger, E. Wayne. Entrepreneurship, equity, and economic development /. Greenwich, Conn. , c1986. xxiii, 308 p. : ISBN 0-89232-711-1 : LC Card 86-20151 DDC 338/.04 19
HB615 .N34 1986 ***NYPL [JLE 87-1672]***

BUSINESSMEN - PAKISTAN - BIOGRAPHY.
Marker, Kekobad Ardeshir, 1896-1984. A petal from the rose /. [Karachi] 1985 (Karachi : Rosette) 2 v. : LC Card 85-932155
HC440.5.M35 A3 1985

BUSINESSMEN - POLAND - BIOGRAPHY.
Wieleżyński, Leszek. Wspólna praca--wspólny plon . London, England [1986], c1985. 295 p., [24] p. of plates : LC Card 87-111287
HD9575.P62 W549 1986

BUSINESSMEN - QUÉBEC (PROVINCE) - BIOGRAPHY.
Richer, Laurette B. Ludger Gravel, 1864-1933 . [Montréal] , c1986. 170 p. : ISBN 2-9800028-1-X LC Card 87-115031
HC112.5.G73 R53 1986

BUSINESSMEN - QUÉBEC (PROVINCE) - INTERVIEWS.
L'Homme d'affaires québécois des années 80 /. Montréal, Québec, Canada , c1983. 418 p., [14] p. of plates : ISBN 2-89045-585-8 LC Card 83-190776
HC117.Q4 H65 1983

BUSINESSMEN - SOUTHERN STATES - BIOGRAPHY.
Mayor, Archer H. Southern timberman . Athens , c1988. p. cm. ISBN 0-8203-0999-0 (alk. paper) LC Card 87-22897 DDC 338.7/63498/0975 19
HD9760.B83 M39 1988

BUSINESSMEN - SPAIN - BIOGRAPHY.
Ekaizer, Ernesto, 1949- José María Ruiz Mateos, el ultimo magnate /. Esplugues de Llobregat, Barcelona , 1985. 833 p., [16] p. of plates : ISBN 84-01-33291-5 LC Card 86-122394 DDC 332.1/6 B 19
HG4216.R85 E38 1985 ***NYPL [JFD 86-6856]***

BUSINESSMEN - SPAIN - VALENCIA - HISTORY - 18TH CENTURY.
Franch Benavent, Ricardo, 1956- Crecimiento comercial y enriquecimiento burgués en la Valencia del siglo XVIII /. Valencia [1986?] 340 p. : ISBN 84-505-4154-9 LC Card 87-110614
HF3690.V3 F7 1986

BUSINESSMEN - SWEDEN - HANDBOOKS, MANUALS, ETC.
Kay-Åberg, K. (Karl), 1861-1927. Sveriges industri . Stockholm , 1898. xvi p., 1054 columns, 1055-1071 p. ; LC Card 85-666356
HC372.2 .K39x 1898

BUSINESSMEN - SWITZERLAND - BIOGRAPHY.
Jéquier, François. Charles Veillon . Zürich , 1985. 142 p. : LC Card 85-139330 DDC 338.092/4 B 19
HC395.5.V45 J45 1985

Riedl-Ehrenberg, Renate. Alfred Kern (1850-1893), Edouard Sandoz (1853-1928) . Zürich , c1986. 90 p. : LC Card 86-159933 DDC 338/.09494 s 338.7/66/0094943 19
HC395.5.A2 S3 no. 44 QD21

Tauber, Herbert. Johann Ulrich Aebi . Zürich , c1983. 84, [2] p. : LC Card 83-192282
HC395.5.A2 S3 no. 38 HD9486.S94A36

BUSINESSMEN - TIME MANAGEMENT.
Bates, Jefferson D., 1920- The portable office . Washington, D.C. , c1987. 262 p. : ISBN 0-87491-491-3 :; 0-87491-841-3 (jacket) LC Card 87-1773 DDC 658.4/093 19
HD38 .B325 1987

BUSINESSMEN - UNITED STATES.
Nader, Ralph. The big boys . New York , c1986. xix, 571 p. ; ISBN 0-394-53338-0 : LC Card 85-25979 DDC 338.6/44/0973 19
HD2785 .N33 1986 ***NYPL [JLE 86-2421]***

BUSINESSMEN - UNITED STATES - ATTITUDES.
Kolarik, William F. A model for the study of international trade politics . New York , 1987. 613 p. : ISBN 0-8240-8086-6 (alk. paper) : LC Card 87-23788 DDC 382/.0947/0730724 19
HF3105 .K64 1987

BUSINESSMEN - UNITED STATES - BIOGRAPHY.
Butcher, Lee. Accidental millionaire . New York , c1988. xii, 224 p., [4] p. of plates : ISBN 0-913729-79-5 LC Card 87-9414 DDC 338.7/61004/0924 B 19
HD9696.C64 A863 1988

Carter, John Mack. Starting at the top . New York [1985] 252 p. ; ISBN 0-688-04520-0 LC Card 85-4826 DDC 338/.04/0922 B 19
HC102.5.A2 C37 1985 ***NYPL [JLD 87-1089]***

Curtis, Jane, 1918- Frederick Billings, Vermonter, pioneer lawyer, business man, conservationist . Woodstock, VT , c1986. 135 p. : ISBN 0-930985-04-4 (pbk.) : LC Card 86-28103 DDC 385/.092/4 B 19
HE2754.B5 C87 1986

Daniels, Leroy Judson, 1882- Tales of an old horsetrader . Iowa City , 1987. viii, 235 p. : ISBN 0-87745-173-7 LC Card 87-10932 DDC 338.1/761/00924 B 19
HD9434.U6 D36 1987

Hammer, Armand, 1897- Hammer /. New York , c1987. 544 p., [32] p. of plates : ISBN 0-399-13275-9 LC Card 86-30289 DDC 338.092/4 B 19
HC102.5.H35 A3 1987

Harris, Kenneth, 1919- The wildcatter . New York , c1987. x, 180 p., [8] p. of plates : ISBN 1-555-84048-5 LC Card 87-8183 DDC 338.7/622338/0924 B 19
HD9570.A53 H37 1987

Iacocca, Lee A. The Iacocca tapes [sound recording] . Chicago, Ill. , c1985. 6 sound cassettes : LC Card 87-750990
HD9710.U I

Kantowicz, Edward R. True Value . Chicago , 1986. 270 p., [16] p. of plates : ISBN 0-89526-580-X : LC Card 86-42795 DDC 381/.45683/0924 B 19
HD9745.U5 C655 1986 ***NYPL [JLE 87-1449]***

Kiam, Victor. Going for it! . New York , c1986. 260 p. ; ISBN 0-688-06060-9 : LC Card 85-61762 DDC 338/.04/0924 B 19
HC102.5.K53 A34 1986 ***NYPL [JLE 86-2954]***

Kingstone, Brett. The dynamos . New York , c1987. xx, 256 p. : ISBN 0-471-85827-7 LC Card 87-1754 DDC 338/.04/0922 B 19
HC102.5.A2 K56 1987

Klein, Maury, 1939- The life and legend of Jay Gould /. Baltimore , c1986. xvi, 595 p., [24] p. of plates : ISBN 0-8018-2880-5 (alk. paper) LC Card 85-24107 DDC 332/.092/4 B 19
HC102.5.G68 K55 1986 ***NYPL [JFE 86-2364]***

Littman, Jonathan, 1958- Once upon a time in ComputerLand . Tucson, AZ , c1987. xiii, 296 p., [8] p. of plates : ISBN 0-89586-502-5 : LC Card 87-3823 DDC 381/.4500416/0973 19
HD9696.C64 C655 1987

Miller, Russell. The house of Getty /. London , 19. 361 p., [32] p. of plates : ISBN 0-7181-2601-7 : LC Card 86-222703 DDC 332/.092/4 B 19
HD9570.G4 M55 1986b

Miller, Russell. The house of Getty /. South Yarmouth, Ma. [1987], c1985. 669 p. [16] p. of plates : ISBN 1-555-04230-9 LC Card 86-24259

DDC 332/.092/4 B 19
HD9570.G4 M55 1987

Minkow, Barry. Making it in America /. [Los Angeles?] , c1985. 136 p. ; LC Card 85-51822 DDC 650.1/092/4 B 19
HC102.5.M5 A3 1985

Sculley, John. Odyssey . New York , c1987. xiv, 450 p., [16] p. of plates : ISBN 0-06-015780-1 : LC Card 87-45142 DDC 331.7/61004165/0924 B 19
HD9696.C62 S38 1987

Trump, Donald, 1946- Trump . New York , 1988. p. cm. ISBN 0-394-55528-7 LC Card 87-42663 DDC 333.33/092/4 B 19
HC102.5.T78 A3 1988

Wells, Della Wager. George Waldo Woodruff . [Macon, Ga.] c1987. x, 167 p. : ISBN 0-86554-298-8 LC Card 87-24700 DDC 338/.04/0924 B 19
HC102.5.W66 W45 1987

Worthy, James C. William C. Norris . Cambridge, Mass. , c1987. xiv, 259 p. : ISBN 0-88730-087-1 LC Card 87-1808 DDC 338.7/61004/0924 B 19
HD9696.C62 N689 1987

Wyden, Peter. The unknown Iacocca /. New York , c1987. 416 p. : ISBN 0-688-06616-X LC Card 87-15240 DDC 338.7/6292/0924 B 19
HD9710.U52 I28 1987

BUSINESSMEN - UNITED STATES - BIOGRAPHY - JUVENILE LITERATURE.
Haddock, Patricia. Standing up for America . Minneapolis, Minn. , c1987. 111 p. : ISBN 0-87518-362-X : LC Card 86-32965 DDC 338.7/6292/0924 B 92 19
HD9710.U52 I246 1987

BUSINESSMEN - UNITED STATES - HISTORY - 20TH CENTURY.
Sanford, William F. The American business community and the European Recovery Program, 1947-1952 /. New York , 1987. xiv, 366 p. ; ISBN 0-8240-8091-2 (alk. paper) LC Card 87-23765 DDC 338.91/73/04 19
HC240 .S259 1987

BUSINESSMEN - VENEZUELA - HISTORY - 20TH CENTURY.
Brito Figueroa, Federico. La aristocracia del dinero en Venezuela actual, 1945-1985 /. Barquisimeto, Venezuela , 1986- v. <1 > ; ISBN 980-608-700-3 (v. 1) : LC Card 87-404343 DDC 305.5/234/0987 19
HG185.V4 B75 1986

BUSINESSMEN - WEST (U. S.) - BIOGRAPHY.
Business entrepreneurs in the West /. Manhattan, Kan. , c1986. 120 p. : ISBN 0-89745-088-4 (pbk.) LC Card 87-135380 DDC 338/.04/0922 B 19
HC102.5.A2 B78 1986

BUSINESSMEN - WEST (U. S.) - HISTORY.
Dary, David. Entrepreneurs of the old West /. New York , c1986. xi, 368 p. : ISBN 0-394-52405-5 LC Card 85-45590 DDC 338/.04/0978 19
HC102.5.A2 D37 1986 ***NYPL [JLE 86-4063]***

Dary, David. Entrepreneurs of the old West /. Lincoln [1987], c1986. xi, 368 p. : ISBN 0-8032-6572-7 (pbk.) LC Card 87-5892 DDC 338/.04/0978 19
HC102.5.A2 D37 1987

BUSINESSWOMEN. see **WOMEN IN BUSINESS.**

Buskirk, Richard Hobart, 1927-
Price, Courtney H. The entrepreneur's resource handbook /. Denver, Colo. , 1987. 178 p. : ISBN 0-944303-00-5 (pbk.) LC Card 87-62190
HD62.5 .P65 1987

Stanton, William J. Management of the sales force /. Homewood, Ill. , 1987. xv, 704 p. : ISBN 0-256-03635-7 LC Card 86-82598 DDC 658.8/1 19
HF5438.4 .S78 1987

Busse, Dieter. Die Wirkungen von Sonderfahrstreifen für Busse auf die Fahrzeiten im Individualverkehr und öffentlichen Personenahverkehr : eine modellgestützte Analyse für einen innerstädtischen Verkehrsengpass in Münster / Dieter Busse. Münster : Lit Verlag, [1985?] xii, 274 p. : ill. ; 20 cm. (Betriebswirtschaftliche Schriftenreihe . Bd. 19) Bibliography: p. 249-274. ISBN 3-88660-264-8 LC Card 86-138804
1. Traffic engineering - Germany (West) - Münster in Westfalen. 2. Transportation - Germany (West) - Münster in Westfalen. 3. Bus lines - Germany (West) - Münster in Westfalen. I. Title. II. Series.
HE363.G34 M933 1985

Busse von Colbe, Walther.
Betriebswirtschaftstheorie / Walther Busse von Colbe, Gert Lassmann. 2., revid. und erw. Aufl. Berlin ; New York : Springer-Verlag, <c1986-> v. <3 > : ill. ; 21 cm. (Heidelberger Taschenbücher. Bd. <242 >) Includes bibliographies and indexes. ISBN 0-387-16407-3 (Bd. 3 : U. S.) LC Card 87-103759
1. Industrial management. I. Lassmann, Gert. II. Title.
HD35 .B88 1986

Bussière, Yves. Vieillissement de la population et demande de transport dans la région de Montréal : 1978-1991 / par Yves Bussière, avec la collaboration de Bernard McCann, Anita Seni. Montréal, Québec : I.N.R.S.-Urbanisation, [1983] 83 p. : ill. ; 28 cm. (Etudes et Documents / I.N.R.S.-Urbanisation . 36) "Mai 1983." Bibliography: p. 75-77. ISBN 2-89228-036-2 LC Card 84-177163
1. Local transit - Québec (Province) - Montréal Region. 2. Age distribution (Demography) - Québec (Province) - Montréal Region. I. McCann, Bernard. II. Seni, Anita. III. Series: Etudes et documents (INRS-Urbanisation) , 36. IV. Title.
HE4509.M68 B88 1983

Busson, Terry. Hackett, Judith C. Managing rural infrastructure . Lexington, Ky. , c1986. iii, 36 p. : ISBN 0-87292-070-4 (pbk.) : LC Card 87-404481 DDC 363/.0973 19
HD3888 .H27 1986

Bussy, Carvel de. Spitzmüller, Alexander, 1862-1953. Memoirs of Alexander Spitzmüller, Freiherr von Harmersbach (1862-1953) . Boulder , New York , 1987. xi, 327 p., [5] p. of plates : ISBN 0-88033-124-0 LC Card 87-80511 DDC 332.3/2/0924 B 19
HG1552.S65 A3 1987

Bustamante G., Jaime. Algunos antecedentes estadísticos sobre las organizaciones económicas populares / Jaime Bustamante G. Santiago, Chile : Programa de Economía del Trabajo, Academia de Humanismo Cristiano, 1986. 23 p. ; 22 cm. "Trabajo preparado especialmente para el Seminario 'El Movimiento Laboral y el Retorno a la Democracia,' organizado por el PET el 24 de mayo de 1986." LC Card 87-101323
1. Cottage industries - Chile. 2. Self-help housing - Chile. 3. Consumer cooperatives - Chile. I. Programa de Economía del Trabajo (Academia de Humanismo Cristiano). II. Title.
HD2346.C53 B87 1986

Bustamante Institute of Public and International Affairs.
Trade, aid, and democracy in the Caribbean . [S.l.] [1986] 68 p. : LC Card 87-400829 DDC 338.91/09729 19
HC151 .T73 1986

Trade unions and democracy . [Kingston, Jamaica] [1986] iii, 52 p. : LC Card 87-133832 DDC 322/.2/09729 19
HD6571 .T72 1986

Bustamante Ramírez, Enrique. La Televisión en España mañana . Madrid , 1986. 331 p. ; ISBN 84-323-0563-X LC Card 86-199326
HE8700.9.S63 T45 1986 ***NYPL [MWGV (Spain) 87-2054]***

Bustelo, Eduardo S.
Política x técnica no planejamento . São Paulo [Brasília] , 1982. 251 p. ; LC Card 86-150182
HD85.P65 P65 1982

Políticas de ajuste y grupos más vulnerables en América Latina . [Bogotá, Colombia] , 1987. 278 p. : ISBN 958-9093-01-9 LC Card 87-404285 DDC 338.98 19
HC125 .P647 1987

Busurin, K. A. Nauchnaia͡ organizat͡sii͡a truda v dorozhnom khozi͡aĭstve / K.A. Busurin, V.I. Parfenova. Moskva : Stroĭizdat, 1981. 159 p. ; 21 cm. Bibliography: p. 157-[158] LC Card 87-461013
1. Road construction industry - Russian S.F.S.R. 2. Road construction workers - Russian S.F.S.R. I. Parfenova, V. I. (Valentina Ivanovna). II. Title.
HD9717.5.R63 S653 1981

Busygin, Vladimir Petrovich. Val'tukh, Konstantin Kurtovich. Matematicheskiĭ i statisticheskiĭ analiz funkt͡sii potreblenii͡a /. Novosibirsk , 1986. 165, [3] p. : LC Card 86-230310
HB801 .V26 1986

But the world goes on the same : changing times in Durham pit villages / compiled, edited and produced by the Durham Strong Words collective. Whitley Bay, Tyne & Wear : Strong Words, Erdesdun Publications, 1979. 106 p. : ill. ; 22 cm. "ISBN 0905274067 (pbk.)"--GB80-34355. LC Card 81-107503
1. Labor and laboring classes - England - Durham (County) - History - 20th century. 2. Coal miners - England - Durham (County) - History - 20th century. 3. Durham (County) - Social conditions. I. Strong Words (Firm).
HD8399.D872 B87 1979

Butcher and Company . Butcher, Jonathan. New York , 1985. 20 p. : LC Card 85-61590 DDC 332.6/06/074811 19
HG5129.P5 B85 1985

BUTCHER AND COMPANY (PHILADELPHIA, PA.)
Butcher, Jonathan. Butcher and Company . New York , 1985. 20 p. : LC Card 85-61590 DDC 332.6/06/074811 19
HG5129.P5 B85 1985

Butcher, Helen. Walsh, Brendan P., 1955- On-line information . Oxford, [Oxfordshire] , New York, NY, USA , 1987. xli, 327 p. : ISBN 0-631-15543-0 : LC Card 87-13154 DDC 025/.04/02465 19
HF5548.2 .W294 1987

Butcher, Jonathan. Butcher and Company : serving the American investment community for 75 years / Jonathan Butcher. New York : Newcomen Society of the United States, 1985. 20 p. : ill. ; 23 cm. (Newcomen publication. no. 1235) Address delivered at a "1985 Philadelphia Meeting" of the Newcomen Society of the United States on January 31, 1985. LC Card 85-61590 DDC 332.6/06/074811 19
1. Butcher and Company (Philadelphia, Pa.). I. Title.
HG5129.P5 B85 1985

Butcher, Lee. Accidental millionaire : the rise and fall of Steve Jobs at Apple Computer / Lee Butcher.1st ed. New York : Paragon House, c1988. xii, 224 p., [4] p. of plates : ports. ; 24 cm. Includes index. ISBN 0-913729-79-5 LC Card 87-9414 DDC 338.7/61004/0924 B 19
1. Apple Computer, Inc. - History. 2. Jobs, Steven, 1955-. 3. Computer industry - United States - History. 4. Businessmen - United States - Biography. I. Title.
HD9696.C64 A863 1988

BUTCHERING. see **SLAUGHTERING AND SLAUGHTER-HOUSES.**

BUTCHERS - ITALY - PRATO REGION - HISTORY.
Nigro, Giampiero. Gli uomini dell'irco . Firenze , 1983. xxii, 184 p. : ISBN 88-00-86022-2 : LC Card 84-238769
HD9425.I83 P76 1983 ***NYPL [JLE 86-2127]***

Buter, Adriaan. De kadans van de getouwen : heren en knechten in de Nederlandse textiel / Adriaan Buter. Amsterdam : Elsevier, 1985. 160 p. : ill. (some col.) ; 28 cm. Bibliography: p. [159] ISBN 90-10-05573-6 LC Card 86-110698
1. Textile industry - Netherlands - History. 2. Textile workers - Netherlands - History. I. Title.
HD9865.N65 B88 1985

Butler, Eamonn. Milton Friedman : a guide to his economic thought / Eamonn Butler. Aldershot, Hants, England : Gower/Maurice Temple Smith, c1985. 272 p. : ill. ; 23 cm. Includes index. Bibliography: p. 263-265. ISBN 0-85117-261-X :
1. Friedman, Milton, 1912-. 2. Economics - History. 3. Monetary policy - History. I. Title.
NYPL [JLD 86-1090]

Butler, Elizabeth M. Alcoholism programs in industry : an Alberta survey / prepared by Elizabeth M. Butler for Medical Services Branch, Occupational Health & Safety Division, Alberta Workers' Health, Safety, and Compensation. Edmonton, Alta. : The Branch, [1982] xiii, 80 p. : ill. ; 28 cm. "September, 1982." Bibliography: p. 54-59. LC Card 86-212872 DDC 331.25/5 19

1. Alcoholism and employment - Alberta. I. Alberta Workers' Health, Safety and Compensation. Medical Services Branch. II. Title.
HF5549.5.A4 B88 1982

Butler, Stephen A. Management incentive compensation plans / Stephen A. Butler, Michael W. Maher. Montvale, N.J. : National Association of Accountants, c1986. v, 55 p. ; 23 cm. Bibliography: p. 45-55. "No. 86196-SP-7M-10/86"--Cover. ISBN 0-86641-140-2 (pbk.) LC Card 86-230062 DDC 658.4/07225 19
1. Executives - Salaries, etc. - United States. 2. Incentives in industry - United States. I. Maher, Michael, 1946-. II. National Association of Accountants. III. Title.
HD4965.5.U6 B86 1986

Butlin, S. J. (Sydney James), d. 1977. The Australian monetary system, 1851 to 1914 / S.J. Butlin. [s.l] : J.F. Butlin, 1986. 404 p. : ill. ; 28 cm. Includes bibliographical references and index. ISBN 1-86252-307-X (pbk.) LC Card 87-154610 DDC 332.4/994 19
1. Money - Australia - History. 2. Banks and banking - Australia - History. I. Title.
HG1394 .B87 1986

Butnik-Siverskiĭ, Aleksandr Borisovich. Ėkonomiko-matematicheskie metody v analize khoziaĭstvennoĭ deiatel'nosti predpriiatiĭ i ob"edineniĭ /. Moskva , 1982. 194, [5] p. : LC Card 83-161166
HD30.25 .E394 1982

Butschek, Felix.
Strukturpolitik als Dimension der Vollbeschäftigungspolitik /. Stuttgart , c1983. 103 p. : ISBN 3-437-50276-X : LC Card 83-233394
HD5706 .S82 1983

Vom Nachzügler zum Vorbild(?) . Stuttgart , c1985. 183 p. : ISBN 3-437-50303-0 LC Card 86-200243
HC265 .V65 1985

Butter and margarine attitude & usage : consumer research from United Dairy Industry Association. Rosemont, Ill. (6300 N. River Rd., Rosemont 60018) : The Association, c1986. 234 p. : ill. ; 28 cm. Cover title: Butter & margarine attitudes & usage. "1986 study (including 1972-1986 trends)"--Cover. LC Card 87-404035 DDC 338.1/772/0973 19
1. Butter trade - United States - Statistics. 2. Margarine industry - United States - Statistics. 3. Consumers' preferences - United States - Statistics. 4. Market surveys - United States. I. United Dairy Industry Association (U. S.). II. Title: Butter and margarine attitude and usage. III. Title: Butter & margarine attitudes & usage.
HD9278.U4 B87 1986

Butter and margarine attitude and usage. Butter and margarine attitude & usage . Rosemont, Ill. (6300 N. River Rd., Rosemont 60018) , c1986. 234 p. : LC Card 87-404035 DDC 338.1/772/0973 19
HD9278.U4 B87 1986

Butter & margarine attitudes & usage. Butter and margarine attitude & usage . Rosemont, Ill. (6300 N. River Rd., Rosemont 60018) , c1986. 234 p. : LC Card 87-404035 DDC 338.1/772/0973 19
HD9278.U4 B87 1986

BUTTER TRADE - UNITED STATES - STATISTICS.
Butter and margarine attitude & usage . Rosemont, Ill. (6300 N. River Rd., Rosemont 60018) , c1986. 234 p. : LC Card 87-404035 DDC 338.1/772/0973 19
HD9278.U4 B87 1986

Butterworth, John E.
Economic analysis of information and contracts . Boston , c1988. p. cm. ISBN 0-89838-252-1 : LC Card 87-22508 DDC 657 19
HF5625 .E28 1988

Financial reporting : theory and application to the oil and gas industry in Canada / by John E. Butterworth and Haim Falk. Hamilton, Ont. : Society of Management Accountants of Canada, 1986. viii, 250 p. : ill. ; 22 cm. "A research monograph prepared for the Accounting Principles and Practices Committee, the Society of Management Accountants of Canada." Includes bibliographies. ISBN 0-920212-52-2 (pbk.) LC Card 87-101758 DDC 657/.86203 19
1. Petroleum industry and trade - Canada - Accounting. 2. Gas industry - Canada - Accounting. I. Falk, Haim. II. Society of Management Accountants of Canada. Accounting Principles and Practices Committee. III. Title.
HF5686.P3 B87 1986

BUTTERWORTH, JOHN E.
Economic analysis of information and contracts . Boston , c1988. p. cm. ISBN 0-89838-252-1 : LC Card 87-22508 DDC 657 19
HF5625 .E28 1988

Butterworths BASIC series.
Mole, R. H. (Richard H.) BASIC business analysis and operations research /. London , Boston , 1987. 136 p. : ISBN 0-408-01590-X (pbk.) : LC Card 86-26398 DDC 658.4/034/0285526 19
HD30.25 .M66 1987

Stratfold, Peter. BASIC business systems simulation /. London , Boston , 1987. viii, 172 p. : ISBN 0-408-01260-9 (pbk.) : LC Card 87-18795 DDC 650/.028/55133 19
HF5548.5.B3 S78 1987

Buttler, Friedrich. Staat und Beschäftigung . Nürnberg , 1985. 471 p. : LC Card 86-674027
HD5713 .S72x 1985

Buttler, Günter. Flexible Arbeitszeit gegen starre Sozialsysteme /. Baden-Baden , 1986. 254 p. ; ISBN 3-7890-1213-0 LC Card 87-101055 DDC 331.25/72/0943 19
HD5109.2.G3 F43 1986

Büttner, Herbert. Die segmentorientierte Marketingplanung im Einzelhandelsbetrieb / von Herbert Büttner. Göttingen : O. Schwartz, 1986. 413 p. : ill. ; 23 cm. (Schriften zur Handelsforschung. Nr. 73) Bibliography: p. 383-413. ISBN 3-509-01424-3 LC Card 87-134581 DDC 658.8/7 19
1. Retail trade - Management. 2. Market segmentation. I. Title.
HF5429 .B87 1986

Button, Joe W. Synthetic fibers in asphalt paving mixtures / by Joe W. Button and Thomas G. Hunter ; sponsored by State Department of Highways and Public Transportation, in cooperation with U. S. Department of Transportation, Federal Highway Administration. College Station, Tex. : Texas Transportation Institute, Texas A&M University, System, [1984] vi, 153 p. : ill. ; 28 cm. (Research report / Texas Transportation Institute, Texas A&M University System . 319-1F) "November 1984." Bibliography: p. 86-90. "Research study 2-9-82-319." LC Card 86-620835 DDC 380.5 s 625.8/5 19
1. Asphalt concrete - Additives. 2. Reinforced concrete, Fiber. I. Hunter, Thomas G. II. Texas. State Dept. of Highways and Public Transportation. III. United States. Federal Highway Administration. IV. Series: Research report (Texas Transportation Institute) , 319-1F. V. Title.
HE203 .T43 no. 319-1F TA443.A7

Bútùn tăshkilatchylyg ishini vă siiasi ishi Sov. IKP XXVI gurultaĭy gărarlarynyn ĭerină ĭetirilmăsină ĭonăltmăli. Aliev, Geĭdar Alievich. Vsiu organizatorskuiu i politicheskuiu rabotu--na vypolnenie reshenii XXVI s"ezda KPSS . Baku , 1981. 50 p. ; LC Card 82-158175
HC337.A9 A683 1981

Buvollen, H. P. (Hans Petter)
The situation of workers in the industrialised countries with special reference to Scandinavia / Hans Petter Buvollen and Ines Vargas. Oslo : International Peace Research Institute, [1985] 24 p. ; 30 cm. (PRIO report, 0333-483X . 6/85) Cover title. Bibliography: p. 23-24. LC Card 86-205580 DDC 331.13/7948 19
1. Labor and laboring classes - Scandinavia. 2. Labor supply - Scandinavia. 3. Unemployment - Scandinavia. I. Vargas, Ines. II. Series: PRIO report , 85/6. III. Title.
HD8540 .B86 1985

Vargas, Ines. The NIEO and the situatuon of workers . Oslo [1985] xiv, 290 p. ; ISBN 82-7288-121-7 (pbk.) LC Card 86-205407 DDC 331/.098 19
HD6530.5 .V36 1985

Buxton . Schwieder, Dorothy, 1933- Ames , 1987. viii, 256 p. : ISBN 0-8138-0246-6 LC Card 87-2929 DDC 305/.9622 19
HD8039.M62 U66825 1987

BUXTON (IOWA) - SOCIAL CONDITIONS.
Schwieder, Dorothy, 1933- Buxton . Ames , 1987. viii, 256 p. : ISBN 0-8138-0246-6 LC Card 87-2929 DDC 305/.9622 19
HD8039.M62 U66825 1987

BUY-MAKE DECISIONS. see **MAKE-OR-BUY DECISIONS.**

Buy more home for less money /. Lohmar, Ceil. Crystal Bay, Minn. (P.O. Box 61, Crystal Bay 55323) , c1987. 121 p. : ISBN 0-940641-00-3 (pbk.) LC Card 87-401647 DDC 643/.12 19
HD1379 .L646 1987

BUY-OR-MAKE DECISIONS. see **MAKE-OR-BUY DECISIONS.**

BUYERS' GUIDES. see **CONSUMER EDUCATION; SHOPPING.**

BUYING. see **INDUSTRIAL PROCUREMENT; PURCHASING.**

Buying and selling a home. The Kiplinger/Changing times guide to buying and selling a home /. Washington, DC , New York, NY , c1987. iii, 311 p. : ISBN 0-938721-02-X (pbk.) : LC Card 87-167806 DDC 643/.12 19
HD1379 .K52 1987

Buying & selling a home. The Kiplinger/Changing times guide to buying and selling a home /. Washington, DC , New York, NY , c1987. iii, 311 p. : ISBN 0-938721-02-X (pbk.) : LC Card 87-167806 DDC 643/.12 19
HD1379 .K52 1987

Buying by mail . Christen, François G. Menlo Park, CA (333 Ravenswood Ave., Menlo Park 94025) , c1986. v, 2, 59, 6 leaves : LC Card 86-209563 DDC 658.8/4 19
HF5415.126 .C48 1986

BUYING, INDUSTRIAL. see **INDUSTRIAL PROCUREMENT.**

Buying into America . Tolchin, Martin. New York , 1988. p. cm. ISBN 0-8129-1667-0 : LC Card 87-40198 DDC 332.6/73/0973 19
HG4910 .T65 1988

Buying or selling a home : tax breaks. Chicago, Ill. (4025 W. Peterson Ave., Chicago 60646) : Commerce Clearing House, c1986. 31 p. : ill. ; 23 cm. (Tax angles and tax savings series) Includes index. LC Card 86-209128 DDC 343.7305/46 347.303546 19
1. Real property tax - United States. 2. Real property and taxation - United States. 3. House buying. 4. House selling. I. Commerce Clearing House. II. Series.
HJ4182.A5 B89 1986

Buying right . Wayner, Stephen A. New York , 1987. 247 p. : ISBN 0-531-15524-2 LC Card 86-32474 DDC 332.63/24 19
HD1382.5 .W38 1987

Buyout! . Logue, John, 1947- [Kent, Ohio] [1986] vi, 98 p. : ISBN 0-933522-15-0 (pbk.) LC Card 86-623028 DDC 658.1/6 19
HD2746.5 .L64 1986

Buza, Márton. A szakszervezetek Magyarországon / Buza Márton. [Budapest] : Kossuth, 1985. 229 p. ; 22 cm. ISBN 963-09-2747-0 : LC Card 86-190979
1. Trade-unions - Hungary. I. Title.
HD6680.5 .B89 1985

Buzzard, Shirley. Monitoring and evaluating small business projects . [New York, NY] , c1987. ix, 262 p. : LC Card 87-6945 DDC 361.7 19
HD2346.5 .M65 1987

Buzzell, Robert D. (Robert Dow), 1933-
Multinational marketing management . Reading, Mass. , c1988. x, 500 p. : ISBN 0-201-07996-8 (pbk.) : LC Card 87-12599 DDC 658.8/48 19
HF1009.5 .M85 1988

The PIMS principles : linking strategy to performance / Robert D. Buzzell, Bradley T. Gale. New York : Free Press ; London : Collier Macmillan, c1987. xiii, 322 p. : ill. ; 25 cm. Bibliography: p. 301-312. Includes index. ISBN 0-02-904430-8 LC Card 87-416 DDC 658.8/02 19
1. Marketing management. 2. Strategic planning. I. Gale, Bradley T. II. Title.
HF5415.13 .B893 1987

Buzzetti, Luciano. Il distaccamento italiano di Palestina, 1917-1921 / Luciano Buzzetti, Silvano Sorani. Milano : S. Sorani, c1976. 55 p. : ill. (some col.) ; 24 cm. + 1 pamphlet, Translation (16 p. ; 22 cm.) LC Card 86-179004
1. Postmarks - Palestine - History. 2. Italy. Esercito - Postal service - History. I. Sorani, Silvano. II. Title.
HE6185.P13 B89 1976

Bwimba Ntaganda. Bahizi, Joseph. Monographie d'unités domestiques. [Bujumbura] [1985] 41 leaves ; LC Card 86-980542
HC880.Z7 M843 1985

By i forvandling : københavnske gadebilleder før og nu / Torben Liebst ... [et al.]. Copenhagen : Sporvejshistorisk selskab, 1984. 93 p. : ill. ; 18 cm. (Sporvejshistorisk selskabs bogserie . bog nr. 18) ISBN 87-87589-42-7 LC Card 87-155193
1. Street-railroads - Denmark - Copenhagen - History. 2. Local transit - Denmark - Copenhagen - History. I. Liebst, Torben. II. Sporvejshistorisk selskab (Denmark). III. Series.
HE4859.C68 B92 1984

Byars, Lloyd L.
Human resource and personnel management.
Byars, Lloyd L. Human resource management / Lloyd L. Byars, Leslie W. Rue. 2nd ed. Homewood, Ill. , 1987. xiii, 540 p. : ISBN 0-256-03630-6 LC Card 86-82596 DDC 658.3 19
HF5549 .B937 1987

Human resource management / Lloyd L. Byars, Leslie W. Rue. 2nd ed. Homewood, Ill. : Irwin, 1987. xiii, 540 p. : ill. (some col.) ; 24 cm. Rev. ed. of: Human resource and personnel management. 1984. Includes bibliographies and indexes. ISBN 0-256-03630-6 LC Card 86-82596 DDC 658.3 19
1. Personnel management. I. Rue, Leslie W. II. Byars, Lloyd L. Human resource and personnel management. III. Title.
HF5549 .B937 1987

BYELORUSSIAN S.S.R. - ECONOMIC CONDITIONS.
I͡Urėvich, Uladzimir Mikhaĭlavich. Syn'ooka sestra Ukraïny /. Kyïv , 1985. 158 p. ; LC Card 87-109673
HC337.B93 I97 1985

Shimov, V. N. (Vladimir Nikolaevich) Regional'nai͡a ėffektivnost' obshchestvennogo proizvodstva . Minsk , 1986. 167 p. ; LC Card 86-204677
HC337.B93 S55 1986

BYELORUSSIAN S.S.R. - ECONOMIC CONDITIONS - 1945-
Sovetskai͡a Belorussii͡a v 11-ĭ pi͡atiletke . Minsk , 1986. 117 p. : LC Card 87-128043
HC337.B93 S677 1986

BYELORUSSIAN S.S.R. - ECONOMIC POLICY.
Babosov, Evgeniĭ Mikhaĭlovich. XXVII s"ezd KPSS o strategii uskorenii͡a sot͡sial'no-ėkonomicheskogo razvitii͡a strany /. Minsk , 1987. 124 p. ; LC Card 87-166221
HC337.B93 B33 1987

Drit͡s, V. I. (Valentin Ivanovich) Intensifikat͡sii͡a--opredeli͡ai͡ushchee napravlenie sovremennogo ėkonomicheskogo razvitii͡a /. Minsk , 1986. 76, [4] p. ; LC Card 87-144484
HC336.25 .D75 1985

OĖkonomicheskie problemy razvitii͡a narodnogo khozi͡aĭstva i povyshenie ėffektivnosti obshchestvennogo proizvodstva /. Minsk , 1984. 148 p. : LC Card 85-147020
HC337.B93 E45 1984

Shimov, V. N. (Vladimir Nikolaevich) Regional'nai͡a ėffektivnost' obshchestvennogo proizvodstva . Minsk , 1986. 167 p. ; LC Card 86-204677
HC337.B93 S55 1986

BYELORUSSIAN S.S.R. - INDUSTRIES - HISTORY.
Kosti͡uk, Mikhail Pavlovich. Trudovoĭ vklad krest'i͡anstva v pobedu i uprochnenie sot͡sializma . Minsk , 1986. 236 p. ; LC Card 86-136452
HD1492.S652 B9252 1986

Byerly, Victoria Morris. Hard times cotton mill girls : personal histories of womanhood and poverty in the south / Victoria Byerly. Ithaca, N.Y. : ILR Press, New York State School of Industrial and Labor Relations, Cornell University, c1986. x, 223 p. : ill., ports. ; 23 cm. Includes index. ISBN 0-87546-128-X : LC Card 86-20082 DDC 331.4/877/00922 B 19
1. Women textile workers - Southern States - Biography. 2. Women - Employment - Southern States. 3. Women - Southern States - Economic conditions. I. Title.
HD6073.T42 A132 1986
NYPL [JLD 87-1241]

Byggnads- och anläggningsindustrin. [Stockholm] : LiberFörlag, [1981] 84 p. : ill. ; 21 cm. By Svenska byggnadsentreprenörföreningen. "LU 80, bilaga 4." "Ds E 1981:2." ISBN 91-38-06015-9 LC Card 84-120446
1. Construction industry - Sweden. I. Svenska byggnadsentreprenörföreningen. II. Sweden. Ekonomidepartementet. Långtidsutredningen 1980.
HD9715.S852 B898 1981

Byggsektorn 1990 : behov av forskning och utveckling under 80-talet. Stockholm : Byggforskningsrådet, [1982] 91 p. : ill. ; 25 cm. "G13:1982"--Verso t.p. LC Card 83-234610
1. Construction industry - Sweden. 2. Construction industry - Research - Sweden. I. Statens råd för byggnadsforskning (Sweden).
HD9715.S852 B93 1982

Bykov, A. N. (Aleksandr Naumovich)
Sot͡sialisticheskai͡a integrat͡sii͡a i nauchno-tekhnicheskai͡a revoli͡ut͡sii͡a / A.N. Bykov, D.A. Lebin ; otvetstvennyĭ redaktor O.A. Chukanov. Moskva : Izd-vo "Nauka", 1981. 343 p. ; 20 cm. At head of title: Akademii͡a nauk SSSR. Institut ėkonomiki mirovoĭ sot͡sialisticheskoĭ sistemy. Includes bibliographical references. LC Card 82-101911
1. Technological innovations - Europe, Eastern. 2. Europe, Eastern - Economic integration. 3. Communist countries - Economic integration. 4. Technological innovations - Communist countries. I. Lebin, Dmitriĭ Alekseevich. II. Chukanov, Olimp Alekseevich. III. Title.
HC244.Z9 T43 1981

Sozialistische ökonomische Integration : Wissenschaft und Technik / Alexander Naumowitsch Bykow ; [Übersetzer, Silvia Müller].1. Aufl. Berlin : Staatsverlag der Deutschen Demokratischen Republik, 1976. 218 p. ; 22 cm. Translation of: Nauchno-tekhnicheskai͡a integrat͡sii͡a sot͡sialisticheskikh stran, of Chapter 5 of Nauchno-tekhnicheskai͡a revoli͡ut͡sii͡a i integrat͡sii͡a stran SĖV, and of two chapters written especially for this edition. Includes bibliographies. LC Card 87-108725
1. Europe, Eastern - Economic integration. I. Title.
HC244 .B94 1976

Byrne, B. Thomas. The stock index futures market : a trader's insights and strategies / B. Thomas Byrne, Jr. Chicago, Ill. : Probus Pub. Co., c1987. vii, 358 p. : ill. ; 24 cm. Includes index. ISBN 0-917253-28-0 LC Card 87-115177 DDC 332.63/222 19
1. Stock index futures. I. Title.
HG6043 .B97 1987

Byrne, John, 1949-
Energy and cities /. New Brunswick, U. S.A. , c1985. 173 p. : ISBN 0-87855-813-6 (pbk.) LC Card 84-24074 DDC 333.79/13/091732 19
HD108.2 .E525 1985 *NYPL [JLE 86-4441]*

Planning for changing energy conditions /. New Brunswick, N.J., U. S.A. , c1988. xiii, 300 p. : ISBN 0-88738-713-6 (pbk.) : LC Card 87-13977 DDC 333.79 19
HD9502.A2 P59 1988

The Politics of energy research and development /. New Brunswick, U. S.A. , c1986. 181 p. : ISBN 0-88738-653-9 (pbk.) LC Card 86-1307 DDC 333.79/0973 19
HD9502.U52 P63 1986
NYPL [JLE 86-3577]

Byrne, John A. Sculley, John. Odyssey . New York , c1987. xiv, 450 p., [16] p. of plates : ISBN 0-06-015780-1 : LC Card 87-45142 DDC 331.7/61004165/0924 B 19
HD9696.C62 S38 1987

Byrns, Ralph T. Great ideas for teaching economics /. Glenview, Ill. , c1987. xxiv, 400 p. : ISBN 0-673-17245-7 (pbk.) LC Card 87-159026 DDC 330/.07 19
HB74.5.G73 1987

Byrski, Bronisław. Ekonomika i programowanie rozwoju przemysłu /. Kraków , 1978. 378 p. : LC Card 81-172485
HD70.P6 E38 1978

Byte books.
Seybold, Patricia B. Integrated desk-top environments . New York , c1985. ix, 181 p. : ISBN 0-07-056324-1 (pbk.) : LC Card 84-27841 DDC 650/.028/5425 19
HF5548.4.S95 S49 1985
NYPL [JSE 86-2011]

BYZANTINE COINS. see **COINS, BYZANTINE.**

BYZANTINE EMPIRE - ECONOMIC CONDITIONS - SOURCES.
Euangelatou-Notara, Phlōrentia. "Sēmeiōmata" Hellēnikōn kōdikōn hōs pēgē dia tēn ereunan tou oikonomikou kai koinōnikou viou tou Vyzantiou, apo tou 9ou aiōnos mechri tou etous 1204 /. Athēnai , 1982. 296 p. ; LC Card 86-212063
HC294 .E9 1982

BYZANTINE EMPIRE - SOCIAL CONDITIONS - SOURCES.
Euangelatou-Notara, Phlōrentia. "Sēmeiōmata" Hellēnikōn kōdikōn hōs pēgē dia tēn ereunan tou oikonomikou kai koinōnikou viou tou Vyzantiou, apo tou 9ou aiōnos mechri tou etous 1204 /. Athēnai , 1982. 296 p. ; LC Card 86-212063
HC294 .E9 1982

C. A. I. see **Community Associations Institute.**

C.A.S.E. & programmers' workstation markets. Norwalk, Conn., U. S.A. (6 Prowitt St., Norwalk 06855) : International Resource Development Inc., c1987. v, 221 leaves : ill. ; 28 cm. (Report / International Resource Development Inc. . #725) "January 1987." LC Card 87-129461 DDC 380.1/450051 19
1. Computer industry. 2. Computer software industry. 3. Market surveys. I. International Resource Development, inc. II. Title: CASE and programmers' workstation markets. III. Series: Report / International Resource Development Inc. , #725.
HD9696.C62 C2 1987

C. A. S. L. E. see **Commonwealth Association of Surveying and Land Economy.**

C. C. O. M. S. ABC de la economía política /. Madrid [1964] 205 p., [1] folded leaf of plates : LC Card 85-106062
HB178.5 .M25 1964

C (COMPUTER PROGRAM LANGUAGE)
Moore, F. Richard. Programming in C with a bit of UNIX /. Englewood Cliffs, NJ , 1985. vii, 193 p. : ISBN 0-13-730102-2 : LC Card 84-26642 DDC 001.64/24 19
QA76.73.C15 M66 1985
NYPL [JSE 86-1377]

Schustack, Steve, 1952- Variations in C . Bellevue, Wash. [New York] , c1985. xiii, 344 p. ; ISBN 0-914845-48-9 : LC Card 85-5033 DDC 650/.028/5425 19
HF5548.5.C12 S38 1985
NYPL [JSE 87-246]

Wortman, Leon A. C programming with business applications /. Blue Ridge Summit, PA , c1987. xii, 231 p. ; ISBN 0-8306-1457-5 : LC Card 86-23090 DDC 005.2/65 19
HF5548.5.C12 W67 1987

C.D. Deshmukh, his contribution to monetary and economic policy /. Narayan Prasad, P. S. New Delhi , c1985. xiv, 54 p., [1] leaf of plates : LC Card 85-905075 DDC 338.954 19
HC432.5.D47 N37 1985
NYPL [JLD 86-3239]

C. E. B. R. A. P. see **Centro Brasileiro de Análise e Planejamento.**

C. E. C. O. D. see **Centre d'étude du commerce et de la distribution.**

C. E. D. see **Committee for Economic Development.**

C. E. D. A. see **Committee for Economic Development of Australia.**

C. E. E. see **European Economic Community.**

C. E. E. P. see **Centre européen de l'entreprise publique.**

C. E. M. L. A. see **Centro de Estudios Monetarios Latinoamericanos.**

C. E. M. T. see **European Conference of Ministers of Transport.**

C. E. P. see **Centro de Estudos de Planeamento; Council on Economic Priorities.**

C. E. P. A. L. see **United Nations. Economic Commission for Latin America.**

C.E.T.A. arts and humanities experience. Startzel, Donna C. The CETA arts and humanities experience [microform] CETA Ahead project (Arts and humanities employment analysis and documentation) /. Columbia, Md. , 1981. 197 p. ; *NYPL [*XME-11,320]*

C.E.T.A. (Comprehensive Employment and Training Act) and the arts and humanities. Startzel, Donna C. CETA (Comprehensive Employment and Training Act) and the arts and humanities [microform] . Columbia, Md. , 1981. 160 p. ; *NYPL [*XME-11,328]*

C.F.A. readings in fixed income securities analysis. CFA readings in fixed income securities analysis /. Charlottesville, VA (P.O. Box 3668, Charlottesville, VA 22903) , c1985. v, 255 p. : *NYPL [JLF 86-1994]*

C. G. I. L. see **Confederazione generale italiana del lavoro.**

C. I. B. see **International Council for Building Research, Studies and Documentation.**

C. I. C. A. see **Canadian Institute of Chartered Accountants.**

C. I. D. A. see **Inter-American Committee for Agricultural Development.**

C. I. E. P. L. A. N. see **Corporación de Investigaciones Económicas para Latinoamérica.**

C. I. I. R. see **Catholic Institute for International Relations.**

C. I. L. S. S. see **Permanent Inter-State Committee for Drought Control in the Sahel.**

C. I. M. see **Canadian Institute of Mining and Metallurgy.**

C. I. M. M. Y. T. see **International Maize and Wheat Improvement Center.**

CIO. see **Congress of Industrial Organizations.**

C. I. P. C. A. see **Centro de Investigación y Promoción del Campesinado.**

C. I. S. L. see **International Confederation of Free Trade Unions.**

C. M. R. A. see **Chemical Marketing Research Association.**

C. N. I. see **Confederação Nacional da Indústria.**

C. O. B. see **Central Obrera Boliviana.**

C. O. D. E. P. L. A. N. see **Companhia do Desenvolvimento do Planalto Central.**

C. O. M. E. C. O. N. see **Sovet ėkonomicheskoĭ vzaimopomoshchi.**

C. O. M. I. B. O. L. see **Corporación Minera de Bolivia.**

C. P. I. see **Communist Party of India.**

C. P. S. U. [i. e. Communist Party of the Soviet Union] see **Kommunisticheskaia partiia Sovetskogo Soiuza.**

C programming with business applications /. Wortman, Leon A. Blue Ridge Summit, PA , c1987. xii, 231 p. ; ISBN 0-8306-1457-5 : LC Card 86-23090 DDC 005.2/65 19
HF5548.5.C12 W67 1987

La C.S.C. et le programme gouvernemental de mars 1984 /. Arcq, Etienne. Bruxelles [1984] 23 leaves ; LC Card 84-171486
HD8502.C62 A73 1984

ČSSR. see **Czechoslovakia.**

C. V. R. D. see **Companhia Vale do Rio Doce.**

C. V. Starr Center Conference on International Comparisons of the Distribution of Household Wealth (1983 : New York, N.Y.) International comparisons of the distribution of household wealth /. Oxford , New York , 1987. xii, 283 p. : ISBN 0-19-828511-6 : LC Card 86-31241 DDC 339.2/2/094 19
HC240.9.I5 I56 1987

Ça va comme un lundi . Dollé, Anne. [Paris] , c1984. 237 p. ; ISBN 2-01-010177-4 : LC Card 85-143058 DDC 650.1/3 19
HF5386 .D63 1984

Caballero, Lorenzo. Mozambique, food and agriculture sector / Lorenzo Caballero, Thomas Thomsen, Arne Andreasson. Uppsala : Swedish University of Agricultural Sciences, International Rural Development Centre, 1984. 223, [30] p. : ill. ; 29 cm. (Rural development studies, 0346-7287 . no. 16) Bibliography: p. [23]-[30] (second group). ISBN 91-576-2129-2 (pbk.) LC Card 86-218958 DDC 338.1/0967/9 19
1. Produce trade - Mozambique. 2. Agricultural industries - Mozambique. 3. Food industry and trade - Mozambique. 4. Agriculture - Economic aspects - Mozambique. 5. Rural development - Mozambique. I. Thomsen, Thomas. II. Andreasson, Arne. III. Series: Rural development studies (Uppsala, Sweden) , no. 16. IV. Title.
HD9017.M86 C33 1984

Cabana, Francesc, 1934- Les multinacionals a Catalunya / Francesc Cabana. 2a ed. corr. i augm. Barcelona : Edicions de la Magrana, 1986. 154 p. ; 20 cm. (Els Orígens . 16) ISBN 84-7410-162-X LC Card 86-222016
1. International business enterprises - Spain - Catalonia Case studies. 2. International business enterprises - Spain - Catalonia - History. I. Title.
HD2888.5.C38 C33 1986

Cabañas, R. Tosco, Manuel. Aprovechamiento y dominio de las tierras en 1950-51 /. Tegucigalpa, D.C., Honduras [1952] 33 p. ; LC Card 85-197157
HD366 .T66 1952

Cabarga, Leslie. 1,001 advertising cuts from the twenties and thirties /. New York , 1987. 103 p. : ISBN 0-486-25490-9 (pbk.) LC Card 87-15546 DDC 659.13/2/0973 19
HF5813.U6 A525 1987

Cabaud, Michel. 1900, la Française au quotidien / Michel Cabaud et Ronald Hubscher, sur une idée et avec la collaboration de Guy Feinstein. Paris : A. Colin, c1985. 204 p. : ill. ; 25 cm. ISBN 2-200-37097-0 LC Card 86-137649
1. Women - Employment - France - History - 19th century. 2. France - Occupations - History - 19th century. 3. Postcards - France - History - 19th century. 4. Women - Employment - France - History - 19th century - Pictorial works. 5. France - Occupations - History - 19th century - Pictorial works. 6. Postcards - France - History - 19th century - Pictorial works. I. Hubscher, Ronald H. II. Feinstein, Guy. III. Title.
HD6059.F8 C33 1985

CABBAGE PATCH KIDS DOLLS.
Hoffman, William, 1937- Fantasy . Dallas, Tex. , c1984. 217 p. : ISBN 0-87833-386-X LC Card 84-8817 DDC 338.4/76887221/0973 19
HD9993.D653 U64 1984
NYPL [JLE 87-218]

Cabello Jurado, Miguel Angel. Martín Rodríguez, Manuel. Las haciendas locales de la Provincia de Granada, 1940-1983 . Granada [1985?] 369 p. ; ISBN 84-338-0266-6 LC Card 86-230887
HJ9527.G7 M37 1985

CABINET OFFICERS - INDIA - BIOGRAPHY.
Kamath, M. V., 1921- The innovative banker, T.A. Pai, his life and times /. Manipal , Bombay , 1983. x, 247 p., [9] p. of plates : LC Card 83-904531 DDC 332.1/2/0924 B 19
HG1552.P4 K36 1983 *NYPL [JFE 87-879]*

CABINET OFFICERS - ITALY - BIOGRAPHY.
Bonelli, Franco. Bonaldo Stringher . [Udine] [c1985] 169 p. : LC Card 85-220896
HJ1156.S77 B66 1985

CABINET OFFICERS - UNITED STATES.
You may call her madam secretary [motion picture] /. West Tisbury, MA , 1987. 1 film reel (57 min., 40 sec.) : LC Card 87-706816 DDC 973.917 11
HD8073.P38

You may call her madam secretary [videorecording] /. West Tisbury, MA , 1987. 1 videocassette (57 min., 40 sec.) : LC Card 87-706817 DDC 973.917 11
HD8073.P38

CABIS, computer-aided bookkeeping instruction system /. Cooper, Robin, 1951- Reading, Mass. , c1987. p. cm. ISBN 0-201-11307-4 (user's manual) LC Card 86-32148 DDC 657/.2/02855369 19
HF5630 .C68 1987

CABIS (COMPUTER PROGRAM)
Cooper, Robin, 1951- CABIS, computer-aided bookkeeping instruction system /. Reading, Mass. , c1987. p. cm. ISBN 0-201-11307-4 (user's manual) LC Card 86-32148 DDC 657/.2/02855369 19
HF5630 .C68 1987

Cable communication /. Baldwin, Thomas F. Englewood Cliffs, N.J. , c1988. p. cm. ISBN 0-13-110263-X : LC Card 87-16109 DDC 384.55/56 19
HE8700.7 .B35 1988

CABLE TELEVISION.
Baldwin, Thomas F. Cable communication /. Englewood Cliffs, N.J. , c1988. p. cm. ISBN 0-13-110263-X : LC Card 87-16109 DDC 384.55/56 19
HE8700.7 .B35 1988

Pigeat, Henri, 1939- La télévision par cable commence demain /. Paris , c1983. 239 p. ; ISBN 2-259-01062-8 : LC Card 83-237808
HE8700.72.F8 P54 1983

CABLE TELEVISION ADVERTISING - RESEARCH - UNITED STATES - TECHNOLOGICAL INNOVATIONS - CONGRESSES.
Advertising Research Foundation Key Issues Workshop (1985 : New York, N.Y.) Transcript proceedings . New York, NY (3 E. 54th St., New York 10022-3180) , c1985. 174 p. : LC Card 86-214476 DDC 659.14/3/0973 19
HF6146.T42 A27 1985a

Advertising Research Foundation Key Issues Workshop (1986 : New York, N.Y.) Transcript proceedings . New York, NY (3 E. 54th St., New York 10022-3180) , c1986. 214 p. : LC Card 87-404527 DDC 659.14/3/0973 19
HF6146.T42 A27 1986

CABLE TELEVISION - AUSTRIA - SALZBURG (LAND)
Lenhardt, Helmut, 1923- Teure neue Medien . Salzburg , 1983. 152 p. ; ISBN 3-85015-012-7 LC Card 84-107910
HE8700.72.A9 L46 1983

CABLE TELEVISION - CANADA - HISTORY.
Hollins, Timothy. Beyond broadcasting . London , 1984. ix, 385 p. ; ISBN 0-85170-148-5 (pbk.) LC Card 84-125713 DDC 384.55/563 19
HE8700.72.G7 H65 1984
NYPL [JLD 86-1057]

CABLE TELEVISION - EUROPE.
Howard-Healy, Marion. Aspects of the new media in Europe /. Menlo Park, CA (333 Ravenswood Ave., Menlo Park 94025) , c1986. 22 leaves : LC Card 86-220771 DDC 384/.094 19
HE8700.72.E85 H69 1986

CABLE TELEVISION - FRANCE.
Pigeat, Henri, 1939- La télévision par cable commence demain /. Paris , c1983. 239 p. ; ISBN 2-259-01062-8 : LC Card 83-237808
HE8700.72.F8 P54 1983

CABLE TELEVISION - GOVERNMENT POLICY - NEW YORK (STATE) - CONGRESSES.
Conference on Cable Television (1981 : Brooklyn College Student Union) Proceedings /. [Albany, N.Y.] (P.O. Box 167, Albany 12248) [1982] 77 p. ; LC Card 86-622177 DDC 384.55/47/09747 19
HE8700.72.U6 C66 1981

CABLE TELEVISION - GREAT BRITAIN - HISTORY.
Hollins, Timothy. Beyond broadcasting . London , 1984. ix, 385 p. ; ISBN 0-85170-148-5 (pbk.) LC Card 84-125713 DDC 384.55/563 19
HE8700.72.G7 H65 1984
NYPL [JLD 86-1057]

CABLE TELEVISION - NEW YORK (STATE) - CONGRESSES.
Conference on Cable Television (1981 : Brooklyn College Student Union) Proceedings /. [Albany, N.Y.] (P.O. Box 167, Albany 12248) [1982] 77 p. ; LC Card 86-622177 DDC 384.55/47/09747 19
HE8700.72.U6 C66 1981

CABLE TELEVISION - SOCIAL ASPECTS - GERMANY (WEST)
Kubicek, Herbert. Kabel im Haus, Satellit überm Dach . Reinbek bei Hamburg , 1984. 189 p. : ISBN 3-499-15528-1 (pbk.) LC Card 87-673204
HE8700.72.G3 K83x 1984

CABLE TELEVISION - UNITED STATES.
Hollander, Richard S. Video democracy . Mt. Airy, Md. , c1985. ix, 161 p. : ISBN 0-912338-51-2 LC Card 85-81818 DDC 384.55/5 19
HE8700.76.U6 H65 1985
NYPL [MWGT 86-1503]

Mair, George, 1929- Inside HBO . New York , c1988. xviii, 204 p. ; ISBN 0-396-08420-6 : LC Card 87-19939 DDC 384.55/47/0973 19
HE8700.72.U6 M34 1988

CABLE TELEVISION - UNITED STATES - HISTORY.
Hollins, Timothy. Beyond broadcasting . London , 1984. ix, 385 p. ; ISBN 0-85170-148-5 (pbk.) LC Card 84-125713 DDC 384.55/563 19
HE8700.72.G7 H65 1984
NYPL [JLD 86-1057]

Cable, Vincent.
The commerce of culture : experience of Indian handicrafts / Vincent Cable, Ann Weston, L.C. Jain.1st ed. New Delhi : Lancer International in association with Indian Council for Research on International Economic Relations, 1986. 237 p. ; 23 cm. Includes bibliographies and index. ISBN 81-7062-004-X : LC Card 86-902899 DDC 338.4/77455/0954 19
1. Handicraft - Economic aspects - India. 2. India - Commerce. I. Weston, Ann. II. Jain, L. C., 1925-. III. Title.
HF5439.H27 C33 1986

Developing with foreign investment /. London , New York , c1987. viii, 327 p. ; ISBN 0-7099-4825-5 LC Card 87-3603 DDC 332.6/73/091724 19
HG5993 .D47 1987

CABO DELGADO (MOZAMBIQUE) - ECONOMIC CONDITIONS - CASE STUDIES.
A Situação nas antigas zonas libertadas de Cabo Delgado /. [Maputo, Mozambique] , 1983. 59 p. ; LC Card 86-980983 DDC 330.967/9805 19
HC890.Z7 C327 1983

CABO DELGADO (MOZAMBIQUE) - HISTORY - CASE STUDIES.
A Situação nas antigas zonas libertadas de Cabo Delgado /. [Maputo, Mozambique] , 1983. 59 p. ; LC Card 86-980983 DDC 330.967/9805 19
HC890.Z7 C327 1983

CABO DELGADO (MOZAMBIQUE) - POLITICS AND GOVERNMENT - CASE STIDIES.
A Situação nas antigas zonas libertadas de Cabo Delgado /. [Maputo, Mozambique] , 1983. 59 p. ; LC Card 86-980983 DDC 330.967/9805 19
HC890.Z7 C327 1983

Cabo Verde . Carreira, António. Lisboa [1984] 207 p., [16] p. of plates : LC Card 87-400337 DDC 363.8/0966/58 19
HC594.Z9 F33 1984

Cabral, Martim. Portugal, 1386-1986 . London [c1987] 156 p. : ISBN 0-947991-01-8 (pbk.) LC Card 87-404164 DDC 382/.09469/04 19
HF3698.E8 P67 1987

Cacciamali, Maria Cristina. Campino, Antonio Carlos Coelho. Recursos e desempenhos dos programas de formação de mão-de-obra /. São Paulo, SP , Brasília, DF , 1985. 78 p. ; ISBN 85-21-30276-2 LC Card 85-187505
HD5754 .C34 1985

Caciari, P. (Paola) Le 150 ore e la formazione professionale in azienda . Milano, Italy , c1985. 178 p. : LC Card 86-141990
HD5716.T242 I82 1985
NYPL [JFD 87-3739]

CADASTERS - ITALY - LOMBARDY - HISTORY - 18TH CENTURY.
La Proprietà fondiaria in Lombardia dal catasto teresiano all'età napoleonica /. Milano , 1986. 2 v. ; ISBN 88-343-0341-5 (set) : LC Card 87-108100
HD679.L6 P76 1986

CADASTERS - ITALY - MILAN - HISTORY - 18TH CENTURY.
Mazzucchelli, Vanna. Catasto e volto urbano . Roma , 1983. 244 p. ; LC Card 86-106099
HD680.M54 M39 1983

CADASTRAL SURVEYS. see REAL PROPERTY.

Cadastro de entidades estatais : Estado de Alagoas / Governo do Estado de Alagoas, Comissão de Controle das Entidades Estatais. [Maceió] : A Comissão, 1985. 77 p. ; 26 cm. LC Card 86-171884
1. Government business enterprises - Brazil - Alagoas - Directories. I. Alagoas (Brazil). Comissão de Controle das Entidades Estatais.
HD4095.A4 C33 1985

Cadastro geral de empregados e desempregados (Lei 4,923/65) : universo completo (base:AGO/83=100). [Brasília, Brazil] : Ministério do Trabalho, Secretaria de Emprego e Salário, Coordenadoria de Análise do Mercado de Trabalho, 1985. [61] leaves ; 32 cm. Cover title: Mercado de trabalho. Chiefly tables. Includes bibliographical references. LC Card 86-178290
1. Labor supply - Brazil - Statistics. I. Brazil. Coordenadoria de Análise de Mercado de Trabalho. II. Title: Mercado de trabalho.
HD5754 .C26 1985

CAD/CAM SYSTEMS.
Ranky, Paul G., 1951- Computer integrated manufacturing . Englewood Cliffs, N.J. , c1986. xiii, 513 p. : ISBN 0-13-165655-4 : LC Card 85-19199 DDC 670.42/7 19
TS155.6 .R36 1985 ***NYPL [JSE 87-587]***

CAD/CAM SYSTEMS - UNITED STATES.
A Competitive assessment of the U. S. computer-aided design and manufacturing industry /. Washington, D.C. [1987] xi, 58 p. ; LC Card 87-601120 DDC 338.4/7670427 19
HD9696.C63 U514932 1987

Caddes, Carolyn, 1935- Portraits of success : impressions of Silicon Valley pioneers / Carolyn Caddes ; research by Barbara Newton ; with a foreword by John Bardeen. Palo Alto, Calif. : Tioga Pub. Co., 1986. viii, 138 p. : ill. ; 28 cm. Includes index. Bibliography: p. 134. ISBN 0-935382-56-9 : LC Card 86-40032 DDC 338.4/7621/0979473 19
1. Microelectronics industry - California - Santa Clara County - History. 2. Semiconductor industry - California - Santa Clara County - History. 3. Computer industry - California - Santa Clara County - History. 4. Executives - California - Santa Clara County - Biography. 5. Success in business - California - Santa Clara County - Case studies. I. Title.
HD9696.A3 U53173 1986
NYPL [MFX (Caddes) 87-542]

Cadena de silos. Estudio de factibilidad para una cadena de silos intercomunales de papa . [Sucre, Bolivia] 1982. 178 p., [2] leaves of plates : LC Card 83-202593 DDC 338.1/6 19
HD9235.P82 B525 1982
NYPL [JLF 87-711]

Caderno CEBRAP .
(nova sér., 3) Müller, Geraldo. Alimentação e agricultura no Brasil . [São Paulo] , 1984. 64 p. : LC Card 86-132127
HD1872 .M85 1984

Caderno (Centro de Estudos Demográficos (Portugal)) .
(no. 2) A População de Portugal /. [Lisbon] , 1976. 116 p., [1] folded leaf of plates : LC Card 85-204353
HB3621 .P67 1976

Caderno de cultura (Porto Velho, Rondônia, Brazil) .
(2) Gonçalves, Sérgio Ricardo Vieira, 1940- Rondônia--política, agrária e transformação . Porto Velho , 1982. 40 p. : LC Card 87-401465 DDC 338.981/75 19
HC188.R6 G66 1982

Caderno (Instituto de Estudos para o Desenvolvimento (Portugal)) .
(11) Maia, Fernando M. Segurança social em Portugal . Lisboa , 1985. 192 p. : LC Card 86-149393
HD7209 .M35 1985

(6) Seminário sobre Crescimento Económico e Dívida Externa (1982) Seminário sobre Crescimento Económico e Dívida Externa, 18 e 19 de março de 1982 . Lisboa , 1983. 163 p. ; LC Card 85-175819 DDC 336.3/4/09469 19
HJ8744 .S46 1982 ***NYPL [JLG 86-189]***

Cadernos COALBRA .
(3) Alcool e emprego . Brasília, DF , 1983. 170 p. : LC Card 86-200307
HD5718.A4852 B63 1983

Cadernos Condição feminina .
(17) Silva, Manuela. A igualdade de oportunidades de formação profissional para as mulheres /. Lisboa , 1983. 51, [1] p. : LC Card 84-238349
HD6179 .S56 1983

Cadernos culturais da Câmara Municipal de Vila Viçosa .
(2a. sér., no. 5) Pestana, M. Inácio. Movimento demográfico da matriz de Vila Viçosa nos séculos XVI e XVII /. [Vila Viçosa, Portugal , 1985] 32 p. : LC Card 86-199468
HB3622.V55 P47 1985

Cadernos da "Seara Nova". Secção de estudos políticos e sociais.
Costa, F. Ramos da. O Plano Beveridge criticado /. Lisboa , 1943. 75 p. ; LC Card 85-211958
HD7165.A72 C66 1943

Cadernos da UnB.
Couri, Sergio, 1948- Ensaios sobre a evolução dos sistemas econômicos /. Brasília-Distrito Federal [1983] 133 p. : LC Card 84-116306 DDC 330.1 19
HB97.5 .C68 1983 ***NYPL [JLE 86-3363]***

A Intervenção do estado na economia . Brasília, D.F. , c1985. 83 p. ; ISBN 85-23-00198-0 : LC Card 87-102646 DDC 338.1/7373/0981 19
HD9199.B7 I628 1985

Cadernos de divulgação cultural (Bauru, Brazil) .
(14) Rocha, José Carlos Rodrigues. O êxodo rural no município de Pirajuí /. Bauru-SP , 1984. iv, 66 p. : LC Card 86-158771
HB2024.P57 R62 1984

Cadernos de educação política. Série Trabalho e capital.
Ibrahim, José. O que todo cidadão precisa saber sobre comissões de fábrica /. São Paulo, SP [1986] 96 p. : ISBN 85-26-00095-0 LC Card 87-402908 DDC 338.6 19
HD5660.B7 I27 1986

Cadernos do CEDI .
(14) Canavieiros em greve . São Paulo , 1985. 105 p. : LC Card 87-104183 DDC 331.88/1361/098134 19
HD6614.S85 C36 1985

Cadernos do mestrado. Série "História do trabalho" .
(no. 1) O Movimento sindical no interior . Piracicaba, SP [19]84. 38, [10] p. : LC Card 86-200279
HD6615.S32 M68 1984

Cadernos do PROPUR .
(1) Clichevsky, Nora. O mercado de terra na região metropolitana de Porto Alegre /. Porto Alegre , 1982. 60 p. : LC Card 84-256219
HD500.P67 C57 1982

Cadernos IFCH-UNICAMP .
(18) A Feira hippie de Campinas . Campinas, SP, Brasil , São Paulo, SP , 1986. 73 p. ; LC Card 87-404187 DDC 381/.18/098161 19
HF5473.B72 C364 1986

Cadillac desert . Reisner, Marc. New York, N.Y., U. S.A. , 1987, c1986. 582 p., [18] p. of plates : ISBN 0-14-010432-1 (pbk.) : LC Card 87-7602 DDC 333.91/00978 19
HD1739.A17 R45 1987

CÁDIZ (SPAIN : PROVINCE) - ECONOMIC CONDITIONS.
Colaboración sindical al estudio sobre la estructura y posibilidad de desarrollo del Campo de Gibraltar, encomendado por la comisión interministerial designada al efecto /. Cádiz , 1965. 89 p. : LC Card 85-104938
HC390.6 .C65 1965

CÁDIZ (SPAIN : PROVINCE) - ECONOMIC POLICY.
Colaboración sindical al estudio sobre la estructura y posibilidad de desarrollo del Campo de Gibraltar, encomendado por la comisión interministerial designada al efecto /. Cádiz , 1965. 89 p. : LC Card 85-104938
HC390.6 .C65 1965

Cadmus' operational auditing /. Kowalczyk, David S., 1946- New York , c1987. x, 422 p. ; ISBN 0-471-82660-X LC Card 87-23267 DDC 657/.458 19
HF5668.25 .K696 1987

Cafasso, José. Ficción y realidad de la economía argentina (1976-1983) / José Cafasso. [Bahía Blanca, Argentina] : Ateneo del Justicialismo, [1983] 61 p. ; 22 cm. Bibliography: p. 61. LC Card 87-400128 DDC 330.982/064 19
1. Argentina - Economic policy. 2. Argentina - Economic conditions - 1945-1983. I. Title.
HC175 .C15 1983

Café, bonanza y realidades /. Atehortúa, Adolfo. [Bogotá, Colombia] [1986] 118 p. : LC Card 87-402940 DDC 338.1/7373/09861 19
HD9199.C62 A74 1986

El café en Costa Rica . Raventos Vorst, Ciska. San José, Costa Rica , 1985. iii, 145 p. : LC Card 86-174756
HD9199.C82 R39 1985

Cafeicultura . Stolcke, Verena. São Paulo, SP , 1986. 410 p. : LC Card 86-208925
HD9195.B72 S76 1986

CAFÉS. see **HOTELS, TAVERNS, ETC; RESTAURANTS, LUNCH ROOMS, ETC.**

CAFETERIAS. see **RESTAURANTS, LUNCH ROOMS, ETC.**

Caffarella, Rosemary S. (Rosemary Shelly), 1946- Program development and evaluation resource book for trainers / Rosemary S. Caffarella. New York : Wiley, c1988. xxi, 266 p. : ill. ; 29 cm. (Wiley series in training and development) Bibliography: p. 257-260. Includes index. ISBN 0-471-84235-4 LC Card 87-15990 DDC 658.3/12404 19
1. Employees, Training of - Evaluation - Handbooks, manuals, etc. 2. Employees, Training of - Case studies. 3. Employees, Training of - Problems, exercises, etc. I. Title. II. Series.
HF5549.5.T7 C23 1988

Cafiero, Salvatore. Il Mezzogiorno nelle politiche nazionali e comunitarie . Milano , 1982. 379 p. ; LC Card 82-230171 DDC 338.945/7 19
HC305 .M42156 1982 ***NYPL [JLE 86-1611]***

Cafruny, Alan W. Ruling the waves : the political economy of international shipping / Alan W. Cafruny. Berkeley : University of California Press, c1987. xvii, 323 p. ; 24 cm. (Studies in international political economy. 17) Bibliography: p. 287-306. Includes index. ISBN 0-520-05968-9 LC Card 86-30889 DDC 387.5/1 19
1. Merchant marine. 2. Shipping. 3. Shipping conferences. 4. Maritime law. I. Title. II. Series.
HE735 .C34 1987

Cagan, Phillip. Contemporary economic problems . Washington, D.C. , c1987. 332 p. : ISBN 0-8447-3621-X (alk. paper) LC Card 87-1395 DDC 330.973/0927 19
HC106.8 .C665 1987

Cage, R. A. The working class in Glasgow, 1750-1914 /. London , Wolfeboro, N.H. , c1987. xix, 203 p. ; ISBN 0-7099-3415-7 : LC Card 86-24059 DDC 305.5/62/0941443 19
HD8400.G57 W67 1987

Cahier de recherche (Association pour la recherche économique dans les petites et moyennes entreprises (Switzerland)) .
(6) Crise de liquidité et gestion de la trésorerie dans les P.M.E. Genève, Suisse , 1985. 32 p. : LC Card 87-138138
HG4027.7 .C75 1985

Cahier (Erasmus Universiteit Rotterdam. Centrum voor Bedrijfsgeschiedenis) .
(nr. 1) Mees en Chabot, twee kassiers te Rotterdam . Delft , c1986. 87 p. : ISBN 90-70879-40-9 : LC Card 86-205783
HG3120.R62 M44 1986

Cahier (Université de Montréal. Département de sciences économiques) .
(8015) Bronsard, Camille. Systems of demand equations (including labour supply) for different states of the markets and for different regimes /. Montréal [198-] 28 p. ; LC Card 83-222220 DDC 338.5/212 19
HB801 .B77 1980z

(8209) Dussault, François. Les modèles scandinaves et la détermination des ententes salariales des industries manufacturières canadiennes . Montréal [1982] 21, [11] p. ; LC Card 82-196710
HD4979 .D875 1982

(8229) Boyer, Marcel. Riscophobie et étalement à moyenne constante . Montréal [1982] 32 p. : LC Card 85-160864
HB615 .B68 1982

(8336) Raynauld, André. L'impact économique et financier de la Caisse de dépôt et placement du Québec /. Montréal [1983?] 23 p. ; LC Card 85-164461
HG5160.Q4 C357 1983

(8511) Jobin, Jacques. Mesure et incidence des dépenses fiscales au Québec /. Montréal [1984] 27 p. ; LC Card 85-169988
HB3 .C3 vol. 8511 HJ4662.A45

(8517) Loranger, Jean Guy, 1938- Lien entre capital fictif, markup flexible et inflation /. Montréal [1985] 30 p. ; LC Card 85-177724 DDC 332.4/1 19
HB3 .C3 vol. 8517 HG229

Cahiers de Bruges. For other vols. in this series, see Old Catalog.
(n.s. 44) The European Community's development policy . Bruges , 19. 285 p. : LC Card 87-135534 DDC 338.94 19
HC60 .E7626 1986

(n.s., 44) The European Community's development policy . Bruges , 19. 285 p. : LC Card 87-135534 DDC 338.94 19
HC60 .E7626 1986

Cahiers de l'IIPE .
(no 68) N'Dzaba, Tobi. L'enseignement technique et professionnel et la satisfaction des besoins en main-d'œuvre . Paris [1983] i, 139 p. : LC Card 85-189543
HD5845.A6 N38 1983

Cahiers de recherche (Ecole des hautes études commerciales (Montréal, Québec). Institut d'économie appliquée) .
(IEA-85-01) Leroux, François, 1945- Que nous a appris la crise de l'endettement international? /. Montréal, Québec, Canada [1985] 41 leaves ; LC Card 86-144447 DDC 336.3/4/091724 19
HJ8899 .L47 1985

Cahiers de recherches en communication. Caron, André H. Les télévisions étrangères . [Montréal] , 1983. ix, 166 p., 12 leaves : ISBN 2-920396-86-2 : LC Card 83-157210 DDC 302.2/345/09714 19
HE8700.9.C2 C37 1983
NYPL [MWGS 86-2473]

Cahiers d'études comtoises. see **Besançon, France. Université. Annales littéraires.**

Cahiers du Département d'histoire et de géographie. Monographies.
Berthiaume, Nicole, 1952- Rouyn-Noranda . Rouyn [Québec] , 1981. xiii, 169 p. : ISBN 2-89073-103-0 LC Card 83-132846
HD9524.C23 R683 1981

Cahill, Lawrence B. Environmental audits / Lawrence B. Cahill, editor, with Raymond W. Kane ; contributing authors, Leonard J. Fleckenstein, Courtney M. Price, Mark M. Morrel. 5th ed. Rockville, Md., U. S.A. : Government Institutes, 1987. xi, 656 p. : ill. ; 23 cm. Bibliography: p. 251-262. ISBN 0-86587-720-3 (soft) LC Card 87-404450 DDC 658.4/08 19
1. Environmental policy - United States. 2. Environmental law - United States. 3. Environmental auditing - United States. I. Kane, Raymond W. II. Government Institutes. III. Title.
HC110.E5 C26 1987

Caiçara . Marcilio, Maria Luiza. São Paulo-SP (Brasil) , c1986. 244 p. : ISBN 85-05-00523-6 LC Card 87-404833 DDC 304.6/0981/61 19
HD1531.B7 M34 1986

Caicedo Licona, Carlos Arturo. El Chocó por dentro / Carlos Arturo Caicedo Licona. 1a ed. Medellín, Colombia : Editorial Lealon, 1980. 118 p. : ill. ; 24 cm. (Colección Periferia . 2) Includes bibliographical references. LC Card 83-105927
1. Chocó, Colombia - Economic conditions. 2. Blacks - Colombia - Chocó - Economic conditions. I. Title. II. Series.
HC198.C48 C33 1980

Caileff, W. D. (Warren D.), 1933- Lynch, Terry, 1948- Kansas City Southern . Boulder, Colo. , c1987. 223 p. : ISBN 0-87108-735-9 LC Card 87-25288 DDC 385/.065/76 19
HE2791.K17 L96 1987

Caille, Pierre. La théorie de l'échange international de produits différenciés / par Pierre Caille. Fribourg, Suisse : Editions universitaires, c1986. 267 p. : ill. ; 21 cm. (Documents économiques . 30) Bibliography: p. 253-260. ISBN 2-8271-0337-0 LC Card 86-210742
1. Commerce. 2. Commerce - Mathematical models. 3. Commercial policy. I. Title. II. Series.
HF1008 .C35 1986

Os caipiras de São Paulo /. Brandão, Carlos Rodrigues. São Paulo-Brasil , 1983. 92, [4] p. : LC Card 84-179661
HD1531.B7 B72 1983

Cairncross, Frances. Guide to the economy / Frances Cairncross and Phil Keeley. London : Methuen, 1987. viii, 161 p. : ill. ; 20 cm. Vol. 3 of two works previously published under title: The Guardian guide to the economy. Includes bibliographies. ISBN 0-416-39600-3 (pbk.) : LC Card 87-138822 DDC 330.941/085 19
1. Great Britain - Economic conditions - 1945-. I. Keeley, Phil. II. Guardian guide to the economy. III. Title.
HC256.6 .C27 1987

Cairns, W. Lasok, Dominik. The customs law of the European Economic Community /. Deventer, Netherlands , Boston , c1983. xxiii, 292 p. : ISBN 90-6544-077-1 (pbk.) : LC Card 84-148702 DDC 343.405/6 344.0356 19
LAW ***NYPL [JLE 86-2073]***

Cairo Demographic Centre. Population and Development Symposium (1985 : Cairo, Egypt) Population and development . Cairo , 1986. 616 p. : LC Card 86-969481 DDC 304.6 19
HB849 .P575 1986

Caisse centrale de coopération économique (France)
Dominique, juin 1985 . [Paris] , c1985. 102 p. : LC Card 86-209026
HC156.5.Z7 D6626 1985

Grenade, juin 1985 . [Paris] , 1985] 124 p. : LC Card 86-209038
HC156.5.Z7 G7465 1985

St.-Vincent et les Grenadines, juin 1985 . Paris , 1985] 85 p. : LC Card 86-209310
HC156.5 .S72 1985

Sainte-Lucie, juin 1985 . [Paris] , 1985] 120 p. : LC Card 86-209048
HC155.5.Z7 S257 1985

CAISSE DE DÉPÔT ET PLACEMENT DU QUÉBEC.
Raynauld, André. L'impact économique et financier de la Caisse de dépôt et placement du Québec /. Montréal [1983?] 23 p. ; LC Card 85-164461
HG5160.Q4 C357 1983

Caisse des dépôts et consignations (France)
Epargne et développement /. Paris , 1985. 410 p. : ISBN 2-7178-0855-8 : LC Card 86-149765
HC59.72.S3 E62 1985

Caixa Econômica do Estado de São Paulo.
Seminário Nacional de Abastecimento Alimentar em Grandes Cidades--a Experiência de São Paulo (1984 : São Paulo, Brazil) Anais /. São Paulo, São Paulo, Brasil , 1984. xii, 421 p. : LC Card 87-404933 DDC 363.8/0981/61 19
HD9014.B83 S447 1984

Caja de Crédito Agrario, Industrial y Minero (Colombia) Plan integral de desarrollo del predio Putumayo. Bogotá [1986] 29 p. : LC Card 87-401011 DDC 338.9861/7 19
HC198.C49 P55 1986

Caja de Pensiones para la Vejez y de Ahorros. Obra Agrícola. Clavera, Joan. La viticultura catalana davant la integració a la Comunitat Europea /. [Barcelona] [1986] 124 p. : ISBN 6-476-84021-8 LC Card 86-200618
HD9259.G7 S693 1986

CAL-OSHA routine compliance inspections . Schaefer, Andrew. [Sacramento, CA , 1986] 25 p. ; LC Card 86-622709 DDC 363.1/164/09796 19
HD7262.5.U62 C573 1986

CALAMITIES. see **DISASTERS.**

Calcagnotto, Gilberto. Brasilien 1974-1981 : externe Schocks und Krisenadministration : Perspektiven eines neuen Sozialpakts / Gilberto

Calcagnotto. Hamburg : Institut für Iberoamerika-Kunde, [1983] xi, 78 p. : ill. ; 30 cm. (Arbeitsunterlagen und Diskussionsbeiträge . Nr. 19 =) "Januar 1983." Table of contents and summary in Portuguese. Bibliography: p. 71-78. LC Card 83-222930
1. Brazil - Economic policy. 2. Economic stabilization - Brazil. 3. Debts, External - Brazil. 4. Loans, Foreign - Brazil. 5. Brazil - Social conditions - 1945-. I. Series. II. Series: Arbeitsunterlagen und Diskussionsbeiträge , Nr. 19. III. Title.
HC187 .C143 1983

Calcaterra, Francesco. Gli agrumi nella storia del Meridione : origini, sviluppo e peripezie di una coltura su documenti inediti / Francesco Calcaterra. Roma : LED, c1986. 95 p. : ill. ; 22 cm. Includes bibliographical references. LC Card 87-133974
1. Citrus fruit industry - Italy, Southern - History. 2. Citrus fruit industry - Italy, Southern - History - Sources. I. Title.
HD9259.C53 I723 1986

Calcolo dei costi nelle imprese industriali /. Spranzi, Aldo, 1932- Milano [1986] viii, 94 p. : ISBN 88-14-00844-2 : LC Card 86-182386
HC79.C7 S67 1986

Calcul économique et résorption des déséquilibres . France. Groupe de travail "Calcul économique." Paris , c1984. 149 p. ; ISBN 2-11-001233-1 : LC Card 84-227039
HB135 .F72 1984

CALCULATING MACHINES, ELECTRONIC. see **ELECTRONIC DIGITAL COMPUTERS.**

CALCULATORS.
De Lisle, Christian. Business interest calculations /. London , c1985. ix, 274 p. ; ISBN 0-08-039231-8 ***NYPL [JLE 87-1030]***

The calculus of international communications . Jussawalla, Meheroo, 1923- Littleton, Colo. , 1987. xiv, 159 p. ; ISBN 0-87287-503-2 : LC Card 87-2640 DDC 384/.068 19
HE7645 .J87 1987

CALCUTTA METROPOLITAN AREA (INDIA) - ECONOMIC CONDITIONS.
An Approach to economic renewal and promotion programme . [Calcutta] , 1977. 55 leaves ; LC Card 83-908562 DDC 338.954/14 19
HC438.C3 A66 1977

CALCUTTA METROPOLITAN AREA (INDIA) - INDUSTRIES.
An Approach to economic renewal and promotion programme . [Calcutta] , 1977. 55 leaves ; LC Card 83-908562 DDC 338.954/14 19
HC438.C3 A66 1977

Calcutta Metropolitan Development Authority. Economic and Social Support Programme Cell. An Approach to economic renewal and promotion programme . [Calcutta] , 1977. 55 leaves ; LC Card 83-908562 DDC 338.954/14 19
HC438.C3 A66 1977

Caldas, Maria das Graças Conde. Laser : perspectivas tecnológicas e de mercado / Maria das Graças Conde Caldas. [São Paulo] : Promoção de Ciência e Tecnologia, Secretaria da Indústria, Comércio, Ciência e Tecnologia, c1986. 95 p. ; 30 cm. Bibliography: p. 93-95. LC Card 87-143863 DDC 338.4/7621366/0981 19
1. Laser industry - Brazil. I. Title.
HD9999.L323 B63 1986

Caldentey, Maritza de. Buroz Castillo, Eduardo. Programa de cooperación técnica Perú-Venezuela-OEA . Caracas , 1976. [11], 62 p. ; LC Card 84-136478
HD1696.P5 B87 1976

Calder, Eugene B. Advising clients on real estate investments / by Eugene B. Calder, Barbara K. Green. New York, NY (11 Penn Plaza, New York 10001) : M. Bender, 1987. 95 p. in various pagings : ill. ; 30 cm. (Accountant's workbook series) Bibliography: p. 80. Includes index. LC Card 87-61983 DDC 332.63/24 19
1. Real estate investment. 2. Real property and taxation. I. Green, Barbara K. II. Title. III. Series.
HD1382.5 .C34 1987

Calderón Berti, Humberto. Petróleo y opinión pública / [Humberto Calderón Berti]. [Caracas?] : Fondo Editorial "Oro Negro", [1983?] 455 p. : ill. ; 23 cm. LC Card 85-119987 DDC 338.2/72/0987 19
1. Organization of Petroleum Exporting Countries - Addresses, essays, lectures. 2. Petroleum industry and trade - Government policy - Venezuela - Addresses, essays, lectures. 3. Petroleum industry and trade - Addresses, essays, lectures. I. Title.
HD9574.V42 C364 1983
NYPL [JLE 86-535]

Calderón Chacón, Godofredo. Monografía de la República de El Salvador / Godofredo Calderón Chacón. 1a ed. San Salvador, El Salvador : Impresos Prisma, 1986. iv, 132 p. : ill. ; 22 cm. Bibliography: p. 131-132. LC Card 87-401545 DDC 330.97284/052 19
1. El Salvador - Economic conditions - 1945-. I. Title.
HC148 .C35 1986

Calderón G., Fernando.
La Cancha : una gran feria campesina en la ciudad de Cochabamba / Fernando Calderón, Alberto Rivera.1a ed. [Cochabamba, Bolivia] : Centro de Estudios de la Realidad Económica y Social, 1984. 208 p. : ill. ; 16 cm. (Serie Cochambamba . 3) Bibliography: p. [203]-208. LC Card 85-238895
1. Markets - Bolivia - La Cancha (Cochabamba). 2. Peasantry - Bolivia - La Cancha (Cochabamba). I. Rivera P., Alberto. II. Title. III. Series.
HF5473.B62 C363 1984

Jatun Llajta : vendedoras y ladrilleros en Cochabamba / Fernando Calderón G., Alberto Rivera P. La Paz, Bolivia : Centro de Estudios de la Realidad Económica y Social, 1982. v, 448 p., [8] leaves of plates : ill. ; 28 cm. (Serie Estudios urbanos. no. 6) Bibliography: p. 442-448. LC Card 83-111937 DDC 381/.1 19
1. Produce trade - Bolivia - Cochabamba (Dept.). 2. Peddlers and peddling - Bolivia - Cochabamba (Dept.). 3. Brickmakers - Bolivia - Cochabamba (Dept.). 4. Family - Bolivia - Cochabamba (Dept.). 5. Cochabamba (Bolivia : Dept.) - Fairs. I. Rivera P., Alberto. II. Series: Serie Estudios urbanos (Centro de Estudios de la Realidad Económica y Social (La Paz, Bolivia)) , no. 6. III. Title.
HF5473.B62 C623 1982
NYPL [JLF 86-1794]

Calderón González, Arnoldo. América Latina y el Caribe : análisis monetario global relacionado con el ingreso / Arnoldo Calderón González. México, D.F. : Centro de Estudios Monetarios Latinoamericanos, Departamento de Investigaciones, 1985. 51, [25] leaves ; 28 cm. (Serie Cuadernos de investigación . núm. 5) Summary also in English, French, and Portuguese. Bibliography: leaf [75]. LC Card 87-121714 DDC 332.4/98 19
1. Monetary policy - Latin America. 2. Monetary policy - Caribbean Area. 3. Money supply - Latin America. 4. Money supply - Caribbean Area. 5. Income distribution - Latin America. 6. Income distribution - Caribbean Area. I. Series: Serie Cuadernos de investigación (Centro de Estudios Monetarios Latinoamericanos, Departamento de Investigaciones) , núm. 5. II. Title.
HG660.5 .C35 1985

Calderón, Humberto. see **Calderón Berti, Humberto.**

Calderón R., Cedric. Contrabando humano en las Californias / Cedric Calderón R. 2a ed. [S.l. : s.n., 1978] (Guatemala : Propsa) 160 p. ; 23 cm. LC Card 86-218852 DDC 331.6/2/720794 19
1. Alien labor, Mexican - California. 2. Aliens, Illegal - California. I. Title.
HD8083.C2 C23 1978

Calderón, René Ballivián. see **Ballivián Calderón, René.**

Caldwell, James C. Needles, Belverd E. Principles of accounting /. Boston, MA , c1987. xx, 1100, [38] p. : ISBN 0-395-35702-0 LC Card 86-80401 DDC 657 19
HF5635 .N35 1987

CALENDARS - UNITED STATES - CATALOGS.
Strauss, Bob. American sporting advertising /. Jefferson, Me. (Box 1060, Jefferson 04348) , 1987- v. <1 > : LC Card 87-155421 DDC 741.67/0973/074013 19
HF6161.S65 S77 1987

Calet, C. Les Protéines françaises, un enjeu économique . Paris [1984] 6, xiii, 258 p. : LC Card 86-187038
HD9019.P753 F76 1984

Calhoun, David E. A step-by-step guide to real estate principles in California : everything you need to know to pass the California real estate examination / David E. Calhoun.1st ed. Los Angeles, Calif. : California Academy of Real Estate, c1987. 351 p. : ill., forms ; 28 cm. Includes index. LC Card 87-403596 DDC 333.33/09794 19
1. Real estate business - Licenses - California - Examinations, questions, etc. 2. Real estate business - Licenses - California - Outlines, syllabi, etc. 3. Real property - California - Examinations, questions, etc. 4. Real property - California - Outlines, syllabi, etc. I. Title. II. Title: Real estate principles in California.
HD266.C2 C22 1987

Calificación ocupacional en la República Federal de Alemania /. Maslankowski, Willi, 1936- [Nachweis beruflicher Qualifikationen. Spanish. Selections.] Montevideo , 1979. 38 p. : LC Card 86-143001
HD5715.5.G4 M372518 1979

California affordable housing legislation : a study of local implementation. [Sacramento] : State of California, Dept. of Housing and Community Development, [1986?] 2 v. ; 28 cm. Cover title. Prepared for the Department by David M. Dornbusch and Company and Blayney-Dyett, Urban and Regional Planners. Includes bibliographical references. LC Card 86-622916 DDC 363.5/8 19
1. Housing policy - California. 2. Housing - Law and legislation - California. 3. Housing - Finance - Law and legislation - California. I. David M. Dornbusch and Company. II. Blayney-Dyett, Urban and Regional Planners. III. California. Dept. of Housing and Community Development.
HD7303.C2 C275 1986

California and the 21st century . California. Legislature. Senate. Select Committee on Long Range Policy Planning. Sacramento, CA [1986] 3 v. : LC Card 86-622352 DDC 338.5/443/09794 19
HC107.C2 C227 1986

California Arabian Standard Oil Company. see **Arabian American Oil Company.**

California. Assembly. see **California. Legislature. Assembly.**

California. Assessment Standards Division.
Assessment practices survey. [Sacramento, Calif.] , 1987- v. ; LC Card 87-167612 DDC 332.22/2 19
HJ4191 .A74 1987

California. Block Grant Advisory Task Force.
Block Grant Advisory Task Force final report to the Governor and the Legislature of the State of California / J. Lewis Associates, consultant. [Sacramento?] : The Task Force, [1984] 36, [7] leaves ; 28 cm. "January 1, 1984." LC Card 86-622537 DDC 336.1/85 19
1. Block grants - California. I. J. Lewis Associates. II. Title.
HJ325 .C32 1984

California. Business and Transportation Agency. Dept. of Transportation. see **California. Dept. of Transportation.**

California. California Highway Patrol, Dept. of the. see **California. Dept. of the California Highway Patrol.**

California. Center for Health Statistics. Medi-Cal fee-for-service eligibles and prepaid health plan enrollees by age group, sex, and county, July 1984. [Sacramento] [1985] 19 p. : LC Card 86-622330 DDC 362.1/04252/09794021 19
HD7102.U6 C345 1985

California. Corporations, Dept. of. see **California. Dept. of Corporations.**

California crude oil production, 1960-1985. Los Angeles, Calif. (417 S. Hill St., Suite 930, Los Angeles 90013) : Conservation Committee of California Oil Producers, c1986. 149 p., [1] folded leaf of plates : map ; 28 cm. Chiefly tables. LC Card 87-150171 DDC 338.2/7282/09794021 19
1. Petroleum industry and trade - California - Statistics. 2. Oil wells - California - Statistics. I. Conservation Committee of California Oil Producers.
HD9567.C2 C385 1986

CALIFORNIA. DEPT. OF CORPORATIONS.
California. Legislature. Assembly. Committee on Finance and Insurance. Health insurance . Sacramento, Calif. [1984] 359 p. : LC Card 87-621024 DDC 368.3/82/009794 19
HG9397.5.C2 C35 1984

California. Dept. of Finance. Program Evaluation Unit. The Conservation and Liquidation Division, Department of Insurance / prepared by State of California, Department of Finance, Program Evaluation Unit. [Sacramento, Calif.] : The Unit, [1985] xii, 62 p. ; 28 cm. (Report / State of California, Department of Finance, Program Evaluation Unit . no. D85-2) "June 1985." Includes bibliographical references. LC Card 85-622857 DDC 353.97940082/55 19
1. California. Dept. of Insurance. Conservation and Liquidation Division. 2. Insurance - California - State supervision. I. Series: Report (California. Dept. of Finance. Program Evaluation Unit) , no. D85-2. II. Title.
HG8538.C2 C35 1985

California. Dept. of Health. Center for Health Statistics. see **California. Center for Health Statistics.**

California. Dept. of Health Services.
Medi-Cal fee-for-service eligibles and prepaid health plan enrollees by age group, sex, and county--July 1983. [Sacramento] [1984] 21 p. : LC Card 86-622329 DDC 362.1/04252/09794021 19
HD7102.U5 C3 1984

Mielke, Robert B. Live births by estimated marital status of mother, California, 1981. [Sacramento] [1984] 22 p. : LC Card 86-622328 DDC 304.6/32/09794 19
HB935.C2 M54 1984

California. Dept. of Highway Patrol. see **California. Dept. of the California Highway Patrol.**

California. Dept. of Insurance. (Old Catalog form: California. Insurance Dept.)
California earthquake zoning and probable maximum loss evaluation program . Los Angeles, Calif. (600 S. Commonwealth Ave., Los Angeles 90005) [1986] 44, 15 p. : LC Card 86-623193 DDC 368.1/22/09794 19
HG9981.35.C2 C35 1986

CALIFORNIA. DEPT. OF INSURANCE.
California. Legislature. Assembly. Committee on Finance and Insurance. Health insurance . Sacramento, Calif. [1984] 359 p. : LC Card 87-621024 DDC 368.3/82/009794 19
HG9397.5.C2 C35 1984

CALIFORNIA. DEPT. OF INSURANCE. CONSERVATION AND LIQUIDATION DIVISION.
California. Dept. of Finance. Program Evaluation Unit. The Conservation and Liquidation Division, Department of Insurance /. [Sacramento, Calif.] [1985] xii, 62 p. ; LC Card 85-622857 DDC 353.97940082/55 19
HG8538.C2 C35 1985

California. Dept. of Motor Vehicles. Research and Development Section. Huston, Ray E. Senior driver facts /. Sacramento, CA , Springfield, VA , 1986. iii, 22 p. : LC Card 86-623189 DDC 363.1/252/09794021 19
HE5614.3.C3 H87 1986

California. Dept. of the California Highway Patrol. (Old Catalog form: California. Highway Patrol)
A special report to the Legislature on the 55 MPH national maximum speed limit. [Sacramento] : State of California, Dept. of the California Highway Patrol : California Dept. of Transportation, [1986] vi, 95, [171] p. : ill. ; 28 cm. At head of title: AB 2477. Cover title: The 55 mph speed limit. "January 1986." LC Card 86-622347 DDC 388.3/144/09794 19
1. Speed limits - California. 2. Speed limits - United States. I. California. Legislature. II. California. Dept. of Transportation. III. Title. IV. Title: AB 2477. V. Title: 55 mph speed limit.
HE5620.S6 C25 1986

California. Dept. of Transportation. California. Dept. of the California Highway Patrol. A special report to the Legislature on the 55 MPH national maximum speed limit. [Sacramento] [1986] vi, 95, [171] p. : LC Card 86-622347 DDC 388.3/144/09794 19
HE5620.S6 C25 1986

The California Disability Insurance Program : report to the Legislature (pursuant to Section 4 of AB 518, Young, Chapter 903, Statutes of 1983) / prepared by Estimates and Economic Research Group, Employment Data and Research Division, Employment Development Department, Health and Welfare Agency, State of California. [Sacramento] : The Group, [1986] 17, 4 leaves ; 28 cm. "February 1986." LC Card 86-622336 DDC 368.3/82/009794 19
1. Insurance, Disability - California. I. California. Employment Data and Research Division. Estimates and Economic Research Group.
HD7105.25.U6 C35 1986

California. Division of Mass Transportation. Rail passenger development plan : 1985 through 1990 fiscal years as required by section 14036 of the Government Code / prepared by Division of Mass Transportation. Sacramento, CA (1120 N St., Sacramento 95814) : State of California, Dept. of Transportation, [1985] x, 98 p. : ill. ; 28 cm. "March 1985." "DMT 139." LC Card 86-622128 DDC 385/.22/09794 19
1. Railroads - California - Passenger traffic. 2. Railroads and state - California. I. Title.
HE2583 .C25 1985

CALIFORNIA. DIVISION OF OCCUPATIONAL SAFETY AND HEALTH.
Schaefer, Andrew. CAL-OSHA routine compliance inspections . [Sacramento, CA , 1986] 25 p. ; LC Card 86-622709 DDC 363.1/164/09796 19
HD7262.5.U62 C573 1986

California earthquake zoning and probable maximum loss evaluation program : an estimate of potential insured earthquake losses from analysis of data submitted by property and casualty companies in California : California Administrative Code, Title 10, chapter 5, subchapter 3, section 2307. Los Angeles, Calif. (600 S. Commonwealth Ave., Los Angeles 90005) : California Dept. of Insurance, [1986] 44, 15 p. : ill., form, maps ; 28 cm. "June 1986." LC Card 86-623193 DDC 368.1/22/09794 19
1. Insurance, Earthquake - California. 2. Earthquakes - California. I. California. Dept. of Insurance.
HG9981.35.C2 C35 1986

CALIFORNIA - ECONOMIC CONDITIONS.
California. Legislature. Senate. Select Committee on Long Range Policy Planning. California and the 21st century . Sacramento, CA [1986] 3 v. : LC Card 86-622352 DDC 338.5/443/09794 19
HC107.C2 C227 1986

CALIFORNIA - ECONOMIC POLICY.
California. Legislature. Senate. Select Committee on Long Range Policy Planning. California and the 21st century . Sacramento, CA [1986] 3 v. : LC Card 86-622352 DDC 338.5/443/09794 19
HC107.C2 C227 1986

California employment and payrolls, April-June, 1985 /. Albano, Tracy. [Sacramento] [1985] iii, 129 p. ; LC Card 86-623197 DDC 331.12/5/09794021 19
HD5725.C2 A614 1985

California. Employment Data and Research Division. Estimates and Economic Research Group. The California Disability Insurance Program . [Sacramento] [1986] 17, 4 leaves ; LC Card 86-622336 DDC 368.3/82/009794 19
HD7105.25.U6 C35 1986

California, final report on the San Diego demonstration. Goldman, Barbara. Final report on the San Diego job search and work experience demonstration /. New York, N.Y. (3 Park Ave., New York 10016) , c1986. xliv, 269 p. : LC Card 87-118376 DDC 331.12/042/0979498 19
HD5713.6.U542 S395 1986

CALIFORNIA - FOREIGN POPULATION - HISTORY.
Muller, Thomas, 1933- The fourth wave . Washington , c1985. xvii, 217 p. ; ISBN 0-87766-349-1 LC Card 85-22646 DDC 331.6/2/720794 19
HD8081.M6 M85 1985 ***NYPL [JLE 86-3014]***

California. Governor's Office. Office of Planning and Research. Barbaria, Janet. The growth revolt . Sacramento, Calif. [1980] 66 p. : LC Card 81-620644 DDC 336.794 19
HJ4191 .B37 1980 ***NYPL [JLF 86-369]***

California. Governor's Office. Planning and Research, Office of. see **California. Governor's Office. Office of Planning and Research.**

California. Governor's Task Force on Toxics, Waste, and Technology. Final report / Governor's Task Force on Toxics, Waste, and Technology. [Sacramento, CA] : The Task Force, [1986] 2 v. : ill. ; 28 cm. "May 1986." Bibliography: v. 1, p. 175. LC Card 86-622772 DDC 363.7/28 19
1. Hazardous wastes - Government policy - California. 2. Hazardous wastes - Law and legislation - California. I. Title.
HC107.C23 P553 1986

California. Highway Patrol. see **California. Dept. of the California Highway Patrol.**

California. Insurance, Dept. of. see **California. Dept. of Insurance.**

California. Legislature.
California. Dept. of the California Highway Patrol. A special report to the Legislature on the 55 MPH national maximum speed limit. [Sacramento] [1986] vi, 95, [171] p. : LC Card 86-622347 DDC 388.3/144/09794 19
HE5620.S6 C25 1986

California. Public Utilities Commission. Report to the Legislature . [San Francisco] [1984] 40 leaves ; LC Card 86-622236 DDC 384.6/09794 19
HE8840.C2 C35 1984

California. Legislature. Assembly. (Old Catalog form: California. Assembly)

California. Legislature. Assembly. Committee on Elections and Reapportionment. California. Legislature. Assembly. Committee on Local Government. The impact of Proposition 13 (the Jarvis-Gann property tax initiative) on local government programs and services /. [Sacramento, CA.] 1978. iv, 367, 108 p. : LC Card 79-621409 DDC 352/.0794
HJ4191 .C34 1978 ***NYPL [JLF 86-1607]***

California. Legislature. Assembly. Committee on Finance and Insurance. Health insurance : overlapping jurisdiction between the Departments of Corporations and Insurance : committee staff report : October 3, 1984 interim hearing / California Legislature, Assembly Committee on Finance and Insurance. Sacramento, Calif. : The Committee : May be purchased from Joint Publications Office, [1984] 359 p. : forms. ; 28 cm. Cover title. LC Card 87-621024 DDC 368.3/82/009794 19
1. Insurance, Health - California. 2. California. Dept. of Corporations. 3. California. Dept. of Insurance. I. Title.
HG9397.5.C2 C35 1984

California. Legislature. Assembly. Committee on Local Government. The impact of Proposition 13 (the Jarvis-Gann property tax initiative) on local government programs and services / [prepared by staff to the Assembly Committees on Local Government and Revenue and Taxation ; contributions by Staff to the Assembly Committees on Elections and Reapportionment ... et al.]. [Sacramento, CA. : The Assembly : may be purchased from the Assembly Publications Office], 1978. iv, 367, 108 p. : ill. ; 28 cm. Cover title. "709" LC Card 79-621409 DDC 352/.0794
1. Real property tax - California. 2. Local finance - California. I. California. Legislature. Assembly. Committee on Revenue and Taxation. II. California. Legislature. Assembly. Committee on Elections and Reapportionment. III. Title.
HJ4191 .C34 1978 ***NYPL [JLF 86-1607]***

California. Legislature. Assembly. Committee on Revenue and Taxation. California. Legislature. Assembly. Committee on Local Government. The impact of Proposition 13 (the Jarvis-Gann property tax initiative) on local government programs and services /. [Sacramento, CA.] 1978. iv, 367, 108 p. : LC Card 79-621409 DDC 352/.0794
HJ4191 .C34 1978 ***NYPL [JLF 86-1607]***

California. Legislature. Finance and Insurance, Committee on. see **California. Legislature. Assembly. Committee on Finance and Insurance.**

California. Legislature. General Assembly. Committee on Labor and Employment. Schaefer, Andrew. CAL-OSHA routine compliance inspections . [Sacramento, CA , 1986] 25 p. ; LC Card 86-622709 DDC

363.1/164/09796 19
HD7262.5.U62 C573 1986

California. Legislature. Joint Committee on Science and Technology. California. Legislature. Senate. Select Committee on Long Range Policy Planning. California and the 21st century . Sacramento, CA [1986] 3 v. : LC Card 86-622352 DDC 338.5/443/09794 19
HC107.C2 C227 1986

California. Legislature. Joint Legislative Budget Committee. Legislative Analyst. Analysis of the 1987-88 tax expenditure budget. Sacramento, Calif. (925 L St., Suite 650, Sacramento 95814) [1987] 2 v. ; LC Card 87-621598 DDC 353.97940072/4 19
HJ4655.C23 A53 1987

A review of Bay Area public transportation financing. Sacramento, Calif. (925 L St., Suite 650, Sacramento 95814) : Legislative Analyst, [1986] 57 p. : ill. ; 28 cm. LC Card 86-621890 DDC 388.4/042 19
1. Local transit - California - San Francisco Bay Area - Finance. I. Title.
HE4491.S45 C33 1986

Vasche, Jon David. The economic and fiscal effects of a primary source law for California wine imports. Sacramento, Calif. (925 L St., Suite 650, Sacramento 95814) [1986] vi, 130 p. : LC Card 86-622342 DDC 338.4/36632/009794 19
HD9377.C2 V37 1986

California. Legislature. Senate. Committee on Budget and Fiscal Review. Report on the 1986-87 Budget Act (as amended May 21, 1986) / Senate Committee on Budget and Fiscal Review. [Sacramento, Calif.] : The Committee, [1986] 3 v. (1105 leaves) ; 28 cm. Cover title. LC Card 86-622935 DDC 336.794 19
1. Budget - California - Statistics. I. Title.
HJ2053.C3 C36 1986

California. Legislature. Senate. Committee on Industrial Relations. Schaefer, Andrew. CAL-OSHA routine compliance inspections . [Sacramento, CA , 1986] 25 p. ; LC Card 86-622709 DDC 363.1/164/09796 19
HD7262.5.U62 C573 1986

California. Legislature. Senate. Office of Research. Shapiro, Michael E. Utility diversification . Sacramento, CA [1986] 50 p. ; LC Card 86-621960 DDC 338.8/3613636/0973 19
HD2766 .S47 1986

California. Legislature. Senate. Select Committee on Long Range Policy Planning. California and the 21st century : foundations for a competitive society : a report of the Senate Select Committee on Long Range Policy Planning. Sacramento, CA : The Committee : Copies may be purchased from Joint Publications, [1986] 3 v. : ill. ; 28 cm. "Prepared by the staff of the Senate Select Committee on Long Range Policy Planning and the Joint Committee on Science and Technology"--P. [i]. Vol. 3 has title: Meeting California's competitiveness challenge. "January 1986." Includes bibliographies. LC Card 86-622352 DDC 338.5/443/09794 19
1. Economic forecasting - California. 2. California - Economic conditions. 3. Population forecasting - California. 4. California - Population. 5. California - Economic policy. I. California. Legislature. Joint Committee on Science and Technology. II. Title.
HC107.C2 C227 1986

California. Office of Planning and Research. see **California. Governor's Office. Office of Planning and Research.**

California Oil Producers, Conservation Committee of. see **Conservation Committee of California Oil Producers.**

CALIFORNIA - POPULATION.
California. Legislature. Senate. Select Committee on Long Range Policy Planning. California and the 21st century . Sacramento, CA [1986] 3 v. : LC Card 86-622352 DDC 338.5/443/09794 19
HC107.C2 C227 1986

California. Public Utilities Commission. Report to the Legislature : new businesses and the structure of telecommunications utilities / California Public Utilities Commission. [San Francisco] : The Commission, [1984] 40 leaves ; 28 cm. "August 1, 1984." LC Card 86-622236 DDC 384.6/09794 19
1. Telephone - California. 2. Telephone - Government policy - California. I. California. Legislature. II. Title. III. Title: New businesses and the structure of telecommunications utilities.
HE8840.C2 C35 1984

CALIFORNIA - PUBLIC WORKS - CORRUPT PRACTICES.
A Practical guide to investigating public works violations /. Oakland, CA (520 3rd St., Suite 204, Oakland 94607) , 1986. 73 p., [3] leaves of plates : LC Card 86-209657 DDC 363.2/5 19
HD3890.C2 P7 1986

CALIFORNIA - PUBLIC WORKS - HISTORY.
Atkinson, Ray N. Guy F. Atkinson Company of California . New York , 1985, c1986. 24 p. : LC Card 86-61271 DDC 338.7/624/0973 19
HD9715.U54 G882 1986

California. Railroad Commission. see **California. Public Utilities Commission.**

California real estate appraisal . Miller, George H. Englewood Cliffs, N.J. , c1987. xiv, 348 p. : ISBN 0-13-112558-3 : LC Card 87-6956 DDC 333.33/2/09794 19
HD1387 .M545 1987

California real estate exam guide /. Lush, Minnie. Chicago , c1987. p. cm. ISBN 0-88462-591-5 LC Card 87-3290 DDC 333.33/09794 19
HD266.C2 L87 1987

California real estate principles / Dennis J. McKenzie ... [et al.]. 3rd ed. New York : J. Wiley, c1987. ix, 364 p. : ill. ; 29 cm. (John Wiley series in California real estate) Includes index. ISBN 0-471-63274-0 LC Card 87-404650 DDC 333.33/09794 19
1. Real estate business - California. I. McKenzie, Dennis J., 1940-. II. Series.
HD266.C2 C25 1987

California real estate principles. Bowman, Arthur G. Glenview, Ill. , c1987. xiv, 368 p. : ISBN 0-673-16667-8 : LC Card 86-25985 DDC 333.33/09794 19
HD266.C2 B68 1987

California real estate principles /. Stapleton, Charles O. Chicago , c1987. xvi, 428, 8 p. : ISBN 0-88462-569-9 (pbk.) LC Card 86-24870 DDC 333.33/09794 19
HD266.C2 S73 1987

California series on social choice and political economy .
(14) Toward a political economy of development . Berkeley , c1988. p. cm. ISBN 0-520-06051-2 (alk. paper) LC Card 87-10870 DDC 338.9/009172/4 19
HC59.7 .T7376 1988

Bates, Robert H. Essays on the political economy of rural Africa /. Berkeley , 1987, c1983. p. cm. ISBN 0-520-06014-8 (pbk. : alk. paper) LC Card 86-25120 DDC 330.96/0328/091734 19
HD2117 .B37 1987

Colburn, Forrest D. Post-revolutionary Nicaragua . Berkeley , c1986. xi, 145 p. : ISBN 0-520-05524-1 LC Card 85-5798 DDC 338.1/097285 19
HD1817 .C63 1986 ***NYPL [JLD 86-2414]***

A California small business handbook /. Koch, Harry Walter, 1909- [San Francisco] , c1986. 174 p. : ISBN 0-910553-06-8 (pbk.) : LC Card 87-167776 DDC 658/.022/09794 19
HD2346.U52 C25 1986

California State Building and Construction Trades Council. A Practical guide to investigating public works violations /. Oakland, CA (520 3rd St., Suite 204, Oakland 94607) , 1986. 73 p., [3] leaves of plates : LC Card 86-209657 DDC 363.2/5 19
HD3890.C2 P7 1986

CALIFORNIA - STATISTICS, VITAL.
Mielke, Robert B. Live births by estimated marital status of mother, California, 1981. [Sacramento] [1984] 22 p. : LC Card 86-622328 DDC 304.6/32/09794 19
HB935.C2 M54 1984

California, the demonstration of state work/welfare initiatives. Goldman, Barbara. Final report on the San Diego job search and work experience demonstration /. New York, N.Y. (3 Park Ave., New York 10016) , c1986. xliv, 269 p. : LC Card 87-118376 DDC 331.12/042/0979498 19
HD5713.6.U542 S395 1986

California. Transportation, Dept. of. see **California. Dept. of Transportation.**

California. University at Los Angeles. see **California. University. University at Los Angeles.**

California. University, Berkeley. see **California. University.**

California. University, Southern branch. see **California. University. University at Los Angeles.**

California. University. University at Los Angeles. Institute of Industrial Relations. Center for Human Resource Management. The Future directions of employee relations /. Los Angeles, Calif. , c1985. xiv, 418 p. ; ISBN 0-89215-132-3
NYPL [JLD 86-3596]

California - Vital statistics. see **California - Statistics, Vital.**

Calked boots and cant hooks /. Corrigan, George A., 1896-1981. Ashland, WI , 1986, c1976. xxi, 265 p. : ISBN 0-9613961-5-6 (pbk.) : LC Card 87-401439 DDC 331.7/634982/0924 B 19
HD8039.L92 U535 1986

Calked boots & cant hooks. Corrigan, George A., 1896-1981. Calked boots and cant hooks /. Ashland, WI , 1986, c1976. xxi, 265 p. : ISBN 0-9613961-5-6 (pbk.) : LC Card 87-401439 DDC 331.7/634982/0924 B 19
HD8039.L92 U535 1986

CALKING.
Caulks & sealants market. New York, N.Y. , c1983. ix, 250 p. : LC Card 87-143824
HD9999.S44453 U53 1983

The Call accounting market in the United States. New York, N.Y. : Frost & Sullivan, c1983. x, 275 p. : ill. ; 29 cm. Spine title: Telephone call accounting market in the U. S. "#A1186." "March 1983." LC Card 87-143500 DDC 381/.45621387 19
1. Telephone supplies industry - United States. 2. Telephone - United States - Accounting - Equipment and supplies. 3. Market surveys - United States. I. Frost & Sullivan. II. Title: Telephone call accounting market in the U. S.
HD9697.T453 U522 1983

Call money garanti. Mercier, Paul. Le marché du call money garanti /. Bruxelles [1983] 64 p. : LC Card 84-210204
HG1055 .M47 1983

Calla, Ricardo. La derrota de Lechín : las luchas políticas en el XXI Congreso Minero, mayo 1986 / Ricardo Calla. La Paz, Bolivia : Ediciones del Tigre de Papel, 1986. 79 p. : ill. ; 20 cm. LC Card 87-105127
1. Congreso Nacional Minero (21th : 1986 : Oruro, Bolivia). 2. Federación Sindical de Trabajadores Mineros de Bolivia. 3. Lechín Oquendo, Pero Juan. 4. Trade-unions - Miners - Bolivia. I. Title.
HD6609.M62 F433 1986

Callado, Antônio. Entre o deus e a vasilha : ensaio sobre a reforma agrária brasileira, a qual nunca foi feita / Antonio Callado ; foto, José Pinto/Afinal. Rio de Janeiro : Editora Nova Fronteira, c1985. 67 p. : map ; 19 cm. LC Card 85-218767
1. Land reform - Brazil. I. Title.
HD496 .C23 1985

Callaghan, Bede, Sir, 1912- The investment theme in Australia's approach to international trade / Sir Bede Callaghan. [Newcastle, N.S.W.] : University of Newcastle, Dept. of Economics and Institute of Industrial Economics, 1979. 16 leaves ; 30 cm. (Discussion paper / University of Newcastle. Institute of Industrial Economics . no. 8) ISBN 0-7259-0361-9 (pbk.) LC Card 82-133660
1. Investments - Australia. 2. Australia - Commerce. I. Series: Discussion paper / University of Newcastle. Institute of Industrial Economics , no. 8. II. Title.
HG5892 .C35 1979

Callahan, Michael J. Mcloughlin, Caven S. Getting employed, staying employed . Baltimore , c1987. xvi, 239 p. ; ISBN 0-933716-70-2 (pbk.) : LC Card 87-13185 DDC 650.1/4/0240816 19
HD7255 .M395 1987

Callanan, Joseph A. Sales management and motivation / Joseph A. Callanan, Porter Henry. New York : F. Watts, 1987. xi, 204 p. : ill. ; 24 cm. Includes index. ISBN 0-531-15516-1 LC Card 86-29020 DDC 658.8/1 19
1. Sales management. 2. Employee motivation. I. Henry, Porter. II. Title.
HF5438.4 .C335 1987

Callao (Peru : Province). Junta Departamental. Memoria que la Junta Departamental del Callao eleva al Congreso de 1887. Callao , 1887. 23 p. ; LC Card 83-191762
HJ979.C34 M45 1887

Callegari Ramírez, Carlos. Historia del Banco de la Nación. 1a ed. Lima, Perú : Centro de Documentación e Información Andina, 1986. 223 p. : ill. ; 27 cm. Bibliography: p. 223. LC Card 87-400236 DDC 332.1/1/0985 19
1. Banco de la Nación (Peru). 2. Banks and banking, Central - Peru. I. Centro de Documentación e Información Andina (Lima, Peru). II. Title.
HG2946 .C35 1986

Calleja, Carlos. see **Calleja Xifré, Carlos.**

Calleja, Carmen. Junta de Andalucía. Grupo de Trabajo 14, Planificación Económica de las Corporaciones Locales y Comarcalización. Plan económico de Andalucía, 1984-1986 /. [Andalucía] , 1983. 133 p. ; ISBN 84-505-1243-3 LC Card 86-223752
HJ1249.A4 J86 1983

Calleja Xifré, Carlos. El Baix Camp : població, economia i territori / [realitzat per Carles Calleja i Xifré, Gabriel Cortés i Marquès, Joan Veciana i Borràs, amb la col·laboració d'Albert Gonzàlez i Algueró]. Barcelona : Caixa d'Estalvis de Catalunya, [1986] xv, 367 p. : ill., col. maps ; 24 cm. (Col·lecció Catalunya comarcal) Bibliography: p. 347-351. ISBN 84-505-3567-9 LC Card 86-205881
1. Reus Region (Spain) - Economic conditions. 2. Reus Region (Spain) - Population. 3. Reus Region (Spain) - Social conditions. 4. Reus Region (Spain) - Politics and government. I. Cortés i Marquès, Gabriel. II. Veciana i Borràs, Joan. III. Title. IV. Series.
HC388.R482 C35 1986

Callies, Albane. France-Japon : confrontation culturelle dans les entreprises mixtes / Albane Callies. Paris : Libr. de Méridiens, 1986. 208 p. ; 21 cm. Bibliography: p. [199]-206. ISBN 2-86563-129-X LC Card 86-165719
1. Industrial relations - France. 2. Industrial relations - Japan. 3. Industrial organization - France. 4. Industrial organization - Japan. I. Title.
HD8431 .C35 1986

CALLS (COMMERCE) see **PUT AND CALL TRANSACTIONS.**

Calmfors, Lars, 1948- The Fight against unemployment . Cambridge, Mass. , 1987. xii, 204 p. : ISBN 0-262-12122-0 LC Card 87-5356 DDC 339.5/094 19
HD5764.A6 F54 1987

Cals, Joan. El Baix Empordà . Barcelona , c1984. xii, 303 p. : ISBN 84-505-0289-6 LC Card 85-186183
HC387.A636 B35 1984

Calsing, Elizeu F.
Dimensionamento e caracterização da pobreza no Brasil. Calsing, Elizeu F. Extensão e características da pobreza no Brasil / Elizeu Francisco Calsing. Brasília , 1983. 44, [1] p. : LC Card 86-178277
HC190.P6 C29 1983

Extensão e características da pobreza no Brasil / Elizeu Francisco Calsing. Brasília : Instituto de Planejamento Econômico e Social, Instituto de Planejamento, Centro Nacional de Recursos Humanos, 1983. 44, [1] p. : ill. ; 30 cm. "Preparado dentro do Projeto de Cooperação Técnica Internacional entre CNRH/IPEA e UNICEF ... a base de dados apresentada em outro trabalho do mesmo autor, intitulado 'Dimensionamento e caracterização da pobreza no Brasil.'" Bibliography: p. [45] LC Card 86-178277
1. Poor - Brazil. 2. Households - Brazil. I. Calsing, Elizeu F. Dimensionamento e caracterização da pobreza no Brasil. II. Centro Nacional de Recursos Humanos. III. Title.
HC190.P6 C29 1983

Calthorpe, Peter. Van der Ryn, Sim. Sustainable communities . San Francisco [1986] xvii, 238 p. : ISBN 0-87156-800-4 LC Card 83-4676 DDC 307/.14 19
HN90.C6 V36 1986 ***NYPL [JLF 86-1241]***

CALVERT ISLAND (B.C.) - PUBLIC LANDS. Calvert Island crown land plan /. [Victoria, B.C.] , 1981. vii, 63 p. : ISBN 0-7719-8637-8 (pbk.) LC Card 82-208343 DDC 333.1/09711/3 19
HD319.B8 C34 1981

Calvert Island crown land plan / prepared by Lands and Housing Regional Operations Division, Cariboo Region. [Victoria, B.C.] : Province of British Columbia, Ministry of Lands, Parks and Housing, 1981. vii, 63 p. : ill. ; 28 cm. ISBN 0-7719-8637-8 (pbk.) LC Card 82-208343 DDC 333.1/09711/3 19
1. Crown lands - British Columbia - Calvert Island. 2. Calvert Island (B.C.) - Public lands. I. British Columbia. Lands and Housing Regional Operations Division. Cariboo Region.
HD319.B8 C34 1981

Calvo, Alfredo Castillero. see **Castillero Calvo, Alfredo, 1937-**

CAM Foundation. Case studies in international marketing /. London , 1982. vii, 391 p. : ISBN 0-434-90370-1 : LC Card 82-241323 DDC 658.8/48 19
HF1009.5 .C34 1982 ***NYPL [JLE 87-1196]***

Camacho Cabello, José. La Siberia extremeña : población, economía y sociedad en la segunda mitad del siglo XVIII / José Camacho Cabello. [Badajoz] : Excma. Diputación Provincial de Badajoz, 1985. 201 p. : ill. ; 24 cm. (Colección Historia. 2) Bibliography: p. 173-178. ISBN 84-505-1266-2 LC Card 86-200856
1. Estremadura (Spain) - Population - History. 2. Estremadura, Spain - Economic conditions. 3. Estremadura, Spain - Social conditions. I. Series: Colección Historia (Badajoz, Spain) , 2. II. Title.
HB3620.E85 C35 1985

Camacho, Martine. Les poubelles de la survie : la décharge municipale de Tananarive / Martine Camacho. Paris : L'Harmattan, c1986. 207 p. : ill. ; 25 cm. (Collection "Villes et entreprises") ISBN 2-85802-590-5 LC Card 86-180208
1. Poor - Madagascar - Antananarivo. 2. Waste disposal sites - Economic aspects - Madagascar - Antananarivo. I. Title. II. Series.
HC895.Z7 A443 1986

Camacho Rueda, Eduardo. Propiedad y explotación agrarias en el aljarafe sevillano : el caso de Pilas, 1760-1925 / Eduardo Camacho Rueda. Sevilla : Excma. Diputación Provincial de Sevilla, 1984. 199 p. : ill. ; 25 cm. (Publicaciones de la Excma. Diputación Provincial de Sevilla. Sección Historia . ser. 1a, no. 27) Spine title: Propiedad y explotación agrarias del aljarafe sevillano. Bibliography: p. [197]-[199] ISBN 84-500-9772-X LC Card 85-135028
1. Land tenure - Spain - Pilas (Seville) - History. 2. Pilas (Seville, Spain) - Population - History. 3. Landowners - Spain - Pilas (Seville) - History. 4. Cattle trade - Spain - Pilas (Seville) - History. I. Title. II. Title: Propiedad y explotación agrarias del aljarafe sevillano. III. Series.
HD773 .C18 1984

Camagni, Roberto. Il Robot italiano . Milano , 1984. 194 p. : LC Card 86-129858
HD9696.R623 I837 1984
NYPL [JLD 87-1277]

Cámara de Comercio de Bogotá. Régimen de zonas francas en Colombia. Bogotá , 1984. 157 leaves ; LC Card 86-185156
HF1418 .R44 1984

Cámara de Comercio de Cali. Perfiles económicos del Valle del Cauca, Colombia. Cali, Colombia [1981?] 40 p. : LC Card 86-120381 DDC 330.9861/520632 19
HC198.V3 P47 1981

Cámara de Comercio, Industria y Navegación de Santander (Spain)
Reunión coloquio sobre como ven nuestros hombres de empresa la economía de Cantabria para 1984 /. [Santander] [1984?] 54 p. ; ISBN 84-505-0186-5 LC Card 86-187513
HF3690.C35 R48 1984

Reunión coloquio sobre como ven nuestros hombres de empresa la economía de Cantabria para 1985 /. [Santander] [1985?] 78 p. ; ISBN 84-505-1440-1 LC Card 86-193783
HF3690.C35 R49 1985

Câmara de Produtores-Exportadores de Insumos Farmacêuticos e Afins (Rio de Janeiro, Brazil) Brasil--guia dos produtores de insumos farmacêuticos /. Rio de Janeiro, Brasil , 1983. 71 p. ; LC Card 86-202196
HD9670.B82 B7 1983

Cámara Nacional de la Industria de la Construcción (Mexico). Dirección Técnica. La Industria mexicana de la construcción. México, D.F. , 1979. 89 p. : LC Card 87-400496 DDC 338.4/7624/0972 19
HD9715.M4 I53 1979

Cámara Ofical de Comercio e Industria de Madrid. P.M.E., ayudas, estímulos e instituciones especializadas en la C.E.E. . [Madrid] [1983?] 141 p. ; ISBN 84-500-8571-3 LC Card 85-135456
HD2346.E93 P16 1983

Camarade travailleur, connais-tu la C.N.T.G.? Confédération nationale des travailleurs de Guinée. Structure /. [Conakry] [1964?] 23 p. : LC Card 82-220475
HD8826.A5 C66 1964

Camargo, Ana Maria M. Pires de. Comportamento dos preços de olerícolas nos mercados atacadistas e fluxo de produção regional no Brasil, 1977-83 / Ana Maria M. Pires de Camargo, Waldemar Pires de Camargo Filho. São Paulo : Governo do Estado de São Paulo, Secretaria de Agricultura e Abastecimento, Instituto de Economia Agrícola, 1986. 79 p. : ill. ; 23 cm. (Relatório de pesquisa, 0101-5109 . 9/86) Bibliography: p. 59-61. LC Card 87-403840 DDC 338.1/35/0981/61021 19
1. Vegetables - Prices - Brazil - Saõ Paulo (State) - Statistics - History - 20th century. I. Camargo Filho, Waldemar Pires de. II. Series: Relatório de pesquisa (São Paulo (Brazil : State). Instituto de Economia Agrícola) , no. 86/9. III. Title.
HD9220.B73 S263 1986

Camargo Filho, Waldemar Pires de. Camargo, Ana Maria M. Pires de. Comportamento dos preços de olerícolas nos mercados atacadistas e fluxo de produção regional no Brasil, 1977-83 /. São Paulo , 1986. 79 p. : LC Card 87-403840 DDC 338.1/35/0981/61021 19
HD9220.B73 S263 1986

Cambio cultural e imagen del hombre / editor, Alberto Dou ; ponentes, Jon Kepa Acordagoikoetxea ... [et al.]. Bilbao, España : Mensajero, c1984. 248 p. ; 22 cm. (Biblioteca Fomento social. 31.) "Actas de la X Reunión Interdisciplinar que tuvo lugar en Jarandilla (Cáceres) del 4 al 8 de septiembre de 1983"--P. 11. Includes bibliographies. ISBN 84-271-1384-6 LC Card 85-234026
1. Civilization, Occidental - Congresses. 2. Values - Congresses. 3. Knowledge, Theory of - Congresses. 4. Technology and civilization - Congresses. I. Dou, Alberto. II. Acordagoikoetxea, Jon Kepa.
CB245 .C29 1984 ***NYPL [JFD 86-6394]***

Cambio regional, mercado de trabajo y vida obrera en Jalisco / Guillermo de la Peña y Agustín Escobar, comps. 1a ed. Guadalajara, Jalisco, México : Colegio de Jalisco, 1986. 363 p. ; 21 cm. (Colección Estudios sociales. 1) Bibliography: p. ISBN 968-614-201-0 LC Card 86-218238
1. Labor supply - Mexico - Jalisco. 2. Labor and laboring classes - Mexico - Jalisco. 3. Jalisco (Mexico) - Industries. I. Peña, Guillermo de la. II. Escobar Latapí, Agustín. III. Series: Colección Estudios sociales (Guadalajara, Mexico) , 1.
HD5731.J35 C36 1986

Cambio técnico, trabajo y educación . Argenti, Gisela. Montevideo , 1985. 91, 70 leaves : LC Card 87-124118
HC235.T4 A74 1985

Cambio y polarización ocupacional en Centroamérica. 1a ed. [San José, Costa Rica?] : PREALC, 1986. 202 p. : ill. ; 19 cm. "Una primera versión de este trabajo fue presentada al 'Coloquio Subregional sobre la Repercusión de la Crisis Económica en los Mercados Laborales Centroamericanos,' organizado por el PREALC y que se celebró en Panamá el 25 y 26 de octubre de 1985"--P. 7. Bibliography: p. 185-189. ISBN 92-2-305432-X LC Card 86-231773
1. Labor supply - Central America. 2. Informal sector (Economics) - Central America. 3. Agricultural laborers - Central America - Supply and demand. I. Regional Employment Program for Latin America and

the Caribbean.
HD5733.A6 C36 1986

CAMBISTRY. see **FOREIGN EXCHANGE.**

Cambra, G. (Gaétan) Le Iniziative locali per l'occupazione . Milano, Italy , c1985. 244 p. : LC Card 85-221711 DDC 331 s 331.12/042 19
HD85.I7 I68 no. 75 HD5713.5
NYPL [JLD 87-446]

Cambranes, J. C. Agrarismo en Guatemala / J.C. Cambranes. 1a ed. Guatemala : Serviprensa Centroamericana, 1986. 255 p. : ill. ; 22 cm. (Monografía / Centro de Estudios Rurales Centroamericanos . 1) Includes bibliographical references. LC Card 87-401042 DDC 322/.2/097281 19
1. Peasantry - Guatemala - Political activity. 2. Girón de León, Andrés de Jesús, 1946-. 3. Church and the poor - Guatemala. 4. Church and social problems - Guatemala. 5. Catholic Church - Guatemala - Political activity. I. Series: Monografía / Centro de Estudios Rurales Centroamericanos , 1. II. Title.
HD1531.G9 C36 1986

Cambridge dizionario italiano-inglese, inglese-italiano, Signorelli . Reynolds, Barbara, 1914- [Cambridge Italian dictionary.] Cambridge [Cambridgeshire] ; New York : 2276 p. ; ISBN 0-521-32702-4 LC Card 86-1898 DDC 453/.21 19
*PC1640 .R4 1986 NYPL [*R-REK 86-3799]*

Cambridge energy forum.
Energy markets after the collapse . Cambridge, MA (56 John F. Kennedy St., Suite 5, Cambridge 02138) , c1987. 164 p. : LC Card 87-142725 DDC 338.2/728 19
HD9560.5 .E54 1987

Cambridge Energy Research Associates.
The Domestic U. S. oil industry and low oil prices . [Cambridge, Mass.] , c1987. v, 61 leaves : LC Card 87-402219 DDC 338.2/7282/0973 19
HD9574.U62 D66 1987

Energy markets after the collapse . Cambridge, MA (56 John F. Kennedy St., Suite 5, Cambridge 02138) , c1987. 164 p. : LC Card 87-142725 DDC 338.2/728 19
HD9560.5 .E54 1987

Cambridge energy studies.
Gordon, Richard L., 1934- World coal . Cambridge [Cambridgeshire] , New York , 1987. xvi, 145 p. : ISBN 0-521-30827-5 LC Card 86-26349 DDC 338.2/724 19
HD9540.5 .G64 1987

Cambridge Middle East library.
Pamuk, Şevket. The Ottoman empire and European capitalism, 1820-1913 . Cambridge [Cambridgeshire] , New York , 1987. xii, 278 p. : ISBN 0-521-33194-3 LC Card 86-28386 DDC 330.956/01 19
HF1583.4 .P36 1987

Schroeter, Daniel J. Merchants of Essaouira . Cambridge , New York , 1988. p. cm. ISBN 0-521-32455-6 LC Card 87-15163 DDC 330.964/6 19
HC810.Z7 E857 1988

The Cambridge multisectoral dynamic model of the British economy / edited by Terry Baker and William Peterson. Cambridge [Cambridgeshire] ; New York : Cambridge University Press, 1988. p. cm. (Cambridge studies in applied econometrics. no. 5) Bibliography: p. Includes indexes. ISBN 0-521-33004-1 LC Card 86-33375 DDC 330.941/00724 19
1. Great Britain - Economic conditions - 1945- - Econometric models. 2. National income - Great Britain - Accounting - Econometric models. I. Barker, Terry. II. Peterson, William A. III. Series.
HC256.6 .C29 1988

CAMBRIDGE SCHOOL OF ECONOMICS. see **NEOCLASSICAL SCHOOL OF ECONOMICS.**

Cambridge studies in agricultural and rural development.
Ellis, Frank. Peasant economics . Cambridge [Cambridgeshire] , New York , 1988. p. cm. ISBN 0-521-32446-7 LC Card 87-14815 DDC 338.1/09172/4 19
HD1542 .E43 1988

Cambridge studies in applied econometrics.
(no. 5) The Cambridge multisectoral dynamic model of the British economy /. Cambridge [Cambridgeshire] , New York , 1988. p. cm. ISBN 0-521-33004-1 LC Card 86-33375 DDC 330.941/00724 19
HC256.6 .C29 1988

Cambridge studies in historical geography .
(8) Watts, David. The West Indies . Cambridge [Cambridgeshire] , New York , 1987. xxii, 609 p. : ISBN 0-521-24555-9 LC Card 87-5156 DDC 330.9729 19
HC151 .W375 1987

Cambridge studies in Islamic civilization.
Saleh, Nabil A. Unlawful gain and legitimate profit in Islamic law . Cambridge [Cambridgeshire] , New York , 1986. xii, 130 p. ; ISBN 0-521-32298-7 LC Card 85-25547 DDC 297/.14 19
LAW NYPL [JLE 86-2377]

Cambridge studies in management .
(11) The process of technological change . Cambridge [Cambridgeshire] , New York , 1988. p. cm. ISBN 0-521-32303-7 LC Card 87-6641 DDC 658.5/14 19
HD45 .P757 1988

Cambridge studies in medieval life and thought.
For other vols. in this series, see Old Catalog. (4th ser., 7) Dean, Trevor. Land and power in late medieval Ferrara . Cambridge , New York , 1988. xiv, 212 p. : ISBN 0-521-33127-7 LC Card 87-6583 DDC 333.3/0945/45 19
HD679.F47 D43 1988

Cambridge studies in modern political economies.
Maier, Charles S. In search of stability . Cambridge [Cambridgeshire] , New York , 1987. x, 291 p. ; ISBN 0-521-23001-2 LC Card 87-6383 DDC 338.94 19
HC240 .M17 1987

Cambridge studies in philosophy and public policy.
Sagoff, Mark. The economy of the earth . Cambridge [Cambridgeshire] , New York , 1988. p. cm. ISBN 0-521-34113-2 LC Card 87-16091 DDC 363.7/056/0973 19
HC110.E5 S34 1988

Cambridge studies in population, economy, and society in past time .
(6) Knodel, John E. Demographic behavior in the past . Cambridge [Cambridgeshire] , New York , 1988. p. cm. ISBN 0-521-32715-6 LC Card 87-20601 DDC 304.6/0943 19
HB3595 .K53 1988

Camden, Thomas M., 1938- How to get a job in Dallas, Fort Worth : the insider's guide / Thomas M. Camden, Nancy Bishop.2nd ed. Chicago, IL : Surrey Books, c1987. viii, 490 p. : ill. ; 22 cm. (The Insider's guide series) Includes bibliographies and index. ISBN 0-9609516-9-5 (pbk.) : LC Card 86-30123 DDC 650.1/4/097642812 19
1. Job hunting - Texas - Dallas - Directories. 2. Job hunting - Texas - Fort Worth - Directories. 3. Dallas (Tex.) - Industries - Directories. 4. Fort Worth (Tex.) - Industries - Directories. I. Bishop, Nancy, 1949-. II. Title. III. Series.
HF5382.75.U6 C353 1987

CAMERA DEL LAVORO DI MILANO - HISTORY - 20TH CENTURY.
Granata, Ivano, 1949- Sindacato e crisi della democrazia . Milano, Italy , c1986. 224 p. ; LC Card 87-103965
HD6714.M54 G724 1986

Camera di commercio, industria, artigianato e agricoltura di Milano.
Industria e commercio . Milano, Italy , c1985. 194 p. : LC Card 86-112174 DDC 658.7/88/0945 19
HF5415.12.I8 I53 1985 NYPL [JLD 87-432]

Il Sistema dei trasporti nello sviluppo della cooperazione economica internazionale . Milano, Italy , c1985. 341 p. ; LC Card 85-218403
HE2449 .S57 1985

CAMERA INDUSTRY - JAPAN - MANAGEMENT - EMPLOYEE PARTICIPATION - CASE STUDIES.
Kyanon no seisan kakushin. English. Canon production system . Stamford, Conn. , c1987. xxi, 230 p. : ISBN 0-915299-06-2 : LC Card 85-63498 DDC 681/.418/0683 19
HD9708.5.C354 K92513 1987

Camerana, Oddone. L'enigma del cavalier Agnelli e altri itinerari / Oddone Camerona. Milano : Serra e Riva, c1985. 117 p. ; 18 cm. (Collier . 7) LC Card 85-191746
1. Agnelli, Giovanni, 1921-. 2. Fiat (Firm) - History. 3. Industrialists - Italy - Biography. 4. Automobile industry and trade - Italy - History. I. Title.
HD9710.I82 A6615 1985
NYPL [JLC 87-25]

Cameron, Duncan, 1944- The Free trade papers /. Toronto , 1986. 1 [i.e. 50], 227 p. : ISBN 0-88862-972-9 LC Card 87-109310 DDC 382.7/1/0971 19
HF1479 .F74 1986

Cameroon. Southern Cameroons, a British trusteeship territory, was administratively attached to the Eastern Region of Nigeria until 1954, when it became a separate government. In 1960 French Cameroons, also a trusteeship territory, became independent as the Republic of Cameroun. Cameroon (Federal Republic of Cameroon) was constituted in 1961 by the union of Cameroun (Republic of Cameroun) and Southern Cameroons. Within the Federal Republic, territories of the former Republic of Cameroun became the federated state of East Cameroon, and territories of the former Southern Cameroons became the federated state of West Cameroon. Works by these bodies are found under the name used at the time of publication.

CAMEROON - COMMERCE.
Kooperationsführer Kamerun /. Köln , 1986. 70 p. : LC Card 87-408425 DDC 330.967/1104 19
HC995 .K66 1986

CAMEROON - CULTURAL POLICY.
Cameroon. Ministry of Planning and Land Management. VIe Plan quinquennal de développement économique, social et culturel . [Yaoundé] [1986?] lxx, 325 p., [19] leaves of plates : LC Card 87-165935
HC995 .C335 1986

CAMEROON - DEPENDENCY ON FOREIGN COUNTRIES.
Ntumazah, Ndeh. France's satrapy in Kamerun is safe /. [London, England , 1985] 22 leaves ; LC Card 87-138988 DDC 337.6711044 19
HC995 .N78 1985

Cameroon. Direction de l'urbanisme et de l'habitat. Yaoundé, typologie de l'habitat . [Yaoundé, Cameroon] [197-?] [26] p. : LC Card 83-106947
HD1019.Z9 Y368 1970z

CAMEROON - ECONOMIC CONDITIONS - 1960-
Kooperationsführer Kamerun /. Köln , 1986. 70 p. : LC Card 87-408425 DDC 330.967/1104 19
HC995 .K66 1986

CAMEROON - ECONOMIC POLICY.
Cameroon. Ministry of Planning and Land Management. VIe Plan quinquennal de développement économique, social et culturel . [Yaoundé] [1986?] lxx, 325 p., [19] leaves of plates : LC Card 87-165935
HC995 .C335 1986

CAMEROON - FOREIGN ECONOMIC RELATIONS - FRANCE.
Ntumazah, Ndeh. France's satrapy in Kamerun is safe /. [London, England , 1985] 22 leaves ; LC Card 87-138988 DDC 337.6711044 19
HC995 .N78 1985

Cameroon. Ministry of Planning and Land Management. VIe Plan quinquennal de développement économique, social et culturel : 1986-1991 / République du Cameroun, Ministère du plan et de l'aménagement du territoire. [Yaoundé] : Le Ministère, [1986?] lxx, 325 p., [19] leaves of plates : ill. (some col.), col. maps ; 32 cm. LC Card 87-165935
1. Cameroon - Economic policy. 2. Cameroon - Social policy. 3. Cameroon - Cultural policy. I. Title. II. Title: 6e Plan quinquennal de développement économique, social et culturel. III. Title: Sixième plan quinquennal de développement économique, social et culturel.
HC995 .C335 1986

CAMEROON - POLITICS AND GOVERNMENT - 1960-
Ntumazah, Ndeh. France's satrapy in Kamerun is safe /. [London, England , 1985] 22 leaves ; LC Card 87-138988 DDC 337.6711044 19
HC995 .N78 1985

CAMEROON - SOCIAL POLICY.
Cameroon. Ministry of Planning and Land Management. VIe Plan quinquennal de développement économique, social et culturel . [Yaoundé] [1986?] lxx, 325 p., [19] leaves of plates : LC Card 87-165935
HC995 .C335 1986

Camm, J. C. R. (Jack Charles Robert)
Hardtimes--a cartographic and graphic representation of selected aspects of the depression years, 1925-1935, in Australia / J.C.R. Camm. [Newcastle, N.S.W.] : University of Newcastle, 1985. 59, iii p. : ill. ; 30 cm. (Research papers in geography . no. 30) Bibliography: p. 59. ISBN 0-7259-0542-5 (pbk.) : LC Card 86-222404 DDC 330.994/042 19
1. Australia - Economic conditions - 1918- - Maps. 2. Depressions - 1929 - Australia - Maps. I. Title. II. Series.
HC603 .C36 1985

Cammack, Andrew. Kentucky. General Assembly. Tobacco Task Force. Final report of the Kentucky Tobacco Task Force /. Frankfort, Ky. [1986] vii, 91 p. : LC Card 86-622267 DDC 338.1/7371/09769 19
HD9137.K4 K45 1986

Cammarosano, Joseph R. The contributions of John Maynard Keynes to foreign trade theory and policy, 1909-1946 / Joseph R. Cammarosano. New York : Garland Pub., 1987. 437 p. ; 23 cm. (Foreign economic policy of the United States) Originally presented as the author's thesis (Ph. D.)--Fordham University, 1956. Bibliography: p. 404-437. ISBN 0-8240-8076-9 (alk. paper) : LC Card 87-23775 DDC 382.1/04 19
1. Commercial policy. 2. International economic relations. 3. Keynes, John Maynard, 1883-1946 - Contributions in commercial policy. I. Title. II. Series.
HF1411 .C323 1987

Camp, Carolyn Beth. Schimmel, Warren T. Communicating /. New York , c1987. xvi, 624 p., [32] p. of plates : ISBN 0-471-84248-6 LC Card 87-111811 DDC 808/.066651 19
HF5718 .S29 1987

Camp, William G. Managing our natural resources / William G. Camp, Thomas B. Daugherty. Albany, N.Y. : Delmar Publishers, c1988. p. cm. Includes index. Examines the nature, history, and management of natural resources ranging from soil and water to forests, wildlife, and marine resources. Includes suggested activities and discussion of occupations in the field. ISBN 0-8273-2986-5 LC Card 87-25056 DDC 333.7/0973 19
1. Natural resources - United States - Management - Juvenile literature. I. Daugherty, Thomas B. II. Title.
HC103.7 .C33 1988

Campagna, Anthony S. U. S. national economic policy, 1917-1985 / Anthony S. Campagna. New York : Praeger, 1987. xix, 642 p. : ill. ; 25 cm. Bibliography: p. 622-630. Includes index. ISBN 0-275-92426-2 (alk. paper) : LC Card 86-30316 DDC 338.973 19
1. United States - Economic policy. I. Title. II. Title: US national economic policy, 1917-1985.
HC106.2 .C26 1987

Campagne e territorio nel Mezzogiorno fra Settecento e Ottocento /. Massafra, Angelo. Bari , c1984. 324 p. : ISBN 88-22-06039-3 : LC Card 85-179303
HC307.S69 M37 1984

Les campagnes angevines à la fin du Moyen Age . Le Mené, Michel. Nantes , c1982. 534 p., [1] folded leaf of plates : LC Card 87-672705
HC277.A55 L45x 1982

CAMPAIGN FUNDS - UNITED STATES.
Matasar, Ann B. Corporate PACs and federal campaign financing laws . New York , 1986. x, 161 p. ; ISBN 0-89930-086-3 (lib. bdg. : alk. paper)
NYPL [JLE 86-2492]

CAMPAIGNS, PRESIDENTIAL. see **PRESIDENTS - UNITED STATES - ELECTION.**

Campanella, Francesco. L'Insegnamento dell'economia politica nella scuola secondaria superiore . Milano, Italy , c1982. 261 p. ; LC Card 87-673404
HB74.9.I8 I57x 1982

Campanha da fraternidade, 1986. Terra de Deus, terra de irmãos . Brasília-DF [1986] 190 p. : LC Card 86-233600
HD1333.B6 T47 1986

A campanha do petróleo /. Moura, Gerson. São Paulo-SP , 1986. 92 p. : LC Card 86-190721
HD9574.B84 P445 1986

Campbell, Andrew. Goold, Michael. Strategies and styles . Oxford, UK , New York, NY, USA , 1988, c1987. p. cm. ISBN 0-631-15829-4 : LC Card 87-12151 DDC 658/.046 19
HD2756 .G66 1988

Campbell, Bob J. Early results of seat belt legislation in the United States of America / by B.J. Campbell, J. Richard Stewart, Frances A. Campbell. Chapel Hill, N.C. : University of North Carolina, Highway Safety Research Center, [1986] 25 p. : ill. ; 28 cm. "July, 1986." "A-123." Bibliography: p. 24-25. LC Card 86-622836 DDC 363.1/2572/0973 19
1. Automobiles - United States - Seat belts. 2. Automobiles - Seat belts - Law and legislation - United States. I. Stewart, J. Richard. II. Campbell, Frances A. III. University of North Carolina (System). Highway Safety Research Center. IV. Title.
HE5614.2 .C35 1986

Campbell, Colin, 1940- The romantic ethic and the spirit of modern consumerism / Colin Campbell. Oxford, UK ; New York, NY, USA : B. Blackwell, 1987. 301 p. ; 24 cm. Bibliography: p. [228]-294. Includes index. ISBN 0-631-15539-2 : LC Card 86-30979 DDC 339.4/7 19
1. Consumption (Economics). 2. Romanticism. 3. Self-interest. 4. Individualism. I. Title.
HC79.C6 C36 1987

Campbell, Colin Dearborn, 1917- Money, banking, and monetary policy / Colin D. Campbell, Rosemary G. Campbell, Edwin G. Dolan. Chicago : Dryden Press, c1988. xx, 617 p. : ill. (some col.) ; 25 cm. (The Dryden Press series in economics) Includes bibliographies and index. ISBN 0-03-009494-1 LC Card 87-6890 DDC 332.1 19
1. Money. 2. Banks and banking. 3. Finance. I. Campbell, Rosemary G. II. Dolan, Edwin G. III. Title. IV. Series.
HG221 .C245 1988

Campbell, Frances A. Campbell, Bob J. Early results of seat belt legislation in the United States of America /. Chapel Hill, N.C. [1986] 25 p. : LC Card 86-622836 DDC 363.1/2572/0973 19
HE5614.2 .C35 1986

Campbell, Mary V.
Mastering Lotus HAL / Mary V. Campbell. San Francisco : Sybex, c1987. xxi, 342 p. : ill. ; 23 cm. Includes index. ISBN 0-89588-422-4 (pbk.) : LC Card 87-60797 DDC 005.36/9 19
1. Lotus HAL (Computer program). 2. Business - Data processing. I. Title.
HF5548.4.L68 C35 1987

1-2-3, the complete reference / Mary Campbell. Berkeley, Calif. : Osborne McGraw-Hill, c1986. xii, 892 p. : ill. ; 24 cm. On t.p. the registered trademark symbol "TM" is superscript following "1-2-3" in the title. Includes index. ISBN 0-07-881005-1 (pbk.) : LC Card 86-230048 DDC 005.36/9 19
1. Lotus 1-2-3 (Computer program). 2. Business - Data processing. I. Title. II. Title: One-two-three, the complete reference.
HF5548.4.L67 C35 1986

Campbell, Nigel. China strategies : the inside story / Nigel Campbell. [Manchester, Greater Manchester] : University of Manchester ; [Hong Kong] : University of Hong Kong, c1986. xxiv, 161 p. : ill. ; 30 cm. (A China research publication) ISBN 0-903808-51-X (pbk.) LC Card 86-235360 DDC 332.6/7314/0951 19
1. Corporations, Foreign - China. 2. Investments, Foreign - China. 3. Joint ventures - China. 4. Negotiation in business - China. I. Title. II. Series.
HD2910 .C36 1986

Campbell, Robert Malcolm. Grand illusions : the politics of the Keynesian experience in Canada, 1945-1975 / Robert Malcolm Campbell. Peterborough, Canada ; Lewiston, N.Y. : Broadview Press, c1987. 270 p. ; 24 cm. Bibliography: p. 235-263. Includes index. ISBN 0-921149-03-4 LC Card 87-147385 DDC 338.971 19
1. Canada - Economic policy. 2. Canada - Economic conditions - 1945-. 3. Keynesian economics. I. Title.
HC115 .C16 1987

Campbell, Rosemary G. Campbell, Colin Dearborn, 1917- Money, banking, and monetary policy /. Chicago , c1988. xx, 617 p. : ISBN 0-03-009494-1 LC Card 87-6890 DDC 332.1 19
HG221 .C245 1988

Campbell, Sally R. The confident consumer / Sally R. Campbell. South Holland, Ill. : Goodheart-Willcox Co., c1988. 368 p. : ill. (some col.) ; 27 cm. Includes index. ISBN 0-87006-635-8 LC Card 87-2 DDC 381/.33 19
1. Finance, Personal. 2. Consumer education. I. Title.
HG179 .C32 1988

Campbell, Sioux Henley. Osher, Bill. The blue-chip graduate . Atlanta, Ga. , c1987. 238 p. : ISBN 0-934601-19-4 (pbk.) : LC Card 86-63534 DDC 650.1/4/024375 19
HF5381 .O889 1987

Campbell, Siri. Sacks, Frank. The new IRA handbook . Chicago [1987], c1986. 126 p. : ISBN 0-911445-05-6 (pbk.) : LC Card 87-130659 DDC 332.024/01 19
HG1660.U5 S23 1987

Campbell-Smith, Duncan. The British Airways story : struggle for take-off / Duncan Campbell-Smith. London : Coronet Books : Hodder and Stoughton, 1986. viii, 327 p. ; 18 cm. Bibliography: p. 317-318. Includes index. ISBN 0-340-39495-1 (pbk.) : LC Card 86-206477 DDC 387.7/065/41 19
1. British Airways - History. 2. Aeronautics, Commercial - Great Britain - History. 3. Airlines - Great Britain - History. I. Title.
HE9843.B7 C36 1986

Campero, Guillermo. El sindicalismo internacional y la redemocratización de Chile / Guillermo Campero Q. Santiago, Chile : Centro de Estudios del Desarrollo, 1984. 77 p. ; 28 cm. (Material para discusión . no. 12) Bibliography: p. 75-76. LC Card 86-139122 DDC 331.88/0983 19
1. Trade-unions - Chile. 2. AFL-CIO. 3. International Confederation of Free Trade Unions. 4. Political participation - Chile. 5. Chile - Politics and government - 1970-. I. Title. II. Series.
HD6617 .C357 1984

Campesinado indígena y el desafío de la modernidad /. Santana, Roberto. [Quito, Ecuador] , 1983. 209 p. : LC Card 84-156117 DDC 330.9866/074/08998 19
F3721.3.E25 S26 1983
NYPL [HBC 86-2225]

Campesinado y capitalismo en Colombia / D. Fajardo ... [et al.]. Bogotá, Colombia : Centro de Investigación y Educación Popular, 1981. 233 p. ; 21 cm. Includes bibliographical references. LC Card 82-141108 DDC 338.1/09861 19
1. Peasantry - Colombia - Addresses, essays, lectures. 2. Agriculture - Economic aspects - Colombia - Addresses, essays, lectures. 3. Capitalism - Addresses, essays, lectures. I. Fajardo M., Darío.
HD516 .C35 1981 ***NYPL [JLD 86-1342]***

Campesinado y organización en Esmeraldas / [Fredy Rivera V. et al.]. [Quito, Ecuador?] : Centro Andino de Acción Popular : Organización Campesina Muisne-Esmeraldas, [1986] 213 p. : ill. ; 22 cm. (Cuaderno de discusión popular . no. 11) Includes bibliographies. LC Card 86-171561
1. Peasantry - Ecuador - Esmeraldas (Province) - Case studies. 2. Agricultural laborers - Ecuador - Esmeraldas (Province) - Case studies. 3. Agriculture - Economic aspects - Ecuador - Esmeraldas (Province) - Case studies. 4. Banana trade - Ecuador - Esmeraldas (Province) - Case studies. 5. Esmeraldas (Ecuador : Province) - Economic conditions - Case studies. I. Rivera V., Fredy (Rivera Vélez). II. Centro Andino de Acción Popular. III. Organización Campesina Muisne-Esmeraldas.
HD1531.E2 C36 1986

Campesinas y políticos, 1986 : lo que las campesinas creen de los políticos y lo que los políticos les ofrecen / [edición, Angela Hernández, Miguelina Crespo, Luz M. Abreu L.]. Santo Domingo, República Dominicana : Mujeres en Desarrollo Dominicana, 1986. 83 p. : ill. ; 21 cm. LC Card 87-102259
1. Women agricultural laborers - Dominican Republic - Political activity. 2. Women farmers - Dominican Republic - Political activity. I. Hernández, Angela. II. Crespo, Miguelina. III. Abrue L., Luz M. IV. Mujeres en Desarrollo, Inc. (Dominican Republic).
HD6073.A292 D653 1986

Campesinato e capitalismo /. Barreiro, José Carlos. Campinas-SP [1986] 128 p. ; LC Card

86-229683
HD1531.B7 B37 1986

Campesinato goiano . Brandão, Carlos Rodrigues. Goiânia , 1986. 156 p. ; ISBN 85-85003-42-1 : LC Card 87-403866 DDC 305.5/63 19
HD1531.B7 B713 1986

Campfens, Mies. Op een beteren weg . Amsterdam , 1985. 239 p. : ISBN 90-6012-654-8 : LC Card 85-236523
HD8516 .O6 1985 *NYPL [JLD 86-3427]*

Campillo Martín, M. L. Ruiz Avilés, Pedro. Estudio integral de la Sierra de Segura . [Jaén] [1985] 130 leaves : ISBN 84-505-1249-2 LC Card 86-187282
HC387.S438 R85 1985

Campino, Antonio Carlos Coelho. Economia da alimentação e nutrição : (noções básicas) / Antonio Carlos Coelho Campino. São Paulo : Instituto de Pesquisas Econômicas, 1985. 238 p. : ill. ; 22 cm. (Série Ensaios econômicos . v. 42) Includes bibliographies. LC Card 86-129956 DDC 338.1/9/81 19
1. Food supply - Brazil. 2. Food consumption - Brazil. I. Series: Ensaios econômicos (Universidade de São Paulo. Instituto de Pesquisas Econômicas) , 42. II. Title.
HD9014.B82 C35 1985
NYPL [JLD 86-4118]

Recursos e desempenhos dos programas de formação de mão-de-obra / Antônio Carlos Coelho Campino, Maria Cristina Cacciamali, Otto Nogami. São Paulo, SP : Nobel ; Brasília, DF : Ministério do Trabalho, 1985. 78 p. ; 21 cm. (Coleção Estudos econômicos e sociais) Includes bibliographical references. ISBN 85-21-30276-2 LC Card 85-187505
1. Manpower policy - Brazil. I. Cacciamali, Maria Cristina. II. Nogami, Otto. III. Title. IV. Series.
HD5754 .C34 1985

Campo, Carlos Patricio del. Oliveira, Plinio Corrêa de, 1908- A propriedade privada e a livre iniciativa no tufão agro-reformista /. [São Paulo] [1985] xvi, 174 p., [16] p. of plates : LC Card 87-104428
HD1333.B6 O385 1985

Campo, Hugo del, 1941- El "Sindicalismo revolucionario," 1905-1945 /. Buenos Aires , c1986. 153 p. ; ISBN 950-25-1424-6 : LC Card 87-125439 DDC 335/.82/0982 19
HD6602 .S49 1986

CAMPOBELLO DI MAZARA (SICILY) - FOREIGN POPULATION - STATISTICS.
Vizzini, Sergio. Indagine socio-demografica sugli immigrati stranieri in Sicilia . Palermo [1983] 108 p. ; LC Card 86-131931
HB3600.M39 V58 1983

Campomanes, Pedro de. see **Campomanes, Pedro Rodríguez, Conde de, 1723-1803.**

Campomanes, Pedro Rodríguez, Conde de, 1723-1803. Bosquejo de política económica española : delineado sobre el estado presente de sus intereses / Conde de Campomanes ; edición preparada por Jorge Cejudo. Madrid : Editora Nacional, c1984. 182 p. ; 19 cm. (Biblioteca de la literatura y el pensamiento hispánicos. 67) Includes bibliographical references. ISBN 84-276-0691-5 : LC Card 86-153508
1. Economics - Spain - History - 18th century. I. Cejudo López, Jorge. II. Title.
HB117.A2 C34 1984

Camponeses /. Moura, Margarida Maria. São Paulo , 1986. 78 p. ; ISBN 85-08-01089-3 LC Card 86-230194
HD1531.B7 M68 1986

Camponeses e economia rural em Moçambique [microform] /. Wuyts, Marc. Maputo , 1978. 31, A1-A6 p. ; LC Card 80-980386 DDC 338.1/0967/9 19
HD2129 .W89 1978
*NYPL [*ZT-1564 no.14]*

Campos, José Hypólito Machado de. BRDE, a ação governamental na promoção do desenvolvimento econômico e social da Região Sul / José Hypólito Machado de Campos. Porto Alegre : Banco Regional de Desenvolvimento do Extremo Sul, [between 1983 and 1985] 51 p. ; 22 cm. Cover title. LC Card 86-143903
1. Banco Regional de Desenvolvimento do Extremo sul. 2. Development banks - Brazil, South. 3. Brazil, South - Economic policy. 4. Brazil, South - Social policy. I. Banco Regional de Desenvolvimento do Extremo sul. II. Title.
HG2889.S6 C36 1983

Campos, Luis A. (Luis Alberto), 1949- Pequeños campesinos y su incertidumbre : estudios regionales sobre el desarrollo socio-económico rural en el Paraguay / Luis A. Campos, Basilio Nikiphoroff, Ricardo Rodríguez Silvero. Asunción, Paraguay : El Lector, [1986] 224 p. : ill. ; 19 cm. (Colección economía. 2) Includes bibliographies. LC Card 87-400281 DDC 305.5/63 19
1. Peasantry - Paraguay - Case studies. 2. Peasantry - Paraguay - Itapúa - Case studies. 3. Peasantry - Paraguay - Guairá. 4. Peasantry - Paraguay - Caazapá (Dept.). 5. Agriculture - Economic aspects - Paraguay - Paraguari (Dept.). I. Nikiphoroff, Basilio, 1945-. II. Rodríguez Silvero, Ricardo. III. Series: Colección Economía (Asunción, Paraguay) , 2. IV. Title.
HD1531.P3 C36 1986

Campos Netto, José Candido de, 1880-1963. O cavvaliere Aristides Germani / Campos Netto ; [capa, Valdir dos Santos]. 3. ed. [Caxias do Sul, Brazil] : Universidade de Caxias do Sul ; [Porto Alegre] : Escola Superior de Teologia São Lourenço de Brindes, 1978. 111 p. : ill. ; 23 cm. (Coleção Imigração e colonização : Imigração italiana ; 27) LC Card 79-121861
1. Germani, Aristides, b. 1863. 2. Flour and feed trade - Brazil. 3. Flour-mills - Brazil - Management. 4. Manufacturers - Brazil - Biography. 5. Businessmen - Brazil - Biography. 6. Industrialists - Brazil - Biography. I. Series: Coleção Imigração italiana, 27. II. Title.
HD9056.B62 C35 1978 *NYPL [JLD 81-342]*

Camposortega Cruz, Sergio. El método de los componentes demográficos para realizar proyecciones de población. México, D.F. : Secretaría de Gobernación, Consejo Nacional de Población, [1984] 35 p. : ill. ; 21 cm. "Trabajo elaborado por Sergio Camposortega Cruz, investigador del Consejo Nacional de Población"--P. 5. "Junio de 1984." "Conferencia Internacional de Población, México, 1984"--P. 4 of cover. Bibliography: p. 35. LC Card 85-164750
1. Population forecasting. I. Consejo Nacional de Población (Mexico). II. Title.
HB849.53 .C36 1984

Campus Forschung. Schwerpunktreihe Hochschulforschung und Hochschuldidaktik. Akademikertätigkeit im Wandel . Frankfurt [am Main] , New York , c1984. 237 p. ; ISBN 3-593-33321-X LC Card 84-176630
HD6278.G4 A36 1984

Campus Forschung. Schwerpunktreihe "Marketing und Verbraucherarbeit" . (Bd. 3) Riemer, Martin. Beschwerdemanagement /. Frankfurt , New York , c1986. 295 p. ; ISBN 3-593-33756-8 LC Card 87-129210 DDC 658.8/12 19
HF5415.3 .R45 1986

The campus troublemakers . Theodore, Athena. Houston, Tex. , c1986. xxiv, 293 p. ; ISBN 0-88105-066-0 : LC Card 85-14973 DDC 378/.12/088042 19
LB2332.3 .T44 1986 *NYPL [JLE 86-4389]*

CAMS [i. e. Council for Asian Manpower Studies] see **Council for Asian Manpower Studies.**

Camus, Michel. L'expérience pénivauxoise, 1971-1982 : de la croissance au développement / Michel Camus, Jean-Marc Fossorier ; préface de Jacques Austruy ; avant-propos de Louis Augier. [Vaux-le-Pénil : La Ville, 1982] 187 p., [8] p. of plates : ill. ; 22 cm. LC Card 84-190663
1. Vaux-le-Pénil (France) - Economic conditions. 2. Vaux-le-Pénil (France) - Politics and government. I. Fossorier, Jean-Marc. II. Title.
HC277.V35 C36 1982

Can international comparisons of air fares be made? /. Forsyth, P. (Peter) Canberra, Australia [1985] 35 p. ; ISBN 0-949293-46-6 (pbk.) LC Card 86-212326 DDC 387.7/12 19
HE9783 .F67 1985

Can rail save the city? . Hall, Peter, 1931- Aldershot, Hants , Brookfield, Vt., U. S.A. , c1985. xii, 241 p. : ISBN 0-566-00947-1 : LC Card 85-17659 DDC 388.4/2/0943 19
HE4774 .H35 1985 *NYPL [JLD 86-2622]*

Can the CAP be reformed? / editor, Jacques Pelkmans. Maastricht, The Netherlands : European Institut of Public Administration, c1985. xii, 127 p. ; 24 cm. (Working papers / European Institute of Public Administration. EIPA 85/02 =) Includes bibliographies. ISBN 90-6779-013-3 (pbk.) LC Card 86-214732 DDC 338.1/84 19
1. Agriculture and state - European Economic Community countries. I. Pelkmans, Jacques. II. Series. III. Series: Documents de travail (European Institute of Public Administration).
HD1920.5 .C36 1985

Canada. Advisory Council on the Status of Women. Armstrong, Pat, 1945- A working majority . Ottawa, Ont. , c1983. v, 280 p. : ISBN 0-660-11314-7 (pbk.) : LC Card 83-158188 DDC 331.4/0971 19
HD6067.2.C2 A75 1983
NYPL [JLD 86-1585]

Canada. Affirmative Action Division. Cohen, Leah. A summary of the American experience with the Federal Contract Compliance Program . [Ottawa] , 1979. 72 leaves ;
NYPL [JLF 86-1657]

Canada. Anti-inflation Board. The Determinants of negotiated wage settlements in Canada (1966-1975) . [Ottawa] , Hull, Quebec , c1979. x, 256 p. : ISBN 0-660-10162-9 : LC Card 79-313202 DDC 331.2/971
HD4979 .D44 *NYPL [JLE 80-447]*

CANADA - APPROPRIATIONS AND EXPENDITURES.
Guide to the policy & expenditure management system. [Ottawa] , c1980. 33, 33 p. ; ISBN 0-662-51109-3 (pbk.) LC Card 81-116818
HJ7660 .G85 1980

CANADA - CENSUS.
Statistics Canada. Demography Division. Population estimation methods, Canada. Ottawa , c1987. 117 p. : ISBN 0-660-12028-3 (pbk.) : LC Card 87-168812 DDC 304.6/0724 19
HB3529 .S73 1987

Canada. Census Division. For publications,see: **Canada. Statistics Canada.**

CANADA - CENSUS, 1981.
Boxhill, Walton O. 1981 Census information on place of birth, citizenship, and immigration . Ottawa , c1986. 67, [4] p. : ISBN 0-660-52864-9 (pbk.) : LC Card 86-192857
HA741.5 1981f

CANADA - COMMERCE.
Daly, D. J. (Donald James), 1922- Canadian manufactured exports . Montreal, Quebec , c1986. xxviii, 180 p. ; ISBN 0-88645-025-X (pbk.) : LC Card 87-142389 DDC 382/.4567/0971 19
HF3226.5 .D26 1986

Technology and commodity trade [microform] /. Ottawa , c1984. 40 p. : ISBN 0-660-11447-X (pbk.) : LC Card 85-132672 DDC 382/.4562/000971 19
HC120.T4 T43 1984
*NYPL [*ZT-1745 no.16]*

CANADA - COMMERCE - HISTORY.
Bliss, Michael. Northern enterprise . Toronto, Ont. , c1987. 640 p. : ISBN 0-7710-1577-1 : LC Card 87-151013 DDC 380.1/0971 19
HF3224 .B65 1987

CANADA - COMMERCE - PACIFIC AREA.
MacKay, Donald, 1925- The Asian dream . Vancouver , c1986. 223 p. : ISBN 0-88894-501-9 LC Card 86-225670 DDC 385/.0971 19
HE2810.C14 M33 1986

CANADA - COMMERCE - UNITED STATES.
Wonnacott, Ronald J. Canada/United States free trade . Toronto, Ont. , c1985. 30 p. ; ISBN 0-7729-0036-1 (pbk.) LC Card 86-673986
HF1480.5.U57 W66x 1985

CANADA - COMMERCIAL POLICY.
Barber, Clarence L., 1917- Manitoba's interest in and attitude towards a proposed Canada-United States free trade area . [Winnipeg , 1985] 35 leaves : LC Card 86-175828 DDC 382/.0971/073 19
HF1479 .B37 1985

The Free trade papers /. Toronto , 1986. l [i.e. 50], 227 p. : ISBN 0-88862-972-9 LC Card 87-109310 DDC 382.7/1/0971 19
HF1479 .F74 1986

MacCharles, Donald C. (Donald Clare), 1935- Trade among multinationals . London , New York , c1987. xiv, 207 p. ; ISBN 0-7099-4618-X

LC Card 87-9077 DDC 382/.3 19
HF1411 .M2325 1987

Mathewson, G. Frank, 1942- Competition policy and vertical exchange /. Toronto , Buffalo , c1985. xvii, 119 p. : ISBN 0-8020-7248-8 (pbk.) LC Card 86-672936 DDC 338.6/048/0971 19
HF1480 .M37 1985 ***NYPL [JLE 87-512]***

Wonnacott, Paul. The United States and Canada . Washington, DC , 1987. xii, 173 p. : ISBN 0-88132-056-0 (pbk.) : LC Card 87-2660 DDC 382.71073 19
HF1456.5.C2 W65 1987

Wonnacott, Ronald J. Canada/United States free trade . Toronto, Ont. , c1985. 30 p. ; ISBN 0-7729-0036-1 (pbk.) LC Card 86-673986
HF1480.5.U57 W66x 1985

CANADA - COMMERCIAL POLICY - HISTORY - 19TH CENTURY.
Forster, Jakob Johann Benjamin. A conjunction of interests . Toronto , Buffalo , c1986. vi, 288 p. ; ISBN 0-8020-5680-6 (alk. paper) LC Card 87-108915 DDC 382.7/0971 19
HF1765 .F67 1986

Canada. Commission de la lutte contre l'inflation. see **Canada. Anti-inflation Board.**

Canada. Commission de lutte contre l'inflation. see **Canada. Anti-inflation Board.**

Canada. Commission of Inquiry on the Pharmaceutical Industry. Martin, Fernand. La localisation de l'industrie pharmaceutique au Canada /. [Ottawa] , c1986. 48 p. ; ISBN 0-662-93544-6 LC Card 86-206756
HD9670.C22 M37 1986

Canada. Commission of Inquiry on Unemployment Insurance. Newfoundland. Submission to the Federal Commission of Inquiry on Unemployment Insurance /. [St. John's] [1985] 63, vi p. : LC Card 86-215851 DDC 368.4/4/009718 19
HD7096.C2 N48 1985

Canada. Commission royale d'enquête sur la situation de la femme au Canada. see **Canada. Royal Commission on the Status of Women in Canada.**

Canada. Conseil consultatif de la situation de la femme. see **Canada. Advisory Council on the Status of Women.**

Canada. Dept. of Fisheries and the Environment. Lands Directorate. see **Canada. Lands Directorate.**

Canada. Dept. of Industry, Trade and Commerce. (Old Catalog form: Canada. Industry, Trade and Commerce, Dept. of)
Incentive and development programs for Canadian industry. Ottawa, Canada , 1973, c1975. 14, 14 p. ; LC Card 85-158119
HC120.I53 I48 1975

Canada. Dept. of the Environment. Lands Directorate. see **Canada. Lands Directorate.**

Canada. Dept. of Transport. Transportation Development Agency. see **Canada. Transportation Development Agency.**

CANADA - ECONOMIC CONDITIONS.
Perspectives on Canadian economic history /. Toronto , c1987. 287 p. : ISBN 0-7730-4679-8 LC Card 87-168012 DDC 330.971 19
HC113 .P47 1987

CANADA - ECONOMIC CONDITIONS - 1945-
The Agenda for economic renewal . [Ottawa] [1987] 25, 26 p. : LC Card 87-140803 DDC 338.971 19
HC115 .A624 1987

Brunelle, Dorval. L'Etat solide . Montréal, Québec , 1982. 174 p. : ISBN 2-89132-677-6 (pbk.) LC Card 87-672120
HC115 .B773x 1982

Campbell, Robert Malcolm. Grand illusions . Peterborough, Canada , Lewiston, N.Y. , c1987. 270 p. ; ISBN 0-921149-03-4 LC Card 87-147385 DDC 338.971 19
HC115 .C16 1987

The Canadian economy . Toronto, Ont., Canada , c1987. xiii, 474 p. ; ISBN 0-7715-5515-6 (pbk.) : LC Card 87-130572 DDC 330.971/0647 19
HC115 .C2463 1987

Gonick, Cy. The great economic debate . Toronto , 1987. xii, 425 p. : ISBN 0-88862-702-5 LC Card 87-144697 DDC 338.971 19
HC115 .G576 1987

Stuber, Gerald. The slowdown in productivity growth in the 1975-83 period . [Ottawa] [1986] 164 p. : LC Card 87-100880 DDC 338/.06/0971 19
HC120.I52 S78 1986

CANADA - ECONOMIC CONDITIONS - 1945- - CONGRESSES.
First Ministers' Conference (1985 : Halifax, N.S.) [Proceedings of the annual conference of First Ministers, held in Halifax, N.S., November 28-29, 1985]. [Canada , 1986-] portfolios <1-4 > : LC Card 86-201687 DDC 338.971 19
HC115 .F485 1985

CANADA - ECONOMIC CONDITIONS - 1945- - REGIONAL DISPARITIES.
Douglas, Gordon W. Energy and regional investment in Canada /. Calgary, Alta. [1983] x, 114 p. : ISBN 0-920522-28-9 (pbk.) : LC Card 83-160268 DDC 332.6/722 19
HD9502.C32 D68 1983 ***NYPL [JLD 87-996]***

CANADA - ECONOMIC CONDITIONS - 1945- - STATISTICS.
Morin, André, analyste en rémunération. Analyse de l'évolution des principaux indicateurs économiques au Québec, en Ontario, au Canada et aux Etats-Unis . [Québec] [1982] 209 p. ; ISBN 2-551-04641-6 LC Card 83-103355
HC117.Q4 M66 1982

CANADA - ECONOMIC POLICY.
The Agenda for economic renewal . [Ottawa] [1987] 25, 26 p. : LC Card 87-140803 DDC 338.971 19
HC115 .A624 1987

Brunelle, Dorval. L'Etat solide . Montréal, Québec , 1982. 174 p. : ISBN 2-89132-677-6 (pbk.) LC Card 87-672120
HC115 .B773x 1982

Campbell, Robert Malcolm. Grand illusions . Peterborough, Canada , Lewiston, N.Y. , c1987. 270 p. ; ISBN 0-921149-03-4 LC Card 87-147385 DDC 338.971 19
HC115 .C16 1987

The Canadian economy . Toronto, Ont., Canada , c1987. xiii, 474 p. ; ISBN 0-7715-5515-6 (pbk.) : LC Card 87-130572 DDC 330.971/0647 19
HC115 .C2463 1987

Canadian industrial policy in action /. Toronto , Buffalo , c1985. xvii, 231 p. : ISBN 0-8020-7244-5 (pbk.) LC Card 86-672572
HD3616.C23 C36x 1985 ***NYPL [JLD 86-2871]***

Daly, D. J. (Donald James), 1922- On real wage unemployment /. Vancouver, B.C., Canada , 1986. vi, 117 p. : ISBN 0-88975-079-3 (pbk.) LC Card 87-142391 DDC 331.13/7971 19
HD4946.C3 D35 1986

Economic and regional development agreements . [Ottawa?] [1985] 11, 12, [8] p. : LC Card 86-214896 DDC 338.971 19
HC113 .E26 1985

Gonick, Cy. The great economic debate . Toronto , 1987. xii, 425 p. : ISBN 0-88862-702-5 LC Card 87-144697 DDC 338.971 19
HC115 .G576 1987

Hampson, Fen Osler. Forming economic policy . London , 1986. x, 161 p. : ISBN 0-86187-628-8 ***NYPL [JLE 86-3813]***

Laxer, James. Leap of faith . Edmonton , c1986. 140 p. ; ISBN 0-88830-298-3 : LC Card 87-101958 DDC 382.7/1/0971 19
HF1480.15.U5 L39 1986

Minding the public's business. [Ottawa] , 1986. xii, 180 p. : ISBN 0-660-12217-0 (pbk.) : LC Card 87-127219 DDC 338.971 19
HD4005 .M53 1986

Schultz, Richard, 1945- Economic regulation and the federal system /. Toronto , Buffalo , c1985. xv, 187 p. : ISBN 0-8020-7287-9 (pbk.) LC Card 86-672574
HD3616.C23 S38x 1985 ***NYPL [JLD 86-2821]***

Securing economic renewal . [Ottawa] [1987] 147, 161 p. : LC Card 87-144360 DDC 336.71 19
HJ793 .S43 1987

Swankey, Ben. The Tory budget and the corporate plan to restructure Canada, and how the system really works /. Vancouver , c1985. xi, 246 p. ; ISBN 0-920879-00-4 (pbk.) LC Card 86-209703 DDC 338.971 19
HJ2055 .S9 1985

CANADA - ECONOMIC POLICY - CONGRESSES.
First Ministers' Conference (1985 : Halifax, N.S.) [Proceedings of the annual conference of First Ministers, held in Halifax, N.S., November 28-29, 1985]. [Canada , 1986-] portfolios <1-4 > : LC Card 86-201687 DDC 338.971 19
HC115 .F485 1985

Canada. Employment and Immigration Canada (Commission). Glossary of terms . [Ottawa] [1981]-1984. 3 v. ; ISBN 0-662-52389-X (v. 2) LC Card 81-180363 DDC 350/.0003/41 19
JA61 .G55 ***NYPL [JLF 87-379]***

Canada. Energy, Mines and Resources Canada. Oil and natural gas industries in Canada, 1978. [Ottawa] , c1978. viii, 104 p. : LC Card 85-187299
HD9574.C22 O39 1978

Canada Environment Canada. Canada's environment . [Ottawa] , 1986. 20 p. : ISBN 0-662-14571-2 (pbk.) LC Card 86-222737 DDC 333.7/0971 19
HC120.E5 C345 1986

Canada. Film board. see **National Film Board of Canada.**

CANADA - FOREIGN ECONOMIC RELATIONS - JAPAN.
Canadian-Japanese economic relations in a triangular perspective /. Toronto , Scarborough, Ont. [1987] vi, 54 p. : ISBN 0-88806-139-0 (pbk.) LC Card 87-169818 DDC 337.52071 19
HF1480.15.J3 C35 1987

CANADA - FOREIGN ECONOMIC RELATIONS - SOVIET UNION.
SSSR, SShA i Kanada . Moskva , 1987. 325 p. ; LC Card 86-205359
HF3628.U5 S77 1987

CANADA - FOREIGN ECONOMIC RELATIONS - UNITED STATES.
Canadian-Japanese economic relations in a triangular perspective /. Toronto , Scarborough, Ont. [1987] vi, 54 p. : ISBN 0-88806-139-0 (pbk.) LC Card 87-169818 DDC 337.52071 19
HF1480.15.J3 C35 1987

Laxer, James. Leap of faith . Edmonton , c1986. 140 p. ; ISBN 0-88830-298-3 : LC Card 87-101958 DDC 382.7/1/0971 19
HF1480.15.U5 L39 1986

Wonnacott, Paul. The United States and Canada . Washington, DC , 1987. xii, 173 p. : ISBN 0-88132-056-0 (pbk.) : LC Card 87-2660 DDC 382.71073 19
HF1456.5.C2 W65 1987

CANADA - FOREIGN ECONOMIC RELATIONS - UNITED STATES - CONGRESSES.
Building a Canadian-American free trade area /. Washington, D.C. , c1987. xii, 217 p. ; ISBN 0-8157-2973-1 (pbk.) LC Card 87-71507 DDC 382/.0971/073 19
HF1480.15.U5 B85 1987

Canada. Foreign Investment Review Agency. Foreign Investment Division. Notes on some definitions of the multinational enterprise. Ottawa [1971] 31 leaves ; LC Card 82-210581
HD2755.5 .N68 1971

CANADA - FOREIGN POPULATION.
Boxhill, Walton O. 1981 Census information on place of birth, citizenship, and immigration . Ottawa , c1986. 67, [4] p. : ISBN 0-660-52864-9 (pbk.) : LC Card 86-192857
HA741.5 1981f

CANADA - FULL EMPLOYMENT POLICIES.
Bellan, Ruben C., 1918- The unnecessary evil . Toronto, Ont. , c1986. 173 p. : ISBN 0-7710-1153-9 : LC Card 86-222233 DDC 331.13/7971 19
HD5728 .B43 1986

CANADA - GENEALOGY - HANDBOOKS, MANUALS, ETC.

Burgess, Michael, 1948- The state and province vital records guide /. San Bernardino, Calif. , 1988. p. cm. ISBN 0-89370-815-1 : LC Card 87-6312 DDC 929/.1/02573 19
HA38 .B87 1988

Canada - Government. see **Canada - Politics and government.**

Canada. Health Manpower Section. For publications, see: **Canada. Statistics Canada.**

Canada. Indian and Northern Affairs Canada.
The Northern mineral sector . Ottawa [1985] 37, 37 p. : ISBN 0-662-53700-9 (pbk.) LC Card 85-162718 DDC 338.2/0971 19
HD9506.C23 N6758 1985 *NYPL [JLF 86-175]*

CANADA - INDUSTRIES.
Technological change in Canadian industry /. Toronto , Buffalo , c1985. xv, 233 p. ; ISBN 0-8020-7243-7 (pbk.) LC Card 86-164766 DDC 338/.06 19
HC120.T4 T42 1985 *NYPL [JLD 87-654]*

CANADA - INDUSTRIES - CLASSIFICATION.
Canadian standard industrial classification for companies and enterprises, 1980. Ottawa , c1986. xii, 381 p. ; ISBN 0-660-11945-5 : LC Card 87-120163 DDC 338/.02/0971 19
HC115 .C417 1986

CANADA - INDUSTRIES - STATISTICS.
Betcherman, Gordon. Working with technology . [Ottawa] , 1986. 43 p. : ISBN 0-660-12174-3 (pbk.) : LC Card 86-224095 DDC 338/.06 19
HC120.A9 B47 1986

Canada. Industry, Trade and Commerce.
Manufacturing performance. [Canada] [1977?] 18 p. : LC Card 85-194098
HD9734.C25 M36 1977

Canada. Industry, Trade and Commerce and Regional Economic Expansion. Canada. Task Force on the Canadian Motor Vehicle and Automotive Parts Industries. An automotive strategy for Canada . [Ottawa] , 1983. xv, 193 p. : ISBN 0-662-12626-2 *NYPL [JLF 86-648]*

Canada. Industry, Trade and Commerce, Dept. of. see **Canada. Dept. of Industry, Trade and Commerce.**

Canada. Labour Canada.
Accident investigation and reporting . [Ottawa] , c1986. 15, 16 p. : ISBN 0-662-54332-7 (pbk.) LC Card 86-201756
HD7262.25 .A28 1986

Employment injuries and occupational illnesses . Ottawa, Ont. , c1986. 92 p. ; ISBN 0-662-54738-1 (pbk.) LC Card 87-147113 DDC 363.1/12/0971 19
HD7262.5.C3 E463 1986

Twentieth joint conference . [Charlottetown, P.E.I. , 1986] 94 p. ; LC Card 87-147512 DDC 338/.06 19
HC120.T4 T84 1986

Canada. Labour Data Branch. Strikes and lockouts in Canada, 1973 /. Ottawa , 1975. 88 p. : ISBN 2-7114-5902-3 (pbk.) LC Card 82-212112
HD5328 .S77 1975

Canada. Lands Directorate.
Occasional paper.
(no.16) Gierman, D. M. Rural to urban land conversion =. [Ottawa] , Hull, Que. , c1977. xvii, 74 p. ; ISBN 0-662-01301-8
NYPL [JLM 80-106 no.16]

CANADA - MANUFACTURES.
Daly, D. J. (Donald James), 1922- Canadian manufactured exports . Montreal, Quebec , c1986. xxviii, 180 p. ; ISBN 0-88645-025-X (pbk.) : LC Card 87-142389 DDC 382/.4567/0971 19
HF3226.5 .D26 1986

Manufacturing performance. [Canada] [1977?] 18 p. : LC Card 85-194098
HD9734.C25 M36 1977

CANADA - MANUFACTURES - ECONOMETRIC MODELS.
Abbott, Michael G. Male and female earnings in Canadian manufacturing, 1931 /. Kingston, Ont., Canada [1986] 82 p. ; LC Card 87-145991 DDC 331.2/87/0971 19
HD4979 .A22 1986

Dussault, François. Les modèles scandinaves et la détermination des ententes salariales des industries manufacturières canadiennes . Montréal [1982] 21, [11] p. ; LC Card 82-196710
HD4979 .D875 1982

CANADA - MANUFACTURES - PRICES.
Industrial product price indexes, 1981=100 . Ottawa , c1986. 216 p. : ISBN 0-660-52876-2 (pbk.) : LC Card 87-168891
HB235.C2 I53 1986

Canada. Minerals. Whillans, Robert T. Mineral exploration expenditures in Canada, 1969-1975 /. [Ottawa] , c1978. vi, 13 p. : LC Card 85-182002 DDC 338.2/3 19
HD9506.C2 W45 1978

Canada. National Film Board. see **National Film Board of Canada.**

CANADA, NORTHERN - ECONOMIC CONDITIONS.
Developing America's northern frontier /. Lanham, MD , c1987. xx, 250 p. ; ISBN 0-8191-6081-4 (alk. paper) : LC Card 86-28233 DDC 338.9719 19
HC117.N48 D48 1987

Saltykovskaīa, L. V. (Liliīa Veniaminovna) Blizhniĭ Sever Kanady . Moskva , 1983. 78, [2] p. : LC Card 83-196848
HC117.N48 S25 1983

CANADA, NORTHERN - ECONOMIC POLICY.
Developing America's northern frontier /. Lanham, MD , c1987. xx, 250 p. ; ISBN 0-8191-6081-4 (alk. paper) : LC Card 86-28233 DDC 338.9719 19
HC117.N48 D48 1987

The Northern mineral sector . Ottawa [1985] 37, 37 p. : ISBN 0-662-53700-9 (pbk.) LC Card 85-162718 DDC 338.2/0971 19
HD9506.C23 N6758 1985
NYPL [JLF 86-175]

Canada. Office national du film. see **National Film Board of Canada.**

Canada. Office of the Senior Advisor on Integration. For publications, see: **Canada. Statistics Canada.**

CANADA - POLITICS AND GOVERNMENT - 20TH CENTURY.
Osborne, Stephen. Social credit for beginners . Vancouver, Canada , c1986. 229, [1] p. : ISBN 0-88978-175-3 (pbk.) LC Card 87-122126 DDC 332.5/6/0971 19
HG355 .O83 1986

CANADA - POLITICS AND GOVERNMENT - 1945-
Brunelle, Dorval. L'Etat solide . Montréal, Québec , 1982. 174 p. : ISBN 2-89132-677-6 (pbk.) LC Card 87-672120
HC115 .B773x 1982

Canada. Population Estimates and Projections Division. For publications, see: **Canada. Statistics Canada.**

CANADA - POPULATION - STATISTICS.
Household and population projections for Canadian provinces and territories, 1981-2046. Edmonton, Alta., Canada , c1984. 53 p. ; LC Card 84-670146 DDC 312/.8/0971 19
HA745 .H69 1984 *NYPL [JLF 86-642]*

Revised annual estimates of population for census divisions, 1971-1976 /. Ottawa , c1979. 21 p. ; LC Card 82-216681
HA745 .R473 1979

Canada. Public Service Staff Relations Board. Bureau de recherches sur les traitements. see **Canada. Public Service Staff Relations Board. Pay Research Bureau.**

Canada. Public Service Staff Relations Board. Pay Research Bureau. Hanson, R. Employee benefits and conditions of employment in Canada . [Ottawa, Ont.] , c1977. iv, 111 p. : ISBN 0-662-00630-5 (pbk.) LC Card 82-136152
HD4928.N62 C225 1977

Canada. Royal Commission on the Status of Women in Canada. Report of the Royal Commission on the Status of Women in Canada. [Ottawa, Ont.] : The Commission, 1970. xii, 488 p. : ill. ; 23 cm.
1. Women - Canada - Social conditions. 2. Women's rights - Canada. I. Title. *NYPL [JLE 73-1102]*

CANADA - SOCIAL POLICY.
Fiscal federalism /. Toronto , Buffalo , c1986. xvi, 211 p. ; ISBN 0-8020-7312-3 (pbk.)
HJ793 .F59 1986 *NYPL [JLE 86-3253]*

CANADA - STATISTICAL SERVICES - HISTORY.
Cook, W. Rupert. Canadian statistical data . [Canada] [1985?] vi, 218 p. : LC Card 87-118992 DDC 354.710081/9 19
HA37.C26 C66 1985

Canada. Statistics Canada. All publications of various subdivisions are entered directly under Statistics Canada.

Canada. Statistics Canada. Agriculture Division. For publications, see: **Canada. Statistics Canada.**

Canada. Statistics Canada. Balance of Payments Section. For publications, see: **Canada. Statistics Canada.**

Canada. Statistics Canada. Census Division. For publications, see: **Canada. Statistics Canada.**

Canada. Statistics Canada. Consumer Finance Research Staff. For publications, see: **Canada. Statistics Canada.**

Canada. Statistics Canada. Consumer Income and Expenditure Division. For publications, see: **Canada. Statistics Canada.**

Canada. Statistics Canada. Crops Section. For publications, see: **Canada. Statistics Canada.**

Canada. Statistics Canada. Cultural Information Section. For publications, see: **Canada. Statistics Canada.**

Canada. Statistics Canada. Education Division. For publications, see: **Canada. Statistics Canada.**

Canada. Statistics Canada. Education, Science and Culture Division. For publications, see: **Canada. Statistics Canada.**

Canada. Statistics Canada. Elementary-Secondary Education Section. For publications, see: **Canada. Statistics Canada.**

Canada. Statistics Canada. Employment Section. For publications, see: **Canada. Statistics Canada.**

Canada. Statistics Canada. External Trade Commission. For publications, see: **Canada. Statistics Canada.**

Canada. Statistics Canada. External Trade Division. For publications, see: **Canada. Statistics Canada.**

Canada. Statistics Canada. Facilities Section. For publications, see: **Canada. Statistics Canada.**

Canada. Statistics Canada. Farm Income and Prices Section. For publications, see: **Canada. Statistics Canada.**

Canada. Statistics Canada. Federal Government Section. For publications, see: **Canada. Statistics Canada.**

Canada. Statistics Canada. Financial Information Section. For publications, see: **Canada. Statistics Canada.**

Canada. Statistics Canada. General Time Series Staff. For publications, see: **Canada. Statistics Canada.**

Canada. Statistics Canada. Governments Division. For publications, see: **Canada. Statistics Canada.**

Canada. Statistics Canada. Industrial Corporations Section. For publications, see: **Canada. Statistics Canada.**

Canada. Statistics Canada. Industrial Output Section. For publications, see: **Canada. Statistics Canada.**

Canada. Statistics Canada. Institutions Section. For publications, see: **Canada. Statistics Canada.**

Canada. Statistics Canada. Job Vacancy Survey section. For publications, see: **Canada. Statistics Canada.**

Canada. Statistics Canada. Judicial Division. For publications, see: **Canada. Statistics Canada.**

Canada. Statistics Canada. Justice Statistics Division. For publications, see: **Canada. Statistics Canada.**

Canada. Statistics Canada. Labour Division. For publications, see: **Canada. Statistics Canada.**

Canada. Statistics Canada. Labour Force Surveys Section. For publications, see: **Canada. Statistics Canada.**

Canada. Statistics Canada. Livestock and Animal Products Section. For publications, see: **Canada. Statistics Canada.**

Canada. Statistics Canada. Manpower Research and Development Section. For publications, see: **Canada. Statistics Canada.**

Canada. Statistics Canada. Manufacturing and Primary Industries Division. For publications, see: **Canada. Statistics Canada.**

Canada. Statistics Canada. Merchandising and Services Division. For publications, see: **Canada. Statistics Canada.**

Canada. Statistics Canada. National Income and Expenditure Division. For publications, see: **Canada. Statistics Canada.**

Canada. Statistics Canada. Pensions Section. For publications, see: **Canada. Statistics Canada.**

Canada. Statistics Canada. Prices Division. For publications, see: **Canada. Statistics Canada.**

Canada. Statistics Canada. Projections Section. For publications, see: **Canada. Statistics Canada.**

Canada. Statistics Canada. Provincial Government Section. For publications, see: **Canada. Statistics Canada.**

Canada. Statistics Canada. Public Finance Division. For publications, see: **Canada. Statistics Canada.**

Canada. Statistics Canada. Public Health Section. For publications, see: **Canada. Statistics Canada.**

Canada. Statistics Canada. Public Utilities Section. For publications, see: **Canada. Statistics Canada.**

Canada. Statistics Canada. Science Statistics Section. For publications, see: **Canada. Statistics Canada.**

Canada. Statistics Canada. Sciences and Technology Statistics Division. Technology and commodity trade [microform] /. Ottawa , c1984. 40 p. : ISBN 0-660-11447-X (pbk.) : LC Card 85-132672 DDC 382/.4562/000971 19
HC120.T4 T43 1984
NYPL [*ZT-1745 no.16]

Canada. Statistics Canada. Special Cate Facilities Section. For publications, see: **Canada. Statistics Canada.**

Canada. Statistics Canada. Special Studies and Publications Section. For publications, see: **Canada. Statistics Canada.**

Canada. Statistics Canada. Special Surveys and Quality Control Section. For publications, see: **Canada. Statistics Canada.**

Canada. Statistics Canada. Statistics Canada. Postsecondary Education Section. For information see: **Canada. Statistics Canada.**

Canada. Statistics Canada. Student Information Section. For publications, see: **Canada. Statistics Canada.**

Canada. Statistics Canada. Surface Transport Section. For publications, see: **Canada. Statistics Canada.**

Canada. Statistics Canada. Teacher Information Section. For publications, see: **Canada. Statistics Canada.**

Canada. Statistics Canada. Transportation Section. For publications, see: **Canada. Statistics Canada.**

Canada. Statistics Canada. Unemployment Insurance and Manpower Section. For publications, see: **Canada. Statistics Canada.**

Canada. Statistics Canada. Vital Statistics Section. For publications, see: **Canada. Statistics Canada.**

Canada. Statistics Canada. Wholesale Trade Section. For publications, see: **Canada. Statistics Canada.**

Canada. Statistics Canafa. Vocational and Continunig Education Section. For publications,see: **Canada. Statistics Canada.**

Canada. Statistique Canada. see **Canada. Statistics Canada.**

Canada. Status of Women, Advisory Council on the. see **Canada. Advisory Council on the Status of Women.**

Canada. Status of Women in Canada, Royal Commission on the. see **Canada. Royal Commission on the Status of Women in Canada.**

Canada. Supply and Services Canada. Guide to the policy & expenditure management system. [Ottawa] , c1980. 33, 33 p. ; ISBN 0-662-51109-3 (pbk.) LC Card 81-116818
HJ7660 .G85 1980

Canada. Tariff Board. Relating to the reinstatement of the general preferential tariff on imports of rubber footwear : [a report / by the Tariff Board]. Ottawa, Canada : Minister of Supply and Services Canada, c1985. vi, 88 p. ; 26 cm. (Reference . 161.1) "Catalogue No. FT 4-161/1E"--T.p. verso. ISBN 0-660-11961-7 (pbk.) : LC Card 87-109471 DDC 382/.0971 s 382/.4568531/00971 19
1. Tariff on rubber footwear - Canada. 2. Footwear industry - Government policy - Canada. I. Series: Reference (Canada. Tariff Board) , 161.1. II. Title.
HF1762 .A3 no. 161, pt. 1 HF2651.F757C22

Canada. Task Force on Broadcasting Policy. Report of the Task Force on Broadcasting Policy. [Toronto] : Minister of Supply and Services Canada, c1986. 730 p. : ill. ; 25 cm. Includes bibliographies. ISBN 0-660-12164-6 (pbk.) : LC Card 86-231885 DDC 384.54/0971 19
1. Radio broadcasting - Government policy - Canada. 2. Television broadcasting - Government policy - Canada. I. Title.
HE8689.9.C3 C37 1986

Canada. Task Force on Program Review. Environmental quality strategic review . [Ottawa, Canada , c1986. 170 p. ; ISBN 0-660-12148-4 (pbk.) : LC Card 86-217056 DDC 363.7/00971 19
HC120.E5 E59 1986

Canada. Task Force on the Canadian Motor Vehicle and Automotive Parts Industries. An automotive strategy for Canada : report of the Federal Task Force on the Canadian Motor Vehicle and Automotive Parts Industries to Hon. Edward C. Lumley, P.C., M.P., Minister of Industry, Trade and Commerce and Regional Economic Expansion. [Ottawa] : Minister of Supply and Services Canada, 1983. xv, 193 p. : ill. ; 28 cm. "May 1983." "Cat. No. C 2-73/1983E." ISBN 0-662-12626-2
1. Automobile industry and trade - Canada. 2. Automobile industry and trade - Government policy - Canada. I. Canada. Industry, Trade and Commerce and Regional Economic Expansion. II. Title.
NYPL [JLF 86-648]

Canada. Transportation Development Agency. Brouillette, Benoît, 1904-1979. [Perspectives de changements dans la manutention des marchandises aux ports canadiens. English.] Prospective changes for handling of commodities in Canadian ports. Montréal, Québec, Canada [1974] iv, 93, [3] p. ; LC Card 82-219246
HE553 .B7613 1974

Canada/United States free trade . Wonnacott, Ronald J. Toronto, Ont. , c1985. 30 p. ; ISBN 0-7729-0036-1 (pbk.) LC Card 86-673986
HF1480.5.U57 W66x 1985

Canada's environment : an overview. [Ottawa] : Environment Canada, 1986. 20 p. : ill. (some col.), maps ; 28 cm. Cover title. "Catalogue No. EN 21-54/1986-IE"--T.p. verso. ISBN 0-662-14571-2 (pbk.) LC Card 86-222737 DDC 333.7/0971 19
1. Environmental policy - Canada. 2. Natural resources - Canada. I. Canada Environment Canada.
HC120.E5 C345 1986

Canada's mystery man of high finance . How, Douglas. [Very private person.] Hantsport, N.S. , 1986. 173 p. : ISBN 0-88999-305-X (pbk.) LC Card 86-207291 DDC 338.092/2 B 19
HG172.K55 H68 1986

Canadian Advisory Council on the Status of Women. see **Canada. Advisory Council on the Status of Women.**

CANADIAN COMMERCIAL BANK.
Estey, Willard Z. Report of the inquiry into the collapse of the CCB and Northland Bank /. Ottawa, Canada , c1986. xiii, 641 p. : ISBN 0-660-12171-9 (pbk.) : LC Card 87-134617 DDC 332.1/2/0971 19
HG2708.C36 E89 1986

Johnson, Arthur, 1951- Breaking the banks /. Toronto, Canada , c1986. xi, 256 p. ; ISBN 0-88619-072-X LC Card 87-120151 DDC 332.1/2/0971 19
HG2708.C36 J64 1986

Canadian commercial lending . Hatch, James E. Toronto , New York , c1986. ix, 262 p. : ISBN 0-458-80270-0 : LC Card 87-130576 DDC 332.1/753/0685 19
HG3754.5.C2 H38 1986

Canadian corporate social performance . Brooks, Leonard J. Hamilton, Ont. , 1986. xii, 267 p. : ISBN 0-920212-54-9 (pbk.) LC Card 87-100492 DDC 658.4/08/0971 19
HD60.5.C2 B76 1986

The Canadian economy : a regional perspective / edited by Donald J. Savoie. Toronto ; New York : Methuen, c1986. 291 p. : ill. ; 23 cm. Includes bibliographies and index. ISBN 0-458-99950-4 (pbk.) : LC Card 86-218828 DDC 338.971 19
1. Regional planning - Canada. 2. Federal government - Canada. I. Savoie, Donald J.
HC113 .C37 1986

The Canadian economy : problems and policies / G.C. Ruggeri.3rd ed. Toronto, Ont., Canada : Gage, c1987. xiii, 474 p. ; 23 cm. Bibliography: p. 468-474. ISBN 0-7715-5515-6 (pbk.) : LC Card 87-130572 DDC 330.971/0647 19
1. Canada - Economic conditions - 1945-. 2. Canada - Economic policy. I. Ruggeri, G. C.
HC115 .C2463 1987

CANADIAN ENERGY RESEARCH INSTITUTE.
Reinsch, Anthony Ernest. Industrial cogeneration in Canada . Calgary, Alta. [1987] xviii, 137 p. : ISBN 0-920522-41-6 (pbk.) : LC Card 87-163062 DDC 333.79/3 19
HD9685.C2 R45 1987

Canadian farming : an encyclopaedia of agriculture / being the report of the Ontario Agricultural Commission. Toronto : C. Blackett Robinson, 1881. 432 p., [4] folded leaves of plates : ill. ; 23 cm. LC Card 85-666092
1. Agriculture - Canada. 2. Crops - Canada. 3. Livestock - Canada. I. Ontario Agricultural Commission.
HD1783 .C3x 1881

Canadian financial markets /. Hunter, W. T. Peterborough, Canada , c1986. 193 p. : ISBN 0-921149-01-8 (pbk.) LC Card 86-206029 DDC 332.6/0973 19
HG185.C2 H86 1986

Canadian industrial policy in action / D.G. McFetridge, research coordinator. Toronto ; Buffalo : University of Toronto Press, c1985. xvii, 231 p. : ill. ; 23 cm. (The Collected research studies, 0829-2396 . vol. 4) "Published ... in cooperation with the Royal Commission on the Economic Union and Development Prospects for Canada and the Canadian Government Publishing Centre, Supply and Services Canada." Includes bibliographies. CONTENTS. - The economics of industrial policy / D.G. McFetridge -- The impact of government intervention on the major appliance industry in Canada / Harold Crookell -- Crown corporations and economic efficiency / Sanford F. Borins and Barry E.C. Boothman -- An agenda for research on financial markets / John Chant -- Economic regulation in Canada / Keith Acheson -- Commercial and political efficiency / D.G. McFetridge. ISBN 0-8020-7244-5 (pbk.) LC Card 86-672572
1. Industry and state - Canada. 2. Government business enterprises - Canada. 3. Canada - Economic policy. I. McFetridge, D. G., 1945-. II. Royal Commission on the Economic Union and Development Prospects for Canada.
HD3616.C23 C36x 1985
NYPL [JLD 86-2871]

Canadian Institute of Chartered Accountants. CICA handbook. Vézina, Pierre, 1935- Foreign currency translation : an analysis of section 1650 of the CICA handbook / Pierre Vézina. Toronto, Canada , c1985. 94 p. ; ISBN 0-88800-133-9 LC Card 86-201703 DDC

657/.48 19
HG3853.7 .V49 1985

Canadian Institute of Mining and Metallurgy. Mineral Economics Committee. Selected readings in mineral economics /. New York , c1987. ix, 399 p. : ISBN 0-08-035864-0 : LC Card 87-8237 DDC 338.2/0971 19
HD9506.C22 S44 1987

Canadian International Development Agency. Ebanks, G. E. Mortality, fertility, and family planning . Santiago, Chile [1985] 123 p. ; LC Card 87-131697 DDC 304.6/2/09729841 19
HB1376.D65 E32 1985

Canadian-Japanese economic relations in a triangular perspective / edited by Wendy Dobson. Toronto : C.D. Howe Institute ; Scarborough, Ont. : Available from Prentice-Hall Canada, [1987] vi, 54 p. : ill. ; 21 cm. (Observation, 0826-9947 . no. 30) Includes bibliographical references. CONTENTS. - A Canadian perspective / by Wendy Dobson -- A Japanese perspective / by Hideo Sato. ISBN 0-88806-139-0 (pbk.) LC Card 87-169818 DDC 337.52071 19
1. Canada - Foreign economic relations - Japan. 2. Japan - Foreign economic relations - Canada. 3. Canada - Foreign economic relations - United States. 4. United States - Foreign economic relations - Canada. 5. Japan - Foreign economic relations - United States. 6. United States - Foreign economic relations - Japan. I. Dobson, Wendy. II. Dobson, Wendy. Canadian perspective. 1987. III. Sato, Hideo, 1942- Japanese perspective. 1987. IV. Series.
HF1480.15.J3 C35 1987

The Canadian library in Ukrainian studies. Famine in Ukraine, 1932-1933 /. Edmonton , Downsview, Ont., Canada , 1986. 192 p. ; ISBN 0-09-286243-8 LC Card 87-148658 DDC 363.8/0947/71 19
HC337.U53 F314 1986

Canadian manufactured exports . Daly, D. J. (Donald James), 1922- Montreal, Quebec , c1986. xxviii, 180 p. ; ISBN 0-88645-025-X (pbk.) : LC Card 87-142389 DDC 382/.4567/0971 19
HF3226.5 .D26 1986

Canadian Mining Institute. see **Canadian Institute of Mining and Metallurgy.**

Canadian mortgage payments /. Solomon, Stephen S. New York , c1987. 302 p. ; ISBN 0-8120-3939-4 (pbk.) LC Card 87-13073 DDC 332.8/0212 19
HG1634 .S654 1987

Canadian mortgage payments. Solomon, Stephen S. Canadian mortgage payments /. New York , c1987. 302 p. ; ISBN 0-8120-3939-4 (pbk.) LC Card 87-13073 DDC 332.8/0212 19
HG1634 .S654 1987

CANADIAN NATIONAL - EMPLOYEES - INTERVIEWS.
Lemieux-Pépin, Madeleine. P'tit train va loin . Ottawa , 1985. vii, 191 p. ; LC Card 86-177382
HE2808.1 .L45 1985

Canadian National Railway Company. see **Canadian National Railways.**

Canadian National Railway System. see **Canadian National Railways.**

CANADIAN NATIONAL RAILWAYS - HISTORY.
MacKay, Donald, 1925- The Asian dream . Vancouver , c1986. 223 p. : ISBN 0-88894-501-9 LC Card 86-225670 DDC 385/.0971 19
HE2810.C14 M33 1986

The Canadian prairie west and the ranching frontier, 1874-1924 /. Breen, David. Toronto , Buffalo , c1983. xiii, 302 p., [4] p. of plates : ISBN 0-8020-5548-6 LC Card 83-143575 DDC 338.1/762/009712 19
HD9433.C22 P733 1983 ***NYPL [HY 87-755]***

Canadian Railway Labour Association. CRLA submission to the government of Canada / Canadian Railway Labour Association. Ottawa : CRLA, [1977] 28, 31 p. ; 22 x 28 cm. English and French. French t.p.: ASCC mémoire au gouvernement du Canada. "March 7, 1977"--Cover. LC Card 84-256714
1. Railroads and state - Canada. 2. Labor policy - Canada. I. Title. II. Title: ASCC mémoire au gouvernement du Canada.
HE2807 .C33 1977

Canadian readings in personnel and human resource management / [edited by] Shimon L. Dolan, Randall S. Schuler. St. Paul, MN : West Pub. Co., c1987. xi, 467 p. ; 26 cm. Includes bibliographies. ISBN 0-314-32487-9 (pbk.) LC Card 87-2211 DDC 658.3/00971 19
1. Personnel management - Canada. 2. Personnel management. I. Dolan, Shimon. II. Schuler, Randall S.
HF5549.2.C3 C36 1987

CANADIAN SEAMEN'S UNION - HISTORY.
Green, Jim. Against the tide . Toronto , 1986. xvii, 324 p., [16] p. of plates : ISBN 0-919396-49-6 (pbk.) LC Card 87-127604 DDC 331.88/113875/0971 19
HD6528.S4 G74 1986

Canadian standard industrial classification for companies and enterprises, 1980. Ottawa : Statistics Canada, Standard Division, c1986. xii, 381 p. ; 30 cm. ISBN 0-660-11945-5 : LC Card 87-120163 DDC 338/.02/0971 19
1. Canada - Industries - Classification. 2. Statistics Canada. Standard Division.
HC115 .C417 1986

Canadian statistical data . Cook, W. Rupert. [Canada] [1985?] vi, 218 p. : LC Card 87-118992 DDC 354.710081/9 19
HA37.C26 C66 1985

Canadian tax papers .
(no. 77) Robinson, Albert J., 1926- The retail sales tax in Canada /. Toronto, Ont. , c1986. viii, 165 p. ; ISBN 0-88808-025-5 (pbk.) : LC Card 86-210098 DDC 336.2/713/0971 19
HJ5715.C2 R63 1986

Canadian trade at a crossroads series.
Wonnacott, Ronald J. Canada/United States free trade . Toronto, Ont. , c1985. 30 p. ; ISBN 0-7729-0036-1 (pbk.) LC Card 86-673986
HF1480.5.U57 W66x 1985

CANADIANS, FRENCH. see **FRENCH-CANADIANS.**

Canais de distribuição na indústria do mobiliário do Rio Grande do Sul /. Dias, Renato Rodrigues. Santa Maria-RS [Brazil] , 1983. 171 p. : LC Card 86-135650
HD9773.B73 R563 1983

CANALS - ENGLAND.
Atterbury, Paul. English rivers and canals /. London , 1984. 152 p. : ISBN 0-297-78318-1
NYPL [JFF 87-598]

CANALS - GOVERNMENT POLICY - OHIO - HISTORY - 19TH CENTURY.
Scheiber, Harry N. Ohio canal era . Athens , 1987. xxvi, 430 p. ; ISBN 0-8214-0048-7 LC Card 86-23800 DDC 386/.48/09771 19
HE395.O34 S34 1987

CANALS, INTEROCEANIC. See also the names of specific interoceanic canals, e.g.: Panama Canal; Suez Canal; etc. For specific treaties regarding interoceanic canals see under names of individual treaties, e.g.: Clayton-Bulwer treaty, 1850; Hay-Pauncefote treaty, 1901; etc.
Foro El Suroeste de Antioquia y el Chocó Norte (1984 : Urrao, Colombia) Foro El Suroeste de Antioquia y el Chocó Norte . [Medellín] [1985] 65 p. : LC Card 87-400457 DDC 338.9861/2 19
HC198.A5 F595 1984

CANALS, INTEROCEANIC - CENTRAL AMERICA.
United States. Congress. House. Committee on Foreign Affairs. Discussion of the Nicaragua ship canal and the Tehuantepec ship railway schemes before the Committee on Foreign Affairs of the House of Representatives. [Washington] [1882?] 80 p. ; LC Card 82-602443
HE536 .U55 1882

CANALS - OHIO - HISTORY - 19TH CENTURY.
Scheiber, Harry N. Ohio canal era . Athens , 1987. xxvi, 430 p. ; ISBN 0-8214-0048-7 LC Card 86-23800 DDC 386/.48/09771 19
HE395.O34 S34 1987

CANALS - PENNSYLVANIA - EASTON REGION - HISTORY - 19TH CENTURY.
Metz, Lance E. Sherman's guide to Hugh Moore Park /. Easton, PA , 1988. p. cm. ISBN 0-930973-07-0 (pbk.) : LC Card 87-25622 DDC 338.09748/22 19
HE395 .P43 1988

CANALS - PENNSYLVANIA - HISTORY.
Shank, William H. The amazing Pennsylvania canals /. York, Pa. [1986], c1981. 128 p. : ISBN 0-933788-37-1 (pbk.) LC Card 87-400232 DDC 386/.48/09748 19
HE395.P47 S5 1986

CANALS - SOUTH AMERICA - PLANNING.
Interconexión de cuencas sudamericanas. [Buenos Aires] , 1986. 159 leaves, [5] leaves of plates : LC Card 86-225024
HE650 .I58 1986

CANALS - UNITED STATES - HISTORY - JUVENILE LITERATURE.
Harlow, Alvin F. (Alvin Fay), 1875-1963. When horses pulled boats . York, PA , c1983. 72 p. : ISBN 0-933788-43-6 (pbk.) LC Card 87-400271 DDC 386/.48/0973 19
HE395.A3 H37 1983

Cañas, Rolando Francisco. Fabián, Miguel Angel. Monografía del café /. [San Salvador] , 1984. 39 leaves : LC Card 86-177543
HD9199.S142 F33 1984

Canavieiros em greve : campanhas salariais e sindicalismo. São Paulo : Centro Ecumênico de Documentação e Informação, 1985. 105 p. : ill. ; 27 cm. (Cadernos do CEDI . 14) LC Card 87-104183 DDC 331.88/1361/098134 19
1. Trade-unions - Sugar workers - Brazil - Paraíba (State) - Congresses. 2. Trade-unions - Sugar workers - Brazil - Pernambuco (State) - Congresses. 3. Trade-unions - Sugar workers - Brazil - São Paulo (State) - Congresses. 4. Wages - Sugar workers - Brazil - Paraíba (State) - Congresses. 5. Wages - Sugar workers - Brazil - Pernambuco (State) - Congresses. 6. Wages - Sugar workers - Brazil - São Paulo (State) - Congresses. I. Centro Ecumênico de Documentação e Informação. II. Series.
HD6614.S85 C36 1985

Cancela Vilanova, Walter, 1948- El programa de la CONAPRO y las perspectivas económicas inmediatas / Walter Cancela. [Montevideo, Uruguay] : Centro Latinoamericano de Economía Humana, [1985] 39 p. ; 28 cm. (Fichas. Serie B, Material de capacitación . 8) Cover title. LC Card 85-235957 DDC 338.9895 19
1. Uruguay - Economic policy. 2. Uruguay - Economic conditions - 1973-. I. Title.
HC232 .C283 1985

CANCELLATIONS (PHILATELY) - ETHIOPIA - HISTORY.
Payne, Eric. Ethiopia /. Hampstead Norreys, Newbury, Berkshire, England , 1981-1982. 8 v. in 1 : LC Card 87-166672
HE6185.E8 P39 1981

CANCELLATIONS (PHILATELY) - ITALY - TRENTINO-ALTO ADIGE - CATALOGS.
Sottoriva, Fabio. Annullamenti del Trentino-Alto Adige, 1850-1883 =. Rovereto , c1981. 184 p., [8] p. of plates : LC Card 86-178380
HE6185.I72 T747 1981

CANCELLATIONS (PHILATELY) - ITALY - TRENTINO-ALTO ADIGE - HISTORY - 19TH CENTURY.
Sottoriva, Fabio. Annullamenti del Trentino-Alto Adige, 1850-1883 =. Rovereto , c1981. 184 p., [8] p. of plates : LC Card 86-178380
HE6185.I72 T747 1981

CANCELLATIONS (PHILATELY) - WISCONSIN - HISTORY - 19TH CENTURY.
Bournique, Raymond A. County & postmaster postmarks of Wisconsin. Madison, WI (5401 Raymond Rd., Madison 53711) , 1985. 12 p. : LC Card 86-174748 DDC 769.56/7/09775 19
HE6185.U7 W573 1985

CANCER DIAGNOSTIC EQUIPMENT INDUSTRY - UNITED STATES.
Strategic marketing of oncology products /. Tustin, CA, U. S.A. (17722 Irvine Blvd., Tustin 92680) , c1987. 242 p. in various pagings : LC Card 87-402026 DDC 381/.45681761 19
HD9995.C353 U67 1987

La Cancha . Calderón G., Fernando. [Cochabamba, Bolivia] , 1984. 208 p. : LC Card 85-238895
HF5473.B62 C363 1984

Candela, Guido, 1943- Balducci, Renato, 1947- Contrattazione salariale e ciclo economico . Roma , 1982. 174 p. : *NYPL [JLD 86-2868]*

CANDLE INDUSTRY - CHINA.
United States. International Trade Commission. Candles from the People's Republic of China . Washington, DC [1985] 13, 37 p. ; LC Card 86-164215 DDC 382/.4574559332/0951 19
HF2651.C254 U55 1985

Candles from the People's Republic of China . United States. International Trade Commission. Washington, DC [1985] 13, 37 p. ; LC Card 86-164215 DDC 382/.4574559332/0951 19
HF2651.C254 U55 1985

Cane farming : centenary brochure. [San Fernando, Trinidad, West Indies : Centenary Committee of the Trinidad Island-Wide Cane Farmers Association, 1983?] 136 p. : ill. ; 28 cm. Cover title. LC Card 86-200484 DDC 338.1/7361/0972983 19
1. Sugarcane industry - Trinidad - History. 2. Sugar workers - Trinidad - History. I. Trinidad Island-Wide Cane Farmers Association. Centenary Committee.
HD9114.T72 C36 1983

CANE SUGAR. see **SUGAR.**

The canecutters /. Burrows, Geoff, 1941- Carlton, Vic. , 1986. xvi, 288 p. : ISBN 0-522-84304-2 LC Card 86-215188 DDC 331.7/6361/0994 19
HD8039.S86 A83 1986

Canestrelli, Elio. Costa, Paolo. Agglomerazione urbana, localizzazione industriale e Mezzogiorno /. Milano , 1983. viii, 240 p. : LC Card 83-186216 DDC 307.2 19
HB2060.S68 C67 1983 *NYPL [JLE 86-3657]*

CANET DE BERENGUER (SPAIN) - POPULATION.
Pellicer Valero, Jesús-Agustín. Sociología del trabajo en Canet de Berenguer /. Valencia , 1984. 80 p. : ISBN 84-600-3540-9 LC Card 86-216439
HD5808.C33 P45 1984

Canitrot, Adolfo. Orden social y monetarismo / Adolfo Canitrot. Buenos Aires, Argentina : Centro de Estudios de Estado y Sociedad, [1982 or 1983] 50 p. ; 22 cm. (Estudios CEDES, 0326-1646 . v. 4, no. 7) Bibliography: p. 50. LC Card 83-213595
1. Argentina - Economic policy. 2. Argentina - Economic conditions - 1945-1983. 3. Monetary policy - Argentina. I. Title. II. Series.
HC173 .C35 1982

CANNED FOODS INDUSTRY - UNITED STATES - HISTORY.
The Burt Olney Canning Company (factories-Oneida, Albion, and Medina, N.Y.). [Oneida, N.Y. , 1911?] (Oneida, N.Y. : Ryan & Burkhart) [63] p. : LC Card 87-115754
HD9321.9.B85 B87 1911

CANNERIES - NEW YORK - HISTORY.
The Burt Olney Canning Company (factories-Oneida, Albion, and Medina, N.Y.). [Oneida, N.Y. , 1911?] (Oneida, N.Y. : Ryan & Burkhart) [63] p. : LC Card 87-115754
HD9321.9.B85 B87 1911

Cannery women, cannery lives . Ruíz, Vicki. Albuquerque , c1987. xviii, 194 p. : ISBN 0-8263-1006-0 LC Card 87-13878 DDC 331.88/1640282/09794 19
HD6515.F72 U547 1987

CANNING AND PRESERVATION - INDUSTRY AND TRADE - SOVIET UNION.
Kharabuga, V. S. (Vasiliĭ Spiridonovich) Ėkonomika, organizatsiia i planirovanie konservnogo proizvodstva /. Moskva , 1977. 349 p. : LC Card 82-122880
HD9326.S62 K42 1977

CANNING AND PRESERVING - INDUSTRY AND TRADE - HUNGARY.
Lányfalvi, Sándor. Adalékok a tartósítóipar hosszútávu fejlesztésének megalapozásához /. Budapest , 1984. 115 p. ; ISBN 963-491-199-4 LC Card 86-199120
HD9326.H82 L36 1984

Cannon, Gwenda L.
Financial planning applications. Ivers, James F. Financial planning applications / James F. Ivers, III. 6th ed. Bryn Mawr, Pa. , c1987. 2 v. : ISBN 0-943590-13-2 (pbk. : v. 1) LC Card 87-71366 DDC 332.024 19
HG179 .C326 1987

Cannon, William B., 1920- New class politics : the polarization of America and what we can do about it / William B. Cannon.1st ed. Washington, D.C. : Institute for Policy Studies, c1986. 137 p. ; 22 cm. Includes bibliographies. ISBN 0-89758-042-7 (pbk.) : LC Card 86-27511 DDC 336.73 19
1. Budget - United States. 2. United States - Politics and government - 1981-. 3. Income distribution - United States. 4. Social classes - United States. 5. Democratic Party (U. S.). I. Title.
HJ2051 .C35 1986

CANO, MARÍA, 1887-1967.
Marín Taborda, Iván. María Cano en el amanecer de la clase obrera /. Bogotá , 1985. 103 p. : LC Card 86-165616
HD6642 .M37 1985 *NYPL [JLD 86-3540]*

Canon production system . Kyanon no seisan kakushin. English. Stamford, Conn. , c1987. xxi, 230 p. : ISBN 0-915299-06-2 : LC Card 85-63498 DDC 681/.418/0683 19
HD9708.5.C354 K92513 1987

Cansier, Dieter. Öffentliche Finanzen, Kredit und Kapital . Berlin , c1985. xvi, 618 p., [1] leaf of plates : ISBN 3-428-05737-6 LC Card 85-164173
HJ161 .O33 1985

CANTABRIA (SPAIN) - COMMERCE - CONGRESSES.
Reunión coloquio sobre como ven nuestros hombres de empresa la economía de Cantabria para 1984 /. [Santander] [1984?] 54 p. ; ISBN 84-505-0186-5 LC Card 86-187513
HF3690.C35 R48 1984

Reunión coloquio sobre como ven nuestros hombres de empresa la economía de Cantabria para 1985 /. [Santander] [1985?] 78 p. ; ISBN 84-505-1440-1 LC Card 86-193783
HF3690.C35 R49 1985

Cantero Desmartines, Pedro. Iniciación a la economía andaluza /. [Seville, Spain] [1986] 196, [4] p. : ISBN 84-7405-343-9 LC Card 87-152155
HC387.A64 I54 1986

Cantó, Leandro. La caída del bolívar / [Leandro Cantó]. Caracas, Venezuela : Publicaciones Seleven, [1983 or 1984] 223 p. ; 20 cm. (Colección Criterios) LC Card 84-186552 DDC 332.4/987 19
1. Money - Venezuela. 2. Monetary policy - Venezuela. I. Title. II. Series.
HG915 .C36 1983 *NYPL [JLD 87-2426]*

Canto, Victor A.
Currency substitution : theory and evidence from Latin America / Victor A. Canto, Gerald Nickelsburg. Boston : Kluwer Academic Publishers, c1987. viii, 196 p. ; 24 cm. Includes bibliographies and index. ISBN 0-89838-195-9 LC Card 86-27747 DDC 332.4/56/098 19
1. Foreign exchange - Mathematical models. 2. Equilibrium (Economics) - Mathematical models. 3. Substitution (Economics) - Mathematical models. 4. Currency question - Latin America - Mathematical models. 5. Money supply - Latin America - Mathematical models. 6. Monetary policy - Latin America - Mathematical models. 7. Inflation (Finance) - Latin America - Mathematical models. I. Nickelsburg, Gerald. II. Title.
HG3823 .C36 1987

Supply-side portfolio strategies /. Westport, Conn. , 1988. xii, 180 p. : ISBN 0-89930-286-6 (lib. bdg. : alk. paper) LC Card 87-13091 DDC 332.6/0973 19
HG4910 .S775 1988

Canton de Berne (n.f.), balance des travailleurs navetteurs, par communes (2. 12. 1980) Kanton Bern (n.G.), Bilanz der erwerbstätigen Pendler, nach Gemeinden (2. 12. 1980) =. Bern , 1983. 16 p. ; LC Card 83-232809 DDC 388.3/14/094945 19
HD5717.5.S92 B46 1983

Cantón, José. see **Cantón Navarro, José, 1925-**

Cantón Navarro, José, 1925- Algunas ideas de José Martí en relación con la clase obrera y el socialismo / José Cantón Navarro. [2a ed., ampliada]. La Habana : Editora Política, 1981, c1980. 174 p. ; 21 cm. (Textos martianos breves) Includes bibliographical references. LC Card 82-233789 DDC 320.5/31/097291 19
1. Socialism - Cuba. 2. Labor and laboring classes - Cuba. I. Title.
HX159 .C33 1981 *NYPL [JLD 86-1423]*

Cantore, Corrado M., 1948- Modelli di programmazione matematica per la pianificazione aziendale / Corrado M. Cantore. Milano : F. Angeli, [1978] 295 p. ; 22 cm. (Collana L'Azienda moderna. 151) Bibliography: p. 293-295. LC Card 79-338281
1. Corporate planning - Mathematical models. 2. Corporate planning - Data processing. I. Title.
HD30.28 .C36 *NYPL [JLD 80-3558]*

Cantrell, Will. 101 ways to find an overseas job / written by Will Cantrell & Terry Marshall ; edited by Francine Modderno. [Merrifield, VA.] : Cantrell Corp., [c1987] 1 v. (various pagings) ; 26 cm. Cover title. ISBN 0-941541-00-2 (pbk.) LC Card 86-73093 DDC 650.1/4 19
1. Americans - Employment - Foreign countries. 2. Job hunting. 3. Marshall, Terry. 4. Modderno, Francine. I. Title. II. Title: One hundred one ways to find an overseas job. III. Title: One hundred and one ways to find an overseas job.
HF5549.5.E45 C33 1987

CANVASSING.
Detroy, Erich-Norbert, 1945- Wie man mit Brief, Telefon und Erstbesuch neue Kunden systematisch und dauerhaft gewinnt /. Zürich , c1982. 216 p. : ISBN 3-478-23510-3 : LC Card 82-242870
HF5446 .D47 1982

Canziani, Arnaldo. La strategia aziendale / Arnaldo Canziani. [Milano] : Giuffrè, 1984. xx, 288 p. ; 24 cm. (Università "L. Bocconi," Dipartimento di economia aziendale . 81. 11.7) Bibliography: p. [247]-280. Includes indexes. ISBN 88-14-00283-5 : LC Card 85-105652 DDC 658.4/012 19
1. Strategic planning. 2. Corporate planning. I. Series: Università "L. Bocconi," Dipartimento di economia aziendale (Series) , 81. II. Title.
HD30.28 .C364 1984

Caoutchouc et produits en matières plastiques au Québec : monographie sectorielle / [sous la direction de Carmen Sabag-Vaillancourt]. [Québec] : Commission de la santé et de la sécurité du travail du Québec, 1984. 249 p. : ill. ; 28 cm. Cover title. Includes bibliographies. ISBN 2-550-10690-3 LC Card 85-155214 DDC 363.1/196684/09714 19
1. Rubber industry and trade - Health aspects - Québec (Province). 2. Plastics industry and trade - Health aspects - Québec (Province). I. Sabag-Vaillancourt, Carmen. II. Commission de la santé et de la sécurité du travail du Québec.
HD7269.R92 C23 1984

CAP International.
Formsmark II, the short-run forms market /. Arlington, VA (1730 N. Lynn St., Arlington 22209) , c1986. 107 leaves : LC Card 87-146216 DDC 381/.4565129 19
HD9800.7.A2 F67 1986

FormsMark III . Arlington, VA (1730 N. Lynn St., Arlington 22209) , c1986. 154 p. : LC Card 87-401995 DDC 381/.4565129 19
HD9802.3.A2 F67 1986

Capacity analysis techniques for signalized intersections /. Leisch, Jack E. Washington, D.C., USA (525 School St., S.W., Suite 410, Washington 20024-2729) , c1986. 46 p. : LC Card 86-212242 DDC 388.3/14 19
HE336.H48 L45 1986

Capacity utilisation in the large-scale manufacturing industry in Bangladesh /. Rahman, Alimur. [Dhaka] [1983] 123 p. ; LC Card 83-903801 DDC 338.6/44/095492 19
HD69.C3 R34 1983 *NYPL [JLE 86-4622]*

CAPD and agricultural development in the Republic of China on Taiwan : March 1979-September 1984. Taipei : Council for Agricultural Planning and Development, [1984] 152 p. : col. ill. ; 28 cm. "September 1984." Bibliography: p. 149-152. LC Card 87-400057 DDC 338.1/851249 19
1. Agriculture and state - Taiwan. 2. Agricultural innovations - Taiwan. 3. Hsing cheng yüan nung yeh fa chan wei yüan hui (China). I. Hsing cheng yüan nung yeh fa chan wei yüan hui (China).
HD2108 .C36 1984

Capdevila Batlles, José. Agricultura e industria española frente a la CEE : aspectos jurídicos,

económicos y políticos / José Capdevila Batlles ; prólogo de Edgard Pisani. Barcelona : Aedos, [1985?] 252 p. : ill. ; 21 cm. (Biblioteca agrícola Aedos) Bibliography: p. 245-250. ISBN 84-7003-282-8 LC Card 86-171577
1. Spain - Economic policy. 2. Agriculture - Economic aspects - Spain. 3. Spain - Industries. 4. European Economic Community - Spain. I. Title. II. Series.
HC385 .C358 1985

Cape, Norman. Payne, Eric. Ethiopia /. Hampstead Norreys, Newbury, Berkshire, England , 1981-1982. 8 v. in 1 : LC Card 87-166672
HE6185.E8 P39 1981

CAPE OF GOOD HOPE (SOUTH AFRICA) - ECONOMIC CONDITIONS - STATISTICS.
Kruger, Gudrun. Development region D . Port Elizabeth [1985] iv, 89 p. : ISBN 0-86988-274-0 (pbk.) LC Card 86-233113 DDC 304.6/09687/5 19
HA4701.Z9 C354 1985

CAPE OF GOOD HOPE (SOUTH AFRICA) - POPULATION - STATISTICS.
Kruger, Gudrun. Development region D . Port Elizabeth [1985] iv, 89 p. : ISBN 0-86988-274-0 (pbk.) LC Card 86-233113 DDC 304.6/09687/5 19
HA4701.Z9 C354 1985

Cape Town (South Africa). City Engineer's Dept. Facing the squatter crisis /. Cape Town , 1977. 21 p. : LC Card 81-194960
HD7374.4.C343 F33 1977

CAPE VERDE - ECONOMIC CONDITIONS.
Carreira, António. Cabo Verde . Lisboa [1984] 207 p., [16] p. of plates : LC Card 87-400337 DDC 363.8/0966/58 19
HC594.Z9 F33 1984

CAPE VERDE - SOCIAL CONDITIONS.
Carreira, António. Cabo Verde . Lisboa [1984] 207 p., [16] p. of plates : LC Card 87-400337 DDC 363.8/0966/58 19
HC594.Z9 F33 1984

Capela, José. O movimento operário em Lourenço Marques, 1898-1927 / José Capela. [Porto?] : Edições Afrontamento, [1981?] 281, [1] p. ; 21 cm. Bibliography: p. 279-[282]. LC Card 87-401260 DDC 331.88/0967/9 19
1. Trade-unions - Mozambique - Maputo - History. 2. Laborand laboring classes - Mozambique - Maputo - History. I. Title.
HD6869.Z8 M363 1981

Capelo C., J. Alejo (J. Alejo Capelo Cabello), d. 1973. El crimen del 15 de noviembre de 1922 / por J. Alejo Capelo C. Rasgos salientes de la tragedia histórica de noviembre de 1922 / por Segundo Ramos. La hora trágica : (15 de noviembre de 1922) y otros apuntes sobre el movimiento obrero / por José I. Guzmán S. [Guayaquil] : Litografía e Impr. de la Universidad de Guayaquil : Librería y distribuidora Continental], 1983. 10, 14, 19 p. : 1 port. ; 22 cm. (Colección Movimiento obrero ecuatoriano . no. 5) Cover title. LC Card 86-114097
1. General Strike, Ecuador, 1922. 2. Socialism - Ecuador - History - 20th century. 3. Trade-unions - Ecuador - History - 20th century. 4. Labor and laboring classes - Ecuador - History - 20th century. I. Ramos, Segundo, d. 1960. Rasgos salientes de la tragedia histórica de noviembre de 1922. 1983. II. Guzmán S., José I. (José Ignacio). Hora trágica. 1983. III. Title. IV. Title: Rasgos salientes de la tragedia histórica de noviembre de 1922. V. Title: Hora trágica. VI. Series.
HD5358.A6 C36 1983

Capie, Forrest. Financial crises and the world banking system /. London , c1986. x, 270 p. : ISBN 0-333-35129-0 ***NYPL [JLD 86-2132]***

"El capital" . Mandel, Ernest. México, D.F. , 1985. 242 p. ; ISBN 968-231-127-6 LC Card 86-158367
HB501.M37 M355 1985

CAPITAL.
Adam, Martin, 1955- Kapitalstock und Nutzungsdauer . Frankfurt am Main , New York , c1985. v, 151 p. : ISBN 3-8204-8860-X LC Card 85-202132 DDC 332/.0414/0943 19
HG4028.C4 A24 1985

Mandel, Ernest. "El capital" . México, D.F. , 1985. 242 p. ; ISBN 968-231-127-6 LC Card 86-158367
HB501.M37 M355 1985

Marchés, capital et incertitude . Paris , c1986. 265 p. : ISBN 2-7178-1002-1 : LC Card 86-160930
HB615 .M37 1986

Owen, Robert R. (Robert Randolph) Arthur Young guide to financing for growth . New York , c1986. xiv, 298 p. ; ISBN 0-471-81946-8 : LC Card 86-1612 DDC 658.1/522 19
HG4027.7 .O94 1986 ***NYPL [JLE 86-2667]***

Pappa, Hellē. Hoi archaioi Hellēnes syngrapheis sto "Kephalaio" tou Marx /. Athēna , 1983. 112 p. ; LC Card 84-128852
HB501 .P24 1983

Wolff, Robert Paul. Moneybags must be so lucky . Amherst , c1988. p. cm. ISBN 0-87023-615-6 (alk. paper) LC Card 87-20580 DDC 335.4/1 19
HB501.M37 W64 1988

CAPITAL ACCUMULATION. see **SAVING AND INVESTMENT.**

CAPITAL - AFRICA, WEST.
Transnationals and development. Manchester, England , 1984. i, 64 p. ; ***NYPL [JLD 86-3224]***

CAPITAL AND LABOR. see **INDUSTRIAL RELATIONS.**

Capital and labour on the Kimberley diamond fields, 1871-1890 /. Turrell, Robert Vicat. Cambridge [Cambridgeshire] , New York , 1987. xviii, 297 p. : ISBN 0-521-33354-7 LC Card 86-32740 DDC 331.7/622382/0968711 19
HD9677.S63 K567 1987

Capital and peasant production : studies in the continuity and discontinuity of agrarian structures in Sri Lanka / edited by Charles Abeysekera. Colombo, Sri Lanka : Social Scientists' Association of Sri Lanka, 1985. xiv, 230 p. ; 25 cm. C-E $ Includes bibliographies. LC Card 86-900809 DDC 338.1/3/095493 19
1. Agriculture - Economic aspects - Sri Lanka. 2. Agricultural productivity - Sri Lanka. 3. Agriculture - Social aspects - Sri Lanka. 4. Plantations - Sri Lanka. 5. Peasantry - Sri Lanka. I. Abeysekera, Charles.
HD2065.8 .C36 1985 ***NYPL [JLE 87-1667]***

Capital and technological progress in the Indian economy, 1950/51-1980/81 /. Hajra, S. (Sridhar), 1936- New Delhi , 1985. xvi, 198 p. : LC Card 85-900681 DDC 338.954 19
HC440.S3 H35 1985 ***NYPL [JLD 87-736]***

Capital and time . Hicks, John Richard, Sir, 1904- Oxford [Oxfordshire] , New York , 1987. p. cm. ISBN 0-19-877286-6 : LC Card 87-20233 DDC 332/.041 19
HB501 .H48 1987

CAPITAL - ARGENTINA.
Goldberg, Samuel. El stock de capital en la Argentina . [Buenos Aires] , 1986. 28 leaves : LC Card 87-403996 DDC 332/.0414 19
HC180.C3 G65 1986

Podestá, Ricardo Augusto. Argentina, país productor de capitales /. Mendoza , 1976. 11 p. ; LC Card 84-196569
HC180.C3 P62 1976

CAPITAL - BRAZIL - ARAPIRACA REGION.
Estudo especial . Maceió, AL. , 1983. 174 leaves : LC Card 86-167829
HC189.A69 E88 1983

CAPITAL - BRAZIL - PARANÁ (STATE)
Paraná, formação de capital . [Pôrto Alegre] , 1965. 185 p. : LC Card 85-131098
HC188.P35 P388 1965

CAPITAL BUDGET.
Bierman, Harold. The capital budgeting decision . New York , London , c1988. xvi, 557 p. : ISBN 0-02-309941-0 LC Card 87-15257 DDC 658.1/52 19
HG4028.C4 B54 1988

Bierman, Harold. Implementation of capital budgeting techniques . Tampa, FL , c1986. i, 69 p. : ISBN 0-936795-01-8 (pbk.) LC Card 86-231118 DDC 658.1/54 19
HG4028.C4 B544 1986

Leichtfuss, Reinhold. Kapitalbudgetierung in divisionalisierten Unternehmen . Wiesbaden , c1984. 389 p. ; ISBN 3-409-13701-7 LC Card 85-231538
HG4028.C4 L387 1984

CAPITAL BUDGET - DECISION MAKING.
Allerkamp, Ferdinand. Tilgungsplanung . Frankfurt am Main , c1983. xii, 288 p. : ISBN 3-7819-0296-X LC Card 85-239167
HD2747 .A53 1983

CAPITAL BUDGET - GERMANY (WEST) - DÜSSELDORF - STATISTICS.
Mehrjahresinvestitionsprogramm (MIP) der Landeshauptstadt Düsseldorf 1978-1982 /. [Düsseldorf] [1978?] 68, 141, 174, 5 p. ; LC Card 85-141884
HJ9494.D87 M44 1978

CAPITAL BUDGET - NEW YORK (N.Y.)
Citizens Budget Commission (New York, N.Y.) New York City's capital program . New York, N.Y. (110 E. 42nd St., New York 10017) [1986] 17 leaves ; LC Card 87-110059 DDC 336.3/9/097471 19
HJ9289.N4 C54 1986a

CAPITAL BUDGET - POLAND.
Kapustka, Aleksander. Inwestycje w reformie . Zielona Góra , 1985. 282 p. ; LC Card 86-125896
HJ2132 .K37 1985

CAPITAL BUDGET - UNITED STATES.
Supplement to special analysis D . Washington, D.C. , 1985. 1 v. (various pagings) ; ***NYPL [JLF 86-603]***

CAPITAL BUDGET - UNITED STATES - MATHEMATICAL MODELS.
Wacht, Richard F. A new approach to capital budgeting for city and county governments /. Atlanta, Ga. , 1987. ix, 149 p. : ISBN 0-88406-190-6 (pbk.) : LC Card 87-21157 DDC 352.1/2 19
HJ9147 .W33 1987

CAPITAL BUDGET - UNITED STATES - STATES.
Hard choices . Washington , 1984. 23 v. : ***NYPL [JLE 87-566 Appendix 1-23]***

Kaplan, Marshall. Hard choices . Washington , 1984. xi, 230 p. : LC Card 84-602470 DDC 338.4/3363/0973 19
HC110.C3 K37 1984 ***NYPL [JLE 87-566]***

The capital budgeting decision . Bierman, Harold. New York , London , c1988. xvi, 557 p. : ISBN 0-02-309941-0 LC Card 87-15257 DDC 658.1/52 19
HG4028.C4 B54 1988

Capital budgeting for city and county governments. Wacht, Richard F. A new approach to capital budgeting for city and county governments /. Atlanta, Ga. , 1987. ix, 149 p. : ISBN 0-88406-190-6 (pbk.) : LC Card 87-21157 DDC 352.1/2 19
HJ9147 .W33 1987

Capital budgeting techniques. Bierman, Harold. Implementation of capital budgeting techniques . Tampa, FL , c1986. i, 69 p. : ISBN 0-936795-01-8 (pbk.) LC Card 86-231118 DDC 658.1/54 19
HG4028.C4 B544 1986

Capital campaign resource guide. San Francisco, Calif. : Public Management Institute, c1984. x, 1229 p. : ill. ; 28 cm. LC Card 87-122608 DDC 658.1/5224 19
1. Fund raising - United States - Handbooks, manuals, etc. 2. Fund raising - United States - Directories. 3. Corporations, Nonprofit - United States - Finance - Handbooks, manuals, etc. 4. Corporations, Nonprofit - United States - Finance - Directories. I. Public Management Institute.
HG177.5.U6 C36 1984

CAPITAL - CANADA.
Carroll, William K. Corporate power and Canadian capitalism /. Vancouver , 1986. xvii, 284 p. : ISBN 0-7748-0246-4 LC Card 86-223683 DDC 338.8/0971 19
HC120.C3 C37 1986

Capital controls under alternative exchange rate and monetary policy regimes /. Kostiainen, Seppo. Joensuu , 1986. 27 p. ; ISBN 951-696-619-5 (pbk.) LC Card 87-100851 DDC 332.4/5 19
HG3823 .K673 1986

CAPITAL - COSTA RICA.
Pucci, Carlos. Los precios sociales en la evaluación de proyectos en Costa Rica /. San José, Costa Rica , 1979. [108] leaves ; LC Card 83-238167
HC143.Z9 L36 1979

CAPITAL - ENGLAND - HISTORY.
Kenwood, A. G. Capital formation in north east England, 1800-1913 /. New York , 1985. xv, 444 p. : ISBN 0-8240-6685-5 : LC Card 84-46005 DDC 332/.0415/09428 19
HC260.S3 K46 1985 NYPL [JLE 86-3900]

CAPITAL EQUIPMENT. see **INDUSTRIAL EQUIPMENT.**

CAPITAL EXPENDITURES. see **CAPITAL INVESTMENTS.**

CAPITAL EXPORTS. see **FOREIGN EXCHANGE; INVESTMENTS, FOREIGN.**

Capital financeiro e agricultura no Brasil, 1965-1985 /. Delgado, Guilherme Costa. S[ão] Paulo, SP, Brasil , Campinas, SP , c1985. 240 p. ; LC Card 87-102748
HD1440.B8 D45 1985

Capital flight . Cuddington, John T. Princeton, N.J. , c1986. 44 p. ; ISBN 0-88165-230-X (pbk.) : LC Card 86-21386 DDC 332/.041 19
HG3891 .C83 1986

Capital flight and economic crisis . De Murguía, Valdemar. La Jolla, Calif. , 1986. 27 p. ; LC Card 87-621351 DDC 332/.042 19
HG3916 .D4 1986

Capital flight and Third World debt / [edited by] John Williamson and Donald Lessard. Washington, D.C. : Institute for International Economics, 1987. p. cm. Bibliography: p. Includes index. ISBN 0-88132-064-1 LC Card 87-17080 DDC 332/.042 19
1. Capital movements - Developing countries. 2. Debts, External - Developing countries. 3. Debts, External - Latin America - Case studies. I. Williamson, John, 1937-. II. Lessard, Donald R. III. Institute for International Economics (U. S.).
HG3891 .C36 1987

CAPITAL FLOWS. see **CAPITAL MOVEMENTS.**

CAPITAL FORMATION. see **SAVING AND INVESTMENT.**

Capital formation in north east England, 1800-1913 /. Kenwood, A. G. New York , 1985. xv, 444 p. : ISBN 0-8240-6685-5 : LC Card 84-46005 DDC 332/.0415/09428 19
HC260.S3 K46 1985 NYPL [JLE 86-3900]

Capital gains tax reductions of 1978. United States. Office of Tax Analysis. Report to Congress on the capital gains tax reductions of 1978. [Washington, D.C.] [1985] xix, 199 p. ; LC Card 85-602710 DDC 336.24/3 19
HJ4653.C3 U55 1985

CAPITAL GAINS TAX - UNITED STATES.
United States. Office of Tax Analysis. Report to Congress on the capital gains tax reductions of 1978. [Washington, D.C.] [1985] xix, 199 p. ; LC Card 85-602710 DDC 336.24/3 19
HJ4653.C3 U55 1985

CAPITAL - GERMANY, EAST.
Bedürfnisse und Interessen als Triebkräfte unseres Handelns /. Berlin , 1984. 155 p. ; LC Card 84-229147
HC290.795.C3 B43 1984

CAPITAL - GERMANY, WEST.
Kapitalbildung und Altersvorsorge . Köln , Bergisch Gladbach [1983?] 95 p. : LC Card 84-180205
HD7105.45.G3 K37 1983

Schoppe, Siegfried, 1944- Determinanten der Eigenkapitalbildung und Konsequenzen für die Wettbewerbsfähigkeit deutscher Grossunternehmen und Mittelbetriebe /. Hamburg , 1986. 24 p. : LC Card 86-185861
HG4156 .S36 1986

CAPITAL - GERMANY, WEST - CONGRESSES.
DIHT-Kongress (1983 : Frankfurt am Main, Germany) Kapital, Zins, Währung . Bonn , 1984. 68 p. : LC Card 84-212399
HC290.5.C3 D53 1983

CAPITAL - GREAT BRITAIN - HISTORY.
Studies in capital formation in Great Britain . Oxford [Oxfordshire] , New York , c1988. p. cm. ISBN 0-19-828408-X : LC Card 87-15196 DDC 332/.0415/0941 19
HC260.S3 S78 1988

CAPITAL - HANDBOOKS, MANUALS, ETC.
Handbook for raising capital . Homewood, Ill. , c1987. xxiv, 666 p. : ISBN 0-87094-705-2 LC Card 86-71216 *NYPL [*R-Econ. 87-1124]*

CAPITAL - HUNGARY - STATISTICS.
A Nemzeti vagyon és az állóeszközállomány 1970-1978 /. [Budapest] [1979] 140 p. ; LC Card 82-193609
HC300.295.W4 N454 1979

CAPITAL IMPORTS. see **FOREIGN EXCHANGE; INVESTMENTS, FOREIGN.**

Capital income taxation and resource allocation /. Sinn, Hans-Werner. [Kapitaleinkommensbesteuerung. English.] Amsterdam ; New York : xiv, 411 p. ; ISBN 0-444-70208-3 LC Card 87-9126 DDC 336.24/3 19
HD2753.A3 S47413 1987

CAPITAL INVESTMENTS - BRAZIL.
Casagrande Neto, Humberto. Abertura do capital de empresas no Brasil . São Paulo , 1985. 143 p. ; ISBN 85-22-40100-4
NYPL [JLD 86-1080]

Tadini, Venilton. O setor de bens de capital sob encomenda . São Paulo , 1986. 142 p. : LC Card 87-154239 DDC 332/.0414/0981 19
HC190.C3 T33 1986

CAPITAL INVESTMENTS - DECISION-MAKING.
Allerkamp, Ferdinand. Tilgungsplanung . Frankfurt am Main , c1983. xii, 288 p. : ISBN 3-7819-0296-X LC Card 85-239167
HD2747 .A53 1983

Barta, Imre. A beruházások döntéselőkészítése /. Budapest , 1986. 185, [1] p. : ISBN 963-05-4182-3 : LC Card 87-408029
HG4028.C4 B335 1986

Grünig, Rudolf. Verfahren zur Erarbeitung eines Grundsatzsystems für den Investitionsbereich /. Bern , c1984. 144 p. : ISBN 3-258-03442-7 : LC Card 85-139475
HG4028.C4 G75 1984

Wittmann, Franz, 1933- Der Einfluss der Steuern auf die Investitionsentscheidungen der Unternehmen . Frankfurt , New York , c1986. 405 p. ; ISBN 3-593-33642-1 LC Card 86-173001
HG4028.C4 W585 1986

CAPITAL INVESTMENTS - EVALUATION.
Bierman, Harold. The capital budgeting decision . New York , London , c1988. xvi, 557 p. : ISBN 0-02-309941-0 LC Card 87-15257 DDC 658.1/52 19
HG4028.C4 B54 1988

Preparación y presentación de proyectos de inversión /. [Santiago] , 1985. v, 138 p. : LC Card 87-116769
HD39 .P72 1985

Rachlin, Robert, 1937- Return on investment strategies for decision-making /. New York , 1987. x, 306 p. : ISBN 0-531-15528-5 LC Card 87-10633 DDC 658.1/52 19
HG4028.C4 R255 1987

Stermole, Franklin J. Economic evaluation and investment decision methods /. Golden, Colo. , c1987. vi, 479 p. : ISBN 0-9603282-8-9 LC Card 86-83278 DDC 332.63 19
HG4028.C4 S714 1987

Stockton, Richard B. ROI, planning for profitable growth /. New York, N.Y., U. S.A. , c1984. x, 141 leaves : ISBN 0-86604-150-8 (pbk.) LC Card 86-232254 DDC 332.63 19
HG4028.C4 S72 1984b

CAPITAL INVESTMENTS - FINLAND - MATHEMATICAL MODELS.
Karhu, Veli. Akseleraatioteoriaan perustuvia investointifunktiokokeiluja yritystason aineistolla /. Vaasa , 1982. 43, [1] leaves ; ISBN 951-683-160-5 LC Card 83-100841 DDC 332/.0415 19
HG4028.C4 K349 1982
NYPL [JLM 73-601 n:o 85]

CAPITAL INVESTMENTS - FRANCE - MATHEMATICAL MODELS.
Artus, Patrick. Investissement et emploi /. Paris , c1986. 260 p. : ISBN 2-7178-1196-6 : LC Card 87-125878
HG4028.C4 A74 1986

CAPITAL INVESTMENTS - GERMANY, EAST.
Investitionsprozess . Leipzig , c1986. 432 p. : LC Card 86-193837
HG4028.C4 I534 1986

CAPITAL INVESTMENTS - GERMANY, WEST.
Adam, Martin, 1955- Kapitalstock und Nutzungsdauer . Frankfurt am Main , New York , c1985. v, 151 p. : ISBN 3-8204-8860-X LC Card 85-202132 DDC 332/.0414/0943 19
HG4028.C4 A24 1985

Analyse der Wirksamkeit der Beschäftigungszulage . München , 1984. vii, 172 p. : LC Card 85-230164
HJ4720.A45 A53 1984

Behrens-Ramberg, Wolfgang. Steuerliche Anreize bei innovativen Investitionen kleiner und mittlerer Industrieunternehmen unter vergleichender Berücksichtigung nichtsteuerlicher Hilfen /. Stuttgart , c1985. 299 p. ; ISBN 3-7910-5007-9 : LC Card 86-124563 DDC 336.24/316 19
HJ2337.G3 B44 1985
NYPL [JLL 73-505 Nr.6]

Heurung, Rainer-Otto, 1952- Wirken Substanzsteuern investitionshemmend? /. Frankfurt am Main , New York , c1986. xvii, 251, [93] p. : ISBN 3-8204-9800-1 LC Card 87-408762 DDC 332.63 19
HG4028.C4 H49 1986

Klose, Roland, 1954- Die Erschliessung des US-Marktes durch Direktinvestitionen mittelständischer deutscher Unternehmungen des Investitionsgüterbereichs /. [Würzburg? , 1983] (Würzburg : Dissertationsdruck, Schmitt & Meyer) v, 307 p. ; LC Card 84-195414
HG4910 .K56 1983

Uhlmann, Luitpold. Instrumentelle Aspekte der Investitionsförderung . München , 1986. vii, 270 p. : ISBN 3-88512-024-0 LC Card 86-215244 DDC 332.63 19
HG4028.C4 U367 1986

Uhlmann, Luitpold. Investitionsverhalten und Unternehmensgrösse /. Berlin , c1986. 307 p. ; ISBN 3-428-06010-5 LC Card 86-216522
HG4028.C4 U37 1986

CAPITAL INVESTMENTS - GERMANY (WEST) - DECISION MAKING.
Wittmann, Franz, 1933- Der Einfluss der Steuern auf die Investitionsentscheidungen der Unternehmen . Frankfurt , New York , c1986. 405 p. ; ISBN 3-593-33642-1 LC Card 86-173001
HG4028.C4 W585 1986

CAPITAL INVESTMENTS - GERMANY (WEST) - DECISION MAKING - ECONOMETRIC MODELS.
Georgi, Andreas A. Steuern in der Investitionsplanung . Hamburg , 1986. vii, 243, 16, xxviii p. : ISBN 3-89161-702-X LC Card 86-227290
HG4028.C4 G46 1986

CAPITAL INVESTMENTS - GERMANY (WEST) - ECONOMETRIC MODELS.
Funke, Michael, 1956- Tobin's q and industry investment in West Germany /. Berlin [1986] 36 p. : LC Card 87-156645 DDC 332.63 19
HC290.5.C3 F86 1986

Jaap, Christiane. Möglichkeiten betriebswirtschaftlicher Beurteilung privater Kapitalanlagen . Berlin , c1986. xxiii, 322 p. : ISBN 3-428-06008-3 LC Card 86-189069
HG4028.C4 J28 1986

CAPITAL INVESTMENTS - GERMANY (WEST) - MATHEMATICAL MODELS.
Hummeltenberg, Rita. Die optimale Wahl steuerbegünstigter Kapitalanlagen unter Berücksichtigung der Einkommensteuerprogression . Berlin , c1984. xi, 276 p. : ISBN 3-503-02437-9 LC Card 85-227381
HJ4719 .H86 1984

CAPITAL INVESTMENTS - GOVERNMENT POLICY - UNITED STATES - STATES - DIRECTORIES.
Guide to state capital formation incentives and innovations /. [Washington, D.C. , 1983] vii, 154 p. ; LC Card 86-673432
HC110.I53 G84x 1983

CAPITAL INVESTMENTS - HUNGARY.
Soós, Károly Attila. Terv, kampány, pénz . Budapest , 1986. 532 p. : ISBN 963-221-575-3 :

LC Card 87-137237
HB3787.5 .S66 1986

CAPITAL INVESTMENTS - HUNGARY - CASE STUDIES.
Szalai, Erzsébet. Kiemelt vállalat, beruházás, érdek /. Budapest , 1981. 140 p. ; ISBN 963-05-2527-5 LC Card 81-170685
HG4028.C4 S96 1981

CAPITAL INVESTMENTS - HUNGARY - MATHEMATICAL MODELS.
Módszerek a beruházási tevékenység kvantitatív elemzéséhez /. Budapest , 1985. 207 p. : ISBN 963-05-3607-2 : LC Card 86-100399
HG4028.C4 M57 1985

CAPITAL INVESTMENTS - ISRAEL - STATISTICS.
Aspler, I. Seḳer melai ha-hon ha-ḳavu'a be-ta'aśiyah, 1.1.1982 /. Yerushalayim , 1986. 80, xvii p. ; LC Card 87-128243
HA1931 .A354 no. 785 HC415.25.Z9C3

CAPITAL INVESTMENTS - ITALY - CONGRESSES.
Il Finanziamento dell'innovazione nelle imprese industriali /. Milano, Italy , c1985. 271 p. : LC Card 86-157239
HC310.T4 F55 1985

CAPITAL INVESTMENTS - ITALY - DECISION MAKING.
Ecchia, Stefano. La destinazione dell'utile nelle società per azioni . Padova , 1985. 133 p. : LC Card 86-214308
HG4028.P7 E23 1985

CAPITAL INVESTMENTS - MATHEMATICAL MODELS.
Módszerek a beruházási tevékenység kvantitatív elemzéséhez /. Budapest , 1985. 207 p. : ISBN 963-05-3607-2 : LC Card 86-100399
HG4028.C4 M57 1985

Mors, Matthias. Planung und Erwartungsbildung in der Investitionsentscheidung . Frankfurt am Main , c1983. 190 p. : ISBN 3-88129-619-0 LC Card 83-174677
HG4028.C4 M65 1983

Püschel, Manfred, 1953- Die Wahl der optimalen Wärmeversorgungskonfiguration als betriebswirtschaftliches Produktions- und Investitionsproblem /. Frankfurt am Main , New York , c1984. iv, 298 p. : ISBN 3-8204-7432-3 LC Card 86-108875
HD30.25 .P87 1984

CAPITAL INVESTMENTS - MEXICO.
Mántey de Anguiano, M. G. Análisis microeconómico de los factores que determinan el valor de mercado de las empresas industriales mexicanas y su tasa de expansión /. [Mexico City] [1986] iv, 63 leaves : LC Card 87-400949 DDC 658.1/5/0972 19
HG4092 .M36 1986

CAPITAL INVESTMENTS - NEW YORK (N. Y.)
Citizens Budget Commission (New York, N.Y.) New York City's capital program . New York, N.Y. (110 E. 42nd St., New York 10017) [1986] 17 leaves ; LC Card 87-110059 DDC 336.3/9/097471 19
HJ9289.N4 C54 1986a

CAPITAL INVESTMENTS - POLAND.
Kapustka, Aleksander. Gospodarka inwestycyjna i remontowa w latach 1984-1985 /. Zielona Góra , 1984. 294 p. ; LC Card 86-670001
HC340.3.Z9 C35 1984

Kapustka, Aleksander. Inwestycje w reformie . Zielona Góra , 1985. 282 p. ; LC Card 86-125896
HJ2132 .K37 1985

CAPITAL INVESTMENTS - RUSSIAN S.F.S.R. - URAL MOUNTAINS REGION.
Ėkonomicheskaia ėffektivnost' rekonstruktsii deĭstvuiushchikh predpriiatiĭ /. Sverdlovsk , 1981. 171 p. ; LC Card 83-192125
HD39.3 .E37 1981

CAPITAL INVESTMENTS - SOUTH AFRICA - STATISTICS.
Van Zyl, S. J. J. Trends in capital expenditure on fixed assets /. Pretoria , 1985. ix, 100 p. : ISBN 0-908408-49-8 (pbk.) LC Card 86-206341 DDC 658.8/3968 s 332/.0414/0968 19
HC517.S7 S48 no. 125 HG4028.C4

CAPITAL INVESTMENTS - SOVIET UNION.
Androsov, V. I. (Vasiliĭ Ivanovich) Ėffektivnost' kapital'nogo stroitel'stva v torgovle /. Moskva , 1980. 213 p. ; LC Card 81-132839
HC340.C3 A65 1980

Braginskiĭ, L. V. (Lev Vol'fovich) Ėffektivnost' kapital'nykh vlozheniĭ i bankovskaia deiatel'nost' /. Moskva , 1981. 186 p. ; LC Card 82-144216
HG186.S55 B72 1981

Cherniavskiĭ, V. O. (Vasiliĭ Osipovich) Ėffektivnost' i optimal'nost' kapital'nykh vlozheniĭ /. Leningrad , 1986. 68, [4] p. ; LC Card 85-179296
HC340.C3 C4 1986

Lenskaia, S. A. (Svetlana Alekseevna) Proizvodstvennye fondy kak ėkonomicheskaia kategoriia /. Moskva , 1982. 126 p. ; LC Card 83-134249
HC340.C3 L396 1982

Palamarchuk, Aleksandr Semenovich. Rekonstruktsiia predpriiatiĭ i ėffektivnost' proizvodstva /. Moskva , 1981. 62, [2] p. ; LC Card 81-179552
HD39.3 .P34 1981

Rezervy intensifikatsii vosproizvodstva osnovnykh fondov i ikh ispol'zovaniia /. Moskva , 1984. 204 p. ; LC Card 85-240369
HC340.C3 R48 1984

CAPITAL INVESTMENTS - SWEDEN.
Olsson, Hans. Industrins lönsamhet, finansiering och investeringar under 1970-talet . [Stockholm] [1981] 58 p. : ISBN 91-38-06530-4 LC Card 84-120594
HG4211 .O45 1981

CAPITAL INVESTMENTS - TAXATION.
Hergarten, Lothar, 1953- Der Prospekt über steuerbegünstigte Kapitalanlagen . Köln , c1986. v, 209 p. ; ISBN 3-924361-18-5 : LC Card 87-103997 DDC 332.63 19
HG4028.C4 H456 1986

CAPITAL INVESTMENTS - UNITED STATES.
Jorgenson, Dale Weldeau, 1933- Productivity and U. S. economic growth /. Cambridge, Mass. , 1987. 567 p. : ISBN 0-674-71175-0 (alk. paper) LC Card 87-12098 DDC 338/.06/0973 19
HC110.I52 J67 1987

Pagano, Michael A. How the public works . Washington, D.C. , c1986. ix, 68, 6 p. : ISBN 0-933729-13-8 (pbk.) : LC Card 87-129719 DDC 338.4/3363/0973 19
HJ9145 .P343 1986

Supplement to special analysis D . Washington, D.C. , 1985. 1 v. (various pagings) ;
NYPL [JLF 86-603]

CAPITAL INVESTMENTS - UNITED STATES - MATHEMATICAL MODELS.
Wacht, Richard F. A new approach to capital budgeting for city and county governments /. Atlanta, Ga. , 1987. ix, 149 p. : ISBN 0-88406-190-6 (pbk.) : LC Card 87-21157 DDC 352.1/2 19
HJ9147 .W33 1987

CAPITAL INVESTMENTS - YUGOSLAVIA.
Soós, Károly Attila. Terv, kampány, pénz . Budapest , 1986. 532 p. : ISBN 963-221-575-3 : LC Card 87-137237
HB3787.5 .S66 1986

CAPITAL LEVY - CANADA.
Davies, James B., 1951- Reforming capital income taxation in Canada . [Ottawa] , c1987. ix, 153 p. : ISBN 0-660-12454-8 (pbk.) : LC Card 87-168079 DDC 336.24/24/0971 19
HJ4133.C2 .D38 1987

CAPITAL LEVY - INDIA.
Saraf, B. P., 1939- Capital taxation in India /. New Delhi , c1983. viii, 268 p. ; LC Card 83-902683 DDC 343.5405/3 345.40353 19
HJ4126.I45 S27 1983 ***NYPL [JLD 86-3821]***

CAPITAL LEVY - SWEDEN - MATHEMATICAL MODELS.
Agell, Jonas. The effects of capital taxation . Uppsala , Stockholm, Sweden , 1986. 123 p. : ISBN 91-554-1938-0 (pbk.) LC Card 87-100538 DDC 330 s 336.2/009481 19
HB51 .S7 no. 9 HJ2838

CAPITAL MARKET.
Crawford, Vincent P., 1950- International lending, long-term credit relationships, and dynamic contract theory /. Princeton, N.J. [1987] c1986. 34 p. ; ISBN 0-88165-231-8 (pbk.) : LC Card 86-33743 DDC 336.3/435 19
HG3891.5 .C7 1987

Gaab, Werner. Devisenmärkte und Wechselkurse . Berlin , New York , 1983. vii, 305 p. : ISBN 0-387-12615-5 (U. S.) : LC Card 83-222336
HG3851 .G25 1983

Grubel, Herbert G. Multinational banking /. Singapore , 1985. iii, 21 p. ; ISBN 997-19-8817-8 (pbk.) LC Card 86-940563 DDC 332.1/6 19
HG3881 .G747 1985

Ibbotson, Roger G. Investment markets . New York , c1987. ix, 294 p. : ISBN 0-07-031673-2 : LC Card 86-33740 DDC 332.6 19
HG4523 .I23 1987

Jander, Sigurd. Der Einfluss der Geldpolitik auf die Kapitalmarktentwicklung /. Berlin , c1986. 176 p. : ISBN 3-428-06122-5 LC Card 87-134174 DDC 332.63/2 19
HG4523 .J36 1986

Kaufman, Henry. Interest rates, the markets, and the new financial world /. New York, N.Y. , 1986, c1985. xiii, 258 p. : ISBN 0-8129-1333-7 LC Card 86-5865 DDC 332 19
HG173 .K364 1986 ***NYPL [JLD 86-2681]***

Pastuszek, Rainer. Leading und Lagging kurzfristig variierbarer gruppeninterner Geldflüsse im Währungsrisikomanagement einer internationalen Unternehmung /. Pfaffenweiler , 1986. xvi, 275 p. : ISBN 3-89085-122-3 LC Card 87-128258 DDC 658.1/55 19
HG3851 .P295 1986

Stock market anomalies /. Cambridge [Cambridgeshire] , New York , 1988. p. cm. ISBN 0-521-34104-3 LC Card 87-6622 DDC 332.63/2 19
HG4551 .S82 1988

Strong, Norman, 1954- Information and capital markets /. Oxford, UK , New York, NY, USA , 1987. x, 222 p. : ISBN 0-631-13834-X : LC Card 86-31721 DDC 332/.041 19
HG4523 .S77 1987

Wahl, Jack. Informationsbewertung und -effizienz auf dem Kapitalmarkt /. Würzburg , 1983. 211 p. : ISBN 3-7908-0308-1 LC Card 84-154688
HG4515 .W34 1983

Wilder, J. Welles. The Adam theory of markets, or, What matters is profit /. McLeansville, N.C. (P.O. Box 128, Mcleansville 27301) , c1987. 131 p. : LC Card 87-166037 DDC 332.64/4 19
HG4523 .W54 1987

CAPITAL MARKET - AUSTRIA.
Speiser, Harald. Das österreichische Foreign Debt Management, 1956-1983 . Regensburg , c1985. 120 p. : ISBN 3-924956-06-5 LC Card 86-222064
HJ8636 .S66 1985

CAPITAL MARKET - BELGIUM.
Hawawini, Gabriel A. Mandatory financial information and capital market equilibrium in Belgium /. New York , 1987. 271 p. : ISBN 0-8240-7852-7 (alk. paper) : LC Card 87-54 DDC 332.63/222/09493 19
HG5553 .H39 1987

CAPITAL MARKET - BRAZIL.
Costa, Roberto Teixeira da. Brazil's experience in creating a capital market /. São Paulo [1985] 114 p. : LC Card 86-207924 DDC 332.6/0981 19
HG4523 .C67 1985

Mercado financeiro e de capitais . [Brasília? , 1978?] 118 leaves, [25] leaves of plates : LC Card 84-184169
HG185.B7 M47 1978

CAPITAL MARKET - BRAZIL - RIO DE JANEIRO - HISTORY - 19TH CENTURY.
Sweigart, Joseph Earl. Coffee factorage and the emergence of a Brazilian capital market, 1850-1888 /. New York , 1987. xvi, 337 p. : ISBN 0-8240-1373-5 (alk. paper) : LC Card 87-8617 DDC 338.1/3373/098153 19
HD9199.B8 R567 1987

CAPITAL MARKET - CONGRESSES.
Mercados de capitales bajo inflación /. New York, N.Y. , c1982. xxi, 471 p. : ISBN 0-910365-00-8 : LC Card 82-50965 DDC 332.64 19
HG4523 .M47 1982 ***NYPL [JLE 86-3568]***

A Reforma do mercado de capitais. [Lisbon] [1985] 143 p. : LC Card 87-127037 DDC 332.63 19
HG4523 .R44 1985

Shifting frontiers in financial markets /. Dordrecht ; Boston : xii, 360 p. : ISBN 90-247-3225-5 LC Card 85-18821 DDC 332 19
HG4523 .S54 1986 ***NYPL [JLE 86-2694]***

World monetary system in a time of change . Budapest [1987] 283 p. ; ISBN 963-01-7937-7 (pbk.) LC Card 87-169001 DDC 332.4/5 19
HG230.3 .W68 1987

Capital market equilibria / edited by Günter Bamberg and Klaus Spremann ; with contributions by G. Bamberg ... [et al.]. Berlin ; New York : Springer-Verlag, c1986. x, 228 p. : ill. ; 25 cm. Includes bibliographies and indexes. ISBN 0-387-16248-8 (U. S.) LC Card 86-10104 DDC 332.6/0724 19
1. Capital market - Mathematical models. 2. Equilibrium (Economics) - Mathematical models. 3. Efficient market theory - Mathematical models. I. Bamberg, Günter, 1940-. II. Spremann, Klaus.
HG4523 .C33 1986 ***NYPL [JLE 86-4309]***

CAPITAL MARKET - EUROPEAN ECONOMIC COMMUNITY COUNTRIES.
The ECU market . Lexington, Mass. , c1987. xiii, 246 p. : ISBN 0-669-13833-9 (alk. paper) LC Card 87-4185 DDC 332.4/56094 19
HG930.5 .E27 1987

CAPITAL MARKET - EUROPEAN ECONOMIC COMMUNITY COUNTRIES - ADDRESSES, ESSAYS, LECTURES.
European equity markets . New York , 1984. 470 p. : ISBN 0-8240-6307-4 (alk. paper) : LC Card 83-49440 DDC 332.64/094
HG5430.5.A3 E84 1984 ***NYPL [JLE 86-4508]***

CAPITAL MARKET - GERMANY, WEST.
Möller, Hans Peter. Bilanzkennzahlen und Ertragsrisiken des Kapitalmarktes . Stuttgart , 1986. xii, 240 p. : ISBN 3-7910-0382-8 LC Card 86-149711
HF5681.C25 M64 1986

Seja, Jürgen, 1953- Selektive Effekte der global orientierten Geldpolitik der Deutschen Bundesbank auf die Marktstruktur im Bankensektor /. Frankfurt am Main , New York , c1983. xiii, 370 p. ; ISBN 3-8204-5282-6 LC Card 86-119382
HG3055 .S5 1983

CAPITAL MARKET - GERMANY (WEST) - CONGRESSES.
Mannheimer Bankenforum (1985) Risikokapital über die Börse . Berlin , New York , c1986. x, 190 p. ; ISBN 0-387-16671-8 (U. S.) LC Card 86-225903
HG5492 .M35 1985

CAPITAL MARKET - GERMANY (WEST) - MATHEMATICAL MODELS.
Rothacker, Hartmut. Zeitstetige Bewertungsmodelle für Tilgungsanleihen . Heidelberg , c1986. xxiv, 350 p. : ISBN 3-7908-0343-X LC Card 86-222052
HG4523 .R68 1986

Winkelmann, Michael. Aktienbewertung in Deutschland /. Königstein/Ts. , c1984. xii, 242 p. : ISBN 3-445-02377-8 LC Card 85-103576
HG4523 .W56 1984

CAPITAL MARKET - GOVERNMENT POLICY - ALBERTA.
Alberta. Position and policy statement on enhancing the Alberta capital market. [Edmonton, Alta.] [1985] iii, 43 p. ; LC Card 86-137218 DDC 332.63/23 19
HG5150 .A42 1985

CAPITAL MARKET - GREAT BRITAIN - HISTORY.
Kennedy, William P. (William Paca), 1944- Industrial structure, capital markets, and the origins of British economic decline /. Cambridge [Cambridgeshire] , New York , 1987. xii, 230 p. ; ISBN 0-521-23018-7 LC Card 86-24411 DDC 330.941 19
HC255 .K45 1987

CAPITAL MARKET - HANDBOOKS, MANUALS, ETC.
Kemp, L. J. (Lynette J.) The Wardley guide to world money and securities markets /. London , 1984. xvii, 472 p. ; ISBN 0-903121-66-2 ***NYPL [JLG 86-203]***

CAPITAL MARKET - HISTORY.
Armstrong, Martin A. The greatest bull market in history . [Princeton?] , <c1986-. v. <2 > : LC Card 87-138809 DDC 332.64 19
HG4516 .A75 1986

CAPITAL MARKET - MATHEMATICAL MODELS.
Capital market equilibria /. Berlin , New York , c1986. x, 228 p. : ISBN 0-387-16248-8 (U. S.) LC Card 86-10104 DDC 332.6/0724 19
HG4523 .C33 1986 ***NYPL [JLE 86-4309]***

Firchau, Volker. Information evaluation in capital markets /. Berlin , New York , c1986. iv, 103 p. : ISBN 0-387-16462-6 (U. S.) : LC Card 86-6655 DDC 332.6/0724 19
HG4523 .F57 1986 ***NYPL [JLM 72-289 v.268]***

Markowitz, H. (Harry), 1927- Mean-variance analysis in portfolio choice and capital markets /. Oxford, OX, UK , New York, NY, USA , 1987. xi, 387 p. : ISBN 0-631-15381-0 : LC Card 87-2975 DDC 332.6 19
HG4529.5 .M37 1987

Ohlson, James A. The theory of financial markets and information /. New York , c1987. xiii, 181 p. ; ISBN 0-444-01161-7 LC Card 87-9100 DDC 332.6 19
HG173 .O34 1987

CAPITAL MARKET - NIGERIA.
Shahi, M. A. (Muslehuddin Akhil) Money and capital markets in Nigeria . Bombay , 1983. xi [i.e. x], 60 p. ; LC Card 83-905358 DDC 332/.0412/09669 19
HG187.5.N6 S5 1983 ***NYPL [JLE 87-691]***

CAPITAL MARKET - PERU.
El Mercado de capitales como instrumento de la política económica /. [Miraflores, Lima] [1987] 111 p. ; LC Card 87-169408 DDC 332.6/0985 19
HG5392 .M43 1987

CAPITAL MARKET - PORTUGAL - CONGRESSES.
A Reforma do mercado de capitais. [Lisbon] [1985] 143 p. : LC Card 87-127037 DDC 332.63 19
HG4523 .R44 1985

CAPITAL MARKET - SWITZERLAND.
Zimmermann, Heinz, 1958- Kapitalerhöhungen und Aktienmarkt . Köln , 1986. 446 p. : ISBN 3-921471-57-5 LC Card 87-407823 DDC 332.63/222/09494 19
HG5653 .Z56 1986

CAPITAL MARKET - TURKEY.
Aşıkoğlu, Rıza. Sermaye piyasası aracı olarak enflasyon ortamında tahvilleri değerleme /. [Eskişehir, Turkey] , 1983. xii, 155 p. : LC Card 85-221546
HG5706.5.A3 A85 1983

CAPITAL MARKET - UNITED STATES.
Gart, Alan. Handbook of the money and capital markets /. New York , c1988. p. cm. ISBN 0-89930-270-X (lib. bdg. : alk. paper) LC Card 87-24938 DDC 332.63/2/0973 19
HG181 .G367 1988

Henning, Charles N. Financial markets and the economy /. Englewood Cliffs, N.J. , c1988. xvi, 638 p. : ISBN 0-13-316894-8 LC Card 87-24413 DDC 332/.0973 19
HG181 .H37 1988

CAPITAL - MATHEMATICAL MODELS.
Helmedag, Fritz, 1953- Die Technikwahl bei linearer Einzelproduktion, oder, Die dritte Krise der Profitrate /. Frankfurt am Main , New York , c1986. viii, 301 p. : ISBN 3-8204-9645-9 LC Card 86-219002
HB601 .H44 1986

Hicks, John Richard, Sir, 1904- Capital and time . Oxford [Oxfordshire] , New York , 1987. p. cm. ISBN 0-19-877286-6 : LC Card 87-20233 DDC 332/.041 19
HB501 .H48 1987

Reiss, Winfried, 1941- Umwegproduktion und Positivität des Zinses . Berlin , c1981. 152 p. : ISBN 3-428-05009-6 LC Card 82-146836 DDC 332.8/2/0724 19
HB539 .R423 1981 ***NYPL [JLE 86-2623]***

Sinn, Hans-Werner. [Kapitaleinkommensbesteuerung. English.] Capital income taxation and resource allocation /. Amsterdam ; New York : xiv, 411 p. ; ISBN 0-444-70208-3 LC Card 87-9126 DDC 336.24/3 19
HD2753.A3 S47413 1987

CAPITAL MOVEMENTS - ARGENTINA.
Conesa, Eduardo R. Fuga de capitales . Buenos Aires , 1986. 78 p. : LC Card 87-400256 DDC 332.4/5 19
HG3931 .C66 1986

CAPITAL MOVEMENTS - CENTRAL AMERICA.
Glower, Carlos J., 1952- La fuga de capital en Centroamérica, 1977-1984 /. Tegucigalpa, D.C., Honduras, C.A. , 1986. 20 p. : LC Card 87-125008 DDC 332/.042 19
HG3917 .G56 1986

CAPITAL MOVEMENTS - CONGRESSES.
Internationaler Kapitalverkehr und Devisenhandel /. Frankfurt am Main , c1986. 133 p. ; ISBN 3-7819-0347-8 LC Card 87-164156 DDC 332/.042 19
HG3891 .I58 1986

Lessard, Donald R. Capital flight . Washington, DC , 1987. x, 64 p. ; ISBN 0-88132-059-5 LC Card 87-17279 DDC 332/.042 19
HG3891 .C367 1987

CAPITAL MOVEMENTS - DEVELOPING COUNTRIES.
Capital flight and Third World debt /. Washington, D.C. , 1987. p. cm. ISBN 0-88132-064-1 LC Card 87-17080 DDC 332/.042 19
HG3891 .C36 1987

Status report on concessional flows, April 1986. Washington, D.C., U. S.A. , 1986. 25 p. ; ISBN 0-8213-0789-4 (pbk.) LC Card 86-214496 DDC 336.3/435/091724
HG3891 .S7 1986

CAPITAL MOVEMENTS - DEVELOPING COUNTRIES - CONGRESSES.
Lessard, Donald R. Capital flight . Washington, DC , 1987. x, 64 p. ; ISBN 0-88132-059-5 LC Card 87-17279 DDC 332/.042 19
HG3891 .C367 1987

CAPITAL MOVEMENTS - ECONOMETRIC MODELS.
Rötheli, Tobias F. Das Volkseinkommen und die internationalen Kapitalbewegungen /. Bern , c1986. 128 p. ; ISBN 3-258-03669-1 LC Card 87-110633 DDC 332.4/5/0724 19
HG3891 .R67 1986

CAPITAL MOVEMENTS - EUROPE, EASTERN.
Sinkovics, Alfréd. Nemzetközi tőkemozgások és a KGST /. Budapest , 1986, c1985. 336, [1] p. : ISBN 963-221-493-5 : LC Card 87-408509
HG3891 .S57 1986

CAPITAL MOVEMENTS - EUROPEAN ECONOMIC COMMUNITY COUNTRIES.
Fernández Ordóñez, Francisco. España y la CEE . Madrid, España , 1985. 74 p. ; ISBN 84-505-4317-0 LC Card 86-151137
HG2980.5.A6 F47 1985

CAPITAL MOVEMENTS - GOVERNMENT POLICY - UNITED STATES - HISTORY - 20TH CENTURY.
Hawley, James P., 1944- Dollars & borders . Armonk, N.Y. , c1987. xi, 204 p. ; ISBN 0-87332-386-6 : LC Card 86-31395 DDC 332/.041 19
HG3891 .H38 1987

CAPITAL MOVEMENTS - LATIN AMERICA.
Conesa, Eduardo R. Fuga de capitales . Buenos Aires , 1986. 78 p. : LC Card 87-400256 DDC 332.4/5 19
HG3931 .C66 1986

CAPITAL MOVEMENTS - MATHEMATICAL MODELS.
Frenkel, Roberto. Mercado financiero, expectativas cambiarias y movimientos de capital /. Buenos Aires, Argentina [1981] 46

p. : LC Card 82-236987 DDC 332/.0724 19
HG173.6.S62 F73 1981
NYPL [JLD 86-2636]

CAPITAL MOVEMENTS - MEXICO.
De Murguía, Valdemar. Capital flight and economic crisis . La Jolla, Calif. , 1986. 27 p. ; LC Card 87-621351 DDC 332/.042 19
HG3916 .D4 1986

CAPITAL MOVEMENTS - SOVIET UNION.
Neu, C. R. (Carl Richard), 1949- Toward a profile of Soviet behavior in international financial markets /. Santa Monica, CA [1987] xv, 58 p. : ISBN 0-8330-0865-X (pbk.) LC Card 87-13084 DDC 332/.042/0947 19
HG3955 .N48 1987

CAPITAL MOVEMENTS - SWITZERLAND.
Jacobi, Klaus, 1929- Der induzierte Kapitalexport /. Zürich , c1959. viii, 106 p. ; LC Card 87-408198 DDC 332.4/5609494 19
HG3891 .J33 1959

CAPITAL MOVEMENTS - UNITED STATES.
Danielian, Ronald L. The forgotten deficit . Boulder , 1987. xii, 84 p. ; ISBN 0-8133-7450-2 (pbk. : alk. paper) LC Card 87-50654 DDC 332.6/7373 19
HG3883.U7 D36 1987

CAPITAL MOVEMENTS - UNITED STATES - HISTORY - 20TH CENTURY.
Hawley, James P., 1944- Dollars & borders . Armonk, N.Y. , c1987. xi, 204 p. ; ISBN 0-87332-386-6 : LC Card 86-31395 DDC 332/.041 19
HG3891 .H38 1987

CAPITAL MOVEMENTS - VENEZUELA.
Ojeda, Roseliano. Cómo se desangra un país-- ! . Valencia [Venezuela] , c1987. 241 p. ; ISBN 980-212-037-5 LC Card 87-169695 DDC 330.987/0633 19
HC237 .O365 1987

CAPITAL - NIGERIA - KANO STATE.
Bashir, Ibrahim Lawan, 1948- Sources of capital formation and accumulation among Kano entrepreneurs, 1950-1980 /. Boston, MA (270 Bay State Rd., Boston 02215) , 1986. 17 leaves ; LC Card 87-156659 DDC 332/.0415/096695 19
HC1055.Z9 S33 1986

Capital output ratio in the Indian economy /. Chitale, V. P. New Delhi , 1986. viii, 106 p. ; ISBN 81-7027-099-5 : LC Card 86-901894 DDC 338/.06/0954 19
HC435.2 .C4872 1986

CAPITAL PRODUCTIVITY.
Friedrich, Horst, 1935- Die Produktionsverhältnisse /. Berlin , 1981. 228 p. ; LC Card 81-175348
HC79.I52 F75 1981

CAPITAL PRODUCTIVITY - BULGARIA.
Kotsev, Tsvetan. Formirane i izpolzvane na parichnite fondove v stopanskite organizatsii /. Varna , 1985. 117 p. ; LC Card 85-213610
HC403.Z9 C347 1985

Nakev, Ĭordan V. (Ĭordan Vladimirov) Intenzifikatsiia i efektivno izpolzuvane na osnovnite fondove /. Sofiia , 1985. 203 p. ; LC Card 85-243258
HC403.Z9 C356 1985

CAPITAL PRODUCTIVITY - COMMUNIST COUNTRIES.
Metodiki opredeleniia ėkonomicheskoĭ ėffektivnosti kapital'nykh vlozheniĭ v sotsialisticheskikh stranakh . Moskva , 1981. 101 p. ; LC Card 82-204402
HC244.Z9 C35 1981

CAPITAL PRODUCTIVITY - EUROPE, EASTERN.
Metodiki opredeleniia ėkonomicheskoĭ ėffektivnosti kapital'nykh vlozheniĭ v sotsialisticheskikh stranakh . Moskva , 1981. 101 p. ; LC Card 82-204402
HC244.Z9 C35 1981

CAPITAL PRODUCTIVITY - INDIA.
Chitale, V. P. Capital output ratio in the Indian economy /. New Delhi , 1986. viii, 106 p. ; ISBN 81-7027-099-5 : LC Card 86-901894 DDC 338/.06/0954 19
HC435.2 .C4872 1986

CAPITAL PRODUCTIVITY - KIRGHIZ S.S.R.
Abdurakhmanov, I. (Ibraim) Ėffektivnost' kapital'nykh vlozheniĭ v promyshlennosti Kirgizii /. Frunze , 1981. 174 p. ; LC Card 82-160618
HC337.K5453 C32 1981

CAPITAL PRODUCTIVITY - RUSSIAN S.F.S.R. - IAKUTSKAIA A.S.S.R.
Ėffektivnost' kapital'nykh vlozheniĭ i novoĭ tekhniki v narodnom khoziaĭstve IAkutskoĭ ASSR . IAkutsk , 1981. 91 p. ; LC Card 82-217455
HC337.I23 C34 1981

CAPITAL PRODUCTIVITY - SOVIET UNION.
Androsov, V. I. (Vasiliĭ Ivanovich) Ėffektivnost' kapital'nogo stroitel'stva v torgovle /. Moskva , 1980. 213 p. ; LC Card 81-132839
HC340.C3 A65 1980

Cherniavskiĭ, V. O. (Vasiliĭ Osipovich) Ėffektivnost' i optimal'nost' kapital'nykh vlozheniĭ /. Leningrad , 1986. 68, [4] p. ; LC Card 85-179296
HC340.C3 C4 1986

Chernoivanov, G. E. (Gennadiĭ Efimovich) Fondoëmkost' produktsii i ėffektivnost' sotsialisticheskogo proizvodstva /. Moskva , 1980. 156 p. ; LC Card 81-134415
HC340.C3 C54 1980

Lenskaia, S. A. (Svetlana Alekseevna) Proizvodstvennye fondy kak ėkonomicheskaia kategoriia /. Moskva , 1982. 126 p. ; LC Card 83-134249
HC340.C3 L396 1982

Problemy povysheniia ėkonomicheskoĭ ėffektivnosti kapital'nykh vlozheniĭ v territorial'nye promyshlennye kompleksy. Moskva , 1983. 170 p. : LC Card 84-202808
HC340.C3 P747 1983

Puzanov, V. D. (Valeriĭ Dmitrievich) Proizvodstvennoe nakoplenie . Moskva , 1983. 109 p. ; LC Card 83-194433
HC340.S3 P89 1983

Rezervy intensifikatsii vosproizvodstva osnovnykh fondov i ikh ispol'zovaniia /. Moskva , 1984. 204 p. ; LC Card 85-240369
HC340.C3 R48 1984

CAPITAL PRODUCTIVITY - SWEDEN - HISTORY.
Magnusson, Lars, 1941- Kapitalbildning i Sverige 1750-1860 . Uppsala , Stockholm , 1983. 95 p. ; ISBN 91-554-1443-5 LC Card 83-228044
HC374 .M34 1983

Capital taxation in India /. Saraf, B. P., 1939- New Delhi , c1983. viii, 268 p. ; LC Card 83-902683 DDC 343.5405/3 345.40353 19
HJ4126.I45 S27 1983 **NYPL [JLD 86-3821]**

CAPITAL - UNITED STATES - HISTORY.
Sklar, Martin J., 1935- The corporate reconstruction of American capitalism, 1890-1916 . Cambridge [Cambridgeshire] , New York , 1987. p. cm. ISBN 0-521-30921-2 LC Card 87-9408 DDC 338.8/0973 19
HC110.C3 S58 1987

Capital y tecnología en México y América Latina /. Wionczek, Miguel S. México , 1981. 413 p. ; ISBN 968-470-018-0 **NYPL [JLE 87-377]**

CAPITALISM.
Abercrombie, Nicholas. Sovereign individuals of capitalism /. London , Boston , 1986. 211 p. ; ISBN 0-04-301230-2 (alk. paper) LC Card 86-1122 DDC 330.12/2 19
HB501 .A23 1986 **NYPL [JLD 86-3686]**

Aktuelle Probleme der Marktwirtschaft in gesamt- und einzelwirtschaftlicher Sicht . Berlin , c1984. 458 p., [1] leaf of plates : ISBN 3-428-05653-1 LC Card 85-128275
HB501 .A514 1984

Amin, Samir. La déconnexion, pour sortir du système mondial /. Paris , 1986, c1985. 333 p. : ISBN 2-7071-1588-6 : LC Card 86-219988
HF1413 .A45 1986

Berberoglu, Berch. The internationalization of capital . New York , 1987. xxi, 223 p. : ISBN 0-275-92169-7 (alk. paper) : LC Card 86-25259 DDC 337 19
HF1411 .B367 1987

Bömer, Hermann. Die drohende Katastrophe . Frankfurt am Main , 1984. 257 p. : ISBN 3-88012-708-5 : LC Card 85-128942
HC59 .B5925 1984

Bowles, Samuel. Democracy and capitalism . New York , c1986. x, 244 p. ; ISBN 0-465-06052-8 : LC Card 85-47991 DDC 321.8 19
JC423 .B76 1986 **NYPL [JLE 86-2928]**

Braudel, Fernand. La dynamique du capitalisme /. Paris , c1985. 120 p. ; ISBN 2-7003-0501-9 : LC Card 86-130442
HC51 .B675 1985

Brenner, Y. S. Capitalism, competition and economic crisis . Brighton, Sussex , Washington, D.C. , 1984. x, 262 p. ; ISBN 0-7108-0722-8 **NYPL [JLD 86-2553]**

Capitalismes fin de siècle /. Paris , c1986. 268 p. : ISBN 2-13-039425-6 : LC Card 86-231136
HC106.8 .C364 1986

Cazadero, Manuel. Desarrollo, crisis e ideología en la formación del capitalismo . México , 1986. 153 p. ; ISBN 968-16-2280-4 LC Card 87-403551 DDC 330.12/2 19
HB501 .C33 1986

Coase, R. H. (Ronald Harry) The firm, the market, and the law /. Chicago , 1988. p. cm. ISBN 0-226-11100-8 LC Card 87-24193 DDC 338.5/142 19
HD2326 .C6 1988

Corbridge, Stuart. Capitalist world development . London , 1986. xi, 295 p. : ISBN 0-333-32405-6 **NYPL [JLD 86-2925]**

Cowling, Keith. Transnational monopoly capitalism /. Sussex [England] , New York , 1987. vii, 178 p. : ISBN 0-312-00954-2 (St. Martin's) : LC Card 87-4965 DDC 338.8/8 19
HD2755.5 .C68 1987

Damus, Renate. Die Legende von der Systemkonkurrenz . Frankfurt , New York , c1986. 245 p. ; ISBN 3-593-33590-5 LC Card 86-196924
HB90 .D36 1986

Denezhnoe obrashchenie i kredit kapitalisticheskikh stran /. Moskva , 1977. 342 p. ; LC Card 82-196677
HG173.6.R8 D46 1977

Diumulen, I. I. (Ippolit Ippolitovich) Sovremennyĭ tarifnyĭ i netarifnyĭ protektsionizm . Moskva , 1975. 277 p. ; LC Card 82-191746
HF1713 .D62 1975

Dolgovremennye tendentsii v kapitalisticheskom vosproizvodstve . Moskva , 1985. 229 p. : LC Card 86-187722
HB3711 .D62 1985

Domdey, Karl Heinz. Weltwirtschaft und Weltwirtschaftslehre . Berlin , 1984. 366 p. : LC Card 84-245611
HC54 .D65 1984

Dubinin, S. K. (Sergeĭ Konstantinovich) Krizis biudzhetno-finansovogo regulirovaniia ėkonomiki kapitalizma /. Moskva , 1984. 100 p. ; LC Card 84-222701
HJ236 .D82 1984

Eichner, Alfred S. The macrodynamics of advanced market economies /. Armonk, N.Y. , c1987. x, 945 p. : ISBN 0-87332-439-0 (pbk.) LC Card 87-9693 DDC 330.12/2 19
HB501 .E4 1987

Faminskiĭ, Igor' Pavlovich. Ėkonomika sovremennogo imperializma . Moskva , 1987. 175 p. ; LC Card 87-170222
HB501 .F275 1987

Foster, John Bellamy. The theory of monopoly capitalism . New York , 1986. 280 p. ; ISBN 0-85345-688-7 : LC Card 85-32097 DDC 330.12/2 19
HB501 .F66 1986 **NYPL [JLD 86-2415]**

Gaillard, Claude, 1930- Economie et droit du développement /. Alger , c1982. 439 p. ; LC Card 83-216670
HD75 .G34 1982

García, Antonio, 1912- [Bases de la economía contemporánea.] Bases de economía política /. [Bogotá] , 1981. 283 p. ; LC Card 82-138900 DDC 330/.098 19
HB122 .G37 1981 **NYPL [JLD 87-868]**

Gorz, André. [Chemins du paradis. English.] Paths to paradise . London , 1985. vii, 120 p. ; ISBN 0-86104-762-1 (pbk.) :
NYPL [JLD 86-3006]

Grasnick, Georg, 1927- Alter Kapitalismus, "neue Armut" /. Berlin , 1985. 78 p. : LC Card 86-132510 DDC 330.12/2 19
HB501 .G64 1985

Guiba (Writer) Por qué nos confunden-- el comunismo, el capitalismo, los economistas, las elites? /. Montevideo , 1981. 211 p. ; LC Card 82-125535 DDC 330.9/04 19
HC54 .G79 1981 ***NYPL [JLC 86-320]***

Heilbroner, Robert L. Behind the veil of economics . New York , 1988. p. cm. ISBN 0-393-02542-X LC Card 87-20392 DDC 330.12/2 19
HB501 .H396 1988

Helmer, Hans-Josef. Merkantilismus und Kapitalismus im modernen Rationalisierungsprozess /. Frankfurt , c1986. iii, 223 p. ; ISBN 3-88323-647-0 LC Card 87-113030 DDC 330.15/13 19
HB91 .H436 1986

Hexē hapla mathēmata . Thessalonikē , 1945. 32, 16 p. ; LC Card 87-122267
HB501 .H475 1945

Holland, Stuart. The market economy . New York , 1987. xiv, 363 p. : ISBN 0-312-01324-8 : LC Card 87-20908 DDC 330.12/2 19
HB501 .H56 1987

International capitalism and industrial restructuring . Boston , 1987. p. cm. ISBN 0-04-338132-4 (alk. paper) LC Card 86-28870 DDC 338.7 19
HD2321 .I58 1987

Itō, Makoto, 1936- The basic theory of capitalism . Totowa, N.J. , 1987. p. cm. ISBN 0-389-20729-2 LC Card 87-905 DDC 330.12/2 19
HB97.5 .I823 1987

Jackson, Robin. Rational economics /. New York , c1987. v, 145 p. ; ISBN 0-8022-2529-2 : LC Card 86-30260 DDC 330.1 19
HB501 .J27 1987

Katzner, Donald W., 1938- Walrasian microeconomics . Reading, Mass. , c1988. xv, 512 p. : ISBN 0-201-10461-X : LC Card 86-26622 DDC 338.5 19
HB172 .K38 1988

Keller, Friedrich Jakob, 1893- Das Ende des Kapitalismus . Lyss [1981] 211 p. : LC Card 84-104878
HB95 .K33 1981

Kleinewefers, Henner. Reformen für Wirtschaft und Gesellschaft . Frankfurt , New York , c1985. 532 p. : ISBN 3-593-33466-6 LC Card 85-143393
HD84 .K543 1985

Korolev, I. S. (Ivan Sergeevich) Valiūtnye otnoshenii͡a kapitalizma . Moskva , 1986. 228 p. ; LC Card 86-232369
HG6230.3 .K66 1986

Kritika antimarksistskikh vzgli͡adov po problemam NTR /. Moskva , 1987. 157 p. ; LC Card 87-164887
HC340.T4 K75 1987

Lapit͡skiĭ, Mark Isaakovich. The tragedy of millions . Moscow , 1985. 54 p., [8] p. of plates : LC Card 87-100047 DDC 331.13/7 19
HD5708 .L36 1985

Lash, Scott. The end of organized capitalism /. Madison, Wis. , c1987. 383 p. : ISBN 0-299-11670-0 : LC Card 87-14248 DDC 330.12/2 19
HB501 .L278 1987

Le Capitalisme monopoliste d'État. Paris [1971] 2 v. LC Card 75-585406
HC59 .C26 ***NYPL [JLC 71-28]***

Lenin, Vladimir Il'ich, 1870-1924. [Imperializm kak Vysshai͡a stadii͡a kapitalizma. Azerbaijani.] Imperijalizm kapitalizmin ăn jeni devri gibi [microform] /. Baqï , 1927. 99 p. ;
NYPL [*ZO-247 no. 1]

Lima, Rômulo de Araújo, 1949- Em busca da dialética . Campina Grande-Paraíba , 1983. 102 p. ; LC Card 86-130003
HB97.5 .L464 1983

López Díaz, Pedro. Crítica de la economía y la política /. México , 1985. 255 p. ; ISBN 968-590-060-4 LC Card 86-156378
HB501 .L856 1985

Martine, Joël. L'or, la parole, l'Etat . Paris , c1983. 296 p. : ISBN 2-7157-1065-8 LC Card 83-133521
HX542 .M32 1983 ***NYPL [JLD 87-872]***

Marxismus-Leninismus, eine immer junge und wissenschaftliche Lehre (Radio Program). Selections. Neue Phänomene der kapitalistischen Gesellschaft ändern nichts an ihrem Wesen . Wien , 1976. 35 p. : LC Card 85-144894
HB501 .M338 1976

Miles, Robert, 1950- Capitalism and unfree labour . London ; New York : 250 p. : ISBN 0-422-61730-X LC Card 87-3599 DDC 331.11/734 19
HB501 .M654 1987

Mirovoe kapitalisticheskoe khozi͡aĭstvo v 80-e gody . Moskva , 1985. 220 p. ; LC Card 87-166175
HC59 .M549 1985

Molina Ibáñez, Mercedes. Capitalismo y socialismo . Madrid , c1984. 128 p. : ISBN 84-7046-358-6 LC Card 85-135836
HB501 .M694 1984

Naím, Moisés. Posibilidades y limitaciones del funcionamiento de los mercados en los países menos desarrollados . Caracas , c1985. 88 p. : ISBN 980-217-006-2 LC Card 86-193990
HB501 .N255 1985

Noble, Charles, 1948- Liberalism at work . Philadelphia , 1986. x, 292 p. : ISBN 0-87722-421-8 (alk. paper) : LC Card 86-1766 DDC 353.0083/0289 19
HD7654 .N63 1986 ***NYPL [JLE 86-4426]***

Nouvelles technologies et enjeux sociaux . Lyon , c1986. 230 p. : ISBN 2-7297-0279-2 : LC Card 86-187357
HC79.T4 N68 1986

Poletti, Ronaldo. Estado, economia e liberdade /. Brasília, DF [1986] 11 p. ; LC Card 87-403230 DDC 330 19
HB179.P75 P65 1986

Potapov, V̲. V. (Viktor Vladimirovich) Modifikat͡sii teorii "poleznosti" /. Moskva , 1984. 132 p. ; LC Card 84-247447
HB201 .P65 1984

Die Protestantische Ethik und der Verfall des Kapitalismus . [Hamburg] , 1985. 31 p. : LC Card 86-112068
HB501 .P76 1985

Resnick, Stephen A. Knowledge and class . Chicago , c1987. vii, 352 p. ; ISBN 0-226-71021-1 LC Card 86-32631 DDC 335.4 19
HB97.5 .R48 1987

Rol' bankov v usilenii gospodstva finansovogo kapitala /. Moskva , 1985. 206 p. ; LC Card 86-102078
HG3881 .R615 1985

Die Rolle der Rüstung in der Wirtschaft des heutigen Kapitalismus /. Berlin [1984] 127 p. ; LC Card 85-135711
HC281 .B39 1984 Heft 4 HC79.D4

Roncolini, Giuliana, 1948- La crisi della legittimità borghese . Napoli , 1978. 115 p. ; ISBN 88-20-70809-4 : LC Card 79-368996
HC54 .R64 ***NYPL [JLD 81-254]***

Rymalov, V. V. (Viktor Vladimirovich) Podryv vekovykh ustoev . Moskva , 1984. 268, [3] p. : LC Card 85-112238
HC59 .R839 1984

Seabrook, Jeremy, 1939- Landscapes of poverty /. Oxford, U.K. , 1985. x, 175 p. ; ISBN 0-631-14508-7 : LC Card 86-673976
HC79.P6 S36x 1985

Serra Ramoneda, Antonio. Sistema económico y empresa /. Barcelona , 1986. 267 p. : ISBN 84-344-2011-2 LC Card 87-122090
HD37.S66 S46 1986

Sherman, Howard J. Foundations of radical political economy /. Armonk, N.Y. , c1987. xi, 425 p. ; ISBN 0-87332-416-1 : LC Card 86-33849 DDC 330.1 19
HB97.5 .S5117 1987

Sixel, Friedrich W. Crisis and critique . Leiden , New York , 1987. p. cm. ISBN 90-04-08284-0 (pbk.) : LC Card 87-17217 DDC 330.12/2 19
HB501 .S618 1987

Sovremennyĭ kapitalizm . Leningrad , 1985. 212 p. ; LC Card 86-117888
HB501 .S824 1985

Sovremennyĭ konservatizm i krizis burzhuaznoĭ ėkonomicheskoĭ nauki . Moskva , 1986. 175 p. ; LC Card 87-165796
HB241 .S673 1986

Sutcliffe, Robert B. Hard times . London , 1983. 118 p. ; ISBN 0-86104-505-X (pbk.) : LC Card 83-126438 DDC 330.9/04 19
HC59 .S8873 1983 ***NYPL [JLD 86-4088]***

Tammer, Hans. Monopole, Profite, Ausbeutung /. Berlin , 1983. 237 p. : LC Card 84-142912
HD2757.2 .T35 1983

T͡Sygankov, P. A. (Pavel Afanas'evich) V bor'be protiv vsevlastii͡a kapitala /. Moskva , 1986. 139 p. ; LC Card 86-132423
HB501 .T78 1986

Upravlenie prot͡sessom novovvedeniĭ v kapitalisticheskoĭ firme /. Moskva , 1985. 228 p. : LC Card 86-151912
HD58.8 .U67 1985

Velarde Fuertes, Juan. El libertino y el nacimiento del capitalismo /. Madrid , c1981. 158 p. ; ISBN 84-368-0178-4 LC Card 82-101990
HB501 .V39 1981

Viotti, Eduardo Baumgratz. A economia e o estado capitalista /. Petrópolis , 1986. 96 p. ; LC Card 87-137699 DDC 338.9 19
HD85.P65 V56 1986

Weingarten, Richard. Eine kapitaltheoretische Untersuchung zum Gesetz vom tendenziellen Fall der Profitrate einschliesslich der Bestimmung seiner empirischen Relevanz /. München , c1982. ix, 342 p. ; ISBN 3-597-10136-4 LC Card 83-134240
HB601 .W37 1982

Wittmann, Walter, 1935- Wider die organisierte Verantwortungslosigkeit . Frauenfeld , c1984. 175 p. ; ISBN 3-7193-0938-X : LC Card 84-234445
HB95 .W57 1984

Wolf, Charles, 1924- Markets or governments . Cambridge, Mass. , c1988. xv, 220 p. : ISBN 0-262-23134-4 LC Card 87-118516 DDC 338.9 19
HB501 .W89 1988

Zinn, Karl Georg. Arbeit, Konsum, Akkumulation . Hamburg , 1986. 243 p. : ISBN 3-87975-347-4 LC Card 86-230933
HB103.K47 Z56 1986

Zur Theorie und Praxis imperialistischer Anpassungs- und Konfrontationspolitik in der Gegenwart /. Berlin [1986] 99 p. ; LC Card 87-409046 DDC 330.12/2 19
HB501 .Z765 1986

Zwass, Adam. Zwei Weltsysteme . Wien , c1985. 264 p. ; ISBN 3-203-50891-5 LC Card 85-240587 DDC 338.9 19
HB501 .Z93 1985 ***NYPL [JLD 87-226]***

CAPITALISM - ADDRESSES, ESSAYS, LECTURES.

Campesinado y capitalismo en Colombia /. Bogotá, Colombia , 1981. 233 p. ; LC Card 82-141108 DDC 338.1/09861 19
HD516 .C35 1981 ***NYPL [JLD 86-1342]***

Capitalismul contemporan şi teoria [microform] . Bucureşti , 1965. 440 p. ; LC Card 77-452767
HB179.R6 C34 ***NYPL [*ZT-1732 no.2]***

Convergenze tra capitalismo e socialismo . Milano , 1978. lxxi, 399 p. ; LC Card 80-478455
HB501 .C727 ***NYPL [JLD 81-646]***

Corporations and the common good /. Notre Dame, Ind. [Boston] , c1986. xii, 147 p. ; ISBN 0-268-00754-3 : LC Card 85-40597 DDC 174/.4 19
HB501 .C7614 1986 ***NYPL [JLD 86-2145]***

Couri, Sergio, 1948- Ensaios sobre a evolução dos sistemas econômicos /. Brasília-Distrito Federal [1983] 133 p. : LC Card 84-116306 DDC 330.1 19
HB97.5 .C68 1983 ***NYPL [JLE 86-3363]***

The Future of private enterprise /. Atlanta, Ga. , 1984-1986. 3 v. ; ISBN 0-88406-164-7 (pbk. : v. 1) LC Card 83-25386 DDC 338.6/1 19
HB501 .F83 1984 ***NYPL [JLK 87-49]***

Harcourt, Geoffrey Colin. Controversies in political economy . New York , 1986. 293 p. ; ISBN 0-8147-3437-5 : LC Card 85-31055 DDC 330.1 19
HB75 .H33 1986 ***NYPL [JLD 86-3571]***

Marcy, Sam, 1911- Anatomy of the economic crisis /. Atlanta , c1982. viii, 120 p. : ISBN 0-89567-077-1 (pbk.) ***NYPL [JLD 86-1329]***

Production, work, territory . Boston , 1986. xix, 344 p. : ISBN 0-04-338126-X (alk. paper) LC Card 85-20006 DDC 330 19
HC59 .P682 1986 ***NYPL [JLE 86-1745]***

CAPITALISM - AFRICA.
Marsden, Keith. Private enterprise in Africa . Washington, D.C. [1987] xiii, 66 p. ; ISBN 0-8213-0945-5 (pbk.) LC Card 87-18419 DDC 330.96/032 19
HC800 .M353 1987

CAPITALISM - AMERICA - HISTORY.
García, Miguel Angel. El nacimiento de América . México, D.F. , 1984. 284 p. : ISBN 968-415-089-X LC Card 87-403199 DDC 332/.0415/091812 19
HC94.Z9 S34 1984

Capitalism and agriculture in the Haouz of Marrakesh /. Pascon, Paul. [Haouz de Marrakech. English.] London ; New York : 248 p. : ISBN 0-7103-0189-8 LC Card 87-100309 DDC 338.1/0964/6 19
HD2121.Z9 M37613 1986

Capitalism and democracy : Schumpeter revisited / edited by Richard D. Coe and Charles K. Wilber. Notre Dame, Ind. : University of Notre Dame Press, c1985. ix, 190 p. : ill. ; 22 cm. Includes bibliographies. ISBN 0-268-00750-0 : LC Card 84-40362 DDC 335 19
1. Schumpeter, Joseph Alois, 1883-1950. Capitalism, socialism, and democracy - Addresses, essays, lectures. 2. Socialism - Addresses, essays, lectures. 3. Capitalism - Addresses, essays, lectures. 4. Democracy - Addresses, essays, lectures. I. Coe, Richard D. II. Wilber, Charles K.
HX72.S383 C36 1985 ***NYPL [JLD 85-1987]***

Capitalism and equality in America / edited by Peter L. Berger. Lanham : Hamilton Press ; [New York] : Institute for Educational Affairs, c1987. ix, 306 p. : ill. ; 24 cm. (Modern capitalism . v. 1) Includes bibliographies. ISBN 0-8191-5572-1 (v. 1 : alk. paper) : LC Card 86-24739 DDC 330.12/2 19
1. Capitalism - United States. 2. Equality - United States. 3. Income distribution - United States. I. Berger, Peter L. II. Institute for Educational Affairs (New York, N.Y.). III. Series.
HB501 .C2423 1987

Capitalism and equality in the Third World / edited by Peter L. Berger. Lanham : Hamilton Press ; [New York] : Institute for Educational Affairs, c1987. 375 p. ; 24 cm. (Modern capitalism . v. 2) Includes bibliographies. ISBN 0-8191-5574-8 (v. 2 : alk. paper) : LC Card 86-24749 DDC 330.12/2 19
1. Capitalism - Developing countries. 2. Equality - Developing countries. 3. Income distribution - Developing countries. 4. Developing countries - Economic conditions. I. Berger, Peter L. II. Institute for Educational Affairs (New York, N.Y.). III. Series.
HB501 .C24234 1987

Capitalism and unfree labor. Miles, Robert, 1950- Capitalism and unfree labour . London ; New York : 250 p. : ISBN 0-422-61730-X LC Card 87-3599 DDC 331.11/734 19
HB501 .M654 1987

Capitalism and unfree labour . Miles, Robert, 1950- London ; New York : 250 p. : ISBN 0-422-61730-X LC Card 87-3599 DDC 331.11/734 19
HB501 .M654 1987

CAPITALISM - ASIA - HISTORY - CONGRESSES.
Europe and the rise of capitalism /. Oxford [Oxfordshire] , New York, NY, USA , 1987. p. cm. ISBN 0-631-15006-4 : LC Card 87-12293 DDC 330.94 19
HC240.9.C3 E97 1987

Capitalism at war . Godfrey, John F. Leamington Spa, UK ; New York : xiv, 313 p. ; ISBN 0-85496-519-X : LC Card 86-32708 DDC 338.944 19
HD3616.F82 G63 1987

CAPITALISM - AUSTRIA.
Armut in Österreich . Graz , c1977. 168 p. : ISBN 3-7011-7080-0 LC Card 86-176543
HC270.P6 A75 1977

Morawetz, Inge, 1955- Die verborgene Macht . Frankfurt , New York , c1986. 200 p. : ISBN 3-593-33662-6 LC Card 86-223864
HG3008 .M67 1986

CAPITALISM - BRAZIL.
Franco, Luiz L. O Brasil que temos, o país que queremos /. Guarulhos, S.P. [Brazil] , c1985. 87 p. ; LC Card 86-223053
HC187 .F7315 1985

Martins, Luciano, 1934- Estado capitalista e burocracia no Brasil pós-64 /. Rio de Janeiro, RJ , 1985. 265 p. ; LC Card 85-232969 DDC 338.981 19
HC187 .M2947 1985 ***NYPL [JLD 86-1691]***

CAPITALISM - BRAZIL - FORTALEZA.
Casimiro, Liana Maria Carleial de. Acumulação capitalista, emprego e crise . São Paulo , 1986. 216 p. : LC Card 87-152202 DDC 331.12/0981/31 19
HD5755.F6 C37 1986

CAPITALISM - BRAZIL - HISTORY.
Barreiro, José Carlos. Campesinato e capitalismo /. Campinas-SP [1986] 128 p. ; LC Card 86-229683
HD1531.B7 B37 1986

CAPITALISM - BRAZIL - PINDARÉ RIVER VALLEY.
Luna, Regina Celi Miranda Reis. A terra era liberta . São Luís, MA , 1985. xxvii, 146 p. : LC Card 87-135907 DDC 333.3/0981/21 19
HD499.P46 L86 1985

CAPITALISM - BRAZIL - RIO GRANDE DO SUL.
Duarte, Laura Maria Goulart. Capitalismo & cooperativismo no R.G.S. /. Porto Alegre-RS , c1986. 96 p. : ISBN 85-25-40088-2 : LC Card 86-150404
HD1491.B82 R563 1986

CAPITALISM - BURKINA FASO.
Berg, Elliot. Mobilization of the private sector in Burkina Faso . [Burkina Faso? , 1985] 21 p. ; LC Card 87-116357 DDC 338.966/25 19
HC1040 .B47 1985

CAPITALISM - CHILE.
Caputo, Orlando. Notas metodológicas para el análisis de la nueva forma de funcionamiento del capitalismo . Cochabamba [1980] 33 leaves ; LC Card 83-204246
HC192 .C216 1980

Fontaine Talavera, Arturo. Pautas para la confección de una política económica . Santiago, Chile , 1984. 92 leaves : LC Card 86-177872
HC192 .F58 1984

CAPITALISM - CHINA - CONGRESSES.
Foreign capital and technology in China /. New York , 1987. xvii, 191 p. : ISBN 0-275-92716-4 (alk. paper) : LC Card 87-2450 DDC 332.6/7314/0951 19
HG5782 .F67 1987

Capitalism, class conflict, and the new middle class /. Carter, Bob, 1949- London , Boston , 1985. vii, 256 p., 15 p. ; ISBN 0-7100-9624-0 : LC Card 84-9956 DDC 305.5/56 19
HD8039.M39 C37 1985
NYPL [JLD 87-115]

CAPITALISM - COLORADO - HISTORY.
Neuschatz, Michael. The golden sword . New York , 1986. xii, 301 p. ; ISBN 0-313-25104-5 (lib. bdg. : alk. Paper) LC Card 85-27026 DDC 331.88/122334/09788 19
HD8039.M61 U48 1986
NYPL [JLE 87-766]

CAPITALISM - COMMUNIST COUNTRIES.
Popov, Nikola Grigorov. Sŭshtnost, formi i nasoki na izzhivi͡avane na chastnata stopanska deĭnost pri sotsializma /. Sofii͡a , 1985. 363 p. ; LC Card 85-169713
HC704 .P66 1985 ***NYPL [*QK 87-1471]***

Capitalism, competition and economic crisis . Brenner, Y. S. Brighton, Sussex , Washington, D.C. , 1984. x, 262 p. ; ISBN 0-7108-0722-8
NYPL [JLD 86-2553]

CAPITALISM - CONGRESSES.
Capitalismo riformato e sinistra . Milano , 1986. 125 p. ; ISBN 88-24-50380-2 : LC Card 86-229688
HB501 .C24265 1986

Democratic capitalism? . Charlottesville , 1986. ix, 210 p. ; ISBN 0-8139-1112-5 LC Card 86-7755 DDC 321.8 19
JC423 .D4416 1986
NYPL [(not yet cat'd 4/16/87)]

Probleme der staatsmonopolistischen Wirtschaftsregulierung . Rostock , 1981. 35 p. ; LC Card 86-211250
HB501 .P694 1981

A 80-as évek kapitalizmusa . [Budapest] , 1985. 406 p. ; ISBN 963-09-2696-2 : LC Card 86-186468
HB501 .A14 1985

CAPITALISM - COSTA RICA - HISTORY.
Esquivel, Francisco. El desarrollo del capital en la industria de Costa Rica, 1950-1970 /. Heredia, Costa Rica , 1985. 197 p. : ISBN 997-7650-16-0 LC Card 86-210026
HC143 .E83 1985

CAPITALISM - DEVELOPING COUNTRIES.
Capitalism and equality in the Third World /. Lanham [New York] , c1987. 375 p. ; ISBN 0-8191-5574-8 (v. 2 : alk. paper) : LC Card 86-24749 DDC 330.12/2 19
HB501 .C24234 1987

Naím, Moisés. Posibilidades y limitaciones del funcionamiento de los mercados en los países menos desarrollados . Caracas , c1985. 88 p. : ISBN 980-217-006-2 LC Card 86-193990
HB501 .N255 1985

Rangel Guevara, Carlos. [Tercermundismo. English.] Third world ideology and Western reality . New Brunswick , c1986. xiii, 180 p. ; ISBN 0-88738-601-6 (pbk.) LC Card 85-24486 DDC 330.9172/4 19
HC59.7 .R26513 1985 ***NYPL [JLE 86-3009]***

Capitalism divided? . Ingham, Geoffrey K. Basingstoke, Hampshire , 1984. viii, 304 p. : ISBN 0-333-30116-1 LC Card 86-673507
HC255 .I495x 1984b

CAPITALISM - DOMINICA - HISTORY.
Trouillot, Michel-Rolph. Peasants and capital . Baltimore , c1988. xiv, 344 p. : ISBN 0-8018-3481-3 (alk. paper) LC Card 87-20018 DDC 305.5/63 19
HD1531.D58 T76 1988

CAPITALISM - DOMINICAN REPUBLIC - CONGRESSES.
Influencia del sector privado sobre la realidad nacional. [Santo Domingo] [1986] 180 p., [1] leaf of plates : LC Card 86-190331
HC153.5 .I53 1986

CAPITALISM - DOMINICAN REPUBLIC - HISTORY.
Bosch, Juan, 1909- Capitalismo tardío en la República Dominicana /. Santo Domingo, República Dominicana , 1986. 238 p. : LC Card 87-401709 DDC 330.97293/054 19
HC153.5 .B665 1986

CAPITALISM - ECUADOR.
Los Grupos monopólicos en el Ecuador . Quito, Ecuador , 1986. 208 p. : LC Card 87-404236 DDC 338.8/2/09866 19
HD2838 .G78 1986

Ycaza, Patricio. Movimiento obrero, estado y modernización capitalista en el Ecuador, 1960-1983 /. Ecuador [1985 or 1986] 38 p. ; LC Card 86-171415
HC202 .Y35 1985

CAPITALISM - ENGLAND - HISTORY.
Lachmann, Richard. From manor to market . Madison, Wis. , 1987. xiv, 166 p. : ISBN 0-299-11420-1 : LC Card 87-40146 DDC 330.942/05 19
HC254 .L33 1987

CAPITALISM - EUROPE - HISTORY.
Day, John, 1924- The medieval market economy /. Oxford, UK , New York, NY, USA , 1987. p. cm. ISBN 0-631-15479-5 : LC Card 86-26862 DDC 330.94/01 19
HC41 .D39 1987

CAPITALISM - EUROPE - HISTORY - 20TH CENTURY.
Lutz, Burkart, 1925- Der kurze Traum immerwährender Prosperität . Frankfurt/Main , New York , c1984. 272 p. ; ISBN 3-593-33418-6 LC Card 85-131822
HC240 .L88 1984

CAPITALISM - EUROPE - HISTORY - CONGRESSES.
Europe and the rise of capitalism /. Oxford [Oxfordshire] , New York, NY, USA , 1987. p. cm. ISBN 0-631-15006-4 : LC Card 87-12293 DDC 330.94 19
HC240.9.C3 E97 1987

CAPITALISM - FRANCE.
Poncins, Michel de. Tous capitalistes, ou, La réponse au socialisme /. Vouillé [France] , c1983. 164 p. ; LC Card 83-244442 DDC 338.944 19
HC276.2 .P63 1983 ***NYPL [JLD 86-427]***

CAPITALISM - GEORGIAN S.S.R. - HISTORY - 19TH CENTURY.
Nac'vlišvili, N. Memamuluri meurneobis kapitalisturi evoluc'ia Aġmosavlet' Sak'art'veloši /. T'bilisi , 1971. 107 p. ; LC Card 86-168887
HC337.G38 N33 1971

CAPITALISM - GERMANY - HISTORY.
Razvitie kapitalisticheskoĭ manufaktury v Anglii i Germanii XVI-XVII vv. . Moskva , 1981. 132 p. : LC Card 83-111684
HD9735.G32 R39 1981

CAPITALISM - GERMANY (WEST)
Das Politische System der BRD . Berlin , 1985. 479 p. ; LC Card 86-123928 DDC 320.943 19
JN3971.A2 P59 1985 ***NYPL [JLD 86-3144]***

Die Rolle der Rüstung in der Wirtschaft des heutigen Kapitalismus /. Berlin [1984] 127 p. ; LC Card 85-135711
HC281 .B39 1984 Heft 4 HC79.D4

CAPITALISM - GREAT BRITAIN - HISTORY.
Razvitie kapitalisticheskoĭ manufaktury v Anglii i Germanii XVI-XVII vv. . Moskva , 1981. 132 p. : LC Card 83-111684
HD9735.G32 R39 1981

CAPITALISM - HISTORY.
Beaud, Michel. [Histoire du capitalisme, 1500-1980. English.] A history of capitalism, 1500-1980 /. London , 1984. 256 p. ; ISBN 0-333-35957-7 LC Card 87-673370
HC51 .B3813x 1984

Capitalismo e classe operária no Brasil /. Petrópolis , 1984. 69 p. ; LC Card 86-222585
HC51 .C35 1984

Cox, Robert W., 1926- Production, power, and world order . New York , 1987. xii, 500 p. ; ISBN 0-231-05808-X LC Card 86-26387
HD6971 .C78 1987

Domínguez, Jaime de Jesús, 1947- Feudalismo, capitalismo mercantil y capitalismo industrial /. Santo Domingo, República Dominicana , 1981. 229 p. ; ISBN 84-89527-00-8 LC Card 82-200900
HC21 .D66 1981

CAPITALISM - HISTORY - 20TH CENTURY.
Hartmann, Wolf-Dietrich, 1946- Kapitale Karrieren . Berlin , c1986. 154 p. : LC Card 86-214325
HG172.A2 H37 1986

CAPITALISM - HUNGARY.
Szelényi, Iván. Socialist entrepreneurs . Madison, Wis. , 1988. p. cm. ISBN 0-299-11360-4 : LC Card 87-16085 DDC 338.1/09439 19
HD1940.5 .S94 1988

CAPITALISM - INDIA.
Patnaik, Utsa. The agrarian question and the development of capitalism in India /. Delhi , New York , 1986. 45 p. ; ISBN 0-19-561954-4 : LC Card 86-900017 DDC 338.1/0954 19
HD2072 .P33 1986

CAPITALISM - INDIA - ANDHRA PRADESH.
Krishna Rao, Y. V. Growth of capitalism in agriculture . Vijayawada , 1984. x, 62 p. ; LC Card 84-900585 DDC 338.1/3/095484 19
HD2075.A5 K75 1984 ***NYPL [JLD 86-4256]***

CAPITALISM - INDIA - CASE STUDIES.
Krishna Rao, Y. V. Growth of capitalism in agriculture . Vijayawada , 1984. x, 62 p. ; LC Card 84-900585 DDC 338.1/3/095484 19
HD2075.A5 K75 1984 ***NYPL [JLD 86-4256]***

CAPITALISM - KENYA.
Kongstad, Per. Industri, fagbevægelse og lønarbejde i Kenya . Roskilde [1983] 76 p. ; LC Card 85-238103
HC865 .K66 1983

Wegner, Gerhard, 1953- Bauern, Kapital und Staat in Kenia . Berlin , c1983. 94 p. : ISBN 3-88619-038-2 : LC Card 85-171380
HD1538.K4 W44 1983

CAPITALISM - LATIN AMERICA.
Benítez, José Antonio, 1921- La dependencia, el subdesarrollo y la publicidad comercial capitalista /. La Habana, Cuba , 1986. 133 p., [2] p. of plates : LC Card 87-404231 DDC 659.1/098 19
HF5813.L29 B46 1986

Chilcote, Ronald H. Latin America . Boulder , 1986. xv, 175 p. ; ISBN 0-8133-0239-0 (pbk.) : LC Card 85-13899 DDC 338.98 19
HC125 .C487 1986 ***NYPL [JLE 86-4264]***

CAPITALISM - MATHEMATICAL MODELS.
Goodwin, Richard M. (Richard Murphey), 1913- The dynamics of a capitalist economy /. Boulder , 1987. p. cm. ISBN 0-8133-0482-2 : LC Card 86-33965 DDC 330.12/2 19
HB501 .G622 1987

CAPITALISM - MEXICO.
Hellman, Judith Adler. Notes on the failure of reformist capitalism in Mexico /. Toronto, Ont., Canada [1976] 24 p ; LC Card 85-155317 DDC 338.972 19
HC135 .H38 1976

Rivera Ríos, Miguel Angel. Crisis y reorganización del capitalismo mexicano, 1960-1985 /. México, D.F. , 1986. 227 p. : ISBN 968-411-149-5 LC Card 87-401541 DDC 330.972/083 19
HC135 .R435 1986

CAPITALISM - MEXICO - FUERTE RIVER VALLEY - HISTORY.
Gill, Mario. La conquista del Valle del Fuerte /. Culiacán, Rosales, Sinaloa, México , c1983. 273 p., [4] folded leaves of plates : LC Card 86-121747
HC137.F84 G54 1983

CAPITALISM - MEXICO - HISTORY - 19TH CENTURY.
Vásquez M., Luis (Vásquez Medina) El mercantilismo mexicano versus el liberalismo inglés /. México, D.F. , 1985. xiii, 215 p., [18] p. of plates : LC Card 87-403512 DDC 380.1/0972 19
HC135 .V34 1985

CAPITALISM - MEXICO - MONTERREY - HISTORY.
Saragoza, Alex. The Monterrey elite and the Mexican State, 1880-1940 /. Austin , c1988. p. cm. ISBN 0-292-71113-1 LC Card 87-23779 DDC 305.5/234/097213 19
HG185.M6 S27 1988

CAPITALISM - MEXICO - TABASCO (STATE) - HISTORY.
Tostado Gutiérrez, Marcela. El Tabasco porfiriano /. Villahermosa [Mexico] , 1985. 179 p. : ISBN 968-88900-7-3 LC Card 86-189960
HC137.T3 T67 1985

CAPITALISM - MORAL AND ETHICAL ASPECTS.
McKenzie, Richard B. The fairness of markets . Lexington, Mass. , c1987. xiv, 235 p. : ISBN 0-669-14801-6 (alk. paper) LC Card 86-45958 DDC 330 19
HB72 .M35 1987

Marktwirtschaft und Gesellschaftsordnung . Berlin , c1983. 220 p., [1] leaf of plates : ISBN 3-428-05365-6 LC Card 83-191615
HB72 .M248 1983

Waibl, Elmar. Ökonomie und Ethik . Stuttgart-Bad Cannstatt , c1984. 429 p. ; ISBN 3-7728-0892-1 LC Card 85-130712
HB501 .W28 1984

CAPITALISM - MOROCCO - ESSAOUIRA - HISTORY - 18TH CENTURY.
Schroeter, Daniel J. Merchants of Essaouira . Cambridge , New York , 1988. p. cm. ISBN 0-521-32455-6 LC Card 87-15163 DDC 330.964/6 19
HC810.Z7 E857 1988

CAPITALISM - MOROCCO - ESSAOUIRA - HISTORY - 19TH CENTURY.
Schroeter, Daniel J. Merchants of Essaouira . Cambridge , New York , 1988. p. cm. ISBN 0-521-32455-6 LC Card 87-15163 DDC 330.964/6 19
HC810.Z7 E857 1988

CAPITALISM - MOROCCO - MARRAKESH REGION - HISTORY.
Pascon, Paul. [Haouz de Marrakech. English.] Capitalism and agriculture in the Haouz of Marrakesh /. London ; New York : 248 p. : ISBN 0-7103-0189-8 LC Card 87-100309 DDC 338.1/0964/6 19
HD2121.Z9 M37613 1986

CAPITALISM - PERU - CUZCO (DEPT.)
Cori Castro, Wilfredo. Mercados y precios en la economía campesina . [Cuzco, Peru] , 1986. 29 p. : LC Card 86-200941
HC228.C8 C59 1986

CAPITALISM - PERU - HISTORY.
Humala Tasso, Ulises. Subdesarrollo o camino al colapso . [S.l. , 1987?] (Lima, Perú : Graphos 100 Editores) 175 p. ; LC Card 87-403093 DDC 330.985/0633 19
HC227 .H86 1987

CAPITALISM - PSYCHOLOGICAL ASPECTS.
Kurthen, Hermann. Politische Ökonomie und Persönlichkeitstheorie . Köln , 1985. 245 p. ; ISBN 3-7609-5181-3 LC Card 85-155083
HB74.P8 K87 1985

CAPITALISM - PUERTO RICO - HISTORY.
Dietz, James L., 1947- Economic history of Puerto Rico . Princeton , c1986. xxiii, 337 p., [11] p. of plates : ISBN 0-691-07716-9 (alk. paper) : LC Card 86-12313 DDC 330.97295 19
HC154.5 .D54 1986 ***NYPL [JLE 87-1592]***

CAPITALISM - RELIGIOUS ASPECTS - CHRISTIANITY.
Griffiths, Brian. The creation of wealth . Downers Grove, Ill. , c1984. 160 p. : ISBN 0-87784-566-2 (pbk.) : LC Card 85-5210 DDC 330.12/2 19
HB72 .G74 1984 ***NYPL [JLD 86-3576]***

Wogaman, J. Philip. Economics and ethics . Philadelphia , c1986. xiii, 145 p. ; ISBN 0-8006-1904-8 (pbk.) LC Card 85-45478 DDC 261.8/5 19
HB72 .W633 1986 ***NYPL [JLD 86-3984]***

CAPITALISM - RELIGIOUS ASPECTS - CONGRESSES.
Morality of the market . Vancouver, B.C., Canada , c1985. xxv, 601 p. ; ISBN 0-88975-074-2 (pbk.) : LC Card 86-158049 DDC 174/.4 19
HB72 .M56 1985

CAPITALISM - RELIGIOUS ASPECTS - PROTESTANT CHURCHES.
Die Protestantische Ethik und der Verfall des Kapitalismus . [Hamburg] , 1985. 31 p. : LC Card 86-112068
HB501 .P76 1985

CAPITALISM - RUSSIAN S.F.S.R. - URAL MOUNTAINS REGION - HISTORIOGRAPHY.
Ural i problemy regional'noĭ istoriografii. Sverdlovsk , 1986. 83 p. ; LC Card 87-159699
HC337.R852 U73853 1986

CAPITALISM - SOCIAL ASPECTS.
Moskovtsev, I. S. (Ivan Sergeevich) Sovremennyĭ imperializm, antogonizmy i krizisy /. Moskva , 1985. 67 p. : LC Card 85-232554
HB501 .M7219 1985

CAPITALISM - SOCIAL ASPECTS - GREAT BRITAIN - HISTORY.
Williamson, Jeffrey G., 1935- Did British capitalism breed inequality? /. Boston , 1985. ix, 270 p. : ISBN 0-04-942186-7 : LC Card 84-20413 DDC 339.2/2/0941 19
HC260.I5 W45 1985 ***NYPL [JLE 86-1361]***

CAPITALISM - SOUTH AFRICA - KIMBERLEY - HISTORY.
Turrell, Robert Vicat. Capital and labour on the Kimberley diamond fields, 1871-1890 /. Cambridge [Cambridgeshire] , New York , 1987. xviii, 297 p. : ISBN 0-521-33354-7 LC Card 86-32740 DDC 331.7/622382/0968711 19
HD9677.S63 K567 1987

CAPITALISM - SOUTH ASIA.
Bhairav, Kalki Kaal. Populist manifesto /. Grand Forks, ND, USA (830 S. 48th St., Grand Forks 58201) [c1986] vii, 85 p. ; LC Card 86-201038 DDC 338.954 19
HC430.6 .B46 1986

CAPITALISM - SOVIET UNION - HISTORY.
Küttler, Wolfgang. Lenins Formationsanalyse

der bürgerlichen Gesellschaft in Russland vor 1905 . Berlin , 1978. 331 p. ; LC Card 86-102733
HC334.5 .K87 1978

CAPITALISM - SOVIET UNION - HISTORY - 19TH CENTURY - COLLECTED WORKS.
Druzhinin, N. M. (Nikolaĭ Mikhaĭlovich) Sotsial'no-ėkonomicheskaia istoriia Rossii . Moskva , 1987. 421 p., [1] leaf of plates : LC Card 87-164847
HC334.5 .D78 1987

CAPITALISM - TURKEY - HISTORY - 19TH CENTURY.
Keyder, Caglar. State and class in Turkey . London ; New York , 1987. 252 p. ; ISBN 0-86091-877-7 (pbk.) : LC Card 87-14992 DDC 338.9561 19
HC492 .K497 1987

Pamuk, Şevket. The Ottoman empire and European capitalism, 1820-1913 . Cambridge [Cambridgeshire] , New York , 1987. xii, 278 p. : ISBN 0-521-33194-3 LC Card 86-28386 DDC 330.956/01 19
HF1583.4 .P36 1987

CAPITALISM - TURKEY - HISTORY - 20TH CENTURY.
Keyder, Caglar. State and class in Turkey . London , New York , 1987. 252 p. ; ISBN 0-86091-877-7 (pbk.) : LC Card 87-14992 DDC 338.9561 19
HC492 .K497 1987

CAPITALISM - UKRAINE - HISTORY - 18TH CENTURY.
Ponomarev, Alekseĭ Mikhaĭlovich. Rozvytok kapitalistychnykh vidnosyn u promyslovosti Ukraïny XVIII st. /. L'viv , 1971. 181 p. ; LC Card 82-105634
HC337.U5 P58 1971

CAPITALISM - UNITED STATES.
Arnold, Ron. Ecology wars . Bellevue, Wash. , c1987. 182 p. ; ISBN 0-939571-00-5 LC Card 87-17 DDC 363.7/00973 19
HC110.E5 A77 1987

Capitalism and equality in America /. Lanham [New York] , c1987. ix, 306 p. : ISBN 0-8191-5572-1 (v. 1 : alk. paper) : LC Card 86-24739 DDC 330.12/2 19
HB501 .C2423 1987

Hodgetts, Richard M. Essentials of economics and free enterprise /. Menlo Park, Calif. , c1987. 437 p. : ISBN 0-201-20719-2 LC Card 86-207031 DDC 330 19
HB171.5 .H677 1987

Hollingsworth, J. Rogers (Joseph Rogers), 1932- The governance of the American economy . Berlin [1985] 60 p. ; LC Card 86-205784 DDC 330.973 19
HC106.8 .H635 1985

Magdoff, Harry. Stagnation and the financial explosion /. New York , c1987. 208 p. : ISBN 0-85345-716-6 : LC Card 86-33129 DDC 330.973/0927 19
HC106.8 .M315 1987b

Plotkin, Sidney. Keep out . Berkeley , c1987. xiii, 360 p. ; ISBN 0-520-05806-2 LC Card 86-30807 DDC 333.3/0973 19
HD205 .P56 1987

Die Rolle der Rüstung in der Wirtschaft des heutigen Kapitalismus /. Berlin [1984] 127 p. ; LC Card 85-135711
HC281 .B39 1984 Heft 4 HC79.D4

Stock, Walter. High Technology . Köln , 1986. 244 p. : ISBN 3-7609-1049-1 : LC Card 86-230225
HC110.H53 S76 1986

CAPITALISM - UNITED STATES - HISTORY.
Chandler, Alfred Dupont. The coming of managerial capitalism . Homewood, Ill. , 1985. xiv, 877 p. : ISBN 0-256-03285-8 LC Card 84-82470 DDC 338.6/44/0973 19
HD2785 .C47 1985 ***NYPL [JLE 86-4418]***

Livingston, James, 1949- Origins of the Federal Reserve System . Ithaca , 1986. 250 p. ; ISBN 0-8014-1844-5 (alk. paper) LC Card 85-48199 DDC 332.1/1/0973 19
HG2563 .L58 1986 ***NYPL [JLE 86-2522]***

CAPITALISM - UNITED STATES - MORAL AND ETHICAL ASPECTS.
The Common good and U. S. capitalism /. Lanham, MD , c1987. viii, 425 p. ; ISBN 0-8191-6364-3 (alk. paper) : LC Card 87-8334 DDC 306/.36/0973 19
HD60.5.U5 C665 1987

CAPITALISM - UNITED STATES - PUBLIC OPINION.
Reinarman, Craig. American states of mind . New Haven , c1987. x, 262 p. ; ISBN 0-300-03817-8 (alk. paper) LC Card 86-26752 DDC 330.12/2/0973 19
HD3616.U47 R1464 1987

CAPITALISM - URUGUAY.
Peirano, Ricardo. El rol del empresario privado en el desarrollo económico y social en democracia /. Montevideo, Uruguay , 1986. 79 leaves ; LC Card 87-404359 DDC 338.9895 19
HC232 .P45 1986

CAPITALISM - VENEZUELA.
Larrazábal, Radamés. Los planes del capitalismo para la década de los 80 /. [Caracas, Venezuela? , 1982] (Caracas, Venezuela : Cooperative Mixta de Trabajadores Gráficos) 81 p. ; LC Card 83-201901
HC237 .L325 1982

CAPITALISM - YUGOSLAVIA.
Der Kapitalistische Charakter der jugoslawischen Arbeiterselbstverwaltung im Lichte des 8. Kongresses des Bundes der Kommunisten Jugoslawiens. Tirana , 1965. 54 p. ; LC Card 85-127335
HD5660.Y8 K27 1965

CAPITALISM - ZAIRE - HAUT-ZAÏRE.
MacGaffey, Janet. Entrepreneurs and parasites . Cambridge [Cambridgeshire] , New York , 1987. xiii, 241 p. : ISBN 0-521-33533-7 LC Card 87-13160 DDC 338.09675/1 19
HC955.Z7 K49956 1987

CAPITALISM - ZAIRE - KISANGANI.
MacGaffey, Janet. Entrepreneurs and parasites . Cambridge [Cambridgeshire] , New York , 1987. xiii, 241 p. : ISBN 0-521-33533-7 LC Card 87-13160 DDC 338.09675/1 19
HC955.Z7 K49956 1987

CAPITALISM - ZAIRE - KIVU.
MacGaffey, Janet. Entrepreneurs and parasites . Cambridge [Cambridgeshire] , New York , 1987. xiii, 241 p. : ISBN 0-521-33533-7 LC Card 87-13160 DDC 338.09675/1 19
HC955.Z7 K49956 1987

Le capitalisme mondial /. Michalet, Charles Albert. Paris [c1985], c1976. 368 p. : ISBN 2-13-039215-6 : LC Card 86-137294 DDC 338.8/8 19
HD2755.5 .M52 1985

Capitalismes fin de siècle / publié sous la direction de Robert Boyer, avec la collaboration de Michel Aglietta ... [et al.]. 1re éd. Paris : Presses universitaires de France, c1986. 268 p. : ill. ; 22 cm. (Economie en liberté, 0768-0988) Includes bibliographies. ISBN 2-13-039425-6 : LC Card 86-231136
1. United States - Economic conditions - 1981-. 2. France - Economic conditions - 1945-. 3. Developing countries - Economic conditions. 4. Capitalism. 5. Economic development. 6. United States - Economic policy - 1981-. 7. France - Economic policy - 1945-. 8. Developing countries - Economic policy. I. Boyer, Robert. II. Aglietta, Michel. III. Series.
HC106.8 .C364 1986

Capitalismo. Caputo, Orlando. Notas metodológicas para el análisis de la nueva forma de funcionamiento del capitalismo . Cochabamba [1980] 33 leaves ; LC Card 83-204246
HC192 .C216 1980

Capitalismo & cooperativismo no R.G.S. /. Duarte, Laura Maria Goulart. Porto Alegre-RS , c1986. 96 p. : ISBN 85-25-40088-2 : LC Card 86-150404
HD1491.B82 R563 1986

Capitalismo de estado, 1927-1956 /. Angueira, María del Carmen. Buenos Aires , c1986. 116 p. : ISBN 950-25-1416-5 LC Card 87-100705
HD9711.A72 A54 1986

El capitalismo dependiente y su incidencia en el problema agrario venezolano /. Portocarrero de Guzmán, Blancanieve. Valencia, Venezuela , c1985. 189 p. : LC Card 86-226697
HD1333.V4 P67 1985

Capitalismo e classe operária no Brasil / Serviço de Educação Popular. 3a. ed. Petrópolis : Vozes, 1984. 69 p. ; 21 cm. (Série "Estudos" / Serviço de Educação Popular . 2) Bibliography: p. 69. LC Card 86-222585
1. Economic history. 2. Capitalism - History. 3. Labor and laboring classes - History. 4. Brazil - Economic conditions. I. Serviço de Educação Popular (Rio de Janeiro, Brazil). II. Series: Série "Estudos" (Serviço de Educação Popular (Rio de Janeiro, Brazil)) , 2.
HC51 .C35 1984

Capitalismo e cooperativismo no R.G.S. Duarte, Laura Maria Goulart. Capitalismo & cooperativismo no R.G.S. /. Porto Alegre-RS , c1986. 96 p. : ISBN 85-25-40088-2 : LC Card 86-150404
HD1491.B82 R563 1986

Capitalismo riformato e sinistra : forum di "Repubblica," 14 febbraio 1986 / i relatori, Giorgio Ruffolo ... [et al.].1a ed. Milano : Comunità, 1986. 125 p. ; 22 cm. ISBN 88-24-50380-2 : LC Card 86-229688
1. Capitalism - Congresses. 2. Economic policy - Congresses. 3. Social policy - Congresses. 4. Socialism - Congresses. 5. Communism - Congresses. I. Ruffolo, Giorgio.
HB501 .C24265 1986

Capitalismo tardío en la República Dominicana /. Bosch, Juan, 1909- Santo Domingo, República Dominicana , 1986. 238 p. : LC Card 87-401709 DDC 330.97293/054 19
HC153.5 .B665 1986

Capitalismo y socialismo . Molina Ibáñez, Mercedes. Madrid , c1984. 128 p. : ISBN 84-7046-358-6 LC Card 85-135836
HB501 .M694 1984

Capitalismul contemporan şi teoria [microform] : studii critice / [Gh.P. Apostol ... et al.]. Bucureşti : Editura politică, 1965. 440 p. ; 20 cm. Table of contents in Romanian, French, German, and Russian. Includes bibliographical references. Microfilm. New York : New York Public Library, 1986. 1 microfilm reel ; 35 mm. (MN *ZZ-26,610) LC Card 77-452767
1. Economics - Addresses, essays, lectures. 2. Economic history - 1945-1971 - Addresses, essays, lectures. 3. Capitalism - Addresses, essays, lectures. I. Apostol, Gheorge.
HB179.R6 C34 ***NYPL [*ZT-1732 no.2]***

CAPITALIST AND FINANCIERS - FRANCE - HISTORY - 18TH CENTURY.
Bruguière, Michel. Gestionnaires et profiteurs de la Révolution . Paris , c1986. 339 p. : ISBN 2-85565-332-0 : LC Card 87-123230
HJ1083 .B78 1986

Capitalist property and financial power . Scott, John, 1912- Brighton, Sussex , 1986. x, 230 p. ; ISBN 0-7450-0047-9 ***NYPL [JLD 86-3078]***

Capitalist world development . Corbridge, Stuart. London , 1986. xi, 295 p. : ISBN 0-333-32405-6 ***NYPL [JLD 86-2925]***

CAPITALISTS AND FINANCIERS.
Intercorporate relations . Cambridge [Cambridgeshire] , New York , 1987. x, 330 p. : ISBN 0-521-33503-5 LC Card 87-6388 DDC 338.7 19
HD2741 .I585 1987

CAPITALISTS AND FINANCIERS - ARAB COUNTRIES - DIRECTORIES.
The APS who's who in Middle East banking & trade. Nicosia, Cyprus , c1984. 2 v. : LC Card 83-149147 ***NYPL [JLF 86-983]***

CAPITALISTS AND FINANCIERS - CANADA.
Francis, Diane. Controlling interest . Toronto, Ont., Canada , c1986. 352 p. ; ISBN 0-7715-9744-4 LC Card 86-218086 DDC 338.8/0971 19
HD2809 .F73 1986

CAPITALISTS AND FINANCIERS - CANADA - BIOGRAPHY.
How, Douglas. [Very private person.] Canada's mystery man of high finance . Hantsport, N.S. , 1986. 173 p. : ISBN 0-88999-305-X (pbk.) LC Card 86-207291 DDC 338.092/2 B 19
HG172.K55 H68 1986

CAPITALISTS AND FINANCIERS - FLORIDA - BIOGRAPHY.
Akin, Edward N. Flagler, Rockefeller partner and Florida baron /. Kent, Ohio , c1988. xiii, 305 p. : ISBN 0-87338-348-6 (alk. paper) LC Card

87-2070 DDC 338/.04/0924 B 19
HC102.5.F55 A75 1988

CAPITALISTS AND FINANCIERS - FRANCE - BIOGRAPHY.
Bruguière, Michel. Gestionnaires et profiteurs de la Révolution . Paris , c1986. 339 p. : ISBN 2-85565-332-0 : LC Card 87-123230
HJ1083 .B78 1986

CAPITALISTS AND FINANCIERS - GREAT BRITAIN - BIOGRAPHY - DICTIONARIES.
Dictionary of business biography . London , 1984. 5 v. : ISBN 0-406-27340-5 (set) LC Card 86-188034 DDC 338/.0092/2 B 19
HC252.5.A2 D53 1984 NYPL [JLM 86-569]

CAPITALISTS AND FINANCIERS - HISTORY - 20TH CENTURY.
Hartmann, Wolf-Dietrich, 1946- Kapitale Karrieren . Berlin , c1986. 154 p. : LC Card 86-214325
HG172.A2 H37 1986

CAPITALISTS AND FINANCIERS - ITALY.
Turani, Giuseppe. Briganti e gentiluomini della finanza italiana /. [Milano] , c1987. 394 p. ; ISBN 88-20-00657-X : LC Card 87-168620
HG186.I8 T86 1987

CAPITALISTS AND FINANCIERS - MEXICO - MONTERREY - HISTORY.
Saragoza, Alex. The Monterrey elite and the Mexican State, 1880-1940 /. Austin , c1988. p. cm. ISBN 0-292-71113-1 LC Card 87-23779 DDC 305.5/234/097213 19
HG185.M6 S27 1988

CAPITALISTS AND FINANCIERS - SOUTH AFRICA - HISTORY - 19TH CENTURY.
Wheatcroft, Geoffrey. The Randlords /. New York , 1987, c1985. xix, 314 p. : ISBN 0-671-63993-5 (pbk.) : LC Card 87-4513 DDC 338.2/0968 19
HD9536.S62 W44 1985

CAPITALISTS AND FINANCIERS - SWEDEN.
Andersson, Dan, 1948- Vad gör kapitalisterna? . Stockholm , c1983. 167 p. : ISBN 91-550-2919-1 : LC Card 84-143408
HG186.S85 A53 1983

CAPITALISTS AND FINANCIERS - SWEDEN - REGISTERS.
Sundqvist, Sven-Ivan, 1939- Ägarna och makten i Sveriges börsföretag 1985 =. [Stockholm] [1985] 318 p. : ISBN 91-7588-085-7 : LC Card 86-105378
HG186.S85 S86 1985 NYPL [JLE 86-3810]

CAPITALISTS AND FINANCIERS - UKRAINE - BIOGRAPHY.
Pamíati Abrama ÍUr'evicha Dobrogo. Pamíati Abrama ÍUr'evicha Dobrago. Parizh , 1939. 101 p., [1] leaf of plates : LC Card 83-136332
HG185.S65 P36 1939

CAPITALISTS AND FINANCIERS - UNITED STATES.
Allen, Frederick Lewis, 1890-1954. The lords of creation. New York, London, 1935. xii, 483 p. LC Card 35-20649 DDC 332.0973
HG181 .A57 NYPL [JLD 86-1097]

Scholl, Heinz. Bilderberger & Trilaterale . Euskirchen, Bundesrepublik Deutschland , c1977. 92 p. ; LC Card 85-199172
HD2785 .S396 1977

Slater, Robert, 1943- The titans of takeover /. Englewood Cliffs, N.J. , c1987. ix, 230 p. : ISBN 0-13-922055-0 LC Card 86-25364 DDC 338.8/3/0973 19
HD2785 .S44 1987

CAPITALISTS AND FINANCIERS - UNITED STATES - BIOGRAPHY.
Browder, Clifford, 1928- The money game in old New York . Lexington, KY , c1986. viii, 319 p., [8] p. of plates : ISBN 0-8131-1573-6 LC Card 85-17938 DDC 332/.092/4 B 19
HG172.D74 B76 1986 NYPL [JFE 86-1911]

Hammer, Armand, 1897- Hammer /. New York , c1987. 544 p., [32] p. of plates : ISBN 0-399-13275-9 LC Card 86-30289 DDC 338.092/4 B 19
HC102.5.H35 A3 1987

Klein, Maury, 1939- The life and legend of Jay Gould /. Baltimore , c1986. xvi, 595 p., [24] p. of plates : ISBN 0-8018-2880-5 (alk. paper) LC Card 85-24107 DDC 332/.092/4 B 19
HC102.5.G68 K55 1986
NYPL [JFE 86-2364]

Matz, Mary Jane. The many lives of Otto Kahn /. New York [1984] x, 299 p., [8] p. of plates : ISBN 0-918728-36-3 : LC Card 83-26326 DDC 361.7/4/0924 B 19
HV28.K32 M37 1984 NYPL [JFD 86-2699]

Shields, Jerry. The invisible billionaire, Daniel Ludwig /. Boston , 1986. xii, 401 p. : ISBN 0-395-35402-1 : LC Card 86-7519 DDC 387.5/092/4 B 19
HE569.L84 S55 1986 NYPL [JFE 86-3861]

Train, John. The midas touch . New York , c1987. xi, 207 p. ; ISBN 0-06-015643-0 : LC Card 86-45157 DDC 332.6/092/4 B 19
HG172.B84 T72 1987

CAPITALISTS AND FINANCIERS - UNITED STATES - HISTORY.
DiBacco, Thomas V. Made in the U. S.A. . New York , c1987. xii, 290 p. ; ISBN 0-06-015624-4 : LC Card 86-45652 DDC 338.0973 19
HC103 .D46 1987 NYPL [JLD 87-1292]

Folsom, Burton W. Entrepreneurs versus the historians /. Washington, DC , New York, NY , c1987. p. cm. ISBN 0-89526-573-7 : LC Card 87-23390 DDC 338/.04/0973 19
HG181 .F647 1987

CAPITALISTS AND FINANCIERS - VENEZUELA - HISTORY - 20TH CENTURY.
Brito Figueroa, Federico. La aristocracia del dinero en Venezuela actual, 1945-1985 /. Barquisimeto, Venezuela , 1986- v. <1 > ; ISBN 980-608-700-3 (v. 1) : LC Card 87-404343 DDC 305.5/234/0987 19
HG185.V4 B75 1986

CAPITALISTS AND FINANCIERS - ZAIRE - CASE STUDIES.
MacGaffey, Janet. Entrepreneurs and parasites . Cambridge [Cambridgeshire] , New York , 1987. xiii, 241 p. : ISBN 0-521-33533-7 LC Card 87-13160 DDC 338.09675/1 19
HC955.Z7 K49956 1987

CAPITALIZATION (FINANCE) see **CORPORATIONS - FINANCE; SECURITIES.**

Capitelli, René. Die Zinsstruktur der Schweiz : ein faktoranalytischer Ansatz im Frequenzbereich / René Capitelli. Frankfurt am Main : Haag + Herchen, c1983. ix, 221 p. : ill. ; 21 cm. (Schriftenreihe des Instituts für Empirische Wirtschaftsforschung der Universität Zürich . Bd. 12) Originally presented as the author's thesis (doctoral)--Universität Zürich. Bibliography: p. 213-220. ISBN 3-88129-700-6 LC Card 84-129042
1. Interest rates - Switzerland. I. Title. II. Series.
HG1623.S9 C36 1983

Caplan, David L. The professional option trader's manual / by David L. Caplan. Malibu, Calif. (P.O. Box 2126, Malibu 90265) : Opportunities in Options, c1987. 2 v. in 1 (viii, 177 p.) : ill. ; 28 cm. Bibliography: p. 139-140. CONTENTS. - v. 1. Basic concepts -- v. 2. Advanced concepts. LC Card 87-116716 DDC 332.64/52 19
1. Put and call transactions. I. Title.
HG6042 .C36 1987

Caple, John. The right work : finding it and making it right / John Caple. New York, N.Y. : Dodd, Mead, 1977. xvi, 269 p. ; 24 cm. "A Gamut book." Includes index. ISBN 0-396-09064-8 LC Card 87-15734 DDC 650.1/4 19
1. Vocational guidance. 2. Career changes. 3. Success in business. 4. Job satisfaction. I. Title.
HF5381 .C2634 1987

Capon, Noel. Corporate strategic planning / Noel Capon, John Farley, and James M. Hulbert. New York : Columbia University Press, 1987. p. cm. (Columbia studies in business, government, and society) Bibliography: p. Includes index. ISBN 0-231-06380-6 LC Card 87-18239 DDC 658.4/012 19
1. Strategic planning. 2. Corporate planning. I. Farley, John U. II. Hulbert, James M. III. Title. IV. Series.
HD30.28 .C375 1987

Cappelen, Ådne, 1942- Gleditsch, Nils Petter, 1942- Economic incentives to arm? . Oslo [1986] 72 p. : ISBN 82-7288-134-9 LC Card 87-163647 DDC 338.4/36234 19
HC79.D4 G54 1986

Capps, Oral. Food demand analysis . Blacksburg, Va. [1986] xii, 292 p. : LC Card 87-620670 DDC 339.4/86413 19
HD9000.5 .F5946 1986

Capsicum y cultura . Long-Solís, Janet. México , 1986. 181 p. : ISBN 968-16-2124-7 LC Card 86-221123
HD9235.P462 M65 1986

Captain David B. Walker, journal and papers, 1864-1869 . Walker, David B., 1841 or 2-ca. 1906. Juneau, Alaska (Pouch G, Juneau 99811) , 1984. 60 p. : LC Card 84-622198
HD9481.U4 W359 1984

Captive insurance companies . Bawcutt, P. A. (Paul A.) Cambridge [Cambridgeshire] , Wolfeboro, N.H. , 1987. xii, 410 p. : ISBN 0-85941-382-9 : LC Card 86-32621 DDC 368/.0068 19
HG8104 .B38 1987

Caputo, Orlando. Notas metodológicas para el análisis de la nueva forma de funcionamiento del capitalismo : (Chile, desde Septiembre de 1973) / Orlando Caputo. Cochabamba : Universidad Mayor de San Simón, Instituto de Estudios Sociales y Económicos, [1980] 33 leaves ; 29 cm. (Serie "Esquemas" . no. 4) Binder's title: Capitalismo. LC Card 83-204246
1. Chile - Economic conditions - 1970-. 2. Capitalism - Chile. I. Title: Nueva forma de funcionamiento del capitalismo. II. Title: Capitalismo. III. Series.
HC192 .C216 1980

Car-free in Boston : the guide to public transit in Greater Boston & New England / editor, Gordon Lewin ; associate editor, Charles Bahne.5th ed. Cambridge, MA (P.O. Box 192, Cambridge 02238) : Association for Public Transportation, c1986. 160 p. : ill. ; 21 cm. Includes index. LC Card 86-231024 DDC 388.4/09744 19
1. Local transit - Massachusetts - Boston Metropolitan Area - Handbooks, manuals, etc. 2. Local transit - New England - Handbooks, manuals, etc. I. Lewin, Gordon, 1951-. II. Bahne, Charles. III. Association for Public Transportation.
HE4491.B8 C37 1986

The Car industry : labour relations and industrial adjustment / David Marsden ... [et al.]. London ; New York : Tavistock, 1985. viii, 210 p. : ill. ; 22 cm. (Social science paperbacks) Includes indexes. Bibliography: p. [197]-201. ISBN 0-422-79550-X LC Card 85-14742 DDC 331/.04292/0941 19
1. Industrial relations - Great Britain. 2. Trade-unions - Automobile industry workers - Great Britain. 3. Automobile industry and trade - Great Britain - Management. I. Marsden, David.
HD6976.A82 G72 1985
NYPL [JLD 87-403]

CAR WASHES - UNITED STATES.
Hess, Alan. Googie . San Francisco, CA [1986]. 144 p. : ISBN 0-87701-334-9 (pbk.) : LC Card 85-17089 DDC 725/.71/0973 19
NA7856 .H47 1986
NYPL [3-MQWO 86-2210]

Carabelli, Umberto. Balducci, Cataldo. Il sindacato /. Torino , c1984. 2 v. ; ISBN 88-02-03818-X (set) : LC Card 85-158972 DDC 344.45/0188 344.504188 19
LAW NYPL [JLE 86-3250]

CARACAS REGION (VENEZUELA) - COMMERCE - HISTORY - 19TH CENTURY.
Lucena Salmoral, Manuel. Vísperas de la independencia americana . Madrid , 1986. vii, 389 p. ; ISBN 84-205-1308-3 LC Card 86-205153
HF3490.C37 L83 1986

Características básicas y evolución reciente del sector externo de El Salvador. San Salvador, El Salvador : Fundación Salvadoreña para el Desarrollo Económico y Social, 1986. 47 p. : ill. ; 29 cm. At head of title: Departamento de Estudios Económicos y Sociales. Errata slip inserted. Includes bibliographical references. LC Card 87-403789 DDC 337.7284 19
1. El Salvador - Foreign economic relations. I. Fundación Salvadoreña para el Desarrollo Económico y Social. Departamento de Estudios Económicos y Sociales.
HF1494 .C37 1986

Características de los instrumentos de ahorro. Santiago, Chile : Dirección de Política Financiera, Banco Central de Chile, 1983. 91 p. ; 26 cm. LC Card 84-119555 DDC 332.63/2/0983 19
1. Securities - Chile. 2. Saving and investment - Chile. I. Banco Central de Chile, Santiago. Dirección de Política Financiera.
HG5342 .C37 1983 ***NYPL [JLF 86-620]***

Características de los instrumentos de ahorro. Santiago, Chile : Banco Central de Chile, Dirección de Estudios, 1986. 115 p. ; 26 cm. Bibliography: p. 115. LC Card 87-403226 DDC 332.63/2/0983 19
1. Securities - Chile. 2. Saving and investment - Chile. I. Banco Central de Chile. Dirección de Estudios.
HG5342 .C37 1986

Caractéristiques des familles à revenu élevé, 1980. Rashid, A. Characteristics of high income families, 1980 /. Ottawa [1986] 97 p. : ISBN 0-660-52875-4 (pbk.) : LC Card 86-210700
HC120.I5 R36 1986

Caractéristiques familiales et activité sur le marché du travail. Family characteristics and labour force activity . Ottawa , c1986. xxii, 131 p. ; ISBN 0-660-52240-3 (pbk.) : LC Card 86-206978
HD5728 .F36 1986

Caracterização da indústria agroalimentar no Paraná / Fundação Edison Vieira, Instituto Paranaense de Desenvolvimento Econômico e Social, IPARDES. Curitiba : IPARDES : Conselho de Desenvolvimento do Extremo Sul, 1985. x, 50 leaves : ill. ; 30 cm. "Convênio, Programa das Nações Unidas para o Desenvolvimento--PNUD, Organização das Nações Unidas para a Agricultura e Alimentação--FAO, Projeto Consolidação e Expansão da Agricultura de Alimentos no Paraná (BRA/82/017), Conselho de Desenvolvimento do Extremo-Sul--Codesul." LC Card 86-202725
1. Food industry and trade - Brazil - Paraná (State). I. Fundação Edison Vieira. II. Codesul.
HD9014.B83 P3718 1985

Caracterização da população do Distrito Federal : aspectos básicos e sócio-econômicos / Governo do Distrito Federal, Secretaria dó Governo, Companhia do Desenvolvimento do Planalto Central. Brasília : CODEPLAN, 1984. 56, [1] p. : ill. ; 21 cm. Bibliography: p. [57] LC Card 86-130173 DDC 331.12/0981/74021 19
1. Distrito Federal (Brazil) - Population - Statistics. 2. Labor supply - Brazil - Distrito Federal - Statistics. I. Companhia do Desenvolvimento do Planalto Central.
HA988.D5 C37 1984

Caraïbe export / Chambre de commerce et d'industrie de Pointe à Pitre. [Pointe à Pitre] : La Chambre, [1984] 129 p. ; 29 cm. Cover title. LC Card 86-155448
1. Caribbean Area - Commerce - Statistics. 2. Caribbean Area - Economic conditions - Statistics. I. Chambre de commerce & d'industrie de Pointe-à-Pitre.
HF3311.5 .C37 1984

Carajas iron ore project. Report to the World Bank, Amazônia Mineração S.A. . London [1979?] v, 57, [31] leaves : LC Card 85-154695
HD9524.B8 R46 1979

Caramanlis, Constantine. see **Karamanlis, Konstantinos, 1907-**

Caras del movimiento. Sandoval, Godofredo. Las mil caras del movimiento social boliviano /. La Paz, Bolivia [1986] 132 p. : LC Card 86-227792
HD6608.5 .S25 1986

Caravantes, Geraldo R. (Geraldo Ronchetti) Administração por objetivos : uma abordagem sócio-técnica / Geraldo Ronchetti Caravantes. Porto Alegre : Editoral McGraw-Hill do Brasil : Fundação para o Desenvolvimento de Recursos Humanos, 1977. 191 p., [1] folded leaf of plates : ill. ; 23 cm. Bibliography: p. 185-191. LC Card 85-211209
1. Management by objectives. 2. System theory. . 3. Decision-making. I. Title.
HD30.65 .C37 1977

Carcano, M. (Marco) Automazione d'ufficio . Roma [1985] 248 p. : LC Card 86-213829
HF1152.P28 A95 1985

Cárdenas, Isabel Laura. Ramona y el robot : el servicio doméstico en barrios prestigiosos de Buenos Aires, 1895-1985 / Isabel Laura Cárdenas.1a ed. Buenos Aires, Argentina : Ediciones Búsqueda, 1986. 155 p. : ill. ; 20 cm. (Colección Perspectivas) Bibliography: p. 147-151. ISBN 950-560-032-1 LC Card 87-100727
1. Women domestics - Argentina - Buenos Aires Metropolitan Area - History. I. Title.
HD6072.2.A72 B843 1986

Cárdenas, Lázaro, 1895-1970. Los ejidos de Yucatán y el henequén : discursos / Lázaro Cárdenas ; prólogo de Francisco Luna Kan. [Mexico City, Mexico] : Centro de Estudios Históricos del Agrarismo en México, c1984. 79 p. : ill. ; 21 cm. (Colección conmemorativa . 14) LC Card 87-403579 DDC 333.3/1/7265 19
1. Land reform - Mexico - Yucatán (State) - History. 2. Henequin industry - Mexico - Yucatán (State) - History. 3. Ejidos - Mexico - Yucatán (State) - History. 4. Mexico - History - 1910-1946. I. Title. II. Series.
HD1333.M62 Y823 1984

Cárdenas, Martha. Política ambiental y desarrollo . [Bogotá, Colombia] , 1986. 221 p. : LC Card 86-207035
HC130.E5 P65 1986

Cardillo, Giovanni. La programmabilità delle gestioni aziendali in tempi di inflazione / Giovanni Cardillo. Milano : Giuffrè, 1983. 118 p. ; 24 cm. (Collana di studi economico-aziendali / Centro universitario studi aziendali . 3) Bibliography: p. [113]-118. LC Card 84-177279 DDC 658.4/012/0945 19
1. Corporate planning - Italy. 2. Inflation (Finance) - Italy. I. Series: Collana di studi studi economico-aziendali (Milan, Italy)) , 3. II. Title.
HD70.I8 C27 1983 ***NYPL [JLD 86-1047]***

CARDIOGRAPHY - DATA PROCESSING - CONGRESSES.
Sistema raspoznavaniía ritmogramm serdtsa . Vil'nius , 1980. 55 p. : LC Card 81-194159
HD38 .S715 vyp. 49 QP112.5.C3

CARDIOVASCULAR EQUIPMENT INDUSTRY.
Cardiovascular therapy market . Tustin, CA, U. S.A. (17722 Irvine Blvd., Tustin 92680) , c1987. 1 v. (various foliations) ; LC Card 87-402037 DDC 380.1/45681761 19
HD9995.C363 U62 1987

Noninvasive cardiovascular and cardiorespiratory diagnostic devices (U. S. and international). Tustin, CA (17722 Irvine Blvd., Tustin 92680) , c1986. 1 v. (various pagings) : LC Card 87-101739 DDC 380.1/45681761 19
HD9995.C363 U65 1986

CARDIOVASCULAR EQUIPMENT INDUSTRY - UNITED STATES.
Cardiovascular surgery products markets in the U. S. New York, N.Y. , c1983. xxiii, 197 p. : LC Card 87-143453
HD9995.S93 U525 1983

Cardiovascular therapy market . Tustin, CA, U. S.A. (17722 Irvine Blvd., Tustin 92680) , c1987. 1 v. (various foliations) ; LC Card 87-402037 DDC 380.1/45681761 19
HD9995.C363 U62 1987

Noninvasive cardiovascular and cardiorespiratory diagnostic devices (U. S. and international). Tustin, CA (17722 Irvine Blvd., Tustin 92680) , c1986. 1 v. (various pagings) : LC Card 87-101739 DDC 380.1/45681761 19
HD9995.C363 U65 1986

Cardiovascular surgery products markets in the U. S. New York, N.Y. : Frost & Sullivan, c1983. xxiii, 197 p. : ill. ; 29 cm. "#A1115." "October 1983." LC Card 87-143453
1. Surgical instruments and apparatus industry - United States. 2. Cardiovascular equipment industry - United States. 3. Market surveys - United States. I. Frost & Sullivan.
HD9995.S93 U525 1983

Cardiovascular therapy market : open heart technology, cardiovascular prostheses, interventional cardiology, cardiac assist devices and heart transplants, cardiac pacemakers, pharmaceuticals / Biomedical Business International.5th revision. Tustin, CA, U. S.A. (17722 Irvine Blvd., Tustin 92680) : BBI, c1987. 1 v. (various foliations) ; 29 cm. (Report / Biomedical Business International . #7027) "Top 100 open heart centers in the U. S.": Appendix A. "April 1987." LC Card 87-402037 DDC 380.1/45681761 19
1. Cardiovascular equipment industry - United States. 2. Cardiovascular equipment industry. 3. Market surveys - United States. I. Biomedical Business International, Inc. II. Series: Report (Biomedical Business International, Inc.) , #7027.
HD9995.C363 U62 1987

Cardoso, Eliana A. Inflation, growth and the real exchange rate : essays on economic history in Brazil and Latin America, 1850-1983 / Eliana A. Cardoso. New York : Garland, 1987. 98 p. : ill. ; 24 cm. (South American and Latin American economic history) Thesis (Ph. D.)--Massachusetts Institute of Technology, 1979. Bibliography: p. 96-98. ISBN 0-8240-1356-5 (alk. paper) : LC Card 87-8570 DDC 330.981 19
1. Brazil - Economic policy. 2. Coffee trade - Government policy - Brazil - History. 3. Agricultural price supports - Brazil - History. 4. Monetary policy - Brazil - History. 5. Foreign exchange - Brazil - History. 6. Inflation (Finance) - Brazil - History. 7. Brazil - Commercial policy - History. 8. Economic stabilization - Latin America - History. I. Title. II. Series.
HC187 .C218 1987

CARDS, ADVERTISING. see **ADVERTISING CARDS.**

Care & feeding of ideas. Adams, James L. The care and feeding of ideas . Reading, Mass. , 1986. xv, 223 p. : ISBN 0-201-10160-2 : LC Card 86-10895 DDC 153.3/5 19
BF408 .A3 1986 ***NYPL [JFE 87-1553]***

The care and feeding of ideas . Adams, James L. Reading, Mass. , 1986. xv, 223 p. : ISBN 0-201-10160-2 : LC Card 86-10895 DDC 153.3/5 19
BF408 .A3 1986 ***NYPL [JFE 87-1553]***

CARE (Firm) Mohamed, Yagoub Abdalla. The North Kordofan rural water supply baseline survey /. Khartoum , 1982. xv, 152 p. : LC Card 85-981166
HD1699.S82 K875 1982

Career Assessment Inventory . Johansson, Charles B. (Charles Berthil) [Minneapolis, Minn.] , c1986. ix, 218 p. : LC Card 87-112723
HF5381.5 .J63 1986

Career Assessment Inventory. Johansson, Charles B. (Charles Berthil) Manual for the Career Assessment Inventory /. [Minneapolis] , c1976. 93 p. : LC Card 86-219030
HF5381.5 .J64 1976

CAREER ASSESSMENT INVENTORY.
Johansson, Charles B. (Charles Berthil) Career Assessment Inventory . [Minneapolis, Minn.] , c1986. ix, 218 p. : LC Card 87-112723
HF5381.5 .J63 1986

Johansson, Charles B. (Charles Berthil) Manual for the Career Assessment Inventory /. [Minneapolis] , c1976. 93 p. : LC Card 86-219030
HF5381.5 .J64 1976

Career blazers.
Lewis, William, 1946- Fast-track careers . New York , c1987. x, 212 p. ; ISBN 0-471-83801-2 (pbk.) : LC Card 87-10045 DDC 331.7/02/0973 19
HF5382.5.U5 L45 1987

Career Center research report.
Friedman, Stewart D. Leadership succession systems and corporate performance /. New York, N.Y. (316 Uris Hall, New York, N.Y. 10027) , c1985. ix, 141 p. :
NYPL [JLF 87-255]

Friedman, Stewart D. Leadership succession systems and corporate performance /. New York, N.Y. (316 Uris Hall, New York 10027) , c1985. ix, 141 p. ; LC Card 86-162460 DDC 331.25/96 19
HD38.2 .F73 1985

Ginzberg, Eli, 1911- Resizing for organizational effectiveness . New York, N.Y. (316 Uris Hall, New York 10027) , c1985. vii, 43 p. ; LC Card 86-162474 DDC 658.1/6 19
HD58.9 .G56 1985

CAREER CHANGES.
Caple, John. The right work . New York, N.Y. , 1977. xvi, 269 p. ; ISBN 0-396-09064-8 LC Card 87-15734 DDC 650.1/4 19
HF5381 .C2634 1987

Falvey, Jack, 1938- What's next? . Charlotte, Vt. , c1987. 189 p. ; ISBN 0-913589-26-8 : LC Card 87-10553 DDC 650.1/4 19
HF5384 .F35 1987

Gerberg, Robert J. [Job changing system.] Robert Gerberg's job changing system . Kansas City , c1986. xxii, 265 p. : ISBN 0-8362-7932-8 : LC Card 86-17298 DDC 650.1/4 19
NYPL [JD 87-125]

Irish, Richard K. Go hire yourself an employer /. New York , 1987. xxviii, 280 ; ISBN 0-385-23378-7 (pbk.) : LC Card 87-6896 DDC 650.1/4 19
HF5382.7 .I74 1987

Kanchier, Carole. Questers . Saratoga, Calif. , c1987. xi, 225 p. ; ISBN 0-88247-767-6 (pbk.) : LC Card 87-60351 DDC 658.4/09 19
HF5384 .K36 1987

Levinson, Jay Conrad. Quit your job! . New York , c1987. 216 p. ; ISBN 0-396-08882-1 LC Card 87-15545 DDC 650.1 19
HF5384 .L48 1987

McAdam, Terry W. [Careers in the nonprofit sector.] Doing well by doing good . New York, N.Y., U. S.A. , 1988, c1986. xxi, 201 p. : ISBN 0-14-046820-X (pbk.) LC Card 87-23602 DDC 650.1/4 19
HF5381 .M12 1988

Nicholson, Nigel. Managerial job change . Cambridge [Cambridgeshire] , New York , 1988. xi, 274 p. : ISBN 0-521-33459-4 LC Card 87-11752 DDC 331.12/72 19
HD38.2 .N53 1988

Plumez, Jacqueline Hornor. Divorcing a corporation . New York, N.Y. , 1985. xxiii, 198 p. : ISBN 0-394-54457-9 : LC Card 85-40183 DDC 650.1/4 19
HF5384 .P58 1986 *NYPL [JLE 86-2346]*

Selles, G. (Gert) Mid career crisis /. Deventer [1985?] 135 p. : ISBN 90-6001-934-2 LC Card 86-163138
HF5384 .S45 1985

CAREER CHANGES - GERMANY (WEST)
Kretschmann, Rolf. Möglichkeiten des Berufswechsels von Haupterwerbslandwirten unter besonderer Berücksichtigung von Agrarstruktur und Arbeitsmarkt /. Göttingen , 1986. xi, 109 p. : LC Card 87-408871 DDC 331.25/924 19
HD1536.G3 K746 1986

CAREER CHANGES - STUDY AND TEACHING - UNITED STATES.
Transitional career counseling from the Air Force to the private sector . Washington, D.C. , c1987. iv, 153 leaves : LC Card 87-401057 DDC 358.4/1154/0973 19
HF5382.75.U6 T7 1987

CAREER CHANGES - UNITED STATES.
Brudney, Juliet F. Forced out . New York , c1987. 208 p. ; ISBN 0-671-64411-4 (pbk.) : LC Card 87-14927 DDC 650.1/4/0240564 19
HD6280 .B78 1987

Career counseling . Yost, Elizabeth B. San Francisco, Calif. , c1987. xvi, 265 p. : ISBN 1-555-42035-4 (alk. paper) LC Card 86-46335 DDC 158.6 19
HF5381 .Y58 1987

CAREER DEVELOPMENT.
Davidson, Jeffrey P. Blow your own horn . New York, NY , c1987. xv, 271 p. : ISBN 0-8144-5908-0 LC Card 86-47809 DDC 650.1/4 19
HF5549.5.C35 D375 1987

Dayhoff, Signe A. Create your own career opportunities /. Andover, Mass. , c1987. x, 111 p. : ISBN 0-931790-75-1 : LC Card 86-26332 DDC 650.1/4 19
HF5549.5.C35 D38 1987

Feldman, Daniel C. Managing careers in organizations /. Glenview, Ill. , c1988. 249 p. : ISBN 0-673-18562-1 (pbk.) : LC Card 87-16580 DDC 650.1/4 19
HF5549 .F386 1988

Future perfect . Columbia, S.C. (P.O. Box 6828, Columbia 29260) , c1987. x, 104 p. : LC Card 87-143129 DDC 650.1 19
HF5549.5.C35 F87 1987

Henry, Lauchland. The professional's guide to working smarter /. Tenafly, N.J. , 1988. xv, 208 p. : ISBN 0-935310-03-7 LC Card 87-23868 DDC 650.1 19
HD8038.A1 H47 1988

London, Manuel. Career management and survival in the workplace . San Francisco , 1987. xviii, 226 p. ; ISBN 1-555-42043-5 (alk. paper) LC Card 86-46334 DDC 658.3/14 19
HF5549.5.C35 L65 1987

Mcunu, Ernest. Top level advice to aspirant black managers /. Braamfontein [1985] 48 p. ; LC Card 87-152084 DDC 658.4/09 19
HD38.2 .M395 1985

Miller-Tiedeman, Anna, 1934- Lifecareer . Vista, CA , c1988. v, 65 p. ; ISBN 0-9613436-3-X (pbk.) LC Card 87-17298 DDC 331.7/02 19
HF5381 .M496 1988

Norris, Kenneth E. Winning at work . Blue Ridge Summit, PA , c1987. viii, 116 p. ; ISBN 0-8306-3077-5 : LC Card 86-27359 DDC 650.1 19
HF5548.83 .N67 1987

Osher, Bill. The blue-chip graduate . Atlanta, Ga. , c1987. 238 p. : ISBN 0-934601-19-4 (pbk.) : LC Card 86-63534 DDC 650.1/4/024375 19
HF5381 .O889 1987

Vaughan, Hap. Your career game /. New York , c1987. x, 240 p. : ISBN 0-471-62949-9 (pbk.) LC Card 87-20964 DDC 650.1/4 19
HF5549.5.C35 V38 1987

Your job [filmstrip] . Pleasantville, NY , 1986. 2 filmstrips (ca. 74 fr. each) : LC Card 86-700184 DDC 650.1 11
HF5549.5.C35

Your job [videorecording] . Pleasantville, NY , 1986. 1 videocassette (30 min.) : LC Card 87-705039 DDC 650.1 11
HF5549.5.C35

CAREER DEVELOPMENT - UNITED STATES - LONGITUDINAL STUDIES.
Hopkins, David M. Changing career values . Bethlehem, PA , 1986. x, 126 p. : ISBN 0-914885-10-3 (pbk.) LC Card 87-112752 DDC 331.25 19
HD8038.U5 H66 1986

CAREER EDUCATION - AUSTRALIA - CONGRESSES.
The Future impact of technology on work and education /. London , New York , 1987. p. cm. ISBN 1-85000-083-2 : LC Card 87-13641 DDC 331.12/0994 19
HD6331.2.A8 F87 1987

CAREER EDUCATION - UNITED STATES - CONGRESSES.
The Future impact of technology on work and education /. London , New York , 1987. p. cm. ISBN 1-85000-083-2 : LC Card 87-13641 DDC 331.12/0994 19
HD6331.2.A8 F87 1987

Career guidance and counseling through the life span . Herr, Edwin L. Glenview, Ill. , c1988. xvi, 576 p. : ISBN 0-673-39726-2 LC Card 87-22748 DDC 331.7/02/0973 19
HF5382.5.U5 H39 1988

Career management and survival in the workplace . London, Manuel. San Francisco , 1987. xviii, 226 p. ; ISBN 1-555-42043-5 (alk. paper) LC Card 86-46334 DDC 658.3/14 19
HF5549.5.C35 L65 1987

Career planning in Bangladesh : proceedings of the seminar held under the auspices of the Bangladesh Public Administration Training Centre, Savar, Dhaka, 21-22 December 1985. Dhaka : Management and Public Administration Division, Bangladesh Public Administration Training Centre, c1986. 159 p. ; 30 cm. "Proceedings of the Seminar on Career Planning in Bangladesh held on December 21 and 22, 1985 at the Bangladesh Public Administration Training Centre, Savar, Dhaka"--Pref. Includes bibliographies. LC Card 86-903477 DDC 331.7/02/095492 19
1. Vocational guidance - Bangladesh - Congresses. 2. Civil service positions - Bangladesh - Congresses. I. Bangladesh Public Administration Training Centre. II. Seminar on Career Planning in Bangladesh (1985 : Bangladesh Public Administration Training Centre).
HF5382.5.B27 C37 1986

Career success. Derr, C. Brooklyn (Clyde Brooklyn) Managing the new careerists /. San Francisco , 1986. xxii, 288 p. ; ISBN 0-87589-677-4 LC Card 85-45901 DDC 658.3/02 19
HF5549.2.U5 D47 1986
NYPL [JLE 86-2427]

Career women and childbearing . Wilk, Carole. New York , c1986. xxii, 304 p. ; ISBN 0-442-29352-6 LC Card 85-9216 DDC 306.8/743 19
HQ759 .W52 1986 *NYPL [JLD 86-1811]*

Careerists. Derr, C. Brooklyn (Clyde Brooklyn) Managing the new careerists /. San Francisco , 1986. xxii, 288 p. ; ISBN 0-87589-677-4 LC Card 85-45901 DDC 658.3/02 19
HF5549.2.U5 D47 1986
NYPL [JLE 86-2427]

CAREERS. see **OCCUPATIONS; PROFESSIONS; VOCATIONAL GUIDANCE.**

Careers encyclopedia. VGM's careers encyclopedia /. Lincolnwood, Ill., U. S.A. , c1988. xi, 484 p. ; ISBN 0-8442-6132-7 LC Card 87-62404 DDC 331.7/02/0973 19
HF5382.5.U5 C337 1988

Careers encyclopedia. VGM's careers encyclopedia /. Lincolnwood, Ill., U. S.A. , c1988. xi, 484 p. ; ISBN 0-8442-6132-7 LC Card 87-62404 DDC 331.7/02/0973 19
HF5382.5.U5 C337 1988

Careers in high tech /. Winkler, Connie. New York, N.Y. , c1987. vi, 220 p. : ISBN 0-668-06537-0 (pbk.) LC Card 86-25277 DDC 331.7/02 19
HD8039.H54 W56 1987

Careers in public accounting 1986/87- . Emerson, James C. Seattle, Wash. (2824 Sahalee Dr. E., Redmond 98053) , c1986. 261 p. ; LC Card 87-71857 DDC 338.7/61657/0973 19
HF5616.U5 E46 1986

Careers in the world of investments /. Epstein, Rachel S. New York , c1988. 47 p. : ISBN 1-555-46631-1 LC Card 87-13182 DDC 332.6/023 19
HG4528 .E67 1988

Careers in trucking /. Schauer, Donald D. New York , 1987. xii, 132 p. : ISBN 0-8239-0748-1 : LC Card 87-4769 DDC 388.3/24/02373 19
HE5623 .S33 1987

Carew, Jack. You'll never get no for an answer / Jack Carew. New York : Simon and Schuster, c1987. 224 p. : ill. ; 23 cm. ISBN 0-671-62495-4 LC Card 87-13043 DDC 658.8/5 19
1. Selling. I. Title.
HF5438.25 .C33 1987

Carey, George Wescott, 1933- Order, freedom, and the polity . Lanham, MD [Bryn Mawr, Pa.] , c1986. x, 184 p. ; ISBN 0-8191-5155-6 (alk. paper) : LC Card 85-26438 DDC 323.44 19
JC571 .O77 1986 *NYPL [JLE 86-3182]*

CAREY, HENRY CHARLES, 1793-1879 - CONTRIBUTIONS IN ECONOMICS.
Morrison, Rodney J., 1934- Henry C. Carey and American economic development /. Philadelphia , 1986. ix, 91 p. : ISBN 0-87169-763-7 (pbk.) LC Card 86-71420 DDC 338.973/0092/4 19
HB119.C3 M67 1986

Carfantan, Jean Yves. L'Europe verte sous influence : l'heure du choix / Jean-Yves Carfantan. Paris : Editions du Seuil, c1985. 282 p. ; 24 cm. Includes bibliographical references. ISBN 2-02-008982-3 : LC Card 86-140900 DDC 338.1/094 19
1. Agriculture - Economic aspects - European Economic Community countries. 2. Agriculture - Political aspects - European Economic Community countries. 3. Agriculture and state - European Economic Community countries. I. Title.
HD1920.5 .C37 1985 *NYPL [JLE 87-526]*

CARGO. see **CARGO HANDLING.**

CARGO GEAR. see **CARGO HANDLING.**

CARGO HANDLING.
Couper, A. D. New cargo-handling techniques . Geneva , 1986. xii, 172 p., [1] folded leaf of plates : ISBN 92-2-105419-5 (pbk.) : LC Card 87-117776 DDC 331.7/61387164 19
HD6331.18.L65 C68 1986

CARGO SHIPS - HISTORY.
Mallett, Alan S. Idyll of the Kings, 1889-1979 . Kendal [Cumbria] , 1980. 64 p. : ISBN 0-905617-10-X (pbk.) LC Card 81-105772 DDC 387.5/065/41 19
HE945.K48 M35 1980

CARGO SHIPS - SOVIET UNION.
Rakhovetskiĭ, A. N. (Anatoliĭ Nikolaevich) Operativnaia frakhtovaia deiatel'nost' na morskom transporte /. Moskva , 1986. 159 p. : LC Card 86-115637
HE597.S615 R36 1986

Cari compagni . Lama, Luciano. Roma , c1986. vii, 184 p. ; LC Card 87-155314
HD6710.L35 A4 1986

CARIBBEAN AREA - COMMERCE - CASE STUDIES.
El Efecto que tendrían los aumentos de los peajes del Canal de Panamá sobre países seleccionados de América Latina y el Caribe . Washington, D.C. [1982] iii, 76 p. ; LC Card 85-176637
HE538.R3 E34 1982

CARIBBEAN AREA - COMMERCE - CONGRESSES.
Trade, aid, and democracy in the Caribbean . [S.l.] [1986] 68 p. : LC Card 87-400829 DDC 338.91/09729 19
HC151 .T73 1986

CARIBBEAN AREA - COMMERCE - STATISTICS.
Caraïbe export /. [Pointe à Pitre] [1984] 129 p. ; LC Card 86-155448
HF3311.5 .C37 1984

CARIBBEAN AREA - COMMERCE - UNITED STATES.
Mukerjee, Dilip. Lessons from the Caribbean Basin initiative /. Kuala Lumpur, Malaysia , c1985. 36 p. ; ISBN 967-99974-6-4 (pbk.) LC Card 87-101396 DDC 338.91/73/0729 19
HF1456.5.C27 M85 1985

CARIBBEAN AREA - DEPENDENCY ON FOREIGN COUNTRIES.
Haas, Hans-Dieter. Karibische Klein- und Mikrostaaten . Tübingen , 1985. xvi, 200 p. : ISBN 3-921552-62-1 LC Card 86-155952
HC141 .H25 1985

CARIBBEAN AREA - ECONOMIC CONDITIONS.
Bonetti, Mario. Staat und Gesellschaft im karibischen Raum im 16. Jahrhundert /. München , 1984. 668 p. : ISBN 3-7705-2162-5 LC Card 85-132458 DDC 330.9729/02 19
HC151 .B66 1984

CARIBBEAN AREA - ECONOMIC CONDITIONS - 1945-
The Caribbean Basin and the changing world economic structure /. Groningen , c1986. 194 p. ; ISBN 90-01-18630-0 (pbk.) : LC Card 87-117415 DDC 330.9729/052 19
HC151 .C26 1986

Caribbean labour and the economic environment. Bri[d]getown, Barbados [1985] i, 40 p. ; LC Card 86-127832 DDC 330.9729/052 19
HC151 .C32 1985

Haas, Hans-Dieter. Karibische Klein- und Mikrostaaten . Tübingen , 1985. xvi, 200 p. : ISBN 3-921552-62-1 LC Card 86-155952
HC141 .H25 1985

Notas críticas sobre el plan Reagan para la cuenca del Caribe /. La Habana , 1982. 84 p. ; LC Card 87-400638 DDC 337.729073 19
HF1456.5.C27 N67 1982

Worrell, DeLisle. Small island economies . New York , 1987. xiv, 289 p. : ISBN 0-275-92795-4 (alk. paper) : LC Card 87-12495 DDC 330.9729/052 19
HC151 .W67 1987

CARIBBEAN AREA - ECONOMIC CONDITIONS - 1945- - CASE STUDIES.
Hope, Kempe R. Development finance and the development process . New York , 1987. 100 p. ; ISBN 0-313-25835-X (lib. bdg. : alk. paper) LC Card 86-29617 DDC 336.729 19
HJ844.3 .H67 1987

CARIBBEAN AREA - ECONOMIC CONDITIONS - 1945- - CONGRESSES.
Current economic and financial issues of the North American and Caribbean countries /. Mexico, D.F. , 1983. 390 p. : LC Card 87-106905 DDC 330.97/00539 19
HC95 .C87 1983

The State in Caribbean society /. Mona, Jamaica , c1986. vii, 157 p. ; ISBN 976-410-001-5 (pbk.) LC Card 87-403404 DDC 330.9729/052 19
HC151 .S73 1986

CARIBBEAN AREA - ECONOMIC CONDITIONS - STATISTICS.
Caraïbe export /. [Pointe à Pitre] [1984] 129 p. ; LC Card 86-155448
HF3311.5 .C37 1984

CARIBBEAN AREA - ECONOMIC INTEGRATION.
Haas, Hans-Dieter. Karibische Klein- und Mikrostaaten . Tübingen , 1985. xvi, 200 p. : ISBN 3-921552-62-1 LC Card 86-155952
HC141 .H25 1985

United Nations. Caribbean Development and Co-operation Committee. Informe final del octavo período de sesiones del Comité de Desarrollo y Cooperación del Caribe (Puerto Príncipe, Haití, 6 al 12 de junio de 1984). [Port-au-Prince?] , 1984. iv, 36 p. ; LC Card 85-187058
HC151 .U54 1984

CARIBBEAN AREA - ECONOMIC INTEGRATION - CONGRESSES.
The Nassau understanding . [Nassau, Bahamas , 1984] 7 p. : LC Card 87-109663 DDC 338.9729 19
HC151 .N37 1984

CARIBBEAN AREA - ECONOMIC POLICY.
United Nations. Caribbean Development and Co-operation Committee. Informe final del octavo período de sesiones del Comité de Desarrollo y Cooperación del Caribe (Puerto Príncipe, Haití, 6 al 12 de junio de 1984). [Port-au-Prince?] , 1984. iv, 36 p. ; LC Card 85-187058
HC151 .U54 1984

CARIBBEAN AREA - ECONOMIC POLICY - CONGRESSES.
The Nassau understanding . [Nassau, Bahamas , 1984] 7 p. : LC Card 87-109663 DDC 338.9729 19
HC151 .N37 1984

The State in Caribbean society /. Mona, Jamaica , c1986. vii, 157 p. ; ISBN 976-410-001-5 (pbk.) LC Card 87-403404 DDC 330.9729/052 19
HC151 .S73 1986

CARIBBEAN AREA - FOREIGN ECONOMIC RELATIONS - EUROPE.
The Caribbean Basin and the changing world economic structure /. Groningen , c1986. 194 p. ; ISBN 90-01-18630-0 (pbk.) : LC Card 87-117415 DDC 330.9729/052 19
HC151 .C26 1986

CARIBBEAN AREA - FOREIGN ECONOMIC RELATIONS - UNITED STATES.
Notas críticas sobre el plan Reagan para la cuenca del Caribe /. La Habana , 1982. 84 p. ; LC Card 87-400638 DDC 337.729073 19
HF1456.5.C27 N67 1982

Caribbean area - Government. see **Caribbean Area - Politics and government.**

CARIBBEAN AREA - POLITICS AND GOVERNMENT - 1945- - CONGRESSES.
The State in Caribbean society /. Mona, Jamaica , c1986. vii, 157 p. ; ISBN 976-410-001-5 (pbk.) LC Card 87-403404 DDC 330.9729/052 19
HC151 .S73 1986

CARIBBEAN AREA - SOCIAL CONDITIONS.
Bonetti, Mario. Staat und Gesellschaft im karibischen Raum im 16. Jahrhundert /. München , 1984. 668 p. : ISBN 3-7705-2162-5 LC Card 85-132458 DDC 330.9729/02 19
HC151 .B66 1984

The Caribbean Basin and the changing world economic structure / edited by Henk E. Chin. Groningen : Wolters-Noordhoff, c1986. 194 p. ; 24 cm. Includes bibliographies. ISBN 90-01-18630-0 (pbk.) : LC Card 87-117415 DDC 330.9729/052 19
1. Caribbean Area - Economic conditions - 1945-. 2. Europe - Foreign economic relations - Caribbean Area. 3. Caribbean Area - Foreign economic relations - Europe. 4. Petroleum industry and trade - Caribbean Area. 5. Bauxite mines and mining - Caribbean Area. I. Chin, H. E.
HC151 .C26 1986

CARIBBEAN BASIN INITIATIVE, 1983-
Agricultural marketing handbook for Caribbean Basin products. Spanish. Manual--mercadeo de productos agrícolas de la Cuenca del Caribe /. San José, Costa Rica . x, 434 p. : ISBN 92-9039-101-4 LC Card 86-204686
HD9014.C442 A4718 1986

Mukerjee, Dilip. Lessons from the Caribbean Basin initiative /. Kuala Lumpur, Malaysia , c1985. 36 p. ; ISBN 967-99974-6-4 (pbk.) LC Card 87-101396 DDC 338.91/73/0729 19
HF1456.5.C27 M85 1985

Notas críticas sobre el plan Reagan para la cuenca del Caribe /. La Habana , 1982. 84 p. ; LC Card 87-400638 DDC 337.729073 19
HF1456.5.C27 N67 1982

Caribbean cases in auditing /. Mendes, Margaret. Kingston, Jamaica , c1986. 58 p. : ISBN 976-8053-00-3 (pbk.) LC Card 87-403426 DDC 657/.45 19
HF5667 .M456 1986

CARIBBEAN COMMUNITY - CONGRESSES.
The Nassau understanding . [Nassau, Bahamas , 1984] 7 p. : LC Card 87-109663 DDC 338.9729 19
HC151 .N37 1984

Caribbean Congress of Labour. Caribbean labour and the economic environment. Bri[d]getown, Barbados [1985] i, 40 p. ; LC Card 86-127832 DDC 330.9729/052 19
HC151 .C32 1985

Caribbean Development Bank. Economics and Programming Dept. Economic memorandum on Anguilla. [Kingston, Jamaica] : Economics and Programming Dept., [1985] 2, 55 p. : ill. ; 28 cm. Cover title. "May 1985." LC Card 86-204700 DDC 330.97297/3 19
1. Anguilla - Economic conditions. 2. Economic development projects - Anguilla. I. Title.
HC156.Z7 A483 1985

Caribbean labour and the economic environment. Bri[d]getown, Barbados : Caribbean Congress of Labour, [1985] i, 40 p. ; 29 cm. Cover title. "March 1985." Includes bibliographical references. LC Card 86-127832 DDC 330.9729/052 19
1. Economic indicators - Caribbean Area. 2. Caribbean Area - Economic conditions - 1945-. I. Caribbean Congress of Labour.
HC151 .C32 1985

Caribbean Research Center, St. Lucia. Search Conference on Energy Futures for St. Lucia (1982 : Castries, Saint Lucia) The energy future for St. Lucia . Castries, St. Lucia [1982] 23 p. ; LC Card 87-400749 DDC 333.79/097298/43 19
HD9502.S0552 S4 1982

Caribbean series (Koninklijk Instituut voor Taal-, Land- en Volkenkunde (Netherlands)) .
(1) Lamur, Carlo. The American takeover . Dordrecht, Holland , Cinnaminson, N.J., U. S.A. , 1985. vi, 209 p., [6] p. of plates : ISBN 90-6765-078-1 (pbk.) : LC Card 86-181373 DDC 338.8/87 19
HD9539.A63 G886 1985

Caribbees. see **Antilles, Lesser.**

CARICOM. see **Caribbean Community.**

C.A.R.I.C.O.M. see **Caribbean Community.**

Carim, Enver. Third world development /. London , New York , 1985. 3 v. : ISBN 0-946027-65-X (v. 1) ***NYPL [JLF 86-626]***

A caring society . Bernstein, Irving, 1916- Boston , 1985. 338 p., [24] p. of plates : ISBN 0-395-33116-1 : LC Card 84-25129 DDC 362.8/5/0973 19
HD8072 .B365 1985 ***NYPL [JLD 86-2102]***

CARINTHIA (AUSTRIA) - OCCUPATIONS - STATISTICS.
Die Entwicklung der Beschäftigungslage in Kärnten seit 1960 /. Klagenfurt [1979] 23 leaves : LC Card 85-143747
HD5772.C37 E57 1979

Cariola, Leonor. Corvalán Vásquez, Oscar E., 1947- Empleo y capacitación en los talleres informales de Santiago /. Montevideo , 1984. 150 p. ; LC Card 86-127324
HD2346.C54 S263 1984

Caris, J. Fuseren in non-profit organisaties : analyse van een complex proces / J. Caris, R. Clarijs, G. Nierman. Nijmegen : Dekker & Van de Vegt, 1986. 107 p. : ill. ; 21 cm. Bibliography: p. 103. ISBN 90-255-0018-8 : LC Card 86-205531
1. Consolidation and merger of corporations -

Netherlands - Case studies. 2. Corporations, Non-profit - Netherlands - Case studies. 3. Interorganizational relations - Netherlands - Case studies. I. Clarijs, R. II. Nierman, G. III. Title.
HD2746.5 .C35 1986

Cáritas Española. Departamento de Investigación Sociológica. La Reconversión industrial, la crisis y reforma agraria. [Madrid] [1984] 148 p. : ISBN 84-398-1197-7 LC Card 86-216324
HC385 .R375 1984

Carl Beck papers in Russian and East European studies .
(paper no. 504) Weinberg, Robert. Social democracy and workers in Odessa . Pittsburgh, Pa. (4E23 Forbes Quad, Pittsburgh 15260) [1986] 34 p. ; LC Card 86-199472
HD8530.O32 W45 1986

Carl Mengers erster Entwurf zu seinem Hauptwerk "Grundsätze" geschrieben als Anmerkungen zu den "Grundsätzen der Volkswirthschaftslehre" von Karl Heinrich Rau. Menger, Carl, 1840-1921. Tokio , 1963. xxviii, 236 p., [3] leaves of plates : LC Card 85-210245
HB175 .M47 1963

Carlen, Louis. Hundert Jahre Rechts- und Wirtschaftsgeschichte an der Rechts-, Wirtschafts- und Sozialwissenschaftlichen Fakultät der Universität Freiburg =. Freiburg, Schweiz , 1982. 96 p., [6] p. of plates : ISBN 3-7278-0277-4 : LC Card 83-108855 DDC 340 19
K296 .H86 1982 ***NYPL [JLD 86-676]***

Carli Ballola, Sandra. La Compagnia lavoratori portuali di Ravenna, 1930-1980 / Sandra Carli Ballola. [Italy : s.n., 1981?] (Imola : Galeati) 208 p. : ill. ; 22 cm. Bibliography: p. 205-208. LC Card 83-206502
1. Compagnia portuale di Ravenna (Italy) - History. 2. Stevedores - Italy - Ravenna - History. 3. Cooperative societies - Italy - Ravenna - History. I. Title.
HD8039.L82 I83 1981

Carlin, Vivian F., 1919- Where can mom live? : a family guide to living arrangements for elderly parents / by Vivian F. Carlin, Ruth Mansberg. Lexington, Mass. : Lexington Books, c1987. viii, 206 p. : ill. ; 24 cm. Bibliography: p. 194-197. Includes index. ISBN 0-669-13665-4 (alk. paper) LC Card 86-45526 DDC 363.5/9 19
1. Aged - United States - Dwellings. 2. Parents, Aged - Care - United States. I. Mansberg, Ruth, 1924-. II. Title.
HD7287.92.U54 C37 1987

Carlsen, Anne Marie Sloth. Køn og ledelse : en sammenlignende undersøgelse af mænds og kvinders adgang til-- og adfærd i-- ledende stillinger / Anne Marie Sloth Carlsen, Lise Toft. København : Politiske studier : [Danske boghandleres kommissionsanstalt], 1986. 251 p. : forms ; 21 cm. A slightly rev. ed. of the authors' special ed., by the same title, issued at the Institut for samfundsfag og forvaltning, University of Copenhagen, September 1986. Bibliography: p. 244-251. ISBN 87-87749-29-7 (pbk.) :kr149.00 LC Card 87-145777
1. Women executives - Denmark. 2. Success in business - Denmark. 3. Sex discrimination in employment - Denmark. I. Toft, Lise. II. Title.
HD6054.4.D4 C37 1986

Carlsen, Melody A. Wendling, Wayne. The regulatory impact on pensions /. Brookfield, Wis. , 1986. xiii, 91 p. : ISBN 0-89154-314-7 (pbk.) : LC Card 87-129712 DDC 331.25/2/0973 19
HD7105.35.U6 W46 1986

Carlson, John A., 1933- Stocks, shocks, and price-output dynamics / by John A. Carlson. West Lafayette, Ind. : Institute for Research in the Behavioral, Economic, and Management Sciences, Krannert Graduate School of Management, Purdue University, [1984] 30, 13 p. ; 28 cm. (Paper / Institute for Research in the Behavioral, Economic, and Management Sciences, Krannert Graduate School of Management, Purdue University . no. 859) "July 1984." Bibliography: p. 28-30. LC Card 84-623131 DDC 658/.001/9 s 332.63/222/0973 19
1. Price policy - United States - Econometric models. 2. Stocks - Prices - United States - Econometric models. I. Series: Paper (Krannert Graduate School of Management. Institute for Research in the Behavioral, Economic, and Management Sciences) , no. 859. II. Title.
HD6483 .P8 no. 859 HF5416.5

Carlson, Patricia M. Darlington, Richard B. Behavioral statistics . New York, N.Y. , London , c1987. xxiv, 628 p. : ISBN 0-02-907860-1 LC Card 87-12040 DDC 519.5 19
HA29 .D246 1987

Carlson, Richard C. Managing the changing work force : work force implications of economic restructuring / Richard C. Carlson, Douglas C. Henton, Diane McGinty Morse. Menlo Park, Calif. (333 Ravenswood Ave., Menlo Park 94025-3476) : SRI International, Business Intelligence Program, c1984. 44 p. : col. ill. ; 28 cm. (Report / SRI International, Business Intelligence Program . no. 709 (fall 1984)) Cover title. LC Card 86-212936 DDC 658.3 19
1. Labor supply. 2. Manpower policy. 3. Economic history - 1971-. 4. Personnel management. I. Henton, Douglas C. II. Morse, Diane McGinty. III. Business Intelligence Program (SRI International). IV. Series: Research report (Business Intelligence Program (SRI International)) , no. 709. V. Title.
HD5706 .C29 1984

Carlsson, C. (Christer), 1946- Datorstöd i mindre företag : 7 praktikfall i administrativa processer / Christer Carlsson. Åbo : Åbo akademi : Distribution, Tidningsbokhandeln, 1983. 248 p. : ill. ; 21 cm. (Meddelanden från Stiftelsens för Åbo akademi forskningsinstitut, 0356-7109 . nr. 80 =) Bibliography: p. [220]-223. ISBN 951-648-877-3 LC Card 83-126466
1. Small business - Sweden - Data processing. I. Series: Meddelanden från Stiftelsens för Åbo akademi forskningsinstitut, nr. 80. II. Title.
HF5548.2 .C286 1983

Carlsson, Jerker, 1950- Newly industrializing countries and the political economy of south-south relations /. New York , 1988. p. cm. ISBN 0-312-01180-6 : LC Card 87-23476 DDC 337/.09172/4 19
HF1413 .N497 1988

Carlton, Thomas W. LeBlond, Geoffrey T. Como usar Lotus 1-2-3 . Miami, Fla. , 1986- p. cm. LC Card 86-23629 DDC 005.36/9 19
HF5548.4.L67 L418 1986

Carlyle, Patrick C. Luskin, Donald L. Index options & futures . New York , c1987. xi, 355 p. : ISBN 0-471-85464-6 LC Card 86-28189 DDC 332.63/222 19
HG6043 .L87 1987

Carlzon, Jan.
Moments of truth / Jan Carlzon. Cambridge, Mass. : Ballinger Pub. Co., c1987. xiii, 135 p. ; 24 cm. ISBN 0-88730-200-9 LC Card 87-1070 DDC 387.7/065/485 19
1. Scandinavian Airlines System - Management. 2. Aeronautics, Commercial - Sweden - Management. 3. Airlines - Sweden - Management. I. Title.
HE9860.S28 C37 1987

Riv pyramiderna! : en bok om den nya människan, chefen och ledaren / Jan Carlzon i samarbete med Tomas Lagerström. [Stockholm] : Bonnier, c1985 219 p. : ill. ; 22 cm. ISBN 91-0-046844-4 LC Card 86-139896
1. Scandinavian Airlines System - Management. 2. Aeronautics, Commercial - Sweden - Management. 3. Airlines - Sweden - Management. I. Lagerström, Tomas, 1939-. II. Title.
HE9860.S28 C375 1986

Carmell, Pamela. Attali, Jacques. [Homme d'influence. English.] A man of influence . London , 1986. 346 p. ; ISBN 0-297-78978-3 ***NYPL [JFE 87-583]***

Carmichael, D. R. Douglas R.), 1941-
Clay, John R. Guide to preparing financial statements /. Fort Worth, Tex. , c1987- 2 v. (loose-leaf) ; LC Card 87-161098 DDC 657/.3 19
HF5681.B2 C565 1987

Guide to audits of local governments / authors, Douglas R. Carmichael, William W. Holder ; contributing authors, A. Lewis Crain, Dennis R. Meals, Meryl L. Reed. 1st ed. Fort Worth, Tex. : Practitioners Pub. Co., 1986- 2 v. (loose-leaf) : ill. ; 30 cm. Includes index. CONTENTS. - v. 1. [no special title] -- v. 2. Practice aids. LC Card 86-206730 DDC 657/.835045 19
1. Local finance - Auditing - Standards - United States - Handbooks, manuals, etc. I. Holder, William W. II. Title. III. Title: Audits of local governments.
HJ9777.A3 C37 1986

Carmichael, K. S. (Keith Stanley) Taxation of Lloyd's underwriters / by K.S. Carmichael and P.H. Wolstenholme. London : HFL Publishers, 1980. xvi, 107 p. : forms ; 22 cm. (Chartac taxation guides) ISBN 0-372-30027-8 (pbk.) : LC Card 81-107459
1. Insurance - Taxation - Great Britain. 2. Insurance - Great Britain - Accounting. 3. Insurance, Marine - Taxation - Great Britain. 4. Insurance, Marine - Great Britain - Accounting. 5. Lloyd's Underwriters' Association. I. Wolstenholme, P. H. II. Title. III. Series.
HG8123.G7 C37 1980

Carmichael, Robert S. Science/earth science on stamps and banknotes [slide] /. Lincoln, Neb. , 1984. 30 slides : LC Card 85-702119 DDC 551 11
HE6183.S36

Carmignani, Fabrizo. Assenteismo e presenteismo : due strategie del comportamento operaio / di Fabrizio Carmignani ; prefazione di Giuseppe Bonazzi. Milano, Italy : F. Angeli, c1984. 211 p. ; 22 cm. At head of title: Cespe-Centro studi di politica economica del Partito comunista italiano. Bibliography: p. [205]-211. LC Card 84-175594 DDC 658.3/14 19
1. Job satisfaction. 2. Railroads - Italy - Employees - Case studies. I. CESPE (Organization). II. Title.
HD5115 .C37 1984 ***NYPL [JLD 86-3383]***

Carmo, Heron Carlos E. do (Heron Carlos Esvael) Endo, Seiti Kaneko. Pesquisa de orçamentos familiares no município de São Paulo /. São Paulo [Rio de Janeiro] , 1984. 131 p. : LC Card 85-136517
HB235.B8 E53 1984

Carmona, Pedro, (Carmona Estanga) Estrategias de desarrollo e integración en el Grupo Andino . Lima, Perú , 1985. 414 p. : LC Card 87-125026 DDC 337.1/8 19
HC167.A5 E87 1985

Carnegie Council on Ethics & International Affairs. In search of an East Asian development model /. New Brunswick, N.J., USA , c1988. xi, 243 p. ; ISBN 0-88738-686-5 (pbk.) LC Card 87-19061 DDC 338.95 19
HC460.5 .I5 1988

Carnegie-Mellon University. Public regulation . Cambridge, Mass. , c1987. xiv, 404 p. ; ISBN 0-262-02258-3 LC Card 86-21302 DDC 338.973 19
HD3616.U47 P83 1987

Carneiro, Ricardo. Política econômica da Nova República /. Rio de Janeiro, RJ [1986] 275 p. : LC Card 87-102398
HC187 .P67 1986

Carnes, William T. Effective meetings for busy people : let's decide it and go home / William T. Carnes.IEEE Press ed. New York : IEEE Press, c1987. xvi, 348 p. ; 24 cm. "Published under the sponsorship of the IEEE Professional Communication Society." Includes bibliographical references and index. "IEEE order number: PC02030"--T.p. verso. ISBN 0-87942-211-4 LC Card 86-27719 DDC 658.4/563 19
1. Corporate meetings. 2. Meetings. I. IEEE Professional Communication Society. II. Title.
HD2743 .C37 1987

Carnet d'adresses / Soderag. [Pointe-à-Pitre, Guadeloupe] : Soderag, [1986?] 64 p. : ill. ; 31 cm. LC Card 87-152834
1. SODERAG. 2. Development credit corporations - Guadeloupe. 3. Development credit corporations - Martinique. 4. Development credit corporations - Guyana. 5. Guadeloupe - Industries - Directories. 6. Martinique - Industries - Directories. 7. Guyana - Industries - Directories. I. SODERAG.
HG3729.G862 C37 1986

Carney, David C. Siegel, Eric S. The Arthur Young business plan guide /. New York , c1987. xii, 184 p. ; ISBN 0-471-85885-4 LC Card 86-32622 DDC 658.4/012 19
HD62.5 .S556 1987

Caro, Jean-Yves. Les économistes distingués : logique sociale d'un champ scientifique / Jean-Yves Caro. Paris : Presses de la Fondation nationale des sciences politiques, c1983. 287 p. : ill. ; 22 cm. Bibliography: p. [271]-287. ISBN 2-7246-0484-9 : LC Card 84-117472
1. Economics. I. Title.
HB71 .C28 1983

Carol, Dan. Financial condition of the U. S. electric utility industry. [Washington] [1986] xviii, 82 p. : *NYPL [JLF 86-1386]*

Caroleo, Anna, 1948- Il movimento cooperativo in Italia nel primo dopoguerra (1918-1925) / Anna Caroleo ; presentazione di Maurizio Degl'Innocenti. Milano, Italy : F. Angeli, c1986. 376 p. ; 22 cm. (Studi e ricerche storiche. 75) Includes bibliographical references and index. LC Card 86-192160
1. Cooperation - Italy - History - 20th century. 2. Reconstruction (1914-1939) - Italy. I. Title.
HD3503 .C36 1986

Carolingia impressa .
(8) Autonomie als arbeidssociologisch vraagstuk . Zeist , 1987. 237 p. : ISBN 90-6720-032-8 : LC Card 87-169950
HD5660.N4 A94 1987

Carolrhoda on my own book.
Brandt, Betty. Special delivery /. Minneapolis, Minn. , c1988. 40 p. : ISBN 0-87614-312-5 (lib. bdg.) LC Card 87-15647 DDC 383/.4973 19
HE6371 .B77 1988

Caron, André H. Les télévisions étrangères : leur impact sur nos images politiques et culturelles / par André H. Caron.1ère éd. [Montréal] : Université de Montréal, Faculté des arts et des sciences, Dép. de communication, 1983. ix, 166 p., 12 leaves : ill. ; 22 cm. (Cahiers de recherches en communication) Bibliography: p. 123-127. ISBN 2-920396-86-2 : LC Card 83-157210 DDC 302.2/345/09714 19
1. Television broadcasting - Social aspects - Québec (Province) - Case studies. 2. Television audiences - Québec (Province) - Case studies. 3. French-Canadians - Québec (Province) - Ethnic identity - Case studies. 4. Television programs, Foreign - Québec (Province). I. Title. II. Series.
HE8700.9.C2 C37 1983
NYPL [MWGS 86-2473]

Caron, Diane. Les postes de traite de fourrure sur la Côte-Nord et dans l'Outaouais / Diane Caron. [Québec] : Gouvernement du Québec, Ministère des affaires culturelles, [1984] xvi, 150 p. : ill. ; 28 cm. (Dossiers. 56) Bibliography: p. 143-150. ISBN 2-551-06277-2 LC Card 84-220957
1. Fur trade - Canada - History. 2. Indians of North America - Canada - Trading posts - History. I. Series: Dossiers (Québec (Province). Ministère des affaires culturelles) , 56. II. Title.
HD9944.C22 C34 1984

CARORA (VENEZUELA) - COMMERCE - HISTORY - 20TH CENTURY.
García Ponce, Antonio, 1929- Crisis oligarquía y latifundio . Barquisimeto, Venezuela , 1986. 104 p., [1] folded leaf of plates : ISBN 980-608-701-1 : LC Card 87-134729 DDC 338.1/762/0098725 19
HF3490.C375 G37 1986

Carpenter, Donna Sammons. Breitbard, Stanley H. The Price Waterhouse book of personal financial planning /. New York , 1988. xi, 447 p. ; ISBN 0-8050-0387-8 LC Card 87-8493 DDC 332.024 19
HG179 .B727 1988

Carpenter, Gregory. Business strategy and the life cycle concept : summary of Marketing Science Institute Conference, December 12, 1985 / Gregory Carpenter, John U. Farley. Cambridge, Mass. (1000 Massachusetts Ave., Cambridge 02138) : Marketing Science Institute, [1985] [19] leaves ; 28 cm. LC Card 87-108925 DDC 658.5/038 19
1. Product life cycle - Congresses. 2. Strategic planning - Congresses. I. Farley, John U. II. Title.
HF5415.155 .C37 1985

Carr, Barry. The Mexican Left, the popular movements, and the politics of austerity /. La Jolla, Calif. , 1986. vi, 96 p. ; LC Card 87-621353 DDC 322/.2/0972 19
HC135 .M525535 1986

Carr, Marilyn. The AT reader . London , 1985. xvii, 468 p. : ISBN 0-946688-10-9
NYPL [JLE 86-2305]

Carraro, Kenneth C. An economic evaluation of alternative sources of funding for agricultural lending by commercial banks / by Kenneth C. Carraro and Eddy L. LaDue. Ithaca, N.Y. : Dept. of Agricultural Economics, Cornell University Agricultural Experiment Station, New York State College of Agriculture and Life Sciences, Cornell University, [1985] 48 p. ; 28 cm. (A.E. research . 85-7) Cover title. "April 1985." LC Card 86-622432 DDC 332.7/1/09747 19
1. Agricultural credit - New York (State). 2. Agricultural credit - United States. I. LaDue, Eddy L. II. Title. III. Series.
HG2051.U6 N53 1985

Carrasco, Hernán. Mariano, Alfonso, José, Lorenzo, Manuel . Quito, Ecuador , 1985. 128 p., [8] leaves of plates : LC Card 86-136793
HD1531.E2 M37 1985

Carrasco, Ramiro. Tendencias sindicales después del VI Congreso de la C.O.B. /. La Paz , c1985. 111 p. ; LC Card 86-137172
HD8272.C65 T45 1985

Carreira, António.
Cabo Verde : aspectos sociais, secas e fomes do século XX / António Carreira. Lisboa : Ulmeiro, [1984] 207 p., [16] p. of plates : ill. ; 21 cm. (Biblioteca Ulmeiro. no. 9) Includes bibliographical references. LC Card 87-400337 DDC 363.8/0966/58 19
1. Famines - Cape Verde - History - 20th century. 2. Droughts - Cape Verde - History - 20th century. 3. Cape Verde - Social conditions. 4. Cape Verde - Economic conditions. I. Title.
HC594.Z9 F33 1984

As companhias pombalinas : de Grão-Pará e Maranhão e Pernambuco e Paraíba / António Carreira.[2a. ed.]. Lisboa : Editorial Presença, [1983] 426 p. : ill. ; 21 cm. (Biblioteca de textos universitários . 57) Rev. ed. of: As companhias pombalinas de navegação, comércio e tráfico de escravos da costa africana para o Nordeste brasileiro. Bibliography: p. 421-424. LC Card 86-146987
1. Companhia Geral do Grão Pará e Maranhão - History. 2. Companhia Geral de Pernambuco e Paraíba - History. 3. Slave-trade - Brazil, Northeast - History. 4. Slave-trade - Africa - History. I. Carreira, António. Companhias pombalinas de navegação, comércio e tráfico de escravos da costa africana para o Nordeste brasileiro. II. Title.
HF491.C592 C37 1983

Companhias pombalinas de navegação, comércio e tráfico de escravos da costa africana para o Nordeste brasileiro.
Carreira, António. As companhias pombalinas : de Grão-Pará e Maranhão e Pernambuco e Paraíba / António Carreira.[2a. ed.]. Lisboa [1983] 426 p. : LC Card 86-146987
HF491.C592 C37 1983

Os portuguêses nos rios de Guiné, 1500-1900 / António Carreira. Lisboa : [A. Carreira], 1984. 205 p. : ill. ; 25 cm. Cover title. Bibliography: p. 188-193. LC Card 85-149851
1. Portugal - Commerce - Africa, West - History. 2. Africa, West - Commerce - Portugal - History. 3. Coastwise shipping - Africa, West - History. I. Title.
HF3698.A358 C37 1984

Carreras, Charles. United States economic penetration of Venezuela and its effects on diplomacy, 1895-1906 / Charles Carreras. New York : Garland Pub., 1987. 252 p. : map ; 23 cm. (Foreign economic policy of the United States) Originally presented as the author's thesis (Ph.D.--University of North Carolina at Chapel Hill, 1971) Bibliography: p. [244]-252. ISBN 0-8240-8077-7 (alk. paper) : LC Card 87-23723 DDC 332.6/7373/087 19
1. Investments, American - Venezuela - History. 2. United States - Foreign economic relations - Venezuela. 3. Venezuela - Foreign economic relations - United States. 4. United States - Foreign relations - 1897-1901. I. Title. II. Series.
HG5412 .C45 1987

Carreras, Rodrigo X. Vivienda y población en Costa Rica : segundo avance, necesidades de vivienda hasta el año 2000 / Rodrigo X. Carreras, Justo Aguilar, Marcos Bogan ; asistentes de investigación, Jorge Segura, Carlos Luis Oses. Heredia, Costa Rica : Instituto de Estudios Sociales en Población, Universidad Nacional, 1979. 203 p. : ill. ; 33 cm. (Informe . no. 19) "Distribución restringida." On t.p.: 1978. Bibliography: p. 200-203. LC Card 87-404329 DDC 363.5/097286 19
1. Housing forecasting - Costa Rica. 2. Housing - Costa Rica. I. Aguilar, Justo. II. Bogan, Marcos. III. Series: Informe (Universidad Nacional (Costa Rica). Instituto de Estudios Sociales en Población) , #19. IV. Title.
HD7308.A3 C37 1979

Carriage of crude oil by sea. Gunner, T. J. Gunner and Edwards on the carriage of crude oil by sea /. London , New York , 1986. xii, 137 p. : ISBN 1-85044-073-5 (pbk.) : LC Card 86-224898 DDC 387.5/448 19
HE595.P4 G86 1986

CARRIAGES AND CARTS - NORWAY - OSLO - HISTORY.
Winge, Harald. Føringaredskaper i Aker fogderi . Oslo , 1976. 105 p. : LC Card 86-460271
HE259.Z7 A48 1976

CARRIAGES AND CARTS - ZAMBIA - EASTERN PROVINCE.
Rajeswaran, K. A feasibility study on the ox-driven scotch cart project . Lusaka, Zambia [1985] vii leaves, 66 p., [3] leaves of plates : LC Card 87-980373 DDC 388.3/41/096894 19
HE153 .R35 1985

Carrier accountability monitoring project. The American Society of Internal Medicine's carrier accountability monitoring project . Washington, DC [1986] 8 p. ; LC Card 86-219845 DDC 368.4/26/0068 19
HD7102.U4 A753 1986

Carrieri, Mimmo. Il mestiere politico del sindacato / Mimmo Carrieri, Carlo Donolo. 1a ed. Roma : Editori riuniti, 1986. 218 p. ; 22 cm. (Politica e società. 57) Bibliography: p. 211-216. ISBN 88-359-2930-X : LC Card 86-200898
1. Trade-unions - Italy - Political activity. I. Donolo, Carlo. II. Title.
HD8485 .C37 1986

CARRIERS - RATES. see
TRANSPORTATION - RATES.

CARRIERS - UNITED STATES.
Barrett, Colin. Practical handbook of transportation contracting and rate negotiations /. Washington , c1987. ix, 269 p. ; ISBN 0-87408-037-1 LC Card 86-50988 DDC 380.5/24/068 19
HE199.U5 B37 1987

Carrilho, Maria José. Análise da idade média ao casamento, 1930-1978 / Maria José Carrilho. Lisboa, Portugal : Instituto Nacional de Estatística, Serviços Centrais, Centro de Estudos Demográficos, 1984. 27 p. : ill. ; 30 cm. Cover title. LC Card 85-124431
1. Marriage - Portugal - Statistics. 2. Middle aged women - Portugal - Statistics. 3. Middle aged men - Portugal - Statistics. I. Title.
HB1241 .C37 1984

Carrillo V., Jorge (Carrillo Viveros)
Conflictos laborales en la industria maquiladora / Jorge Carrillo V. 1a ed. Tijuana, Baja California : Centro de Estudios Fronterizos del Norte de México, 1985. 55 p. : ill. ; 23 cm. (Cuadernos CEFNOMEX) Bibliography: p. 53-55. ISBN 968-607-504-6 LC Card 87-117557 DDC 331.4/87/09721 19
1. Strikes and lockouts - Offshore assembly industry - Mexican-American Border Region. I. Title. II. Series.
HD5331.O33 C37 1985

Mujeres fronterizas en la industria maquiladora / Jorge Carrillo V., Alberto Hernández. 1a ed. [Mexico City] : Secretaría de Educación Pública ; Tijuana, B.C.N. : Centro de Estudios Fronterizos del Norte de México, 1985. 216 p. : ill. ; 21 cm. (Colección Frontera) Bibliography: p. 195-216. ISBN 968-290-389-0 LC Card 87-400964 DDC 331.4 19
1. Women offshore assembly industry workers - Mexican-American Border Region. I. Hernández H., Alberto (Hernández Hernández). II. Series: Frontera. III. Title.
HD6073.O332 M483 1985

Carrión, Diego. Tierras para asentamientos populares . Quito, Ecuador , 1985. 378 p. : LC Card 87-400165 DDC 333.77/13/0986613 19
HD530.Q58 T54 1985

Carrión, Julio. Galin, Pedro. Asalariados y clases populares en Lima /. Lima [1986] 127 p. ; LC Card 87-400199 DDC 331/.0985/25 19
HD8350.L562 G35 1986

Carrion Júnior, Francisco M. (Francisco Machado), 1944- O Rio Grande em busca de novos caminhos por um projeto regional / Carrion Jr. Porto Alegre, RS : Mercado Aberto, 1986. 78 p. : ill. ; 22 cm. (Série Depoimentos) "Roteiro bibliográfico": p. [76]-78. LC Card 87-129162 DDC 330.981/65063 19

1. Rio Grande do Sul (Brazil) - Economic conditions. 2. Unemployment, Structural - Brazil - Rio Grande do Sul. I. Title.
HC188.R4 C35 1986

Carrion, Rosinha Machado. Participação ou manipulação : um estudo de caso / Rosinha Machado Carrion. Porto Alegre, RS : Fundação de Economia e Estatística, 1984. 111 p. : forms ; 23 cm. (Teses. n. 8) Originally presented as the author's thesis (master's--Pontificia Universidade Católica do Rio Grande do Sul, 1982) Bibliography: p. [109]-111. LC Card 84-209842 DDC 658 19
1. Industrial management - Employee participation. 2. Organizational behavior. I. Series: Teses (Rio Grande do Sul (Brazil). Fundação de Economia e Estatística) , n. 8. II. Title.
HD37.P63 C29 1984 NYPL [JLE 86-2263]

Carroll, Barry J. Private means--public ends . New York , 1987. xiii, 187 p. ; ISBN 0-275-92429-7 (alk. paper) : LC Card 86-25251 DDC 361.6/1/0973 19
HN65 .P69 1987 NYPL [JLE 87-1390]

Carroll, Joe.
Lewis, Diane, 1936- The insider's guide to finding the right job /. Nashville , c1987. 190 p. ; ISBN 0-8407-3107-8 (pbk.) : LC Card 86-33305 DDC 650.1/4 19
HF5382.75.U6 L49 1987

Lewis, Diane, 1936- Why women fail in business /. Nashville , c1987. p. cm. ISBN 0-8407-4219-3 : LC Card 87-15370 DDC 658.4/09088042 19
HD6054.3 .L48 1987

Carroll, John Millar. Computer security / John M. Carroll. 2nd ed. Boston : Butterworths, c1987. xv, 446 p. : ill. ; 25 cm. Bibliography: p. 431-436. Includes index. ISBN 0-409-90032-X LC Card 86-29901 DDC 658.4/78 19
1. Electronic data processing departments - Security measures. 2. Computers - Access control. 3. Computer crimes. I. Title.
HF5548.2 .C29 1987

Carroll, Thomas M. Brennan, Michael Joseph, 1928- Preface to quantitative economics & econometrics. Cincinnati , c1987. x, 580 p. : ISBN 0-538-08230-5 (pbk.) LC Card 86-60209 DDC 330/.028 19
HB139 .B74 1987

Carroll, William K. Corporate power and Canadian capitalism / William K. Carroll. Vancouver : University of British Columbia Press, 1986. xvii, 284 p. : ill. ; 24 cm. Bibliography: p. [257]-276. Includes index. ISBN 0-7748-0246-4 LC Card 86-223683 DDC 338.8/0971 19
1. Capital - Canada. 2. Corporations - Canada. 3. Elite (Social sciences) - Canada. I. Title.
HC120.C3 C37 1986

Carron, Andrew S. Bosworth, Barry, 1942- The economics of federal credit programs /. Washington, D.C. , c1987. xii, 214 p. : ISBN 0-8157-1038-0 : LC Card 85-48205 DDC 336.3/44/0973 19
HJ8119 .B67 1987

Carrying capacities of nation-states /. McCoid, Catherine Hodge. New Haven, Conn. (P.O. Box 2015, Yale Station, New Haven 06520) , 1984. x, 198 leaves : LC Card 84-152784 DDC 304.6/2 19
GN33.5 .M38 1984 NYPL [JFE 86-2142]

CARS (AUTOMOBILES) see **AUTOMOBILES.**

Carson, Carol S. The use of national income and product accounts for public policy : our successes and failures / by Carol S. Carson and George Jaszi. Washington, D.C. : U. S. Dept. of Commerce, Bureau of Economic Analysis : For sale by the Supt. of Docs., U. S. G.P.O., 1986. 26 p. : ill. ; 28 cm. (Bureau of Economic Analysis staff paper . 43) Paper presented at the American Statistical Association meetings, Las Vegas, Nev., Aug. 5, 1985. "January 1986." Includes bibliographical references. "BEA-SP86-043"--Cover. LC Card 86-601338 DDC 339.5/0973 19
1. National income - United States - Accounting - Congresses. 2. Political planning - United States - Congresses. 3. United States - Economic policy - 1981- - Congresses. I. Jaszi, George. II. Title. III. Series.
HC110.I5 C37 1986

Carta Punta del Este. Mesa Redonda sobre la Carta de Punta del Este (1961 : Universidad Nacional Autónoma de México) Memoria del ciclo de conferencias de Mesa Redonda sobre la Carta de Punta del Este /. México , 1962. 224 p. : LC Card 85-105213
HC125 .M48 1961

Cartagena Agreement. see **Acuerdo de Cartagena.**

CARTAGENA (COLOMBIA) - COMMERCE.
Pombo, José Ignacio de, 1761-1815. Comercio y contrabando en Cartagena de Indias, 2 de junio de 1800 /. Bogotá, Colombia , 1986. 124 p. ; LC Card 87-107126
HJ6864 .P66 1986

Cartas, José María. Precondiciones para la implementación de la economía social de mercado en América Latina : un estudio de casos, Panamá y Uruguay / por José María Cartas y Helmut Wittelsbürger. Buenos Aires, República Argentina : Centro Interdisciplinario de Estudios sobre el Desarrollo Latinoamericano, c1985. 80 p. ; 29 cm. Summaries also in English and German. Bibliography: p. 77-80. LC Card 87-101628
1. Latin America - Economic policy - Case studies. 2. Uruguay - Economic policy - Case studies. 3. Panama - Economic policy - Case studies. I. Wittelsbürger, Helmut. II. Centro Interdisciplinario de Estudios sobre el Desarrollo Latinoamericano. III. Title.
HC125 .C374 1985

Cartay Angulo, Rafael, 1941- La transición del feudalismo al capitalismo y la revolución industrial / Rafael Cartay Angulo. [Mérida? : s.n., 1983] (Mérida, Venezuela : Tall. Gráf. Universitarios) 258 p. ; 23 cm. Bibliography: p. 237-258. LC Card 84-188666
1. Economic history. I. Title.
HC51 .C363 1983

CARTELS.
Ghanem, Shukri Mohammed. OPEC, the rise and fall of an exclusive club /. London ; New York : x, 233 p. ; ISBN 0-7103-0175-8 LC Card 87-131574 DDC 341.7/5472282 19
HD9560.1.O66 G55 1986

Holloway, Steven Kendall, 1951- The aluminum multinationals and the bauxite cartel /. New York , 1988. vii, 93 p. : ISBN 0-312-00939-9 : LC Card 87-12991 DDC 338.8/87 19
HD9539.A62 H64 1988

CARTELS - GERMANY - HISTORY.
Bechtold, Hartmut. Die Kartellierung der deutschen Volkswirtschaft und die sozialdemokratische Theorie-Diskussion vor 1933 /. Frankfurt am Main , c1986. 291 p. ; ISBN 3-89228-000-2 LC Card 86-193858
HD2757.5 .B43 1986

Carter, Bob, 1949- Capitalism, class conflict, and the new middle class / Bob Carter. London ; Boston : Routledge & Kegan Paul, 1985. vii, 256 p., 15 p. ; 23 cm. (International library of sociology) Based on the author's thesis (doctoral)--University of Bristol, 1980. Includes bibliography and index. ISBN 0-7100-9624-0 : LC Card 84-9956 DDC 305.5/56 19
1. White collar workers. 2. Class consciousness. 3. Marxian school of sociology. I. Title.
HD8039.M39 C37 1985 NYPL [JLD 87-115]

Carter, D. D. The changing face of Canadian labour relations law / Donald D. Carter. Kingston, Ont., Canada : Industrial Relations Centre, Queen's University, 1985. 15 p. ; 29 cm. (Reprint series, 0075-6156 . no. 54) Cover title. Paper presented at the annual Fall Industrial Relations Seminar, Industrial Relations Centre, Queen's University , Kingston, Ont., Oct. 20-25, 1985. Bibliography: p. 14-15. ISBN 0-88886-126-5 (pbk.) LC Card 86-145328 DDC 331 s 344.71/01 331 s 347.1041 19
1. Labor laws and legislation - Canada. 2. Civil rights - Canada. I. Fall Industrial Relations Seminar (1985 : Industrial Relations Centre, Queen's University, Kingston, Ont.). II. Series: Reprint series (Queen's University (Kingston, Ont.). Industrial Relations Centre) , no. 54. III. Title.
HD8102 .K52 no. 54 KE3009

Carter, Harold O. Eidman, Vernon R., 1936- Decision models for California turkey growers /. Berkeley, Calif. [1968] ii, 80 p. : LC Card 87-401009 DDC 338.1/09794 s 636.5/92/0068 19
HD1407 .C27 no. 21 HD9437.U63C3

Carter, John Mack. Starting at the top : America's new achievers : twenty-three success stories told by men and women whose dreams of being boss came true / John Mack Carter and Joan Feeney. New York : Morrow, [1985] 252 p. ; 22 cm. Includes index. ISBN 0-688-04520-0 LC Card 85-4826 DDC 338/.04/0922 B 19
1. Businessmen - United States - Biography. 2. Success in business - United States - Case studies. I. Feeney, Joan. II. Title.
HC102.5.A2 C37 1985
NYPL [JLD 87-1089]

Carter, Luther J. Nuclear imperatives and public trust : dealing with radioactive waste / Luther J. Carter. Washington, D.C. : Resources for the Future ; [Baltimore, Md.] : distributed worldwide by the Johns Hopkins University Press, c1987. xii, 473 p. ; 25 cm. Includes bibliographical references and indexes. ISBN 0-915707-29-2 : LC Card 87-4706 DDC 363.7/28 19
1. Radioactive waste disposal - Government policy - United States. 2. Radioactive waste disposal - Government policy - Case studies. I. Title.
HC110.E5 C358 1987

Carter, R. L. Personal financial markets . Deddington, Oxford , Atlantic Highlands, N.J. , 1986. viii, 279 p. : ISBN 0-86003-540-9 LC Card 86-235455 DDC 332.1/7 19
HG186.G7 P38 1986

Cartillas turolenses .
(no. 3) Infante Díaz, Jorge. Aproximación a la estructura económica de la provincia de Teruel /. [Teruel] , 1986. 59 p. : ISBN 84-505-3546-8 LC Card 87-105066
HC387.T4 I53 1986

Caruth, Donald L.
Compensation management for banks / Donald L. Caruth. Boston : Bankers Pub. Co., c1986. viii, 312 p. : ill. ; 25 cm. Includes index. Bibliography: p. [301]-308. ISBN 0-87267-060-0 LC Card 86-3543 DDC 332.1/068/3 19
1. Banks and banking - Personnel management. 2. Wages - Bank employees. I. Title.
HG1615.7.C65 C37 1986
NYPL [JLE 87-828]

Staffing the contemporary organization : a guide to planning, recruiting, and selecting for human resource professionals / Donald L. Caruth, Robert M. Noe, III, and R. Wayne Mondy. New York : Quorum Books, 1988. xii, 309 p. : ill. ; 25 cm. Bibliography: p. 301-304. Includes index. ISBN 0-89930-236-X (lib. bdg. : alk. paper) LC Card 87-13092 DDC 658.3 19
1. Personnel management. 2. Manpower planning. 3. Recruiting of employees. 4. Employee selection. I. Noe, Robert M. II. Mondy, R. Wayne, 1940-. III. Title.
HF5549 .C296 1988

Carvalho, Flávio Condé de. Desgualdo Netto, Domingos. Aspectos agroeconômicos da soja /. São Paulo , 1985. 139 p. ; LC Card 86-158570
HD9235.S62 B74 1985

Carvalho, José António Segueira. A adesão de Portugal à C.E.E. : uma opção histórica, um imperativo de desenvolvimento / José António Sequeira Carvalho. [Lisbon, Portugal] : Associação dos Estudantes do Instituto Superior de Economia, 1985. 97 p. : ill. ; 20 cm. Bibliography: p. 91-93. LC Card 86-150962
1. European Economic Community - Portugal. I. Title.
HC241.25.P6 C38 1985

Carvalho, Osvaldo Ferraro de. Ensaio sôbre a problemática dos transportes / Osvaldo Ferraro de Carvalho. Rio de Janeiro : Biblioteca do Exército, 1957. 324 p., [5] folded leaves of plates : ill., maps (some col.) ; 19 cm. (Biblioteca do exército. vol. 231) Includes bibliographical references. LC Card 85-197985
1. Transportation - Brazil. I. Series: Publicação (Biblioteca do Exército (Brazil)) , 231. II. Title.
HE233 .C345 1957

Carvão mineral / equipe, Leosergio Angheben, coordenador ; Evaldo José Kummer ... [et al.]. [Porto Alegre] : Banco Regional de Desenvolvimento do Extremo Sul, [19]84. 56 p. ; 22 cm. Cover title: Carvão mineral na região Sul. LC Card 86-163115
1. Coal trade - Brazil, South. I. Angheben, Leosergio. II. Kummer, Evaldo José. III. Banco Regional de Desenvolvimento do Extremo sul. IV. Title: Carvão

mineral na região Sul.
HD9554.B83 S683 1984

Carvão mineral na região Sul. Carvão mineral /. [Porto Alegre] [19]84. 56 p. ; LC Card 86-163115
HD9554.B83 S683 1984

Carvell, Steven. Strebel, Paul. In the shadows of Wall Street . Englewood Cliffs, N.J. , c1988. xii, 228 p. : ISBN 0-13-455999-1 LC Card 87-42680 DDC 332.63/22 19
HG4921 .S84 1988

Carvounis, Chris C. The United States trade deficit of the 1980s : origins, meanings, and policy responses / Chris C. Carvounis. New York : Quorum Books, 1987. vi, 190 p. ; 22 cm. Bibliography: p. [175]-184. Includes index. ISBN 0-89930-219-X (lib. bdg. : alk. paper) LC Card 87-2561 DDC 382.1/7/0973 19
1. Balance of trade - United States. 2. United States - Commerce. I. Title. II. Title: Trade deficit of the 1980's.
HF3031 .C37 1987

Casa de la Cultura Ecuatoriana. (Old Catalog form: Casa de la Cultura Ecuatoriana, Quito) Guzmán Ortega, Gonzalo. Superestructuras y subdesarrollo . Quito , 1985. 178 p. : LC Card 86-132144
HC59.7 .G86 1985

CASA DE MONEDA DE MÉXICO - HISTORY - 18TH CENTURY.
Cortina Portilla, Manuel. Algo sobre la plata en México en el siglo XVIII /. México , 1986. 48 p., [1] folded leaf of plates : LC Card 87-404604 DDC 332.4/042/097253 19
HG661 .C67 1986

La casa dividida . López Castro, Gustavo. Zamora, Mich. [i.e. Michoacán] [S.l.] , 1986. 169 p. : ISBN 968-7230-19-3 LC Card 87-400954 DDC 304.8/73/07237 19
HB3532.G66 L66 1986

Casaca, José Paulo Martins. O papel do sector leiteiro no desenvolvimento económico dos Açores : uma perspectiva de integração económica / José Paulo Martins Casaca. Ponta Delgada : Universidade dos Açores, 1985. 260, [16] p., [1] leaf of plates : ill. (some col.) ; 23 cm. Abstract in English. Bibliography: p. 153-179. LC Card 86-167454
1. Milk trade - Government policy - Azores. 2. Milk trade - Azores. 3. Azores - Economic policy. I. Title.
HD9282.A962 C37 1985

Casagrande Neto, Humberto. Abertura do capital de empresas no Brasil : um enfoque prático / Humberto Casagrande Neto. São Paulo : Atlas, 1985. 143 p. ; 22 cm. Bibliography: p. 143. ISBN 85-22-40100-4
1. Capital investments - Brazil. 2. Corporations, Brazilian. 3. Securities - Brazil. I. Title.
NYPL [JLD 86-1080]

Casares, Gabriel Tortella. see **Tortella Casares, Gabriel.**

Casas Grieve, Luis Felipe de las. Economía y frustración social : balance económico del gobierno de acción popular (1980-1981) / por Luis F. de las Casas Grieve, Milton Guerrero Rodríguez, Manuel Martínez Alvarado. Lima, Perú : Instituto de Estudios e Investigación Política, Económica y Social, [1982?] 128 p. : ill. ; 21 cm. LC Card 83-104684
1. Peru - Economic policy. 2. Peru - Economic conditions - 1968-. 3. Acción Popular (Peru) - Platforms. I. Guerrero Rodríguez, Milton. II. Martínez Alvarado, Manuel, 1914-. III. Title.
HC227 .C27 1982

Cascarini, Daniel C. Costeo y evaluación de la producción conjunta : teoría y práctica / Daniel C. Cascarini. Buenos Aires : Editorial El Coloquio, [1985] 206 p. : ill. ; 22 cm. Bibliography: p. [205]-206. ISBN 950-593-015-1 LC Card 86-133889 DDC 338/.06 19
1. Industrial productivity. I. Title.
HD56 .C37 1985

Cascella, Pasquale. Lama, Luciano. Cari compagni . Roma , c1986. vii, 184 p. ; LC Card 87-155314
HD6710.L35 A4 1986

Cascio, Wayne F.
Applied psychology in personnel management / Wayne F. Cascio. 3rd ed. Englewood Cliffs, NJ : Prentice-Hall, c1987. xv, 510 p. : ill. ; 25 cm. Bibliography: p. 462-497. Includes indexes. ISBN 0-13-041427-1 : LC Card 86-25253 DDC 658.3/001/9 19
1. Personnel management. 2. Psychology, Industrial. I. Title.
HF5549 .C297 1987

Costing human resources : the financial impact of behavior in organizations / Wayne F. Cascio.2nd ed. Boston, Mass. : PWS-Kent Pub. Co., c1987. xiv, 274 p. : ill. ; 21 cm. (Kent human resource management series) Includes bibliographies and index. ISBN 0-534-08034-0 (pbk.) : LC Card 87-2501 DDC 658.1/553 19
1. Labor costs - Accounting. I. Title. II. Series.
HF5681.L2 C37 1987

CASE and programmers' workstation markets. C.A.S.E. & programmers' workstation markets. Norwalk, Conn., U. S.A. (6 Prowitt St., Norwalk 06855) , c1987. v, 221 leaves : LC Card 87-129461 DDC 380.1/450051 19
HD9696.C62 C2 1987

The case for South African gold mining stocks . Rosenthal, Daniel M. Bethel, CT , c1987. vi, 57 p. : ISBN 0-938689-05-3 (pbk.) LC Card 87-160603 DDC 332.63/22 19
HG293 .R676 1987

Case, Frederick E. Investing in real estate / Fred E. Vase. 2nd rev. ed. New York : Prentice Hall, 1988. p. cm. Includes index. ISBN 0-13-503260-1 : LC Card 87-19269 DDC 332.63/24 19
1. Real estate investment. I. Title.
HD1382.5 .C365 1988

CASE METHOD.
A Casebook for systems development /. London , Baltimore, Md., USA , 1986. iv, 88, [1] p. : ISBN 0-7131-3600-6 LC Card 87-114266 DDC 658 19
HD31 .C3554 1986

A case of inequity [microform] . Coalition of Northeast Governors. Policy Research Center. [New York] , 1977. 39 p. ;
NYPL [*ZT-1564 no.21]

Case studies in ergonomics practice . (v. 3) Fallik, Fred. Managing organizational change . Philadelphia , 1988. p. cm. ISBN 0-85066-430-6 : LC Card 87-18027 DDC 658.3 19
HF5548 .F274 1988

Case studies in international business /. Grosse, Christine Uber. Englewood Cliffs, N.J. , c1988. xv, 155 p. : ISBN 0-13-119314-7 (pbk.) LC Card 87-22307 DDC 658/.049 19
HD62.4 .G76 1988

Case studies in international management /. Sawyer-Lauçanno, Christopher, 1951- Englewood Cliffs, N.J. , c1987. xvii, 138 p. : ISBN 0-13-119298-1 (pbk.) LC Card 86-22724 DDC 658/.049 19
HD62.4 .S29 1987

Case studies in international marketing / edited by Peter Doyle and Norman A. Hart. London : Published on behalf of the CAM Foundation and the Institute of Marketing [by] Heinemann, 1982. vii, 391 p. : ill. ; 24 cm. ISBN 0-434-90370-1 : LC Card 82-241323 DDC 658.8/48 19
1. Export marketing - Great Britain - Case studies. 2. Export marketing - Europe - Case studies. I. Doyle, Peter. II. Hart, Norman A. III. CAM Foundation.
HF1009.5 .C34 1982 ***NYPL [JLE 87-1196]***

Case study series (NGO Water Supply & Sanitation Decade Service (Sri Lanka)) . (no. 2) Fernando, Vijita. Punchiwilaththawa, household study of a dry zone village /. Colombo, Sri Lanka , 1986. 36 p. : LC Card 86-902299 DDC 330.9549/3 19
HC424.Z7 P864 1986

A Casebook for systems development / S. Rogerson ... [et al.]. London ; Baltimore, Md., USA : E. Arnold, 1986. iv, 88, [1] p. : ill. ; 25 cm. Bibliography: p. [89] ISBN 0-7131-3600-6 LC Card 87-114266 DDC 658 19
1. Management - Case studies. 2. Business - Case studies. 3. Systems analysis - Case studies. 4. Case method. I. Rogerson, S.
HD31 .C3554 1986

Caselli, Clara.
L'internationalisation bancaire en Egypte / Clara Caselli. Milano : Finafrica-Cariplo : Giuffrè, [1982] 223 p. ; 25 cm. (Marchés du crédit des pays d'Afrique . 17) Bibliography: p. [213]-214. LC Card 83-132087 DDC 332.1/5/0962 19
1. Banks and banking, Foreign - Egypt. 2. Investments, Foreign - Egypt. 3. Egypt - Foreign economic relations. I. Title. II. Series.
HG3386.A6 C37 1982 ***NYPL [JLE 86-1969]***

Mauri, Arnaldo. Moneta e banca in Etiopia /. Milano [1986] xi, 316 p. : ISBN 88-14-00769-1 LC Card 86-182310
HG3389.A6 M38 1986
NYPL [JLE 87-1721]

Caselli, Lorenzo. Le Strategie di acquisto della grande impresa nell'evoluzione dei sistemi produttivi . Milano, Italy , c1985. 223 p. : LC Card 85-233748
HD85.I7 I68 no. 76 HD39.5
NYPL [JLD 87-426]

Caselli, Mario, 1944- La gestione marketing nella banca : cosa significa, perchè e come realizzare razionali e dinamiche politiche di mercato negli istituti di credito / Mario Caselli ; prefazione di Roberto Ruozi. Milano : F. Angeli, [1977] 332 p. : ill. ; 22 cm. (Collana L'Azienda moderna ; 141) Includes bibliographical references. LC Card 77-553379
1. Bank marketing. 2. Credit - Italy. I. Title.
HG1616.M3 C37 ***NYPL [JLD 80-3228]***

Cases and classics in marketing management / Dennis H. Tootelian, Ralph M. Gaedeke. San Diego : Harcourt Brace Jovanovich, c1986. ix, 513 p. : ill. ; 25 cm. Rev. ed. of: Marketing management. c1980. Includes bibliographies and index. ISBN 0-15-505775-8 LC Card 85-80071 DDC 658.8/00973 19
1. Marketing - United States - Management. 2. Marketing - United States - Management - Case studies. I. Tootelian, Dennis H. II. Gaedeke, Ralph M.
HF5415.13 .C28 1986 ***NYPL [JLE 86-3101]***

Cases and readings for marketing for nonprofit organizations. Strategic marketing for nonprofit organizations . Englewood Cliffs, NJ , c1987. x, 386 p. : ISBN 0-13-851312-0 (pbk.) : LC Card 86-25262 DDC 658.8 19
HF5415 .C2854 1987

Cases in advertising and promotion management /. Quelch, John A. Plano, Tex. , 1987. xv, 759 p. : ISBN 0-256-03713-2 LC Card 86-72244 DDC 659.1 19
HF5823 .Q44 1987

Cases in business decision making / Education Development Center, Inc. (EDC) ; David A. Garvin, project director. Chicago : Dryden Press, c1987. ix, 102 p. : ill. ; 24 cm. Bibliography: p. 35. ISBN 0-03-009108-X (pbk.) LC Card 86-29131 DDC 658.4/033 19
1. Decision-making - Case studies. I. Garvin, David A. II. Education Development Center.
HD30.23 .C375 1987

Cases in business policy / Brian Kenny ... [et al.]. Oxford, UK ; New York : B. Blackwell, 1987. ix, 538 p. : ill. ; 23 cm. Includes bibliographical references. ISBN 0-631-15544-9 (pbk.) : LC Card 87-6607 DDC 658.4/012 19
1. Strategic planning - Case studies. 2. Management - Case studies. I. Kenny, Brian.
HD30.28 .C379 1987

Cases in consumer behavior /. Tongren, Hale N., 1921- Englewood Cliffs, N.J. , c1987. xiii, 224 p. : ISBN 0-13-115346-3 (pbk.) LC Card 86-25547 DDC 658.8/342 19
HF5415.3 .T64 1987

Cases in corporate finance /. Dimson, Elroy, 1947- Chichester [West Sussex] , New York , c1988. xxiv, 412 p. : ISBN 0-471-91764-8 : LC Card 87-6299 DDC 658.1/5 19
HG4015.5 .D56 1988

Cases in marketing management /. Bernhardt, Kenneth L., 1944- Plano, Tex. , 1985. xiii, 705 p. : ISBN 0-256-03055-3 LC Card 84-70994 DDC 658.8 19
HF5415.13 .B448 1985
NYPL [JLE 86-2513]

Cases in strategic management /. Boseman, F. Glenn. New York , c1988. ix, 476 p. : ISBN 0-471-85463-8 (pbk.) LC Card 87-24261 DDC 658.4/012 19
HD30.28 .B67 1988

Cases in strategic management . Mescon, Timothy S. New York , c1988. ix, 725 p. : ISBN 0-06-044465-7 (pbk.) LC Card 87-25141

DDC 658.4/012 19
HD30.28 .M46 1988

Cases in strategic management and business policy /. Wheelen, Thomas L. Reading, Mass. , c1987. xii, 530 p. : ISBN 0-201-09134-8 (pbk.) : LC Card 86-26501 DDC 658.4/012 19
HD30.28 .W428 1987

Cases in strategic management for business /. Bartlett, Hale C. Chicago , c1988. xiii, 784 p. : ISBN 0-03-007183-6 (pbk.) LC Card 87-20208 DDC 658.4/012 19
HD30.28 .B369 1988

Casey, Bernard. Early retirement schemes with a replacement condition : programmes and experiences in Belgium, France, Great Britain, and the Federal Republic of Germany / Bernard Casey. Berlin : IIM Labour Market Policy, Wissenschaftszentrum Berlin, [1985] 44 p. ; 30 cm. (Discussion papers, 0722-673X . IIM/LMP 85-6a) "August 1985." Bibliography: p. 42-44. LC Card 86-205942 DDC 331.25/2 19
1. Early retirement - Belgium. 2. Early retirement - France. 3. Early retirement - Great Britain. 4. Early retirement - Germany (West). I. Series: Discussion papers (International Institute of Management. Labour Market Policy) , IIM/LMP 85-6a. II. Title.
HD7110.B4 C37 1985

Casey, Douglas R. Two new investment reports from Doug Casey. Arlington, VA (1300 N. 17th St., Suite 1660, Arlington 22209) : Alexandria House Books, c1985. 64, 65 p. : ill. ; 28 cm. Cover title. CONTENTS. - What the smart money is betting on in 1985--Doug Casey's predictions for 1985-1986. LC Card 86-230393 DDC 332.6/78 19
1. Investments - United States - Handbooks, manuals, etc. I. Title.
HG4921 .C35 1985

Cash, Adam. Guerrilla capitalism : how to practice free enterprise in an unfree economy / Adam Cash. Port Townsend, Wash. : Loompanics Unlimited, c1984. 172 p. : ill. ; 22 cm. Bibliography: p. 163-172. ISBN 0-915179-16-4 (pbk.) LC Card 84-81910 DDC 343.7305/23 347.303523 19
1. Informal sector (Economics) - United States. 2. Tax evasion - United States. I. Title.
HD2346.U5 C34 1984 ***NYPL [JLD 86-2946]***

CASH FLOW.
Allen, David. Funds flow management . London , 1980. x, 84 p. :
NYPL [JLD 86-2760]

Credit analysis . Philadelphia, Pa. , c1987. 146 p. : ISBN 0-936742-38-0 (pbk.) : LC Card 86-28628 DDC 332.1/753/0685 19
HG1641 .C66 1987

Effective cash flow management. New York, N.Y., U. S.A. , c1985. x, 223 p. : ISBN 0-86604-176-1 (pbk.) LC Card 86-205438 DDC 658.1/5244 19
HG4028.C45 E34 1985

Helfert, Erich A. Techniques of financial analysis /. Homewood, Ill. , 1987. xiii, 458 p. : ISBN 0-256-03625-X (pbk.) LC Card 86-82589 DDC 658.1/51 19
HG4026 .H44 1987

Kelly, John M. Managing cash flow /. New York , 1986. xii, 210 p. : ISBN 0-531-15509-9 LC Card 86-5657 DDC 658.1/5244 19
HG4028.C45 K453 1986
NYPL [JLE 86-4460]

Toncré, Emery. Maximizing cash flow . New York , c1986. ix, 210 p. : ISBN 0-471-80744-3 : LC Card 85-29643 DDC 658.1/5244 19
HG4028.C45 T66 1986
NYPL [JLE 86-3140]

CASH FLOW - GERMANY, WEST.
Schneider, Pia, 1956- Finanzwirtschaftliche Nebenrechnungen . Frankfurt am Main , New York , c1985. xiii, 303 p. : ISBN 3-8204-8472-8 LC Card 85-190966
HF5686.C7 S354 1985

CASH FLOW - MINNESOTA.
Minnesota. Dept. of Finance. Cash flow report. [St. Paul] [1986] 26, [4] leaves : LC Card 86-622795 DDC 336.776 19
HJ515 .M56 1986

Cash flow report. Minnesota. Dept. of Finance. [St. Paul] [1986] 26, [4] leaves : LC Card 86-622795 DDC 336.776 19
HJ515 .M56 1986

The cash incentive . Philp, Norman E. Canberra , 1986. xii, 135 p. : ISBN 0-86784-984-3 (pbk.) LC Card 87-150813
HD2346.P37 P46 1986

Cash Management . Tüchter, Ulrich. Köln , c1985. 122 p. : ISBN 3-87951-126-8 LC Card 87-152212 DDC 332.1/2/0681 19
HG4028.C45 T83 1985

CASH MANAGEMENT.
Allen, David. Funds flow management . London , 1980. x, 84 p. :
NYPL [JLD 86-2760]

Chastain, Clark E. Corporate asset management . New York , 1987. xxiii, 345 p. : ISBN 0-89930-237-8 (lib. bdg. : alk. paper) LC Card 87-2493 DDC 658.1/5244 19
HG4026 .C458 1987

Effective cash flow management. New York, N.Y., U. S.A. , c1985. x, 223 p. : ISBN 0-86604-176-1 (pbk.) LC Card 86-205438 DDC 658.1/5244 19
HG4028.C45 E34 1985

Kelly, John M. Managing cash flow /. New York , 1986. xii, 210 p. : ISBN 0-531-15509-9 LC Card 86-5657 DDC 658.1/5244 19
HG4028.C45 K453 1986
NYPL [JLE 86-4460]

Nunes, Morris A., 1949- Balance sheet management . New York , c1987. xvi, 288 p. : ISBN 0-471-62956-1 (pbk.) LC Card 87-23093 DDC 658.1/51 19
HF5681.B2 N86 1987

Ross, Derek. International treasury management /. New York, N.Y. , c1988. p. cm. ISBN 0-13-473968-X : LC Card 87-16118 DDC 658.1/599 19
HG4027.5 .R67 1988

Toncré, Emery. Maximizing cash flow . New York , c1986. ix, 210 p. : ISBN 0-471-80744-3 : LC Card 85-29643 DDC 658.1/5244 19
HG4028.C45 T66 1986
NYPL [JLE 86-3140]

Tüchter, Ulrich. Cash Management . Köln , c1985. 122 p. : ISBN 3-87951-126-8 LC Card 87-152212 DDC 332.1/2/0681 19
HG4028.C45 T83 1985

Cash management and the payments system : ground rules, costs, and risks? / The Globecon Group. Morristown, N.J. : Financial Executives Research Foundation, c1986. viii, 102 p. : ill. ; 23 cm. ISBN 0-910586-62-4 (pbk.) LC Card 86-82305 DDC 658.1/5244 19
1. Cash management - United States. 2. Payment - United States. I. Globecon Group. II. Financial Executives Research Foundation.
HG4028.C45 C359 1986

CASH MANAGEMENT - MATHEMATICAL MODELS.
Fietz, Günter. Kurzfristige Finanzplanung und Grossprojektfertigung /. Frankfurt am Main , New York , c1986. iv, 269 p. : ISBN 3-8204-9322-0 LC Card 86-156212
HG4012 .F53 1986

CASH MANAGEMENT - UNITED STATES.
Cash management and the payments system . Morristown, N.J. , c1986. viii, 102 p. : ISBN 0-910586-62-4 (pbk.) LC Card 86-82305 DDC 658.1/5244 19
HG4028.C45 C359 1986

CASH MANAGEMENT - UNITED STATES - DATA PROCESSING.
ACH marketing handbook. [Washington, DC] (1901 L St., NW, Suite 640, Washington 20036) [c1987] 123, [24] p. ; LC Card 87-130512 DDC 332.1/028 19
HG4028.C45 A28 1987

CASH POSITION (CORPORATION FINANCE) see CORPORATIONS - CASH POSITION.

Cash, R. Patrick. Improving apparel shop profits : a professional approach / R. Patrick Cash, Harold H. Frankel]. [New York, N.Y.] : National Retail Merchants Association, [c1986] 285 p. : ill. ; 25 cm. Includes index. ISBN 0-87102-131-5 LC Card 86-61313 DDC 687/.068/8 19
1. Clothing trade - Management. 2. Stores, Retail - Management. I. Frankel, Harold H. II. National Retail Merchants Association. III. Title.
HD9940.A2 C37 1986

CASH TAKEOVER BID. see TENDER OFFERS (SECURITIES)

Cashew Export Promotion Council. Directory of exporters of cashew from India. Cochin, India [1986?] 138 p. ; LC Card 87-901352 DDC 382/.414573/02554 19
HD9259.C33 I423 1986

CASHEW NUT INDUSTRY - INDIA - DIRECTORIES.
Directory of exporters of cashew from India. Cochin, India [1986?] 138 p. ; LC Card 87-901352 DDC 382/.414573/02554 19
HD9259.C33 I423 1986

Cashing in at the checkout /. Samtur, Susan J. New York , c1979. 152 p. : ISBN 0-448-15704-7 : LC Card 79-51120 DDC 381/.1 19
HF6127 .S25 ***NYPL [JLD 81-566]***

Casillas, Rex J. Oil and diplomacy : the evolution of American foreign policy in Saudi Arabia, 1933-1945 / Rex J. Casillas. New York : Garland Pub., 1987. p. cm. (Foreign economic policy of the United States) Bibliography: p. Includes index. ISBN 0-8240-8078-5 : LC Card 87-23769 DDC 337.730538 19
1. United States - Foreign economic relations - Saudi Arabia. 2. Saudi Arabia - Foreign economic relations - United States. 3. Petroleum industry and trade - Saudi Arabia - History. 4. Arabian American Oil Company - History. I. Title. II. Series.
HF1456.5.S33 C37 1987

Casimiro, Liana Maria Carleial de.
Acumulação capitalista, emprego e crise : um estudo de caso / Liana Maria Carleial de Casimiro. São Paulo : Instituto de Pesquisas Econômicas, 1986. 216 p. : ill. ; 23 cm. (Série Ensaios econômicos . no. 59) Bibliography: p. 176-189. LC Card 87-152202 DDC 331.12/0981/31 19
1. Labor supply - Brazil - Fortaleza. 2. Capitalism - Brazil - Fortaleza. 3. Fortaleza (Brazil) - Economic conditions. I. Series: Ensaios econômicos (Universidade de São Paulo. Instituto de Pesquisas Econômicas) , 59. II. Title.
HD5755.F6 C37 1986

Avaliação da política industrial do Ceará : uma contribuição ao debate. Fortaleza : Instituto Euvaldo Lodi, Núcleo Regional do Ceará, 1983. 58 p. ; 21 cm. Includes bibliographical references. LC Card 86-129541
1. Industry and state - Brazil - Ceará (State). I. Instituto Euvaldo Lodi. Núcleo Regional do Ceará. II. Title.
HD3616.B84 C422 1983

Seca : momento para repensar a pobreza do Nordeste : uma análise a partir do Estado do Ceará / Liana Maria Carleial de Casimiro. Fortaleza-Ceará : Federação das Indústrias do Estado do Ceará : Instituto Euvaldo Lodi-Núcleo Regional do Ceará, [19]84. 63 p. ; 21 cm. Bibliography: p. 61-63. LC Card 86-130055 DDC 330.981/31063 19
1. Ceará, Brazil (State) - Economic conditions. 2. Arid regions agriculture - Brazil - Ceará (State). 3. Agriculture - Economic aspects - Brazil - Ceará (State). I. Title.
HC188.C4 C29 1984

Casley, D. J.
Data collection in developing countries / D.J. Casley and D.A. Lury. 2nd ed. Oxford [Oxfordshire] ; New York : Clarendon Press, 1987. p. cm. Includes index. ISBN 0-19-442425-1 (pbk.) : LC Card 87-12574 DDC 001.4/222/091724 19
1. Sampling (Statistics). 2. Developing countries - Statistical services. I. Lury, D. A. II. Title.
HA31.2 .C37 1987

Project monitoring and evaluation in agriculture / Dennis J. Casley and Krishna Kumar. Baltimore : published for the World Bank [by] the Johns Hopkins University Press, c1987. xiii, 159 p. : ill. ; 24 cm. "Published for the World Bank." "A joint study: the World Bank, International Fund for Agricultural Development, Food and Agriculture Organization of the United Nations"--P. [4] of cover. Bibliography: p. 155-156. Includes index. ISBN 0-8018-3616-6 (pbk.) LC Card 87-22632 DDC 351.82/33 19
1. Agricultural development projects - Management. 2. Agricultural development projects - Evaluation. I.

Kumar, Krishna, 1940-. II. International Bank for Reconstruction and Development. III. International Fund for Agricultural Development. IV. Food and Agriculture Organization of the United Nations. V. Title.
HD1415 .C335 1987

Caslin, Terry. Current controversies in economics /. Oxford [Oxfordshire] UK , New York, NY, USA , 1987. xii, 319 p. : ISBN 0-631-15157-5 : LC Card 86-29928 DDC 338.941 19
HB171.5 .C975 1987

Caspari, Manfred. Was trennt Europa? /. Baden-Baden , 1986. 147 p. ; ISBN 3-7890-1320-X LC Card 87-108024 DDC 337.1/42 19
HC241.2 .W394 1986

Cass, Bettina. Income support for families with children / Bettina Cass. Canberra : Australian Govt. Pub. Service, [1986] xiii, 126 p. : ill. ; 25 cm. (Issues paper / Social Security Review . no. 1) Bibliography: p. 115-120. ISBN 0-644-05378-X (pbk.) LC Card 87-103419 DDC 362.5/82 19
1. Family allowances - Australia. 2. Income maintenance programs - Australia. I. Series: Issues paper (Australia. Social Security Review) , no. 1. II. Title.
HD4925.5.A8 C37 1986

Cass, Eugene Louis. Man and work in society . New York , c1975. xiv, 313 p. : ISBN 0-442-29359-3 LC Card 75-26866 DDC 658.3
HF5549 .M299 ***NYPL [JLE 76-2406]***

CASSAVA INDUSTRY - EUROPEAN ECONOMIC COMMUNITY COUNTRIES.
Schneider, Karl Josef. Das Selbstbeschränkungsabkommen zwischen Thailand und der Europäischen Gemeinschaft . Kiel , 1986. x, 192, 30 p. ; ISBN 3-922553-82-6 LC Card 87-408324 DDC 382/.413682/09593 19
HF3800.55.Z7 E867 1986

CASSAVA INDUSTRY - THAILAND.
Schneider, Karl Josef. Das Selbstbeschränkungsabkommen zwischen Thailand und der Europäischen Gemeinschaft . Kiel , 1986. x, 192, 30 p. ; ISBN 3-922553-82-6 LC Card 87-408324 DDC 382/.413682/09593 19
HF3800.55.Z7 E867 1986

Cassel, H. (Hjalmar), b. 1868. Amerikanisches Geschäftsleben / H. Cassel. 7. Aufl. Berlin : Karl Curtius, 1908. vi, 110 p. ; 20 cm. LC Card 85-666349
1. United States - Industries. I. Title.
HC106 .C37x 1908

Cassel, Jules M. Amble, Joan Lordi. A guide to implementation of Statement 87 on employer's accounting for pensions . Stamford, Conn. (High Ridge Park, P.O. Box 3821, Stamford 06905-0821) , c1986. vii, 106 p. : LC Card 87-133173 DDC 657/.75
HF5686.O5 A56 1986

Cassell's German-English, English-German dictionary =. Betteridge, Harold T. New York , 1978. xx, 1580 p. ; ISBN 0-02-522920-6 (standard) LC Card 77-18452 DDC 433/.21 19
PF3640 .B453 1978
NYPL [*P-Desk 86-5858]

Cassell's New English-Croatian and Croatian-English dictionary /. Bogadek, F. A. (Francis Aloysius), 1882- [New English-Croatian and Croatian-English dictionary.] New York [c1985] vii, 531, 497, 46, 7 p. ; ISBN 0-02-512140-5 LC Card 85-23140 DDC 491.8/2321 19
PG1377 .B72 1985 ***NYPL [*QAD 87-600]***

La Cassetta degli strumenti : ideologie e modelli sociali nell'industrialismo italiano / a cura di Valerio Castronovo ; scritti di P. Audenino ... [et al.]. Milano, Italy : F. Angeli, c1986. 305 p. : ill. ; 22 cm. (Studi e ricerche storiche. 67) Includes bibliographical references. LC Card 86-160695
1. Italy - Industries - History. 2. Industry - Social aspects - Italy - History. I. Castronovo, Valerio. II. Audenino, Patrizia.
HC304 .C37 1986

Cassiano, Paulo. Clichevsky, Nora. O mercado de terra na região metropolitana de Porto Alegre /. Porto Alegre , 1982. 60 p. : LC Card 84-256219
HD500.P67 C57 1982

Cassidy, Henry J. Studenmund, A. H. Using econometrics . Boston , c1987. xii, 440 p. : ISBN 0-316-82010-5 LC Card 86-21382 DDC 330/.028 19
HB139 .S795 1987

Casson, Mark, 1945-
The firm and the market : studies on multinational enterprise and the scope of the firm / Mark Casson.1st MIT Press ed. Cambridge, Mass. : MIT Press, 1987. xii, 283 p. : ill. ; 24 cm. Bibliography: p. [262]-273. Includes index. ISBN 0-262-03129-9 LC Card 86-27199 DDC 658/.049 19
1. International business enterprises. I. Title.
HD2755.5 .C392 1987

Multinationals and world trade : vertical integration and the division of labour in world industries / Mark Casson in association with David Barry ... [et al.]. London ; Boston : Allen & Unwin, 1986. xi, 401 p. : ill. ; 23 cm. Includes index. Bibliography: p. [372]-388. ISBN 0-04-338125-1 (alk. paper) LC Card 85-15734 DDC 338.8/8 19
1. Vertical integration. 2. International division of labor. 3. Vertical integration - Case studies. 4. International business enterprises - Case studies. I. Title.
HD2748 .C37 1986 ***NYPL [JLD 86-1224]***

Cast in a racial mould . Webster, Eddie. Johannesburg , 1985. xv, 299 p., [8] p. of plates : ISBN 0-86975-285-5
NYPL [JLD 87-780]

Cast in a racial mould . Webster, Eddie. Johannesburg , 1985. xv, 299 p., [6] p. of plates : ISBN 0-86975-285-5 (pbk.) : LC Card 86-213551 DDC 331.88/1712/0968 19
HD6870.5.Z7 F758 1985

Castán, Carlos. Cayón, Juan Ramón. Billetes españoles, 1783-1983 . Madrid, España [1983?] 82 p. : ISBN 88-300-9799-6 LC Card 85-232320
HG1137 .C38 1983

Castañeda, María Eugenia. Información básica sobre el GATT y el desarrollo industrial y comercial de México. México , c1985. 79, 62 p. ; LC Card 87-400559 DDC 338.0972 19
HC135 .I53 1985

Castanhar, José Cezar. Cavalcanti, Bianor Scelza. Administração da política industrial no Brasil . Rio de Janeiro , 1986. ii, 87, 10 p. : LC Card 87-102756 DDC 338.981 19
HD3616.B83 C28 1986

Castanho Filho, Eduardo Pires. A questão energética / Eduardo Pires Castanho Filho. São Paulo : Governo do Estado de São Paulo, Secretaria de Agricultura e Abastecimento, Instituto de Economia Agrícola, 1984. 15 p. ; 23 cm. (Relatório de pesquesa, 0101-5109 . 14/84) Bibliography: p. 15. LC Card 86-159794
1. Energy consumption. 2. Petroleum industry and trade. I. Series: Relatório de pesquisa (São Paulo (Brazil : State). Instituto de Economia Agrícola) , no. 84/14. II. Title.
HD9502.A2 C385 1984

Castanias, Richard P. Griffin, Paul A. Accounting for the translation of foreign currencies . Stamford, Conn. , c1987. viii, 112 p. : ISBN 0-910065-22-5 (pbk.) LC Card 86-81640 DDC 657/.48 19
HG3853.7 .G75 1987

CASTE - INDIA - KARNATAKA.
Hanumantha Rayappa, P. (Pullikunta), 1938- Backwardness and welfare of scheduled castes and scheduled tribes in India /. New Delhi , 1986. xi, 121 p. ; ISBN 81-7024-059-X : LC Card 86-902970
HC437.K27 H36 1986

Parvathamma, C., 1928- Scheduled castes and tribes . New Delhi , 1984. xiii, 310 p. ;
NYPL [JLD 87-707]

CASTE - NEPAL.

Castellani, Maurice. French solo / Maurice Castellani. Paris : J. Picollec, c1985. 262 p. ; 21 cm. In French. ISBN 2-86477-063-6 : LC Card 85-205040
1. Castellani, Maurice. 2. Black marketeers - France - Marseille - Biography. 3. Marseille (France) - Biography. I. Title.
HF5482.65.F7 C373 1985

CASTELLANI, MAURICE.
Castellani, Maurice. French solo /. Paris , c1985. 262 p. ; ISBN 2-86477-063-6 : LC Card 85-205040
HF5482.65.F7 C373 1985

Castelli, Joseph. Christen, François G. Buying by mail . Menlo Park, CA (333 Ravenswood Ave., Menlo Park 94025) , c1986. v, 2, 59, 6 leaves : LC Card 86-209563 DDC 658.8/4 19
HF5415.126 .C48 1986

Castellino, Onorato. Che cosa si produce, come e per chi . Torino , 1983. 514 p. : LC Card 85-167580
HB177 .C46 1983

Castells, Antoni, 1950- Bricall, Josep Maria, 1936- Estat autonòmic i finances públiques . [Barcelona] , 1984. 358 p. : ISBN 84-500-9868-8 LC Card 85-106586
HJ1000 .B75 1984 ***NYPL [JLE 86-3989]***

Castells, Manuel. Nuevas tecnologías, economía y sociedad en España /. Madrid , c1986. 2 v. (xvi, 1056 p.) : ISBN 84-206-9495-9 (set) LC Card 86-205429
HC390.T4 N84 1986

Castiglia, Miguel Angel. Aumento del ingreso y mejoramiento de las condiciones de trabajo del sector informal urbano en sietes ciudades del Perú /. [Lima, Perú?] , 1986. ii, 69, [25] leaves : LC Card 87-106249
HD2346.P4 A85 1986

CASTILE (SPAIN) - SOCIAL CONDITIONS.
López Alonso, Carmen. Los rostros y la realidad de la pobreza en la sociedad castellana medieval (siglos XIII-XV) /. Madrid [1983?] 54 p. ; ISBN 84-7075-284-7 LC Card 87-110606
HC387.C244 L66 1983

CASTILIAN LANGUAGE. see **SPANISH LANGUAGE.**

Castilla-La Mancha en la época contemporánea, 1808-1939 /. Sánchez Sánchez, Isidro. [Castilla-La Mancha] [1986] iii, 204 p. : ISBN 84-505-3538-7 LC Card 87-122049
HC387.C245 S36 1986

CASTILLA-LA MANCHA (SPAIN) - ECONOMIC CONDITIONS.
Sánchez Sánchez, Isidro. Castilla-La Mancha en la época contemporánea, 1808-1939 /. [Castilla-La Mancha] [1986] iii, 204 p. : ISBN 84-505-3538-7 LC Card 87-122049
HC387.C245 S36 1986

CASTILLA-LA MANCHA (SPAIN) - SOCIAL CONDITIONS.
Sánchez Sánchez, Isidro. Castilla-La Mancha en la época contemporánea, 1808-1939 /. [Castilla-La Mancha] [1986] iii, 204 p. : ISBN 84-505-3538-7 LC Card 87-122049
HC387.C245 S36 1986

Castilla y León (Spain). Departamento de Economía y Hacienda. García Villarejo, Avelino. Estructura financiera y actividad inversora de las administraciones públicas en Castilla y León /. Valladolid , 1984. 431 p. : ISBN 84-505-0331-0 LC Card 87-108720
HJ1249.C29 G37 1984

Castillero, Alfredo. see **Castillero Calvo, Alfredo, 1937-**

Castillero Calvo, Alfredo, 1937- La ruta transístmica y las comunicaciones marítimas hispanas, siglos XVI a XIX / Alfredo Castillero Calvo. Panamá : Ediciones Nari, 1984. 35 p. ; 22 cm. "Este trabajo fue presentado como ponencia en el Seminario sobre Puertos y Fortificaciones en América y Filipinas, organizado por la Comisión de Estudios Históricos del Ministerio de Obras Públicas y Urbanismo de España, en el marco de las conmemoraciones del Vo centenario del descubrimiento de América. Dicho seminario se celebró en Madrid del 11 al 13 de junio de 1984 en la Sala de Actos del Ministerio de Obras Públicas y Urbanismo." LC Card 84-219993
1. Trade routes - Panana - Canal Zone - History. 2. Spain - Colonies - Commerce - History. I. Title.
HE326 .C37 1984

Castillo Falcato, Norma. Pereira, Nilda. Economía, organización y planificación de la producción industrial /. La Habana , 1984. 2 v. : LC Card 87-401248
HD2328 .P47 1984

Castillo, Julián. La amortización de deudas en Colombia : cómo generar sistemas nuevos para una economía inflacionaria, cómo controlar préstamos en Upac / Julián Castillo.1a ed. Bogotá, Colombia : Legis, 1985. 162 leaves ; 28

cm. (Papeles de trabajo para la gerencia) LC Card 86-204058 DDC 332.7/09861 19
1. Amortization - Colombia. 2. Loans - Colombia. 3. Inflation (Finance) - Colombia. I. Title. II. Series.
HG4028.A5 C37 1985

Castillo, Oscar. Galin, Pedro. Asalariados y clases populares en Lima /. Lima [1986] 127 p. ; LC Card 87-400199 DDC 331/.0985/25 19
HD8350.L562 G35 1986

Castle, Gray. The Business insurance handbook /. Homewood, Ill. , c1981. xvii, 753 p. : ISBN 0-87094-237-9 LC Card 80-70437 DDC 368.8/1/00202 19
*HG8059 .B87 NYPL [*R-Econ. 86-2502]*

Castle, Robert. Work, leisure, and technology /. Melbourne, Australia , 1986. vi, 273 p. : ISBN 0-582-71151-7 (pbk.) LC Card 87-105477 DDC 303.4/83/0994 19
HD6331.2.A8 W67 1986

Castrillo M., Hugo. Reseña histórica del petróleo en Bolivia / Hugo Castrillo M. 1a ed. La Paz, Bolivia : [Yacimientos Petrolíferos Fiscales Bolivianos], 1986. 82 p., [1] leaf of plates : ill. ; 21 cm. "En homenaje al cincuentenario de Yacimientos Petrolíferos Fiscales Bolivianos." Bibliography: p. 79-82. LC Card 87-403504 DDC 338.2/7282/0984 19
1. Yacimientos Petrolíferos Fiscales Bolivianos - History. 2. Petroleum industry and trade - Government ownership - Bolivia - History. I. Yacimientos Petrolíferos Fiscales Bolivianos. II. Title.
HD9574.B64 Y294 1986

Castro and the Cuban labor movement . Córdova, Efrén. Lanham, MD , c1987. xii, 341 p. ; ISBN 0-8191-5952-2 (alk. paper) : LC Card 86-28159 DDC 322/.2/097291 19
HD6578.5 .C67 1987

Castro, Aníbal de. R.D., frente a su propia realidad : conferencias y editoriales / Aníbal de Castro. [Santo Domingo, Dominican Republic? : s.n., 1986] 450, [2] p. ; 20 cm. Bibliography: p. [451]. LC Card 87-115306 DDC 330.97293/054 19
1. Dominican Republic - Economic conditions - 1961-. 2. Dominican Republic - Politics and government - 1961-. I. Title. II. Title: RD, frente a su propia realidad.
HC153.5 .C383 1986

Castro, Anna Maria de. Castro, Josué de, 1908-1973. Fome, um tema proibido . Petrópolis , 1983. 154 p. ; LC Card 83-224629
HD9000.5 .C28 1983

Castro, Armando. Lições de economia II : a economia mundial contemporânea / Armando Castro. Lisboa : Caminho, c1986. 223 p. ; 21 cm. (Biblioteca Universidade Popular . 6) Bibliography: p. 211-217. LC Card 87-106195 DDC 330 19
1. Economics. I. Title. II. Series.
HB178.5 .C37 1986

Castro, Fidel, 1927-
[Nada podrá detener la marcha de la historia. Selections]
Si no hay solución a la crisis, habrá explosiones sociales generalizadas de carácter revolucionario. La Habana : Editora Política, 1985. 97 p. ; 21 cm. Selections from an interview given by Fidel Castro to Jeffrey M. Elliot and Mervin M. Dymally, in Mar. 1985, and published in full under title: Nada podrá detener la marcha de la historia. LC Card 87-115245 DDC 338.9 19
1. Latin America - Economic conditions - 1945-. 2. Castro, Fidel, 1927- - Interviews. I. Elliot, Jeffrey M. II. Dymally, Mervyn M., 1926-. III. Title.
HC125 .C37825 1985

CASTRO, FIDEL, 1927- - INTERVIEWS.
Castro, Fidel, 1927- [Nada podrá detener la marcha de la historia. Selections.] Si no hay solución a la crisis, habrá explosiones sociales generalizadas de carácter revolucionario. La Habana , 1985. 97 p. ; LC Card 87-115245 DDC 338.9 19
HC125 .C37825 1985

[Crisis económica y social del mundo. English]
The world economic and social crisis : its impact on the underdeveloped countries, its somber prospects and the need to struggle if we are to survive : report to the Seventh Summit Conference of Non-aligned Countries / Fidel Castro. New Delhi : People's Pub. House, 1983. 224 p. : ill. ; 23 cm. Bibliography: p. 221-224. LC Card 83-908475 DDC 337/.097172/4 19
1. International economic relations - Congresses. 2. Developing countries - Economic conditions - Congresses. I. Conference of Heads of State or Government of Non-aligned Countries (7th : 1983 : New Delhi, India). II. Title.
HC59.7 .C31472 1983 NYPL [JLD 87-486]

Castro Gutiérrez, Felipe. La extinción de la artesanía gremial / Felipe Castro Gutiérrez. 1a ed. México : Universidad Nacional Autónoma de México, Instituto de Investigaciones Históricas, 1986. 188 p. ; 23 cm. (Serie Historia novohispana . 35) Originally presented as the author's thesis (licenciado en historia), 1982. Bibliography: p. [183]-186. ISBN 968-8374-01-6 LC Card 87-104891
1. Guilds - Mexico - Mexico City - History. 2. Guilds - New Spain - History. 3. Artisans - New Spain - History. 4. Artisans - Mexico - Mexico City - History. I. Series: Serie de historia novohispana, 35. II. Title.
HD6473.M64 M483 1986

Castro, J. As instituições para-estatais no estado novo / J. Castro. Rio de Janeiro, Brasil : [s.n.], 1939 (Rio [de Janeiro] : Companhia Carioca) 225 p., [2] leaves of plates : ports. ; 20 cm. Bibliography: p. 225. LC Card 85-222446
1. Government business enterprises - Brazil. 2. Corporate state - Brazil. 3. Banks and banking - Government ownership - Brazil. 4. Coffee trade - Government ownership - Brazil. I. Title.
HD4094 .C35 1939

Castro, Josué de, 1908-1973. Fome, um tema proibido : últimos escritos de Josué de Castro / organizadora, Anna Maria de Castro. Petrópolis : Vozes, 1983. 154 p. ; 21 cm. List of works by Josué de Castro: p. 153-154. LC Card 83-224629
1. Food supply. 2. Famines. 3. Starvation. 4. Hunger. I. Castro, Anna Maria de. II. Title.
HD9000.5 .C28 1983

CASTRO, JOSUÉDE, 1908-1973.
Semana Josué de Castro e a nova geografia da fome, Rio de Janeiro, 19-24 de setembro de 1983 . [S.l. , 1983] 90 leaves : LC Card 86-201115
HD9000.5 .S3968 1983

Castro, Paulo Furtado de. Modelo estocástico para a estimação do produto potencial "IPEA/Depto. de Economia-UnB.". [Brasília, Brazil] : Fundação Universidade de Brasília, Departamento de Economia, [1981] 12, [16] : ill. ; 30 cm. (Texto para discussão . no. 072) Prepared by: Paulo Furtado de Castro, Mary de Melo Souza. Bibliography: p. [28] LC Card 85-210547
1. Gross national product - Brazil - Econometric models. I. Souza, Mary de Melo. II. Universidade de Brasília. Departamento de Economia. III. Series: Texto para discussão (Universidade de Brasília. Departamento de Economia) , no. 72. IV. Title.
HC190.I5 C37 1981

Castro, Paulo Rabello de.
Novos espaços do estado na gestão econômica. 1986. Setor público, reordenamento e privatização / Paulo Rabello de Castro, Carlos von Doellinger. [Rio de Janeiro, RJ , 1986] 47 p. : LC Card 87-403308 DDC 338.981 19
HC187 .S436 1986

Castro, Pedro. Greve, fatos e significados / Pedro Castro. São Paulo : Editora Atica, 1986. 72 p. ; 19 cm. (Série Princípios . 63) Bibliography: p. [62]-72. ISBN 85-08-01170-9 : LC Card 86-230606
1. Strikes and lockouts - Brazil. I. Title.
HD5353 .C37 1986

Castro Ruz, Fidel. see Castro, Fidel, 1927-

Castronovo, Valerio.
La Cassetta degli strumenti . Milano, Italy , c1986. 305 p. : LC Card 86-160695
HC304 .C37 1986

Immagini di industria in Italia . Roma , c1985. [128] p. : LC Card 86-145396
HC305 .I46 1985

Castrovilla, Joseph A. The printed circuit board industry / Joseph A. Castrovilla, project analyst. Stamford, Conn., U. S.A. : Business Communications Co., c1985. ix, 116 leaves : ill. ; 29 cm. (Business opportunity report . G-067R) "September 1985"--T.p. verso. ISBN 0-89336-451-7 (soft) LC Card 87-403911 DDC 381/.4562138174/0973 19
1. Printed circuits industry - United States. I. Business Communications Co. II. Title. III. Series.
HD9696.P743 U634 1985

Caswell, Julie A. Issues after a century of federal competition policy /. Lexington, Mass. , c1987. vii, 387 p. ; ISBN 0-669-13320-5 (alk. paper) LC Card 86-45377 DDC 338.6/048/0973 19
HD3616.U47 I77 1987

The catalog of catalogs . Palder, Edward L. Kensington, Md. , 1987. xxxiv, 423 p. ; ISBN 0-933149-11-5 (pbk.) : LC Card 86-51220 DDC 381/.14/029473 19
HF5466 .P35 1987

Catálogo da indústria têxtil e do vestuário do Rio Grande do Sul / [elaborado por Secretaria da Indústria e Comércio do Rio Grande do Sul, Departamento Técnico, Divisão de Estudos Especiais]. [Porto Alegre] : A Secretaria, 1985. 96 p. ; 22 cm. LC Card 86-209398
1. Textile industry - Brazil - Rio Grande do Sul - Directories. 2. Clothing trade - Brazil - Rio Grande do Sul - Directories. I. Rio Grande do Sul (Brazil). Secretaria da Indústria e Comércio. Departamento Técnico. Divisão de Estudos Especiais.
HD9864.B83 R593 1985

Catálogo de informações sócio-econômicas dos municípios, Bahia / Governo do Estado da Bahia, Secretaria da Fazenda, Escola de Administração Fazendária, Coordenadoria de Programas Especiais. Salvador, BA : EAF, [1984] 354 p. ; 31 cm. LC Card 86-210868
1. Bahia (Brazil : State) - Statistics. 2. Municipal government - Brazil - Bahia (State) - Statistics. I. Bahia (Brazil : State). Escola de Administração Fazendária. Coordenadoria de Programas Especiais. II. Title: Bahia, catálogo de informações sócio-econômicas dos municípios.
HA988.B3 C38 1984

Catálogo de ocupações pesquisadas em Fortaleza. [Fortaleza] : Superintendência do Desenvolvimento do Estado do Ceará : Secretaria de Educação do Estado do Ceará : 111, [1] p. ; 29 cm. Bibliography: p. [112] Includes index. LC Card 83-222529
1. Vocational guidance - Brazil - Fortaleza. 2. Personality and occupation. 3. Job descriptions. I. Superintendência do Desenvolvimento do Estado do Ceará. II. Ceará (Brazil : State). Secretaria de Educação. III. PREMEN. Gerência do Ceará.
HF5382.5.B7 C38 1972

Catálogo de tarifas postales y telegráficas. Madrid : RGPT, [1964?] 256, [42] p. : ill. (some col.) ; 28 cm. On cover: Reparto Guía Postal y Telegráfica. LC Card 85-106223
1. Telegraph - Spain - Rates. 2. Postal service - Spain - Rates. 3. Telegraph code addresses - Directories. I. Reparto Guía Postal y Telegráfica (Spain).
HE8277 .C37 1964

CATALOGS.
Bly, Robert W. Create the perfect sales piece . New York , c1985. xii, 242 p. : ISBN 0-471-82525-5 (pbk.) : LC Card 85-12457 DDC 659.13/2 19
HF5823 .B635 1985 NYPL [JLE 86-3454]

CATALOGS, COMMERCIAL - DIRECTORIES.
Gottlieb, Richard. The directory of mail order catalogs /. [New York, N.Y.] , Sharon, CT , c1987. xi, 385 p. ; ISBN 0-8160-1740-9 LC Card 86-31959 DDC 016.381/14/0973 19
HF5466 .G63 1987

Palder, Edward L. The catalog of catalogs . Kensington, Md. , 1987. xxxiv, 423 p. ; ISBN 0-933149-11-5 (pbk.) : LC Card 86-51220 DDC 381/.14/029473 19
HF5466 .P35 1987

Wathey, Patricia Wogen. The international mail-order shopping guide /. Englewood Cliffs, N.J. , 1984. 338 p. : ISBN 0-13-473083-6 LC Card 84-8390 DDC 381/.14/025 19
HF5466 .W38 1984
*NYPL [*R-Econ. 84-3915]*

Catalogue de la Cinémathèque national des relations industrielles. National industrial relations film catalogue. [Ottawa, Ont.] , c1986. 31, 21 p. ; ISBN 0-662-54352-1 (pbk.) LC Card 86-203066 DDC 016.331 19
HD6971 .N24 1986

Catalogue des timbres fiscaux et sociaux de France / Association française des collectionneurs de timbres fiscaux (ARA-France). Le Havre : Editions Loisirs et culture, 1982. 135 p. : ill. ; 24 cm. One leaf describing history of ARA-France inserted. LC Card

86-159729
1. Revenue-stamps - France - Catalogs. I. Association française des collectionneurs de timbres fiscaux.
HJ5412 .C37 1982

Catalogue des timbres-poste de la France et des colonies françaises. Southfield, MI (15565 Northland Dr., Suite 605 West, Southfield 48075-5308) : R. Koerber, <[1985]- > v. <2 > : ill. ; 30 cm. (Postilion publications) At head of title: Yvert & Tellier. Reprint. Originally published: Amiens : Yvert, 1936. CONTENTS. - -- t. 2. Colonies françaises, pays de protectorat, pays sous mandat, bureaux indochinois. LC Card 86-210422
1. Postage-stamps - France - Territories and possessions - Catalogs. 2. Postmarks - France - Territories and possessions - Catalogs. 3. Postal service - France - Territories and possessions. 4. Postage-stamps - France - Colonies - Catalogs. 5. Postmarks - France - Colonies - Catalogs. 6. Postal service - France - Colonies. I. Yvert & Tellier (Firm). II. Series.
HE6185.F82 C37 1985

Catalogue des vignettes françaises de Croix-Rouge /. Granger, Louis. [Aurillac] [1964] 117 p. ; LC Card 68-39071
HE6184.S42 G7 1964

Catalogue of interviews . Palmer, Michele. [Storrs, Conn.] , 1983. ii, 79 p. ; LC Card 86-621476 DDC 331.12/09746 19
HD6331.2.U52 C86 1983

Catalogue of state shared revenue sources distributed between 1973-1986. Sapolsky, Joann. Tallahassee, Fla. (House Office Bldg., Tallahassee 32301) [1986] v, 76 leaves : LC Card 86-623224 DDC 336.1/85/09759 19
HJ375 .S26 1986

CATALONIA (SPAIN) - COMMERCE - AMERICA - HISTORY.
El Comerç entre Catalunya i Amèrica (segles XVIII i XIX) /. Barcelona , 1986. 173 p. : ISBN 84-85905-24-5 LC Card 86-204187
HF3689.C3 C39 1986

Catalonia (Spain). Departament d'Agricultura, Ramaderia i Pesca. L'IVA en els sectors agrari i pesquer catalans. [Barcelona] , 1985. 49 p. ; ISBN 84-393-0632-6 LC Card 86-165858
HJ5715.S7 L58 1985

Catalonia (Spain). Departament de Cultura. Catalunya, la fàbrica d'Espanya . [Barcelona] , 1985. 201 p. : LC Card 86-185178
HC387.C25 C336 1985

Catalonia (Spain). Departament d'Indústria i Energia. Catalunya, la fàbrica d'Espanya . [Barcelona] , 1985. 201 p. : LC Card 86-185178
HC387.C25 C336 1985

Catalonia (Spain). Direcció General de Transports. Estudi motivacional i d'opinió sobre els transports públics a la conurbació barcelonina ; Estudi de comunicació per a la campanya publicitària del foment de l'ús del transport col·lectiu /. [Barcelona] [1982?] 80 p. : ISBN 84-393-0087-5 LC Card 86-209206
HE4899.B43 E87 1982

CATALONIA (SPAIN) - ECONOMIC POLICY.
Conte, Jesús. La Catalunya a mig fer /. Barcelona , c1985. 259 p. ; ISBN 84-86006-64-5X LC Card 86-164880
HC387.C25 C57 1985

CATALONIA (SPAIN) - HISTORY - AUTONOMY AND INDEPENDENCE MOVEMENTS.
Sabater, Jordi, 1958- Anarquisme i catalanisme . Barcelona , 1986. 231 p. ; ISBN 84-297-2490-7 LC Card 87-108668
HD8582.C583 S24 1986

CATALONIA (SPAIN) - INDUSTRIES - HISTORY - EXHIBITIONS.
Catalunya, la fàbrica d'Espanya . [Barcelona] , 1985. 201 p. : LC Card 86-185178
HC387.C25 C336 1985

CATALONIA (SPAIN) - MANUFACTURES - HISTORY - EXHIBITIONS.
Catalunya, la fàbrica d'Espanya . [Barcelona] , 1985. 201 p. : LC Card 86-185178
HC387.C25 C336 1985

CATALONIA (SPAIN) - POPULATION - HISTORY.
Iglésies, Josep, 1902- El moviment de població de les comarques de la Catalunya de sobirania francesa en el curs dels segles XIX i XX /. Barcelona , 1979. 63 p. ; LC Card 81-120813
HB3620.C3 I325 1979

La Catalunya a mig fer /. Conte, Jesús. Barcelona , c1985. 259 p. ; ISBN 84-86006-64-5X LC Card 86-164880
HC387.C25 C57 1985

Catalunya, la fàbrica d'Espanya : un segle d'industrialització catalana, 1833-1936 / [C.I.R.I.T., el Departament de Cultur ai el Departament d'Indústria de la Generalitat de Catalunya]. [Barcelona] : Ajuntament de Barcelona, 1985. 201 p. : ill. (some col.), ports. ; 30 x 31 cm. "Antic Mercat del Born, 1985"--Cover. LC Card 86-185178
1. Catalonia (Spain) - Industries - History - Exhibitions. 2. Catalonia (Spain) - Manufactures - History - Exhibitions. I. Comissió Interdepartemental de Recerca i Innovació Tecnològica (Barcelona, Spain). II. Catalonia (Spain). Departament de Cultura. III. Catalonia (Spain). Departament d'Indústria i Energia. IV. Barcelona (Spain). Ayuntamiento.
HC387.C25 C336 1985

Catalyst, inc. The Corporate guide to parental leaves, including Catalyst's Report on a national study of parental leaves /. New York, NY (250 Park Ave. South, New York 10003) , c1986. 145 p. : LC Card 87-161920 DDC 658.3/122 19
HD6065.5.U6 C67 1986

Catania, Patrick J. Speculating in futures. [Chicago] , c1986. v, 65 p. : LC Card 87-100478 DDC 332.64/4 19
HG6046 .S63 1986

Catasto e volto urbano . Mazzucchelli, Vanna. Roma , 1983. 244 p. ; LC Card 86-106099
HD680.M54 M39 1983

CATASTRAL SURVEYS. see **REAL PROPERTY.**

CATASTROPHES. see **DISASTERS.**

Catastrophic health insurance : the "Medigap" crisis : a report / by the Chairman of the Subcommittee on Health and Long-Term Care of the Select Committee on Aging, House of Representatives, Ninety-ninth Congress, second session. Washington : U. S. G.P.O., 1986. iii, 278 p. : ill., forms ; 24 cm. At head of title: Committee print. Distributed to some depository libraries in microfiche. Shipping list no.: 86-695-P. "August 1986." "Comm. pub. no. 99-576." Item 1009-B-2, 1009-C-2 (microfiche) LC Card 86-603399 DDC 368.3/82/00973 19
1. Medigap. 2. Medigap - Law and legislation. I. United States. Congress. House. Select Committee on Aging. Subcommittee on Health and Long-Term Care. II. Title: The "Medigap" crisis.
HD7102.U4 C37 1986

Catastrophic losses : how the insurance system would handle two $7 billion hurricanes. Oak Brook, Ill. (1200 Harger Rd., Suite 222, Oak Brook 60521) : All-Industry Research Advisory Council, c1986. vi, 73 p. : ill. ; 28 cm. "November 1986." LC Card 87-106114 DDC 368.1/22014/0973 19
1. Insurance, Disaster - United States - Adjustment of claims. 2. Insurance, Disaster - Adjustment of claims. 3. Storms - United States. 4. Risk (Insurance). 5. Reinsurance - United States. I. All-Industry Research Advisory Council.
HG9979.3 .C38 1986

Cateora, Philip R. Marketing : an international perspective / Philip R. Cateora, Susan M. Keaveney. Homewood, Ill. : Irwin, 1987. xi, 172 p. : ill. ; 23 cm. (Irwin perspectives in international business) Includes bibliographies and index. ISBN 0-256-05626-9 (pbk.) LC Card 86-83392 DDC 658.8/48 19
1. Export marketing. 2. Export marketing - United States. I. Keaveney, Susan M. II. Title. III. Series.
HF1009.5 .C37 1987

Cater, Nick. Sudan : the roots of famine : a report for Oxfam / by Nick Cater. Oxford : Oxfam, c1986. i, 36 p. : ill., map ; 30 cm. Bibliography: p. [35]-36. ISBN 0-85598-075-3 (pbk.) : LC Card 86-234718 DDC 363.8/09624 19
1. Famines - Sudan. 2. Sudan - Economic conditions. I. Oxfam. II. Title.
HC835.Z9 F33 1986

CATERPILLAR TRACTOR COMPANY.
Zinman, Michael. The history of the decline and fall of the Raterpillar Tractor Company . Ardsley, N.Y. , c1986. 231 p. : ISBN 0-937704-03-2 (pbk.) : LC Card 86-82887 DDC 338.7/629225 19
HD9710.4.U64 R388 1986

Cathelat, Marie-France.
Crecimiento e información. 1985. Comunicación y tecnología en la investigación demográfica / Centro Peruano de Investigación Aplicada. Lima , 1985. vi, 38 p. ; LC Card 86-168814
HB849.6 .C65 1985

Catheter devices for interventional cardiology, angiography, and radiology--U. S. and international. 2nd revision. Tustin, CA, U. S.A. (17722 Irvine Blvd., Tustin 92680) : Biomedical Business International, c1987. 1 v. (various foliations) : ill. ; 29 cm. (Report / Biomedical Business International . #7021) Rev. ed. of: Catheter devices for interventional radiology, cardiology, and angiography. c1984. "May 1987." LC Card 87-168823 DDC 381/.45681761 19
1. Catheter industry - United States. 2. Catheter industry. 3. Market surveys - United States. 4. Market surveys. I. Biomedical Business International, Inc. II. Catheter devices for interventional radiology, cardiology, and angiography. III. Series: Report (Biomedical Business International, Inc.) , #7021.
HD9995.C383 U628 1987

Catheter devices for interventional radiology, cardiology, and angiography. Catheter devices for interventional cardiology, angiography, and radiology--U. S. and international. Tustin, CA, U. S.A. (17722 Irvine Blvd., Tustin 92680) , c1987. 1 v. (various foliations) : LC Card 87-168823 DDC 381/.45681761 19
HD9995.C383 U628 1987

CATHETER INDUSTRY.
Catheter devices for interventional cardiology, angiography, and radiology--U. S. and international. Tustin, CA, U. S.A. (17722 Irvine Blvd., Tustin 92680) , c1987. 1 v. (various foliations) : LC Card 87-168823 DDC 381/.45681761 19
HD9995.C383 U628 1987

CATHETER INDUSTRY - UNITED STATES.
Catheter devices for interventional cardiology, angiography, and radiology--U. S. and international. Tustin, CA, U. S.A. (17722 Irvine Blvd., Tustin 92680) , c1987. 1 v. (various foliations) : LC Card 87-168823 DDC 381/.45681761 19
HD9995.C383 U628 1987

Catholic Church. (Old Catalog form: Catholic Church, Roman)

CATHOLIC CHURCH - ADDRESSES, ESSAYS, LECTURES.
Gonella, Guido, 1905- Contestazioni /. Roma , 1983. 3 v. ; LC Card 84-237282 DDC 945.092 19
JN5451 .G57 1983 ***NYPL [JFE 86-1367]***

CATHOLIC CHURCH AND LABOR. see **CHURCH AND LABOR.**

CATHOLIC CHURCH - BRAZIL - CONCEIÇÃO DO ARAGUAIA - CLERGY - POLITICAL ACTIVITY.
Figueira, Ricardo Rezende, 1952- A justiça do lobo . Petrópolis , 1986. 115 p. ; LC Card 87-137552 DDC 305.5/63 19
HD500.C74 F54 1986

Catholic Church. Comissão Pastoral da Terra (Brazil) CPT : pastoral e compromisso / Comissão Pastoral da Terra. Petrópolis : Editora Vozes, em co-edição com Comissão Pastoral da Terra, 1983. 105 p. ; 23 cm. Includes bibliographical references. LC Card 86-209008
1. Land tenure - Brazil - Goiás (State). 2. Land use - Brazil - Goiás (State). 3. Peasantry - Brazil - Goiás (State) - Political activity. 4. Land reform - Brazil - Goiás (State). 5. Catholic Church. Comissão Pastoral da Terra (Brazil). I. Title.
HD499.G65 C38 1983

CATHOLIC CHURCH. COMISSÃO PASTORAL DA TERRA (BRAZIL)
Catholic Church. Comissão Pastoral da Terra (Brazil) CPT . Petrópolis , 1983. 105 p. ; LC Card 86-209008
HD499.G65 C38 1983

Catholic Church. Conferencia Episcopal Paraguaya. Equipo Nacional de Pastoral Social. El Fenómeno migratorio en el Paraguay /. Asunción, Paraguay [1985] 258 p. : LC Card 86-100044
HB2033 .F45 1985

Catholic Church. Conferência Nacional dos Bispos do Brasil. Terra de Deus, terra de irmãos . Brasília-DF [1986] 190 p. : LC Card 86-233600
HD1333.B6 T47 1986

CATHOLIC CHURCH - DOCTRINES.
The Best of This world /. Lanham, MD , c1986. x, 405 p. ; ISBN 0-8191-5605-1 (alk. paper) : LC Card 86-22411 DDC 261.8 19
HB72 .B5 1987 ***NYPL [JFE 86-5571]***

McLean, Edward B. Roman Catholicism and the right to work /. Lanham , c1985. ix, 175 p. ; ISBN 0-8191-5009-6 (alk. paper) : LC Card 85-20379 DDC 261.8/5 19
HD6338 .M436 1985 ***NYPL [JLD 86-2803]***

Sullivan, Patrick J., 1929- Blue collar, Roman collar, white collar . Lanham, MD , c1987. xii, 346 p. ; ISBN 0-8191-5704-X (alk. paper) : LC Card 86-24593 DDC 261.85 19
HD6338.2.U5 S85 1987

Weigel, George. Tranquillitas ordinis . Oxford , New York , 1987. xiii, 489 p. ; ISBN 0-19-504193-3 (alk. paper) : LC Card 86-12742 DDC 261.8/73/08822 19
BX1795.P43 W45 1987
NYPL [JFE 87-1638]

CATHOLIC CHURCH - GUATEMALA - POLITICAL ACTIVITY.
Cambranes, J. C. Agrarismo en Guatemala /. Guatemala , 1986. 255 p. : LC Card 87-401042 DDC 322/.2/097281 19
HD1531.G9 C36 1986

CATHOLIC CHURCH - LATIN AMERICA.
Antoncich, Ricardo. [Cristianos ante la injusticia. English.] Christians in the face of injustice . Maryknoll, N.Y. , c1987. xvi, 181 p. ; ISBN 0-88344-413-5 (pbk.) LC Card 86-23529 DDC 261.8 19
BX1753 .A5813 1987 ***NYPL [JLE 87-1051]***

Junto a nuestro pueblo. [Lima, Perú] [1979 or 1980] 71 p. : LC Card 82-100009
BX1426.2 .J86 1979 ***NYPL [JLF 86-1152]***

Pérez Aguirre, Luis. Predicaciones en la plaza /. Montevideo , 1985. 228 p. ; LC Card 85-225854 DDC 282/.8 19
BX1426.2 .P46 1985 ***NYPL [JLE 87-456]***

Catholic Church. Pope (1978- : John Paul II) LABOREM EXERCENS.
Arbeit, mehr als Kapital . Wuppertal , c1983. 191 p. ; ISBN 3-87294-224-7 LC Card 84-182379
HD6338 .A69 1983

Catholic Church. Pope (1978- : John Paul II) [Laborem exercens. Spanish.] Juan Pablo II y el trabajo . [Santiago, Chile] , 1984. 135 p. ; LC Card 85-197537
HD6338 .C277 1984

Máspero, Emilio. Importancia y significado de la encíclica sobre el trabajo humano del papa Juan Pablo II para el movimiento obrero latinoamericano /. [Caracas, Venezuela] [1984] 159 p. : LC Card 87-404543 DDC 261.8/5 19
HD6338 .M425 1984

LABOREM EXERCENS - CONGRESSES.
Encuentro Latinoamericano de Pastoral Social (1986 : Bogotá, Colombia) El mundo del trabajo . Bogotá , 1986. 92 p. ; ISBN 958-625-053-9 LC Card 87-400623 DDC 261.8/5 19
HD6338 .C277 1981 Suppl.

[Laborem exercens. Spanish]
Juan Pablo II y el trabajo : la encíclica Laborem exercens, textos y comentarios. 1a ed. [Santiago, Chile] : Instituto Latinoamericano de Doctrina y Estudios Sociales : Editorial Salesiana, 1984. 135 p. ; 21 cm. Includes bibliographical references and index. LC Card 85-197537
1. Catholic Church. Pope (1978- : John Paul II) Laborem exercens. 2. Church and labor. I. Instituto Latinoamericano de Estudios Sociales. II. Title. III. Title: Juan Pablo Segundo y el trabajo.
HD6338 .C277 1984

Catholic Church, Roman. see **Catholic Church.**

Catholic Fund for Overseas Development. The Common agricultural policy and the Third World . London , 1986. 97 p. : ISBN 0-946848-79-3 (pbk.) : LC Card 87-150069 DDC 338.1/81/094 19
HD9015.E82 C665 1986

Catholic Institute for International Relations. The Common agricultural policy and the Third World . London , 1986. 97 p. : ISBN 0-946848-79-3 (pbk.) : LC Card 87-150069 DDC 338.1/81/094 19
HD9015.E82 C665 1986

Catin, Maurice. Effets externes : marché et systèmes de décision collective / Maurice Catin ; préface de Gérard Bramoullé. Paris : Editions Cujas, c1985. 455 p. : ill. ; 24 cm. (Collection de la Faculté d'économie appliquée d'Aix-Marseille III) Originally presented as the author's thesis (doctoral)--Université de droit, d'économie et des sciences d'Aix-Marseille, 1980. Bibliography: p. [435]-450. ISBN 2-254-85071-2 : LC Card 86-186253
1. Externalities (Economics). I. Title. II. Series.
HB846.3 .C37 1985

Catrina, Werner. Der Eternit-Report : Stephan Schmidheinys schweres Erbe / Werner Catrina. Zürich : Orell Füssli, c1985. 244 p. : ill. ; 23 cm. Bibliography: p. 243-244. ISBN 3-280-01615-0 LC Card 85-225903
1. Schweiz. Eternit Holding. 2. Asbestos industry - Employees - Diseases and hygiene - Switzerland. 3. Asbestos industry - Hygienic aspects - Switzerland. 4. Asbestos industry - Employees - Diseases and hygiene. 5. Asbestos industry - Hygienic aspects. I. Title.
HD7269.A552 S93 1985 ***NYPL [JLD 87-38]***

CATS - GREAT BRITAIN - HISTORY.
Dear cats . London , 1986. 128 p. : LC Card 87-126969 DDC 628.9/693 19
HE6939.S42 D42 1986

Cattani, V. (Venerio) Bilancio della socialdemocrazia . Napoli , 1984. 156 p. ; LC Card 84-249837
HX73 .B55 1984 ***NYPL [JLD 87-1536]***

Catterall, D. M. Rankin, H. C. D. Corporation tax for students /. Wokingham, Berkshire, England , 1985. x, 230 p. : ISBN 0-85258-242-0 (pbk.) LC Card 85-3272 DDC 657/.46/0941 19
HD2753.G7 R36 1985

Cattini, Marco. I contadini di San Felice : metamorfosi di un mondo rurale nell'Emilia dell'età moderna / Marco Cattini. Torino : G. Einaudi, c1984. xvii, 364 p., [2] leaves of plates : ill. ; 21 cm. (Studi / Fondazione Luigi Einaudi . 3) Includes bibliographical references. ISBN 88-06-05682-4 : LC Card 84-189545
1. Peasantry - Italy - San Felice sul Panaro - History. 2. San Felice sul Panaro (Italy) - Rural conditions. I. Series: Studi / Fondazione Luigi Einaudi , 3. II. Title.
HD1536.I8 C34 1984

CATTLE BREEDERS - OREGON - HARNEY COUNTY - HISTORY.
Simpson, Peter K., 1930- The community of cattlemen . Moscow, Idaho , c1987. xiv, 228 p. ; ISBN 0-89301-117-7 (pbk.) LC Card 87-5855 DDC 338.1/762/00979595 19
HD9433.U5 H277 1987

Cattle marketing in Lesotho /. Swallow, Brent M. Maseru, Lesotho [1986] iv, 75 leaves : LC Card 87-132309 DDC 381/.416213/096816 19
HD9433.L452 S9 1986

CATTLE - SOUTH AFRICA - TRANSKEI - MARKETING.
Tapson, D. R. Proposals for a cattle marketing strategy for Transkei /. [Fort Hare] [1982] ii, 45 leaves, 4 leaves of plates : ISBN 0-949974-68-4 LC Card 86-209520 DDC 381/.4162/00968791 19
HD9433.S643 T77 1982

CATTLE TRADE - BOTSWANA.
Hubbard, Michael. Agricultural exports and economic growth . London , New York , 1986. xx, 284 p. : ISBN 0-7103-0121-9
NYPL [Sc D 86-967]

CATTLE TRADE - BRAZIL, NORTHEAST.
Barbosa, Túlio. Expansión del cultivo de la caña de azúcar y de la ganadería en el Nordeste del Brasil . Santiago de Chile , Nueva York, NY, Estados Unidos de América , 1986. 170 p. : ISBN 92-1-321209-7 LC Card 87-400309 DDC 338.1/7361/09813 19
HD9114.B7 N67943 1986

CATTLE TRADE - CENTRAL AMERICA.
Williams, Robert G. (Robert Gregory), 1948- Export agriculture and the crisis in Central America /. Chapel Hill , c1986. xvi, 257 p. : ISBN 0-8078-1693-0 LC Card 85-20978 DDC 382/.41/09728 19
HD9884.C352 W55 1986
NYPL [JLE 86-3412]

CATTLE TRADE - COLOMBIA.
Kalmanovitz, Salomón. El desarrollo de la ganadería en Colombia, 1950-1972 . [Bogotá, Colombia] [1978] p. 195-238 : LC Card 86-157918
HD9433.C62 K35 1978

CATTLE TRADE - GOVERNMENT POLICY - BRAZIL, NORTHEAST.
Barbosa, Túlio. Expansión del cultivo de la caña de azúcar y de la ganadería en el Nordeste del Brasil . Santiago de Chile , Nueva York, NY, Estados Unidos de América , 1986. 170 p. : ISBN 92-1-321209-7 LC Card 87-400309 DDC 338.1/7361/09813 19
HD9114.B7 N67943 1986

CATTLE TRADE - LATIN AMERICA.
Shane, Douglas R. Hoofprints on the forest . Philadelphia , c1986. xvi, 159 p. ; ISBN 0-89727-054-1 : LC Card 83-26585 DDC 338.1/76213/098 19
HD9433.L292 S53 1984
NYPL [JLD 86-2289]

CATTLE TRADE - LLANOS ORIENTALES (COLOMBIA AND VENEZUELA)
Pedraja Tomán, René de la. Los Llanos . Bogotá, Colombia , 1984. 101 p. : LC Card 84-221343
HC198.L56 P4 1984

CATTLE TRADE - OREGON - HARNEY COUNTY - HISTORY.
Simpson, Peter K., 1930- The community of cattlemen . Moscow, Idaho , c1987. xiv, 228 p. ; ISBN 0-89301-117-7 (pbk.) LC Card 87-5855 DDC 338.1/762/00979595 19
HD9433.U5 H277 1987

CATTLE TRADE - PRAIRIE PROVINCES - HISTORY.
Breen, David. The Canadian prairie west and the ranching frontier, 1874-1924 /. Toronto , Buffalo , c1983. xiii, 302 p., [4] p. of plates : ISBN 0-8020-5548-6 LC Card 83-143575 DDC 338.1/762/009712 19
HD9433.C22 P733 1983 ***NYPL [HY 87-755]***

CATTLE TRADE - SPAIN - PILAS (SEVILLE) - HISTORY.
Camacho Rueda, Eduardo. Propiedad y explotación agrarias en el aljarafe sevillano . Sevilla , 1984. 199 p. : ISBN 84-500-9772-X LC Card 85-135028
HD773 .C18 1984

CATTLE TRADE - UNITED STATES.
Angell, George. Agricultural options . New York, NY , c1986. ix, 230 p. : ISBN 0-8144-5822-X LC Card 85-48215 DDC 332.64/25 19
HG6047.G8 A54 1986 ***NYPL [JLE 86-2854]***

CATTLE TRADE - UNITED STATES - HISTORY.
Skaggs, Jimmy M. Prime cut . College Station , c1986. xiii, 263 p., [8] p. of plates : ISBN 0-89096-249-9 : LC Card 85-40742 DDC 338.1/76213/0973 19
HD9415 .S58 1986 ***NYPL [JLE 86-3913]***

CATTLE TRADE - URUGUAY.
Barbato de Silva, Celia. La ganadería vacuna uruguaya . Montevideo, Uruguay [1980] 77 leaves ; ***NYPL [JLF 86-1101]***

CATTLE TRADE - URUGUAY - STATISTICS.
Encuesta pecuaria en profundidad . Montevideo, Uruguay [1977-1978] 2 v. ; LC Card 87-402173 DDC 338.1/762/009895021 19
HD9433.U82 E53 1979

CATTLE TRADE - VENEZUELA - CARACAS REGION - HISTORY - 19TH CENTURY.
Lucena Salmoral, Manuel. Vísperas de la independencia americana . Madrid , 1986. vii, 389 p. ; ISBN 84-205-1308-3 LC Card 86-205153
HF3490.C37 L83 1986

CATTLE TRADE - VENEZUELA - CARORA - HISTORY - 20TH CENTURY.
García Ponce, Antonio, 1929- Crisis oligarquía y latifundio . Barquisimeto, Venezuela , 1986. 104 p., [1] folded leaf of plates : ISBN 980-608-701-1 : LC Card 87-134729 DDC

338.1/762/0098725 19
HF3490.C375 G37 1986

CAUCA RIVER REGION (COLOMBIA) - INDUSTRIES.
Vellinga, Menno. Industrialization and regional development in Colombia /. Amsterdam, The Netherlands , 1983. 183 p. : ISBN 90-70280-80-9 LC Card 83-209247 DDC 338.09861/26 19
HC198.C296 V45 1983

CAUE de l'Ile de la Réunion. L'Habitat réunionnais /. Saint-Denis [1983] 73 p., A-T leaves of plates : LC Card 84-981007
HD7378.9.A3 H33 1983

Cauet, Sylvie. Le Renouvellement du tissu industriel . Paris [1986] 130 p. ; ISBN 2-11-001568-3 : LC Card 86-191910
HD3616.F83 R46 1986

CAULKING. see **CALKING.**

Caulks & sealants market. New York, N.Y. : Frost & Sullivan, c1983. ix, 250 p. : ill. ; 29 cm. "September 1983." "#A1226." LC Card 87-143824
1. Sealing compounds industry - United States. 2. Calking. 3. Market surveys - United States. I. Frost & Sullivan. II. Title: Caulks and sealants market.
HD9999.S44453 U53 1983

Caulks and sealants market. Caulks & sealants market. New York, N.Y. , c1983. ix, 250 p. : LC Card 87-143824
HD9999.S44453 U53 1983

Causal structure. Discovering causal structure . Orlando , 1987. xvii, 394 p. : ISBN 0-12-286962-1 (alk. paper) LC Card 87-1860 DDC 300/.1/51 19
HA29 .D495 1987

Causas de evasão. Azevedo, Edilza Araújo. [Campina Grande, Brasil] , 1984. 104 leaves : LC Card 85-203901
HD5715.5.B69 P335 1984

Causas y efectos de la crisis económica en México /. García Alba Iduñate, Pascual, 1948- [Financial aspects of macroeconomic management in Mexico. Spanish.] México, D.F. , 1984. 124 p. : ISBN 968-12-0285-6 LC Card 86-138030
HC135 .G29818 1984

Causas y manejo de la crisis económica dominicana, 1974-1984 / [editor, Frank Moya Pons]. Santo Domingo, República Dominicana : Forum, 1986. 184 p. : ill. ; 22 cm. (Forum. 18) Spine title: Crisis económica. Papers presented at a meeting of FORUM, held Nov. 21, 1981 at the Hotel Santo Domingo Sur. LC Card 86-208551
1. Dominican Republic - Economic conditions - 1961- - Congresses. 2. Dominican Republic - Economic policy - Congresses. I. Moya Pons, Frank, 1944-. II. FORUM (Debating society). III. Title: Crisis económica. IV. Series: FORUM (Series : Santo Domingo, Dominican Republic) , 18.
HC153.5 .C385 1986

Causes and remedies for displacement of steel workers : an analysis of the characteristics of displaced steel workers and of programs designed to assist their readjustment, including a policy agenda developed by the administration : a report submitted to Congress pursuant a request made in the Trade and Tariff Act of 1984. [Washington, D.C.? : s.n., 1985] iv, 83, 2, 2 p. ; 28 cm. "April 1985." LC Card 86-601602 DDC 331.13/704 19
1. Iron and steel workers - United States. 2. Iron and steel workers - Government policy - United States. 3. Steel industry and trade - United States. 4. Trade adjustment assistance - United States. I. United States. Congress.
HD8039.I52 U524 1985

Cauwenberghe, Eddy van. International Congress on Economic History (8th : 1982 : Budapest, Hungary) Münzprägung, Geldumlauf und Wechselkurse . Trier , 1984. 421 p. : ISBN 3-923087-06-3 (pbk.)
HG205 1982 .I53 ***NYPL [JLE 86-3176]***

Cauwet, Martine. Images économiques des entreprises : énergie au 1-1-1983 / Martine Cauwet, Bruno Lutinier. Paris : INSEE, [1986] 41 p. ; 30 cm. (Archives & documents . no 147) Dossier sectoriel ; no 2 "Janvier 1986." Includes bibliographical references. Chiefly tables. ISBN 2-11-064902-X : LC Card 86-229455
1. Energy industries - France - Statistics. I. Lutinier, Bruno. II. Series: Archives & documents (Institut national de la statistique et des études économiques (France)) , no 147. III. Title.
HD9502.F72 C38 1986

Cavaco, Carminda. A mulher na agricultura portuguesa : comunicação / apresentada por Carminda Cavaco. [Lisbon] : Centro de Estudos Geográficos, Universidade de Lisboa, I.N.I.C., 1981. 34 leaves : maps ; 30 cm. (Estudos de geografia humana e regional . B4) "Seminário Internacional sobre as Agriculturas da Europa Mediterrânea: os Homens e o Trabalho." LC Card 85-216534
1. Women farmers - Portugal. 2. Farmers' wives - Portugal. 3. Women in agriculture - Portugal. I. Series: Estudos de geografia humana e regional , no. B4. II. Title.
HD6073.F32 P83 1981

Cavaco Silva, Aníbal A. (Aníbal António), 1939- O mercado financeiro português em 1966 / por Aníbal A. Cavaco Silva. Lisboa : Centro de Economia e Finanças, 1968. xiv, 104 p. : ill. ; 25 cm. (Estudos e seminários / Instituto Gulbenkian de Ciência, Centro de Economia e Finanças) Summary in English and French. Includes bibliographical references. LC Card 85-133959
1. Financial institutions - Portugal. 2. Banks and banking - Portugal. I. Series: Estudos e seminários. II. Title.
HG186.P8 C38 1968

Cavalcante, José Cândido Marques. Dicionário inglês-português de termos econômicos & comerciais / José Cândido Marques Cavalcante. [Fortaleza] : Banco do Nordeste do Brasil ; Petrópolis : Editora Vozes, 1979. 408 p. ; 23 cm. LC Card 80-113110
1. Economics - Dictionaries. 2. Commerce - Dictionaries. 3. English language - Dictionaries - Portuguese. I. Title.
HB61 .C37 ***NYPL [JLE 81-244]***

Cavalcanti, Amaro, 1849-1922. O meio circulante nacional : (1808-1835) / Amaro Cavalcanti. Brasília-Distrito Federal : Editora Universidade de Brasília, 1983- v. : ill. ; 23 cm. (Coleção Temas brasileiros . v. 53-) "Com o apoio Fundação Roberto Marinho." LC Card 84-160002
1. Money - Brazil - History. 2. Money - Law and legislation - Brazil - History. I. Title.
HG833 .C38 1983 ***NYPL [JLL 85-246]***

Cavalcanti, Bianor Scelza. Administração da política industrial no Brasil : relatório final / Bianor Scelza Cavalcanti, Jorge Vianna Monteiro, José Cezar Castanhar. Rio de Janeiro : IPEA/INPES, 1986. ii, 87, 10 p. : ill. ; 30 cm. (Série Estudos de política industrial e comércio exterior . no. 8) "Tiragem, 250 exemplares"--Verso t.p. Bibliography: p. 84-87. LC Card 87-102756 DDC 338.981 19
1. Industry and state - Brazil. I. Monteiro, Jorge Vianna. II. Castanhar, José Cezar. III. Title. IV. Series.
HD3616.B83 C28 1986

Cavalcanti, Maria Luisa, 1943- La politica commerciale italiana, 1945-1952 : uomini e fatti / Maria Luisa Cavalcanti. Napoli : Edizioni scientifiche italiane, c1984. 288 p. ; 24 cm. (Biblioteca di storia economica e sociale. Saggi . 2) Bibliography: p. [267]-276. Includes index. LC Card 86-121609 DDC 380.1/3/0945 19
1. Italy - Commercial policy - History - 20th century. I. Title. II. Series.
HF1549 .C38 1984

Cavanagh, Gerald F. Ethical dilemmas in the modern corporation / Gerald F. Cavanagh, Arthur F. McGovern. Englewood Cliffs, NJ : Prentice Hall, c1988. x, 198 p. : ill. ; 23 cm. Includes bibliographies and index. ISBN 0-13-290058-0 (pbk.) LC Card 87-25726 DDC 174/.4 19
1. Business ethics. 2. Corporations - Moral and ethical aspects. I. McGovern, Arthur F. II. Title.
HF5387 .C38 1988

Cavanna, Henry. Public sector deficits in OECD countries . New York , 1987. p. cm. ISBN 0-312-00533-4 : LC Card 87-11876 DDC 339.5/23/091724 19
HJ2043 .P8 1987

Cavazzuti, Filippo, 1942- Lezioni di economia . Milano , 1979. 195 p. ; LC Card 80-451708
HG1029.5 .L49 ***NYPL [JLC 86-357]***

Cavelti, Peter C., 1947- New profits in gold, silver, strategic metals : the complete investment guide / Peter C. Cavelti.1st McGraw-Hill ed. New York : McGraw-Hill, 1984, c1985. 221 p. : ill. ; 24 cm. Includes index. Bibliography: p. 209-212. ISBN 0-07-010288-0 LC Card 84-12268 DDC 332.63 19
1. Precious metals - Handbooks, manuals, etc. 2. Strategic materials - Handbooks, manuals, etc. I. Title.
HG261 .C38 1985 ***NYPL [JLE 84-2956]***

Caves, Richard E.
American industry : structure, conduct, performance / Richard Caves.6th ed. Englewood Cliffs, N.J. : Prentice-Hall, c1987. x, 124 p. : ill. ; 24 cm. (Foundations of modern economics series) Bibliography: p. 117-118. Includes index. ISBN 0-13-027665-0 (pbk.) : LC Card 86-22706 DDC 338.0973 19
1. United States - Industries. 2. Industrial concentration - United States. 3. Restraint of trade - United States. I. Title.
HC106.5 .C34 1987

American industry: structure, conduct, performance [by] Richard Caves. 3d ed. Englewood Cliffs, N.J., Prentice-Hall [c1972] vii, 117 p. illus. 24 cm. (Foundations of modern economics series) Bibliography: p. 111-112. ISBN 0-13-027573-5 LC Card 72-170034 DDC 338/.0973
1. United States - Industries. 2. Restraint of trade - United States. I. Title.
HC106.5 .C34 1972

Cavuoto, James. LaserWrite it! : [a desktop publishing guide to reports, resumes, newsletters, directories, business forms, and more] / James Cavuoto. Reading, Mass. : Addison-Wesley, 1986. viii, 198 p. : ill. ; 24 cm. Includes index. ISBN 0-201-11327-9 : LC Card 86-3406 DDC 070.5/028/5 19
1. Electronic publishing. 2. Self-publishing - Data processing. 3. LaserWriter (Printer). 4. Macintosh (Computer) - Programming. 5. Business - Data processing. I. Title.
Z286.E43 C38 1986 ***NYPL [JSE 86-1226]***

Cayman Islands. Dept. of Finance and Development. Statistics Unit.
A Guide to the new consumer price index. [George Town, Grand Caymon, B.W.I.] [1985] 26 leaves ; LC Card 86-221984 DDC 338.5/28/0972921 19
HB235.C29 G85 1985

Population, birth, death, and marriage statistics of the Cayman Islands . [George Town] [1987] 10 leaves ; LC Card 87-403402 DDC 304.6/097292/1021 19
HA916.Z9 C2968 1987

CAYMAN ISLANDS - STATISTICS, VITAL.
Population, birth, death, and marriage statistics of the Cayman Islands . [George Town] [1987] 10 leaves ; LC Card 87-403402 DDC 304.6/097292/1021 19
HA916.Z9 C2968 1987

Cayón, Juan Ramón. Billetes españoles, 1783-1983 : Carlos III a Juan Carlos I / Juan R. Cayón, Carlos Castán. Madrid, España : C. Castán : J.R. Cayón, [1983?] 82 p. : ill. ; 22 cm. ISBN 88-300-9799-6 LC Card 85-232320
1. Bank-notes - Spain - Catalogs. I. Castán, Carlos. II. Title.
HG1137 .C38 1983

Cazacu, Honorina. Democrația socialistă în acțiune : o perspectivă sociologică asupra conducerii întreprinderii industriale / Honorina Cazacu (coordonator), Ion Glodeanu, Sorin Mitulescu. București : Editura Academiei Republicii Socialiste România, 1985. 192 p. : ill. ; 21 cm. At head of title: Academia de Științe Sociale și Politice a Republicii Socialiste România. Universitatea București. Centrul de Cercetări Sociologice. Table of contents in English, Romanian, and Russian. Summary in English. Includes bibliographical references. CONTENTS. - Democrație și conducere / Honorina Cazacu -- Conducerea colectivă și baza ei de masă / Honorina Cazacu -- Conducerea colectivă și sistemul informațional al întreprinderii / Sorin Mitulescu, Ion Glodeanu -- Particularități în procesul participării la conducere / Sorin Mitulescu -- Consiliul oamenilor muncii în mecanismul conducerii colective / Ion Glodeanu -- Conducerea colectivă / Honorina Cazacu. LC Card 86-216024
1. Industrial management - Romania - Employee participation. I. Glodeanu, Ion. II. Mitulescu, Sorin. III. Title.
HD5660.R6 C39 1985

Cazadero, Manuel. Desarrollo, crisis e ideología en la formación del capitalismo : un estudio sobre la Ley de correspondencia / Manuel Cazadero.1a ed. México : Fondo de Cultura Económica, 1986. 153 p. ; 23 cm. (Sección de obras de economía) Bibliography: p. 147-152. ISBN 968-16-2280-4 LC Card 87-403551 DDC 330.12/2 19
1. Capitalism. 2. Marxian economics. I. Series: Sección de obras de economía (Fondo de Cultura Económica (Mexico)). II. Title.
HB501 .C33 1986

Cazals, Michel. Bourguinat, Henri. L'entreprise française face aux variations de change . Paris , c1985. vi, 123 p. : ISBN 2-7178-0899-X : LC Card 85-190582 DDC 332.4/5 19
HG3815 .B68 1985 NYPL [JLE 86-494]

Cazorla, José. see **Cazorla Pérez, José.**

Cazorla Pérez, José. Emigración y retorno . [Madrid] , 1981. 325 p., [2] folded leaves of plates : ISBN 84-500-5097-9 LC Card 82-145134 DDC 325.46 19
JV8251 .E49 1981 NYPL [JLE 86-3179]

CBO study.
Earnings sharing options for the social security system. [Washington, D.C.?] [1986] xxv, 137 p. : LC Card 86-601147 DDC 368.4/3015/0973 19
HD7125 .E227 1986 NYPL [JLF 86-1058]

Kaplan, Daniel P. Has trade protection revitalized domestic industries? Washington, D.C. [1986] xvi, 111 p. : LC Card 86-603423 DDC 382.7/3/0973 19
HF1421 .K36 1986

Webre, Philip. The budgetary and economic effects of oil taxes. Washington, DC , 19. xvi, 55 p. ; *NYPL [JLF 86-1354]*

CBS computer books.
Wolenik, Robert. MacWrite made easier /. New York , 1985. xiv, 210 p. : ISBN 0-03-001763-7 LC Card 84-19781 DDC 652/.5 19
Z52.5.M32 W64 1985 NYPL [JLE 85-1535]

CBS INC. - BIOGRAPHY.
Paper, Lewis J. Empire . New York , 1987. x, 384 p., [16] p. of plates : ISBN 0-312-00591-1 : LC Card 87-4368 DDC 384.54/092/4 B 19
HE8689.8.P34 P36 1987

CBS schoolbreak special (Television program)
Contract for life, the S.A.D.D. story [motion picture] /. Los Angeles, CA , 1985. 1 film reel (31 min.) : LC Card 85-700743 DDC 363.1 11
HE5620.D7

Contract for life, the S.A.D.D story [videorecording] /. Los Angeles, CA , 1985. 1 videocassette (31 min.) : LC Card 85-700744 DDC 363.1 11
HE5620.D7

CCPD documents. Justice and development .
(no. 6) The Debt crisis and the Third World. Geneva [1986] 54 p. ; LC Card 87-114938 DDC 336.3/435/091724 19
HJ8899 .D426 1986

CD-ROM INDUSTRY - UNITED STATES.
CD ROM markets. Norwalk, Conn., U. S.A. (6 Prowitt St., Norwalk 06855) , c1986. v, 201 leaves : LC Card 86-227050 DDC 381/.4500456 19
HD9696.O673 U627 1986

CD ROM markets. Norwalk, Conn., U. S.A. (6 Prowitt St., Norwalk 06855) : International Resource Development Inc., c1986. v, 201 leaves : ill. ; 28 cm. (Report / International Resource Development Inc. . #697) "June 1986." LC Card 86-227050 DDC 381/.4500456 19
1. CD-ROM industry - United States. 2. Market surveys - United States. I. International Resource Development, inc. II. Series: Report / International Resource Development Inc. , #697. III. Title.
HD9696.O673 U627 1986

CDA Investment Technologies, Inc. Equity performance 1977-1986 . Washington, D.C. , c1987. 28, [A-Q] p. : LC Card 87-159010 DDC 332.1/754/0973 19
HG1616.I5 E68 1987

CEARÁ (BRAZIL : STATE) - POPULATION.
O Norte cearense /. Recife , 1985. 303 p. : LC Card 86-209022
HD1875.C4 N67 1985

Ceará (Brazil : State). Secretaria de Educação. Catálogo de ocupações pesquisadas em Fortaleza. [Fortaleza] . 111, [1] p. ; LC Card 83-222529
HF5382.5.B7 C38 1972

Ceará, Brazil (City) see Fortaleza (Brazil)

CEARÁ, BRAZIL (STATE) - ECONOMIC CONDITIONS.
Casimiro, Liana Maria Carleial de. Seca . Fortaleza-Ceará [19]84. 63 p. ; LC Card 86-130055 DDC 330.981/31063 19
HC188.C4 C29 1984

CEARÁ, BRAZIL (STATE) - INDUSTRIES.
O Norte cearense /. Recife , 1985. 303 p. : LC Card 86-209022
HD1875.C4 N67 1985

Ceara Hatton, Miguel. Hacia una reestructuración dirigida de la economía dominicana /. Santo Domingo, República Dominicana , c1986. 355 p. : LC Card 87-402158 DDC 338.97293 19
HC153.5 .H33 1986

Cearley, George Walker. American Airlines : America's leading airline / written by George Walker Cearley, Jr. Dallas, Tex. (P.O. Box 12312, Dallas, 75225) : G.W. Cearley, Jr., c1987. 136 p. : ill. ; 28 cm. Bibliography: p. 134-135. LC Card 87-132433 DDC 387.7/065/73 19
1. American Airlines, inc. - History. 2. Airlines - United States - History. 3. Aeronautics, Commercial - United States - History. I. Title.
HE9803.A95 C4 1987

Ceaușescu, Nicolae.
Cuvîntare la Plenara Consiliului Național al Oamenilor Muncii, din 19-20 ianuarie 1981 / Nicolae Ceaușescu. București : Editura Politică, 1981. 31 p. ; 20 cm. LC Card 81-153290
1. Romania - Economic policy - 1945-. 2. Communism - Romania. I. Title.
HC405 .C4215 1981

Romania from the perspective opened by the 1986-1990 five-year plan. Bucharest [1986?] iii, 119 p. ; LC Card 87-124268 DDC 338.9498 19
HC405 .R563 1986

Cebrap. see **Centro Brasileiro de Análise e Planejamento.**

Cebula, Richard J. The deficit problem in perspective / Richard J. Cebula. Lexington, Mass. : Lexington Books, c1987. x, 106 p. : ill. ; 23 cm Includes bibliographies and index. ISBN 0-669-14303-0 (pbk. : alk. paper) LC Card 86-45792 DDC 339.5/23/0973 19
1. Budget deficits - United States. 2. Fiscal policy - United States. 3. Budget - Law and legislation - United States. I. Title.
HJ2052 .C42 1987

CEDA. see **Committee for Economic Development of Australia.**

CEDA information paper.
Skully, Michael T. American depositary receipts . [Melbourne] [1986] 44 leaves : LC Card 86-229206 DDC 332.6/7373/094 19
HG5892 .S58 1986

CEDEFOP document.
Equal opportunity counsellors . Berlin , Washington, DC , 1986. 50 p. : ISBN 92-825-6559-9 : LC Card 87-136233 DDC 331.13/3/094 19
HD4903.5.E8 E79 1986

Promotion of cooperation amongst research and development organizations in the field of vocational training . Berlin , Washington, DC , 1986. 111 p. ; ISBN 92-825-6570-X (pbk.) : LC Card 87-133749 DDC 331.25/92/094
HD5715.5.E78 P77 1986

Raimond, Jean-Marie. Vocational training of young migrants in France /. Berlin , 1986. x, 101 p. : ISBN 92-825-6118-6
NYPL [JLG 87-134]

Wagner, Karin. Relation between education, employment, and productivity and their impact on education and labour market policies . Berlin , Washington, DC , 1986. ix, 80 p. ; ISBN 92-825-6371-5 : LC Card 87-136255 DDC 331.12/042/0941 19
HD5715.5.G4 W35 1986

CEDEX (Organization) Formas alternativas de negociação das exportações brasileiras . Belo Horizonte, MG , c1984. 122 p. ; LC Card 86-200391
HF1513 .F67 1984

CEDIS (Organization)
Los Grupos monopólicos en el Ecuador . Quito, Ecuador , 1986. 208 p. : LC Card 87-404236 DDC 338.8/2/09866 19
HD2838 .G78 1986

La Política económica del gobierno de Febres Cordero. Quito, Ecuador [1986] 84 p. : LC Card 87-403470
HC202 .P65 1986

CEDLA incidentele publicaties .
(26) Vellinga, Menno. Industrialization and regional development in Colombia /. Amsterdam, The Netherlands , 1983. 183 p. : ISBN 90-70280-80-9 LC Card 83-209247 DDC 338.09861/26 19
HC198.C296 V45 1983

CEDLA (Organization) Segunda reforma agraria . La Paz, Bolivia [1987] 287 p. : LC Card 87-403057 DDC 333.3/1/84 19
HD1333.B5 S44 1987

CEDSI (Center) L'Effort économique de défense . [Grenoble] , 1985. 235 p. : LC Card 86-199399
HC280.D4 E38 1985

CEDU (Organization : Rio Grande do Sul, Brazil) Energia e assentamentos humanos. Porto Alegre , 1983. 40 p. : LC Card 86-200513
HD9502.A2 E513 1983

Cédulas brasileiras da República : emissões do Tesouro Nacional / Banco do Brasil S.A., Museu e Arquivo Histórico. Rio de Janeiro : O Museu, 1965. 111 p. : ill. ; 31 cm. LC Card 85-119119
1. Paper money - Brazil - History. I. Brazil. Tesouro Nacional. II. Banco do Brasil (1905-). Museu, Arquivo Histórico e Biblioteca.
HG837 .C43 1965

Cegos Management Development (Firm : London, England) Bauwens, Jan G., 1924- Industrial co-operation and investment in Yugoslavia /. Luxembourg , Washington, D.C. , 1986. viii, 161 p. : ISBN 92-825-6410-X (pbk.) : LC Card 86-216364 DDC 332.6/73/09497 19
HG5682 .B38 1986

Cejan, Samo, 1949- Družba, znanost, tehnologija . Ljubljana , 1982. 472 p. ; LC Card 84-235191
HC407.Z9 T434 1982

Cejudo, Jorge. see **Cejudo López, Jorge.**

Cejudo López, Jorge. Campomanes, Pedro Rodríguez, Conde de, 1723-1803. Bosquejo de política económica española . Madrid , c1984. 182 p. ; ISBN 84-276-0691-5 : LC Card 86-153508
HB117.A2 C34 1984

CELADE (Organization)
Bolivia . [La Paz, Bolivia] [Santiago, Chile] [1985] 107 p. : LC Card 86-160849
HA954 .B64 1985

Ebanks, G. E. Mortality, fertility, and family planning . Santiago, Chile [1985] 123 p. ; LC Card 87-131697 DDC 304.6/2/09729841 19
HB1376.D65 E32 1985

Estimaciones y proyecciones de población, 1950-2025 /. [Caracas] , 1985-[1987] 2 v. : ISBN 980-280-006-6 (set) LC Card 87-123959 DDC 304.6/2/0987021 19
HA1095 .E885 1985

Guatemala . [Guatemala] , San José, Costa Rica [1984] vii, 73 p. : LC Card 86-158744
HA755 .U5 no. 1045 HB949.A3

Čelenković, Teodosije. Radna snaga u samoupravnom društvu : teorijsko-metodološka rasprava / Teodosije Čelenković. Beograd : Izdavačka radna organizacija "Rad," 1980. 241 p. ; 20cm. (Teorijski spisi) In Serbo-Croatian (Roman) Bibliography: p. 232-240. LC Card 82-166188
1. Labor supply - Yugoslavia. 2. Management - Yugoslavia - Employee participation. I. Title. II. Series.
HD5811.6.A6 C45 1980

Celis, Adán. 5 momentos, 5 planteamientos : Adán Celis, presidente de "FEDECAMARAS," 1983-1985 : recopilación de sus más destacadas intervenciones. Puerto la Cruz [Venezuela] : [s.n.], 1985. 99 p. ; 22 cm. LC Card 87-401953 DDC 338.987 19
1. Venezuela - Economic conditions - 1958-. 2. Venezuela - Social conditions - 1958-. 3. Federación Venezolana de Cámaras y Asociaciones de Comercio y Producción. I. Title. II. Title: Cinco momentos, cinco

planteamientos.
HC237 .C445 1985

The cellular communications industry /. Leibowitz, Dennis. New York, N.Y. (140 Broadway, New York 10005) , c1985. ii, 67 p. : LC Card 86-201572 DDC 384.5/33/0973 19
HD9696.R363 U65 1985

CELLULAR RADIO EQUIPMENT INDUSTRY - EUROPE.
The Mobile radio market in Western Europe. New York, N.Y. , c1982. x, 283 p. : LC Card 87-141850 DDC 380.1/45621384165/094 19
HD9696.R363 E855 1982

CELLULAR RADIO EQUIPMENT INDUSTRY - UNITED STATES.
Leibowitz, Dennis. The cellular communications industry /. New York, N.Y. (140 Broadway, New York 10005) , c1985. ii, 67 p. : LC Card 86-201572 DDC 384.5/33/0973 19
HD9696.R363 U65 1985

The U. S. mobile radio communications equipment market. New York, N.Y. , c1983. viii, 253 p. : LC Card 87-142226 DDC 384.5/3 19
HD9696.R363 U684 1983

CELLULOSE INDUSTRY - BRAZIL.
Mercado brasileiro de celulose e papel /. Brasília, D.F. , 1982. vii, 224 leaves : LC Card 84-210712
HD9660.C43 B75 1982

CEMENT INDUSTRIES - AFRICA.
The Cement industry in the African region /. Addis Ababa , 1983. 36, [40] p. ; LC Card 86-201071 DDC 338.4/766694/096 19
HD9622.A42 C46 1983

CEMENT INDUSTRIES - BRAZIL - MINAS GERAIS - ENERGY CONSUMPTION.
Uso de energia na indústria de cimento em Minas Gerais, 1980-1983. [Belo Horizonte] , 1985. 146 p. : LC Card 86-152639
HD9622.B73 M569 1985

CEMENT INDUSTRIES - INDIA.
Das, Kumar Bar. Cement industry of India /. New Delhi , 1987. xxi, 465 p. : ISBN 81-7024-083-2 : LC Card 87-900765 DDC 338.4/766694/0954 19
HD9622.I52 D37 1987

CEMENT INDUSTRIES - INDIA - CONGRESSES.
National Workshop on Productivity Enhancement in Indian Cement Industry-- a Pragmatic Approach to Modernisation (1986 : New Delhi, India) National Workshop on Productivity Enhancement in Indian Cement Industry-- a Pragmatic Approach to Modernisation, 19-20 March 1986 . New Delhi [1986] 42 p. : LC Card 87-901966 DDC 338.4/766694/0954 19
HD9622.I52 N34 1986

CEMENT INDUSTRIES - URUGUAY.
Uruguay. Asemblea General. Cámara de Representantes. Investigación en la Administración, Nacional de Combustibles, Alcohol y Portland /. [Montevideo] , 1935. 352 p. ; LC Card 85-105071
HD9574.U72 U78 1935

The Cement industry in the African region / Economic Commission for Africa. Addis Ababa : The Commission, 1983. 36, [40] p. ; 28 cm. Corrigendum sheet laid in. LC Card 86-201071 DDC 338.4/766694/096 19
1. Cement industries - Africa. I. Economic Commission for Africa.
HD9622.A42 C46 1983

Cement industry of India /. Das, Kumar Bar. New Delhi , 1987. xxi, 465 p. : ISBN 81-7024-083-2 : LC Card 87-900765 DDC 338.4/766694/0954 19
HD9622.I52 D37 1987

Cement Manufacturers' Association (India) National Workshop on Productivity Enhancement in Indian Cement Industry-- a Pragmatic Approach to Modernisation (1986 : New Delhi, India) National Workshop on Productivity Enhancement in Indian Cement Industry-- a Pragmatic Approach to Modernisation, 19-20 March 1986 . New Delhi [1986] 42 p. : LC Card 87-901966 DDC 338.4/766694/0954 19
HD9622.I52 N34 1986

CEMLA. see Centro de Estudios Monetarios Latinoamericanos.

Cenários para a economia brasileira, 1984-1990. [Rio de Janeiro] : Presidência da República, Secretaria de Planejamento, Banco Nacional de Desenvolvimento Econômico e Social, Area de Planejamento, Departamento de Planejamento, 1984. 81 p. : ill. ; 30 cm. LC Card 85-209337
1. Brazil - Economic conditions - 1985-. 2. Brazil - Economic conditions - 1964-1985. 3. Economic forecasting - Brazil. I. Banco Nacional de Desenvolvimento Econômico e Social (Brazil). Departamento de Planejamento.
HC187 .C28 1984

CENCEP (Center : France) Epargne et développement /. Paris , 1985. 410 p. : ISBN 2-7178-0855-8 : LC Card 86-149765
HC59.72.S3 E62 1985

Cencini, Alvaro. Money, income, and time : a quantum-theoretical approach / Alvaro Cencini. London ; New York : Pinter Publishers, 1988. p. cm. Includes index. ISBN 0-86187-943-0 : LC Card 87-7279 DDC 332.4 19
1. Money. 2. Quantity theory of money. 3. Income. 4. Time and economic reactions. I. Title.
HG221 .C39 1988

Cens d'edificis, 1970 / Subdepartament d'Estadistica. [Barcelona] : El Subdepartament, [1979?] 5, 9 leaves ; 22 x 30 cm. Cover title. LC Card 84-131679
1. Housing - Spain - Barcelona - Statistics. 2. Buildings - Spain - Barcelona - Statistics. 3. Barcelona (Spain) - Census, 1970. I. Barcelona (Spain). Subdepartamento de Estadística.
HD7351.B3 C45 1979

Cens vivendas 1970 / Subdepartament d'Estadistica. [Barcelona] : Subdepartament d'Estadistica, [1979?] 4, 9 leaves ; 22 x 30 cm. Cover title. LC Card 84-131705
1. Housing - Spain - Barcelona - Statistics. 2. Barcelona (Spain) - Census, 1970. I. Barcelona (Spain). Subdepartamento de Estadística.
HD7351.B3 C47 1979

CENSIS (Series) .
(1) A metà decennio . Milano, Italy , c1986. 355 p. ; LC Card 86-224676
HA1374 .A19 1986

Censo agrario 1982 : programa de imputación automática. Madrid : Instituto Nacional de Estadística, 1983. 104, 8 p. : ill. ; 25 cm. ISBN 84-260-0803-8 LC Card 84-134551
1. Agriculture - Economic aspects - Spain - Data processing. 2. System design. 3. Spain - Census, 1982. I. Instituto Nacional de Estadística (Spain).
HD2022 .C45 1983

Censo de población, 1984. San José, Costa Rica : Ministerio de Gobernación y Policía, Impr. Nacional, 1987. 2 v. : ill. ; 27 cm. República de Costa Rica, Ministerio de Economía, Industria y Comercio, Dirección General de Estadística y Censos"--Cover. "Noviembre 1986" LC Card 87-402193 DDC 304.6/097286/021 19
1. Costa Rica - Census, 1984. 2. Costa Rica - Population - Statistics. I. Costa Rica. Dirección General de Estadística y Censos.
HA801.5 1984

Censo de vivienda, 1984 / [República de Costa Rica, Ministerio de Economía, Industria y Comercio, Dirección General de Estadística y Censos]. San José, Costa Rica : Ministerio de Gobernación y Policía : Impr. Nacional, 1987. xxxiii, 335 p. : ill. ; 28 cm. Date on t.p.: 1986. Chiefly tables. LC Card 87-402910 DDC 363.5/097286/021 19
1. Housing - Costa Rica - Statistics. 2. Costa Rica - Census, 1984. I. Costa Rica. Dirección General de Estadística y Censos. II. Costa Rica. Ministerio de Gobernación y Policía.
HD7308.A3 C46 1987

Censo nacional de población y vivienda, 1981 : resultados definitivos. Santo Domingo, Distrito Nacional, República Dominicana : Oficina Nacional de Estadística, 1985- v. <1 > : forms, maps ; 28 cm. Spine title: República Dominicana. Chiefly tables. CONTENTS. - v. 1. Distrito Nacional. LC Card 86-223758
1. Dominican Republic - Census, 1981. 2. Dominican Republic - Population - Statistics. 3. Households - Dominican Republic - Statistics. 4. Housing - Dominican Republic - Statistics. I. Dominican Republic. Oficina Nacional de Estadística. II. Title: República Dominicana.
HA886.5 1981c

Censo 85. XV censo nacional de población y IV de vivienda. Bogotá , 1986- v. <1-5, 7 > : LC Card 87-402787 DDC 304.6/09861/021 19
HA1011.5 1985a

CENSUS.
Population geography . London , Dover, N.H. , c1986. 322 p. : ISBN 0-7099-4045-9 : LC Card 86-6210 DDC 304.6 19
HB1951 .P653 1986 **NYPL [JLD 86-3692]**

Statistics Canada. Statistical Services Field. A compendium of methods of error evaluation in censuses and surveys /. Ottawa , 1978. 25 p. ; LC Card 80-499370 DDC 001.4/225 19
HA31.2 .C36 1978 **NYPL [JLF 81-125]**

CENSUS DISTRICTS - CANADA - STATISTICS.
Revised annual estimates of population for census divisions, 1971-1976 /. Ottawa , c1979. 21 p. ; LC Card 82-216681
HA745 .R473 1979

CENSUS DISTRICTS - TRINIDAD AND TOBAGO.
1980 population and housing census . Trinidad and Tobago , c1986. 15 p. : LC Card 87-402815 DDC 304.6/097298/3 19
HA867 .A4 1980b

CENSUS DISTRICTS - VENEZUELA.
Nomenclador de centros poblados. [Caracas] [1986-1987] 7 v. : LC Card 87-119549
HA1091.5 1981a

Census eighty. Census '80 . Baltimore, Md. (2225 N. Charles St., Baltimore 21218) [1983] xv, 106 leaves : LC Card 83-622347 DDC 339.2/2/097526 19
HC108.B2 C46 1983 **NYPL [JLF 86-1594]**

Census mapping survey / edited by Prithvish Nag for International Geographical Union Commission on Population Geography. New Delhi : Concept, 1984. xxiii, 299 p. : ill., maps ; 25 cm. Map on lining papers. Country reports, with reference to selected countries from all the continents. Includes bibliographies. LC Card 84-902653 DDC 304.6 19
1. Census - Maps. 2. Population - Maps. I. Nag, Prithvish.
HA31.25 .C46 1984 **NYPL [JLE 85-3881]**

CENSUS - MAPS.
Census mapping survey /. New Delhi , 1984. xxiii, 299 p. : LC Card 84-902653 DDC 304.6 19
HA31.25 .C46 1984 **NYPL [JLE 85-3881]**

Census monograph (Singapore) .
(no. 3) Saw, Swee-Hock, 1931- The labour force of Singapore /. Singapore [1984] xi, 78 p. : ISBN 997-19-1416-6 (pbk.) LC Card 86-946447 DDC 331.11/09595/7 19
HD5823.A6 S28 1984

Census of agricultural and pastoral production, 1979. Sensus van landbou- en veeteelproduksie, 1979 =. Pretoria [1985?] xiv, 266 p. ; ISBN 0-621-09380-7 : LC Card 86-150362 DDC 338.1/0968/021 19
HD2130.5 .S48 1985

Census of agriculture, 1978-1979 : preliminary report. [Kingston] : Jamaica Dept. of Statistics, [1983] vi, ix, 167 p. : ill. ; 28 cm. Chiefly tables. LC Card 83-242227 DDC 338.1/097292 19
1. Agriculture - Economic aspects - Jamaica - Statistics. 2. Farms, Size of - Jamaica - Statistics. I. Jamaica. Dept. of Statistics.
HD1847 .C46 1983 **NYPL [JLF 86-1028]**

Census of distribution, 1977-78 : general regional summary : New Zealand distribution industries. Wellington, N.Z. : The Dept., [1980]-<[1981] > v. <11 > : ill. ; 30 cm. (Statistics bulletin / Department of Statistics) Cover title. CONTENTS. - Series A, no. 1. General statistics -- Series A, no. 2. Link data 1972-73 and 1977-78 censuses concentration ratios -- Series B, no. 1. Wholesale trade & retail trade -- Series B, no. 2. Restaurants and hotels, personal and household services -- Series B, no. 3. North Island regional statistics -- Series B, no. 4. South Island regional statistics -- Series C, no. 1. Wholesale trade -- Series C, no. 2. Wholesale trade -- Series C, no. 3. Retail trade -- Series C, no. 4. Retail trade -- Series C, no. 5. Restaurants and hotels. LC Card 86-204705
1. Retail trade - New Zealand - Statistics. 2. Wholesale trade - New Zealand - Statistics. 3. Service industries - New Zealand - Statistics. I. New Zealand. Dept. of

Statistics. II. Series: Statistics bulletin (New Zealand. Dept. of Statistics).
HF5429.6.N47 C46 1980

Census of India. SRS based abridged life tables, 1976-80. New Delhi , 1986. v, 37 p. : LC Card 87-901200
HB1470 .S77 1986

Census of India, 1981. Series 6, Haryana. Delhi : Controller of Publications, Govt. of India, <1981-1983 > v. in : ill., maps ; 30 cm. Issued by Registrar General & Census Commissioner, India; some vols. by Director of Census Operations, Haryana. CONTENTS. - -- pt. 2A. General population tables and pt. 2B. Primary census abstract -- pt. 2, special. Report and tables 5 per cent sample data -- pt. 7. Tables on houses and disabled population -- pt. 10A. Town directory -- pt. 13. District census handbook. A & B. Village & town directory ; Village & townwise primary census abstract (12 v.): [1] Ambala. [2] Bhiwani. [3] Faridabad. [4] Gurgaon. [5] Hisar. [6] Jind. [7] Karnal. [8] Kurukshetra. [9] Mahendragarh. [10] Rohtak. [11] Sirsa. [12] Sonpat. LC Card 87-915014
1. Haryana (India) - Census, 1981. 2. India - Census, 1981. I. India. Office of the Registrar General. II. India. Census Commissioner. III. India. Director of Census Operations, Haryana.
HA4587.H37 C46 1981

Census of India, 1981. Series 16, Orissa. Delhi : Controller of Publications, <[1982]-1986 > v. in : ill., maps ; 30 cm. Some vols. have text in English and Hindi. Some vols. have title also in Hindi: Bhārata kī janagaṇanā, 1981. Śṛṅkhalā 16, Uṛīsā. Issued by A.R. Nanda, Director of Census Operations, Orissa. CONTENTS. - -- pt. 2A. General population tables -- pt. 3A & B. <i-ii > General economic tables (2 v.) -- pt. 4A. Social and cultural tables -- pt. 5A & B. Migration tables <1 v. > -- pt. 6A & B. Fertility tables -- pt. 13. District census handbook. B, Village and townwise primary census abstract 3 v.: [5] Dhenkanal <pt. B > [8] Kendujhar <pt. B > [13] Sundargarh <pt. B > LC Card 87-915022 DDC 315.4/13 19
1. Orissa (India) - Census, 1981. 2. India - Census, 1981. I. India. Director of Census Operations, Orissa. II. Title: Bhārata kī janagaṇanā, 1981.
HA4587.O74 C46 1982

Census of India, 1981. Series 7, Himachal Pradesh. Delhi : Controller of Publications, <1982-1986 > <v. in > : ill., maps ; 30 cm. Issued by K.L. Negi, Director of Census Operations, Himachal Pradesh. CONTENTS. - -- pt. 2A. General population tables -- pt. 2B. Primary census abstract -- pt. 3A & B & pt. 4A. General economic tables ; Social and cultural tables. 1 v. -- pt. 5A & B. Migration tables -- pt. 6A & B. Fertility tables -- pt. 7. Tables on houses and disabled population -- pt. 10A. Town directory -- pts. 13. District census handbook. A & B. Village & town directory ; Village & townwise primary census abstract <10 > v.: [1] Bilaspur. [2] Chamba. [3] Hamirpur. -- [6] Kullu. [7] Lahul & Spiti. [8] Mandi. [9] Shimla. [10] Sirmaur. [11] Solan. [12] Una. LC Card 87-915013
1. Himachal Pradesh (India) - Census, 1981. 2. India - Census, 1981. I. India. Director of Census Operations, Himachal Pradesh.
HA4587.H54 C45 1982

Census of India, 1981. Series 17, Punjab. Delhi : Controller of Publications, <[1982]-[1983?] > v. in : maps ; 31 cm. Issued by Director of Census Operations, Punjab. CONTENTS. - -- pt. 2A and pt. 2B. General population tables and Primary census abstract -- pt. 7. Tables on houses and disabled population -- pt. 10A. Town directory -- pt. 13. District census handbook. A & B, Village & town directory ; Village & townwise primary census abstract <8 > v.: [1] Amritsar. [2] Bathinda. [3] Faridkot. [6] Hoshiarpur. [7] Jalandhar. [8] Kapurthala. [10] Patiala. [11] Rupnagar. LC Card 87-915023 DDC 304.6/0954/552021 19
1. Punjab (India) - Census, 1981. 2. India - Census, 1981. I. India. Director of Census Operations, Punjab.
HA4587.P86 C46 1982

Census of India, 1981. Series 19, Sikkim. Delhi : Controller of Publications, <[1982]-1985 > v. in : ill., maps ; 28 cm. Issued by J.K. Thapa, Director of Census Operations, Sikkim. CONTENTS. - -- pt. 2A and 2B. General population tables and Primary census abstract -- pt. 3A & B. General economic tables and pt. 4A. Social and cultural tables 1 v. -- pt. 5A & B. Migration tables -- pt. 6A & B. Fertility tables -- pt. 7. Tables on houses and disabled population with analytical notes -- pt. 13. District census handbook. A & B., Village and town directory ; Village and townwise primary census abstract: North, East, South & West districts. LC Card 87-915025 DDC 304.6/0954/167021 19
1. Sikkim (India) - Census, 1981. 2. India - Census, 1981. I. India. Director of Census Operations, Sikkim.
HA4587.S55 C46 1982

Census of India, 1981. Series 32, Pondicherry. New Delhi : Controller of Publications, <1982-[1985] > v. in : ill., maps ; 28-31 cm. Issued by P.L. Samy, Director of Census Operations, Pondicherry. CONTENTS. - -- pt. 2A & B. General population tables and primary census abstract -- pt. 3A & B. General economic tables and pt. 4A. Social and cultural tables -- pt. 5A & B. Migration tables -- pt. 6A & B. Fertility tables -- pt. 7. Tables on houses and disabled population -- pt. 13. District census handbook. A & B. Village & town directory ; Village & townwise primary census abstract. LC Card 87-915039 DDC 304.6/0954/86021 19
1. Pondicherry (India) - Census, 1981. 2. India - Census, 1981. I. India. Directorate of Census Operations, Pondicherry.
HA4587.P647 C46 1982

Census of India, 1981. Series 15, Nagaland. Delhi : Controller of Publications, <1983-1985 > v. in : ill., maps ; 31 cm. Issued by Daniel Kent, Director of Census Operations, Nagaland. CONTENTS. - -- pt. 2A. General population tables -- pt. 2B. Primary census abstract -- pt. 3A & B.-pt. 4A. General economic tables. Social and cultural tables -- pt. 5A & B. Migration tables -- pt. 6A & B. Fertility tables -- pt. 7. Tables on houses and disabled population -- pt. 13. District census handbook. A & B. Village & town directory ; Village & town primary census abstract and scheduled tribes primary census abstract. 7 v.: [1] Kohima. [2] Mokokchung. [3] Mon. [4] Phek. [5] Tuensang. [6] Wokha. [7] Zunheboto. LC Card 87-915021 DDC 304.6/0954/165021 19
1. Nāgāland (India) - Census, 1981. 2. India - Census, 1981. I. India. Director of Census Operations, Nagaland.
HA4587.N33 C46 1983

Census of India, 1981. Series 29, Goa, Daman & Diu. Delhi : Controller of Publications, <1983-[1985] > v. in : map ; 29-31 cm. Issued by S.K. Gandhe, Director of Census Operations, Goa, Daman & Diu. CONTENTS. - -- pt. 2A-2B. General population tables and Primary census abstract -- pt. 3A & B-pt. 4A. General economic tables. Social and cultural tables -- pt. 5A & B. Migration tables -- pt. 6A & B. Fertility tables -- pt. 7. Tables on houses and disabled population -- pt. 13. District census handbook. A and B. Village and town directory and Village and townwise primary census abstract: Goa, Daman, Diu. LC Card 87-915036 DDC 304.6/0954/799021 19
1. Goa, Daman and Diu (India) - Census, 1981. 2. India - Census, 1981. I. India. Director of Census Operations, Goa, Daman & Diu.
HA4587.W47 C46 1983

Census of India, 1981. Series 11, Madhya Pradesh. Delhi : Controller of Publications, <[1983]-[1986] > v. in : ill., maps ; 31 cm. Some vols. have text in English and Hindi. Some vols. have title also in Hindi: Bhārata kī janagaṇanā, 1981. Śṛṅkhalā 11, Madhya Pradeśa. Issued by K.C. Dubey, Director of Census Operations, Madhya Pradesh; some vols. by Registrar General & Census Commissioner, India. CONTENTS. - -- pt. 2A. General population tables -- pt. 2B. Primary census abstract -- pt. 2, special. Report and tables based on 5 per cent sample data -- pt. 3A & B. General economic tables (7 v.) -- pt. 4A. Social and cultural tables -- pt. 5A & B. Migration tables -- pt. 6A & B. Fertility tables -- pt. 7. Tables on houses and disabled population -- pt. 13. District census handbook. A, Village & town directory ; B, Village & townwise primary census abstract <10 > v.: [10] Datia, A-B (2 v.) [15] Gwalior, A-B (2 v.) [25] Narsimhapur, A-B (2 v.) [26] Panna, A-B (2 v.) [29] Raisen, A-B (2 v.) LC Card 87-915017 DDC 304.6/0954/3021 19
1. Madhya Pradesh (India) - Census, 1981. 2. India - Census, 1981. I. India. Director of Census Operations, Madhya Pradesh. II. India. Office of the Registrar General. III. India. Census Commissioner. IV. Title: Bhārata kī janagaṇanā, 1981. Śṛṅkhalā 11, Madhya Pradeśa.
HA4587.M32 C46 1983

Census of India, 1981. Series 5, Gujarat. Delhi : Controller of Publications, <1983-1986 > v. in : maps ; 30 cm. Some vols. have text in English and Hindi. Some vols. have title also in Hindi: Bhārata kī janagaṇanā, 1981. Śṛṅkhalā 5, Gujarāta. Issued by R.S. Chhaya, Director of Census Operations, Gujarat. CONTENTS. - pt. 2A. General population tables -- pt. 2B. General population tables (4 v.) -- 4A. Social and cultural tables -- pt. 5A & B. Migration tables -- pt. 6A & B. Fertility tables -- pt. 13. District census handbook. A & B. village and town directory ; Village & townwise primary census abstract <18 > v.: [1] Ahmadabad. [2] Amreli. [3] Banas Kantha. [4] Bharuch. [5] Bhavnagar. [6] The Dangs. [7] Gandhinagar. [8] Jamnagar. [9] Junagadh. [10] Kheda. [11] Kachchh. [12] Mahesana. [13] Panch Mahals. [14] Rajkot. [15] Sabar Kantha. [17] Surendranagar. [18] Vadodara. [19] Valsad. LC Card 87-915012 DDC 304.6/0954/75021 19
1. Gujarat (India) - Census, 1981. 2. India - Census, 1981. I. India. Director of Census Operations, Gujarat. II. Title: Bhārata kī janagaṇanā, 1981.
HA4587.G84 C46 1983

Census of India, 1981. Series 26, Chandigarh. Delhi : Controller of Publications, <1983-[1985] > v. in : ill., maps ; 30 cm. Issued by Ardaman Singh, Director of Census Operations, Chandigarh. CONTENTS. - -- pt. 2A. General population tables & pt. 2B. Primary census abstracts -- pt. 3A & B. General economic tables and pt. 4A. Social and cultural tables -- pt. 5A & B. Migration tables -- pt. 6A & B. Fertility tables -- pt. 7. Tables on houses and disabled population -- pt. 13. District census handbook. A & B, Village & town directory ; Village & townwise primary census abstract: Chandigarh. LC Card 87-915033 DDC 304.6/0954/552 19
1. Chandigarh (India : Union Territory) - Census, 1981. 2. India - Census, 1981. I. India. Director, Census Operations, Union Territory, Chandigarh.
HA4587.C52 C46 1983

Census of India, 1981. Series 1, India. Delhi : Controller of Publications, <1983-1985 > v. in : ill., maps (some col.) ; 28 cm. Some vols. have text in English and Hindi. Some vols. have title also in Hindi: Bhārata kī janagaṇanā, 1981. Śṛṅkhalā 1, Bhārata. Issued by P. Padmanabha, Registrar General & Census Commissioner for India. CONTENTS. - -- pt. 2A (i). General population tables -- pt. 2B. Primary census abstract. (i) General population. (ii) Scheduled castes. (2 v.) -- pt. 2, special. Report & tables based on 5 per cent sample data -- pt. 7A. Uses to which census houses are put. -- pt. 7B. The physically handicapped. LC Card 87-915010 DDC 304.6/0954/021 19
1. India - Census, 1981. I. India. Office of the Registrar General. II. India. Census Commissioner. III. Title: Bhārata kī janagaṇanā, 1981.
HA4581.5 1981g

Census of India, 1981. Series 4, Bihar. Delhi : Controller of Publications, <1983-1987 > v. in : ill., maps ; 30 cm. Some vols. have text in English and Hindi. Some vols. have title also in Hindi: Bhārata kī janagaṇanā, 1981. Śṛṅkhalā 4, Bihāra. Issued by Registrar General & Census Commissioner, India, and some vols. by Director of Census Operations, Bihar. CONTENTS. - -- pt. 2B. Primary census abstract -- pt. 2, special. Report and tables based on 5 per cent sample data -- pt. 3A & B. General economic tables. (4 v.)--pt. 4A. Social and cultural tables -- pt. 5A & B. Migration tables -- pt. 6A & B. Fertility tables -- pt. 7. Tables on houses and disabled population -- pt. 10A. Town directory. -- pts. 13. District census handbook. A & B. Village & town directory ; Village & townwise primary census abstract <22 > v.: [1] Aurangabad. [2] Begusarai. [3] Bhagalpur. [4] Bhojpur. [5] Darbhanga. [9] Gopalganj. [10] Hazaribag. [14] Madhubani. [15] Munger. [17] Nalanda. [18] Nawada. [19] Palamu. [20] Paschim Champaran. [21] Patna. [22] Purba Champaran. [23] Purnia. [25] Rohtas. [26] Saharsa. [29] Saran. [31] Sitarmahi. [32] Siwan.[33] Vaishali. LC Card 87-915011 DDC 304.6/0954/12021 19
1. Bihar (India) - Census, 1981. 2. India - Census, 1981. I. India. Office of the Registrar General. II. India. Census Commissioner. III. India. Director of Census Operations, Bihar. IV. Title: Bhārata kī janagaṇanā, 1981.
HA4587.B53 C46 1983

Census of India, 1981. Series 21, Tripura. Gangtok, Sikkim : Printed by Govt. of India Press, <1983-1986 > v. in : ill., maps ; 31 cm. Issued by S.R. Chakraborty, Director of Census Operations, Tripura. CONTENTS. - -- 2A. General population tables -- pt. 2B. Primary census abstract -- pt. 3A & B-pt. 4A. General economic tables. Social and cultural tables. 1 v. -- pt. 5A & B. Migration tables -- pt. 7. Tables on houses and disabled population -- pt. 13. District census handbook. A & B, Village and town directory ; Village & townwise primary census abstract

<1 > v.: [1] North Tripura. LC Card 87-915028 DDC 315.4/15 19

1. Tripura (India) - Census, 1981. 2. India - Census, 1981. I. India. Director of Census Operations, Tripura.

HA4587.T74 C46 1983

Census of India, 1981. Series 30, Lakshadweep. Delhi : Controller of Publications, <1984-1986 > v. in : ill., maps ; 28-31 cm. Issued by Director of Census Operations, Lakshadweep. CONTENTS. - -- 2A & B. General population tables and primary census abstract -- pt. 3A & B-pt. 4A. General economic tables. Social and cultural tables -- pt. 5A & B. Migration tables -- pt. 6A & B. Fertility tables -- pt. 7. Tables on houses and disabled population. LC Card 87-915037 DDC 304.6/0954/81021 19

1. Lakshadweep (India) - Census, 1981. 2. India - Census, 1981. I. India. Director of Census Operations, Lakshadweep.

HA4587.L34 C46 1984

Census of India, 1981. Series 27, Dadra & Nagar Haveli. Delhi : Controller of Publications, <1984-1985 > v. in : maps ; 30 cm. Issued by S.K. Gandhe, Director of Census Operations, Goa, Daman & Diu and Dadra & Nagar Haveli. CONTENTS. - -- pt. 2A. General population tables and pt. 2B. Primary census abstract -- pt. 3A & B-pt. 4A. General economic tables. Social and cultural tables -- pt. 5A & B. Migration tables -- pt. 6A & B. Fertility tables -- pt. 13. District census handbook. A and B, Village and town directory and village and townwise primary census abstract: Dadra & Nagar Haveli. LC Card 87-915034 DDC 304.6/0954/796021 19

1. Dādra and Nagar Haveli (India) - Census, 1981. I. India. Diector of Census Operations, Dadra and Nagar Haveli.

HA4587.D33 C46 1984

Census of India, 1981. Series 25, Arunachal Pradesh. Delhi : Controller of Publications, <1984-1986 > v. in : ill., maps ; 31 cm. Issued by M.B. Rai, Director of Census Operations Arunachal Pradesh. CONTENTS. - -- pt. 3A & B.-pt. 4A. General economic tables and Social and cultural tables -- pt. 5A & B. Migration tables -- pt. 6A & B. Fertility tables -- pt. 7. Tables on houses and disabled population -- pt. 13. District census handbook. A & B. Village & town directory ; Village & townwise primary census abstract <7 > v.: [1] Dibang Valley. [3] East Siang. [4] Lohit. [6] Tirap. [7] Upper Subansiri. [8] West Kameng. [9] West Siang. LC Card 87-915032 DDC 304.6/0954/163021 19

1. Arunachal Pradesh (India) - Census, 1981. 2. India - Census, 1981. I. India. Director of Census Operations, Arunachal Pradesh.

HA4587.A78 C47 1984

Census of India, 1981. Series 10, Kerala. Delhi : Controller of Publications, <1984-1987 > v. in : ill., maps (some col.) ; 30 cm. Some vols. have text in English and Hindi. Some vols. have title also in Hindi: Bhārata kī janagaṇanā, 1981. Śṛṅkhalā 10, Kerala. Issued by M. Vijayanunni, Director of Census Operations, Kerala. CONTENTS. - -- pt. 2A. General population tables -- pt. 2B. Primary census abstract -- pt. 3A & B. <i-iii > General economic tables (3 v.) -- pt. 4A. Social and cultural tables -- pt. 5A & B. Migration tables -- pt. 6A & B. Fertility tables -- pt. 7. Houses and disabled persons -- pt. 13A & B. Village directory and town directory ; Primary census abstract <1 > v.: [2] Cannanore. LC Card 87-915015 DDC 304.6/0954/83021 19

1. Kerala (India) - Census, 1981. 2. India - Census, 1981. I. India. Director of Census Operations, Kerala. II. Title: Bhārata kī janagaṇanā, 1981. Śṛṅkhalā 10, Kerala.

HA4587.K47 C46 1984

Census of India, 1981. Series 2, Andhra Pradesh. Delhi : Controller of Publications, <1984-1986 > v. in : maps ; 30 cm. Some vols. have text in English and Hindi. Some vols. have title also in Hindi: Bhārata kī janagaṇanā, 1981. Śṛṅkhalā 2, Āndhra Pradeśa. Issued by Registrar General & Census Commissioner, India: some vols. by Director of Census Operations, Andhra Pradesh. CONTENTS. - -- pt. 2B. Primary census abstract -- pt. 2, special. Report and tables based on 5 per cent sample data -- pt. 3A & B. General economic tables (4 v.) -- pt. 4A. Social and cultural tables -- pt. 5A & B. Migration tables -- pt. 6A & B. Fertility tables -- pt. 7. Houses and disabled population -- pt. 13. District census handbook. A & B, Village & town directory ; Village & town primary census abstract <18 > v.: [1] Adilabad. [2] Anantapur. [3] Chittoor. [4] Cuddapah. [5] East Godavari. [6] Guntur. [8] Karimnagar. [9] Khammam. [10] Krishna. [11] Kurnool. [12] Mahabubnagar. [13] Medak. [14] Nalgonda. [16] Nizamabad. [19] Srikakulam. [21] Vizianagaram. [22] Warangal. [23] West Godavari. LC Card 87-915009 DDC 304.6/0954/84021 19

1. Andhra Pradesh (India) - Census, 1981. 2. India - Census, 1981. I. India. Office of the Registrar General. II. India. Census Commissioner. III. India. Director of Census Operations, Andhra Pradesh. IV. Title: Bhārata kī janagaṇanā, 1981.

HA4587.A52 C46 1984

Census of India, 1981. Series 23, West Bengal. Delhi : Controller of Publications, <1985-[1987] > v. in : maps (some folded) ; 30 cm. Some vols. have text in English and Hindi. Some vols. have also title in Hindi: Bhārata kī janagaṇanā, 1981. Śṛṅkhalā 23, Paścima Bangāla. Issued by Director of Census Operations, West Bengal. CONTENTS. - -- pt. 2, special. Report and tables 5 per cent sample data -- pt. 3A & B. General economic tables (4 v.) -- pt. 4A. Social and cultural tables -- pt. 5A & B. Migration tables -- pt. 6 A & B. Fertility tables -- pt. 13. District census handbook. A-B. Village & town directory ; Village & townwise primary census abstract <4 > v.: [5] Calcutta, A&B. [11] Maldah <v. B > [12] Medinipur <v. B > [15] Puruliya <v. B > LC Card 87-915030 DDC 304.6/0954/14021 19

1. West Bengal (India) - Census, 1981. 2. India - Census, 1981. I. India. Director of Census Operations, West Bengal. II. Title: Bhārata kī janagaṇanā, 1981. Śṛṅkhalā 23, Paścima Bangāla.

HA4587.W47 C46 1985

Census of India, 1981. Series 13, Manipur. Delhi : Manager of Publications, Civil Line, <1985-1987 > v. in : ill., maps ; 29 cm. Issued by R.K. Birendra Singh, Director of Census Operations, Manipur. CONTENTS. - -- pt. 2B. Primary census abstract -- pt. 3A & B.-pt. 4A. General economic tables. Social and cultural tables (1 v.) -- pt. 5A & B. Migration tables -- 6A & B. Fertility tables -- pt. 13. District census handbook. A & B. Villige & town directory ; Village & townwise primary census abstract <2 > v.: [5] Manipur North. [8] Tengnoupal. LC Card 87-915019 DDC 304.6/0954/17021 19

1. Manipur (India) - Census, 1981. 2. India - Census, 1981. I. India. Director of Census Operations, Manipur.

HA4587.M36 C46 1985

Census of India, 1981. Household population by religion of head of household, up to C.D. block and town level, series 14, Meghalaya . New Delhi , 1986. iii, 70 p. ; LC Card 87-901361 DDC 304.6/0954/164021 19

HA4587.M43 H68 1986

Census of India, 1981. Household population by religion of head of household, upto C.D. block and town level, series 31, Mizoram . Delhi , 1986. xiii, 17 p. ; LC Card 87-900232 DDC 304.6/0954/166021 19

HA4587.M58 H68 1986

Census of India, 1981. Jilā janagaṇanā hastapustikā . [Lakhanaū] [1983] xi, 174, ii p., [5] folded leaves of plates : LC Card 86-903117

HA4587.J48 J55 1983

Census of India, 1981. Census monograph . (no. 1) Sinha, Sunil Kumar. Urban growth in India, 1951-81 . New Delhi , 1986. vi, 72 p. : LC Card 86-902819

HA4581.5 1981e

Census of laundry, cleaning and dyeing services, 1980. Sensus van wassery-, skoonmaak- en kleurdienste, 1980 =. Pretoria [1984?] xiv, 59 p., [1] folded leaf of plates : ISBN 0-621-08730-0 : LC Card 86-122444

HD9999.L383 S67 1984

A census of one billion people . International Seminar on China's 1982 Population Census (1982 : Peking, China) [Wanchai, Hongkong , Boulder, Colo. , 1986, c1987] 704 p., [4] leaves of plates : LC Card 87-2131 DDC 304.6/0723 19

HA4631.5 .I57 1982

Census of population and housing (1980). Evaluation and research reports. Programs to improve coverage in the 1980 census. 1980 census of population and housing. Evaluation and research reports. Programs to improve coverage in the 1980 census. Washington, D.C. : U. S. Dept. of Commerce, Bureau of the Census : For sale by the Supt. of Docs., U. S. G.P.O., [1987] 83 p. : forms ; 28 cm. Distributed to depository libraries in microfiche. "Issued January 1987." Includes bibliographies. "PHC80-E3." S/N 003-024-06237-2 Item 154 (microfiche) LC Card 87-601259

1. United States - Census, 20th, 1980 - Evaluation. I. United States. Bureau of the Census. II. Title. III. Title: Evaluation and research reports. IV. Title: Programs to improve coverage in the 1980 census.

HA201 1980aa

Census of population and housing, 1981. V. 3, General report. [Colombo] : Dept. of Census Statistics, Ministry of Plan Implementation, [1986] iv, 232 p. : ill., maps ; 29 cm. Cover title: Sri Lanka census of population and housing, 1981, general report, volume 3. LC Card 87-901055

1. Sri Lanka - Population - Statistics. 2. Housing - Sri Lanka - Statistics. 3. Sri Lanka - Census, 1981. I. Sri Lanka. Jalalēkhana hā Saṅkhyālēkhana Depārtamēntuva. II. Title: Sri Lanka census of population and housing 1981.

HA4570.8 .A4 1981c

Census of the motor trade and repair services, 1977. Sensus van motorhandel en hersteldienste, 1977 =. Pretoria [1982?] xiv, 166 p. : ISBN 0-621-07034-3 : LC Card 82-240419

HD9710.S72 S46 1982

Census of 1,000,000,000 people. International Seminar on China's 1982 Population Census (1982 : Peking, China) A census of one billion people . [Wanchai, Hongkong , Boulder, Colo. , 1986, c1987] 704 p., [4] leaves of plates : LC Card 87-2131 DDC 304.6/0723 19

HA4631.5 .I57 1982

Census of 1985 dry milk distribution & production trends / compiled by American Dry Milk Institute, Inc. Chicago, Ill. (130 N. Franklin St., Chicago 60606) : American Dairy Products Institute, c1986. 13 p. ; 28 cm. (Bulletin / American Dairy Products Institute . no. 1000) Cover title. Chiefly tables. LC Card 86-208490 DDC 338.1/77143/0973021 19

1. Dried milk industry - United States - Statistics. I. American Dry Milk Institute. II. Series: Bulletin / American Dairy Products Institute , no. 1000.

HD9282.U4 C463 1986

Census supplement (Ethiopia. Central Statistical Office) .

(1) Population of weredas and towns, by sex and average household size, based on the preliminary census results, and population projections by age, sex groups, and rural-urban, for total country and regions, 1984-1995 /. Addis Ababa [1985] 370 p. ; LC Card 86-980450 DDC 304.6/0963/021 19

HA4689 .P67 1985

Census, 1981. Jilā janagaṇanā hastapustikā . [Lakhanaū] [1983] xi, 174, ii p., [5] folded leaves of plates : LC Card 86-903117

HA4587.J48 J55 1983

Census '80 : income and poverty status report for regional planning districts. Baltimore, Md. (2225 N. Charles St., Baltimore 21218) : Regional Planning Council, [1983] xv, 106 leaves : ill. (some col.) ; 29 cm. "January 1983." "ERIS 83-02." LC Card 83-622347 DDC 339.2/2/097526 19

1. Income - Maryland - Baltimore Metropolitan Area - Statistics. 2. Poor - Maryland - Baltimore Metropolitan Area - Statistics. 3. Baltimore Metropolitan Area - Census. 4. United States - Census, 20th, 1980. I. Maryland. Regional Planning Council. II. Title: Census eighty. III. Title: Income and poverty status report for regional planning districts.

HC108.B2 C46 1983 ***NYPL [JLF 86-1594]***

Cent ans d'histoire du droit et d'histoire économique à la Faculté de droit et des sciences économiques de l'Université de Fribourg. Hundert Jahre Rechts- und Wirtschaftsgeschichte an der Rechts-, Wirtschafts- und Sozialwissenschaftlichen Fakultät der Universität Freiburg =. Freiburg, Schweiz , 1982. 96 p., [6] p. of plates : ISBN 3-7278-0277-4 : LC Card 83-108855 DDC 340 19

K296 .H86 1982 ***NYPL [JLD 86-676]***

Cent-cinquante meilleures entreprises françaises. 150 meilleures entreprises françaises /. Paris , c1986. 313 p. ; ISBN 2-234-01894-3 : LC Card 87-107207

HF5382.75.F8 A13 1986

Cent un réseaux urbains de transports collectifs : informations statistiques, évolution 1975-1981, situation 1981. [Paris] : Ministère des transports, Direction des transports terrestres, Service des transports urbains régionaux et départementaux, [1982] 48 p. : ill. ; 21 x 30 cm. "Décembre 1982." LC Card 83-227229

1. Local transit - France - Statistics. I. France. Service des transports urbains régionaux et départementaux.
HE4764 .C45 1982

Centar CK SKH za idejno-teorijski rad "Vladimir Bakarić." Društvena reprodukcija u djelu Vladimira Bakarića /. Zagreb , 1985 printing. 204 p. ; LC Card 86-233326
HD5650 .D68 1985

Centelleo de la industria en Panamá /. Correa V., Virgilio (Correa Vásquez) [Panama?] 1986 ([Panama, Panama] : Tall. Gráf. del Centro de Impresión Educativa) 279 p., [6] p. of plates : LC Card 87-404562 DDC 338.097287 19
HC147 .C67 1986

Centennial histories series.
Kincaid, William M. A history of the Oklahoma State University, College of Business Administration /. Stillwater, Okla. , c1987. x, 227 p. : ISBN 0-914956-31-0 LC Card 87-11046 DDC 650/.07/1176634 19
HF1134.O57 K55 1987

Center for Agriculture and Rural Development. Hackett, Judith C. Managing rural infrastructure . Lexington, Ky. , c1986. iii, 36 p. : ISBN 0-87292-070-4 (pbk.) : LC Card 87-404481 DDC 363/.0973 19
HD3888 .H27 1986

Center for Applied Economic Research. University. Kentucky. Ware, Ray M. Piggybacking--the federal-state collection act of 1972 /. Lexington, Ky. , 1980. ix leaves, 35 p. ;
NYPL [JLM 79-1230 no.10]

Center for Creative Leadership. Morrison, Ann M. Breaking the glass ceiling . Reading, Mass. , c1987. ix, 229 p. : ISBN 0-201-15787-X : LC Card 87-1853 DDC 658.4/09/024042 19
HD6054.4.U6 M67 1987

Center for Health Promotion and Education (U. S.) Violence Epidemiology Branch. Centers for Disease Control suicide surveillance . Atlanta, GA [1985] ii, 33 p. : LC Card 86-602520 DDC 362.2 19
HB1323.S82 U53 1985

Center for International Research (U. S.) Hobbs, Frank. Demographic estimates, projections, and selected social characteristics of the population of India /. Washington, D.C. [1986] vii, 148 p. : LC Card 87-601294 DDC 304.6/0954/021 19
HA4585 .H63 1986

Center for National Policy (U. S.) Dealing with farm sector debt . Washington, D.C. (317 Massachusetts Ave., N.E., Washington 20002) , c1986. 47 p. : LC Card 86-71068 DDC 332.7/1/0973 19
HD1440.U6 D4 1986

Center for Popular Economics (U. S.)
Economic report of the people /. Boston , c1986. xvii, 260 p. : ISBN 0-89608-315-2 (pbk.) : LC Card 85-30342 DDC 330.973/0927 19
HC106.8 .E29 1986 *NYPL [JLD 87-301]*

Folbre, Nancy. A field guide to the U. S. economy /. New York , c1987. 1 v. (various pagings) : ISBN 0-394-75047-0 (pbk.) : LC Card 86-42974 DDC 330.973 19
HC103 .F59 1987

Center for Southeast Asian Studies, Kyoto. see **Kyōto Daigaku. Tōnan Ajia Kenkyū Sentā.**

Center for Strategic and International Studies (Washington, D.C.) Shinn, William T., 1936- The decline of the Russian peasant household /. New York , 1987. xvii, 122 p. ; ISBN 0-275-92767-9 (alk. paper) LC Card 87-2554 DDC 338.1/0947 19
HD1992 .S4735 1987

Center for the Study of Foreign Affairs (U. S.)
Black labor unions in South Africa . Washington, D.C. , 1987. vi, 63 p. ; LC Card 86-600599 DDC 331.6/9/968 19
HD6870.5 .B53 1987

New dimensions in foreign economic policy . Washington, DC , 1986. xiii, 118 p. ; LC Card 86-600514 DDC 337.73 19
HF1410.5 .N488 1986

Center for the Study of Opposition in Poland. Twierdochlebow, W. J. Solidarność . Menlo Park, CA , 1985. 72, v leaves ; LC Card 86-221919 DDC 331.89/28238204/094382 19
HD5397.7.S512 1980 .G358 1985

Center for the Study of the Recent History of the United States (Iowa City, Iowa) Agricultural distress in the Midwest, past & present /. Iowa City , 1986. ix, 111 p. : ISBN 0-87414-049-8 : LC Card 86-29932 DDC 338.1/0977 19
HD1773.A3 A37 1986

Center for the Utilization of Federal Technology (U. S.) Directory of federal & state business assistance . Springfield, VA , c1986. xii, 159 p. : ISBN 0-934213-03-8 (pbk.) : LC Card 86-601675 DDC 353.0082/025 19
HC110.I53 D57 1986

Center for United Labor Action. Lapides, Kenneth. The battle of the boycott . New York, N.Y. , 1974. 22 p., [3] p. of plates : LC Card 87-125953 DDC 331.89/3 19
HD5325.C62 1972 .L36 1974

Center of Latin American Monetary Studies. see **Centro de Estudios Monetarios Latinoamericanos.**

Center of Planning and Economic Research. see **Kentron Programmatismou kai Oikonomikōn Ereunōn.**

Centers for Disease Control suicide surveillance : summary 1970-80 / Violence Epidemiology Branch, Center for Health Promotion and Education. Atlanta, GA : U. S. Dept. of Health and Human Services, Public Health Service, Centers for Disease Control, Center for Health Promotion and Education, [1985] ii, 33 p. : ill., 1 map ; 28 cm. Cover title. Caption title: Suicide surveillance report, United States, 1970-1980. "This report analyzes national vital statistics data from the National Center for Health Statistics on suicide deaths in the United States for the period 1970-1980"--P. [2] of cover. Distributed to depository libraries in microfiche. "Issued: March 1985." Includes bibliographies. Item 505-A-19 (microfiche) LC Card 86-602520 DDC 362.2 19
1. Suicide - United States - Statistics. I. Center for Health Promotion and Education (U. S.) Violence Epidemiology Branch. II. National Center for Health Statistics (U. S.). III. Title: Suicide surveillance. IV. Title: Suicide surveillance report, United States, 1970-1980.
HB1323.S82 U53 1985

Centocinquante ore e la formazione professionale in azienda. Le 150 ore e la formazione professionale in azienda . Milano, Italy , c1985. 178 p. : LC Card 86-141990
HD5716.T242 I82 1985
NYPL [JFD 87-3739]

Centrais Elétricas Brasileiras. see **Eletrobrás.**

Central African Republic. International Labour Organisation. Organisation de l'Institut national de formation et de perfectionnement professionnels de Bangui (INFPP) . Genève , 1980. 14 p. ; ISBN 92-2-202448-6 LC Card 82-214934
HD5716.M342 C335 1980

Central agencies, intergovernmental managers, and Australian federal-state relations /. Warhurst, John. Canberra , 1983. vi, 27 p. : ISBN 0-86784-318-7 (pbk.) LC Card 85-217351
JQ4020.S8 W28 1983
NYPL [JLL 82-87 no.29]

CENTRAL AMERICA - COMMERCE - UNITED STATES.
Mukerjee, Dilip. Lessons from the Caribbean Basin initiative /. Kuala Lumpur, Malaysia , c1985. 36 p. ; ISBN 967-99974-6-4 (pbk.) LC Card 87-101396 DDC 338.91/73/0729 19
HF1456.5.C27 M85 1985

CENTRAL AMERICA - ECONOMIC CONDITIONS.
Aguilera Peralta, Gabriel Edgardo. Raíces y perspectivas de la crisis económica /. San José, Costa Rica , 1986. 297 p. ; ISBN 997-7990-33-6 LC Card 87-404300 DDC 330.9728/053 19
HC141 .A63 1986

Lohmann, Jens. Den mellemamerikanske drøm . [Copenhagen] , c1984. 184 p. : ISBN 87-7456-194-4 LC Card 84-193120
HC141 .L64 1984

López, Roberto. Los orígenes económicos de la crisis en Centroamérica /. San José, Costa Rica [1986] 134 p. : LC Card 87-106423
HC141 .L67 1986

Mayorga Quirós, Román. El crecimiento desigual en Centroamérica (1950-2000) /. México, D.F. , 1983. 125 p. : ISBN 968-12-0238-4 LC Card 85-242511
HC141 .M39 1983

CENTRAL AMERICA - ECONOMIC CONDITIONS - 1979-
Leonard, H. Jeffrey. Natural resources and economic development in Central America . New Brunswick, N.J., U. S.A. , c1987. xxii, 279 p. : ISBN 0-88738-722-5 (pbk.) LC Card 87-10871 DDC 333.7/09728 19
HC141 .L44 1987

Matz, Manfred. Briefe aus Mittelamerika . Hameln , c1981. 59 p. : LC Card 83-204578
HC141 .M38 1981

Rivera, Eugenio. Centroamérica, política económica y crisis /. San José, Costa Rica , c1986. 201 p. : ISBN 997-7904-37-5 LC Card 87-404079 DDC 338.9728 19
HC141 .R58 1986

CENTRAL AMERICA - ECONOMIC CONDITIONS - REGIONAL DISPARITIES.
El Crecimiento desigual en Centroamérica, 1950-2000. [Buenos Aires, Argentina] [between 1982 and 1986] 133 leaves ; LC Card 86-200824
HC141 .C73 1982

CENTRAL AMERICA - ECONOMIC INTEGRATION.
El Crecimiento desigual en Centroamérica, 1950-2000. [Buenos Aires, Argentina] [between 1982 and 1986] 133 leaves ; LC Card 86-200824
HC141 .C73 1982

Esser, Klaus. Zentralamerika, USA, EG und Bundesrepublik Deutschland /. Berlin , 1987. xi, 137 p. : ISBN 3-88985-043-X LC Card 87-401334 DDC 337.1/728 19
HC141 .E86 1987

CENTRAL AMERICA - ECONOMIC POLICY.
Bulmer-Thomas, V. The political economy of Central America since 1920 /. Cambridge , New York , 1987. xxiii, 416 p. : ISBN 0-521-34284-8 LC Card 87-11779 DDC 338.9728 19
HC141 .B78 1987

Leonard, H. Jeffrey. Natural resources and economic development in Central America . New Brunswick, N.J., U. S.A. , c1987. xxii, 279 p. : ISBN 0-88738-722-5 (pbk.) LC Card 87-10871 DDC 333.7/09728 19
HC141 .L44 1987

Rivera, Eugenio. Centroamérica, política económica y crisis /. San José, Costa Rica , c1986. 201 p. : ISBN 997-7904-37-5 LC Card 87-404079 DDC 338.9728 19
HC141 .R58 1986

CENTRAL AMERICA - FOREIGN RELATIONS - 1979-
Esser, Klaus. Zentralamerika, USA, EG und Bundesrepublik Deutschland /. Berlin , 1987. xi, 137 p. : ISBN 3-88985-043-X LC Card 87-401334 DDC 337.1/728 19
HC141 .E86 1987

CENTRAL AMERICA - FOREIGN RELATIONS - UNITED STATES.
Barry, Tom, 1950- The soft war . New York , 1988. xv, 304 p. ; ISBN 0-8021-0003-1 LC Card 87-13238 DDC 338.91/73/0728 19
HC141 .B375 1988

Implications of population trends for U. S. foreign policy in Central America . Washington , 1984. iii, 16 p. : LC Card 86-602534 DDC 304.6/09728 19
HB3533 .I55 1984

Williams, Robert G. (Robert Gregory), 1948- Export agriculture and the crisis in Central America /. Chapel Hill , c1986. xvi, 257 p. : ISBN 0-8078-1693-0 LC Card 85-20978 DDC 382/.41/09728 19
HD9884.C352 W55 1986
NYPL [JLE 86-3412]

Central America - Government. see **Central America - Politics and government.**

CENTRAL AMERICA - HISTORY - 1951-
McCann, Thomas P. On the inside . Boston , c1987. p. cm. ISBN 0-933341-53-9 : LC Card 87-43040 DDC 338.7/634 19
HD9249.U6 M23 1987

CENTRAL AMERICA - POLITICS AND GOVERNMENT - 1979-
Esser, Klaus. Zentralamerika, USA, EG und Bundesrepublik Deutschland /. Berlin , 1987. xi, 137 p. : ISBN 3-88985-043-X LC Card 87-401334 DDC 337.1/728 19
HC141 .E86 1987

Williams, Robert G. (Robert Gregory), 1948- Export agriculture and the crisis in Central America /. Chapel Hill , c1986. xvi, 257 p. : ISBN 0-8078-1693-0 LC Card 85-20978 DDC 382/.41/09728 19
HD9884.C352 W55 1986 *NYPL [JLE 86-3412]*

CENTRAL AMERICA - POPULATION.
Diaz-Briquets, Sergio. Conflict in Central America . Washington, D.C. (777 14th St. NW, Washington 20005) , 1986. 16 p. : LC Card 87-401095 DDC 304.6/09728 19
HB3533 .D5 1986

Implications of population trends for U. S. foreign policy in Central America . Washington , 1984. iii, 16 p. : LC Card 86-602534 DDC 304.6/09728 19
HB3533 .I55 1984

Leonard, H. Jeffrey. Natural resources and economic development in Central America . New Brunswick, N.J., U. S.A. , c1987. xxii, 279 p. : ISBN 0-88738-722-5 (pbk.) LC Card 87-10871 DDC 333.7/09728 19
HC141 .L44 1987

Mayorga Quirós, Román. El crecimiento desigual en Centroamérica (1950-2000) /. México, D.F. , 1983. 125 p. : ISBN 968-12-0238-4 LC Card 85-242511
HC141 .M39 1983

Central America postal history. Central America postal history and a listing of prephilatelic postmarks =. New York [Yonkers, N.Y.?] , 1986. xiv, 142 p. : ISBN 0-912574-41-0 (pbk.) LC Card 87-402819 DDC 383/.49728 19
HE6674 .C46 1986

Central America postal history and a listing of prephilatelic postmarks = Centro América historia postal y catálogo de marcas prefilatélicas / Leo J. Harris, editor.Paperback English ed. New York : Collectors Club ; [Yonkers, N.Y.?] : Federación Interamericana de Filatelia, 1986. xiv, 142 p. : ill. ; 23 cm. English text with notes and captions also in Spanish. Spine title: Central America postal history. Bibliography: p. 133-135. Includes index. ISBN 0-912574-41-0 (pbk.) LC Card 87-402819 DDC 383/.49728 19
1. Postal service - Central America - History. 2. Postmarks - Central America - History. I. Harris, Leo J. II. Collectors Club (New York, N.Y.). III. Federación Interamericana de Filatelia. IV. Title: Centro América historia postal y catálogo de marcas prefilatélicas. V. Title: Central America postal history.
HE6674 .C46 1986

CENTRAL AMERICA - RURAL CONDITIONS.
Brockett, Charles D., 1946- Land, power, and poverty . Boston , c1988. p. cm. ISBN 0-04-497027-7 LC Card 87-22746 DDC 338.1/09728 19
HD1797 .B76 1988

CENTRAL AMERICA - SOCIAL CONDITIONS.
Lohmann, Jens. Den mellemamerikanske drøm . [Copenhagen] , c1984. 184 p. : ISBN 87-7456-194-4 LC Card 84-193120
HC141 .L64 1984

CENTRAL AMERICA - SOCIAL CONDITIONS - 1979-
Matz, Manfred. Briefe aus Mittelamerika . Hameln , c1981. 59 p. : LC Card 83-204578
HC141 .M38 1981

Central American Program for Development of Social Sciences. see **Programa Centroamericano de Desarrollo de las Ciencias Sociales.**

Central Bank of Sri Lanka : functions and working. [Colombo] : The Bank, [1986] 238 p. : col. ill. ; 23 cm. LC Card 86-903712 DDC 332.1/1/095493 19
1. Sri Laṅkā Maha Bāṅkuva. 2. Banks and banking, Central - Sri Lanka. I. Sri Laṅkā Maha Bāṅkuva.
HG3270.8.A7 C47 1986

Central Bank of the Bahamas. Economic Intelligence Dept. A General information guide on the economy of the Bahamas /. Nassau, Bahamas [1986] x, 60 p. ; LC Card 87-400226 DDC 330.97296 19
HC152 .G46 1986

CENTRAL BANK OF THE GAMBIA.
Faal, A. A. Money and capital markets in the Gambia and United Kingdom, and the problem of economic management at central bank level . [S.l. , 198-] 27 leaves ; LC Card 87-400415 DDC 332.1/0966/51 19
HG187.5.G25 F3 1980z

Central Bank of the Philippines. Performance report, 1949-1954. [Manila, 1955] 39 p. illus. 23 cm. Cover title. LC Card 72-222290
HG3316 .A535

Central bankers, bureaucratic incentives, and monetary policy / edited by Eugenia Froedge Toma, Mark Toma. Dordrecht ; Boston : Martinus Nijhoff ; xiv, 251 p. : ill. ; 25 cm. (Financial and monetary policy studies. v. 13) Includes bibliographies. ISBN 90-247-3366-9 LC Card 86-12572 DDC 332.1/12/0973 19
1. Board of Governors of the Federal Reserve System (U. S.). 2. Monetary policy - United States. 3. Banks and banking, Central - Decision making. I. Toma, Mark. II. Toma, Eugenia Froedge.
HG2565 .C33 1986 *NYPL [JLE 87-394]*

CENTRAL BANKING. see **BANKS AND BANKING, CENTRAL.**

Central banking in Latin America /. Tamagna, Frank M. [Banca central en América Latina. English.] México , 1965. xii, 285 p. ; LC Card 87-403322 DDC 332.1/1/098 19
HG2710.5.A7 T3513 1965

CENTRAL BANKS. see **BANKS AND BANKING, CENTRAL.**

CENTRAL BUSINESS DISTRICTS - GERMANY (WEST) - CASE STUDIES.
Hall, Peter, 1931- Can rail save the city? . Aldershot, Hants , Brookfield, Vt., U. S.A. , c1985. xii, 241 p. : ISBN 0-566-00947-1 : LC Card 85-17659 DDC 388.4/2/0943 19
HE4774 .H35 1985 *NYPL [JLD 86-2622]*

CENTRAL BUSINESS DISTRICTS - GREAT BRITAIN - CASE STUDIES.
Hall, Peter, 1931- Can rail save the city? . Aldershot, Hants , Brookfield, Vt., U. S.A. , c1985. xii, 241 p. : ISBN 0-566-00947-1 : LC Card 85-17659 DDC 388.4/2/0943 19
HE4774 .H35 1985 *NYPL [JLD 86-2622]*

CENTRAL BUSINESS DISTRICTS - MANITOBA - WINNIPEG.
Downtown and regional shopping centre retailing in Winnipeg /. Winnipeg, Man., Canada , 1985. x, 90, [8] p. : ISBN 0-920213-22-7 (pbk.) LC Card 86-137592 DDC 381/.1/0971274 19
HF5429.6.C3 D69 1985 *NYPL [JLF 86-1331]*

Central city terminus . Pearson, Charles, 1794-1862. [S.l.] 1845 (London : Richard and John E. Taylor) 20 p. ; LC Card 85-666155
HE3019.L8 P42x 1845

Central Committee of California Oil Producers. see **Conservation Committee of California Oil Producers.**

Central Cooperative Union, Sofia. see **Tsentralen kooperativen si͡uz.**

Central Cotton Research Institute, Multan.
Galal, M. F. Pakistan . Rome [i.e. Multan] , 1978. vii, 36 p. ; LC Card 83-931176
HD9086.P32 G35 1978

Central Council for Agricultural and Horticultural Co-operation. Gasson, Ruth M. Labour sharing in agriculture /. [London] [1979] 117 p. ; ISBN 0-901859-82-6 (pbk.) LC Card 83-226074 DDC 331.25/72 19
HD5119.A292 G744 1979

Central Council of Hungarian Trade Unions. see **Szakszervezetek Országos Tanácsa.**

Central Council of the Trade Unions (Hungary) see **Szakszervezetek Országos Tanácsa.**

CENTRAL DE ABASTECIMENTO DE GÊNEROS ALIMENTÍCIOS DA REGIÃO METROPOLITANA DE FORTALEZA.
Reestudo da parte de cereais e estivas relacionado com a viabilidade técnico-econômico-financeira da Central de Abastecimento de Gêneros Alimentícios da Região Metropolitana de Fortaleza. [Fortaleza] , 1973. 72 leaves : LC Card 82-147387
HD9014.B83 F587 1973

CENTRAL DE TRABAJADORES DE CUBA - HISTORY.
Córdova, Efrén. Castro and the Cuban labor movement . Lanham, MD , c1987. xii, 341 p. ; ISBN 0-8191-5952-2 (alk. paper) : LC Card 86-28159 DDC 322/.2/097291 19
HD6578.5 .C67 1987

Central El Palmar (Caracas, Venezuela)
Quintas reuniones técnicas de información, evaluación y perspectivas de las empresas /. [Caracas, Venezuela] [1984?] 245 p. : LC Card 87-404408 DDC 338.8/6/09877 19
HD2843.Z75 C467 1984

CENTRAL EL PALMAR (CARACAS, VENEZUELA) - MANAGEMENT.
Quintas reuniones técnicas de información, evaluación y perspectivas de las empresas /. [Caracas, Venezuela] [1984?] 245 p. : LC Card 87-404408 DDC 338.8/6/09877 19
HD2843.Z75 C467 1984

CENTRAL EUROPE - COMMERCE - AUSTRIA - HISTORY - 18TH CENTURY - SOURCES.
Prokopp, Ludwig Ferdinand. Europäische Commerzreisen um die Mitte des 18. Jahrhunderts /. Linz , c1982. xiii, 446 p., [1] folded leaf of plates : ISBN 3-85320-296-1 LC Card 83-150921
HF3548.C36 P76 1982

CENTRAL EUROPE - COMMERCE - HISTORY.
Der Handel des frühen Mittelalters . Göttingen , 1985. 510 p. : ISBN 3-525-82433-5 (Deut. Bibl.) LC Card 86-209040
HF3495 .U57 1985 t. 3

CENTRAL EUROPE - COMMERCIAL POLICY - HISTORY - CONGRESSES.
Städtewesen und Merkantilismus in Mitteleuropa /. Köln , 1983. xii, 333 p. : ISBN 3-412-00382-4 LC Card 83-155285
HF1531 .S688 1983

CENTRAL EUROPE - DESCRIPTION AND TRAVEL - SOURCES.
Prokopp, Ludwig Ferdinand. Europäische Commerzreisen um die Mitte des 18. Jahrhunderts /. Linz , c1982. xiii, 446 p., [1] folded leaf of plates : ISBN 3-85320-296-1 LC Card 83-150921
HF3548.C36 P76 1982

CENTRAL EUROPE - ECONOMIC CONDITIONS.
Festschrift für Univ.-Prof. Dr. Georg Zwanowetz anlässlich der Vollendung des 65. Lebensjahres /. [Innsbruck] , c1984. 332 p. : LC Card 84-183487
HC244 .F48 1984

Paskaleva-Zakharieva, Virzhinii͡a. Sredna Evropa i zemite po Dolnii͡a Dunav prez XVIII-XIX v. . Sofii͡a , 1986. 317 p. : LC Card 86-219994
HC244 .P29 1986

CENTRAL EUROPE - ECONOMIC CONDITIONS - CONGRESSES.
Methoden der Politikberatung im wirtschaftspolitischen Bereich /. Wien , 1984. 116 p. ; LC Card 84-222756
HC265 .M39 1984

CENTRAL EUROPE - INDUSTRIES.
Seidenfus, Hellmuth Stefan. Die Bedeutung der Seehäfen für die Industrialisierung Mitteleuropas /. Göttingen , 1979. 20 p. ; ISBN 3-525-85769-1 LC Card 86-194319
HE131 .M84 Heft 18 HE557.A3

CENTRAL EUROPE - SOCIAL CONDITIONS.
Paskaleva-Zakharieva, Virzhinii͡a. Sredna Evropa i zemite po Dolnii͡a Dunav prez XVIII-XIX v. . Sofii͡a , 1986. 317 p. : LC Card 86-219994
HC244 .P29 1986

The central Florida career guide /. Fencl, George. Altamonte Springs, FL. , c1987. 56, 48 p. : ISBN 0-942827-00-7 (pbk.) : LC Card 87-402073 DDC 650.1/4/09759 19
HF5382.75.U62 F64 1987

Central Globo de Comercialização. Divisão de Marketing. Atlas de cobertura 1985/86. [Rio de Janeiro] [1985?] ca. 100 p. : LC Card 86-201241
HE8700.66.B7 A74 1985

Central government expenditure . Reddy, K. N. (Kaipa Narayana), 1936- New Delhi , 1984. xvi, 175 p. ; LC Card 84-901866 DDC 336.3/9/0954 19
HJ2157 .R43 1984 *NYPL [JLD 87-66]*

CENTRAL HEATING PLANTS. see **HEATING FROM CENTRAL STATIONS.**

Central Illinois Light Company (East Peoria, Ill.) Urban Land Institute. R.S. Wallace Station, East Peoria, Illinois . Washington, D.C. (1090 Vermont Ave., N.W., Washington 20005) , c1986. 36 p. : LC Card 86-216045 DDC 333.77/17/0977352 19
HD268.E26 U73 1986

Central Industrial Region. Morrison, Daniel, 1945- "Trading peasants" and urbanization in eighteenth-century Russia . New York , 1987. 415 p. ; ISBN 0-8240-8059-9 (alk. paper) : LC Card 87-7425 DDC 307.2 19
HB2068.S65 M67 1987

Central Institute for Research and Training in Employment Service (India) Workshop on Promotion of Self-Employment in Rural Areas (1982 : Allahabad, India) Workshop on Promotion of Self-employment in Rural Areas, Allahabad, 26-30 November 1982 . New Delhi [1983] iii, 186 p. ; LC Card 83-906671 DDC 338.6/42 19
HD8037.I4 W67 1982

Central Java develops, 1979-1980. Jawa Tengah membangun =. [Semarang] [1985] iii, 37 leaves : LC Card 86-943679
HC437.J39 J39 1985

CENTRAL LATINOAMERICANO DE TRABAJADORES - CONGRESSES.
Máspero, Emilio. Informe político y de orientación ante el VIIIo Congreso de la CLAT . [Caracas] , 1983. 122 p. : LC Card 87-403072 DDC 305.5/62/098 19
HD8110.5.A5 C466 1983

CENTRAL-LOCAL GOVERNMENT RELATIONS - UGANDA.
Bunker, Stephen G., 1944- Double dependency and constraints on class formation in Bugisu, Uganda /. Urbana, Ill. , 1983. v, 88 p. : LC Card 86-229748 DDC 303.3/09676/1 19
HD1538.U43 B86 1983

CENTRAL OBRERA BOLIVIANA - CONGRESSES.
Tendencias sindicales después del VI Congreso de la C.O.B. /. La Paz , c1985. 111 p. ; LC Card 86-137172
HD8272.C65 T45 1985

CENTRAL PLACES.
Rizzieri, Juarez Alexandre Baldini. Desenvolvimento econômico e urbanização . São Paulo , 1982. 219 p. : LC Card 83-150574 DDC 330.9173/2 19
HT321 .R59 1982 *NYPL [JLD 86-3817]*

CENTRAL PLACES - GERMANY (WEST) - MIESBACH.
Gräf, Peter. Zur Raumrelevanz infrastruktureller Massnahmen . Kallmünz/Regensburg , 1978. xxxvii, 259 p., [9] leaves of plates (7 folded) : ISBN 3-7847-6518-1 LC Card 85-205909
HC281 .M8 Bd. 18 HC288.M53

CENTRAL PLACES - HUNGARY - STATISTICS.
Budapest és a jelentősebb városok napi munkaerővonzási körzete népességének főbb jellemzői, 1980. január 1. /. Budapest , 1986. 106 p. : ISBN 963-02-4578-7 LC Card 87-407674
HA1205 .B83 1986

CENTRAL PLANNING.
Bokros, Lajos. Piac és pénz a modern gazdaságban /. Budapest , 1985. 340, [1] p. ; ISBN 963-221-551-6 : LC Card 86-185991
HB95 .B65 1985

Ficzere, Lajos. A gazdaság irányításának jellege, az irányítás szervezete, eszközei és módszerei /. Budapest , 1984. 112 p. ; ISBN 963-02-3265-0 (Magy. nemz. bibl.) LC Card 85-130150
HD87.5 .F53 1984

Hartwig, Karl-Hans. Monetäre Steuerungsprobleme in sozialistischen Planwirtschaften /. Stuttgart , New York , 1987. vi, 146 p. ; ISBN 3-437-50295-6 LC Card 87-136038 DDC 339.5/3/0947 19
HG925 .H37 1987

Nörenberg, Günther. Planwirtschaft im Zerrspiegel des Linksradikalismus /. Berlin , 1984. 108 p. ; LC Card 84-196372
HC59 .N652 1984

Sachs, Ignacy. [Développer les champs de planification. English.] Development and planning /. Cambridge [Cambridgeshire] ; New York : ix, 134 p. ; ISBN 0-521-33454-3 LC Card 87-11780 DDC 338.9 19
HD82 .S23313 1987

Zur Interdependenz von Unternehmens- und Wirtschaftsordnung /. Stuttgart , New York , 1986. x, 280 p. ; ISBN 3-437-50296-4 LC Card 87-134241 DDC 338.9 19
HB95 .Z87 1986

CENTRAL PLANNING - BURKINA FASO.
Conseil national de la révolution (Burkina Faso) Programme populaire de développement, octobre 1984 décembre 1985 /. [Ouagadougou, Burkina Faso] [1985?] 1 v. (various pagings) : LC Card 87-160992
HC1040 .C66 1985

Conseil national de la révolution (Burkina Faso) Programme populaire de développement, octobre 1984-décembre 1985 . [Ouagadougou] [1986] 2 v. : LC Card 87-158925
HC1040 .C66 1986

CENTRAL PLANNING - COMMUNIST COUNTRIES.
Die Übergangsperiode . [Leipzig] , 1986. 80 p. ; LC Card 87-407523 DDC 338.9/009171/7 19
HC704 .U24 1986

CENTRAL PLANNING - CUBA.
Cuba's socialist economy toward the 1990s /. Boulder, Colo. , 1987. ix, 188 p. : ISBN 1-555-87080-5 (lib. bdg. : alk. paper) : LC Card 87-12867 DDC 338.97291 19
HC152.5 .C824 1987

El Sistema de dirección y planificación de la economía en las empresas. La Habana , 1981. xi, 203 p. : LC Card 83-212653
HC152.5 .S57 1981

CENTRAL PLANNING - CZECHOSLOVAKIA.
Fusko, Zoltán. Koncepcia ďalšieho rozvoja plánovitého riadenia efektívneho využívania pracovnej sily . Bratislava , 1982. 62 p. ; LC Card 83-113861
HD5772.3.A6 F87 1982

Klusoň, Václav. Teoretické otázky formování plánovitého řízení národního hospodářství ČSSR /. Praha , 1986- v. <1 > ; LC Card 87-167771
HC270.28 .K58 1986

Planomernoe razvitie sotsialisticheskoĭ ėkonomiki /. Moskva , Bratislava , 1977. 262 p. ; LC Card 87-100683
HC336.25 .P448 1977

CENTRAL PLANNING - DEVELOPING COUNTRIES - MATHEMATICAL MODELS.
Martens, André. La planification économique du développement . Montréal [1982] 2 v. : LC Card 83-178486
HC59.7 .M323 1982

CENTRAL PLANNING - EUROPE, EASTERN.
Soós, Károly Attila. Terv, kampány, pénz . Budapest , 1986. 532 p. : ISBN 963-221-575-3 : LC Card 87-137237
HB3787.5 .S66 1986

Sovershenstvovanie sistemy narodnokhoziaĭstvennogo upravleniia v sotsialisticheskikh stranakh . Moskva , 1986. 196 p. ; LC Card 87-163453
HC244 .S595115 1986

Winiecki, Jan. The distorted world of Soviet type economies /. Pittsburgh, Pa. , 1988. p. cm. ISBN 0-8229-1149-3 LC Card 87-25193 DDC 338.947 19
HC244 .W573 1988

CENTRAL PLANNING - EUROPE, EASTERN - ECONOMETRIC MODELS - CONGRESSES.
Macromodels and forecasts of national economy . Warszawa , 1986. 284 p. : ISBN 83-01-06464-1 (pbk.) : LC Card 86-226942 DDC 338.947 19
HC244 .M227 1986

CENTRAL PLANNING - FRANCE.
Bauchet, Pierre. Le plan dans l'économie française /. Paris , c1986. 246 p. : ISBN 2-7246-0532-2 : LC Card 86-223474
HC276.2 .B292 1986

CENTRAL PLANNING - GERMANY (EAST)
Mit qualitativ neuen Schritten zu höchsten Leistungen . Berlin , 1986. 80 p. ; ISBN 3-320-00807-2 LC Card 87-144292 DDC 338.9431 19
HC290.78 .M567 1986

Otto, Wolfgang, Diplom-Staatswissenschaftler. Ökonomische Strategie und volkswirtschaftliche Masseninitiative /. Berlin , 1984. 61 p. : LC Card 85-189271
HC290.78 .O88 1984

Produktion, Intensivierung, Effektivität /. Jena , 1978. 180 p. : LC Card 85-183724
HC290.795.I52 P75 1978

Waterkamp, Rainer. Das zentralstaatliche Planungssystem der DDR . Berlin , c1983. 194 p. : ISBN 3-428-05405-9 LC Card 83-217231
HC290.78 .W38 1983

CENTRAL PLANNING - GERMANY (EAST) - ECONOMETRIC MODELS.
Collier, Irwin L., 1951- Connections, effective purchasing power, and real product in the German Democratic Republic /. Berlin , 1985. ix, 216 p. : ISBN 3-921374-34-0 (pbk.) LC Card 86-229298 DDC 330 s 338.9431/00724 19
HC244.A1 B4 Nr. 44 HC290.78

CENTRAL PLANNING - HUNGARY.
A Gazdaságirányítás és a szakszervezetek /. Budapest , 1985. 191 p. ; ISBN 963-322-253-2 : LC Card 86-104573
HC300.28 .G349 1985

Gazdaságirányítás, 1985 /. Budapest , 1984. 175 p. ; ISBN 963-221-540-0 : LC Card 85-229856
HC300.28 .G338 1984

Nyitrai, Ferencné. Prioritások gazdaságunk fejlesztésében /. [Budapest] , 1986. 270 p. ; ISBN 963-09-2782-9 : LC Card 87-408568
HC300.28 .N954 1986

La Voie hongroise . [Paris] , c1986. 319 p. : ISBN 2-7021-1378-8 : LC Card 86-221784
HC300.28 .V65 1986

CENTRAL PLANNING - HUNGARY - HISTORY.
Vigvári, András. A gazdaságirányítási rendszer egyes kérdései, elmélettörténeti megközelítésben /. [Budapest] , 1985. 87 p. ; ISBN 963-673-302-3 LC Card 85-231820
HC300.28 .V53 1985

CENTRAL PLANNING - HUNGARY - MATHEMATICAL MODELS.
Kovács, Kálmán. Tervezési szintek érdekeltségének összehangolása gazdaságszabályozási eszközökkel . Budapest , 1984. 50 p. : ISBN 963-491-189-7 LC Card 86-198789
HD1940.5.Z8 K68 1984

CENTRAL PLANNING - INDIA.
Venkateswaran, R. J. Decision-making in Indian economy . Bombay , 1986. vii, 199 p. ; LC Card 86-902861 DDC 338.954 19
HC435.2 .V457 1986

CENTRAL PLANNING - MATHEMATICAL MODELS.
Opyt razrabotki i realizatsii sistemy ukrupnennykh modeleĭ perspektivnogo planirovaniia /. Moskva , 1984. 216 p. : LC Card 85-199888
HD75.5 .O69 1984

CENTRAL PLANNING - NICARAGUA.
Bereciuk, Román M. Introducción en la teoría de la planificación de la economía nacional /. [Managua] , 1986. 93 leaves ; LC Card 87-403888 DDC 338.97285 19
HC146 .B47 1986

CENTRAL PLANNING - ROMANIA.
Romania from the perspective opened by the 1986-1990 five-year plan. Bucharest [1986?] iii, 119 p. ; LC Card 87-124268 DDC 338.9498 19
HC405 .R563 1986

CENTRAL PLANNING - RUSSIAN S.F.S.R. - TIKHVIN REGION.
Dolgosrochnoe sotsial′no-ėkonomicheskoe

planirovanie /. Leningrad , 1986. 165 p. : LC Card 87-146872
HC338.T5 D65 1986

CENTRAL PLANNING - SOVIET UNION.
Aktual'nye problemy planomernogo razvitiia narodnogo khoziaistva /. Moskva , 1980. 247 p. ; LC Card 81-131558
HC336.25 .A455 1980

Braginskiĭ, L. V. (Lev Vol'fovich) Ėffektivnost' kapital'nykh vlozheniĭ i bankovskaia deiatel'nost' /. Moskva , 1981. 186 p. ; LC Card 82-144216
HG186.S55 B72 1981

Chistiakov, E. G. (Evgeniĭ Gavrilovich) Metody sochetaniia otraslevogo i territorial'nogo planirovaniia /. Moskva , 1982. 147, [3] p. : LC Card 82-189489
HC336.25 .C516 1982

Efimov, A. N. (Anatoliĭ Nikolaevich) Problemy obosnovaniia gosudarstvennogo plana /. Moskva , 1980. 197, [3] p. ; LC Card 81-135658
HC336.25 .E346 1980

Ėkonomicheskie sviazi i sovershenstvovanie khoziaistvennogo mekhanizma . Kursk , 1985. 107 p. ; LC Card 86-235039
HC340.I57 E37 1985

Granick, David. Job rights in the Soviet Union . Cambridge , New York , 1987. ix, 344 p. ; ISBN 0-521-33295-8 LC Card 86-26392 DDC 331.11/0947 19
HD5796 .G72 1987

Guber, A. A. (Aleksandr Andreevich) Industry /. Moscow , 1985. 46 p., [16] p. of plates : LC Card 86-208070 DDC 338.947 19
HC336.25 .G8 1985

Kuromiya, Hiroaki. Stalin's industrial revolution . Cambridge [Cambridgeshire] , New York , 1988. p. cm. ISBN 0-521-35157-X LC Card 87-25010 DDC 338.947 19
HC335.4 .K87 1988

Martyniuk, S. M. (Stanislav Mikhaĭlovich) Planomernost' i ėffektivnost' sotsialisticheskogo obshchestvennogo proizvodstva /. Kiev , 1982. 141 p. ; LC Card 83-219823
HC335 .M3675 1982

Planomernoe razvitie sotsialisticheskoĭ ėkonomiki /. Moskva , Bratislava , 1977. 262 p. ; LC Card 87-100683
HC336.25 .P448 1977

Sovershenstvovanie proizvodstvennykh otnosheniĭ sotsializma /. Moskva , 1986. 203 p. ; ***NYPL [*QIP 87-2800]***

The Soviet economy on the brink of reform . Boston , 1988. p. cm. ISBN 0-04-335063-1 (alk. paper) LC Card 87-19514 DDC 338.947 19
HC335 .C626 1988

Tesler, Edward. Soviet economic planning . Falls Church, VA (7700 Leesburg Pike, #250, Falls Church 22043) , c1986. ix, 88 leaves : LC Card 87-403383 DDC 338.947 19
HC335 .T425 1986

CENTRAL PLANNING - SOVIET UNION - HISTORY.
Rukopozhatie piatiletok /. Moskva , 1981. 237 p. : LC Card 82-103792
HC335 .R76 1981

Strumilin, S. G. (Stanislav Gustavovich), 1877-1974. Na planovom fronte /. Moskva , 1980. 463 p. ; LC Card 81-135522
HC335.2 .S83 1980

CENTRAL PLANNING - SOVIET UNION - MATHEMATICAL MODELS.
Sheviakov, Alekseĭ IUr'evich. Modelirovanie sbalansirovannosti i soglasovaniia planovykh resheniĭ v sfere narodnogo blagosostoianiia /. Moskva , 1986. 211 p. : LC Card 86-177908
HC336.25 .S525 1986

Zauberman, Alfred. Planning under indeterminacy /. Bielefeld, Federal Republic of Germany [1976] 153, 5 p. ; LC Card 85-127554
HC336.25 .Z38 1976

CENTRAL PLANNING - TURKEY.
Planned development in Turkey and the State Planning Organization. [Ankara] [1986] 47 p. : LC Card 87-151757 DDC 338.9561 19
HC492 .P63 1986

The Central south region statistical tables, 1960/61 to 1973/74. [Perth] : Dept. of Industrial Development, Research Section, [1976] 188 p. ; 34 cm. Cover title. "September 1976." LC Card 84-255738 DDC 330.9941/063/021 19
1. Western Australia - Economic conditions - Statistics. I. Western Australia. Dept. of Industrial Development. Research Section.
HC607.W47 C448 1976

CENTRAL STATION HEATING. see **HEATING FROM CENTRAL STATIONS.**

Central taxation of income in India since 1951 . Mittal, Satya Narayan, 1947- Delhi , New Delhi , 1986. 321 p. ; ISBN 81-7018-327-8 : LC Card 86-902918 DDC 336.24/0954 19
HJ4766 .M58 1986

The Central Workers' Circle of St. Petersburg, 1889-1894 . Share, Michael. New York , 1987. xi, 396 p., [6] p. of plates : ISBN 0-8240-8063-7 (alk. paper) : LC Card 87-374 DDC 305.5/62/0947453 19
HD8522.T753 S53 1987

Centrales nucleares en España . Costa Morata, Pedro. Madrid [1987?] 51 p. : ISBN 84-398-8834-1 LC Card 87-165955
HD9698.S72 C62 1987

CENTRALIZATION IN GOVERNMENT. see **DECENTRALIZATION IN GOVERNMENT.**

CENTRALIZATION IN MANAGEMENT. see **DECENTRALIZATION IN MANAGEMENT.**

Centre de perfectionnement et de formation en cours d'emploi (Bujumbura, Burundi) Comment acheter, produire et vendre dans les entreprises africaines . [Bujumbura?] [1984 or 1985] 122 p. : LC Card 85-981488
HD29 .C624 1984

Formation des cadres supérieurs féminins / République du Burundi, Ministère de la fonction publique, Centre de perfectionnement et de formation en cours d'emploi, 1983. [Bujumbura?] : Programme des Nations Unies pour le développement, 1983. 2 v. : ill. ; 29 cm. Bibliography: v. 2, p. 178. CONTENTS. - [1] Cours initial -- [2] Cours final. LC Card 87-104998
1. Women executives - Training of - Burundi. 2. Women in management - Burundi. I. Title.
HD6054.4.B94 C46 1983

Gahungu, Fidèle. Document d'initiation à l'informatique des organisations /. [Bujumbura?] [1983- v. <1> : LC Card 86-980527
HD30.2 .G34 1983

Centre de perfectionnement et de formation en cours d'emploi (Burundi) Simard, Jean-Guy. Comptabilité analytique /. [Bujumbura?] [1983] 120 p. : LC Card 85-981500
HF5642 .S54 1983

[Publication] see **Besançon, France. Université. Annales littéraires.**

[Publication] see **Besançon, France. Université. Annales littéraires.**

Centre de recherches en économie appliquée (Algiers, Algeria) Les Modèles de consommation et les politiques alimentaires dans les pays du Maghreb . Alger [1985?] 401 p. : LC Card 87-132818
HD9017.A24 M63 1985

Centre de recherches et d'études sur les sociétés méditerranéennes. Bernard, Chantal. La politique de l'emploi-formation au Maghreb, 1970-1980 /. Paris , 1982. 472 p. ; ***NYPL [JLE 86-568]***

Centre de recherches pour le développement international. see **International Development Research Centre.**

Centre de Treball i Documentació (Barcelona, Spain) Terra, treball i propietat . Barcelona , c1986. 346 p. ; ISBN 84-7423-287-2 LC Card 86-216973
HD2025.C35 T47 1986

Centre départemental de documentation pédagogique de la Réunion. L'Habitat réunionnais /. Saint-Denis [1983] 73 p., A-T leaves of plates : LC Card 84-981007
HD7378.9.A3 H33 1983

Centre d'Estudis de l'Hospitalet (Series) .
(3) Massana i Llorens, Ma. Pilar. L'Hospitalet a l'inici del S. XVIII . L'Hospitalet de Llobregat , 1985. 116 p. : LC Card 86-230458
HD779.H67 M37 1985

Centre d'Estudis Urbanístics, Municipals i Territorials (Barcelona, Spain) Manual de servicios municipales . Barcelona , 1982. 340 p. ; ISBN 84-500-5399-4 LC Card 82-214246 DDC 363/.0946 19
HD4687 .M36 1982 ***NYPL [JLC 86-139]***

Centre d'étude du commerce et de la distribution. (Old Catalog form: France. Centre d'Étude du Commerce et de la Distribution) Dix années d'espaces-piétons . Paris [1984] 191 p. : ISBN 2-85723-124-5 LC Card 85-104132
HE336.P43 D59 1984

Centre d'études, de recherches et de formation institutionnelles du Sud-Est (France) Legay, Marie-Agnès. Réduction de la durée du travail et changement des modes de vie . Aix-en-Provence [1984] ix, 366 p. : LC Card 86-185902
HD6066.F8 L44 1984

Centre d'études des revenus et des coûts. Constat de l'évolution récente des revenus en France . Paris [1984] 220 p. : LC Card 85-127672
HC280.I5 C67 1984

Centre d'études des transports urbains. Les Rues mixtes . [Bagneux] [1982] 40 p. : ISBN 2-11-083325-4 : LC Card 84-104398
HE363.F72 P437 1982

Centre d'études économiques et sociales du pays de Rennes. Elections prud'homales . Rennes [1983] 92 p. : LC Card 85-136661
HD5554.A3 E44 1983

Centre d'études européennes de Waterloo. L'Information financière . Bruxelles , 1983. 220 p. ; ISBN 2-8027-0298-X LC Card 84-104169
HG151.5 .I56 1983

Centre d'études prospectives et d'informations internationales (France) Economie mondiale 1980-1990, la fracture? . Paris , c1984. x, 406 p. : ISBN 2-7178-0803-5 : LC Card 85-105930
HC59 .E384 1984

Centre d'histoire contemporaine du Languedoc méditerranéen et du Roussillon. Mélanges Robert Laurent . Montpellier , 1980. xxi, 296 p. : LC Card 83-151672
HC273 .M43 1980

Centre européen de coordination de recherche et de documentation en sciences sociales. see **European Centre for the Co-ordination of Research and Documentation in Social Sciences.**

Centre européen de l'entreprise publique. Seminario sobre Consequencias para las Entidades Oficiales de Crédito de la Entrada de España en las Comunidades Europeas (1984 : Madrid, Spain) Seminario sobre Consequencias para las Entidades Oficiales de Crédito de la Entrada de España en las Comunidades Europeas /. [Madrid] [1984?] 270 p. ; ISBN 84-505-0963-7 LC Card 85-186710
HG1642.E86 S46 1984

Centre for Business Research (Manchester, Greater Manchester) Ohinata, Yo. The lending procedures of commercial banks in the United States, the United Kingdom, Japan, Germany and France /. [Manchester] [1983] 138 p. ; ISBN 0-903808-34-X (pbk.) LC Card 86-132282 DDC 332.1/753 19
HG1642.U5 O35 1983

Centre for Economic Policy Research (Great Britain) Natural resources and the macroeconomy /. Oxford, UK , 1986. xvi, 352 p. : ISBN 0-631-15087-0 LC Card 86-673943
HC59 .N3194x 1986b

Centre for Employment Initiatives (Great Britain) Cooperation in the field of employment : local employment initiatives : report on a second series of local consultations held in European countries, 1984-1985 : final report / by the Centre for Employment Initiatives, London. Luxembourg : Office for Official Publications of the European Communities ; Washington, DC : European Community Information Service, 1986. 55 p. ; 30 cm. (Document / Commission of the European Communities) "Project manager: P. Kuenstler." At head of title: Commission of the European Communities. ISBN 92-825-6086-4 (pbk.) : LC Card 87-134296 DDC 331.12/042/094 19

1. Labor supply - Europe - Congresses. 2. Manpower policy - Europe - Congresses. I. Kuenstler, P. II. Commission of the European Communities. III. Series: Document / Commission of the European Communities. IV. Title.
HD5764.A6 C45 1986

Centre for European Policy Studies (Louvain-la-Neuve, Belgium) The Fight against unemployment . Cambridge, Mass. , 1987. xii, 204 p. : ISBN 0-262-12122-0 LC Card 87-5356 DDC 339.5/094 19
HD5764.A6 F54 1987

Centre for Middle Eastern and Islamic Studies) . Occasional papers series.
(no. 11) Seccombe, Ian J. Manpower and migration . [Durham, England] , c1981. viii, 110 p. : LC Card 84-673623
HD5812.25.A6 S42x 1981
NYPL [JLD 86-2457]

Centre for Public Sector Studies (India)
Government media and the public sector . New Delhi , 1983. 270 p. ; LC Card 83-907479 DDC 302.3/24/0954 19
HD59 .G62 1983 ***NYPL [JLD 86-3767]***

Centre for Research on European Women. The Viability of employment initiatives involving women . Luxembourg , Washington, DC , 1986. 1 v. (various pagings) ; ISBN 92-825-6088-0 (pbk.) : LC Card 87-137342 DDC 331.4/12/094 19
HD3423.5.E86 V5 1986

Centre français du commerce extérieur. Direction des produits agro-alimentaires. Pezet, P. (Pierre) Les opérateurs français du commerce international agro-alimentaire /. Paris , c1984. 85 p. : ISBN 2-279-52812-6 LC Card 85-136648 DDC 382/.456413/00944 19
HD9012.5 .P43 1984

Centre Guillaume Jacquemyns. La Statistique en France . Bruxelles [1980] 194 p. ; LC Card 84-147748
HA19 .S73 1980

Centre international de hautes études agronomiques méditerranéennes. Institut agronomique méditerranéen de Montpellier. see **Institut agronomique méditerranéen de Montpellier.**

Centre ivoirien de recherches économiques et sociales. A Critical appraisal of the economic and social conditions in the west African subregion /. [Lagos , 1979-1980] 10 v. : LC Card 87-159535 DDC 330.966 19
HC1000 .C75 1979

Centre national de la recherche scientifique (France)
Europe and the rise of capitalism /. Oxford [Oxfordshire] , New York, NY, USA , 1987. p. cm. ISBN 0-631-15006-4 : LC Card 87-12293 DDC 330.94 19
HC240.9.C3 E97 1987

The Foundations of Keynesian analysis . New York , 1988. xlvi, 267 p. ; ISBN 0-312-00985-2 : LC Card 87-13048 DDC 330.15/6 19
HB99.7 .F68 1988

Le Travail . Paris , c1986. iv, 370 p. ; ISBN 2-7178-1138-9 : LC Card 87-123294
HD8428 .T72 1986

Centre national de la recherche scientifique (France). Laboratoire associé 111. Les Phénomènes de "frontière" dans les pays tropicaux . Paris , 1981. vii, 456 p. : LC Card 83-122397
HD1131 .P47 1981

Centre on Transnational Corporations (United Nations)
Foreign direct investment in Latin America . New York , c1986. iv, 28 p ; ISBN 92-1-104189-9 (pbk.) LC Card 87-104207 DDC 332.6/73/098 19
HG5160.5.A3 F67 1986

Transnational corporations in South Africa and Namibia . New York , 1986-<1987. v. <1-2, 4 > ; ISBN 92-1-104190-2 (pbk. : set) LC Card 87-403059 DDC 338.8/8868 19
HD2922 .T72 1986

Centre régional de documentation pédagogique de Lyon. Transports et échanges . [Lyon] , 1979. 64 p. ; LC Card 80-125866
HE192.F8 T73 1979

Centre régional d'études et de documentation économiques. Trade unionism in the republic of Mali . [Lome, Togo] [1983] 78 p. : LC Card 87-107028 DDC 331.88/0966/23 19
HD8827.A5 U557 1983

Centre-state financial relations and finance commissions /. Gaur, Achal Kumar, 1959- Allahabad, India , 1985. x, 364 p. ; LC Card 85-904373 DDC 336.54 19
HJ1334 .G38 1985

Centre tricontinental (Louvain-la-Neuve, Belgium) La Politique agraire en Chine . Ottignies, Louvain-la-Neuve, Belgique [1981] 84 leaves ; LC Card 86-203953
HD926 .P65 1981

Centro América historia postal y catálogo de marcas prefilatélicas. Central America postal history and a listing of prephilatelic postmarks =. New York [Yonkers, N.Y.?] , 1986. xiv, 142 p. : ISBN 0-912574-41-0 (pbk.) LC Card 87-402819 DDC 383/.49728 19
HE6674 .C46 1986

Centro Andino de Acción Popular. Campesinado y organización en Esmeraldas /. [Quito, Ecuador?] [1986] 213 p. : LC Card 86-171561
HD1531.E2 C36 1986

Centro Argentino de Ingenieros. Hacia un planeamiento de la industria de la construcción en la Argentina /. Buenos Aires , 1943. 289 p. : LC Card 85-104409
HD9715.A72 H33 1943

CENTRO ARTÍSTICO E OPERÁRIO MARANHENSE - HISTORY.
Corrêa, Rossini. Mudança social no Nordeste . São Luís , 1986. 176 p., [6] p. of plates : LC Card 87-152221 DDC 322/.2/098121 19
HD8289.M37 C67 1986

Centro Brasileiro de Análise e Planejamento. Müller, Geraldo. Alimentação e agricultura no Brasil . [São Paulo] , 1984. 64 p. : LC Card 86-132127
HD1872 .M85 1984

A Renda da terra . [São Paulo, Brazil] , Petrópolis , c1980. 152 p. : LC Card 81-214665
HC186 .C36a no. 27 HB401

Centro de Capacitación para el Desarrollo (San José, Costa Rica)
Guadamuz López, Ernesto. La política agraria actual . San José, Costa Rica , 1986. 33 p. ; LC Card 87-402782 DDC 338.1/87286 19
HD1803 .G83 1986

Historia gráfica de las luchas populares en Costa Rica, 1870-1930. San José, Costa Rica , 1986- v. <1 > : ISBN 997-7944-12-1 (v. 1) LC Card 87-158835 DDC 305.5/62/097286 19
HD8138 .H57 1986

Centro de Desenvolvimento Cívico e Municipal do IBAM. Encontro de Trabalho sobre Descentralização dos Serviços Municipais (1983 : Rio de Janeiro, Brazil) Relatório final /. [Rio de Janeiro] [1983] 60 leaves ; LC Card 84-160735
HD4634 .E53 1983

Centro de Desenvolvimento, Pesquisa e Tecnologia do Estado do Amazonas. Coordenadoria de Estudos e Pesquisas. Projeção da população do Estado do Amazonas e seus municípios /. Manaus, Amazonas , 1984. 37 leaves ; LC Card 87-402133 DDC 304.6/0981/13021 19
HA988.A5 P76 1984

Centro de Divulgación de Historia Popular (Lima, Peru) Taller Alternativas de Cambio de Modelo Empresarial (1985 : Cooperativa San Bartolo del Valle del Santa (Peru)) Taller Alternativas de Cambio de Modelo Empresarial, San Bartolo, Valle del Santa. Lima, Perú [1986] 40 p. : LC Card 87-136317 DDC 334/.683/0985 19
HD1491.P4 T35 1985

Centro de Documentación e Información Andina (Lima, Peru) Callegari Ramírez, Carlos. Historia del Banco de la Nación. Lima, Perú , 1986. 223 p. : LC Card 87-400236 DDC 332.1/1/0985 19
HG2946 .C35 1986

Centro de Ecodesarrollo. Ortiz de Montellano, Ana. Tecnologías pesqueras en el trópico húmedo de México /. México, D.F. , 1985. 146 p. : LC Card 86-208331
HD9464.M42 O77 1985

Centro de Economía Transnacional.
Feldman, Ernesto V. (Ernesto Víctor) Crisis financiera y endeudamiento externo en la Argentina /. [Buenos Aires] , c1986. 184 p. ; ISBN 950-25-1313-4 LC Card 86-182663
HG185.A7 F45 1986

Lichtensztejn, Samuel, 1934- Fondo Monetario Internacional y Banco Mundial . San José, Costa Rica , Buenos Aires, Argentina , 1986. 215 p. : LC Card 86-233561
HG3881.5.I58 L527 1986

Centro de Estudios de Comercialización Agropecuaria y Agroindustrial (Argentina)
Anuario estadístico agropecuario argentino, 1930-1984 . [Buenos Aires] [1984] 2 v. (480 leaves) ; LC Card 86-177130
HD1862 .A69 1984

Centro de Estudios del Cobre y la Minería (Santiago, Chile) Chile y CIPEC ante la crisis del cobre /. Santiago de Chile , 1985. 74 p. ; LC Card 86-144485
HD9539.C7 C526 1985 ***NYPL [JLD 87-363]***

Centro de Estudios del Desarrollo (Santiago, Chile)
Fontaine Talavera, Arturo. Pautas para la confección de una política económica . Santiago, Chile , 1984. 92 leaves : LC Card 86-177872
HC192 .F58 1984

Mannarelli M., Virgilio B. Organización institucional del sector agrícola /. Santiago, Chile , 1985. 81, [3] p. : LC Card 86-115545 DDC 338.1/883 19
HD1878 .M35 1985

Centro de Estudios del Trabajo. El Terremoto del 19 de septiembre y los trabajadores mexicanos. [Mexico City, Mexico?] [1985] 114 p. ; LC Card 86-144990
HC138.M4 T47 1985 ***NYPL [JLC 87-130]***

Centro de Estudios del Trabajo (Nicaragua)
D'Ciófalo V., Giovanni. El trabajo infantil urbano en Managua /. Managua , 1986. ii, 76, 3, [33] leaves ; LC Card 87-403894 DDC 331.3/1/09728513 19
HD6250.N5 M363 1986

Centro de Estudios Demográficos (Portugal) A População de Portugal /. [Lisbon] , 1976. 116 p., [1] folded leaf of plates : LC Card 85-204353
HB3621 .P67 1976

Centro de Estudios Monetarios Latinoamericanos. (Old Catalog form: Centro de Estudios Monetarios Latinoamericanos, Mexico)
Financiamiento agrícola. México, D.F. , 1985. i, 156 p. ; LC Card 86-156375
HG2051.L26 F55 1985

Centro de Estudios Rurales Andinos Bartolomé de las Casas. Estrategias para el desarrollo de la Sierra /. Cusco , c1986. 418 p. : LC Card 86-199393
HC228.A54 E87 1986

Centro de Estudios sobre América.
Fernández Tabío, Luis René. Apuntes sobre el capital financiero en Estados Unidos . La Habana , 1981 [i.e. 1982] ii, 74 p. : LC Card 87-401153
HG5851.A3 F47 1982

Fernández Tabío, Luis René. Los intereses económicos en la producción militar de los Estados Unidos /. La Habana , 1982. ii, 87 p. : LC Card 87-400639 DDC 338.4/76234/0973 19
HD9743.U6 F46 1982

Notas críticas sobre el plan Reagan para la cuenca del Caribe /. La Habana , 1982. 84 p. ; LC Card 87-400638 DDC 337.729073 19
HF1456.5.C27 N67 1982

Centro de Estudos Agrícolas (Instituto Brasileiro de Economia) Balanço e disponibilidade interna de gêneros alimentícios de origem vegetal, 1979 a 1983 /. Rio de Janeiro, Brasil , 1985. 67 p. ; LC Card 87-404963 DDC 339.4/86413/00981021 19
HD9014.B82 B345 1985

Centro de Estudos da Dependência (Lisbon, Portugal) Ferreira, Eduardo de Sousa, 1936- Reintegração dos emigrantes portugueses .

[Lisbon] , 1984. xiv, 137 p. ; LC Card 86-132652
HD8380.5 .F47 1984

Centro de Estudos de Planeamento. Lei das finanças locais . [Lisbon] [1980] 56 leaves ; LC Card 83-223473
HJ9529 .L45 1980

Centro de Estudos Humanísticos (Porto, Portugal) Perspectivas sobre o norte de Portugal. Porto , 1981. 242 p. : LC Card 83-163948
HC393.M55 P47 1981

Centro de Informaciones y Estudios del Uruguay. Lombardi, Nelly Niedworok de. Algunas cifras sobre la fuerza de trabajo en el Uruguay /. [Montevideo] [1979] 18 leaves : LC Card 86-164130
HD5762.A6 L66 1979

Centro de Investigación y Adiestramiento Político Administrativo (San José, Costa Rica) Daremblum, Jaime. Del cacao al colón . San José, Costa Rica [1977?- v. <1- > ; LC Card 87-402194 DDC 332.4/97286 19
HG682 .D37 1977

Centro de Investigación y Consultoría (La Paz, Bolivia) Tendencias sindicales después del VI Congreso de la C.O.B. /. La Paz , c1985. 111 p. ; LC Card 86-137172
HD8272.C65 T45 1985

Centro de Investigación y Docencia Económicas. Sacristán, Antonio. Disertaciones sobre economía mexicana /. México, D.F. , 1982. 39 p. ; LC Card 87-123937 DDC 332.1/0972 19
HG2714 .S23 1982

Centro de Investigación y Promoción del Campesinado. Reforma agraria como proceso social . Piura, Perú [1984] 163 p. : LC Card 84-232526 DDC 333.3/1/85 19
HD1333.P4 R44 1984 ***NYPL [JLD 86-2537]***

Centro de Investigaciones Agrarias (Mexico City, Mexico) Estructura agraria y desarrollo agrícola en México . México , 1974 (1979 printing) xvi, 1174 p. : LC Card 81-126616 DDC 338.1/0972 19
HD1792 .E85 1974 ***NYPL [JLE 81-372]***

Centro de Investigaciones CIUDAD. Transports urbains et services en Amérique latine . Arcueil, France , Quito [1985- v. <1 > : ISBN 2-85782-137-9 (set) LC Card 87-153020
HE311.L29 T73 1985

Centro de Investigaciones CIUDAD (Quito, Ecuador) Tierras para asentamientos populares . Quito, Ecuador , 1985. 378 p. : LC Card 87-400165 DDC 333.77/13/0986613 19
HD530.Q58 T54 1985

Centro de Investigaciones Ecológicas del Sureste (San Cristóbal de Las Casas, Mexico) Thompson G., Roberto. Problemática agraria y política petrolera en Chiapas /. Tuxtla Gutiérrez, Chiapas , 1983. 37 p., [1] leaf of plates : LC Card 84-243074
HD9574.M63 C457 1983

Centro de Investigaciones Económicas (Uruguay) Barbato de Silva, Celia. La ganadería vacuna uruguaya . Montevideo, Uruguay [1980] 77 leaves ; ***NYPL [JLF 86-1101]***

Forteza, Alvaro. Efectos de la política económica en el mercado de leche fluida /. Montevideo, Uruguay [1986] 126 p. : LC Card 87-121158
HD9282.U72 F67 1986

Centro de Memória Sindical (São Paulo, Brazil) Roio, José Luiz del. 1o. de maio /. São Paulo , 1986. 152, [16] p. : LC Card 86-197367
HD7791 .R59 1986

Centro de Pesquisas e Desenvolvimento (Brazil) Substituição de óleo diesel . [Brasília, Brazil] [19]84. 84 p. : LC Card 87-404960 DDC 338.4/76553 19
HD9579.D53 B737 1984

Centro de Projetos e Estudos (Bahia, Brazil) Análise da citricultura na Bahia . Salvador , 1986. 88 p. : LC Card 86-221439
HD9259.C53 B63 1986

Empresas estatais na Bahia. Salvador, Bahia, Brasil , 1986. 134 p. : LC Card 87-137490 DDC 338.6/2/098142 19
HD4095.B33 E47 1986

A Evolução dos setores secundário e terciário da economia baiana na década de 70 /. Salvador , 1985. 80 p. : LC Card 87-124067 DDC 338.4/7/00098142 19
HD9734.B73 B334 1985

Centro de Promoción Minera (Bolivia) La Nueva política económica . La Paz, Bolivia , 1986. 57 p. : LC Card 87-403839 DDC 338.984 19
HC182 .N84 1986

Centro de Promoción Popular (La Paz, Bolivia) La Artesanía de tejidos en la ciudad de La Paz /. La Paz, Bolivia , 1986. 74, [6] p. : LC Card 87-101929
HD8039.T42 B525 1986

Centro de Prospectiva y Estudios Nacionales (Bolivia) Bolivia en el año 2010. [La Paz, Bolivia?] , 1986. ii, 325 p. : LC Card 87-101220
HC182 .B564 1986

Centro di studi sociali e sindacali (Rome, Italy) L'Europa sindacale agli inizi degli anni '80 . Bologna , c1982. 385 p. : LC Card 84-140478 DDC 331.88/094 19
HD6657 .E89 1982

Regalia, Ida, 1946- Eletti e abbandonati . Bologna , c1984. 355 p. : ISBN 88-15-00592-7 : LC Card 84-250543 DDC 331.87/33/0945 19
HD6490.O42 I87 1984 ***NYPL [JLD 86-211]***

Centro Dominicano de Promoción de Exportaciones. División de Producción. Informe final "estudio de oferta exportable" /. Santo Domingo, República Dominicana [1985] 101, [57] p. ; LC Card 85-203743
HC153.5 .I54 1985

Centro Ecumênico de Documentação e Informação. Canavieiros em greve . São Paulo , 1985. 105 p. : LC Card 87-104183 DDC 331.88/1361/098134 19
HD6614.S85 C36 1985

Centro Español de Gestión. Cómo establecer el control presupuestario /. Madrid , 1983. 95 p. : ISBN 84-256-0387-0 LC Card 85-221532
HG4026 .C56 1983

Centro estero camere commercio lombarde. Conferenza internazionale sul tema Le zone franche industriali, nuove forme di investimento, l'America latina (1985 : Milan, Italy) Le zone franche industriali nei paesi emergenti . Milano, Italy , c1986. 207 p. ; LC Card 86-223193
HF1418 .C525 1985

Centro Europa ricerche (Rome, Italy) Quale strategia per l'industria? . Bologna , c1986. 221 p. : ISBN 88-15-00975-2 : LC Card 86-182300
HC310.I53 Q35 1986

Centro europea dell'impresa Pubblica. see **Centre européen de l'entreprise publique.**

Centro Europeo de Coordinación de Estudios y de Documentación en las Ciencias Sociales. see **European Centre for the Co-ordination of Research and Documentation in Social Sciences.**

Centro Interamericano de Estudios Tributarios. La Política tributaria en Latinoamérica . Washington, D.C. , 1986. ix, 180 p. ; ISBN 0-8270-2496-7 (pbk.) LC Card 87-403563 DDC 336.2/0098 19
HJ3374.5 .P65 1986

Centro Interdisciplinario de Estudios sobre el Desarrollo Latinoamericano.
Cartas, José María. Precondiciones para la implementación de la economía social de mercado en América Latina . Buenos Aires, República Argentina , c1985. 80 p. ; LC Card 87-101628
HC125 .C374 1985

La Economía social de mercado . Buenos Aires, República Argentina [1984], c1983. 109 p. ; ISBN 950-9431-00-1 LC Card 86-120441 DDC 338.9 19
HD85.S7 E36 1983

Centro Interdisciplinario de Estudios sobre el Desarrollo Uruguay.
Martorelli, Horacio. Nuevo estilo de desarrollo para Uruguay . Montevideo, Uruguay , 1982. 2 v. : LC Card 85-167867 DDC 338.1/09895 19
HD1907 .M376 1982 ***NYPL [JLF 86-935]***

Taller "Perspectivas y Alternativas de la Agricultura Familiar" (1983 : Montevideo, Uruguay) Taller "Perspectivas y Alternativas de la Agricultura Familiar". Montevideo, Uruguay [1984] 1 v. (various pagings) : LC Card 85-203149 DDC 338.1/6 19
HD1476.L29 T35 1983 ***NYPL [JLF 86-884]***

Taller sobre Identificación de Políticas que Permitan Dinamizar el Complejo de Producción y Comercialización de Carnes Rojas, con Enfasis en la Industria Frigorífica (1984 : Montevideo, Uruguay) Taller sobre Identificación de Políticas que Permitan Dinamizar el Complejo de Producción y Comercialización de Carnes Rojas, con Enfasis en la Industria Frigorífica. Montevideo, Uruguay [1985] 13, 18, 16 p. : LC Card 85-236237
HD9440.U82 T35 1984

Centro Internacional de Formación en Ciencias Ambientales. Diez años después de Estocolmo . Madrid [1983?] 285 p. : ISBN 84-85633-26-3 LC Card 84-122682 DDC 304.2 19
GF49 .D54 1983 ***NYPL [JLE 86-1307]***

Centro Internacional de Investigaciones para el Desarrollo. see **International Development Research Centre.**

Centro Montañés de Investigación y Desarrollo Empresarial (Santander, Spain) Reunión coloquio sobre como ven nuestros hombres de empresa la economía de Cantabria para 1984 /. [Santander] [1984?] 54 p. ; ISBN 84-505-0186-5 LC Card 86-187513
HF3690.C35 R48 1984

Centro Nacional de Desarrollo de Personal (Colombia) Breve reseña histórica de la formación profesional y del trabajo /. Bogotá [1973] 29, [1] leaves ; LC Card 85-208500
HD5715 .B74 1973

Centro Nacional de Información y Estadísticas del Trabajo (Mexico) Pedrero, Mercedes. Indicadores para el estudio de la población económicamente activa basados en la información censal de 1970 /. México, D.F. [1977] 495 p. ; LC Card 85-202779
HA765 .P43 1977

Centro-Oeste : convite ao investidor. [Brasília] : Superintendência do Desenvolvimento da Região Centro-Oeste, [1983] 196 p., [3] leaves of plates : ill. ; 32 cm. Bibliography: p. 195-196. LC Card 85-208305
1. Industrial promotion - Brazil, Central West - Handbooks, manuals, etc. 2. Investments - Brazil, Central West - Handbooks, manuals, etc. 3. Tax incentives - Brazil, Central West - Handbooks, manuals, etc. I. Brazil. Superintendência do Desenvolvimento da Região Centro-Oeste.
HC188.C46 C47 1983

Centro-Oeste brasileiro / Ministério do Interior, Superintendência do Desenvolvimento da Região Centro-Oeste. [Brasília] : SUDECO, 1981. 9 v. : ill., maps ; 22 x 32 cm. Title from v. 1. CONTENTS. - 1. Centro-Oeste brasileiro -- 2. Aspectos sociais -- 3. Aspectos econômicos -- 4. Potencial agrícola e agroindustrial -- 5. Potencial energético -- 6. Potencial mineralógico -- 7. Potencial turístico -- 8. Aparato institucional -- 9. Crédito, financiamentos e incentivos fiscais. LC Card 87-405115 DDC 330.981/7063 19
1. Brazil, Central West - Economic conditions. 2. Brazil, Central West - Social conditions. I. Brazil. Superintendência do Desenvolvimento da Região Centro-Oeste.
HC188.C46 C465 1981

O Centro-Oeste e a retomada do desenvolvimento nacional . Mato Grosso do Sul (Brazil). Fundação Instituto de Apoio ao Planejamento do Estado. [Campo Grande] , 1985. 113 p., [1] folded leaf : LC Card 87-404972 DDC 338.981/71 19
HC188.C46 M37 1985

Centro para el Desarrollo Económico y Social de América Latina. ACLO (Organization) "Estudio de participación campesina en la estructura y acción de ACLO" . [Sucre, Bolivia] , 1980. 94 leaves ; LC Card 83-203590
HD1531.B6 A24 1980

CENTRO PARA LA PROMOCIÓN DE LAS EXPORTACIONES Y LAS INVERSIONES (COSTA RICA)
Hallauer, Robert. Export promotion policies in Costa Rica . Austin , 1985. 17 p. ; LC Card 86-622254 DDC 382/.63/097286 19
HF1487 .H35 1985

Centro Paraguayo de Estudios Sociológicos. Foro de Economía. Economía paraguaya, 1985. Asunción, Paraguay , 1986. 285 p. : LC Card 86-182987
HC222 .E27 1986

Centro Peruano de Investigación Aplicada. Comunicación y tecnología en la investigación demográfica /. Lima , 1985. vi, 38 p. ; LC Card 86-168814
HB849.6 .C65 1985

Centro ricerche economiche e sociali per il Meridionale (Naples, Italy) Terremoto e crisi urbana . Napoli , 1981. 207 p. ;
NYPL [JLE 86-4532]

Centro studi Confindustria. L'Economia in cifre, 1971-1985 /. Roma [1986] viii, 154 p. ; LC Card 86-233222
HC305 .E246 1986

Centro Uruguay Independiente. Lucha y polémica sindical, 1968-1973. [Montevideo?] , 1985. 4 v. ; LC Card 86-107744 DDC 322/.2/09895 19
HD6647 .L83 1985 *NYPL [JLC 86-368]*

Centroamérica . Gallardo, María Eugenia. San José, Costa Rica , 1986. 259 p. : ISBN 92-9039-110-3 LC Card 87-401731 DDC 330.9728/053 19
HC141 .G35 1986

Centroamérica, política económica y crisis /. Rivera, Eugenio. San José, Costa Rica , c1986. 201 p. : ISBN 997-7904-37-5 LC Card 87-404079 DDC 338.9728 19
HC141 .R58 1986

Centrum voor Studie en Documentatie van Latijns Amerika (Amsterdam, Netherlands) El Sector informal en Bolivia /. [La Paz, Bolivia?] [1986] 323 p. : LC Card 87-100849
HD2346.B6 S43 1986

A Century of service : the Puget Power story / by Robert C. Wing, editor ; Robert C. Cumbow, associate editor ; Julie Springer, designer.1st ed. Bellevue, Wash. : Puget Sound Power & Light Co., c1987. 178 p. : ill. ; 28 cm. Bibliography: p. 167. Includes index. ISBN 0-9619061-0-3 (pbk.) : LC Card 87-16582 DDC 338.7/6136362/097977 19
1. Puget Sound Power and Light Company - History. 2. Electric utilities - Northwest, Pacific - History. I. Wing, Robert C., 1921-. II. Cumbow, Robert C., 1946-.
HD9685.U7 P923 1987

Century twenty-one accounting. Swanson, Robert M. Century 21 accounting . Cincinnati , c1988. xi, 653 p. : ISBN 0-538-02470-4 LC Card 87-60958 DDC 657/.046 19
HF5635 .C4228 1988

Century 21 accounting . Swanson, Robert M. Cincinnati , c1988. xi, 653 p. : ISBN 0-538-02470-4 LC Card 87-60958 DDC 657/.046 19
HF5635 .C4228 1988

Century 21 accounting. Swanson, Robert M. Century 21 accounting . Cincinnati , c1988. xi, 653 p. : ISBN 0-538-02470-4 LC Card 87-60958 DDC 657/.046 19
HF5635 .C4228 1988

Ceny detaliczne 1971-1985 / [komitet redakcyjny Głównego Urzędu Statystycznego, przewodniczący Wiesław Sadowski ; redaktor główny Lech Gradowski]. Warszawa : Główny Urząd Statystyczny, 1985. 160 p. ; 24 cm. (Statystyka Polski. Seria Materiały statystyczne . 37) LC Card 86-196060
1. Prices - Poland - Statistics. 2. Retail trade - Poland - Statistics. I. Sadowski, Wiesław. II. Gradowski, Lech. III. Poland. Główny Urząd Statystyczny. IV. Series.
HB235.P6 C45 1985

CEPAL. see **United Nations. Economic Commission for Latin America.**

CERAMIC INDUSTRIES.
Advanced ceramics market opportunities. Norwalk, Conn., U. S.A. (6 Prowitt St., Norwalk 06855) , c1986. iv, 223 leaves ; LC Card 87-162866 DDC 380.1/45666 19
HD9590.5 .A38 1986

CERAMIC INDUSTRIES - IZERSKIE MOUNTAINS (POLAND AND CZECHOSLOVAKIA) - HISTORY.
John, Walter. Glasspinnerei im Isergebirge /. Schwäbisch-Gmünd , 1984, c1974. 78 p. : LC Card 85-135799
HD9623.I94 J64 1984

CERAMIC INDUSTRIES - TECHNOLOGICAL INNOVATIONS.
The World market for high technology industrial ceramics. New York, N.Y. [1985] 1 v. (various pagings) ; ISBN 0-931634-52-0 (pbk.) LC Card 86-201912 DDC 382/.45666 19
HD9590.5 .W67 1985

Cercle amical des P.T.T. de Lille (France) Histoire de la poste et des télécommunications dans la région Nord-Pas-de-Calais . [Lille] , c1983. 156 p. : LC Card 86-115052
HE6986.N67 H57 1983

Cercle de la cité (Paris, France) Projet pour la France . Paris , c1983. 196 p. ; ISBN 2-7340-0032-6 : LC Card 83-196098
HC276.2 .P767 1983

Cercola, Raffaele. L'intervento esterno nello sviluppo industriale del Mezzogiorno : analisi della situazione attuale e delle tendenze recenti / Raffaele Cercola. Napoli : Guida, c1984. 252 p. ; 23 cm. Bibliography: p. [247]-250. ISBN 88-7042-861-3 : LC Card 86-192219
1. Investments, Foreign - Italy, Southern. I. Title.
HG5533.S68 C47 1984

Cereal feed use in the Third World . Sarma, J. S. Washington, D.C. , c1986. 68 p. : ISBN 0-89629-058-1 (pbk.) LC Card 86-27355 DDC 338.1/7325/091724 19
HD9052.D44 S27 1986

CEREAL PRODUCTS - EUROPEAN ECONOMIC COMMUNITY COUNTRIES - COSTS.
Stanton, B. F. (Bernard Freeland), 1925- Production costs for cereals in the European community . Ithaca, N.Y. [1986] 178 p., 2 p. of plates : LC Card 86-622607 DDC 338.1/331/094 19
HD9045.E82 S73 1986

CEREAL PRODUCTS - UNITED STATES - COSTS.
Stanton, B. F. (Bernard Freeland), 1925- Production costs for cereals in the European community . Ithaca, N.Y. [1986] 178 p., 2 p. of plates : LC Card 86-622607 DDC 338.1/331/094 19
HD9045.E82 S73 1986

The cereals dilemma . Stanton, B. F. (Bernard Freeland), 1925- Ithaca, N.Y. [1986] 50 p. : LC Card 86-622419 DDC 338.1/731/094 19
HD9045.A2 S7 1986

Černa, Milada. Your trade partners in Czechoslovakia /. Praha , 1986. 187 p. : LC Card 87-127524 DDC 382/.025/437 19
HF3550.3.A48 Y58 1986

Cernea, Michael M. Measuring project impact : monitoring and evaluation in the PIDER Rural Development Project, Mexico / prepared by Michael M. Cernea. Washington, D.C., U. S.A. : World Bank, c1979. vi, 93 p. ; 28 cm. (World Bank staff working paper . no. 332) Cover title. "June 1979." Includes bibliographical references. LC Card 81-170764
1. Programa de Inversiones para el Desarrollo Rural (Mexico). 2. Agricultural development projects - Mexico. 3. Rural development projects - Mexico. 4. Mexico - Rural conditions. 5. Mexico - Economic conditions - 1970-. I. Title. II. Series.
HD1792 .C43 1979

Cernovodeanu, Paul. Relaţiile comerciale româno-engleze în contextul politicii orientale a Marii Britanii : 1803-1878 / Paul Cernovodeanu. Cluj-Napoca : Dacia, 1986. 404 p. ; 21 cm. Summary in English. Includes bibliographical references and index. LC Card 87-143711
1. Great Britain - Commerce - Romania - History - 19th century. 2. Romania - Commerce - Great Britain - History - 19th century. 3. Great Britain - Commerce - Balkan Peninsula - History - 19th century. 4. Balkan Peninsula - Commerce - Great Britain - History - 19th century. I. Title.
HF3508.R6 C47 1986

Cerón Solarte, Benhur. Contexto socioeconómico de las migraciones internas en Nariño / Benhur Cerón Solarte. Pasto [Colombia] : Universidad de Nariño, 1985. i, 276, 51 p. : ill. ; 24 cm. Includes bibliographical references. LC Card 87-102199
1. Migration, Internal - Colombia - Nariño (Dept.). 2. Land settlement - Colombia - Nariño (Dept.). I. Title.
HB2028.N37 C47 1985

Cerrado : a Brazilian grain project for domestic and foreign markets. [Rio de Janeiro] : Companhia Vale do Rio Doce, Secretaria Técnica da Presidência, 1984. 53 p., [2] leaves of plates : ill. (some col.), col. maps ; 30 cm. LC Card 87-132493 DDC 380.1/4131/0981 19
1. Grain trade - Brazil. 2. Grain trade - Government policy - Brazil. 3. Grain trade - Brazil - Transportation - Costs. 4. Balance of payments - Brazil. 5. Cerrados - Brazil - Goiás (State). 6. Cerrados - Brazil - Minas Gerais. I. Companhia Vale do Rio Doce.
HD9044.B682 C47 1984

CERRADOS - BRAZIL - GOIÁS (STATE)
Cerrado . [Rio de Janeiro] , 1984. 53 p., [2] leaves of plates : LC Card 87-132493 DDC 380.1/4131/0981 19
HD9044.B682 C47 1984

CERRADOS - BRAZIL - MINAS GERAIS.
Cerrado . [Rio de Janeiro] , 1984. 53 p., [2] leaves of plates : LC Card 87-132493 DDC 380.1/4131/0981 19
HD9044.B682 C47 1984

Cerri, Marianela. Corvalán Vásquez, Oscar E., 1947- Empleo y capacitación en los talleres informales de Santiago /. Montevideo , 1984. 150 p. ; LC Card 86-127324
HD2346.C54 S263 1984

CERRO CORPORATION STRIKE, 1971.
Cobriza, Cobriza, 1971 /. [Lima? Peru] , 1981. 136 p. ; LC Card 83-106108
HD5361 .M612 1971

CERRO DE PASCO MINING COMPANY - HISTORY.
DeWind, Josh. Peasants become miners . New York , 1987. vii, 421 p. : ISBN 0-8240-1358-1 (alk. paper) LC Card 87-8361 DDC 338.2/0985/23 19
HD8039.M61 P44 1987

Certain tobacco . United States. International Trade Commission. Washington, DC [1985] 1 v. (various pagings) ; LC Card 87-600640 DDC 338.1/7371/0973 19
HD9136 .U55 1985

Certificación ocupacional : experiencias y logros / CINTERFOR.1a ed. Ciudad de México : Organización Internacional del Trabajo, CINTERFOR, 1981. 76 p. ; 23 cm. (Informes. no. 106) "Proyecto 128." Bibliography: p. 75-76. ISBN 968-8290-30-0 LC Card 86-142976
1. Occupational training - Latin America. 2. Occupational training - Research - Latin America. I. CINTERFOR (Organization). II. Series: Informes (CINTERFOR (Organization)) , no. 106.
HD5715.5.L3 C47 1981

CERTIFICATES OF SHARE. see **STOCK CERTIFICATES.**

CERTIFICATES OF STOCK. see **STOCK CERTIFICATES.**

Certified Professional Secretary® examination. Lindsell, Sheryl L. CPS®--Certified Professional Secretary® examination /. New York, N.Y. , c1987. xxx, 286 p. : ISBN 0-13-122805-6 (pbk.) : LC Card 87-11381 DDC 651.3/741/076 19
HF5547.5 .L554 1987

Certified professional secretary examination review series. 2nd ed. [Kansas City, Mo.?] : Professional Secretaries International ; New York : Wiley, c1986- v. <1, 6 > : ill. ; 28 cm. CONTENTS. - module 1. Behavioral science in business / Wilma D. Stricklin, Deborah Lauer -- module 6. Office technology / Betty L. Schroeder, Diane Routhier Graf. ISBN 0-471-84353-9 (pbk. : v. 1) LC Card 87-100577 DDC 651.3/74/076 19
1. Office practice - Problems, exercises, etc. I. Stricklin, Wilma D. II. Lauer, Deborah. III. Professional Secretaries International.
HF5547.5 .C44 1986

CERTIFIED PUBLIC ACCOUNTANTS. see **ACCOUNTANTS.**

Certo, Samuel C. Strategic management : concepts and applications / Samuel C. Certo, J. Paul Peter.1st ed. New York : Random House, c1988. p. cm. ISBN 0-394-35920-8 : LC Card 87-23565 DDC 658.4/012 19
1. Corporate planning - United States. 2. Corporate planning - United States - Case studies. I. Peter, J. Paul. II. Title.
HD30.28 .C43 1988.

Cerutti, Mario. Burguesía y capitalismo en Monterrey, 1850-1910 / Mario Cerutti. 1a ed.

México, D.F. : Claves Latinoamericanas, 1983. 214 p. ; 20 cm. Includes bibliographical references. ISBN 968-8430-10-2 LC Card 86-221932
1. Monterrey (Mexico) - Industries - History. 2. Saving and investment - Mexico - Monterrey - History. 3. Industrialists - Mexico - Monterrey - History. 4. Industry and state - Mexico - Monterrey - History. 5. Labor supply - Mexico - Monterrey - History. I. Title.
HC138.M6 C47 1983

Cervantes Corona, José Guadalupe. Zacatecas (Mexico : State). Governor (1980- : Cervantes Corona) Tercer informe de gobierno. Zacatecas , 1983. 350 p. : LC Card 86-202257
HJ15.Z3 Z33 1980

Cervantes Islas, Joel.
Glower, Carlos J., 1952- América Latina y el sistema monetario internacional /. [Mexico City, Mexico] [1986] iv, 28 leaves : LC Card 87-400944 DDC 332.4/56098 29
HG3881 .G577 1986

La inflación en dos marcos cambiarios : el caso de seis países latinoamericanos en el período 1960-1980 / Joel Cervantes Islas. México, D.F. : Centro de Estudios Monetarios Latinoamericanos, Departamento de Investigaciones, 1985. iv, 67 leaves ; 28 cm. (Serie Cuadernos de investigación . núm. 2) Summary also in English, French, and Portuguese. Collaborator, Carlos J. Glower. Bibliography: leaves 64-67. LC Card 87-108752 DDC 332.4/1/098 19
1. Inflation (Finance) - Latin America - Case studies. 2. Foreign exchange administration - Latin America - Case studies. I. Glower, Carlos J., 1952-. II. Series: Serie Cuadernos de investigación (Centro de Estudios Monetarios Latinoamericanos, Departamento de Investigaciones) , núm. 2. III. Title.
HG660.5 .C43 1985

Cervero, Robert. Suburban gridlock / Robert Cervero. New Brunswick, N.J. : Center for Urban Policy Research, c1986. xxiii, 248 p. : ill. ; 24 cm. Includes index. Bibliography: p.235-236. ISBN 0-88285-115-2 : LC Card 86-2628 DDC 388.4/13142/0973 19
1. Traffic congestion - United States. 2. Traffic flow - United States. 3. Land use - United States - Planning. 4. Suburbs - United States. I. Title.
HE355.3.C64 C47 1986
NYPL [JLE 86-4446]

Ces patrons qui gagnent /. Baumier, Jean. Paris , c1986. 262 p. ; ISBN 2-259-01532-8 : LC Card 87-106535
HD2855 .B38 1986

Cesare Zavattini presenta La civiltà delle acque : dall'acqua la vita e la morte : Sant'Alberto di Ravenna / a cura della Cooperativa culturale "Un paese vuole conoscersi.". [Bologna] : Cappelli, [1985] 272 p., 24 p. of plates : ill. ; 20 cm. (Universale il portolano . 17) Bibliography: p. [267]-272. LC Card 86-105989 DDC 945/.47 19
1. Sant'Alberto (Ravenna, Italy) - Economic conditions. 2. Sant'Alberto (Ravenna, Italy) - Industries - History. 3. Sant'Alberto (Ravenna, Italy) - Social conditions. 4. Sant'Alberto (Ravenna, Italy) - History. I. Zavattini, Cesare, 1902-. II. Cooperativa culturale "Un paese vuole conoscersi" (Sant'Alberto (Ravenna, Italy)).
HC308.S33 C47 1985

Česko-ruský ekonomický slovník.
Cheshsko-russkiĭ ėkonomicheskiĭ slovar′ . Moskva , Praga , 1986. 300 p. ; LC Card 85-146401
HB61 .C453 1986 ***NYPL [*QAD 87-1680]***

Československá akademie věd. Československá demografická společnost. see **Československá demografická společnost.**

Československá demografická společnost.
Migrace a osídlení v socialistických zemích =. Praha , 1984- v. <1 > : LC Card 87-160334
HB2041 .M526 1984

20 let Československé demografické společnosti při ČSAV / [zpracoval kolektiv pod vedením V. Roubíčka]. Praha : ČSDS, 1985. 198 p. : ill. ; 20 cm. Includes bibliographical references. Errata slip inserted. LC Card 86-208016
1. Československá demografická společnost. 2. Demography - Czechoslovakia - Societies. 3. Demographers - Czechoslovakia - Directories. I. Roubíček, V. (Vladimír). II. Title. III. Title: Dvacet let Československé demografické společnosti při ČSAV.
HB3592.3.A3 C47 1985

ČESKOSLOVENSKÁ DEMOGRAFICKÁ SPOLEČNOST.
Československá demografická společnost. 20 let Československé demografické společnosti při ČSAV /. Praha , 1985. 198 p. : LC Card 86-208016
HB3592.3.A3 C47 1985

Československá geografická společnost. Migrace a osídlení v socialistických zemích =. Praha , 1984- v. <1 > : LC Card 87-160334
HB2041 .M526 1984

Československá obchodní a průmyslová komora.
Your trade partners in Czechoslovakia /. Praha , 1986. 187 p. : LC Card 87-127524 DDC 382/.025/437 19
HF3550.3.A48 Y58 1986

Československá Republika. see **Czechoslovakia.**

Československá Socialistická Republika. see **Czechoslovakia.**

Český statistický úřad. Městská správa. Sčítání lidu, domů a bytů 1970. Praha [1970?] 132, [64] p. ; LC Card 82-143437
HA1198.P7 S38 1970

CESPE (Organization)
Carmignani, Fabrizo. Assenteismo e presenteismo . Milano, Italy , c1984. 211 p. ; LC Card 84-175594 DDC 658.3/14 19
HD5115 .C37 1984 ***NYPL [JLD 86-3383]***

La Riconversione produttiva nell'edilizia /. Milano , 1984, c1981. 319 p. :
NYPL [JLD 86-3381]

Politica monetaria e debito pubblico . Milano, Italy , c1984. 209 p. : LC Card 85-111306 DDC 332.4/945 19
HJ8678 .P65 1984 ***NYPL [JLD 86-1207]***

Ricerca sociale e movimento operaio . Milano , c1982. 294 p. ; LC Card 82-246648 DDC 331/.0945 19
HD8481 .R53 1982 ***NYPL [JLD 86-3380]***

Cespedes S., Víctor Hugo.
Costa Rica : la economía en 1985 / Víctor Hugo Céspedes, Alberto Di Mare, Ronulfo Jiménez.1a ed. San José, Costa Rica : Academia de Centroamérica, 1986. 208 p. : ill. ; 21 cm. Includes bibliographies. ISBN 997-7210-06-3 LC Card 87-404067 DDC 330.97286/053 19
1. Costa Rica - Economic conditions - 1948-. I. Di Mare, Alberto. II. Jiménez R., Ronulfo. III. Title.
HC143 .C483 1986

Costa Rica--recuperación sin reactivación : evolución de la economía en 1984 / Víctor Hugo Céspedes, Alberto Di Mare, Ronulfo Jiménez ; con la colaboración de Edna Camacho Mejía.1a ed. San José, Costa Rica : Academia de Centroamérica, 1985. 238 p. : ill. ; 21 cm. Includes bibliographical references. ISBN 997-7210-05-5 LC Card 86-208956
1. Costa Rica - Economic conditions - 1948-. 2. Debts, External - Costa Rica. 3. Costa Rica - Economic Policy. I. Di Mare, Alberto. II. Jiménez R., Ronulfo. III. Title.
HC143 .C484 1985

CESSIO BONORUM. see **BANKRUPTCY.**

The CETA arts and humanities experience [microform] CETA Ahead project (Arts and humanities employment analysis and documentation) /. Startzel, Donna C. Columbia, Md. , 1981. 197 p. ; ***NYPL [*XME-11,320]***

CETA (Comprehensive Employment and Training Act) and the arts and humanities [microform] . Startzel, Donna C. Columbia, Md. , 1981. 160 p. ; ***NYPL [*XME-11,328]***

CETA (Comprehensive Employment and Training Act) arts and humanities experience -- CETA Ahead project. Startzel, Donna C. The CETA arts and humanities experience [microform] CETA Ahead project (Arts and humanities employment analysis and documentation) /. Columbia, Md. , 1981. 197 p. ;
NYPL [*XME-11,320]

Ceti medi e ricostruzione . D'Angelo, Lucio. [Milano] , 1981. vi, 287 p. ; LC Card 81-213297
JN5657.D45 D36 1981
NYPL [JLE 86-3459]

Ceylan, Sadi, 1951- Die geschichtliche Umwandlung der ökonomischen Gesellschaftsformation der Türkei / Sadi Ceylan. Berlin : EXpress Edition, c1985. 270 p. ; 21 cm. (X-Publikationen) Bibliography: p. 265-270. ISBN 3-88548-482-X LC Card 86-221332
1. Turkey - Economic conditions. 2. Turkey - Social conditions. 3. Turkey - Industries - History. I. Title.
HC492 .C49 1985

CFA readings in fixed income securities analysis / the Institute of Chartered Financial Analysts. Charlottesville, VA (P.O. Box 3668, Charlottesville, VA 22903) : The Institute, c1985. v, 255 p. : ill. ; 28 cm. Bibliography: p. 249-255.
1. Investment analysis - Addresses, essays, lectures. 2. Securities - Addresses, essays, lectures. 3. Portfolio management - Addresses, essays, lectures. 4. Bonds - Addresses, essays, lectures. I. Institute of Chartered Financial Analysts. II. Title: C.F.A. readings in fixed income securities analysis. III. Title: Fixed income securities analysis. ***NYPL [JLF 86-1994]***

CFEC report .
(no. 84-13) Focht, Rick. Employment and gross earnings of Washington residents in Alaska's commercial fisheries, 1977-1982 /. Juneau, AK [1984] v leaves, 126 p. ; LC Card 86-622318 DDC 331.2/8392/09797021 19
HD4966.F542 U554 1984

(no. 84-14) Focht, Rick. Employment and gross earnings of Oregon residents in Alaska's commercial fisheries, 1977-1982 /. Juneau, AK [1984] v, 69 p. : LC Card 86-622319 DDC 331.12/5392/09798021 19
HD4966.F652 U54 1984b

(no. 84-15) Focht, Rick. Employment and gross earnings of California residents in Alaska's commercial fisheries, 1977-1982 /. Juneau, AK [1984] v, 53 p. : LC Card 86-622320 DDC 331.12/5392/09798021 19
HD4966.F652 U54 1984c

La Cgil nei suoi congressi /. Piccioni, Alessandro. Roma , c1986. 168 p. ; LC Card 87-103188
HD8473 .P53 1986

CGT-FO (UNION) - HISTORY.
Validire, Jean-Louis. André Bergeron, une force ouvrière /. Paris , c1984. 244 p. ; ISBN 2-259-01206-X : LC Card 85-105625 DDC 331.88/0944 19
HD6684 .V35 1984

CGTP-Intersindical. Seminário sobre Política Fiscal (1984? : CGTP-IN) Contribuições para a reforma do sistema fiscal português . Lisboa , 1985. 226 p. : LC Card 87-107879 DDC 336.469 19
HJ1252 .S46 1984

Ch Trng, H Hà N 1982-1983. 2 v. ; LC Card 87-142403
HD890.5 .T78 1982

Chabaud-Rychter, Danielle. Espace et temps du travail domestique / Danielle Chabaud-Rychter, Dominique Fougeyrollas-Schwebel, Françoise Sonthonnax. Paris : Libr. des Méridiens, 1985. 156 p. ; 21 cm. (Collection "Réponses sociologiques", 0761-6252) Includes bibliographical references. ISBN 2-86563-127-3 LC Card 86-165713
1. Housewives. 2. Sexual division of labor. I. Fougeyrollas-Schwebel, Dominique. II. Sonthonnax, Françoise. III. Title. IV. Series.
HD6055 .C45 1985

Chackiel, Juan. La fuerza de trabajo en los países de la Cuenca del Plata según los censos de 1960 / Juan Chackiel. San José, Costa Rica : Centro Latinoamericano de Demografía, 1976. iv, 81 p. : ill. ; 27 cm. (Serie A / CELADE . no. 1022) Bibliography: p. [79]-81. LC Card 83-169596
1. Labor supply - Río de la Plata Region (Argentina and Uruguay). 2. Argentina - Census, 1960. 3. Bolivia - Census, 1960. 4. Brazil - Census, 1960. 5. Paraguay - Census, 1960. 6. Uruguay - Census, 1960. I. Series: Serie A (CELADE (Organization)) , no. 1022. II. Title.
HD5746.A6 C42 1976

Chacko, George Kuttickal, 1930-
Robotics/artificial intelligence/productivity : U. S.--Japan concomitant coalitions / George K. Chacko. Princeton, N.J. : Petrocelli Books, c1986. 2 v. in 1 (xvii, 335 p.) : ill. ; 24 cm. Includes bibliographical references and index. CONTENTS. - Book 1. Productivity promises of robotics and artificial intelligence. -- Book 2. Concomitant coalitions in cars and computers. ISBN 0-89433-228-7 LC Card 86-12177 DDC 658.5/14 19
1. Flexible manufacturing systems - United States. 2. Flexible manufacturing systems - Japan. 3. Robotics - United States. 4. Robotics - Japan. 5. Computer industry - United States - Automation. 6. Computer industry - Japan - Automation. 7. Automobile industry

and trade - United States - Automation. 8. Automobile industry and trade - Japan - Automation. I. Title.
HD9725 .C48 1986 ***NYPL [JLE 87-1001]***

CHACO BOREAL WAR, 1932-1935. see **CHACO WAR, 1932-1935.**

CHACO DISPUTE. see **CHACO WAR, 1932-1935.**

CHACO WAR, 1932-1935 - FINANCE - BOLIVIA.
Seiferheld, Alfredo M., 1950- Economía y petróleo durante la Guerra del Chaco . Asunción , 1983. 535 p. : LC Card 84-121699 DDC 330.9892/071 19
HC222 .S36 1983 ***NYPL [JLD 85-1032]***

CHACO WAR, 1932-1935 - FINANCE - PARAGUAY.
Seiferheld, Alfredo M., 1950- Economía y petróleo durante la Guerra del Chaco . Asunción , 1983. 535 p. : LC Card 84-121699 DDC 330.9892/071 19
HC222 .S36 1983 ***NYPL [JLD 85-1032]***

Chacón, Francisco. see **Chacón Jiménez, Francisco.**

Chacón Jiménez, Francisco. Murcia, un modelo económico en el mundo mediterráneo durante el siglo XVI / Francisco Chacón Jímenez. [Murcia] : Universidad de Murcia, Facultad de Filosofía y Letras, 1978. 29 p., [7] folded leaves of plates : ill. ; 25 cm. (Publicaciones de la Universidad de Murcia) Abridgement of thesis (doctoral)--Universidad Central de Barcelona, 1977. Includes bibliographical references. ISBN 84-600-1243-3 LC Card 86-133743
1. Murcia, Spain (Province) - Economic conditions. 2. Murcia (Spain : Province) - Population - History. 3. Murcia, Spain (Province) - History. I. Title. II. Series.
HC387.M8 C48 1978

Chacon, Vamireh. Kultur und Entwicklung in Brasilien : von der Monokultur zur Industrialiserung / Vamireh Chacon. Dortmund : Sozialforschungsstelle an der Universität Münster, 1970. v, 308 p. ; 21 cm. (Arbeitsunterlage 40/41 zur Lateinamerikaforschung) Includes bibliographies. LC Card 86-172094
1. Brazil - Economic conditions. 2. Brazil - Industries - History. 3. Brazil - Politics and government. I. Series: Arbeitsunterlage zur Lateinamerikaforschung, 40/41. II. Title.
HC187 .C44 1970

CHAD - ECONOMIC CONDITIONS.
Bureau de zone UNICEF de Yaoundé. Eléments du rapport annuel de la zone de Yaoundé /. N'Djaména [1984] [43] leaves : LC Card 86-980240
HC990 .B87 1984

CHAD - SOCIAL CONDITIONS.
Bureau de zone UNICEF de Yaoundé. Eléments du rapport annuel de la zone de Yaoundé /. N'Djaména [1984] [43] leaves : LC Card 86-980240
HC990 .B87 1984

Chadbourne, Bruce D. Wells, Alexander T. General aviation marketing /. Malabar, Fla. , 1987. viii, 268 p. : ISBN 0-89874-987-5 LC Card 86-21504 DDC 629.133/340422/0688 19
HD9711.A2 W45 1987

Chadeau, Emmanuel, 1956- Les inspecteurs des finances au XIXe siècle (1850-1914) : profil social et rôle économique / Emmanuel Chadeau. Paris : Economica, c1986. iii, 184 p. : ill., maps ; 24 cm. (Collection Histoire) Bibliography: p. [91]-96. ISBN 2-7178-1175-3 : LC Card 87-131650
1. Finance, Public - France - Auditing - History - 19th century. 2. Auditors - France - History - 19th century. 3. Finance, Public - France - Auditing - History - 20th century. 4. Auditing - France - History - 20th century. I. Title.
HJ9925.F8 C42 1986

Chaderton, Robertine. Mendes, Margaret. Caribbean cases in auditing /. Kingston, Jamaica , c1986. 58 p. : ISBN 976-8053-00-3 (pbk.) LC Card 87-403426 DDC 657/.45 19
HF5667 .M456 1986

Chadsri Bunnag. Housing in urban development : Thailand country monograph / by Chadsri Bunnag. [Bangkok] : Centre for Housing and Human Settlements Studies, National Housing Authority ; [Rotterdam] Netherlands : Institute for Housing Studies, [1985] 49, [2] leaves : map ; 30 cm. (Research report . no. 7) Cover title. Bibliography: leaves [50]-[51]. LC Card 86-915989 DDC 363.5/09593 19
1. Housing - Thailand. 2. Housing policy - Thailand. 3. Urbanization - Thailand. I. Sūn Wichākān Thīyū'āsai læ Kāntang Thinthān Manut (Thailand). II. Institute for Housing Studies (Netherlands). III. Series: Research report (Sūn Wichākān Thīyū'āsai læ Kāntang Thinthān Manut (Thailand)) , no. 7. IV. Title.
HD7363.55.A3 C46 1985

Chahad, José Paulo Zeetano.
Macedo, Roberto Brás Matos. FGTS e a rotatividade /. São Paulo-SP , Brasília-DF , 1985. 231 p. : ISBN 85-21-30271-1 LC Card 85-187484
HD7096.B6 M33 1985

O Mercado de trabalho no Brasil . São Paulo , 1986. 263 p. : LC Card 86-221361
HD5754 .M47 1986

Chaikind, Stephen. Paying for social security : funding options for the near term / Congress of the United States, Congressional Budget Office. [Washington, D.C.]: The Office : [Supt. of Docs., U. S. G.P.O., distributor], 1981. xix, 47 p. ; 26 cm. (A CBO study) "Written by Stephen Chaikind ... and by Hyman Sanders." "February 1981"--Cover. Includes bibliographical references. LC Card 81-601225 DDC 353.0082/56 19
1. Social security - United States - Finance. 2. Social security taxes - United States. I. Sanders, Hyman. II. Title.
HD7125 .C47 ***NYPL [JLF 86-252]***

Chaîneau, André. Mécanismes et politique monétaires : économie du système bancaire français / André Chaîneau.7e éd. mise à jour. Paris : Presses universitaires de France, 1979, c1968 311 p. : ill. ; 21 cm. (L'Économiste. 1) Includes index. Bibliography: p. [295]-305. ISBN 2-13-036227-3
1. Money - France. 2. Monetary policy - France. I. Title. ***NYPL [JLD 86-2730]***

Chaĭnikov, I͡U. V. Perspektivy reshenii͡a prodovol'stvennoĭ problemy v razvivai͡ushchikhsi͡a stranakh . Moskva , 1985. 142 p. ; LC Card 85-188217
HD9018.D44 P47 1985

Chakrabarti, Rajendra M. Underdevelopment and choices in agriculture : the Indian perspective / Rajendra M. Chakrabarti. New Delhi : Heritage Publishers, India, 1986. xv, 322 p. : ill. ; 22 cm. In the Indian context. Bibliography: p. [305]-319. Includes index. LC Card 86-903184 DDC 338.1/0954 19
1. India - Economic conditions - 1947-. 2. Agriculture - Economic aspects - India. I. Title.
HC435.2 .C466 1986

Chakrabarti, S. B., 1943- Around the plough : socio-cultural context of agricultural farming in an Indian village / S.B. Chakrabarti. Calcutta : Anthropological Survey of India, Ministry of Human Resource Development, Dept. of Culture, Govt. of India, 1986. xviii, 203 p., 8 p. of plates : ill., maps ; 25 cm. (Memoir / Anthropoligical Survey of India . no. 67) Originally presented as author's thesis (Ph. D.--University of Calcutta, 1982) Includes index. Bibliography: p. [177]-184. LC Card 86-902283
1. Agriculture - Social aspects - India - Panchra. 2. Agricultural innovations - Social aspects - India - Panchra. I. Series: India (Republic). Anthropological Survey. Memoir ; no. 67. II. Title.
HD2075.P36 C48 1986
NYPL [L-10 8468 no.67]

Chakraborty, D. (Debesh) Contribution to national and regional planning problems /. Calcutta , 1983. vii, 174 p., [2] leaves of plates (some folded) : LC Card 83-907550 DDC 338.954 19
HC435.2 .C63 1983 ***NYPL [JLD 86-3868]***

Chakraborty, S. K. Human response in organizations : towards the Indian ethos / S.K. Chakraborty. Calcutta, India : Vivekananda Nidhi : Exclusive distributors, Standard Literature Co., [1985] xv, 228 p. : ill. ; 25 cm. Includes bibliographies and index. LC Card 87-901782 DDC 658/.00954 19
1. Organizational behavior. 2. Management - India. I. Title.
HD58.7 .C44 1985

Chakravarty, Sukhamoy.
Development planning : the Indian experience / Sukhamoy Chakravarty. Oxford [Oxfordshire] : Clarendon Press ; New York : Oxford University Press, 1987. viii, 137 p. ; 23 cm. Bibliography: p. [91]-102. Includes indexes. ISBN 0-19-828555-8 : LC Card 87-1554 DDC 338.954 19
1. India - Economic policy - 1947-. 2. India - Social policy. I. Title.
HC435.2 .C467 1987

Monetary policy . New Delhi , c1986. 70 p. ; LC Card 87-900210 DDC 332.4/954 19
HG1235 .M66 1986

Chala, Pierre Tucoo- see **Tucoo-Chala, Pierre.**

Chalandon, Albin. Quitte ou double / Albin Chalandon. Paris : B. Grasset, c1986. 317 p. ; 24 cm. ISBN 2-246-37401-4 : LC Card 86-170477
1. Privatization - France. 2. France - Economic conditions - 1945-. I. Title.
HD4165 .C47 1986

Chalfin, Robert J. Seminar material for understanding and using financial statements / Robert J. Chalfin. Newark, N.J. (15 Washington St., Newark 07102) : New Jersey Institute for Continuing Legal Education, c1987. 95, [43] leaves ; 28 cm. LC Card 87-402010 DDC 657/.33/024344 19
1. Financial statements. I. New Jersey Institute for Continuing Legal Education. II. Title. III. Title: Understanding and using financial statements.
HF5681.B2 C415 1987

The challenge /. Allen, Robert G. New York , c1987. 301 p. ; ISBN 0-671-52618-9 LC Card 87-4317 DDC 650.1 19
HF5386 .A543 1987

Challenge & change . Kaufman, Stuart Bruce. Kensington, Md. , c1986. ix, 163 p. : LC Card 86-229223 DDC 331.88/1797/0973 19
HD6515.T6 K38 1986

Challenge and change. Kaufman, Stuart Bruce. Challenge & change . Kensington, Md. , c1986. ix, 163 p. : LC Card 86-229223 DDC 331.88/1797/0973 19
HD6515.T6 K38 1986

The Challenge of new technology : innovation in British business since 1850 / edited by Jonathan Liebenau. Aldershot, Hants, England ; Brookfield, Vt., U. S.A. : Gower, c1988. x, 155 p. : ill. ; 24 cm. (Business history series) Includes bibliographical references and index. ISBN 0-566-05147-8 : LC Card 87-8592 DDC 338/.06 19
1. Technological innovations - Economic aspects - Great Britain. 2. Great Britain - Industries. I. Liebenau, Jonathan. II. Series.
HC260.T4 C46 1988

A challenge of the 1980s . Foot, David K. [Toronto] , c1981. 99 p. in various pagings :
NYPL [JLF 86-1304]

The challenge to multilateralism . United Nations. Economic and Social Council. Committee for Development Planning. New York , 1985. ix, 39 p. : ISBN 92-1-109109-8 (pbk.) LC Card 86-105993 DDC 382.9/1 19
HF1411 .U5383 1985

Challenging unions . Edelson, Miriam. Ottawa, Ont. , 1987. 28 p. ; ISBN 0-919653-64-2 (pbk.) : LC Card 87-165425 DDC 331.88/088042 19
HD6079.2.C2 E34 1987

Challet, Louis. Plessy, Bernard, 1939- La vie quotidienne des mineurs au temps de Germinal /. [Paris] , c1984. 339 p. : ISBN 2-01-009272-4 : LC Card 85-160775
HD8039.M6152 F86 1984

Challier, Marie-Christine. La fécondité en France : analyse microéconomique / Marie-Christine Challier. Paris : Editions du CNRS, 1985. 196 p. : ill. ; 24 cm. (Sciences sociales / Centre national de la recherche scientifique, Centre régional de publications de Toulouse) Bibliography: p. [185]-196. ISBN 2-222-03773-5 : LC Card 86-234728
1. Fertility, Human - Economic aspects - France. 2. France - Population. I. Series: Sciences sociales (Centre régional de publications de Toulouse). II. Title.
HB1003 .C46 1985

Chalmin, Philippe. Négociants et chargeurs : la saga du négoce international des matières premières / Philippe Chalmin.2e éd. rev. et augm. Paris : Economica, 1985. 299 p. : ill. ; 24 cm. (Collection Bibliothèque des matières premières) Bibliography: p. [286]-289. Includes index. ISBN

2-7178-0851-5 : LC Card 85-149921 DDC 333.7 19
1. Raw materials. 2. Commerce. I. Series: Bibliothèque des matières premières. II. Title.
HF1051 .C42 1985

Chamber of Commerce of the United States of America.
Contact : a directory of business and economic education programs / Chamber of Commerce of the United States.2d ed. Washington, D.C. : The Chamber, c1980. v, 129 p. : ill. ; 28 cm. ISBN 0-89834-024-1 (pbk.) LC Card 80-80440 DDC 650/.07/073 19
1. Business - Information services. - Directories. 2. Public relations - United States. 3. Industry - Social aspects - United States. I. Title.
HF5351 .C46 1980 ***NYPL [JLF 86-1414]***

Chamber of Commerce of the United States of America. Council on Trends and Perspective. Government regulation of business : its growth, impact, and future : papers / by Paul W. MacAvoy ... [et al.]. Washington, D.C. : Council on Trends and Perspective, Chamber of Commerce of the United States, c1979. x, 108 p. ; 23 cm. Includes bibliographical references. ISBN 0-89834-018-7(pbk.) : LC Card 79-91604 DDC 338.973
1. Industry and state - United States. 2. Trade regulation - United States. I. MacAvoy, Paul W. II. Title.
HD3616.U46 C44 1979
NYPL [JLE 80-2446]

Chamberlain, Robert W. Mosich, Donna M. Mastering Dac-Easy . Glenview, Ill. , c1988. p. cm. ISBN 0-673-18735-7 LC Card 87-4847 DDC 657/.028/55369 19
HF5679 .M64 1988

Chamberlin, John H., 1950- Gellings, Clark W. Demand-side management . Lilburn, GA , c1988. xi, 465 p. : ISBN 0-88173-027-0 : LC Card 86-46131 DDC 363.6/2/068 19
HD9685.A2 G45 1988

Chambers, Robert, 1932- Managing canal irrigation : practical analysis from South Asia / Robert Chambers. Cambridge [Cambridgeshire] ; New York : Cambridge University Press, 1988. p. cm. (Wye studies in agricultural and rural development) Bibliography: p. Includes index. ISBN 0-521-34554-5 LC Card 87-16738 DDC 333.91/3/0954 19
1. Irrigation - India - Management. 2. Irrigation - Sri Lanka - Management. 3. Irrigation - Philippines - Management. 4. Irrigation - Management. I. Title. II. Series.
HD1741.I29 C45 1988

Chambers, Robert G.
Applied production analysis / Robert G. Chambers. Cambridge [Cambridgeshire] ; New York : Cambridge University Press, 1988. p. cm. ISBN 0-521-30699-X LC Card 87-12511 DDC 338.5 19
1. Production (Economic theory). I. Title.
HB241 .C452 1988

Coyle, Barry. Economic gains from agricultural trade . Washington, D.C. [Springfield, VA , 1986] iii, 41 p. : LC Card 86-602417 DDC 382/.41/0973 19
HD9005 .C86 1986

Chambliss, William J. (joint author) Block, Alan A. Organizing crime /. New York, N.Y. , c1981. 238 p. ; ISBN 0-444-99079-8 LC Card 80-25099 DDC 364.1/06 19
HV6030 .B55 ***NYPL [JLE 86-4076]***

Chambost, Édouard. Guide de la banque suisse et de ses secrets / Edouard Chambost. [Paris] : Balland, c1987. 317 p. : ill. ; 30 cm. Bibliography: p. 303-312. ISBN 2-7158-0626-4 : LC Card 87-132185
1. Banks and banking - Switzerland. I. Title. II. Title: Banque suisse.
HG3204 .C43 1987

Chambre de commerce & d'industrie de Pointe-à-Pitre. Caraïbe export /. [Pointe à Pitre] [1984] 129 p. ; LC Card 86-155448
HF3311.5 .C37 1984

Chambre de commerce, d'industrie et d'artisanat du Burkina. Berg, Elliot. Mobilization of the private sector in Burkina Faso . [Burkina Faso? , 1985] 21 p. ; LC Card 87-116357 DDC 338.966/25 19
HC1040 .B47 1985

Chambre de commerce et d'industrie de Pointe-à-Pitre. Le Lolo . Pointe-à-Pitre [1984?] 63 p. : LC Card 86-155167
HF5473.G83 L65 1984

Champagne, la coupe est pleine . Bergeot, Paul. [Paris] , c1980. 185 p. ; ISBN 2-86510-001-4 : LC Card 80-120736
HD9382.7.C5 B468 1980

Champagne, Paul J. McAfee, R. Bruce. Organizational behavior . St. Paul , c1987. xviii, 489 p. : ISBN 0-314-93201-1 : LC Card 86-24745 DDC 658.3 19
HD58.7 .M38 1987

Champaud, Jacques. Barbier, J. C. Migrations et développement . Paris , 1983, c1984. 372 p. : ISBN 2-7099-0711-7
NYPL [M-11 4991 no.170]

Champion, A. G. (Anthony Gerard) Changing places . London , Baltimore, Md., USA , 1987. xv, 144 p. : ISBN 0-7131-6498-0 (pbk.) : LC Card 87-148942 DDC 331.12/5/0941 19
HD5765.A6 C49 1987

Champness, Michael. Oil tanker databook, 1985 / Michael Champness and Gilbert Jenkins. London ; New York : Elsevier Applied Science Publishers ; vii, 347 p. ; 28 cm. ISBN 0-85334-311-X LC Card 86-217414 DDC 387.5/448 19
1. Tankers - Statistics. 2. Petroleum industry and trade - Statistics. I. Jenkins, Gilbert. II. Title.
HE566.T3 C42 1985

Chan, Yupo. Facility location and land use . New York, N.Y. , c1986. vii, 40 p. : ISBN 0-87262-574-5 (pbk.) LC Card 86-25926 DDC 338.6/042 19
HD171.A15 F33 1986

Chanana, Charanjit. Industrial economics in developing countries, India : a case study / Charanjit Chanana. New Delhi : Marketing and Economic Research Bureau, 1983. 113 p. : ill. ; 23 cm. "Published for Indian Institute of Industrial Economics, New Delhi." LC Card 83-903832 DDC 338.0954 19
1. Manpower policy - India. 2. Industrial organization - Developing countries - Case study. 3. India - Industries. 4. India - Economic policy. I. Indian Institute of Industrial Economics. II. Title.
HC435.2 .C4717 1983 ***NYPL [JLD 87-674]***

Chancen für einen langen Aufschwung / Sachverständigenrat zur Begutachtung der Gesamtwirtschaftlichen Entwicklung. Stuttgart : Kohlhammer, 1984. xvii, 350 p. : ill. ; 27 cm. (Jahresgutachten / Sachverständigenrat zur Begutachtung der Gesamtwirtschaftlichen Entwicklung . 1984/85) Includes index. ISBN 3-17-003288-7 : LC Card 86-178498
1. Economic forecasting - Germany, West. 2. Germany, West - Economic conditions - 1974-. 3. Germany, West - Economic policy - 1974-. I. Sachverständigenrat zur Begutachtung der Gesamtwirtschaftlichen Entwicklung (Germany). II. Series.
HC286.7 .C48 1984

Chander Bhan, 1949- Farm mechanisation and social change / Chander Bhan. New Delhi : Northern Book Centre, c1987. x, 125 p. ; 23 cm. Revision of the author's thesis (Ph. D.--Haryana Agricultural University, Hisar, India) Study, with reference to Karnal, Bhiwani, and Hisar districts, Haryana, conducted during 1981-1982. Bibliography: p. [117]-120. Includes indexes. ISBN 81-85119-24-4 : LC Card 87-902310 DDC 338.1/61/0954558 19
1. Farm mechanization - India - Bhiwani (District). 2. Farm mechanization - India - Karnāl (District). 3. Farm mechanization - India - Hisar (District). 4. Social change. I. Title.
HD2075.B48 C42 1987

CHANDĪGARH (INDIA : UNION TERRITORY) - CENSUS, 1981.
Census of India, 1981. Delhi , <1983-[1985]. v. in : LC Card 87-915033 DDC 304.6/0954/552 19
HA4587.C52 C46 1983

Chandler, Alfred Dupont. The coming of managerial capitalism : a casebook on the history of American economic institutions / Alfred D. Chandler, Jr., Richard S. Tedlow. Homewood, Ill. : R.D. Irwin, 1985. xiv, 877 p. : ill. ; 25 cm. (The Irwin series in management and the behavioral sciences) Includes bibliographical references and index. ISBN 0-256-03285-8 LC Card 84-82470 DDC 338.6/44/0973 19
1. Business enterprises - United States - History. 2. Industrial concentration - United States - History. 3. Industry and state - United States - History. 4. Capitalism - United States - History. I. Tedlow, Richard S. II. Title.
HD2785 .C47 1985 ***NYPL [JLE 86-4418]***

Chandler, John. Practical business planning / John Chandler. London ; New York : McGraw-Hill, c1987. 210 p. ; 23 cm. "Published in association with the Institute of Chartered Accountants in England and Wales." Includes bibliographies and index. ISBN 0-07-084172-1 (pbk.) : LC Card 87-3240 DDC 658.4/012 19
1. Corporate planning. 2. Managerial accounting. I. Institute of Chartered Accountants in England and Wales. II. Title.
HD30.28 .C45 1987

Chandler, Tertius. Four thousand years of urban growth : an historical census / Tertius Chandler. Lewiston, N.Y., U. S.A. : St. David's University Press, c1987. xiii, 656 p. : maps ; 26 cm. Bibliography: p. [577]-639. Includes index. ISBN 0-88946-207-0 (alk. paper) LC Card 86-31122 DDC 307.1/4 19
1. Cities and towns - Growth. 2. Population. I. Title.
HB2161 .C46 1987

Chandola, L. M. Juyal, B. N. Child labour . Varanasi , 1985. xiii, 161 p. ; LC Card 87-901161 DDC 331.3/1/0954 19
HD6250.I42 J89 1985

Chandra Joshi, Navin. see **Joshi, Navin Chandra.**

Chandra Mukhopadhyay, Subhas. see **Mukhopadhyay, Subhas Chandra, 1938-**

Chaney, Dale. Selling your house without a broker : the complete guide to saving thousands of dollars in commissions by selling your own home / Dale Chaney and Mary Beth Libbey. Chicago : Contemporary Books, c1986. 98 p. : forms ; 21 cm. Includes index. ISBN 0-8092-4833-6 (pbk.) : LC Card 86-24043 DDC 333.33/8 19
1. House selling. I. Libbey, Mary Beth. II. Title.
HD1379 .C48 1986

Chaney, Elsa. Bunster, Ximena. Sellers & servants . New York , 1985. x, 258 p. : ISBN 0-03-060543-1 (alk. paper) : LC Card 85-6259 DDC 331.4/0985/25 19
HD6072.2.P42 L563 1985
NYPL [JLE 86-910]

Change agent skills in helping and human service settings /. Egan, Gerard. Monterey, Calif. , c1985. xi, 306 p. : ISBN 0-534-03624-4 : LC Card 84-7804 DDC 361.3/07 19
HV11 .E43 1985 ***NYPL [JLE 86-1963]***

Change and continuity among the scheduled caste leather workers /. Prasad, R. R., 1955- Hyderabad , 1986. 132 p., [4] leaves of plates : LC Card 87-902216
HD8039.L42 I575 1986

Change master companies [videorecording] : putting the theory into action / produced for Encyclopaedia Britannica Educational Corp. by Chuck Olin Associates. Chicago, IL : The Corporation, 1987. 1 videocassette (42 min.) : sd., col. Title from data sheet. Based on the book: The change masters / Rosabeth Moss Kanter. Issued as U-matic 3/4 in. or Beta II 1/2 in. or VHS 1/2 in. Shows how Hewlett-Packard, Security Pacific Bank, and the Stanley Works have refocused their business and personnel strategies by using the concepts developed by Dr. Rosabeth Moss Kanter. LC Card 87-705608 DDC 658.3 11
1. Technological innovations - United States - Employee participation. 2. Organizational change - United States. 3. Hewlett-Packard Company. 4. Security Pacific National Bank. 5. Stanley Works Inc. I. Kanter, Rosabeth Moss. Change masters. II. Encyclopaedia Britannica Educational Corporation. III. Chuck Olin Associates.
HD45

The Change masters [motion picture] : understanding the theory / Rosabeth Moss Kanter ; [produced by] Chuck Olin Associates, Inc. Chicago, Ill. : Encyclopaedia Britannica Educational Corp., 1987. 1 film reel (29 min.) : sd., col. ; 16 mm. + 1 teacher's guide. Title from data sheet. Based on the book: The change masters / Rosabeth Moss Kanter. Business and industrial companies and individuals. Issued also as videorecording. Dr. Rosabeth Moss Kanter identifies "change masters" as individuals and companies who anticipate change and respond with new ideas. She describes the seven ingredients that are essential to

successful change masters, and explains how to create the kind of environment that builds innovation and permits acceptance to change. LC Card 87-705269 DDC 658.3 11
1. Technological innovations - United States - Employee participation. 2. Organizational change. I. Kanter, Rosabeth Moss. II. Kanter, Rosabeth Moss. Change masters. III. Chuck Olin Associates. IV. Encyclopaedia Britannica Educational Corporation.
HD45

The Change masters [videorecording] : understanding the theory / Rosabeth Moss Kanter ; [produced by] Chuck Olin Associates, Inc. Chicago, Ill. : Encyclopaedia Britannica Educational Corp., 1987. 1 videocassette (29 min.) : sd., col. + 1 teacher's guide. Title from data sheet. Based on the book: The change masters / Rosabeth Moss Kanter. Business and industrial companies and individuals. Issued as U-matic 3/4 in. or Beta 1/2 in. or VHS 1/2 in. Issued also as motion picture. Dr. Rosabeth Moss Kanter identifies "change masters" as individuals and companies who anticipate change and respond with new ideas. She describes the seven ingredients that are essential to successful change masters, and explains how to create the kind of environment that builds innovation and permits acceptance to change. LC Card 86-707881 DDC 658.3 11
1. Technological innovations - United States - Employee participation. 2. Organizational change. I. Kanter, Rosabeth Moss. II. Kanter, Rosabeth Moss. Change masters. III. Chuck Olin Associates. IV. Encyclopaedia Britannica Educational Corporation.
HD45

CHANGE (PSYCHOLOGY)
Adams, James L. The care and feeding of ideas . Reading, Mass. , 1986. xv, 223 p. : ISBN 0-201-10160-2 : LC Card 86-10895 DDC 153.3/5 19
BF408 .A3 1986 ***NYPL [JFE 87-1553]***

CHANGE, SOCIAL. see **SOCIAL CHANGE.**

Changement de technologie en économie et société. Technologischer Wandel in Wirtschaft und Gesellschaft =. Freiburg, Schweiz , 1985. 316 p., [1] leaf of plates : ISBN 3-7278-0347-9 : LC Card 86-129382
HC79.T4 T436 1985

Changer la Martinique . Crusol, Jean. Paris , c1986. 91 p. : ISBN 2-903033-73-0 : LC Card 86-210884
HC158.6 .C78 1986

Changing alliances /. Dyer, Davis. Boston, Mass. , c1987. xvi, 333 p. ; ISBN 0-87584-175-9 LC Card 86-33619 DDC 338.4/76292/0973 19
HD9710.U52 D94 1987

Changing auditors and the effect on earnings, auditors' opinions, and stock prices /. Mangold, Nancy R. (Nancy Rueyhwa), 1949- Ann Arbor, Mich. , c1987. viii, 165 p. ; ISBN 0-8357-1786-0 (alk. paper) LC Card 87-19128 DDC 338.7/4/0973 19
HF5686.C7 M3295 1987

Changing career values . Hopkins, David M. Bethlehem, PA , 1986. x, 126 p. : ISBN 0-914885-10-3 (pbk.) LC Card 87-112752 DDC 331.25 19
HD8038.U5 H66 1986

The changing culture of a factory /. Jaques, Elliott. New York , 1987. xvii, 341 p. ; ISBN 0-8240-8212-5 (alk. paper) : LC Card 86-25815 DDC 671/.068 19
HD8039.M5 J37 1987

The Changing domestic priorities series. Holahan, John. Medicaid . Washington, D.C. , c1986. xvii, 124 p. ; ISBN 0-87766-406-4 LC Card 86-28100 DDC 353.0084/1045 19
HD7102.U4 H59 1986

The changing face of Canadian labour relations law /. Carter, D. D. Kingston, Ont., Canada , 1985. 15 p. ; ISBN 0-88886-126-5 (pbk.) LC Card 86-145328 DDC 331 s 344.71/01 331 s 347.1041 19
HD8102 .K52 no. 54 KE3009

Changing fertility patterns in Vermont. Burlington, Vt. (Box 70, 60 Main St., Burlington 05402) : Vermont Dept. of Health, [1986] 18 p. : ill. ; 28 cm. (Public health statistics bulletin) Caption title. "July 1986." Bibliography: p. 18. LC Card 86-622900 DDC 304.6/32/09743 19
1. Fertility, Human - Vermont. I. Vermont. Dept. of Health. II. Series.
HB935.V4 C46 1986

Changing fortunes . Tigges, Leann M. New York , 1987. xvi, 174 p. : ISBN 0-275-92580-3 (alk. paper) : LC Card 87-2357 DDC 331.2/973 19
HD4975 .T5 1987

The Changing labor market : a longitudinal study of young men / edited by Stephen M. Hills ; with contributions by David Ball ... [et al.]. Lexington, Mass. : Lexington Books, c1986. x, 166 p. : ill. ; 24 cm. Includes bibliographies and index. ISBN 0-669-11943-1 (alk. paper) LC Card 85-45710 DDC 331.12/0973 19
1. Labor supply - United States - Effect of technological innovations on. 2. Employment of men - United States - Longitudinal studies. 3. Insurance, Unemployment - United States. 4. Young men - Employment - United States. I. Ball, David. II. Hills, Stephen M.
HD6331.2.U5 C47 1986 ***NYPL [JLE 86-1069]***

The changing labour market for postsecondary graduates, 1975-1984 /. Picot, W. Garnett. Ottawa , c1987. 86, 94 p. : ISBN 0-660-52896-7 (pbk.) : LC Card 87-169612 DDC 331.11/423 19
HD6278.C3 P52 1987

Changing money : financial innovation in developed countries / edited by Marcello de Cecco. New York, NY, USA : B. Blackwell, 1987. p. cm. Bibliography: p. Includes index. ISBN 0-631-15501-5 :$60.00 LC Card 86-28317 DDC 332 19
1. Finance. I. De Cecco, Marcello.
HG175 .C445 1987

Changing occupational structure of scheduled tribes /. Singh, R. S. (Rama Shankar), 1950- New Delhi, India , 1986. 291 p. : ISBN 81-210-0175-7 : LC Card 86-903755
HB3640.C48 S56 1986

The Changing passenger car markets : the new role for plastics / Peter J. Mooney, project analyst. Stamford, Conn., U. S.A. : Business Communications Co., c1985. viii, 227 leaves : ill. ; 29 cm. (Business opportunity report . P-069) ISBN 0-89336-479-7 (pbk.) LC Card 87-404429 DDC 381/.4566849 19
1. Automobile industry and trade - United States. 2. Automobile industry and trade. 3. Plastics in automobiles. I. Mooney, Peter. II. Business Communications Co. III. Series.
HD9710.U52 C385 1985

Changing places : Britain's demographic, economic, and social complexion / A.G. Champion ... [et al.]. London ; Baltimore, Md., USA : E. Arnold, 1987. xv, 144 p. : ill. ; 25 cm. Bibliography: p. [131]-135. Includes index. ISBN 0-7131-6498-0 (pbk.) : LC Card 87-148942 DDC 331.12/5/0941 19
1. Labor supply - Great Britain. 2. Great Britain - Population. 3. Great Britain - Economic conditions - 1945-. 4. Great Britain - Social conditions - 1945-. 5. Unemployment - Great Britain. I. Champion, A. G. (Anthony Gerard).
HD5765.A6 C49 1987

The changing profile of pensions in America /. Andrews, Emily S. Washington, DC , c1985. xxvii, 234 p. ; ISBN 0-86643-038-5 (pbk.) LC Card 85-25296 DDC 332.6/7254 19
HD7105.45.U6 A53 1985 ***NYPL [JLE 87-62]***

Changing status of educated working women . Raghunadha Reddy, C. (Chinnathimmanna), 1950- Delhi , New Delhi , 1986. 210 p. ; ISBN 81-7018-379-0 : LC Card 86-902900 DDC 305.4/3/0095484 19
HD6190.A5 R34 1986

The changing structure of South Carolina agriculture since 1959 /. Lyson, Thomas A. Clemson, S.C. [1986] 29 p. : LC Card 87-620716 DDC 338.1/09757 19
HD1775.S6 L97 1986

Changing the course : federal grants-in-aid funding, 1964-83 : the effects of the Reagan administration budget cuts on the District of Columbia and other urban centers : staff report for the Committee on the District of Columbia, House of Representatives, Ninety-ninth Congress, second session. Washington : U. S. G.P.O. : For sale by the Supt. of Docs., Congressional Sales Office, U. S. G.P.O., 1986. xvii, 142 p. : ill., maps ; 24 cm. At head of title: Committee print. "A supplement to Problems in urban centers, vols. I and II, serial nos. 96-17 and 97-15." Distributed to some depository libraries in microfiche. Shipping list no.: 86-559-P. "March 1, 1986." Bibliography: p. 131-135. "Serial no. S-5." Item 1014-A, 1014-B (microfiche) LC Card 86-603365 DDC 336.1/85 19
1. Grants-in-aid - United States. 2. Federal-city relations - United States. 3. Municipal finance - United States. 4. Finance, Public - Washington (D.C.). I. United States. Congress. House. Committee on the District of Columbia. II. Title: Federal grants-in-aid funding, 1964-83.
HJ275 .C455 1986

Changing the definition of a household . Todd, Jean Elizabeth. London , 1986. viii, 43 p. : ISBN 0-11-691071-2 (pbk.) : LC Card 87-132272
HB849.49 .T63 1986

Changing the game . Wilson, Larry. New York , c1987. 286 p. : ISBN 0-671-61313-8 LC Card 87-12900 DDC 658.8/5 19
HF5438.25 .W299 1987

Changing times. The Kiplinger/Changing times guide to buying and selling a home /. Washington, DC , New York, NY , c1987. iii, 311 p. : ISBN 0-938721-02-X (pbk.) : LC Card 87-167806 DDC 643/.12 19
HD1379 .K52 1987

Changing Times Education Service. Risks & rewards of entrepreneurship /. Saint Paul, Minn. , c1988. 123 p. : ISBN 0-8219-0323-3 (pbk.) LC Card 87-21787 DDC 338/.04 19
HB615 .R56 1988

Changing trends in women's employment . Savara, Mira. Bombay , 1986. xii, 137 p. ; LC Card 86-902789 DDC 331.4/877/00954792 19
HD6073.T42 I47 1986

The Changing workplace : new directions in staffing and scheduling. Washington, D.C. : Bureau of National Affairs ; [Rockville, Md.] : Copies obtained from the BNA Response Center, c1986. iv, 140 p. : ill. ; 28 cm. (A BNA special report) "45-LDSR-47"--P. 4 of cover. ISBN 0-87179-910-3 (pbk.) LC Card 86-221689 DDC 331.25/72 19
1. Hours of labor - United States. 2. Hours of labor, Flexible - United States. 3. Part-time employment - United States. 4. Temporary employment - United States. 5. Subcontracting - United States. I. Bureau of National Affairs, Washington, D. C. II. Series.
HD5124 .C46 1986

The Changing world of work, major issues ahead : report of the Director-General. Geneva : International Labour Office, 1986- v. <1 > : ill. ; 24 cm. At head of title: International Labour Conference, 72nd session, 1986. ISBN 92-2-105165-X (pbk. : pt. 1) : LC Card 86-214807 DDC 331 19
1. Labor and laboring classes - 1970-. 2. Labor policy. 3. Industrial relations. I. International Labour Office.
HD4854 .C42 1986

CHANNELS, MARKETING. see **MARKETING CHANNELS.**

Channels to employment for the disabled and ex-offenders /. Rugh, Jack Leighton, 1911- San Gabriel, Calif. (5555 N. Charlotte Ave., San Gabriel 91776) , c1987. 89 p. : LC Card 87-402897 DDC 362.4/0484/02573 19
HD7256.U5 R75 1987

Chant, Verne G. Two global scenarios : the evolution of energy use and the economy to 2030 / Verne G. Chant. Laxenburg, Austria : International Institute for Applied Systems Analysis, c1981. vi, 75 p. : ill. ; 24 cm. (Research reports / International Institute for Applied Systems Analysis . RR 81-35) "November 1981." Bibliography: p. 58. ISBN 3-7045-0026-7 (pbk.) LC Card 83-130587 DDC 333.79/12 19
1. Energy consumption - Forecasting. 2. Energy industries - Forecasting. 3. Energy development - Forecasting. 4. Twenty-first century - Forecasts. I. Title. II. Title: 2 global scenarios. III. Series: Research reports / International Institute for Applied Systems Analysis , RR 81-35.
HD9502.A2 C45 1981 ***NYPL [JLE 86-595]***

Čhanthiphā Sukhumālachāt. Ngopprамān phǣndin phǣn mai : witthayāniphon / sanǟ t [Bangkok? : Chanthiphā Sukhumālachāt], 2521

[1978] 173 (some folded), [3] leaves : charts ; 30 cm. Cover title: Witthayāniphon r LC Card 81-917611
1. Budget - Thailand. I. Title. II. Title: Witthayāniphon r
HJ2162.55 .C47 1978

Chantraine, Heinrich. Frieden und Friedenssicherung in Vergangenheit und Gegenwart . München , 1984. 115 p. ; ISBN 3-7705-2147-1 (pbk.) :
NYPL [JFL 76-295 Bd. 7]

Chanturiia, V. K. (Vladimir Kapitonovich) Molodezh′ i udarnyĭ kommunisticheskiĭ trud : posobie dlia uchashchikhsia / V.K. Chanturiia ; pod red. O.A. Omel′chenko. Moskva : "Prosveshchenie", 1981. 205 p. : ill. (some col.), col. map ; 16 cm. (Moia Sovetskaia Rodina) Authorized for instructional purposes. LC Card 82-178361
1. Youth - Employment - Soviet Union. I. Omel′chenko, O. A. II. Title.
HD6276.S592 C46 1981

Stroitsia Nechernozem′e / V. Chanturiia. Moskva : Stroĭizdat, 1980. 94 p. ; 20 cm. LC Card 81-135603
1. Construction industry - Russian S.F.S.R. - Non-Chernozem Region. 2. Rural development - Russian S.F.S.R. - Non-Chernozem Region. I. Title.
HD9715.S73 N63 1980

Chao, Tzu-yuan.
[Hsin lao tung chia chih li lun. German] Neue Arbeitswerttheorie : der Weg nach Utopia / von Chao Tzu-yuan. ; aus dem Chinesischen übertragen von Christian Gries in Zusammenarbeit mit dem Autor.Deutsche Erstausgabe. Hamburg : [s.n.], 1974. x, 173 p. ; 21 cm. Includes the preface of the original Chinese ed., and also a summary in English. Translation of Hsin lao tung chai chih li lun. LC Card 74-351429 DDC 335.4/12 19
1. Work. 2. Marxian economics. I. Title.
HD4904 .C45715

"Ein Chaos wollen wir nicht" : 18 Gespräche im Klartext zur Schweizer Medienpolitik / herausgegeben von Max Jaggi ; die Gesprächsteilnehmer, Hans Werner Binz ... [et al.]. Basel : Lenos Verlag, c1985. 223 p. : ill. ; 21 cm. (Bd. 9 der Reihe Mediaprint) "Die in diesem Band versammelten Gespräche erschienen erstmals im Schweizer Medien-Magazin Klartext"--T.p. verso. ISBN 3-85787-141-5 : LC Card 86-128638
1. Broadcasting policy - Switzerland. 2. Broadcasters - Switzerland - Interviews. I. Jäggi, Max. II. Binz, Hans Werner, 1925-. III. Klartext (Basel, Switzerland). IV. Series: Mediaprint , Bd. 9.
HE8689.9.S95 C57 1985

Chapel Hill, N. C. University of North Carolina. see **University of North Carolina at Chapel Hill.**

Chapman and Hall computing.
Gilder, Jules H., 1947- Apple IIc and IIe assembly language /. New York , 1986. 178 p. : ISBN 0-412-01121-2 (pbk.) : LC Card 86-2592 DDC 005.265 19
QA76.8.A66225 G55 1986
NYPL [JSE 87-575]

Chapman, Brian A. Shuker, Iain G. W. Economic analysis of the cost structure of commercial sugar cane farms in Louisiana /. Baton Rouge, La. [1986] vi, 50 p. : LC Card 86-622542 DDC 338.1/09763 s 338.1/7361/09763021 19
HD1775.L8 L7 no. 651 HD9107.L8

Chapman, Edward A. Exhibit marketing : a survival guide for managers / Edward A. Chapman, Jr. New York : McGraw-Hill, c1987. x, 309 p. : ill., forms ; 24 cm. Bibliography: p. 299-306. Includes index. ISBN 0-07-010669-X : LC Card 87-2621 DDC 659.1/52 19
1. Exhibitions. 2. Merchandising. 3. Marketing. I. Title.
HF5845 .C47 1987

Chapman, Elwood N. Your attitude is showing : a primer of human relations / Elwood N. Chapman.5th ed. Chicago : Science Research Associates, c1987. vii, 194 p. ; 23 cm. Includes index. ISBN 0-574-20905-0 (pbk.) LC Card 86-26318 DDC 158.7 19
1. Psychology, Industrial. 2. Industrial sociology. 3. Interpersonal relations. I. Title.
HF5548.8 .C36 1987

Chapman, Jack, 1945- How to make $1,000 a minute : negotiating salaries & raises / by Jack Chapman with Steve Sanders. Berkeley, Calif. : Ten Speed Press, c1987. xii, 90 p. : ill. ; 28 cm. Cover title: How to make $1000 a minute. ISBN 0-89815-191-0 (pbk.) : LC Card 86-23099 DDC 650.1/4 19
1. Promotions. 2. Wages. 3. Negotiation in business. 4. Interpersonal relations. I. Title. II. Title: How to make one thousand dollars a minute.
HF5549.5.P7 C48 1987

Chapman, Jeffrey I. Long-term financial planning . Washington, D.C. , 1987. 188 p. ; ISBN 0-87326-076-7 (pbk.) : LC Card 87-2613 DDC 352.1/0973 19
HJ275 .L66 1987

Chapman, Paul G., 1952- The youth training scheme in the United Kingdom / Paul G. Chapman and Michael J. Tooze. Aldershot, Hants, England ; Brookfield, Vt., U. S.A. : Avebury, c1987. x, 124 p. ; 23 cm. Bibliography: p. 80-85. Includes indexes. ISBN 0-566-05360-8 : LC Card 86-29604 DDC 331.3/42592/0941 19
1. Occupational training - Great Britain. 2. Youth - Employment - Great Britain. I. Tooze, Michael J., 1942-. II. Title.
HD5715.5.G7 C47 1987

Chapman, Simon. Great expectorations : advertising and the tobacco industry / by Simon Chapman. London : Comedia Pub. Group, 1986. 158 p. : ill. ; 22 cm. (Comedia series . no. 35) Bibliography: p. [152]-158. ISBN 0-906890-86-1 (pbk.) : LC Card 86-204305 DDC 659.1/96797 19
1. Advertising - Tobacco trade. I. Title. II. Series.
HF6161.T6 C48 1986

Chaponnière, R. Les fonctions des agents économiques exportant des biens d'équipement, dans le cadre des relations est-ouest et nord-sud, depuis 1970 / R. Chaponnière, J. Perrin, B. Réal. [Paris] : Ministère des transports, [1981] 159 leaves : ill. ; 30 cm. At head of title: Université des sciences sociales de Grenoble, Institut de recherche économique et de planification de développement. Includes bibliographical references. LC Card 82-180468 DDC 382/.456817 19
1. Industrial equipment industry - Agents. 2. Industrial equipment industry - Developing countries. 3. Industrial equipment industry - Communist countries. 4. Industrial equipment industry - France. I. Perrin, J. II. Réal, Bernard. III. Université des sciences sociales de Grenoble. Institut de recherche économique et de planification du développement. IV. Title.
HD9705.A2 C55 1981 ***NYPL [JLG 86-212]***

Chapple, Jonathan. Porter, James. Integrating the computer with your business . London , 1980. 308 p. ; ISBN 0-372-30032-4
NYPL [JLD 86-2442]

Chapter management techniques : proceedings from the 1987 conference / presented by the American Production and Inventory Control Society, Inc. Falls Church, VA : The Society, c1987. iv, 64 p. : ill. ; 28 cm. ISBN 0-935406-96-4 (pbk.) LC Card 87-72230 DDC 658.5/06/073 19
1. American Production and Inventory Control Society. I. American Production and Inventory Control Society.
HD40 .C45 1987

Characteristics of high income families, 1980 /. Rashid, A. Ottawa [1986] 97 p. : ISBN 0-660-52875-4 (pbk.) : LC Card 86-210700
HC120.I5 R36 1986

Characteristics of occupational injuries and illnesses in New Mexico, 1982 / prepared by New Mexico Occupational Health and Safety Bureau, Data Management Section in cooperation with U. S. Department of Labor, Bureau of Labor Statistics and New Mexico Labor and Industrial Commission, Office of the Labor Commissioner. Santa Fe, N.M. : State of New Mexico, Environmental Improvement Division, [1983?] 43 p. : ill. ; 28 cm. (EID report . no. EID/OHS/85-3) LC Card 86-621034 DDC 363.1/12/09789021 19
1. Industrial accidents - New Mexico - Statistics. 2. Occupational diseases - New Mexico - Statistics. I. New Mexico. Occupational Health and Safety Bureau. Data Management Section. II. Series: EID report (New Mexico. Environmental Improvement Division) , no. EID/OHS/85-3.
HD7262.5.U62 N625 1983

Characteristics of occupational injuries and illnesses in New Mexico, 1983 / prepared by Patrick Jennings ... [et al.] in cooperation with the U. S. Department of Labor, Bureau of Labor Statistics and New Mexico Labor and Industrial Commission, Office of the Labor Commissioner. Santa Fe, N.M. : State of New Mexico, Environmental Improvement Division, New Mexico Occupational Health and Safety Bureau, Data Management Section, [1983] 47 p. : ill. ; 28 cm. (EID report . no. EID/OHS/85-4) LC Card 86-620786 DDC 363.1/12/09789021 19
1. Industrial accidents - New Mexico - Statistics. 2. Occupational diseases - New Mexico - Statistics. I. Jennings, Patrick C. II. United States. Bureau of Labor Statistics. III. New Mexico Labor and Industrial Commission. Office of the Labor Commissioner. IV. New Mexico. Occupational Health and Safety Bureau. Data Management Section.
HD7262.5.U62 N626 1983

Characteristics of poverty in nonmetro counties /. Morrissey, Elizabeth S. Washington, D.C. , 1985. iv, 10 p. : LC Card 86-602555 DDC 362.5/0973 19
HC110.P6 M67 1985

Charanjit Chanana. see **Chanana, Charanjit.**

Charbit, Yves. Enfants, familles, migrations dans le bassin méditerranéen / Yves Charbit et Catherine Bertrand. [Paris] : Presses universitaires de France, 1985. viii, 195 p. ; 24 cm. (Travaux et documents / Institut national d'études démographiques, 0071-8823 . cahier no 110) Title on spine: Enfants, familles, migrations. "Bibliographie générale": p. [149]-158. "Bibliographie commentée": p. [159]-177. ISBN 2-7332-0110-7 (pbk.)
1. Children of alien laborers - Europe. 2. Children of alien laborers - Mediterranean Region. 3. Alien labor - Europe. 4. Europe - Foreign population. I. Bertrand, Catherine. II. Title. III. Title: Enfants, familles, migrations. IV. Series: France. Institut national d'études démographiques. Travaux et documents, cahier no 110.
HQ792.E8 C47 1985
NYPL [JLL 72-295 cahier no 110]

Charbon, Paul. Le facteur et ses métamorphoses / Paul Charbon, Pierre Nougaret. Barembach : J.-P. Gyss, c1984. 266 p., [24] p. of plates : ill. (some col.) ; 33 cm. Includes index. Bibliography: p. 259-266. ISBN 2-902912-40-4 LC Card 85-118656 DDC 383/.4944 19
1. Postal service - France - Letter carriers - History. 2. Postal service - France - History. I. Nougaret, Pierre. II. Title.
HE6989.P4 C48 1984 ***NYPL [JLG 86-165]***

CHARBONNEAUX-B.S.N. (FIRM) - HISTORY.
La Verrerie champenoise, Charbonneaux-B.S.N. Reims, de 1870 à nos jours /. Die , c1984. 279 p. : ISBN 2-904638-12-1 : LC Card 84-247744
HD9623.F8 V47 1984

CHARCOAL INDUSTRY - DELAWARE RIVER VALLEY (N.Y.-DEL. AND N.J.) - HISTORY.
Myers, Frank Daniel. The wood chemical industry in the Delaware Valley /. Middletown, N.Y. , 1986. [160] p. : LC Card 87-108267
HD9660.M573 U616 1986

Chardonnens, Jean-Pierre. Le financement de l'entreprise en période de récession économique / par Jean-Pierre Chardonnens. [Fribourg] : Editions universitaires Fribourg Suisse, c1984. 269 p. : ill. ; 21 cm. (Documents économiques . 24) Bibliography: p. 261-269. ISBN 2-8271-0281-1 : LC Card 84-225557 DDC 658.1/5 19
1. Business enterprises - Finance. 2. Business cycles. I. Title. II. Series.
HG4026 .C457 1984

Charged bodies . Mahon, Thomas. New York , c1985. 339 p. : ISBN 0-453-00487-3 LC Card 84-18957 DDC 338.4/76213817/0979473 19
HD9696.A3 U5666 1985
NYPL [JLD 86-1109]

CHARITABLE INSTITUTIONS. see **CHARITIES.**

CHARITIES - EUROPE - HISTORY.
La Storia dei poveri . Roma , c1985. xii, 300 p. ; ISBN 88-382-3530-9 : LC Card 86-198943
HC240.9.P6 S76 1985

CHARITIES, FOOD PRODUCING. see **FOOD RELIEF.**

CHARITIES - ITALY - LOMBARDY - HISTORY.
Bressan, E. (Edoardo) Povertà e assistenza in

Lombardia nell'età napoleonica /. [Milano] , Bari , c1985. viii, 339 p. : ISBN 88-420-2653-0 : LC Card 86-162978
HC307.L8 B74 1985

CHARITY.
Garczyński, Stefan. O dawaniu /. Warszawa , 1985. 172 p. ; ISBN 83-10-08676-8
NYPL [*QO 87-1235]

En charkuterifabrik med tradition .
Grenander-Nyberg, Gertrud, 1912- Stockholm , c1985. 207 p. : ISBN 91-38-09206-9 LC Card 86-159511
HD9145.S88 E544 1985

Charles Creel, Pilar. Pontones S., Jaime. Condicionantes estructurales del desarrollo tecnológico /. [Mexico City, Mexico] [1982] 27, [2] leaves ; LC Card 85-203882
HC79.T4 P66 1982

Charles, Patricia. Search Conference on Energy Futures for St. Lucia (1982 : Castries, Saint Lucia) The energy future for St. Lucia . Castries, St. Lucia [1982] 23 p. ; LC Card 87-400749 DDC 333.79/097298/43 19
HD9502.S0552 S4 1982

Charles Redd monographs in western history. (no. 17) Layton, Stanford J., 1941- To no privileged class . Provo, Utah , Salt Lake City, Utah , c1987. p. cm. ISBN 0-941214-59-1 : LC Card 87-14299 DDC 333.1/6/0978 19
HD1339.U5 L39 1987

Charles River Associates. Analysis of the federal residential energy tax credits [microform] . Boston, Mass. , 1982. v, 102 p. :
NYPL [*XME-11,559]

Charles Veillon . Jéquier, François. Zürich , 1985. 142 p. : LC Card 85-139330 DDC 338.092/4 B 19
HC395.5.V45 J45 1985

Charnay, Annie. Transports et échanges . [Lyon] , 1979. 64 p. ; LC Card 80-125866
HE192.F8 T73 1979

Charnov, Bruce H.
Management report : how to hire a consultant / by Bruce H. Charnov. Westbury, N.Y. : Asher-Gallant Press, c1987. 63 p. : ill. ; 28 cm. ISBN 0-87280-120-9 (pbk.) : LC Card 87-24106 DDC 658.4/6 19
1. Business consultants. I. Title. II. Title: How to hire a consultant.
HD69.C6 C36 1987

Montana, Patrick J. Management /. New York , c1987. xi, 466 p. : ISBN 0-8120-3559-3 (pbk.) : LC Card 87-1376 DDC 658 19
HD31 .M618 1987

Charoon Vitiprod. Rapid population growth, living conditions, and fertility reduction implication (Bangkok metropolis) / Charoon Vitiprod. Edited version. [Singapore : s.n.], 1979. ii, 41 leaves : maps ; 29 cm. (SEAPRAP research report . no. 37) Cover title. Includes bibliographical references. LC Card 82-940038
1. Bangkok Metropolitan Area (Thailand) - Population. 2. Fertility, Human - Thailand - Bangkok Metropolitan Area. 3. Housing - Thailand - Bangkok Metropolitan Area. 4. Quality of life - Thailand - Bangkok Metropolitan Area. 5. Birth control - Thailand - Bangkok Metropolitan Area. I. Title. II. Series.
HB3644.55.B36 C48 1979

Charoux, J. A. E. (J. A. Eric) The integration of the Black manager into South African organizations / by J.A.E. Charoux. Cape Town : Juta & Co., 1986. xi, 178 p. : ill. ; 21 cm. Bibliography: p. 165-173. Includes index. ISBN 0-7021-1706-4 (pbk.) LC Card 87-113544 DDC 331.6/3/968 19
1. Executives, Black - South Africa - Case studies. 2. Blacks - Employment - South Africa - Case studies. I. Title.
HD38.25.S6 C53 1986

Charpentier, Silvia. Lizano Fait, Eduardo. La condicionalidad cruzada y la deuda externa /. [San José] , 1986. 16, [1] leaves : LC Card 87-127835 DDC 336.3/435/091724 19
HJ8899 .L59 1986

Charro Valls, José María. Sociedades de garantía recíproca : situación actual / José María Charro Valls, María Isabel Sánchez Bernal. Salamanca, España : Ediciones Universidad de Salamanca, 1985. 73 p. ; 22 cm. (Acta Salmanticensia. Científicos y literarios . 61) Bibliography: p. 73. ISBN 84-7481-349-2 LC Card 87-133330
1. Mutual funds - Spain. 2. Mutual funds - Europe. 3. Mutual funds - Japan. I. Sánchez Bernal, María Isabel. II. Title. III. Series.
HG5634.5 .C47 1985

Charron, Marie-France, 1952- Le suicide au Québec : analyse statistique / Marie-France Charron. [Quebec] : Gouvernement du Québec, Ministère des affaires sociales, Direction générale des programmes de santé, Direction des politiques de santé, 1983. 221 p. : ill. ; 22 cm. Includes bibliographical references. ISBN 2-551-05209-2 LC Card 83-168606
1. Suicide - Québec (Province) - Statistics. I. Québec (Province). Direction des politiques de santé. II. Title.
HB1323.S82 C352 1983

Chartac taxation guides.
Carmichael, K. S. (Keith Stanley) Taxation of Lloyd's underwriters /. London , 1980. xvi, 107 p. : ISBN 0-372-30027-8 (pbk.) : LC Card 81-107459
HG8123.G7 C37 1980

A Chartbook from the Conference Board.
Collins, Lora S. The U. S. economy to 1990 /. New York, N.Y. , c1985. 21 p. : ISBN 0-8237-0307-X (pbk.) LC Card 86-200284 DDC 338.5/443/0973 19
HC106.8 .C636 1985

CHARTISM.
Chartism and Christianity. New York , 1986. 45, 24, 90 p. ; ISBN 0-8240-5593-4 (alk. paper) : LC Card 86-25705 DDC 322/.2 19
HD8396 .C483 1986

Chartism in Wales and Ireland. New York , 1986. 15, 32, 16, 18, 20 p. : ISBN 0-8240-5594-2 (alk. paper) : LC Card 86-25706 DDC 322/.2/0941 19
HD8396 .C494 1986

Saville, John. 1848 . Cambridge [Cambridgeshire] , New York , 1987. ix, 310 p. ; ISBN 0-521-33341-5 LC Card 86-29975 DDC 322/.2/0941 19
HD8396 .S28 1987

CHARTISM - BIOGRAPHY.
Chartist biographies and autobiographies. New York , 1986. 90 p. ; ISBN 0-8240-5599-3 : LC Card 86-33612 DDC 322.4/4/0922 B 19
HD8396 .C528 1986

CHARTISM - HISTORY.
Rothstein, Theodore. From chartism to labourism /. New York , 1984. vi, 365 p. ; ISBN 0-8240-5722-8 (alk. paper) : LC Card 83-48495 DDC 335/.1 19
HX249 .R68 1984 ***NYPL [JLD 86-1828]***

CHARTISM - SOURCES.
Chartist and anti-Chartist pamphlets. New York , 1986. ca. 300 p. : ISBN 0-8240-5583-7 (alk. paper) : LC Card 86-27144 DDC 322/.2 19
HD8396 .C527 1986

Chartist biographies and autobiographies. New York , 1986. 90 p. ; ISBN 0-8240-5599-3 : LC Card 86-33612 DDC 322.4/4/0922 B 19
HD8396 .C528 1986

Feargus O'Connor, attack and defense. New York , 1986. 1 v. (various pagings) ; ISBN 0-8240-5592-6 (alk. paper) : LC Card 86-27131 DDC 322/.2/0924 19
HD8396 .F43 1986

Working Men's Association, the first convention, and the National Association. New York , 1986. 1 v. (various pagings) : ISBN 0-8240-5586-1 : LC Card 86-33479 DDC 322/.2/0942 19
HD8396 .W67 1986

Chartist and anti-Chartist pamphlets. New York : Garland Pub. Co., 1986. ca. 300 p. : ill. ; 23 cm. (Chartism : working-class politics in the Industrial Revolution) Reprint of pamphlets published 1838-1844. CONTENTS. - An address to the working men of England / Peter Bussey -- An address on the people's charter / Humphrey Price -- A glance at the present times / Humphrey Price -- The question "What is a Chartist?" answered the Finsbury Tract Society -- The designs of the Chartists and their probable consequences / Edward Baines -- Warnings to the people on street warfare / Alexander Somerville -- The rights of woman / R.J. Richardson -- An examination of the Corn and Provision laws / John Campbell -- Letters to the Manchester Chartists / P.M. McDouall -- Stubborn facts from the factories / William Rashleigh. ISBN 0-8240-5583-7 (alk. paper) : LC Card 86-27144 DDC 322/.2 19
1. Chartism - Sources.
HD8396 .C527 1986

Charvet, Jean-Paul. Les greniers du monde / Jean-Paul Charvet. Paris : Economica, c1985. 368 p. : ill., maps ; 24 cm. (Collection Economie agricole & agro-alimentaire) Bibliography: p. [347]-357. ISBN 2-7178-0925-2 : LC Card 85-191889 DDC 338.1/731 19
1. Grain trade - Illinois. 2. Grain trade - France - Beauce. I. Title.
HD9030.5 .C47 1985 ***NYPL [JLE 86-488]***

Chase, C. David. Mugged on Wall Street : an insider shows you how to protect yourself from the financial pros / C. David Chase. New York : Simon and Schuster, c1987. 349 p. : ill. ; 25 cm. Includes index. ISBN 0-671-62706-6 LC Card 87-4707 DDC 332.6/78 19
1. Investments - United States. 2. Finance, Personal - United States. I. Title.
HG4910 .C52 1987

Chase Econometrics (Firm)
The Next oil shock . Bala Cynwyd, PA (150 Monument Rd., Bala Cynwyd 19004) , 1986. 2 v. : LC Card 87-109243 DDC 333.82/32 19
HD9560.5 .N47 1986

U. S. economic review . Bala Cynwyd, Pa., USA (150 Monument Rd., Bala Cynwyd 19004-1790) , c1985. 7, 28 p. : LC Card 87-145506 DDC 338.5/443/0973 19
HC106.8 .U18 1985

CHASE, THE. see **HUNTING.**

Chase World Information Corporation. Bazarian, Carl J. The Gulf States =. New York, N.Y. , c1980. 577 p. : ISBN 0-916006-07-7 LC Card 80-65496
HC415.3 .B39 1980

The Chase World Information series on developing business in the Middle East and North Africa.
Bazarian, Carl J. The Gulf States =. New York, N.Y. , c1980. 577 p. : ISBN 0-916006-07-7 LC Card 80-65496
HC415.3 .B39 1980

Chastain, Clark E. Corporate asset management : a guide for financial and accounting professionals / Clark E. Chastain. New York : Quorum Books, 1987. xxiii, 345 p. : ill. ; 24 cm. Includes bibliographies and index. ISBN 0-89930-237-8 (lib. bdg. : alk. paper) LC Card 87-2493 DDC 658.1/5244 19
1. Corporations - Finance. 2. Assets (Accounting). 3. Cash management. 4. Consolidation and merger of corporations - Finance. I. Title.
HG4026 .C458 1987

Chasteen, Lanny G., 1942- Intermediate accounting / Lanny G. Chasteen, Richard E. Flaherty, Melvin C. O'Connor. 2nd ed. New York : Random House, Business Division, c1987. xxviii, 1328 p. : ill. ; 27 cm. Includes index. ISBN 0-394-35802-3 : LC Card 86-29865 DDC 657/.044 19
1. Accounting. I. Flaherty, Richard E., 1944-. II. O'Connor, Melvin C. III. Title.
HF5635 .C474 1987

"Chastit͡sa serdt͡sa moego--" : dokumental'nye rasskazy o leningradskikh rabochikh--laureatakh Gosudarstvennoĭ premii SSSR / [sostavitel' knigi A.S. Osipov]. Leningrad : Lenizdat, 1981. 331 p. : ports. ; 22 cm. LC Card 82-179000
1. Labor and laboring classes - Russian S.F.S.R. - Leningrad - Biography. I. Osipov, A. S. (Aleksandr Sergeevich).
HD8530.L5 C42 1981

Chastotnyĭ anglo-russkiĭ slovar'. Kadieva, D. A. Leningrad , 1986. 126 p. ; LC Card 87-146427
HB61 .K23 1986

Chatelain, Jacky. Les trous du commerce extérieur / Jacky Chatelain. Paris : Syros, c1984. 170 p. : ill. ; 19 cm. (Collection "Alternatives économiques") Bibliography: p. 167-168. ISBN 2-86738-031-1 : LC Card 84-241861
1. Balance of trade - France. I. Series: Collection "Alternatives économiques". II. Title.
HF3556.5 .C42 1984

Chatham House paper .
(34) Turner, Louis, 1942- Industrial collaboration with Japan /. London , New York , 1987. 117 p. ; ISBN 0-7102-1109-0 (pbk.) :

LC Card 86-26048 DDC 338.8/8 19
HD62.47 .T87 1987

Chatham House papers .
(no. 35) Holley, H. A., 1924- Developing country debt . London : London ; 85 p. ; ISBN 0-7102-1211-9 (pbk.) : LC Card 86-29838 DDC 336.3/435/091724 19
HG3891.5 .H65 1987

(35) Holley, H. A., 1924- Developing country debt . London : London ; 85 p. ; ISBN 0-7102-1211-9 (pbk.) : LC Card 86-29838 DDC 336.3/435/091724 19
HG3891.5 .H65 1987

Chatterji, P. C. (Probhat Chandra), 1921- Broadcasting in India / P.C. Chatterji. New Delhi ; Newbury Park Calif. : Sage, 1987. 210 p. ; 23 cm. (Case studies on broadcasting systems) In association with the International Institute of Communications." Includes index. ISBN 0-8039-9529-6 (U. S.) LC Card 87-4336 DDC 384.54/0954 19
1. Broadcasting - India. 2. Broadcasting policy - India. I. Title.
HE8689.9.I4 C49 1987

Chatterji, Rakhahari, 1943- Working class and the nationalist movement in India : the critical years / Rakhahari Chatterji. New Delhi : South Asian Publishers, c1984. ix, 215 p. ; 22 cm. Includes bibliographical references and index. LC Card 84-902674 DDC 322.4/4/0954 19
1. Labor and laboring classes - India - Political activity. 2. Nationalism - India - History. 3. India - Politics and government - 1919-1947. 4. India - Politics and government - 1857-1919. I. Title.
HD8686 .C47 1984 ***NYPL [JLD 87-709]***

Chattopadhyay, Gouranga P., 1931- When the twain meet . Allahabad , 1986. vi, 170 p. ; LC Card 87-900706 DDC 658/.00954 19
HD70.I4 W54 1986

Châu, Lê- see **Lê-Châu.**

Chaudhary, S. K. Planning and employment trends in India / S.K. Chaudhary. New Delhi : Deep & Deep Publications, c1987. 300 p. ; 23 cm. With special reference to Bihar. Bibliography: p. [290]-298. Includes index. LC Card 86-903543 DDC 331.11/0954/12 19
1. Labor supply - India. 2. Unemployment - India. 3. Manpower policy - India. 4. Labor supply - India - Bihar. 5. Unemployment - India - Bihar. 6. Manpower policy - India - Bihar. I. Title.
HD5819 .C47 1987

Chaudhry-Lawton, Rani. Hastings, Colin. The superteam solution . San Diego, Calif. , c1987. x, 182 p. : ISBN 0-88390-206-0 (pbk.) : LC Card 87-19185 DDC 658.4/036 19
HD66 .H38 1987

Chauhan, Indira, 1949-
The dilemma of working women hostelers : with special reference to Maharashtra / Indira Chauhan. Delhi : B.R. Pub. Corp. ; New Delhi : Distributed by D.K. Publishers' Distributors, 1986. 70 p. : ill. ; 23 cm. Bibliography: p. [66]-67. Includes index. ISBN 81-7018-374-X : LC Card 86-902619 DDC 305.4/0954/792 19
1. Women - Employment - India. 2. Women - Employment - India - Maharashtra. 3. Women - Housing - India. 4. Women - Housing - India - Maharashtra. 5. Lodging-houses - India. 6. Lodging-houses - India - Maharashtra. I. Title.
HD6189 .C42 1986

Purdah to profession : a case study of working women in M.P / Indira Chauhan. Delhi : B.R. Pub. Corp. ; New Delhi : Distributed by D.K. Publishers' Distributors, 1986. vi, 295 p. ; 23 cm. Socioeconomic conditions, with reference to Bhopal City, Madhya Pradesh. Bibliography: p. [285]-292. Includes index. ISBN 81-7018-375-8 : LC Card 86-902846 DDC 331.4/0954/3 19
1. Women - Employment - India - Bhopal - Case studies. 2. Women - Employment - India - Case studies. 3. Women - India - Bhopal - Social conditions - Case studies. 4. Women - India - Social conditions - Case studies. I. Title.
HD6190.B48 C47 1986

Chaurasia, B. P. (Bhanu Pratap) Urban land use and planning / B.P. Chaurasia. Allahabad, India : Chugh Publications, 1987. xxiii, 347 p. : ill., maps ; 22 cm. Study with reference to Ganga-Ghaghra Doab East Region, eastern Uttar Pradesh. Bibliography: p. [295]-304. Includes index. ISBN 81-85076-20-0 : LC Card 87-900386 DDC 333.77/17/09542 19
1. Land use, Urban - India - Uttar Pradesh. 2. City planning - India - Uttar Pradesh. I. Title.
HD879.U8 C53 1987

Chavane, Laurence. Le phénomène Leclerc : de Landerneau à l'an 2000 / Laurence Chavane. Paris : Plon, c1986. 253 p., [16] p. of plates : ill. ; 23 cm. Includes bibliographical references. ISBN 2-259-01481-X : LC Card 86-186372
1. Leclerc, Edouard, 1926-. 2. Leclerc, Michel-Edouard. 3. Supermarkets - France - History. 4. Businessmen - France - Biography. I. Title.
HF5469.23.F72 L422 1986

Chavangi, Noel A.
Cultural aspects of fuelwood procurement in Kakamega District / Noel Chavangi. Nairobi : Beijer Institute, [1984] 13 leaves ; 30 cm. (Working paper / Kenya Woodfuel Development Programme . no. 4) Cover title. At head of title: KWDP. "October 1984." LC Card 87-112356 DDC 333.75 19
1. Fuelwood industry - Kenya - Kakamega District. 2. Agricultural development projects - Kenya - Kakamega District. 3. Tree planting - Kenya - Kakamega District. 4. Sexual division of labor - Kenya - Kakamega District. I. Series: Working paper / Kenya Woodfuel Development Programme , no. 4. II. Title.
HD9769.F843 K43 1984

Culture as the basis for implementing self-sustaining wood fuel development programmes / Noel A. Chavangi, Rutger J. Engelhard, Valerie Jones. Nairobi, Kenya : Beijer Institute, [1985] 24 leaves ; 30 cm. Cover title. At head of title: KWDP. "October 1985"--Cover. Bibliography: leaf 23. LC Card 87-111963 DDC 333.75 19
1. Fuelwood industry - Kenya. 2. Agricultural development projects - Kenya. 3. Tree planting - Kenya. 4. Sexual division of labor - Kenya. I. Engelhard, Rutger J. II. Jones, Valerie. III. Kenya Woodfuel Development Programme. IV. Title.
HD9769.F843 K433 1985

CHAVERS, P. W.
Chavers-Wright, Madrue, 1916- The guarantee . New York , 1985. xix, 425 p. : ISBN 0-931505-02-X (pbk.) : LC Card 84-51854 DDC 338/.04/0924 B 19
HG2463.C48 C48 1985
NYPL [Sc D 86-412]

Chavers-Wright, Madrue, 1916- The guarantee . New York , 1987, c1985. xix, 427 p. : ISBN 0-931505-05-4 : LC Card 86-51447 DDC 338/.04/0924 B 19
HG2463.C48 C48 1987

Chavers-Wright, Madrue, 1916-
The guarantee : P.W. Chavers, banker, entrepreneur, philanthropist in Chicago's Black Belt of the twenties / by Madrue Chavers-Wright.1st ed. New York : Wright-Armstead Associates, 1985. xix, 425 p. : ill. ; 22 cm. Includes index. Bibliography: p. 413-418. ISBN 0-931505-02-X (pbk.) : LC Card 84-51854 DDC 338/.04/0924 B 19
1. Chavers, P. W. 2. Bankers - Illinois - Chicago - Biography. 3. Afro-Americans in business - Illinois - Chicago - Biography. 4. Entrepreneur - Biography. 5. Philanthropists - Illinois - Chicago - Biography. 6. Chicago - Race relations - 20th century. I. Title.
HG2463.C48 C48 1985
NYPL [Sc D 86-412]

The guarantee : P.W. Chavers, banker, entrepreneur, philanthropist in Chicago's Black Belt of the twenties / by Madrue Chavers-Wright.2nd ed. New York : Wright-Armstead Associates, 1987, c1985. xix, 427 p. : ill. ; 23 cm. Bibliography: p. 413-418. Includes index. ISBN 0-931505-05-4 : LC Card 86-51447 DDC 338/.04/0924 B 19
1. Chavers, P. W. 2. Bankers - Illinois - Chicago - Biography. 3. Afro-Americans in business - Illinois - Chicago - Biography. 4. Philanthropists - Illinois - Chicago - Biography. 5. Chicago (Ill.) - Race relations. I. Title.
HG2463.C48 C48 1987

Chaves, Fernando Luis. Tierras para asentamientos populares . Quito, Ecuador , 1985. 378 p. : LC Card 87-400165 DDC 333.77/13/0986613 19
HD530.Q58 T54 1985

Chavez, Valerie Taliman. Roberts, Malcolm B. Senate Transportation Committee, RS 2477 Task Force report /. [Anchorage, Alaska] [1986] 121 leaves, 27 p. : LC Card 86-622718 DDC 333.78/09798 19
HE356.A4 R63 1986

Chavunduka, G. L. Report of the Commission of Inquiry into the Agricultural Industry /. [Harare?] [1982] ix, 205 p. : LC Card 85-980325 DDC 338.1/096891 19
HD2131 .R47 1982

Chawluk, A. Unemployment, hysteresis, and the natural rate hypothesis . Oxford, UK , New York, NY, USA , 1987. p. cm. ISBN 0-631-15688-7 : LC Card 87-14071 DDC 331.13/7 19
HD5707.5 .U555 1987

Che-Alford, Janet. Mortgagor [sic] households in Canada : their geographic and household characteristics, affordability and housing problems / by Janet Che-Alford = Ménages débiteurs hypothécaires au Canada : caractéristiques géographiques, caractéristiques du ménage, degré d'accessibilité à la propriété et problèmes liés au logement / par Janet Che-Alford. Ottawa : Statistics Canada, Housing Family and Social Statistics Division, c1986. 100 p. : ill. ; 28 cm. English and French. Includes bibliographies. ISBN 0-660-52986-6 (pbk.) : LC Card 86-202749 DDC 332.7/22/0971 19
1. Home ownership - Canada. 2. Mortgage loans - Canada. 3. Households - Canada. I. Title. II. Title: Ménages débiteurs hypothécaires au Canada.
HD7287.82.C2 C48 1986

Che cosa si produce, come e per chi : manuale italiano di microeconomia / a cura di Onorato Castellino con Daniele Ciravegna ... [et al.].2a ed. riv. e ampliata. Torino : G. Giappichelli, 1983. 514 p. : ill. ; 25 cm. Includes bibliographical references. LC Card 85-167580
1. Microeconomics. 2. Economics. I. Castellino, Onorato. II. Ciravegna, Daniele.
HB177 .C46 1983

Cheah, Chee-Wah. Jussawalla, Meheroo, 1923- The calculus of international communications . Littleton, Colo. , 1987. xiv, 159 p. ; ISBN 0-87287-503-2 : LC Card 87-2640 DDC 384/.068 19
HE7645 .J87 1987

Cheaper transportation . Farley, H. W. Yorkville, Ill. , 1874. 10 p. ; LC Card 85-665909
HE199.U6 F3x 1874

The cheapskate's handbook . Lowe, Mifflin. Los Angeles , 1986. 104 p. : ISBN 0-8431-1246-8 (pbk.): LC Card 86-207189 DDC 332.024 19
HG7931 .L68 1986

Chebanenko, Vladimir Mikhaĭlovich. Sistema planirovaniia tekhnicheskogo urovnia otrasli / V.M. Chebanenko. Moskva : "Ėkonomika", 1985. 118, [7] p. : ill. ; 21 cm. Bibliography: p. [124] LC Card 85-241451
1. Industrial management - Soviet Union. 2. Efficiency, Industrial - Soviet Union. 3. Technological innovations - Soviet Union. I. Title.
HD70.S63 C45 1985

Cheblokov, A. T. (Andreĭ Timofeevich)
Finansovoe planirovanie v promyshlennosti / A.T. Cheblokov. Moskva : "Finansy i statistika", 1983. 133, [2] p. ; 20 cm. Bibliography: p. 133-[134] LC Card 84-134674
1. Soviet Union - Industries - Finance - Planning. 2. Finance - Soviet Union. I. Title.
HC336.25 .C48 1983

CHECK COLLECTION SYSTEMS - GERMANY (WEST)
Vajc, Klaus, 1958- Ausgliederung des Zahlungsverkehrs aus dem Universalbankbereich /. Frankfurt am Main , New York , c1986. viii, 238 p. : ISBN 3-8204-8825-1 LC Card 86-220359
HG1692 .V34 1986

CHECK FLOAT - UNITED STATES.
Thomas, O. Tom. Trimming float to build earnings . Chicago, Ill. (111 E. Wacker Dr., Chicago 60601) , c1986. iv, 104 p. : LC Card 86-233102 DDC 332.1/752 19
HG1692 .T46 1986

Checketts, Darby. Take pride in your work and build team effectiveness / Darby Checketts. Provo, Utah : Cornerstone Professional Development, c1987. v, 132 p. : ill. ; 22 cm. Bibliography: p. 131-132. ISBN 0-9618170-0-3 (pbk.) LC Card 87-70380 DDC 658.4/036 19
1. Employee motivation. 2. Work groups. I. Title.
HF5549.5.M63 C45 1987

CHECKS - BRAZIL - RIO GRANDE DO SUL.
Michel, Nelson Emílio. Evolução dos índices do número e do valor de cheques compensados no Rio Grande do Sul, período de 1960-7, e sua análise estatística /. Porto Alegre , 1976. 79 leaves : LC Card 82-159893
HG1692 .M53 1976

CHECKS - CRIMINAL PROVISIONS - ECONOMIC ASPECTS - BRAZIL.
Iorio de Souza, Ubiratan Jorge, 1946- Uma análise econômica do problema do cheque sem fundos no Brasil /. Rio de Janeiro [Brasília] , 1985. 204 p. : LC Card 87-141390 DDC 332.7/6 19
HG1691 .I58 1985

CHECKS - UNITED STATES.
Story, Joseph, 1779-1845. Commentaries on the law of promissory notes [microform]. Boston, 1868. xliv, 739 p. LC Card 12-34848
*NYPL [*ZT-1734]*

Cheeks, James E. Keoghs : keys to security and wealth / James E. Cheeks. New York : F. Watts, c1986. xviii, 248 p. ; 22 cm. Includes index. ISBN 0-531-15505-6 LC Card 85-31753 DDC 332.024/01 19
1. Retirement income - United States. 2. Finance, Personal - United States. I. Title.
HG1660.U5 C48 1986 NYPL [JLD 86-3669]

Cheema, G. Shabbir. Urban shelter and services : public policies and management approaches / G. Shabbir Cheema. New York : Praeger, 1987. x, 220 p. ; 25 cm. Bibliography: p. 203-211. Includes index. ISBN 0-275-92653-2 (alk. paper) : LC Card 87-6982 DDC 363.5/8 19
1. Poor - Housing - Government policy - Developing countries.
HD7287.96.D44 C47 1987

CHEESE INDUSTRY - VENEZUELA - LARA.
Naranjo M., José R. La artesanía del queso larense /. Caracas , 1985. 202 p., [16] p. of plates : ISBN 980-265-223-7 LC Card 87-403552 DDC 338.1/773/098725 19
HD9280.V43 L376 1985

CHEESEMAKERS - VENEZUELA - LARA.
Naranjo M., José R. La artesanía del queso larense /. Caracas , 1985. 202 p., [16] p. of plates : ISBN 980-265-223-7 LC Card 87-403552 DDC 338.1/773/098725 19
HD9280.V43 L376 1985

Chekeres, A. I. (Aleksandr Ivanovich)
Ėffektivnost′ territorial′noĭ organizatsii promyshlennogo proizvodstva v Kazakhstane /. Alma-Ata , 1980. 190 p. ; LC Card 82-164638
HC337.K33 D53 1980

Chekhutov, A. I. Razvivaiushchiesia strany . Moskva , 1982. 307 p. ; LC Card 85-115259
HC59.7 .R33858 1982

CHELIABINSKAIA OBLAST′ (R.S.F.S.R.) - INDUSTRIES.
Osobennosti razvitiia i puti povysheniia ėffektivnosti proizvoditel′nykh sil regiona /. Sverdlovsk , 1984. 141 p. ; LC Card 86-135171
HC337.R852 C456 1984

Chelmēs, D. (Dēmētrios), 1894-1967. Ekthesis tou dioikētou k-ou Dēmētriou E. Chelmē ex onomatos tou Dioikētikou Symvouliou tēs Trapezēs kata tēn genikēn syneleusin tōn metochōn tēs 25ēs Maiou 1964. Athēnai : Ethnikē Trapeza tēs Hellados, 1964. 55 p. ; 29 cm. "Ethnikē Trapeza tēs Hellados: Hē drastēriotēs kata ta etē 1957-1963": ([1] folded leaf, [2] p.) laid in. LC Card 87-109901
1. Greece - Economic conditions - 1918-1974. 2. Ethnikē Trapeza tēs Hellados. I. Ethnikē Trapeza tēs Hellados. II. Ethnikē Trapeza tēs Hellados. Dioikētikon Symvoulion. III. Title.
HC295 .C45 1964

Chelovecheskiĭ faktor--zaniatost′, blagosostoianie /. Kostakov, V. G. (Vladimir Georgievich) Moskva , 1981. 78 p. : LC Card 82-164831
HD5796 .K567 1981

Chelovek, svobodnoe vremia i profsoiuzy / pod redaktsieĭ N.P. Pishchulina. Moskva : Profizdat, 1980. 256 p., [32] p. of plates : col. ill. ; 18 cm. Title on added t.p.: Chovek, svobodno vreme i profsŭiuzi. Includes bibliographical references. LC Card 81-137052
1. Industrial recreation. 2. Industrial recreation - Soviet Union. 3. Industrial recreation - Bulgaria. I. Pishchulin, N. P. II. Title: Chovek, svobodno vreme i profsŭiuzi.
HD7395.R4 C42 1980

Chemical Bank (New York, N.Y.) Guide to state capital formation incentives and innovations /. [Washington, D.C. , 1983] vii, 154 p. ; LC Card 86-673432
HC110.I53 G84x 1983

CHEMICAL INDUSTRIES - GERMANY, WEST.
Welzmüller, Rudolf. Preispolitik und Akkumulation . Köln , c1982. 283 p. : ISBN 3-7663-0522-0 : LC Card 82-140922 DDC 338.8/266/00943 19
HD9654.5 .W44 1982 NYPL [JLD 86-2908]

The chemical industry . World Chemical Congress of Marketing and Business Research (1986 : Newport Beach, Calif.) [Staten Island, N.Y.] , c1986. 435 p. : LC Card 86-72599 DDC 338.4/766 19
HD9650 .W67 1986

CHEMICAL INDUSTRY - BRAZIL.
Figueiredo, João Kubitschek de. A situação das indústrias de base, TT1-39-59 /. [S.l.] [1960?] 75, [2] p. : LC Card 85-144484
HD9524.B82 F54 1960

CHEMICAL INDUSTRY - BULGARIA.
Buchvarov, Stoyan. Bulgaria's chemical industry /. Sofia , 1986. 60 p., [16] p. of plates : LC Card 87-111684 DDC 338.4/766/0094977 19
HD9666.B92 B83 1986

CHEMICAL INDUSTRY - BULGARIA - DIRECTORIES.
Naĭdenov, Naĭden, Kh. (Naĭden Khristov) Bulgarian chemical industry /. Sofia , 1985. 59 p. : LC Card 86-218952 DDC 338.7/66/00254977 19
HD9656.B82 N35 1985

CHEMICAL INDUSTRY - COSTA RICA - TECHNOLOGICAL INNOVATIONS.
Morales C., Pedro A. Política industrial y adquisición de tecnología en la actividad química en Costa Rica /. [San José, Costa Rica] [1984] ii, 55 p. ; LC Card 86-199221
HD9655.C82 M67 1984

CHEMICAL INDUSTRY - DELAWARE RIVER VALLEY (N.Y.-DEL. AND N.J.) - HISTORY.
Myers, Frank Daniel. The wood chemical industry in the Delaware Valley /. Middletown, N.Y. , 1986. [160] p. : LC Card 87-108267
HD9660.M573 U616 1986

CHEMICAL INDUSTRY - DICTIONARIES - RUSSIAN.
Kuznetsov, IU. I. (IUriĭ Igorevich) Russko-angliĭskiĭ razgovornik dlia neftekhimikov i khimikov-neorganikov /. Moskva , 1985. 359 p. ; LC Card 86-138945 DDC 660/.03/9171 19
HD9579.C32 K88 1985
*NYPL [*QAD 86-3599]*

CHEMICAL INDUSTRY - GERMANY - HISTORY.
Köhler, Otto, 1935- --und heute die ganze Welt . Hamburg , c1986. 350 p. : ISBN 3-89136-081-9 LC Card 87-116787
HD9654.9.I5 K64 1986

Stratmann, Friedrich. Chemische Industrie unter Zwang? . Stuttgart , 1985. xiv, 531 p. : ISBN 3-515-04399-3 LC Card 86-205409 DDC 338.4/766/0943 19
HD9654.5 .S77 1985

CHEMICAL INDUSTRY - GERMANY (WEST)
Specht, Günter. Industrielles Beschaffungsverhalten . Frankfurt am Main , New York , c1985. iii, 167 p. : ISBN 3-8204-8938-X LC Card 86-120719
HD9654.5 .S64 1985

CHEMICAL INDUSTRY - GERMANY (WEST) - DÜSSELDORF - HISTORY.
Schöne, Manfred, 1935- Stammwerk Henkel, 80 Jahre in Düsseldorf-Holthausen /. Düsseldorf , 1981. 148 p. : LC Card 86-216690
HD9654.9.H444 S36 1981

CHEMICAL INDUSTRY - GERMANY (WEST) - HISTORY.
Goosmann, Cornelia. Ein Jahrhundert Wasserglas von Henkel /. Düsseldorf , c1985. 76 p. : ISBN 3-923324-67-8 LC Card 86-171258
HD9654.9.H444 G66 1985

Heintzeler, Wolfgang. Der rote Faden . Stuttgart , c1983. 292 p. ; ISBN 3-512-00664-7 LC Card 83-183709
HD9654.9.B27 H45 1983

Schöne, Manfred, 1935- Von der Leimabteilung zum grössten Klebstoffwerk Europas /. Düsseldorf , 1979. 68 p. : LC Card 86-216773
HD9654.9.H444 S37 1979

Stratmann, Friedrich. Chemische Industrie unter Zwang? . Stuttgart , 1985. xiv, 531 p. : ISBN 3-515-04399-3 LC Card 86-205409 DDC 338.4/766/0943 19
HD9654.5 .S77 1985

CHEMICAL INDUSTRY - GERMANY (WEST) - HISTORY - SOURCES.
US-Administration . Frankfurt (M) , 1976. 153 p. : LC Card 85-224662
HD9654.9.H64 U7 1976

CHEMICAL INDUSTRY - GOVERNMENT POLICY - COSTA RICA.
Morales C., Pedro A. Política industrial y adquisición de tecnología en la actividad química en Costa Rica /. [San José, Costa Rica] [1984] ii, 55 p. ; LC Card 86-199221
HD9655.C82 M67 1984

CHEMICAL INDUSTRY - GOVERNMENT POLICY - GERMANY - HISTORY.
Stratmann, Friedrich. Chemische Industrie unter Zwang? . Stuttgart , 1985. xiv, 531 p. : ISBN 3-515-04399-3 LC Card 86-205409 DDC 338.4/766/0943 19
HD9654.5 .S77 1985

CHEMICAL INDUSTRY - GOVERNMENT POLICY - GERMANY (WEST) - HISTORY.
Stratmann, Friedrich. Chemische Industrie unter Zwang? . Stuttgart , 1985. xiv, 531 p. : ISBN 3-515-04399-3 LC Card 86-205409 DDC 338.4/766/0943 19
HD9654.5 .S77 1985

CHEMICAL INDUSTRY - GREAT BRITAIN - HISTORY.
Kennedy, Carol. ICI . London , 1986. xii, 209 p., [20] p. of plates : ISBN 0-09-167300-3 : LC Card 87-121862 DDC 338.7/66/00941 19
HD9652.9.I5 K46 1986

CHEMICAL INDUSTRY - HUNGARY.
Specht, Günter. Industrielles Beschaffungsverhalten . Frankfurt am Main , New York , c1985. iii, 167 p. : ISBN 3-8204-8938-X LC Card 86-120719
HD9654.5 .S64 1985

Szekér, Gyula. A kemizálás és a magyar vegyipar /. Budapest , 1985. 340 p. : ISBN 963-10-6508-1 : LC Card 86-127325
HD9656.H92 S86 1985

CHEMICAL INDUSTRY - HUNGARY - HISTORY.
Halkovics, László. A magyar vegyipar fejlődése, 1945-1980 között és eredményei a magyar népgazdaság szolgálatában /. Budapest [1985] 50 p. ; ISBN 963-8191-50-3 (Magy. nmz. bibl.) LC Card 86-148561
HD9656.H92 H35 1985

CHEMICAL INDUSTRY - NEW YORK (STATE) - ACCIDENTS.
Jaffe, Susan. Toxic chemical accidents in New York State . New York, N.Y. (2 World Trade Center, New York 10047) [1986] 27, 13, 33 p. ; LC Card 86-622820 DDC 363.1/79 19
HD7269.C452 U54 1986

CHEMICAL INDUSTRY - POLITICAL ASPECTS - GERMANY - HISTORY - 20TH CENTURY.
Hayes, Peter, 1946- Industry and ideology . Cambridge [Cambridgeshire] , New York , 1987. xxviii, 411 p. : ISBN 0-521-32948-5 LC Card 86-28388 DDC 338.7/66/00943 19
HD9654.9.I5 H39 1987

CHEMICAL INDUSTRY - RUSSIAN S.F.S.R. - SIBERIA - CONGRESSES.
Vsesoiuznaia konferentsiia "Razvitie proizvoditel′nykh sil Sibiri i zadachi uskoreniia nauchno-tekhnicheskogo progressa" (1985 : Tomsk, R.S.F.S.R.). Sektsiia "Khimicheskaia promyshlennost′." Razvitie khimicheskoĭ promyshlennosti Sibiri . Tomsk , 1985. 177 p. : LC Card 86-176713
HD9656.S56 S538 1985

CHEMICAL INDUSTRY - SOVIET UNION.
Avrekh, G. L. (Gennadiĭ Lipanovich) Ėkonomika na urovne molekul /. Moskva ,

1986. 141 p. : LC Card 86-179247
HD9656.S55 A95 1986

Zalevskiĭ, A. A. (Andreĭ Andreevich) Ėkonomika khimicheskoĭ promyshlennosti /. Moskva , 1986. 189 p. ; LC Card 86-225661
HD9656.S55 Z36 1986

CHEMICAL INDUSTRY - SOVIET UNION - MANAGEMENT.
Cherednichenko, K. K. (Konstantin Konstantinovich) Sovershenstvovanie organizatsii truda i upravleniia v khimicheskoĭ promyshlennosti /. Moskva , 1982. 203 p. ; LC Card 83-125684
HD9656.S55 C48 1982

Ėkonomika, organizatsiia i planirovanie proizvodstva v khimicheskoĭ promyshlennosti /. Moskva , 1986. 254 p. : LC Card 86-227240
HD9656.S55 E38 1986

CHEMICAL INDUSTRY - TECHNOLOGICAL INNOVATIONS - CONGRESSES.
World Chemical Congress of Marketing and Business Research (1986 : Newport Beach, Calif.) The chemical industry . [Staten Island, N.Y.] , c1986. 435 p. : LC Card 86-72599 DDC 338.4/766 19
HD9650 .W67 1986

CHEMICAL INDUSTRY - UKRAINE - HISTORY.
Sokolov, V. N. (Viacheslav Nikolaevich) Kursom na sotsialisticheskuiu industrializatsiiu /. Kiev , 1985. 158, [2] p. ; LC Card 87-113771
HD9656.S56 U377 1985

Chemical Market Research Association. see **Chemical Marketing Research Association.**

Chemical Marketing Research Association. (Old Catalog form: Chemical market research association)
World Chemical Congress of Marketing and Business Research (1986 : Newport Beach, Calif.) The chemical industry . [Staten Island, N.Y.] , c1986. 435 p. : LC Card 86-72599 DDC 338.4/766 19
HD9650 .W67 1986

Chemical Marketing Research Association. Meeting (1985 : San Antonio, Tex.) World petrochemicals . [Staten Island, N.Y. (139 Chestnut Ave., Staten Island 10305)] , c1985. 279 p. : LC Card 85-71088 DDC 338.4/7661804 19
HD9579.C32 W68 1985 ***NYPL [JLD 86-2185]***

CHEMICAL PLANT EQUIPMENT INDUSTRY - TECHNOLOGICAL INNOVATIONS - EVALUATION - STANDARDS - SOVIET UNION.
Kogan, Ninel. New standards for evaluating technological innovation in the USSR . Falls Church, VA (7700 Leesburg Pike, #250, Falls Church 22043) , c1986. xii, 103 leaves (some folded) : LC Card 87-151964 DDC 338.4/7681766/0947 19
HD9579.C33 S654 1986

CHEMICAL PLANT EQUIPMENT INDUSTRY - UNITED STATES.
The U. S. market for hazardous duty liquid pumps and valves. New York, N.Y. , c1983. 2 v. (viii, 343 leaves) : LC Card 87-401677 DDC 381/.456216 19
HD9651.5 .U16 1983

Chemin de fer de Paris à Lyon par Troyes et Dijon . Berthelin, E. (Egmont), 1807-1860. Troyes , 1843. 54, [2] p. ; LC Card 85-665948
HE3068 .B47x 1843

CHEMIN DE FER FRANCO-ÉTHIOPIEN.
Rosso, Max. Le rail franco-éthiopien en détresse /. Paris , c1983. 311 p. : ISBN 2-214-04961-4 : LC Card 83-173267
HE3416.Z8 F737 1983

Chemin Dupontès, P. Les Petites Antilles : étude sur leur évolution économique, 1820-1908 / P. Chemin Dupontès ; préface de Marcel Dubois. [Fort-de-France] : Désormeaux ; [Paris] : L'Harmattan, [1979] x, 318 p., [10] p. of plates : ill. ; 22 cm. (Collection Les Antilles après l'abolition) Bibliography: p. [311]-312. Includes index. ISBN 2-85275-105-4 LC Card 84-164674
1. Antilles, Lesser - Economic conditions. I. Title. II. Series.
HC151 .C49 1979

Un Chemin pour sortir de la crise / Paul Boccara ... [et al.] ; [Philippe Herzog et un collectif d'économistes]. Paris : Messidor/Editions sociales, c1985. 249 p. ; 22 cm. (Gestion) "Ce livre est le fruit d'un travail collectif de tous les collaborateurs de la Section économique du Comité central du Parti communiste français"--P. 7. ISBN 2-209-05753-1 LC Card 86-154397
1. France - Economic policy - 1945-. 2. Parti communiste français - Platforms. 3. Communism - France. I. Boccara, Paul. II. Herzog, Philippe. III. Parti communiste français. Section économique.
HC276.2 .C517 1985

Chemineau, Laurent. Tout sur la France en 100 graphiques /. Paris , c1986. 113 p. : ISBN 2-86260-154-3 : LC Card 87-106635
HA1224 .T68 1986

Chemische Industrie unter Zwang? . Stratmann, Friedrich. Stuttgart , 1985. xiv, 531 p. : ISBN 3-515-04399-3 LC Card 86-205409 DDC 338.4/766/0943 19
HD9654.5 .S77 1985

CHEMISTS - GREAT BRITAIN - BIOGRAPHY.
Lischka, J. R. (Johannes Richard), 1933- Ludwig Mond and the British alkali industry /. New York , 1985. 233 p. ; ISBN 0-8240-6686-3 (alk. paper) : LC Card 84-46006 DDC 338.4/7673725/0924 19
HD9660.A43 G75 1985 ***NYPL [JSD 86-547]***

CHEMISTS - SWITZERLAND - BIOGRAPHY.
Riedl-Ehrenberg, Renate. Alfred Kern (1850-1893), Edouard Sandoz (1853-1928) . Zürich , c1986. 90 p. : LC Card 86-159933 DDC 338/.09494 s 338.7/66/0094943 19
HC395.5.A2 S3 no. 44 QD21

Chemu uchit opyt druzeĭ /. Utkin, Ė. A. (Ėduard Andreevich) Moskva , 1987. 141 p. ; LC Card 87-120824 DDC 658/.009171/7 19
HD70.C725 U85 1987

CH'EN, CHIA-KENG, 1874-1961.
Yong, C. F. (Ching Fatt) Tan Kah-kee, the making of an overseas Chinese legend /. Singapore , 1987 [i.e. 1986] xix, 391 p., [16] p. of plates : ISBN 0-19-582678-7 LC Card 86-946451 DDC 338/.04/0924 B 19
HC445.8.C47 Y66 1986

Chen, Edward K. Y. The markets of Asia/Pacific--People's Republic of China / the Asia Pacific Centre ; Edward Chen and Steve Chin. London : APC ; Aldershot, Hants, England : Gower, c1984. 124 p., [1] leaf of plates : map ; 30 cm. Includes index. ISBN 0-566-02316-4 LC Card 87-672541
1. China - Economic conditions - 1976-. 2. China - Commerce. I. Chin, Steve S. K. II. Asia Pacific Centre. III. Title.
HC427.92 .C353x 1984b

Chen hsing Chung-hua chih lu--kai ko ti sung ko / chu pien Juan Po, Wang Chi-k'uan, Chuang K'ai-hsün. 880-02 Pei-ching ti 1 pan. Pei-ching : Chung-kuo chan wang ch'u pan she : Pei-ching shih hsin hua shu tien fa hsing, 1985. 4, 3, 385 p. ; 19 cm. In Chinese. LC Card 86-106324
1. Industrial management - China. 2. Management - China. I. Juan, Po. II. Wang, Chi-k'uan. III. Chuang, K'ai-hsün. ***NYPL [*OVY 86-3099]***

Chen, Jai-Sheng. Mathur, Iqbal. Strategies for joint ventures in the People's Republic of China /. New York , 1987. viii, 196 p. ; ISBN 0-275-92354-1 (alk. paper) : LC Card 87-7033 DDC 338.8/8851 19
HD62.47 .M38 1987

Chen, Jiyuan. China's industrial reform /. New York , c1987. xii, 378 p. ; ISBN 0-19-520592-8 : LC Card 87-5616 DDC 338.951 19
HD3616.C63 C495 1987

Chen, Phillip M., 1935- Sea lane security studies . Taipei, Taiwan, Republic of China , 1986. 100 p. ; LC Card 87-133640 DDC 359/.03 19
HE327 .S435 1986

Chen, Sheng Li, 1945- Coale, Ansley J. Basic data on fertility in the provinces of China, 1940-82 /. Honolulu, HI [1987] xvii, 366 p. : ISBN 0-86638-088-4 (pbk.) : LC Card 86-32765 DDC 304.6/32/0951 19
HB1064.A3 C63 1987

Chêng, Chu-yüan. The demand and supply of primary energy in mainland China / Chu-yuan Cheng. Taipei, Taiwan, Republic of China : Chung-Hua Institution for Economic Research ; Seattle : Distributed by University of Washington Press, c1984. viii, 178 p. ; 26 cm. (Mainland China economic series . no. 3) Page 178 blank. Bibliography: p. 171-177. LC Card 84-231216 DDC 333.79/11/0951 19
1. Energy industries - China. 2. Energy consumption - China. I. Title. II. Series.
HD9502.C62 C49 1984 ***NYPL [JLF 87-21]***

Chêng, Tso-yüan. see **Chêng, Chu-yüan.**

Cheque sem fundos. Iorio de Souza, Ubiratan Jorge, 1946- Uma análise econômica do problema do cheque sem fundos no Brasil /. Rio de Janeiro [Brasília] , 1985. 204 p. : LC Card 87-141390 DDC 332.7/6 19
HG1691 .I58 1985

Cherednichenko, K. K. (Konstantin Konstantinovich) Sovershenstvovanie organizatsii truda i upravleniia v khimicheskoĭ promyshlennosti / K.K. Cherednichenko. Moskva : Khimiia, 1982. 203 p. ; 23 cm. Includes bibliographical references and index. LC Card 83-125684
1. Chemical industry - Soviet Union - Management. I. Title.
HD9656.S55 C48 1982

Cherevik, E. D. (Evgeniĭ Dmitrievich) IAshkin, V. A. (Vladimir Andreevich) Planirovanie ėkonomicheskogo rosta v razvivaiushchikhsia stranakh . Moskva , 1986. 120 p. ; LC Card 86-220878
HC59.7 .I13 1986

Cherkasov, N. A. Osobennosti khoziaĭstvennogo mekhanizma v zarubezhnykh stranakh--chlenakh SĖV . Leningrad , 1984. 54 p. ; LC Card 85-153742
HC244 .O723 1984

Cherkovets, Viktor Nikitich.
"Kapital" K. Marksa i ėkonomicheskie problemy razvitogo sotsializma /. Moskva , 1980. 260 p. ; LC Card 81-134413
HB501 .K248 1980

Obshchestvennyĭ kharakter proizvodstva i sotsialisticheskaia sobstvennost' /. Moskva , 1985. 286 p. ; LC Card 85-173513
HC340.I52 O27 1985

Chernetsova, V. I. Piatiletka, god vtoroĭ . Petrozavodsk , 1977. 101 p. ; LC Card 81-161405
HC337.K265 P52 1977

Cherniak, V. K. Teoriia i praktika ėkonomiki demoprotsessa . Kiev , 1982. 181 p., [2] folded leaves of plates : LC Card 83-145373
HB883.5 .T46 1982

Cherniakhovskaia, N. I. "Problema neftedollarov" . Moskva , 1984. 231 p. ; LC Card 85-189000
HC498 .P75 1984

Cherniavskiĭ, A. A. Spravochnik rukovoditelia srednego zvena kolkhoza, sovkhoza /. Minsk , 1981. 518 p. ; LC Card 82-147885
HD1492.S65 S67 1981

Cherniavskiĭ, A. V. (Andreĭ Vasil'evich) Cherniavskiĭ, V. O. (Vasiliĭ Osipovich) Ėffektivnost' i optimal'nost' kapital'nykh vlozheniĭ /. Leningrad , 1986. 68, [4] p. ; LC Card 85-179296
HC340.C3 C4 1986

Cherniavskiĭ, V. O. (Vasiliĭ Osipovich) Ėffektivnost' i optimal'nost' kapital'nykh vlozheniĭ / V.O. Cherniavskiĭ, A.V. Cherniavskiĭ. Leningrad : Stroĭizdat, Leningradskoe otd-nie, 1986. 68, [4] p. ; 22 cm. Bibliography: p. [70] LC Card 85-179296
1. Capital productivity - Soviet Union. 2. Capital investments - Soviet Union. I. Cherniavskiĭ, A. V. (Andreĭ Vasil'evich). II. Title.
HC340.C3 C4 1986

CHERNOBYL NUCLEAR ACCIDENT, CHERNOBYL', UKRAINE, 1986.
Tschernobyl hat unser Leben verändert . Reinbek bei Hamburg , 1986. 203 p. : ISBN 3-499-15922-8 : LC Card 87-123041 DDC 363.1/79 19
HD9698.G42 T73 1986

Chernoivanov, G. E. (Gennadiĭ Efimovich) Fondoёmkost' produktsii i ėffektivnost'

sotsialisticheskogo proizvodstva / G.E. Chernoivanov. Moskva : "Mysl′", 1980. 156 p. ; 20 cm. (Ėkonomicheskaia teoriia i khoziaistvennaia praktika) Includes bibliographical references. LC Card 81-134415
1. Capital productivity - Soviet Union. 2. Industrial productivity - Soviet Union. I. Series: Ėkonomicheskiia teoriia i khoziaistvennaia praktika (Moscow, R.S.F.S.R. : 1981). II. Title.
HC340.C3 C54 1980

Chernova, F. I. (Faina Ivanovna) Zubets, V. M. (Vasiliĭ Mikhaĭlovich) Rezervy povysheniia ėffektivnosti proizvodstva na magnitogorskom metallurgicheskom kombinate /. Cheliabinsk , 1975. 183 p. ; LC Card 81-170397
HD9525.S653 M39 1975

Chernovolenko, V. F. (Vilen Filippovich) Sem′ia i vosproizvodstvo struktury trudovoĭ zaniatosti . Kiev , 1984. 238 p. : LC Card 86-142706
HB2698.U38 S46 1984

Cherol, Rachelle. Seminar on Economic Integration (1982 : Inter-American Development Bank) The economic integration process of Latin America in the 1980's . Washington, D.C. [1984] 318 p. : ISBN 0-940602-17-2 (pbk.) LC Card 87-159367
HC125 .S3973 1982

Cherrington, J. Owen.
The Complete CPA examination review, auduiing, 1986-1987 /. Boston , c1986. 42, 237, 177, 12 p. : ISBN 0-395-41132-7 (pbk.) LC Card 86-80561 DDC 657/.45/076 19
HF5667 .C5852 1986

Cost and managerial accounting / J. Owen Cherrington, E. Dee Hubbard, David H. Luthy. St. Paul : West Pub. Co., c1988. p. cm. Reprint. Originally published: Dubuque, Iowa : Wm. C. Brown, 1985. Includes bibliographies and index. ISBN 0-314-25327-0 : LC Card 86-24753 DDC 657/.42 19
1. Cost accounting. 2. Managerial accounting. I. Hubbard, E. Dee. II. Luthy, David H. III. Title.
HF5686.C8 C475 1988

Cherry Hill, N. J. Management Information Corporation. see **Management Information Corporation.**

Chertan, S. E. (Sergeĭ Evgen′evich) Sistema natural′no-stoimostnykh mezhotraslevykh balansov soiuznoĭ respubliki : problemy razrabotki i vnedreniia v planirovanie / S.E. Chertan ; otvetstvennyĭ redaktor P.S. Soltan. Kishinev : "Shtiintsa", 1984. 242, [6] p., [2] folded leaves of plates : ill. ; 22 cm. At head of title: Gosplan Moldavskoĭ SSR. Nauchno-issledovatel′skiĭ institut planirovaniia. Summary in English and French. Bibliography: p. 236-[243] LC Card 85-130960
1. Material balances - Moldavian S.S.R. 2. Moldavian S.S.R. - Economic policy. I. Soltan, Petr Semenovich. II. Title.
HC337.M55 C46 1984

Cheru, Fantu. Dependence, underdevelopment, and unemployment in Kenya : school leavers in a peripheral capitalist political economy / Fantu Cheru. Lanham, MD : University Press of America, c1987. xvii, 198 p. : ill. ; 24 cm. Bibliography: p. 179-183. Includes index. ISBN 0-8191-6539-5 (alk. paper) : LC Card 87-13710 DDC 331.13/77/096762 19
1. High school graduates - Employment - Kenya. 2. Labor policy - Kenya. 3. Kenya - Economic policy. 4. Education and state - Kenya. I. Title.
HD6276.K42 C46 1987

Cherunilam, Francis. Housing in India / Francis Cherunilam & Odeyar D. Heggade. 1st ed. Bombay : Himalaya Pub. House, 1987. vi, 168 p. ; 23 cm. Bibliography: p. [158]-168. LC Card 86-903722 DDC 363.5/0954 19
1. Housing - India. I. Heggade, Odeyar D. II. Title.
HD7361.A3 C46 1987

CHESAPEAKE AND OHIO CANAL (MD. AND WASHINGTON, D.C.)
Internal Improvement Convention (1834 : Baltimore, Md.) Journal of the Internal improvement convention. Baltimore, 1835. 93 p., 1 l. LC Card 06-22129
HE396.C5 I6

Cheshsko-russkiĭ ėkonomicheskiĭ slovar′ : okolo 20,000 terminov / pod redaktsieĭ M.N. Os′movoĭ ; [avtory, IA. Vydrova ... et al.]. Moskva : "Russkiĭ iazyk" ; Praga : SNTL, Izd-vo tekhn. lit-ry, 1986. 300 p. ; 21 cm. Title on added t.p.: Česko-ruský ekonomický slovník. LC Card 85-146401
1. Economics - Dictionaries - Czech. 2. Czech language - Dictionaries - Russian. I. Os′mova, Markiana Nikolaevna. II. Vydrova, IA. (IArushe). III. Title: Česko-ruský ekonomický slovník.
HB61 .C453 1986 ***NYPL [*QAD 87-1680]***

Chesley, Agnes. Lucier, Gary. Farm income data . Washington, DC [1986] iv, 311 p. : LC Card 86-602022 DDC 338.1/0973 s 338.1/3/0973021 19
HD1751 .A5 no. 740 HD1769

Chesnokov, N. I. (Nikolaĭ Ivanovich) Ėkonomicheskie problemy osvoeniia Ural′skogo Severa /. Sverdlovsk , 1982. 69 p. : LC Card 83-188353
HC336.9.N65 E37 1982

Chesnokov, S. V. (Sergeĭ Valerianovich) Determinatsionnyĭ analiz sotsial′no-ėkonomicheskikh dannykh / S.V. Chesnokov. Moskva : "Nauka," Glav. red. fiziko-matematicheskoĭ lit-ry, 1982. 167, [1] p. : ill. ; 22 cm. (Teoriia i metody sistemnogo analiza) Bibliography: p. 165-[168] LC Card 83-173210
1. Social sciences - Statistical methods. I. Title. II. Series.
HA29.5.R9 C52 1982

Chesterton, Gilbert Keith, 1874-1936. [Crimes of England. French]
Les crimes de l'Angleterre [microform]; introduction de Charles Sarolea, traduction de Charles Grolleau. Paris, G. Crès et Cie, 1916. 273 p. front. (port.) 21 cm. Translation of The Crimes of England. Microfilm. New York: New York Public Library, 1986. 1 microfilm reel; 35 mm. (MN *ZZ-26036) LC Card 19-16286
1. Irish question. 2. World War, 1914-1918. 3. Great Britain - Relations (genera) with Germany. 4. Germany - Relations (general) with Great Britain. I. Grolleau, Charles, 1867- tr. II. Title.
DA47.2 .C55 ***NYPL [*Z-4049 no.7]***

Chetirideset brigadirski leta. 40 brigadirski leta /. Sofiia , 1986. 173 p., [12] p. of plates : LC Card 87-103049
HD4870.B9 A15 1986

Chetley, Andrew. The politics of baby foods : successful challenges to an international marketing strategy / Andrew Chetley. London : Frances Pinter, 1986. xv, 189 p. ; 24 cm. (Global politics) Includes index. Bibliography: p. [166]-184. ISBN 0-86187-293-2
1. Dried milk industry - Political aspects. 2. Baby foods industry - Political aspects. 3. Infants - Developing countries - Nutrition. 4. Advertising - Baby foods - Developing countries - Moral and ethical aspects. I. Title. ***NYPL [JLE 86-2969]***

Chetvernina, T. IA. Bukhval′d, E. M. Povyshenie proizvoditel′nosti truda--kliuchevaia zadacha sovetskoĭ ėkonomiki . Moskva , 1984. 63 p. ; LC Card 85-188977
HC340.L3 B85 1984

Chetyrkin, Evgeniĭ Mikhaĭlovich. Klimenko, B. I. Mezhotraslevye balansy kapitalisticheskikh stran . Moskva , 1986. 150 p. ; LC Card 86-231527
HC110.I57 K65 1986

Chevalier, Gérard. Introduction à la gestion prévisionnelle /. Lyon , c1985. 337 p. : ISBN 2-7297-0268-7 : LC Card 86-132861 DDC 658.4/0355 19
HD30.28 .I56 1985

Chevalier, Paul. Los problemas del socialismo en nuestra tiempo [microform]. México, 1944. 119 p. DDC 335.082
HX40 .P73 ***NYPL [*ZT-1711 no.21]***

Chevènement, Jean-Pierre. France. Mission "Recherche, technologie et progrès en coopération." Recherche et coopération avec le Tiers Monde . Paris , c1983. 120 p. ; ISBN 2-11-001071-1 : LC Card 83-196852
HC60 .F727 1983

Chew, T. A. The off-farm labour supply of padi farmers in Kelantan, Malaysia [microform] / T.A. Chew and R.T. Shand. [Canberra] : Australian National University, c1984. 19 p. ; 30 cm. (Working paper, 0814-1266 . no. 38) Bibliography: p. 13-14. Microfilm. New York : New York Public Library, 1986. 1 microfilm reel ; 35 mm. (MN *ZZ-26,873) ISBN 0-86784-513-9 (pbk.) LC Card 85-670027 DDC 331.12/93318/095951 19
1. Supplementary employment - Malaysia - Kelantan - Case studies. 2. Rice farmers - Malaysia - Kelantan - Supplementary employment. 3. Farmers, Part-time - Malaysia - Kelantan. I. Shand, Richard Tregurtha. II. Series: Working paper (Australian National University. Development Studies Centre : 1984) , no. 38. III. Title.
HD5854.55.M4 C47 1984
NYPL [*ZF-1745 no.58]

Chiang, Hsüeh-mo. She hui chu i so yu chih yen chiu / Chiang Hsüeh-mo chu. 880-03 Ti 1 pan. Hang-chou : Che-chiang jen min ch'u pan she : Che-chiang sheng Hsin hua shu tien fa hsing, 1985. [3], 211 p. ; 21 cm. Cover title also in pinyin: Shehuizhuyi suoyouzhi yanjiu. In Chinese. Includes bibliographical reference.
1. Production (Economic theory). 2. Marxian economics. I. Title. II. Title: Shehuizhuyi suoyouzhi yanjiu. ***NYPL [*OVL 86-3601]***

Chiapas (Mexico). Congreso. Thompson G., Roberto. Problemática agraria y política petrolera en Chiapas /. Tuxtla Gutiérrez, Chiapas , 1983. 37 p., [1] leaf of plates : LC Card 84-243074
HD9574.M63 C457 1983

CHIAPAS. MEXICO - ECONOMIC CONDITIONS.
Bennholdt-Thomsen, Veronika. Bauern in Mexiko . Frankfurt [am Main] , New York , c1982. 214 p. ; ISBN 3-593-33167-5 LC Card 83-139124 DDC 305.5/63 19
HD1531.M6 B46 1982

Chibnik, Michael, 1946- Farm work and fieldwork . Ithaca , 1987. 293 p. : ISBN 0-8014-9446-X (pbk. : alk. paper) LC Card 86-19960 DDC 305.5/55/0973 19
HD8039.F32 U635 1987

Chicago. Board of Trade.
Speculating in futures. [Chicago] , c1986. v, 65 p. : LC Card 87-100478 DDC 332.64/4 19
HG6046 .S63 1986

Chicago Board of Trade. Education and Publication Services Dept. Trading in soybean complex futures /. [Chicago] , c1986. v, 53 p. ; LC Card 87-101090 DDC 332.64/4 19
HG6047.S6 T73 1986

CHICAGO (ILL.) - RACE RELATIONS.
Chavers-Wright, Madrue, 1916- The guarantee . New York , 1987, c1985. xix, 427 p. : ISBN 0-931505-05-4 : LC Card 86-51447 DDC 338/.04/0924 B 19
HG2463.C48 C48 1987

Chicago Project (Universität München) German workers in Chicago . Urbana , c1988. p. cm. ISBN 0-252-01458-8 (alk. paper) LC Card 87-10780 DDC 331.6/2/43077311 19
HD8081.G4 G46 1988

CHICAGO - RACE RELATIONS - 20TH CENTURY.
Chavers-Wright, Madrue, 1916- The guarantee . New York , 1985. xix, 425 p. : ISBN 0-931505-02-X (pbk.) : LC Card 84-51854 DDC 338/.04/0924 B 19
HG2463.C48 C48 1985
NYPL [Sc D 86-412]

Die Chicago School of Antitrust Analysis .
Schmidt, Ingo. Baden-Baden , 1986. 119 p. : ISBN 3-7890-1285-8 LC Card 87-409043 DDC 330.15/6 19
HB98.3 .S35 1986

CHICAGO SCHOOL OF ECONOMICS.
Brighton on the rocks . Brighton [1983?] 192 p. : ISBN 0-904733-00-4 (pbk.) : LC Card 84-173777 DDC 336.3/9/0942256 19
HJ9438.B75 B75 1983 ***NYPL [JLD 87-104]***

Brink, Helge. Monetarisme og økonomisk politik /. [Copenhagen] , c1984. 125 p. ; ISBN 87-574-4380-7 : LC Card 84-253099
HG1092 .B75 1984

Jiménez, Félix. Perú, economía no-neoclásica, modelo de acumulación, crisis y alternativa de desarrollo no-monetarista /. Lima, Perú , 1986. 107 p. : LC Card 87-404229 DDC 338.985 19
HC227 .J53 1986

Kaldor, Nicholas, 1908- The scourge of monetarism /. Oxford , New York , 1986. xxv, 112 p. : ISBN 0-19-877248-3
NYPL [JLD 86-2212]

Makasheva, N. A. Sovremennyĭ monetarizm i krizis burzhuaznoĭ ėkonomicheskoĭ teorii .

Moskva , 1985. 47 p. ; LC Card 86-187688
HB98.3 .M35 1985

Managing the UK economy . Cambridge, UK , 1987. xxvii, 328 p. : ISBN 0-7456-0316-5 : LC Card 86-26860 DDC 338.941 19
HC256.5 .M392 1987

Menkhoff, Lukas. Zur Theorie der nicht-monetär verursachten Inflation /. Berlin , c1986. 222 p. : ISBN 3-428-06051-2 LC Card 86-215073
HG229 .M524 1986

Modelo económico chileno . Santiago, Chile [1982] 606 p. ; LC Card 83-201307
HC192 .M63 1982

La Nouvelle économie libérale /. Paris , c1983. 280 p. : ISBN 2-7246-0487-3 : LC Card 84-140644
HB95 .N63 1983

Políticas macro-económicas . Santiago de Chile [1986] 409 p. : LC Card 87-403669 DDC 338.98 19
HC125 .P657 1986

Rousseas, Stephen William. Post Keynesian monetary economics /. Armonk, N.Y. , c1986. x, 126 p.; ISBN 0-87332-355-6 LC Card 85-14181 DDC 332.4/6 19
HG230.3 .R68 1986 ***NYPL [JLE 86-4326]***

Schmidt, Ingo. Die Chicago School of Antitrust Analysis . Baden-Baden , 1986. 119 p. : ISBN 3-7890-1285-8 LC Card 87-409043 DDC 330.15/6 19
HB98.3 .S35 1986

CHICAGO SCHOOL OF ECONOMICS - CONGRESSES.
Friedman, Milton, 1912- Politics and tyranny . San Francisco, Calif. , c1984. 68 p. ; ISBN 0-936488-00-X (pbk.) : LC Card 84-61364 DDC 330 19
HB98.3 .F75 1984 ***NYPL [JLE 87-857]***

Chicago. University. Dept. of geography. Research paper .
(no. 217-218) World patterns of modern urban change . Chicago , 1986. x, 479 p. : ISBN 0-89065-122-1 : LC Card 85-23231 DDC 910 s 307.7/6 19
H31 .C514 no.217-218 ***NYPL [JFM 72-132 no.217-218]***

CHICANOS. see **MEXICAN AMERICANS.**

CHIEF EXECUTIVE OFFICERS.
Robert, Michel, 1941- The strategist CEO . New York , 1988. viii, 140 p. : ISBN 0-89930-268-8 (lib. bdg. : alk. paper) LC Card 87-10945 DDC 658.4/012 19
HD30.28 .R63 1988

CHIEF EXECUTIVE OFFICERS - CASE STUDIES.
Aguilar, Francis J. (Francis Joseph) General managers in action /. New York , 1988. viii, 498 p. : ISBN 0-19-504083-X (alk. paper) LC Card 87-12503 DDC 658.4 19
HD38.2 .A39 1987

CHIEF EXECUTIVE OFFICERS - RECRUITING.
Korn, Lester. The winning edge . New York , c1988. p. cm. ISBN 0-671-55263-5 LC Card 87-23249 DDC 658.4/09 19
HD38.2 .K67 1988

CHIEF EXECUTIVE OFFICERS - UNITED STATES - SUCCESSION.
Leadership succession /. New Brunswick, [N.J.], U. S.A. , 1987. x, 157 p. : ISBN 0-88738-162-6 : LC Card 87-10947 DDC 658.4 19
HD38.25.U6 L43 1987

Vancil, Richard F. Passing the baton . Boston, Mass. , c1987. xxii, 318 p. : ISBN 0-87584-182-1 LC Card 87-11962 DDC 658.4 19
HD38.25.U6 V36 1987

Chief financial officer . Deschamps, Benoit. New York , c1988. xxvii, 582, [165] p. ; ISBN 0-471-84892-1 LC Card 87-21656 DDC 658.1/5 19
HG4026 .D48 1988

CHIEF FINANCIAL OFFICERS.
Deschamps, Benoit. Chief financial officer . New York , c1988. xxvii, 582, [165] p. ; ISBN 0-471-84892-1 LC Card 87-21656 DDC 658.1/5 19
HG4026 .D48 1988

CHIHUAHUA (MEXICO) - SOCIAL CONDITIONS.
Verbeek, Henk. Residentiële mobiliteit in Ciudad Chihuahua, Mexico /. Utrecht [1986] iii, 142 p. : LC Card 86-172646
HD7288.92.M62 C488 1986

CHILCHOTA REGION (MEXICO) - ECONOMIC CONDITIONS.
Ramírez C., Luis Alfonso. Chilchota, un pueblo al pie de la sierra . Zamora, Mich. [i.e. Michoacán] [Morelia, Mexico] , 1986. 306 p. : ISBN 968-7230-23-1 LC Card 87-401034 DDC 330.972/37 19
HC138.C45 R36 1986

Chilchota, un pueblo al pie de la sierra . Ramírez C., Luis Alfonso. Zamora, Mich. [i.e. Michoacán] [Morelia, Mexico] , 1986. 306 p. : ISBN 968-7230-23-1 LC Card 87-401034 DDC 330.972/37 19
HC138.C45 R36 1986

Chilcote, Ronald H. Latin America : capitalist and socialist perspectives of development and underdevelopment / Ronald H. Chilcote and Joel C. Edelstein. Boulder : Westview Press, 1986. xv, 175 p. ; 23 cm. (Latin American perspectives series . no. 3) "This is a complete revision and expansion of our introduction to Latin America : the struggle with dependency and beyond, published in 1974"--Pref. Includes index. Bibliography: p. 153-164.
ISBN 0-8133-0239-0 (pbk.) : LC Card 85-13899 DDC 338.98 19
1. Capitalism - Latin America. 2. Socialism - Latin America. 3. Latin America - Economic conditions - 1945-. 4. Latin America - Social conditions - 1945-. I. Edelstein, Joel C. II. Title. III. Series.
HC125 .C487 1986 ***NYPL [JLE 86-4264]***

CHILD AND PARENT. see **PARENT AND CHILD.**

CHILD BIRTH. see **CHILDBIRTH.**

CHILD CARE CENTERS. see **DAY CARE CENTERS.**

CHILD CARE SERVICES - UNITED STATES.
The Business of caring [videorecording] /. Washington, DC , 1984. 1 videocassette (23 min.) : LC Card 84-707513 DDC 362.7 11
HF5549.5.D39

CHILD HEALTH. see **CHILD WELFARE.**

Child, John, 1940- Organization of innovation . Berlin , New York , 1987. x, 238 p. : ISBN 0-89925-167-6 (U. S.) : LC Card 87-19936 DDC 658.4/06 19
HD45 .O73 1987

CHILD LABOR. see **YOUTH - EMPLOYMENT; CHILDREN - EMPLOYMENT.**

Child labour . Juyal, B. N. Varanasi , 1985. xiii, 161 p. ; LC Card 87-901161 DDC 331.3/1/0954 19
HD6250.I42 J89 1985

Child labour . Nangia, Parveen. New Delhi , c1987. ix, 295 p. : ISBN 81-85146-00-4 : LC Card 86-903812 DDC 331.3/1/0954 19
HD6250.I42 N35 1987

Child labour and exploitation in the carpet industry . Juyal, B. N. New Delhi , c1987. 49, [1] p. ; LC Card 87-900920 DDC 331.3/1/0954 19
HD6250.I42 J87 1987

Child labour and health : problems and prospects / editors, Usha S. Naidu, Kamini R. Kapadia. Bombay : Tata Institute of Social Sciences, c1985. xi, 287 p. ; 23 cm. (T.I.S.S. series . no. 54) With reference to India; proceedings of a seminar jointly organized by the Unit for Child and Youth Research, Tata Institute of Social Sciences, Bombay, and Maternal and Child Health Unit, World Health Organization, Geneva, held in Bombay, April 20-22, 1982. Bibliography: p. 276-287. LC Card 86-900928 DDC 331.3/1/0956 19
1. Children - Employment - India. 2. Children - Care and hygiene - India. I. Naidu, Usha Sidana, 1947-. II. Kapadia, Kamini R. III. World Health Organization. Maternal and Child Health Unit. IV. Tata Institute of Social Sciences. Unit for Child and Youth Research. V. Series.
HD6250.I42 C46 1985 ***NYPL [JLD 87-1553]***

The child of an eagle . White, Bob. [Cape Girardeau, Mo. , c1980] v, 78 p. : LC Card 87-405068 DDC 386/.22436 19
HE630.M6 W48 1980

CHILD REARING.
Wilk, Carole. Career women and childbearing . New York , c1986. xxii, 304 p. ; ISBN 0-442-29352-6 LC Card 85-9216 DDC 306.8/743 19
HQ759 .W52 1986 ***NYPL [JLD 86-1811]***

CHILD WELFARE - ADDRESSES, ESSAYS, LECTURES.
The Impact of world recession on children /. Oxford [Oxfordshire] , New York , 1984. xiv, 221 p. : ISBN 0-08-031329-9 : LC Card 84-14694 DDC 362.7/042 19
HV715 .I475 1984 ***NYPL [JLE 86-2315]***

CHILDBIRTH - BERMUDA ISLANDS - STATISTICS.
A Review of birth statistics, Bermuda, 1971-1978 /. [Hamilton] [1980] 62 p. ; LC Card 85-189032 DDC 304.6/3/097299021 19
HB1078.A3 R48 1980 ***NYPL [JLF 85-3121]***

CHILDBIRTH - CALIFORNIA - STATISTICS.
Mielke, Robert B. Live births by estimated marital status of mother, California, 1981. [Sacramento] [1984] 22 p. : LC Card 86-622328 DDC 304.6/32/09794 19
HB935.C2 M54 1984

CHILDBIRTH - HUNGARY - STATISTICS.
Egységes szülészeti adatszolgáltatási rendszer . Budapest , 1986. 102 p. ; LC Card 86-233497
HB1002.5.A3 E39 1986

CHILDBIRTH - MICHIGAN - STATISTICS.
Southeastern Michigan minor civil divisions . Detroit, Mich. (1200 Book Bldg., Detroit 48226) , c1986. i, 285 p. : LC Card 87-105776 DDC 304.6/3/09774021 19
HB935.M5 S68 1986

CHILDBIRTH - SWITZERLAND.
Entwicklung der Geburtenhäufigkeit in der Schweiz nach Wochentag und Stunden /. Bern , 1984. 40 p. : LC Card 85-163580
HA1593 .B45 Heft 114 HB1033

Children at work in Kenya /. Kayongo-Male, Diane. Nairobi , New York , 1984. x, 187 p. : ISBN 0-19-572546-8 (pbk.) LC Card 85-980979 DDC 331.3/1/096761 19
HD6250.K4 K39 1984 ***NYPL [Sc D 86-960]***

CHILDREN - CARE AND HYGIENE - INDIA.
Child labour and health . Bombay , c1985. xi, 287 p. ; LC Card 86-900928 DDC 331.3/1/0956 19
HD6250.I42 C46 1985 ***NYPL [JLD 87-1553]***

CHILDREN - CHARITIES. see **CHILD WELFARE.**

CHILDREN - ECONOMIC CONDITIONS - ADDRESSES, ESSAYS, LECTURES.
The Impact of world recession on children /. Oxford [Oxfordshire] , New York , 1984. xiv, 221 p. : ISBN 0-08-031329-9 : LC Card 84-14694 DDC 362.7/042 19
HV715 .I475 1984 ***NYPL [JLE 86-2315]***

CHILDREN - EMPLOYMENT - BRAZIL.
Spindel, Cheywa R. Espaços de socialização e exploração do menor assalariado . São Paulo, SP , 1986. 254 p. ; LC Card 87-405001 DDC 331.3/1/0981 19
HD6276.B72 S67 1986

CHILDREN - EMPLOYMENT - BRAZIL - HISTORY.
Dal-Rosso, Sadi. As condições de emprego do menor trabalhador . [Brasília] , c1986. 114 p. ; LC Card 86-224647
HD6231 .D35 1986

CHILDREN - EMPLOYMENT - DENMARK - HISTORY.
Weinreich, Torben. Arbejdet . [Copenhagen] , c1984. 64 p. : ISBN 87-591-0003-6 : LC Card 84-197811
HD6250.D42 W45 1984

CHILDREN - EMPLOYMENT - GREAT BRITAIN.
Great Britain. Health and Safety Commission. Proposal to review the minimum age at which children may drive or ride on agricultural machinery /. London [1982] 12 p. ; ISBN 0-11-883635-8 (pbk.) LC Card 82-214120 DDC 363.1/89 19
HD6247.A4 G74 1982

CHILDREN - EMPLOYMENT - HISTORY.
Dal-Rosso, Sadi. As condições de emprego do

menor trabalhador . [Brasília] , c1986. 114 p. ; LC Card 86-224647
HD6231 .D35 1986

CHILDREN - EMPLOYMENT - INDIA.
Child labour and health . Bombay , c1985. xi, 287 p. ; LC Card 86-900928 DDC 331.3/1/0956 19
HD6250.I42 C46 1985 ***NYPL [JLD 87-1553]***

Juyal, B. N. Child labour . Varanasi , 1985. xiii, 161 p. ; LC Card 87-901161 DDC 331.3/1/0954 19
HD6250.I42 J89 1985

Nangia, Parveen. Child labour . New Delhi , c1987. ix, 295 p. : ISBN 81-85146-00-4 : LC Card 86-903812 DDC 331.3/1/0954 19
HD6250.I42 N35 1987

CHILDREN - EMPLOYMENT - INDIA - ADDRESSES, ESSAYS, LECTURES.
Women and child workers in unorganised sector . New Delhi , 1983. xii, 104 p. ; LC Card 83-906999 DDC 331.3/1/0954 19
HD6189 .W64 1983 ***NYPL [JLD 87-730]***

CHILDREN - EMPLOYMENT - INDIA - CASE STUDIES.
Juyal, B. N. Child labour and exploitation in the carpet industry . New Delhi , c1987. 49, [1] p. ; LC Card 87-900920 DDC 331.3/1/0954 19
HD6250.I42 J87 1987

CHILDREN - EMPLOYMENT - KENYA.
Kayongo-Male, Diane. Children at work in Kenya /. Nairobi , New York , 1984. x, 187 p. : ISBN 0-19-572546-8 (pbk.) LC Card 85-980979 DDC 331.3/1/096761 19
HD6250.K4 K39 1984 ***NYPL [Sc D 86-960]***

CHILDREN - EMPLOYMENT - KENYA - NAIROBI.
Nakhisa, Sellah A. Parking boys in the city of Kenya "Nairobi" /. [Nairobi , 1981?] ii, 27 leaves ; LC Card 82-980697 DDC 331.3/1 19
HE367.K43 P376 1981

CHILDREN - EMPLOYMENT - NICARAGUA - MANAGUA.
D'Ciófalo V., Giovanni. El trabajo infantil urbano en Managua /. Managua , 1986. ii, 76, 3, [33] leaves ; LC Card 87-403894 DDC 331.3/1/09728513 19
HD6250.N5 M363 1986

CHILDREN - EMPLOYMENT - THAILAND.
Föste, Wolfgang. Verkaufte Träume . München , c1982. 53 p. : ISBN 3-88676-011-1 (pbk.) LC Card 87-672593
HD6250.T52 F67x 1982

CHILDREN - EMPLOYMENT - WYOMING.
Wyoming. Dept. of Labor and Statistics. Wyoming child labor, 1985. Cheyenne, Wyo. , 1985. vi, 71 p. : LC Card 86-622187 DDC 331.3/1/09787 19
HD6250.U4 W85 1985a

CHILDREN - FINANCE, PERSONAL - STUDY AND TEACHING.
Nichols, Harwood, 1942- Money sense . Washington, DC , 1987. p. cm. ISBN 0-87491-871-5 (pbk.) : LC Card 87-24129 DDC 332.024/007 19
HG179 .N53 1987

CHILDREN - HEALTH. see **CHILDREN - CARE AND HYGIENE.**

CHILDREN - HOURS OF LABOR. see **HOURS OF LABOR.**

CHILDREN - HYGIENE. see **CHILDREN - CARE AND HYGIENE.**

CHILDREN IN ADVERTISING - MALAYSIA.
Selling dreams . Penang, Malaysia , c1986. 149 p. : ISBN 967-99502-0-4 (pbk.) LC Card 87-940287 DDC 659.1 19
HF5823 .S46 1986

CHILDREN - INDIA - MORTALITY.
Infant and childhood mortality in India . Delhi, India , c1985. xiv, 120 p. : LC Card 85-905202
NYPL [JLD 87-517]

CHILDREN - MALAYSIA - MORTALITY.
Why were infant and child mortality rates highest in the poorest states of Peninsular Malaysia, 1941-75? /. Santa Monica, CA (P.O. Box 2138, Santa Monica 90406-2138) [1986] xi, 45 p. ; LC Card 86-210106 DDC 304.6/4/088054 19
HB1323.I42 M49 1986

CHILDREN OF ALIEN LABORERS - EUROPE.
Charbit, Yves. Enfants, familles, migrations dans le bassin méditerranéen /. [Paris] , 1985. viii, 195 p. ; ISBN 2-7332-0110-7 (pbk.)
HQ792.E8 C47 1985
NYPL [JLL 72-295 cahier no 110]

CHILDREN OF ALIEN LABORERS - MEDITERRANEAN REGION.
Charbit, Yves. Enfants, familles, migrations dans le bassin méditerranéen /. [Paris] , 1985. viii, 195 p. ; ISBN 2-7332-0110-7 (pbk.)
HQ792.E8 C47 1985
NYPL [JLL 72-295 cahier no 110]

CHILDREN OF ALIEN LABORERS - VOCATIONAL EDUCATION - FRANCE.
Raimond, Jean-Marie. Vocational training of young migrants in France /. Berlin , 1986. x, 101 p. : ISBN 92-825-6118-6
NYPL [JLG 87-134]

CHILDREN OF ALIEN LABORERS - VOCATIONAL EDUCATION - GERMANY (WEST)
Arnold-Rösner, Regina. Berufliche Integration junger Türken . Hamburg , 1986. 122 p. : ISBN 3-925408-05-3 LC Card 86-223625
HD8458.T9 A76 1986

CHILDREN - PROTECTION. see **CHILD WELFARE.**

CHILDREN - RECREATION. see **GAMES.**

CHILDREN - ZAMBIA - KEEMBE (CENTRAL PROVINCE) - MORTALITY.
Interrelationships among infant and childhood mortality, socio-economic factors and fertility in Zambia . Lusaka , Addis Ababa [1984?] 300 p. : LC Card 87-105950 DDC 304.6/32/096894 19
HB1323.I42 Z335 1984

CHILDREN - ZAMBIA - LUSAKA - MORTALITY.
Interrelationships among infant and childhood mortality, socio-economic factors and fertility in Zambia . Lusaka , Addis Ababa [1984?] 300 p. : LC Card 87-105950 DDC 304.6/32/096894 19
HB1323.I42 Z335 1984

CHILDREN'S ACCIDENTS - GERMANY (WEST) - STATISTICS.
Arbeitssicherheit '86 . Bonn [1986] 47, 46, 22 p. : LC Card 87-409083 DDC 363.1/12/0943 19
HD7708 .A7 1986

CHILDREN'S DAY CARE CENTERS. see **DAY CARE CENTERS.**

CHILDREN'S GAMES. see **GAMES.**

CHILE - CENSUS, 1982.
XV censo nacional de población y IV de vivienda--Chile, Abril 1982. [Santiago] , <[1983]-[1986]. <v. 3-14; in 15 > : LC Card 87-110013
HA994 1982d

XV Censo nacional de población y IV de vivienda--Chile, abril 1982. [Santiago] [1985-<1986]. v. <1-13 > : LC Card 87-109976
HA994 1982c

Chile. Comisión Nacional de Energía. Balance de energía, 1965-1984 . Santiago, Chile [1985 or 1986] 191 p. : LC Card 87-401010 DDC 333.79/0983 19
HD9502.C52 B35 1985

CHILE - COMMERCE.
Desormeaux J., Jorge. Determinación de precios del sector exportador chileno, 1978-1982 /. Santiago, Chile , 1983. 88 p. : LC Card 87-403699 DDC 338.5/2/0983 19
HB235.C57 D47 1983

Ffrench-Davis, Ricardo. Origen y destino de las exportaciones chilenas, 1965-80 /. Santiago, Chile , 1981. 22, 6, [27] leaves ; LC Card 83-182100
HF3416.5 .F46 1981b

CHILE - COMMERCE - ARGENTINA.
Argerich, Federico Raúl. Posibilidades de intercambio compensado entre Argentina y Chile y exportaciones graníferas al area del Pacífico, ambos por el paso de San Francisco /. Córdoba , 1985. 35 p. ; LC Card 87-402749 DDC 382/.0983/082 19
HF3418.A7 A8 1985

CHILE - COMMERCIAL POLICY.
Coloma C., Fernando. Credibilidad de la política comercial /. Santiago, Chile , 1986. 43 p. : LC Card 87-102077
HF1515 .C64 1986

CHILE - COMMERCIAL POLICY - ECONOMETRIC MODELS.
Coloma C., Fernando. Algunas consideraciones sobre los efectos distributivos del proceso de liberalización comercial /. Santiago , 1982. 31 leaves ; LC Card 87-102072
HF1713 .C617 1982

CHILE - COMMERCIAL POLICY - MATHEMATICAL MODELS.
Aedo, Cristián. Protección efectiva en Chile, 1974-1979 /. Santiago [1984] 56 leaves ; LC Card 85-152465
HF1956 .A35 1984

CHILE - ECONOMIC CONDITIONS - 1918-1970.
Pisciotta, John L. (John Lee) Development policy, inflation, and politics in Chile, 1938-1958 . New York , 1987. v, 188 p. ; ISBN 0-8240-1367-0 (alk. paper) : LC Card 87-7617 DDC 338.983 19
HC192 .P625 1987

CHILE - ECONOMIC CONDITIONS - 1970-
Büchi Buc, Hernán. Exposición sobre el estado de la hacienda pública /. [Santiago] , 1985. 92 p. ; LC Card 87-105088 DDC 338.983 19
HC192 .B83 1985

Caputo, Orlando. Notas metodológicas para el análisis de la nueva forma de funcionamiento del capitalismo . Cochabamba [1980] 33 leaves ; LC Card 83-204246
HC192 .C216 1980

Edwards, Sebastián. Monetarism and liberalization . Cambridge, MA , c1987. xxi, 233 p. : ISBN 0-88730-105-3 LC Card 86-25959 DDC 338.983 19
HC192 .E249 1987 ***NYPL [JLE 87-1485]***

Fontaine Talavera, Arturo. Pautas para la confección de una política económica . Santiago, Chile , 1984. 92 leaves : LC Card 86-177872
HC192 .F58 1984

Larraín P., Christian. Subsidiariedad o intervencionismo? . [Santiago, Chile] [1986] 137 p. ; LC Card 87-401544 DDC 338.983 19
HC192 .L36 1986

Vega F., Humberto (Vega Fernández) Política económica y movimiento laboral . Santiago, Chile , 1986. 52 p. : LC Card 87-101128
HC192 .V355 1986

CHILE - ECONOMIC CONDITIONS - 1973-
Modelo económico chileno . Santiago, Chile [1982] 606 p. ; LC Card 83-201307
HC192 .M63 1982

CHILE - ECONOMIC CONDITIONS - STATISTICS.
Indicadores económicos y sociales, 1960-1985 /. Santiago, Chile , c1986. xvi, 415 p. : LC Card 87-120338
HC192 .I52 1986

CHILE - ECONOMIC POLICY.
Büchi Buc, Hernán. Exposición sobre el estado de la hacienda pública /. [Santiago] , 1985. 92 p. ; LC Card 87-105088 DDC 338.983 19
HC192 .B83 1985

Edwards, Sebastián. Monetarism and liberalization . Cambridge, MA , c1987. xxi, 233 p. : ISBN 0-88730-105-3 LC Card 86-25959 DDC 338.983 19
HC192 .E249 1987 ***NYPL [JLE 87-1485]***

Fontaine Talavera, Arturo. Pautas para la confección de una política económica . Santiago, Chile , 1984. 92 leaves : LC Card 86-177872
HC192 .F58 1984

Gatica, Jaime. Deindustrialization in Chile /. Boulder , 1988. p. cm. ISBN 0-8133-7392-1 : LC Card 86-32513 DDC 338.983 19
HD9734.C52 G37 1988

Gómez de Reyes, María Teresa. Experiencias de políticas de estabilización . México, D.F. , 1985. iv, 66 leaves ; LC Card 87-122042 DDC 338.982 19
HC125 .G57 1985

Larraín P., Christian. Subsidiariedad o intervencionismo? . [Santiago, Chile] [1986]

137 p. ; LC Card 87-401544 DDC 338.983 19
HC192 .L36 1986

Modelo económico chileno . Santiago, Chile [1982] 606 p. ; LC Card 83-201307
HC192 .M63 1982

Nowak, Felicitas. Financial liberalization revisited . Göttingen [1986] 49 p. : LC Card 87-121206 DDC 332/.0983 19
HG185.C5 N69 1986

Pisciotta, John L. (John Lee) Development policy, inflation, and politics in Chile, 1938-1958 . New York , 1987. v, 188 p. ; ISBN 0-8240-1367-0 (alk. paper) : LC Card 87-7617 DDC 338.983 19
HC192 .P625 1987

Pitts, Mary Anne, 1927- Economic development in Chile under two growth strategies, 1925-1968 /. New York , 1987. vii, 246 p. ; ISBN 0-8240-1368-9 (alk. paper) : LC Card 87-7618 DDC 338.983 19
HC192 .P627 1987

Reactivación con transformación . [Santiago, Chile] [c1984] 29 leaves ; LC Card 85-156967
HD5708.47.C5 R43 1984

Vega F., Humberto (Vega Fernández) Política económica y movimiento laboral . Santiago, Chile , 1986. 52 p. : LC Card 87-101128
HC192 .V355 1986

Vega Tapia, Héctor. L'économie du populisme et le projet de passage au socialisme proposé par l'Unité populaire au Chili /. [Brussels] , 1984. 511 p. ; LC Card 85-146534 DDC 338.983 19
HC192 .V37 1984 ***NYPL [JLE 86-3663]***

CHILE - ECONOMIC POLICY - CONGRESSES.
Economic liberalization in developing countries /. Oxford [Oxfordshire] , New York , 1986. vi, 278 p. : ISBN 0-631-15023-4 : LC Card 86-6153 DDC 338.9/009172/4 19
HC59.7 .E3116 1986 ***NYPL [JLE 86-4644]***

CHILE - ECONOMIC POLICY - ECONOMETRIC MODELS.
Lagos, Luis Felipe. El efecto de los shocks externos sobre el producto . Santiago, Chile , 1985. 15, [8] leaves : LC Card 87-404321 DDC 339.383 19
HC195.I5 L34 1985

CHILE - FOREIGN ECONOMIC RELATIONS - GREAT BRITAIN.
Couyoumdjian, Juan Ricardo. Chile y Gran Bretaña . [Santiago] [1986] xvi, 340 p., [4] p. of plates : LC Card 86-222403
HF1516.5.G72 C68 1986

CHILE - FOREIGN RELATIONS.
Bernstein Carabantes, Enrique. Recuerdos de un diplomático /. Santiago de Chile [1984- v. : LC Card 84-172336 DDC 327.83 19
F3099 .B43 1984 ***NYPL [JFL 84-297]***

CHILE - FULL EMPLOYMENT POLICIES.
Ruiz-Tagle P., Jaime. Los trabajadores del Programa del Empleo Mínimo . Santiago , 1984. 179 p. : LC Card 84-234738
HD5756.A6 R86 1984

Chile - Government. see **Chile - Politics and government.**

CHILE - HISTORY - 1824-1920.
Couyoumdjian, Juan Ricardo. Chile y Gran Bretaña . [Santiago] [1986] xvi, 340 p., [4] p. of plates : LC Card 86-222403
HF1516.5.G72 C68 1986

CHILE - HISTORY - 1920-
Winn, Peter. Weavers of revolution . New York , 1986. xiv, 328 p. : ISBN 0-19-503960-2 : LC Card 85-18832 DDC 338.7/67721/098331 19
HD8039.T42 C478 1986
NYPL [JLE 86-1973]

CHILE - INDUSTRIES.
Gatica, Jaime. Deindustrialization in Chile /. Boulder , 1988. p. cm. ISBN 0-8133-7392-1 : LC Card 86-32513 DDC 338.983 19
HD9734.C52 G37 1988

CHILE - MANUFACTURES.
Gatica, Jaime. Deindustrialization in Chile /. Boulder , 1988. p. cm. ISBN 0-8133-7392-1 : LC Card 86-32513 DDC 338.983 19
HD9734.C52 G37 1988

Weinstein L., Jacqueline. La industria en una estrategia de desarrollo para Chile /. Santiago, Chile , 1984. 50 leaves ; LC Card 86-139143
HD3616.C52 W45 1984

Chile. Ministerio de Hacienda. Büchi Buc, Hernán. Exposición sobre el estado de la hacienda pública /. [Santiago] , 1985. 92 p. ; LC Card 87-105088 DDC 338.983 19
HC192 .B83 1985

Chile. Oficina de Planificación Nacional. Preparación y presentación de proyectos de inversión /. [Santiago] , 1985. v, 138 p. : LC Card 87-116769
HD39 .P72 1985

Chile. Oficina de Planificación Nacional. Departamento de Contabilidad Social. Matriz de insumo-producto de la economía chilena, 1977. [Santiago] [1980 or 1981] 85 p. ; LC Card 82-199199
HC195.I57 M37 1980

Chile--opciones y desafíos del sindicalismo rural, 1973-1985 /. Cruz, María Elena. Santiago, Chile , 1985. 57 p. ; LC Card 87-100897
HD6619.A29 C78 1985

Chile. Planificación Nacional, Oficina de. see **Chile. Oficina de Planificación Nacional.**

CHILE - POLITICS AND GOVERNMENT - 1920-1970.
Pisciotta, John L. (John Lee) Development policy, inflation, and politics in Chile, 1938-1958 . New York , 1987. v, 188 p. ; ISBN 0-8240-1367-0 (alk. paper) : LC Card 87-7617 DDC 338.983 19
HC192 .P625 1987

Vega Tapia, Héctor. L'économie du populisme et le projet de passage au socialisme proposé par l'Unité populaire au Chili /. [Brussels] , 1984. 511 p. ; LC Card 85-146534 DDC 338.983 19
HC192 .V37 1984 ***NYPL [JLE 86-3663]***

CHILE - POLITICS AND GOVERNMENT - 1970-
Campero, Guillermo. El sindicalismo internacional y la redemocratización de Chile /. Santiago, Chile , 1984. 77 p. ; LC Card 86-139122 DDC 331.88/0983 19
HD6617 .C357 1984

Lechner, Norbert, 1939- La conflictiva y nunca acabada construcción del orden deseado /. [Santiago, Chile] [1984] 204 p. ; ISBN 84-89401-05-5 LC Card 84-227472 DDC 320.982 19
JL2624 .L43 1984 ***NYPL [JLE 87-2137]***

Ruiz-Tagle P., Jaime. El sindicalismo chileno después del plan laboral /. Santiago, Chile [1985?] 211 p. ; ***NYPL [JLD 87-1182]***

Vega Tapia, Héctor. L'économie du populisme et le projet de passage au socialisme proposé par l'Unité populaire au Chili /. [Brussels] , 1984. 511 p. ; LC Card 85-146534 DDC 338.983 19
HC192 .V37 1984 ***NYPL [JLE 86-3663]***

CHILE - POLITICS AND GOVERNMENT - 1970-1973.
Bossle, Lothar. Allende und der europäische Sozialismus /. Würzburg [1981?] 146 p. ; ISBN 3-88567-026-7 (pbk.) LC Card 82-149701 DDC 983/.0646/0924 19
HX197.A44 B67 1981 ***NYPL [HIF 86-2151]***

CHILE - POLITICS AND GOVERNMENT - 1973-
Cruz, María Elena. Chile--opciones y desafíos del sindicalismo rural, 1973-1985 /. Santiago, Chile , 1985. 57 p. ; LC Card 87-100897
HD6619.A29 C78 1985

CHILE - POPULATION, RURAL.
Lira, Luis Felipe. Estructura agraria, crecimiento de la población y migraciones . Santiago, Chile , 1976. 90 p. ; LC Card 83-169710
HB2025 .L57 1976

CHILE - POPULATION - STATISTICS.
XV censo nacional de población y IV de vivienda--Chile, Abril 1982. [Santiago] , <[1983]-[1986]. <v. 3-14; in 15 > : LC Card 87-110013
HA994 1982d

XV Censo nacional de población y IV de vivienda--Chile, abril 1982. [Santiago] [1985-<1986]. v. <1-13 > : LC Card 87-109976
HA994 1982c

Chile. Presidencia de la República. Oficina de Planificación Nacional. see **Chile. Oficina de Planificación Nacional.**

CHILE - RURAL CONDITIONS.
Problemas metodológicos de una encuesta rural en Chile y estructura del empleo /. [Santiago, Chile] [c1983] ii, 27 leaves ; LC Card 84-225128
HD1531.C5 P76 1983

CHILE - SOCIAL CONDITIONS - STATISTICS.
Indicadores económicos y sociales, 1960-1985 /. Santiago, Chile , c1986. xvi, 415 p. : LC Card 87-120338
HC192 .I52 1986

Chile. Superintendencia de Valores y Seguros. Producción corredores de seguros 1985. [Chile] , 1986. 390 p. ; LC Card 87-403786 DDC 368/.0025/83 19
HG8576 .P76 1986

Chile y CIPEC ante la crisis del cobre / Jorge Bande ... [et al.]. Santiago de Chile : Centro de Estudios del Cobre y la Minería, 1985. 74 p. ; 21 cm. (Cuadernos de CESCO . no. 1) Revised papers from a seminar entitled "La crisis del cobre, alternatives para Chile y CIPEC" held in Aug. 1984. Includes bibliographical references. LC Card 86-144485
1. Intergovernmental Council of Copper Exporting Countries - Congresses. 2. Copper industry and trade - Government policy - Chile - Congresses. 3. Copper industry and trade - Congresses. I. Bande B., Jorge. II. Centro de Estudios del Cobre y la Minería (Santiago, Chile). III. Series.
HD9539.C7 C526 1985 ***NYPL [JLD 87-363]***

Chile y Gran Bretaña . Couyoumdjian, Juan Ricardo. [Santiago] [1986] xvi, 340 p., [4] p. of plates : LC Card 86-222403
HF1516.5.G72 C68 1986

Chilivumbo, Alifeyo.
Communal agrarian cooperative societies : an experiment in rural socialism / by A. Chilivumbo. Lusaka : National Commission for Development Planning : University of Zambia, [1986] iii, 134 p. ; 30 cm. At head of title: Republic of Zambia. "A report prepared for National Commission for Development Planning, Lusaka and University of Zambia, Lusaka." LC Card 86-981399 DDC 334/.683/096894 19
1. Agriculture, Cooperative - Zambia. 2. Agriculture, Cooperative - Zambia - Case studies. 3. Socialism - Zambia. 4. Agriculture and state - Zambia. I. Zambia. National Commission for Development Planning. II. University of Zambia. III. Title.
HD1491.Z35 C45 1986

Migration and uneven rural development in Africa : the case of Zambia / Alifeyo Chilivumbo. Lanham, MD : University Press of America, c1985. xx, 118 p. : maps ; 21 cm. Bibliography: p. 113-118. ISBN 0-8191-4929-2 (alk. paper) : LC Card 85-17908 DDC 307.2 19
1. Rural-urban migration - Zambia. 2. Urban-rural migration - Zambia. 3. Rural development - Zambia. I. Title.
HB2123.6.A3 C47 1985
NYPL [JLD 86-1953]

Strengthening women's participation in food and agricultural marketing . [Lusaka] [1984] 78 p. ; LC Card 86-980282 DDC 331.4/83/096894 19
HD6073.A292 Z3374 1984

Chilnick, Lawrence D. The complete guide to drug testing : a Random House professional books report / Lawrence D. Chilnick.1st ed. New York, N.Y. : Random House, c1987. p. cm. Bibliography: p. Includes index. ISBN 0-394-56058-2 : LC Card 87-9631 DDC 658.3/82 19
1. Drug testing - United States. 2. Drugs and employment - United States. 3. Drug abuse - United States - Prevention. 4. Labor discipline - Law and legislation - United States. I. Random House (Firm). II. Title.
HF5549.5.D7 C46 1987

Chilton, Kenneth. Public policy toward corporate takeovers /. New Brunswick (USA) , c1988. xvi, 176 p. ; ISBN 0-88738-166-9 : LC Card 87-10750 DDC 338.8/3/0973 19
HD2795 .P825 1988

Chimanlal Lalbhai Centre for Management. Industrial sickness . Ahmedabad , c1984. xv, 459 p. ; LC Card 87-902007 DDC 363.1/19677/00954 19
HD9866.I63 A385 1984

Issues in modernization of the textile industry . Ahmedabad , 1985. 87 p. : LC Card 87-902140 DDC 338.4/7677/00954 19
HD9866.I62 I58 1985

Chimerine, Lawrence. Handbook for raising capital . Homewood, Ill. , c1987. xxiv, 666 p. : ISBN 0-87094-705-2 LC Card 86-71216
NYPL [*R-Econ. 87-1124]

Chimitdorzhiev, Sh. B. Ulymzhiev, D. B. (Dashi Batuevich) Put′ mongol′skogo aratstva k sotsializmu /. Novosibirsk , 1987. 283, [5] p. ; LC Card 87-159668
HD1491.M55 U49 1987

CHIMNEY-SWEEPS - GREAT BRITAIN - HISTORY.
Strange, K. H. (Kathleen H.), 1904- Climbing boys . London ; New York : xiv, 146 p. : ISBN 0-85031-431-3 : LC Card 83-143704 DDC 331.5/5 19
HD8039.C482 G77 1982
NYPL [JLD 85-681]

Chin, H. E. The Caribbean Basin and the changing world economic structure /. Groningen , c1986. 194 p. ; ISBN 90-01-18630-0 (pbk.) : LC Card 87-117415 DDC 330.9729/052 19
HC151 .C26 1986

Chin, Ssu-K'ai. see **Chin, Steve S. K.**

Chin, Steve S. K. Chen, Edward K. Y. The markets of Asia/Pacific--People's Republic of China /. London , Aldershot, Hants, England , c1984. 124 p., [1] leaf of plates : ISBN 0-566-02316-4 LC Card 87-672541
HC427.92 .C353x 1984b

China and the future . Hamrin, Carol Lee. Boulder, Colo. , 1986. p. cm. ISBN 0-8133-7364-6 : LC Card 86-28960 DDC 338.951 19
HC427.92 .H34 1986

CHINA - CENSUS, 1982 - CONGRESSES.
International Seminar on China's 1982 Population Census (1982 : Peking, China) A census of one billion people . [Wanchai, Hongkong , Boulder, Colo. , 1986, c1987] 704 p., [4] leaves of plates : LC Card 87-2131 DDC 304.6/0723 19
HA4631.5 .I57 1982

CHINA - COMMERCE.
Chen, Edward K. Y. The markets of Asia/Pacific--People's Republic of China /. London , Aldershot, Hants, England , c1984. 124 p., [1] leaf of plates : ISBN 0-566-02316-4 LC Card 87-672541
HC427.92 .C353x 1984b

Kathuria, Sanjay. India's exports, the challenge from China /. New Delhi , 1986. 106 p. ; LC Card 86-902526 DDC 382/.6/0954 19
HF3836.5 .K37 1986

The Open policy at work /. Beijing, China [1985] 281 p. ; LC Card 86-219666 DDC 337.51 19
HF1604 .O63 1985

Tsao, James T. H. China's development strategies and foreign trade /. Lexington, Mass. , c1987. xii, 209 p. : ISBN 0-669-13954-8 (alk. paper) LC Card 86-45590 DDC 338.951 19
HC427.9 .T689 1987

CHINA - COMMERCE - ASIA, SOUTHEASTERN.
Manezhev, S. A. (Sergeĭ Aleksandrovich) Ėkonomicheskie otnoshenii͡a KNR so stranami I͡Ugo-Vostochnoĭ Azii /. Moskva , 1980. 191 p. ; LC Card 81-130904
HF1604.Z4 A7856 1980

CHINA - COMMERCE - BRITISH COLUMBIA.
China economic overview . [Victoria] [1985?] 111, [2] p. : ISBN 0-7726-0465-7 (pbk.) LC Card 86-202984 DDC 330.951/058 19
HC427.92 .C68 1985

CHINA - COMMERCE - EAST ASIA.
Lardy, Nicholas R. China's entry into the world economy . Lanham, MD , New York, N.Y. , c1987. xviii, 57 p. : ISBN 0-8191-6371-6 (alk. paper) : LC Card 87-10625 DDC 382/.0951 19
HF3820.5 .L37 1987

CHINA - COMMERCE - EUROPE, EASTERN.
Lardy, Nicholas R. China's entry into the world economy . Lanham, MD , New York, N.Y. , c1987. xviii, 57 p. : ISBN 0-8191-6371-6 (alk. paper) : LC Card 87-10625 DDC 382/.0951 19
HF3820.5 .L37 1987

CHINA - COMMERCE - HISTORY.
So, Alvin Y., 1953- The South China silk district . Albany, N.Y. , c1986. xii, 206 p. : ISBN 0-88706-322-5 LC Card 86-14575 DDC 338.4/7677391/095127 19
HD9926.C63 S637 1986
NYPL [JLE 87-1448]

CHINA - COMMERCE - SPAIN.
La Economía china de la revolución a las cuatro modernizaciones /. Madrid [1986?] 181 p. : LC Card 86-229994
HC427.9 .E319 1986

CHINA - COMMERCE - SWITZERLAND.
Yang, Yuming. L'industrie horlogère suisse et ses relations avec la Chine de 1949 à 1982 /. Geneve , 1984. 186 leaves : LC Card 85-104853
HD9999.C583 S99 1984

CHINA - COMMERCE - UNITED STATES.
Lardy, Nicholas R. China's entry into the world economy . Lanham, MD , New York, N.Y. , c1987. xviii, 57 p. : ISBN 0-8191-6371-6 (alk. paper) : LC Card 87-10625 DDC 382/.0951 19
HF3820.5 .L37 1987

Tsao, James T. H. China's development strategies and foreign trade /. Lexington, Mass. , c1987. xii, 209 p. : ISBN 0-669-13954-8 (alk. paper) LC Card 86-45590 DDC 338.951 19
HC427.9 .T689 1987

CHINA - COMMERCIAL POLICY.
Kathuria, Sanjay. India's exports, the challenge from China /. New Delhi , 1986. 106 p. ; LC Card 86-902526 DDC 382/.6/0954 19
HF3836.5 .K37 1986

Mathur, Iqbal. Strategies for joint ventures in the People's Republic of China /. New York , 1987. viii, 196 p. ; ISBN 0-275-92354-1 (alk. paper) : LC Card 87-7033 DDC 338.8/8851 19
HD62.47 .M38 1987

Tsao, James T. H. China's development strategies and foreign trade /. Lexington, Mass. , c1987. xii, 209 p. : ISBN 0-669-13954-8 (alk. paper) LC Card 86-45590 DDC 338.951 19
HC427.9 .T689 1987

CHINA - COMMERCIAL POLICY - CONGRESSES.
Foreign capital and technology in China /. New York , 1987. xvii, 191 p. : ISBN 0-275-92716-4 (alk. paper) : LC Card 87-2450 DDC 332.6/7314/0951 19
HG5782 .F67 1987

CHINA - ECONOMIC CONDITIONS - 1912-1949.
Honig, Emily. Sisters and strangers . Stanford, Calif. , 1986. ix, 299 p. : ISBN 0-8047-1274-3 (alk. paper) : LC Card 84-51711 DDC 331.4/87721/0951132 19
HD6073.T42 C64 1986
NYPL [JLD 86-3016]

CHINA - ECONOMIC CONDITIONS - 1949-
La Economía china de la revolución a las cuatro modernizaciones /. Madrid [1986?] 181 p. : LC Card 86-229994
HC427.9 .E319 1986

Lyons, Thomas P. Economic integration and planning in Maoist China /. New York , 1987. xiii, 376 p. ; ISBN 0-231-06542-6 LC Card 87-5414 DDC 338.951 19
HC427.9 .L96 1987

CHINA - ECONOMIC CONDITIONS - 1949- - CONGRESSES.
China im Konflikt zwischen verschiedenen Ordnungskonzeptionen /. Berlin , c1985. 157 p. : ISBN 3-428-05923-9 LC Card 86-164406
HC427.9 .C56525 1985

CHINA - ECONOMIC CONDITIONS - 1976-
Chen, Edward K. Y. The markets of Asia/Pacific--People's Republic of China /. London , Aldershot, Hants, England , c1984. 124 p., [1] leaf of plates : ISBN 0-566-02316-4 LC Card 87-672541
HC427.92 .C353x 1984b

China economic overview . [Victoria] [1985?] 111, [2] p. : ISBN 0-7726-0465-7 (pbk.) LC Card 86-202984 DDC 330.951/058 19
HC427.92 .C68 1985

The Chinese economy since 1978 /. Boulder , 1988. p. cm. ISBN 0-8133-0555-1 (v. 1) : LC Card 87-10631 DDC 330.951/058 19
HC427.92 .C4674 1988

CHINA - ECONOMIC CONDITIONS - 1976- - CONGRESSES.
Wirtschaftsreformen und neue Entwicklungsstrategien in der Volksrepublik China /. Frankfurt am Main , New York , c1986. 185 p. ; ISBN 3-8204-9101-5 LC Card 86-220822
HC427.92 .W56 1986

CHINA - ECONOMIC CONDITIONS - 1976- - STATISTICS.
Toussaint, Marcel. China market atlas /. Hong Kong , c1986. ix, 222 p. : LC Card 86-218633 DDC 330.951/058 19
HC427.92 .T69 1986

China economic overview : a British Columbia perspective. [Rev. ed.] [Victoria] : Province of British Columbia, Ministry of International Trade and Investment, [1985?] 111, [2] p. : ill. ; 28 cm. Cover title. Rev. ed. of: China economic overview / Madelaine Cox. 1981? Bibliography: p. [112]-[113] ISBN 0-7726-0465-7 (pbk.) LC Card 86-202984 DDC 330.951/058 19
1. China - Economic conditions - 1976-. 2. China - Economic policy - 1976-. 3. Investments, Foreign - China. 4. China - Commerce - British Columbia. 5. British Columbia - Commerce - China. I. Cox, Madelaine. China economic overview. II. British Columbia. Ministry of International Trade and Investment.
HC427.92 .C68 1985

CHINA - ECONOMIC POLICY.
Azqueta Oyarzun, Diego. Teoría económica de la acumulación socialista . Madrid , 1983. 224 p. ; ISBN 84-7214-279-5 LC Card 84-140278 DDC 332/.0415/091717 19
HC710.S3 A97 1983 ***NYPL [JLD 86-1859]***

So, Alvin Y., 1953- The South China silk district . Albany, N.Y. , c1986. xii, 206 p. : ISBN 0-88706-322-5 LC Card 86-14575 DDC 338.4/7677391/095127 19
HD9926.C63 S637 1986
NYPL [JLE 87-1448]

CHINA - ECONOMIC POLICY - 1949-
La Economía china de la revolución a las cuatro modernizaciones /. Madrid [1986?] 181 p. : LC Card 86-229994
HC427.9 .E319 1986

Lee, Peter N. S., 1940- Industrial management and economic reform in China, 1949-1984 /. Hong Kong , New York , 1987. x, 335 p. ; ISBN 0-19-584118-2 : LC Card 87-13748 DDC 338.951 19
HD70.C5 L44 1987

Liu, Alan P. L., 1937- Phoenix and the lame lion . Stanford, Calif. , c1987. x, 182 p. ; ISBN 0-8179-8581-6 LC Card 87-13555 DDC 338.951 19
HC430.5 .L568 1987

Lyons, Thomas P. Economic integration and planning in Maoist China /. New York , 1987. xiii, 376 p. ; ISBN 0-231-06542-6 LC Card 87-5414 DDC 338.951 19
HC427.9 .L96 1987

Tsao, James T. H. China's development strategies and foreign trade /. Lexington, Mass. , c1987. xii, 209 p. : ISBN 0-669-13954-8 (alk. paper) LC Card 86-45590 DDC 338.951 19
HC427.9 .T689 1987

CHINA - ECONOMIC POLICY - 1949- - CONGRESSES.
China im Konflikt zwischen verschiedenen Ordnungskonzeptionen /. Berlin , c1985. 157 p. : ISBN 3-428-05923-9 LC Card 86-164406
HC427.9 .C56525 1985

CHINA - ECONOMIC POLICY - 1976-
China economic overview . [Victoria] [1985?] 111, [2] p. : ISBN 0-7726-0465-7 (pbk.) LC Card

86-202984 DDC 330.951/058 19
HC427.92 .C68 1985

Hamrin, Carol Lee. China and the future . Boulder, Colo. , 1986. p. cm. ISBN 0-8133-7364-6 : LC Card 86-28960 DDC 338.951 19
HC427.92 .H34 1986

Kai ko. English. Reform in China . Armonk, N.Y., USA , c1987. p. cm. ISBN 0-87332-458-7 : LC Card 87-23537 DDC 338.951 19
HC427.92 .K32 1987

Mathur, Iqbal. Strategies for joint ventures in the People's Republic of China /. New York , 1987. viii, 196 p. ; ISBN 0-275-92354-1 (alk. paper) : LC Card 87-7033 DDC 338.8/8851 19
HD62.47 .M38 1987

Oborne, Michael West. China's special economic zones /. Paris [Washington, D.C.] 1986. 185 p. : ISBN 92-64-12801-8 (pbk.) : LC Card 86-217671 DDC 338.6/042/0951 19
HC427.92 .O27 1986

Rabushka, Alvin. The new China . San Francisco , Boulder, Colo. , 1987. xii, 254 p. ; ISBN 0-936488-15-8 (pbk. : alk. paper) LC Card 87-10574 DDC 338.951 19
HC427.92 .R33 1987

CHINA - ECONOMIC POLICY - 1976- - CONGRESSES.
Foreign capital and technology in China /. New York , 1987. xvii, 191 p. : ISBN 0-275-92716-4 (alk. paper) : LC Card 87-2450 DDC 332.6/7314/0951 19
HG5782 .F67 1987

Wirtschaftsreformen und neue Entwicklungsstrategien in der Volksrepublik China /. Frankfurt am Main , New York , c1986. 185 p. ; ISBN 3-8204-9101-5 LC Card 86-220822
HC427.92 .W56 1986

China Energy Workshop I: Petroleum Processing (1985 : Honolulu, Hawaii) China's petroleum industry in the international context : proceedings from the China Energy Workshop I: Petroleum Processing / Fereidun Fesharaki, David Fridley, editors. Boulder [Colo.] : Westview Press, 1986. xvii, 166 p. : ill., maps ; 22 cm. "Conducted at the East-West Center, Honolulu, Hawaii, 25-26 April 1985, organized by the Resource Systems Institute of the East-West Center." ISBN 0-86638-072-8 (pbk.) LC Card 86-50695 DDC 338.2/7282/0951 19
1. Petroleum industry and trade - China - Congresses. 2. Petroleum chemicals industry - China - Congresses. I. Fesharaki, Fereidun. II. Fridley, David, 1956-. III. East-West Resource Systems Institute. IV. Title.
HD9576.C52 C524 1985
NYPL [JLD 86-3885]

CHINA - FOREIGN ECONOMIC RELATIONS.
Oborne, Michael West. China's special economic zones /. Paris [Washington, D.C.] 1986. 185 p. : ISBN 92-64-12801-8 (pbk.) : LC Card 86-217671 DDC 338.6/042/0951 19
HC427.92 .O27 1986

The Open policy at work /. Beijing, China [1985] 281 p. ; LC Card 86-219666 DDC 337.51 19
HF1604 .O63 1985

CHINA - FOREIGN ECONOMIC RELATIONS - ASIA, SOUTHEASTERN.
Manezhev, S. A. (Sergeĭ Aleksandrovich) Ėkonomicheskie otnoshenii͡a KNR so stranami I͡Ugo-Vostochnoĭ Azii /. Moskva , 1980. 191 p. ; LC Card 81-130904
HF1604.Z4 A7856 1980

CHINA - FOREIGN ECONOMIC RELATIONS - EUROPEAN ECONOMIC COMMUNITY COUNTRIES.
Wiesegart, Kurt. Wirtschaftskooperation mit China . Hamburg , 1984. 126 p. ; ISBN 3-87895-260-0 LC Card 85-146617
HF1604.Z4 E869 1984

CHINA - FOREIGN ECONOMIC RELATIONS - GERMANY, WEST.
Wiesegart, Kurt. Wirtschaftskooperation mit China . Hamburg , 1984. 126 p. ; ISBN 3-87895-260-0 LC Card 85-146617
HF1604.Z4 E869 1984

CHINA - FOREIGN ECONOMIC RELATIONS - GERMANY (WEST) - CONGRESSES.
Wirtschaftsreformen und neue Entwicklungsstrategien in der Volksrepublik China /. Frankfurt am Main , New York , c1986. 185 p. ; ISBN 3-8204-9101-5 LC Card 86-220822
HC427.92 .W56 1986

CHINA - FOREIGN ECONOMIC RELATIONS - GREAT BRITAIN.
Edwards, E. W. British diplomacy and finance in China, 1895-1914 /. Oxford [Oxfordshire] , New York , 1987. 212 p. : ISBN 0-19-822916-X : LC Card 86-28567 DDC 337.41051 19
HF1534.5.C5 E39 1987

CHINA - FOREIGN ECONOMIC RELATIONS - UNITED STATES.
Cosgrove, Julia Fukuda. United States foreign economic policy toward China, 1943-1946 . New York , 1987. 235 p. ; ISBN 0-8240-8079-3 (alk. paper) : LC Card 87-23791 DDC 337.73051 19
HF1456.5.C6 C67 1987

CHINA - FOREIGN RELATIONS - 1912-1949.
Cosgrove, Julia Fukuda. United States foreign economic policy toward China, 1943-1946 . New York , 1987. 235 p. ; ISBN 0-8240-8079-3 (alk. paper) : LC Card 87-23791 DDC 337.73051 19
HF1456.5.C6 C67 1987

CHINA - FOREIGN RELATIONS - GREAT BRITAIN.
Edwards, E. W. British diplomacy and finance in China, 1895-1914 /. Oxford [Oxfordshire] , New York , 1987. 212 p. : ISBN 0-19-822916-X : LC Card 86-28567 DDC 337.41051 19
HF1534.5.C5 E39 1987

China - Government. see **China - Politics and government.**

China im Konflikt zwischen verschiedenen Ordnungskonzeptionen / von Armin Bohnet ... [et al.] ; herausgegeben von Alfred Schüller. Berlin : Duncker & Humblot, c1985. 157 p. : ill. ; 24 cm. (Schriften des Vereins für Socialpolitik, Gesellschaft für Wirtschafts- und Sozialwissenschaften . n.F., Bd. 150) Reports presented at a meeting of the Ausschuss zum Vergleich von Wirtschaftssystemen which was held Sept. 20-21, 1984 in Hamburg. Includes bibliographies. CONTENTS. - Der Plan-Markt-Mechanismus Chinas / von Norbert Kloten -- Reformen des Planungs- und Leitungssystemens in der Industrie der VR China / von Armin Bohnert und Günter Jaehne -- Beschäftigungsprobleme und Beschäftigungspolitik in China / von Jiří Kosta -- Der Agrarsektor in der Volksrepublik China / von Eberhard Schinke. ISBN 3-428-05923-9 LC Card 86-164406
1. China - Economic policy - 1949- - Congresses. 2. China - Economic conditions - 1949- - Congresses. I. Bohnet, Armin. II. Schüller, Alfred. III. Gesellschaft für Wirtschafts- und Sozialwissenschaften, Verein für Socialpolitik. Ausschuss zum Vergleich von Wirtschaftssystemen. IV. Series.
HC427.9 .C56525 1985

CHINA - INDUSTRIES.
Business opportunities in China . Menlo Park, Calif. (333 Ravenswood Ave., Menlo Park 94025-3476) , c1984. 32 p. : LC Card 86-210279 DDC 338.8/8851 19
HC427.92 .B85 1984

China. Kuo chia t'ung chi chü. Jen k'ou t'ung chi ssu. International Seminar on China's 1982 Population Census (1982 : Peking, China) A census of one billion people . [Wanchai, Hongkong , Boulder, Colo. , 1986, c1987] 704 p., [4] leaves of plates : LC Card 87-2131 DDC 304.6/0723 19
HA4631.5 .I57 1982

China. Kuo min ching chi p'ing heng t'ung chi ssu. Ch'üan kuo t'ou ju ch'an ch'u piao, 1981. English. Input-output tables of China, 1981 /. Beijing , Honolulu , 1987. p. cm. ISBN 0-86638-104-X (East-West Population Institute) LC Card 87-24457 DDC 339.2/3/0951 19
HC430.I57 C5813 1981

China. Kuo wu yüan. Jen k'ou p'u ch'a pan kung shih. International Seminar on China's 1982 Population Census (1982 : Peking, China) A census of one billion people . [Wanchai, Hongkong , Boulder, Colo. , 1986, c1987] 704 p., [4] leaves of plates : LC Card 87-2131 DDC 304.6/0723 19
HA4631.5 .I57 1982

China market atlas /. Toussaint, Marcel. Hong Kong , c1986. ix, 222 p. : LC Card 86-218633 DDC 330.951/058 19
HC427.92 .T69 1986

CHINA - POLITICS AND GOVERNMENT - 1976-
Hamrin, Carol Lee. China and the future . Boulder, Colo. , 1986. p. cm. ISBN 0-8133-7364-6 : LC Card 86-28960 DDC 338.951 19
HC427.92 .H34 1986

Lieberthal, Kenneth. Bureaucratic politics and Chinese energy development /. [Washington, D.C.] [1986] xii, 405 p. ; LC Card 86-602422 DDC 333.79/0951 19
HD9502.C62 L54 1986

CHINA - POPULATION.
Banister, Judith, 1943- China's changing population /. Stanford, Calif. , 1987. xiii, 488 p. : ISBN 0-8047-1155-0 (alk. paper) : LC Card 82-60105 DDC 304.6/0951 19
HB3654.A3 B36 1987

CHINA - POPULATION POLICY.
Banister, Judith, 1943- China's changing population /. Stanford, Calif. , 1987. xiii, 488 p. : ISBN 0-8047-1155-0 (alk. paper) : LC Card 82-60105 DDC 304.6/0951 19
HB3654.A3 B36 1987

Greenhalgh, Susan. Fertility policy in China . New York, N.Y. [1986] 31 p. ; LC Card 87-154581 DDC 304.6/6/0951 19
HB1064.A3 G74 1986

A China research publication.
Campbell, Nigel. China strategies . [Manchester, Greater Manchester] [Hong Kong] , c1986. xxiv, 161 p. : ISBN 0-903808-51-X (pbk.) LC Card 86-235360 DDC 332.6/7314/0951 19
HD2910 .C36 1986

CHINA - RURAL CONDITIONS.
La Politique agraire en Chine . Ottignies, Louvain-la-Neuve, Belgique [1981] 84 leaves ; LC Card 86-203953
HD926 .P65 1981

CHINA - SOCIAL LIFE AND CUSTOMS - 1912-1949.
Barth, Johannes, 1891- Als deutscher Kaufmann in Fernost . Berlin , c1984. 206 p. : ISBN 3-503-02366-6 LC Card 84-143117
HC289.B7 B373 1984

CHINA - STATISTICS.
Statisztikai idősorok a Kínai Népköztársaságról. Budapest , 1986. 119 p. ; ISBN 963-02-4495-0 LC Card 86-217703
HA4635 .S73 1986

China strategies . Campbell, Nigel. [Manchester, Greater Manchester] [Hong Kong] , c1986. xxiv, 161 p. : ISBN 0-903808-51-X (pbk.) LC Card 86-235360 DDC 332.6/7314/0951 19
HD2910 .C36 1986

China, the livestock sector. Washington, D.C., U. S.A. : World Bank, 1987. vii, 195 p. ; 28 cm. (A World Bank country study) ISBN 0-8213-0940-4 (pbk.) LC Card 87-16089 DDC 338.1/76/00951 19
1. Animal industry - China. 2. Livestock - China. I. International Bank for Reconstruction and Development. II. Series.
HD9426.C62 C475 1987

China today .
(10) The Open policy at work /. Beijing, China [1985] 281 p. ; LC Card 86-219666 DDC 337.51 19
HF1604 .O63 1985

(9) On rolls the green revolution /. Beijing, China [1984] 142 p., [36] p. of plates : LC Card 86-115054 DDC 338.1/0951 19
HD2097 .O5 1984 ***NYPL [JLK 83-122 no.9]***

China today (Peking, China) .
(9) On rolls the green revolution /. Beijing, China [1984] 142 p., [36] p. of plates : LC Card 86-115054 DDC 338.1/0951 19
HD2097 .O5 1984 ***NYPL [JLK 83-122 no.9]***

China. Wai tzu kuan li chü. Guide to China's foreign economic relations and trade. Investment special /. Hong Kong , 1983. 342 p. : ISBN 0-9627063-8-8 : LC Card 84-177660 DDC 346.51/07 345.1067 19
HG5784 .G835 1983 ***NYPL [*OVY 86-3398]***

CHINANTEC INDIANS.
Ewell, Peter T., 1947- Uxpanapa . Ithaca, N.Y. [1982] xiv, 218 p., [35] leaves of plates : LC Card 84-621492 DDC 338.1/0972/6 19
HD1795.P3 E94 1982

China's changing population /. Banister, Judith, 1943- Stanford, Calif. , 1987. xiii, 488 p. : ISBN 0-8047-1155-0 (alk. paper) : LC Card 82-60105 DDC 304.6/0951 19
HB3654.A3 B36 1987

China's dairy and food processing industries . Keidel, Albert. Washington, D.C. , c1986. ii, 65 leaves ; LC Card 86-233105 DDC 338.1/77/0951 19
HD9275.C62 K45 1986

China's development strategies and foreign trade /. Tsao, James T. H. Lexington, Mass. , c1987. xii, 209 p. : ISBN 0-669-13954-8 (alk. paper) LC Card 86-45590 DDC 338.951 19
HC427.9 .T689 1987

China's entry into the world economy . Lardy, Nicholas R. Lanham, MD , New York, N.Y. , c1987. xviii, 57 p. : ISBN 0-8191-6371-6 (alk. paper) : LC Card 87-10625 DDC 382/.0951 19
HF3820.5 .L37 1987

China's industrial reform / Gene Tidrick and Chen Jiyuan, editors. New York : Oxford University Press, c1987. xii, 378 p. ; 25 cm. (A World Bank research publication) "Published for the World Bank." Includes bibliographies and index. ISBN 0-19-520592-8 : LC Card 87-5616 DDC 338.951 19
1. Industry and state - China. 2. Industrial management - China. I. Tidrick, Gene, 1942-. II. Chen, Jiyuan. III. International Bank for Reconstruction and Development.
HD3616.C63 C495 1987

China's petroleum industry in the international context . China Energy Workshop I: Petroleum Processing (1985 : Honolulu, Hawaii) Boulder [Colo.] , 1986. xvii, 166 p. : ISBN 0-86638-072-8 (pbk.) LC Card 86-50695 DDC 338.2/7282/0951 19
HD9576.C52 C524 1985
NYPL [JLD 86-3885]

China's special economic zones /. Oborne, Michael West. Paris [Washington, D.C.] 1986. 185 p. : ISBN 92-64-12801-8 (pbk.) : LC Card 86-217671 DDC 338.6/042/0951 19
HC427.92 .O27 1986

CHINAWARE. see **POTTERY.**

Chinello, Cesco. Operai e scelte politiche . Milano, Italy , c1986. 267 p., 45 p. of plates : LC Card 86-169148
HD8439.V462 O64 1986

CHINESE AMERICANS - SOCIAL CONDITIONS.
Siu, Paul C. P. (Paul Chan Pang), 1906- The Chinese laundryman . New York , c1987. xlii, 311 p. : ISBN 0-8147-7859-3 : LC Card 87-5609 DDC 331.6/2/51073 19
HD8039.L32 U675 1987

Chinese Economic System Reform Research Institute. Kai ko. English. Reform in China . Armonk, N.Y., USA , c1987. p. cm. ISBN 0-87332-458-7 : LC Card 87-23537 DDC 338.951 19
HC427.92 .K32 1987

The Chinese economy since 1978 / edited by Stephan Feuchtwang. Boulder : Westview Press, 1988. p. cm. Bibliography: p. Includes indexes. CONTENTS. - v. 1. Rural economy -- v. 2. Urban economy. ISBN 0-8133-0555-1 (v. 1) : LC Card 87-10631 DDC 330.951/058 19
1. China - Economic conditions - 1976-. I. Feuchtwang, Stephan.
HC427.92 .C4674 1988

The Chinese laundryman . Siu, Paul C. P. (Paul Chan Pang), 1906- New York , c1987. xlii, 311 p. : ISBN 0-8147-7859-3 : LC Card 87-5609 DDC 331.6/2/51073 19
HD8039.L32 U675 1987

Chinloy, Peter, 1950- Real estate : investment and financial strategy / Peter Chinloy ; Zachary Rolnik, editor. Boston, Mass. : Kluwer Academic Publishers, c1987. p. cm. Bibliography: p. Includes index. ISBN 0-89838-237-8 LC Card 87-3249 DDC 332.63/24 19
1. Real estate investment. 2. Mortgages. 3. Housing - Finance. 4. Real property. I. Title.
HD1382.5 .C475 1987

Chiplin, Brian. Personal financial markets . Deddington, Oxford , Atlantic Highlands, N.J. , 1986. viii, 279 p. : ISBN 0-86003-540-9 LC Card 86-235455 DDC 332.1/7 19
HG186.G7 P38 1986

CHIPPEWA FALLS (WIS.) - DESCRIPTION - VIEWS.
Friedlander, Lee. Cray at Chippewa Falls /. Minneapolis, Minn. (608 2nd Ave., S., Minneapolis 55402) , 1987. 96 p. : LC Card 86-73134
HD9696.C64 C734 1987

Chips! . Oppenheimer, Max Stul. Homewood, Ill. , c1987. xii, 203 p. : ISBN 0-87094-942-X (pbk.) LC Card 86-72272 DDC 004/.068/7 19
HD9696.C62 O665 1987

CHIPS, the Consolidated Local Street and Highway Improvement Program . New York (State). Legislature. Legislative Commission on Critical Transportation Choices. [Albany, N.Y.] [1986] i, 18 leaves ; LC Card 87-620568 DDC 388.1/12 19
HE356.N7 N37 1986

Chiras, Daniel D. Environmental science : a framework for decision making / Daniel D. Chiras.2nd ed. Menlo Park, Calif. : Benjamin/Cummings Pub. Co., c1988. xxiii, 531 p., [16] p. of plates : ill. (some col.) ; 29 cm. (Benjamin/Cummings series in the life sciences) Includes bibliographies and index. ISBN 0-8053-2257-4 LC Card 87-13906 DDC 363.7 19
1. Environmental policy. 2. Environmental protection. I. Title. II. Series.
HC79.E5 C485 1988

Chisholm, Anthony. Land degradation . Cambridge [Cambridgeshire] , New York , c1987. p. cm. ISBN 0-521-34079-9 LC Card 87-13170 DDC 333.73/16 19
HD1036 .L36 1987

Chishti, Anees, 1941-
Dateline Bhopal : a newsman's diary of the gas disaster / Anees Chishti. New Delhi : Concept Pub. Co., 1986. 160 p. ; 23 cm. Includes index. LC Card 86-901993 DDC 363.1/79
1. Chishti, Anees, 1941- - Diaries. 2. Journalists - India - Diaries. 3. Bhopal Union Carbide Plant Disaster, Bhopal, India, 1984. 4. Industrial toxicology - India - Bhopal. 5. Pesticides industry - India - Bhopal - Accidents. 6. Methyl isocyanate - Environmental aspects - India - Bhopal. I. Title.
HD7269.C452 I5225 1986
NYPL [JLD 87-1050]

CHISHTI, ANEES, 1941- - DIARIES.
Chishti, Anees, 1941- Dateline Bhopal . New Delhi , 1986. 160 p. ; LC Card 86-901993 DDC 363.1/79
HD7269.C452 I5225 1986
NYPL [JLD 87-1050]

Chislennye metody v zadachakh optimal'nogo ėkonomicheskogo planirovaniia / [otvetstvennye redaktory IU.N. Ivanov i A.E. Iliutovich]. Moskva : Vses. nauch.-issl. in-t sistemnykh issledovaniĭ, 1983. 158 p. : ill. ; 26 cm. (Sbornik trudov / VNII sistemnykh issledovaniĭ . vyp. 1) Includes bibliographies. LC Card 84-128729
1. Soviet Union - Economic policy - 1981- - Mathematical models. I. Ivanov, IU. N., d.f.-m.n. II. Iliutovich, A. E. III. Series: Sbornik trudov (Vsesoiuznyĭ nauchno-issledovatel'skiĭ institut sistemnykh issledovaniĭ) , 1983, vyp. 1.
HC336.25 .C515 1983

Chisnall, Peter M. Small firms in action : case histories in entrepreneurship / Peter M. Chisnall. London ; New York : McGraw-Hill Book Co., c1987. vii, 149 p. ; 21 cm. Includes index. ISBN 0-07-084180-2 (pbk.) : LC Card 87-21518 DDC 658/.022 19
1. Small business - Great Britain - Case studies. 2. New business enterprises - Great Britain - Case studies. 3. Entrepreneurship - Great Britain - Case studies. I. Title.
HD2346.G7 C55 1987

Chistiakov, E. G. (Evgeniĭ Gavrilovich) Metody sochetaniia otraslevogo i territorial'nogo planirovaniia / E.G. Chistiakov. Moskva : Izd-vo "Nauka", 1982. 147, [3] p. : ill. ; 20 cm. (Problemy sovetskoĭ ėkonomiki) Bibliography: p. 146-[148] LC Card 82-189489
1. Soviet Union - Economic policy - 1981-. 2. Central planning - Soviet Union. 3. Regional planning - Soviet Union. I. Title.
HC336.25 .C516 1982

Chistobaev, A. I. (Anatoliĭ Ivanovich) Bugaev, V. K. (Vladimir Konstantinovich) Territorial'naia struktura ėkonomicheskogo raĭona . Leningrad , 1986. 164, [3] p. : LC Card 87-120624
HC336.25 .B84 1986

Chistov, Kirill Vasil'evich. IUkhneva, N. V. Ėtnicheskiĭ sostav i ėtnosotsial'naia struktura naseleniia Peterburga . Leningrad , 1984. 220 p., [1] folded leaf of plates : LC Card 85-116858
HB3608.L4 I94 1984 ***NYPL [*QGK 87-925]***

Chitale, V. P. Capital output ratio in the Indian economy / by V.P. Chitale ; [sponsored by] Economic and Scientific Research Foundation. New Delhi : Radiant Publishers, 1986. viii, 106 p. ; 22 cm. ISBN 81-7027-099-5 : LC Card 86-901894 DDC 338/.06/0954 19
1. Capital productivity - India. 2. Cost effectiveness. 3. India - Economic policy - 1980-. I. Economic and Scientific Research Foundation (India). II. Title.
HC435.2 .C4872 1986

Chittharanjan Felix Amerasinghe. see **Amerasinghe, Chittharanjan Felix, 1933-**

Chizhov, IU. A. (IUriĭ Alekseevich) Problemy modelirovaniia makroėkonomicheskikh sistem . Kiev , 1982. 100 p. ; LC Card 83-144893
HB139 .P755 1982

Chlanda, Henry. Manuscript post offices of New York State /. [Richford, N.Y.?] , 1984. xii, 54 p., [12] p. of plates : LC Card 86-213682 DDC 383/.49747 19
HE6376.A1 N729 1984

Chlumský, Jiří. Hospodářská politika USA v oblasti energetiky / Jiří Chlumský. Praha : Ekonomický ustav ČSAV, 1986. 134 p. ; 20 cm. (Výzkum. publ. VP . č. 237) Summary in English and Russian. Bibliography: p. 123-126. LC Card 86-215183
1. Energy policy - United States. I. Series: Výzk. publ. (Ekonomicko-matematická laboratoř (Ekonomický ústav ČSAV)) , č. 237. II. Title.
HD9502.U52 C526 1986

Chmielewicz, Klaus. Entwicklungslinien der Kosten- und Erlösrechnung /. Stuttgart , c1983. viii, 232 p. : ISBN 3-7910-0304-6 : LC Card 83-200474
HF5686.C8 E65 1983

Chocano, Guillermo Molina. see **Molina Chocano, Guillermo.**

El Chocó--ayer, hoy y mañana /. Cuesta Moreno, Marco Tobías. Bogotá, Colombia , 1986. 131 p., [5] leaves of plates : LC Card 87-115171 DDC 330.9861/270632 19
HC198.C48 C84 1986

CHOCÓ, COLOMBIA - ECONOMIC CONDITIONS.
Caicedo Licona, Carlos Arturo. El Chocó por dentro /. Medellín, Colombia , 1980. 118 p. : LC Card 83-105927
HC198.C48 C33 1980

Cuesta Moreno, Marco Tobías. El Chocó--ayer, hoy y mañana /. Bogotá, Colombia , 1986. 131 p., [5] leaves of plates : LC Card 87-115171 DDC 330.9861/270632 19
HC198.C48 C84 1986

CHOCO (COLOMBIA) - HISTORY.
Cuesta Moreno, Marco Tobías. El Chocó--ayer, hoy y mañana /. Bogotá, Colombia , 1986. 131 p., [5] leaves of plates : LC Card 87-115171 DDC 330.9861/270632 19
HC198.C48 C84 1986

CHOCÓ, COLOMBIA - SOCIAL CONDITIONS.
Cuesta Moreno, Marco Tobías. El Chocó--ayer, hoy y mañana /. Bogotá, Colombia , 1986. 131 p., [5] leaves of plates : LC Card 87-115171 DDC 330.9861/270632 19
HC198.C48 C84 1986

El Chocó por dentro /. Caicedo Licona, Carlos Arturo. Medellín, Colombia , 1980. 118 p. : LC Card 83-105927
HC198.C48 C33 1980

CHOCOLATE INDUSTRY - FRANCE - HISTORY.
Marrey, Bernard. Un capitalisme idéal /. Paris , c1984. 236 p., [24] p. of plates : ISBN 2-86215-060-6 : LC Card 84-252196 DDC

338.7/6413374/0944 19
HD9200.F74 M356 1984
NYPL [JLD 87-1579]

Choguill, Charles L. New communities for urban squatters : lessons from the plan that failed in Dhaka, Bangladesh / Charles L. Choguill. New York : Plenum Press, c1987. xiv, 213 p. : ill. ; 24 cm. (Urban innovation abroad) Bibliography: p. 188-203. Includes index. ISBN 0-306-42545-9 LC Card 86-30501 DDC 307.3/36 19
1. Squatter settlements - Bangladesh - Dhaka. 2. Urban policy - Bangladesh - Dhaka. 3. Housing policy - Bangladesh - Dhaka. 4. City planning - Bangladesh - Dhaka. I. Title. II. Series.
HD7361.6.D57 C46 1987

Choice of careers.
(29) Great Britain. Central Youth Employment Executive. Company secretary. [London, 1970] 15 p. ISBN 0-11-360036-4 : LC Card 72-534885 DDC 331.702 s
HF5381.A1 G73 no. 29, 1970

The choice of discount rate applicable to government resource use . Quirk, James P. Santa Monica, CA [1987] xviii, 52 p. : ISBN 0-8330-0849-8 (pbk.) LC Card 87-9867 DDC 336.3/9 19
HJ7451 .Q57 1987

CHOICE OF PROFESSION. see VOCATIONAL GUIDANCE.

CHOICE OF TRANSPORTATION.
Mackie, Peter J., 1947- The British transport industry and the European Community . Aldershot, Hampshire, England , Brookfield, Vt., U. S.A. , c1987. xvi, 184 p. : ISBN 0-566-05368-3 : LC Card 86-24186 DDC 380.5/24/0941 19
HE199.G5 M33 1987

CHOICE OF TRANSPORTATION - STATISTICS.
Briggs, Dwight. Journey-to-work trends . Washington, D.C. , Springfield, VA [1986] 1 v. (various pagings) : LC Card 86-602387 DDC 388.4/1314/0973 19
HE371.A3 B75 1986

CHOICE (PSYCHOLOGY) - CONGRESSES.
Behavioral foundations of economic theory. Rational choice . Chicago , 1987. ix, 332 p. : ISBN 0-226-34857-1 (alk. paper) LC Card 86-27241 DDC 330/.01/9 19
HB74.P8 B44 1987

The Reasoning criminal . New York , c1986. xiv, 246 p. : ISBN 0-387-96272-7 : LC Card 86-1275 DDC 364.3 19
HV6080 .R38 1986 ***NYPL [JLE 86-3522]***

CHOICE, SOCIAL. see SOCIAL CHOICE.

Choice under uncertainty and the demand for health insurance /. Marquis, M. Susan. Santa Monica, CA (P.O. Box 2138, Santa Monica 90406-2138) [1986] ix, 50 p. ; LC Card 87-118503 DDC 368.3/8/00973 19
HG9396 .M268 1986

Chojnacki, Jakub. Petrochemia a rozwój Płocka / Jakub Chojnacki. Wyd. 2., zmienione i uzup. Płock : Tow. Nauk. Płockie, 1977. [4], 290, [1] p., [76] p. of plates : ill. (some col.), facsims. ; 25 cm. Polish, English, German, and Russian. Bibliography: p. [220]-228. LC Card 81-200767
1. Płock, Poland - Economic conditions. 2. Petroleum industry and trade - Poland - Płock - History. I. Title.
HC340.3.Z7 P573 1977

Choksi, Armeane M., 1944- Economic liberalization in developing countries /. Oxford [Oxfordshire] , New York , 1986. vi, 278 p. : ISBN 0-631-15023-4 : LC Card 86-6153 DDC 338.9/009172/4 19
HC59.7 .E3116 1986 ***NYPL [JLE 86-4644]***

Cholmar, Sidney. New directions in microwave ovens : packaging and cookware / Sidney Cholmar. Stamford, Conn., U. S.A. : Business Communications Co., c1985. x, 119 leaves ; 29 cm. (Business opportunity report . GA-055) "August 1985"--T.p. verso. ISBN 0-89336-459-2 (pbk.) LC Card 87-163958 DDC 381/.4568388 19
1. Microwave oven industry - United States. 2. Food container industry - United States. 3. Cookware industry - United States. 4. Market surveys - United States. I. Title. II. Series.
HD9971.5.S763 U53 1985

Le chômage /. Freyssinet, Jacques. Paris , 1984. 128 p. : ISBN 2-7071-1478-2 LC Card 85-115448 DDC 331.13/7 19
HD5707.5 .F74 1984

Le chômage, c'est les autres /. Vasseur, Philippe. Paris , c1985. 224 p. ; ISBN 2-7144-1867-8 : LC Card 86-120821 DDC 331.13/7944 19
HD5775 .V37 1985

Chômage des jeunes : aperçu de l'évolution de 1970 à 1982. Bruxelles : Direction Statistiques, études, information, Service Etudes, [1984] 49 p. : ill. ; 30 cm. (Collection "Etudes économiques et sociales") Cover title. LC Card 84-222918
1. Youth - Employment - Belgium. 2. Unemployed - Belgium. I. Belgium. Direction Statistiques, études, information. Service Etudes. II. Series.
HD6276.B42 C48 1984

Chômage, inflation et régulation de la conjoncture au Québec /. Fortin, Pierre. [Unemployment, inflation, and economic stabilization in Quebec. French.] Montréal, Québec [1980] viii, 144 p. : ISBN 0-88806-063-7 (pbk.) LC Card 87-673448
HC117.Q4 F63x 1980

Chŏn'guk Ŭnhaeng Yŏnhaphoe (Korea)
Internationalization of banking . Seoul, Korea , c1986. 300 p. : LC Card 87-114642 DDC 332.1/5 19
HG3881 .I496 1986

Chonov, Nikola. Inflat͡siia v sŭvremennoto kapitalistichesko obshtestvo / Nikola Chonov. 1. izd. Sofii͡a : Partizdat, 1985. 168 p. ; 18 cm. (Ikonomikata na kapitalizma dnes) Includes bibliographical references. LC Card 85-243423
1. Inflation (Finance). I. Title. II. Series.
HG229 .C534 1985

Choosing an investment company /. Seligman, Barnard. Cambridge, Mass. , c1987. xvii, 174 p. : ISBN 0-88730-094-4 LC Card 87-1437 DDC 332.6 19
HG4930 .S45 1987

Choosing effective development programs . Gardner, James E. New York , 1987. x, 194 p. ; ISBN 0-89930-182-7 (lib. bdg. : alk. paper) LC Card 86-30604 DDC 658.4/071245 19
HF5549.15 .G36 1987

Chopra, Kiran. Managing profits, profitability & productivity in public sector banking / Kiran Chopra. 1st ed. Jalandhar : ABS Publications, 1987. 320 p. : ill. ; 22 cm. Study of five selected public sector banks from Punjab, Haryana, Himachal Pradesh, Jammu and Kashmir, and the Union Territory of Chandigarh, 1969-1981. Bibliography: p. [312]-318. Includes index. ISBN 81-7072-012-5 : LC Card 87-901014 DDC 332.1/0954 19
1. Banks and banking - Government ownership - India. 2. Profit - India. I. Title.
HG3284 .C56 1987

Chopra, O. P. (Om Prakash), 1941- Tax ethics, unaccounted income : some tax reforms, or, Black money, the norm of the day / O.P. Chopra. New Delhi : Inter-India Publications, 1985, c1984. vi, 119 p. ; 25 cm. Spine title: Tax ethics, or, Black money. Bibliography: p. [113]-115. LC Card 85-900955 DDC 336.2/06 19
1. Tax evasion - India. 2. Spendings tax - India. 3. Value-added tax - India. I. Title. II. Title: Tax ethics, or, Black money.
HJ2348.5 .C46 1985 ***NYPL [JLE 87-1297]***

Chorafas, Dimitris N. Applying expert systems in business / Dimitris N. Chorafas. New York : McGraw-Hill, c1987. xii, 232 p. : ill. ; 24 cm. Includes bibliographical references and index. ISBN 0-07-010880-3 : LC Card 86-2794 DDC 658/.05633 19
1. Management - Data processing. 2. Business - Data processing. 3. Expert systems (Computer science). I. Title.
HD30.2 .C475 1987 ***NYPL [JLE 86-3893]***

CHOTA NAGPUR (INDIA) - OCCUPATIONS.
Singh, R. S. (Rama Shankar), 1950- Changing occupational structure of scheduled tribes /. New Delhi, India , 1986. 291 p. : ISBN 81-210-0175-7 : LC Card 86-903755
HB3640.C48 S56 1986

CHOTA NAGPUR (INDIA) - SCHEDULED TRIBES - EMPLOYMENT.
Singh, R. S. (Rama Shankar), 1950- Changing occupational structure of scheduled tribes /. New Delhi, India , 1986. 291 p. : ISBN 81-210-0175-7 : LC Card 86-903755
HB3640.C48 S56 1986

Chotard, Yvon, 1921- Les patrons et le patronat / Yvon Chotard. [Paris] : Calmann-Lévy, c1986. 231 p. ; 23 cm. ISBN 2-7021-1538-1 : LC Card 87-167099
1. Employers' associations - France. 2. France - Politics and government - 1981-. 3. Industrial relations - France. I. Title.
HD6948.F8 C46 1986

Čhotmāihēt kānsāng Phraphutthar̄up phra prathān Phutthamonthon /. Songsan Ninkamhǣng. Krung Thēp , 2525 [1982] 172 p. : ISBN 974-7921-05-7 LC Card 83-916060
HB1912.G38 S66 1982

Choudhury, Masudul Alam, 1948- Contributions to Islamic economic theory : a study in social economics / Masudul Alam Choudhury. Houndmills, Basingstoke, Hampshire : Macmillan, 1986. xvii, 241 p. : ill. ; 23 cm. Includes bibliographical references and index. ISBN 0-333-38507-1
1. Economics - Religious aspects - Islam. 2. Islam - Economic aspects. I. Title. ***NYPL [JLD 86-3601]***

Chouinard, Jacques, 1944-
Morin, André, analyste en rémunération. Analyse de l'évolution des principaux indicateurs économiques au Québec, en Ontario, au Canada et aux Etats-Unis . [Québec] [1982] 209 p. ; ISBN 2-551-04641-6 LC Card 83-103355
HC117.Q4 M66 1982

Nadeau, Jean. Les indicateurs globaux de la productivité . Québec [1982] 41 p. : ISBN 2-551-05072-3 LC Card 83-221751
HC120.I52 N33 1982

Chouraqui, Jean Claude.
Atkinson, Paul. The formulation of monetary policy . [Paris, France] [1986, c1985] 41 p. : LC Card 86-212837 DDC 332.4/6 19
HG230.3 .A75 1986

Public debt in a medium-term context and its implications for fiscal policy / by Jean-Claude Chouraqui, Brian Jones, and Robert Bruce Montador. [Paris, France] : OECD, c1986. 67 p. : ill. ; 30 cm. (Working papers / OECD, Department of Economics and Statistics . no. 30) Summary in French. Cover title. Bibliography: p. 32-37. LC Card 86-218210 DDC 339.5 19
1. Debts, Public. 2. Fiscal policy. I. Jones, Brian. II. Montador, Robert Bruce. III. Series: Working papers (Organisation for Economic Co-operation and Development. Dept. of Economics and Statistics) , no. 30. IV. Title.
HJ8030 .C48 1986

Chouteau, Eujenio. Informe sobre la provincia de Coquimbo / presentado al supremo gobierno por Eujenio Chouteau. Santiago de Chile : Impr. Nacional, 1887. 262 p. ; 23 cm. Spine title: La provincia de Coquimbo. Includes bibliographical references. LC Card 85-165581
1. Coquimbo, Chile (Province) - Economic conditions. 2. Mines and mineral resources - Chile - Coquimbo (Province). I. Title. II. Title: Provincia de Coquimbo.
HC193.C64 C46 1887

Chovek, svobodno vreme i profsŭi͡uzi. Chelovek, svobodnoe vremi͡a i profsoi͡uzy /. Moskva , 1980. 256 p., [32] p. of plates : LC Card 81-137052
HD7395.R4 C42 1980

Chow, Kit Boey. Vente, Rolf E. Education and training for industrial development in Singapore and other ASEAN countries . Baden-Baden , Singapore , 1984. 175 p. : ISBN 3-7890-0941-5 LC Card 84-186381 DDC 331.25/92/0959 19
HD5715.5.S55 V46 1984
NYPL [JLD 86-2773]

Chowdhry, D. Paul. Profile of social welfare and development in India / by D. Paul Chowdhry. New Delhi : M.N. Publishers & Distributors, 1985. viii, 340 p. ; 22 cm. Includes bibliographical references and index. LC Card 85-901093 DDC 362/.954 19
1. Public welfare - India. 2. Volunteer workers in social service - India. 3. Social security - India. 4. Rural development - India. I. Title.
HV393 .C515 1985 ***NYPL [JLD 86-2575]***

Chowdhury, Ashraf U. Norway's commodity assistance and import support to Bangladesh : a study commissioned by the Norwegian Ministry of Development Cooperation / prepared by Chr. Michelsen Institute, Development Research and Action Programme (DERAP), Bergen, Norway ; responsible authors, Ashraf

U. Chowdhury, Eirik G. Jansen, Ole David Koht Norbye. [Oslo, Norway] : Royal Norwegian Ministry of Development Cooperation, [1986] 83 p. : ill. ; 30 cm. (Evaluation report . 7.86) "January 1986." Includes bibliographical references. LC Card 87-150872 DDC 338.91/481/05492 19
1. Economic assistance, Norwegian - Bangladesh. I. Jansen, Eirik G. II. Norbye, Ole David Koht, 1919-. III. Norway. Departementet for utviklingshjelp. IV. Chr. Michelsens institutt. Forskings- og aksjonsprogrammet for utviklingsland. V. Series: Evaluation report (Oslo, Norway) , 86.7. VI. Title.
HC440.8 .C48 1986

Chr. Michelsens institutt.
Norsk industris internasjonalisering, rettet mot utviklingslandene . Bergen [1982] vi, 57 p. ; LC Card 83-139811
HD2932 .N67 1982

Chr. Michelsens institutt. Avdeling for samfunnsvitenskap og utvikling. Zambia, country study and Norwegian aid review. Fantoft, Norway , 1986. xxi, 202 p., [1] leaf of plates : ISBN 82-905840-6-7 (pbk.) LC Card 87-105777 DDC 338.91/481/06894 19
HC915 .Z36 1986

Chr. Michelsens institutt. Forskings- og aksjonsprogrammet for utviklingsland. Chowdhury, Ashraf U. Norway's commodity assistance and import support to Bangladesh . [Oslo, Norway] [1986] 83 p. : LC Card 87-150872 DDC 338.91/481/05492 19
HC440.8 .C48 1986

Chr. Michelsens institutt. Forsknings- og aksjonsprogrammet for utviklingsland. Bangladesh . Fantoft, Norway , 1986. xxxiii, 353 p. : ISBN 82-905840-8-3 (pbk.) LC Card 87-128545 DDC 330.9549/205 19
HC440.8 .B352 1986

Chrēmatodotēsē ependyseōn tou agrotikou tomea . Baltas, Nik. K. Athēna , 1984. 142 p. ; LC Card 86-201892
HD2055.5 .B35 1984

Christainsen, Gregory. (joint author) Haveman, Robert H. Jobs and the environment /. Scarsdale, N.Y. , c1979. 32 p. ; LC Card 79-15418 DDC 301.31/0973
HC110.E5 H38 ***NYPL [JLM 83-380 no.10]***

CHRISTELIJK NATIONAAL VAKVERBOND IN NEDERLAND.
Vakbeweging in verandering . Deventer , 1986. 191 p. : ISBN 90-267-1082-8 : LC Card 86-224831
HD6727 .V29 1986

Christen, François G. Buying by mail : VALS looks at direct marketing / by François Christen and Joseph Castelli. Menlo Park, CA (333 Ravenswood Ave., Menlo Park 94025) : Values and Lifestyles Program, c1986. v, 2, 59, 6 leaves : ill. ; 28 cm. (VALS report . no. 66) On t.p. the registered trademark symbol "TM" is superscript following "VALS." "July 1986." Includes bibliographical references. LC Card 86-209563 DDC 658.8/4 19
1. Direct marketing - United States. 2. Market surveys - United States. I. Castelli, Joseph. II. Values and Lifestyles Program (SRI International). III. Title. IV. Series.
HF5415.126 .C48 1986

Christensen, C. Roland (Carl Roland), 1919- Business policy . Homewood, Ill. , 1987. xx, 940 p. : ISBN 0-256-03358-7 LC Card 86-82216 DDC 658.4/012 19
HD2785 .B78 1987

Christensen, K. (Kathleen) Women and home-based work : the unspoken contract / Kathleen Christensen.1st ed. New York : Holt, c1988. xv, 201 p. ; 22 cm. Bibliography: p. 185-195. Includes index. ISBN 0-8050-0386-X LC Card 87-8527 DDC 305.4/3 19
1. Self-employed women - United States. 2. Home-based businesses - United States. 3. Work and family - United States. I. Title.
HD6072.6.U5 C47 1988

Christiaans, H. H. C. M. Ondernemen en vernieuwen . Delft, Netherlands , 1985. 240 p. : ISBN 90-6275-189-X LC Card 86-113900
HD2346.N4 O53 1985

CHRISTIAN COMMUNES. see **CHRISTIAN COMMUNITIES.**

CHRISTIAN COMMUNITIES - CATHOLIC CHURCH - BRAZIL, NORTHEAST.
Malvezzi, Roberto. Mil quatrocentos e sessenta dias no império do sol . São Paulo , 1985. 197 p. : ISBN 85-05-00296-2 : LC Card 85-200637
HC188.N6 M34 1985

CHRISTIAN DEMOCRACY.
Keller, Friedrich Jakob, 1893- Das Ende des Kapitalismus . Lyss [1981] 211 p. : LC Card 84-104878
HB95 .K33 1981

Christian Democrats (Italy) see **Partito della democrazia cristiana.**

Christian ethics and economics : the North-South conflict / edited by Dietmar Mieth and Jacques Pohier ; English Language editor, Marcus Lefébure. Edinburgh : T. & T. Clark ; New York : Seabury Press, c1980. xii, 114 p. ; 22 cm. (Concilium . 140) Includes bibliographies. ISBN 0-8164-2282-6 (Seabury Press : pbk.) LC Card 80-50892
1. International economic relations. 2. Economics - Religious aspects - Christianity. I. Mieth, Dietmar. II. Pohier, Jacques Marie. III. Lefébure, Marcus. IV. Series: Concilium (Glen Rock, N.J.) , v. 140.
HF1411 .C422 1980

CHRISTIAN GIVING.
Perry, Richard D. Money problems /. Elgin, Ill. , c1987. 111 p. ; ISBN 1-555-13797-0 (pbk.) LC Card 86-73209 DDC 332.024 19
HG179 .P367 1987

CHRISTIAN LIFE - 1960-
Follis, Anne Bowen, 1947- I'm not a women's libber, but--and other confessions of a Christian feminist /. Nashville , c1981. 128 p. ; ISBN 0-687-18687-0 LC Card 81-1241
HQ1426 .F75 ***NYPL [JLD 85-1976]***

CHRISTIAN SOCIALISM. see **SOCIALISM, CHRISTIAN.**

CHRISTIAN SOCIOLOGY. see **SOCIOLOGY, CHRISTIAN.**

CHRISTIANITY - 19TH CENTURY.
Chartism and Christianity. New York , 1986. 45, 24, 90 p. ; ISBN 0-8240-5593-4 (alk. paper) : LC Card 86-25705 DDC 322/.2 19
HD8396 .C483 1986

CHRISTIANITY AND JUSTICE - LATIN AMERICA.
Antoncich, Ricardo. [Cristianos ante la injusticia. English.] Christians in the face of injustice . Maryknoll, N.Y. , c1987. xvi, 181 p. ; ISBN 0-88344-413-5 (pbk.) LC Card 86-23529 DDC 261.8 19
BX1753 .A5813 1987 ***NYPL [JLE 87-1051]***

Christiano, David, 1948- The Cold war against labor . Berkeley, CA , c1987. 2 v. (xxii, 915 p.) : ISBN 0-913876-19-4 (set); 0-913876-20-4 (set) : LC Card 87-18510 DDC 331.88/0973 19
HD6508 .C62 1987

Christians in the face of injustice . Antoncich, Ricardo. [Cristianos ante la injusticia. English.] Maryknoll, N.Y. , c1987. xvi, 181 p. ; ISBN 0-88344-413-5 (pbk.) LC Card 86-23529 DDC 261.8 19
BX1753 .A5813 1987 ***NYPL [JLE 87-1051]***

Christians, Uwe, 1957- Entwicklung und empirische Überprüfung eines konjunkturgerechten Erfolgsprognosemodells zur Unterstützung der Kreditwürdigkeitsprüfung : eine Untersuchung unter besonderer Berücksichtigung wissenschaftstheoretischer Aspekte / Uwe Christians. München : V. Florentz, c1986. xiv, 412 p. : ill. ; 21 cm. (Hochschulschriften zur Betriebswirtschaftslehre . Bd. 45) Bibliography: p. 372-409. Includes index. ISBN 3-88259-430-6 (Deut. Bibl.) LC Card 87-409324 DDC 332.7/0943 19
1. Credit - Germany (West) - Econometric models. 2. Business cycles - Germany (West) - Econometric models. 3. Bankruptcy - Germany (West) - Econometric models. I. Title. II. Series.
HG3754.5.G3 C48 1986

Christians, Volker C. Neue Zahlungsverkehrsinstrumente : eine Untersuchung über mögliche Auswirkungen ihres Einsatzes auf das Mengengeschäft der Kreditinstitute / von Volker C. Christians. Frankfurt am Main : Barudio & Hess, 1985. 216 p. ; 21 cm. (Reihe Oikos . Bd. 17) Originally presented as the author's thesis (doctoral)--Universität zu Köln. Bibliography: p. 185-216. ISBN 3-922182-17-8 : LC Card 86-100407
1. Electronic funds transfers - Germany (West). 2. Banks and banking - Germany (West) - Automation. I. Title. II. Series.
HG1710 .C48 1985

Christiansen, Niels Finn. Arbejderbevægelsens forhistorie : træk af den tidlige danske arbejderbevægelses politiske og sociale udvikling 1848 til 1880 / Niels Finn Christiansen. [Copenhagen] : Selskabet til forskning i arbejderbevægelsens historie, 1986. 188 p. : ill. ; 21 cm. (SFAH skriftserie . nr. 18) Summary in English and German. Bibliography: p. 177-182. ISBN 87-87739-21-6 : LC Card 87-145749
1. Trade-unions - Denmark - History - 19th century. 2. Labor and laboring classes - Denmark - History - 19th century. I. Title. II. Series.
HD6742 .C495 1986

Christie, Alan R. An account of major activities in the Canterbury Labour and Trades Council District, 1929-1936 / by Alan R. Christie. [Wellington] : Victoria University of Wellington, Industrial Relations Centre, 1980. 38, [3] p. ; 30 cm. (Student research papers in industrial relations. no. 7) "Paper prepared as part requirement for Diploma in industrial relations at Victoria University of Wellington." Bibliography: p. [41] LC Card 81-120047
1. Industrial relations - New Zealand - Canterbury - History. I. Title. II. Series.
HD8930.5.Z8 C3623 1980

Christie, Renfrew. Electricity, industry, and class in South Africa / Renfrew Christie. London : Macmillan in association with St. Antony's College, Oxford, 1984. xiii, 241 p. : ill. ; 23 cm. (St Antony's/Macmillan series) Bibliography: p. 207-235. Includes index. ISBN 0-333-36288-8 LC Card 87-673182
1. Electric utilities - South Africa - History. 2. Electrification - South Africa - History. 3. Social class - South Africa - History. 4. South Africa - Industries - History. I. Title.
HD9685.S582 C47x 1984b

CHRISTLICH-DEMOKRATISCHE UNION DEUTSCHLANDS (GERMANY : WEST) - PLATFORMS.
Biedenkopf, Kurt H. Die neue Sicht der Dinge . München , c1985. 458 p. ; ISBN 3-492-02813-6 LC Card 86-105815
HB95 .B53 1985

Der christlich-nationale Deutsche Gewerkschaftsbund (DGB) im politisch-ökonomischen Kräftefeld der Weimarer Republik . Roder, Hartmut, 1951- Frankfurt am Main , New York , c1986. 804 p. : ISBN 3-8204-9325-5 LC Card 86-194815
HD8443.D457 R63 1986

Christliche Motive auf Briefmarken . Schönen, Hans G. Rommerskirchen-Oekoven , 1984, c1983. xv, 830 p. ; ISBN 3-9800824-0-7 : LC Card 84-208011
HE6183.C47 S36 1984

Christman, John H. Business Mexico /. México, D.F. , 1978. 343 p. : LC Card 87-405299 DDC 332.1/732272 19
HF3237 .B87 1978

Christoffersen, Mads. Fysisk planlægning og samfundsmæssige reproduktionsproblemer : træk af den offentlige fysiske planlægnings udvikling i Danmark i perioden fra 1922 til 1978 / Mads Christoffersen, Hanne Topsøe-Jensen.2. opl. København : Akademisk forlag, 1980, c1979. 317 p. ; 22 cm. (Kultursociologiske skrifter. bd. 8) Revision of thesis (master's) -- Københavens universitet, 1979. Bibliography: p. 307-317. ISBN 87-500-1922-8
1. Regional planning - Denmark. 2. Production (Economic theory). 3. Marxian economics. 4. Denmark - Economic policy. I. Topsøe-Jensen, Hanne. II. Title. III. Series. ***NYPL [JLD 86-2303]***

Christopher, A. J. The Crown lands of British South Africa, 1853-1914 / by A.J. Christopher. Kingston, Ont., Canada : Limestone Press, 1984. vii, 247 p., [8] p. of plates : ill., maps ; 24 cm. (Modern Africa series. no. 4) Map on lining papers. Includes bibliographical references and index. ISBN 0-919642-04-7 LC Card 85-125786 DDC 333.1/0968 19
1. Crown lands - South Africa - History. 2. Land settlement - South Africa - History. 3. South Africa - Public lands - History. I. Title.
HD991 .C49 1984 ***NYPL [Sc E 85-373]***

Christopher, Elizabeth M. Leadership training through gaming : power, people, and problem solving / Elizabeth M. Christopher and Larry

E. Smith. New York : Nichols Pub. Co., 1987. 187 p. : ill. ; 24 cm. Bibliography: p. [183]-184. Includes index. ISBN 0-89397-284-3 : LC Card 87-12362 DDC 658.4/07353 19
1. Leadership - Simulation methods. 2. Management games. 3. Management - Simulation methods. I. Smith, Larry E. II. Title.
HD57.7 .C53 1987

CHROMATOGRAPHIC ANALYSIS EQUIPMENT INDUSTRY - EUROPE. Analytical instruments markets in Europe. New York, N.Y. , c1983. xii, 253 p. ; LC Card 87-141819 DDC 380.1/45681754 19
HD9706.65.C573 E82 1983

Chronicle Guidance Publications, inc. Chronicle occupational briefs and occupational reprints. Moravia, NY [1986- 4 v. (loose-leaf) : LC Card 86-231523 DDC 331.7/02/0973 19
HF5382.5.U5 C49 1986

Chronicle occupational briefs and occupational reprints. Moravia, NY [1987]- 4 v. (loose-leaf) : LC Card 87-403954 DDC 331.7/02/0973 19
HF5382.5.U5 C49 1987

Chronicle occupational briefs. Chronicle occupational briefs and occupational reprints. Moravia, NY [1986- 4 v. (loose-leaf) : LC Card 86-231523 DDC 331.7/02/0973 19
HF5382.5.U5 C49 1986

Chronicle occupational briefs. Chronicle occupational briefs and occupational reprints. Moravia, NY [1987]- 4 v. (loose-leaf) : LC Card 87-403954 DDC 331.7/02/0973 19
HF5382.5.U5 C49 1987

Chronicle occupational briefs and occupational reprints. Rev. through Aug. 1986. Moravia, NY : Chronicle Guidance Publications, [1986- 4 v. (loose-leaf) : ill. ; 30 cm. Caption title. Cover title: Chronicle occupational briefs. Spine title: Occupational briefs. Includes bibliographies and index. LC Card 86-231523 DDC 331.7/02/0973 19
1. Vocational guidance - United States. 2. United States - Occupations. I. Chronicle Guidance Publications, inc. II. Title: Occupational briefs. III. Title: Chronicle occupational briefs.
HF5382.5.U5 C49 1986

Chronicle occupational briefs and occupational reprints. Rev. through Aug. 1987. Moravia, NY : Chronicle Guidance Publications, [1987]- 4 v. (loose-leaf) : ill. ; 30 cm. Caption title. Cover title: Chronicle occupational briefs. Spine title: Occupational briefs. Includes bibliographies. LC Card 87-403954 DDC 331.7/02/0973 19
1. Vocational guidance - United States. 2. United States - Occupations. I. Chronicle Guidance Publications, inc. II. Title: Chronicle occupational briefs. III. Title: Occupational briefs.
HF5382.5.U5 C49 1987

Chronicles of corporate change : management lessons from AT&T and its offspring / Leonard A. Schlesinger ... [et al.]. Lexington, Mass. : Lexington Books, c1987. xiv, 254 p. : ill. ; 24 cm. Bibliography: p. [233]-238. Includes index. ISBN 0-669-13685-9 (alk. paper) LC Card 86-45555 DDC 384.6/065/73 19
1. American Telephone and Telegraph Company - Reorganization. 2. Northwestern Bell Telephone Company. 3. Telephone - United States. 4. Telecommunication - United States. 5. Organizational effectiveness. I. Schlesinger, Leonard A. II. American Telephone and Telegraph Company.
HE8846.A55 C47 1987

Chronicles of hunger /. Pike, Clarence Edward, 1917- Millwood, N.Y. , 1988. p. cm. ISBN 0-8046-9410-9 LC Card 87-12332 DDC 363.8 19
HD9000.5 .P55 1988

Chrześcijaństwo a związki zawodowe /. Markiewicz, Stanisław. Warszawa , 1985. 618 p. : ISBN 83-202-0352-X (pbk.) :
NYPL [*QO 86-2625]

Chua, Jess H. Gains from stock-market timing / by Jess H. Chua and Richard S. Woodward. New York, N.Y. (90 Trinity Pl., New York 10006) : Salomon Brothers Center for the Study of Financial Institutions, Graduate School of Business Administration, New York University, [c1986] 75 p. ; 23 cm. (Monograph series in finance and economics . monograph 1986-2) Bibliography: p. 72-73. LC Card 87-129798 DDC 332.63/222 19
1. Stock price forecasting. I. Woodward, Richard S. II. Title. III. Title: Market timing. IV. Series.
HG4637 .C48 1986

Ch'üan kuo t'ou ju ch'an ch'u piao, 1981. English. Input-output tables of China, 1981 / compiled by the Centre of Economic Forecasting, State Planning Commission of China and Department of Statistics on Balances of National Economy, State Statistical Bureau, People's Republic of China. Beijing : China Statistical Information and Consultancy Service Centre ; Honolulu : East-West Population Institute, East-West Center, 1987. p. cm. Translation of: Ch'üan kuo t'ou ju ch'an ch'u piao, 1981 (shih pien). ISBN 0-86638-104-X (East-West Population Institute) LC Card 87-24457 DDC 339.2/3/0951 19
1. Input-output tables - China. I. Kuo chia chi hua wei yüan hui ching chi yü ts'e chung hsin (China). II. China. Kuo min ching chi p'ing heng t'ung chi ssu. III. Title.
HC430.I57 C5813 1981

Chuang, K'ai-hsün. Chen hsing Chung-hua chih lu--kai ko ti sung ko /. Pei-ching , 1985. 4, 3, 385 p. ; LC Card 86-106324
NYPL [*OVY 86-3099]

Chuck Olin Associates.
Change master companies [videorecording] . Chicago, IL , 1987. 1 videocassette (42 min.) : LC Card 87-705608 DDC 658.3 11
HD45

The Change masters [motion picture] . Chicago, Ill. , 1987. 1 film reel (29 min.) : LC Card 87-705269 DDC 658.3 11
HD45

The Change masters [videorecording] . Chicago, Ill. , 1987. 1 videocassette (29 min.) : LC Card 86-707881 DDC 658.3 11
HD45

Roadmap for change. Chicago, Ill. , 1987. 1 film reel (28 min.) : LC Card 87-705133 DDC 658 11
HD9710

Chudleigh, P. D. Copeland, M. C. (Michael Campbell) Transport energy in New Zealand's overseas trade . Auckland, N.Z. [1982] iv, 130 p. : LC Card 84-159485 DDC 387.5/1 19
HE597.N4 C63 1982
NYPL [JSK 82-15 no.80]

Chuecos, Héctor García. see **García Chuecos, Héctor.**

Chufrin, Gennadiĭ Illarionovich. Sverkhmonopolii v I͡Ugo-Vostochnoĭ Azii /. Moskva , 1983. 219 p. ; LC Card 83-223670
HD2901 .S84 1983

Chuĭkov, V. I. (Vasiliĭ Ivanovich), 1900- Ot Stalingrada do Berlina / V.I. Chuĭkov. Moskva : Sovetskai͡a Rossii͡a, 1985. 699 p. : port. ; 21 cm. (Voennye memuary) Previous ed.: Moskva : Voenizdat, 1980.
1. Chuĭkov, V. I. (Vasiliĭ Ivanovich), 1900-. 2. World War, 1939-1945 - Biography. 3. World War, 1939-1945 - Soviet Union. 4. Stalingrad, Battle of, 1942-1943. 5. World War, 1939-1945 - Personal narratives, Russian. I. Title.
NYPL [*QGR 87-2179]

CHUĬKOV, V. I. (VASILIĬ IVANOVICH), 1900-
Chuĭkov, V. I. (Vasiliĭ Ivanovich), 1900- Ot Stalingrada do Berlina /. Moskva , 1985. 699 p. :
NYPL [*QGR 87-2179]

Chukanov, Olimp Alekseevich. Bykov, A. N. (Aleksandr Naumovich) Sotsialisticheskai͡a integratsii͡a i nauchno-tekhnicheskai͡a revoli͡utsii͡a /. Moskva , 1981. 343 p. ; LC Card 82-101911
HC244.Z9 T43 1981

Chumacero, Antonio. Origen de una empresa pública : el caso de Tabacos Mexicanos / Antonio Chumacero ; introducción de Víctor Alvarez Trasviña.1a ed. Tepic, Nayarit : Universidad Autónoma de Nayarit, 1985 [i.e. 1986] xviii, 279 p. : ill., ports. ; 21 cm. Includes bibliographical references. LC Card 87-145432 DDC 338.7/6371/0972 19
1. Tabacos Mexicanos, S.A. de C.V. - History. 2. Tobacco industry - Mexico - History. I. Title.
HD9144.M44 T333 1986

Chumachenko, Nikolaĭ Grigor′evich. Upravlenie nauchno-tekhnicheskim progressom v soi͡uznykh respublikakh /. Tallin , 1986. 158 p. ; LC Card 87-123175
HC340.T4 U77 1986

Chumanova, N. I. Nakoplenie i ego rol′ v obshchestvennom vosproizvodstve Uzbekskoĭ SSR / N.I. Chumanova. Tashkent : Izd-vo "Fan" Uzbekskoĭ SSR, 1982. 116 p. ; 22 cm. At head of title: Akademii͡a nauk Uzbekskoĭ SSR. Institut ėkonomiki. Includes bibliographical references. LC Card 83-193447
1. Saving and investment - Uzbek S.S.R. I. Title.
HC337.U963 S33 1982

Chumbley, Richard L. Texas real estate finance /. New York , c1987. xviii, 365 p. : ISBN 0-471-82300-7 (pbk.) LC Card 86-29004 DDC 332.7/2/09764 19
HD266.T4 T5 1987

Chung-kuo ch'uan t'ung nung yeh yü hsien tai nungyeh / Kao Wen-t'ao... [et al.]. 880-02 Ti 1 pan. Pei-ching : Chung-kuo nung yeh k'o chi ch'u pan she : Hsin hua shu tien Pei-ching fa hsing so fa hsing, 1986. 312 p. : ill. ; 21 cm. In Chinese.
1. Agriculture - China - History. 2. Agriculture - China. I. Kuo, Wen-t'ao. ***NYPL [*OVL 87-1966]***

Chung-kuo kung jen yün tung ti hsien ch'ü. 880-02 Pei-ching ti 1 pan. Pei-ching : Kung jen ch'u pan she : Hsin hua shu tien Pei-ching fa hsing so fa hsing, 1983- v. : ports. ; 21 cm. Vol. 3 has edition statement: Ti 1 pan. In Chinese. Includes bibliographical references. LC Card 84-231479 DDC 322/.2/0951 19
1. Labor and laboring classes - China - History - 20th century. 2. Trade-unions - China - History - 20th century.
HD8736 .C496 1983 <Orien China>
NYPL [*OVY 87-4134]

Chung-kuo kuo chi ching chi tzu hsün kung ssu. Business opportunities in China . Menlo Park, Calif. (333 Ravenswood Ave., Menlo Park 94025-3476) , c1984. 32 p. : LC Card 86-210279 DDC 338.8/8851 19
HC427.92 .B85 1984

Chung-kuo li tai huo pi. English. A History of Chinese currency : 16th century BC-20th century AD. [Peking] : Xinhua (New China) Pub. House ; Kowloon, Hong Kong : M.A.O. Management Group, 1983. 220 p. : col. ill. ; 26 cm. Translation of: Chung-kuo li tai huo pi shih. Includes index. ISBN 962-7094-01-3 LC Card 86-233155 DDC 769.5/5951 19
1. Money - China - History.
HG1282 .C4913 1983

Chung-kuo sheng ch'an li ching chi hsüeh yen chiu hui.
Sheng ch'an li kuei lü yen chiu /. Pei-ching , 1985. 5, 3, 466 p. : LC Card 85-242399 DDC 335.4/12 19
HB241 .S519 1985 <Orien China>
NYPL [*OVL 87-507]

Chung-kuo sheng ch'an li ching chi hsüeh yen chiu hui. Nien hui (2nd : 1983 : K'un-ming shih, China) Sheng ch'an li kuei lü yen chiu /. Pei-ching , 1985. 5, 3, 466 p. : LC Card 85-242399 DDC 335.4/12 19
HB241 .S519 1985 <Orien China>
NYPL [*OVL 87-507]

Chung-kuo tui wai ching chi kuan hsi erh shih liu t'iao. The Open policy at work /. Beijing, China [1985] 281 p. ; LC Card 86-219666 DDC 337.51 19
HF1604 .O63 1985

Chung-kuo tui wai ching chi mao i chih nan. Hsin k'ai fang ch'eng shih chuan chi. Guide to China's foreign economic relations and trade. Cities newly opened to foreign investors /. Hong Kong , 1985. 385 p. : ISBN 962-7063-19-3
NYPL [*OVY 86-3400]

Chung-kuo tui wai ching chi mao i chih nan. T'ou tzu chuan chi. Guide to China's foreign economic relations and trade. Investment special /. Hong Kong , 1983. 342 p. : ISBN 0-9627063-8-8 : LC Card 84-177660 DDC 346.51/07 345.1067 19
HG5784 .G835 1983 ***NYPL [*OVY 86-3398]***

Chung-kuo tui wai ching chi mao i pu cheng ts'e yen chiu shih.
Guide to China's foreign economic relations and trade. Cities newly opened to foreign investors /. Hong Kong , 1985. 385 p. : ISBN 962-7063-19-3
NYPL [*OVY 86-3400]

Guide to China's foreign economic relations and trade. Investment special /. Hong Kong , 1983. 342 p. : ISBN 0-9627063-8-8 : LC Card

84-177660 DDC 346.51/07 345.1067 19
HG5784 .G835 1983 ***NYPL [*OVY 86-3398]***

Chung, Shin-Yung, d. 1962. Der Zwangssparprozess als Werkzeug der Entwicklungspolitik : dargestellt am Beispiel der Republik Korea / von Shin-Yung Chung. Bonn : Gesellschaft für Wirtschafts- und Verkehrswissenschaftliche Forschung, c1982. xiv, 204 p., [1] leaf of plates : ill. ; 21 cm. (Entwicklungspolitische Schriften des Instituts für Industrie- und Verkehrspolitik der Universität Bonn und der Gesellschaft für Wirtschafts- u. Verkehrswissenschaftliche Forschung) "Erstellt und vervollständigt aus den Unterlagen, die Shin-Yung Chung für seine Promotion zum Dr. rer. pol. an der Universität Hamburg erarbeitet hat"--1st prelim. p. Bibliography: p. 190-204. LC Card 83-214728
1. Saving and investment - Korea (South). 2. Economic development. 3. Korea (South) - Economic conditions - 1945-. 4. Saving and investment - Developing countries. I. Title. II. Series.
HC470.S3 C48 1982

Chung yang yen chiu yüan. Ching chi yen chiu so. Symposium on Monetary Theory (1986 : Institute of Economics, Academia Sinica) Symposium on Monetary Theory, January 3-8, 1986 =. Taipei, Taiwan, Republic of China [1986?] 2 v. (iv, 630 p.) : LC Card 87-152394 DDC 332.4 19
HG203 .S96 1986

Chung yang yen chiu yüan. Institute of Economics. see **Chung yang yen chiu yüan. Ching chi yen chiu so.**

Čhunlasān wichākān . (pī thī 1, chabap thī 1) Rǣngngān Thai. Krung Thēp , 2528 [1985] 53 p. ; LC Card 86-915944
HD5822.55.A6 R35 1985

Chuntulov, V. T. (Vladimir Timofeevich) Aktual′nye problemy sotsial′no-ėkonomicheskogo razvitiia SSSR v sovremennyĭ period /. Moskva , 1984. 153 p. ; LC Card 85-205938
HC336.25 .A46 1984

Chuo Kikuu cha Dar es Salaam. Bureau of Resource Assessment and Land Use Planning. Workshop on the Institutionalization of the Shallow Wells Programme under Tanzanian Administration (1981 : University of Dar es Salaam) Proceedings of the Workshop on the Institutionalization of the Shallow Wells Programme under Tanzanian Administration /. [Dar es Salaam?] , 1981. 3, 16, 12 p. ; LC Card 85-980881 DDC 333.7/09678 s 333.91/22/09678 19
HD107 .D36 no. 71 HD1699.T33

Chuo Kikuu cha Dar es Salaam. Economic Research Bureau. Hyuha, Mukwanason. Financial structure and economic development in Africa . Dar-es-Salaam, Tanzania , c1983. 43 p. : LC Card 85-981441 DDC 332/.096 19
HG187.5.A2 H98 1983

Chupeev, V. A. (Vladimir Alekseevich) Sazonov, S. N. (Sergeĭ Nikolaevich) Oplata truda v sel′skom khoziaĭstve . Moskva , 1984. 268 p. ; LC Card 84-244595
HD4966.A292 S6574 1984

CHURCH ADMINISTRATION. see **CHURCH MANAGEMENT.**

CHURCH AND INDUSTRY - DOMINICAN REPUBLIC - CONGRESSES.
Influencia del sector privado sobre la realidad nacional. [Santo Domingo] [1986] 180 p., [1] leaf of plates : LC Card 86-190331
HC153.5 .I53 1986

CHURCH AND LABOR - FRANCE - HISTORY.
Debès, Joseph. L'appel de la J.O.C., 1926-1928 /. Paris , 1986. 292 p. : ISBN 2-204-02529-1 : LC Card 86-189508
HD8430 .D37 1986

CHURCH AND LABOR - GERMANY (WEST) - ADDRESSES, ESSAYS, LECTURES.
Aussperrung und Streik . Mainz , 1981, c1980. 173 p. ; ISBN 3-7867-0854-1 LC Card 81-101514 DDC 331.89/2943 19
HD5378 .A97 1981 ***NYPL [JLD 86-2787]***

CHURCH AND LABOR - GERMANY (WEST) - CONGRESSES.
Soziallehre der Kirche und katholische Verbände /. Köln , 1980. 244 p. ; ISBN 3-7616-0568-4 (pbk.) : LC Card 81-122896 DDC 306/.6/0943 19
HN39.G3 S693 ***NYPL [JLC 86-231]***

CHURCH AND LABOR - GERMANY (WEST) - SPEYER.
Kirchen kämpfen mit . Mainz , 1981. 106 p. : ISBN 3-7867-0873-8 LC Card 81-188986 DDC 261.8/34562/094343 19
HD6338.2.G32 S634 1981
NYPL [JLD 86-2786]

CHURCH AND LABOR - NETHERLANDS - MAASTRICHT - HISTORY.
Perry, Jos. Roomsche kinine tegen roode koorts . Amsterdam , 1983. 334 p. : ISBN 90-6012-571-1 : LC Card 83-240733
HD6481.2.N4 P47 1983
NYPL [JLD 86-3418]

CHURCH AND LABOR - UNITED STATES.
Sullivan, Patrick J., 1929- Blue collar, Roman collar, white collar . Lanham, MD , c1987. xii, 346 p. ; ISBN 0-8191-5704-X (alk. paper) : LC Card 86-24593 DDC 261.85 19
HD6338.2.U5 S85 1987

CHURCH AND LABOR - UNITED STATES - HISTORY.
Winters, Donald E. The soul of the wobblies . Westport, Conn. , 1985. 159 p. ; ISBN 0-313-24472-3 (lib. bdg.) LC Card 84-27973 DDC 331.88/6 19
HD8055.I5 W56 1985 ***NYPL [JLD 87-775]***

CHURCH AND LABOR - UNITED STATES - HISTORY - 20TH CENTURY.
Sullivan, Patrick J., 1929- U. S. Catholic institutions and labor unions, 1960-1980 /. Lanham, MD , c1985. 545 p. ; ISBN 0-8191-4970-5 (alk. paper) : LC Card 85-20171 DDC 331.88/1128273 19
HD6481.2.U6 S85 1985
NYPL [JLE 86-2407]

CHURCH AND SOCIAL PROBLEMS - BRAZIL.
Terra de Deus, terra de irmãos . Brasília-DF [1986] 190 p. : LC Card 86-233600
HD1333.B6 T47 1986

CHURCH AND SOCIAL PROBLEMS - GERMANY (WEST) - CATHOLIC CHURCH - CONGRESSES.
Soziallehre der Kirche und katholische Verbände /. Köln , 1980. 244 p. ; ISBN 3-7616-0568-4 (pbk.) : LC Card 81-122896 DDC 306/.6/0943 19
HN39.G3 S693 ***NYPL [JLC 86-231]***

CHURCH AND SOCIAL PROBLEMS - GUATEMALA.
Cambranes, J. C. Agrarismo en Guatemala /. Guatemala , 1986. 255 p. : LC Card 87-401042 DDC 322/.2/097281 19
HD1531.G9 C36 1986

CHURCH AND SOCIAL PROBLEMS - LATIN AMERICA.
Antoncich, Ricardo. [Cristianos ante la injusticia. English.] Christians in the face of injustice . Maryknoll, N.Y. , c1987. xvi, 181 p. ; ISBN 0-88344-413-5 (pbk.) LC Card 86-23529 DDC 261.8 19
BX1753 .A5813 1987 ***NYPL [JLE 87-1051]***

Junto a nuestro pueblo. [Lima, Perú] [1979 or 1980] 71 p. : LC Card 82-100009
BX1426.2 .J86 1979 ***NYPL [JLF 86-1152]***

Pérez Aguirre, Luis. Predicaciones en la plaza /. Montevideo , 1985. 228 p. ; LC Card 85-225854 DDC 282/.8 19
BX1426.2 .P46 1985 ***NYPL [JLE 87-456]***

CHURCH AND SOCIAL PROBLEMS - LATIN AMERICA - CATHOLIC CHURCH.
Lay, Jean-Benoît. Vers la libération de l'Amérique latine /. Paris , c1985. 215 p. : ISBN 2-85802-433-X LC Card 85-136403
HC123 .L39 1985

CHURCH AND THE POOR - GUATEMALA.
Cambranes, J. C. Agrarismo en Guatemala /. Guatemala , 1986. 255 p. : LC Card 87-401042 DDC 322/.2/097281 19
HD1531.G9 C36 1986

CHURCH AND THE POOR - LATIN AMERICA.
Junto a nuestro pueblo. [Lima, Perú] [1979 or 1980] 71 p. : LC Card 82-100009
BX1426.2 .J86 1979 ***NYPL [JLF 86-1152]***

CHURCH LANDS - FRANCE - HISTORY - 18TH CENTURY.
Arsac, Pierre. La vente des biens de la Grande Chartreuse sous la Révolution /. Grenoble , 1984. 104 p. : ISBN 2-904661-02-6 LC Card 86-118639
HD643 .A77 1984

CHURCH LANDS - ITALY - SIENA REGION - HISTORY.
Epstein, Stephan R., 1960- Alle origini della fattoria toscana . Firenze , c1986. 315 p. : LC Card 87-104355
HD1470.5.I82 S544 1986

CHURCH LANDS - SPAIN - ANDALUSIA - HISTORY - 19TH CENTURY.
González do Molina Navarro, Manuel. Desamortización, deuda pública y crecimiento económico, Andalucía, 1820/1823 /. Granada , Córdoba :bFundación Paco Natera [1985?] 443 p. : ISBN 84-505-1053-8 LC Card 86-210676
HD779.A4 G66 1985

CHURCH LANDS - SPAIN - GRANADA (PROVINCE) - HISTORY - 19TH CENTURY.
Gómez Oliver, Miguel. La desamortización de Mendizábal en Granada /. Granada [1983] 226 p. : LC Card 85-135214
HD479.G73 G65 1983

CHURCH LANDS - SPAIN - HISTORY.
Rueda Hernanz, Germán. La desamortización de Mendizábal y Espartero en España /. Madrid , c1986. 200 p. ; ISBN 84-376-0592-X LC Card 86-216590
HD774 .R84 1986

CHURCH LANDS - SPAIN - JAÉN (PROVINCE) - HISTORY - 18TH CENTURY.
Herr, Richard. Rural change and royal finances in Spain at the end of the old regime /. Berkeley , c1987. p. cm. ISBN 0-520-05948-4 (alk. paper) LC Card 86-25027 DDC 333.3/0946/25 19
HD779.J34 H47 1987

CHURCH LANDS - SPAIN - SALAMANCA (PROVINCE) - HISTORY - 18TH CENTURY.
Herr, Richard. Rural change and royal finances in Spain at the end of the old regime /. Berkeley , c1987. p. cm. ISBN 0-520-05948-4 (alk. paper) LC Card 86-25027 DDC 333.3/0946/25 19
HD779.J34 H47 1987

CHURCH LANDS - SPAIN - TIERRA DE CAMPOS REGION - HISTORY.
Martínez Sopena, Pascual. La Tierra de Campos occidental . [Valladolid] , 1985. 843 p. : ISBN 84-505-1390-1 LC Card 86-231937
HD779.T54 M37 1985

CHURCH MANAGEMENT.
Just treatment for those who work for the church. Cincinnati, OH (100 E. 8th St., Cincinnati 45202) , c1986. ix, 21 p. ; LC Card 86-228672 DDC 254/.0068/3 19
HF5549 .J87 1986

Church of Christ of Latter-Day Saints. see **Church of Jesus Christ of Latter-Day Saints.**

CHURCH OF JESUS CHRIST OF LATTER-DAY SAINTS - BIOGRAPHY.
Hickman, Martin Berkeley, 1925- David Matthew Kennedy . Salt Lake City, Utah , c1987. xi, 403 p. : ISBN 0-87579-093-3 : LC Card 87-19898 DDC 332.1/092/4 B 19
HG2463.K46 H53 1987

CHURCH PROPERTY - FRANCE - HISTORY - 18TH CENTURY.
Arsac, Pierre. La vente des biens de la Grande Chartreuse sous la Révolution /. Grenoble , 1984. 104 p. : ISBN 2-904661-02-6 LC Card 86-118639
HD643 .A77 1984

Church, Roy. The history of the British coal industry. Oxford [Oxfordshire] , New York , c1983- v. : ISBN 0-19-828283-4 (v. 2) : LC Card 83-4194 DDC 338.2/724/0941 19
HD9551.5 .F58 1983 ***NYPL [JLL 84-138]***

Church, Roy A. Herbert Austin : the British motor car industry to 1941 / Roy Church. London : Europa Publications, c1979. lii, 233

p., [3] leaves of plates : ill. ; 23 cm. (The Europa library of business biography) Includes index. Bibliography: p. 217-224. ISBN 0-905118-29-4 : LC Card 79-317202 DDC 338.7/62/920924 B
1. Austin, Herbert, Baron Austin of Longbridge, 1866-1941. 2. Businessmen - Great Britain - Biography. 3. Automobile industry and trade - Great Britain - History.
HD9710.G72 A93 ***NYPL [JFD 86-9452]***

CHURCH WORK, SOCIAL. see **CHURCH AND SOCIAL PROBLEMS.**

CHURCHES - ADMINISTRATION. see **CHURCH MANAGEMENT.**

CHURCHES - MANAGEMENT. see **CHURCH MANAGEMENT.**

Churchill, Anthony A., 1938- Rural water supply and sanitation : time for a change / Anthony A. Churchill with the assistance of David de Ferranti ... [et al.]. Washington, D.C. : World Bank, c1987. xvi, 111 p. : ill. ; 28 cm. (World Bank discussion papers . 18) Bibliography: p. 107-111. ISBN 0-8213-0950-1 (pbk.) LC Card 87-23005 DDC 338.4/336361/091724 19
1. Water-supply, Rural - Developing countries - Finance. 2. Sanitation, Rural - Developing countries - Finance. I. Series.
HD1702 .C48 1987

Churchill Films.
Contract for life, the S.A.D.D. story [motion picture] /. Los Angeles, CA , 1985. 1 film reel (31 min.) : LC Card 85-700743 DDC 363.1 11
HE5620.D7

Contract for life, the S.A.D.D story [videorecording] /. Los Angeles, CA , 1985. 1 videocassette (31 min.) : LC Card 85-700744 DDC 363.1 11
HE5620.D7

Churchill, Gilbert A. Basic marketing research / Gilbert A. Churchill, Jr. Chicago : Dryden Press, [1987], c1988. xvii, 765 p. : ill. ; 27 cm. (Dryden Press series in marketing) Includes bibliographies and index. ISBN 0-03-007278-6 LC Card 87-5288 DDC 658.8/3 19
1. Marketing research. I. Title. II. Series.
HF5415.2 .C49 1988

Chūtō Kyōryoku Sentā. Joint Symposium on the Energy Industries: Prospects of Co-operation Between Arab Gulf States and Japan (1984 : Tokyo, Japan) The Arab Gulf States and Japan . London , Dover, N.H. , c1986. xiv, 216 p. : ISBN 0-7099-3393-2 : LC Card 85-12819 DDC 338.2/728/0952 19
HD9576.P52 J65 1984 ***NYPL [JLD 86-1669]***

CHUVASHSKAI͡A A.S.S.R. (R.S.F.S.R.) - ECONOMIC POLICY.
XXVI s″ezd KPSS i voprosy ėkonomiki narodnogo khozi͡aĭstva Chuvashskoĭ ASSR. Cheboksary , 1982. 157 p. ; LC Card 83-128420
HC337.C46 A17 1982

Chuvashskai͡a A.S.S.R. (R.S.F.S.R.). Nauchno-issledovatel′skiĭ institut i͡azyka, literatury, istorii i ėkonomiki.
Ėffektivnost′ proizvodstva v agropromyshlennom komplekse Chuvashskoĭ ASSR /. Cheboksary , 1985. 198 p. ; LC Card 86-203897
HD9015.S653 C483 1985

Sot͡sial′no-ėkonomicheskie problemy ispol′zovanii͡a trudovykh resursov /. Cheboksary , 1986. 70 p. ; LC Card 87-137786
HD5797.C56 S68 1986

Voprosy istorii sot͡sialisticheskogo preobrazovanii͡a i razvitii͡a sel′skogo khozi͡aĭstva Chuvashskoĭ ASSR /. Cheboksary , 1985. 176 p. ; LC Card 86-100164
HD1492.5.S65 C488 1985

XXVI s″ezd KPSS i voprosy ėkonomiki narodnogo khozi͡aĭstva Chuvashskoĭ ASSR. Cheboksary , 1982. 157 p. ; LC Card 83-128420
HC337.C46 A17 1982

Cia. Brasileira de Alimentos. Debate Nacional sobre Abastecimento Popular (1986) Documento final /. Brasília, DF , 1986. 51 leaves : LC Card 87-146594 DDC 363.8/0981 19
HD9014.B82 D43 1986

Ciabattoni, Francis. Rice, Jonathan. How to survive and profit from the coming currency recall /. Chicago , c1986. xiii, 258 p. : ISBN 0-8092-4998-7 : LC Card 86-6215 DDC 332.4/973 19
HG540 .R53 1986 ***NYPL [JLE 86-3508]***

Cibin, Renato. Le Iniziative locali per l'occupazione . Milano, Italy , c1985. 244 p. : LC Card 85-221711 DDC 331 s 331.12/042 19
HD85.I7 I68 no. 75 HD5713.5 ***NYPL [JLD 87-446]***

Cibreiros, Sérgio Augusto. Mercado financeiro e de capitais . [Brasília? , 1978?] 118 leaves, [25] leaves of plates : LC Card 84-184169
HG185.B7 M47 1978

Cichy, E. Ulrich. Probleme monetärer und finanzwirtschaftlicher Steuerung im Systemvergleich /. Duisburg , c1986. 175 p. : ISBN 3-921473-43-8 LC Card 86-211745
HC286.6 .P754 1986

Ciclo da mineração / Ministério da Fazenda, Delegacia do Ministério da Fazenda no Estado do Rio de Janeiro, Divisão de Administração, Setor de Documentação, Museu da Fazenda Federal. Rio de Janeiro-RJ : O Museu, 1984. 95 p. : ill. ; 23 cm. Bibliography: p. 87-95. LC Card 85-186500
1. Gold mines and mining - Brazil - History. 2. Diamond industry and trade - Brazil - History. I. Museu da Fazenda Federal.
HD9536.B82 C56 1984

Ciclo de Conferencias sobre "La Empresa" (1961-1962 : Instituto de Estudios Políticos) La Empresa. Madrid , 1962. 348 p. : LC Card 85-108024
HD2326 .E47 1962

Ciclo de debates .
(no. 6-7) Lopes, Marcos José. Atendimento ao mercado de energia elétrica do Nordeste /. Recife, PE [1984] 2 v. in 4 : LC Card 86-166126
HD9685.B83 N675 1984

El Ciclo industrial en España : series históricas de las encuestas de coyuntura industrial / Ministerio de Industria y Energía, Secretaría General Técnica. Madrid : Servicio de Publicaciones, Ministerio de Industria y Energía, [1984?] 436 p. : ill. ; 23 cm. (Colección Economía e industria . 3) Includes bibliographies. ISBN 84-7474-282-X LC Card 87-113099
1. Spain - Industries. 2. Industrial surveys - Spain. 3. Business cycles - Spain. I. Spain. Ministerio de Industria y Energía. Secretaría General Técnica. II. Series.
HC385 .C49 1984

Ciclo Integrado sobre Administração Financeira /. Ciclo Integrado sobre Administração Financeira (1983 : Escola de Administração Fazendária) Salvador, BA [1984] 53 p. : LC Card 86-157989
HG185.B7 C52 1983

Ciclo Integrado sobre Administração Financeira (1983 : Escola de Administração Fazendária) Ciclo Integrado sobre Administração Financeira / Governo do Estado da Bahia, Secretaria da Fazenda, Escola de Administração Fazendária, Coordenadoria de Programas Especiais. Salvador, BA : A Coordenadoria, [1984] 53 p. : ill. ; 26 cm. CONTENTS. - As necessidades de financiamento e as limitações do sistema financeiro nacional / Antônio Carlos Magalhães Júnior -- Planejamento financeiro de empresas governamentais / Edilson Souto Freire -- Análise das demonstrações financeiras / Jorge Antonio Barros Cerqueira. LC Card 86-157989
1. Finance - Brazil - Congresses. 2. Government business enterprises - Brazil - Finance - Congresses. I. Bahia (Brazil : State). Escola de Administração Fazendária. II. Title.
HG185.B7 C52 1983

Ciclos productivos en el espacio peruano colonial, siglos XVI-XIX . Ríos Burga, Jaime R. Lima, Perú , 1986. 70 p. : LC Card 87-401070 DDC 338.5/42/0983 19
HC227 .R456 1986

CIDA. see **Inter-American Committee for Agricultural Development.**

Cidadão, estado e políticas no Brasil contemporâneo / Departamento de Sociologia da Universidade de Brasília ; coordenação geral, Wilma de M. Figueiredo. Brasília-Distrito Federal : Programa Nacional de Desburocratização : Editora Universidade de Brasília, c1986. 290 p. : ill. ; 23 cm. Includes bibliographies. CONTENTS. - Reforma agrária e cidadania / Elizabeth S. Freitas, Isabelle B.P. da Silva -- A Nova República e os pequenos produtores rurais nordestinos / Yves Chaloult -- Prespectivas de um planejamento democrático na Nova República / José Estêvão Machado Arcanjo -- A atualização do discurso liberal no Programa Nacional de Desburocratização / Maria Cilene M. Sales dos Santos -- Previdência social e sociedade em período de crise / Vicente de Paula Faleiros -- O modelo energético no Brasil democrático / Paulo Augusto Leonelli -- A reforma tributária e a Constituinte / Mário Tinoco da Silva -- O município brasileiro e a descentralização governamental / Elizeu Francisco Calsing -- A luta pela terra / Ivan Sergio Freire de Souza, Michelangelo Giotto S. Trigueiro. ISBN 85-23-00214-6 LC Card 87-405054 DDC 338.981 19
1. Agriculture and state - Brazil. 2. Brazil - Politics and government - 1985-. 3. Brazil - Economic policy. 4. Brazil - Social policy. I. Figueiredo, Vilma. II. Programa Nacional de Desburocratização (Brazil). III. Universidade de Brasília. Departamento de Sociologia.
HD1873 .C53 1986

A cidade invade as águas . Sócrates, Jodete Rios. [São Paulo] , 1985. 296 p., [2] folded leaves of plates : LC Card 87-118596 DDC 333.91/00981/61 19
HD1696.B84 S427 1985

Cidambi, Raghu. Command area development, successes and learnings . Hyderabad , c1980. iii, 138 p. ; LC Card 83-906246 DDC 338.1/854 19
HD1741.I29 C65 1980 ***NYPL [JLD 87-597]***

CIDER INDUSTRY - ENGLAND.
Rendell, John. An economic survey of intensive bush cider orchards, 1972-1981 . [Reading, Berks.] [1984] 24 p. : ISBN 0-7049-0814-X (pbk.) : LC Card 85-111963 DDC 338.1/74117 19
HD9398.G83 E57 1984

Cien años de la Bolsa de Comercio de Rosario.
De Marco, Miguel Ángel. 1884-1984, los cien años de la Bolsa de Comercio de Rosario /. [S.l. , 1984?] (Rosario : Escuela de Artes Gráficas del Colegio San José de Rosario) 167 p. : LC Card 87-115398 DDC 332.64/28224 19
HG5320.R67 D4 1984

CIEN (Organization) Vides de Orive, Enna. Análisis de la situación económica de Guatemala, 1965-1984 /. Guatemala, Guatemala , 1985. ii leaves, 118 p. : LC Card 86-205265 DDC 330.97281/053 19
HC144 .V53 1985

Ciencia y transformación social . Baez, René. Quito, Ecuador , 1986. 141 p. ; LC Card 86-214736 DDC 330.9/0038 19
HC125 .B195 1986

Ciencias económicas, políticas y sociales.
Consuegra Higgins, José. El pensamiento económico colombiano /. Bogotá, Colombia , 1984. 216 p. ; LC Card 84-200191 DDC 330/.09861 19
HB123.C6 C662 1984 ***NYPL [JLC 87-88]***

Ciencias económicas y empresariales. see **Serie: Ciencias económicas y empresariales.**

Ciencias sociales (Mexico City, Mexico)
Los Sindicatos nacionales en el México contemporáneo /. [México, D.F.] , 1986- v. <1 > ; ISBN 968-498-020-5 (set) LC Card 87-401211 DDC 331.88/0972 19
HD6532 .S55 1986

Ciento cinco años de vida bancaria en Costa Rica /. Gil Pacheco, Rufino. San José , 1982. 406 p. : LC Card 83-228041 DDC 332.1/097286 19
HG2734 .G55 1982 ***NYPL [JLD 86-3356]***

Cieplan. see **Corporación de Investigaciones Económicas para Latinoamérica.**

CIGAR INDUSTRY - CUBA - HISTORY - 19TH CENTURY.
Westfall, L. Glenn, 1943- Don Vicente Martinez Ybor, the man and his empire . New York , 1987. vii, 214 p. : ISBN 0-8240-1374-3 (alk. paper) : LC Card 87-8690 DDC 338.7/67972/0924 19
HD9149.C5 U777 1987

CIGAR INDUSTRY - FLORIDA - HISTORY - 19TH CENTURY.
Westfall, L. Glenn, 1943- Don Vicente Martinez Ybor, the man and his empire . New York , 1987. vii, 214 p. : ISBN 0-8240-1374-3 (alk. paper) : LC Card 87-8690 DDC 338.7/67972/0924 19
HD9149.C5 U777 1987

CIGNA Worldwide (Firm) CIGNA Worldwide guide : a perspective on global facilities. [S.l.] : CIGNA Worldwide, [c1985] [218] p. ; 30 cm. Cover title. LC Card 86-206403 DDC 368.8/1 19
1. CIGNA Worldwide (Firm). 2. Insurance, Business. I. Title.
HG8059 .C53 1985

CIGNA WORLDWIDE (FIRM)
CIGNA Worldwide (Firm) CIGNA Worldwide guide . [S.l.] [c1985] [218] p. ; LC Card 86-206403 DDC 368.8/1 19
HG8059 .C53 1985

CIGNA Worldwide guide . CIGNA Worldwide (Firm) [S.l.] [c1985] [218] p. ; LC Card 86-206403 DDC 368.8/1 19
HG8059 .C53 1985

Cilliers, S. P. Patterns of migration and settlement in rural South Africa / by S.P. Cilliers & L.P. Raubenheimer. [Stellenbosch] : Research Unit for Sociology of Development, University of Stellenbosch, 1986. 19, 13 leaves, 5 folded leaves of plates : maps ; 30 cm. (Occasional paper / Department of Sociology . no. 10) "May 1986." Bibliography: leaves 18-19. ISBN 0-908422-81-4 (pbk.) : LC Card 87-126315 DDC 304.8/0968 19
1. Rural-urban migration - South Africa - Statistics. 2. South Africa - Population, Rural - Statistics. 3. Blacks - South Africa - Migrations - Statistics. 4. Colored people (South Africa) - Migrations - Statistics. 5. East Asians - South Africa - Migrations - Statistics. I. Raubenheimer, L. P. II. Series: Geleentheidstuk , no. 10. III. Title.
HB2123.4.A3 C56 1986

Cimillo, Elsa. La terciarización del empleo en la Argentina. El sector del comercio minorista / Elsa Cimillo. [Buenos Aires] : República Argentina, Ministerio de Trabajo y Seguridad Social : Secretaría de Planificación, [1985] 23, [41], 3 p. ; 31 cm. (Estudios y documentos de trabajo sobre empleo, remuneraciones y recursos humanos) "Proyecto Gobierno Argentino, Programa de las Naciones Unidas para el Desarrollo, Organización Internacional del Trabajo, ARG/84/029, octubre 1985." Bibliography: p. [2] (2nd group). LC Card 87-123708 DDC 381/.1/0982 19
1. Retail trade - Argentina. 2. Retail trade - Argentina - Employees. 3. Retail trade - Argentina - Buenos Aires Metropolitan Area. 4. Retail trade - Argentina - Buenos Aires Metropolitan Area - Employees. I. Argentina. II. United Nations. Development Programme. III. International Labour Organisation. IV. Title. V. Series.
HF5429.6.A7 C56 1985

Cimmyt. see **International Maize and Wheat Improvement Center.**

CINANTEC INDIANS. see **CHINANTEC INDIANS.**

Cinco anos de migração em Rondônia 1979/83. 5 anos de migração em Rondônia, 1979/83 /. Porto Velho , 1984. 7, [19] leaves : LC Card 87-151286 DDC 304.8/0981/75 19
HB2024.R65 A12 1984

Cinco momentos, cinco planteamientos. Celis, Adán. 5 momentos, 5 planteamientos . Puerto la Cruz [Venezuela] , 1985. 99 p. ; LC Card 87-401953 DDC 338.987 19
HC237 .C445 1985

Cincuenta años de la CTV, 1936-1986. Godio, Julio. 50 años de la C.T.V., 1936-1986 . Caracas, Venezuela [1986] 149 p. ; ISBN 980-607-709-1 LC Card 87-401745 DDC 331.88/0987 19
HD8362.C68 G63 1986

CINDERELLA MATERIALS (PHILATELY) - EUROPE.
Maier, Lotte. Militärmarken /. Dortmund , 1981. 158 p. : ISBN 3-88379-253-5 (kart.) : LC Card 81-180793
HE6184.S42 M35 1981

Cinquante mots clefs de la consommation. Balfet, Michel. Les 50 mots clefs de la consommation /. Toulouse , c1985. 310 p. : ISBN 2-7089-1969-5 : LC Card 86-140639 DDC 339.4/7 19
HB801 .B276 1985

CINTERFOR (Organization)
Agudelo Mejía, Santiago. Lineamientos para la implantación de un servicio de certificación ocupacional /. Montevideo , 1983. 67 p. : LC Card 86-142627
HD5715.5.L3 A348 1983

Certificación ocupacional . Ciudad de México , 1981. 76 p. ; ISBN 968-8290-30-0 LC Card 86-142976
HD5715.5.L3 C47 1981

Concepto y aplicación del enfoque de sistemas en los procesos y técnicas de instrucción. Montevideo , 1980. 283 p. : LC Card 86-143811
HD5715.5.L29 C66 1980

La Formación profesional ante las exigencias del desarrollo. Montevideo , 1980. 98 p. ; LC Card 86-139077
HD5715.5.L3 F664 1980

Ciocca, Pierluigi, 1941- Interesse e profitto : saggi sul sistema creditizio / Pierluigi Ciocca. Bologna : Il Mulino, c1982. 245 p. : ill. ; 22 cm. (Studi e ricerche. 132) Includes bibliographical references and index. LC Card 84-139966 DDC 332/.0945 19
1. Finance - Italy - History - 20th century. 2. Banks and banking - Italy - History - 20th century. 3. Monetary policy - Italy - History - 20th century. 4. Credit - Italy - History - 20th century. I. Title.
HG186.I8 C56 1982

Cipca. see **Centro de Investigación y Promoción del Campesinado.**

Cipolletta, Innocenzo. Struttura industriale e politiche macroeconomiche in Italia /. Bologna , c1986. 152 p. : ISBN 88-15-01193-5 : LC Card 87-100465
HC305 .S845 1986

CIQRO (Organization) Quintana Roo . Puerto Morelos, Q.R. , 1980. iv, 203 p., [32] leaves of plates : LC Card 84-222175
HC137.Q5 Q55 1980

CIR staff paper .
(no. 10) Rapawy, Stephen. Civilian employment in the U. S.S.R., 1950 to 1983 /. Washington, D.C. [1985] 35 leaves ; LC Card 87-601284 DDC 331.12/5/0947021 19
HD5796 .R358 1985

(no. 11) Sagers, Matthew J. The freight rate structure on Soviet railroads /. Washington, D.C. [1985] vii, 28 p. : LC Card 87-601285 DDC 385/.12/0947 19
HE1895 .S25 1985

(no. 13) Heinemeier, Meredith M. 1977 consumption by industrial sector /. Washington, D.C. [1986] vii, 148 p. ; LC Card 87-601286 DDC 339.2/3/0947 19
HC340.I57 H45 1986

(no. 14) Sagers, Matthew J. Natural gas liquids and the Soviet gas processing industry /. Washington, D.C. [1986] viii, 72, 2 p. : LC Card 87-601287 DDC 338.4/766573 19
HD9581.2.L573 S657 1986

(no. 16) Taylor, Jeffrey R., 1954- Employment outlook for China to the year 2000 /. Washington, D.C. [1986] 43 leaves, 2 p. ; LC Card 87-601289 DDC 331.12/3/0951021 19
HD5830.A6 T375 1986

(no. 17) Treml, Vladimir G. Soviet foreign trade in foodstuffs . Washington, D.C. [1986] viii, 69, 2 p. ; LC Card 87-601290 DDC 382/.45664/00947 19
HD9015.S65 T74 1986

(no. 19) Tretyakova, Albina. Cost estimates for the Soviet gas industry, 1970 to 1990 /. Washington, D.C. [1986] vii, 116 p. ; LC Card 87-601292 DDC 338.2/3 19
HD9581.S652 T74 1986

(no. 2) Sagers, Matthew J. Refinery throughput in the U. S.S.R. /. Washington, D.C. [1984] v, 81, 2 p. : LC Card 87-601276 DDC 338.4/766553/0947 19
HD9575.S652 S25 1984

(no. 21) Hobbs, Frank. Demographic estimates, projections, and selected social characteristics of the population of India /. Washington, D.C. [1986] vii, 148 p. : LC Card 87-601294 DDC 304.6/0954/021 19
HA4585 .H63 1986

(no. 4) Sagers, Matthew J. Restructuring the Soviet petroleum refining industry /. Washington, D.C. [1985] v, 57 p. ; LC Card 87-601278 DDC 338.4/766553/0947 19
HD9575.S652 S254 1985

Ciravegna, Daniele. Che cosa si produce, come e per chi . Torino , 1983. 514 p. : LC Card 85-167580
HB177 .C46 1983

I circoli di qualità . Nicoletti, Bernardo. Milano, Italy , c1986. 249 p. ; LC Card 86-207976
HD66 .N53 1986

Les circuits économiques en Afrique noire /. Albagli, Claude. Abidjan , c1983. 67 p. : ISBN 2-7236-0585-X LC Card 86-179144
HB74.9.A357 A43 1983

CIRCUITS, INTEGRATED. see **INTEGRATED CIRCUITS.**

CIRCULAR VELOCITY OF MONEY - ECONOMETRIC MODELS.
Bordo, Michael D. The long-run behavior of the velocity of circulation . Cambridge [Cambridgeshire] , New York , 1987. xiv, 181 p. : ISBN 0-521-32633-8 LC Card 86-32628 DDC 332.4/14 19
HG226.6 .B67 1987

CIREBON (INDONESIA : KABUPATEN) - RURAL CONDITIONS.
Breman, Jan. Control of land and labour in colonial Java . Dordrecht, Netherlands , Cinnaminson, N.J., U. S.A. , 1983. xi, 158 p. : ISBN 90-6765-048-X (pbk.) LC Card 86-145678 DDC 333.3/1/5982 19
HD1333.I52 C573 1983

CIRET-Studien, 0170-5679 .
(36) Essays on the performance of leading indicators based on qualitative data /. Munich , 1985. 148 p. : ISBN 3-88512-009-7 (pbk.) : LC Card 86-181861 DDC 330/.0724 19
HB3730 .E78 1985

Ciriquiain-Gaiztarro, M. Los puertos marítimos del País Vasco / por M. Ciriquiain-Gaiztarro. San Sebastián : Txertoa, [1986?] 270 p. : ill. ; 22 cm. (Colección Ipar haizea. 23) Bibliography: p. [263]-268. ISBN 84-7148-180-4 LC Card 87-105513
1. Harbors - Spain - País Vasco. I. Title.
HE558.P15 C57 1986

CISKEI (SOUTH AFRICA) - ECONOMIC CONDITIONS - STATISTICS.
Kruger, Gudrun. Development region D . Port Elizabeth [1985] iv, 89 p. : ISBN 0-86988-274-0 (pbk.) LC Card 86-233113 DDC 304.6/09687/5 19
HA4701.Z9 C354 1985

CISKEI (SOUTH AFRICA) - POPULATION - STATISTICS.
Kruger, Gudrun. Development region D . Port Elizabeth [1985] iv, 89 p. : ISBN 0-86988-274-0 (pbk.) LC Card 86-233113 DDC 304.6/09687/5 19
HA4701.Z9 C354 1985

Cisneros C., Antonio. La mujer trabajadora : sus necesidades y criterios sobre la vida familiar / Antonio J. Cisneros, Carlos Koch, Germán La Fuente. La Paz, Bolivia : Centro de Investigaciones Sociales, [1984] 131 leaves : ill. ; 28 cm. (Série Estudios de promoción femenina . no. 3) "Febrero 1984." Bibliography: leaves 130-131. LC Card 85-129000 DDC 331.4/0984 19
1. Women - Employment - Bolivia. 2. Family - Bolivia. 3. Birth control - Bolivia. 4. Women - Health and hygiene - Bolivia. 5. Women - Medical care - Bolivia. I. Koch, Carlos. II. La Fuente, Germán. III. Title.
HD6121 .C58 1984 ***NYPL [JLF 86-1704]***

Cisneros Orna, Manuel H. Minería, riqueza y pobreza del Perú / Manuel H. Cisneros Orna. [Lima, Peru] : Instituto Cultural José María Arguedas, [1986] 205 p. : ill. ; 21 cm. Includes bibliographical references. LC Card 87-100765
1. Mineral industries - Peru. I. Title.
HD9506.P42 C57 1986

CISOC Bellarmino. La Opción preferencial por los pobres . [Santiago] [1987] 360 p. : LC Card 87-403060 DDC 362.5/098 19
HC130.P6 O63 1987

Cistelecan, Lazăr M. Procesul investițional / Lazăr M. Cistelecan. București : Editura Academiei Republicii Socialiste România, 1983. 264 p. : ill. ; 21 cm. One folded leaf of plates inserted. Summary in English and Russian. Bibliography: p. 251-255. LC Card 84-135967
1. Investments - Romania. 2. Investments. I. Title.
HG5692 .C57 1983

CITIES AND STATE. see **URBAN POLICY.**

CITIES AND TOWN - FRANCE - GROWTH - CONGRESSES.
Colloque Les Périphéries urbaines (1984 :

Angers, France) Actes du Colloque Les Périphéries urbaines . Caen , c1985. 270 p. : ISBN 2-905461-03-9 : LC Card 86-173712
HB2263 .C65 1984

CITIES AND TOWNS - ADDRESSES, ESSAYS, LECTURES.
World patterns of modern urban change . Chicago , 1986. x, 479 p. : ISBN 0-89065-122-1 : LC Card 85-23231 DDC 910 s 307.7/6 19
H31 .C514 no.217-218
NYPL [JFM 72-132 no.217-218]

CITIES AND TOWNS - AFGHANISTAN - SAR-E POL.
Jebens, Albrecht. Wirtschafts- und sozialgeographische Untersuchung über das Heimgewerbe in Nordafghanistan unter besonderer Berücksichtigung der Mittelstadt Sar-e-Pul . Tübingen , 1983. xii, 415 p., [2] folded leaves of plates : LC Card 86-128235
HD2346.A52 S275 1983

CITIES AND TOWNS - AFRICA - ADDRESSES, ESSAYS, LECTURES.
Struggle for the city . Beverly Hills , c1983. 319 p. : ISBN 0-8039-2067-9 LC Card 83-11196 DDC 305.5/62/096 19
HD8774 .S87 1983 ***NYPL [JLD 83-3496]***

CITIES AND TOWNS - AFRICA - GROWTH.
Feeding African cities . Bloomington , c1987. x, 249 p. ; ISBN 0-253-32102-6 LC Card 86-46323 DDC 338.1/9/6 19
HD9017.A2 F44 1987

CITIES AND TOWNS - ALABAMA - STATISTICS.
Gilder, Gilford C. Alabama municipal data book, 1985 /. Montgomery, Ala. (State Capitol, Montgomery 36130) [1986] 97 p. : LC Card 86-622909 DDC 307.7/6/09761021 19
HA225 .G55 1986

CITIES AND TOWNS - ARGENTINA - GROWTH - CASE STUDIES.
Toledo, Nora Elena. El tamaño de las ciudades y la distribución de los ingresos (Argentina y Colombia) /. San Juan, Argentina , 1985. 63 p. : LC Card 87-400258 DDC 339.2/2/09861 19
HC200.I5 T65 1985

CITIES AND TOWNS - BRAZIL - CEARÁ (STATE)
O Norte cearense /. Recife , 1985. 303 p. : LC Card 86-209022
HD1875.C4 N67 1985

CITIES AND TOWNS - BRAZIL - ENERGY CONSUMPTION.
Energia e assentamentos humanos. Porto Alegre , 1983. 40 p. : LC Card 86-200513
HD9502.A2 E513 1983

CITIES AND TOWNS - BRAZIL - GROWTH.
Estudos e propostas para a organização territorial e desenvolvimento urbano do Brasil. Brasilia , 1981. 126 leaves, [7] folded leaves of plates : ***NYPL [JLG 86-151]***

CITIES AND TOWNS - BRAZIL - RIO GRANDE DO SUL - STATISTICS.
Os Municípios do Rio Grande do Sul . [Porto Alegre] , 1985. 250, [7] p. : LC Card 87-401216 DDC 318.1/65 19
HA988.R8 M86 1985

CITIES AND TOWNS - CENTRAL EUROPE - HISTORY - CONGRESSES.
Städtewesen und Merkantilismus in Mitteleuropa /. Köln , 1983. xii, 333 p. : ISBN 3-412-00382-4 LC Card 83-155285
HF1531 .S688 1983

CITIES AND TOWNS - COLOMBIA - GROWTH - CASE STUDIES.
Toledo, Nora Elena. El tamaño de las ciudades y la distribución de los ingresos (Argentina y Colombia) /. San Juan, Argentina , 1985. 63 p. : LC Card 87-400258 DDC 339.2/2/09861 19
HC200.I5 T65 1985

CITIES AND TOWNS - DEVELOPING COUNTRIES - CONGRESSES.
Urbanisation in the developing world /. London , Dover, N.H. , c1986. 265 p. ; ISBN 0-7099-0884-9 : LC Card 86-4551 DDC 307.7/6/091724 19
HT149.5 .U74 1986 ***NYPL [JLD 86-2402]***

CITIES AND TOWNS - DEVELOPING COUNTRIES - GROWTH - CONGRESSES.
Urbanisation in the developing world /. London , Dover, N.H. , c1986. 265 p. ; ISBN 0-7099-0884-9 : LC Card 86-4551 DDC 307.7/6/091724 19
HT149.5 .U74 1986 ***NYPL [JLD 86-2402]***

CITIES AND TOWNS - ECONOMIC ASPECTS. see **URBAN ECONOMICS.**

CITIES AND TOWNS - ENERGY CONSUMPTION.
Energia e assentamentos humanos. Porto Alegre , 1983. 40 p. : LC Card 86-200513
HD9502.A2 E513 1983

CITIES AND TOWNS - EUROPE - GROWTH - HISTORY.
Russell, Josiah Cox, 1900- The control of late ancient and medieval population /. Philadelphia , 1985. xv, 272 p. ; ISBN 0-87169-160-4 LC Card 83-71298
NYPL [JLF 85-844]

CITIES AND TOWNS - GERMANY (WEST) - NORTH RHINE-WESTPHALIA - STATISTICS.
Vorausberechnung der Bevölkerung in den kreisfreien Städten und Kreisen Nordrhein-Westfalens . Düsseldorf [1983] 103 p. : LC Card 86-202728
HA1320.N6 A32 Heft 500

CITIES AND TOWNS - GROWTH - GREAT BRITAIN.
Herington, John. The outer city /. London , New York , 1984. 205 p. : ISBN 0-06-318237-8
NYPL [JLE 86-1465]

CITIES AND TOWNS - INDIA - GROWTH.
Mills, Edwin S. Studies in Indian urban development /. New York , 1986. viii, 214 p. ; ISBN 0-19-520507-3 : LC Card 86-2489 DDC 307.1/4/0954 19
HT147.I5 M56 1986 ***NYPL [JLE 86-3750]***

CITIES AND TOWNS - INDIA - GROWTH - STATISTICS.
Sinha, Sunil Kumar. Urban growth in India, 1951-81 . New Delhi , 1986. vi, 72 p. : LC Card 86-902819
HA4581.5 1981e

CITIES AND TOWNS - ITALY - CONGRESSES.
L'Analisi degli insediamenti umani e produttivi /. Milano, Italy , c1984. 295 p. : LC Card 84-179265 DDC 330.945/0928 19
HC305 .A6618 1984 ***NYPL [JLD 86-3298]***

CITIES AND TOWNS - ITALY - SICILY - STATISTICS.
Greco, Eugenio. Storia demografica dei comuni siciliani dal 1832 al 1858 /. Palermo [1982] 60, [61] p. ; LC Card 85-103229
HB2270.S5 G74 1982

Storia demografica dei comuni siciliani dal 1862 al 1971 /. Palermo [1979] 294 p. ; LC Card 86-131917
HB2270.S5 S76 1979

CITIES AND TOWNS - LAW AND LEGISLATION. see **MUNICIPAL CORPORATIONS.**

CITIES AND TOWNS, MOVEMENT TO. see **CITIES AND TOWNS - GROWTH; URBANIZATION.**

CITIES AND TOWNS - PLANNING. see **CITY PLANNING.**

CITIES AND TOWNS - POLAND.
Bonenberg, Wojciech. Przemysł w mieście . Gliwice , 1985. 181 p., [8] folded leaves of plates : LC Card 86-219523
HC340.3.Z9 D52 1985

CITIES AND TOWNS - RUSSIAN S.F.S.R.
Problemy rasseleniia v SSSR . Moskva , 1980. 254 p. : LC Card 81-135093
HB2068.S65 P76 1980

CITIES AND TOWNS - RUSSIAN S.F.S.R. - HISTORY - 18TH CENTURY.
Morrison, Daniel, 1945- "Trading peasants" and urbanization in eighteenth-century Russia . New York , 1987. 415 p. ; ISBN 0-8240-8059-9 (alk. paper) : LC Card 87-7425 DDC 307.2 19
HB2068.S65 M67 1987

CITIES AND TOWNS - SOVIET UNION.
Problemy rasseleniia v SSSR . Moskva , 1980. 254 p. : LC Card 81-135093
HB2068.S65 P76 1980

CITIES AND TOWNS - SURVEYING. see **SURVEYING.**

CITIES AND TOWNS - SWEDEN.
Kommunerna och framtiden . [Stockholm] , 1984] 224 p. : ISBN 91-38-08484-8 : LC Card 85-107984
HC375 .K654 1984

Kommunerna och näringslivet . Stockholm , c1984. 173 p. : ISBN 91-38-90331-8 : LC Card 84-253511
HC375 .K655 1984

CITIES AND TOWNS - UNITED STATES.
Bowman, Thomas F. Finding your best place to live in America /. New York , c1981. xiii, 337 p. : ISBN 0-940162-00-8 (pbk.) : LC Card 81-51506 DDC 973.927 19
HT123 .B665 ***NYPL [Pub. Cat. 86-574]***

Cutter, Susan L. Rating places . Washington, D.C. , c1985. viii, 76 p. : ISBN 0-89291-191-3 (pbk.) : LC Card 85-13469 DDC 307/.0973 19
GF503 .C87 1985 ***NYPL [JLD 86-2715]***

CITIES AND TOWNS - UNITED STATES - CIVIC IMPROVEMENT.
McNulty, Robert H., 1940- The economics of amenity . Washington, D.C. , c1985. xvi, 157 p. : ISBN 0-941182-15-0 (pbk.) LC Card 85-6545 DDC 307.7/6/0973 19
HT321 .M36 1985 ***NYPL [JLE 86-4519]***

CITIES AND TOWNS - UNITED STATES - GROWTH - CASE STUDIES.
Growth management . Washington, D.C. , c1986. iv, 218 p. : ISBN 0-87420-655-3 (pbk.) LC Card 86-50332 DDC 307.1/4/0973 19
HD205 .G76 1986 ***NYPL [JLE 87-558]***

CITIES AND TOWNS - VENEZUELA - HISTORY.
Estaba, Rosa M. Geografía de los paisajes urbanos e industriales de Venezuela /. Caracas , c1985. 291 p., [4] folded leaves : ISBN 980-271-006-7 LC Card 86-148810 DDC 307.7/6/0987 19
HC237 .E766 1985 ***NYPL [JLD 86-2340]***

Citizen participation in public decision making / edited by Jack DeSario and Stuart Langton. Westport, Conn. : Greenwood Press, 1987. xii, 237 p. ; 22 cm. (Contributions in political science, 0147-1066 . no. 158) "Prepared under the auspices of the Policy Studies Organization." Includes index. Bibliography: p. [223]-228. ISBN 0-313-25478-8 (lib. bdg. : alk. paper) : LC Card 86-7571 DDC 323/.042/0973 19
1. Political participation - United States. 2. Technocracy. I. DeSario, Jack. II. Langton, Stuart. III. Policy Studies Organization. IV. Series.
JK1764 .C525 1987 ***NYPL [JLD 87-932]***

Citizens Budget Commission (New York, N.Y.)
Green, Cynthia B. Reducing New York State's deficit /. New York, N.Y. (110 E. 42nd St., New York 10017) [1986] ii leaves, 33 p. ; LC Card 87-108691 DDC 336.747 19
HJ2053.N7 G74 1986

Municipal tax policy in New York City : opportunities for reform / Citizens Budget Commission. New York, N.Y. (110 E. 42nd St., New York 10017) : The Commission, [1986] iii leaves, 25 p. ; 28 cm. "June 1986, volume 53, no. 4." Bibliography: p. 24-25. LC Card 87-110053 DDC 336.2/0097471 19
1. Taxation - New York (N.Y.). I. Title.
HJ9289.N4 C54 1986

New York City's capital program : how are the dollars being spent? / Citizens Budget Commission. New York, N.Y. (110 E. 42nd St., New York 10017) : The Commission, [1986] 17 leaves ; 28 cm. "January 1986." "Volume 53, no. 2." Bibliography: leaf 16. LC Card 87-110059 DDC 336.3/9/097471 19
1. Capital budget - New York (N.Y.). 2. Capital investments - New York (N.Y.). 3. New York (N.Y.) - Public works - Finance. I. Title.
HJ9289.N4 C54 1986a

Citizen's Clearinghouse for Hazardous Wastes (Arlington, Va.) Petersen, Sybil. Transportation . Arlington, Va. (P.O. Box 926, Arlington 22216) [1986] [8], 40 p. : LC Card 87-401670 DDC 363.1/7 19
HE199.5.D3 P48 1986

Citizens slaves, guest-workers . Gilani, Ijaz. Islamabad, Pakistan , c1985. 84 p. ; LC Card

85-931825 DDC 331.6/2/54 19
HD5856.S64 G55 1985

Un citoyen aux Etats-Généraux. Paris : Edhis, [1976] (Milan : Graphica Sipiel) 46 p. ; 23 cm. Facsim. Originally published: 1788. "Le tirage a été limité à 150 exemplaires numérotés sur papier verge à la main et 30 exemplaires hors commerce." LC Card 87-672450
1. Finance, Public - France - To 1789. 2. Confiscations - France.
HJ1082 .C57x 1976

CITRUS FRUIT INDUSTRY - BRAZIL - BAHIA (STATE)
Análise da citricultura na Bahia . Salvador , 1986. 88 p. : LC Card 86-221439
HD9259.C53 B63 1986

CITRUS FRUIT INDUSTRY - FLORIDA - FORECASTING.
Fairchild, Gary F. Florida citrus production trends 1986-87 through 1995-96. Gainesville, Fla. [1985] iv, 35 p. : LC Card 86-622647 DDC 338.1/7435/09759 19
HD9259.C53 U553 1985

CITRUS FRUIT INDUSTRY - ITALY, SOUTHERN - HISTORY.
Calcaterra, Francesco. Gli agrumi nella storia del Meridione . Roma , c1986. 95 p. : LC Card 87-133974
HD9259.C53 I723 1986

CITRUS FRUIT INDUSTRY - ITALY, SOUTHERN - HISTORY - SOURCES.
Calcaterra, Francesco. Gli agrumi nella storia del Meridione . Roma , c1986. 95 p. : LC Card 87-133974
HD9259.C53 I723 1986

Una città in cerca d'identità . Vernuccio, Pietro, 1947- Modica , 1984. 201 p., [12] p. of plates : LC Card 86-164886
HC308.M53 V47 1984

CITY AND TOWN LIFE.
Sequera, Armando José, 1953- Alegato contra el automóvil /. Caracas , 1985. 157 p. ; ISBN 980-222-019-1 : LC Card 87-107528 DDC 388.3/21 19
HE5613 .S46 1985

CITY AND TOWN LIFE - UNITED STATES.
Stirrings of culture /. Dallas, Tex. , 1986. xix, 250 p. ; ISBN 0-911005-07-2 : LC Card 86-24028 DDC 306 19
HM101 .S786 1986 *NYPL [JFF 87-151]*

CITY GOVERNMENT. see **MUNICIPAL GOVERNMENT.**

CITY LIFE. see **CITY AND TOWN LIFE.**

City of women . Stansell, Christine. Urbana , 1987, c1986. xiv, 301 p. ; ISBN 0-252-01481-2 (pbk.) LC Card 87-16163 DDC 305.4/2/097471 19
HD6096.N6 S8 1987

CITY PLANNING - ADDRESSES, ESSAYS, LECTURES.
Singer, Paul Israel, 1932- Economia politica e processi di urbanizzazione /. Venezia , 1978. xx, 132 p. ; *NYPL [JLD 86-786]*

CITY PLANNING - BANGLADESH - DHAKA.
Choguill, Charles L. New communities for urban squatters . New York , c1987. xiv, 213 p. : ISBN 0-306-42545-9 LC Card 86-30501 DDC 307.3/36 19
HD7361.6.D57 C46 1987

CITY PLANNING - BERLIN (GERMANY)
Homfeld, Wolfgang. Verkehrsberuhigung in Berlin (West) . Berlin , c1984. 306 p. : ISBN 3-496-00782-6 LC Card 84-212018
HE311.G32 B4753 1984

CITY PLANNING - BRAZIL - ADDRESSES, ESSAYS, LECTURES.
A Produção capitalista da casa (e da cidade) no Brasil industrial /. São Paulo , 1979. 166 p. : LC Card 80-100793
HD7323.A3 P76 1979 *NYPL [JLD 80-3858]*

CITY PLANNING - CALIFORNIA.
Local government mobilehome and mobilehome park policies in California . [Sacramento, Calif.] [1986] iii, 70 p. ; LC Card 86-622920 DDC 333.33/8 19
HD7289.62.U6 L63 1986

CITY PLANNING - CALIFORNIA - LOS ANGELES.
Bottles, Scott L. Los Angeles and the automobile . Berkeley , c1987. xiii, 301 p. : ISBN 0-520-05795-3 (alk. paper) LC Card 86-14660 DDC 388.4/1321/0979494 19
HE5634.L7 B68 1987

CITY PLANNING - DEVELOPING COUNTRIES.
Cubukgil, Adil. Urbanization in developing countries . [Toronto] , 1981. ii, 77 p. ; *NYPL [JLF 87-277]*

CITY PLANNING - FRANCE.
Lacour, Claude. Croissance urbaine . Paris , 1981. 219 p. : ISBN 2-222-02928-7 (pbk.) : LC Card 82-153821 DDC 388.4/068 19
HE4764 .L3 1981 *NYPL [JLG 86-56]*

CITY PLANNING - GERMANY, WEST - CITIZEN PARTICIPATION.
Herzog, Werner. Kartographie und Bürgerbeteiligung im Rahmen der vorbereitenden Bauleitplanung . Paderborn , 1986. xi, 164 p. : ISBN 3-506-71256-X LC Card 87-401386 DDC 333.73/17/028 19
HD108.6 .H47 1986

CITY PLANNING - GREAT BRITAIN.
Bruton, Michael J. Local planning in practice /. London , 1987. 452 p. : ISBN 0-09-165381-9 *NYPL [JLE 87-1201]*

Herington, John. The outer city /. London , New York , 1984. 205 p. : ISBN 0-06-318237-8 *NYPL [JLE 86-1465]*

Parker, Dennis J. Urban flood protection benefits . Aldershot, Hants, England , Brookfield, Vt., U. S.A. , c1987. xvii, 284 p. : ISBN 0-291-39707-7 LC Card 87-147842 DDC 363.3/49372 19
HD1676.G7 P37 1987

CITY PLANNING - INDIA.
Mills, Edwin S. Studies in Indian urban development /. New York , 1986. viii, 214 p. ; ISBN 0-19-520507-3 : LC Card 86-2489 DDC 307.1/4/0954 19
HT147.I5 M56 1986 *NYPL [JLE 86-3750]*

CITY PLANNING - INDIA - UTTAR PRADESH.
Chaurasia, B. P. (Bhanu Pratap) Urban land use and planning /. Allahabad, India , 1987. xxiii, 347 p. : ISBN 81-85076-20-0 : LC Card 87-900386 DDC 333.77/17/09542 19
HD879.U8 C53 1987

CITY PLANNING - ITALY - CONGRESSES.
La Politica comunitaria della casa. Roma, 1971. 227 p. LC Card 74-883223 *NYPL [JLD 72-3595]*

CITY PLANNING - ITALY - NAPLES.
Terremoto e crisi urbana . Napoli , 1981. 207 p. ; *NYPL [JLE 86-4532]*

CITY PLANNING - MEXICO - MEXICO CITY - HISTORY.
López Monjardín, Adriana. Hacia la ciudad del capital--México, 1790-1870 /. México, D.F. , 1985. 193 p. : LC Card 87-124857 DDC 330.972/53 19
HC138.M4 L66 1985

CITY PLANNING - NEW JERSEY.
Hudson Waterfront Walkway plan and design guidelines /. [Trenton, N.J.] , 1984] 136 p. : *NYPL [JLF 87-913]*

CITY PLANNING - RUSSIAN S.F.S.R. - MOSCOW - HISTORY.
Kreis, Barbara, 1947- Moskau, 1917-35 . [Germany] , c1985. 243 p., [3] p. of plates : ISBN 3-921420-26-1 : LC Card 86-170426
HD7345.M6 K73 1985

CITY PLANNING - RUSSIAN S.F.S.R. - MOSCOW REGION.
Geograficheskie problemy razvitiia narodnogo khoziaistva Moskovskogo regiona /. Moskva , 1986. 104 p. : LC Card 87-135959
HC338.M6 G46 1986

CITY PLANNING - SOUTH AFRICA - PINETOWN.
Stretch, C. The effectiveness of town planning in Natal . Pietermaritzburg, Natal, South Africa , 1986. 35 p. ; LC Card 86-159747 DDC 361.2/5/09684 s 307.1/2/096845 19
HC517.N3 A44 vol. 64 HT169.S62P56

CITY PLANNING - SOUTH AFRICA - UMHLANGA ROCKS.
Stretch, C. The effectiveness of town planning in Natal . Pietermaritzburg, Natal, South Africa , 1986. 35 p. ; LC Card 86-159747 DDC 361.2/5/09684 s 307.1/2/096845 19
HC517.N3 A44 vol. 64 HT169.S62P56

CITY PLANNING - SOVIET UNION.
Novikov, È. A. (Ènergiĭ Alekseevich) Gorod i prirodopol'zovanie /. Leningrad , 1984. 143 p. ; LC Card 85-125032
HC333.5 .N68 1984

CITY PLANNING - SPAIN - CONGRESSES.
Manual de servicios municipales . Barcelona , 1982. 340 p. ; ISBN 84-500-5399-4 LC Card 82-214246 DDC 363/.0946 19
HD4687 .M36 1982 *NYPL [JLC 86-139]*

CITY PLANNING - UNITED STATES.
Frieden, Bernard J. The politics of neglect . Cambridge, Mass. [1975] x, 281 p. ; ISBN 0-262-06061-2 LC Card 75-6792 DDC 309.2/62/0973
HT167 .F74 *NYPL [JLE 80-1135]*

McNulty, Robert H., 1940- The economics of amenity . Washington, D.C. , c1985. xvi, 157 p. : ISBN 0-941182-15-0 (pbk.) LC Card 85-6545 DDC 307.7/6/0973 19
HT321 .M36 1985 *NYPL [JLE 86-4519]*

Mayer, Harold Melvin, 1916- Land uses in American cities /. Champaign, Ill. [c1983] vi, 176 p. : ISBN 0-941226-02-6 (pbk.) LC Card 82-81036 DDC 333.77/13/0973 19
HD257 .M39 1983 *NYPL [JLD 86-3126]*

Tomioka, Seishiro. Planned unit developments . New York , c1984. xviii, 192 p. : ISBN 0-471-08595-2 : LC Card 82-13419 DDC 307/.12/0973 19
HD257 .T65 1984 *NYPL [JLF 86-1316]*

Weiss, Marc A. (Marc Allan) The rise of the community builders . New York , 1987. xii, 228 p. : ISBN 0-231-06504-3 LC Card 87-5115 DDC 333.77/17/0973 19
HD257 .W46 1987

CITY PLANNING - VENEZUELA.
Gilbert, Alan, 1944- The political economy of land . Aldershot, Hants , Brookfield, Vt., U. S.A. , c1985. xv, 163 p. : ISBN 0-566-00507-2 : LC Card 85-17535 DDC 333.77/13/0987 19
HD576 .G54 1985 *NYPL [JLD 86-3632]*

The city revolution . Hall, Maximilian. New York , 1987. xiii, 147 p. ; ISBN 0-312-00986-0 : LC Card 87-9684 DDC 332.6/0941 19
HG186.G7 H35 1987

CITY SURVEYING. see **SURVEYING.**

CITY TRAFFIC - BERLIN (GERMANY) - ENVIRONMENTAL ASPECTS.
Homfeld, Wolfgang. Verkehrsberuhigung in Berlin (West) . Berlin , c1984. 306 p. : ISBN 3-496-00782-6 LC Card 84-212018
HE311.G32 B4753 1984

CITY TRAFFIC - DENMARK.
Larsen, Flemming. Parkeringsbehov i ældre tætte bydele . København , 1985. 250 p. : LC Card 86-165642
HE336.P37 L37 1985

CITY TRAFFIC - ENVIRONMENTAL ASPECTS - BERLIN (GERMANY)
Homfeld, Wolfgang. Verkehrsberuhigung in Berlin (West) . Berlin , c1984. 306 p. : ISBN 3-496-00782-6 LC Card 84-212018
HE311.G32 B4753 1984

CITY TRAFFIC - MATHEMATICAL MODELS.
Pauck, Reinhard. Mikroökonomische Modelle des städtischen Verkehrs . Baden-Baden , 1983. 295 p. : ISBN 3-7890-0779-X LC Card 83-157997 DDC 388.4/0724 19
HE305 .P39 1983 *NYPL [JLD 87-977]*

CITY TRAFFIC - TEXAS.
Lomax, Timothy J. Relative mobility in Texas cities, 1975 to 1984 /. College Station, Tex. [1986] xiii, 30, 9 p. : LC Card 87-620994 DDC 380.5 s 388.4/1314/09764 19
HE203 .T43 no. 339-8 HE356.T4

CITY TRANSIT. see **LOCAL TRANSIT.**

City transport in developed and developing countries /. Rallis, Tom. New York , 1988. xiv, 202 p. : ISBN 0-312-00450-8 : LC Card 86-29789 DDC 388.4 19
HE305 .R35 1988

CITY TRANSPORTATION. see **URBAN TRANSPORTATION.**

City unions . Maier, Mark. New Brunswick [N.J.] , c1987. xii, 221 p. ; ISBN 0-8135-1229-8 (pbk.) : LC Card 86-26031 DDC 331.88/113520747/1 19
HD8005.2.U53 N46 1987

City University (London, England). Centre for the Study of Financial Institutions. Rutterford, Janette. The securities industry . [London] [1986] 93 p. : LC Card 87-160412 DDC 332.63/2/0941 19
HG5432 .R87 1986

CIVIC PLANNING. see **CITY PLANNING.**

CIVIC RIGHTS. see **POLITICAL RIGHTS.**

CIVICS, AMERICAN. see **CIVICS.**

CIVICS - STUDY AND TEACHING - SOUTHERN STATES - HISTORY - 19TH CENTURY.
Mitchell, Theodore R. Political education in the Southern Farmers' Alliance, 1887-1900 /. Madison, Wis. , 1987. xiv, 242 p. : ISBN 0-299-11470-8 : LC Card 87-40141 DDC 338.1/06/075 19
HD1485.N35 M58 1987

CIVIL ENGINEERING - MANAGEMENT. see **ENGINEERING - MANAGEMENT.**

CIVIL GOVERNMENT. see **POLITICAL SCIENCE.**

CIVIL LIBERTY. see **LIBERTY.**

CIVIL RIGHTS - CANADA.
Carter, D. D. The changing face of Canadian labour relations law /. Kingston, Ont., Canada , 1985. 15 p. ; ISBN 0-88886-126-5 (pbk.) LC Card 86-145328 DDC 331 s 344.71/01 331 s 347.1041 19
HD8102 .K52 no. 54 KE3009

Salhany, Roger E. The origin of rights /. Toronto , 1986. viii, 175 p. ; ISBN 0-459-38750-2 LC Card 86-177651 DDC 342.71/085 347.10285 19
KDZ574 .S25 1986 ***NYPL [JLE 87-1679]***

CIVIL RIGHTS - DEVELOPING COUNTRIES - CONGRESSES.
Les Libéraux et le dialogue Nord-Sud . Bonn , c1982. 220 p. ; ISBN 3-920590-36-8 LC Card 84-204748
HC59.7 .L4177 1982

CIVIL RIGHTS (INTERNATIONAL LAW)
Mower, A. Glenn (Alfred Glenn) International cooperation for social justice . Westport, Conn. , c1985. x, 271 p. ; ISBN 0-313-24702-1 (lib. bdg.) LC Card 84-27954 DDC 341.4/81 19
K3240.4 .M676 1985 ***NYPL [JLD 85-3575]***

CIVIL RIGHTS MOVEMENTS - SOUTH AFRICA.
Mandela, Winnie. Part of my soul /. Harmondsworth , 1985. 163 p., [8] p. of plates :
NYPL [Sc C 86-121]

Mandela, Winnie. Part of my soul went with him /. New York , 1985, c1984. 163 p., [8] p. of plates : ISBN 0-393-02215-3 : LC Card 85-21632 DDC 968/.00496 19
DT779.955.M36 A35 1985
NYPL [JFD 86-7717]

CIVIL RIGHTS - UNITED STATES.
Moral rights in the workplace /. Albany , c1987. xii, 312 p. ; ISBN 0-88706-362-4 LC Card 86-6949 DDC 331.25 19
HD6957.U6 M67 1987
NYPL [JLE 87-1197]

Salhany, Roger E. The origin of rights /. Toronto , 1986. viii, 175 p. ; ISBN 0-459-38750-2 LC Card 86-177651 DDC 342.71/085 347.10285 19
KDZ574 .S25 1986 ***NYPL [JLE 87-1679]***

Selected affirmative action topics in employment and business set-asides . Washington, D.C. , 1985-1986. 2 v. :
NYPL [JLM 86-600]

CIVIL SERVICE - CONGRESSES.
Public expenditure . Dublin, Ireland , 1986. 138 p. ; ISBN 0-906980-56-9 (pbk.) : LC Card 86-143826 DDC 336.3/9 19
HJ7461 .P83 1986 ***NYPL [JLD 87-553]***

CIVIL SERVICE PENSIONS - GERMANY, WEST.
Infratest Sozialforschung. Datenlage zur Alterssicherung . Bonn , 1984. 330 p. : LC Card 86-132439 DDC 331.25/2/0943 19
HD7105.35.G3 I54 1984

CIVIL SERVICE POSITIONS - BANGLADESH - CONGRESSES.
Career planning in Bangladesh . Dhaka , c1986. 159 p. ; LC Card 86-903477 DDC 331.7/02/095492 19
HF5382.5.B27 C37 1986

CIVIL SERVICE RECRUITING.
Aoiz Iriarte, María Rosario. Técnicas psicosociales en la administración pública . Alcalá de Henares, Madrid, España [1984] 238 p. : ISBN 84-7351-179-4 LC Card 85-189583
HF5549.5.S38 A57 1984

CIVIL SERVICE REFORM - UNITED STATES.
Fraud, waste, and abuse in government . Philadelphia , c1986. x, 159 p. ; ISBN 0-89727-058-4 LC Card 86-2967 DDC 336.73 19
HJ257.2 .F72 1986 ***NYPL [JLE 86-4153]***

CIVIL SERVICE - UNITED STATES - EXAMINATIONS.
Czukor, John C. Beginning office worker /. New York , c1988. 291 p. ; ISBN 0-13-072018-6 (pbk.) : LC Card 87-20740 DDC 651.3/7/076 19
HF5547.5 .B414 1988

CIVIL SERVICE - UNITED STATES - PERSONNEL MANAGEMENT.
Morrisey, George L. Performance appraisals in the public sector . Reading, Mass. , 1983. xiii, 172 p. ; ISBN 0-201-04847-7 (pbk.) : LC Card 83-6049 DDC 353.001/42 19
JK766.6 .M67 1983 ***NYPL [JLE 83-3164]***

CIVIL WAR - UNITED STATES. see **UNITED STATES - HISTORY - CIVIL WAR, 1861-1865.**

Civilian employment in the U. S.S.R., 1950 to 1983 /. Rapawy, Stephen. Washington, D.C. [1985] 35 leaves ; LC Card 87-601284 DDC 331.12/5/0947021 19
HD5796 .R358 1985

Civilisations et sociétés. For other vols. in this series, see entry in Old Catalog: Ecole pratique des hautes études, Paris. Sciences économiques et sociales, Section des. Civilisations et societés.
(71) Woronoff, Denis, 1939- L'industrie sidérurgique en France pendant la Révolution et l'Empire /. Paris , c1984. 592 p. : ISBN 2-7132-0843-2 LC Card 85-138825 DDC 338.4/76691/0944 19
HD9522.5 .W64 1984 ***NYPL [JLE 86-3532]***

A civilização da seca . Guerra, Paulo de Brito, 1914- Fortaleza , 1981. 324 p. : LC Card 82-231215 DDC 361.6/0981/3 19
HT395.B72 N63 1981 ***NYPL [JLD 86-2873]***

Civilizația socialistă : dimensiuni și confruntări contemporane / coordonator Al. Tănase. București : Editura Academiei Republicii Socialiste România, 1979. 289, [2] p., [1] leaf of plates : col. ill. ; 21 cm. At head of title: Academia de Științe Sociale și Politice. Institutul de Filozofie. Table of contents in Romanian, English, and Russian. Bibliography: p. 286-[290] LC Card 80-460491
1. Socialism - Addresses, essays, lectures. 2. Civilization, Modern - 1950- - Addresses, essays, lectures. I. Tănase, Alexandru.
HX56 .C48 ***NYPL [JLD 81-195]***

CIVILIZATION AND MACHINERY. see **TECHNOLOGY AND CIVILIZATION.**

CIVILIZATION AND TECHNOLOGY. see **TECHNOLOGY AND CIVILIZATION.**

CIVILIZATION, MODERN - 1950-
Lindner, Eberhard. Ausweg aus der Weltkrise . Karlsruhe , 1984. 319 p. : ISBN 3-921653-15-0 LC Card 85-104217 DDC 363.7 19
HD75.6 .L56 1984 ***NYPL [JLD 87-484]***

Toffler, Alvin. Previews & premises /. Montréal, Québec , 1984, c1983. 230 p. ; ISBN 0-920057-37-3 (pbk.)
NYPL [JFD 86-3191]

CIVILIZATION, MODERN - 1950- - ADDRESSES, ESSAYS, LECTURES.
Civilizația socialistă . București , 1979. 289, [2] p., [1] leaf of plates : LC Card 80-460491
HX56 .C48 ***NYPL [JLD 81-195]***

Comunicazione come dominio? /. Milano [1979] 147 p. ; ISBN 88-20-41548-8 : LC Card 79-395059 DDC 302.2/3
HM258 .C5896 ***NYPL [JLD 86-3359]***

CIVILIZATION, OCCIDENTAL - CONGRESSES.
Cambio cultural e imagen del hombre /. Bilbao, España , c1984. 248 p. ; ISBN 84-271-1384-6 LC Card 85-234026
CB245 .C29 1984 ***NYPL [JFD 86-6394]***

CIVILIZATION, WESTERN. see **CIVILIZATION, OCCIDENTAL.**

El civisme mundial i la pau /. Fontan, Pere. Barcelona , 1986. 104 p. : ISBN 84-7263-417-5 LC Card 86-186325
HF1411 .F592 1986

Civitas Resultate .
(v. 7) Economics and philosophy /. Tübingen , 1985. ix, 284 p. : ISBN 3-16-244944-8 LC Card 85-236925 DDC 330 19
HB72 .E27 1985 ***NYPL [JFE 86-2159]***

Civitas (Society) Economics and philosophy /. Tübingen , 1985. ix, 284 p. : ISBN 3-16-244944-8 LC Card 85-236925 DDC 330 19
HB72 .E27 1985 ***NYPL [JFE 86-2159]***

Claims processing for benefit plans, 1983 . Benefits Processing Institute (1983 : Hollywood, Fla.) Brookfield, Wis. , 1984. x, 82 p. : ISBN 0-89154-220-5 (pbk.) : LC Card 84-80454 DDC 331.25/5 19
HG9396 .B47 1984 ***NYPL [JLD 86-3940]***

Clandestine radio broadcasting . Soley, Lawrence C. New York , 1987. xiv, 384 p. ; ISBN 0-275-92259-6 (alk. paper) : LC Card 86-21169 DDC 384.54 19
HE8697.P6 S59 1986
NYPL [MWGH 87-1678]

Clapham, David. Public housing . London , Wolfeboro, N.H. , c1987. 174 p. : ISBN 0-7099-4826-3 : LC Card 86-24056 DDC 363.5/8 19
HD7288.78.G7 P83 1987

Clapp, John M. Real estate market analysis . New York , 1988. xvii, 350 p. : ISBN 0-275-92414-9 (alk. paper) : LC Card 87-15832 DDC 333.33/22 19
HD1382.5 .R396 1988

Clarijs, R. Caris, J. Fuseren in non-profit organisaties . Nijmegen , 1986. 107 p. : ISBN 90-255-0018-8 : LC Card 86-205531
HD2746.5 .C35 1986

Clark, Colin, 1905- National income and economic progress . New York , 1988. p. cm. ISBN 0-312-01566-6 : LC Card 87-24063 DDC 339.3 19
HB141.5 .N375 1988

CLARK, COLIN, 1905-
National income and economic progress . New York , 1988. p. cm. ISBN 0-312-01566-6 : LC Card 87-24063 DDC 339.3 19
HB141.5 .N375 1988

Clark, Colin Whitcomb, 1931- Conrad, Jon M. Natural resource economics . Cambridge [Cambridgeshire] , New York , 1987. x, 231 p. : ISBN 0-521-33188-9 LC Card 87-11582 DDC 333.7 19
HC59 .C693 1987

Clark, David, Ph. D. Information services in rural areas : prospects for telecommunications access / D. Clark, K.I. Unwin. Norwich [Norfolk] : Geo Books, c1980. x, 122 p. : ill., maps, forms ; 24 cm. Bibliography: p. 119-122. ISBN 0-86094-058-6 (pbk.) LC Card 81-149488
1. Telecommunication - England - Lincolnshire. 2. Communication and traffic - England - Lincolnshire. 3. Lincolnshire - Rural conditions. I. Unwin, K. I. II. Title.
HE8109.L55 C55 1980

Clark, Gordon L. Judges and the cities : interpreting local autonomy / Gordon L. Clark. Chicago : University of Chicago Press, c1985. xv, 247 p. ; 24 cm. Includes index. Bibliography: p. 231-242. ISBN 0-226-10753-1 : LC Card 85-1018 DDC 306/.0973 19
1. Social institutions - United States. 2. Local government - United States. 3. Social structure - United States. 4. Local government - Law and legislation - United States - Interpretation and construction. 5. Judicial process - United States. 6. Urban policy - United States. I. Title.
HN59.2 .C57 1985 ***NYPL [JLE 86-1068]***

Clark, Hal G. Illustrations of accounting for pensions and for settlements and curtailments of defined benefit pension plans : a survey of the application of FASB Statement nos. 87 & 88 / Hal G. Clark, Leonard Lorensen. New York, N.Y. (1211 Ave. of the Americas, New York 10036-8775) : American Institute of Certified Public Accountants, c1987. 34 p. ; 28 cm. (Financial report survey. [33]) Spine title: Illustrations of accounting for pensions. "March 1987"--Cover. LC Card 87-401762 DDC 657/.75 19
1. Pension trusts - United States - Accounting. 2. Old age pensions - United States - Accounting. I. Lorensen, Leonard. II. Title.
HF5686.O5 C56 1987

Clark, Ira G. Water in New Mexico : a history of its management and use / Ira G. Clark.1st ed. Albuquerque : University of New Mexico Press, c1987. xviii, 839 p. : ill. ; 27 cm. Bibliography: p. 787-808. Includes index. ISBN 0-8263-0923-2 LC Card 86-30819 DDC 333.91/009789 19
1. Water resources development - Government policy - New Mexico - History. I. Title.
HD1694.N6 C42 1987

Clark, J. R. (Jeff R.)
Macroeconomics : cost and choice / J.R. Clark, Michael Veseth. San Diego : Harcourt Brace Jovanovich, c1987. xv, 574 p. : ill. (some col.) ; 28 cm. Includes bibliographies and index. ISBN 0-15-551226-9 (pbk.) LC Card 86-83043 DDC 339 19
1. Macroeconomics. I. Veseth, Michael. II. Title.
HB172.5 .C585 1987

Microeconomics : cost and choice / J.R. Clark, Michael Veseth. San Diego : Harcourt Brace Jovanovich, c1987. xii, 454 p. : ill. ; 28 cm. Includes bibliographies and index. ISBN 0-15-551225-0 (pbk.) LC Card 86-83044 DDC 338.5 19
1. Microeconomics. I. Veseth, Michael. II. Title.
HB172 .C543 1987

Clark, James Leland, 1929-
HOW 4. Clark, James Leland, 1929- HOW 5 : a handbook for office workers / James L. Clark, Lyn R. Clark.5th ed. Boston, Mass. , c1988. ix, 370 p. : ISBN 0-534-87144-5 (pbk.) : LC Card 87-20155 DDC 651.7/402 19
HF5726 .C55 1988

HOW 5 : a handbook for office workers / James L. Clark, Lyn R. Clark.5th ed. Boston, Mass. : PWS-Kent Pub. Co., c1988. ix, 370 p. : ill. ; 23 cm. Rev. ed. of: HOW 4. 4th ed. c1985. Includes index. ISBN 0-534-87144-5 (pbk.) : LC Card 87-20155 DDC 651.7/402 19
1. Commercial correspondence - Handbooks, Manuals, etc. I. Clark, Lyn. II. Clark, James Leland, 1929- HOW 4. III. Title. IV. Title: HOW five.
HF5726 .C55 1988

Clark-James, Suzanne. Providing personal financial planning services in your CPA practice / by Suzanne Clark-James. New York, NY (11 Penn Plaza, New York 10001) : M. Bender, 1987. 1 v. (various pagings) : ill. ; 30 cm. (Accountant's workbook series) Includes index. LC Card 87-61984 DDC 657/.068/5 19
1. Finance, Personal. 2. Accountants. 3. Financial planners. I. Title. II. Series.
HG179 .C59 1987

Clark, John Garretson, 1932- Energy and the federal government : fossil fuel policies, 1900-1946 / John G. Clark. Urbana : University of Illinois Press, c1987. xxiii, 511 p. : ill. ; 24 cm. Includes index. Bibliography: p. 391-496. ISBN 0-252-01295-X LC Card 85-20505 DDC 333.8/2/0973 19
1. Energy policy - United States - History - 20th century. 2. Fuel trade - Government policy - United States - History - 20th century. 3. Fossil fuels - Government policy - United States - History - 20th century. I. Title.
HD9502.U52 C57 1987 ***NYPL [JLE 87-736]***

Clark, Jon, Ph.D. The process of technological change . Cambridge [Cambridgeshire] , New York , 1988. p. cm. ISBN 0-521-32303-7 LC Card 87-6641 DDC 658.5/14 19
HD45 .P757 1988

Clark, Kim B. The Uneasy alliance . Boston, Mass. , c1985. x, 485 p. : ISBN 0-87584-172-4 LC Card 85-8709 DDC 658.5 19
HD56 .U53 1985 ***NYPL [JLE 86-2361]***

Clark, Lyn. Clark, James Leland, 1929- HOW 5 . Boston, Mass. , c1988. ix, 370 p. : ISBN 0-534-87144-5 (pbk.) : LC Card 87-20155 DDC 651.7/402 19
HF5726 .C55 1988

Clark, Paul F., 1954- Forging a union of steel . Ithaca, N.Y. , c1987. vii, 153 p. : ISBN 0-87546-135-2 (pbk.) LC Card 87-21508 DDC 331.88/169142/0973 19
HD6515.I5 F58 1987

Clark, Peter A. Anglo-American innovation / Peter A. Clark. Berlin ; New York : Walter de Gruyter, 1987. ix, 404 p. : ill. ; 24 cm. (De Gruyter studies in organization . 9) Bibliography: p. [383]-400. Includes indexes. ISBN 0-89925-164-1 (U. S.) : LC Card 87-22221 DDC 338/.06 19
1. Technological innovations - Great Britain - Management. 2. Technological innovations - United States - Management. I. Title. II. Series.
HD45 .C52 1987

Clark, Rodney, 1945- Venture capital in Britain, America, and Japan / Rodney Clark. New York : St. Martin's Press, 1987. p. cm. Bibliography: p. Includes index. ISBN 0-312-00505-9 : LC Card 86-28001 DDC 332/.0415 19
1. Venture capital - Great Britain. 2. Venture capital - United States. 3. Venture capital - Japan. I. Title.
HG5432 .C58 1987

Clark, Susan E. Newman, Marie Mastin. The vital link . Washington, DC , c1986. vii, 48 p. : ISBN 0-931032-21-0 (pbk.) LC Card 86-200991 DDC 363.6/2/0973 19
HD9685.U5 N493 1986

Clark University (Worcester, Mass.). Program for International Development. Mohamed, Yagoub Abdalla. The North Kordofan rural water supply baseline survey /. Khartoum , 1982. xv, 152 p. : LC Card 85-981166
HD1699.S82 K875 1982

Clark, Wallace, 1926- Linen on the green : an Irish mill village, 1730-1982 / by Wallace Clark.2nd ed. Belfast : Universities Press (Belfast), 1983, c1982. xii, 183 p., [16] p. of plates : ill. ; 22 cm. Maps on lining papers. Bibliography: p. 172-173. Includes index. ISBN 0-9509042-0-1 LC Card 84-242010 DDC 338.4/76771164/0941629 19
1. Linen industry - Northern Ireland - Maghera Region (Londonderry) - History. 2. Maghera (Londonderry, Northern Ireland) - History. I. Title.
HD9930.G73 N625 1983

Clarke, John Innes. Population and development projects in Africa /. Cambridge [Cambridgeshire] , New York , 1985. xvi, 329 p. : ISBN 0-521-30527-6 LC Card 84-29323 DDC 304.6/096 19
HB2121.A3 P67 1985 ***NYPL [JLF 86-186]***

Clarke, Michael, 1945- Regulating the city : competition, scandal, and reform / Michael Clarke. Milton Keynes, Eng. ; Philadelphia, Pa. : Open University Press, 1986. 194 p. ; 24 cm. Includes bibliographical references and index. ISBN 0-335-15381-X LC Card 85-29715 DDC 332.1/09421/2 19
1. Financial institutions - England - London - Corrupt practices. 2. Financial institutions - Government policy - England - London. I. Title.
HG186.G7 C53 1985 ***NYPL [JLE 86-3357]***

Clarke, Peter S., 1941- Complete guide to loan documentation / Peter S. Clarke. Englewood Cliffs, N.J. : Prentice-Hall, c1986. xvii, 494 p. : forms ; 29 cm. Includes index. ISBN 0-13-160615-8 : LC Card 85-3519 DDC 332.1/753 19
1. Bank loans. 2. Bank loans - Forms. I. Title.
HG1641 .C55 1986 ***NYPL [JLF 86-1464]***

Clarke, R. V. G. The Reasoning criminal . New York , c1986. xiv, 246 p. : ISBN 0-387-96272-7 : LC Card 86-1275 DDC 364.3 19
HV6080 .R38 1986 ***NYPL [JLE 86-3522]***

Clarke, Roger. The Economics of the firm /. Oxford [Oxfordshire] , New York, NY, USA , 1987. p. cm. ISBN 0-631-14075-1 : LC Card 86-27057 DDC 338.6 19
HD2326 .E243 1987

La Clase obrera argentina : cambios y tendencias. Buenos Aires : Editorial Anteo, 1986. 136 p. ; 20 cm. "Trabajo realizado por el Seminario 'Sobre la Clase Obrera en la Argentina' realizado por el Centro de Estudios Marxistas-Leninistas 'Victorio Codovilla' en común con Revista internacional, los días 26, 27 y 28 de junio de 1985, coordinador, Amado Heller"--T.p. verso. Includes bibliographical references. LC Card 86-206788
1. Labor and laboring classes - Argentina - Congresses. 2. Trade-unions - Argentina - Congresses. I. Seminario "Sobre la Clase Obrera en la Argentina" (1985 : Buenos Aires, Argentina).
HD8266.5 .C57 1986

Clases, segregación y barrios /. Mosquera Torres, Gilma. Cali, Colombia , 1984. 126 p. : LC Card 86-218143
HD7325.V35 M67 1984

Clases sociales y acción obrera en Chile / Francisco Zapata, compilador. 1a ed. México, D.F. : Colegio de México, Centro de Estudios Sociológicos, 1986. 230 p. ; 17 cm. (Jornadas. 110) Includes bibliographies. ISBN 968-12-0326-7 LC Card 87-404023 DDC 331/.0983 19
1. Labor and laboring classes - Chile. 2. Trade-unions - Chile. I. Zapata, Francisco. II. Series.
HD8296.5 .C57 1986

Clasicos agrarios.
George, Henry, 1839-1897. [Progress and poverty. Spanish.] Progreso y miseria /. [Madrid , 1985?] cxv, 384 p. : ISBN 84-7479-375-0 : LC Card 87-112201
HB171 .G276 1985

Clasing, Henry K. The secrets of a professional futures trader / by Henry Clasing. Brightwaters, N.Y. : Windsor Books, c1987. 231 p. : ill. ; 29 cm. ISBN 0-930233-15-8 LC Card 87-166047 DDC 332.64/4 19
1. Financial futures. 2. Commodity exchanges. 3. Put and call transactions. I. Title.
HG6024.A3 C58 1987

Class and culture.
Edsforth, Ronald, 1948- Class conflict and cultural consensus . New Brunswick, N.J. , c1987. xvi, 294 p. ; ISBN 0-8135-1184-4 LC Card 86-7955 DDC 330.9774/37 19
HC108.F55 E37 1987 ***NYPL [JLE 87-978]***

Gabler, Edwin, 1949- The American telegrapher . New Brunswick, NJ , c1988. p. cm. ISBN 0-8135-1284-0 : LC Card 87-19878 DDC 331.89/2813841/0973 19
HD5325 .T252 1883

Janiewski, Dolores E., 1948- Sisterhood denied . Philadelphia , 1985. xvii, 248 p. : ISBN 0-87722-361-0 : LC Card 84-2640 DDC 305.4/2/09756563 19
HD6073.T62 U65 1985
NYPL [Sc E 86-322]

Class and health : research and longitudinal data / edited by Richard G. Wilkinson. London ; New York : Tavistock Publications, 1986. x, 223 p. : ill. ; 25 cm. Includes bibliographies and indexes. ISBN 0-422-60360-0 : LC Card 86-5972 DDC 362.1/0941 19
1. Social medicine - Great Britain. 2. Mortality - Great Britain. 3. Social classes - Great Britain. 4. Social medicine - Great Britain - Longitudinal studies. 5. Mortality - Great Britain - Longitudinal studies. 6. Social classes - Great Britain - Longitudinal studies. I. Wilkinson, Richard G.
RA418.3.G7 C56 1986 ***NYPL [JLE 87-505]***

CLASS CONFLICT. see SOCIAL CONFLICT.

Class conflict and cultural consensus . Edsforth, Ronald, 1948- New Brunswick, N.J. , c1987. xvi, 294 p. ; ISBN 0-8135-1184-4 LC Card 86-7955 DDC 330.9774/37 19
HC108.F55 E37 1987 ***NYPL [JLE 87-978]***

Class conflict and the crisis of feudalism . Hilton, R. H. (Rodney Howard), 1916- London , Ronceverte, W. Va. , 1985. 349 p. ; ISBN 0-907628-36-2 : LC Card 85-21855 DDC 305.5/0942 19
HD604 .H48 1985 ***NYPL [JFE 87-391]***

CLASS CONSCIOUSNESS.
Carter, Bob, 1949- Capitalism, class conflict, and the new middle class /. London , Boston , 1985. vii, 256 p., 15 p. ; ISBN 0-7100-9624-0 : LC Card 84-9956 DDC 305.5/56 19
HD8039.M39 C37 1985
NYPL [JLD 87-115]

CLASS CONSCIOUSNESS - GERMANY (WEST)
Voss, G. Günter. Bewusstsein ohne Subjekt? . Grosshesselohe , 1984. vi, 512 p. : ISBN 3-924346-07-0 : LC Card 85-131494
HD6957.G35 V67 1984

CLASS CONSCIOUSNESS - UNITED STATES - HISTORY - 20TH CENTURY.

Fantasia, Rick. Cultures of solidarity . Berkeley , c1988. p. cm. ISBN 0-520-06053-9 (alk. paper) LC Card 87-16748 DDC 331.8/0973 19
HD8072.5 .F36 1988

CLASS DISTINCTION. see **SOCIAL CLASSES.**

Class formation in the plantation system /. Bhowmik, Sharit, 1948- New Delhi , 1981. xix, 263 p. : LC Card 81-903777 DDC 305/.93633 19
HD1470.5.I42 J342 1981
NYPL [JLD 86-2612]

Class, politics and the economy /. Clegg, Stewart. London , Boston , 1986. viii, 451 p. ; ISBN 0-7102-0452-3 : LC Card 85-8369 DDC 305.5 19
HT609 .C62 1986 *NYPL [JLD 87-459]*

Class, structure, and knowledge . Abercrombie, Nicholas. London , 1980. 196 p. ; ISBN 0-8147-0571-5 : *NYPL [JLD 80-2963]*

CLASS STRUGGLE. see **SOCIAL CONFLICT.**

Classes sociais e agricultura no Nordeste /. Andrade, Manuel Correia de Oliveira. Recife , 1985. 105 p. ; ISBN 85-7019-096-4 LC Card 87-119335
HD1875.P4 A84 1985

Classes sociais nos campos . Almeida, João Ferreira de. Lisboa [1986] 544 p. : LC Card 87-400121 DDC 305.5/63 19
HD1536.P77 A44 1986

CLASSES, SOCIAL. see **SOCIAL CLASSES.**

Classical economics /. Hollander, Samuel. Oxford [Oxfordshire] , New York, NY, USA , 1987. xiv, 485 p. : ISBN 0-631-13435-2 : LC Card 87-8004 DDC 330.15/3 19
HB94 .H65 1987

Classical political economy : a survey of recent literature / edited by William O. Thweatt. Boston : Kluwer Academic Publishers, c1988. viii, 275 p. : ill. ; 24 cm. (Recent economic thought) Includes bibliographies and indexes. ISBN 0-89838-229-7 : LC Card 87-3394 DDC 330.15/3 19
1. Classical school of economics. 2. Marxian economics. I. Thweatt, William O. II. Series.
HB94 .C42 1988

CLASSICAL SCHOOL OF ECONOMICS.

Classical political economy . Boston , c1988. viii, 275 p. : ISBN 0-89838-229-7 : LC Card 87-3394 DDC 330.15/3 19
HB94 .C42 1988

Elsner, Wolfram. Ökonomische Institutionenanalyse . Berlin , c1986. xv, 469 p. : ISBN 3-428-06035-0 LC Card 86-206447
HB99.5 .E47 1986

Gomes, Leonard. Foreign trade and the national economy . New York , 1987. viii, 323 p. ; ISBN 0-312-00765-5 : LC Card 87-4674 DDC 382 19
HF1008 .G65 1987

Hollander, Samuel. Classical economics /. Oxford [Oxfordshire] , New York, NY, USA , 1987. xiv, 485 p. : ISBN 0-631-13435-2 : LC Card 87-8004 DDC 330.15/3 19
HB94 .H65 1987

Hsieh, Ching-Yao, 1917- A search for synthesis in economic theory /. Armonk, N.Y. , c1985. xii, 268 p. : ISBN 0-87332-328-9 LC Card 84-29816 DDC 330.1 19
HB71 .H73 1985 *NYPL [JLE 87-315]*

Malthus, T. R. (Thomas Robert, 1766-1834. Essays on political economy /. London , 1986. 327 p. : ISBN 1-85196-107-0 LC Card 87-672114
HB861 .A2x 1986 vol. 7

Malthus, T. R. (Thomas Robert, 1766-1834. Principles of political economy . London , 1986. 2 v. (18, x, 439 p.) : ISBN 1-85196-105-4 (v. 1) LC Card 87-672115
HB861 .A2x 1986 vol. 5-6

Malthus, T. R. (Thomas Robert, 1766-1834. Principles of political economy /. Cambridge , New York , 1987. p. cm. ISBN 0-521-32363-0 (set) LC Card 86-32742 DDC 330.15/3 19
HB161 .M25 1987

Porta, Pier Luigi. Scuola classica e teoria economica /. Milano , 1984. xi, 145 p. ; ISBN 88-14-00004-2 : LC Card 84-177305 DDC 330.15/3 19
HB167 .P67 1984 *NYPL [JLE 86-4055]*

Schmidt, Christian, 1950- Essai sur l'économie ricardienne /. Paris , 1984. 168 p. ; ISBN 2-7178-0693-8 : LC Card 84-218068
HB103.R5 S25 1984

CLASSICAL SCHOOL OF ECONOMICS - CONGRESSES.

Studien zur Entwicklung der ökonomischen Theorie /. Berlin , c1981- v. ; ISBN 3-428-04862-8 (v. 1) : LC Card 81-154218 DDC 330/.09 19
HB75 .S787 1981
NYPL [JLL 73-186 Bd.115]

Classification by broad economic categories : defined in terms of SITC rev. 3 / Department of International Economic and Social Affairs, Statistical Office. New York : United Nations, 1986. x, 68 p. ; 28 cm. (Statistical papers. Series M . no. 53, rev. 2) "ST/ESA/STAT/SER.M/53/rev. 2." "United Nations publication sales no. E.86.XVII.24"--T.p. verso. ISBN 92-1-161276-4 (pbk.) LC Card 87-401426 DDC 338/.02/012 19
1. Commercial products - Classification. I. United Nations. Statistical Office. II. Standard international trade classification revision 3. III. Series: Statistical papers. Series M , no. 53.
HF1041 .C53 1986

Classification guide for commercial building construction. 3rd ed. [New York, N.Y.?] : Premium Audit Advisory Service, c1986. 72 p. : ill. ; 28 cm. Page 72 blank. Includes index. LC Card 87-119406 DDC 368.4/1 19
1. Construction workers - United States - Classification. 2. Construction workers - United States - Code numbers. 3. Workers' compensation - United States - Classification. 4. Workers' compensation - United States - Code numbers. I. Premium Audit Advisory Service.
HD7116.R3152 U63 1986

Classification guide for street and road construction / [Premium Audit Advisory Service]. 2nd ed. New York, NY : American Insurance Services Group, c1986. 44 p. : ill. ; 28 cm. Includes index. LC Card 86-232165 DDC 368.4/1 19
1. Road construction workers - United States - Classification - Code numbers. 2. Workers' compensation - United States - Classification - Code numbers. I. Premium Audit Advisory Service.
HD7116.R62 U63 1986

Clatanoff, Robert M. Patterns of property tax administration in the United States / by Robert M. Clatanoff. Chicago, Ill. : International Association of Assessing Officers, Research and Technical Services Dept., 1986. x, 178 p. : col. maps ; 28 cm. (Research and information series . no. 5) "June 1986." Bibliography: p. 177-178. ISBN 0-88329-145-2 (pbk.) LC Card 86-7240 DDC 353.9/37242 19
1. Property tax - United States - States. 2. Assessment - United States - States. 3. Tax administration and procedure - United States - States. I. Title. II. Series.
HJ4120 .C528 1986 *NYPL [JLF 87-464]*

Clausen, Hermann. Landwirtschaftliche Übergangsbetriebe in Niedersachsen . Göttingen , 1985. xiii, 105 p. ; LC Card 86-185987
HD9013.7.L68 L36 1985

Clauss, Rüdiger, 1952- Marketing der Unternehmen des öffentlichen Personen, nahverkehrs im Spannungsfeld erwerbswirtschaftlicher und gemeinwirtschaftlicher Ziele / Rüdiger Clauss. 1. Aufl. Bergisch Gladbach : J. Eul, 1985. xiii, 308 p. : ill. ; 21 cm. Originally presented as the author's thesis (doctoral--Universität Köln, 1984) Bibliography: p. 292-308. ISBN 3-89012-019-9 LC Card 85-175468
1. Transportation - Germany (West) - Marketing. 2. Transportation - Germany, West - Passenger traffic. 3. Transportation and state - Germany, West. I. Title.
HE249 .C42 1985

Clavera, Joan.

Clavera, Joan. La viticultura catalana davant la integració a la Comunitat Europea /. [Barcelona] [1986] 124 p. : ISBN 6-476-84021-8 LC Card 86-200618
HD9259.G7 S693 1986

La viticultura catalana davant la integració a la Comunitat Europea / Joan Clavera, Jordi Bacaria. [Barcelona] : Caixa de Pensions, Obra Social, Agrícola, [1986] 124 p. : ill. (some col.) ; 25 cm. "Obra Agrícola de la Caixa de Pensions." Bibliography: p. 119. ISBN 6-476-84021-8 LC Card 86-200618
1. Grape industry - Spain - Catalonia. 2. Wine industry - Spain - Catalonia. 3. European Economic Community - Spain - Catalonia. I. Clavera, Joan. II. Bacaria, Jordi. III. Caja de Pensiones para la Vejez y de Ahorros. Obra Agrícola. IV. Title.
HD9259.G7 S693 1986

CLAY INDUSTRIES - PORTUGAL - FINANCE.

Almeida, João Carreira. Fabricação de materiais de barro para construção . Lisboa , 1978. 186 p., [3] leaves of plates (one folded) : LC Card 82-112167 DDC 338.4/36914/09469 19
HD9596.P82 A85 1978

Clay, Jason W. Politics and the Ethiopian famine, 1984-1985 / by Jason W. Clay and Bonnie K. Holcomb. Cambridge, MA (11 Divinity Ave., Cambridge 02138) : Cultural Survival, 1985. xi, 250 p. : ill. ; 28 cm. (Occasional papers . 20) Bibliography: p. 247-250. LC Card 86-153948 DDC 363.8/56/0963 19
1. Famines - Ethiopia. 2. Refugees - Ethiopia. 3. Agriculture and state - Ethiopia. 4. Ethiopia - Politics and government - 1974-. I. Holcomb, Bonnie K. II. Series: Occasional paper / Cultural Survival Inc. , 20. III. Title.
HC845.Z9 F33 1985 *NYPL [JLF 87-364]*

Clay, John R.

Accounting for S corporations and noncorporate entities : a self-study course based upon Guide to compilation and review engagements / authors John R. Clay, Marilyn Rutledge, Barbara Gargiulo ; contributing authors Dennis R. Meals, Dan M. Guy. Fort Worth, Tex. : PPC-CPE, c1987. 1 v. (various pagings) ; 28 cm. (PPC self-study library) LC Card 87-163295 DDC 657/.95/076 19
1. Corporations - United States - Accounting. 2. Accounting - Problems, exercises, etc. I. Rutledge, Marilyn. II. Gargiulo, Barbara. III. Meals, Dennis R. Guide to compilation and review engagements. IV. Title. V. Title: S corporations and noncorporate entities. VI. Series.
HF5686.C7 C58 1987

Advanced compilation and review : practice problems and solutions : a self-study course based upon Guide to compilation and review engagements / authors, John R. Clay, Marilyn Rutledge, Barbara Gargiulo ; contributing authors, Dennis R. Meals, Dan M. Guy. Fort Worth, Tex. : Practitioners Pub. Co., c1987. 1 v. (various pagings) : ill. ; 28 cm. (PPC self-study CPE) Cover title: Advanced compilation & review. Includes bibliographies. LC Card 87-160681 DDC 657/.3 19
1. Financial statements, Unaudited. 2. Financial statements, Unaudited - Problems, exercises, etc. I. Rutledge, Marilyn. II. Gargiulo, Barbara. III. Meals, Dennis R. Guide to compilation and review engagements. IV. Title. V. Title: Advanced compilation & review. VI. Series.
HF5667.65 .M42 1986 Suppl.

Guide to preparing financial statements / by John R. Clay, Stephen D. Holton ; with contributing editors, Doug Carmichael, Marilyn Rutledge. 1987 ed. Fort Worth, Tex. : Practitioners Pub. Co., c1987- 2 v. (loose-leaf) ; 30 cm. + trends volume. Includes index. LC Card 87-161098 DDC 657/.3 19
1. Financial statements. I. Holton, Stephen D. II. Carmichael, D. R. Douglas R.), 1941-. III. Rutledge, Marilyn. IV. Title.
HF5681.B2 C565 1987

Meals, Dennis R. Guide to compilation and review engagements /. Fort Worth, Tex. , c1986- 3 v. (loose-leaf) : LC Card 86-224183 DDC 657/.3 19
HF5667.65 .M42 1986

Clayton, E. (Eric) Agriculture, poverty, and freedom in developing countries / Eric Clayton. London : Macmillan, 1983. x, 277 p. : ill. ; 23 cm. (Macmillan international college edition) Bibliography: p. [240]-258. Includes index. ISBN 0-333-36100-8 LC Card 86-673664
1. Agriculture - Economic aspects - Developing countries. I. Title.
HD1417 .C52x 1983

Clayton, Lawrence A. Grace : W.R. Grace & Co. : the formative years, 1850-1930 / Lawrence A. Clayton. Ottawa, Ill. : Jameson

Books, c1985. xiii, 403 p., [32] p. of plates : ill., maps ; 23 cm. Includes index. Bibliography: p. 387-394. ISBN 0-915463-25-3 LC Card 85-14856 DDC 338.8/8885 19
1. W.R. Grace & Co. - History. 2. International business enterprises - Peru - History. 3. International business enterprises - Latin America - History. 4. United States - Foreign economic relations - Latin America. 5. Latin America - Foreign economic relations - United States. I. Title.
HD9505.P4 C43 1986 ***NYPL [JLE 86-3892]***

CLEANERS (COMPOUNDS) see **CLEANING COMPOUNDS.**

Cleaning and contaminant monitoring systems for the semiconductor industry : a business opportunity analysis. San Jose, CA (1754 Technology Dr., Suite 226, San Jose 95110) : VLSI Research, c1986. 1 v. (various pagings) : ill. ; 28 cm. "April 1986." Includes bibliographies. LC Card 87-114689 DDC 380.1/4562138152
1. Cleaning compounds industry. 2. Cleaning machinery and appliances industry. 3. Semiconductors - Cleaning - Equipment and supplies. 4. Market surveys. I. VLSI Research, Inc.
HD9999.C4862 C55 1986

CLEANING AND DYEING INDUSTRY - SOUTH AFRICA - STATISTICS.
Sensus van wassery-, skoonmaak- en kleurdienste, 1980 =. Pretoria [1984?] xiv, 59 p., [1] folded leaf of plates : ISBN 0-621-08730-0 : LC Card 86-122444
HD9999.L383 S67 1984

CLEANING COMPOUNDS INDUSTRY.
Cleaning and contaminant monitoring systems for the semiconductor industry . San Jose, CA (1754 Technology Dr., Suite 226, San Jose 95110) , c1986. 1 v. (various pagings) : LC Card 87-114689 DDC 380.1/4562138152
HD9999.C4862 C55 1986

CLEANING COMPOUNDS INDUSTRY - UNITED STATES.
Promotion strategies for household cleaning products. New York, N.Y. , c1983. 2 v. (xx, 635 p.) ; LC Card 87-142358 DDC 381/.456671/0973 19
HD9999.C4863 U56 1983

CLEANING COMPOUNDS - MARKETING.
Promotion strategies for household cleaning products. New York, N.Y. , c1983. 2 v. (xx, 635 p.) ; LC Card 87-142358 DDC 381/.456671/0973 19
HD9999.C4863 U56 1983

CLEANING MACHINERY AND APPLIANCES INDUSTRY.
Cleaning and contaminant monitoring systems for the semiconductor industry . San Jose, CA (1754 Technology Dr., Suite 226, San Jose 95110) , c1986. 1 v. (various pagings) : LC Card 87-114689 DDC 380.1/4562138152
HD9999.C4862 C55 1986

CLEANING PREPARATIONS. see **CLEANING COMPOUNDS.**

CLEANLINESS. see **SANITATION.**

Clear & simple filing and records management /. Taylor, Mary Sue, 1938- New York, NY , c1987. 171 p. : ISBN 0-671-62397-4 (pbk.) : LC Card 86-28534 DDC 651.5 19
HF5736 .T388 1987

Clear and simple filing and records management. Taylor, Mary Sue, 1938- Clear & simple filing and records management /. New York, NY , c1987. 171 p. : ISBN 0-671-62397-4 (pbk.) : LC Card 86-28534 DDC 651.5 19
HF5736 .T388 1987

CLEAR-CUTTING - LATIN AMERICA.
Shane, Douglas R. Hoofprints on the forest . Philadelphia , c1986. xvi, 159 p. ; ISBN 0-89727-054-1 : LC Card 83-26585 DDC 338.1/76213/098 19
HD9433.L292 S53 1984
NYPL [JLD 86-2289]

CLEARING AGREEMENTS. see **INTERNATIONAL CLEARING.**

CLEARING-HOUSE. see **CLEARINGHOUSE.**

CLEARING, INTERNATIONAL. see **INTERNATIONAL CLEARING.**

CLEARING OF SECURITIES - UNITED STATES.
Financial Industry Securities Council Same Day Funds Settlement Task Force. Same day funds settlement for securities transactions . [New York, N.Y.] [S.l.] , c1985. 61 leaves in various foliations : LC Card 85-193287 DDC 332.64 19
HG4631 .F56 1985 ***NYPL [JLF 86-919]***

CLEARINGHOUSE.
Vrsaljko, Krešimir. Teorija i praksa domaćih i medunarodnih plaćanja /. Zagreb , 1982. xiv, 460 p. ; LC Card 84-160248
HG2341.Y82 V77 1982

CLEARINGHOUSE - DATA PROCESSING.
ACH receivers handbook. Washington, D.C. (1901 L St., N.W., Suite 640, Washington 20036) , c1986. 104 p. : LC Card 87-112783 DDC 332.1/028 19
HG2306 .A25 1986

CLEARINGHOUSE - UNITED STATES.
Introduction to ACH corporate payments /. Washington, D.C. (1901 L St., N.W., Suite 640, Washington 20036) [c1986] 90 p. : LC Card 86-222675 DDC 332.1/028 19
HG1710 .I58 1986

CLEARINGHOUSE - UNITED STATES - DATA PROCESSING.
ACH marketing handbook. [Washington, DC] (1901 L St., NW, Suite 640, Washington 20036) [c1987] 123, [24] p. ; LC Card 87-130512 DDC 332.1/028 19
HG4028.C45 A28 1987

CLEARINGHOUSE - UNITED STATES - EVALUATION.
Guide to ACH processor selection & evaluation . Washington, D.C. (Suite 640, 1901 L St., N.W., Washington 20036) , c1987. v, 199 p. ; LC Card 87-402621 DDC 332.1/028 19
HG2322 .G85 1987

CLEARINGHOUSE - YUGOSLAVIA.
Vrsaljko, Krešimir. Teorija i praksa domaćih i medunarodnih plaćanja /. Zagreb , 1982. xiv, 460 p. ; LC Card 84-160248
HG2341.Y82 V77 1982

Cleaves, Peter S. Professions and the state : the Mexican case / Peter S. Cleaves. Tucson : University of Arizona Press, c1987. xv, 147 p. : ill. ; 24 cm. (Profmex monograph series) Bibliography: p. 131-144. Includes index. ISBN 0-8165-1016-4 (alk. paper) LC Card 87-5911 DDC 331.7/12/0972 19
1. Professional employees - Government policy - Mexico. 2. Professions - Government policy - Mexico. 3. Professional education - Mexico. 4. Economists - Mexico - Political activity. 5. Petroleum engineers - Mexico - Political activity. 6. Agriculturists - Mexico - Political activity. 7. Physicians - Mexico - Political activity. 8. Trade and professional associations - Mexico. 9. Trade-unions - Professional employees - Mexico. I. Title. II. Series.
HD8038.M6 C55 1987

Clegg, Chris W. The Human side of advanced manufacturing technology /. Chichester [West Sussex] , New York , c1987. xi, 205 p. : ISBN 0-471-90867-3 : LC Card 86-32554 DDC 331.25 19
HD9720.5 .H85 1987

Clegg, Hugh Armstrong. A history of British trade unions since 1889 / by Hugh Armstrong Clegg. Oxford : Clarendon Press ; New York : Oxford University Press, <1987- c1985- > p. cm. Bibliography: v. 2, p. Includes index. CONTENTS. - -- v. 2. 1911-1933. ISBN 0-19-828307-5 (pbk. : v. 2) : LC Card 87-15229 DDC 331.88/0941 19
1. Trade-unions - Great Britain - History. I. Title.
HD6664 .C3864 1987

Clegg, James. The Bolton Gas Company, 1818-1872 : an historical retrospect / by James Clegg. Bolton : Daily Chronicle Steam-Printing Works, 1872. 46 p. ; 22 cm. "Re-printed, with additions, from the Bolton Chronicle of Sept. 7, 14, and 21, 1872." LC Card 85-666285
1. Bolton Gas Company (Bolton, Greater Manchester) - History. 2. Gas companies - England - Bolton (Greater Manchester). I. Title.
HD9581.G74 B64x 1872

Clegg, Jeremy, 1955- Multinational enterprise and world competition : a comparative study of the USA, Japan, the UK, Sweden, and West Germany / Jeremy Clegg ; foreword by John H. Dunning. New York : St. Martin's Press, 1987. xiv, 206 p. : ill. ; 23 cm. Based on the author's thesis (Ph. D.)--Reading University, 1985. Bibliography: p. 194-202. Includes index. ISBN 0-312-00852-X : LC Card 87-4735 DDC 338.8/8 19
1. International business enterprises - Case studies. 2. Competition, International - Case studies. I. Title.
HD2755.5 .C54 1987

Clegg, Stewart. Class, politics and the economy / Stewart Clegg, Paul Boreham, Geoff Dow. London ; Boston : Routledge & K. Paul, 1986. viii, 451 p. ; 23 cm. Includes indexes. Bibliography: p. 391-428. ISBN 0-7102-0452-3 : LC Card 85-8369 DDC 305.5 19
1. Marxian school of sociology. 2. Marxian economics. I. Boreham, Paul. II. Dow, Geoff. III. Title.
HT609 .C62 1986 ***NYPL [JLD 87-459]***

Cleland, David I. Project management handbook /. New York , 1988. p. cm. ISBN 0-442-22114-2 LC Card 87-23151 DDC 658.4/04 19
HD69.P75 P75 1988

Cleland, J. G. (John G.) World Fertility Survey . Oxford [Oxfordshire] , New York , 1986. p. cm. ISBN 0-19-828525-6 : LC Card 86-23483 DDC 304.6/32/0732 19
HB901 .H664 1986

Clemens, Reinhard.
Albach, Horst. Kosten der Arbeit . Stuttgart , c1985. xi, 179 p. : ISBN 3-7910-5003-6 : LC Card 86-162885 DDC 658.3/00943 19
HD5029 .A43 1985
NYPL [JLL 73-505 Nr.2]

Standortprobleme von Industrieunternehmen in Ballungsräumen : eine empirische Untersuchung im IHK-Bezirk Dortmund unter besonderer Berücksichtigung der Unternehmensgrösse / Reinhard Clemens, Hermann Tengler. Göttingen : O. Schwartz, c1983. xviii, 257 p. : ill. ; 21 cm. (Beiträge zur Mittelstandsforschung . Heft 93) Bibliography: p. 253-257. ISBN 3-509-01330-1 LC Card 83-198706
1. Dortmund Metropolitan Area (Germany) - Economic conditions. 2. Dortmund Metropolitan Area (Germany) - Industries. 3. Dortmund Metropolitan Area (Germany) - Economic policy. I. Tengler, Hermann. II. Title. III. Series.
HC289.D6 C54 1983

Clemensen, A. Berle. Illinois and Michigan Canal National Heritage Corridor, Illinois : historical inventory, history, and significance / by A. Berle Clemensen. [Denver, Colo.] : National Park Service, Denver Service Center, [1985] ix, 109 p. : map ; 28 cm. "July 1985." Bibliography: p. 98-108. LC Card 85-603278 DDC 386/.48/097732 19
1. Illinois and Michigan Canal (Ill.) - History. 2. Illinois and Michigan Canal National Heritage Corridor (Ill.) - Economic conditions. I. United States. National Park Service. Denver Service Center. II. Title.
HE396.I4 C56 1985

Clement, Hermann. Entwicklungsmöglichkeiten des deutsch-sowjetischen Handels in der zweiten Hälfte der 80er Jahre vor dem Hintergrund der sowjetischen Planung / Hermann Clement. München : Osteuropa-Institut München, 1986. 14 leaves ; 29 cm. (Arbeiten aus dem Osteuropa-Institut München . Nr. 112) "Vortrag gehalten vor der Arbeitsgruppe der Kommission der Bundesrepublik Deutschland und der Union der Sozialistischen Sowjetrepubliken für Wirtschaftliche und Wissenschaftlich-Technische Zusammenarbeit am 10. Januar 1986 in Moskau." Includes bibliographical references. LC Card 86-167481
1. Germany (West) - Commerce - Soviet Union - Congresses. 2. Soviet Union - Commerce - Germany (West) - Congresses. 3. Soviet Union - Economic policy - 1981- - Congresses. I. Title.
HF3568.S66 C58 1986

Clement, Werner. Einkommensverteilung und Qualifikation : empirische Ergebnisse aus dem österreichischen Mikrozensus 1981 / Werner Clement ; unter Mitarbeit von Norbert Rainer und Peter Weiss. Wien : Signum-Verlag, 1984. vi, 201 p. : ill. ; 21 cm. Bibliography: p. 193-197. ISBN 3-85436-020-7 LC Card 84-191161
1. Income distribution - Austria. 2. Income distribution - Statistical methods. 3. Austria - Census, 1981. I. Rainer, Norbert. II. Weiss, Peter. III. Title.
HC270.I5 C56 1984

Clementi, Alberto. Abitazione e periferie urbane nei paesi in via di sviluppo . Milano, Italy ,

c1985. 450 p. : LC Card 86-132019
HD7287.96.L29 A25 1985
NYPL [JLD 87-1173]

Clements, Kenneth W., 1950- Theil, Henri. Applied demand analysis . Cambridge, Mass. , 1987. xxi, 279 p. : ISBN 0-88730-217-3 LC Card 86-32230 DDC 338.5/212 19
HB801 .T489 1987

Clements, R. T. The Reserve Bank econometric model of the New Zealand economy : Model XI / R.T. Clements (ed.) C.D. Hansen, M.J. Hames. Wellington : Reserve Bank of New Zealand, [1986] 62 p., [2] leaves of plates : ill. ; 30 cm. (Research paper . no. 40) "September 1986." Bibliography: p. 43. LC Card 87-142103 DDC 330.9931/00724 19
1. New Zealand - Economic conditions - 1945- - Econometric models. I. Hansen, C. D. II. Hames, M. J. III. Series: Research paper (Reserve Bank of New Zealand) , no. 40. IV. Title.
HC665 .C54 1986

Clements, Robert W. Tetreault, Wilfred F., 1927- Starting right in your new business /. Reading, Mass. , c1987. ix, 226 p. ; ISBN 0-201-07795-7 (pbk.) : LC Card 87-19464 DDC 658.1/141 19
HD62.7 .T47 1987

Clementson Electronic Services. International telecommunications markets, production & trade /. New York, N.Y. , 1986. 317 p. : ISBN 0-935859-11-X (pbk.) LC Card 86-23052 DDC 338.7/62138 19
HD9696.T442 I578 1986

Clerc, Denis. L'inflation / Denis Clerc. Paris : Syros, c1984. 126 p. : ill. ; 19 cm. (Collection "Alternatives économiques") Includes bibliographical references. ISBN 2-86738-041-3 : LC Card 84-241799 DDC 332.4/1 19
1. Inflation (Finance). I. Series: Collection "Alternatives économiques". II. Title.
HG229 .C548 1984

CLERGY - MAJOR ORDERS. see **CLERGY.**

CLERGY - SPAIN - STATISTICS - HISTORY - 18TH CENTURY.
Pérez de Guinea, María del Carmen. Estudio sobre la sociedad soriana en el siglo XVIII . [Spain] [1982?] 296 p. ; LC Card 85-136714
HA1559.S65 P47 1982

CLERGYMEN. see **CLERGY.**

Clerical employment and technological change /. Hunt, H. Allan. Kalamazoo, Mich. , 1986. x, 296 p. : ISBN 0-88099-042-2 (pbk.) LC Card 86-26556 DDC 331.12/5165137/0973 19
HD5718.M392 U65 1986

CLERICAL OCCUPATIONS.
Women, clerical work, and office automation . Washington, D.C. , 1986. vi, 64 p. ; LC Card 86-602559 DDC 331.4/8165137/0973 19
HD6095 .W685 1986

CLERKS - BRAZIL - FORTALEZA - RECREATION.
Situação de saúde e lazer do comerciário de Fortaleza /. Fortaleza-CE , 1977/1978 [i.e. 1978] 66 leaves ; LC Card 83-116799
HD5755.F6 S58 1978

CLERKS - EFFECT OF AUTOMATION ON.
Baethge, Martin. Zukunft der Angestellten . Frankfurt , New York , c1986. 460 p. : ISBN 3-593-33368-6 (pbk.) LC Card 87-673317
HD5707 .B28x 1986

CLERKS - EFFECT OF AUTOMATION ON - ADDRESSES, ESSAYS, LECTURES.
Human aspects in office automation /. Amsterdam , New York , 1984. xv, 322 p. : ISBN 0-444-42327-3 : LC Card 84-5917 DDC 363.1/19651 19
HF5547.5 .H85 1984 ***NYPL [JLF 86-892]***

CLERKS - GERMANY - HISTORY.
Speier, Hans. German white-collar workers and the rise of Hitler /. New Haven , 1986. xv, 208 p. ; ISBN 0-300-03701-5 LC Card 86-9120 DDC 331.7/92/0943 19
HD8039.M4 G3639413 1986
NYPL [JLE 87-909]

CLERKS - HEALTH AND HYGIENE - BRAZIL - FORTALEZA.
Situação de saúde e lazer do comerciário de Fortaleza /. Fortaleza-CE , 1977/1978 [i.e. 1978] 66 leaves ; LC Card 83-116799
HD5755.F6 S58 1978

CLERKS - UNITED STATES - EFFECT OF TECHNOLOGICAL INNOVATIONS ON.
Hunt, H. Allan. Clerical employment and technological change /. Kalamazoo, Mich. , 1986. x, 296 p. : ISBN 0-88099-042-2 (pbk.) LC Card 86-26556 DDC 331.12/5165137/0973 19
HD5718.M392 U65 1986

CLERKS - UNITED STATES - EFFECTS OF AUTOMATION ON.
Women, clerical work, and office automation . Washington, D.C. , 1986. vi, 64 p. ; LC Card 86-602559 DDC 331.4/8165137/0973 19
HD6095 .W685 1986

CLERKS - UNITED STATES - SUPPLY AND DEMAND.
Hunt, H. Allan. Clerical employment and technological change /. Kalamazoo, Mich. , 1986. x, 296 p. : ISBN 0-88099-042-2 (pbk.) LC Card 86-26556 DDC 331.12/5165137/0973 19
HD5718.M392 U65 1986

CLERKS - VOCATIONAL GUIDANCE. see **CLERICAL OCCUPATIONS.**

Clés pour une stratégie nouvelle du développement / Anouar Abdel-Malek ... [et al.]. Paris : Editions ouvrières : Unesco, c1984. 226 p. : ill. ; 21 cm. Includes bibliographies. ISBN 2-7082-2365-7 : LC Card 85-116966 DDC 338.9/009172/4 19
1. Developing countries - Economic conditions. 2. Developing countries - Economic policy. 3. Economic development. I. Abdel-Malek, Anouar, 1924-.
HC59.7 .C584 1984

Cleto, Romeo B. The Ilocos and Cordillera provinces : a general physical and socio-economic profile / by Romeo B. Cleto, with Christoph J. Dehn, Hilario J. Padilla. Baguio City [Philippines] : Katinnulong Daguiti Umili Iti Amianan, Inc. (KADUAMI) ; Manila : Sibol ng Agham at Akmang Teknolohiya (SIBAT), National Secretariat, [1986] xvii, 265 p. : maps ; 22 cm. Page 123a, inserted. Bibliography: p. 231-240. LC Card 87-111697 DDC 330.9599/1 19
1. Luzon (Philippines) - Economic conditions. 2. Luzon (Philippines) - Social conditions. I. Dehn, Christoph H. II. Padilla, Hilario J. III. Katinnulong Daguiti Umili Iti Amianan, Inc. IV. Sibol ng Agham at Akamang Teknolohiya (Organization). National Secretariat. V. Title.
HC457.L8 C56 1986

Cleveland, Robert W. Income nonresponses : March 1983 CPS. [Washington] : U. S. Dept. of Commerce, Bureau of the Census : For sale by Supt. of Docs., U. S. G.P.O., [1985] iv, 87 p. : ill. ; 28 cm. (Technical paper . 54) "Prepared by Robert W. Cleveland and Mary F. Henson"--Acknowledgments. "Issued September 1985." Bibliography: p. 9. LC Card 85-603179 DDC 339.2/2/0973021 19
1. Income - United States - Statistics. 2. Household surveys - United States - Response rate. I. Henson, Mary F. II. Series: Technical paper (United States. Bureau of the Census) , 54. III. Title.
HC110.I5 C44 1985

Cléves S., Rodrigo. Rendimientos de beneficiado de café : cosecha 1985-1986 / Rodrigo Cléves S., Rolando Vásquez M., Martín Montero H. San José, Costa Rica : Instituto del Café de Costa Rica, Centro de Investigaciones en Café, 1986. 35 leaves : col. ill. ; 28 cm. LC Card 87-403521 DDC 338.1/6 19
1. Coffee trade - Costa Rica - Capital productivity. 2. Coffee trade - Costa Rica - Labor productivity. I. Vásquez M., Rolando. II. Montero H., Martín. III. Title.
HD9199.C82 C57 1986

Clichevsky, Nora.
Habitat popular . Buenos Aires , 1986. 162 p. : LC Card 87-404028 DDC 363.5/8 19
HD7305.5 .H32 1986

O mercado de terra na região metropolitana de Porto Alegre / Nora Clichevsky, Nirce Saffer, Paulo Cassiano. Porto Alegre : Programa de Pós-Graduação em Planejamento Urbano e Regional, Faculdade de Arquitetura, Universidade Federal do Rio Grande do Sul, 1982. 60 p. : ill. ; 30 cm. (Cadernos do PROPUR . 1) Includes bibliographies. LC Card 84-256219
1. Land use, Urban - Brazil - Porto Alegre. 2. Real estate business - Brazil - Port Alegre. I. Saffer, Nirce. II. Cassiano, Paulo. III. Title. IV. Series.
HD500.P67 C57 1982

Cliffe, Lionel. Experiences of agricultural and rural cooperatives in socialist countries in Africa / prepared for FAO by Lionel Cliffe. [S.l.] : FAO, [1985?] 40 p. ; 30 cm. Cover title. Background paper for the Regional Expert Consultation on the Role of Rural Cooperatives in the Production Sectors in Africa, ECA, Addis Ababa, Ethiopia, 7-11 Oct. 1985. Bibliography: p. 38-40. LC Card 87-104467 DDC 334/.683/096 19
1. Agriculture, Cooperative - Africa - Congresses. I. Food and Agriculture Organization of the United Nations. II. Title.
HD1491.A48 C55 1985

Clifton-Brown, E. Project 1.04 : African co-operative societies in Rhodesia : a survey of African co-operatives in Rhodesia undertaken from January to April 1976. Salisbury, Zimbabwe : Whitsun Foundation, [1977] 46 leaves ; 30 cm. "September 1977." LC Card 84-256608
1. Cooperative societies - Zimbabwe. 2. Cooperation - Zimbabwe. I. Whitsun Foundation. II. Title. III. Title: African co-operative societies in Rhodesia.
HD3562.3.A4 C55 1977

CLIMATE AND CROPS. see **CROPS AND CLIMATE.**

CLIMATE, GREENHOUSE. see **GREENHOUSES.**

The Climate of persuasion : a study of the public image of advertising media. [Richmond, VA.] : Richmond Newspapers, 1959. 58 p. : ill. ; 28 cm.
1. Advertising - Psychological aspects. 2. Motivation research (Marketing). I. Richmond Newspapers, Inc.
NYPL [JLF 86-1150]

CLIMATOLOGY, AGRICULTURAL. see **CROPS AND CLIMATE.**

Climbing boys . Strange, K. H. (Kathleen H.), 1904- London ; New York : xiv, 146 p. : ISBN 0-85031-431-3 : LC Card 83-143704 DDC 331.5/5 19
HD8039.C482 G77 1982
NYPL [JLD 85-681]

Cline, Carolyn Garrett, 1947- The velvet ghetto . San Francisco , 1986. 147 leaves in various foliations : LC Card 86-161157 DDC 331.4/816592/0973 19
HD6054.2.U6 V45 1986

Cline, Ray S. U. S. ASEAN relations . Washington, D.C. , 1987. xxii, 222 p. ; ISBN 0-943057-00-0 (pbk.) LC Card 87-50526 DDC 337.59073 19
HF1456.5.A7 U72 1987

Cline, William R.
Bergsten, C. Fred, 1941- The United States-Japan economic problem /. Washington, D.C. , c1985. x, 164 p. : ISBN 0-262-52108-3 LC Card 85-18106 DDC 382/.0973/052 19
HF3127 .B47 1985 ***NYPL [JLE 87-19]***

The future of world trade in textiles and apparel / William R. Cline. Washington, DC : Institute for International Economics, 1987. xiv, 325 p. : ill. ; 23 cm. Includes bibliographical references and index. ISBN 0-88132-025-0 (pbk.) : LC Card 87-17068 DDC 382/.45677 19
1. Textile industry. 2. Clothing trade. 3. Textile industry - Government policy - United States. 4. Clothing trade - Government policy - United States. I. Title.
HD9850.5 .C55 1987

Informatics and development : trade and industrial policy in Argentina, Brazil, and Mexico / by William R. Cline. Washington, D.C. (9416 Friendship Station, Washington 20016) : Economics International, [1987] vi, 161 p. ; 23 cm. "February 1987." Includes bibliographical references. LC Card 87-6819 DDC 338.4/7004/0981 19
1. Computer industry - Government policy - Brazil. 2. Computer industry - Government policy - Argentina. 3. Computer industry - Government policy - Mexico. 4. Computer software industry - Government policy - Brazil. 5. Computer software industry - Government policy - Argentina. 6. Computer software industry - Government policy - Mexico. I. Title.
HD9696.C63 B728 1987

Mobilizing bank lending to debtor countries / William R. Cline. Washington, DC : Institute for International Economics, 1987. viii, 92 p. : ill. ; 23 cm. (Policy analyses in international economics . 18) Includes bibliographical references.

ISBN 0-88132-062-5 (pbk.) LC Card 87-16857 DDC 332.1/5 19
1. Loans, Foreign - Developing countries. 2. Debts, External - Developing countries. 3. Banks and banking, International. I. Title. II. Series.
HG3891.5 .C58 1987

Clinton, James Edson. Lieberman, Anne M. Mastering money . Chicago, Ill. , Naperville, IL , c1987. xi, 267 p. : ISBN 0-88462-589-3 (pbk.) : LC Card 87-3655 DDC 332.024 19
HG179 .L486 1987

CLOCK AND WATCH MAKING - CHINA.
Yang, Yuming. L'industrie horlogère suisse et ses relations avec la Chine de 1949 à 1982 /. Geneve , 1984. 186 leaves : LC Card 85-104853
HD9999.C583 S99 1984

CLOCK AND WATCH MAKING - SWITZERLAND.
Yang, Yuming. L'industrie horlogère suisse et ses relations avec la Chine de 1949 à 1982 /. Geneve , 1984. 186 leaves : LC Card 85-104853
HD9999.C583 S99 1984

CLOSE CORPORATIONS - NEW YORK (STATE) - ERIE COUNTY - LEGAL RESEARCH.
Law, Gordon T., 1945- A guide to information on closely held corporations /. Buffalo, N.Y. , c1986. p. cm. ISBN 0-9615917-1-4 : LC Card 86-32812 DDC 338.7/4/072073 19
HD2785 .L38 1986

CLOSE CORPORATIONS - TAXATION - UNITED STATES.
Silton, Lawrence C. How to buy or sell the closely held corporation /. Englewood Cliffs, N.J. , c1987. xi, 308 p. ; ISBN 0-13-403064-8 LC Card 87-14433 DDC 658.1/6 19
HG4028.V3 S54 1987

CLOSE CORPORATIONS - UNITED STATES.
Silton, Lawrence C. How to buy or sell the closely held corporation /. Englewood Cliffs, N.J. , c1987. xi, 308 p. ; ISBN 0-13-403064-8 LC Card 87-14433 DDC 658.1/6 19
HG4028.V3 S54 1987

CLOSE CORPORATIONS - UNITED STATES - INFORMATION SERVICES.
Law, Gordon T., 1945- A guide to information on closely held corporations /. Buffalo, N.Y. , c1986. p. cm. ISBN 0-9615917-1-4 : LC Card 86-32812 DDC 338.7/4/072073 19
HD2785 .L38 1986

CLOSE CORPORATIONS - UNITED STATES - LEGAL RESEARCH.
Law, Gordon T., 1945- A guide to information on closely held corporations /. Buffalo, N.Y. , c1986. p. cm. ISBN 0-9615917-1-4 : LC Card 86-32812 DDC 338.7/4/072073 19
HD2785 .L38 1986

CLOSE CORPORATIONS - UNITED STATES - VALUATION.
Valuation of a closely held business. New York, N.Y. (1211 Ave. of the Americas, New York 10036-8775) , c1987. 44 p. : LC Card 87-402129 DDC 658.1/522 19
HF5681.V3 V35 1987

CLOSE CORPORATIONS - VALUATION.
Silton, Lawrence C. How to buy or sell the closely held corporation /. Englewood Cliffs, N.J. , c1987. xi, 308 p. ; ISBN 0-13-403064-8 LC Card 87-14433 DDC 658.1/6 19
HG4028.V3 S54 1987

Close, Paul. Family and economy in modern society /. Basingstoke, Hampshire , 1985. xvi, 234 p. ; ISBN 0-333-37437-1 LC Card 86-674026
HD4904.25 .F35x 1985

Close to the customer : an American Management Association research report on consumer affairs / foreword by John Guaspari. New York, N.Y. : AMA Membership Publications Division, American Management Association, c1987. 96 p. ; 28 cm. (AMA briefings & surveys) Bibliography: p. 94-96. ISBN 0-8144-3513-0 (pbk.) : LC Card 87-12558 DDC 658.8/12 19
1. Customer relations. I. American Management Association. II. Series.
HF5415.5 .C57 1987

Close Up Foundation. Economic choices . Arlington, Va. , c1987. 73 p. : ISBN 0-932765-08-4 (pbk.) : LC Card 87-686 DDC 338.973 19
HC106 .E24 1987

CLOSED-END FUNDS. see **INVESTMENT TRUSTS.**

Closed labor markets . Stafford, Walter W. New York, N.Y. (105 E. 22nd St., New York 10010) , c1985. xvi, 203, 3, [2] p. ; LC Card 85-186853 DDC 331.12/09747/1 19
HD5726.N5 S73 1985 ***NYPL [Sc F 86-274]***

CLOSED SEA (MARE CLAUSUM) see **FREEDOM OF THE SEAS.**

The closed shop in British industry /. Dunn, Stephen. London , 1984. xii, 181 p. ; ISBN 0-333-26202-6 LC Card 87-673181
HD6488.2.G7 D86x 1984

CLOSING COSTS. see **SETTLEMENT COSTS.**

Closing the door on a nuclear future : an Earthwatch campaign against British nuclear expansion. [Harbour View, Bantry, Co. Cork : Earthwatch, 1986] [7] leaves : ill. ; 32 cm. Cover title. Issued in portfolio. "Autumn 1986." LC Card 87-111333 DDC 333.79/27/0941 19
1. Nuclear industry - Government policy - Great Britain. 2. Nuclear power plants - Environmental aspects - Great Britain. 3. Nuclear power plants - Environmental aspects - Ireland. 4. Antinuclear movement - Ireland. 5. Radioactive pollution - Ireland. 6. Earthwatch (Organization : Ireland). I. Earthwatch (Organization : Ireland).
HD9698.G72 C56 1986

CLOTH. see **TEXTILE FABRICS.**

CLOTHIERS. see **CLOTHING TRADE.**

CLOTHING AND DRESS - TARIFF. see **TARIFF ON CLOTHING.**

CLOTHING FACTORIES - AUTOMATION.
Hoffman, Kurt. Micro-electronics and clothing . New York , 1988. xxxii, 253 p. ; ISBN 0-275-92798-9 (alk. paper) : LC Card 87-25736 DDC 338.4/5687 19
HD9940.A2 H63 1988

CLOTHING TRADE - BRAZIL.
Ribeiro, Lêda Cristina de O. Santana Cançado. Considerações sobre o mercado das indústrias de confecções brasileiras. Belo Horizonte [Brazil] , 1985. 66 leaves : LC Card 87-404932 DDC 338.4/7687/0981 19
HD9940.B82 R53 1985

CLOTHING TRADE - BRAZIL - BAHIA (STATE)
A Indústria de confecções na Bahia. [Salvador] [1981] 40 p. ; LC Card 87-400671
HD9940.B83 B345 1981

CLOTHING TRADE - BRAZIL - MINAS GERAIS.
Ribeiro, Lêda Cristina de O. Santana Cançado. Considerações sobre o mercado das indústrias de confecções brasileiras. Belo Horizonte [Brazil] , 1985. 66 leaves : LC Card 87-404932 DDC 338.4/7687/0981 19
HD9940.B82 R53 1985

CLOTHING TRADE - BRAZIL - RIO GRANDE DO SUL - DIRECTORIES.
Catálogo da indústria têxtil e do vestuário do Rio Grande do Sul /. [Porto Alegre] , 1985. 96 p. ; LC Card 86-209398
HD9864.B83 R593 1985

CLOTHING TRADE - CANADA - CONGRESSES.
Table de concertation sur l'industrie du vêtement (1985 : Montréal, Québec) Rapport de la Table de concertation sur l'industrie du vêtement . [Québec] [1985] v, 174, 12 p. ; LC Card 87-103889
HD9940.C22 Q847 1985

CLOTHING TRADE - GERMANY (WEST) - LABOR PRODUCTIVITY.
Fischer, Joachim, 1948- Neue Leistungspolitik in der Bekleidungsindustrie . Frankfurt/Main , New York , c1986. 264 p. : ISBN 3-593-33635-9 LC Card 86-197222
HD9940.G32 F57 1986

CLOTHING TRADE - GERMANY (WEST) - PERSONNEL MANAGEMENT.
Fischer, Joachim, 1948- Neue Leistungspolitik in der Bekleidungsindustrie . Frankfurt/Main , New York , c1986. 264 p. : ISBN 3-593-33635-9 LC Card 86-197222
HD9940.G32 F57 1986

CLOTHING TRADE - GOVERNMENT POLICY.
The Textile and apparel trade crisis . Washington, D.C. (1775 Pennsylvania Ave., N.W., Washington 20006) , c1985. vi, 200, [23] p. : LC Card 87-122082 DDC 382/.45677 19
HD9850.6 .T475 1985

CLOTHING TRADE - GOVERNMENT POLICY - DEVELOPING COUNTRIES.
Howell, Thomas R., 1949- The EEC and the third Multifiber Arrangement . Washington, DC , 1986. [14], 126, [12] p. : LC Card 86-224652 DDC 382/.45677/0094 19
HD9865.E852 H68 1986

CLOTHING TRADE - GOVERNMENT POLICY - EUROPEAN ECONOMIC COMMUNITY COUNTRIES.
Howell, Thomas R., 1949- The EEC and the third Multifiber Arrangement . Washington, DC , 1986. [14], 126, [12] p. : LC Card 86-224652 DDC 382/.45677/0094 19
HD9865.E852 H68 1986

CLOTHING TRADE - GOVERNMENT POLICY - UNITED STATES.
Cline, William R. The future of world trade in textiles and apparel /. Washington, DC , 1987. xiv, 325 p. : ISBN 0-88132-025-0 (pbk.) : LC Card 87-17068 DDC 382/.45677 19
HD9850.5 .C55 1987

CLOTHING TRADE - INTERNATIONAL COOPERATION.
Planning & implementing an apparel sourcing strategy . Arlington, Va. (2500 Wilson Blvd., Suite 301, Arlington 22209) , c1986. 41 p. : LC Card 87-107327 DDC 687/.068/7 19
HD9940.U4 P52 1986

CLOTHING TRADE - ITALY.
McKnight, Gerald. Gucci . New York , c1987. xi, 362 p. : ISBN 1-556-11037-5 (alk. paper) : LC Card 86-46390 DDC 338.7/687/0945 19
HD9940.I84 G86 1987

CLOTHING TRADE - MANAGEMENT.
Cash, R. Patrick. Improving apparel shop profits] [New York, N.Y.] [c1986] 285 p. : ISBN 0-87102-131-5 LC Card 86-61313 DDC 687/.068/8 19
HD9940.A2 C37 1986

CLOTHING TRADE - MANAGEMENT - DATA PROCESSING.
McPherson, Edwin M. Apparel manufacturing management systems . Park Ridge, N.J., U. S.A. , c1987. xiv, 392 p. : ISBN 0-8155-1141-8 : LC Card 87-12239 DDC 687/.068 19
HD9940.A2 M42 1987

CLOTHING TRADE - MANAGEMENT - DATA PROCESSING - EQUIPMENT AND SUPPLIES.
Acquiring, enhancing, replacing apparel systems . Arlington, VA (2500 Wilson Blvd., Suite 301, Arlington 22201) , 1986. iii, 28 p. : LC Card 87-107487 DDC 687/.028/5 19
HD9940.A2 A26 1986

CLOTHING TRADE - MEXICO - STATISTICS.
La Industria textil y del vestido en México, 1970-1982. México, D.F. , 1984. 77 p. : ISBN 968-8097-69-1 LC Card 85-203070 DDC 338.4/7677/00972021 19
HD9864.M62 I53 1984 ***NYPL [JLF 87-363]***

CLOTHING TRADE - QUALITY CONTROL.
Boeker, Heiner, 1955- Qualitätspolitik in der industriellen Beschaffung . Bochum , 1986. ix, 296 p. ; ISBN 3-88339-525-0 LC Card 87-127490 DDC 687/.068/5 19
HD9940.A2 B64 1986

CLOTHING TRADE - QUÉBEC (PROVINCE) - CONGRESSES.
Table de concertation sur l'industrie du vêtement (1985 : Montréal, Québec) Rapport de la Table de concertation sur l'industrie du vêtement . [Québec] [1985] v, 174, 12 p. ; LC Card 87-103889
HD9940.C22 Q847 1985

CLOTHING TRADE - SOUTH AFRICA.
South Africa. Committee of Inquiry into the Textile and Clothing Industries. The policy of protection in regard to textiles and clothing . Pretoria , 1982?] ix, 110, [28] p. ; ISBN 0-621-08170-1 (pbk.) : LC Card 86-207580 DDC 382/.45677/00968 19
HF2651.C635 S627 1982

CLOTHING TRADE - STATISTICS.
La Industria textil y del vestido en México, 1970-1982. México, D.F. , 1984. 77 p. : ISBN 968-8097-69-1 LC Card 85-203070 DDC 338.4/7677/00972021 19
HD9864.M62 I53 1984 ***NYPL [JLF 87-363]***

CLOTHING TRADE - SWEDEN.
Tekoindustrierna . Stockholm , 1980. 189 p. : ISBN 91-38-05813-8 LC Card 82-236884
HD9865.S86 T45 1980

CLOTHING TRADE - SWITZERLAND - DIRECTORIES.
Handbuch der schweizerischen Textil-, Bekleidungs- und Lederwirtschaft =. Zürich , 1986. 214 p. : ISBN 3-909214-07-X LC Card 86-221803
HD9940.S93 H36 1986

CLOTHING TRADE - UNITED STATES.
Foreign regulations affecting U. S. textile/apparel exports. [Washington, D.C.] [1986] 283 p. ; LC Card 86-601588
HF2651.T42 F67 1986

Ghadar, Fariborz. U. S. industrial competitiveness . Lexington, Mass. , c1987. x, 114 p. : ISBN 0-669-15689-2 (alk. paper) LC Card 86-46341 DDC 338.4/7677/00973 19
HD9855 .G47 1987

International trade in textiles & apparel . [Washington, D.C.] , c1987. 1 v. (various foliations) : LC Card 87-404516 DDC 382/.45677/00973 19
HD9850.5 .I43 1987

Planning & implementing an apparel sourcing strategy . Arlington, Va. (2500 Wilson Blvd., Suite 301, Arlington 22209) , c1986. 41 p. : LC Card 87-107327 DDC 687/.068/7 19
HD9940.U4 P52 1986

CLOTHING TRADE - UNITED STATES - FORECASTING.
Special analysis and outlook for E.I. Du Pont De Nemours & Company (Inc.), Chemicals and Pigments Department. Boston, Mass. (7 Liberty Sq., Boston 02109) [1986] 17, [6] p. : LC Card 86-205857 DDC 338.4/766/00973 19
HD9660.P253 U672 1986

CLOTHING TRADE - UNITED STATES - STATISTICS.
Taylor, John A. (John Alvin), 1930- U. S. imports of textile and apparel products under the multifiber arrangement, 1981-84 /. Washington, D.C. [1985] v, 136 p. ; LC Card 86-601665 DDC 382/.45677/00973021 19
HD9940.U4 T38 1985

CLOTHING TRADE - VIRGINIA - DIRECTORIES.
Haigh, Robert William, 1926- Leading Virginia industries . Charlottesville, Va. [1986] 161 p. : LC Card 87-620837 DDC 338.4/7677/009755 19
HD9857.V8 H35 1986

CLOTHING TRADE - VIRGINIA - FINANCE - STATISTICS.
Haigh, Robert William, 1926- Leading Virginia industries . Charlottesville, Va. [1986] 161 p. : LC Card 87-620837 DDC 338.4/7677/009755 19
HD9857.V8 H35 1986

CLOTHING TRADE - VIRGINIA - STATISTICS.
Haigh, Robert William, 1926- Leading Virginia industries . Charlottesville, Va. [1986] 161 p. : LC Card 87-620837 DDC 338.4/7677/009755 19
HD9857.V8 H35 1986

CLOTHING TRADE - ZIMBABWE.
Investment opportunity in textiles & clothing, Zimbabwe. [Harare, Zimbabwe] [1985?] 72 p., [12] leaves of plates : LC Card 87-400412 DDC 338.4/7677/0096891 19
HD9867.Z552 I58 1985

CLOTHING WORKERS - BULGARIA - VARNA - HISTORY.
Khadzhiev, Stefan. Zavod "Druzhba" . Varna , 1985. 161 p., [3] leaves of plates : LC Card 86-140096
HD8039.C62 B95 1985

CLOTHING WORKERS - BULGARIA - VIDIN.
Po visochinite na sŭrtseto . Sofiia , 1986. 75 p., [16] p. of plates : LC Card 87-101682
HD8039.C62 B97 1986

CLOTHING WORKERS - JUVENILE LITERATURE.
Fitz-Gerald, Christine Maloney. I can be a textile worker /. Chicago , c1987. 29 p. : ISBN 0-516-01912-0 (lib bdg.) LC Card 87-10716 DDC 677/.0023/73 19
HD8039.C6 F57 1987

CLOVERLEAF (HIGHWAY ENGINEERING) see **ROADS - INTERCHANGES AND INTERSECTIONS.**

Club de l'astrolabe (Lyon, France) Projet pour la France . Paris , c1983. 196 p. ; ISBN 2-7340-0032-6 : LC Card 83-196098
HC276.2 .P767 1983

Club de Rome. see **Club of Rome.**

Club of Rome Conference (1984 : Helsinki, Finland) Managing global issues : reasons for encouragement : proceedings of the Club of Rome Conference, Helsinki, 1984 / Club of Rome, Finland Committee ; [editor, Vuokko Jarva, researcher]. [Lahti] : University of Helsinki, Lahti Research and Training Centre, [1985] 216 p. : ill. (some col.) ; 25 cm. The Club's 1984 conference was held in Helsinki, July 9-12th. Includes bibliographies. ISBN 951-45-3807-2 (pbk.) LC Card 87-140928 DDC 909.82/8 19
1. Economic history - 1971- - Congresses. 2. Economic forecasting - Congresses. 3. Social history - 1970- - Congresses. 4. Economic development - Congresses. 5. Peace - Congresses. I. Jarva, Vuokko. II. Club of Rome. Finland Committee.
HC13 .C56 1984

Club of Rome. Finland Committee. Club of Rome Conference (1984 : Helsinki, Finland) Managing global issues . [Lahti] [1985] 216 p. : ISBN 951-45-3807-2 (pbk.) LC Card 87-140928 DDC 909.82/8 19
HC13 .C56 1984

Club van Rome. see **Club of Rome.**

Clukey, Lee Paul. UNIX and XENIX demystified / Lee Paul Clukey. 1st ed. Blue Ridge Summit, Pa. : Tab Books, 1985. xii, 243 p. ; ill. ; 24 cm. On t.p. the registered trademark symbol "TM" is superscript following "UNIX" in title and registered trademark symbol "R" is superscript following "XENIX" in title. Includes index. ISBN 0-8306-0874-5 : LC Card 85-2658 DDC 001.64/2 19
1. UNIX (Computer operating system). 2. XENIX (Computer operating system). I. Title.
QA76.6 .C57 1985 ***NYPL [JSE 86-1905]***

CLUSTER ANALYSIS.
Kiffe, Ulrich. Die Klassifizierung in der Bundesrepublik Deutschland angebotener Personenkraftwagen mit multivariaten Analysemethoden /. Münster , 1984. xx, 24, 340 p. : ISBN 3-88660-148-8 LC Card 84-208133
HD9710.G42 K48 1984

Stahl, Herbert. Clusteranalyse grosser Objektmengen mit problemorientierten Distanzmassen /. Thun , c1985. ii, vi, 323 p. : ISBN 3-87144-908-3 LC Card 86-112498
HA29.5.G4 S68 1985

Umani, Mario. Un procedimento per la ripartizione ottimale di una collettività in classi . [Trieste] , 1978. 19 p. ; LC Card 81-111875 DDC 368/.092 19
HG9970 .U46 1978 ***NYPL [TB (Triesta. Università Istituto do statistica. Pubblicazioni. n.17)]***

Clusteranalyse grosser Objektmengen mit problemorientierten Distanzmassen /. Stahl, Herbert. Thun , c1985. ii, vi, 323 p. : ISBN 3-87144-908-3 LC Card 86-112498
HA29.5.G4 S68 1985

Clyde (Alta.)
McCully, Al. Clyde growth report, 1985 /. [Edmonton] [1985] iii, 66 p. : LC Card 86-228996 DDC 338.97123/3 19
HD320.C5 M33 1985

CLYDE (ALTA.) - ECONOMIC POLICY.
McCully, Al. Clyde growth report, 1985 /. [Edmonton] [1985] iii, 66 p. : LC Card 86-228996 DDC 338.97123/3 19
HD320.C5 M33 1985

Clyde growth report, 1985 /. McCully, Al. [Edmonton] [1985] iii, 66 p. : LC Card 86-228996 DDC 338.97123/3 19
HD320.C5 M33 1985

CMA examination review /. Gleim, Irvin N. Gainesville, Fla. , c1987. 2 v. : ISBN 0-917537-21-1 (pbk. : v. 1) LC Card 87-70930 DDC 658.1/511/076 19
HF5661 .G42 1987

CME white paper series .
(no. 5) Futures and options trading for commercial banks . Chicago, Ill. (30 S. Wacker Dr., Chicago 60606) , c1986. 14 p. : LC Card 87-131777 DDC 332.1/754 19
HG2491 .F87 1986

CMS occasional papers and documentation.
Miller, Mark J. Employer sanctions in Western Europe /. Staten Island, N.Y. , 1987. viii, 67 p. ; ISBN 0-934733-20-1 (pbk.) : LC Card 86-31739 DDC 331.6/2/094 19
HD8378.5.A2 M5395 1987

CMTC (Firm : São Paulo, Brazil) Intervenção no transporte . [São Paulo, SP, Brasil , 1985?] 31 leaves ; LC Card 86-171230
HE5653.S23 I58 1985

CMTC (FIRM : SÃO PAULO, BRAZIL)
Intervenção no transporte . [São Paulo, SP, Brasil , 1985?] 31 leaves ; LC Card 86-171230
HE5653.S23 I58 1985

Lopes, Miriam B. P. Oelsner (Miriam Bettina Paulina Oelsner) Pequena história dos transportes públicos de São Paulo. São Paulo [1985] 91 p. : LC Card 86-158179
HE5653.Z7 C675 1985

Coaching for improved work performance /. Fournies, Ferdinand F. Blue Ridge Summit, PA , c1987. x, 214 p. : ISBN 0-8306-3054-6 (pbk.) : LC Card 86-23098 DDC 658.3/14 19
HF5549 .F65 1987

COACHING - GERMANY - HISTORY.
Beyrer, Klaus. Die Postkutschenreise /. Tübingen , 1985. 284 p. : ISBN 3-925340-35-1 LC Card 86-198761
HE6995 .B49 1985

COACHING - OREGON - UNION COUNTY - HISTORY.
Barklow, Irene. From trails to rails . Enterprise, Or. , c1987. ix, 300 p. : ISBN 0-9618185-2-2 : LC Card 87-15709 DDC 383/.4979571 19
HE6376.A1 O727 1987

COACHING - TEXAS - HISTORY - 19TH CENTURY.
Austerman, Wayne R. (Wayne Randolph), 1948- Sharps rifles and Spanish mules . College Station , c1985. x, 367 p., [8] p. of plates : ISBN 0-89096-220-0 : LC Card 84-40557 DDC 383/.49764 19
HE6376.A1 T417 1985 ***NYPL [JLE 85-3346]***

Coal : environmental policies and institutions. Paris : Organisation for Economic Co-operation and Development ; [Washington, D.C. : OECD Publications and Information Centre, distributor], 1987. 108 p. ; 23 cm. Includes bibliographies. ISBN 92-64-12909-X (pbk.) : LC Card 87-163847 DDC 363.7/31 19
1. Coal trade - Environmental aspects - Government policy. 2. Air - Pollution - Law and legislation. 3. Coal - Combustion - Environmental aspects. I. Organisation for Economic Co-operation and Development.
HD9540.6 .C63 1987

Coal after nationalisation / edited by S. S. Parikh. 1st ed. Calcutta : Coal Consumers Association of India, 1977. 676, [122] p. : ill., maps ; 26 cm. "A survey of coal industry, reliable and authentic articles, directory for the consumers, the trade and the industry and a compendium of statistics before and after coal nationalisation." Advertising matter included in paging. LC Card 77-905030
1. Coal trade - India. 2. Coal mines and mining - India. I. Parikh, S. S.
HD9556.I42 C57 ***NYPL [JLF 78-1568]***

COAL - ALASKA.
Arctic Slope Consulting Engineers. Western Arctic Coal Development Project . Anchorage, Alaska [1986] 2 v. : LC Card 87-621058 DDC 333.8/22/09798 19
HD9547.A4 A85 1986

Coal bulk handling equipment market. New York, N.Y. : Frost & Sullivan, c1984. iv, 243 p. : ill. ; 29 cm. "September 1984." "#A1194." LC Card 87-142522 DDC 380.1/45622334/028 19
1. Coal-handling machinery industry - United States. 2.

Market surveys. I. Frost & Sullivan.
HD9545 .C578 1984

COAL - COMBUSTION - ENVIRONMENTAL ASPECTS.
Coal . Paris [Washington, D.C.] 1987. 108 p. ; ISBN 92-64-12909-X (pbk.) : LC Card 87-163847 DDC 363.7/31 19
HD9540.6 .C63 1987

COAL - GEOLOGY - COLOMBIA - VALLE DEL CAUCA - MAPS.
Estudio del Plan de desarrollo carbonífero de la zona de Valle del Cauca en la República de Colombia. Tokio, Japon , 1977. v, 149 leaves : LC Card 84-244429
HD9554.C63 V34 1977

COAL-HANDLING MACHINERY INDUSTRY - UNITED STATES.
Coal bulk handling equipment market. New York, N.Y. , c1984. iv, 243 p. : LC Card 87-142522 DDC 380.1/45622334/028 19
HD9545 .C578 1984

Coal industry examination : final report, 1974. London : Dept. of Energy, [1974] 35 p. ; 24 cm. Cover title. LC Card 85-192146 DDC 338.2/724/0941 19
1. Coal trade - Great Britain. I. Great Britain. Dept. of Energy.
HD9551.5 .C43 1974

Coal industry of India /. Prasad, Anubhuti Ranjan. New Delhi , 1986. xxvi, 516 p. : ISBN 81-7024-055-7 : LC Card 86-902669 DDC 338.2/724/0954 19
HD9556.I42 P72 1986

COAL LANDS. see **COAL.**

COAL LEASES - UNITED STATES.
Potential effects of section 3 of the Federal Coal Leasing Amendments Act of 1976. Washington, D.C. , 1986. vii, 186 p. : LC Card 86-600512 DDC 333.33/9 19
HD242.3 .P68 1986 ***NYPL [JLF 86-1368]***

COAL MINERS - BRAZIL - CRICIÚMA.
Volpato, Terezinha Gascho. A pirita humana . Florianópolis , 1984. 159 p. : LC Card 85-150574
HD8039.M62 B78 1984

COAL MINERS - ENGLAND - DURHAM (COUNTY) - HISTORY - 20TH CENTURY.
But the world goes on the same . Whitley Bay, Tyne & Wear , 1979. 106 p. : LC Card 81-107503
HD8399.D872 B87 1979

COAL MINERS - ENGLAND, NORTHERN - HISTORY - 19TH CENTURY.
Colls, Robert. The pitmen of the northern coalfield . Manchester, UK , Wolfeboro, NH, USA , c1987. xv, 386 p., [2] p. of plates : ISBN 0-7190-2202-9 (U. S.) : LC Card 87-11029 DDC 305/.9622/09427 19
HD8039.M62 G737 1987

COAL MINERS - ENGLAND - THURCROFT (SOUTH YORKSHIRE) - INTERVIEWS.
Thurcroft, a village and the miners' strike . Nottingham [Nottinghamshire] , Atlantic Highlands, NJ , 1986. 276 p. : ISBN 0-85124-441-6 LC Card 86-21887 DDC 331.89/2822334/0942823 19
HD5346.M6152 1984 .T48 1987
NYPL [JLD 87-985]

COAL MINERS - FRANCE - HISTORY - 19TH CENTURY.
Plessy, Bernard, 1939- La vie quotidienne des mineurs au temps de Germinal /. [Paris] , c1984. 339 p. : ISBN 2-01-009272-4 : LC Card 85-160775
HD8039.M6152 F86 1984

COAL MINERS - FRANCE - LORRAINE - HISTORY - PICTORIAL WORKS.
Glück auf! . Paris [1986] 117 p. : ISBN 2-86738-115-0 : LC Card 86-178958
HD8039.M6152 F84 1986

COAL-MINERS - GERMANY, WEST.
Peter, Gerd, 1941- Der Arbeitsschutzbeauftragte . Frankfurt , New York , c1986. 344 p. : ISBN 3-593-33633-2 LC Card 86-160932
HD6490.S52 G365 1986

COAL-MINERS - GERMANY (WEST) - DORTMUND - HISTORY - EXHIBITIONS.
Leben mit Gneisenau, hundert Jahre-- . Dortmund , Essen [1986?] 317 p. : ISBN 3-88474-323-6 LC Card 87-408388 DDC 331.7/622334/094355 19
HD8039.M62 G335 1986

COAL MINERS - GERMANY (WEST) - PENZBERG - HISTORY - 20TH CENTURY.
Tenfelde, Klaus. Proletarische Provinz . München , 1982. xvii, 409 p. : ISBN 3-486-50701-X : LC Card 83-124119
HD8460.P452 T46 1982

COAL MINERS - GERMANY (WEST) - RUHR (REGION) - HISTORY.
Berg, Werner. Wirtschaft und Gesellschaft in Deutschland und Grossbritannien im Übergang zum "organisierten Kapitalismus" . Berlin , c1984. 888 p. : ISBN 3-428-05495-4 LC Card 84-222230
HD9553.7.R8 B47 1984

COAL MINERS - HUNGARY - BORSOD MEGYE - HISTORY.
200 éves a borsodi szénbányászat, 1786-1986 /. [Miskolc , 1986] 223 p. : ISBN 963-02-4565-5 (Magy. nemz. bibl.) LC Card 87-150976
HD9555.H83 B6715 1986

COAL-MINERS - INDIA.
Basurāẏa, Sunīla. Kaẏalā śramika, jībana o saṃgrāma /. Durgāpura , Kalikātā , 1986. 239 p. ; LC Card 86-903821
HD8039.M62 I394 1986

COAL MINERS - IOWA - BUXTON.
Schwieder, Dorothy, 1933- Buxton . Ames , 1987. viii, 256 p. : ISBN 0-8138-0246-6 LC Card 87-2929 DDC 305/.9622 19
HD8039.M62 U66825 1987

COAL MINERS - MEXICO - BARROTERÁN.
Arenal, Sandra. Barroterán! . [Mexico City?] , c1984. 116 p. ; ISBN 968-495-016-0 LC Card 85-195552
HD8039.M62 M63 1984

COAL MINERS - PENNSYLVANIA - SAINT CLAIR (SCHUYLKILL COUNTY) - HISTORY - 19TH CENTURY.
Wallace, Anthony F. C., 1923- St. Clair . New York , 1987. xvii, 519 p. : ISBN 0-394-52867-0 : LC Card 86-46120 DDC 307.7/66/0974817 19
HD8039.M62 U6699 1987

COAL MINERS - PENNSYLVANIA - SCRANTON REGION - HISTORY - ADDRESSES, ESSAYS, LECTURES.
Hard coal, hard times . Scranton , 1984, c1983. xv, 193 p. ; ISBN 0-917445-00-7 LC Card 85-156422 DDC 331.7/622335/0974837
HD8039.M62 U633 1984
NYPL [JLE 87-1218]

COAL MINERS - SPAIN - ASTURIAS - HISTORY - 20TH CENTURY.
Shubert, Adrian, 1953- The road to revolution in Spain . Urbana , c1987. 183 p. : ISBN 0-252-01368-9 (alk. paper) LC Card 86-24998 DDC 331.7/622334/094615 19
HD8039.M62 S68 1987

COAL-MINERS - UNITED STATES.
Miernyk, William H. The coalmining industry in the United States /. Geneva , 1986. 53, ix p. : ISBN 92-9014-409-2 (pbk.)
NYPL [JLE 87-1534]

COAL MINERS - WALES, SOUTH - HISTORY.
Berg, Werner. Wirtschaft und Gesellschaft in Deutschland und Grossbritannien im Übergang zum "organisierten Kapitalismus" . Berlin , c1984. 888 p. : ISBN 3-428-05495-4 LC Card 84-222230
HD9553.7.R8 B47 1984

COAL MINERS' WIVES - WALES - ABERTILLERY (GWENT) - BIOGRAPHY.
Miller, Jill. You can't kill the spirit . London , c1986. 142 p. : ISBN 0-7043-4021-6 (pbk.) : LC Card 87-100804 DDC 305.4/2/0942995 19
HD5365.M6152 1984 .W345 1986

COAL MINES AND MINING - ALASKA.
Arctic Slope Consulting Engineers. Western Arctic Coal Development Project . Anchorage, Alaska [1986] 2 v. : LC Card 87-621058 DDC 333.8/22/09798 19
HD9547.A4 A85 1986

COAL MINES AND MINING - ALASKA - CHICKALOON REGION - HISTORY.
Bauer, Mary Cracraft. A history of coal-mining in the Sutton-Chickaloon area prior to WW II /. [Anchorage, Alaska] [1985] ii, 47 leaves : LC Card 86-620606 DDC 338.2/724/097983 19
HD9548.S87 B38 1985

COAL MINES AND MINING - ALASKA - SUTTON REGION - HISTORY.
Bauer, Mary Cracraft. A history of coal-mining in the Sutton-Chickaloon area prior to WW II /. [Anchorage, Alaska] [1985] ii, 47 leaves : LC Card 86-620606 DDC 338.2/724/097983 19
HD9548.S87 B38 1985

COAL MINES AND MINING - BRAZIL - CRICIÚMA.
Volpato, Terezinha Gascho. A pirita humana . Florianópolis , 1984. 159 p. : LC Card 85-150574
HD8039.M62 B78 1984

COAL MINES AND MINING - COLOMBIA - VALLE DEL CAUCA - MAPS.
Estudio del Plan de desarrollo carbonífero de la zona de Valle del Cauca en la República de Colombia. Tokio, Japon , 1977. v, 149 leaves : LC Card 84-244429
HD9554.C63 V34 1977

COAL MINES AND MINING - ENVIRONMENTAL ASPECTS - UNITED STATES.
Energy and Environmental Analysis, inc. Benefit/cost analyses of laws and regulations affecting coal . Washington , 1977. ca. 750 p. : LC Card 77-603790 DDC 363.6
TD195.C58 E53 1977 ***NYPL [JLF 81-219]***

COAL MINES AND MINING - GERMANY (WEST) - RUHR (REGION) - HISTORY.
Berg, Werner. Wirtschaft und Gesellschaft in Deutschland und Grossbritannien im Übergang zum "organisierten Kapitalismus" . Berlin , c1984. 888 p. : ISBN 3-428-05495-4 LC Card 84-222230
HD9553.7.R8 B47 1984

COAL MINES AND MINING - GOVERNMENT POLICY - GERMANY (WEST) - RUHR (REGION) - HISTORY.
Berg, Werner. Wirtschaft und Gesellschaft in Deutschland und Grossbritannien im Übergang zum "organisierten Kapitalismus" . Berlin , c1984. 888 p. : ISBN 3-428-05495-4 LC Card 84-222230
HD9553.7.R8 B47 1984

COAL MINES AND MINING - GOVERNMENT POLICY - WALES, SOUTH - HISTORY.
Berg, Werner. Wirtschaft und Gesellschaft in Deutschland und Grossbritannien im Übergang zum "organisierten Kapitalismus" . Berlin , c1984. 888 p. : ISBN 3-428-05495-4 LC Card 84-222230
HD9553.7.R8 B47 1984

COAL MINES AND MINING - GREAT BRITAIN - HISTORY.
The history of the British coal industry. Oxford [Oxfordshire] , New York , c1983- v. : ISBN 0-19-828283-4 (v. 2) : LC Card 83-4194 DDC 338.2/724/0941 19
HD9551.5 .F58 1983 ***NYPL [JLL 84-138]***

COAL MINES AND MINING - HUNGARY - BORSOD MEGYE - HISTORY.
200 éves a borsodi szénbányászat, 1786-1986 /. [Miskolc , 1986] 223 p. : ISBN 963-02-4565-5 (Magy. nemz. bibl.) LC Card 87-150976
HD9555.H83 B6715 1986

COAL MINES AND MINING - INDIA.
Coal after nationalisation /. Calcutta , 1977. 676, [122] p. : LC Card 77-905030
HD9556.I42 C57 ***NYPL [JLF 78-1568]***

COAL MINES AND MINING - PENNSYLVANIA - SAINT CLAIR (SCHUYLKILL COUNTY) - HISTORY - 19TH CENTURY.
Wallace, Anthony F. C., 1923- St. Clair . New York , 1987. xvii, 519 p. : ISBN 0-394-52867-0 : LC Card 86-46120 DDC 307.7/66/0974817 19
HD8039.M62 U6699 1987

COAL MINES AND MINING - SOVIET UNION - ACCOUNTING.
Shvarts, M. A. (Mikhail Aleksandrovich) Ėkonomicheskiĭ analiz deiatel'nosti proizvodstvennogo ob"edineniia po dobyche uglia /. Moskva , 1986. 222 p. ; LC Card

85-236907
HF5686.M6 S48 1986

COAL MINES AND MINING - WALES, SOUTH - HISTORY.
Berg, Werner. Wirtschaft und Gesellschaft in Deutschland und Grossbritannien im Übergang zum "organisierten Kapitalismus" . Berlin , c1984. 888 p. : ISBN 3-428-05495-4 LC Card 84-222230
HD9553.7.R8 B47 1984

The coal of El Cerrejón . Kline, Harvey F. University Park , c1987. viii, 216 p. : ISBN 0-271-00491-6 : LC Card 86-43038 DDC 333.8/2215/09861 19
HD9554.C63 E3748 1987

COAL-OIL. see **PETROLEUM.**

COAL STRIKE, GREAT BRITAIN, 1984-1985.
Digging deeper . London , 1985. xiv, 252 p. : ISBN 0-86091-820-3 (pbk.) : LC Card 87-118973 DDC 331.89/2822334/0941 19
HD5365.M6152 1984 .D54 1985

The Enemy within . London , New York , 1986. xxiii, 260 p. : ISBN 0-7102-0888-X (pbk.) : LC Card 86-12192 DDC 331.89/2822334/0941 19
HD5365.M6152 1984 .E54 1986

Miller, Jill. You can't kill the spirit . London , c1986. 142 p. : ISBN 0-7043-4021-6 (pbk.) : LC Card 87-100804 DDC 305.4/2/0942995 19
HD5365.M6152 1984 .W345 1986

Thurcroft, a village and the miners' strike . Nottingham [Nottinghamshire] , Atlantic Highlands, NJ , 1986. 276 p. : ISBN 0-85124-441-6 LC Card 86-21887 DDC 331.89/2822334/0942823 19
HD5346.M6152 1984 .T48 1987
NYPL [JLD 87-985]

Wilsher, Peter. Strike . London [1985] xiii, 284 p., [16] p. of plates : ISBN 0-233-97825-9 : LC Card 86-221981 DDC 331.89/2822334/0941 19
HD5365.M6152 1984 .W55 1985b

COAL STRIKE, W. VA., 1920-1921.
Savage, Lon, 1928- Thunder in the mountains /. Elliston, Va. , 1986. iv, 160 p. : ISBN 0-9617256-0-5 (pbk.) : LC Card 87-7634 DDC 331.89/2822334/097543 19
HD5325.M63 1920 .W47

COAL-TAR INDUSTRY - SOVIET CENTRAL ASIA.
Ulitskiĭ, L. I. (Lazar′ Ioakhimovich) K organizatsii koksokhimicheskoĭ promyshlennosti v Sredneĭ Azii. Tashkent, 1945. 63 p. LC Card 51-55383
HD9559 .C7S68

COAL TRADE.
Gordon, Richard L., 1934- World coal . Cambridge [Cambridgeshire] , New York , 1987. xvi, 145 p. : ISBN 0-521-30827-5 LC Card 86-26349 DDC 338.2/724 19
HD9540.5 .G64 1987

COAL TRADE - AFRICA, SOUTHERN.
Lange, G. F. Summary report on a mission to southern Africa from 9 July to 21 August 1985 for the development of coal resources in Malawi, Swaziland, Mozambique, Zambia, and Zimbabwe. [Addis Ababa] [1985] ii, 60 p. ; LC Card 85-981333 DDC 338.2/724/0968 19
HD9557.A356 L36 1985

COAL TRADE - ALASKA.
Arctic Slope Consulting Engineers. Western Arctic Coal Development Project . Anchorage, Alaska [1986] 2 v. : LC Card 87-621058 DDC 333.8/22/09798 19
HD9547.A4 A85 1986

COAL TRADE - ALASKA - CHICKALOON REGION - HISTORY.
Bauer, Mary Cracraft. A history of coal-mining in the Sutton-Chickaloon area prior to WW II /. [Anchorage, Alaska] [1985] ii, 47 leaves : LC Card 86-620606 DDC 338.2/724/097983 19
HD9548.S87 B38 1985

COAL TRADE - ALASKA - SUTTON REGION - HISTORY.
Bauer, Mary Cracraft. A history of coal-mining in the Sutton-Chickaloon area prior to WW II /. [Anchorage, Alaska] [1985] ii, 47 leaves : LC Card 86-620606 DDC 338.2/724/097983 19
HD9548.S87 B38 1985

COAL TRADE - AUSTRALIA - HISTORY - SOURCES.
Pemberton, P. A. Pure merinos and others . Canberra , c1986. 125 p. : ISBN 0-86784-796-4 (pbk.) LC Card 87-164515 DDC 382/.41636/0994 19
HE565.G7 P46 1986

COAL TRADE - BRAZIL - ARROIO DOS RATOS - HISTORY.
Sulzbach, Ervino Lothar. Arroio dos Ratos, berço da indústria carbonífera nacional . [Rio Grande do Sul] c1985 (Rio Grande do Sul : Flores Linotipia) 163 p. : LC Card 86-150014
HD9554.B83 A777 1985

COAL TRADE - BRAZIL, SOUTH.
Carvão mineral /. [Porto Alegre] [19]84. 56 p. ; LC Card 86-163115
HD9554.B83 S683 1984

COAL TRADE - COLOMBIA - EJÓN HILL.
Acosta M., Amylkar (Acosta Medina), 1950- [Selections. 1986.] Escritos, 1978-1986 /. Medellín, Colombia , 1986. 201 p. ; LC Card 87-404338 DDC 330.9861/0632 19
HC197 .A5562 1986

COAL TRADE - COLOMBIA - VALLE DEL CAUCA.
Estudio del Plan de desarrollo carbonífero de la zona de Valle del Cauca en la República de Colombia. Tokio, Japon , 1977. v, 149 leaves : LC Card 84-244429
HD9554.C63 V34 1977

COAL TRADE - ENVIRONMENTAL ASPECTS - GOVERNMENT POLICY.
Coal . Paris [Washington, D.C.] 1987. 108 p. ; ISBN 92-64-12909-X (pbk.) : LC Card 87-163847 DDC 363.7/31 19
HD9540.6 .C63 1987

COAL TRADE - GOVERNMENT POLICY - AUSTRALIA - COLLIE (W.A.)
Taylor, Neil. Collie, coal, and energy policy in Western Australia /. Murdoch, W.A. [1985] 56 p. : ISBN 0-86905-080-X (pbk.) LC Card 87-116549 DDC 333.8/22/099412 19
HD9558.A83 C657 1985

COAL TRADE - GOVERNMENT POLICY - COLOMBIA - EJÓN HILL REGION.
Kline, Harvey F. The coal of El Cerrejón . University Park , c1987. viii, 216 p. : ISBN 0-271-00491-6 : LC Card 86-43038 DDC 333.8/2215/09861 19
HD9554.C63 E3748 1987

COAL TRADE - GREAT BRITAIN.
Coal industry examination . London [1974] 35 p. ; LC Card 85-192146 DDC 338.2/724/0941 19
HD9551.5 .C43 1974

COAL TRADE - GREAT BRITAIN - HISTORY.
The history of the British coal industry. Oxford [Oxfordshire] , New York , c1983- v. : ISBN 0-19-828283-4 (v. 2) : LC Card 83-4194 DDC 338.2/724/0941 19
HD9551.5 .F58 1983 ***NYPL [JLL 84-138]***

COAL TRADE - GREAT BRITAIN - HISTORY - 20TH CENTURY.
Robertson, Alex. The bleak midwinter, 1947 /. Manchester, U.K. , Wolfeboro, N.H., U. S.A. , 1987. x, 207 p. : ISBN 0-7190-1902-8 : LC Card 87-11085 DDC 333.8/22/0941 19
HD9551.5 .R56 1987

COAL TRADE - GREAT BRITAIN - HISTORY - SOURCES.
Pemberton, P. A. Pure merinos and others . Canberra , c1986. 125 p. : ISBN 0-86784-796-4 (pbk.) LC Card 87-164515 DDC 382/.41636/0994 19
HE565.G7 P46 1986

COAL TRADE - HUNGARY - BORSOD MEGYE - HISTORY.
200 éves a borsodi szénbányászat, 1786-1986 /. [Miskolc , 1986] 223 p. : ISBN 963-02-4565-5 (Magy. nemz. bibl.) LC Card 87-150976
HD9555.H83 B6715 1986

COAL TRADE - INDIA.
Coal after nationalisation /. Calcutta , 1977. 676, [122] p. : LC Card 77-905030
HD9556.I42 C57 ***NYPL [JLF 78-1568]***

Prasad, Anubhuti Ranjan. Coal industry of India /. New Delhi , 1986. xxvi, 516 p. : ISBN 81-7024-055-7 : LC Card 86-902669 DDC 338.2/724/0954 19
HD9556.I42 P72 1986

COAL TRADE - MONTANA.
Brower, John C. The economic impact of coal mining in Montana /. Missoula, Mont. [1985] 31 p. : LC Card 87-620608 DDC 338.2/724/09786 19
HD9547.M6 B76 1985

COAL TRADE - SPAIN - ASTURIAS - HISTORY - 20TH CENTURY.
Shubert, Adrian, 1953- The road to revolution in Spain . Urbana , c1987. 183 p. : ISBN 0-252-01368-9 (alk. paper) LC Card 86-24998 DDC 331.7/622334/094615 19
HD8039.M62 S68 1987

COAL TRADE - UNITED STATES.
Potential effects of section 3 of the Federal Coal Leasing Amendments Act of 1976. Washington, D.C. , 1986. vii, 186 p. : LC Card 86-600512 DDC 333.33/9 19
HD242.3 .P68 1986 ***NYPL [JLF 86-1368]***

COAL TRADE - VENEZUELA - ZULIA.
Sánchez Meleán, Jorge. Reflexiones para la acción /. [Venezuela?] , 1986. xv, 322 p. : ISBN 980-232-049-8 LC Card 87-134702 DDC 338.987 19
HC237 .S275 1986

COAL TRADE - VIRGINIA.
Hibbard, W. R. (Walter Rollo) The Virginia coal industry . Blacksburg, Va. (617 N. Main St., Blacksburg 24061) [1986] ii, 46 leaves ; LC Card 87-620671 DDC 338.2/724/09755 19
HD9547.V8 H523 1986

The Virginia coal industry . Blacksburg, Va. [1986] [15] leaves ; LC Card 86-622456 DDC 381/.4224/09755 19
HD9547.V8 V57 1986

COALBRA Coque e Alcool da Madeira (Brazil)
Alcool e emprego . Brasília, DF , 1983. 170 p. : LC Card 86-200307
HD5718.A4852 B63 1983

Coale, Ansley J. Basic data on fertility in the provinces of China, 1940-82 / Ansley J. Coale and Chen Sheng Li. Honolulu, HI : East-West Population Institute, East-West Center, [1987] xvii, 366 p. : ill. ; 23 cm. (Papers of the East-West Population Institute, 0732-0531 . no. 104) Chiefly tables. "January 1987." ISBN 0-86638-088-4 (pbk.) : LC Card 86-32765 DDC 304.6/32/0951 19
1. Fertility, Human - China - Provinces - History. I. Chen, Sheng Li, 1945-. II. Title. III. Series.
HB1064.A3 C63 1987

Coalition forming behavior / edited by Heinz Sauermann. Tübingen : Mohr, 1978. viii, 375 p. : ill. ; 24 cm. (Contributions to experimental economics . 8 = 8) Papers presented at the second Conference on Experimental Economics, Winzenhohl, Germany, August 28th to September 2nd, 1977. Includes bibliographies and indexes. ISBN 3-16-340982-2 LC Card 86-227555 DDC 330 s 658.4 19
1. Negotiation in business - Congresses. 2. Negotiation - Congresses. 3. Coalition (Social sciences) - Congresses. I. Sauermann, Heinz. II. Conference on Experimental Economics (2nd : 1977 : Winzenhohl, Germany). III. Series: Beiträge zur experimentellen Wirtschaftsforschung, 8. Bd.
HB41 .B29 1967 vol. 8 HD58.6

Coalition of Northeast Governors. Policy Research Center. A case of inequity [microform] : regional patterns in defense expenditures, 1950-1977 / a joint study by the Coneg Policy Research Center, inc. and the Northeast-Midwest Research Institute. [New York] : The Center, 1977. 39 p. ; 28 cm. Cover title. "August 1977." Errata sheet inserted. Microfilm. New York : New York Public Library, 1985. 1 microfilm reel ; 35 mm. (MN *ZZ-25,047)
1. Defense contracts - United States. 2. Disarmament - Economic aspects - United States. 3. United States - Armed Forces - Procurement. I. Northeast-Midwest Research Institute. II. Title.
NYPL [*ZT-1564 no.21]

COALITION (SOCIAL SCIENCES) - CONGRESSES.
Coalition forming behavior /. Tübingen , 1978. viii, 375 p. : ISBN 3-16-340982-2 LC Card 86-227555 DDC 330 s 658.4 19
HB41 .B29 1967 vol. 8 HD58.6

The coalmining industry in the United States /. Miernyk, William H. Geneva , 1986. 53, ix p. :

ISBN 92-9014-409-2 (pbk.)
NYPL [JLE 87-1534]

Coase, R. H. (Ronald Harry) The firm, the market, and the law / R.H. Coase. Chicago : University of Chicago Press, 1988. p. cm. Includes index. ISBN 0-226-11100-8 LC Card 87-24193 DDC 338.5/142 19
1. Industrial organization (Economic theory). 2. Externalities (Economics). 3. Capitalism. I. Title.
HD2326 .C6 1988

Coast Community College District. Marketing. Fountain Valley, CA , 1985. 1 videocassette (30 min.) : LC Card 87-705967 DDC 658.8 11
HF5415

Coast Telecourses (Firm) Marketing. Fountain Valley, CA , 1985. 1 videocassette (30 min.) : LC Card 87-705967 DDC 658.8 11
HF5415

COASTAL ZONE MANAGEMENT - BRITISH COLUMBIA.
Dorcey, Anthony H. J., 1944- Bargaining in the governance of Pacific coastal resources . Vancouver, B.C. , c1986. xvi, 219 p. : ISBN 0-920146-34-1 (pbk.) LC Card 86-222720 DDC 333.91/7/09711 19
HC117.B8 D67 1986

COASTAL ZONE MANAGEMENT - DEVELOPING COUNTRIES.
Alternative Hafen- und Küstenpolitik /. Hamburg , 1985. 260 p. : ISBN 3-88876-034-8 LC Card 87-133678 DDC 387.1/094 19
HE557.G3 A55 1985

COASTAL ZONE MANAGEMENT - EUROPE.
Alternative Hafen- und Küstenpolitik /. Hamburg , 1985. 260 p. : ISBN 3-88876-034-8 LC Card 87-133678 DDC 387.1/094 19
HE557.G3 A55 1985

COASTAL ZONE MANAGEMENT - GERMANY (WEST)
Alternative Hafen- und Küstenpolitik /. Hamburg , 1985. 260 p. : ISBN 3-88876-034-8 LC Card 87-133678 DDC 387.1/094 19
HE557.G3 A55 1985

COASTWISE SHIPPING - AFRICA, WEST - HISTORY.
Carreira, António. Os portuguêses nos rios de Guiné, 1500-1900 /. Lisboa , 1984. 205 p. : LC Card 85-149851
HF3698.A358 C37 1984

COASTWISE SHIPPING - BRAZIL.
Estudo preliminar para o establecimento de prioridades no financiamento para construção de embarcações para a navegação interior /. [Rio de Janeiro] , 1985. [84] leaves : LC Card 87-403936 DDC 386/.0981 19
HE653 .E88 1985

COASTWISE SHIPPING - TEXAS.
The Gulf Intracoastal Waterway in Texas . [Austin] , 1982. 1 v. (various pagings) : LC Card 83-620632
HE631.T4 G44 1982

Coates, Austin. The commerce in rubber : the first 250 years / Austin Coates. Singapore ; New York : Oxford University Press, 1987. xv, 380 p., [32] p. of plates : ill., maps ; 24 cm. Maps on lining papers. Bibliography: p. [373]-375. Includes index. ISBN 0-19-588868-5 : LC Card 87-20332 DDC 338.1/738952 19
1. Rubber industry and trade - History. I. Title.
HD9161.A2 C62 1987

Coates, David. The Economic revival of modern Britain . Aldershot, Hants, England , c1987. xv, 349 p. : ISBN 1-85278-000-2 (pbk.) : LC Card 87-170031 DDC 338.941 19
HC256.6 .E227 1987

Coates, Ken.
Freedom and fairness . Nottingham, England , Atlantic Highlands, N.J. , 1986. 157 p. ; ISBN 0-85124-440-8 LC Card 86-28038 DDC 331.88/0942 19
HD6664 .F763 1986

Trade unions and politics / Ken Coates and Tony Topham. Oxford, OX, UK ; New York, NY, USA : Blackwell, 1986. ix, 268 p. : ill. ; 24 cm. Includes bibliographical references and index. ISBN 0-631-13752-1 : LC Card 85-22959 DDC 322/.2/0941 19
1. Trade-unions - Great Britain - Political activity. 2. Unemployment - Great Britain. 3. Manpower policy - Great Britain. I. Topham, Anthony. II. Title.
HD6667 .C63 1986 NYPL [JLE 86-1729]

Trade unions in Britain / Ken Coates and Tony Topham. Nottingham : Spokesman, 1980. xii, 385 p. : ill. ; 23 cm. (Spokesman university paperback . no. 23) Bibliography: p. [370]-378. Includes indexes. ISBN 0-85124-293-6 LC Card 86-673477 DDC 331.88/0941 19
1. Trade-unions - Great Britain. I. Topham, Tony. II. Title.
HD6664 .C38765 1980

Coates, Mary Lou. Employment equity : issues, approaches, and public policy framework / Mary Lou Coates. Kingston, Ont., Canada : Industrial Relations Centre, Queen's University at Kingston, 1986. 109 p. : ill. ; 28 cm. (Research and current issues series, 0317-2546 . no. 44) Bibliography: p. 56-60. ISBN 0-88886-131-1 (pbk.) LC Card 86-182985 DDC 331.13/3/0971 19
1. Discrimination in employment - Government policy - Canada. 2. Affirmative action programs - Canada. I. Title. II. Series.
HD4903.5.C2 C6 1986

Cobb, Douglas Ford. LeBlond, Geoffrey T. Como usar Lotus 1-2-3 . Miami, Fla. , 1986- p. cm. LC Card 86-23629 DDC 005.36/9 19
HF5548.4.L67 L418 1986

Cobham, David P. Macroeconomic analysis : an intermediate text / David Cobham. London ; New York : Longman, 1987. viii, 159 p. : ill. ; 24 cm. (Longman economics series) Bibliography: p. 154-155. Includes index. ISBN 0-582-29708-7 (pbk.) LC Card 86-27825 DDC 339 19
1. Macroeconomics. I. Title. II. Series.
HB172.5 .C63 1987

COBRA (ORGANIZATION) - HISTORY.
Silvia Helena. Rastro de Cobra /. [Brazil , 1984] (Rio de Janeiro, RJ : Alphaset Gráfica e Editora) 124 p., [4] p. of plates : LC Card 87-130372 DDC 338.4/7004/0981 19
HD9696.C63 B77 1984

Cobriza, Cobriza, 1971 / equipo de investigación, Miguel Gutiérrez, Vilma Aguilar, Ana María Mur ; colabora, Gregorio Martínez ; textos, crónica, Miguel Gutiérrez, testimonios, Vilma Aguilar ; colabora, Ana María Mur. 1a ed. [Lima? Peru] : Ediciones Nueva Crónica, 1981. 136 p. ; 21 cm. (Serie Nueva crónica y buen gobierno) Bibliography: p. [131]-134. LC Card 83-106108
1. Cerro Corporation Strike, 1971. I. Gutiérrez, Miguel. II. Aguilar, Vilma. III. Mur, Ana María.
HD5361 .M612 1971

Coca-Cola . Hoy, Anne H. Atlanta, Ga. , c1986. 159 p. : LC Card 86-209155 DDC 338.7/66362/0973 19
HD9349.S634 C64 1986

Coca-Cola Company.
Hoy, Anne H. Coca-Cola . Atlanta, Ga. , c1986. 159 p. : LC Card 86-209155 DDC 338.7/66362/0973 19
HD9349.S634 C64 1986

COCA-COLA COMPANY.
Oliver, Thomas, 1950- The real Coke, the real story /. New York , 1986. 195 p. ; ISBN 0-394-55273-3 : LC Card 86-10151 DDC 338.7/66362/0973 19
HD9349.S634 C67 1986
NYPL [JLE 86-4489]

Oliver, Thomas, 1950- The real Coke, the real story /. New York , 1987, c1986. 234 p., [9] p. of plates : ISBN 0-14-010408-9 (pbk.) LC Card 87-11836 DDC 338.7/66362/0973 19
HD9349.S634 C67 1987

COCA-COLA COMPANY - HISTORY.
Hoy, Anne H. Coca-Cola . Atlanta, Ga. , c1986. 159 p. : LC Card 86-209155 DDC 338.7/66362/0973 19
HD9349.S634 C64 1986

Oliver, Thomas, 1950- The real Coke, the real story /. New York , 1986. 195 p. ; ISBN 0-394-55273-3 : LC Card 86-10151 DDC 338.7/66362/0973 19
HD9349.S634 C67 1986
NYPL [JLE 86-4489]

Oliver, Thomas, 1950- The real Coke, the real story /. New York , 1987, c1986. 234 p., [9] p. of plates : ISBN 0-14-010408-9 (pbk.) LC Card 87-11836 DDC 338.7/66362/0973 19
HD9349.S634 C67 1987

COCA-COLA COMPANY - PICTORIAL WORKS.
Hoy, Anne H. Coca-Cola . Atlanta, Ga. , c1986. 159 p. : LC Card 86-209155 DDC 338.7/66362/0973 19
HD9349.S634 C64 1986

COCA INDUSTRY - BOLIVIA - CHAPARÉ.
Producción y comercialización de la coca . Cochabamba, Bolivia , 1972. 92 leaves in various foliations, [3] folded leaves of plates : LC Card 85-138614
HD9019.C632 B646 1972

COCA INDUSTRY - BOLIVIA - YUNGAS.
Producción y comercialización de la coca . Cochabamba, Bolivia , 1972. 92 leaves in various foliations, [3] folded leaves of plates : LC Card 85-138614
HD9019.C632 B646 1972

COCHABAMBA (BOLIVIA : DEPT.) - FAIRS.
Calderón G., Fernando. Jatun Llajta . La Paz, Bolivia , 1982. v, 448 p., [8] leaves of plates : LC Card 83-111937 DDC 381/.1 19
HF5473.B62 C623 1982
NYPL [JLF 86-1794]

COCHIN PORT - HISTORY.
Paul, D. Babu (Daniel Babu), 1941- A queen's story . New Delhi , c1987. xix, 132 p. : ISBN 0-7069-3376-1 : LC Card 86-903827 DDC 387.1/0954/83 19
HE560.C56 P38 1987

Cochrane, Allan. Developing local economic strategies . Milton Keynes [England] , Philadelphia , 1987. p. cm. ISBN 0-335-15522-7 LC Card 87-22681 DDC 338.941 19
HC256.6 .D48 1987

Cochrane, John. Plaxico, James Sam, 1924- Financial status of Oklahoma farmers and ranchers, 1985 . [Stillwater] [1986] 42 p. ; LC Card 86-622478 DDC 338.1/3/09766021 19
HD1775.O5 P57 1986

Cockburn, Cynthia. Machinery of dominance : women, men, and technical know-how / Cynthia Cockburn. London ; Dover, N.H. : Pluto Press, 1985. 282 p. ; 20 cm. Bibliography: p. [258]-277. Includes index. ISBN 0-7453-0065-0 (pbk.) : LC Card 86-204262 DDC 331.13/3/0941 19
1. Sex discrimination in employment - Great Britain. 2. Technicians in industry - Great Britain. I. Title.
HD6060.5.G7 C63 1985

Cockcroft, James D. Outlaws in the promised land : Mexican immigrant workers and America's future / James D. Cockcroft.1st Grove Press ed. New York : Grove Press, 1986. 306 p. ; 25 cm. Includes index. Bibliography: p. 288-298. ISBN 0-394-54592-3 : LC Card 84-73206 DDC 331.6/2/72073 19
1. Alien labor, Mexican - United States. 2. Alien labor, Mexican - United States - Forecasting. I. Title.
HD8081.M6 C63 1986
NYPL [JLE 86-2776]

Cocklin, Chris. Demands on rural lands . Boulder, Colo. , 1987. xvi, 336 p. : ISBN 0-8133-7361-1 (pbk. : alk. paper) LC Card 87-50751 DDC 333.76/13 19
HD105 .D43 1987

Cockrill, Philip.
Liberia / Philip Cockrill. Newbury, Berkshire, England : P. Cockrill, [198-?] 15 v. in 2 : ill. ; 21 cm. (Series booklet . no. 1-10, 21-25) LC Card 86-217641
1. Postage stamps - Liberia - History. 2. Postmarks - Liberia - History. 3. Postal service - Liberia - History. I. Series: Cockrill, Philip. Series booklet , no. 1, etc. II. Title.
HE6185.L49 C63 1980z

Series booklet .
(no. 1, etc) Cockrill, Philip. Liberia /. Newbury, Berkshire, England [198-?] 15 v. in 2 : LC Card 86-217641
HE6185.L49 C63 1980z

Cockrill series booklet .
(no. 13-20) Payne, Eric. Ethiopia /. Hampstead Norreys, Newbury, Berkshire, England , 1981-1982. 8 v. in 1 : LC Card 87-166672
HE6185.E8 P39 1981

COCOA FARMERS - GHANA.
Arhin, Kwame. The expansion of cocoa production in Ghana . [Ghana] [1985] xiii, 137 p., [5] p. of plates : LC Card 86-222543 DDC

338.1/7374/09667 19
HD8039.C6362 G42 1985

COCOA FARMERS - GHANA - SUPPLEMENTARY EMPLOYMENT - CASE STUDIES.
Nyanteng, V. K. Supplementary occupations and incomes of cocoa farmers in the Suhum agricultural district of Ghana /. Legon , 1979. 17 p. ; LC Card 87-402747 DDC 331.7/63374/09667 19
HD8039.C6362 G46 1979

COCOA TRADE - DEVELOPING COUNTRIES.
Short, Joseph N. American business and foreign policy . New York , 1987. 340 p. : ISBN 0-8240-8093-9 (alk. paper) : LC Card 87-23792 DDC 382/.41373/0973 19
HD9199.U48 S46 1987

COCOA TRADE - GHANA.
Konings, Piet. The state and rural class formation in Ghana . London ; Boston : xvi, 391 p. : ISBN 0-7103-0117-0 LC Card 85-28109 DDC 305.5/09667 19
HN832.Z9 S65 1986 ***NYPL [Sc D 86-574]***

COCOA TRADE - UNITED STATES.
Short, Joseph N. American business and foreign policy . New York , 1987. 340 p. : ISBN 0-8240-8093-9 (alk. paper) : LC Card 87-23792 DDC 382/.41373/0973 19
HD9199.U48 S46 1987

COCONUT INDUSTRY - PHILIPPINES.
Hawes, Gary, 1950- The Philippine State and the Marcos regime . Ithaca , 1987. 196 p. ; ISBN 0-8014-2012-1 (alk. paper) LC Card 86-29237 DDC 382/.41/09599 19
HD9016.P52 H38 1987

Codeplan. see **Companhia do Desenvolvimento do Planalto Central.**

Codesria.
Inventaire . Paris [Washington, D.C.] 1986. xxvii, 262 p. ; ISBN 92-64-02871-4 : LC Card 87-129509
HD77.5.A34 I58 1986

Organisation for Economic Co-operation and Development. Development Centre. Répertoire . Paris , Washington, D.C. , 1986. xxiv, 523 p. ; ISBN 92-64-02872-2 : LC Card 87-146730
HD77.5.A34 O75 1986

Codesul.
Caracterização da indústria agroalimentar no Paraná /. Curitiba , 1985. x, 50 leaves : LC Card 86-202725
HD9014.B83 P3718 1985

Paraná, formação de capital . [Pôrto Alegre] , 1965. 185 p. : LC Card 85-131098
HC188.P35 P388 1965

Código de productos y materias primas / Instituto Nacional de Estadística, Departamento de Estadísticas Económicas, División de Estadísticas Productivas. La Paz, Bolivia : La División, 1981. 129 leaves ; 32 cm. Cover title. LC Card 85-129059
1. Commercial products - Bolivia - Classification. I. Instituto Nacional de Estadística (Bolivia). División de Estadísticas Productivas.
HF1044.B5 C63 1981

Cody, Seamus. The Parliament of labour : 100 years of the Dublin Council of Trade Unions / Seamus Cody, John O'Dowd, Peter Rigney. Dublin, Ireland : Dublin Council Of Trade Unions, 1986. 253 p. : ill. ; 21 cm. Bibliography: p. 243-250. LC Card 87-102467 DDC 331.88/09418/35 19
1. Dublin Council of Trade Unions - History. I. O'Dowd, John. II. Rigney, Peter. III. Title.
HD8400.3.A5 D833 1986

Coe, Richard D. Capitalism and democracy . Notre Dame, Ind. , c1985. ix, 190 p. : ISBN 0-268-00750-0 : LC Card 84-40362 DDC 335 19
HX72.S383 C36 1985 ***NYPL [JLD 85-1987]***

COEFFICIENT OF ELASTICITY. see **ELASTICITY (ECONOMICS)**

Coelho, Antonio Borges. Quadros para uma viagem a Portugal no Sec. XVI / António Borges Coelho. Lisboa : Caminho, c1986. 403 p., [2] folded leaves of plates : maps ; 21 cm. (Colecção universitária . 13) LC Card 87-401474
1. Portugal - Economic conditions. 2. Portugal - Social conditions. 3. Portugal - Population - History - 16th century. 4. Portugal - Description and travel. I. Title. II. Series.
HC392 .C573 1986

Coelho, Carlos Nayro de Azevedo. Opções de política econômica / Carlos Nayro Coelho. Brasília : Ministério da Agricultura, Companhia de Financiamento da Produção, 1986. 137 p. ; 22 cm. (Estudos especiais . v. 19) Bibliography: p. 137. LC Card 87-403318 DDC 338.981 19
1. Brazil - Economic policy. I. Series: Estudos especiais (Brasília, Brazil) , v. 19. II. Title.
HC187 .C565 1986

La coerción económica internacional . Mac Lean U., Roberto. [Lima, Perú] [1986] 28 p. ; LC Card 87-142994 DDC 337 19
HF1411 .M218 1986

Coers, Hermann Max. El Banco Central Latinaoamericano : una "utopía" en busca de su realización / Hermann Max Coers.1a ed. México : Centro de Estudios Monetarios Latinoamericanos, 1972. xv, 78 p. ; 17 cm. (Ensayos. 31) Bibliography: p. 75-76. LC Card 87-401518 DDC 332.1/1/098 19
1. Banks and banking, Central - Latin America. 2. Latin America - Economic integration. I. Series: Ensayos (Centro de Estudios Monetarios Latinoamericanos) , 31. II. Title.
HG2710.5.A7 C6 1972

Coes, Donald V., 1943- O Brasil na economia internacional. [Salvador, Brazil] : Fundação Bahiana para Estudos Econômicos e Sociais, [1984?] 55 p. : ports. ; 23 cm. "Conferência do Prof. Donald Vinton Coes, da Universidade de Illinois, EUA, tendo como debatedores os economistas Paulo Guedes e Moisés Glatt, da Fundação Getúlio Vargas do Rio de Janeiro e Reub Celestino, Superintendente do Desenbanco--no auditório do Desenbanco, em 11 de maio d 1984." LC Card 86-234065
1. Brazil - Foreign economic relations. 2. Brazil - Foreign economic relations - United States. 3. United States - Foreign economic relations - Brazil. 4. Brazil - Economic policy. I. Title.
HF1513 .C64 1984

Coetzee, Jan Karel. Development is for people /. Braamfontein, Johannesburg , 1986. 253 p. : ISBN 0-86954-274-5 (pbk.) : LC Card 86-200074 DDC 338.9 19
HD75 .D488 1986

Coetzee, S. F. Regional economic development in the Southern African development area / S.F. Coetzee, G.F. Geringer, A.M. Thompson. Sandton, Republic of South Africa : Development Bank of Southern Africa, 1985. xvi, 105 p. : ill. ; 30 cm. (Position paper . no. 2) Bibliography: p. 97-105. LC Card 87-150264 DDC 338.968 19
1. South Africa - Economic policy. 2. Regional planning - South Africa. I. Geringer, G. F. II. Thompson, A. M. III. Series: Position paper (Development Bank of Southern Africa) , no. 2. IV. Title.
HC905 .C64 1985

Coeymans, Juan Eduardo. Determinants of sectoral annual real wages in a developing economy / Juan Eduardo Coeymans A. Santiago : Pontificia Universidad Católica de Chile, Instituto de Economía, Oficina de Publicaciones, 1986. 32, [4] leaves : ill. ; 27 cm. (Documento de trabajo / Pontificia Universidad Católica de Chile, Instituto de Economía . no. 106) Bibliography: leaf [36]. LC Card 87-404007 DDC 331.12/5/0983 19
1. Wages - Chile - Econometric models. 2. Labor supply - Chile - Econometric models. 3. Unemployment - Chile - Econometric models. I. Series: Documento de trabajo (Universidad Católica de Chile. Instituto de Economía) , no. 106. II. Title.
HD5006 .C64 1986

COFFEE BREWING.
Report on the coffee service industry /. Columbus, Ohio [1984] 1 v. (various foliations) : LC Card 87-100404 DDC 381/.4566393 19
HD9199.U48 R47 1984

Coffee Development Group (U. S.)
Bruskin, R. H. A market strategy study of the whole bean coffee market . [New Brunswick, N.J.] [1985] 1 v. (various pagings) : LC Card 87-100003 DDC 381/.41373/0971 19
HD9199.U48 B84 1985

Iced coffee taste test . Van Nuys, CA (14416 Victory Blvd. Van Nuys 91401) [1985] 132 p., 6, 6 leaves : LC Card 87-100181 DDC 381/.4566393/0973 19
HD9199.U48 I25 1985

Report on the coffee service industry /. Columbus, Ohio [1984] 1 v. (various foliations) : LC Card 87-100404 DDC 381/.4566393 19
HD9199.U48 R47 1984

COFFEE - EL SALVADOR.
Fabián, Miguel Angel. Monografía del café /. [San Salvador] , 1984. 39 leaves : LC Card 86-177543
HD9199.S142 F33 1984

Coffee factorage and the emergence of a Brazilian capital market, 1850-1888 /. Sweigart, Joseph Earl. New York , 1987. xvi, 337 p. : ISBN 0-8240-1373-5 (alk. paper) : LC Card 87-8617 DDC 338.1/3373/098153 19
HD9199.B8 R567 1987

COFFEE-HOUSES - UNITED STATES.
Hess, Alan. Googie . San Francisco, CA [1986]. 144 p. : ISBN 0-87701-334-9 (pbk.) : LC Card 85-17089 DDC 725/.71/0973 19
NA7856 .H47 1986
NYPL [3-MQWO 86-2210]

COFFEE INDUSTRY - BRAZIL.
Tsunechiro, Alfredo. O desempenho dos mercados a termo . São Paulo , 1986. xi, 123 p. : LC Card 87-404554 DDC 332.64/4 19
HG6046 .T75 1986

COFFEE, INSTANT.
Report on the coffee service industry /. Columbus, Ohio [1984] 1 v. (various foliations) : LC Card 87-100404 DDC 381/.4566393 19
HD9199.U48 R47 1984

Coffee, John C., 1944- Knights, raiders, and targets . New York , 1987. p. cm. ISBN 0-19-504405-3 (alk. paper) LC Card 86-33293 DDC 338.8/3 19
HD2746.5 .K58 1987

COFFEE PLANTATION WORKERS - BRAZIL - HISTORY.
Stolcke, Verena. Cafeicultura . São Paulo, SP , 1986. 410 p. : LC Card 86-208925
HD9195.B72 S76 1986

COFFEE PLANTATION WORKERS - BRAZIL - SÃO PAULO (STATE) - HISTORY - 19TH CENTURY.
Salles, Iraci Galvão. Trabalho, progresso e a sociedade civilizada . São Paulo [Brasília] , 1986. 145 p. ; LC Card 86-224281
HD8289.S282 S24 1986

Ziegler, Béatrice. Schweizer statt Sklaven . Stuttgart , c1985. 466 p., [16] p. of plates : ISBN 3-515-04174-5 : LC Card 85-133062 DDC 331.6/2/49408161 19
HD8289.S283 Z54 1985
NYPL [JLE 87-1222]

COFFEE TRADE - BRAZIL - COSTS.
Custo de produção de café /. Curitiba-Paraná [19]84. 47 p. ; LC Card 85-211612
HD9199.B7 C93 1984

COFFEE TRADE - BRAZIL - HISTORY.
Stolcke, Verena. Cafeicultura . São Paulo, SP , 1986. 410 p. : LC Card 86-208925
HD9195.B72 S76 1986

Topik, Steven. The political economy of the Brazilian State, 1889-1930 /. Austin , 1987. xii, 241 p. : ISBN 0-292-76500-2 LC Card 87-5835 DDC 338.981 19
HC187 .T558 1987

COFFEE TRADE - BRAZIL - RIO DE JANEIRO - HISTORY - 19TH CENTURY.
Sweigart, Joseph Earl. Coffee factorage and the emergence of a Brazilian capital market, 1850-1888 /. New York , 1987. xvi, 337 p. : ISBN 0-8240-1373-5 (alk. paper) : LC Card 87-8617 DDC 338.1/3373/098153 19
HD9199.B8 R567 1987

COFFEE TRADE - BRAZIL - SÃO PAULO (STATE) - HISTORY.
Barreiro, José Carlos. Campesinato e capitalismo /. Campinas-SP [1986] 128 p. ; LC Card 86-229683
HD1531.B7 B37 1986

Heipel, Gerd. Nichtkapitalistische Produktionsverhältnisse und Konkurrenz .

Pfaffenweiler , 1986. vii, 459 p. ; ISBN 3-89085-116-9 LC Card 86-171832
HD9199.B8 S22 1986

COFFEE TRADE - BRAZIL - SÃO PAULO (STATE) - HISTORY - 19TH CENTURY - CASE STUDIES.
Witter, José Sebastião. A Revolta dos Parceiros /. São Paulo, SP , 1986. 77 p. : LC Card 87-102716
HD4875.B8 W58 1986

COFFEE TRADE - BURUNDI.
Les Cultures industrielles du Burundi . Bujumbura [1985] 63 p. : LC Card 85-981329
HD9195.B942 C85 1985

COFFEE TRADE - COLOMBIA.
Atehortúa, Adolfo. Café, bonanza y realidades /. [Bogotá, Colombia] [1986] 118 p. : LC Card 87-402940 DDC 338.1/7373/09861 19
HD9199.C62 A74 1986

Echavarría Olózaga, Hernán. El hueco negro . [S.l. , 1986] (Bogotá, Colombia : Editorial Andes) 244 p., [7] p. of plates : LC Card 86-209093
HC197 .E34 1986

Leibovich, José. Comercio exterior y distribución de ingresos . Bogotá, Colombia , 1984. vii, 221 p. : LC Card 87-402975 DDC 382/.41373/09861 19
HD9199.C62 L45 1984

COFFEE TRADE - COLOMBIA - ADDRESSES, ESSAYS, LECTURES.
Thomas, Vinod, 1949- Linking macroeconomic and agricultural policies for adjustment with growth . Baltimore , c1985. xv, 252 p. ; ISBN 0-8018-3121-0 : LC Card 85-45105 DDC 338.9861 19
HC197 .T38 1985 ***NYPL [JLE 86-1438]***

COFFEE TRADE - COSTA RICA.
Paz Cárcamo, Guillermo. El universo del café /. Heredia [1983] 145 p. ; LC Card 87-400683 DDC 338.1/7373/097286 19
HD9195.C82 P39 1983

COFFEE TRADE - COSTA RICA - CAPITAL PRODUCTIVITY.
Cléves S., Rodrigo. Rendimientos de beneficiado de café . San José, Costa Rica , 1986. 35 leaves : LC Card 87-403521 DDC 338.1/6 19
HD9199.C82 C57 1986

Rojas Rojas, Edgar. Indices de eficiencia económica para la industria beneficiadora de café . San José, Costa Rica , 1986. 14 leaves : LC Card 87-403520 DDC 338.1/6 19
HD9199.C82 R65 1986

COFFEE TRADE - COSTA RICA - HISTORY.
Daremblum, Jaime. El auge del café y la apertura de la economía costarricense /. San José, Costa Rica , 1980. 62 p. ; LC Card 84-247131
HF3255 .D37 1980

Raventos Vorst, Ciska. El café en Costa Rica . San José, Costa Rica , 1985. iii, 145 p. : LC Card 86-174756
HD9199.C82 R39 1985

COFFEE TRADE - COSTA RICA - LABOR PRODUCTIVITY.
Cléves S., Rodrigo. Rendimientos de beneficiado de café . San José, Costa Rica , 1986. 35 leaves : LC Card 87-403521 DDC 338.1/6 19
HD9199.C82 C57 1986

Rojas Rojas, Edgar. Indices de eficiencia económica para la industria beneficiadora de café . San José, Costa Rica , 1986. 14 leaves : LC Card 87-403520 DDC 338.1/6 19
HD9199.C82 R65 1986

COFFEE TRADE - DEVELOPING COUNTRIES.
Short, Joseph N. American business and foreign policy . New York , 1987. 340 p. : ISBN 0-8240-8093-9 (alk. paper) : LC Card 87-23792 DDC 382/.41373/0973 19
HD9199.U48 S46 1987

COFFEE TRADE - EL SALVADOR.
Fabián, Miguel Angel. Monografía del café /. [San Salvador] , 1984. 39 leaves : LC Card 86-177543
HD9199.S142 F33 1984

COFFEE TRADE - GOVERNMENT OWNERSHIP - BRAZIL.
Castro, J. As instituições para-estatais no estado novo /. Rio de Janeiro, Brasil , 1939 (Rio [de Janeiro] : Companhia Carioca) 225 p., [2] leaves of plates : LC Card 85-222446
HD4094 .C35 1939

COFFEE TRADE - GOVERNMENT POLICY - BRAZIL.
A Intervenção do estado na economia . Brasília, D.F. , c1985. 83 p. ; ISBN 85-23-00198-0 : LC Card 87-102646 DDC 338.1/7373/0981 19
HD9199.B7 I628 1985

COFFEE TRADE - GOVERNMENT POLICY - BRAZIL - HISTORY.
Cardoso, Eliana A. Inflation, growth and the real exchange rate . New York , 1987. 98 p. : ISBN 0-8240-1356-5 (alk. paper) : LC Card 87-8570 DDC 330.981 19
HC187 .C218 1987

COFFEE TRADE - GOVERNMENT POLICY - BRAZIL - HISTORY - 20TH CENTURY.
Fritsch, Winston. External constraints on economic policy in Brazil, 1889-1930 /. Pittsburgh, PA , 1988. p. cm. ISBN 0-8229-1147-7 LC Card 87-19209 DDC 338.981 19
HC187 .F757 1988

COFFEE TRADE - HAITI.
Girault, Christian A. [Commerce du café en Haïti. Spanish.] El comercio del café en Haití . Santo Domingo, República Dominicana , c1985. 426 p. : LC Card 86-200427
HD9199.H22 G5518 1985

COFFEE TRADE - NICARAGUA.
Gariazzo, Alicia. El café en Nicaragua . Managua, Nicaragua , 1984. 175 p. : LC Card 85-192390
HD9199.N52 G37 1984 ***NYPL [JLF 86-1521]***

COFFEE TRADE - NICARAGUA - CARAZO.
Gariazzo, Alicia. El café en Nicaragua . Managua, Nicaragua , 1984. 175 p. : LC Card 85-192390
HD9199.N52 G37 1984 ***NYPL [JLF 86-1521]***

COFFEE TRADE - NICARAGUA - MATAGALPA (DEPT.)
Gariazzo, Alicia. El café en Nicaragua . Managua, Nicaragua , 1984. 175 p. : LC Card 85-192390
HD9199.N52 G37 1984 ***NYPL [JLF 86-1521]***

COFFEE TRADE - UNITED STATES.
Attitudes toward vended coffee /. [Chicago? , 1983] 1 v. (various pagings) : LC Card 86-235525 DDC 381/.4566393 19
HD9199.U48 A88 1983

Bruskin, R. H. A market strategy study of the whole bean coffee market . [New Brunswick, N.J.] [1985] 1 v. (various pagings) : LC Card 87-100003 DDC 381/.41373/0971 19
HD9199.U48 B84 1985

Iced coffee taste test . Van Nuys, CA (14416 Victory Blvd. Van Nuys 91401) [1985] 132 p., 6, 6 leaves : LC Card 87-100181 DDC 381/.4566393/0973 19
HD9199.U48 I25 1985

Report on the coffee service industry /. Columbus, Ohio [1984] 1 v. (various foliations) : LC Card 87-100404 DDC 381/.4566393 19
HD9199.U48 R47 1984

Short, Joseph N. American business and foreign policy . New York , 1987. 340 p. : ISBN 0-8240-8093-9 (alk. paper) : LC Card 87-23792 DDC 382/.41373/0973 19
HD9199.U48 S46 1987

COFFEE TRADE - VENEZUELA - HISTORY.
Estaba, Rosa M. Geografía de los paisajes urbanos e industriales de Venezuela /. Caracas , c1985. 291 p., [4] folded leaves : ISBN 980-271-006-7 LC Card 86-148810 DDC 307.7/6/0987 19
HC237 .E766 1985 ***NYPL [JLD 86-2340]***

COFFEE - UNITED STATES.
Attitudes toward vended coffee /. [Chicago? , 1983] 1 v. (various pagings) : LC Card 86-235525 DDC 381/.4566393 19
HD9199.U48 A88 1983

COFFEE - UNITED STATES - MARKETING.
Bruskin, R. H. A market strategy study of the whole bean coffee market . [New Brunswick, N.J.] [1985] 1 v. (various pagings) : LC Card 87-100003 DDC 381/.41373/0971 19
HD9199.U48 B84 1985

Coffey, Peter. The European monetary system--past, present, and future / by Peter Coffey. 2nd rev. ed. Dordrecht ; Boston : M. Nijhoff ; p. cm. Includes bibliographical references and index. ISBN 90-247-3446-0 LC Card 86-23833 DDC 332.4/5/094 19
1. Money - European Economic Community countries. I. Title.
HG930.5 .C63 1987

Cogan, Douglas. Generating energy alternatives : demand-side management, renewable energy at America's electric utilities / Douglas Cogan, Susan Williams.1987 ed. Washington, D.C. : Investor Responsibility Research Center, c1987. xi, 358 p. : ill. ; 28 cm. ISBN 0-931035-16-3 (pbk.) LC Card 87-403993 DDC 333.79 19
1. Electric utilities - United States - Energy conservation. 2. Renewable energy sources - United States. I. Williams, Susan. II. Investor Responsibility Research Center. III. Title.
HD9685.U5 C588 1987

The Cogeneration equipment and services market in the U. S. New York, N.Y. : Frost & Sullivan, c1983. 2 v. (ix, 306 leaves) : ill. ; 29 cm. "May 1983." "#A1202." LC Card 87-138703 DDC 381/.456213141 19
1. Electric generator industry - United States. 2. Cogeneration of electric power and heat - United States. 3. Market surveys - United States. I. Frost & Sullivan.
HD9695.U52 C64 1983

COGENERATION OF ELECTRIC POWER AND HEAT - ECONOMIC ASPECTS - CANADA.
Reinsch, Anthony Ernest. Industrial cogeneration in Canada . Calgary, Alta. [1987] xviii, 137 p. : ISBN 0-920522-41-6 (pbk.) : LC Card 87-163062 DDC 333.79/3 19
HD9685.C2 R45 1987

COGENERATION OF ELECTRIC POWER AND HEAT - ILLINOIS.
Illinois. Commerce Commission. Independent power production in Illinois /. Springfield, Ill. (P.O. Box 4905, Springfield 62708) [1986- v. <1 > : LC Card 86-622355 DDC 338.4/762131/09773 19
HD9685.U6 I263 1986

COGENERATION OF ELECTRIC POWER AND HEAT - UNITED STATES.
The Cogeneration equipment and services market in the U. S. New York, N.Y. , c1983. 2 v. (ix, 306 leaves) : LC Card 87-138703 DDC 381/.456213141 19
HD9695.U52 C64 1983

Illinois. Commerce Commission. Independent power production in Illinois /. Springfield, Ill. (P.O. Box 4905, Springfield 62708) [1986- v. <1 > : LC Card 86-622355 DDC 338.4/762131/09773 19
HD9685.U6 I263 1986

Cogestión en la empresa . Mantero, Osvaldo. Caracas, Venezuela [1986] 215 p. : ISBN 0-9806771-1-3 LC Card 87-401945 DDC 658.3/152/0987 19
HD5660.V4 M36 1986

COGNITION.
Halpern, Diane F. Sex differences in cognitive abilities /. Hillsdale, N.J. , 1986. x, 189 p. : ISBN 0-89859-579-7 LC Card 86-11506 DDC 155.3/3 19
BF311 .H295 1986 ***NYPL [JFE 86-4001]***

Handbook of motivation and cognition . New York , c1986. x, 610 p. : ISBN 0-89862-667-6 LC Card 85-24916 DDC 153.8 19
BF503 .H36 1986 ***NYPL [JFE 86-2410]***

Kahney, Hank. Problem solving . Milton Keynes , Philadelphia , 1986. 155 p. : ISBN 0-335-15327-5 (pbk.) LC Card 85-21651 DDC 153.4/3 19
BF441 .K24 1986 ***NYPL [JFE 86-1837]***

Nuttin, Jozef, 1909- [Théorie de la motivation humaine. English.] Motivation, planning, and action . Leuven, Belgium , Hillsdale, N.J. , c1984. viii, 251 p. ; ISBN 0-89859-332-8 (L.

Erlbaum) LC Card 83-16416 DDC 153.8 19
BF503 .N8713 1984 ***NYPL [JFE 86-2315]***

Sims, Henry P., 1939- The thinking organization /. San Francisco , 1986. xxvii, 375 p. : ISBN 0-87589-690-1 LC Card 85-45913 DDC 302.3/5 19
HD58.7 .S584 1986 ***NYPL [JLE 86-2921]***

Sperber, Dan. Relevance . Oxford [Oxfordshire] , 1986. viii, 279 p. : ISBN 0-631-13756-4 ***NYPL [JFE 86-1728]***

Cohen, Allen R. Effective behavior in organizations . Homewood, Ill. , 1988. xxvi, 959 p. : ISBN 0-256-05967-5 LC Card 87-82176 DDC 658.4 19
HD58.7 .E35 1988

Cohen, Barbara G. F. Human aspects in office automation /. Amsterdam , New York , 1984. xv, 322 p. : ISBN 0-444-42327-3 : LC Card 84-5917 DDC 363.1/19651 19
HF5547.5 .H85 1984 ***NYPL [JLF 86-892]***

Cohen, Carol E. 1983 tax capacity of the states : an information report. Washington, D.C. (1111 20th St., NW, Washington 20575) : Advisory Commission on Intergovernmental Relations, [1986] ix, 111 p. : ill. ; 28 cm. Spine title: Tax capacity of the states. "Prepared by Carol E. Cohen and Mark David Menchik, with technical assistance provided by Robert Lucke of the Congressional Budget Office"--P. v. "April 1986." Bibliography: p. 11. "M-148." LC Card 86-601628 DDC 336.2/013/73
1. Taxation, State. I. Menchik, Mark D. II. Lucke, Robert, 1955-. III. United States. Advisory Commission on Intergovernmental Relations. IV. Title. V. Title: Tax capacity of the states.
HJ2385 .C59 1986

Cohen, Dorothy. Advertising / Dorothy Cohen. Glenview, Ill. : Scott, Foresman, c1988. 626, [28] p. : ill. (some col.) ; 26 cm. Includes bibliographical references and indexes. ISBN 0-673-18255-X LC Card 87-15933 DDC 659.1 19
1. Advertising. I. Title.
HF5821 .C56 1988

Cohen, Eli B. Business BASIC for the IBM PC with cases / Eli B. Cohen, Jeff Alger, Elizabeth C. Boyd. 1st ed. St. Louis : Times Mirror/Mosby College Pub., 1987. xxiv, 634 p. : ill. ; 24 cm. (Times Mirror/Mosby data processing and information systems series) Includes index. ISBN 0-8016-1244-6 (pbk.) LC Card 86-23100 DDC 005.2/165 19
1. Basic (Computer program language). 2. IBM Personal Computer. 3. Business - Data processing. I. Alger, Jeff. II. Boyd, Elizabeth C. III. Title. IV. Series.
HF5548.5.B3 C64 1987

Cohen, Jacob, 1918- The flow of funds in theory and practice : a flow-constrained approach to monetary theory and policy / by Jacob Cohen. Dordrecht ; Boston : Kluwer Academic Publishers, 1987. viii, 341 p. : ill. ; 25 cm. (Financial and monetary policy studies. 15) Bibliography: p. 310-329. Includes indexes. ISBN 90-247-3601-3 LC Card 87-21316 DDC 332.4 19
1. Money. 2. Monetary policy. 3. Flow of funds. I. Title.
HG221 .C678 1987

Cohen, Jeffrey E. Economics and politics of industrial policy . Boulder , 1986. xi, 120 p. ; ISBN 0-8133-7140-6 (pbk. : alk. paper) : LC Card 85-26478 DDC 338.94 19
HD3616.U47 E34 1986
NYPL [JLE 86-4353]

Cohen, Jerome Bernard, 1915-
Investment analysis and portfolio management [by] Jerome B. Cohen, Edward D. Zinbarg [and] Arthur Zeikel. Rev. ed. Homewood, Ill., R. D. Irwin, 1973. xiv, 946 p. illus. 24 cm. Includes bibliographies. ISBN 0-256-01429-9 LC Card 72-98120
1. Saving and investment - United States. 2. Securities - United States. I. Zinbarg, Edward D., joint author. II. Zeikel, Arthur, joint author. III. Title.
HG4521 .C5296 1973 ***NYPL [JLE 74-744]***

Investment analysis and portfolio management / Jerome B. Cohen, Edward D. Zinbarg, Arthur Zeikel. 3d ed. Homewood, Ill. : R. D. Irwin, 1977. xvi, 819 p. : ill. ; 24 cm. Includes bibliographies and index. ISBN 0-256-01883-9 LC Card 76-15739
1. Investments - United States. 2. Securities - United States. I. Zinbarg, Edward D., joint author. II. Zeikel, Arthur, joint author. III. Title.
HG4521 .C5296 1977
NYPL [*R-Econ. 78-1366]

Cohen, Joel W., 1952- Holahan, John. Medicaid . Washington, D.C. , c1986. xvii, 124 p. ; ISBN 0-87766-406-4 LC Card 86-28100 DDC 353.0084/1045 19
HD7102.U4 H59 1986

Cohen, Jon S. International monetary problems and supply-side economics . Houndmills, Basingstoke, Hampshire , 1986. viii, 162 p. : ISBN 0-333-36200-4 ***NYPL [JLD 86-4356]***

Cohen, Kalman J. The Microstructure of securities markets /. Englewood Cliffs, N.J. , c1986. ix, 254 p. ; ISBN 0-13-581794-3 LC Card 85-28265 DDC 332.64 19
HG4661 .M53 1986 ***NYPL [JLE 86-2001]***

Cohen, Larry. Basic concepts of accounting and taxation of property/casualty insurance companies /. New York, N.Y. , c1984. 66 p. : ISBN 0-932387-01-2 :
NYPL [JLE 86-2615]

Cohen, Leah. A summary of the American experience with the Federal Contract Compliance Program : executive summary submitted to the Affirmative Action Division, the Special Client Needs Branch, Canada Employment and Immigration Commission / Leah Cohen. [Ottawa] : Employment and Immigration Canada, 1979. 72 leaves ; 28 cm. Cover title.
1. Affirmative action programs - United States. 2. Public contracts - United States. I. Canada. Affirmative Action Division. II. Title. ***NYPL [JLF 86-1657]***

Cohen, M. Bruce. Jones, Seymour, 1931- The Coopers & Lybrand guide to growing your business /. New York , c1988. xiii, 477 p. ; ISBN 0-471-85941-9 LC Card 87-21688 DDC 658 19
HD31 .J627 1988

Cohen, Noemí. Trabajadores y seguridad social en América Latina / Noemí Cohen, Sara Gutiérrez. 1a ed. México, D.F. : Instituto Mexicano del Seguro Social, Secretaría General, Departamento de Asuntos Internacionales, [1982], c1981. 146 p. ; 21 cm. Bibliography: p. 141-146. ISBN 968-8241-38-5 LC Card 83-140620 DDC 368.4/0098 19
1. Social security - Latin America. 2. Trade-unions - Latin America. 3. Labor supply - Latin America. I. Gutiérrez, Sara. II. Instituto Mexicano del Seguro Social. Departamento de Asuntos Internacionales. III. Title.
HD7130.5 .C63 1982 ***NYPL [JLD 86-2768]***

Cohen, Richard, 1946- Bailey, Norman A. The Mexican time bomb /. New York , 1987. vi, 61 p. ; ISBN 0-87078-209-6 (pbk.) : LC Card 87-400092 DDC 336.3/4/0972 19
HJ8519 .B26 1987

Cohen, Robin.
International labour and the Third World . Aldershot, Hants, England , c1987. xii, 283 p. ; ISBN 0-566-00971-4 : LC Card 86-31791 DDC 331/.09172/4 19
HD8943 .I55 1987

The new helots : migrants in the international division of labour / Robin Cohen. Aldershot, Hants, England : Avebury ; Brookfield, Vt., USA : Gower Pub. Co., c1987. xiii, 290 p. : ill. ; 23 cm. (Research in ethnic relations series) Bibliography: p. 257-280. Includes index. ISBN 0-566-00932-3 : LC Card 87-19807 DDC 331.6/2 19
1. Alien labor. 2. Developing countries - Emigration and immigration. I. Title. II. Series.
HD6304 .C64 1987

Cohen, Ronald L. (Ronald Lee), 1944- Justice . New York , c1986. xii, 283 p. ; ISBN 0-306-42256-5 LC Card 86-20503 DDC 320/.01/1 19
JC578 .J89 1986 ***NYPL [JLE 87-304]***

Cohen-Rosenthal, Edward. Mutual gains : a guide to union-management cooperation / Edward Cohen-Rosenthal and Cynthia E. Burton. New York : Praeger, 1987. xv, 287 p. : ill. ; 25 cm. Includes bibliographies and index. ISBN 0-275-92204-9 (alk. paper) : LC Card 86-25249 DDC 331/.01/12 19
1. Labor-management committees - United States. 2. Industrial relations - United States. I. Burton, Cynthia E. II. Title.
HD6490.L33 C64 1987

Cohen, Stephen D. The making of United States international economic policy : principles, problems, and proposals for reform / Stephen D. Cohen.3rd ed. New York : Praeger, 1987. p. cm. Includes bibliographies and index. ISBN 0-275-92334-7 (alk. paper) : LC Card 87-24082 DDC 382/.3/0973 19
1. United States - Foreign economic relations. I. Title.
HF1455 .C576 1987

Cohen, Stephen S. Manufacturing matters : the myth of the post-industrial economy / Stephen S. Cohen, John Zysman. New York : Basic Books, c1987. xiv, 297 p. : ill. ; 24 cm. "A Council on Foreign Relations Book." Bibliography: p. [267]-285. Includes index. ISBN 0-465-04384-4 : LC Card 86-47737 DDC 338.4/767/0973 19
1. United States - Manufactures. I. Zysman, John. II. Title.
HD9725 .C58 1987

Cohen, Steve, 1950- Getting to the right job / Steve Cohen and Paulo de Oliveira. New York : Workman Pub., 1987. 288 p. ; 23 cm. Includes index. ISBN 0-89480-040-X (pbk.) : LC Card 85-40899 DDC 650.1/4 19
1. Vocational guidance. 2. Job hunting. 3. College graduates - Employment. I. De Oliveira, Paulo. II. Title.
HF5381 .C6814 1987

Cohen, William A., 1937-
Developing a winning marketing plan / William A. Cohen. New York : Wiley, c1987. ix, 324 p. : ill. ; 24 cm. (Wiley series on business strategy) Bibliography: p. 283. ISBN 0-471-84529-9 LC Card 86-32402 DDC 658.8/02 19
1. Marketing. I. Title. II. Series.
HF5415 .C54247 1987

The practice of marketing management : analysis, planning, and implementation / William A. Cohen. New York : Macmillan ; London : Collier Macmillan, c1988. xix, 695 p. : ill. ; 24 cm. Includes bibliographical references and indexes. ISBN 0-02-323150-5 LC Card 87-11281 DDC 658.8 19
1. Marketing management. I. Title.
HF5415.13 .C635 1988

The student's guide to finding a superior job / William A. Cohen. San Diego : Slawson Communication, c1987. ix, 144 p. ; 23 cm. "An Avant book." ISBN 0-932238-41-6 (pbk.) : LC Card 87-4487 DDC 650.1/4 19
1. Job hunting. 2. College graduates - Employment. 3. Students - Employment. I. Title.
HF5382.7 .C64 1987

Cohn, Samuel, 1954- The process of occupational sex-typing : the feminization of clerical labor in Great Britain / Samuel Cohn. Philadelphia : Temple University Press, 1985. viii, 279 p. ; 24 cm. (Women in the political economy) Includes index. Bibliography: p. 253-266. ISBN 0-87722-402-1 : LC Card 85-14864 DDC 331.4/8165137/0941 19
1. Sexual division of labor - Great Britain - History. 2. Women clerks - Great Britain - History. 3. Women - Employment - Great Britain - History. I. Title. II. Title: Occupational sex-typing. III. Series.
HD6060.65.G7 C64 1985
NYPL [JLE 86-917]

Cohn, Steven. Energy economics . Englewood Cliffs, N.J. , c1987. viii, 328 p. : ISBN 0-13-277245-0 : LC Card 86-25254 DDC 333.79/0973 19
HD9502.U52 E4874 1987

COHORT ANALYSIS.
Az 1937-68 években született nők kohorsz-termékenysége /. Budapest [1986] 77 p. ; LC Card 87-407670
HB1002.5.A3 A15 1986

COHORT ANALYSIS - CONGRESSES.
Recent advances in the techniques for demographic analysis /. Bombay , 1987. xiv, 456 p. ; LC Card 87-900498
HB849 .R42 1987

COIMBATORE, INDIA (DISTRICT) - INDUSTRIES.
Thanulingom Nadar, N. Small scale industry . Coimbatore, Tamil Nadu , 1985. 194 p. ; LC Card 85-903280 DDC 338.6/42/095482 19
HD2346.I52 C648 1985
NYPL [JLD 86-1411]

Coimbatore Krishnarao Prahalad. see **Prahalad, C. K.**

Coin and conscience : popular views of money, credit, and speculation, sixteenth through nineteenth centuries : catalog of an exhibition of prints from the Bleichroeder Collection, Kress Library of Business and Economics. [Boston, Mass.] : Baker Library, Harvard Business School, 1986. [28] p. : ill. ; 27 cm. Bibliography: p. [28] Includes index. LC Card 86-203197 DDC 332.4/94 19
1. Money - Europe - History - Exhibitions - Catalogs. 2. Kress Library of Business and Economics - Catalogs. I. Kress Library of Business and Economics. II. Baker Library.
HG925 .C65 1986

COINAGE, INTERNATIONAL.
Masera, R. S. L'unificazione monetaria e lo SME /. Bologna , c1980. 220 p. ; LC Card 82-150717 DDC 332.4/566/094 19
HG930.5.Z8 M37 1980 ***NYPL [JLD 87-902]***

COINAGE - STATISTICS.
World coinage report, 1980-1984. Washington, D.C. [1986?] vi, 114 p. : LC Card 86-602440 DDC 737.4/021 19
HG327 .W67 1986

COINAGE - UNITED STATES - HISTORY.
Wolman, Paul. The U. S. Mint /. New York , c1987. 92 p. : ISBN 0-87754-829-3 (lib. bdg.) : LC Card 86-31720 DDC 353.0082/2 19
HG459 .W65 1987

COINAGE - UNITED STATES - HISTORY - 19TH CENTURY.
Head, Sylvia. The neighborhood mint . Macon, Ga. , c1986. xviii, 206 p. : ISBN 0-86554-240-6 (alk. paper) : LC Card 86-23500 DDC 737.49758/273 19
HG461.D342 H4 1986

COINING, ILLICIT. see **COUNTERFEITS AND COUNTERFEITING.**

COINS, BYZANTINE - HISTORY - SOURCES.
Euangelatou-Notara, Phlōrentia. "Sēmeiōmata" Hellēnikōn kōdikōn hōs pēgē dia tēn ereunan tou oikonomikou kai koinōnikou viou tou Vyzantiou, apo tou 9ou aiōnos mechri tou etous 1204 /. Athēnai , 1982. 296 p. ; LC Card 86-212063
HC294 .E9 1982

COINS, POLISH - HISTORY.
Cywiński, Henryk. Dziesięć wieków pieniądza polskiego 980-1980 /. Warszawa , 1982. 243 p., [24] p. of plates : ISBN 83-205-3413-5 LC Card 83-119732
HG1087 .C98 1982

COINS - WEIGHTS AND MEASURES - TABLES.
World coinage report, 1980-1984. Washington, D.C. [1986?] vi, 114 p. : LC Card 86-602440 DDC 737.4/021 19
HG327 .W67 1986

Cointreau, Edouard. Privatisation . Paris , c1986. 188 p. ; ISBN 2-85802-651-3 : LC Card 86-161183
HD3854 .P75 1986

COKE INDUSTRY - SOVIET CENTRAL ASIA.
Ulitskiĭ, L. I. (Lazar′ Ioakhimovich) K organizatsii koksokhimicheskoĭ promyshlennosti v Sredneĭ Azii. Tashkent, 1945. 63 p. LC Card 51-55383
HD9559 .C7S68

Colaboración sindical al estudio sobre la estructura y posibilidad de desarrollo del Campo de Gibraltar, encomendado por la comisión interministerial designada al efecto / Organización Sindical. Cádiz : Consejo Económico Sindical del Campo de Gibraltar, 1965. 89 p. : ill. (some col.) ; 27 cm. Cover title: Estructura y posibilidad de desarrollo del Campo de Gibraltar. LC Card 85-104938
1. Gibraltar - Economic policy. 2. Gibraltar - Economic conditions. 3. Cádiz (Spain : Province) - Economic policy. 4. Cádiz (Spain : Province) - Economic conditions. I. Consejo Económico Sindical del Campo de Gibraltar. II. Title: Estructura y posibilidad de desarrollo del Campo de Gibraltar.
HC390.6 .C65 1965

Colaiácovo, Juan Luis. Trading companies : experiencia internacional : textos y casos / Juan Luis Colaiácovo.1a ed. Rio de Janeiro, RJ : Ph. D. Editora, c1986. 448 p. : ill. ; 22 cm. In Spanish. Bibliography: p. 430-448. ISBN 85-85037-07-5; 85-05-37070-5 LC Card 87-135895 DDC 382/.06/01 19
1. Trading companies. 2. Trading companies - Case studies. I. Title.
HF1009.5 .C575 1986

Čolak, Nikola. Regesti marittimi croati /. Padova , 1985- v. <v. 1, pt. 1 > : LC Card 86-215640
HE565.Y8 R42 1985

Colander, David C. Incentive-based incomes policies . Cambridge, Mass. , c1986. xxi, 263 p. : ISBN 0-88730-082-0 LC Card 85-20090 DDC 331.2/9 19
HC79.W24 I465 1986 ***NYPL [JLE 86-3724]***

Colasanto, Michele. Sul "movimento" della qualità della vita di lavoro /. Milano , c1982. 117 p. ; LC Card 82-246606
HD6955 .S94 1982 ***NYPL [JLD 87-1159]***

Colbe, Walther Busse von. see **Busse von Colbe, Walther.**

Colbjørnsen, Tom. Så samles vi på valen--? : en rapport fra FAFOs organisasjonsundersøkelse / av Tom Colbjørnsen, Arvid Fennefoss, Gudmund Hernes. [Oslo?] : FAFO, [1985] 88 p. : ill. ; 24 cm. Bibliography: p. 88. ISBN 82-991187-5-1 LC Card 85-220350
1. Trade-unions - Norway - Public opinion. 2. Public opinion - Norway. I. Fennefoss, Arvid. II. Hernes, Gudmund, 1941-. III. Title.
HD6752 .C644 1985

Colburn, Forrest D. Post-revolutionary Nicaragua : state, class, and the dilemmas of agrarian policy / Forrest D. Colburn. Berkeley : University of California Press, c1986. xi, 145 p. : ill. ; 22 cm. (California series on social choice and political economy) Includes index. Bibliography: p. 133-138. ISBN 0-520-05524-1 LC Card 85-5798 DDC 338.1/097285 19
1. Agriculture - Economic aspects - Nicaragua. 2. Social classes - Nicaragua. 3. Nicaragua - Rural conditions. 4. Nicaragua - Politics and government - 1979-. I. Title. II. Series.
HD1817 .C63 1986 ***NYPL [JLD 86-2414]***

Colchester, Marcus. Ethiopia's bitter medicine, settling for disaster . London , 1986. 55 p. : ISBN 0-946592-01-2 (pbk.) LC Card 86-232852 DDC 333.3/1/63
HD979.Z63 E74 1986

The Cold war against labor : an anthology / edited by Ann Fagan Ginger and David Christiano. Berkeley, CA : Meiklejohn Civil Liberties Institute, c1987. 2 v. (xxii, 915 p.) : ill. ; 23 cm. (Studies in law and social change . no. 3) Includes bibliographies and index. ISBN 0-913876-19-4 (set); 0-913876-20-4 (set) : LC Card 87-18510 DDC 331.88/0973 19
1. Trade-unions - United States - History - 20th century. 2. Trade-unions - Law and legislation - United States - History - 20th century. 3. Labor laws and legislation - United States - History - 20th century. I. Ginger, Ann Fagan. II. Christiano, David, 1948-. III. Meiklejohn Civil Liberties Institute. IV. Series.
HD6508 .C62 1987

Cole, George Douglas Howard, 1889-1959. The next ten years in British social and economic policy / G.D.H. Cole. New York : Garland Pub., 1985. xxi, 459 p. ; 22 cm. (English workers and the coming of the welfare state, 1918-1945) Includes index. Reprint. Originally published: London : Macmillan, 1929. ISBN 0-8240-7607-9 (alk. paper) : LC Card 85-13055 DDC 338.941 19
1. Socialism - Great Britain. 2. Great Britain - Economic policy - 1918-1945. 3. Great Britain - Economic conditions - 1918-1945. I. Title. II. Series.
HC256.3 .C6 1985 ***NYPL [JLD 86-3300]***

Cole, J. P. (John Peter), 1928-
Buck, Trevor. Modern Soviet economic performance /. New York, NY , 1987. viii, 192 p. ; ISBN 0-631-14417-X : LC Card 86-24457 DDC 330.947/085 19
HC336.25 .B826 1987

Development and underdevelopment : a profile of the Third World / John Cole. London ; New York : Methuen, 1987. vi, 104 p. : ill. ; 21 cm. (Methuen introductions to development) Bibliography: p. [99]-100. Includes index. ISBN 0-416-92080-2 (pbk.) LC Card 86-23758 DDC 338.9/009172/4 19
1. Developing countries - Economic conditions. 2. Economic development - Case studies. I. Title. II. Series.
HC59.7 .C59 1987

Cole, Julio Harold, 1955- Latin American inflation : theoretical interpretations and empirical results / Julio Harold Cole. New York : Praeger, 1987. xv, 89 p. : ill. ; 25 cm. Bibliography: p. 81-85. Includes index. ISBN 0-275-92809-8 (alk. paper) : LC Card 87-15156 DDC 332.4/1/098 19
1. Latin America - Economic conditions - 1945-. 2. Inflation (Finance) - Latin America. 3. Bolivia - Economic conditions - 1982-. 4. Inflation (Finance) - Bolivia. I. Title.
HC125 .C62 1987

Cole, Victoria A. Bauer, Mary Cracraft. A history of coal-mining in the Sutton-Chickaloon area prior to WW II /. [Anchorage, Alaska] [1985] ii, 47 leaves : LC Card 86-620606 DDC 338.2/724/097983 19
HD9548.S87 B38 1985

Coleção Albano Franco .
(2) Silva, Angela Inês Gandra e. Os acordos SENAI/empresa . Rio de Janeiro-RJ-Brasil , 1985. xvii, 97 p. ; LC Card 86-176735
HD5715.5.B68 S55 1985

Coleção América Latina (Icone Editora (São Paulo))
Delgado, Guilherme Costa. Capital financeiro e agricultura no Brasil, 1965-1985 /. S[ão] Paulo, SP, Brasil , Campinas, SP , c1985. 240 p. ; LC Card 87-102748
HD1440.B8 D45 1985

Coleção Ciências sociais. Série Questão agrária .
(1) Luna, Regina Celi Miranda Reis. A terra era liberta . São Luís, MA , 1985. xxvii, 146 p. : LC Card 87-135907 DDC 333.3/0981/21 19
HD499.P46 L86 1985

Coleção Coroa vermelha. Estudos brasileiros .
(v. 12) Costa, Sérgio Amad, 1958- Estado e controle sindical no Brasil . São Paulo , 1986. xiv, 192 p. : ISBN 85-85008-48-2 : LC Card 87-154269 DDC 331.88/0981 19
HD6612 .C67 1986

Coleção Estudos brasileiros (Paz e Terra (Firm)) .
(v. 93-94) A Transição incompleta . Rio de Janeiro-RJ , 1986. 2 v. ; LC Card 86-224684
HC187 .T72 1986

Coleção Estudos econômicos e sociais.
Campino, Antonio Carlos Coelho. Recursos e desempenhos dos programas de formação de mão-de-obra /. São Paulo, SP , Brasília, DF , 1985. 78 p. ; ISBN 85-21-30276-2 LC Card 85-187505
HD5754 .C34 1985

Macedo, Roberto Brás Matos. FGTS e a rotatividade /. São Paulo-SP , Brasília-DF , 1985. 231 p. : ISBN 85-21-30271-1 LC Card 85-187484
HD7096.B6 M33 1985

Coleção Estudos históricos.
Mello, Zélia Maria Cardoso de. Metamorfoses da riqueza, São Paulo, 1845-1895 . São Paulo , 1985. 188 p. : LC Card 85-207635
HC188.S3 M49 1985

Salles, Iraci Galvão. Trabalho, progresso e a sociedade civilizada . São Paulo [Brasília] , 1986. 145 p. ; LC Card 86-224281
HD8289.S282 S24 1986

Coleção Fonte de informação.
Nassif, Luís. O cruzado . São Paulo/SP , 1986. 255 p. : LC Card 86-224110
HG835 .N37 1986

Coleção Gerson Augusto da Silva .
(16) Machado, Vera Barrouin Crivano. O diálogo norte-sul /. Brasília, DF , 1983. 58 p. ; LC Card 86-171831
HF1412 .M33 1983

(9) Silva, Gerson Augusto da. Estudos tributários /. Brasília, DF , 1983. 139 p. : LC Card 84-127110
HJ2525 .S49 1983

Coleção Hipólito José da Costa .
(v. 10) Formiga, Marcone. Personagens da crise /. Brasília , 1984. 160 p. : LC Card 86-157831
HC187 .F636 1984

Coleção ILDES .
(1) Schwarz, Manfred, 1910- Social security in Brazil . Rio de Janeiro, Brasil [1980] [14], 161 p. : LC Card 87-123549 DDC 368.4/00981 19
HD7154 .S36 1980

Coleção IV centenário .
(10) Leite, José Alfredo A. A sócio-economia do semi-árido /. João Pessoa , 1985. 47 p. : LC Card 87-141315 DDC 330.981/33/063 19
HD1875.P34 L45 1985

Coleção O Povo quer viver .
(13) Malvezzi, Roberto. Mil quatrocentos e sessenta dias no império do sol . São Paulo , 1985. 197 p. : ISBN 85-05-00296-2 : LC Card 85-200637
HC188.N6 M34 1985

Coleção Sopral .
(5) O Proálcool vale? /. [São Paulo-SP (Brasil)] , 1985. 52 p. : LC Card 86-220396
HD9502.5.A433 B645 1985

(8) Aspectos econômicos, jurídicos e sociais da Reforma Agrária /. São Paulo-SP Brasil [1985] 75 p. ; LC Card 86-220237
HD1333.B6 A85 1985

Coleção Temas & teses. Transição para o desenvolvimento .
(1) Setor público, reordenamento e privatização /. [Rio de Janeiro, RJ , 1986] 47 p. : LC Card 87-403308 DDC 338.981 19
HC187 .S436 1986

Coleção Temas brasileiros (Universidade de Brasília. Editora) .
(v. 59) Década republicana /. Brasília, Distrito Federal , c1986. 2 v. ; ISBN 85-23-00062-3 (set) LC Card 86-211423
HJ923 .D38 1986

Coleção Tempo municipal .
(4) Pôrto, Josè da Costa, 1909- O açúcar num documento colonial /. Recife , 1984. 116 p. ; LC Card 87-102690
HD9114.B7 P448 1984

Coleção Teoria e prática sociais.
Khoury, Yara Aun. As greves de 1917 em São Paulo e o processo de organização proletária /. São Paulo , 1981. 221 p. ; LC Card 81-210934 DDC 331.2/98161 19
HD5355.S26 K48 1981
NYPL [JLD 86-3514]

Colecção Biblioteca das ciências do homem. Antropologia .
(2) Portela, José, 1950- Trabalho cooperativo em duas aldeias de Trás-os-Montes /. Porto , 1986. 79 p., [4] p. of plates : LC Card 87-400109 DDC 334/.683/094692 19
HD1491.P82 T736 1986

Colecção Manuais de fiscalidade.
Seminário sobre Política Fiscal (1984? : CGTP-IN) Contribuições para a reforma do sistema fiscal português . Lisboa , 1985. 226 p. : LC Card 87-107879 DDC 336.469 19
HJ1252 .S46 1984

Colecção Temas de cultura portuguesa .
(no. 9) Reflexões sobre história e cultura portuguesa . Lisboa , 1985. 286 p. ; LC Card 86-135021 DDC 946.9 19
HC392 .R34 1985

Colecção Teses e teorias .
(1) Mónica, Maria Filomena, 1943- Artesãos e operários . Lisboa [1986] 228 p., [24] p. of plates : LC Card 86-229921
HD8596 .M65 1986

(2) Almeida, João Ferreira de. Classes sociais nos campos . Lisboa [1986] 544 p. : LC Card 87-400121 DDC 305.5/63 19
HD1536.P77 A44 1986

Colecção universitária .
(13) Coelho, Antonio Borges. Quadros para uma viagem a Portugal no Sec. XVI /. Lisboa , c1986. 403 p., [2] folded leaves of plates : LC Card 87-401474
HC392 .C573 1986

Colección Ambito Castilla y León .
(35) Pastor Antolín, Luis J., 1958- La red de transporte en Castilla y León /. Valladolid [1986?] 161 p. : ISBN 84-86047-71-4 LC Card 86-231524
HE363.S64 C376 1986

Colección Análisis histórica .
(no. 1) Ycaza, Patricio. Historia del movimiento obrero ecuatoriano . Quito , 1984. 371 p. :
NYPL [JLB 86-21]

Colección Aportaciones.
Tamayo Rodríguez, Jaime E. La estructura del sindicalismo en Jalisco /. Guadalajara, Jalisco, México [1985] 224 p. ; ISBN 968-570-147-4 LC Card 86-208258
HD6535.J35 T36 1985

Colección Argumentos (Montevideo, Uruguay) .
(no. 2) El Primer batllismo . Montevideo [1985] 159 p. : LC Card 85-233561 DDC 338.9895 19
HC232 .P75 1985 ***NYPL [JLC 86-259]***

Colección Arqueología, antropología e historia. Serie Historia.
Tostado Gutiérrez, Marcela. El Tabasco porfiriano /. Villahermosa [Mexico] , 1985. 179 p. : ISBN 968-88900-7-3 LC Card 86-189960
HC137.T3 T67 1985

Colección Arzans y Vela.
Escobari de Querejazu, Laura. Producción y comercio en el espacio sur andino en el siglo XVII . La Paz , 1985. 218 p., [12] p. of plates : LC Card 86-174929
HC167.A5 E83 1985

Colección Barva. Serie Pensamiento. Subserie Ensayo.
Esquivel, Francisco. El desarrollo del capital en la industria de Costa Rica, 1950-1970 /. Heredia, Costa Rica , 1985. 197 p. : ISBN 997-7650-16-0 LC Card 86-210026
HC143 .E83 1985

Colección Biblioteca básica de administración pública. Serie especial.
Aoiz Iriarte, María Rosario. Técnicas psicosociales en la administración pública . Alcalá de Henares, Madrid, España [1984] 238 p. : ISBN 84-7351-179-4 LC Card 85-189583
HF5549.5.S38 A57 1984

Azqueta Oyarzun, Diego. Teoría de los precios sociales /. Alcala de Henares-Madrid, España [1985?] 250 p. : ISBN 84-7351-181-6 : LC Card 87-105447
HB846.3 .A97 1985

Colección Biblioteca bśica de administración pública. Serie especial.
Herrero Suazo, Santiago. Técnicas presupuestarias en la administración pública /. Alcalá de Henares-Madrid, España [1984?] 382 p. : ISBN 84-7351-173-5 LC Card 85-185202
HJ1248 .H47 1984

Colección Biblioteca economistas aragoneses .
(1) Normante y Carcavilla, Lorenzo. Discurso sobre la utilidad de los conocimientos económico-políticos y la necesidad de su estudio metódico ; Proposiciones de economía civil y comercio ; Espíritu del señor Melón en su ensayo político sobre el comercio /. [Aragón] [1984?] 1 v. (various pagings) ; ISBN 84-505-0473-2 LC Card 87-104302
HC385 .N57 1984

Colección Biblioteca SENALDE .
(v. 3-4) Transición demográfica y oferta de fuerza de trabajo en Colombia /. [Bogotá], República de Colombia , 1986. 2 v. : ISBN 958-95096-0-6 (set) LC Card 87-113652 DDC 331.11/09861 19
HD5757.A6 T7 1986

Colección Bicentenario (Caracas, Venezuela)
Nweihed, Kaldone G., 1929- Bolívar y el Tercer Mundo . Caracas, Venezuela , c1984. 400 p. : ISBN 84-499-7056-3 LC Card 85-136718
F2235.3 .N98 1984 ***NYPL [JFE 86-1176]***

Colección Charlas con trabajadores.
Arenal, Sandra. Sangre joven . México, D.F. , 1986. 130 p., [2] p. of plates : ISBN 968-427-128-X LC Card 87-139058 DDC 331.4/87/0972 19
HD6073.O332 M4953 1986

Colección CLAT.
Máspero, Emilio. Importancia y significado de la encíclica sobre el trabajo humano del papa Juan Pablo II para el movimiento obrero latinoamericano /. [Caracas, Venezuela] [1984] 159 p. : LC Card 87-404543 DDC 261.8/5 19
HD6338 .M425 1984

Máspero, Emilio. Informe político y de orientación ante el VIIIo Congreso de la CLAT . [Caracas] , 1983. 122 p. : LC Card 87-403072 DDC 305.5/62/098 19
HD8110.5.A5 C466 1983

Colección conmemorativa .
(14) Cárdenas, Lázaro, 1895-1970. Los ejidos de Yucatán y el henequén . [Mexico City, Mexico] , c1984. 79 p. : LC Card 87-403579 DDC 333.3/1/7265 19
HD1333.M62 Y823 1984

Colección Criterios.
Cantó, Leandro. La caída del bolívar /. Caracas, Venezuela [1983 or 1984] 223 p. ; LC Card 84-186552 DDC 332.4/987 19
HG915 .C36 1983 ***NYPL [JLD 87-2426]***

Colección Cuadernos CEDAL .
(7) Arias Sánchez, Oscar. Democracia, independencia y sociedad latinoamericana /. San José, Costa Rica , 1985. 100 p. ; ISBN 997-7956-09-X LC Card 87-400690 DDC 320.97286 19
HC143 .A773 1985

Colección Cuadernos universitarios. Serie Ciencias sociales .
(no. 5) Serrano Gálvez, Enrique. Economía de la actividad forestal /. México , 1983. 139 p. : LC Card 86-200927
HD9764.M62 S47 1983

Colección de bolsillo (Universidad Autónoma de Madrid) .
(1) La Amenaza de guerra nuclear /. Madrid , 1985. 129 p. ; ISBN 84-7477-027-0 LC Card 86-100273 DDC 355/.0217 19
U263 .A44 1985 ***NYPL [JLD 86-2519]***

Colección Debates-CEDE .
(no. 5) Deuda externa latinoamericana y proceso de ajuste . Bogotá, Colombia , 1985. 335 p. : LC Card 86-164491
HJ8514.5 .D484 1985

Colección Divulgación.
Villanueva, Eric. Crisis henequenera y movimientos campesinos en Yucatán, 1966-1983 /. México, D.F. , 1985. 220 p., [10] p. of plates : ISBN 968-603-803-5 LC Card 86-118134 DDC 304.8/0972/65 19
HD9156.H463 M67 1985
NYPL [JLD 87-342]

Colección Documentos (Colombia. Departamento Administrativo Nacional de Estadística) .
(3) Metodología de las cuentas nacionales de Colombia. Bogotá, D.E. [1986] 291 p. ; LC Card 87-403848 DDC 339.3861 19
HC200.I5 M47 1986

Colección Economía (Asunción, Paraguay) .
(2) Campos, Luis A. (Luis Alberto), 1949- Pequeños campesinos y su incertidumbre . Asunción, Paraguay [1986] 224 p. : LC Card 87-400281 DDC 305.5/63 19
HD1531.P3 C36 1986

Colección Economía e industria .
(3) El Ciclo industrial en España . Madrid [1984?] 436 p. : ISBN 84-7474-282-X LC Card 87-113099
HC385 .C49 1984

Colección Economía paraguaya.
Martínez Díaz, Nicasio. Economía y política . [Asunción] 1986 ([Asunción] : El Gráfico) 54 p. ; LC Card 87-400204 DDC 338.9892 19
HC222 .M38 1986

Colección Ecuador/hoy.
Pérez Sáinz, Juan Pablo. Entre la fábrica y la ciudad /. Quito, Ecuador , 1986, c1985. 87, [6] p. ; LC Card 87-403298 DDC 331.7/677/00986613 19
HD8039.T42 E26 1986

Colección Ediciones de la Revista de trabajo .
(11) Biglino Campos, Paloma. El socialismo español y la cuestión agraria (1890-1936) /. Madrid [1986?] 564 p. ; ISBN 84-7434-368-2 LC Card 87-136300
HD6764.A29 B54 1986

Colección El Overol azul.
Arenal, Sandra. Barroterán! . [Mexico City?] , c1984. 116 p. ; ISBN 968-495-016-0 LC Card 85-195552
HD8039.M62 M63 1984

Colección Estudio (Universidad Central de Venezuela. Fondo Editorial de Humanidades y Educación)
Arcila Farías, Eduardo, 1913- Fundamentos económicos del Imperio Español en América /. Caracas , 1985. 133 p. : LC Card 85-242008
HC389 .A73 1985

Fernández Russo, Omar. Elementos de economía para uso de no economistas /. Caracas , 1985. 226 p. : LC Card 85-240123
HB178.5 .F38 1985

Colección Estudios e investigaciones.
García Murcia, Joaquín. El fondo de garantía salarial /. Madrid , 1983. 454 p. ; ISBN 84-7434-201-5 LC Card 85-194099
HD7096.S7 G37 1983

Colección Estudios económicos .
(1) Larraín P., Christian. Subsidiariedad o intervencionismo? . [Santiago, Chile] [1986] 137 p. ; LC Card 87-401544 DDC 338.983 19
HC192 .L36 1986

Colección Estudios históricos (Santiago, Chile)
Pizarro, Crisóstomo. La huelga obrera en Chile, 1890-1970 /. Santiago, Chile [1986] 227 p. : LC Card 87-115190 DDC 331.89/2983 19
HD5356.A6 P59 1986

Colección Estudios internacionales (Universidad de Chile. Instituto de Estudios Internacionales)
Estudios sobre integración económica y cooperación regional en el Cono Sur . Santiago de Chile , c1985. 283 p. ; LC Card 86-174604
HC167.S67 E78 1985

Colección Estudios sectoriales .
(no. 3) Errázuriz, Enrique. Industria eléctrica, 1960-1985 . [Santiago, Chile] [1986] 243 p. : LC Card 87-403870 DDC 338.4/762131/0983 19
HD9685.C52 E77 1986

Colección Estudios sociales (Guadalajara, Mexico)
(1) Cambio regional, mercado de trabajo y vida obrera en Jalisco /. Guadalajara, Jalisco, México , 1986. 363 p. ; ISBN 968-614-201-0 LC Card 86-218238
HD5731.J35 C36 1986

(2) Escobar Latapí, Agustín. Con el sudor de tu frente . Guadalajara, Jalisco, México , c1986. 312 p. ; ISBN 968-614-200-2 LC Card 86-209222
HD5731.G84 E83 1986

Colección Experiencias populares .
(3) Hardy, Clarisa. Hambre + dignidad=ollas comunes /. [Santiago, Chile] , 1986. 282 p., [16] p. of plates : *NYPL [JLD 87-334]*

Colección Formación. Serie Legislación cooperativa.
Manual de interpretación de estados financieros /. [Santiago, Chile] [1984] 49 p. : LC Card 85-150204
HD2965 .M35 1984

Colección Guidance.

Colección Historia (Badajoz, Spain) .
(2) Camacho Cabello, José. La Siberia extremeña . [Badajoz] , 1985. 201 p. : ISBN 84-505-1266-2 LC Card 86-200856
HB3620.E85 C35 1985

(3) Rodríguez Grajera, Alfonso. La población de Mérida en el siglo XVII /. [Badajoz] , 1985. xv, 162 p. : ISBN 84-505-1500-9 LC Card 86-232003
HB3620.M47 R63 1985

Colección Historia de los trabajadores de América Latina .
(2) Vilas, Carlos María. Democracia y participación obrera en la Revolución Sandinista /. Morelia, Michoacán , 1985. 44 p., [6] p. of plates : LC Card 87-128110 DDC 322/.2/097285 19
HD8168 .V55 1985

Colección Historia. Serie Estadísticas básicas .
(no. 2) Gutiérrez y Ulloa, Antonio. Libro de la razón general de hacienda nacional . Guadalajara, Jalisco, México , 1983. 222 p. ; ISBN 968-8320-48-X LC Card 87-401751 DDC 336.72/35 19
HJ805.J3 G87 1983

Colección Historia (Toluca de Lerdo, Mexico) .
(1) García Luna O., Margarita (García Luna Ortega) El movimiento obrero en el Estado de México . Toluca, Estado de México , 1984. 302 p. : ISBN 968-514-014-6 LC Card 86-173738
HC137.M473 G37 1984

Colección Latinoamérica. Serie Ensayo .
(12) García, Miguel Angel. El nacimiento de América . México, D.F. , 1984. 284 p. : ISBN 968-415-089-X LC Card 87-403199 DDC 332/.0415/091812 19
HC94.Z9 S34 1984

Colección Libros de bolsillo (Instituto de Estudios Fiscales (Spain)) .
(55) Cuadrado Roura, Juan R. Política de rentas . [Madrid] [1980?] 471 p. : ISBN 84-7196-297-7 LC Card 85-131138
HC390.I5 C8 1980

Colección Manuales de finanzas públicas .
(17) Ross, Jaime. Instrumentos tributarios de financiamientos coadyuvantes a la producción agraria de alimentos /. Santo Domingo, R.D. [1983] i, 229 p. ; LC Card 84-159753
HJ4308 .R67 1983

Colección Monografías (Fundación Forum (Argentina))
Más allá del salario . [Buenos Aires] , 1983] 30 p. ; ISBN 950-9209-03-1 LC Card 84-126229
HB701 .M36 1983

Yornet, Mario E. Combustibles . Buenos Aires [1980] 105, viii leaves : LC Card 84-134419
HD9574.A72 Y67 1980

Colección Movimiento obrero ecuatoriano .
(no. 2) Puig Vilazar, Carlos. Sacrificio de un pueblo, 15 de noviembre de 1922 /. [Guayaquil, Ecuador] , 1983. 88 p. ; LC Card 86-115462
HD5358.A6 P85 1983

(no. 5) Capelo C., J. Alejo (J. Alejo Capelo Cabello), d. 1973. El crimen del 15 de noviembre de 1922 /. [Guayaquil] , 1983. 10, 14, 19 p. : LC Card 86-114097
HD5358.A6 C36 1983

(no. 7) Movimiento obrero del Ecuador, 1970-1979 . Guayaquil, Ecuador [1985] 300 p. ; LC Card 86-105256 DDC 331.88/09866 19
HD6627 .M68 1985 *NYPL [JLD 86-3140]*

(no. 8) Masas, luchas, solidaridad /. [S.l. , 1985] ([Guayaquil] : Litografía e Impr. de la Universidad de Guayaquil) 298 p. : LC Card 86-177888
HD8316 .M37 1985

Colección múltiple. Testimonio.
Andrión Alabarca, Aurelio, 1924- Sobre el surco reviven las esperanzas /. Panamá, R. de P. [1978] 84 p. : LC Card 82-100242
HD1531.P2 A53 1978

Colección "Pensadores políticos colombianos" .
(t. 9) López, Alejandro, 1876-1940. [Selections. 1983.] Obras selectas /. Bogotá, D.E. , 1983. xiii, 458 p. ; LC Card 86-233252
HC197 .L6172 1983

Colección Pensamiento económico .
(2) Quijano, José Manuel. Finanzas, desarrollo económico y penetración extranjera /. Puebla, Pue. , 1985. 395 p. : LC Card 86-112589 DDC 332/.0972 19
HG185.M6 Q55 1985 *NYPL [JLD 86-2195]*

Colección Pensamiento social (Quito, Ecuador)
Baez, René. Ciencia y transformación social . Quito, Ecuador , 1986. 141 p. ; LC Card 86-214736 DDC 330.9/0038 19
HC125 .B195 1986

Pacheco, Lucas. La política económica en el Ecuador . Quito, Ecuador , 1985. 219 p. ; LC Card 87-400294 DDC 338.9866 19
HC202 .P26 1985

Colección Periferia .
(2) Caicedo Licona, Carlos Arturo. El Chocó por dentro /. Medellín, Colombia , 1980. 118 p. : LC Card 83-105927
HC198.C48 C33 1980

Colección Periodismo de hoy.
Donadío, Alberto, 1953- Por qué cayó Jaime Michelsen? /. Bogotá , c1984. 142 p. : ISBN 84-89209-42-1 LC Card 85-122262
HG2908.C65 D66 1984

Colección Peruanicemos el Perú.
Iguíñiz, Javier. Crisis y fluctuaciones en la economía peruana, 1950-1983 . Jesús María [Peru] [1985] 245 p. : LC Card 86-116792 DDC 338.5/42/0985 19
HB3779 .I35 1985 *NYPL [JLC 86-268]*

Colección Problemas de México (Ediciones Era)
Astorga Lira, Enrique. Mercado de trabajo rural en México . México, D.F. , 1985. 127 p. : ISBN 968-411-139-8 LC Card 86-141300 DDC 331.7/63/0972 19
HD1531.M6 A88 1985 *NYPL [JLC 87-68]*

Rivera Ríos, Miguel Angel. Crisis y reorganización del capitalismo mexicano, 1960-1985 /. México, D.F. , 1986. 227 p. : ISBN 968-411-149-5 LC Card 87-401541 DDC 330.972/083 19
HC135 .R435 1986

Colección Rafael María Baralt.
Crisis y control de cambio /. Maracaibo, Venezuela , 1984. 101 p. ; LC Card 87-400572 DDC 332.4/560987 19
HG3941 .C74 1984

Colección Realidad nacional (Tegucigalpa, Honduras) .
(no. 4) Molina Chocano, Guillermo. Estado liberal y desarrollo capitalista en Honduras /. Tegucigalpa, Honduras , 1985. 136 p. : LC Card 86-233622
HG5202 .M65 1985

Colección realizarse. Biblioteca Educación y acción social.
Domínguez, Javier. Organizaciones obreras cristianas en la oposición al franquismo (1951-1975) . Bilbao [1985?] 479 p. ; ISBN 84-271-1431-1 LC Card 87-153234
HD6481.2.S7 D65 1985

Colección Rescate (Culiacán, Mexico) .
(19) Gill, Mario. La conquista del Valle del Fuerte /. Culiacán, Rosales, Sinaloa, México , c1983. 273 p., [4] folded leaves of plates : LC Card 86-121747
HC137.F84 G54 1983

Colección Soria existe.
Romero, Carmelo, 1950- Historia contemporánea de Soria, 1860-1936 . [Soria] , 1982. 510 p. : ISBN 84-85792-02-5 LC Card 85-136084
HC387.S67 R66 1982

Colección Status quaestionis.
Aguirre, Mariano A. De Hiroshima a los euromisiles /. Madrid , c1984. 254 p. : ISBN 84-309-1062-X LC Card 85-215587
U264 .A39 1984 *NYPL [JFC 86-1643]*

Colección Temas (Bogotá, Colombia)
La Ocupación y su remuneración en las empresas petroleras en Colombia, 1977-1984. Bogotá, D.E. [1986] 37 p. : LC Card 87-402964 DDC 331.12/5223382/09861 19
HD8039.P42 V446 1986

Colección Temas de política internacional.
Problemas económicos del Tercer Mundo /. Buenos Aires, República Argentina , c1983. 210 p. : ISBN 950-577-070-7 LC Card 84-120737 DDC 337/.09172/4 19
HF1413 .P75 1983 *NYPL [JLC 86-394]*

Colección Temas (Editorial Universitaria de Buenos Aires)
Ferrucci, Ricardo Jorge. La promoción industrial en Argentina /. [Buenos Aires] , c1986. 274 p. : ISBN 950-23-0307-5 LC Card 87-124151 DDC 338.982 19
HD3616.A73 F47 1986

Quadri Castillo, Mario. La Argentina descentralizada /. [Buenos Aires] , c1986. 236 p. : ISBN 950-23-0322-9 LC Card 87-402244 DDC 330.982/064 19
HC175 .Q33 1986

Colección Temas sociales (Santiago, Chile) .
(1) Schkolnik, Mariana. Sobrevivir en la población José M. Caro y en Lo Hermida /. [Santiago, Chile] [1986] 150 p., [20] p. of plates : LC Card 87-400080 DDC 362.5/8/098331 19
HC193.S2 S35 1986

Colección Tesis doctorales (Spain. Ministerio de Trabajo y Seguridad Social)
Vara Miranda, Ma. Jesús (María Jesús) Análisis de las cooperativas de trabajo asociado en Madrid /. [Madrid] , c1985. 463 p. : ISBN 84-7434-332-1 LC Card 87-109103 DDC 334/.6/094643 19
HD3218.M38 V37 1985

Colección TN .
(14) Lanzaro, Jorge Luis. Sindicatos y sistema político . Montevideo, Uruguay , 1986. 132 p. ; LC Card 87-403149 DDC 322/.2/09895 19
HD3616.U72 L36 1986

Colección universitaria (San José, Costa Rica)
López, José Roberto. La economía del banano en Centroamérica /. San José, Costa Rica , c1986. 236 p. : ISBN 997-7904-31-6 LC Card 87-404078 DDC 338.1/74772/09728 19
HD9259.B3 C4554 1986

Rivera, Eugenio. Centroamérica, política económica y crisis /. San José, Costa Rica , c1986. 201 p. : ISBN 997-7904-37-5 LC Card

87-404079 DDC 338.9728 19
HC141 .R58 1986

Colecciones paralelas. Historia .
(3) Herrera García, Antonio. El Aljarafe durante el antiguo régimen /. Sevilla , 1981. 147 p., [3] leaves of plates : ISBN 84-500-4850-8 LC Card 82-142028 DDC 333.3/0946/86 19
HD779.A39 H47 1981 NYPL [JLC 86-126]

Colegio de Graduados en Ciencias Económicas del Paraguay.
Política internacional, economía e integración /. Asunción del Paraguay [1985] 178 p. ; LC Card 86-122468
HF1523 .P65 1985

Seminario Estrategia de Desarrollo en Condiciones de Oferta Abundante de Energía Eléctrica (1980 : Asunción, Paraguay) Memoria del Seminario Estrategia de Desarrollo en Condiciones de Oferta Abundante de Energía Eléctrica . Asunción, Paraguay [s.l.] , 1980. 165 p., [18] leaves of plates : LC Card 83-169471 DDC 363.6/2 19
HD9685.P32 S45 1980 NYPL [JLE 87-995]

Colegio de México. Programa de Energéticos. Mercados mundiales de hidrocarburos . México, D.F. , 1983. 377 p. : ISBN 968-12-0231-7 LC Card 84-222729
HD9560.5 .M39 1983

Colegio de Michoacán. Guadalajara, la gran ciudad de la pequeña industria /. Zamora, Mich. , c1985. 301 p. : ISBN 968-7230-12-6 LC Card 86-191608
HD2346.M42 G824 1985

Colegio Nacional de Economistas (Mexico) México, una economía en transición /. México, D.F. , 1984-1985. 3 v. ; ISBN 968-18-1900-4 (v. 1) LC Card 86-235462
HC135 .M549 1985

Coleman, D. C. (Donald Cuthbert), 1920- History and the economic past : an account of the rise and decline of economic history in Britain / D.C. Coleman. Oxford : Clarendon Press ; New York : Oxford University Press, 1987. 150 p.; 23 cm. Includes bibliographical references and index. ISBN 0-19-828305-9 LC Card 86-28543 DDC 330/.07/1041 19
1. Economic history - Study and teaching - Great Britain. I. Title.
HC28.5.G7 C65 1987

Coleman, David. The State of population theory . Oxford, OX , New York, NY, USA , 1986. 311 p. : ISBN 0-631-13975-3 : LC Card 85-26668 DDC 304.6/01 19
HB849.4 .S73 1986 NYPL [JLE 86-2411]

Coles, Adrian, 1954- Boléat, Mark. The mortgage market /. London , Boston , 1987. x, 176 p. ; ISBN 0-04-334011-3 (alk. paper) LC Card 86-28875 DDC 332.7/22 19
HG2040.5.G7 B65 1987

COLES COUNTY (ILL.) - HISTORY.
Redlich, Paul R. The postal history of Coles County, Illinois . Des Plaines, Ill. (P.O. Box 1513, Des Plaines 60018) , c1986. v, 175 p. : LC Card 87-400110 DDC 383/.4977372 19
HE6376.A1 I58 1986

Colgan, Charles S. The natural resource industries of Maine : an assessment and statistical portrait / Charles S. Colgan, Lloyd C. Irland, Joyce Benson. [Augusta, Me.] : Executive Dept., Maine State Planning Office : Finance Authority of Maine, [1986] 135 p. : ill. ; 28 cm. "May 1986." Bibliography: p. 125-126. LC Card 87-620550 DDC 338.09741 19
1. Agricultural industries - Maine. 2. Fish trade - Maine. 3. Forest products industry - Maine. I. Irland, Lloyd C. II. Benson, Joyce. III. Maine. State Planning Office. IV. Finance Authority of Maine. V. Title.
HD9007.M2 C64 1986

Colihan, Mary Ann. Haley, Stephen W. Effective credit management in the equipment leasing and finance industry /. Arlington, VA , c1986. ix, 121 p. : ISBN 0-912413-01-8 (pbk.) LC Card 87-105306 DDC 658.1/5242 19
HD39.4 .H35 1986

Coll, Steve.
The deal of the century : the breakup of AT&T / Steve Coll.1st Touchstone ed. New York : Simon & Schuster, 1988, c1986. xv, 400 p. : 1 ill. ; 22 cm. (A Touchstone book) Bibliography: p. 381-385. Includes index. ISBN 0-671-64592-7 (pbk.) : LC Card 87-23410 DDC 384.6/065/73 19
1. American Telephone and Telegraph Company - Reorganization - History. 2. Telephone - United States - History. I. Title.
HE8846.A55 C58 1988

The taking of Getty Oil : the full story of the most spectacular--& catastrophic--takeover of all time / Steve Coll. New York : Atheneum, 1987. xiii, 528 p. ; 25 cm. Bibliography: p. 487-517. Includes index. ISBN 0-689-11860-0 LC Card 87-11467 DDC 338.8/3622338/0973 19
1. Getty Oil Company. 2. Getty family. 3. Petroleum industry and trade - United States - History. I. Title.
HD9569.G48 C65 1987

Collado, Faustino, 1954- Crisis y situación política en República Dominicana / Faustino Collado. Santo Domingo, República Dominicana : Editora Universitaria-UASD, [1985] 69 p. ; 21 cm. (Publicaciones de la Universidad Autónoma de Santo Domingo . vol. 360) Bibliography: p. 68. LC Card 87-115929
1. Dominican Republic - Economic conditions - 1961-. 2. Dominican Republic - Politics and government - 1961-. 3. Communism. I. Series: Publicaciones de la Universidad Autónoma de Santo Domingo , v. 360. II. Title.
HC153.5 .C65 1985

Collana "Ca' Bembo" .
(7) Di Bernardo, Barbara. Transizione tecnologica e strategie evolutive . Padova , 1985. xiii, 432 p. : LC Card 86-214184
HD45 .D47 1985

Collana del Centro di studi sulle crisi d'impresa e sulle ristrutturazioni industriali .
(2) Guatri, Luigi. Crisi e risanamento delle imprese /. Milano , 1986. viii, 339 p. : ISBN 88-14-00914-7 : LC Card 86-228719
HD58.8 .G82 1986

Collana di diritto ed economia .
(11) Strategie industriali e prospettive di sviluppo nel settore automobilistico /. Milano [1985] 235 p. : ISBN 88-14-00541-9 (pbk.) : LC Card 85-183335 DDC 338.4/76292/0945 19
HD9710.A2 S86 1985 NYPL [JLE 87-493]

(13) L'Industria siderurgica . Milano [1986] 193 p. : ISBN 88-14-00787-X : LC Card 86-222572
HD9510.5 .I473 1986

(3) Fruscio, Dario. Il sistema distributivo italiano . [Milano] , 1983. vii, 184 p. ; LC Card 83-233439 DDC 380.1/0945 19
HF5415.6 .F78 1983 NYPL [JLE 86-3650]

(4) Moro, Domenico. Crisi e ristrutturazione dell'industria siderurgica italiana /. [Milano] [1984] 256 p. : LC Card 84-181172 DDC 338.4/76691/0945 19
HD9525.I82 M67 1984 NYPL [JLE 86-3649]

(7) Sviluppo della finanza internazionale e interdipendenza dei sistemi finanziari . [Italy] [1984] iv, 204 p. : ISBN 88-14-00203-7 : LC Card 84-238589 DDC 332/.042 19
HG205.S85 S85 1984 NYPL [JLE 86-482]

(8) Il Leasing e il mercato del credito in Italia /. [Milano] [1984] iv, 82 p. : ISBN 88-14-00263-0 (pbk.) : LC Card 84-250907
HD39.4 .L37 1984 NYPL [JLE 87-509]

Collana di economia e politica dell'energia .
(22) Ascari, Sergio. Il metano in Italia . Milano, Italy , c1985. 292 p. : LC Card 86-135353
HD9579.M43 I82 1985

Collana di finanza locale .
(3) La Potestà impositiva dei comuni e delle province /. Rimini , c1985. 109 p. ; LC Card 85-194391 DDC 336.2/014/45 19
HJ9498 .P68 1985 NYPL [JLE 86-4120]

Collana di marketing .
(7) De Luca, Amedeo, 1945- Le applicazioni dei metodi statistici alle analisi di mercato /. Milano, Italy , c1984. 341 p. : LC Card 85-185924 DDC 380.1/01/5195 19
HF1017 .D4 1984

Collana di "monografie" (Associazione per lo sviluppo dell'industria nel Mezzogiorno) .
(47) Il Mezzogiorno nelle politiche nazionali e comunitarie . Milano , 1982. 379 p. ; LC Card 82-230171 DDC 338.945/7 19
HC305 .M42156 1982 NYPL [JLE 86-1611]

Collana di politiche del lavoro .
(3) Runggaldier, Ulrich. Le politiche regionali del lavoro . Milano, Italy , c1986. 160 p. ; LC Card 86-169484
HD8376.5 .R93 1986

Collana di psicologia del lavoro. Sezione Ricerche e studi .
(3) Petrillo, Giovanna, 1952- Produttività e improduttività del lavoro domestico . Bologna , 1985. 139 p. ; LC Card 86-132212
HD8039.H842 I87 1985

Collana di psicologia (Raffaello Cortina editore) .
(8) Frontori, Laura. Il mercato dei segni . Milano , c1986. xv, 186 p., [8] p. of plates : ISBN 88-7078-040-6 : LC Card 86-161029
HF5822 .F74 1986

Collana di pubblicazioni dell'Istituto di politica economica e finanziaria della Facoltà di economia e commercio della Università di Roma .
(9) Romagnoli, Gian Cesare, 1948- Nuove politiche di finanziamento degli enti locali in Italia . Milano, Italy , c1985. 260 p. : LC Card 86-169439
HJ9497 .R65 1985

Collana di scienza politica .
(4) Convegno "La scienza politica in Italia, bilancio e prospettive" (1984 : Milan, Italy) Politica ed economia . Milano, Italy , c1987. 159 p. ; LC Card 87-139661
HC305 .C6767 1984

Collana di studi demografici. For additional listing of contents, see Old Catalog.
(12) Storia demografica dei comuni siciliani dal 1862 al 1971 /. Palermo [1979] 294 p. ; LC Card 86-131917
HB2270.S5 S76 1979

(13) Greco, Eugenio. Storia demografica dei comuni siciliani dal 1832 al 1858 /. Palermo [1982] 60, [61] p. ; LC Card 85-103229
HB2270.S5 G74 1982

(14) Vizzini, Sergio. Indagine socio-demografica sugli immigrati stranieri in Sicilia . Palermo [1983] 108 p. ; LC Card 86-131931
HB3600.M39 V58 1983

Collana di studi di tecnica aziendale .
(1) Cuomo, Gennaro. Funzioni, strutture, strategie delle imprese commerciali complesse /. Padova , 1984. 236 p. : LC Card 86-214195
HD38.5 .C86 1984

Collana di studi e ricerche (Italy. Ministero degli affari esteri. Dipartimento per la cooperazione allo sviluppo) .
(2) D'Angelo, Massimo. Criteri per una cooperazione industriale con i paesi in via di sviluppo /. Milano , c1981. 294 p. ; ISBN 88-20-42145-3 : LC Card 82-113466
HF1549 .D36 1981 NYPL [JLD 86-3318]

(4) Guida alla valorizzazione agricola nei paesi in via di sviluppo /. Milano, Italy , c1983. 434 p. : LC Card 83-144803 DDC 338.1/09172/4 19
HD1417 .G85 1983 NYPL [JLD 86-3296]

(7) Abitazione e periferie urbane nei paesi in via di sviluppo . Milano, Italy , c1985. 450 p. : LC Card 86-132019
HD7287.96.L29 A25 1985 NYPL [JLD 87-1173]

Collana di studi studi economico-aziendali (Milan, Italy)) .
(3) Cardillo, Giovanni. La programmabilità delle gestioni aziendali in tempi di inflazione /. Milano , 1983. 118 p. ; LC Card 84-177279 DDC 658.4/012/0945 19
HD70.I8 C27 1983 NYPL [JLD 86-1047]

Collana Fondazione Giulio Pastore. Sezione Economia e sociologia del lavoro .
(1) Sul "movimento" della qualità della vita di lavoro /. Milano , c1982. 117 p. ; LC Card 82-246606
HD6955 .S94 1982 NYPL [JLD 87-1159]

Collana Insor .
(14) Barberis, Corrado. Agricoltura e strati sociali /. Milano, Italy , c1986. 269 p. ; LC Card 86-214233
HD1536.I8 B328 1986

Collana IReR .
(12) Conto consolidato della spesa pubblica in Lombardia /. Milano, Italy , c1982. 234 p. ; LC Card 85-147746
HJ9925.I8 C63 1982

(22) Lavoro femminile, sviluppo tecnologico e

segregazione occupazionale /. Milano, Italy , c1984. 458 p. : LC Card 84-190076 DDC 331.4/0945 19
HD6154 .L385 1984 ***NYPL [*QO 87-1143]***

(29) Scelte strategiche e riorganizzazione aziendale . Milano, Italy , c1985. 312 p. ; LC Card 86-146459
HD2864 .S36 1985 ***NYPL [JLD 87-1549]***

(33) Gario, Giuseppe. Discontinuità e permanenza . Milano, Italy , c1986. 262 p. : LC Card 87-149940
HC307.L8 G37 1986

Collana Ires/Cgil (Milan, Italy) .
(9) Valvo, Tino, 1948- Retribuzioni a confronto . Milano, Italy , c1986. 247 p. : LC Card 86-170001
HD5035.T87 V34 1986

Collana Università .
(11) Romitelli, Valerio. Critica dell'economia politica e teoria delle forze produttive /. Milano , c1982. 241 p. ; LC Card 82-200332 DDC 338.5 19
HB241 .R66 1982 ***NYPL [JLD 87-812]***

(14) Tasgian, Astrig. L'imposta e il deposito previo sugli acquisti di valuta e la crisi della lira del 1976 . Milano , c1983. 139 p. : LC Card 83-187693 DDC 332.4/945 19
HG1029.5 .T37 1983 ***NYPL [JLD 87-813]***

(15) Economia tra teoria e politica /. Milano , c1984. 295 p. ; LC Card 84-171327 DDC 330/.09 19
HB75 .E28 1984 ***NYPL [JLD 87-819]***

(4) Moro, Beniamino, 1945- Programmazione lineare e teoria dell'impresa /. Milano [1980] 182 p. : ISBN 88-20-41708-1 : LC Card 80-489699
T57.74 .M67 ***NYPL [JLD 87-792]***

(9) Magni, Carlo. I mercati regionali del lavoro e il problema degli indicatori . Milano [1981] 133, [3] p. : ISBN 88-20-42109-7 : LC Card 81-194409
HD5784 .M3 1981 ***NYPL [JLD 87-815]***

The collapse of the Weimar Republic . Abraham, David, 1946- New York , 1986. liii, 352 p. ; ISBN 0-8419-1083-9 LC Card 86-27033 DDC 338.0943 19
HD3616.G35 A27 1986

Collar, George. An industrial and social history of England / by George Collar. London ; New York : Sir I. Pitman & Sons, [1912] 283 p. : ill. ; 19 cm. Cover title: Industrial and social history. Illustrations on lining papers. LC Card 85-666355
1. Great Britain - Economic conditions. 2. Great Britain - Industries - History. I. Title. II. Title: Industrial and social history.
HC253 .C65x 1912

Collard, David A. Economics, growth, and sustainable environments . New York , 1988. viii, 205 p. : ISBN 0-312-01240-3 : LC Card 87-12520 DDC 363.7 19
HC79.E5 E2774 1988

Col·lecció Catalunya comarcal.
El Baix Empordà . Barcelona , c1984. xii, 303 p. : ISBN 84-505-0289-6 LC Card 85-186183
HC387.A636 B35 1984

Calleja Xifré, Carlos. El Baix Camp . Barcelona [1986] xv, 367 p. : ISBN 84-505-3567-9 LC Card 86-205881
HC388.R482 C35 1986

La Garrotxa . [Barcelona , c1983. xv, 323 p. : ISBN 84-7231-912-1 LC Card 85-184803
HC387.G34 G37 1983

Col·lecció Clio .
(1) Huertas, Josep Maria. Obrers a Catalunya . Barcelona , 1982. 409 p. : ISBN 84-85905-06-7 LC Card 83-101512
HD8589.C32 H83 1982
NYPL [JLD 86-3659]

(5) Barrull Pelegrí, Jaume, 1947- Les comarques de Lleida durant la segona república, 1930-1936 /. Barcelona , 1986. 503 p. : ISBN 84-85905-23-7 LC Card 86-203986
HC388.L4 B37 1986

(6) El Comerç entre Catalunya i Amèrica (segles XVIII i XIX) /. Barcelona , 1986. 173 p. : ISBN 84-85905-24-5 LC Card 86-204187
HF3689.C3 C39 1986

Col·lecció Miquel Santaló i Parvorell .
(1) Medir i Huerta, Rosa M. Les comarques gironines . Girona , 1986. 211 p. : ISBN 84-505-3103-9 LC Card 87-101047
HC387.G4 M43 1986

Col·lecció Prat de la Riba .
(1) Bricall, Josep Maria, 1936- Estat autonòmic i finances públiques . [Barcelona] , 1984. 358 p. : ISBN 84-500-9868-8 LC Card 85-106586
HJ1000 .B75 1984 ***NYPL [JLE 86-3989]***

(2) Las Finanzas municipales en el estado de las autonomías . [Barcelona] , 1985. 178 p. ; ISBN 84-505-1593-9 LC Card 85-240344
HJ9525 .F55 1985

The collected papers of James Meade /. Meade, J. E. (James Edward), 1907- [Works. 1988.] London , Boston , 1988- p. cm. ISBN 0-04-445073-7 (v. 1. : alk. paper) LC Card 87-15288 DDC 330.1 19
HD5710 .M43 1988

Collected papers of the National Workshop on Project Evaluation, held at the National Institute for Public Administration, 10-14 December, 1984. National Workshop on Project Evaluation (1984 : National Institute for Public Administration, Lusaka, Zambia) [Lusaka] , 1985. 1 v. in various pagings ; LC Card 85-981123 DDC 338.96894/0068 19
HC915.Z9 E446 1984

Collected research papers .
(v. 7) Mathewson, G. Frank, 1942- Competition policy and vertical exchange /. Toronto , Buffalo , c1985. xvii, 119 p. : ISBN 0-8020-7248-8 (pbk.) LC Card 86-672936 DDC 338.6/048/0971 19
HF1480 .M37 1985 ***NYPL [JLE 87-512]***

Collected research studies .
(v. 1) Income distribution and economic security in Canada /. Toronto , Buffalo , c1985. xv, 321 p. : ISBN 0-8020-7241-0 (pbk.) LC Card 85-227851 DDC 330.971/064 19
HC120.I5 I53 1985 ***NYPL [JLE 86-1881]***

(v. 21) Fiscal and monetary policy /. Toronto , Buffalo , c1986. xviii, 339 p. : ISBN 0-8020-7263-1 (pbk.) LC Card 86-672943 DDC 336.3/0971 19
HJ793 .F55 1986 ***NYPL [JLE 87-511]***

(v. 3) Technological change in Canadian industry /. Toronto , Buffalo , c1985. xv, 233 p. ; ISBN 0-8020-7243-7 (pbk.) LC Card 86-164766 DDC 338/.06 19
HC120.T4 T42 1985 ***NYPL [JLD 87-654]***

(v. 42) Schultz, Richard, 1945- Economic regulation and the federal system /. Toronto , Buffalo , c1985. xv, 187 p. : ISBN 0-8020-7287-9 (pbk.) LC Card 86-672574
HD3616.C23 S38x 1985
NYPL [JLD 86-2821]

Collected works of Leif Johansen /. Johansen, Leif. [Essays. Selections.] Amsterdam ; New York : 2 v. (xiii, 974 p.) ; ISBN 0-444-87833-5 (set) LC Card 87-6814 DDC 330.1 19
HB171 .J59725 1987

COLLECTIBLES AS AN INVESTMENT - JUVENILE LITERATURE.
Epstein, Rachel S. Alternative investments /. New York , c1988. 47 p. : ISBN 1-555-46633-8 LC Card 87-21766 DDC 332.6/78 19
HG4521 .E685 1988

COLLECTING OF ACCOUNTS - UNITED STATES.
President's Private Sector Survey on Cost Control (U. S.) President's private sector survey on cost control . Washington, D.C. , 1983. viii, 320 p. ; ***NYPL [JLF 86-727]***

Stelter, Thomas. Complete guide to skip tracing . Eau Claire, Wis. , c1987. 143 p. : ISBN 0-941161-16-1 (pbk.) LC Card 87-124276 DDC 658.8/8 19
HG3752.7.U6 S74 1987

Winston, Arthur. Complete guide to tested telephone collection techniques /. Englewood Cliffs, N.J. , c1988. p. cm. ISBN 0-13-160185-7 : LC Card 87-22321 DDC 658.8/8 19
HG3752.7.U6 W56 1988

Collection "Action et gestion"
Genzel, David. De la publicité à la communication /. Paris [1984?] 271 p. : ISBN 2-86737-005-1 LC Card 84-175281
HF5813.F8 G46 1984

COLLECTION AGENCIES.
Dietrich, Bernhard R. Inkasso Unternehmungen /. Neuried , c1986. xxxv, 200 p. ; ISBN 3-88893-050-2 LC Card 87-133343 DDC 658.8/8 19
HG3752.5 .D54 1986

COLLECTION AGENCIES - LAW AND LEGISLATION.
Dietrich, Bernhard R. Inkasso Unternehmungen /. Neuried , c1986. xxxv, 200 p. ; ISBN 3-88893-050-2 LC Card 87-133343 DDC 658.8/8 19
HG3752.5 .D54 1986

Collection Alternatives paysannes.
N'Kaloulou, Bernard, 1952- Dynamique paysanne et développement rural au Congo /. Paris , c1984. 260 p. : ISBN 2-85802-416-X LC Card 84-246506 DDC 305.5/63 19
HD1006 .N57 1984 ***NYPL [JLD 87-304]***

Collection Avis et recommandations.
Conseil de planification et de développement du Québec. Le réseau décisionnel en agro-alimentation au Québec . [Québec] [1979] 29 p. ; LC Card 85-102587
HD9014.C4 Q425 1979

Collection Bibliothèque de gestion. Série Enseignement.
Lamorlette, Corine. 10 études de cas de fiscalité avec corrigés détaillés . Paris , 1984. 95 p. : ISBN 2-7178-0802-7 : LC Card 85-129474
HF5681.T3 L28 1984

Collection C.E.S.B.
Bizot, Alain. La pratique bancaire française en matière de financement sur le marché intérieur /. Paris , c1985. 238 p. : ISBN 2-86325-033-7 : LC Card 86-159009
HG1642.F8 B59 1985

Collection Colloques et séminaires (O.R.S.T.O.M. (Agency : France))
Séminaire international sur la place des femmes dans l'autosuffisance et les stratégies alimentaires (1985 : Paris, France) Femmes et politiques alimentaires . Paris , 1985. 741 p. : ISBN 2-7099-0763-1 LC Card 86-205282
HD6073.A292 D4477 1985

Collection Coopération et développement.
Delalande, Philippe, 1937- Science économique et maîtrise de l'avenir /. Paris , 1984. 305 p. : ISBN 2-7178-0790-X : LC Card 85-104627
HB71 .D45 1984

Collection de la Faculté d'économie appliquée d'Aix-Marseille III.
Catin, Maurice. Effets externes . Paris , c1985. 455 p. : ISBN 2-254-85071-2 : LC Card 86-186253
HB846.3 .C37 1985

Collection de la Faculté des sciences juridiques, économiques et sociales. Série de langue française .
(28) Berrada, Abdelkader. Le crédit agricole au Maroc, 1917-1977 /. [Rabat] , 1979. 264 p. ; LC Card 82-136521 DDC 332.7/1/0964 19
HG2051.M8 B47 1979

Collection de la Maison des pays ibériques .
(4) Les Communications dans la péninsule Ibérique au Moyen-Age . Paris , 1981. 208 p. : ISBN 2-222-02922-8 : LC Card 81-213698 DDC 380.5/0946 19
HE261.A5 C65 1981 ***NYPL [JLG 86-113]***

Collection de la RPP.
Johanet, Gilles. Contes et mécomptes de la protection sociale /. Paris , c1986. 175 p. : ISBN 2-86702-024-4 : LC Card 86-179065
HD7175 .J64 1986

Collection de l'Ecole française de Rome, 0223-5099 .
(85) Dewerpe, Alain. L'industrie aux champs . Roma , 1985. xxxv, 543 p. : ISBN 2-7283-0081-X LC Card 86-221375
HC307.N58 D48 1985

Collection de l'I.M.E. .
(no 27) Offant, Pierre. Adaptation structurelle de l'économie française à la limitation de la consommation d'énergie /. Dijon , c1984. 224, iii p. : ISBN 2-85975-026-6 LC Card 85-205959
HD9502.F72 O33 1984

Collection de l'Institut de recherche et d'information sur les multinationales.
L'Information et la consultation des travailleurs dans les enterprises multinationales /. [Paris] [Genève?] , 1984. 290 p. ; ISBN 2-13-038651-2

(pbk.)
HD62.4 .I53 1984 ***NYPL [JLD 87-60]***

Collection des A. T. P. - Sciences humaines. see **Actions thématiques programmées. A. T. P.: Sciences humaines.**

Collection des actions thématiques programmées: Sciences humaines. see **Actions thématiques programmées. A. T. P.: Sciences humaines.**

Collection des ateliers du développement .
(no 5) Promotion de la petite industrie dans les pays en développement /. Paris , c1985. 103 p. : ISBN 2-86844-008-8 LC Card 85-242526 DDC 338.6/42/0943 19
HD2346.5 .P76 1985 ***NYPL [JLD 86-3171]***

Collection des ateliers Technologie et développement .
(no 1) Politiques vivrières, dépendances alimentaires et développement /. [Paris] , c1984. iv, 129 p. : ISBN 2-86844-000-2 : LC Card 84-248912
HD9017.S152 P65 1984

(no 3) Stratégies d'industrialisation et maîtrise du développement. Paris , c1984. 115, [3] p. : ISBN 2-86844-002-9 LC Card 84-248894
HC59.7 .S854 1984

Collection des rapports officiels.
Comptes de l'emploi . Paris , c1984. 219 p. : ISBN 2-11-001264-1 : LC Card 85-132416
HD5775 .C5344 1984

France. Mission "Recherche, technologie et progrès en coopération." Recherche et coopération avec le Tiers Monde . Paris , c1983. 120 p. ; ISBN 2-11-001071-1 : LC Card 83-196852
HC60 .F727 1983

Germon, Claude. La normalisation, clé d'un nouvel essor . Paris , c1983. 156 p. ; ISBN 2-11-001026-6 : LC Card 83-217768
HD3616.F83 G47 1983

Pastré, Olivier. La modernisation des banques françaises . Paris [1985] 234 p. : ISBN 2-11-001537-3 : LC Card 86-179536
HG3026 .P37 1985

Le Transport fluvial . Paris , c1983. 108 p. : ISBN 2-11-001087-8 : LC Card 83-170808
HE668 .T73 1983

Collection des thèses de la Faculté des sciences économiques et sociales, 0271-7146 .
(thèse no 278) Huber, Gérard. Les conséquences à long terme de la politique macroéconomique /. Berne , 1982. 449 p. ; ISBN 3-261-04985-5 LC Card 87-672303
HB172.5 .H82x 1982

Collection du Centre de recherches d'histoire des mouvements sociaux et du syndicalisme.
Fourcaut, Annie, 1950- Femmes à l'usine . Paris , 1982. 268 p. : ISBN 2-7071-1258-5 : LC Card 82-151587
HD6145 .F65 1982

Collection du COPS.
Privatisation . Paris , c1986. 188 p. ; ISBN 2-85802-651-3 : LC Card 86-161183
HD3854 .P75 1986

Collection Economie.
Collection "Economie et statistiques avancées." Série Ecole nationale de la statistique et de l'administration économique et Centre d'études des programmes économiques.
Pisani-Ferry, Jean. Problèmes de macroéconomie /. Paris , 1984. 452 p. : ISBN 2-7178-0801-9 : LC Card 85-100663 DDC 339 19
HB173 .P534 1984

Collection "Encyclopédie pratique complète de la V.P.C. et de la publicité directe" .
(2) Grémillard, Roger. 75 moyens qui ont fait leurs preuves d'augmenter vos rendements et diminuer vos coûts en publicité et en V.P.C. /. Créteil , c1982. 158 p. ; LC Card 82-238594
HF5466 .G718 1982

Collection "Etudes de l'Annuaire de l'Afrique du Nord"
Bernard, Chantal. La politique de l'emploi-formation au Maghreb, 1970-1980 /. Paris , 1982. 472 p. ; ***NYPL [JLE 86-568]***

La Politique de l'emploi-formation au Maghreb, 1970-1980 /. Paris , 1982. 472 p. : ISBN 2-222-03122-2 LC Card 84-222103 DDC 331.11/0961 19
HD5838 .P65 1982

Collection "Etudes économiques et sociales"
Chômage des jeunes . Bruxelles [1984] 49 p. : LC Card 84-222918
HD6276.B42 C48 1984

Collection Gestion (Economica (Firm)). Série Politique générale, finance et marketing.
Augros, Jean-Claude. Finance . Paris , c1985. 320 p. : ISBN 2-7178-0911-2 : LC Card 85-219227 DDC 332.64/52/0944 19
HG6042 .A94 1985 ***NYPL [JLE 87-295]***

Vatteville, Éric. Mesure des ressources humaines et gestion de l'entreprise /. Paris , c1985. 286 p. : ISBN 2-7178-0969-4 : LC Card 86-137038 DDC 658.3 19
HF5549 .V382 1985

Collection Gestion (Economica (Firm)). Série Production et techniques quantitatives appliquées à la gestion.
Roy, B. (Bernard), 1934- Méthodologie multicritère d'aide à la décision /. Paris , c1985. xxii, 423 p. : ISBN 2-7178-0901-5 : LC Card 86-166619
HD30.25 .R68 1985

Collection Gestion (Presses universitaires de France)
Maricourt, Renaud de. La prévision des ventes /. Paris , c1985. 159 p. : ISBN 2-13-039013-7 : LC Card 86-138110 DDC 658.8/18 19
HF5415 .M2794 1985

Collection "Histoire du papier monnaie français" .
(v. 2) Muszynski, Maurice. Les assignats de la Révolution française /. Bruyères-le-Châtel , c1981. 163 p. : LC Card 87-672912
HG978 .M87x 1981

(1) Muszynski, Maurice. Les billets de la Banque de France ; Les émissions du Trésor /. Bruyères-le-Châtel , 1985. 160 p. : LC Card 83-132282
HG985 .M88 1985

(2) Muszynski, Maurice. Les assignats de la Révolution française /. Bruyères-le-Châtel , c1981. 163 p. : LC Card 87-672912
HG978 .M87x 1981

Collection Histoire et théorie.
Duboin, Marie-Louise. Les affranchis de l'an 2000 /. Paris , c1984. 303 p. ; ISBN 2-86738-026-X : LC Card 84-203792
HD83 .D74 1984

Les Aventures du marxisme /. Paris , c1984. 415 p. ; ISBN 2-86738-025-1 (pbk.)
NYPL [JLD 87-212]

Collection Institut technique de banque, 0293-8030.
Barbier, André. Guide pratique de l'analyse financière à l'usage des banquiers /. Paris , c1985. viii, 313 p. : ISBN 2-86325-038-8 : LC Card 86-165653
HF5686.C7 B32 1985

Collection J. Brémond.
Brémond, Janine. L'économie française face aux défis mondiaux . Paris , c1985. 320 p. : ISBN 2-218-07456-7 LC Card 86-168427
HC276.2 .B657 1985

Collection Latomus. For other vols. in this series, see Old Catalog.
(v. 194) Pack, Edgar. Städte und Steuern in der Politik Julians . Bruxelles , 1986. 420 p. ; ISBN 2-87031-134-6 LC Card 87-105922 DDC 336.2/014/37 19
HJ9497.A3 P33 1986

COLLECTION LAWS.
Dietrich, Bernhard R. Inkasso Unternehmungen /. Neuried , c1986. xxxv, 200 p. ; ISBN 3-88893-050-2 LC Card 87-133343 DDC 658.8/8 19
HG3752.5 .D54 1986

COLLECTION LAWS - UNITED STATES.
Stelter, Thomas. Complete guide to skip tracing . Eau Claire, Wis. , c1987. 143 p. : ISBN 0-941161-16-1 (pbk.) LC Card 87-124276 DDC 658.8/8 19
HG3752.7.U6 S74 1987

Collection Les Antilles après l'abolition.
Chemin Dupontès, P. Les Petites Antilles . [Fort-de-France] [Paris] [1979] x, 318 p., [10] p. of plates : ISBN 2-85275-105-4 LC Card 84-164674
HC151 .C49 1979

Collection Les Publications de la Maison des sciences de l'homme de Strasbourg.
Réformisme et révisionnisme dans les socialismes allemand, autrichien et français /. Paris , c1984. 195 p. ; ISBN 2-7351-0053-7 : LC Card 85-105830
HX273 .R39 1984 ***NYPL [JLE 86-4752]***

COLLECTION LETTERS. see **COLLECTING OF ACCOUNTS.**

Collection L'Etudiant pratique, 0759-9064 .
(19) Placier, Anne. Les métiers de la publicité /. Paris , c1984. 247 p., [15] p. of plates : ISBN 2-86745-019-5 LC Card 85-118630
HF5828.4 .P58 1984

Collection Liberté sans frantières.
Le Tiers-mondisme en question /. Paris , c1986. 225 p. ; ISBN 2-85565-299-5 : LC Card 86-185503
HC60 .T518 1986

Collection Management 2000.
Enrègle, Yves. Du conflit à la motivation . Paris , 1985. 196 p. : ISBN 2-7081-0642-2 : LC Card 85-231586
HF5549.5.M63 E57 1985

Collection Mathématiques appliquées pour la maîtrise.
Aubin, Jean-Pierre. L'analyse non linéaire et ses motivations économiques /. Paris , New York , 1984. x, 214 p. : ISBN 2-225-79541-X : LC Card 86-135801
HB135 .A86 1984

Collection "Modèles et macroéconomie appliquée. " Série "Etudes et recherches" .
(no 1) Serra, Daniel. Monnaie, inflation et croissance /. Paris , 1982. xi, 306 p. : ISBN 2-7178-0478-1 : LC Card 82-153767 DDC 332.4/0724 19
HG221 .S485 1982 ***NYPL [JLE 86-1903]***

Collection "Nouvelles pratiques sociales", 0762-0810.
Tozzi, Michel. Militer autrement /. Bruxelles, Belgique , Lyon, France [1985] 162 p. ; ISBN 2-85008-067-5 : LC Card 86-178750
HD6684 .T66 1985

COLLECTION OF ACCOUNTS. . see **COLLECTING OF ACCOUNTS.**

A Collection of cases in marketing management / [edited by] H. Robert Dodge, William G. Zikmund. 2nd ed. St. Paul : West Pub. Co., c1987. xix, 344 p. ; 25 cm. Rev. ed. of: A Collection of outstanding cases in marketing management. c1979. Includes bibliographical references. ISBN 0-314-85313-8 (pbk.) LC Card 87-6072 DDC 658.8/00973 19
1. Marketing - United States - Management - Case studies. I. Dodge, H. Robert, 1929-. II. Zikmund, William G. III. Collection of outstanding cases in marketing management.
HF5415.13 .C64 1987

Collection of data of agriculture and food industry from the liberation till now /.
Mezőgazdasági és élelmiszeripari adattár a felszabadulástól napjainkig. English. Budapest , 1985. 85 p. ; ISBN 963-502-393-6 LC Card 86-230345
HD1940.5 .M49713 1985

Collection of outstanding cases in marketing management. A Collection of cases in marketing management /. St. Paul , c1987. xix, 344 p. ; ISBN 0-314-85313-8 (pbk.) LC Card 87-6072 DDC 658.8/00973 19
HF5415.13 .C64 1987

Collection Politique sociale, 0243-3265.
Galland, Olivier. Jeunes en transit . Paris , c1984. 236 p. ; ISBN 2-7082-2405-0 : LC Card 85-102779 DDC 367/.94486 19
HD6276.F72 G35 1984

Collection Repères. Série "Structures économiques."
Baslé, Maurice. Le budget de l'Etat /. Paris , 1985. 127 p. : ISBN 2-7071-1534-7 LC Card 86-161271
HJ2106 .B37 1985

Pastré, Olivier. L'informatisation et l'emploi /. Paris , 1983. 127 p. : ISBN 2-7071-1387-5 LC Card 83-161919 DDC 331.12/0944 19
HD6331.2.F8 P37 1983

Collection Repères. Série "Travail et emploi."
Freyssinet, Jacques. Le chômage /. Paris , 1984. 128 p. : ISBN 2-7071-1478-2 LC Card 85-115448 DDC 331.13/7 19
HD5707.5 .F74 1984

Collection "Réponses sociologiques", 0761-6252.
Chabaud-Rychter, Danielle. Espace et temps du travail domestique /. Paris , 1985. 156 p. ; ISBN 2-86563-127-3 LC Card 86-165713
HD6055 .C45 1985

Collection Tiers monde, 0223-5870.
L'Hériteau, Marie France. Le Fonds monétaire international et les pays du Tiers-monde /. Paris , c1986. 277 p. : ISBN 2-13-039203-2 : LC Card 86-165389
HG3881.5.I58 L52 1986

Collection Vie et économie.
Deiss, Joseph. Economie politique et politique économique de la Suisse /. Fribourg , c1979. 412 p. : LC Card 86-673870
HC397 .D387x 1979

Collection "Villes et entreprises"
Camacho, Martine. Les poubelles de la survie . Paris , c1986. 207 p. : ISBN 2-85802-590-5 LC Card 86-180208
HC895.Z7 A443 1986

Dijk, Meine Pieter van. Burkina-Faso . Paris , c1986. 203 p. ; ISBN 2-85802-638-6 LC Card 86-221033
HD2346.B822 O933 1986

Dijk, Meine Pieter van. Sénégal . Paris [1986] 164 p. ; ISBN 2-85802-637-8 LC Card 86-221017
HD2346.S42 D343 1986

Durand-Lasserve, Alain. L'exclusion des pauvres dans les villes du Tiers-Monde . Paris , c1986. 198 p. : ISBN 2-85802-613-8 LC Card 87-111461
HD7391 .D79 1986

Nourrir les villes en Afrique sub-saharienne /. Paris , c1985. 421 p. : ISBN 2-85802-562-X LC Card 86-222243
HD9017.S82 N68 1985

Collections de l'INSEE .
(no 440-441) Sources et méthodes d'élaboration des comptes nationaux. [Paris] [1983] 481 p. ; LC Card 84-161813
HC271 .A218 no. 440-441 HJ9925.F8

Collections de statistique agricole, 0336-5638 .
(étude no 228) Colliez, Jean-Paul. Les salariés agricoles permanents, leur rémunération en octobre 1982. Paris [1984] 62 p. : ISBN 2-11-083969-4 LC Card 85-108387
HD4966.A292 F73 1984

Collections statistiques du Ministère de l'urbanisme et du logement. Statistiques et études générales, 0184-6892 .
(no 79) Les Logements neufs en 1978 . Paris , 1982. 40 p. : LC Card 83-176727
HD7338.A4 L64 1982

COLLECTIVE AGREEMENTS. see COLLECTIVE LABOR AGREEMENTS.

Collective bargaining . International Labour Office. Geneva , 1986. ix, 112 p. ; ISBN 92-2-105284-2 (pbk.) : LC Card 86-208328 DDC 331.89 19
HD6971.5 .I57 1986

COLLECTIVE BARGAINING - AGRICULTURE - SPAIN.
González Rodríguez, Juan Jesús. La patronal agraria . Madrid [1986?] 46 p. ; ISBN 84-7075-335-3 LC Card 87-111477
HD6976.A292 S74 1986

COLLECTIVE BARGAINING - AUSTRALIA.
Niland, John R. Control, consensus, or chaos? . Sydney , Boston , 1985. xiv, 330 p. : ISBN 0-86861-447-5 (pbk.) LC Card 85-70461 DDC 331.89/0994 19
HD8846.5 .N55 1985 ***NYPL [JLD 87-354]***

COLLECTIVE BARGAINING - AUTOMOBILE INDUSTRY - GERMANY (WEST)
Streeck, Wolfgang, 1946- Industrial relations in West Germany . London , 1984. 178 p. ; ISBN 0-435-83839-3 LC Card 87-673421
HD6698.A8 S77x 1984b

COLLECTIVE BARGAINING - AUTOMOBILE INDUSTRY - GERMANY (WEST) - CASE STUDIES.
Industrial relations and technical change in the British, Italian, and German automobile industry . Berlin [1985] 1 v. (various pagings) : LC Card 86-206613 DDC 338/.04292/094 19
HD6976.A82 G75 1985

COLLECTIVE BARGAINING - AUTOMOBILE INDUSTRY - GREAT BRITAIN - CASE STUDIES.
Industrial relations and technical change in the British, Italian, and German automobile industry . Berlin [1985] 1 v. (various pagings) : LC Card 86-206613 DDC 338/.04292/094 19
HD6976.A82 G75 1985

COLLECTIVE BARGAINING - AUTOMOBILE INDUSTRY - ITALY - CASE STUDIES.
Industrial relations and technical change in the British, Italian, and German automobile industry . Berlin [1985] 1 v. (various pagings) : LC Card 86-206613 DDC 338/.04292/094 19
HD6976.A82 G75 1985

COLLECTIVE BARGAINING - AUTOMOBILE INDUSTRY - UNITED STATES - HISTORY.
Katz, Harry Charles, 1951- Shifting gears . Cambridge, Mass. , c1985. xii, 230 p. : ISBN 0-262-11098-9 LC Card 84-26105 DDC 331/.04292/0973 19
HD6976.A82 U528 1985 ***NYPL [JLE 85-2260]***

COLLECTIVE BARGAINING - BRAZIL - HISTORY - 20TH CENTURY.
Sousa, Amaury de. A nova política salarial e as negociações coletivas de trabalho no Brasil, 1979-1982 . [Brazil?] 1983. 109 leaves ; LC Card 87-404781 DDC 331.2/981 19
HD5004 .S675 1983

COLLECTIVE BARGAINING - CALIFORNIA.
Seider, Maynard, 1943- A year in the life of a factory /. San Pedro, Calif. , 1984. 152 p. ; ISBN 0-917300-16-5 (pbk.) : LC Card 83-50914 DDC 331.89/28621381/0979466 19
HD8039.E38 U67 1984 ***NYPL [JLD 86-4400]***

COLLECTIVE BARGAINING - CHILE.
Barrera, Manuel. Trade unions and the state in the present day Chile . Geneva, Switzerland , Santiago, Chile , 1986. xx, 154 p. : LC Card 87-128364 DDC 331.89/0983 19
HD6617 .B273 1986

COLLECTIVE BARGAINING - COAL MINING INDUSTRY - UNITED STATES.
Miernyk, William H. The coalmining industry in the United States /. Geneva , 1986. 53, ix p. : ISBN 92-9014-409-2 (pbk.)
NYPL [JLE 87-1534]

COLLECTIVE BARGAINING - CONSTRUCTION INDUSTRY - GERMANY (WEST)
Rahmentarifverträge, Gehaltstarifverträge, Vermögensbildungstarifverträge, Tabelle der Kündigungsfristen, Auslösungssätze für die technischen und kaufmännischen Angestellten und für die Poliere und Schachtmeister des Baugewerbes im Gebiet der Bundesrepublik Deutschland /. Düsseldorf , 1977. 102 p. ; ISBN 3-8041-1158-0 LC Card 85-166026
HD6698.R315 R34 1977

COLLECTIVE BARGAINING - CONSTRUCTION INDUSTRY - UNITED STATES - HANDBOOKS, MANUALS, ETC.
Manual for collective bargaining /. Washington, D.C. (Suite 1040, 1101 15th St., N.W., Washington 20005) , 1987. 1 v. (various pagings) ; LC Card 87-150563 DDC 331.8/90424/0973 19
HD6515.B9 M36 1987

COLLECTIVE BARGAINING - EUROPE - CASE STUDIES.
Collective bargaining in industrialised market economies . Geneva , 1987. xii, 333 p. ; ISBN 92-2-105606-6 (pbk.) : LC Card 87-170568 DDC 331.89 19
HD6971.5 .C63 1987

COLLECTIVE BARGAINING - FRANCE.
Mothé-Gautrat, Daniel, 1924- Pour une nouvelle culture d'entreprise /. Paris , 1986. 173 p. ; ISBN 2-7071-1596-7 : LC Card 86-185142
HD8431 .M63 1986

COLLECTIVE BARGAINING - GERMANY, WEST.
Berghahn, Volker Rolf. Industrial relations in West Germany /. Leamington Spa, UK ; New York : p. cm. ISBN 0-907582-64-8 : LC Card 87-9359 DDC 331/.0943 19
HD8451 .B45 1988

Vajna, Thomas. Das Kaufkraftargument /. Köln , c1982. 52 p. ; ISBN 3-602-24710-4 : LC Card 83-193844
HD5029 .V35 1982

COLLECTIVE BARGAINING - GOVERNMENT EMPLOYEES - UNITED STATES.
Public sector labor relations . Lexington, Mass. , c1988. xi, 648 p. ; ISBN 0-669-12893-7 (alk. paper) LC Card 82-64038 DDC 331.89/041353 19
HD8005.6.U5 P83 1988

COLLECTIVE BARGAINING - HANDBOOKS, MANUALS, ETC.
International Labour Office. Collective bargaining . Geneva , 1986. ix, 112 p. ; ISBN 92-2-105284-2 (pbk.) : LC Card 86-208328 DDC 331.89 19
HD6971.5 .I57 1986

Collective bargaining in American industry : contemporary perspectives and future directions / edited by David B. Lipsky, Clifford B. Donn. Lexington, Mass. : Lexington Books, c1987. ix, 351 p. ; 24 cm. Based on papers presented at a conference held at Cornell University on Mar. 7-9, 1986; co-sponsored by the New York State School of Industrial and Labor Relations at Cornell and the Institute of Industrial Relations at Le Moyne College. Includes bibliographies and index. ISBN 0-669-12594-6 (alk. paper) LC Card 85-45936 DDC 331.89/0973 19
1. Collective bargaining - United States - Congresses. I. Lipsky, David B., 1939-. II. Donn, Clifford B. III. New York State School of Industrial and Labor Relations. IV. Le Moyne College. Institute of Industrial Relations.
HD6508 .C656 1987

Collective bargaining in industrialised market economies : a reappraisal / John P. Windmuller ... [et al.]. Geneva : International Labour Office, 1987. xii, 333 p. ; 24 cm. Includes bibliographies. ISBN 92-2-105606-6 (pbk.) : LC Card 87-170568 DDC 331.89 19
1. Collective bargaining. 2. Collective bargaining - Europe - Case studies. I. Windmuller, John P.
HD6971.5 .C63 1987

Collective bargaining in South Africa /. Jones, Robert A., MSc. Johannesburg , 1984. 104 p. ; ISBN 0-86954-173-0 ***NYPL [JLD 85-1003]***

COLLECTIVE BARGAINING - INTERNATIONAL BUSINESS ENTERPRISES - EUROPE - ADDRESSES, ESSAYS, LECTURES.
Employee consultation and information in multinational corporations /. London , Dover, N.H. , c1986. 265 p. ; ISBN 0-7099-2624-3 : LC Card 85-21264 DDC 331.25 19
NYPL [JLD 86-1612]

COLLECTIVE BARGAINING - IRON INDUSTRY.
International Labour Organisation. Iron and Steel Committee. Policies for maintaining social development through collective bargaining, legislation, and adequate social security protection to cope with structural change in the iron and steel industry /. Geneva , 1986. 45 p. ; ISBN 92-2-105497-7 (pbk.) : LC Card 86-222047 DDC 331.89/0469142 19
HD8039.I5 I6 1986

COLLECTIVE BARGAINING - ITALY.
Nacamulli, Raoul C. D. La razionalità contrattata . Bologna , c1986. 166 p. : ISBN 88-15-01189-7 : LC Card 87-122104
HD6709 .N296 1986

COLLECTIVE BARGAINING - ITALY - CONGRESSES.
La Riforma del salario /. Milano , c1984. 150 p. ; LC Card 84-251133 DDC 331.2/945 19
HD5034 .R54 1984 ***NYPL [JLD 86-1082]***

COLLECTIVE BARGAINING - MANUALS. see COLLECTIVE BARGAINING - HANDBOOKS, MANUALS, ETC.

COLLECTIVE BARGAINING - MONONGAHELA RIVER REGION (W. VA. AND PA.)
Hoerr, John P., 1930- And the wolf finally came . Pittsburgh, PA , 1988. p. cm. ISBN

0-8229-3572-4 LC Card 87-24932 DDC 338.4/7669142/097488 19
HD9517.M85 H64 1988

COLLECTIVE BARGAINING - PENNSYLVANIA.
Hoerr, John P., 1930- And the wolf finally came . Pittsburgh, PA , 1988. p. cm. ISBN 0-8229-3572-4 LC Card 87-24932 DDC 338.4/7669142/097488 19
HD9517.M85 H64 1988

COLLECTIVE BARGAINING - SOUTH AFRICA.
Jones, Robert A., MSc. Collective bargaining in South Africa /. Johannesburg , 1984. 104 p. ; ISBN 0-86954-173-0 ***NYPL [JLD 85-1003]***

COLLECTIVE BARGAINING - STEEL INDUSTRY.
International Labour Organisation. Iron and Steel Committee. Policies for maintaining social development through collective bargaining, legislation, and adequate social security protection to cope with structural change in the iron and steel industry /. Geneva , 1986. 45 p. ; ISBN 92-2-105497-7 (pbk.) : LC Card 86-222047 DDC 331.89/0469142 19
HD8039.I5 I6 1986

COLLECTIVE BARGAINING - STEEL INDUSTRY - ILLINOIS - CHICAGO.
Whyte, William Foote, 1914- Pattern for industrial peace /. New York , 1987, c1951. ix, 245 p. : ISBN 0-8240-8227-3 (alk. paper) : LC Card 86-25790 DDC 331.89/0469142/0977/311 19
HD6515.I52 C48 1987

COLLECTIVE BARGAINING - TEXTILE INDUSTRY - ITALY - LOMBARDY.
Guidotti, Daniela. Strategia generale e azione decentrata . Milano, Italy , c1986. 216 p. ; LC Card 86-193797
HD6976.T42 I764 1986

COLLECTIVE BARGAINING - UNITED STATES.
Allen, Robert E. (Robert Edward), 1946- Contemporary labor relations /. Reading, Mass. , c1988. xi, 724 p. : ISBN 0-201-10083-5 : LC Card 87-24128 DDC 331/.0973 19
HD8072.5 .A43 1988

Balliet, Lee. Survey of labor relations /. Washington, D.C. , c1981. ix, 198 p. : ISBN 0-87179-347-4 LC Card 80-26863 DDC 331/.0973
HD8072.5 .B34 ***NYPL [JLE 86-4719]***

Balliet, Lee. Survey of labor relations /. Washington, D.C. , c1987. xi, 212 p. : ISBN 0-87179-544-2 (pbk.) LC Card 87-864 DDC 331/.0973 19
HD8072.5 .B34 1987

Beal, Edwin Fletcher. The practice of collective bargaining /. Homewood, Ill. , 1985. xvi, 560 p. : ISBN 0-256-03214-9 LC Card 84-82023 DDC 331.89 19
HD6508 .B375 1985
NYPL [*R-Econ. 86-3458]

Marshall, F. Ray. Unheard voices . New York , c1987. xi, 339 p. : ISBN 0-465-08869-4 : LC Card 83-46084 DDC 338.6 19
HD5660.U5 M36 1987

New York (State). Legislature. Assembly. Standing Committee on Labor. A report on the plight of the collective bargaining system /. [Albany] [1984] 64 p. ; LC Card 86-622572 DDC 331.89/0973 19
HD6508 .N49 1984

Sandver, Marcus H. Labor relations . Boston , c1987. xxii, 529 p. : ISBN 0-316-77024-8 LC Card 86-27314 DDC 331/.0973 19
HD8072.5 .S32 1987

Sauer, Robert L. Labor relations . Columbus, Ohio , c1987. x, 518 p. : ISBN 0-675-20207-8 LC Card 87-134391 DDC 331/.0973 19
HD8066 .S28 1987

Sloane, Arthur A. Labor relations /. Englewood Cliffs, N.J. , c1988. xiv, 543 p. : ISBN 0-13-519604-3 LC Card 87-14535 DDC 331.89/0973 19
HD8072 .S6185 1988

Sullivan, Patrick J., 1929- Blue collar, Roman collar, white collar . Lanham, MD , c1987. xii, 346 p. ; ISBN 0-8191-5704-X (alk. paper) : LC Card 86-24593 DDC 261.85 19
HD6338.2.U5 S85 1987

COLLECTIVE BARGAINING - UNITED STATES - CONGRESSES.
Collective bargaining in American industry . Lexington, Mass. , c1987. ix, 351 p. ; ISBN 0-669-12594-6 (alk. paper) LC Card 85-45936 DDC 331.89/0973 19
HD6508 .C656 1987

COLLECTIVE BARGAINING - UNITED STATES - HISTORY.
Balfour, Alan. Union-management relations in a changing economy /. Englewood Cliffs, N.J. , c1987. xiv, 482 p. : ISBN 0-13-938804-4 LC Card 86-30495 DDC 331/.0973 19
HD8066 .B34 1987

COLLECTIVE BARGAINING - WEST VIRGINIA.
Hoerr, John P., 1930- And the wolf finally came . Pittsburgh, PA , 1988. p. cm. ISBN 0-8229-3572-4 LC Card 87-24932 DDC 338.4/7669142/097488 19
HD9517.M85 H64 1988

COLLECTIVE CHOICE. see **SOCIAL CHOICE.**

COLLECTIVE FARMS - BYELORUSSIAN S.S.R. - CAPITAL INVESTMENTS.
Golovko, N. A. (Nikolaĭ Anatol′evich) Osnovnye neproizvodstvennye fondy kolkhozov /cN.A. Golovko ; nauchnyĭ redaktor F.S. Martinkevich. Minsk , 1984. 94, [2] p. ; LC Card 84-177536
HD1492.S652 B9237 1984

COLLECTIVE FARMS - BYELORUSSIAN S.S.R. - FINANCE.
Golovko, N. A. (Nikolaĭ Anatol′evich) Osnovnye neproizvodstvennye fondy kolkhozov /cN.A. Golovko ; nauchnyĭ redaktor F.S. Martinkevich. Minsk , 1984. 94, [2] p. ; LC Card 84-177536
HD1492.S652 B9237 1984

COLLECTIVE FARMS - ESTONIA - MANAGEMENT.
Luukas, Ants. [Majandi parteigrupid. Russian.] Partiĭnye gruppy v kolkhozakh i sovkhozakh /. Tallin , 1984. 77 p., [8] p. of plates : LC Card 87-115056
HD1492.S652 E85517 1984

COLLECTIVE FARMS - ETHIOPIA.
Alemneh Dejene. Peasants, agrarian socialism, and rural development in Ethiopia /. Boulder , 1987. xiii, 162 p. : ISBN 0-8133-7247-X (pbk. : alk. paper) LC Card 86-51527 DDC 338.1/0963 19
HD2124.5 .A79 1987

COLLECTIVE FARMS - GERMANY, EAST.
Rosenkranz, Otto. (ed) Handbuch des Genossenschaftsbauern. [Berlin, 1954-<1959. v. <v. 1, pt. 1-2; v. 3; in 3 > LC Card 60-21317
HD1491.G33 R6

COLLECTIVE FARMS - HUNGARY.
A Mezőgazdasági szövetkezetek szabályozó rendszere /. [Budapest] , 1979. 119 p. ; LC Card 86-187443
HD1492.H8 M417 1979

Vályi, Éva. A mezőgazdasági vállalati szervezet fejlődésének és fejlesztésének törvényszerűségei /. Budapest , 1985. 107, [1] p. : ISBN 963-05-3468-1 : LC Card 86-137169
HD1492.H8 V33 1985

COLLECTIVE FARMS - HUNGARY - BORSOD-ABAÚJ-ZEMPLÉN MEGYE - OFFICIALS AND EMPLOYEES.
Ivanics, András. A termelőszövetkezeti termelésirányitókról . Budapest , 1984. 83 p. ; ISBN 963-491-179-X LC Card 86-198816
HD1492.H82 B675 1984

COLLECTIVE FARMS - HUNGARY - CSONGRÁD MEGYE - HISTORY.
Két évtized . Szeged , 1987. 116 p., [67] p. of plates : LC Card 87-407665
HD1492.H82 C765 1987

COLLECTIVE FARMS - HUNGARY - FINANCE.
Pilling, András. Az önelszámoló rendszer alkalmazásának, a kistermelők integrálásának és a kihelyezett részlegeknek a hatása a mezőgazdasági vállalatok szervezeti felépítésére, s annak müködésére /. Budapest , 1985. 89 p. ; ISBN 963-491-206-0 LC Card 86-196755
HD1492.H8 P55 1985

COLLECTIVE FARMS - HUNGARY - FINANCE - STATISTICS.
A Szocialista nagyüzemek főbb ágazatainak költség- és jövedelemhelyzete 1984-ben /. Budapest , 1985. 35, [46] p. ; LC Card 85-177804
HD1492.H8 S93 1985

COLLECTIVE FARMS - HUNGARY - HISTORY.
Simon, Péter, 1926- A magyar parasztság sorsfordulója, 1946-1949 /. [Budapest] , 1984. 212 p. : ISBN 963-09-2475-7 :
HD1333.H9 S57 1984 ***NYPL [JLD 86-3163]***

COLLECTIVE FARMS - HUNGARY - MANAGEMENT.
A Szabályozórendszerre történő reagálás főbb termelőszövetkezeti tapasztalatai /. Budapest , 1985. 68 p. ; LC Card 87-408583
HD1492.H8 S92 1985

COLLECTIVE FARMS - HUNGARY - OFFICIALS AND EMPLOYEES.
Meszticzky, András. Termelőszövetkezeti szakemberek munkahelyváltoztatása . [Budapest] , 1985. 165 p. : LC Card 86-218526
HD1492.H8 M37 1985

Simó, Tibor. Metszetek az agrártársadalom struktúrájából /. Budapest , 1985. 167 p. ; ISBN 963-7700-25-0 : LC Card 86-232606
HD1536.H9 S56 1985

COLLECTIVE FARMS - HUNGARY - OFFICIALS AND EMPLOYEES - TIME MANAGEMENT - STATISTICS.
A Háztáji és kisegitő gazdaság szerepe az életmód alakulásában . Budapest , 1983. 263 p. ; ISBN 963-02-2948-X (Magy. nemz. bibl.) LC Card 84-216989
HD1476.H8 H28 1983

COLLECTIVE FARMS - HUNGARY - PERSONNEL MANAGEMENT.
Németi, László. A személyzeti munka gyakorlati kérdései a mezőgazdasági termelőszövetkezetekben /. [Budapest] , 1984. 243 p. ; ISBN 963-502-370-7 LC Card 86-147870
HD1492.H8 N43 1984

COLLECTIVE FARMS - HUNGARY - PEST MEGYE.
Mezőgazdasági szövetkezetek Pest megyében, 1985 . Budapest , 1985. 442 p. : ISBN 963-02-4206-0 LC Card 87-137365
HD1492.H82 P475 1985

COLLECTIVE FARMS - HUNGARY - PUTNOK REGION.
Dobrossy, István. Termelés és életmód . Debrecen , 1983. 282 p. : ISBN 963-471-276-2 LC Card 86-100359
HD1492.H82 P873 1983

COLLECTIVE FARMS - HUNGARY - SOMOGY MEGYE - OFFICIALS AND EMPLOYEES.
Lugossy, Györgyi. Szándékok és lehetőségek . Budapest , 1985. 85 p. : ISBN 963-491-215-X LC Card 86-199350
HD1492.H82 S665 1985

COLLECTIVE FARMS - LATVIA - ACCOUNTING.
Vaikulis, J. (Jānis) Lauksaimniecības uzņēmumu saimnieciskās darbības analīze /. Riga , 1986. 185 p. ; LC Card 86-199301
HD1492.S652 L38 1986

COLLECTIVE FARMS - LAW AND LEGISLATION - HUNGARY.
A Mezőgazdasági szövetkezetek szabályozó rendszere /. [Budapest] , 1979. 119 p. ; LC Card 86-187443
HD1492.H8 M417 1979

COLLECTIVE FARMS - NICARAGUA.
Hintermeister, Alberto. El empleo agrícola en una estructra en transformación . [Santiago, Chile] , 1982. 27 p. ; LC Card 87-403249 DDC 331.7/63/097285 19
HD1531.N5 H56 1982

COLLECTIVE FARMS - RUSSIAN S.F.S.R. - CAUCASUS, NORTHERN.
Krivoded, V. V. KPSS i kolkhoznoe krest′ianstvo v 1945-1959 gg. /. Rostov-na-Donu , 1984. 190 p. ; LC Card 87-100194
HD1492.S652 C384 1984

COLLECTIVE FARMS - RUSSIAN S.F.S.R. - KRASNODARSKIĬ KRAĬ.
Rotov, Viktor. Li͡ubimoe pole /. Moskva , 1980. 149 p. ; LC Card 81-143989
HD1492.S652 K76 1980

COLLECTIVE FARMS - RUSSIAN S.F.S.R. - SIBERIA.
Smirnov, V. D. (Vasiliĭ Dmitrievich) Sotsial′no-ėkonomicheskiĭ ėksperiment v kolkhoze /. Novosibirsk , 1986. 111 p. : LC Card 86-171536
HD1492.S652 S527 1986

COLLECTIVE FARMS - SOVIET UNION - MANAGEMENT.
Spravochnik rukovoditeli͡a srednego zvena kolkhoza, sovkhoza /. Minsk , 1981. 518 p. ; LC Card 82-147885
HD1492.S65 S67 1981

COLLECTIVE FARMS - TURKMEN S.S.R. - HISTORY.
Berdiev, G. Tagtabazar raĭonynyn͡g Kirov adyndaky kolkhozynyn͡g tarykhy /. Ashgabat , 1986. 79 p. : LC Card 86-198891
HD1492.S652 T873 1986

COLLECTIVE FARMS - UKRAINE - HISTORY.
Istorii͡a kolhospu "Zdobutok ZHovtni͡a" /. Kyïv , 1986. 188 p., [8] p. of plates : LC Card 87-161618
HD1492.S652 U3835 1986

COLLECTIVE FARMS - UKRAINE - MANAGEMENT.
Zakharchenko, A. G. (Alekseĭ Gavrilovich) Kollektivnyĭ podri͡ad v sel′skom khozi͡aĭstve /. Kiev , 1985. 107 p. : LC Card 86-222274
HD1492.S652 U389 1985

COLLECTIVE FARMS - UZBEK S.S.R.
Aminova, R. Kh. Kolkhoznoe krest′i͡anstvo Uzbekistana na puti k razvitomu sotsializmu /. Tashkent , 1983. 358 p. ; LC Card 84-192680
HD1492.S652 U922 1983

COLLECTIVE FARMS - UZBEK S.S.R. - PERSONNEL MANAGEMENT.
Aminova, R. Kh. Kolkhoznoe krest′i͡anstvo Uzbekistana na puti k razvitomu sotsializmu /. Tashkent , 1983. 358 p. ; LC Card 84-192680
HD1492.S652 U922 1983

COLLECTIVE LABOR AGREEMENTS - AGRICULTURE - UKRAINE.
Zakharchenko, A. G. (Alekseĭ Gavrilovich) Kollektivnyĭ podri͡ad v sel′skom khozi͡aĭstve /. Kiev , 1985. 107 p. : LC Card 86-222274
HD1492.S652 U389 1985

COLLECTIVE LABOR AGREEMENTS - CONSTRUCTION INDUSTRY - GERMANY (WEST)
Rahmentarifverträge, Gehaltstarifverträge, Vermögensbildungstarifverträge, Tabelle der Kündigungsfristen, Auslösungssätze für die technischen und kaufmännischen Angestellten und für die Poliere und Schachtmeister des Baugewerbes im Gebiet der Bundesrepublik Deutschland /. Düsseldorf , 1977. 102 p. ; ISBN 3-8041-1158-0 LC Card 85-166026
HD6698.R315 R34 1977

COLLECTIVE LABOR AGREEMENTS - CONSTRUCTION INDUSTRY - QUÉBEC (PROVINCE)
Leclerc, Claudine. La sécurité d'emploi dans l'industrie de la construction au Québec . [Quebec] , c1983. xii, 275 p. : ISBN 2-7637-7028-2 LC Card 84-126505 DDC 331.25/96 19
HD5718.B92 C248 1983
NYPL [JLE 86-3170]

COLLECTIVE LABOR AGREEMENTS - CONSTRUCTION INDUSTRY - UNITED STATES - STATISTICS.
Wage and benefit settlements in construction, 1986. Washington, D.C. (1101 15th St., N.W., Suite 1040, Washington 20005) , c1986. 10 p. : LC Card 87-139726 DDC 331.2/824/0973021 19
HD4966.B892 U685 1986

COLLECTIVE LABOR AGREEMENTS - ITALY.
Balducci, Cataldo. Il sindacato /. Torino , c1984. 2 v. ; ISBN 88-02-03818-X (set) : LC Card 85-158972 DDC 344.45/0188 344.504188 19
LAW ***NYPL [JLE 86-3250]***

Nacamulli, Raoul C. D. La razionalità contrattata . Bologna , c1986. 166 p. : ISBN 88-15-01189-7 : LC Card 87-122104
HD6709 .N296 1986

Organizzazione del lavoro, mobilità e aspetti formativi nella contrattazione . Milano, Italy , c1982. 172 p. ; LC Card 83-106874
HD6709 .O73 1982

COLLECTIVE LABOR AGREEMENTS - ITALY - ADDRESSES, ESSAYS, LECTURES.
La Vertenza sul costo del lavoro e le relazioni industriali /. Milano, Italy , c1984. 243 p. : LC Card 84-144150 DDC 338.5/1/0945 19
HD5034 .V47 1984 ***NYPL [JLD 86-2858]***

COLLECTIVE LABOR AGREEMENTS - TELEVISION BROADCASTING - GERMANY (WEST)
Heinrich, Herbert, 1938- Arbeitsbewertung und Disziplinierung . Spardorf , c1985. v, 281 p. ; ISBN 3-922919-67-7 LC Card 86-162759
HF5549.5.J62 H36 1985

COLLECTIVE LABOR AGREEMENTS - TEXTILE INDUSTRY - INDIA - PUNJAB.
Asdhir, Vijay, 1947- Industrial relations in India . New Delhi , c1987. 376 p. ; LC Card 86-903540 DDC 331.89/2877/00954552 19
HD8686.5 .A85 1987

COLLECTIVE LABOR AGREEMENTS - TEXTILE INDUSTRY - ITALY - LOMBARDY.
Guidotti, Daniela. Strategia generale e azione decentrata . Milano, Italy , c1986. 216 p. ; LC Card 86-193797
HD6976.T42 I764 1986

COLLECTIVE LABOR AGREEMENTS - UNITED STATES.
Gassner, Peter, 1941- Kollektivmacht und Individualschutz im amerikanischen Arbeitsrecht /. Frankfurt am Main , c1981. 155 p. ; ISBN 3-8204-6119-1 : LC Card 82-164604 DDC 344.73/0189 347.304189 19
KF3408.Z94 G474 1981
NYPL [JLD 86-1212]

COLLECTIVE SECURITY. see **SECURITY, INTERNATIONAL.**

COLLECTIVE SETTLEMENTS - ECUADOR - HISTORY.
González S., Víctor A. Las tierras comunales en el Ecuador /. Guayaquil, Ecuador , 1982. 109 p. ; LC Card 87-672596
HD1289.E2 G66x 1982

COLLECTIVE SETTLEMENTS - MEXICO - FUERTE RIVER VALLEY - HISTORY.
Gill, Mario. La conquista del Valle del Fuerte /. Culiacán, Rosales, Sinaloa, México , c1983. 273 p., [4] folded leaves of plates : LC Card 86-121747
HC137.F84 G54 1983

COLLECTIVISM.
Pérez Baró, Albert. Trenta mesos de col·lectivisme a Catalunya, cinquanta anys després /. Barcelona , 1986. 283 p. : ISBN 84-297-2412-5 LC Card 86-186185
HD4245.C3 P45 1986

COLLECTIVIZATION OF AGRICULTURE - BYELORUSSIAN S.S.R. - HISTORY.
Kosti͡uk, Mikhail Pavlovich. Trudovoĭ vklad krest′i͡anstva v pobedu i uprochnenie sotsializma . Minsk , 1986. 236 p. ; LC Card 86-136452
HD1492.S652 B9252 1986

COLLECTIVIZATION OF AGRICULTURE - HUNGARY.
Vasary, Ildiko. Beyond the plan . Boulder , 1987. xvii, 308 p. : ISBN 0-8133-7412-X (soft : alk. paper) : LC Card 87-8219 DDC 307.7/2/09439 19
HD1492.H8 V35 1987

COLLECTIVIZATION OF AGRICULTURE - HUNGARY - HISTORY - CONGRESSES.
Agrárgazdaság, agrártársadalom, agrárpolitika /. Szeged , 1985. 338 p. : ISBN 963-481-548-0 : LC Card 86-143859
HD1940.5 .A78 1985

COLLECTIVIZATION OF AGRICULTURE - KAZAKH S.S.R. - HISTORY.
Tulepbaev, B. A. [Sotsialisticheskie agrarnye preobrazovanii͡a v Sredneĭ Azii i Kazakhstane. English.] Socialist Agrarian reforms in Central Asia and Kazakhstan /. Moscow , 1986. 231, [1] p. ; LC Card 86-171559
HD1995.C4 T8313 1986

COLLECTIVIZATION OF AGRICULTURE - MONGOLIA - HISTORY.
Ulymzhiev, D. B. (Dashi Batuevich) Put′ mongol′skogo aratstva k sotsializmu /. Novosibirsk , 1987. 283, [5] p. ; LC Card 87-159668
HD1491.M55 U49 1987

COLLECTIVIZATION OF AGRICULTURE - RUSSIAN S.F.S.R. - CHUVASHSKAI͡A A. S.S.R. - HISTORY.
Voprosy istorii sotsialisticheskogo preobrazovanii͡a i razvitii͡a sel′skogo khozi͡aĭstva Chuvashskoĭ ASSR /. Cheboksary , 1985. 176 p. ; LC Card 86-100164
HD1492.5.S65 C488 1985

COLLECTIVIZATION OF AGRICULTURE - RUSSIAN S.F.S.R. - HISTORY.
Agrarnai͡a revoli͡utsii͡a i sotsialisticheskie preobrazovanii͡a v sovetskoĭ derevne . Gor′kiĭ , 1980. 84 p. ; LC Card 82-141565
HD1995.R8 A68 1980

Ivanov, E. P. (Evgeniĭ Pavlovich) Kollektivizatsii͡a krest′i͡anskikh khozi͡aĭstv i likvidatsii͡a kulachestva kak klassa na Severo-Zapade RSFSR, 1927-1937 gg. . Leningrad , 1983. 91 p. ; LC Card 84-190520
HD1492.S652 R875 1983
NYPL [*QI 87-3170]

Iz istorii krest′i͡anstva Evropeĭskogo Severa, Verkhnego Povolzh′i͡a i Urala v period Velikoĭ Okti͡abr′skoĭ sotsialisticheskoĭ revoli͡utsii i pobedy sotsializma v SSSR, 1917-1937 gg. /. Kirov , 1979. 170 p. ; LC Card 82-103738
HD1492.S652 R8755 1979

Seleznev, V. A. (Valeriĭ Aleksandrovich) Pervye shagi sotsialisticheskikh preobrazovaniĭ v sel′skom khozi͡aĭstve Severo-Zapada RSFSR, 1917-1929 gg. . Leningrad , 1983. 198 p. ; LC Card 83-197523
HD1492.S652 R877 1983
NYPL [*QIP 87-1327]

Veselov, A. P. (Anatoliĭ Pavlovich) Bor′ba Kommunisticheskoĭ partii za provedenie kul′turnoĭ revoli͡utsii v derevne v gody kollektivizatsii /. Leningrad , 1978. 127 p. ; LC Card 81-166878
HD1492.S652 R878 1978

COLLECTIVIZATION OF AGRICULTURE - RUSSIAN S.F.S.R. - KALININ REGION - HISTORY - 20TH CENTURY.
Altrichter, Helmut, 1945- Die Bauern von Tver . München , 1984. 373 p. : ISBN 3-486-52071-7 LC Card 84-162284
HD1536.S65 A47 1984

COLLECTIVIZATION OF AGRICULTURE - RUSSIAN S.F.S.R. - SIBERIA - HISTORY.
Kooperativnoe dvizhenie v Sibiri . Ti͡umen′ , 1984. 72 p. ; LC Card 85-179545
HD3517.A3 R875 1984

COLLECTIVIZATION OF AGRICULTURE - SOVIET CENTRAL ASIA - HISTORY.
Tulepbaev, B. A. [Sotsialisticheskie agrarnye preobrazovanii͡a v Sredneĭ Azii i Kazakhstane. English.] Socialist Agrarian reforms in Central Asia and Kazakhstan /. Moscow , 1986. 231, [1] p. ; LC Card 86-171559
HD1995.C4 T8313 1986

COLLECTIVIZATION OF AGRICULTURE - SOVIET UNION.
Agrarnai͡a politika Kommunisticheskoĭ partii na ėtape stroitel′stva MTS, 1929-1939 . Vladimir , 1985. 132 p. ; ***NYPL [*QIK 87-3394]***

Bogoli͡ubov, Klavdiĭ Mikhaĭlovich. Vernym kursom /. Moskva , 1984. 287 p. ; LC Card 85-164820
HD1492.S65 B64 1984

COLLECTIVIZATION OF AGRICULTURE - SOVIET UNION - HISTORY.
Istorii͡a sovetskogo krest′i͡anstva . Moskva , 1986- v. : ***NYPL [*QG 87-3228]***

Istorii͡a sovetskogo krest′i͡anstva /. Moskva , 1986-<1987. v. <1-3 > : LC Card 86-230318
HD1492.S65 I88 1986

COLLECTIVIZATION OF AGRICULTURE - SOVIET UNION, NORTHWESTERN -

HISTORY.
Ivanov, E. P. (Evgeniĭ Pavlovich) Kollektivizatsiia krest'ianskikh khoziaĭstv i likvidatsiia kulachestva kak klassa na Severo-Zapade RSFSR, 1927-1937 gg. . Leningrad , 1983. 91 p. ; LC Card 84-190520
HD1492.S652 R875 1983
NYPL [*QI 87-3170]

COLLECTIVIZATION OF AGRICULTURE - UKRAINE - HISTORY.

COLLECTIVIZATION OF AGRICULTURE - UZBEK S.S.R. - HISTORY.
Aminova, R. Kh. Pobeda kolkhoznogo stroia v Uzbekistane . Tashkent , 1981. 289 p. ; LC Card 82-161362
HD1492.S652 U9226 1981

The collectors . McIntosh, Dave. Toronto, Ont., Canada , c1984. 414 p. : ISBN 0-920053-29-7 LC Card 85-162089 DDC 354.710072/46/09 19
HJ6751.A6 M35 1984 ***NYPL [JLE 86-2880]***

COLLECTORS AND COLLECTING - QUÉBEC (PROVINCE) - BIOGRAPHY.
Richer, Laurette B. Ludger Gravel, 1864-1933 . [Montréal] , c1986. 170 p. : ISBN 2-9800028-1-X LC Card 87-115031
HC112.5.G73 R53 1986

Collectors Club (New York, N.Y.) Central America postal history and a listing of prephilatelic postmarks =. New York [Yonkers, N.Y.?] , 1986. xiv, 142 p. : ISBN 0-912574-41-0 (pbk.) LC Card 87-402819 DDC 383/.49728 19
HE6674 .C46 1986

College accounting . Slater, Jeffrey, 1947- Englewood Cliffs, N.J. , c1988. p. cm. ISBN 0-13-140708-2 LC Card 87-7343 DDC 657 19
HF5635 .S6315 1988c

College accounting . Slater, Jeffrey, 1947- Englewood Cliffs, N.J. , c1988. p. cm. ISBN 0-13-140716-3 LC Card 87-21879 DDC 657 19
HF5635 .S6315 1988

College accounting . Slater, Jeffrey, 1947- Englewood Cliffs, N.J. , c1988. p. cm. ISBN 0-13-140906-9 LC Card 87-21878 DDC 657 19
HF5635 .S6315 1988b

College cash . Hutchinson, Van. San Diego , 1987. p. cm. ISBN 0-15-619150-4 (pbk.) : LC Card 87-8666 DDC 658.4/2 19
HD62.5 .H88 1987

COLLEGE GRADUATES - EMPLOYMENT.
Cohen, Steve, 1950- Getting to the right job /. New York , 1987. 288 p. ; ISBN 0-89480-040-X (pbk.) : LC Card 85-40899 DDC 650.1/4 19
HF5381 .C6814 1987

Cohen, William A., 1937- The student's guide to finding a superior job /. San Diego , c1987. ix, 144 p. ; ISBN 0-932238-41-6 (pbk.) : LC Card 87-4487 DDC 650.1/4 19
HF5382.7 .C64 1987

Lento-McGovern, Diane, 1956- Life after college . White Hall, Va. , c1987. 179 p. ; ISBN 0-932620-77-9 (pbk.) : LC Card 87-6412 DDC 331.7/02 19
HF5381 .L354 1987

Osher, Bill. The blue-chip graduate . Atlanta, Ga. , c1987. 238 p. : ISBN 0-934601-19-4 (pbk.) : LC Card 86-63534 DDC 650.1/4/024375 19
HF5381 .O889 1987

COLLEGE GRADUATES - EMPLOYMENT - CANADA.
Picot, W. Garnett. The changing labour market for postsecondary graduates, 1975-1984 /. Ottawa , c1987. 86, 94 p. : ISBN 0-660-52896-7 (pbk.) : LC Card 87-169612 DDC 331.11/423 19
HD6278.C3 P52 1987

COLLEGE GRADUATES - EMPLOYMENT - DENMARK - STATISTICS.
De Nyuddannedes indplacering på arbejdsmarkedet 1981-1983 . [Copenhagen , 1986] 1 v. (various pagings) : ISBN 87-503-6320-4 LC Card 87-127126
HD6278.D4 N98 1986

COLLEGE GRADUATES - EMPLOYMENT - GERMANY, WEST.
Abiturienten und Hochschulabsolventen beim Übergang vom Studium in den Beruf . Nürnberg , 1983. 407 p. : LC Card 84-140881
HD6278.G4 A25 1983

Akademikertätigkeit im Wandel . Frankfurt [am Main] , New York , c1984. 237 p. ; ISBN 3-593-33321-X LC Card 84-176630
HD6278.G4 A36 1984

COLLEGE GRADUATES - EMPLOYMENT - HUNGARY.
Szilágyi, Klára J. A pályafejlődés vizsgálatának módszertani lehetőségei a felsőoktatásban /. Budapest , 1985. 110 p. ; ISBN 963-404-020-9 LC Card 86-174899
HF5429.6.H8 S95 1985

COLLEGE GRADUATES - EMPLOYMENT - INDIA - WEST BENGAL.
Bose, P. K. Graduate employment and higher education in West Bengal /. Paris , New Delhi , 1983. vi, 288, [1] p. : ISBN 0-85226-078-4 (pbk.) LC Card 83-163900 DDC 331.11/423 19
HD6278.I52 W473 1983
NYPL [JLD 86-2269]

COLLEGE GRADUATES - EMPLOYMENT - SWEDEN.
Studerandepopulation och arbetsmarknad . [Stockholm] [1986] 78 p. : ISBN 91-38-09464-9 LC Card 87-106834
HD6278.S75 S78 1986

COLLEGE GRADUATES - EMPLOYMENT - UNITED STATES.
Leape, Martha P. The Harvard guide to careers /. Cambridge, Mass. , 1987. ix, 181 p. ; ISBN 0-674-37564-5 (pbk.) LC Card 87-8409 DDC 331.7/02 19
HF5382.5.U5 L36 1987

Phillips, Jack J., 1945- Recruiting, training, and retaining new employees . San Francisco , 1987. xxii, 324 p. ; ISBN 1-555-42042-7 (alk. paper) LC Card 86-46332 DDC 658.3/14 19
HF5549.5.R44 P49 1987

Salzman, Marian L. Wanted, liberal arts graduates . New York , 1987. xvi, 341 p. ; ISBN 0-385-24008-2 (pbk.) : LC Card 87-8846 DDC 650.1/4 19
HF5382.75.U6 S27 1987

COLLEGE GRADUATES - ESTONIA.
Osobennosti popolneniia osnovnykh otriadov intelligentsii /. Tallin , 1981. 131 p. : LC Card 82-125732
HD8038.S652 E775 1981

COLLEGE GRADUATES - UNITED STATES - ATTITUDES - LONGITUDINAL STUDIES.
Hopkins, David M. Changing career values . Bethlehem, PA , 1986. x, 126 p. : ISBN 0-914885-10-3 (pbk.) LC Card 87-112752 DDC 331.25 19
HD8038.U5 H66 1986

College keyboarding/typewriting : complete course / Charles H. Duncan ... [et al.].11th ed. Cincinnati : South-Western Pub. Co., c1985. 396, xvi p. : ill. (some col.) ; 23 x 30 cm. At head of title: Keyboarding, formatting, communication skills, document production. Rev. ed. of: College typewriting / D.D. Lessenberry, S.J. Wanous, C.H. Duncan. 8th ed. 1969. Includes index. ISBN 0-538-20750-7 LC Card 84-50474 DDC 652.3 19
1. Typewriting. 2. Electronic data processing - Keyboarding. I. Duncan, C. H. (Charles Howard), 1924-. II. Lessenberry, D. D. (David Daniel), 1896- College typewriting.
Z49 .C65 1985 ***NYPL [JSF 86-1142]***

College of William and Mary. Dept. of Anthropology. The Economic demography of mass poverty. [Williamsburg, Va., U. S.A. , c1986] xiv, 142 p. : LC Card 85-73339 DDC 339.4/6/091724 19
HB884 .E36 1986

COLLEGE STUDENTS AS CONSUMERS - UNITED STATES.
Telecommunications opportunities for colleges and universities /. McLean, Va. (1355 Beverly Rd., Suite 100, McLean 22101) , c1986. 208 p. ; LC Card 86-231086 DDC 384.6/3 19
HD9696.T443 U572 1986

COLLEGE STUDENTS - BRAZIL.
Fundação Projeto Rondon. Diretrizes de planejamento . [Brasília , 1982] [21] leaves ; LC Card 85-186578
HD4870.B6 F86 1982

COLLEGE STUDENTS - EMPLOYMENT - UNITED STATES.
Hutchinson, Van. College cash . San Diego , 1987. p. cm. ISBN 0-15-619150-4 (pbk.) : LC Card 87-8666 DDC 658.4/2 19
HD62.5 .H88 1987

COLLEGE STUDENTS - SAUDI ARABIA - INTERVIEWS.
Viola, Joy Winkie. Human resources development in Saudi Arabia . Boston , c1986. xxvi, 291 p. : ISBN 0-88746-070-4 (IHRDC) LC Card 85-19694 DDC 303.4/8273/0538 19
HD5812.35.A6 V56 1986
NYPL [JLE 86-2188]

COLLEGE STUDENTS - UNITED STATES - INTERVIEWS.
Viola, Joy Winkie. Human resources development in Saudi Arabia . Boston , c1986. xxvi, 291 p. : ISBN 0-88746-070-4 (IHRDC) LC Card 85-19694 DDC 303.4/8273/0538 19
HD5812.35.A6 V56 1986
NYPL [JLE 86-2188]

COLLEGES. see UNIVERSITIES AND COLLEGES.

COLLEGES AND UNIVERSITIES - SOUTHERN CONE OF SOUTH AMERICA.
Estudios sobre integración económica y cooperación regional en el Cono Sur . Santiago de Chile , c1985. 283 p. ; LC Card 86-174604
HC167.S67 E78 1985

Collegiate School, New Haven. see **Yale University.**

Collegiate School of Connecticut. see **Yale University.**

Collette, Will. Petersen, Sybil. Transportation . Arlington, Va. (P.O. Box 926, Arlington 22216) [1986] [8], 40 p. : LC Card 87-401670 DDC 363.1/7 19
HE199.5.D3 P48 1986

Collie, coal, and energy policy in Western Australia /. Taylor, Neil. Murdoch, W.A. [1985] 56 p. : ISBN 0-86905-080-X (pbk.) LC Card 87-116549 DDC 333.8/22/099412 19
HD9558.A83 C657 1985

Collier, David A. Service management : operating decisions / David A. Collier. Englewood Cliffs, N.J. : Prentice-Hall, c1987. xiii, 300 p. : ill. ; 25 cm. Includes bibliographies. ISBN 0-13-806977-8 (pbk.) LC Card 86-30365 DDC 658.5 19
1. Service industries - Management. I. Title.
HD9980.5 .C655 1987

Collier, Irwin L., 1951- Connections, effective purchasing power, and real product in the German Democratic Republic / Irwin L. Collier, Jr. Berlin : Osteuropa-Institut, 1985. ix, 216 p. : ill. ; 21 cm. (Berichte des Osteuropa-Instituts an der Freien Universität Berlin, 0409-1477 . Heft 135. Nr. 44.) English and German. Includes bibliographies. ISBN 3-921374-34-0 (pbk.) LC Card 86-229298 DDC 330 s 338.9431/00724 19
1. Central planning - Germany (East) - Econometric models. 2. Germany (East) - Economic policy - Econometric models. I. Series: Berichte des Osteuropa-Instituts an der Freien Universität Berlin , Heft 135. II. Title.
HC244.A1 B4 Nr. 44 HC290.78

Collier, Paul.
Labour and poverty in Kenya, 1900-1980 / Paul Collier and Deepak Lal. Oxford : Clarendon Press ; New York : Oxford University Press, 1986. xi, 296 p. : ill. ; 25 cm. Includes index. Bibliography: p. [279]-288. ISBN 0-19-828505-1 : LC Card 86-1352 DDC 331.12/09676/2 19
1. Labor supply - Kenya. 2. Poor - Kenya. 3. Income distribution - Kenya. I. Lal, Deepak. II. Title.
HD5840.5.A6 C65 1986
NYPL [JLE 86-3282]

Labour and poverty in rural Tanzania : ujamaa and rural development in the United Republic of Tanzania / Paul Collier, Samir Radwan, and Samuel Wangwe, with Albert Wagner. Oxford [Oxfordhire] : Clarendon Press ; New York : Oxford University Press, 1986. vii, 143 p. : map ; 23 cm. "A study prepared for the International Labour Office within the framework of the World

Employment Programme." Includes bibliographies and index. ISBN 0-19-828531-0 : LC Card 86-5303 DDC 307.1/4/09678 19
1. Rural development - Tanzania. 2. Ujamaa villages - Tanzania. 3. Households - Tanzania. 4. Peasantry - Tanzania. 5. Poor - Tanzania. I. Raḍwān, Samīr Muḥammad. II. Wangwe, S. M. III. Title.
HN797.Z9 C625 1986 NYPL [JLD 87-511]

Collier, William L. Budidaya padi di Jawa /. Jakarta , 1986. x, 339 p. : LC Card 87-941451
HD9066.I63 J3493 1986

Colliez, Jean-Paul. Les salariés agricoles permanents, leur rémunération en octobre 1982. Paris : Ministère de l'agriculture, Service central des enquêtes et études statistiques, [1984] 62 p. : ill. ; 30 cm. (Collections de statistique agricole, 0336-5638 . étude no 228) "Résultats de l'enquête d'octobre 1982 sur les salaires et la main-d'œuvre salariée dans l'agriculture." "Etude réalisée par Jean-Paul Colliez"--P. 3. "Mai 1984"--Cover. ISBN 2-11-083969-4 LC Card 85-108387
1. Agricultural wages - France - Statistics. I. Title. II. Title: Salariés agricoles permanents. III. Series.
HD4966.A292 F73 1984

Collings, Jesse, 1831-1920. The great war, its lessons and its warnings [microform], by Jesse Collings. London, The Rural World Pub. Co. [1915] 113 p. front., pl. 20 cm. Microfilm. New York: New York Public Library, 1986. 1 microfilm reel; 35 mm. (MN *ZZ-26154) LC Card 16-1094
1. Agriculture - Great Britain. 2. World War, 1914-1918 - Economic aspects - Great Britain. I. Title.
*HC256.2 .C55 NYPL [*Z-4053 no.6]*

Collins English-German dictionary = Pons Englisch-Deutsch Globalwörterbuch / by Roland Breitsprecher ... [et al.].1. Aufl. London : Collins ; Stuttgart : Klett, 1986, c1983. 2 v. (xviii, 1390, xxiii, 1380 p.) ; 20 cm. Vol. 2 has title: Collins German-English dictionary = Pons Deutsch-Englisch Globalwörterbuch. Half title, vol. 1: Globalwörterbuch Englisch-Deutsch, German-English dictionary; vol. 2: Globalwörterbuch Deutsch-Englisch, German-English dictionary. Based on Pens-Collins Grosswörterbuch. ISBN 3-12-517131-8 (v. 1)
1. German language - Dictionaries - English. 2. English language - Dictionaries - German. I. Breitsprecher, Roland. II. Title: Pons Englisch-Deutsch Globalwörterbuch. III. Title: Collins German-English dictionary. IV. Title: Pons Deutsch-Englisch Globalwörterbuch. V. Title: Globalwörterbuch Englisch-Deutsch. VI. Title: Globalwörterbuch Deutsch-Englisch. NYPL [JFC 86-2613]

Collins German-English dictionary. Collins English-German dictionary =. London , Stuttgart , 1986, c1983. 2 v. (xviii, 1390, xxiii, 1380 p.) ; ISBN 3-12-517131-8 (v. 1)
NYPL [JFC 86-2613]

Collins, James B. Fiscal limits of absolutism : direct taxation in early seventeenth-century France / James B. Collins. Berkeley : University of California Press, c1987. p. cm. Bibliography: p. Includes index. ISBN 0-520-05911-5 (alk. paper) LC Card 87-19090 DDC 336.2/00944 19
1. Taxation - France - History - 17th century. 2. Tax administration and procedure - History - 17th century. 3. France - Politics and government - 17th century. 4. Elite (Social sciences) - France - History - 17th century. 5. Despotism - History - 17th century. I. Title.
HJ2648 .C65 1987

Collins, Lora S. The U. S. economy to 1990 / by Lora S. Collins, with contributions from Eva Culen and Ken Goldstein. New York, N.Y. : Conference Board, c1985. 21 p. : ill. (some col.) ; 28 cm. (A Chartbook from the Conference Board) Conference Board report ; no. 864 ISBN 0-8237-0307-X (pbk.) LC Card 86-200284 DDC 338.5/443/0973 19
1. Economic forecasting - United States. 2. United States - Economic conditions - 1981-. I. Culen, Eva. II. Goldstein, Ken. III. Title. IV. Title: US economy to 1990. V. Series.
HC106.8 .C636 1985

Collins, Norman J. Palestine Mandate issues, 1921-1948 : the Crown Agents requisition books / Norman J. Collins. [New York] : Society of Israel Philatelists Educational Fund, c1987. 52 p. : ill. ; 26 cm. LC Card 87-400470 DDC 383/.495694 19
1. Postal service - Palestine - History - 20th century. 2. Postage-stamps - Palestine - History - 20th century. I. Title.
HE7186 .C65 1987

Collins, Norman R. Dean, Gerald W. World trade in fresh oranges . Berkeley, Calif. [1967] 70 p. : LC Card 87-401008 DDC 338.1/09794 s 382/.41431 19
HD1407 .C27 no. 18 HD9259.O7

Collins, Paul D. Brazil in Africa : perspectives on the growth and prospects of economic cooperation between newly industrialized and developing countries / Paul D. Collins. Austin : Office for Public Sector Studies, Institute for Latin American Studies, University of Texas at Austin, 1986. 16 p. ; 28 cm. (Technical papers series . no. 49) Bibliography: p. 13-16. LC Card 86-622252 DDC 337.8106 19
1. Brazil - Foreign economic relations - Africa. 2. Africa - Foreign economic relations - Brazil. I. Title. II. Series.
HF1514.5.A35 C65 1986

Collins, Rip, 1947- Double your sales commission using a personal computer / Rip Collins, Steve Whitehead. Dubuque, Iowa : W.C. Brown, c1986. ix, 155 p. ; 23 cm. Includes index. ISBN 0-697-00802-9 (pbk.) : LC Card 85-71486 DDC 658.8/1/00285536 19
1. Selling - Data processing. 2. Microcomputers - Programming. I. Whitehead, Steve. II. Title.
HF5438.35 .C65 1986 NYPL [JLE 86-1773]

Collins, Rosemary. Family and economy in modern society /. Basingstoke, Hampshire , 1985. xvi, 234 p. ; ISBN 0-333-37437-1 LC Card 86-674026
HD4904.25 .F35x 1985

COLLISIONS, AUTOMOBILE. see **TRAFFIC ACCIDENTS.**

Colloque d'étude des politiques économiques Récession et relance (1984 : Paris, France) Récession et relance / Vincent Ansquer ... [et al.] ; [édité par] Tovy Grjebine. Paris : Economica, 1984. 218 p. : ill. ; 24 cm. "Colloque d'étude des politiques économiques Récession et relance, tenue dans les salles de l'Assemblée nationale"--P. opp. t.p. Includes bibliographical references. ISBN 2-7178-0690-3 : LC Card 85-158199 DDC 338.5/42 19
1. Business cycles - Congresses. 2. Economic forecasting - Congresses. I. Grjebine, Tovy. II. Ansquer, Vincent. III. Title.
HB3711 .C59 1984

Colloque international. Dix années d'espaces-piétons . Paris [1984] 191 p. : ISBN 2-85723-124-5 LC Card 85-104132
HE336.P43 D59 1984

Colloque Les Périphéries urbaines (1984 : Angers, France) Actes du Colloque Les Périphéries urbaines : quelles sociétés? quels espaces? quels dynamismes? : Angers, 6 et 7 décembre 1984 / [organisé par] UA-CNRS 915 Espaces géographiques et sociétés localisées dans la France de L'Ouest. Caen : Centre de publications de l'Université de Caen, c1985. 270 p. : ill. ; 30 cm. (Géographie sociale, 0766-9267 . 2) Cover title: Les périphéries urbaines. "Septembre 1985." Includes bibliographies. ISBN 2-905461-03-9 : LC Card 86-173712
1. Migration, Internal - France - Congresses. 2. Metropolitan areas - France - Congresses. 3. Cities and town - France - Growth - Congresses. 4. Suburbs - France - Congresses. I. UA-CNRS 915 Espaces géographiques et sociétés localisées dans la France de l'Ouest. II. Title. III. Title: Périphéries urbaines. IV. Series.
HB2263 .C65 1984

Colloque "Poitiers 1981" (1981 : Université de Poitiers) Actes du Colloque "Poitiers 1981" : 14-16 octobre 1981 / organisé par le Centre de géographie humaine et sociale (Département de géographie). Poitiers [France] : Centre de géographie humaine et sociale, [1983] 472 p. : ill. ; 30 cm. (Travaux du Centre de géographie humaine et sociale, 0223-9272 . no 7) At head of title: Université de Poitiers, 550e anniversaire. Bibliography: p. 333-449. LC Card 84-119227
1. Poitiers (France) - Population - Congresses. 2. Poitiers (France) - Economic conditions - Congresses. 3. Community and college - France - Poitiers - Congresses. I. Université de Poitiers. Centre de géographie humaine et sociale. II. Title. III. Title: "Poitiers 1981.". IV. Series.
HB3594.P65 C65 1981

Colloque sur l'histoire de la sécurité sociale . Colloque sur l'histoire de la sécurité sociale (1980 : Caen, France) Paris , 1981. 263 p. ; LC Card 81-201274
HD7175 .C58 1980

Colloque sur l'histoire de la sécurité sociale (1980 : Caen, France) Colloque sur l'histoire de la sécurité sociale : actes du 105e Congrès national des sociétés savantes, Caen, 1980. Paris : Association pour l'étude de l'histoire de la sécurité sociale, 1981. 263 p. ; 24 cm. At head of title: Comité des travaux historiques et scientifiques. Comité d'histoire de la sécurité sociale. Includes bibliographical references. LC Card 81-201274
1. Social security - France - History - Congresses. I. Congrès national des sociétés savantes (105th : 1980 : Caen, France). II. France. Comité des travaux historiques et scientifiques. III. France. Comité d'histoire de la sécurité sociale. IV. Association pour l'étude de l'histoire de la sécurité sociale. V. Title.
HD7175 .C58 1980

Colloquium geographicum, 0588-3253 . (Bd. 19) Beiträge zur empirischen Wirtschaftsgeographie /. Bonn , c1986. 238 p. : ISBN 3-427-74191-5 LC Card 87-104279 DDC 330.9 19
HF1025 .B3495 1986

Colloquium on New Forms of Work and Activity (1986 : Brussels, Belgium) Neue Arbeits- und Tätigkeitsformen . Dublin, Ireland [Washington, D.C.] c1986. xvi, 339 p. ; ISBN 92-825-6418-5 LC Card 87-408469 DDC 306/.36/094 19
HD6957.E86 N48 1986

Colls, Robert. The pitmen of the northern coalfield : work, culture, and protest, 1790-1850 / Robert Colls. Manchester, UK ; Wolfeboro, NH, USA : Manchester University Press, c1987. xv, 386 p., [2] p. of plates : maps ; 23 cm. Bibliography: p. [308]-373. Includes index. ISBN 0-7190-2202-9 (U. S.) : LC Card 87-11029 DDC 305/.9622/09427 19
1. Coal miners - England, Northern - History - 19th century. 2. England, Northern - Social conditions. I. Title.
HD8039.M62 G737 1987

Colman, David.
Food and agricultural exports from less-developed countries. Transnationals and development. Manchester, England , 1984. i, 64 p. ; *NYPL [JLD 86-3224]*

Colman, Robert Douglas. Modern business financing : a guide to innovative strategies and techniques / Robert Douglas Colman. Englewood Cliffs, N.J. : Prentice-Hall, c1986. xxi, 281 p. : ill. ; 29 cm. Includes index. ISBN 0-13-589060-8 LC Card 85-20490 DDC 658.1/5 19
1. Business enterprises - Finance - Handbooks, manuals, etc. 2. Corporations - Finance - Handbooks, manuals, etc. I. Title.
HG4027.3 .C64 1986 NYPL [JLF 86-616]

Colman Sercovich, Francisco. see **Sercovich, Francisco Colman.**

Cologne Radio. see **Westdeutscher Rundfunk.**

Aktuelle Fragen der Energiewirtschaft. see **Aktuelle Fragen der Energiewirtschaft.**

Cologne. Westdeutscher Rundfunk. see **Westdeutscher Rundfunk.**

Coloma C., Fernando.
Algunas consideraciones sobre los efectos distributivos del proceso de liberalización comercial / Fernando Coloma C., Luis Felipe Lagos M. Santiago : Pontificia Universidad Católica de Chile, Instituto de Economía, 1982. 31 leaves ; 28 cm. (Documento de trabajo . no. 101) Includes bibliographical references. LC Card 87-102072
1. Free trade and protection - Free trade - Econometric models. 2. Tariff - Econometric models. 3. Chile - Commercial policy - Econometric models. I. Lagos, Luis Felipe. II. Series: Documento de trabajo (Universidad Católica de Chile. Instituto de Economía) , no. 101. III. Title.
HF1713 .C617 1982

Credibilidad de la política comercial / Fernando Coloma C., Pablo González S. Santiago, Chile : Pontificia Universidad Católica de Chile, Instituto de Economía, 1986. 43 p. : ill. ; 28 cm. (Documento de trabajo . no. 102) Includes bibliographical references. LC Card 87-102077
1. Chile - Commercial policy. I. González S., Pablo. II.

Series: Documento de trabajo (Universidad Católica de Chile. Instituto de Economía) , no. 102. III. Title.
HF1515 .C64 1986

Los efectos de una desgravación arancelaria en el contexto de una economía con movilidad imperfecta de trabajo / Fernando Coloma C., Luis Felipe Lagos M. Santiago : Pontificia Universidad Católica de Chile, Instituto de Economía, Oficina de Publicaciones, 1985. 46 leaves : ill. ; 27 cm. (Documento de trabajo / Pontificia Universidad Católica de Chile, Instituto de Economía, Oficina de Publicaciones . no. 96) Includes bibliographical references. LC Card 85-203579
1. Tariff - Econometric models. 2. Labor mobility - Econometric models. 3. Commercial policy - Econometric models. 4. Income distribution - Econometric models. I. Lagos, Luis Felipe. II. Series: Documento de trabajo (Universidad Católica de Chile. Instituto de Economía) , no. 96. III. Title.
HF1713 .C618 1985

Endeudamiento externo y tasa de descuento social : un ejercicio / Fernando Coloma C. Santiago, Chile : Pontificia Universidad Católica de Chile, Instituto de Economía, 1986. 66 leaves : ill. ; 28 cm. (Documento de trabajo . no. 103) Includes bibliographical references. LC Card 87-102066
1. Debts, External - Social aspects - Econometric models. 2. Debts, External - Social aspects - Evaluation - Econometric models. I. Title. II. Title: Tasa de descuento social. III. Series: Documento de trabajo (Universidad Católica de Chile. Instituto de Economía) , no. 103.
HJ8083 .C65 1986

Colombia : reseña de su estructura económica. Bogotá, Colombia : Banco de la República, Departamento de Investigaciones Económicas, c1985. 109 p. : col. ill. ; 20 cm. "Esta publicación fue elaborada por el Departamento de Investigaciones Económicas del Banco de la República, con la valiosa colaboración de otras dependencias de la entidad, tales coma la de Asuntos Culturales, Jurídica y Oficina de Cambios." ISBN 958-9028-00-4 LC Card 86-179279
1. Colombia - Economic conditions - 1970-. 2. Colombia - Industries. 3. Colombia - Foreign economic relations. I. Banco de la República (Colombia). Departamento de Investigaciones Económicas.
HC197 .C627 1985

Colombia.
Ley 42 de 1985 (febrero 11). 1986. Colombia. Ministerio de Comunicaciones. Una revolución en las comunicaciones : memoria al Congreso / Noemí Sanín Posada. [Bogotá] 1986. 307 p., [5] leaves of plates : LC Card 87-401464 DDC 384/.09861 19
HE8011 .C65 1986

Colombia agraria .
(7) Rivera Cusicanqui, Silvia. Política e ideología en el movimiento campesino colombiano . [Bogotá] [s.l.] , 1982. 188 p. ; LC Card 84-155496
HD511.5.A87 R58 1982 ***NYPL [JLD 86-1208]***

COLOMBIA - APPROPRIATIONS AND EXPENDITURES - STATISTICS.
Hacienda y crédito público . [Bogotá, Colombia] [1986] 94 p. : LC Card 87-404281 DDC 336.861 19
HJ2083 .H33 1986

COLOMBIA - BOUNDARIES - VENEZUELA.
Foro de Proyectos de Inversión Colombo-Venezolanos (1986 : Cúcuta, Colombia) La frontera colombo-venezolana, una región donde invertir /. Bogotá, D.E. [1986] 96 p. ; LC Card 87-403851 DDC 332.6/09861 19
HG5352 .F67 1986

Colombia. Cámara de Representantes. see **Colombia. Congreso. Cámara de Representantes.**

COLOMBIA - CENSUS, 1985.
XV censo nacional de población y IV de vivienda. Bogotá , 1986- v. <1-5, 7 > : LC Card 87-402787 DDC 304.6/09861/021 19
HA1011.5 1985a

COLOMBIA - CENSUS, 1985 - CONGRESSES.
Seminario Taller sobre el XV Censo Nacional de Población y IV de Vivienda, 1985 (1986 : Girardot, Colombia) Seminario Taller sobre el XV Censo Nacional de Población y IV de Vivienda, 1985 /. Girardot [Colombia] , 1986. 327 p. : ISBN 958-608-038-2 LC Card 87-403863 DDC 304.6/0723 19
HA1011.5 1985b

COLOMBIA - COMMERCE.
Leibovich, José. Comercio exterior y distribución de ingresos . Bogotá, Colombia , 1984. vii, 221 p. : LC Card 87-402975 DDC 382/.41373/09861 19
HD9199.C62 L45 1984

COLOMBIA - COMMERCE - HISTORY - 20TH CENTURY.
Rodríguez, Luis Hernando. Análisis descriptivo de las exportaciones colombianas, 1950-1980 /. Bogotá, Colombia , 1985. 3, 169 p. : LC Card 87-402978 DDC 382/.6/09861 19
HF3426.5 .R63 1985

COLOMBIA - COMMERCE - MATHEMATICAL MODELS.
Mayer, Thomas, 1927- Instabile Exportmärkte und wirtschaftliche Entwicklung . Tübingen , c1983. vii, 181 p. : ISBN 3-16-344673-6 LC Card 83-218666
HF3426.5 .M39 1983

COLOMBIA - COMMERCE - UNITED STATES.
Matz, Viktor, 1947- Entwicklungsländer im internationalen Konjunkturzusammenhang . Bergisch Gladbach , c1986. 199, lxxvi p. ; ISBN 3-89012-052-0 LC Card 86-227998
HF3408.U5 M37 1986

COLOMBIA - COMMERCIAL POLICY - ADDRESSES, ESSAYS, LECTURES.
Thomas, Vinod, 1949- Linking macroeconomic and agricultural policies for adjustment with growth . Baltimore , c1985. xv, 252 p. ; ISBN 0-8018-3121-0 : LC Card 85-45105 DDC 338.9861 19
HC197 .T38 1985 ***NYPL [JLE 86-1438]***

Colombia. Comunicaciones, Ministerio de. see **Colombia. Ministerio de Comunicaciones.**

Colombia. Congreso. Cámara de Representantes. (Old Catalog form: Colombia. Cámara de Representantes)

Colombia. Congreso. Cámara de Representantes. Comisión Nombrada para Estudiar el Conflicto Surgido entre la United Fruit Company y la Cooperativa Bananera Colombiana. Informe de la Comisión Nombrada para Estudiar el Conflicto Surgido entre la United Fruit Company y la Cooperativa Bananera Colombiana. Bogotá : Impr. Nacional, 1930. 32 p. ; 25 cm. At head of title: República de Colombia. Cámara de Representantes. LC Card 83-189629
1. Banana trade - Colombia. 2. United Fruit Company. 3. Cooperativa Bananera Colombiana. 4. Governmental investigations - Colombia. I. Title.
HD9259.B3 C728 1930

Colombia. Consejo de Ministros. Foro de la Esperanza (1985 : Ibagué, Colombia) Foro de la Esperanza . [Bogotá?] [1985] 154 p. ; LC Card 87-401285 DDC 338.9861 19
HC197 .F59 1985

Colombia. Departamento Nacional de Planeación.
Foro de Proyectos de Inversión Colombo-Venezolanos (1986 : Cúcuta, Colombia) La frontera colombo-venezolana, una región donde invertir /. Bogotá, D.E. [1986] 96 p. ; LC Card 87-403851 DDC 332.6/09861 19
HG5352 .F67 1986

Plan nacional de rehabilitación . [Bogotá, Colombia] , 1985. 86 leaves : LC Card 87-103481 DDC 338.9861 19
HC197 .P59 1985

Políticas de ajuste y grupos más vulnerables en América Latina . [Bogotá, Colombia] , 1987. 278 p. : ISBN 958-9093-01-9 LC Card 87-404285 DDC 338.98 19
HC125 .P647 1987

Seminario Taller sobre el XV Censo Nacional de Población y IV de Vivienda, 1985 (1986 : Girardot, Colombia) Seminario Taller sobre el XV Censo Nacional de Población y IV de Vivienda, 1985 /. Girardot [Colombia] , 1986. 327 p. : ISBN 958-608-038-2 LC Card 87-403863 DDC 304.6/0723 19
HA1011.5 1985b

Colombia. Departmento Administrativo Nacional de Cooperativas. Una Obra cooperativa /. Bogotá, Colombia [1982] 276 p. ; LC Card 86-226857
HD3477.A4 O27 1982

COLOMBIA. DEPARTMENTO ADMINISTRATIVO NACIONAL DE COOPERATIVAS.
Una Obra cooperativa /. Bogotá, Colombia [1982] 276 p. ; LC Card 86-226857
HD3477.A4 O27 1982

Colombia. Desarrollo Económico, Ministerio de. see **Colombia. Ministerio de Desarrollo Económico.**

COLOMBIA - ECONOMIC CONDITIONS - 1918-
Las Empresas transnacionales en el desarrollo colombiano. Santiago de Chile , Nueva York, NY , 1986. 218 p. : ISBN 92-1-321213-5 LC Card 87-402186 DDC 338.8/88861 19
HD2837 .E47 1986

Síntesis de la economía colombiana, 1959-1974 /. Bogotá, D.E. , 1974. vii, 90 leaves, [6] leaves of plates : LC Card 87-403567 DDC 330.9861/0632 19
HC197 .S56 1974

COLOMBIA - ECONOMIC CONDITIONS - 1918-1970.
López, Alejandro, 1876-1940. [Selections. 1983.] Obras selectas /. Bogotá, D.E. , 1983. xiii, 458 p. ; LC Card 86-233252
HC197 .L6172 1983

COLOMBIA - ECONOMIC CONDITIONS - 1970-
Acosta M., Amylkar (Acosta Medina), 1950- [Selections. 1986.] Escritos, 1978-1986 /. Medellín, Colombia , 1986. 201 p. ; LC Card 87-404338 DDC 330.9861/0632 19
HC197 .A5562 1986

Barco, Virgilio. La lucha contra la pobreza /. [Bogotá] , 1985. 193 p. ; ISBN 958-9044-11-5 LC Card 85-239429
HC197 .B2765 1985

Colombia . Bogotá, Colombia , c1985. 109 p. : ISBN 958-9028-00-4 LC Card 86-179279
HC197 .C627 1985

Eastman, Jorge Mario. Hacia un populismo petrolero? y otros temas /. Bogotá, Colombia , 1986. viii, 145 p., [8] p. of plates : LC Card 86-227075
HD9574.C52 E18 1986

Echavarría Olózaga, Hernán. El hueco negro . [S.l. , 1986] (Bogotá, Colombia : Editorial Andes) 244 p., [7] p. of plates : LC Card 86-209093
HC197 .E34 1986

Giraldo Valencia, Federico, 1950- Una crítica puntual . Medellín , 1986. 204 p. ; LC Card 87-400327 DDC 338.9861 19
HC197 .G52 1986

Pedraja Tomán, René de la. Los Llanos . Bogotá, Colombia , 1984. 101 p. : LC Card 84-221343
HC198.L56 P4 1984

COLOMBIA - ECONOMIC CONDITIONS - 1970- - CONGRESSES.
Perspectivas de la economía mundial y colombiana /. Bogotá, Colombia , 1986. 106 p. ; ISBN 958-616-044-0 LC Card 87-115573 DDC 330.9861/0632 19
HC197 .P35 1986

COLOMBIA - ECONOMIC POLICY.
Agudelo Villa, Hernando. (comp) La política del Ministerio de Desarrollo. Bogotá, 1972-73. 3 v. LC Card 73-208936
HC197 .A63

Barco, Virgilio. La lucha contra la pobreza /. [Bogotá] , 1985. 193 p. ; ISBN 958-9044-11-5 LC Card 85-239429
HC197 .B2765 1985

Echavarría Olózaga, Hernán. El hueco negro . [S.l. , 1986] (Bogotá, Colombia : Editorial Andes) 244 p., [7] p. of plates : LC Card 86-209093
HC197 .E34 1986

Gallón Giraldo, Gustavo. Concertación simple y concertación ampliada /. Bogotá, Colombia [between 1982 and 1985] 62 p. ; LC Card 85-147865
HC197 .G25 1982

Giraldo Valencia, Federico, 1950- Una crítica

puntual . Medellín , 1986. 204 p. ; LC Card 87-400327 DDC 338.9861 19
HC197 .G52 1986

Gómez Buendía, Hernando. Sindicalismo y política económica /. Bogotá, Colombia , 1986. 324 p. : ISBN 958-9061-16-8 LC Card 87-401441 DDC 331.88/09861 19
HD6622 .G64 1986

Hopkins, Mike. Alternatives to unemployment and underemployment . Boulder , 1985. xiv, 129 p. : ISBN 0-8133-0200-5 (pbk.) LC Card 85-45007 DDC 331.13/79861 19
HD5757.A6 H67 1985 **NYPL [JLD 86-2149]**

Jiménez, Margarita. Historia del desarrollo regional en Colombia /. Bogotá, Colombia , 1985. 338 p. ; ISBN 958-9061-04-4 LC Card 85-242811
HC197 .J57 1985

Plan nacional de rehabilitación . [Bogotá, Colombia] , 1985. 86 leaves : LC Card 87-103481 DDC 338.9861 19
HC197 .P59 1985

Yepes C., Alfonso. Del caos al orden . [S.l. , 1986] ([S.l.] : Editorial Nomos) 239 p., [1] leaf of plates : LC Card 87-400255 DDC 331.1/1/09861 19
HD5757.A6 Y46 1986

COLOMBIA - ECONOMIC POLICY - ADDRESSES, ESSAYS, LECTURES.
Thomas, Vinod, 1949- Linking macroeconomic and agricultural policies for adjustment with growth . Baltimore , c1985. xv, 252 p. ; ISBN 0-8018-3121-0 : LC Card 85-45105 DDC 338.9861 19
HC197 .T38 1985 **NYPL [JLE 86-1438]**

COLOMBIA - ECONOMIC POLICY - CONGRESSES.
Foro de la Esperanza (1985 : Ibagué, Colombia) Foro de la Esperanza . [Bogotá?] [1985] 154 p. ; LC Card 87-401285 DDC 338.9861 19
HC197 .F59 1985

COLOMBIA - FOREIGN ECONOMIC RELATIONS.
Colombia . Bogotá, Colombia , c1985. 109 p. : ISBN 958-9028-00-4 LC Card 86-179279
HC197 .C627 1985

Colombia. Gobierno, Ministerio de. see **Colombia. Ministerio de Gobierno.**

Colombia - Government. see **Colombia - Politics and government.**

Colombia. Hacienda, Ministerio de. see **Colombia. Ministerio de Hacienda.**

COLOMBIA - INDUSTRIES.
Colombia . Bogotá, Colombia , c1985. 109 p. : ISBN 958-9028-00-4 LC Card 86-179279
HC197 .C627 1985

Cortes, Mariluz. Success in small and medium-scale enterprises . New York , c1987. xiii, 289 p. ; ISBN 0-19-520593-6 : LC Card 86-46296 DDC 338.6/42/09861 19
HD2346.C7 C69 1987

COLOMBIA - INDUSTRIES - CONGRESSES.
La Industria colombiana y la "ALALC.". [Medellín] [1964] 112 p. ; LC Card 85-111774
HC197 .I36 1964

COLOMBIA - MANUFACTURES.
Wallace, Brian F. Ownership and development . Athens, Ohio , 1987. ix, 176 p. ; ISBN 0-89680-145-4 (pbk.) LC Card 86-33255 DDC 332.6/7322861 19
HD9734.C62 W35 1987

Colombia. Ministerio de Comunicaciones. Una revolución en las comunicaciones : memoria al Congreso / Noemí Sanín Posada. [Bogotá : Ministerio de Comunicaciones], 1986. 307 p., [5] leaves of plates : ill. ; 21 cm. Spine title: Memorias del Ministerio de Comunicaciones, 1982-1986. "Ley 42 de 1985": p. 277-305. LC Card 87-401464 DDC 384/.09861 19
1. Telecommunication - Colombia. 2. Telecommunication policy - Colombia. I. Sanín Posada, Noemí. II. Colombia. Ley 42 de 1985 (febrero 11). 1986. III. Title. IV. Title: Memoria al Congreso. V. Title: Memorias del Ministerio de Comunicaciones, 1982-1986.
HE8011 .C65 1986

COLOMBIA. MINISTERIO DE DESARROLLO ECONÓMICO.
Agudelo Villa, Hernando. (comp) La política del Ministerio de Desarrollo. Bogotá, 1972-73. 3 v. LC Card 73-208936
HC197 .A63

Colombia. Ministerio de Gobierno. Plan nacional de rehabilitación . [Bogotá, Colombia] , 1985. 86 leaves : LC Card 87-103481 DDC 338.9861 19
HC197 .P59 1985

COLOMBIA. MINISTERIO DE HACIENDA.
(Old Catalog form: Colombia. Hacienda, Ministerio de.)
Murillo Toro, Manuel, 1816-1880. Escritos económicos /. Bogotá, Colombia , 1985. 120 p. ; LC Card 86-165762
HJ943 .M87 1985

Colombia. Ministerio de Hacienda y Crédito Público. Hacienda y crédito público . [Bogotá, Colombia] [1986] 94 p. : LC Card 87-404281 DDC 336.861 19
HJ2083 .H33 1986

Colombia. Ministerio de Hacienda y Crédito Públio. Oficina Económica. Síntesis de la economía colombiana, 1959-1974 /. Bogotá, D.E. , 1974. vii, 90 leaves, [6] leaves of plates : LC Card 87-403567 DDC 330.9861/0632 19
HC197 .S56 1974

Colombia. Ministerio de Salud Pública. Departamento Nacional de Planeación. see **Colombia. Departamento Nacional de Planeación.**

Colombia. Planeación, Departamento Nacional de. see **Colombia. Departamento Nacional de Planeación.**

COLOMBIA - POLITICS AND GOVERNMENT - 1974-
Kline, Harvey F. The coal of El Cerrejón . University Park , c1987. viii, 216 p. : ISBN 0-271-00491-6 : LC Card 86-43038 DDC 333.8/2215/09861 19
HD9554.C63 E3748 1987

Plan nacional de rehabilitación . [Bogotá, Colombia] , 1985. 86 leaves : LC Card 87-103481 DDC 338.9861 19
HC197 .P59 1985

COLOMBIA - POPULATION.
Transición demográfica y oferta de fuerza de trabajo en Colombia /. [Bogotá], República de Colombia , 1986. 2 v. : ISBN 958-95096-0-6 (set) LC Card 87-113652 DDC 331.11/09861 19
HD5757.A6 T7 1986

COLOMBIA - POPULATION, RURAL.
Ordóñez G., Myriam. Población y familia rural en Colombia /. Bogotá , 1986. 179 p. : LC Card 86-208940
HB2447 .O73 1986

Colombia. Presidencia de la República.
Plan nacional de rehabilitación . [Bogotá, Colombia] , 1985. 86 leaves : LC Card 87-103481 DDC 338.9861 19
HC197 .P59 1985

Colombia. Presidencia de la República. Secretaría de Información y Prensa. Betancur, Belisario, 1923- Un semáforo en rojo . [Bogotá] [1984] 12, 12, 12 p. ; LC Card 87-125515 DDC 338.98 19
HC125 .B42 1984

COLOMBIA - RURAL CONDITIONS.
Reproducción de fuerza de trabajo, educación y migración en el sector rural colombiano /. Bogotá, Colombia , 1985. 98, [52] p. : LC Card 87-402979 DDC 331.1/09861 19
HD5757.A6 R46 1985

Colombia. Servicio Nacional de Empleo. Dirección General. Transición demográfica y oferta de fuerza de trabajo en Colombia /. [Bogotá], República de Colombia , 1986. 2 v. : ISBN 958-95096-0-6 (set) LC Card 87-113652 DDC 331.11/09861 19
HD5757.A6 T7 1986

COLOMBIA - SOCIAL CONDITIONS.
Acosta M., Amylkar (Acosta Medina), 1950- [Selections. 1986.] Escritos, 1978-1986 /. Medellín, Colombia , 1986. 201 p. ; LC Card 87-404338 DDC 330.9861/0632 19
HC197 .A5562 1986

COLOMBIA - SOCIAL POLICY.
Gallón Giraldo, Gustavo. Concertación simple y concertación ampliada /. Bogotá, Colombia [between 1982 and 1985] 62 p. ; LC Card 85-147865
HC197 .G25 1982

Plan nacional de rehabilitación . [Bogotá, Colombia] , 1985. 86 leaves : LC Card 87-103481 DDC 338.9861 19
HC197 .P59 1985

Yepes C., Alfonso. Del caos al orden . [S.l. , 1986] ([S.l.] : Editorial Nomos) 239 p., [1] leaf of plates : LC Card 87-400255 DDC 331.1/1/09861 19
HD5757.A6 Y46 1986

COLOMBIA - STATISTICS, VITAL.
Flórez Nieto, Carmen Elisa. The existence of a Latin American mortality pattern . Bogotá, Colombia , 1985. 153 p. : LC Card 87-145922
HB1397 .F56 1985

Colombo, Giuseppe, 1836-1921. Industria e politica nella storia d'Italia : scritti scelti, 1861-1916 / Giuseppe Colombo ; a cura di Carlo G. Lacaita. [Milano] : Cariplo ; Roma : Laterza, c1985. 497 p. : ill. ; 24 cm. (Economia e società in Lombardia dall'età delle riforme alla grande crisi . 1) Includes bibliographical references and index. ISBN 88-420-2555-0 : LC Card 85-180231 DDC 338.945 19
1. Industrial promotion - Italy - History - Sources. 2. Industry and state - Italy - History - Sources. 3. Italy - Economic policy - Sources. I. Lacaita, Carlo G. II. Title. III. Series.
HC310.I53 C65 1985 **NYPL [JLE 86-2517]**

COLONIA DEL SACRAMENTO (URUGUAY) - HISTORY - 18TH CENTURY.
Santos, Corcino Medeiros dos. Economia e sociedade do Rio Grande do Sul . São Paulo, SP, Brasil , 1984. xxi, 216 p. : ISBN 85-04-00203-9 : LC Card 85-199838
HF3409.R56 S25 1984

COLONIAL AFFAIRS. see **COLONIES.**

Colonial entrepreneurs, families and business in Bourbon Mexico City /. Kicza, John E., 1947- Albuquerque , c1983. 1 v. : ISBN 0-8263-0655-1 (v. 1) LC Card 82-21962 DDC 305.5/54/097253 19
HF3240.M5 K52 1983 **NYPL [JLL 83-164]**

COLONIALISM. see **IMPERIALISM; COLONIES.**

Colonialism and migration : indentured labour before and after slavery / edited by P.C. Emmer ; contribution by E. van den Boogaart ... [et al.]. Dordrecht : M. Nijhoff ; Higham, MA, USA : Distributors for the U. S. and Canada, Kluwer Boston, 1986. vi, 303 p. : ill., maps ; 25 cm. (Comparative studies in overseas history. 7) Includes bibliography and index. ISBN 90-247-3253-0 LC Card 85-21809 DDC 331.11/73 19
1. Indentured servants - America - History - Congresses. 2. Labor supply - America - History - Congresses. 3. America - Emigration and immigration - History - Congresses. 4. America - Population - History - Congresses. I. Emmer, P. C. II. Boogaart, E. van den. III. Series. IV. Series: Comparative studies in overseas history, v. 7.
HD4875.A837 C65 1986
NYPL [JLE 86-3920]

COLONIES.
Nweihed, Kaldone G., 1929- Bolívar y el Tercer Mundo . Caracas, Venezuela , c1984. 400 p. : ISBN 84-499-7056-3 LC Card 85-136718
F2235.3 .N98 1984 **NYPL [JFE 86-1176]**

COLONIES AND COLONIZATION. see **COLONIES.**

COLONIES AND COLONIZATION, BRITISH. see **GREAT BRITAIN - COLONIES.**

COLONIES AND COLONIZATION, SPANISH. see **SPAIN - COLONIES.**

COLONIES - ECONOMIC CONDITIONS.
Die Peripherie in der Weltwirtschaftskrise, Afrika, Asien und Lateinamerika, 1929-1939 /. Paderborn , c1982. 295 p. : ISBN 3-506-77461-1 LC Card 83-167120 DDC 330.9172/4 19
HC59.7 .P457 1982 **NYPL [JLE 87-1202]**

Colonisation et régionalisme . Trincaz, Pierre Xavier. Paris , 1984. 270 p. : ISBN 2-7099-0713-5 LC Card 86-148748 DDC 330.966/3 19
HC1045.Z7 Z548 1984

La colonización antioqueña y la fundación de Manizales /. Giraldo Zuluaga, Luisa Fernanda, 1957- Manizales, Colombia [1983] 217 p. : LC Card 84-107745
HD519.C35 G57 1983

Colonización en Bolivia /. Wiggins, Steve. Sucre, Bolivia [1976?] iv, 112 p. : LC Card 83-203672
HD486 .W54 1976

COLONIZATION - TROPICS.
Les Phénomènes de "frontière" dans les pays tropicaux . Paris , 1981. vii, 456 p. : LC Card 83-122397
HD1131 .P47 1981

Coloquio Internacional, Política Petrolera: Respuestas del Mundo (1985 : Lima, Peru) Situación petrolera peruana . [Lima, Perú] [1985] iii, 102 leaves : LC Card 86-193466
HD9574.P52 S58 1985

Color coding for filing systems. Barber, Donald T. Filing dynamics . Emeryville, Calif. , 1987. 92 p. : ISBN 0-941151-00-X LC Card 87-60316 DDC 651.5/3 19
HF5741 .B44 1987

COLOR IN ADVERTISING.
Danger, Eric P. (Eric Paxton) Selecting colour for print /. Aldershot, Hants, England , Brookfield, Vt., U. S.A. , c1987. x, 164 p. ; ISBN 0-291-39715-8 (U. S.) : LC Card 86-23060 DDC 659.13/23 19
HF5839 .D36 1987

Color machine vision . Miller, Richard Kendall, 1946- Madison, GA [c1986] 174 leaves : ISBN 0-89671-079-3 (pbk.) LC Card 87-116822 DDC 380.1/4500637 19
HD9696.C62 M55 1986

COLOR PRINTER INDUSTRY - UNITED STATES.
Color printer markets. Norwalk, Conn., U. S.A. (6 Prowitt St., Norwalk 06855) , c1987. vi, 188 leaves ; LC Card 87-401926 DDC 381/.456213987/0973 19
HD9696.C63 U514916 1987

Color printer markets. Norwalk, Conn., U. S.A. (6 Prowitt St., Norwalk 06855) : International Resource Development Inc., c1987. vi, 188 leaves ; 28 cm. (Report / International Resource Development Inc. . #728 (Feb. 1987)) LC Card 87-401926 DDC 381/.456213987/0973 19
1. Color printer industry - United States. 2. Market surveys - United States. I. International Resource Development, inc. II. Series: Report / International Resource Development Inc. , #728.
HD9696.C63 U514916 1987

COLOR PRINTING.
Danger, Eric P. (Eric Paxton) Selecting colour for print /. Aldershot, Hants, England , Brookfield, Vt., U. S.A. , c1987. x, 164 p. ; ISBN 0-291-39715-8 (U. S.) : LC Card 86-23060 DDC 659.13/23 19
HF5839 .D36 1987

COLORADO - ECONOMIC CONDITIONS.
Neuschatz, Michael. The golden sword . New York , 1986. xii, 301 p. ; ISBN 0-313-25104-5 (lib. bdg. : alk. Paper) LC Card 85-27026 DDC 331.88/122334/09788 19
HD8039.M61 U48 1986
NYPL [JLE 87-766]

COLORADO RIVER - WATER-RIGHTS - CONGRESSES.
New courses for the Colorado River . Albuquerque , c1986. xx, 253 p. : ISBN 0-8263-0854-6 LC Card 85-24577 DDC 333.91/009791/3 19
HD1695.C7 N49 1986 ***NYPL [JLE 86-1736]***

Colorado River Working Symposium (1983 : Santa Fe, N.M.) New courses for the Colorado River . Albuquerque , c1986. xx, 253 p. : ISBN 0-8263-0854-6 LC Card 85-24577 DDC 333.91/009791/3 19
HD1695.C7 N49 1986 ***NYPL [JLE 86-1736]***

COLORED PEOPLE (SOUTH AFRICA) - EMPLOYMENT - SOUTH AFRICA - CAPE OF GOOD HOPE.
Goldin, Ian. The poverty of Coloured labour preference . Cape Town [1984] ii, 97 p. : ISBN 0-7992-0570-2 (pbk.) LC Card 84-195453
HD8801.Z8 C324 1984

COLORED PEOPLE (SOUTH AFRICA) - MIGRATIONS - STATISTICS.
Cilliers, S. P. Patterns of migration and settlement in rural South Africa /. [Stellenbosch] , 1986. 19, 13 leaves, 5 folded leaves of plates : ISBN 0-908422-81-4 (pbk.) : LC Card 87-126315 DDC 304.8/0968 19
HB2123.4.A3 C56 1986

COLORED PEOPLE (UNITED STATES) see AFRO-AMERICANS.

Colours. Frontrunners. Chapel Hill, NC , 1987. 1 videocassette (28 min., 50 sec.) : LC Card 87-706853 DDC 338.6 11
HD9940

Colson, Elizabeth, 1917- Scudder, Thayer. An evaluation of the Gwembe South Development Project, Zambia /. Binghamton, N.Y., USA [1982] 48 p. ; LC Card 87-119502 DDC 338.96894 19
HC915.Z7 G846 1982

Coltman, Michael M., 1930- Hospitality management accounting / Michael M. Coltman. 3rd ed. New York : Van Nostrand Reinhold, c1987. xi, 449 p. : ill. ; 25 cm. "A CBI book." Includes index. ISBN 0-442-21777-3 : LC Card 86-28201 DDC 657/.837 19
1. Hotels, taverns, etc. - Accounting. 2. Food service - Accounting. 3. Managerial accounting. I. Title.
HF5686.H75 C53 1987

The Columbia history of urban life.
Weiss, Marc A. (Marc Allan) The rise of the community builders . New York , 1987. xii, 228 p. : ISBN 0-231-06504-3 LC Card 87-5115 DDC 333.77/17/0973 19
HD257 .W46 1987

Columbia Law School Alumni Association. International Law Symposium (1984 : Cambridge, Cambridgeshire) The United States, transnational business, and the law . New York , c1985. x, 132 p. ; ISBN 0-379-20783-4 LC Card 85-61594 DDC 346/.07 342.67 19
K1004.6 1984 ***NYPL [JLF 86-1046]***

Columbia Law School Association of the United Kingdom. International Law Symposium (1984 : Cambridge, Cambridgeshire) The United States, transnational business, and the law . New York , c1985. x, 132 p. ; ISBN 0-379-20783-4 LC Card 85-61594 DDC 346/.07 342.67 19
K1004.6 1984 ***NYPL [JLF 86-1046]***

Columbia studies in business, government, and society.
Capon, Noel. Corporate strategic planning /. New York , 1987. p. cm. ISBN 0-231-06380-6 LC Card 87-18239 DDC 658.4/012 19
HD30.28 .C375 1987

Quinn, Dennis Patrick, 1955- Restructuring the automobile industry . New York , 1988. p. cm. ISBN 0-231-06524-8 LC Card 87-15919 DDC 338.4/76292/0941 19
HD9710.U52 Q56 1988

Columbia University. Center for Career Research and Human Resource Management. Friedman, Stewart D. Leadership succession systems and corporate performance /. New York, N.Y. (316 Uris Hall, New York, N.Y. 10027) , c1985. ix, 141 p. :
NYPL [JLF 87-255]

Ginzberg, Eli, 1911- Resizing for organizational effectiveness . New York, N.Y. (316 Uris Hall, New York 10027) , c1985. vii, 43 p. ; LC Card 86-162474 DDC 658.1/6 19
HD58.9 .G56 1985

Columbia University. Center for Futures Market Studies. The Industrial organization of futures markets /. Lexington, Mass. , c1984. vii, 312 p. : ISBN 0-669-06836-5 LC Card 83-48029 DDC 332.64/4 19
HG6024.A3 I52 1984 ***NYPL [JLE 86-4471]***

Columbia University. Center on Japanese Economy and Business. Japan and the United States today . New York , 1986, c1987. vii, 234 p. : ISBN 0-231-06575-2 LC Card 86-32640 DDC 332/.042/0952 19
HG3903 .J35 1987

Columbia University. Graduate School of Business. Center for Operations. Starr, Martin Kenneth, 1927- The performance of Japanese-owned firms in America, 1982-1985 /. [New York, NY] , c1987. ii, 41 leaves : LC Card 87-145262 DDC 338.8/8952/073 19
HD2785 .S66 1987

Colummi, Cristiana. --Anche l'uomo doveva essere di ferro . Milano, Italy , c1986. 441 p. : LC Card 86-213675
HD8490.T742 A53 1986

COM (Commission of the European Communities) .

Les comarques de Lleida durant la segona república, 1930-1936 /. Barrull Pelegrí, Jaume, 1947- Barcelona , 1986. 503 p. : ISBN 84-85905-23-7 LC Card 86-203986
HC388.L4 B37 1986

Les comarques gironines . Medir i Huerta, Rosa M. Girona , 1986. 211 p. : ISBN 84-505-3103-9 LC Card 87-101047
HC387.G4 M43 1986

Combating takeover attempts. Washington, D.C. : National Association of Manufacturers : Order from Publications Coordinator, National Association of Manufacturers, c1986. xi, 12 p. : ill. ; 23 cm. Comments of NAM's 1985 board of directors' panel discussion. "March 1986"--Cover. CONTENTS. - Recognizing the threat / Paul H. Elicker -- Planning the defense / Richard L. Berry -- Surviving the attack / Fred L. Hartley -- Identifying the real enemy / Parker G. Montgomery. LC Card 86-224303 DDC 658.1/6 19
1. Consolidation and merger of corporations - United States - Prevention. 2. Tender offers (Securities) - United States. I. National Association of Manufactures (U. S.).
HD2746.5 .C645 1986

Combatting the effects of cyclical drought in Ethiopia. Addis Ababa, Ethiopia : Relief and Rehabilitation Commission, [1985] 56 p. : ill. ; 24 cm. "January 1985." Bibliography: p. 56. LC Card 86-224201 DDC 363.8/83/0963 19
1. Droughts - Ethiopia. 2. Famines - Ethiopia. 3. Disaster relief - Ethiopia. I. Ethiopia. Relief and Rehabilitation Commission.
HC845.Z9 F332 1985

COMBINATIONS IN RESTRAINT OF TRADE. see MONOPOLIES; RESTRAINT OF TRADE.

COMBINATIONS OF LABOR. see STRIKES AND LOCKOUTS.

Combustibles . Yornet, Mario E. Buenos Aires [1980] 105, viii leaves : LC Card 84-134419
HD9574.A72 Y67 1980

Comcorde. Secretaría Técnica. Estadísticas agropecuarias. Montevideo, República Oriental del Uruguay , 1979. [79] p. ; LC Card 82-209370
HD9014.U82 E78 1979

Come parla la pubblicità . Grandi, Roberto. Milano , 1987. 175 p. ; LC Card 87-168680
HF6146.T42 G7 1987

Comeau, John, 1952- Communication on the job : a practical approach / John Comeau, Gwen Diehn. Englewood Cliffs, N.J. : Prentice-Hall, c1987. xxvi, 356 p. : ill. ; 23 cm. Includes index. ISBN 0-13-153685-0 (pbk.) : LC Card 86-30555 DDC 651.7 19
1. Communication in management. 2. Communication in organizations. 3. Commercial correspondence. I. Diehn, Gwen, 1943-. II. Title.
HD30.3 .C62 1987

Comeback, case by case . Vogel, Ezra F. New York , c1985. 320 p. ; ISBN 0-671-46079-X LC Card 84-22232 DDC 338.952 19
HD3616.U47 V64 1985
NYPL [JLE 85-2275]

COMECON. see Sovet ėkonomicheskoĭ vzaimopomoshchi.

Comedia series .
(no. 34) Root, Jane. Open the box . London , 1986. 126 p. : ISBN 0-906890-78-0 (pbk.) : LC Card 86-206072 DDC 302.2/345/0941 19
HE8700.9.G7 R66 1986

(no. 35) Chapman, Simon. Great expectorations . London , 1986. 158 p. : ISBN 0-906890-86-1 (pbk.) : LC Card 86-204305 DDC 659.1/96797 19
HF6161.T6 C48 1986

Comeliau, Christian. L'Impasse Nord-Sud . Paris , c1984. 103 p. : ISBN 2-11-001207-2 : LC Card 84-163951
HC59 .I44 1984

Comentário sôbre os balanços gerais da União de 1963 /. Cotia, Raul Fontes. [Brasília] [1964]

45 p. ; LC Card 85-194302
HJ2079 .C68 1964

Comentarios económicos /. Salvador Ortíz, S., 1917-1983. Santo Domingo, República Dominicana , 1984- v. ; LC Card 85-118318 DDC 330.9 19
HC125 .S2615 1984 ***NYPL [JLK 85-83]***

Comer, Michael J. Corporate fraud / Michael J. Comer. 2nd ed. London ; New York : McGraw-Hill, 1985. xvi, 453 p. : ill. ; 24 cm. Includes index. Bibliography: p. 434-435. ISBN 0-07-084791-6 : LC Card 85-11686 DDC 364.1/63 19
1. Corporations - Corrupt practices. 2. Fraud investigation. 3. Computer crimes - Prevention. I. Title.
HV6768 .C65 1985 ***NYPL [JLE 86-909]***

El Comerç entre Catalunya i Amèrica (segles XVIII i XIX) / Josep M. Delgado ... [et al.]. 1a ed. Barcelona : L'Avenç, 1986. 173 p. : ill. ; 22 cm. (Col·lecció Clio . 6) Bibliography: p. 165-169. ISBN 84-85905-24-5 LC Card 86-204187
1. Catalonia (Spain) - Commerce - America - History. 2. America - Commerce - Spain - Catalonia - History. 3. Spain - Colonies - America - Commerce - History. I. Delgado, Josep M. (Maria). II. Series.
HF3689.C3 C39 1986

Comercialização de alimentos na região norte, 1985 / Ministério da Indústria e do Comércio, Conselho de Desenvolvimento Comercial, Coordenadoria de Projetos Especiais ; equipe técnica, Almir Freire Lima ... [et al.]. Brasília, DF : CPE, 1985. 51 p. ; 22 cm. (Série Cadernos técnicos . no. 24) Includes bibliographical references. LC Card 86-129086
1. Food industry and trade - Brazil, North. I. Lima, Almir Freire. II. Conselho de Desenvolvimento Comercial. Coordenadoria de Projetos Especiais. III. Series.
HD9014.B83 N673 1985

Comercialización de artesanías /. Sandoval H., Orlando. [Quito, Ecuador] , 1985. 231 p. : LC Card 87-400169 DDC 331.7/94 19
HD2346.E2 S26 1985

Comercialización interna de los alimentos en América Latina : problemas, productos y políticas : selección de las ponencias presentadas en un seminario internacional celebrado en el Centro Internacional de Agricultura Tropical en Cali, Colombia, 11-13 julio 1984 / redactores, Gregory J. Scott y M. Gary Costello. Ottawa, Canada : International Development Research Centre, c1985. 253 p. : ill., maps ; 23 cm. (IDRC. 243s) "Informes"--Cover. Bibliography: p. 245-253. ISBN 0-88936-448-6 LC Card 87-118494 DDC 338.1/9/8 19
1. Food industry and trade - Latin America - Congresses. 2. Farm produce - Latin America - Congresses. 3. Food consumption - Latin America - Congresses. I. Scott, Gregory J. II. Costello, M. Gary (Michael Gary). III. International Development Research Centre (Canada). IV. Series: IDRC (Series) , 243s.
HD9014.L32 C66 1985

El comercio callejero en la ciudad de Medellín . López Castaño, Hugo. Medellín , 1983. xv, 194 leaves : LC Card 85-131765
HF5459.C7 L67 1983

Comercio de granos entre la Argentina y los países del Grupo Andino. [Buenos Aires, Argentina] : Bolsa de Cereales de Buenos Aires : Instituto para la Integración de América Latina, 1983. ii, 154 p. : ill. ; 28 cm. Bibliography: p. [153]-154. LC Card 86-201891
1. Grain Trade - Argentina. 2. Grain trade - Andes Region. 3. Argentina - Commerce - Andes Region. 4. Andes Region - Commerce - Argentina. I. Bolsa de Cereales de Buenos Aires. II. Institute for Latin American Integration.
HD9044.A8 C65 1983

El comercio del café en Haití . Girault, Christian A. [Commerce du café en Haïti. Spanish.] Santo Domingo, República Dominicana , c1985. 426 p. : LC Card 86-200427
HD9199.H22 G5518 1985

Comercio exterior . Fumero Marta, Julio, 1934- La Habana , 1985. vii, 210 p. : LC Card 87-107270
HF1008 .F86 1985

Comercio exterior y distribución de ingresos . Leibovich, José. Bogotá, Colombia , 1984. vii, 221 p. : LC Card 87-402975 DDC 382/.41373/09861 19
HD9199.C62 L45 1984

Comércio externo do Maranhão /. Costa Filho, João Evangelista da. [São Luís, Maranhão] [1982] 72 p. : LC Card 87-404935 DDC 382/.098121 19
HF3409.M3 C67 1982

El comercio intrarregional de alimentos básicos. Basco, Carlos A. [S.l.] , 1986. xi, 558 p. : LC Card 87-404784 DDC 382/.41/098 19
HD9014.L32 B37 1986

Comercio y contrabando en Cartagena de Indias, 2 de junio de 1800 /. Pombo, José Ignacio de, 1761-1815. Bogotá, Colombia , 1986. 124 p. ; LC Card 87-107126
HJ6864 .P66 1986

COMFORT, STANDARD OF. see **COST AND STANDARD OF LIVING.**

COMIBOL. see **Corporación Minera de Bolivia.**

Comín, Alfonso C. Noticia de Andalucía / Alfonso C. Comín ; introducción, Felipe González Márquez. Sevilla : Editoriales Andaluzas Unidas, [1985] 338 p. ; 19 cm. (Biblioteca de la cultura andaluza . 29.) Includes bibliographical references. ISBN 84-7587-037-6 LC Card 86-219377
1. Andalusia (Spain) - Economic conditions. 2. Andalusia (Spain) - Rural conditions. 3. Andalusia (Spain) - Social conditions. I. Series: Biblioteca de la cultura andaluza , 29. II. Title.
HC387.A64 C62 1985

The coming of age of political economy, 1815-1825 /. Langer, Gary F. New York , 1987. x, 224 p. : ISBN 0-313-25645-4 (lib. bdg. : alk. paper) LC Card 86-31802 DDC 330/.0941 19
HB103.A2 L36 1987

The coming of managerial capitalism . Chandler, Alfred Dupont. Homewood, Ill. , 1985. xiv, 877 p. : ISBN 0-256-03285-8 LC Card 84-82470 DDC 338.6/44/0973 19
HD2785 .C47 1985 ***NYPL [JLE 86-4418]***

Coming to grips with the internal market / Jacques Pelkmans & Marc Vanheukelen, editors. Maastricht, The Netherlands : European Institute of Public Administration, c1986. viii, 136 p. ; 24 cm. (Working papers / European Institute of Public Administration) English and French. Includes bibliographies. ISBN 90-6779-019-2 (pbk.) LC Card 86-222624 DDC 337.1/42 19
1. European Economic Community. 2. Tariff - European Economic Community countries. 3. Technology - European Economic Community countries - International cooperation. I. Pelkmans, Jacques. II. Vanheukelen, Marc. III. European Institute of Public Administration. IV. Series. V. Series: Documents de travail (European Institute of Public Administration).
HC241.2 .C5548 1986

Comisión Económica para América Latina. see **United Nations. Economic Commission for Latin America.**

Comisión Energía y Recursos de AEPDEN-Amigos de la Tierra. Modelo energético de tránsito / Comisión Energía y Recursos de AEPDEN-Amigos de la Tierra. Madrid : Miraguano, [1979?] 136 p. ; 18 cm. (Colección Amigos de la tierra . 3) Bibliography: p. 133-134. ISBN 84-85639-02-2 LC Card 79-126051
1. Power resources - Spain. 2. Energy policy - Spain. 3. Energy conservation - Spain. I. Title.
HD9502.S662 C66 1979 ***NYPL [JLC 87-71]***

Comisión Evangélica Latinoamericana de Educación Cristiana. Junto a nuestro pueblo. [Lima, Perú] [1979 or 1980] 71 p. : LC Card 82-100009
BX1426.2 .J86 1979 ***NYPL [JLF 86-1152]***

Comisión Nacional de Rehabilitación del Lisiado. Argentina. Comisión Nacional de Rehabilitación del Lisiado. [Buenos Aires] , 1965. [24] leaves ; LC Card 85-110867
HD7256.A7 A74 1965

COMISIÓN NACIONAL DE REHABILITACIÓN DEL LISIADO. Argentina. Comisión Nacional de Rehabilitación del Lisiado. Comisión Nacional de Rehabilitación del Lisiado. [Buenos Aires] , 1965. [24] leaves ; LC Card 85-110867
HD7256.A7 A74 1965

COMISIÓN TÉCNICA MIXTA DE SALTO GRANDE. Obras hidroeléctricas binacionales en América Latina. [Buenos Aires, Argentina] , 1985. vii leaves, 385 p., 3 leaves of plates : LC Card 86-180644
HD1696.A7 O27 1985

Comissão de fábrica : uma forma de organização operária / Oposição Sindical Metalúrgica. Petrópolis : Vozes, 1981. 60 p. ; 21 cm. "Esta pesquisa contou com a colaboração da Equipe da FASE/São Paulo." LC Card 86-190732
1. Works councils - Brazil - Case studies. 2. Management - Brazil - Employee participation - Case studies. I. Oposição Sindical Metalúrgica (São Paulo, Brazil). II. Equipe da FASE/São Paulo.
HD5660.B7 C66 1981

Comissão Estadual de Planejamento Agrícola de Sergipe. Projeto Tabuleiros Norte de Sergipe /. Aracaju , 1977. 521 p. : LC Card 86-131158
HD1875.S4 P76 1977

Comissió Interdepartemental de Recerca i Innovació Tecnològica (Barcelona, Spain) Catalunya, la fàbrica d'Espanya . [Barcelona] , 1985. 201 p. : LC Card 86-185178
HC387.C25 C336 1985

Comissões de fábrica. Ibrahim, José. O que todo cidadão precisa saber sobre comissões de fábrica /. São Paulo, SP [1986] 96 p. : ISBN 85-26-00095-0 LC Card 87-402908 DDC 338.6 19
HD5660.B7 I27 1986

Comité de Acción para la Seguridad Alimentaria Regional (Sistema Económico Latinoamericano) Basco, Carlos A. El comercio intrarregional de alimentos básicos. [S.l.] , 1986. xi, 558 p. : LC Card 87-404784 DDC 382/.41/098 19
HD9014.L32 B37 1986

Comitê de Divulgação do Mercado de Capitais (Brazil) Guia ação . RJ [i.e. Rio de Janeiro] [1985 or 1986] 285 p. ; LC Card 87-405004 DDC 332.6/78/0981 19
HG5334.5 .G85 1985

Comité Delaney. Le Projet Delaney . [St-Raymond, Québec] [1983] 76 leaves in various foliations : LC Card 84-224364
HD9685.C3 Q456 1983

Comité d'entreprise et formation /. Nallet, Jean François. Paris-La Défense (Tour Europe, 92080 cedex 07) , 1977. 140 p. (1 fold.) ; LC Card 78-358400
HD5660.F7 N34

Comité d'entreprise et formation /. Nallet, Jean François. Paris-la-Défense , 1979. 181 p. ;
NYPL [JLF 81-80]

Comité d'expansion de la Loire. Bilan socio-économique de la Loire / Comité d'expansion de la Loire. Saint Etienne : Le Comité, [1983] 270 p., [2] leaves of plates : ill. ; 30 cm. "Décembre 1983." Bibliography: p. 269. LC Card 85-104338
1. Loire, France (Dept.) - Economic conditions. 2. Loire, France (Dept.) - Social conditions. 3. Loire (France : Dept.) - Industries. 4. Loire (France : Dept.) - Economic policy. 5. Loire (France : Dept.) - Social policy. I. Title.
HC277.L6 C66 1983

Comité Interamericana de Desarrollo Agrícola. see **Inter-American Committee for Agricultural Development.**

Comité international d'enregistrement des fréquences. see **International Frequency Registration Board.**

Comité permanent interétats de lutte contre la sécheresse dans la Sahel. see **Permanent Inter-State Committee for Drought Control in the Sahel.**

Comité Promotor de Investigaciones para el Desarrollo Rural (Mexico) Por una nueva política alimentaria /. [México, D.F.] , 1984. 114 p. ; LC Card 85-131176 DDC 338.1/9/72 19
HD9014.M62 P67 1984 ***NYPL [JLC 86-348]***

Command Area Development programme in India : achievements and perspective. New Delhi : Central Board of Irrigation and Power, 1981. ii, 62 p. ; 29 cm. At head of title: Government of India, Ministry of Irrigation. "Command Area Development and Water Management Division, New Delhi." LC Card 83-907584

1. Irrigation - India. 2. Agriculture - India. I. India (Republic). Ministry of Irrigation.
NYPL [JLF 86-818]

Command area development, successes and learnings : proceedings of a seminar, held at Hyderabad, November 6-8, 1977 / K.K. Singh, Raghu Cidambi, editors. Hyderabad : Administrative Staff College of India for Training Division, Dept. of Personnel and Administrative Reforms, Govt. of India, c1980. iii, 138 p. ; 23 cm. LC Card 83-906246 DDC 338.1/854 19
1. Irrigation districts - India - Planning - Congresses. 2. Communication in rural development - India - Congresses. 3. Rural development - India - Finance - Congresses. I. Singh, K. K. (Kailash Kumar), 1930-. II. Cidambi, Raghu. III. India. Dept. of Personnel & Administrative Reforms. Training Division.
HD1741.I29 C65 1980 NYPL [JLD 87-597]

Commander, Simon. The state and agricultural development in Egypt since 1973 / Simon Commander. London ; Atlantic Highlands, NJ : Ithaca Press in association with the Overseas Development Institute, 1988. p. cm. (Middle East science policy studies . no. 11) Bibliography: p. Includes index. ISBN 0-86372-080-3 LC Card 87-3616 DDC 338.1/862 19
1. Agriculture and state - Egypt. I. Overseas Development Institute (London, England). II. Title. III. Series.
HD2123.Z8 C66 1988

COMMEMORATIVE POSTAGE STAMPS.
Gees, René. Schweiz UPU 1900 . Bern [1976?] 56 p. : LC Card 86-170456
HE6271 .G44 1976

COMMEMORATIVE POSTAGE STAMPS - CATALOGS.
Sieger (Firm) Weltpostverein (UPU) . Lorch/Württemberg , c1982. 408 p. : LC Card 83-224689
HE6271 .S55 1982

Comment acheter, produire et vendre dans les entreprises africaines : séminaire tenu [à Bujumbura] du 11 au 20 avril 1984 / République du Burundi, Ministère de la fonction publique, C.P.F., Centre de perfectionnement et de formation en cours d'emploi. [Bujumbura?] : Programme des Nations Unies pour le développement, [1984 or 1985] 122 p. : ill. ; 29 cm. Includes bibliographies. LC Card 85-981488
1. Industrial management - Congresses. 2. Industrial management - Burundi - Congresses. I. Centre de perfectionnement et de formation en cours d'emploi (Bujumbura, Burundi). II. United Nations. Development Programme.
HD29 .C624 1984

A comment on the goals and potential implications of Finnish average cost price regulation /. Wahlroos, Björn. Helsingfors , 1978. 12, [1] leaves : ISBN 951-555-053-X LC Card 85-192907
HB236.F55 W328 1978

COMMERCE - ADDRESSES, ESSAYS, LECTURES.
Economía internacional /. México , 1979- v. in : *NYPL [JLK 86-184]*

Kuo wai shang yeh yen chiu tzu liao /. [Peking] , 1984. 3, 604 p. ;
*NYPL [*OVY 86-3606]*

Commerce and morality / edited by Tibor R. Machan. Totowa, N.J. : Rowman & Littlefield, 1987. p. cm. Includes index. ISBN 0-8476-7586-6 LC Card 87-16635 DDC 174/.4 19
1. Business ethics. 2. Industry and state. I. Machan, Tibor R.
HF5387 .C65 1987

COMMERCE CLAUSE (U. S. CONSTITUTION) see INTERSTATE COMMERCE.

COMMERCE - CONGRESSES.
Global economic imbalances /. Washington, DC , 1985. x, 116 p. ; ISBN 0-88132-038-2 (pbk.) LC Card 85-8279 DDC 330.9/048 19
HD73 .G56 1985 NYPL [JLE 87-1314]

International trade and exchange rates in the late eighties /. Amsterdam ; New York : xii, 418 p. : ISBN 0-444-87941-2 LC Card 86-223111 DDC 382.4/5 19
HG203 .I58 1985

COMMERCE - DICTIONARIES.
Abdel Haleem, M. A. English-Arabic business dictionary /. London , 1984. xxxii, 263 p. ; ISBN 0-86010-448-6 : LC Card 83-228731 DDC 650/.03/21 19
HF1002 .A23 1984 NYPL [JLD 86-2048]

Cavalcante, José Cândido Marques. Dicionário inglês-português de termos econômicos & comerciais /. [Fortaleza] , Petrópolis , 1979. 408 p. ; LC Card 80-113110
HB61 .C37 NYPL [JLE 81-244]

A Dictionary of economics & commerce . Beirut , 1983. 383 p. ; LC Card 83-961782 DDC 330/.03/21 19
*HB61 .D4896 1983 NYPL [*OEO 87-1397]*

Dietl, Clara-Erika. Commercial dictionary . Wiesbaden , c1985-c1987. 2 v. ; ISBN 3-409-19900-4 (v. 1) LC Card 86-160868
HF1002 .D493 1985
*NYPL [*R-Econ. 87-1271]*

Organisation for European Economic Co-operation. Terminologie des échanges et paiements internationaux et de la comptabilité nationale. Paris [1958] 146, [6] p. LC Card 58-47135 DDC 382.03
HF1002 .O7 NYPL [JLF 87-128]

Picchi, Fernando. Economics and business . Bologna , 1986. 1333 p. ; ISBN 88-08-04550-1 LC Card 86-201141 DDC 330/.03/51 19
HB61 .P49 1986

Spinelli, Nicola, 1881- Dizionario commerciale, italiano-inglese e inglese-italiano . Torino , 1957. 464, 683, 138 p. ;
NYPL [JLD 85-226]

Strutz, Henry. Talking business in German . Woodbury, N.Y. , c1987. iv, 256 p. : ISBN 0-8120-3747-2 (pbk.) LC Card 86-22360 DDC 650/.03/31 19
HF1002 .S79 1987

COMMERCE - DICTIONARIES - FRENCH.
Emolumento, Vincenzo. Dizionario commerciale . Milano , 1983. 1150 p. ; ISBN 88-7075-068-X : LC Card 84-151136 DDC 380.1/03/41 19
HF1002 .E57 1983 NYPL [JLD 86-1323]

Organisation for European Economic Co-operation. Terminologie des échanges et paiements internationaux et de la comptabilité nationale. Paris [1958] 146, [6] p. LC Card 58-47135 DDC 382.03
HF1002 .O7 NYPL [JLF 87-128]

COMMERCE - DICTIONARIES - GERMAN.
Aussenwirtschafts-Alphabet . Frankfurt am Main , c1986. 396 p. ; LC Card 87-401369 DDC 382/.03/31 19
HF1001 .A86 1986

Dietl, Clara-Erika. Commercial dictionary . Wiesbaden , c1985-c1987. 2 v. ; ISBN 3-409-19900-4 (v. 1) LC Card 86-160868
HF1002 .D493 1985
*NYPL [*R-Econ. 87-1271]*

Koschnick, Wolfgang J., 1942- Standard-Lexikon für Marketing, Marktkommunikation, Markt- und Mediaforschung /. München , New York , 1987. vi, 940 p. : ISBN 3-598-10583-5 LC Card 87-143648 DDC 380.1/03/31 19
HF5415 .K617 1987

Strutz, Henry. Talking business in German . Woodbury, N.Y. , c1987. iv, 256 p. : ISBN 0-8120-3747-2 (pbk.) LC Card 86-22360 DDC 650/.03/31 19
HF1002 .S79 1987

COMMERCE - DICTIONARIES - HUNGARIAN.
Mádai, Edit. Külkereskedelmi tevékenységhez kapcsolódó általános fogalommeghatározások /. [Budapest , 1984] (Budapest : Datorg Nyomda) 177 p. ; ISBN 963-02-2359-7 LC Card 87-409581
HF1001 .M27 1984

COMMERCE - DICTIONARIES - ITALIAN.
Emolumento, Vincenzo. Dizionario commerciale . Milano , 1983. 1150 p. ; ISBN 88-7075-068-X : LC Card 84-151136 DDC 380.1/03/41 19
HF1002 .E57 1983 NYPL [JLD 86-1323]

Picchi, Fernando. Economics and business . Bologna , 1986. 1333 p. ; ISBN 88-08-04550-1 LC Card 86-201141 DDC 330/.03/51 19
HB61 .P49 1986

Spinelli, Nicola, 1881- Dizionario commerciale, italiano-inglese e inglese-italiano . Torino , 1957. 464, 683, 138 p. ;
NYPL [JLD 85-226]

COMMERCE - DICTIONARIES - POLISH.
Białecki, Klemens. Słownik handlu zagranicznego /. Warszawa , 1986. 359 p. ; ISBN 83-208-0112-5 : LC Card 86-221378
HF1001 .B47 1986

COMMERCE - DICTIONARIES - RUSSIAN.
Kratkiĭ vneshneėkonomicheskiĭ slovar′ /. Moskva , 1984. 244 p. ; LC Card 85-156834
*HF1001 .K7 1984 NYPL [*QCK 86-3635]*

COMMERCE - EARLY WORKS TO 1800.
Pinto, Isaac de, 1715-1787. [Selections. 1960.] O economista Isaac de Pinto, o seu "Tratado da circulação e do crédito," e outros escritos económicos /. Lisboa , 1960. 247 p. : LC Card 85-125396
HJ150 .P552 1960

COMMERCE - EDUCATION. see BUSINESS EDUCATION.

COMMERCE - GEOGRAPHY. see GEOGRAPHY, COMMERCIAL.

COMMERCE - HISTORY.
Müller, Karlhans, 1938- Vom Tauschhandel zur Weltwirtschaft . Reutlingen , c1984. 320 p. : ISBN 3-7709-0564-4 LC Card 87-673138
HC21 .M85x 1984

COMMERCE - HISTORY - MEDIEVAL, 500-1500.
Kürtz, Hans Joachim. Zu Zeiten der Hanse . Lübeck , c1983. 128 p. : ISBN 3-87498-330-7 LC Card 87-672840
HF455 .K87x 1983

COMMERCE - HISTORY - 19TH CENTURY.
Jones, Charles A., 1949- International business in the nineteenth century . New York , c1987. xi, 260 p. ; ISBN 0-8147-4172-X : LC Card 87-11321 DDC 338.8/8/09034 19
HF497 .J66 1987

COMMERCE - HISTORY - 20TH CENTURY.
Rosecrance, Richard N. The rise of the trading state . New York , c1986. xiii, 268 p. : ISBN 0-465-07035-3 : LC Card 85-47558 DDC 382/.09/04 19
HF1007 .R549 1985 NYPL [JLE 86-951]

The commerce in rubber . Coates, Austin. Singapore , New York , 1987. xv, 380 p., [32] p. of plates : ISBN 0-19-588868-5 : LC Card 87-20332 DDC 338.1/738952 19
HD9161.A2 C62 1987

COMMERCE - INFORMATION SERVICES - BIBLIOGRAPHY.
Grist, John. The Grist guide . Amherst, MA, U. S.A. (P.O. Box 227, Amherst 01004) , c1984. ii, 48 p. ; LC Card 85-108426 DDC 382/.025/73 19
HF294 .G75 1984
*NYPL [*R-Econ. 87-1266]*

COMMERCE - JURISPRUDENCE. see COMMERCIAL LAW.

COMMERCE - MATHEMATICAL MODELS.
Caille, Pierre. La théorie de l'échange international de produits différenciés /. Fribourg, Suisse , c1986. 267 p. : ISBN 2-8271-0337-0 LC Card 86-210742
HF1008 .C35 1986

Kattermann, Dieter. Neoricardianische Modelle zur Theorie des internationalen Handels und ihre Kritik der neoklassischen Aussenhandelstheorie . Bremen , 1981. 135, A-G p. : ISBN 3-88722-039-0 LC Card 82-177622 DDC 337/.0724 19
HF1412 .K37 1981 NYPL [JLD 86-2740]

Sgro, Pasquale M. The theory of duality & international trade /. London , c1986. 307 p. : ISBN 0-7099-3307-X *NYPL [JLD 86-3202]*

Withagen, Cees, 1950- Economic theory and international trade in natural exhaustible resources /. Berlin , New York , 1985. vi, 172 p. : ISBN 0-387-15970-3 LC Card 85-22101 DDC 333.7 19
HC59 .W55 1985
NYPL [JLM 72-289 no.253]

The commerce of culture . Cable, Vincent. New

Delhi , 1986. 237 p. ; ISBN 81-7062-004-X : LC Card 86-902899 DDC 338.4/77455/0954 19
HF5439.H27 C33 1986

COMMERCE - STATISTICAL METHODS. see **COMMERCIAL STATISTICS.**

COMMERCE - STATISTICS.
Brodin, Anders. The OECD Compatible Trade and Production data base, 1970-1983 /. [Paris, France] , c1986. ii, 81 p. ; LC Card 86-213116 DDC 382/.021 19
HF1016 .B68 1986

Commodity trade (by sea) statistics . New York , 1980. v, 396 p. ; LC Card 87-112992 DDC 387.5/55/021 19
HE562.8 .C667 1980

COMMERCIAL AERONAUTICS. see **AERONAUTICS, COMMERCIAL.**

Commercial and industrial activities in space. L'Attività commerciale e industriale nello spazio . [Trieste] [1986] 192 p. : LC Card 86-215438
HD9711.75.A2 A77 1986

Commercial and industrial enzymes /. Crull, Anna W. Stamford, Conn., U. S.A. , c1986. xiii, 160 leaves : ISBN 0-89336-492-4 (pbk.) LC Card 87-164403 DDC 380.1/4566063 19
HD9660.E582 C783 1986

COMMERCIAL ARITHMETIC. see **BUSINESS MATHEMATICS.**

COMMERCIAL ART - COLOMBIA.
1880-1980, un siglo de publicidad gráfica en Colombia /. [Bogotá?] [1984] 286 p. : LC Card 84-202348 DDC 659.1/09861 19
HF5813.C63 A16 1984
NYPL [3-MDW+ 86-17]

COMMERCIAL ASSOCIATIONS.
Business interests, organizational development, and private interest government . Berlin , New York , 1987. viii, 232 p. ; ISBN 0-89925-380-6 (U. S.) : LC Card 87-21403 DDC 338.4/7664 19
HD9000.5 .B87 1987

COMMERCIAL ATTACHÉS - UNITED STATES - CONGRESSES.
The Role of embassies in promoting business . Lanham, MD , 1987, c1981. p. cm. ISBN 0-8191-5053-3 (pbk. : alk. paper) LC Card 87-14027 DDC 382/.3/0973 19
HF1417.5 .R64 1987

Commercial banking /. Abrol, Prem Nath. Delhi, India , 1987. viii, 224 p. ; LC Card 87-900129 DDC 332.1/2/09546 19
HG3289.J35 A37 1987

Commercial banks amid the financial revolution . Ballarín, Eduard. Cambridge, Mass. , 1986. xvi, 248 p. : ISBN 0-88730-081-2 LC Card 85-23299 DDC 332.1/2/0973 19
HG1616.C87 B35 1986
NYPL [JLE 86-2810]

COMMERCIAL BUDGET. see **BUDGET IN BUSINESS.**

COMMERCIAL BUILDINGS.
Commercial real estate . Dallas, Tex. , c1986. 219 p. : ISBN 0-87833-459-9 : LC Card 85-27108 DDC 332.63/243 19
HD1393.25 .C65 1986 *NYPL [JLE 86-4267]*

Small business incubators . Washington, D.C. , c1984. 32 p. : LC Card 86-233015 DDC 333.33/8 19
HD1393.25 .S63 1984

COMMERCIAL CATALOGS. see **CATALOGS, COMMERCIAL.**

Commercial conflict and foreign policy . Rowland, Benjamin M. New York , 1987. 431 p. ; ISBN 0-8240-8090-4 (alk. paper) : LC Card 87-23787 DDC 337.73041 19
HF1456.5.G7 R68 1987

COMMERCIAL CORNERS. see **MONOPOLIES; SPECULATION; STOCK-EXCHANGE.**

COMMERCIAL CORRESPONDENCE - DICTIONARIES - GERMAN.
Roessler, Helmut R. Deutsche Geschäftskorrespondenz . Lanham, MD , c1987. xii, 218 p. : ISBN 0-8191-6277-9 (alk. paper) : LC Card 87-6086 DDC 658.4/53 19
HF5728.G3 R64 1987

COMMERCIAL CORRESPONDENCE, FRENCH.
Geoghegan, C., 1945- Handbook of commercial French /. London , New York , 1988. p. cm. ISBN 0-7102-0857-X LC Card 87-16320 DDC 448/.002465 19
HF5728.F8 G46 1988

COMMERCIAL CORRESPONDENCE, GERMAN.
Seddig, Gert. Lehrbuch der Altenpflege. Hannover , c1983. 95 p. : ISBN 3-87870-204-3 LC Card 83-230557
HF5728.G3 S49 1983

COMMERCIAL CORRESPONDENCE, GERMAN - HANDBOOKS, MANUALS, ETC.
Roessler, Helmut R. Deutsche Geschäftskorrespondenz . Lanham, MD , c1987. xii, 218 p. : ISBN 0-8191-6277-9 (alk. paper) : LC Card 87-6086 DDC 658.4/53 19
HF5728.G3 R64 1987

COMMERCIAL CORRESPONDENCE - HANDBOOKS, MANUALS, ETC.
Brusaw, Charles T. The business writer's handbook /. New York , c1987. xxviii, 764 p. : ISBN 0-312-00571-7 : LC Card 87-4361 DDC 651.7/5 19
HF5726 .B874 1987

Clark, James Leland, 1929- HOW 5 . Boston, Mass. , c1988. ix, 370 p. : ISBN 0-534-87144-5 (pbk.) : LC Card 87-20155 DDC 651.7/402 19
HF5726 .C55 1988

COMMERCIAL CREDIT.
Baross, Jenő. A kereskedelmi hitel és a váltó gyakorlata /. Budapest , 1985. 123 p. ; LC Card 86-228454
HG3754.5.H9 B37 1985

COMMERCIAL CREDIT - COLOMBIA.
Restrepo Correa, Alejandro. Manual de crédito industrial y agropecuario . [Bogotá, D.E. , 1985] 270, 30, 4 p. : LC Card 86-110073
HG3751.9.C7 R47 1985

COMMERCIAL CREDIT - GOVERNMENT POLICY - ITALY - CONGRESSES.
Convegno C.I.D.I.S. (1980 : Iesolo, Italy) Credito e finanziarie regionali . Padova , c1983. vi, 148 p. ; LC Card 85-215231
HG3729.I72 C66 1980

COMMERCIAL CREDIT - HUNGARY.
Baross, Jenő. A kereskedelmi hitel és a váltó gyakorlata /. Budapest , 1985. 123 p. ; LC Card 86-228454
HG3754.5.H9 B37 1985

Lovassné Szecső, Judit. A kereskedelmi hitel és a váltó alkalmazásának 1985. évi tapasztalatai /. Budapest [1986] 62 p. ; ISBN 963-7202-84-6 LC Card 87-151536
HG3754.5.H9 L68 1986

COMMERCIAL CREDIT - NIGERIA.
Akwaeze, G. C. Practical steps in raising business finance from banks /. Enugu, Nigeria , 1985. 290 p. : ISBN 978-15-6214-5 (pbk.) LC Card 87-118106 DDC 658.1/5224 19
HG3754.5.N6 A38 1985

COMMERCIAL CREDIT - PERU.
Hinojosa Tapia, Juan. La problemática de los almacenes generales de depósito como instituciones financieras no bancarias en el Perú (1970-1983) /. Lima, Perú , 1985. iii, 29, [43] p. : LC Card 86-218257
HG3751.9.P4 H56 1985

COMMERCIAL CRIMES - GREAT BRITAIN - CASE STUDIES.
Sherrard, Michael. London Capital Group Limited (formerly British Bangladesh Trust Limited) . London , 1977. vi, 376 p. : ISBN 0-11-512127-7 (pbk.) LC Card 85-164377
HG4135 .S46 1977

COMMERCIAL CRIMES - ITALY.
Turani, Giuseppe. Briganti e gentiluomini della finanza italiana /. [Milano] , c1987. 394 p. ; ISBN 88-20-00657-X : LC Card 87-168620
HG186.I8 T86 1987

COMMERCIAL CRISES. see **DEPRESSIONS.**

COMMERCIAL DESIGN. see **COMMERCIAL ART.**

Commercial dictionary . Dietl, Clara-Erika. Wiesbaden , c1985-c1987. 2 v. ; ISBN 3-409-19900-4 (v. 1) LC Card 86-160868
HF1002 .D493 1985
*NYPL [*R-Econ. 87-1271]*

COMMERCIAL DOCUMENTS - HISTORY.
McCusker, John J. European bills of entry and marine lists . Cambridge, Mass. , 1985. 75 p. : LC Card 86-673685
HE565.A3 M32 1985

COMMERCIAL EDUCATION. see **BUSINESS EDUCATION.**

COMMERCIAL ETHICS. see **BUSINESS ETHICS.**

COMMERCIAL FINANCE COMPANIES - ITALY.
Bagella, Michele. Gli istituti di credito speciale e il mercato finanziario, 1947-1962 /. Milano, Italy , c1986. 289 p. ; LC Card 86-232526
HG3729.I7 B34 1986

Commercial fisherman. Klein, John F. (John Frederick), 1950- A day in the life of a commercial fisherman /. Mahwah, N.J. , c1988. 32 p. : ISBN 0-8167-1109-7 (lib. bdg.) : LC Card 87-10949 DDC 639/.2/02373 19
HD8039.F65 K57 1988

COMMERCIAL GEOGRAPHY. see **GEOGRAPHY, COMMERCIAL.**

The Commercial greenhouses & associated equipment & agrochemicals market. New York, N.Y. : Frost & Sullivan, c1983. vii, 274 leaves : ill. ; 29 cm. "#A1196." "July 1983." LC Card 87-143480
1. Farm supply industries - United States. 2. Market surveys - United States. I. Frost & Sullivan. II. Title: Commercial greenhouses and associated equipment and agrochemicals market.
HD9475.U52 C66 1983

Commercial greenhouses and associated equipment and agrochemicals market. The Commercial greenhouses & associated equipment & agrochemicals market. New York, N.Y. , c1983. vii, 274 leaves : LC Card 87-143480
HD9475.U52 C66 1983

COMMERCIAL JOURNALISM. see **JOURNALISM, COMMERCIAL.**

COMMERCIAL LAW - ADDRESSES, ESSAYS, LECTURES.
Hundert Jahre Rechts- und Wirtschaftsgeschichte an der Rechts-, Wirtschafts- und Sozialwissenschaftlichen Fakultät der Universität Freiburg =. Freiburg, Schweiz , 1982. 96 p., [6] p. of plates : ISBN 3-7278-0277-4 : LC Card 83-108855 DDC 340 19
K296 .H86 1982 *NYPL [JLD 86-676]*

COMMERCIAL LAW - CONGRESSES.
International Law Symposium (1984 : Cambridge, Cambridgeshire) The United States, transnational business, and the law . New York , c1985. x, 132 p. ; ISBN 0-379-20783-4 LC Card 85-61594 DDC 346/.07 342.67 19
K1004.6 1984 *NYPL [JLF 86-1046]*

Tariff, legal, and credit constraints on East-West commercial relations /. Ottawa , 1975. 101 p. ; LC Card 76-379543 DDC 382.1
K3823.A55 T3 *NYPL [JLD 86-1752]*

COMMERCIAL LAW - UNITED ARAB EMIRATES - ABŪ ẒABY (EMIRATE)
Dalīl rajul al-aʻmāl fī al-ṣināʻah wa-al-tijārah . [Abu Ẓaby] , 1984. 305 p. : LC Card 86-965166
HF5233.A56 D35 1984

COMMERCIAL LAW - UNITED STATES.
Howell, Rate A. The legal environment of business /. Chicago , c1987. xiv, 783 p. : ISBN 0-03-008369-9 LC Card 86-4503 DDC 346.73/07 347.3067 19
KF1600 .H68 1987 *NYPL [JLE 87-911]*

COMMERCIAL LAW - UNITED STATES - CONGRESSES.
International Law Symposium (1984 : Cambridge, Cambridgeshire) The United States, transnational business, and the law . New York , c1985. x, 132 p. ; ISBN 0-379-20783-4 LC Card 85-61594 DDC 346/.07 342.67 19
K1004.6 1984 *NYPL [JLF 86-1046]*

COMMERCIAL LEASES - GERMANY (WEST) - DECISION MAKING - ECONOMETRIC MODELS.
Slotta, Gerd. Die Entscheidung über die

Betriebspacht bzw. Betriebsverpachtung /. Hamburg , c1986. xi, 374 p. : ISBN 3-925630-00-7 LC Card 86-152904
HD39.4 .S56 1986

Commercial lending /. Ruth, George E. Washington, D.C. (1120 Connecticut Ave., N.W., Washington 20036) , c1987. vi, 427 p. : LC Card 87-405117 DDC 332.1/753/0685 19
HG1642.U5 R88 1987

Commercial lending by thrift institutions . Dickerson, Charles S. Philadelphia, Pa. , c1987. 50 p. ; ISBN 0-936742-39-9 (pbk.) LC Card 87-161133 DDC 332.7 19
HG3751 .D53 1987

Commercial liability risk management and insurance / Donald S. Malecki ... [et al.]. 2nd ed. Malvern, Pa. : American Institute for Property and Liability Underwriters, 1986. 2 v. : ill. ; 24 cm. Rev. ed. of: Commercial liability risk management and insurance / Donald S. Malecki, James H. Donaldson, Ronald C. Horn. 1st ed. 1978. "CPCU 4"--Spine. Includes indexes. Bibliography: v. 2, p. 423-426. ISBN 0-89463-049-0 (set) LC Card 86-72708 DDC 368.8/1 19
1. Insurance, Business. 2. Insurance, Liability. 3. Risk management. I. Malecki, Donald S. II. American Institute for Property and Liability Underwriters.
HG8059 .C64 1986

COMMERCIAL LOANS.
Dickerson, Charles S. Commercial lending by thrift institutions . Philadelphia, Pa. , c1987. 50 p. ; ISBN 0-936742-39-9 (pbk.) LC Card 87-161133 DDC 332.7 19
HG3751 .D53 1987

COMMERCIAL LOANS - INDIA.
COMMERCIAL LOANS - STUDY AND TEACHING - UNITED STATES.
Pace, Edmond E. Developing a basic loan training program /. Philadelphia, Pa. , c1987. 108 p. ; ISBN 0-936742-41-0 (pbk.) : LC Card 87-7936 DDC 332.1/753/0683 19
HG1642.U5 P33 1987

COMMERCIAL LOANS - UNITED STATES.
Dickerson, Charles S. Current approaches to grading commercial loans /. Philadelphia, Pa. , c1987. 42 p. ; ISBN 0-936742-43-7 (pbk.) LC Card 87-18458 DDC 332.1/753/0685 19
HG1642.U5 D53 1987

Small business financing . Philadelphia, Pa. , c1987. 118 p. ; ISBN 0-936742-40-2 (pbk.) : LC Card 87-5534 DDC 332.1/753/0685 19
HG3754.5.U6 S6 1987

COMMERCIAL LOANS - UNITED STATES - DIRECTORIES.
Blum, Laurie. Free money for small businesses and entrepreneurs /. New York , c1988. ix, 229 p. ; ISBN 0-471-85803-X : LC Card 87-20978 DDC 658.1/5224 19
HG4027.7 .B58 1988

Commercial newsgathering from space. Washington, DC : Congress of the U. S., Office of Technology Assessment : For sale by the Supt. of Docs., U. S. G.P.O., [1987] ix, 51 p. : ill., maps ; 26 cm. (A technical memorandum) Shipping list no.: 87-319-P. "May 1987." Includes bibliographical references. "OTA-TM-ISC-40"--P. [4] of cover. S/N 052-003-01066-6 Item 1070-M LC Card 87-619818 DDC 070.4/3 19
1. Artificial satellites in telecommunication - United States. 2. Reporters and reporting - United States. 3. Artificial satellites in remote sensing - United States. 4. Remote sensing - Government policy - United States. I. United States. Congress. Office of Technology Assessment. II. Series: Technical memoranda (United States. Congress. Office of Technology Assessment).
HE9721.U5 C65 1987

COMMERCIAL ORGANIZATIONS. see **COMMERCIAL ASSOCIATIONS.**

COMMERCIAL PAPER. see **NEGOTIABLE INSTRUMENTS.**

COMMERCIAL POLICY - ADDRESSES, ESSAYS, LECTURES.
Kuo wai shang yeh yen chiu tzu liao /. [Peking] , 1984. 3, 604 p. ;
*NYPL [*OVY 86-3606]*

Strategic trade policy and the new international economics /. Cambridge, Mass. , c1986. 313 p. ; ISBN 0-262-11112-8 LC Card 86-2758 DDC 382/.3 19
HF1411 .S82 1986 *NYPL [JLE 86-3896]*

COMMERCIAL POLICY - CONGRESSES.
Free trade in the world economy . Boulder , 1987. p. cm. ISBN 0-8133-0596-9 LC Card 87-20148 DDC 382.7/1 19
HF1703 .F74 1987

International trade and the consumer . Paris [Washington, D.C. , 1986. 296 p. ; ISBN 92-64-12813-1 (pbk.) : LC Card 86-216097 DDC 382/.3 19
HF1410.5 .I585 1986 *NYPL [JLE 87-1541]*

Schmidtchen, Dieter. Property rights, Freiheit und Wettbewerbspolitik /. Tübingen , 1983. 71 p. ; ISBN 3-16-344630-2 (Deut. Bibl.) LC Card 84-100421
HF1410.5 .S36 1983

Varna Forum (2nd : 1985 : Varna, Bulgaria) Varna Forum II . [Varna?] [s.n.] [1985] 166 p. ; LC Card 86-220415 DDC 382/.091713/01717 19
HF1410.5 .V37 1985

COMMERCIAL POLICY - ECONOMETRIC MODELS.
Coloma C., Fernando. Los efectos de una desgravación arancelaria en el contexto de una economía con movilidad imperfecta de trabajo /. Santiago , 1985. 46 leaves : LC Card 85-203579
HF1713 .C618 1985

COMMERCIAL POLICY - ITALY.
Quale strategia per l'industria? . Bologna , c1986. 221 p. : ISBN 88-15-00975-2 : LC Card 86-182300
HC310.I53 Q35 1986

COMMERCIAL POLICY - MATHEMATICAL MODELS - CONGRESSES.
General equilibrium trade policy modeling /. Cambridge, Mass. , c1986. vii, 360 p. : ISBN 0-262-19245-4 LC Card 85-19144 DDC 382/.3/0724 19
HF1410.5 .G46 1986 *NYPL [JLE 86-4456]*

COMMERCIAL PRODUCTS - AFRICA, SOUTHERN - STATISTICS.
Consumer markets in Southern Africa. London , 1986. 173 p., [1] p. of plates : ISBN 0-86338-095-6 LC Card 87-160745 DDC 330.968/063 19
HF3900 .C66 1986

COMMERCIAL PRODUCTS - AUSTRIA.
Hutter, Monika, 1950- Die Warenstruktur des Aussenhandels . Frankfurt am Main , New York , c1987. 216 p. ; ISBN 3-8204-8810-3 LC Card 87-407938 DDC 382/.09436 19
HF3546.5 .H87 1987

COMMERCIAL PRODUCTS - BOLIVIA - CLASSIFICATION.
Código de productos y materias primas /. La Paz, Bolivia , 1981. 129 leaves ; LC Card 85-129059
HF1044.B5 C63 1981

COMMERCIAL PRODUCTS - BRAZIL.
Neustadt, Peter. Wachstum und Strukturwandlungen Brasiliens in ihrer Bedeutung für die strategische Marketingplanung von Konsumgüterunternehmungen /. Diessenhofen , cop. 1979. ix, 463 p. : ISBN 3-7253-0092-5 : LC Card 80-469750
HF5415.12.B7 N48 1979
NYPL [JLD 80-3357]

COMMERCIAL PRODUCTS - CHILE.
Ffrench-Davis, Ricardo. Origen y destino de las exportaciones chilenas, 1965-80 /. Santiago, Chile , 1981. 22, 6, [27] leaves ; LC Card 83-182100
HF3416.5 .F46 1981b

COMMERCIAL PRODUCTS - CLASSIFICATION.
Classification by broad economic categories . New York , 1986. x, 68 p. ; ISBN 92-1-161276-4 (pbk.) LC Card 87-401426 DDC 338/.02/012 19
HF1041 .C53 1986

United Nations. Statistical Office. Standard international trade classification revision 3 /. New York , 1986. xvi, 106, 31, 25 p. ; ISBN 92-1-161265-9 (pbk.) LC Card 86-226177 DDC 338/.02/012 19
HF1041 .U56 1986

COMMERCIAL PRODUCTS - DEVELOPING COUNTRIES - CLASSIFICATION.
Handbook of state trading organizations of developing countries =. New York , 1985. clxxxix, 542 p. : ISBN 92-1-012014-0 (pbk.) LC Card 86-233995
HF1009.7.D44 H35 1985

COMMERCIAL PRODUCTS - ECUADOR - DIRECTORIES.
Directorio nacional de pequeñas industrias . [Quito] , 1985. 264 p. ; LC Card 86-192239
HF3433 .D59 1985

COMMERCIAL PRODUCTS - FRANCE - TERMINOLOGY.
Tarifs routiers de marchandises. Paris [1986] 201 p. ; ISBN 2-7212-0295-2 LC Card 87-123802
HE5668.A6 T37 1986

COMMERCIAL PRODUCTS - GERMANY, WEST.
Kornhardt, Ullrich. Entwicklungstendenzen im Konsumgüterhandwerk /. Göttingen , 1986. 385 p. : ISBN 3-509-01418-9 LC Card 86-197187
HD2341.A1 G6 Bd. 37 HD2346.G3

COMMERCIAL PRODUCTS - GERMANY (WEST) - TESTING.
Warentest und Konsument . Frankfurt/Main , New York , c1984. 268 p. : ISBN 3-593-33295-7 LC Card 84-150919
HF1040.9.G3 W37 1984

COMMERCIAL PRODUCTS - INDIA.
India. Planning Commission. Programme Evaluation Organisation. Evaluation report on essential supplies programme. New Delhi , 1985. vii, 121 p. ; LC Card 87-902422 DDC 381/.41/0954 19
HF1040.9.I4 I46 1985

Raza, Moonis. Transport geography of India . New Delhi , 1986. xii, 299 p. : LC Card 86-903251 DDC 380.5/0954 19
HE3298 .R39 1986

COMMERCIAL PRODUCTS - INDIA - DICTIONARIES.
The Wealth of India . New Delhi , c1985- v. <1- > : ISBN 81-85038-00-7 (set) LC Card 87-900740 DDC 333.7/0954 19
HF1054.I5 W4 1985

COMMERCIAL PRODUCTS - MEXICO - HISTORY - 19TH CENTURY.
Alvarado Gómez, Armando. Principales productos del comercio exterior mexicano del siglo XIX /. México, D.F. , 1985. v. <1 > ; LC Card 87-401206 DDC 382/.0972 19
HF3236 .A5 1985

COMMERCIAL PRODUCTS - POLAND - CLASSIFICATION.
Nomenklatura artykułów i usług do badania spożycia (NAS). Warszawa , 1980. 87 p. ; LC Card 81-109132
HF1044.P6 N66 1980

COMMERCIAL PRODUCTS - QUALITY. see **QUALITY CONTROL; QUALITY OF PRODUCTS.**

COMMERCIAL PRODUCTS - SOVIET UNION.
Kostin, Leonid Alekseevich. Proizvodstvo tovarov narodnogo potrebleniia . Moskva , 1980. 212 p. ; LC Card 87-107901
HF1040.9.S65 K67 1980

Levin, A. I. (Aleksandr Ivanovich) Tovarnoe obrashchenie . Moskva , 1980. 286 p. ; LC Card 81-141540
HF1040.9.S65 L48 1980

COMMERCIAL PRODUCTS - TESTING.
Fritz, Wolfgang, Dipl.-Kfm. Warentest und Konsumgüter-Marketing . Wiesbaden , c1984. 596 p. : ISBN 3-409-13600-2 LC Card 84-207784
HF5415.2 .F75 1984

COMMERCIAL PRODUCTS - THAILAND - DIRECTORIES.
Thailand, its economic products. [Bangkok] , 1961, 1962 printing. 68 p. : LC Card 82-122480
HF1040.9.T5 T53 1962

COMMERCIAL PRODUCTS - YUGOSLAVIA.
Review of exporters and importers of Yugoslavia . Zagreb , 1965. ca. 650 p. : LC Card 84-149403
HF3732.3 .R46 1965

Commercial real estate : how to buy, build, manage, sell, and profit from it / edited by Jack Corgan. Dallas, Tex. : Taylor Pub. Co., c1986. 219 p. : ill. ; 24 cm. ISBN 0-87833-459-9 : LC

Card 85-27108 DDC 332.63/243 19
1. Commercial buildings. 2. Real estate business. I. Corgan, Jack.
HD1393.25 .C65 1986 ***NYPL [JLE 86-4267]***

COMMERCIAL RECORDS. see **BUSINESS RECORDS.**

COMMERCIAL ROUTES. see **TRADE ROUTES.**

COMMERCIAL SCHOOLS. see **BUSINESS EDUCATION.**

COMMERCIAL STATISTICS - COMPUTER PROGRAMS.
O'Keeffe, Linda. Statistical packages for the IBM PC family /. New York , c1986. x, 162 p. : ISBN 0-07-056320-9 : LC Card 85-18213 DDC 658/.055365 19
HF1017 .O39 1986 ***NYPL [JSE 86-1876]***

COMMERCIAL STATISTICS - DATA PROCESSING.
Bond, Kenneth M. Essential business statistics . Boston , c1988. xiii, 332 p. : ISBN 0-534-91530-2 LC Card 87-25652 DDC 519.5/028/55369 19
HF1017 .B63 1988

Bowerman, Bruce L. Computer modeling for business and industry /. New York , c1984. vii, 219 p. : ISBN 0-8247-7296-2 LC Card 84-17063 DDC 519.5/0285425 19
HF1017 .B655 1984 ***NYPL [JSE 86-623]***

Kilpatrick, Michael, 1952- Business statistics using Lotus 1-2-3 /. New York , c1987. ix, 326 p. : ISBN 0-471-84525-6 (pbk.) : LC Card 86-24737 DDC 519.5/028/55369 19
HF1017 .K55 1987

Levine, David M., 1946- Using Minitab with Basic business statistics /. Englewood Cliffs, N.J. , c1986. viii, 160 p. : ISBN 0-13-057779-0 (pbk.) LC Card 87-400304 DDC 519.5/028/55369 19
HF1017 .L425 1986

Ross, Steven S. SPREADSTAT . New York , c1988. p. cm. ISBN 0-07-053909-X : LC Card 87-22811 DDC 005.36/9 19
HF1017 .R67 1988

COMMERCIAL STATISTICS - DATA PROCESSING - HANDBOOKS, MANUALS, ETC.
Miller, Robert B. (Robert Burnham), 1942- Minitab handbook for business and economics /. Boston , c1988. x, 331 p. : ISBN 0-87150-092-2 (pbk.) LC Card 86-32830 DDC 519.5/02855369 19
HF1017 .M494 1988

COMMERCIAL TREATIES.
Pfeiffer, Gabrielle. Mountains of butter, lakes of milk . Genève , 1986. 78, [4] p. : LC Card 87-109400 DDC 382/.417 19
HD9275.A2 P48 1986

Commercializing SDI technologies / edited by Stewart Nozette & Robert Lawrence Kuhn. New York : Praeger, 1987. xvi, 246 p. : ill. ; 25 cm. Includes bibliographies and index. ISBN 0-275-92332-0 (alk. paper) : LC Card 87-18333 DDC 338.4/762 19
1. High technology industries - United States. 2. Strategic Defense Initiative. I. Nozette, Stewart, 1957-. II. Kuhn, Robert Lawrence.
HC110.H53 C65 1987

COMMERCIALS, TELEVISION. see **TELEVISION ADVERTISING.**

Il commercio estero delle tecnologie, dei progetti industriali e dei know how /. Foglio, Antonio, 1940- Milano, Italy , 1984. 269 p. ; LC Card 86-102943
HC79.H53 F64 1984

Commercio in Lombardia / a cura di Giorgio Taborelli ; saggi di Marica Milanesi ... [et al.] ; fotografie di Giorgio Majno. Milano : Mediocredito lombardo, c1986- v. <1 > : col. ill. ; 35 cm. Includes bibliographies. LC Card 87-158732
1. Lombardy (Italy) - Commerce - History. 2. Lombardy (Italy) - Industries - History. I. Taborelli, Giorgio. II. Milanesi, Marica, 1947-.
HF3589.L65 C65 1986

Commission "Avenir économique de la Belgique." L'Avenir économique de la Belgique . [Bruxelles , 1981] 155 p. ; LC Card 87-672443
HC315 .A93x 1981

Commission de la santé et de la sécurité du travail du Québec. Caoutchouc et produits en matières plastiques au Québec . [Québec] , 1984. 249 p. : ISBN 2-550-10690-3 LC Card 85-155214 DDC 363.1/196684/09714 19
HD7269.R92 C23 1984

Commission de lutte contre l'inflation. see **Canada. Anti-inflation Board.**

Commission des Communautés européennes. see **Commission of the European Communities.**

Commission européenne pour l'étude de l'opinion publique et des marchés. see **Esomar.**

Commission of the European Communities. (Old Catalog form: European Communities. Commission)

Commission of the European Communities. Bureau de recherches d'analyses et d'études coordonnées. La Formation des syndicalistes aux nouvelles technologies de l'information et à leur introduction dans les entreprises . Luxembourg , Washington, D.C. , 1986. 52, 13, 7 p. : ISBN 92-825-5881-9 : LC Card 86-179989
HD6331.2.E86 F67 1986

COMMISSION OF THE EUROPEAN COMMUNITIES. COMMUNITY BUREAU OF REFERENCE - CONGRESSES.
Lauer, Karl Friedrich. Das Referenzbüro der Gemeinschaften /. [Dortmund?] , 1976. 76 p. ; LC Card 85-241026
HD30 .A7 Heft 171 T59.A1

Commission of the European Communities. Directorate-General of Information. A Community research policy for development. Brussels : Commission of the European Communities, Directorate-General for Information, [1983] 21 p. ; 30 cm. (Europe information. Development) Cover title. "March 1983." "DE 44." "X/114/83." LC Card 85-166173 DDC 338.91/4/01724 19
1. European Economic Community - Economic assistance. 2. European Economic Community - Technical assistance. 3. Economic assistance - Developing countries. 4. Technical assistance - Developing countries. I. Title. II. Series.
HC60 .C584 1983

Commission of the European Communities. Information, Directorate-General on. see **Commission of the European Communities. Directorate-General of Information.**

Commission of the European Communities. Joint Research Centre.

COMMISSION OF THE EUROPEAN COMMUNITIES. JOINT RESEARCH CENTRE.

Commission of the European Communities. Monetary Committee. Die Währungspolitik in den Ländern der Europäischen Wirtschaftsgemeinschaft . Luxembourg , Washington, D.C. , 1972. 451 p. ; LC Card 85-116654
HG930.5 .W34 1972

Commission on California State Government Organization and Economy. A study of the organization and coordination of electric energy planning and electric utility regulation in California : a report of the Commission on California State Government Organization and Economy. [Sacramento] (11th & L Bldg., Suite 550, Sacramento 95814) : The Commission, [1984] 3, x leaves, 54 p. ; 28 cm. "February 1984." LC Card 85-623154 DDC 333.79/32/09794 19
1. Electric utilities - Government policy - California. I. Title.
HD9685.U6 C325 1984

Commission régionale du plan pour le développement des réseaux des télécommunications en Afrique. Plan général de développement du réseau régional en Afrique =. Genève , 1983. 134 p. : ISBN 92-71-02066-9 LC Card 85-146412
HE8465 .P54 1983

COMMISSIONS OF INQUIRY. see **GOVERNMENTAL INVESTIGATIONS.**

Commit to quality /. Townsend, Patrick L. New York , c1986. xvii, 189 p. : ISBN 0-471-83953-1 LC Card 85-29639 DDC 658.5/62 19
HD66 .T65 1986 ***NYPL [JLE 86-3004]***

Committee for Economic Development. The New economic role of American states . New York , 1988. x, 370 p. ; ISBN 0-19-505003-7 LC Card 87-12499 DDC 338.973 19
HC106.8 .N495 1988

Committee for Economic Development of Australia. Niland, John R. Control, consensus, or chaos? . Sydney , Boston , 1985. xiv, 330 p. : ISBN 0-86861-447-5 (pbk.) LC Card 85-70461 DDC 331.89/0994 19
HD8846.5 .N55 1985 ***NYPL [JLD 87-354]***

Committee for Economic Development. Research and Policy Committee.
Leadership for dynamic state economies : a statement / by the Research and Policy Committee of the Committee for Economic Development. New York, N.Y. : Committee for Economic Development, 1986. xii, 104 p. ; 27 cm. Includes bibliographical references. ISBN 0-87186-782-6 LC Card 86-20760 DDC 338.973 19
1. Industry and state - United States - States. 2. Intergovernmental fiscal relations - United States. 3. United States - Economic policy. I. Title.
HC103 .C734 1986 ***NYPL [JLF 86-1832]***

Work and change : labor market adjustment policies in a competitive world : a statement / by the Research and Policy Committee of the Committee for Economic Development. New York, N.Y. : Committee for Economic Development, 1987 printing. iv, 76 p. : ill. ; 28 cm. Bibliography: p. 59-66. ISBN 0-87186-083-X (pbk.) : LC Card 87-694 DDC 331.12/042/0973 19
1. Manpower policy - United States. 2. Manpower planning - United States. 3. Competition, International. I. Title.
HD5724 .C6647 1987

Committee of Industrial Organizations. see **Congress of Industrial Organizations.**

Committee on African Development Strategies (U. S.) Compact for African development : report of the Committee on African Development Strategies : a joint project of the Council on Foreign Relations and the Overseas Development Council. Berkeley, CA (2120 Berkeley Way, Berkeley 94720) : University of California Press, [1985] 24 p. : ill. (some col.) ; 28 cm. Cover title. LC Card 86-200473 DDC 338.967 19
1. Africa, Sub-Saharan - Economic policy. 2. Economic assistance, American - Africa, Sub-Saharan. 3. Food relief - Africa, Sub-Saharan. I. Council on Foreign Relations. II. Overseas Development Council. III. Title.
HC800 .C645 1985

Committee on Science, Engineering, and Public Policy (U. S.). Panel on Technology and Employment. Technology and employment . Washington, D.C. , 1987. xiii, 225 p. : ISBN 0-309-03744-1 (pbk.) : LC Card 87-42807 DDC 331.12/0973 19
HD6331.2.U5 T43 1987

Committee on Science, Engineering, and Public Policy (U. S.). Panel on the Impact of National Security Controls on International Technology Transfer. Balancing the national interest : U. S. national security export controls and global economic competition / Panel on the Impact of National Security Controls on International Technology Transfer, Committee on Science, Engineering, and Public Policy, National Academy of Sciences, National Academy of Engineering, Institute of Medicine. Washington, D.C. : National Academy Press, 1987. xiii, 321 p. : ill. ; 24 cm. Bibliography: p. 297-309. Includes index. ISBN 0-309-03738-7 LC Card 87-60020 DDC 337.73 19
1. United States - Foreign economic relations. 2. Technology transfer - Government policy - United States. 3. United States - National security. 4. Export controls - United States. I. Title.
HF1456 .C65 1987

Committee on Science, Technology, and Regional Economic Development. The impact of science and technology on regional economic development; an assessment of national policies regarding research and development in the context of regional economic development. Washington, National Academy of Sciences, 1969. xi, 111 p. 23 cm. Bibliography: p. 98-105. LC Card 72-604009 DDC 338.973
1. Research - Economic aspects - United States. 2.

Regional planning - United States. I. Title.
HC110.R4 C65 1969b *NYPL [JLE 87-898]*

Committee on Studies for Cooperation in Development in South Asia. Ghafoor, Abdul. Development of human resources . Islamabad [1984] v, ii leaves, 99 p., v, ii leaves ; LC Card 85-932024 DDC 331.11/09549/1 19
HD5819 .G48 1984

Committee on Taxation, Resources and Economic Development. State and local finance . Madison, Wis. , 1983. x, 243 p. : ISBN 0-299-09340-9 : LC Card 83-47757 DDC 336.73 19
HJ275 .S675 1983 *NYPL [JLE 86-4001]*

COMMITTEES.
Bacon, Jeremy. Board committees in European companies /. New York, N.Y. , c1986. vii, 16 p. ; ISBN 0-8237-0325-8 (pbk.) LC Card 86-207711 DDC 658.4/22/094 19
HD2745 .B14 1986

Committees & consultation : 1986-87 service directory. Tallahassee, Fla. (325 W. College Ave., Tallahassee 32314) : Florida Institute of Certified Public Accountants, c1986. 76 p. : ill. ; 28 cm. Cover title. LC Card 87-109390 DDC 657/.025/759 19
1. Florida Institute of Certified Public Accountants - Directories. I. Florida Institute of Certified Public Accountants. II. Title: Committees and consultation.
HF5616.U6 F63 1986

Committees and consultation. Committees & consultation . Tallahassee, Fla. (325 W. College Ave., Tallahassee 32314) , c1986. 76 p. : LC Card 87-109390 DDC 657/.025/759 19
HF5616.U6 F63 1986

COMMITTEES IN MANAGEMENT. see **MANAGEMENT COMMITTEES.**

COMMODITY CONTROL.
Atsé, David. Commodity futures trading and international market stabilization /. Uppsala , Stockholm, Sweden , 1986. 151 p. : ISBN 91-554-1961-5 (pbk.) LC Card 87-148645 DDC 330 s 332.64/42 19
HB51 .S7 no. 10 HG6046

Delmas, Philippe. La stabilisation des prix des matières premières . Paris , 1983. vii, 359 p. : ISBN 2-7178-0657-1 : LC Card 84-116258
HF1051 .D38 1983

MacBean, Alasdair I. Commodity policies . London , New York , c1987. 438 p. : ISBN 0-7099-1708-2 LC Card 87-9069 DDC 382/.3/091724 19
HF1428 .M29 1987

COMMODITY CONTROL - DEVELOPING COUNTRIES.
Herrmann, Roland. The compensatory financing system of the International Monetary Fund . Kiel, West-Germany , 1983. iii, 85 p. ; ISBN 3-922553-18-4 (pbk.) LC Card 83-227524 DDC 332.1/52 19
HG3881.5.I58 H47 1983 *NYPL [JLD 97-7]*

COMMODITY EXCHANGES - ADDRESSES, ESSAYS, LECTURES.
Firms and markets . London , c1986. xiii, 271 p. : ISBN 0-7099-2446-1
NYPL [JLD 86-2134]

COMMODITY EXCHANGES - ARGENTINA - ROSARIO ((SANTE FE) - HISTORY.
De Marco, Miguel Ángel. 1884-1984, los cien años de la Bolsa de Comercio de Rosario /. [S.l. , 1984?] (Rosario : Escuela de Artes Gráficas del Colegio San José de Rosario) 167 p. : LC Card 87-115398 DDC 332.64/28224 19
HG5320.R67 D4 1984

COMMODITY EXCHANGES - BIBLIOGRAPHY.
Woy, James B. Commodity futures trading . New York , 1976. x, 206 p. ; ISBN 0-8352-0899-0 LC Card 76-23430 DDC 016.3326/44
Z7164.C83 W69 HG6046
NYPL [JLE 86-473]

COMMODITY EXCHANGES - BRAZIL.
Pereira, Eduardo Novo da Costa. Bolsa de commodities . Rio de Janeiro, RJ , 1985. ix, 69 p. ; LC Card 86-129753
HG6024.B7 P47 1985

COMMODITY EXCHANGES - BRAZIL - SÃO PAULO.
Tsunechiro, Alfredo. O desempenho dos mercados a termo . São Paulo , 1986. xi, 123 p. : LC Card 87-404554 DDC 332.64/4 19
HG6046 .T75 1986

COMMODITY EXCHANGES - CONGRESSES.
The Industrial organization of futures markets /. Lexington, Mass. , c1984. vii, 312 p. : ISBN 0-669-06836-5 LC Card 83-48029 DDC 332.64/4 19
HG6024.A3 I52 1984 *NYPL [JLE 86-4471]*

COMMODITY EXCHANGES - DICTIONARIES.
Woy, James B. Commodity futures trading . New York , 1976. x, 206 p. ; ISBN 0-8352-0899-0 LC Card 76-23430 DDC 016.3326/44
Z7164.C83 W69 HG6046
NYPL [JLE 86-473]

COMMODITY EXCHANGES - HANDBOOKS, MANUALS, ETC.
Handbook of financial markets . Homewood, Ill. , c1986. xix, 785 p. : ISBN 0-87094-600-5 LC Card 85-71920 DDC 332.6/78 19
HG4527 .H25 1986
*NYPL [*R-Econ 86-3815]*

Handbook of financial markets--securities, options, futures /. Homewood, Ill. , c1981. xxiii, 794 p. : ISBN 0-87094-216-6 LC Card 80-70448 DDC 332.6/78 19
HG4527 .H25 *NYPL [JLE 86-1500]*

COMMODITY EXCHANGES - LAW AND LEGISLATION - UNITED STATES.
Futures markets . Washington, D.C. , c1985. xiii, 325 p. : ISBN 0-8447-3592-2 LC Card 85-26705 DDC 332.64/4 19
HG6049 .F86 1985 *NYPL [JLE 86-1532]*

COMMODITY EXCHANGES - LAW AND LEGISLATION - UNITED STATES - HISTORY.
Markham, Jerry W. The history of commodity futures trading and its regulation /. New York , 1987. xiv, 305 p. ; ISBN 0-275-92313-4 (alk. paper) : LC Card 86-25246 DDC 332.64/4 19
HG6049 .M37 1986 *NYPL [JLE 87-819]*

COMMODITY EXCHANGES - MATHEMATICAL MODELS.
Ghosh, S. Stabilizing speculative commodity markets /. Oxford [Oxfordshire] , New York , 1987. xiii, 437 p. : ISBN 0-19-828472-1 : LC Card 86-32654 DDC 332.64/4 19
HG6046 .G485 1987

COMMODITY EXCHANGES - STATISTICAL METHODS.
Kaufman, Perry J. The new commodity trading systems and methods /. New York , c1987. xvi, 521 p. : ISBN 0-471-87879-0 LC Card 87-6073 DDC 332.64/4 19
HG6036 .K38 1987

COMMODITY EXCHANGES - UNITED STATES.
Black, Deborah G. Success and failure of futures contracts . New York, N.Y. (90 Trinity Pl., New York 10006) [c1986] 70 p. ; LC Card 87-129777 DDC 332.64/4 19
HG6046 .B52 1986

Futures markets . Washington, D.C. , c1985. xiii, 325 p. : ISBN 0-8447-3592-2 LC Card 85-26705 DDC 332.64/4 19
HG6049 .F86 1985 *NYPL [JLE 86-1532]*

Hadady, R. Earl (Robert Earl), 1920- Winning with the insiders /. West Palm Beach, Fla. , c1987. vi, 115 p. : ISBN 0-9613048-8-X : LC Card 87-40003 DDC 332.64/4 19
HG4910 .H18 1987

Speculating in futures. [Chicago] , c1986. v, 65 p. : LC Card 87-100478 DDC 332.64/4 19
HG6046 .S63 1986

Stocks, bonds, options, futures . New York, N.Y. [Englewood Cliffs, N.J.] , c1987. 332 p. : ISBN 0-13-846718-8 : LC Card 87-11324 DDC 332.6/78 19
HG4921 .S7945 1987

Trading in soybean complex futures /. [Chicago] , c1986. v, 53 p. ; LC Card 87-101090 DDC 332.64/4 19
HG6047.S6 T73 1986

Weiss, David M., 1938- After the trade is made . New York, N.Y. , c1986. xii, 436 p. : ISBN 0-13-018581-7 : LC Card 85-30997 DDC 332.64/273 19
HG4910 .W365 1986 *NYPL [JLE 86-4304]*

COMMODITY EXCHANGES - UNITED STATES - HISTORY.
Markham, Jerry W. The history of commodity futures trading and its regulation /. New York , 1987. xiv, 305 p. ; ISBN 0-275-92313-4 (alk. paper) : LC Card 86-25246 DDC 332.64/4 19
HG6049 .M37 1986 *NYPL [JLE 87-819]*

Commodity futures trading . Woy, James B. New York , 1976. x, 206 p. ; ISBN 0-8352-0899-0 LC Card 76-23430 DDC 016.3326/44
Z7164.C83 W69 HG6046
NYPL [JLE 86-473]

Commodity futures trading and international market stabilization /. Atsé, David. Uppsala , Stockholm, Sweden , 1986. 151 p. : ISBN 91-554-1961-5 (pbk.) LC Card 87-148645 DDC 330 s 332.64/42 19
HB51 .S7 no. 10 HG6046

Commodity policies . MacBean, Alasdair I. London , New York , c1987. 438 p. : ISBN 0-7099-1708-2 LC Card 87-9069 DDC 382/.3/091724 19
HF1428 .M29 1987

Commodity Research Bureau (Chicago, Ill.) Understanding the securities markets . Jersey City, NJ (75 Montgomery St., Jersey City 07302) , c1986. 36 p. ; LC Card 87-130670 DDC 332.63/2 19
HG4910 .U53 1986

Commodity Research Bureau (New York, N.Y.) Understanding the futures markets. New York, NY (100 Church St., Suite 1850 New York 10007) , c1987. 61 p. ; LC Card 87-129996 DDC 332.64/4 19
HG6024.A3 U64 1987

Commodity taxation and India's fiscal policy /. Agarwala, N. L. (Natwar Lal) New Delhi , c1985. 294 p. ; LC Card 85-904360 DDC 339.5/25/0954 19
HJ5715.I4 A73 1985 *NYPL [JLD 87-610]*

Commodity trade (by sea) statistics : results of the maritime transport study for the years 1972-1975 : analysis by type of goods moved during 1972-1975 between regions of the world / Department of International Economic and Social Affairs, Statistical Office. New York : United Nations, 1980. v, 396 p. ; 28 cm. (Statistical papers. Series D . vol. 23-26, no. 2) Tables. "ST/ESA/STAT/SER.D/72, 73, 74, 75." "United Nations publication. Sales no. E.80.XVII.14"--T.p. verso. LC Card 87-112992 DDC 387.5/55/021 19
1. Shipping - Statistics. 2. Commerce - Statistics. I. United Nations. Statistical Office. II. Title: Results of the maritime transport study for the years 1972-1975. III. Series: Statistical papers. Series D , v. 23-26, no. 2.
HE562.8 .C667 1980

Commodore sixty-four/one hundred twenty-eight graphics and sound programming. Krute, Stan. Commodore 64/128 graphics and sound programming /. Blue Ridge Summit, PA , 1986. xv, 253 p. : ISBN 0-8306-0440-5 : LC Card 85-14694 DDC 006.6/765 19
T385 .K77 1986 *NYPL [JSE 87-266]*

COMMODORE 128 (COMPUTER) - PROGRAMMING.
Krute, Stan. Commodore 64/128 graphics and sound programming /. Blue Ridge Summit, PA , 1986. xv, 253 p. : ISBN 0-8306-0440-5 : LC Card 85-14694 DDC 006.6/765 19
T385 .K77 1986 *NYPL [JSE 87-266]*

COMMODORE 64 (COMPUTER) - PROGRAMMING.
Krute, Stan. Commodore 64/128 graphics and sound programming /. Blue Ridge Summit, PA , 1986. xv, 253 p. : ISBN 0-8306-0440-5 : LC Card 85-14694 DDC 006.6/765 19
T385 .K77 1986 *NYPL [JSE 87-266]*

Commodore 64/128 graphics and sound programming /. Krute, Stan. Blue Ridge Summit, PA , 1986. xv, 253 p. : ISBN 0-8306-0440-5 : LC Card 85-14694 DDC 006.6/765 19
T385 .K77 1986 *NYPL [JSE 87-266]*

The Common agricultural policy and the Third World : a conference / sponsored by CAFOD ... [et al.], London, 23 June 1986. London : Catholic Institute for International Relations, 1986. 97 p. : ill. ; 21 cm. Includes bibliographical references. CONTENTS. - The reform of the CAP and the developing countries / Alan Matthews -- Food strategies for tomorrow / Susan

George -- The EEC and ACP / Sipke Brouwer, Marc Franco, Edwin Carrington -- Botswana's beef industry and the CAP / Michael Hubbard -- The CAP and the oilseeds economies of the developing countries / Geoffrey Bastin -- The EEC and the world sugar crisis / Belinda Coote -- Agriculture in the new GATT round / Murray Cobban -- Summary of the debate / Colm Regan. ISBN 0-946848-79-3 (pbk.) : LC Card 87-150069 DDC 338.1/81/094 19
1. Produce trade - Government policy - European Economic Community countries - Congresses. 2. Produce trade - Developing countries - Congresses. 3. European Economic Community countries - Foreign economic relations - Developing countries - Congresses. 4. Developing countries - Foreign economic relations - European Economic Community countries - Congresses. 5. Agriculture and state - European Economic Community countries - Congresses. I. Catholic Fund for Overseas Development. II. Catholic Institute for International Relations.
HD9015.E82 C665 1986

Common agricultural policy of the European Community and implications for U. S. agricultural trade. Japanese import barriers to U. S. agricultural exports and the Common agricultural policy of the European Community and implications for U. S. agricultural trade . Washington , 1986. vii, 65 p. : LC Card 87-601384 DDC 382/.5/0952 19
HF1601 .J363 1986

COMMON CARRIERS. see **CARRIERS.**

Common fate, common bond . Mitter, Swasti, 1939- London , Wolfeboro, N.H., USA , 1986. 184 p. : ISBN 0-7453-0026-X (pbk.) : LC Card 87-101525 DDC 331.4/2 19
HD6053 .M54 1986

COMMON GOOD.
The Common good and U. S. capitalism /. Lanham, MD , c1987. viii, 425 p. ; ISBN 0-8191-6364-3 (alk. paper) : LC Card 87-8334 DDC 306/.36/0973 19
HD60.5.U5 C665 1987

The Common good and U. S. capitalism / Oliver F. Williams and John W. Houck, editors. Lanham, MD : University Press of America, c1987. viii, 425 p. ; 24 cm. "Co-published by arrangement with the Notre Dame Center for Ethics and Religious Values in Business"--T.p. verso. Includes bibliographies and index. ISBN 0-8191-6364-3 (alk. paper) : LC Card 87-8334 DDC 306/.36/0973 19
1. Industry - Social aspects - United States. 2. Capitalism - United States - Moral and ethical aspects. 3. Business ethics. 4. Common good. I. Williams, Oliver F. II. Houck, John W., 1951-. III. Title: Common good and United States capitalism.
HD60.5.U5 C665 1987

Common good and United States capitalism. The Common good and U. S. capitalism /. Lanham, MD , c1987. viii, 425 p. ; ISBN 0-8191-6364-3 (alk. paper) : LC Card 87-8334 DDC 306/.36/0973 19
HD60.5.U5 C665 1987

The common people of Great Britain . Harrison, J. F. C. (John Fletcher Clews) Bloomington , 1985. 445 p. : ISBN 0-253-20357-0 (pbk.) LC Card 84-48820 DDC 305.5/62/0942 19
HD8388 .H36 1985 ***NYPL [JLD 86-3656]***

The common-sense mortgage . Miller, Peter G. New York , c1987. xvi, 285 p. ; ISBN 0-06-055081-3 : LC Card 86-46265 DDC 332.7/22 19
HG2040 .M54 1987

Common sense real estate /. Ochsner, Neal. New York , c1987. xi, 239 p. : ISBN 0-8050-0509-9 LC Card 87-8420 DDC 332.63/24 19
HD1382.5 .O36 1987

Common stock price histories, 1910-1986. Morristown, N.J. : WIT Financial Publishers, c1987. 208 p. : all ill. ; 28 cm. ISBN 0-9618454-0-6 (pbk.) LC Card 87-158025 DDC 332.63/222/0973 19
1. Stocks - Prices - United States - History - Charts, diagrams, etc. I. WIT Financial Publishers.
HG4916 .C65 1987

COMMONS - ECUADOR - HISTORY.
González S., Víctor A. Las tierras comunales en el Ecuador /. Guayaquil, Ecuador , 1982. 109 p. ; LC Card 87-672596
HD1289.E2 G66x 1982

COMMONS (SOCIAL ORDER) see **LABOR AND LABORING CLASSES; MIDDLE CLASSES.**

Commonwealth Association of Surveying and Land Economy.
The management and development of land and seabed resources . London [1985] 139 p. : ISBN 0-903577-29-1 (pbk.) LC Card 86-104896 DDC 333.7 19
HD105 .M36 1985

The Management and development of natural resources . London [1985] 192 p. : ISBN 0-903577-33-X (pbk.) LC Card 86-206154 DDC 333.7 19
HC13 .M35 1985

Commonwealth Geographical Bureau. Remote sensing and tropical land management /. [New York] , c1986. xii, 365 p., [16] p. of plates : ISBN 0-471-90889-4 : LC Card 85-17932 DDC 333.73/13/028 19
HD108.8 .R45 1986 ***NYPL [JLE 87-943]***

Commonwealth Scientific and Industrial Research Organization (Australia). Division of Groundwater Research. National Workshop on Urban Water Demand Management (1986 : Alexander Library, Perth Cultural Centre) Working papers for the National Workshop on Urban Water Demand Management . Leederville, WA [1986] xii, 657 p. : LC Card 87-119946 DDC 333.91/2/0994 19
HD4465.A8 N37 1986

COMMONWEALTH, THE. see **POLITICAL SCIENCE; STATE, THE.**

Communal agrarian cooperative societies . Chilivumbo, Alifeyo. Lusaka [1986] iii, 134 p. ; LC Card 86-981399 DDC 334/.683/096894 19
HD1491.Z35 C45 1986

COMMUNAL LIVING - DENMARK.
Nørrung, Per. The producing commune /. Aalborg Ø., Denmark , 1985. 39 p. ; ISBN 87-88353-11-7 (pbk.) LC Card 87-100060 DDC 334/.6/09489 19
HD3209.A4 N67 1985

Communauté des radios publiques de langue française. La Guerre des ondes . Paris , Lausanne , c1985. 382 p. : ISBN 2-601-00475-4 (Payot) ***NYPL [MWGK (France) 87-550]***

Communauté économique européenne. see **European Economic Community.**

COMMUNES, CHRISTIAN. see **CHRISTIAN COMMUNITIES.**

Communicating /. Schimmel, Warren T. New York , c1987. xvi, 624 p., [32] p. of plates : ISBN 0-471-84248-6 LC Card 87-111811 DDC 808/.066651 19
HF5718 .S29 1987

Communicating effectively . Dellinger, Susan. Millwood, N.Y., 1987, c1982. p. cm. ISBN 0-916667-14-6 LC Card 87-20830 DDC 658.4/5 19
HF5718 .D44 1987

Communicating employee responsibilities and rights : a modern management mandate / edited by Chimezie A.B. Osigweh, Yg. New York Quorum Books, c1987. xiv, 254 p. ; 25 cm. Bibliography: p. [221]-236. Includes index. ISBN 0-89930-200-9 (lib. bdg. : alk. paper) LC Card 86-25281 DDC 658.3/15 19
1. Communication in personnel management. 2. Employee rights. I. Osigweh, Chimezie A. B., 1955-.
HF5549.5.C6 C5825 1987

Communicating for results . Hamilton, Cheryl. Belmont, Calif. , c1987. xiii, 418 p. : ISBN 0-534-07956-3 (pbk.) LC Card 86-28108 DDC 658.4/5 19
HD30.3 .H35 1987

Communicating for survival . Brody, E. W. New York , 1987. xi, 264 p. : ISBN 0-275-92652-4 (alk. paper) : LC Card 87-11774 DDC 658.3/00141 19
HF5549.5.C6 B69 1987

Communicating in business and professional settings /. Hanna, Michael S., 1939- New York , c1988. p. cm. ISBN 0-394-36447-3 LC Card 87-12713 DDC 658.4/5 19
HD30.3 .H36 1988

Communicating with clients . Pulvino, Charles J. Paramus, NJ , c1987. ix, 194 p. : ISBN 0-13-153578-1 (pbk.) LC Card 87-153498 DDC 332.1/068/8 19
HG179.5 .P86 1987

Communicating with security analysts /. Weber, Nathan. New York, N.Y. (845 3rd Ave., New York 10022) , c1985. 22 p. : LC Card 86-212395 DDC 658.4/5 19
HD59 .W36 1985

COMMUNICATION, ADMINISTRATIVE. see **COMMUNICATION IN MANAGEMENT.**

COMMUNICATION AND STATE. see **COMMUNICATION POLICY.**

COMMUNICATION AND TRAFFIC.
Martin, James, 1933- The wired world . Carnforth, Lancashire, England , 1986. xiii, 140 p. : ISBN 0-906774-49-7 (pbk.) LC Card 87-157689 DDC 384 19
HE7631 .M373 1986

COMMUNICATION AND TRAFFIC - ENGLAND - LINCOLNSHIRE.
Clark, David, Ph. D. Information services in rural areas . Norwich [Norfolk] , c1980. x, 122 p. : ISBN 0-86094-058-6 (pbk.) LC Card 81-149488
HE8109.L55 C55 1980

COMMUNICATION AND TRAFFIC - INDIA.
Sukhwal, B. L., 1929- India . New York , 1987. viii, 200 p. : ISBN 0-938719-13-0 LC Card 86-81410 DDC 333.7/0954 19
HC433.5 .S85 1987

COMMUNICATION AND TRAFFIC - NORTH AMERICA - HISTORY.
Steele, Ian Kenneth. The English Atlantic, 1675-1740 . New York , 1986. xii, 400 p. ISBN 0-19-503968-8 LC Card 85-25828 DDC 380.3/09171/241 19
HE202 .S74 1986 ***NYPL [JLE 86-4056]***

COMMUNICATION AND TRAFFIC - NORWAY - HISTORY.
Bjørnland, Dag, 1935- Fra dampmaskin til jetfly . [Oslo] , c1982. 104 p. : ISBN 82-508-0180-6 : LC Card 83-134968
HE259 .B5 1982

COMMUNICATION AND TRAFFIC - SPAIN - ASTURIAS.
Argüelles, Alfonso. Los Oscos y la Cuenca del Eo . [Asturias] [1984?] ix, 317 p. : ISBN 84-505-0237-3 LC Card 86-174593
HC387.A7 A74 1984

COMMUNICATION AND TRAFFIC - WEST INDIES, BRITISH - HISTORY.
Steele, Ian Kenneth. The English Atlantic, 1675-1740 . New York , 1986. xii, 400 p. ISBN 0-19-503968-8 LC Card 85-25828 DDC 380.3/09171/241 19
HE202 .S74 1986 ***NYPL [JLE 86-4056]***

A communication audit handbook . Hamilton, Seymour, 1941- New York , c1987. x, 197 p. : ISBN 0-8013-0061-4 : LC Card 87-3743 DDC 658.4/5 19
HD30.3 .H353 1987

COMMUNICATION, EMPLOYEE. see **COMMUNICATION IN MANAGEMENT; COMMUNICATION IN PERSONNEL MANAGEMENT.**

Communication (Hillsdale, N.J.)
Beville, Hugh Malcolm. Audience ratings . Hillsdale, N.J. , 1987. p. cm. ISBN 0-8058-0175-8 LC Card 87-21001 DDC 384.54/3 19
HE8697.A8 B46 1987

Olasky, Marvin N. Corporate public relations and American private enterprise . Hillsdale, NJ , 1987. p. cm. ISBN 0-8058-0052-2 LC Card 87-3551 DDC 659.2/0973 19
HD59.6.U6 O4 1987

COMMUNICATION IN ACCOUNTING - UNITED STATES.
Written communication of results in MAS engagements. New York, N.Y. (1211 Ave. of the Americas, New York 10036-8775) , c1987. 7 p. ; LC Card 87-159283 DDC 808/.066657 19
HF5719 .W74 1987

COMMUNICATION IN AGRICULTURE - ITALY.
Strategia dei servizi per l'agricoltura . [Roma] [1983] 158 p. : LC Card 85-155420
HD9475.I82 S77 1983

COMMUNICATION IN DEMOGRAPHY - PERU.
Comunicación y tecnología en la investigación

demográfica /. Lima , 1985. vi, 38 p. ; LC Card 86-168814
HB849.6 .C65 1985

COMMUNICATION IN ECONOMIC DEVELOPMENT.
Constantino, Renato. Synthetic culture and development /. Quezon City , c1985. iv, 72 p. ; ISBN 971-10-5803-0 (pbk.) LC Card 85-234601 DDC 302.2 19
HD76. C66 1985 *NYPL [JLD 87-27]*

Ernst, Mario, 1953- Demokratische Wirtschaftspolitik . Bern , New York , c1986. x, 178 p. : ISBN 3-261-03571-4 LC Card 86-198029
HD76 .E76 1986

COMMUNICATION IN ECONOMIC DEVELOPMENT - PHILLIPINES.
Constantino, Renato. Synthetic culture and development /. Quezon City , c1985. iv, 72 p. ; ISBN 971-10-5803-0 (pbk.) LC Card 85-234601 DDC 302.2 19
HD76. C66 1985 *NYPL [JLD 87-27]*

COMMUNICATION IN FINANCIAL INSTITUTIONS - EUROPE - CONGRESSES.
L'Information financière . Bruxelles , 1983. 220 p. ; ISBN 2-8027-0298-X LC Card 84-104169
HG151.5 .I56 1983

COMMUNICATION IN FOREIGN TRADE.
Ōmae, Ken'ichi, 1943- Beyond national borders . Homewood, Ill. , c1987. xi, 128 p. : ISBN 1-556-23017-6 LC Card 86-72864 DDC 337.52 19
HF1602.15.U6 O4 1987

COMMUNICATION IN INDUSTRY. see **COMMUNICATION IN MANAGEMENT.**

COMMUNICATION IN MANAGEMENT - CASE STUDIES.
Braehmer, Uwe. Nachrichtendiffusion in Grossunternehmen . Münster [1983?] 271 p. : ISBN 3-88660-090-0 LC Card 83-206152
HD30.3 .B69 1983

COMMUNICATION IN MANAGEMENT - GERMANY (WEST)
Haag, Ingeborg. Arbeitskommunikation, Kommunikationsarbeit . Berlin , 1986. viii, 258 p. ; ISBN 3-923024-08-8 LC Card 86-226373
HD6957.G35 H33 1986

COMMUNICATION IN MANAGEMENT - ITALY.
Pacifici, Giorgio. Il futuro presente . Milano, Italy , c1985. 201 p. ; LC Card 86-127322 DDC 384/.0945 19
HE8174 .P33 1985

COMMUNICATION IN MANAGEMENT - SIMULATION METHODS.
Melrose, John. BUCOMCO . Chicago , c1987. vii, 187 p. : ISBN 0-574-20070-3 (pbk.) : LC Card 86-31585 DDC 651.7/4 19
HF5718 .M44 1987

COMMUNICATION IN MANAGEMENT - UNITED STATES.
Selnow, Gary W. Planning, implementing, and evaluating targeted communication programs . New York , 1987. vi, 291 p. : ISBN 0-89930-208-4 (lib. bdg. : alk. paper) LC Card 86-30418 DDC 659.1 19
HD30.3 .S46 1987

COMMUNICATION IN MANAGEMENT - UNITED STATES - EVALUATION.
The velvet ghetto . San Francisco , 1986. 147 leaves in various foliations : LC Card 86-161157 DDC 331.4/816592/0973 19
HD6054.2.U6 V45 1986

COMMUNICATION IN MARKETING.
Communicators' guide to marketing /. New York , c1987. xii, 226 p. : ISBN 0-582-28645-X LC Card 86-27787 DDC 658.8 19
HF5415.123 .C66 1987

Foote, Cameron S. The fourth medium . Homewood, Ill. , c1986. xxix, 226 p. : ISBN 0-87094-913-6 LC Card 86-70966 DDC 658.8/2 19
HF5438.5 .F66 1986 *NYPL [JLE 87-1433]*

COMMUNICATION IN MARKETING - GERMANY, WEST.
Weis, Hans Christian. Marketingkommunikation in der Investitionsgüterindustrie . Thun , c1983. v, 319, xxxix p. : ISBN 3-87144-741-2 : LC Card 83-159201
HF5415.123 .W45 1983

COMMUNICATION IN MARKETING - GERMANY, WEST - CASE STUDIES.
Weis, Hans Christian. Marketingkommunikation in der Investitionsgüterindustrie . Thun , c1983. v, 319, xxxix p. : ISBN 3-87144-741-2 : LC Card 83-159201
HF5415.123 .W45 1983

COMMUNICATION IN MARKETING - ITALY.
Industria e commercio . Milano, Italy , c1985. 194 p. : LC Card 86-112174 DDC 658.7/88/0945 19
HF5415.12.I8 I53 1985 *NYPL [JLD 87-432]*

COMMUNICATION IN ORGANIZATION.
Owen, Harrison, 1936- Spirit . Potomac, Md. , 1987. viii, 245 p. : ISBN 0-9618205-0-0 (pbk.) LC Card 87-70469 DDC 658.4/06 19
HD58.8 .O94 1987

COMMUNICATION IN ORGANIZATIONS.
Brody, E. W. Communicating for survival . New York , 1987. xi, 264 p. : ISBN 0-275-92652-4 (alk. paper) : LC Card 87-11774 DDC 658.3/00141 19
HF5549.5.C6 B69 1987

Brown, David S. (David Springer), 1915- Management's hidden enemy . Mt. Airy, Md. , 1987. viii, 123 p. ; ISBN 0-912338-59-8 LC Card 86-82670 DDC 658.4/5 19
HD30.3 .B76 1987

Comeau, John, 1952- Communication on the job . Englewood Cliffs, N.J. , c1987. xxvi, 356 p. : ISBN 0-13-153685-0 (pbk.) : LC Card 86-30555 DDC 651.7 19
HD30.3 .C62 1987

Daniels, Tom D. Perspectives on organizational communication /. Dubuque, Iowa , c1987. xiv, 288 p. : ISBN 0-697-00444-9 LC Card 86-72711 DDC 658.4/5 19
HD30.3 .D33 1987

Francis, Dave. Unblocking organizational communication . Aldershot, Hants, England , Brookfield, Vt. , c1987. xiv, 185 p. ; ISBN 0-566-02572-8 : LC Card 87-14836 DDC 658.4/5 19
HD30.3 .F73 1987

Francis, Dave. 50 activities for unblocking organizational communication /. Aldershot, Hants, England , Brookfield, Vt., U. S.A. , c1987. p. cm. ISBN 0-566-02571-X : LC Card 87-14079 DDC 658.4/5 19
HD30.3 .F7 1987

Handbook of organizational communication . Newbury Park, Calif. , c1987. 781 p. : ISBN 0-8039-2387-2 : LC Card 87-23417 DDC 658.4/5 19
HD30.3 .H3575 1987

Handbook of organizational communication /. Norwood, N.J. , c1988. 502 p. : ISBN 0-89391-446-0 LC Card 87-19380 DDC 658.4/5 19
HD30.3 .H357 1988

Hanna, Michael S., 1939- Communicating in business and professional settings /. New York , c1988. p. cm. ISBN 0-394-36447-3 LC Card 87-12713 DDC 658.4/5 19
HD30.3 .H36 1988

Mayntz, Renate. Dokumentation und Organisation . Bergisch Gladbach , 1984. 132 p. : ISBN 3-89012-008-3 : LC Card 85-131112
HD30.3 .M394 1984

Organizational communication /. New Brunswick, N.J., U. S.A. , c1987. p. cm. ISBN 0-88738-164-2 : LC Card 87-13856 DDC 658.4/5 19
HD30.3 .O72 1987

Schlesinger, James R. Organizational structures and planning /. [Santa Monica, Calif. , 1966] iii, 45 p. : LC Card 87-404140 DDC 353.6 19
HD58.9 .S35 1966

Shockley-Zalabak, Pamela. Fundamentals of organizational communication . New York , c1988. xii, 445 p. : ISBN 0-582-28636-0 LC Card 87-3323 DDC 658.4/5 19
HD30.3 .S55 1988

Wilson, Gerald L., 1943- Organizational communication /. New York , c1986. xiv, 322 p. : ISBN 0-06-042387-0 LC Card 85-8723 DDC 658.4/5 19
HD58.7 .W55 1986 *NYPL [JLE 86-2600]*

COMMUNICATION IN ORGANIZATIONS - ADDRESSES, ESSAYS, LECTURES.
Organization--communication . Norwood, N.J. , c1986- v. : ISBN 0-89391-274-3 (v. 1) LC Card 85-6159 DDC 302.3/5 19
HD31 .O727 1986 *NYPL [JLL 86-382]*

COMMUNICATION IN ORGANIZATIONS - AUDITING.
Hamilton, Seymour, 1941- A communication audit handbook . New York , c1987. x, 197 p. : ISBN 0-8013-0061-4 : LC Card 87-3743 DDC 658.4/5 19
HD30.3 .H353 1987

COMMUNICATION IN PERSONNEL MANAGEMENT - GERMANY (WEST)
Zangl, Hans. Durchlaufzeiten im Büro . Berlin , c1985. xvii, 365 p. : ISBN 3-503-02458-1 LC Card 85-137750
HF5549.5.C6 Z33 1985

COMMUNICATION IN PUBLIC ADMINISTRATION.
Mayntz, Renate. Dokumentation und Organisation . Bergisch Gladbach , 1984. 132 p. : ISBN 3-89012-008-3 : LC Card 85-131112
HD30.3 .M394 1984

COMMUNICATION IN RESEARCH. see **COMMUNICATION IN SCIENCE.**

COMMUNICATION IN RURAL DEVELOPMENT - INDIA - CONGRESSES.
Command area development, successes and learnings . Hyderabad , c1980. iii, 138 p. ; LC Card 83-906246 DDC 338.1/854 19
HD1741.I29 C65 1980 *NYPL [JLD 87-597]*

COMMUNICATION IN SCIENCE.
Mayntz, Renate. Dokumentation und Organisation . Bergisch Gladbach , 1984. 132 p. : ISBN 3-89012-008-3 : LC Card 85-131112
HD30.3 .M394 1984

COMMUNICATION IN SOCIAL WORK - UNITED STATES - CASE STUDIES.
Egan, Gerard. Change agent skills in helping and human service settings /. Monterey, Calif. , c1985. xi, 306 p. : ISBN 0-534-03624-4 : LC Card 84-7804 DDC 361.3/07 19
HV11 .E43 1985 *NYPL [JLE 86-1963]*

COMMUNICATION, INDUSTRIAL. see **COMMUNICATION IN MANAGEMENT.**

Communication on the job . Comeau, John, 1952- Englewood Cliffs, N.J. , c1987. xxvi, 356 p. : ISBN 0-13-153685-0 (pbk.) : LC Card 86-30555 DDC 651.7 19
HD30.3 .C62 1987

COMMUNICATION POLICY.
Kleinmann, Klaus, 1956- Die langfristige Entwicklung von Kommunikation und Staatsausgaben /. Frankfurt am Main , New York , c1985. v, 194 p. : ISBN 3-8204-8873-1 LC Card 85-200073
HJ131 .K56 1985

COMMUNICATION SATELLITES. see **ARTIFICIAL SATELLITES IN TELECOMMUNICATION.**

COMMUNICATION SYSTEMS, COMPUTER. see **COMPUTER NETWORKS.**

Communication technology . Rogers, Everett M. New York , London , c1986. xii, 273 p. : ISBN 0-02-927110-X LC Card 85-27555 DDC 621.38 19
TK5102.5 .R55 1986 *NYPL [JSE 86-1913]*

Communications.
Snow, Marcellus S. Telecommunications . Amsterdam , New York , 1986. xvi, 304 p. : ISBN 0-444-87926-9 LC Card 86-224686 DDC 384/.041 19
HE7645 .S58 1986

Communications (Annenberg School of Communications (University of Pennsylvania))
Snow, Marcellus S. Telecommunications . Amsterdam , New York , 1986. xvi, 304 p. : ISBN 0-444-87926-9 LC Card 86-224686 DDC 384/.041 19
HE7645 .S58 1986

Communications deregulation . Tunstall, Jeremy. Oxford, UK , New York, NY, USA , 1986. xi, 324 p. ; ISBN 0-631-14819-1 : LC Card 85-22983

DDC 343.73/0994 347.303994 19
KF2765 .T86 1986 **NYPL [JLE 86-2991]**

Communications in business /. Wells, Walter. Boston , c1988. xvi, 632 p. : ISBN 0-534-87167-4 LC Card 87-22721 DDC 651.7/4 19
HF5721 .W36 1988

Communications in the modern corporate environment /. Abelow, Daniel. Englewood Cliffs, NJ , c1986. xviii, 236 p. : ISBN 0-13-153842-X LC Card 85-16942 DDC 658/.0546 19
HF5548.2 .A24 1986 **NYPL [JLE 86-1992]**

Communications/Information Systems Planning Service : office systems software : distributed systems. Boston, MA (89 Broad St., Boston 02110) : Yankee Group, c1986. ii, 78 p. ; 28 cm. "August 1986." LC Card 86-225335 DDC 381/.45651853 19
1. Computer software industry - United States. 2. Electronic data processing - United States - Distributed processing. 3. Office practice - Automation. 4. Market surveys - United States. I. Yankee Group. II. Title: Office systems software.
HD9696.C63 U51492 1986

COMMUNICATIONS-RELAY SATELLITES. see **ARTIFICIAL SATELLITES IN TELECOMMUNICATION.**

Communications systems. Business guide to communications systems /. London , 1987. x, 230 p. : ISBN 0-273-02671-2 (pbk.) : LC Card 87-147021 DDC 651.7 19
HD30.335 .B85 1987

Communications Systems & Services.
Beyond private lines . Boston, MA (200 Portland St., Boston 02114) , c1987. iv, 117 p. : LC Card 87-144067 DDC 384.3/0973 19
HE7775 .B46 1987

Fiber optics after long distance /. Boston, Mass. (89 Broad St., Boston 02110) , c1986. vii, 114 p. : LC Card 86-220473 DDC 381/.456213692/0973 19
HD9696.F523 U5429 1986

ISDN . Boston, MA (200 Portland St., Boston 02114) , c1987. iv, 118 p. : LC Card 87-159823 DDC 380.1/450046 19
HD9696.D382 I82 1987

Communications Systems & Services (Series)
Integrated voice/data PBXs /. Boston, MA (200 Portland St., Boston 02114) , c1987. iv, 102 p. : LC Card 87-402843 DDC 381/.45621385 19
HE8817 .I57 1987

New RHC strategies /. Boston, MA (200 Portland St., Boston 02114) , c1987. iii, 117 p. ; LC Card 87-147694 DDC 384.6/065/73 19
HE8846.A55 N497 1987

Communications/Information Systems (Firm : Yankee Group)
Beyond private lines . Boston, MA (200 Portland St., Boston 02114) , c1987. iv, 117 p. : LC Card 87-144067 DDC 384.3/0973 19
HE7775 .B46 1987

IBM's evolving mainframes . Boston, Mass. (200 Portland St., Boston 02114) , c1986. iii, 45 p. : LC Card 86-231231 DDC 381/.4500412/0973 19
HD9696.C64 I48466 1986

Integrated voice/data PBXs /. Boston, MA (200 Portland St., Boston 02114) , c1987. iv, 102 p. : LC Card 87-402843 DDC 381/.45621385 19
HE8817 .I57 1987

ISDN . Boston, MA (200 Portland St., Boston 02114) , c1987. iv, 118 p. : LC Card 87-159823 DDC 380.1/450046 19
HD9696.D382 I82 1987

Managing corporate data centers . Boston, MA (200 Portland St., Boston 02114) , c1987. ii, 34 p. : LC Card 87-148811 DDC 658/.055133 19
HF5548.2 .M2955 1987

Mandela, Audrey L. Electronic mail update . Boston, Mass. (200 Portland St., Boston 02114) , c1986. ii, 135 p. : LC Card 87-124538 DDC 384.3/4/0973 19
HD9696.M353 U56 1986

Market leaders . Boston, MA (200 Portland St., Boston 02114) , c1987. v, 123 p. : LC Card 87-402841 DDC 381/.4500416/0973 19
HD9696.C63 U52476 1987

New RHC strategies /. Boston, MA (200 Portland St., Boston 02114) , c1987. iii, 117 p. ; LC Card 87-147694 DDC 384.6/065/73 19
HE8846.A55 N497 1987

Communications/Information Systems Planning Service and Critical Path Planning Service (Form : Yankee Group) Living with SNA /. Boston, MA (89 Broad St., Boston 02110) [1986] 60 p. : LC Card 86-201765 DDC 381/.4500468/0973 19
HD9696.C63 U5223 1986

Communicators' guide to marketing / International Association of Business Communicators ; edited by Clara Degen. New York : Longman, c1987. xii, 226 p. : ill. ; 24 cm. (Longman series in public communication) Includes bibliographies and index. ISBN 0-582-28645-X LC Card 86-27787 DDC 658.8 19
1. Communication in marketing. 2. Marketing. I. Degen, Clara. II. International Association of Business Communicators. III. Series.
HF5415.123 .C66 1987

COMMUNISM - ADDRESSES, ESSAYS, LECTURES.
Analytical Marxism /. Cambridge, CB ; New York : viii, 313 p. : ISBN 0-521-30025-8 LC Card 85-11697 DDC 335.4 19
HB97.5 .A487 1986 **NYPL [JLE 86-1742]**

Wolf, Hanna. Ausgewählte Reden und Aufsätze /. Berlin , 1979. 439 p. ; LC Card 80-478273 DDC 335.43/09431
HX280.5.A6 W64 **NYPL [JLD 81-322]**

COMMUNISM - AFRICA, SUB-SAHARAN.
Görgens, Egon, 1941- Entwicklungshilfe und Ordnungspolitik . Bern , c1983. 111 p. ; ISBN 3-258-03324-2 : LC Card 84-108530
HC800 .G67 1983

COMMUNISM - ALBANIA - HISTORY - 20TH CENTURY.
Fishta, Iljaz. Ekonomia e Shqipërisë në vitet e para të ndërtimit socialist, 1944-1948 /. Tiranë , 1984. 489 p. ; LC Card 85-163026
HC402 .F55 1984

COMMUNISM AND AGRICULTURE - GERMANY.
Kautsky, Karl, 1854-1938. [Agrarfrage. English.] The agrarian question /. London , Atlantic Highlands, N.J. , 1988- p. cm. ISBN 1-85305-024-5 (v. 2) LC Card 87-20593 DDC 338.1 19
HD1306.G3 K315 1988

COMMUNISM AND AGRICULTURE - SOVIET UNION.
Bogoliubov, Klavdiĭ Mikhaĭlovich. Vernym kursom /. Moskva , 1984. 287 p. ; LC Card 85-164820
HD1492.S65 B64 1984

COMMUNISM AND TECHNOLOGY.
Politökonomische Probleme des Gebrauchswerts, der Nützlichkeit und der Bewertung von Gebrauchswerten /. Karl-Marx-Stadt [1983] 92 p. ; LC Card 84-167577
HB201 .P63 1983

Soziale Aspekte der Mikroelektronik /. Berlin , 1985. 122 p. ; LC Card 87-409418 DDC 306/.46 19
HD6331 .S683 1985

COMMUNISM AND TECHNOLOGY - GERMANY (EAST)
Ökonomische und soziale Wirksamkeit des wissenschaftlich-technischen Fortschritts /. Berlin , 1986. 314 p. ; ISBN 3-320-00713-0 LC Card 87-100866 DDC 338/.06 19
HC290.795.T4 O38 1986

COMMUNISM AND TRADE UNIONS. see **TRADE-UNIONS AND COMMUNISM.**

COMMUNISM AND YOUTH. see **SOCIALISM AND YOUTH.**

COMMUNISM - CHINA.
Walder, Andrew George. Communist neo-traditionalism . Berkeley , c1986. xxi, 302 p. ; ISBN 0-520-05439-3 (alk. paper) LC Card 85-27093 DDC 306/.36/0951 19
HD8736.5 .W34 1986 **NYPL [JLD 86-3749]**

COMMUNISM - CONGRESSES.
Capitalismo riformato e sinistra . Milano , 1986. 125 p. ; ISBN 88-24-50380-2 : LC Card 86-229688
HB501 .C24265 1986

Les Aventures du marxisme /. Paris , c1984. 415 p. ; ISBN 2-86738-025-1 (pbk.)
NYPL [JLD 87-212]

COMMUNISM - DEVELOPING COUNTRIES.
Az Elmélet és a fegyverek kritikája . Budapest [1981] xxv, 509 p. ; ISBN 963-461-775-1 (Magy. nemz. bibl.) LC Card 85-139263
HC59.7 .E45 1981

Marxian theory and the third world /. New Delhi , Beverly Hills , 1985. 325 p. ; ISBN 0-8039-9489-3 LC Card 85-1863 DDC 335.43/09172/4 19
HX517.8 .M37 1985 **NYPL [JLE 86-3088]**

Transition and development . New York, NY [Berkeley, Calif.] , c1986. 352 p. ; ISBN 0-85345-705-0 (pbk.) : LC Card 86-12579 DDC 335.43/09172/4 19
HX517.8 .T73 1986 **NYPL [JLD 86-3907]**

COMMUNISM - DEVELOPING COUNTRIES - CONGRESSES.
Les Aventures du marxisme /. Paris , c1984. 415 p. ; ISBN 2-86738-025-1 (pbk.)
NYPL [JLD 87-212]

COMMUNISM - EGYPT.
Goldberg, Ellis. Tinker, tailor, and textile worker . Berkeley , 1986. xiii, 234 p. : ISBN 0-520-05353-2 (alk. paper) LC Card 85-16472 DDC 322.4/4/0962 19
HD8786 .G65 1986 **NYPL [JLE 87-500]**

COMMUNISM - EUROPE.
La Izquierda europea . Barcelona , 1985. 282 p. ; ISBN 84-307-7438-6 LC Card 86-186087
HX238.5 .I97 1985 **NYPL [JLD 86-4090]**

Salvadori, Massimo L., 1908- Eurocomunismo e socialismo sovietico . Torino , 1978. xxvii, 161 p. ; LC Card 80-497655 DDC 324.245075 19
JN5657.C63 S24 **NYPL [JLC 81-75]**

Sarlēs, Dēmētrēs. Hoi politikes pleures tēs entaxēs tēs Helladas stēn EOK . Athēna , 1981. 212 p. ; LC Card 83-170595
HC241.25.G8 S27 1981

COMMUNISM - FRANCE.
Un Chemin pour sortir de la crise /. Paris , c1985. 249 p. ; ISBN 2-209-05753-1 LC Card 86-154397
HC276.2 .C517 1985

Walter, Jean Jacques, 1932- Main basse sur la France /. Paris , c1984. 252 p. ; ISBN 2-7103-0188-1 LC Card 84-231340 DDC 335/.00944 19
HX264 .W36 1984 **NYPL [JLD 86-1773]**

COMMUNISM - FRANCE - HISTORY.
Rice-Maximin, Edward Francis, 1941- Accomodation and resistance . New York , 1986. xi, 175 p. ; ISBN 0-313-25355-2 (lib. bdg. : alk. paper) LC Card 86-4624 DDC 959.704/1 19
DS553.1 .R53 1986 **NYPL [JFE 87-1024]**

COMMUNISM - GERMANY - ADDRESSES, ESSAYS, LECTURES.
Wozu noch in die Parlamente? /. [Reutlingen] , 1978. 81 p. : LC Card 82-223081 DDC 322/.2/0943 19
HD6697 .W69 1978 **NYPL [JLD 87-886]**

COMMUNISM - GERMANY, EAST.
Die DDR in der Welt des Sozialismus /. Berlin , 1985. 237 p. ; LC Card 85-188821 DDC 335.43/09431 19
HX280.5.A6 D38 1985
NYPL [JLD 87-1167]

30 Jahre DDR und das Fiasko imperialistischer Prognosen, Pläne und Propheten . [Berlin] , 1979. 40 p. ; LC Card 83-198579
HC290.78 .A14 1979

COMMUNISM - GERMANY, EAST - ADDRESSES, ESSAYS, LECTURES.
Wolf, Hanna. Ausgewählte Reden und Aufsätze /. Berlin , 1979. 439 p. ; LC Card 80-478273 DDC 335.43/09431
HX280.5.A6 W64 **NYPL [JLD 81-322]**

COMMUNISM - GERMANY (EAST) - HISTORY - 20TH CENTURY - SOURCES.
Wie wir angefangen haben . Berlin , 1985. 326

p. : LC Card 85-217979
HD1333.G35 W54 1985

COMMUNISM - GERMANY - HISTORY - ADDRESSES, ESSAYS, LECTURES.
Solidargemeinschaft und Klassenkampf . Frankfurt am Main , 1986. 382 p. ; ISBN 3-518-11363-1 *NYPL [JLC 86-423]*

COMMUNISM - GREAT BRITAIN - HISTORY.
Shipway, Mark. Anti-parliamentary communism . New York , 1988. p. cm. ISBN 0-312-01265-9 : LC Card 87-23083 DDC 338.6 19
HD5660.G7 S48 1988

COMMUNISM - GREECE.
Sarlēs, Dēmētrēs. Hoi politikes pleures tēs entaxēs tēs Helladas stēn EOK . Athēna , 1981. 212 p. ; LC Card 83-170595
HC241.25.G8 S27 1981

COMMUNISM - HISTORY.
Berg, Hermann von, 1933- Marxismus-Leninismus . Köln , 1986. 335 p. : ISBN 3-7663-0982-X *NYPL [JLD 86-4000]*

Kautsky, Karl, 1854-1938. Die Vorläufer des neueren Sozialismus /. Stuttgart , 1895. 2 v. ; *NYPL [JLF 85-168]*

COMMUNISM - HISTORY - 20TH CENTURY.
Haug, Wolfgang Fritz. Pluraler Marxismus . Berlin , 1985- v. ; ISBN 3-88619-303-9 (Bd. 1) LC Card 86-119293 DDC 355.43/09/04 19
HX40 .H27 1985 NYPL [JLK 86-57]

COMMUNISM - HUNGARY.
Szelényi, Iván. Socialist entrepreneurs . Madison, Wis. , 1988. p. cm. ISBN 0-299-11360-4 : LC Card 87-16085 DDC 338.1/09439 19
HD1940.5 .S94 1988

Communism in unions. Boulware, Lemuel Richetts, 1895- What to do about communism in unions . [Schenectady, N.Y.?] [1952?] 62 p. ; *NYPL [JLD 86-247]*

COMMUNISM - ITALY.
Keszthelyi, Csaba. Az autonómia kérdése az olasz szakszervezeti egységért folytatott küzdelemben /. [Budapest] , 1985. 75 p. ; ISBN 963-673-322-8 LC Card 86-185901
HD6680.5.Z65 K47 1985

COMMUNISM - LATIN AMERICA.
Transition and development . New York, NY [Berkeley, Calif.] , c1986. 352 p. ; ISBN 0-85345-705-0 (pbk.) : LC Card 86-12579 DDC 335.43/09172/4 19
HX517.8 .T73 1986 NYPL [JLD 86-3907]

COMMUNISM - NICARAGUA.
Transition and development . New York, NY [Berkeley, Calif.] , c1986. 352 p. ; ISBN 0-85345-705-0 (pbk.) : LC Card 86-12579 DDC 335.43/09172/4 19
HX517.8 .T73 1986 NYPL [JLD 86-3907]

COMMUNISM - PHILOSOPHY.
Berg, Hermann von, 1933- Marxismus-Leninismus . Köln , 1986. 335 p. : ISBN 3-7663-0982-X *NYPL [JLD 86-4000]*

COMMUNISM - ROMANIA.
Ceaușescu, Nicolae. Cuvîntare la Plenara Consiliului Național al Oamenilor Muncii, din 19-20 ianuarie 1981 /. București , 1981. 31 p. ; LC Card 81-153290
HC405 .C4215 1981

COMMUNISM - ROMANIA - HISTORY - 19TH CENTURY.
Condițiile istorice ale apariției și dezvoltării clasei muncitoare din România . București , 1984. 652 p. ; LC Card 84-234192
HD8648 .C65 1984

COMMUNISM - SOVIET UNION.
Ratiu, Ion. Moscow challenges the world /. London , 1986. 410 p. ; ISBN 0-907671-23-5 *NYPL [JLE 87-1665]*

Salvadori, Massimo L., 1908- Eurocomunismo e socialismo sovietico . Torino , 1978. xxvii, 161 p. ; LC Card 80-497655 DDC 324.245075 19
JN5657.C63 S24 NYPL [JLC 81-75]

COMMUNISM - SOVIET UNION - CONGRESSES.
Les Aventures du marxisme /. Paris , c1984. 415 p. ; ISBN 2-86738-025-1 (pbk.) *NYPL [JLD 87-212]*

Uchenie K. Marksa ob ėtapakh razvitiia sposoba proizvodstva i problemy zrelogo sotsializma . Leningrad , 1985. 150 p. ; LC Card 86-140577
HB97.5 .U24 1985

COMMUNISM - SOVIET UNION - HISTORY - 20TH CENTURY.
Shturman, Dora, 1923- Nash novyĭ mir . Ierusalim , 1986. 464 p. : LC Card 87-114263
HB97.5 .S5155 1986

COMMUNISM - SPAIN - CÓRDOBA (PROVINCE) - HISTORY - 20TH CENTURY.
Díaz del Moral, Juan, 1870-1948. Las agitaciones campesinas del período bolchevista, 1918-1920 /. Sevilla [1985?] 230 p. ; ISBN 84-7587-031-7 LC Card 86-181529
HD1536.S7 D48 1985

COMMUNISM - SPAIN - MONTIJO - HISTORY - 19TH CENTURY.
Introducción a la historia del movimiento obrero en Montijo . [Montijo?] [1982?] 103 p., 48 p. of plates : ISBN 84-300-6966-6 LC Card 85-177027
HD8590.M65 I57 1982

COMMUNISM - UNITED STATES - 1917-
Boulware, Lemuel Richetts, 1895- What to do about communism in unions . [Schenectady, N.Y.?] [1952?] 62 p. ; *NYPL [JLD 86-247]*

COMMUNIST COUNTRIES - COMMERCE.
The New Communist Third World . London , c1982. 392 p. ; ISBN 0-7099-2709-6 LC Card 86-673518
HF1413 .N495x 1982b

COMMUNIST COUNTRIES - COMMERCE - GERMANY (WEST)
Wolff von Amerongen, Otto, 1918- Trendwende im Osthandel /. Bonn , 1977. 23 p. ; LC Card 85-141570
HF1411 .W583 1977

COMMUNIST COUNTRIES - ECONOMIC CONDITIONS.
Crisis and reform in socialist economies /. Boulder , 1987. xi, 196 p. ; ISBN 0-8133-7332-8 (pbk. : alk. paper) : LC Card 86-32602 DDC 338.9/009171/7 19
HC704 .C75 1987

Eberstadt, Nick, 1955- The poverty of communism /. New Brunswick, N.J., U. S.A. , c1987. p. cm. ISBN 0-88738-188-X : LC Card 87-19097 DDC 362.5/09171/7 19
HC710.P6 E24 1987

International Bank for Economic Co-operation. IBEC, 10 years. Moscow [1973] [27] p. : LC Card 82-216202
HG3881.5.I55 I58 1973

Socialist economy and economic policy /. Wien , New York , 1985. 279 p. : ISBN 0-387-81903-7 (pbk.) LC Card 86-201536
HC704 .S557 1985

Die Wirtschaftliche Entwicklung in den sozialistischen Ländern Osteuropas zur Jahreswende 1985/86 /. Hamburg , 1986. 336 p. ; ISBN 3-87895-295-3 LC Card 86-185852
HC244 .W5776 1986

COMMUNIST COUNTRIES - ECONOMIC CONDITIONS - REGIONAL DISPARITIES.
Regionale Aspekte der Wirtschaftsplanung in den Mitteleuropäischen RGW-Staaten. Marburg/Lahn , 1983. 95 p. : ISBN 3-87969-178-9 LC Card 84-249235
HC270.28 .R42 1983

COMMUNIST COUNTRIES - ECONOMIC INTEGRATION.
Burova, S. E. (Stella Efimovna) Kritika burzhuaznykh vzgliadov na ėkonomicheskoe sotrudnichestvo stran SĖV /. Moskva , 1986. 154 p. ; LC Card 86-232355
HC243.5 .B87 1986

Bykov, A. N. (Aleksandr Naumovich) Sotsialisticheskaia integratsiia i nauchno-tekhnicheskaia revoliutsiia /. Moskva , 1981. 343 p. ; LC Card 82-101911
HC244.Z9 T43 1981

Die DDR in der Welt des Sozialismus /. Berlin , 1985. 237 p. ; LC Card 85-188821 DDC 335.43/09431 19
HX280.5.A6 D38 1985 NYPL [JLD 87-1167]

Fingerland, Jaroslav. Mezinárodní socialistická ekonomická integrace a předmětné sféry specializace národohospodářského komplexu ČSSR /. Praha , 1985. 169 p. ; LC Card 86-215200
HF1542.3.Z4 C654 1985

COMMUNIST COUNTRIES - ECONOMIC INTEGRATION - HISTORY.
Ladygin, Boris Nikolaevich. Istoricheskiĭ opyt sotrudnichestva stran SĖV /. Moskva , 1980. 284 p. ; LC Card 81-130900
HC244 .L282 1980

COMMUNIST COUNTRIES - ECONOMIC POLICY.
Crisis and reform in socialist economies /. Boulder , 1987. xi, 196 p. ; ISBN 0-8133-7332-8 (pbk. : alk. paper) : LC Card 86-32602 DDC 338.9/009171/7 19
HC704 .C75 1987

Domdey, Karl Heinz. Weltwirtschaft und Weltwirtschaftslehre . Berlin , 1984. 366 p. : LC Card 84-245611
HC54 .D65 1984

Eremin, A. M. (Al'bert Mikhaĭlovich) Metodologiia opredeleniia osnovnogo i iskhodnogo otnosheniĭ ėkonomiki sotsializma /. Kazan' , 1980. 157, [3] p. ; LC Card 81-134646
HB97.5 .E665 1980

Hospodářský mechanismus fungování socialistické ekonomiky /. Praha , 1985. 238 p. ; LC Card 86-203712
HC704 .H65 1985

Khoziaĭstvennyĭ mekhanizm funktsionirovaniia sotsialisticheskoĭ ėkonomiki /. Moskva , 1982. 358 p. ; LC Card 83-134242
HC243.5 .K47 1982

Regionale Aspekte der Wirtschaftsplanung in den Mitteleuropäischen RGW-Staaten. Marburg/Lahn , 1983. 95 p. : ISBN 3-87969-178-9 LC Card 84-249235
HC270.28 .R42 1983

Socialist economy and economic policy /. Wien , New York , 1985. 279 p. : ISBN 0-387-81903-7 (pbk.) LC Card 86-201536
HC704 .S557 1985

Die Übergangsperiode . [Leipzig] , 1986. 80 p. ; LC Card 87-407523 DDC 338.9/009171/7 19
HC704 .U24 1986

The World socialist economy. Moscow , 1986. 279 p. ; LC Card 86-231463 DDC 338.9/009171/7 19
HC704 .W67 1986

COMMUNIST COUNTRIES - FOREIGN ECONOMIC RELATIONS.
Socialist economy and economic policy /. Wien , New York , 1985. 279 p. : ISBN 0-387-81903-7 (pbk.) LC Card 86-201536
HC704 .S557 1985

COMMUNIST COUNTRIES - FOREIGN ECONOMIC RELATIONS - CZECHOSLOVAKIA.
Fingerland, Jaroslav. Mezinárodní socialistická ekonomická integrace a předmětné sféry specializace národohospodářského komplexu ČSSR /. Praha , 1985. 169 p. ; LC Card 86-215200
HF1542.3.Z4 C654 1985

COMMUNIST COUNTRIES - FOREIGN ECONOMIC RELATIONS - DEVELOPING COUNTRIES.
Kupriianov, A. B. (Alekseĭ Borisovich) Razvivaiushchiesia strany i mezhdunarodnoe sotrudnichestvo . Moskva , 1980. 262 p. ; LC Card 81-131557
HC59.7 .K863 1980

COMMUNIST COUNTRIES - FOREIGN RELATIONS - GERMANY (EAST)
Die DDR in der Welt des Sozialismus /. Berlin , 1985. 237 p. ; LC Card 85-188821 DDC 335.43/09431 19
HX280.5.A6 D38 1985
NYPL [JLD 87-1167]

COMMUNIST COUNTRIES - POPULATION POLICY - CASE STUDIES.
Working women in socialist countries . Geneva , 1985. xvi, 234 p. : ISBN 92-2-103910-2 (pbk.) : LC Card 85-181464 DDC 304.6/32/091717 19
HB901 .W657 1985 NYPL [JLE 86-1433]

Communist countries - Propaganda. see **Propaganda, Communist.**

COMMUNIST COUNTRIES - SOCIAL CONDITIONS.
Eberstadt, Nick, 1955- The poverty of communism /. New Brunswick, N.J., U. S.A. , c1987. p. cm. ISBN 0-88738-188-X : LC Card 87-19097 DDC 362.5/09171/7 19
HC710.P6 E24 1987

COMMUNIST LEADERSHIP - RUSSIAN S.F. S.R. - HISTORY.
Krasnykh, L. M. (Leonid Mikhaĭlovich) Partiĭnoe rukovodstvo sovershenstvovaniem upravleniia promyshlennost'iu v period stroitel'stva sotsializma, 1926-1937 . Krasnoiarsk , 1986. 150, [2] p. ; LC Card 86-226013
HD70.S63 K73 1986

Communist neo-traditionalism . Walder, Andrew George. Berkeley , c1986. xxi, 302 p. ; ISBN 0-520-05439-3 (alk. paper) LC Card 85-27093 DDC 306/.36/0951 19
HD8736.5 .W34 1986 NYPL [JLD 86-3749]

Communist Party (Branch of the Communist International) see **Communist Party of the United States of America.**

Communist Party (France) see **Parti communiste français.**

Communist Party (Germany) see **Kommunistische Partei Deutschlands.**

Communist Party of Bulgaria. see **Bŭlgarska komunisticheska partiia.**

Communist Party of France. see **Parti communiste français.**

Communist Party of Germany. see **Kommunistische Partei Deutschlands.**

COMMUNIST PARTY OF INDIA - BIOGRAPHY.
Sen, P. K. (Prabhat Kumar), 1905- Purono dinera kathā /. Kalakātā , 1985. 49 p. ; LC Card 85-904772
HD6812.5.S46 A3 1985

Communist Party of Russia. see **Kommunisticheskaia partiia Sovetskogo Soiuza.**

Communist Party of Spain. see **Partido Comunista de España.**

Communist Party of the Soviet Union. see **Kommunisticheskaia partiia Sovetskogo Soiuza.**

COMMUNIST PARTY OF THE UNITED STATES OF AMERICA - HISTORY.
Hall, Gus. Working class USA . New York , 1987. 392 p. : ISBN 0-7178-0660-X : LC Card 87-3232 DDC 305.5/62/0973 19
HD8066 .H29 1987

Communist Party (United States) see **Communist Party of the United States of America.**

COMMUNIST PROPAGANDA. see **PROPAGANDA, COMMUNIST.**

COMMUNIST REVISIONISM - HISTORY.
Vŭznikvane, razvitie i zalez na oportiunizma v bŭlgarskoto rabotnichesko dvizhenie, 1891/1948 /. Sofiia , 1986. 696 p. ; LC Card 86-200229
HD8628 .V89 1986

Communist states and international change . Linden, Ronald Haly. Boston , c1987. xviii, 201 p. ; ISBN 0-04-497050-1 : LC Card 87-11389 DDC 337.497 19
HF1581 .L56 1987

COMMUNISTS - HUNGARY - INTERVIEWS.
Gáspár, Sándor. A munkásosztály szolgálatában /. [Budapest] , c1983. 326 p., [26] p. of plates : ISBN 963-322-025-4 : LC Card 84-129952
HD6680.5.Z55 G375 1983

COMMUNISTS - INDIA - BIOGRAPHY.
Sen, P. K. (Prabhat Kumar), 1905- Purono dinera kathā /. Kalakātā , 1985. 49 p. ; LC Card 85-904772
HD6812.5.S46 A3 1985

COMMUNITIES, CHRISTIAN. see **CHRISTIAN COMMUNITIES.**

COMMUNITY.
Ideology and national competitiveness . Boston, Mass. , c1987. x, 350 p. ; ISBN 0-87584-147-3 LC Card 86-19569 DDC 338.6/048 19
HF1414 .I34 1987 NYPL [JLE 87-1046]

Community Agency for Social Enquiry (South Africa) Orkin, Mark. Disinvestment, the struggle, and the future . Johannesburg , 1986. xii, 78 p. : ISBN 0-86975-305-3 (pbk.) LC Card 87-100474 DDC 332.6/73/0968 19
HG5851.A3 O47 1986

COMMUNITY AND COLLEGE - FRANCE - POITIERS - CONGRESSES.
Colloque "Poitiers 1981" (1981 : Université de Poitiers) Actes du Colloque "Poitiers 1981" . Poitiers [France] [1983] 472 p. : LC Card 84-119227
HB3594.P65 C65 1981

COMMUNITY AND COLLEGE - SWITZERLAND - BASELLAND.
Frey, René Leo. Die regionale Ausstrahlung der Universität Basel /. Basel , c1984. 73 p. : LC Card 84-166545 DDC 378/.103 19
HC395 .A75 no. 8 LC238.4.S92B37

COMMUNITY ANTENNA TELEVISION - UNITED STATES - MANAGEMENT.
Marcus, Norman, 1934- Broadcast and cable management /. Englewood Cliffs, N.J. , c1986. xii, 308 p. : ISBN 0-13-083577-3 LC Card 85-3565 DDC 384.54/068 19
HE8700.8 .M37 1986 NYPL [JLE 86-3127]

Community Associations Institute. Dowden, C. James. Creating a community association . Washington, D.C. , Alexandria, Va. , 1986. vii, 76 p. : ISBN 0-87420-659-6 (pbk.) LC Card 86-50785 DDC 643/.2 19
HD7287.67.U5 C73 1986

Community bank guide to asset/liability management policies / prepared by Olson Research Associates, Inc. Washington, D.C. (1120 Connecticut Ave., N.W., Washington 20036) : American Bankers Association, c1987. v, 241 p. : ill. ; 28 cm. LC Card 87-167068 DDC 332.1/2/0681 19
1. Asset-liability management (Banking). I. Olson Research Associates. II. American Bankers Association.
HG1615.25 .C65 1987

COMMUNITY COUNCILS. see **COMMUNITY ORGANIZATION.**

COMMUNITY DEVELOPMENT.
Community management . West Hartford, Conn. , c1986. xxii, 328 p. : ISBN 0-931816-40-8 (pbk.) LC Card 86-27691 DDC 338.95 19
HD75.6 .C65 1986

Community Development Block Grant Program (U. S.) Nolon, John R. Housing rehabilitation under the Community Development Block Grant Program . [New York, N.Y.] [1984] 150 p. in various pagings ; LC Card 86-622826 DDC 363.5/8 19
HD7303.N7 N65 1984

COMMUNITY DEVELOPMENT - BRAZIL - MINAS GERAIS.
Haddad, Paulo Roberto. Dimensões do planejamento estadual no Brasil . Rio de Janeiro , 1985. 188 p. : LC Card 86-195636
HC188.M6 H33 1985

COMMUNITY DEVELOPMENT - BRAZIL, NORTHEAST.
Aspectos gerais da economia e da sociedade do Nordeste. Recife , 1984. 318 p. : LC Card 86-159446
HC188.N6 A75 1984

COMMUNITY DEVELOPMENT - BRAZIL - SÃO PAULO (STATE) - HISTORY.
Kuznesof, Elizabeth Anne. Household economy and urban development . Boulder , 1986. 216 p. : ISBN 0-8133-7181-3 : LC Card 85-31491 DDC 307.7/64/098161 19
HC188.S3 K89 1986 NYPL [JLE 87-711]

COMMUNITY DEVELOPMENT CONSULTANTS.
Scott-Stevens, Susan. Foreign consultants and counterparts . Boulder , 1987. xvii, 229 p. : ISBN 0-8133-7370-0 (pbk. : alk. paper) LC Card 87-50750 DDC 306/.46 19
HC79.T4 S36 1987

COMMUNITY DEVELOPMENT CORPORATIONS - MICHIGAN.
Michigan. Dept. of Labor. An assessment of the effectiveness of the Bureau of Community Services, Michigan Economic and Social Opportunity Commission, and community action agencies /. [Lansing, Mich.] [1986] 56 p. : LC Card 87-620767 DDC 362/.9774 19
HC107.M53 P6333 1986

COMMUNITY DEVELOPMENT - FEDERAL AID. see **FEDERAL AID TO COMMUNITY DEVELOPMENT.**

COMMUNITY DEVELOPMENT - FLORIDA.
Tax incentives for community revitalization in Florida /. Tallahassee, Fla. [1983] 45 p. ; LC Card 86-623222 DDC 343.75906/6 347.590366 19
HJ4655.F64 T39 1983

COMMUNITY DEVELOPMENT - FRANCE.
Projet pour la France . Paris , c1983. 196 p. ; ISBN 2-7340-0032-6 : LC Card 83-196098
HC276.2 .P767 1983

COMMUNITY DEVELOPMENT - LAW AND LEGISLATION - FLORIDA.
Tax incentives for community revitalization in Florida /. Tallahassee, Fla. [1983] 45 p. ; LC Card 86-623222 DDC 343.75906/6 347.590366 19
HJ4655.F64 T39 1983

COMMUNITY DEVELOPMENT - NEW YORK (N.Y.)
New York City Partnership. The Partnership. New York, N.Y. , c1986. 44 p. : LC Card 86-223138 DDC 380.1/06/07471 19
HF296.N4 N48 1986

COMMUNITY DEVELOPMENT - NEW YORK (STATE) - FINANCE - HANDBOOKS, MANUALS, ETC.
A Step-by-step guide to resources for economic development /. Albany, N.Y. [New York, N.Y.] , 1983, c1980. 195 p. : LC Card 85-621196 DDC 353.0082/09747 19
HC107.N73 P6353 1983 NYPL [JLF 86-638]

COMMUNITY DEVELOPMENT - UNITED STATES.
United States. Congress. House. Committee on Banking, Currency and Housing. Subcommittee on Historic Preservation and Coinage. Preservation programs of the Federal government in the area of housing and community development /. Washington , 1976. vi, 86 p. ; LC Card 77-601749
HT175 .U583 1976 NYPL [JLE 78-1181]

United States. National Commission on Neighborhoods. People, building neighborhoods . [Washington?] , Washington [1979] xi, 358 p. : LC Card 79-602955 DDC 307.7/6/0973
HN90.C6 U66 1979 NYPL [JLM 81-194]

COMMUNITY DEVELOPMENT - UNITED STATES - CONGRESSES.
Community energy management as an economic development strategy . [Lincoln, Neb.] (Box 95085, Lincoln 68509-5085) [1984 or 1985] iv, 396 p. : LC Card 86-622211 DDC 333.79/0973 19
HD9502.U52 C656 1984

National Conference on Rural Development, Des Moines, 1973. Proceedings. Washington, 1974. iii, 108 p. LC Card 74-600918 DDC 309.2/63/0973
HN65 .N35 1973 NYPL [JLE 81-564 no.2]

COMMUNITY DEVELOPMENT, URBAN - BRAZIL - FORTALEZA.
Fernandes, Adelita Neto Carleial. Condições de vida nos bairros de Fortaleza, nov/84 a mar/85 . Fortaleza , 1986. 92 p. : LC Card 86-196902
HC189.F67 F47 1986

COMMUNITY DEVELOPMENT, URBAN - DEVELOPING COUNTRIES.
Laquian, Aprodicio A. Basic housing . Ottawa, Canada , c1983. 163 p. : ISBN 0-88936-370-6 (pbk.) LC Card 83-231129 DDC 363.5/8/091724 19
HD7391 .L36 1983 NYPL [JLE 86-1376]

COMMUNITY DEVELOPMENT, URBAN - ECUADOR - QUITO REGION - CITIZEN PARTICIPATION.
Tierras para asentamientos populares . Quito, Ecuador , 1985. 378 p. : LC Card 87-400165 DDC 333.77/13/0986613 19
HD530.Q58 T54 1985

COMMUNITY DEVELOPMENT, URBAN - UNITED STATES.
Ferguson, Gary D. Evaluation of the small

cities community development block grant program--the role of the counties [microform] /. Cambridge, Mass. , 1981. vii, vi, 186 p. ; *NYPL [*XME-11,283]*

Industrial democracy . Beverly Hills , c1985. 308 p. : ISBN 0-8039-2476-3 LC Card 85-11741 DDC 338.973/009173/2 19
HT321 .I53 1985 NYPL [JLD 86-3621]

Meyers, Edward M. Rebuilding America's cities . Cambridge, Mass. , c1986. xxi, 290 p. : ISBN 0-88730-051-0 LC Card 85-30780 DDC 307.3/4/0973 19
HT175 .U59 1986 NYPL [JLE 86-2874]

Newman & Hermanson Company. Evaluation of the small cities component of the community development block grant program [microform] . Cambridge, Mass. , 1981. viii, xvii, 147 p. ; *NYPL [*XME-11,274]*

Varady, David P. Neighborhood upgrading . Albany , c1986. x, 184 p. : ISBN 0-88706-299-7 LC Card 85-30392 DDC 307.3/362/0973 19
HT175 .V37 1986 NYPL [JLE 87-373]

COMMUNITY DEVELOPMENT, URBAN - UNITED STATES - CASE STUDIES.
Van der Ryn, Sim. Sustainable communities . San Francisco [1986] xvii, 238 p. : ISBN 0-87156-800-4 LC Card 83-4676 DDC 307/.14 19
HN90.C6 V36 1986 NYPL [JLF 86-1241]

Community energy management as an economic development strategy : a national colloquium, October 14-16, 1984, Lincoln, Nebraska : proceedings. [Lincoln, Neb.] (Box 95085, Lincoln 68509-5085) : [Nebraska Energy Office, 1984 or 1985] iv, 396 p. : ill. ; 28 cm. Cover title. Sponsored by Nebraska Energy Office, the Department of Community and Regional Planning, and the Community Resource and Research Center both departments of the College of Architecture, University of Nebraska-Lincoln. LC Card 86-622211 DDC 333.79/0973 19
1. Energy policy - United States - Congresses. 2. United States - Economic conditions - 1981- - Congresses. 3. Energy conservation - United States - Congresses. 4. Community development - United States - Congresses. I. Nebraska Energy Office. II. University of Nebraska--Lincoln. Dept. of Community and Regional Planning. III. University of Nebraska--Lincoln. Community Resource and Research Center.
HD9502.U52 C656 1984

Community grazing . Eastman, Clyde, 1936- Albuquerque , c1987. xiii, 176 p. : ISBN 0-8263-0936-4 LC Card 86-25058 DDC 333.74/09789 19
HD243.N74 E18 1987

COMMUNITY HEALTH. see **PUBLIC HEALTH.**

Community helpers series (New York, N.Y.)
Johnson, Jean, 1943- Sanitation workers, A to Z /. New York, N.Y. , 1988. p. cm. ISBN 0-8027-6772-9 LC Card 87-23129 DDC 628/.4/02373 19
HD8039.S257 J64 1988

Community Information Exchange (National Urban Coalition (U. S.)) Corporate support for community development. Washington, D.C. , c1984. 15 p. ; LC Card 87-100348 DDC 361.7/65/0973 19
HD60.5.U5 C689 1984

Community Information Exchange (U. S.) Small business incubators . Washington, D.C. , c1984. 32 p. : LC Card 86-233015 DDC 333.33/8 19
HD1393.25 .S63 1984

COMMUNITY LEADERSHIP - INDONESIA - NAMPU.
Purwanto, Bambang. Kepemimpinan dan masalah pertanahan di pedesaan Jawa . [Yogyakarta] , 1985. ix, 58 p. : LC Card 86-943756
HD900.N36 P87 1985

COMMUNITY LEADERSHIP - INDONESIA - NGANDAGAN.
Purwanto, Bambang. Kepemimpinan dan masalah pertanahan di pedesaan Jawa . [Yogyakarta] , 1985. ix, 58 p. : LC Card 86-943756
HD900.N36 P87 1985

COMMUNITY LIFE.
Harper, Douglas A. Working knowledge . Chicago , 1987. x, 214 p. : ISBN 0-226-31688-2 LC Card 86-30708 DDC 302.3/4 19
HD4904 .H335 1987

Petersen, Paul. Wohngemeinschaft oder Grossfamilie. [Wuppertal, c1972] 224 p. LC Card 72-375103 *NYPL [JLD 77-3003]*

Community management : Asian experience and perspectives / edited by David C. Korten. West Hartford, Conn. : Kumarian Press, c1986. xxii, 328 p. : ill. ; 23 cm. (Kumarian Press library of management for development) Includes bibliographies. ISBN 0-931816-40-8 (pbk.) LC Card 86-27691 DDC 338.95 19
1. Economic development - Environmental aspects. 2. Economic development - Social aspects. 3. Community development. I. Korten, David C. II. Series.
HD75.6 .C65 1986

Community nutrition /. Obert, Jessie Craig, 1911- New York , c1986. xviii, 478 p. : ISBN 0-471-82187-X LC Card 85-16910 DDC 363.8/8/0973 19
HV696.F6 O23 1986 NYPL [JLE 86-1398]

The community of cattlemen . Simpson, Peter K., 1930- Moscow, Idaho , c1987. xiv, 228 p. ; ISBN 0-89301-117-7 (pbk.) LC Card 87-5855 DDC 338.1/762/00979595 19
HD9433.U5 H277 1987

COMMUNITY ORGANIZATION - GERMANY (WEST) - NORTH RHINE-WESTPHALIA.
Anders leben . Berlin , 1985. 231 p. : ISBN 3-8012-0107-4 LC Card 85-189669
HD7287.72.G32 N6725 1985

Community participation for road planning in squatter settlement upgrading : training module. Nairobi, Kenya : United Nations Centre for Human Settlements, 1983. 56 leaves : ill., maps ; 30 cm. + 4 road maps. Includes bibliographical references. LC Card 86-980653 DDC 388.1/09676/2 19
1. Highway planning - Kenya - Citizen participation. 2. Squatter settlements - Kenya. I. United Nations Centre for Human Settlements.
HE367.K43 C584 1983

Community participation in development projects . Paul, Samuel, 1930- Washington, D.C. [1987]. v, 37 p. : ISBN 0-8213-0886-6 (pbk.) LC Card 87-2183 DDC 338.9/009172/4 19
HD75.8 .P38 1987

Community piped water supply systems in developing countries . Okun, Daniel Alexander. Washington, D.C. , 1987. xi, 249 p. : ISBN 0-8213-0896-3 (pbk.) LC Card 87-8161 DDC 363.6/1/091724 19
HD4465.D44 O38 1987

COMMUNITY POWER.
Oettinger, Craig Milton, 1945- The politics of excluded groups . 1978. xvi, 454 leaves : *NYPL [Sc Micro R-4615]*

COMMUNITY POWER - UGANDA - BUGISU (DISTRICT)
Bunker, Stephen G., 1944- Double dependency and constraints on class formation in Bugisu, Uganda /. Urbana, Ill. , 1983. v, 88 p. : LC Card 86-229748 DDC 303.3/09676/1 19
HD1538.U43 B86 1983

A Community research policy for development. Commission of the European Communities. Directorate-General of Information. Brussels [1983] 21 p. ; LC Card 85-166173 DDC 338.91/4/01724 19
HC60 .C584 1983

COMMUNITY SURVEYS. see **SOCIAL SURVEYS.**

COMMUTERS - HUNGARY.
Bőhm, Antal. Társadalmunk ingázói, az ingázók társadalma /. [Budapest] , 1985. 166, [I] p. ; ISBN 963-09-2654-7 : LC Card 86-185996
HD5717.5.H9 B64 1985

Commuting in America . Pisarski, Alan. Westport, Conn. (P.O. Box 2055, Westport 06880-2055) , c1987. 78 p. : LC Card 86-82787 DDC 388.3/14/0973 19
HD5717.5.U6 P57 1987

COMMUTING - SWITZERLAND - BERN (CANTON) - STATISTICS.
Kanton Bern (n.G.), Bilanz der erwerbstätigen Pendler, nach Gemeinden (2. 12. 1980) =. Bern , 1983. 16 p. ; LC Card 83-232809 DDC 388.3/14/094945 19
HD5717.5.S92 B46 1983

COMMUTING - UNITED STATES.
Pisarski, Alan. Commuting in America . Westport, Conn. (P.O. Box 2055, Westport 06880-2055) , c1987. 78 p. : LC Card 86-82787 DDC 388.3/14/0973 19
HD5717.5.U6 P57 1987

COMMUTING - UNITED STATES - STATISTICS.
Briggs, Dwight. Journey-to-work trends . Washington, D.C. , Springfield, VA [1986] 1 v. (various pagings) : LC Card 86-602387 DDC 388.4/1314/0973 19
HE371.A3 B75 1986

Cómo establecer el control presupuestario / Centro Español de Gestión. 1a ed. Madrid : Ibérico Europea de Ediciones, 1983. 95 p. : ill. ; 21 cm. (Cómo) ISBN 84-256-0387-0 LC Card 85-221532
1. Business enterprises - Finance. 2. Budget in business. I. Centro Español de Gestión.
HG4026 .C56 1983

Cómo mejorar el nivel de vida /. Ayau, Manuel F. [Guatemala , 1982] (Guatemala : Editorial Piedra Santa) 91 p. : LC Card 86-174413
HB178.5 .A93 1982

Cómo se desangra un país-- ! . Ojeda, Roseliano. Valencia [Venezuela] , c1987. 241 p. ; ISBN 980-212-037-5 LC Card 87-169695 DDC 330.987/0633 19
HC237 .O365 1987

Como usar Lotus 1-2-3 . LeBlond, Geoffrey T. Miami, Fla. , 1986- p. cm. LC Card 86-23629 DDC 005.36/9 19
HF5548.4.L67 L418 1986

Como ven nuestros hombres de empresa la economía de Cantabria para 1984. Reunión coloquio sobre como ven nuestros hombres de empresa la economía de Cantabria para 1984 /. [Santander] [1984?] 54 p. ; ISBN 84-505-0186-5 LC Card 86-187513
HF3690.C35 R48 1984

Como ven nuestros hombres de empresa la economía de Cantabria para 1985. Reunión coloquio sobre como ven nuestros hombres de empresa la economía de Cantabria para 1985 /. [Santander] [1985?] 78 p. ; ISBN 84-505-1440-1 LC Card 86-193783
HF3690.C35 R49 1985

COMPACT DISC INDUSTRY - UNITED STATES.
The Compact disc market--phase II . New York, N.Y. (444 Madison Ave., New York 10022) , c1986. viii, 57, [13] p. : LC Card 86-227224 DDC 381/.4562138933 19
HD9697.P563 U526 1986

The Compact disc market--phase II : includes automotive market data : a Newsweek study / conducted by the Data Group Inc. New York, N.Y. (444 Madison Ave., New York 10022) : Additional copies, Advertising Resource Center, Newsweek, c1986. viii, 57, [13] p. : ill. ; 28 cm. LC Card 86-227224 DDC 381/.4562138933 19
1. Compact disc industry - United States. 2. Sound recording industry - United States. 3. Market surveys - United States. 4. Consumers' preferences - United States. I. Newsweek, inc. II. Data Group (U. S.).
HD9697.P563 U526 1986

Compact for African development . Committee on African Development Strategies (U. S.) Berkeley, CA (2120 Berkeley Way, Berkeley 94720) [1985] 24 p. : LC Card 86-200473 DDC 338.967 19
HC800 .C645 1985

Compagnia di Giesù. see **Jesuits.**

La Compagnia lavoratori portuali di Ravenna, 1930-1980 /. Carli Ballola, Sandra. [Italy , 1981?] (Imola : Galeati) 208 p. : LC Card 83-206502
HD8039.L82 I83 1981

COMPAGNIA PORTUALE DI RAVENNA (ITALY) - HISTORY.
Carli Ballola, Sandra. La Compagnia lavoratori portuali di Ravenna, 1930-1980 /. [Italy , 1981?] (Imola : Galeati) 208 p. : LC Card 83-206502
HD8039.L82 I83 1981

Compagnie de Jésus. see **Jesuits.**

COMPAGNIE GÉNÉRALE AÉROPOSTALE - HISTORY.
Danel, Raymond. Les lignes Latécoère . Toulouse , c1986. 208 p., [16] p. of plates : ISBN 2-7089-8611-2 : LC Card 87-165510
HE9848.C66 D36 1986 vol. 1

Compagnie hollandaise des Indes orientales. see **Nederlandsche Oost-Indische Compagnie.**

Compagnie nationale des commissaires aux comptes (France) Le Contrôle de qualité . [Paris] [1983] 297 p. : ISBN 2-900670-20-9 : LC Card 85-106388
HF5616.F7 C66 1983

Companhia Brasileira de Armazenamento. Plano nacional de armazenagem, 1985 / CIBRAZEM, Companhia Brasileira de Armazenamento. Brasília, DF : CIBRAZEM, [1985 or 1986] 1 v. (various foliations) : ill. ; 30 cm. LC Card 87-403918 DDC 381 19
1. Warehouses - Government policy - Brazil. I. Title.
HF5489.B73 C66 1985

Companhia de Distritos Industriais de Sta. Catarina. Sinopse de informações dos municípios catarinenses. Florianópolis, SC , 1986. 155 leaves : LC Card 87-403943 DDC 330.981/64063 19
HC188.S26 S555 1986

Companhia de Financiamento da Produção (Brazil) Análise das distorções dos preços domésticos em relação aos preços de fronteira . Brasília , 1983. 125 p. : LC Card 86-200859
HD9014.B82 A66 1983

Companhia de Viação São Paulo-Mato Grosso. Ante-projeto do núcleo de colonização "Presidente Kennedy" / elaborado por Jan A. Bata, Nélson V. de Oliveira ; com a colaboração de Vladimir Kubik ... [et al.]. Mato Grosso, Brasil : Companhia de Viação São Paulo-Mato Grosso, 1962. 40 p., [15] leaves of plates : ill. (some col.) ; 32 cm. LC Card 85-135105
1. Agricultural colonies - Brazil - Bataiporã. I. Bata, Jan A. II. Oliveira, Nélson V. de. III. Title.
HD1516.B8 C64 1962

Companhia do Desenvolvimento do Planalto Central. Caracterização da população do Distrito Federal . Brasília , 1984. 56, [1] p. : LC Card 86-130173 DDC 331.12/0981/74021 19
HA988.D5 C37 1984

Companhia Energética de Minas Gerais. Diagnóstico energético, 1978/1983 /. Belo Horizonte , 1985. 177 p. : LC Card 87-121240 DDC 333.79/0981/51 19
HD9502.B73 M563 1985

Fluxo energético estadual, 1983 /. [Belo Horizonte, Brazil] , 1985. 105 p. : LC Card 87-404947 DDC 333.79/0981/51 19
HD9502.B73 M5646 1985

Seminário de Energia de Biomassa (1985? : Belo Horizonte, Brazil?) Seminário de Energia de Biomassa . [Belo Horizonte?] , <[1986?-. v. <[1-2] > : LC Card 87-107998
HD9502.5.B543 B67 1985

Seminários sobre Perspectivas dos Setores Produtivos de Minas Gerais (1986 : Belo Horizonte, Brazil) Seminários sobre Perspectivas dos Setores Produtivos de Minas Gerais . Belo Horizonte , 1986. 124 leaves ; LC Card 87-108000 DDC 338.0981/51 19
HC188.M6 S46 1986

Uso de energia na indústria de cimento em Minas Gerais, 1980-1983. [Belo Horizonte] , 1985. 146 p. : LC Card 86-152639
HD9622.B73 M569 1985

Companhia Energética de São Paulo. Marsiglia, Cecília. S/A Central Elétrica Rio Claro /. São Paulo , 1986. 105 p. : LC Card 87-404945 DDC 363.6/2/098161 19
HD9685.B83 C4886 1986

COMPANHIA GERAL DE PERNAMBUCO E PARAÍBA - HISTORY.
Carreira, António. As companhias pombalinas . Lisboa [1983] 426 p. : LC Card 86-146987
HF491.C592 C37 1983

COMPANHIA GERAL DO GRÃO PARÁ E MARANHÃO - HISTORY.
Carreira, António. As companhias pombalinas . Lisboa [1983] 426 p. : LC Card 86-146987
HF491.C592 C37 1983

COMPANHIA GERAL DO GRÃO PARÁ E MARANHÃO - HISTORY - 18TH CENTURY.
Diário da navegação de Macau, 1759-1761 . Lisboa , 1970. 274 p. ; LC Card 86-201114
HF1009.7.M25 D53 1970

COMPANHIA PAULISTA DE ESTRADAS DE FERRO - HISTORY.
Leme, Dulce M. Pompêo C. (Dulce Maria Pompêo de Camargo) Trabalhadores ferroviários em greve /. Campinas [Brazil] , 1986. 269 p. : ISBN 85-26-80007-8 : LC Card 87-102922 DDC 331.89/281385/098161 19
HD5354.R12 1906 .S365 1986

COMPANHIA PAULISTA DE ESTRADAS DE FERRO STRIKE, 1906.
Leme, Dulce M. Pompêo C. (Dulce Maria Pompêo de Camargo) Trabalhadores ferroviários em greve /. Campinas [Brazil] , 1986. 269 p. : ISBN 85-26-80007-8 : LC Card 87-102922 DDC 331.89/281385/098161 19
HD5354.R12 1906 .S365 1986

Companhia Vale do Rio Doce.
Cerrado . [Rio de Janeiro] , 1984. 53 p., [2] leaves of plates : LC Card 87-132493 DDC 380.1/4131/0981 19
HD9044.B682 C47 1984

Report to the World Bank, Amazônia Mineração S.A. . London [1979?] v, 57, [31] leaves : LC Card 85-154695
HD9524.B8 R46 1979

COMPANHIA VALE DO RIO DOCE - EMPLOYEES.
Minayo, Maria Cecília de Souza. Os homens de ferro . Rio de Janeiro , 1986. 244 p. : LC Card 87-129149 DDC 331.7/622341/098151 19
HD8039.M72 B86 1986

As companhias pombalinas . Carreira, António. Lisboa [1983] 426 p. : LC Card 86-146987
HF491.C592 C37 1983

Compañía de Jesús. see **Jesuits.**

COMPAÑÍA REAL DEL MONTE Y PACHUCA - HISTORY - 18TH CENTURY.
Ladd, Doris M. The making of a strike . Lincoln , c1988. x, 205 p. ; ISBN 0-8032-2876-7 (alk. paper) LC Card 87-5897 DDC 331.8/928223423/097246 19
HD5331.M72 1766 .P325 1988

Compañía Telefónica Nacional de España. Spain and the telephone . New York , 1925. 16 p., [1] folded leaf of plates : LC Card 85-666351
HE9324 .S63x 1925

COMPANIES. see **CORPORATIONS; PARTNERSHIP.**

COMPANIES, PRIVATE. see **PRIVATE COMPANIES.**

COMPANIES, SUBSIDIARY. see **SUBSIDIARY CORPORATIONS.**

Company administration handbook. 5th ed. Aldershot, Hants, England : Gower, 1982. xxiv, 770 p. : ill. ; 24 cm. Includes bibliographies and index. ISBN 0-566-02352-0 LC Card 83-111544 DDC 658/.00941 19
1. Industrial management - Great Britain - Handbooks, manuals, etc. 2. Corporation law - Great Britain - Handbooks, manuals, etc. 3. Corporation secretaries - Great Britain - Handbooks, manuals, etc.
HD70.G7 C57 1982 ***NYPL [JLE 86-2558]***

Company administration handbook / edited by Derek Beattie. 6th ed. Aldershot, Hants, England ; Brookfield, Vt., U. S.A. : Gower Pub., 1988. xxiv, 737 p. : ill. ; 24 cm. Includes bibliographies and index. ISBN 0-566-02667-8 : LC Card 86-31876 DDC 658/.00941 19
1. Industrial management - Great Britain - Handbooks, manuals, etc. 2. Corporation law - Great Britain - Handbooks, manuals, etc. 3. Corporation secretaries - Great Britain - Handbooks, manuals, etc. I. Beattie, Derek.
HD70.G7 C57 1988

Company and industry cases in strategy and policy /. Pearce, John A. Homewood, IL , 1986. xiv, 711 p. : ISBN 0-256-03558-X : LC Card 85-82002 ***NYPL [JLE 87-993]***

Company auditing /. Lee, Thomas Alexander. Wokingham, Berkshire, England , 1986. x, 197 p. ; ISBN 0-85258-243-9 (pbk.) LC Card 85-22537 DDC 657/.45 19
HF5667 .L387 1986 ***NYPL [JLD 86-3477]***

COMPANY INSURANCE. see **INSURANCE, BUSINESS.**

COMPANY LAW. see **CORPORATION LAW.**

Company loyalty . Shea, Gordon F., 1925- New York, N.Y. , c1987. 86 p. : ISBN 0-8144-2331-0 (pbk.) : LC Card 86-28883 DDC 650.1 19
HD58.9 .S48 1987

COMPANY MEETINGS. see **CORPORATE MEETINGS.**

Company of Jesus. see **Jesuits.**

Company policy manual. The IFM guide to the preparation of a company policy manual. Greenvale, N.Y. , c1987. xv, 412 p. ; ISBN 0-916592-71-5 (loose-leaf) LC Card 87-22258 DDC 658.3/01 19
HF5549 .I5643 1987

Company programs to ease the impact of shutdowns /. Berenbeim, Ronald. New York, N.Y. , c1986. ix, 57 p. : ISBN 0-8237-0320-7 (pbk.) LC Card 86-207794 DDC 331.25 19
HF5549.5.D55 B47 1986

COMPANY REPORTS. see **CORPORATION REPORTS.**

Company secretary. Great Britain. Central Youth Employment Executive. [London, 1970] 15 p. ISBN 0-11-360036-4 : LC Card 72-534885 DDC 331.702 s
HF5381.A1 G73 no. 29, 1970

A company that cares . Foster, Lawrence G., 1925- New Brunswick, N.J. , c1986. 175 p. : ISBN 0-9617676-1-8 LC Card 86-27478 DDC 338.7/616151/0973 19
HD9666.9.J6 F67 1986

Company town . Petersen, Keith. Pullman, Wash. , Moscow, Idaho , 1987. xix, 284 p., [32] p. of plates : ISBN 0-87422-036-X (alk. paper) : LC Card 87-14980 DDC 307.7/67/0979686 19
HD9759.P63 P47 1987

COMPANY TOWN ARCHITECTURE - GERMANY (WEST) - SCHIFFWEILER.
Habicht, Werner. Werkssiedlung Madenfelderhof bei Landsweiler-Reden . Saarbrücken , 1985. 54 p., [52] p. of plates : LC Card 87-408673 DDC 330.943/42 19
HD7289.5.A3 G437 1985

COMPANY TOWNS - GERMANY (WEST) - SCHIFFWEILER.
Habicht, Werner. Werkssiedlung Madenfelderhof bei Landsweiler-Reden . Saarbrücken , 1985. 54 p., [52] p. of plates : LC Card 87-408673 DDC 330.943/42 19
HD7289.5.A3 G437 1985

COMPANY TOWNS - IDAHO - HISTORY.
Petersen, Keith. Company town . Pullman, Wash. , Moscow, Idaho , 1987. xix, 284 p., [32] p. of plates : ISBN 0-87422-036-X (alk. paper) : LC Card 87-14980 DDC 307.7/67/0979686 19
HD9759.P63 P47 1987

COMPANY TOWNS - SOUTHERN STATES - HISTORY.
Mayor, Archer H. Southern timberman . Athens , c1988. p. cm. ISBN 0-8203-0999-0 (alk. paper) LC Card 87-22897 DDC 338.7/63498/0975 19
HD9760.B83 M39 1988

COMPANY UNIONS - JAPAN.
Iida, Tsuneo, 1932- What is really unique about the Japanese economy? /. Nagoya, Japan , 1985. 13 leaves ; LC Card 87-109242 DDC 331.25 19
HF5549.5.S4 I35 1985

Comparable worth . Kondratas, S. Anna. Washington, D.C. [c1986] 16 p. ; LC Card 86-212973 DDC 331.2/1 19
HD6061 .K66 1986

Comparable worth, pay equity, and public policy / edited by Rita Mae Kelly and Jane Bayes ; prepared under the auspices of the Policy Studies Organization. New York : Greenwood Press, 1988. xi, 280 p. ; 24 cm. (Contributions in labor studies, 0886-8239 . no. 22) Bibliography: p. [247]-267. Includes index. ISBN 0-313-26014-1 (lib. bdg. : alk. paper) LC Card 87-17735 DDC 331.2/1 19
1. Pay equity - Government policy - United States. I.

Kelly, Rita Mae. II. Bayes, Jane H., 1939-. III. Series.
HD6061.2.U6 C656 1988

COMPARATIVE ACCOUNTING.
The Accounting profession in [name of country] . New York, N.Y. , c1987- v. <1-5 > ; LC Card 87-150526 DDC 657 19
HF5611 .A34 1987

Belkaoui, Ahmed, 1943- The new environment in international accounting . New York , c1988. p. cm. ISBN 0-89930-267-X (lib. bdg. : alk. paper) LC Card 87-7252 DDC 657/.95 19
HF5686.I56 B45 1988

The Fourth company accounts directive of 1978 and the accounting systems of the Federal Republic of Germany, France, Italy, the United Kingdom, the United States, and Japan. Luxembourg , Washington, DC , 1986. 164, [47] p. ; ISBN 92-825-6454-1 (pbk.) : LC Card 87-134287 DDC 657 19
HF5611 .F686 1986

Frattini, Giovanni. Contabilità e bilancio . Milano [1986] xiii, 317 p. : ISBN 88-14-00831-0 : LC Card 86-182373
HF5625 .F73 1986

Harmonization of accounting standards . Paris , Washington, D.C. , 1986. 147 p. ; ISBN 92-64-12895-6 (pbk.) : LC Card 87-124490 DDC 657/.0218 19
HF5611 .H37 1986

Orsini, Larry L. World accounting /. New York, NY (11 Penn Plaza, New York 10001) , 1987- c1986- 2 v. (loose-leaf) ; LC Card 86-73012 DDC 657 19
HF5611 .O75 1987

Zeff, Stephen A. Forging accounting principles in five countries . Champaign, Ill. , 1971, c1972. xvii, 332 p. ; LC Card 86-226472
HF5605 .Z44 1972

COMPARATIVE ADVANTAGE (COMMERCE)
Albuquerque, Marcos Cintra Cavalcanti de. Riscos e perspectivas da divisão internacional do trabalho =. Brasília, DF [1986] 19, 17, [2] p. ; LC Card 87-403241 DDC 331/.01 19
HF1411 .A3984 1986

Evans, H. David (Henry David) The political economy of trade and development /. New York , 1988- p. cm. ISBN 0-312-00955-0 (v. 1) : LC Card 87-16370 DDC 382 19
HF1008 .E83 1988

International comparative advantage in manufacturing . Vienna , 1986. xii, 226 p. : ISBN 92-1-106210-1 (pbk.) LC Card 86-214978 DDC 382.1/042 19
HF1412 .I57 1986

Leonard, H. Jeffrey. Pollution and the struggle for the world product . Cambridge [Cambridgeshire] , New York , 1988. p. cm. ISBN 0-521-34042-X LC Card 87-17766 DDC 338.6/042 19
HD75.6 .L46 1988

Mohs, Ralf-Matthias. Exporte, komparative Vorteile und wirtschaftliche Entwicklung in den Schwellenländern . Göttingen [1983] 236 p. : ISBN 3-509-01345-X LC Card 84-126961
HF4055 .M64 1983

Török, Ádám. Komparatív előnyök . Budapest , 1986, c1985. 225, [1] p. ; ISBN 963-221-579-6 : LC Card 87-105362
HF1412 .T67 1986

COMPARATIVE ADVANTAGE (COMMERCE) - CASE STUDIES.
States versus markets in the world-system /. Beverly Hills, Calif. , c1985. 295 p. ; ISBN 0-8039-2510-7 LC Card 85-11716 DDC 338.9 19
HD3611 .S76 1985 ***NYPL [JLD 86-3227]***

COMPARATIVE ADVANTAGE (COMMERCE) - STATISTICS.
International comparative advantage in manufacturing . Vienna , 1986. xii, 226 p. : ISBN 92-1-106210-1 (pbk.) LC Card 86-214978 DDC 382.1/042 19
HF1412 .I57 1986

COMPARATIVE COSTS. see **COMPARATIVE ADVANTAGE (COMMERCE)**

COMPARATIVE ECONOMIC SYSTEMS. see **COMPARATIVE ECONOMICS.**

COMPARATIVE ECONOMICS - ADDRESSES, ESSAYS, LECTURES.
Couri, Sergio, 1948- Ensaios sobre a evolução dos sistemas econômicos /. Brasília-Distrito Federal [1983] 133 p. : LC Card 84-116306 DDC 330.1 19
HB97.5 .C68 1983 ***NYPL [JLE 86-3363]***

Wachstumsverlangsamung und Konjunkturzyklen in unterschiedlichen Wirtschaftssystemen /. Berlin , c1984. 191 p. : ISBN 3-428-05626-4
NYPL [JLL 73-186 Bd. 142]

COMPARATIVE ECONOMICS - CONGRESSES.
Economic incentives . London , 1986. xiii, 497 p. ; ISBN 0-333-40473-4 ***NYPL [JLD 87-367]***

The comparative economics of research development in East and West . Hanson, Philip. Chur, Switzerland , New York , c1987. viii, 101 ; ISBN 3-7186-0419-1 (pbk.) LC Card 87-23623 DDC 338/.06 19
HC79.T4 H355 1987

Comparative ethnic and race relations.
Jenkins, Richard, 1952- Racism and recruitment . Cambridge [Cambridgeshire] , New York , 1986. xi, 281 p. ; ISBN 0-521-32028-3 LC Card 85-17483 DDC 331.13/3/0941 19
HG4903.5.G7 J46 1986
NYPL [JLE 86-3305]

COMPARATIVE GOVERNMENT - ADDRESSES, ESSAYS, LECTURES.
The Rise of the modern state /. Brighton, Sussex , 1986. viii, 255 p. ; ISBN 0-7450-0059-2
NYPL [JLD 86-2353]

The State in global perspective /. Aldershot, Hants, Eng. ; Brookfield, Vt., USA : xx, 300 p. : ISBN 0-566-05160-5 (U. S.) : LC Card 85-31741 DDC 320.1 19
NYPL [JLD 86-3236]

Comparative government-industry relations : Western Europe, the United States, and Japan / edited by Stephen Wilks, Maurice Wright. Oxford : Clarendon Press ; New York : Oxford University Press, 1987. xiii, 321 p. ; 23 cm. (Government-industry relations) ISBN 0-19-827493-9 : LC Card 86-28631 DDC 338.9 19
1. Industry and state - Europe. 2. Industry and state - United States. 3. Industry and state - Japan. I. Wilks, Stephen. II. Wright, Maurice. III. Series.
HD3611 .C63 1987

Comparative labour law and industrial relations / editor, Blanpain, R. ; [contributors] Aaron, B. ... [et al.]. 2nd rev. ed. Deventer [Netherlands] ; Boston : Kluwer Law and Taxation Publishers, c1985. xiii, 527 p. ; 25 cm. Includes bibliographies and indexes. ISBN 90-6544-236-7 (pbk.) LC Card 85-10000 DDC 344/.01 342.41 19
1. Labor laws and legislation - Addresses, essays, lectures. 2. Industrial relations - Addresses, essays, lectures. I. Blanpain, Roger. II. Aaron, Benjamin.
K1705.6 .C65 1985 ***NYPL [JLE 86-2420]***

Comparative local statistics /. Melbourne and Metropolitan Board of Works. Statistical Division. [Melbourne] [1983] 135, [2] p. : LC Card 86-228235 DDC 319.45/1 19
HA3008.M45 M45 1983

Comparative management : a regional view / edited by Raghu Nath. Cambridge, Mass. : Ballinger Pub. Co., c1988. xv, 321 p. : ill. ; 24 cm. (Ballinger series in business in a global environment) Includes bibliographies and indexes. ISBN 0-88730-136-3 LC Card 87-17459 DDC 658 19
1. Comparative management. I. Nath, Raghu. II. Series.
HD30.55 .C656 1988

COMPARATIVE MANAGEMENT - ADDRESSES, ESSAYS, LECTURES.
Bjørn-Andersen, Niels. Managing computer impact . Norwood, N.J. , c1986. viii, 248 p. : ISBN 0-89391-358-8 LC Card 85-30754 DDC 658/.05 19
HD30.2 .B55 1986 ***NYPL [JLE 86-2806]***

COMPARATIVE MANAGEMENT - CONGRESSES.
Organization of innovation . Berlin , New York , 1987. x, 238 p. : ISBN 0-89925-167-6 (U. S.) : LC Card 87-19936 DDC 658.4/06 19
HD45 .O73 1987

COMPARATIVE ORGANIZATION.
Comparative studies in administration /. New York , 1987. xiv, 224, 40 p. : ISBN 0-8240-8220-6 (alk. paper) : LC Card 86-27017 DDC 658 19
HD30.55 .C66 1987

Littler, Craig R. The development of the labour process in capitalist societies . London , Exeter, N.H. , 1982. 226 p. : ISBN 0-435-82540-2 : LC Card 82-210245 DDC 306/.36 19
HD8390 .L48 1982 ***NYPL [JLD 87-1005]***

Comparative patterns of economic development, 1850-1914 /. Morris, Cynthia Taft. Baltimore , c1988. xi, 575 p. ; ISBN 0-8018-3507-0 (alk. paper) LC Card 87-45480 DDC 338.9/009 19
HC51 .M645 1988

Comparative studies in administration / James D. Thompson ... [et al.]. Management and technology / Joan Woodward. New York : Garland, 1987. xiv, 224, 40 p. : ill. ; 23 cm. (Continuity in administrative science) Reprint (1st work). Originally published: Pittsburgh : University of Pittsburgh Press, c1959. Reprint (2nd work). Originally published: London, H.M.S.O., 1958. Includes index. ISBN 0-8240-8220-6 (alk. paper) : LC Card 86-27017 DDC 658 19
1. Comparative management. 2. Comparative organization. I. Thompson, James D. II. Woodward, Joan, M.A. Management and technology. III. Series.
HD30.55 .C66 1987

Comparative studies in history, institutions, and public policy.
Solberg, Carl E. The prairies and the pampas . Stanford, Calif. , 1987. xii, 297 p. : ISBN 0-8047-1346-4 (alk. paper) : LC Card 86-27854 DDC 338.1/8 19
HD9049.W5 C297 1987

Comparative studies in overseas history.
(v. 7) Colonialism and migration . Dordrecht , Higham, MA, USA , 1986. vi, 303 p. : ISBN 90-247-3253-0 LC Card 85-21809 DDC 331.11/73 19
HD4875.A837 C65 1986
NYPL [JLE 86-3920]

(7) Colonialism and migration . Dordrecht , Higham, MA, USA , 1986. vi, 303 p. : ISBN 90-247-3253-0 LC Card 85-21809 DDC 331.11/73 19
HD4875.A837 C65 1986
NYPL [JLE 86-3920]

A Comparative study on accounting policy between Japanese and the U. S. companies / project members, leader, Aishi Imafuku ... [et al.]. Tokyo, Japan : Institute of Business Research, College of Economics, Nihon University, c1986. iv, 56 p. : ill. ; 26 cm. (Survey report . no. 7) LC Card 87-169003 DDC 657/.0952 19
1. Corporations - United States - Accounting - Public opinion. 2. Corporations - Japan - Accounting - Public opinion. 3. Managerial accounting - Decision making - Public opinion. 4. Public opinion - United States. 5. Public opinion - Japan. I. Imafuku, Aishi, 1941-. II. Series: Survey report (Nihon Daigaku. Sangyō Keiei Kenkyūjo) , no. 7.
HF5686.C7 C635 1986

Comparative tax systems : Europe, Canada, and Japan / Joseph A. Pechman, editor ; contributing authors, Krister Andersson ... [et al.]. Arlington, Va. : Tax Analysts, 1987. xiv, 447 p. : ill. ; 23 cm. Includes bibliographies and index. CONTENTS. - Introduction / by Joseph A. Pechman -- Sweden / by Krister Andersson -- Netherlands / by Flip de Kam -- France / by Jean-Louis Lienard, Kenneth C. Messere, and Jeffrey Owens -- Italy / by Laura Castellucci -- Federal Republic of Germany / by Annette Dengel ; translated by Birgit Schneider -- United Kingdom / by Nick Morris -- Canada / by Harry M. Kitchen -- Japan / by M. Homma, T. Maeda, and K. Hashimoto. ISBN 0-918255-05-8 (pbk.) : LC Card 87-50143 DDC 336.2 19
1. Taxation - Europe. 2. Taxation - Japan. 3. Taxation - Canada. I. Pechman, Joseph A., 1918-. II. Andersson, Krister.
HJ2599.5 .C65 1987

Comparative technology choice in development . Otsuka, Keijiro. New York , 1988. viii, 247 p. : ISBN 0-312-00516-4 : LC Card 86-29666 DDC 338.4/567721/0952 19
HD9886.I42 O87 1988

Comparative work systems . Matejko, Aleksander.

New York , 1986. xx, 237 p. ; ISBN 0-03-004492-8 (alk. paper) : LC Card 85-6354 DDC 306/.36/0947 19
HD6957.E82 M37 1985 ***NYPL [JLE 86-1083]***

COMPARATIVES ADVANTAGE (COMMERCE)
Moldau, Juan Hersztajn. Custo dos recursos domésticos /. Rio de Janeiro , 1985. 94, 4 p. ; LC Card 86-200395
HC190.C7 M64 1985

COMPARISON ADVERTISING. see **ADVERTISING, COMPARISON.**

A comparison of Alaska's wholesale trade sector with other states /. Schiller, Robert, 1950- [Juneau, Alaska] [1984] vi, 104 p. : LC Card 86-620623 DDC 381/.2/09798 19
HF5421 .S33 1984

A comparison of some land-use allocation/interaction models [microform] /. Foot, David H.S. Reading [Berkshire] , 1974. 36 p. : ISBN 0-7049-0338-5 ***NYPL [*ZT-1712 no.13]***

Comparison of the insurance loss experience of unibody and frame construction cars after a collision repair, 1981-82 models. Washington, D.C. (Watergate 600, Washington 20037) : Highway Loss Data Institute, c1985. 10 p. : ill. ; 28 cm. (Research report HLDI . A-24 (Oct. 1985)) Insurance special report / Highway Loss Data Institute LC Card 87-107697 DDC 368.5/72/00973 19
1. Insurance, Automobile - United States. 2. Traffic accidents - United States. I. Highway Loss Data Institute. II. Series: Research report HLDI , A-24.
HG9970.3 .C65 1985

Compendio estadístico / Gobierno de Córdoba, Secretaría Ministerio de Planeamiento y Coordinación, Dirección de Estadística y Censos. Córdoba, República Argentina : La Dirección, [1984] 110 leaves : ill ; 21 x 30 cm. Chiefly tables. LC Card 87-400414 DDC 304.6/0982/54021 19
1. Córdoba (Argentina : Province) - Population - Statistics. 2. Households - Argentina - Córdoba (Province) - Statistics. 3. Córdoba (Argentina : Province) - Economic conditions - Statistics. 4. Gross national product - Argentina - Córdoba (Province) - Statistics. I. Córdoba (Argentina : Province). Dirección de Estadística y Censos.
HA958.C6 C64 1984

A compendium of methods of error evaluation in censuses and surveys /. Statistics Canada. Statistical Services Field. Ottawa , 1978. 25 p. ; LC Card 80-499370 DDC 001.4/225 19
HA31.2 .C36 1978 ***NYPL [JLF 81-125]***

Compendium of state fiscal information / prepared by Maine State Legislature, Office of Fiscal and Program Review. [Augusta?] : The Office, [1985] 40 leaves : ill. ; 28 cm. "December, 1985." "Pub. #17." LC Card 86-621730 DDC 336.741/021 19
1. Revenue - Maine - Statistics. 2. Taxation - Maine - Statistics. 3. Maine - Appropriations and expenditures - Statistics. I. Maine. Legislature. Office of Fiscal and Program Review.
HJ2410 .C65 1985

Compendium of studies of international income and taxes. Statistics of income . Washington, D.C. , 1985. iii, 516 p. : ***NYPL [JLF 86-833]***

A compendium of the law and practice of vendors and purchasers of real estate [microform]. Dart, Joseph Henry, 1817-1887. New York, Albany, 1851. civ, 665 (i.e. 856) p. LC Card 17-19132 ***NYPL [*ZT-1719]***

Compensation /. Milkovich, George T. Plano, Tex. , 1987. xiv, 655 p. : ISBN 0-256-03709-4 LC Card 86-72247 DDC 658.3/2 19
HF5549.5.C67 M54 1987

COMPENSATION. see **WAGES.**

Compensation administration /. Belcher, David W. Englewood Cliffs, N.J. , c1987. xv, 464 p. : ISBN 0-13-154790-9 : LC Card 86-25494 DDC 658.3/2 19
HF5549.5.C67 B45 1987

COMPENSATION ADMINISTRATION. see **COMPENSATION MANAGEMENT.**

Compensation and benefits in research & development / directed by Steven Langer. Crete, IL : Abbott, Langer & Associates, c1987. 692 p. ; 28 cm. ISBN 0-916506-34-7 (pbk.) LC Card 87-403067 DDC 331.2/816584/00973021 19
1. Executives - Salaries ,etc. - United States - Statistics. 2. Employee fringe benefits - United States - Statistics. I. Langer, Steven. II. Abbott, Langer & Associates.
HD4965.5.U6 C656 1987

La Compensation des charges familiales au Québec / Raynald Leblanc ... [et al.]. [Quebec] : Régie des rentes du Québec, [1986] xxi, 197 p. ; 28 cm. (Les Publications du Québec) Collection Etude et recherche ; no 3 Bibliography: p. 191-197. ISBN 2-551-08707-4 LC Card 86-179318
1. Family allowances - Québec (Province). 2. Social security - Québec (Province). I. Leblanc, Raynald. II. Régie des rentes du Québec.
HD4925.5.C2 C65 1986

Compensation in the accounting/financial field / directed by Steven Langer. 8th ed. Crete, IL : Abbott, Langer & Associates, c1987. 489 p. ; 28 cm. ISBN 0-916506-36-3 (pbk.) LC Card 87-153325 DDC 331.12/81657/0973021 19
1. Accountants - Salaries, etc. - United States - Statistics. 2. Auditors - Salaries, etc. - United States - Statistics. I. Langer, Steven. II. Abbott, Langer & Associates.
HF5627 .C57 1987

COMPENSATION MANAGEMENT - CONGRESSES.
Incentives, cooperation, and risk sharing . Totowa, N.J. , 1987. xvi, 239 p. : ISBN 0-8476-7464-9 LC Card 87-4558 DDC 658.3/22 19
HF5549.5.C67 I56 1987

Compensation management for banks /. Caruth, Donald L. Boston , c1986. viii, 312 p. : ISBN 0-87267-060-0 LC Card 86-3543 DDC 332.1/068/3 19
HG1615.7.C65 C37 1986 ***NYPL [JLE 87-828]***

COMPENSATION MANAGEMENT - GERMANY (WEST) - CONGRESSES.
Neue Entwicklungen bei Arbeit, Entgelt und Führung /. Freiburg im Breisgau , c1984. 169 p. : ISBN 3-448-01480-X : LC Card 84-249237
HF5549.2.G3 N48 1984

COMPENSATION MANAGEMENT - HUNGARY.
Ott, György. A vállalati bértarifarendszer /. [Budapest] , 1984. 110 p. ; ISBN 963-322-158-7 : LC Card 85-176915
HD5022.5 .O77 1984

COMPENSATION MANAGEMENT - JAPAN.
Ballon, Robert J. Salary administration in Japan . Tokyo , 1985. 44 p. ; ISBN 4-88168-100-1 LC Card 86-115944 DDC 331.2/952 19
HD5077 .B3454 1985

COMPENSATION MANAGEMENT - UNITED STATES.
McFadden, John J. Retirement plans for employees /. Homewood, Ill. , 1988. xviii, 326 p. : ISBN 0-256-05588-2 LC Card 87-81436 DDC 658.3/253 19
HD7105.35.U6 M33 1988

COMPENSATION MANAGEMENT - UNITED STATES - HANDBOOKS, MANUALS, ETC.
Plunkett, Jack W. The almanac of American employers . Chicago , 1985. 340 p. ; ISBN 0-8092-5407-7 LC Card 85-14908 DDC 331.2/0973 19
HF5549.5.C67 P58 1985 ***NYPL [*R-Econ. 85-3166]***

The compensatory financing system of the International Monetary Fund . Herrmann, Roland. Kiel, West-Germany , 1983. iii, 85 p. ; ISBN 3-922553-18-4 (pbk.) LC Card 83-227524 DDC 332.1/52 19
HG3881.5.I58 H47 1983 ***NYPL [JLD 97-7]***

COMPENSATORY SPENDING. see **DEFICIT FINANCING.**

Competitief ondernemen : een handreiking voor hedendaags management / André Vlerick ... [et al.]. Antwerpen : Kluwer, 1983. vi, 233 p. : ill. ; 25 cm. (Bibliotheek wetenschappelijk bedrijfsbeheer) Includes bibliographies. ISBN 90-6716-301-5 LC Card 85-177786
1. Competition. 2. Competition - Belgium. 3. Industrial management. I. Vlerick, A. J. II. Series.
HD41 .C64 1983

COMPETITION.
Arndt, Helmut, 1911- Leistungswettbewerb und ruinöse Konkurrenz in ihrem Einfluss auf Wohlfahrt und Beschäftigung . Berlin , c1986. 147 p. ; ISBN 3-428-06078-4 LC Card 87-112253 DDC 338.9 19
HD41 .A755 1986

Ballarín, Eduard. Estrategias competitivas para la banca . Barcelona , 1985. 277 p. : ISBN 84-344-1040-0 LC Card 85-241009
HG1607.S7 B35 1985

Böbel, Ingo. Wettbewerb und Industriestruktur . Berlin , New York , 1984. xiv, 336 p. : ISBN 0-387-13143-4 (U. S.) LC Card 85-111698
HD2757 .B63 1984

Brenner, Reuven. Rivalry . Cambridge , New York , 1987. xi, 244 p. ; ISBN 0-521-33187-0 LC Card 86-24415 DDC 338.6/048 19
HD41 .B743 1987

Competitief ondernemen . Antwerpen , 1983. vi, 233 p. : ISBN 90-6716-301-5 LC Card 85-177786
HD41 .C64 1983

Competition policy and deregulation . Paris , 1986. 35 p. ; LC Card 86-217040 DDC 338.6/048 19
HD3612 .C65 1986

Farzin, Yeganeh Hossein, 1950- Competition and substitutes in the market for an exhaustible resource /. Greenwich, Conn. , c1985. xvi, 209 : ISBN 0-89232-604-2 : LC Card 85-23765 DDC 338.2/7282/0724 19
HD9560.5 .F385 1985 ***NYPL [JLE 86-1585]***

Fronhoff, Bernd, 1956- Die Gestaltung von Marketingstrategien . Bergisch Gladbach , 1986. ix, 369 p. : ISBN 3-89012-067-9 LC Card 87-122913 DDC 658.8/02 19
HF5415.135 .F76 1986

Geroski, Paul A. Do dominant firms decline? /. Berlin [1985] 23, [8] p. ; LC Card 86-213583 DDC 338.6/44 19
HD2757 .G47 1985

Hainzl, Martin. Konkurrenzanalyse in der strategischen Planung /. Wien , 1985. 143 p. : ISBN 3-85436-027-4 LC Card 86-127579 DDC 658.4/012 19
HD30.28 .H334 1985

Ireland, Norman J. Product differentiation and non-price competition /. Oxford, UK , New York, NY, USA , 1987. 192 p. : ISBN 0-631-13846-3 : LC Card 86-24504 DDC 658.8/16 19
HF5415.15 .I74 1987

Kelly, John M., 1949- How to check out your competition . New York , c1987. xii, 349 p. : ISBN 0-471-85670-3 (pbk.) LC Card 86-32408 DDC 658.8/02 19
HD41 .K44 1987

Langenbach, Peter. Wettbewerb und staatliche Sachausgaben /. Bochum , 1981. viii, 316 p. ; ISBN 3-88339-194-8 : LC Card 81-205020 DDC 336.3/9 19
HJ7461 .L36 1981 ***NYPL [JLD 86-2579]***

Maxeiner, Dirk, 1953- Testfahrer und Autospione . Stuttgart , 1985. 214 p. : ISBN 3-613-01022-4 : LC Card 85-170273
HD9710.A2 M385 1985

Morse, Diane McGinty. Managing competitive intelligence . Menlo Park, Calif. , c1985. 36 p. : LC Card 87-404501 DDC 658.4/7 19
HD38.7 .M674 1985

Neumann, Carl Wolfgang. Historische Entwicklung und heutiger Stand der Wettbewerbstheorie . Königstein/Ts. , 1982. 318 p. ; ISBN 3-7610-6362-8 : LC Card 83-154547
HB238 .N48 1982

Niemeier, Joachim, 1955- Wettbewerbsumwelt und interne Konfigurationen . Frankfurt am Main , New York , c1986. xv, 412 p. : ISBN 3-8204-9541-X LC Card 87-407931 DDC 338.6/048 19
HD41 .N54 1986

Product standardization and competitive strategy /. Amsterdam ; New York : xii, 316 p. : ISBN 0-444-70232-6(U. S.) LC Card 87-8849 DDC 338/.02 19
HD62 .P75 1987

Reheis, Fritz. Konkurrenz und Gleichgewicht

als Fundamente von Gesellschaft . Berlin , c1986. xi, 401 p. : ISBN 3-428-06102-0 LC Card 87-131057 DDC 339.5 19
HB238 .R44 1986

Ricketts, Martin J. The economics of business enterprise . Brighton, Sussex , 1987. xii, 306 p. : ISBN 0-7108-0221-8 : LC Card 87-104594 DDC 338.5 19
HD2731 .R53 1987

Vella, Carolyn M. Competitive intelligence in the computer age /. New York , 1987. xv, 189 p. ; ISBN 0-89930-169-X (lib. bdg. : alk. paper) LC Card 86-25565 DDC 651.8 19
HF5548.2 .V38 1987

COMPETITION - ADDRESSES, ESSAYS, LECTURES.
Competitiveness through technology . Lexington, Mass. , c1986. xix, 215 p. : ISBN 0-669-11604-1 (alk. paper) LC Card 85-45379 DDC 338.97306 19
T185 .C67 1986 ***NYPL [JLE 86-1968]***

Firms and markets . London , c1986. xiii, 271 p. : ISBN 0-7099-2446-1
NYPL [JLD 86-2134]

Competition among international airlines /. Pryke, Richard. Aldershot , Brookfield, USA , 1987. xi, 113 p. : ISBN 0-566-05333-0 : LC Card 86-31877 DDC 387.7/1 19
HE9780 .P79 1987

Competition and substitutes in the market for an exhaustible resource /. Farzin, Yeganeh Hossein, 1950- Greenwich, Conn. , c1985. xvi, 209 : ISBN 0-89232-604-2 : LC Card 85-23765 DDC 338.2/7282/0724 19
HD9560.5 .F385 1985 ***NYPL [JLE 86-1585]***

COMPETITION - BELGIUM.
Competitief ondernemen . Antwerpen , 1983. vi, 233 p. : ISBN 90-6716-301-5 LC Card 85-177786
HD41 .C64 1983

COMPETITION - BERLIN (GERMANY)
Ring, Peter. Regionale Besonderheiten der Preisbildung und Ansätze zur Förderung des Wettbewerbs auf dem Berliner Baustoffmarkt /. Berlin , 1986. 187 p. : ISBN 3-428-06112-8 LC Card 87-114036 DDC 330 s 338.4/3691/09431554 19
HC281 .B33 Heft 91 HD9715.G33B52

COMPETITION - CONGRESSES.
Dauderstädt, Michael. Wettbewerbsfähig durch soziale Disziplin? . Bonn [1981] 38 p. ; LC Card 85-137321
HD41 .D38 1981

Innovation and entrepreneurship in organizations . Amsterdam ; New York : vii, 207 p. : ISBN 0-444-42716-3 (U. S.) : LC Card 86-24207 DDC 658.4/012 19
HD41 .I56 1986

New developments in the analysis of market structure . Cambridge, Mass. , 1986. xxiv, 559 p. : ISBN 0-262-19241-1 LC Card 85-4246 DDC 338.8 19
HD2326 .N43 1986 ***NYPL [JLD 86-3570]***

Schmidtchen, Dieter. Property rights, Freiheit und Wettbewerbspolitik /. Tübingen , 1983. 71 p. ; ISBN 3-16-344630-2 (Deut. Bibl.) LC Card 84-100421
HF1410.5 .S36 1983

COMPETITION - ECONOMETRIC MODELS.
Vilks, Arnis. Aggregation und Kausalität im Modell des allgemeinen Konkurrenzgleichgewichts . Göttingen , c1984. 141 p. ; ISBN 3-525-11287-4 (Deut. Bibl.) LC Card 84-225754
HB842 .V55 1984

COMPETITION - EUROPEAN ECONOMIC COMMUNITY COUNTRIES.
Yamawaki, Hideki. Industry competition and the formation of the European common market /. Berlin [1986] 34, 3 p. ; LC Card 87-156700 DDC 341.24/22 19
HD41 .Y35 1986

COMPETITION - FLORIDA.
Florida and Mexico competition for the winter fresh vegetable market /. Washington, D.C. [1986] v, 101 p. : LC Card 86-602381 DDC 338.1 s 381/.415/0973 19
HD1751 .A91854 no. 556 HD9225.U53F5

Competition for land in the American South . Healy, Robert G. Washington, D.C. , c1985. xxxii, 333 p. : ISBN 0-89164-094-0 (pbk.) LC Card 85-25459 DDC 333.76/13/0975 19
HD266.A13 H43 1985 ***NYPL [JLE 86-2724]***

COMPETITION - GERMANY, WEST.
Baum, Herbert, Dr. Wettbewerbspolitik auf dem Treibstoffmarkt /. Baden-Baden , c1983. 97 p. ; ISBN 3-7890-0881-8 LC Card 83-187053
HD9573.5 .B38 1983

Der Einfluss des Staates auf den Wettbewerb /. Berlin , c1986. 101 p. ; ISBN 3-428-06084-9 LC Card 87-132303 DDC 338.943 19
HD3616.G35 E38 1986

Langenbach, Peter. Wettbewerb und staatliche Sachausgaben /. Bochum , 1981. viii, 316 p. ; ISBN 3-88339-194-8 : LC Card 81-205020 DDC 336.3/9 19
HJ7461 .L36 1981 ***NYPL [JLD 86-2579]***

Lipfert, Helmut. Mitgliederförderndes Kooperations- und Konkurrenzmanagement in genossenschaftlichen Systemen /. Göttingen , c1986. xvii, 302 p. : ISBN 3-525-12754-5 LC Card 86-235180 DDC 334/.068 19
HD3498 .L53 1986

Wettbewerbsbeschränkung in der Nachfrage. Köln , 1985. vii, 145 p. ; ISBN 3-452-20479-0
NYPL [JLE 86-2774]

Zörgiebel, Wilhelm W. Technologie in der Wettbewerbsstrategie . Berlin , c1983. xv, 322 p. : ISBN 3-503-02361-5 LC Card 84-158275
HD9703.G42 Z67 1983

COMPETITION - GOVERNMENT POLICY - CANADA.
Mathewson, G. Frank, 1942- Competition policy and vertical exchange /. Toronto , Buffalo , c1985. xvii, 119 p. : ISBN 0-8020-7248-8 (pbk.) LC Card 86-672936 DDC 338.6/048/0971 19
HF1480 .M37 1985 ***NYPL [JLE 87-512]***

COMPETITION - GOVERNMENT POLICY - MASSACHUSETTS - WORCESTER COUNTY.
Doeringer, Peter B. Invisible factors in local economic development /. New York , 1987. vii, 144 p. : ISBN 0-19-504965-9 (alk. paper) LC Card 87-13550 DDC 338.9744/3 19
HC107.M42 W674 1987

COMPETITION - GOVERNMENT POLICY - UNITED STATES.
Issues after a century of federal competition policy /. Lexington, Mass. , c1987. vii, 387 p. ; ISBN 0-669-13320-5 (alk. paper) LC Card 86-45377 DDC 338.6/048/0973 19
HD3616.U47 I77 1987

COMPETITION, IMPERFECT.
Greenhut, Melvin L. The economics of imperfect competition . Cambridge [Cambridgeshire] , New York , 1987. xix, 408 p. : ISBN 0-521-30552-7 LC Card 86-11707 DDC 338.6/048 19
HB238 .G74 1987 ***NYPL [JLE 87-1413]***

Kriesler, Peter. Kalecki's microanalysis . Cambridge , New York , 1987. xii, 132 p. : ISBN 0-521-33145-5 LC Card 86-24414 DDC 338.5/21 19
HB238 .K75 1987

Leibenstein, Harvey. Inside the firm . Cambridge, Mass. , 1987. xiv, 276 p. : ISBN 0-674-45515-0 (alk. paper) LC Card 87-8426 DDC 302.3/5 19
HD2326 .L45 1987

Ohta, H. (Hiroshi), 1940- Spatial price theory of imperfect competition /. College Station , c1988. p. cm. ISBN 0-89096-372-X : LC Card 87-22333 DDC 338.5/2 19
HB221 .O385 1988

COMPETITION, IMPERFECT - CONGRESSES.
Imperfect competition and international trade . Brighton, Sussex , Atlantic Highlands, N.J. , c1986. xiv, 242 p. : ISBN 0-391-03403-0 (Humanities Press) LC Card 86-660 DDC 382 19
HF1411 .I354 1986 ***NYPL [JLD 86-2120]***

COMPETITION, IMPERFECT - GERMANY (WEST)
Schröter, Klaus, 1953- Die wettbewerbspolitische Behandlung der leitungsgebundenen Energiewirtschaft . Frankfurt am Main , New York , c1986. viii, 300 p. ; ISBN 3-8204-9551-7 LC Card 87-407422 DDC 363.6/2/0943 19
HD9685.G3 S375 1986

COMPETITION, IMPERFECT - MATHEMATICAL MODELS.
Meade, James Edward, 1907- Alternative systems of business organization and of worker's remuneration /. London , Boston , 1986. x, 144 p. : ISBN 0-04-331112-1 (alk. paper) LC Card 85-26734 DDC 330/.1 19
HB238 .M4 1986 ***NYPL [JLD 86-2943]***

Thimrén, Claes. Imperfectly competitive markets for exhaustible resources . Stockholm, Sweden [1986] 94 p. : ISBN 91-7258-212-X (pbk.) LC Card 87-151530 DDC 333.7/0724 19
HB238 .T54 1986

Willner, Johan. Economic policy under imperfect competition /. Åbo [Finland] 1983. 34 p. ; ISBN 951-648-926-5 (pbk.) LC Card 84-137942 DDC 338.9/00724 19
HB238 .W539 1983
NYPL [JLL 77-251 no.187]

Competition in a dual economy /. Bowring, Joseph. Princeton, N.J. , c1986. vi, 208 p. ; ISBN 0-691-04234-9 (alk. paper) : LC Card 85-43271 DDC 338.6/048/0724 19
HD41 .B687 1986 ***NYPL [JLD 86-3314]***

Competition in the oil pipeline industry . Untiet, Charles J. [Washington, D.C.] [1984] iii leaves, 73, [332] p., [10] p. of plates : LC Card 84-602723 DDC 388.5 19
HD9580.U5 U58 1984 ***NYPL [JLF 85-864]***

COMPETITION, INTERNATIONAL - CASE STUDIES.
Clegg, Jeremy, 1955- Multinational enterprise and world competition . New York , 1987. xiv, 206 p. : ISBN 0-312-00852-X : LC Card 87-4735 DDC 338.8/8 19
HD2755.5 .C54 1987

Ramsey, Douglas K. The corporate warriors /. Boston , 1987. xxi, 261 p. ; ISBN 0-395-35487-0 : LC Card 86-20954 DDC 338.8/3/0973 19
HD41 .R27 1987 ***NYPL [JLE 87-1347]***

COMPETITION, INTERNATIONAL - CONGRESSES.
EPHMRA/ESOMAR Seminar (1985 : Lisbon, Portugal) Pharmaceutical competitor analysis . Brooklands, Sale, Cheshire, U.K. [1985] iv, 390 p. : ISBN 92-831-1103-6 (pbk.) : LC Card 86-202276 DDC 338.4/76151 19
HD9665.5 .E64 1985

Imperfect competition and international trade . Brighton, Sussex , Atlantic Highlands, N.J. , c1986. xiv, 242 p. : ISBN 0-391-03403-0 (Humanities Press) LC Card 86-660 DDC 382 19
HF1411 .I354 1986 ***NYPL [JLD 86-2120]***

Internationale Wettbewerbsfähigkeit des Finanzplatzes Schweiz /. Bern , c1987. 131 p. : ISBN 3-258-03806-6 LC Card 87-114764 DDC 332.1 s 332.1/09494 19
HG1526 .B27 Bd. 101 HG3206

Proceedings of a symposium on competitiveness of U. S. grains in international markets /. Fargo, N.D. [1986] ii leaves, 67 p. : LC Card 86-622839 DDC 382/.4131/0973 19
HD9035 .P76 1986

U. S. agriculture and Third World economic development . Washington, D.C. , c1987. xv, 103 p. : ISBN 0-89068-086-8 (pbk.): LC Card 86-62757 DDC 338.9/009172/4 19
HD1755 .U173 1987

World petrochemicals . [Staten Island, N.Y. (139 Chestnut Ave., Staten Island 10305)] , c1985. 279 p. : LC Card 85-71088 DDC 338.4/7661804 19
HD9579.C32 W68 1985
NYPL [JLD 86-2185]

COMPETITION, INTERNATIONAL - HISTORY.
Conybeare, John A. C. Trade wars . New York , 1987. xv, 319 p. ; ISBN 0-231-06234-6 LC Card 87-8097 DDC 382 19
HF1414 .C665 1987

COMPETITION, INTERNATIONAL - HISTORY - 20TH CENTURY.
Maione, Giuseppe, 1942- Tecnocrati e mercanti . Milano, Italia , c1986. 354 p. ; LC

Card 86-194293
HC305 .M274 1986

Von der Konkurrenz zur Rivalität . Stuttgart , 1986. 186 p. ; ISBN 3-515-04760-3 LC Card 87-134320 DDC 337/.09/04 19
HF1411 .V665 1986

COMPETITION, INTERNATIONAL - MATHEMATICAL MODELS.
Menzler-Hokkanen, Ingeborg. Measuring changes in intra-industry competitiveness /. Helsingfors [1986] 39 p. ; ISBN 951-555-247-8 (pbk.) LC Card 87-170429 DDC 338.6/048 19
HC79.I52 M46 1986

COMPETITION - MATHEMATICAL MODELS.
Bowring, Joseph. Competition in a dual economy /. Princeton, N.J. , c1986. vi, 208 p. ; ISBN 0-691-04234-9 (alk. paper) : LC Card 85-43271 DDC 338.6/048/0724 19
HD41 .B687 1986 ***NYPL [JLD 86-3314]***

Telser, Lester G., 1931- A theory of efficient cooperation and competition /. Cambridge , New York , 1987. xii, 306 p. : ISBN 0-521-30619-1 LC Card 87-5114 DDC 338.6/042/0724 19
HD41 .T43 1987

COMPETITION - MEXICO.
Florida and Mexico competition for the winter fresh vegetable market /. Washington, D.C. [1986] v, 101 p. : LC Card 86-602381 DDC 338.1 s 381/.415/0973 19
HD1751 .A91854 no. 556 HD9225.U53F5

Competition policy and deregulation : developments since the adoption of the 1979 council recommendation on competition policy and exempted or regulated sectors : report / by the Committee of Experts on Restrictive Business Practices. Paris : Organisation for Economic Co-operation and Development, 1986. 35 p. ; 30 cm. LC Card 86-217040 DDC 338.6/048 19
1. Trade regulation. 2. Competition. 3. Privatization. I. Organisation for Economic Co-operation and Development. Committee of Experts on Restrictive Business Practices.
HD3612 .C65 1986

Competition policy and vertical exchange /. Mathewson, G. Frank, 1942- Toronto , Buffalo , c1985. xvii, 119 p. : ISBN 0-8020-7248-8 (pbk.) LC Card 86-672936 DDC 338.6/048/0971 19
HF1480 .M37 1985 ***NYPL [JLE 87-512]***

COMPETITION, SOCIALIST. see **SOCIALIST COMPETITION.**

COMPETITION, UNFAIR - ASIA.
U. S. trade relations with Asia . Washington , 1987. vii, 85 p. ; LC Card 87-601359 DDC 382/.0973/05 19
HF3118 .U15 1987

COMPETITION, UNFAIR - CASE STUDIES.
Oppenheimer, Michael F. Nontariff barriers . Boulder , 1987. xiii, 203 p. ; ISBN 0-8133-7403-0 (pbk. : alk. paper) LC Card 87-50073 DDC 338.4/762/000973 19
HC110.H53 O66 1987

COMPETITION, UNFAIR - CONGRESSES.
Oligopoly, competition, and welfare /. Oxford, OX, UK , New York, NY, USA , 1985. 191 p. : ISBN 0-631-14479-X (pbk.) LC Card 85-11200 DDC 338.8/2 19
HD2757.3 .O44 1985 ***NYPL [JLE 86-1961]***

COMPETITION, UNFAIR - EAST ASIA.
Unfair foreign trade practices . Washington , 1986. v, 27 p. ; LC Card 86-603374 DDC 382/.0973/05 19
HF3126.5 .U53 1986

COMPETITION, UNFAIR - UNITED STATES.
Oster, Sharon. The strategic use of regulatory investment by industry sub-groups [microform] . New Haven, Ct. , 1980. 39 p. ;
NYPL [*XME-11,347]

COMPETITION - UNITED STATES.
Adams, Walter, 1922 (Aug. 27)- The bigness complex . New York , 1986. xiii, 426 p. ; ISBN 0-394-54721-7 : LC Card 86-42624 DDC 338.6/44/0973 19
HD2785 .A68 1986 ***NYPL [JLE 87-1432]***

Asch, Peter. Economic theory and the antitrust dilemma /. Malabar, Fla. , 1984, c1970. x, 414 p. : ISBN 0-89874-699-X LC Card 83-19947 DDC 338.8/0973 19
HD2785 .A78 1984 ***NYPL [JLE 86-4132]***

Bhote, Keki R., 1925- Supply management . New York, N.Y. , c1987. 150 p. : ISBN 0-8144-2330-2 (pbk.) : LC Card 86-28795 DDC 658.7/2/0973 19
HD39.5 .B49 1987

Economic competitiveness promoting America's living standard /] Washington , 1986 [i.e. 1987] vii, 34 p. : LC Card 87-601340 DDC 338.973 19
HC106.8 .E2745 1987

Florida and Mexico competition for the winter fresh vegetable market /. Washington, D.C. [1986] v, 101 p. : LC Card 86-602381 DDC 338.1 s 381/.415/0973 19
HD1751 .A91854 no. 556 HD9225.U53F5

Langwell, Kathryn M. A synthesis of research on competition in the financing and delivery of health services /. Hyattsville, MD. , Springfield, VA , 1982. 85 p. ; LC Card 82-600612 DDC 338.4/73621/0973 19
RA410.53 .L36 1982 ***NYPL [JLF 86-422]***

McAuliffe, Robert E. Advertising, competition, and public policy . Lexington, Mass. , c1987. vi, 116 p. ; ISBN 0-669-12391-9 (alk. paper) LC Card 85-45896 DDC 659.1/0973 19
HF5813.U6 M33 1987 ***NYPL [JLE 87-1426]***

Miller, Irwin. The health care survival curve . Homewood, Ill. , c1984. xv, 144 p. ; ISBN 0-87094-481-9 LC Card 83-73714 DDC 338.4/73621/0973 19
RA410.53 .M55 1984 ***NYPL [JLE 86-4362]***

Primeaux, Walter J. Direct electric utility competition . New York, NY, USA , 1986. xiii, 297 p. ; ISBN 0-03-004858-3 (alk. paper) : LC Card 85-20487 DDC 338.8/26136362/0973 19
HD9685.U5 P74 1985 ***NYPL [JLE 86-4075]***

Strickland, Allyn D. Firm diversification, mutual forbearance behavior and price-cost margins /. New York , 1984. 155 p. ; ISBN 0-8240-4159-3 (alk. paper) LC Card 79-53209 DDC 338.8/3/0973
HD2756.U5 S76 1984 ***NYPL [JLE 86-3907]***

Trade policy and U. S. competitiveness /. Washington, D.C. , Lanham, Md. , c1987. xvi, 144 p. ; ISBN 0-8447-3633-3 (alk. paper) LC Card 87-18831 DDC 382/.3/0973 19
HF1455 .T65 1987

Untiet, Charles J. Competition in the oil pipeline industry . [Washington, D.C.] [1984] iii leaves, 73, [332] p., [10] p. of plates : LC Card 84-602723 DDC 388.5 19
HD9580.U5 U58 1984 ***NYPL [JLF 85-864]***

COMPETITION - UNITED STATES - CASE STUDIES.
Ramsey, Douglas K. The corporate warriors /. Boston , 1987. xxi, 261 p. ; ISBN 0-395-35487-0 : LC Card 86-20954 DDC 338.8/3/0973 19
HD41 .R27 1987 ***NYPL [JLE 87-1347]***

COMPETITION - UNITED STATES - HISTORY.
Folsom, Burton W. Entrepreneurs versus the historians /. Washington, DC , New York, NY , c1987. p. cm. ISBN 0-89526-573-7 : LC Card 87-23390 DDC 338/.04/0973 19
HG181 .F647 1987

A Competitive assessment of the U. S. computer-aided design and manufacturing industry / prepared by Capital Goods and International Construction Sector Group. Washington, D.C. : U. S. Dept. of Commerce, International Trade Administration : For sale by the Supt. of Docs., U. S. G.P.O., [1987] xi, 58 p. ; 28 cm. Shipping list no.: 87-135-P. "February 1987." S/N 003-009-00498-5 Item 231-B-1 Includes bibliographical references. LC Card 87-601120 DDC 338.4/7670427 19
1. Computer industry - United States. 2. Computer service industry - United States. 3. CAD/CAM systems - United States. I. United States. International Trade Administration. Capital Goods and International Construction Sector Group. II. Title: Competitive assessment of the US computer-aid design and manufacturing systems industry.
HD9696.C63 U514932 1987

A Competitive assessment of the U. S. digital central office switch industry / prepared by Office of Telecommunications. Washington, D.C. : Dept. of Commerce, International Trade Administration : [Supt. of Docs., U. S. G.P.O., U. S. G.P.O., distributor], 1986. xv, 106 p. : ill., 28 cm. Shipping list no.: 86-848-P. "September 1986." Bibliography: p. 103-106. S/N 003-009-00486-1 Item 231-B-1 LC Card 86-603064 DDC 382/.456321387 19
1. Telecommunication switching systems equipment industry - United States. 2. Market surveys - United States. I. United States. International Trade Administration. Office of Telecommunications.
HD9696.T443 U5225 1986

Competitive assessment of the U. S. equipment leasing industry. A Competitive assessment of the United States equipment leasing industry. Washington, D.C. [1985] xvi, 116 p. : LC Card 85-601661 DDC 382/.45 19
HD9999.L4363 U63 1985
NYPL [JLF 86-1710]

A Competitive assessment of the U. S. general aviation aircraft industry / prepared by Trade Development, Office of Aerospace. Washington, D.C. : U. S. Dept. of Commerce, International Trade Administration : For sale by the Supt. of Docs., U. S. G.P.O., 1986. xix, 69 p. : ill. ; 28 cm. Shipping list no.: 86-705-P. "June 1986." Bibliography: p. 67-69. S/N 003-009-00484-5 Item 231-B-1 LC Card 86-602548 DDC 338.4/762913334/0973 19
1. Aircraft industry - United States. I. United States. Trade Development. Office of Aerospace.
HD9711.U6 C636 1986

Competitive assessment of the U. S. microcomputer industry. A Competitive assessment of the United States microcomputer industry . Washington, D.C. [1986] xiv, 123 p. : LC Card 86-602781 DDC 338.4/700416/0973 19
HD9696.C63 U514937 1986

Competitive assessment of the U. S. microcomputer industry: business/professional systems. A Competitive assessment of the United States microcomputer industry . Washington, D.C. [1986] xiv, 123 p. :
NYPL [JLF 87-251]

A Competitive assessment of the U. S. robotics industry / prepared by Capital Goods and International Construction Sector Group. Washington, D.C. : U. S. Dept. of Commerce, International Trade Administration : For sale by the Supt. of Docs., U. S. G.P.O., [1987] xiii, 85 p. ; 28 cm. Shipping list no.: 87-197-P. "March 1987." Includes bibliographical references. S/N 003-009-00499-3 Item 231-B-1 LC Card 87-601316 DDC 338.4/7629892 19
1. Robot industry - United States. 2. Robotics - United States. 3. Competition, International. I. United States. International Trade Administration. Capital Goods and International Construction Sector Group. II. Title: Competitive assessment of the US robotics industry.
HD9696.R623 U615 1987

A Competitive assessment of the U. S. transformer industry / prepared by Capital Goods and International Construction Sector Group, International Trade Administration, U. S. Dept. of Commerce. Washington, D.C. : The Administration : For Sale by the Supt. of Docs., U. S. G.P.O, [1986] xii, 82 p. : ill. ; 28 cm. "February 1986". Bibliography: p. 81-82.
1. Electric transformers - Economic aspects - United States. 2. Electric transformers - Economic aspects. 3. Electric machinery industry - United States. 4. Electric machinery industry. I. United States. International Trade Administration. Capital Goods and International Construction Sector Group. ***NYPL [JSF 86-672]***

A Competitive assessment of the United States equipment leasing industry. Washington, D.C. : Office of Service Industries, Deputy Assistant Secretary for Services, Assistant Secretary for Trade Development, [1985] xvi, 116 p. : ill. ; 28 cm. "March 1985." Cover title: A Competitive assessment of the U. S. equipment leasing industry. Bibliography: p. 111-116. LC Card 85-601661 DDC 382/.45 19
1. Lease and rental services - United States. 2. Industrial equipment leases - United States. I. United States. International Trade Administration Office of Service Industries. II. United States. International Trade Administration. Assistant Secretary for Trade Development. III. Title: Competitive assessment of the U. S. equipment leasing industry.
HD9999.L4363 U63 1985
NYPL [JLF 86-1710]

A Competitive assessment of the United States microcomputer industry : business/professional systems / prepared by the Office of Computers and Business Equipment, Science and Electronics. Washington, D.C. : U. S. Dept. of Commerce, International Trade Administration : For sale by the Supt. of Docs., U. S. G.P.O., [1986] xiv, 123 p. : ill. ; 28 cm. Cover title: A competitive assessment of the U. S. microcomputer industry. Shipping list no.: 86-792-P. "August 1986." S/N 003-009-00485-3 Item 231-B-1 LC Card 86-602781 DDC 338.4/700416/0973 19
1. Computer industry - United States. 2. Microcomputers - United States. 3. Competition, International. I. United States. International Trade Administration. Office of Computers and Business Equipment. II. Title: Competitive assessment of the U. S. microcomputer industry.
HD9696.C63 U514937 1986

A Competitive assessment of the United States microcomputer industry : business/professional systems / prepared by the Office of Computers and Business Equipment, Science and Electronics. Washington, D.C. : U. S. Dept. of Commerce, International Trade Administration : For sale by the Superintendent of Documents, U. S. G.P.O., [1986] xiv, 123 p. : ill. ; 28 cm. Title on cover: A competitive assessment of the U. S. microcomputer industry: business/professional systems. "August 1986."
1. Computer industry - United States. 2. Microcomputers - Economic aspects - United States. 3. Business - Data processing. I. United States. International Trade Administration. Office of Computers and Business Equipment. II. Title: Competitive assessment of the U. S. microcomputer industry: business/professional systems.
NYPL [JLF 87-251]

Competitive assessment of the US computer-aid design and manufacturing systems industry. A Competitive assessment of the U. S. computer-aided design and manufacturing industry /. Washington, D.C. [1987] xi, 58 p. ; LC Card 87-601120 DDC 338.4/7670427 19
HD9696.C63 U514932 1987

Competitive assessment of the US robotics industry. A Competitive assessment of the U. S. robotics industry /. Washington, D.C. [1987] xiii, 85 p. ; LC Card 87-601316 DDC 338.4/7629892 19
HD9696.R623 U615 1987

COMPETITIVE BIDDING. see **CONTRACTS, LETTING OF.**

The Competitive challenge : strategies for industrial innovation and renewal / edited by David J. Teece. Cambridge, Mass. : Ballinger Pub. Co., c1987. xii, 256 p. : ill. ; 24 cm. (Ballinger series on innovation and organizational change) "The Transamerica lectures in corporate strategy, School of Business, University of California, Berkeley." Includes index. ISBN 0-88730-178-9 LC Card 87-1190 DDC 658.4/06 19
1. Industrial management - United States. 2. Strategic planning - United States. 3. Technological innovations - United States - Management. 4. Competition, International. I. Teece, David J. II. Transamerica Corporation. III. Series.
HD70.U5 C58 1987

Competitive employment issues and strategies / edited by Frank R. Rusch. Baltimore : P.H. Brookes Pub. Co., c1986. xvii, 363 p. : ill. ; 26 cm. Includes bibliographies and indexes. ISBN 0-933716-59-1 : LC Card 85-30929 DDC 362/.0425 19
1. Handicapped - Employment - United States - Addresses, essays, lectures. 2. Vocational rehabilitation - United States - Addresses, essays, lectures. I. Rusch, Frank R.
HD7256.U5 C4655 1986 ***NYPL [JLF 87-19]***

A Competitive future for Europe? : towards a new European industrial policy / edited by P.R. Beije ... [et al.]. London ; New York : Croom Helm, c1987. 324 p. : ill. ; 23 cm. "Published in the USA by Croom Helm in association with Methuen, Inc."--T.p. verso. Includes bibliographies and index. ISBN 0-7099-5032-2 LC Card 87-9096 DDC 338.94 19
1. Industry and state - European Economic Community countries. I. Beije, P. R. (Paul R.), 1952-.
HD3616.E833 C66 1987

Competitive intelligence in the computer age /. Vella, Carolyn M. New York , 1987. xv, 189 p. ; ISBN 0-89930-169-X (lib. bdg. : alk. paper) LC Card 86-25565 DDC 651.8 19
HF5548.2 .V38 1987

Competitive manufacturing . Miller, Stanley S. New York , c1988. ix, 245 p. : ISBN 0-442-26395-3 LC Card 87-10484 DDC 658.5/03 19
HD30.28 .M52 1988

The competitive position of U. S. and European Community pork and the United States and third-country markets . Ludwick, David E. Washington, DC [1985] xxiii, 341 p. : LC Card 86-601366 DDC 380.1/4566492/0973 19
HD9435.U52 L83 1985

Competitiveness . Arndt, Sven W. Washington, D.C. , Lanham, MD , c1987. 120 p. : ISBN 0-8447-3625-2 (alk. paper) LC Card 87-1250 DDC 382/.0973 19
HF3031 .A83 1987

The Competitiveness of American metal mining and processing : a report / prepared by the Congressional Research Service for the use of the Subcommittee on Oversight and Investigations of the Committee on Energy and Commerce, U. S. House of Representatives. Washington : U. S. G.P.O. : For sale by the Supt. of Docs., Congressional Sales Office, U. S. G.P.O., 1986. x, 186 p. ; 24 cm. At head of title: 99th Congress, 2d session. Committee print. Distributed to some depository libraries in microfiche. Shipping list no.: 86-577-P. "July 1986." Includes bibliographical references. "Committee print 99-FF." 1019-A, 1019-B (microfiche) LC Card 86-603391 DDC 338.2/74/0973 19
1. Metal trade - United States. 2. Mineral industries - United States. I. Library of Congress. Congressional Research Service. II. United States. Congress. House. Committee on Energy and Commerce. Subcommittee on Oversight and Investigations.
HD9506.U62 C63 1986

Competitiveness through technology : what business needs from government / edited by Jerry Dermer. Lexington, Mass. : Lexington Books, c1986. xix, 215 p. : ill. ; 24 cm. Includes bibliographies and index. CONTENTS. - Government policy and the competitive effects of innovation / Alan Kantrow -- Computer-integrated manufacturing (CIM) and the next industrial revolution / Robert U. Ayres -- Competing through technology / Bruce Rubinger -- The blending of two paradigms for private-sector technology strategy / Mel Horwitch -- Frameworks to increase trade / Clive Simmonds -- The role of government action in formulating competitive strategies / Michael Cassidy -- Technological change and re-industrialization / Ray Rothwell -- Strengthening the technological competitiveness of industries / Bela Gold -- Government policies in support of automated manufacturing / Jack Baranson -- Locational perspectives on policies for innovation / John Britton and Meric Gertler -- Cooperative research and development centres / Bill Hetzner and J.D. Eveland -- State-level manufacturing technology initiatives / Louis Tornatzky. ISBN 0-669-11604-1 (alk. paper) LC Card 85-45379 DDC 338.97306 19
1. Technology - Addresses, essays, lectures. 2. Technology and state - Addresses, essays, lectures. 3. Competition - Addresses, essays, lectures. I. Dermer, Jerry.
T185 .C67 1986 ***NYPL [JLE 86-1968]***

Compilation and review engagements. Meals, Dennis R. Guide to compilation and review engagements /. Fort Worth, Tex. , c1986- 3 v. (loose-leaf) : LC Card 86-224183 DDC 657/.3 19
HF5667.65 .M42 1986

Compilation and review manual /. Perry, Larry L. Englewood Cliffs, N.J. , c1987- 1 v. (loose-leaf) : ISBN 0-13-162934-4 (loose-leaf) LC Card 86-63240 DDC 657/.3 19
HF5681.B2 P42185 1987

Compilation and review practice manual, 1987 /. Afterman, Allan B. Boston , c1986. 1 v. (various pagings) : ISBN 0-88712-706-1 (pbk.) LC Card 87-105236 DDC 657/.3 19
HF5681.B2 A5914 1986

COMPLEMENTARY METAL OXIDE SEMICONDUCTORS. see **METAL OXIDE SEMICONDUCTORS, COMPLEMENTARY.**

The complete book of Excel macros /. Benjamin, Louis. Berkeley, Calif. , c1986. xviii, 123 p. : ISBN 0-07-881214-3 (pbk.) LC Card 86-106041 DDC 650/.028/55369 19
HF5548.4.E93 B46 1986
NYPL [JSE 87-239]

The complete book of product publicity /. Barhydt, James D. New York, NY , c1987. xi, 308 p. : ISBN 0-8144-5668-5 LC Card 86-47592 DDC 659.2 19
HD59 .B35 1987

The complete book of training . Mayo, G. Douglas. San Diego, Calif. , c1987. ix, 217 p. : ISBN 0-88390-208-7 : LC Card 87-14090 DDC 658.3/124 19
HF5549.5.T7 M369 1987

The Complete CPA examination review, auduiing, 1986-1987 / editors, Belverd E. Needles, Jr, Doyle Z. Williams ; contributing authors, J. Owen Cherrington ... [et al.]. 7th ed. Boston : Houghton Mifflin Co., c1986. 42, 237, 177, 12 p. : ill. ; 28 cm. ISBN 0-395-41132-7 (pbk.) LC Card 86-80561 DDC 657/.45/076 19
1. Auditing - Examinations, questions, etc. I. Needles, Belverd E. II. Williams, Doyle Z. III. Cherrington, J. Owen.
HF5667 .C5852 1986

The complete dictionary of media terms /. Brown, William P. Chicago, IL , c1986. vii, 151 p. ; ISBN 0-913247-01-4 (pbk.) LC Card 86-70712 DDC 302.2/34/0321 19
HF5826.5 .B77 1986

The complete franchise book . Foster, Dennis L. Rocklin, Calif. , c1988. 249 p. ; ISBN 0-914629-24-7 : LC Card 87-2471 DDC 658.8/708 19
HF5429.23 .F67 1988

The complete guide to buying, selling, and investing in undeveloped land /. Sheerin, James J. Chicago, Ill. , c1987. xiii, 339 p. : ISBN 0-917253-57-4 : LC Card 86-25460 DDC 346.04/3 342.643 19
HD1382.5 .S46 1987 ***NYPL [JLE 87-1118]***

Complete guide to cost-effective employee benefit programs /. Kozlowski, Joseph G. Englewood Cliffs, N.J. , c1987. xix, 276 p. : ISBN 0-13-160037-0 LC Card 87-11816 DDC 658.3/25 19
HD4928.N62 U636 1987

The complete guide to drug testing . Chilnick, Lawrence D. New York, N.Y. , c1987. p. cm. ISBN 0-394-56058-2 : LC Card 87-9631 DDC 658.3/82 19
HF5549.5.D7 C46 1987

Complete guide to loan documentation /. Clarke, Peter S., 1941- Englewood Cliffs, N.J. , c1986. xvii, 494 p. : ISBN 0-13-160615-8 : LC Card 85-3519 DDC 332.1/753 19
HG1641 .C55 1986 ***NYPL [JLF 86-1464]***

Complete guide to making a public stock offering. Winter, Elmer L. Englewood Cliffs, N.J. [1972] 295 p. ISBN 0-13-160192-X LC Card 70-164924 DDC 658.1/52
HG4028.S7 W5 1972 ***NYPL [JLF 86-390]***

Complete guide to skip tracing . Stelter, Thomas. Eau Claire, Wis. , c1987. 143 p. : ISBN 0-941161-16-1 (pbk.) LC Card 87-124276 DDC 658.8/8 19
HG3752.7.U6 S74 1987

Complete guide to tested telephone collection techniques /. Winston, Arthur. Englewood Cliffs, N.J. , c1988. p. cm. ISBN 0-13-160185-7 : LC Card 87-22321 DDC 658.8/8 19
HG3752.7.U6 W56 1988

Complete guide to venture capital. Richardson, Clinton. The Venture magazine complete guide to venture capital /. New York , c1987. xxiv, 261 p. : ISBN 0-452-25918-5 (pbk.) : LC Card 87-5721 DDC 332/.0415 19
HG4751 .R52 1987

The complete portfolio of sales personnel tests with recruiting, screening, and selecting guidelines /. Rosenthal, Walter, 1929- Westbury, N.Y. , c1987. p. cm. ISBN 0-87280-011-3 LC Card 87-17523 DDC 658.3/1125 19
HF5439.65 .R67 1987

The complete real estate math book /. Sussex, Margie. Englewood Cliffs, N.J. , c1988. vii, 288 p. : ISBN 0-13-162298-6 (pbk.) LC Card 87-14397 DDC 513/.02433 19
HF5695.5.R3 S935 1988

Complete sourcebook of personal computing 1985. Bowker's complete sourcebook of personal computing 1985. New York , c1984. lxviii, 1050 p. ; ISBN 0-8352-1931-3 (pbk.) : LC Card 84-20460 DDC 001.64 19
QA76.5 .B669 1984 ***NYPL [JSE 86-443]***

Completing the youth agenda . United States. Employment and Training Administration. Office of Youth Program. Washington , 1979. 73 p. ; ***NYPL [JLF 86-454]***

COMPLEXION. see COSMETICS.

Compliance costs and consumer benefits of the Electronic Fund Transfer Act . Schroeder, Frederick J. Washington, D.C. , 1985. 23 p. : LC Card 86-603417 DDC 332.1/028 19
HG1710 .S38 1985

COMPONENTS CONSTRUCTION. see BUILDINGS, PREFABRICATED.

Comportamento dos preços de olerícolas nos mercados atacadistas e fluxo de produção regional no Brasil, 1977-83 /. Camargo, Ana Maria M. Pires de. São Paulo , 1986. 79 p. : LC Card 87-403840 DDC 338.1/35/0981/61021 19
HD9220.B73 S263 1986

Comportement électoral au Québec / sous la direction de Jean Crête. Chicoutimi, Québec, Canada : G. Morin, c1984. xv, 447 p. : ill. ; 22 cm. Includes index. Bibliography: p. 18-21. PARTIAL CONTENTS. - Vingt ans de sondage d'opinion politique au Québec / Jean-Pierre Beaud -- La simulation de la rationalité économique du comportement électoral des Québécois, 1970-1981 / Réjean Landry -- Conjoncture économique et élections / Jean Crête -- La participation politique des femmes au Québec, 1965-1977 / Carole Uhlaner -- Le réalignement fédéral-provincial et l'interaction électorale au Québec, 1962-1979 / Neil Nevitte -- L'appui au parti québécois : l'évolution de la clientèle de 1970 à 1981 / André Blais, Richard Nadeau -- La clientèle du OUI / André Blais, Richard Nadeau -- Les Québécois votent non / Maurice Pinard, Richard Hamilton -- Soutien politique et comportement électoral lors du référendum québécois / Jon H. Pammet ... et al. -- Les élections, les études électorales et la théorie politique / Koula Mellos. ISBN 2-89105-063-0 LC Card 85-177886 DDC 324.9714 19
1. Elections - Quebec (Province). 2. Voting - Quebec (Province). 3. Referendum - Québec (Province). 4. Public opinion - Quebec (Province). I. Crête, Jean.
JL258 .C65 1984 ***NYPL [JLD 87-1351]***

A composite algorithm for the concave-cost LTL consolidation problem /. Balakrishnan, Anantaram. West Lafayette, Ind. [1985] 43, 14 p. : LC Card 86-139493
HD6483 .P8 no. 877 T57.85

COMPOSITE MATERIALS INDUSTRY.
Advanced composites . Stamford, Conn. , c1985. x, 206 leaves : ISBN 0-89336-442-8 (soft) LC Card 87-166023 DDC 338.4/7620118 19
HD9999.C7152 A38 1985

The composition and distribution of British investment in Latin America, 1865 to 1913 /. Stone, Irving, 1923- New York , 1987. xi, 502 p. : ISBN 0-8240-1372-7 : LC Card 87-8540 DDC 332.6/7341/08 19
HG5160.5.A3 S76 1987

Compra de carteras : crisis del sistema bancario uruguayo : estudio y documentos / Luis Stolovich ... [et al.]. Montevideo : Ediciones de la Banda Oriental, [1986] 188 p. : ill. ; 19 cm. (Temas del siglo XX . 37) Includes bibliographical references. LC Card 87-403157 DDC 332.1/09895 19
1. Banks and banking - Uruguay. 2. Banks and banking, Central - Uruguay. 3. Investment banking - Uruguay. 4. Loans, Foreign - Uruguay. I. Stolovich, Luis. II. Series.
HG2954 .C66 1986

Compraventas de tierras en el Cuzco, 1825-1869 /. Mörner, Magnus. Estocolmo , 1984. 66 p. : LC Card 87-403757 DDC 333.3/0985/37 19
HD559.C87 M67 1984

The comprehensibility of taxation . James, Simon R. Aldershot, Hants, England , Brookfield, Vt., USA , c1987. xiii, 314 p. : ISBN 0-566-05348-9 : LC Card 86-25690 DDC 336.2/00941 19
HJ2619 .J36 1987

The comprehension and miscomprehension of print communications . Jacoby, Jacob. New York, N.Y. , Hillsdale, N.J. , c1987. xvii, 273 p. : ISBN 0-8058-0087-5 (L. Erlbaum Associates) LC Card 87-1366 DDC 659.13/2 19
HF6107 .J32 1987

Comprehensive ARM payment tables. Financial comprehensive ARM payment tables /. Boston, Mass. , Philadelphia, PA , c1985. 255 p. ; ISBN 0-89471-379-5 (pbk.) : LC Card 85-206951 DDC 332.8/2/021 19
HG1634 .F44 1985

Comprehensive compound interest tables /. Sherman, Michael. Chicago , c1986. 280 p. ; ISBN 0-8092-4875-1 (pbk.) : LC Card 86-208382 DDC 332.8/2/021 19
HG1632 .S54 1986

A comprehensive English-Hindi dictionary of governmental & educational words & phrases ... /. Raghu Vira. New Delhi , 1962. 189, 1572 p. ; ***NYPL [JLF 87-203]***

Comprehensive Health Planning Council of Southeastern Michigan. Southeastern Michigan minor civil divisions . Detroit, Mich. (1200 Book Bldg., Detroit 48226) , c1986. i, 285 p. : LC Card 87-105776 DDC 304.6/3/09774021 19
HB935.M5 S68 1986

Comprendre et gérer la fiscalité de l'entreprise /. Mallard, Jean-Claude, 1947- La Tronche , Paris [1985] 255 p. : LC Card 86-166702
HD2753.F8 M34 1985

Comprendre l'économie africaine / textes choisis et présentés par Frédéric Gagey. Paris : L'Harmattan, c1985. 566 p. : ill. ; 24 cm. (Bibliothèque du développement) Bibliography: p. 561-562. ISBN 2-85802-566-2 LC Card 86-222248
1. Africa - Economic conditions. 2. Developing countries - Economic conditions. I. Gagey, F. II. Series.
HC800 .C654 1985

Comprendre les problèmes de population . Locoh, Thérèse. Lomé, Togo , 1984. 72, [3], 3 p. : LC Card 87-131146
HB871 .L57 1984

COMPRESSOR INDUSTRY - UNITED STATES.
The Portable compressor market. New York, N.Y. (106 Fulton St., New York 10038) , c1983. xi, 254 p. : LC Card 87-142051
HD9705.5.C643 U66 1983

U. S. stationary compressors market. New York, N.Y. , c1983. xi, 271 p. : LC Card 87-143527 DDC 380.1/4562153/0973 19
HD9705.5.C643 U648 1983

Compromisso com o povo . Agripino, Jose. [Natal, Brazil] [1983?] 19 p. ; LC Card 86-215313
HC188.R38 A54 1983

Comptabilité analytique /. Simard, Jean-Guy. [Bujumbura?] [1983] 120 p. : LC Card 85-981500
HF5642 .S54 1983

Comptabilité analytique de gestion . Dubrulle, Louis. [Paris] , c1985-c1987. 2 v. : ISBN 2-04-015766-2 (v. 2) : LC Card 86-149033 DDC 668/.65/0681 19
HF5642 .D74 1985

Comptabilité des sociétés . Garnier, Pierre, 1899- [Paris] , c1985. xxiv, 344 p. : ISBN 2-04-015767-0 : LC Card 85-221781 DDC 657 19
HF5642 .G273 1985

Comptabilité nationale /. Labidi, M. (Mourad) Alger , 1982. 381 p. : LC Card 84-237940
HC815.Z9 I515 1982

Les comptes consolidés . Raffegeau, Jean. Paris , c1984. 971 p. : ISBN 2-85115-064-2 : LC Card 84-245353 DDC 657/.3 19
HF5681.B2 R25 1984

Comptes de l'emploi : données physico-financières, 1980-1982 : rapport au ministre délégué auprès du ministre des affaires sociales et de la solidarité nationale chargé de l'emploi. Paris : Documentation française, c1984. 219 p. : ill. ; 24 cm. (Collection des rapports officiels) Bibliography: p. 219. ISBN 2-11-001264-1 : LC Card 85-132416
1. Labor supply - France. 2. Manpower policy - France. I. France. Ministre délégué auprès du ministre des affaires sociales et de la solidarité nationale, chargé de l'emploi. II. Series.
HD5775 .C5344 1984

Comptes de l'hôtel des rois de France aux XIVe et XVe siècles. Douët-d'Arcq, L. (Louis), 1808-1882. (ed) Paris, 1865. 3 p.l., xlii p., 1 l., 437 p., 1 l. LC Card 05-5875
HJ1077 .D6

Comptes économiques de la Réunion, série 1975-1980 . Abramovici, G. Ste Clotilde, [Réunion] [1983?] 133 p. ; LC Card 86-980541
HC598 .A37 1983

Compton, Eric N., 1925- The new world of commercial banking / Eric N. Compton. Lexington, Mass. : Lexington Books, c1987. xvi, 316 p. : ill. ; 24 cm. Bibliography: p. [307]-310. Includes index. ISBN 0-669-14017-1 (alk. paper) LC Card 86-45002 DDC 332.1/2/068 19
1. Banks and banking - United States. 2. Bank management - United States. I. Title.
HG2491 .C646 1987

COMPTROLLERSHIP. see CONTROLLERSHIP.

Computador faz política /. Paim, Gilberto. Rio de Janeiro, RJ-Brasil [1985] 164 p. ; LC Card 86-128056
HD9696.C63 B75 1985

The Computation and modelling of economic equilibria / edited by Dolf Talman and Gerard van der Laan. Amsterdam ; New York : North-Holland ; xiv, 229 p. : ill. ; 23 cm. (Contributions to economic analysis. 167) "Papers delivered at a conference entitled Economic Equilibria: Computation and Modelling, held at Tilburg University in 1985."--Pref. Includes bibliographies. ISBN 0-444-70285-7 LC Card 87-15666 DDC 339/.0724 19
1. Equilibrium (Economics) - Mathematical models - Congresses. I. Talman, Dolf, 1952-. II. Laan, G. van der. III. Series.
HB145 .C64 1987

Computational handbook of statistics /. Bruning, James L. Glenview, Ill. , c1987. 372 p. ; ISBN 0-673-18407-2 (pbk.) LC Card 86-31593 DDC 519.5 19
HA29 .B835 1987

Computational methods for population projections . Shorter, Frederic Claiborne. New York , 1987, c1974. vii, 192 p. : ISBN 0-87834-056-4 (pbk.) LC Card 87-9303 DDC 304.6/2/0285 19
HB849.53 .S54 1987

Compute! library selection.
Rozells, Gia L. Making dollars and cents with dollars and sense /. Greensboro, N.C. , c1987. ix, 207 p. : ISBN 0-87455-101-3 (pbk.) : LC Card 87-160661 DDC 332.024/0028/55369 19
HG179 .R74 1987

Compute!'s quick & easy guide to learning Lotus 1-2-3 /. Wolf, Douglas, 1948- Greensboro, N.C. , c1987. vi, 139 p. : ISBN 0-87455-106-4 (pbk.) : LC Card 87-163385 DDC 005.36/9 19
HF5548.4.L67 W65 1987

Compute!'s quick and easy guide to learning Lotus 1-2-3. Wolf, Douglas, 1948- Compute!'s quick & easy guide to learning Lotus 1-2-3 /. Greensboro, N.C. , c1987. vi, 139 p. : ISBN 0-87455-106-4 (pbk.) : LC Card 87-163385 DDC 005.36/9 19
HF5548.4.L67 W65 1987

COMPUTER AIDED DESIGN.
Anderka, Siegfried. Computerunterstützte ökonometrische Modellerstellung in Lehre und Forschung . Idstein , 1985. 407 p. : ISBN 3-925196-11-0 LC Card 85-237458
HB141 .A56 1985

The computer and telecommunications industry in Japan, 1986 /. Salvaggio, Jerry Lee. Houston, Tex. , Arlington, Va. [c1986] 2 v. : LC Card 86-214521 DDC 338.4/7004/0952 19
HD9696.C63 J364 1986

Computer anxiety and the use of microcomputers in management /. Howard, Geoffry S. Ann Arbor, Mich. , c1986. xii, 137 p. ; ISBN 0-8357-1759-3 (alk. paper) LC Card 86-6904 DDC 658.4/0028/5 19
HD30.2 .H69 1986 ***NYPL [JLE 86-3451]***

COMPUTER-ASSISTED INSTRUCTION.
(1987) Gery, Gloria, 1944- Making CBT happen . Boston , 1987. xiv, 225 p. : ISBN 0-9617968-0-4 (pbk.) : LC Card 86-51671 DDC 658.3/12404 19
HF5549.5.T7 G42 1987

COMPUTER-ASSISTED INSTRUCTION - PROGRAMMING.
Ireland. Courseware Committee. Report of the Courseware Committee . Dublin [1986] vii, 79 p. ; LC Card 86-226148 DDC 338.4/70053 19
HD9811.I732 I74 1986

COMPUTER BULLETIN BOARDS.
Simon, Sam, 1945- Phonewriting . [Washington, D.C.] , c1986. iv, 92 p., [4] p. of plates : ISBN 0-943444-03-9 (pbk.) LC Card 86-214171 DDC 004.6 19
HE6239.E54 S56 1986

COMPUTER CENTERS. see **DATA PROCESSING SERVICE CENTERS.**

Computer chips and paper clips . National Research Council (U. S.). Committee on Women's Employment and Related Social Issues. Panel on Technology and Women's Employment. Washington, D.C. , 1986. v. : ISBN 0-309-03688-7 (v. 1) LC Card 86-18113 DDC 331.4/8165137/0973 19
HD6331.18.M39 N38 1986
NYPL [JLL 87-129]

COMPUTER COMMUNICATION SYSTEMS. see **COMPUTER NETWORKS.**

Computer concepts for agribusiness /. Woolverton, Michael W. Westport, Conn. , 1985. xii, 311 p. : ISBN 0-87055-510-3 : LC Card 85-23043 DDC 631 19
HD1433 .W66 1985 ***NYPL [JLE 86-1534]***

COMPUTER CONTROL. see **AUTOMATION.**

COMPUTER CRIMES - PREVENTION.
Comer, Michael J. Corporate fraud /. London , New York , 1985. xvi, 453 p. : ISBN 0-07-084791-6 : LC Card 85-11686 DDC 364.1/63 19
HV6768 .C65 1985 ***NYPL [JLE 86-909]***

Computer data center design . Halper, Robert F. New York , c1985. xv, 189 p. : ISBN 0-471-82579-4 : LC Card 85-5347 DDC 658/.054 19
HD9696.C62 H24 1985
NYPL [JSE 86-1294]

COMPUTER DEPARTMENT SECURITY MEASURES. see **ELECTRONIC DATA PROCESSING DEPARTMENTS - SECURITY MEASURES.**

Computer essays for management /. Kanter, Jerome. Englewood Cliffs, N.J. , 1987, c1986. xi, 109 p. ; ISBN 0-13-165994-4 : LC Card 86-30651 DDC 658/.05 19
HD30.2 .K36 1987

COMPUTER FRAUD. see **COMPUTER CRIMES.**

COMPUTER INDUSTRY.
Add-on boards & peripherals for the IBM PC & compatibles. Norwalk, Conn., U. S.A. (6 Prowitt St., Norwalk 06855) , c1986. x, 320 leaves ; LC Card 86-235156 DDC 380.1/456213984 19
HD9696.C62 A34 1986

C.A.S.E. & programmers' workstation markets. Norwalk, Conn., U. S.A. (6 Prowitt St., Norwalk 06855) , c1987. v, 221 leaves : LC Card 87-129461 DDC 380.1/450051 19
HD9696.C62 C2 1987

Computer security markets. Norwalk, Conn., U. S.A. (6 Prowitt St., Norwalk 06855) , c1987. vii, 163 leaves ; LC Card 87-151110 DDC 380.1/450058 19
HD9696.C62 C6436 1987

Converging voice/data/video technologies at the workstation /. Stamford, Conn., U. S.A. , c1986. v, 119 leaves ; ISBN 0-89336-466-5 (pbk.) LC Card 87-168057 DDC 380.1/45004 19
HD9801.A2 C66 1986

Glücksmann, Riccardo. Telematica . Milano , 1982. xii, 273 p., [4] p. of plates : ISBN 88-7056-120-8 LC Card 84-184344
HD9696.D383 I84 1982

Information activities, electronics, and telecommunications technologies . Paris , Washington, D.C.] 1981- v. : ISBN 92-64-12241-9 (pbk. : v. 1) LC Card 81-211344 DDC 338.4/700151 19
HD9696.C62 I53 ***NYPL [JLL 86-393]***

The Markets and competitive environment for portable computers. New York, N.Y. , c1983. xii, 356 p. : LC Card 87-143515 DDC 380.1/4500416 19
HD9696.C62 M369 1983

Miller, Richard Kendall, 1946- Color machine vision . Madison, GA [c1986] 174 leaves : ISBN 0-89671-079-3 (pbk.) LC Card 87-116822 DDC 380.1/4500637 19
HD9696.C62 M55 1986

Non-keyboard data entry. Norwalk, Conn., U. S.A. (6 Prowitt St., Norwalk 06855) , c1986. vii, 306 leaves : LC Card 86-224995 DDC 380.1/4500476 19
HD9696.C62 N665 1986

Opitz, Otto. Zur Analyse des Personal Computer Marktes 1985 . Augsburg [1986] 35 leaves : LC Card 87-407365 DDC 380.1/4500416 19
HD9696.C62 O664 1986

Oppenheimer, Max Stul. Chips! . Homewood, Ill. , c1987. xii, 203 p. : ISBN 0-87094-942-X (pbk.) LC Card 86-72272 DDC 004/.068/7 19
HD9696.C62 O665 1987

Poppel, Harvey L. Information technology . New York , c1987. xx, 207 p. : ISBN 0-07-050511-X : LC Card 86-27782 DDC 338.4/7004/0973 19
HD9696.C62 P623 1987

Powell, James B. The Dow Jones-Irwin guide to high tech investing . Homewood, Ill. , c1986. xix, 356 p. : ISBN 0-87094-596-3 : LC Card 85-72178 DDC 332.6/7253 19
HG4521 .P63 1986 ***NYPL [JLE 86-2261]***

Rattner, Henrique. Informática e sociedade /. São Paulo-SP , 1985. 219 p. : LC Card 85-221850
HC79.T4 R387 1985

COMPUTER INDUSTRY - BRAZIL.
Paim, Gilberto. Computador faz política /. Rio de Janeiro, RJ-Brasil [1985] 164 p. ; LC Card 86-128056
HD9696.C63 B75 1985

COMPUTER INDUSTRY - BRAZIL - HISTORY.
Silvia Helena. Rastro de Cobra /. [Brazil , 1984] (Rio de Janeiro, RJ : Alphaset Gráfica e Editora) 124 p., [4] p. of plates : LC Card 87-130372 DDC 338.4/7004/0981 19
HD9696.C63 B77 1984

COMPUTER INDUSTRY - CALIFORNIA - SANTA CLARA COUNTY - BIOGRAPHY.
Mahon, Thomas. Charged bodies . New York , c1985. 339 p. : ISBN 0-453-00487-3 LC Card 84-18957 DDC 338.4/76213817/0979473 19
HD9696.A3 U5666 1985
NYPL [JLD 86-1109]

COMPUTER INDUSTRY - CALIFORNIA - SANTA CLARA COUNTY - HISTORY.
Caddes, Carolyn, 1935- Portraits of success . Palo Alto, Calif. , 1986. viii, 138 p. : ISBN 0-935382-56-9 : LC Card 86-40032 DDC 338.4/7621/0979473 19
HD9696.A3 U53173 1986
NYPL [MFX (Caddes) 87-542]

COMPUTER INDUSTRY - DATA BASES - HANDBOOKS, MANUALS, ETC.
Search ACT . Louisville, Ky. , c1986. 1 v. (various pagings) ; ISBN 0-914604-27-9 LC Card 86-215617 DDC 025/.06004 19
HD9696.C62 S43 1986

COMPUTER INDUSTRY - DIRECTORIES.
Bowker's complete sourcebook of personal computing 1985. New York , c1984. lxviii, 1050 p. ; ISBN 0-8352-1931-3 (pbk.) : LC Card 84-20460 DDC 001.64 19
QA76.5 .B669 1984 ***NYPL [JSE 86-443]***

International directory of suppliers and agents for information handling equipment and logistical support services /. Zagreb , 1985. iii, 418 p. ; LC Card 86-220527 DDC 338.7/61004/025 19
HD9696.A2 I595 1985

COMPUTER INDUSTRY - EUROPE.
The IBM market in Europe. New York, N.Y. , c1983. 2 v. (xv, 573, 9 p.) ; LC Card 87-146364 DDC 380.1/45004/094 19
HD9696.C64 I4846 1983

Mackintosh, Ian, 1927- Sunrise Europe . Oxford, UK , New York, NY, USA , 1986. xx, 288 p. : ISBN 0-631-14406-4 : LC Card 86-6077 DDC 338.4/7004/094 19
HD9696.C63 E8547 1986
NYPL [JLE 86-3364]

The Microprocessor development systems market in West Europe. New York, N.Y. (106 Fulton St., New York 10038) , c1983. 2 v. : LC Card 87-401674 DDC 380.1/4500416/094 19
HD9696.C63 E765 1983

COMPUTER INDUSTRY - EUROPEAN ECONOMIC COMMUNITY COUNTRIES.
Baquiast, Jean-Paul. La France dans la bataille des technologies de l'intelligence /. Paris , c1985. 221 p. ; ISBN 2-11-001440-7 : LC Card 86-126853 DDC 338.4/7004/094 19
HD9696.C63 F72 1985

COMPUTER INDUSTRY - FORECASTING.
Anderla, Georges. Computer strategies, 1990-9 . Chichester [West Sussex] , New York , c1987. xxi, 299 p. : ISBN 0-471-91585-8 : LC Card 87-8173 DDC 338.4/7004 19
HD9696.C62 A53 1987

COMPUTER INDUSTRY - FRANCE.
Baquiast, Jean-Paul. La France dans la bataille des technologies de l'intelligence /. Paris , c1985. 221 p. ; ISBN 2-11-001440-7 : LC Card 86-126853 DDC 338.4/7004/094 19
HD9696.C63 F72 1985

COMPUTER INDUSTRY - GERMANY, WEST.
Büromaschinen, Datenverarbeitungsgeräte und -einrichtungen . Berlin [1984] xxi, 400 p. : ISBN 3-428-05740-6 LC Card 86-139011
HC281 .B33 Heft 82 HD9800.G3

COMPUTER INDUSTRY - GOVERNMENT POLICY.
Software . Paris , 1985. 203 p. : ISBN 92-64-12755-0 (pbk.) ***NYPL [JLE 86-2914]***

COMPUTER INDUSTRY - GOVERNMENT POLICY - ARGENTINA.
Cline, William R. Informatics and development . Washington, D.C. (9416 Friendship Station, Washington 20016) [1987] vi, 161 p. ; LC Card 87-6819 DDC 338.4/7004/0981 19
HD9696.C63 B728 1987

COMPUTER INDUSTRY - GOVERNMENT POLICY - BRAZIL.
Cline, William R. Informatics and development . Washington, D.C. (9416 Friendship Station, Washington 20016) [1987] vi, 161 p. ; LC Card 87-6819 DDC 338.4/7004/0981 19
HD9696.C63 B728 1987

COMPUTER INDUSTRY - GOVERNMENT POLICY - MEXICO.
Cline, William R. Informatics and development . Washington, D.C. (9416 Friendship Station, Washington 20016) [1987] vi, 161 p. ; LC Card 87-6819 DDC 338.4/7004/0981 19
HD9696.C63 B728 1987

COMPUTER INDUSTRY - GOVERNMENT POLICY - UNITED STATES.
Flamm, Kenneth, 1951- Targeting the computer . Washington, D.C. , c1987. xiii, 266 p. ; ISBN 0-8157-2852-2 : LC Card 87-11706 DDC 338.4/7004/0973 19
HD9696.C63 U516466 1987

COMPUTER INDUSTRY - GREAT BRITAIN.
Kelly, Tim. The British computer industry . New York, NY , c19. 267 p. : ISBN 0-7099-3123-9 : LC Card 87-569 DDC 338.4/7004/0941 19
HD9696.C63 G765 1987

COMPUTER INDUSTRY - ITALY.
Glücksmann, Riccardo. Telematica . Milano , 1982. xii, 273 p., [4] p. of plates : ISBN 88-7056-120-8 LC Card 84-184344
HD9696.D383 I84 1982

L'Informatica nella società italiana, 1984 . Milano [1984] 257 p. ; LC Card 84-249272 DDC 338.4/7004/0945 19
HD9696.C63 I85 1984
NYPL [JLD 86-3303]

COMPUTER INDUSTRY - JAPAN.
Salvaggio, Jerry Lee. The computer and telecommunications industry in Japan, 1986 /. Houston, Tex. , Arlington, Va. [c1986] 2 v. :

LC Card 86-214521 DDC 338.4/7004/0952 19
HD9696.C63 J364 1986

COMPUTER INDUSTRY - JAPAN - ADDRESSES, ESSAYS, LECTURES.
Plan for information society-a national goal toward year 2000. Italian. Verso una società dell'informazione . Milano , 1974. 157 p. : ***NYPL [TB (Studi e ricerche di scienze sociali. v.60)]***

COMPUTER INDUSTRY - JAPAN - AUTOMATION.
Chacko, George Kuttickal, 1930- Robotics/artificial intelligence/productivity . Princeton, N.J. , c1986. 2 v. in 1 (xvii, 335 p.) : ISBN 0-89433-228-7 LC Card 86-12177 DDC 658.5/14 19
HD9725 .C48 1986 ***NYPL [JLE 87-1001]***

COMPUTER INDUSTRY - JAPAN - DIRECTORIES.
Salvaggio, Jerry Lee. The computer and telecommunications industry in Japan, 1986 /. Houston, Tex. , Arlington, Va. [c1986] 2 v. : LC Card 86-214521 DDC 338.4/7004/0952 19
HD9696.C63 J364 1986

COMPUTER INDUSTRY - MANAGEMENT - HISTORY.
Mercer, David (David Steuart) IBM . London , 1987. 306 p. ; ISBN 1-85091-287-4 : LC Card 87-138763 DDC 338.7/61004/0973 19
HD9696.C64 I4855 1987

COMPUTER INDUSTRY - MEXICO.
Quibrera Matienzo, Enrique. La informática nacional . [Xochimilco, Mexico] , 1984. 133 p. ; LC Card 86-124964 DDC 338.4/7004/0972 19
HD9696.C63 M617 1984

COMPUTER INDUSTRY - PLANNING.
Anderla, Georges. Computer strategies, 1990-9 . Chichester [West Sussex] , New York , c1987. xxi, 299 p. : ISBN 0-471-91585-8 : LC Card 87-8173 DDC 338.4/7004 19
HD9696.C62 A53 1987

COMPUTER INDUSTRY - SOUTH AFRICA.
Automating apartheid . Philadelphia , c19. ix, 107 p. : ISBN 0-910082-00-6 (pbk.) : LC Card 86-201384 DDC 382/.45004/0968 19
HD9696.C63 S62 1984

COMPUTER INDUSTRY - UNITED STATES.
Artificial intelligence markets. Norwalk, Conn., U. S.A. (6 Prowitt St., Norwalk 06855) , c1986. vii, 215 leaves ; LC Card 86-227054 DDC 380.1/450063 19
HD9696.C63 U5118 1986

Automating apartheid . Philadelphia , c19. ix, 107 p. : ISBN 0-910082-00-6 (pbk.) : LC Card 86-201384 DDC 382/.45004/0968 19
HD9696.C63 S62 1984

A Competitive assessment of the U. S. computer-aided design and manufacturing industry /. Washington, D.C. [1987] xi, 58 p. ; LC Card 87-601120 DDC 338.4/7670427 19
HD9696.C63 U514932 1987

A Competitive assessment of the United States microcomputer industry . Washington, D.C. [1986] xiv, 123 p. : ***NYPL [JLF 87-251]***

A Competitive assessment of the United States microcomputer industry . Washington, D.C. [1986] xiv, 123 p. : LC Card 86-602781 DDC 338.4/700416/0973 19
HD9696.C63 U514937 1986

Consolidated data base . San Jose, Calif. (1290 Ridder Park Dr., San Jose 95131-2398) , c1986. ii, 94 p. ; LC Card 87-108611 DDC 381/.45004/0973
HD9696.C63 U515626 1986

Database management systems. Norwalk, Conn., U. S.A. (6 Prowitt St., Norwalk 06855) , c1986. iv, 149 leaves ; LC Card 86-226965 DDC 381/.4500574/0973
HD9696.C63 U515925 1986

Dressler, Fritz R. S. The entrepreneurial age . Media, PA , c1985. ii, 228, 5 p. ; ISBN 0-918514-10-X (pbk.) LC Card 85-232719 DDC 338.04/0973 19
HB615 .D73 1985 ***NYPL [JLD 86-3104]***

IBM's evolving mainframes . Boston, Mass. (200 Portland St., Boston 02114) , c1986. iii, 45 p. : LC Card 86-231231 DDC 381/.4500412/0973 19
HD9696.C64 I48466 1986

Living with SNA /. Boston, MA (89 Broad St., Boston 02110) [1986] 60 p. : LC Card 86-201765 DDC 381/.4500468/0973 19
HD9696.C63 U5223 1986

Manufacturing database management systems /. Boston, MA (89 Broad St., Boston 02110) , c1986. vii, 216 p. : LC Card 86-210661 DDC 381/.4500574/0973 19
HD9696.C63 U5226 1986

Market leaders . Boston, MA (200 Portland St., Boston 02114) , c1987. v, 123 p. : LC Card 87-402841 DDC 381/.4500416/0973 19
HD9696.C63 U52476 1987

The Markets and competitive environment for portable computers. New York, N.Y. , c1983. xii, 356 p. : LC Card 87-143515 DDC 380.1/4500416 19
HD9696.C62 M369 1983

The Mini-microcomputer turnkey engineering systems market. New York, N.Y. , c1983. vi, 228 p. ; LC Card 87-142400 DDC 381/.4500416 19
HD9696.C63 U5262 1983

Non-intelligent terminal market in the U. S. New York, N.Y. , c1983. vi, 197 p. : LC Card 87-143735 DDC 381/.456213985/0973 19
HD9696.C63 U52637 1983

The Office automation market in the U. S. New York, N.Y. , <c1983-. v. <2 > : LC Card 87-166011 DDC 381/.456816/0973 19
HD9801.U542 O34 1983

The Optical memory media market in the U. S. New York, N.Y. , c1983. iv, 218 leaves : LC Card 87-143513 DDC 381/.4562139767/0973 19
HD9696.C63 U52734 1983

The Personal computer hardware add-on device market. New York, N.Y. , c1983. viii, 2, 228 p. : LC Card 87-143524
HD9696.C63 U52783 1983

Sculley, John. Odyssey . New York , c1987. xiv, 450 p., [16] p. of plates : ISBN 0-06-015780-1 : LC Card 87-45142 DDC 331.7/61004165/0924 B 19
HD9696.C62 S38 1987

The U. S. market for intelligent terminals. New York, N.Y. , c1983. vi, 195 p. : LC Card 87-143740 DDC 381/.456213985/0973 19
HD9696.C63 U5885 1983

COMPUTER INDUSTRY - UNITED STATES - AUTOMATION.
Chacko, George Kuttickal, 1930- Robotics/artificial intelligence/productivity . Princeton, N.J. , c1986. 2 v. in 1 (xvii, 335 p.) : ISBN 0-89433-228-7 LC Card 86-12177 DDC 658.5/14 19
HD9725 .C48 1986 ***NYPL [JLE 87-1001]***

COMPUTER INDUSTRY - UNITED STATES - DIRECTORIES.
Pathways through data processing, small business systems. Cherry Hill, N.J. (140 Barclay Center, Cherry Hill 08034) , c1980. 182 p. : LC Card 81-118723 DDC 001.64/04/029473 19
HF5548.2 P295 1980 ***NYPL [JLF 86-351]***

COMPUTER INDUSTRY - UNITED STATES - HISTORY.
Butcher, Lee. Accidental millionaire . New York , c1988. xii, 224 p., [4] p. of plates : ISBN 0-913729-79-5 LC Card 87-9414 DDC 338.7/61004/0924 B 19
HD9696.C64 A863 1988

Littman, Jonathan, 1958- Once upon a time in ComputerLand . Tucson, AZ , c1987. xiii, 296 p., [8] p. of plates : ISBN 0-89586-502-5 : LC Card 87-3823 DDC 381/.4500416/0973 19
HD9696.C64 C655 1987

Wang, An, 1920- Lessons . Reading, Mass. , 1986. 248 p., [28] p. of plates : ISBN 0-201-09400-2 LC Card 86-10768 DDC 338.7/61004/0924 B 19
HD9696.C62 A3 1986 ***NYPL [JFE 86-5201]***

Worthy, James C. William C. Norris . Cambridge, Mass. , c1987. xiv, 259 p. : ISBN 0-88730-087-1 LC Card 87-1808 DDC 338.7/61004/0924 B 19
HD9696.C62 N689 1987

COMPUTER INDUSTRY - UNITED STATES - STATISTICS.
The Home terminal II . [Boston, Ma.] (89 Broad St., Boston 02110) [1986] 63 leaves : LC Card 86-211108 DDC 381/.45621396/0973 19
HD9696.C63 U518327 1986

COMPUTER INDUSTRY - UNITED STATES - TECHNOLOGICAL INNOVATIONS.
Flamm, Kenneth, 1951- Targeting the computer . Washington, D.C. , c1987. xiii, 266 p. ; ISBN 0-8157-2852-2 : LC Card 87-11706 DDC 338.4/7004/0973 19
HD9696.C63 U516466 1987

COMPUTER INDUSTRY - WISCONSIN - CHIPPEWA FALLS - EMPLOYEES - PICTORIAL WORKS.
Friedlander, Lee. Cray at Chippewa Falls /. Minneapolis, Minn. (608 2nd Ave., S., Minneapolis 55402) , 1987. 96 p. : LC Card 86-73134
HD9696.C64 C734 1987

Computer information systems for business.
Simkin, Mark G. Introduction to computer information systems for business /. Dubuque, Iowa , c1987. xxvi, 678 p. : ISBN 0-697-00125-3 LC Card 86-72218 DDC 658/.05 19
HF5548.2 .S4498 1987

Computer integrated manufacturing . Ranky, Paul G., 1951- Englewood Cliffs, N.J. , c1986. xiii, 513 p. : ISBN 0-13-165655-4 : LC Card 85-19199 DDC 670.42/7 19
TS155.6 .R36 1985 ***NYPL [JSE 87-587]***

COMPUTER INTEGRATED MANUFACTURING SYSTEMS.
Ranky, Paul G., 1951- Computer integrated manufacturing . Englewood Cliffs, N.J. , c1986. xiii, 513 p. : ISBN 0-13-165655-4 : LC Card 85-19199 DDC 670.42/7 19
TS155.6 .R36 1985 ***NYPL [JSE 87-587]***

COMPUTER INTEGRATED MANUFACTURING SYSTEMS - UNITED STATES.
Delson, Erwin B. The factory automation industry /. New York, N.Y. , c1985. 1 v. (various pagings) : ISBN 0-931634-16-4 (pbk.) LC Card 86-203033 DDC 338.4/76298/0973 19
HD9696.A963 U635 1985

COMPUTER LITERACY.
Howard, Geoffry S. Computer anxiety and the use of microcomputers in management /. Ann Arbor, Mich. , c1986. xii, 137 p. ; ISBN 0-8357-1759-3 (alk. paper) LC Card 86-6904 DDC 658.4/0028/5 19
HD30.2 .H69 1986 ***NYPL [JLE 86-3451]***

COMPUTER LITERACY - UNITED STATES.
Goldstein, Harold. Training for work in the computer age . Washington, D.C. , 1986. iv, 109 p. ; LC Card 86-601422 DDC 331.25/92 19
HD5715.2 .G63 1986

Computer modeling for business and industry /.
Bowerman, Bruce L. New York , c1984. vii, 219 p. : ISBN 0-8247-7296-2 LC Card 84-17063 DDC 519.5/0285425 19
HF1017 .B655 1984 ***NYPL [JSE 86-623]***

Computer models for production and inventory control / edited by Haluk Bekiroglu. La Jolla, Calif. : Society for Computer Simulation, c1984. ix, 148 p. : ill. ; 29 cm. (Simulation series, 0735-9276 . v. 12, no. 2 (Jan. 1984)) Includes bibliographies. LC Card 84-189641 DDC 658.5/0028/54 19
1. Production control - Data processing. 2. Production control - Mathematical models. 3. Inventory control - Data processing. 4. Inventory control - Mathematical models. I. Bekiroglu, Haluk. II. Series: Simulation series , v. 12, no. 2.
TS157 .C63 1984 ***NYPL [JSF 86-930]***

COMPUTER NETWORKS - CONGRESSES.
International Conference on Networks and Electronic Office Systems (1983 : University of Reading) Networks and electronic office systems . London , c1983. 240 p. : ISBN 0-903748-52-5 ***NYPL [JSG 86-298]***

International Conference on Networks and Electronic Office Systems (1985 : London, England) Networks and electronic office systems . London , c1985. 166 p. : ISBN 0-903748-60-6 ***NYPL [JSG 86-264]***

COMPUTER NETWORKS - GOVERNMENT POLICY.
Jussawalla, Meheroo, 1923- The calculus of international communications . Littleton, Colo. ,

1987. xiv, 159 p. ; ISBN 0-87287-503-2 : LC Card 87-2640 DDC 384/.068 19
HE7645 .J87 1987

COMPUTER NETWORKS - UNITED STATES.
The Online commercial database business /. Stamford, Conn., U. S.A. , c1985. xxi, 230 leaves : ISBN 0-89336-320-0 (pbk.) LC Card 87-40457 DDC 381/.4500574/0973 19
HD9696.D363 U66 1985

COMPUTER PRINTER SUPPLIES INDUSTRY - UNITED STATES.
O'Reilly, Francis J. Computer printers . Stamford, Conn., U. S.A. , c1985. iv, 103 leaves ; ISBN 0-89336-460-6 (pbk.) LC Card 87-163961 DDC 338.4/76213987 19
HD9696.C63 U52737 1985

Computer printers . O'Reilly, Francis J. Stamford, Conn., U. S.A. , c1985. iv, 103 leaves ; ISBN 0-89336-460-6 (pbk.) LC Card 87-163961 DDC 338.4/76213987 19
HD9696.C63 U52737 1985

COMPUTER PROGRAMS - DEBUGGING. see **DEBUGGING IN COMPUTER SCIENCE.**

COMPUTER PROGRAMS - DIRECTORIES.
Nicholson, Norm. The individual investor's microcomputer resource guide /. Chicago , c1986. viii, 216 p. ; ISBN 0-930369-17-3 (pbk.) LC Card 86-204335 DDC 332.6/028/553 19
HG4515.5 .N53 1986

COMPUTER PROGRAMS - PURCHASING.
Oppenheimer, Max Stul. Chips! . Homewood, Ill. , c1987. xii, 203 p. : ISBN 0-87094-942-X (pbk.) LC Card 86-72272 DDC 004/.068/7 19
HD9696.C62 O665 1987

COMPUTER-RELATED SERVICES INDUSTRY. see **COMPUTER SERVICE INDUSTRY.**

Computer security /. Carroll, John Millar. Boston , c1987. xv, 446 p. : ISBN 0-409-90032-X LC Card 86-29901 DDC 658.4/78 19
HF5548.2 .C29 1987

Computer security handbook / editors, Arthur E. Hutt, Seymour Bosworth, Douglas B. Hoyt. 2nd ed. New York, N.Y. : Macmillan Pub. Co., c1987. p. cm. Includes index. ISBN 0-02-915300-X LC Card 87-1735 DDC 658.4/78 19
1. Electronic data processing departments - Security measures. I. Hutt, Arthur E. II. Bosworth, Seymour. III. Hoyt, Douglas B.
HF5548.37 .C64 1987

Computer security markets. Norwalk, Conn., U. S.A. (6 Prowitt St., Norwalk 06855) : International Resource Development, c1987. vii, 163 leaves ; 28 cm. (Report / International Resource Development Inc. . #731) "April 1987." LC Card 87-151110 DDC 380.1/450058 19
1. Computer industry. 2. Computers - Access control - Equipment and supplies. 3. Electronic data processing departments - Security measures - Equipment and supplies. 4. Market surveys. I. International Resource Development, inc. II. Series: Report / International Resource Development Inc. , #731.
HD9696.C62 C6436 1987

COMPUTER SECURITY MEASURES. see **ELECTRONIC DATA PROCESSING DEPARTMENTS - SECURITY MEASURES.**

COMPUTER SERVICE INDUSTRY.
On-line database services markets. Norwalk, Conn., U. S.A. (6 Prowitt St., Norwalk 06855) , c1984. v, 207 leaves ; LC Card 86-233709 DDC 381/.4502504/0973 19
HD9696.C62 O66 1984

Oppenheimer, Max Stul. Chips! . Homewood, Ill. , c1987. xii, 203 p. : ISBN 0-87094-942-X (pbk.) LC Card 86-72272 DDC 004/.068/7 19
HD9696.C62 O665 1987

Third-party maintenance of computer and datacom equipment. Norwalk, Conn., U. S.A. (6 Prowitt St., Norwalk 06855) , c1987. vi, 180 leaves ; LC Card 87-129551 DDC 381/.45004/0973 19
HD9696.C62 T45 1987

COMPUTER SERVICE INDUSTRY - CALIFORNIA, SOUTHERN - DIRECTORIES.
Horner, Ken. Guide to computer installations in southern California . Palo Alto, Calif. , c1986. iv, 750 p. : LC Card 87-134229 DDC 004/.025/7949 19
HD9696.C63 U518343 1986

COMPUTER SERVICE INDUSTRY - DIRECTORIES.
International directory of suppliers and agents for information handling equipment and logistical support services /. Zagreb , 1985. iii, 418 p. ; LC Card 86-220527 DDC 338.7/61004/025 19
HD9696.A2 I595 1985

COMPUTER SERVICE INDUSTRY - UNITED STATES.
ADAPSO guide to market research for the computer software and services industry. Arlington, Va. (1300 N. 17th St., Suite 300, Arlington 22209) , c1985. 71 p. ; LC Card 87-402047 DDC 005/.068/8 19
HD9696.C63 U511235 1985

A Competitive assessment of the U. S. computer-aided design and manufacturing industry /. Washington, D.C. [1987] xi, 58 p. ; LC Card 87-601120 DDC 338.4/7670427 19
HD9696.C63 U514932 1987

MSA, the software company. New York, N.Y. , c1982. v, 73 leaves : LC Card 87-143692 DDC 338.7/610053/0973 19
HD9696.C64 M355 1982

Third party maintenance of computers and data terminals in the United States. New York, N.Y. , c1983. vi, 269 leaves ; LC Card 87-142515 DDC 381/.4562139/0973 19
HD9696.C63 U5874 1983

COMPUTER SERVICE INDUSTRY - UNITED STATES - DIRECTORIES.
Third party maintenance of computers and data terminals in the United States. New York, N.Y. , c1983. vi, 269 leaves ; LC Card 87-142515 DDC 381/.4562139/0973 19
HD9696.C63 U5874 1983

COMPUTER SIMULATION.
Jennergren, L. Peter (Lars Peter), 1944- Discrete-events simulations models in PASCAL/MT+ on a microcomputer /. Lund, Sweden , c1984. 135 p. ; ISBN 91-44-22221-1 (pbk.) : ***NYPL [JSD 86-366]***

COMPUTER SOFTWARE.
Breslin, Jud. Selecting and installing software packages . New York , 1986. xviii, 242 p. : ISBN 0-89930-158-4 (lib. bdg. : alk. paper) LC Card 86-12403 DDC 658.4/038 19
QA76.754 .B74 1986 ***NYPL [JLE 87-1133]***

Burton, Kevin R. Advanced applications for PFS and the IBM assistant series /. Blue Ridge Summit, PA , c1985. x, 213 p. : ISBN 0-8306-0989-X : LC Card 85-9885 DDC 001.64/25 19
QA76.754 .B87 1985 ***NYPL [JSE 86-2148]***

COMPUTER SOFTWARE - DEVELOPMENT.
Holliday, Paul, 1938- A handbook of software development and operating procedures for microcomputers /. New York , c1985. xix, 181 p. : ISBN 0-02-949510-5 : LC Card 84-19384 DDC 001.64/2 19
QA76.6 .H645 1985 ***NYPL [JSE 87-332]***

Smith, Kenneth, 1932- Corporate accounting systems . Workingham, England , Reading, Mass. , c1988. p. cm. ISBN 0-201-17824-9 LC Card 87-24130 DDC 657/.028/55 19
HF5679 .S645 1988

COMPUTER SOFTWARE INDUSTRY.
C.A.S.E. & programmers' workstation markets. Norwalk, Conn., U. S.A. (6 Prowitt St., Norwalk 06855) , c1987. v, 221 leaves : LC Card 87-129461 DDC 380.1/450051 19
HD9696.C62 C2 1987

Kaiser, Martin. The New Zealand software industry . Wellington, N.Z. , c1986. 110 p. : ISBN 0-477-06781-6 (pbk.) LC Card 86-212814 DDC 338.4/70053/09931 19
HD9696.C63 N454 1986

Software . Paris , 1985. 203 p. : ISBN 92-64-12755-0 (pbk.) ***NYPL [JLE 86-2914]***

COMPUTER SOFTWARE INDUSTRY - ACCOUNTING.
McGee, Robert W. Accounting and tax aspects of computer software manufacturing /. New York , 1987. viii, 162 p. ; ISBN 0-275-92273-1 (alk. paper) : LC Card 87-15140 DDC 657/.73 19
HF5686.C54 M38 1987

COMPUTER SOFTWARE INDUSTRY - DIRECTORIES.
Guide to real estate and mortgage banking software /. Washington, D.C. , 1986. 3 v. ; ISBN 0-917935-14-4 (pbk. : set) LC Card 86-63061 DDC 333.3/028/553 19
HD1380 .G85 1986a

COMPUTER SOFTWARE INDUSTRY - EUROPE.
The Office systems software market in Europe. New York, N.Y. , c1983. xv, 256 p. : LC Card 87-144095 DDC 380.1/450053/094 19
HD9696.C63 E8555 1983

COMPUTER SOFTWARE INDUSTRY - GERMANY (WEST)
Maenner, Ulrike. Der deutsche Software-Markt und die internationale Wettbewerbsfähigkeit deutscher Anbieter /. Hamburg , 1986. 94 p. : ISBN 3-87895-320-8 LC Card 87-407404 DDC 338.4/70053/0943 19
HD9696.C63 G446 1986

COMPUTER SOFTWARE INDUSTRY - GOVERNMENT POLICY - ARGENTINA.
Cline, William R. Informatics and development . Washington, D.C. (9416 Friendship Station, Washington 20016) [1987] vi, 161 p. ; LC Card 87-6819 DDC 338.4/7004/0981 19
HD9696.C63 B728 1987

COMPUTER SOFTWARE INDUSTRY - GOVERNMENT POLICY - BRAZIL.
Cline, William R. Informatics and development . Washington, D.C. (9416 Friendship Station, Washington 20016) [1987] vi, 161 p. ; LC Card 87-6819 DDC 338.4/7004/0981 19
HD9696.C63 B728 1987

COMPUTER SOFTWARE INDUSTRY - GOVERNMENT POLICY - MEXICO.
Cline, William R. Informatics and development . Washington, D.C. (9416 Friendship Station, Washington 20016) [1987] vi, 161 p. ; LC Card 87-6819 DDC 338.4/7004/0981 19
HD9696.C63 B728 1987

COMPUTER SOFTWARE INDUSTRY - GREAT BRITAIN.
Great Britain. Advisory Council for Applied Research and Development. Software, a vital key to UK competitiveness /. London , 1986. viii, 87 p. : ISBN 0-11-630829-X (pbk.) : LC Card 86-209046 DDC 338.4/70053/0941 19
HD9696.C63 G74 1986

COMPUTER SOFTWARE INDUSTRY - IRELAND.
Ireland. Courseware Committee. Report of the Courseware Committee . Dublin [1986] vii, 79 p. ; LC Card 86-226148 DDC 338.4/70053 19
HD9811.I732 I74 1986

COMPUTER SOFTWARE INDUSTRY - NEW ZEALAND.
Kaiser, Martin. The New Zealand software industry . Wellington, N.Z. , c1986. 1 v. (various pagings) : ISBN 0-477-06783-2 (pbk.) LC Card 86-212843 DDC 381/.450053/09931 19
HD9696.C63 N455 1986

Kaiser, Martin. The New Zealand software industry . Wellington, N.Z. , c1986. 110 p. : ISBN 0-477-06781-6 (pbk.) LC Card 86-212814 DDC 338.4/70053/09931 19
HD9696.C63 N454 1986

COMPUTER SOFTWARE INDUSTRY - TAXATION - LAW AND LEGISLATION.
McGee, Robert W. Accounting and tax aspects of computer software manufacturing /. New York , 1987. viii, 162 p. ; ISBN 0-275-92273-1 (alk. paper) : LC Card 87-15140 DDC 657/.73 19
HF5686.C54 M38 1987

COMPUTER SOFTWARE INDUSTRY - UNITED STATES.
Ada military & commercial markets. Norwalk, Conn., U. S.A. (6 Prowitt St., Norwalk 06855) , c1986. vii, 196 leaves ; LC Card 87-400056 DDC 381/.45005133/0973 19
HD9696.C63 U51123 1986

ADAPSO guide to market research for the computer software and services industry. Arlington, Va. (1300 N. 17th St., Suite 300, Arlington 22209) , c1985. 71 p. ; LC Card

87-402047 DDC 005/.068/8 19
HD9696.C63 U511235 1985

Communications/Information Systems Planning Service . Boston, MA (89 Broad St., Boston 02110) , c1986. ii, 78 p. ; LC Card 86-225335 DDC 381/.45651853 19
HD9696.C63 U51492 1986

Database management systems. Norwalk, Conn., U. S.A. (6 Prowitt St., Norwalk 06855) , c1986. iv, 149 leaves ; LC Card 86-226965 DDC 381/.4500574/0973
HD9696.C63 U515925 1986

Expert systems. Boston, Mass. (89 Broad St., 14th Floor, Boston 02110) , c1985. 61 p. : LC Card 87-400871 DDC 381/.4500633/0973 19
HD9696.C63 U516435 1985

The Home computer software market. New York, N.Y. , c1983. iv, 212 p. : LC Card 87-141858 DDC 381/.45004/0973 19
HD9696.C63 U5183245 1983

Interactive videodisk software market. New York, N.Y. , c1983. iv, 228 leaves ; LC Card 87-143767
HD9696.C63 U518378 1983

Manufacturing database management systems /. Boston, MA (89 Broad St., Boston 02110) , c1986. vii, 216 p. : LC Card 86-210661 DDC 381/.4500574/0973 19
HD9696.C63 U5226 1986

The Mini-microcomputer turnkey engineering systems market. New York, N.Y. , c1983. vi, 228 p. ; LC Card 87-142400 DDC 381/.4500416 19
HD9696.C63 U5262 1983

MSA, the software company. New York, N.Y. , c1982. v, 73 leaves ; LC Card 87-143692 DDC 338.7/610053/0973 19
HD9696.C64 M355 1982

COMPUTER SOFTWARE INDUSTRY - UNITED STATES - DIRECTORIES.
Directory of software producers. Fairfax, Va. (3150 Spring St., Fairfax 22031-2399) , c1986. [28] p. ; LC Card 87-109219 DDC 338.7/6137139445 19
HD9696.C63 U515957 1986

Computer solutions for business . Dayton, Doug, 1951- Redmond, Wash. [New York] , c1987. xi, 274 p. : ISBN 0-914845-98-5 (pbk.) : LC Card 87-23957 DDC 651.8 19
HF5548.2 .D377 1987

Computer strategies, 1990-9 . Anderla, Georges. Chichester [West Sussex] , New York , c1987. xxi, 299 p. : ISBN 0-471-91585-8 : LC Card 87-8173 DDC 338.4/7004 19
HD9696.C62 A53 1987

Computer studies series.
Burn, Janice. Information analysis /. London , 1987. x, 260 p. : ISBN 0-948825-50-2 (pbk.) : LC Card 87-166130 DDC 658.4/038 19
HD30.35 .B87 1987

Computer technology in construction : proceedings of a conference / organized by the Institution of Civil Engineers and held in London on 25-27 September, 1984. London : T. Telford, 1985. 308 p. : ill. ; 24 cm. Includes bibliographical references. ISBN 0-7277-0234-3 LC Card 85-670263 DDC 338.4/5624 19
1. Construction industry - Great Britain - Data processing - Congresses. 2. Building - Great Britain - Data processing - Congresses. I. Institution of Civil Engineers, London.
HD9715.G72 C64 1985
NYPL [JLE 86-2586]

COMPUTER TERMINALS.
Non-intelligent terminal market in the U. S. New York, N.Y. , c1983. vi, 197 p. : LC Card 87-143735 DDC 381/.456213985/0973 19
HD9696.C63 U52637 1983

The U. S. market for intelligent terminals. New York, N.Y. , c1983. vi, 195 p. : LC Card 87-143740 DDC 381/.456213985/0973 19
HD9696.C63 U5885 1983

Computer und Partizipation . Mambrey, Peter. Opladen , c1986. xiv, 271 p. : ISBN 3-531-11851-X LC Card 87-122986 DDC 650/.028/5 19
HF5548.2 .M27 1986

COMPUTER VISION.
Miller, Richard Kendall, 1946- Color machine vision . Madison, GA [c1986] 174 leaves : ISBN 0-89671-079-3 (pbk.) LC Card 87-116822 DDC 380.1/4500637 19
HD9696.C62 M55 1986

Computergestützte Auswahl interkontinentaler Distributionsverfahren /. Krieger, Winfried. Berlin , c1984. 143 p. : ISBN 3-428-05617-5 LC Card 84-219069
HF5765 .K75 1984

Computergestütztes Ertragsteuersimulationsmodell der deutschen internationalen Kapitalgesellschaft . Hölter, Erich, 1955- Giessen , c1986. xxv, 383 p. : ISBN 3-922730-67-1 LC Card 87-116057 DDC 336.24/3/0943 19
HJ4720.A7 H65 1986

Computerized manufacturing automation [microform] : employment, education, and the workplace : summary. Washington, D.C. : Congress of the United States, Office of Technology Assessment : For sale by the Supt. of Docs., U. S. G.P.O., 1984. 35 p. : ill. ; 23 cm. (OTA reports) "OTA-CIT-236"--p. 4 of cover. "April 1984"--p. 4 of cover. Microfilm. New York : New York Public Library, 1986. 1 microfilm reel ; 35 mm. (MN *ZZ-26,054)
1. Manufacturing processes - Automation. 2. Production engineering - Data processing. 3. Robots, Industrial. I. Series. ***NYPL [*ZV-326 no.31]***

COMPUTERLAND (FIRM) - HISTORY.
Littman, Jonathan, 1958- Once upon a time in ComputerLand . Tucson, AZ , c1987. xiii, 296 p., [8] p. of plates : ISBN 0-89586-502-5 : LC Card 87-3823 DDC 381/.4500416/0973 19
HD9696.C64 C655 1987

COMPUTERS - ACCESS CONTROL.
Carroll, John Millar. Computer security /. Boston , c1987. xv, 446 p. : ISBN 0-409-90032-X LC Card 86-29901 DDC 658.4/78 19
HF5548.2 .C29 1987

Doswell, R. T. Word processing [microform] . [Manchester, Greater Manchester] , 1983. 30 p. ; ISBN 0-85012-361-5
NYPL [*ZT-1554 no.46]

COMPUTERS - ACCESS CONTROL - EQUIPMENT AND SUPPLIES.
Computer security markets. Norwalk, Conn., U. S.A. (6 Prowitt St., Norwalk 06855) , c1987. vii, 163 leaves ; LC Card 87-151110 DDC 380.1/450058 19
HD9696.C62 C6436 1987

COMPUTERS AND CRIME. see **COMPUTER CRIMES.**

Computers and democracy : a Scandinavian challenge / edited by Gro Bjerknes, Pelle Ehn, Morten Kyng. Aldershot [Hants, England] ; Brookfield [Vt.], USA : Avebury, c1987. x, 434 p. : ill. ; 23 cm. "This 'festschrift to' ... Kristen Nygaard represents selected material from the working conference entitled 'Development and use of computer-based systems and tools, in the context of democratization of work' ... held at the Computer Science Department at Aarhus University"--Pref. Includes bibliographies. ISBN 0-566-05476-0 : LC Card 87-8398 DDC 338/.06 19
1. Management - Employee participation - Congresses. 2. Computers - Social aspects - Congresses. 3. Industrial relations - Effect of technological innovations on - Congresses. I. Bjerknes, Gro. II. Ehn, Pelle, 1948-. III. Kyng, Morten, 1950-. IV. Nygaard, Kristen, 1926-.
HD5650 .C65 1987

Computers and information systems in business . Gremillion, Lee L. (Lee Louis) New York , c1988. xxi, 359 p., [16] p. of plates : ISBN 0-07-051007-5 (pbk.) LC Card 87-20300 DDC 650/.028/5 19
HF5548.2 .G7196 1988

Computers and the sales effort . Wallis, Louis A. New York, N.Y. , c1986. v, 26 p. : ISBN 0-8237-0326-6 (pbk.) LC Card 87-404503 DDC 658.8/1/00285416 19
HF5438.35 .W35 1986

COMPUTERS, ELECTRONIC. see **COMPUTERS.**

COMPUTERS, ELECTRONIC DIGITAL. see **ELECTRONIC DIGITAL COMPUTERS.**

Computers for managing information /. Bergerud, Marly, 1942- New York , c1988. xvi, 480 p., [32] p. of plates : ISBN 0-471-84441-1 LC Card 87-20979 DDC 650/.028/5 19
HF5548.2 .B387 1988

Computers in business /. Long, Larry E. Englewood Cliffs, N.J. , c1987. xxv, 609 p. : ISBN 0-13-164294-4 LC Card 86-30412 DDC 650/.028/5 19
HF5548.2 .L586 1987

Computers in purchasing [microform] /. Sinkel, Dimitri. New York , c1984. 48 p. : ISBN 0-8144-2305-1 : LC Card 84-9034 DDC 658.7/2/02854 19
HF5437 .S52 1984 ***NYPL [*ZT-1565 no.12]***

COMPUTERS - MARKETING - CASE STUDIES.
Rodgers, F. G. (Francis G.) The IBM way . New York , c1986. xiv, 235 p. ; ISBN 0-06-015522-1 : LC Card 85-45223 DDC 338.7/61004/0973 19
HD9696.C64 I4875 1986
NYPL [JLE 86-1374]

COMPUTERS - PURCHASING.
Dayton, Doug, 1951- Computer solutions for business . Redmond, Wash. [New York] , c1987. xi, 274 p. : ISBN 0-914845-98-5 (pbk.) : LC Card 87-23957 DDC 651.8 19
HF5548.2 .D377 1987

Oppenheimer, Max Stul. Chips! . Homewood, Ill. , c1987. xii, 203 p. : ISBN 0-87094-942-X (pbk.) LC Card 86-72272 DDC 004/.068/7 19
HD9696.C62 O665 1987

Pathways through data processing, small business systems. Cherry Hill, N.J. (140 Barclay Center, Cherry Hill 08034) , c1980. 182 p. : LC Card 81-118723 DDC 001.64/04/029473 19
HF5548.2 P295 1980 ***NYPL [JLF 86-351]***

COMPUTERS - RESEARCH - GOVERNMENT POLICY - UNITED STATES.
Flamm, Kenneth, 1951- Targeting the computer . Washington, D.C. , c1987. xiii, 266 p. ; ISBN 0-8157-2852-2 : LC Card 87-11706 DDC 338.4/7004/0973 19
HD9696.C63 U516466 1987

COMPUTERS - SOCIAL ASPECTS - CONGRESSES.
Computers and democracy . Aldershot [Hants, England] , Brookfield [Vt.], USA , c1987. x, 434 p. : ISBN 0-566-05476-0 : LC Card 87-8398 DDC 338/.06 19
HD5650 .C65 1987

COMPUTERS - SOCIAL ASPECTS - UNITED STATES.
EAPs and the information revolution . New York , c1987. 106 p. ; ISBN 0-86656-606-6 LC Card 86-33519 DDC 331.25 19
HF5549.5.E42 E37 1987

Computerunterstützte ökonometrische Modellerstellung in Lehre und Forschung . Anderka, Siegfried. Idstein , 1985. 407 p. : ISBN 3-925196-11-0 LC Card 85-237458
HB141 .A56 1985

COMPUTING MACHINES (COMPUTERS) see **COMPUTERS.**

Comsis Corporation. Klinger, Dieter. Personal travel in the U. S. . Washington, D.C. , Springfield, Va. [1986] 2 v. : LC Card 86-603072 DDC 380.5/22/0973021 19
HE199.9 .K535 1986

Comstock, Gary, 1954- Is there a moral obligation to save the family farm? /. Ames , 1987. xxvii, 427 p. : ISBN 0-8138-1000-0 (pbk.) LC Card 87-13399 DDC 338.1/0973 19
HD1476.U5 I8 1987

COMTAP (INFORMATION RETRIEVAL SYSTEM)
Brodin, Anders. The OECD Compatible Trade and Production data base, 1970-1983 /. [Paris, France] , c1986. ii, 81 p. ; LC Card 86-213116 DDC 382/.021 19
HF1016 .B68 1986

Com/tech report series .
(vol. 1, no. 2) Frank, Peter. Business opportunities for broadcasters in MDS pay television /. Washington, DC [c1982] 29 p. ; LC Card 86-201299
HE8700.72.U6 F73 1982

Comunicação (Brazil. Museu Nacional. Programa de Pós-Graduação em Antropologia Social) .
(no. 9) Sigaud, Lygia. Efeitos sociais de grandes projetos hidrelétricos . [Rio de Janeiro] , 1986.

116 p. ; LC Card 87-120281 DDC 333.91/4 19
HD1696.B84 S346 1986

Comunicação mercadológica em tempo de incertezas /. Galindo, Daniel dos Santos. S. Paulo-SP , c1986. 167 p. : LC Card 86-224127
HF5415.12.B7 G35 1986

Comunicación social, poder y democracia en México /. Arredondo Ramírez, Pablo. Guadalajara, Jalisco, México , c1986. 214 p. : LC Card 86-227944
HE8689.9.M6 A77 1986

Comunicación y tecnología en la investigación demográfica / Centro Peruano de Investigación Aplicada. Lima : El Centro, 1985. vi, 38 p. ; 22 cm. CONTENTS. - Crecimiento e información / Marie-France Cathelat -- Población y tecnología / Víctor Carlos Lora. LC Card 86-168814
1. Communication in demography - Peru. I. Cathelat, Marie-France. Crecimiento e información. 1985. II. Lora, Víctor Carlos. Población y tecnología. 1985. III. Centro Peruano de Investigación Aplicada.
HB849.6 .C65 1985

Comunicazione come dominio? / [scritti di] A. Abruzzese ... [et al.] ; introduzione di Giovanni Cesareo. Milano : F. Angeli, [1979] 147 p. ; 22 cm. (I Quaderni di Ikon . 1) Includes bibliographical references. ISBN 88-20-41548-8 : LC Card 79-395059 DDC 302.2/3
1. Mass media - Social aspects - Addresses, essays, lectures. 2. Civilization, Modern - 1950- - Addresses, essays, lectures. I. Abruzzese, Alberto. II. Series.
HM258 .C5896 ***NYPL [JLD 86-3359]***

Comunicazione e marketing. Grandi, Roberto. Come parla la pubblicità . Milano , 1987. 175 p. ; LC Card 87-168680
HF6146.T42 G7 1987

Comunidad económica europea. see **European Economic Community.**

Comunità economica europea. see **European Economic Community.**

Con el sudor de tu frente . Escobar Latapí, Agustín. Guadalajara, Jalisco, México , c1986. 312 p. ; ISBN 968-614-200-2 LC Card 86-209222
HD5731.G84 E83 1986

Con esta sangre obrera /. García-Salve, Francisco. Madrid , 1980. 197 p., 1 leaf ; ISBN 84-85759-08-7 : LC Card 81-141428
HD6477 .G37 1980

Con la vida a cuestas . Moscoso Pacheco, Arturo C. Oruro, Bolivia , 1987. 122 p. : LC Card 87-403838 DDC 362.2/922/088388 19
HD8039.P66 B56 1987

Conant, Melvin. Critique of Energy security, a report to the President of the United States by the U. S. Department of Energy / Melvin A. Conant. Washington, D.C., U. S.A. (1511 K St., NW, Suite #725, Washington 20005) : Conant and Associates, c1987. 23 leaves ; 28 cm. "March 25, 1987." LC Card 87-401127 DDC 333.79/0973 19
1. Energy policy - United States. 2. Energy industries - United States. I. Title.
HD9502.U52 C658 1987

Conant, Ralph Wendell, 1926- Private means--public ends . New York , 1987. xiii, 187 p. ; ISBN 0-275-92429-7 (alk. paper) : LC Card 86-25251 DDC 361.6/1/0973 19
HN65 .P69 1987 ***NYPL [JLE 87-1390]***

La concentration des emplois féminins . Huet, Maryse. Paris [1983] 138 p. : ISBN 2-11-064535-0 : LC Card 85-176290 DDC 331.4/12/0944 19
HD6145 .H79 1983

CONCENTRATION. INDUSTRIAL. see **INDUSTRIAL CONCENTRATION.**

Concepção anarquista do sindicalismo /. Vasco, Neno. Porto , 1984. 209 p. ; LC Card 84-256086 DDC 320.5/7 19
HX833 .V37 1984 ***NYPL [JLD 86-2525]***

Concepciones del desarrollo social. Kontseptsii obshchestvennogo razvitiia. Spanish. Moscú , <1984-. v. <2 > ; LC Card 87-124757
HC125 .K65517 1984

The concept of leisure. Duncan, A. R. C. (Alastair Robert Campbell), 1915- Kingston, Ont. [1970?] 8 p. LC Card 70-534907 DDC 331/.08 s
HD8102 .K52 no. 5

Concepto y aplicación del enfoque de sistemas en los procesos y técnicas de instrucción. 1a ed. Montevideo : Organización Internacional del Trabajo, Centro Interamericano de Investigación y Documentación sobre Formación Profesional, 1980. 283 p. : ill. ; 23 cm. (Informes. no. 100) Product of a meeting held Oct. 22-24, 1979 in Caracas, sponsored by the Instituto Nacional de Cooperación Educativa and CINTERFOR. "Proyecto 065." Includes bibliographical references. LC Card 86-143811
1. Occupational training - Latin America - Planning. I. CINTERFOR (Organization). II. Instituto Nacional de Cooperación Educativa. III. Series: Informes (CINTERFOR (Organization)) , no. 100.
HD5715.5.L29 C66 1980

Los conceptos básicos del transporte marítimo y la situación de la actividad en América Latina. Sepúlveda Whittle, Tomás. Santiago de Chile , Nueva York, NY , 1986. 118 p. ; ISBN 92-1-321211-9 LC Card 87-400454 DDC 387.5/098 19
HE571 .S45 1986

Concepts in Marketing Research (Firm) Ricke, Keith G. Credit union membership study, 1986 /. St. Paul, Minn. [c1987] 72 leaves : LC Card 87-154030 DDC 334/.22 19
HG2037 .R54 1987

Concepts in social policy .
(2) Page, Robert M. Stigma /. London , Boston , 1984. xii, 207 p. ; ISBN 0-7100-9786-7 : LC Card 83-24638 DDC 302/.12 19
HM291 .P25 1984 ***NYPL [JLD 86-3113]***

Conceptual and methodological issues on agricultural marketing research in Zambia /. Harbans Singh, 1940- [Lusaka, Zambia] [1979?] 19, [2] leaves ; LC Card 85-980091
HD9017.Z32 H37 1979

Conceptual blockbusting . Adams, James L. Reading, Mass. , c1986. xi, 161 p. : ISBN 0-201-10149-1 LC Card 85-28722 DDC 153.4 19
BF441 .A28 1986 ***NYPL [JFE 86-4947]***

Conceptual management of top-level managers /. Smrčka, Jaroslav. Prague , 1977. 57 p. ; LC Card 85-139531
HD30.23 .S665 1977

Conceptual selling . Miller, Robert B. (Robert Bruce), 1931- Berkeley, Calif. , New York, N.Y. , c1987. 320 p. : ISBN 0-8050-0410-6 LC Card 86-29428 DDC 658.8/5 19
HF5438.25 .M566 1987

Concertación simple y concertación ampliada /. Gallón Giraldo, Gustavo. Bogotá, Colombia [between 1982 and 1985] 62 p. ; LC Card 85-147865
HC197 .G25 1982

CONCESSIONS - MEXICO - HISTORY - SOURCES.
Diversos documentos y datos relativos al proyectado ferrocarril de Chamela a Aguascalientes /. Guadalajara, México , 1982. 24, iii, 98 p. : LC Card 86-115748 DDC 385/.0972 19
HE2818 .D58 1982

CONCESSIONS - MEXICO - NUEVO LEÓN (STATE)
Nuevo León (Mexico : State). Archivo General del Estado. Permisos y concesiones, 1890-1912 /. [Monterrey, Mexico] [1981] 43 leaves ; LC Card 81-216459
HD3616.M44 N866 1981

Il concetto di equilibrio nella teoria economica neoclassica /. Donzelli, Franco. Roma , 1986. 518 p. ; LC Card 86-192826
HB145 .D65 1986

Conciliation and adjudication today /. Kher, Manik. Pune , c1985. 99 : LC Card 85-903388 DDC 344.54/0189143 345.404189143 19
LAW ***NYPL [JLE 86-1567]***

Concilium (Glen Rock, N.J.) .
(v. 140) Christian ethics and economics . Edinburgh , New York , c1980. xii, 114 p. ; ISBN 0-8164-2282-6 (Seabury Press : pbk.) LC Card 80-50892
HF1411 .C422 1980

(v. 160) Unemployment and the right to work /. Edinburgh , New York , c1982. x, 98 p. ; ISBN 0-8164-2391-1 (Seabury Press : pbk.) LC Card 87-150638
HD5707.5 .U544 1982

Conclusiones y recomendaciones propuestas por la Federación Sindical de Trabajadores Mineros de Bolivia para aplicación. Diagnóstico general de la Corporación Minera de Bolivia, 1985 . La Paz, Bolivia , 1986. 2 v. ; LC Card 87-401587 DDC 338.2/0984 19
HD9506.B64 C646 1986

Conclusions from "The NIEO and the situation of workers" . Vargas, Ines. Oslo :International Peace Research Institute, [1986] 21 p. ; LC Card 87-128390 DDC 337.8 19
HF1480.5 .V37 1986

Conclusions of the government on the report and recommendations of the committee set up to study and recommend ways of solving the financial and administrative problems of the Agricultural Development Corporation /. South-Eastern State, Nigeria. Calabar [Nigeria] [1971?] 5 p. ; LC Card 87-404113
HG2051.N62 C767 1971

Concours publics à l'agriculture par régions ou catégories d'exploitations en 1981. Savignac, Philippe. Paris [1984] 81 p. : ISBN 2-11-083993-7 LC Card 85-168478
HD1947 .S29 1984

CONCRETE, FIBER REINFORCED. see **REINFORCED CONCRETE, FIBER.**

CONCRETE, FIBROUS. see **REINFORCED CONCRETE, FIBER.**

CONCRETE PRODUCTS INDUSTRY - QUÉBEC (PROVINCE)
Ristic, Veselin. Profil de l'industrie québécoise des éléments d'architecture et de structure préfabriqués en béton /. [Québec] , c1983. 168 p. : LC Card 85-100163
HD9622.C23 Q437 1983

La condicionalidad cruzada y la deuda externa /. Lizano Fait, Eduardo. [San José] , 1986. 16, [1] leaves : LC Card 87-127835 DDC 336.3/435/091724 19
HJ8899 .L59 1986

Condicionantes da modernização do pequeno agricultor /. Gomes, Sebastião Teixeira. São Paulo , 1986. 181 p. : LC Card 87-153609 DDC 338.1/0981/51 19
HD1875.M5 G65 1986

Condicionantes estructurales del desarrollo tecnológico /. Pontones S., Jaime. [Mexico City, Mexico] [1982] 27, [2] leaves ; LC Card 85-203882
HC79.T4 P66 1982

Condicionantes físicos del asentamiento humano en el norte de la Patagonia /. Reboratti, Carlos E. Buenos Aires , 1982. 47 p. : LC Card 83-185201
HD479.C57 R43 1982

Condiciones de trabajo y coordinación de las inspecciones /. Galin, Pedro. Lima, Perú , 1986. 19 p. ; LC Card 87-401748 DDC 331.25 19
HD6957.L29 G35 1986

Las condiciones de vida y de trabajo de los tamberos de la pampa húmeda . Solé, Miguel José. Stockholm , 1983. 33 p. ; LC Card 84-107283
HD1865.P35 S65 1983

Condiciones socioeconómicas de la mujer trabajadora en la República Dominicana / [editor, Frank Moya Pons]. Santo Domingo, República Dominicana : FORUM, 1986. 150 p. ; 22 cm. (Forum. 21) Spine title: La mujer trabajadora. "Este libro recoge las exposiciones que fueron presentadas en el encuentro sobre las condiciones socioeconómicas de la mujer trabajadora en la República Dominicana, celebrado en el Hotel Santo Domingo Sur, el lunes 3 de junio de 1985"--P. 9. LC Card 86-208584
1. Women - Employment - Dominican Republic - Congresses. I. Moya Pons, Frank, 1944-. II. FORUM (Debating society). III. Title: Mujer trabajadora. IV. Series: FORUM (Series : Santo Domingo, Dominican Republic) , 21.
HD6112.5 .C65 1986

As condições de emprego do menor trabalhador . Dal-Rosso, Sadi. [Brasília] , c1986. 114 p. ; LC Card 86-224647
HD6231 .D35 1986

Condições de vida nos bairros de Fortaleza, nov/84 a mar/85 . Fernandes, Adelita Neto Carleial. Fortaleza , 1986. 92 p. : LC Card

86-196902
HC189.F67 F47 1986

Condições de vida nos municípios paraibanos /. Santos, Madalena Herculano dos. João Pessoa (PB) : Brasília, DF : 103 p. : LC Card 87-403990 DDC 330.981/33063 19
HC188.P343 S26 1986

CONDIMENTS - SOVIET UNION.
Korobkina, Z. V. (Zoia Vasil'evna) Tovarovedenie vkusovykh tovarov /. Moskva , 1986. 207 p. ; LC Card 86-220308
HD9015.S652 K67 1986

Condițiile istorice ale apariției și dezvoltării clasei muncitoare din România : făurirea și afirmarea partidului său politic : 1821-1893 / [prefață de Ion Popescu-Puțuri ; autori, Nicolae Copoiu, Augustin Deac (coordonator) et al.]. București : Editura Politică, 1984. 652 p. ; 22 cm. At head of title: Institutul de Studii Istorice și Social-Politice de pe lîngă C.C. al P.C.R. Includes bibliographical references and index. LC Card 84-234192
1. Labor and laboring classes - Romania - Political activity - History - 19th century. 2. Romania - Politics and government - 19th century. 3. Social conflict - Romania - History - 19th century. 4. Communism - Romania - History - 19th century. 5. Political parties - Romania - History - 19th century. I. Copoiu, Nicolae. II. Deac, Augustin. III. Institutul de Studii Istorice și Social-Politice de pe lîngă C.C. al P.C.R.
HD8648 .C65 1984

Conditions de travail en agriculture . Nicourt, Christian. Paris , <1985-. v. <2 > : ISBN 2-85340-585-0 (v. 2) LC Card 86-218948
HD1536.F8 N53 1985

Conditions of employment . Schroeder, Ighsaan. Cape Town [1985]- 1 v. (loose-leaf) ; ISBN 0-7992-1002-1 (loose-leaf) LC Card 86-232933 DDC 331.2/0968 19
HD4927.S6 S37 1985

Conditions of life among the cotton workers of southeastern Lancashire, 1780-1850 /. Fleischman, Richard K. New York , 1985. 475 p. ; ISBN 0-8240-6681-2 (alk. paper) : LC Card 84-46001 DDC 305/.9677/094276 19
HD8039.T42 G74 1985
NYPL [JLE 86-3899]

Conditions of work and quality of working life : a directory of institutions / edited by Linda Stoddart assisted by Kristine Falciola.2nd rev. ed. Geneva : International Labour Office, 1986. xxi, 306 p. ; 24 cm. ISBN 92-2-105328-8 (pbk.) : LC Card 86-215659 DDC 306/.36/025 19
1. Industrial hygiene - Societies, etc. - Directories. 2. Industrial safety - Societies, etc. - Directories. 3. Work environment - Societies, etc. - Directories. 4. Quality of work life - Societies, etc. - Directories. I. Stoddart, L. II. Falciola, Kristine.
HD7260 .C64 1986

La condizione degli immigrati stranieri in Italia . Hornziel, Ijola Maria. Milano, Italy , c1986. 166 p. : LC Card 86-181215
HD8488.A2 H67 1986

Le Condizioni industriali della provincia di Bergamo, 1891 : riedizione promossa dalla Unione degli industriali della provincia di Bergamo. Bologna : Li Causi, [1983] 130 p., [1] leaf of plates : col. map ; 21 cm. (Archivio storico dell'industria italiana. Le Fonti) Reprint. Originally published: Roma : Tip. nazionale di G. Bertero, 1891. LC Card 85-235349
1. Bergamo (Italy : Province) - Industries - Statistics. I. Unione degli industriali della provincia di Bergamo (Italy). II. Series: Archivio storico dell'industria italiana. Fonti.
HC307.B5 C59 1983

The condominium and cooperative apartment buyer's and seller's guide /. Kennedy, David W. New York , c1987. viii, 312 p. : ISBN 0-471-62732-1 (pbk.) LC Card 87-21548 DDC 333.33/8 19
HD1390.5 .K46 1987

CONDOMINIUM ASSOCIATIONS - UNITED STATES.
Dowden, C. James. Creating a community association . Washington, D.C. , Alexandria, Va. , 1986. vii, 76 p. : ISBN 0-87420-659-6 (pbk.) LC Card 86-50785 DDC 643/.2 19
HD7287.67.U5 C73 1986

Condominium development guide . Romney, Keith B. Boston , c1984- v. ; ISBN 0-88712-195-0 LC Card 83-50498 ***NYPL [JLL 87-76]***

CONDOMINIUM (HOUSING) - UNITED STATES.
United States. Dept. of Housing and Urban Development. Office of Policy Development and Research. Division of Policy Studies. The conversion of rental housing to condominiums and cooperatives . [Washington, D.C.] , 1982. 95 p. : ***NYPL [JLF 86-442]***

CONDOMINIUMS.
Bloch, H. I. Sonny. Inside real estate . New York , c1987. xx, 375 p. ; ISBN 1-555-84030-2 LC Card 86-28303 DDC 333.33/8 19
HD1379 .B515 1987

Kennedy, David W. The condominium and cooperative apartment buyer's and seller's guide /. New York , c1987. viii, 312 p. : ISBN 0-471-62732-1 (pbk.) LC Card 87-21548 DDC 333.33/8 19
HD1390.5 .K46 1987

CONDOMINIUMS - HANDBOOKS, MANUALS, ETC.
Romney, Keith B. Condominium development guide . Boston , c1984- v. ; ISBN 0-88712-195-0 LC Card 83-50498 ***NYPL [JLL 87-76]***

CONDOMINIUMS - UNITED STATES - HANDBOOKS, MANUALS, ETC.
Romney, Keith B. Condominium development guide . Boston , c1984- v. ; ISBN 0-88712-195-0 LC Card 83-50498 ***NYPL [JLL 87-76]***

Conen, Dieter, 1951- Wirkung von Werbesprache : eine experimentelle Untersuchung zur Interaktion von Bild und Text / Dieter Conen. München : GBI-Verlag, c1985. iii, 162 p., [7] p. of plates : ill. ; 21 cm. (Betriebswirtschaftliche Forschungsbeiträge . Bd. 21) Bibliography: p. 116-127. Includes index. ISBN 3-89003-021-1 LC Card 86-159595
1. Advertising - Psychological aspects. 2. Labels. I. Title. II. Series.
HF5822 .C58 1985

Conesa, Eduardo R.
Bases y puntos de partida para la recuperación de la economía argentina : una propuesta de ajuste estructural con desarrollo económico dentro del sistema económico de la Constitución de 1853 / Eduardo R. Conesa. Buenos Aires, Argentina : Ediciones Macchi, c1986. 178 p. : ill. ; 22 cm. Cover title: Economía argentina, bases y puntos para su recuperación. Includes bibliographical references and index. ISBN 950-53-7109-8 LC Card 87-400257 DDC 338.982 19
1. Argentina - Economic policy. 2. Economic stabilization - Argentina. 3. Fiscal policy - Argentina. 4. Monetary policy - Argentina. I. Title. II. Title: Economía argentina, bases y puntos para su recuperación.
HC175 .C6145 1986

Fuga de capitales : política económica argentina y latinoamericana : un análisis comparativo / Eduardo Conesa. Buenos Aires : Instituto de Política Económica y Social, 1986. 78 p. : ill. ; 22 cm. (Serie Estudios) Includes bibliographical references. LC Card 87-400256 DDC 332.4/5 19
1. Capital movements - Argentina. 2. Capital movements - Latin America. 3. Argentina - Economic policy. 4. Latin America - Economic policy. I. Series: Serie Estudios (Buenos Aires, Argentina). II. Title.
HG3931 .C66 1986

Confalonieri, Antonio. La politica del debito pubblico in Italia, 1919-1943 / Antonio Confalonieri, Ettore Gatti. Milano : Cariplo ; Roma : Laterza, c1986. 2 v. (536 p.) ; 24 cm. (Studi di storia monetaria e finanziaria moderna . 4) Includes bibliographical references and index. ISBN 88-420-2794-4 : LC Card 87-125992
1. Debts, Public - Italy - History - 20th century. 2. Fiscal policy - Italy - History - 20th century. I. Gatti, Ettore. II. Title. III. Series.
HJ8678 .C64 1986

Confcoltivatori.
L'Imprenditore coltivatore nella società che cambia . [Italy] [1983] (Roma : Arti grafiche Jasillo) 364 p. : LC Card 86-185731
HD1972 .I44 1983

Confcoltivatori. Centro istruzione professionale agricola e assistenza tecnica. Strategia dei servizi per l'agricoltura . [Roma] [1983] 158 p. : LC Card 85-155420
HD9475.I82 S77 1983

CONFCOLTIVATORI - CONGRESSES.
L'Imprenditore coltivatore nella società che cambia . [Italy] [1983] (Roma : Arti grafiche Jasillo) 364 p. : LC Card 86-185731
HD1972 .I44 1983

Confederação Nacional da Indústria. Custos e tarifas de energia elétrica . [Rio de Janeiro] , 1982. 40 p. ; LC Card 86-146330
HD9685.B8 C87 1982

Confederación de Empresarios Privados de Bolivia. Pensamiento de la empresa privada boliviana : (documentos emitidos de febrero 1977 a marzo 1981) / Confederación de Empresarios Privados de Bolivia. La Paz, Bolivia : La Confederación, [1981] 274 p. : ill. ; 28 cm. Cover title. LC Card 82-138113 DDC 322/.3/0984 19
1. Confederación de Empresarios Privados de Bolivia. 2. Business and politics - Bolivia. 3. Business enterprises - Bolivia. I. Title.
HC181 .C6426 1981 ***NYPL [JLF 86-1617]***

CONFEDERACIÓN DE EMPRESARIOS PRIVADOS DE BOLIVIA.
Confederación de Empresarios Privados de Bolivia. Pensamiento de la empresa privada boliviana . La Paz, Bolivia [1981] 274 p. : LC Card 82-138113 DDC 322/.3/0984 19
HC181 .C6426 1981 ***NYPL [JLF 86-1617]***

Confederación de Trabajadores de México. Reunión Nacional para el Desarrollo de la Industria, el Comercio, la Distribución y Otros Servicios (1981 : Mexico City, Mexico) Memoria /. [Mexico City] , 1981. 428 p., [4] folded leaves of plates : LC Card 84-228700
HD3616.M42 R46 1981

CONFEDERACIÓN DE TRABAJADORES DE MEXICO - HISTORY.
Velasco, Carlos. Fidel Velázquez /. [Mexico City, Mexico] , 1986. 150 p. : ISBN 968-85606-1-8 LC Card 87-403697 DDC 331.88/0972 19
HD8112.C563 V45 1986

CONFEDERACIÓN DE TRABAJADORES DE VENEZUELA - HISTORY - 20TH CENTURY.
Godio, Julio. 50 años de la C.T.V., 1936-1986 . Caracas, Venezuela [1986] 149 p. ; ISBN 980-607-709-1 LC Card 87-401745 DDC 331.88/0987 19
HD8362.C68 G63 1986

Confederación Granadina. see **Colombia.**

Confederación Internacional de Organizaciones Syndicales Libres. see **International Confederation of Free Trade Unions.**

CONFEDERACIÓN NACIONAL DEL TRABAJO (SPAIN) - HISTORY - 20TH CENTURY.
Sabater, Jordi, 1958- Anarquisme i catalanisme . Barcelona , 1986. 231 p. ; ISBN 84-297-2490-7 LC Card 87-108668
HD8582.C583 S24 1986

CONFÉDÉRATION DES SYNDICATS CHRÉTIENS (BELGIUM)
Arcq, Etienne. La C.S.C. et le programme gouvernemental de mars 1984 /. Bruxelles [1984] 23 leaves ; LC Card 84-171486
HD8502.C62 A73 1984

Confédération des syndicats nationaux. Comité de la condition féminine. Les Effets des conditions de travail sur la santé des travailleuses . [Montréal] [1984] 230 p., [5] p. of plates : ISBN 2-920658-00-X : LC Card 86-158040
HD6067 .E34 1984

Confédération internationale des syndicats libres. see **International Confederation of Free Trade Unions.**

Confédération nationale des travailleurs de Guinée. Structure / Confédération nationale des travailleurs de Guinée, C.N.T.G.-U. S.P.A. [Conakry] : C.N.T.G., [1964?] 23 p. : ill. ; 24 cm. "Camarade travailleur, connais-tu la C.N.T.G.?"--P. [1] LC Card 82-220475
1. Confédération nationale des travailleurs de Guinée. 2. Trade-unions - Guinea. I. Title. II. Title: Camarade travailleur, connais-tu la C.N.T.G.?.
HD8826.A5 C66 1964

CONFÉDÉRATION NATIONALE DES TRAVAILLEURS DE GUINÉE.
Confédération nationale des travailleurs de Guinée. Structure /. [Conakry] [1964?] 23 p. : LC Card 82-220475
HD8826.A5 C66 1964

Confederation of German Employers' Associations. see **Bundesvereinigung der Deutschen Arbeitgeberverbände.**

CONFEDERAZIONE GENERALE ITALIANA DEL LAVORO - HISTORY - 20TH CENTURY.
Piccioni, Alessandro. La Cgil nei suoi congressi /. Roma , c1986. 168 p. ; LC Card 87-103188
HD8473 .P53 1986

CONFEDERAZIONE GENERALE ITALIANA DEL LAVORO - OFFICIALS AND EMPLOYEES - CORRESPONDENCE.
Lama, Luciano. Cari compagni . Roma , c1986. vii, 184 p. ; LC Card 87-155314
HD6710.L35 A4 1986

Conference on Mainstreams in Industrial Organization, (1985 : University of Amsterdam) Mainstreams in industrial organization /. Dordrecht , Boston , 1986. 2 v. (x, 465 p.) ; ISBN 90-247-3363-4 LC Card 86-12345 DDC 338.6 19
HD29 .M25 1986 ***NYPL [JLE 87-457]***

Conference Board briefing charts / Office of the Senior Fellow and Economic Counsellor, the Conference Board. Interim ed. New York, N.Y. (845 3rd Ave., New York 10022) : The Board, c1986. 42, 8 leaves : chiefly ill. ; 28 cm. Cover title. LC Card 87-104050 DDC 330.973/0927 19
1. Economic indicators - United States. I. Conference Board. Office of the Senior Fellow and Economic Counsellor.
HC106.8 .C663 1986

Conference Board. Corporate Relations Program. Weber, Nathan. Communicating with security analysts /. New York, N.Y. (845 3rd Ave., New York 10022) , c1985. 22 p. : LC Card 86-212395 DDC 658.4/5 19
HD59 .W36 1985

Conference Board. Economic Forum. The 1986-87 outlook . New York, N.Y. (845 3rd Ave., New York 10022) , c1986. 18 p. : LC Card 86-212392 DDC 338.5/443/0973 19
HC106.8 .A14 1986

Conference Board. Office of the Senior Fellow and Economic Counsellor. Conference Board briefing charts /. New York, N.Y. (845 3rd Ave., New York 10022) , c1986. 42, 8 leaves : LC Card 87-104050 DDC 330.973/0927 19
HC106.8 .C663 1986

The Conference Board report .
(no. 881) Troy, Kathryn. Meeting human needs . New York, NY , c1986. vii, 55 p. ; ISBN 0-8237-0323-1 (pbk.) LC Card 86-207649 DDC 658.3/8 19
HD7654 .T73 1986

Conférence des donateurs (1983 : Djibouti, Djibouti) Djibouti, ville et pays en voie de développement . Djibouti [c1983] 2 v. : LC Card 87-131462
HC855.Z9 E443 1983

Conférence des Nations Unies sur le commerce et le développement. see **United Nations. Conference on Trade and Development.**

Conférence européenne des horaires des trains de voyageurs (1984 : Paris, France)
Procès-verbaux de la Conférence européenne des horaires des trains de voyageurs pour les années 1985/87 : Paris du 18 au 27 septembre 1984 = Niederschriften der Europäischen Reisezugfahrplankonferenz für die Jahre 1985/87 : Paris vom 18. bis 27. September 1984. Paris : La Conférence, 1984. 619 p. ; 30 cm. French and German. LC Card 85-152699
1. Railroads - Europe - Time-tables - Congresses. I. Title. II. Title: Niederschriften der Europäischen Reisezugfahrplankonferenz für die Jahre 1985/87.
HE3004 .C64 1984

Conférence européenne des ministers des transports. see **European Conference of Ministers of Transport.**

CONFERENCE LINES. see **SHIPPING CONFERENCES.**

Conference of First Ministers (1985 : Halifax, N. S.) Economic and regional development agreements . [Ottawa?] [1985] 11, 12, [8] p. : LC Card 86-214896 DDC 338.971 19
HC113 .E26 1985

Conference of Heads of State or Government of Non-aligned Countries (7th : 1983 : New Delhi, India)
Castro, Fidel, 1927- [Crisis económica y social del mundo. English.] The world economic and social crisis . New Delhi , 1983. 224 p. : LC Card 83-908475 DDC 337/.097172/4 19
HC59.7 .C31472 1983 ***NYPL [JLD 87-486]***

Directions for reform . New Delhi [1984] x, 78 p. ; ISBN 0-7069-2692-7 : LC Card 84-903168 DDC 332/.042 19
HG3881 .D57 1984 ***NYPL [JLD 86-4409]***

Conference of Heads of State or Government of Non-aligned Countries (8th : 1986 : Harare, Zimbabwe) World economy in the mid-eighties . New Delhi, India , c1986. xii, 222 p. ; LC Card 86-903369 DDC 330.9/048 19
HB171 .W83 1986

Conference of Mayors. see **United States Conference of Mayors.**

Conference of National Experts on the Future of Migration (1986 : Paris, France) The Future of migration. Paris , Washington, D.C. , 1987. 319 p. : ISBN 92-64-12949-9 (pbk.) : LC Card 87-163484 DDC 304.8/094 19
HB1952 .F88 1987

Conference of the Mayors of the World's Major Cities (13th : 1984 : Milan, Italy) Afghani, Abdus Sattar. Traffic growth in Karachi . [Karachi] [1985] [25] leaves : LC Card 85-931413 DDC 388.4/13142/09549183 19
HE373.P183 K372 1985

Conference on Africa and the Market Economy. Conference on Africa and the Market Economy (1985 : University of London) London , 1985. 1 v. (various pagings) ; LC Card 86-218280 DDC 330.96/0328 19
HC800 .C657 1985

Conference on Africa and the Market Economy (1985 : University of London) Conference on Africa and the Market Economy. London : Centre of African Studies, School of Oriental and African Studies, University of London, 1985. 1 v. (various pagings) ; 30 cm. Includes bibliographies. LC Card 86-218280 DDC 330.96/0328 19
1. Africa - Economic conditions - 1960- - Congresses. 2. Africa - Commerce - Congresses. 3. Africa - Foreign economic relations - Congresses. I. University of London. School of Oriental and African Studies. II. Title.
HC800 .C657 1985

Conference on Agriculture and the Environment (1986 : Resources for the Future) Agriculture and the environment /. Washington, D.C. , c1986. xvii, 298 p. : ISBN 0-915707-33-0 (pbk.) : LC Card 87-43010 DDC 363.7/31 19
HD1755 .P47 1986

Conference on Cable Television (1981 : Brooklyn College Student Union) Proceedings / Conference on Cable Television at Brooklyn College Student Union, November 19, 1981 ; conference coordinator, Marilyn M. DuBois. [Albany, N.Y.] (P.O. Box 167, Albany 12248) : New York State Legislative Commission on Science and Technology, [1982] 77 p. ; 28 cm. "Co-sponsored by the Humanities Institute of Brooklyn College"--Cover. LC Card 86-622177 DDC 384.55/47/09747 19
1. Cable television - New York (State) - Congresses. 2. Cable television - Government policy - New York (State) - Congresses. I. DuBois, Marilyn M. II. New York (State). Legislature. Legislative Commission on Science & Technology. III. Brooklyn College. Humanities Institute. IV. Title.
HE8700.72.U6 C66 1981

Conference on Experimental Economics (2nd : 1977 : Winzenhohl, Germany)
Bargaining behavior /. Tübingen , 1978. x, 383 p. : ISBN 3-16-340972-5 LC Card 86-227549 DDC 330 s 658.4 19
HB41 .B29 1967 Bd. 7 HD58.6

Coalition forming behavior /. Tübingen , 1978. viii, 375 p. : ISBN 3-16-340982-2 LC Card 86-227555 DDC 330 s 658.4 19
HB41 .B29 1967 vol. 8 HD58.6

Conference on General Equilibrium Trade Policy Modeling (1984 : Columbia University) General equilibrium trade policy modeling /. Cambridge, Mass. , c1986. vii, 360 p. : ISBN 0-262-19245-4 LC Card 85-19144 DDC 382/.3/0724 19
HF1410.5 .G46 1986 ***NYPL [JLE 86-4456]***

Conference on Housing and Urban Development in Sub-Saharan Africa (10th : 1986 : Harare, Zimbabwe) Report on housing and urban development in Zimbabwe . [Harare, Zimbabwe , 1986] vi, 46 p., [1] folded leaf of plates : LC Card 87-980381 DDC 363.5/8 19
HD7374.5.A3 R46 1986

Conference on International Banking (1985 : Pace University) The Debt crisis and financial stability . New York, NY (Attn: Comptroller, Pace Plaza, 10038) , 1985. xi, 157 p. : ISBN 0-88239-017-1 : LC Card 85-19243 DDC 336.3/435/091724 19
HG3891.5 .D4 1985 ***NYPL [JLE 86-3911]***

Conference on International Banking (1986 : Pace University) International banking and world economic growth . New York , 1987. xviii, 183 p. : ISBN 0-275-92669-9 (alk. paper) : LC Card 87-7353 DDC 332.1/5 19
HG3881 .I575133 1987

Conference on Key Problems of Latin America (4th : 1985 : Miami, Fla.) Foreign investment, debt, and economic growth in Latin America /. New York , 1988. xix, 250 p. : ISBN 0-312-00936-4 : LC Card 87-18808 DDC 332.6/73/098 19
HG5160.5.A3 F675 1988

Conference on Keynes and Public Policy after Fifty Years (1986 : Glendon College) Keynes and public policy after fifty years /. New York , <c1988-. v. <2 > : ISBN 0-8147-3444-8 (v. 1) : LC Card 87-20368 DDC 330.15/6 19
HB99.7 .K3815 1988

Conference on Local Economic Strategies (1986 : Parsifal College) Developing local economic strategies . Milton Keynes [England] , Philadelphia , 1987. p. cm. ISBN 0-335-15522-7 LC Card 87-22681 DDC 338.941 19
HC256.6 .D48 1987

Conference on Rural Development, National. see **National Conference on Rural Development, Des Moines, 1973.**

Conference on Tax Administration Research, January 1985. Conference on Tax Administration Research Strategies (1985 : Washington, D.C.) Washington, D.C. [1985] 2 v. : LC Card 86-601369 DDC 353.0072/4 19
HJ3252 .C66 1985 ***NYPL [JLF 86-1791]***

Conference on Tax Administration Research Strategies (1985 : Washington, D.C.)
Conference on Tax Administration Research, January 1985. Washington, D.C. : Office of the Assistant Commissioner (Planning, Finance and Research), Internal Revenue Service, [1985] 2 v. : ill. ; 28 cm. Includes bibliographies. CONTENTS. - v. 1. Summary -- v. 2. Proceedings. LC Card 86-601369 DDC 353.0072/4 19
1. Tax administration and procedure - United States - Congresses. 2. Tax collection - United States - Congresses. 3. Taxpayer compliance - United States - Congresses. I. United States. Internal Revenue Service. Office of the Assistant Commissioner (Planning, Finance, and Research). II. Title.
HJ3252 .C66 1985 ***NYPL [JLF 86-1791]***

Conference on the Development of Amazonia in Seven Countries (1979 : University of Cambridge, Centre of Latin American Studies) Land, people, and planning in contemporary Amazonia /. [Cambridge, Cambridgeshire] , 1980. xvi, 313 p. : LC Card 87-672189
HC167.A42 L36x 1980

Conference on the Effects of Taxation on Capital Formation (1986 : Palm Beach, Fla.) Taxes and capital formation. Cambridge, Mass. (1050 Massachusetts Ave., Cambridge 02138) : National Bureau of Economic Research, 1986. 40 p. ; 23 cm. (NBER summary report) "Summarizes the papers discussed at the NBER's Conference on the Effects of Taxation on Capital Formation held on February 13-16, 1986, in Palm Beach, Florida." Edited by Donna Zerwitz. LC Card 87-101954 DDC 336.2/00973 19
1. Fiscal policy - United States - Congresses. 2.

Taxation - United States - Congresses. 3. Saving and investment - United States - Congresses. I. Zerwitz, Donna. II. National Bureau of Economic Research. III. Title. IV. Series.
HJ2381 .C6974 1986

Conference on Trade and Development. see **United Nations. Conference on Trade and Development.**

Conference on Transportation in Nigeria (1977 : University of Ibadan) Transportation in Nigerian national development . Ibadan , c1981. xi, 602 p. : ISBN 978-18-1010-6 (pbk.) LC Card 82-196087 DDC 380.5/09669 19
HE287.7 .T72 1981 ***NYPL [Sc E 86-178]***

Conference papers (University of London. Australian Studies Centre)
Australian industrial relations . London [1986] 24 p. ; ISBN 0-902499-56-4 (pbk.) : LC Card 86-233230 DDC 331/.0994 19
HD8846.5 .A96 1986

Conference report (National Bureau of Economic Research)
Exchange rates and international macroeconomics /. Chicago , 1983. x, 382 p. : ISBN 0-226-26249-9 LC Card 83-14524 DDC 332.4/56 19
HG205 1981c ***NYPL [JLE 86-3231]***

La Conférence sur les communications . Conférence sur les communications (1983 : Montréal, Québec) [Québec] [1984] ix, 489 p. ; ISBN 2-551-06176-8 LC Card 85-103400
HE7818.Q4 C46 1983

Conférence sur les communications (1983 : Montréal, Québec) La Conférence sur les communications : Montréal, 4, 5, 6 octobre 1983 : rapport. [Québec] : Secrétariat permanent des conférences socio-économiques du Québec, [1984] ix, 489 p. ; 25 cm. (Les Conférences socio-économiques du Québec) Includes indexes. ISBN 2-551-06176-8 LC Card 85-103400
1. Telecommunication - Québec (Province) - Congresses. I. Title. II. Series.
HE7818.Q4 C46 1983

CONFERENCES. see **CONGRESSES AND CONVENTIONS.**

Conférences prononcées à l'occasion de l'assemblée des délégués du 27 mai 1978. Vorträge gehalten anlässlich der Abgeordnetenversammlung vom 27. Mai 1978 =. [Bern] , 1978. 44 p. : LC Card 84-115871
HC397 .V67 1978

Conferencia de las Naciones Unidas sobre Comercio y Desarrollo. see **United Nations. Conference on Trade and Development.**

Conferência do Ministro dos Transportes na Escola Superior de Guerra : política de transportes : Rio de Janeiro, 15 julio 1981. [Brasília] : Ministério dos Transportes, [198-] [61] p. : ill. ; 22 cm. LC Card 86-193198
1. Transportation and state - Brazil - Congresses. I. Brazil. Ministério dos Transportes. II. Title: Política de transportes.
HE233 .C59 1980z

Conferencia Económica Latinoamericana (1984 : Quito, Ecuador) Documentación relacionada con la Conferencia Económica Latino Americana, Quito, 9-13 enero, 1984. [Rome, Italy] : Instituto Italo Latino Americano, Vice Secretaría Socio-Económica, 1984. 62 p. ; 27 cm. Cover title. LC Card 86-134389 DDC 338.98 19
1. Latin America - Economic policy - Congresses. I. Title.
HC125 .C6555 1984

Conferência Internacional sobre Integração de Portugal na CEE (1985 : Lisbon, Portugal) Custos certos, beneficios incertos . [Lisboa] [1986] 307 p. : LC Card 87-127179 DDC 341.24/22 19
HC241.25.P6 C87 1986

Conferencia sobre Financiación y Administración de los Asentamientos Humanos (1982 : Mexico City, Mexico) Vivienda rural, México. [Mexico City] [1982?] 40 p. : LC Card 86-174056
HD7289.M6 V58 1982

Conferencias sobre desarrollo económico, presupuesto, estabilización y nacionalización de empresas económicas. La Paz, Bolivia : Universidad Mayor de "San Andrés," 1955. 180 p. : ill. ; 27 cm. (Publicaciones de la Facultad de Derecho. Cuaderno . no. 15) "Separata de Revista de derecho no. 18, La Paz--marzo 1954." LC Card 86-167406
1. Bolivia - Economic policy. 2. Budget - Bolivia. 3. Economic stabilization - Bolivia. 4. Government business enterprises - Bolivia. I. Universidad Mayor de San Andrés. Facultad de Derecho. II. Series.
HC182 .C54 1955

Conferencias sobre la Carta de Punta del Este. Mesa Redonda sobre la Carta de Punta del Este (1961 : Universidad Nacional Autónoma de México) Memoria del ciclo de conferencias de Mesa Redonda sobre la Carta de Punta del Este /. México , 1962. 224 p. : LC Card 85-105213
HC125 .M48 1961

Conferenza economica dell'area pisana (1984 : Pisa, Italy) Atti / Conferenza economica dell'area pisana : Pisa 23-24 maggio 1984, Pisa 10 dicembre 1984 ; a cura del Comune di Pisa. Pisa : Pacini, [1985-1986], c1985. 2 v. : ill. ; 24 cm. LC Card 86-223161
1. Pisa Region (Italy) - Economic conditions - Congresses. 2. Pisa Region (Italy) - Economic policy - Congresses. I. Pisa (Italy). II. Title.
HC308.P58 C66 1984

Conferenza internazionale Costi e relativi finanziamenti dei sistemi pensionistici nei paesi europei (1982 : Rome, Italy) Costi e relativi finanziamenti dei sistemi pensionistici nei paesi europei . Roma , 1985. xi, 486 p. : LC Card 86-206925
HD7164 .C67 1985

Conferenza internazionale sul tema Le zone franche industriali, nuove forme di investimento, l'America latina (1985 : Milan, Italy) Le zone franche industriali nei paesi emergenti : l'America latina / F. Bortolotti ... [et al.] / a cura di Giuseppe Vimercati, E.A. Fiera di Milano, Contrade. Milano, Italy : F. Angeli, c1986. 207 p. ; 22 cm. "Atti della Conferenza internazionale sul tema 'Le zone franche industriali, nuove forme di investimento, l'America latina' ... organizzata dall'E.A. Fiera Milano in collaborazione con Contrade S.P.A. e il Centro estero camere commercio lombarde si è svolta a Milano il 17 aprile 1985"--T.p. verso. English, Italian, and Spanish. Includes bibliographical references. LC Card 86-223193
1. Free ports and zones - Latin America - Congresses. 2. Export processing zones - Latin America - Congresses. 3. Investments - Latin America - Congresses. I. Bortolotti, F. (Fabio). II. Vimercati, Giuseppe. III. Ente autonomo Fiera di Milano. IV. Contrade (Firm). V. Centro estero camere commercio lombarde. VI. Title.
HF1418 .C525 1985

Conferenza nazionale sull'energia . Conferenza nazionale sull'energia (1987 : Rome, Italy) Roma [1987]- v. <1-2 > : LC Card 87-167955
HD9502.I82 C63 1987

Conferenza nazionale sull'energia (1987 : Rome, Italy) Conferenza nazionale sull'energia : Roma, 24-27 febbraio 1987. Roma : Istituto Poligrafico e Zecca dello Stato, [1987]- v. <1-2 > : ill. ; 29 cm. At head of title: Ministero dell'industria, del commercio e dell'artigianato. Includes documents in English. LC Card 87-167955
1. Energy policy - Italy - Congresses. I. Italy. Ministero dell'industria, del commercio e dell'artigianato. II. Title.
HD9502.I82 C63 1987

The confidence gap . Lipset, Seymour Martin. Baltimore , 1987. xxiv, 460 p. : ISBN 0-8018-3044-3 (pbk.) LC Card 86-27416 DDC 303.3/8/0973 19
HD2785 .L53 1987

The confident consumer /. Campbell, Sally R. South Holland, Ill. , c1988. 368 p. : ISBN 0-87006-635-8 LC Card 87-2 DDC 381/.33 19
HG179 .C32 1988

Confidential--information security [motion picture] / AIMS Media ; director, writer, John Ralmon. Van Nuys, CA : AIMS Media, 1986. 1 film reel (22 min.) : sd., col. ; 16 mm. Title from data sheet. Management, employees, security officers. Issued also as videorecording. A con man, by demonstrating the tricks of his trade, shows ways industrial spies can extract sensitive information from a company. Explains how employees could prevent such theft and how security awareness serves the interest of employees as well as management. LC Card 87-705606 DDC 658.4 11
1. Business intelligence. 2. Trade secrets. I. AIMS Media.
HD38.7

Confidential--information security [videorecording] / AIMS Media ; director, writer, John Ralmon. Van Nuys, CA : AIMS Media, 1986. 1 videocassette (22 min.) : sd., col. Title from data sheet. Management, employees, security officers. Issued as U-matic 3/4 in. or Beta 1/2 in. or VHS 1/2 in. Issued also as motion picture. A con man, by demonstrating the tricks of his trade, shows ways industrial spies can extract sensitive information from a company. Explains how employees could prevent such theft and how security awareness serves the interest of employees as well as management. LC Card 87-705607 DDC 658.4 11
1. Business intelligence. 2. Trade secrets. I. AIMS Media.
HD38.7

CONFISCATIONS - FRANCE.
Un citoyen aux Etats-Généraux. Paris [1976] (Milan : Graphica Sipiel) 46 p. ; LC Card 87-672450
HJ1082 .C57x 1976

CONFISCATIONS - FRANCE - HISTORY - 18TH CENTURY.
Arsac, Pierre. La vente des biens de la Grande Chartreuse sous la Révolution /. Grenoble , 1984. 104 p. : ISBN 2-904661-02-6 LC Card 86-118639
HD643 .A77 1984

Conflict and crisis in rural America /. Waterfield, Larry W. New York , 1986. iv, 235 p. : ISBN 0-03-006074-5 (alk. paper) : LC Card 85-19366 DDC 333.76/0973 19
HD256 .W35 1986 ***NYPL [JLE 86-2792]***

Conflict and order . Morgan, Jane. Oxford [Oxfordshire] , New York , c1987. p. cm. ISBN 0-19-820128-1 : LC Card 87-11027 DDC 331.89/2942 19
HD5366.A6 M67 1987

Conflict in Central America . Diaz-Briquets, Sergio. Washington, D.C. (777 14th St. NW, Washington 20005) , 1986. 16 p. : LC Card 87-401095 DDC 304.6/09728 19
HB3533 .D5 1986

CONFLICT MANAGEMENT.
Berkel, Karl. Konflikttraining /. Heidelberg , c1985. 82 p. : ISBN 3-7938-7735-3 LC Card 85-188803
HD42 .B47 1985

Burton, John W. (John Wear), 1915- Resolving deep-rooted conflict . Lanham, MD , c1987. vii, 74 p. ; ISBN 0-8191-6284-1 (alk. paper) : LC Card 87-6144 DDC 658.4 19
HD42 .B87 1987

Conflict management and problem solving . New York , 1987. x, 321 p. : ISBN 0-8147-7866-6 : LC Card 87-11072 DDC 658.4 19
HD42 .C65 1987

Enrègle, Yves. Du conflit à la motivation . Paris , 1985. 196 p. : ISBN 2-7081-0642-2 : LC Card 85-231586
HF5549.5.M63 E57 1985

Escalation and intervention . Boulder, Colo. , 1986. x, 181 p. ; ISBN 0-8133-7200-3 : LC Card 86-4020 DDC 327.1/6 19
U104 .E83 1986 ***NYPL [JLE 86-4131]***

Gerstein, Arnold, 1940- Win-win approaches to conflict avoidance /. Salt Lake City, Utah , 1986. xvii, 110 p. : ISBN 0-87905-215-5 LC Card 85-26261 DDC 303.6 19
HM136 .G46 1986 ***NYPL [JLD 86-2104]***

Mastenbroek, W. F. G. [Conflicthantering en organisatie-ontwikkeling. English.] Conflict management and organization development /. Chichester , New York , c1987. x, 166 p. ; ISBN 0-471-91415-0 : LC Card 87-10463 DDC 302.3/5 19
HD58.8 .M32513 1987

Moore, Christopher W., 1947- The mediation process . San Francisco , 1986. xxii, 348 p. ; ISBN 0-87589-673-1 (alk. paper) LC Card 85-23675 DDC 302.3 19
HM136 .M684 1986 ***NYPL [JLE 86-3017]***

Stulberg, Joseph B. Taking charge/managing conflict /. Lexington, Mass. , c1987. xii, 175 p. ; ISBN 0-669-14014-7 (alk. paper) LC Card

86-45597 DDC 658.4 19
HD42 .S78 1987

Weiss, Donald H., 1936- How to deal with difficult people /. New York, N.Y. , c1987. 57 p. ; ISBN 0-8144-7674-0 (pbk.) : LC Card 86-47827 DDC 158/.2 19
HD42 .W45 1987

Conflict management and organization development /. Mastenbroek, W. F. G. [Conflicthantering en organisatie-ontwikkeling. English.] Chichester , New York , c1987. x, 166 p. ; ISBN 0-471-91415-0 : LC Card 87-10463 DDC 302.3/5 19
HD58.8 .M32513 1987

Conflict management and problem solving : interpersonal to international applications / edited by Dennis J.D. Sandole and Ingrid Sandole-Staroste ; foreword by Kenneth E. Boulding. New York : New York University Press, 1987. x, 321 p. : ill. ; 24 cm. Bibliography: p. [298]-306. Includes index. ISBN 0-8147-7866-6 : LC Card 87-11072 DDC 658.4 19
1. Conflict management. 2. Problem solving. I. Sandole, Dennis J. D., 1941-. II. Sandole-Staroste, Ingrid, 1948-.
HD42 .C65 1987

CONFLICT MANAGEMENT - GERMANY (WEST)
Kauer, Christian, 1951- Konfliktregelung und Mitbestimmung . Frankfurt am Main , New York , c1985. 393 p. : ISBN 3-8204-5626-0 (pbk.) LC Card 87-672045
HD5660.G4 K37x 1985

CONFLICT MANAGEMENT - MATHEMATICAL MODELS.
Analysing conflict and its resolution . Oxford [Oxfordshire] , New York , 1987. xvi, 349 p. : ISBN 0-19-853611-9 : LC Card 86-31108 DDC 658.4 19
HD42 .A52 1987

CONFLICT MANAGEMENT - UNITED STATES.
Alternative environmental conflict management approaches . [Ann Arbor, MI] (Dana Bldg., Ann Arbor 48109-1115) [1986] 252 p. : LC Card 86-225219 DDC 363.7/058/0973 19
HC110.E5 A643 1986

CONFLICT MANAGEMENT - YUGOSLAVIA.
Korać, Slobodan. Konflikti razvojnih ciljeva u samoupravnom društvu /. Beograd , 1981. 304 p. : LC Card 82-166028
HD42 .K67 1981

CONFLICT OF GENERATIONS - GERMANY (WEST) - CASE STUDIES.
Steinrücke, Margareta, 1953- Generationen im Betrieb . Frankfurt , New York , c1986. 343 p. ; ISBN 3-593-33639-1 LC Card 87-137842 DDC 331.3/0943 19
HD6283.G4 S74 1986

A conflict of visions /. Sowell, Thomas, 1930- New York , c1987. 273 p. ; ISBN 0-688-06912-6 LC Card 86-18187 DDC 303.3/72 19
HM73 .S68 1987 ***NYPL [JLD 87-823]***

CONFLICT, SOCIAL. see **SOCIAL CONFLICT.**

Conflicting paradigms in the economics of developing nations /. David, Wilfred L. New York , 1986. xix, 215 p. : ISBN 0-275-92108-5 (alk. paper) : LC Card 86-16906 DDC 330.9172/4 19
HC59.7 .D335 1986 ***NYPL [JLE 86-4423]***

Conflicto estado-empresarios en los gobiernos de Cárdenas, López Mateos y Echeverría /. Martínez Nava, Juan Manuel. México , 1984. 240 p. ; ISBN 968-429-411-5 LC Card 85-240016
HD3616.M43 M37 1984

El conflicto sindical en América Latina /. Zapata, Francisco. México, D.F. , 1986. 228 p. : ISBN 968-12-0323-2 LC Card 87-105269
HD5330.5.A6 Z36 1986

Conflictos laborales en la industria maquiladora /. Carrillo V., Jorge (Carrillo Viveros) Tijuana, Baja California , 1985. 55 p. : ISBN 968-607-504-6 LC Card 87-117557 DDC 331.4/87/09721 19
HD5331.O33 C37 1985

Conflicts of interest in the proxy voting system /. Heard, James E. Washington, D.C. , c1987. 100 p. : ISBN 0-931035-18-X (pbk.) LC Card 87-404270 DDC 338.8/3/0973 19
HD2743 .H43 1987

Conflicts over closure . Love, Cohn, 1938- Aldershot, Hants, England , Brookfield, Vt., U. S.A. [1987] p. cm. ISBN 0-566-05367-5 : LC Card 86-29496 DDC 338.6/042 19
HD5708.55.G7 L68 1987

CONFORMITY.
Lenssen, Adolf K. Konformität und Nichtkonformität im Betrieb . Konstanz , 1986. 400 p. : ISBN 3-89191-064-9 (p. 4. of cover); 3-89191-064-7 LC Card 87-109576 DDC 658.3/001/9 19
HF5549 .L4619 1986

Confrontation, class consciousness, and the labor process : studies in proletarian class formation / edited by Michael Hanagan and Charles Stephenson. Westport, Conn. : Greenwood Press, 1986. viii, 261 p. ; 24 cm. (Contributions in labor studies, 0886-8239 . no. 18) Includes index. Bibliography: p. [241]-253. ISBN 0-313-25140-1 (lib. bdg. : alk. paper) LC Card 85-17734 DDC 305.5/62 19
1. Labor and laboring classes - Addresses, essays, lectures. 2. Proletariat - Addresses, essays, lectures. 3. Industrial sociology - Addresses, essays, lectures. 4. Labor economics - Addresses, essays, lectures. I. Hanagan, Michael P., 1947-. II. Stephenson, Charles. III. Series.
HD4851 .C63 1986 ***NYPL [JLE 86-3558]***

Confrontation or negotiation : United States policy and European agriculture : reports from a public policy study of the Curry Foundation. Millwood, N.Y. : Associated Faculty Press, 1985. xvi, 303 p. : ill. ; 24 cm. Includes bibliographies. ISBN 0-8046-9397-8 : LC Card 85-18667 DDC 382/.41/094 19
1. Produce trade - Government policy - European Economic Community countries - Congresses. 2. Produce trade - Government policy - United States - Congresses. 3. Agriculture and state - European Economic Community countries - Congresses. 4. Agriculture and state - United States - Congresses. 5. Free trade and protection - Congresses. 6. United States - Foreign economic relations - European Economic Community countries - Congresses. 7. European Economic Community countries - Foreign economic relations - United States - Congresses. I. Curry Foundation.
HD9015.E82 C67 1985
NYPL [JLE 86-4594]

Confronting the world food crisis /. Stevens, Charles J. Muscatine, Iowa [1981] 24 p. : LC Card 82-127279 DDC 338.1/9 19
HD9000.6 .S73 ***NYPL [JLK 75-198 no. 27]***

CONGLOMERATE CORPORATIONS.
Goold, Michael. Strategies and styles . Oxford, UK , New York, NY, USA , 1988, cl987. p. cm. ISBN 0-631-15829-4 : LC Card 87-12151 DDC 658/.046 19
HD2756 .G66 1988

CONGLOMERATE CORPORATIONS - GERMANY - HISTORY.
Meyer, August. Das Syndikat . Braunschweig , c1986. 348 p. ; ISBN 3-925151-18-4 LC Card 87-129940 DDC 338.2/73/0943 19
HD9523.9.R45 M49 1986

CONGLOMERATE CORPORATIONS - GERMANY, WEST.
Wolf, Martin, 1954- Erfahrungen mit der Profit-Center-Organisation /. Frankfurt am Main , New York , c1985. viii, 285 p. : ISBN 3-8204-8746-8 LC Card 85-243838
HD2756.2.G3 W65 1985

CONGLOMERATE CORPORATIONS - GERMANY, WEST - HISTORY.
Maisel, Helmut. Diversifikation und konglomerate Interdependenz . Frankfurt , c1984. 237 p. : ISBN 3-88323-518-0 LC Card 84-213494
HD2756.2.G3 M34 1984

CONGLOMERATE CORPORATIONS - GREAT BRITAIN - HISTORY.
Reader, W. J. (William Joseph), 1920- Grand Metropolitan . Oxford [Oxfordshire] , New York , 1988. p. cm. ISBN 0-19-822976-3 : LC Card 87-21942 DDC 338.8/8941 19
HD2845.Z75 G77 1988

CONGLOMERATE CORPORATIONS - ITALY - ACCOUNTING.
Mella, Piero. Contabilità delle aziende divise /. [Milan] , c1983. 281 p. : ISBN 88-21-70036-4 LC Card 85-151879
HF5686.C7 M427 1983

CONGLOMERATE CORPORATIONS - JAPAN.
Futatsugi, Yūsaku, 1935- [Gendai Nihon no kigyō shūdan. English.] Japanese enterprise groups /. [Kobe] , 1986. 179 p. : LC Card 86-220427 DDC 338.8/0952 19
HD2756.2.J3 F8813 1986

CONGLOMERATE CORPORATIONS - UNITED STATES.
Gort, Michael, 1923- Diversification and integration in American industry /. Westport, Conn. , 1984, c1962. xxi, 238 p. ; ISBN 0-313-24423-5 (lib. bdg.) LC Card 84-10730 DDC 338.8/0973 19
HD2756.2.U5 G67 1984
NYPL [JLE 86-4435]

Strickland, Allyn D. Firm diversification, mutual forbearance behavior and price-cost margins /. New York , 1984. 155 p. ; ISBN 0-8240-4159-3 (alk. paper) LC Card 79-53209 DDC 338.8/3/0973
HD2756.U5 S76 1984 ***NYPL [JLE 86-3907]***

CONGLOMERATE MERGERS. see **CONGLOMERATE CORPORATIONS.**

Congo : du pétrole et des dettes. Paris : L'Harmattan [distributor, 1983] 19 p. : ill. ; 21 cm. Cover title. Distributor from label on p. [1] of cover. LC Card 85-118609
1. Petroleum industry and trade - Congo (Brazzaville) - Economic aspects.
HD9577.C62 C65 1983

CONGO (BRAZZAVILLE) - ECONOMIC CONDITIONS.
Migrations rurales et urbanisation en République populaire du Congo. Addis Ababa , 1984. x, 168 p. : LC Card 84-980878
HB2125.A3 M54 1984

CONGO (BRAZZAVILLE) - ECONOMIC CONDITIONS - REGIONAL DISPARITIES.
N'Kaloulou, Bernard, 1952- Dynamique paysanne et développement rural au Congo /. Paris , c1984. 260 p. : ISBN 2-85802-416-X LC Card 84-246506 DDC 305.5/63 19
HD1006 .N57 1984 ***NYPL [JLD 87-304]***

CONGO (BRAZZAVILLE) - POPULATION, RURAL.
Migrations rurales et urbanisation en République populaire du Congo. Addis Ababa , 1984. x, 168 p. : LC Card 84-980878
HB2125.A3 M54 1984

CONGO (BRAZZAVILLE) - RURAL CONDITIONS.
N'Kaloulou, Bernard, 1952- Dynamique paysanne et développement rural au Congo /. Paris , c1984. 260 p. : ISBN 2-85802-416-X LC Card 84-246506 DDC 305.5/63 19
HD1006 .N57 1984 ***NYPL [JLD 87-304]***

Congram, Carole A. The Services challenge . Chicago, Ill. , 1987. vi, 108 p. : ISBN 0-87757-188-0 (pbk.) LC Card 87-12543 DDC 658.8 19
HD9980.5 .S4255 1987

Congrès international de la population, Florence 1985, 5-12 juin. International Population Conference (1985 : Florence, Italy) International Population Conference, Florence 1985, 5-12 June =. Liège, Belgium , c1985- v. : ISBN 2-87108-004-6 (set) LC Card 86-113476 DDC 304.6 19
HB849 .I616 1985 ***NYPL [JLL 86-265]***

Congrès national des sociétés savantes (105th : 1980 : Caen, France) Colloque sur l'histoire de la sécurité sociale (1980 : Caen, France) Colloque sur l'histoire de la sécurité sociale . Paris , 1981. 263 p. ; LC Card 81-201274
HD7175 .C58 1980

CONGRESO DE LA COB (6TH : 1984 : COCHABAMBA, BOLIVIA) - CONGRESSES.
Tendencias sindicales después del VI Congreso de la C.O.B. /. La Paz , c1985. 111 p. ; LC Card 86-137172
HD8272.C65 T45 1985

Congreso Nacional de Investigación Histórica (1st : 1984 : Lima, Peru?) Las Crisis económicas en la historia del Perú /. [Lima, Perú] [s.l.] , 1986. 376 p. : LC Card 87-400306 DDC 330.985 19
HC227 .C744 1986

CONGRESO NACIONAL MINERO (20TH : 1984 : DISTRITO MINERO DE MATILDE, BOLIVIA)
Lazarte, Jorge. Crisis de identidad y centralidad minera . [La Paz, Bolivia] [1986] 37 p. : LC Card 87-401455 DDC 331.88/122/0984 19
HD8039.M61 B586 1986

CONGRESO NACIONAL MINERO (21TH : 1986 : ORURO, BOLIVIA)
Calla, Ricardo. La derrota de Lechín . La Paz, Bolivia , 1986. 79 p. : LC Card 87-105127
HD6609.M62 F433 1986

Congress and economic policy making. West, Darrell M., 1954- Congress and economic policymaking /. Pittsburgh, Pa. , c1987. xiv, 203 p. ; ISBN 0-8229-5396-X (pbk.) LC Card 87-40160 DDC 338.973 19
HC106.8 .W45 1987

Congress and economic policymaking /. West, Darrell M., 1954- Pittsburgh, Pa. , c1987. xiv, 203 p. ; ISBN 0-8229-5396-X (pbk.) LC Card 87-40160 DDC 338.973 19
HC106.8 .W45 1987

Congress and the Executive . Barrie, Robert W. New York , 1987. 347 p. ; ISBN 0-8240-8071-8 (alk. paper) LC Card 87-23814 DDC 382/.3/0973 19
HF1455 .B317 1987

CONGRESS OF INDUSTRIAL ORGANIZATIONS.
Boulware, Lemuel Richetts, 1895- What to do about communism in unions . [Schenectady, N.Y.?] [1952?] 62 p. ; ***NYPL [JLD 86-247]***

CONGRESS OF INDUSTRIAL ORGANIZATIONS (U. S.) - BIOGRAPHY.
Salmond, John A. Miss Lucy of the CIO . Athens , c1988. p. cm. ISBN 0-8203-0956-7 (alk. paper) LC Card 87-5822 DDC 331.88/33/0924 B 19
HD6509.M375 S25 1988

CONGRESS OF INDUSTRIAL ORGANIZATIONS (U. S.) - HISTORY.
Griffith, Barbara S. The crisis of American labor . Philadelphia , 1988. xvi, 239 p. : ISBN 0-87722-503-6 (alk. paper) : LC Card 87-9998 DDC 331.88/33/0975 19
HD8055.C75 G75 1988

Congress of Working People of Romania (3rd : 1986 : Bucharest, Romania) Third Congress of Working People of Romania. Bucharest : Agerpres, [1986?] ii, 56 p. ; 21 cm. Cover title. LC Card 86-225999 DDC 331/.09498 19
1. Congress of Working People of Romania (3rd : 1986 : Bucharest, Romania). 2. Labor and laboring classes - Romania - Congresses. 3. Labor policy - Romania - Congresses. 4. Romania - Economic policy - 1945- - Congresses. 5. Romania - Social policy - Congresses. I. Title.
HD8642 .C59 1986

CONGRESS OF WORKING PEOPLE OF ROMANIA (3RD : 1986 : BUCHAREST, ROMANIA)
Congress of Working People of Romania (3rd : 1986 : Bucharest, Romania) Third Congress of Working People of Romania. Bucharest [1986?] ii, 56 p. ; LC Card 86-225999 DDC 331/.09498 19
HD8642 .C59 1986

CONGRESSES AND CONVENTIONS - HANDBOOKS, MANUALS, ETC.
Lant, Jeffrey L. Money talks . Cambridge, Mass. , c1985. vii, 302 p. : ISBN 0-940374-08-0 (pbk.) LC Card 87-105725 DDC 001 19
HD69.C6 L27 1985

Congressional Delegation to the World Food Conference. see United States. Congressional Delegation to the World Food Conference.

Congressional Quarterly, inc.
Beyond Reagan . Washington, D.C. , c1987. v, 209 p. : ISBN 0-87187-437-7 (pbk.) : LC Card 87-3057 DDC 338.973 19
HC106.8 .B47 1987

Editorial research reports on the American work ethic. Washington [1973] iii, 180 p. ISBN 0-87187-042-8 LC Card 72-94080 DDC 331.1/1/0973
HD8072 .E34 ***NYPL [JLD 86-1374]***

Energy and environment . Washington, D.C. , c1985. x, 190 p. : ISBN 0-87187-360-5 : LC Card 85-25471 DDC 333.79/0973 19
HD9502.U52 E4524 1985
NYPL [JLE 86-2859]

La Conjoncture économique en Europe : automne 1982 : rapport général à la réunion de l'Association des instituts européens de conjoncture économique ... Bruxelles, 28-29 octobre 1982 / rédigé par Maria Eugénia Pires ... [et al.]. Lisboa, Portugal : Instituto de Análise da Conjuntura e Estudos de Planeamento, [1982] 78 p. : ill. ; 30 cm. LC Card 83-181663
1. Europe - Economic conditions - 1945-. 2. Economic forecasting - Europe. I. Pires, Maria Eugénia. II. Association des instituts européens de conjoncture économique. III. Instituto de Análise da Conjuntura e Estudos de Planeamento (Portugal).
HC240 .C588 1982

A conjunction of interests . Forster, Jakob Johann Benjamin. Toronto , Buffalo , c1986. vi, 288 p. ; ISBN 0-8020-5680-6 (alk. paper) LC Card 87-108915 DDC 382.7/0971 19
HF1765 .F67 1986

Conkling, Edgar C. Berry, Brian Joe Lobley, 1934- Economic geography . Englewood Cliffs, N.J. , c1987. xi, 447 p. : ISBN 0-13-231440-1 : LC Card 87-2250 DDC 330.9 19
HC59 .B52 1987

Conley, Chip. Godin, Seth. Business rules of thumb /. New York, NY , c1987. x, 165 p. ; ISBN 0-446-37026-6 (pbk.) LC Card 87-6262 DDC 650.1 19
HF5386 .G55 1987

CONNECTICUT - ECONOMIC CONDITIONS.
Hadden, Kenneth. Poverty in Connecticut, 1979 /. Storrs, CT [1986] 24 p. : LC Card 86-623148 DDC 362.5/09746 19
HC107.C8 H33 1986

Connecticut. Governor (1980- : O'Neill)
Infrastructure revitalization status report, October, 1985 /. [Hartford, Conn.] [1986?] 23 leaves ; LC Card 86-622547 DDC 363/.09746 19
HC107.C83 C35 1986

Connecticut. Intergovernmental Relations Division. Tax districts. [Hartford, Conn.] [1985] 53 p. ; LC Card 86-620827 DDC 352.1/3/09746 19
HJ9210 .T39 1985

CONNECTICUT - SOCIAL CONDITIONS.
Hadden, Kenneth. Poverty in Connecticut, 1979 /. Storrs, CT [1986] 24 p. : LC Card 86-623148 DDC 362.5/09746 19
HC107.C8 H33 1986

Connecticut workers and a half century of technological change, 1930-1980, oral history project. Palmer, Michele. Catalogue of interviews . [Storrs, Conn.] , 1983. ii, 79 p. ; LC Card 86-621476 DDC 331.12/09746 19
HD6331.2.U52 C86 1983

Connecticut workers and technological change . Asher, Robert. Storrs , c1983. 100 p. : LC Card 83-62409 DDC 306/.3/09746 19
HD8083.C7 A83 1983 ***NYPL [JLE 86-1507]***

Connections : an energy strategy for the future / Economic Council of Canada. [Ottawa] : The Council ; Ottawa, Canada : Canadian Govt. Pub. Centre, Supply and Services Canada [distributor], 1985. x, 207 p. : ill. ; 27 cm. Includes bibliographical references. ISBN 0-660-11743-6 (pbk.) : LC Card 85-136746 DDC 333.79/0971 19
1. Power resources - Canada. 2. Energy policy - Canada.
TJ163.25.C2 C66 1985 ***NYPL [JLF 87-326]***

Connections, effective purchasing power, and real product in the German Democratic Republic /. Collier, Irwin L., 1951- Berlin , 1985. ix, 216 p. : ISBN 3-921374-34-0 (pbk.) LC Card 86-229298 DDC 330 s 338.9431/00724 19
HC244.A1 B4 Nr. 44 HC290.78

Conneely, Joe M. Tiner, John I. Accounting for treasury products . Cambridge, England , Wolfeboro, N.H., USA , 1988. p. cm. ISBN 0-85941-389-6 : LC Card 87-12531 DDC 657/.833 19
HG1708 .T56 1988

Connell, John R. Touche Ross guide to personal financial management /. Englewood Cliffs, N.J. , c1987. xviii, 332 p. ; ISBN 0-13-925413-7 : LC Card 87-2470 DDC 332.024 19
HG179 .P5729 1987

Conning & Company.
Directors and officers liability . Hartford, Conn. (101 Pearl St., Hartford 06103) , c1986. 53 p. ; LC Card 86-211342
HG8053.8 .D57 1986

Life solvency monitor. Hartford, Conn. (41 Lewis St., Hartford 06103) , 1985. 201 p. : LC Card 86-215848 DDC 368.3/2/006 19
HG8955 .L55 1985

Life solvency monitor. Hartford, Conn. (101 Pearl St., Hartford 06103) , 1986. 227 p. : LC Card 86-209963 DDC 368.3/2/006 19
HG8955 .L55 1986

1986 ordinary life insurance reference manual . Hartford, Conn. (101 Pearl St., Hartford 06103) [1986] 88 p. ; LC Card 87-163896 DDC 368/.006/073 19
HG8955 .A56 1986

Connolly, Michael B. (Michael Bahaamonde), 1941- Economic reform and stabilization in Latin America /. New York , c1986. xxiii, 348 p. : ISBN 0-275-92307-X (alk. paper) : LC Card 86-9405 DDC 338.98 19
HC125 .E374 1986 ***NYPL [JLE 87-1073]***

Connolly, Paul M. Promotional practices and policies : career building in the '80s :highlights of the literature / by Paul M. Connolly.1st ed. New York : Pergamon, c1985. 52 p. ; 29 cm. (Work in America Institute studies in productivity, 0149-8703 . 41) Bibliography: p. 43-52. ISBN 0-08-029515-0 (pbk.) : LC Card 85-3421 DDC 658.3/142 19
1. Personnel management - United States. 2. Job enrichment - United States. 3. Job satisfaction - United States. I. Title. II. Series.
HF5549.2.U5 C66 1985
NYPL [JLM 83-380 no.41]

Connolly, Seamus G. Finding, entering, and succeeding in a foreign market / Seamus G. Connolly. Englewood Cliffs, N.J. : Prentice-Hall, c1987. xiii, 274 p. : ill. ; 24 cm. Includes index. Bibliography: p. 266. ISBN 0-13-316951-0 LC Card 86-25395 DDC 658.8/48 19
1. Export marketing - Management. 2. International business enterprises - Management. I. Title.
HF1009.5 .C59 1986 ***NYPL [JLE 87-1310]***

Connor, Patrick E. Managing organizational change / Patrick E. Connor & Linda K. Lake. New York : Praeger, 1988. xii, 192 p. : ill. ; 24 cm. Bibliography: p. [181]-183. Includes index. ISBN 0-275-92335-5 (alk. paper) : LC Card 87-12475 DDC 658.4/06 19
1. Organizational change. I. Lake, Linda K. II. Title.
HD58.8 .C653 1988

Connor, Richard A. Getting new clients / Richard A. Connor, Jr., Jeffrey P. Davidson. New York : Wiley, c1987. xxiii, 305 p. : ill. ; 24 cm. Includes index. ISBN 0-471-62778-X LC Card 87-21657 DDC 658.8 19
1. Professions - Marketing. I. Davidson, Jeffrey P. II. Title.
HD8038.A1 C665 1987

Conover, Ted. Coyotes : a journey through the secret world of America's illegal aliens / by Ted Conover.1st ed. New York : Vintage Books, 1987. xix, 264 p. : port. ; 21 cm. (Vintage departures) ISBN 0-394-75518-9 (pbk.) : LC Card 87-6101 DDC 331.6/2/72073 19
1. Alien labor, Mexican - United States. 2. Aliens, Illegal - United States. I. Title.
HD8081.M6 C65 1987

La conquista del espacio territorial sanjuanino /. Marzo, Miguel. Mendoza , 1968. 89 p., [12] leaves of plates : LC Card 82-166187
HD479.S25 M37 1968

La conquista del Valle del Fuerte /. Gill, Mario. Culiacán, Rosales, Sinaloa, México , c1983. 273 p., [4] folded leaves of plates : LC Card 86-121747
HC137.F84 G54 1983

Conrad, Jon M. Natural resource economics : notes and problems / Jon M. Conrad and Colin W. Clark. Cambridge [Cambridgeshire] ; New York : Cambridge University Press, 1987. x, 231 p. : ill. ; 24 cm. Bibliography: p. [225]-228. Includes index. ISBN 0-521-33188-9 LC Card 87-11582 DDC 333.7 19

1. Natural resources. 2. Environmental policy. I. Clark, Colin Whitcomb, 1931-. II. Title.
HC59 .C693 1987

Conrad, Klaus, 1940- Produktivitätslücken nach Wirtschaftszweigen im internationalen Vergleich : Beschreibung und ökonometrische Ursachenanalyse für die USA, Japan und die Bundesrepublik Deutschland, 1960-1979 / Klaus Conrad. Berlin ; New York : Springer-Verlag, c1985. 165 p. ; 25 cm. (Studies in contemporary economics . 17) Bibliography: p. [163]-165. ISBN 0-387-15571-6 (U. S.) LC Card 85-233665
1. Industrial productivity - United States - Econometric models. 2. Industrial productivity - Japan - Econometric models. 3. Industrial productivity - Germany (West) - Econometric models. I. Title. II. Series.
HC110.I52 C67 1985

Conrad, Leo M. Zimmerman, Steven M. Understanding and using microcomputers /. St. Paul , c1988. xxvi, 371 p. : ISBN 0-314-60096-5 (pbk.) LC Card 87-19044 DDC 650/.028/5416 19
HF5548.2 .Z58 1988

Conrail . New York (State). Legislature. Legislative Commission on Critical Transportation Choices. [Albany] [1986] i, 134 p. ; LC Card 87-620569 DDC 385/.065/73 19
HE2791.C899 N48 1986

CONRAIL - FINANCE.
Dayton, Mark R. Economic viability of Conrail. Washington, D.C. [1986] xvii, 85 p. : LC Card 86-602852 DDC 385/.1 19
HE2791.C8994 D39 1986

Conroy, Hilary, 1919- New tides in the Pacific . New York , 1987. xiii, 216 p. ; ISBN 0-313-25625-X (lib. bdg. : alk. paper) LC Card 87-8406 DDC 337.1/9 19
HC681 .N48 1987

CONSCIENTIOUS OBJECTORS - GERMANY, WEST.
Wer fürchtet sich vor'm schwarzen Mann? niemand! und wenn er kommt? dann lesen wir . Velbert , c1985. 95 p. : ISBN 3-922319-08-4 : LC Card 86-206116 DDC 355.2/2363/0943 19
HD4870.G3 W47 1985

Conseil d'assistance économique mutuelle. see **Sovet ėkonomicheskoĭ vzaimopomoshchi.**

Conseil de l'Europe. see **Council of Europe.**

Conseil de planification et de développement du Québec. Le réseau décisionnel en agro-alimentation au Québec : adopté à la 36e Assemblée régulière le 19 octobre 1979 / Conseil de planification et de développement du Québec. [Québec] : Le Conseil, [1979] 29 p. ; 29 cm. (Collection Avis et recommandations) On cover: Avis et recommandations au Premier ministre et au Ministre de l'agriculture et de l'alimentation. LC Card 85-102587
1. Agricultural industries - Government policy - Québec (Province). 2. Agriculture and state - Québec (Province). 3. Industrial promotion - Québec (Province). I. Québec (Province). Premier ministre. II. Québec (Province). Ministère de l'agriculture et de l'alimentation. III. Title. IV. Title: Avis et recommandations au Premier ministre et au Ministre de l'agriculture et de l'alimentation. V. Series.
HD9014.C4 Q425 1979

Conseil international de l'étain. see **International Tin Council.**

Conseil international du bâtiment pour la recherche, l'étude et de la documentation. see **International Council for Building Research, Studies and Documentation.**

Conseil national de la révolution (Burkina Faso) Programme populaire de développement, octobre 1984 décembre 1985 / Burkina Faso, Ministère de la planification et du développement populaire, Conseil national de la révolution. [Ouagadougou, Burkina Faso] : Le Conseil, [1985?] 1 v. (various pagings) : col. map ; 30 cm. "An II." LC Card 87-160992
1. Burkina Faso - Economic policy. 2. Central planning - Burkina Faso. I. Title.
HC1040 .C66 1985

Programme populaire de développement, octobre 1984-décembre 1985 : bilan final / Burkina Faso, Ministère de la planification et du développement populaire, Conseil national de la Révolution. [Ouagadougou] : Le Conseil Ministère de la planification et du développement populaire, [1986] 2 v. : maps ; 30 cm. "An II." "Juin 1986." CONTENTS. - t. 1. Analyses -- t. 2. Annexes. LC Card 87-158925
1. Burkina Faso - Economic policy. 2. Central planning - Burkina Faso. I. Title.
HC1040 .C66 1986

Conseil scientifique hongrois d'économie mondiale. see **Magyar Tudományos Akadémia, Budapest. Világgazdasági Kutató Intézet.**

Consejería de Agricultura y Pesca del Principado de Asturias. Argüelles, Alfonso. Los Oscos y la Cuenca del Eo . [Asturias] [1984?] ix, 317 p. : ISBN 84-505-0237-3 LC Card 86-174593
HC387.A7 A74 1984

Consejo de Europa. see **Council of Europe.**

Consejo Económico Sindical del Campo de Gibraltar. Colaboración sindical al estudio sobre la estructura y posibilidad de desarrollo del Campo de Gibraltar, encomendado por la comisión interministerial designada al efecto /. Cádiz , 1965. 89 p. : LC Card 85-104938
HC390.6 .C65 1965

Consejo Económico Sindical Provincial (Cuenca, Spain) IV pleno del Consejo Económico Sindical de Cuenca : gráficos, estadísticas y conclusiones / Consejo Económico Sindical Provincial. [Cuenca] : El Consejo, 1965. 128 p. : ill. ; 29 cm. LC Card 85-105812
1. Agriculture - Economic aspects - Spain - Cuenca. 2. Cuenca (Spain) - Industries. 3. Cuenca (Spain) - Economic conditions. 4. Cuenca (Spain) - Social conditions. I. Title. II. Title: Cuarto pleno del Consejo Económico Sindical de Cuenca. III. Title: 4o pleno del Consejo Económico Sindical de Cuenca.
HD2025.C84 C65 1965

Consejo Económico Sindical Provincial (Teruel, Spain) Estudio para el desarrollo de las zonas económicas de la Provincia de Teruel /. [Teruel] , 1965. 75, 61, 63, 65, 74, 61 p. ; LC Card 85-110389
HC387.T4 E886 1965

Consejo Interamericano Económico y Social. see **Inter-American Economic and Social Council.**

Consejo Internacional del Estaño. see **International Tin Council.**

Consejo Latinoamericano de Ciencias Sociales. Comisión de Demografía. Elizaga, Juan C. (Juan Carlos) Investigaciones sobre recursos humanos en América Latina . Santiago de Chile , 1972. 16 p. ; LC Card 83-103424
HA755 .U5 no. 91 HD5730.5.A6

Consejo Nacional de Ciencia y Tecnología (Peru) Las Crisis económicas en la historia del Perú /. [Lima, Perú] [s.l.] , 1986. 376 p. : LC Card 87-400306 DDC 330.985 19
HC227 .C744 1986

Consejo Nacional de Desarrollo (Argentina). Sector Presupuesto Económico Nacional. Resultados de la encuesta sobre expectativas de producción e inversión de las empresas industriales /. Buenos Aires , 1965. 81 leaves : LC Card 85-114982
HC180.I52 R47 1965

Consejo Nacional de Desarrollo (Ecuador). Sección Programación del Sector Público. Estadísticas financieras del sector público ecuatoriano, años 1975-1981 /. [Quito] [1983] 316 p. ; LC Card 86-179747
HJ955 .E792 1983

Consejo Nacional de Desarrollo (Ecuador). Secretaría General de Planificación. Lineamientos generales para el Plan de Desarrollo, 1984-1988. Quito, Ecuador , 1985. ii, 42 leaves ; LC Card 86-149211
HC202 .L52 1985

Plan Nacional de Desarrollo, 1985-1988 / Consejo Nacional de Desarrollo, Secretaría General de Planificación. [Quito, Ecuador] : La Secretaría, [1985] 3 leaves, iv, 218 p. : ill. ; 29 cm. Cover title: Ecuador, Plan Nacional de Desarrollo, 1985-1988. Accompanied by anexo 1 "Programas y proyectos para el desarrollo de los sectores productivos" (204 p. ; 21 x 29 cm); anexo 2 "Programas y proyectos para la integración espacial y organización del territorio" (112 p. ; 21 x 29 cm.); anexo 3 "Programas y proyectos para el desarrollo de los recursos humanos" (319 p. ; 21 x 29 cm.); and anexo 4 "Otras políticas y programas" (96 p. ; 21 x 29 cm.) LC Card 86-146646 DDC 338.9866 19
1. Ecuador - Economic policy. I. Title. II. Title: Ecuador, Plan Nacional de Desarrollo, 1985-1988.
HC202 .C675 1985b

Consejo Nacional de Población (Mexico) Camposortega Cruz, Sergio. El método de los componentes demográficos para realizar proyecciones de población. México, D.F. [1984] 35 p. : LC Card 85-164750
HB849.53 .C36 1984

Proyecciones de la población de México y de las entidades federativas, 1980-2010. México, D.F. , c1985. xiii, 134 p. ; ISBN 968-8097-66-7 LC Card 86-223751
HB3531 .P78 1985

Consejo Nacional de Política Económica y Social (Colombia) Foro de la Esperanza (1985 : Ibagué, Colombia) Foro de la Esperanza . [Bogotá?] [1985] 154 p. ; LC Card 87-401285 DDC 338.9861 19
HC197 .F59 1985

Consejo Superior de Planificación Económica (Honduras)
Situación actual y perspectivas económicas, 1972 : informe de la Comisión del Consejo Superior de Planificación Económica / integrada por Rubén Mondragón C. ... [et al.]. Tegucigalpa, D.C., Honduras, C.A. : El Consejo, 1972. 38, [18] leaves ; 28 cm. LC Card 86-158684
1. Honduras - Economic conditions - 1918-1980. 2. Economic forecasting - Honduras. I. Mondragón, Rubén. II. Title.
HC145 .C66 1972

Consejo Superior de Planificación Económica (Honduras). Secretaría Técnica.
Honduras, informe general de la situación socioeconómica. Tegucigalpa, D.C., Honduras, C.A. , 1971. 2, 6, 155 leaves ; LC Card 86-120957
HC145 .H665 1971

Imagen de la estructura económica-social y explotación de los recursos naturales /. Tegucigalpa, D.C., Honduras, C.A. , 1973. viii, 334 p. : LC Card 86-177356
HC145 .I52 1973

Proyecto de desarrollo local de La Paz, Intibucá / República de Honduras, Secretaría Técnica del Consejo Superior de Planificación Económica, CONSUPLANE. [Tegucigalpa, Honduras] : Secretaría General de la Organización de los Estados Americanos, [1984- v. <1 > : ill., maps ; 28 cm. CONTENTS. - t. 1. Diagnóstico del área local. LC Card 86-213886
1. Economic development projects - Honduras - La Paz (Dept.). 2. Economic development projects - Honduras - Intibucá (Dept.). 3. Agricultural productivity - Honduras - La Paz (Dept.). 4. Agricultural productivity - Honduras - Intibucá (Dept.). 5. Forest productivity - Honduras - La Paz (Dept.). 6. Forest productivity - Honduras - Intibucá (Dept.). 7. Handicrafts - Honduras - La Paz (Dept.). 8. Handicrafts - Honduras - Intibucá (Dept.). I. Organization of American States. General Secretariat. II. Title.
HC145.Z9 E443 1984

Consejo Superior Universitario Centroamericano. Central American Program for Development of Social Sciences. see **Programa Centroamericano de Desarrollo de las Ciencias Sociales.**

Consejo Superior Universitario Centroamericano. Programa Centroamericano de Desarrollo de las Ciencias Sociales. see **Programa Centroamericano de Desarrollo de las Ciencias Sociales.**

Consejo Venezolano de la Industria. Comité Ejecutivo. Belardi C., Arturo. La industria frente a la inflación . Valencia [Venezuela] , 1981. 92 leaves : LC Card 85-187972
HG915 .B44 1981

Conselho Coordenador de Recenseamento (Mozambique) Os Distritos em números /. [Maputo?] [1983-1985] 10 v. ; LC Card 86-980977 DDC 330.67/905021 19
HC890 .D57 1983

Conselho de Desenvolvimento Comercial. Coordenadoria de Projetos Especiais. Comercialização de alimentos na região norte, 1985 /. Brasília, DF , 1985. 51 p. ; LC Card

86-129086
HD9014.B83 N673 1985

Conselho de Desenvolvimento Industrial (Brazil). Secretaria Executiva. Mercado brasileiro de celulose e papel /. Brasília, D.F. , 1982. vii, 224 leaves : LC Card 84-210712
HD9660.C43 B75 1982

CONSELHO MONETÁRIO NACIONAL (BRAZIL) - HISTORY.
Vianna, Maria Lúcia Teixeira Werneck. A administração do "milagre" . Petrópolis , 1987. 180 p. ; LC Card 87-403982 DDC 332.4/981 19
HG835 .V527 1987

Conselho Nacional de Desenvolvimento Urbano (Brazil) Estudos e propostas para a organização territorial e desenvolvimento urbano do Brasil. Brasilia , 1981. 126 leaves, [7] folded leaves of plates : ***NYPL [JLG 86-151]***

Conselho Nacional de Informática e Automação (Brazil). Comissão Especial de Automação Bancária. Relatório da Comissão Especial de Automação Bancária. Brasília , 1985. 304 p. : LC Card 86-230558
HG1709 .R35 1985

Consensus, control, and critique . Alvesson, Mats, 1956- Aldershot, Hants, England , Brookfield, Vt., USA , c1987. viii, 162 p. : ISBN 0-566-05285-7 : LC Card 87-8427 DDC 306/.36 19
HD6955 .A442 1987

Les conséquences à long terme de la politique macroéconomique /. Huber, Gérard. Berne , 1982. 449 p. ; ISBN 3-261-04985-5 LC Card 87-672303
HB172.5 .H82x 1982

Les conséquences économiques de l'investissement étranger en France . Savary, Julien, 1944- Toulouse [1984] 24 p. ; LC Card 85-143217
HG5472 .S28 1984

Conséquences économiques et sociales de la course aux armements /. United Nations. Secretary-General. [Economic and social consequences of the arms race and of military expenditures. French.] Paris , 1983. 121 p. : ISBN 2-7178-0645-8 : LC Card 84-136625
HC79.D4 U52 1983

The Conservation and Liquidation Division, Department of Insurance /. California. Dept. of Finance. Program Evaluation Unit. [Sacramento, Calif.] [1985] xii, 62 p. ; LC Card 85-622857 DDC 353.97940082/55 19
HG8538.C2 C35 1985

Conservation Committee of California Oil Producers. California crude oil production, 1960-1985. Los Angeles, Calif. (417 S. Hill St., Suite 930, Los Angeles 90013) , c1986. 149 p., [1] folded leaf of plates : LC Card 87-150171 DDC 338.2/7282/09794021 19
HD9567.C2 C385 1986

Conservation Foundation.
Agriculture and the environment in a changing world economy. Washington, D.C. , c1986. xi, 66 p. : ISBN 0-89164-099-1 (pbk.) LC Card 86-24088 DDC 338.1/873 19
HD1761 .A6228 1986

State of the environment . Washington, D.C. , c1984. xxxiv, 586 p. : ISBN 0-89164-084-3 LC Card 84-12651 DDC 363.7/00973 19
TD171 .S74 1984 ***NYPL [JLD 86-3097]***

CONSERVATION OF ENERGY RESOURCES. see **ENERGY CONSERVATION.**

Conservation of Human Resources studies in the new economy.
Bailey, Thomas Raymond. Immigrant and native workers . Boulder , 1987. xvi, 168 p. : ISBN 0-8133-7349-2 : LC Card 86-28205 DDC 331.6/2/0973 19
HD8081.A5 B35 1987

CONSERVATION OF NATURAL RESOURCES - ASIA, SOUTHEASTERN - CONGRESSES.
Environment and resources in the Pacific /. Geneva, Switzerland , 1985. iv, 294 p. : LC Card 86-217776 DDC 333.7/2/099 19
HC681.3.E5 E58 1985

CONSERVATION OF NATURAL RESOURCES - CONGRESSES.
Demands on rural lands . Boulder, Colo. , 1987. xvi, 336 p. : ISBN 0-8133-7361-1 (pbk. : alk. paper) LC Card 87-50751 DDC 333.76/13 19
HD105 .D43 1987

CONSERVATION OF NATURAL RESOURCES - GOVERNMENT POLICY - GERMANY (WEST)
Paul, Joachim, 1956- Zur politischen Durchsetzungsfähigkeit einer ökologisch orientierten Marktwirtschaft . Frankfurt am Main , New York , c1986. xvii, 569 p. ; ISBN 3-8204-9810-9 LC Card 87-407614 DDC 363.7/056/0943 19
HC290.5.E5 P38 1986

CONSERVATION OF NATURAL RESOURCES - GOVERNMENT POLICY - ITALY - MILAN REGION.
Metropoli e agricoltura /. Milano , c1982. 319 p. : LC Card 82-246692 DDC 333.76/13/094521 19
HD680.M54 M47 1982 ***NYPL [JLD 86-3678]***

CONSERVATION OF NATURAL RESOURCES - GOVERNMENT POLICY - UNITED STATES.
Kloepfer, Deanne. The Watt record . Washington, D.C. [1983] ii, 66, 9, 3 p. : LC Card 86-232533 DDC 333.1/0973 19
HD183.L3 K58 1983

Social science in natural resource management systems /. Boulder , 1987. xii, 265 p. : ISBN 0-8133-7485-5 (pbk. : alk. paper) LC Card 87-23138 DDC 333.7/0973 19
HC103.7 .S62 1987

CONSERVATION OF NATURAL RESOURCES - GREAT BRITAIN.
Countryside conflicts . Aldershot, Hants, England , Brookfield, Vt., U. S.A. , c1986. vi, 378 p. [4] leaves of plates : ISBN 0-566-05088-9 : LC Card 85-24603 DDC 333.76/17/0941 19
HD596 .C675 1986 ***NYPL [JLD 86-2487]***

CONSERVATION OF NATURAL RESOURCES - LATIN AMERICA.
Bordering on trouble . Bethesda, Md. , 1986. xii, 448 p. : ISBN 0-917561-25-2 (pbk.) LC Card 86-7941 DDC 338.98 19
HC125 .B594 1986 ***NYPL [JLE 86-4501]***

CONSERVATION OF NATURAL RESOURCES - OCEANIA - CONGRESSES.
Environment and resources in the Pacific /. Geneva, Switzerland , 1985. iv, 294 p. : LC Card 86-217776 DDC 333.7/2/099 19
HC681.3.E5 E58 1985

CONSERVATION OF NATURAL RESOURCES - SOUTHERN STATES.
Healy, Robert G. Competition for land in the American South . Washington, D.C. , c1985. xxxii, 333 p. : ISBN 0-89164-090-0 (pbk.) LC Card 85-25459 DDC 333.76/13/0975 19
HD266.A13 H43 1985 ***NYPL [JLE 86-2724]***

CONSERVATION OF NATURAL RESOURCES - UNITED STATES.
An Environmental agenda for the future /. Washington, D.C. , c1985. viii, 155 p. ; ISBN 0-933280-29-7 (pbk.) : LC Card 85-19760 DDC 304.2 19
TD171 .E56 1985 ***NYPL [JLE 86-2773]***

Waterfield, Larry W. Conflict and crisis in rural America /. New York , 1986. iv, 235 p. : ISBN 0-03-006074-5 (alk. paper) : LC Card 85-19366 DDC 333.76/0973 19
HD256 .W35 1986 ***NYPL [JLE 86-2792]***

CONSERVATION OF NATURAL RESOURCES - UNITED STATES - CONGRESSES.
Population change, natural resources, and regionalism /. Milford, Pa. , c1986. viii, 104 p. : ISBN 0-938549-00-6 (pbk.) LC Card 86-25682 DDC 304.6/0973 19
HB3505 .P62 1986

CONSERVATION OF NATURAL RESOURCES - UNITED STATES - HISTORY.
West, Patrick C. Natural resource bureaucracy and rural poverty . Ann Arbor, MI , c1982. xiii, 168 p. : LC Card 83-102928 DDC 333.7/16/0973 19
HD1761 .W423 1982 ***NYPL [JLE 86-4095]***

CONSERVATION OF PETROLEUM. see **PETROLEUM CONSERVATION.**

CONSERVATION OF POWER RESOURCES. see **ENERGY CONSERVATION.**

CONSERVATION OF RESOURCES. see **CONSERVATION OF NATURAL RESOURCES.**

CONSERVATION OF THE SOIL. see **SOIL CONSERVATION.**

CONSERVATION OF WATER. see **WATER CONSERVATION.**

Conservation of water and related land resources /. Black, Peter E. Totowa, N.J. , 1987. xvi, 336 p. : ISBN 0-8476-7567-X LC Card 87-4770 DDC 333.91/16/0973 19
HD1694 .A5105 1987

CONSERVATION OF WILDLIFE. see **WILDLIFE CONSERVATION.**

CONSERVATISM.
Achminow, Herman F., 1921- Am grossen Krieg "vorbeischleichen"? . Bonn , c1983. 304 p. ; ISBN 3-923920-00-8 LC Card 84-150915 DDC 355/.03304 19
UA646 .A38 1983 ***NYPL [JFD 87-1743]***

Wohlfarth, Karl Anton. Leistung und Ethos . Paderborn , 1984. 266 p. ; ISBN 3-506-70223-8 LC Card 84-238158
HD60 .W64 1984

CONSERVATISM - FRANCE - HISTORY.
Lebovics, Herman. The alliance of iron and wheat in the Third French Republic, 1860-1914 . Baton Rouge , c1988. p. cm. ISBN 0-8071-1350-6 LC Card 87-21386 DDC 338.944 19
HC276 .L354 1988

CONSERVATISM - GREAT BRITAIN.
Nuscheler, Franz. Die Entwicklungspolitik der Regierung Thatcher . [Bonn] [1986] 93 p. : LC Card 86-186261
HC60 .N87 1986

CONSERVATISM - UNITED STATES.
Brick, Howard, 1953- Daniel Bell and the decline of intellectual radicalism . Madison, Wis. , 1986. 215-266. ISBN 0-299-10550-4 : LC Card 85-40757 DDC 300/.92/4 19
H59.B42 B75 1986 ***NYPL [JLE 86-3046]***

Falik, Marilyn. Ideology and abortion policy politics /. New York, N.Y. , 1983. 228 p. ; ISBN 0-03-062813-X LC Card 83-2402 DDC 363.4/6 19
HQ767.5.U5 F34 1983 ***NYPL [JLE 85-1581]***

Nuscheler, Franz. Die Entwicklungspolitik der Regierung Thatcher . [Bonn] [1986] 93 p. : LC Card 86-186261
HC60 .N87 1986

Osiatyński, Wiktor, 1945- Współczesny konserwatyzm i liberalizm amerykański /. Warszawa , 1984. 552 p. ; ISBN 83-01-04929-4 (pbk.) : ***NYPL [*QO 86-3450]***

CONSERVATISM - UNITED STATES - HISTORY - 20TH CENTURY.
Withers, William, 1905-1987. Politics and economic policy . New York, N.Y. , c1986. 240 p. : ISBN 0-8062-2722-2 : LC Card 86-201185 DDC 338.973 19
HC106 .W82 1986

Consideraciones acerca del estado del debate en teoría macroeconómica /. Rosende Ramírez, Francisco. Santiago , 1986. 51 leaves ; LC Card 87-116226 DDC 339 19
HB178.5 .R67 1986

Consideraciones aproximativas en torno a la investigación laboral en América Latina /. Feuer, Björn. Stockholm [1985] 18 p. ; LC Card 85-205735
HD4824.5.L29 F48 1985

Considerações sobre o mercado das indústrias de confecções brasileiras. Ribeiro, Lêda Cristina de O. Santana Cançado. Belo Horizonte [Brazil] , 1985. 66 leaves : LC Card 87-404932 DDC 338.4/7687/0981 19
HD9940.B82 R53 1985

Consiglio dell'Europa. see **Council of Europe.**

Consiglio nazionale delle ricerche (Italy) IFIP TC 8/WG 8.4 Working Conference on Methods and Tools for Office Systems (1986 : Pisa, Italy) Office systems . Amsterdam ; New York : xi, 347 p. : ISBN 0-444-70241-5 (U. S.) LC Card 87-8916 DDC 651.8 19
HF5548.2 .I285 1986

Consiglio nazionale dell'economia e del lavoro (Italy)
Italia multinazionale . Milano , 1986. 2 v. : LC Card 87-158571
HD2864 .I82 1986

Rapporto CNEL su risparmio e borsa : Assemblea, 6 giugno, 1984. Roma : Consiglio nazionale dell'economia e del lavoro : "L'Erma" di Bretschneider [distributor], 1984. 308 p. : ill. ; 24 cm. Distributor stamped on t.p. Chiefly tables. LC Card 85-242331 DDC 332/.0415/0945021 19
1. Saving and investment - Italy - Statistics. 2. Stocks - Italy - Statistics. I. Title.
HC310.S3 C66 1984

Consistency of model year injury claim frequency results for selected 1981-1983 models. Washington, D.C (Watergate 600, Washington 20037) : Highway Loss Data Institute, c1986. 11 p. ; 28 cm. (Research report HLDI . A-26 (May 1986)) Insurance special report / Highway Loss Data Institute LC Card 87-107714 DDC 368.5/72/00973 19
1. Insurance, Automobile - United States. 2. Traffic accidents - United States. I. Highway Loss Data Institute. II. Series: Research report HLDI , A-26.
HG9970.3 .C66 1986

Consistent correction of census and vital registration data for Thailand, 1960-80 /. Luther, Norman Y., 1936- Honolulu, Hawaii [1986] vii, 39 p. ; ISBN 0-86638-089-2 (pbk.) : LC Card 86-32807 DDC 304.6/0723 19
HA39.T4 L87 1986

Il consolidamento strutturale dell'occupazione in specifiche aree con particolare riguardo alla provincia di Gorizia /. Albertini, Sergio. Milano , c1984. 184 p. ; LC Card 84-234951 DDC 331.12/0945/392 19
HD5785.G67 A42 1984

Consolidated data base : U. S. markets, 1981-1990 / Dataquest. San Jose, Calif. (1290 Ridder Park Dr., San Jose 95131-2398) : Dataquest, c1986. ii, 94 p. ; 28 cm. "September 1986." LC Card 87-108611 DDC 381/.45004/0973
1. Computer industry - United States. 2. Electronic office machine industry - United States. 3. Telecommunication equipment industry - United States. 4. Semiconductor industry - United States. 5. Market surveys - United States. I. Dataquest (Firm).
HD9696.C63 U515626 1986

Consolidated Gold Fields . Johnson, Paul (Paul A.) New York , 1987. p. cm. ISBN 0-312-00549-0 : LC Card 86-31307 DDC 338.7/6223422/0968 19
HD9536.S64 C665 1987

CONSOLIDATED GOLD FIELDS LIMITED - HISTORY.
Johnson, Paul (Paul A.) Consolidated Gold Fields . New York , 1987. p. cm. ISBN 0-312-00549-0 : LC Card 86-31307 DDC 338.7/6223422/0968 19
HD9536.S64 C665 1987

Consolidated Rail Corporation. see Conrail.

CONSOLIDATION AND MERGER OF CORPORATIONS - CONGRESSES.
Mergers and acquisitions /. Chicago , 1988. xi, 108 p. : ISBN 0-226-03209-4 LC Card 87-19035 DDC 658.1/6 19
HD2746.5 .M45 1988

CONSOLIDATION AND MERGER OF CORPORATIONS - ECONOMIC ASPECTS - UNITED STATES.
Corporate takeovers . Washington , 1987. viii, 126 p. ; LC Card 87-601347 DDC 338.8/3/0973 19
HD2746.5 .C676 1987

CONSOLIDATION AND MERGER OF CORPORATIONS - FINANCE.
Chastain, Clark E. Corporate asset management . New York , 1987. xxiii, 345 p. : ISBN 0-89930-237-8 (lib. bdg. : alk. paper) LC Card 87-2493 DDC 658.1/5244 19
HG4026 .C458 1987

CONSOLIDATION AND MERGER OF CORPORATIONS - GERMANY, WEST.
Drukarczyk, Jochen. Credit contracts, collateral-based security agreements, and bankruptcy /. Regensburg [1983?] 25 leaves ; LC Card 84-181506 DDC 332.7/5/0943 19
HG3769.G34 D78 1983

Feldmann, Berthold. Unternehmenskonzentration, Marktmacht und Lohnniveau . Göttingen , c1984. xii, 260 p. : ISBN 3-525-12269-1 LC Card 85-162393
HD2746.5 .F45 1984

Möller, Wolf-Peter. Der Erfolg von Unternehmenszusammenschlüssen . München , c1983. 403 p. : ISBN 3-597-10456-8 LC Card 83-227517
HD2746.5 .M65 1983

CONSOLIDATION AND MERGER OF CORPORATIONS - GOVERNMENT POLICY - UNITED STATES.
Public policy toward corporate takeovers /. New Brunswick (USA) , c1988. xvi, 176 p. ; ISBN 0-88738-166-9 : LC Card 87-10750 DDC 338.8/3/0973 19
HD2795 .P825 1988

CONSOLIDATION AND MERGER OF CORPORATIONS - INFORMATION SERVICES - UNITED STATES.
Rosenberg, Gerald I. How to find information about acquisition candidates /. Washington, D.C. , c1987. 79 p. ; ISBN 0-934940-45-2 LC Card 86-51570 DDC 016.3387/4/0973 19
HD2785 .R58 1987

CONSOLIDATION AND MERGER OF CORPORATIONS - ITALY.
Le Strategie di acquisto della grande impresa nell'evoluzione dei sistemi produttivi . Milano, Italy , c1985. 223 p. : LC Card 85-233748
HD85.I7 I68 no. 76 HD39.5 ***NYPL [JLD 87-426]***

CONSOLIDATION AND MERGER OF CORPORATIONS - MATHEMATICAL MODELS.
Hörnig, Bodo. Beteiligungs- und Fusionsvorhaben . Berlin , c1985. xvi, 357 p. : ISBN 3-428-05786-4 LC Card 85-168610
HD2746.5 .H67 1985

CONSOLIDATION AND MERGER OF CORPORATIONS - NETHERLANDS - CASE STUDIES.
Caris, J. Fuseren in non-profit organisaties . Nijmegen , 1986. 107 p. : ISBN 90-255-0018-8 : LC Card 86-205531
HD2746.5 .C35 1986

CONSOLIDATION AND MERGER OF CORPORATIONS - TAXATION - CONGRESSES.
Mergers and acquisitions /. Chicago , 1988. xi, 108 p. : ISBN 0-226-03209-4 LC Card 87-19035 DDC 658.1/6 19
HD2746.5 .M45 1988

CONSOLIDATION AND MERGER OF CORPORATIONS - TAXATION - UNITED STATES.
Smirlock, Michael. Taxes and mergers . New York, N.Y. (90 Trinity Place, New York 10006) [c1986] 42 p. : LC Card 86-210061 DDC 336.24/3 19
HD2746.5 .S64 1986

Tax, SEC, and accounting aspects of corporate acquisitions, 1984 /. New York, N.Y. (810 Seventh Ave., New York 10019) , c1984. 584 p. : LC Card 84-231882 DDC 343.7306/7 347.30367 19
KF6499.M4 T39 1984 ***NYPL [JLD 87-57]***

CONSOLIDATION AND MERGER OF CORPORATIONS - UNITED STATES.
Brooks, John, 1920- The takeover game /. New York , c1987. x, 390 p. ; ISBN 0-525-24586-3 : LC Card 87-5967 DDC 338.8/3/0973 19
HD2746.5 .B76 1987

Corporate mergers and high yield (junk) bonds . Washington , 1986. vi, 57 p. ; LC Card 87-601339 DDC 332.63/22 19
HD2746.5 .C67 1986

Corporate takeovers . Washington , 1987. viii, 126 p. ; LC Card 87-601347 DDC 338.8/3/0973 19
HD2746.5 .C676 1987

Gort, Michael, 1923- Diversification and integration in American industry /. Westport, Conn. , 1984, c1962. xxi, 238 p. ; ISBN 0-313-24423-5 (lib. bdg.) LC Card 84-10730 DDC 338.8/0973 19
HD2756.2.U5 G67 1984 ***NYPL [JLE 86-4435]***

Hirsch, Paul Morris. Pack your own parachute . Reading, Mass. , c1987. xix, 197 p. ; ISBN 0-201-12205-7 (pbk.) : LC Card 87-14388 DDC 658.4/09 19
HD38.25.U6 H578 1987

Johnston, Moira, 1934- Takeover . New York , c1986. xv, 395 p. ; ISBN 0-87795-784-3 : LC Card 86-10818 DDC 338.8/3/0973 19
HD2746.5 .J64 1986 ***NYPL [JLE 86-3932]***

Johnston, Moira, 1934- Takeover /. New York, N.Y. , 1987, c1986. xiii, 418 p. ; ISBN 0-14-010505-0 (pbk.) LC Card 87-8560 DDC 338.8/3/0973 19
HD2746.5 .J64 1987

Madrick, Jeffrey G. Taking America . Toronto , New York , 1987. 310 p. ; ISBN 0-553-05229-2 LC Card 87-928 DDC 338.8/3/0973 19
HG4028.T4 M33 1987

Meek, Christopher. Managing by the numbers . Reading, Mass. , c1988. ix, 293 p. : ISBN 0-201-16129-X : LC Card 87-16088 DDC 338.7/4/0973 19
HD70.U5 M413 1988

Petzinger, Thomas. Oil & honor . New York , c1987. 495 p., [8] p. of plates : ISBN 0-399-13276-7 LC Card 87-2255 DDC 338.8/3622338/0973 19
HD9569.T4 P48 1987

Ravenscraft, David J., 1952- Mergers, sell-offs, and economic efficiency /. Washington, D.C. , c1987. xiii, 290 p. : ISBN 0-8157-7348-X : LC Card 87-14018 DDC 338.8/3/0973 19
HD2746.5 .R38 1987

Slater, Robert, 1943- The titans of takeover /. Englewood Cliffs, N.J. , c1987. ix, 230 p. : ISBN 0-13-922055-0 LC Card 86-25364 DDC 338.8/3/0973 19
HD2785 .S44 1987

Stevens, Mark, 1947- The insiders . New York , c1987. 256 p. ; LC Card 87-2537 DDC 364.1/68 19
HG4910 .S67 1987

Tax, SEC, and accounting aspects of corporate acquisitions, 1984 /. New York, N.Y. (810 Seventh Ave., New York 10019) , c1984. 584 p. : LC Card 84-231882 DDC 343.7306/7 347.30367 19
KF6499.M4 T39 1984 ***NYPL [JLD 87-57]***

US-Fusionsrichtlinien, 1984 /. Köln , c1985. 83 p. ; ISBN 3-452-20248-8 : LC Card 86-100251
HB41 .F63 Heft 6 KF1477

Zinman, Michael. The history of the decline and fall of the Raterpillar Tractor Company . Ardsley, N.Y. , c1986. 231 p. : ISBN 0-937704-03-2 (pbk.) : LC Card 86-82887 DDC 338.7/629225 19
HD9710.4.U64 R388 1986

CONSOLIDATION AND MERGER OF CORPORATIONS - UNITED STATES - DIRECTORIES.
Rosenbaum, Virginia K. Antitakeover charter amendments . Washington, D.C. , 1986. 100 p. : ISBN 0-931035-07-4
NYPL [JLF 86-1964]

Rosenberg, Gerald I. How to find information about acquisition candidates /. Washington, D.C. , c1987. 79 p. ; ISBN 0-934940-45-2 LC Card 86-51570 DDC 016.3387/4/0973 19
HD2785 .R58 1987

CONSOLIDATION AND MERGER OF CORPORATIONS - UNITED STATES - HANDBOOKS, MANUALS, ETC.
Scharf, Charles A. Acquisitions, mergers, sales, buyouts, and takeovers . Englewood Cliffs, N.J. , c1985. xi, 452 p. : ISBN 0-13-003120-8 LC Card 85-6566 DDC 658.1/6/0973 19
HD2741 .S35 1985 ***NYPL [JLF 86-611]***

CONSOLIDATION AND MERGER OF CORPORATIONS - UNITED STATES - PREVENTION.
Combating takeover attempts. Washington, D.C. , c1986. xi, 12 p. : LC Card 86-224303 DDC 658.1/6 19
HD2746.5 .C645 1986

CONSOLIDATION AND MERGER OF CORPORATIONS - UNITED STATES - PREVENTION - CASE STUDIES.
Michel, Allen, 1945- Takeover madness . New York , c1986. xii, 397 p. : ISBN 0-471-01079-0

LC Card 85-32315 DDC 658.1/8 19
HD2746.5 .M53 1986 ***NYPL [JLE 86-2989]***

CONSOLIDATION AND MERGER OF CORPORATIONS - UNITED STATES - PREVENTION - DIRECTORIES.
Rosenbaum, Virginia. Takeover defenses . Washington, D.C. , c1987. 227 p. ; ISBN 0-931035-13-9 (pbk.) LC Card 87-400095 DDC 338.7/4/02573 19
HD2746.5 .R67 1987

Consolidation policies in OECD countries : report / by the Working Group on Accounting Standards. Paris : Organisation for Economic Co-operation and Development, 1987. 60, 63 p. ; 27 cm. (Accounting standards harmonization . no. 2) English and French. Added t.p. has title: Les méthodes de consolidation des comptes dans les pays de l'OCDE. ISBN 92-64-02876-5 : LC Card 87-168671 DDC 657/.3 19
1. Financial statements, Consolidated. 2. Financial statements, Consolidated - Standards. 3. Organisation for Economic Co-operation and Development. I. Organisation for Economic Co-operation and Development. Working Group on Accounting Standards. II. Title: Méthodes de consolidation des comptes dans les pays de l'OCDE. III. Series.
HF5681.B2 C593 1987

Consommation. Balfet, Michel. Les 50 mots clefs de la consommation /. Toulouse , c1985. 310 p. : ISBN 2-7089-1969-5 : LC Card 86-140639 DDC 339.4/7 19
HB801 .B276 1985

Consortium for International Cooperation in Higher Education. Solving world hunger, the U. S. stake /. Cabin John, MD , 1986. ix, 102 p. : ISBN 0-932020-42-9 (pbk.) : LC Card 86-17665 DDC 363.8/526/0973 19
HV696.F6 S65 1986 ***NYPL [JLF 87-531]***

CONSPIRACIES - UNITED STATES.
Scholl, Heinz. Bilderberger & Trilaterale . Euskirchen, Bundesrepublik Deutschland , c1977. 92 p. ; LC Card 85-199172
HD2785 .S396 1977

Conspiracy of giants . Fridjhon, Michael. Johannesburg , c1986. xii, 419 p. : ISBN 0-947012-34-6 LC Card 87-139111 DDC 338.4/76631/0968 19
HD9367.S7 F75 1986

CONSTANTINE (ALGERIA : WILĀYAH) - ECONOMIC CONDITIONS.
Meuleman, Johan H. Le Constantinois entre les deux guerres mondiales . Assen, Pays-Bas , 1985. 296 p., [1] folded leaf of plates : ISBN 90-232-2093-5 : LC Card 86-119662
HC815.Z7 C666 1985

CONSTANTINE (ALGERIA : WILĀYAH) - RURAL CONDITIONS.
Meuleman, Johan H. Le Constantinois entre les deux guerres mondiales . Assen, Pays-Bas , 1985. 296 p., [1] folded leaf of plates : ISBN 90-232-2093-5 : LC Card 86-119662
HC815.Z7 C666 1985

Constantino, Renato. Synthetic culture and development / Renato Constantino. Quezon City : Foundation for Nationalist Studies, c1985. iv, 72 p. ; 22 cm. Bibliography: p. [67]-72. ISBN 971-10-5803-0 (pbk.) LC Card 85-234601 DDC 302.2 19
1. Communication in economic development. 2. Communication in economic development - Phillipines. I. Title.
HD76. C66 1985 ***NYPL [JLD 87-27]***

Le Constantinois entre les deux guerres mondiales . Meuleman, Johan H. Assen, Pays-Bas , 1985. 296 p., [1] folded leaf of plates : ISBN 90-232-2093-5 : LC Card 86-119662
HC815.Z7 C666 1985

Constat de l'évolution récente des revenus en France : 1980-1983. Paris : Centre d'études des revenus et des coûts : Documentation française, [1984] 220 p. : ill. ; 27 cm. (Documents du Centre d'étude des revenus et des coûts, 0336-1470 . no 71) Includes bibliographical references. "Numéro spécial"--Cover. LC Card 85-127672
1. Income - France. I. Centre d'études des revenus et des coûts. II. Series.
HC280.I5 C67 1984

The constraints of corporate tradition . Kantrow, Alan M., 1947- New York , c1987. xvii, 216 p. ; ISBN 0-06-015753-4 : LC Card 86-46075 DDC 302.3/5 19
HD58.7 .K375 1987

Construção de habitações na zona rural da microrregião do São Francisco / Governo do Estado de Pernambuco, Secretaria de Planejamento--SEPLAN, Instituto de Desenvolvimento de Pernambuco--CONDEPE. Recife : CONDEPE, 1982. 23 leaves ; 30 cm. (Série Projetos sócio-econômicos . no. 4) LC Card 86-175009
1. Housing, Rural - Brazil - São Francisco River Region. 2. Housing, Rural - Brazil - Pernambuco - Case studies. I. Instituto de Desenvolvimento de Pernambuco. II. Series.
HD7289.B72 S263 1982

CONSTRUCTION, HOUSE. see **HOUSE CONSTRUCTION.**

CONSTRUCTION INDUSTRY.
Employment policy and job creation in and through the construction industry . Geneva , 1986. vi, 110 p. : ISBN 92-2-105709-7 (pbk.) : LC Card 87-167960 DDC 331.12/924 19
HD9715.A2 E42 1986

Seymour, Howard, 1961- The multinational construction industry /. London , New York , c1987. 295 p. ; ISBN 0-7099-5438-7 LC Card 87-21720 DDC 338.8/87 19
HD9715.A2 S49 1987

CONSTRUCTION INDUSTRY - ACCOUNTING.
Thomsett, Michael C. Builder's guide to accounting /. Carlsbad, CA , c1987. 302 p. : ISBN 0-934041-18-0 (pbk.) : LC Card 87-6817 DDC 657/.869 19
HF5686.B7 T47 1987

CONSTRUCTION INDUSTRY - ACCOUNTING - DATA PROCESSING.
Grout, Gary. Business computing for small contractors /. Berkeley, Calif. , c1986. xv, 314 p. : ISBN 0-07-881229-1 (pbk.) LC Card 86-206636 DDC 690/.8/0285536 19
HF5686.B7 G75 1986

CONSTRUCTION INDUSTRY - ARGENTINA.
Hacia un planeamiento de la industria de la construcción en la Argentina /. Buenos Aires , 1943. 289 p. : LC Card 85-104409
HD9715.A72 H33 1943

CONSTRUCTION INDUSTRY - ARGENTINA - STATISTICS.
Edificación, 1972-1984. Buenos Aires , 1986. 36 p. : LC Card 87-404780 DDC 338.4/7624/0982021 19
HD9715.A72 E35 1986

CONSTRUCTION INDUSTRY - BYELORUSSIAN S.S.R. - CAPITAL PRODUCTIVITY.
Shevchuk, L. V. (Līūdmila Vladimirovna) Metodicheskie osnovy analiza i prognozirovaniīā fondootdachi . Minsk , 1983. 118 p. : LC Card 84-118665
HD9715.S73 B9465 1983

Sovershenstvovanie khoziāīstvennogo mekhanizma v stroitel'stve /. Minsk , 1984. 111 p. : LC Card 86-220340
HD9715.S73 B947 1984

CONSTRUCTION INDUSTRY - BYELORUSSIAN S.S.R. - CAPITAL PRODUCTIVITY - ECONOMETRIC MODELS.
Shevchuk, L. V. (Līūdmila Vladimirovna) Metodicheskie osnovy analiza i prognozirovaniīā fondootdachi . Minsk , 1983. 118 p. : LC Card 84-118665
HD9715.S73 B9465 1983

CONSTRUCTION INDUSTRY - BYELORUSSIAN S.S.R. - TECHNOLOGICAL INNOVATIONS.
Sovershenstvovanie khoziāīstvennogo mekhanizma v stroitel'stve /. Minsk , 1984. 111 p. : LC Card 86-220340
HD9715.S73 B947 1984

CONSTRUCTION INDUSTRY - CALIFORNIA - HISTORY.
Atkinson, Ray N. Guy F. Atkinson Company of California . New York , 1985, c1986. 24 p. : LC Card 86-61271 DDC 338.7/624/0973 19
HD9715.U54 G882 1986

CONSTRUCTION INDUSTRY - CONTRACTS AND SPECIFICATIONS. see **BUILDING - CONTRACTS AND SPECIFICATIONS.**

CONSTRUCTION INDUSTRY - COSTA RICA - STATISTICS.
Mulquin, Marie Eve. Las estadísticas del sector construcción en Costa Rica . [San José] , 1981. 39 p. ; LC Card 81-216965
HD9715.C82 M85 1981

CONSTRUCTION INDUSTRY - DATA PROCESSING.
Grout, Gary. Business computing for small contractors /. Berkeley, Calif. , c1986. xv, 314 p. : ISBN 0-07-881229-1 (pbk.) LC Card 86-206636 DDC 690/.8/0285536 19
HF5686.B7 G75 1986

CONSTRUCTION INDUSTRY - DEVELOPING COUNTRIES.
Moavenzadeh, Fred, 1935- The construction industry in developing countries. Nairobi , 1984. 2 v. ; LC Card 85-980242 DDC 338.4/767/091724 19
HD9715.D44 M63 1984

CONSTRUCTION INDUSTRY - EUROPE.
Surrey, John. The European power plant industry . [Brighton, Sussex] , c1981. viii, 90 p. ; ISBN 0-903422-31-X (pbk.) : LC Card 83-130609 DDC 338.4/76213121/094 19
HD9695.E92 S87 1981
NYPL [JLD 86-4078]

CONSTRUCTION INDUSTRY - FINANCE.
Unger, Maurice Albert, 1917- Real estate finance /. Cincinnati , c1984. vi, 426 p. : ISBN 0-538-19630-0 LC Card 83-61343 DDC 332.7/2 19
HG2040 .U53 1984 ***NYPL [JLE 86-4718]***

CONSTRUCTION INDUSTRY - GERMANY - NUREMBERG - HISTORY.
Gömmel, Rainer. Vorindustrielle Bauwirtschaft in der Reichsstadt Nürnberg und ihrem Umland (16.-18. Jh.) /. [Stuttgart] , 1985. xii, 300 p. : ISBN 3-515-04481-7 LC Card 86-122013
HD9715.G33 N874 1985

CONSTRUCTION INDUSTRY - GERMANY, WEST.
Mayer, Ralph-Dieter. Stahl- und Leichtmetallbau, Schienenfahrzeugbau . Berlin , c1985. 352 p. : ISBN 3-428-05771-6 LC Card 85-161158
HD9523.5 .M3 1985

CONSTRUCTION INDUSTRY - GERMANY (WEST) - ECONOMETRIC MODELS.
Jaap, Christiane. Möglichkeiten betriebswirtschaftlicher Beurteilung privater Kapitalanlagen . Berlin , c1986. xxiii, 322 p. : ISBN 3-428-06008-3 LC Card 86-189069
HG4028.C4 J28 1986

CONSTRUCTION INDUSTRY - GERMANY (WEST) - FINANCE.
Gisteren, Roland van, 1950- Branchenorientierte Bonitätsanalyse mit Früherkennungseigenschaften . München , c1986. 2, xi, 393 p. : ISBN 3-88259-370-9 LC Card 86-173025
HD9715.G32 G57 1986

CONSTRUCTION INDUSTRY - GERMANY (WEST) - LEVERKUSEN - STATISTICS.
Marx, G. Die Entwicklung der Wohnungsbautätigkeit in Leverkusen /. Leverkusen [1984] 37 p., [1] folded leaf of plates : LC Card 84-183932
HD9715.G33 L575 1984

CONSTRUCTION INDUSTRY - GREAT BRITAIN - DATA PROCESSING - CONGRESSES.
Computer technology in construction . London , 1985. 308 p. : ISBN 0-7277-0234-3 LC Card 85-670263 DDC 338.4/5624 19
HD9715.G72 C64 1985
NYPL [JLE 86-2586]

CONSTRUCTION INDUSTRY - GUATEMALA - GUATEMALA - COSTS.
Revisión del índice del costo de la construcción de vivienda en la Ciudad de Guatemala, años 1975-1979. Guatemala , 1979. 35 p. : LC Card 82-182718
HD9715.G983 G827 1979

The construction industry in developing countries. Moavenzadeh, Fred, 1935- Nairobi , 1984. 2 v. ; LC Card 85-980242 DDC 338.4/767/091724 19
HD9715.D44 M63 1984

CONSTRUCTION INDUSTRY - ITALY.
La Riconversione produttiva nell'edilizia /. Milano , 1984, c1981. 319 p. :
NYPL [JLD 86-3381]

CONSTRUCTION INDUSTRY - ITALY - CONGRESSES.
Seminario di aggiornamento per i quadri sindacali della categoria (1985 : Rome, Italy) Evoluzione del processo produttivo nelle construzioni . Milano, Italy , c1986. 142 p. : LC Card 86-210757
HD9715.I82 S46 1985

CONSTRUCTION INDUSTRY - LABOR PRODUCTIVITY.
Adrian, James J. Construction productivity improvement /. New York , c1987. xiii, 303 p. : ISBN 0-444-01121-8 LC Card 86-24172 DDC 624/.068/3 19
HD9715.A2 A353 1987

CONSTRUCTION INDUSTRY - LABOR PRODUCTIVITY - CASE STUDIES - CONGRESSES.
Productivity and human factors in construction /. London , New York , 1987. p. cm. ISBN 0-419-14010-7 LC Card 87-20547 DDC 624/.068 s 624/.068/3 19
HD9715.A2 M296 vol. 2

CONSTRUCTION INDUSTRY - LABOR PRODUCTIVITY - CONGRESSES.
Productivity and human factors in construction /. London , New York , 1987. p. cm. ISBN 0-419-14010-7 LC Card 87-20547 DDC 624/.068 s 624/.068/3 19
HD9715.A2 M296 vol. 2

CONSTRUCTION INDUSTRY - LAW AND LEGISLATION - GERMANY, WEST.
Gisteren, Roland van, 1950- Branchenorientierte Bonitätsanalyse mit Früherkennungseigenschaften . München , c1986. 2, xi, 393 p. : ISBN 3-88259-370-9 LC Card 86-173025
HD9715.G32 G57 1986

CONSTRUCTION INDUSTRY - MANAGEMENT - CASE STUDIES - CONGRESSES.
Construction management and organisation in perspective /. London , New York , 1987. p. cm. ISBN 0-419-14020-4 LC Card 87-20548 DDC 624/.068 s 624/.068 19
HD9715.A2 M296 vol. 3

Managing construction worldwide /. London , New York , 1987. p. cm. ISBN 0-419-14030-1 (set) LC Card 87-20545 DDC 624/.068 19
HD9715.A2 M296

Systems for managing construction /. London , New York , 1987. p. cm. ISBN 0-419-14000-X LC Card 87-20546 DDC 624/.068 s 624/.068 19
HD9715.A2 M296 vol. 1

CONSTRUCTION INDUSTRY - MANAGEMENT - CONGRESSES.
Construction management and organisation in perspective /. London , New York , 1987. p. cm. ISBN 0-419-14020-4 LC Card 87-20548 DDC 624/.068 s 624/.068 19
HD9715.A2 M296 vol. 3

Managing construction worldwide /. London , New York , 1987. p. cm. ISBN 0-419-14030-1 (set) LC Card 87-20545 DDC 624/.068 19
HD9715.A2 M296

Specialty Conference on Engineering and Construction Projects (1982 : New Orleans, La.) Proceedings of the Specialty Conference on Engineering and Construction Projects . New York, N.Y. , c1982. vi, 329 p. : ISBN 0-87262-299-1 (pbk.) LC Card 82-70492 DDC 658.5 19
TA190 .S67 1982 *NYPL [JLD 86-1905]*

Systems for managing construction /. London , New York , 1987. p. cm. ISBN 0-419-14000-X LC Card 87-20546 DDC 624/.068 s 624/.068 19
HD9715.A2 M296 vol. 1

CONSTRUCTION INDUSTRY - MEXICO.
La Industria mexicana de la construcción. México, D.F. , 1979. 89 p. : LC Card 87-400496 DDC 338.4/7624/0972 19
HD9715.M4 I53 1979

CONSTRUCTION INDUSTRY - PANAMA - PANAMA (DISTRICT)
Pacheco D., Rubén. Industria de la construcción . [Panamá] , 1974. 17, [1] leaves, [4] leaves of plates : LC Card 87-400643
HD9715.P223 P367 1974

CONSTRUCTION INDUSTRY - PERSONNEL MANAGEMENT.
Anderson, S. D. (Stuart D.) Project manpower management . New York , c1987. ix, 509 p. : ISBN 0-471-86189-8 LC Card 86-26728 DDC 624/.068 19
HD9715.A2 A515 1987

Measures to overcome obstacles to the observance in the construction industry of ILO standards . Geneva , 1986. v, 89 p. : ISBN 92-2-105710-0 (pbk.) : LC Card 87-167948 DDC 331.25 19
HD9715.A2 M36 1986

CONSTRUCTION INDUSTRY - QUÉBEC (PROVINCE) - ACCIDENTS.
Les Accidents du travail dans la construction au Québec /. [Quebec] [1983] vii, 256 p. : ISBN 2-550-10554-0 LC Card 85-100967
HD9715.C33 Q42 1983

CONSTRUCTION INDUSTRY - QUÉBEC (PROVINCE) - EMPLOYEES - SUPPLY AND DEMAND.
Leclerc, Claudine. La sécurité d'emploi dans l'industrie de la construction au Québec . [Quebec] , c1983. xii, 275 p. : ISBN 2-7637-7028-2 LC Card 84-126505 DDC 331.25/96 19
HD5718.B92 C248 1983
NYPL [JLE 86-3170]

CONSTRUCTION INDUSTRY - QUÉBEC (PROVINCE) - SEASONAL VARIATIONS.
Leclerc, Claudine. La sécurité d'emploi dans l'industrie de la construction au Québec . [Quebec] , c1983. xii, 275 p. : ISBN 2-7637-7028-2 LC Card 84-126505 DDC 331.25/96 19
HD5718.B92 C248 1983
NYPL [JLE 86-3170]

CONSTRUCTION INDUSTRY - RESEARCH - SWEDEN.
Byggsektorn 1990 . Stockholm [1982] 91 p. : LC Card 83-234610
HD9715.S852 B93 1982

CONSTRUCTION INDUSTRY - RUSSIAN S.F.S.R. - NON-CHERNOZEM REGION.
Chanturii͡a, V. K. (Vladimir Kapitonovich) Stroit͡sii͡a Nechernozem'e /. Moskva , 1980. 94 p. ; LC Card 81-135603
HD9715.S73 N63 1980

CONSTRUCTION INDUSTRY - RUSSIAN S.F.S.R. - SIBERIA, WESTERN.
Khaĭtun, A. D. (Alekseĭ Davydovich) Ėkspeditsionno-vakhtovoe stroitel'stvo v Zapadnoĭ Sibiri /. Leningrad , 1982. 175, [1] p. : LC Card 83-165812
HD9715.S73 S565 1982

CONSTRUCTION INDUSTRY - SAFETY MEASURES.
Goldsmith, David, 1946- Safety management in construction and industry /. New York , c1987. viii, 120 p. : ISBN 0-07-023677-1 LC Card 86-27733 DDC 363.1/19624 19
HD7262 .G58 1987

CONSTRUCTION INDUSTRY - SOCIAL ASPECTS - UNITED STATES.
Silver, Marc L., 1950- Under construction . Albany , c1986. xi, 251 p. ; ISBN 0-88706-308-X LC Card 85-30447 DDC 331.7/624/0973 19
HD6956.B92 U67 1986
NYPL [JLE 86-4616]

CONSTRUCTION INDUSTRY - SOVIET UNION - CAPITAL INVESTMENTS.
I͡Armolovich, M. V. (Mikhail Viktorovich) Finansovye rychagi i material'nye stimuly sovershenstvovanii͡a stroitel'nogo proizvodstva /. Moskva , 1982. 196 p. ; LC Card 83-167253
HD9715.S72 I27 1982

CONSTRUCTION INDUSTRY - SOVIET UNION - CAPITAL PRODUCTIVITY.
Muzhit͡skikh, V. V. (Viktor Vasil'evich) Finansirovanie i kreditovanie kapital'nogo stroitel'stva v usloviiakh ėkonomicheskogo ėksperimenta /. Moskva , 1985. 157 p. ; LC Card 86-169842
HD9715.S72 M894 1985

CONSTRUCTION INDUSTRY - SOVIET UNION - EMPLOYEES.
Piskunov, F. F. (Fedor Fedorovich) Zabota o stroitel'nykh kadrakh /. Moskva , 1986. 71 p. : LC Card 86-220202
HD8039.B92 S686 1986

CONSTRUCTION INDUSTRY - SOVIET UNION - FINANCE.
Galkin, I. G. (Il'i͡a Grigor'evich) Sovershenstvovanie planirovanii͡a stroitel'nogo proizvodstva /. Moskva , 1986. 167 p. : LC Card 85-178938
HD9715.S72 G35 1986

I͡Armolovich, M. V. (Mikhail Viktorovich) Finansovye rychagi i material'nye stimuly sovershenstvovanii͡a stroitel'nogo proizvodstva /. Moskva , 1982. 196 p. ; LC Card 83-167253
HD9715.S72 I27 1982

Muzhit͡skikh, V. V. (Viktor Vasil'evich) Finansirovanie i kreditovanie kapital'nogo stroitel'stva v usloviiakh ėkonomicheskogo ėksperimenta /. Moskva , 1985. 157 p. ; LC Card 86-169842
HD9715.S72 M894 1985

CONSTRUCTION INDUSTRY - SOVIET UNION - LABOR PRODUCTIVITY.
Borisov, I͡U. D. (I͡Uriĭ Dmitrievich) Ėkonomicheskie problemy povyshenii͡a proizvoditel'nosti truda v stroitel'stve /. Moskva , 1985. 183 p. ; LC Card 86-208622
HD9715.S72 B67 1985

Serov, V. M. (Viktor Mikhaĭlovich) Proizvoditel'nost' truda v stroitel'stve . Moskva , 1986. 253 p. : LC Card 85-179119
HD9715.S72 S47 1986

Taganskiĭ, B. M. (Boris Mikhaĭlovich) Ėkonomicheskiĭ analiz v stroitel'stve /. Moskva , 1986. 148, [4] p. : LC Card 86-227177
HD9715.S72 T35 1986

Zarubin, Vadim Nikolaevich. Intensifikat͡sii͡a i trudoemkost' stroitel'nogo proizvodstva /. Moskva , 1986. 183, [1] p. ; LC Card 85-178984
HD9715.S72 Z37 1986

CONSTRUCTION INDUSTRY - SOVIET UNION - LABOR PRODUCTIVITY - MATHEMATICAL MODELS.
Ivanov, V. R. (Vladimir Romanovich) Proizvoditel'nost' truda i zarabotnai͡a plata v stroitel'stve sooruzheniĭ svi͡azi /. Moskva , 1985. 159 p. : LC Card 85-224803
HD9715.S72 I9 1985

CONSTRUCTION INDUSTRY - SOVIET UNION - MANAGEMENT.
Osnovy ėkonomiki i upravlenii͡a stroitel'nym proizvodstvom /. Moskva , 1978. 285 p. ; LC Card 81-171493
HD9715.S72 O86 1978

Sidorov, A. I. (Alekseĭ Ivanovich) Kompleksnyĭ analiz proektnogo proizvodstva na primere promyshlennogo proektirovanii͡a /. Moskva , 1985. 197, [3] p. : LC Card 86-129875
HD9715.S72 S57 1985

CONSTRUCTION INDUSTRY - SOVIET UNION, NORTHERN - CAPITAL INVESTMENTS.
Kaplan, L. M. (Lev Moiseevich) Ėkonomicheskie problemy upravlenii͡a stroitel'nym proizvodstvom na Severe /. Leningrad , 1983. 167 p. : LC Card 84-113191
HD9715.S73 N675 1983

CONSTRUCTION INDUSTRY - SOVIET UNION - PLANNING.
Kompleksinis subalansuotas statybos planavimas /. Vilnius , 1983. 115 p. : LC Card 83-187666
HD9715.S72 K66 1983

Sidorov, A. I. (Alekseĭ Ivanovich) Kompleksnyĭ analiz proektnogo proizvodstva na primere promyshlennogo proektirovanii͡a /. Moskva , 1985. 197, [3] p. : LC Card 86-129875
HD9715.S72 S57 1985

CONSTRUCTION INDUSTRY - SPAIN.
El Libro blanco de la promoción-construcción. [Barcelona] , 1985. 141 p. : LC Card 86-188032
HD7351.A3 L53 1985

CONSTRUCTION INDUSTRY - SPAIN - CATALONIA.
El Libro blanco de la promoción-construcción. [Barcelona] , 1985. 141 p. : LC Card 86-188032
HD7351.A3 L53 1985

CONSTRUCTION INDUSTRY - SWEDEN.
Byggnads- och anläggningsindustrin. [Stockholm] [1981] 84 p. : ISBN 91-38-06015-9 LC Card 84-120446
HD9715.S852 B898 1981

Byggsektorn 1990 . Stockholm [1982] 91 p. : LC Card 83-234610
HD9715.S852 B93 1982

CONSTRUCTION INDUSTRY - SWITZERLAND.
Finsinger, Jörg. Der Submissionswettbewerb . Bern , c1986. 104 p. : ISBN 3-258-03617-9 : LC Card 86-224617
HD9715.S92 F56 1986

CONSTRUCTION INDUSTRY - SWITZERLAND - FINANCE.
Schweizer, Max. Investieren und Finanzieren . Zürich , c1984. 176 p. : ISBN 3-85565-209-0 : LC Card 84-244976
HD9715.S92 S38 1984

CONSTRUCTION INDUSTRY - TURKEY - MATHEMATICAL MODELS.
Boratav, Korkut. Housing yearbook /. Ankara, Turkey , 1985. 32, [2] p. ; LC Card 87-403323 DDC 363.5/09561 19
HD7358.25.A3 B67 1985

CONSTRUCTION INDUSTRY - UKRAINE - CAPITAL INVESTMENTS.
I͡Akovlev, I͡U. P. (I͡Uriĭ Prokofʹevich) Ėffektivnoe ispolʹzovanie kapitalʹnykh vlozheniĭ v selʹskom stroitelʹstve /. Kiev , 1985. 104 p. : LC Card 86-214694
HD9715.S73 U383 1985

CONSTRUCTION INDUSTRY - UNITED STATES.
Technology, trade, and the U.S residential construction industry . Washington, D.C. , 1986. x, 91 p. : LC Card 86-600575 DDC 338.4/769083/0973 19
HD9715.U52 T43 1986

CONSTRUCTION INDUSTRY - UNITED STATES - EMPLOYEES - STATISTICS.
Occupational employment in mining, construction, finance, and services. Washington, D.C. [1986] vi, 141 p. ; LC Card 86-603149 DDC 331.12/51/000973021 19
HD9506.U62 O23 1986

CONSTRUCTION INDUSTRY - UNITED STATES - FINANCE.
Construction lending for income-producing properties . Washington, D.C. (1120 Connecticut Ave., N.W. Washington 20036) , c1986. xiv, 163 p. : LC Card 86-209027 DDC 332.1/753 19
HG2040.5.U5 M49 1986

CONSTRUCTION INDUSTRY - UNITED STATES - FORECASTING.
Stotter, James. Intelligent buildings . Stamford, Conn., U. S.A. , c1986. ix, 127 leaves : ISBN 0-89336-414-2 (pbk.) LC Card 87-165953 DDC 338.4/769/0973 19
HD9715.U52 S76 1986

CONSTRUCTION INDUSTRY - UNITED STATES - MANAGEMENT.
Levine, Stuart M. The construction manager . [Washington, D.C.] (1120 20th St., NW, Washington 20036) , c1986. ii, 218 p. : LC Card 87-109137 DDC 624/.068 19
HD9715.A2 L43 1986

CONSTRUCTION INDUSTRY - UNITED STATES - PERSONNEL MANAGEMENT.
Northrup, Herbert Roof, 1918- Doublebreasted operations and pre-hire agreements in construction . Philadelphia, Penn., USA , c1987. viii, 127 p. : ISBN 0-89546-067-X (pbk.) LC Card 87-81475 DDC 331.88/92 19
HD9715.U52 N67 1984 Suppl.

Northrup, Herbert Roof, 1918- Open shop construction revisited /. Philadelphia, Pa., U. S.A. , c1984. xxxv, 674 p. : ISBN 0-89546-047-5 : LC Card 84-48502 DDC 331.88/92 19
HD9715.U52 N67 1984 ***NYPL [TB (Pennsylvania. University. Wharton School of Finance and Commerce. Industrial Research Unit. Industrial Research Unit Study. no. 62)]***

CONSTRUCTION INDUSTRY - UNITED STATES - TECHNOLOGICAL INNOVATIONS.
Stotter, James. Intelligent buildings . Stamford, Conn., U. S.A. , c1986. ix, 127 leaves : ISBN 0-89336-414-2 (pbk.) LC Card 87-165953 DDC 338.4/769/0973 19
HD9715.U52 S76 1986

Technology, trade, and the U.S residential construction industry . Washington, D.C. , 1986. x, 91 p. : LC Card 86-600575 DDC 338.4/769083/0973 19
HD9715.U52 T43 1986

CONSTRUCTION INDUSTRY - WEST (U. S.) - HISTORY.
Atkinson, Ray N. Guy F. Atkinson Company of California . New York , 1985, c1986. 24 p. : LC Card 86-61271 DDC 338.7/624/0973 19
HD9715.U54 G882 1986

Construction Labor Research Council. Wage and benefit settlements in construction, 1986. Washington, D.C. (1101 15th St., N.W., Suite 1040, Washington 20005) , c1986. 10 p. : LC Card 87-139726 DDC 331.2/824/0973021 19
HD4966.B892 U685 1986

Construction lending for income-producing properties : real estate mortgage lending for bankers. Washington, D.C. (1120 Connecticut Ave., N.W. Washington 20036) : American Bankers Association, c1986. xiv, 163 p. : ill. ; 28 cm. Rev. ed. of: Construction lending for income-producing property by Thomas C. Miller, F. Weller Meyer, and John W. Starke. LC Card 86-209027 DDC 332.1/753 19
1. Mortgage loans - United States. 2. Construction industry - United States - Finance. I. Miller, Thomas C. Construction lending for income-producing property. II. American Bankers Association. III. Title: Real estate mortgage lending for bankers.
HG2040.5.U5 M49 1986

Construction management and organisation in perspective / edited by Peter R. Lansley and Peter A. Harlow. London ; New York : E. & F.N. Spon, 1987. p. cm. (Managing construction worldwide . v. 3) Bibliography: p. Includes index. ISBN 0-419-14020-4 LC Card 87-20548 DDC 624/.068 s 624/.068 19
1. Construction industry - Management - Congresses. 2. Construction industry - Management - Case studies - Congresses. I. Lansley, Peter R. II. Harlow, P. A. (Peter Alan). III. Series.
HD9715.A2 M296 vol. 3

The construction manager . Levine, Stuart M. [Washington, D.C.] (1120 20th St., NW, Washington 20036) , c1986. ii, 218 p. : LC Card 87-109137 DDC 624/.068 19
HD9715.A2 L43 1986

CONSTRUCTION, MODULAR. see **MODULAR CONSTRUCTION.**

CONSTRUCTION OF ROADS. see **ROAD CONSTRUCTION.**

Construction productivity improvement /. Adrian, James J. New York , c1987. xiii, 303 p. : ISBN 0-444-01121-8 LC Card 86-24172 DDC 624/.068/3 19
HD9715.A2 A353 1987

Construction profit management . Brunotte, Leonard. Englewood Cliffs, N.J. , c1987. xxvii, 324 p. : ISBN 0-13-168980-0 : LC Card 87-1168 DDC 692/.8 19
HD9715.A2 B78 1987

CONSTRUCTION WORKERS - EUROPEAN ECONOMIC COMMUNITY COUNTRIES - SUPPLY AND DEMAND.
Employment and housing renovation in Europe /. Luxembourg , Washington, DC , 1986. 89 p. : ISBN 92-825-6422-3 : LC Card 87-136222 DDC 331.2/89/083094 19
HD5718.B92 E863 1986

CONSTRUCTION WORKERS - GERMANY - NUREMBERG - HISTORY.
Gömmel, Rainer. Vorindustrielle Bauwirtschaft in der Reichsstadt Nürnberg und ihrem Umland (16.-18. Jh.) /. [Stuttgart] , 1985. xii, 300 p. : ISBN 3-515-04481-7 LC Card 86-122013
HD9715.G33 N874 1985

CONSTRUCTION WORKERS - ITALY - CONGRESSES.
Seminario di aggiornamento per i quadri sindacali della categoria (1985 : Rome, Italy) Evoluzione del processo produttivo nelle construzioni . Milano, Italy , c1986. 142 p. : LC Card 86-210757
HD9715.I82 S46 1985

CONSTRUCTION WORKERS - LEGAL STATUS, LAWS, ETC. - UNITED STATES.
Northrup, Herbert Roof, 1918- Doublebreasted operations and pre-hire agreements in construction . Philadelphia, Penn., USA , c1987. viii, 127 p. : ISBN 0-89546-067-X (pbk.) LC Card 87-81475 DDC 331.88/92 19
HD9715.U52 N67 1984 Suppl.

CONSTRUCTION WORKERS - QUÉBEC (PROVINCE) - SUPPLY AND DEMAND.
Leclerc, Claudine. La sécurité d'emploi dans l'industrie de la construction au Québec . [Quebec] , c1983. xii, 275 p. : ISBN 2-7637-7028-2 LC Card 84-126505 DDC 331.25/96 19
HD5718.B92 C248 1983 ***NYPL [JLE 86-3170]***

CONSTRUCTION WORKERS - SERVICES FOR - SOVIET UNION.
Piskunov, F. F. (Fedor Fedorovich) Zabota o stroitelʹnykh kadrakh /. Moskva , 1986. 71 p. : LC Card 86-220202
HD8039.B92 S686 1986

CONSTRUCTION WORKERS - SUPPLY AND DEMAND.
Employment policy and job creation in and through the construction industry . Geneva , 1986. vi, 110 p. : ISBN 92-2-105709-7 (pbk.) : LC Card 87-167960 DDC 331.12/924 19
HD9715.A2 E42 1986

CONSTRUCTION WORKERS - TRAINING OF - ITALY.
Franciosi, Franco B. Professionalità e formazione nel settore delle costruzioni . Venezia , 1985. 178 p. ; ISBN 88-317-4781-9 : LC Card 86-234138
HD5716.B92 I724 1985

CONSTRUCTION WORKERS - UNITED STATES.
Silver, Marc L., 1950- Under construction . Albany , c1986. xi, 251 p. ; ISBN 0-88706-308-X LC Card 85-30447 DDC 331.7/624/0973 19
HD6956.B92 U67 1986 ***NYPL [JLE 86-4616]***

CONSTRUCTION WORKERS - UNITED STATES - CLASSIFICATION.
Classification guide for commercial building construction. [New York, N.Y.?] , c1986. 72 p. : LC Card 87-119406 DDC 368.4/1 19
HD7116.R3152 U63 1986

CONSTRUCTION WORKERS - UNITED STATES - CODE NUMBERS.
Classification guide for commercial building construction. [New York, N.Y.?] , c1986. 72 p. : LC Card 87-119406 DDC 368.4/1 19
HD7116.R3152 U63 1986

Los Constructores de la ciudad : tradiciones de lucha y de trabajo del Sindicato Central de Constructores y Albañiles de La Paz, 1908-1980. La Paz : Taller de Historia Oral Andina, UMSA : El Sindacato, 1986. 84 p. : ill. ; 23 cm. LC Card 86-234740
1. Sindicato Central de Constructores y Albañiles de La Paz - History. 2. Trade-unions - Construction workers - Bolivia - La Paz - History. 3. Trade-unions - Bricklayers - Bolivia - La Paz - History. I. Universidad Mayor de San Andrés. Taller de Historia Oral Andina.
HD6609.B892 S563 1986

Consuegra Higgins, José. El pensamiento económico colombiano / José Consuegra Higgins. 1a ed. Bogotá, Colombia : Plaza & Janés, 1984. 216 p. ; 20 cm. (Ciencias económicas, políticas y sociales) Bibliography: p. [215]-216. LC Card 84-200191 DDC 330/.09861 19
1. Economics - Colombia - History. 2. Sociology - Colombia - History. I. Title. II. Series.
HB123.C6 C662 1984 ***NYPL [JLC 87-88]***

Consuegra, José. see **Consuegra Higgins, José.**

Consular conference in Denmark, June 76. [Copenhagen] : Danish Ministry of Foreign Affairs, [1976] 47 p. : ill. ; 20 x 21 cm. LC Card 85-189659
1. Denmark - Foreign economic relations - Congresses. 2. Denmark - Foreign relations - Congresses. 3. European Economic Community - Denmark - Congresses. 4. Denmark - Diplomatic and consular service - Congresses. I. Denmark. Udenrigsministeriet.
HF1561 .C66 1976

CONSULECTRA Unternehmungsberatung. Neue Entwicklungen bei Arbeit, Entgelt und Führung /. Freiburg im Breisgau , c1984. 169 p. : ISBN 3-448-01480-X : LC Card 84-249237
HF5549.2.G3 N48 1984

Consulta sobre el GATT . Mexico. Congreso. Cámara de Senadores. México , c1986. v, 540 p. ; LC Card 87-114865 DDC 382/.0972 19
HF1481 .M45 1986

Consultant compendium. Wellesley, MA : Consultant Compendium, c1986. 1 v. (various pagings) : ill. ; 30 cm. Loose-leaf. Includes indexes. LC Card 87-115215 DDC 332.6/2 19
1. Investment advisers - United States - Directories. I. Consultant Compendium, Inc.
HG4907 .C66 1986

Consultant Compendium, Inc. Consultant compendium. Wellesley, MA , c1986. 1 v. (various pagings) : LC Card 87-115215 DDC 332.6/2 19
HG4907 .C66 1986

Consultant report (Food and Agriculture Organization of the United Nations) . (1) Galal, M. F. Pakistan . Rome [i.e. Multan] , 1978. vii, 36 p. ; LC Card 83-931176
HD9086.P32 G35 1978

CONSULTANTS.
Czander, William M. The application of social systems thinking to organizational consulting /. Lanham , c1986. 243 p. ; ISBN 0-8191-5183-1 (alk. paper) : LC Card 85-29508 DDC 658.4/6 19
HD69.C6 C9 1986 ***NYPL [JLE 86-3269]***

Holtz, Herman. The consultant's guide to winning clients /. New York , c1988. ix, 262 p. ; ISBN 0-471-62759-3 : LC Card 87-24945 DDC 658.4/6 19
HD69.C6 H623 1988

Holtz, Herman. Expanding your consulting practice with seminars /. New York , c1987. xvi, 240 p. : ISBN 0-471-85899-4 LC Card 87-14231 DDC 658.4/6 19
HD69.C6 H625 1987

CONSULTANTS, BUSINESS. see **BUSINESS CONSULTANTS.**

CONSULTANTS - DEVELOPING COUNTRIES.
Wells, Jeremy. The export marketing of technical consulting services from developing countries /. Geneva , 1986. vi, 127 p. : LC Card 87-168669 DDC 658.4/6/091724 19
HD9989.D44 W46 1986

The consultant's guide to winning clients /. Holtz, Herman. New York , c1988. ix, 262 p. ; ISBN 0-471-62759-3 : LC Card 87-24945 DDC 658.4/6 19
HD69.C6 H623 1988

CONSULTANTS - HANDBOOKS, MANUALS, ETC.
Lant, Jeffrey L. Money talks . Cambridge, Mass. , c1985. vii, 302 p. : ISBN 0-940374-08-0 (pbk.) LC Card 87-105725 DDC 001 19
HD69.C6 L27 1985

CONSULTANTS - MARKETING.
Holtz, Herman. Advice, a high profit business . Englewood Cliffs, N.J. , c1986. xii, 242 p. : ISBN 0-13-011958-X LC Card 85-24405 DDC 658.4/6/0688 19
HD69.C6 H618 1986 ***NYPL [JLE 86-3858]***

The consultant's problem solving workbook /. Tepper, Ron, 1937- New York , c1987. xiv, 323 p. : ISBN 0-471-84682-1 LC Card 86-24728 DDC 658.4/6 19
HD69.C6 T47 1987

CONSUMER ADVERTISING. see **ADVERTISING.**

Consumer & catering disposable products market in Europe. New York, N.Y. : Frost & Sullivan, c1983. [29], 386 p. ; 29 cm. Spine title: Disposable products market in Europe. "December 1983." "#E636." LC Card 87-142586 DDC 380.1/4568 19
1. Disposable tableware industry - Europe. 2. Market surveys - Europe. I. Frost & Sullivan. II. Title: Consumer and catering disposable products market in Europe. III. Title: Disposable products market in Europe.
HD9971.5.T323 E853 1983

Consumer and catering disposable products market in Europe. Consumer & catering disposable products market in Europe. New York, N.Y. , c1983. [29], 386 p. ; LC Card 87-142586 DDC 380.1/4568 19
HD9971.5.T323 E853 1983

Consumer automobile leasing study /. Stellman, Caroline B. Baltimore, Md. (7 N. Calvert St., Baltimore 21202) , 1986. ii, 59 p. ; LC Card 87-620899 DDC 388.3/2 19
HE5633.M3 S74 1986

Consumer behavior . Peter, J. Paul. Homewood, Ill. , 1987. xvii, 698 p., [16] p. of plates : ISBN 0-256-03177-0 LC Card 86-81801 DDC 658.8/342 19
HF5415.3 .P468 1987

Consumer behavior /. Schiffman, Leon G. Englewood Cliffs, N.J. , c1987. xviii, 724 p. : ISBN 0-13-169020-5 LC Card 86-25224 DDC 658.8/342 19
HF5415.3 .S29 1987

Consumer behavior . Zaltman, Gerald. Malabar, Fla. , 1987, c1983. p. cm. ISBN 0-89874-989-1 LC Card 86-21297 DDC 658.8/342 19
HF5415.3 .Z28 1987

Consumer behavior and marketing action /. Assael, Henry. Boston, Mass. , c1987. xix, 700 p., [8] p. of plates : ISBN 0-534-07530-4 : LC Card 86-21336 DDC 658.8/342 19
HF5415.3 .A83 1987

Consumer behavior and the practice of marketing /. Runyon, Kenneth E. Columbus , c1987. xv, 776 p. : ISBN 0-675-20463-1 LC Card 86-62987 DDC 658.8/342 19
HF5415.3 .R86 1987

CONSUMER COMPLAINTS.
Riemer, Martin. Beschwerdemanagement /. Frankfurt , New York , c1986. 295 p. ; ISBN 3-593-33756-8 LC Card 87-129210 DDC 658.8/12 19
HF5415.3 .R45 1986

CONSUMER COOPERATIVES - BURUNDI.
Coopératives et populations rurales . [Bujumbura] [1986] ix, 64 leaves : LC Card 86-981185
HD3561.A4 C66 1986

CONSUMER COOPERATIVES - CHILE.
Bustamante G., Jaime. Algunos antecedentes estadísticos sobre las organizaciones económicas populares /. Santiago, Chile , 1986. 23 p. ; LC Card 87-101323
HD2346.C53 B87 1986

Razeto M., Luis, 1945- Las organizaciones económicas populares en la nueva coyuntura económica /. Santiago, Chile , 1984. 23 p. ; LC Card 84-227565
HD2346.C53 R39 1984

CONSUMER COOPERATIVES - GERMANY.
Stuchlik, Karl-Heinz. Die Arbeitsverhältnisse in deutschen Konsumgenossenschaften . Berlin , c1983. 533 p. : ISBN 3-428-05355-9 LC Card 83-191612
HD3338 .S88 1983

CONSUMER COOPERATIVES - GERMANY - EMPLOYEES.
Stuchlik, Karl-Heinz. Die Arbeitsverhältnisse in deutschen Konsumgenossenschaften . Berlin , c1983. 533 p. : ISBN 3-428-05355-9 LC Card 83-191612
HD3338 .S88 1983

CONSUMER COOPERATIVES - GERMANY (WEST)
Jösch, Jutta. Konsumgenossenschaften und Food-Cooperatives . Berlin , c1983. 126 p. : ISBN 3-428-05423-7 LC Card 83-231020
HD3338 .J67 1983

CONSUMER COOPERATIVES - GERMANY (WEST) - HISTORY.
Aschhoff, Gunther, 1934- Das deutsche Genossenschaftswesen . Frankfurt am Main , 1985. 167 p. : ISBN 3-7819-0345-1 LC Card 86-145522
HD3038 .A77 1985

CONSUMER COOPERATIVES - HUNGARY.
Működési forma, belső mechanizmus . Budapest , 1985. 208 p. : LC Card 87-408582
HD3332.5.A4 M85 1985

CONSUMER COOPERATIVES - HUNGARY - AUDITING.
Mészáros, Sándor. Felügyelőbizottságok az ÁFÉSZ-ekben /. [Budapest] [1976] 58 p. ; LC Card 86-187734
HD3332.5.A5 M47 1976

CONSUMER COOPERATIVES - HUNGARY - FINANCE.
Marty, János. A jövedelmezőség számításának és elemzésének módszerei az ÁFÉSZ-nél /. Budapest , 1984. 228 p. : ISBN 963-7006-05-2 : LC Card 85-176220
HD3492.5.A4 M37 1984

A Tagsági vagyoni hozzájárulás feltételrendszere . Budapest , 1984. 69 p. ; ISBN 963-7006-29-X : LC Card 85-185839
HD3332.5.A4 T34 1984

CONSUMER COOPERATIVES - HUNGARY - STATISTICS.
Gazdálkodási és jövedelmezőségi adatok, mutatószámok a szövetkezeti bolti kiskereskedelemben /. Budapest , 1984. 113 p. ; ISBN 963-7006-24-9 : LC Card 85-154737
HF5429.6.H8 G39 1984

CONSUMER COOPERATIVES - HUNGARY - SZOLNOK MEGYE - HISTORY.
Urbán, László. A földmüvesszövetkezetek, fogyasztási szövetkezetek négy évtizede Szolnok megyében /. Szolnok , 1985 ([Szolnok] : Készült a Damjanich János Múzeum Rota Gépén) 435 p. ; ISBN 963-01-6642-9 LC Card 87-407748
HD3332.5.A6 S98 1985

CONSUMER COOPERATIVES - QUÉBEC (PROVINCE)
Fortin, Andrée. Le Rézo . Québec, Québec , 1985. 282 p. : ISBN 2-89224-052-2 LC Card 86-225353
HD3290.A3 Q435 1985

CONSUMER COOPERATIVES - SOVIET CENTRAL ASIA.
Istamov, D. I. (Damir Istamovich) Ėkonomicheskie problemy razvitiia promyshlennogo proizvodstva potrebitel´skoĭ kooperatsii . Tashkent , 1982. 126 p. ; LC Card 82-200979
HD3517.A3 C475 1982

CONSUMER COOPERATIVES - SOVIET UNION.
Smirnov, A. A. (Alekseĭ Alekseevich) Potrebitel´skaia kooperatsiia v odinnadtsatoĭ piatiletke /. Moskva , 1981. 88 p. : LC Card 82-106193
HD3355 .S65 1981

Consumer Council of Maryland. Stellman, Caroline B. Consumer automobile leasing study /. Baltimore, Md. (7 N. Calvert St., Baltimore 21202) , 1986. ii, 59 p. ; LC Card 87-620899 DDC 388.3/2 19
HE5633.M3 S74 1986

Consumer credit in the United States. United States. National Commission on Consumer Finance. [Washington] 1972 [i.e. 1973] xxv, 294 p. LC Card 72-600335 DDC 332.7/43
HG3755 .U59 1972 ***NYPL [JLF 74-435]***

CONSUMER CREDIT - KENYA - CONGRESSES.
Women and credit . [Nairobi?] [1985] 17, 2 p. ; LC Card 85-981504 DDC 332.7/088042 19
HG3756.K4 W65 1985

CONSUMER CREDIT - LAW AND LEGISLATION - UNITED STATES.
Walker, Glen. Credit where credit is due . New York , c1979. ix, 198 p. ; ISBN 0-03-042356-2 LC Card 79-4201 DDC 332.7/43
HG3756.U54 W34 ***NYPL [JLD 86-1388]***

CONSUMER CREDIT - PANAMA.
Conte Porras, J. El crédito, la banca y la moneda panameña /. Panamá, Panamá , 1983. 204 p. : ***NYPL [JLE 86-3126]***

CONSUMER CREDIT - UNITED STATES.
Beares, Paul. Consumer lending /. Washington, D.C. (1120 Connecticut Ave., N.W., Washington 20036) , c1987. xi, 335 p. : LC Card 87-410019 DDC 332.1/753/0685 19
HG3755 .B39 1987

James, Christopher. How to get credit and loans . Austin, TX , 1987. viii, 179 p. : ISBN 0-9618114-0-4 (pbk.) : LC Card 87-71591 DDC 332.7/43 19
HG3756.U54 J36 1987

Pricing consumer credit . Washington, D.C. (1120 Connecticut Ave., N.W., Washington 20036) , c1986. 136 p. : LC Card 86-209981

DDC 332.1/753 19
HG1642.U5 P75 1986

United States. National Commission on Consumer Finance. Consumer credit in the United States. [Washington] 1972 [i.e. 1973] xxv, 294 p. LC Card 72-600335 DDC 332.7/43
HG3755 .U59 1972 ***NYPL [JLF 74-435]***

Walker, Glen. Credit where credit is due . New York , c1979. ix, 198 p. ; ISBN 0-03-042356-2 LC Card 79-4201 DDC 332.7/43
HG3756.U54 W34 ***NYPL [JLD 86-1388]***

Consumer economics after Keynes . Hadjimatheou, George. New York , 1987. viii, 280 p. : ISBN 0-312-00478-8 : LC Card 87-9427 DDC 339.4/7 19
HB801 .H245 1987

CONSUMER EDUCATION - GERMANY, WEST.
Warentest und Konsument . Frankfurt/Main , New York , c1984. 268 p. : ISBN 3-593-33295-7 LC Card 84-150919
HF1040.9.G3 W37 1984

Consumer expenditure survey : interview survey, 1982-83. Washington, D.C. : U. S. Dept. of Labor, Bureau of Labor Statistics : For sale by the Supt. of Docs. U. S. G.P.O., [1986] vi, 193 p. : ill. ; 21 x 28 cm. (Bulletin / U. S. Dept. of Labor, Bureau of Labor Statistics . 2246) LC Card 86-602456 DDC 339.4/1/0973 19
1. Consumption (Economics) - United States - Statistics. 2. Income distribution - United States - Statistics. 3. Cost and standard of living - United States - Statistics. I. United States. Bureau of Labor Statistics. II. Series: Bulletin (United States. Bureau of Labor Statistics) , 2246.
HC110.C6 C5647 1986

Consumer Federation of America. Hoffman, Naphtali. The bank book . San Diego , 1986. xiii, 222 p. ; ISBN 0-15-610676-0 (pbk.) : LC Card 85-27271 DDC 332.1/7/0973 19
HG1616.C87 H64 1986
NYPL [JLE 86-3189]

Consumer financial services : delivering financial services : new technologies, new opportunities / Consumer & Technology Division. Boston, MA (200 Portland St., Boston 02114) : Yankee Group, 1986. xvi, 83 p. : ill. ; 28 cm. (Industry research report) LC Card 86-230330 DDC 332.1/028 19
1. Automatic banking equipment industry - United States. 2. Market surveys - United States. I. Yankee Group. Consumer & Technology Division. II. Series.
HD9696.B363 U543 1986

Consumer guide . Miller, Lynn Orr. [Skokie, IL] , c1986. 64 p. ; LC Card 86-219152 DDC 332.63/27 19
HG4530 .M56 1986

Consumer guide. Getting the most from social security . Skokie, IL (3841 W. Oakton St., Skokie 60076) , c1986. 192 p. : LC Card 86-219986 DDC 344.73/023 347.30423 19
HD7125 .G43 1986

Consumer guide investment series .
(no. 3) Getting the most from social security . Skokie, IL (3841 W. Oakton St., Skokie 60076) , c1986. 192 p. : LC Card 86-219986 DDC 344.73/023 347.30423 19
HD7125 .G43 1986

(no. 3) Miller, Lynn Orr. Consumer guide . [Skokie, IL] , c1986. 64 p. ; LC Card 86-219152 DDC 332.63/27 19
HG4530 .M56 1986

Consumer healthcare. Healthcare electronics /. Boston, MA (89 Broad St., Boston 02110) , c1986. iv, 79 p. : LC Card 86-212563 DDC 381/.45681761 19
HD9995.E43 U55 1986

The consumer interest . Forbes, J. D. (James D.), 1932- London , New York , c1987. 341 p. : ISBN 0-7099-1063-0 LC Card 87-12947 DDC 381/.34 19
HF5415.3 .F598 1987

Consumer lending /. Beares, Paul. Washington, D.C. (1120 Connecticut Ave., N.W., Washington 20036) , c1987. xi, 335 p. : LC Card 87-410019 DDC 332.1/753/0685 19
HG3755 .B39 1987

Consumer markets in Southern Africa. London : Euromonitor, 1986. 173 p., [1] p. of plates : map ; 31 cm. ISBN 0-86338-095-6 LC Card 87-160745 DDC 330.968/063 19
1. Africa, Southern - Commerce - Statistics. 2. Africa, Southern - Economic conditions, 1975- - Statistics. 3. Commercial products - Africa, Southern - Statistics. I. Euromonitor Publications Limited.
HF3900 .C66 1986

CONSUMER PANELS - GERMANY (WEST)
Weissman, Arnold. Verbraucherpanel, Informationen als Grundlage für Marketingentscheidungen im Einzelhandel /. München , c1983. xxviii, 194, [4] p. : ISBN 3-88259-242-7 LC Card 83-161472
HF5415.3 .W437 1983

CONSUMER PRICE INDEX. see **COST AND STANDARD OF LIVING.**

Consumer price index numbers of Pakistan, 1980-81 = 100 / Federal Bureau of Statistics, Statistics Division, Government of Pakistan. Karachi : Manager of Publications, [1985] 118 p. ; 21 x 28 cm. "FBS-166/500." Chiefly tables. LC Card 86-930250 DDC 338.5/28/095491 19
1. Consumer price indexes - Pakistan. 2. Prices - Pakistan. I. Pakistan. Federal Bureau of Statistics.
HB235.P25 C65 1985

CONSUMER PRICE INDEXES.
Kirsten, José Tiacci. Custo de vida . São Paulo , 1985. xi, 158 p. : LC Card 86-143942
HB235.B8 K57 1985

Mulquin, Marie Eve. Empalme del índice de precios al consumidor . [San José] , 1981. 15 leaves ; LC Card 81-216387
HB221 .M774 1981

CONSUMER PRICE INDEXES - BRAZIL.
Kirsten, José Tiacci. Custo de vida . São Paulo , 1985. xi, 158 p. : LC Card 86-143942
HB235.B8 K57 1985

CONSUMER PRICE INDEXES - BRAZIL - SÃO PAULO.
Endo, Seiti Kaneko. Pesquisa de orçamentos familiares no município de São Paulo /. São Paulo [Rio de Janeiro] , 1984. 131 p. : LC Card 85-136517
HB235.B8 E53 1984

CONSUMER PRICE INDEXES - CAYMAN ISLANDS.
A Guide to the new consumer price index. [George Town, Grand Caymon, B.W.I.] [1985] 26 leaves ; LC Card 86-221984 DDC 338.5/28/0972921 19
HB235.C29 G85 1985

CONSUMER PRICE INDEXES - COSTA RICA.
Mulquin, Marie Eve. Empalme del índice de precios al consumidor . [San José] , 1981. 15 leaves ; LC Card 81-216387
HB221 .M774 1981

CONSUMER PRICE INDEXES - GERMANY (WEST) - STATISTICS.
Döhrn, Roland. Privater Verbrauch und Einzelhandel in der Bundesrepublik Deutschland . Essen , 1981. 280 p. ; LC Card 87-408859 DDC 338.5/28/0943 19
HB235.G3 D57 1981

CONSUMER PRICE INDEXES - HAWAII.
The Honolulu consumer price index, 1940-1986. [Honolulu] [1986] 19 p. ; LC Card 86-622085 DDC 319.69 s 338.5/28/09969 19
HA329.1 .A25 no. 187 HB235.U6

CONSUMER PRICE INDEXES - HUNGARY.
Kiskereskedelmi áralakulás, 1981-1985 /. Budapest , 1986. 81 p. ; LC Card 86-202239
HB235.H8 K56 1986

CONSUMER PRICE INDEXES - MARTINIQUE.
Guglielmetti, Francis. L'indice des prix de la Martinique, base 100 en 1979 . [Fort de France?] [1985] 130, xxiii p. : ISBN 2-11-062943-6 : LC Card 86-176702
HB235.M37 G83 1985

CONSUMER PRICE INDEXES - PAKISTAN.
Consumer price index numbers of Pakistan, 1980-81 =. Karachi [1985] 118 p. ; LC Card 86-930250 DDC 338.5/28/095491 19
HB235.P25 C65 1985

CONSUMER PRICE INDEXES - SWEDEN.
Isacsson, Göthe. Index för prisregleringar. Stockholm [1985?] 80 p. : ISBN 91-618-0082-1 LC Card 85-206079
HB235.S8 I83 1985

CONSUMER PRICE INDEXES - UNITED STATES.
DeMilner, Lawrence E. Indexing with the consumer price index . [Washington, D.C.] , 1981. xx, 123 p. : LC Card 81-602368 DDC 338.5/28/0973 19
HG229.5 .D45 ***NYPL [JLF 85-3118]***

CONSUMER PROTECTION.
Forbes, J. D. (James D.), 1932- The consumer interest . London , New York , c1987. 341 p. : ISBN 0-7099-1063-0 LC Card 87-12947 DDC 381/.34 19
HF5415.3 .F598 1987

Neirynck, Jacques. Le Consommateur averti /. Lausanne , 1979. 173 p. ; ISBN 2-8289-0029-X : LC Card 79-394845 DDC 381/.34
HC79.C63 N43 ***NYPL [JLD 86-2606]***

CONSUMER PROTECTION - AUSTRIA.
Bauer, Fritz. Konsumenteninformation und ihre Nutzer /. Linz , 1986. ii, 113 p. : ISBN 3-85320-388-4 LC Card 87-134585 DDC 381/.3/09436 19
HC270.C6 B38 1986

CONSUMER PROTECTION - BRAZIL.
Neves, Tancredo, 1910- Tancredo Neves na defesa do consumidor /. Brasília , 1985. 48 p. : LC Card 86-129214
HC190.C63 N48 1985

CONSUMER PROTECTION - CONGRESSES.
Empirical approaches to consumer protection economics . Washington, D.C. [1986] ii, 484 p. : ***NYPL [JLE 86-3552]***

International trade and the consumer . Paris [Washington, D.C. , 1986. 296 p. ; ISBN 92-64-12813-1 (pbk.) : LC Card 86-216097 DDC 382/.3 19
HF1410.5 .I585 1986 ***NYPL [JLE 87-1541]***

Consumer protection economics. Empirical approaches to consumer protection economics . Washington, D.C. [1986] ii, 484 p. : LC Card 86-602207 DDC 381/.34/0973 19
HC110.C63 E46 1986

Consumer protection economics. Empirical approaches to consumer protection economics . Washington, D.C. [1986] ii, 484 p. :
NYPL [JLE 86-3552]

CONSUMER PROTECTION - EUROPEAN ECONOMIC COMMUNITY COUNTRIES.
Producer consumer dialogue . Brussels [1984] ii, 55 p. ; LC Card 85-178866 DDC 381/.34/094 19
HC240.9.C63 P77 1984
NYPL [JLD 86-2369]

Verbraucherpolitik in der sozialen Marktwirtschaft . Bonn , c1984. 146 p. ; ISBN 3-922335-04-7 LC Card 85-228004
HC240.9.C63 V47 1984

CONSUMER PROTECTION - GERMANY, WEST.
Ambros, Werner. Verbraucherinteressen und Agrarpolitik /. Krefeld , 1986. x, 260 p. : ISBN 3-88358-068-6 LC Card 87-122729 DDC 338.1/843 19
HD1957 .A63 1986

Berücksichtigung von Verbraucherinteressen bei staatlichen Anbietern /. Frankfurt , New York , c1984. x, 241 p. : ISBN 3-593-33291-4 LC Card 84-147664
HC290.5.C63 B47 1984

Schatz, Heribert. Verbraucherinteressen im politischen Entscheidungsprozess /. Frankfurt/Main , New York , c1984. 275 p. ; ISBN 3-593-33293-0 LC Card 84-212024
HC290.5.C63 S33 1984

Warentest und Konsument . Frankfurt/Main , New York , c1984. 268 p. : ISBN 3-593-33295-7 LC Card 84-150919
HF1040.9.G3 W37 1984

CONSUMER PROTECTION - GERMANY (WEST) - CITIZEN PARTICIPATION.
Bürgerbeteiligung in der Verbraucherinformationspolitik . Frankfurt , New York , c1986. 241 p. : ISBN 3-593-33681-2 LC Card 86-230016
HC290.5.C63 B87 1986

CONSUMER PROTECTION - GERMANY, WEST - NORTH RHINE-WESTPHALIA.
Schatz, Heribert. Verbraucherinteressen im politischen Entscheidungsprozess /.

Frankfurt/Main , New York , c1984. 275 p. ; ISBN 3-593-33293-0 LC Card 84-212024
HC290.5.C63 S33 1984

CONSUMER PROTECTION - LAW AND LEGISLATION - GERMANY, WEST.
Schatz, Heribert. Verbraucherinteressen im politischen Entscheidungsprozess /. Frankfurt/Main , New York , c1984. 275 p. ; ISBN 3-593-33293-0 LC Card 84-212024
HC290.5.C63 S33 1984

CONSUMER PROTECTION - SWEDEN.
Wolvén, Lars-Erik. Konsumenter, konsumentpolitik, rationalitet och välfärd . Umeå , 1981. 83 leaves ; LC Card 82-105540 DDC 658.8/342/09485 19
HC380.C63 W64 NYPL [JLM 74-106 no.61]

CONSUMER PROTECTION - UNITED STATES.
Gordon, Leland James, 1897- Economics for consumers /. New York , c1977. ix, 693 p. : ISBN 0-442-22242-4 LC Card 76-50515 DDC 381/.3/0973 19
HB801 .G6 1977 NYPL [JLE 86-1506]

Lee, Stewart Munro. Personal finance for consumers /. Columbus, Ohio , c1987. xiii, 518 p. : ISBN 0-942280-33-4 : LC Card 86-30503 DDC 381/.3/0973 19
HB301 .L256 1987

United States. Congress. House. Committee on Energy and Commerce. Subcommittee on Oversight and Investigations. Dangerous medicine . Washington , 1986. v, 31 p. ; LC Card 86-602099 DDC 363.1/942/0973 19
HD9665.9.U6 U55 1986

United States. National Commission on Consumer Finance. Consumer credit in the United States. [Washington] 1972 [i.e. 1973] xxv, 294 p. LC Card 72-600335 DDC 332.7/43
HG3755 .U59 1972 NYPL [JLF 74-435]

CONSUMER PROTECTION - UNITED STATES - CONGRESSES.
Empirical approaches to consumer protection economics . Washington, D.C. [1986] ii, 484 p. : LC Card 86-602207 DDC 381/.34/0973 19
HC110.C63 E46 1986

Consumer reports. I'll buy that! . New York , c1986. 240 p. : ISBN 0-89043-046-2 LC Card 86-1281 DDC 303.4/83 19
HF5415.153 .I45 1986 NYPL [JLG 87-125]

Consumer Review Systems. Berdie, Douglas R. The Yellow Pages report . St. Paul, Minn. (905 Raymond Ave., St. Paul 55114) , c1986. 109 p. ; LC Card 86-209709 DDC 659.13/2 19
HF6146.T4 B45 1986

CONSUMER SATISFACTION.
Lele, Milind M. The customer is key . New York , c1987. xii, 260 p. : ISBN 0-471-82859-9 LC Card 87-21549 DDC 658.8/12 19
HF5415.3 .L45 1987

Riemer, Martin. Beschwerdemanagement /. Frankfurt , New York , c1986. 295 p. ; ISBN 3-593-33756-8 LC Card 87-129210 DDC 658.8/12 19
HF5415.3 .R45 1986

CONSUMER SATISFACTION - GERMANY (WEST)
Bruhn, Manfred. Konsumentenzufriedenheit und Beschwerden . Frankfurt am Main , Bern , 1982. xiv, 211 p. ; ISBN 3-8204-5712-7 LC Card 82-131889
HF5415.3 .B78 1982

CONSUMER SATISFACTION - UNITED STATES.
Market leaders . Boston, MA (200 Portland St., Boston 02114) , c1987. v, 123 p. : LC Card 87-402841 DDC 381/.4500416/0973 19
HD9696.C63 U52476 1987

CONSUMER SATISFACTION - UNITED STATES - STATISTICS.
Auto outlook IV /. [New York] , c1986. 60 leaves ; LC Card 86-231268 DDC 381/.456292/0973 19
HD9710.U52 A76 1986

Consumer socialization . Moschis, George P., 1944- Lexington, Mass. , 1987. xiii, 353 p. ; ISBN 0-669-11244-5 (alk. paper) LC Card 85-45165 DDC 658.8/342 19
HF5415.3 .M66 1987 NYPL [JLE 87-1666]

Consumer sovereignty and human interests /. Penz, G. Peter. Cambridge [Cambridgeshire] , New York , 1986. xiv, 242 p. ; ISBN 0-521-26571-1 LC Card 85-22407 DDC 330.15/5 19
HB846 .P46 1986 NYPL [JLE 86-3311]

CONSUMER STATISFACTION - UNITED STATES.
Hessick, Michael H. Achieving quality in financial service organizations . New York , c1988. p. cm. ISBN 0-89930-231-9 (lib. bdg. : alk. paper) LC Card 87-24937 DDC 332.1/2/0688 19
HG181 .H44 1988

CONSUMERS.
Assael, Henry. Consumer behavior and marketing action /. Boston, Mass. , c1987. xix, 700 p., [8] p. of plates : ISBN 0-534-07530-4 : LC Card 86-21336 DDC 658.8/342 19
HF5415.3 .A83 1987

Balfet, Michel. Les 50 mots clefs de la consommation /. Toulouse , c1985. 310 p. : ISBN 2-7089-1969-5 : LC Card 86-140639 DDC 339.4/7 19
HB801 .B276 1985

Berndt, Hermann, 1956- Konsumentscheidung und Informationsüberlastung . München , c1983. 368 p. : ISBN 3-89003-002-5 LC Card 84-192993
HF5821 .B42 1983

Courchaure, Stéphane. Les riches . [Paris] , c1985. 261 p. ; ISBN 2-7158-0537-3 : LC Card 86-111316 DDC 305.5/234 19
HC79.C6 C68 1985 NYPL [JLD 86-4451]

Earl, Peter E. Lifestyle economics . Brighton, Sussex , 1986. xiii, 314 p. : ISBN 0-7450-0083-5
NYPL [JLD 86-3424]

Enke, Harald. Der Konsumeffekt der Investitionen . Tübingen , 1986. xii, 114 p. ; ISBN 3-88573-026-X LC Card 87-407594 DDC 339.4/3 19
HG4521 .E63 1986

Forbes, J. D. (James D.), 1932- The consumer interest . London , New York , c1987. 341 p. : ISBN 0-7099-1063-0 LC Card 87-12947 DDC 381/.34 19
HF5415.3 .F598 1987

Fritz, Wolfgang, Dipl.-Kfm. Warentest und Konsumgüter-Marketing . Wiesbaden , c1984. 596 p. : ISBN 3-409-13600-2 LC Card 84-207784
HF5415.2 .F75 1984

Katz, Reinhard. Informationsquellen der Konsumenten . Wiesbaden , c1983. xxix, 297 p. : ISBN 3-409-13602-9 LC Card 84-118615
HF5415.3 .K35 1983

Mähling, Friedrich W. (Friedrich Wilhelm), 1952- Werbung, Wettbewerb und Verbraucherpolitik /. München , c1983. xii, 477 p. : ISBN 3-88259-258-3 LC Card 84-144205
HF5822 .M34 1983

Moschis, George P., 1944- Consumer socialization . Lexington, Mass. , 1987. xiii, 353 p. ; ISBN 0-669-11244-5 (alk. paper) LC Card 85-45165 DDC 658.8/342 19
HF5415.3 .M66 1987 NYPL [JLE 87-1666]

Mullen, Brian. The psychology of consumer behavior /. Hillsdale, N.J. , 1988. p. cm. ISBN 0-89859-857-5 LC Card 87-15601 DDC 658.8/342 19
HF5415.3 .M85 1988

Neirynck, Jacques. Le Consommateur averti /. Lausanne , 1979. 173 p. ; ISBN 2-8289-0029-X : LC Card 79-394845 DDC 381/.34
HC79.C63 N43 NYPL [JLD 86-2606]

Peter, J. Paul. Consumer behavior . Homewood, Ill. , 1987. xvii, 698 p., [16] p. of plates : ISBN 0-256-03177-0 LC Card 86-81801 DDC 658.8/342 19
HF5415.3 .P468 1987

Philosophical and radical thought in marketing /. Lexington, Mass. , c1987. xxi, 392 p. : ISBN 0-669-14301-4 (alk. paper) LC Card 86-45791 DDC 658.8 19
HF5415 .P485 1987

Ringbeck, Jürgen. Qualitäts- und Werbestrategien bei Qualitätsunsicherheit der Konsumenten /. Wiesbaden , c1986. 256 p. ; ISBN 3-409-13612-6 LC Card 87-111545 DDC 658.8/02 19
HF5415.135 .R56 1986

Runyon, Kenneth E. Consumer behavior and the practice of marketing /. Columbus , c1987. xv, 776 p. : ISBN 0-675-20463-1 LC Card 86-62987 DDC 658.8/342 19
HF5415.3 .R86 1987

Schiffman, Leon G. Consumer behavior /. Englewood Cliffs, N.J. , c1987. xviii, 724 p. : ISBN 0-13-169020-5 LC Card 86-25224 DDC 658.8/342 19
HF5415.3 .S29 1987

Zaltman, Gerald. Consumer behavior . Malabar, Fla. , 1987, c1983. p. cm. ISBN 0-89874-989-1 LC Card 86-21297 DDC 658.8/342 19
HF5415.3 .Z28 1987

Consumers and life insurance /. Organisation for Economic Co-operation and Development. Committee on Consumer Policy. Paris , Washington, D.C. , 1987. 79 p. ; ISBN 92-64-12920-0 (pbk.) : LC Card 87-163859 DDC 368.3/2 19
HG8771 .O73 1987

Consumers Association of Penang. Selling dreams . Penang, Malaysia , c1986. 149 p. : ISBN 967-99502-0-4 (pbk.) LC Card 87-940287 DDC 659.1 19
HF5823 .S46 1986

CONSUMERS - ATTITUDES.
Bleicker, Ulrike. Produktbeurteilung der Konsumenten . Würzburg , c1983. 245 p. : ISBN 3-7908-0292-1 LC Card 83-191583
HF5415.3 .B52 1983

Katzev, Richard D. Promoting energy conservation . Boulder , 1987. xvi, 218 p. : ISBN 0-8133-7337-9 (pbk.) : LC Card 86-32587 DDC 333.79/16 19
HD9502.A2 K38 1987

Organisation for Economic Co-operation and Development. Committee on Consumer Policy. Consumers and life insurance /. Paris , Washington, D.C. , 1987. 79 p. ; ISBN 92-64-12920-0 (pbk.) : LC Card 87-163859 DDC 368.3/2 19
HG8771 .O73 1987

CONSUMERS - AUSTRIA.
Bauer, Fritz. Konsumenteninformation und ihre Nutzer /. Linz , 1986. ii, 113 p. : ISBN 3-85320-388-4 LC Card 87-134585 DDC 381/.3/09436 19
HC270.C6 B38 1986

CONSUMERS - BRAZIL.
Neustadt, Peter. Wachstum und Strukturwandlungen Brasiliens in ihrer Bedeutung für die strategische Marketingplanung von Konsumgüterunternehmungen /. Diessenhofen , cop. 1979. ix, 463 p. : ISBN 3-7253-0092-5 : LC Card 80-469750
HF5415.12.B7 N48 1979
NYPL [JLD 80-3357]

CONSUMERS - CASE STUDIES.
Tongren, Hale N., 1921- Cases in consumer behavior /. Englewood Cliffs, N.J. , c1987. xiii, 224 p. : ISBN 0-13-115346-3 (pbk.) LC Card 86-25547 DDC 658.8/342 19
HF5415.3 .T64 1987

CONSUMERS - COLOMBIA - CALI.
Salazar T., Boris. Las formas de consumo en Colombia . [Cali, Colombia] [1982] 118, [45] p. ; LC Card 85-192219 DDC 658.8/343/0986152 19
HC200.C6 S25 1982 NYPL [JLD 86-1935]

CONSUMERS - CONGRESSES.
The Role of affect in consumer behavior . Lexington, Mass. , c1986. ix, 196 p. : ISBN 0-669-12874-0 (alk. paper) LC Card 85-46042 DDC 658.8/342 19
HF5415.3 .R65 1986 NYPL [JLE 86-3376]

CONSUMERS COOPERATIVES - CHILE.
Hardy, Clarisa. Hambre + dignidad=ollas comunes /. [Santiago, Chile] , 1986. 282 p., [16] p. of plates : *NYPL [JLD 87-334]*

CONSUMERS - ECONOMETRIC MODELS.
Gerhardt, Gisela, 1955- Konsumverhalten und wirtschaftliche Entwicklung . München , c1984. 224 p. : ISBN 3-88259-278-8 LC Card 84-220049
HC79.C6 G47 1984

CONSUMERS - EUROPE, WEST.
Katona, George, 1901- [Aspirations and affluence. Dutch.] Het psychologisch klimaat van de economie in de Verenigde Staten en

West-Europa /. Utrecht , 1974. 247 p. ; ISBN 90-274-5826-X *NYPL [JLD 86-295]*

CONSUMERS - EUROPEAN ECONOMIC COMMUNITY COUNTRIES.
Verbraucherpolitik in der sozialen Marktwirtschaft . Bonn , c1984. 146 p. ; ISBN 3-922335-04-7 LC Card 85-228004
HC240.9.C63 V47 1984

CONSUMERS - GERMANY, WEST.
Berndt, Hermann, 1956- Konsumentscheidung und Informationsüberlastung . München , c1983. 368 p. : ISBN 3-89003-002-5 LC Card 84-192993
HF5821 .B42 1983

Berücksichtigung von Verbraucherinteressen bei staatlichen Anbietern /. Frankfurt , New York , c1984. x, 241 p. : ISBN 3-593-33291-4 LC Card 84-147664
HC290.5.C63 B47 1984

Bopp-Schmehl, Annemarie, 1946- Technische Normung und Verbraucherinteressen im gesellschaftlichen Wandel /. Frankfurt am Main , c1984. iii, 269 p. ; ISBN 3-88129-834-7 : LC Card 85-119483
HC290.5.C6 B66 1984

Bruhn, Manfred. Konsumentenzufriedenheit und Beschwerden . Frankfurt am Main , Bern , 1982. xiv, 211 p. ; ISBN 3-8204-5712-7 LC Card 82-131889
HF5415.3 .B78 1982

Meier, Bernd, 1952- Verbraucherpolitik in der Bundesrepublik Deutschland . Frankfurt am Main , New York , c1984. iii, 256 p. : ISBN 3-8204-8404-3 (pbk.) LC Card 87-672663
HC290.5.C6 M36x 1984

Rösch, Willi. Das tägliche Duell zwischen Handel und Verbraucher . [München-Gräfelfing] , c1975. 110 p. : LC Card 84-121903
HF5429.6.G42 R67 1975

Schöll, Wolfgang. Konsumentenverhalten in der Bundesrepublik Deutschland 1958-1982 . Thun , c1985. 226, 70, [9] p. : ISBN 3-87144-900-8 (Deut. Bibl.) : LC Card 85-232693
HC290.5.C6 S35 1985

Windhorst, Karl-Götz. Wertewandel und Konsumentenverhalten . Münster , c1985. xxi, 299 p. : ISBN 3-7923-0520-8 LC Card 85-171929 DDC 338.5/21/0943 19
HB201 .W663 1985 *NYPL [JLE 87-369]*

CONSUMERS - GERMANY (WEST) - ATTITUDES.
Warentest und Konsument . Frankfurt/Main , New York , c1984. 268 p. : ISBN 3-593-33295-7 LC Card 84-150919
HF1040.9.G3 W37 1984

CONSUMERS - GERMANY, WEST - MATHEMATICAL MODELS.
Horn, Christel-Margret. Feldtheorie und Konsumverhalten /. Freiburg im Breisgau , c1983. 121 p. : ISBN 3-448-01293-9 LC Card 84-136042
HF5415.3 .H65 1983

CONSUMERS - GERMANY (WEST) - NORTH RHINE-WESTPHALIA.
Döhne, Ulrich. Analyse der Ansiedlung von Einkaufszentren und Verbrauchermärkten in Nordrhein-Westfalen /. Dortmund , Essen , 1977. 39 p. : LC Card 86-181973
HF5429.6.G42 D64 1977

CONSUMERS' GOODS. see **MANUFACTURES.**

A consumer's guide to financial planning . Dowd, Merle E. New York , 1987. 296 p. : ISBN 0-531-15517-X LC Card 86-32491 DDC 332.024 19
HG179 .D68 1987

Consumers guide to Social Security benefits . Berko, Robert L. South Orange, N.J. , 1986. p. cm. ISBN 0-934873-04-6 (pbk.) : LC Card 86-23933 DDC 344.73/023 347.30423 19
HD7125 .B47 1986

The Consumers' League of New York : behind the scenes of women's work / edited by David J. Rothman and Sheila M. Rothman. New York : Garland, 1987. 47, 47, 55 p. : ill. ; 22 cm. (Women & children first) Reprint (1st work). Originally published: Behind the scenes in a restaurant. [New York] : Consumers' League of New York City, 1916. Reprint (2nd work). Originally published: Behind the scenes in a hotel. New York City : Consumers' League of New York, 1922. Reprint (3rd work). Originally published: Behind the scenes in canneries. New York City : Consumers' League of New York, 1930. Includes bibliographical references. ISBN 0-8240-7684-2 (alk. paper) : LC Card 87-19804 DDC 331.4/2/09747 19
1. Women - Employment - New York (State). I. Rothman, David J. II. Rothman, Sheila M. III. Consumers' League of New York City. IV. Behind the scenes in a restaurant. 1987. V. Behind the scenes in a hotel. 1987. VI. Behind the scenes in canneries. 1987. VII. Series.
HD6096.N6 C66 1987

Consumers' League of New York City. The Consumers' League of New York . New York , 1987. 47, 47, 55 p. : ISBN 0-8240-7684-2 (alk. paper) : LC Card 87-19804 DDC 331.4/2/09747 19
HD6096.N6 C66 1987

CONSUMERS - MATHEMATICAL MODELS.
Balderjahn, Ingo. Das umweltbewusste Konsumentenverhalten . Berlin , c1986. ix, 277 p. ; ISBN 3-428-06107-1 LC Card 87-113640 DDC 658.8/34/0724 19
HF5415.3 .B316 1986

Hertrich, Roland, 1954- Die Reihenfolge der Informationssuche von Konsumenten . Frankfurt am Main , New York , c1985. iv, 272 p. ; ISBN 3-8204-8594-5 LC Card 85-230707
HB801 .H43 1985

Horn, Christel-Margret. Feldtheorie und Konsumverhalten /. Freiburg im Breisgau , c1983. 121 p. : ISBN 3-448-01293-9 LC Card 84-136042
HF5415.3 .H65 1983

Kucher, Eckhard. Scannerdaten und Preissensitivität bei Konsumgütern /. Wiesbaden , c1985. 282 p. : ISBN 3-409-13608-8 LC Card 86-128961
HB801 .K789 1985

Riepe, Claudia. Produkteigenschaften und das Nachfrageverhalten von Konsumenten . Thun , c1984. 341 p. : ISBN 3-87144-841-9 LC Card 85-113523
HB801 .R45 1984

CONSUMERS POWER COMPANY.
Michigan. Legislature. House of Representatives. Special House Committee to Study Consumers Power Company. Report of the Special House Committee to Study Consumers Power Company . Lansing, Mich. (The Capitol, Lansing 48909) [1985] iv leaves, 57 p. ; LC Card 86-622638 DDC 338.7/6136362/09774 19
HD9685.U7 C785 1985

CONSUMERS' PREFERENCE - CONGRESSES.
Wert- und Präferenzprobleme in den Sozialwissenschaften /. Berlin , c1981. 268 p. : ISBN 3-428-05013-4 LC Card 86-230716
HF5415.3 .W47 1981

CONSUMERS' PREFERENCES.
Bauer, Hans H. Die Entscheidung des Handels über die Aufnahme neuer Produkte . Berlin , c1980. xxiii, 479 p. ; ISBN 3-428-04702-8 LC Card 87-408771 DDC 658.8 s 658.8/343 19
HF5415.A2 S37 Bd. 10 HF5415.153

Bleicker, Ulrike. Produktbeurteilung der Konsumenten . Würzburg , c1983. 245 p. : ISBN 3-7908-0292-1 LC Card 83-191583
HF5415.3 .B52 1983

Kiffe, Ulrich. Die Klassifizierung in der Bundesrepublik Deutschland angebotener Personenkraftwagen mit multivariaten Analysemethoden /. Münster , 1984. xx, 24, 340 p. : ISBN 3-88660-148-8 LC Card 84-208133
HD9710.G42 K48 1984

Knorr, Peter. Messwerte der Informationsnachfrage in komplexen Beurteilungsprozessen /. Kiel , 1986. xvi, 241 p. : ISBN 3-922553-77-X LC Card 86-149044
HB133 .K59 1986

Penz, G. Peter. Consumer sovereignty and human interests /. Cambridge [Cambridgeshire] , New York , 1986. xiv, 242 p. ; ISBN 0-521-26571-1 LC Card 85-22407 DDC 330.15/5 19
HB846 .P46 1986 *NYPL [JLE 86-3311]*

Wong, Stanley. The foundations of Paul Samuelson's revealed preference theory . London , Boston , 1978. x, 148 p. : ISBN 0-7100-8643-1 : LC Card 78-40600 DDC 339.4/7
HB801 .W594 *NYPL [JLD 87-1092]*

CONSUMERS' PREFERENCES - COLOMBIA - CALI.
Salazar T., Boris. Las formas de consumo en Colombia . [Cali, Colombia] [1982] 118, [45] p. ; LC Card 85-192219 DDC 658.8/343/0986152 19
HC200.C6 S25 1982 *NYPL [JLD 86-1935]*

CONSUMERS' PREFERENCES - ECONOMETRIC MODELS.
Langkamp, Peter. Die Erfassung von Carryover-Effekten im Marketing . Thun , c1984. 335 p. : ISBN 3-87144-844-3 : LC Card 85-113501
HF5415.3 .L36 1984

CONSUMERS' PREFERENCES - HISTORY.
Bayley, Stephen. Sex, drink, and fast cars . London , Boston , 1986. 112 p. ; ISBN 0-571-14526-4 (pbk.) : LC Card 87-672358
HD9710.U52 B34 1986

CONSUMERS' PREFERENCES - MATHEMATICAL MODELS - CONGRESSES.
Innovation diffusion models of new product acceptance /. Cambridge, Mass. , 1986. xvi, 318 p. : ISBN 0-88730-076-6 LC Card 85-23300 DDC 658.8/343 19
HF5415.153 .I55 1986 *NYPL [JLE 86-3235]*

CONSUMERS' PREFERENCES - UNITED STATES.
Attitudes toward vended coffee /. [Chicago? , 1983] 1 v. (various pagings) : LC Card 86-235525 DDC 381/.4566393 19
HD9199.U48 A88 1983

Bruskin, R. H. A market strategy study of the whole bean coffee market . [New Brunswick, N.J.] [1985] 1 v. (various pagings) : LC Card 87-100003 DDC 381/.41373/0971 19
HD9199.U48 B84 1985

The Compact disc market--phase II . New York, N.Y. (444 Madison Ave., New York 10022) , c1986. viii, 57, [13] p. : LC Card 86-227224 DDC 381/.4562138933 19
HD9697.P563 U526 1986

Iced coffee taste test . Van Nuys, CA (14416 Victory Blvd. Van Nuys 91401) [1985] 132 p., 6, 6 leaves : LC Card 87-100181 DDC 381/.4566393/0973 19
HD9199.U48 I25 1985

McAlpine, Pamela J. The air freight industry . Menlo Park, CA (333 Ravenswood Ave., Menlo Park 94025) , c1986. 12 leaves ; LC Card 87-402973 DDC 387.7/44/0973 19
HE9788.5.U5 M37 1986

Report on the coffee service industry /. Columbus, Ohio [1984] 1 v. (various foliations) : LC Card 87-100404 DDC 381/.4566393 19
HD9199.U48 R47 1984

Settle, Robert B. Why they buy . New York , c1986. xvi, 351 p. ; ISBN 0-471-84457-8 : LC Card 86-13303 DDC 658.8/343/0973 19
HC110.C6 S48 1986 *NYPL [JLE 86-4432]*

Understanding first-time recreation vehicle buyers . Reston, VA (P.O. Box 2999, Prepared for Recreation Vehicle Industry Association, c1986. xxvi, 80 p. ; LC Card 87-108982 DDC 381/45629226/0973 19
HD9710.37.U62 U53 1986

CONSUMERS' PREFERENCES - UNITED STATES - ECONOMETRIC MODELS.
Marquis, M. Susan. Choice under uncertainty and the demand for health insurance /. Santa Monica, CA (P.O. Box 2138, Santa Monica 90406-2138) [1986] ix, 50 p. ; LC Card 87-118503 DDC 368.3/8/00973 19
HG9396 .M268 1986

CONSUMERS' PREFERENCES - UNITED STATES - STATISTICS.
Butter and margarine attitude & usage . Rosemont, Ill. (6300 N. River Rd., Rosemont 60018) , c1986. 234 p. : LC Card 87-404035

DDC 338.1/772/0973 19
HD9278.U4 B87 1986

Fresh trends, 1987 . [Lincolnshire, Ill.] (400 Knightsbridge Pkwy., Lincolnshire 60069) , c1987. 4 v. ; LC Card 87-162047 DDC 381/.415/0973 19
HD9244 .F73 1987

1986 buyers of new cars . New York, N.Y. (444 Madison Ave., New York 10022) , c1986. 2 v. : LC Card 86-229142 DDC 381/.456292/0973021 19
HD9710.U52 A17 1986

CONSUMERS' RESEARCH.

Feider, Josef. Konsumentenreaktion auf Preise /. Göttingen , c1985. xii, 303 p. : ISBN 3-525-12667-0 LC Card 85-203330
HF5415.3 .F39 1985

Hildebrandt, Lutz. Konfirmatorische Analysen von Modellen des Konsumentenverhaltens /. Berlin , c1983. xii, 307 p. : ISBN 3-428-05381-8 LC Card 83-190106
HF5415.3 .H55 1983

CONSUMERS - RESEARCH - ADDRESSES, ESSAYS, LECTURES.

Perspectives on methodology in consumer research /. New York , c1986. xi, 301 p. : ISBN 0-387-96238-7 : LC Card 85-26047 DDC 658.8/34 19
HF5415.3 .P464 1986 NYPL [JLE 86-4371]

CONSUMERS' SURPLUS.

Johansson, Per-Olov, 1949- The economic theory and measurement of environmental benefits /. Cambridge [Cambridgeshire] , New York , 1987. x, 223 p. : ISBN 0-521-32877-2 LC Card 86-33364 DDC 339.4 19
HB825 .J64 1987

CONSUMERS' SURPLUS - ECONOMETRIC MODELS.

Johansson, Per-Olov, 1949- The economic theory and measurement of environmental benefits /. Cambridge [Cambridgeshire] , New York , 1987. x, 223 p. : ISBN 0-521-32877-2 LC Card 86-33364 DDC 339.4 19
HB825 .J64 1987

CONSUMERS - SWEDEN.

Konsumtion i förändring . Vällingby [1985] 87 p. : LC Card 86-224791
HC380.C6 K675 1985

CONSUMERS - SWEDEN - CASE STUDIES.

Wolvén, Lars-Erik. Konsumenter, konsumentpolitik, rationalitet och välfärd . Umeå , 1981. 83 leaves ; LC Card 82-105540 DDC 658.8/342/09485 19
HC380.C63 W64 NYPL [JLM 74-106 no.61]

CONSUMERS - UNITED STATES.

The Affluent market. New York, N.Y. (500 5th Ave., New York 10110) [1984] 227 leaves : LC Card 86-201904 DDC 658.8/348 19
HC110.C6 A63 1984

Energy efficiency . Washington, D.C. , 1987, c1986. 333 p. : ISBN 0-918249-05-8 (pbk.) LC Card 86-28817 DDC 333.79/16/0973 19
HD9502.U52 E4883 1987

Gordon, Leland James, 1897- Economics for consumers /. New York , c1977. ix, 693 p. : ISBN 0-442-22242-4 LC Card 76-50515 DDC 381/.3/0973 19
HB801 .G6 1977 NYPL [JLE 86-1506]

Katona, George, 1901- [Aspirations and affluence. Dutch.] Het psychologisch klimaat van de economie in de Verenigde Staten en West-Europa /. Utrecht , 1974. 247 p. ; ISBN 90-274-5826-X *NYPL [JLD 86-295]*

Lazer, William. Handbook of demographics for marketing and advertising . Lexington, Mass. , c1987. xxi, 211 p. : ISBN 0-669-16013-X (alk. paper) LC Card 86-46440 DDC 304.6/0973 19
HC110.C6 L39 1987

Lee, Stewart Munro. Personal finance for consumers /. Columbus, Ohio , c1987. xiii, 518 p. : ISBN 0-942280-33-4 : LC Card 86-30503 DDC 381/.3/0973 19
HB301 .L256 1987

Mariger, Randall P., 1954- Consumption behavior and the effects of government fiscal policies /. Cambridge, Mass. , 1986. xi, 265 p. ; ISBN 0-674-16635-3 (alk. paper) LC Card 85-17550 DDC 339.4/7/0973 19
HC110.C6 M287 1986 NYPL [JLE 86-3315]

Settle, Robert B. Why they buy . New York , c1986. xvi, 351 p. ; ISBN 0-471-84457-8 : LC Card 86-13303 DDC 658.8/343/0973 19
HC110.C6 S48 1986 NYPL [JLE 86-4432]

CONSUMERS - UNITED STATES - ATTITUDES.

Attitudes toward vended coffee /. [Chicago? , 1983] 1 v. (various pagings) : LC Card 86-235525 DDC 381/.4566393 19
HD9199.U48 A88 1983

Iced coffee taste test . Van Nuys, CA (14416 Victory Blvd. Van Nuys 91401) [1985] 132 p., 6, 6 leaves : LC Card 87-100181 DDC 381/.4566393/0973 19
HD9199.U48 I25 1985

Report on the coffee service industry /. Columbus, Ohio [1984] 1 v. (various foliations) : LC Card 87-100404 DDC 381/.4566393 19
HD9199.U48 R47 1984

Understanding first-time recreation vehicle buyers . Reston, VA (P.O. Box 2999, Prepared for Recreation Vehicle Industry Association, c1986. xxvi, 80 p. ; LC Card 87-108982 DDC 381/45629226/0973 19
HD9710.37.U62 U53 1986

CONSUMERS - UNITED STATES - ATTITUDES - STATISTICS.

Auto outlook IV /. [New York] , c1986. 60 leaves ; LC Card 86-231268 DDC 381/.456292/0973 19
HD9710.U52 A76 1986

CONSUMERS - UNITED STATES - CASE STUDIES.

Tongren, Hale N., 1921- Cases in consumer behavior /. Englewood Cliffs, N.J. , c1987. xiii, 224 p. : ISBN 0-13-115346-3 (pbk.) LC Card 86-25547 DDC 658.8/342 19
HF5415.3 .T64 1987

CONSUMERS - UNITED STATES - HISTORY - 20TH CENTURY.

Economics U$A. Chicago, IL , 1986. 1 videocassette (28 min.) : LC Card 86-708020 DDC 330.15 11
HB99.7

El consumidor como agente económico /. Fonseca Zamora, Jorge. Cartago , 1985. 196 p. : ISBN 997-7660-05-0 LC Card 87-116492 DDC 339.4/7 19
HB801 .F57 1985

Il Consumo dell'audiovisivo / scritti di G. Airenti ... [et al.]. Milano, Italy : F. Angeli, c1984. 173 p. : ill. ; 22 cm. (I Quaderni di Ikon . 7) English and Italian. Includes bibliographies. LC Card 85-178903
1. Television audiences - Italy. 2. Television industry - Italy. 3. Video tape industry - Italy. I. Airenti, Gabriella. II. Series.
HE8700.66.I8 C66 1984

Consumption behavior and the effects of government fiscal policies /. Mariger, Randall P., 1954- Cambridge, Mass. , 1986. xi, 265 p. ; ISBN 0-674-16635-3 (alk. paper) LC Card 85-17550 DDC 339.4/7/0973 19
HC110.C6 M287 1986 NYPL [JLE 86-3315]

CONSUMPTION (ECONOMICS)

Balfet, Michel. Les 50 mots clefs de la consommation /. Toulouse , c1985. 310 p. : ISBN 2-7089-1969-5 : LC Card 86-140639 DDC 339.4/7 19
HB801 .B276 1985

Campbell, Colin, 1940- The romantic ethic and the spirit of modern consumerism /. Oxford, UK , New York, NY, USA , 1987. 301 p. ; ISBN 0-631-15539-2 : LC Card 86-30979 DDC 339.4/7 19
HC79.C6 C36 1987

Enke, Harald. Konsumtive Arbeit . Freiburg im Breisgau , c1983. 354 p. : ISBN 3-448-01239-4 LC Card 83-224110
HF5549.5.J63 E54 1983

Fonseca Zamora, Jorge. El consumidor como agente económico /. Cartago , 1985. 196 p. : ISBN 997-7660-05-0 LC Card 87-116492 DDC 339.4/7 19
HB801 .F57 1985

Gordon, Leland James, 1897- Economics for consumers /. New York , c1977. ix, 693 p. : ISBN 0-442-22242-4 LC Card 76-50515 DDC 381/.3/0973 19
HB801 .G6 1977 NYPL [JLE 86-1506]

Hicks, John Richard, Sir, 1940- A revision of demand theory /. Oxford [Oxfordshire] , New York , 1986, c1956. vii, 196 p. : ISBN 0-19-828110-2 LC Card 86-154241 DDC 338.5/212 19
HB801 .H48 1986 NYPL [JLD 86-3663]

Hobson, J. A. (John Atkinson), 1858-1940. The economics of unemployment /. New York , 1985. 157 p. ; ISBN 0-8240-7615-X : LC Card 85-13053 DDC 331.13/7 19
HB822 .H63 1985 NYPL [JLC 86-452]

Lee, Stewart Munro. Personal finance for consumers /. Columbus, Ohio , c1987. xiii, 518 p. : ISBN 0-942280-33-4 : LC Card 86-30503 DDC 381/.3/0973 19
HB301 .L256 1987

M. S. ABC de la economía política /. Madrid [1964] 205 p., [1] folded leaf of plates : LC Card 85-106062
HB178.5 .M25 1964

Maierbeck, Marianne. Nutzen- und Zielprobleme privater Haushalte . Berlin , 1978. 203 p. : ISBN 3-428-04220-4 : LC Card 79-356181
TX7 .B4 Heft 13 HB201 NYPL [JLE 86-3431]

Melišek, František. Ekonomický rast a štrukturálne zmeny v socialistickej ekonomike /. Bratislava , 1980. 175 p. : LC Card 82-464724 DDC 338.9 19
*HD84.5 .M379 1980 NYPL [*QT 87-1737]*

Pflaumer, Peter, 1947- Bevölkerung, Haushalte, Konsum . Frankfurt , New York , c1986. iv, 218 p. : ISBN 3-593-33674-X LC Card 87-408990 DDC 339.4/7 19
HB849.53 .P49 1986

Roth, Timothy P. The present state of consumer theory /. Lanham, MD , c1987. vi, 168 p. ; ISBN 0-8191-5708-2 (alk. paper) : LC Card 86-24619 DDC 339.4/7/01 19
HB801 .R687 1987

Wong, Stanley. The foundations of Paul Samuelson's revealed preference theory . London , Boston , 1978. x, 148 p. : ISBN 0-7100-8643-1 : LC Card 78-40600 DDC 339.4/7
HB801 .W594 NYPL [JLD 87-1092]

Zinn, Karl Georg. Arbeit, Konsum, Akkumulation . Hamburg , 1986. 243 p. : ISBN 3-87975-347-4 LC Card 86-230933
HB103.K47 Z56 1986

CONSUMPTION (ECONOMICS) - BULGARIA.

Upravlenie na narodnoto potreblenie /. Sofiia , 1984. 235 p. : LC Card 85-212359
HC403.Z9 C628 1984

CONSUMPTION (ECONOMICS) - COMMUNIST COUNTRIES.

Libura, Urszula. Konsumpcja a wykorzystanie możliwości produkcyjnej w gospodarce socjalistycznej /. Warszawa , 1979. 242 p. ; ISBN 83-01-00103-8 LC Card 81-192720
HC710.C6 L53 1979

CONSUMPTION (ECONOMICS) - CONGRESSES.

Empirical approaches to consumer protection economics . Washington, D.C. [1986] ii, 484 p. : *NYPL [JLE 86-3552]*

CONSUMPTION (ECONOMICS) - ECONOMETRIC MODELS.

Theil, Henri. Applied demand analysis . Cambridge, Mass. , 1987. xxi, 279 p. : ISBN 0-88730-217-3 LC Card 86-32230 DDC 338.5/212 19
HB801 .T489 1987

Tobin, James, 1918- Essays in economics. Cambridge, Mass. , 1987. vii, 492 p. : ISBN 0-262-20064-3 LC Card 87-3913 DDC 330/.028 19
HB801 .T6 1987

CONSUMPTION (ECONOMICS) - ESTONIA.

Voprosy razvitiia obsluzhivaniia naseleniia . Tallin , 1985. 140 p. : LC Card 85-158428
HD9986.S683 E888 1985

CONSUMPTION (ECONOMICS) - EUROPE, EASTERN.

Bondarenko, E. L. (Evgeniia Lavrent'eva) Lichnoe potreblenie v usloviiakh

ėkonomicheskoĭ integrat͡sii stran--chlenov SĖV /. Moskva , 1984. 110 p. ; LC Card 84-222687
HC244.Z9 C613 1984

CONSUMPTION (ECONOMICS) - GERMANY, EAST.
Kaufmann, Manfred. Die persönliche materielle Interessiertheit an der Material- und Energieökonomie /. Jena , 1984. 112 p. : LC Card 85-224317
HF1054.G42 K38 1984

CONSUMPTION (ECONOMICS) - GERMANY (EAST) - CONGRESSES.
"Ökonomische Probleme der bedarfsorientierten Produktionsdurchführung" . Karl-Marx-Stadt , 1984. 139 p. : LC Card 84-245348
HD70.G22 O35 1984

CONSUMPTION (ECONOMICS) - GERMANY, WEST.
Meier, Bernd, 1952- Verbraucherpolitik in der Bundesrepublik Deutschland . Frankfurt am Main , New York , c1984. iii, 256 p. : ISBN 3-8204-8404-3 (pbk.) LC Card 87-672663
HC290.5.C6 M36x 1984

Schmucker, Helga. Studien zur empirischen Haushalts- und Verbrauchsforschung /. Berlin , 1980. xiv, 357 p. : ISBN 3-428-04657-9 LC Card 80-153661
TX7 .B4 Heft 15 HD7029 ***NYPL [JLE 86-3430]***

Schöll, Wolfgang. Konsumentenverhalten in der Bundesrepublik Deutschland 1958-1982 . Thun , c1985. 226, 70, [9] p. : ISBN 3-87144-900-8 (Deut. Bibl.) : LC Card 85-232693
HC290.5.C6 S35 1985

CONSUMPTION (ECONOMICS) - HISTORY.
McCracken, Grant David, 1951- Culture and consumption . Bloomington , c1988. xv, 174 p. ; ISBN 0-253-31526-3 LC Card 87-45394 DDC 339.4/7 19
HC79.C6 M385 1988

CONSUMPTION (ECONOMICS) - HUNGARY - STATISTICS.
A Lakosság jövedelme és fogyasztása, 1960-1973 /. [Budapest] , c1975. 91 p. ; ISBN 963-340-048-1 LC Card 86-196944
HC300.295.I5 L32 1975

A Lakosság jövedelme és fogyasztása, 1960-1983 /. Budapest , 1984. 118 p. ; ISBN 963-340-740-0 : LC Card 85-155585
HC300.295.I5 L3315 1984 ***NYPL [JLF 86-672]***

A Lakosság jövedelme és fogyasztása, 1970-1984 . Budapest , 1985. 83 p. ; LC Card 86-217829
HC300.295.I5 L3316 1985

CONSUMPTION (ECONOMICS) - LATVIA.
Ėkonomicheskie svi͡azi proizvodstva i potreblenii͡a pri sotsializme . Riga , 1978. 152 p. ; LC Card 81-168062
HF1040.9.S65 E36 1978

CONSUMPTION (ECONOMICS) - MATHEMATICAL MODELS.
Hadjimatheou, George. Consumer economics after Keynes . New York , 1987. viii, 280 p. : ISBN 0-312-00478-8 : LC Card 87-9427 DDC 339.4/7 19
HB801 .H245 1987

Owen, Dorian, 1953- Money, wealth, and expenditure . Cambridge [Cambridgeshire] , New York , 1986. xi, 210 p. ; ISBN 0-521-26761-7 LC Card 85-19009 DDC 339.4/7/0724 19
HB820 .O94 1986 ***NYPL [JLE 87-1594]***

Sell, Friedrich L. Der Konsumcharakter der Einkommensentstehung . Freiburg im Breisgau , c1982. 221 p. : ISBN 3-448-01269-6 LC Card 82-233541 DDC 339.4/7/0724 19
HB820 .S44 1982 ***NYPL [JLD 87-1580]***

Val´tukh, Konstantin Kurtovich. Matematicheskiĭ i statisticheskiĭ analiz funkt͡sii potreblenii͡a /. Novosibirsk , 1986. 165, [3] p. : LC Card 86-230310
HB801 .V26 1986

Val´tukh, Konstantin Kurtovich. T͡Selevai͡a funkt͡sii͡a potreblenii͡a . Novosibirsk , 1980. 381, [3] p. ; LC Card 81-134031
HB801 .V265 1980

CONSUMPTION (ECONOMICS) - NEPAL.
Employment, income distribution, and consumption patterns in Nepal . Kathmandu, Nepal , 1983. xiv, 122 p. ; LC Card 84-901199 DDC 330.9549/6 19
HD5812.9.A6 E47 1983 ***NYPL [JLF 86-1993]***

CONSUMPTION (ECONOMICS) - POLAND.
Rudnicki, Leszek. Zróżnicowania wzorców konsumpcji ludności rolniczej dwuzawodowej /. Kraków , 1985. 313 p. : LC Card 86-174377
HC340.3.Z9 C6177 1985

CONSUMPTION (ECONOMICS) - POLAND - KRAKÓW.
Prace z zakresu socjologii /. Kraków , 1979. 137 p. ; LC Card 80-129964
HB9 .K53 nr. 117 HC340.3.Z7K7

CONSUMPTION (ECONOMICS) - POLAND - ŁÓDŹ REGION.
Problemy rynku i handlu w Łodzi i regionie łódzkim /. [Łódź] , 1978. 193 p. : LC Card 80-129744
HD9986.P72 L636 1978

CONSUMPTION (ECONOMICS) - SOUTH AFRICA - DURBAN - STATISTICS.
Van Wyk, H. de J. Income and expenditure patterns of urban Black multiple households in Durban, 1985 /. Pretoria , 1986. xi, 130 p. : ISBN 0-908408-59-5 (pbk.) LC Card 87-151639 DDC 658.8/3968 s 339.4/1/0968455021 19
HC517.S7 S48 no. 130, pt. 4 HD7064.4.Z8D8

CONSUMPTION (ECONOMICS) - SOVIET UNION.
Beli͡aevskiĭ, I. K. (Igor´ Konstantinovich) Naselenie i tovarooborot . Moskva , 1980. 144 p. : LC Card 81-135180
HB801 .B377 1980

Ėkonomicheskoe stimulirovanie truda v uslovii͡akh sotsializma . Moskva , 1986. 179 p. ; LC Card 87-166364
HD5046 .E47 1986

Heinemeier, Meredith M. 1977 consumption by industrial sector /. Washington, D.C. [1986] vii, 148 p. ; LC Card 87-601286 DDC 339.2/3/0947 19
HC340.I57 H45 1986

Intensifikat͡sii͡a ėkonomiki i narodnoe potreblenie /. Moskva , 1983. 166 p. ; LC Card 84-227789
HC340.C6 I58 1983

Kont͡sept͡sii͡a i napravlenii͡a rat͡sionalizat͡sii narodnogo potreblenii͡a /. Moskva , 1985. 172 p. : LC Card 86-193920
HC340.C6 K573 1985

Kostin, Leonid Alekseevich. Proizvodstvo tovarov narodnogo potreblenii͡a . Moskva , 1980. 212 p. ; LC Card 87-107901
HF1040.9.S65 K67 1980

Kurochkin, I͡U. P. (I͡Uriĭ Petrovich) Sotsial´no-ėkonomicheskai͡a priroda i formy neobkhodimogo produkta pri sotsializme /. Leningrad , 1984. 135 p. ; LC Card 84-218003
HC340.B38 K87 1984

Levin, A. I. (Aleksandr Ivanovich) Tovarnoe obrashchenie . Moskva , 1980. 286 p. ; LC Card 81-141540
HF1040.9.S65 L48 1980

Lipko, A. G. (Alekseĭ Gennad´evich) Proizvodstvo i potreblenie v regione /. Moskva , 1986. 142 p. : LC Card 86-211374
HC336.25 .L56 1986

Makhmutov, A. Kh. (Anas Khusainovich) Lichnoe potreblenie v uslovii͡akh razvitogo sotsializma /. Kazan´ , 1980. 249 p. ; LC Card 82-162621
HC340.C6 M29 1980

Tret´i͡ak, V. P. (Vladimir Petrovich) Pri͡amye khozi͡aĭstvennye svi͡azi v sotsialisticheskoĭ ėkonomike /. Leningrad , 1986. 141 p. : LC Card 87-146709
HF5415.6 .T74 1986

CONSUMPTION (ECONOMICS) - SOVIET UNION - MATHEMATICAL MODELS.
Val´tukh, Konstantin Kurtovich. Matematicheskiĭ i statisticheskiĭ analiz funkt͡sii potreblenii͡a /. Novosibirsk , 1986. 165, [3] p. : LC Card 86-230310
HB801 .V26 1986

Val´tukh, Konstantin Kurtovich. T͡Selevai͡a funkt͡sii͡a potreblenii͡a . Novosibirsk , 1980. 381, [3] p. ; LC Card 81-134031
HB801 .V265 1980

CONSUMPTION (ECONOMICS) - SWEDEN.
Konsumtion i förändring . Vällingby [1985] 87 p. : LC Card 86-224791
HC380.C6 K675 1985

CONSUMPTION (ECONOMICS) - TAXATION. see **TAXATION OF ARTICLES OF CONSUMPTION.**

CONSUMPTION (ECONOMICS) - UKRAINE - FORECASTING.
I͡Ukhimenko, V. V. (Vladimir Vasil´evich) Izuchenie i prognozirovanie sprosa na bytovye uslugi /. Kiev , 1983. 103 p. ; LC Card 83-218585
HD9986.S683 U385 1983

CONSUMPTION (ECONOMICS) - UNITED STATES.
Mariger, Randall P., 1954- Consumption behavior and the effects of government fiscal policies /. Cambridge, Mass. , 1986. xi, 265 p. ; ISBN 0-674-16635-3 (alk. paper) LC Card 85-17550 DDC 339.4/7/0973 19
HC110.C6 M287 1986 ***NYPL [JLE 86-3315]***

CONSUMPTION (ECONOMICS) - UNITED STATES - CONGRESSES.
Empirical approaches to consumer protection economics . Washington, D.C. [1986] ii, 484 p. : LC Card 86-602207 DDC 381/.34/0973 19
HC110.C63 E46 1986

CONSUMPTION (ECONOMICS) - UNITED STATES - ECONOMETRIC MODELS.
Gylfason, Thorvaldur. Interest, inflation, and the aggregate consumption function /. Stockholm, Sweden [1979] 44 leaves : LC Card 81-114286
HC110.C6 G95 1979

CONSUMPTION (ECONOMICS) - UNITED STATES - STATISTICS.
Consumer expenditure survey . Washington, D.C. [1986] vi, 193 p. : LC Card 86-602456 DDC 339.4/1/0973 19
HC110.C6 C5647 1986

CONSUMPTION - GERMANY (EAST)
Bedürfnisse und Interessen als Triebkräfte unseres Handelns /. Berlin , 1984. 155 p. ; LC Card 84-229147
HC290.795.C3 B43 1984

CONSUMPTION - HUNGARY - STATISTICS.
A Lakosság jövedelme és fogyasztása, 1970-1985 /. Budapest , 1986. 97 p. ; ISBN 963-340-805-9 : LC Card 87-408026
HC300.295.I5 L3317 1986

CONSUMPTION OF ENERGY. see **ENERGY CONSUMPTION.**

The Consumption tax : a better alternative? / edited by Charls E. Walker and Mark A. Bloomfield. Cambridge, Mass. : Ballinger Pub. Co., c1987. xviii, 382 p. : ill. ; 24 cm. "American Council for Capital Formation-- Center for Policy Research." Includes bibliographies and index. ISBN 0-88730-159-2 LC Card 87-17838 DDC 336.2/71/0973 19
1. Spendings tax - United States. I. Walker, Charls E. (Charls Edward), 1923-. II. Bloomfield, Mark A. III. American Council for Capital Formation. Center for Policy Research.
HJ5715.U6 C658 1987

Contabilidad general . Orozco Cadena, José. Quito, Ecuador , 1986. xii, 551, [1] p. : LC Card 86-218544 DDC 657/.09866 19
HF5616.E2 O76 1986

A contabilidade após a reforma monetária /. Marion, José Carlos. São Paulo , 1986. 196 p. : ISBN 85-22-40175-6 : LC Card 86-222982
HG835 .M37 1986

La contabilità analitica dei costi . Mancini, Andrea, 1954- [Torino] , 1986. 53 p. : ISBN 88-85851-00-2 : LC Card 87-114718
HF5686.C8 M265 1986

Contabilità delle aziende divise /. Mella, Piero. [Milan] , c1983. 281 p. : ISBN 88-21-70036-4 LC Card 85-151879
HF5686.C7 M427 1983

Contabilità e bilancio . Frattini, Giovanni. Milano [1986] xiii, 317 p. : ISBN 88-14-00831-0 : LC Card 86-182373
HF5625 .F73 1986

Contabilità e bilancio.
Mella, Piero. Contabilità delle aziende divise /. [Milan] , c1983. 281 p. : ISBN 88-21-70036-4 LC Card 85-151879
HF5686.C7 M427 1983

Contact . Chamber of Commerce of the United States of America. Washington, D.C. , c1980. v, 129 p. : ISBN 0-89834-024-1 (pbk.) LC Card 80-80440 DDC 650/.07/073 19
HF5351 .C46 1980 ***NYPL [JLF 86-1414]***

Contacts : the firms, the people, in electronic banking / [Ben Parsons, editor & publisher ; Kelly LaMotte, assistant editor]. San Rafael, CA (1724 Lincoln Ave., San Rafael 94901) : DataPlus Research & Pub. Co., [c1986] 252 p. ; 28 cm. Includes index. LC Card 86-217208 DDC 332.1/028 19
1. Electronic funds transfers - United States - Directories. I. Parsons, Ben. II. LaMotte, Kelly. III. DataPlus Research & Publishing Company.
HG1710 .C66 1986

I contadini di San Felice . Cattini, Marco. Torino , c1984. xvii, 364 p., [2] leaves of plates : ISBN 88-06-05682-4 : LC Card 84-189545
HD1536.I8 C34 1984

CONTAINER CARGO. see **UNITIZED CARGO SYSTEMS.**

CONTAINER-SHIP OPERATIONS. see **UNITIZED CARGO SYSTEMS.**

CONTAINER SHIPS.
Koch, Hasso B. Funktions- und Sozialstrukturen auf Containerschiffen /. Frankfurt am Main , New York , c1986. vi, 542 p. : ISBN 3-8204-9334-4 LC Card 86-194048
HE566.C6 K63 1986

CONTAINERIZATION - BELGIUM - ANTWERP.
Mester, Bernt. Marktchancen der Binnenschiffahrt im Container-Hinterlandverkehr der Häfen der Hamburg-Antwerpen-Range /. Düsseldorf , 1986. xii, 304 p. ; LC Card 87-409549
HE5 .C6 Nr. 47 HE558.H3

CONTAINERIZATION - CANADA.
Brouillette, Benoît, 1904-1979. [Perspectives de changements dans la manutention des marchandises aux ports canadiens. English.] Prospective changes for handling of commodities in Canadian ports. Montréal, Québec, Canada [1974] iv, 93, [3] p. ; LC Card 82-219246
HE553 .B7613 1974

CONTAINERIZATION - GERMANY (WEST) - HAMBURG REGION.
Mester, Bernt. Marktchancen der Binnenschiffahrt im Container-Hinterlandverkehr der Häfen der Hamburg-Antwerpen-Range /. Düsseldorf , 1986. xii, 304 p. ; LC Card 87-409549
HE5 .C6 Nr. 47 HE558.H3

CONTAMINATED FOOD. see **FOOD CONTAMINATION.**

CONTAMINATION OF ENVIRONMENT. see **POLLUTION.**

Conte, J. see **Conte Porras, J.**

Conte, Jesús. La Catalunya a mig fer / Jesús Conte ; pròleg, Jordi Pujol. 1a ed. Barcelona : El Llamp, c1985. 259 p. ; 20 cm. (Col·lecció "La Rella") Bibliography: p. 257-259. Includes indexes. ISBN 84-86006-64-5X LC Card 86-164880
1. Catalonia (Spain) - Economic policy. 2. Infrastructure (Economics) - Spain - Catalonia. 3. Regional planning - Spain - Catalonia. I. Title.
HC387.C25 C57 1985

Conte Porras, J. El crédito, la banca y la moneda panameña / J. Conte-Porras. Ed. oficial, 4a ed. Panamá, Panamá : Banco Nacional de Panamá, 1983. 204 p. : ill. (some col.) ; 23 cm. (Boletín cultural / Ediciones Biblioteca José Agustín Arango Ch . v. 6) "Edición conmemorativa del septuagésimo novena aniversario de la fundación del Banco Nacional de Panamá."--colophon.
1. Banco Nacional de Panamá. 2. Banks and banking, Central - Panama. 3. Banks and banking, Central - Panama - History. 4. Credit - Panama. 5. Consumer credit - Panama. I. Series: Boletín cultural (Panama, Panama) , v. 6. II. Title. ***NYPL [JLE 86-3126]***

Conte, Stephane. Lord, Montague J. Market price models for Latin America's major commodity exports /. Washington, D.C. [1986] vii, 219 p. : LC Card 87-115208 DDC 338.5/2/098 19
HD9014.A2 L67 1986

Contemporary business planning . Giesen, David. Chicago, IL (111 E. Wacker Dr., Chicago 60601) , c1987. 128 p. : LC Card 87-401916 DDC 332.3/2/068 19
HG1897 .G54 1987

Contemporary economic problems : deficits, taxes, and economic adjustments / Phillip Cagan, editor ; Eduardo Somensatto, associate editor. Washington, D.C. : American Enterprise Institute, c1987. 332 p. : ill. ; 24 cm. (AEI studies, 0892-3981 . 455) Includes bibliographies. ISBN 0-8447-3621-X (alk. paper) LC Card 87-1395 DDC 330.973/0927 19
1. United States - Economic conditions - 1981-. 2. United States - Economic policy - 1981-. 3. Budget - United States. 4. Taxation - United States. 5. Balance of trade - United States. I. Cagan, Phillip. II. Somensatto, Eduardo. III. Title: Deficits, taxes, and economic adjustments. IV. Series.
HC106.8 .C665 1987

Contemporary financial management /. Moyer, R. Charles, 1945- St. Paul , c1988. xxiv, 793, 24 p. : ISBN 0-314-64227-7 LC Card 87-24201 DDC 658.1/5 19
HG4026 .M68 1988

Contemporary issues .
(no. 4) Rosenblatt, Samuel M. East-West trade in technology . Washington, D.C. , c1980. viii, 64 p. ; LC Card 80-81923 DDC 382/.4560973 19
HF1414.5 .R67 ***NYPL [JLD 81-233]***

Contemporary issues and practices in marketing / [compiled by] Robert F. Hoel. 1987/88 ed. Boston : Allyn and Bacon, 1987. p. cm. ISBN 0-205-10545-9 LC Card 87-1062 DDC 658.8 19
1. Marketing. I. Hoel, Robert F.
HF5415 .C5475 1987

Contemporary labor relations /. Allen, Robert E. (Robert Edward), 1946- Reading, Mass. , c1988. xi, 724 p. : ISBN 0-201-10083-5 : LC Card 87-24128 DDC 331/.0973 19
HD8072.5 .A43 1988

Contemporary problems in Nigerian industrial relations / edited by Ukandi G. Damachi, Tayo Fashoyin. Lagos, Nigeria : Development Press, 1986. xii, 150 p. ; 22 cm. Bibliography: p. 143-147. ISBN 978-252-200-7 LC Card 87-139560 DDC 331/.09669 19
1. Industrial relations - Nigeria. I. Damachi, Ukandi Godwin. II. Fashoyin, Tayo.
HD8831 .C65 1986

Contemporary real estate principles /. Danks, Lawrence J. Medford, N.J. , c1987. x, 439 p. : ISBN 0-9610624-1-X (pbk.) LC Card 86-63861 DDC 333.33 19
HD1375 .D25 1987

Contemporary retailing /. Bolen, William H., 1943- Englewood Cliffs, N.J. , c1988. xviii, 622 p. : ISBN 0-13-170309-9 LC Card 87-17514 DDC 658.8/7 19
HF5429 .B595 1988

Contemporary social theory (London, England)
Ingham, Geoffrey K. Capitalism divided? . Basingstoke, Hampshire , 1984. viii, 304 p. : ISBN 0-333-30116-1 LC Card 86-673507
HC255 .I495x 1984b

Contemporary studies in energy analysis and policy .
(v 6) Farzin, Yeganeh Hossein, 1950- Competition and substitutes in the market for an exhaustible resource /. Greenwich, Conn. , c1985. xvi, 209 : ISBN 0-89232-604-2 : LC Card 85-23765 DDC 338.2/7282/0724 19
HD9560.5 .F385 1985 ***NYPL [JLE 86-1585]***

(v. 8) Khazzoom, J. Daniel. An econometric model integrating conservation measures in the residential demand for electricity /. Greenwich, Conn. , c1986. xx, 305 p. : ISBN 0-89232-606-9 : LC Card 86-7173 DDC 333.79/3216/0724 19
HD9685.A2 K54 1986 ***NYPL [JLE 86-4174]***

Contemporary views on marketing practice / edited by Gary L. Frazier, Jagdish N. Sheth. Lexington, Mass. : Lexington Books, c1987. vi, 282 p. : ill. ; 24 cm. Based on papers presented at the First Stellner Symposium on Theories of Marketing Practice, held at the University of Illinois at Champaign-Urbana, May 23-25, 1985. Includes bibliographies. ISBN 0-669-15120-3 (alk. paper) LC Card 86-46218 DDC 658.8 19
1. Marketing - Congresses. I. Frazier, Gary L. II. Sheth, Jagdish N. III. Stellner Symposium on Theories of Marketing Practice (1st : 1985 : University of Illinois at Champaign-Urbana).
HF5411 .C66 1987

Contending approaches to the political economy of Taiwan / edited by Edwin A. Winckler and Susan M. Greenhalgh. Armonk, N.Y. : M.E. Sharpe, c1988. p. cm. Bibliography: p. Includes index. ISBN 0-87332-440-4 : LC Card 87-16413 DDC 338.951/249 19
1. Taiwan - Economic conditions. I. Winckler, Edwin A. II. Greenhalgh, Susan.
HC430.5 .C75 1988

Contes et mécomptes de la protection sociale /. Johanet, Gilles. Paris , c1986. 175 p. : ISBN 2-86702-024-4 : LC Card 86-179065
HD7175 .J64 1986

Contesse, L. (Luis), 1948- IFIP Working Conference on System Modelling and Optimization (1984 : Santiago, Chile) Recent advances in system modelling and optimization . Berlin , New York , c1986. 199 p. : ISBN 0-387-17083-9 (U. S.) LC Card 86-29770 DDC 003 19
QA402 .I43 1984 ***NYPL [JSE 87-639]***

Contestazioni /. Gonella, Guido, 1905- Roma , 1983. 3 v. ; LC Card 84-237282 DDC 945.092 19
JN5451 .G57 1983 ***NYPL [JFE 86-1367]***

Contexto socioeconómico de las migraciones internas en Nariño /. Cerón Solarte, Benhur. Pasto [Colombia] , 1985. i, 276, 51 p. : LC Card 87-102199
HB2028.N37 C47 1985

Conti, Elio. L'imposta diretta a Firenze nel Quattrocento (1427-1494) / di Elio Conti. Roma : Nella sede dell'Istituto, 1984. 406 p. ; 26 cm. (Studi storici. fasc. 136-139) Bibliography: p. [371]-373. Includes indexes. LC Card 86-171245
1. Taxation - Italy - Florence - History. 2. Finance, Public - Italy - Florence - History. 3. Florence (Italy) - History - 1421-1737. I. Series: Studi storici (Istituto storico italiano per il Medio Evo) , fasc. 136-139. II. Title.
HJ9500.F562 C65 1984

The Continental affair . McCollom, James P. New York , c1987. xv, 393 p. ; ISBN 0-396-08809-0 : LC Card 87-21471 DDC 332.1/223/0977311 19
HG2613.C44 C686 1987

CONTINENTAL ILLINOIS NATIONAL BANK AND TRUST COMPANY OF CHICAGO.
McCollom, James P. The Continental affair . New York , c1987. xv, 393 p. ; ISBN 0-396-08809-0 : LC Card 87-21471 DDC 332.1/223/0977311 19
HG2613.C44 C686 1987

CONTINENTAL SHELF - PACIFIC COAST (U. S.)
Webster, Frank L. Pacific OCS lease sale, October 1, 1964, Oregon and Washington /. [Washington] [1985] iii, 36 p. : LC Card 86-601138 DDC 333.33/9 19
HD243.A18 W43 1985

CONTINENTAL SHELF - UNITED STATES.
Offshore lands . San Francisco, Calif. , c1985. xxviii, 169 p. : ISBN 0-936488-10-7 (alk. paper) : LC Card 85-63548 DDC 333.8/23/0973 19
HD242.5 .O34 1985 ***NYPL [JLE 86-2726]***

CONTINUING EDUCATION.
National CPE curriculum . New York, N.Y. , c1987- 1 v. (loose-leaf) : ISBN 0-87051-001-0 (loose-leaf : CIP data sheet) : LC Card 87-18832 DDC 657/.07/15 19
HF5635 .N25 1987

CONTINUING EDUCATION - BURUNDI.
Formation des adultes . [Bujumbura] [1984- v. <1 > : LC Card 86-980941
HD5715.5.B94 F67 1984

CONTINUING EDUCATION - GERMANY, WEST.
Angsturlaub statt Bildungsurlaub . Frankfurt am Main , c1979. 179 p. : ISBN 3-88203-044-5 LC Card 85-167471
HD5257.2.G3 A54 1979

CONTINUING EDUCATION - GERMANY (WEST) - HESSE - CASE STUDIES.
Dobischat, Rolf, 1950- Berufliche

Weiterbildung, Arbeitsmarkt und Region . Frankfurt am Main , New York , c1985. 691 p. : ISBN 3-8204-5673-2 LC Card 86-158931
HD5715.5.G42 H473 1985

CONTINUING EDUCATION - GERMANY (WEST) - NORTH RHINE-WESTPHALIA - CASE STUDIES.
Dobischat, Rolf, 1950- Berufliche Weiterbildung, Arbeitsmarkt und Region . Frankfurt am Main , New York , c1985. 691 p. : ISBN 3-8204-5673-2 LC Card 86-158931
HD5715.5.G42 H473 1985

CONTINUING EDUCATION - ITALY - MILAN.
Le 150 ore e la formazione professionale in azienda . Milano, Italy , c1985. 178 p. : LC Card 86-141990
HD5716.T242 I82 1985
NYPL [JFD 87-3739]

CONTINUING EDUCATION - UNITED STATES - DIRECTORIES.
Jones, Constance. Beat the MBAs to the top! . Reading, Mass. , c1987. vii, 360 p. ; ISBN 0-201-11310-4 (pbk.) : LC Card 87-11363 DDC 650/.07/15 19
HF1131 .J756 1987

Continuing the commitment : agricultural development in the Sahel. Washington, D.C. : Congress of the U. S., Office of Technology Assessment : For sale by the Supt. of Docs., U. S. G.P.O., [1986] ix, 164 p. : ill., maps ; 26 cm. At head of title: OTA special report. Distributed to depository libraries in microfiche. "August 1986"--P. [4] of cover. Bibliography: p. 137-142. "OTA-F-308"--P. [4] of cover. S/N 052-003-01043-7 Item 1070-M LC Card 86-600555 DDC 338.1/8 19
1. Agricultural assistance - Sahel. 2. Agricultural development projects - Sahel. 3. Sahel - Economic conditions. I. United States. Congress. Office of Technology Assessment. II. Title: Agricultural development in the Sahel.
HD2120.S15 C66 1986

Continuity in administrative science.
Argyris, Chris, 1923- Personality and organization . New York , 1987, c1957. xiii, 291 p. ; ISBN 0-8240-8200-1 (alk. paper) : LC Card 86-27054 DDC 658.4 19
HD58.7 .A75 1987

Comparative studies in administration /. New York , 1987. xiv, 224, 40 p. : ISBN 0-8240-8220-6 (alk. paper) : LC Card 86-27017 DDC 658 19
HD30.55 .C66 1987

Costello, Timothy W. Psychology in administration . New York , 1987. xii, 500 p. : ISBN 0-8240-8202-8 (alk. paper) : LC Card 86-25805 DDC 658/.001/9 19
HF5548.8 .C6 1987

Dalton, Melville. Men who manage . New York , 1987. xi, 318 p., [1] leaf of plates : ISBN 0-8240-8203-6 (alk. paper) : LC Card 86-25801 DDC 658.4 19
HD31 .D2 1987

Dubin, Robert. The world of work . New York , 1987. xiii, 448 p. : ISBN 0-8240-8204-4 (alk. paper) : LC Card 86-25791 DDC 306/.36 19
HD6955 .D817 1987

Follett, Mary Parker, 1868-1933. Freedom & co-ordination . New York , 1987. xvii, 89 p. ; ISBN 0-8240-8229-X (alk. paper) : LC Card 86-27079 DDC 658.4/092 19
HD57.7 .F66 1987

Gordon, Robert Aaron. Higher education for business /. New York , 1987, c1959. xi, 491 p. ; ISBN 0-8240-8207-9 (alk. paper) : LC Card 86-25813 DDC 650/.07/1173 19
HF1131 .G6 1987

Handbook of organizations /. New York , 1987, c1965. 2 v. (xvi, 1247 p.) : ISBN 0-8240-8215-X (set : alk. paper) : LC Card 86-25797 DDC 658.4 19
HD58.7 .H365 1987

Hemphill, John K. (John Knox), 1919- Dimensions of executive positions . New York , 1987, c1960. xiv, 103 p. ; ISBN 0-8240-8209-5 (alk. paper) : LC Card 86-27078 DDC 658.4 19
HD38.2 .H46 1987

Jaques, Elliott. The changing culture of a factory /. New York , 1987. xvii, 341 p. ; ISBN 0-8240-8212-5 (alk. paper) : LC Card 86-25815 DDC 671/.068 19
HD8039.M5 J37 1987

Job attitudes . New York , 1987. xii, 279 p. ; ISBN 0-8240-8210-9 (alk. paper) : LC Card 86-26935 DDC 331.25 19
HF5549.5.J63 J57 1987

Katz, Daniel, 1903- Productivity, supervision, and morale in an office situation, part I /. New York , 1987, c1950. vii, 84 p. ; ISBN 0-8240-8211-7 (alk. paper) : LC Card 86-25804 DDC 658.3 19
HF5549 .K282 1987

Likert, Rensis, 1903- New patterns of management /. New York , 1987. vii, 279 p. : ISBN 0-8240-8214-1 (alk. paper) : LC Card 86-25800 DDC 658.4 19
HD31 .L43 1987

Modern organization theory . New York , 1987, c1959. x, 324 p. : ISBN 0-8240-8208-7 (alk. paper) : LC Card 86-27072 DDC 658 19
HD31 .M614 1987

Social science approaches to business behavior /. New York , 1987. vii, 183 p. : ISBN 0-8240-8201-X (alk. paper) : LC Card 86-25802 DDC 658.4 19
HD58.7 .S66 1987

The Social science of organization[s] . New York , 1987. ix, 182 p. : ISBN 0-8240-8213-3 (alk. paper) : LC Card 86-27069 DDC 658.4/03 19
HD58.7 .S67 1987

Stagner, Ross, 1909- Psychology of industrial conflict /. New York , 1987, c1956. ix, 550 p. : ISBN 0-8240-8218-4 (alk. paper) : LC Card 86-27080 DDC 158.7 19
HF5548.8 .S713 1987

Tannenbaum, Robert. Leadership and organization . New York , 1987, c1961. xiv, 456 p. : ISBN 0-8240-8219-2 (alk. paper) : LC Card 86-27019 DDC 303.3/4 19
HD57.7 .T36 1987

Tiffin, Joseph, 1905- Industrial psychology /. New York , 1987, [c1942] xvi, 386 p. : ISBN 0-8240-8221-4 (alk. paper) : LC Card 86-25803 DDC 158.7 19
HF5548.8 .T5 1987

Viteles, Morris S. (Morris Simon), 1898- Industrial psychology /. New York , 1987, c1932. xviii, 652 p., 8 p. of plates : ISBN 0-8240-8224-9 (alk. paper) : LC Card 86-25817 DDC 158.7 19
HF5548.8 .V55 1987

Vroom, Victor Harold, 1932- Some personality determinants of the effects of participation /. New York , 1987, c1960. x, 91 p. ; ISBN 0-8240-8225-7 (alk. paper) : LC Card 86-27081 DDC 158.7 19
HF5548.8 .V695 1987

Whyte, William Foote, 1914- Pattern for industrial peace /. New York , 1987, c1951. ix, 245 p. : ISBN 0-8240-8227-3 (alk. paper) : LC Card 86-25790 DDC 331.89/0469142/0977/311 19
HD6515.I52 C48 1987

Conto consolidato della spesa pubblica in Lombardia / IReR ; ricerca condotta da Piero Giarda. Milano, Italy : F. Angeli, c1982. 234 p. ; 22 cm. (Collana IReR . 12) Includes bibliographical references. LC Card 85-147746
1. Lombardy (Italy) - Appropriations and expenditures - Accounting. 2. Finance, Public - Italy - Lombardy - Accounting. 3. Financial statements, Consolidated - Italy - Lombardy. I. Giarda, Piero D. II. I.Re.R. III. Series.
HJ9925.I8 C63 1982

CONTRABAND TRADE. see **SMUGGLING.**

Contrabando humano en las Californias /. Calderón R., Cedric. [S.l. , 1978] (Guatemala : Propsa) 160 p. ; LC Card 86-218852 DDC 331.6/2/720794 19
HD8083.C2 C23 1978

Contrabbando di fatica. Soldini, Bruno, 1939- Uomini da soma . [Lugano] , c1985. 289 p. : LC Card 86-136358
HJ6947 .S65 1985

Contract for life, the S.A.D.D. story [motion picture] / a Helios production ; producer, Paul Deason ; director, Joseph Pevney ; writer, Peter Silverman. Los Angeles, CA : Churchill Films, 1985. 1 film reel (31 min.) : sd., col. ; 16 mm. + 1 teacher's guide. Title from data sheet. Stephen Macht. Photographer, Hanania Baer ; film editor, Ed Cotter ; music, Misha Segal. Originally shown on the television program: CBS schoolbreak special. Junior and senior high school students. Issued also as videorecording. Tells how, in 1981, two members of the same high school hockey team were killed in separate automobile accidents in which liquor was involved and, spurred by the tragedy, the boys' coach and friends formed Students Against Driving Drunk, which now has several thousand chapters around the United States. LC Card 85-700743 DDC 363.1 11
1. Students Against Driving Drunk (Organization). 2. Drunk driving - Prevention - Societies, etc. I. Macht, Stephen. II. Helios Productions. III. Churchill Films. IV. CBS schoolbreak special (Television program). V. Title: Contract for life, the SADD story.
HE5620.D7

Contract for life, the S.A.D.D story [videorecording] / a Helios production ; producer, Paul Deason ; director, Joseph Peveny ; writer, Peter Silverman. Los Angeles, CA : Churchill Films, 1985. 1 videocassette (31 min.) : sd., col. + 1 teacher's guide. Title from data sheet. Stephen Macht. Photographer, Hanania Baer ; film editor, Ed Cotter ; music, Misha Segal. Originally shown on the television program: CBS schoolbreak special. Junior and senior high school students. Issued as U-matic 3/4 in. or Beta 1/2 in. or VHS 1/2 in. Issued also as motion picture. Tells how, in 1981, two members of the same high school hockey team were killed in separate automobile accidents in which liquor was involved and, spurred by the tragedy, the boys' coach and friends formed Students Against Driving Drunk, which now has several thousand chapters around the United States. LC Card 85-700744 DDC 363.1 11
1. Students Against Driving Drunk (Organization). 2. Drunk driving - Prevention - Societies, etc. I. Macht, Stephen. II. Helios Productions. III. Churchill Films. IV. CBS schoolbreak special (Television program). V. Title: Contract for life, the SADD story.
HE5620.D7

Contract for life, the SADD story. Contract for life, the S.A.D.D. story [motion picture] /. Los Angeles, CA , 1985. 1 film reel (31 min.) : LC Card 85-700743 DDC 363.1 11
HE5620.D7

Contract for life, the SADD story. Contract for life, the S.A.D.D story [videorecording] /. Los Angeles, CA , 1985. 1 videocassette (31 min.) : LC Card 85-700744 DDC 363.1 11
HE5620.D7

CONTRACT LABOR - DOMINICAN REPUBLIC.
Lemoine, Maurice. [Sucre amer. English.] Bitter sugar /. London , 1985. 308 p., [17] p. of plates : ISBN 0-86232-445-9 LC Card 87-672356
HD4875.D44 L4513x 1985b

Lemoine, Maurice. [Sucre amer. English.] Bitter sugar /. London , c1985. 308 p., [17] p. of plates : ISBN 0-86232-445-9
NYPL [JLD 86-814]

CONTRACT LABOR - HAWAII - HISTORY.
Ewanchuk, Michael, 1908- Hawaiian ordeal . Winnipeg, Man. , c1986. xii, 180 p. : ISBN 0-9690768-7-8 (pbk.) : LC Card 87-156576
HD4875.U5 E93x 1986

CONTRACT LABOR - SOUTHWEST, NEW - HISTORY - 20TH CENTURY.
Driscoll, Bárbara A. El programa de braceros ferroviarios /. Tijuana, Baja California , 1985. 45 p. ; ISBN 968-607-501-1 LC Card 86-188661
HD8039.R432 U62 1985

CONTRACT RESEARCH. see **RESEARCH, INDUSTRIAL.**

CONTRACT SYSTEM (LABOR) - SWEDEN.
Sweden. Rekryteringsutredningen. Arbetsförmedlingskontrakt . [Stockholm] [1983] 195, 9, 2 p. ; ISBN 91-38-07728-0 LC Card 84-218571
HD4875.S8 S94 1983

CONTRACTING OUT - FLORIDA.
The Role of privatization in Florida's growth /. [Tallahassee?] , c1987. iv, 474 p. ; LC Card 87-403210 DDC 338.9 19
HD3865.F6 R65 1987

Contracting with the United States Department of Transportation [microform]. United States. Dept. of Transportation. Office of the Secretary. Washington, D.C. , 1984. iii, 40 p. :
*NYPL [*ZT-1711 no.25]*

Contractor, Farok J. Cooperative strategies in international business /. Lexington, Mass. , c1988. xxix, 513 p. : ISBN 0-669-14927-6 (alk. paper) LC Card 86-46160 DDC 338.8/8 19
HD2755.5 .C645 1988

CONTRACTORS - GREAT BRITAIN - HISTORY - 19TH CENTURY.
Joby, R. S. The railway builders . Newton Abbot [Devon] , North Pomfret, Vt. , c1983. 200 p. : ISBN 0-7153-7959-3 : LC Card 84-147746 DDC 338.7/6251/00941 19
HE3018 .J63 1983 NYPL [JLD 86-918]

CONTRACTORS' OPERATIONS - ACCOUNTING. see **CONSTRUCTION INDUSTRY - ACCOUNTING.**

CONTRACTS, AGRICULTURAL - FRANCE - CHAMPAGNE-ARDENNE.
Berger, Alain. Les récoltants vendeurs au kilo champenois face au contrat interprofessionnel /. Paris , Epernay [1984] 45, 63 p. : ISBN 2-85340-534-6 LC Card 85-111856
HD9382.7.C5 B47 1984

CONTRACTS FOR WORK AND LABOR.
Rizzo, Michael R. How to make profits with service contracts /. New York, NY , c1987. xii, 367 p. ; ISBN 0-8144-5807-6 LC Card 86-47590 DDC 658 19
HD9980.5 .R59 1987

CONTRACTS FOR WORK, LABOR, AND MATERIALS. see **CONTRACTS FOR WORK AND LABOR.**

CONTRACTS, GOVERNMENT. see **PUBLIC CONTRACTS.**

CONTRACTS, LETTING OF.
Barrmeyer, Martin-Christian. Die Angebotsplanung bei Submission /. Münster [1982?] xii, 198 p. : ISBN 3-88660-081-5 : LC Card 83-227153
HD2365 .B36 1982

Bidding & estimating in the building service industry. Fairfax, VA , c1983. v, 10 p. : LC Card 87-110623 DDC 648/.068/1 19
HD9999.B882 B53 1983

Marsh, P. D. V. The art of tendering /. Aldershot, Hants, England , Brookfield, Vt. , c1987. ix, 171 p. ; ISBN 0-291-39736-0 : LC Card 87-7429 DDC 658.7/23 19
HD2365 .M37 1987

CONTRACTS, LETTING OF - CONGRESSES.
Bidding for projects financed by international lending agencies /. Aldershot, Hants. , c1982. vii, 345 p. : ISBN 0-566-03033-0 LC Card 82-210482 DDC 332.1/53 19
HD2365 .B52 1982 NYPL [JLG 85-120]

CONTRACTS, LETTING OF - ECONOMETRIC MODELS.
Barrmeyer, Martin-Christian. Die Angebotsplanung bei Submission /. Münster [1982?] xii, 198 p. : ISBN 3-88660-081-5 : LC Card 83-227153
HD2365 .B36 1982

CONTRACTS, LETTING OF - SWITZERLAND.
Finsinger, Jörg. Der Submissionswettbewerb . Bern , c1986. 104 p. : ISBN 3-258-03617-9 : LC Card 86-224617
HD9715.S92 F56 1986

CONTRACTS, PUBLIC. see **PUBLIC CONTRACTS.**

CONTRACTS - UNITED STATES - FORMS.
Burns, Robert, 1938- Master forms & contracts from your copier . Tucson, AZ , c1987. 160 p. : ISBN 0-89586-513-0 (pbk.) : LC Card 86-82238 DDC 651/.29 19
HF5371 .B845 1987

Contractual arrangements for intertemporal trade / edited by Edward C. Prescott and Neil Wallace. Minneapolis, MN : University of Minnesota Press, c1987. p. cm. (Minnesota studies in macroeconomics . v. 1) Bibliography: p. ISBN 0-8166-1533-0 : LC Card 86-24888 DDC 332.64/4/0724 19
1. Demand functions (Economic theory) - Congresses. 2. Speculation - Congresses. 3. Equilibrium (Economics) - Congresses. 4. Exchange - Congresses. I. Prescott, Edward C. II. Wallace, Neil. III. Series.
HB801 .C629 1987

CONTRACTUAL LIMITATIONS. see **CONTRACTS.**

Contrade (Firm) Conferenza internazionale sul tema Le zone franche industriali, nuove forme di investimento, l'America latina (1985 : Milan, Italy) Le zone franche industriali nei paesi emergenti . Milano, Italy , c1986. 207 p. ; LC Card 86-223193
HF1418 .C525 1985

Contradictions and dilemmas . Kornai, János. [Ellentmondások és dilemmák. English.] Cambridge, Mass. , 1986, c1983. ix, 165 p. : ISBN 0-262-11107-1 LC Card 85-5168 DDC 330.9439/053 19
HC300.28 .K67213 1986
NYPL [JLC 86-254]

Contrary investing . Band, Richard E. New York , c1985. viii, 197 p. : ISBN 0-07-003604-7 : LC Card 85-99 DDC 332.6/78 19
HG4527 .B233 1985 NYPL [JLE 86-1234]

Contrattazione salariale e ciclo economico . Balducci, Renato, 1947- Roma , 1982. 174 p. :
NYPL [JLD 86-2868]

Contribuição de melhoria . Biava, Adriano Henrique Rebelo. São Paulo-SP , 1987. 243 p. : LC Card 87-404978 DDC 339.5/2/0981 19
HJ2525 .B5 1987

Contribuições para a reforma do sistema fiscal português . Seminário sobre Política Fiscal (1984? : CGTP-IN) Lisboa , 1985. 226 p. : LC Card 87-107879 DDC 336.469 19
HJ1252 .S46 1984

Contributed papers to the National Seminar on Population, Employment, and Development Planning in Sierra Leone . National Seminar on Population, Employment, and Development Planning in Sierra Leone (1980 : Freetown, Sierra Leone) Freetown, Sierra Leone , <[1980-. v. <2 > : LC Card 87-163849 DDC 304.6/0966/4 19
HB3666.9.A3 N38 1980

Contribution à l'étude des migrations au Togo /. Akakpo-Ahianyo, Anani. Lomé , 1976. 108 p., [5] p. of plates : LC Card 87-150756
HB2125.8.A3 A38 1976

Contribution des Italiens au XX Congrès général de l'UIESP, Firenze, 5-12 giugno 1985. Contribution of Italian scholars to the IUSSP XX General Conference =. Roma [1985?] 320 p. : LC Card 87-169376 DDC 304.6/0945 19
HB3599 .C647 1985

Contribution of exports to U. S. employment . Davis, Lester A. Washington, D.C. , 1986. 33 p. : LC Card 86-602848 DDC 331.12/0973 19
HD5710.75.U6 D38 1986

Contribution of Italian scholars to the IUSSP XX General Conference = Contribution des Italiens au XX Congrès Général de l'UIESP, Firenze, 5-12 giugno 1985. Roma : Consiglio Nazionale delle ricerche, Istituto di ricerche sulla popolazione, [1985?] 320 p. : ill. ; 24 cm. Papers in English and French. Papers presented at the General Conference of the International Union for the Scientific Study of Population held in Florence 6/5-12/85 under the sponsorship of the IRP. Includes bibliographies. LC Card 87-169376 DDC 304.6/0945 19
1. Italy - Population. 2. Fertility, Human - Italy. I. Title: Contribution des Italiens au XX Congrès général de l'UIESP, Firenze, 5-12 giugno 1985.
HB3599 .C647 1985

Contribution of state-directed land settlement to agricultural development . Klempin, Arno. Saarbrücken , Fort Launderdale, 1979. viii, 169 p. : ISBN 3-88156-121-8 LC Card 80-464363 DDC 333.3/1/593
HD890.55 .K57 NYPL [JLE 80-1270]

Contribution to national and regional planning problems / editors, A Ghosh, D. Chakraborty. Calcutta : K.P. Bagchi, 1983. vii, 174 p., [2] leaves of plates (some folded) : ill. ; 23 cm. Includes bibliographical references and index. LC Card 83-907550 DDC 338.954 19
1. Metropolitan areas - Government policy - India. 2. Regional planning - Iran. 3. India - Economic policy - 1947-. I. Ghosh, A., 1921-. II. Chakraborty, D. (Debesh).
HC435.2 .C63 1983 NYPL [JLD 86-3868]

Contribution to the study of world history, 0885-9159 .
(no. 2) Rice-Maximin, Edward Francis, 1941- Accomodation and resistance . New York , 1986. xi, 175 p. ; ISBN 0-313-25355-2 (lib. bdg. : alk. paper) LC Card 86-4624 DDC 959.704/1 19
DS553.1 .R53 1986 NYPL [JFE 87-1024]

Contributions in American studies, 0084-9227 .
(no. 81) Winters, Donald E. The soul of the wobblies . Westport, Conn. , 1985. 159 p. ; ISBN 0-313-24472-3 (lib. bdg.) LC Card 84-27973 DDC 331.88/6 19
HD8055.I5 W56 1985 NYPL [JLD 87-775]

(no. 84) Neuschatz, Michael. The golden sword . New York , 1986. xii, 301 p. ; ISBN 0-313-25104-5 (lib. bdg. : alk. Paper) LC Card 85-27026 DDC 331.88/122334/09788 19
HD8039.M61 U48 1986
NYPL [JLE 87-766]

Contributions in economics and economic history, 0084-9235 .
(no. 68) DiFilippo, Anthony, 1950- Military spending and industrial decline . Westport, Conn. , c1986. x, 199 p. ; ISBN 0-313-25179-7 (lib bdg. : alk. paper) LC Card 85-27144 DDC 338.4/7621902/0973 19
HD9703.U5 D54 1986
NYPL [JLD 86-2930]

(no. 69) Gillis, R. Peter. Lost initiatives . New York , 1986. 326 p. : ISBN 0-313-25415-X (lib. bdg. : alk. paper) LC Card 86-3122 DDC 333.75/0971 19
HD9764.C3 G55 1986 NYPL [JLE 87-947]

(no. 71) Gruchy, Allan Garfield, 1906- The reconstruction of economics . New York , 1987. xx, 173 p. ; ISBN 0-313-25679-9 (lib. bdg. : alk. paper) LC Card 86-25721 DDC 330 19
HB99.5 .G79 1987

(no. 72) Langer, Gary F. The coming of age of political economy, 1815-1825 /. New York , 1987. x, 224 p. : ISBN 0-313-25645-4 (lib. bdg. : alk. paper) LC Card 86-31802 DDC 330/.0941 19
HB103.A2 L36 1987

(no. 73) Sorge, Friedrich A. (Friedrich Adolf), 1828-1906. Friedrich A. Sorge's labor movement in the United States . New York , c1987. xiii, 196 p. ; ISBN 0-313-25518-0 (lib. bdg. : alk. paper) LC Card 86-31792 DDC 331/.0973 19
HD8072 .S7175 1987

(no. 74) Hope, Kempe R. Development finance and the development process . New York , 1987. 100 p. ; ISBN 0-313-25835-X (lib. bdg. : alk. paper) LC Card 86-29617 DDC 336.729 19
HJ844.3 .H67 1987

(no. 75) Godfried, Nathan. Bridging the gap between rich and poor . New York , 1987. xii, 225 p. ; ISBN 0-313-25648-9 (lib. bdg. : alk. paper) LC Card 87-8471 DDC 338.91/73/056 19
HC415.15 .G63 1987

(no. 76) Rethinking the nineteenth century . New York , c1988. p. cm. ISBN 0-313-25997-6 (lib. bdg. : alk. paper) LC Card 87-17791 DDC 330.9/034 19
HC53 .R48 1988

(no. 78) Stockhausen, Gerard Lawrence. Threats of quotas in international trade, their effect on the exporting country /. New York , 1988. 170 p. : ISBN 0-313-25785-X (lib. bdg. : alk. paper) LC Card 87-23682 DDC 382/.64 19
HF1430 .S86 1988

(no. 79) Kane, Nancy Frances, 1954- Textiles in transition . New York , c1988. p. cm. ISBN 0-313-25529-6 (lib. bdg. : alk. paper) LC Card 87-24950 DDC 338.4/767721/0973 19
HD9875 .K3 1988

Contributions in ethnic studies, 0196-7088 .
(no. 16) Race, ethnicity, and minority housing in the United States /. New York , 1986. xxv, 224 p. ; ISBN 0-313-24848-6 (lib. bdg. : alk. paper) LC Card 86-9971 DDC 363.5/9 19
HD7288.72.U5 R33 1986
NYPL [JLE 87-946]

Contributions in labor studies, 0886-8239 .
(no. 18) Confrontation, class consciousness, and the labor process . Westport, Conn. , 1986. viii,

261 p. ; ISBN 0-313-25140-1 (lib. bdg. : alk. paper) LC Card 85-17734 DDC 305.5/62 19
HD4851 .C63 1986 ***NYPL [JLE 86-3558]***

(no. 21) Lane, A. T. Solidarity or survival? . New York , 1987. xii, 230 p. ; ISBN 0-313-25544-X (lib. bdg. : alk. paper) LC Card 86-25735 DDC 331.6/2/0973 19
HD8081.A5 L36 1987

(no. 22) Comparable worth, pay equity, and public policy /. New York , 1988. xi, 280 p. ; ISBN 0-313-26014-1 (lib. bdg. : alk. paper) LC Card 87-17735 DDC 331.2/1 19
HD6061.2.U6 C656 1988

Contributions in political science, 0147-1066 .
(no. 140) Dependency theory and the return of high politics /. Westport, Conn. , 1986. xii, 270 p. : ISBN 0-313-24860-5 (lib. bdg. : alk. paper) LC Card 85-17745 DDC 337 19
HF1411 .D35 1986 ***NYPL [JLE 86-2911]***

(no. 153) Rural public administration . Westport, Conn. , 1986. ix, 208 p. ; ISBN 0-313-25246-7 (lib. bdg. : alk. paper) LC Card 85-27253 DDC 352/.00722/0973 19
JS425 .R87 1986 ***NYPL [JLE 86-4005]***

(no. 158) Citizen participation in public decision making /. Westport, Conn. , 1987. xii, 237 p. ; ISBN 0-313-25478-8 (lib. bdg. : alk. paper) : LC Card 86-7571 DDC 323/.042/0973 19
JK1764 .C525 1987 ***NYPL [JLD 87-932]***

(no. 174) The French socialists in power, 1981-1986 /. New York , c1987. xii, 212 p. ; ISBN 0-313-25407-9 (lib. bdg. : alk. paper) LC Card 86-33569 DDC 338.944 19
HC276.2 .F699 1987

(no. 179) The Unfulfilled promise of synthetic fuels . New York , 1987. xxii, 225 p. ; ISBN 0-313-25666-7 (lib. bdg. : alk. paper) LC Card 87-247 DDC 338.4/766266/0973 19
HD9502.5.S963 U5475 1987

(no. 181) Hurwitz, Leon. The European Community and the management of international cooperation /. New York , 1987. xvii, 267 p. ; ISBN 0-313-25030-8 (lib. bdg. : alk. paper) LC Card 87-229 DDC 337.1/4 19
HC241.2 .H87 1987

(no. 188) New tides in the Pacific . New York , 1987. xiii, 216 p. ; ISBN 0-313-25625-X (lib. bdg. : alk. paper) LC Card 87-8406 DDC 337.1/9 19
HC681 .N48 1987

(no. 200) Dimensions of hazardous waste politics and policy /. New York , c1988. p. cm. ISBN 0-313-25989-5 (lib. bdg. : alk. paper) LC Card 87-17792 DDC 363.7/28 19
HC110.E5 D56 1988

Contributions in sociology, 0084-9278 .
(no. 62) Housing markets and policies under fiscal austerity /. New York , 1987. x, 263 p. : ISBN 0-313-25409-5 (lib. bdg. : alk. paper) LC Card 86-29603 DDC 363.5 19
HD7287 .H67 1987

(no. 66) Housing and neighborhoods . New York , 1987. xii, 319 p. : ISBN 0-313-25459-1 (lib. bdg. : alk. paper) LC Card 87-7527 DDC 307.3/36 19
HD7287.5 .H47 1987

The contributions of John Maynard Keynes to foreign trade theory and policy, 1909-1946 /. Cammarosano, Joseph R. New York , 1987. 437 p. ; ISBN 0-8240-8076-9 (alk. paper) : LC Card 87-23775 DDC 382.1/04 19
HF1411 .C323 1987

Contributions to econometrics /. Sargan, John Denis. Cambridge , New York , 1988- p. cm. ISBN 0-521-32570-6 (v. 1) LC Card 87-6328 DDC 330/.028 19
HB139 .S37 1988

Contributions to economic analysis. For additional listing of contents, see Old Catalog.
(153 153) Stabilization policy in France and the Federal Republic of Germany /. Amsterdam ; New York : xii, 379 p. : ISBN 0-444-87529-8 LC Card 84-28614 DDC 338.943 19
HC276.2 .S77 1985 ***NYPL [TB (Contributions to economic analysis. no.153)]***

(160) Manohar Rao, M. J. Filtering and control of macroeconomic systems . Amsterdam ; New York : xii, 279 p. : ISBN 0-444-70188-5 (Elsevier Science Pub. Co.) LC Card 86-32928 DDC 339.5/0954 19
HC435.2 .M34 1987

(161) Natural gas markets and contracts /. Amsterdam ; New York : x, 320 p. : ISBN 0-444-70206-7 (U. S.) LC Card 87-5061 DDC 380.1/42285/094 19
HD9581.E82 N37 1987 ***NYPL [TB (Contributions to economic analysis. v.161)]***

(162) The International monetary system and its reform . Amsterdam ; New York : 3 v. : ISBN 0-444-70227-X LC Card 87-6737 DDC 332.4/5 19
HG3881 .I57672 1987

(163) Macroeconomics [i.e. Macroeconomic] impacts of energy shocks /. Amsterdam ; New York : xvi, 331 p. : ISBN 0-444-70247-4 (U. S.) LC Card 87-9035 DDC 338.4/36655/0724 19
HG229 .M315 1987

(164) Macroeconomic medium-term models in the Nordic countries /. Amsterdam ; New York : x, 324 p. : ISBN 0-444-70262-8 (U. S.) LC Card 87-13422 DDC 330.948/00724 19
HC345 .M33 1987

(165) Epstein, Roy J. (Roy Jacob), 1954- A history of econometrics /. Amsterdam ; New York : x, 254 p. ; ISBN 0-444-70267-9 LC Card 87-15308 DDC 330/.028 19
HB139 .E67 1987

(166) Conway, Patrick J. Economic shocks and structural adjustments . Amsterdam ; New York : xiv, 219 p. : ISBN 0-444-70281-4 LC Card 87-15667 DDC 338.9561 19
HC492 .C65 1987

(167) The Computation and modelling of economic equilibria /. Amsterdam ; New York : xiv, 229 p. : ISBN 0-444-70285-7 LC Card 87-15666 DDC 339/.0724 19
HB145 .C64 1987

(168) Regional labour markets . Amsterdam ; New York : xvii, 500 p. : ISBN 0-444-70323-3 LC Card 87-22200 DDC 331.12 19
HD5707 .R37 1987

Contributions to experimental economics. Beiträge zur experimentellen Wirtschaftsforschung. Tübingen, 1967-<78. v. <1-2, 4-8 > LC Card 68-85600 DDC 330 19
HB41 .B29 1967

Contributions to Islamic economic theory . Choudhury, Masudul Alam, 1948- Houndmills, Basingstoke, Hampshire , 1986. xvii, 241 p. : ISBN 0-333-38507-1 ***NYPL [JLD 86-3601]***

Contributions to the study of music and dance, 0193-9041 .
(no. 8) Perris, Arnold. Music as propaganda . Westport, Conn. , c1985. x, 247 p. ; ISBN 0-313-24505-3 (lib. bdg.) LC Card 84-27969 DDC 781/.15 19
ML3838 .P43 1985 ***NYPL [JMD 86-149]***

Control, consensus, or chaos? . Niland, John R. Sydney , Boston , 1985. xiv, 330 p. : ISBN 0-86861-447-5 (pbk.) LC Card 85-70461 DDC 331.89/0994 19
HD8846.5 .N55 1985 ***NYPL [JLD 87-354]***

CONTROL DATA CORPORATION - HISTORY.
Worthy, James C. William C. Norris . Cambridge, Mass. , c1987. xiv, 259 p. : ISBN 0-88730-087-1 LC Card 87-1808 DDC 338.7/61004/0924 B 19
HD9696.C62 N689 1987

El control de gestión en la empresa moderna /. Banegas Banegas, Benito. Madrid , c1985. 127 p. : ISBN 84-256-0432-X LC Card 86-194934
HD37.S66 B36 1985

CONTROL, INVENTORY. see **INVENTORY CONTROL.**

Control obrero colectivo y co-gestión . Lora, Guillermo. La Paz, Bolivia , 1982. 45 p. ; LC Card 83-204234
HD5650 .L73 1982

Control of land and labour in colonial Java . Breman, Jan. Dordrecht, Netherlands , Cinnaminson, N.J., U. S.A. , 1983. xi, 158 p. : ISBN 90-6765-048-X (pbk.) LC Card 86-145678 DDC 333.3/1/5982 19
HD1333.I52 C573 1983

The control of late ancient and medieval population /. Russell, Josiah Cox, 1900- Philadelphia , 1985. xv, 272 p. ; ISBN 0-87169-160-4 LC Card 83-71298
NYPL [JLF 85-844]

The control of municipal budgets . Merriman, David. New York , c1987. x, 170 p. : ISBN 0-89930-217-3 (lib. bdg. : alk. paper) LC Card 87-2495 DDC 352.1/2/0973 19
HJ9157 .M47 1987

CONTROL, PRODUCTION. see **PRODUCTION CONTROL.**

CONTROL (PSYCHOLOGY)
Perris, Arnold. Music as propaganda . Westport, Conn. , c1985. x, 247 p. ; ISBN 0-313-24505-3 (lib. bdg.) LC Card 84-27969 DDC 781/.15 19
ML3838 .P43 1985 ***NYPL [JMD 86-149]***

Winn, Denise, 1950- The manipulated mind . London , c1983. 217 p. ; ISBN 0-86304-025-X LC Card 83-184383 DDC 302.3/3 19
BF632.5 .W56 1983 ***NYPL [JFD 87-1158]***

CONTROL THEORY.
(1982) Murata, Yasuo, 1931- Optimal control methods for linear discrete-time economic systems /. New York , c1982. x, 202 p. ; ISBN 0-387-90709-2 LC Card 82-19137 DDC 338.9/00724 19
HD75.5 .M87 1982 ***NYPL [JLE 87-95]***

(1984) Tu, Pierre N. V. (Pierre Ninh Van) Introductory optimization dynamics . Berlin , New York , 1984. xiii, 387 p. : ISBN 0-387-13305-4 (U. S.)
NYPL [JSE 86-1520]

(1985) Eppers, Jürgen. Zur Feinsteuerung ökonomischer Entscheidungsfolgen /. Frankfurt am Main , c1985. 87 p. : ISBN 3-88129-950-5 : LC Card 86-149502
HD30.23 .E66 1985

(1987) Manohar Rao, M. J. Filtering and control of macroeconomic systems . Amsterdam ; New York : xii, 279 p. : ISBN 0-444-70188-5 (Elsevier Science Pub. Co.) LC Card 86-32928 DDC 339.5/0954 19
HC435.2 .M34 1987

(1987) Seierstad, Atle. Optimal control theory with economic applications /. Amsterdam ; New York : xvi, 445 p. : ISBN 0-444-87923-4 (Elsevier Science Pub. Co.) LC Card 86-16504 DDC 629.8/312 19
QA402.3 .S4 1986 ***NYPL [JLE 87-1123]***

(1988) Kendrick, David A. Feedback . Dordrecht , Boston , 1988. vi, 147 p. : ISBN 90-247-3593-9 LC Card 87-20990 DDC 339.5 19
HB172.5 .K45 1988

CONTROL THEORY - CONGRESSES.
Stochastic optimization . Berlin , New York , c1985. x, 754 p. : ISBN 0-387-16659-9 (U. S.) LC Card 86-11865 DDC 629.8/312 19
QA402.3 .S778 1985 ***NYPL [JSE 86-1596]***

CONTROL THEORY - ECONOMETRIC MODELS.
Kontrolltheoretische Ansätze in makroökonometrischen Modellen /. Frankfurt am Main , New York , c1985. 170 p. : ISBN 3-8204-8314-4 LC Card 86-156081
HB3732 .K68 1985

O controle da base monetária e as flutuações dos multiplicadores monetários e creditícios /. Lemgruber, Antonio Carlos. [Brasília] [1981?] 118 p. : LC Card 85-154853
HG835 .L35 1981

Le Contrôle de qualité : étude présentée à l'occasion du XXXVIIIe congrès national / Conseil supérieur de l'Ordre des experts-comptables et des comptables agréés, avec la participation de la Compagnie nationale des commissaires aux comptes. [Paris] : Le Conseil, [1983] 297 p. : forms ; 24 cm. Includes bibliographical references. ISBN 2-900670-20-9 : LC Card 85-106388
1. Accounting - France - Quality control - Congresses. I. Ordre des experts comptables et des comptables agréés (France). Conseil supérieur. II. Compagnie nationale des commissaires aux comptes (France).
HF5616.F7 C66 1983

CONTROLLERSHIP - CONGRESSES.
Langfristiges Anlagengeschäft, Risiko-Management und Controlling /. Düsseldorf , c1986. 148 p. : ISBN 3-7754-0016-8

LC Card 86-227044
HG4534 .L36 1986

Controlling /. Bramsemann, Rainer, 1942- Wiesbaden , 1980. 238 p. : ISBN 3-409-30592-0 LC Card 85-122847
HG4026 .B664 1980

Controlling in Versorgungsunternehmen /. Bozem, Karlheinz. München , 1986. xiv, 468, 10 p. : ISBN 3-486-26236-X LC Card 87-135246 DDC 363.6/2/0681 19
HD2763 .B66 1986

Controlling interest . Francis, Diane. Toronto, Ont., Canada , c1986. 352 p. ; ISBN 0-7715-9744-4 LC Card 86-218086 DDC 338.8/0971 19
HD2809 .F73 1986

Controlling interest rate risk : new techniques and applications formoney managements / [edited by] Robert B. Platt. New York : Wiley, c1986. xv, 414 p. : ill. ; 24 cm. (Wiley professional banking and finance series, 0733-8945) Includes bibliographies and index. ISBN 0-471-82354-6 : LC Card 85-22504 DDC 332.8/2 19
1. Interest rates - Addresses, essays, lectures. 2. Investments - Addresses, essays, lectures. 3. Risk - Addresses, essays, lectures. I. Platt, Robert B., 1936-. II. Series.
HG1621 .C6 1986 ***NYPL [JLE 86-2850]***

Controlling-Praxis .
(CP 12) Posselt, Siegfried G. Budgetkontrolle als Instrument zur Unternehmungssteuerung /. Darmstadt , c1986. 272 p. : ISBN 3-87820-068-4 LC Card 87-113335 DDC 658.1/54 19
HG4028.B8 P67 1986

(CP 5) Melcher, Horst. Aufbau eines Controllingsystems für Consulting-Unternehmen /. Darmstadt , c1982. 276 p. : ISBN 3-87820-052-8 LC Card 83-110639
HD69.C6 M45 1982

Controlling the federal bureaucracy /. Riley, Dennis D. Philadelphia , 1987. xiv, 200 ; ISBN 0-87722-455-2 (alk. paper) : LC Card 86-14469 DDC 353.07/5 19
JK421 .R52 1987 ***NYPL [JLD 87-1396]***

Controlling the growth of monetary aggregates /. Rasche, Robert H. Boston , c1987. xviii, 212 p. : ISBN 0-89838-226-2 : LC Card 87-3737 DDC 332.4/6 19
HG230.3 .R37 1987

Controlling work stress . Matteson, Michael T. San Francisco, Calif. , 1987. xx, 378 p. ; ISBN 1-555-42062-1 (alk. paper) LC Card 87-45503 DDC 658.3/82 19
HF5548.85 .M378 1987

Il controllo degli inquinamenti delle acque . Lewanski, Rodolfo. Milano , 1986. 194 p. : ISBN 88-14-00753-5 : LC Card 86-160300
HC310.W32 L48 1986

Controversies in political economy . Harcourt, Geoffrey Colin. New York , 1986. 293 p. ; ISBN 0-8147-3437-5 : LC Card 85-31055 DDC 330.1 19
HB75 .H33 1986 ***NYPL [JLD 86-3571]***

CONURBATIONS. see **METROPOLITAN AREAS.**

Convegno C.I.D.I.S. (1980 : Iesolo, Italy) Credito e finanziarie regionali : atti del Convegno C.I.D.I.S., Centro internazionale di studi giuridici : Jesolo, 19-21 settembre, 1980. Padova : CEDAM : Giunta regionale del Veneto, c1983. vi, 148 p. ; 24 cm. Includes bibliographical references. LC Card 85-215231
1. Commercial credit - Government policy - Italy - Congresses. 2. Credit - Law and legislation - Italy - Congresses. 3. Industrial promotion - Italy - Congresses. 4. Italy - Economic conditions - 1976- - Regional disparities - Congresses. I. Title.
HG3729.I72 C66 1980

Convegno Genova nell'economia marittimo/portuale in Europa e nel mondo (1982 : Genoa, Italy) Atti del Convegno Genova nell'economia marittimo/portuale in Europa e nel mondo : innovazione, competitività, occupazione : Genova, 17-18-19 giugno 1982. Genova : Comune di Genova, [1982?] 135 p. : col. ill., ports. ; 29 cm. LC Card 86-105783
1. Harbors - Italy - Genoa - Congresses. 2. Shipping - Italy - Genoa - Congresses. 3. Genoa (Italy) - Commerce - Congresses. I. Genoa (Italy).
HE558.G3 C66 1982

Convegno "Il lavoro si crea" (1985 : Ravenna, Italy) Il lavoro si crea : impresa e lavoro : job creation in Europa : atti del Convegno, Ravenna, 24-25 ottobre 1985 / presentazione di Gianni De Michelis. Milano, Italy : F. Angeli, c1986. 305 p. : ill. ; 22 cm. Sponsored by the Cooperativa muratori & cementisti. LC Card 86-232529
1. Labor supply - Europe - Congresses. 2. Unemployment - Europe - Congresses. I. Cooperativa muratori & cementisti (Ravenna, Italy). II. Title.
HD5764.A6 C68 1985

Convegno "La scienza politica in Italia, bilancio e prospettive" (1984 : Milan, Italy) Politica ed economia : fenomenti politici e analisi economiche : atti del Convegno "La scienza politica in Italia, bilancio e prospettive", Milano, maggio 1984. Milano, Italy : F. Angeli, c1987. 159 p. ; 22 cm. (Collana di scienza politica . 4) Includes bibliographies. LC Card 87-139661
1. Italy - Economic policy - Congresses. 2. Italy - Social policy - Congresses. 3. Italy - Politics and government - 1976- - Congresses. I. Title. II. Series.
HC305 .C6767 1984

Convegno nazionale del PCI (1982 : Milan, Italy) Le nuove frontiere dello sviluppo : informatica, microelettronica e tecnologie associate, quale futuro per l'Italia? / Convegno nazionale del PCI, Dipartimento economico e problemi sociali ; a cura di Mario Grasso. Milano, Italy : F. Angeli, c1983. 368 p. ; 22 cm. LC Card 85-174697
1. Electronic industries - Italy - Congresses. 2. Microelectronics industry - Italy - Congresses. I. Grasso, Mario. II. Partito comunista italiano. Dipartimento economico e problemi sociali. III. Title.
HD9696.A3 I727 1982

Convegno nazionale di studi storici (1979 : Schio, Italy) Schio e Alessandro Rossi : imprenditorialità, politica, cultura e paesaggi sociali del secondo Ottocento / a cura di Giovanni L. Fontana. Roma : Edizioni di storia e letteratura, 1985-1986. 2 v. (1487 p., [1] folded leaf of plates) : ill. (some col.) ; 25 cm. (Storia ed economia . 18-19) "Atti del Convegno nazionale di studi storici, Schio, 14-16 dicembre 1979"--T.p. verso. Folded leaf of plates mounted on p. [3] of cover, v. 2. Includes bibliographical references and indexes. LC Card 87-110167
1. Rossi, Alessandro, 1819-1898 - Congresses. 2. Industrialists - Italy - Biography - Congresses. 3. Schio (Italy) - Industries - History - 19th century - Congresses. 4. Labor and laboring classes - Italy - Schio - History - 19th century - Congresses. 5. Textile industry - Italy - Schio - History - 19th century - Congresses. I. Fontana, Giovanni L. II. Title. III. Series.
HC302.5.R6 C66 1979

Convegno nazionale "Qualche idea sui fiumi" (1983 : Iesi, Italy) Atti del Convegno nazionale "Qualche idea sui fiumi," Jesi, aprile 1983. Ancona : Lavoro editoriale, c1983-c1984. 2 v. ; 21 cm. (Dibattiti contemporanei) Includes bibliographies. CONTENTS. - v. 1. La risorsa fiume -- v. 2. Progetto fiume. ISBN 88-7663-030-9 (v. 1) : LC Card 84-119835
1. Water resources development - Italy - Congresses. 2. Rivers - Italy - Regulation - Congresses. I. Title. II. Series.
HD1697.I8 C62 1983 ***NYPL [JLK 87-40]***

Convegno "Sviluppo della finanza internazionale e interdipendenza dei sistemi finanziari" (1983 : Università di Pavia) Sviluppo della finanza internazionale e interdipendenza dei sistemi finanziari . [Italy] [1984] iv, 204 p. : ISBN 88-14-00203-7 : LC Card 84-238589 DDC 332/.042 19
HG205.S85 S85 1984 ***NYPL [JLE 86-482]***

La Convención, el trabajo y sus luchas sociales / Marco Aurelio Ugarte Ochoa [editor]. [Peru? : s.n., 1983] (Cusco, Perú : Impr. AMAUTA) 152, vii p., [12] leaves of plates : ill. ; 20 cm. "Homenaje en su 126 aniversario." Includes bibliographies. LC Card 87-127171 DDC 330.985/3 19
1. La Convención (Peru) - Economic conditions. 2. Labor and laboring classes - Peru - La Convención - History. 3. La Convención (Peru) - Biography. 4. La Convención (Peru) - History. I. Ugarte Ochoa, Marco Aurelio.
HC228.C65 C66 1983

CONVENIENCE STORES - UNITED STATES.
NACS convenience store customer purchasing patterns research report /. [Falls Church, Va. , 1985?] vi, 76 p. : LC Card 86-157648 DDC 381/.1 19
HF5469.55.U62 N33 1985
NYPL [JLF 87-810]

CONVENIENCE STORES - UNITED STATES - AUTOMATION.
Survey of automation in the convenience store industry /. Alexandria, Va. (1605 King St., Alexandria 22314-2792) , c1986. vii, 39, 9 p. : LC Card 87-147614 DDC 381/.1 19
HF5469.55.U62 S87 1986

CONVENIENCE STORES - UNITED STATES - AUTOMATION - STATISTICS.
Survey of automation in the convenience store industry /. Alexandria, Va. (1605 King St., Alexandria 22314-2792) , c1986. vii, 39, 9 p. : LC Card 87-147614 DDC 381/.1 19
HF5469.55.U62 S87 1986

CONVENTIONS (CONGRESSES) see **CONGRESSES AND CONVENTIONS.**

Convergenze tra capitalismo e socialismo : quindici anni di discussioni / a cura di Carlo Schneider. Milano : Giuffrè, 1978. lxxi, 399 p. ; 23 cm. Includes bibliographical references and index. LC Card 80-478455
1. Capitalism - Addresses, essays, lectures. 2. Socialism - Addresses, essays, lectures. I. Schneider, Carlo.
HB501 .C727 ***NYPL [JLD 81-646]***

The Converging technologies series.
Meyer, N. Dean. The information edge /. New York , c1987. xvii, 333 p. ; ISBN 0-07-041782-2 LC Card 86-222546 DDC 651.8 19
HF5547.5 .M495 1987

Converging voice/data/video technologies at the workstation / Robert Moran, project analyst. Stamford, Conn., U. S.A. : Business Communications Co., c1986. v, 119 leaves ; 29 cm. (Business opportunity report . G-096) "March 1986"--T.p. verso. ISBN 0-89336-466-5 (pbk.) LC Card 87-168057 DDC 380.1/45004 19
1. Electronic office machine industry. 2. Computer industry. 3. Data transmission equipment industry. 4. Word processing equipment industry. 5. Market surveys. I. Moran, Robert, 1928-. II. Series.
HD9801.A2 C66 1986

CONVERSATION PIECE (PORTRAIT PAINTING) - MEXICO - MEXICO CITY.
Cortina Portilla, Manuel. Algo sobre la plata en México en el siglo XVIII /. México , 1986. 48 p., [1] folded leaf of plates : LC Card 87-404604 DDC 332.4/042/097253 19
HG661 .C67 1986

Conversion of accounting records. Great Britain. Decimal Currency Board. London, 1969. [1], 33 p. ISBN 0-11-700407-3 : LC Card 77-489376 DDC 657
HF5635 .G777

The conversion of rental housing to condominiums and cooperatives . United States. Dept. of Housing and Urban Development. Office of Policy Development and Research. Division of Policy Studies. [Washington, D.C.] , 1982. 95 p. : ***NYPL [JLF 86-442]***

CONVERSION OF WASTE PRODUCTS. see **RECYCLING (WASTE, ETC.)**

CONVERTIBLE BONDS - FRANCE.
Augros, Jean-Claude. Finance . Paris , c1985. 320 p. : ISBN 2-7178-0911-2 : LC Card 85-219227 DDC 332.64/52/0944 19
HG6042 .A94 1985 ***NYPL [JLE 87-295]***

CONVERTIBLE BONDS - GERMANY (WEST)
Janssen, Friedrich, 1948- Bedeutung und Ausstattung von Wandel- und Optionsanleihen /. Göttingen , 1982. 279 p. : ISBN 3-509-01319-0 LC Card 83-240528
HG5501 .J35 1982

CONVERTIBLE BONDS - INDIA.
CONVERTIBLE BONDS - UNITED STATES.
Wilson, Richard S. Corporate senior securities . Chicago, Ill. , c1987. xiv, 459 p. : ISBN 0-917253-79-5 : LC Card 87-6980 DDC 332.63/2 19
HG4963 .W56 1987

CONVERTIBLE PREFERRED STOCKS - GERMANY (WEST)

Janssen, Friedrich, 1948- Bedeutung und Ausstattung von Wandel- und Optionsanleihen /. Göttingen , 1982. 279 p. : ISBN 3-509-01319-0 LC Card 83-240528
HG5501 .J35 1982

CONVERTIBLE PREFERRED STOCKS - UNITED STATES.
Wilson, Richard S. Corporate senior securities . Chicago, Ill. , c1987. xiv, 459 p. : ISBN 0-917253-79-5 : LC Card 87-6980 DDC 332.63/2 19
HG4963 .W56 1987

Convivência do homem com a seca e irrigação no Nordeste / conferências de Raymundo Fonseca Souza ... [et al.], no auditório do Desenbanco, em 26 de janeiro de 1984. [Salvador, Brazil] : Fundação Bahiana para Estudos Econômicos e Sociais, [1984] 76 p. : ill. ; 23 cm. LC Card 87-130774 DDC 333.91/3/09813 19
1. Irrigation - Brazil, Northeast - Congresses. 2. Seca - Congresses. I. Souza, Raymundo Fonseca. II. Fundação Bahiana para Estudos Econômicos e Sociais.
HD1741.B82 N624 1984

Conway, H. McKinley (Hobart McKinley), 1920- Facility planning technology /. Norcross, Ga. , c1987. viii, 935 p. : ISBN 0-910436-26-6 LC Card 86-72097 DDC 658.2/1 19
HD30.28 .F33 1987

Conway, Patrick J. Economic shocks and structural adjustments : Turkey after 1973 / Patrick J. Conway. Amsterdam ; New York : North-Holland ; xiv, 219 p. : ill. ; 23 cm. (Contributions to economic analysis. 166) Bibliography: p. 207-219. ISBN 0-444-70281-4 LC Card 87-15667 DDC 338.9561 19
1. Turkey - Economic conditions - 1960- - Econometric models. 2. Turkey - Economic policy - Econometric models. I. Title. II. Series.
HC492 .C65 1987

Conybeare, John A. C. Trade wars : the theory and practice of international commercial rivalry / John A.C. Conybeare. New York : Columbia University Press, 1987. xv, 319 p. ; 24 cm. (The Political economy of international change) Bibliography: p. [295]-313. Includes index. ISBN 0-231-06234-6 LC Card 87-8097 DDC 382 19
1. Competition, International. 2. Competition, International - History. I. Title. II. Series.
HF1414 .C665 1987

COOK, A. J. (ARTHUR JAMES)
Davies, Paul, 1951- A.J. Cook /. Wolfeboro, NH , c1987. p. cm. ISBN 0-7190-2160-X LC Card 87-11114 DDC 331.88/122/0924 B 19
HD8393.C63 D38 1987

Cook, Alice. Greenham women everywhere : dreams, ideas and actions from the women's peace movement / Alice Cook & Gwyn Kirk. Boston, Mass. : South End Press, 1984, c1983. 127, [1] p. : ill. ; 20 cm. Bibliography: p. [128] ISBN 0-89608-199-0
1. Antinuclear movement - Great Britain. 2. Antinuclear movement. 3. Nuclear disarmament. I. Kirk, Gwyn. II. Title. ***NYPL [JLD 87-215]***

Cook, Barbara Ensor, 1950- Rothberg, Diane S., 1930- Part-time professional /. Washington, D.C. , c1985. 158 p. ; ISBN 0-87491-786-7 (pbk.) : LC Card 85-19964 DDC 650.1/4 19
HD5110.2.U5 R67 1985
NYPL [JLE 86-2582]

Cook, Harold F., 1929- Pioneer American businessman in Korea : the life and times of Walter Davis Townsend / by Harold F. Cook. Seoul, Korea : Published for Royal Asiatic Society, Korea Branch by Seoul Computer Press, 1981. ix, 104 p. : port. ; 24 cm. (Monograph series / Royal Asiatic Society, Korea Branch . no. 5) Includes index. Bibliography: p. 96-100. LC Card 83-140523 DDC 382/.09519/0730924 B 19
1. Townsend, Walter Davis, 1856-1918. 2. Merchants - United States - Biography. 3. Merchants - Korea - Biography. 4. Korea - History - 1864-1910. I. Series: Royal Asiatic Society of Great Britain and Ireland. Korea Branch. Monograph series , no. 5. II. Title.
HF3023.T68 C66 1981
NYPL [JFE 86-4650]

Cook, James R., 1938- The start-up entrepreneur : how you can succeed in building your own company into a major enterprise starting from scratch / James R. Cook.1st Perennial Library ed. New York : Perennial Library, 1987, c1986. xii, 306 p. ; 20 cm. Bibliography: p. 293-296. Includes index. ISBN 0-06-097070-7 (pbk.) : LC Card 86-45650 DDC 658.4/2 19
1. New business enterprises. 2. Entrepreneur. I. Title.
HD62.5 .C664 1987

Cook, Mark. Personnel selection and productivity / Mark Cook. Chichester [West Sussex] ; New York : Wiley, c1988. p. cm. (Wiley series in psychology and productivity at work) Bibliography: p. Includes index. ISBN 0-471-91148-8 : LC Card 87-21070 DDC 658.3/112 19
1. Employee selection. I. Title. II. Series.
HF5549.5.S38 C66 1988

Cook, Mary F., 1937- New directions in human resources : a handbook / Mary F. Cook. Englewood Cliffs, N.J. : Prentice-Hall, c1987. xxx, 466 p. : ill. ; 29 cm. Includes index. ISBN 0-13-612433-X LC Card 87-1286 DDC 658.3 19
1. Personnel management. I. Title.
HF5549 .C7244 1987

Cook, Noble David. Numeracion general de todas las personas de ambos sexos, edades y calidades q[ue] se hà hecho en esta ciudad de Lima, año de 1700 /. Lima , 1985. xv, 358 p. : LC Card 87-400680
HA1069.L7 N86 1985

Cook, P. (Paul).
State, foreign enterprise and industrial capitalism in West Africa. Transnationals and development. Manchester, England , 1984. i, 64 p. ; ***NYPL [JLD 86-3224]***

Cook, Robert F., 1943- Public service employment : the experience of a decade / Robert F. Cook, Charles F. Adams Jr., V. Lane Rawlins, and associates. Kalamazoo, Mich. : W.E. Upjohn Institute for Employment Research, 1985. xiii, 131 p. ; 23 cm. Includes bibliographies. ISBN 0-88099-031-7 (pbk.) LC Card 85-22495 DDC 331.13/77/0973 19
1. Public service employment - United States. 2. Manpower policy - United States. 3. Occupational training - United States. 4. United States - Full employment policies. I. Adams, Charles F., 1945-. II. Rawlins, V. Lane. III. Title.
HD5713.6.U54 C66 1985
NYPL [JLE 86-3877]

Cook, W. Rupert. Canadian statistical data : an introduction to sources and interpretation / by W. Rupert Cook and Joan Mount. [Canada] : Micromedia Ltd., [1985?] vi, 218 p. : ill. ; 28 cm. Includes bibliographies and index. LC Card 87-118992 DDC 354.710081/9 19
1. Canada - Statistical services - History. 2. Statistics Canada - History. I. Mount, Joan. II. Title.
HA37.C26 C66 1985

Cook, Wade.
Pay no taxes with real estate / Wade B. Cook. 1984 rev. ed. Orem, Utah : Investment and Tax Publications, c1982. xvii, 152, [7] p. : ill. ; 28 cm. Bibliography: p. [153]-[159] ISBN 0-910019-09-6 (pbk.) LC Card 86-228579 DDC 343.7305/46 347.303546 19
1. Real property tax - United States. 2. Tax shelters - United States. 3. Income tax - United States. I. Title.
HJ4181 .C66 1982

Real estate : the best game in town / Wade B. Cook. Orem, Utah : ITP, c1983. 142 p. : ill. ; 21 cm. Bibliography : p. 137-142. ISBN 0-910019-10-X (pbk.) LC Card 86-220658 DDC 332.63/24 19
1. Real eatate investment. I. Title.
HD1382.5 .C6697 1983

Cook, Wade B. How to pick up foreclosures : a step-by-step guide for getting there before the auction / Wade B. Cook. Tempe, AZ : Regency Books ; New York : Distributed by Kampmann, c1983. xviii, 130 p. : ill. ; 25 cm. ISBN 0-910019-04-5 LC Card 86-218222 DDC 332.63/244 19
1. Real estate investment. 2. House buying. 3. Foreclosure. I. Title.
HD1382.5 .C6694 1983

Cooke, Philip. Global restructuring local response . London , Merstham, Redhill, Surrey , c1986. 308 p. : ISBN 0-86226-174-0 (pbk.) LC Card 86-197207 DDC 331.12/0941 19
HD6331.2.G7 G57 1986

COOKERY, LOW-CALORIE. see **LOW-CALORIE DIET.**

COOKERY - PICKLES. see **CANNING AND PRESERVING.**

COOKERY - PRESERVES. see **CANNING AND PRESERVING.**

COOKERY (SEA FOOD)
(1984) Dore, Ian, 1941- Fresh seafood, the commercial buyer's guide . Huntington, N.Y. , c1984. 375 p. : ISBN 0-943738-07-5 : LC Card 84-5174 DDC 641.3/92/0687 19
HD9450.5 .D67 1984 ***NYPL [JSD 86-449]***

COOKIE INDUSTRY - UNITED STATES.
Fields, Debbi. "One smart cookie" . New York , c1987. 173 p., [16] p. of plates : ISBN 0-671-61838-5 LC Card 87-15172 DDC 338.7/6647525/0924 B 19
HD9058.C65 F544 1987

COOKWARE INDUSTRY - UNITED STATES.
Cholmar, Sidney. New directions in microwave ovens . Stamford, Conn., U. S.A. , c1985. x, 119 leaves ; ISBN 0-89336-459-2 (pbk.) LC Card 87-163958 DDC 381/.4568388 19
HD9971.5.S763 U53 1985

Cooley, Philip L. Business financial management / Philip L. Cooley, Peyton Foster Roden. Chicago : Dryden Press, c1988. xxv, 924, [34] p. : ill. (some col.) ; 24 cm. Includes bibliographies and index. ISBN 0-03-009979-X LC Card 87-20079 DDC 658.1/5 19
1. Corporations - Finance. 2. Business enterprises - Finance. I. Roden, Peyton Foster. II. Title.
HG4026 .C63 1988

Cooley, Walter L. Vermont's urban population, 1950 to 1985 / Walter L. Cooley. Burlington, Vt. (Box 70, 60 Main St., Burlington 05402) : Vermont Dept. of Health, [1986] 9 leaves : ill. ; 28 cm. (Public health statistics bulletin) Caption title. "May 1986." Includes bibliographical references. LC Card 86-622184 DDC 304.6/09743 19
1. Vermont - Population - Statistics. I. Title. II. Series.
HA675 .C66 1986

COOLGARDIE (W.A.) - HISTORY.
Wattone, Mike, 1939- Quest for gold /. Scarborough, W.A. , 1985. 103 p. : ISBN 0-949731-03-X (pbk.) LC Card 86-142484 DDC 338.2/741/09941 19
HD9536.A83 C669 1985
NYPL [JLE 87-662]

Coomans, Géry, 1949- La production sociale des femmes / Géry Coomans. Bruxelles : Editions de l'Université de Bruxelles, c1983. 223 p. : ill. ; 24 cm. "Centre d'histoire économique et sociale." Bibliography: p. 211-218. ISBN 2-8004-0820-0 : LC Card 84-199167
1. Women - Employment - Belgium. 2. Wages - Women - Belgium. 3. Family - Belgium. I. Title.
HD6158 .C66 1983

Coombs, Rod. Economics and technological change / Rod Coombs, Paolo Saviotti, and Vivien Walsh. Totowa, N.J. : Rowman & Littlefield, 1987. xv, 296 p. : ill. ; 23 cm. Bibliography: p. 279-292. Includes index. ISBN 0-8476-7545-9 : LC Card 86-28000 DDC 338/.06 19
1. Technological innovations - Economic aspects. 2. Industrial organization. 3. Technological innovations - Government policy. 4. Technology and state - Citizen participation. I. Saviotti, Paolo. II. Walsh, Vivien. III. Title.
HC79.T4 C67 1987

Coon, Randal C. North Dakota lignite industry's contribution to the state economy / Randal C. Coon and F. Larry Leistritz. Fargo, N.D. : Dept. of Agricultural Economics, Agricultural Experiment Station, North Dakota State University, [1986] v, 40 p. : ill. ; 28 cm. (Agricultural economics miscellaneous report . no 99) Cover title. "June 1986." Bibliography: p. [39]-40. LC Card 86-623006 DDC 338.2/722/09784 19
1. Lignite industry - North Dakota. 2. North Dakota - Economic conditions. I. Leistritz, F. Larry. II. Series: Agricultural economics miscellaneous report (Fargo, N.D.) , no. 99. III. Title.
HD9559.L6 U5525 1986

Cooner, James J. Investing in municipal bonds : balancing risks and rewards / James J. Cooner. New York : Wiley, c1987. xvi, 233 p. : ill. ; 25 cm. Bibliography: p. 226-227. Includes index. ISBN 0-471-84941-3 LC Card 86-28911 DDC 332.63/233/0973 19
1. Municipal bonds - United States. I. Title.
HG4952 .C66 1987

Coop image series.
Glimpses of cooperatives through press . New Delhi , 1986- v. <1- > ; LC Card 87-900398 DDC 334/.0954 19
HD3538 .G55 1986

Cooper, Alison. Bowers, Cathy. U. S. and Canadian investment in South Africa and Namibia . Washington, D.C. , c1986. xiii, 238 p. ; ISBN 0-931035-10-4 (pbk.) LC Card 86-209149 DDC 338.8/8973/068025 19
HG5851.A3 B69 1986

Cooper & Lybrand. Tax incentives for community revitalization in Florida /. Tallahassee, Fla. [1983] 45 p. ; LC Card 86-623222 DDC 343.75906/6 347.590366 19
HJ4655.F64 T39 1983

Cooper, Arnold C. Smith, Clayton G. Established companies diversifying into young industries . West Lafayette, Ind. [1986] 27, 15 p. ; LC Card 86-621740 DDC 658/.001/9 s 338.8/3 19
HD6483 .P8 no. 893 HD2755.8

Cooper Brothers & Co.
A History of Cooper Brothers & Co., 1854-1954. New York , 1986, c1954. xi, 116 p., [13] leaves of plates : ISBN 0-8240-7881-0 (alk. paper) : LC Card 86-25720 DDC 338.7/61657/0941 19
HF5616.G73 C665 1986

COOPER BROTHERS & CO. - HISTORY.
A History of Cooper Brothers & Co., 1854-1954. New York , 1986, c1954. xi, 116 p., [13] leaves of plates : ISBN 0-8240-7881-0 (alk. paper) : LC Card 86-25720 DDC 338.7/61657/0941 19
HF5616.G73 C665 1986

Cooper, C. J. Kotzé, D. J. (David Jacobus) Energy projections for South Africa /. Johannesburg, Republic of South Africa , 1985. 125 p. : ISBN 0-86970-259-9 (pbk.) : LC Card 86-219416 DDC 333.79/13/0968 19
HD9502.S56 K68 1985

Cooper, Cary L.
Davidson, Marilyn. Stress and the woman manager /. Oxford [Oxfordshire], 1983. 230 p. ; ISBN 0-85520-623-3 ***NYPL [JLE 85-1426]***

Job stress and blue collar work /. Chichester [West Sussex] , New York , c1985. ix, 243 p. : ISBN 0-471-90811-8 : LC Card 85-12022 DDC 158.7 19
HF5548.85 .J64 1985 ***NYPL [JLE 86-2412]***

Women and information technology /. Chichester , New York , c1987. viii, 283 p. : ISBN 0-471-91603-X : LC Card 87-10554 DDC 331.4 19
HD6053 .W636 1987

Cooper, Frederick, 1947- Struggle for the city . Beverly Hills , c1983. 319 p. : ISBN 0-8039-2067-9 LC Card 83-11196 DDC 305.5/62/096 19
HD8774 .S87 1983 ***NYPL [JLD 83-3496]***

Cooper, George. Land and power in Hawaii : the Democratic years / George Cooper, Gavan Daws. Honolulu, Hawaii : Benchmark Books, c1985. x, 518 p. ; 25 cm. Includes index. Bibliography: p. [460]-487. ISBN 0-9615052-0-6 : LC Card 85-72037 DDC 333.73/13/09969 19
1. Democratic Party (Hawaii). 2. Land use - Government policy - Hawaii. 3. Real estate development - Government policy - Hawaii. 4. Hawaii - Politics and government - 1900-1959. 5. Hawaii - Politics and government - 1959-. I. Daws, Gavan. II. Title.
HD266.H3 C66 1985 ***NYPL [JLE 87-361]***

Cooper, Robin, 1951- CABIS, computer-aided bookkeeping instruction system / by Robin Cooper, Michael Vitale, and Harvard Business School. Reading, Mass. : Addison-Wesley, c1987. p. cm. ISBN 0-201-11307-4 (user's manual) LC Card 86-32148 DDC 657/.2/02855369 19
1. CABIS (Computer program). 2. Bookkeeping - Computer-assisted instruction. 3. Accounting - Computer-assisted instruction. I. Vitale, Michael. II. Harvard University. Graduate School of Business Administration. III. Title.
HF5630 .C68 1987

Cooper, Russell W., 1955- Wage and employment patterns in labor contracts : microfoundations and macroeconomic implications / Russell W. Cooper. Chur, Switzerland ; New York : Harwood Academic, c1987. viii, 80 p. : ill. ; 22 cm. (Fundamentals of pure and applied economics, 0191-1708 . v. 19.) Bibliography: p. 71-75. Includes index. ISBN 3-7186-0378-0 (pbk.) LC Card 86-31947 DDC 331.12/5 19
1. Wages. 2. Employment (Economic theory). 3. Labor contract. I. Series: Fundamentals of pure and applied economics , v. 19. II. Title.
HD4909 .C57 1987

Cooper, Thomas W.
State highway finance trends. Highway finance : two reports on highway finance / prepared by the Office of Highway Planning. [Washington] [1983] iii, 96 p. ;
NYPL [JLF 87-431]

Cooperação e coexistência /. Pinto, L. M. Teixeira (Luis Maria Teixeira) [Lisboa] , 1965. 205 p., [1] folded leaf of plates : LC Card 85-205639
HF1411 .P52 1965

Cooperación empresaria--estudios.
Sourrouille, Juan V. Inversiones extranjeras en América Latina . Buenos Aires [1984] viii, 142 p. : LC Card 86-183036
HG5160.5.A3 S64 1984

La Cooperación empresarial argentino-brasileña : estudio de las posibilidades y contribuciones de las inversiones conjuntas y transferencia de tecnología entre la Argentina y Brasil. [Buenos Aires] : BID/INTAL, 1983. viii, 160 p. ; 28 cm. Includes bibliographical references. LC Card 87-125370 DDC 338.8/8/0981 19
1. Business enterprises - Argentina. 2. Business enterprises - Brazil. 3. Joint ventures - Argentina. 4. Joint ventures - Brazil. 5. Technology transfer - Argentina. 6. Technology transfer - Brazil. I. Institute for Latin American Integration.
HD2829 .C66 1983

Cooperación empresarial--estudios.
Exenciones arancelarias e integración /. [Buenos Aires] , 1986. 273 p. ; LC Card 87-400577 DDC 382.7/1/098 19
HF1733.L29 E96 1986

Cooperación Técnica Suiza. International Labour Organisation. Desarrollo de la formación profesional rural . Ginebra , 1982. ii, 30 p. : ISBN 92-2-303048-X LC Card 84-113985
HD5715.5.H8 I58 1982

Cooperare e competere / testi di Lorenzo Sintini ... [et al.]. 1a ed. in "Campi del sapere". Milano : Feltrinelli, 1986. 2 v. : ill. ; 23 cm. (Campi del sapere) Includes bibliographical references. ISBN 88-07-10058-4 (v. 1) : LC Card 87-125969
1. Cooperation - Congresses. 2. Cooperation - Italy - Congresses. I. Sintini, Lorenzo.
HD2953 .C66 1986

Co-operation and nationality . Russell, George William, 1867-1935. Dublin , c1982. 103 p. ; ISBN 0-7165-0335-2 (pbk.) LC Card 82-192895 DDC 334/.683/09417 19
HD1491.I6 R87 1982 ***NYPL [JLD 86-2358]***

COOPERATION - AUSTRALIA - VICTORIA.
Victoria. Ministerial Advisory Committee on Co-operation. The co-operative way . Melbourne , 1986. viii, 151 p. : ISBN 0-7241-5172-9 (pbk.) LC Card 87-158122 DDC 334/.09945 19
HD3570.A6 V538 1986

COOPERATION - BRAZIL - PARANÁ (STATE) - CONGRESSES.
Encontro Estadual de Cooperativismo (1979 : Curitiba, Brazil) Anais /. [Curitiba] [1979] 41 leaves : LC Card 84-223142
HD3475.A3 P364 1979

COOPERATION - BULGARIA - HISTORY.
Istoriia na kooperativnoto dvizhenie v Bŭlgariia /. Sofiia , 1986- v. <1 > ; LC Card 87-158327
HD3531.5.A4 I87 1986

COOPERATION - CONGRESSES.
Cooperare e competere /. Milano , 1986. 2 v. : ISBN 88-07-10058-4 (v. 1) : LC Card 87-125969
HD2953 .C66 1986

COOPERATION - DENMARK - RIBE (AMT) - HISTORY.
Just, Flemming. Brugsforeningsbevægelsen 1866-1920 . Esbjerg , 1984. 192 p. : ISBN 87-88521-04-4 LC Card 85-114707
HD3059.A6 R524 1984

COOPERATION - DEVELOPING COUNTRIES.
Klöwer, Gerd Günter. Genossenschaften in Entwicklungsländern . Göttingen , 1981. 56 p. ; ISBN 3-509-01085-X LC Card 82-174706 DDC 334/.09172/4 19
HD3575 .K58 1981 ***NYPL [JLE 86-3343]***

COOPERATION - ECUADOR.
Garzón L., Isaías. Manual de cooperativismo estudiantil ecuatoriano /. Riobamba, Ecuador [1983?] 244 p. : LC Card 86-134182
HD2965 .G38 1983

Coopération et aménagement (France) Laborie, Jean Paul. La politique française d'amenagement du territoire de 1950 à 1985 /. Paris , 1985. 176 p., [8] p. of plates : ISBN 2-11-001488-1(pbk.) : ***NYPL [JLG 87-38]***

COOPERATION - FRANCE.
Boursier, François, 1947- L'économie sociale, mythes et réalités /. Lyon [1984] 108 p. : ISBN 2-85008-045-4 : LC Card 84-154709 DDC 334/.0944 19
HD3494 .B63 1984 ***NYPL [JLD 87-330]***

COOPERATION - FRANCE - HISTORY.
Boursier, François, 1947- L'économie sociale, mythes et réalités /. Lyon [1984] 108 p. : ISBN 2-85008-045-4 : LC Card 84-154709 DDC 334/.0944 19
HD3494 .B63 1984 ***NYPL [JLD 87-330]***

COOPERATION - GERMANY.
Novy, Klaus. Illustrierte Geschichte der Gemeinwirtschaft . Berlin , c1985. 239 p. : ISBN 3-8012-0111-2 LC Card 86-122604
HD3498 .N68 1985

COOPERATION - GERMANY (WEST) - HISTORY.
Aschhoff, Gunther, 1934- Das deutsche Genossenschaftswesen . Frankfurt am Main , 1985. 167 p. : ISBN 3-7819-0345-1 LC Card 86-145522
HD3038 .A77 1985

Köhler, Holm-Detlev, 1956- Ökonomie und Autonomie . Frankfurt , c1986. 213 p. ; ISBN 3-925798-24-2 LC Card 87-108165 DDC 334/.0943 19
HD3498 .K63 1986

COOPERATION - GERMANY (WEST) - MANAGEMENT.
Lipfert, Helmut. Mitgliederförderndes Kooperations- und Konkurrenzmanagement in genossenschaftlichen Systemen /. Göttingen , c1986. xvii, 302 p. : ISBN 3-525-12754-5 LC Card 86-235180 DDC 334/.068 19
HD3498 .L53 1986

COOPERATION - GREAT BRITAIN.
Dunman, Jack. Co-ops--the future. London [1969] 20 p. ISBN 0-900302-01-1 : LC Card 77-428347 DDC 334/.5/0942
HD3486 .D84

COOPERATION - HISTORY.
Nagy, László, 1914- Szövetkezetelmélet, szövetkezetpolitika, szövetkezeti jog /. Budapest , 1986. 299, [1] p. ; ISBN 963-221-904-X : LC Card 87-138020 DDC 334/.09439 19
HD3492.5.A4 N34 1986

COOPERATION - HUNGARY.
Gyenes, Antal. Szövetkezetipolitikai, szövetkezetelméleti ismeretek /. Budapest , 1974. 217 p. ; LC Card 87-113832
HD3492.5.A4 G94 1974

COOPERATION - HUNGARY - HISTORY.
Nagy, László, 1914- Szövetkezetelmélet, szövetkezetpolitika, szövetkezeti jog /. Budapest , 1986. 299, [1] p. ; ISBN 963-221-904-X : LC Card 87-138020 DDC 334/.09439 19
HD3492.5.A4 N34 1986

Cooperation in development and humanitarian assistance. Islamabad, Pakistan : UNDP, [1985] 50 p. : ill. ; 25 cm. Subtitle on cover: Pakistan & the United Nations. "October 1985." LC Card 86-930251 DDC 338.91/09549/1 19
1. Economic assistance - Pakistan. 2. Technical assistance - Pakistan. 3. United Nations - Economic assistance. 4. United Nations - Technical assistance. I. United Nations. Development Programme.
HC440.5 .C66 1985

Cooperation in the field of employment . Centre for Employment Initiatives (Great Britain) Luxembourg , Washington, DC , 1986. 55 p. ; ISBN 92-825-6086-4 (pbk.) : LC Card

87-134296 DDC 331.12/042/094 19
HD5764.A6 C45 1986

COOPERATION - INDIA.
Glimpses of cooperatives through press . New Delhi , 1986- v. <1- > ; LC Card 87-900398 DDC 334/.0954 19
HD3538 .G55 1986

Sami Uddin. Cooperative sector in India after independence /. New Delhi , 1983. vi, 597 p. ; LC Card 83-903263 DDC 334/.0954 19
HD3538 .S25 1983 ***NYPL [JLD 86-3874]***

COOPERATION, INTERNATIONAL. see **INTERNATIONAL COOPERATION.**

COOPERATION - ITALY - CONGRESSES.
Cooperare e competere /. Milano , 1986. 2 v. : ISBN 88-07-10058-4 (v. 1) : LC Card 87-125969
HD2953 .C66 1986

COOPERATION - ITALY - HISTORY - 20TH CENTURY.
Caroleo, Anna, 1948- Il movimento cooperativo in Italia nel primo dopoguerra (1918-1925) /. Milano, Italy , c1986. 376 p. ; LC Card 86-192160
HD3503 .C36 1986

COOPERATION - NEPAL - CONGRESSES.
Cooperative development and basic needs /. Kathmandu, Nepal , 1985. iii, 238 p. ; LC Card 86-900318 DDC 338.9549/3 19
HC425 .C66 1985

COOPERATION - OUTLINES, SYLLABI, ETC.
Bragulat, Jorge. La enseñanza del cooperativismo en la Universidad /. Madrid [1982] 119 p. : LC Card 85-203554
HD2955 .B72 1982

COOPERATION - PERU.
Wester León, Humberto. Diagnóstico situacional del movimiento cooperativo peruano /. [Lima] , 1981- v. : ***NYPL [JLL 86-146]***

COOPERATION - POLAND.
Boczar, Kazimierz. Spółdzielczość . Warszawa , 1986. 398 p. ; ISBN 83-208-0500-7 : LC Card 86-176276
HD3057.7.A4 B63 1986

Samborska-Boć, Elżbieta. Układy powiązań w kooperacji przemysłowej /. Wrocław , 1982. 103 p. ; LC Card 83-109302
HD3517.7.A4 S28 1982

COOPERATION - QUÉBEC (PROVINCE) - GUYENNE - HISTORY.
Desharnais, Marcel, 1924- Guyenne . Montréal, Québec , c1983. 182 p. : ISBN 2-89035-062-2 LC Card 84-127460
HD3450.G89 D47 1983

COOPERATION - RESEARCH - COSTA RICA.
Propuesta para el desarrollo de un programa de investigación sobre propiedad social con énfasis en cooperativismo /. San José, Costa Rica , 1986. ii, 70 p. : LC Card 87-125056 DDC 334/.097286 19
HD3454.A4 P76 1986

COOPERATION - RUSSIAN S.F.S.R. - SIBERIA - HISTORY.
Kooperativnoe dvizhenie v Sibiri . Tiumen´ , 1984. 72 p. ; LC Card 85-179545
HD3517.A3 R875 1984

COOPERATION - SENEGAL.
Sourang, Abdou. Le rôle du mouvement coopératif dans le développement du Sénégal . [Dakar] [1981] 44 leaves : LC Card 85-207626
HD3567.7.A4 S67 1981

COOPERATION - SOVIET CENTRAL ASIA.
Istamov, D. I. (Damir Istamovich) Ėkonomicheskie problemy razvitiia promyshlennogo proizvodstva potrebitel´skoĭ kooperatsii . Tashkent , 1982. 126 p. ; LC Card 82-200979
HD3517.A3 C475 1982

COOPERATION - SOVIET UNION.
Smirnov, A. A. (Alekseĭ Alekseevich) Potrebitel´skaia kooperatsiia v odinnadtsatoĭ piatiletke /. Moskva , 1981. 88 p. : LC Card 82-106193
HD3355 .S65 1981

COOPERATION - STUDY AND TEACHING (HIGHER)
Bragulat, Jorge. La enseñanza del cooperativismo en la Universidad /. Madrid [1982] 119 p. : LC Card 85-203554
HD2955 .B72 1982

COOPERATION - SWEDEN.
Dellenbrant, Jan Åke, 1946- Föreningsdemokrati och företagsdemokrati . [Stockholm] [1981] 85 p. ; ISBN 91-38-06488-X LC Card 83-245188
HD5660.S9 D44 1981

Fredriksson, Carl, 1947- Kooperationens industrisektor i 1980-talets industri-Sverige . [Stockholm] [1981] iv, 196, 24, 11 p. : ISBN 91-38-06535-5 LC Card 83-147552
HD3522 .F74 1981

COOPERATION - SWEDEN - HISTORY - 20TH CENTURY.
Kylebäck, Hugo, 1930- Konsument- och lantbrukskooperation i Sverige . Stockholm [1984] 277 p. ; ISBN 91-85196-18-5 : LC Card 86-120646
HD3524.A1 K663 1984

Cooperation under anarchy / edited by Kenneth A. Oye. Princeton, N.J. : Princeton University Press, 1986. 260 p. ; 24 cm. ISBN 0-691-07695-2 : LC Card 85-42936 DDC 327.1/1 19
1. World politics - 20th century - Addresses, essays, lectures. 2. International relations - Addresses, essays, lectures. 3. International economic relations - Addresses, essays, lectures. 4. International cooperation - Addresses, essays, lectures. I. Oye, Kenneth A., 1949-.
D445 .C736 1986 ***NYPL [JLE 86-1938]***

COOPERATION - URUGUAY - HISTORY.
Terra, Juan Pablo, 1924. Proceso y significado del cooperativismo uruguayo /. Montevideo [1986] 171 p. ; LC Card 87-403179 DDC 334/.09885 19
HD3482.A4 T47 1986

COOPERATION - ZIMBABWE.
Clifton-Brown, E. Project 1.04 . Salisbury, Zimbabwe [1977] 46 leaves ; LC Card 84-256608
HD3562.3.A4 C55 1977

COOPERATIVA BANANERA COLOMBIANA.
Colombia. Congreso. Cámara de Representantes. Comisión Nombrada para Estudiar el Conflicto Surgido entre la United Fruit Company y la Cooperativa Bananera Colombiana. Informe de la Comisión Nombrada para Estudiar el Conflicto Surgido entre la United Fruit Company y la Cooperativa Bananera Colombiana. Bogotá , 1930. 32 p. ; LC Card 83-189629
HD9259.B3 C728 1930

Cooperativa culturale "Un paese vuole conoscersi" (Sant'Alberto (Ravenna, Italy)) Cesare Zavattini presenta La civiltà delle acque . [Bologna] [1985] 272 p., 24 p. of plates : LC Card 86-105989 DDC 945/.47 19
HC308.S33 C47 1985

Cooperativa muratori & cementisti (Ravenna, Italy) Convegno "Il lavoro si crea" (1985 : Ravenna, Italy) Il lavoro si crea . Milano, Italy , c1986. 305 p. : LC Card 86-232529
HD5764.A6 C68 1985

COOPERATIVA SAN BARTOLO DEL VALLE DEL SANTA (PERU) - CONGRESSES.
Taller Alternativas de Cambio de Modelo Empresarial (1985 : Cooperativa San Bartolo del Valle del Santa (Peru)) Taller Alternativas de Cambio de Modelo Empresarial, San Bartolo, Valle del Santa. Lima, Perú [1986] 40 p. : LC Card 87-136317 DDC 334/.683/0985 19
HD1491.P4 T35 1985

Cooperativas agrarias y conflictos políticos en el sur de Jalisco / Esteban Krotz ... [et al.]. 1a ed. México, D.F. : Universidad Autónoma Metropolitana, Unidad Iztapalapa, 1985 [i.e. 1986] 201 p. ; 17 cm. (Cuadernos universitarios / División de Ciencias Sociales y Humanidades, Departamento de Antropología, Area de Relaciones Políticas . 24) Bibliography: p. 197-201. ISBN 968-8401-93-5 LC Card 87-405021 DDC 334/.683/097235 19
1. Agriculture, Cooperative - Mexico - Jalisco. 2. Peasantry - Mexico - Jalisco - Political activity. I. Krotz, Esteban. II. Series: Cuadernos universitarios (Universidad Autónoma Metropolitana. Unidad Iztapalapa) , 24.
HD1491.M42 J353 1986

As Cooperativas na balança comercial brasileira : ano base 1985. [Brasília] : Organização das Cooperativas Brasileiras : Secretaria Nacional de Cooperativismo, Ministério da Agricultura, [1986] 98 p. : ill. ; 15 x 22 cm. (Série Cadernos econômicos . 29) Cover title. "Elaboração do trabalho, Departamento Econômico"--P. [3] of cover. Tables. Errata slip inserted. LC Card 87-403826 DDC 334/.63/0981021 19
1. Brazil - Commerce - Statistics. 2. Cooperative marketing of farm produce - Brazil - Statistics. 3. Producer cooperatives - Brazil - Statistics. I. Organização das Cooperativas Brasileiras. Depto. Econômico. II. Series.
HF3401.5 .C66 1986

Co-operative agricultural development banks . Obul Reddy, D. (Donthi Reddy), 1946- Delhi , New Delhi , 1986. 429 p. ; ISBN 81-7018-378-2 : LC Card 86-902655 DDC 334/.2 19
HG2051.I5 A646 1986 ***NYPL [JLD 87-1527]***

Co-operative agricultural finance . Partap Singh, 1948- New Delhi , 1986. xiii, 188 p. : LC Card 86-903067
HG2051.I5 P376 1986

COOPERATIVE APARTMENT HOUSES. see **APARTMENT HOUSES, COOPERATIVE.**

COOPERATIVE ASSOCIATIONS. see **COOPERATIVE SOCIETIES.**

Cooperative bank : abstracts of the annual reports : contains locations of main offices and branches of banks, as well as names of officers and directors. [Boston] : M.J. Connolly, Secretary of State, [1986] p. A-G, 99, 42 p. ; 28 cm. Cover title. At head of title: The Commonwealth of Massachusetts, Office of the Commissioner of Banks. "April 1986." LC Card 87-620912 DDC 334/.2/025744 19
1. Banks and banking, Cooperative - Massachusetts. I. Massachusetts. Office of the Commissioner of Banks.
HG2038.M4 C58 1986

Co-operative banking and economic development /. Bhorali, Devadas. New Delhi , c1987. 424 p. : LC Card 87-900825 DDC 334/.2/0954162 19
HG2039.I4 B47 1987

COOPERATIVE BANKS. see **BANKS AND BANKING, COOPERATIVE.**

COOPERATIVE BUILDING ASSOCIATIONS. see **BUILDING AND LOAN ASSOCIATIONS.**

Cooperative development and basic needs / editors, Govind Ram Agrawal, Neeru Shrestha. Kathmandu, Nepal : Centre for Economic Development and Administration, Tribhuvan University, Kirtipur, 1985. iii, 238 p. ; 29 cm. "March 1985." Includes bibliographies. LC Card 86-900318 DDC 338.9549/3 19
1. Nepal - Economic policy - Congresses. 2. Cooperation - Nepal - Congresses. I. Agrawal, Govind Ram. II. Shrestha, Neeru. III. Centre for Economic Development and Administration.
HC425 .C66 1985

COOPERATIVE DISTRIBUTION. see **COOPERATION; COOPERATIVE SOCIETIES.**

Cooperative forms of organization in the taxicab industry [microform] . Bergman, Edward M. Washington, D.C. , Springfield, Va. , 1984. 87 p. : ***NYPL [*XME-11,917]***

Co-operative housing development in Kenya . Gatabaki-Kamau, Rose. Nairobi, Kenya [1985] vi leaves, 131 p. : LC Card 86-980648 DDC 334/.1/096762 19
HD7287.72.K4 G37 1985

Cooperative housing development in Kenya. Gatabaki-Kamau, Rose. Co-operative housing development in Kenya . Nairobi, Kenya [1985] vi leaves, 131 p. : LC Card 86-980648 DDC 334/.1/096762 19
HD7287.72.K4 G37 1985

Cooperative involvement in issues of domestic farm policy /. Knutson, Ronald D. College Station, Tex. , 1986. 59 p. : LC Card 86-623063 DDC 338.1/8764 19
HD1491.U6 T45 1986

Cooperative League of the U. S. A. (Old Catalog form: Cooperative League of the United States of America)
How to organize a co-op : moving ahead together / [prepared by the Cooperative League of the U. S.A. and Office of Economic

Opportunity]. Washington : Executive Office of the President, Office of Economic Opportunity, 1969. 53 p. : ill. ; 27 cm. (OEO guidance . 6148-1) Cover title.
1. Agriculture, Cooperative - United States. 2. Cooperative marketing of farm produce - United States. I. United States. Office of Economic Opportunity. II. Title. III. Title: Moving ahead together.
NYPL [JLF 86-590]

Cooperative League of the United States of America. see **Cooperative League of the U. S. A.**

Cooperative long term finance . Reddy, C. R. Delhi, India , 1987. ix, 128 p. : LC Card 87-900729 DDC 334/.2/095484 19
HG2051.I5 A652 1987

COOPERATIVE MARKETING OF FARM PRODUCE - BRAZIL - STATISTICS.
As Cooperativas na balança comercial brasileira . [Brasília] [1986] 98 p. : LC Card 87-403826 DDC 334/.63/0981021 19
HF3401.5 .C66 1986

COOPERATIVE MARKETING OF FARM PRODUCE - UNITED STATES.
Cooperative League of the U. S. A. How to organize a co-op . Washington , 1969. 53 p. :
NYPL [JLF 86-590]

The co-operative movement in Singapore /. Koh, Cher Siang. Singapore [1970] 26 p. ; LC Card 87-121945 DDC 334/.09595/7 19
HD3543.A4 K64 1970

Co-operative principles . Watkins, William Pascoe. Manchester [Greater Manchester] , 1986. xiii, 168 p. ; ISBN 0-85195-140-6 (pbk.) : LC Card 86-216664 DDC 334 19
HD2961 .W448 1986

COOPERATIVE PRODUCTION. see **COOPERATION; COOPERATIVE SOCIETIES; PRODUCER COOPERATIVES.**

Cooperative Republic of Guyana. see **Guyana.**

Cooperative sector in India after independence /. Sami Uddin. New Delhi , 1983. vi, 597 p. ; LC Card 83-903263 DDC 334/.0954 19
HD3538 .S25 1983 NYPL [JLD 86-3874]

COOPERATIVE SOCIETIES - ARGENTINA - CÓRDOBA (PROVINCE) - MANAGEMENT - CASE STUDIES.
La Gestión en empresas cooperativas . Buenos Aires, Argentina [1985] 146 p. ; ISBN 950-0-01257-11 LC Card 87-115117 DDC 334/.0982/54 19
HD3470.A3 C674 1985

COOPERATIVE SOCIETIES - AUSTRALIA - VICTORIA.
Victoria. Ministerial Advisory Committee on Co-operation. The co-operative way . Melbourne , 1986. viii, 151 p. : ISBN 0-7241-5172-9 (pbk.) LC Card 87-158122 DDC 334/.09945 19
HD3570.A6 V538 1986

COOPERATIVE SOCIETIES - AUSTRIA.
Perspektiven der Genossenschaftsrevision . Wien , 1986. x, 322 p. : ISBN 3-85368-775-X LC Card 87-138767 DDC 334/.09436 19
HD3490 .P47 1986

COOPERATIVE SOCIETIES - BARBADOS - DIRECTORIES.
Blondel, Eaulin. Credit unions, co-operatives, trade unions, and friendly societies in Barbados . St. Augustine, Trinidad, Trinidad and Tobago [1986] v, 102 p. ; LC Card 87-403330 DDC 334/.025/72981 19
HD3464.9.A6 B353 1986

COOPERATIVE SOCIETIES - BRAZIL.
Economia informal, tecnologia apropriada e associativismo /. São Paulo , 1986. 176 p. : LC Card 86-233370
HC190.P6 E34 1986

COOPERATIVE SOCIETIES - BRAZIL - PARANÁ - CONGRESSES.
Propostas cooperativistas /. Curitiba , 1986. 56 p. : LC Card 87-403655 DDC 334 19
HD2953 .P76 1986

COOPERATIVE SOCIETIES - CHILE.
Hardy, Clarisa. Hambre + dignidad=ollas comunes /. [Santiago, Chile] , 1986. 282 p., [16] p. of plates : *NYPL [JLD 87-334]*

COOPERATIVE SOCIETIES - COLOMBIA.
Una Obra cooperativa /. Bogotá, Colombia [1982] 276 p. ; LC Card 86-226857
HD3477.A4 O27 1982

COOPERATIVE SOCIETIES - CONGRESSES.
Propostas cooperativistas /. Curitiba , 1986. 56 p. : LC Card 87-403655 DDC 334 19
HD2953 .P76 1986

COOPERATIVE SOCIETIES - DENMARK - RIBE (AMT) - HISTORY.
Just, Flemming. Brugsforeningsbevægelsen 1866-1920 . Esbjerg , 1984. 192 p. : ISBN 87-88521-04-4 LC Card 85-114707
HD3059.A6 R524 1984

COOPERATIVE SOCIETIES - DEVELOPING COUNTRIES.
Klöwer, Gerd Günter. Genossenschaften in Entwicklungsländern . Göttingen , 1981. 56 p. ; ISBN 3-509-01085-X LC Card 82-174706 DDC 334/.09172/4 19
HD3575 .K58 1981 NYPL [JLE 86-3343]

COOPERATIVE SOCIETIES - ECUADOR - MANAGEMENT.
Garzón L., Isaías. Manual de cooperativismo estudiantil ecuatoriano /. Riobamba, Ecuador [1983?] 244 p. : LC Card 86-134182
HD2965 .G38 1983

COOPERATIVE SOCIETIES - FINANCE - HANDBOOKS, MANUALS, ETC.
Manual de interpretación de estados financieros /. [Santiago, Chile] [1984] 49 p. : LC Card 85-150204
HD2965 .M35 1984

COOPERATIVE SOCIETIES - FRANCE - CONGRESSES.
Economie sociale et cycle de vie des institutions /. Paris , 1983. 162 p. : ISBN 2-7178-0631-8 : LC Card 83-174618 DDC 334/.0944 19
HD3494 .E26 1983 NYPL [JLE 86-537]

COOPERATIVE SOCIETIES - GERMANY, WEST.
Bänsch, Axel. Operationalisierung des Unternehmenszieles Mitgliederförderung /. Göttingen , c1983. xv, 245 p. ; ISBN 3-525-12750-2 LC Card 83-199427
HD3498 .B35 1983

Schwenk, Andreas. Die Kreditwürdigkeit der eingetragenen Genossenschaft /. Göttingen , c1984. xiv, 287 p. ; ISBN 3-525-12752-9 LC Card 86-139501
HG3711.G3 S36 1984

COOPERATIVE SOCIETIES - GHANA.
Dadson, J. A. Production co-operatives and rural development in Ghana /. [Addis Ababa] [1985] 53 p. ; LC Card 87-105501 DDC 334/.6/09667 19
HD3258.3.A4 D34 1985

COOPERATIVE SOCIETIES - GOVERNMENT POLICY - COLOMBIA.
Una Obra cooperativa /. Bogotá, Colombia [1982] 276 p. ; LC Card 86-226857
HD3477.A4 O27 1982

COOPERATIVE SOCIETIES - GREECE - HISTORY.
Klēmēs, Arist. N. (Aristeidēs N.), 1915- Hoi synetairismoi stēn Hellada /. Athēna , 1985- v. <1> : LC Card 86-228137
HD3531.83.A4 K56 1985

COOPERATIVE SOCIETIES - HUNGARY.
Gyenes, Antal. Szövetkezetipolitikai, szövetkezetelméleti ismeretek /. Budapest , 1974. 217 p. ; LC Card 87-113832
HD3492.5.A4 G94 1974

COOPERATIVE SOCIETIES - HUNGARY - ACCOUNTING.
Lukács, Lajos. Szövetkezeti gazdálkodás elemzése /. Budapest , 1983. 155 p. : ISBN 963-03-2028-2 (Magy. nemz. bibl.) LC Card 85-184472
HF5686.C67 L84 1983

COOPERATIVE SOCIETIES - INDIA.
Sami Uddin. Cooperative sector in India after independence /. New Delhi , 1983. vi, 597 p. ; LC Card 83-903263 DDC 334/.0954 19
HD3538 .S25 1983 NYPL [JLD 86-3874]

COOPERATIVE SOCIETIES - INDIA - JAMMU AND KASHMIR - DIRECTORIES.
Directory of cooperative societies, 1986. Srinagar [1986] 131 p. ; LC Card 87-900324 DDC 334/.025/546 19
HD3540.A3 J353 1986

COOPERATIVE SOCIETIES - ITALY - RAVENNA - HISTORY.
Carli Ballola, Sandra. La Compagnia lavoratori portuali di Ravenna, 1930-1980 /. [Italy , 1981?] (Imola : Galeati) 208 p. : LC Card 83-206502
HD8039.L82 I83 1981

COOPERATIVE SOCIETIES - KENYA - EMPLOYEES - TRAINING OF.
Training needs for co-operative movement staff . [Nairobi?] [1984] [166] p. : LC Card 86-980729 DDC 331.12/51334/096762 19
HD3560.5.A4 T73 1984

COOPERATIVE SOCIETIES - LATIN AMERICA - CASE STUDIES.
Grassroots development in Latin America & the Caribbean . New York , 1985. vii, 197 p. : ISBN 0-03-001689-4 (alk. paper) : LC Card 84-18180 DDC 334/.098 19
HD3450.5.A4 G72 1985

COOPERATIVE SOCIETIES - LAW AND LEGISLATION - AUSTRIA.
Perspektiven der Genossenschaftsrevision . Wien , 1986. x, 322 p. : ISBN 3-85368-775-X LC Card 87-138767 DDC 334/.09436 19
HD3490 .P47 1986

COOPERATIVE SOCIETIES - LAW AND LEGISLATION - HUNGARY.
Nagy, László, 1914- Szövetkezetelmélet, szövetkezetpolitika, szövetkezeti jog /. Budapest , 1986. 299, [1] p. ; ISBN 963-221-904-X : LC Card 87-138020 DDC 334/.09439 19
HD3492.5.A4 N34 1986

COOPERATIVE SOCIETIES - LAW AND LEGISLATION - PERU.
Torres y Torres Lara, Carlos. Las cooperativas en el Perú, su situación actual y legislación vigente /. Lima, Perú , 1985. 144 p. ; LC Card 86-110544 DDC 346.85/0668 348.506668 19
KHQ1370 .T67 1985 NYPL [JLD 86-2183]

COOPERATIVE SOCIETIES - MANAGEMENT.
Garzón L., Isaías. Manual de cooperativismo estudiantil ecuatoriano /. Riobamba, Ecuador [1983?] 244 p. : LC Card 86-134182
HD2965 .G38 1983

COOPERATIVE SOCIETIES - PERU.
Torres y Torres Lara, Carlos. Las cooperativas en el Perú, su situación actual y legislación vigente /. Lima, Perú , 1985. 144 p. ; LC Card 86-110544 DDC 346.85/0668 348.506668 19
KHQ1370 .T67 1985 NYPL [JLD 86-2183]

Wester León, Humberto. Diagnóstico situacional del movimiento cooperativo peruano /. [Lima] , 1981- v. : *NYPL [JLL 86-146]*

COOPERATIVE SOCIETIES - PORTUGAL - HISTORY.
Goodolphim, Costa, 1842-1910. A associação . Lisboa, Portugal , 1974. 206 p. ; LC Card 87-401116 DDC 334/.09494 19
HD3529.A4 G66 1974

COOPERATIVE SOCIETIES - RESEARCH - COSTA RICA.
Propuesta para el desarrollo de un programa de investigación sobre propiedad social con énfasis en cooperativismo /. San José, Costa Rica , 1986. ii, 70 p. : LC Card 87-125056 DDC 334/.097286 19
HD3454.A4 P76 1986

COOPERATIVE SOCIETIES - SINGAPORE.
Koh, Cher Siang. The co-operative movement in Singapore /. Singapore [1970] 26 p. ; LC Card 87-121945 DDC 334/.09595/7 19
HD3543.A4 K64 1970

COOPERATIVE SOCIETIES - SOVIET UNION.
Kudri͡avt͡sev, A. A. (Alekseĭ Andreevich) Analiz khozi͡aĭstvennoĭ dei͡atelʹnosti kooperativnykh organizat͡siĭ /. Moskva , 1977. 262 p. ; LC Card 82-124930
HD3515 .K78 1977

COOPERATIVE SOCIETIES - SPAIN - ACCOUNTING.
Soto Carniago, Juan José de. Sociedades cooperativas, plan de cuentas . Cáceres , 1984. xv, 150 p. ; ISBN 84-600-3441-0 LC Card

84-221264
HF5686.C67 S67 1984

COOPERATIVE SOCIETIES - SPAIN - CATALONIA.
Rendé, Josep M. Pla d'organització social agrària de Catalunya /. Barcelona , 1924. 138 p., [1] folded leaf of plates : LC Card 86-202164 DDC 334/.683/09467 19
HD1491.S82 C317 1924

COOPERATIVE SOCIETIES - SWEDEN.
Fredriksson, Carl, 1947- Kooperationens industrisektor i 1980-talets industri-Sverige . [Stockholm] [1981] iv, 196, 24, 11 p. : ISBN 91-38-06535-5 LC Card 83-147552
HD3522 .F74 1981

COOPERATIVE SOCIETIES - UNITED STATES.
Bergman, Edward M. Cooperative forms of organization in the taxicab industry [microform] . Washington, D.C. , Springfield, Va. , 1984. 87 p. : ***NYPL [*XME-11,917]***

COOPERATIVE SOCIETIES - ZIMBABWE.
Clifton-Brown, E. Project 1.04 . Salisbury, Zimbabwe [1977] 46 leaves ; LC Card 84-256608
HD3562.3.A4 C55 1977

COOPERATIVE STORES. see **COOPERATIVE SOCIETIES.**

Cooperative strategies in international business / [edited by] Farok J. Contractor, Peter Lorange. Lexington, Mass. : Lexington Books, c1988. xxix, 513 p. : ill. ; 24 cm. Based on papers presented in Oct. 1986 at a colloquium organized by the Graduate School of Management at Rutgers University and the Wharton School of the University of Pennsylvania. Includes bibliographies and index. ISBN 0-669-14927-6 (alk. paper) LC Card 86-46160 DDC 338.8/8 19
1. International business enterprises - Congresses. 2. Joint ventures - Congresses. I. Contractor, Farok J. II. Lorange, Peter. III. Rutgers University. Graduate School of Management. IV. Wharton School.
HD2755.5 .C645 1988

Cooperative studies .
(1) Russell, George William, 1867-1935. Co-operation and nationality . Dublin , c1982. 103 p. ; ISBN 0-7165-0335-2 (pbk.) LC Card 82-192895 DDC 334/.683/09417 19
HD1491.I6 R87 1982 ***NYPL [JLD 86-2358]***

The co-operative way . Victoria. Ministerial Advisory Committee on Co-operation. Melbourne , 1986. viii, 151 p. : ISBN 0-7241-5172-9 (pbk.) LC Card 87-158122 DDC 334/.09945 19
HD3570.A6 V538 1986

Cooperatives and national development . Tegegne Teke. Addis Ababa, Ethiopia [1984] iii, 57 leaves ; LC Card 85-980411 DDC 334/.683/0963 19
HD1491.E83 T44 1984 ***NYPL [JLG 86-173]***

Coopératives et populations rurales : enquête / réalisée par le Centre universitaire de recherche pour le développement économique et social (CURDES). [Bujumbura] : CURDES, [1986] ix, 64 leaves : ill. ; 30 cm. At head of title: République du Burundi, Ministère du développement rural, Département des coopératives. "Mars 1986." "Cette étude a été réalisée par le Laboratoire Logique paysanne et pratiques sociales du C.U.R.D.E.S."--7th prelim. p. LC Card 86-981185
1. Consumer cooperatives - Burundi. 2. Burundi - Population, Rural. I. Université du Burundi. Centre universitaire de recherche pour le développement économique et social. II. Université du Burundi. Laboratoire Logique paysanne et pratiques sociales.
HD3561.A4 C66 1986

El cooperativismo de ahorro y crédito en el Ecuador /. Da Ros, Giuseppina. Quito , 1985. 89 p. : LC Card 86-169048
HG2156.E22 D37 1985

Cooperativismo, desnivelamento e reprodução do campesinato. Estudo especial . Maceió, AL. , 1983. 174 leaves : LC Card 86-167829
HC189.A69 E88 1983

Cooperazione di credito e sviluppo sociale ed economico delle campagne in Emilia Romagna : dalle origini all'avvento del fascismo / a cura di A. Cova, G. Scidà ; contributi di A. Cova ... [et al.] ; presentazione di P. Colliva. Bologna : Federazione delle casse rurali ed artigiane dell'Emilia-Romagna, c1983. 173 p. : ill. ; 24 cm. At head of title: Istituto regionale di studi politici Alcide de Gasperi. Includes bibliographical references. LC Card 85-156690
1. Agricultural cooperative credit associations - Italy - Emilia-Romagna - History. 2. Emilia-Romagna (Italy) - Rural conditions. 3. Emilia-Romagna, Italy - Economic conditions. 4. Agriculture - Italy - Emilia-Romagna - Finance - History. 5. Small business - Italy - Emilia-Romagna - Finance - History. I. Cova, Alberto. II. Scidà, Giuseppe. III. Istituto regionale di studi politici Alcide De Gasperi. IV. Federazione delle casse rurali ed artigiane dell'Emilia-Romagna.
HG2051.I82 E433 1983

Cooperazione italiana allo sviluppo : il problema dei bisogni fondamentali / a cura di Massimo D'Angelo. Roma : Fratelli Palombi, [1984] 144 p. ; 24 cm. (I Quaderni di Cooperazione . 1) Includes bibliographical references. ISBN 88-7621-170-5 : LC Card 85-223760 DDC 338.91/45/01724 19
1. Economic assistance, Italian - Developing countries. 2. Basic needs - Developing countries. I. D'Angelo, Massimo. II. Series.
HC60 .C65757 1984

The Coopers & Lybrand guide to growing your business /. Jones, Seymour, 1931- New York , c1988. xiii, 477 p. ; ISBN 0-471-85941-9 LC Card 87-21688 DDC 658 19
HD31 .J627 1988

Coopers and Lybrand guide to growing your business. Jones, Seymour, 1931- The Coopers & Lybrand guide to growing your business /. New York , c1988. xiii, 477 p. ; ISBN 0-471-85941-9 LC Card 87-21688 DDC 658 19
HD31 .J627 1988

Coopers & Lybrand WD Scott. Jones, Seymour, 1931- The Coopers & Lybrand guide to growing your business /. New York , c1988. xiii, 477 p. ; ISBN 0-471-85941-9 LC Card 87-21688 DDC 658 19
HD31 .J627 1988

Co-ops--the future. Dunman, Jack. London [1969] 20 p. ISBN 0-900302-01-1 : LC Card 77-428347 DDC 334/.5/0942
HD3486 .D84

La coordinación como consecuencia de razones y pasiones . Mejías, Tulio. Caracas, Venezuela , c1983. 37, [2] p. : ISBN 980-217-002-X LC Card 86-193647
HD37.S66 M37 1983

Coordinadora Regional de Investigaciones Económicas y Sociales. Gariazzo, Alicia. El café en Nicaragua . Managua, Nicaragua , 1984. 175 p. : LC Card 85-192390
HD9199.N52 G37 1984
NYPL [JLF 86-1521]

Co-ordinated urban transport pricing : report / prepared by an OECD Scientific Expert/Group. Paris : Organisation for Economic Co-operation and Development ; [Washington, D.C. : OEDC Publications and Information Center, distributor], 1985. 151 p. : ill. ; 27 cm. (Road transport research) Includes bibliographies. ISBN 92-64-12692-9 (pbk.) : LC Card 86-125699 DDC 388.4/042 19
1. Urban transportation - Finance. 2. Urban transportation - Taxation. 3. Urban transportation policy. 4. Local transit - Fares. I. Organisation for Economic Co-operation and Development. II. Series.
HE305 .C58 1985

COORDINATION OF INDUSTRIAL DESIGNS. see **INDUSTRIAL DESIGN COORDINATION.**

Copans, Jean. Balandier, Georges. Sociologie des Brazzavilles noires /. Paris , c1985. xviii, 306 p., [2] leaves of plates : ISBN 2-7246-0524-1 : LC Card 86-138199
HB2125.B73 B34 1985

Cope, Gail W. Warmbrod, Catharine P. Skills for the changing workplace . Columbus, Ohio (1960 Kenny Rd., Columbus 43210-1090) , 1985. ix, 93 p. ; LC Card 86-205907 DDC 651/.07/15 19
HF1106 .W36 1985

Cope, Thom K. Executive guide to employment practices : a practical approach to avoiding unintended discrimination / by Thom K. Cope. Lincoln, Neb. : Media Pub. & Marketing, c1984. vii, 163 p. : forms ; 23 cm. ISBN 0-939644-14-2 (pbk.) : LC Card 84-62043 DDC 344.73/01133 347.3041133 19
1. Discrimination in employment - Law and legislation - United States. 2. Affirmative action programs - Law and legislation - United States. I. Title.
KF3464.Z9 C65 1984 ***NYPL [JLE 87-75]***

Copeland, M. C. (Michael Campbell) Transport energy in New Zealand's overseas trade : a review up to 1980 / M.C. Copeland and A.K. Horsfield, P.D. Chudleigh. Auckland, N.Z. : New Zealand Energy Research and Development Committee, University of Auckland, [1982] iv, 130 p. : ill. ; 30 cm. (Report, 0110-1692 . no. 80 (Oct. 1982)) Study covers the period up to 1980; the first draft was presented to the Committee in April 1980 and the edited version in February 1981. Bibliography: p. 129-130. LC Card 84-159485 DDC 387.5/1 19
1. Shipping - New Zealand - Rates. 2. Shipping - New Zealand - Energy consumption - Costs. 3. Aeronautics, Commercial - New Zealand - Freight - Energy consumption - Costs. I. Horsfield, A. K. (Anne K.). II. Chudleigh, P. D. III. Series: Report (New Zealand Energy Research and Development Committee) , no. 80. IV. Title.
HE597.N4 C63 1982
NYPL [JSK 82-15 no.80]

Copeland, Thomas E., 1946- Financial theory and corporate policy / Thomas E. Copeland, J. Fred Weston. 3rd ed. Reading, Mass. : Addison-Wesley, c1988. xiv, 946 p. : ill. ; 24 cm. Includes bibliographies and indexes. ISBN 0-201-10648-5 : LC Card 87-12595 DDC 658.1/5 19
1. Corporations - Finance. 2. Finance. I. Weston, J. Fred (John Fred), 1916-. II. Title.
HG4011 .C833 1988

Copeland, Vincent.
The blast furnace brothers / by Vincent Copeland. New York, N.Y. : Center for United Labor Action, 1973. iv, 33 p. : ill. ; 22 cm. LC Card 87-125932 DDC 331.13/3 19
1. Discrimination in employment - United States - Case studies. 2. Iron and steel workers - United States - Case studies. 3. Bethlehem Steel Corporation - Personnel management - Case studies. 4. Trade-unions - United States - Minority membership - Case studies. I. Title.
HD4903.3.B582 U63 1973

Expanding empire : the global war drive of big business and the forces that will stop it / by Vincent Copeland.4th ed. New York, N.Y. : Workers World Press, 1972. 62 p. ; 22 cm. LC Card 87-404126 DDC 338.8/8973 19
1. Investments, American. 2. Corporations, American. I. Title.
HG4538 .C668 1972

Kultursociologiske skrifter. see **Kultursociologiske skrifter.**

Copernico, Nicolas. see **Copernicus, Nicolaus, 1473-1543.**

Copernicus, Nicolaus, 1473-1543.
DE MONETAE CUDENDAE RATIONE.
Montanari, Augusto, b. 1843. Nicolò Copernico ed il suo libro De monetae cudendae ratione . Padova , 1877. 70 p. ; LC Card 85-666421
HG220.P6 C636x 1877

Coping with poverty . Rubenstein, Hymie. Boulder, Colo. , 1987. xx, 389 p. : ISBN 0-8133-7387-5 (pbk. : alk. paper) : LC Card 86-32530 DDC 972.98/4400496 19
HC156.5.Z7 S296 1987

Coping with sexual harassment /. Black, Beryl. New York , 1987. 149 p. ; ISBN 0-8239-0732-5 : LC Card 86-26245 DDC 331.13/3 19
HD6060.3 .B55 1987

Copoiu, Nicolae. Condițiile istorice ale apariției și dezvoltării clasei muncitoare din România . București , 1984. 652 p. ; LC Card 84-234192
HD8648 .C65 1984

COPPER INDUSTRY AND TRADE - AFRICA - CONGRESSES.
Regional Workshop on the Role and Prospects of Copper and Aluminium in African Development (1985 : Lusaka, Zambia) Final report /. [Addis Ababa] , 1985. 9 p. ; LC Card 86-980966 DDC 338.2/743/096 19
HD9539.C7 A427 1985

COPPER INDUSTRY AND TRADE - CONGRESSES.
Chile y CIPEC ante la crisis del cobre /. Santiago de Chile , 1985. 74 p. ; LC Card 86-144485
HD9539.C7 C526 1985 ***NYPL [JLD 87-363]***

COPPER INDUSTRY AND TRADE - GERMANY (WEST) - ESSEN - EMPLOYEES.
So schaffen wir! . [Germany , 193-?] (München : F. Bruckmann) [51] leaves : LC Card 86-213082
HD9539.C7 G57 1930z

COPPER INDUSTRY AND TRADE - GOVERNMENT POLICY - CHILE - CONGRESSES.
Chile y CIPEC ante la crisis del cobre /. Santiago de Chile , 1985. 74 p. ; LC Card 86-144485
HD9539.C7 C526 1985 NYPL [JLD 87-363]

COPPER INDUSTRY AND TRADE - GREAT BRITAIN - HISTORY.
Toomey, Robert R., 1949- Vivian and Sons, 1809-1924 . New York , 1985. 427 p. ; ISBN 0-8240-6692-8 (alk. paper) : LC Card 84-46012 DDC 338.7/622343/0941 19
HD9539.C7 G778 1985
NYPL [JLE 86-4440]

COPPER INDUSTRY AND TRADE - MATHEMATICAL MODELS.
Ghosh, S. Stabilizing speculative commodity markets /. Oxford [Oxfordshire] , New York , 1987. xiii, 437 p. : ISBN 0-19-828472-1 : LC Card 86-32654 DDC 332.64/4 19
HG6046 .G485 1987

Toward a new Iron Age? . Cambridge, Mass. , 1987. vi, 173 p. : ISBN 0-674-89818-4 (alk. paper) LC Card 86-22923 DDC 333.8/5 19
HC59 .T63 1987

COPPER INDUSTRY AND TRADE - MEXICO - HISTORY.
Barrett, Elinore M. The Mexican colonial copper industry /. Albuquerque , c1987. xi, 143 p. : ISBN 0-8263-0929-1 LC Card 86-24991 DDC 338.2/743/0972 19
HD9539.C7 M417 1987

COPPER INDUSTRY AND TRADE - NEW SPAIN - HISTORY.
Barrett, Elinore M. The Mexican colonial copper industry /. Albuquerque , c1987. xi, 143 p. : ISBN 0-8263-0929-1 LC Card 86-24991 DDC 338.2/743/0972 19
HD9539.C7 M417 1987

COPPER INDUSTRY AND TRADE - PERU - CASE STUDIES.
Alarcón Aliaga, Carlos. Privilegios y capital transnacional . [Peru?] [1985 or 1986] 168 p. : LC Card 87-127159 DDC 338.8/87 19
HD2841.Z75 S683 1985

COPPER INDUSTRY AND TRADE - YUGOSLAVIA.
Yugoslav copper and copper products =. Beograd , 1986. 83 p. : LC Card 87-108608
HD9539.C7 Y87 1986

COPPER - PRICES - LATIN AMERICA - ECONOMETRIC MODELS.
Lord, Montague J. Market price models for Latin America's major commodity exports /. Washington, D.C. [1986] vii, 219 p. : LC Card 87-115208 DDC 338.5/2/098 19
HD9014.A2 L67 1986

COPPER - TRADE AND STATISTICS. see **COPPER INDUSTRY AND TRADE.**

Coppola, Victor V. Jones, Seymour, 1931- The Coopers & Lybrand guide to growing your business /. New York , c1988. xiii, 477 p. ; ISBN 0-471-85941-9 LC Card 87-21688 DDC 658 19
HD31 .J627 1988

Copsey, S. M. Shiftwork review : research of the European foundation, 1981-1984. Luxembourg : Office for Official Publications of the European Communities ; Washington, DC : European Community Information Service [distributor], 1986. xi, 122 p. : ill. ; 30 cm. (Research report / European Foundation for the Improvement of Living and Working Conditions) "Review of the European Foundation's research into shiftwork, 1981-1984, by S.M. Copsey and E.N. Corlett, with Y. Queinnec."--Title on added t.p. Bibliography: p. vii-x. ISBN 92-825-6419-3 (pbk.) : LC Card 87-137298 DDC 331.25/72 19
1. Shift systems - European Economic Community countries. 2. Night work - European Economic Community countries. I. Corlett, E. N. (Esmond Nigel). II. Quéinnec, Y. (Yvon). III. European Foundation for the Improvement of Living and Working Conditions. IV. Title. V. Title: Review of the European Foundation's research into shiftwork, 1981-1984. VI. Series: Research report / European Foundation for the Improvement of Living and Working Conditions.
HD5111.6.E86 C66 1986

Copublications series .
(3) Hirschman, Albert O. The political economy of Latin American development . La Jolla, Calif. [1986] 57 p. ; LC Card 87-621614 DDC 338.98 19
HC125 .H544 1986

COPY, ADVERTISING. see **ADVERTISING COPY.**

COPY WRITING. see **ADVERTISING COPY.**

COPYING MACHINE EQUIPMENT INDUSTRY.
FormsMark III . Arlington, VA (1730 N. Lynn St., Arlington 22209) , c1986. 154 p. : LC Card 87-401995 DDC 381/.4565129 19
HD9802.3.A2 F67 1986

COPYING MACHINE INDUSTRY.
Electronic copy boards--local & remote. Norwalk, Conn., U. S.A. (6 Prowitt St., Norwalk 06855) , c1986. iii, 101 leaves : LC Card 86-224860 DDC 381/.45621380414 19
HD9802.3.A2 E45 1986

FormsMark III . Arlington, VA (1730 N. Lynn St., Arlington 22209) , c1986. 154 p. : LC Card 87-401995 DDC 381/.4565129 19
HD9802.3.A2 F67 1986

COPYING MACHINE INDUSTRY - UNITED STATES.
Jacobson, Gary. Xerox . New York , c1986. ix, 338 p. ; ISBN 0-02-551600-0 LC Card 85-30922 DDC 338.7/68644 19
HD9802.3.U64 X475 1986
NYPL [JLE 86-2982]

Jacobson, Gary. Xerox . New York , 1987, c1986. xii, 338 p. ; ISBN 0-02-033830-9 (pbk.) LC Card 86-31009 DDC 338.7/68644 19
HD9802.3.U64 X475 1986b

Coquery, Catherine. see **Coquery-Vidrovitch, Catherine.**

Coquery-Vidrovitch, Catherine.
[Afrique noire. English]
Africa : endurance and change south of the Sahara / Catherine Coquery-Vidrovitch ; translated by David Maisel. Berkeley : University of California Press, c1988. p. cm. Translation of: Afrique noire. Bibliography: p. Includes index. ISBN 0-520-05679-5 (alk. paper) LC Card 87-15316 DDC 967 19
1. Africa, Sub-Saharan - Economic conditions. 2. Africa, Sub-Saharan - Population - History. 3. Africa, Sub-Saharan - Colonial influence - History. 4. Africa, Sub-Saharan - Politics and government. 5. Africa, Sub-Saharan - Rural conditions. 6. Labor and laboring classes - Africa, Sub-Saharan - History. I. Title.
HC800 .C67513 1988

COQUIMBO, CHILE (PROVINCE) - ECONOMIC CONDITIONS.
Chouteau, Eujenio. Informe sobre la provincia de Coquimbo /. Santiago de Chile , 1887. 262 p. ; LC Card 85-165581
HC193.C64 C46 1887

Coraggio, José Luis. Transition and development . New York, NY [Berkeley, Calif.] , c1986. 352 p. ; ISBN 0-85345-705-0 (pbk.) : LC Card 86-12579 DDC 335.43/09172/4 19
HX517.8 .T73 1986 NYPL [JLD 86-3907]

El coraje de las mineras . Hernández, Zoila. Lima, Perú , 1986. 184 p. : LC Card 86-232046
HD5361.Z9 C35 1986

Corazzol, Gigi, 1945- Livelli stipulati a Venezia nel 1591 : studio storico / Gigi Corazzol. Pisa : Giardini editori e stampatori in Pisa, c1986. 167 p., [8] leaves of plates : ill. ; 25 cm. (Supplementi di studi veneziani) Bibliography: p. 155-167. LC Card 86-192693
1. Land tenure - Italy - Venice Region - History - 16th century. 2. Emphyteusis - Italy - Venice Region - History - 16th century. I. Title. II. Series.
HD680.V4 C67 1986

Corben, Christopher W. Fairfield on-scene study of collisions . [Sydney?] [1977] 120 p. : LC Card 85-170609
HE5614.5.A8 F37 1977

Corbishley, M. Anne. Yost, Elizabeth B. Career counseling . San Francisco, Calif. , c1987. xvi, 265 p. : ISBN 1-555-42035-4 (alk. paper) LC Card 86-46335 DDC 158.6 19
HF5381 .Y58 1987

Corbo, Vittorio. Growth-oriented adjustment programs /. Washington, D.C. , 1987. xiii, 537 p. : ISBN 0-939934-92-2 (pbk.) LC Card 87-21361 DDC 338.9 19
HD73 .G76 1987

Corbridge, Stuart. Capitalist world development : a critique of radical development geography / Stuart Corbridge. London : Macmillan, 1986. xi, 295 p. : ill. ; 23 cm. (Critical human geography) Includes indexes. Bibliography: p. 262-284. ISBN 0-333-32405-6
1. Capitalism. 2. Marxian economics. 3. Developing countries - Dependency on foreign countries. I. Title. II. Series. ***NYPL [JLD 86-2925]***

La corde pour les pendre-- . Laurent, Eric. Paris , c1985. 304 p. ; ISBN 2-213-01550-3 : LC Card 85-231994
HF1411 .L3645 1985

Corden, W. M. (Warner Max)
Protection and competition in international trade . Oxford [Oxfordshire] , New York, NY, USA , 1987. vi, 242 p. : ISBN 0-631-15004-8 : LC Card 86-29915 DDC 382/.3 19
HF1411 .P697 1987

Protection and liberalization : a review of analytical issues / by W. Max Corden. Washington, D.C. : International Monetary Fund, c1987. v, 28 p. ; 28 cm. (Occasional papers of the International Monetary Fund, 0251-6365 . no. 54) "August 1987." Bibliography: p. 28. ISBN 0-939934-95-7 (pbk.) : LC Card 87-16932 DDC 382.7 19
1. Commercial policy. 2. Free trade and protection. I. Series: Occasional paper (International Monetary Fund) , no. 54. II. Title.
HF1411 .C5954 1987

CORDEN, W. M. (WARNER MAX)
Protection and competition in international trade . Oxford [Oxfordshire] , New York, NY, USA , 1987. vi, 242 p. : ISBN 0-631-15004-8 : LC Card 86-29915 DDC 382/.3 19
HF1411 .P697 1987

Cordero, Ricardo. Der Financial Futures Markt / von Ricardo Cordero. Bern : P. Haupt, c1986. xii, 200 p. : ill. ; 23 cm. (Bankwirtschaftliche Forschungen. Bd. 97) Bibliography: p. 195-200. ISBN 3-258-03638-1 LC Card 87-408496 DDC 332.1 s 332.64/4 19
1. Financial futures. I. Title. II. Series.
HG1526 .B27 Bd. 97 HG6024.3

CORDES . Ortiz, Rolando. Lima, Perú , 1987. 96 p. ; LC Card 87-405059 DDC 338.985 19
HC227 .O73 1987

Cordes, Walter, 1907- Eugen Schmalenbach . Stuttgart , 1984. xvii, 478 p. : ISBN 3-8202-0295-1 LC Card 84-215889
HF5616.G3 E93 1984

Cordewener, Karl-Friedrich, 1951-
Kundenbediente Datenstationen als marktpolitische Instrumente des Bankbetriebs / von Karl-Friedrich Cordewener. Göttingen : O. Schwartz, 1982. 268 p. : ill. ; 20 cm. (Göttinger Hefte zur Bankbetriebslehre und Unternehmungsfinanzierung . Heft 10) Bibliography: p. 236-263. Includes indexes. ISBN 3-509-01312-3 LC Card 84-182492
1. Banks and banking - Germany (West) - Customer services. 2. Banks and banking - Germany (West) - Automation. I. Title. II. Series.
HG3048 .C67 1982

Cordini, Mabel. A Mulher rural e mudanças no processo de produção agrícola . [Brasília] [1984] i, 161 p. ; LC Card 86-150197
HD6073.A292 L295 1984

Córdoba (Argentina : Province)
Plandecor, Plan de desarrollo de Córdoba : diagnóstico preliminar. Córdoba : Gobierno de Córdoba, 1981-<1982 > v. <1-3 > : ill. ; 30 cm. CONTENTS. - [1] Area aspectos productivos -- [2] Area aspectos sociales -- [3] Area ordenamiento territorial. LC Card 87-401182 DDC 330.982/54064 19
1. Córdoba (Argentina : Province) - Economic conditions. I. Title.
HC177.C7 C66 1981

Córdoba (Argentina : Province). Dirección de Estadística y Censos. Compendio estadístico /. Córdoba, República Argentina [1984] 110 leaves : LC Card 87-400414 DDC 304.6/0982/54021 19
HA958.C6 C64 1984

CÓRDOBA (ARGENTINA : PROVINCE) - ECONOMIC CONDITIONS.
Córdoba (Argentina : Province) Plandecor, Plan de desarrollo de Córdoba . Córdoba , 1981-<1982. v. <1-3 > : LC Card 87-401182 DDC 330.982/54064 19
HC177.C7 C66 1981

CÓRDOBA (ARGENTINA : PROVINCE) - ECONOMIC CONDITIONS - STATISTICS.
Compendio estadístico /. Córdoba, República Argentina [1984] 110 leaves : LC Card 87-400414 DDC 304.6/0982/54021 19
HA958.C6 C64 1984

CÓRDOBA (ARGENTINA : PROVINCE) - POPULATION - STATISTICS.
Compendio estadístico /. Córdoba, República Argentina [1984] 110 leaves : LC Card 87-400414 DDC 304.6/0982/54021 19
HA958.C6 C64 1984

CÓRDOBA (ARGENTINA) - ADMINISTRATIVE AND POLITICAL DIVISIONS - STATISTICS.
León Almeida, Pedro. Ensayo de categorización de los municipios de Córdoba /. Córdoba, Argentina , 1984. 74 leaves : LC Card 87-403755 DDC 330.982/54062/021 19
HC177.C7 L46 1984

CÓRDOBA (ARGENTINA) - ECONOMIC CONDITIONS - STATISTICS.
León Almeida, Pedro. Ensayo de categorización de los municipios de Córdoba /. Córdoba, Argentina , 1984. 74 leaves : LC Card 87-403755 DDC 330.982/54062/021 19
HC177.C7 L46 1984

CÓRDOBA (SPAIN : PROVINCE) - ECONOMIC CONDITIONS.
Barroso Rodríguez, Antonio. Estudio de las comarcas Campiña Alta y Penibética de Córdoba . Córdoba , 1984. 268 p. : ISBN 84-505-0166-0 LC Card 85-182568
HC387.C58 B37 1984

CÓRDOBA (SPAIN : PROVINCE) - RURAL CONDITIONS.
Díaz del Moral, Juan, 1870-1948. Las agitaciones campesinas del período bolchevista, 1918-1920 /. Sevilla [1985?] 230 p. ; ISBN 84-7587-031-7 LC Card 86-181529
HD1536.S7 D48 1985

Córdoba (Spain). Delegación de Cultura. Seis estudios sobre el proletariado andaluz (1868-1939). [Córdoba] , 1984. 247 p. ; ISBN 84-500-9584-0 LC Card 86-142680 DDC 305.5/62/09468 19
HD8589.A52 S45 1984
NYPL [JLD 87-1550]

Cordón Munilla, Publio, 1935- España y las inversiones extranjeras / Publio Cordón Munilla. Zaragoza : Cámara Oficial de Comercio e Industria, [1968?] 79 p. ; 22 cm. Bibliography: p. 78-79. LC Card 86-144082 DDC 332.6/73/0946 19
1. Investments, Foreign - Spain. I. Title.
HG5632 .C66 1968

Córdova, Armando. Crisis y control de cambio /. Maracaibo, Venezuela , 1984. 101 p. ; LC Card 87-400572 DDC 332.4/560987 19
HG3941 .C74 1984

Córdova, Efrén.
Castro and the Cuban labor movement : statecraft and society in a revolutionary period (1959-1961) / Efrén Córdova. Lanham, MD : University Press of America, c1987. xii, 341 p. ; 23 cm. Includes bibliographies and index. ISBN 0-8191-5952-2 (alk. paper) : LC Card 86-28159 DDC 322/.2/097291 19
1. Trade-unions - Cuba - Political activity - History. 2. Central de Trabajadores de Cuba - History. 3. Labor and laboring classes - Cuba - History. 4. Cuba - History - Revolution, 1959. I. Title.
HD6578.5 .C67 1987

Relaciones colectivas del trabajo en América Latina. Portuguese. As relações coletivas de trabalho na América Latina . São Paulo . 327 p. ; LC Card 87-151930 DDC 331/.098 19
HD8110.5 .R3817 1985

Cordts, Willi. Intrasektorale Einkommensstreuung in der Landwirtschaft /. Münster-Hiltrup , 1983. 177 p. : ISBN 3-7843-0281-5 : LC Card 83-236007
HD1955 .I57 1983

Corgan, Jack. Commercial real estate . Dallas, Tex. , c1986. 219 p. : ISBN 0-87833-459-9 : LC Card 85-27108 DDC 332.63/243 19
HD1393.25 .C65 1986 ***NYPL [JLE 86-4267]***

Cori Castro, Wilfredo. Mercados y precios en la economía campesina : el caso de las Provincias Atlas / Wilfredo Cori Castro. [Cuzco, Peru] : Universidad Nacional San Antonio Abad del Cusco, Instituto de Investigación UNSAAC-NUFFIC, 1986. 29 p. : ill. ; 31 cm. (Serie Avances de investigación) "El presente documento es parte del proyecto la economía campesina de las provincias altas." "Convenio de Cooperación Inter Universitaria Peruano-Holandés"--Cover. Includes bibliographical references. LC Card 86-200941
1. Cuzco, Peru (Dept.) - Economic conditions. 2. Capitalism - Peru - Cuzco (Dept.). 3. Peasantry - Peru - Cuzco (Dept.). 4. Farm produce - Peru - Cuzco (Dept.) - Marketing. I. Instituto de Investigación UNSAAC-NUFFIC. II. Series: Serie Avances de Investigación (Cuzco, Peru). III. Title.
HC228.C8 C59 1986

Corlett, E. N. (Esmond Nigel) Copsey, S. M. Shiftwork review . Luxembourg , Washington, DC , 1986. xi, 122 p. : ISBN 92-825-6419-3 (pbk.) : LC Card 87-137298 DDC 331.25/72 19
HD5111.6.E86 C66 1986

Cormier, P. (Pierre) Lépine, Ginette. Vous autres au syndicat-- /. Montréal, Québec , c1984. 179 p. ; ISBN 2-89037-214-6 LC Card 85-101458
HD8005.2.C23 M665 1984

CORN INDUSTRY - BRAZIL - ARAGUAIA RIVER WATERSHED.
Perfis indicativos para a industrialização do arroz, milho e soja. Brasília , 1985. 189 p. : LC Card 86-195651
HD9066.B83 A737 1985

CORN INDUSTRY - BRAZIL - PARANÁ (STATE)
Avila, Luiz Gonçalves. Desenvolvimento industrial e rendimento da terra . Rio de Janeiro, RJ , 1985. 111 p. : LC Card 86-233493
HD1875.S26 A95 1985

CORN INDUSTRY - BRAZIL - SANATA CATARINA (STATE)
Avila, Luiz Gonçalves. Desenvolvimento industrial e rendimento da terra . Rio de Janeiro, RJ , 1985. 111 p. : LC Card 86-233493
HD1875.S26 A95 1985

CORN INDUSTRY - BRAZIL - TOCANTINS RIVER WATERSHED.
Perfis indicativos para a industrialização do arroz, milho e soja. Brasília , 1985. 189 p. : LC Card 86-195651
HD9066.B83 A737 1985

CORN INDUSTRY - HUNGARY.
Ár- és külkereskedelmi tanulmány a buzára és kukoricára, Magyarország /. Budapest , 1984. 93 p. ; ISBN 963-491-218-4 (Magy. nemz. bibl.) LC Card 86-147569
HD9049.W5 H93 1984

CORN INDUSTRY - PHILIPPINES - HISTORY - STATISTICS.
Selected statistics on rice & corn . Diliman, Quezon City [1969] xxix, 306 p. : LC Card 87-400545 DDC 338.1/7315/09599021 19
HD9066.P62 S45 1969

CORN - PRICES - HUNGARY.
Ár- és külkereskedelmi tanulmány a buzára és kukoricára, Magyarország /. Budapest , 1984. 93 p. ; ISBN 963-491-218-4 (Magy. nemz. bibl.) LC Card 86-147569
HD9049.W5 H93 1984

CORN TRADE - ZAMBIA - MPIKA DISTRICT.
Agricultural commercialisation and the allocation of labour time in Mpika District, northern Zambia. Mpika, Zambia [1986?] iii, 42 leaves : LC Card 86-981249 DDC 338.1/096894 19
HD2131.5.Z9 M653 1986

CORN - ZAMBIA - MPIKA DISTRICT.
Agricultural commercialisation and the allocation of labour time in Mpika District, northern Zambia. Mpika, Zambia [1986?] iii, 42 leaves : LC Card 86-981249 DDC 338.1/096894 19
HD2131.5.Z9 M653 1986

Cornblit, Oscar. Sindicatos obreros y asociaciones empresarias hasta la década del centenario / Oscar Cornblit. Buenos Aires, Argentina : Instituto Torcuato Di Tella, Centro de Investigaciones Sociales, 1984. 109 p. ; 26 cm. (Documento de trabajo / Instituto Torcuato Di Tella, Centro de Investigaciones Sociales . no. 94) Bibliography: p. 72-109. LC Card 87-401262 DDC 331.88/0982 19
1. Trade-unions - Argentina - History. 2. Employers' associations - Argentina - History. I. Series: Documento de trabajo (Centro de Investigaciones Sociales (Instituto Torcuato Di Tella)) , no. 94. II. Title.
HD6602 .C665 1984

Cornejo Ramírez, Enrique. Rebolledo Soberón, Luis. Deuda externa . [Lima] , c1985. 58 p. : LC Card 86-120059
HJ8514.5 .R43 1985

Cornelius, Wayne A., 1945- The political economy of Mexico under de la Madrid : the crisis deepens, 1985-1986 / by Wayne A. Cornelius. La Jolla, Calif. : Center for U. S.-Mexican Studies, University of California, San Diego, 1986. 50 p. ; 23 cm. (Research report series / Center for U. S.-Mexican Studies, University of California, San Diego . 43) Includes bibliographical references. LC Card 87-621352 DDC 330.972/0834 19
1. Mexico - Economic policy 1970-. 2. Mexico - Economic conditions - 1970-. 3. Madrid Hurtado, Miguel de la. I. Series: Research report series (University of California, San Diego. Center for U. S.-Mexican Studies) , 43. II. Title.
HC135 .C7185 1986

Corneliussen, Lene. 90 plus 10 /. [Copenhagen] [1986] 39 p. : ISBN 87-7002-353-0 LC Card 86-197313
HD5799.A6 A12 1986

Cornell international industrial and labor relations reports .
(no. 13) Semyonov, Moshe. Hewers of wood and drawers of water . Ithaca, NY , c1987. xii, 152 p. : ISBN 0-87546-133-6 (pbk. : alk. paper) LC Card 87-2682 DDC 331.6/99275695 19
HD8660 .S45 1987

Cornell, Lasse. Arbete och arbetsformernas utveckling / Lars Cornell. Göteborg : [Ekonomisk-historiska institutionen, Göteborgs universitet], 1986. 161 p. : ill. ; 23 cm. (Meddelanden från Ekonomisk-historiska institutionen vid Göteborgs universitet, 0072-5080 . 55) Bibliography: p. 145-157. ISBN 91-85196-27-4 LC Card 86-212110
1. Labor and laboring classes - History. I. Title. II. Series.
HD4851 .C67 1986

Cornell studies in political economy.
Hawes, Gary, 1950- The Philippine State and the Marcos regime . Ithaca , 1987. 196 p. ; ISBN 0-8014-2012-1 (alk. paper) LC Card 86-29237 DDC 382/.41/09599 19
HD9016.P52 H38 1987

Laux, Jeanne Kirk, 1942- State capitalism . Ithaca , 1988. ix, 250 p. ; ISBN 0-8014-2079-2 (alk. paper) LC Card 87-47600 DDC 338.6/2/0971 19
HD4005 .L38 1988

The Political economy of the new Asian industrialism /. Ithaca, N.Y. , 1987. 252 p. ; ISBN 0-8014-1948-4 (alk. paper) LC Card 86-29103 DDC 338.95 19
HC460.5 .P65 1987

The Politics of international debt /. Ithaca , 1986. 272 p. ; ISBN 0-8014-1911-5 (alk. paper) LC Card 85-48243 DDC 327.1/11 19
HJ8083 .P65 1986 ***NYPL [JLE 86-2405]***

Samuels, Richard J. The business of the Japanese state . Ithaca , 1987. xii, 359 p. : ISBN 0-8014-2022-9 (alk. paper) LC Card 87-5230 DDC 338.4/7621042/0952 19
HD9502.J32 S27 1987

Vogel, David, 1947- National styles of regulation . Ithaca, N.Y. , 1986. 325 p. ; ISBN 0-8014-1658-2 LC Card 85-21332 DDC

363.7/056/0941 19
HC260.E5 V64 1986 ***NYPL [JLE 86-2434]***

Cornell University. Audio-Visual Resource Center. Take control of your finances [slide] . Ithaca, NY , 1984. 66 slides : LC Card 87-705083 DDC 640 11
HG179

Cornell University. Center for International Studies. Rural Development Committee. see **Cornell University. Rural Development Committee.**

Cornell University. China-Japan Program. Kelly, William W. (William Wright), 1946- Water control in Tokugawa Japan . Ithaca, N.Y. , c1982. ix, 260 p. : LC Card 83-126822
HD1741.J32 A325 1982

Cornell University. College of Agriculture and Life Sciences. see **New York State College of Agriculture and Life Sciences.**

Cornell University. Cooperative Extension. Take control of your finances [slide] . Ithaca, NY , 1984. 66 slides : LC Card 87-705083 DDC 640 11
HG179

Cornell University East Asia papers . (no. 31) Kelly, William W. (William Wright), 1946- Water control in Tokugawa Japan . Ithaca, N.Y. , c1982. ix, 260 p. : LC Card 83-126822
HD1741.J32 A325 1982

Cornell University East Asia papers, 8756-5293 . (no. 45) Pauly, Louis W. Regulatory politics in Japan . Ithaca, N.Y. , c1987. vi, 82 p. ; ISBN 0-939657-45-7 (pbk.) LC Card 87-403245 DDC 332.1/5/0952 19
HG3324 .P38 1987

Cornell University. Media Services. Take control of your finances [slide] . Ithaca, NY , 1984. 66 slides : LC Card 87-705083 DDC 640 11
HG179

Cornell University. New York State College of Agriculture and Life Sciences. see **New York State College of Agriculture and Life Sciences.**

Cornell University. Rural Development Committee. Uphoff, Norman Thomas. Local institutional development . West Hartford, CT , c1986. xv, 421 p. ; ISBN 0-931816-45-9 LC Card 86-15288 DDC 302.3/5 19
HC59.7 .U64 1986 ***NYPL [JLE 87-1200]***

Cornell/international agricultural economics study.
Ewell, Peter T., 1947- Uxpanapa . Ithaca, N.Y. [1982] xiv, 218 p., [35] leaves of plates : LC Card 84-621492 DDC 338.1/0972/6 19
HD1795.P3 E94 1982

CORNERS, COMMERCIAL. see **MONOPOLIES; SPECULATION; STOCK-EXCHANGE.**

Cornfield, Daniel B. Workers, managers, and technological change . New York , c1987. xxii, 362 p. : ISBN 0-306-42450-9 LC Card 87-2327 DDC 331/.0973 19
HD6331.2.U5 W67 1987

Cornia, Giovanni Andrea. The Impact of world recession on children /. Oxford [Oxfordshire] , New York , 1984. xiv, 221 p. : ISBN 0-08-031329-9 : LC Card 84-14694 DDC 362.7/042 19
HV715 .I475 1984 ***NYPL [JLE 86-2315]***

CORNISH - AUSTRALIA - HISTORY.
Payton, Philip, 1953- The Cornish miner in Australia . Trewolsta, Trewirgie, Kernow [Cornwall] , 1984. xi, 242 p. : ISBN 0-907566-51-0 : LC Card 85-202456 DDC 305.8/9167094 19
HD8039.M62 A87 1984
NYPL [JLD 86-4079]

Cornish, Derek B. (Derek Blaikie), 1939- The Reasoning criminal . New York , c1986. xiv, 246 p. : ISBN 0-387-96272-7 : LC Card 86-1275 DDC 364.3 19
HV6080 .R38 1986 ***NYPL [JLE 86-3522]***

The Cornish miner in Australia . Payton, Philip, 1953- Trewolsta, Trewirgie, Kernow [Cornwall] , 1984. xi, 242 p. : ISBN 0-907566-51-0 : LC Card 85-202456 DDC 305.8/9167094 19
HD8039.M62 A87 1984
NYPL [JLD 86-4079]

Cornyn-Selby, Alyce, 1946- Take your hands off my attitude! : your right to a bad attitude--the only remaining hope for sanity in service industries / by Alyce P. Cornyn-Selby. Portland, Or. : Beynch Press, 1987. p. cm. ISBN 0-941383-02-4 : LC Card 87-15074 DDC 158.7 19
1. Organizational effectiveness. 2. Attitude (Psychology). 3. Attitude change. I. Title.
HD58.9 .C67 1987

COROMANDEL COAST (INDIA) - COMMERCE - HISTORY.
Arasaratnam, Sinnappah. Merchants, companies, and commerce on the Coromandel Coast, 1650-1740 /. Delhi , New York , 1986. x, 407 p. : ISBN 0-19-561873-4 : LC Card 86-900014 DDC 380.1/0954 19
HF3789.C67 A73 1986

Corona V., Rodolfo. Evaluación de los datos censales de 1980 : población residente y migración en Baja California / Rodolfo Corona.1a ed. Tijuana, Baja California : Centro de Estudios Fronterizos del Norte de México, 1986. 172 p. : ill. ; 23 cm. (Cuadernos CEFNOMEX) Includes bibliographical references. ISBN 968-607-510-0 LC Card 87-117630 DDC 304.6/0723 19
1. Baja California Norte (Mexico) - Census, 1980 - Evaluation. 2. Baja California Sur (Mexico) - Census, 1980 - Evaluation. I. Title. II. Series.
HA767.B34 C67 1986

Coronet/MTI Film and Video. Billion dollar day [videorecording] /. Deerfield, IL , 1986. 1 videocassette (30 min.) : LC Card 86-700167 DDC 332.4 11
HG3903

Corporación de Estudios Ganaderos y Agrícolas (Bogotá, Colombia) Problemas agrarios colombianos /. [Bogotá, Colombia] , México, D.F. , 1986. 467 p. : ISBN 958-606-005-5 LC Card 86-221632
HD1882 .P75 1986

Corporación de Estudios para el Desarrollo (Ecuador)
Análisis del presupuesto general del estado de 1986. [Quito, Ecuador] [1986] ii, 2, 26, 8 p. ; LC Card 87-115859
HJ955 .A523 1986

Coyuntura económica ecuatoriana, 1985-1986. [Quito, Ecuador] [1986] i, 39 p. ; LC Card 86-217289
HC202 .C73 1986

Resultados y perspectivas de la economía ecuatoriana, 1984-1985. Quito, Ecuador [1985] 27, 7 p. ; LC Card 85-215488
HC202 .R47 1985

Corporación de Investigaciones Económicas para Latinoamérica. Políticas macro-económicas . Santiago de Chile [1986] 409 p. : LC Card 87-403669 DDC 338.98 19
HC125 .P657 1986

Corporación de los Andes. Universidad de los Andes (Mérida, Venezuela). Instituto de Investigaciones Económicas. Plan de desarrollo regional /. Mérida , 1973- v. <1-5 > : LC Card 86-202604
HC238.A683 U55 1973

Corporación Editora Nacional (Quito, Ecuador)
La Crisis de la economía ecuatoriana . Quito , 1986. 232 p. : LC Card 87-400395 DDC 330.9866/074 19
HC202 .C755 1986

El Ecuador en la encrucijada . Quito , 1986. 307 p. : LC Card 87-400394 DDC 331.12/09866 19
HD5758.A6 E28 1986

Corporación Financiera de Desarrollo (Peru). Oficina de Asuntos Culturales. Numeracion general de todas las personas de ambos sexos, edades y calidades q[ue] se hà hecho en esta ciudad de Lima, año de 1700 /. Lima , 1985. xv, 358 p. : LC Card 87-400680
HA1069.L7 N86 1985

CORPORACIÓN MINERA DE BOLIVIA.
Diagnóstico general de la Corporación Minera de Bolivia, 1985 . La Paz, Bolivia , 1986. 2 v. ; LC Card 87-401587 DDC 338.2/0984 19
HD9506.B64 C646 1986

CORPORACIÓN MINERA DE BOLIVIA - HISTORY.
Tórrez G. O., José Guillermo (Torrez Gómez Ortega) Minería e integración boliviana /. La Paz, Bolivia , 1986. 181 p., [8] leaves of plates : LC Card 87-400195 DDC 338.2/0984 19
HD9506.B64 C67 1986

Corporate accounting systems . Smith, Kenneth, 1932- Workingham, England , Reading, Mass. , c1988. p. cm. ISBN 0-201-17824-9 LC Card 87-24130 DDC 657/.028/55 19
HF5679 .S645 1988

The corporate address book . Levine, Michael. New York, N.Y. , c1987. 268 p. ; ISBN 0-399-51384-1 (pbk.) LC Card 87-11162 DDC 338.7/4/02573 19
HG4057 .A288 1987

Corporate asset management . Chastain, Clark E. New York , 1987. xxiii, 345 p. : ISBN 0-89930-237-8 (lib. bdg. : alk. paper) LC Card 87-2493 DDC 658.1/5244 19
HG4026 .C458 1987

Corporate Benefits Management Conferences (1986 : Phoenix, Ariz., etc.) Managing corporate benefit plans, 1986 / edited by Mary E. Brennan. Brookfield, Wis. : International Foundation of Employee Benefit Plans, 1986. x, 129 p. : ill. ; 23 cm. "1986 Corporate Benefits Management Conferences, sponsored by the International Foundation of Employee Benefit Plans, April 2-5, Phoenix, Ariz.; May 7-10, Atlantic City, N.J.; August 3-6, Monterey, Calif." Bibliography: p. 20-23. ISBN 0-89154-318-X (pbk.) : LC Card 87-403111 DDC 332.6/7254 19
1. Pension trusts - United States - Management - Congresses. 2. Employee fringe benefits - United States - Management - Congresses. I. Brennan, Mary E. II. International Foundation of Employee Benefit Plans. III. Title.
HD7105.45.U6 C67 1986

The corporate board . Hall, R. Duane. New York , c1987. p. cm. ISBN 0-394-55327-6 : LC Card 87-4937 DDC 658.4/22 19
HD2745 .H34 1987

Corporate capital . Pitelis, Christos. Cambridge [Cambridgeshire] , New York , 1987. viii, 136 p. ; ISBN 0-521-32848-9 LC Card 86-26807 DDC 658.1/5 19
HG4026 .P575 1987

Corporate credit assessment. Bathory, Alexander. The analysis of credit . London , New York , c1987. xiii, 385 p. ; ISBN 0-07-084938-2 : LC Card 87-2060 DDC 658.8/8 19
HG3751 .B385 1987

CORPORATE CULTURE.
Albrecht, Karl. The creative corporation /. Homewood, Ill. , c1987. x, 218 p. ; ISBN 0-87094-929-2 LC Card 86-51668 DDC 302.3/5 19
HD53 .A42 1987

Baba, Marietta L. Business and industrial anthropology . Washington, D.C. , c1986. vii, 48 p. ; ISBN 0-913167-16-9 (pbk.) : LC Card 86-26602 DDC 302.3/5 19
HD58.7 .B33 1986

Dyer, W. Gibb, 1954- Cultural change in family firms . San Francisco , 1986. xxi, 179 p. ; ISBN 1-555-42007-9 (alk. paper) LC Card 86-10585 DDC 658/.045 19
HD62.25 .D94 1986 ***NYPL [JLE 87-1079]***

Ebers, Mark. Organisationskultur, ein neues Forschungsprogramm? /. Wiesbaden , c1985. 223 p. ; ISBN 3-409-13105-1 LC Card 86-135588
HD58.8 .E24 1985

Harris, Philip R. (Philip Robert), 1926- Management in transition . San Francisco, Calif. , c1985. xxvii, 404 p. : ISBN 0-87589-660-X (alk. paper) LC Card 85-45055 DDC 658.4 19
HD58.7 .H3695 1985 ***NYPL [JLE 85-3954]***

Kantrow, Alan M., 1947- The constraints of corporate tradition . New York , c1987. xvii, 216 p. ; ISBN 0-06-015753-4 : LC Card 86-46075 DDC 302.3/5 19
HD58.7 .K375 1987

Korn, Lester. The winning edge . New York , c1988. p. cm. ISBN 0-671-55263-5 LC Card

87-23249 DDC 658.4/09 19
HD38.2 .K67 1988

Poiani, Mario, 1934- La cultura d'impresa . Milano, Italy , c1986. 212, [1] p. ; LC Card 86-221350
HD58.7 .P63 1986

Schuster, Fred E. The Schuster report . New York , c1986. xvi, 200 p. : ISBN 0-471-83293-6 : LC Card 86-9190 DDC 658.3/14 19
HD58.8 .S38 1986 *NYPL [JLE 86-3973]*

Werder, Axel von. Organisationsstruktur und Rechtsnorm . Wiesbaden , c1986. 564 p. : ISBN 3-409-13107-8 LC Card 86-224483
HD58.7 .W35 1986

Westoff, Leslie Aldridge. Corporate romance . New York, NY , c1985. xiii, 246 p. ; ISBN 0-8129-1257-8 : LC Card 85-40284 DDC 658.4/095 19
HD6054.3 .W47 1985 *NYPL [JLD 86-1042]*

CORPORATE CULTURE - FRANCE.
Mothé-Gautrat, Daniel, 1924- Pour une nouvelle culture d'entreprise /. Paris , 1986. 173 p. ; ISBN 2-7071-1596-7 : LC Card 86-185142
HD8431 .M63 1986

CORPORATE CULTURE - GERMANY (WEST)
Arbeitsgestaltung in der Serienfertigung . Frankfurt [am Main] , New York , c1984. 315 p. : ISBN 3-593-32733-3 LC Card 84-230390
HD58.8 .A73 1984

CORPORATE CULTURE - SWITZERLAND - CASE STUDIES.
Kurmann, Bernadette, 1950- Firmenkultur am Beispiel der Sarna /. Bern [1985] 119 p. ; ISBN 3-258-03560-1 : LC Card 86-123837 DDC 338.7/6684/09494 19
HD9661.S94 S275 1985
NYPL [JLD 86-4028]

CORPORATE CULTURE - UNITED STATES.
Hirsch, Paul Morris. Pack your own parachute . Reading, Mass. , c1987. xix, 197 p. ; ISBN 0-201-12205-7 (pbk.) : LC Card 87-14388 DDC 658.4/09 19
HD38.25.U6 H578 1987

Corporate debt : a profile of major indicators : a report / prepared by the Congressional Research Service for the use of the Subcommittee on Telecommunications, Consumer Protection, and Finance of the Committee on Energy and Commerce, U. S. House of Representatives. Washington : U. S. G.P.O. : For sale by the Supt. of Docs., Congressional Sales Office, U. S. G.P.O., 1986. v, 31 p. : ill. ; 24 cm. At head of title: 99th Congress, 2d session. Committee print. Distributed to some depository libraries in microfiche. Shipping list no.: 86-801-P. "September 1986." Includes bibliographical references. "Committee print 99-KK." Item 1019-A, 1019-B (microfiche) LC Card 86-603382 DDC 338.7/4/0973 19
1. Corporate debt - United States. I. Library of Congress. Congressional Research Service. II. United States. Congress. House. Committee on Energy and Commerce. Subcommittee on Telecommunications, Consumer Protection, and Finance.
HG4028.D3 C67 1986

CORPORATE DEBT - UNITED STATES.
Corporate debt . Washington , 1986. v, 31 p. : LC Card 86-603382 DDC 338.7/4/0973 19
HG4028.D3 C67 1986

CORPORATE DESIGN COORDINATION. see **INDUSTRIAL DESIGN COORDINATION.**

CORPORATE DIVESTITURE - DEVELOPING COUNTRIES.
Berg, Elliot. Divestiture in developing countries /. Washington, D.C. , 1987. vii, 30 p. : ISBN 0-8213-0917-X (pbk.) LC Card 87-14235 DDC 338.9/009172/4 19
HD4420.8 .B45 1987

CORPORATE DIVESTITURE - SOUTH AFRICA.
Voorhes, Meg. Black South African views on disinvestment /. Washington, D.C. (Suite 600, 1755 Massachusetts Ave., N.W., Washington 20036) [1986] 36 p. ; LC Card 86-209279 DDC 332.6/73/0968 19
HG5851.A3 V66 1986

CORPORATE DIVESTITURE - UNITED STATES.
Hauck, David. U. S. corporate withdrawal from South Africa . Washington, D.C. (Suite 600, 1755 Massachusetts Ave., N.W., Washington 20036) [1986] 22 p. ; LC Card 86-209299 DDC 332.6/7373/068 19
HG5851.A3 H39 1986

Ravenscraft, David J., 1952- Mergers, sell-offs, and economic efficiency /. Washington, D.C. , c1987. xiii, 290 p. : ISBN 0-8157-7348-X : LC Card 87-14018 DDC 338.8/3/0973 19
HD2746.5 .R38 1987

Corporate finance /. Ross, Stephen A. St. Louis , 1988. xxvii, 857 p. : ISBN 0-8016-4211-6 (pbk.) LC Card 87-18076 DDC 658.1/5 19
HG4026 .R675 1988

CORPORATE FINANCE. see **CORPORATIONS - FINANCE.**

Corporate finance and accounting. Woelfel, Charles J. The desktop encyclopedia of corporate finance & accounting /. Chicago, Ill. , c1987. viii, 518 p. : ISBN 0-917253-65-5 : LC Card 87-2302 DDC 658.1/5 19
HG4027.3 .W64 1987

Corporate finance & accounting. Woelfel, Charles J. The desktop encyclopedia of corporate finance & accounting /. Chicago, Ill. , c1987. viii, 518 p. : ISBN 0-917253-65-5 : LC Card 87-2302 DDC 658.1/5 19
HG4027.3 .W64 1987

Corporate finance and fiscal policy in Ireland /. Stewart, J. C., 1949- Aldershot, Hants, England , Brookfield, Vt., USA , c1987. x, 166 p. ; ISBN 0-566-05441-8 : LC Card 87-14908 DDC 658.1/5/09415 19
HG4144 .S74 1987

Corporate financial planning and management in a deficit economy /. Nevaer, Louis E. V. New York , 1987. 171 p. : ISBN 0-89930-202-5 (lib. bdg. : alk. paper) LC Card 86-25582 DDC 658.1/145 19
HG4063 .N48 1987

Corporate financing in international markets /. Davey, Patrick J. New York, N.Y. (845 3rd Ave., New York 10022) , c1986. 15 p. ; LC Card 86-212373 DDC 658.1/599 19
HG4061 .D384 1986

Corporate financing, 1960-1969. Hillstrom, Roger. 1960-1969, a decade of corporate and international finance. New York [1972] 381 p. LC Card 72-175335 DDC 332
HG4907 .H54 *NYPL [JLG 73-17]*

Corporate fraud /. Comer, Michael J. London , New York , 1985. xvi, 453 p. : ISBN 0-07-084791-6 : LC Card 85-11686 DDC 364.1/63 19
HV6768 .C65 1985 *NYPL [JLE 86-909]*

Corporate governance and shareholder rights . Mathiasen, Karen. Washington, DC (1755 Massachusetts Ave., N.W., Suite 600, Washington 20036) , c1986. 96 p. ; LC Card 86-230362 DDC 346.73/0666 347.306666 19
HD2743 .M34 1986

Corporate governance service.
Mathiasen, Karen. Corporate governance and shareholder rights . Washington, DC (1755 Massachusetts Ave., N.W., Suite 600, Washington 20036) , c1986. 96 p. ; LC Card 86-230362 DDC 346.73/0666 347.306666 19
HD2743 .M34 1986

The Corporate guide to parental leaves, including Catalyst's Report on a national study of parental leaves / by the staff of Catalyst. New York, NY (250 Park Ave. South, New York 10003) : Catalyst, c1986. 145 p. : ill. ; 30 cm. "Report on a national study of parental leaves" (82 p. : ill. ; 28 cm.) inserted in pocket. LC Card 87-161920 DDC 658.3/122 19
1. Parental leave - United States. 2. Corporate planning - United States. I. Catalyst, inc. II. Report on a national study of parental leaves. 1986.
HD6065.5.U6 C67 1986

Corporate identity design /. Napoles, Veronica, 1951- New York , c1988. 144 p. : ISBN 0-442-26844-0 (pbk.) : LC Card 87-6190 DDC 659.2/85 19
HD59.2 .N36 1988

CORPORATE IMAGE.
Napoles, Veronica, 1951- Corporate identity design /. New York , c1988. 144 p. : ISBN 0-442-26844-0 (pbk.) : LC Card 87-6190 DDC 659.2/85 19
HD59.2 .N36 1988

CORPORATE IMAGE AND DESIGN. see **INDUSTRIAL DESIGN COORDINATION.**

Corporate income tax and profit rates . Sen, Tapas Kumar, 1956- New Delhi , c1984. xiii, 267 p. ; LC Card 84-900209 DDC 336.24/3/0954 19
HJ4766.Z7 S46 1984 *NYPL [JLD 86-4138]*

The corporate infighter's handbook . Davis, William, 1933- London , 1984. 144 p. : ISBN 0-283-99133-X (pbk.) : LC Card 85-240558 DDC 650.1 19
HF5386 .D325 1984 *NYPL [JLE 87-618]*

CORPORATE INSURANCE. see **INSURANCE, BUSINESS.**

CORPORATE INVESTMENT RESEARCH AND CONSULTANCY BUREAU (INDIA)
Structure and management of the gilt-edged securities market in India. New Delhi , 1983. v, 186 p. : LC Card 84-901424 DDC 332.63/2044 19
HG5735 .S77 1983 *NYPL [JLD 87-871]*

CORPORATE MANAGEMENT.
Schwenk, Charles R. The essence of strategic decision making /. Lexington, Mass. , c1988. xii, 138 p. : ISBN 0-669-13023-0 (alk. paper) LC Card 86-80040 DDC 658.4/03 19
HD30.23 .S39 1988

CORPORATE MANAGEMENT - CASE STUDIES.
Schwenk, Charles R. The essence of strategic decision making /. Lexington, Mass. , c1988. xii, 138 p. : ISBN 0-669-13023-0 (alk. paper) LC Card 86-80040 DDC 658.4/03 19
HD30.23 .S39 1988

Corporate Management Tax Conference (1986)
Income tax considerations in corporate financing. Toronto, Canada : Canadian Tax Foundation, c1986. xv, 475 p. : ill. ; 23 cm. Includes bibliographical references. ISBN 0-88808-027-1 : LC Card 87-153466 DDC 658.1/53 19
1. Corporations - Canada - Finance - Congresses. 2. Corporations - Taxation - Canada - Congresses. I. Canadian Tax Foundation. II. Title.
HG4090 .C67 1986

CORPORATE MEETINGS.
Carnes, William T. Effective meetings for busy people . New York , c1987. xvi, 348 p. ; ISBN 0-87942-211-4 LC Card 86-27719 DDC 658.4/563 19
HD2743 .C37 1987

CORPORATE MEETINGS - UNITED STATES.
Epstein, Edward Jay, 1935- Who owns the corporation? . New York , 1986. vi, 69 p. ; ISBN 0-87078-208-8 (pbk.) : LC Card 87-101003 DDC 338.7/4/0973 19
HD2743 .E67 1986

CORPORATE MERGERS. see **CONSOLIDATION AND MERGER OF CORPORATIONS.**

Corporate mergers and high yield (junk) bonds : recent market trends and regulatory developments : a report / prepared by the Congressional Research Service for the use of the Subcommittee on Telecommunications, Consumer Protection, and Finance of the Committee on Energy and Commerce, U. S. House of Representatives. Washington : U. S. G.P.O. : For sale by the Supt. of Docs., Congressional Sales Office, U. S. G.P.O., 1986. vi, 57 p. ; 24 cm. At head of title: 99th Congress, 2d session. Committee print. Distributed to some depository libraries in microfiche. Shipping list no.: 86-1001-P. "December 1986." Includes bibliographical references. "Committee print 99-00." Item 1019-A, 1019-B (microfiche) LC Card 87-601339 DDC 332.63/22 19
1. Consolidation and merger of corporations - United States. 2. Junk bonds - United States. 3. Bonds - United States. 4. Securities - United States. I. Library of Congress. Congressional Research Service. II. United States. Congress. House. Committee on Energy and Commerce. Subcommittee on Telecommunications, Consumer Protection, and Finance.
HD2746.5 .C67 1986

Corporate P.A.C's and federal campaign financing laws. Matasar, Ann B. Corporate PACs and federal campaign financing laws . New York , 1986. x, 161 p. ; ISBN 0-89930-086-3 (lib. bdg. : alk. paper) *NYPL [JLE 86-2492]*

Corporate PACs and federal campaign financing laws . Matasar, Ann B. New York , 1986. x, 161 p. ; ISBN 0-89930-086-3 (lib. bdg. : alk. paper) *NYPL [JLE 86-2492]*

Corporate Ph. D. Groneman, Carol. [Corporate Ph. D.] Corporate PhD . New York, N.Y., U. S.A. , 1987, c1985. xx, 156 p. ; ISBN 0-14-010123-3 (pbk.) LC Card 86-30654 DDC 658.4/09 19
HD38.25.U6 G76 1987

Corporate PhD . Groneman, Carol. [Corporate Ph. D.] New York, N.Y., U. S.A. , 1987, c1985. xx, 156 p. ; ISBN 0-14-010123-3 (pbk.) LC Card 86-30654 DDC 658.4/09 19
HD38.25.U6 G76 1987

Corporate planning and strategies in forest industries /. Sierila, Pentti, 1934- Atlanta, GA, USA , c1987. vii, 138 p. : ISBN 0-89852-441-5 (pbk.) LC Card 87-50439 DDC 634.9/8/068 19
HD9750.5 .S54 1987

CORPORATE PLANNING - CASE STUDIES.
Bartlett, Hale C. Cases in strategic management for business /. Chicago , c1988. xiii, 784 p. : ISBN 0-03-007183-6 (pbk.) LC Card 87-20208 DDC 658.4/012 19
HD30.28 .B369 1988

Pearce, John A. Company and industry cases in strategy and policy /. Homewood, IL , 1986. xiv, 711 p. : ISBN 0-256-03558-X : LC Card 85-82002 *NYPL [JLE 87-993]*

CORPORATE PLANNING - CONGRESSES.
The Management of strategic change /. Oxford [Oxfordshire] , New York, NY , 1988, c1987. p. cm. ISBN 0-631-15695-X : LC Card 87-15634 DDC 658.4/012 19
HD30.28 .M344 1988

A Vállalati tervezés uj módszere . [Pécs] [1985?] 167 p. : LC Card 86-187131
HD29 .V35 1985

CORPORATE PLANNING - DATA PROCESSING.
Barakonyi, Károly. Számítógépes vállalati tervezés /. Budapest , 1984. 320, [1] p. : ISBN 963-221-456-0 (Magy. nemz. bibl.) : LC Card 85-174882
HD30.2 .B36 1984

Cantore, Corrado M., 1948- Modelli di programmazione matematica per la pianificazione aziendale /. Milano [1978] 295 p. ; LC Card 79-338281
HD30.28 .C36 *NYPL [JLD 80-3558]*

CORPORATE PLANNING - FRANCE.
Zémor, Pierre. Un bon conseil . Paris , c1986. 278 p. : ISBN 2-85565-300-2 : LC Card 86-174727
HD69.C6 Z4 1986

CORPORATE PLANNING - HANDBOOKS, MANUALS, ETC.
Business planning guide . Dover, N.H. (50 Mill St., Dover 03820) , c1985. vii, 115 p. : LC Card 86-622397 DDC 658.4/01 19
HD30.28 .B85 1985

CORPORATE PLANNING - ITALY.
Cardillo, Giovanni. La programmabilità delle gestioni aziendali in tempi di inflazione /. Milano , 1983. 118 p. ; LC Card 84-177279 DDC 658.4/012/0945 19
HD70.I8 C27 1983 *NYPL [JLD 86-1047]*

Scelte strategiche e riorganizzazione aziendale . Milano, Italy , c1985. 312 p. ; LC Card 86-146459
HD2864 .S36 1985 *NYPL [JLD 87-1549]*

CORPORATE PLANNING - ITALY - CASE STUDIES.
Società di terziario avanzato e professionalità . Roma [1984] 159 p. : LC Card 85-232870
HD69.C6 S66 1984

CORPORATE PLANNING - JAPAN.
Hirono, Ryōkichi. Factors which hinder or help productivity improvement in the Asian region, a review and the prospect . Tokyo, Japan , c1980. v, 111 p. ; ISBN 92-833-1470-0 LC Card 81-174179 DDC 338/.06/0952 19
HD56 .H57 1980 *NYPL [JLE 86-2287]*

CORPORATE PLANNING - MATHEMATICAL MODELS.
Cantore, Corrado M., 1948- Modelli di programmazione matematica per la pianificazione aziendale /. Milano [1978] 295 p. ; LC Card 79-338281
HD30.28 .C36 *NYPL [JLD 80-3558]*

Hilfer, Rudolf. Stochastische Modelle für die betriebliche Planung /. München , c1985. ii, 191 p. : ISBN 3-89003-015-7 LC Card 85-189343
HD30.25 .H55 1985

Meijboom, Bert R., 1957- Planning in decentralized firms . Berlin , New York , c1987. x, 168 p. : ISBN 0-387-17795-7 (U. S. : pbk.) : LC Card 87-9824 DDC 658.4/012 19
HD30.28 .M43 1987

CORPORATE PLANNING - NETHERLANDS.
Ondernemingsstrategie, theorie en praktijk . Leiden , c1986. xi, 346 p. : ISBN 90-207-1424-4 : LC Card 86-199689
HD37.D8 O54 1986

CORPORATE PLANNING - UNITED STATES.
Certo, Samuel C. Strategic management . New York , c1988. p. cm. ISBN 0-394-35920-8 : LC Card 87-23565 DDC 658.4/012 19
HD30.28 .C43 1988.

The Corporate guide to parental leaves, including Catalyst's Report on a national study of parental leaves /. New York, NY (250 Park Ave. South, New York 10003) , c1986. 145 p. : LC Card 87-161920 DDC 658.3/122 19
HD6065.5.U6 C67 1986

Friedman, Stewart D. Leadership succession systems and corporate performance /. New York, N.Y. (316 Uris Hall, New York, N.Y. 10027) , c1985. ix, 141 p. : *NYPL [JLF 87-255]*

Nevaer, Louis E. V. Corporate financial planning and management in a deficit economy /. New York , 1987. 171 p. : ISBN 0-89930-202-5 (lib. bdg. : alk. paper) LC Card 86-25582 DDC 658.1/145 19
HG4063 .N48 1987

CORPORATE PLANNING - UNITED STATES - CASE STUDIES.
Certo, Samuel C. Strategic management . New York , c1988. p. cm. ISBN 0-394-35920-8 : LC Card 87-23565 DDC 658.4/012 19
HD30.28 .C43 1988.

Mescon, Timothy S. Cases in strategic management . New York , c1988. ix, 725 p. : ISBN 0-06-044465-7 (pbk.) LC Card 87-25141 DDC 658.4/012 19
HD30.28 .M46 1988

Corporate power and Canadian capitalism /. Carroll, William K. Vancouver , 1986. xvii, 284 p. : ISBN 0-7748-0246-4 LC Card 86-223683 DDC 338.8/0971 19
HC120.C3 C37 1986

Corporate productivity in action . Martin, Doris. Wailuku, Hawaii , c1987. 89 p. ; ISBN 0-9615541-0-X (pbk.) LC Card 85-90446 DDC 658.3/14 19
HC110.I52 M37 1987

CORPORATE PROFITS.
Davis, Marvin A. Turn-around . Chicago , c1987. 194 p. ; ISBN 0-8092-4780-1 : LC Card 86-29285 DDC 658.4/06 19
HD58.8 .D38 1987

Nunes, Morris A., 1949- Balance sheet management . New York , c1987. xvi, 288 p. : ISBN 0-471-62956-1 (pbk.) LC Card 87-23093 DDC 658.1/51 19
HF5681.B2 N86 1987

CORPORATE PROFITS - IRELAND - EFFECT OF INFLATION ON.
Stewart, J. C., 1949- Corporate finance and fiscal policy in Ireland /. Aldershot, Hants, England , Brookfield, Vt., USA , c1987. x, 166 p. ; ISBN 0-566-05441-8 : LC Card 87-14908 DDC 658.1/5/09415 19
HG4144 .S74 1987

CORPORATE PROFITS - ITALY.
Ecchia, Stefano. La destinazione dell'utile nelle società per azioni . Padova , 1985. 133 p. : LC Card 86-214308
HG4028.P7 E23 1985

CORPORATE PROFITS - JAPAN - MATHEMATICAL MODELS.
Odagiri, Hiroyuki, 1946- A study of company profit-rate time series . Berlin [1986] 15, 5 p. ; LC Card 87-165037 DDC 338.7/4/0952 19
HG4028.P7 O33 1986

CORPORATE PROFITS - MATHEMATICAL MODELS.
Geroski, Paul. The persistence of profits . Berlin [1985] 35, 6 p. : LC Card 86-212315 DDC 338.5/16/0724 19
HG4028.P7 G47 1985

Odagiri, Hiroyuki, 1946- A study of company profit-rate time series . Berlin [1986] 15, 5 p. ; LC Card 87-165037 DDC 338.7/4/0952 19
HG4028.P7 O33 1986

CORPORATE PROFITS - SWEDEN.
Olsson, Hans. Industrins lönsamhet, finansiering och investeringar under 1970-talet . [Stockholm] [1981] 58 p. : ISBN 91-38-06530-4 LC Card 84-120594
HG4211 .O45 1981

CORPORATE PROFITS - UNITED STATES - ACCOUNTING.
Mangold, Nancy R. (Nancy Rueyhwa), 1949- Changing auditors and the effect on earnings, auditors' opinions, and stock prices /. Ann Arbor, Mich. , c1987. viii, 165 p. ; ISBN 0-8357-1786-0 (alk. paper) LC Card 87-19128 DDC 338.7/4/0973 19
HF5686.C7 M3295 1987

Corporate protocol . Grant-Sokolosky, Valerie. Tulsa , c1986. 203 p. : ISBN 0-89274-417-0 (pbk.): LC Card 86-205553 DDC 174/.4 19
HF5387 .G7 1986

Corporate public relations and American private enterprise . Olasky, Marvin N. Hillsdale, NJ , 1987. p. cm. ISBN 0-8058-0052-2 LC Card 87-3551 DDC 659.2/0973 19
HD59.6.U6 O4 1987

The corporate reconstruction of American capitalism, 1890-1916 . Sklar, Martin J., 1935- Cambridge [Cambridgeshire] , New York , 1987. p. cm. ISBN 0-521-30921-2 LC Card 87-9408 DDC 338.8/0973 19
HC110.C3 S58 1987

CORPORATE REORGANIZATIONS - CONGRESSES.
Ginzberg, Eli, 1911- Resizing for organizational effectiveness . New York, N.Y. (316 Uris Hall, New York 10027) , c1985. vii, 43 p. ; LC Card 86-162474 DDC 658.1/6 19
HD58.9 .G56 1985

CORPORATE REORGANIZATIONS - GREAT BRITAIN.
Global restructuring local response . London , Merstham, Redhill, Surrey , c1986. 308 p. : ISBN 0-86226-174-0 (pbk.) LC Card 86-197207 DDC 331.12/0941 19
HD6331.2.G7 G57 1986

CORPORATE REORGANIZATIONS - ITALY.
Guatri, Luigi. Crisi e risanamento delle imprese /. Milano , 1986. viii, 339 p. : ISBN 88-14-00914-7 : LC Card 86-228719
HD58.8 .G82 1986

Scelte strategiche e riorganizzazione aziendale . Milano, Italy , c1985. 312 p. ; LC Card 86-146459
HD2864 .S36 1985 *NYPL [JLD 87-1549]*

Corporate romance . Westoff, Leslie Aldridge. New York, NY , c1985. xiii, 246 p. ; ISBN 0-8129-1257-8 : LC Card 85-40284 DDC 658.4/095 19
HD6054.3 .W47 1985 *NYPL [JLD 86-1042]*

Corporate sector and agriculture : proceedings of Assocham Workshop. New Delhi : Associated Chambers of Commerce and Industry of India, [1985] 88 p. ; 26 cm. On the role of corporations in agricultural development in India. LC Card 87-902181 DDC 338.1/0954 19
1. Farm corporations - India. 2. Agriculture, Cooperative - India. I. Associated Chambers of Commerce & Industry of India.
HD2072 .C65 1985

Corporate senior securities . Wilson, Richard S. Chicago, Ill. , c1987. xiv, 459 p. : ISBN 0-917253-79-5 : LC Card 87-6980 DDC 332.63/2 19
HG4963 .W56 1987

Corporate social responsibility : contemporary viewpoints / Suzanne Robitaille Ontiveros, editor ; foreword by Joan L. Bavaria. Santa Barbara, Calif. : ABC-CLIO, c1986. xv, 229 p. ;

24 cm. (The Dynamic organization series) Includes bibliographical references and indexes. ISBN 0-87436-469-8 (alk. paper) : LC Card 86-3416 DDC 658.4/08 19
1. Industry - Social aspects. 2. Corporations - Social aspects. I. Ontiveros, Suzanne R. II. Series.
HD60 .C693 1986 ***NYPL [JLE 86-3089]***

CORPORATE STATE - BRAZIL.
Castro, J. As instituições para-estatais no estado novo /. Rio de Janeiro, Brasil , 1939 (Rio [de Janeiro] : Companhia Carioca) 225 p., [2] leaves of plates : LC Card 85-222446
HD4094 .C35 1939

CORPORATE STATE - EUROPE.
Political stability and neo-corporatism . London , Beverly Hills , 1987. x, 276 p. ; ISBN 0-8039-8028-0 LC Card 86-63492 DDC 321.9 19
HD3616.E8 P64 1987

Wilensky, Harold L. Democratic corporatism and policy linkages . Berkeley , c1987. ix, 97 p. ; ISBN 0-87725-169-X (pbk.) : LC Card 87-3525 DDC 338.9 19
HD3616.E8 W54 1987

CORPORATE STATE - GERMANY (WEST)
Hüttig, Christoph. Gemeinwirtschaft im Sozialstaat . Frankfurt am Main , c1986. vi, 355 p. : ISBN 3-88129-990-4 : LC Card 86-223747
HD4175 .H83 1986

CORPORATE STATE - JAPAN.
Wilensky, Harold L. Democratic corporatism and policy linkages . Berkeley , c1987. ix, 97 p. ; ISBN 0-87725-169-X (pbk.) : LC Card 87-3525 DDC 338.9 19
HD3616.E8 W54 1987

CORPORATE STATE - PHILIPPINES.
Stauffer, Robert B. The Philippines under Marcos . Sydney [1986] 207 p. ; ISBN 0-908470-69-X (pbk.) LC Card 87-123266 DDC 338.9599 19
HD3616.P62 S7 1986

CORPORATE STATE - SWEDEN.
Micheletti, Michele. Organizing interest and organized protest . [Stockholm] , 1985. vii, 253 p. ; ISBN 91-7146-451-4 (pbk.) LC Card 86-145828 DDC 322/.2/09481 19
HD8572.T5 M53 1985
NYPL [JLL 74-316 no.29]

CORPORATE STATE - SWITZERLAND.
Farago, Peter. Verbände als Träger öffentlicher Politik . Grüsch , c1987. xi, 185 p. : ISBN 3-7253-0290-1 LC Card 87-140606 DDC 322/.3/09494 19
HD2429.S92 F37 1987

CORPORATE STATE - UNITED STATES.
Wilensky, Harold L. Democratic corporatism and policy linkages . Berkeley , c1987. ix, 97 p. ; ISBN 0-87725-169-X (pbk.) : LC Card 87-3525 DDC 338.9 19
HD3616.E8 W54 1987

CORPORATE STATE - URUGUAY - HISTORY - 20TH CENTURY.
Lanzaro, Jorge Luis. Sindicatos y sistema político . Montevideo, Uruguay , 1986. 132 p. ; LC Card 87-403149 DDC 322/.2/09895 19
HD3616.U72 L36 1986

Corporate staying power . Hobbs, James B. Lexington, Mass. , c1987. xi, 178 p. ; ISBN 0-669-11153-8 (alk. paper) LC Card 85-45096 DDC 338.7/4/0973 19
HD58.9 .H62 1987 ***NYPL [JLE 87-1125]***

Corporate strategic planning /. Capon, Noel. New York , 1987. p. cm. ISBN 0-231-06380-6 LC Card 87-18239 DDC 658.4/012 19
HD30.28 .C375 1987

Corporate strategies for controlling substance abuse / edited by Helen Axel. New York, N.Y. : Conference Board, c1986. xi, 50 p. ; 28 cm. (Conference Board report. no. 883) Includes bibliographical references. ISBN 0-8237-0327-4 (pbk.) LC Card 86-207704 DDC 658.3/82 19
1. Employee assistance programs - United States. 2. Drugs and employment - United States. 3. Alcoholism and employment - United States. 4. Drug abuse - United States - Prevention. I. Axel, Helen.
HF5549.5.E42 C66 1986

Corporate strategy, organization, and change. Johnson, Gerry. Strategic change and the management process /. Oxford, OX, UK , New York, NY, USA , 1987. xv, 319 p. : ISBN 0-631-14717-9 : LC Card 87-5152 DDC 658.4/012 19
HD30.28 .J65 1987

CORPORATE STYLE. see **INDUSTRIAL DESIGN COORDINATION.**

Corporate support for community development. Washington, D.C. : Community Information Exchange, National Urban Coalition, c1984. 15 p. ; 28 cm. (Technical bulletin) Bibliography: p. 7-12. LC Card 87-100348 DDC 361.7/65/0973 19
1. Industry - Social aspects - United States. 2. Industry - Social aspects - United States - Bibliography. 3. Fund raising - United States - Bibliography. I. Community Information Exchange (National Urban Coalition (U. S.)). II. Series: Technical bulletin (Community Information Exchange (U. S.)).
HD60.5.U5 C689 1984

The corporate survivors /. Stine, G. Harry (George Harry), 1928- New York, N.Y. , c1986. 230 p. : ISBN 0-8144-5831-9 LC Card 86-47597 DDC 338.7/4/0973 19
HD2785 .S73 1986 ***NYPL [JLE 86-4469]***

Corporate takeovers : public policy implications for the economy and corporate governance : a report from the chairman of the Subcommittee on Telecommunications, Consumer Protection, and Finance of the Committee on Energy and Commerce, U. S. House of Representatives. Washington : U. S. G.P.O. : For sale by the Supt. of Docs., U. S. G.P.O., 1987. viii, 126 p. ; 24 cm. At head of title: 99th Congress, 2d session. Committee print. Distributed to some depository libraries in microfiche. Shipping list no.: 86-193-P. "December 1986." Includes bibliographical references. "Committee print 99-QQ." S/N 052-070-06272-0 Item 1019-A, 1019-B (microfiche) LC Card 87-601347 DDC 338.8/3/0973 19
1. Consolidation and merger of corporations - United States. 2. Consolidation and merger of corporations - Economic aspects - United States.
HD2746.5 .C676 1987

Corporate taxation and investment . Morgan, Eleanor. Haldershot, Hants Gull, England , Brookfield, Vt., USA , c1986. x, 220 p. ; ISBN 0-566-05265-2 : LC Card 86-25642 DDC 336.24/3/0941 19
HJ4708.A7 M63 1986

Corporate transformation : revitalizing organizations for a competitive world / [edited by] Ralph H. Kilmann, Teresa Joyce Covin, and associates.1st ed. San Francisco : Jossey-Bass, 1988. xxxi, 553 p. : ill. ; 24 cm. (The Jossey-Bass management series) Based on a conference held Oct. 22-25, 1986, sponsored by the Program in Corporate Culture in the Joseph M. Katz Graduate School of Business, University of Pittsburgh. Includes bibliographies and indexes. ISBN 1-555-42060-5 (alk. paper) LC Card 87-45427 DDC 658.4/063 19
1. Organizational change. 2. Corporate reorganizations. I. Kilmann, Ralph H. II. Covin, Teresa Joyce, 1959-. III. Joseph M. Katz Graduate School of Business. Program in Corporate Culture. IV. Series.
HD58.8 .C66 1988

Corporate valuation . Smith, Gordon V., 1937- New York , c1988. xiv, 224 p. : ISBN 0-471-85826-9 LC Card 87-23114 DDC 658.1/522 19
HG4028.V3 S58 1988

The Corporate view : how business executives rate their trade associations / a survey conducted by the Gallup Organization, Inc., on behalf of the ASAE Foundation ... . Washington, DC : The Foundation, c1982. vii, 92 p. ; 29 cm.
1. Trade and professional associations - United States. 2. Executives - United States - Attitudes. I. Gallup Organization. II. Foundation of the American Society of Association Executives. ***NYPL [JLF 87-940]***

The corporate warriors /. Ramsey, Douglas K. Boston , 1987. xxi, 261 p. ; ISBN 0-395-35487-0 : LC Card 86-20954 DDC 338.8/3/0973 19
HD41 .R27 1987 ***NYPL [JLE 87-1347]***

CORPORATION ACCOUNTING. see **CORPORATIONS - ACCOUNTING.**

CORPORATION DIRECTORS. see **DIRECTORS OF CORPORATIONS.**

CORPORATION EXECUTIVES. see **EXECUTIVES.**

CORPORATION FINANCE. see **CORPORATIONS - FINANCE.**

Corporation for Enterprise Development. Building the new economy : states in the lead / the Corporation for Enterprise Development ; with the assistance of the Council of State Planning Agencies ; edited by David R. Jones. Washington, D.C. : The Corporation, 1986. iv, 178 p. ; 28 cm. Bibliography: p. 174-178. CONTENTS. - Introduction ; Investing in entrepreneurship ; Investing in people / Robert E. Friedman and William Schweke -- Investing in innovation / John P. Campbell -- Investing in public works / Barbara Dyer and Robert Pollard -- Investing in mature industries / William Schweke -- Investing in natural resources / William Northdurft -- Investing in poor communities / William Schweke. ISBN 0-9605804-2-5 (pbk.) LC Card 86-61273 DDC 338.973 19
1. Industrial promotion - United States - States. 2. United States - Economic policy - 1981-. 3. New business enterprises - United States - States. 4. Technological innovation - United States - States. 5. Investments - United States - States. I. Jones, David, 1954-. II. Council of State Planning Agencies. III. Title.
HC110.I53 C67 1986

Making the grade . Washington, D.C. , c1987. ii, 142 p. : ISBN 0-9605804-4-1 (pbk.) LC Card 87-70671 DDC 330.973/0927 19
HC106.8 .M318 1987

CORPORATION INCOME TAX. see **CORPORATIONS - TAXATION.**

CORPORATION LAW.
Werder, Axel von. Organisationsstruktur und Rechtsnorm . Wiesbaden , c1986. 564 p. : ISBN 3-409-13107-8 LC Card 86-224483
HD58.7 .W35 1986

CORPORATION LAW - GERMANY, WEST.
Kastner, Friedrich, 1951- Entscheidungsansätze zur Rechtsformwahl . München , c1984. xviii, 631 p. : ISBN 3-87821-200-3 LC Card 87-136549 DDC 658.4/03/0943 19
HD2859 .K37 1984

Kroneberg, Jürgen. Die mitbestimmte selbständige Aktiengesellschaft /. Göttingen , 1982. xii, 211 p. ; ISBN 3-88415-554-7 : LC Card 83-159183 DDC 346.43/0664 344.306664 19
KK3000 .K76 1982 ***NYPL [JLD 86-1552]***

Werner, Horst S. Der aktienrechtliche Abhängigkeitstatbestand . Göttingen , 1979. xxxix, 214 p. ; ISBN 3-88415-560-1 : LC Card 80-452340 DDC 346.43/066
LAW ***NYPL [JLD 86-1592]***

CORPORATION LAW - GREAT BRITAIN - HANDBOOKS, MANUALS, ETC.
Company administration handbook. Aldershot, Hants, England , 1982. xxiv, 770 p. : ISBN 0-566-02352-0 LC Card 83-111544 DDC 658/.00941 19
HD70.G7 C57 1982 ***NYPL [JLE 86-2558]***

Company administration handbook /. Aldershot, Hants, England , Brookfield, Vt., U. S.A. , 1988. xxiv, 737 p. : ISBN 0-566-02667-8 : LC Card 86-31876 DDC 658/.00941 19
HD70.G7 C57 1988

CORPORATION LAW - INDIA - CONGRESSES.
Workshop on Impact of Regulatory Mechanism on Corporate Sector (1984 : Bangalore, India) Workshop on Impact of Regulatory Mechanism on Corporate Sector . New Delhi [1985] 104 p. : LC Card 87-902536 DDC 338.954 19
HC435.2 .W67 1984

CORPORATION LAW - SWEDEN.
Dahlgren, Bo, 1924- Nyckeln til styrelserummet . Stockholm [1983] 182 p. : ISBN 91-1-837051-9 : LC Card 83-210185
HD2883 .D34 1983

CORPORATION LAW - UNITED STATES.
Angell, Joseph Kinnicut, 1794-1857. Treatise on the law of private corporations aggregate [microform] /. Boston , 1855. lv, 939 p. ;
NYPL [*ZT-1731]

CORPORATION MEETINGS. see **CORPORATE MEETINGS.**

CORPORATION - REORGANIZATION. see **CORPORATE REORGANIZATIONS.**

CORPORATION REPORTS - CASE STUDIES.

Ferris, Kenneth R. Financial accounting and corporate reporting . Plano, Tex. , 1987. xi, 422 p. : ISBN 0-256-03554-7 (pbk.) LC Card 86-71236 DDC 657/.3 19
HF5686.C7 F455 1987

CORPORATION REPORTS - HANDBOOKS, MANUALS, ETC.
Vickman, Thomas M. Handbook of model accounting reports and formats /. Englewood Cliffs, N.J. , c1987. xvii, 350 p. : ISBN 0-13-380338-4 : LC Card 86-15068 DDC 658.1/512 19
HF5635 .V53 1987 ***NYPL [JLF 87-214]***

CORPORATION RESERVES - ITALY - DECISION MAKING.
Ecchia, Stefano. La destinazione dell'utile nelle società per azioni . Padova , 1985. 133 p. : LC Card 86-214308
HG4028.P7 E23 1985

CORPORATION SECRETARIES - GREAT BRITAIN.
Great Britain. Central Youth Employment Executive. Company secretary. [London, 1970] 15 p. ISBN 0-11-360036-4 : LC Card 72-534885 DDC 331.702 s
HF5381.A1 G73 no. 29, 1970

CORPORATION SECRETARIES - GREAT BRITAIN - HANDBOOKS, MANUALS, ETC.
Company administration handbook. Aldershot, Hants, England , 1982. xxiv, 770 p. : ISBN 0-566-02352-0 LC Card 83-111544 DDC 658/.00941 19
HD70.G7 C57 1982 ***NYPL [JLE 86-2558]***

Company administration handbook /. Aldershot, Hants, England , Brookfield, Vt., U. S.A. , 1988. xxiv, 737 p. : ISBN 0-566-02667-8 : LC Card 86-31876 DDC 658/.00941 19
HD70.G7 C57 1988

CORPORATION TAX. see **CORPORATIONS - TAXATION.**

Corporation tax for students /. Rankin, H. C. D. Wokingham, Berkshire, England , 1985. x, 230 p. : ISBN 0-85258-242-0 (pbk.) LC Card 85-3272 DDC 657/.46/0941 19
HD2753.G7 R36 1985

CORPORATIONS - ACCOUNTING.
Baillie, John. Systems of profit measurement /. New York , 1985. viii, 112 p. ; ISBN 0-85258-234-X (pbk.) LC Card 84-21578 DDC 657/.48 19
HF5681.I48 B34 1985

Barbier, André. Guide pratique de l'analyse financière à l'usage des banquiers /. Paris , c1985. viii, 313 p. : ISBN 2-86325-038-8 : LC Card 86-165653
HF5686.C7 B32 1985

Edwards, J. S. S. (Jeremy S. S.) The economic analysis of accounting profitability /. Oxford , New York , 1987. 133 p. : ISBN 0-19-877241-6 : LC Card 87-5575 DDC 657/.95 19
HF5686.C7 E34 1987

The Institute of Internal Auditors reports on fraud . Altamonte Springs, Fla. , c1987. xv, 74 p. : ISBN 0-89413-164-8 (pbk.) LC Card 87-401942 DDC 657/.3 19
HF5686.C7 I53 1987

Merchant, Kenneth A. Fraudulent and questionable financial reporting . Morristown, N.J. , c1987. iv, 48, [36] p. ; ISBN 0-910586-64-0 (pbk.) LC Card 87-80813 DDC 657/.3 19
HF5686.C7 M44 1987

CORPORATIONS - ACCOUNTING - CASE STUDIES.
Ferris, Kenneth R. Financial accounting and corporate reporting . Plano, Tex. , 1987. xi, 422 p. : ISBN 0-256-03554-7 (pbk.) LC Card 86-71236 DDC 657/.3 19
HF5686.C7 F455 1987

CORPORATIONS - ACCOUNTING - CORRUPT PRACTICES.
The Institute of Internal Auditors reports on fraud . Altamonte Springs, Fla. , c1987. xv, 74 p. : ISBN 0-89413-164-8 (pbk.) LC Card 87-401942 DDC 657/.3 19
HF5686.C7 I53 1987

Merchant, Kenneth A. Fraudulent and questionable financial reporting . Morristown, N.J. , c1987. iv, 48, [36] p. ; ISBN 0-910586-64-0 (pbk.) LC Card 87-80813 DDC 657/.3 19
HF5686.C7 M44 1987

CORPORATIONS - ACCOUNTING - HISTORY - ADDRESSES, ESSAYS, LECTURES.
Lee, Thomas Alexander. The evolution of corporate financial reporting /. New York , 1984. x, 307 p. ; ISBN 0-8240-6332-5 (alk. paper) : LC Card 83-49431 DDC 657/.3 19
HF5686.C7 L43 1984 ***NYPL [JLD 86-2835]***

CORPORATIONS - ACCOUNTING - LAW AND LEGISLATION - AUSTRIA.
Nadvornik, Wolfgang. Konzernrechnungslegung in Österreich . Linz , c1985. ii, 109 p. ; ISBN 3-85320-341-8 : LC Card 85-218757
HF5686.C7 N27 1985

CORPORATIONS - ACCOUNTING - LAW AND LEGISLATION - BELGIUM.
Hawawini, Gabriel A. Mandatory financial information and capital market equilibrium in Belgium /. New York , 1987. 271 p. : ISBN 0-8240-7852-7 (alk. paper) : LC Card 87-54 DDC 332.63/222/09493 19
HG5553 .H39 1987

CORPORATIONS - ACCOUNTING - LAW AND LEGISLATION - BRAZIL.
Marion, José Carlos. A contabilidade após a reforma monetária /. São Paulo , 1986. 196 p. : ISBN 85-22-40175-6 : LC Card 86-222982
HG835 .M37 1986

CORPORATIONS - ACCOUNTING - LAW AND LEGISLATION - GERMANY (WEST)
Kohlmann, Ulrike, 1954- Möglichkeiten und Grenzen der Aussagefähigkeit von Teilkonzernabschlüssen /. München , c1986. viii, 180 p. ; ISBN 3-88259-419-5 LC Card 87-121768 DDC 657/.95/0943 19
HF5686.C7 K644 1986

Schulte, Karl-Werner. Bilanzpolitik und Publizitätsverhalten deutscher Aktiengesellschaften . Bergisch Gladbach , c1986. xx, 553 p. : ISBN 3-89012-070-9 LC Card 87-122912 DDC 658.1/5/0943 19
HF5686.C7 S357 1986

Veit, Klaus-Rüdiger. Die Konkursrechnungslegung . Köln , c1982. xiv, 221 p. ; ISBN 3-452-19273-3 LC Card 83-130656 DDC 346.43/078 344.30678 19
KK4290 .V44 1982 ***NYPL [JLE 87-1129]***

CORPORATIONS - ADDRESSES, ESSAYS, LECTURES.
Corporations and the common good /. Notre Dame, Ind. [Boston] , c1986. xii, 147 p. ; ISBN 0-268-00754-3 : LC Card 85-40597 DDC 174/.4 19
HB501 .C7614 1986 ***NYPL [JLD 86-2145]***

CORPORATIONS, AMERICAN.
Copeland, Vincent. Expanding empire . New York, N.Y. , 1972. 62 p. ; LC Card 87-404126 DDC 338.8/8973 19
HG4538 .C668 1972

Kennedy, Charles R. Political risk management . New York , 1987. xiv, 163 p. : ISBN 0-89930-157-6 (lib. bdg. : alk. paper) LC Card 86-25588 DDC 332.6/7373 19
HG4538 .K44 1987

CORPORATIONS, AMERICAN - ACCOUNTING.
Evans, Thomas G. Foreign exchange risk management under statement 52 /. Stamford, Conn. , c1986. ix, 133 p. : ISBN 0-910065-21-7 (pbk.) LC Card 86-91435 DDC 657/.48 19
HG3853.7 .E935 1986

CORPORATIONS, AMERICAN - INDIA - DIRECTORIES.
Indo-U. S. cooperation in business and industry, 1986. [New Delhi] [1986] 166 p. ; LC Card 86-903197
HG4242 .I44 1986

CORPORATIONS, AMERICAN - NAMIBIA - DIRECTORIES.
Bowers, Cathy. U. S. and Canadian investment in South Africa and Namibia . Washington, D.C. , c1986. xiii, 238 p. ; ISBN 0-931035-10-4 (pbk.) LC Card 86-209149 DDC 338.8/8973/068025 19
HG5851.A3 B69 1986

CORPORATIONS, AMERICAN - PHILIPPINES.
Stauffer, Robert B. The Philippines under Marcos . Sydney [1986] 207 p. ; ISBN 0-908470-69-X (pbk.) LC Card 87-123266 DDC 338.9599 19
HD3616.P62 S7 1986

CORPORATIONS, AMERICAN - SOUTH AFRICA.
Hauck, David. U. S. corporate withdrawal from South Africa . Washington, D.C. (Suite 600, 1755 Massachusetts Ave., N.W., Washington 20036) [1986] 22 p. ; LC Card 86-209299 DDC 332.6/7373/068 19
HG5851.A3 H39 1986

Hauck, David. What happens when U. S. companies sell their South African operations? /. Washington, D.C. (Suite 600, 1755 Massachusetts Ave., N.W., Washington 20036) , c1987. 16 p. ; LC Card 87-163729 DDC 338.8/8973/068 19
HG5851.A3 H392 1987

Williams, Oliver F. The apartheid crisis . San Francisco , 1986. xiv, 124 p. : ISBN 0-06-250951-9 (pbk.) : LC Card 85-45726 DDC 332.6/7373/068 19
HG5851.A3 W55 1986 ***NYPL [JLD 86-4023]***

CORPORATIONS, AMERICAN - SOUTH AFRICA - DIRECTORIES.
Bowers, Cathy. U. S. and Canadian investment in South Africa and Namibia . Washington, D.C. , c1986. xiii, 238 p. ; ISBN 0-931035-10-4 (pbk.) LC Card 86-209149 DDC 338.8/8973/068025 19
HG5851.A3 B69 1986

Newman, Anne, 1951- Foreign investment in South Africa and Namibia . Washington, D.C. [1984] ii, 279 p. ; ISBN 0-931035-00-7 (pbk.) LC Card 85-130985 DDC 332.6/73/0968 19
HG5851.A3 N49 1984 ***NYPL [Sc F 85-173]***

CORPORATIONS, AMERICAN - TAXATION - UNITED STATES - STATISTICS.
Statistics of income . Washington, D.C. , 1985. iii, 516 p. : ***NYPL [JLF 86-833]***

Corporations and the common good / edited by Robert B. Dickie and Leroy S. Rouner. Notre Dame, Ind. : University of Notre Dame Press ; [Boston] : School of Management, Boston University, c1986. xii, 147 p. ; 23 cm. Includes bibliographies. CONTENTS. - Introduction -- The moral crisis of capitalism / Peter Berger -- Realities and appearances in capitalism / Robert Heilbroner -- Perfecting capitalism / James E. Post -- The large corporation and the new American ideology / George C. Lodge -- The multinational corporation / Kenneth Mason -- Ethics and corporate strategy / Edwin A. Murray, Jr. -- Sanctions, incentives, and corporate behavior / Peter T. Jones -- Epilogue : can managers be taught to be ethical? / Henry Morgan. ISBN 0-268-00754-3 : LC Card 85-40597 DDC 174/.4 19
1. Capitalism - Addresses, essays, lectures. 2. Corporations - Addresses, essays, lectures. 3. Business ethics - Addresses, essays, lectures. I. Dickie, Robert B. II. Rouner, Leroy S.
HB501 .C7614 1986 ***NYPL [JLD 86-2145]***

CORPORATIONS - AUDITING.
Lee, Thomas Alexander. Company auditing /. Wokingham, Berkshire, England , 1986. x, 197 p. ; ISBN 0-85258-243-9 (pbk.) LC Card 85-22537 DDC 657/.45 19
HF5667 .L387 1986 ***NYPL [JLD 86-3477]***

Lubos, Günter, 1958- Die Berichterstattung der internen Revision im Grossbetrieb /. München , c1986. xxvii, 207 p. ; ISBN 3-88259-421-7 LC Card 87-121827 DDC 657/.458 19
HF5668.25 .L82 1986

CORPORATIONS - AUSTRALIA - FINANCE.
Skully, Michael T. American depositary receipts . [Melbourne] [1986] 44 leaves : LC Card 86-229206 DDC 332.6/7373/094 19
HG5892 .S58 1986

CORPORATIONS - AUSTRALIA - HISTORY.
Sykes, Trevor. Two centuries of panic . Sydney , Boston , 1987. p. cm. ISBN 0-04-176013-1 LC Card 87-16107 DDC 338.7/4/0994 19
HD2747 .S95 1987

CORPORATIONS - AUSTRIA.
Morawetz, Inge, 1955- Die verborgene Macht .

Frankfurt , New York , c1986. 200 p. : ISBN 3-593-33662-6 LC Card 86-223864
HG3008 .M67 1986

CORPORATIONS - AUSTRIA - ACCOUNTING.
Nadvornik, Wolfgang. Konzernrechnungslegung in Österreich . Linz , c1985. ii, 109 p. ; ISBN 3-85320-341-8 : LC Card 85-218757
HF5686.C7 N27 1985

CORPORATIONS - BELGIUM - BRABANT - DIRECTORIES.
Adresboek "Bedrijven in Vlaams-Brabant" =. Vilvoorde , 1985. lxi, 186, 62, 63 p. : LC Card 87-111619
HC317.B7 A37 1985

CORPORATIONS - BRAZIL.
Banas, Geraldo. Os donos do Brasil . São Paulo , 1984. 330 p. ; LC Card 87-673258
HD2834 .B34 1984

CORPORATIONS - BRAZIL - ACCOUNTING.
Marion, José Carlos. A contabilidade após a reforma monetária /. São Paulo , 1986. 196 p. : ISBN 85-22-40175-6 : LC Card 86-222982
HG835 .M37 1986

CORPORATIONS - BRAZIL, NORTHEAST - FINANCE - DIRECTORIES.
Perfil de empresas. Fortaleza-CE [1984] 248 p. ; LC Card 85-191373
HG4111.5.N67 P47 1984

CORPORATIONS, BRAZILIAN.
Casagrande Neto, Humberto. Abertura do capital de empresas no Brasil . São Paulo , 1985. 143 p. ; ISBN 85-22-40100-4
NYPL [JLD 86-1080]

CORPORATIONS, BRITISH - AFRICA - HISTORY - 19TH CENTURY.
Parfënov, I. D. (Igor′ Danilovich) Monopolii͡a i imperii͡a . Saratov , 1980. 191, [1] p. ; LC Card 81-142784
HD2845 .P36 1980

CORPORATIONS, BRITISH - HISTORY.
British multinationals . Aldershot, Hants , Brookfield, Vt., USA , c1986. xi, 212 p. : ISBN 0-566-00997-8 LC Card 86-222817 DDC 338.8/8941 19
HD2755.5 .B75 1986

CORPORATIONS, BUSINESS. see **CORPORATIONS.**

CORPORATIONS - CANADA.
Carroll, William K. Corporate power and Canadian capitalism /. Vancouver , 1986. xvii, 284 p. : ISBN 0-7748-0246-4 LC Card 86-223683 DDC 338.8/0971 19
HC120.C3 C37 1986

CORPORATIONS - CANADA - FINANCE - CONGRESSES.
Corporate Management Tax Conference (1986) Income tax considerations in corporate financing. Toronto, Canada , c1986. xv, 475 p. : ISBN 0-88808-027-1 : LC Card 87-153466 DDC 658.1/53 19
HG4090 .C67 1986

CORPORATIONS, CANADIAN - NAMIBIA - DIRECTORIES.
Bowers, Cathy. U. S. and Canadian investment in South Africa and Namibia . Washington, D.C. , c1986. xiii, 238 p. ; ISBN 0-931035-10-4 (pbk.) LC Card 86-209149 DDC 338.8/8973/068025 19
HG5851.A3 B69 1986

CORPORATIONS, CANADIAN - SOUTH AFRICA - DIRECTORIES.
Bowers, Cathy. U. S. and Canadian investment in South Africa and Namibia . Washington, D.C. , c1986. xiii, 238 p. ; ISBN 0-931035-10-4 (pbk.) LC Card 86-209149 DDC 338.8/8973/068025 19
HG5851.A3 B69 1986

CORPORATIONS - CASH POSITION.
Wuillemin, Lucien. Eléments d'analyse et de gestion financières de l'entreprise en déficit /. Genève , c1982. 191 p. : ISBN 2-8257-0090-8 : LC Card 82-228134 DDC 658.1/5 19
HD49 .W84 1982 ***NYPL [JLE 87-1142]***

CORPORATIONS, CONGLOMERATE. see **CONGLOMERATE CORPORATIONS.**

CORPORATIONS - CONSOLIDATION. see **CONSOLIDATION AND MERGER OF CORPORATIONS.**

CORPORATIONS (CORPORATE STATE) see **CORPORATE STATE.**

CORPORATIONS - CORRUPT PRACTICES.
Comer, Michael J. Corporate fraud /. London , New York , 1985. xvi, 453 p. : ISBN 0-07-084791-6 : LC Card 85-11686 DDC 364.1/63 19
HV6768 .C65 1985 ***NYPL [JLE 86-909]***

CORPORATIONS - CZECHOSLOVAKIA - BOHEMIA - HISTORY.
Brousek, Karl M. Die Grossindustrie Böhmens, 1848-1918 /. München , 1987. 223 p., 8 leaves of plates : ISBN 3-486-51871-2 LC Card 87-142819 DDC 338.6/44/094371 19
HD2356.C96 B643 1987

CORPORATIONS - DIRECTORIES.
How to find information about foreign firms /. Washington, D.C. , c1987. 93 p. ; ISBN 0-934940-46-0 (pbk.) : LC Card 86-51568 DDC 016.3388/8873 19
HD2785 .H69 1987

CORPORATIONS - EUROPE, NORTHERN - HISTORY.
Gilde und Korporation in den nordeuropäischen Städten des späten Mittelalters /. Köln , 1984. 114 p. ; ISBN 3-412-06883-3 LC Card 84-194645
HD6473.E853 G55 1984

CORPORATIONS, FAMILY. see **FAMILY CORPORATIONS.**

CORPORATIONS - FINANCE - CASE STUDIES.
Dimson, Elroy, 1947- Cases in corporate finance /. Chichester [West Sussex] , New York , c1988. xxiv, 412 p. : ISBN 0-471-91764-8 : LC Card 87-6299 DDC 658.1/5 19
HG4015.5 .D56 1988

CORPORATIONS - FINANCE - COMPUTER PROGRAMS.
Shuster, Harvey L. The financial manager's guide to microsoftware /. New York , 1988. p. cm. ISBN 0-471-81176-9 LC Card 87-21663 DDC 658.1/5/0285536 19
HG4012.5 .S47 1988

CORPORATIONS - FINANCE - CONGRESSES.
Financing new technology . London , 1984. 124 p. : ISBN 0-85297-126-5 (pbk.) LC Card 86-117401 DDC 338.6/041 19
HG4027.6 .F55 1984 ***NYPL [JLD 87-1346]***

CORPORATIONS - FINANCE - DATA PROCESSING.
Drew, Rodney. Microcomputers for financial planning /. Aldershot, Hampshire, England , Brookfield, Vt., U. S.A. , c1987. x, 105 p. : ISBN 0-566-02579-5 (pbk.) : LC Card 87-8405 DDC 658.1/5/0285416 19
HG4012.5 .D73 1987

Shuster, Harvey L. The financial manager's guide to microsoftware /. New York , 1988. p. cm. ISBN 0-471-81176-9 LC Card 87-21663 DDC 658.1/5/0285536 19
HG4012.5 .S47 1988

CORPORATIONS - FINANCE - HANDBOOKS, MANUALS, ETC.
Colman, Robert Douglas. Modern business financing . Englewood Cliffs, N.J. , c1986. xxi, 281 p. : ISBN 0-13-589060-8 LC Card 85-20490 DDC 658.1/5 19
HG4027.3 .C64 1986 ***NYPL [JLF 86-616]***

Financial management handbook /. Aldershot, Hants, England , c1987. p. cm. ISBN 0-566-02623-6 : LC Card 87-40 DDC 658.1/5 19
HG4027.3 .F53 1987

Woelfel, Charles J. The desktop encyclopedia of corporate finance & accounting /. Chicago, Ill. , c1987. viii, 518 p. : ISBN 0-917253-65-5 : LC Card 87-2302 DDC 658.1/5 19
HG4027.3 .W64 1987

CORPORATIONS - FINANCE - JUVENILE LITERATURE.
Little, Jeffrey B. Understanding a company /. New York , c1988. 47 p. : ISBN 1-555-46622-2 LC Card 87-17654 DDC 657/.33 19
HG4028.B2 L57 1988

CORPORATIONS - FINANCE - LAW AND LEGISLATION - CANADA.
Bréard, Jean-Pierre. Les contrats de souscription à forfait de valeurs mobilières /. Montréal , 1984. xv, 158 p. : ISBN 2-89266-018-1 (pbk.) :
NYPL [JLD 87-662]

CORPORATIONS - FINANCE - LAW AND LEGISLATION - INDIA.
Kulshreshtha, V. D. (Visheshwar Dayal), 1922- Government regulation of financial management of private corporate sector in India /. Bombay , 1986. xxiv, 306 p. ; LC Card 87-902600
HG4241 .K85 1986

CORPORATIONS - FINANCE - LAW AND LEGISLATION - UNITED STATES.
Bréard, Jean-Pierre. Les contrats de souscription à forfait de valeurs mobilières /. Montréal , 1984. xv, 158 p. : ISBN 2-89266-018-1 (pbk.) :
NYPL [JLD 87-662]

CORPORATIONS - FINANCE - MATHEMATICAL MODELS.
Financial modelling in corporate management /. Chichester [West Sussex] , New York , c1987. xv, 404 p. : ISBN 0-471-91476-2 : LC Card 86-32446 DDC 658.1/5/0724 19
HG4012 .F54 1987

Shim, Jae K. Handbook of financial analysis, forecasting, and modeling /. Englewood Cliffs, NJ , c1988. p. cm. ISBN 0-13-377995-5 : LC Card 87-14325 DDC 658.1/5 19
HG4011 .S46 1988

Tuovila, Olavi. Optimal financing policy of the firm . Vaasa , 1983. 127 p. : ISBN 951-683-199-0 (pbk.) LC Card 84-204398
HG4012 .T86 1983

CORPORATIONS, FOREIGN - CHINA.
Campbell, Nigel. China strategies . [Manchester, Greater Manchester] [Hong Kong] , c1986. xxiv, 161 p. : ISBN 0-903808-51-X (pbk.) LC Card 86-235360 DDC 332.6/7314/0951 19
HD2910 .C36 1986

CORPORATIONS, FOREIGN - CHINA - CONGRESSES.
Foreign capital and technology in China /. New York , 1987. xvii, 191 p. : ISBN 0-275-92716-4 (alk. paper) : LC Card 87-2450 DDC 332.6/7314/0951 19
HG5782 .F67 1987

CORPORATIONS, FOREIGN - EUROPE, EASTERN - HISTORY - ADDRESSES, ESSAYS, LECTURES.
International business and Central Europe, 1918-1939 /. [Leicester, Leicestershire] , New York , 1983. xxvii, 459 p. : ISBN 0-312-41982-1 : LC Card 83-13956 DDC 338.8/8843 19
HD2844 .I57 1983 ***NYPL [JLE 86-3697]***

CORPORATIONS, FOREIGN - INDIA - MANAGEMENT.
Johri, Lalit M. Business strategies of multinational corporations in India . New Delhi , 1983. v, 172 p. ; LC Card 83-906128 DDC 338.8/87 19
HD9672.I52 J63 1983 ***NYPL [JLD 86-4081]***

CORPORATIONS, FOREIGN - INFORMATION SERVICES - UNITED STATES.
How to find information about foreign firms /. Washington, D.C. , c1987. 93 p. ; ISBN 0-934940-46-0 (pbk.) : LC Card 86-51568 DDC 016.3388/8873 19
HD2785 .H69 1987

CORPORATIONS, FOREIGN - NIGERIA.
Onimode, Bade. MNC's in Nigeria . Ibadan , 1983. ix, 144 p. ; ISBN 978-231-800-0 (pbk.) LC Card 86-195403 DDC 338.8/88669 19
HD2928 .O55 1983

CORPORATIONS, FOREIGN - SOUTH AFRICA - DIRECTORIES.
Newman, Anne, 1951- Foreign investment in South Africa and Namibia . Washington, D.C. [1984] ii, 279 p. ; ISBN 0-931035-00-7 (pbk.) LC Card 85-130985 DDC 332.6/73/0968 19
HG5851.A3 N49 1984 ***NYPL [Sc F 85-173]***

CORPORATIONS, FOREIGN - TAXATION - UNITED STATES - STATISTICS.
Statistics of income . Washington, D.C. , 1985. iii, 516 p. : ***NYPL [JLF 86-833]***

CORPORATIONS, FOREIGN - UNITED STATES - DIRECTORIES.
How to find information about foreign firms /. Washington, D.C. , c1987. 93 p. ; ISBN 0-934940-46-0 (pbk.) : LC Card 86-51568

DDC 016.3388/8873 19
HD2785 .H69 1987

CORPORATIONS - FRANCE - DIRECTORIES.
150 meilleures entreprises françaises /. Paris , c1986. 313 p. ; ISBN 2-234-01894-3 : LC Card 87-107207
HF5382.75.F8 A13 1986

CORPORATIONS - FRANCE - HISTORY.
Baumier, Jean. Ces patrons qui gagnent /. Paris , c1986. 262 p. ; ISBN 2-259-01532-8 : LC Card 87-106535
HD2855 .B38 1986

Bouchary, Jean. Les compagnies financières à Paris à la fin du XVIIIe siècle--tome II [microform] ... /. Paris , 1941. 212 p. ;
*NYPL [*ZT-1711 no.28]*

CORPORATIONS, GERMAN - LATIN AMERICA.
Wolffsohn, Michael. Politik als Investitionsmotor? . Frankfurt am Main , New York , c1985. 141 p. : ISBN 3-8204-7487-0 (pbk.) LC Card 87-672289
HD2810.5 W64x 1985

CORPORATIONS - GERMANY - HISTORY - STATISTICAL METHODS - STUDY AND TEACHING - CONGRESSES.
Beiträge zur quantitativen vergleichenden Unternehmensgeschichte /. Stuttgart , c1985. 206 p. : ISBN 3-608-91325-4 LC Card 85-233589
HD2734 .B32 1985

CORPORATIONS - GERMANY, WEST - ACCOUNTING.
Fangl, Hans. Zum Kostencharakter von Ertragsteuern /. Berlin , c1986. 208 p. : ISBN 3-428-06032-6 LC Card 86-219710 DDC 336.24/3/0943 19
HD2753.G3 F26 1986

Kohlmann, Ulrike, 1954- Möglichkeiten und Grenzen der Aussagefähigkeit von Teilkonzernabschlüssen /. München , c1986. viii, 180 p. ; ISBN 3-88259-419-5 LC Card 87-121768 DDC 657/.95/0943 19
HF5686.C7 K644 1986

Schneider, Pia, 1956- Finanzwirtschaftliche Nebenrechnungen . Frankfurt am Main , New York , c1985. xiii, 303 p. : ISBN 3-8204-8472-8 LC Card 85-190966
HF5686.C7 S354 1985

Schulte, Karl-Werner. Bilanzpolitik und Publizitätsverhalten deutscher Aktiengesellschaften . Bergisch Gladbach , c1986. xx, 553 p. : ISBN 3-89012-070-9 LC Card 87-122912 DDC 658.1/5/0943 19
HF5686.C7 S357 1986

CORPORATIONS - GERMANY (WEST) - DECISION MAKING.
Kastner, Friedrich, 1951- Entscheidungsansätze zur Rechtsformwahl . München , c1984. xviii, 631 p. : ISBN 3-87821-200-3 LC Card 87-136549 DDC 658.4/03/0943 19
HD2859 .K37 1984

CORPORATIONS - GERMANY, WEST - FINANCE.
Jäger, Hubert. Die Bewertung von konzerninternen Lieferungen und Leistungen in der operativen Planung /. Heidelberg , c1987. xii, 345 p. ; ISBN 3-7908-0367-7 LC Card 87-145912 DDC 658.1/5/0943 19
HG4156 .J336 1987

Schulte, Karl-Werner. Bilanzpolitik und Publizitätsverhalten deutscher Aktiengesellschaften . Bergisch Gladbach , c1986. xx, 553 p. : ISBN 3-89012-070-9 LC Card 87-122912 DDC 658.1/5/0943 19
HF5686.C7 S357 1986

Uhlmann, Luitpold. Investitionsverhalten und Unternehmensgrösse /. Berlin , c1986. 307 p. ; ISBN 3-428-06010-5 LC Card 86-216522
HG4028.C4 U37 1986

CORPORATIONS - GERMANY (WEST) - FINANCE - CONGRESSES.
DIHT-Kongress (1983 : Frankfurt am Main, Germany) Kapital, Zins, Währung . Bonn , 1984. 68 p. : LC Card 84-212399
HC290.5.C3 D53 1983

CORPORATIONS - GERMANY (WEST) - MANAGEMENT.
Massenberg, Jost A., 1956- Strategie und Entwicklung deutscher Grossunternehmen . Frankfurt am Main , New York , c1986. xi, 398 p. : ISBN 3-8204-9666-1 LC Card 86-220603
HD70.G2 M37 1986

CORPORATIONS, GOVERNMENT - CANADA.
Stewart, Walter. Uneasy lies the head . Toronto , 1987. 266 p. ; ISBN 0-00-217757-9 LC Card 87-144685 DDC 354.7109/2 19
HD4005 .S74 1987

CORPORATIONS, GOVERNMENT - CANADA - PERSONNEL MANAGEMENT.
Employment equity for crown corporations . Ottawa , 1986. 17, 18 p. ; ISBN 0-662-54400-5 (pbk.) LC Card 86-207179 DDC 354.71001/04 19
HD4903.5.C2 E47 1986

CORPORATIONS, GOVERNMENT - CANADA - PROVINCES.
Stewart, Walter. Uneasy lies the head . Toronto , 1987. 266 p. ; ISBN 0-00-217757-9 LC Card 87-144685 DDC 354.7109/2 19
HD4005 .S74 1987

CORPORATIONS, GOVERNMENT - GERMANY (WEST) - MANAGEMENT - EMPLOYEE PARTICIPATION.
Süllow, Bernd. Korporative Repräsentation der Gewerkschaften . Frankfurt , New York , c1982. 146 p. ; ISBN 3-593-33169-1 LC Card 83-153450
HD4177 .S85 1982

CORPORATIONS, GOVERNMENT - GREAT BRITAIN - EVALUATION.
Day, Patricia. Accountabilities . London , New York , 1987. 259 p. : ISBN 0-422-79340-X : LC Card 87-164015 DDC 354.4109/2 19
HD4147 .D39 1987

CORPORATIONS, GOVERNMENT - INDIA - BIHAR - FINANCE.
Sahay, S. N. (Surendra Nath) Financial management of public enterprises /. New Delhi , 1984. xiii, 216 p. ; LC Card 84-900657 DDC 354.54/12092/0681 19
HD4295.B5 S24 1984 *NYPL [JLD 86-4430]*

CORPORATIONS, GOVERNMENT - INDIA - FINANCE - CASE STUDIES.
Sahay, S. N. (Surendra Nath) Financial management of public enterprises /. New Delhi , 1984. xiii, 216 p. ; LC Card 84-900657 DDC 354.54/12092/0681 19
HD4295.B5 S24 1984 *NYPL [JLD 86-4430]*

CORPORATIONS, GOVERNMENT - POLAND - ADDRESSES, ESSAYS, LECTURES.
Ekonomiczne i prawne problemy przedsiębiorstwa uspołecznionego /. Poznań , 1981. 137 p. ; LC Card 83-167540
HB54 .P6 nr. 101 HD4215.7

CORPORATIONS, GOVERNMENT - QUÉBEC (PROVINCE)
Privatisation de sociétés d'Etat. English. Privatization of Crown corporations . [Québec] [1986] 71 p. : LC Card 86-220606 DDC 338.9714 19
HD4010.Q4 P7513 1986

CORPORATIONS, GOVERNMENT - UNITED STATES - CORRUPT PRACTICES.
Henriques, Diana B. The machinery of greed . Lexington, Mass. , c1986. x, 161 p. ; ISBN 0-669-09809-4 (alk. paper) LC Card 85-23841 DDC 364.1/68 19
HD3885 .H45 1986 *NYPL [JLE 86-2739]*

CORPORATIONS - GREAT BRITAIN - ACCOUNTING.
The Regulatory framework of accounting /. Estover, Plymouth , 1985. [12], 391 p. : ISBN 0-7121-0491-7 *NYPL [JLF 87-84]*

CORPORATIONS - GREAT BRITAIN - CORRUPT PRACTICES - CASE STUDIES.
Sherrard, Michael. London Capital Group Limited (formerly British Bangladesh Trust Limited) . London , 1977. vi, 376 p. : ISBN 0-11-512127-7 (pbk.) LC Card 85-164377
HG4135 .S46 1977

CORPORATIONS - GREAT BRITAIN - FINANCE.
Scott, John, 1912- Capitalist property and financial power . Brighton, Sussex , 1986. x, 230 p. ; ISBN 0-7450-0047-9
NYPL [JLD 86-3078]

Sudarsanam, P. S. Market and industry structure and corporate cost of capital . London [1986] 33 p. ; LC Card 86-208314 DDC 338.7/4/0941 19
HG4135 .S83 1986

CORPORATIONS - GREAT BRITAIN - INFORMATION SERVICES.
Norkett, P. T. C. Guide to company information in Great Britain /. Burnt Mill, Harlow, Essex, U.K. , c1986. xi, 208 p. : ISBN 0-582-97820-3 (pbk.) : LC Card 86-220140 DDC 338.7/4/072041 19
HD2845 .N67 1986

CORPORATIONS - HISTORY.
Baumier, Jean. Ces patrons qui gagnent /. Paris , c1986. 262 p. ; ISBN 2-259-01532-8 : LC Card 87-106535
HD2855 .B38 1986

Jacobson, Gary. Xerox . New York , c1986. ix, 338 p. ; ISBN 0-02-551600-0 LC Card 85-30922 DDC 338.7/68644 19
HD9802.3.U64 X475 1986
NYPL [JLE 86-2982]

CORPORATIONS - HISTORY - STATISTICAL METHODS - STUDY AND TEACHING - CONGRESSES.
Beiträge zur quantitativen vergleichenden Unternehmensgeschichte /. Stuttgart , c1985. 206 p. : ISBN 3-608-91325-4 LC Card 85-233589
HD2734 .B32 1985

CORPORATIONS - INDIA - DIRECTORIES.
Indo-U. S. cooperation in business and industry, 1986. [New Delhi] [1986] 166 p. ; LC Card 86-903197
HG4242 .I44 1986

CORPORATIONS - INDIA - FINANCE.
Kulshreshtha, V. D. (Visheshwar Dayal), 1922- Government regulation of financial management of private corporate sector in India /. Bombay , 1986. xxiv, 306 p. ; LC Card 87-902600
HG4241 .K85 1986

Public limited companies in India, 1980-82 . Bombay , 1986. xvi, 359 p. ; LC Card 87-902505 DDC 338.7/4/0954021 19
HG4242 .P83 1986

Yadav, R. A. (Ram Avtar), 1949- Financial ratios and the prediction of corporate failure /. New Delhi , 1986. xvi, 196 p. ; LC Card 86-903341 DDC 338.7/4/0954 19
HF5681.R25 Y33 1986

CORPORATIONS - INDIA - ORISSA - GROWTH.
Sahu, Promod K. (Promod Kumar), 1942- Industrial economy of Orissa /. Delhi , New Delhi , 1986. viii, 152 p. ; ISBN 81-7018-401-0 : LC Card 86-903551 DDC 338.0954/13 19
HC437.O7 S24 1986

CORPORATIONS - INFORMATION SERVICES - UNITED STATES - HANDBOOKS, MANUALS, ETC.
How to find information about private companies /. Washington, DC , c1987. iii, 149 p. ; ISBN 0-934940-47-9 (pbk.) : LC Card 86-51566 DDC 016.3387/4/0973 19
HG4013.5 .H69 1987

CORPORATIONS - INVESTOR RELATIONS.
Altman, Richard M. Creating investor demand for company stock . New York , c1988. p. cm. ISBN 0-89930-173-8 (lib. bdg. : alk. paper) LC Card 86-25566 DDC 332.6/42 19
HG4661 .A57 1988

Bänsch, Axel. Operationalisierung des Unternehmenszieles, Mitgliederförderung /. Göttingen , 1983. xv, 245 p. ; ISBN 3-525-12750-2 *NYPL [JLE 86-1770]*

CORPORATIONS - IRELAND - FINANCE.
Stewart, J. C., 1949- Corporate finance and fiscal policy in Ireland /. Aldershot, Hants, England , Brookfield, Vt., USA , c1987. x, 166 p. ; ISBN 0-566-05441-8 : LC Card 87-14908 DDC 658.1/5/09415 19
HG4144 .S74 1987

CORPORATIONS, ITALIAN - FOREIGN COUNTRIES.
Italia multinazionale . Milano , 1986. 2 v. : LC Card 87-158571
HD2864 .I82 1986

CORPORATIONS - ITALY - ACCOUNTING.
Leccisotti, Mario. Politiche dell'impresa e sistema tributario /. Napoli , 1984. 174 p. : ISBN 88-20-70883-3 : *NYPL [JLD 86-3651]*

CORPORATIONS - ITALY - CORRUPT PRACTICES.
Risanamento e riordino delle partecipazioni statali . Milano, Italy , c1986. 429 p. : LC Card 86-169331
HC310.I53 R57 1986

CORPORATIONS - ITALY - FINANCE.
Leccisotti, Mario. Politiche dell'impresa e sistema tributario /. Napoli , 1984. 174 p. : ISBN 88-20-70883-3 : *NYPL [JLD 86-3651]*

CORPORATIONS - ITALY - FINANCE - STATISTICS.
Dati cumulativi di 1356 società italiane, 1968-1983 /. [Italy , 1984] (Milano : O. Capriolo) xxvi, 258 p. ; LC Card 86-229023
HG4166 .D39 1984

CORPORATIONS - JAPAN - ACCOUNTING - PUBLIC OPINION.
A Comparative study on accounting policy between Japanese and the U. S. companies /. Tokyo, Japan , c1986. iv, 56 p. : LC Card 87-169003 DDC 657/.0952 19
HF5686.C7 C635 1986

CORPORATIONS - JAPAN - FINANCE.
Scott, John, 1912- Capitalist property and financial power . Brighton, Sussex , 1986. x, 230 p. ; ISBN 0-7450-0047-9 *NYPL [JLD 86-3078]*

CORPORATIONS, JAPANESE.
Woronoff, Jon. Japan's commercial empire /. Armonk, N.Y. , c1984. 415 p. : ISBN 0-87332-312-2 LC Card 84-22146 DDC 337.52 19
HF1601 .W66 1984 *NYPL [JLD 87-761]*

CORPORATIONS, JAPANESE - EUROPEAN ECONOMIC COMMUNITY COUNTRIES.
The Internationalization of Japanese business . Boulder , 1986. p. cm. ISBN 0-8133-0531-4 : LC Card 87-8186 DDC 338.8/8952/04 19
HD2844.5 .I567 1986

CORPORATIONS, JAPANESE - UNITED STATES.
Starr, Martin Kenneth, 1927- The performance of Japanese-owned firms in America, 1982-1985 /. [New York, NY] , c1987. ii, 41 leaves : LC Card 87-145262 DDC 338.8/8952/073 19
HD2785 .S66 1987

Yoshida, Mamoru. Japanese direct manufacturing investment in the United States /. New York , 1987. xiv, 220 p. : ISBN 0-275-92347-9 (alk. paper) : LC Card 86-22689 DDC 332.6/7352/073 19
HG4910 .Y58 1986 *NYPL [JLE 87-1122]*

CORPORATIONS, JAPANESE - UNITED STATES - CASE STUDIES.
Kujawa, Duane. Japanese multinationals in the United States . New York , 1986. xii, 291 p. ; ISBN 0-03-006718-9 (alk. paper) : LC Card 85-28310 DDC 338.8/8952/073 19
HF5549.2.U5 K84 1986
NYPL [JLE 86-3833]

CORPORATIONS, JAPANESE - UNITED STATES - PERSONNEL MANAGEMENT - CASE STUDIES.
Kujawa, Duane. Japanese multinationals in the United States . New York , 1986. xii, 291 p. ; ISBN 0-03-006718-9 (alk. paper) : LC Card 85-28310 DDC 338.8/8952/073 19
HF5549.2.U5 K84 1986
NYPL [JLE 86-3833]

CORPORATIONS - JURISPRUDENCE. see **CORPORATION LAW.**

CORPORATIONS - LAWS AND LEGISLATION. see **CORPORATION LAW.**

CORPORATIONS - MANAGEMENT.
Jagoe, A. L. (Armiger L.), 1921- The winning corporation . Washington, D.C. , c1987. xviii, 232 p. ; ISBN 0-87491-858-9 : LC Card 87-1766 DDC 658.4 19
HD31 .J245 1987

CORPORATIONS - MEETINGS. see **CORPORATE MEETINGS.**

CORPORATIONS, MEMBERSHIP. see **CORPORATIONS, NONPROFIT.**

CORPORATIONS - MERGER. see **CONSOLIDATION AND MERGER OF CORPORATIONS.**

CORPORATIONS - MORAL AND ETHICAL ASPECTS.
Cavanagh, Gerald F. Ethical dilemmas in the modern corporation /. Englewood Cliffs, NJ , c1988. x, 198 p. : ISBN 0-13-290058-0 (pbk.) LC Card 87-25726 DDC 174/.4 19
HF5387 .C38 1988

CORPORATIONS - NEPAL - FINANCE.
Pradhan, Radhe S. Public corporations of Nepal . New Delhi, India , 1986. xiii, 173 p. ; LC Card 86-903436 DDC 338.7/4/095496 19
HF5681.R25 P73 1986

CORPORATIONS - NETHERLANDS - FINANCE.
Omgeving, doelstellingen en organisatie . Assen , 1986. viii, 464 p. : ISBN 90-232-2208-3 : LC Card 86-182876
HG4181 .O44 1986

CORPORATIONS - NEW YORK (N.Y.) - DIRECTORIES.
Major employers in and around New York City. Hillsdale, N.J. (P.O. Box 294, Hillsdale 07642-0294) , c1986. iv, 112 p. ; LC Card 86-211679 DDC 338.7/4/025741 19
HF5382.75.U62 N56 1986

CORPORATIONS - NIGERIA - FINANCE.
Osubor, John Uche. Business finance and banking in Nigeria /. Owerri, Imo State, Nigeria , 1984. vii, 209 p. : ISBN 978-235-700-13 (pbk.) LC Card 86-207599 DDC 332.1/09669 19
HG3431.A6 O85 1984

CORPORATIONS, NONPROFIT - ACCOUNTING.
Henke, Emerson O. Introduction to nonprofit organization accounting /. Boston , c1988. xvi, 670 p. : ISBN 0-534-08322-6 LC Card 87-7330 DDC 657/.98 19
HF5686.N56 H45 1988

CORPORATIONS, NONPROFIT - CALIFORNIA - SAN FRANCISCO METROPOLITAN AREA - FINANCE.
Salamon, Lester M. San Francisco Bay Area nonprofit organizations . Washington, D.C. (2100 M St., N.W., Washington 20037) , c1987. vi, 26 p. : LC Card 87-403000 DDC 338.7/4/0979461 19
HJ9205.S3 S34 1987

CORPORATIONS, NONPROFIT - FINANCE.
Bryce, Herrington J. Financial and strategic management for nonprofit organizations /. Englewood Cliffs, N.J. , c1987. xviii, 395 p. : ISBN 0-13-316597-3 LC Card 86-30454 DDC 658/.049 19
HG4027.65 .B78 1987

Groot, T. L. C. M. Financieël management van non-profit organisaties /. Groningen , c1985. 200 p. : ISBN 90-01-30316-1 : LC Card 85-214807
HG4027.65 .G76 1985

CORPORATIONS, NONPROFIT - GERMANY - HISTORY.
Vereinswesen und bürgerliche Gesellschaft in Deutschland /. München , 1984. 180 p. ; ISBN 3-486-52081-4 LC Card 84-205111
HD2429.G3 V46 1984

CORPORATIONS, NONPROFIT - MANAGEMENT.
Brown, Kathleen M. Applied empirical research on nonprofit organization management . San Francisco, CA , c1986. 38 p. ; LC Card 86-207093 DDC 658/.048 19
HD62.6 .B76 1986

Bryce, Herrington J. Financial and strategic management for nonprofit organizations /. Englewood Cliffs, N.J. , c1987. xviii, 395 p. : ISBN 0-13-316597-3 LC Card 86-30454 DDC 658/.049 19
HG4027.65 .B78 1987

Espy, Siri N. Handbook of strategic planning for nonprofit organizations /. New York , 1986. ix, 131 p. ; ISBN 0-275-92342-8 (alk. paper) LC Card 86-21192 DDC 658.1/148 19
HD62.6 .E86 1986 *NYPL [JLE 87-874]*

Fram, Eugene H. Policy vs. paper clips . Milwaukee, Wis. , 1988. p. cm. ISBN 0-87304-227-1 LC Card 87-24377 DDC 658/.048 19
HD62.6 .F73 1988

Nonprofit organizational effectiveness study . Washington, D.C. (1828 L St., N.W., Washington 20036) , c1986. v, 125 p. ; LC Card 87-141542 DDC 658/.048 19
HD31 .N57 1986

Promoting issues & ideas . New York, N.Y. , 1987. 183 p. : ISBN 0-87954-192-X (pbk.) : LC Card 87-7600 DDC 659.2/88 19
HD62.6 .P76 1987

CORPORATIONS, NONPROFIT - MANAGEMENT - EVALUATION - ADDRESSES, ESSAYS, LECTURES.
Performance and credibility . Lexington, Mass. , c1986. x, 307 p. : ISBN 0-669-11037-X (alk. paper) LC Card 85-50707 DDC 658/.048 19
HD62.6 .P47 1986 *NYPL [JLE 86-1159]*

CORPORATIONS, NONPROFIT - MARKETING.
Kotler, Philip. Strategic marketing for nonprofit organizations /. Englewood Cliffs, N.J. , c1987. xvi, 670 p. : LC Card 86-25538 DDC 658.8 19
HF5415 .K6312 1987

Strategic marketing for nonprofit organizations . Englewood Cliffs, NJ , c1987. x, 386 p. : ISBN 0-13-851312-0 (pbk.) : LC Card 86-25262 DDC 658.8 19
HF5415 .C2854 1987

CORPORATIONS, NONPROFIT - MARKETING - CASE STUDIES.
Marketing. Fountain Valley, CA , 1985. 1 videocassette (30 min.) : LC Card 87-705967 DDC 658.8 11
HF5415

Strategic marketing for nonprofit organizations . Englewood Cliffs, NJ , c1987. x, 386 p. : ISBN 0-13-851312-0 (pbk.) : LC Card 86-25262 DDC 658.8 19
HF5415 .C2854 1987

CORPORATIONS, NON-PROFIT - NETHERLANDS - CASE STUDIES.
Caris, J. Fuseren in non-profit organisaties . Nijmegen , 1986. 107 p. : ISBN 90-255-0018-8 : LC Card 86-205531
HD2746.5 .C35 1986

CORPORATIONS, NONPROFIT - NEW YORK (STATE) - FINANCE.
Altschuler, David M. New York nonprofit organizations . Washington, D.C. (2100 M St., N.W., Washington 20037) , c1987. vii, 43 p. : LC Card 87-159600 DDC 658.1/5 19
HD2769.2.U6 A48 1987

CORPORATIONS, NONPROFIT - PLANNING.
Barry, Bryan W. Strategic planning workbook for nonprofit organizations /. St. Paul, MN , c1986. 72 p., [8] leaves of plates : ISBN 0-940069-00-8 (pbk.) LC Card 87-153976 DDC 658.4/012 19
HD62.6 .B37 1986

Espy, Siri N. Handbook of strategic planning for nonprofit organizations /. New York , 1986. ix, 131 p. ; ISBN 0-275-92342-8 (alk. paper) LC Card 86-21192 DDC 658.1/148 19
HD62.6 .E86 1986 *NYPL [JLE 87-874]*

CORPORATIONS, NONPROFIT - RHODE ISLAND - FINANCE.
Salamon, Lester M. Rhode Island nonprofit organizations . Washington, D.C. , Providence, RI , c1987. vii, 40 p. : LC Card 87-148803 DDC 338.7/4/09745 19
HD2769.2.U6 S25 1987

CORPORATIONS, NONPROFIT - SWITZERLAND - ACCOUNTING - CASE STUDIES.
Egger, Emil. Management Accounting in öffentlichen nichtgewinnorientierten Organisationen . Zürich , c1985. xii, 220 p. : ISBN 3-7255-2410-6 LC Card 85-132536
HF5686.N56 E33 1985

CORPORATIONS, NONPROFIT - UNITED STATES.
Lewis, William, 1946- Profitable careers in nonprofit /. New York , c1987. vi, 202 p. ; ISBN 0-471-83699-0 (pbk.) : LC Card 87-6102 DDC 331.7/02 19
HF5382.5.U5 L44 1987

Nonprofit organizations, a government

management tool /. New York , 1980. xxi, 173 p. ; ISBN 0-03-053966-8 : LC Card 79-23632 DDC 350 19
JK468.R45 N66 ***NYPL [JLE 80-1874]***

Weisbrod, Burton Allen, 1931- The nonprofit economy /. Cambridge, Mass. , 1988. p. cm. ISBN 0-674-62625-7 (alk. paper) LC Card 87-23718 DDC 338.7/4 19
HD2769.2.U6 W45 1988

CORPORATIONS, NONPROFIT - UNITED STATES - ACCOUNTING.
Hay, Leon Edwards, 1923- Essentials of accounting for governmental and not-for-profit organizations /. Homewood, Ill. , 1987. x, 310 p. ; ISBN 0-256-03454-0 (pbk.) LC Card 86-82587 DDC 657/.98 19
HJ9801 .H39 1987

CORPORATIONS, NONPROFIT - UNITED STATES - FINANCE.
Abramson, Alan J. The nonprofit sector and the new federal budget /. Washington, D.C. , c1986. xviii, 138 p. : ISBN 0-87766-401-3 (pbk.) : LC Card 87-154012 DDC 361.7/63/0973 19
HJ2052 .A54 1986

The [Name of community] nonprofit sector in a time of government retrenchment. Washington, D.C. , c1984-<c1986. v. <1-2, 5-6, 9-11, 13-15 > : LC Card 87-167661 DDC 338.7/4/0973 19
HG4061 .N36 1984

CORPORATIONS, NONPROFIT - UNITED STATES - FINANCE - COLLECTED WORKS.
Government spending and the nonprofit sector in [name of community]. Washington, D.C. , <c1984-c1985. v. <1-11 > ; LC Card 87-168173 DDC 339.5/22/0973 19
HJ2052 .G67 1984

CORPORATIONS, NONPROFIT - UNITED STATES - FINANCE - DIRECTORIES.
Capital campaign resource guide. San Francisco, Calif. , c1984. x, 1229 p. : LC Card 87-122608 DDC 658.1/5224 19
HG177.5.U6 C36 1984

CORPORATIONS, NONPROFIT - UNITED STATES - FINANCE - HANDBOOKS, MANUALS, ETC.
Capital campaign resource guide. San Francisco, Calif. , c1984. x, 1229 p. : LC Card 87-122608 DDC 658.1/5224 19
HG177.5.U6 C36 1984

CORPORATIONS, NONPROFIT - UNITED STATES - MARKETING - CASE STUDIES.
Kotler, Philip. Strategic marketing for nonprofit organizations /. Englewood Cliffs, N.J. , c1987. xvi, 670 p. : LC Card 86-25538 DDC 658.8 19
HF5415 .K6312 1987

CORPORATIONS - NORWAY - CORRUPT PRACTICES - CASE STUDIES.
Jacobsen, Alf R., 1950- Eventyret Anders Jahre /. Oslo , c1982. 303 p., [16] p. of plates : ISBN 82-7094-311-8 : LC Card 83-168197
HE569.J34 J33 1982 ***NYPL [JFD 87-4754]***

CORPORATIONS, NORWEGIAN - DEVELOPING COUNTRIES - CONGRESSES.
Norsk industris internasjonalisering, rettet mot utviklingslandene . Bergen [1982] vi, 57 p. ; LC Card 83-139811
HD2932 .N67 1982

CORPORATIONS - PAKISTAN - FINANCE - STATISTICS.
Financial performance of PICIC assisted companies ... [Karachi] [198-?] v. <1 > ; LC Card 85-931756
HG4244.5 .F56 1980z

CORPORATIONS - PAPERS, REPORTS, ETC. see **CORPORATION REPORTS.**

CORPORATIONS - PUBLIC RELATIONS. see **PUBLIC RELATIONS - CORPORATIONS.**

CORPORATIONS - RECORDS AND CORRESPONDENCE. see **BUSINESS RECORDS.**

CORPORATIONS - SENEGAL - AUDITING.
Sougue, Matthieu Kounabé. La pratique de l'audit financier dans les entreprises au Sénégal, à travers le cabinet Helios . [Dakar] [1983?] 194, [18] leaves : LC Card 85-121418
HF5686.C7 S67 1984

CORPORATIONS - SOCIAL ASPECTS.
Corporate social responsibility . Santa Barbara, Calif. , c1986. xv, 229 p. ; ISBN 0-87436-469-8 (alk. paper) : LC Card 86-3416 DDC 658.4/08 19
HD60 .C693 1986 ***NYPL [JLE 86-3089]***

CORPORATIONS - SOUTH AFRICA.
Ontleding van genoteerde maatskappye JEB industriële afdelingsgemiddeldes . Pretoria , 1984. iv, 163 p. ; ISBN 0-86979-588-0 LC Card 85-156278
HD2922 .O57 1984

CORPORATIONS, SUBSIDIARY. see **SUBSIDIARY CORPORATIONS.**

CORPORATIONS - SWEDEN.
Dahlgren, Bo, 1924- Nyckeln til styrelserummet . Stockholm [1983] 182 p. : ISBN 91-1-837051-9 : LC Card 83-210185
HD2883 .D34 1983

Edgren, Jan, 1940- Divisionalisering och därefter . Stockholm , c1983. 157 p. : ISBN 91-7722-013-7 : LC Card 83-186664
HD50 .E34 1983

CORPORATIONS - SWEDEN - FINANCE.
Olsson, Hans. Industrins lönsamhet, finansiering och investeringar under 1970-talet . [Stockholm] [1981] 58 p. : ISBN 91-38-06530-4 LC Card 84-120594
HG4211 .O45 1981

CORPORATIONS, SWEDISH - DEVELOPING COUNTRIES.
Mattsson, Jan. Nationella övertaganden av utländska dotterbolag . Stockholm [1982] 213 p. : ISBN 91-1-827592-3 LC Card 83-122459
HD2932 .M38 1982

CORPORATIONS, SWISS.
Hämisegger, Kuno, 1956- Neue Formen des Auslandengagements . Bern , New York , c1986. 292 p. : ISBN 3-261-03598-6 LC Card 86-208515
HF1411 .H253 1986

CORPORATIONS - TAXATION.
Sinn, Hans-Werner. Kapitaleinkommensbesteuerung . Tübingen , 1985. xv, 352 p. : ISBN 3-16-344827-5 LC Card 85-164588
HD2753.A3 S48 1985

Wittmann, Franz, 1933- Der Einfluss der Steuern auf die Investitionsentscheidungen der Unternehmen . Frankfurt , New York , c1986. 405 p. ; ISBN 3-593-33642-1 LC Card 86-173001
HG4028.C4 W585 1986

CORPORATIONS - TAXATION - BERLIN (GERMANY)
Hecker, Christian. Abschreibungsgesellschaften in Berlin (West) . Köln , c1982. viii, 236, xix, 78 p. : ISBN 3-921379-96-2 LC Card 83-197457
HJ4720.B45 H43 1982

CORPORATIONS - TAXATION - CANADA - CONGRESSES.
Corporate Management Tax Conference (1986) Income tax considerations in corporate financing. Toronto, Canada , c1986. xv, 475 p. : ISBN 0-88808-027-1 : LC Card 87-153466 DDC 658.1/53 19
HG4090 .C67 1986

CORPORATIONS - TAXATION - ECONOMETRIC MODELS.
Hamm, Rüdiger. Die Inzidenz sektorspezifischer Kapitalbesteuerung /. Krefeld , 1983. 296 p. : ISBN 3-88358-034-1 LC Card 83-218772
HD2753.A3 H36 1983

CORPORATIONS - TAXATION - EUROPEAN ECONOMIC COMMUNITY COUNTRIES.
Lutz, Stefan. Die Körperschaftsteuer in der Europäischen Gemeinschaft . Pfaffenweiler , 1984. xii, 346 p. : ISBN 3-89085-037-5 : LC Card 85-142851
HD2753.E8 L87 1984

CORPORATIONS - TAXATION - FINLAND.
Ekholm, Bo-Göran. Skattetryckets fördelning inom finländska industriföretag /. Helsingfors [1985] 39 p. ; ISBN 951-555-222-2 LC Card 85-214497
HD2753.F5 E38 1985

CORPORATIONS - TAXATION - FRANCE.
Mallard, Jean-Claude, 1947- Comprendre et gérer la fiscalité de l'entreprise /. La Tronche , Paris [1985] 255 p. : LC Card 86-166702
HD2753.F8 M34 1985

CORPORATIONS - TAXATION - GERMANY, WEST.
Döring, Ulrich. Kostensteuern, der Einfluss von Steuern auf kurzfristige Produktions- und Absatzentscheidungen /. Stuttgart , c1984. x, 228 p. ; ISBN 3-7910-0369-0 LC Card 86-134925
HD2753.G3 D73 1984

Esser, Carsten, 1960- Das Fremdkapital im Unternehmen als Insolvenzursache und die Möglichkeiten rechtlicher Steuerung der Finanzierungsgrundlagen /. Frankfurt am Main , New York , c1986. xvi, 131 p. (1 folded) ; ISBN 3-8204-9398-0 LC Card 86-229108
HG5501 .E85 1986

Fangl, Hans. Zum Kostencharakter von Ertragsteuern /. Berlin , c1986. 208 p. : ISBN 3-428-06032-6 LC Card 86-219710 DDC 336.24/3/0943 19
HD2753.G3 F26 1986

Heurung, Rainer-Otto, 1952- Wirken Substanzsteuern investitionshemmend? /. Frankfurt am Main , New York , c1986. xvii, 251, [93] p. : ISBN 3-8204-9800-1 LC Card 87-408762 DDC 332.63 19
HG4028.C4 H49 1986

Wittmann, Franz, 1933- Der Einfluss der Steuern auf die Investitionsentscheidungen der Unternehmen . Frankfurt , New York , c1986. 405 p. ; ISBN 3-593-33642-1 LC Card 86-173001
HG4028.C4 W585 1986

CORPORATIONS - TAXATION - GERMANY (WEST) - DATA PROCESSING.
Hölter, Erich, 1955- Computergestütztes Ertragsteuersimulationsmodell der deutschen internationalen Kapitalgesellschaft . Giessen , c1986. xxv, 383 p. : ISBN 3-922730-67-1 LC Card 87-116057 DDC 336.24/3/0943 19
HJ4720.A7 H65 1986

Storz, Peter, 1954- Steuerplanung im Unternehmen mit einem computergestützten Modell /. München , c1984. vii, 657 p. : ISBN 3-88259-282-6 LC Card 84-174173 DDC 336.24/3/0943 19
HD2753.G3 S76 1984

CORPORATIONS - TAXATION - GERMANY (WEST) - ECONOMETRIC MODELS.
Georgi, Andreas A. Steuern in der Investitionsplanung . Hamburg , 1986. vii, 243, 16, xxviii p. : ISBN 3-89161-702-X LC Card 86-227290
HG4028.C4 G46 1986

CORPORATIONS - TAXATION - GERMANY (WEST) - MATHEMATICAL MODELS.
Hölter, Erich, 1955- Computergestütztes Ertragsteuersimulationsmodell der deutschen internationalen Kapitalgesellschaft . Giessen , c1986. xxv, 383 p. : ISBN 3-922730-67-1 LC Card 87-116057 DDC 336.24/3/0943 19
HJ4720.A7 H65 1986

CORPORATIONS - TAXATION - GREAT BRITAIN.
Knightley, Phillip. The Vestey affair /. London , 1981. 159 p., [8] p. of plates : ISBN 0-354-04708-6 : LC Card 81-193209 DDC 343.4104/092/2 344.10340922 19
HD2753.G7 K55 1981

Rankin, H. C. D. Corporation tax for students /. Wokingham, Berkshire, England , 1985. x, 230 p. : ISBN 0-85258-242-0 (pbk.) LC Card 85-3272 DDC 657/.46/0941 19
HD2753.G7 R36 1985

CORPORATIONS - TAXATION - GREAT BRITAIN - CASE STUDIES.
Morgan, Eleanor. Corporate taxation and investment . Haldershot, Hants Gull, England , Brookfield, Vt., USA , c1986. x, 220 p. ; ISBN 0-566-05265-2 : LC Card 86-25642 DDC 336.24/3/0941 19
HJ4708.A7 M63 1986

CORPORATIONS - TAXATION - INDIA.
Sen, Tapas Kumar, 1956- Corporate income tax and profit rates . New Delhi , c1984. xiii, 267 p. ; LC Card 84-900209 DDC 336.24/3/0954 19
HJ4766.Z7 S46 1984 ***NYPL [JLD 86-4138]***

CORPORATIONS - TAXATION - IRELAND.
Stewart, J. C., 1949- Corporate finance and fiscal policy in Ireland /. Aldershot, Hants,

England , Brookfield, Vt., USA , c1987. x, 166 p. ; ISBN 0-566-05441-8 : LC Card 87-14908 DDC 658.1/5/09415 19
HG4144 .S74 1987

CORPORATIONS - TAXATION - ITALY.
Leccisotti, Mario. Politiche dell'impresa e sistema tributario /. Napoli , 1984. 174 p. : ISBN 88-20-70883-3 :
NYPL [JLD 86-3651]

Politiche tributarie e struttura industriale in Italia /. Bologna , c1986. 118 p. ; ISBN 88-15-01224-9 : LC Card 86-224989
HD2753.I7 P65 1986

CORPORATIONS - TAXATION - LAW AND LEGISLATION - GERMANY (WEST)
Esser, Carsten, 1960- Das Fremdkapital im Unternehmen als Insolvenzursache und die Möglichkeiten rechtlicher Steuerung der Finanzierungsgrundlagen /. Frankfurt am Main , New York , c1986. xvi, 131 p. (1 folded) ; ISBN 3-8204-9398-0 LC Card 86-229108
HG5501 .E85 1986

Piltz, Detlev Jürgen. Vorschlag zur Verbesserung der Behandlung nichtabziehbarer Ausgaben im KStG 1977 /. Bonn , 1987. 42 leaves ; LC Card 87-401366 DDC 332 s 343.4305/267 332 s 344.3035267 19
HJ1120 .B65 Nr. 263 KK7226

CORPORATIONS - TAXATION - LAW AND LEGISLATION - LIECHTENSTEIN.
Walser, Olaf. Buchführungspflicht und Besteuerung der Sitzunternehmungen und Holdinggesellschaften in Liechtenstein /. Vaduz, Fürstentum Liechtenstein [1983] 31 p. ; LC Card 85-226619
HD2753.L76 W35 1983

CORPORATIONS - TAXATION - LIECHTENSTEIN.
Walser, Olaf. Buchführungspflicht und Besteuerung der Sitzunternehmungen und Holdinggesellschaften in Liechtenstein /. Vaduz, Fürstentum Liechtenstein [1983] 31 p. ; LC Card 85-226619
HD2753.L76 W35 1983

CORPORATIONS - TAXATION - MATHEMATICAL MODELS.
Sinn, Hans-Werner. [Kapitaleinkommensbesteuerung. English.] Capital income taxation and resource allocation /. Amsterdam ; New York : xiv, 411 p. ; ISBN 0-444-70208-3 LC Card 87-9126 DDC 336.24/3 19
HD2753.A3 S47413 1987

CORPORATIONS - TAXATION - UNITED STATES.
Block, Stanley B. The Tax Reform Act of 1986 . Homewood, Ill. , 1987. v, 26 p. ; ISBN 0-256-06055-X (pbk.) LC Card 87-403584 DDC 658.1/5 19
HG4026 .B589 1987 Suppl.

Federal tax reform and the states . Washington, D.C. (1616 H St., N.W., Suite 600, Washington 20006) , c1987. 84 p. ; LC Card 87-404532 DDC 336.2/05/0973 19
HJ2381 .F37 1987

CORPORATIONS - TAXATION - UNITED STATES - HANDBOOKS, MANUALS, ETC.
The Book of business knowledge /. New York, N.Y. , c1987. p. cm. ISBN 0-932648-83-5 : LC Card 86-30962 DDC 658 19
HF5356 .B72 1987

The Boss's encyclopedia /. New York, N.Y. , c1987. xxvi, 594 p. ; ISBN 0-932648-75-4 LC Card 86-30961 DDC 658 19
HF5356 .B735 1987

Business confidential. New York, N.Y. , c1987. xi, 504 p. ; ISBN 0-932648-82-7 LC Card 86-30963 DDC 650 19
HF5356 .B9259 1987

CORPORATIONS - TAXATION - UNITED STATES - STATISTICS.
Starcher, Mark L. Quantifying the impact of the Tax Reform Act of 1986 on effective corporate tax rates /. [Arlington, Va.] , c1986. 45, 3 leaves, 12 leaves of plates : LC Card 87-402048 DDC 336.24/3/0973021 19
HJ4653.C7 S675 1986

Statistics of income . Washington, D.C. , 1985. iii, 516 p. : ***NYPL [JLF 86-833]***

CORPORATIONS - UNITED STATES.
Allen, Frederick Lewis, 1890-1954. The lords of creation. New York, London, 1935. xii, 483 p. LC Card 35-20649 DDC 332.0973
HG181 .A57 ***NYPL [JLD 86-1097]***

Angell, Joseph Kinnicut, 1794-1857. Treatise on the law of private corporations aggregate [microform] /. Boston , 1855. lv, 939 p. ;
NYPL [*ZT-1731]

Kirichenko, È. V. (Èlina Vsevolodovna) Korporatsii SShA v bor'be za vneshnie rynki sbyta /. Moskva , 1981. 196 p. ; LC Card 82-152673
HD2766 .K53 1981

O'Reilly, James T., 1947- Unions' rights to company information /. Philadelphia, Pa. , c1987. xiii, 312 p. ; ISBN 0-89546-060-2 LC Card 85-82257 ***NYPL [JLL 74-174 no.21]***

Scholl, Heinz. Bilderberger & Trilaterale . Euskirchen, Bundesrepublik Deutschland , c1977. 92 p. ; LC Card 85-199172
HD2785 .S396 1977

Sealy, Albert H. Macro blueprint . New York , 1986. viii, 407, 232 p. ; ISBN 0-89192-390-X LC Card 86-218989 DDC 338.973 19
HD2785 .S412 1986

Tomasko, Robert M. Downsizing . New York , c1987. p. cm. ISBN 0-8144-5907-2 LC Card 87-47709 DDC 338.6/4 19
HD69.S5 T59 1987

CORPORATIONS - UNITED STATES - ACCOUNTING.
Clay, John R. Accounting for S corporations and noncorporate entities . Fort Worth, Tex. , c1987. 1 v. (various pagings) ; LC Card 87-163295 DDC 657/.95/076 19
HF5686.C7 C58 1987

Hill, Henry P. Accounting principles for the autonomous corporate entity /. New York , 1987. xii, 144 p. : ISBN 0-89930-212-2 (lib. bdg. : alk. paper) LC Card 86-25587 DDC 657/.95 19
HF5686.C7 H55 1987

CORPORATIONS - UNITED STATES - ACCOUNTING - PUBLIC OPINION.
A Comparative study on accounting policy between Japanese and the U. S. companies /. Tokyo, Japan , c1986. iv, 56 p. : LC Card 87-169003 DDC 657/.0952 19
HF5686.C7 C635 1986

CORPORATIONS - UNITED STATES - AUDITING.
Mangold, Nancy R. (Nancy Rueyhwa), 1949- Changing auditors and the effect on earnings, auditors' opinions, and stock prices /. Ann Arbor, Mich. , c1987. viii, 165 p. ; ISBN 0-8357-1786-0 (alk. paper) LC Card 87-19128 DDC 338.7/4/0973 19
HF5686.C7 M3295 1987

CORPORATIONS - UNITED STATES - CASE STUDIES.
Business policy . Homewood, Ill. , 1987. xx, 940 p. : ISBN 0-256-03358-7 LC Card 86-82216 DDC 658.4/012 19
HD2785 .B78 1987

Paul, Ronald N. The 101 best performing companies in America /. Chicago, Ill. , c1986. vii, 382 p. ; ISBN 0-917253-39-6 : LC Card 86-4947 DDC 338.7/4/0973 19
HD2785 .P38 1986 ***NYPL [JLE 86-3151]***

CORPORATIONS - UNITED STATES - CHARITABLE CONTRIBUTIONS.
Zhurikhin, È. A. (Èduard Alekseevich) "Filantropicheskie" fondy SShA v sisteme vlasti monopoliĭ /. Moskva , 1978. 182, [2] p. ; LC Card 81-160810
HG4028.C6 Z48 1978

CORPORATIONS - UNITED STATES - DIRECTORIES.
Bard, Ray. Breaking in . New York , 1985. 256 p. ; ISBN 0-688-05893-0 (pbk.) LC Card 85-6571 DDC 331.25/92/02573 19
HF5549.5.T7 B29 1985
NYPL [*R-Econ. 86-248]

Davidson, Jeffrey P. Marketing to the Fortune 500 and other corporations /. Homewood, Ill. , c1987. xv, 291 p. : ISBN 0-87094-984-5 LC Card 86-51669 DDC 658.8 19
HF5415.1 .D28 1987

Levine, Michael. The corporate address book . New York, N.Y. , c1987. 268 p. ; ISBN 0-399-51384-1 (pbk.) LC Card 87-11162 DDC 338.7/4/02573 19
HG4057 .A288 1987

Rosenbaum, Virginia K. Antitakeover charter amendments . Washington, D.C. , 1986. 100 p. : ISBN 0-931035-07-4
NYPL [JLF 86-1964]

Rosenberg, Gerald I. How to find information about acquisition candidates /. Washington, D.C. , c1987. 79 p. ; ISBN 0-934940-45-2 LC Card 86-51570 DDC 016.3387/4/0973 19
HD2785 .R58 1987

CORPORATIONS - UNITED STATES - FINANCE.
Davey, Patrick J. Corporate financing in international markets /. New York, N.Y. (845 3rd Ave., New York 10022) , c1986. 15 p. ; LC Card 86-212373 DDC 658.1/599 19
HG4061 .D384 1986

Hillstrom, Roger. 1960-1969, a decade of corporate and international finance. New York [1972] 381 p. LC Card 72-175335 DDC 332
HG4907 .H54 ***NYPL [JLG 73-17]***

Introduction to ACH corporate payments /. Washington, D.C. (1901 L St., N.W., Suite 640, Washington 20036) [c1986] 90 p. : LC Card 86-222675 DDC 332.1/028 19
HG1710 .I58 1986

Nevaer, Louis E. V. Corporate financial planning and management in a deficit economy /. New York , 1987. 171 p. : ISBN 0-89930-202-5 (lib. bdg. : alk. paper) LC Card 86-25582 DDC 658.1/145 19
HG4063 .N48 1987

Scott, John, 1912- Capitalist property and financial power . Brighton, Sussex , 1986. x, 230 p. ; ISBN 0-7450-0047-9
NYPL [JLD 86-3078]

Winter, Elmer L. Complete guide to making a public stock offering. Englewood Cliffs, N.J. [1972] 295 p. ISBN 0-13-160192-X LC Card 70-164924 DDC 658.1/52
HG4028.S7 W5 1972 ***NYPL [JLF 86-390]***

CORPORATIONS - UNITED STATES - FINANCE - DIRECTORIES.
Metzger, Bertram L. Profit sharing in 38 large companies . Evanston, Ill. , 1975-78. 2 v. : ISBN 0-911192-25-5 : LC Card 75-39379 DDC 658.32/25
HD2984 .M47 ***NYPL [JLF 86-389]***

CORPORATIONS - UNITED STATES - FINANCE - PLANNING.
Umapathy, Srinivasan. Current budgeting practices in U. S. industry . New York , 1987. xxxix, 176 p. ; ISBN 0-89930-250-5 (lib. bdg. : alk. paper) LC Card 87-5969 DDC 658.1/54 19
HG4028.B8 U46 1987

CORPORATIONS - UNITED STATES - HANDBOOKS, MANUALS, ETC.
Plunkett, Jack W. The almanac of American employers . Chicago , 1985. 340 p. ; ISBN 0-8092-5407-7 LC Card 85-14908 DDC 331.2/0973 19
HF5549.5.C67 P58 1985
NYPL [*R-Econ. 85-3166]

CORPORATIONS - UNITED STATES - HISTORY.
Blackford, Mansel G., 1944- Business enterprise in American history /. Boston , c1986. xi, 456 p. : ISBN 0-395-35155-3 (pbk.) LC Card 85-60780 DDC 338.7/4/0973 19
HD2785 .B52 1986 ***NYPL [JLE 86-3008]***

Bunting, David G. The rise of large American corporations, 1889-1919 /. New York , 1986, c1987. 224 p. ; ISBN 0-8240-8353-9 (alk. paper) : LC Card 86-29527 DDC 338.6/44 19
HD2785 .B76 1987

Managing big business . Boston, Mass. , c1986. xxvii, 425 p. ; ISBN 0-87584-142-2 LC Card 86-7683 DDC 338.6/44/0973 19
HD2785 .M353 1986 ***NYPL [JLE 87-1360]***

Weaver, Paul, 1942 Oct. 18- The suicidal corporation /. New York , c1988. p. cm. ISBN 0-671-52378-3 LC Card 87-23468 DDC 338.7/4/0973 19
HD2785 .W38 1988

CORPORATIONS - UNITED STATES - HISTORY - 20TH CENTURY.
Stine, G. Harry (George Harry), 1928- The corporate survivors /. New York, N.Y. , c1986. 230 p. : ISBN 0-8144-5831-9 LC Card 86-47597 DDC 338.7/4/0973 19
HD2785 .S73 1986 ***NYPL [JLE 86-4469]***

CORPORATIONS - UNITED STATES - INFORMATION SERVICES - UNITED STATES - DIRECTORIES.
How to find company intelligence in state documents /. Washington, D.C. , c1986. 110 p. ; ISBN 0-934940-38-X (pbk.) LC Card 86-218108 DDC 016.3387/4/0973 19
HD2785 .H67 1986

CORPORATIONS - UNITED STATES - INVESTOR RELATIONS - CASE STUDIES.
Weber, Nathan. Communicating with security analysts /. New York, N.Y. (845 3rd Ave., New York 10022) , c1985. 22 p. : LC Card 86-212395 DDC 658.4/5 19
HD59 .W36 1985

CORPORATIONS - UNITED STATES - INVESTOR RELATIONS - DIRECTORIES.
Investor relations directory . Highland Park, Ill., U. S.A. (P.O. Box 1037, Highland Park 60035) , c1986. 166 p. ; LC Card 86-228008 DDC 338.7/61659285/02573 19
HD59 .I568 1986

CORPORATIONS - UNITED STATES - POLITICAL ACTIVITY.
Matasar, Ann B. Corporate PACs and federal campaign financing laws . New York , 1986. x, 161 p. ; ISBN 0-89930-086-3 (lib. bdg. : alk. paper)
NYPL [JLE 86-2492]

CORPORATIONS - UNITED STATES - PUBLIC OPINION.
Lipset, Seymour Martin. The confidence gap . Baltimore , 1987. xxiv, 460 p. : ISBN 0-8018-3044-3 (pbk.) LC Card 86-27416 DDC 303.3/8/0973 19
HD2785 .L53 1987

CORPORATIONS, WEST GERMAN - ADDRESSES, ESSAYS, LECTURES.
Multinationale Konzerne . Köln , c1982. 478 p. : ISBN 3-7663-0506-9 LC Card 82-196963 DDC 332.6/73/0943 19
HD5710.75.G3 M84 1982
NYPL [JLD 86-2753]

CORPORATIONS, WEST GERMAN - EUROPEAN ECONOMIC COMMUNITY COUNTRIES.
Urban, Sabine M.-L. Entreprises allemandes et coopération industrielle à l'échelle européenne . Paris , c1986. 162 p. : ISBN 2-11-001580-2 : LC Card 86-175800
HD2844 .U7 1986

CORPORATIONS, WEST GERMAN - TAXATION - DATA PROCESSING.
Hölter, Erich, 1955- Computergestütztes Ertragsteuersimulationsmodell der deutschen internationalen Kapitalgesellschaft . Giessen , c1986. xxv, 383 p. : ISBN 3-922730-67-1 LC Card 87-116057 DDC 336.24/3/0943 19
HJ4720.A7 H65 1986

CORPORATIONS, WEST GERMAN - TAXATION - MATHEMATICAL MODELS.
Hölter, Erich, 1955- Computergestütztes Ertragsteuersimulationsmodell der deutschen internationalen Kapitalgesellschaft . Giessen , c1986. xxv, 383 p. : ISBN 3-922730-67-1 LC Card 87-116057 DDC 336.24/3/0943 19
HJ4720.A7 H65 1986

CORPORATIONS - YUGOSLAVIA - FINANCE - MATHEMATICAL MODELS.
Smiljanić, Slobodan. Sistem upravljanja investicijama /. Kragujevac , 1984. 185 p. : LC Card 86-115123
HG4234.6 .S65 1984

CORPORATISM. see **CORPORATE STATE.**

CORPORATIVE STATE. see **CORPORATE STATE.**

CORPORATIVISM. see **CORPORATE STATE.**

CORPS (computing, organizations, policy, and society) series.
Johnson, Bonnie McDaniel, 1944- Managing organizational innovation . New York , 1987. xiv, 242 p. ; ISBN 0-231-06398-9 LC Card 87-307 DDC 652/.5 19
HF5548.115 .J64 1987

Corre, Jean. Raffegeau, Jean. Les comptes consolidés . Paris , c1984. 971 p. : ISBN 2-85115-064-2 : LC Card 84-245353 DDC 657/.3 19
HF5681.B2 R25 1984

Correa, Jorge Lois. Sistemas y equipos de desmedulado en la industria del bagazo de la caña de azúcar / Jorge Lois Correa. Ciudad de La Habana : Editorial Científico-Técnica, c1982. 77 p. : ill. ; 23 cm. At head of title: Instituto Cubano de Investigaciones sobre los Derivados de la Caña de Azúcar. Bibliography: p. [73]-77. LC Card 85-198777
1. Bagasse industry - Cuba - Equipment and supplies. 2. Sugarcane industry - Cuba - Equipment and supplies. I. ICIDCA. II. Title.
HD9119.B4 C83 1982

Correa, R. (Rafael), 1947- IFIP Working Conference on System Modelling and Optimization (1984 : Santiago, Chile) Recent advances in system modelling and optimization . Berlin , New York , c1986. 199 p. : ISBN 0-387-17083-9 (U. S.) LC Card 86-29770 DDC 003 19
QA402 .I43 1984 ***NYPL [JSE 87-639]***

Corrêa, Rossini. Mudança social no Nordeste : conflitos de trabalho, luta de classes e poder político em 1900 : uma biografia institucional do Centro Artístico e Operário Maranhense / Rossini Corrêa. São Luís : Serviço de Impr. e Obras Gráficas do Estado, 1986. 176 p., [6] p. of plates : facsims. ; 22 cm. Bibliography: p. 171-176. LC Card 87-152221 DDC 322/.2/098121 19
1. Centro Artístico e Operário Maranhense - History. 2. Labor and laboring classes - Brazil - Maranhão - Political activity - History. 3. Artisans - Brazil - Maranhão - Political activity - History. 4. Socialism - Brazil - Maranhão - History. I. Title.
HD8289.M37 C67 1986

Correa V., Virgilio (Correa Vásquez) Centelleo de la industria en Panamá / Virgilio Correa V. 1era ed. [Panama? : s.n.], 1986 ([Panama, Panama] : Tall. Gráf. del Centro de Impresión Educativa) 279 p., [6] p. of plates : ill. ; 21 cm. Bibliography: p. 264-266. LC Card 87-404562 DDC 338.097287 19
1. Panama - Industries. 2. Industry and state - Panama. 3. Petroleum industry and trade - Panama. I. Title.
HC147 .C67 1986

Correia de Andrade, Manuel. see **Andrade, Manuel Correia de Oliveira.**

Correia de Oliveira Andrade, Manuel. see **Andrade, Manuel Correia de Oliveira.**

CORRELATION (STATISTICS)
Schroeder, Larry D. Understanding regression analysis . Beverly Hills , c1986. 95 p. : ISBN 0-8039-2758-4 LC Card 85-63790
NYPL [JLK 77-39 no.57]

West, Bruce J. An essay on the importance of being nonlinear /. Berlin , New York , c1985. viii, 204 p. : ISBN 0-387-16038-8 (U. S.)
NYPL [JSK 75-186 v.62]

El correo marítimo en el Río de la Plata /.
Marcó del Pont, José. Buenos Aires , 1913. 161 p. : LC Card 85-125707
HE6819.M3 M37 1913

CORRESPONDENCE. see **COMMERCIAL CORRESPONDENCE.**

CORRIENTES (ARGENTINA) - CENSUS, 1850.
Sonzogni, Cristina María. La población de la ciudad de Corrientes a mediados del siglo XIX /. Corrientes , 1980. 50, [4] leaves, [14] leaves of plates : LC Card 85-209374
HB3560.C67 S65 1980

CORRIENTES (ARGENTINA) - CENSUS, 1857.
Sonzogni, Cristina María. La población de la ciudad de Corrientes a mediados del siglo XIX /. Corrientes , 1980. 50, [4] leaves, [14] leaves of plates : LC Card 85-209374
HB3560.C67 S65 1980

CORRIENTES (ARGENTINA) - POPULATION - HISTORY - 19TH CENTURY.
Sonzogni, Cristina María. La población de la ciudad de Corrientes a mediados del siglo XIX /. Corrientes , 1980. 50, [4] leaves, [14] leaves of plates : LC Card 85-209374
HB3560.C67 S65 1980

Corrigan, George A., 1896-1981. Calked boots and cant hooks / George A. Corrigan ; L.G. Sorden, editor ; Charles Twining, foreword. 2nd ed. Ashland, WI : Northword, 1986, c1976. xxi, 265 p. : ill., map, ports. ; 23 cm. Cover title: Calked boots & cant hooks. ISBN 0-9613961-5-6 (pbk.) : LC Card 87-401439 DDC 331.7/634982/0924 B 19
1. Corrigan, George A., 1896-1981. 2. Loggers - Wisconsin - Biography. 3. Loggers - Michigan - Biography. I. Sorden, L. G. (Leland George). II. Title. III. Title: Calked boots & cant hooks.
HD8039.L92 U535 1986

CORRIGAN, GEORGE A., 1896-1981.
Corrigan, George A., 1896-1981. Calked boots and cant hooks /. Ashland, WI , 1986, c1976. xxi, 265 p. : ISBN 0-9613961-5-6 (pbk.) : LC Card 87-401439 DDC 331.7/634982/0924 B 19
HD8039.L92 U535 1986

CORRUPTION (IN POLITICS) - BRAZIL.
Tibiriçá, Luiz Caldas. Brasil . São Paulo, SP , 1984. 159 p. ; LC Card 84-215785
HC187 .T5 1984 ***NYPL [JLD 87-507]***

CORRUPTION (IN POLITICS) - GERMANY (WEST) - HAMBURG.
Neue Heimat . Hamburg , 1983. 231 p. : ISBN 3-87975-238-9 LC Card 83-150360
HD7339.H3 N48 1983

CORRUPTION (IN POLITICS) - INDIA.
Mehta, Vadilal Lallubhai, 1903- Unemployment, inequality, parallel economy . Ahmedabad , 1982. viii, 141 p., [1] leaf of plates : LC Card 82-900764 DDC 331.13/7954 19
HD5819 .M43 1982 ***NYPL [JLD 85-2751]***

CORRUPTION (IN POLITICS) - ITALY.
Risanamento e riordino delle partecipazioni statali . Milano, Italy , c1986. 429 p. : LC Card 86-169331
HC310.I53 R57 1986

CORRUPTION (IN POLITICS) - MEXICO.
Mexican topics . [México, D.F.] [1986] 2 portfolios : LC Card 86-221843 DDC 972.08/3 19
HC135 .M52554 1986

Serrano Illescas, Alfonso. Pobre patria! /. México, D.F. , 1982. 132 p. ; ISBN 968-409-161-3 LC Card 85-122377
HC135 .S368 1982

CORRUPTION (IN POLITICS) - NIGERIA - EAST-CENTRAL STATE.
Anambra State, Nigeria. Government white paper on the report of the Administrative Board of Inquiry on Ministry of Works /. [Enugu, Nigeria] [1976?] 100 p. ; LC Card 86-205027 DDC 354.669/4 19
HD4365.5.Z8 E373 1976

CORRUPTION (IN POLITICS) - UNITED STATES.
Fraud, waste, and abuse in government . Philadelphia , c1986. x, 159 p. ; ISBN 0-89727-058-4 LC Card 86-2967 DDC 336.73 19
HJ257.2 .F72 1986 ***NYPL [JLE 86-4153]***

CORRUPTION (IN POLITICS) - VENEZUELA.
Ojeda, Roseliano. Cómo se desangra un país-- ! . Valencia [Venezuela] , c1987. 241 p. ; ISBN 980-212-037-5 LC Card 87-169695 DDC 330.987/0633 19
HC237 .O365 1987

CORRUPTION (IN POLITICS) - WEST (U. S.) - HISTORY.
Reisner, Marc. Cadillac desert . New York, N.Y., U. S.A. , 1987, c1986. 582 p., [18] p. of plates : ISBN 0-14-010432-1 (pbk.) : LC Card 87-7602 DDC 333.91/00978 19
HD1739.A17 R45 1987

CORRUPTION INVESTIGATION - CALIFORNIA.
A Practical guide to investigating public works violations /. Oakland, CA (520 3rd St., Suite 204, Oakland 94607) , 1986. 73 p., [3] leaves of plates : LC Card 86-209657 DDC 363.2/5 19
HD3890.C2 P7 1986

Corsi, Jerome R. Marketing life insurance in a bank or thrift /. Boulder, Colo. , 1986. xii, 233 p. ; ISBN 0-8133-7205-4 : LC Card 86-1644

DDC 332.1/7 19
HG1616.I47 M37 1986
NYPL [JLD 86-3992]

Corsten, Hans. Die Produktion von Dienstleistungen : Grundzüge einer Produktionswirtschaftslehre des tertiären Sektors / von Hans Corsten. Berlin : E. Schmidt, c1985. xii, 439 p. : ill. ; 21 cm. (Betriebswirtschaftliche Studien. 51) Bibliography: p. 406-435. Includes index. ISBN 3-503-02523-5 LC Card 86-113978 DDC 658 19
1. Service industries - Management. I. Title.
HD9980.5 .C67 1985

Cortázar, René. Políticas macro-económicas . Santiago de Chile [1986] 409 p. : LC Card 87-403669 DDC 338.98 19
HC125 .P657 1986

Corten, André. Duarte, Isis. Trabajadores urbanos . Santo Domingo, República Dominicana , c1986. 314 p. ; LC Card 87-402153 DDC 331/.097293 19
HD8218.5 .D83 1986

Cortés A., Guadalupe. Las Derrotas obreras, 1946-1952 /. México , 1984. 204 p. ; ISBN 968-580-647-0 LC Card 84-255708 DDC 331.88/0972 19
HD6532 .D36 1984 *NYPL [JLE 86-4685]*

Cortés de Pinzón, Magdalena. Bases de contabilidad nacional / Magdalena Cortés de Pinzón, Rómulo Enrique Pinzón Santos. [Bogotá, Colombia] : República de Colombia, Departamento Administrativo Nacional de Estadística, [1982] 96 p. : ill. ; 21 cm. Errata slip inserted. Bibliography: p. 95-96. LC Card 82-216044
1. National income - Accounting. 2. National income - Colombia - Accounting. I. Pinzón Santos, Rómulo Enrique. II. Title.
HC79.I5 C675 1982

Cortés, Fernando, 1941- Análisis del cambio en la concentración a través del coeficiente de Gini / Fernando Cortés, Rosa Ma. Rubalcava. México, D.F. : Facultad Latinoamericana de Ciencias Sociales, Sede Académica de México, [1982] 55 leaves : ill. ; 28 cm. (Doc. . 1/82) Includes bibliographical references. LC Card 83-111847
1. Gini coefficient. I. Rubalcava, Rosa María. II. Series: Doc. (Facultad Latinoamericana de Ciencias Sociales. Sede Académica de México) , 82/1. III. Title.
HB523 .C67 1982

Cortés i Marqués, Gabriel. Calleja Xifré, Carlos. El Baix Camp . Barcelona [1986] xv, 367 p. : ISBN 84-505-3567-9 LC Card 86-205881
HC388.R482 C35 1986

Cortes, Mariluz. Success in small and medium-scale enterprises : the evidence from Colombia / Mariluz Cortes, Albert Berry, and Ashfaq Ishaq. New York : Published for the World Bank [by] Oxford University Press, c1987. xiii, 289 p. ; 25 cm. (A World Bank research publication) Bibliography: p. 275-282. Includes index. ISBN 0-19-520593-6 : LC Card 86-46296 DDC 338.6/42/09861 19
1. Small business - Colombia. 2. Colombia - Industries. I. Berry R., Albert. II. Ishaq, Ashfaq, 1953-. III. Title.
HD2346.C7 C69 1987

Cortiços em São Paulo : frente e verso / Município de São Paulo, Secretaria Municipal do Planejamento. São Paulo : A Secretaria, 1986. 195, [2] p. : ill. (some folded) ; 31 cm. (Serie Documentos) Bibliography: p. [196]-[197]. LC Card 87-119201 DDC 363.5/8 19
1. Urban poor - Housing - Brazil - São Paulo. 2. Slums - Brazil - São Paulo. I. São Paulo (Brazil). Secretaria Municipal do Planejamento. II. Series: Série Documentos (São Paulo (Brazil). Secretaria Municipal do Planejamento).
HD7287.96.B62 S263 1986

Cortina Portilla, Manuel. Algo sobre la plata en México en el siglo XVIII / Manuel Cortina Portilla. México : Grupo Consa, 1986. 48 p., [1] folded leaf of plates : col. port. ; 34 cm. "Edición privada ... fuera del comercio." LC Card 87-404604 DDC 332.4/042/097253 19
1. Casa de Moneda de México - History - 18th century. 2. Mints - Mexico - Mexico City - History - 18th century. 3. Fagoaga Iragorri, Francisco, 1679-1736 - Portraits. 4. Fagoaga family - Portraits. 5. Conversation piece (Portrait painting) - Mexico - Mexico City. 6. Portrait paintings - 18th century - Mexico - Mexico City. I. Title.
HG661 .C67 1986

Corugedo, Rosa González. see **González Corugedo, Rosa.**

Corvalán Vásquez, Oscar E., 1947- Empleo y capacitación en los talleres informales de Santiago / Oscar Corvalán, Leonor Cariola, Marianela Cerri. 1a ed. Montevideo : CINTERFOR/OIT, 1984. 150 p. ; 23 cm. (Estudios y monografías . no. 67) Includes bibliographical references. LC Card 86-127324
1. Small business - Chile - Santiago. 2. Informal sector (Economics) - Chile - Santiago. 3. Labor supply - Chile - Santiago. 4. Occupational training - Chile - Santiago. 5. Apprentices - Chile - Santiago. I. Cariola, Leonor. II. Cerri, Marianela. III. Series: Estudios y monografías (CINTERFOR (Organization)) , no. 67. IV. Title.
HD2346.C54 S263 1984

Corwen, Leonard. Brandt, Ed. Fifty and fired . Bedford, Mass. , c1987. xii, 242 p. ; ISBN 0-938179-07-1 : LC Card 87-12150 DDC 650.1/4/0240564 19
HD38.25.U6 B7 1987

Cos'e il sindacato. Roma : Edizioni lavoro, c1986. 76 p. : ill. (some col.) ; 25 cm. ISBN 88-7910-145-5 : LC Card 86-163777
1. Trade-unions - Italy. I. Edizioni del lavoro.
HD6709 .C675 1986

Cosenza, Teresa. Shapiro, H. Jack (Harris Jack) Reviving industry in America . Cambridge, Mass. , c1987. xii, 204 p. : ISBN 0-88730-118-5 LC Card 87-17585 DDC 338.4/767/0973 19
HD9725 .S46 1987

Cosgrove, Denis E. Social formation and symbolic landscape / Denis E. Cosgrove. Totowa, N.J. : Barnes & Noble Books, 1985, c1984. 293 p. : ill., maps, plans ; 23 cm. Includes index. Bibliography: p. 272-283. ISBN 0-389-20540-0 LC Card 84-21629 DDC 304.2 19
1. Landscape assessment - History. 2. Social history - Modern, 1500-. 3. Land use - History. I. Title.
GF90 .C67 1985 *NYPL [JLD 86-2206]*

Cosgrove, Julia Fukuda. United States foreign economic policy toward China, 1943-1946 : from the end of extraterritoriality to the Sino-American Commercial Treaty of 1946 / Julia Fukuda Cosgrove. New York : Garland Pub., 1987. 235 p. ; 23 cm. (Foreign economic policy of the United States) Originally presented as the author's thesis (Ph. D.--Washington University, Saint Louis, Mo., 1980) Bibliography: p. 221-228. ISBN 0-8240-8079-3 (alk. paper) : LC Card 87-23791 DDC 337.73051 19
1. United States - Foreign economic relations - China. 2. China - Foreign economic relations - United States. 3. United States - Foreign relations - 1933-1945. 4. United States - Foreign relations - 1945-1953. 5. China - Foreign relations - 1912-1949. I. Title. II. Series.
HF1456.5.C6 C67 1987

Cosgrove Twitchett, Carol. The European Community's development policy . Bruges , 19. 285 p. : LC Card 87-135534 DDC 338.94 19
HC60 .E7626 1986

Cosmetics & toiletries marketing strategies in Europe. Marketing strategies for selling cosmetics & toiletries in Europe. New York, N.Y. , c1983. 381 p. ; LC Card 87-141847 DDC 380.1/456685/094 19
HD9970.5.C673 E8555 1983

Cosmetics and toiletries marketing strategies in Europe. Marketing strategies for selling cosmetics & toiletries in Europe. New York, N.Y. , c1983. 381 p. ; LC Card 87-141847 DDC 380.1/456685/094 19
HD9970.5.C673 E8555 1983

COSMETICS - EUROPE - MARKETING.
Marketing strategies for selling cosmetics & toiletries in Europe. New York, N.Y. , c1983. 381 p. ; LC Card 87-141847 DDC 380.1/456685/094 19
HD9970.5.C673 E8555 1983

COSMETICS INDUSTRY - EUROPE.
Marketing strategies for selling cosmetics & toiletries in Europe. New York, N.Y. , c1983. 381 p. ; LC Card 87-141847 DDC 380.1/456685/094 19
HD9970.5.C673 E8555 1983

Cosse, Gustavo. Estado y agro en el Ecuador, 1960-1980 / Gustavo Cosse. Quito : Corporación Editora Nacional, 1984. 112 p. : ill. ; 21 cm. (Biblioteca de ciencias sociales. v. 1) Bibliography: p. [111]-112. LC Card 85-119842 DDC 338.1/8866 19
1. Agriculture and state - Ecuador. 2. Agriculture - Economic aspects - Ecuador. I. Series: Biblioteca de ciencias sociales (Quito, Ecuador) , v. 1. II. Title.
HD1888 .C67 1984 *NYPL [JLD 86-2738]*

Cost accounting . Killough, Larry N. St. Paul , c1987. xxii, 870 p. : ISBN 0-314-25865-5 : LC Card 86-26677 DDC 658.1/511 19
HF5686.C8 K488 1987

Cost accounting . Oliver, E. Eugene. Englewood Cliffs, NJ , c1987. xv, 352 p. : ISBN 0-13-179979-7 LC Card 86-25225 DDC 657/.42 19
HF5686.C8 O45 1987

COST ACCOUNTING.
Cherrington, J. Owen. Cost and managerial accounting /. St. Paul , c1988. p. cm. ISBN 0-314-25327-0 : LC Card 86-24753 DDC 657/.42 19
HF5686.C8 C475 1988

Daff, Trevor. Cost and management accounting /. London , New York , 1988. p. cm. ISBN 0-582-46924-4 LC Card 87-3715 DDC 657/.42 19
HF5686.C8 D17 1988

Dieterle, Robert. Kostenrechnung . Bern , c1983. 258 p. : ISBN 3-258-03210-6 : LC Card 83-185404
HF5686.C8 D53 1983

Drury, Colin. Management and cost accounting /. Workingham, Berkshire, England , 19. xv, 599 p. : ISBN 0-442-30637-7 (pbk.) LC Card 85-3266 DDC 658.1/511 19
HF5635 .D798 1986

Entwicklungslinien der Kosten- und Erlösrechnung /. Stuttgart , c1983. viii, 232 p. : ISBN 3-7910-0304-6 : LC Card 83-200474
HF5686.C8 E65 1983

Geiss, Wilfried. Betriebswirtschaftliche Kennzahlen . Frankfurt am Main , New York , c1986. 405 p. : ISBN 3-8204-9629-7 LC Card 87-407301 DDC 657/.42 19
HF5686.C8 G384 1986

Karpunin, M. G. (Mikhail Grigor′evich) Funktsional′no-stoimostnoĭ analiz v otraslevom upravlenii ėffektivnost′iu /. Moskva , 1983. 199 p. : LC Card 84-120682
HF5686.C8 K275 1983

Killough, Larry N. Cost accounting . St. Paul , c1987. xxii, 870 p. : ISBN 0-314-25865-5 : LC Card 86-26677 DDC 658.1/511 19
HF5686.C8 K488 1987

Oliver, E. Eugene. Cost accounting . Englewood Cliffs, NJ , c1987. xv, 352 p. : ISBN 0-13-179979-7 LC Card 86-25225 DDC 657/.42 19
HF5686.C8 O45 1987

Persoglia, Johann. Projectcontrolling als Subsystem des Rechnungswesens /. Graz , c1986. 238 p. ; ISBN 3-7041-0149-4 LC Card 87-407965 DDC 657/.42 19
HF5686.C8 P475 1986

Röhrenbacher, Hans. Die Kosten- und Leistungsrechnung im Handelsbetrieb . Berlin , c1985. 176 p. : ISBN 3-428-05808-9 LC Card 86-129151 DDC 657/.42 19
HF5686.C8 R583 1985

Rotch, William. The executive's guide to management accounting and control systems /. Houston, Tex. , 1987. ix, 225 p. : ISBN 0-87393-044-4 LC Card 87-163287 DDC 658.1/511 19
HF5635 .R829 1987

Winkler, Wigbert M. Kostenrechnung in Klein- und Mittelbetrieben . Graz , c1986. vi, 287 p. : ISBN 3-7041-0150-8 LC Card 87-409225
HF5686.C8 W683 1986

COST ACCOUNTING - CASE STUDIES.
Mancini, Andrea, 1954- La contabilità analitica dei costi . [Torino] , 1986. 53 p. : ISBN 88-85851-00-2 : LC Card 87-114718
HF5686.C8 M265 1986

COST ACCOUNTING - DATA PROCESSING.
Knoop, Jens. Online-Kostenrechnung für die CIM-Planung . Berlin , c1986. 242 p. : ISBN 3-503-02569-3 LC Card 86-227596
HF5686.C8 K5835 1986

Lehman, Mark W. Using the microcomputer in cost accounting . St. Paul , c1988. x, 396 p. : ISBN 0-314-34729-1 (pbk.) LC Card 87-10632 DDC 657/.42/02855369 19
HF5686.C8 L34 1988

COST ACCOUNTING - PROBLEMS, EXERCISES, ETC.
Dieterle, Robert. Kostenrechnung . Bern , c1983. 258 p. : ISBN 3-258-03210-6 : LC Card 83-185404
HF5686.C8 D53 1983

COST ACCOUNTING - SOVIET UNION.
Karpunin, M. G. (Mikhail Grigor′evich) Funktsional′no-stoimostnoĭ analiz v otraslevom upravlenii ėffektivnost′iu /. Moskva , 1983. 199 p. : LC Card 84-120682
HF5686.C8 K275 1983

Cost and management accounting /. Daff, Trevor. London , New York , 1988. p. cm. ISBN 0-582-46924-4 LC Card 87-3715 DDC 657/.42 19
HF5686.C8 D17 1988

Cost and managerial accounting /. Cherrington, J. Owen. St. Paul , c1988. p. cm. ISBN 0-314-25327-0 : LC Card 86-24753 DDC 657/.42 19
HF5686.C8 C475 1988

COST AND STANDARD OF LIVING - BANGLADESH - STATISTICS.
Bangladesh household expenditure survey, 1981-82. Dhaka, Bangladesh , 1986. 160 p., [13] leaves of plates : LC Card 86-902560 DDC 339.4/1/095492021 19
HD7051.6 .B36 1986

COST AND STANDARD OF LIVING - BELGIUM - STATISTICS.
Familiebudgetter . Luxembourg , Washington, D.C. , c1986. 279 p. ; ISBN 92-825-5583-6 : LC Card 86-213531
HD7033 .F35 1986

COST AND STANDARD OF LIVING - BRAZIL.
Vieira, Cláudio Afonso. Urbanização e custo de reprodução da força de trabalho /. São Paulo , 1984. 175 p., [5] folded leaves of plates :

COST AND STANDARD OF LIVING - BRAZIL - FORTALEZA.
Fernandes, Adelita Neto Carleial. Condições de vida nos bairros de Fortaleza, nov/84 a mar/85 . Fortaleza , 1986. 92 p. : LC Card 86-196902
HC189.F67 F47 1986

COST AND STANDARD OF LIVING - BRAZIL - SÃO PAULO.
Vieira, Cláudio Afonso. Urbanização e custo de reprodução da força de trabalho /. São Paulo , 1984. 175 p., [5] folded leaves ; LC Card 85-136502
HD5755.S3 V54 1984

COST AND STANDARD OF LIVING - CZECHOSLOVAKIA - MATHEMATICAL MODELS.
Sistema ėkonomiko-matematicheskikh modeleĭ dlia analiza i prognoza urovnia zhizni /. Moskva , 1986. 262 p. : LC Card 86-232874
HD6978 .S56 1986

COST AND STANDARD OF LIVING - DENMARK - STATISTICS.
Familiebudgetter . Luxembourg , Washington, D.C. , c1986. 279 p. ; ISBN 92-825-5583-6 : LC Card 86-213531
HD7033 .F35 1986

COST AND STANDARD OF LIVING - DEVELOPING COUNTRIES.
Grootaert, Christiaan, 1950- Measuring and analyzing levels of living in developing countries . Washington, D.C., U. S.A. , c1986. x, 139 p. : ISBN 0-8213-0758-4 (pbk.) LC Card 86-5611 DDC 339.4/7/091724 19
HD7067 .G76 1986b

COST AND STANDARD OF LIVING - ECUADOR.
Coyuntura económica ecuatoriana, 1985-1986. [Quito, Ecuador] [1986] i, 39 p. ; LC Card 86-217289
HC202 .C73 1986

COST AND STANDARD OF LIVING - ENGLAND - LONDON.
Wilson, Gail. Money in the family . Aldershot, Hants., England , Brookfield, USA , c1987. ix, 271 p. ; ISBN 0-566-05389-6 : LC Card 87-7402 DDC 339.2/2 19
HG179 .W53517 1987

COST AND STANDARD OF LIVING - GERMANY, EAST.
Lebenshaltung und Lebensniveau in der DDR /. Bonn , c1986. 64 p. ; LC Card 87-409446 DDC 339.4/4/09431 19
HD7029.5 .L386 1986

COST AND STANDARD OF LIVING - GERMANY, WEST.
Demographische Probleme der Haushaltsökonomie /. Bochum , 1986. vii, 212 p. : ISBN 3-88339-534-X LC Card 87-137970 DDC 339.4/1/0943 19
HD7029 .D37 1986

Krause, Detlef. Einkommensquellen und Lebenschancen . Berlin , c1986. 189 p. : ISBN 3-428-06114-4 LC Card 87-130932 DDC 339.2/2/0943 19
HC290.5.I5 K7 1986

Schmucker, Helga. Studien zur empirischen Haushalts- und Verbrauchsforschung /. Berlin , 1980. xiv, 357 p. : ISBN 3-428-04657-9 LC Card 80-153661
TX7 .B4 Heft 15 HD7029
NYPL [JLE 86-3430]

COST AND STANDARD OF LIVING - GERMANY (WEST) - DUISBURG.
Ölçen, Ali Nejat. Türken und Rückkehr . Frankfurt a.M. , 1986. 132 p. ; ISBN 3-924320-51-9 LC Card 87-138316 DDC 331.6/2/56104355 19
HD8458.T9 O43 1986

COST AND STANDARD OF LIVING - GREECE - STATISTICS.
Familiebudgetter . Luxembourg , Washington, D.C. , c1986. 279 p. ; ISBN 92-825-5583-6 : LC Card 86-213531
HD7033 .F35 1986

COST AND STANDARD OF LIVING - GRENADA.
Burpee, C. Gaye. 1985 household survey of Grenada . Ann Arbor, Mich. , 1986. 168 p. : ISBN 0-87944-317-0 (pbk.) LC Card 86-217405 DDC 339.4/1/0723 19
HD7009.9.Z8 G843 1986

COST AND STANDARD OF LIVING - HUNGARY.
Életszínvonal és közhangulat /. Budapest , 1984. 69 p. ; LC Card 86-147705
HD7027.5 .E44 1984

COST AND STANDARD OF LIVING - HUNGARY - PUBLIC OPINION.
Salamin, Pálné. Vélemények az életszínvonalról /. Budapest , 1986. 88 p. : LC Card 86-218875
HD7027.5 .S25 1986

COST AND STANDARD OF LIVING - HUNGARY - STATISTICS.
Az Ipari nagyüzemi munkásság jövedelmi viszonyai, élet- és munkakörülményei /. [Budapest] [1985] 94 p. ; LC Card 85-210330
HD8420.5 .I63 1985

COST AND STANDARD OF LIVING - IRELAND - STATISTICS.
Familiebudgetter . Luxembourg , Washington, D.C. , c1986. 279 p. ; ISBN 92-825-5583-6 : LC Card 86-213531
HD7033 .F35 1986

COST AND STANDARD OF LIVING - IVORY COAST.
Grootaert, Christiaan, 1950- Measuring and analyzing levels of living in developing countries . Washington, D.C., U. S.A. , c1986. x, 139 p. : ISBN 0-8213-0758-4 (pbk.) LC Card 86-5611 DDC 339.4/7/091724 19
HD7067 .G76 1986b

COST AND STANDARD OF LIVING - LATIN AMERICA.
Egner, Erich, 1901- Hauswirtschaft und Lebenshaltung . Berlin , 1974. 249 p. ; ISBN 3-428-03093-1 : LC Card 76-511945
TX7 .B4 Heft 9 HD6995.5
NYPL [JLE 86-3436]

COST AND STANDARD OF LIVING - LATVIA.
Problemy urovnia zhizni i demografii . Riga , 1979. 175 p. ; LC Card 82-106660
HD7035.Z8 L376 1979

COST AND STANDARD OF LIVING - MATHEMATICAL MODELS.
Sistema ėkonomiko-matematicheskikh modeleĭ dlia analiza i prognoza urovnia zhizni /. Moskva , 1986. 262 p. : LC Card 86-232874
HD6978 .S56 1986

COST AND STANDARD OF LIVING - MEXICO.
Madrigal Pana, Johnny. Metodología y construcción de un indicador del ingreso familiar . San José, Costa Rica , 1986. 43 p. ; LC Card 87-404395 DDC 339.4/2/0972 19
HD6996 .M33 1986

COST AND STANDARD OF LIVING - NEBRASKA.
Love, Douglas O. The minimum cost of living in Nebraska /. [Lincoln] [1986] 2 v. : LC Card 87-620964 DDC 339.4/2/09782 19
HD6993.N4 L68 1986

COST AND STANDARD OF LIVING - NETHERLANDS - STATISTICS.
Familiebudgetter . Luxembourg , Washington, D.C. , c1986. 279 p. ; ISBN 92-825-5583-6 : LC Card 86-213531
HD7033 .F35 1986

COST AND STANDARD OF LIVING - PARAGUAY.
Flecha, Agustín Oscar. La economía nacional y el costo de vida /. Asunción, Paraguay , 1986. 49 p. ; LC Card 87-122881 DDC 330.9892/073 19
HD7018 .F57 1986

COST AND STANDARD OF LIVING - PARAGUAY - CONGRESSES.
Flecha, Agustín Oscar. Crisis económica . [Asunción] [1987] 65 p. ; LC Card 87-404003 DDC 331.2/3/09892 19
HD4920.P2 F57 1987

COST AND STANDARD OF LIVING - PERU - DEPARTMENTS.
Migraciones laborales en el Perú . [Monterrico] [c1984] 47 p. : LC Card 84-235623 DDC 331.12/7985 19
HD5761 .M53 1984 ***NYPL [JLF 86-799]***

COST AND STANDARD OF LIVING - PHILIPPINES - BAYAWAN.
Socio-economic and marketing study of municipal fishing households, Bayawan, Negros Oriental, Philippines. Manila, Philippines [1983] vii, 94, 7 p. : LC Card 86-225887
HD8039.F652 P67 1983

COST AND STANDARD OF LIVING - POLAND - STATISTICS.
Warunki życia ludności w 1984 r. /. Warszawa , 1985. 108 p. ; LC Card 86-225456
HD7035.7 .W35 1985

COST AND STANDARD OF LIVING - SEYCHELLES - STATISTICS.
The Household expenditure survey, 1983-1984. Mahé, Seychelles [1986] 74 p. : LC Card 86-981214 DDC 339.4/7/09696 19
HD7068.8 .H68 1986

COST AND STANDARD OF LIVING - SOUTH AFRICA - DURBAN - STATISTICS.
Martins, J. H. Income and expenditure patterns of urban Indian multiple households in Durban, 1985 /. Pretoria , 1986. xi, 126 p. : ISBN 0-908408-54-4 (pbk.) LC Card 86-208481 DDC 658.8/3968 s 339.4/1/09684 19
HC517.S7 S48 no. 130, pt. 1 HD7064.4.Z8D8

Van Wyk, H. de J. Income and expenditure patterns of urban Black multiple households in Durban, 1985 /. Pretoria , 1986. xi, 130 p. : ISBN 0-908408-59-5 (pbk.) LC Card 87-151639 DDC 658.8/3968 s 339.4/1/0968455021 19
HC517.S7 S48 no. 130, pt. 4 HD7064.4.Z8D8

COST AND STANDARD OF LIVING - SOUTH AFRICA - PIETERMARITZBURG - STATISTICS.
Martins, J. H. Income and expenditure patterns of urban Indian households in Pietermaritzburg, 1985 /. Pretoria , 1986. xi, 126 p. : ISBN 0-908408-60-9 (pbk.) LC Card 87-140863 DDC 658.8/3968 s 339.4/1/0968475 19
HC517.S7 S48 no. 130, pt. 5 HD7064.4.Z8P54

COST AND STANDARD OF LIVING - SOUTH AFRICA - PRETORIA - STATISTICS.
Martins, J. H. Income and expenditure patterns of urban black multiple households in Pretoria,

1985 /. Pretoria , 1986. xi, 128 p. : ISBN 0-908408-57-9 (pbk.) LC Card 86-220725 DDC 658.8/3968 s 339.4/1/0968235 19
HC517.S7 S48 no. 130, pt. 2 HD7064.4.Z8P74

COST AND STANDARD OF LIVING - SOVIET UNION.
Matthews, Mervyn. Poverty in the Soviet Union . Cambridge [Cambridgeshire] , New York , 1986. xv, 227 p. ; ISBN 0-521-32544-7 LC Card 86-993 DDC 305.5/69/0947 19
HC340.P6 M38 1986 ***NYPL [JLD 87-262]***

COST AND STANDARD OF LIVING - SOVIET UNION - MATHEMATICAL MODELS.
Sistema ėkonomiko-matematicheskikh modeleĭ dli͡a analiza i prognoza urovni͡a zhizni /. Moskva , 1986. 262 p. : LC Card 86-232874
HD6978 .S56 1986

COST AND STANDARD OF LIVING - SOVIET UNION - STATISTICAL METHODS.
Statisticheskie metody v issledovanii͡akh truda, dokhodov i potreblenii͡a /. Moskva , 1981. 382 p. : LC Card 82-155399
HA1.A38 A15 t. 42 HD7035

COST AND STANDARD OF LIVING - SPAIN - STATISTICS.
Familiebudgetter . Luxembourg , Washington, D.C. , c1986. 279 p. ; ISBN 92-825-5583-6 : LC Card 86-213531
HD7033 .F35 1986

COST AND STANDARD OF LIVING - SWEDEN - HISTORY.
Lagerqvist, Lars O. Vad kostade det? . Stockholm , c18. 115 p. : ISBN 91-36-02399-X : LC Card 86-158743
HD7040 .L34 1985

COST AND STANDARD OF LIVING - UNITED STATES.
Davidson, James Dale. The squeeze /. New York , c1980. 281 p. ; ISBN 0-671-40084-3 LC Card 79-28411 DDC 330.973
HC106.7 .D38 ***NYPL [JLE 80-1960]***

Economic competitiveness promoting America's living standard /] Washington , 1986 [i.e. 1987] vii, 34 p. : LC Card 87-601340 DDC 338.973 19
HC106.8 .E2745 1987

England, Paula. Households, employment, and gender . New York , c1986. ix, 237 p. : ISBN 0-202-30322-5 (lib. bdg.) LC Card 85-18628 DDC 304.6 19
HQ536 .E54 1986 ***NYPL [JLE 86-2828]***

COST AND STANDARD OF LIVING - UNITED STATES - STATISTICS.
Consumer expenditure survey . Washington, D.C. [1986] vi, 193 p. : LC Card 86-602456 DDC 339.4/1/0973 19
HC110.C6 C5647 1986

COST AND STANDARD OF LIVING - URUGUAY - STATISTICS.
Encuesta de gastos e ingresos de los hogares, 1982-1983 . [Montevideo] [1986] 76, 96, 120 p. : LC Card 87-403151 DDC 339.4/2/09895 19
HD7020 .E53 1986

COST AND STANDARD OF LIVING - UZBEK S.S.R.
Ul′masov, Akhmed Ul′masovich. Uzbekistan--ėkonomicheskiĭ rost i blagosostoi͡anie naselenii͡a /. Tashkent , 1978. 182 p. ; LC Card 81-145788
HC337.U96 U95 1978

COST CONTROL - DICTIONARIES.
Woelfel, Charles J. Budgeting, pricing, and cost controls . Chicago, Ill. , c1987. p. cm. ISBN 0-917253-91-4 : LC Card 87-17921 DDC 658.1/5/0321 19
HG151 .W63 1987

Cost-effective management for today's public affairs, or, How to succeed as a PAO in an era of constraints / edited by Wesley Pedersen. Washington, D.C. (1255 Twenty-third St., N.W., Suite 750, Washington 20037) : Public Affairs Council, [c1987] xiii, 109 p. : ill. ; 28 cm. (A Public Affairs Council handbook) LC Card 87-135276 DDC 659.2 19
1. Public relations. 2. Industrial publicity. I. Pedersen, Wesley. II. Title: How to succeed as a PAO in an era of constraints. III. Series.
HD59 .C645 1987

Cost estimates for the Soviet gas industry, 1970 to 1990 /. Tretyakova, Albina. Washington, D.C. [1986] vii, 116 p. ; LC Card 87-601292 DDC 338.2/3 19
HD9581.S652 T74 1986

Cost estimating for government contracts : course manual. [Washington, D.C.] (1120 20th St., NW, Washington 20036) : Federal Publications, c1986. 1 v. (various pagings) : ill. ; 28 cm. LC Card 87-100120 DDC 658.1/552 19
1. Public contracts - Estimates - United States. I. Federal Publications Inc.
HD3860 .C67 1986

COST - MATHEMATICAL MODELS.
Heathfield, David F. An introduction to cost and production functions /. Atlantic Highlands, NJ , 1987. xv, 193 p. : ISBN 0-391-03506-1 LC Card 86-27587 DDC 338.5 19
HB241 .H39 1987

The cost of occupational accidents and diseases /. Andreoni, Diego. Geneva , c1986. viii, 142 p. : ISBN 92-2-103758-4 (pbk.) : LC Card 87-119442 DDC 338.4/336311 19
HD7262 .A73 1986

The Cost of thinking : information economies of ten Pacific countries / edited by Meheroo Jussawalla, Donald M. Lamberton, and Neil D. Karunaratne. Norwood, N.J. : Ablex Pub. Corp., c1988. xii, 249 p. : ill. ; 24 cm. (Communication and information science) Includes bibliographies and indexes. ISBN 0-89391-419-3 LC Card 87-22937 DDC 338.4/7004/099 19
1. Information technology - Economic aspects - Pacific Area. I. Jussawalla, Meheroo, 1923-. II. Lamberton, D. M. (Donald McLean), 1927-. III. Karunaratne, Neil Dias, 1937-.
HC681.3.I55 C67 1988

COST OF WAR. see **WAR, COST OF.**

Cost reduction. 1st ed. Oxford ; New York : Published for the National Examinations Board for Supervisory Studies in conjunction with the Northern Regional Management Centre by Pergamon Press, 1986. ix, 65 p. : ill. ; 30 cm. (Super series : open learning for supervisory management. Economic and financial aspects . no. 402) Includes bibliographies. ISBN 0-08-034177-2 (pbk.) LC Card 87-100499 DDC 658.1/552 19
1. Cost control. I. National Examinations Board for Supervisory Studies (Great Britain). II. Northern Regional Management Centre (Great Britain). III. Series: Super series. Economic and financial aspects , no. 402.
HD47.3 .C67 1986

COST REDUCTION. see **COST CONTROL.**

Costa, Beatriz B. O trabalhador e a produção hoje : um ponto de vista / Beatriz Costa. Petrópolis : Editora Vozes ; Rio de Janeiro, RJ, Brasil : NOVA, 1985. 78 p. ; 23 cm. (Cadernos de educação popular. 9) Includes bibliographical references. LC Card 86-150042 DDC 331.11/8 19
1. Labor productivity. 2. Production (Economic theory). I. Title.
HC79.L3 C67 1985

Costa, F. Ramos da.
Inquérito à habitação rural : crítica a obra : estudo e soluções do problema / por F. Ramos da Costa. Lisboa : Seara Nova, 1944. 57 p. : ill. ; 19 cm. (Cadernos da "Seara Nova") LC Card 86-137838
1. Housing, Rural - Portugal. I. Title.
HD7289.P67 C67 1944

O Plano Beveridge criticado / por F. Ramos da Costa. Lisboa : Seara Nova : [Distribuidores, Editorial Organizações], 1943. 75 p. ; 19 cm. (Cadernos da "Seara Nova." Estudos políticos e sociais) Distributor from inserted label. LC Card 85-211958
1. Great Britain. Inter-departmental Committee on Social Insurance and Allied Services. Social insurance and allied services. 2. Social security - Great Britain. I. Series: Cadernos da "Seara Nova". Secção de estudos políticos e sociais. II. Title.
HD7165.A72 C66 1943

Costa Filho, João Evangelista da. Comércio externo do Maranhão / [João Evangelista da Costa Filho]. [São Luís, Maranhão] : Instituto de Pesquisas Econômicas e Sociais, [1982] 72 p. : ill. ; 29 cm. (Série Estudos monográficos . 4) Bibliography: p. 78-79. LC Card 87-404935 DDC 382/.098121 19
1. Maranhão (Brazil) - Commerce. I. Title. II. Series.
HF3409.M3 C67 1982

Costa, G. (Giovanni) Nacamulli, Raoul C. D. La razionalità contrattata . Bologna , c1986. 166 p. : ISBN 88-15-01189-7 : LC Card 87-122104
HD6709 .N296 1986

Costa, Iraci del Nero da.
Lima, José Luiz. Estatísticas básicas do setor agrícola no Brasil /. São Paulo , 1983- v. : LC Card 83-219032 DDC 338.1/0981 19
HD9014.B82 L55 1983 ***NYPL [JLL 86-432]***

Paraná : mapas de habitantes, 1798-1830 / Iraci del Nero da Costa, Horácio Gutiérrez. São Paulo : Instituto de Pesquisas Econômicas, 1985. 185 p. : ill., map ; 14 x 21 cm. (Série Estatísticas básicas da economia brasileira . no. 4) Chiefly tables. Includes bibliographical references. LC Card 86-158196
1. Parana (Brazil : State) - Population - Statistics - History - 19th century. I. Gutiérrez, Horácio. II. Title. III. Series.
HA984 .C67 1985

Costa, José Pereira da. Livros de contas da ilha da Madeira, 1504-1537 /. Coimbra , 1985- v. <1 > ; LC Card 86-232733
HJ9930.3.M33 L58 1985

Costa, Manoel Augusto. Política demográfica /. Salvador [1983] 82 p. : LC Card 87-138903 DDC 304.6/0981 19
HB3563 .P65 1983

Costa, Marcia Regina da. As vítimas do capital : os acidentados do trabalho / Marcia Regina da Costa. Rio de Janeiro : Achiamé, 1981. 117 p. ; 22 cm. Originally presented as the author's thesis (mestrado--Pontifícia Universidade Católica de São Paulo, 1979) under the title: Relações de produção e acidentes do trabalho em São Paulo. Bibliography: p. 115-117. LC Card 82-149102
1. Industrial accidents - Brazil. 2. Industrial accidents - Brazil - São Paulo (State). 3. Industrial safety - Law and legislation - Brazil. I. Title.
HD7262.5.B7 C67 1981
NYPL [JLD 86-2852]

Costa Morata, Pedro. Centrales nucleares en España : significación energética y posibilidades de sustitución / Pedro Costa Morata. Madrid : Fundación IESA, [1987?] 51 p. : ill. ; 21 cm. (Economía. no. 1) Bibliography: p. 51. ISBN 84-398-8834-1 LC Card 87-165955
1. Nuclear power industry - Spain. 2. Energy policy - Spain. 3. Electric utilities - Spain. I. Series: Economía (Fundación Investigaciones Económicas y Sociales Aplicadas) , no. 1. II. Title.
HD9698.S72 C62 1987

Costa, Nelson. Custo de produção de café /. Curitiba-Paraná [19]84. 47 p. ; LC Card 85-211612
HD9199.B7 C93 1984

Costa, Paolo. Agglomerazione urbana, localizzazione industriale e Mezzogiorno / Paolo Costa, Elio Canestrelli. Milano : Giuffrè, 1983. viii, 240 p. : ill. ; 25 cm. (Collana di "Monografie". 49) Bibliography: p. [235]-240. LC Card 83-186216 DDC 307.2 19
1. Rural-urban migration - Italy, Southern. 2. Urbanization - Italy, Southern. 3. Italy, Southern - Industries - Location. I. Canestrelli, Elio. II. Series: Associazione per lo sviluppo dell'industria nel Mezzogiorno. Centro per gli studi sullo sviluppo economico. Collana di "Monografie." 49. III. Title.
HB2060.S68 C67 1983 ***NYPL [JLE 86-3657]***

Costa, Pedro. see **Costa Morata, Pedro.**

Costa Pôrto, José da. see **Pôrto, Josè da Costa, 1909-**

Costa Rica . Cespedes S., Víctor Hugo. San José, Costa Rica , 1986. 208 p. : ISBN 997-7210-06-3 LC Card 87-404067 DDC 330.97286/053 19
HC143 .C483 1986

COSTA RICA - CENSUS, 1968.
Pantelides, Edith A. El hogar como unidad de análisis de los datos censales . Santiago de Chile , 1972. ii, 48 p. : LC Card 83-169482
HA755 .U53 no. 147 HB849.49

COSTA RICA - CENSUS, 1984.
Censo de población, 1984. San José, Costa Rica , 1987. 2 v. : LC Card 87-402193 DDC 304.6/097286/021 19
HA801.5 1984

Censo de vivienda, 1984 /. San José, Costa Rica , 1987. xxxiii, 335 p. : LC Card 87-402910 DDC 363.5/097286/021 19
HD7308.A3 C46 1987

COSTA RICA - CIVILIZATION.
Las Instituciones costarricenses del siglo XX /. [San José] , 1986. 376 p. ; ISBN 997-7232-96-5 LC Card 86-231789
HC143 .I54 1986

Costa Rica colonial : tres ensayos / Juan Carlos Solórzano, Luis Fernando Sibaja. [San José, Costa Rica : Programa Centroamericano de Ciencias Sociales del CSUCA, 1984] 83 p. ; 21 cm. (Cuadernos centroamericanos de ciencias sociales . 11) Limited edition of 500 copies. Includes bibliographies. CONTENTS. - Hispanoamérica y la expansión europea, siglos XV al XVIII / Juan Carlos Solórzano Fonseca -- Costa Rica colonial / Juan Carlos Solórzano Fonseca -- La encomienda de tributo en el Valle Central de Costa Rica (1569-1683) / Luis Fernando Sibaja. LC Card 86-173945
1. Spain - Colonies - America - Economic policy. 2. America - Economic conditions. 3. Costa Rica - Economic conditions. 4. Costa Rica - Politics and government - To 1821. 5. Tax collection - Costa Rica - History - 16th century. 6. Tax collection - Costa Rica - History - 17th century. I. Solórzano, Juan Carlos. Hispanoamérica y la expansión europea, siglos XV al XVIII. 1984. II. Solórzano, Juan Carlos. Costa Rica colonial. 1984. III. Sibaja Chacón, Luis Fernando. Encomienda de tributo en el Valle Central de Costa Rica (1569-1683). 1984. IV. Programa Centroamericano de Desarrollo de las Ciencias Sociales. V. Series.
HC389 .C67 1984

COSTA RICA - COMMERCE.
Las Exportaciones y la incidencia del sector externo en el desarrollo económico. [San José] , 1984. 32, [8], [7], 4 leaves ; LC Card 87-115490 DDC 338.1/097286 19
HD9014.C772 E95 1984

COSTA RICA - COMMERCE - HISTORY.
Daremblum, Jaime. El auge del café y la apertura de la economía costarricense /. San José, Costa Rica , 1980. 62 p. ; LC Card 84-247131
HF3255 .D37 1980

Costa Rica. Dirección General de Planificación del Trabajo y el Empleo. Encuesta nacional de hogares, empleo y desempleo . San José, Costa Rica , 1982. xi, xi, 86 p. ; LC Card 82-202317
HD5734.A6 E53 1982

Costa Rica. Dirección Sectorial de Energía.
Hernández C., Alexandra. Encuesta de consumo energético en el sector transporte /. San José, Costa Rica , 1985. 68, [137] p. : LC Card 86-218227
HE5638 .H37 1985

Obando S., Marta. Encuesta residencial de consumo energético /. San José, Costa Rica , 1985. iv, 56, [71] p. : LC Card 86-219603
HD9502.C82 O23 1985

Costa Rica. División de Planificación y Coordinación Regional. Análisis de indicadores socioeconómicos, Subregión Limón . [San José] [1981] 26 p. ; LC Card 83-240958
HC143.Z7 L554 1981

COSTA RICA - ECONOMIC CONDITIONS.
Acuña Ortega, Víctor H. El desarrollo económico y social de Costa Rica . [San José, Costa Rica] , 1986. vi, 135 p. ; ISBN 997-7440-08-5 LC Card 87-100815
HC143 .A54 1986

Costa Rica colonial . [San José, Costa Rica , 1984] 83 p. ; LC Card 86-173945
HC389 .C67 1984

Daremblum, Jaime. Crisis internacionales y economía nacional . San José, Costa Rica , 1982. 62 p. ; LC Card 84-247158
HC143 .D36 1982

Daremblum, Jaime. Del cacao al colón . San José, Costa Rica [1977?- v. <1- > ; LC Card 87-402194 DDC 332.4/97286 19
HG682 .D37 1977

Las Instituciones costarricenses del siglo XX /. [San José] , 1986. 376 p. ; ISBN 997-7232-96-5 LC Card 86-231789
HC143 .I54 1986

COSTA RICA - ECONOMIC CONDITIONS - 1948-
Arias Sánchez, Oscar. Democracia, independencia y sociedad latinoamericana /. San José, Costa Rica , 1985. 100 p. ; ISBN 997-7956-09-X LC Card 87-400690 DDC 320.97286 19
HC143 .A773 1985

Cespedes S., Víctor Hugo. Costa Rica . San José, Costa Rica , 1986. 208 p. : ISBN 997-7210-06-3 LC Card 87-404067 DDC 330.97286/053 19
HC143 .C483 1986

Cespedes S., Víctor Hugo. Costa Rica--recuperación sin reactivación . San José, Costa Rica , 1985. 238 p. : ISBN 997-7210-05-5 LC Card 86-208956
HC143 .C484 1985

Costa Rica--respuesta al cuestionario del Banco Interamericano de Desarrollo /. [San José] [1962] 69 leaves (some folded) ; LC Card 85-117361
HC143 .C685 1962

Jacobstein, Helen L., 1925- The process of economic development in Costa Rica, 1948-1970 . New York , 1987. 338 p. : ISBN 0-8240-1363-8 (alk. paper) : LC Card 87-8519 DDC 338.97286 19
HC143 .J28 1987

Matarrita Mena, José Joaquín. Areas industriales de Costa Rica /. San José, Costa Rica, América Central [1986] 151 p. : ISBN 997-7500-01-0 LC Card 87-404258 DDC 338.097286 19
HC143 .M38 1986

Picado Hidalgo, Roberto. La inflación y la política económica, el caso de Costa Rica . [San José] , 1985. 16, 20 p. ; LC Card 86-219388
HC143 .P52 1985

Rovira Mas, Jorge, 1950- La crisis de Costa Rica /. San José, Costa Rica , 1986. 175 p. ; LC Card 87-125520 DDC 338.97286 19
HC143 .R667 1986

Sandoval Aguilar, Guillermo. El desarrollo costarricense y la fecundidad del hombre /. Heredia , 1985. 233 p. ; LC Card 86-117576
HB947 .S26 1985

COSTA RICA - ECONOMIC CONDITIONS - 1948- - STATISTICS.
Estadísticas, 1950-1985. San José, Costa Rica , 1986. 221 p. ; LC Card 87-404209 DDC 332/.097286/021 19
HG185.C7 E84 1986

COSTA RICA - ECONOMIC POLICY.
Cespedes S., Víctor Hugo. Costa Rica--recuperación sin reactivación . San José, Costa Rica , 1985. 238 p. : ISBN 997-7210-05-5 LC Card 86-208956
HC143 .C484 1985

Daremblum, Jaime. Crisis internacionales y economía nacional . San José, Costa Rica , 1982. 62 p. ; LC Card 84-247158
HC143 .D36 1982

Delgado Q., Félix. Programas de estabilización y condicionalidad en Costa Rica /. San José, Costa Rica , 1986. 30, [6] leaves ; LC Card 87-404196 DDC 338.97286 19
HC143 .D45 1986

Denton L., Carlos F. Población, fecundidad y desarrollo en Costa Rica, 1950-1970 /. [Heredia, Costa Rica] , 1984. iv, 150 p. : LC Card 86-117583 DDC 304.6/097286 19
HB3531 .D44 1984 ***NYPL [JLF 87-144]***

Jacobstein, Helen L., 1925- The process of economic development in Costa Rica, 1948-1970 . New York , 1987. 338 p. : ISBN 0-8240-1363-8 (alk. paper) : LC Card 87-8519 DDC 338.97286 19
HC143 .J28 1987

Picado Hidalgo, Roberto. La inflación y la política económica, el caso de Costa Rica . [San José] , 1985. 16, 20 p. ; LC Card 86-219388
HC143 .P52 1985

Rovira Mas, Jorge, 1950- La crisis de Costa Rica /. San José, Costa Rica , 1986. 175 p. ; LC Card 87-125520 DDC 338.97286 19
HC143 .R667 1986

COSTA RICA - ECONOMIC POLICY - EVALUATION.
Gamboa Conejo, Rita Ma. (Rita María) Resultados preliminares del análisis metodológico de los planes nacionales de desarrollo, 1974-1982 /. Heredia , 1985. 1 v. (various pagings) : LC Card 87-402159 DDC 338.97286 19
HC143 .G36 1985

Costa Rica - Government. see **Costa Rica - Politics and government.**

COSTA RICA - INDUSTRIES.
Matarrita Mena, José Joaquín. Areas industriales de Costa Rica /. San José, Costa Rica, América Central [1986] 151 p. : ISBN 997-7500-01-0 LC Card 87-404258 DDC 338.097286 19
HC143 .M38 1986

COSTA RICA - INDUSTRIES - HISTORY.
Esquivel, Francisco. El desarrollo del capital en la industria de Costa Rica, 1950-1970 /. Heredia, Costa Rica , 1985. 197 p. : ISBN 997-7650-16-0 LC Card 86-210026
HC143 .E83 1985

COSTA RICA - INDUSTRIES - HISTORY - 20TH CENTURY.
Las Instituciones costarricenses del siglo XX /. [San José] , 1986. 376 p. ; ISBN 997-7232-96-5 LC Card 86-231789
HC143 .I54 1986

Costa Rica. Ministerio de Gobernación y Policía.
Censo de vivienda, 1984 /. San José, Costa Rica , 1987. xxxiii, 335 p. : LC Card 87-402910 DDC 363.5/097286/021 19
HD7308.A3 C46 1987

Costa Rica. Oficina de Planificación Nacional y Política Económica. Análisis de indicadores socioeconómicos, Subregión Limón . [San José] [1981] 26 p. ; LC Card 83-240958
HC143.Z7 L554 1981

COSTA RICA - POLITICS AND GOVERNMENT.
Las Instituciones costarricenses del siglo XX /. [San José] , 1986. 376 p. ; ISBN 997-7232-96-5 LC Card 86-231789
HC143 .I54 1986

COSTA RICA - POLITICS AND GOVERNMENT - TO 1821.
Costa Rica colonial . [San José, Costa Rica , 1984] 83 p. ; LC Card 86-173945
HC389 .C67 1984

COSTA RICA - POLITICS AND GOVERNMENT - 1821-1948.
Daremblum, Jaime. Crisis internacionales y economía nacional . San José, Costa Rica , 1982. 62 p. ; LC Card 84-247158
HC143 .D36 1982

COSTA RICA - POLITICS AND GOVERNMENT - 1948-
Arias Sánchez, Oscar. Democracia, independencia y sociedad latinoamericana /. San José, Costa Rica , 1985. 100 p. ; ISBN 997-7956-09-X LC Card 87-400690 DDC 320.97286 19
HC143 .A773 1985

Daremblum, Jaime. Crisis internacionales y economía nacional . San José, Costa Rica , 1982. 62 p. ; LC Card 84-247158
HC143 .D36 1982

Jacobstein, Helen L., 1925- The process of economic development in Costa Rica, 1948-1970 . New York , 1987. 338 p. : ISBN 0-8240-1363-8 (alk. paper) : LC Card 87-8519 DDC 338.97286 19
HC143 .J28 1987

COSTA RICA - POPULATION.
Denton L., Carlos F. Población, fecundidad y desarrollo en Costa Rica, 1950-1970 /. [Heredia, Costa Rica] , 1984. iv, 150 p. : LC Card 86-117583 DDC 304.6/097286 19
HB3531 .D44 1984 ***NYPL [JLF 87-144]***

COSTA RICA - POPULATION - STATISTICS.
Censo de población, 1984. San José, Costa Rica , 1987. 2 v. : LC Card 87-402193 DDC 304.6/097286/021 19
HA801.5 1984

Costa Rica--recuperación sin reactivación .
Cespedes S., Víctor Hugo. San José, Costa Rica , 1985. 238 p. : ISBN 997-7210-05-5 LC Card 86-208956
HC143 .C484 1985

Costa Rica--respuesta al cuestionario del Banco Interamericano de Desarrollo / Banco Central de Costa Rica, Departamento de Estudios Económicos. [San José] : El Departamento, [1962] 69 leaves (some folded) ; 27 cm. Cover

title. "Diciembre de 1961." Includes bibliographical references. LC Card 85-117361
1. Costa Rica - Economic conditions - 1948-. 2. Finance, Public - Costa Rica. 3. Costa Rica - Rural conditions. 4. Land tenure - Costa Rica. 5. Housing - Costa Rica. 6. Education - Costa Rica. I. Inter-American Development Bank. II. Banco Central de Costa Rica. Departamento de Estudios Económicos.
HC143 .C685 1962

COSTA RICA - RURAL CONDITIONS.
Costa Rica--respuesta al cuestionario del Banco Interamericano de Desarrollo /. [San José] [1962] 69 leaves (some folded) ; LC Card 85-117361
HC143 .C685 1962

Costa Rica. Secretaría Ejecutiva de Planificación del Subsector Industrial. Inversión industrial en Costa Rica . [San José] , 1986. 171 p., [1] folded leaf of plates : LC Card 87-400481 DDC 338.97286 19
HC143.Z9 I535 1986

COSTA RICA - SOCIAL CONDITIONS.
Acuña Ortega, Víctor H. El desarrollo económico y social de Costa Rica . [San José, Costa Rica] , 1986. vi, 135 p. ; ISBN 997-7440-08-5 LC Card 87-100815
HC143 .A54 1986

Las Instituciones costarricenses del siglo XX /. [San José] , 1986. 376 p. ; ISBN 997-7232-96-5 LC Card 86-231789
HC143 .I54 1986

Sandoval Aguilar, Guillermo. El desarrollo costarricense y la fecundidad del hombre /. Heredia , 1985. 233 p. ; LC Card 86-117576
HB947 .S26 1985

Costa, Ricardo L. La Gestión en empresas cooperativas . Buenos Aires, Argentina [1985] 146 p. ; ISBN 950-0-01257-11 LC Card 87-115117 DDC 334/.0982/54 19
HD3470.A3 C674 1985

Costa, Roberto Teixeira da. Brazil's experience in creating a capital market / Roberto Teixeira da Costa. São Paulo : BOVESPA, [1985] 114 p. : ill. ; 22 cm. LC Card 86-207924 DDC 332.6/0981 19
1. Capital market - Brazil. 2. Financial institutions - Brazil. I. Title.
HG4523 .C67 1985

Costa, Sérgio Amad, 1958- Estado e controle sindical no Brasil : um estudo sobre três mecanismos de coerção, 1960/64 / Sérgio Amad Costa. São Paulo : T.A. Queiroz, 1986. xiv, 192 p. : ill. ; 21 cm. (Coleção Coroa vermelha. Estudos brasileiros . v. 12) Originally presented as the author's thesis (mestrado em ciência política)--Universidade de São Paulo, 1985. Bibliography: p. [185]-192. ISBN 85-85008-48-2 : LC Card 87-154269 DDC 331.88/0981 19
1. Trade-unions - Government policy - Brazil. 2. Trade-unions - Law and legislation - Brazil. I. Title. II. Series.
HD6612 .C67 1986

Costa, Tereza Cristina N. Araújo. Oliveira, Lúcia Elena Garcia de. O lugar do negro na força de trabalho /. Rio de Janeiro , 1983. 86 p. ; ISBN 85-24-00024-4 LC Card 86-129924
HD8288.5.B55 O45 1983

Costello, Cynthia B. (Cynthia Butler)
Home-based employment : implications for working women / by Cynthia B. Costello. Washington, D.C. (1700 18th St., N.W., Washington 20009) : Women's Research and Education Institute, 1987. iii, 20 p. ; 23 cm. Bibliography: p. 18-20. LC Card 87-403088 DDC 331.4/0973 19
1. Home-based businesses - United States. 2. Home labor - Government policy - United States. 3. Self-employed women - United States. I. Title.
HD2336.U5 C58 1987

Costello, M. Gary (Michael Gary)
Comercialización interna de los alimentos en América Latina . Ottawa, Canada , c1985. 253 p. : ISBN 0-88936-448-6 LC Card 87-118494 DDC 338.1/9/8 19
HD9014.L32 C66 1985

Costello, Michael A. Mobility and employment in urban Southeast Asia : examples from Indonesia and the Philippines / edited by Michael A. Costello, Thomas R. Leinbach, and Richard Ulack, with Marliou Palabrica-Costello and Bambang Suwarno. Boulder : Westview Press, 1987. xvi, 190 p. : maps ; 23 cm. (International studies in migration) Bibliography: p. 171-187. Includes index. ISBN 0-8133-7352-2 (pbk. : alk. paper) : LC Card 87-10649 DDC 307.2 19
1. Rural-urban migration - Indonesia - Case studies. 2. Rural-urban migration - Philippines - Case studies. 3. Labor supply - Indonesia - Case studies. 4. Labor supply - Philippines - Case studies. 5. Urbanization - Indonesia - Case studies. 6. Urbanization - Philippines - Case studies. I. Leinbach, Thomas R., 1941-. II. Ulack, Richard, 1942-. III. Title. IV. Series.
HB2107 .C67 1987

Costello, Timothy W. Psychology in administration : a research orientation / Timothy W. Costello, Sheldon S. Zalkind. New York : Garland Pub., 1987. xii, 500 p. : ill. ; 24 cm. (Continuity in administrative science) Reprint. Originally published: Englewood Cliffs, N.J. : Prentice-Hall, 1963. (Behavioral sciences in business series) Bibliography: p. 465-486. Includes indexes. ISBN 0-8240-8202-8 (alk. paper) : LC Card 86-25805 DDC 658/.001/9 19
1. Psychology, Industrial. 2. Industrial management. 3. Communication in personnel management. I. Zalkind, Sheldon S. II. Series. III. Series: Prentice-Hall behavioral sciences in business series. IV. Title.
HF5548.8 .C6 1987

Costeo y evaluación de la producción conjunta . Cascarini, Daniel C. Buenos Aires [1985] 206 p. : ISBN 950-593-015-1 LC Card 86-133889 DDC 338/.06 19
HD56 .C37 1985

Los costes de las obras a cargo del sector público . López Nieto, Antonio. Madrid , 1962. xiv, 214 p. : LC Card 85-107655
HD3856.S7 L66 1962

I costi dell'adempimento tributario in Italia . Scanu, Salvatore. [Cagliari] , Milano, Italy , c1984. 153 p. ; LC Card 85-118845
HD9326.I82 S32 1984

Costi e relativi finanziamenti dei sistemi pensionistici nei paesi europei : conferenza internazionale, 11-12-13 ottobre 1982. Roma : Istituto nazionale della previdenza sociale, 1985. xi, 486 p. : col. ill. ; 24 cm. In Italian, with some contributions in English, French, and German, with Italian translations. "Conferenza internazionale Costi e relativi finanziamenti dei sistemi pensionistici nei paesi europei, Roma, 11-12-13 ottobre 1982"--P. [iii] Errata slip inserted. Includes bibliographies. LC Card 86-206925
1. Pensions - Europe - Finance - Congresses. 2. Social security - Europe - Finance - Congresses. I. Conferenza internazionale Costi e relativi finanziamenti dei sistemi pensionistici nei paesi europei (1982 : Rome, Italy). II. Istituto nazionale della previdenza sociale (Italy).
HD7164 .C67 1985

Costing human resources . Cascio, Wayne F. Boston, Mass. , c1987. xiv, 274 p. : ISBN 0-534-08034-0 (pbk.) : LC Card 87-2501 DDC 658.1/553 19
HF5681.L2 C37 1987

Costo real del crédito en 1984 /. Valenzuela Cornejo, Ignacio. Santiago , 1985. 28 p. ; LC Card 86-106375 DDC 332.7/0983 19
HG3729.C52 V35 1985

COSTS, INDUSTRIAL - BRAZIL.
Moldau, Juan Hersztajn. Custo dos recursos domésticos /. Rio de Janeiro , 1985. 94, 4 p. ; LC Card 86-200395
HC190.C7 M64 1985

COSTS, INDUSTRIAL - ECONOMETRIC MODELS.
Spranzi, Aldo, 1932- Calcolo dei costi nelle imprese industriali /. Milano [1986] viii, 94 p. : ISBN 88-14-00844-2 : LC Card 86-182386
HC79.C7 S67 1986

Winkelmann, Jürgen. Die Planung langfristiger Kosten . Thun , c1982. 281 p. : ISBN 3-87144-702-1 LC Card 83-129316
HD47 .W54 1982

COSTS, INDUSTRIAL - GERMANY, EAST.
Brandt, Horst. Kostensenkung und Gewinn /. Berlin , 1985. 100 p. ; LC Card 87-144350 DDC 338.5/1/09431 19
HC290.795.C7 B7 1985

COSTS, INDUSTRIAL - GERMANY, WEST.
Döring, Ulrich. Kostensteuern, der Einfluss von Steuern auf kurzfristige Produktions- und Absatzentscheidungen /. Stuttgart , c1984. x, 228 p. ; ISBN 3-7910-0369-0 LC Card 86-134925
HD2753.G3 D73 1984

COSTS, INDUSTRIAL - ITALY - ADDRESSES, ESSAYS, LECTURES.
La Vertenza sul costo del lavoro e le relazioni industriali /. Milano, Italy , c1984. 243 p. : LC Card 84-144150 DDC 338.5/1/0945 19
HD5034 .V47 1984 ***NYPL [JLD 86-2858]***

COSTS, INDUSTRIAL - PORTUGAL - STATISTICS.
Indicadores económicos e financeiros da Central de Balanços (1978-1980). [Porto] [1982] 204 p. : LC Card 85-166692
HC394.5.C7 I53 1982

COSTS, INDUSTRIAL - SOVIET UNION.
Igumnov, I͡U. S. (I͡Uriĭ Stepanovich) Sebestoimostʹ i puti ee snizhenii͡a v promyshlennosti /. Kiev , 1986. 223 p. ; LC Card 87-126676
HC340.C7 I38 1986

Kirillov, S. R. (Sergeĭ Rufovich) Soizmerenie zatrat i rezulʹtatov v teorii planovogo tsenoobrazovanii͡a /. Moskva , 1987. 188 p. ; LC Card 87-157208
HB235.S73 K57 1987

Tishkov, I. E. (Ivan Efremovich) Uchet i kalʹkulirovanie sebestoimosti produkt͡sii vspomogatelʹnykh proizvodstv /. Moskva , 1980. 110 p. ; LC Card 81-143226
HC340.C7 T57 1980

T͡Sena i khozraschet /. Moskva , 1986. 144 p. ; LC Card 87-163568
HB235.S73 T72 1986

COSTS, INDUSTRIAL - SOVIET UNION - ACCOUNTING.
Borodkin, Alekseĭ Sergeevich. Uchet zatrat na osvoenie novoĭ tekhniki /. Moskva , 1985. 142 p. : LC Card 86-219761
HF5686.C8 B597 1985

COSTS, INDUSTRIAL - UNITED STATES.
Leone, Robert A. Who profits . New York , 1986. xiii, 248 p. ; ISBN 0-465-09183-0 : LC Card 85-47992 DDC 338.973 19
HD3616.U47 L44 1986
NYPL [JLD 86-2410]

COSTS, LABOR. see **LABOR COSTS.**

COSTS, SOCIAL. see **EXTERNALITIES (ECONOMICS)**

Côte-d'Ivoire . International Labour Organisation. Genève , 1984. 94 p. : ISBN 92-2-203860-6 LC Card 86-219971
HD5846.9.A6 I57 1984

Côte d'Ivoire. see **Ivory Coast.**

Cote, Raymond. Understanding hospitality accounting I / Raymond Cote. East Lansing, Mich. : Educational Institute of the American Hotel & Motel Association, c1987. p. cm. Includes index. ISBN 0-86612-035-1 : LC Card 87-15724 DDC 657/.837 19
1. Hotels, taverns, etc. - Accounting. 2. Motels - Accounting. 3. Restaurants, lunch rooms, etc. - Accounting. 4. Food service - Accounting. I. Title.
HF5686.H75 C63 1987

Cotia, Raul Fontes. Comentário sôbre os balanços gerais da União de 1963 / Raul Fontes Cotia. [Brasília] : Ministério da Fazenda, [1964] 45 p. ; 23 cm. LC Card 85-194302
1. Budget - Brazil. 2. Brazil - Appropriations and expenditures. I. Brazil. Ministério da Fazenda. II. Title.
HJ2079 .C68 1964

COTTAGE INDUSTRIES - AFGHANISTAN - SAR-E POL.
Jebens, Albrecht. Wirtschafts- und sozialgeographische Untersuchung über das Heimgewerbe in Nordafghanistan unter besonderer Berücksichtigung der Mittelstadt Sar-e-Pul . Tübingen , 1983. xii, 415 p., [2] folded leaves of plates : LC Card 86-128235
HD2346.A52 S275 1983

COTTAGE INDUSTRIES - ASIA - CONGRESSES.
Invisible hands . New Delhi , Newbury Park, Calif. , 1987. 273 p. ; ISBN 0-8039-9524-5 (U. S.) LC Card 87-4337 DDC 331.4/0954 19
HD6181.85 .A85 1987

COTTAGE INDUSTRIES - CHILE.
Bustamante G., Jaime. Algunos antecedentes estadísticos sobre las organizaciones económicas populares /. Santiago, Chile , 1986. 23 p. ; LC

Card 87-101323
HD2346.C53 B87 1986

Razeto M., Luis, 1945- Las organizaciones económicas populares en la nueva coyuntura económica /. Santiago, Chile , 1984. 23 p. ; LC Card 84-227565
HD2346.C53 R39 1984

COTTAGE INDUSTRIES - GOVERNMENT POLICY - BRAZIL - CEARÁ (STATE)
Estudos fundamentais . Fortaleza , 1986. 120 p. : LC Card 87-120224
HD2346.B72 C44 1986

COTTAGE INDUSTRIES - GUATEMALA - DIRECTORIES.
Directorio artesanal, 1978 /. Guatemala , 1981. 6 v. ; LC Card 87-403025
HD2346.G8 D57 1981

COTTAGE INDUSTRIES - GUATEMALA - STATISTICS.
Principales indicadores económicos . Guatemala , 1982. 487 p. ; LC Card 87-403026 DDC 331.7/94 19
HD2346.G8 P75 1982

Cottage industries in Nepal /. Palikhe, Komal Prasad. Kathmandu, Nepal , 1986. 93 p. ; LC Card 86-903473 DDC 338.6/34/095493 19
HD2346.N36 P35 1986

COTTAGE INDUSTRIES - INDIA.
Mishra, G. P. Village industries and agriculture in changing agrarian situation /. New Delhi , c1985. 120 p. ; ISBN 81-7024-010-7 LC Card 85-904926 DDC 338.6/34/0954 19
HD2346.I5 M49 1985 ***NYPL [JLD 86-3746]***

COTTAGE INDUSTRIES - ITALY.
Esposito, Gennaro, 1956- Decentramento produttivo, lavoro a domicilio e sindacato /. Milano [1983] 109 p. ; LC Card 85-150186
HD2336.I8 E86 1983

COTTAGE INDUSTRIES - MEXICO - NAHUATZEN REGION.
García López, Lucía. Nahuatzen, agricultura y comercio en una comunidad serrana /. Zamora, Mich. , México, D.F. , c1984. 115 p. : ISBN 968-7230-03-7 LC Card 85-154045 DDC 338.1/0972/37 19
HD1795.N34 G37 1984 ***NYPL [JLD 87-16]***

COTTAGE INDUSTRIES - NEPAL.
Palikhe, Komal Prasad. Cottage industries in Nepal /. Kathmandu, Nepal , 1986. 93 p. ; LC Card 86-903473 DDC 338.6/34/095493 19
HD2346.N36 P35 1986

COTTAGE INDUSTRIES - PAPUA NEW GUINEA.
Philp, Norman E. The cash incentive . Canberra , 1986. xii, 135 p. : ISBN 0-86784-984-3 (pbk.) LC Card 87-150813
HD2346.P37 P46 1986

COTTAGE INDUSTRIES - RUSSIAN S.F.S.R. - SIBERIA - HISTORY - 19TH CENTURY.
Solov′eva, E. I., d-r ist. nauk. Promysly sibirskogo krest′i͡anstva v poreformennyĭ period /. Novosibirsk , 1981. 327 p. : LC Card 82-111175
HD2346.S652 S527 1981

COTTAGE INDUSTRIES - SWEDEN - MARKS HÄRAD - HISTORY - 19TH CENTURY.
Andersson-Palmqvist, Lena. Decentraliserad textilindustri . Stockholm , 1979/80 [i.e. 1980] 68 p. : ISBN 91-86016-06-7 LC Card 81-138133
HD9865.S87 M373 1980

COTTER & COMPANY - HISTORY.
Kantowicz, Edward R. True Value . Chicago , 1986. 270 p., [16] p. of plates : ISBN 0-89526-580-X : LC Card 86-42795 DDC 381/.45683/0924 B 19
HD9745.U5 C655 1986
NYPL [JLE 87-1449]

COTTER, JOHN, 1904-
Kantowicz, Edward R. True Value . Chicago , 1986. 270 p., [16] p. of plates : ISBN 0-89526-580-X : LC Card 86-42795 DDC 381/.45683/0924 B 19
HD9745.U5 C655 1986
NYPL [JLE 87-1449]

Cottle, Sidney. Graham, Benjamin, 1894- [Security analysis.] Graham and Dodd's security analysis. New York , c1988. xiii, 656 p. : ISBN 0-07-013235-6 : LC Card 87-19990 DDC 332.63/2 19
HG4529 .G7 1988

Cotton and wheat production in the Egyptian agriculture . Eckstein, Zvi. [Tel Aviv] [1984] 40 leaves : LC Card 84-186315 DDC 338.1/711/0962 19
HD9087.E42 E35 1984

COTTON GROWING - NICARAGUA.
Hintermeister, Alberto. El empleo agrícola en una estructra en transformación . [Santiago, Chile] , 1982. 27 p. ; LC Card 87-403249 DDC 331.7/63/097285 19
HD1531.N5 H56 1982

COTTON - PAKISTAN - GRADING.
Galal, M. F. Pakistan . Rome [i.e. Multan] , 1978. vii, 36 p. ; LC Card 83-931176
HD9086.P32 G35 1978

COTTON - PAKISTAN - MARKETING.
Galal, M. F. Pakistan . Rome [i.e. Multan] , 1978. vii, 36 p. ; LC Card 83-931176
HD9086.P32 G35 1978

COTTON PICKING - BRAZIL - SÃO PAULO (STATE)
Fleury, Maria Tereza Leme. A organização do trabalho na lavoura algodoeira paulista /. [São Paulo, Brasil] 1984. 208 p. : LC Card 85-145302 DDC 338.1/7351/098161 19
HD9084.B62 S264 1984
NYPL [JLE 86-1740]

COTTON - PRICES - LATIN AMERICA - ECONOMETRIC MODELS.
Lord, Montague J. Market price models for Latin America's major commodity exports /. Washington, D.C. [1986] vii, 219 p. : LC Card 87-115208 DDC 338.5/2/098 19
HD9014.A2 L67 1986

COTTON - PRICES - PAKISTAN.
Galal, M. F. Pakistan . Rome [i.e. Multan] , 1978. vii, 36 p. ; LC Card 83-931176
HD9086.P32 G35 1978

Cotton, Richard, 1944- Energy conservation . Washington, D.C. , c1986. xii, 270 p. : ISBN 0-8157-7716-7 : LC Card 85-26894 DDC 333.79/16/0973 19
HD9502.U62 E478 1986
NYPL [JLE 86-4084]

COTTON TEXTILE INDUSTRY - ENGLAND - LANCASHIRE - HISTORY.
Fleischman, Richard K. Conditions of life among the cotton workers of southeastern Lancashire, 1780-1850 /. New York , 1985. 475 p. ; ISBN 0-8240-6681-2 (alk. paper) : LC Card 84-46001 DDC 305/.9677/094276 19
HD8039.T42 G74 1985
NYPL [JLE 86-3899]

COTTON TEXTILE INDUSTRY - ENGLAND - LANCASHIRE - HISTORY - 20TH CENTURY.
Streat, Raymond, Sir. Lancashire and Whitehall . Manchester [Greater Manchester] , c1987. 2 v. : ISBN 0-7190-2390-4 (v. 1) LC Card 87-11026 DDC 338.7/67721/0924 B 19
HD9881.5.S77 A3 1987

COTTON TEXTILE INDUSTRY - GOVERNMENT POLICY - GREAT BRITAIN - HISTORY - 20TH CENTURY.
Streat, Raymond, Sir. Lancashire and Whitehall . Manchester [Greater Manchester] , c1987. 2 v. : ISBN 0-7190-2390-4 (v. 1) LC Card 87-11026 DDC 338.7/67721/0924 B 19
HD9881.5.S77 A3 1987

The cotton textile industry in Porfiriato, Mexico, 1870-1910 /. Keremitsis, Dawn, 1921- New York , 1987. 232 p. : ISBN 0-8240-1364-6 (alk. paper) : LC Card 87-7619 DDC 338.4/767721/0972 19
HD9884.M42 K47 1987

COTTON TEXTILE INDUSTRY - INDIA.
Otsuka, Keijiro. Comparative technology choice in development . New York , 1988. viii, 247 p. : ISBN 0-312-00516-4 : LC Card 86-29666 DDC 338.4/567721/0952 19
HD9886.I42 O87 1988

COTTON TEXTILE INDUSTRY - INDIA - FINANCE.
Gupta, S. C., 1954- Institutional financing and industrial growth . Jaipur , 1987. xx, 316 p. (some folded) : LC Card 87-900864
HD9886.I42 G83 1987

Gurdev Singh. Financing of kapas-cloth system /. New Delhi , c1987. xi, 59 p. ; ISBN 81-204-0217-0 : LC Card 87-902510 DDC 338.4/367721/0954 19
HD9886.I42 G87 1987

COTTON TEXTILE INDUSTRY - INDIA - ORISSA.
Mahapatro, P. C. (Poorna Chandra), 1944- Economics of cotton handloom industry in India /. New Delhi , 1986. xvi, 277 p. ; ISBN 81-7024-060-3 : LC Card 86-903087 DDC 338.4/774614/0954
HD9866.I63 O745 1986

COTTON TEXTILE INDUSTRY - INDIA - TECHNOLOGICAL INNOVATIONS.
Otsuka, Keijiro. Comparative technology choice in development . New York , 1988. viii, 247 p. : ISBN 0-312-00516-4 : LC Card 86-29666 DDC 338.4/567721/0952 19
HD9886.I42 O87 1988

COTTON TEXTILE INDUSTRY - JAPAN.
Otsuka, Keijiro. Comparative technology choice in development . New York , 1988. viii, 247 p. : ISBN 0-312-00516-4 : LC Card 86-29666 DDC 338.4/567721/0952 19
HD9886.I42 O87 1988

COTTON TEXTILE INDUSTRY - JAPAN - HISTORY - 20TH CENTURY.
Bauge, Kenneth L. (Kenneth LeRoy) Voluntary export restriction as a foreign commercial policy with special reference to Japanese cotton textiles, 1930-1962 /. New York , 1987. 277 p. ; ISBN 0-8240-8072-6 LC Card 87-23717 DDC 382/.4567721/0952 19
HD9886.J3 B38 1987

COTTON TEXTILE INDUSTRY - JAPAN - TECHNOLOGICAL INNOVATIONS.
Otsuka, Keijiro. Comparative technology choice in development . New York , 1988. viii, 247 p. : ISBN 0-312-00516-4 : LC Card 86-29666 DDC 338.4/567721/0952 19
HD9886.I42 O87 1988

COTTON TEXTILE INDUSTRY - LABOR PRODUCTIVITY - CASE STUDIES.
Pack, Howard. Productivity, technology, and industrial development . New York , c1987. x, 193 p. : ISBN 0-19-520543-X : LC Card 86-33271 DDC 331.11/8 19
HD9870.5 .P25 1987

COTTON TEXTILE INDUSTRY - MEXICO - HISTORY - 19TH CENTURY.
Keremitsis, Dawn, 1921- The cotton textile industry in Porfiriato, Mexico, 1870-1910 /. New York , 1987. 232 p. : ISBN 0-8240-1364-6 (alk. paper) : LC Card 87-7619 DDC 338.4/767721/0972 19
HD9884.M42 K47 1987

COTTON TEXTILE INDUSTRY - SOUTHERN STATES - EMPLOYEES - HISTORY.
Hodges, James A., 1932- New deal labor policy and the southern cotton textile industry, 1933-1941 /. Knoxville , c1986. xii, 252 p. : ISBN 0-87049-496-1 (alk. paper) : LC Card 85-20368 DDC 338.4/767721/0975 19
HD8039.T42 U652 1986
NYPL [JLE 86-3477]

McHugh, Cathy. Mill family . New York , 1988. p. cm. ISBN 0-19-504299-9 LC Card 87-7832 DDC 331.7/67721/0975 19
HD8039.T42 U654 1988

COTTON TEXTILE INDUSTRY - SOUTHERN STATES - HISTORY.
McHugh, Cathy. Mill family . New York , 1988. p. cm. ISBN 0-19-504299-9 LC Card 87-7832 DDC 331.7/67721/0975 19
HD8039.T42 U654 1988

COTTON TEXTILE INDUSTRY - UNITED STATES.
Horne, M. K. (McDonald Kelso), 1909- The economic outlook for U. S. cotton . Memphis, Tenn. , 1962. 32 p. : LC Card 86-162675
HD9075 .H73 1962

COTTON TEXTILE INDUSTRY - UNITED STATES - HISTORY.
Davis, Burke, 1913- War bird . Chapel Hill , c1987. viii, 267 p., [26] p. of plates : ISBN 0-8078-1752-X (alk. paper) LC Card 87-5934 DDC 338.7/67721/0924 B 19
HD9880.S67 D38 1987

Kane, Nancy Frances, 1954- Textiles in

transition . New York , c1988. p. cm. ISBN 0-313-25529-6 (lib. bdg. : alk. paper) LC Card 87-24950 DDC 338.4/767721/0973 19
HD9875 .K3 1988

COTTON TEXTILE INDUSTRY - UNITED STATES - HISTORY - 20TH CENTURY.
Bauge, Kenneth L. (Kenneth LeRoy) Voluntary export restriction as a foreign commercial policy with special reference to Japanese cotton textiles, 1930-1962 /. New York , 1987. 277 p. ; ISBN 0-8240-8072-6 LC Card 87-23717 DDC 382/.4567721/0952 19
HD9886.J3 B38 1987

COTTON TRADE - ARGENTINE REPUBLIC.
América Latina y la economía mundial del algodón. Santiago de Chile , 1985. 128 p. : ISBN 92-1-321189-9 LC Card 85-230001 DDC 338.1/7351/098 19
HD9884.L3 A46 1985 NYPL [JLE 86-3341]

COTTON TRADE - BRAZIL - RIO GRANDE DO NORTE - HISTORY.
Takeya, Denise Monteiro. Um outro Nordeste . Fortaleza , 1985. 137 p. : LC Card 86-232681
HD9084.B62 R568 1985

COTTON TRADE - BRAZIL - SÃO PAULO (STATE)
Fleury, Maria Tereza Leme. A organização do trabalho na lavoura algodoeira paulista /. [São Paulo, Brasil] 1984. 208 p. : LC Card 85-145302 DDC 338.1/7351/098161 19
HD9084.B62 S264 1984
NYPL [JLE 86-1740]

COTTON TRADE - BURUNDI.
Les Cultures industrielles du Burundi . Bujumbura [1985] 63 p. : LC Card 85-981329
HD9195.B942 C85 1985

COTTON TRADE - CENTRAL AMERICA.
Williams, Robert G. (Robert Gregory), 1948- Export agriculture and the crisis in Central America /. Chapel Hill , c1986. xvi, 257 p. : ISBN 0-8078-1693-0 LC Card 85-20978 DDC 382/.41/09728 19
HD9884.C352 W55 1986
NYPL [JLE 86-3412]

COTTON TRADE - CHAD.
Société cotonnière du Tchad. Direction générale. Douze années de Cotontchad, 1971-1983 . N'Djaména [1984] 30 leaves ; LC Card 86-980210
HD9087.C474 S637 1984

COTTON TRADE - DEVELOPING COUNTRIES.
Third World countries in the international cotton economy /. [Nyon, Switzerland?] , 1979. i, 61 p. : LC Card 86-223016
HD9088.D44 T47 1979

COTTON TRADE - EGYPT - ECONOMETRIC MODELS.
Eckstein, Zvi. Cotton and wheat production in the Egyptian agriculture . [Tel Aviv] [1984] 40 leaves : LC Card 84-186315 DDC 338.1/711/0962 19
HD9087.E42 E35 1984

COTTON TRADE - GUATEMALA.
América Latina y la economía mundial del algodón. Santiago de Chile , 1985. 128 p. : ISBN 92-1-321189-9 LC Card 85-230001 DDC 338.1/7351/098 19
HD9884.L3 A46 1985 NYPL [JLE 86-3341]

COTTON TRADE - MEXICO.
América Latina y la economía mundial del algodón. Santiago de Chile , 1985. 128 p. : ISBN 92-1-321189-9 LC Card 85-230001 DDC 338.1/7351/098 19
HD9884.L3 A46 1985 NYPL [JLE 86-3341]

COTTON TRADE - MISSISSIPPI - HISTORY.
Moore, John Hebron. The emergence of the Cotton Kingdom in the Old Southwest . Baton Rouge , c1988. xii, 323 p. : ISBN 0-8071-1404-9 (pbk.) LC Card 87-2803 DDC 330.9762 19
HC107.M7 M66 1988

COTTON TRADE - NICARAGUA.
América Latina y la economía mundial del algodón. Santiago de Chile , 1985. 128 p. : ISBN 92-1-321189-9 LC Card 85-230001 DDC 338.1/7351/098 19
HD9884.L3 A46 1985 NYPL [JLE 86-3341]

COTTON TRADE - PARAGUAY.
América Latina y la economía mundial del algodón. Santiago de Chile , 1985. 128 p. : ISBN 92-1-321189-9 LC Card 85-230001 DDC 338.1/7351/098 19
HD9884.L3 A46 1985 NYPL [JLE 86-3341]

Palau, Tomás. El cultivo del algodón y la soya en el Paraguay y sus derivaciones sociales. Santiago de Chile , 1986. 148 p. ; ISBN 92-1-321207-0 LC Card 87-400251 DDC 338.1/7351/09892 19
HD9084.P25 P35 1986

COTTON TRADE - SOUTHERN STATES - EMPLOYEES - HISTORY.
Like a family . Chapel Hill , c1987. xxiii, 468 p. : ISBN 0-8078-1754-6 (alk. paper) LC Card 87-40135 DDC 305/.9677 19
HD9077.A13 L55 1987

COTTON TRADE - SOUTHERN STATES - HISTORY.
Like a family . Chapel Hill , c1987. xxiii, 468 p. : ISBN 0-8078-1754-6 (alk. paper) LC Card 87-40135 DDC 305/.9677 19
HD9077.A13 L55 1987

COTTON TRADE - UNITED STATES.
Horne, M. K. (McDonald Kelso), 1909- The economic outlook for U. S. cotton . Memphis, Tenn. , 1962. 32 p. : LC Card 86-162675
HD9075 .H73 1962

COTTONSEED - PAKISTAN.
Galal, M. F. Pakistan . Rome [i.e. Multan] , 1978. vii, 36 p. ; LC Card 83-931176
HD9086.P32 G35 1978

Cottrell, P. L. International business and Central Europe, 1918-1939 /. [Leicester, Leicestershire] , New York , 1983. xxvii, 459 p. : ISBN 0-312-41982-1 : LC Card 83-13956 DDC 338.8/8843 19
HD2844 .I57 1983 NYPL [JLE 86-3697]

Coudroglou, Aliki. Employee assistance programs within the context of personnel policies / Aliki Coudroglou. Brookfield, Wis. : International Foundation of Employee Benefit Plans, c1986. 26 p. ; 28 cm. (Research report . 86-4) "December 1986." Bibliography: p. 24-26. ISBN 0-89154-322-8 (pbk.) LC Card 87-158924 DDC 658.3/82 19
1. Employee assistance programs. I. Series: Research report (International Foundation of Employee Benefit Plans) , rpt. 86-4. II. Title.
HF5549.5.E42 C676 1986

Coulson, Robert D. The intelligent investor's guide to profiting from stock market inefficiencies / by D. Robert Coulson. Chicago, Ill. : Probus, c1987. xii, 261 p. : ill. ; 24 cm. Bibliography: p. 209-212. Includes index. ISBN 0-917253-46-9 : LC Card 86-25341 DDC 332.6 19
1. Portfolio management. 2. Investment analysis. 3. Stock-exchange. I. Title.
HG4529.5 .C68 1987

Council for Asian Manpower Studies. The Motor vehicle industry in Asia . [Singapore] [1983] xxv, 419 p. : ISBN 997-16-9057-8 LC Card 83-941793 DDC 338.4/76292/095 19
HD9710.3.A78 M67 1983
NYPL [JLE 85-1592]

Council for Economic Opportunities in Greater Cleveland (Cleveland, Ohio) Ohio poverty indicators. Cleveland, Ohio (668 Euclid Ave, Suite 700, Cleveland 44114) , c1986-<c1987. v. <1-2 > : LC Card 87-107608 DDC 362.5/2/09771 19
HC107.O323 P6355 1986

Council for Mutual Economic Aid. see **Sovet ėkonomicheskoĭ vzaimopomoshchi.**

Council for Mutual Economic Assistance.
Brabant, Jozef M. van. Regional price formation in Eastern Europe . Boston ; Dordrecht : xiv, 290 p. ; ISBN 90-247-3540-8 LC Card 87-12238 DDC 338.5/26/0947 19
HB235.E8 B73 1987

COUNCIL FOR MUTUAL ECONOMIC ASSISTANCE.
Altmann, Franz-Lothar. Die tschechoslowakische Volkswirtschaft und der Rat für gegenseitige Wirtschaftshilfe (RGW) /. München [1986] 31 leaves ; LC Card 86-203484
HF3550.3.Z7 E8523 1986

Belichenko, A. N. (Al′bert Nikolaevich) Kreditnye otnoshenii͡a mezhdu stranami-chlenami SĖV /. Moskva , 1983. 134 p. : LC Card 84-171632
HG3729.E932 B45 1983

Bondarenko, E. L. (Evgenii͡a Lavrent′evna) Zakonomernosti razvitii͡a sotsialisticheskikh mezhdunarodnykh proizvodstvennykh otnosheniĭ /. Moskva , 1983. 127 p. ; LC Card 84-200940
HC244 .B694 1983

Brabant, Jozef M. van. Adjustment, structural change, and economic efficiency . Cambridge [Cambridgeshire] , New York , 1987. xviii, 480 p. ; ISBN 0-521-33455-1 LC Card 87-785 DDC 332.4/947 19
HG186.E82 B7 1987

Burova, S. E. (Stella Efimovna) Kritika burzhuaznykh vzgli͡adov na ėkonomicheskoe sotrudnichestvo stran SĖV /. Moskva , 1986. 154 p. ; LC Card 86-232355
HC243.5 .B87 1986

Gabrisch, Hubert. Polen im RGW . Hamburg , 1986. 308 p. ; ISBN 3-87895-316-X LC Card 87-407406 DDC 330.9438/056 19
HC340.3 .G34 1986

The Hungarian enterprise in the context of intra-CMEA relations /. Budapest , 1986. 93 p. ; ISBN 963-301-138-8 (pbk.) LC Card 87-101284 DDC 337.439 19
HF1542.5.H8 H85 1986

Indo-CMEA economic relations /. New Delhi , 1987. xviii, 263 p. ; ISBN 81-7024-078-6 : LC Card 87-901620 DDC 337.54047 19
HC433 .I535 1987

Kállay, Georges Christophe de. L'importance des marchés de l'Europe de l'Est . Genève , 1986. 247 p. ; LC Card 86-179357
HF3408.Z7 E8525 1986

Kozlov, I. D. (Igor′ Dmitrievich) Ėnergeticheskoe khozi͡aĭstvo stran SĖV . Moskva , 1980. 158 p. ; LC Card 87-107887
HD9502.E83 K686 1980

Leznik, A. D. (Aleksandr Davidovich) Upravlenie mezhdunarodnoĭ spetsializatsieĭ proizvodstva stran SĖV /. Moskva , 1982. 143 p. ; LC Card 83-123508
HC244 .L466 1982

Machowski, Heinrich. RGW-Staaten und Dritte Welt . Bonn , 1981. iii, 84 p. ; ISBN 3-7713-0167-X LC Card 85-224767
HF1532.15.D44 M33 1981

Quilitzsch, Siegmar. Die sozialistische Gemeinschaft zu Beginn der 80er Jahre . Berlin , 1984. 141 p. : LC Card 84-180106
HC243.5 .Q55 1984

SĖV -- osnovnye napravlenii͡a sotrudnichestva . Moskva , 1984. 203 p. ; LC Card 85-177814
HC243.5 .S48 1984

Sinkovics, Alfréd. Nemzetközi tőkemozgások és a KGST /. Budapest , 1986, c1985. 336, [1] p. : ISBN 963-221-493-5 : LC Card 87-408509
HG3891 .S57 1986

Sovet ėkonomicheskoĭ vzaimopomoshchi . Moskva , 1984. 29 p. : LC Card 86-203121
HC243.5 .S683 1984

Die Sozialistische Gemeinschaft . Berlin , 1985. 238 p. ; LC Card 86-120025 DDC 337.1/1717 19
HC243.5 .S685 1985

Szelecki, György. Mit kell tudni a KGST-ről? /. [Budapest] , 1986. 126, [5] p. : ISBN 963-09-2731-4 : LC Card 86-210839
HC243.5 .S94 1986

T͡Sarevski, Nesho Vŭlev. The People's Republic of Bulgaria . Sofia , 1986. 102 p. ; LC Card 87-123346 DDC 337.1/4977 19
HC403 .T748 1986

Vneshneėkonomicheskie svi͡azi stran-chlenov SĖV v uslovii͡akh sotsialisticheskoĭ integratsii /. Kiev , 1983. 245 p. ; LC Card 83-189711
HC243.5 .V54 1983

Vŭlkovski, Georgi Danov. Mezhdunarodni ikonomicheski otnoshenii͡a pri sottsializma . Sofii͡a , 1985 [i.e. 1986] 151 p. ; LC Card 87-134453
HC244 .V84 1986

The World socialist economy. Moscow , 1986. 279 p. ; LC Card 86-231463 DDC 338.9/009171/7 19
HC704 .W67 1986

Council for Mutual Economic Assistance. Secretariat. Sovet ėkonomicheskoĭ vzaimopomoshchi . Moskva , 1984. 29 p. : LC Card 86-203121
HC243.5 .S683 1984

Council of Europe. Committee of Experts on Local and Regional Finance.
Kelly, G. Financial resources for local and regional authorities /. Strasbourg , 1985. 79 p. ; LC Card 86-206535 DDC 336/.014/4 19
HJ9420 .K45 1985

Meadows, W. J. The response of local authorities to central government incitement to reduce expenditure . Strasbourg , 1986. 33 p. ; LC Card 87-135687 DDC 336.3/9/094 19
HJ9415 .M43 1986

Council of Europe. Committee of Experts on Local and Regional Finances. Policies with regard to grants to local authorities . Strasbourg , 1986. 35 p. : LC Card 86-218329 DDC 336.1/85 19
HJ1000 .P65 1986

Council of Europe. Steering Committee for Regional Planning. The Regionalisation of transport and regional planning in practice . Paris, France [Washington, D.C.] c1984. 199 p. : ISBN 92-821-1091-5 (pbk.) : LC Card 85-180250 DDC 380.5/068 19
HE242 .R44 1984 ***NYPL [JLG 86-138]***

Council of Scientific & Industrial Research (India). Publications & Information Directorate. The Wealth of India . New Delhi , c1985- v. <1- > : ISBN 81-85038-00-7 (set) LC Card 87-900740 DDC 333.7/0954 19
HF1054.I5 W4 1985

Council of State Governments.
The State of the states . Lexington, KY , c1986. 56 p. ; ISBN 0-87292-064-X (pbk.) LC Card 87-162324 DDC 330.973/0927 19
HC106.8 .S735 1986

Council of State Governments. Western Office.
Fairfax, Sally K. Federal lands . Washington, D.C. , c1987. xviii, 252 p. : ISBN 0-933280-33-5 (pbk.) :$ LC Card 86-27512 DDC 333.1/0978 19
HD243.A17 F35 1987

Council of State Housing Agencies (U. S.) Tiven, Marjorie. State initiatives in elderly housing . Washington, DC , c1987. xviii, 79 p. ; LC Card 87-154352 DDC 363.5/9 19
HD7287.92.U54 T58 1987

Council of State Planning Agencies. Corporation for Enterprise Development. Building the new economy . Washington, D.C. , 1986. iv, 178 p. ; ISBN 0-9605804-2-5 (pbk.) LC Card 86-61273 DDC 338.973 19
HC110.I53 C67 1986

COUNCIL OF THE EUROPEAN COMMUNITIES - DICTIONARIES.
Glossaire des Communautés européennes . Luxembourg , 1987, c1986. 706 p. ; ISBN 92-824-0410-2 : ***NYPL [JLF 87-217]***

Council of the European Communities. General Secretariat. Glossaire des Communautés européennes . Luxembourg , 1987, c1986. 706 p. ; ISBN 92-824-0410-2 :
NYPL [JLF 87-217]

Council of the European Communities. Terminology Dept. EG-Wörterverzeichnis . Luxembourg , 1984. 1 v. (various pagings) ; ISBN 92-824-0123-5 LC Card 85-131398
KJE926.5 .E35 1984 ***NYPL [JLF 86-1818]***

Council on Economic Priorities.
Goldman, Benjamin A. Hazardous waste management . Washington, D.C. , c1986. xx, 316 p. : ISBN 0-933280-30-0 : LC Card 86-2748 DDC 363.7/28 19
HD9975.U52 G65 1986
NYPL [JLE 87-1159]

Lydenberg, Steven D. Rating America's corporate conscience . Reading, Mass. , c1986. x, 499 p. : ISBN 0-201-15886-8 : LC Card 86-8064 DDC 338.7/4/0973 19
HD60.5.U5 L93 1986
NYPL [*R-Econ. 87-1830]

Council on Environmental Quality. see **United States. Council on Environmental Quality.**

Council on Foreign Relations.
Committee on African Development Strategies (U. S.) Compact for African development . Berkeley, CA (2120 Berkeley Way, Berkeley 94720) [1985] 24 p. : LC Card 86-200473 DDC 338.967 19
HC800 .C645 1985

Unemployment and growth in the Western economies /. New York, N.Y. , c1984. x, 142 p. ; ISBN 0-87609-001-3 (pbk.) : LC Card 84-9415 DDC 331.13/791812 19
HD5707.5 .U54 1984 ***NYPL [JLE 86-1564]***

The Council on Foreign Relations series on international trade.
Paarlberg, Robert L. Fixing farm trade . Cambridge, Mass. , c1988. xiv, 159 p. ; ISBN 0-88730-196-7 LC Card 87-24118 DDC 382/.41/0973 19
HD9006 .P27 1988

COUNSELING - ADDRESSES, ESSAYS, LECTURES.
Employee problem prevention and counseling . Westport, Conn. , 1985. xii, 338 p. ; ISBN 0-89930-084-7 (lib. bdg.) LC Card 84-26499 DDC 658.3/85 19
HF5549.5.C8 E47 1985
NYPL [JLE 86-1105]

COUNSELING, EMPLOYEE. see **EMPLOYEE COUNSELING.**

COUNSELORS - EUROPEAN ECONOMIC COMMUNITY COUNTRIES.
Equal opportunity counsellors . Berlin , Washington, DC , 1986. 50 p. : ISBN 92-825-6559-9 : LC Card 87-136233 DDC 331.13/3/094 19
HD4903.5.E8 E79 1986

COUNTER CULTURE. see **RADICALISM.**

Counter cultures . Benson, Susan Porter, 1943- Urbana , c1986. xvi, 322 p. : ISBN 0-252-01252-6 (alk. paper) LC Card 85-21012 DDC 381/.1/0973 19
HF5465.U5 B45 1986 ***NYPL [JLE 87-1091]***

Counter merchandising . Pfeiffer, Paul L. Chicago, Ill. (Suite 2260, 20 N. Wacker Dr., Chicago 60606) , c1986. 84 p., [1] leaf of plates : LC Card 87-404047 DDC 658.8/5 19
HF5438.25 .P49 1986

COUNTER TRADE.
Iske, Thorsten, 1960- Verbundgeschäfte . Frankfurt am Main , New York , c1986. v, 267 p. : ISBN 3-8204-9756-0 LC Card 86-218131
HF1019 .I85 1986

COUNTERFEITS AND COUNTERFEITING.
Tazwīr al-mustanadāt wa-tazyīf al-ʻumlāt wa-al-asālīb al-ʻilmīyah lil-kashf ʻanhā. [Cairo] [1978] 296 p., [1] leaf of plates : ISBN 977-7049-73-0 LC Card 79-961630
HG335 .T3 1978

COUNTERFEITS AND COUNTERFEITING - HISTORY.
Rochette, Edward C., 1927- Making money /. Frederick, CO , c1986. 107 p. : ISBN 0-939650-25-8 (pbk.) : LC Card 86-22120 DDC 364.1/33/09 19
HG335 .R63 1986

COUNTERFEITS AND COUNTERFEITING - UNITED STATES.
United States. Congress. House. Committee on Energy and Commerce. Subcommittee on Oversight and Investigations. Dangerous medicine . Washington , 1986. v, 31 p. ; LC Card 86-602099 DDC 363.1/942/0973 19
HD9665.9.U6 U55 1986

Counterpart GmbH. Guinea (Revolutionäre Volksrepublik Guinea) . Köln , 1983. viii, 89 p. : LC Card 85-104313
HC1030 .G83 1983

COUNTERREVOLUTIONS.
Soley, Lawrence C. Clandestine radio broadcasting . New York , 1987. xiv, 384 p. ; ISBN 0-275-92259-6 (alk. paper) : LC Card 86-21169 DDC 384.54 19
HE8697.P6 S59 1986
NYPL [MWGH 87-1678]

Countertrade . Alexandrides, Costas G. New York , c1987. xx, 235 p. ; ISBN 0-471-84711-9 LC Card 87-12966 DDC 382 19
HF1414.3 .A44 1987

Countertrade . Bürgin, Rolf, 1956- Bern , New York , c1986. x, 253 p. : ISBN 3-261-03584-6 LC Card 86-195899
HF1573 .B79 1986

COUNTERTRADE.
Alexandrides, Costas G. Countertrade . New York , c1987. xx, 235 p. ; ISBN 0-471-84711-9 LC Card 87-12966 DDC 382 19
HF1414.3 .A44 1987

Countertrade and trading companies . New York, N.Y. , c1984. iv, 283 p. : LC Card 84-196766 DDC 343.73/0878 347.303878 19
KF1976 .C68 1984 ***NYPL [JLD 86-4098]***

Francis, Dick. The countertrade handbook /. New York , 1987. ix, 270 p. : ISBN 0-89930-320-X (lib. bdg. : alk. paper) LC Card 87-11867 DDC 382 19
HF1414.3 .F72 1987

Jones, Stephen F. North/south countertrade . London , c1984. 97 p. : LC Card 85-239985 DDC 382/.091722/01724 19
HF1414.3 .J65 1984

Samsinger, Berndt R. Countertrade, eine alternative Marketing-Strategie /. Bern , c1986. xiii, 285 p. : ISBN 3-258-03597-0 : LC Card 86-191674
HF1412 .S26 1986

Countertrade and trading companies : trade trends in the '80s / chairman, Peter D. Ehrenhaft. New York, N.Y. : Law & Business/Harcourt, Brace, Jovanovich, c1984. iv, 283 p. : ill. ; 22 cm. Includes bibliographical references. LC Card 84-196766 DDC 343.73/0878 347.303878 19
1. Countertrade - United States. 2. Export trading companies - Law and legislation - United States. 3. Countertrade. 4. Export trading companies - Law and legislation. I. Ehrenhaft, Peter D.
KF1976 .C68 1984 ***NYPL [JLD 86-4098]***

COUNTERTRADE - CONGRESSES.
International countertrade /. New York , 1987. xii, 191 p. : ISBN 0-89930-213-0 (lib. bdg. : alk. paper) LC Card 86-25319 DDC 382 19
HF1410.5 .I5716 1987

Countertrade, eine alternative Marketing-Strategie /. Samsinger, Berndt R. Bern , c1986. xiii, 285 p. : ISBN 3-258-03597-0 : LC Card 86-191674
HF1412 .S26 1986

The countertrade handbook /. Francis, Dick. New York , 1987. ix, 270 p. : ISBN 0-89930-320-X (lib. bdg. : alk. paper) LC Card 87-11867 DDC 382 19
HF1414.3 .F72 1987

COUNTERTRADE - SWITZERLAND.
Bürgin, Rolf, 1956- Countertrade . Bern , New York , c1986. x, 253 p. : ISBN 3-261-03584-6 LC Card 86-195899
HF1573 .B79 1986

COUNTERTRADE - UNITED STATES.
Countertrade and trading companies . New York, N.Y. , c1984. iv, 283 p. : LC Card 84-196766 DDC 343.73/0878 347.303878 19
KF1976 .C68 1984 ***NYPL [JLD 86-4098]***

The Counting instrument market in the U. S. New York, N.Y. : Frost & Sullivan, c1983. v, 197 p. : ill. ; 29 cm. "September, 1983." "(#A1175)." LC Card 87-143757 DDC 381/.4568114 19
1. Digital counter industry - United States. 2. Market surveys - United States. I. Frost & Sullivan.
HD9696.D543 U63 1983

COUNTRY AND WESTERN MUSIC. see **COUNTRY MUSIC.**

Country commitment to development projects /. Heaver, Richard, 1952- Washington, D.C., U.S.A. [1986] 32 p. ; ISBN 0-8213-0860-2 (pbk.) LC Card 86-28114 DDC 338.91 19
HC59.72.E44 H43 1986

COUNTRY HOMES - CANADA - PURCHASING.
Scher, Les. Finding and buying your place in the country /. New York , London , c1987. p. cm. ISBN 0-02-008400-5 LC Card 87-24246 DDC 643/.2 19
HD256 .S27 1987

COUNTRY HOMES - UNITED STATES - PURCHASING.
Scher, Les. Finding and buying your place in the country /. New York , London , c1987. p. cm. ISBN 0-02-008400-5 LC Card 87-24246

DDC 643/.2 19
HD256 .S27 1987

COUNTRY HOUSES. see **COUNTRY HOMES.**

COUNTRY MUSIC - UNITED STATES.
Wacholtz, Larry E. Inside country music /. New York , 1986. 254 p. ; ISBN 0-8230-7532-X (pbk. : alk. paper) LC Card 86-4234 DDC 784.5/2/002373 19
ML3790 .W24 1986 ***NYPL [JNE 86-18]***

COUNTRY RISK.
Dworak, Brigitte M. Das Länderrisiko als bankbetriebliches Problem /. Berlin , c1985. 168 p. : ISBN 3-428-05761-9 LC Card 85-213576
HG5993 .D86 1985

Goldberg, Ellen S. On edge . New York , 1987. ix, 116 p. ; ISBN 0-275-92604-4 (alk. paper) : LC Card 86-25324 DDC 332.1/5 19
HG3881 .G6142 1987

Kennedy, Charles R. Political risk management . New York , 1987. xiv, 163 p. : ISBN 0-89930-157-6 (lib. bdg. : alk. paper) LC Card 86-25588 DDC 332.6/7373 19
HG4538 .K44 1987

Oxelheim, Lars. Macroeconomic uncertainty . Chichester [West Sussex] , New York , c1987. xv, 251 p. : ISBN 0-471-91480-0 : LC Card 87-8333 DDC 658.1/55 19
HG3821 .O894 1987

Solberg, Ronald L., 1953- Sovereign rescheduling . London , Boston , 1988. p. cm. ISBN 0-04-332122-4 (alk. paper) LC Card 87-18805 DDC 336.3/435 19
HG3891.5 .S65 1988

Ting, Wenlee. Multinational risk assessment and management . New York , c1987. p. cm. ISBN 0-89930-175-4 (lib. bdg. : alk. paper) LC Card 87-5970 DDC 658 19
HD61 .T56 1987

Countryside conflicts : the politics of farming, forestry, and conservation / Philip Lowe ... [et al.]. Aldershot, Hants, England ; Brookfield, Vt., U. S.A. : Gower/M.T. Smith, c1986. vi, 378 p. [4] leaves of plates : ill., map ; 23 cm. ISBN 0-566-05088-9 : LC Card 85-24603 DDC 333.76/17/0941 19
1. Land use, Rural - Great Britain. 2. Land use, Rural - Government policy - Great Britain. 3. Agriculture - Economic aspects - Great Britain. 4. Forests and forestry - Economic aspects - Great Britain. 5. Soil conservation - Great Britain. 6. Conservation of natural resources - Great Britain. I. Lowe, Philip.
HD596 .C675 1986 ***NYPL [JLD 86-2487]***

County & postmaster postmarks of Wisconsin. Bournique, Raymond A. Madison, WI (5401 Raymond Rd., Madison 53711) , 1985. 12 p. : LC Card 86-174748 DDC 769.56/7/09775 19
HE6185.U7 W573 1985

County and postmaster postmarks of Wisconsin. Bournique, Raymond A. County & postmaster postmarks of Wisconsin. Madison, WI (5401 Raymond Rd., Madison 53711) , 1985. 12 p. : LC Card 86-174748 DDC 769.56/7/09775 19
HE6185.U7 W573 1985

County business growth. Trenton, N.J. (CN 824, Trenton 08625-0824) : Dept. of Commerce and Economic Development, Office of Economic Research, [1987] 2 v. : ill., maps ; 28 cm. Cover title. "January 1987"--V. 2. LC Card 87-404521 DDC 331.12/09749/021 19
1. Labor supply - New Jersey - Statistics. 2. New Jersey - Economic conditions - Statistics. 3. New Jersey - Industries - Statistics. I. New Jersey. Dept. of Commerce and Economic Development. Office of Economic Research.
HD5725.N5 C68 1987

COUNTY FINANCE. see **LOCAL FINANCE.**

County profiles : socio-economic characteristics. Albany, N.Y. : New York State Dept. of Labor, Division of Research and Statistics, Bureau of Labor Market Information, [1984-<1985 > v. : ill. ; 28 cm. (Bureau of Labor Market Information report . FYI1985, no. 9, <12, 15 >) LC Card 84-623501 DDC 330.9747/043 19
1. New York (State) - Economic conditions. 2. New York (State) - Social conditions. I. New York (State). Bureau of Labor Market Information. II. Series: BLMI report , FY1985, no. 9, etc.
HC107.N7 C64 1984

Couper, A. D. New cargo-handling techniques : implications for port employment and skills / A.D. Couper. Geneva : International Labour Office, 1986. xii, 172 p., [1] folded leaf of plates : ill. ; 24 cm. Bibliography: p. 167-172. ISBN 92-2-105419-5 (pbk.) : LC Card 87-117776 DDC 331.7/61387164 19
1. Stevedores - Effect of technological innovations on. 2. Cargo handling. I. Title.
HD6331.18.L65 C68 1986

Couplepower . Krupa, Arlene. New York , c1987. 227 p. ; ISBN 0-396-09029-X (pbk.) : LC Card 87-20065 DDC 658.4/09 19
HD62.25 .K78 1987

COUPONS (RETAIL TRADE)
Samtur, Susan J. Cashing in at the checkout /. New York , c1979. 152 p. : ISBN 0-448-15704-7 : LC Card 79-51120 DDC 381/.1 19
HF6127 .S25 ***NYPL [JLD 81-566]***

Courchaure, Stéphane. Les riches : comment ils dépensent leur argent / Stéphane Courchaure et François Marot. [Paris] : Balland, c1985. 261 p. ; 22 cm. Includes index. Bibliography: p. 253. ISBN 2-7158-0537-3 : LC Card 86-111316 DDC 305.5/234 19
1. Consumers. 2. Millionaires. I. Marot, François. II. Title.
HC79.C6 C68 1985 ***NYPL [JLD 86-4451]***

Courchene, Thomas J. Ontario's proposals for the Canadian securities industry / Thomas J. Courchene, with John D. Todd and Lawrence P. Schwartz. Toronto : C.D. Howe Institute ; Scarborough, Ont. : Available from Prentice-Hall Canada, [1986] 39 p. : ill. ; 21 cm. (Observation, 0826-9947 . no. 29) Includes bibliographical references. ISBN 0-88806-137-4 (pbk.) LC Card 87-133168 DDC 332.63/2 19
1. Securities - Canada. 2. Brokers - Canada. 3. Securities - Government policy - Canada. 4. Securities - Government policy - Ontario. I. Todd, John D. II. Schwartz, Lawrence P., 1948-. III. Title. IV. Series.
HG5158 .C68 1986

Courcoux, Etienne. Mallard, Jean-Claude, 1947- Comprendre et gérer la fiscalité de l'entreprise /. La Tronche , Paris [1985] 255 p. : LC Card 86-166702
HD2753.F8 M34 1985

Coureau, Serge. Savoir vendre pour vendre plus / Serge Coureau. Paris : Dunod, c1986. 147 p. ; 22 cm. Bibliography: p. 145. Includes index. ISBN 2-04-016534-7 LC Card 87-122332
1. Selling. I. Title.
HF5438.25 .C68 1986

Couri, Sergio, 1948- Ensaios sobre a evolução dos sistemas econômicos / Sergio Couri. Brasília-Distrito Federal : Editora Universidade de Brasília, [1983] 133 p. : ill. ; 23 cm. (Cadernos da UnB) Errata slip inserted. Includes bibliographical references. LC Card 84-116306 DDC 330.1 19
1. Marxian economics - Addresses, essays, lectures. 2. Keynesian economics - Addresses, essays, lectures. 3. Capitalism - Addresses, essays, lectures. 4. Economic history - 1750-1918 - Addresses, essays, lectures. 5. Economic history - 1918- - Addresses, essays, lectures. 6. Comparative economics - Addresses, essays, lectures. I. Title. II. Series.
HB97.5 .C68 1983 ***NYPL [JLE 86-3363]***

Courlet, Claude. L'Europe du sud au milieu du gué / Claude Courlet, Jean Laganier. Grenoble : Presses universitaires de Grenoble, 1984. 122 p. ; 22 cm. (Influences) Includes bibliographies. ISBN 2-7061-0243-8 : LC Card 85-116696
1. Europe, Southern - Economic conditions. 2. Europe, Southern - Economic policy. I. Laganier, Jean. II. Title. III. Series.
HC244.5 .C68 1984

Courrier hebdomadaire du CRISP, 0008-9664 . (no 1032) Arcq, Etienne. La C.S.C. et le programme gouvernemental de mars 1984 /. Bruxelles [1984] 23 leaves ; LC Card 84-171486
HD8502.C62 A73 1984

Cours de droit. Licence.
Jessua, Claude. Histoire de la pensée économique /. Paris , 1981. 494, viii p. : LC Card 87-672485
HB75 .J47x 1981

A course in business statistics /. Mendenhall, William. Boston, Mass. [1988] p. cm. ISBN 0-534-91488-8 LC Card 87-20731 DDC 519.5 19
HF1017 .M458 1988

Course module series.
Goodpaster, Kenneth E., 1944- Ethics in management /. Boston , c1984. 154 p. : ISBN 0-87584-165-1 (course module : pbk.) LC Card 84-12847 DDC 174/.4 19
HF5387 .G66 1984

COURT, JOHAN DE LA, 1622-1660.
Wildenberg, Ivo W. (Ivo Willibrord) Johan & Pieter de la Court, 1622-1660 & 1618-1685 . Amsterdam , 1986. xiii, 180 p., [21] p. of plates : ISBN 90-302-1162-8 : LC Card 87-141484
HC322.5.A2 W55 1986

COURT, PIETER DE LA, 1618?-1685.
Wildenberg, Ivo W. (Ivo Willibrord) Johan & Pieter de la Court, 1622-1660 & 1618-1685 . Amsterdam , 1986. xiii, 180 p., [21] p. of plates : ISBN 90-302-1162-8 : LC Card 87-141484
HC322.5.A2 W55 1986

Court, W. H. B. (William Henry Bassano) Scarcity and choice in history, by W.H.B. Court. London, Edward Arnold, 1970. viii, 256 p. 23 cm. Includes bibliographical references. Index. LC Card 79-488977 DDC 330.9
1. Great Britain - Economic conditions - Addresses, essays, lectures. 2. Economic history - Addresses, essays, lectures. I. Title.
HC253 .C675

The courtiers of American business /. Brahmstedt, W. T. (William T.), 1924- Palm Springs, Calif. , c1987. 190 p. : ISBN 0-88280-118-X (pbk.) : LC Card 86-29078 DDC 650.1/3 19
HF5386 .B777 1987

COURTS, INDUSTRIAL. see **LABOR COURTS.**

COURTS, LABOR. see **LABOR COURTS.**

Couyoumdjian, Juan Ricardo. Chile y Gran Bretaña : durante la Primera Guerra Mundial y la postguerra, 1914-1921 / Juan Ricardo Couyoumdjian. [Santiago] : Editorial Andres Bello : Ediciones Universidad Católica de Chile, [1986] xvi, 340 p., [4] p. of plates : ill. ; 23 cm. Bibliography: p. 329-340. LC Card 86-222403
1. Chile - Foreign economic relations - Great Britain. 2. Great Britain - Foreign economic relations - Chile. 3. Saltpeter industry - Chile - History - 20th century. 4. Investments, British - Chile - History - 20th century. 5. World War, 1914-1918 - Chile. 6. World War, 1914-1918 - Great Britain. 7. Chile - History - 1824-1920. 8. Great Britain - History - George V, 1910-1936. I. Title.
HF1516.5.G72 C68 1986

Cova, Alberto.
Cooperazione di credito e sviluppo sociale ed economico delle campagne in Emilia Romagna . Bologna , c1983. 173 p. : LC Card 85-156690
HG2051.I82 E433 1983

Cremona e la sua provincia nell'Italia unita. Milano , 1984. 2 v. : ISBN 88-14-00552-4 : LC Card 86-207553
HC308.C74 C74 1984

Čovekova životna sredina i ekonomski razvoj /. Crnobrnja, Mihailo. Beograd [1984?] 206 p. : LC Card 86-184927
HC407.Z9 E55 1984

Covello, Vincent T. Society for Risk Analysis International Workshop on Uncertainty in Risk Assessment, Risk Management, and Decision Making (1984 : Knoxville, Tenn.) Uncertainty in risk assessment, risk management, and decision making /. New York , c1987. x, 538 p. : ISBN 0-306-42557-2 LC Card 87-2403 DDC 658 19
HD61 .S625 1984

Coventry transport . Denton, A. S. Birmingham [West Midlands, England] , c1985- v. <1 > : ISBN 0-905103-05-X (pbk.) : LC Card 86-224227 DDC 388.4/09424/98 19
HE4719.C68 D46 1985

Coventry transport, 1884-1940. Denton, A. S. Coventry transport . Birmingham [West Midlands, England] , c1985- v. <1 > : ISBN 0-905103-05-X (pbk.) : LC Card 86-224227 DDC 388.4/09424/98 19
HE4719.C68 D46 1985

COVENTRY (WEST MIDLANDS, ENGLAND) - ECONOMIC CONDITIONS.
Beechey, Veronica. A matter of hours .

Minneapolis, MN , c1987. 212 p. ; ISBN 0-8166-1641-8 : LC Card 87-12459 DDC 331.4/12/0942498 19
HD6136.Z6 C683 1987

COVERTURE. see **MARRIED WOMEN.**

Covin, Teresa Joyce, 1959- Corporate transformation . San Francisco , 1988. xxxi, 553 p. : ISBN 1-555-42060-5 (alk. paper) LC Card 87-45427 DDC 658.4/063 19
HD58.8 .C66 1988

Cowan, William C. Kaplan, Howard J. Scouts on stamps of the world /. [Hicksville, N.Y.] , c1986. 1 v. (loose-leaf) : LC Card 86-224816 DDC 769.56/3 19
HE6183.B63 K36 1986

Cowbells and coffins . Beverley, Mary Frances. Austin, Tex. , c1987. xi, 63 p. : ISBN 0-89015-593-3 (pbk.) : LC Card 87-6711 DDC 381/.1 19
HF5429.3 .B49 1987

Cowe, Roger, 1951- Handbook of management accounting. Aldershot, Hants, England , Brookfield, Vt., U. S.A. , c1988. xxvi, 468 p. : ISBN 0-566-02615-5 : LC Card 86-29616 DDC 658.1/511 19
HF5635 .H228 1988

COWLEY (OXFORD, ENG.)
Making cars . London , Boston , c1985. ix, 131 p. : ISBN 0-7102-0272-5 : LC Card 84-13398 DDC 338.4/76292/0942574 19
HD8039.A82 G75 1984
NYPL [JLE 86-2303]

Cowling, Keith. Transnational monopoly capitalism / Keith Cowling and Roger Sugden. Sussex [England] : Wheatsheaf Books ; New York : St. Martin's Press, 1987. vii, 178 p. : ill. ; 23 cm. Bibliography: p. 163-173. Includes index. ISBN 0-312-00954-2 (St. Martin's) : LC Card 87-4965 DDC 338.8/8 19
1. International business enterprises. 2. Capitalism. 3. Monopolies. 4. International division of labor. 5. Income distribution. I. Sugden, Roger. II. Title.
HD2755.5 .C68 1987

Cox, Andrew W. State, finance, and industry . Brighton, Sussex , 1986. ix, 292 p. ; ISBN 0-7108-0219-6 ***NYPL [JLD 86-2997]***

Cox, Edwin Burk, 1950- The Bank director's handbook /. Dover, Mass. , c1986. xxiii, 294 p. : ISBN 0-86569-145-2 : LC Card 86-3592 DDC 332.1/068 19
HG1615 .B34 1986 ***NYPL [JLE 86-4332]***

Cox, Keith Kohn. Marketing management and strategy . Englewood Cliffs, NJ , c1988. x, 406 p. : ISBN 0-13-558453-1 (pbk.) LC Card 87-18849 DDC 658.8 19
HF5415.13 .M3524 1988

Cox, Madelaine.
China economic overview. China economic overview : a British Columbia perspective. [Rev. ed.] [Victoria] [1985?] 111, [2] p. : ISBN 0-7726-0465-7 (pbk.) LC Card 86-202984 DDC 330.951/058 19
HC427.92 .C68 1985

Cox, Robert W., 1926-
Power and production .
(v. 1) Cox, Robert W., 1926- Production, power, and world order . New York , 1987. xii, 500 p. ; ISBN 0-231-05808-X LC Card 86-26387
HD6971 .C78 1987

(v. 2) Harrod, Jeffrey. Power, production, and the unprotected worker /. New York , 1987. xviii, 347 p. ; ISBN 0-231-05844-6 (alk. paper) LC Card 86-26374 DDC 306/.36 19
HD6971 .H287 1987

Production, power, and world order : social forces in the making of history / Robert W. Cox. New York : Columbia University Press, 1987. xii, 500 p. ; 24 cm. (Power and production . v. 1) The political economy of international change Bibliography: p. [463]-487. Includes index. ISBN 0-231-05808-X LC Card 86-26387
1. Industrial relations - History. 2. Power (Social sciences) - History. 3. Capitalism - History. 4. International economic relations. I. Series: Cox, Robert W., 1926- Power and production , v. 1. II. Title.
HD6971 .C78 1987

Cox, Samuel H., Jr. Martin, John D., 1945- The theory of finance . Chicago , c1988. xxvi, 709 p. : ISBN 0-03-063854-2 LC Card 87-496 DDC 332/.01 19
HG173 .M353 1988

Cox, Terry. Peasants, class, and capitalism : the rural research of L.N. Kritsman and his school / Terry Cox. Oxford [Oxfordshire] ; New York : Clarendon Press ; xii, 271 p. ; 23 cm. Includes index. Bibliography: p. [251]-268. ISBN 0-19-878014-1 : LC Card 86-2362 DDC 305.5/63 19
1. Kritsman, L. (Lev), 1890-1938. 2. Peasantry - Soviet Union - Historiography. 3. Social classes - Soviet Union - Historiography. 4. Agriculture and state - Soviet Union - Historiography. 5. Soviet Union - Rural conditions - Historiography. I. Title.
HD1536.S65 C69 1986
NYPL [JLD 86-3986]

Coxall, W. N. Parties and pressure groups / W.N. Coxall. 2nd ed. London ; New York : Longman, 1986. iv, 196 p. ; 20 cm. (Political realities) Examines the structure of the British political system and the role of the major and minor parties and pressure groups. Includes bibliographical references and index. ISBN 0-582-35189-8
1. Political parties - Great Britain. 2. Pressure groups - Great Britain. I. Title. ***NYPL [JLD 86-2729]***

Coyle, Angela. Redundant women / Angela Coyle. London : Women's Press, 1984. 154 p. : port. ; 20 cm. Bibliography: p. 151-154. ISBN 0-7043-3923-4 (pbk.) : LC Card 84-100906 DDC 331.4/137941 19
1. Employees, Dismissal of - Great Britain. 2. Women textile workers - Great Britain. I. Title.
HD5708.55.G7 C68 1984
NYPL [JLD 86-3916]

Coyle, Barry. Economic gains from agricultural trade : a review and bibliography / Barry Coyle, Robert G. Chambers, and Andrew Schmitz. Washington, D.C. : U. S. Dept. of Agriculture, Economic Research Service ; [Springfield, VA : Available from National Technical Information Service, 1986] iii, 41 p. : ill. ; 28 cm. (Bibliographies and literature of agriculture . no. 48) Cover title. Shipping list no.: 86-571-P. "July 1986"--p. [2] of cover. Bibliography: p. 28-41. Item 32-B-1 LC Card 86-602417 DDC 382/.41/0973 19
1. Produce trade - United States. 2. Agriculture - Economic aspects - United States. I. Chambers, Robert G. II. Schmitz, Andrew. III. United States. Dept. of Agriculture. Economic Research Service. IV. Title. V. Series.
HD9005 .C86 1986

Coyotes . Conover, Ted. New York , 1987. xix, 264 p. : ISBN 0-394-75518-9 (pbk.) : LC Card 87-6101 DDC 331.6/2/72073 19
HD8081.M6 C65 1987

Coyuntura económica /. Morales, Juan Antonio. La Paz , 1987. 99 p. : LC Card 87-403036 DDC 330.984/052 19
HC182 .M66 1987

Coyuntura económica ecuatoriana, 1985-1986. [Quito, Ecuador] : Corporación de Estudios para el Desarrollo, [1986] i, 39 p. ; 29 cm. (Apunte técnico . no. 5) LC Card 86-217289
1. Ecuador - Economic conditions - 1972-. 2. Gross national product - Ecuador. 3. Finance, Public - Ecuador. 4. Ecuador - Commerce. 5. Cost and standard of living - Ecuador. I. Corporación de Estudios para el Desarrollo (Ecuador). II. Series.
HC202 .C73 1986

Cozen, Michael P. World patterns of modern urban change . Chicago , 1986. x, 479 p. : ISBN 0-89065-122-1 : LC Card 85-23231 DDC 910 s 307.7/6 19
H31 .C514 no.217-218
NYPL [JFM 72-132 no.217-218]

Cozian, Maurice. Annales de fiscalité : D.E.C.S. / par Maurice Cozian.3e éd. Paris : Librairies techniques, 1981. 127 p. ; 21 cm. (Collection Expertise comptable, 0150-8814) "Sujets d'examen et corrigés détaillés"--Cover. ISBN 2-7111-0289-0 : LC Card 81-150065
1. Taxation - France - Examinations, questions, etc. I. Series: Expertise comptable. II. Title.
HJ2659 .C65 1981

Cozzetto, Fausto. Mezzogiorno e demografia nel XV secolo / Fausto Cozzetto. Soveria M.lli, CZ : Rubbettino, c1986. ix, 202 p. ; 22 cm. (Biblioteca di storia e cultura meridionale. Saggi . 3) Italian and Latin. "Liber focorum Regni Neapolis": p. 55-172. Includes bibliographical references and index. LC Card 86-213782
1. Naples (Kingdom) - Population - History - Sources. 2. Taxation - Italy - Naples (Kingdom) - Lists. I. Liber focorum Regni Neapolis. 1986. II. Title. III. Title: Mezzogiorno e demografia nel 15_o secolo. IV. Title: Mezzogiorno e demografia nel entésimoquinto secolo. V. Series.
HB3600.N37 C69 1986

CPA exam questions on accounting practice /. Francisco, Albert K. Belmont, CA , c1987. 1 v. (various pagings) ; ISBN 0-932276-80-6 (pbk.) LC Card 87-62331 DDC 657/.076 19
HF5661 .F67 1987

CPA exam questions on accounting theory /. Francisco, Albert K. Belmont, CA. , c1987. 1 v. (various pagings) ; ISBN 0-932276-79-2 (pbk.) LC Card 87-62332 DDC 657/.076 19
HF5661 .F675 1987

CPC Foundation. Hopkins, David M. Changing career values . Bethlehem, PA , 1986. x, 126 p. : ISBN 0-914885-10-3 (pbk.) LC Card 87-112752 DDC 331.25 19
HD8038.U5 H66 1986

CP/M (COMPUTER OPERATING SYSTEM)
Townsend, Carl, 1938- Exploring word processors . Beaverton, Or. , c1984. viii, 239 p. : ISBN 0-88056-104-1 (pbk.) : LC Card 83-26259 DDC 652 19
Z52.5.C65 T68 1984 ***NYPL [JSD 86-495]***

CPS®--Certified Professional Secretary® examination /. Lindsell, Sheryl L. New York, N.Y. , c1987. xxx, 286 p. : ISBN 0-13-122805-6 (pbk.) : LC Card 87-11381 DDC 651.3/741/076 19
HF5547.5 .L554 1987

CPT . Catholic Church. Comissão Pastoral da Terra (Brazil) Petrópolis , 1983. 105 p. ; LC Card 86-209008
HD499.G65 C38 1983

Crabb-Velez, Connie Ann. Wendling, Wayne. The regulatory impact on pensions /. Brookfield, Wis. , 1986. xiii, 91 p. : ISBN 0-89154-314-7 (pbk.) : LC Card 87-129712 DDC 331.25/2/0973 19
HD7105.35.U6 W46 1986

"Crackie" . Belliveau, John Edward, 1913- Hantsport, N.S. , 1986. 192 p. : ISBN 0-88999-315-7 (pbk.) LC Card 87-120170 DDC 338.092/2 B 19
HC112.5.A2 B44 1986

Cracking the global market . Nadel, Jack. New York, NY , c1987. ix, 246 p. ; ISBN 0-8144-5911-0 LC Card 87-47703 DDC 658.8/48 19
HF1008 .N33 1987

Crafts and small-scale industries in Lesotho : an empirical study of problems and promotion / Thomas Fues ... [et al.]. Berlin : German Development Institute, [1982] vi, 60, 16 p., [1] leaf of plates : ill. ; 30 cm. Bibliography: p. 60. LC Card 84-215894 DDC 338.6/42/096816 19
1. Small business - Lesotho. 2. Handicraft - Lesotho. 3. Industrial promotion - Lesotho. I. Fues, Thomas.
HD2346.L44 C73 1982 ***NYPL [Sc F 86-141]***

CRAFTS (HANDICRAFTS) see **HANDICRAFT.**

Craig, Malcolm. Successful investment strategy / Malcolm Craig. 2nd ed. Cambridge, England ; Wolfeboro, N.H., USA. : Woodhead-Faulkner, 1988. p. cm. Includes index. ISBN 0-85941-383-7 : LC Card 87-8325 DDC 332.6/78 19
1. Investments. 2. Investments - Great Britain. I. Title.
HG4521 .C858 1988

Craig, Robert L. Training and development handbook . New York , c1987. xiv, 878 p. : ISBN 0-07-013353-0 : LC Card 87-2629 DDC 658.3/124 19
HF5549.5.T7 T6648 1987

Craig, Susan.
Germs of an idea. 1977. Lewis, W. Arthur (William Arthur), 1915- Labour in the West Indies : the birth of a worker's movement / by W. Arthur Lewis ; with an afterwork "Germs of an Idea" by Susan Craig. London , 1977. 104 p., [12] p. of plates : ISBN 0-901241-25-3 (pbk.) LC Card 86-232414
HD6595.4 .L49 1977

Crain, Sharon. Deal me in! : the game plan for career success for women / by Sharon Crain. Boulder, Colo. : Daskam Pub., c1987. vi, 185 p. : ill. ; 24 cm. LC Card 87-19904 DDC 650.1

19
1. Success in business. 2. Women in business. I. Title.
HF5386 .C893 1987

Cramer, J. S. (Jan Salomon), 1928- The Practice of econometrics . Dordrecht , Boston , 1987. xii, 273 p. : ISBN 90-247-3502-5 LC Card 87-4054 DDC 330/.028 19
HB139 .P7 1987

Cramer, Stanley H. Herr, Edwin L. Career guidance and counseling through the life span . Glenview, Ill. , c1988. xvi, 576 p. : ISBN 0-673-39726-2 LC Card 87-22748 DDC 331.7/02/0973 19
HF5382.5.U5 H39 1988

Crandall, Robert W. Regulating the automobile /. Washington, D.C. , c1986. xiii, 202 p. ; ISBN 0-8157-1594-3 : LC Card 85-48171 DDC 343.73/078629222 347.30378629222 19
HD9710.U52 R39 1986 *NYPL [JLE 86-3240]*

Cranfill, Steven L. Small business banking : assessing needs and establishing strategies / by Management Advisory Services, Inc., Steven L. Cranfill, David A. Duryee, Mark D. Schmitz. Washington, D.C. (1120 Connecticut Ave. N.W., Washington, D.C.) : American Bankers Association, c1987. ix, 78 p. : ill. ; 28 cm. Bibliography: p. 72-78. LC Card 87-135069 DDC 332.1/753 19
1. Small business - United States - Finance. 2. Bank loans - United States. 3. Banks and banking - United States - Customer services. I. Duryee, David A. II. Schmitz, Mark D. III. Management Advisory Services (Seattle, Wash.). IV. American Bankers Association. V. Title.
HG4027.7 .C7 1987

Crano, William D., 1942- Selnow, Gary W. Planning, implementing, and evaluating targeted communication programs . New York , 1987. vi, 291 p. : ISBN 0-89930-208-4 (lib. bdg. : alk. paper) LC Card 86-30418 DDC 659.1 19
HD30.3 .S46 1987

Cravens, David W. Readings and cases in marketing management /. Homewood, Ill. , 1987. xv, 443 p. : ISBN 0-256-03161-4 (pbk.) LC Card 86-82585 DDC 658.8 19
HF5415.13 .R362 1987

Crawford, Bill, 1955- Fowler, Gene, 1950- Border radio . Austin, Tex. , c1987. p. cm. ISBN 0-87719-066-6 : LC Card 87-17975 DDC 384.54/53/09721 19
HE8699.M4 F68 1987

Crawford, Bill, 1929- Wray, William C. What every engineer should know about microcomputer systems design and debugging /. New York, N.Y. , c1984. ix, 183 p. : ISBN 0-8247-7160-5 LC Card 83-25204 DDC 001.64 19
QA76.6 .W73 1984 *NYPL [JSE 86-1632]*

Crawford, Edward K., 1933- A management guide to leveraged buyouts / Edward K. Crawford. New York : Wiley, c1987. x, 257 p. ; 24 cm. (Wiley professional banking and finance series, 0733-8945) Includes index. ISBN 0-471-83232-4 LC Card 86-32390 DDC 658.1/6 19
1. Leveraged buyouts. 2. Leveraged buyouts - Case studies. I. Title. II. Series.
HD2746.5 .C7 1987

Crawford, H. W. (Hollie W.), 1919- McDowell, M. C. (Milton C.), 1920- Math workbook for foodservice/lodging /. New York , c1988. v, 265 p. : ISBN 0-442-21872-9 (pbk.) : LC Card 87-15960 DDC 513/.93/024642 19
HF5695.5.F616 M317 1988

Crawford, Vincent P., 1950- International lending, long-term credit relationships, and dynamic contract theory / Vincent P. Crawford. Princeton, N.J. : International Finance Section, Dept. of Economics, Princeton University, [1987] c1986. 34 p. ; 23 cm. (Princeton studies in international finance, 0081-8070 . no. 59 (Mar. 1987)) Bibliography: p. 27-29. ISBN 0-88165-231-8 (pbk.) : LC Card 86-33743 DDC 336.3/435 19
1. Loans, Foreign. 2. Capital market. 3. Credit. 4. Contracts. I. Series: Princeton studies in international finance, no. 59. II. Title.
HG3891.5 .C7 1987

Cray at Chippewa Falls /. Friedlander, Lee. Minneapolis, Minn. (608 2nd Ave., S., Minneapolis 55402) , 1987. 96 p. : LC Card 86-73134
HD9696.C64 C734 1987

Cray Research, Inc.
Friedlander, Lee. Cray at Chippewa Falls /. Minneapolis, Minn. (608 2nd Ave., S., Minneapolis 55402) , 1987. 96 p. : LC Card 86-73134
HD9696.C64 C734 1987

CRAY RESEARCH, INC. - PICTORIAL WORKS.
Friedlander, Lee. Cray at Chippewa Falls /. Minneapolis, Minn. (608 2nd Ave., S., Minneapolis 55402) , 1987. 96 p. : LC Card 86-73134
HD9696.C64 C734 1987

Crazy business . Stai, Anette. Oslo , c1984. 146 p., [48] p. of plates : ISBN 82-09-10210-9 LC Card 85-160098
HD6073.M772 N677 1984

Create and deliver dynamite presentations /. Wall, William C. Huntsville, Ala. , c1987. p. cm. ISBN 0-938745-02-6 : LC Card 87-14130 DDC 658.8/5 19
HF5438.25 .W275 1987

Create the perfect sales piece . Bly, Robert W. New York , c1985. xii, 242 p. : ISBN 0-471-82525-5 (pbk.) : LC Card 85-12457 DDC 659.13/2 19
HF5823 .B635 1985 *NYPL [JLE 86-3454]*

Create your own career opportunities /. Dayhoff, Signe A. Andover, Mass. , c1987. x, 111 p. : ISBN 0-931790-75-1 : LC Card 86-26332 DDC 650.1/4 19
HF5549.5.C35 D38 1987

Creating a community association . Dowden, C. James. Washington, D.C. , Alexandria, Va. , 1986. vii, 76 p. : ISBN 0-87420-659-6 (pbk.) LC Card 86-50785 DDC 643/.2 19
HD7287.67.U5 C73 1986

Creating a community association. Dowden, C. James. Creating a community association . Washington, D.C. , Alexandria, Va. , 1986. vii, 76 p. : ISBN 0-87420-659-6 (pbk.) LC Card 86-50785 DDC 643/.2 19
HD7287.67.U5 C73 1986

Creating investor demand for company stock . Altman, Richard M. New York , c1988. p. cm. ISBN 0-89930-173-8 (lib. bdg. : alk. paper) LC Card 86-25566 DDC 332.6/42 19
HG4661 .A57 1988

Creating opportunities for change . White, Louise G. Boulder, Colo. , 1987. xvii, 283 p. : ISBN 1-555-87031-7 (lib. bdg.) : LC Card 87-4557 DDC 338.9/0068 19
HD75.8 .W47 1987

Creating the high performance team /. Buchholz, Steve. New York , c1987. xiii, 202 p. : ISBN 0-471-85672-X : LC Card 86-32623 DDC 658.4/02 19
HD66 .B82 1987a

The creation of wealth . Griffiths, Brian. Downers Grove, Ill. , c1984. 160 p. : ISBN 0-87784-566-2 (pbk.) : LC Card 85-5210 DDC 330.12/2 19
HB72 .G74 1984 *NYPL [JLD 86-3576]*

CREATIVE ABILITY IN BUSINESS - CONGRESSES.
Frontiers in creative and innovative management /. Cambridge, Mass. , 1985, c1986. xxv, 391 p. : ISBN 0-88730-057-X LC Card 85-15125 DDC 658.4 19
HD53 .F76 1986 *NYPL [JLE 86-3614]*

CREATIVE ABILITY IN BUSINESS - MANAGEMENT.
Wijvekate, M. L. (Maren L.) De tweede taakdimensie . Naarden , c1986. 343 p. : ISBN 90-6010-628-8 : LC Card 86-199762
HD53 .W55 1986

CREATIVE ABILITY IN BUSINESS - NETHERLANDS - MANAGEMENT.
Wijvekate, M. L. (Maren L.) De tweede taakdimensie . Naarden , c1986. 343 p. : ISBN 90-6010-628-8 : LC Card 86-199762
HD53 .W55 1986

The creative corporation /. Albrecht, Karl. Homewood, Ill. , c1987. x, 218 p. ; ISBN 0-87094-929-2 LC Card 86-51668 DDC 302.3/5 19
HD53 .A42 1987

Creative modelling with Lotus 1-2-3 /. Jackson, Mary, 1936- Chichester , New York , c1985. ix, 169 p. : ISBN 0-471-90796-0 (pbk.) LC Card 86-228784 DDC 005.36/9 19
HF5548.4.L67 J33 1985b

CREATIVE THINKING.
Adams, James L. The care and feeding of ideas . Reading, Mass. , 1986. xv, 223 p. : ISBN 0-201-10160-2 : LC Card 86-10895 DDC 153.3/5 19
BF408 .A3 1986 *NYPL [JFE 87-1553]*

Adams, James L. Conceptual blockbusting . Reading, Mass. , c1986. xi, 161 p. : ISBN 0-201-10149-1 LC Card 85-28722 DDC 153.4 19
BF441 .A28 1986 *NYPL [JFE 86-4947]*

Miller, Arthur I. Imagery in scientific thought . Boston , c1984. xiv, 355 p. : ISBN 0-8176-3196-8 LC Card 83-26649 DDC 502.8 19
Q175 .M628 1984 *NYPL [JSE 86-1114]*

Miller, Arthur I. Imagery in scientific thought . Cambridge, Mass. , 1986, c1984. xiv, 355 p. : ISBN 0-262-63104-0 (pbk.) : LC Card 85-23212 DDC 502.8 19
Q175 .M628 1986 *NYPL [JSE 87-67]*

Creativity / [edited by] A. Dale Timpe. New York, N.Y. : Facts on File Publications, c1987. xvi, 383 p. : ill. ; 23 cm. (The Art and science of business management . v. 4) Bibliography: p. 372-376. Includes index. ISBN 0-8160-1463-9 : LC Card 86-29320 DDC 650.1 19
1. Creative ability in business. I. Timpe, A. Dale. II. Series.
HD53 .C745 1987

Creativity and intuition in business . Harman, Willis W. Menlo Park, Calif. (333 Ravenswood Ave., Menlo Park 94025-3476) , c1985. 28 p. : LC Card 86-232128 DDC 658.4/09 19
HD53 .H37 1985

Creativity in services marketing : what's new, what works, what's developing / edited by M. Venkatesan, Diane M. Schmalensee, and Claudia Marshall. Chicago, IL : American Marketing Association, 1986. 175 p. : ill. ; 28 cm. (Proceedings series - American Marketing Association) Papers presented at AMA's Services Marketing Conference held in San Francisco, September 8-11, 1985. Includes bibliographies. ISBN 0-87757-179-1 (pbk.) LC Card 85-26785 DDC 658.8 19
1. Service industries - Congresses. 2. Marketing - Congresses. I. Venkatesan, M., 1936-. II. Schmalensee, Diane H. III. Marshall, Claudia. IV. American Marketing Association. V. Services Marketing Conference (4th : 1985 : San Francisco, Calif.).
HD9980.5 .C74 1986 *NYPL [JLF 86-1783]*

CRÈCHES (DAY NURSERIES) see **DAY CARE CENTERS.**

Crecimiento comercial y enriquecimiento burgués en la Valencia del siglo XVIII /. Franch Benavent, Ricardo, 1956- Valencia [1986?] 340 p. : ISBN 84-505-4154-9 LC Card 87-110614
HF3690.V3 F7 1986

El Crecimiento desigual en Centroamérica, 1950-2000. [Buenos Aires, Argentina] : Banco Interamericano de Desarrollo, Instituto para la Integración de América Latina, [between 1982 and 1986] 133 leaves ; 29 cm. Includes bibliographical references. LC Card 86-200824
1. Central America - Economic conditions - Regional disparities. 2. Central America - Economic integration. 3. Economic forecasting - Central America. I. Institute for Latin American Integration.
HC141 .C73 1982

El crecimiento desigual en Centroamérica (1950-2000) /. Mayorga Quirós, Román. México, D.F. , 1983. 125 p. : ISBN 968-12-0238-4 LC Card 85-242511
HC141 .M39 1983

Credibilidad de la política comercial /. Coloma C., Fernando. Santiago, Chile , 1986. 43 p. : LC Card 87-102077
HF1515 .C64 1986

CREDIT ADMINISTRATION. see **CREDIT MANAGEMENT.**

Le crédit agricole au Maroc, 1917-1977 /. Berrada, Abdelkader. [Rabat] , 1979. 264 p. ; LC Card 82-136521 DDC 332.7/1/0964 19
HG2051.M8 B47 1979

CREDIT, AGRICULTURAL. see **AGRICULTURAL CREDIT.**

CREDIT ALLOCATION. see **CREDIT CONTROL.**

Credit analysis : a special collection from the Journal of commercial bank lending. Philadelphia, Pa. : R. Morris Associates, c1987. 146 p. : ill. ; 23 cm. Includes bibliographical references. CONTENTS. - Credit analysis, tying it all together, part I ; Credit analysis, tying it all together, part II / Dennis C. Eisenreich -- A philosophical foundation for credit analysis / David B. Still -- Working capital theory revisited / Jeffey W. Miller -- Cash flow, the most critical issue of the 1980s / James E. Perry -- Cash flow from operations and liquidity analysis / Lyn M. Fraser -- Analyzing the quantity and quality of cash flow for long-term borrowing / Dev Strischek -- The recession-sensitive borrower / John R. Carter -- Examining personal financial statements / Christopher Volk -- Using tax returns as credit analysis tools / Maurice F. Claeys -- Break-even analysis and operating leverage / Dev Strischek -- More on break-even analysis / Venkatesan Srinivasan. ISBN 0-936742-38-0 (pbk.) : LC Card 86-28628 DDC 332.1/753/0685 19
1. Credit management. 2. Bank loans. 3. Cash flow. I. Robert Morris Associates. II. Journal of commercial bank lending.
HG1641 .C66 1987

Credit and collections problem solver . Andover, James J. New York, NY, U. S.A. , c1987. x, 175 p. : ISBN 0-86604-219-9 (pbk.) LC Card 87-156416 DDC 658.8/8 19
HG3751 .A53 1987

CREDIT - ARGENTINA - HISTORY - 20TH CENTURY.
García, Valeriano F. A critical inquiry into Argentine economic history, 1946-1970 /. New York , 1987. vi, 127 p. : ISBN 0-8240-1361-1 (alk. paper) : LC Card 87-7620 DDC 330.982/062 19
HG815 .G27 1987

CREDIT - AUSTRIA.
Pernsteiner, August W. Gestaltkonforme partnerschaftliche "Beteiligungs-" und "Kreditfinanzierung" von "Klein-" und "Mittelbetrieben" /. Wien , 1983. 355, xxx p. : ISBN 3-85369-536-1 LC Card 83-206156
HG4027.7 .P47 1983

Le crédit-bail . France. Conseil économique et social. [Paris] [1985] 90 p. in various pagings : LC Card 86-184049
HD39.4 .F73 1985

CREDIT - BELGIUM.
Verheirstraeten, A. Geld, krediet en intrest in de Belgische financiële sector /. Leuven , 1977. xxii, 337 p. : LC Card 78-345984
HG1055 .V47 ***NYPL [JLM 86-1310 nr.23]***

CREDIT - BRAZIL.
National Monetary Council (Brazil) Brazil-- money and credit programming in 1983 /. Brazil [1982] 38 p. ; LC Card 87-131446
HG835 .N36 1982

CREDIT - BRAZIL - ARAPIRACA REGION.
Estudo especial . Maceió, AL. , 1983. 174 leaves : LC Card 86-167829
HC189.A69 E88 1983

CREDIT - BRAZIL - SÃO PAULO (STATE) - HISTORY.
Saes, Flávio Azevedo Marques de, 1948- Crédito e bancos no desenvolvimento da economia paulista, 1850-1930 /. São Paulo , 1986. 238 p. : LC Card 87-144659 DDC 332.1/0981/61 19
HG2889.S25 S24 1986

CREDIT BUREAUS.
Büchner, Robert. Grundzüge der Finanzanalyse /. München , c1981. x, 426 p. : ISBN 3-8006-0885-5 LC Card 82-156543
HF5693.G47 B83 1981

Lehner, Susanna Walpurga. Unternehmensanalyse . Wien , c1984. 243 p. : ISBN 3-85428-023-8 : LC Card 84-173011
HG3751.5 .L44 1984

CREDIT BUREAUS - GERMANY, WEST.
Heno, Rudolf. Kreditwürdigkeitsprüfung mit Hilfe von Verfahren der Mustererkennung /. Bern , c1983. vi, 317 p. : ISBN 3-258-03245-9 : LC Card 83-228668
HG1526 .B27 Bd. 81 HG3751.9.G3

CREDIT - CANADA - MANAGEMENT.
Hatch, James E. Canadian commercial lending . Toronto , New York , c1986. ix, 262 p. : ISBN 0-458-80270-0 : LC Card 87-130576 DDC 332.1/753/0685 19
HG3754.5.C2 H38 1986

CREDIT CARDS - DENMARK.
Rapport om betalingskort . [Copenhagen] [1982] 302, 4, 17 p. ; ISBN 87-503-4413-7 LC Card 83-243151
HG3756.D4 R36 1982

CREDIT CARDS - GERMANY, WEST.
Beck, Peter. Einwendungen bei Eurocheque und Kreditkarte /. [S.l. , 1986] (Köln : Druck und Verarbeitung, Druck- + Verlagshaus Wienand) xv, 146, 31 p. ; LC Card 86-233484
HG3756.G3 B43 1986

CREDIT CARDS - GREAT BRITAIN.
Frazer, P. A. T. Plastic and electronic money . Cambridge [Cambridgeshire] , Dover, NH. USA , 1985. x, 294 p. ; ISBN 0-85941-290-3 : LC Card 85-22552 DDC 332.1/028 19
HG1710 .F73 1985 ***NYPL [JLE 86-1401]***

CREDIT - CHILE - ECONOMETRIC MODELS.
Valenzuela Cornejo, Ignacio. Costo real del crédito en 1984 /. Santiago , 1985. 28 p. ; LC Card 86-106375 DDC 332.7/0983 19
HG3729.C52 V35 1985

CREDIT - COLOMBIA - STATISTICS.
Hacienda y crédito público . [Bogotá, Colombia] [1986] 94 p. : LC Card 87-404281 DDC 336.861 19
HJ2083 .H33 1986

Credit contracts, collateral-based security agreements, and bankruptcy /. Drukarczyk, Jochen. Regensburg [1983?] 25 leaves ; LC Card 84-181506 DDC 332.7/5/0943 19
HG3769.G34 D78 1983

CREDIT CONTROL.
Dierkes, Friedhelm. Die Kreditüberwachung im Bankbetrieb . Berlin , c1986. 139 p. : ISBN 3-428-05987-5 LC Card 86-161146
HG3705 .D54 1986

CREDIT CONTROL - BRAZIL.
Lemgruber, Antonio Carlos. O controle da base monetária e as flutuações dos multiplicadores monetários e creditícios /. [Brasília] [1981?] 118 p. : LC Card 85-154853
HG835 .L35 1981

CREDIT CONTROL - DEVELOPING COUNTRIES.
Gylfason, Thorvaldur. Credit policy and economic activity in developing countries with IMF stabilization programs /. Princeton, N.J. , c1987. 44 p. ; ISBN 0-88165-232-6 (pbk.) : LC Card 87-3389 DDC 332.7/09172/4 19
HG3711.D48 G94 1987

CREDIT CONTROL - MATHEMATICAL MODELS.
Eichberger, Jürgen, 1952- Geld und Kredit in einer Ökonomie mit festen Preisen . Frankfurt am Main , New York , c1984. 152 p. : ISBN 3-8204-5441-1 LC Card 85-191492
HG230.3 .E53 1984

CREDIT CONTROL - UNITED STATES.
Bosworth, Barry, 1942- The economics of federal credit programs /. Washington, D.C. , c1987. xii, 214 p. : ISBN 0-8157-1038-0 : LC Card 85-48205 DDC 336.3/44/0973 19
HJ8119 .B67 1987

CREDIT COOPERATIVES. see **BANKS AND BANKING, COOPERATIVE.**

CREDIT - DICTIONARIES - RUSSIAN.
Finansovo-kreditnyĭ slovar′ /. Moskva , 1984- v. ; LC Card 84-203984
HG151 .F53 1984 ***NYPL [*QAC 85-1247]***

CREDIT - DOMINICAN REPUBLIC.
Mercados financieros y distribución del ingreso /. Santo Domingo, República Dominicana , 1986. 117 p. : LC Card 87-405027 DDC 332.1/097293 19
HG185.D65 M47 1986

CREDIT - EUROPE, EASTERN.
Belichenko, A. N. (Al′bert Nikolaevich) Kreditnye otnoshenii͡a mezhdu stranami-chlenami SĖV /. Moskva , 1983. 134 p. : LC Card 84-171632
HG3729.E932 B45 1983

CREDIT - EUROPEAN ECONOMIC COMMUNITY COUNTRIES.
Seminario sobre Consequencias para las Entidades Oficiales de Crédito de la Entrada de España en las Comunidades Europeas (1984 : Madrid, Spain) Seminario sobre Consequencias para las Entidades Oficiales de Crédito de la Entrada de España en las Comunidades Europeas /. [Madrid] [1984?] 270 p. ; ISBN 84-505-0963-7 LC Card 85-186710
HG1642.E86 S46 1984

CREDIT, EXPORT. see **EXPORT CREDIT.**

CRÉDIT FONCIER. see **AGRICULTURAL CREDIT.**

CREDIT - GERMANY, WEST.
Drukarczyk, Jochen. Credit contracts, collateral-based security agreements, and bankruptcy /. Regensburg [1983?] 25 leaves ; LC Card 84-181506 DDC 332.7/5/0943 19
HG3769.G34 D78 1983

Duttle, Josef. Ökonomische Analyse dinglicher Sicherheiten . Krefeld , 1986. xvii, 417 p. : ISBN 3-88358-062-7 LC Card 87-104300
HG3711.G3 D87 1986

Kupitz, Rolf. Die Kreditwirtschaft als wettbewerbspolitischer Ausnahmebereich . Thun , c1983. 300 p. ; ISBN 3-87144-773-0 : LC Card 84-129435
HG3754.5.G3 K86 1983

Schwenk, Andreas. Die Kreditwürdigkeit der eingetragenen Genossenschaft /. Göttingen , c1984. xiv, 287 p. ; ISBN 3-525-12752-9 LC Card 86-139501
HG3711.G3 S36 1984

Zessin, Axel, 1953- Unternehmungsbewertung von Kreditinstituten /. Göttingen , 1982. 296 p. : ISBN 3-509-01313-1 LC Card 84-109138
HG4028.V3 Z47 1982

CREDIT - GERMANY (WEST) - ECONOMETRIC MODELS.
Christians, Uwe, 1957- Entwicklung und empirische Überprüfung eines konjunkturgerechten Erfolgsprognosemodells zur Unterstützung der Kreditwürdigkeitsprüfung . München , c1986. xiv, 412 p. : ISBN 3-88259-430-6 (Deut. Bibl.) LC Card 87-409324 DDC 332.7/0943 19
HG3754.5.G3 C48 1986

CREDIT - GREAT BRITAIN.
Blake, Hubert, 1893- Currency and credit before and since 1914 [microform] /. London , 1923. viii, 91 p. ; ***NYPL [*ZT-1736 no.1]***

CREDIT - GREAT BRITAIN - MANAGEMENT.
Crichton, Susan. Understanding factoring and trade credit /. London , 1986. xv, 199 p. : ISBN 0-08-039204-0 (pbk.) : LC Card 87-122377 DDC 658.8/8 19
HG3752.3 .C75 1986

CREDIT - GREECE - ATHENS - HISTORY.
Finley, M. I. (Moses I.), 1912- Studies in land and credit in ancient Athens, 500-200 B.C. . New Brunswick, U. S.A. , c1985. xli, 332 p. ; ISBN 0-88738-066-2 : LC Card 85-14091 DDC 333.3/0938/5 19
HD134 .F5 1985 ***NYPL [JLE 86-4293]***

Credit guarantee schemes for small and medium enterprises /. Levitsky, Jacob, 1924- Washington, D.C. , 1987. vi, 91 p. ; ISBN 0-8213-0866-1 (pbk.) LC Card 86-32571 DDC 658.8/7 19
HG9977 .L48 1987

CREDIT GUIDES.
Lehner, Susanna Walpurga. Unternehmensanalyse . Wien , c1984. 243 p. : ISBN 3-85428-023-8 : LC Card 84-173011
HG3751.5 .L44 1984

CREDIT GUIDES - GERMANY (WEST)
Heno, Rudolf. Kreditwürdigkeitsprüfung mit Hilfe von Verfahren der Mustererkennung /. Bern , c1983. vi, 317 p. : ISBN 3-258-03245-9 : LC Card 83-228668
HG1526 .B27 Bd. 81 HG3751.9.G3

CREDIT - INDIA.
Ramachandra Rao, B. All about priority sector advances /. New Delhi , 1984. 350 p. : LC Card 84-901313 DDC 332.7/0954 19
HG3729.I42 R36 1984 ***NYPL [JLD 87-574]***

CREDIT - INDIA - VADODARA.
Agrawal, R. B. L. Financing of the urban poor & small borrowers by commercial banks . Baroda , 1983. 108 p. ; LC Card 83-906426 DDC 332.1/753/095475 19
HG1642.I5 A38 1983 ***NYPL [JLD 86-4318]***

CREDIT - INFORMATION SERVICES. see **CREDIT BUREAUS.**

CREDIT - ITALY.
Allegri, Vincenzo. Credito di scopo e finanziamento bancario delle imprese /. Milano [1984] 166 p. ; ISBN 88-14-00299-1 : LC Card 85-187365 DDC 332.7/0945 19
HG1642.I8 A44 1984 ***NYPL [JLE 86-3661]***

Bagella, Michele. Gli istituti di credito speciale e il mercato finanziario, 1947-1962 /. Milano, Italy , c1986. 289 p. ; LC Card 86-232526
HG3729.I7 B34 1986

Caselli, Mario, 1944- La gestione marketing nella banca . Milano [1977] 332 p. : LC Card 77-553379
HG1616.M3 C37 ***NYPL [JLD 80-3228]***

CREDIT - ITALY - ADDRESSES, ESSAYS, LECTURES.
Il Leasing e il mercato del credito in Italia /. [Milano] [1984] iv, 82 p. : ISBN 88-14-00263-0 (pbk.) : LC Card 84-250907
HD39.4 .L37 1984 ***NYPL [JLE 87-509]***

Per una ristrutturazione e riconversione dell'industria italiana /. Bologna , 1980. 244 p. ; LC Card 82-102594 DDC 338.945 19
HD3616.I83 P43 ***NYPL [JLD 86-599]***

CREDIT - ITALY - EMILIA-ROMAGNA - STATISTICS.
I Conti finanziari dell'Emilia-Romagna /. [Bologna] , c1984. 157 p. : ISBN 88-15-00522-6 : LC Card 84-235593 DDC 332.1/0945/4 19
HG3089.E45 C66 1984
NYPL [JLE 86-3198]

CREDIT - ITALY - HISTORY - 20TH CENTURY.
Ciocca, Pierluigi, 1941- Interesse e profitto . Bologna , c1982. 245 p. : LC Card 84-139966 DDC 332/.0945 19
HG186.I8 C56 1982

CREDIT - LAW AND LEGISLATION - GERMANY (WEST)
Drukarczyk, Jochen. Credit contracts, collateral-based security agreements, and bankruptcy /. Regensburg [1983?] 25 leaves ; LC Card 84-181506 DDC 332.7/5/0943 19
HG3769.G34 D78 1983

Duttle, Josef. Ökonomische Analyse dinglicher Sicherheiten . Krefeld , 1986. xvii, 417 p. : ISBN 3-88358-062-7 LC Card 87-104300
HG3711.G3 D87 1986

Kupitz, Rolf. Die Kreditwirtschaft als wettbewerbspolitischer Ausnahmebereich . Thun , c1983. 300 p. ; ISBN 3-87144-773-0 : LC Card 84-129435
HG3754.5.G3 K86 1983

Schwenk, Andreas. Die Kreditwürdigkeit der eingetragenen Genossenschaft /. Göttingen , c1984. xiv, 287 p. ; ISBN 3-525-12752-9 LC Card 86-139501
HG3711.G3 S36 1984

CREDIT - LAW AND LEGISLATION - ITALY.
Allegri, Vincenzo. Credito di scopo e finanziamento bancario delle imprese /. Milano [1984] 166 p. ; ISBN 88-14-00299-1 : LC Card 85-187365 DDC 332.7/0945 19
HG1642.I8 A44 1984 ***NYPL [JLE 86-3661]***

La Riforma della legge bancaria . Milano [1984] 283 p. ; ISBN 88-14-00126-X : LC Card 84-190853 DDC 346.45/082 344.50682 19
LAW ***NYPL [JLE 86-3654]***

CREDIT - LAW AND LEGISLATION - ITALY - CONGRESSES.
Convegno C.I.D.I.S. (1980 : Iesolo, Italy) Credito e finanziarie regionali . Padova , c1983. vi, 148 p. ; LC Card 85-215231
HG3729.I72 C66 1980

CRÉDIT LYONNAIS - HISTORY.
Morin, Jean, 1875-1969. Souvenirs d'un banquier français . Paris , c1983. 326 p., [8] p. of plates : ISBN 2-207-22988-2 : LC Card 84-172168
HG1552.M67 A3 1983

CREDIT MANAGEMENT.
Andover, James J. Credit and collections problem solver . New York, NY, U. S.A. , c1987. x, 175 p. : ISBN 0-86604-219-9 (pbk.) LC Card 87-156416 DDC 658.8/8 19
HG3751 .A53 1987

Bathory, Alexander. The analysis of credit . London , New York , c1987. xiii, 385 p. ; ISBN 0-07-084938-2 : LC Card 87-2060 DDC 658.8/8 19
HG3751 .B385 1987

Bukics, Rosie L. The handbook of credit and accounts receivable management /. Chicago, Ill. , c1987. xi, 252 p. : ISBN 0-917253-67-1 : LC Card 87-7008 DDC 658.8/8 19
HG3751 .B85 1987

Credit analysis . Philadelphia, Pa. , c1987. 146 p. : ISBN 0-936742-38-0 (pbk.) : LC Card 86-28628 DDC 332.1/753/0685 19
HG1641 .C66 1987

Crichton, Susan. Understanding factoring and trade credit /. London , 1986. xv, 199 p. : ISBN 0-08-039204-0 (pbk.) : LC Card 87-122377 DDC 658.8/8 19
HG3752.3 .C75 1986

Franchini, Augusto. Le aziende di credito . Bologna , <1986-. v. <2 > ; LC Card 87-170318
HG3751 .F73 1986

La Gestione degli istituti di credito industriale /. Milano [1985] xviii, 868 p. : ISBN 88-14-00665-2 : LC Card 86-170383
HG3726 .G47 1985

Griffin, Paul A. Usefulness to investors and creditors of information provided by financial reporting /. Stamford, Conn. , c1987. xii, 294 p. ; ISBN 0-910065-24-1 (pbk.) LC Card 87-81637 DDC 657/.3 19
HF5681.B2 G79 1987

CREDIT - MATHEMATICAL MODELS.
Nowak, Felicitas. The allocation of bank credit and the efficiency of investment /. Göttingen, Rep. Fed. de Alemania [1986] 23 p. : LC Card 87-121215 DDC 332.7/0724 19
HG1641 .N68 1986

CREDIT - PANAMA.
Conte Porras, J. El crédito, la banca y la moneda panameña /. Panamá, Panamá , 1983. 204 p. : ***NYPL [JLE 86-3126]***

CREDIT - PERU.
Zúñiga A., Remigio. Banca nacional /. Chimbote, Perú , c1986. 478 p. ; LC Card 87-403541 DDC 332.1/0985 19
HG2944 .Z86 1986

Credit policy and economic activity in developing countries with IMF stabilization programs /. Gylfason, Thorvaldur. Princeton, N.J. , c1987. 44 p. ; ISBN 0-88165-232-6 (pbk.) : LC Card 87-3389 DDC 332.7/09172/4 19
HG3711.D48 G94 1987

Credit policy of the firm and issues in cost of financing accounts receivable . Walia, Tirlochan S. Lake Success, N.Y. (3000 Marcus Ave., Lake Success 11042) , c1986. [16] p. : LC Card 86-212977 DDC 658.1/5244 19
HG3752.3 .W35 1986

CREDIT - SOVIET UNION.
Braginskiĭ, L. V. (Lev Vol′fovich) Ėffektivnost′ kapital′nykh vlozheniĭ i bankovskaia deiatel′nost′ /. Moskva , 1981. 186 p. ; LC Card 82-144216
HG186.S55 B72 1981

Denezhnoe obrashchenie i kredit SSSR /. Moskva , 1986. 374 p. : LC Card 87-157773
HG3729.S632 D46 1986

Konnik, I. I. (Iosif Isaakovich) Denezhnoe obrashchenie v protsesse rasshirennogo sotsialisticheskogo vosproizvodstva /. Moskva , 1982. 269 p. ; LC Card 83-165373
HG186.S55 K65 1982

Organizatsiia i planirovanie kredita i denezhnogo obrashcheniia /. Moskva , 1984. 350 p. ; LC Card 85-108172
HG3729.S632 O74 1984

CREDIT - SOVIET UNION - CONGRESSES.
Rol′ finansovo-kreditnogo mekhanizma v povyshenii ėffektivnosti obshchestvennykh zatrat . Moskva , 1984. 153 p. ; LC Card 86-113408
HG186.S55 R64 1984

Sbalansirovannost′ sotsialisticheskoĭ ėkonomiki i finansovo-kreditnyĭ mekhanizm /. Moskva , 1984. 108 p. ; LC Card 85-240300
HG186.S55 S27 1984

CREDIT - SWITZERLAND - MANAGEMENT.
Zellweger, Bruno. Ueberwachung kommerzieller Bankkredite /. Bern , c1983. xx, 330 p. : ISBN 3-258-03246-7 : LC Card 83-214274
HG1526 .B27 Bd. 77 HG1642.S95

Credit union membership study, 1986 /. Ricke, Keith G. St. Paul, Minn. [c1987] 72 leaves : LC Card 87-154030 DDC 334/.22 19
HG2037 .R54 1987

CREDIT UNIONS - BARBADOS - DIRECTORIES.
Blondel, Eaulin. Credit unions, co-operatives, trade unions, and friendly societies in Barbados . St. Augustine, Trinidad, Trinidad and Tobago [1986] v, 102 p. ; LC Card 87-403330 DDC 334/.025/72981 19
HD3464.9.A6 B353 1986

Credit unions, co-operatives, trade unions, and friendly societies in Barbados . Blondel, Eaulin. St. Augustine, Trinidad, Trinidad and Tobago [1986] v, 102 p. ; LC Card 87-403330 DDC 334/.025/72981 19
HD3464.9.A6 B353 1986

CREDIT UNIONS - MALAWI - EVALUATION.
Dublin, Jack. Mid-term evaluation of the Malawi Union of Savings and Credit Co-operatives Project (612-0205) /. Lilongwe, Malawi , 1983. x, 84, [29] leaves ; LC Card 85-981350 DDC 334/.22/096897 19
HG2039.M29 D83 1983

CREDIT UNIONS - UNITED STATES.
Ricke, Keith G. Credit union membership study, 1986 /. St. Paul, Minn. [c1987] 72 leaves : LC Card 87-154030 DDC 334/.22 19
HG2037 .R54 1987

CREDIT UNIONS - UNITED STATES - PUBLIC OPINION.
How consumers view credit unions . New York, NY (1 Penn Plaza, Suite 1631, New York 10119) , c1986. 37, 7 leaves, [166] p. ; LC Card 87-111937 DDC 334/.22/0973 19
HG2037 .H68 1986

CREDIT - UNITED STATES.
Davis, John A., 1947- A look at the credit approval process /. Philadelphia, Pa. , c1987. 55 p. : ISBN 0-936742-36-4 (pbk.) LC Card 86-23855 DDC 332.7 19
HG1642.U5 D38 1987

CREDIT - UNITED STATES - MANAGEMENT.
Haley, Stephen W. Effective credit management in the equipment leasing and finance industry /. Arlington, VA , c1986. ix, 121 p. : ISBN 0-912413-01-8 (pbk.) LC Card 87-105306 DDC 658.1/5242 19
HD39.4 .H35 1986

CREDIT - URUGUAY.
González, José I. (José Iván), 1944- La segmentación del mercado del crédito y sus impactos sobre la distribución del ingreso /. Montevideo, Uruguay , 1984. ii, 5, 123 p. : LC Card 85-236586
HG3754.5.U8 G66 1984

Credit where credit is due . Walker, Glen. New York , c1979. ix, 198 p. ; ISBN 0-03-042356-2 LC Card 79-4201 DDC 332.7/43
HG3756.U54 W34 ***NYPL [JLD 86-1388]***

CREDITANSTALT-BANKVEREIN (AUSTRIA) - HISTORY.
Spitzmüller, Alexander, 1862-1953. Memoirs of Alexander Spitzmüller, Freiherr von Harmersbach (1862-1953) . Boulder , New York , 1987. xi, 327 p., [5] p. of plates : ISBN 0-88033-124-0 LC Card 87-80511 DDC 332.3/2/0924 B 19
HG1552.S65 A3 1987

Credito di scopo e finanziamento bancario delle imprese /. Allegri, Vincenzo. Milano [1984] 166 p. ; ISBN 88-14-00299-1 : LC Card 85-187365 DDC 332.7/0945 19
HG1642.I8 A44 1984 ***NYPL [JLE 86-3661]***

Crédito e bancos no desenvolvimento da economia paulista, 1850-1930 /. Saes, Flávio

Azevedo Marques de, 1948- São Paulo , 1986. 238 p. : LC Card 87-144659 DDC 332.1/0981/61 19
HG2889.S25 S24 1986

Credito e finanziarie regionali . Convegno C.I.D.I.S. (1980 : Iesolo, Italy) Padova , c1983. vi, 148 p. ; LC Card 85-215231
HG3729.I72 C66 1980

Crédito y seguro agrícola . Tejada C., Frank A. Santo Domingo, República Dominicana , 1986. 104 p. : LC Card 87-400183 DDC 332.7/1/097293 19
HG2051.D6 T45 1986

Cremer, Hans Diedrich, 1910- Handbuch der Landwirtschaft und Ernährung in den Entwicklungsländern /. Stuttgart , c1982- v. : ISBN 3-8001-3059-9 (Bd. 1) LC Card 84-155503 DDC 338.1/09172/4 19
HD1417 .H24 1982 ***NYPL [JLL 86-257]***

Cremona e la sua provincia nell'Italia unita. Milano : A. Giuffrè, 1984. 2 v. : ill. ; 24 cm. At head of title: Camera di commercio, industria, artigianato e agricoltura, Cremona. Includes bibliographical references and indexes. CONTENTS. - v. 1. La storia economica / di Alberto Cova -- v. 2. Le fonti per la storia economica e sociale / di Sauro Medici. ISBN 88-14-00552-4 : LC Card 86-207553
1. Cremona (Italy) - Economic conditions. 2. Cremona (Italy : Province) - Economic conditions. I. Cova, Alberto. II. Medici, Sauro.
HC308.C74 C74 1984

CREMONA (ITALY : PROVINCE) - ECONOMIC CONDITIONS.
Cremona e la sua provincia nell'Italia unita. Milano , 1984. 2 v. : ISBN 88-14-00552-4 : LC Card 86-207553
HC308.C74 C74 1984

CREMONA (ITALY) - ECONOMIC CONDITIONS.
Cremona e la sua provincia nell'Italia unita. Milano , 1984. 2 v. : ISBN 88-14-00552-4 : LC Card 86-207553
HC308.C74 C74 1984

CRES monograph .
(no. 18) Land degradation . Cambridge [Cambridgeshire] , New York , c1987. p. cm. ISBN 0-521-34079-9 LC Card 87-13170 DDC 333.73/16 19
HD1036 .L36 1987

Crescimento ou economia estacionária. Daly, Herman E. [Salvador] [1983] 56 p. : LC Card 87-127979 DDC 338.9 19
HD85.S7 D35 1983

Cresheim management books.
Bencin, Richard L., 1935- Strategic telemarketing . Philadelphia, Pa., USA , c1987. xviii, 182 p. : ISBN 0-915601-02-8 LC Card 86-30057 DDC 658.8/5 19
HF5415.1265 .B46 1987

Crespo, Miguelina. Campesinas y políticos, 1986 . Santo Domingo, República Dominicana , 1986. 83 p. : LC Card 87-102259
HD6073.A292 D653 1986

Cresta, Jean-Paul. Théorie des marchés d'assurance / Jean-Paul Cresta ; préface Jean-Jacques Laffont. Paris : Economica, 1984. vii, 231 p. : ill. ; 24 cm. (Collection Approfondissement de la connaissance économique) Bibliography: p. [219]-225. ISBN 2-7178-0696-2 : LC Card 84-235141
1. Risk (Insurance) - Mathematical models. 2. Insurance - Mathematical models. 3. Equilibrium (Economics) - Mathematical models. I. Title.
HG8054.5 .C74 1984

Creşterea eficienţei mijloacelor circulante, cerinţă actuală /. Roşca, Teodor. Bucureşti , 1983. 234 p. : LC Card 84-152999
HG4028.W65 R67 1983 ***NYPL [JLD 87-49]***

Crête, Jean. Comportement électoral au Québec /. Chicoutimi, Québec, Canada , c1984. xv, 447 p. : ISBN 2-89105-063-0 LC Card 85-177886 DDC 324.9714 19
JL258 .C65 1984 ***NYPL [JLD 87-1351]***

CREUSE (FRANCE) - ECONOMIC CONDITIONS.
Bandy de Nalèche, Louis. Les Maçons de la Creuse /. Limoges , 1984. 99 p., [16] p. of plates : ISBN 2-85521-059-3 : LC Card 85-169794 DDC 331.7/69321/094468 19
HB2054.C74 B36 1984

CREUSE (FRANCE) - POPULATION - HISTORY.
Bandy de Nalèche, Louis. Les Maçons de la Creuse /. Limoges , 1984. 99 p., [16] p. of plates : ISBN 2-85521-059-3 : LC Card 85-169794 DDC 331.7/69321/094468 19
HB2054.C74 B36 1984

Crew, Michael. Boxhill, Walton O. 1981 Census information on place of birth, citizenship, and immigration . Ottawa , c1986. 67, [4] p. : ISBN 0-660-52864-9 (pbk.) : LC Card 86-192857
HA741.5 1981f

Crew, Michael A. Regulating utilities in an era of deregulation /. New York , 1987. xii, 201 p. : ISBN 0-312-00527-X : LC Card 86-29639 DDC 363.6/0973 19
HD2763 .R43 1987

Criação de empresas de alta tecnologia : capital de risco e os bancos de desenvolvimento / coordenador, Silvio Aparecido dos Santos. São Paulo : Instituto de Administração-FEA-USP : Banco de Desenvolvimento do Estado de São Paulo : 192, [1] p. ; 22 cm. (Coleção Novos umbrais) Bibliography: p. 191-[193]. LC Card 87-403991 DDC 338.4/362/000981 19
1. High technology industries - Brazil - Finance. 2. Venture capital - Brazil. 3. Development banks - Brazil. I. Santos, Silvio Aparecido dos. II. Universidade de São Paulo. Instituto de Administração. III. Banco de Desenvolvimento do Estado de São Paulo.
HC190.H53 C75 1987

Crichton, Susan. Understanding factoring and trade credit / Susan Crichton and Charles Ferrier. 1st ed. London : Waterlow, 1986. xv, 199 p. : ill. ; 21 cm. (Waterlow's business library) Bibliography: p. 187-189. Includes index. ISBN 0-08-039204-0 (pbk.) : LC Card 87-122377 DDC 658.8/8 19
1. Factoring (Finance). 2. Factoring (Finance) - Great Britain. 3. Credit management. 4. Credit - Great Britain - Management. 5. Factoring (Finance) - Law and legislation - Great Britain. I. Ferrier, Charles W. II. Title. III. Series.
HG3752.3 .C75 1986

CRIME AND CRIMINALS - ADDRESSES, ESSAYS, LECTURES.
Barbara Wootton--social science and public policy . London , New York , 1986. xi, 291 p. ; ISBN 0-422-79690-5 LC Card 85-27650 DDC 330 19
HB171 .B248 1985 ***NYPL [JLE 86-1743]***

CRIME AND CRIMINALS - CANADA - BIOGRAPHY.
Edwards, Peter, 1956- Waterfront warlord . Toronto, Ont., Canada , c1987. ix, 213 p. : ISBN 1-550-13013-7 : LC Card 87-150705 DDC 331.88/113875/0924 B 19
HD6525.B36 E39 1987

CRIME AND CRIMINALS - CONGRESSES.
The Reasoning criminal . New York , c1986. xiv, 246 p. : ISBN 0-387-96272-7 : LC Card 86-1275 DDC 364.3 19
HV6080 .R38 1986 ***NYPL [JLE 86-3522]***

CRIME AND CRIMINALS - ECONOMIC ASPECTS - SWEDEN.
Schuller, Bernd-Joachim. Ekonomi och kriminalitet . [Göteborg , 1986] ix, 250 p. : LC Card 86-212186
HB54 .G65 no. 17 HV6171

CRIME AND CRIMINALS - SWEDEN - NORRKÖPING - HISTORY - 19TH CENTURY.
Horgby, Björn. Den disciplinerade arbetaren . Stockholm [1986] 322 p. : ISBN 91-22-00804-7 LC Card 87-105821
HC378.N67 H67 1986

CRIME AND CRIMINALS - UNITED STATES.
Bennett, Georgette. Crimewarps . Garden City, N.Y. , 1987. xix, 435 p. ; ISBN 0-385-23090-7 : LC Card 86-10885 DDC 364/.973 19
HV6791 .B45 1987 ***NYPL [JLE 87-1261]***

Block, Alan A. Organizing crime /. New York, N.Y. , c1981. 238 p. ; ISBN 0-444-99079-8 LC Card 80-25099 DDC 364.1/06 19
HV6030 .B55 ***NYPL [JLE 86-4076]***

CRIME DETECTION. see **CRIMINAL INVESTIGATION.**

Crime e castigo da dívida externa /. Nery, Sebastião. Brasília-Distrito Federal [1986] 170 p. ; LC Card 86-208917
HJ8579 .N47 1986

CRIME FORECASTING - UNITED STATES.
Bennett, Georgette. Crimewarps . Garden City, N.Y. , 1987. xix, 435 p. ; ISBN 0-385-23090-7 : LC Card 86-10885 DDC 364/.973 19
HV6791 .B45 1987 ***NYPL [JLE 87-1261]***

CRIME PHOTOGRAPHY. see **PHOTOGRAPHY, LEGAL.**

CRIME SYNDICATES. see **ORGANIZED CRIME.**

El crimen del 15 de noviembre de 1922 /. Capelo C., J. Alejo (J. Alejo Capelo Cabello), d. 1973. [Guayaquil] , 1983. 10, 14, 19 p. : LC Card 86-114097
HD5358.A6 C36 1983

CRIMES, COMMERCIAL. see **COMMERCIAL CRIMES.**

The crimes of patriots . Kwitny, Jonathan. New York , c1987. 424 p., [8] p. of plates : ISBN 0-393-02387-7 : LC Card 87-22032 DDC 364.1/0994 19
HG3448.N846 K95 1987

Crimewarps . Bennett, Georgette. Garden City, N.Y. , 1987. xix, 435 p. ; ISBN 0-385-23090-7 : LC Card 86-10885 DDC 364/.973 19
HV6791 .B45 1987 ***NYPL [JLE 87-1261]***

CRIMINAL INVESTIGATION - ARAB COUNTRIES.
Tazwīr al-mustanadāt wa-tazyīf al-ʻumlāt wa-al-asālīb al-ʻilmīyah lil-kashf ʻanhā. [Cairo] [1978] 296 p., [1] leaf of plates : ISBN 977-7049-73-0 LC Card 79-961630
HG335 .T3 1978

CRIMINAL INVESTIGATION - INDIA.
India. Parliament. Committee on Public Undertakings. Action taken by Government on the recommendations contained in the sixteenth report of the Committee on Public Undertakings (Sixth Lok Sabha) on Jute Corporation of India Ltd. . New Delhi , 1979. vii, 82 p. ; LC Card 79-906770
HD9156.J8 I355 1979

CRIMINAL JUSTICE, ADMINISTRATION OF - ECONOMIC ASPECTS - SWEDEN.
Schuller, Bernd-Joachim. Ekonomi och kriminalitet . [Göteborg , 1986] ix, 250 p. : LC Card 86-212186
HB54 .G65 no. 17 HV6171

CRIMINAL PSYCHOLOGY - CONGRESSES.
The Reasoning criminal . New York , c1986. xiv, 246 p. : ISBN 0-387-96272-7 : LC Card 86-1275 DDC 364.3 19
HV6080 .R38 1986 ***NYPL [JLE 86-3522]***

CRIMINALS. see **CRIME AND CRIMINALS.**

CRIMINOLOGY. see **CRIME AND CRIMINALS.**

Criquillion, Ana. Revolución y mujeres del campo . Managua [1985] 46 p. : LC Card 86-231936
HD1333.N5 R48 1985

La Crise de l'endettement international : acte II : colloque du GRECO, CNRS, EFIQ. Paris : Economica, c1986. 410 p. : ill. ; 24 cm. (Collection Approfondissement de la connaissance économique) "Publié à l'initiative de Henri Bourguinat, Jacques Mistral." "L'ouvrage qu'on lira ci-après reprend le plus grand nombre des contributions présentées au troisième colloque du GRECO 'Economie et finances internationales quantitatives' organisés à Paris dans les locaux de L'ENSAE les 3 et 4 juillet 1985"--P. 3. Bibliography: p. [399]-406. Includes index. ISBN 2-7178-1127-3 : LC Card 86-222862
1. Debts, External - Congresses. 2. Loans, Foreign - Congresses. 3. International finance - Congresses. I. Bourguinat, Henri. II. Mistral, Jacques. III. GRECO CNRS EFIQ (Group).
HJ8017 .C74 1986

Crise de liquidité et gestion de la trésorerie dans les P.M.E. Genève, Suisse : Association pour la recherche économique dans les petites et moyennes entreprises, 1985. 32 p. : ill. ; 30 cm. (Cahier de recherche . 6) Cover title. Bibliography: p. 32. LC Card 87-138138
1. Small business - Finance. 2. Small business - Cash position. I. Series: Cahier de recherche (Association pour la recherche économique dans les petites et

moyennes entreprises (Switzerland)) , 6.
HG4027.7 .C75 1985

La crise des motivations /. Lévy-Leboyer, Claude. Paris , c1984. 135 p. ; ISBN 2-13-038772-1 : LC Card 85-115430
HF5549.5.M63 L47 1984

A crise do desenvolvimento, uma estratégia para o futuro /. Langoni, Carlos Geraldo. Rio de Janeiro , 1985. xix, 176 p. : ISBN 85-03-00001-6 : LC Card 85-151246 DDC 338.981 19
HG835 .L36 1985 ***NYPL [JLD 86-288]***

A crise do petróleo e a economia brasileira /. O'Keefe, Hsu Yuet Heung. São Paulo , 1984. 137 p. : LC Card 85-143617 DDC 338.2/3 19
HD9574.B82 O43 1984
NYPL [JLD 86-2712]

A crise econômica e o flagelo do desemprego /. Serra, José. São Paulo , 1984. 27 p. : LC Card 87-124054 DDC 331.13/704 19
HD5708.47.B6 S47 1984

Crise et pauvreté en Afrique.
Gozo, K. M. Crise et pauvreté en Côte d'Ivoire . Addis Abéba , c1983. iv, 84 p. ; ISBN 92-2-203648-4 LC Card 85-981192
HC1025 .G69 1983

Gozo, K. M. Effets de la récession sur l'économie togolaise . Addis Abéba , 1985. 50, 24 p. ; ISBN 92-2-205044-4 LC Card 86-159834 DDC 330.966/8104 19
HC1015 .G69 1985

Mamder, Josué Sandjiman. Les effets de la crise mondiale actuelle sur l'économie et la population gabonaises /. Addis Abéba , c1984. 34 p. ; ISBN 92-2-203795-2 LC Card 86-215256
HC975 .M36 1984

Crise et pauvreté en Côte d'Ivoire . Gozo, K. M. Addis Abéba , c1983. iv, 84 p. ; ISBN 92-2-203648-4 LC Card 85-981192
HC1025 .G69 1983

CRISES AND PANICS. see **DEPRESSIONS.**

CRISES, COMMERCIAL. see **DEPRESSIONS.**

Crisi di impresa . Masciocchi, Giuseppe. Milano , 1983. viii, 112 p. ; LC Card 84-141092 DDC 657/.73 19
HD2747 .M37 1983 ***NYPL [JLE 86-4053]***

Crisi e risanamento delle imprese /. Guatri, Luigi. Milano , 1986. viii, 339 p. : ISBN 88-14-00914-7 : LC Card 86-228719
HD58.8 .G82 1986

Crisi e ristrutturazione dell'industria siderurgica italiana /. Moro, Domenico. [Milano] [1984] 256 p. : LC Card 84-181172 DDC 338.4/76691/0945 19
HD9525.I82 M67 1984
NYPL [JLE 86-3649]

Le Crisi finanziarie / a cura di Giancarlo Martinengo e Pietro Carlo Padoan. Bologna : Il Mulino, c1985. 348 p. : ill. ; 22 cm. (Problemi e prospettive. Serie di economia) Bibliography: p. 345-348. ISBN 88-15-00807-1 : LC Card 85-201934 DDC 332.1 19
1. Banks and banking - Case studies. 2. Financial institutions - Case studies. 3. Bank investments - Case studies. 4. Bank failures - Case studies. 5. Business cycles - Case studies. I. Martinengo, Giancarlo. II. Padoan, Pietro Carlo. III. Series.
HG1591 .C75 1985

Crisis accountability and development in the Third World . Ghartey, J. B., 1944- Aldershot, Hants, England , Brookfield, Vt., USA , c1987. x, 170 p. ; ISBN 0-566-05290-3 : LC Card 86-25777 DDC 338.91/096 19
HC800 .G52 1987

Crisis and critique . Sixel, Friedrich W. Leiden , New York , 1987. p. cm. ISBN 90-04-08284-0 (pbk.) : LC Card 87-17217 DDC 330.12/2 19
HB501 .S618 1987

Crisis and reform in socialist economies / edited by Peter Gey, Jiří Kosta, and Wolfgang Quaisser. Boulder : Westview Press, 1987. xi, 196 p. ; 23 cm. (Westview special studies in international economics) Based on papers presented at an international conference held in Freudenberg, Oct. 3-5, 1986. Includes bibliographies. ISBN 0-8133-7332-8 (pbk. : alk. paper) : LC Card 86-32602 DDC 338.9/009171/7 19
1. Communist countries - Economic policy. 2. Economic forecasting - Communist countries. 3. Communist countries - Economic conditions. I. Gey, Peter. II. Kosta, H. G., Jiří, 1921-. III. Quaisser, Wolfgang, 1955-.
HC704 .C75 1987

La crisis de Costa Rica /. Rovira Mas, Jorge, 1950- San José, Costa Rica , 1986. 175 p. ; LC Card 87-125520 DDC 338.97286 19
HC143 .R667 1986

Crisis de identidad y centralidad minera . Lazarte, Jorge. [La Paz, Bolivia] [1986] 37 p. : LC Card 87-401455 DDC 331.88/122/0984 19
HD8039.M61 B586 1986

La crisis de la deuda en América Latina /. Rey Salgado, Rafael del. [Spain] [1985] ii, 88 p. ; LC Card 86-131407
HJ8514.5 .R49 1985

La Crisis de la economía ecuatoriana : elementos para su interpretación. Quito : Corporación Editora Nacional, 1986. 232 p. : ill. ; 22 cm. (Biblioteca de ciencias sociales. v. 12) Papers presented at the V Encuentro de Historia y Realidad Económica y Social del Ecuador held in Cuenca on November 17-21, 1986, organized by the Instituto de Investigaciones Sociales de la Universidad de Cuenca. Includes bibliographical references. LC Card 87-400395 DDC 330.9866/074 19
1. Ecuador - Economic conditions - 1972- - Congresses. I. Corporación Editora Nacional (Quito, Ecuador). II. Encuentro de Historia y Realidad Económica y Social del Ecuador (5th : 1986 : Cuenca, Ecuador). III. Universidad de Cuenca. Instituto de Investigaciones Sociales. IV. Series: Biblioteca de ciencias sociales (Quito, Ecuador) , v. 12.
HC202 .C755 1986

La crisis del desarrollo argentino . Prebisch, Raúl. Buenos Aires , c1986. 195 p. ; ISBN 950-0-26293-2 LC Card 86-229773
HC180.S3 P74 1986

La crisis del empresariado nacional /. Abusada-Salah, Roberto. [Lima] [1983] 41 p. ; LC Card 84-236119
HC227 .A57 1983

Crisis económica. Causas y manejo de la crisis económica dominicana, 1974-1984 /. Santo Domingo, República Dominicana , 1986. 184 p. : LC Card 86-208551
HC153.5 .C385 1986

Crisis económica . Flecha, Agustín Oscar. [Asunción] [1987] 65 p. ; LC Card 87-404003 DDC 331.2/3/09892 19
HD4920.P2 F57 1987

Crisis económica mundial, 1974-1975 . Alvarado U., Hernán (Alvarado Ugarte) Heredia, Costa Rica , 1980. 62 p. ; LC Card 87-402100 DDC 330.9/047 19
HC59 .A765 1980

Las Crisis económicas en la historia del Perú / Heraclio Bonilla, editor ; [Efraín Trelles ... et al.]. 1era. ed. [Lima, Perú] : Centro Latinoamericano de Historia Económica y Social ; [s.l.] : Fundación Friedrich Ebert, 1986. 376 p. : ill. ; 21 cm. Contains papers from the Primer Congreso Nacional de Investigación Histórica, held on Nov. 11-16, 1984 in Lima and sponsored by the Consejo Nacional de Ciencia y Tecnología. Includes bibliographies. LC Card 87-400306 DDC 330.985 19
1. Peru - Economic conditions. I. Bonilla, Heraclio. II. Trelles Aréstegui, Efraín. III. Consejo Nacional de Ciencia y Tecnología (Peru). IV. Congreso Nacional de Investigación Histórica (1st : 1984 : Lima, Peru?).
HC227 .C744 1986

La crisis financiera en México /. Dávila Flores, Alejandro, 1956- [Mexico City, Mexico] , 1986. 228 p. : LC Card 87-401258 DDC 330.972/0834 19
HG185.M6 D33 1986

Crisis financiera y endeudamiento externo en la Argentina /. Feldman, Ernesto V. (Ernesto Víctor) [Buenos Aires] , c1986. 184 p. ; ISBN 950-25-1313-4 LC Card 86-182663
HG185.A7 F45 1986

Crisis henequenera y movimientos campesinos en Yucatán, 1966-1983 /. Villanueva, Eric. México, D.F. , 1985. 220 p., [10] p. of plates : ISBN 968-603-803-5 LC Card 86-118134 DDC 304.8/0972/65 19
HD9156.H463 M67 1985
NYPL [JLD 87-342]

The crisis in African agriculture /. Gakou, Mohamed Lamine. [Crise de l'agriculture africaine. English.] London ; Atlantic Highlands, N.J., USA : xii, 100 p. ; ISBN 0-86232-732-6 : LC Card 87-13355 DDC 338.1/096 19
HD2117 .G3513 1987

Crisis in Bethlehem . Strohmeyer, John, 1924- New York, N.Y., U. S.A. , 1987, c1986. xii, 244 p. ; ISBN 0-14-010370-8 (pbk.) LC Card 87-11835 DDC 338.7/669142/0974822 19
HD9519.B4 S87 1987

Crisis internacionales y economía nacional . Daremblum, Jaime. San José, Costa Rica , 1982. 62 p. ; LC Card 84-247158
HC143 .D36 1982

CRISIS MANAGEMENT.
Bridges, William, 1933- Surviving corporate transition . New York , 1988. xii, 227 p. ; ISBN 0-385-23761-8 : LC Card 87-19978 DDC 658.4/06 19
HD31 .B7395 1988

CRISIS MANAGEMENT - GERMANY (WEST)
Müller, Rainer, 1953- Krisenmanagement in der Unternehmung . Frankfurt am Main , New York , c1986. xxvii, 773 p. : ISBN 3-8204-7479-X LC Card 87-409055 DDC 658.4 19
HD49 .M84 1986

CRISIS MANAGEMENT - ITALY.
Guatri, Luigi. Crisi e risanamento delle imprese /. Milano , 1986. viii, 339 p. : ISBN 88-14-00914-7 : LC Card 86-228719
HD58.8 .G82 1986

The crisis of American labor . Griffith, Barbara S. Philadelphia , 1988. xvi, 239 p. : ISBN 0-87722-503-6 (alk. paper) : LC Card 87-9998 DDC 331.88/33/0975 19
HD8055.C75 G75 1988

A crisis of the welfare state? . Hadenius, Axel, 1945- Stockholm, Sweden , c1986. 151 p. : ISBN 91-22-00821-7 (pbk.) : LC Card 87-127805 DDC 339.5/22/09485 19
HJ2837 .H34 1986

Crisis oligarquía y latifundio . García Ponce, Antonio, 1929- Barquisimeto, Venezuela , 1986. 104 p., [1] folded leaf of plates : ISBN 980-608-701-1 : LC Card 87-134729 DDC 338.1/762/0098725 19
HF3490.C375 G37 1986

Crisis, producción y desarrollo . Najri, José Antonio, 1948- Santo Domingo, Repúblic Dominicana , 1986 (Santo Domingo, República Dominicana : Editora Corripio) ix, 248 p. ; LC Card 87-102092
HF1502 .N34 1986

Crisis, quién la provoca y a quién beneficia. Ideas para la cultura europea . Barcelona [1980?] 64 p. : ISBN 84-300-3210-X LC Card 85-105410
HC57 .I24 1980

Crisis y control de cambio / Armando Córdova ... [et al.]. 1a ed. Maracaibo, Venezuela : Editorial de la Universidad del Zulia, 1984. 101 p. ; 22 cm. (Colección Rafael María Baralt) Papers presented at a meeting organized by the Centro Programa de Estudios Latinoamericanos de la Universidad del Zulia, held in Maracaibo in May 1983. LC Card 87-400572 DDC 332.4/560987 19
1. Foreign exchange problem - Venezuela - Congresses. 2. Venezuela - Economic policy - Congresses. I. Córdova, Armando. II. Universidad del Zulia. Centro Programa de Estudios Latinoamericanos. III. Series.
HG3941 .C74 1984

Crisis y fluctuaciones en la economía peruana, 1950-1983 . Iguíñiz, Javier. Jesús María [Peru] [1985] 245 p. : LC Card 86-116792 DDC 338.5/42/0985 19
HB3779 .I35 1985 ***NYPL [JLC 86-268]***

Crisis y reorganización del capitalismo mexicano, 1960-1985 /. Rivera Ríos, Miguel Angel. México, D.F. , 1986. 227 p. : ISBN 968-411-149-5 LC Card 87-401541 DDC 330.972/083 19
HC135 .R435 1986

Crisis y situación política en República Dominicana /. Collado, Faustino, 1954- Santo Domingo, República Dominicana [1985] 69 p. ; LC Card 87-115929
HC153.5 .C65 1985

Cristofano, Sam M. Management of local public works /. Washington, D.C. , c1986. xvii, 402 p. : ISBN 0-87326-048-1 : LC Card 86-125 DDC 363/.068 19
HD4431 .M35 1986 *NYPL [JLF 86-1543]*

Cristol, Steven M. Barban, Arnold M. Essentials of media planning . Lincolnwood, Ill., U. S.A. , c1987. xii, 160 p. : ISBN 0-8442-3018-9 (pbk.) : LC Card 86-51055 DDC 659.1/11 19
HF5826.5 .B37 1987

Critchfield, Richard. The golden bowl be broken : peasant life in four cultures / Richard Critchfield.2nd ed. / with a new preface and afterword. Bloomington : Indiana University Press, 1988. p. cm. Originally published in 1973. ISBN 0-253-32554-4 LC Card 87-3690 DDC 305.5/63 19
1. Peasantry - Developing countries - Case studies. 2. Developing countries - Rural conditions - Case studies. 3. Villages - Developing countries - Case studies. 4. Agriculture - Developing countries - Case studies. I. Title.
HD1542 .C75 1988

Criteri per una cooperazione industriale con i paesi in via di sviluppo /. D'Angelo, Massimo. Milano , c1981. 294 p. ; ISBN 88-20-42145-3 : LC Card 82-113466
HF1549 .D36 1981 *NYPL [JLD 86-3318]*

Criteria for energy pricing policy . Energy Pricing Policy Workshop (1984 : Bangkok, Thailand) London , Gaithersburg, MD, USA , 1985. 247 p. : ISBN 0-86010-618-1 : LC Card 86-147259 DDC 333.79/17 19
HD9502.D442 E56 1984

Crítica de la economía y la política /. López Díaz, Pedro. México , 1985. 255 p. ; ISBN 968-590-060-4 LC Card 86-156378
HB501 .L856 1985

Critica dell'economia politica e teoria delle forze produttive /. Romitelli, Valerio. Milano , c1982. 241 p. ; LC Card 82-200332 DDC 338.5 19
HB241 .R66 1982 *NYPL [JLD 87-812]*

Una crítica puntual . Giraldo Valencia, Federico, 1950- Medellín , 1986. 204 p. ; LC Card 87-400327 DDC 338.9861 19
HC197 .G52 1986

A Critical appraisal of the economic and social conditions in the west African subregion / conducted by the Nigerian Institute of Social and Economic Research (NISER) Ivorian Centre for Economic and Social Research (CIRES) Rev. [Lagos : Economic Community of West African State, 1979-1980] 10 v. : ill. ; 33 cm. Cover title. CONTENTS. - [1] [without special title] -- [2] Population profile -- [3] Education and manpower development -- [4] Health -- [5] Industrial development -- [6] Review of river/lake basin development projects -- [7] Agricultural development, crops and livestock -- [8] Energy -- [9] International assistance -- [10] Other multilateral, bilateral, and special arrangements. LC Card 87-159535 DDC 330.966 19
1. Africa, West - Economic conditions. 2. Africa, West - Social conditions. I. Nigerian Institute of Social and Economic Research. II. Centre ivoirien de recherches économiques et sociales. III. Economic Community of West African States.
HC1000 .C75 1979

Critical employment issues facing the Southeast / edited by Bruce E. Kaufman, William T. Rutherford. Atlanta, Ga. : College of Business Administration, Georgia State University, 1986. xv, 156 p. ; 22 cm. (Research monograph . no. 98) Papers originally presented at a conference held at Georgia State University, Feb. 22, 1983. Includes bibliographical references. ISBN 0-88406-191-4 LC Card 85-31410 DDC 331.12/5/0975 19
1. Employment forecasting - Southern States - Congresses. 2. Foreign trade and employment - Southern States - Congresses. I. Kaufman, Bruce E. II. Rutherford, William T. III. Georgia State University. College of Business Administration.
HD5725.S85 C75 1986
NYPL [JLD 86-2441]

Critical human geography.
Corbridge, Stuart. Capitalist world development . London , 1986. xi, 295 p. : ISBN 0-333-32405-6 *NYPL [JLD 86-2925]*

Short, John R. The urban arena . London , 1984. viii, 202 p. : ISBN 0-333-36139-3 LC Card 87-672913
HC256.6 .S49x 1984

A critical inquiry into Argentine economic history, 1946-1970 /. García, Valeriano F. New York , 1987. vi, 127 p. : ISBN 0-8240-1361-1 (alk. paper) : LC Card 87-7620 DDC 330.982/062 19
HG815 .G27 1987

Critical issues in social justice.
Justice . New York , c1986. xii, 283 p. ; ISBN 0-306-42256-5 LC Card 86-20503 DDC 320/.01/1 19
JC578 .J89 1986 *NYPL [JLE 87-304]*

CRITICAL MATERIALS. see **STRATEGIC MATERIALS.**

Critical perspectives on housing / edited by Rachel G. Bratt, Chester Hartman, Ann Meyerson. Philadelphia : Temple University Press, 1986. xxi, 686 p. : ill. ; 24 cm. Includes index. Bibliography: p. 634-674. ISBN 0-87722-395-5 LC Card 85-17274 DDC 363.5/0973 19
1. Housing - United States - Addresses, essays, lectures. 2. Public housing - United States - Addresses, essays, lectures. 3. Labor and laboring classes - Dwellings - United States - Addresses, essays, lectures. I. Bratt, Rachel G., 1946-. II. Hartman, Chester W. III. Meyerson, Ann, 1949-.
HD7293 .C738 1986 *NYPL [JLE 86-3639]*

Critical social thought.
Valli, Linda, 1947- Becoming clerical workers /. Boston , 1986. xv, 261 p. ; ISBN 0-7102-0336-5 *NYPL [JLD 86-1147]*

CRITICISM (PHILOSOPHY)
Alvesson, Mats, 1956- [Organisationsteori och teknokratiskt medvetande. English.] Organization theory and technocratic consciousness . Berlin , New York , 1987. ix, 286 p. : ISBN 0-89925-165-X : LC Card 86-24057 DDC 306/.36 19
HD6955 .A44313 1987

Lloyd, Christopher, 1950- Explanation in social history /. Oxford, UK , New York, NY, USA , 1986. xi, 375 p. : ISBN 0-631-13113-2 : LC Card 85-13359 DDC 301/.09 19
HN28 .L58 1986 *NYPL [JLE 86-1677]*

Critique of Energy security, a report to the President of the United States by the U. S. Department of Energy /. Conant, Melvin. Washington, D.C., U. S.A. (1511 K St., NW, Suite #725, Washington 20005) , c1987. 23 leaves ; LC Card 87-401127 DDC 333.79/0973 19
HD9502.U52 C658 1987

Crittenden, Vicky L. Jazz : a case study / Vicky L. Crittenden. Reading, Mass. : Addison-Wesley Pub. Co., c1986. 62 p. : ill. ; 28 cm. ISBN 0-201-11365-1 (pbk.) LC Card 86-211796 DDC 658.8/0028/55369 19
1. Jazz (Computer program). 2. Selling - Computer programs. I. Title.
HF5439.C67 C75 1986

CRLA submission to the government of Canada /. Canadian Railway Labour Association. Ottawa [1977] 28, 31 p. ; LC Card 84-256714
HE2807 .C33 1977

CRM Productions.
Customer service [motion picture] . Del Mar, CA , 1985. 1 film reel (13 min.) : ISBN 0-07-620872-9 LC Card 86-708025 DDC 658.8 11
HF5415.5

Customer service [videorecording] . Del Mar, CA , 1985. 1 videocassette (13 min.) : ISBN 0-07-109048-7 (3/4 in.) LC Card 86-708026 DDC 658.8 11
HF5415.5

Dealing with difficult customers [motion picture] /. Del Mar, CA , 1986. 1 film reel (13 min.) : ISBN 0-07-620875-3 LC Card 86-708027 DDC 658.8 11
HF5415.5

Dealing with difficult customers [videorecording] /. Del Mar, CA , 1986. 1 videocassette (13 min.) : ISBN 0-07-109068-1 (3/4 in.) LC Card 86-708028 DDC 658.8 11
HF5415.5

How to define goals and objectives [videorecording] /. Del Mar, CA , 1986. 1 videocassette (18 min.) : ISBN 0-07-109094-0 (3/4 in.) LC Card 86-700128 DDC 658.4 11
HF5549.5.G6

How to influence motivation [videorecording] /. Del Mar, CA , 1986. 1 videocassette (31 min.) : ISBN 0-07-109093-2 (3/4 in.) LC Card 86-700127 DDC 658.3 11
HF5549.5.M63

How to lead effectively [videorecording] /. Del Mar, CA , 1986. 1 videocassette (19 min.) : ISBN 0-07-109095-9 (3/4 in.) LC Card 86-700130 DDC 658.4 11
HD57.7

How to solve problems [videorecording] /. Del Mar, CA , 1986. 1 videocassette (22 min.) : ISBN 0-07-109096-7 (3/4 in.) LC Card 86-700129 DDC 658.4 11
HD30.29

An Introduction to communication on the telephone [videorecording] /. Del Mar, CA , 1987. 1 videocassette (7 min.) : LC Card 87-700082 DDC 658.8 11
HF5415.1265

The Meeting robbers [motion picture] /. Del Mar, CA , 1985. 1 film reel (20 min.) : ISBN 0-07-620874-5 LC Card 85-702616 DDC 658.4 11
HD30.3

The Meeting robbers [videorecording] /. Del Mar, CA , 1985. 1 videocassette (20 min.) : ISBN 0-07-109067-3 (3/4 in.) LC Card 85-702617 DDC 658.4 11
HD30.3

Productivity and the self-fulfilling prophecy [motion picture] . Del Mar, CA , 1987. 1 film reel (27 min.) : LC Card 87-700078 DDC 658.4 11
HF5549.5.I5

Productivity and the self-fulfilling prophecy [videorecording] . Del Mar, CA , 1987. 1 videocassette (27 min.) : LC Card 87-700079 DDC 658.4 11
HF5549.5.I5

Questions and recommendations on the telephone [videorecording] /. Del Mar, CA , 1987. 1 videocassette (13 min.) : LC Card 87-700084 DDC 658.8 11
HF5415.1265

Crnobrnja, Mihailo. Čovekova životna sredina i ekonomski razvoj / Mihailo Crnobrnja. Beograd : NIO Poslovna politika, [1984?] 206 p. : ill. ; 24 cm. In Serbo-Croatian (roman) Includes bibliographies. LC Card 86-184927
1. Environmental policy - Yugoslavia. 2. Yugoslavia - Economic conditions - 1945-. I. Title.
HC407.Z9 E55 1984

CROATIA - COMMERCE - HISTORY - GERMANY.
Sundhaussen, Holm. Wirtschaftsgeschichte Kroatiens im nationalsozialistischen Grossraum 1941-1945 . Stuttgart , 1983. 386 p. : ISBN 3-421-06150-5 LC Card 83-242921
HC407.Z7 C7678 1983

CROATIA - ECONOMIC CONDITIONS.
Sundhaussen, Holm. Wirtschaftsgeschichte Kroatiens im nationalsozialistischen Grossraum 1941-1945 . Stuttgart , 1983. 386 p. : ISBN 3-421-06150-5 LC Card 83-242921
HC407.Z7 C7678 1983

CROATIA - ECONOMIC CONDITIONS - CONGRESSES.
Kongres privrednih stručnjaka Hrvatske (1943-1944 : Otočac and Čazma, Croatia) Kongres privrednih stručnjaka Hrvatske . Zagreb , 1985. 252 p., [16] p. of plates : ISBN 86-80359-01-7 LC Card 86-176200
HC407.Z7 C7637 1943

CROATIA - ECONOMIC POLICY.
Osnove dugoročnog razvoja SR Hrvatske--svodna studija /. Zagreb , 1984. 437 p. ; LC Card 87-151188
HC407.Z7 C7647 1984

Croatia (Province) see **Croatia.**

CROATIAN LANGUAGE. see **SERBO-CROATIAN LANGUAGE.**

CROATO-SERBIAN LANGUAGE. see **SERBO-CROATIAN LANGUAGE.**

Crocker, Olga L. Incidents and cases in Canadian personnel administration / Olga L. Crocker and Susan A. Fekete. Toronto ; New York : Methuen, c1986. 216 p. : ill. ; 23 cm. ISBN 0-458-98690-9 (pbk.) : LC Card 86-218837

DDC 658.3/00971 19
1. Personnel management - Canada - Case studies. I. Fekete, Susan A. II. Title.
HF5549.2.C3 C76 1986

CROCKERY. see **POTTERY.**

Crockett, Andrew. Strengthening the international monetary system : exchange rates, surveillance, and objective indicators / by Andrew Crockett and Morris Goldstein. Washington, D.C. : International Monetary Fund, c1987. vii, 84 p. ; 28 cm. (Occasional paper (International Monetary Fund) . no. 50) "February 1987." Bibliography: p. 83-84. LC Card 86-33750 DDC 332.4/5 19
1. International finance. 2. Foreign exchange problem. 3. Monetary policy. I. Goldstein, Morris, 1944- II. International Monetary Fund. III. Series. IV. Series: Occasional paper (International Monetary Fund) , no. 50. V. Title.
HG3881 .C694 1987

Crockford, Neil. The administration of insurance / Neil Crockford. Cambridge [Cambridgeshire] ; Wolfeboro, N.H., USA : ICSA Pub., 1987. x, 134 p. : ill. ; 24 cm. Includes index. ISBN 0-902197-42-8 : LC Card 86-27596 DDC 368/.0068 19
1. Insurance. 2. Insurance companies - Management. I. Title.
HG8051 .C84 1987

CROFTERS - HISTORY.
Richards, Eric. A history of the Highland clearances /. London , c1982-1985. 2 v. : ISBN 0-85664-496-X : LC Card 81-208122 DDC 333.33/5 19
HD1511.G7 R53 1982 ***NYPL [JLL 82-171]***

Croissance, échange et monnaie en économie internationale : mélanges en l'honneur de Monsieur le Professeur Jean Weiller. Paris : Economica, c1985. 604 p. : ill. ; 24 cm. "Contributions de: Michel Aglietta" ... [et al.]--P. [4] of cover. "Principales publications de Jean Weiller": p. [589]-595. Includes bibliographies. ISBN 2-7178-0912-0 (pbk.) :
1. Weiller, Jean, 1905-. 2. International economic relations - Addresses, essays, lectures. 3. International finance - Addresses, essays, lectures. I. Weiller, Jean, 1905-. ***NYPL [JLE 86-1157]***

Croissance économique et espace urbain dans le Sahel tunisien depuis l'indépendance /. Jedidi, Mohammed. [Tunis] , 1986. 2 v. : LC Card 87-123401
HC820 .J43 1986

Croissance urbaine . Lacour, Claude. Paris , 1981. 219 p. : ISBN 2-222-02928-7 (pbk.) : LC Card 82-153821 DDC 388.4/068 19
HE4764 .L3 1981 ***NYPL [JLG 86-56]***

CROIX-ROUGE FRANÇAISE - MISCELLANEA.
Granger, Louis. Catalogue des vignettes françaises de Croix-Rouge /. [Aurillac] [1964] 117 p. ; LC Card 68-39071
HE6184.S42 G7 1964

Crome, Erhard. Quilitzsch, Siegmar. Die sozialistische Gemeinschaft zu Beginn der 80er Jahre . Berlin , 1984. 141 p. : LC Card 84-180106
HC243.5 .Q55 1984

Crompton, Cathy. Too old for a job, too young for a pension? : income support for older people out of work / Cathy Crompton. Canberra : Australian Govt. Pub. Service, 1986. x, 69 p. ; 25 cm. (Issues paper / Social Security Review . no. 2) Bibliography: p. 67-69. ISBN 0-644-05599-5 LC Card 87-150775 DDC 368.4/4/00880564 19
1. Age and employment - Australia. 2. Aged - Australia - Economic conditions. 3. Insurance, Unemployment - Australia. 4. Retirement income - Australia. 5. Income maintenance programs - Australia. I. Series: Issue paper (Australia. Social Security Review) , no. 2. II. Title.
HD6283.A8 C76 1986

Crompton, Rosemary. Gender and stratification /. Cambridge, CB, UK , Oxford, OX, UK , 1986. viii, 271 p. ; ISBN 0-7456-0167-7 : LC Card 85-28342 DDC 305.3 19
HQ1075 .G46 1986 ***NYPL [JLE 86-2966]***

Cronin, Thomas E. Burns, James MacGregor. State and local politics . Englewood Cliffs, N.J. , c1984. xi, 266 p. : ISBN 0-13-843524-3 (pbk.) LC Card 83-21259 DDC 320.973 19
JK2408 .B87 1984 ***NYPL [JLE 87-142]***

Crook, Clive. Pennant-Rea, Rupert. The Economist economics /. Harmondsworth, Middlesex, England , New York, U. S.A. , 1986. 197 p. : ISBN 0-14-022703-2 (pbk.) : LC Card 86-219602 DDC 330 19
HB171 .P458 1986

Crook, Jonathan N. Reekie, W. Duncan. Managerial economics /. Oxford [Oxfordshire] , Atlantic Highlands, N.J. , 1987. xi, 522 p. : ISBN 0-86003-070-9 LC Card 87-12627 DDC 338.5/024/658 19
HD30.22 .R39 1987

The Croom Helm critical assessments of leading economists.
Thomas Robert Malthus, critical assessments /. London , Dover, N.H. , c1986. 4 v. : ISBN 0-7099-3650-8 (set) : LC Card 85-22412 DDC 304.6/092/4 19
HB863 .T38 1986 ***NYPL [JFF 86-588]***

Croom Helm industrial geography series.
Rich, D. C. The industrial geography of Australia /. London , Wolfeboro, N.H. , c1987. xvi, 384 p. : ISBN 0-7099-2214-0 : LC Card 86-29383 DDC 338.0994 19
HC610.D5 R53 1987

Croom Helm progress in geography series.
Population geography . London , Dover, N.H. , c1986. 322 p. : ISBN 0-7099-4045-9 : LC Card 86-6210 DDC 304.6 19
HB1951 .P653 1986 ***NYPL [JLD 86-3692]***

The Croom Helm series in international business.
MacCharles, Donald C. (Donald Clare), 1935- Trade among multinationals . London , New York , c1987. xiv, 207 p. ; ISBN 0-7099-4618-X LC Card 87-9077 DDC 382/.3 19
HF1411 .M2325 1987

Croom Helm series on the contemporary economic history of Europe.
Berend, T. Iván (Tibor Iván), 1930- The Hungarian economy in the twentieth century /. London , c1985. 316 p. ; ISBN 0-7099-2209-4 LC Card 86-673483
HC300.24 .B44 1985b

Harrison, Joseph, 1944- The Spanish economy in the twentieth century /. London , c1985. 207 p. : ISBN 0-85664-721-7 : LC Card 86-674012
HC385 .H34x 1985b

Lampe, John R. The Bulgarian economy in the twentieth century /. London , c1986. x, 245 p. : ISBN 0-7099-1644-2 LC Card 86-673485
HC403 .L36x 1986b

Landau, Zbigniew. The Polish economy in the twentieth century /. London , c1985. vi, 346 p. ; ISBN 0-7099-1607-8 LC Card 86-673496
HC340.3 .L36x 1985b

Croom Helm series on theory and practice of adult education in North America.
Learning in the workplace /. London , New York , c1987. 217 p. ; ISBN 0-7099-4659-7 LC Card 87-20062 DDC 658.3/1243 19
HF5549.5.T7 L38 1987

Croom Helm small business series.
Hull, Christopher J. Helping small firms grow . New York , c1987. 228 p. : ISBN 0-7099-4791-7 LC Card 87-15728 DDC 338.6/42 19
HD2346.G3 .H786 1987

Crop insurance for agricultural development : issues and experience / edited by Peter Hazell, Carlos Pomareda, and Alberto Valdés ; with the assistance of Joan Straker Hazell. Baltimore : Published for the International Food Policy Research Institute by the Johns Hopkins University Press, c1986. xviii, 322 p. ill. ; 24 cm. "This publication is the outcome of collaboration between the International Food Policy Research Institute and the Inter-American Institute for Cooperation on Agriculture." Includes index. Bibliography: p. 299-309. ISBN 0-8018-2673-X (alk. paper) LC Card 85-9810 DDC 368.1/22 19
1. Insurance, Agricultural - Crops - Addresses, essays, lectures. 2. Agriculture and state - Addresses, essays, lectures. 3. Agricultural credit - Addresses, essays, lectures. I. Hazell, P. B. R. II. Pomareda, Carlos. III. Valdés, Alberto, 1935-. IV. International Food Policy Research Institute. V. Inter-American Institute for Cooperation on Agriculture.
HG9968 .C76 1985 ***NYPL [JLE 86-1082]***

CROP REPORTS. see **AGRICULTURE - STATISTICS.**

CROPPING SYSTEMS - AUSTRIA.
Landwirtschaftliche Produktionsalternativen am Beispiel Ethanol, Ölsaaten und Eiweissfutterpflanzen /. Wien , 1985. 141 p. : LC Card 86-108149 DDC 338.1/09436 19
HD1935 .L33 1985

CROPPING SYSTEMS - ECONOMIC ASPECTS - SIERRA LEONE.
Kireta-Katewu, Patrick R., 1953- Economic analyses of the farmer cropping system under risks and uncertainties in Sierra Leone /. Hamburg , 1985. xviii, 245 p. : ISBN 3-87895-266-X (pbk.) LC Card 87-103068 DDC 338.1/62 19
HD2146.5 .K57 1985

CROPS AND CLIMATE - INDIA - PUNJAB.
Rachhpal Singh, 1944- Farm production in rainfed sub-mountainous Punjab /. Delhi , New Delhi , 1987. vi, 349 p. ; ISBN 81-7018-450-9 : LC Card 87-902161 DDC 338.1/0954/552 19
HD2075.P8 R33 1987

CROPS - CANADA.
Canadian farming . Toronto , 1881. 432 p., [4] folded leaves of plates : LC Card 85-666092
HD1783 .C3x 1881

CROPS - STATISTICS. see **AGRICULTURE - STATISTICS.**

Crosby, Philip B. Running things : the art of making things happen / Philip B. Crosby. New York : New American Library, 1987, c1986. p. cm. Reprint. Originally published: New York : McGraw-Hill, c1986. Includes index. ISBN 0-452-25915-0 LC Card 86-28508 DDC 658.4/092 19
1. Leadership. 2. Management. I. Title.
HD57.7 .C76 1987

Cross-country trucker. Bourne, Miriam Anne. A day in the life of a cross-country trucker /. Mahwah, N.J. , c1988. 32 p. : ISBN 0-8167-1117-8 (lib. bdg.) : LC Card 87-13582 DDC 388.3/24/02373 19
HD8039.M795 B68 1988

CROSS-CULTURAL ORIENTATION.
Scott-Stevens, Susan. Foreign consultants and counterparts . Boulder , 1987. xvii, 229 p. : ISBN 0-8133-7370-0 (pbk. : alk. paper) LC Card 87-50750 DDC 306/.46 19
HC79.T4 S36 1987

Cross, Mary. Persuasive business writing : creating better letters, memos, reports, and more / Mary Cross. New York, NY : American Management Association, c1987. x, 179 p. : ill. ; 24 cm. Bibliography: p. 171-172. Includes index. ISBN 0-8144-5898-X LC Card 86-47808 DDC 808/.066651 19
1. Business writing. I. Title.
HF5718.3 .C76 1987

Cross, Rod. Unemployment, hysteresis, and the natural rate hypothesis . Oxford, UK , New York, NY, USA , 1987. p. cm. ISBN 0-631-15688-7 : LC Card 87-14071 DDC 331.13/7 19
HD5707.5 .U555 1987

Crosson, Pierre R. Agriculture and the environment /. Washington, D.C. , c1986. xvii, 298 p. : ISBN 0-915707-33-0 (pbk.) : LC Card 87-43010 DDC 363.7/31 19
HD1755 .P47 1986

Crouch, Susan C. (Susan Catherine), 1958- Western responses to Tanzanian socialism, 1967-83 / Susan C. Crouch. Aldershot, Hants, England ; Brookfield, Vt., USA : Avebury, c1987. x, 194 p. ; 23 cm. Originally presented as the author's thesis (Ph. D.)--London School of Economics, 1986. Bibliography: p. 181-194. ISBN 0-566-05455-8 : LC Card 87-15018 DDC 337.678 19
1. Tanzania - Foreign economic relations. 2. Tanzania - Foreign relations. 3. Tanzania - Politics and government - 1964-. 4. Tanzania - Economic policy. 5. Socialism - Tanzania. I. Title.
HF1612.9 .C76 1987

Crousse, Bernard. Espaces disputés en Afrique noire . Paris , c1986. 426 p., [8] p. of plates : ISBN 2-86537-146-8 LC Card 86-210958
HD965 .E86 1986

CROWDING OUT (ECONOMICS) - GERMANY (WEST)
Hunger, Carola, 1956- Crowding-out in einem Modell mit Mengenrationierung . Idstein ,

1985. x, 251 p. : ISBN 3-925196-06-4 LC Card 86-136872
HJ1120 .H85 1985

Crowding-out in einem Modell mit Mengenrationierung . Hunger, Carola, 1956- Idstein , 1985. x, 251 p. : ISBN 3-925196-06-4 LC Card 86-136872
HJ1120 .H85 1985

Crowe, Robert M. Time and money : using time value analysis in financial planning / Robert M. Crowe. Homewood, Ill. : Dow Jones-Irwin, c1987. 1 v. (various pagings) : ill. ; 28 cm. ISBN 1-556-23051-6 (pbk.) LC Card 87-70621 DDC 332.024 19
1. Interest. 2. Annuities. 3. Discounted cash flow. I. Title.
HG1621 .C76 1987

Crowley, Charles. Income and poverty in New Jersey [microform] : 1980 census of population and housing / State Data Center. Trenton, N.J. : State of New Jersey, Dept. of Labor, Division of Planning and Research, Office of Demographic and Economic Analysis, [1982] 32 p. ; 22 x 28 cm. "CN388." "October 1982." "This publication was prepared by Charles Crowley." -- p. [1] Microfilm. New York : New York Public Library, 1986. 1 microfilm reel ; 35 mm. (MN *ZZ-26,234) LC Card 83-620831 DDC 339.2/2/09749 19
1. Income - New Jersey - Statistics. 2. Poor - New Jersey - Statistics. 3. New Jersey - Census, 1980. 4. United States - Census, 20th, 1980. I. New Jersey State Data Center. II. Title.
HC107.N53 I5113 1982
NYPL [*ZT-1712 no.31]

CROWN LANDS - BRITISH COLUMBIA - CALVERT ISLAND.
Calvert Island crown land plan /. [Victoria, B.C.] , 1981. vii, 63 p. : ISBN 0-7719-8637-8 (pbk.) LC Card 82-208343 DDC 333.1/09711/3 19
HD319.B8 C34 1981

The Crown lands of British South Africa, 1853-1914 /. Christopher, A. J. Kingston, Ont., Canada , 1984. vii, 247 p., [8] p. of plates : ISBN 0-919642-04-7 LC Card 85-125786 DDC 333.1/0968 19
HD991 .C49 1984 ***NYPL [Sc E 85-373]***

CROWN LANDS - SOUTH AFRICA - HISTORY.
Christopher, A. J. The Crown lands of British South Africa, 1853-1914 /. Kingston, Ont., Canada , 1984. vii, 247 p., [8] p. of plates : ISBN 0-919642-04-7 LC Card 85-125786 DDC 333.1/0968 19
HD991 .C49 1984 ***NYPL [Sc E 85-373]***

Crozat, Marie-Louise. Friedman, Janet T. (Janet Teri), 1957- Safecracking the mortgage secrets . Houston, Tex. , c1987. 141 p. : ISBN 0-942037-00-6 (pbk.) : LC Card 87-13357 DDC 332.7/22/0973 19
HG2040.5.U5 F75 1987

Crozier, Brian. Ratiu, Ion. Moscow challenges the world /. London , 1986. 410 p. ; ISBN 0-907671-23-5 ***NYPL [JLE 87-1665]***

Crucible . Kaufmann, Dwight W., 1919- [Pittsburgh? Pa.] , c1986. x, 298 p. : LC Card 86-224545 DDC 338.7/669142/0973 19
HD9519.C7 K38 1986

CRUCIBLE STEEL COMPANY OF AMERICA - HISTORY.
Kaufmann, Dwight W., 1919- Crucible . [Pittsburgh? Pa.] , c1986. x, 298 p. : LC Card 86-224545 DDC 338.7/669142/0973 19
HD9519.C7 K38 1986

Cruickshank, A. A. Kubálková, V. International inequality /. London , c1981. 293 p. : ISBN 0-7099-0221-2 LC Card 86-673398
HF1411 .K819x 1981b

Cruise ship employment directory /. Schultz, Gordon F. Centralia, Wash. (131 Elma Dr., Centralia 98531) , c1987. 102 p. ; LC Card 87-166826 DDC 385/.22/02373 19
HE566.E9 S38 1987

CRUISE SHIPS - NORTH AMERICA.
Murphy, Michael, 1927- Ferryliner vacations in North America . New York , c1988. ix, 277 p. : ISBN 0-525-48355-1 (pbk.) : LC Card 87-13640 DDC 910/.2/02 19
HE5772.A3 M87 1988

CRUISE SHIPS - VOCATIONAL GUIDANCE - DIRECTORIES.
Schultz, Gordon F. Cruise ship employment directory /. Centralia, Wash. (131 Elma Dr., Centralia 98531) , c1987. 102 p. ; LC Card 87-166826 DDC 385/.22/02373 19
HE566.E9 S38 1987

Crull, Anna W.
Commercial and industrial enzymes / Anna W. Crull, Patricia Ruffio. Stamford, Conn., U. S.A. : Business Communications Co., c1986. xiii, 160 leaves : ill. ; 29 cm. (Business opportunity report . C-067) "March 1986"--T.p. verso. Bibliography: leaves 151-160. ISBN 0-89336-492-4 (pbk.) LC Card 87-164403 DDC 380.1/4566063 19
1. Enzymes industry. 2. Market surveys. I. Ruffio, Patricia. II. Title. III. Series.
HD9660.E582 C783 1986

Geotextiles, geomembranes, geomatrices . Stamford, Conn., U. S.A. , c1986. xii, 133 leaves : ISBN 0-89336-496-7 (pbk.) LC Card 87-403913 DDC 668.9 19
HD9869.I533 U64 1986

New trends in gas separations : highlighting membrane developments / Anna W. Crull. Stamford, Conn., U. S.A. : Business Communications Co., c1986. xvi, 222 leaves : ill. ; 29 cm. (Business opportunity report . C-062) "January 1986"--T.p. verso. ISBN 0-89336-422-3 (pbk.) LC Card 87-165549 DDC 660.2/842 19
1. Gas separation membrane industry - United States. 2. Market surveys - United States. I. Business Communications Co. II. Title. III. Series.
HD9660.G372 C78 1986

Crumbley, D. Larry. Handbook of governmental accounting and finance /. New York , c1988. 1 v. (various pagings) ; ISBN 0-471-84741-0 LC Card 87-23092 DDC 350.72/31 19
HJ9801 .H36 1988

Crump, Stuart. Bates, Jefferson D., 1920- The portable office . Washington, D.C. , c1987. 262 p. : ISBN 0-87491-491-3 :; 0-87491-841-3 (jacket) LC Card 87-1773 DDC 658.4/093 19
HD38 .B325 1987

Crusol, Jean. Changer la Martinique : initiation à l'économie des Antilles / Jean Crusol. Paris : Editions caribéennes, c1986. 91 p. : ill. ; 20 cm. ISBN 2-903033-73-0 : LC Card 86-210884
1. Martinique - Economic conditions. I. Title.
HC158.6 .C78 1986

Cruz, María Elena. Chile--opciones y desafíos del sindicalismo rural, 1973-1985 / María Elena Cruz D., Arturo Sáez Ch. Santiago, Chile : Grupo de Investigaciones Agrarias, Academia de Humanismo Cristiano, 1985. 57 p. ; 25 cm. (Serie Documentos de trabajo . no. 23) Bibliography: p. 55-57. LC Card 87-100897
1. Trade-unions - Agricultural laborers - Chile. 2. Chile - Politics and government - 1973-. 3. Labor policy - Chile. 4. Peasantry - Chile - Political activity. I. Sáez Ch., Arturo. II. Series: Serie Documentos de trabajo (Academia de Humanismo Cristiano (Santiago, Chile). Grupo de Investigaciones Agrarias) , no. 23. III. Title.
HD6619.A29 C78 1985

Cruz, Marina. 1,001 advertising cuts from the twenties and thirties /. New York , 1987. 103 p. : ISBN 0-486-25490-9 (pbk.) LC Card 87-15546 DDC 659.13/2/0973 19
HF5813.U6 A525 1987

O cruzado . Nassif, Luís. São Paulo/SP , 1986. 255 p. : LC Card 86-224110
HG835 .N37 1986

O cruzado e o austral . Peláez, Carlos Manuel. São Paulo , 1986. 174 p. : ISBN 85-22-40173-X LC Card 87-102770 DDC 332.4/981 19
HG835 .P43 1986

Család, háztartás és a városi cselédség /. Gyáni, Gábor. Budapest , c1983. 251, [1] p. ; ISBN 963-271-955-7 : LC Card 84-129676
HD6072.2.H8 G92 1983

A családok és háztartások előreszámítása, 1981-2001 /. Csernák, Józsefné. Budapest , 1985. 125 p. : LC Card 86-166603
HA1201 .A64 no. 59 HA1205

Csatorday, Géza. A szállitási rendszer fejlesztési lehetőségeinek vizsgálata a tejiparban / Csatorday Géza. Budapest : Agrárgazdasági Kutató Intézet, 1985. 94 p. : ill. ; 28 cm. (Agrárgazdasági Kutató Intézet, 0209-5696 . 1985/15) Bibliography: p. 93. ISBN 963-491-216-8 LC Card 86-199210
1. Milk - Transportation. 2. Milk trade - Hungary. I. Series: Agrárgazdasági Kutató Intézet (Series) , 1985/15. II. Title.
HE199.5.M5 C73 1985

CSC et le programme gouvernemental de mars 1984. Arcq, Etienne. La C.S.C. et le programme gouvernemental de mars 1984 /. Bruxelles [1984] 23 leaves ; LC Card 84-171486
HD8502.C62 A73 1984

Csemniczky, Jánosné. Bontó, László. Iparfejlesztés a hetedik ötéves terv időszakában /. [Budapest] , 1986. 170, [4] p. : ISBN 963-09-3001-3 : LC Card 87-138631
HC300.28 .B659 1986

Csendes, Béla. Az Élelmiszer-gazdaság távlati fejlesztése /. Budapest , 1984. 163 p. ; ISBN 963-231-717-3 : LC Card 85-194280
HD1940.5.Z8 E54 1984

CSER reprint .
(no. 13) Beckman, Björn, 1938- Public investment and agrarian transformation in northern Nigeria /. [Zaria , 1983] 33 p. ; LC Card 87-402849 DDC 338.1/8669 19
HD2145.5 .B43 1983

CSER research report .
(no. 6) Jaworek, Rudolf. The development of small scale industry in Kaduna State . Zaria [1980] vii, 162, [44] p., [2] leaves of plates : LC Card 84-256006
HD2356.N62 K34 1980

C.S.E.R. research series .
(11) Ogwude, Innocent C. (Innocent Chuka) Industrial demand for freight transport in Kaduna State /. Zaria [Nigeria] [1984] 101 p. : LC Card 86-152627 DDC 380.5/24/096695 19
HE287.7.Z7 K336 1984

Cserhalmi, Imre. Ha nincs fék, gáz van : szabálytalan útinapló / Cserhalmi Imre. [Budapest] : Kossuth, 1984. 294 p. ; 20 cm. LC Card 85-183756
1. Trucking - Hungary - Anecdotes, facetiae, satire, etc. 2. Truck drivers - Hungary - Anecdotes, facetiae, satire, etc. I. Title.
HE5667.5.A6 C74 1984

Csermák, Béla. A Vízgazdálkodás távlati fejlesztésének prognózisai /. Budapest , 1983. 176 p. : ISBN 963-602-278-X LC Card 85-109619
HD1697.H8 V59 1983

Csernák, Józsefné. A családok és háztartások előreszámítása, 1981-2001 / irták, Csernák Józsefné, Szabó Kálmán. Budapest : Központi Statisztikai Hivatal Népességtudományi Kutató Intézet, 1985. 125 p. : ill. ; 29 cm. (A Központi Statisztikai Hivatal Népességtudományi Kutató Intézetének és a Magyar Tudományos Akadémia Demográfiai Bizottságának közleményei, 0134-0093 . 59) Bibliography: p. 53. LC Card 86-166603
1. Households - Hungary - Statistics. 2. Family - Hungary - Statistics. 3. Hungary - Population - Statistics. 4. Population forecasting - Hungary - Statistics. I. Szabó, Kálmán. II. Title. III. Series.
HA1201 .A64 no. 59 HA1205

Csete, László.
A Mezőgazdasági és élelmiszeripari vállalatok gazdálkodása /. Budapest , 1984. 315, [1] p. : ISBN 963-231-968-0 : LC Card 85-230887
HD1493.H8 M48 1984

Összefoglalás, Szolnok megye agroökológiai potenciálja az ezredfordulón /. Budapest , 1984. 115 p. : ISBN 963-491-193-5 LC Card 86-198809
HD1940.5.Z9 S966 1984

CSP International (Firm) Deregulation of the radio spectrum in the UK / by CSP International. London : H.M.S.O., 1987. vi, 182, [30] p. : ill. ; 30 cm. "Radiocommunications Division, Department of Trade and Industry"--Cover. Bibliography: p. [1]-[8] (second set). ISBN 0-11-513979-6 (pbk.) : LC Card 87-170465 DDC 384.54/52 19
1. Radio frequency allocation - Great Britain. 2. Television frequency allocation - Great Britain. I. Great Britain. Dept. of Trade and Industry. Radiocommunications Division. II. Title.
HE8689.9.G7 C76 1987

CSS working papers.
Baxter, Ellen. The Heights . New York, N.Y. [1986] 69 leaves : LC Card 87-401534 DDC

363.5/8 19
HD7287.96.U62 N683 1986

Csúcs, Andrásné. Az OKBT Tudományos Kutatási Szakbizottság kezdeményezése, illetve megbízása alapján készült kutatások, 1973-1983 /. [Budapest] , 1983. 124 p. : ISBN 963-02-3169-7 (Magy. nemz. bibl.) LC Card 85-126922
HE5614.5.H8 O38 1983
NYPL [JLD 87-1181]

Cuaderno de formación .
(no. 6) La Nueva política económica . La Paz, Bolivia , 1986. 57 p. : LC Card 87-403839 DDC 338.984 19
HC182 .N84 1986

Cuaderno de trabajo (Instituto Libertad y Democracia (Lima, Peru)) .
(2) Las Leyes de estabilidad laboral y sus efectos económicos /. Lima, Perú [1986?] 67 p. : LC Card 87-403254 DDC 331.11/0985 19
HD8344 .L49 1986

Cuaderno de trabajo (Instituto Nacional de Antropología e Historia (Mexico). Dirección de Estudios Históricos) .
(no. 46) López Monjardín, Adriana. Hacia la ciudad del capital--México, 1790-1870 /. México, D.F. , 1985. 193 p. : LC Card 87-124857 DDC 330.972/53 19
HC138.M4 L66 1985

(no. 47) Flores Clair, Eduardo. Estadísticas mineras de México en el siglo XIX /. México, D.F. , 1985. 181 p. ; LC Card 87-401718 DDC 338.2/0972 19
HD9506.M62 F57 1985

(47) Alvarado Gómez, Armando. Principales productos del comercio exterior mexicano del siglo XIX /. México, D.F. , 1985. v. <1 > ; LC Card 87-401206 DDC 382/.0972 19
HF3236 .A5 1985

(47) Ramírez Bautista, Elia. Estadísticas bancarias . México, D.F. , 1985. 10, ca. 200 p. ; ISBN 968-603-813-2 LC Card 87-401719 DDC 332.1/0972/021 19
HG2714 .R36 1985

Cuadernos administrativos .
(1) Mock Cedeño, Ariel. Las empresas públicas en Panamá . Panamá, Rep. de Panamá , 1986. vi, 89, [5] p. ; LC Card 87-400433 DDC 338.97287 19
HD4043 .M63 1986

Cuadernos CEFNOMEX.
Bilbao, Elena. La frontera de San Ysidro . Tijuana, Baja California , 1986. 27 p. ; ISBN 968-607-513-5 LC Card 87-125801 DDC 330.9794/98 19
HC108.S65 B55 1986

Carrillo V., Jorge (Carrillo Viveros) Conflictos laborales en la industria maquiladora /. Tijuana, Baja California , 1985. 55 p. : ISBN 968-607-504-6 LC Card 87-117557 DDC 331.4/87/09721 19
HD5331.O33 C37 1985

Corona V., Rodolfo. Evaluación de los datos censales de 1980 . Tijuana, Baja California , 1986. 172 p. : ISBN 968-607-510-0 LC Card 87-117630 DDC 304.6/0723 19
HA767.B34 C67 1986

Driscoll, Bárbara A. El programa de braceros ferroviarios /. Tijuana, Baja California , 1985. 45 p. ; ISBN 968-607-501-1 LC Card 86-188661
HD8039.R432 U62 1985

González-Aréchiga, Bernardo. Vinculación fronteriza a Estados Unidos y su cambio con la crisis /. Tijuana, Baja California , 1985. 54 p. ; ISBN 968-607-500-3 LC Card 86-187758
HF3239.M49 G66 1985

Cuadernos centroamericanos de ciencias sociales .
(11) Costa Rica colonial . [San José, Costa Rica , 1984] 83 p. ; LC Card 86-173945
HC389 .C67 1984

(12) Raventos Vorst, Ciska. El café en Costa Rica . San José, Costa Rica , 1985. iii, 145 p. : LC Card 86-174756
HD9199.C82 R39 1985

Cuadernos de administración pública.
(no. 43) Funciones y servicios de competencia municipal /. Córdoba, República Argentina , 1984. 94 leaves ; LC Card 87-121632 DDC 352.082 19
HD4629 .F86 1984

Cuadernos de administración pública (Universidad Católica de Córdoba. Centro de Investigación y Perfeccionamiento en Ciencias Económicas y Administración Pública) .
(39) León Almeida, Pedro. Ensayo de categorización de los municipios de Córdoba /. Córdoba, Argentina , 1984. 74 leaves : LC Card 87-403755 DDC 330.982/54062/021 19
HC177.C7 L46 1984

(43) Funciones y servicios de competencia municipal /. Córdoba, República Argentina , 1984. 94 leaves ; LC Card 87-121632 DDC 352.082 19
HD4629 .F86 1984

Cuadernos de CESCO .
(no. 1) Chile y CIPEC ante la crisis del cobre /. Santiago de Chile , 1985. 74 p. ; LC Card 86-144485
HD9539.C7 C526 1985 *NYPL [JLD 87-363]*

Cuadernos de ciencia política (Santiago, Chile) .
(no. 7) Israel Zipper, Ricardo. Democracia y liberalismo /. Santiago de Chile , 1984. 56 p. ; LC Card 85-197546
HB95 .I87 1984

Cuadernos de ciencias sociales. Serie Testeos teóricos .
(1) Toledo, Nora Elena. El tamaño de las ciudades y la distribución de los ingresos (Argentina y Colombia) /. San Juan, Argentina , 1985. 63 p. : LC Card 87-400258 DDC 339.2/2/09861 19
HC200.I5 T65 1985

Cuadernos de economía aplicada.
Ahijado, Manuel. Piero Sraffa . Madrid , 1985. 90 p. ; ISBN 84-85942-31-0 LC Card 87-104173
HB109.S73 A35 1985

Cuadernos de economía y finanzas .
(cuaderno no. 1) Glower, Carlos J., 1952- La fuga de capital en Centroamérica, 1977-1984 /. Tegucigalpa, D.C., Honduras, C.A. , 1986. 20 p. : LC Card 87-125008 DDC 332/.042 19
HG3917 .G56 1986

Cuadernos de estudio. Serie Geografía .
(16) Molina Ibáñez, Mercedes. Capitalismo y socialismo . Madrid , c1984. 128 p. : ISBN 84-7046-358-6 LC Card 85-135836
HB501 .M694 1984

Cuadernos de formación tributaria.
Esparza Cervera, José Ramón. Impuesto sobre la renta . Valencia [1982?] 1 v. (various pagings) ; ISBN 84-85672-11-9 LC Card 83-134521
HJ4744 .E86 1982

Cuadernos de geohistoria regional, 0325-8246 .
(no. 2) Sonzogni, Cristina María. La población de la ciudad de Corrientes a mediados del siglo XIX /. Corrientes , 1980. 50, [4] leaves, [14] leaves of plates : LC Card 85-209374
HB3560.C67 S65 1980

(no. 5) Borrini, Héctor R. El proceso de colonización en el impenetrable chaqueño /. Corrientes , 1981. 60 leaves : LC Card 86-204205 DDC 333.3/1/8234 19
HD479.C47 B67 1981

Cuadernos de investigación (Centro de Investigación y Promoción del Campesinado) .
(no. 27) Escóbar, Filemón, 1936- La mina vista desde el guardatojo . La Paz, Bolivia , 1986. 77 p. ; LC Card 87-118481 DDC 331.7/622/0984 19
HD8039.M61 B57 1986

Cuadernos de investigación (Chiclayo, Lambayeque, Peru) .
Cuadernos de investigación (Confederación Universitaria Centroamericana) .
(#2) Lungo, Mario. El problema de la tierra urbana . Ciudad Universitaria Rodrigo Facio [Costa Rica] , 1986. 42 p. ; LC Card 87-127789 DDC 333.77/13 19
HD1391 .L86 1986

(#5) Lungo, Mario. El terremoto de octubre de 1986 en San Salvador y la situación habitacional de los sectores populares /. Ciudad Universitaria Rodrigo Facio [Costa Rica] , 1987. 26 leaves ; LC Card 87-125001 DDC 363.3/495 19
HD7287.96.S22 S265 1987

Cuadernos de investigación social (Iquique, Chile) .
(vol. 1, no. 14) González M., Sergio (González Miranda) ZOFRI, un enclave comercial /. Iquique, Chile [1985] 38, [2] p. ; LC Card 86-167491
HF1418 .G66 1985

Cuadernos de la Biblioteca FELABAN .
(no. 19) El Manejo de los riesgos de la informática . Bogotá, D.E. [1984?] 61 p. : LC Card 85-183870
HF5548.2 .M2985 1984

Cuadernos de la CEPAL .
(no. 52) Sepúlveda Whittle, Tomás. Los conceptos básicos del transporte marítimo y la situación de la actividad en América Latina. Santiago de Chile , Nueva York, NY , 1986. 118 p. ; ISBN 92-1-321211-9 LC Card 87-400454 DDC 387.5/098 19
HE571 .S45 1986

Cuadernos de la CEPAL, 0252-2195 .
(52) Sepúlveda Whittle, Tomás. Los conceptos básicos del transporte marítimo y la situación de la actividad en América Latina. Santiago de Chile , Nueva York, NY , 1986. 118 p. ; ISBN 92-1-321211-9 LC Card 87-400454 DDC 387.5/098 19
HE571 .S45 1986

(54) The Economic crisis . Santiago, Chile , New York, NY, USA , 1986. 132 p. : ISBN 92-1-121132-8 (pbk.) LC Card 87-404540 DDC 338.98 19
HC125 .E368 1986

Cuadernos de pastoral social .
(5) El Fenómeno migratorio en el Paraguay /. Asunción, Paraguay [1985] 258 p. : LC Card 86-100044
HB2033 .F45 1985

Cuadernos de pensamiento propio. Serie Avances .
(2) Gariazzo, Alicia. El café en Nicaragua . Managua, Nicaragua , 1984. 175 p. : LC Card 85-192390
HD9199.N52 G37 1984
NYPL [JLF 86-1521]

Cuadernos de planificación y promoción social. Serie Avance de investigación .
(2) Gamboa Conejo, Rita Ma. (Rita María) Resultados preliminares del análisis metodológico de los planes nacionales de desarrollo, 1974-1982 /. Heredia , 1985. 1 v. (various pagings) : LC Card 87-402159 DDC 338.97286 19
HC143 .G36 1985

Cuadernos de trabajo (Asociación Mexicana de Investigadores de la Comunicación) .
(1) Medios de comunicación, hegemonía y proyectos de desarrollo. [Mexico City] [between 1982 and 1987] 179 p. ; LC Card 87-127821 DDC 338.9/007/1 19
HD77 .M43 1982

Cuadernos de trabajo (Instituto Nacional de Antropología e Historia (Mexico). Departamento de Etnología y Antropología Social) .
(30) Mora, Teresa. La Mixteca baja, su migración . México, D.F. , 1982. 129, [84] leaves ; LC Card 87-122391 DDC 304.6/0972/74 19
HB3532.O18 M67 1982

Cuadernos del Centro de Servicio y Promoción Social. Serie Investigación .
(no. 3) Pontones S., Jaime. Condicionantes estructurales del desarrollo tecnológico /. [Mexico City, Mexico] [1982] 27, [2] leaves ; LC Card 85-203882
HC79.T4 P66 1982

Cuadernos del CEUR, 0326-1417 .
(no. 5) Reboratti, Carlos E. Condicionantes físicos del asentamiento humano en el norte de la Patagonia /. Buenos Aires , 1982. 47 p. : LC Card 83-185201
HD479.C57 R43 1982

(16) Habitat popular . Buenos Aires , 1986. 162 p. : LC Card 87-404028 DDC 363.5/8 19
HD7305.5 .H32 1986

Cuadernos del I.D.R. .
(1) Jordá Borrell, Rosa Ma. (Rosa Maria) Dinámica y distribución recientes de la población andaluza /. [Sevilla] [1985?] 80 p. :

ISBN 84-600-3827-0 LC Card 87-124031
HB3620.A5 J67 1985

Cuadernos del Instituto de Investigaciones Políticas y Sociales. Estudios económico-sociales.
Marzo, Miguel. La conquista del espacio territorial sanjuanino /. Mendoza , 1968. 89 p., [12] leaves of plates : LC Card 82-166187
HD479.S25 M37 1968

Cuadernos del Senado .
(55) Información básica sobre el GATT y el desarrollo industrial y comercial de México. México , c1985. 79, 62 p. ; LC Card 87-400559 DDC 338.0972 19
HC135 .I53 1985

(59) Mexico. Congreso. Cámara de Senadores. Consulta sobre el GATT . México , c1986. v, 540 p. ; LC Card 87-114865 DDC 382/.0972 19
HF1481 .M45 1986

Cuadernos del TICOM .
(no. 32) Quibrera Matienzo, Enrique. La informática nacional . [Xochimilco, Mexico] , 1984. 133 p. ; LC Card 86-124964 DDC 338.4/7004/0972 19
HD9696.C63 M617 1984

(no. 35) Esparza Oteo T., Luis. La política cultural del estado mexicano y el desarrollo de la T.V. /. México, D.F. , 1984. 116 p. ; LC Card 87-404017 DDC 384.55/4/0972 19
HE8700.9.M6 E84 1984

Cuadernos laborales (Mexico City, Mexico) .
(31) La Mujer y el trabajo en México . México , 1986. 346 p. : ISBN 968-8132-48-9 LC Card 87-101329
HD6101 .M86 1986

Cuadernos laborales. Serie Relaciones del trabajo.
Pérez Menayo, Vicente. La protección del desempleo en España y en los países de las Comunidades Europeas /. [Madrid] [1980?] 303 p. : ISBN 84-500-3715-8 LC Card 83-240633 DDC 368.4/4/00946 19
HD7096.S7 P47 1980 ***NYPL [JLE 87-705]***

Cuadernos Teoría y sociedad .
(4) El Proceso de trabajo en México /. [Iztapalapa, Mexico] [1983 or 1984] 227 p. : LC Card 87-401038 DDC 331/.0972 19
HD8116.5 .P76 1983

Cuadernos universitarios (Universidad Autónoma Metropolitana. Unidad Iztapalapa) .
(24) Cooperativas agrarias y conflictos políticos en el sur de Jalisco /. México, D.F. , 1985 [i.e. 1986] 201 p. ; ISBN 968-8401-93-5 LC Card 87-405021 DDC 334/.683/097235 19
HD1491.M42 J353 1986

Cuadrado Roura, Juan R. Política de rentas : objetivos e instrumentación, experiencia internacional, el caso español / Juan R. Cuadrado Roura y José E. Villena Peña. [Madrid] : Ministerio de Hacienda, Instituto de Estudios Fiscales, [1980?] 471 p. : ill. ; 19 cm. (Colección Libros de bolsillo. 55) Bibliography: p. 449-463. ISBN 84-7196-297-7 LC Card 85-131138
1. Income - Government policy - Spain. 2. Income - Government policy - Case studies. I. Villena Peña, José E. II. Series: Colección Libros de bolsillo (Instituto de Estudios Fiscales (Spain)) , 55. III. Title.
HC390.I5 C8 1980

Cuarenta años de inflación en la argentina, 1945-1985 /. Vitelli, Guillermo. Buenos Aires [1986] 239 p. : ISBN 950-600-086-7 LC Card 87-124167 DDC 332.4/1/0982 19
HG815 .V57 1986

Cuarto pleno del Consejo Económico Sindical de Cuenca. Consejo Económico Sindical Provincial (Cuenca, Spain) IV pleno del Consejo Económico Sindical de Cuenca . [Cuenca] , 1965. 128 p. : LC Card 85-105812
HD2025.C84 C65 1965

Cuatro lecciones de William Brass . Arretx, Carmen. Santiago de Chile , 1977. 88 p. : LC Card 83-169600
HB1321.B73 A77 1977

CUBA - DEPENDENCY ON FOREIGN COUNTRIES - HISTORY.
Goizueta-Mimó, Félix. [Effects of sugar monoculture upon colonial Cuba.] Bitter Cuban sugar . New York , 1987. xvii, 287 p. : ISBN 0-8240-1362-X (alk. paper) : LC Card 87-8632 DDC 338.1/7361/097291 19
HD9114.C89 G6419 1987

Cuba. Dirección de Perfeccionamiento del SDPE.
El Sistema de dirección y planificación de la economía en las empresas. La Habana , 1981. xi, 203 p. : LC Card 83-212653
HC152.5 .S57 1981

CUBA - ECONOMIC CONDITIONS.
Goizueta-Mimó, Félix. [Effects of sugar monoculture upon colonial Cuba.] Bitter Cuban sugar . New York , 1987. xvii, 287 p. : ISBN 0-8240-1362-X (alk. paper) : LC Card 87-8632 DDC 338.1/7361/097291 19
HD9114.C89 G6419 1987

CUBA - ECONOMIC CONDITIONS - 1918-1959.
Jorge, Antonio, 1931- An evaluation of Cuba's post-revolutionary socioeconomic models /. Coral Gables, Fla. [1984?] 26 p. ; LC Card 87-124135 DDC 330.97291/064 19
HC152.5 .J66 1984

Torras de la Luz, Jacinto, 1909-1963. [Selections. 1984.] Obras escogidas /. La Habana , 1984- v. <1 > : LC Card 87-125434 DDC 338.97291 19
HC152.5 .T662 1984

CUBA - ECONOMIC CONDITIONS - 1959-
Banco Nacional de Cuba (Founded 1948) Cuba's financial crisis . Washington, D.C. (1000 Thomas Jefferson St., N.W., Suite 601, Washington 20007) , 1985. vii, 64, [19] p. : LC Card 86-105593 DDC 330.97291/064 19
HC152.5 .B36 1985 ***NYPL [JLE 86-3732]***

Cuba's socialist economy toward the 1990s /. Boulder, Colo. , 1987. ix, 188 p. : ISBN 1-555-87080-5 (lib. bdg. : alk. paper) : LC Card 87-12867 DDC 338.97291 19
HC152.5 .C824 1987

Jorge, Antonio, 1931- An evaluation of Cuba's post-revolutionary socioeconomic models /. Coral Gables, Fla. [1984?] 26 p. ; LC Card 87-124135 DDC 330.97291/064 19
HC152.5 .J66 1984

Pérez-López, Jorge F. Measuring Cuban economic performance /. Austin , 1987. xii, 202 p. : ISBN 0-292-75092-7 LC Card 86-24907 DDC 339.37291 19
HC152.5 .P47 1987

Torras de la Luz, Jacinto, 1909-1963. [Selections. 1984.] Obras escogidas /. La Habana , 1984- v. <1 > : LC Card 87-125434 DDC 338.97291 19
HC152.5 .T662 1984

CUBA - ECONOMIC POLICY.
Goizueta-Mimó, Félix. [Effects of sugar monoculture upon colonial Cuba.] Bitter Cuban sugar . New York , 1987. xvii, 287 p. : ISBN 0-8240-1362-X (alk. paper) : LC Card 87-8632 DDC 338.1/7361/097291 19
HD9114.C89 G6419 1987

El Sistema de dirección y planificación de la economía en las empresas. La Habana , 1981. xi, 203 p. : LC Card 83-212653
HC152.5 .S57 1981

Torras de la Luz, Jacinto, 1909-1963. [Selections. 1984.] Obras escogidas /. La Habana , 1984- v. <1 > : LC Card 87-125434 DDC 338.97291 19
HC152.5 .T662 1984

Cuba, el movimiento obrero y su entorno socio-politico, 1865-1983 /. Riesgo, Rodolfo. Miami , 1985. 251 p. ; ISBN 0-917049-02-0 (pbk.) LC Card 86-673864
HD6578.5 .R53x 1985

CUBA - FOREIGN ECONOMIC RELATIONS - EUROPE, EASTERN.
Kuba v mezhdunarodnom sotsialisticheskom razdelenii truda /. Moskva , 1986. 146 p. : LC Card 86-232928
HF1500.5.E852 K83 1986

CUBA - HISTORY - REVOLUTION, 1959.
Córdova, Efrén. Castro and the Cuban labor movement . Lanham, MD , c1987. xii, 341 p. ; ISBN 0-8191-5952-2 (alk. paper) : LC Card 86-28159 DDC 322/.2/097291 19
HD6578.5 .C67 1987

CUBA - RURAL CONDITIONS.
CUBA - STATISTICAL SERVICES.
Silva Fernández, Ricardo. Organización de la estadística en Cuba /. Playa, Ciudad de La Habana , 1985 printing, c1980. 136 p. : LC Card 87-115269 DDC 354.72910081/9 19
HA37.C866 S55 1985

Cuban-American National Foundation Inc. .
(12) Banco Nacional de Cuba (Founded 1948) Cuba's financial crisis . Washington, D.C. (1000 Thomas Jefferson St., N.W., Suite 601, Washington 20007) , 1985. vii, 64, [19] p. : LC Card 86-105593 DDC 330.97291/064 19
HC152.5 .B36 1985 ***NYPL [JLE 86-3732]***

CUBAN AMERICANS - FLORIDA - MIAMI.
Botifoll, Luis J. How Miami's new image was created /. Coral Gables, Fla. [1985?] 16 p. ; LC Card 87-124138
HC108.M5 B68 1985

Cuba's financial crisis . Banco Nacional de Cuba (Founded 1948) Washington, D.C. (1000 Thomas Jefferson St., N.W., Suite 601, Washington 20007) , 1985. vii, 64, [19] p. : LC Card 86-105593 DDC 330.97291/064 19
HC152.5 .B36 1985 ***NYPL [JLE 86-3732]***

Cuba's socialist economy toward the 1990s / edited by Andrew Zimbalist. Boulder, Colo. : L. Rienner Publishers, 1987. ix, 188 p. : ill. ; 26 cm. "First published as volume 15, number 1 (January 1987) of World development"--T.P. verso. Includes bibliographies and index. ISBN 1-555-87080-5 (lib. bdg. : alk. paper) : LC Card 87-12867 DDC 338.97291 19
1. Cuba - Economic conditions - 1959-. 2. Agriculture and state - Cuba. 3. Industry and state - Cuba. 4. Public health - Cuba. 5. Central planning - Cuba. I. Zimbalist, Andrew S.
HC152.5 .C824 1987

Čubra, Nikola. Naučnoistraživački i razvojni rad u organizacijama udruženog rada / Nikola Čubra. Beograd : NIRO "Književne novine," 1982. 165 p. : ill. ; 24 cm. In Serbo-Croatian (Roman) On t.p., cover, and spine: 04. Bibliography: p. 159-161. LC Card 82-166181
1. Industrial organization - Yugoslavia - Research - Methodology. 2. Research, Industrial - Yugoslavia. I. Title.
HD30 .C83 1982

Cubukgil, Adil. Urbanization in developing countries : some reflections on the literature / Adil Cubukgil. [Toronto] : University of Toronto, Urban and Regional Planning, 1981. ii, 77 p. ; 28 cm. (Papers on planning and design . no. 30) Bibliography: p. 71-77.
1. Urbanization - Developing countries. 2. City planning - Developing countries. 3. Regional planning - Developing countries. I. Title. II. Series.
NYPL [JLF 87-277]

Cúcuta y sus servicios públicos básicos /. Buenahora Febres-Cordero, Norma. Bogotá, D.E. , 1984. 136 p. ; LC Card 85-205425
HD4637.A5 B84 1984

Cuddington, John T.
Budget deficits and the current account in the presence of classical unemployment / John T. Cuddington, José M. Viñals. [Madrid] : Banco de España, Servicio de Estudios, [1984] 47 p. : ill. ; 27 cm. (Documento de trabajo / Banco de España, Servicio de Estudios . no. 8418) "November 1984." Bibliography: p. 35-37. ISBN 84-505-0847-9 (pbk.) LC Card 86-215031 DDC 339.5/23/0724 19
1. Budget deficits - Mathematical models. 2. Balance of trade - Mathematical models. 3. Unemployment - Mathematical models. 4. Equilibrium (Economics) - Mathematical models. I. Viñals, José M. II. Series: Documento de trabajo / Banco de España, Servicio de Estudios , no. 8418. III. Title.
HJ2005 .C83 1984

Capital flight : estimates, issues, and explanations / John T. Cuddington. Princeton, N.J. : International Finance Section, Dept. of Economics, Princeton University, c1986. 44 p. ; 23 cm. (Princeton studies in international finance, 0081-8070 . no. 58 (Dec. 1986) Bibliography: p. 39-40. ISBN 0-88165-230-X (pbk.) : LC Card 86-21386 DDC 332/.041 19
1. Capital movements. 2. International finance. 3. Debts, External - Developing countries. I. Series: Princeton studies in international finance, no. 58. II. Title.
HG3891 .C83 1986

Cuenca García, Eduardo. Las intervenciones financieras comunitarias / Eduardo Cuenca García. Madrid : Ministerio de Economía y

Hacienda, Instituto de Estudios Fiscales, [1985?] 53 p. ; 24 cm. (Monografía / Instituto de Estudios Fiscales . no. 4.) Includes bibliographical references. ISBN 84-7196-523-2 LC Card 85-200493
1. European Economic Community - Finance. 2. European Coal and Steel Community. 3. European Agricultural Guidance and Guarantee Fund. 4. European Social Fund. 5. European Regional Development Fund. I. Series: Monografías (Instituto de Estudios Fiscales (Spain)) , no. 4. II. Title.
HJ2094.5 .C84 1985

CUENCA (SPAIN) - ECONOMIC CONDITIONS.
Consejo Económico Sindical Provincial (Cuenca, Spain) IV pleno del Consejo Económico Sindical de Cuenca . [Cuenca] , 1965. 128 p. : LC Card 85-105812
HD2025.C84 C65 1965

CUENCA (SPAIN) - INDUSTRIES.
Consejo Económico Sindical Provincial (Cuenca, Spain) IV pleno del Consejo Económico Sindical de Cuenca . [Cuenca] , 1965. 128 p. : LC Card 85-105812
HD2025.C84 C65 1965

CUENCA (SPAIN) - SOCIAL CONDITIONS.
Consejo Económico Sindical Provincial (Cuenca, Spain) IV pleno del Consejo Económico Sindical de Cuenca . [Cuenca] , 1965. 128 p. : LC Card 85-105812
HD2025.C84 C65 1965

Cuentas financieras de la economía española, 1972-1982 / Banco de España. [Madrid] : Banco de España, Servicio de Estudios, 1984. 157 p. ; 26 cm. ISBN 84-500-9729-0 LC Card 86-205358
1. Flow of funds - Spain - Accounting. I. Banco de España.
HC390.F55 C84 1984

Cuenya, Beatriz. Habitat popular . Buenos Aires , 1986. 162 p. : LC Card 87-404028 DDC 363.5/8 19
HD7305.5 .H32 1986

Cuervo García, Alvaro. Manual de sistema financiero : instituciones, mercados y medios en España / Alvaro Cuervo, Luis Rodríguez Sáiz y José Alberto Parejo.1a ed. Barcelona : Ariel, 1987. 427 p. : ill. ; 24 cm. (Ariel economía. Serie Ciencias empresariales) Bibliography: p. [415]-421. ISBN 84-344-2013-9 LC Card 87-135198
1. Finance - Spain. 2. Banks and banking - Spain. 3. Financial institutions - Spain. 4. Monetary policy - Spain. I. Rodríguez Sáiz, L. (Luis). II. Parejo Gamir, Alberto. III. Title. IV. Series.
HG186.S6 C84 1987

Cuervo, Luis Mauricio. Jaramillo, Samuel. Análisis de las condiciones de vivienda de los hogares colombianos, a partir de los resultados de la encuesta nacional de hogares, etapa 33, 1981 /. Bogotá, Colombia , 1985. ii, 166 p. ; LC Card 87-403605 DDC 363.5/1/09861 19
HD7325.A3 J37 1985

Cuesta Moreno, Marco Tobías. El Chocó--ayer, hoy y mañana / Marco Tobías Cuesta Moreno ; prólogo de Jorge Mario Eastman. 1a ed. Bogotá, Colombia : Fundación Publicaciones Consigna, 1986. 131 p., [5] leaves of plates : ill. ; 21 cm. (Colección Fundación Publicaciones Consigna) Bibliography: p. 130-131. LC Card 87-115171 DDC 330.9861/270632 19
1. Chocó, Colombia - Economic conditions. 2. Chocó, Colombia - Social conditions. 3. Choco (Colombia) - History. I. Title.
HC198.C48 C84 1986

Cuevas, Enrique de las. Las industrias forestales en la Provincia de Huesca / por Enrique de las Cuevas. Huesca : Tip. de Modesto Aguarón, 1919. 58 p. ; 20 cm. LC Card 84-100478
1. Forest products industry - Spain - Huesca (Province). I. Title.
HD9765.S7 H833 1919

Culbertson, John. Issues after a century of federal competition policy /. Lexington, Mass. , c1987. vii, 387 p. ; ISBN 0-669-13320-5 (alk. paper) LC Card 86-45377 DDC 338.6/048/0973 19
HD3616.U47 I77 1987

Culen, Eva. Collins, Lora S. The U. S. economy to 1990 /. New York, N.Y. , c1985. 21 p. : ISBN 0-8237-0307-X (pbk.) LC Card 86-200284 DDC 338.5/443/0973 19
HC106.8 .C636 1985

Cullis, John C. Microeconomics and the public economy : a defence of Leviathan / John G. Cullis and Philip R. Jones. Oxford, OX, UK ; New York, NY, USA : B. Blackwell, 1987. xx, 251 p. : ill. ; 24 cm. Spine title: Microeconomics & the public economy. Includes bibliographies and indexes. ISBN 0-631-15552-X : LC Card 87-5169 DDC 338.5 19
1. Microeconomics. 2. Finance, Public. 3. Expenditures, Public. I. Jones, Philip R., 1948-. II. Title. III. Title: Micro-economics and the public economy. IV. Title: Microeconomics & the public economy.
HB172 .C85 1987

Culp, Dwyer, Guterson & Grader. Joint development financing for public works . Olympia, Wash. (9th & Columbia Bldg., MS/GH-51, Olympia 98504) [1986] 1 v. (various pagings) : LC Card 86-622101 DDC 338.4/3363/09797 19
HD3890.W2 J65 1986

El cultivo del algodón y la soya en el Paraguay y sus derivaciones sociales. Palau, Tomás. Santiago de Chile , 1986. 148 p. ; ISBN 92-1-321207-0 LC Card 87-400251 DDC 338.1/7351/09892 19
HD9084.P25 P35 1986

A cultura da vinha na região do Redondo /. Pereira, Francisco José Piteira. [Lisbon] , 1983. 11, 4, 30, 21 leaves, [2] leaves of plates : LC Card 84-238378
HD9259.G7 P47 1983

La cultura d'impresa . Poiani, Mario, 1934- Milano, Italy , c1986. 212, [1] p. ; LC Card 86-221350
HD58.7 .P63 1986

Cultura e vita civile nel Settecento. Monti, Aldino. Alle origini della borghesia urbana . Bologna , c1985. 469 p. : ISBN 88-15-00833-0 : LC Card 86-110136 DDC 333.3/0945/41 19
HD680.B65 M66 1985 ***NYPL [JLD 87-481]***

Cultura fondamentale. Unità didattiche . (3) Guarracino, Scipione, 1943- Le origini dell'industria /. Milano, Italy , c1985. 83 p. : LC Card 86-157399
HD2321 .G78 1985

Cultura tairona.
Foro de la Esperanza (1985 : Ibagué, Colombia) Foro de la Esperanza . [Bogotá?] [1985] 154 p. ; LC Card 87-401285 DDC 338.9861 19
HC197 .F59 1985

Cultural and economic factors in the fertility of Thai women /. Hogan, Dennis P. Honolulu, HI [1987] p. cm. ISBN 0-86638-103-1 : LC Card 87-21459 DDC 304.6/32/09593 19
HB1054.55.A3 H64 1987

CULTURAL ANTHROPOLOGY. see **ETHNOLOGY.**

Cultural aspects of fuelwood procurement in Kakamega District /. Chavangi, Noel A. Nairobi [1984] 13 leaves ; LC Card 87-112356 DDC 333.75 19
HD9769.F843 K43 1984

CULTURAL CHANGE. see **SOCIAL CHANGE.**

Cultural change in family firms . Dyer, W. Gibb, 1954- San Francisco , 1986. xxi, 179 p. ; ISBN 1-555-42007-9 (alk. paper) LC Card 86-10585 DDC 658/.045 19
HD62.25 .D94 1986 ***NYPL [JLE 87-1079]***

CULTURAL EVOLUTION. see **SOCIAL CHANGE.**

Cultural resource management study . (no. 11) Weinbaum, Paul O. Hoosac docks . Boston, Mass. , 1985. vi, 95 p. : LC Card 85-603289 DDC 387.1/64/0974461 19
HE554.B6 W45 1985

CULTURE.
Harrison, Lawrence E. Underdevelopment is a state of mind . [Cambridge, Mass.] , Lanham, MD , 1988, c1985. p. cm. ISBN 0-8191-6490-9 (pbk. : alk. paper) : LC Card 87-24678 DDC 330.98/0038 19
HC125 .H384 1988

Huxley, Aldous, 1894-1963. [Brave new world.] Brave new world ; and, Brave new world revisited /. London , 1984. xxii, 387 p. ; ISBN 0-7011-2769-4 : LC Card 84-134715 DDC 823/.912 19
PR6015.U9 B65 1984 ***NYPL [JFE 86-4706]***

McCoid, Catherine Hodge. Carrying capacities of nation-states /. New Haven, Conn. (P.O. Box 2015, Yale Station, New Haven 06520) , 1984. x, 198 leaves : LC Card 84-152784 DDC 304.6/2 19
GN33.5 .M38 1984 ***NYPL [JFE 86-2142]***

Stirrings of culture /. Dallas, Tex. , 1986. xix, 250 p. ; ISBN 0-911005-07-2 : LC Card 86-24028 DDC 306 19
HM101 .S786 1986 ***NYPL [JFF 87-151]***

Thompson, Kenneth, 1937- Beliefs and ideology /. Chichester, West Sussex : London ; 135 p. ; ISBN 0-85312-858-8 : LC Card 86-2984 DDC 306/.4 19
BL60 .T49 1986 ***NYPL [JLD 86-2479]***

Culture and consumption . McCracken, Grant David, 1951- Bloomington , c1988. xv, 174 p. ; ISBN 0-253-31526-3 LC Card 87-45394 DDC 339.4/7 19
HC79.C6 M385 1988

Culture and context in Sudan . Tully, Dennis. Albany, N.Y. , c1988. p. cm. ISBN 0-88706-502-3 LC Card 86-23180 DDC 338.1/09627 19
HC835.Z7 D377 1988

Culture and reproduction : an anthropological critique of demographic transition theory / edited by W. Penn Handwerker. Boulder, Colo. : Westview Press, 1986. xix, 389 p. : ill. ; 23 cm. Based on papers presented at a conference held Dec. 2, 1981 at the University of California, Los Angeles. Includes index. Bibliography: p. 350-382. ISBN 0-8133-7199-6 (pbk. : alk. paper) : LC Card 86-5671 DDC 304.6/32 19
1. Demographic transition. 2. Fertility, Human. 3. Demographic anthropology. I. Handwerker, W. Penn.
HB887 .C85 1986 ***NYPL [JLE 86-3842]***

Culture as the basis for implementing self-sustaining wood fuel development programmes /. Chavangi, Noel A. Nairobi, Kenya [1985] 24 leaves ; LC Card 87-111963 DDC 333.75 19
HD9769.F843 K433 1985

CULTURE - CONGRESSES.
Travail, loisirs, culture. [Bruxelles] [Zwevegem]] 1970. ix, 163 p. LC Card 71-856101
HD4904.7 .T7 1970

CULTURE DIFFUSION - ITALY - ADDRESSES, ESSAYS, LECTURES.
Il Territorio immaginario /. Milano [1980] 106 p. ; ISBN 88-20-41848-7 : LC Card 81-123209 DDC 302.2/34/0945 19
HE8700.9.I8 T47 1980
NYPL [JFD 86-8337]

The culture facade . Rigdon, Susan M., 1943- Urbana , c1988. p. cm. ISBN 0-252-01495-2 (alk. paper) LC Card 87-19063 DDC 305.5/69 19
HC79.P6 R57 1988

CULTURE - HISTORY.
McCracken, Grant David, 1951- Culture and consumption . Bloomington , c1988. xv, 174 p. ; ISBN 0-253-31526-3 LC Card 87-45394 DDC 339.4/7 19
HC79.C6 M385 1988

Les Cultures industrielles du Burundi : le café, le thé, le coton / République du Burundi, Ministère de l'information, Direction générale des publications de presse burundaise. Bujumbura : Dép. de la documentation, [1985] 63 p. : ill. ; 23 cm. "Juin 1985"--Cover. Bibliography: p. 63. LC Card 85-981329
1. Coffee trade - Burundi. 2. Tea trade - Burundi. 3. Cotton trade - Burundi. 4. Burundi - Economic conditions. I. Burundi. Direction générale des publications de la presse burundaise.
HD9195.B942 C85 1985

Cultures of solidarity . Fantasia, Rick. Berkeley , c1988. p. cm. ISBN 0-520-06053-9 (alk. paper) LC Card 87-16748 DDC 331.8/0973 19
HD8072.5 .F36 1988

Cumbow, Robert C., 1946- A Century of service . Bellevue, Wash. , c1987. 178 p. : ISBN 0-9619061-0-3 (pbk.) : LC Card 87-16582 DDC 338.7/6136362/097977 19
HD9685.U7 P923 1987

Cummins, David E. (David Earl), 1938- Yager, Francis P. Financial profile of cooperatives handling grain . [Washington, D.C.] [1986] vii, 24 p. : LC Card 86-601622 DDC

334/.6831/0973021 19
HD9034 .Y34 1986

CUNARD STEAMSHIP COMPANY, LTD. - HISTORY.
Arnell, J. C. Steam and the North Atlantic mails . Toronto, Ont. , c1986. x, 295 p. : ISBN 0-919801-36-6 : LC Card 87-127353 DDC 383/.142/091631 19
HE6233 .A76 1986

Cunha, Paulo Vieira da. Grupos homogêneos no mercado de trabalho assalariado . Brasília , 1985. 56 p. : LC Card 85-231654
HD5004 .G78 1985

Cunha, Rafael Alves de. Duas décadas da produção e do produto da agropecuária RS, 1964-84 / Rafael Alves da Cunha. Porto Alegre : Secretaria de Coordenação e Planejamento, Fundação de Economia e Estatística, 1986- v. <1 > : ill. ; 30 cm. (Agregados econômicos, RS . n. 1. v. 1) Bibliography: v. 1, p. [179]-181. Errata slip inserted in v. 1. CONTENTS. - t. 1. Produção LC Card 87-404979 DDC 338.1/0981/65 19
1. Farm produce - Brazil - Rio Grande do Sul. 2. Agriculture - Economic aspects - Brazil - Rio Grande do Sul. I. Rio Grande do Sul (Brazil). Fundação de Economia e Estatística. II. Series: Agregados econômicos, RS , n. 1. III. Title.
HD9014.B83 R5416 1986

Cunningham, Jan. All about multi-level marketing : the wave of the future, with 5 steps to success / by Jan Cunningham. Denver, CO (1020 15th St., Suite 41C, Denver 80202) : CMC Multi-Level Marketing, c1986. 173 p. : ill. ; 22 cm. LC Card 86-213072 DDC 658.8/4 19
1. Multilevel marketing. 2. Success in business. I. Title. II. Title: Multi-level marketing.
HF5415.126 .C85 1986

Cuomo, Gennaro. Funzioni, strutture, strategie delle imprese commerciali complesse / Gennaro Cuomo. Padova : CEDAM, 1984. 236 p. : ill. ; 25 cm. (Collana di studi di tecnica aziendale . 1) Bibliography: p. [233]-236. LC Card 86-214195
1. Business logistics. I. Title. II. Series.
HD38.5 .C86 1984

Curatola, Anthony P. State income tax consequences of retirement plan distributions / Anthony P. Curatola. Brookfield, Wis. : International Foundation of Employee Benefit Plans, c1986. 20 p. ; 28 cm. (Research report . 86-5) "December 1986." Bibliography: p. 19-20. ISBN 0-89154-324-4 (pbk.) LC Card 87-158902 DDC 336.24/16 19
1. Pension trusts - Taxation - United States. 2. Income tax - United States - Deductions - Retirement contributions. 3. Taxation, State. I. Series: Research report (International Foundation of Employee Benefit Plans) , rept. 86-5. II. Title.
HJ4653.P5 C87 1986

Curet, Eliezer. Puerto Rico : development by integration to the U. S. / Eliezer Curet. Rio Piedras, P.R. (Calle Roble No. 51, Rio Piedras 00925) : Editorial Cultural, 1986. xiii, 257 p. : ill. ; 23 cm. Bibliography: p. 249-257. LC Card 87-100359 DDC 338.97295 19
1. Puerto Rico - Economic conditions - 1952-. 2. Puerto Rico - Economic policy. I. Title.
HC154.5 .C87 1986

Curran, James. Survival of the small firm /. Aldershot, Hants, England , Brookfield, Vt., U. S.A. , c1986. 2 v. : ISBN 0-566-00725-8 (v. 1) : LC Card 85-27035 DDC 338.6/42 19
HD2341 .S87 1986 ***NYPL [JLD 86-2643]***

CURRENCY. see **MONEY.**

Currency and credit before and since 1914 [microform] /. Blake, Hubert, 1893- London , 1923. viii, 91 p. ; ***NYPL [*ZT-1736 no.1]***

Currency and interest rate hedging . Andersen, Torben Juul. New York, N.Y. , c1987. viii, 272 p. : ISBN 0-13-195645-0 LC Card 87-7758 DDC 332.64/5 19
HG3853 .A53 1987

CURRENCY QUESTION - EUROPE.
Grabbe, J. Orlin. International financial markets /. New York , c1986. xi, 347 p. : ISBN 0-444-01032-7 LC Card 85-32545 DDC 332.4/5 19
HG3851 .G64 1986 ***NYPL [JLF 87-82]***

CURRENCY QUESTION - EUROPE, EASTERN.
Konstantinov, ÎU. A. (ÎUriĭ Anatol′evich) Mezhdunarodnaia valiutnaia sistema stran--chlenov SĖV /. Moskva , 1982. 231 p. ; LC Card 82-210094
HG3942 .K67 1982

CURRENCY QUESTION - EUROPEAN ECONOMIC COMMUNITY COUNTRIES - CONGRESSES.
Problemy valiutnogo soiuza stran-chlenov Evropeĭskogo ėkonomicheskogo soobshchestva i razvitie mezhdunarodnoĭ valiutnoĭ sistemy kapitalizma . Sofiia , 1984. 151 p. ; LC Card 85-224144
HG3942.8 .P76 1984

CURRENCY QUESTION - GREAT BRITAIN.
Malthus, T. R. (Thomas Robert, 1766-1834. The measure of value stated and illustrated . Fairfield, NJ , 1988. p. cm. ISBN 0-678-00603-2 LC Card 87-17246 DDC 332.4/1 19
HB201 .M297 1988

Ricardo, David, 1772-1823. Scritti monetari /. Roma [1985] 495 p. ; LC Card 86-207988
HG938 .R63 1985

CURRENCY QUESTION - INDIA.
Keynes, John Maynard, 1883-1946. Indian currency and finance /. London , 1913 (Edinburgh : R. & R. Clark) viii, 263 p., [1] folded leaf of plates ; LC Card A13-2169 DDC 332.4/954
HG1234 .K4 ***NYPL [*KF 1913 87-34]***

CURRENCY QUESTION - ITALY.
Tasgian, Astrig. L'imposta e il deposito previo sugli acquisti di valuta e la crisi della lira del 1976 . Milano , c1983. 139 p. : LC Card 83-187693 DDC 332.4/945 19
HG1029.5 .T37 1983 ***NYPL [JLD 87-813]***

CURRENCY QUESTION - LATIN AMERICA - MATHEMATICAL MODELS.
Canto, Victor A. Currency substitution . Boston , c1987. viii, 196 p. ; ISBN 0-89838-195-9 LC Card 86-27747 DDC 332.4/56/098 19
HG3823 .C36 1987

CURRENCY QUESTION - MATHEMATICAL MODELS.
Nyberg, Peter. On the choice of optimal central bank currency baskets /. Åbo , 1982. 24 p. ; ***NYPL [JLL 77-251 no. 181]***

CURRENCY QUESTION - UNITED STATES.
Rice, Jonathan. How to survive and profit from the coming currency recall /. Chicago , c1986. xiii, 258 p. : ISBN 0-8092-4998-7 : LC Card 86-6215 DDC 332.4/973 19
HG540 .R53 1986 ***NYPL [JLE 86-3508]***

Currency substitution . Canto, Victor A. Boston , c1987. viii, 196 p. ; ISBN 0-89838-195-9 LC Card 86-27747 DDC 332.4/56/098 19
HG3823 .C36 1987

Current account in asset market models of exchange rate determination. Gross, Alexander, 1953- The role of the current account in asset market models of exchange rate determination /. Berlin , New York , 1987. xiii, 391 p. : ISBN 0-89925-373-3 (U. S.) : LC Card 87-8852 DDC 332.4/56 19
HG3882 .G75 1987

Current approaches to grading commercial loans /. Dickerson, Charles S. Philadelphia, Pa. , c1987. 42 p. ; ISBN 0-936742-43-7 (pbk.) LC Card 87-18458 DDC 332.1/753/0685 19
HG1642.U5 D53 1987

Current budgeting practices in U. S. industry . Umapathy, Srinivasan. New York , 1987. xxxix, 176 p. ; ISBN 0-89930-250-5 (lib. bdg. : alk. paper) LC Card 87-5969 DDC 658.1/54 19
HG4028.B8 U46 1987

Current concepts in nutrition .
(v. 7) American Jewish Joint Distribution Committee. [Choroba głodowa. English.] Hunger disease . New York , c1979. xiv, 261 p. : ISBN 0-471-05003-2 LC Card 78-26397 DDC 616.3/9
RC627.S7 A43 1979
NYPL [*PXV (Warsaw) 86-3505]

Current controversies in economics / edited by Howard Vane and Terry Caslin. Oxford [Oxfordshire] UK ; New York, NY, USA : B. Blackwell, 1987. xii, 319 p. : ill. ; 24 cm. Includes bibliographies and index. ISBN 0-631-15157-5 : LC Card 86-29928 DDC 338.941 19
1. Economics. 2. Economic policy. 3. Neoclassical school of economics. 4. Great Britain - Economic policy - 1945-. 5. Great Britain - Economic conditions - 1945-. I. Vane, Howard R. II. Caslin, Terry.
HB171.5 .C975 1987

Current economic and financial issues of the North American and Caribbean countries / edited by Edgar Ortiz. Mexico, D.F. : North American Economics and Finance Association, 1983. 390 p. : ill. ; 28 cm. A selection of rev. papers presented at the North American Economics and Finance Association Annual Meeting held on Dec. 28-30, 1982 in New York City. Includes bibliographies. LC Card 87-106905 DDC 330.97/00539 19
1. North America - Economic conditions - Congresses. 2. Caribbean Area - Economic conditions - 1945- - Congresses. 3. Finance - North America - Congresses. 4. Finance - Caribbean area - Congresses. I. Ortiz, Edgar. II. North American Economics and Finance Association.
HC95 .C87 1983

Current issues brief .
(1986-87/2) McCormick, William A. The export woodchip industry of south east NSW . Barton, A.C.T. , 1986. 23 p. : LC Card 87-163674 DDC 333.75/09944 19
HD9769.W383 A85 1986

(1986-87/3) Kopras, Andrew. Trading with South Africa /. [Canberra] , 1986. 14 p. ; LC Card 87-164241 DDC 382/.0968/094021 19
HF3901.A45 K66 1986

Current issues in human-resource management /. Schein, Lawrence. New York, N.Y. (845 3rd Ave., New York 10022) , c1986. 17 p. : LC Card 86-212364 DDC 658.3/01 19
HF5549.5.M3 S34 1986

Current issues (Institute of Southeast Asian Studies. ASEAN Economic Research Unit) .
(no. 9) K. A. Mohamed Ariff, 1940- Malaysia and ASEAN economic cooperation /. Singapore , 1980, cover 1981. 177 p. ; ISBN 997-19-0207-9 LC Card 82-940035
HC441 .K18 1981

Current problems of economic integration : the problems of promoting and financing integration projects / United Nations Conference on Trade and Development. New York : United Nations, 1986. viii, 115 p. ; 30 cm. "TD/B/C.7/79"--T.p. verso. "United Nations publication sales no. E.86.II.D.1"--T.p. verso. Includes bibliographical references. ISBN 92-1-112216-3 (pbk.) LC Card 87-106405 DDC 337.1/1724 19
1. Developing countries - Economic integration. 2. International economic integration. 3. Development banks - Developing countries. I. United Nations. Conference on Trade and Development.
HC59.7 .C845 1986

Current readings on money, banking, and financial markets / edited by James A. Wilcox ; Frederic S. Mishkin, consulting editor. 1987 ed. Boston : Little, Brown, c1987. xii, 356 p. : ill. ; 28 cm. Includes bibliographies. ISBN 0-316-94020-8 (pbk.) LC Card 87-4116 DDC 332 19
1. Finance. 2. Money. 3. Banks and banking. 4. International finance. I. Wilcox, James Allen, 1952-. II. Mishkin, Frederic S.
HG175 .C87 1987

Current trends in water-supply planning . Prasifka, David W., 1951- New York , c1988. xi, 266 p. : ISBN 0-442-27511-0 : LC Card 87-12157 DDC 333.91/212 19
HD1691 .P7 1988

Current U. S. trade policy : analysis, agenda, and administration / Robert E. Baldwin, J. David Richardson, editors. Cambridge, Mass. (1050 Massachusetts Ave., Cambridge 02138) : National Bureau of Economic Research, 1986. iii, 128 p. ; 23 cm. (NBER conference report) "Based on papers presented at the National Bureau of Economic Research Conference on Current Trade Policy Issues, which was held in Cambridge, Massachusetts, on August 8, 1985"--Pref. Includes bibliographies. LC Card 86-201110 DDC 382/.3/0973 19
1. United States - Commercial policy - Congresses. I. Baldwin, Robert E. II. Richardson, J. David. III. National Bureau of Economic Research. IV. National Bureau of Economic Research Conference on Current Trade Policy Issues (1985 : Cambridge, Mass.). V. Title:

Current United States trade policy. VI. Series.
HF1455 .C87 1986

Current United States trade policy. Current U. S. trade policy . Cambridge, Mass. (1050 Massachusetts Ave., Cambridge 02138) , 1986. iii, 128 p. ; LC Card 86-201110 DDC 382/.3/0973 19
HF1455 .C87 1986

CURRENT VALUE ACCOUNTING - GREAT BRITAIN.
Accounting for economic costs and changing prices . London , 1986. 2 v. : ISBN 0-11-560004-3 (pbk. : v. 1) : LC Card 86-216162 DDC 657/.42 19
HF5658.5 .A22 1986

Currie, Ian. Durkacz, Victor Edward. Financial planning for new businesses /. Chichester [West Sussex] , New York , c1985. 257 p. : ISBN 0-471-90843-6 (pbk.) : LC Card 85-17927 DDC 658.1/5 19
HG4027.6 .D87 1985 ***NYPL [JLE 86-929]***

Currie, Lawrence A., 1949- A time for change : industrial relations and the Digby strike, 1979-1983 / by Lawrence A. Currie. Halifax, N.S. : Dalhousie Labour-University Committee, Henson College of Public Affairs and Continuing Education, Dalhousie University, c1986. 64 p. : ill. ; 20 cm. ISBN 0-88926-031-1 (pbk.) LC Card 86-230034 DDC 331.89/281388322 19
1. School Bus Drivers' Strike, Digby, N.S., 1979-1983. 2. Industrial relations - Nova Scotia. I. Title.
HD5329.M82 1979 .D543 1986

Currier, Chet. No cost/low cost investing / Chet Currier, David Smyth. New York : F. Watts, 1987. 240 p. ; 24 cm. Includes index. ISBN 0-531-15527-7 LC Card 87-13690 DDC 332.6/78 19
1. Investments - United States. 2. Securities - United States. I. Smyth, David, 1929-. II. Title. III. Title: Low cost investing.
HG4910 .C86 1987

Curry Foundation. Confrontation or negotiation . Millwood, N.Y. , 1985. xvi, 303 p. : ISBN 0-8046-9397-8 : LC Card 85-18667 DDC 382/.41/094 19
HD9015.E82 C67 1985
NYPL [JLE 86-4594]

Curso de formação superior. Mercado financeiro e de capitais . [Brasília? , 1978?] 118 leaves, [25] leaves of plates : LC Card 84-184169
HG185.B7 M47 1978

Curtis, Fred A. (Fred Allen), 1946- ENERGEX '84 (1984 : Regina, Sask.) Energy developments . Toronto , New York , 1984. xxiv, 1026 p. : ISBN 0-08-025407-1 LC Card 85-122124 DDC 333.79 19
TJ163.15 .E46 1984 ***NYPL [JSF 86-799]***

Curtis, Jane, 1918- Frederick Billings, Vermonter, pioneer lawyer, business man, conservationist : an illustrated biography / by Jane Curtis, Peter Jennison, and Frank Lieberman. Woodstock, VT : Woodstock Foundation, c1986. 135 p. : ill., ports. ; 28 cm. Includes index. ISBN 0-930985-04-4 (pbk.) : LC Card 86-28103 DDC 385/.092/4 B 19
1. Billings, Frederick, 1823-1890. 2. Businessmen - United States - Biography. 3. Northern Pacific Railway Company - History. I. Jennison, Peter S. II. Lieberman, Frank. III. Title.
HE2754.B5 C87 1986

Curtis, Richard (Richard E.) Affording access to quality care . Washington, D.C. (444 N. Capitol St., N.W., Suite 250, Washington 20001) , c1986. xx, 245 p. ; LC Card 87-127057 DDC 338.4/336210452/0973 19
HD7102.U4 A66 1986

Curwen, Peter J.
Goacher, D. J. (David J.) British non-bank financial intermediaries /. London , Boston , 1987. xxiv, 460 p. : ISBN 0-04-332109-7 (alk. paper) LC Card 86-32146 DDC 332.1/0941 19
HG186.G7 B73 1987

Public enterprise : a modern approach / by Peter J. Curwen. Brighton, Sussex : Wheatsheaf Books, 1986. xvii, 318 p. : ill. ; 23 cm. Includes index. Bibliography: p. 306-313. ISBN 0-312-65435-9 : LC Card 85-26234 DDC 354.4109/2 19
1. Government business enterprises - Great Britain. 2. Government ownership - Great Britain. 3. Privatization - Great Britain. I. Title.
HD4145 .C87 1986 ***NYPL [JLD 86-1636]***

Curwin, Jon.
Business studies in context : an assignment-based business simulation / John Curwin, Debbie Goodkin, Roger Slater. London ; New York : McGraw-Hill, 1987. p. cm. "Students' book." Teacher's manual includes v. for Appendices. ISBN 0-07-707034-8 : LC Card 87-22560 DDC 658.4/0352 19
1. Industrial management - Mathematical models. 2. Industrial management - Data processing. 3. Business - Mathematical models. 4. Business - Data processing. I. Goodkin, Debbie. II. Slater, Roger. III. Title.
HD30.25 .C87 1987

Quantitative methods for business decisions / Jon Curwin and Roger Slater. New York : Van Nostrand Reinhold Co., 1985. xii, 343 p. : ill. ; 24 cm. Includes index. ISBN 0-442-30640-7 (pbk.) LC Card 85-3267 DDC 519.5/024658 19
1. Business mathematics. 2. Statistics. I. Slater, Roger. II. Title.
HF5691 .C87 1985

Cusco . Barrenechea Lercari, Carlos. Cusco [Peru] 1986. 77 p. ; LC Card 87-400243 DDC 338.1/88537 19
HD1905.C87 B37 1986

Cushing, Barry E. Accounting information systems . Reading, Mass. , c1987. p. cm. ISBN 0-201-10376-1 : LC Card 87-1155 DDC 657/.028/5 19
HF5679 .A34 1987

Cushman, Robert Frank, 1931-
The Business insurance handbook /. Homewood, Ill. , c1981. xvii, 753 p. : ISBN 0-87094-237-9 LC Card 80-70437 DDC 368.8/1/00202 19
HG8059 .B87 ***NYPL [*R-Econ. 86-2502]***

Handbook for raising capital . Homewood, Ill. , c1987. xxiv, 666 p. : ISBN 0-87094-705-2 LC Card 86-71216 ***NYPL [*R-Econ. 87-1124]***

Cussianovich, Pedro. Economía y energía en Costa Rica : bases para el planteamiento de alternativas agroenergéticas / Pedro Cussianovich, Juan Antonio Aguirre. San José, Costa Rica : Instituto Interamericano de Cooperación para la Agricultura, Comité de Trópicos y División de Agroenergía, 1982. viii, 71, [10] leaves : ill. ; 28 cm. (Serie Publicaciones misceláneas, 0534-5391 . no. 313) Bibliography: leaf [72] LC Card 86-179795
1. Energy industries - Costa Rica. 2. Energy policy - Costa Rica. I. Aguirre, Juan Antonio. II. Series: Série Publicações misceláneas , no. 313. III. Title.
HD9502.C82 C87 1982

Cust, Richard. The forced loan and English politics, 1626-1628 / Richard Cust. Oxford [Oxfordshire] : Clarendon Press ; New York : Oxford University Press, 1987. x, 358 p. ; 23 cm. Bibliography: p. [338]-345. Includes index. ISBN 0-19-822951-8 : LC Card 87-7977 DDC 336.42 19
1. Finance, Public - Great Britain - To 1688. 2. Intergovernmental fiscal relations - Great Britain - History - 17th century. 3. Great Britain - Politics and government - 1625-1649. I. Title.
HJ1012 .C87 1987

Custo de produção : leite. Curitiba, Paraná : Organização das Cooperativas do Estado do Paraná, 1987. 88 p. ; 22 cm. Bibliography: p. 88. LC Card 87-405296 DDC 338.1/371/098162 19
1. Milk trade - Brazil - Paraná (State) - Costs. I. Organização das Cooperativas do Estado do Paraná.
HD9282.B73 P3435 1987

Custo de produção de café /
OCEPAR--Organização das Cooperativas do Estado do Paraná. Curitiba-Paraná : OCEPAR, [19]84. 47 p. ; 22 cm. Prepared by Nelson Costa, Flávio Enir Turra, and Gilberto Borges da Silveira. Limited edition of 300 copies. Bibliography: p. 47. LC Card 85-211612
1. Coffee trade - Brazil - Costs. I. Costa, Nelson. II. Turra, Flávio Enir. III. Silveira, Gilberto Borges da. IV. Organização das Cooperativas do Estado do Paraná.
HD9199.B7 C93 1984

Custo de vida . Kirsten, José Tiacci. São Paulo , 1985. xi, 158 p. : LC Card 86-143942
HB235.B8 K57 1985

Custo dos recursos domésticos /. Moldau, Juan Hersztajn. Rio de Janeiro , 1985. 94, 4 p. ; LC Card 86-200395
HC190.C7 M64 1985

Custom and contract . Schweitzer, Mary M. New York , 1987. xii, 271 p. : ISBN 0-231-06288-5 LC Card 87-8003 DDC 338.9748 19
HC107.P4 S417 1987

The customer is key . Lele, Milind M. New York , c1987. xii, 260 p. : ISBN 0-471-82859-9 LC Card 87-21549 DDC 658.8/12 19
HF5415.3 .L45 1987

Customer premises telecom equipment & the regional Bell companies. Norwalk, Conn., U. S.A. (6 Prowitt St., Norwalk 06855) : International Resource Development Inc., c1987. ix, 193 leaves ; 28 cm. (Report / International Resource Development Inc. . #736 (May 1987)) LC Card 87-403216 DDC 381/.45621385 19
1. Private branch exchange telephone equipment industry - United States. 2. Market surveys - United States. 3. American Telephone and Telegraph Company. I. International Resource Development, inc. II. Title: Customer premises telecom equipment and the regional Bell companies. III. Series: Report / International Resource Development Inc. , #736.
HD9697.T453 U5245 1987

Customer premises telecom equipment and the regional Bell companies. Customer premises telecom equipment & the regional Bell companies. Norwalk, Conn., U. S.A. (6 Prowitt St., Norwalk 06855) , c1987. ix, 193 leaves ; LC Card 87-403216 DDC 381/.45621385 19
HD9697.T453 U5245 1987

CUSTOMER RELATIONS.
Close to the customer . New York, N.Y. , c1987. 96 p. ; ISBN 0-8144-3513-0 (pbk.) : LC Card 87-12558 DDC 658.8/12 19
HF5415.5 .C57 1987

Customer service [motion picture] . Del Mar, CA , 1985. 1 film reel (13 min.) : ISBN 0-07-620872-9 LC Card 86-708025 DDC 658.8 11
HF5415.5

Customer service [videorecording] . Del Mar, CA , 1985. 1 videocassette (13 min.) : ISBN 0-07-109048-7 (3/4 in.) LC Card 86-708026 DDC 658.8 11
HF5415.5

Dealing with difficult customers [motion picture] /. Del Mar, CA , 1986. 1 film reel (13 min.) : ISBN 0-07-620875-3 LC Card 86-708027 DDC 658.8 11
HF5415.5

Dealing with difficult customers [videorecording] /. Del Mar, CA , 1986. 1 videocassette (13 min.) : ISBN 0-07-109068-1 (3/4 in.) LC Card 86-708028 DDC 658.8 11
HF5415.5

Desatnick, Robert L. Managing to keep the customer . San Francisco , 1987. xvi, 163 p. ; ISBN 1-555-42027-3 (alk. paper) LC Card 86-21399 DDC 658.8/12 19
HF5415.5 .D47 1987

LeBoeuf, Michael. How to win customers and keep them for life /. New York , c1987. 190 p. ; ISBN 0-399-13301-1 LC Card 87-13892 DDC 658.8/12 19
HF5415.5 .L4 1987

Metz, Matthias. Kundenfreundliches Verhalten . Frankfurt am Main , c1985. xxi, 349 p. : ISBN 3-7819-0326-5 LC Card 85-202352
HG1616.P8 M47 1985

Poppe, Fred C. 50 rules to keep a client happy /. New York , c1987. 90 p. : ISBN 0-06-015779-8 : LC Card 87-45139 DDC 659.1/125 19
HF6178 .P66 1987

CUSTOMER RELATIONS - CASE STUDIES.
Strategies for international industrial marketing . London , Dover, N.H. , c1986. 310 p. : ISBN 0-7099-2494-1 : LC Card 85-29047 DDC 658.8/48 19
HF1009.7.E85 S77 1986
NYPL [JLD 86-1596]

Customer service [motion picture] : strategies for success / produced by CRM Productions, Inc. Del Mar, CA : McGraw-Hill Training Systems, 1985. 1 film reel (13 min.) : sd., col. ; 16 mm. + 1 leader's guide. Title from data sheet. College students and adults. Issued also as videorecording. Emphasizes that courteous, efficient customer service is

critical to the operation of a successful organization. Focusing on the actions of several employees in a department store, illustrates a four-step customer service transaction model for use in the field, on the telephone, and over the counter. ISBN 0-07-620872-9 LC Card 86-708025 DDC 658.8 11
1. Customer service. 2. Customer relations. I. CRM Productions. II. McGraw-Hill Training Systems (Firm).
HF5415.5

Customer service [motion picture] : the film / Barr Films ; producers, Ron Walsh and Mike Sedan ; director, Ron Walsh. Pasadena, CA : Barr Films, 1987. 1 film reel (24 min.) : sd., col. ; 16 mm. + 1 guide. Title from data sheet. Ages 15 through adults. Issued also as videorecording. Gives effective methods of customer relations by showing amusing scenes of waitresses, receptionists, salespeople, insurance, and bank personnel, and depicts how they should not do their jobs. LC Card 87-706736 DDC 658.8 11
1. Customer service. I. Barr Films.
HF5415.5

CUSTOMER SERVICE - SOVIET UNION.
Bel'chikov, ÎA. M. Prodavets i Pokupatel', ili rasskaz o tom, kakimi mogli by stat' ikh otnosheniîa, bud' rîadom Psikholog /. Riga , 1986. 157, [3] p. : LC Card 87-129915
HF5438.8.P75 B45 1986

Customer service [videorecording] : strategies for success / produced by CRM Productions, Inc. Del Mar, CA : McGraw-Hill Training Systems, 1985. 1 videocassette (13 min.) : sd., col. + 1 leader's guide. Title from data sheet. College students and adults. Issued as U-matic 3/4 in. or VHS 1/2 in. Issued also as motion picture. Emphasizes that courteous, efficient customer service is critical to the operation of a successful organization. Focusing on the actions of several employees in a department store, illustrates a four-step customer service transaction model for use in the field, on the telephone, and over the counter. ISBN 0-07-109048-7 (3/4 in.) LC Card 86-708026 DDC 658.8 11
1. Customer service. 2. Customer relations. I. CRM Productions. II. McGraw-Hill Training Systems (Firm).
HF5415.5

Customer service [videorecording] : the film / Barr Films ; producers, Ron Walsh and Mike Sedan ; director, Ron Walsh. Pasadena, CA : Barr Films, 1987. 1 videocassette (24 min.) : sd., col. + 1 guide. Title from data sheet. Ages 15 through adults. Issued as U-matic 3/4 in. or Beta 1/2 in. or VHS 1/2 in. Issued also as motion picture. Gives effective methods of customer relations by showing amusing scenes of waitresses, receptionists, salespeople, insurance, and bank personnel, and depicts how they should not do their jobs. LC Card 87-706737 DDC 658.8 11
1. Customer service. I. Barr Films.
HF5415.5

CUSTOMS ADMINISTRATION - CANADA - HISTORY.
McIntosh, Dave. The collectors . Toronto, Ont., Canada , c1984. 414 p. : ISBN 0-920053-29-7 LC Card 85-162089 DDC 354.710072/46/09 19
HJ6751.A6 M35 1984 ***NYPL [JLE 86-2880]***

CUSTOMS ADMINISTRATION - DENMARK.
Denmark. Direktoratet for toldvæsenet. Information og kontrol . [Copenhagen] [1985] 125, [49] p. : LC Card 86-209910
HJ6971 .D46 1985

CUSTOMS ADMINISTRATION - DENMARK - HISTORY.
Eliassen, Peter. Kongeåen, eller, Den gamle grænse /. [København, Amaliegade 44, 1256 K] [Esbjerg] , 1980. 357, [4] p. : ISBN 87-87796-02-3 : LC Card 81-107972
HJ6971 .E45 1980

CUSTOMS ADMINISTRATION - LAW AND LEGISLATION - EUROPEAN ECONOMIC COMMUNITY COUNTRIES.
Lasok, Dominik. The customs law of the European Economic Community /. Deventer, Netherlands , Boston , c1983. xxiii, 292 p. : ISBN 90-6544-077-1 (pbk.) : LC Card 84-148702 DDC 343.405/6 344.0356 19
LAW ***NYPL [JLE 86-2073]***

CUSTOMS ADMINISTRATION - MADEIRA ISLANDS - HISTORY - 16TH CENTURY.
Livros de contas da ilha da Madeira, 1504-1537 /. Coimbra , 1985- v. <1 > ; LC Card 86-232733
HJ9930.3.M33 L58 1985

CUSTOMS ADMINSITRATION - PORTUGAL - HISTORY.
Santos, Pedro Ribeiro dos. Génese e estrutura da Guarda Fiscal . [Lisbon] [1985] 193 p., [9] leaves of plates : LC Card 87-400399 DDC 354.4690072/46 19
HJ6996 .A25 1985

CUSTOMS DUTIES. see **TARIFF.**

Customs law of the E.E.C. Lasok, Dominik. The customs law of the European Economic Community /. Deventer, Netherlands , Boston , c1983. xxiii, 292 p. : ISBN 90-6544-077-1 (pbk.) : LC Card 84-148702 DDC 343.405/6 344.0356 19
LAW ***NYPL [JLE 86-2073]***

Customs law of the EEC. Lasok, Dominik. The customs law of the European Economic Community /. Deventer, Netherlands , Boston , c1983. xxiii, 292 p. : ISBN 90-6544-077-1 (pbk.) : LC Card 84-148702 DDC 343.405/6 344.0356 19
LAW ***NYPL [JLE 86-2073]***

The customs law of the European Economic Community /. Lasok, Dominik. Deventer, Netherlands , Boston , c1983. xxiii, 292 p. : ISBN 90-6544-077-1 (pbk.) : LC Card 84-148702 DDC 343.405/6 344.0356 19
LAW ***NYPL [JLE 86-2073]***

CUSTOMS (TARIFF) see **TARIFF.**

CUSTOMS UNIONS.
Sousa, Fernando Freire de. A adesão de Portugal à CEE . [Porto] [1985] 96 p. ; LC Card 86-174408
HF2236 .S68 1985

Williamson B., Carlos. La teoría sobre preferencias arancelarias . Santiago, Chile , 1985. 35 leaves : LC Card 85-202146
HF1733.L29 W54 1985

CUSTOMS UNIONS - LATIN AMERICA.
Aragão, José María. La Asociación Latinoamericana de Libre Comercio (ALALC) y la Asociación Latinoamericana de Integración (ALADI) . Buenos Aires, Argentina [1984] xiii, 172 p. ; LC Card 86-201881
HC125 .A69 1984

CUSTOMS UNIONS - LATIN AMERICA - CONGRESSES.
La Industria colombiana y la "ALALC.". [Medellín] [1964] 112 p. ; LC Card 85-111774
HC197 .I36 1964

Custos certos, benefícios incertos : políticas públicas portuguesas na CEE / edição coordenada por Jorge Braga de Macedo. [Lisboa] : Associação Portuguesa para o Estudo das Relações Internacionais, [1986] 307 p. : ill. ; 21 cm. Papers presented at a panel discussion held Mar. 5-6, 1985 at the Fundação Calouste Gulbenkian in Lisbon as part of the Conferência Internacional sobre Integração de Portugal na CEE. Bibliography: p. 298-301. LC Card 87-127179 DDC 341.24/22 19
1. European Economic Community - Portugal - Congresses. I. Macedo, Jorge Braga de. II. Associação Portuguesa para o Estudo das Relações Internacionais. III. Conferência Internacional sobre Integração de Portugal na CEE (1985 : Lisbon, Portugal).
HC241.25.P6 C87 1986

Custos e tarifas de energia elétrica : breve estudo comparativo / Confederação Nacional da Indústria. [Rio de Janeiro] : A Confederação, 1982. 40 p. ; 21 cm. LC Card 86-146330
1. Electric utilities - Brazil - Costs. 2. Electric utilities - Brazil - Rates. I. Confederação Nacional da Indústria.
HD9685.B8 C87 1982

Custos operacionais no SBPE /. Dantas Neto, Antônio da Costa. Rio de Janeiro/RJ , 1983. 67 p. : LC Card 85-108995
HG2156.B8 D36 1983

Cuthbertson, Keith. Macroeconomic systems / Keith Cuthbertson and Mark P. Taylor. Oxford, UK ; New York, NY, USA : Basil Blackwell, 1987. ix, 278 p. : ill. ; 24 cm. Bibliography: p. [264]-273. Includes indexes. ISBN 0-631-14341-6 : LC Card 87-10332 DDC 339 19
1. Macroeconomics. I. Taylor, Mark P., 1958-. II. Title.
HB172.5 .C87 1987

Cutrona, Cheryl. The Department of Labor / Cheryl Cutrona ; introduction by Arthur M. Schlesinger, Jr. [New York] : Chelsea House, c1988. 95 p. : ill. ; 24 cm. (Know your government) Bibliography: p. 92. Includes index. Surveys the history of the Department of Labor, describing its structure, current function, and influence on American society. ISBN 0-87754-844-7 LC Card 87-24906 DDC 353.83 19
1. United States. Dept. of Labor - History - Juvenile literature. I. Series: Know your government (New York, N.Y.). II. Title.
HD8066 .C85 1988

Cutter, Susan L. Rating places : a geographer's view on quality of life / Susan L. Cutter. Washington, D.C. : Association of American Geographers, c1985. viii, 76 p. : ill., maps ; 22 cm. (Resource publications in geography) Bibliography: p. [71]-76. ISBN 0-89291-191-3 (pbk.) : LC Card 85-13469 DDC 307/.0973 19
1. Anthropo-geography - United States. 2. Quality of life - United States. 3. Cities and towns - United States. I. Title.
GF503 .C87 1985 ***NYPL [JLD 86-2715]***

CUTTING OF METALS. see **METAL-CUTTING.**

Cuvîntare la Plenara Consiliului Național al Oamenilor Muncii, din 19-20 ianuarie 1981 /. Ceaușescu, Nicolae. București , 1981. 31 p. ; LC Card 81-153290
HC405 .C4215 1981

CUYO (ARGENTINA) - ECONOMIC CONDITIONS.
Fleming, William J. Region vs nation . Tempe , c1986. 82 p. ; ISBN 0-87918-066-8 LC Card 86-29919 DDC 330.982/64 19
HC177.M4 F55 1986

CUZCO (PERU : DEPT.) - POPULATION.
Díaz Gómez, Jorge. Deterioro de los términos de intercambio, migración eventual y pobreza campesina en el departamento del Cusco /. [Cuzco, Peru] , 1986. 17, 3 leaves, 2 leaves of plates : LC Card 86-200938
HD1531.P4 D52 1986

CUZCO, PERU (DEPT.) - ECONOMIC CONDITIONS.
Cori Castro, Wilfredo. Mercados y precios en la economía campesina . [Cuzco, Peru] , 1986. 29 p. : LC Card 86-200941
HC228.C8 C59 1986

C.V. Starr Center for Applied Economics (New York University) Incentives, cooperation, and risk sharing . Totowa, N.J. , 1987. xvi, 239 p. : ISBN 0-8476-7464-9 LC Card 87-4558 DDC 658.3/22 19
HF5549.5.C67 I56 1987

CYBERNETICS - CONGRESSES.
Kybernetik und Management . Berlin , c1983. viii, 131 p. : ISBN 3-428-05448-2 LC Card 84-109870
HD29 .K92 1983

CYCLES (BICYCLES) see **BICYCLES.**

Cyclic analysis in futures trading . Bernstein, Jacob, 1946- New York , c1988. p. cm. ISBN 0-471-01185-1 LC Card 87-26350 DDC 332.64/4 19
HG6024.A3 B48 1988

CYCLING PATHS - AUSTRIA.
Bauer, Helfried. Fahrradfreundliche Verkehrspolitik in Stadt und Land . Wien , 1984. 87 p. : LC Card 85-150945
HE5739.A9 B38 1984

CYCLING PATHS - SCANDINAVIA.
Cykeltrafik i nordiske byer /. København , 1982. 207 p. : ISBN 87-7303-045-7 LC Card 83-242616
HE5739.S34 C94 1982

Cyert, Richard Michael, 1921- Technology and employment . Washington, D.C. , 1987. xiii, 225 p. : ISBN 0-309-03744-1 (pbk.) : LC Card 87-42807 DDC 331.12/0973 19
HD6331.2.U5 T43 1987

Cykeltrafik i nordiske byer / Nordisk embedsmandskomité for transportspørgsmål, Arbejdsgruppen vedrørende cykeltrafik. København : Nordisk ministerråd, 1982. 207 p. : ill. ; 30 cm. Bibliography: p. 102-107. Includes index. ISBN 87-7303-045-7 LC Card 83-242616
1. Bicycle commuting - Scandinavia. 2. Cycling paths - Scandinavia. I. Nordiska ämbetsmannakommittén för transportfrågor. Arbejdsgruppen vedrørende cykeltrafik.
HE5739.S34 C94 1982

Cyprus, a long-term development perspective. Washington, D.C., U. S.A. : World Bank,

[1987] xvii, 79 p., [1] folded leaf of plates : ill., col. map ; 28 cm. (A World Bank country study, 0253-2123) Includes bibliographical references. ISBN 0-8213-0931-5 (pbk.) LC Card 87-15988 DDC 338.95645 19
1. Cyprus - Economic conditions. 2. Cyprus - Economic policy. I. International Bank for Reconstruction and Development. II. Series.
HC415.2 .C956 1987

CYPRUS - ECONOMIC CONDITIONS.
Cyprus, a long-term development perspective. Washington, D.C., U. S.A. [1987] xvii, 79 p., [1] folded leaf of plates : ISBN 0-8213-0931-5 (pbk.) LC Card 87-15988 DDC 338.95645 19
HC415.2 .C956 1987

Trito Ektakto Schedio Oikonomikēs Draseōs, 1979-1981. Leukōsia [1981?] xv, 398 p. ; LC Card 86-192190
HC415.2 .T75 1981

CYPRUS - ECONOMIC POLICY.
Cyprus, a long-term development perspective. Washington, D.C., U. S.A. [1987] xvii, 79 p., [1] folded leaf of plates : ISBN 0-8213-0931-5 (pbk.) LC Card 87-15988 DDC 338.95645 19
HC415.2 .C956 1987

Trito Ektakto Schedio Oikonomikēs Draseōs, 1979-1981. Leukōsia [1981?] xv, 398 p. ; LC Card 86-192190
HC415.2 .T75 1981

Cyprus. Grapheio Programmatismou. Epitropē Programmatismou. Trito Ektakto Schedio Oikonomikēs Draseōs, 1979-1981. Leukōsia [1981?] xv, 398 p. ; LC Card 86-192190
HC415.2 .T75 1981

Cyr, François, 1952- Eléments d'histoire de la FTQ : la FTQ et la question nationale / François Cyr, Rémi Roy. [Laval] : Editions coopératives Albert Saint-Martin, [1981] 205 p. ; 21 cm. (Collection Recherches et documents) Includes bibliographical references. ISBN 2-89035-045-2 : LC Card 82-105783 DDC 331.88/09714 19
1. Fédération des travailleurs du Québec. 2. Trade unions - Québec (Province) - Québec. I. Roy, Rémi, 1950-. II. Title.
HD8102.F43 C97 1981

Cyr, John E. Real estate brokerage : a success guide / John E. Cyr & Joan m. Sobeck.2nd ed. Chicago : Real Estate Education Co., c1988. xiii, 367 p. : ill., forms ; 24 cm. Includes index. ISBN 0-88462-674-1 (pbk.) LC Card 87-16650 DDC 333.33/068 19
1. Real estate agents - United States. 2. Real estate business - United States. I. Sobeck, Joan m. II. Title.
HD278 .C95 1988

Cysne, Rubens Penha.
Breve retrospecto da economia brasileira entre 1979 e 1984 / Rubens Penha Cysne. [Rio de Janeiro] : Escola de Pós-Graduação em Economia do Instituto Brasileiro de Economia da Fundação Getúlio Vargas, [1985] 30 leaves ; 30 cm. (Ensaios econômicos / EPGE . no. 66) Bibliography: leaf 30. LC Card 86-176751
1. Brazil - Economic conditions - 1964-1985. 2. Indexation (Economics) - Brazil. I. Series: Ensaios econômicos (Escola de Pós-Graduação em Economia), no. 66. II. Title.
HC187 .C98 1985

Política macroeconômica no Brasil, 1964/66 e 1980/84 / Rubens Penha Cysne. Rio de Janeiro, RJ : Fundação Getúlio Vargas, [1986?] 125 p. : ill. ; 21 cm. Cover title. At head of title: Prêmio Losango de apoio a teses em economia, 84, 85. Errata slip inserted. Bibliography: p. 124-125. LC Card 86-229936
1. Brazil - Economic policy. 2. Indexation (Economics) - Brazil. 3. Macroeconomics. I. Title.
HC187 .C983 1986

Cywiński, Henryk. Dziesięć wieków pieniądza polskiego 980-1980 / Henryk Cywiński. Wyd. 1. Warszawa : Ludowa Spółdzielnia Wydawnicza, 1982. 243 p., [24] p. of plates : ill. ; 19 cm. Bibliography: p. 239-[242] ISBN 83-205-3413-5 LC Card 83-119732
1. Money - Poland - History. 2. Coins, Polish - History. I. Title. II. Title: 10 wieków pieniądza polskiego 980-1980.
HG1087 .C98 1982

Czander, William M. The application of social systems thinking to organizational consulting / William M. Czander. Lanham : University Press of America, c1986. 243 p. ; 24 cm. Includes index. Bibliography: p. 235-243. ISBN 0-8191-5183-1 (alk. paper) : LC Card 85-29508 DDC 658.4/6 19
1. Consultants. 2. Social systems. 3. Organizational effectiveness. I. Title.
HD69.C6 C9 1986 NYPL [JLE 86-3269]

Czasny, Karl. Lehrjahre bei Bau-Holz : Erfahrungen in einer Gewerkschaftszentrale / K. Czasny, R. Kende. Wien : Verlag für Gesellschaftskritik, c1985. ix, 148 p. ; 20 cm. (Aufrisse-Buch . 4) Bibliography: p. 139-148. ISBN 3-900351-34-1 LC Card 86-227367 DDC 331.88/174/09436 19
1. Gewerkschaft der Bau- und Holzarbeiter (Austria). 2. Trade-unions - Woodworkers - Austria. I. Kende, R. (Richard). II. Title. III. Series.
HD6678.W62 G493 1985

CZECH LANGUAGE - DICTIONARIES - RUSSIAN.
Cheshsko-russkiĭ ėkonomicheskiĭ slovar′. Moskva , Praga , 1986. 300 p. ; LC Card 85-146401
*HB61 .C453 1986 NYPL [*QAD 87-1680]*

Czechoslovak agriculture /. Kutil, Jaroslav. Prague , 1983. 125 p., [48] p. of plates : LC Card 84-109068 DDC 338.1/09437 19
HD1940.3.Z8 K87 1983
NYPL [JLD 86-2294]

Czechoslovak Republic. see **Czechoslovakia.**

Czechoslovak Socialist Republic. see **Czechoslovakia.**

CZECHOSLOVAKIA - CENSUS, 1970.
Sčítání lidu, domů a bytů 1970. Praha [1970?] 132, [64] p. ; LC Card 82-143437
HA1198.P7 S38 1970

CZECHOSLOVAKIA - CENSUS, 1980.
Vývoj společnosti ČSSR, podle výsledků sčítání lidu, domů a bytů 1980. [Prague] , 1985. 2 v. ; LC Card 86-185144
HA1191.5 1980b

CZECHOSLOVAKIA - COMMERCE.
Altmann, Franz-Lothar. Tschechoslowakei 1984/85 . München , 1985. 31 leaves ; LC Card 85-179408
HC270.28 .A415 1985

CZECHOSLOVAKIA - COMMERCE - DIRECTORIES.
Your trade partners in Czechoslovakia /. Praha , 1986. 187 p. : LC Card 87-127524 DDC 382/.025/437 19
HF3550.3.A48 Y58 1986

CZECHOSLOVAKIA - COMMERCE - EUROPE, EASTERN.
Altmann, Franz-Lothar. Die tschechoslowakische Volkswirtschaft und der Rat für gegenseitige Wirtschaftshilfe (RGW) /. München [1986] 31 leaves ; LC Card 86-203484
HF3550.3.Z7 E8523 1986

CZECHOSLOVAKIA - ECONOMIC CONDITIONS - 1945-
Altmann, Franz-Lothar. Tschechoslowakei 1984/85 . München , 1985. 31 leaves ; LC Card 85-179408
HC270.28 .A415 1985

Batt, Judy. Economic reform and political change in eastern Europe . New York , 1987. p. cm. ISBN 0-312-01196-2 : LC Card 87-24065 DDC 338.9437 19
HC270.28 .B37 1987

Kazimour, Jan, engineer. Rezervy v ekonomice /. Praha , 1981. 227 p. ; LC Card 81-208368
HC270.28 .K38 1981

Závada, Josef. Perspektivy hospodářského a sociálního rozvoje ČSSR /. Praha , 1986. 134 p. ; LC Card 87-161408
HC270.28 .Z38 1986

CZECHOSLOVAKIA - ECONOMIC CONDITIONS - 1945- - REGIONAL DISPARITIES.
Regionale Aspekte der Wirtschaftsplanung in den Mitteleuropäischen RGW-Staaten. Marburg/Lahn , 1983. 95 p. : ISBN 3-87969-178-9 LC Card 84-249235
HC270.28 .R42 1983

CZECHOSLOVAKIA - ECONOMIC POLICY - 1945-
Batt, Judy. Economic reform and political change in eastern Europe . New York , 1987. p. cm. ISBN 0-312-01196-2 : LC Card 87-24065 DDC 338.9437 19
HC270.28 .B37 1987

Fusko, Zoltán. Koncepcia ďalšieho rozvoja plánovitého riadenia efektívneho využívania pracovnej sily . Bratislava , 1982. 62 p. ; LC Card 83-113861
HD5772.3.A6 F87 1982

Murashko, G. P. (Galina Pavlovna) Politicheskaia bor′ba v Chekhoslovakii v 1944-1948 gg. i natsionalizatsiia sredstv proizvodstva /. Moskva , 1986. 326, [2] p. ; LC Card 86-202951
HC270.28 .M87 1986

Regionale Aspekte der Wirtschaftsplanung in den Mitteleuropäischen RGW-Staaten. Marburg/Lahn , 1983. 95 p. : ISBN 3-87969-178-9 LC Card 84-249235
HC270.28 .R42 1983

CZECHOSLOVAKIA - ECONOMIC POLICY - 1965-
Altmann, Franz-Lothar. Tschechoslowakei 1984/85 . München , 1985. 31 leaves ; LC Card 85-179408
HC270.28 .A415 1985

Klusoň, Václav. Teoretické otázky formování plánovitého řízení národního hospodářství ČSSR /. Praha , 1986- v. <1 > ; LC Card 87-167771
HC270.28 .K58 1986

Planomernoe razvitie sotsialisticheskoĭ ėkonomiki /. Moskva , Bratislava , 1977. 262 p. ; LC Card 87-100683
HC336.25 .P448 1977

Závada, Josef. Perspektivy hospodářského a sociálního rozvoje ČSSR /. Praha , 1986. 134 p. ; LC Card 87-161408
HC270.28 .Z38 1986

Czechoslovakia. Federální statistický úřad. Vývoj společnosti ČSSR, podle výsledků sčítání lidu, domů a bytů 1980. [Prague] , 1985. 2 v. ; LC Card 86-185144
HA1191.5 1980b

CZECHOSLOVAKIA - FOREIGN ECONOMIC RELATIONS - COMMUNIST COUNTRIES.
Fingerland, Jaroslav. Mezinárodní socialistická ekonomická integrace a předmětné sféry specializace národohospodářského komplexu ČSSR /. Praha , 1985. 169 p. ; LC Card 86-215200
HF1542.3.Z4 C654 1985

CZECHOSLOVAKIA - FOREIGN ECONOMIC RELATIONS - FRANCE.
Segal, Paul Harold, 1946- The French state and French private investment in Czechoslovakia, 1918-1938 . New York , 1987. vi, 379 p. ; ISBN 0-8240-8041-6 (alk. paper) : LC Card 87-252 DDC 332.6/7344/0437 19
HG5470.3.A3 S44 1987

CZECHOSLOVAKIA - INDUSTRIES.
Altmann, Franz-Lothar. Tschechoslowakei 1984/85 . München , 1985. 31 leaves ; LC Card 85-179408
HC270.28 .A415 1985

CZECHOSLOVAKIA - POLITICS AND GOVERNMENT - 1945-
Batt, Judy. Economic reform and political change in eastern Europe . New York , 1987. p. cm. ISBN 0-312-01196-2 : LC Card 87-24065 DDC 338.9437 19
HC270.28 .B37 1987

Murashko, G. P. (Galina Pavlovna) Politicheskaia bor′ba v Chekhoslovakii v 1944-1948 gg. i natsionalizatsiia sredstv proizvodstva /. Moskva , 1986. 326, [2] p. ; LC Card 86-202951
HC270.28 .M87 1986

CZECHOSLOVAKIA - POPULATION - STATISTICS.
Vývoj společnosti ČSSR, podle výsledků sčítání lidu, domů a bytů 1980. [Prague] , 1985. 2 v. ; LC Card 86-185144
HA1191.5 1980b

CZECHOSLOVAKIA - SOCIAL CONDITIONS.
Riesenfellner, Stefan. Der Sozialreporter . Wien , c1987. vi, 278 p. ; ISBN 3-900351-67-8 LC Card 87-137993 DDC 305.5/62/09436 19
HD8410 .R54 1987

Czego można oczekiwać od ekonomii /. Samecki, Wiesław. Warszawa , 1981. 35 p. ; ISBN 83-202-0150-0 LC Card 86-150577
HC340.3 .S24 1981

Czepiel, John A. The Services challenge . Chicago, Ill. , 1987. vi, 108 p. : ISBN 0-87757-188-0 (pbk.) LC Card 87-12543 DDC 658.8 19
HD9980.5 .S4255 1987

Czinkota, Michael R. International marketing / Michael R. Czinkota, Ilkka A. Ronkainen. Chicago : Dryden Press, c1988. xxi, 649 p. : ill. (some col.) ; 24 cm. Includes bibliographies and indexes. ISBN 0-03-070297-6 LC Card 86-32959 DDC 658.8/48 19
1. Export marketing. I. Ronkainen, Ilkka A. II. Title.
HF1009.5 .C95 1988

Czukor, John C. Beginning office worker / John C. Czukor. 11th ed. New York : Arco : Distributed by Prentice Hall Trade, c1988. 291 p. ; 28 cm. (Arco civil service test tutor) Spine title: Arco's beginning office worker. ISBN 0-13-072018-6 (pbk.) : LC Card 87-20740 DDC 651.3/7/076 19
1. Office practice - Examinations, questions, etc. 2. Civil Service - United States - Examinations. I. Title: Arco's beginning office worker. II. Series.
HF5547.5 .B414 1988

Czynniki kształtujące poziom dochodów w gospodarstwach indywidualnych /. Klank, Leszek. Warszawa , 1985. 176 p. ; ISBN 83-01-05449-2 : *NYPL [*QO 86-2601]*

D. Alvaro Pais e o pensamento económico em Portugal na Idade Média /. Amzalak, Moses Bensabat, 1892- Lisboa , 1954. 71 p. : LC Card 84-213332
HB79.P45 A49 1954

Đ ' ANG C
Đ ' ang c Hà N 1985. 88 p. ; LC Card 87-153845
HD6820.5 .D36 1985

Đ ' ang c Hà N Lao đ 1985. 88 p. ; 19 cm. LC Card 87-153845
1. Trade-unions - Vietnam. 2. Đ ' ang c
HD6820.5 .D36 1985

d.B.A.S.E. II for beginners. Lima, Tony. dBASE II for beginners /. Englewood Cliffs, N.J. , c1985. xix, 234 p. : ISBN 0-13-196098-9 : LC Card 84-22897 DDC 001.64/2 19
QA76.9.D3 L56 1985 NYPL [JSE 87-247]

D. C. see **Partito della democrazia cristiana.**

D. E. S. A. L. see **Centro para el Desarrollo Económico y Social de América Latina.**

D. G. B. see **Deutscher Gewerkschaftsbund.**

D. G. F. K. see **Deutsche Gesellschaft für Friedens- und Konfliktforschung.**

D. I. E. see **Deutsches Institut für Entwicklungspolitik.**

DIE Schriften. see **Deutsches Institut für Entwicklungspolitik. Schriften.**

D. I. F. U. see **Deutsches Institut für Urbanistik.**

D. I. H. T. For corporate body represented by these initials, see: **Deutscher Industrie- und Handelstag.**

D.I.H.T.-Meinung, 1982. Deutscher Industrie- und Handelstag. DIHT-Meinung, 1982 /. Bonn , 1982. 104 p. ; LC Card 83-206569
HC286.7 .D47 1982

D.I.W.-Symposion. DIW-Symposion (1983 : Berlin, Germany) Strategien für mehr Arbeitsplätze in Berlin . Berlin , c1984. 209 p. : ISBN 3-87061-277-0 LC Card 84-202956
HD5780.B4 D58 1983

D. K. M. S. see **Dimitrovski komunisticheski mladezhki sŭiuz.**

D. O. E. see **United States. Dept. of Energy.**

D. P. see **Partito della democrazia cristiana.**

D. S. E. see **Deutsche Stiftung für Entwicklungsländer.**

Da Danmark igen sagde ja til det fælles-- /. Ellemann-Jensen, Uffe, 1941- [Copenhagen] , c1987. 157 p. : ISBN 87-569-2234-5 : LC Card 87-163358
HC241.25.D4 E45 1987

Da inflação ao cruzado . Modiano, Eduardo Marco. Rio de Janeiro , c1986. 126 p. : ISBN 85-7001-362-0 : LC Card 87-102624
HC187 .M593 1986

Da Ros, Giuseppina. El cooperativismo de ahorro y crédito en el Ecuador / Giuseppina Da Ros. Quito : Pontificia Universidad Católica del Ecuador, 1985. 89 p. : ill. ; 19 cm. (Documentos de análisis . no. 3) Bibliography: p. 85-89. LC Card 86-169048
1. Building and loan associations - Ecuador. 2. Banks and banking, Cooperative - Ecuador. I. Title.
HG2156.E22 D37 1985

Dabat, Christine. As mulheres nas organizações profissionais / Christine Dabat e Georgina Oliveira. Recife : Associação dos Sociólogos de Pernambuco, Centro de Estudos da Mulher, 1985. 21 p. ; 32 cm. Includes bibliographical references. LC Card 86-177927
1. Trade and professional associations - Brazil, Northeast. 2. Sex discrimination in employment - Brazil, Northeast. 3. Women in the professions - Brazil, Northeast - Interviews. I. Oliveira, Georgina. II. Title.
HD2429.B6 D33 1985

Dabbāgh, Ṭāhir Husayn. 'Alāqī, Madanī 'Abd al-Qādir. al-Idārah wa-al-bī'ah . [Jiddah] , 1985. 136 p. : LC Card 86-200390
HD70.S28 A422 1985

Dąbrowski, Marek. Ekonomiczne konsekwencje samorządności pracowniczej / Marek Dąbrowski. Wrocław : Zakład Narodowy im. Ossolińskich, 1986. 140 p. ; 24 cm. (Prace habilitacyjne) At head of title: Polska Akademia Nauk. Instytut Nauk Ekonomicznych. Includes bibliographical references. ISBN 83-04-02213-3 : LC Card 86-199502
1. Industrial management - Poland - Employee participation. I. Series: Prace habilitacyjne (Wrocław, Poland). II. Title.
HD5660.P6 D33 1986

DĄBROWSKI, PRZEMYSŁAW.
Przestrzenne aspekty gospodarki żywnościowej do 2000 r. . Warszawa , 1986. 166 p. : ISBN 83-208-0497-3 : LC Card 86-223691
HD9015.P72 P72 1986

Dac-Easy accounting and payroll made easy /. West, Gary, 1947- Blue Ridge Summit, PA , c1987. ix, 261 p. : ISBN 0-8306-2914-9 (pbk.) : LC Card 87-10056 DDC 657/.028/55369 19
HF5679 .W47 1987

DAC-EASY ACCOUNTING (COMPUTER PROGRAM)
Mosich, Donna M. Mastering Dac-Easy . Glenview, Ill. , c1988. p. cm. ISBN 0-673-18735-7 LC Card 87-4847 DDC 657/.028/55369 19
HF5679 .M64 1988

West, Gary, 1947- Dac-Easy accounting and payroll made easy /. Blue Ridge Summit, PA , c1987. ix, 261 p. : ISBN 0-8306-2914-9 (pbk.) : LC Card 87-10056 DDC 657/.028/55369 19
HF5679 .W47 1987

DAC-EASY PAYROLL (COMPUTER PROGRAM)
Mosich, Donna M. Mastering Dac-Easy . Glenview, Ill. , c1988. p. cm. ISBN 0-673-18735-7 LC Card 87-4847 DDC 657/.028/55369 19
HF5679 .M64 1988

West, Gary, 1947- Dac-Easy accounting and payroll made easy /. Blue Ridge Summit, PA , c1987. ix, 261 p. : ISBN 0-8306-2914-9 (pbk.) : LC Card 87-10056 DDC 657/.028/55369 19
HF5679 .W47 1987

Dachary, Alfredo César. El Caribe mexicano : hombres e historias / Alfredo César Dachary, Stella Maris Arnáiz Burne.1a ed. México, D.F. : SEP Cultura, Centro de Investigaciones y Estudios Superiores en Antropología Social : Museo Nacional de Culturas Populares, 1985. 110 p. : ill., 9 maps ; 23 cm. (Serie Los Pescadores de México . v. 8) Cuadernos de la Casa Chata ; 117 ISBN 968-496-069-7 LC Card 86-118335 DDC 338.3/7270972 19
1. Fishers - Mexico - Quintana Roo (State). 2. Fishing - Mexico - Quintana Roo (State). I. Arnáiz Burne, Stella Maris. II. Title. III. Series.
HD8039.F66 M426 1985
NYPL [JLD 87-1321]

Dachrodt, Heinz-G., 1944- Arbeit und Gesellschaft im Umbruch : Zukunft ohne Arbeit, Arbeit ohne Zukunft? / Heinz-G. Dachrodt. Köln : Bund-Verlag, [1987], c1986. 128 p. : ill. ; 19 cm. ISBN 3-7663-0961-7 LC Card 87-139264 DDC 331.12/0943 19
1. Labor supply - Germany (West) - Effect of technological innovations on. 2. Germany, West - Population. 3. Germany, West - Moral conditions. I. Title.
HD6331.2.G28 D33 1987

Dacier, Pierre. Les dossiers noirs de l'industrie française / Pierre Dacier, Jean-Louis Levet, Jean-Claude Tourret. [Paris] : Fayard, c1985. 414 p. ; 24 cm. (L'Esprit d'entreprise) ISBN 2-213-01659-3 : LC Card 86-178468
1. France - Industries. 2. France - Economic conditions - 1945-. 3. Industry and state - France. I. Levet, Jean-Louis. II. Tourret, Jean-Claude. III. Title. IV. Series.
HC276.2 .D2 1985

Dadaîan, V. S. (Vladislav Surenovich), 1933-
Global'nye ėkonomicheskie modeli / V.S. Dadaîan. Moskva : Izd-vo "Nauka", 1981. 214 p. : ill. ; 22 cm. At head of title: Akademiîa nauk SSSR. TSentral'nyĭ ėkonomiko-matematicheskiĭ institut. Includes bibliographical references. LC Card 82-117634
1. Economic development - Mathematical models. I. Title.
HD75.5 .D33 1981

Voprosy stranovogo makromodelirovaniîa /. Moskva , 1984. 177 p. : LC Card 86-144302
HB141 .V665 1984

Dadibhavi, R. V. Income, productivity, and industrial structure / R.V. Dadibhavi ; foreword by D.M. Nanjundappa. Allahabad, India : Chugh Publications, 1986. xx, 295 p. ; 22 cm. Revision of the author's thesis (Ph. D.--M.S. University, 1984) Study of Karnataka, based on 1960/61-1975/76 data. Bibliography: p. 274-292. Includes index. ISBN 81-85076-02-2 : LC Card 86-902847 DDC 339.2/0954/87 19
1. Income - India - Karnataka. 2. Agricultural productivity - India - Karnataka. 3. Industrial productivity - India - Karnataka. 4. Karnataka, India - Economic conditions. I. Title.
HC437.K27 D33 1986

DADRA AND NAGAR HAVELI (INDIA) - CENSUS, 1981.
Census of India, 1981. Delhi , <1984-1985. v. in : LC Card 87-915034 DDC 304.6/0954/796021 19
HA4587.D33 C46 1984

Dadson, J. A. Production co-operatives and rural development in Ghana / J.A. Dadson. [Addis Ababa] : Economic Commission for Africa, [1985] 53 p. ; 28 cm. "Regional Expert Consultation on the Role of Rural Co-operatives in the Productive Sectors in Africa, Addis Ababa, 7-11, October 1985." "ECA/SDEHSD/IRD/85/WP.3." "October 1985." Bibliography: leaves 42-45. LC Card 87-105501 DDC 334/.6/09667 19
1. Producer cooperatives - Ghana. 2. Rural development - Ghana. 3. Agriculture, Cooperative - Ghana. 4. Cooperative societies - Ghana. I. United Nations Industrial Development Organization. Regional Expert Consultation on the Role of Rural Co-operatives in the Productive Sectors in Africa. II. Title.
HD3258.3.A4 D34 1985

D.A.E. research report .
(no. 651) Shuker, Iain G. W. Economic analysis of the cost structure of commercial sugar cane farms in Louisiana /. Baton Rouge, La. [1986] vi, 50 p. : LC Card 86-622542 DDC 338.1/09763 s 338.1/7361/09763021 19
HD1775.L8 L7 no. 651 HD9107.L8

(no. 659) Fielder, Lonnie L. Agricultural statistics and prices for Louisiana, 1909-1985 /. [Baton Rouge, LA] [1986] iv, [122] p. : LC Card 87-620749 DDC 338.1/09763 s 338.1/09763/021 19
HD1775.L8 L7 no. 659

(no. 661) Traylor, Harlon D. An analysis of grain elevator bankruptcies in Louisiana /. [Baton Rouge?] [1986] iii, 77 p. ; LC Card 87-620885 DDC 338.1/09763 s 338.1/6 19
HD1775.L8 L7 no. 661 HD9037.L6

(no. 662) Wharton, Robert B. Analysis of rice export flows from southern states /. [Baton Rouge?] [1986] iii, 44 p. ; LC Card 87-620886 DDC 338.1/09763 s 382/.41318/0975021 19
HD1775.L8 L7 no. 662 HD9066.U46A13

Dähne, Eberhard. SPD wohin? . Frankfurt/Main , c1987. 114 p. ; ISBN 3-88807-047-3 LC Card

87-401340 DDC 330 s 324.243/072 19
HB97.5 .I53 Nr. 44 JN3971.A98S571712

Daff, Trevor. Cost and management accounting / Trevor Daff. London ; New York : Longman, 1988. p. cm. (Longman exam guides) Includes index. ISBN 0-582-46924-4 LC Card 87-3715 DDC 657/.42 19
1. Cost accounting. 2. Managerial accounting. I. Title. II. Series.
HF5686.C8 D17 1988

Daft, Richard L.
Management / Richard L. Daft. Chicago : Dryden Press, c1988. xxv, 787 p., [1] p. of plates : ill. (some col.) ; 26 cm. (The Dryden Press series in management) Bibliography: p. [724]-746. Includes indexes. ISBN 0-03-009473-9 LC Card 87-6820 DDC 658 19
1. Industrial management. I. Title.
HD31 .D134 1988

Organization theory : cases and applications / Richard L. Daft, Kristen D. Skivington, Mark P. Sharfman.2nd ed. St. Paul : West Pub. Co., c1987. xxviii, 338 p. : ill. ; 25 cm. ISBN 0-314-28488-5 (pbk.) LC Card 86-28965 DDC 658.4 19
1. Organization - Case studies. 2. Management - Case studies. I. Skivington, Kristen D. II. Sharfman, Mark P. III. Title.
HD31 .D136 1987

Dagbok frå bondekongressen i Moskva, oktober 1923 /. Hovda, Gudmund. Oslo , 1984. 46 p. ; ISBN 82-902503-1-2 LC Card 85-190754
HD1405 .H68 1984

DAGESTANSKAI͡A A.S.S.R. (R.S.F.S.R.) - COMMERCE.
Gadzhiev, B. U. (Bagautdin Ustaevich) Ėkonomicheskie problemy sovershenstvovanii͡a torgovli na osnove kompleksnoĭ ratsionalizatsii /. Makhachkala , 1984. 282 p. ; LC Card 86-213223
HF3629.D34 G33 1984

DAGESTANSKAI͡A A.S.S.R. (R.S.F.S.R.) - COMMERCIAL POLICY.
Gadzhiev, B. U. (Bagautdin Ustaevich) Ėkonomicheskie problemy sovershenstvovanii͡a torgovli na osnove kompleksnoĭ ratsionalizatsii /. Makhachkala , 1984. 282 p. ; LC Card 86-213223
HF3629.D34 G33 1984

Dagum, Estela Bee. The X-II-ARIMA seasonal adjustment method / by Estela Bee Dagum. Ottawa : Statistics Canada, Seasonal Adjustment and Time Series Staff, c1980. 119 p. : ill. ; 29 cm. "February 1980." "3-0002-511." "Catalogue 12-564E Occasional"--Cover. Bibliography: p. [117]-119. LC Card 83-225028
1. Seasonal variations (Economics) - Mathematical models. 2. Time-series analysis - Mathematical models. I. Statistics Canada. Seasonal Adjustment and Time Series Analysis Staff. II. Title.
HB137 .D34 1980

Dahal, Kishor. Indo-Nepal trade : problems and prospects / Kishor Dahal. Kathmandu, Nepal : Ratna Pustak Bhandar, c1987. x, 66, [9] p. ; 23 cm. Bibliography: p. [75] LC Card 87-902005 DDC 382/.0954/05496 19
1. India - Commerce - Nepal. 2. Nepal - Commerce - India. I. Title.
HF3788.N45 D34 1987

Dahlgren, Bo, 1924- Nyckeln til styrelserummet : praktik och juridik för bolagsstyrelsen / Bo Dahlgren, Krister Moberg. Stockholm : Norstedt, [1983] 182 p. : ill. ; 21 cm. Bibliography: p. 171-176. Includes index. ISBN 91-1-837051-9 : LC Card 83-210185
1. Corporations - Sweden. 2. Corporation law - Sweden. I. Moberg, Krister, 1950-. II. Title.
HD2883 .D34 1983

DAHLONEGA (GA.) - HISTORY.
Head, Sylvia. The neighborhood mint . Macon, Ga. , c1986. xviii, 206 p. : ISBN 0-86554-240-6 (alk. paper) : LC Card 86-23500 DDC 737.49758/273 19
HG461.D342 H4 1986

Dahmani, Mohamed. L'occidentalisation des pays du Tiers Monde : mythes et réalités / Mohamed Dahmani. Paris : Economica ; Alger : Office des publications universitaires, c1983. 217 p. ; 24 cm. Bibliography: p. [213]-214. ISBN 2-7178-0623-7 : LC Card 83-162697 DDC 909/.09724082 19
1. Developing countries - Economic policy. 2. Developing countries - Politics and government. 3. Developing countries - Civilization - Occidental influences. I. Title.
HC59.7 .D273 1983 ***NYPL [JLE 86-566]***

Dahrendorf, Ralf.
Die Chancen der Krise : über die Zukunft des Liberalismus / Ralf Dahrendorf. Stuttgart : Deutsche Verlags-Anstalt, c1983. 240 p. ; 21 cm. ISBN 3-421-06148-3
1. Liberalism. 2. Economic history - 1971-. 3. World politics - 1945-. 4. Germany, West - Politics and government. I. Title. ***NYPL [JFD 87-2528]***

Neue Arbeits- und Tätigkeitsformen . Dublin, Ireland [Washington, D.C.] c1986. xvi, 339 p. ; ISBN 92-825-6418-5 LC Card 87-408469 DDC 306/.36/094 19
HD6957.E86 N48 1986

Dai porti al sistema portuale . Vallega, Adalberto. Savona , 1985. 320 p. : LC Card 87-139096
HE558.L44 V35 1985

Daibert, José Ricardo Motta. Avaliação do desempenho de transporte coletivo por ônibus / José Ricardo Motta Daibert. Brasília, DF : EBTU, 1985. 73 p. : ill. ; 28 cm. (Série Teses. 6) Summary in English. Originally presented as the author's thesis (master's)--Instituto Militar de Engenharia, Rio de Janeiro, 1983. Bibliography: p. 73. LC Card 87-113224 DDC 388.4/1322/0981 19
1. Bus lines - Brazil - Evaluation. 2. Local transit - Brazil - Evaluation. I. Empresa Brasileira dos Transportes Urbanos. II. Series: Série Teses / Empresa Brasileira dos Transportes Urbanos , 6. III. Title.
HE5653.A6 D35 1985

Daiches, David, 1912- Sozialreform und Rhetorik =. Wiesbaden , 1984. 174 p. ; ISBN 3-515-02857-9 ***NYPL [L-11 3778 Bd. 4]***

Daicoff, Darwin W. The Kansas retail liquor industry : final report to the Department of Revenue, State of Kansas / Darwin W. Daicoff, Douglas C. Houston. [Lawrence, Kan.] : Institute for Public Policy and Business Research, University of Kansas, [1985] 53 leaves ; 29 cm. "December 1985." Bibliography: leaves 51-53. "No. 100." LC Card 86-622263 DDC 381/.456631/09781 19
1. Liquor industry - Kansas. I. Houston, Douglas C. II. Kansas. Dept. of Revenue. III. Title.
HD9390.U63 K23 1985

Dailey, Robert C. Understanding people in organizations / Robert C. Dailey in collaboration with Daniel S. Fogel. St. Paul, MN : West Pub. Co., c1988. xviii, 525 p. : ill. ; 26 cm. Includes bibliographies and index. ISBN 0-314-24254-6 LC Card 86-32460 DDC 658.4 19
1. Organizational behavior. 2. Organizational change. I. Fogel, Daniel S. II. Title.
HD58.7 .D34 1988

DAIMLER-BENZ AKTIENGESELLSCHAFT.
Osswald, Richard, 1917- Lebendige Arbeitswelt . Stuttgart , c1986. 394 p. : ISBN 3-421-06309-5 LC Card 86-148169
HD9710.G44 D385 1986

Daimler-Motoren-Gesellschaft in Berlin-Stuttgart. see **Daimler-Benz Aktiengesellschaft.**

Daire Tolmo, Alonso. Gonzales Torres, Rodrigo. Los paros nacionales en Chile, 1919-1973 /. Santiago [Chile] , 1984. 234 p. ; LC Card 86-200794
HD5356.A6 G66 1984

Dairy & Food Industries Supply Association.
Keidel, Albert. China's dairy and food processing industries . Washington, D.C. , c1986. ii, 65 leaves ; LC Card 86-233105 DDC 338.1/77/0951 19
HD9275.C62 K45 1986

Dairy development . Ratnam, C. Allahabad, India , 1986. xii, 168 p., [2] p. of plates : ISBN 81-85076-06-5 : LC Card 86-903085 DDC 338.1/77/095484 19
HD9275.I53 V587 1986

Dairy development and milk cooperatives . Mergos, George, 1948- Washington, D.C. [1987] xiv, 140 p. : ISBN 0-8213-0932-3 (pbk.) LC Card 87-15976 DDC 334/.68371/09543 19
HD9282.I53 M286 1987

Dairy development, marketing, and economic growth /. Bedi, M. S., 1946- New Delhi , c1987. 255 p. : LC Card 87-901246 DDC 338.1/77/0954552 19
HD9275.I53 P852 1987

Dairy imports and import policy in Mali and their implications for the dairy sector in the Bamako area /. Massow, Valentin von, 1925- Addis Ababa, Ethiopia [1985] v leaves, 57 p., [12] leaves ; LC Card 86-981009 DDC 382/.417/096623 19
HD9275.M423 B366 1985

DAIRY LAWS - UNITED STATES - STATES.
State milk regulation . [Washington, D.C.] (1301 New York Ave., N.W., Washington 20005-4788) [1986] viii, 62 p. ; LC Card 86-602413 DDC 338.1/771/0973 19
HD9282.U4 S72 1986

DAIRY PLANTS - URUGUAY.
Producción y exportación de lácteos /. Montevideo, Uruguay , 1977. 21 p. ; LC Card 85-205438
HD9275.U92 P76 1977

DAIRY PRODUCTS - INDIA - MARKETING.
Surendar Singh, 1946- Agro-economics of dairy development in India /. New Delhi , 1986. xii, 188 p. ; LC Card 86-902764 DDC 338.1/77/0954 19
HD9275.I52 S87 1986

DAIRY PRODUCTS - INDIA - VISHAKHAPATNAM (DISTRICT) - MARKETING.
Ratnam, C. Dairy development . Allahabad, India , 1986. xii, 168 p., [2] p. of plates : ISBN 81-85076-06-5 : LC Card 86-903085 DDC 338.1/77/095484 19
HD9275.I53 V587 1986

DAIRY PRODUCTS INDUSTRY.
Pfeiffer, Gabrielle. Mountains of butter, lakes of milk . Genève , 1986. 78, [4] p. : LC Card 87-109400 DDC 382/.417 19
HD9275.A2 P48 1986

DAIRY PRODUCTS INDUSTRY - BRAZIL - PARANÁ (STATE)
Estudo sobre o setor de laticínios no Estado do Paraná /. Curitiba , 1980. iii, 47 leaves : LC Card 86-201233
HD9275.B73 P34 1980

DAIRY PRODUCTS INDUSTRY - CHINA.
Keidel, Albert. China's dairy and food processing industries . Washington, D.C. , c1986. ii, 65 leaves ; LC Card 86-233105 DDC 338.1/77/0951 19
HD9275.C62 K45 1986

DAIRY PRODUCTS INDUSTRY - DENMARK.
Kóbor, Kálmán. A hús- és a tejgazdaság jellemző vonásai Dániában /. Budapest , 1984. 111 p. : ISBN 963-491-183-8 LC Card 86-198770
HD9425.D4 K6 1984

DAIRY PRODUCTS INDUSTRY - GOVERNMENT POLICY.
Pfeiffer, Gabrielle. Mountains of butter, lakes of milk . Genève , 1986. 78, [4] p. : LC Card 87-109400 DDC 382/.417 19
HD9275.A2 P48 1986

DAIRY PRODUCTS INDUSTRY - GOVERNMENT POLICY - MALI.
Massow, Valentin von, 1925- Dairy imports and import policy in Mali and their implications for the dairy sector in the Bamako area /. Addis Ababa, Ethiopia [1985] v leaves, 57 p., [12] leaves ; LC Card 86-981009 DDC 382/.417/096623 19
HD9275.M423 B366 1985

DAIRY PRODUCTS INDUSTRY - INDIA - VISHAKHAPATNAM (DISTRICT)
Ratnam, C. Dairy development . Allahabad, India , 1986. xii, 168 p., [2] p. of plates : ISBN 81-85076-06-5 : LC Card 86-903085 DDC 338.1/77/095484 19
HD9275.I53 V587 1986

DAIRY PRODUCTS INDUSTRY - MALAWI.
Rhodesia and Nyasaland. Commission of Inquiry into the Dairy Industry. Report of the Commission of Inquiry into the Dairy Industry, 1961 /. Salisbury , 1962. 91 p., [1] folded leaf of plates : LC Card 86-105139
HD9275.Z552 R46 1962

DAIRY PRODUCTS INDUSTRY - MALI - BAMAKO REGION.
Massow, Valentin von, 1925- Dairy imports and import policy in Mali and their implications for the dairy sector in the Bamako area /. Addis Ababa, Ethiopia [1985] v leaves, 57 p., [12] leaves ; LC Card 86-981009 DDC 382/.417/096623 19
HD9275.M423 B366 1985

DAIRY PRODUCTS INDUSTRY - URUGUAY.
Producción y exportación de lácteos /. Montevideo, Uruguay , 1977. 21 p. ; LC Card 85-205438
HD9275.U92 P76 1977

DAIRY PRODUCTS INDUSTRY - ZAMBIA.
Rhodesia and Nyasaland. Commission of Inquiry into the Dairy Industry. Report of the Commission of Inquiry into the Dairy Industry, 1961 /. Salisbury , 1962. 91 p., [1] folded leaf of plates : LC Card 86-105139
HD9275.Z552 R46 1962

DAIRY PRODUCTS INDUSTRY - ZIMBABWE.
Rhodesia and Nyasaland. Commission of Inquiry into the Dairy Industry. Report of the Commission of Inquiry into the Dairy Industry, 1961 /. Salisbury , 1962. 91 p., [1] folded leaf of plates : LC Card 86-105139
HD9275.Z552 R46 1962

DAIRY PRODUCTS - PRICES - GOVERNMENT POLICY - GERMANY (WEST)
Schmidt, Erich, 1941- Milcherzeugnis-Nachfrage unter veränderten Marktbedingungen . Münster-Hiltrup , 1985. vii, 89 p. : ISBN 3-7843-0320-X : LC Card 87-408713 DDC 338.1/8 19
HD9282.G2 S29 1985

DAIRYING, COOPERATIVE - INDIA - MADHYA PRADESH.
Mergos, George, 1948- Dairy development and milk cooperatives . Washington, D.C. [1987] xiv, 140 p. : ISBN 0-8213-0932-3 (pbk.) LC Card 87-15976 DDC 334/.68371/09543 19
HD9282.I53 M286 1987

DAIRYING - ECONOMIC ASPECTS - INDIA.
Surendar Singh, 1946- Agro-economics of dairy development in India /. New Delhi , 1986. xii, 188 p. ; LC Card 86-902764 DDC 338.1/77/0954 19
HD9275.I52 S87 1986

DAIRYING - ECONOMIC ASPECTS - INDIA - PUNJAB.
Bedi, M. S., 1946- Dairy development, marketing, and economic growth /. New Delhi , c1987. 255 p. : LC Card 87-901246 DDC 338.1/77/0954552 19
HD9275.I53 P852 1987

DAIRYING - GOVERNMENT POLICY - INDIA.
Surendar Singh, 1946- Agro-economics of dairy development in India /. New Delhi , 1986. xii, 188 p. ; LC Card 86-902764 DDC 338.1/77/0954 19
HD9275.I52 S87 1986

DAIRYING - INDIA - VISHĀKHAPATNAM (DISTRICT)
Ratnam, C. Dairy development . Allahabad, India , 1986. xii, 168 p., [2] p. of plates : ISBN 81-85076-06-5 : LC Card 86-903085 DDC 338.1/77/095484 19
HD9275.I53 V587 1986

Dal-Rosso, Sadi. As condições de emprego do menor trabalhador : comerás o pão com o suor do teu rosto / Sadi Dal-Rosso, Mara Lúcia S. Resende. [Brasília] : Thesaurus, c1986. 114 p. ; 21 cm. Bibliography: p. 109-114. LC Card 86-224647
1. Children - Employment - History. 2. Children - Employment - Brazil - History. I. Resende, Mara Lúcia S. II. Title.
HD6231 .D35 1986

Dalal-Clayton, D. B. (D. Barry) Lupande Development Workshop (1983 : Nyamaluma Wildlife Conservation Camp) Proceedings of the Lupande Development Workshop . Chipata, Zambia , 1984. x, 121 p. : LC Card 84-980605 DDC 333.73/17/096894 19
HD993.Z8 L835 1983 ***NYPL [JLG 87-67]***

Dale Carnegie & Associates. Managing through people /. Garden City, NY (1475 Franklin Ave., Garden City 11530) , c1987. 345 p. ; LC Card 87-167705 DDC 658.4 19
HD31 .M29427 1987

Dale, Richard. Financial deregulation . Cambridge , Wolfeboro, N.H., USA , 1986. xiii, 88 p. ; ISBN 0-85941-366-7 : LC Card 87-104563 DDC 332/.0941 19
HG186.G7 F546 1986

D'Aleo, Richard J., 1943-
Federal statistical directory 1984. Evinger, William R., 1943- Federal statistical directory : the guide to personnel and data sources / William R. Evinger.28th ed. Phoenix, Ariz. , 1987. iv, 127 p. ; ISBN 0-89774-398-9 (pbk.) LC Card 87-12359 DDC 353.0081/9 19
HA37.U55 E85 1987

Dalgaard, Bruce R. Money, financial institutions, and economic activity / Bruce R. Dalgaard. Glenview, Ill. : Scott, Foresman, c1987. 560 p. : ill. ; 24 cm. Includes bibliographies and index. ISBN 0-673-15876-4 LC Card 87-4851 DDC 332.1 19
1. Finance. 2. Money. 3. Banks and banking. 4. Economics. I. Title.
HG173 .D28 1987

Dalhousie College and University. see **Dalhousie University.**

Dalhousie University. Centre for International Business Studies. New theories of the multinational enterprise /. London , c1982. 303 p. : ISBN 0-7099-2224-8 LC Card 86-673671
HD2755.5 .N485x 1982

Dalhousie University. International Business Studies, Centre for. see **Dalhousie University. Centre for International Business Studies.**

Dalīl al-hay'āt al-tijārīyah al-ḥukūmīyah fī al-buldān al-nāmiyah. Handbook of state trading organizations of developing countries =. New York , 1985. clxxxix, 542 p. : ISBN 92-1-012014-0 (pbk.) LC Card 86-233995
HF1009.7.D44 H35 1985

Dalīl rajul al-a'māl fī al-ṣinā'ah wa-al-tijārah : Imārat Abū Ẓaby / i'dād Qism al-Dirāsāt wa-al-Buḥūth al-Iqtiṣādīyah. [Abu Ẓaby] : Ghurfat Tijārat wa-Ṣinā'at Abū Ẓaby, 1984. 305 p. : ill. (some col.), forms, col. ports. ; 24 cm. Bibliography: p. 305. LC Card 86-965166
1. Abū Ẓaby (United Arab Emirates : Emirate) - Commerce - Directories. 2. Abū Ẓaby (United Arab Emirates : Emirate) - Industries - Directories. 3. Abū Ẓaby (United Arab Emirates : Emirate) - Manufactures - Directories. 4. Commercial law - United Arab Emirates - Abū Ẓaby (Emirate). 5. Industrial laws and legislation - United Arab Emirates - Abū Ẓaby (Emirate). I. Ghurfat Tijārat wa-Ṣinā'at Abū Ẓaby. Qism al-Dirāsāt wa-al-Buḥūth al-Iqtiṣādīyah.
HF5233.A56 D35 1984

Dalin, V. M. (Viktor Moiseevich) Trunskiĭ, I͡U. G. Frantsuzskai͡a derevni͡a v XIX-XX vekakh . Moskva , 1986. 283 p. ; LC Card 86-201573
HD1945 .T78 1986

DALKON SHIELD (INTRAUTERINE CONTRACEPTIVE)
Perry, Susan. Nightmare . New York , c1985. xvii, 261 p. ; ISBN 0-02-595930-1 : LC Card 85-13710 DDC 338.7/616139435 19
HD9995.C64 A236 1985
NYPL [JLE 85-3950]

Dall, C. H. A., Mrs. see **Dall, Caroline Wells (Healey), 1822-1912.**

Dall, Caroline Wells (Healey), 1822-1912. "Woman's right to labor," or, Low wages and hard work : in three lectures, delivered in Boston, November, 1859 / by Caroline H. Dall. Boston : Walker, Wise, and Co., 1860. xv, 184 p. ; 18 cm. LC Card 87-162350
1. Women - Employment - History. I. Title. II. Title: Low wages and hard work.
HD6053 .D27 1860

Dalla grande associazione degli operai di Novara al Circolo operaio agricolo della Bicocca . Bermani, Cesare, 1937- Novara [1983] 345 p., [31] p. of plates : LC Card 85-148843
HD6714.N68 B47 1983

Dalla Valle, F. Energiaottanta . Milano , 1980. [xv] 284 p. ; ***NYPL [JLD 86-3690]***

Dallago, Bruno, 1950- The Unofficial economy . Aldershot, Hants, England , Brookfield, Vt., USA , c1987. 345 p. : ISBN 0-566-05131-1 : LC Card 86-25634 DDC 381 19
HD2341 .U56 1987

DALLAS (TEX.) - INDUSTRIES - DIRECTORIES.
Camden, Thomas M., 1938- How to get a job in Dallas, Fort Worth . Chicago, IL , c1987. viii, 490 p. : ISBN 0-9609516-9-5 (pbk.) : LC Card 86-30123 DDC 650.1/4/097642812 19
HF5382.75.U6 C353 1987

DALLAS (TEX.) - SOCIAL CONDITIONS.
Stirrings of culture /. Dallas, Tex. , 1986. xix, 250 p. ; ISBN 0-911005-07-2 : LC Card 86-24028 DDC 306 19
HM101 .S786 1986 ***NYPL [JFF 87-151]***

Dall'interno della UIL (1950-1985) /. Simoncini, Franco. Milano, Italy , c1986. 274 p. ; LC Card 86-169848
HD8473.U533 S56 1986

Dalloz gestion. Management.
Tixier, Maud. Dictionnaire américain-anglais-français du management /. Paris , 1985. 381 p. ; ISBN 2-247-00647-7 : LC Card 86-160705
HD30.15 .T59 1985 ***NYPL [JLD 86-3975]***

Dalloz Gestion. Vie internationale de l'entreprise.
Gestion internationale de l'entreprise /. Paris , 1984. 393 p. : ISBN 2-247-00496-2 : LC Card 85-114907
HD62.4 .G47 1984

DALMATIAN LANGUAGE (SLAVIC) see **SERBO-CROATIAN LANGUAGE.**

D'Almeida, Ayite-Fily, 1949- Kjellstrom, Sven B., 1945- Institutional development and technical assistance in macro-economic policy formulation . Washington, D.C., U. S.A. [1987] 69 p. ; ISBN 0-8213-0919-6 (pbk.) LC Card 87-14021 DDC 339.5/0966/81 19
HC1015 .K58 1987

Dalrymple, Douglas J. Sales management : concepts and cases / Douglas J. Dalrymple.3rd ed. New York : Wiley, c1988. p. cm. Bibliography: p. Includes indexes. ISBN 0-471-62495-0 LC Card 87-23749 DDC 658.8/1 19
1. Sales management. 2. Sales management - Case studies. I. Title.
HF5438.4 .D34 1988

Dalton, Melville. Men who manage : fusions of feeling and theory in administration / Melville Dalton. New York : Garland Pub., 1987. xi, 318 p., [1] leaf of plates : ill. ; 23 cm. (Continuity in administrative science) Reprint. Originally published: New York : Wiley, 1959. Bibliography: p. 287-299. Includes indexes. ISBN 0-8240-8203-6 (alk. paper) : LC Card 86-25801 DDC 658.4 19
1. Industrial management. 2. Industrial sociology. I. Title. II. Series.
HD31 .D2 1987

Dalwick, Robert Elgar Richard.
Newfoundland air mails, 1919-1939. Harmer, C. H. C. (Cyril Henry Carrington) Newfoundland air mails : air stamps and flight covers from 1919 through March 31, 1949 : an update of 1953 edition / by C.H.C. Harmer ; edited by Joseph L. Eisendrath.Rev. and updated. Cinnaminson, N.J., U. S.A. , 1984. x, 181 p. : LC Card 87-147693 DDC 383/.144/09718 19
HE6185.C23 N475 1984

Daly, D. J. (Donald James), 1922-
Canadian manufactured exports : constraints and opportunities / D.J. Daly, D.C. MacCharles. Montreal, Quebec : Institute for Research on Public Policy, c1986. xxviii, 180 p. ; 23 cm. (Essays in international economics, 0826-4384) Bibliography: p. 155-168. ISBN 0-88645-025-X (pbk.) : LC Card 87-142389 DDC 382/.4567/0971 19
1. Exports - Canada. 2. Canada - Commerce. 3. Canada - Manufactures. I. MacCharles, Donald C. (Donald Clare), 1935-. II. Title. III. Series.
HF3226.5 .D26 1986

Managerial macroeconomics : a Canadian perspective / Donald J. Daly. Homewood, Ill. : Irwin, 1988. xvi, 383 p. : ill. ; 25 cm. Includes index. Bibliography: p. 345-352. ISBN 0-256-06000-2 LC Card 87-80950 DDC 339/.024658 19
1. Managerial economics - Canada. 2. Management - Canada - Decision making. 3. Macroeconomics. I. Title.
HD30.22 .D35 1988

On real wage unemployment / D.J. Daly and D.C. MacCharles. Vancouver, B.C., Canada : Fraser Institute, 1986. vi, 117 p. : ill. ; 22 cm. (Focus, 0715-5417 . no. 18) Bibliography: p. 111-117. ISBN 0-88975-079-3 (pbk.) LC Card 87-142391 DDC 331.13/7971 19
1. Wages and labor productivity - Canada. 2. Unemployment - Canada. 3. Supply-side economics - Canada. 4. Canada - Economic policy. I. MacCharles, D. C. (Donald C.), 1935-. II. Series: Focus (Fraser Institute (Vancouver, B.C.)) , 18. III. Title.
HD4946.C3 D35 1986

Daly, Herman E. Crescimento ou economia estacionária. [Salvador] : Fundação Bahiana para Estudos Econômicos e Sociais, [1983] 56 p. : ill., ports. ; 23 cm. "Conferência do Prof. Herman Edward Daly, da Universidade de Louisiana, tendo como debatedores os professores Antônio Carlos Lemgruber e Moisés Glatt, da Fundação Getúlio Vargas, no auditório do Desenbanco, em 5 de agosto de 1983." LC Card 87-127979 DDC 338.9 19
1. Economic policy - Congresses. I. Lemgruber, Antonio Carlos. II. Glatt, Moisés. III. Fundação Bahiana para Estudos Econômicos e Sociais. IV. Title.
HD85.S7 D35 1983

Daly, J. Bowles (John Bowles) Glimpses of Irish industries / by J. Bowles Daly. London : Ward and Downey, 1889. xvi, 219, 16 p. ; 20 cm. "Wards & Downey's catalogue": 16 p. at end. LC Card 85-666357
1. Ireland - Industries. I. Title.
HC260.5 .D35x 1889

Dalzell, Robert F. Enterprising elite : the Boston Associates and the world they made / Robert F. Dalzell, Jr. Cambridge, Mass. : Harvard University Press, 1987. xviii, 298 p., [11] p. of plates : ill. ; 24 cm. (Harvard studies in business history. 40) Bibliography: p. 239-289. Includes index. ISBN 0-674-25765-0 (alk. paper) LC Card 86-33649 DDC 338.4/7677/0097444 19
1. Textile industry - Massachusetts - Lowell - History - 19th century. 2. Textile industry - Massachusetts - Waltham - History - 19th century. 3. Boston Region (Mass.) - Industries - History - 19th century. I. Title. II. Title: Boston Associates. III. Series.
HD9858.L9 D35 1987

DAMAGES - UNITED STATES.
Breit, William. Antitrust penalty reform . Washington, D.C. , c1986. x, 83 p. : ISBN 0-8447-3600-7 (alk. paper) LC Card 86-3203 DDC 343.73/072/0269 347.303720269 19
KF1657.T7 B74 1986 ***NYPL [JLE 86-3948]***

Damanik, Konta I. Kurs mata uang sebagai alat kebijakan di negara sedang berkembang (NSB) / oleh Konta I. Damanik. Salatiga : Fakultas Ekonomi, Universitas Kristen Satya Wacana, 1980. ii, 21 leaves ; 29 cm. (Seri monografi / Fakultas Ekonomi, Universitas Kristen Satya Wacana . no. 1) LC Card 85-941470
1. Monetary policy - Developing countries. I. Series: Seri monografi (Universitas/I.K.I.P. Kristen Satya Wacana. Fakultas Ekonomi) , no. 1. II. Title.
HG1496 .D35 1980

D'Ambrósio, Ubiratan. World peace and the developing countries . Basingstoke, Hampshire , 1986. xix, 272 p. ; ISBN 0-333-43636-9
NYPL [JLD 87-1192]

Damian-Knight, Guy. The I Ching on business and decision making : successful management strategy based on the ancient oracle of China / by Guy Damian-Knight. Rochester, VT : Destiny Books, 1987. p. cm. ISBN 0-89281-173-0 : LC Card 87-15440 DDC 658.4/03 19
1. Industrial management - Decision making. 2. I ching. I. Title.
HD37.C47 D35 1987

Damit es nicht verloren geht-- .
(5) Mägde . Wien , 1985. 211 p. : ISBN 3-205-06154-3 LC Card 86-127196
HD6072.2.A9 M34 1985

A Damjanich János Múzeum közleményei .
(15-18) Szabó, László. Munkaszervezet és termelékenység a magyar parasztságnál a XIX-XX. században /. Szolnok , 1968 (Debrecen : Szabadság Lapnyomda) 167 p. : LC Card 86-188720
HD1536.H9 S89 1968

Dämpfling, Björn, 1949- Die Marxsche Theorie der Grundrente : eine kritische Studie / Björn Dämpfling. Hamburg : VSA-Verlag, 1985. 161 p. ; 24 cm. Bibliography: p. 154-161. ISBN 3-87975-302-4 LC Card 86-172913
1. Rent (Economic theory). 2. Marxian economics. I. Title.
HB401 .D35 1985

DAMS - ENVIRONMENTAL ASPECTS - GOVERNMENT POLICY - AUSTRALIA - TASMANIA.
Lowe, D. A. (Douglas Ackley), 1942- The price of power . South Melbourne , 1984. viii, 184 p., [12] p. of plates : ISBN 0-333-38088-6 LC Card 84-254286 DDC 333.91/62/099466 19
HD9685.A83 T385 1984
NYPL [JLD 87-795]

Damus, Renate. Die Legende von der Systemkonkurrenz : kapitalistische und realsozialistische Industriegesellschaft / Renate Damus. Frankfurt ; New York : Campus, c1986. 245 p. ; 21 cm. Bibliography: p. 243-245. ISBN 3-593-33590-5 LC Card 86-196924
1. Comparative economics. 2. Capitalism. 3. Socialism. I. Title.
HB90 .D36 1986

Danaher, Kevin. Lappé, Frances Moore. Betraying the national interest /. New York , 1987, c1986. p. cm. ISBN 0-8021-0012-0 LC Card 87-12067 DDC 338.91 19
HC60 .L325 1987

A Dance along the precipice : the political and economic dimensions of the international debt problem / edited by William N. Eskridge, Jr. Lexington, Mass. : Lexington Books, c1985. xxxii, 283 p. : ill. ; 24 cm. Papers presented at the Eighth Sokol Colloquium, held at the University of Virginia, March 1984. Includes bibliographical references and index. ISBN 0-669-10899-5 (alk. paper) LC Card 85-5789 DDC 336.3/435/091724 19
1. Debts, External - Developing countries - Congresses. 2. Debt relief - Developing countries - Congresses. I. Eskridge, William N. II. Sokol Colloquium (8th : 1984 : University of Virginia).
HJ8899 .D36 1985 ***NYPL [JLE 86-2308]***

Danchenko, M. I. (Mykola Ivanovych)
Dystsyplina pratsi / M.I. Danchenko, A.R. Matsiuk. Kyïv : Nauk. dumka, 1983. 110 p. ; 20 cm. (Naukovo-populiarna literatura) Title in colophon: Distsiplina truda. Includes bibliographical references. LC Card 83-215106
1. Labor discipline - Ukraine. 2. Employee motivation - Ukraine. I. Matsiuk, A. R. (Anatoliĭ Romanovich). II. Title. III. Title: Distsiplina truda.
HF5549.5.L3 D34 1983

Danel, J. M. Evaluation du développement rural /. [Paris] , c1982. 201 p. : ISBN 2-11-084484-1 LC Card 84-134740
HC59.72.E44 E93 1982

Danel, Raymond.
Les lignes Latécoère : 1918-1927 / Raymond Danel. Toulouse : Privat, c1986. 208 p., [16] p. of plates : ill. ; 24 cm. (Les Pionniers de l'aviation commerciale . 1) Le Midi et son histoire Bibliography: p. [207]-208. ISBN 2-7089-8611-2 : LC Card 87-165510
1. Compagnie générale aéropostale - History. 2. Aeronautics, Commercial - France - History. I. Series: Danel, Raymond. Pionniers de l'aviation commerciale , 1. II. Title.
HE9848.C66 D36 1986 vol. 1

Pionniers de l'aviation commerciale .
(1) Danel, Raymond. Les lignes Latécoère . Toulouse , c1986. 208 p., [16] p. of plates : ISBN 2-7089-8611-2 : LC Card 87-165510
HE9848.C66 D36 1986 vol. 1

Daneri, Oscar. El atípico caso argentino : del desarrollo al subdesarrollo : teoría y realidad de la política económica del sector externo, la economía social cristiana, inflación y deuda externa como efecto del desequilibrio estructural de la economía, la nueva estrategia del desarrollo para el siglo XXI / Oscar Daneri. Buenos Aires : [s.n.], 1986. 412 p. : ill. ; 20 cm. Bibliography: p. 405-410. ISBN 950-43-0291-4 LC Card 87-400194 DDC 338.982 19
1. Argentina - Economic conditions - 1945-. 2. Argentina - Economic policy. I. Title.
HC175 .D26 1986

Danesh, Abol Hassan, 1952- Rural exodus & squatter settlements in the Third World : case of Iran / Abol Hassan Danesh. Lanham, MD : University Press of America, c1987. xii, 168 p. : ill. ; 24 cm. Bibliography: p. 158-167. ISBN 0-8191-6443-7 (alk. paper) : LC Card 87-10627 DDC 307.2 19
1. Rural-urban migration - Iran. 2. Urban-rural migration - Iran. 3. Urbanization - Iran. 4. Squatter settlements - Iran. I. Title. II. Title: Rural exodus and squatter settlements in the Third World.
HB2096.4.A3 D36 1987

Dangat, S. B., 1942- Farm income stabilization in dry farming areas / S.B. Dangat ; foreword by D.K. Salunkhe. Delhi, India : Mittal Publications, 1986. xi, 237 p. ; 22 cm. Originally presented as the author's thesis (Ph. D.--Mahatma Phule Agricultural University, 1984) Study based on data collected from the Ahmednagar District, Maharashtra, for the year 1981-82. Bibliography: p. [229]-234. Includes index. LC Card 86-903137 DDC 338.1/3/0954792 19
1. Dry farming - Economic aspects - India - Ahmadnagar District - Case studies. 2. Dry farming - Economic aspects - India - Case studies. 3. Farm income - India - Ahmadnagar District - Case studies. 4. Farm income - India - Case studies. I. Title.
HD2075.A36 D35 1986

Dange, Manohar N. Theory and practice of urban land values in India / M.N. Dange. Bombay : Tripathi, 1983. xii, 132 p. ; 22 cm. Includes index. LC Card 83-903969 DDC 333.33/2/0954 19
1. Real property - Valuation - India. 2. Land use, Urban - India. I. Title.
HD878 .D36 1983 ***NYPL [JLD 87-729]***

D'Angelillo, Massimo, 1956- Job creation : il sostegno alle nuove imprese in Europa / Massimo D'Angelillo ; prefazione de Mario Zigarella. Milano, Italy : F. Angeli, c1985. 231 p. ; 22 cm. Includes bibliographical references. LC Card 86-156936
1. New business enterprises - Government policy - Europe. 2. Industrial promotion - Europe. 3. Europe - Full employment policies. I. Title.
HD5764.A6 D418 1985
NYPL [JLD 86-3248]

D'Angelo, Lucio. Ceti medi e ricostruzione : il partito democratico del lavoro (1943-1948) / Lucio D'Angelo. [Milano] : Giuffrè, 1981. vi, 287 p. ; 25 cm. (Università di Roma, Facoltà di scienze politiche . 34) Includes bibliographical references and index. LC Card 81-213297
1. Partito democratico del lavoro - History. 2. Middle classes - Italy - History - 20th century. 3. Labor and laboring classes - Italy - History - 20th century. 4. Reconstruction (1939-1951) - Italy. 5. Italy - Politics and government - 1943-1947. I. Title.
JN5657.D45 D36 1981
NYPL [JLE 86-3459]

D'Angelo, Massimo.
Cooperazione italiana allo sviluppo . Roma [1984] 144 p. ; ISBN 88-7621-170-5 : LC Card 85-223760 DDC 338.91/45/01724 19
HC60 .C65757 1984

Criteri per una cooperazione industriale con i paesi in via di sviluppo / di Massimo D'Angelo e Richard Walker ; coordinamento, Paolo Basurto. Milano : F. Angeli, c1981. 294 p. ; 22 cm. (Studi e ricerche / Ministero degli affari esteri, Dipartimento per la cooperazione allo sviluppo . 2) At head of title: Ministero degli affari esteri, Dipartimento per la cooperazione allo sviluppo; Iai, Istituto affari internazionali. Includes index. ISBN 88-20-42145-3 : LC Card 82-113466
1. Industry and state - Italy. 2. Industry and state - Developing countries. 3. Italy - Foreign economic relations - Developing countries. 4. Developing Countries - Foreign economic relations - Italy. 5. Italy - Commercial policy. 6. Developing countries - Commercial policy. I. Walker, Richard. II. Italy. Ministero degli affari esteri. Dipartimento per la cooperazione allo sviluppo. III. Series: Collana di studi e ricerche (Italy. Ministero degli affari esteri. Dipartimento per la cooperazione allo sviluppo) , 2. IV. Title.
HF1549 .D36 1981 ***NYPL [JLD 86-3318]***

Danger, Eric P. (Eric Paxton) Selecting colour for print / E.P. Danger. Aldershot, Hants, England : Gover Technical Press ; Brookfield, Vt., U. S.A. : Gower Pub. Co., c1987. x, 164 p. ; 26 cm. Bibliography: p. [163]-164. ISBN 0-291-39715-8 (U. S.) : LC Card 86-23060 DDC 659.13/23 19
1. Color in advertising. 2. Color printing. I. Title.
HF5839 .D36 1987

DANGEROUS GOODS. see **HAZARDOUS SUBSTANCES.**

DANGEROUS MATERIALS. see **HAZARDOUS SUBSTANCES.**

Dangerous medicine . United States. Congress. House. Committee on Energy and Commerce. Subcommittee on Oversight and Investigations. Washington , 1986. v, 31 p. ; LC Card 86-602099 DDC 363.1/942/0973 19
HD9665.9.U6 U55 1986

Daniel Bell and the decline of intellectual radicalism . Brick, Howard, 1953- Madison, Wis. , 1986. 215-266. ISBN 0-299-10550-4 : LC Card 85-40757 DDC 300/.92/4 19
H59.B42 B75 1986 ***NYPL [JLE 86-3046]***

Daniel, James, 1916- International Industrial Conference, 1st, San Francisco, 1957. Private investment /. New York , 1980, c1958. xi, 282 p. ; ISBN 0-405-13355-3 LC Card 80-606 DDC 332.6/7314
HG4538 .I537 1957d ***NYPL [JLD 81-249]***

Daniel, Philip. Foreign investment in Papua New Guinea : policies and practices / Philip Daniel and Rod Sims. Canberra : National Centre for Development Studies, The Australian National University, 1986. x, 144 p. : ill. ; 25 cm. (Pacific research monograph, 0155-9060 . 12) Bibliography: p. 141-144. ISBN 0-86784-761-1 (pbk.) LC Card 87-151193 DDC 332.6/7322953 19
1. Investments, Foreign - Papua New Guinea. 2. Investments, Foreign - Government policy - Papua New Guinea. I. Sims, Rod. II. Title. III. Series.
HG5982.A3 D36 1986

Daniel Thorner memorial lecture. Patnaik, Utsa. The agrarian question and the development of capitalism in India /. Delhi , New York , 1986. 45 p. ; ISBN 0-19-561954-4 : LC Card 86-900017 DDC 338.1/0954 19
HD2072 .P33 1986

Daniel, Troy E.
Lehman, Mark W. Using the microcomputer in cost accounting . St. Paul , c1988. x, 396 p. : ISBN 0-314-34729-1 (pbk.) LC Card 87-10632 DDC 657/.42/02855369 19
HF5686.C8 L34 1988

Lehman, Mark W. Using the microcomputer in managerial accounting . St. Paul , c1987. x, 406 p. : ISBN 0-314-98515-8 (pbk.) LC Card 87-2194 DDC 658.1/511/02855369 19
HF5657.4 .L44 1987

Daniel, W. W. (William Wentworth), 1938- Workplace industrial relations and technical change / W.W. Daniel. London : F. Pinter in association with Policy Studies Institute, c1987. 312 p. : ill. ; 23 cm. Includes bibliographical references and index. ISBN 0-86187-917-1 LC Card 87-154801 DDC 331/.0941 19
1. Industrial relations - Great Britain - Effect of technological innovations on. I. Policy Studies Institute. II. Title.
HD8391 .D3535 1987

Daniel, Wayne W., 1929- Essentials of business statistics / Wayne W. Daniel. 2nd ed. Boston : Houghton Mifflin, c1988. xvi, 426, 99, 4 p. : col. ill. ; 25 cm. Includes index. ISBN 0-395-35650-4 LC Card 87-80109 DDC 519.5/024658 19
1. Commercial statistics. I. Title.
HF1017 .D28 1988

Danielian, Ronald L. The forgotten deficit : America's addiction to foreign capital / Ronald L. Danielian and Stephen E. Thomsen. Boulder : Westview Press, 1987. xii, 84 p. ; 22 cm. (Studies in American business and the international economy) "Published in cooperation with the International Economic Policy Association." Includes bibliographical references and index. ISBN 0-8133-7450-2 (pbk. : alk. paper) LC Card 87-50654 DDC 332.6/7373 19
1. Balance of payments - United States. 2. Investments, American. 3. Capital movements - United States. 4. Investments, Foreign - United States. 5. United States - Foreign economic relations. I. Thomsen, Stephen E. II. International Economic Policy Association. III. Title. IV. Series.
HG3883.U7 D36 1987

Daniels, Leroy Judson, 1882- Tales of an old horsetrader : the first hundred years / by Leroy Judson Daniels ; as told to Helen S. Herrick.1st ed. Iowa City : University of Iowa Press, 1987. viii, 235 p. : ill. ; 23 cm. (A Bur oak original) ISBN 0-87745-173-7 LC Card 87-10932 DDC 338.1/761/00924 B 19
1. Daniels, Leroy Judson, 1882-. 2. Businessmen - United States - Biography. 3. Horse industry - United States - History. I. Herrick, Helen S. II. Title. III. Series.
HD9434.U6 D36 1987

DANIELS, LEROY JUDSON, 1882-
Daniels, Leroy Judson, 1882- Tales of an old horsetrader . Iowa City , 1987. viii, 235 p. : ISBN 0-87745-173-7 LC Card 87-10932 DDC 338.1/761/00924 B 19
HD9434.U6 D36 1987

Daniels, Tom D. Perspectives on organizational communication / Tom D. Daniels, Barry K. Spiker. Dubuque, Iowa : W.C. Brown, c1987. xiv, 288 p. : ill. ; 24 cm. Includes bibliographies and indices. ISBN 0-697-00444-9 LC Card 86-72711 DDC 658.4/5 19
1. Communication in organizations. I. Spiker, Barry K. II. Title.
HD30.3 .D33 1987

Daniels, William R. (William Roy), 1941- Group power : a manager's guide to using meetings / William R. Daniels. San Diego, Calif. : University Associates, c1986. vi, 94 p. : ill. ; 23 cm. Bibliography: p. 93-94. ISBN 0-88390-204-4 (pbk.) : LC Card 86-24955 DDC 658.4/563 19
1. Communication in management. 2. Meetings. 3. Social groups. I. Title.
HD30.3 .D34 1986

Danilin, Vi͡acheslav Ivanovich. Modin, Anatoliĭ Andreevich. Dinamika proizvodstvennykh ob"edineniĭ i modeli planirovanii͡a ikh dei͡atel'nosti /. Moskva , 1984. 231 p. : LC Card 84-195690
HD9705.S595 M62 1984

Danilov, L. L. (Leonid Luk'i͡anvich), 1914- USSR, the 12th five-year plan period / Leonid Danilov ; [translated form the Russian by Oleg Svetlov]. Moscow : Novosti Press Agency Pub. House, 1986. 55 p. : ill. ; 19 cm. Title on t.p. verso: SSSR v XII pi͡atiletke. LC Card 87-123056 DDC 338.947 19
1. Soviet Union - Economic policy - 1986-. I. Title. II. Title: SSSR v XII pi͡atiletke.
HC336.25 .D378 1986

Danish economic survey. [Copenhagen] : Ministry for Economic Affairs, Economic Secretariat, [1984] 72 p. : ill. ; 22 cm. "Translation of Chapter I to IV if Økonomisk oversigt, Oktober, 1984"--Pref. "October 1984." LC Card 86-220598 DDC 330.9489/058 19
1. Economic forecasting - Denmark. 2. Denmark - Economic conditions - 1945-. I. Denmark. Økonomiske sekretariat. II. Økonomisk oversigt.
HC355 .D226 1984

Danish Employers' Confederation. see **Dansk arbejdsgiverforening.**

Dankovits, László. A Gazdaságirányítás és a szakszervezetek /. Budapest , 1985. 191 p. ; ISBN 963-322-253-2 : LC Card 86-104573
HC300.28 .G349 1985

Danks, Lawrence J. Contemporary real estate principles / Lawrence J. Danks. Medford, N.J. : Pilgrim Books, c1987. x, 439 p. : ill. ; 28 cm. ISBN 0-9610624-1-X (pbk.) LC Card 86-63861 DDC 333.33 19
1. Real estate business. I. Title.
HD1375 .D25 1987

Danmark. see **Denmark.**

Danmarks areal. København : Danmarks statistik, 1968. 228 p., [1] folded leaf of plates : map ; 23 cm. (Statistiske meddelelser . 1968:4) Includes index. LC Card 83-223613
1. Real property - Denmark - Statistics. I. Danmarks statistik. II. Series.
HD736 .D36 1968

Danmarks forvaltningshøjskole. Rapporter udarbejdet af Forvaltningshøjskolen og Miljøstyrelsens økonomifunktion. København [1983] 59 p. : ISBN 87-503-4574-5 LC Card 85-150558
HD4465.D4 R36 1983

Danmarks statistik.
Danmarks areal. København , 1968. 228 p., [1] folded leaf of plates : LC Card 83-223613
HD736 .D36 1968

Metodologi for Danmarks betalingsbalance =. Luxembourg , Washington, D.C. , 1985. 181 p. ; ISBN 92-825-4927-5 : LC Card 86-122287
HG3883.D4 M48 1985

Regionale dødelighedsforskelle i Danmark 1971-79. København , 1983. 136 p. : ISBN 87-501-0582-5 : LC Card 84-169325
HA1473 .A35 nr. 39 HB1441

Dann, Otto. Vereinswesen und bürgerliche Gesellschaft in Deutschland /. München , 1984. 180 p. ; ISBN 3-486-52081-4 LC Card 84-205111
HD2429.G3 V46 1984

Dannenberg, Gabriele. Wer steuert die "Anti-Kernkraft-Bewegung"-- und mit welchem Ziel? /. Wiesbaden [1977] 38 p. : LC Card 86-140106 DDC 333.79/24 19
HD9698.A2 W44 1977

Danner, David, 1948- Mundel, Marvin Everett, 1916- BASIC, a personal computer language for improving productivity /. Tokyo, Japan , c1986. v, 322 p. ; ISBN 92-833-1089-0 LC Card 86-211814 DDC 005.26 19
HF5548.5.B3 M86 1986

Danos, Paul, 1942-
Intermediate accounting. Martin, Dale R. Lotus 1-2-3 applications with disk / Dale R. Martin, A. Scott Preston. Englewood Cliffs, N.J. , c1986. viii, 120 p. : ISBN 0-13-540717-6 (pbk.) LC Card 86-200542 DDC 657/.044/02855369 19
HF5679 .M37 1986

Dansk arbejdsgiverforening. 90 plus 10 /. [Copenhagen] [1986] 39 p. : ISBN 87-7002-353-0 LC Card 86-197313
HD5799.A6 A12 1986

Dansk industripolitik : en førlængelse af økonomien / Anne Hyldegård Jensen ... [et al.]. [Århus] : Geografisk institut, Aarhus universitet, 1983. 143 p. : ill. ; 30 cm. (Notat / Geografisk institut, Aarhus universitet, 0106-9047 . 36) Includes bibliography. LC Card 84-164502
1. Industry and state - Denmark. 2. Denmark - Economic conditions - 1945-. I. Jensen, Anne Hyldegård. II. Series: Notat (Aarhus universitet. Geografisk institut) , 36.
HD3616.D43 D35 1983

Dansk ledelse halvfems i et internationalt perspektiv. Dansk ledelse '90 i et internationalt perspektiv . [Copenhagen] , 1983. 226 p. : ISBN 87-7553-128-3 : LC Card 83-185958
HD57.7 .D38 1983

Dansk ledelse '90 i et internationalt perspektiv : et udviklingsprojekt fra Dansk Management Center / redigeret af Per Thygesen Poulsen.1. udg. [Copenhagen] : Børsen, 1983. 226 p. : ill. ; 22 cm. Includes bibliographical references. ISBN 87-7553-128-3 : LC Card 83-185958
1. Leadership. 2. Management - Denmark. I. Poulsen, Per Thygesen. II. Dansk Management Center. III. Title: Dansk ledelse halvfems i et internationalt perspektiv.
HD57.7 .D38 1983

Dansk Management Center. Dansk ledelse '90 i et internationalt perspektiv . [Copenhagen] , 1983. 226 p. : ISBN 87-7553-128-3 : LC Card 83-185958
HD57.7 .D38 1983

Den danske fjerkræsektor 1985, en beskrivelse . Landsudvalget for fjerkræ (Denmark) [Denmark? , 1986] 152 p. ; LC Card 86-224129
HD9437.D42 L35 1986

Det danske valutamarked /. Kolte, Lars. København , 1984, c1983. 215 p. : ISBN 87-17-03415-9 LC Card 85-127552
HG3957 .K64 1984

Danson, Mike. Redundancy and recession . Norwich, England , c1986. xii, 174 p. : ISBN 0-86094-201-5 : LC Card 86-218942 DDC 330.941/0858 19
HC256.6 .R44 1986

Dantas Junior, Altino. Lula, 1945- Lula sem censura . Petrópolis [Brazil] , 1981. 101 p. ;
NYPL [JLC 86-389]

Dantas Neto, Antônio da Costa. Custos operacionais no SBPE / Antônio da Costa Dantas Neto. Rio de Janeiro/RJ : Escola Nacional de Habitiação e Poupança, 1983. 67 p. : ill. ; 30 cm. Bibliography: p. 43. LC Card 85-108995
1. Building and loan associations - Brazil - Costs - Mathematical models. I. Title.
HG2156.B8 D36 1983

Dantwala, M. L. (Mohanlal Lalloobhai), 1909- Indian agricultural development since independence . New Delhi , c1986. viii, 519

p. ; ISBN 81-204-0118-2 : LC Card 86-902551 DDC 338.1/0954 19
HD2072 .I526 1986

DANUBE RIVER REGION - COMMERCE.
Petrov, Vladimir. Izpolzuvaneto na reka Dunav za prevoz na tovari za i ot Sredna i Zapadna Evropa /. Sofiia, 1985. 71 p. ; LC Card 86-105301
HE387.D2 P36 1985

DANUBE RIVER VALLEY - ECONOMIC CONDITIONS.
Paskaleva-Zakharieva, Virzhiniia. Sredna Evropa i zemite po Dolniia Dunav prez XVIII-XIX v. . Sofiia, 1986. 317 p. : LC Card 86-219994
HC244 .P29 1986

DANUBE RIVER VALLEY - SOCIAL CONDITIONS.
Paskaleva-Zakharieva, Virzhiniia. Sredna Evropa i zemite po Dolniia Dunav prez XVIII-XIX v. . Sofiia, 1986. 317 p. : LC Card 86-219994
HC244 .P29 1986

Danyi, Pál. Múlt, jelen, jövő a műszaki haladás szolgálatában . Pécs , 1985. 305 p. : LC Card 87-408539
HC300.29.B37 M86 1985

Danziger, Sheldon.
The Distributional impacts of public policies /. New York , 1988. xvii, 257 p. ; ISBN 0-312-00749-3 : LC Card 87-11877 DDC 339.2/0973 19
HC110.I5 D535 1988

Fighting poverty . Cambridge, Mass. , 1986. viii, 418 p. : ISBN 0-674-30085-8 (alk. paper) LC Card 85-24848 DDC 362.5/8/0973 19
HC110.P63 F54 1986 ***NYPL [JLE 86-4089]***

Dapaah, S. K. Ewusi, Kodwo. The development and resettlement of oncho-freed zones in the Volta River Basin of West Africa . [Legon, Ghana] [1985] 89 p. ; LC Card 87-127503 DDC 333.3/1/667 19
HD1022.Z8 V654 1985

Dar al-Saʻūdīyah lil-Khadamāt al-Istishārīyah. A Guide to industrial investment /. Riyadh , 1986. vi, 286 p., [4] leaves of plates : LC Card 87-400301 DDC 332.6/7322538 19
HC415.33.Z9 I534 1986

DAR MASALIT (SUDAN) - ECONOMIC CONDITIONS.
Tully, Dennis. Culture and context in Sudan . Albany, N.Y. , c1988. p. cm. ISBN 0-88706-502-3 LC Card 86-23180 DDC 338.1/09627 19
HC835.Z7 D377 1988

Darabont, Árpád. A Nemzeti vagyon és az állóeszközállomány 1970-1978 /. [Budapest] [1979] 140 p. ; LC Card 82-193609
HC300.295.W4 N454 1979

Darai, Lajos Mihály. Görög, Tibor. Ökopesszimizmus, technooptimizmus és korunk globális problémái /. [Budapest] , 1984. 85 p. : ISBN 963-673-290-6 LC Card 85-130717
HC59 .G6226 1984

Darbéra, Richard. Le planificateur et le cyclopousse : les avatars de la politique des transports urbains en Inde / Richard Darbéra, Bernard Henri Nicot ; préface de Ralph Gakenheimer. Caen : Paradigme, 1986. xiii, 190 p. : ill. (some col.) ; 21 cm. (Transports & communication, 0760-9922 . 4) Bibliography: p. 135-142. ISBN 2-86878-015-6 : LC Card 86-192929
1. Urban transportation - India. 2. Pedicabs - India. 3. Urban transportation policy - India. I. Nicot, Bernard Henri. II. Title. III. Series.
HE311.I4 D36 1986

Darby, D. S. Verma, Gajendra K. Race, training, and employment /. London , New York , 1987. vi, 134 p. : ISBN 1-85000-243-6 : LC Card 87-15470 DDC 331.3/46/0941 19
HD5715.5.G7 V47 1987

Dare to change your job and your life. Kanchier, Carole. Questers . Saratoga, Calif. , c1987. xi, 225 p. ; ISBN 0-88247-767-6 (pbk.) : LC Card 87-60351 DDC 658.4/09 19
HF5384 .K36 1987

Daremblum, Jaime.
El auge del café y la apertura de la economía costarricense / por Jaime Daremblum. El registro civil y el proceso electoral en Costa Rica : bases de un sistema político democrático / por Rafael Villegas. 1a ed. San José, Costa Rica : Centro de Investigación y Adiestramiento Político Administrativo, 1980. 62 p. ; 25 x 11 cm. (Estudios del Centro de Investigación y Adiestramiento Político Administrativo . nos. 2-3 (dic. 1979)) Includes bibliographies. LC Card 84-247131
1. Costa Rica - Commerce - History. 2. Coffee trade - Costa Rica - History. 3. Registers of births, etc. - Costa Rica - History. I. Villegas, Rafael. Registro civil y el proceso electoral en Costa Rica. 1980. II. Title. III. Title: Registro civil y el processo electoral en Costa Rica. IV. Series: Estudios del Centro de Investigación y Adiestramiento Político Administrativo , no. 2-3.
HF3255 .D37 1980

Crisis internacionales y economía nacional : Costa Rica ante las dos guerras mundiales y la gran depresión / por Jaime Daremblum.1a ed. San José, Costa Rica : Centro de Investigación y Adiestramiento Político Administrativo, 1982. 62 p. ; 25 x 12 cm. (Estudios del Centro de Investigación y Adiestramiento Político Administrativo . no. 6 (enero 1982)) Bibliography: p. 60-62. LC Card 84-247158
1. Costa Rica - Economic conditions. 2. Costa Rica - Economic Policy. 3. Costa Rica - Politics and government - 1821-1948. 4. Costa Rica - Politics and government - 1948-. I. Series: Estudios del Centro de Investigación y Adiestramiento Político Administrativo , no. 6. II. Title.
HC143 .D36 1982

Del cacao al colón : el desarrollo de la moneda y la banca en Costa Rica / Jaime Daremblum. San José, Costa Rica : Centro de Investigación y Adiestramiento Político-Administrativo, [1977?- v. <1- > ; 28 cm. Includes bibliographical references. LC Card 87-402194 DDC 332.4/97286 19
1. Money - Costa Rica - History. 2. Monetary policy - Costa Rica - History. 3. Banks and banking - Costa Rica - History. 4. Costa Rica - Economic conditions. I. Centro de Investigación y Adiestramiento Político Administrativo (San José, Costa Rica). II. Title.
HG682 .D37 1977

DARFUR - COMMERCE.
Doornbos, Paul. Some aspects of smuggling between Chad and Sudan [microform] /. Khartoum [1983] 19 leaves, [1] leaf of plates : LC Card 84-980097 DDC 364.1/33 19
HF3887.Z8 D373 1983
NYPL [*ZT-1646 no.52]

Dargoltz, Raúl E. (Raúl Eduardo) La alianza anglo argentina : historia de la destrucción de una provincia / Raúl E. Dargoltz. Buenos Aires : Ediciones del Mar Dulce, [1983] 168 p. : ill. ; 18 cm. Includes bibliographical references. LC Card 84-117468
1. Lumber trade - Argentina - Santiago del Estero (Province) - History. 2. Quebracho. 3. Railroads - Argentina - Santiago del Estero (Province) - History. 4. Investments, European - Argentina - Santiago del Estero (Province) - History. I. Title.
HD9764.A73 S353 1983

DARK AGES. see **MIDDLE AGES.**

Darkness to daylight . Romeo, Mary Ellen. Harrisburg, Pa. , c1986. 152 p. : LC Card 86-216619 DDC 621.319/09748 19
HD9688.U53 P46 1986

Darlington, Richard B. Behavioral statistics : logic and methods / Richard B. Darlington, Patricia M. Carlson, with contributions by Ronald G. Nathan and Katherine B. Koffel. New York, N.Y. : Free Press ; London : Collier Macmillan, c1987. xxiv, 628 p. : ill. ; 24 cm. Bibliography: p. 615. Includes indexes. ISBN 0-02-907860-1 LC Card 87-12040 DDC 519.5 19
1. Social sciences - Statistical methods. 2. Psychometrics. I. Carlson, Patricia M. II. Title.
HA29 .D246 1987

Darlow, Clive. The London property market in AD 2000 /. London , New York , 1986. xi, 155 p. : ISBN 0-419-14100-6 : LC Card 86-217227 DDC 333.33/22/09421 19
HD610.L6 L66 1986

Darmawan, Daidumi. Kamus istilah ekonomi /. Jakarta , 1984. v, 216 p. ; LC Card 85-941380
HB61 .K26 1984

Darmon, Jacques. Le grand dérangement : la guerre du téléphone / Jacques Darmon. [Paris] : J.C. Lattès, c1985. 269 p. : ill. ; 23 cm. LC Card 85-242541 DDC 384/.068 19
1. Telecommunication - France. 2. Telecommunication policy - France. I. Title. II. Title: Guerre du téléphone.
HE8144 .D37 1985 ***NYPL [JLE 87-363]***

DAROCA REGION (SPAIN) - RURAL CONDITIONS.
DAROCA (SPAIN) - ECONOMIC CONDITIONS.
DAROCA (SPAIN) - POPULATION.
DARPASILA (INDIA) - ECONOMIC CONDITIONS.
Majumder, Arun. Poverty, development, and exchange relations . New Delhi , 1987. xiii, 141 p. : ISBN 81-7027-108-8 : LC Card 87-900910
HC438.B24 M35 1987

Darst, David M., 1947- The handbook of the bond and money markets / David M. Darst. New York : McGraw-Hill, c1981. xv, 461 p. : ill. ; 24 cm. Includes index. ISBN 0-07-015401-5 LC Card 80-36816 DDC 332.63/23
1. Bonds - Handbooks, manuals, etc. 2. Investments - Handbooks, manuals, etc. 3. Money market - Handbooks, manuals, etc. I. Title.
HG4527 .D37 ***NYPL [JLE 87-568]***

Darstellungen zur internationalen Politik und Entwicklungspolitik, 0173-1270 .
(Bd. 6) Hanisch, Rolf, 1942- Der Staat, ländliche Armutsgruppen und legale Bauernbewegung in den Philippinen /. Baden-Baden , 1983. xii, 432 p. ; ISBN 3-7890-0980-6 LC Card 84-143058
HD1537.P5 H35 1983

(Bd. 7) Strukturelemente der Weltgesellschaft . Frankfurt am Main , 1981. v, 356 p. : ISBN 3-7875-1727-8 LC Card 83-190809
HF1411 .S845 1981

Darstellungskonzepte der Input-Output-Rechnung /. Reich, Utz-Peter. Stuttgart , 1984. 185 p. : ISBN 3-17-003301-8 ***NYPL [JLE 86-1264]***

Dart, Joseph Henry, 1817-1887. A compendium of the law and practice of vendors and purchasers of real estate [microform]. By J. Henry Dart. With copious notes and references to the American and English decisions. Also, a prefactory view of the existing law of real property in England and the United States. By Thomas W. Waterman. New York, Banks, Gould ; Albany, Gould, Banks, 1851. civ, 665 (i.e. 856) p. 24 cm. Paging irregular following starred paging of the earlier edition, inset in the margin of the text. Microfilm. New York : New York Public Library, 1982. 1 microfilm reel ; 35 mm. (MN *ZZ-20719) LC Card 17-19132
1. Vendors and purchasers - Great Britain. 2. Real property - Great Britain. 3. Real property - United States. I. Waterman, Thomas Whitney, 1821-1898, ed. II. Title. ***NYPL [*ZT-1719]***

Daru, M. le comte (Napoléon), 1807-1890. Berthelin, E. (Egmont), 1807-1860. Chemin de fer de Paris à Lyon par Troyes et Dijon . Troyes , 1843. 54, [2] p. ; LC Card 85-665948
HE3068 .B47x 1843

Daruwala, Rusi J. The Bombay Chamber story : 150 years / Rusi J. Daruwala. Bombay : Bombay Chamber of Commerce & Industry, c1986. xvii, 312 p., [19] p. of plates : ill., map, ports. ; 23 cm. "Bombay Chamber, 1936-1986." Includes index. Bibliography: p. 301. LC Card 86-902920 DDC 380.1/06/054792 19
1. Bombay Chamber of Commerce & Industry - History. 2. Bombay (India) - Economic conditions. I. Title.
HF331.I4 D37 1986

Darwin Rebellion, 1911-1919 /. Alcorta, F. X. (Frank X.) [Darwin, N.T.] , 1984. xiv, 115 p., [8] p. of plates : ISBN 0-7245-0492-3 : LC Card 84-220611 DDC 331.89/294295 19
HD5450.Z9 D373 1984 ***NYPL [JLF 87-405]***

Dary, David.
Entrepreneurs of the old West / David Dary ; pen-and-ink drawings by Al M. Napoletano. 1st American ed. New York : Knopf : Distributed by Random House, c1986. xi, 368 p. : ill., map, ports. ; 25 cm. Includes index. Map on lining papers. Bibliography: p. [341]-350. ISBN 0-394-52405-5 LC Card 85-45590 DDC 338/.04/0978 19
1. Businessmen - West (U. S.) - History. 2. Entrepreneur - History. I. Title.
HC102.5.A2 D37 1986
NYPL [JLE 86-4063]

Entrepreneurs of the old West / David Dary ; pen-and-ink d0awings by Al.M. Napoletano. Lincoln : University of Nebraska Press, [1987],

c1986. xi, 368 p. : ill., ports. ; 23 cm. Reprint. Originally published: New York : Knopf, 1986. Bibliography: p. [341]-350. Includes index. ISBN 0-8032-6572-7 (pbk.) LC Card 87-5892 DDC 338/.04/0978 19
1. Businessmen - West (U. S.) - History. 2. Entrepreneur - History. I. Title.
HC102.5.A2 D37 1987

Das, Arjun, 1946- Economic philosophy of ancient India / Arjun Das. Delhi : Agam Kala Prakashan, 1986. vi, 224 p. : ill. ; 25 cm. Bibliography: p. [217]-219. Includes index. LC Card 86-903116 DDC 330/.0954 19
1. Economics - India - History. I. Title.
HB126.I4 D36 1986

Das Bedienungsstandard-Konzept als Instrument zur Bewertung des ÖPNV in ländlichen Räumen, exemplarisch dargestellt am Einkaufsverkehr /. Tiedtke, Hans-Ullrich. Bochum , 1981. viii, 274 p. ; ISBN 3-88339-192-1 : LC Card 81-205962 DDC 388/.0943 19
HE152.5 .T53 1981 ***NYPL [JLD 86-2578]***

Das Foto-Taschenbuch .
(2) Hallensleben, Ruth. Frauenarbeit in der Industrie . Berlin-Kreuzberg , c1985. 157 p. : ISBN 3-88940-602-5 : LC Card 86-201457
HD6149 .H27 1985

Das Frankreichbild der deutschen Arbeiterbewegung 1859-1865 /. Simon, Dan, 1937- [Gerlingen] , 1984. 334 p. ; ISBN 3-88350-451-3 LC Card 84-173175
HD8450 .S56 1984 ***NYPL [JLD 86-2711]***

Das, Kumar Bar. Cement industry of India / Kumar Bar Das. New Delhi : Ashish Pub. House, 1987. xxi, 465 p. : ill., folded map ; 23 cm. Bibliography: p. [380]-394. Includes index. ISBN 81-7024-083-2 : LC Card 87-900765 DDC 338.4/766694/0954 19
1. Cement industries - India. I. Title.
HD9622.I52 D37 1987

Das, Nagen C., 1943- Development of handloom industry : organisation, production, marketing / Nagen C. Das ; foreword by A.K. Sarma. New Delhi : Deep & Deep Publications, c1986. 264 p. : ill. ; 22 cm. With reference to Assam. Bibliography: p. [257]-262. Includes index. LC Card 86-903222 DDC 338.4/767702822/0954162 19
1. Handloom industry - India - Assam. I. Title.
HD9866.I63 A874 1986

Das oligarquias agrárias ao predomínio urbano-industrial . Mueller, Charles Curt. Rio de Janeiro , 1983. 363 p. ; LC Card 87-403875 DDC 305.5/232/0981 19
HC187 .M76 1983

Das Politische System der BRD : Geschichte und Gegenwart / [Autorenkollektiv unter Leitung von Karl-Heinz Röder].1. Aufl. Berlin : Staatsverlag der Deutschen Demokratischen Republik, 1985. 479 p. ; 23 cm. (Studien zum politischen System des Imperialismus . Bd. 3) Includes bibliographical references and index. LC Card 86-123928 DDC 320.943 19
1. Political parties - Germany, West. 2. Capitalism - Germany (West). 3. Germany, West - Politics and government. 4. Germany, West - Economic conditions. I. Röder, Karl Heinz. II. Title: Politische System der B.R.D. III. Series.
JN3971.A2 P59 1985 ***NYPL [JLD 86-3144]***

Dâsagupta, Pânnâlâla, 1909- Production by the masses : search for an alternative / by Pannalal Dasgupta.1st ed. Calcutta : Sribhumi, 1983. vi, 54 p. ; 23 cm. LC Card 83-906787 DDC 331.11/8/0954 19
1. Industrial productivity - India. 2. Manpower policy - India. 3. Surplus agricultural commodities - Government policy - India. I. Title.
HC440.I52 D37 1983 ***NYPL [JLD 87-708]***

Dasar-dasar ekonomi Mahathir / editor, Jomo. Kuala Lumpur : Institut Analisa Sosial, 1986. xvi, 187 p. : ill. ; 22 cm. In Malay. Includes bibliographical references. LC Card 86-943311
1. Malaysia - Economic policy. 2. Mahathir bin Mohamad, 1925-. I. Jomo K. S. (Jomo Kwame Sundaram). II. Mahathir bin Mohamad, 1925-.
HC445.5 .D37 1986

Dasgupta, Sugata, 1926- Movement for a no poverty society . Calcutta , 1980. 78 p. ; LC Card 81-902107
HC415.P6 M68 1980

Data analysis. Norušis, M. J. (Marija J.), 1948- The SPSS guide to data analysis for SPSS with additional instructions for SPSS/PC /. Chicago, IL , c1987. xiii, 428 p. : ISBN 0-918469-42-2 (pbk.) LC Card 87-60776 DDC 001.4/22 19
HA32 .N6519 1987

Data analysis . Perkinson, Richard C. Wellesley, Mass. , c1984. xvii, 285 p. : ISBN 0-89435-105-2 LC Card 83-63212 DDC 001.64 19
QA76.9.D3 P46 1984 ***NYPL [JSE 85-1742]***

Data-base : Estado de São Paulo / [Lúcia Bastos Ribeiro de Sena, assessora responsavel]. [São Paulo] : Secretaria de Estado de Relações do Trabalho, Governo do Estado de São Paulo, 1986. 259 p. : ill. ; 22 x 28 cm. LC Card 87-403668 DDC 331.88/025/8161 19
1. Trade-unions - Brazil - São Paulo (State) - Directories. 2. Labor disputes - Brazil - São Paulo (State) - Directories. I. Sena, Lúcia Bastos Ribeiro de. II. São Paulo (Brazil : State). Secretaria de Estado de Relações do Trabalho.
HD6615.S32 D37 1986

DATA BASE INDUSTRY.
Hartley, Jill. New electronic information services . Aldershot, Hants, England , Brookfield, Vt., USA , c1987. 147 p. : ISBN 0-566-05489-2 (pbk.) : LC Card 87-23600 DDC 338.4/700574/0941 19
HD9696.D364 G74 1987

DATA BASE INDUSTRY - GREAT BRITAIN.
Hartley, Jill. New electronic information services . Aldershot, Hants, England , Brookfield, Vt., USA , c1987. 147 p. : ISBN 0-566-05489-2 (pbk.) : LC Card 87-23600 DDC 338.4/700574/0941 19
HD9696.D364 G74 1987

DATA BASE INDUSTRY - UNITED STATES.
The Online commercial database business /. Stamford, Conn., U. S.A. , c1985. xxi, 230 leaves : ISBN 0-89336-320-0 (pbk.) LC Card 87-40457 DDC 381/.4500574/0973 19
HD9696.D363 U66 1985

DATA BASE MANAGEMENT.
Bradley, James, 1942- Introduction to data base management in business /. New York , c1987. xii, 669 p. : ISBN 0-03-011924-3 LC Card 86-22914 DDC 658/.054 19
HF5548.2 .B678 1987

Database management systems. Norwalk, Conn., U. S.A. (6 Prowitt St., Norwalk 06855) , c1986. iv, 149 leaves ; LC Card 86-226965 DDC 381/.4500574/0973
HD9696.C63 U515925 1986

Frost, R. A. (Richard A.) Introduction to knowledge base systems /. London , 1986. xxi, 677 p. : ISBN 0-00-383114-0
NYPL [JFE 86-3366]

Hawryszkiewycz, I. T. Database analysis and design /. Chicago , c1984. xx, 578 p. : ISBN 0-574-21485-2 : LC Card 84-1341 DDC 001.64/2 19
QA76.9.D3 H386 1984
NYPL [JSE 86-2113]

The IAS-System data base . Wien, Austria [1982] ii, 151, 3 p. : ***NYPL [JSG 86-170]***

Lima, Tony. dBASE II for beginners /. Englewood Cliffs, N.J. , c1985. xix, 234 p. : ISBN 0-13-196098-9 : LC Card 84-22897 DDC 001.64/2 19
QA76.9.D3 L56 1985 ***NYPL [JSE 87-247]***

Maller, Steven. Mastering Omnis 3 /. Blue Ridge Summit, PA , 1986. xi, 207 p. : ISBN 0-8306-0374-3 : LC Card 86-5758 DDC 658/.05574 19
HF5548.4.O55 M35 1986
NYPL [JSE 87-264]

Moore, James M. (James Mendon), 1925- An engineers guide to spreadsheets, word processors & data base managers /. Norcross, GA , c1986. xi, 154 p. : ISBN 0-89806-081-8 (pbk.) LC Card 87-157586 DDC 620/.0028/553 19
HF5548 .M566 1986

Perkinson, Richard C. Data analysis . Wellesley, Mass. , c1984. xvii, 285 p. : ISBN 0-89435-105-2 LC Card 83-63212 DDC 001.64 19
QA76.9.D3 P46 1984 ***NYPL [JSE 85-1742]***

Prague, Cary N. Programming with dBase III /. Blue Ridge Summit, Pa. , 1985. ix, 292 p. ; ISBN 0-8306-0976-8 : LC Card 84-23979 DDC 001.64/2 19
QA76.9.D3 P728 1985 ***NYPL [JSE 87-75]***

Prague, N. Cary. Programming with dBASE III PLUS /. Blue Ridge Summit, PA , c1986. vi, 375 p. : ISBN 0-8306-0326-3 : LC Card 86-5736 DDC 005.74 19
QA76.9.D3 P729 1986 ***NYPL [JSE 87-539]***

DATA BASE SEARCHING.
Walsh, Brendan P., 1955- On-line information . Oxford, [Oxfordshire] , New York, NY, USA , 1987. xli, 327 p. : ISBN 0-631-15543-0 : LC Card 87-13154 DDC 025/.04/02465 19
HF5548.2 .W294 1987

Wasik, John F. The electronic business information sourcebook /. New York , c1987. xvi, 208 p. ; ISBN 0-471-62464-0 : LC Card 87-8289 DDC 026/.65 19
HF5548.2 .W324 1987

Data collection in developing countries /. Casley, D. J. Oxford [Oxfordshire] , New York , 1987. p. cm. ISBN 0-19-442425-1 (pbk.) : LC Card 87-12574 DDC 001.4/222/091724 19
HA31.2 .C37 1987

Data communications for business /. Lientz, Bennet P. St. Louis , 1987. xx, 326 p. : ISBN 0-8016-3013-4 LC Card 86-23012 DDC 650/.028/546 19
HF5548.2 .L535 1987

DATA COMPRESSION (TELECOMMUNICATION)
Voice compression technology . Stamford, Conn., U. S.A. , c1985. xii, 146 leaves ; ISBN 0-89336-430-4 (soft) LC Card 87-165256 DDC 380.1/45621389 19
HD9696.T442 V65 1985

Data Courier, inc. Search ACT . Louisville, Ky. , c1986. 1 v. (various pagings) ; ISBN 0-914604-27-9 LC Card 86-215617 DDC 025/.06004 19
HD9696.C62 S43 1986

Data Group (U. S.) The Compact disc market--phase II . New York, N.Y. (444 Madison Ave., New York 10022) , c1986. viii, 57, [13] p. : LC Card 86-227224 DDC 381/.4562138933 19
HD9697.P563 U526 1986

Data matters topical reports.
Medi-Cal fee-for-service eligibles and prepaid health plan enrollees by age group, sex, and county--July 1983. [Sacramento] [1984] 21 p. : LC Card 86-622329 DDC 362.1/04252/09794021 19
HD7102.U5 C3 1984

Medi-Cal fee-for-service eligibles and prepaid health plan enrollees by age group, sex, and county, July 1984. [Sacramento] [1985] 19 p. : LC Card 86-622330 DDC 362.1/04252/09794021 19
HD7102.U6 C345 1985

Mielke, Robert B. Live births by estimated marital status of mother, California, 1981. [Sacramento] [1984] 22 p. : LC Card 86-622328 DDC 304.6/32/09794 19
HB935.C2 M54 1984

DATA NETWORKS, COMPUTER. see **COMPUTER NETWORKS.**

Data preview .
(no. 23) Farley, Pamela J. Private health insurance in the United States . Rockville, MD , Springfield, VA [1986] 106 p. : LC Card 86-23618 DDC 368.3/82/00973 19
HG9396 .F3 1986

DATA PROCESSING. see **ELECTRONIC DATA PROCESSING; INFORMATION STORAGE AND RETRIEVAL SYSTEMS.**

DATA PROCESSING SERVICE CENTERS.
Oppenheimer, Max Stul. Chips! . Homewood, Ill. , c1987. xii, 203 p. : ISBN 0-87094-942-X (pbk.) LC Card 86-72272 DDC 004/.068/7 19
HD9696.C62 O665 1987

Third-party maintenance of computer and datacom equipment. Norwalk, Conn., U. S.A. (6 Prowitt St., Norwalk 06855) , c1987. vi, 180 leaves ; LC Card 87-129551 DDC 381/.45004/0973 19
HD9696.C62 T45 1987

DATA PROCESSING SERVICE CENTERS - CALIFORNIA, SOUTHERN - DIRECTORIES.

Horner, Ken. Guide to computer installations in southern California . Palo Alto, Calif. , c1986. iv, 750 p. : LC Card 87-134229 DDC 004/.025/7949 19
HD9696.C63 U518343 1986

DATA PROCESSING SERVICE CENTERS - DESIGN AND CONSTRUCTION.
Halper, Robert F. Computer data center design . New York , c1985. xv, 189 p. : ISBN 0-471-82579-4 : LC Card 85-5347 DDC 658/.054 19
HD9696.C62 H24 1985
NYPL [JSE 86-1294]

DATA PROCESSING SERVICE CENTERS - PLANNING.
Halper, Robert F. Computer data center design . New York , c1985. xv, 189 p. : ISBN 0-471-82579-4 : LC Card 85-5347 DDC 658/.054 19
HD9696.C62 H24 1985
NYPL [JSE 86-1294]

DATA PROTECTION - GOVERNMENT POLICY.
Jussawalla, Meheroo, 1923- The calculus of international communications . Littleton, Colo. , 1987. xiv, 159 p. ; ISBN 0-87287-503-2 : LC Card 87-2640 DDC 384/.068 19
HE7645 .J87 1987

DATA PROTECTION - LATVIA.
Pravovye voprosy RASU . Riga , 1979. 109, [3] p. ; LC Card 82-100548
HC337.L3 P722 1979

DATA PROTECTION - UKRAINE.
Pravovye problemy RASU /. Kiev , 1985. 303 p. : LC Card 86-139849
HC337.U5 P65 1985

Data sources on residential change and the housing market . Morrison, Philip S., 1947- [Toronto] [1977] 76 p. : LC Card 85-158244
HD7305.T68 M67 1977

DATA STORAGE AND RETRIEVAL SYSTEMS. see **INFORMATION STORAGE AND RETRIEVAL SYSTEMS.**

DATA TERMINALS (COMPUTERS) see **COMPUTER TERMINALS.**

DATA TRANSMISSION EQUIPMENT INDUSTRY.
Converging voice/data/video technologies at the workstation /. Stamford, Conn., U. S.A. , c1986. v, 119 leaves ; ISBN 0-89336-466-5 (pbk.) LC Card 87-168057 DDC 380.1/45004 19
HD9801.A2 C66 1986

Electronic copy boards--local & remote. Norwalk, Conn., U. S.A. (6 Prowitt St., Norwalk 06855) , c1986. iii, 101 leaves : LC Card 86-224860 DDC 381/.45621380414 19
HD9802.3.A2 E45 1986

Electronic document interchange markets . Norwalk, Conn., U. S.A. (6 Prowitt St., Norwalk 06855) , c1987. v, 192 leaves : LC Card 87-403217 DDC 384.3/1 19
HD9696.D382 E44 1987

Glücksmann, Riccardo. Telematica . Milano , 1982. xii, 273 p., [4] p. of plates : ISBN 88-7056-120-8 LC Card 84-184344
HD9696.D383 I84 1982

ISDN . Boston, MA (200 Portland St., Boston 02114) , c1987. iv, 118 p. : LC Card 87-159823 DDC 380.1/450046 19
HD9696.D382 I82 1987

Peripherals for the ISDN D-channel. Norwalk, Conn., U. S.A. (6 Prowitt St., Norwalk 06855) , c1986. iv, 153 leaves : LC Card 87-129535 DDC 380.1/45621385 19
HD9696.D382 P46 1986

Voice compression technology . Stamford, Conn., U. S.A. , c1985. xii, 146 leaves ; ISBN 0-89336-430-4 (soft) LC Card 87-165256 DDC 380.1/45621389 19
HD9696.T442 V65 1985

DATA TRANSMISSION EQUIPMENT INDUSTRY - ITALY.
Glücksmann, Riccardo. Telematica . Milano , 1982. xii, 273 p., [4] p. of plates : ISBN 88-7056-120-8 LC Card 84-184344
HD9696.D383 I84 1982

DATA TRANSMISSION EQUIPMENT INDUSTRY - JAPAN.
Japanese penetration into the United States communications data processing and office equipment markets. New York, N.Y. , c1983. v, 308 p. ; LC Card 87-143908 DDC 381/.45004/0973 19
HD9696.D383 U635 1983

DATA TRANSMISSION EQUIPMENT INDUSTRY - UNITED STATES.
The Enhanced data network (van) market. New York, N.Y. , c1983. v, 258 p. : LC Card 87-143825
HD9696.D383 U6344 1983

Japanese penetration into the United States communications data processing and office equipment markets. New York, N.Y. , c1983. v, 308 p. ; LC Card 87-143908 DDC 381/.45004/0973 19
HD9696.D383 U635 1983

Local area networks . Stamford, Conn., U. S.A. , c1986. xvi, 186 leaves : ISBN 0-89336-438-X (pbk.) LC Card 87-404428 DDC 381/.4500468/0973 19
HD9696.C63 U52253 1986

The Market for advanced business communications in the United States. New York, N.Y. , c1983. 2 v. (x, 365 leaves) : LC Card 87-144924 DDC 384/.041 19
HD9696.T443 U5465 1983

The Online commercial database business /. Stamford, Conn., U. S.A. , c1985. xxi, 230 leaves : ISBN 0-89336-320-0 (pbk.) LC Card 87-40457 DDC 381/.4500574/0973 19
HD9696.D363 U66 1985

Packet switching equipment markets /. Stamford, Conn., U. S.A. , c1985. v, 205 leaves : ISBN 0-89336-465-7 (pbk.) LC Card 87-403884 DDC 381/.456213878 19
HD9696.T443 U556 1985

The Videotex marketplace. Bethesda, Md. , c1984. 203 p. : ISBN 0-934960-17-8 (pbk.) : LC Card 84-201507 DDC 384 19
HD9696.D383 U638 1984
NYPL [JSF 86-430]

DATA TRANSMISSION EQUIPMENT INDUSTRY - UNITED STATES - DIRECTORIES.
The Videotex marketplace. Bethesda, Md. , c1984. 203 p. : ISBN 0-934960-17-8 (pbk.) : LC Card 84-201507 DDC 384 19
HD9696.D383 U638 1984
NYPL [JSF 86-430]

DATA TRANSMISSION SYSTEMS - CONGRESSES.
International Conference on Networks and Electronic Office Systems (1983 : University of Reading) Networks and electronic office systems . London , c1983. 240 p. : ISBN 0-903748-52-5 ***NYPL [JSG 86-298]***

International Conference on Networks and Electronic Office Systems (1985 : London, England) Networks and electronic office systems . London , c1985. 166 p. : ISBN 0-903748-60-6 ***NYPL [JSG 86-264]***

DATA TRANSMISSION SYSTEMS - LAW AND LEGISLATION.
Issues in international telecommunications policy . Washington, D.C. , c1983. xviii, 260 p. ; ISBN 0-9612072-0-5 (pbk.) LC Card 83-82231 DDC 343.73/0994 347.303994 19
KF2765 .I85 1983 ***NYPL [JLF 86-1125]***

DATA TRANSMISSION SYSTEMS - LAW AND LEGISLATION - UNITED STATES.
Issues in international telecommunications policy . Washington, D.C. , c1983. xviii, 260 p. ; ISBN 0-9612072-0-5 (pbk.) LC Card 83-82231 DDC 343.73/0994 347.303994 19
KF2765 .I85 1983 ***NYPL [JLF 86-1125]***

Database analysis and design /. Hawryszkiewycz, I. T. Chicago , c1984. xx, 578 p. : ISBN 0-574-21485-2 : LC Card 84-1341 DDC 001.64/2 19
QA76.9.D3 H386 1984
NYPL [JSE 86-2113]

Database management systems. Norwalk, Conn., U. S.A. (6 Prowitt St., Norwalk 06855) : International Resource Development Inc., c1986. iv, 149 leaves ; 28 cm. (Report / International Resource Development Inc. . #703) "July 1986." LC Card 86-226965 DDC 381/.4500574/0973
1. Computer software industry - United States. 2. Computer industry - United States. 3. Market surveys - United States. 4. Data base management. I. International Resource Development, inc. II. Series: Report (International Resources Development, inc.) , #703.
HD9696.C63 U515925 1986

Datalog file .
(no. 86-1025) Morse, Diane McGinty. Involving managers in competitive analysis /. Menlo Park, CA (333 Ravenswood Ave., Menlo Park 94025) , c1986. 11 leaves : LC Card 86-220559 DDC 658.4/012 19
HD38.7 .M67 1986

(no. 86-1052) Howard-Healy, Marion. Aspects of the new media in Europe /. Menlo Park, CA (333 Ravenswood Ave., Menlo Park 94025) , c1986. 22 leaves : LC Card 86-220771 DDC 384/.094 19
HE8700.72.E85 H69 1986

(no. 86-1055) Shelton, Robert D. Hazardous waste management market assessment /. Menlo Park, CA (333 Ravenswood Ave., Menlo Park 94025) , c1986. 19 p. : LC Card 86-220787 DDC 338.4/7363728 19
HD9975.U52 S54 1986

(no. 86-1062) Woodward, Maria Lourdes. Business issues for the Asia-Pacific region /. Menlo Park, CA (333 Ravenswood Ave., Menlo Park 94025) , c1986. 14 p. ; LC Card 86-220779 DDC 330.95/0428
HC413.A78 W66 1986

(no. 86-1102) Hollyer, Mark. Maritime shipping in the 1980s /. Menlo Park, CA (333 Ravenswood Ave., Menlo Park 94025) , c1986. 18 leaves : LC Card 87-150588 DDC 387.5 19
HE735 .H57 1986

(no. 86-1103) Light, Donald H. Adding value to product through service /. Menlo Park, CA (333 Ravenswood Ave., Menlo Park 94025) , c1986. 21 leaves : LC Card 87-149955 DDC 658.8/12 19
HF5415.5 .L54 1986

DataPlus Research & Publishing Company. Contacts . San Rafael, CA (1724 Lincoln Ave., San Rafael 94901) [c1986] 252 p. ; LC Card 86-217208 DDC 332.1/028 19
HG1710 .C66 1986

Dataquest (Firm) Consolidated data base . San Jose, Calif. (1290 Ridder Park Dr., San Jose 95131-2398) , c1986. ii, 94 p. ; LC Card 87-108611 DDC 381/.45004/0973
HD9696.C63 U515626 1986

Datateknik i industriproduktionen . Sweden. Data- och elektronikkommittén. [Stockholm] [1981] 182 p. : ISBN 91-38-06456-1 LC Card 84-113236
HD30.2 .S92 1981

Dateline Bhopal . Chishti, Anees, 1941- New Delhi , 1986. 160 p. ; LC Card 86-901993 DDC 363.1/79
HD7269.C452 I5225 1986
NYPL [JLD 87-1050]

Daten zum Finanzausgleich : Entwicklung seit 1972 / Herausgeber, Verbindungsstelle der Bundesländer beim Amt der Niederösterreichischen Landesregierung. Wien : Die Verbindungsstelle, [1986] xx, 331 p. : col. charts ; 30 cm. Chiefly tables. Includes index. LC Card 86-209464
1. Revenue sharing - Austria - Provinces - Statistics. I. Verbindungsstelle der Bundesländer beim Amt der Niederösterreichischen Landesregierung.
HJ1066 .D37 1986

Datenlage zur Alterssicherung . Infratest Sozialforschung. Bonn , 1984. 330 p. : LC Card 86-132439 DDC 331.25/2/0943 19
HD7105.35.G3 I54 1984

DATES, BOOKS OF. see **CALENDARS.**

Dati cumulativi di 1356 società italiane, 1968-1983 / a cura di "Mediobanca.". [Italy : s.n., 1984] (Milano : O. Capriolo) xxvi, 258 p. ; 24 cm. LC Card 86-229023
1. Corporations - Italy - Finance - Statistics. I. Mediobanca.
HG4166 .D39 1984

Datola, Stefano. Bezza, Bruno. Le lotte degli elettromeccanici /. Milano , c1981. 179 p. : ISBN 88-20-42149-6 : LC Card 81-200954 DDC 331.89/282131/0945 19
HD5384.E3 B49 1981 ***NYPL [JLD 86-2898]***

Datorer och decentralisering : en sekretariatsrapport från Dataeffektutredningen. [Stockholm] : LiberFörlag, [1983] 52 p. : ill. ; 21 cm. "Ds A 1983.11." Bibliography: p. 51-52. ISBN 91-38-07877-5 LC Card 84-219052
1. Business - Sweden - Data processing. 2. Decentralization in management - Sweden. I. Sweden. Dataeffektutredningen.
HF5548.2 .D3715 1983

DATORG Tanácsadó Iroda. Tanácsadó Szolgálat. Pálfi, Sándor. Nemzetközi biztosítás a külkereskedelem szolgálatában /. [Budapest] [1986] 63 p. ; ISBN 963-02-4369-5 LC Card 87-425585
HG8059 .P35 1986

Datoriseringen i försäkringsbranschen . Handelshögskolan i Stockholm. Ekonomiska forskningsinstitutet. [Stockholm] [1981] 81, [36] p. : ISBN 91-38-06574-6 LC Card 82-244714
HG8673 .H35 1981

Datorstöd i mindre företag . Carlsson, C. (Christer), 1946- Åbo , 1983. 248 p. : ISBN 951-648-877-3 LC Card 83-126466
HF5548.2 .C286 1983

Datos básicos para el estudio de la población en la región de Murcia /. Bel Adell, María del Carmen. [Murcia] , c1985. 223 p. ; ISBN 84-600-3907-2 LC Card 86-218876
HA1558.M8 B44 1985

Datos distritales para fines de desarrollo. [Lima] : Cooperación Popular, [1964] 92 p. : 24 maps ; 21 x 33 cm. Cover title. "Alianza para el Progreso." "... resultado de la colaboración entre la Comisión Ejecutiva Interministerial de Cooperación Popular y la Agencia Internacional de Desarrollo (A.I.D.)"--Cover p. 2. Chiefly tables. LC Card 85-134068 DDC 318.5 19
1. Peru - Statistics. I. Peru. Cooperación Popular. II. United States. Agency for International Development.
HA1064 .D37 1964

Datta, Anindya. Growth and equity : a critique of the Lewis-Kuznets tradition with special reference to India / Anindya Datta. Calcutta ; New York : Oxford University Press, 1986. xii, 119 p. : ill. ; 22 cm. Critique of the theories of William Arthur Lewis, b. 1915 and Simon Smith Kuznets, b. 1901, development economists. Bibliography: p. [105]-115. Includes index. ISBN 0-19-561882-3 : LC Card 87-900001 DDC 338.954 19
1. Economic development. 2. India - Economic conditions - 1947-. 3. Lewis, W. Arthur (William Arthur), 1915-. 4. Kuznets, Simon Smith, 1901-. I. Title.
HD82 .D334 1986

Datta, Bhabatosh, 1911- Social justice in a mixed economy / Bhabatosh Datta. Calcutta : Calcutta University, 1982. ii, 64 p. ; 22 cm. (Professor Monimohan Sen memorial lectures . 1980) Includes bibliographical references. LC Card 82-905698 DDC 338.954 19
1. Social justice. 2. Distributive justice. 3. India - Economic policy - 1947-. I. Title. II. Title: Professor Monimohan Sen memorial lectures.
HC435.2 .D353 1982 ***NYPL [JLD 86-3172]***

Datta-Ray, B., 1925- The Pattern & problems of population in north-east India /. New Delhi , 1986. xv, 433 p. ; ISBN 81-85024-03-0 : LC Card 86-902123 DDC 304.6/0954/1 19
HA4587.I44 P37 1986

Datta, Śekhara. Tebhāgā āndolana / Śekhara Datta. Ḍhākā : Bāṃlā Ekāḍemī, 1985. 103, [1] p. ; 19 cm. (Bhāshā-śahīda granthamālā) In Bengali. On the 1946-1947 peasant movement in Bengal claiming for the tillers a larger share of produce. Bibliography: p. [104] LC Card 86-902072
1. Peasantry - India - Bengal - Political activity. I. Title. II. Series.
HD1537.I4 D34 1985

Datz, Stephen R. Errors : inverts, imperforates, colors omitted on United States postage stamps / Stephen R. Datz.1986 ed. Loveland, Colo. (P.O. Box 402, Loveland 80537) : General Philatelic Corp., 1986. vi, 100 p. : ill. ; 23 cm. Cover title: U. S. errors. LC Card 87-128178 DDC 769.56973 19
1. Postage-stamps - United States - Flaws. I. Title. II. Title: U. S. errors.
HE6184.E7 D38 1986

Dau, Michele. L'Informatica nella società italiana, 1984 . Milano [1984] 257 p. ; LC Card 84-249272 DDC 338.4/7004/0945 19
HD9696.C63 I85 1984
NYPL [JLD 86-3303]

Dauderstädt, Michael.
Entwicklungspolitik, Politik ohne Entwicklung : Eigenanstrengungen, Ordnungspolitik und Politikdialog im Nord-Süd-Verhältnis / Michael Dauderstädt. Bonn : Forschungsinstitut der Friedrich-Ebert-Stiftung, Abt. Entwicklungsländerforschung, [1984] 38 p. ; 21 cm. (Internationale Politik, 0174-5204 . 29) Internationale Wirtschaft Based on the result of a meeting held 2/8/84 which was sponsored by the Friedrich-Ebert-Stiftung. LC Card 85-136902
1. Developing countries - Economic policy. 2. Economic development. 3. Dependency. I. Friedrich-Ebert-Stiftung. II. Series: Internationale Politik (Bonn, Germany) , 29. III. Title.
HC59.7 .D327 1984

Las relaciones hispano-portuguesas y la integración europea / M. Dauderstädt. Madrid : Fundación IESA, [1987?] 36 p. ; 21 cm. (Economía. no. 2) Includes bibliographical references. ISBN 84-398-8593-8 LC Card 87-161277
1. Spain - Foreign economic relations - Portugal. 2. Portugal - Foreign economic relations - Spain. 3. European Economic Community - Spain. 4. European Economic Community - Portugal. I. Series: Economía (Fundación IESA) , no 2. II. Title.
HF1570.15.P8 D38 1987

Wettbewerbsfähig durch soziale Disziplin? : Gesellschaften im internationalen Konkurrenzkampf : Expertengespräch in Bonn, 14. Oktober 1981 / Michael Dauderstädt. Bonn : Forschungsinstitut der Friedrich-Ebert-Stiftung, [1981] 38 p. ; 21 cm. (Internationale Wirtschaft) The author's report of the conference which was sponsored by the Friedrich-Ebert-Stiftung. LC Card 85-137321
1. Competition - Congresses. 2. Economic policy - Congresses. I. Friedrich-Ebert-Stiftung. II. Series: Internationale Wirtschaft (Bonn, Germany). III. Title.
HD41 .D38 1981

Daugherty, Thomas B. Camp, William G. Managing our natural resources /. Albany, N.Y. , c1988. p. cm. ISBN 0-8273-2986-5 LC Card 87-25056 DDC 333.7/0973 19
HC103.7 .C33 1988

"Daughters of Jefferson, daughters of bootblacks" . Andolsen, Barbara Hilkert. Macon, GA , c1986. xiv, 130 p. ; ISBN 0-86554-204-X : LC Card 86-816 DDC 305.4/2/0973 19
HQ1426 .A6827 1986 ***NYPL [JLE 86-3359]***

Dauhajre, Andrés. Reforma financiera en pequeñas economías abiertas / Andrés Dauhajre, hijo. 1a ed. Santo Domingo, República Dominicana : Centro de Estudios Monetarios y Bancarios, 1986. 97 p. : ill. ; 21 cm. (Biblioteca Mercados financieros . 4) Serie Estudios Bibliography: p. 97. LC Card 87-402920 DDC 332.4/56097293 19
1. Foreign exchange administration - Dominican Republic - Mathematical models. 2. Finance - Dominican Republic - Mathematical models. 3. Economic stabilization - Dominican Republic - Mathematical models. I. Series. II. Series: Serie Estudios (Centro de Estudios Monetarios y Bancarios (Santo Domingo, Dominican Republic)). III. Title.
HG3926.5 .D38 1986

Dauser, R. Bendeich, E. (Eugen), 1945- Wirtschaftliche Datenerfassung in Klein- und Mittelbetrieben . München , c1979. 211 p. : ISBN 3-478-41740-6 LC Card 85-171162
HD62.7 .B4 1979

Dautriat, Pierre. Vignes et vignerons d'autrefois dans le Barséquanais : un village type, Neuville-sur-Seine / Pierre Dautriat. Saint-Seine-l'Abbaye : Editions de Saint-Seine-l'Abbaye, c1984. 70 p. : ill. ; 22 cm. ISBN 2-86701-018-7 : LC Card 85-117852
1. Wine industry - France - Neuville-sur-Seine - History. 2. Viticulture - France - Neuville-sur-Seine - History. 3. Neuville-sur-Seine (France) - Economic conditions. I. Title.
HD9385.F82 N483 1984

Dave, Nalini V. Industrial sickness and key areas of management : planning, finance, marketing, technology, labour-management relations / Nalini V. Dave ; foreword by N.M. Khandelwal. New Delhi : Deep & Deep Publications, c1987. 523 p. : ill. ; 23 cm. Originally presented as the author's thesis (Ph. D.--Saurashtra University) under the title: Industrial sickness and some key areas of management : a study of textile industry, Gujarat. Bibliography: p. [516]-520. Includes index. LC Card 87-901105 DDC 658/.00954/75 19
1. Business mortality - India - Gujarat. 2. Industrial management - India - Gujarat. 3. Textile industry - India - Gujarat - Management. I. Title.
HD2747 .D32 1987

Davenport-Hines, R. P. T. (Richard Peter Treadwell), 1953- Markets and bagmen . Aldershot, Hants, England , Brookfield, Vt., USA , c1986. xii, 204 p. : ISBN 0-566-05066-8 : LC Card 86-22951 DDC 380.1/0941 19
HF5415.12.G7 M37 1986

Davenport, Michael, 1940- Trade policy, protectionism, and the Third World / Michael Davenport. London ; Dover, N.H. : Croom Helm, c1986. 152 p. : ill. ; 22 cm. Includes index. Bibliography: p. 139-143. ISBN 0-7099-4516-7 : LC Card 86-6192 DDC 382.7/53 19
1. Tariff preferences - European Economic Community countries. 2. European Economic Community countries - Commerce - Developing countries. 3. Developing countries - Commerce - European Economic Community countries. I. Title.
HF2039.5.Z7 D38 1986
NYPL [JLD 86-2759]

Davey, Patrick J.
Corporate financing in international markets / by Patrick J. Davey. New York, N.Y. (845 3rd Ave., New York 10022) : Conference Board, c1986. 15 p. ; 28 cm. (Research bulletin / The Conference Board . no. 196) Bibliography: p. 15. LC Card 86-212373 DDC 658.1/599 19
1. Corporations - United States - Finance. 2. International finance. I. Series: Research bulletin (Conference Board) , no. 196. II. Title.
HG4061 .D384 1986

High interest rates and tight money, by Patrick J. Davey and Francis J. Walsh, Jr. [New York, National Industrial Conference Board, 1969] 25 p. 23 cm. (Managing the financial function. no. 6) LC Card 70-9411 DDC 332.8/0973
1. Interest and usury - United States. I. Walsh, Francis J., joint author. II. Series. III. Series: Managing the financial function, report no. 6. IV. Title.
HB545 .D38

David Hume Institute. Financial deregulation . Cambridge , Wolfeboro, N.H., USA , 1986. xiii, 88 p. ; ISBN 0-85941-366-7 : LC Card 87-104563 DDC 332/.0941 19
HG186.G7 F546 1986

Dávid, László, Dr. A Vízgazdálkodás távlati fejlesztésének prognózisai /. Budapest , 1983. 176 p. : ISBN 963-602-278-X LC Card 85-109619
HD1697.H8 V59 1983

David M. Dornbusch and Company. California affordable housing legislation . [Sacramento] [1986?] 2 v. ; LC Card 86-622916 DDC 363.5/8 19
HD7303.C2 C275 1986

David Matthew Kennedy . Hickman, Martin Berkeley, 1925- Salt Lake City, Utah , c1987. xi, 403 p. : ISBN 0-87579-093-3 : LC Card 87-19898 DDC 332.1/092/4 B 19
HG2463.K46 H53 1987

David, Michiel, 1930- (joint author) De Vos, Wouter. Point de mire . Antwerpen, Belgiëlai 147 a , 1977. 125 p. : ISBN 90-02-01132-6 : LC Card 78-370280 DDC 309.1
HC59 .D464 ***NYPL [JLD 80-3135]***

David, Wilfred L. Conflicting paradigms in the economics of developing nations / Wilfred L. David. New York : Praeger, 1986. xix, 215 p. : ill. ; 25 cm. Includes index. Bibliography: p. 191-211. ISBN 0-275-92108-5 (alk. paper) : LC Card 86-16906 DDC 330.9172/4 19
1. Dependency. 2. Developing countries - Economic conditions. I. Title.
HC59.7 .D335 1986 ***NYPL [JLE 86-4423]***

Davidoff, Leonore. Our work, our lives, our words . Basingstoke, Hampshire , 1986. xiii, 189 p. : ISBN 0-333-36598-4
NYPL [JLD 86-4220]

Davidovich, I͡A. A. Rabochai͡a molodezh′ SSSR v period razvitogo sotsializma : sovetskie istoriko-sotsiologicheskie issledovanii͡a : nauchno-analiticheskiĭ obzor / [avtor obzora I͡A.A. Davidovich ; otvetstvennyĭ redaktor V.M.

Shevyrin]. Moskva : Akademiia nauk SSSR, In-t nauch. informatsii po obshchestvennym naukam, 1985. 37 p. ; 20 cm. Bibliography: p. 34-37. LC Card 86-187709
1. Youth - Employment - Soviet Union. 2. Young adults - Employment - Soviet Union. I. Shevyrin, V. M. II. Institut nauchnoĭ informatsii po obshchestvennym naukam (Akademiia nauk SSSR). III. Title.
HD6276.S59 D38 1985

Davidson, Donald A. Vink, A. P. A. [Landschapsecologie en landgebruik. English.] Landscape ecology and land use /. London , New York , 1983, c1980. vi, 264 p. : ISBN 0-582-30077-0 (pbk.) : LC Card 82-10030 DDC 333.73/13 19
HD108.6 .V5613 1983 NYPL [JLE 86-3886]

Davidson, George, 1943- The ABC's of air travel / by George Davidson. Scottsdale, Ariz. : ABC's of Air Travel, c1984. iv, 89 p. : ill. ; 22 cm. Includes index. ISBN 0-931921-00-7 (pbk.) : LC Card 84-71960 DDC 387.7/42/0973 19
1. Aeronautics, Commercial - United States - Passenger traffic - Handbooks, manuals, etc. 2. Air travel - Handbooks, manuals, etc. I. Title. II. Title: A.B.C.'s of air travel.
HE9787.5.U5 D38 1984
NYPL [JLD 86-2219]

Davidson, James Dale.
Blood in the streets : investment profits in a world gone mad / James Dale Davidson, in collaboration with Sir William Rees-Mogg. New York : Summit Books, c1987. 386 p. ; 22 cm. Includes bibliographical references and index. ISBN 0-671-62735-X : LC Card 87-9935 DDC 332.6 19
1. Investments. 2. World politics. 3. Economic history. I. Rees-Mogg, William, 1928-. II. Title.
HG4516 .D38 1987

The squeeze / James Dale Davidson. New York : Summit Books, c1980. 281 p. ; 24 cm. Includes bibliographical references. ISBN 0-671-40084-3 LC Card 79-28411 DDC 330.973
1. Cost and standard of living - United States. 2. Middle classes - United States. 3. United States - Economic conditions - 1971-1981. I. Title.
HC106.7 .D38 NYPL [JLE 80-1960]

Davidson, Jeffrey P.
Blow your own horn : how to market yourself and your career / Jeffrey P. Davidson. New York, NY : American Management Association, c1987. xv, 271 p. : ill. ; 24 cm. Bibliography: p. 252-259. Includes index. ISBN 0-8144-5908-0 LC Card 86-47809 DDC 650.1/4 19
1. Career development. 2. Professions - Marketing. I. Title.
HF5549.5.C35 D375 1987

Connor, Richard A. Getting new clients /. New York , c1987. xxiii, 305 p. : ISBN 0-471-62778-X LC Card 87-21657 DDC 658.8 19
HD8038.A1 C665 1987

Look before you leap : entrepreneurial pitfalls you don't want to land in / Jeffrey P. Davidson. New York : Walker, 1988. p. cm. Bibliography: p. Includes index. ISBN 0-8027-1012-3 LC Card 87-23274 DDC 658.4/2 19
1. New business enterprises - United States - Management. 2. Small business - United States - Management. I. Title.
HD62.5 .D38 1988

Marketing to the Fortune 500 and other corporations / Jeffrey P. Davidson. Homewood, Ill. : Dow Jones-Irwin, c1987. xv, 291 p. : ill. ; 24 cm. Includes bibliographies and index. ISBN 0-87094-984-5 LC Card 86-51669 DDC 658.8 19
1. Marketing - United States. 2. Small business - United States - Management. 3. Corporations - United States - Directories. 4. Purchasing - United States - Directories. I. Title.
HF5415.1 .D28 1987

Davidson, Marilyn.
Stress and the woman manager / Marilyn Davidson and Cary Cooper. Oxford [Oxfordshire]: M. Robertson. 1983. 230 p. ; 24 cm. Includes index. Bibliography: p. [217]-225. ISBN 0-85520-623-3
1. Job stress - Great Britain. 2. Women executives - Great Britain. 3. Women middle managers - Great Britain. I. Cooper, Cary L. II. Title.
NYPL [JLE 85-1426]

Women and information technology /. Chichester , New York , c1987. viii, 283 p. : ISBN 0-471-91603-X : LC Card 87-10554 DDC 331.4 19
HD6053 .W636 1987

Davidson, Sidney, 1919-
Financial accounting : an introduction to concepts, methods, and uses / Sidney Davidson, Clyde P. Stickney, Roman L. Weil.5th ed. Chicago : Dryden Press, c1988. xvi, 800 p. ; 24 cm. (The Dryden Press series in accounting) Includes bibliographical references and index. ISBN 0-03-011522-1 LC Card 87-9135 DDC 657 19
1. Accounting. I. Stickney, Clyde P., 1944-. II. Weil, Roman L. III. Title. IV. Series.
HF5635 .D228 1988

Managerial accounting . Chicago , c1988. xii, 926 p. : ISBN 0-03-011964-2 LC Card 87-18469 DDC 658.1/511 19
HF5635 .M2358 1988

Davidson, William Harley, 1951- Ghadar, Fariborz. U. S. industrial competitiveness . Lexington, Mass. , c1987. x, 114 p. : ISBN 0-669-15689-2 (alk. paper) LC Card 86-46341 DDC 338.4/7677/00973 19
HD9855 .G47 1987

Davidson, William R. Retailing management / William R. Davidson, Daniel J. Sweeney, Ronald W. Stampfl. 6th ed. New York : Wiley, c1988. xix, 876 p. : ill. ; 25 cm. Bibliography: p. 835-860. Includes index. ISBN 0-471-85094-2 LC Card 87-10555 DDC 658.8/7 19
1. Retail trade - Management. I. Sweeney, Daniel J. (Daniel Joseph), 1943-. II. Stampfl, Ronald W. III. Title.
HF5429 .D334 1988

Davies, Garth W. P. Bingham, John E. A handbook of systems analysis /. London , 1978. ix, 229 p. : ISBN 0-333-24198-3 : LC Card 79-309251
HF5548.2 .B47 1978b NYPL [JLE 80-2972]

Davies, James B., 1951- Reforming capital income taxation in Canada : efficiency and distributional effects of alternative options / James B. Davies, France St-Hilaire. [Ottawa] : Economic Council of Canada : available from Canadian Govt. Pub. Centre, Supply and Services Canada, c1987. ix, 153 p. : ill. ; 27 cm. Bibliography: p. [149]-153. ISBN 0-660-12454-8 (pbk.) : LC Card 87-168079 DDC 336.24/24/0971 19
1. Capital levy - Canada. 2. Income tax - Canada. 3. Spendings tax - Canada. 4. Tax incidence - Canada. I. St-Hilaire, France. II. Economic Council of Canada. III. Title.
HJ4133.C2 .D38 1987

Davies, Omar.
The Debt problem in Jamaica . Mona, Jamaica , c1986. viii, 125 p. : ISBN 976-410-002-3 (pbk.) LC Card 87-403413 DDC 336.3/4/097292 19
HJ8552 .D43 1986

The State in Caribbean society /. Mona, Jamaica , c1986. vii, 157 p. ; ISBN 976-410-001-5 (pbk.) LC Card 87-403404 DDC 330.9729/052 19
HC151 .S73 1986

Davies, Paul, 1951- A.J. Cook / Paul Davies. Wolfeboro, NH : Manchester University Press, c1987. p. cm. (Lives of the left) Bibliography: p. Includes index. ISBN 0-7190-2160-X LC Card 87-11114 DDC 331.88/122/0924 B 19
1. Cook, A. J. (Arthur James). 2. Labor and laboring classes - Great Britain - Biography. 3. Labor disputes - Great Britain - History - 20th century. I. Title. II. Series.
HD8393.C63 D38 1987

Davies, R. E. G. (Ronald Edward George)
Pan Am : an airline and its aircraft / by R.E.G. Davies ; illustrated by Mike Machat.1st ed. New York : Orion Books, c1987. vi, 90 p. : ill. (some col.) ; 23 x 29 cm. Bibliography: p. vi. Includes index. ISBN 0-517-56639-7 : LC Card 87-5581 DDC 387.7/065/73 19
1. Pan American World Airways, inc. - History. 2. Aeronautics, Commercial - United States - History. 3. Airlines - United States - History. I. Title.
HE9803.P36 D38 1987

Rebels and reformers of the airways / R.E.G. Davies. Washington, D.C. : Smithsonian Institution Press, c1987. xvi, 440 p. : ill. ; 24 cm. Bibliography: p. 413-415. Includes index. ISBN 0-87474-354-0 (alk. paper) LC Card 86-26243 DDC 387.7/092/2 19
1. Aeronautics, Commercial - History. 2. Air lines - History. 3. Aeronautics, Commercial - Biography. I. Title.
HE9775 .D38 1987

Dávila Andrade, Oswaldo. El Grupo Andino : hacia una integración distinta / [Oswaldo Dávila Andrade]. [Lima? : s.n., 1985] ([Lima?] : Oficina de Publicaciones) 110 p. ; 22 cm. Bibliography: p. 105-110. LC Card 86-158814
1. Andes region - Economic integration. 2. Grupo Andino. I. Title.
HC167.A5 D38 1985

Davila, Carlos. Gramley, Lyle E. Real estate finance and housing . Washington, D.C. (1125 15th St., N.W., Washington 20005) , c1987. vii, 132 p. : LC Card 87-124264 DDC 332.7/2/0973021 19
HG2040.5.U5 G73 1987

Dávila Flores, Alejandro, 1956- La crisis financiera en México / Alejandro Dávila Flores. 1a ed. [Mexico City, Mexico] : Ediciones de Cultura Popular, 1986. 228 p. : ill. ; 21 cm. (Economía) Bibliography: p. 225-228. LC Card 87-401258 DDC 330.972/0834 19
1. Finance - Mexico. 2. Mexico - Economic conditions - 1970-. I. Series: Economía (Ediciones de Cultura Popular). II. Title.
HG185.M6 D33 1986

Dávila L. de Guevara, Carlos. Productividad y participación . [Bucaramanga, Colombia] , c1985. 165 p. : ISBN 958-9302-15-6 LC Card 86-166141
HD5660.C7 P76 1985

Dávila, Roberto. México, una economía en transición /. México, D.F. , 1984-1985. 3 v. ; ISBN 968-18-1900-4 (v. 1) LC Card 86-235462
HC135 .M549 1985

Davis, Bertha, 1910- The national debt / Bertha Davis ; [illustrations by Anne Canevari Green]. New York : F. Watts, c1987. 112 p. ; 25 cm. (An Impact book) Bibliography: p 107-109. Includes index. Discusses the current federal budget deficit, defines national debt, money supply, and other economic terms, chronicles the history of federal spending, and proposes solutions to the problem. ISBN 0-531-10415-X LC Card 87-10441 DDC 336.3/4/0973 19
1. Budget deficits - United States - Juvenile literature. I. Green, Anne Canevari, ill. II. Title.
HJ2052 .D38 1987

Davis, Burke, 1913- War bird : the life and times of Elliott White Springs / by Burke Davis. Chapel Hill : University of North Carolina Press, c1987. viii, 267 p., [26] p. of plates : ill. ; 24 cm. Bibliography: p. [244]-258. Includes index. ISBN 0-8078-1752-X (alk. paper) LC Card 87-5934 DDC 338.7/67721/0924 B 19
1. Springs, Elliott White. 2. Springs Industries - History. 3. Cotton textile industry - United States - History. 4. Industrialists - United States - Biography. 5. World War, 1914-1918 - Biography. 6. Novelists, American - 20th century - Biography. I. Title.
HD9880.S67 D38 1987

Davis, Charles E., 1947- Dimensions of hazardous waste politics and policy /. New York , c1988. p. cm. ISBN 0-313-25989-5 (lib. bdg. : alk. paper) LC Card 87-17792 DDC 363.7/28 19
HC110.E5 D56 1988

Davis, Charlotte. Ports of California, by Charlotte Davis and Lois Trainor. Illustrated with photos. and illus. by Jim Gindraux. Los Angeles, Elk Grove Press [1970] 80 p. illus. (part col.) 27 cm. Describes the most important small and large seaports in California, their effect on nearby cities, and the most important kinds of cargo each handles. LC Card 79-114863 DDC 387.1/09794
1. Harbors - California - Juvenile literature. I. Trainor, Lois, joint author. II. Gindraux, Jim, illus. III. Title.
HE554.C16 D3

Davis, Dan J. The disposition and sentencing of operating while intoxicated (OWI) offenders in Iowa : preliminary summary data for state fiscal year 1985 / prepared by Dan J. Davis. [Des Moines, Iowa] (523 E. 12th St., Des Moines 50319) : Iowa Statistical Analysis Center, Office for Planning and Programming, State of Iowa, [1986] 29 leaves : ill. ; 28 cm. Cover title. Prepared for the Governor's Highway Safety Office. "March 1986." Chiefly tables. LC Card 86-621927

DDC 364.1/47 19
1. Drunk driving - Iowa - Statistics. I. Iowa. Office for Planning and Programming. Statistical Analysis Center. II. Iowa. Governor's Highway Safety Office. III. Title.
HE5620.D7 D37 1986

Davis, Donald D., 1950- Managing technological innovation / Donald D. Davis and associates. 1st ed. San Francisco : Jossey-Bass, 1986. xxi, 302 p. : ill. ; 24 cm. (The Jossey-Bass management series) Includes bibliographical references and index. ISBN 1-555-42008-7 LC Card 86-15378 DDC 658.5/14 19
1. Technological innovations - Management. 2. Manufacturing processes - Technological innovations - Management. I. Title. II. Series.
HD45 .D34 1986 *NYPL [JLE 87-862]*

Davis, Ed. Democracy and control in the workplace /. Melbourne, Australia , 1986. 388 p. ; ISBN 0-582-71159-2 (pbk.) LC Card 87-102095 DDC 331.01/12 19
HD5660.A8 D46 1986

Davis, Frank Green, 1913- The Black community's social security / Frank G. Davis. Washington : University Press of America, c1977. xiii, 189 p. : graphs ; 22 cm. Includes bibliographical references. ISBN 0-8191-0282-2 LC Card 78-304298
1. Afro-Americans - Economic conditions. 2. Afro-Americans - Social conditions - 1975-. 3. Afro-Americans - Social conditions - 1964-1975. 4. Social security - United States. I. Title.
E185.8 .D237 *NYPL [JLD 78-1907]*

Davis, Gregg. Rose, Adam Zachery. Natural resource policy and income distribution /. Baltimore , c1988. xvi, 139 p. : ISBN 0-8018-3523-2 (alk. paper) LC Card 87-2788 DDC 333.7/0973 19
HC103.7 .R67 1988

Davis, James C. (James Cushman) Rise from want : a peasant family in the machine age / James C. Davis. Philadelphia : University of Pennsylvania Press, 1986. xv, 165 p. : ill. ; 24 cm. Includes index. Bibliography: p. [153]-161. ISBN 0-8122-8034-2 : LC Card 86-19228 DDC 305.5/63 19
1. Žužek family. 2. Peasantry - Yugoslavia - Slovenia - Case studies. 3. Peasantry - Karst (Yugoslavia and Italy). 4. Karst (Yugoslavia and Italy) - Social conditions. 5. Karst (Yugoslavia and Italy) - Economic conditions. I. Title.
HD1536.Y8 D38 1986 *NYPL [JLE 87-710]*

Davis, James E. (James Edwin), 1940-
Economics : a resource book for secondary schools / James E. Davis, Regina McCormick. Santa Barbara, Calif. : ABC-CLIO, c1988. xv, 354 p. : ill. ; 24 cm. (Social studies resources for secondary school librarians, teachers, and students) Includes index. ISBN 0-87436-479-5 (alk. paper) LC Card 87-18670 DDC 330/.07/1273 19
1. Economics - Study and teaching (Secondary). I. McCormick, Regina. II. Title. III. Series.
HB74.5 .D39 1988

World economic data . Santa Barbara, Calif. , c1987. x, 231 p. ; ISBN 0-87436-485-X (alk. paper) : LC Card 87-14508 DDC 330.9/04 19
HC59 .W643 1987

Davis, James Richard, 1947-
Accounting information systems . Reading, Mass. , c1987. p. cm. ISBN 0-201-10376-1 : LC Card 87-1155 DDC 657/.028/5 19
HF5679 .A34 1987

Morse, Wayne J. Management accounting /. Reading, Mass. , c1988. xxiii, 840 p. : ISBN 0-201-15760-8 : LC Card 87-11570 DDC 658.1/511 19
HF5635 .M864 1988

Davis, John A., 1947- A look at the credit approval process / John A. Davis, Jr. Philadelphia, Pa. : R. Morris Associates, c1987. 55 p. : ill. ; 23 cm. Includes bibliographical references. ISBN 0-936742-36-4 (pbk.) LC Card 86-23855 DDC 332.7 19
1. Bank loans - United States. 2. Credit - United States. I. Title.
HG1642.U5 D38 1987

Davis, Karen, 1942- Medicare policy : new directions for health and long-term care / Karen Davis, Diane Rowland. Baltimore : Johns Hopkins University Press, c1986. xiii, 137 p. ; 23 cm. Includes index. Bibliography: p.125-132. ISBN 0-8018-2874-0 (alk. paper) LC Card 85-45048 DDC 368.4/26/00973 19
1. Insurance, Health - United States. 2. Medicare. 3. Medicaid. 4. Medical care, Cost of - United States. 5. Long-term care facilities - United States. I. Rowland, Diane. II. Title.
HD7102.U4 D279 1986
NYPL [JLE 86-3782]

Davis, Keith, 1918- Frederick, William Crittenden, 1925- Business and society . New York , c1988. xxvii, 626 p. : ISBN 0-07-015561-5 : LC Card 87-21436 DDC 658.4/08 19
HD60 .F72 1988

Davis, Kevin. Lewis, Mervyn. Domestic and international banking /. Cambridge, Mass. , 1987. ix, 440 p. : ISBN 0-262-12126-3 LC Card 87-2962 DDC 332.1 19
HG1586 .L39 1987

Davis, Kingsley, 1908-
Below-replacement fertility in industrial societies . Cambridge [Cambridgeshire] , New York , c1987. x, 360 p. : ISBN 0-521-34324-0 LC Card 87-6371 DDC 304.6/32 19
HB901 .B45 1987b

Below-replacement fertility in industrial societies . New York, N.Y., USA , c1987. x, 360 p. : LC Card 87-2458 DDC 304.6/32 19
HB901 .B45 1987

Davis, Lester A. Contribution of exports to U. S. employment : staff report / prepared by Lester A. Davis. Washington, D.C. : Office of Trade and Investment Analysis, Trade Information and Analysis, International Trade Administration, U. S. Dept. of Commerce : For sale by the Supt. of Docs., U. S. G.P.O., 1986. 33 p. : ill. ; 28 cm. Shipping list no.: 86-476-P. "March 1986." Bibliography: p. 33. "Project CTR-008-86." S/N 003-009-00476-4 LC Card 86-602848 DDC 331.12/0973 19
1. Foreign trade and employment - United States. I. United States. International Trade Administration. Office of Trade and Investment Analysis. II. Title.
HD5710.75.U6 D38 1986

Davis, Marvin A. Turn-around : the no-nonsense guide to corporate renewal / Marvin A. Davis. Chicago : Contemporary Books, c1987. 194 p. ; 24 cm. Includes index. ISBN 0-8092-4780-1 : LC Card 86-29285 DDC 658.4/06 19
1. Organizational change. 2. Organizational effectiveness. 3. Corporate profits. I. Title.
HD58.8 .D38 1987

Davis, Michael C., 1953-
International trade [microform] . Frederick, MD , 1987. microfilm reel ISBN 0-89093-551-3 (microfilm) : LC Card 87-6240 DDC 382 19
HF1008

Multinational corporations, OPEC, cartels, foreign investment, and technology transfer [microform] . Frederick, MD , 1987. microfilm reel ISBN 0-89093-552-1 (microfilm) : LC Card 87-6249 DDC 338.8 19
HD2755.5

Davis, Nancy Yaw. Research and consulting as a business / Nancy Yaw Davis, Rodger P. McConochie, David R. Stevenson. Washington, D.C. : National Association for the Practice of Anthropology, c1987. v, 41 p. : map ; 23 cm. (NAPA bulletin . 4) Includes bibliographies. ISBN 0-913167-21-5 (pbk.) LC Card 87-20254 DDC 658.4/6 19
1. Business consultants - Case studies. 2. Small business - Case studies. I. McConochie, Rodger P. II. Stevenson, David R. III. Title. IV. Series.
HD69.C6 D38 1987

Davis, R. Mack. Price, Courtney H. The entrepreneur's resource handbook /. Denver, Colo. , 1987. 178 p. : ISBN 0-944303-00-5 (pbk.) LC Card 87-62190
HD62.5 .P65 1987

Davis, Roy B. Knutson, Ronald D. Cooperative involvement in issues of domestic farm policy /. College Station, Tex. , 1986. 59 p. : LC Card 86-623063 DDC 338.1/8764 19
HD1491.U6 T45 1986

Davis, Stanley M. Future perfect / Stanley M. Davis. Reading, Mass. : Addison-Wesley, c1987. 243 p. : ill. ; 22 cm. Bibliography: p. 229-[232]. Includes index. ISBN 0-201-11513-1 : LC Card 87-18669 DDC 658 19
1. Management. 2. Organization. I. Title.
HD31 .D325 1987

Davis, Steve, 1953- The electric mailbox / Steve Davis, Candy Travis. 1st ed. Dallas, Tex. : S. Davis Pub., c1986. 286 p. ; 23 cm. Includes index. ISBN 0-911061-14-2 (pbk.) LC Card 84-91756 DDC 384.3/4 19
1. Electronic mail systems - Handbooks, manuals, etc. I. Travis, A. B., 1929-. II. Title.
HE6239.E54 D38 1986

Davis, William, 1933- The corporate infighter's handbook : winning the office war / William Davis ; illustrations by John Jensen. London : Sidgwick & Jackson, 1984. 144 p. : ill. ; 24 cm. ISBN 0-283-99133-X (pbk.) : LC Card 85-240558 DDC 650.1 19
1. Success in business. 2. Office politics. I. Jensen, John, 1930-. II. Title.
HF5386 .D325 1984 *NYPL [JLE 87-618]*

Davison, Ian Hay. Sherrard, Michael. London Capital Group Limited (formerly British Bangladesh Trust Limited) . London , 1977. vi, 376 p. : ISBN 0-11-512127-7 (pbk.) LC Card 85-164377
HG4135 .S46 1977

Davydov, I. (Iosif) Rabochie dinastii Urala /. Sverdlovsk , 1977. 340 p. : LC Card 81-170557
HD8527.A1 R33 1977

Dawes, Frank Victor. Not in front of the servants : a true portrait of Upstairs, downstairs life / Frank Victor Dawes.Rev. and expanded ed. London : Hutchinson, 1984. 178 p., [16] p. of plates : ill. ; 22 cm. Includes index. Bibliography: p. 172-174. ISBN 0-09-155291-5 (pbk.) : LC Card 84-195925 DDC 640/.46/0942 19
1. Servants - England - History. 2. Upper classes - England - History. I. Title.
HD8039.D52 G718 1984
NYPL [JLD 86-1944]

Dawood, Nawaz. Tea and poverty : plantations and the political economy of Sri Lanka / Nawaz Dawood. Kowloon, Hong Kong : Urban Rural Mission, Christian Conference of Asia, 1980. xii, 166 p. ; 23 cm. Bibliography: p. 151-157. LC Card 80-154803 DDC 338.1/7372/095493 19
1. Sri Lanka - Economic conditions. 2. Sri Lanka - Social conditions. 3. Plantation life - Sri Lanka. 4. Sri Lanka - Commerce. I. Title.
HC424 .D36 1980

Daws, Gavan. Cooper, George. Land and power in Hawaii . Honolulu, Hawaii , c1985. x, 518 p. ; ISBN 0-9615052-0-6 : LC Card 85-72037 DDC 333.73/13/09969 19
HD266.H3 C66 1985 *NYPL [JLE 87-361]*

Dawson, George Glenn, 1925- Gordon, Sanford D. Introductory economics /. Lexington, Mass. , c1987. xviii, 490 p. : ISBN 0-669-09119-7 LC Card 86-80503 DDC 330.973/092 19
HB171.5 .G648 1987

Dawson, Jim (James L.) Perry, Susan. Nightmare . New York , c1985. xvii, 261 p. ; ISBN 0-02-595930-1 : LC Card 85-13710 DDC 338.7/616139435 19
HD9995.C64 A236 1985
NYPL [JLE 85-3950]

Day, Alan J. (Alan John) Government economic agencies of the world . Detroit , c1985. x, 546 p. ; ISBN 0-8103-2104-1 (Gale) LC Card 84-26861 DDC 351.82/025 19
HD87.25 .G68 1985
*NYPL [*R-Econ 86-6573]*

Day, Arthur R. Escalation and intervention . Boulder, Colo. , 1986. x, 181 p. ; ISBN 0-8133-7200-3 : LC Card 86-4020 DDC 327.1/6 19
U104 .E83 1986 *NYPL [JLE 86-4131]*

DAY CARE CENTERS AND INDUSTRY - UNITED STATES.
The Business of caring [videorecording] /. Washington, DC , 1984. 1 videocassette (23 min.) : LC Card 84-707513 DDC 362.7 11
HF5549.5.D39

DAY CARE CENTERS - INDIA.
Mina Swaminathan, 1933- Who cares? . New Delhi , 1985. xi, 159 p. : LC Card 86-900126
HV861.I4 M56 1985 *NYPL [JLD 86-3265]*

Day, Denis W. How to cut business travel costs / Denis W. Day. New York : Wiley, c1986. ix, 207 p. : ill. ; 24 cm. (The Wiley/Ronald-National Association of Accountants professional book series) "A

Ronald Press publication." Includes index. ISBN 0-471-83633-8 : LC Card 86-9277 DDC 658.1/553 19
1. Business travel - United States - Management. 2. Business travel - United States - Costs. I. Title. II. Series.
HD38 .D39 1986 NYPL [JLE 86-4235]

A day in the life of a commercial fisherman /. Klein, John F. (John Frederick), 1950- Mahwah, N.J. , c1988. 32 p. : ISBN 0-8167-1109-7 (lib. bdg.) : LC Card 87-10949 DDC 639/.2/02373 19
HD8039.F65 K57 1988

A day in the life of a cross-country trucker /. Bourne, Miriam Anne. Mahwah, N.J. , c1988. 32 p. : ISBN 0-8167-1117-8 (lib. bdg.) : LC Card 87-13582 DDC 388.3/24/02373 19
HD8039.M795 B68 1988

Day, John, 1924- The medieval market economy / John Day. Oxford, UK ; New York, NY, USA : B. Blackwell, 1987. p. cm. "A collection of essays (many previously available only in French or Italian)"--Info. fr. publ. Bibliography: p. Includes index. ISBN 0-631-15479-5 : LC Card 86-26862 DDC 330.94/01 19
1. Economic history - Medieval, 500-1500. 2. Europe - Economic conditions - To 1492. 3. Capitalism - Europe - History. I. Title.
HC41 .D39 1987

Day-Lower, Donna C., 1951- Raines, John C. Modern work and human meaning /. Philadelphia , c1986. 150 p. ; ISBN 0-664-24703-2 (pbk.) LC Card 85-26370 DDC 241/.64 19
BJ1498 .R335 1986 NYPL [JLD 86-2382]

DAY NURSERIES. see **DAY CARE CENTERS.**

Day, Patricia. Accountabilities : five public services / Patricia Day, Rudolf Klein. London ; New York : Tavistock, 1987. 259 p. : ill. ; 23 cm. Includes bibliographies and index. ISBN 0-422-79340-X : LC Card 87-164015 DDC 354.4109/2 19
1. Corporations, Government - Great Britain - Evaluation. 2. Administrative responsibility - Great Britain. I. Klein, Rudolf. II. Title.
HD4147 .D39 1987

Day, Stuart. Bundy, Darcie. Total coverage . New York , c1987. xiv, 224 p. ; ISBN 0-06-055077-5 : LC Card 86-46050 DDC 368/.0029 19
HG8051 .B846 1987

Dayhoff, Signe A. Create your own career opportunities / Signe A. Dayhoff. Andover, Mass. : Brick House Pub. Co., c1987. x, 111 p. : ill. ; 24 cm. Includes bibliographies and index. ISBN 0-931790-75-1 : LC Card 86-26332 DDC 650.1/4 19
1. Career development. 2. Interpersonal relations. 3. Success in business. 4. Assertiveness (Psychology). I. Title.
HF5549.5.C35 D38 1987

Dayton, Doug, 1951- Computer solutions for business : planning and implementing a successful computer environment / Doug Dayton. Redmond, Wash. : Microsoft Press ; [New York] : Distributed to the book trade in the United States by Harper & Row, c1987. xi, 274 p. : ill. ; 24 cm. Includes index. ISBN 0-914845-98-5 (pbk.) : LC Card 87-23957 DDC 651.8 19
1. Business - Data processing. 2. Computers - Purchasing. I. Title.
HF5548.2 .D377 1987

Dayton, Mark R. Economic viability of Conrail. Washington, D.C. : Congress of the U. S., Congressional Budget Office, [1986] xvii, 85 p. : ill. ; 28 cm. (A special study) Shipping list no.: 86-760-P. "August 1986"--Cover. Item 1005-C LC Card 86-602852 DDC 385/.1 19
1. Conrail. 2. ConRail - Finance. I. United States. Congressional Budget Office. II. Series: Special study (United States. Congressional Budget Office). III. Title.
HE2791.C8994 D39 1986

Daza Vaca, Ernesto. Informe general y proyecto de parcelación, Antioquia # 2 (Barbosa y Santo Domingo) /. Bogotá, D.E. , 1964. 2, 73, 16 leaves, [1] leaf of plates : LC Card 85-107102
HD1476.C72 B375 1964

dBASE II--a comprehensive user's manual /. Bharucha, Kerman D. Blue Ridge Summit, Pa. , c1985. xi, 305 p. ; ISBN 0-8306-0884-2 : LC Card 84-23959 DDC 001.64/25 19
HF5548.4.D22 B43 1985 NYPL [JSE 87-19]

DBASE II (COMPUTER PROGRAM)
Bharucha, Kerman D. dBASE II--a comprehensive user's manual /. Blue Ridge Summit, Pa. , c1985. xi, 305 p. ; ISBN 0-8306-0884-2 : LC Card 84-23959 DDC 001.64/25 19
HF5548.4.D22 B43 1985 NYPL [JSE 87-19]

Lima, Tony. dBASE II for beginners /. Englewood Cliffs, N.J. , c1985. xix, 234 p. : ISBN 0-13-196098-9 : LC Card 84-22897 DDC 001.64/2 19
QA76.9.D3 L56 1985 NYPL [JSE 87-247]

dBASE II for beginners /. Lima, Tony. Englewood Cliffs, N.J. , c1985. xix, 234 p. : ISBN 0-13-196098-9 : LC Card 84-22897 DDC 001.64/2 19
QA76.9.D3 L56 1985 NYPL [JSE 87-247]

DBASE III (COMPUTER PROGRAM)
Prague, Cary N. Programming with dBase III /. Blue Ridge Summit, Pa. , 1985. ix, 292 p. ; ISBN 0-8306-0976-8 : LC Card 84-23979 DDC 001.64/2 19
QA76.9.D3 P728 1985 NYPL [JSE 87-75]

DBASE III PLUS (COMPUTER PROGRAM)
Prague, N. Cary. Programming with dBASE III PLUS /. Blue Ridge Summit, PA , c1986. vi, 375 p. : ISBN 0-8306-0326-3 : LC Card 86-5736 DDC 005.74 19
QA76.9.D3 P729 1986 NYPL [JSE 87-539]

dBASE two--a comprehensive user's manual. Bharucha, Kerman D. dBASE II--a comprehensive user's manual /. Blue Ridge Summit, Pa. , c1985. xi, 305 p. ; ISBN 0-8306-0884-2 : LC Card 84-23959 DDC 001.64/25 19
HF5548.4.D22 B43 1985 NYPL [JSE 87-19]

dBASE two for beginners. Lima, Tony. dBASE II for beginners /. Englewood Cliffs, N.J. , c1985. xix, 234 p. : ISBN 0-13-196098-9 : LC Card 84-22897 DDC 001.64/2 19
QA76.9.D3 L56 1985 NYPL [JSE 87-247]

dBASE 2 for beginners. Lima, Tony. dBASE II for beginners /. Englewood Cliffs, N.J. , c1985. xix, 234 p. : ISBN 0-13-196098-9 : LC Card 84-22897 DDC 001.64/2 19
QA76.9.D3 L56 1985 NYPL [JSE 87-247]

dBASE2-a comprehensive user's manual. Bharucha, Kerman D. dBASE II--a comprehensive user's manual /. Blue Ridge Summit, Pa. , c1985. xi, 305 p. ; ISBN 0-8306-0884-2 : LC Card 84-23959 DDC 001.64/25 19
HF5548.4.D22 B43 1985 NYPL [JSE 87-19]

DBSA in the southern African development framework /. La Grange, A. B. Sandton, Republic of South Africa [1985] 36 p. : LC Card 87-150256 DDC 332.2 19
HC900 .L3 1985

D'Ciófalo V., Giovanni. El trabajo infantil urbano en Managua / autor, Giovanni D'Ciófalo V. Managua : Ediciones CETRA, 1986. ii, 76, 3, [33] leaves ; 28 cm. "Esta investigación fue realizada con la colaboración de los siguientes funcionarios del Centro de Estudios del Trabajo (CETRA): Cro. Danny Sáenz Navarrete, Alberto Mayorga Aguilar, María de los Angeles Pizzí Acevedo e Ivania Jiménez Calderón." Bibliography: leaf [33] (4th group). LC Card 87-403894 DDC 331.3/1/09728513 19
1. Children - Employment - Nicaragua - Managua. 2. Youth - Employment - Nicaragua - Managua. I. Centro de Estudios del Trabajo (Nicaragua). II. Title.
HD6250.N5 M363 1986

DDC spreadsheets. Blanc, Iris. [New York, N.Y.] [c1986] 161 p. : LC Card 87-159255 DDC 005.3/07/1273 19
HF5548.2 .B527 1986

DDR im Überblick. English. How socialist competition is run / [translated by Intertext]. Berlin : Panorama DDR, 1983. 64 p. : ill. ; 20 cm. (Experiences, results, prospects) Translation of: DDR im Überblick. LC Card 86-201752 DDC 338.6/048/09431 19
1. Socialist competition - Germany (East). I. Title.
HC290.795.S6 D3713 1983

De Bilbao y de Vizcaya sobre sus orígenes históricos y económicos /. Lafarga Lozano, Adolfo. [Bilbao? , 1976?] (Bilbao : Gráficas Loroño) 310 p. : ISBN 84-400-1414-7 LC Card 85-142805
HF3690.B5 L34 1976

Dé Carli, Gileno.
Desafio energético / Gileno Dé Carli ; prefácio, Aureliano Chaves. Recife : [s.n.], 1981 (Recife : Companhia Editora de Pernambuco) 309 p. ; 23 cm. LC Card 86-129710
1. Energy policy Brazil. 2. Alcohol fuel industry - Government policy - Brazil. I. Title.
HD9502.B72 D4 1981

História da reforma agrária / Gileno Dé Carli. [Recife?] : Editora ASA Pernambuco, 1985. 524 p. ; 21 cm. Publisher from stamp on t.p. Includes bibliographical references and index. LC Card 87-102928 DDC 333.3/1/81 19
1. Land reform - Brazil - History. I. Title.
HD1333.B6 D4 1985

De Caro, Gaspare. Walras, Léon, 1834-1910. L'economia monetaria /. Roma [1985] 2 v. (949 p.) : LC Card 87-140163
HG221 .W219 1985

De Castro, Steve. "Turnpikes for small open economies : Jamaica, Minas Gerais, Nova Scotia, Puerto Rico and Trinidad and Tobago : a dynamic comparison of input-output structure" / Steve de Castro. [Brasília] : Fundação Universidade de Brasília, [1982] 22 leaves ; 30 cm. "Nov. 82." Bibliography: leaves 21-22. LC Card 83-156613 DDC 339.2/3/091724 19
1. Turnpike theory (Economics) - Case studies. 2. Input-output analysis - Developing countries - Case studies. I. Title.
HD82 .D376 1982

De Cecco, Marcello.
Changing money . New York, NY, USA , 1987. p. cm. ISBN 0-631-15501-5 :$60.00 LC Card 86-28317 DDC 332 19
HG175 .C445 1987

Monetary theory and economic institutions . New York , 1987. ix, 349 p. : ISBN 0-312-00407-9 : LC Card 86-26069 DDC 332.4/01 19
HG203 .M68 1987

De Franchis, Carlo. Giammaria Ortes : un sistema d'economia matematica nel '700 / Carlo De Franchis. Napoli : A. Chiurazzi & Figlio, 1930. 165 p. ; 19 cm. (Politica, economia, corporativismo . v. 3) Bibliography: p. [163]-165. LC Card 87-139766
1. Ortes, Giammaria, 1713-1790. 2. Economists - Italy - Biography. 3. Economics - Italy - History - 18th century. 4. Economics, Mathematical - Italy - History - 18th century. I. Title. II. Series.
HB109.O68 D4 1930

De Geer, Hans, 1944- Bättre eller sämre med datorer? : fem arbetsplatser och datoriseringens problem / Hans de Greer. Stockholm : LiberFörlag, c1982. 112 p. ; 21 cm. (Publica) ISBN 91-38-90157-9 : LC Card 82-187964
1. Business - Sweden - Data processing - Case studies. I. Title.
HF5548.2 .D378 1982

De gehuwde vrouw en haar kindertal anno 1975 /. Netherlands (Kingdom, 1815-). Centraal Bureau voor de Statistiek. Hoofdafdeling Bevolkingsstatistieken. 's-Gravenhage , 1980. 78 p. : LC Card 81-100844
HB1015 .N47 1980
NYPL [JLM 78-1515 nr.9]

De-Gennin, Vil'gel'm, 1676-1750.
[Opisanie ural'skikh i sibirskikh zavodov 1735. English]
Description of Ural and Siberian factories in 1735 / by G.W. de-Hennin ; Edwin A. Battison, scientific editor ; [translated from the Russian by A.S. Deshpande and W.V. Nabar]. [Washington, D.C.] : Smithsonian Institution Libraries and National Science Foundation, 1987. p. cm. Translation of: Opisanie ural'skikh i sibirskikh zavodov 1735. LC Card 87-600052 DDC 338.0947/87 19
1. Ural Mountains Region (R.S.F.S.R.) - Industries. 2. Siberia (R.S.F.S.R.) - Industries. 3. Mineral industries - Russian S.F.S.R. - Ural Mountains Region. 4. Mineral industries - Russian S.F.S.R. - Siberia. I. Battison, Edwin A. II. Title.
HC337.R852 U733613 1987

De Gijsel, Peter. Schattenwirtschaft und alternative Ökonomie . Regensburg , c1984. 268 p. : ISBN 3-924956-00-6 LC Card 86-224071
HD2341 .S337 1984

De Grauwe, Paul. see Grauwe, Paul de.

De Gruyter studies in organization .
(10) Unemployment . Berlin , New York , 1987. xx, 353 p. : ISBN 0-89925-277-X : LC Card 87-24369 DDC 331.13/7 19
HD5701.3 .U53 1987

(11) Organization of innovation . Berlin , New York , 1987. x, 238 p. : ISBN 0-89925-167-6 (U. S.) : LC Card 87-19936 DDC 658.4/06 19
HD45 .O73 1987

(7) Organizing industrial development /. Berlin , New York , 1986. xi, 391 p. : ISBN 0-89925-168-4 (U. S.) LC Card 86-24074 DDC 338.9 19
HD31 .O783 1986 ***NYPL [JLE 87-789]***

(8) Alvesson, Mats, 1956- [Organisationsteori och teknokratiskt medvetande. English.] Organization theory and technocratic consciousness . Berlin , New York , 1987. ix, 286 p. : ISBN 0-89925-165-X : LC Card 86-24057 DDC 306/.36 19
HD6955 .A44313 1987

(9) Clark, Peter A. Anglo-American innovation /. Berlin , New York , 1987. ix, 404 p. : ISBN 0-89925-164-1 (U. S.) : LC Card 87-22221 DDC 338/.06 19
HD45 .C52 1987

De Hiroshima a los euromisiles /. Aguirre, Mariano A. Madrid , c1984. 254 p. : ISBN 84-309-1062-X LC Card 85-215587
U264 .A39 1984 ***NYPL [JFC 86-1643]***

De-industrialization and foreign trade /. Rowthorn, Bob. Cambridge [Cambridgeshire] , New York , 1987. xi, 422 p. : ISBN 0-521-26360-3 LC Card 87-6331 DDC 338.0941 19
HC256.5 .R683 1987

De Janvry, Alain.

De Jesus, Ed. C. Beyond bureaucracy . West Hartford, Conn. , c1986. xii, 256 p. : ISBN 0-931816-44-0 LC Card 86-34420 DDC 338.9/0068 19
HC59.72.E44 B48 1986

De la dictadura al socialismo democrático . Nieto de Alba, Ubaldo, 1931- Madrid , c1984. 269 p. ; ISBN 84-7209-177-5 LC Card 86-146735 DDC 338.946 19
HC385 .N49 1984 ***NYPL [JLD 86-2390]***

De la publicité à la communication /. Genzel, David. Paris [1984?] 271 p. : ISBN 2-86737-005-1 LC Card 84-175281
HF5813.F8 G46 1984

De Lisle, Christian. Business interest calculations / Christian de Lisle. London : Waterlow Pub., c1985. ix, 274 p. ; 23 cm. ([Waterlow practitioner's library]) Includes index. ISBN 0-08-039231-8
1. Business mathematics - Problems, exercises, etc. 2. Calculators. 3. Interest - Problems, exercises, etc. I. Title. II. Series. ***NYPL [JLE 87-1030]***

De Luca, A. Richard. Project management. Chicago, Ill. , 1987, c1985. 1 videocassette (30 min.) : LC Card 87-705140 DDC 658.4 11
HD69.P75

De Luca, Amedeo, 1945- Le applicazioni dei metodi statistici alle analisi di mercato / Amedeo De Luca ; prefazione di Luigi Muttarini. Milano, Italy : F. Angeli, c1984. 341 p. : ill. ; 22 cm. (Collana di marketing . 7) Bibliography: p. [335]-341. Includes index. LC Card 85-185924 DDC 380.1/01/5195 19
1. Commercial statistics. I. Title. II. Series.
HF1017 .D4 1984

De Marco, Maria. Intervento straordinario e amministrazione locale nel mezzogiorno /. Milano, Italy , c1985. 348 p. ; LC Card 86-144245
HC310.I53 I58 1985

De Marco, Miguel Ángel. 1884-1984, los cien años de la Bolsa de Comercio de Rosario / [investigación y redacción, Miguel Angel De Marco y Oscar Luis Ensinck ; coordinación general, Raúl N. Gardelli]. [S.l. : s.n., 1984?] (Rosario : Escuela de Artes Gráficas del Colegio San José de Rosario) 167 p. : ill. (some col.) ; 29 cm. Cover title: Los cien años de la Bolsa de Comercio de Rosario. Errata slip inserted. Bibliography: p. 167. LC Card 87-115398 DDC 332.64/28224 19
1. Bolsa de Comercio de Rosario - History. 2. Stock-exchange - Argentina - Rosario (Sante Fe) - History. 3. Commodity exchanges - Argentina - Rosario ((Sante Fe) - History. 4. Grain trade - Argentina - Rosario (Sante Fe) - History. I. Ensinck, Oscar Luis. II. Gardelli, Raúl N. III. Title. IV. Title: Cien años de la Bolsa de Comercio de Rosario.
HG5320.R67 D4 1984

De Masi, Domenico. Manuale di ricerca sul lavoro e sulle organizzazioni /. Roma , 1985. 384 p. : LC Card 86-118313 DDC 306/.36/072 19
HD4824 .M32 1985 ***NYPL [JLD 87-1160]***

De Menil, George, 1940-
Stabilization policy in France and the Federal Republic of Germany /. Amsterdam ; New York : xii, 379 p. : ISBN 0-444-87529-8 LC Card 84-28614 DDC 338.943 19
HC276.2 .S77 1985 ***NYPL [TB (Contributions to economic analysis. no.153)]***

Weltwirtschaftsgipfel / George de Menil, Anthony M. Solomon ; mit einem Vorwort von Helmut Schmidt. Bonn : Forschungsinstitut der Deutschen Gesellschaft für Auswärtige Politik : Vertrieb, Europa Union, [1983] iv, 130 p. ; 21 cm. (Arbeitspapiere zur Internationalen Politik, 0344-9815 . 26) Includes bibliographical references. ISBN 3-7713-0203-X LC Card 85-224780
1. International economic relations. I. Solomon, Anthony M. II. Title. III. Series.
HF1411 .D345 1983

De Mente, Boye.
How to do business with the Japanese : a complete guide to Japanese customs and business practices / Boye De Mente. Lincolnwood, Ill., U. S.A. : NTC Business Books, c1987. vi, 269 p. ; 23 cm. Includes bibliographical references. ISBN 0-8442-8509-9 (pbk.) LC Card 86-62724 DDC 395/.52 19
1. Business etiquette - Japan. 2. National characteristics, Japanese. 3. United States - Commerce - Japan. 4. Japan - Commerce - United States. 5. Japan - Economic conditions - 1945-. I. Title.
HF5387 .D3835 1987

Japanese etiquette & ethics in business / Boye de Mente. 5th ed. Lincolnwood, Ill. : Passport Books, c1987. ix, 182 p. : ill. ; 23 cm. ISBN 0-8442-8507-2 (pbk.) : LC Card 86-60830 DDC 395/.52 19
1. Business etiquette - Japan. 2. Business ethics - Japan. 3. Industrial management - Japan. 4. National characteristics, Japanese. I. Title. II. Title: Japanese etiquette and ethics in business.
HF5387 .D384 1987

De Michelis, G. (Gianni)
Il piano del lavoro / Gianni De Michelis. 1a ed. Roma : Laterza, 1986. xii, 267 p. : ill. ; 22 cm. (Libri del tempo Laterza. 204) Bibliography: p. 245-[252] Includes index. ISBN 88-420-2753-7 : LC Card 86-219772
1. Labor policy - Italy. 2. Labor and laboring classes - Italy. I. Title.
HD8481 .D42 1986

Rapporto sulle partecipazioni statali /. Milano [1981] 1 v. (in various pagings) ; ISBN 88-20-42161-5 : LC Card 81-199972 DDC 338.945 19
HC310.I53 R35 ***NYPL [JLD 83-2970]***

De Murguía, Valdemar. Capital flight and economic crisis : Mexican post-devaluation exiles in a California community / by Valdemar de Murguía. La Jolla, Calif. : Center for U. S.-Mexican Studies, University of California, San Diego, 1986. 27 p. ; 23 cm. (Research report series / Center for U. S.-Mexican Studies, University of California, San Diego . 44) Includes bibliographical references. LC Card 87-621351 DDC 332/.042 19
1. Capital movements - Mexico. 2. Bank deposits - United States. 3. Devaluation of currency - Mexico. 4. Mexicans - California - La Jolla (San Diego). I. Series: Research report series (University of California, San Diego. Center for U. S.-Mexican Studies) , 44. II. Title.
HG3916 .D4 1986

De Narbonne à Bordeaux . Roman, Yves. Lyon , c1983. 333 p. : ISBN 2-7297-0200-8 : LC Card 84-179554
HF377 .R65 1983

De Old, Alan R. Transportation : the technology of moving people and products / Alan R. De Old, Everett Sheets, William Alexander. Worcester, Mass. : Davis Publications, c1986. x, 534 p. : ill. (some col.) ; 24 cm. Includes index. ISBN 0-87192-126-X LC Card 86-70174 DDC 380.5 19
1. Transportation. I. Sheets, Everett. II. Alexander, William. III. Title.
HE151 .D42 1986

De Oliveira, Paulo. Cohen, Steve, 1950- Getting to the right job /. New York , 1987. 288 p. ; ISBN 0-89480-040-X (pbk.) : LC Card 85-40899 DDC 650.1/4 19
HF5381 .C6814 1987

De protesta a rebelión--la "subversión" (Rosario, mayo 1969) /. Balvé, Beba. Buenos Aires, Argentina [1985] xvii, 123 p. ; LC Card 86-162379
HD5350.R67 B35 1985

De que adoecem e morrem os trabalhadores / [organizadores] Herval Pina Ribeiro, Francisco Antonio de Castor Lacaz. São Paulo : Diesat : IMESP, 1985. 236 p. ; 23 cm. Cover title. Includes bibliographies. LC Card 85-231487
1. Industrial hygiene - Brazil. 2. Occupational diseases - Brazil. 3. Quality of work life - Brazil. I. Ribeiro, Herval Pina. II. Lacaz, Francisco A. de Castro (Francisco Antonio de Castro). III. DIESAT (Organization).
HD7683 .D4 1985

De Renzo, D. J. Pharmaceutical manufacturers of the United States /. Park Ridge, N.J., U. S.A. , 1987. vi, 300 p. ; ISBN 0-8155-1109-4 : LC Card 86-33276 DDC 338.7/616151/02573 19
HD9666.3 .P47 1987

De Roo, Priscilla. Laborie, Jean Paul. La politique française d'amenagement du territoire de 1950 à 1985 /. Paris , 1985. 176 p., [8] p. of plates : ISBN 2-11-001488-1(pbk.) :
NYPL [JLG 87-38]

De Siervo, Ugo. Intervento straordinario e amministrazione locale nel mezzogiorno /. Milano, Italy , c1985. 348 p. ; LC Card 86-144245
HC310.I53 I58 1985

De Silva, Leelananda. Oteiza, Enrique. Technical co-operation among Third World countries and the international order /. Mexico, D.F. , 1978. 72 p. ; LC Card 86-223022 DDC 338.9/26 19
HC60 .O838 1978

De Vita, Carol J.
Altschuler, David M. New York nonprofit organizations . Washington, D.C. (2100 M St., N.W., Washington 20037) , c1987. vii, 43 p. : LC Card 87-159600 DDC 658.1/5 19
HD2769.2.U6 A48 1987

Salamon, Lester M. Rhode Island nonprofit organizations . Washington, D.C. , Providence, RI , c1987. vii, 40 p. : LC Card 87-148803 DDC 338.7/4/09745 19
HD2769.2.U6 S25 1987

Salamon, Lester M. San Francisco Bay Area nonprofit organizations . Washington, D.C. (2100 M St., N.W., Washington 20037) , c1987. vi, 26 p. : LC Card 87-403000 DDC 338.7/4/0979461 19
HJ9205.S3 S34 1987

De Vos, Wouter. Point de mire : l'actualité / W. Devos, R. Geivers, M. David. Antwerpen, Belgiëlai 147 a : Erasme, 1977. 125 p. : col. ill. ; 22 cm. Includes index. ISBN 90-02-01132-6 : LC Card 78-370280 DDC 309.1
1. Economic history - 1971-. 2. Social history - 1945-. 3. World politics - 1945-. I. Geivers, R., joint author. II. David, Michiel, 1930- joint author. III. Title.
HC59 .D464 ***NYPL [JLD 80-3135]***

De Vries, Barend A. Remaking the World Bank / Barend A. de Vries ; foreword by I.G. Patel. Washington, DC : Seven Locks Press ; Lanham, Md. : Distributed by National Book Network, c1987. xvi, 184 p. ; 21 cm. Bibliography: p. 162-176. Includes index. ISBN 0-932020-49-6 (pbk.) LC Card 87-23406 DDC 332.1/532 19
1. World Bank. I. Title.
HG3881.5.W57 D4 1987

De Vries, Margaret Garritsen, 1922- Balance of payments adjustment, 1945 to 1986 : the IMF experience / Margaret Garritsen de Vries. Washington, D.C. : International Monetary Fund, 1987. xi, 336 p. ; 23 cm. Bibliography: p. 310-322. Includes index. ISBN 0-939934-93-0 (pbk.) : LC Card 87-17242 DDC 332.1/52 19
1. Balance of payments - Developing countries. 2. International Monetary Fund. 3. International finance. I. International Monetary Fund. II. Title.
HG3890 .D4 1987

Deac, Augustin. Condițiile istorice ale apariției și dezvoltării clasei muncitoare din România . București , 1984. 652 p. ; LC Card 84-234192
HD8648 .C65 1984

DEAF SMITH ELECTRIC COOPERATIVE - HISTORY.
Guy, Duane F. Texas 47--Deaf Smith . [Hereford, Tex.] , c1986. vii, 160 p. : LC Card 86-210662 DDC 334/.682131/09764835 19
HD9688.U54 D434 1986

Deal maker. Kuhn, Robert Lawrence. Dealmaker . New York , c1988. xi, 316 p. : ISBN 0-471-62465-9 LC Card 87-21543 DDC 658 19
HD58.6 .K84 1988

Deal me in! . Crain, Sharon. Boulder, Colo. , c1987. vi, 185 p. : LC Card 87-19904 DDC 650.1 19
HF5386 .C893 1987

The deal of the century . Coll, Steve. New York , 1988, c1986. xv, 400 p. : ISBN 0-671-64592-7 (pbk.) : LC Card 87-23410 DDC 384.6/065/73 19
HE8846.A55 C58 1988

Dealing with difficult customers [motion picture] / produced by CRM Productions, Inc. Del Mar, CA : McGraw-Hill Training Systems, 1986. 1 film reel (13 min.) : sd., col. ; 16 mm. + 1 leader's guide. Title from data sheet. College students and adults. Issued also as videorecording. Using a series of vignettes, shows appropriate steps that customer service representatives can take to resolve customer problems, turning dissatisfied customers into satisfied ones. ISBN 0-07-620875-3 LC Card 86-708027 DDC 658.8 11
1. Customer service. 2. Customer relations. I. CRM Productions. II. McGraw-Hill Training Systems (Firm).
HF5415.5

Dealing with difficult customers [videorecording] / produced by CRM Productions, Inc. Del Mar, CA : McGraw-Hill Training Systems, 1986. 1 videocassette (13 min.) : sd., col. + 1 leader's guide. Title from data sheet. College students and adults. Issued as U-matic 3/4 in. or VHS 1/2 in. Issued also as motion picture. Using a series of vignettes, shows appropriate steps that customer service representatives can take to resolve customer problems, turning dissatisfied customers into satisfied ones. ISBN 0-07-109068-1 (3/4 in.) LC Card 86-708028 DDC 658.8 11
1. Customer service. 2. Customer relations. I. CRM Productions. II. McGraw-Hill Training Systems (Firm).
HF5415.5

Dealing with farm sector debt : toward a solution : a report from the food and agriculture policy study project. Washington, D.C. (317 Massachusetts Ave., N.E., Washington 20002) : Center for National Policy, c1986. 47 p. : ill. ; 28 cm. (Alternatives for the 1980's . no. 19) LC Card 86-71068 DDC 332.7/1/0973 19
1. Agricultural credit - Government policy - United States. 2. Debt - Government policy - United States. I. Center for National Policy (U. S.). II. Series.
HD1440.U6 D4 1986

Dealing with objections and irate customers. People skills in action, for loan officers and processors. Chicago, Ill. , 1986. 1 videocassette (20 min.) : LC Card 86-707349 DDC 658.8 11
HG1641

Dealmaker . Kuhn, Robert Lawrence. New York , c1988. xi, 316 p. : ISBN 0-471-62465-9 LC Card 87-21543 DDC 658 19
HD58.6 .K84 1988

DEALS.
Kuhn, Robert Lawrence. Dealmaker . New York , c1988. xi, 316 p. : ISBN 0-471-62465-9 LC Card 87-21543 DDC 658 19
HD58.6 .K84 1988

Dean, Gerald W.
Eidman, Vernon R., 1936- Decision models for California turkey growers /. Berkeley, Calif. [1968] ii, 80 p. : LC Card 87-401009 DDC 338.1/09794 s 636.5/92/0068 19
HD1407 .C27 no. 21 HD9437.U63C3

World trade in fresh oranges : an analysis of the effect of European Economic Community tariff policies / Gerald W. Dean and Norman R. Collins. Berkeley, Calif. : University of California Division of Agricultural Sciences, Giannini Foundation of Agricultural Economics, California Agricultural Experiment Station, [1967] 70 p. : ill. ; 26 cm. (Giannini Foundation monograph . no. 18) Cover title. "January 1967." Bibliography: p. 69-70. LC Card 87-401008 DDC 338.1/09794 s 382/.41431 19
1. Orange trade. 2. Tariff on oranges - European Economic Community countries. I. Collins, Norman R. II. Title. III. Series.
HD1407 .C27 no. 18 HD9259.O7

Dean, James W., 1956- Deciding to innovate : how firms justify advanced technology / James W. Dean, Jr. Cambridge, Mass. : Ballinger, c1987. xviii, 165 p. ; 24 cm. Includes bibliographies and index. ISBN 0-88730-189-4 LC Card 87-17432 DDC 658.5/14 19
1. United States - Manufactures - Technological innovations - Decision making - Case studies. 2. Technological innovations - Management - Case studies. I. Title.
HD9725 .D35 1987

Dean, John, B. App. Sc. Design for diversification /. Canberra , Portland, OR. [1985] 57 p. : ISBN 0-909724-68-7 (pbk.) LC Card 86-222390 DDC 363.5/0994 19
HD7379.A3 D47 1985

Dean, Trevor. Land and power in late medieval Ferrara : the rule of the Este, 1350-1450 / Trevor Dean. Cambridge ; New York : Cambridge University Press, 1988. xiv, 212 p. : maps ; 23 cm. (Cambridge studies in medieval life and thought. 4th ser., 7) Based on the author's thesis (doctoral)--University of Oxford, 1982. Bibliography: p. 189-207. Includes index. ISBN 0-521-33127-7 LC Card 87-6583 DDC 333.3/0945/45 19
1. Land tenure - Italy - Ferrara (Province) - History. 2. Land tenure - Italy - Emilia-Romagna - History. 3. Ferrara (Italy : Province) - History. 4. Emilia-Romagna, Italy - History. 5. Este family. I. Title. II. Series.
HD679.F47 D43 1988

The Dean Witter guide for today's investor /. Gardiner, Robert M. New York, NY , c1988. p. cm. ISBN 0-453-00582-9 LC Card 87-24168 DDC 332.6/78 19
HG4527 .G37 1988

Deane, Barbara. Dellinger, Susan. Communicating effectively . Millwood, N.Y., 1987, c1982. p. cm. ISBN 0-916667-14-6 LC Card 87-20830 DDC 658.4/5 19
HF5718 .D44 1987

Dear cats : the Post Office letters / edited by Russell Ash ; illustrated by Kevin W. Maddison. London : Pavilion : M. Joseph, 1986. 128 p. : ill. ; 19 cm. LC Card 87-126969 DDC 628.9/693 19
1. Great Britain. Post Office - Security measures - History. 2. Postal service - Great Britain - Security measures - History. 3. Rodents - Control - Great Britain - History. 4. Cats - Great Britain - History. I. Ash, Russell.
HE6939.S42 D42 1986

Dearden, John. Management accounting : text and cases / John Dearden. Englewood Cliffs, N.J. : Prentice Hall, c1988. xiv, 639 p. : ill. ; 24 cm. Includes bibliographical references and index. ISBN 0-13-549123-1 LC Card 87-19300 DDC 658.1/511 19
1. Managerial accounting. 2. Managerial accunting - Case studies. I. Title.
HF5657.4 .D42 1988

DEATH RATE. see **MORTALITY.**

Death tribute. Mouat, Frederic J. (Frederic John), 1816-1897. The death tribute of England to India . London , 1875. 14 p. ; LC Card 87-168950
HB1469 .M67 1875

The death tribute of England to India . Mouat, Frederic J. (Frederic John), 1816-1897. London , 1875. 14 p. ; LC Card 87-168950
HB1469 .M67 1875

DEATH - WASHINGTON (STATE) - STATISTICS.
Injury deaths in Washington State, 1968-1983 . Seattle, Wash. (1610 NE 150th, Seattle 98155) [1985] 49, [78] p. : LC Card 86-623057 DDC 363.1/02/09797021 19
HB1323.A22 U65 1985

Deaton, Brady J. Local infrastructure investment in rural America /. Boulder , 1988. xxi, 291 p. ; ISBN 0-8133-7460-X (soft : alk. paper) LC Card 87-21606 DDC 332.6/7252 19
HC110.P83 L63 1988

DeBat, Don. The mortgage manual : the complete guide to choosing the real estate loan that's best for you / Don DeBat ; edited by Thomas A. Kelly. Chicago : Contemporary Books, c1986. ix, 154 p. ; 21 cm. Includes index. ISBN 0-8092-4890-5 (pbk.) : LC Card 86-23972 DDC 332.7/22 19
1. Mortgage loans - United States. 2. House buying - United States. I. Kelly, Thomas A. (Thomas Alfred). II. Title.
HG2040.5.U5 D423 1986

Debate Nacional sobre Abastecimento Popular (1986) Documento final / Debate Nacional sobre Abastecimento Popular, 26/janeiro/86 ; Ministério da Agricultura, COBAL-Cia. Brasileira de Alimentos. Brasília, DF : Ministério da Agricultura, Cia. Brasileira de Alimentos, Diretoria de Planejamento, 1986. 51 leaves : ill., ports. ; 30 cm. Cover title. Spine title: Documento final do Debate Nacional sobre Abastecimento Popular. "As organizações populares de todo o Brasil, interessadas na democratização do abastecimento alimentar, vão discutir uma nova prática para o setor." LC Card 87-146594 DDC 363.8/0981 19
1. Food supply - Brazil - Congresses. I. Cia. Brasileira de Alimentos. II. Title. III. Title: Documento final do Debate Nacional sobre Abastecimento Popular.
HD9014.B82 D43 1986

The Debate over stabilization policy / [edited by] Franco Modigliani. Cambridge [Cambridgeshire] ; New York : Cambridge University Press, 1986. xiv, 270 p. : ill. ; 25 cm. (Raffaele Mattioli lectures) At head of title: Raffaele Mattioli Foundation. Includes index. Bibliography: p. 253-262. ISBN 0-521-26790-0 LC Card 84-21366 DDC 338.9 19
1. Economic stabilization - Addresses, essays, lectures. 2. Economic policy - Addresses, essays, lectures. I. Modigliani, Franco. II. Raffaele Mattioli Foundation. III. Series.
HB3732 .D43 1986 ***NYPL [JLF 86-1945]***

DEBATES AND DEBATING - UNITED STATES.
Debating United States agricultural policy . Kansas City, Mo. (P.O. Box 20626, Kansas City 64195) , c1986. 111 p. ; LC Card 86-224267 DDC 338.1/873 19
HD1761 .D37 1986b

DEBATING. see **DEBATES AND DEBATING.**

Debating United States agricultural policy : a preliminary analysis / Richard G. Fawcett, editor. Kansas City, Mo. (P.O. Box 20626, Kansas City 64195) : National Federation of State High School Associations, c1986. 111 p. ; 24 cm. (National Federation publications) Includes bibliographies. LC Card 86-224267 DDC 338.1/873 19
1. Agriculture and state - United States. 2. Debates and debating - United States. I. Fawcett, Richard G.
HD1761 .D37 1986b

Debattserien (Stiftelsen Marknadsekonomiskt alternativ för Sverige) .
(6) Söderström, Lars, 1940- Perspektiv på fördelningspolitiken /. [Stockholm] [1984] 83 p. : ISBN 91-7566-068-7 LC Card 85-108552
HC380.I5 S62 1984

Debeir, Jean-Claude. Les servitudes de la puissance : une histoire de l'énergie / Jean-Claude Debeir, Jean-Paul Deléage, Daniel Hémery. [Paris] : Flammarion, c1986. 428 p. : ill. ; 22 cm. (Nouvelle bibliothèque scientifique) Bibliography: p. [379]-409. ISBN 2-08-211163-6 : LC Card 87-121577
1. Energy policy. 2. Industry - Power supply. 3. Energy development. I. Deléage, Jean-Paul. II. Hémery, Daniel. III. Title.
HD9502.A2 D43 1986

DEBENTURES. see **BONDS.**

Debès, Joseph. L'appel de la J.O.C., 1926-1928 / Joseph Debès, Emile Poulat. Paris : Editions du Cerf, 1986. 292 p. : ill. ; 24 cm. (Histoires, 0769-2633) Bibliography: p. [277]-285. Includes index. ISBN 2-204-02529-1 : LC Card 86-189508
1. Jeunesse ouvrière chrétienne (France) - History. 2. Labor and laboring classes - France - History. 3. Church and labor - France - History. 4. Youth - Employment - France - History. I. Poulat, Émile. II. Title.
HD8430 .D37 1986

DEBIT CARDS - UNITED STATES.
American Bankers Association. Retail Payments

Task Force. Ad Hoc Committee. Implementation guidelines for online debit card systems at the point of sale /. [Washington, D.C.] , c1986. 1 v. (various pagings) : LC Card 86-224882 DDC 332.1/028 19
HG1710.5 .A47 1986

DEBT.
Thaker, B. C. Fiscal policy, monetary analysis, and debt management . New Delhi , 1985. xvi, 356 p. : LC Card 85-903636 DDC 339.5/2/0954 19
HG230.3 .T46 1985 NYPL [JLD 86-1324]

Debt, adjustment, and renegotiation in Latin America : orthodox and alternative approaches / Economic Commission for Latin America and the Caribbean (ECLAC). Boulder, Colo. : L. Rienner Publishers, 1986. x, 171 p. : ill. ; 24 cm. "Published in cooperation with the United Nations." Includes index. Bibliography: p. 159-167. ISBN 0-931477-72-7 : LC Card 85-30098 DDC 336.3/435/098 19
1. International Monetary Fund - Latin America - Addresses, essays, lectures. 2. Debts, External - Latin America - Addresses, essays, lectures. 3. Debt relief - Latin America - Addresses, essays, lectures. I. United Nations. Economic Commission for Latin America and the Caribbean.
HJ8514.5 .D44 1986 NYPL [JLE 87-781]

The Debt crisis and financial stability : the future : proceedings of a conference held at Pace University, New York City, in March 1985 / edited by S.K. Kaushik ; [contributions by Ravi Batra ... et al.]. New York, NY (Attn: Comptroller, Pace Plaza, 10038) : Pace University, 1985. xi, 157 p. : ill. ; 24 cm. Papers from the Conference on International Banking. Includes index. Bibliography: p. 143-151. ISBN 0-88239-017-1 : LC Card 85-19243 DDC 336.3/435/091724 19
1. Loans, Foreign - Developing countries - Congresses. 2. Debts, External - Developing countries - Congresses. 3. International finance - Congresses. I. Kaushik, S. K., 1944-. II. Batra, Raveendra N. III. Conference on International Banking (1985 : Pace University).
HG3891.5 .D4 1985 NYPL [JLE 86-3911]

The Debt crisis and the Third World. Geneva : World Council of Churches, Programme Unit on Justice and Service, Commission on the Churches' Participation in Development, [1986] 54 p. ; 21 cm. (CCPD documents. Justice and development . no. 6) Oikoumene "January 1986"--Cover. Bibliography: p. [53] LC Card 87-114938 DDC 336.3/435/091724 19
1. Debts, External - Developing countries. I. World Council of Churches. Commission on the Churches' Participation in Development. II. Series.
HJ8899 .D426 1986

The Debt crisis in Latin America. Stockholm : Institute of Latin American Studies, 1986. 199 p. : charts ; 22 cm. (Monographs / Institute of Latin American Studies . no. 13) Includes bibliographies. ISBN 91-87134-01-2 LC Card 87-108739 DDC 336.3/435/098 19
1. Debts, External - Latin America. 2. Loans, Foreign - Latin America. 3. Debt relief - Latin America. I. Latinamerika-institutet i Stockholm.
HJ8514.5 .D45 1986

DEBT - GOVERNMENT POLICY - UNITED STATES.
Dealing with farm sector debt . Washington, D.C. (317 Massachusetts Ave., N.E., Washington 20002) , c1986. 47 p. : LC Card 86-71068 DDC 332.7/1/0973 19
HD1440.U6 D4 1986

DEBT - INDIA.
Thaker, B. C. Fiscal policy, monetary analysis, and debt management . New Delhi , 1985. xvi, 356 p. : LC Card 85-903636 DDC 339.5/2/0954 19
HG230.3 .T46 1985 NYPL [JLD 86-1324]

The Debt problem in Jamaica : situation and solutions / edited by Omar Davies.New ed. Mona, Jamaica : University of the West Indies, Dept. of Economics, c1986. viii, 125 p. : ill. ; 21 cm. (Monograph / Economics Dept., U.W.I., Mona . #1) Edited papers presented at a symposium held on May 10, 1985, sponsored by the Dept. of Economics. "September 1986"--T.p. verso. Includes bibliographies. ISBN 976-410-002-3 (pbk.) LC Card 87-403413 DDC 336.3/4/097292 19
1. Debts, External - Jamaica. 2. Debt relief - Jamaica. I. Davies, Omar. II. University of the West Indies (Mona, Jamaica). Dept. of Economics. III. Series: Monograph (University of the West Indies (Mona, Jamaica). Dept. of Economics) , #1.
HJ8552 .D43 1986

The debt problems of Eastern Europe /. Zloch-Christy, Iliana, 1953- Cambridge [Cambridgeshire] , New York , 1987. xix, 220 p. ; ISBN 0-521-33542-6 LC Card 87-11634 DDC 336.3/435/0947 19
HJ8615 .Z57 1987

DEBT, PUBLIC.
Pinto, Isaac de, 1715-1787. [Selections. 1960.] O economista Isaac de Pinto, o seu "Tratado da circulação e do crédito," e outros escritos económicos /. Lisboa , 1960. 247 p. : LC Card 85-125396
HJ150 .P552 1960

Debt ratings criteria. Standard & Poor's debt ratings criteria . New York, N.Y. (25 Broadway, New York 10004) , c1986. viii, 68 p. : LC Card 87-102292 DDC 338.7/4/0973 19
HG4521 .S729 1986

DEBT RELIEF.
Dillon, K. Burke. Recent experience with multilateral official debt rescheduling /. Washington, D.C. , c1987. v, 22 p. : LC Card 87-2633 DDC 336.3/435 19
HG3891.5 .D55 1987

Solberg, Ronald L., 1953- Sovereign rescheduling . London , Boston , 1988. p. cm. ISBN 0-04-332122-4 (alk. paper) LC Card 87-18805 DDC 336.3/435 19
HG3891.5 .S65 1988

DEBT RELIEF - AFRICA, SUB-SAHARAN - CASE STUDIES.
Foreign indebtedness and basic human needs in four African countries . Washington , 1986. ii, 54 p. : LC Card 86-603396 DDC 336.3/435/0967
HC800 .F67 1986

DEBT RELIEF - BRAZIL.
Alcalde Cardoza, Xavier. El poder norteamericano y la renegociación de la deuda externa brasileña, 1982-1983 /. Lima, Perú , 1985. 62 p. ; LC Card 86-223475
HJ8579 .A44 1985

Batista Júnior, Paulo Nogueira. International financial flows to Brazil since the late 1960s . Washington, D.C. , 1987. 66 p. ; ISBN 0-8213-0891-2 (pbk.) LC Card 87-6065 DDC 336.3/4/0981 19
HJ8579 .B369 1987

DEBT RELIEF - DEVELOPING COUNTRIES.
Aggarwal, Vinod K. International debt threat . Berkeley , c1987. vii, 71 p. ; ISBN 0-87725-529-6 (pbk.) LC Card 87-80549 DDC 336.3/435 19
HG3891.5 .A38 1987

Dillon, K. Burke. Recent experience with multilateral official debt rescheduling /. Washington, D.C. , c1987. v, 22 p. : LC Card 87-2633 DDC 336.3/435 19
HG3891.5 .D55 1987

International borrowing . Washington, D.C. , c1986. 499 p. : ISBN 0-935328-40-8 LC Card 86-82157 DDC 341.7/51 19
K4450 .I576 1986 NYPL [JLF 86-1814]

Leroux, François, 1945- Que nous a appris la crise de l'endettement international? /. Montréal, Québec, Canada [1985] 41 leaves ; LC Card 86-144447 DDC 336.3/4/091724 19
HJ8899 .L47 1985

A Strategy for restoration of growth in middle-income countries that face debt-servicing difficulties. Washington, D.C., U. S.A. , 1986. 43 p. : ISBN 0-8213-0811-4 (pbk.) LC Card 86-214478 DDC 338.9/009172/4 19
HJ8899 .S77 1986

DEBT RELIEF - DEVELOPING COUNTRIES - CONGRESSES.
A Dance along the precipice . Lexington, Mass. , c1985. xxxii, 283 p. : ISBN 0-669-10899-5 (alk. paper) LC Card 85-5789 DDC 336.3/435/091724 19
HJ8899 .D36 1985 NYPL [JLE 86-2308]

DEBT RELIEF - DEVELOPING COUNTRIES - STATISTICS - FORECASTING.
Status report . Philadelphia, PA (3624 Science Center, Philadelphia 19104) , c1987. iii, 67 p. : LC Card 87-153448 DDC 336.3/435/091724 19
HJ8899 .S72 1987

DEBT RELIEF - DICTIONARIES.
Guiliani Cury, Hugo. Glosario de terminos de renegociacíon de deuda externa =. Santo Domingo, República Dominicana , 1985. 68 p. ; LC Card 86-184550
HJ8046 .G85 1985

DEBT RELIEF - DICTIONARIES - SPANISH.
Guiliani Cury, Hugo. Glosario de terminos de renegociacíon de deuda externa =. Santo Domingo, República Dominicana , 1985. 68 p. ; LC Card 86-184550
HJ8046 .G85 1985

DEBT RELIEF - DOMINICAN REPUBLIC.
Renegociación de la deuda externa, 1985 /. Santo Domingo, República Dominicana , 1985. iv, 168 p. ; LC Card 86-186407
HJ8548 .R46 1985

DEBT RELIEF - JAMAICA.
The Debt problem in Jamaica . Mona, Jamaica , c1986. viii, 125 p. : ISBN 976-410-002-3 (pbk.) LC Card 87-403413 DDC 336.3/4/097292 19
HJ8552 .D43 1986

DEBT RELIEF - LATIN AMERICA.
The Debt crisis in Latin America. Stockholm , 1986. 199 p. : ISBN 91-87134-01-2 LC Card 87-108739 DDC 336.3/435/098 19
HJ8514.5 .D45 1986

Deuda externa latinoamericana y proceso de ajuste . Bogotá, Colombia , 1985. 335 p. : LC Card 86-164491
HJ8514.5 .D484 1985

Rebolledo Soberón, Luis. Deuda externa . [Lima] , c1985. 58 p. : LC Card 86-120059
HJ8514.5 .R43 1985

Report on the medium term prospects for Latin American countries. Roma , 1986. 109 p. : LC Card 86-223594 DDC 336.3/435/098 19
HJ8514.5 .R46 1986

DEBT RELIEF - LATIN AMERICA - ADDRESSES, ESSAYS, LECTURES.
Debt, adjustment, and renegotiation in Latin America . Boulder, Colo. , 1986. x, 171 p. : ISBN 0-931477-72-7 : LC Card 85-30098 DDC 336.3/435/098 19
HJ8514.5 .D44 1986 NYPL [JLE 87-781]

DEBT RELIEF - MEXICO.
Aschentrupp Toledo, Hermann. La dimensión política de la crisis y renegociación de la deuda externa mexicana /. México, D.F. [1985] 229 p. ; LC Card 87-401754 DDC 336.3/4/0972 19
HJ8519 .A8 1985

The debt rescheduling process /. Milivojević, Marko, 1957- London , 1985. xvi, 240 p. : ISBN 0-86187-575-3 LC Card 87-672863
HG3891.5 .M55x 1985b

DEBT - VENEZUELA.
Ojeda, Roseliano. Cómo se desangra un país-- ! . Valencia [Venezuela] , c1987. 241 p. ; ISBN 980-212-037-5 LC Card 87-169695 DDC 330.987/0633 19
HC237 .O365 1987

Debtor countries after the debt crisis. Status report . Philadelphia, PA (3624 Science Center, Philadelphia 19104) , c1987. iii, 67 p. : LC Card 87-153448 DDC 336.3/435/091724 19
HJ8899 .S72 1987

DEBTS, EXTERNAL - AFRICA, SUB-SAHARAN.
Green, Reginald Herbold. The IMF and stabilisation in sub-Saharan Africa . Brighton, England [1986] ii, 70 p. ; LC Card 86-208478 DDC 332.1/52 19
HC800 .G72 1986

DEBTS, EXTERNAL - ARAB COUNTRIES.
Zakī, Ramzī. al-Duyūn wa-al-tanmiyah . al-Qāhirah , 1985. 271 p. : LC Card 86-960543
HJ8824 .Z34 1985

DEBTS, EXTERNAL - ARGENTINA.
Argentina 1984 . [Buenos Aires?] [1984] 95 p. ; LC Card 85-132860
HJ8569 .A75 1984

Feldman, Ernesto V. (Ernesto Víctor) Crisis financiera y endeudamiento externo en la Argentina /. [Buenos Aires] , c1986. 184 p. ; ISBN 950-25-1313-4 LC Card 86-182663
HG185.A7 F45 1986

Perdía, Roberto Cirilo. Existe otra Argentina posible /. Buenos Aires , 1986. 276 p. : ISBN

950-97640-0-0 LC Card 87-139879 DDC 336.3/4/0982 19
HG3881.5.I58 P47 1986

DEBTS, EXTERNAL - ARGENTINA - HISTORY.
Vitale, Luis. Historia de la deuda externa latinoamericana y entretelones del endeudamiento argentino /. Buenos Aires, Argentina , c1986. 351 p. ; ISBN 950-37-0223-2 LC Card 87-100729
HJ8514.5 .V57 1986

DEBTS, EXTERNAL - AUSTRALIA - VICTORIA.
Victorian public sector debt. [Melbourne, Vic.] [1986] vii, 57, [1] p. ; LC Card 87-165135 DDC 336.3/4/09945 19
HJ8857.V53 V53 1986

DEBTS, EXTERNAL - AUSTRIA.
Speiser, Harald. Das österreichische Foreign Debt Management, 1956-1983 . Regensburg , c1985. 120 p. : ISBN 3-924956-06-5 LC Card 86-222064
HJ8636 .S66 1985

DEBTS, EXTERNAL - BOLIVIA.
Devlin, Robert. External debt in Bolivia /. Boulder, Colo. , 1987. p. cm. ISBN 0-8133-7366-2 : LC Card 87-2088 DDC 336.3/4/0984 19
HJ8574 .D48 1987

DEBTS, EXTERNAL - BRAZIL.
Alcalde Cardoza, Xavier. El poder norteamericano y la renegociación de la deuda externa brasileña, 1982-1983 /. Lima, Perú , 1985. 62 p. ; LC Card 86-223475
HJ8579 .A44 1985

Baer, Mônica. A internacionalização financeira no Brasil /. Petrópolis , 1986. 159 p. ; LC Card 86-200812
HG185.B7 B28 1986

Batista Júnior, Paulo Nogueira. International financial flows to Brazil since the late 1960s . Washington, D.C. , 1987. 66 p. ; ISBN 0-8213-0891-2 (pbk.) LC Card 87-6065 DDC 336.3/4/0981 19
HJ8579 .B369 1987

Calcagnotto, Gilberto. Brasilien 1974-1981 . Hamburg [1983] xi, 78 p. : LC Card 83-222930
HC187 .C143 1983

Delfim Netto, Antônio. Só o político pode salvar o economista /. Rio de Janeiro , 1986. xvii, 146 p. ; LC Card 87-137681 DDC 338.981 19
HC187 .D565 1986

Martone, Celso L. (Celso Luiz) Macroeconomic policies, debt accumulation, and adjustment in Brazil, 1965-84 /. Washington, D.C. , 1987. vii, 43 p. ; ISBN 0-8213-0892-0 (pbk.) LC Card 86-1527 DDC 336.3/4/0981 19
HJ8579 .M37 1987

Moreira, Marcílio Marques. The Brazilian quandary /. New York , 1986. vi, 87 p. : ISBN 0-87078-171-5 (pbk.) : LC Card 86-210942 DDC 332.3/4/0981 19
HJ8579 .M66 1986

Nery, Sebastiáo. Crime e castigo da dívida externa /. Brasília-Distrito Federal [1986] 170 p. ; LC Card 86-208917
HJ8579 .N47 1986

DEBTS, EXTERNAL - CHILE.
La Deuda externa . [Santiago, Chile] , 1985. 105 leaves : LC Card 86-171251
HJ8514.5 .D47 1985

DEBTS, EXTERNAL - COLOMBIA.
Echavarría Olózaga, Hernán. El hueco negro . [S.l. , 1986] (Bogotá, Colombia : Editorial Andes) 244 p., [7] p. of plates : LC Card 86-209093
HC197 .E34 1986

Pérez Triana, Santiago, 1858-1916. Unificación de deudas . Londres , 1912. 81 p. ; LC Card 85-111033
HJ8589 .P47 1912

DEBTS, EXTERNAL - CONGRESSES.
La Crise de l'endettement international . Paris , c1986. 410 p. : ISBN 2-7178-1127-3 : LC Card 86-222862
HJ8017 .C74 1986

Global economic imbalances /. Washington, DC , 1985. x, 116 p. ; ISBN 0-88132-038-2 (pbk.) LC Card 85-8279 DDC 330.9/048 19
HD73 .G56 1985 ***NYPL [JLE 87-1314]***

The International debt problem . Tübingen , 1986. vi, 193 p. : ISBN 3-16-345084-9 (pbk.) LC Card 86-201893 DDC 336.3/435 19
HG3891.5 .I557 1986

The International debt problem . Boulder , 1987. p. cm. ISBN 0-8133-0595-0 LC Card 87-20149 DDC 336.3/435 19
HG3891.5 .I557 1987

Die Internationale Finanzierungskrise /. Frankfurt am Main , c1985. 153 p. ; ISBN 3-7819-2536-6 LC Card 87-146671 DDC 336.3/435 19
HG3891.5 .I587 1985

DEBTS, EXTERNAL - COSTA RICA.
Cespedes S., Víctor Hugo. Costa Rica--recuperación sin reactivación . San José, Costa Rica , 1985. 238 p. : ISBN 997-7210-05-5 LC Card 86-208956
HC143 .C484 1985

DEBTS, EXTERNAL - CUBA.
Banco Nacional de Cuba (Founded 1948) Cuba's financial crisis . Washington, D.C. (1000 Thomas Jefferson St., N.W., Suite 601, Washington 20007) , 1985. vii, 64, [19] p. : LC Card 86-105593 DDC 330.97291/064 19
HC152.5 .B36 1985 ***NYPL [JLE 86-3732]***

DEBTS, EXTERNAL - DEVELOPING COUNTRIES.
Aggarwal, Vinod K. International debt threat . Berkeley , c1987. vii, 71 p. ; ISBN 0-87725-529-6 (pbk.) LC Card 87-80549 DDC 336.3/435 19
HG3891.5 .A38 1987

Barth, James R. International debt . Fairfax, Va. , 1984. 36 p. ; ***NYPL [*ZT-1554 no.21]***

Brimmer, Andrew F. The world banking system . New York , 1985. 59 p. ; ISBN 0-8147-1068-9 : LC Card 85-5115 DDC 332.1/5 19
HG3881 .B677 1985 ***NYPL [JLD 86-2189]***

Capital flight and Third World debt /. Washington, D.C. , 1987. p. cm. ISBN 0-88132-064-1 LC Card 87-17080 DDC 332/.042 19
HG3891 .C36 1987

Cline, William R. Mobilizing bank lending to debtor countries /. Washington, DC , 1987. viii, 92 p. : ISBN 0-88132-062-5 (pbk.) LC Card 87-16857 DDC 332.1/5 19
HG3891.5 .C58 1987

Cuddington, John T. Capital flight . Princeton, N.J. , c1986. 44 p. ; ISBN 0-88165-230-X (pbk.) : LC Card 86-21386 DDC 332/.041 19
HG3891 .C83 1986

The Debt crisis and the Third World. Geneva [1986] 54 p. ; LC Card 87-114938 DDC 336.3/435/091724 19
HJ8899 .D426 1986

Dillon, K. Burke. Recent experience with multilateral official debt rescheduling /. Washington, D.C. , c1987. v, 22 p. : LC Card 87-2633 DDC 336.3/435 19
HG3891.5 .D55 1987

Dworak, Brigitte M. Das Länderrisiko als bankbetriebliches Problem /. Berlin , c1985. 168 p. : ISBN 3-428-05761-9 LC Card 85-213576
HG5993 .D86 1985

Economic report of the people /. Boston , c1986. xvii, 260 p. : ISBN 0-89608-315-2 (pbk.) : LC Card 85-30342 DDC 330.973/0927 19
HC106.8 .E29 1986 ***NYPL [JLD 87-301]***

Fuchs, Nikolaus, 1955- Ursachen- und Krisenanalyse der Verschuldung von Entwicklungsländern . Berlin , c1986. 258 p. : ISBN 3-925410-05-8 LC Card 87-124994 DDC 336.3/435/091724 19
HJ8899 .F83 1986

Griffin, Keith B. World hunger and the world economy . New York , 1987. xvi, 274 p. ; ISBN 0-8419-1128-2 LC Card 86-33626 DDC 330.9172/4 19
HC59.7 .G749 1987

Hedström, Håkan, 1960- Die internationale Verschuldungskrise . Heidelberg [1985] xvi, 273 p. : ISBN 3-920431-50-2 LC Card 86-122591
HJ8899 .H43 1985

Holley, H. A., 1924- Developing country debt . London : London ; 85 p. ; ISBN 0-7102-1211-9 (pbk.) : LC Card 86-29838 DDC 336.3/435/091724 19
HG3891.5 .H65 1987

Im Teufelskreis der Verschuldung . Hamburg , 1984. 261 p. : ISBN 3-88506-126-0 LC Card 85-131681
HG3881.5.I58 I37 1984

International borrowing . Washington, D.C. , c1986. 499 p. : ISBN 0-935328-40-8 LC Card 86-82157 DDC 341.7/51 19
K4450 .I576 1986 ***NYPL [JLF 86-1814]***

Die Internationale Schuldenkrise . Berlin , 1986. 179 p. : ISBN 3-428-05972-7 LC Card 86-172589
HJ8899 .I58 1986

Katash, S. S. Mezhdunarodnyĭ kredit i vneshnia͡ia zadolzhennost′ razvivaiu͡shchikhsi͡a stran /. Moskva , 1984. 43 p. ; LC Card 87-100185
HG3877 .K37 1984

Leroux, François, 1945- Que nous a appris la crise de l'endettement international? /. Montréal, Québec, Canada [1985] 41 leaves ; LC Card 86-144447 DDC 336.3/4/091724 19
HJ8899 .L47 1985

Lizano Fait, Eduardo. La condicionalidad cruzada y la deuda externa /. [San José] , 1986. 16, [1] leaves : LC Card 87-127835 DDC 336.3/435/091724 19
HJ8899 .L59 1986

Löschner, Ernst. Souveräne Risken und internationale Verschuldung /. Wien , 1983. 187 p. : ISBN 3-214-06553-X : LC Card 84-152762 DDC 336.3/435/091724 19
HJ8899 .L67 1983 ***NYPL [JLE 86-1553]***

Lomax, David F. The developing country debt crisis /. London , 1986. xxiv, 317 p. ; ISBN 0-333-38581-0 ***NYPL [JLD 86-3497]***

Lomax, David F. The developing country debt crisis /. Basingstoke, Hampshire , 1986. xxiv, 317 p. : ISBN 0-333-38581-0 LC Card 86-674010
HJ8899 .L64x 1986b

Milivojević, Marko, 1957- The debt rescheduling process /. London , 1985. xvi, 240 p. : ISBN 0-86187-575-3 LC Card 87-672863
HG3891.5 .M55x 1985b

Mugglin, Markus. Exportrisikogarantie, internationale Verschuldung und schweizerische Entwicklungspolitik /. Adliswil , 1985. 56 p. : ISBN 3-7229-4036-X LC Card 85-148130
HF1574.5.D44 M84 1985

Naylor, R. T., 1945- Hot money and the politics of debt /. New York, N.Y. , 1987. 463 p. ; ISBN 0-671-62319-2 LC Card 86-33739 DDC 364.1/68 19
HG3891 .N39 1987

Nossiter, Bernard D. The global struggle for more . New York , c1987. xvi, 254 p. ; ISBN 0-06-435851-8 : LC Card 86-45762 DDC 337/.09172/4 19
HC59.7 .N676 1987

Nunnenkamp, Peter. The international debt crisis of the Third World . New York , 1986. xvi, 205 p. ; ISBN 0-312-42003-X : LC Card 85-2008 DDC 336.3/435/091724 19
HJ8899 .N86 1985 ***NYPL [JLD 86-2529]***

Pool, John Charles. The ABCs of international finance . Lexington, Mass. , c1987. xii, 138 p. ; ISBN 0-669-15605-1 (alk. paper) LC Card 86-45933 DDC 332/.042 19
HG3851 .P66 1987

Restoring growth in the debt-laden Third World . New York , 1987. x, 82 p. : ISBN 0-930503-02-3 : LC Card 87-23778 DDC 336.3/435/091724 19
HJ8899 .R47 1987

A Strategy for restoration of growth in middle-income countries that face debt-servicing difficulties. Washington, D.C., U. S.A. , 1986. 43 p. : ISBN 0-8213-0811-4 (pbk.) LC Card 86-214478 DDC 338.9/009172/4 19
HJ8899 .S77 1986

Wellons, Philip A. Passing the buck . Boston, Mass. , c1987. xiv, 342 p. : ISBN 0-87584-146-5 (alk. paper) LC Card 86-19508 DDC 332.1/53

19
HG3891.5 .W46 1987 ***NYPL [JLE 87-1072]***

DEBTS, EXTERNAL - DEVELOPING COUNTRIES - ADDRESSES, ESSAYS, LECTURES.

Adjustment crisis in the Third World /. New Brunswick, USA , c1984. x, 186 p. ; ISBN 0-88738-040-9 LC Card 84-8690 DDC 337/.09172/4 19
HC59.7 .A733 1984 ***NYPL [JLE 86-2491]***

Stagflation, savings, and the state . New York , 1986. xii, 402 p. : ISBN 0-19-520496-4 LC Card 85-31981 DDC 330.9172/4 19
HG229 .S74 1986 ***NYPL [JLE 86-2621]***

Uncertain future . New Brunswick, N.J. , c1984. x, 129 p. ; ISBN 0-88738-041-7 : LC Card 84-16240 DDC 332.1/5 19
HG3891.5 .U53 1984 ***NYPL [JLE 86-2494]***

DEBTS, EXTERNAL - DEVELOPING COUNTRIES - CASE STUDIES.

Indebtedness and growth in developing countries /. Hamburg , 1986. 344 p. ; ISBN 3-87895-300-3 (pbk.) LC Card 86-213057 DDC 336.3/435/091724 19
HJ8899 .I53 1986

DEBTS, EXTERNAL - DEVELOPING COUNTRIES - CONGRESSES.

A Dance along the precipice . Lexington, Mass. , c1985. xxxii, 283 p. : ISBN 0-669-10899-5 (alk. paper) LC Card 85-5789 DDC 336.3/435/091724 19
HJ8899 .D36 1985 ***NYPL [JLE 86-2308]***

The Debt crisis and financial stability . New York, NY (Attn: Comptroller, Pace Plaza, 10038) , 1985. xi, 157 p. : ISBN 0-88239-017-1 : LC Card 85-19243 DDC 336.3/435/091724 19
HG3891.5 .D4 1985 ***NYPL [JLE 86-3911]***

Deuda externa y reforma del sistema monetario internacional . Bogotá, D.E., Colombia , 1986. 235 p. ; ISBN 958-608-037-4 LC Card 87-400468 DDC 336.3/435/098 19
HJ8514.5 .D487 1986

International debt and central banking in the 1980s /. New York , 1987. viii, 234 p. ; ISBN 0-312-00530-X : LC Card 87-4300 DDC 336.3/435/091724 19
HJ8899 .I574 1987

DEBTS, EXTERNAL - DEVELOPING COUNTRIES - STATISTICS.

Developing country debt . Washington, D.C. , c1987. xliii, 29 p. : ISBN 0-8213-0889-0 LC Card 87-2074 DDC 336.3/435/091724021 19
HJ8899 .D483 1987

Statistics on external indebtedness . Paris , 1985. 27 p. ; LC Card 86-204760 DDC 336.3/435/091724 19
HJ8899 .S7 1985

DEBTS, EXTERNAL - DEVELOPING COUNTRIES - STATISTICS - FORECASTING.

Status report . Philadelphia, PA (3624 Science Center, Philadelphia 19104) , c1987. iii, 67 p. : LC Card 87-153448 DDC 336.3/435/091724 19
HJ8899 .S72 1987

DEBTS, EXTERNAL - DICTIONARIES.

Guiliani Cury, Hugo. Glosario de terminos de renegociacíon de deuda externa =. Santo Domingo, República Dominicana , 1985. 68 p. ; LC Card 86-184550
HJ8046 .G85 1985

DEBTS, EXTERNAL - DICTIONARIES - SPANISH.

Guiliani Cury, Hugo. Glosario de terminos de renegociacíon de deuda externa =. Santo Domingo, República Dominicana , 1985. 68 p. ; LC Card 86-184550
HJ8046 .G85 1985

DEBTS, EXTERNAL - DOMINICAN REPUBLIC.

Renegociación de la deuda externa, 1985 /. Santo Domingo, República Dominicana , 1985. iv, 168 p. ; LC Card 86-186407
HJ8548 .R46 1985

DEBTS, EXTERNAL - EUROPE, EASTERN.

Barth, James R. International debt . Fairfax, Va. , 1984. 36 p. ; ***NYPL [*ZT-1554 no.21]***

Zloch-Christy, Iliana, 1953- The debt problems of Eastern Europe /. Cambridge [Cambridgeshire] , New York , 1987. xix, 220 p. ; ISBN 0-521-33542-6 LC Card 87-11634 DDC 336.3/435/0947 19
HJ8615 .Z57 1987

DEBTS, EXTERNAL - HAITI - HISTORY.

Mathon, Alix. [Haïti, un cas.] Haïti, un cas /. [Port-au-Prince? , 1985] (Port-au-Prince, Haïti : Impr. Le Natal) 172, 271 p. ; LC Card 86-139806 DDC 330.97294 19
HC153 .M38 1985 ***NYPL [Sc D 86-555]***

DEBTS, EXTERNAL - JAMAICA.

The Debt problem in Jamaica . Mona, Jamaica , c1986. viii, 125 p. : ISBN 976-410-002-3 (pbk.) LC Card 87-403413 DDC 336.3/4/097292 19
HJ8552 .D43 1986

DEBTS, EXTERNAL - LATIN AMERICA.

The Debt crisis in Latin America. Stockholm , 1986. 199 p. : ISBN 91-87134-01-2 LC Card 87-108739 DDC 336.3/435/098 19
HJ8514.5 .D45 1986

La Deuda externa . [Santiago, Chile] , 1985. 105 leaves : LC Card 86-171251
HJ8514.5 .D47 1985

Deuda externa latinoamericana y proceso de ajuste . Bogotá, Colombia , 1985. 335 p. : LC Card 86-164491
HJ8514.5 .D484 1985

The Economy of Latin America and the Caribbean . Washington, D.C. [1986] v, 30 p. ; ISBN 0-8270-2333-2 (pbk.) : LC Card 86-203268 DDC 336.3/435/09729 19
HJ8514.5 .E34 1986

Gavagnin Taffarel, Osvaldo. La deuda externa de América Latina . Lima, Perú , 1986. 157 p. : LC Card 86-235251
HJ8514.5 .G37 1986

Gómez Pérez, José Antonio, 1950- Desarrollo, crisis, deuda y política económica en Panamá . Panamá , 1985. vii, 168 p. : LC Card 86-122320 DDC 338.97287 19
HC147 .G66 1985 ***NYPL [JLD 86-2899]***

Kisic Wagner, Drago. Reflexiones en torno al proceso de coordinación latinoamericano sobre la deuda externa /. [Lima, Perú] [1985] 29 p. ; LC Card 87-403187 DDC 336.3/435/098 19
HJ8514.5 .K57 1985

Köhn, Doris. Die Verschuldung lateinamerikanischer Länder /. Hamburg , 1984. 148 p. ; ISBN 3-87895-259-7 LC Card 85-134749
HJ8514.5 .K64 1984

La Problemática del endeudamiento externo y el financiamiento del desarrollo agropecuario latinoamericano. Lima, Perú [1985] 131 p. : LC Card 86-122361 DDC 336.3/435/098 19
HJ8514.5 .P76 1985 ***NYPL [JLD 86-3143]***

López Hurtado, José. Latinoamérica, su deuda externa . Bogotá, D.E., Colombia , 1987. xxii, 156 p. : ISBN 958-9074-43-X LC Card 87-404201 DDC 336.3/435/098 19
HJ8514.5 .L66 1987

Pastor, Manuel. The International Monetary Fund and Latin America . Boulder, Colo. , 1987. xvi, 228 p. : ISBN 0-8133-7373-5 (pbk. : alk. paper) : LC Card 86-32575 DDC 332.4/98 19
HG660.5 .P33 1987

Políticas macro-económicas . Santiago de Chile [1986] 409 p. : LC Card 87-403669 DDC 338.98 19
HC125 .P657 1986

Rebolledo Soberón, Luis. Deuda externa . [Lima] , c1985. 58 p. : LC Card 86-120059
HJ8514.5 .R43 1985

Report on the medium term prospects for Latin American countries. Roma , 1986. 109 p. : LC Card 86-223594 DDC 336.3/435/098 19
HJ8514.5 .R46 1986

Rey Salgado, Rafael del. La crisis de la deuda en América Latina /. [Spain] [1985] ii, 88 p. ; LC Card 86-131407
HJ8514.5 .R49 1985

Schatan, Jacobo. [América Latina, deuda externa y desarrollo. English.] World debt . London , Atlantic Highlands, N.J., USA , 1987. xv, 126 p. ; ISBN 0-86232-688-5 : LC Card 87-13330 DDC 336.3/435/098 19
HJ8514.5 .S313 1987

Schinke, Rolf. Ursachen der Verschuldungskrise . Göttingen [1987] 33 p. : LC Card 87-409568 DDC 336.3/435/098 19
HJ8514.5 .S34 1987

Vela, Gil. Deuda externa latinoamericana /. Ecuador , 1984. 180 p. ; LC Card 85-180466 DDC 336.3/435/098 19
HJ8514.5 .V45 1984 ***NYPL [JLD 86-308]***

Wiarda, Howard J., 1939- Latin America at the crossroads . Boulder, Colo. , Washington, D.C. , 1987. xiii, 114 p. ; ISBN 0-8133-0423-7 (alk. paper) : LC Card 86-18997 DDC 330.98/003 19
HC125 .W47 1987 ***NYPL [JLE 87-835]***

DEBTS, EXTERNAL - LATIN AMERICA - ADDRESSES, ESSAYS, LECTURES.

Debt, adjustment, and renegotiation in Latin America . Boulder, Colo. , 1986. x, 171 p. : ISBN 0-931477-72-7 : LC Card 85-30098 DDC 336.3/435/098 19
HJ8514.5 .D44 1986 ***NYPL [JLE 87-781]***

Petras, James F., 1937- Latin America . Totowa, N.J. , 1986. xi, 187 p. ; ISBN 0-8476-7505-X : LC Card 86-1885 DDC 337.8 19
HC125 .P4643 1986 ***NYPL [JLE 86-4366]***

DEBTS, EXTERNAL - LATIN AMERICA - CASE STUDIES.

Capital flight and Third World debt /. Washington, D.C. , 1987. p. cm. ISBN 0-88132-064-1 LC Card 87-17080 DDC 332/.042 19
HG3891 .C36 1987

Deuda externa latinoamericana y proceso de ajuste . Bogotá, Colombia , 1985. 335 p. : LC Card 86-164491
HJ8514.5 .D484 1985

DEBTS, EXTERNAL - LATIN AMERICA - CONGRESSES.

Deuda externa y reforma del sistema monetario internacional . Bogotá, D.E., Colombia , 1986. 235 p. ; ISBN 958-608-037-4 LC Card 87-400468 DDC 336.3/435/098 19
HJ8514.5 .D487 1986

El Perú frente al capital extranjero . Lima, Perú [1985] xl, 399 p. : LC Card 86-109611 DDC 332.6/73/0985 19
HG5392 .P47 1985 ***NYPL [JLD 87-384]***

External debt, savings, and growth in Latin America . Washington, D.C. , Buenos Aires , 1987. xv, 207 p. ; ISBN 0-939934-95-7 (pbk.) : LC Card 87-21422 DDC 336.3/435/098 19
HJ8514.5 .E984 1987

Foreign investment, debt, and economic growth in Latin America /. New York , 1988. xix, 250 p. : ISBN 0-312-00936-4 : LC Card 87-18808 DDC 332.6/73/098 19
HG5160.5.A3 F675 1988

Latin America's debt crisis . Boulder, Colo. , 1987. xiii, 176 p. ; ISBN 1-555-87053-8 (lib. bdg. : alk. paper) : LC Card 87-4956 DDC 336.3/435/098 19
HJ8514.5 .L395 1987

Política internacional, economía e integración /. Asunción del Paraguay [1985] 178 p. ; LC Card 86-122468
HF1523 .P65 1985

Silva Ruete, Javier. La respuesta de Latinoamérica a la crisis internacional /. [Lima, Peru?] [1984] 99 p. ; LC Card 86-154728
HF1480.5 .S55 1984

DEBTS, EXTERNAL - LATIN AMERICA - HISTORY.

Vitale, Luis. Historia de la deuda externa latinoamericana y entretelones del endeudamiento argentino /. Buenos Aires, Argentina , c1986. 351 p. ; ISBN 950-37-0223-2 LC Card 87-100729
HJ8514.5 .V57 1986

DEBTS, EXTERNAL - MEXICO.

Aschentrupp Toledo, Hermann. La dimensión política de la crisis y renegociación de la deuda externa mexicana /. México, D.F. [1985] 229 p. ; LC Card 87-401754 DDC 336.3/4/0972 19
HJ8519 .A8 1985

Bailey, Norman A. The Mexican time bomb /. New York , 1987. vi, 61 p. ; ISBN 0-87078-209-6 (pbk.) : LC Card 87-400092 DDC 336.3/4/0972 19
HJ8519 .B26 1987

Kraft, Joseph. The Mexican rescue /. New

York , 1984. 66 p. ; LC Card 84-10354 DDC 336.3/4/0972 19
HJ8519 .K73 1984 ***NYPL [JLE 86-2931]***

Mexican topics . [México, D.F.] [1986] 2 portfolios : LC Card 86-221843 DDC 972.08/3 19
HC135 .M52554 1986

Rubio F., Luis. A Mexican response /. New York , 1987. vi, 72 p. ; ISBN 0-87078-215-0 (pbk.) LC Card 87-162458 DDC 336.3/4/0972 19
HJ8519 .R83 1987

Sacristán, Antonio. Disertaciones sobre economía mexicana /. México, D.F. , 1982. 39 p. ; LC Card 87-123937 DDC 332.1/0972 19
HG2714 .S23 1982

DEBTS, EXTERNAL - MEXICO - CONGRESSES.
Mexiko . Bonn [1983?] 127, [2] p. ; LC Card 85-206583
HC135 .M585 1983

DEBTS, EXTERNAL - MEXICO - HISTORY.
Quijano, José Manuel. Finanzas, desarrollo económico y penetración extranjera /. Puebla, Pue. , 1985. 395 p. : LC Card 86-112589 DDC 332/.0972 19
HG185.M6 Q55 1985 ***NYPL [JLD 86-2195]***

DEBTS, EXTERNAL - MOROCCO.
Benazzou, Chaouki, 1936- Le Maroc face à l'endettement extérieur . [Rabat] 1986 ([Rabat] : Imprimé aux Editions maghrébines) 151 p. : LC Card 87-967050
HG3883.M8 B46 1986

DEBTS, EXTERNAL - NEPAL.
Upadhyaya, Kamal Prasad. External debt and debt servicing in Nepal /. Kathmandu , 1985. ii, 67, [1] p. ; LC Card 86-902874 DDC 336.3/4/095496 19
HJ8777.9 .U62 1985

DEBTS, EXTERNAL - PAKISTAN.
Ahrens, Heinz-Dietmar. Towards reducing the dependence on capital imports . Wiesbaden , 1982. xvi, 337 p. : ISBN 3-515-03853-1 (pbk.) LC Card 86-214363 DDC 338.9549/1 19
HC440.5 .A726 1982

DEBTS, EXTERNAL - PANAMA.
Gómez Pérez, José Antonio, 1950- Desarrollo, crisis, deuda y política económica en Panamá . Panamá , 1985. vii, 168 p. : LC Card 86-122320 DDC 338.97287 19
HC147 .G66 1985 ***NYPL [JLD 86-2899]***

DEBTS, EXTERNAL - PARAGUAY.
Palacios, Eulalio R. Reflexiones sobre economia nacional e internacional /. [S.l.] 1986 (Asunción, Paraguay : Tall. Gráf. de la Impr. Nacional) 333 p. ; LC Card 86-226634
HC222 .P36 1986

DEBTS, EXTERNAL - PARAGUAY - CONGRESSES.
Política internacional, economía e integración /. Asunción del Paraguay [1985] 178 p. ; LC Card 86-122468
HF1523 .P65 1985

DEBTS, EXTERNAL - PERU.
Alva Castro, Luis. Deuda o desarrollo . Lima, Perú , 1987. 127 p. : LC Card 87-403115 DDC 336.3/4/0985 19
HJ8604 .A75 1987

Uriarte, J. Manuel. Transnational banks and the dynamics of the Peruvian foreign debt and inflation /. New York , c1986. x, 195 p. : ISBN 0-03-002599-0 (alk. paper) : LC Card 84-26307 DDC 336.3/4/0985 19
HJ8604 .U75 1985 ***NYPL [JLE 86-1384]***

DEBTS, EXTERNAL - PERU - CONGRESSES.
El Perú frente al capital extranjero . Lima, Perú [1985] xl, 399 p. : LC Card 86-109611 DDC 332.6/73/0985 19
HG5392 .P47 1985 ***NYPL [JLD 87-384]***

DEBTS, EXTERNAL - POLITICAL ASPECTS - ADDRESSES, ESSAYS, LECTURES.
The Politics of international debt /. Ithaca , 1986. 272 p. ; ISBN 0-8014-1911-5 (alk. paper) LC Card 85-48243 DDC 327.1/11 19
HJ8083 .P65 1986 ***NYPL [JLE 86-2405]***

DEBTS, EXTERNAL - PORTUGAL - CONGRESSES.
Seminário sobre Crescimento Económico e Dívida Externa (1982) Seminário sobre Crescimento Económico e Dívida Externa, 18 e 19 de março de 1982 . Lisboa , 1983. 163 p. ; LC Card 85-175819 DDC 336.3/4/09469 19
HJ8744 .S46 1982 ***NYPL [JLG 86-189]***

DEBTS, EXTERNAL - SOCIAL ASPECTS - ECONOMETRIC MODELS.
Coloma C., Fernando. Endeudamiento externo y tasa de descuento social . Santiago, Chile , 1986. 66 leaves : LC Card 87-102066
HJ8083 .C65 1986

DEBTS, EXTERNAL - SOCIAL ASPECTS - EVALUATION - ECONOMETRIC MODELS.
Coloma C., Fernando. Endeudamiento externo y tasa de descuento social . Santiago, Chile , 1986. 66 leaves : LC Card 87-102066
HJ8083 .C65 1986

DEBTS, EXTERNAL - SPAIN.
Albentosa Puche, Luis. El sector exterior en España /. Madrid , c1984. 343 p. : ISBN 84-85719-40-9 LC Card 85-214668 DDC 336.3/4/0946 19
HG3883.S69 A45 1984 ***NYPL [JLC 86-251]***

DEBTS, EXTERNAL - SPAIN - HISTORY.
Martín Martín, Victoriano. Los Rothschild y las minas de Almadén . Madrid , 1980. xiv, 639 p. ; ISBN 84-7196-338-8 LC Card 83-149823
HJ8738 .M37 1980

DEBTS, EXTERNAL - TANZANIA.
Green, Reginald Herbold. The IMF and stabilisation in sub-Saharan Africa . Brighton, England [1986] ii, 70 p. ; LC Card 86-208478 DDC 332.1/52 19
HC800 .G72 1986

DEBTS, EXTERNAL - UNITED STATES.
Solomon, Anthony M. The dollar, debt, and the trade deficit /. New York , 1987. 55 p. ; ISBN 0-8147-7863-1 : LC Card 86-23651 DDC 382.1/7/0973 19
HF3031 .S65 1987

DEBTS, EXTERNAL - VENEZUELA.
Echevarría Salvat, Oscar A., 1935- Deuda--crisis cambiaria . Caracas , 1986. xx, 248 p. : ISBN 980-265-224-5 LC Card 87-400245 DDC 336.3/4/0987 19
HG3883.V4 E28 1986

DEBTS, INTERNATIONAL. see **DEBTS, EXTERNAL.**

DEBTS, PUBLIC - AFRICA, SUB-SAHARAN - CASE STUDIES.
Foreign indebtedness and basic human needs in four African countries . Washington , 1986. ii, 54 p. : LC Card 86-603396 DDC 336.3/435/0967
HC800 .F67 1986

DEBTS, PUBLIC - AUSTRALIA - VICTORIA.
Victorian public sector debt. [Melbourne, Vic.] [1986] vii, 57, [1] p. ; LC Card 87-165135 DDC 336.3/4/09945 19
HJ8857.V53 V53 1986

DEBTS, PUBLIC - CONGRESSES.
Public expenditure . Dublin, Ireland , 1986. 138 p. ; ISBN 0-906980-56-9 (pbk.) : LC Card 86-143826 DDC 336.3/9 19
HJ7461 .P83 1986 ***NYPL [JLD 87-553]***

DEBTS, PUBLIC - DEVELOPING COUNTRIES.
Löschner, Ernst. Souveräne Risken und internationale Verschuldung /. Wien , 1983. 187 p. : ISBN 3-214-06553-X : LC Card 84-152762 DDC 336.3/435/091724 19
HJ8899 .L67 1983 ***NYPL [JLE 86-1553]***

DEBTS, PUBLIC - GERMANY - HISTORY - 19TH CENTURY.
Ahrens, Gerhard, 1939- Staatsverschuldung ohne Ende? /. Hamburg [1984] 37 leaves ; LC Card 85-166341
HJ8650 .A37 1984

DEBTS, PUBLIC - GERMANY, WEST.
Piel, Manfred, 1945- [Staatsverschuldung, Schicksalsfrage der Nation?] Staatsverschuldung, Hintergründe und Probleme /. Stuttgart [1982] 128 p. ; LC Card 83-118137
HJ8654 .P52 1982

DEBTS, PUBLIC - GERMANY (WEST) - BADEN - HISTORY.
Ullmann, Hans-Peter. Staatsschulden und Reformpolitik . Göttingen , c1986. 2 v. (842 p.) ; ISBN 3-525-35398-7 LC Card 86-210338
HJ8655.B38 U55 1986

DEBTS, PUBLIC - GERMANY (WEST) - BAVARIA - HISTORY.
Ullmann, Hans-Peter. Staatsschulden und Reformpolitik . Göttingen , c1986. 2 v. (842 p.) ; ISBN 3-525-35398-7 LC Card 86-210338
HJ8655.B38 U55 1986

DEBTS, PUBLIC - GERMANY (WEST) - ECONOMETRIC MODELS.
Francke, Hans-Hermann. Zinswirkungen der Staatsverschuldung . Berlin , c1984. 138 p. : ISBN 3-428-05727-9 LC Card 86-107232
HJ8654 .F73 1984

DEBTS, PUBLIC - GREECE - HISTORY - 19TH CENTURY.
Andreadēs, Andreas Michaēl, 1876-1935. Historia tōn ethnikōn daneiōn /. Athēna , 1986- v. <1 > ; LC Card 87-112859
HJ8672 .A53 1986

DEBTS, PUBLIC - IRELAND.
FitzGerald, John D. The national debt and economic policy in the medium term /. Dublin , c1986. 62 p. : ISBN 0-7070-0089-0 (pbk.) : LC Card 87-110464 DDC 336.3/4/09417 19
HJ8630.A2 F58 1986

DEBTS, PUBLIC - ITALY - CONGRESSES.
Politica monetaria e debito pubblico . Milano, Italy , c1984. 209 p. : LC Card 85-111306 DDC 332.4/945 19
HJ8678 .P65 1984 ***NYPL [JLD 86-1207]***

DEBTS, PUBLIC - ITALY - HISTORY - 20TH CENTURY.
Confalonieri, Antonio. La politica del debito pubblico in Italia, 1919-1943 /. Milano , Roma , c1986. 2 v. (536 p.) ; ISBN 88-420-2794-4 : LC Card 87-125992
HJ8678 .C64 1986

DEBTS, PUBLIC - MATHEMATICAL MODELS.
Meyer-Cording, Claus, 1953- Die Auswirkungen kreditfinanzierter Staatsausgaben auf das Volkseinkommen . Frankfurt am Main , New York , c1986. v, 256 p. : ISBN 3-8204-9634-3 LC Card 86-204989
HB141.5 .M49 1986

DEBTS, PUBLIC - MEXICO - HISTORY - 19TH CENTURY.
Tenenbaum, Barbara, 1946- The politics of penury . Albuquerque , c1986. xviii, 250 p. ; ISBN 0-8263-0890-2 : LC Card 86-16027 DDC 336.72 19
HJ802 .T46 1986 ***NYPL [JLE 87-482]***

DEBTS, PUBLIC - PERU.
Ycaza Clerc, Mónica de. Política de endeudamiento público interno en el Perú . Lima, Perú , 1985. ii, 23, [39] p. : LC Card 86-223472
HJ8604 .Y33 1985

DEBTS, PUBLIC - SPAIN.
Sala Garrido, Ramón. El mercado de deuda pública /. [Valencia] [1984] 163 p. : ISBN 84-505-0146-6 LC Card 86-213799
HJ8739 .S25 1984

DEBTS, PUBLIC - SPAIN - ANDALUSIA - HISTORY - 19TH CENTURY.
González do Molina Navarro, Manuel. Desamortización, deuda pública y crecimiento económico, Andalucía, 1820/1823 /. Granada , Córdoba :bFundación Paco Natera [1985?] 443 p. : ISBN 84-505-1053-8 LC Card 86-210676
HD779.A4 G66 1985

DEBTS, PUBLIC - SPAIN - HISTORY.
Martín Martín, Victoriano. Los Rothschild y las minas de Almadén . Madrid , 1980. xiv, 639 p. ; ISBN 84-7196-338-8 LC Card 83-149823
HJ8738 .M37 1980

Spain. Tribunal de Cuentas. Memoria relativa a las cuentas generales del estado, 1935-1960 /. Madrid , 1964. 221 p. ; LC Card 85-104523
HJ1244 .S72 1964

DEBTS, PUBLIC - SPAIN - MADRID.
Madrid (Spain). Alcaldía. Situación de crédito, hacienda y presupuesto del Municipio de Madrid en 1907 . Madrid , 1907. viii, 137 p. ; LC Card 85-131486
HJ9528.M38 M34 1907

DEBTS, PUBLIC - SWITZERLAND.
Hablützel, Peter. Staatsverschuldung . Basel , c1984. 96 p. : ISBN 3-7190-0864-9 LC Card

84-159813
HJ8749 .H33 1984

DEBTS, PUBLIC - UNITED STATES.
Infrastructure financing [microform] . [New York] , c1983. 22, 7, 17 p. :
NYPL [*ZT-1565 no.20]

Malkin, Lawrence. The national debt /. New York , c1987. ix, 309 p. ; ISBN 0-8050-0382-7 LC Card 86-27347 DDC 336.3/4/0973 19
HJ8119 .M34 1987

A Nation in debt . Frederick, Md. , c1987. p. cm. ISBN 0-89093-963-2 : LC Card 86-28254 DDC 339.5/23/0973 19
HJ2052 .N36 1987

La Nueva política económica . La Paz, Bolivia , 1986. 57 p. : LC Card 87-403839 DDC 338.984 19
HC182 .N84 1986

Petersen, John E. Innovative capital financing /. Chicago, IL (1313 E. 60th St., Chicago 60637) , 1985. ii, 38 p. : LC Card 86-175368 DDC 336.73 19
HG4936 .P424 1985

The debugger's handbook . McKelvey, James. Belmont, Calif. , c1986. xvi, 138 p. : ISBN 0-534-06432-9 LC Card 85-22628 DDC 005.13/3 19
QA76.73.U25 M34 1986 ***NYPL [JSE 87-65]***

DEBUGGING IN COMPUTER SCIENCE.
McKelvey, James. The debugger's handbook . Belmont, Calif. , c1986. xvi, 138 p. : ISBN 0-534-06432-9 LC Card 85-22628 DDC 005.13/3 19
QA76.73.U25 M34 1986 ***NYPL [JSE 87-65]***

Wray, William C. What every engineer should know about microcomputer systems design and debugging /. New York, N.Y. , c1984. ix, 183 p. : ISBN 0-8247-7160-5 LC Card 83-25204 DDC 001.64 19
QA76.6 .W73 1984 ***NYPL [JSE 86-1632]***

Debunne, Georges. Vakbonden en Europa : verleden en toekomst / Georges Debunne. Leuven : Kritak, c1987. 206 p. ; 21 cm. ISBN 90-6303-228-5 : LC Card 87-157537
1. European Trade Union Confederation - History. 2. Trade-unions - European Economic Community countries - Political activity. I. Title.
HD8372.E86 D43 1987

Debus, Günter. West European Conference on the Psychology of Work and Organization (1985 : Aachen, Germany) The psychology of work and organization . Amsterdam ; New York : xi, 407 p. : ISBN 0-444-70029-3 (U. S.) LC Card 86-8947 DDC 158.7 19
HF5548.8 .W475 1985 ***NYPL [JLE 86-4341]***

Una década de la economía jiennense, 1969-1979 /. Ortega Campos, Pedro. [Jaén] [1984] 122 leaves : ISBN 84-505-0662-X LC Card 86-187312
HC387.J3 O76 1984

Década republicana / Visconde de Ouro Preto ... [et al.]. Nova ed., rev. e atualizada. Brasília, Distrito Federal : Editora Universidade de Brasília : Instituto Nacional do Livro, c1986. 2 v. ; 23 cm. (Coleção Temas brasileiros . v. 59) Includes bibliographies. Vol. 2 by Cândido de Oliveira and others. ISBN 85-23-00062-3 (set) LC Card 86-211423
1. Finance, Public - Brazil - History - 19th century. 2. Education - Brazil - History - 19th century. 3. Freedom of the press - Brazil - History - 19th century. I. Ouro Preto, Affonso Celso de Assis Figueiredo, Visconde de, 1836-1912. II. Series: Coleção Temas brasileiros (Universidade de Brasília. Editora) , v. 59.
HJ923 .D38 1986

Decade of discontent . Gardner, Nick. Oxford, OX, UK , New York, NY, USA , 1987. 236 p. : ISBN 0-631-15307-1 : LC Card 86-30949 DDC 338.941 19
HC256.6 .G36 1987

DECEIT. see **FRAUD.**

Decelles, Paul G. Hester, Edward J. Predicting which disabled employees will return to work . Topeka, Kan. (700 Jackson, 9th floor, Topeka 66603) , c1986. x, 86 p. : LC Card 86-231920 DDC 331.5/9 19
HD7256.U5 H43 1986

Decentraliserad textilindustri .
Andersson-Palmqvist, Lena. Stockholm , 1979/80 [i.e. 1980] 68 p. : ISBN 91-86016-06-7 LC Card 81-138133
HD9865.S87 M373 1980

DECENTRALIZATION. see **DECENTRALIZATION IN GOVERNMENT.**

DECENTRALIZATION IN GOVERNMENT - ARGENTINA - HISTORY.
Quadri Castillo, Mario. La Argentina descentralizada /. [Buenos Aires] , c1986. 236 p. : ISBN 950-23-0322-9 LC Card 87-402244 DDC 330.982/064 19
HC175 .Q33 1986

DECENTRALIZATION IN GOVERNMENT - BRAZIL - CONGRESSES.
Encontro de Trabalho sobre Descentralização dos Serviços Municipais (1983 : Rio de Janeiro, Brazil) Relatório final /. [Rio de Janeiro] [1983] 60 leaves ; LC Card 84-160735
HD4634 .E53 1983

DECENTRALIZATION IN GOVERNMENT - FRANCE.
Laborie, Jean Paul. La politique française d'amenagement du territoire de 1950 à 1985 /. Paris , 1985. 176 p., [8] p. of plates : ISBN 2-11-001488-1(pbk.) : ***NYPL [JLG 87-38]***

Lanier, Lucien. Les entreprises dans la décentralisation /. Paris [1985] xvi, 217 p. ; ISBN 2-86658-028-1 : LC Card 85-217648 DDC 338.944 19
HD3616.F83 L28 1985 ***NYPL [JLD 87-546]***

Lefebvre, André, docteur en droit. Planification et aménagement des communes, des départements et des régions /. Paris , c1985. 335 p. : ISBN 2-7013-0620-5 : LC Card 86-113657 DDC 338.944 19
HT395.F7 L43 1985 ***NYPL [JLD 87-1577]***

DECENTRALIZATION IN GOVERNMENT - FRANCE - AQUITAINE.
Savary, Gilles. Naissance d'une région, rue Esprit-des-lois . [Bordeaux] [1986] 274 p. : ISBN 2-904506-06-5 : LC Card 86-165118
HC277.A6 S28 1986

DECENTRALIZATION IN GOVERNMENT - FRANCE - CONGRESSES.
Energie et décentralisation /. Paris , 1984. 297 p. : ISBN 2-7178-0782-9 : LC Card 84-249613
HD9502.F72 E5334 1984

DECENTRALIZATION IN GOVERNMENT - PERU.
Lizárraga Bobbio, Raúl. Estrategias para la descentralización y el desarrollo regional /. Lima, Perú , c1985. 356 p. : LC Card 86-146658
HT395.P4 L59 1985 ***NYPL [JLD 87-1315]***

DECENTRALIZATION IN GOVERNMENT - SPAIN.
Gimeno Ullastres, Juan Antonio. El nuevo Estado fiscal español . Madrid , 1981. xx, 315 p. : ISBN 84-7214-219-1 LC Card 85-176738
HJ1249.A1 G56 1981

DECENTRALIZATION IN GOVERNMENT - SWEDEN.
Öhman, Berndt, 1940- Kommunerna och sysselsättningspolitiken . [Stockholm] [1985] 212 p. ; ISBN 91-38-08745-6 LC Card 86-114034
HD5803 .O36 1985

DECENTRALIZATION IN GOVERNMENT - VENEZUELA.
Sánchez Meleán, Jorge. Reflexiones para la acción /. [Venezuela?] , 1986. xv, 322 p. : ISBN 980-232-049-8 LC Card 87-134702 DDC 338.987 19
HC237 .S275 1986

DECENTRALIZATION IN MANAGEMENT.
Lash, Scott. The end of organized capitalism /. Madison, Wis. , c1987. 383 p. : ISBN 0-299-11670-0 : LC Card 87-14248 DDC 330.12/2 19
HB501 .L278 1987

Lehr, Jay H., 1936- Orbital management . Lanham, MD [Cambridge, MA] , c1987. xvi, 104 p. : ISBN 0-8191-6264-7 (alk. paper) : LC Card 87-143 DDC 658.4/02 19
HD50 .L44 1987

DECENTRALIZATION IN MANAGEMENT - MATHEMATICAL MODELS.
Meijboom, Bert R., 1957- Planning in decentralized firms . Berlin , New York , c1987. x, 168 p. : ISBN 0-387-17795-7 (U. S. : pbk.) : LC Card 87-9824 DDC 658.4/012 19
HD30.28 .M43 1987

DECENTRALIZATION IN MANAGEMENT - SWEDEN.
Datorer och decentralisering . [Stockholm] [1983] 52 p. : ISBN 91-38-07877-5 LC Card 84-219052
HF5548.2 .D3715 1983

Edgren, Jan, 1940- Divisionalisering och därefter . Stockholm , c1983. 157 p. : ISBN 91-7722-013-7 : LC Card 83-186664
HD50 .E34 1983

DECENTRALIZATION OF GOVERNMENT.
Rosenfeld, Martin. Ausgabeneffekte kommunaler Funktionalreformen . Baden-Baden , 1985. 395 p. : ISBN 3-7890-1077-4 LC Card 86-156503
HJ9493.5.L6 R67 1985

DECENTRALIZATION OF GOVERNMENT - GERMANY (WEST) - LOWER SAXONY.
Rosenfeld, Martin. Ausgabeneffekte kommunaler Funktionalreformen . Baden-Baden , 1985. 395 p. : ISBN 3-7890-1077-4 LC Card 86-156503
HJ9493.5.L6 R67 1985

Decentramento produttivo, lavoro a domicilio e sindacato /. Esposito, Gennaro, 1956- Milano [1983] 109 p. ; LC Card 85-150186
HD2336.I8 E86 1983

DeCenzo, David A. Personnel/human resource management. 3rd ed. / David A. DeCenzo, Stephen P. Robbins. Englewood Cliffs, N.J. : Prentice-Hall, c1988. xvii, 637 p. : ill. ; 25 cm. Second ed. / Stephen P. Robbins. Includes bibliographies and indexes. ISBN 0-13-657198-0 LC Card 87-6983 DDC 658.3 19
1. Personnel management. I. Robbins, Stephen P., 1943-. II. Title.
HF5549 .D396 1988

Deciding to innovate . Dean, James W., 1956- Cambridge, Mass. , c1987. xviii, 165 p. ; ISBN 0-88730-189-4 LC Card 87-17432 DDC 658.5/14 19
HD9725 .D35 1987

DECIMAL SYSTEM - GREAT BRITAIN.
Great Britain. Decimal Currency Board. Conversion of accounting records. London, 1969. [1], 33 p. ISBN 0-11-700407-3 : LC Card 77-489376 DDC 657
HF5635 .G777

Décimo censo general de población y vivienda, 1980. X censo general de población y vivienda, 1980 . México, D.F. , c1985- v. < 1-6 > : ISBN 968-8099-30-9 (v. 1) LC Card 86-226718
HA761.5 1980d

Decimoquinto censo nacional de población y cuarto de vivienda. XV censo nacional de población y IV de vivienda. Bogotá , 1986- v. < 1-5, 7 > : LC Card 87-402787 DDC 304.6/09861/021 19
HA1011.5 1985a

Décimoquinto Censo nacional de Población y cuarto de vivienda--Chile, abril 1982. XV Censo nacional de población y IV de vivienda--Chile, abril 1982. [Santiago] [1985- < 1986]. v. < 1-13 > : LC Card 87-109976
HA994 1982c

Décimoquinto censo nacional de población y quarto de vivienda. XV censo nacional de población y IV de vivienda--Chile, Abril 1982. [Santiago] , < [1983]-[1986]. < v. 3-14; in 15 > : LC Card 87-110013
HA994 1982d

A decision-centred view of environmental planning /. Faludi, Andreas. Oxford [Oxfordshire] , New York , 1987. xiii, 240 p. ; ISBN 0-08-032698-6 : LC Card 87-10414 DDC 333.7 19
HC79.E5 F28 1987

La décision du dividende en Suisse /. Vieli, Mario. [Fribourg] , c1984. 187 p. : ISBN 2-8271-0282-X : LC Card 84-225559 DDC 658.1/55 19
HG4028.D5 V54 1984

The decision maker's guide to applied planning, organization, administration, research, evaluation, information processing and analysis techniques. Dumas, Neil S. [Gainesville] 1970. 191 p. LC Card 75-633083 DDC 016.6584
HD69.D4 D78

DECISION-MAKING - ABSTRACTS.
Dumas, Neil S. The decision maker's guide to applied planning, organization, administration, research, evaluation, information processing and analysis techniques. [Gainesville] 1970. 191 p. LC Card 75-633083 DDC 016.6584
HD69.D4 D78

DECISION-MAKING - CASE STUDIES.
Cases in business decision making /. Chicago , c1987. ix, 102 p. : ISBN 0-03-009108-X (pbk.) LC Card 86-29131 DDC 658.4/033 19
HD30.23 .C375 1987

Nelson, Robert B. Decision point . New York, NY , c1987. x, 278 p. : ISBN 0-8144-7659-7 (pbk.) : LC Card 86-47820 DDC 658.4/03 19
HD30.23 .N44 1987

Schwenk, Charles R. The essence of strategic decision making /. Lexington, Mass. , c1988. xii, 138 p. : ISBN 0-669-13023-0 (alk. paper) LC Card 86-80040 DDC 658.4/03 19
HD30.23 .S39 1988

DECISION-MAKING - CONGRESSES.
Behavioral foundations of economic theory. Rational choice . Chicago , 1987. ix, 332 p. : ISBN 0-226-34857-1 (alk. paper) LC Card 86-27241 DDC 330/.01/9 19
HB74.P8 B44 1987

Large-scale modelling and interactive decision analysis . Berlin , New York , c1986. vii, 362 p. : ISBN 3-540-16785-4 : LC Card 86-20205 DDC 658.4/03 19
T57.6 .L34 1986 ***NYPL [JLM 72-289 v. 273]***

NATO Advanced Study Institute on Intelligent Decision Support in Process Environments (1985 : San Miniato, Italy) Intelligent decision support in process environments /. Berlin , New York , c1986. xv, 524 p. : ISBN 0-387-13922-2 (U. S.) LC Card 86-6742 DDC 658.4/03 19
T57.95 .N37 1985 ***NYPL [JFE 86-4847]***

The Reasoning criminal . New York , c1986. xiv, 246 p. : ISBN 0-387-96272-7 : LC Card 86-1275 DDC 364.3 19
HV6080 .R38 1986 ***NYPL [JLE 86-3522]***

DECISION-MAKING - ECONOMETRIC MODELS.
Eppers, Jürgen. Zur Feinsteuerung ökonomischer Entscheidungsfolgen /. Frankfurt am Main , c1985. 87 p. : ISBN 3-88129-950-5 : LC Card 86-149502
HD30.23 .E66 1985

Decision making for bankers . Kiczek, Paul. Washington, D.C. (1120 Connecticut Ave., NW, Washington 20036) , c1986. 89 p. : LC Card 87-115307 DDC 332.1/2/02855369 19
HG1709 .K53 1986

DECISION MAKING, GROUP.
Brightman, Harvey J. Group problem solving . Atlanta, Ga. , 1987. p. cm. ISBN 0-88406-201-5 : LC Card 87-21876 DDC 658.4/036 19
HD30.29 .B735 1987

DECISION MAKING, GROUP - BULGARIA.
Nikolaev, Ivan. Izrabotvane na kolektivnite resheniia /. Sofiia , 1985. 69 p. ; LC Card 86-174800
HD30.23 .N55 1985

DECISION-MAKING, GROUP - CONGRESSES.
Experimental social dilemmas /. Frankfurt am Main , New York , c1986. vi, 234 p. : ISBN 3-8204-8574-0 (pbk.) : LC Card 86-10307 DDC 302 19
HM132 .E96 1986 ***NYPL [JLD 87-1177]***

DECISION-MAKING, GROUP - MATHEMATICAL MODELS.
Hwang, C. L. (Ching-Lai), 1929- Group decision making under multiple criteria . Berlin , New York , c1987. xi, 400 p. : ISBN 0-387-17177-0 (U. S. : pbk.) : LC Card 86-29729 DDC 658.4/036 19
HD30.23 .H87 1987

Kim, Ki Hang. Team theory /. Chichester , New York , 1987. viii, 246 p. ; ISBN 0-7458-0154-4 : LC Card 87-4137 DDC 658.4/036 19
HD30.23 .K396 1987

DECISION-MAKING - HANDBOOKS, MANUALS, ETC.
Wells, Richard C. The right choice . New York, N.Y., U. S.A. , c1985. viii, 178 p. : ISBN 0-86604-198-2 (pbk.) LC Card 86-201105 DDC 658.4/033 19
HD31 .W457 1985

Decision making in complex times . Burke, Richard C. Hamilton, Ont. , 1984. xii, 185 p. : ISBN 0-920212-27-1 (pbk.) LC Card 85-154342 DDC 658.4/08 19
HD60 .B86 1984 ***NYPL [JLD 86-2720]***

Decision-making in Indian economy . Venkateswaran, R. J. Bombay , 1986. vii, 199 p. ; LC Card 86-902861 DDC 338.954 19
HC435.2 .V457 1986

Decision-making in multinational enterprises . Ghertman, Michel. Geneva , 1984. v, 62 p. : ISBN 92-2-103831-9 (pbk.) : LC Card 86-213603 DDC 658.4/03 19
HD62.4 .G48 1984

Decision-making in the Soviet energy industry : selected papers with analysis / David Katsman ... [et al.] ; with a foreword by Judith Record McKinney ; edited by Katherine E. Young ; translated by Vladimir Talmy. Falls Church, VA (7700 Leesburg Pike, #250, Falls Church 22043) : Delphic Associates, c1986. ix, 166 leaves ; 28 cm. "October, 1986." Includes bibliographies. LC Card 87-401592 DDC 333.79/0947 19
1. Energy industries - Soviet Union - Management. 2. Energy policy - Soviet Union. 3. Industrial management - Soviet Union - Decision making. I. Katsman, David. II. Young, Katherine E. III. Delphic Associates.
HD9502.S652 D43 1986

DECISION-MAKING, JUDICIAL. see **JUDICIAL PROCESS.**

DECISION-MAKING - MATHEMATICAL MODELS.
Arrow, Kenneth Joseph, 1921- Social choice and multicriterion decision-making /. Cambridge, Mass. , c1986. vii, 127 p. : ISBN 0-262-01087-9 LC Card 85-19913 DDC 302/.13 19
HM271 .A73 1986 ***NYPL [JLD 86-3628]***

Ballot, Michael. Decision-making models in production & operations management /. Malabar, Fla. , 1986. xi, 295 p. : ISBN 0-89874-825-9 LC Card 84-29740 DDC 658.5/036 19
TS155 .B2435 1984 ***NYPL [JLF 86-1851]***

Bartels, Sibylle, 1955- Entwicklung und Beurteilung von Aggregationsstrategien für lineare Entscheidungsmodelle /. Frankfurt am Main , New York , c1986. xv, 265 p. : ISBN 3-8204-9190-2 LC Card 86-146466
HD30.25 .B365 1986

Burn, Janice. Information analysis /. London , 1987. x, 260 p. : ISBN 0-948825-50-2 (pbk.) : LC Card 87-166130 DDC 658.4/038 19
HD30.35 .B87 1987

Fischer, Thomas. Kontrolltheoretische Entscheidungsmodelle . Berlin , c1982. x, 343 p. : ISBN 3-428-05111-4 :
NYPL [JLE 86-3084]

Kim, Ki Hang. Team theory /. Chichester , New York , 1987. viii, 246 p. ; ISBN 0-7458-0154-4 : LC Card 87-4137 DDC 658.4/036 19
HD30.23 .K396 1987

Mälich, Wolfgang. Informationstheoretische Lösung ausgewählter Entscheidungsprobleme /. Göttingen , c1984. vi, 269 p. : ISBN 3-525-12314-0 LC Card 84-162246
HD30.23 .M345 1984

Management decision support systems using fuzzy sets and possibility theory /. Köln , c1985. xi, 350 p. : ISBN 3-88585-143-1 (pbk.) LC Card 85-217558 DDC 658.4/033 19
HD30.23 .M353 1985 ***NYPL [JLE 86-4562]***

Meijboom, Bert R., 1957- Planning in decentralized firms . Berlin , New York , c1987. x, 168 p. : ISBN 0-387-17795-7 (U. S. : pbk.) : LC Card 87-9824 DDC 658.4/012 19
HD30.28 .M43 1987

Mors, Matthias. Planung und Erwartungsbildung in der Investitionsentscheidung . Frankfurt am Main , c1983. 190 p. : ISBN 3-88129-619-0 LC Card 83-174677
HG4028.C4 M65 1983

Pinney, William E., 1941- Management science . New York , c1987. xvii, 620 p. : ISBN 0-06-045229-3 LC Card 86-22933 DDC 658.4/033 19
HD30.25 .P56 1987

Roy, B. (Bernard), 1934- Méthodologie multicritère d'aide à la décision /. Paris , c1985. xxii, 423 p. : ISBN 2-7178-0901-5 : LC Card 86-166619
HD30.25 .R68 1985

Sengupta, Jatikumar. Optimal decisions under uncertainty . Berlin , New York , 1985. 286 p. ; ISBN 0-387-15032-3 (U. S.) LC Card 84-26683 DDC 658.4/033 19
HD30.23 .S46 1985 ***NYPL [JLE 86-4652]***

Decision-making models in production & operations management /. Ballot, Michael. Malabar, Fla. , 1986. xi, 295 p. : ISBN 0-89874-825-9 LC Card 84-29740 DDC 658.5/036 19
TS155 .B2435 1984 ***NYPL [JLF 86-1851]***

Decision-making models in production and operations management. Ballot, Michael. Decision-making models in production & operations management /. Malabar, Fla. , 1986. xi, 295 p. : ISBN 0-89874-825-9 LC Card 84-29740 DDC 658.5/036 19
TS155 .B2435 1984 ***NYPL [JLF 86-1851]***

DECISION-MAKING - RESEARCH - ADDRESSES, ESSAYS, LECTURES.
Der Praktische Nutzen empirischer Forschung /. Tübingen , 1981. viii, 324 p. ; ISBN 3-16-344392-3 : LC Card 81-197515 DDC 658.4/03 19
HD30.4 .P7 1981 ***NYPL [JLE 86-1360]***

DECISION-MAKING - SIMULATION METHODS.
Simulation als betriebliche Entscheidungshilfe . Berlin , New York , 1987. xi, 282 p. : ISBN 0-387-17353-6 LC Card 87-121884 DDC 658.4/0352 19
HD30.23 .S56 1987

Decision models for California turkey growers /. Eidman, Vernon R., 1936- Berkeley, Calif. [1968] ii, 80 p. : LC Card 87-401009 DDC 338.1/09794 s 636.5/92/0068 19
HD1407 .C27 no. 21 HD9437.U63C3

Decision point . Nelson, Robert B. New York, NY , c1987. x, 278 p. : ISBN 0-8144-7659-7 (pbk.) : LC Card 86-47820 DDC 658.4/03 19
HD30.23 .N44 1987

DECISION PROCESSES. see **DECISION-MAKING.**

DECISION (PSYCHOLOGY) see **DECISION-MAKING.**

Decision support and expert systems . Turban, Efraim. New York , London , c1988. xxi, 697 p. : ISBN 0-02-421650-X LC Card 87-23911 DDC 658.4/03 19
HD30.2 .T87 1988

DECISION SUPPORT SYSTEMS.
Gessford, John Evans. Modern information systems . Reading, Mass. , c1980. xii, 512 p. : ISBN 0-201-03099-3 : LC Card 78-74684 DDC 658/.05/4
HF5548.2 .G48 ***NYPL [JLE 80-1913]***

Turban, Efraim. Decision support and expert systems . New York , London , c1988. xxi, 697 p. : ISBN 0-02-421650-X LC Card 87-23911 DDC 658.4/03 19
HD30.2 .T87 1988

Decision synthesis . Watson, Stephen R. Cambridge [Cambridgeshire] , New York , 1987. xvi, 299 p. : ISBN 0-521-32569-2 LC Card 87-10270 DDC 658.4/03 19
HD30.23 .W38 1987

Decision-theoretic analysis of envisaged income tax reforms for FRG and U. S. /. Bamberg, Günter, 1940- [Augsburg] [1986] 11 leaves : LC Card 87-101962 DDC 336.24/0724 19
HJ4719 .B35 1986

Decisiones de precio en alta inflación /. Frenkel, Roberto. Buenos Aires, Argentina , 1979. 58 p. ; LC Card 80-125798 DDC 332.4/15 19
HF5416.5 .F73 ***NYPL [JLD 86-2701]***

Decisionmakers bookshelf.
Newman, Marie Mastin. The vital link . Washington, DC , c1986. vii, 48 p. : ISBN 0-931032-21-0 (pbk.) LC Card 86-200991

DDC 363.6/2/0973 19
HD9685.U5 N493 1986

DECK-CARGO. see **SHIPS - CARGO.**

Deck, Steven A. Nevaer, Louis E. V. Corporate financial planning and management in a deficit economy /. New York , 1987. 171 p. : ISBN 0-89930-202-5 (lib. bdg. : alk. paper) LC Card 86-25582 DDC 658.1/145 19
HG4063 .N48 1987

Decker, Hedwig. Standortverlagerungen der Industrie in der Region München / von Hedwig Decker. Kallmünz/Regensburg : M. Lassleben, 1984. xxvi, 92 p. : ill., maps ; 30 cm. (Münchner Studien zur Sozial- und Wirtschaftsgeographie. Bd. 25) Originally presented as the author's thesis (doctoral)--Universität München, 1984. Summaries in English, French, and Russian. Bibliography: p. xiv-xx. Eight folded maps in pocket. ISBN 3-7847-6525-4 LC Card 86-136483 DDC 304.2/0943 s 338.6/042/094336 19
1. Munich (Germany) - Industries - Location. I. Title. II. Series.
HC281 .M8 Bd. 25 HC289.M86

Le déclin des marchands privilégiés en Corée . Yu, Wŏn-dong. [Paris] , 1984. 104 p. : ISBN 2-905358-03-3 : LC Card 85-131336
HF3830.5 .Y78 1984

The decline of American steel . Tiffany, Paul A. New York , 1988. p. cm. ISBN 0-19-504382-0 (alk. paper) LC Card 87-5782 DDC 338.4/7669142/0973 19
HD9515 .T54 1988

The decline of organized labor in the United States /. Goldfield, Michael. Chicago , 1987. xv, 294 p. : ISBN 0-226-30102-8 LC Card 86-24890 DDC 331.88/0973 19
HD6508 .G683 1987

The Decline of the British economy / [edited by] Bernard Elbaum and William Lazonick. Oxford [Oxfordshire] : Clarendon Press ; New York : Oxford University Press, 1987, c1986. vii, 310 p. ; 24 cm. Includes bibliographies and index. ISBN 0-19-877281-5 (pbk.) : LC Card 87-5479 DDC 330.941/08 19
1. Great Britain - Economic conditions - 19th century. 2. Great Britain - Economic conditions - 20th century. 3. Great Britain - Economic policy. I. Elbaum, Bernard. II. Lazonick, William.
HC255 .D43 1987

The decline of the Russian peasant household /. Shinn, William T., 1936- New York , 1987. xvii, 122 p. ; ISBN 0-275-92767-9 (alk. paper) LC Card 87-2554 DDC 338.1/0947 19
HD1992 .S4735 1987

Décolonisations et nouvelles dépendances : modèles et contre-modèles idéologiques et culturels dans le Tiers-Monde : textes / réunis par Catherine Coquery-Vidrovitch & Alain Forest. [Lille] : Presses universitaires de Lille, c1986. 282 p. : ill. ; 24 cm. (Economies et sociétés) Includes bibliographical references. ISBN 2-85939-287-4 : LC Card 87-104133
1. Developing countries - Economic conditions. 2. Decolonization - Developing countries. 3. Developing countries - Politics and government. 4. Developing countries - Social conditions. 5. Developing countries - Dependency on foreign countries. I. Coquery-Vidrovitch, Catherine. II. Forest, Alain. III. Series: Economies et sociétés (Lille, France).
HC59.7 .D354 1986

DECOLONIZATION.
Nweihed, Kaldone G., 1929- Bolívar y el Tercer Mundo . Caracas, Venezuela , c1984. 400 p. : ISBN 84-499-7056-3 LC Card 85-136718
F2235.3 .N98 1984 ***NYPL [JFE 86-1176]***

DECOLONIZATION - DEVELOPING COUNTRIES.
Décolonisations et nouvelles dépendances . [Lille] , c1986. 282 p. : ISBN 2-85939-287-4 : LC Card 87-104133
HC59.7 .D354 1986

Protz, Michael. Administrative Zusammenarbeit in der Entwicklungspolitik . Speyer , 1982. ix, 382, 2 p. ; LC Card 86-218043
HC60 .P77 1982

DeConcini, Dennis.
La déconnexion, pour sortir du système mondial /. Amin, Samir. Paris , 1986, c1985. 333 p. : ISBN 2-7071-1588-6 : LC Card 86-219988
HF1413 .A45 1986

Decouvrez la Province du Nord-Ouest. Discover the North West of Cameroon . [Bamenda? , 1984] 197 p., [2] p. of plates : LC Card 87-101117 DDC 330.967/11204 19
HC995.Z7 N673 1984

Decyzje w organizacjach gospodarczych /. Sterniczuk, Henryk. Warszawa , 1980. 167 p. ; ISBN 83-208-0052-8 LC Card 81-109564
HD30.23 .S726 1980

Dedijer, Stevan. Intelligence for economic development . Leamington Spa, [Warwickshire] ; New York : xiii, 264 p. : ISBN 0-85496-520-3 : LC Card 86-32250 DDC 025/.063389 19
HD76.2 .I58 1987

The deductibility of state and local taxes . Dilger, Robert Jay, 1954- Washington, D.C. [1985] 1 v. (various pagings) ; ISBN 0-933729-02-2 (pbk.) : LC Card 85-155605 DDC 336.24/216 19
HJ4653.D4 D55 1985 ***NYPL [JLF 86-412]***

Dee, Philippa S. Financial markets and economic development : the economics and politics of Korean financial reform / Philippa S. Dee. Tübingen : Mohr, c1986. ix, 131 p. ; 24 cm. (Kieler Studien, 0340-6989 . 198) Bibliography: p. 124-[131] ISBN 3-16-345086-5 LC Card 86-190926 DDC 338.9519/5 19
1. Korea (South) - Economic policy - 1960-. 2. Korea (South) - Economic conditions - 1960-. 3. Finance - Korea (South). I. Title. II. Series.
HC467 .D44 1986

Deerberg, Karl-Heinrich. Intrasektorale Einkommensstreuung in der Landwirtschaft /. Münster-Hiltrup , 1983. 177 p. : ISBN 3-7843-0281-5 : LC Card 83-236007
HD1955 .I57 1983

DEERE & COMPANY - HISTORY.
Nelson, Selmer, 1917- Grossenburg's fifty years with John Deere /. Freeman, S.D. , c1987. viii, 167 p. : LC Card 87-80826 DDC 338.7/681763/0978361 19
HD9486.U6 G766 1987

Deere, Carmen Diana.
The peasantry in political economy : trends of the 1980s / Carmen Diana Deere. [Amherst, MA] : International Area Studies Program, University of Massachusetts at Amherst, 1987. 76 p. ; 22 cm. (Occasional papers / University of Massachusetts, Amherst, Latin American Studies Program . no. 19) Bibliography: p. 68-76. LC Card 87-404080 DDC 305.5/63 19
1. Peasantry - Latin America. 2. Agriculture - Economic aspects - Latin America. 3. Latin America - Economic policy. I. Series: Occasional papers series (University of Massachusetts at Amherst. Program in Latin American Studies) , no. 19. II. Title.
HD1531.L3 D44 1987

Transition and development . New York, NY [Berkeley, Calif.] , c1986. 352 p. ; ISBN 0-85345-705-0 (pbk.) : LC Card 86-12579 DDC 335.43/09172/4 19
HX517.8 .T73 1986 ***NYPL [JLD 86-3907]***

DEFAULT (FINANCE) - DEVELOPING COUNTRIES.
Brimmer, Andrew F. The world banking system . New York , 1985. 59 p. ; ISBN 0-8147-1068-9 : LC Card 85-5115 DDC 332.1/5 19
HG3881 .B677 1985 ***NYPL [JLD 86-2189]***

Defence, security, and development / edited by Saadet Deger and Robert West. New York : St. Martin's Press, 1987. xiii, 219 p. : ill. ; 23 cm. Bibliography: p. [207]-214. Includes indexes. CONTENTS. - Defence expenditure, national security, and economic development in the Third World / Saadet Deger and Robert L. West -- Improved measures of the defence burden in developing countries / Robert L. West -- Security expenditure / Nicole Ball -- Capital-labour substitution in defence provision / Ron Smith, Anthony Humm, and Jacques Fontanel -- Defence, entitlement, and development / Saadet Deger and Somnath Sen -- Security and development in the Third World / W. Scott Thompson -- The creative of an international disarmament fund for development / Jacques Fontanel and Ron Smith -- The causes of military expenditure in developing countries / Alfred Maizels and Machiko K. Nissanke -- National security, domestic resource constraints, and elite choices in the Third World / Robert L. Rothstein -- Current trends in arms transfers / Michael Brzoska -- Arms trade and the Third World / Arcadi Oliveres -- Arms transfer control / Herbert Wulf. ISBN 0-312-01243-8 : LC Card 87-12129 DDC 338.4/76234/091724 19
1. Developing countries - National security - Economic aspects. 2. Disarmament - Economic aspects - Developing countries. 3. Munitions - Developing countries. I. Deger, Saadet, 1950-. II. West, Robert, 1925-.
HC59.72.D4 D436 1987

DEFENSE CONTRACTS - UNITED STATES.
Coalition of Northeast Governors. Policy Research Center. A case of inequity [microform] . [New York] , 1977. 39 p. ;
NYPL [*ZT-1564 no.21]

DEFENSE (LAW) see **ACTIONS AND DEFENSES.**

Defense Marketing Services, inc.
Aerospace markets /. Greenwich, CT, U. S.A. (100 Northfield St., Greenwich 06830) , c1987. 1 v. (various pagings) : LC Card 87-156000 DDC 380.1/456291 19
HD9711.5.A2 A37 1987

Precision guided munitions . Greenwich, CT., U. S.A. (P.O. Box 4585, Greenwich 06830) , c1986. 606, 4 p. ; LC Card 86-207047 DDC 380.1/456234 19
HD9744.P732 P74 1986

Top 500 RDT&E companies /. Greenwich, CT, U. S.A. (100 Northfield St., Greenwich 06830) , c1986. 721, [50] p. : LC Card 87-120786 DDC 338.7/6234/02573 19
HD9743.U6 T66 1986

DEFENSES. see **INDUSTRIAL MOBILIZATION.**

DEFERRED COMPENSATION - UNITED STATES.
Dunn, Pat. Script for an employee flipchart presentation titled The 401(k) plan . Chicago, Ill. , c1986. [40] p. : ISBN 0-88462-610-5 (pbk.) LC Card 86-201609 DDC 331.25/5 19
HG1660.U5 D86 1986

DEFERRED TAX.
Edwards, J. S. S. (Jeremy S. S.) The economic analysis of accounting profitability /. Oxford , New York , 1987. 133 p. : ISBN 0-19-877241-6 : LC Card 87-5575 DDC 657/.95 19
HF5686.C7 E34 1987

DEFICIENCY APPROPRIATIONS BILLS. see **UNITED STATES - APPROPRIATIONS AND EXPENDITURES.**

DEFICIT FINANCING.
Wenzel, Heinz-Dieter. Defizitfinanzierung als Instrument einer zielorientierten Finanzpolitik . Baden-Baden , 1983. 249 p. : ISBN 3-7890-0869-9 : LC Card 83-240582
HJ8019 .W45 1983

DEFICIT FINANCING - CANADA.
Bellan, Ruben C., 1918- The unnecessary evil . Toronto, Ont. , c1986. 173 p. : ISBN 0-7710-1153-9 : LC Card 86-222233 DDC 331.13/7971 19
HD5728 .B43 1986

DEFICIT FINANCING - EUROPE - HISTORY - 18TH CENTURY.
Stolleis, Michael, 1941- Pecunia nervus rerum . Frankfurt am Main , c1983. 184 p. ; ISBN 3-465-01590-8 (Deut Bibl.) LC Card 83-183704
HJ1000 .S76 1983

DEFICIT FINANCING - GERMANY - HISTORY - 19TH CENTURY.
Ahrens, Gerhard, 1939- Staatsverschuldung ohne Ende? /. Hamburg [1984] 37 leaves ; LC Card 85-166341
HJ8650 .A37 1984

DEFICIT FINANCING - MATHEMATICAL MODELS.
Weigert, Edmund. Defizitfinanzierte Fiskalpolitik in einer kleinen offenen Volkswirtschaft bei flexiblen Wechselkursen . Krefeld , 1987, c1986. iii, 211 p. ; ISBN 3-88358-071-6 LC Card 87-146660 DDC 339.5/2/0724 19
HJ161 .W44 1987

DEFICIT FINANCING - UNITED STATES.
Economic choices 1987 /. Washington, D.C. , 1986. xii, 126 p. ; ISBN 0-8157-1040-2 LC Card 85-48278 ***NYPL [JLE 86-2737]***

Reducing the federal deficit . Washington, D.C. , 1982. 1 v. (various pagings) :
NYPL [JLF 86-1219]

DEFICIT FINANCING - UNITED STATES - HISTORY.
Savage, James D., 1951- Balanced budgets and American politics /. Ithaca, N.Y. , c1988. p. cm. ISBN 0-8014-2047-4 LC Card 87-25061 DDC 339.5/23/0973 19
HJ2050 .S28 1988

The deficit problem in perspective /. Cebula, Richard J. Lexington, Mass. , c1987. x, 106 p. : ISBN 0-669-14303-0 (pbk. : alk. paper) LC Card 86-45792 DDC 339.5/23/0973 19
HJ2052 .C42 1987

DEFICIT SPENDING. see **DEFICIT FINANCING.**

Deficits, taxes, and economic adjustments. Contemporary economic problems . Washington, D.C. , c1987. 332 p. : ISBN 0-8447-3621-X (alk. paper) LC Card 87-1395 DDC 330.973/0927 19
HC106.8 .C665 1987

Definicje pojęć ekonomicznych stosowanych w planowaniu i statystyce . (zbiór 9) Definicje z zakresu inwestycji . Warszawa , 1977. 42 p. ; LC Card 81-172624
HG4528 .D44 1977

Definicje z zakresu inwestycji : według stanu prawnego w dniu 31 III 1977 r. Warszawa : Zarząd Wydawn. Statystycznych i Druk., 1977. 42 p. ; 24 cm. (Definicje pojęć ekonomicznych stosowanych w planowaniu i statystyce . zbiór 9) Zeszyty metodyczne ; nr 23 At head of title: Główny Urząd Statystyczny. Bibliography: p. 38-[41] LC Card 81-172624
1. Investments - Terminology. I. Poland. Główny Urząd Statystyczny. II. Series.
HG4528 .D44 1977

Defizitfinanzierte Fiskalpolitik in einer kleinen offenen Volkswirtschaft bei flexiblen Wechselkursen . Weigert, Edmund. Krefeld , 1987, c1986. iii, 211 p. ; ISBN 3-88358-071-6 LC Card 87-146660 DDC 339.5/2/0724 19
HJ161 .W44 1987

Defizitfinanzierung als Instrument einer zielorientierten Finanzpolitik . Wenzel, Heinz-Dieter. Baden-Baden , 1983. 249 p. : ISBN 3-7890-0869-9 : LC Card 83-240582
HJ8019 .W45 1983

DEFLATION (FINANCE) - UNITED STATES.
Wanniski, Jude, 1936- The political economy in perspective [microform] . Morristown, N.J. (66 Macculloch Ave., Morristown 07960) [1983] 5 p. ; LC Card 83-239685 DDC 332.4/973 19
HG540 .W36 1983 ***NYPL [*ZT-1708 no.21]***

Defliese, Philip L. Montgomery, Robert Hiester, 1872-1953. [Auditing.] Montgomery's Auditing. New York , c1987. xxv, 896 p. : ISBN 0-471-85423-9 LC Card 86-28938 DDC 657/.45 19
HF5667 .M7 1987

Defoe and economics . Dijkstra, Bram. New York , 1987. xvi, 247 p. ; ISBN 0-312-00535-0 : LC Card 86-29691 DDC 330.1 19
HB103.D4 D56 1987

DEFOE, DANIEL, 1661?-1731 - VIEWS ON ECONOMICS.
Dijkstra, Bram. Defoe and economics . New York , 1987. xvi, 247 p. ; ISBN 0-312-00535-0 : LC Card 86-29691 DDC 330.1 19
HB103.D4 D56 1987

Degen, Bernard, 1952- Das Basel der andern : Geschichte der Basler Gewerkschaftsbewegung / Bernard Degen ; herausgegeben vom Basler Gewerkschaftsbund anlässlich seines hundertjährigen Bestehens.1. Aufl. Basel : Z-Verlag, 1986. 199 p. : ill. ; 21 cm. Bibliography: p. 192-197. ISBN 3-85990-073-6 LC Card 87-137650 DDC 331.88/09494/3 19
1. Trade-unions - Switzerland - Basel - History. 2. Labor and laboring classes - Switzerland -Basel - History. I. Basler Gewerkschaftsbund. II. Title.
HD6775.B29 D44 1986

Degen, Clara. Communicators' guide to marketing /. New York , c1987. xii, 226 p. : ISBN 0-582-28645-X LC Card 86-27787 DDC 658.8 19
HF5415.123 .C66 1987

Degen, Robert A. The American monetary system : a concise survey of its evolution since 1896 / Robert A. Degen. Lexington, Mass. : Lexington Books, c1987. x, 242 p. ; 24 cm. Bibliography: p. [233]-237. Includes index. ISBN 0-669-15827-5 (alk. paper) LC Card 86-46363 DDC 332.4/973 19
1. Money - United States - History. 2. Monetary policy - United States - History. 3. Banks and banking - United States - History. I. Title.
HG501 .D44 1987

Deger, Saadet, 1950- Defence, security, and development /. New York , 1987. xiii, 219 p. : ISBN 0-312-01243-8 : LC Card 87-12129 DDC 338.4/76234/091724 19
HC59.72.D4 D436 1987

DeGooyer, Janice. Women's work, undervalued, underpaid : a report on pay equity [microform] / written by Janice DeGooyer, Laurie Westley ; edited by Sally Steenland.Rev. April 1984. Washington, D.C. : National Commission on Working Women, 1984, c1982. 27, [4] leaves : 29 cm. Bibliography: leaves [2-3]. Microfilm. New York : New York Public Library, 1986. 1 microfilm reel ; 35 mm. (MN *ZZ-26,374)
1. Equal pay for equal work - United States. 2. Wages - Women - United States. 3. Women - Employment - United States. I. Westley, Laurie A. II. Steenland, Sally. III. National Commission on Working Women. IV. Title. ***NYPL [*ZT-1708 no.39]***

DeGroh, Teresa. Standards for self-service storage facilities / Teresa deGroh, Rachel German. Chicago, IL (1313 E. 60th St., Chicago 60637) : American Planning Association, c1986. 22 p. : ill. ; 28 cm. (Report / American Planning Association, Planning Advisory Service . no. 396) Cover title. LC Card 86-227124 DDC 658.7/85 19
1. Self-service storage facilities - Standards - United States. I. German, Rachel. II. Series: Report / American Planning Association, Planning Advisory Service , no. 396. III. Title.
HF5487 .D44 1986

Degrotte, Jean-André, 1947- L'économie bafouée, ou, Les hommes politiques au créneau / Jean-André Degrotte, Emmanuel Euverte. Paris : Editions Entente, c1985. 130, [11] p. : ill. ; 20 cm. (Vivre demain, 0336-7959) Bibliography: p. 127-[131] ISBN 2-7266-0074-3 LC Card 85-230533
1. Hours of labor. 2. Unemployment. I. Euverte, Emmanuel, 1948-. II. Title. III. Title: Economie bafouée.
HD5106 .D42 1985

Dehlin, Dale R. North Dakota employment and wages, 1984 /. Bismarck, N.D. (1000 E. Divide, Bismarck 58501) [1985] [3], 13, 13 leaves ; LC Card 86-623005 DDC 331.12/5/09784021 19
HD5725.N84 N73 1985

Dehmel, Alexander. Die Struktur der internationalen Liquiditätskrise seit dem ersten Ölpreisschub, 1973/1974 : Ursachen, Schuldner- und Gläubigerstruktur, Lösungsansätze / Alexander Dehmel. Frankfurt am Main ; New York : P. Lang, c1985. x, 221 p. : ill. ; 21 cm. (Europäische Hochschulschriften. Reihe V, Volks- und Betriebswirtschaft, 0531-7339 . Bd. 676 = vol. 676 = vol. 676) Originally presented as the author's thesis (doctoral)--Johann Wolfgang Goethe-Universität Frankfurt am Main. Bibliography: p. 207-221. ISBN 3-8204-8941-X LC Card 86-108628
1. Liquidity (Economics). 2. Petroleum products - Prices. 3. International finance. 4. Debts, External. 5. Economic history - 1971-. I. Series: Europäische Hochschulschriften. Reihe V, Volks- und Betriebswirtschaft , Bd. 676. II. Title.
HG178 .D44 1985

Dehn, Christoph H. Cleto, Romeo B. The Ilocos and Cordillera provinces . Baguio City [Philippines] , Manila [1986] xvii, 265 p. : LC Card 87-111697 DDC 330.9599/1 19
HC457.L8 C56 1986

Deiatel'nost' partiĭnykh organizatsiĭ po razvitiiu promyshlennosti Urala v period razvitogo sotsializma : mezhvuzovskiĭ sbornik nauchnykh trudov / [redaktsionnaia kollegiia V.P. Lanin ... et al.]. Perm' : Permskiĭ gos. universitet, 1984. 96 p. ; 22 cm. At head of title: Ministerstvo vysshego i srednego spetsial'nogo obrazovaniia RSFSR. Permskiĭ ordena Trudovogo Krasnogo Znameni gosudarstvennyĭ universitet imeni A.M. Gor'kogo. Includes bibliographical references. LC Card 86-181271
1. Ural Mountains Region (R.S.F.S.R.) - Industries. 2. Ural Mountains Region (R.S.F.S.R.) - Economic policy. I. Lanin, V. P. (Vladimir Petrovich). II. Permskiĭ gosudarstvennyĭ universitet imeni A.M. Gor'kogo.
HC337.R852 U734 1984

Deimer, Klaus. Berücksichtigung von Verbraucherinteressen bei staatlichen Anbietern /. Frankfurt , New York , c1984. x, 241 p. : ISBN 3-593-33291-4 LC Card 84-147664
HC290.5.C63 B47 1984

Deindustrialization in Chile /. Gatica, Jaime. Boulder , 1988. p. cm. ISBN 0-8133-7392-1 : LC Card 86-32513 DDC 338.983 19
HD9734.C52 G37 1988

Deĭneko, O. A. (Oleg Aleksandrovich) Sovremennyĭ organizator proizvodstva / O.A. Deĭneko. Moskva : Ėkonomika, 1984. 172, [2] p. : ill. ; 20 cm. Bibliography: p. 170-[173] LC Card 85-112451
1. Executives - Soviet Union. 2. Industrial management - Soviet Union. I. Title.
HD38.25.S65 D45 1984

Deiss, Joseph. Economie politique et politique économique de la Suisse / Joseph Deiss. Fribourg : Fragnière, c1979. 412 p. : ill. ; 24 cm. (Collection Vie et économie) Bibliography: p. 406. Includes index. LC Card 86-673870
1. Switzerland - Economic conditions - 1945-. 2. Switzerland - Economic policy. I. Title. II. Series.
HC397 .D387x 1979

Deissmann, Gerhard. Wachsende Städte an der Unterweser . Bremen , 1965. xii, 243 p., [7] folded leaves of plates : LC Card 85-122713
HC289.B7 W33 1965

Deĭstvena organizatorska i ideĭno-vŭzpitatelna rabota za izpŭlnenie resheniiata na Fevruarskiia plenum na TSK na BKP / [sŭstavitel Iliia Borisov]. Vedomstveno izd. Vratsa : Okrŭzhen kom-t na BKP--Vratsa, 1985. 56 p. : ill. ; 20 cm. LC Card 86-172762
1. Bulgaria - Economic policy - 1944-. 2. Bulgaria - Politics and government - 1944-. I. Borisov, Iliia. II. Okrŭzhen komitet na BKP--Vratsa.
HC403 .D45 1985

Dejene Aredo. Economic study of the establishment of sorghum mill and dehuller in Ethiopia : final research report : (draft) / by Dejene Aredo. [Addis Ababa?] : Institute of Development Research, Addis Ababa University, [1986] 37 leaves ; 30 cm. "October 1986." Includes bibliographical references. LC Card 87-980144 DDC 338.1/73174/0963 19
1. Sorghum industry - Ethiopia. I. Title.
HD9049.S6 E83 1986

Deka, P. (Phani), 1945- Industrial development in north east India /. Guwahati , 1987. xx, 179 p. : LC Card 87-902151 DDC 338.0954/1 19
HC437.N57 I55 1987

Dekaexaselida tēs Komep. Hexē hapla mathēmata . Thessalonikē , 1945. 32, 16 p. ; LC Card 87-122267
HB501 .H475 1945

Del actor racional al cesto de basura . Kelly de Escobar, Janet. Caracas, Venezuela , c1983. 31 p., 3 leaves : ISBN 980-217-003-8 LC Card 86-201788
HD30.23 .K363 1983

Dél-alföldi évszázadok, 0237-4587.
Blazovich, László. A Körös-Tisza-Maros köz középkori településrendje /. Békéscsaba , Szeged , 1985. 207 p., [9] folded leaves of plates : ISBN 963-01-6828-6 LC Card 87-408571
HD640.5.Z8 G743 1985

Del Boca, Frances K. The Social psychology of female-male relations . Orlando , 1986. xvi, 351 p. ; ISBN 0-12-065280-3 (alk. paper) LC Card 85-9138 DDC 305.3 19
HM132 .S569 1986 ***NYPL [JLE 86-1746]***

Del cacao al colón . Daremblum, Jaime. San José, Costa Rica [1977?- v. <1- > ; LC Card 87-402194 DDC 332.4/97286 19
HG682 .D37 1977

Del caos al orden . Yepes C., Alfonso. [S.l. , 1986] ([S.l.] : Editorial Nomos) 239 p., [1] leaf of plates : LC Card 87-400255 DDC 331.1/1/09861 19
HD5757.A6 Y46 1986

Del Casale, Mary. Ladbrook, Denis A. Disadvantaged youth in an isolated region . [Pilbara, W.A.] [1985] ix, 125 p. : LC Card 87-121044 DDC 331.3/4/099413 19
HD6276.A83 P555 1985

Del desierto a la selva /. López Serrano, Francisco. México , 1984. 215 p. : ISBN

968-13-1608-8 LC Card 86-189936
HD1516.M5 L66 1984

Del Rosario, Rody. Unyon! / Rody del Rosario at Rosario del Rosario. Malate, Manila : Aklat Pilipino, [1985] 65 p. : ill. ; 22 cm. In Tagalog. "May 1, 1985"--T.p. verso. LC Card 85-184386
1. Trade-unions - Philippines - Handbooks, manuals, etc. I. Del Rosario, Rosario. II. Title.
HD6828 .D45 1985

Del Rosario, Rosario. Del Rosario, Rody. Unyon! /. Malate, Manila [1985] 65 p. : LC Card 85-184386
HD6828 .D45 1985

Dela (Slovenska akademija znanosti in umetnosti. Razred za zgodovinske in družbene vede) . (27) Mihelič, Darja. Neagrarno gospodarstvo Pirana od 1280 do 1340 =. Ljubljana , 1985. 244 p., [12] p. on folded leaves : LC Card 86-202646
HC407.Z7 P576 1985

Delahaye, Brian L., 1946- Smith, Barry J., 1947- How to be an effective trainer . New York , c1987. 404 p. : ISBN 0-471-85239-2 (pbk.) LC Card 86-26774 DDC 658.3/1243 19
HF5549.5.T7 S642 1987

Delalande, Philippe, 1937- Science économique et maîtrise de l'avenir / Philippe Delalande. Paris : Economica : Agence de coopération culturelle & technique, 1984. 305 p. : ill. ; 24 cm. (Collection Coopération et développement) Bibliography: p. [295]-297. ISBN 2-7178-0790-X : LC Card 85-104627
1. Economics - Philosophy. 2. Economic history. 3. History - Philosophy. I. Title. II. Series.
HB71 .D45 1984

Delany, George. The #1 home business book : sound advice and ideas for extra income at home / George & Sandra Delany.1st ed. Blue Ridge Summit, PA : Liberty House, [1987] 168 p. : ill. ; 21 cm. Reprint. Originally published: Cockeysville, Md. : Liberty Pub. Co., c1981. Includes index. ISBN 0-8306-3022-8 (pbk.) : LC Card 87-2936 DDC 658/.041 19
1. Self-employed. 2. Supplementary employment. 3. New business enterprises - Management. 4. Small business - Management. 5. Occupations. I. Delany, Sandra. II. Title. III. Title: Number one home business book.
HD8036 .D44 1987

Delany, Sandra. Delany, George. The #1 home business book . Blue Ridge Summit, PA [1987] 168 p. : ISBN 0-8306-3022-8 (pbk.) : LC Card 87-2936 DDC 658/.041 19
HD8036 .D44 1987

Delatouche, Raymond. Pernoud, Régine, 1909- Le Moyen Age pour quoi faire? /. [Paris] , c1986. 315 p. : ISBN 2-234-01940-0 : LC Card 86-189820
HC41 .P46 1986

Delaunay, Jean Claude. Salariat et plus-value en France depuis la fin du XIXe siècle / Jean-Claude Delaunay. Paris : Presses de la Fondation nationale des sciences politiques, c1984. xiv, 304 p. : ill. ; 22 cm. Includes index. Bibliography: p. [283]-291. ISBN 2-7246-0488-1 : LC Card 84-172193 DDC 331.2/944 19
1. Surplus value - France - History - 20th century. 2. Wages - France - History - 20th century. 3. Labor and laboring classes - France - History - 20th century. I. Title. II. Title: Salariat et plus-value en France depuis la fin du dix-neuvième siècle. III. Title: Salariat.
HB206 .D45 1984 ***NYPL [JLD 86-426]***

Delaware data book. Dover, Del. : Delaware Development Office, 1984- 1 v. (loose-leaf) : ill., maps ; 30 cm. Cover title. LC Card 87-622062 DDC 330.9751/043 19
1. Delaware - Economic conditions. I. Delaware Development Office.
HC107.D3 D435 1984

Delaware data book. [Dover, Del.] (P.O. Box 1401, Dover 19903) : [State of Delaware, Executive Dept., Delaware Development Office, 1986] 1 v. (various pagings) : ill. ; 29 cm. LC Card 86-621752 DDC 330.9751/043 19
1. Delaware - Economic conditions. I. Delaware Development Office. Executive Dept.
HC107.D3 D435 1986

Delaware Development Office.
Delaware data book. Dover, Del. , 1984- 1 v. (loose-leaf) : LC Card 87-622062 DDC 330.9751/043 19
HC107.D3 D435 1984

Delaware Development Office. Executive Dept. Delaware data book. [Dover, Del.] (P.O. Box 1401, Dover 19903) [1986] 1 v. (various pagings) : LC Card 86-621752 DDC 330.9751/043 19
HC107.D3 D435 1986

DELAWARE - ECONOMIC CONDITIONS.
Delaware data book. Dover, Del. , 1984- 1 v. (loose-leaf) : LC Card 87-622062 DDC 330.9751/043 19
HC107.D3 D435 1984

Delaware data book. [Dover, Del.] (P.O. Box 1401, Dover 19903) [1986] 1 v. (various pagings) : LC Card 86-621752 DDC 330.9751/043 19
HC107.D3 D435 1986

Delden, P. J. van, 1949- De toekomst van de vrije tijd / Pieterjan van Delden. [Deventer] : Van Loghum Slaterus, c1986. 102 p. ; 22 cm. Bibliography: p. 101-102. ISBN 90-6001-973-3 : LC Card 86-199367
1. Leisure. 2. Leisure - Netherlands. 3. Time management. 4. Time management - Netherlands. I. Title.
HD4904.6 .D45 1986

Deléage, Jean-Paul. Debeir, Jean-Claude. Les servitudes de la puissance . [Paris] , c1986. 428 p. : ISBN 2-08-211163-6 : LC Card 87-121577
HD9502.A2 D43 1986

DELEGATING OF AUTHORITY. see **DELEGATION OF AUTHORITY.**

Délégation à l'aménagement du territoire et à l'action régionale. see **France. Délégation à l'aménagement du territoire et à l'action régionale.**

DELEGATION OF AUTHORITY.
Goodworth, Clive T. Effective delegation /. London , Brookfield, Vt., USA , 1985. 148 p. : ISBN 0-09-161781-2 (pbk.) : LC Card 86-204300 DDC 658.4/02 19
HD50 .G66 1985

Rowbottom, Ralph William. Organisational design . Aldershot, Hants, England , Brookfield, Vt., USA , 1987. 165 p. : ISBN 0-566-05408-6 : LC Card 86-31946 DDC 658.4/02 19
HD50 .R68 1987

Delegation of the Commission of the European Communities for South Asia. South Asian cooperation in industry, energy, and technology /. New Delhi , Newbury Park, Calif. , 1987. p. cm. ISBN 0-8039-9538-5 (pbk.) LC Card 87-14994 DDC 337.1/54 19
HC430.6 .S675 1987

Ḏelēs, Dēmētrēs I. Hē anaptyxē tēs hellēnikēs geōrgias : hē periptōsē tēs Thessalias / Dēmētrē I. Ḏelē. Athēna : Agrotikē Trapeza Hellados, Dieuthynsē Meletōn & Programmatismou, 1985. 3 v. in 2 : ill. ; 24 cm. (Meletes gia tēn agrotikē oikonomia . 20) Bibliography: v. 2, p. 319-322. LC Card 86-203175
1. Agriculture - Economic aspects - Greece. 2. Produce trade - Greece. 3. Agriculture and state - Greece. I. Title. II. Series.
HD2055.5 .D44 1985

Delfim Netto, Antônio.
Brasil 82, a grande luta para manter o espaço para crescer : palestra do ministro A. Delfim Netto, Escola de Guerra Naval, Rio de Janeiro, 15 de setembro de 1982. Brasília : Presidência da República, Secretaria de Planejamento, 1982. 37 p. : ill. ; 22 cm. (Publicação / Coordenadoria de Comunicação Social, Secretaria de Planejamento da Presidência da República . 07/82) LC Card 84-249919
1. Brazil - Economic policy. I. Brazil. Secretaria de Planejamento. II. Series: Publicação (Brazil. Secretaria de Planejamento. Coordenadoria de Comunicação Social) , 82/07. III. Title.
HC187 .D552 1982

Só o político pode salvar o economista / Delfim Netto. Rio de Janeiro : Delfim Netto, 1986. xvii, 146 p. ; 21 cm. LC Card 87-137681 DDC 338.981 19
1. Brazil - Economic policy. 2. Debts, External - Brazil. 3. Free trade and protection - Free trade. I. Title.
HC187 .D565 1986

Delgado, Christopher L. Accelerating food production in Sub-Saharan Africa /. Baltimore , c1987. xix, 417 p. ; ISBN 0-8018-3390-6 (alk. paper) LC Card 86-10684 DDC 338.1/9/67 19
HD2117 .A33 1987 ***NYPL [JLE 87-1366]***

Delgado, Guilherme Costa. Capital financeiro e agricultura no Brasil, 1965-1985 / Guilherme Costa Delgado. S[ão] Paulo, SP, Brasil : Icone Editora ; Campinas, SP : Editora da UNICAMP, c1985. 240 p. ; 21 cm. (Coleção América Latina) Bibliography: p. 237-240. LC Card 87-102748
1. Agricultural credit - Brazil. 2. Agriculture - Economic aspects - Brazil. 3. Agriculture - Brazil - Finance. I. Series: Coleção América Latina (Icone Editora (São Paulo)). II. Title.
HD1440.B8 D45 1985

Delgado, Josep M. (Maria) El Comerç entre Catalunya i Amèrica (segles XVIII i XIX) /. Barcelona , 1986. 173 p. : ISBN 84-85905-24-5 LC Card 86-204187
HF3689.C3 C39 1986

Delgado Q., Félix. Programas de estabilización y condicionalidad en Costa Rica / Félix Delgado Q. San José, Costa Rica : Banco Central de Costa Rica, 1986. 30, [6] leaves ; 28 cm. (Serie "Comentarios sobre asuntos económicos" . no. 64) Bibliography: leaves [35]-[36]. LC Card 87-404196 DDC 338.97286 19
1. Costa Rica - Economic Policy. 2. Economic stabilization - Costa Rica. I. Title. II. Series.
HC143 .D45 1986

DELHI (INDIA) - ECONOMIC CONDITIONS.
Vinze, Medha Dubhashi, 1958- Women entrepreneurs in India . Delhi, India , 1987. ix, 238 p. ; LC Card 86-903594 DDC 305.4/3338 19
HD6190.D44 V55 1987

DELHI (INDIA) - SOCIAL CONDITIONS.
Vinze, Medha Dubhashi, 1958- Women entrepreneurs in India . Delhi, India , 1987. ix, 238 p. ; LC Card 86-903594 DDC 305.4/3338 19
HD6190.D44 V55 1987

Delhi. Indian Council of World Affairs. see **Indian Council of World Affairs.**

Delhi. Indian Institute of Foreign Trade. see **Indian Institute of Foreign Trade.**

Delhi Science Forum. "All India Seminar on National Drug Policy" (1986 : New Delhi, India) Drug industry and the Indian people . New Delhi , Patna , 1986. 333 p. : LC Card 87-900874 DDC 338.4/76151/0954 19
HD9611.I52 A44 1986

De Deli Spoorweg Maatschappij . Meijer, H., 1904- Zutphen , c1987. 152 p. : ISBN 90-6011-540-6 : LC Card 87-157915
HE3340.D45 M45 1987

DELI SPOORWEG MAATSCHAPPIJ - HISTORY.
Meijer, H., 1904- De Deli Spoorweg Maatschappij . Zutphen , c1987. 152 p. : ISBN 90-6011-540-6 : LC Card 87-157915
HE3340.D45 M45 1987

Delitev po delu v socialistični družbi /. Glas, Miroslav, 1950- Ljubljana , 1986. 631 p. : LC Card 87-147216
HC407.Z9 I51473 1986

DELIVERY OF GOODS - ITALY.
Industria e commercio . Milano, Italy , c1985. 194 p. : LC Card 86-112174 DDC 658.7/88/0945 19
HF5415.12.I8 I53 1985 ***NYPL [JLD 87-432]***

DELIVERY OF GOODS - POLAND.
Blotko, Kazimierz. Racjonalny podział przewozów ładunków między gałęzie transportu /. Warszawa , 1978. 126 p. ; LC Card 81-206824
HF5780.P7 B57 1978

Marciniak-Neider, Danuta. Spedycja lądowa /. Gdańsk , 1979- v. <1 > ; LC Card 81-181249
HF5780.P7 M37 1979

Délivrez-nous des cadres /. Bondt, Frank de. [Paris] , c1984. 248 p. ; LC Card 85-103087 DDC 331.7/12/0944 19
HD8038.F7 B65 1984

Dell, Edmund. The politics of economic interdependence / Edmund Dell. New York : St. Martin's Press, 1987. x, 268 p. ; 23 cm. Bibliography: p. 258-262. Includes index. ISBN 0-312-00526-1 : LC Card 86-31345 DDC 337 19
1. International economic relations. 2. Free trade and

protection - Free trade. 3. Economic policy. I. Title.
HF1411 .D332 1987

Dell, Sidney Samuel. The International monetary system and its reform . Amsterdam ; New York : 3 v. : ISBN 0-444-70227-X LC Card 87-6737 DDC 332.4/5 19
HG3881 .I57672 1987

Della strada ferrata Pia-Cassia da citta della Pieve a Civitavecchia e del ristauro del Porto Neroniano in Anzio . Blasi, Benedetto. Roma , 1846. 56 p., [3] folded leaves of plates : LC Card 85-665949
HE3098 .B51x 1846

Dellenbrant, Jan Åke, 1946- Föreningsdemokrati och företagsdemokrati : två vägar till ekonomisk demokrati : en studie / utförd på uppdrag av Kooperationsutredningen av Jan Åke Dellenbrant. [Stockholm] : LiberFörlag, [1981] 85 p. ; 21 cm. At head of title: Industridepartementet. Bibliography: p. 81-85. "Ds I 1981:13." ISBN 91-38-06488-X LC Card 83-245188
1. Industrial management - Sweden - Employee participation. 2. Cooperation - Sweden. I. Sweden. Kooperationsutredningen. II. Title.
HD5660.S9 D44 1981

Delli Carpini, Michael X., 1953- Stability and change in American politics : the coming of age of the generation of the 1960s / Michael X. Delli Carpini. New York : New York University Press, 1986. xxv, 374 p. ; 24 cm. Includes bibliographies and index. ISBN 0-8147-1780-2 (alk. paper) : LC Card 85-15348 DDC 323/.042/0973 19
1. Political participation - United States. 2. Baby boom generation - United States. 3. United States - Politics and government - 1945-. I. Title.
JK1764 .D45 1986 ***NYPL [JLE 86-2183]***

Dellinger, Susan. Communicating effectively : a complete guide for better managing / Susan Dellinger, Barbara Deane. Millwood, N.Y.: Buckley-Little Book Catalogue, 1987, c1982. p. cm. Reprint. Originally published: Radnor, Pa. : Chilton Book Co., c1980. Bibliography: p. Includes index. ISBN 0-916667-14-6 LC Card 87-20830 DDC 658.4/5 19
1. Business communication. I. Deane, Barbara. II. Title.
HF5718 .D44 1987

Delmas, Philippe. La stabilisation des prix des matières premières : un dialogue manqué / Philippe Delmas, Christophe Guillemin ; préface de Edgard Pisani. Paris : Economica, 1983. vii, 359 p. : ill. ; 24 cm. Includes bibliographical references. ISBN 2-7178-0657-1 : LC Card 84-116258
1. Raw materials - Prices. 2. Commodity control. I. Guillemin, Christophe. II. Title.
HF1051 .D38 1983

Deloitte, Haskins & Sells. Stringer, Kenneth W. Statistical techniques for analytical review in auditing /. New York , c1986. xii, 301 p. : ISBN 0-471-86076-X : LC Card 85-17874 DDC 657/.45/0285536 19
HF5667 .S85 1986 ***NYPL [JLE 86-2704]***

DeLorme, Charles D. Ekelund, Robert B. (Robert Burton), 1940- Macroeconomics. Plano, Tex. , 1987. xvi, 536 p. : ISBN 0-256-03678-0 LC Card 86-71959 DDC 339 19
HB172.5 .D44 1987

Delphic Associates. Decision-making in the Soviet energy industry . Falls Church, VA (7700 Leesburg Pike, #250, Falls Church 22043) , c1986. ix, 166 leaves ; LC Card 87-401592 DDC 333.79/0947 19
HD9502.S652 D43 1986

Delson, Erwin B.
The bar coding systems industry. New York, N.Y. : Find/SVP, c1986. 1 v. (various pagings) : ill. ; 29 cm. (A Business information report) "April 1986." ISBN 0-931634-64-4 (pbk.) LC Card 87-156445 DDC 380.1/45621399 19
1. Product coding equipment industry. 2. Market surveys. I. Find/SVP (Firm). II. Title. III. Series.
HD9801.6.P762 D45 1986

The factory automation industry / [author, Erwin B. Delson]. New York, N.Y. : Find/SVP, c1985. 1 v. (various pagings) : ill. ; 29 cm. (A Business information report) ISBN 0-931634-16-4 (pbk.) LC Card 86-203033 DDC 338.4/76298/0973 19
1. Automatic control equipment industry - United States. 2. Robot industry - United States. 3. Computer integrated manufacturing systems - United States. 4. Market surveys - United States. I. Find/SVP (Firm). II. Title. III. Series.
HD9696.A963 U635 1985

Demaegdt, Philippe. Le Renouvellement du tissu industriel . Paris [1986] 130 p. ; ISBN 2-11-001568-3 : LC Card 86-191910
HD3616.F83 R46 1986

Demain la France : une enquête de l'Expansion. Paris : Hachette, c1986. 423 p., [32] p. of plates : ill. (some col.) ; 18 cm. (Collection Pluriel, 0296-2063 . 8476) ISBN 2-01-011955-X LC Card 86-174163
1. France - Economic conditions - 1945-. 2. France - Economic policy - 1945-. 3. Economic forecasting - France.
HC276.2 .D42 1986

Demain l'acier français /. Masson, Jean Louis. Paris , c1986. 404 p. : ISBN 2-254-86071-1 : LC Card 86-190326
HD9522.5 .M37 1986

Demanche, Georges, b. 1855. En Espagne : les chemins de fer en montagne Gibraltar / Georges Demanche. Paris : G. Chamerot, 1883. 40 p. ; 24 cm. "Extrait de l'Annuaire du Club alpin français." LC Card 85-665876
1. Railroads - Spain. 2. Railroad travel - Spain. I. Title.
HE3195 .D45x 1883

DEMAND AND SUPPLY. see **SUPPLY AND DEMAND.**

The demand and supply of primary energy in mainland China /. Chêng, Chu-yüan. Taipei, Taiwan, Republic of China , Seattle , c1984. viii, 178 p. ; LC Card 84-231216 DDC 333.79/11/0951 19
HD9502.C62 C49 1984 ***NYPL [JLF 87-21]***

DEMAND CURVES (ECONOMIC THEORY) see **DEMAND FUNCTIONS (ECONOMIC THEORY)**

DEMAND (ECONOMIC THEORY)
Beliaevskiĭ, I. K. (Igor´ Konstantinovich) Naselenie i tovarooborot . Moskva , 1980. 144 p. : LC Card 81-135180
HB801 .B377 1980

Demand, equilibrium, and trade . London , 1984. xx, 256 p. : ISBN 0-333-33184-2 LC Card 87-673439
HB34 .D45x 1984b

Hicks, John Richard, Sir, 1940- A revision of demand theory /. Oxford [Oxfordshire] , New York , 1986, c1956. vii, 196 p. : ISBN 0-19-828110-2 LC Card 86-154241 DDC 338.5/212 19
HB801 .H48 1986 ***NYPL [JLD 86-3663]***

Sardoni, Claudio. Marx and Keynes on economic recession . New York , 1987. xiv, 152 p. ; ISBN 0-8147-7871-2 : LC Card 87-13749 DDC 338.5/42 19
HB3714 .S27 1987

DEMAND (ECONOMIC THEORY) - ECONOMETRIC MODELS.
Vilks, Arnis. Aggregation und Kausalität im Modell des allgemeinen Konkurrenzgleichgewichts . Göttingen , c1984. 141 p. ; ISBN 3-525-11287-4 (Deut. Bibl.) LC Card 84-225754
HB842 .V55 1984

Demand, equilibrium, and trade : essays in honour of Ivor F. Pearce / edited by A. Ingham and A.M. Ulph. London : Macmillan, 1984. xx, 256 p. : ill., port. ; 23 cm. Includes bibliographies and indexes. ISBN 0-333-33184-2 LC Card 87-673439
1. Economics. 2. Demand (Economic theory). 3. Equilibrium (Economics). 4. International economic relations. 5. Pearce, I. F. (Ivor F.). I. Pearce, I. F. (Ivor F.). II. Ingham, A. III. Ulph, Alistair.
HB34 .D45x 1984b

The demand for fertility control in Sub-Saharan Africa /. Frank, Odile. New York, N.Y., U. S.A. (1 Dag Hammarskjold Plaza, New York 10017) [1985] 50 p. ; LC Card 86-204127 DDC 363.9/6/09624 19
HB1071.A3 F69 1985

DEMAND FOR MONEY - BANGLADESH - MATHEMATICAL MODELS.
Hossain, Md. Akhtar. The short-run demand for real money balances in the Bangladesh economy . Bundoora, Vic., Australia [1986] 90 p. ; ISBN 0-85816-784-0 (pbk.) LC Card 86-228714 DDC 332.4/14 19
HG1240.6 .H67 1986

DEMAND FOR MONEY - BRAZIL - ECONOMETRIC MODELS.
Melo, Valdir Ramalho de. Seleção de agregados monetários /. [Brasília] [1981] 136 p. : LC Card 85-161532
HG835 .M45 1981

DEMAND FOR MONEY - ECONOMETRIC MODELS.
Bordo, Michael D. The long-run behavior of the velocity of circulation . Cambridge [Cambridgeshire] , New York , 1987. xiv, 181 p. : ISBN 0-521-32633-8 LC Card 86-32628 DDC 332.4/14 19
HG226.6 .B67 1987

The demand for money in Sweden, 1970-1983 /. Krusell, Per. Stockholm, Sweden [1986] 91 p. ; ISBN 0-917258-21-5 (pbk.) LC Card 87-151531 DDC 332.4/14 19
HG1125 .K78 1986

DEMAND FOR MONEY - SWEDEN - ECONOMETRIC MODELS.
Krusell, Per. The demand for money in Sweden, 1970-1983 /. Stockholm, Sweden [1986] 91 p. ; ISBN 0-917258-21-5 (pbk.) LC Card 87-151531 DDC 332.4/14 19
HG1125 .K78 1986

DEMAND FOR MONEY - SWITZERLAND.
Heri, Erwin W. Die Geldnachfrage . Berlin , New York , c1986. 226 p. : ISBN 0-387-17157-6 (U. S.) LC Card 86-232268
HG226.5 .H47 1986

DEMAND FUNCTIONS (ECONOMIC THEORY) - CONGRESSES.
Contractual arrangements for intertemporal trade /. Minneapolis, MN , c1987. p. cm. ISBN 0-8166-1533-0 : LC Card 86-24888 DDC 332.64/4/0724 19
HB801 .C629 1987

Demand-side management . Gellings, Clark W. Lilburn, GA , c1988. xi, 465 p. : ISBN 0-88173-027-0 : LC Card 86-46131 DDC 363.6/2/068 19
HD9685.A2 G45 1988

Demand-supply gap and public distribution of foodgrains in India /. Narayanan, S. New Delhi , 1986. xii, 166 p. ; ISBN 81-85005-00-1 : LC Card 86-902667 DDC 338.1/731/0954 19
HD9046.I4 N28 1986

Demanda de fatores e ofertas na agricultura brasileira . Santos, José Carlos de Souza. Rio de Janeiro , 1983. 110 p. ; LC Card 87-403023 DDC 338.1/0981 19
HD1872 .S25 1983

Demanda de fatores, energia e substituição na indústria brasileira, 1970/79 /. Santos, José Carlos de Souza. São Paulo , 1986. 183 p. : LC Card 86-234783
HB241 .S26 1986

Demanda dinámica por trabajo /. Rojas Ramos, Patricio. Santiago , 1986. 58 p. : LC Card 87-404328 DDC 331.12/5/0983 19
HD5756.A6 R65 1986

Demands on rural lands : planning for resource use / edited by Chris Cocklin, Barry Smit, and Tom Johnston. Boulder, Colo. : Westview Press, 1987. xvi, 336 p. : ill. ; 23 cm. (Westview special studies in natural resources and energy management) Includes bibliographies and index. ISBN 0-8133-7361-1 (pbk. : alk. paper) LC Card 87-50751 DDC 333.76/13 19
1. Land use, Rural - Congresses. 2. Land use, Rural - Planning - Congresses. 3. Natural resources - Congresses. 4. Conservation of natural resources - Congresses. I. Cocklin, Chris. II. Smit, Barry. III. Johnston, Tom.
HD105 .D43 1987

DeMarco, Tom. Peopleware : productive projects and teams / Tom DeMarco & Timothy Lister. New York, NY : Dorset House Pub. Co., c1987. x, 188 p. : ill. ; 23 cm. Bibliography: p. 179-184. Includes index. ISBN 0-932633-05-6 (pbk.) : LC Card 87-22293 DDC 658.3/14 19
1. Management. 2. Organizational behavior. 3. Organizational effectiveness. 4. Industrial project management. I. Lister, Timothy R. II. Title.
HD31 .D42185 1987

Dembner, Steve. Information note on the technical cooperation programme /. Rome

[1985?] 29 p. : LC Card 87-122600 DDC 338.9/26/091724 19
HC60 .I477 1985

Demenev, Anatoliĭ Iosifovich. Metodicheskie rekomendatsii po issledovaniiu proizvodstvennoĭ infrastruktury territorial'no-proizvodstvennykh kompleksov i promyshlennykh uzlov /. Sverdlovsk , 1983. 79 p. (some folded) ; LC Card 86-113572
HC340.C3 M416 1983

Dement'ev, N. P. Val'tukh, Konstantin Kurtovich. Matematicheskiĭ i statisticheskiĭ analiz funktsii potrebleniia /. Novosibirsk , 1986. 165, [3] p. : LC Card 86-230310
HB801 .V26 1986

Dementsev, V. V. (Viktor Vladimirovich) O Gosudarstvennom biudzhete SSSR na 1986 god i ob ispolnenii Gosudarstvennogo biudzheta SSSR za 1984 god : doklad i zakliuchitel'noe slovo na sovmestnykh zasedaniiakh Soveta Soiuza i Soveta Natsional'nosteĭ chetvertoĭ sessii Verkhovnogo Soveta SSSR odinnadtsatogo sozyva / V.V. Dementsev. Zakon Soiuza Sovetskikh Sotsialisticheskikh Respublik o Gosudarstvennom biudzhete SSSR na 1986 god. Postanovlenie Verkhovnogo Soveta SSSR ob utverzhdenii otcheta ob ispolnenii Gosudarstvennogo biudzheta SSSR za 1984 god. Moskva : Izd-vo polit. lit-ry, 1985. 28 p. ; 20 cm. LC Card 86-203425
1. Budget - Soviet Union. I. Soviet Union. Zakon Soiuza Sovetskikh Sotsialisticheskikh Respublik o Gosudarstvennom biudzhete SSSR na 1986 god. 1985. II. Soviet Union. Verkhovnyĭ Sovet. Postanovlenie Verkhovnogo Soveta SSSR ob utverzhdenii otcheta ob ispolnenii Gosudarstvennogo biudzheta USSR za 1984 god. 1985. III. Title. IV. Title: Zakon Soiuza Sovetskikh Sotsialisticheskikh Respublik o Gosudarstvennom biudzhete SSSR na 1986 god. V. Title: Postanovlenie Verkhovnogo Soveta SSSR ob utverzhdenii otcheta ob ispolnenii Gosudarstvennogo biudzheta SSSR za 1984 god.
HJ2129 .D46 1985

Demeny, Paul George, 1932- The world demographic situation / Paul Demeny. New York, N.Y., U. S.A. (One Dag Hammarskjold Plaza, New York 10017) : Population Council, [1985] 52 p. : ill. ; 23 cm. (Working papers / Center for Policy Studies . no. 121) Cover title. Prepared for the 71st American Assembly on United States International Population Policy held at Harriman, N.Y., Apr. 17-20, 1986. "December 1985." LC Card 87-402019 DDC 304.6 19
1. Population. 2. Population forecasting. I. Series: Working papers (Population Council. Center for Policy Studies) , no. 121. II. Title.
HB871 .D386 1985

Dēmētrakopoulos, Odysseas. Hē Hellēnikē viomēchania apo ton 19o ston 20o aiōna /. Athēna , 1985. 32 p., [22] p. of plates : LC Card 86-212947
HC295 .H373 1985

Dem'ianov, Vladimir Fedorovich. IIASA (International Institute for Applied Systems Analysis) Workshop on Nondifferentiable Optimization (1984 : Sopron, Hungary) Nondifferentiable optimization . Berlin , New York , 1985. vi, 349 p. : ISBN 0-387-15979-7 (U. S.) LC Card 85-25029 DDC 658.4/03/4 19
T57.6 .I46 1984
NYPL [JLM 72-289 no.255]

DeMilner, Lawrence E. Indexing with the consumer price index : problems and alternatives / the Congress of the United States, Congressional Budget Office. [Washington, D.C.] : The Office : For sale by the Supt. of Docs., U. S. G.P.O., 1981. xx, 123 p. : ill. ; 26 cm. "June 1981"--Cover. Includes bibliographical references. LC Card 81-602368 DDC 338.5/28/0973 19
1. Indexation (Economics) - United States. 2. Consumer price indexes - United States. 3. Food stamp program - United States. I. Title.
HG229.5 .D45 ***NYPL [JLF 85-3118]***

Deming legacy. Roadmap for change. Chicago, Ill. , 1987. 1 film reel (28 min.) : LC Card 87-705133 DDC 658 11
HD9710

DEMING, W. EDWARDS (WILLIAM EDWARDS), 1900-
Roadmap for change. Chicago, Ill. , 1987. 1 film reel (28 min.) : LC Card 87-705133 DDC 658 11
HD9710

Democracia económica.
Godio, Julio. Sindicalismo y política en América Latina /. Caracas, Venezuela [1983] 315 p. ; LC Card 83-157510 DDC 322/.2/098 19
HD8110.5 .G64 1983 ***NYPL [JLD 86-1758]***

Democracia, independencia y sociedad latinoamericana /. Arias Sánchez, Oscar. San José, Costa Rica , 1985. 100 p. ; ISBN 997-7956-09-X LC Card 87-400690 DDC 320.97286 19
HC143 .A773 1985

Democracia real y renovación del movimiento de los trabajadores. Máspero, Emilio. Informe político y de orientación ante el VIIIo Congreso de la CLAT . [Caracas] , 1983. 122 p. : LC Card 87-403072 DDC 305.5/62/098 19
HD8110.5.A5 C466 1983

Democracia y liberalismo /. Israel Zipper, Ricardo. Santiago de Chile , 1984. 56 p. ; LC Card 85-197546
HB95 .I87 1984

Democracia y participación obrera en la Revolución Sandinista /. Vilas, Carlos María. Morelia, Michoacán , 1985. 44 p., [6] p. of plates : LC Card 87-128110 DDC 322/.2/097285 19
HD8168 .V55 1985

DEMOCRACY - ADDRESSES, ESSAYS, LECTURES.
Demokratie . Berlin , 1981. 188 p. ; LC Card 81-149074 DDC 320.5/315 19
HX73 .D45 1981 ***NYPL [JLD 86-3341]***

Karpiński, Wojciech. Szkice o wolności /. Chicago, Ill. (2886 Milwaukee Ave., Chicago, Ill. 60618) , 1980. 95 p. ; LC Card 81-201974
JC585 .K32 1980 ***NYPL [*QR 86-4376]***

Rationalism, humanism, and democracy . Meerut , 1985. xcii, 514 p., [2] p. of plates : LC Card 85-901252 DDC 144 19
B833 .R29 1985 ***NYPL [JFD 86-3589]***

Democracy and capitalism . Bowles, Samuel. New York , c1986. x, 244 p. ; ISBN 0-465-06052-8 : LC Card 85-47991 DDC 321.8 19
JC423 .B76 1986 ***NYPL [JLE 86-2928]***

Democracy and control in the workplace / edited by Ed. Davis and Russell Lansbury. Melbourne, Australia : Longman Cheshire, 1986. 388 p. ; 22 cm. (Australian management studies) Bibliography: p. [358]-373. Includes indexes. ISBN 0-582-71159-2 (pbk.) LC Card 87-102095 DDC 331.01/12 19
1. Industrial management - Australia - Employee participation. 2. Industrial management - Employee participation. I. Davis, Ed. II. Lansbury, Russell D.
HD5660.A8 D46 1986

Democracy and economic power . Kelso, Louis O. Cambridge, Mass. , 1986. xii, 175 p. : ISBN 0-88730-115-0 : LC Card 86-14027 DDC 338.6 19
HD5660.U5 K45 1986 ***NYPL [JLE 86-4658]***

Democracy and public choice : essays in honor of Gordon Tullock / edited by and with contributions from Charles K. Rowley. Oxford [Oxfordshire] ; New York, NY, USA : Blackwell, 1987. x, 265 p. : ill., ports. ; 24 cm. Articles are from "A conference held at Colonial Williamsburg 9-11 April 1986, entitled 'Towards a Freer Society: Some Unintended Consequences of Tullock's Scholarship'"--Pref. Includes bibliographies and index. ISBN 0-631-15029-3 : LC Card 87-6402 DDC 302/.13 19
1. Social choice. 2. Democracy. 3. Tullock, Gordon. I. Rowley, Charles Kershaw. II. Tullock, Gordon.
HB846.8 .D46 1987

Democracy at work /. Burns, Patrick. London , 1981. 164 p. : ISBN 0-330-26478-8 (pbk.) LC Card 86-673620
HD6664 .B845x 1981

DEMOCRACY - CONGRESSES.
Democratic capitalism? . Charlottesville , 1986. ix, 210 p. ; ISBN 0-8139-1112-5 LC Card 86-7755 DDC 321.8 19
JC423 .D4416 1986
NYPL [(not yet cat'd 4/16/87)]

Freedom and control in a democratic society /. New York , c1976. 107 p. ;
NYPL [JLD 80-3590]

Order, freedom, and the polity . Lanham, MD [Bryn Mawr, Pa.] , c1986. x, 184 p. ; ISBN 0-8191-5155-6 (alk. paper) : LC Card 85-26438 DDC 323.44 19
JC571 .O77 1986 ***NYPL [JLE 86-3182]***

Trade unions and democracy . [Kingston, Jamaica] [1986] iii, 52 p. : LC Card 87-133832 DDC 322/.2/09729 19
HD6571 .T72 1986

DEMOCRACY - HISTORY.
Kloppenberg, James T. Uncertain victory . New York , 1986. x, 546 p. ; ISBN 0-19-503749-9 : LC Card 85-21636 DDC 320.5/315/094 19
JA84.E9 K57 1986 ***NYPL [JLE 86-2574]***

DEMOCRACY - MORAL AND ETHICAL ASPECTS.
Marktwirtschaft und Gesellschaftsordnung . Berlin , c1983. 220 p., [1] leaf of plates : ISBN 3-428-05365-6 LC Card 83-191615
HB72 .M248 1983

Democrația socialistă în acțiune . Cazacu, Honorina. București , 1985. 192 p. : LC Card 86-216024
HD5660.R6 C39 1985

Democratic capitalism? : essays in search of a concept / edited by Fred E. Baumann. Charlottesville : Published for the Public Affairs Conference Center, Kenyon College, by the University Press of Virginia, 1986. ix, 210 p. ; 24 cm. Includes bibliographies and indexes. ISBN 0-8139-1112-5 LC Card 86-7755 DDC 321.8 19
1. Democracy - Congresses. 2. Capitalism - Congresses. I. Baumann, Fred E.
JC423 .D4416 1986
NYPL [(not yet cat'd 4/16/87)]

DEMOCRATIC CENTRALISM - GERMANY (EAST)
Otto, Wolfgang, Diplom-Staatswissenschaftler. Ökonomische Strategie und volkswirtschaftliche Masseninitiative /. Berlin , 1984. 61 p. : LC Card 85-189271
HC290.78 .O88 1984

Democratic corporatism and policy linkages . Wilensky, Harold L. Berkeley , c1987. ix, 97 p. ; ISBN 0-87725-169-X (pbk.) : LC Card 87-3525 DDC 338.9 19
HD3616.E8 W54 1987

DEMOCRATIC PARTY (HAWAII)
Cooper, George. Land and power in Hawaii . Honolulu, Hawaii , c1985. x, 518 p. ; ISBN 0-9615052-0-6 : LC Card 85-72037 DDC 333.73/13/09969 19
HD266.H3 C66 1985 ***NYPL [JLE 87-361]***

DEMOCRATIC PARTY (U. S.)
Cannon, William B., 1920- New class politics . Washington, D.C. , c1986. 137 p. ; ISBN 0-89758-042-7 (pbk.) : LC Card 86-27511 DDC 336.73 19
HJ2051 .C35 1986

La Démocratisation du secteur public : liste des entreprises / [préparé et réalisé par le Secrétariat général du Haut conseil]. Paris : Haut conseil du secteur public, [1984] 87 p. ; 30 cm. Cover title. "Janvier 1984." Includes index. LC Card 84-233767
1. Government business enterprises - France - Directories. 2. Government business enterprises - France - Management - Employee participation. 3. Government business enterprises - Employees - Legal status, laws, etc. - France. 4. Government business enterprises - Law and legislation - France. I. France. Haut conseil du secteur public.
HD4165 .D46 1984

Democrazia cristiana. see **Partito della democrazia cristiana.**

Demografía de la Alpujarra . Luna, Paco. [Granada] [1984] 301 p., [3] leaves of plates : ISBN 84-338-0205-4 LC Card 85-221373
HB3620.A45 L85 1984

Demografia teritorială a României /. Trebici, Vladimir. București , 1986. 160 p. : LC Card 87-151036
HB3631 .T72 1986

Demográficas e sociais =. Macao. Repartição dos Serviços de Estatística. Macau [1984] [28] p. ; LC Card 86-162433
HA4643 .M33 1984

Demograficheskaia politika : opyt sotsialisticheskikh stran : sbornik stateĭ / pod redaktsieĭ A.G. Volkova. Moskva : "Finansy i

statistika", 1983. 187 p. : ill. ; 21 cm. (Novoe v zarubezhnoĭ demografii) Includes bibliographies. LC Card 84-145010
1. Europe, Eastern - Population policy. I. Volkov, A. G. (Andreĭ Gavrilovich).
HB3581 .D44 1983

Demograficheskaia politika sotsialisticheskogo obshchestva / otvetstvennyĭ redaktor T.V. Riabushkin. Moskva : "Nauka", 1986. 190 p. : ill. ; 22 cm. At head of title: Akademiia nauk SSSR. Nauchnyĭ sovet "Sotsial'no-ėkonomicheskie problemy narodonaseleniia." TSentral'nyĭ ėkonomiko-matematicheskiĭ institut. Includes bibliographical references. LC Card 87-120466
1. Soviet Union - Population policy. I. Riabushkin, T. V. (Timon Vasil'evich). II. Nauchnyĭ sovet "Sotsial'no-ėkonomicheskie problemy narodonaseleniia" (Akademiia nauk SSSR). III. TSentral'nyĭ ėkonomiko-matematicheskiĭ institut (Akademiia nauk SSSR).
HB3607 .D425 1986

Demograficheskaia politika sotsialisticheskogo obshchestva / otvetstvennyĭ redaktor T.V. Riabushkin. Moskva : "Nauka", 1986. 190 p. ; 22 cm. At head of title: Akademiia nauk SSSR. Nauchnyĭ sovet "Sotsial'no-ėkonomicheskie problemy narodonaseleniia." TSentral'nyĭ ėkonomiko-matematicheskiĭ institut. Includes bibliographical references.
1. Population policy. 2. Demography. 3. Soviet Union - Population policy. I. Riabushkin, T. V. (Timon Vasil'evich). II. Nauchnyĭ sovet "Sotsial'no-ėkonomicheskie problemy narodonaseleniia" (Akademiia nauk SSSR). III. TSentral'nyĭ ėkonomiko-matematicheskiĭ institut (Akademiia nauk SSSR). ***NYPL [*QIP 87-2842]***

Demograficheskie protsessy v sotsialisticheskom obshchestve. Hungarian. Demográfiai folyamatok a szocialista társadalomban az európai KGST országok példáján / [forditotta a Népesedésstatisztikai Főosztály]. Budapest : Statisztikai Kiadó Vállalat, 1984. 136 p. ; 24 cm. Translation of: Demograficheskie protsessy v sotsialisticheskom obshchestve. LC Card 85-154859
1. Europe, Eastern - Population. I. Hungary. Központi Statisztikai Hivatal. Népesedésstatisztikai Főosztály.
HB3581 .D4515 1984

Demograficheskoe modelirovanie . Iskakov, B. I. (Boris Ivanovich) Moskva , 1982. 75 p. ; LC Card 83-179019
HB849.51 .I85 1982

Demograficheskoe razvitie v SSSR / [redaktsionnaia kollegiia L.L. Rybakovskiĭ ... et al. ; redaktor-sostavitel' L.L. Rybakovskiĭ]. Moskva : "Mysl'", 1985. 126 p. ; 20 cm. (Demografiia--problemy i perspektivy) Summaries in English. Includes bibliographical references. LC Card 85-170633
1. Soviet Union - Population. I. Rybakovskiĭ, Leonid Leonidovich. II. Series.
HB3607 .D445 1985

Demografiia v zerkale istorii nauki. Shelestov, D. K. (Dmitriĭ Kuz'mich) Demography in the mirror of history /. Moscow , c1987. 214 p. ; LC Card 86-201399 DDC 304.6/0947 19
HB853.S65 S54 1983

Demografiia--problemy i perspektivy.
Demograficheskoe razvitie v SSSR /. Moskva , 1985. 126 p. ; LC Card 85-170633
HB3607 .D445 1985

Detnost' semi'i--vchera, segodnia, zavtra /. Moskva , 1986. 205 p. : LC Card 87-109456 DDC 304.6/32/0947 19
HB1017 .D47 1986

DEMOGRAPHERS - CZECHOSLOVAKIA - DIRECTORIES.
Československá demografická společnost. 20 let Československé demografické společnosti při ČSAV /. Praha , 1985. 198 p. : LC Card 86-208016
HB3592.3.A3 C47 1985

DEMOGRAPHERS - GREAT BRITAIN - BIOGRAPHY.
Thomas Robert Malthus, critical assessments /. London , Dover, N.H. , c1986. 4 v. : ISBN 0-7099-3650-8 (set) : LC Card 85-22412 DDC 304.6/092/4 19
HB863 .T38 1986 ***NYPL [JFF 86-588]***

DEMOGRAPHIC ANTHROPOLOGY.
Culture and reproduction . Boulder, Colo. , 1986. xix, 389 p. : ISBN 0-8133-7199-6 (pbk. : alk. paper) : LC Card 86-5671 DDC 304.6/32 19
HB887 .C85 1986 ***NYPL [JLE 86-3842]***

McCoid, Catherine Hodge. Carrying capacities of nation-states /. New Haven, Conn. (P.O. Box 2015, Yale Station, New Haven 06520) , 1984. x, 198 leaves : LC Card 84-152784 DDC 304.6/2 19
GN33.5 .M38 1984 ***NYPL [JFE 86-2142]***

Demographic behavior in the past . Knodel, John E. Cambridge [Cambridgeshire] , New York , 1988. p. cm. ISBN 0-521-32715-6 LC Card 87-20601 DDC 304.6/0943 19
HB3595 .K53 1988

Demographic characteristics of the population. Tekhunot demografiyot shel ha-ukhlusiyah . Yerushalayim , 1985. 31, 175, xxxiv p. : LC Card 86-204169
HA4560 .A4 1983

The Demographic dimension in Indonesian development / Graeme J. Hugo ... [et al.]. Singapore ; New York : Oxford University Press, 1987. xxv, 417 p. : ill., maps ; 25 cm. (East Asian social science monographs) Bibliography: p. [379]-404. Includes index. ISBN 0-19-582699-X : LC Card 87-11021 DDC 304.6/09598 19
1. Indonesia - Population. I. Hugo, Graeme.
HB3647 .D45 1987

Demographic estimates, projections, and selected social characteristics of the population of India /. Hobbs, Frank. Washington, D.C. [1986] vii, 148 p. : LC Card 87-601294 DDC 304.6/0954/021 19
HA4585 .H63 1986

Demographic situation in the Community : information report / rapporteur, Roger Burnel. Brussels : Economic and Social Consultative Assembly, 1986. ii, 40 p. : ill. ; 30 cm. "CES 602/84 fin." LC Card 87-135237 DDC 304.6/094 19
1. European Economic Community countries - Population. I. Burnel, Roger. II. Economic and Social Committee of the European Communities.
HB3582.5 .D46 1986

DEMOGRAPHIC SURVEYS - BOTSWANA.
Botswana. Central Statistics Office. Guideline for designing and executing small scale surveys in Botswana. [Gaborone] [1982] 53 p. in various pagings : LC Card 83-154943 DDC 304.6/0723 19
HB849.49 .B68 1982 ***NYPL [JLG 86-217]***

DEMOGRAPHIC SURVEYS - DEVELOPING COUNTRIES.
Acsádi, György. Policy relevance of findings of the world fertility survey for developing countries /. New York , 1986. vi, 160 p. ; LC Card 85-37681 DDC 304.6/32/091724 19
HB1108 .A28 1986

DEMOGRAPHIC SURVEYS - GERMANY (WEST)
Schaefer, Felix, 1950- Muster-Stichproben-Pläne für Bevölkerungs-Stichproben in der Bundesrepublik Deutschland und West-Berlin /. München , c1979. 160 p. : ISBN 3-478-39760-X; 3-478-39760-1 LC Card 84-135457
HB3595 .S29 1979

DEMOGRAPHIC SURVEYS - IVORY COAST.
Enquête démographique à passages répétés, 1978-1979 . [Abidjan] [1980?] 270 p. : LC Card 85-213692 DDC 304.6/09666/8 19
HB3666.A3 E57 1980 ***NYPL [JLF 86-1023]***

DEMOGRAPHIC TRANSITION.
Brown, Lester Russell, 1934- Our demographically divided world /. Washington, D.C. , c1986. 54 p. : ISBN 0-916468-75-5 (pbk.) LC Card 86-51475 DDC 304.6 19
HB871 .B744 1986

Culture and reproduction . Boulder, Colo. , 1986. xix, 389 p. : ISBN 0-8133-7199-6 (pbk. : alk. paper) : LC Card 86-5671 DDC 304.6/32 19
HB887 .C85 1986 ***NYPL [JLE 86-3842]***

DEMOGRAPHIC TRANSITION - COLOMBIA.
Transición demográfica y oferta de fuerza de trabajo en Colombia /. [Bogotá], República de Colombia , 1986. 2 v. : ISBN 958-95096-0-6 (set) LC Card 87-113652 DDC 331.11/09861 19
HD5757.A6 T7 1986

DEMOGRAPHIC TRANSITION - ECONOMETRIC MODELS.
Zimmermann, Rainer. Demographische Variablen in linearen Produktionsmodellen /. Bochum , 1983. 263 p. : ISBN 3-88339-327-4 LC Card 84-107454
HB241 .Z56 1983

DEMOGRAPHIC TRANSITION - ENGLAND.
Levine, David, 1946- Reproducing families . Cambridge [Cambridgeshire] , New York , 1987. ix, 251 p. ; ISBN 0-521-33256-7 LC Card 86-26372 DDC 304.6/0942 19
HB3585 .L48 1987

DEMOGRAPHIC TRANSITION - THAILAND.
Knodel, John E. Thailand's reproductive revolution . Madison, Wis. , c1987. xiii, 251 p. : ISBN 0-299-11050-8 LC Card 87-8172 DDC 304.6/32/09593 19
HB1054.55.A3 K576 1987

Démographie et emploi en Guadeloupe : informations disponibles en 1976. Basse-Terre : I.N.S.E.E., Service départemental de la Guadeloupe, [1977?] 3, xix leaves, [6] leaves of plates : ill. ; 30 cm. Chiefly tables. ISBN 2-11-062928-2 LC Card 85-230531
1. Guadeloupe - Population - Statistics. 2. Labor supply - Guadeloupe - Statistics. I. Institut national de la statistique et des études économiques (France). Service départemental de la Guadeloupe.
HA918.7 .D46 1977

Dēmographikē Hēmerida (1984 : Athens, Greece) Hē Dēmographikē krisē stēn Hellada : ethnikes, oikonomikes kai koinōnikes epiptōseis : Dēmographikē Hēmerida 29ēs Noemvriou 1984 hypo tēn aigida tou Hypourgeiou Politismou kai Epistēmōn. Athēna : Hellēnikē Hetairia Dēmographikōn Meletōn, 1985. 205 p. : ill. ; 24 cm. Title on added t.p.: La crise démographique en Grèce. Summaries in English and French. Includes bibliographies. LC Card 86-192606
1. Greece - Population - Congresses. I. Greece. Hypourgeion Politismou kai Epistēmōn. II. Hellēnikē Hetairia Dēmographikōn Meletōn. III. Title. IV. Title: La crise démographique en Grèce.
HB3632.5.A3 D45 1984

Hē Dēmographikē krisē stēn Hellada : ethnikes, oikonomikes kai koinōnikes epiptōseis : Dēmographikē Hēmerida 29ēs Noemvriou 1984 Hypo tēn aigida tou Hypourgeiou Politismou kai Epistēmōn. 2. ekdosē. Athēna : Hellēnikē Hetairia Dēmographikōn Meletōn, 1986. 205 p. : ill. ; 24 cm. Added t.p. in French. Summaries in English and French. Bibliography: p. 93-94. LC Card 86-201713
1. Greece - Population - Congresses. 2. Greece - Population policy - Congresses. I. Hellēnikē Hetairia Dēmographikōn Meletōn (Greece). II. Greece. Hypourgeion Politismou kai Epistēmōn. III. Title. IV. Title: La crise démographique en Grèce.
HB3632.5.A3 D45 1986

Hē Dēmographikē krisē stēn Hellada . Dēmographikē Hēmerida (1984 : Athens, Greece) Athēna , 1985. 205 p. : LC Card 86-192606
HB3632.5.A3 D45 1984

Hē Dēmographikē krisē stēn Hellada . Dēmographikē Hēmerida (1984 : Athens, Greece) Athēna , 1986. 205 p. : LC Card 86-201713
HB3632.5.A3 D45 1986

Demographische Entwicklung und kapitalbildende Altersversorgungssysteme / [Herausgeber, Gesellschaft für Versicherungswissenschaft und -gestaltung e.V., Köln ; Redaktion, Volker Leienbach]. Bergisch Gladbach : I. Vollmer, 1984. iii, 67 p. ; 21 cm. (Schriftenreihe der Gesellschaft für Versicherungswissenschaft und -gestaltung e.V. Köln . Bd. 6) LC Card 85-154174
1. Old age pensions. 2. Population forecasting. 3. Saving and investment. I. Leienbach, Volker. II. Gesellschaft für Versicherungswissenschaft und -gestaltung e.V. Köln. III. Series.
HD7091 .D46 1984

Demographische Probleme der Haushaltsökonomie / Klaus F. Zimmermann (Hrsg.). Bochum : Studienverlag N. Brockmeyer, 1986. vii, 212 p. : ill. ; 21 cm. (Contributions to quantitative economics . vol. 9 =) Includes bibliographies. CONTENTS. - Der Auszug von Kindern aus dem elterlichen Haushalt / Karl Ulrich Mayer und Michael Wagner -- Ausscheiden erwachsener Kinder aus dem elterlichen Haushalt / Notburga Ott -- Produktionsverlagerung vom Markt

zurück in die privaten Haushalte? / Ronald Schettkat -- Quellen des Wachstums / Klaus F. Zimmermann und Christoph M. Schmidt -- Effiziente Allokation des Familienbudgets / Klaus F. Zimmermann -- Zeitliche Verteilung der Geburten im Familienzyklus und Frauenerwerbstätigkeit / K. Peter Strohmeier -- Zur Lebenssituation älterer Bürger in einer Münchener Vorortgemeinde / Ingeborg Nerlich und Wilfried Schulz. ISBN 3-88339-534-X LC Card 87-137970 DDC 339.4/1/0943 19
1. Cost and standard of living - Germany, West. 2. Households - Economic aspects - Germany (West). 3. Family - Economic aspects - Germany (West). I. Zimmermann, Klaus F. II. Series: Contributions to quantitative economics , vol. 9.
HD7029 .D37 1986

Demographische Variablen in linearen Produktionsmodellen /. Zimmermann, Rainer. Bochum , 1983. 263 p. : ISBN 3-88339-327-4 LC Card 84-107454
HB241 .Z56 1983

DEMOGRAPHY.
Demograficheskaia politika sotsialisticheskogo obshchestva /. Moskva , 1986. 190 p. ;
NYPL [*QIP 87-2842]

Pol, Louis G. Business demography . New York , c1987. p. cm. ISBN 0-89930-218-1 (lib. bdg. : alk. paper) LC Card 87-2494 DDC 304.6 19
HB849.41 .P63 1987

DEMOGRAPHY - ADDRESSES, ESSAYS, LECTURES.
The State of population theory . Oxford, OX , New York, NY, USA , 1986. 311 p. : ISBN 0-631-13975-3 : LC Card 85-26668 DDC 304.6/01 19
HB849.4 .S73 1986 ***NYPL [JLE 86-2411]***

DEMOGRAPHY - CONGRESSES.
International Population Conference (1985 : Florence, Italy) International Population Conference, Florence 1985, 5-12 June =. Liège, Belgium , c1985- v. : ISBN 2-87108-004-6 (set) LC Card 86-113476 DDC 304.6 19
HB849 .I616 1985 ***NYPL [JLL 86-265]***

Recent advances in the techniques for demographic analysis /. Bombay , 1987. xiv, 456 p. ; LC Card 87-900498
HB849 .R42 1987

DEMOGRAPHY - CROSS-CULTURAL STUDIES.
Migration and settlement . Dordrecht ; Boston : xix, 496 p. ; ISBN 90-277-2119-X LC Card 85-25626 DDC 304.8 19
HB1952 .M539 1986 ***NYPL [JLE 86-4091]***

DEMOGRAPHY - CZECHOSLOVAKIA - SOCIETIES.
Československá demografická společnost. 20 let Československé demografické společnosti při ČSAV /. Praha , 1985. 198 p. : LC Card 86-208016
HB3592.3.A3 C47 1985

DEMOGRAPHY - DICTIONARIES - INDONESIAN.
Kamus istilah demografi /. Jakarta , 1985. vi, 119 p. ; LC Card 86-941191
HB849.2 .K35 1985

DEMOGRAPHY - HISTORY.
Korostelev, Gennadiĭ Mikhaĭlovich. Burzhuaznye kontseptsii narodonaseleniia . Moskva , 1981. 158 p. ; LC Card 82-140945
HB851 .K65 1981

Shelestov, D. K. (Dmitriĭ Kuz'mich) Demography in the mirror of history /. Moscow , c1987. 214 p. ; LC Card 86-201399 DDC 304.6/0947 19
HB853.S65 S54 1983

Demography in the mirror of history /. Shelestov, D. K. (Dmitriĭ Kuz'mich) Moscow , c1987. 214 p. ; LC Card 86-201399 DDC 304.6/0947 19
HB853.S65 S54 1983

DEMOGRAPHY - SOVIET UNION - HISTORY.
Shelestov, D. K. (Dmitriĭ Kuz'mich) Demography in the mirror of history /. Moscow , c1987. 214 p. ; LC Card 86-201399 DDC 304.6/0947 19
HB853.S65 S54 1983

DEMOGRAPHY - STUDY AND TEACHING - ESTONIA.
Izuchenie problem narodonaseleniia v Institute ėkonomiki AN Ėstonskoĭ SSR . Tallin , 1979. 78 p. ; LC Card 81-198604
HB850.5.S65 I97 1979

Demokratie : Entwicklungsgesetz des sozialistischen Staates / [Herausgeber, Institut für Theorie des Staates und des Rechts der Akademie der Wissenschaften der DDR, Institut für Staat und Recht der Akademie der Wissenschaften der UdSSR ; Redaktionskollegium, N.P. Farberow ... et al.].1. Aufl. Berlin : Staatsverlag der Deutschen Demokratischen Republik, 1981. 188 p. ; 21 cm. Includes bibliographical references. LC Card 81-149074 DDC 320.5/315 19
1. Socialism - Addresses, essays, lectures. 2. Democracy - Addresses, essays, lectures. I. Farberov, N. P. II. Akademie der Wissenschaften der DDR. Institut für Theorie des Staates und des Rechts. III. Akademiia nauk SSSR. Institut gosudarstva i prava.
HX73 .D45 1981 ***NYPL [JLD 86-3341]***

Demokratie bleibt auf der Strecke. Studer, Stefan. Nationalstrasse, Nationalstrafe, oder, Die Demokratie bleibt auf der Strecke /. Zürich , 1985. 191 p. : ISBN 3-85869-037-6 : LC Card 86-129406
HE363.S92 S83 1985

Demokratische Wirtschaftspolitik . Ernst, Mario, 1953- Bern , New York , c1986. x, 178 p. : ISBN 3-261-03571-4 LC Card 86-198029
HD76 .E76 1986

DeMong, Richard F.
Atchison, Michael D. New financial instruments . Charlottesville, Va. (P.O. Box 3665, Charlottesville 22903) , c1985. viii, 108 p. ; LC Card 85-195578 DDC 332.63 19
HG6024.3 .A83 1985
NYPL [JLL 81-133 no.21]

Broader perspectives on the interest of pension plan participants /. Charlottesville, Va. (P.O. Box 3665, Charlottesville 22903) , c1985. vii, 43 p. : LC Card 85-196669 DDC 332.6/7254 19
HD7105.45.U6 B76 1985
NYPL [JLL 81-133 no. 22]

DEMONSTRATIONS - SWEDEN - STOCKHOLM.
Larsson, Janerik, 1944- Vändpunkten . [Stockholm] [1983] 125 p. : ISBN 91-7566-040-7 : LC Card 84-189468
HD5660.S9 L35 1983

Demontage des Sozialstaats : verfassungsrechtliche Grenzen staatlicher Sparpolitik / Charlotte Niess-Mache, Joachim Schwammborn (Hg.) ; Vorwort von Detlef Hensche. Köln : R. Theurer, 1986. 177 p. ; 21 cm. (Rechtspolitische Schriften . 7) Includes bibliographies. ISBN 3-8161-0107-0 LC Card 87-104505 DDC 338.943 19
1. Germany, West - Economic policy - 1974-. 2. Germany, West - Economic conditions - 1974-. 3. Germany, West - Social policy. I. Niess-Mache, Charlotte. II. Schwammborn, Joachim. III. Series.
HC286.7 .D455 1986

DeMontmollin, Richard Hall. The SCOJA story : jobbers working together / by Richard Hall deMontmollin. [Columbia, S.C.] : South Carolina Petroleum Marketers Association, c1986. xi, 191 p. : ill. ; 29 cm. ISBN 0-9617613-0-X LC Card 86-62676 DDC 381/.456655/060757 19
1. South Carolina Oil Jobbers Association - History. 2. Petroleum industry and trade - South Carolina - History. 3. Gasoline industry - South Carolina - History. 4. Fuel trade - South Carolina - History. I. South Carolina Petroleum Marketers Association. II. Title.
HD9569.S663 D46 1986

Demornex, Jacqueline. Lancôme / Jacqueline Demornex, avec la collaboration de Jean-Claude Hervé ; préface, François Dalle ; photographies, Jacques Boulay. Paris : Editions du Regard, c1985. 189 p. : ill. (some col.) ; 31 cm. ISBN 2-903370-23-0 LC Card 86-201508
1. Lancôme (Firm) - History. 2. Perfumes industry - France - History. I. Hervé, Jean-Claude. II. Title.
HD9999.P3934 L363 1985
NYPL [JSG 87-24]

Dēmosieuma (Hellēnikē Geōgraphikē Hetaireia (Athens, Greece)) .
(4) Moustakas, Dion. E. Hai ploutoparagōgikai dynameis tēs nēsou Androu /. En Athēnais , 1924. 25 p. : LC Card 87-100195
HC297.A53 M68 1924

DemoSystems (Firm) Household and population projections for Canadian provinces and territories, 1981-2046. Edmonton, Alta., Canada , c1984. 53 p. ; LC Card 84-670146 DDC 312/.8/0971 19
HA745 .H69 1984 ***NYPL [JLF 86-642]***

DEMOUNTABLE BUILDINGS. see **BUILDINGS, PREFABRICATED.**

DEMOUNTABLE HOUSES. see **PREFABRICATED HOUSES.**

Den Staat erneuern, den Markt retten /. Engels, Wolfram. Köln , c1983. 228 p. ; ISBN 3-602-34836-9 LC Card 84-182378
HC286 .E54 1983

Denaro . Brera, Paolo. [Brescia] [1984] 110 p. ; LC Card 86-102925
HB49 .B74 1984

Denby, Charles. Indignant heart : a black worker's journal / by Charles Denby (Matthew Ward).1st ed. Montréal : Black Rose Books, 1979. 295 p. : ill. ; 21 cm. ISBN 0-919618-93-6 LC Card 87-672793
1. Denby, Charles. 2. Afro-American automobile industry workers - Biography. 3. Afro-American communists - Biography. 4. International Union, United Automobile, Aerospace, and Agricultural Implement Workers of America - History. 5. United States - Race relations - History. I. Title.
HD8039.A82 U633x 1979

DENBY, CHARLES.
Denby, Charles. Indignant heart . Montréal , 1979. 295 p. : ISBN 0-919618-93-6 LC Card 87-672793
HD8039.A82 U633x 1979

Dende Galicia, Marx : homenaxe a Marx no 1.o centenario da súa morte / edición de Carlos Barros e J. Vilas Nogueira. Sada, A Coruña : Ediciós do Castro, [1985?] 258 p. : port. ; 24 cm. (Ensaio) Includes bibliographical references. ISBN 84-7492-241-0 LC Card 86-215077
1. Marxian economics. 2. Marx, Karl, 1818-1883. 3. Labor and laboring classes - Spain - Galicia (Region) - History. I. Marx, Karl, 1818-1883. II. Barros, Carlos. III. Vilas Nogueira, J.
HB97.5 .D413 1985

Denenberg, R. V., 1942- Denenberg, Tia Schneider. Alcohol and drugs . Washington, D.C. , c1983. xv, 201 p. : ISBN 0-87179-410-1 LC Card 83-7560 DDC 344.73/01255 347.3041255 19
KF3540 .D46 1983 ***NYPL [JLE 86-2348]***

Denenberg, Tia Schneider. Alcohol and drugs : issues in the workplace / Tia Schneider Denenberg, R.V. Denenberg. Washington, D.C. : Bureau of National Affairs, c1983. xv, 201 p. : ill. ; 24 cm. Includes bibliographical references and index. ISBN 0-87179-410-1 LC Card 83-7560 DDC 344.73/01255 347.3041255 19
1. Employee assistance programs - Law and legislation - United States. 2. Labor discipline - Law and legislation - United States. 3. Alcoholism and employment - United States. 4. Drugs and employment - United States. I. Denenberg, R. V., 1942-. II. Title.
KF3540 .D46 1983 ***NYPL [JLE 86-2348]***

Dénes, Katalin. A Szabolcs-Szatmár megyei télialma-termelés, -feldolgozás és -értékesítés rendszerének fejlesztése /. Budapest , 1985. 144 p. : ISBN 963-491-208-7 LC Card 86-196831
HD9259.A6 H87 1985

Denev, Doncho. Aktivizirane na mladezhkoto nauchno i tekhnichesko tvorchestvo /. Sofiia , 1985. 135 p. : LC Card 86-220354
HC403.Z9 T419 1985

Denezhno-kreditnye i finansovye otnosheniia v sisteme sovremennogo gosudarstvenno-monopolisticheskogo kapitalizma. Parichno-kreditni i finansovi otnosheniia v sistemata na sŭvremenniia dŭrzhavno-monopolisticheski kapitalizŭm /. Sofiia , 1985. 245 p. : LC Card 86-153156
HG3881 .P2936 1985

Denezhnoe obrashchenie i kredit kapitalisticheskikh stran / pod redaktsieĭ L.N. Krasavinoĭ. Moskva : "Finansy," 1977. 342 p. ; 23 cm. Authorized for instructional purposes. Includes bibliographical references and index. LC Card 82-196677

1. Finance. 2. Credit. 3. Money. 4. Banks and banking. 5. Capitalism. I. Krasavina, L. N.
HG173.6.R8 D46 1977

Denezhnoe obrashchenie i kredit SSSR / pod redaktsieĭ V.S. Gerashchenko. Izd. 4-e, perer. i dop. Moskva : "Finansy i statistika", 1986. 374 p. : ill. ; 23 cm. Includes bibliographical references and index. LC Card 87-157773
1. Credit - Soviet Union. 2. Money - Soviet Union. 3. Banks and banking - Soviet Union. I. Gerashchenko, V. S. (Vladimir Sergeevich).
HG3729.S632 D46 1986

Denezhnoe obrashchenie v protsesse rasshirennogo sotsialisticheskogo vosproizvodstva /. Konnik, I. I. (Iosif Isaakovich) Moskva , 1982. 269 p. ; LC Card 83-165373
HG186.S55 K65 1982

Denial of maternity benefits to women workers . Hirway, Indira. New Delhi , c1986. iv, 151 p. ; ISBN 81-204-0154-9 : LC Card 86-903013 DDC 331.4/25763 19
HD6065.5.I4 H57 1986

Denis, Pierre. L'ASEAN (Association des pays de l'Asie et du Sud-Est) : ses structures, ses objectifs, ses réalisations / dossier réalisé par Pierre Denis, Feike Reitsma. Ottignies, Louvain-la-Neuve : Centre tricontinental, [1981] 61 p., [3] leaves of plates : ill. ; 30 cm. Includes bibliography. LC Card 86-204495
1. ASEAN. 2. Asia, Southeastern - Economic integration. 3. Asia, Southeastern - Foreign economic relations. I. Reitsma, Feike. II. Title.
HC441 .D45 1981

Deniskin, V. V. (Viktor Vasil'evich) Voronin, V. G. (Valeriĭ Grigor'evich) Ėkonomiko-matematicheskie metody planirovaniia na predpriiatiiakh pishchevoĭ promyshlennosti /. Moskva , 1981. 270 p. : LC Card 82-103139
HD9015.S65 V67 1981

Denisova, N. F. (Nina Fedorovna) Planirovanie otdelochnogo proizvodstva s primeneniem matematicheskikh metodov i ĖVM : na baze trudoemkosti produktsii / N.F. Denisova, V.D. Ivanova, N.A. Tokareva. Moskva : "Legkaia i pishchevaia promyshl.", 1984. 59, [5] p. : ill. ; 21 cm. Bibliography: p. [61] LC Card 85-131509
1. Textile industry - Soviet Union - Planning - Mathematical models. 2. Textile industry - Soviet Union - Planning - Data processing. 3. Textile industry - Soviet Union - Labor productivity. I. Ivanova, V. D. (Valentina Dmitrievna). II. Tokareva, N. A. (Nadezhda Andreevna). III. Title.
HD9865.S652 D46 1984

Denizet, Jean. Le dollar : histoire du système monétaire international depuis 1945 / Jean Denizet. Paris : Fayard, c1985. 259 p. ; 22 cm. Includes indexes. Bibliography: p. [237]-243. ISBN 2-213-01626-7 : LC Card 86-148501 DDC 332.4/560973 19
1. International finance - History. 2. Dollar, American - History. 3. Foreign exchange - History. I. Title.
HG3881 .D344 1985 ***NYPL [JLD 87-337]***

Denk ja nicht, Du bist selber schuld . Fokkink, Manfred, 1955- Gelsenkirchen-Buer , 1980. 180 p. : LC Card 82-114713
HD6276.G4 F6 1980 ***NYPL [JLE 86-1457]***

DENMARK - COMMERCE - HISTORY.
Glamann, Kristof. Studier i dansk merkantilisme . [Copenhagen] , c1983. 243 p. ; ISBN 87-500-2476-0 LC Card 85-125251
HB91 .G57 1983

DENMARK - COMMERCIAL POLICY - HISTORY.
Eriksen, August Wiemann. Eksportrådgivning i Danmark 1910-1921 . [Copenhagen] , 1984. 198 p. : ISBN 87-7497-075-5 LC Card 84-231455
HF1561 .E75 1984

DENMARK - DIPLOMATIC AND CONSULAR SERVICE - CONGRESSES.
Consular conference in Denmark, June 76. [Copenhagen] [1976] 47 p. : LC Card 85-189659
HF1561 .C66 1976

Denmark. Direktoratet for toldvæsenet. Information og kontrol : overvejelser og forslag vedrørende forbedring af toldvæsenets information og kontrol over virksomheder og borgere. [Copenhagen] : Direktoratet for toldvæsenet, [1985] 125, [49] p. : ill. ; 24 cm. (Rapport . 2) "Oktober 1985." LC Card 86-209910
1. Customs administration - Denmark. 2. Denmark. Direktoratet for toldvæsenet. I. Series: Rapport (Denmark. Direktoratet for toldvæsenet) , 2. II. Title.
HJ6971 .D46 1985

DENMARK. DIREKTORATET FOR TOLDVÆSENET.
Denmark. Direktoratet for toldvæsenet. Information og kontrol . [Copenhagen] [1985] 125, [49] p. : LC Card 86-209910
HJ6971 .D46 1985

DENMARK - ECONOMIC CONDITIONS.
Jespersen, Jesper, 1948- Lille Danmark hva'nu? . [Copenhagen] , c1985. 128 p. : ISBN 87-500-2594-5 LC Card 85-243948
HC353 .J47 1985

DENMARK - ECONOMIC CONDITIONS - 1918-1945.
Topp, Niels-Henrik. Udviklingen i de finanspolitiske ideer i Danmark 1930-1945 /. [Copenhagen] [1987] 437 p. ; ISBN 87-574-5100-1 : LC Card 87-149164
HB51 .C63 nr. 30 HJ1222

Ulrichsen, Niels. J.A.K.--en dansk krisebevægelse /. København , 1978. 202 p. ; ISBN 87-87462-13-3 LC Card 87-462108
HD2002 .U45 1978

DENMARK - ECONOMIC CONDITIONS - 1945-
Danish economic survey. [Copenhagen] [1984] 72 p. : LC Card 86-220598 DDC 330.9489/058 19
HC355 .D226 1984

Dansk industripolitik . [Århus] , 1983. 143 p. : LC Card 84-164502
HD3616.D43 D35 1983

Sadolin, Pia. Regional udvikling i Danmark /. [Aarhus] , 1983. 92 p. : LC Card 84-164625
HC355 .S26 1983

Tholstrup, Knud. Tale er sølv, tavshed er underkastelse /. [Copenhagen] [1986] 179 p. : ISBN 87-416-1329-5 : LC Card 86-215991
HC355 .T37 1986

Vor tids fattigdom /. [Copenhagen] , c1986. 130 p. : ISBN 87-412-3897-4 : LC Card 86-214667
HC79.P6 V67 1986

DENMARK - ECONOMIC CONDITIONS - MATHEMATICAL MODELS.
Sørensen, Peter Birch. Økonomisk politik i en åben økonomi /. København , 1985. vi, 179 p. : LC Card 86-135751
HB135 .S575 1985

DENMARK - ECONOMIC POLICY.
Brink, Helge. Monetarisme og økonomisk politik /. [Copenhagen] , c1984. 125 p. ; ISBN 87-574-4380-7 : LC Card 84-253099
HG1092 .B75 1984

Christoffersen, Mads. Fysisk planlægning og samfundsmæssige reproduktionsproblemer . København , 1980, c1979. 317 p. ; ISBN 87-500-1922-8 ***NYPL [JLD 86-2303]***

Jespersen, Jesper, 1948- Lille Danmark hva'nu? . [Copenhagen] , c1985. 128 p. : ISBN 87-500-2594-5 LC Card 85-243948
HC353 .J47 1985

Denmark. Fællesudgiftsudvalget. Rapport om administrationsbudgettering. [Copenhagen] [1984] 85, 33 p. ; LC Card 85-129140
HJ2133 .R36 1984

DENMARK - FOREIGN ECONOMIC RELATIONS - CONGRESSES.
Consular conference in Denmark, June 76. [Copenhagen] [1976] 47 p. : LC Card 85-189659
HF1561 .C66 1976

DENMARK - FOREIGN RELATIONS - CONGRESSES.
Consular conference in Denmark, June 76. [Copenhagen] [1976] 47 p. : LC Card 85-189659
HF1561 .C66 1976

DENMARK - INDUSTRIES.
Andersen, Kirsten Gøgsig. Det skal stampes halv stamp presses og klædeskæres . København [1984] 179 columns : LC Card 85-242146
HD9999.C483 D43 1984

Denmark. Industriministeriet. Rapport om betalingskort . [Copenhagen] [1982] 302, 4, 17 p. ; ISBN 87-503-4413-7 LC Card 83-243151
HG3756.D4 R36 1982

Denmark. Mediekommissionen. Betænkning om et øget dansk tv-udbud. [København] : Direktoratet for statens indkøb, 1983. 168 p. : ill. ; 24 cm. (Mediekommissionens betænkning . nr. 5) "Betænkning nr. 986." ISBN 87-503-4624-5 LC Card 85-128700
1. Television broadcasting - Denmark. 2. Broadcasting policy - Denmark. I. Title. II. Series.
HE8700.9.D4 D45 1983

Denmark. Miljøstyrelsen. Rapporter udarbejdet af Forvaltningshøjskolen og Miljøstyrelsens økonomifunktion. København [1983] 59 p. : ISBN 87-503-4574-5 LC Card 85-150558
HD4465.D4 R36 1983

Denmark. Monopoltilsynet. Discountbutikker i dagligvarehandelen . København , 1983. 175 p. : ISBN 87-88149-11-0 : LC Card 83-237411
HF5429.215.D4 D57 1983

Rugbrødsbranchen . København , 1985. 112 p. : ISBN 87-88149-23-4 : LC Card 86-161889
HD9058.B743 D47 1985

Denmark. Økonomiske sekretariat. Danish economic survey. [Copenhagen] [1984] 72 p. : LC Card 86-220598 DDC 330.9489/058 19
HC355 .D226 1984

Denmark. Planstyrelsen. Larsen, Flemming. Parkeringsbehov i ældre tætte bydele . København , 1985. 250 p. : LC Card 86-165642
HE336.P37 L37 1985

DENMARK - POPULATION.
Mørch, Henning. Befolkningsbeskrivelse . [Copenhagen] , Brenderup , 1982. 160 p. : ISBN 87-87601-58-1 LC Card 83-195528
HB871 .M27 1982

Denmark. Privatiseringsudvalget. Rapport afgivet af Privatiseringsudvalget. [Copenhagen] : Administrationsdepartementet, [1983] 2, 243, [65] p. ; 30 cm. At head of title: Finansministeriet. LC Card 85-134270
1. Privatization - Denmark. I. Title.
HD4224 .D45 1983

DENMARK - STATISTICS, VITAL.
Regionale dødelighedsforskelle i Danmark 1971-79. København , 1983. 136 p. : ISBN 87-501-0582-5 : LC Card 84-169325
HA1473 .A35 nr. 39 HB1441

Denmark. Statsskattedirektoratet. Vurderingen af landets faste ejendomme pr. 1 april 1981 . København [1982] 225 p. ; ISBN 87-503-4048-4 LC Card 82-232266
HD736 .V87 1982

Denmark. Udenrigsministeriet. Consular conference in Denmark, June 76. [Copenhagen] [1976] 47 p. : LC Card 85-189659
HF1561 .C66 1976

Denmark. Udvalget til undersøgelse af vandforsyningernes økonomiske baggrund. Vandpriser : betænkning / afgivet af Udvalget til undersøgelse af vandforsyningernes økonomiske baggrund, nedsat af Miljøministeren den 3. februar 1981. København : Miljøministeriet, [1983] 108 p. ; 24 cm. "April 1983." ISBN 87-503-4559-1 LC Card 84-169901
1. Municipal water supply - Denmark - Rates. 2. Water - Law and legislation - Denmark. I. Title.
HD4465.D4 D46 1983

Denmark. Udvalget til undersøgelse af vandforsyningernes økonomiske baggrund. Vandpriser.
Lauritzen, Niels, 1947- Rapporter /. København [1983] 59 p. : ISBN 87-503-4574-5 LC Card 84-169893
HD4465.D4 L38 1983

Rapporter udarbejdet af Forvaltningshøjskolen og Miljøstyrelsens økonomifunktion. København [1983] 59 p. : ISBN 87-503-4574-5 LC Card 85-150558
HD4465.D4 R36 1983

Teknisk-økonomisk-organisatorisk analyse /. København [1983] 131 p. : ISBN 87-503-4561-3 LC Card 84-169883
HD4465.D4 T44 1983

Denmark. Udvalget vedrørende byfornyelse og støtte til ejerboliger. Redegørelse om støtte til ejerboliger i forbindelse med byfornyelse : nogle modeller / afgivet af Udvalget vedrørende byfornyelse og støtte til ejerboliger. København : Boligministeriet, [1981] 128 p. : ill. ; 24 cm. (Publikationer fra Boligministeriet, Boligstyrelsen og Byggestyrelsen . 41) "September 1981." ISBN 87-503-3873-0 LC Card 82-194685

1. Housing policy - Denmark. 2. Housing - Denmark - Finance. 3. Urban renewal - Denmark. I. Title. II. Series.
HD7347.A4 D455 1981

Denmark. Udvalget vedrørende dansk bistandspolitik. Betænkning om principperne for den danske bistand til udviklingslandene / afgivet af det af regeringen i december 1980 nedsatte udvalg. København : Direktoratet for statens indkøb, 1982. 224 p. ; 24 cm. "Betænkning nr. 958." ISBN 87-503-4037-9 LC Card 84-103068
1. Economic assistance, Danish - Developing countries. I. Title.
HC60 .D435 1982

Denmark. Vejdirektoratet. Økonomisk-statistisk afdeling.
Trafikanalyse Randers 1.-2. december 1982. [Copenhagen] [1983] 64 p. : LC Card 84-169856
HE373.D43 R368 1983

60-punkts tællinger 1983. [Copenhagen] , 1984. 36 p. : LC Card 85-156478
HE373.D4 A6 1984

Dennis, Helen. Fourteen steps in managing an aging work force /. Lexington, Mass. , c1988. xi, [247] p. : ISBN 0-669-13206-3 (alk. paper) LC Card 87-3322 DDC 658.3/042 19
HF5549.5.O44 F68 1988

Denoon, David B. H. Devaluation under pressure : Indian, Indonesia, and Ghana / David B.H. Denoon. Cambridge, Mass. : MIT Press, c1986. xi, 260 p.; 24 cm. Includes index. Bibliography: p. [247]-254. ISBN 0-262-04083-2 LC Card 85-15314 DDC 332.4/14 19
1. Devaluation of currency - India. 2. Devaluation of currency - Indonesia. 3. Devaluation of currency - Ghana. I. Title.
HG1235 .D37 1985 NYPL [JLE 86-2836]

DENSITY, POPULATION. see **POPULATION DENSITY.**

Denslow, David, 1942- Sugar production in northeastern Brazil and Cuba, 1858-1908 / David Denslow. New York : Garland, 1987. 172 p. : ill. ; 24 cm. (South American and Latin American economic history) Thesis (Ph. D.)--Yale University,1974. Bibliography: p. 168-172. ISBN 0-8240-1357-3 (alk. paper) : LC Card 87-8525 DDC 338.1/7361/097291 19
1. Sugarcane industry - Cuba - History. 2. Sugarcane industry - Brazil, Northeast - History. 3. Sugarcane - Cuba - Processing - History. 4. Sugarcane - Brazil, Northeast - Processing - History. I. Title. II. Series.
HD9114.C89 D45 1987

DENTAL INSTRUMENTS AND APPARATUS INDUSTRY.
Growth areas in dentistry . Tustin, CA (17722 Irvine Blvd., Tustin 92680) , c1986. 1 v. (various foliations) : LC Card 86-212546 DDC 381/.45681761 19
HD9995.D42 G76 1986

DENTAL INSTRUMENTS AND APPARATUS INDUSTRY - UNITED STATES - STATISTICS.
Marketing communications effectiveness to the dentist. Tustin, CA (17722 Irvine Blvd., Tustin 92680) , c1986. 130 leaves in various foliations : LC Card 86-231569 DDC 681/.761 19
HD9995.D43 U55 1986

Sales representative effectiveness to the dentist. Tustin, CA (17722 Irvine Blvd., Tustin 92680) , c1986. 113 leaves in various foliations : LC Card 86-231841 DDC 681/.761 19
HD9995.D43 U56 1986

DENTAL INSTRUMENTS AND APPARATUS - UNITED STATES - MARKETING - STATISTICS.
Marketing communications effectiveness to the dentist. Tustin, CA (17722 Irvine Blvd., Tustin 92680) , c1986. 130 leaves in various foliations : LC Card 86-231569 DDC 681/.761 19
HD9995.D43 U55 1986

DENTISTS - UNITED STATES - ATTITUDES - STATISTICS.
Marketing communications effectiveness to the dentist. Tustin, CA (17722 Irvine Blvd., Tustin 92680) , c1986. 130 leaves in various foliations : LC Card 86-231569 DDC 681/.761 19
HD9995.D43 U55 1986

Sales representative effectiveness to the dentist. Tustin, CA (17722 Irvine Blvd., Tustin 92680) , c1986. 113 leaves in various foliations : LC Card 86-231841 DDC 681/.761 19
HD9995.D43 U56 1986

Denton, A. S. Coventry transport : West Midlands transport in words and pictures / A.S. Denton, F.P. Groves. Birmingham [West Midlands, England] : Birmingham Transport Historical Group, c1985- v. <1 > : ill. ; 21 cm. CONTENTS. - pt. 1. 1884-1940. ISBN 0-905103-05-X (pbk.) : LC Card 86-224227 DDC 388.4/09424/98 19
1. Local transit - England - Coventry (West Midlands) - History. I. Groves, F. P. II. Birmingham Transport Historical Group. III. Title. IV. Title: Coventry transport, 1884-1940.
HE4719.C68 D46 1985

Denton L., Carlos F. Población, fecundidad y desarrollo en Costa Rica, 1950-1970 / preparado por Carlos Denton, Olda Ma. Acuña ; con la colaboración de Miguel Gómez B. ... [et al.]. [Heredia, Costa Rica] : Instituto de Estudios Sociales en Población, Facultad de Ciencias Sociales, Universidad Nacional, 1984. iv, 150 p. : ill. ; 28 cm. (Informe de trabajo . #39) Bibliography: p. 145-150. LC Card 86-117583 DDC 304.6/097286 19
1. Fertility, Human - Costa Rica. 2. Costa Rica - Population. 3. Costa Rica - Economic Policy. I. Acuña B., Olda M. II. Series: Informe de trabajo (Universidad Nacional (Costa Rica). Instituto de Estudios Sociales en Población) , no. 39. III. Title.
HB3531 .D44 1984 NYPL [JLF 87-144]

Denton, Peter, 1955- Elliott : a biography of John D. Elliott / by Peter Denton. Bedford, U.K. : Little Hills Press, c1986. 266 p. : ill. ; 23 cm. Includes index. ISBN 0-949773-47-6 LC Card 87-100702 DDC 338/.04/0924 B 19
1. Elliott, John D. (John Dorman), 1941-. 2. Businessmen - Australia - Biography. I. Title.
HC602.5.E45 D45 1986

Les dents du géant . Sautter, Christian. Paris , c1987. 323 p. ; ISBN 2-85565-362-2 : LC Card 87-169635
HC462.9 .S277 1987

DENVER & INTERURBAN RAILROAD - HISTORY.
Jones, William C., 1937- The kite route . Boulder, Colo. , c1986. 159 p. : ISBN 0-87108-721-9 LC Card 86-25190 DDC 385/.5 19
HE2791.D383 J66 1986

Deocadiz, Leo A. RP-Japan relations and ADB . Metro Manila, Philippines , 1986. x, 137 p. : ISBN 971-08-3156-9 (pbk.) LC Card 86-211088 DDC 337.520599 19
HF1600.15.J3 R68 1986

DEONTOLOGY. see **ETHICS.**

Department of Geography publication series . (no. 26) Manufacturing in Kitchener-Waterloo . [Waterloo] , c1987. xiii, 220 p. : ISBN 0-921083-22-X (pbk.) LC Card 87-168616 DDC 338.4/767/0971344 19
HD9734.C3 K56 1987

The Department of Labor /. Cutrona, Cheryl. [New York] , c1988. 95 p. : ISBN 0-87754-844-7 LC Card 87-24906 DDC 353.83 19
HD8066 .C85 1988

Department of Political Science seminar series . (vol. 2) Rural underdevelopment in Nigeria, 1900-1980. Zaria, Nigeria , 1985. iv, 102 p. ; LC Card 86-154806 DDC 338.1/8669 19
HD2145.5.Z8 R87 1985

The Department of Transportation /. Stefany, Wallace Charles. New York, NY , c1988. p. cm. ISBN 0-87754-847-1 LC Card 87-24924 DDC 353.86 19
HE206.3 .S73 1988

DEPARTMENT STORES - EMPLOYEES - UNITED STATES - HISTORY.
Benson, Susan Porter, 1943- Counter cultures . Urbana , c1986. xvi, 322 p. : ISBN 0-252-01252-6 (alk. paper) LC Card 85-21012 DDC 381/.1/0973 19
HF5465.U5 B45 1986 NYPL [JLE 87-1091]

DEPARTMENT STORES - OHIO - CLEVELAND - HISTORY.
Wood, James M., 1939- Halle's . Cleveland, Ohio , 1987. 223 p. : ISBN 0-940601-02-8 : LC Card 87-15010 DDC 381/.45/000977132 19
HF5465.U6 H359 1987

DEPARTMENT STORES - UNITED STATES - HISTORY.
Benson, Susan Porter, 1943- Counter cultures . Urbana , c1986. xvi, 322 p. : ISBN 0-252-01252-6 (alk. paper) LC Card 85-21012 DDC 381/.1/0973 19
HF5465.U5 B45 1986 NYPL [JLE 87-1091]

Departmental information report (Texas Agricultural Experiment Station. Dept. of Agricultural Economics) .
(DIR 86-4) Knutson, Ronald D. Cooperative involvement in issues of domestic farm policy /. College Station, Tex. , 1986. 59 p. : LC Card 86-623063 DDC 338.1/8764 19
HD1491.U6 T45 1986

Dependence, underdevelopment, and unemployment in Kenya . Cheru, Fantu. Lanham, MD , c1987. xvii, 198 p. : ISBN 0-8191-6539-5 (alk. paper) : LC Card 87-13710 DDC 331.13/77/096762 19
HD6276.K42 C46 1987

La dependencia, el subdesarrollo y la publicidad comercial capitalista /. Benítez, José Antonio, 1921- La Habana, Cuba , 1986. 133 p., [2] p. of plates : LC Card 87-404231 DDC 659.1/098 19
HF5813.L29 B46 1986

La dependencia tecnológica española . Sánchez Muñoz, María Paloma. [Madrid] [1984?] xi, 591 p. : ISBN 84-7415-170-8 : LC Card 86-212990
HC390.T4 S26 1984

Dependencia y brechas entre ricos y pobres /. Abreu, Antonio. Bogotá , 1987. 112 p. ; ISBN 958-625-058-X LC Card 87-403548 DDC 337.8 19
HC125 .A23 1987

DEPENDENCIES. see **COLONIES.**

DEPENDENCY.
Apter, David Ernest, 1924- Rethinking development . Newbury Park, Calif. , c1987. 326 p. : ISBN 0-8039-2971-4 LC Card 86-29642 DDC 338.9 19
HD82 .A657 1987

Dauderstädt, Michael. Entwicklungspolitik, Politik ohne Entwicklung . Bonn [1984] 38 p. ; LC Card 85-136902
HC59.7 .D327 1984

David, Wilfred L. Conflicting paradigms in the economics of developing nations /. New York , 1986. xix, 215 p. : ISBN 0-275-92108-5 (alk. paper) : LC Card 86-16906 DDC 330.9172/4 19
HC59.7 .D335 1986 NYPL [JLE 86-4423]

Kalmanovitz, Salomón. El desarrollo tardío del capitalismo . [Bogotá] , 1983. 285 p. ; LC Card 84-155755 DDC 338.9/009172/4 19
HC59.7 .K246 1983 NYPL [JLD 85-2613]

Kannapin, Klaus. Imperialistische Strategie gegen die neue Internationale Wirtschaftsordnung /. Berlin , 1984. 180 p. : LC Card 85-147404
HD84 .K28 1984

Moser, Beat. Konflikt und Kooperation der Dritten Welt mit Industrieländern /. Diessenhofen , c1985. xi, 352 p. : ISBN 3-7253-0236-7 : LC Card 85-139491
HF1413 .M66 1985

DEPENDENCY - ADDRESSES, ESSAYS, LECTURES.
Dependency theory and the return of high politics /. Westport, Conn. , 1986. xii, 270 p. : ISBN 0-313-24860-5 (lib. bdg. : alk. paper) LC Card 85-17745 DDC 337 19
HF1411 .D35 1986 NYPL [JLE 86-2911]

International dimension of development problems . Amsterdam , New York , 1984. 103 p. ; ISBN 0-444-85621-8 (pbk.) LC Card 85-209291 DDC 338.9 19
HD75 .I59 1984 NYPL [JLE 86-1391]

DEPENDENCY (PSYCHOLOGY)
Alarcón, Reynaldo. Psicología, pobreza y subdesarrollo /. Lima, Perú , 1986. 153 p. ; LC Card 87-126266 DDC 155.9/2 19
HC79.P6 A55 1986

Dependency theory and the return of high politics / edited by Mary Ann Tétreault and Charles Frederick Abel. Westport, Conn. : Greenwood Press, 1986. xii, 270 p. : ill. ; 25 cm. (Contributions in political science, 0147-1066 . no. 140) Includes index. "Bibliographic essay": p. 256-260.

ISBN 0-313-24860-5 (lib. bdg. : alk. paper) LC Card 85-17745 DDC 337 19
1. International economic relations - Addresses, essays, lectures. 2. Dependency - Addresses, essays, lectures. 3. International relations - Addresses, essays, lectures. I. Tétreault, Mary Ann, 1942-. II. Abel, Charles. III. Series.
HF1411 .D35 1986 *NYPL [JLE 86-2911]*

Dependent wives. Lopata, Helena Znaniecka, 1925- Widows and dependent wives . New York , 1986. xxi, 242 p. ; ISBN 0-03-046301-7 (alk. paper) : LC Card 85-16753 DDC 362.8/382 19
HV699 .L67 1985 *NYPL [JLE 86-2182]*

Déplante, Henri, 1907- A la conquête du ciel / Henri Déplante. Aix-en-Provence : Edisud, [1985] 233 p. ; 24 cm. LC Card 86-159140
1. Avions Marcel Dassault Breguet aviation - History. 2. Aircraft industry - France - Military aspects - History. 3. Aircraft industry - France - History. I. Title.
HD9711.F74 D374 1985

DEPOSIT BANKING - ITALY.
Fabrizi, Pier Luigi. La politica degli investimenti in titoli nelle banche di deposito /. [Milano] , 1982. xii, 138 p. ; LC Card 82-165568
HG1616.I5 F33 1982

DEPOSIT BANKING - UNITED STATES.
Friedman, David H., 1942- Deposit operations /. Washington, D.C. (1120 Connecticut Ave., N.W., Washington 20036) , c1987. xii, 354 p. : LC Card 87-165558 DDC 332.1/752 19
HG1660.U5 F75 1987

Deposit operations /. Friedman, David H., 1942- Washington, D.C. (1120 Connecticut Ave., N.W., Washington 20036) , c1987. xii, 354 p. : LC Card 87-165558 DDC 332.1/752 19
HG1660.U5 F75 1987

Deppe, Frank. Arbeiterklasse, gibt's die noch? /. Wien , c1985. 246 p. : ISBN 3-900351-46-5 LC Card 86-123225
HD8451 .A836 1985

Deppe, Wilfried. Drei Generationen Arbeiterleben : eine sozio-biographische Darstellung / Wilfried Deppe ; Vorwort von Hans Paul Bahrdt. Frankfurt/Main ; New York : Campus, c1982. 419 p. ; 21 cm. (Studienreihe des Soziologischen Forschungsinstituts Göttingen) Bibliography: p. 409-419. ISBN 3-593-33018-0 LC Card 82-167833 DDC 305.5/62/0922 19
1. Labor and laboring classes - Germany (West) - Interviews. 2. Labor and laboring classes - Germany (West) - Biography. 3. Sociology - Biographical methods. I. Title. II. Title: 3 Generationen Arbeiterleben.
HD6957.G3 D38 1982
NYPL [JLD 86-2569]

Deppenkemper, Bernhard.
Mitgliederversammlungen und Willensbildung in Genossenschaften / Bernhard Deppenkemper. Gelsenkirchen : Mannhold, 1984. 316 p. : ill. ; 21 cm. (Kölner Genossenschaftswissenschaft, 0175-9582 . Bd. 8) Bibliography: p. 286-305. ISBN 3-88485-473-9 LC Card 85-114636
1. Banks and banking, Cooperative - Germany, West. 2. Banks and banking, Cooperative - Law and legislation - Germany (West). I. Title. II. Series.
HG2039.G4 D45 1984

DEPRECIATION.
Normen voor nieuwwaarde en afschrijving van slijtende duurzame produktiemiddelen in de fruitteelt alsmede voor de grondwaarde . Den Haag [1986] 67 p. ; LC Card 86-234475
HF5686.F7 N67 1986

DEPRECIATION - ADDRESSES, ESSAYS, LECTURES.
Depreciation and capital maintenance /. New York , 1984. xi, 137 p. : ISBN 0-8240-6304-X (alk. paper) : LC Card 83-49437 DDC 657/.73 19
HF5681.D5 D45 1984 *NYPL [JLE 86-1715]*

DEPRECIATION ALLOWANCES - BERLIN (GERMANY)
Hecker, Christian. Abschreibungsgesellschaften in Berlin (West) . Köln , c1982. viii, 236, xix, 78 p. : ISBN 3-921379-96-2 LC Card 83-197457
HJ4720.B45 H43 1982

DEPRECIATION ALLOWANCES - LAW AND LEGISLATION - BERLIN (GERMANY)
Hecker, Christian. Abschreibungsgesellschaften in Berlin (West) . Köln , c1982. viii, 236, xix, 78 p. : ISBN 3-921379-96-2 LC Card 83-197457
HJ4720.B45 H43 1982

Depreciation and capital maintenance / edited by Richard P. Brief. New York : Garland Pub., 1984. xi, 137 p. : ill. ; 24 cm. (Accounting history and the development of a profession) Includes bibliographical references. ISBN 0-8240-6304-X (alk. paper) : LC Card 83-49437 DDC 657/.73 19
1. Depreciation - Addresses, essays, lectures. 2. Plant maintenance - Accounting - Addresses, essays, lectures. 3. Industrial equipment - Maintenance and repair - Accounting - Addresses, essays, lectures. I. Brief, Richard P., 1933-. II. Series.
HF5681.D5 D45 1984 *NYPL [JLE 86-1715]*

DEPRESSED CLASSES OF INDIA. see **UNTOUCHABLES.**

DEPRESSIONS - 1857 - GERMANY (WEST) - HAMBURG.
Ahrens, Gerhard, 1939- Krisenmanagement 1857 . Hamburg , 1986. 136 p. ; ISBN 3-923356-11-0 LC Card 87-127645 DDC 338.5/4 19
HB3717 1857 .A38 1986

DEPRESSIONS - 1857 - UNITED STATES.
Huston, James L., 1947- The panic of 1857 and the coming of the Civil War /. Baton Rouge , c1987. xviii, 315 p. ; ISBN 0-8071-1368-9 LC Card 87-2705 DDC 338.5/42 19
HB3717 1857 .H87 1987

DEPRESSIONS - 1929.
Garraty, John Arthur, 1920- The Great Depression . New York, N.Y. , 1987. x, 292 p. : ISBN 0-385-24085-6 (pbk.) : LC Card 87-5458 DDC 338.5/42 19
HB3717 1929 .G36 1987

Ideas para la cultura europea . Barcelona [1980?] 64 p. : ISBN 84-300-3210-X LC Card 85-105410
HC57 .I24 1980

Schmid, Hanspeter, 1951- Wirtschaft, Staat und Macht . Zürich [c1983] 432 p. : ISBN 3-85791-073-9 (Schw. Buch) LC Card 83-244266
HF1573 .S335 1983

DEPRESSIONS - 1929 - AUSTRALIA - MAPS.
Camm, J. C. R. (Jack Charles Robert) Hardtimes--a cartographic and graphic representation of selected aspects of the depression years, 1925-1935, in Australia /. [Newcastle, N.S.W.] , 1985. 59, iii p. : ISBN 0-7259-0542-5 (pbk.) : LC Card 86-222404 DDC 330.994/042 19
HC603 .C36 1985

DEPRESSIONS - 1929 - DEVELOPING COUNTRIES.
Die Peripherie in der Weltwirtschaftskrise, Afrika, Asien und Lateinamerika, 1929-1939 /. Paderborn , c1982. 295 p. : ISBN 3-506-77461-1 LC Card 83-167120 DDC 330.9172/4 19
HC59.7 .P457 1982 *NYPL [JLE 87-1202]*

DEPRESSIONS - 1929 - GREAT BRITAIN.
The Worst of times . London , 1985. 201 p., [8] p. of plates : ISBN 0-7045-0513-4
NYPL [JLD 86-1799]

DEPRESSIONS - 1929 - ICELAND.
Kjartan Jónasson. Kreppuárin á Íslandi 1930-1939 /. [Reykjavik] , 1986- v. <1 > : LC Card 87-117468
HB3717 1929 .K58 1986

DEPRESSIONS - 1929 - INDIA.
Singh, Kanti. The great depression and agrarian economy . Delhi, India , 1987. xii, 206 p. ; LC Card 86-903533 DDC 338.1/0954/12 19
HC437.B47 S53 1987

DEPRESSIONS - 1929 - KANSAS.
Making do and doing without . [Lawrence, Kan.] , 1985, c1983. 98 p. ; LC Card 86-622703 DDC 330.9781/032 19
HC107.K2 M35 1985

DEPRESSIONS - 1929 - SPAIN.
DEPRESSIONS - 1929 - SWITZERLAND.
Schmid, Hanspeter, 1951- Wirtschaft, Staat und Macht . Zürich [c1983] 432 p. : ISBN 3-85791-073-9 (Schw. Buch) LC Card 83-244266
HF1573 .S335 1983

DEPRESSIONS - 1929 - UNITED STATES.
Bernstein, Michael A. (Michael Alan), 1954- The Great Depression . Cambridge [Cambridgeshire] , New York , 1987. xvii, 269 p. : ISBN 0-521-34048-9 LC Card 87-6403 DDC 338.5/42 19
HB3717 1929 .B37 1987

Biles, Roger, 1950- Memphis in the Great Depression /. Knoxville , c1986. 174 p. : ISBN 0-87049-497-X (alk. paper) : LC Card 85-22575 DDC 330.9768/19 19
HC108.M417 B55 1986 *NYPL [JLD 87-34]*

Economics U$A. Chicago, IL , 1986. 1 videocassette (28 min.) : LC Card 86-708020 DDC 330.15 11
HB99.7

The Farmer is the man [sound recording]. Los Angeles, Calif. , p1983. 1 sound cassette (58 min.) : LC Card 87-751678
HD8039.F3

Granville, Joseph Ensign, 1923- The warning . New York , c1985. xvi, 397 p. ; ISBN 0-88191-034-1 : LC Card 85-13107 DDC 332.64/273 19
HG4910 .G76 1985 *NYPL [JLE 86-3122]*

Haley, Charles T. To do good and do well [microform] . 1980. x, 233 leaves ;
NYPL [Sc Micro R-4654]

DEPRESSIONS - 1929 - UNITED STATES - SOURCES.
Slaves of the Depression . Ithaca, N.Y. , 1987. x, 229 p. ; ISBN 0-8014-9464-8 (pbk. : alk. paper) LC Card 87-6671 DDC 331.25/0973 19
HD8072 .S6164 1987

DEPRESSIONS - 1929 - VENEZUELA.
García Ponce, Antonio, 1929- Crisis oligarquía y latifundio . Barquisimeto, Venezuela , 1986. 104 p., [1] folded leaf of plates : ISBN 980-608-701-1 : LC Card 87-134729 DDC 338.1/762/0098725 19
HF3490.C375 G37 1986

DEPRESSIONS - ADDRESSES, ESSAYS, LECTURES.
The Impact of world recession on children /. Oxford [Oxfordshire] , New York , 1984. xiv, 221 p. : ISBN 0-08-031329-9 : LC Card 84-14694 DDC 362.7/042 19
HV715 .I475 1984 *NYPL [JLE 86-2315]*

DEPRESSIONS - HISTORY - CONGRESSES.
Financial crises and the world banking system /. London , c1986. x, 270 p. : ISBN 0-333-35129-0 *NYPL [JLD 86-2132]*

DEPTS, EXTERNAL - DEVELOPING COUNTRIES.
Wood, Robert Everett, 1944- From Marshall Plan to debt crisis . Berkeley , c1986. xviii, 400 p. ; ISBN 0-520-05526-8 (alk. paper) LC Card 86-6934 DDC 338.9/009172/4 19
HC60 .W62 1986 *NYPL [JLE 86-4443]*

Der aktienrechtliche Abhängigkeitstatbestand . Werner, Horst S. Göttingen , 1979. xxxix, 214 p. ; ISBN 3-88415-560-1 : LC Card 80-452340 DDC 346.43/066
LAW *NYPL [JLD 86-1592]*

Der Aufbruch . Guiton, R. J. (Raymond J.), 1915- Rheinfelden , c1984. 2 v. : ISBN 3-87718-746-3 (Bd. 1) LC Card 85-181833 DDC 325/.344/09 19
JV1818 .G85 1984 *NYPL [JFK 86-364]*

Der Eternit-Report . Catrina, Werner. Zürich , c1985. 244 p. : ISBN 3-280-01615-0 LC Card 85-225903
HD7269.A552 S93 1985 *NYPL [JLD 87-38]*

Der Konsumcharakter der Einkommensentstehung . Sell, Friedrich L. Freiburg im Breisgau , c1982. 221 p. : ISBN 3-448-01269-6 LC Card 82-233541 DDC 339.4/7/0724 19
HB820 .S44 1982 *NYPL [JLD 87-1580]*

Der Nord-Süd-Dialog zu Beginn der 80er Jahre = North-South dialogue at the beginning of the 1980's / Alexander G. Friedrich, Hrsg.1. Aufl. Baden-Baden : Nomos Verlagsgesellschaft ; 1982. 99 p. ; 23 cm. (Schriftenreihe der Deutschen Stiftung für Internationale Entwicklung . Dok.Nr. 1097 A, 1097 A/a) Text in German and English. International Symposium with the Members of the Independent Commission on International Development Issues (ICIDI) and with Representatives of the UN System: North-South Dialogue at the Beginning of the 1980's, organized by the Development Policy Forum of the German Foundation for International Development (DSE) in cooperation with the Technical University of Berlin and the Senat of Berlin, Berlin (West), 27 to 31 May 1981. ISBN 3-7890-0774-9

1. International economic relations - Congresses. 2. Economic development - International cooperation - Congresses. I. Friedrich, Alexander G. II. Independent Commission on International Development Issues. III. International Symposium "North-South Dialogue at the beginning of the 1980s" (1981 : Berlin, Germany). IV. Title: North-South dialogue at the beginning of the 1980's. ***NYPL [JLE 87-1282]***

Der Praktische Nutzen empirischer Forschung / herausgegeben von Eberhard Witte. Tübingen : J.C.B. Mohr, 1981. viii, 324 p. ; 24 cm. (Empirische Theorie der Unternehmung, 0340-6814 . Bd. 14) Includes bibliographies. CONTENTS. - Zur praktischen Nutzung von Forschungsergebnissen / Otto H. Poensgen -- Nutzungsanspruch und Nutzungsvielfalt / Eberhard Witte -- Zur Verknüpfung von empirischer Forschung und Hochschulausbildung in der Betriebswirtschaftslehre / Hartmut Kreikebaum -- Entscheidungsforschung und Entscheidungstechnologie / Klaus Brockhoff -- Wege zur praxisorientierten Erfassung der formalen Organisationsstruktur / Herbert Kubicek, Michael Wollnik und Alfred Kieser -- Einsatzbedingungen von Planungs- und Entscheidungstechniken / Richard Köhler und Herbert Uebele -- Zur technologischen Orientierung der empirischen Forschung / Norbert Szyperski und Detlef Müller-Böling -- Über den Sinn der empirischen Forschung in der angewandten Betriebswirtschaftslehre / Werner Kirsch -- Operations research und verhaltenswissenschaftliche Erkenntnisse / Reinhart Schmidt -- Der Bedarf des Operations research an empirischer Forschung / Heiner Müller-Merbach und Hans-Joachim Golling -- Zum Nutzen empirischer Untersuchungen für normative Modelle / Hans-Jürgen Zimmermann -- "Ziel-Klarheit" oder "kontrollierte Ziel-Unklarheit" in Entscheidungen? / Jürgen Hauschildt. ISBN 3-16-344392-3 : LC Card 81-197515 DDC 658.4/03 19
1. Industrial management - Research - Addresses, essays, lectures. 2. Industrial organization - Research - Addresses, essays, lectures. 3. Decision-making - Research - Addresses, essays, lectures. 4. Operations research - Addresses, essays, lectures. I. Witte, Eberhard.
HD30.4 .P7 1981 ***NYPL [JLE 86-1360]***

Der wichtige Grund bei der personengesellschaftlichen Auflösungs- und Ausschliessungsklage . Stauf, Wolfgang. Göttingen , 1980. xiv, 80 p. ; ISBN 3-88415-549-0 : LC Card 80-150978 DDC 346.73/07 347.3067 19
KK2435.7 .S7 1980 ***NYPL [JLD 86-1591]***

Deran, Elisabeth. Low-cost marketing strategies : field-tested techniques for tight budgets / Elisabeth Deran. New York : Praeger, 1987. ix, 151 p. ; 26 cm. Includes bibliographies and index. ISBN 0-275-92341-X (alk. paper) : LC Card 86-30640 DDC 658.8 19
1. Marketing. 2. Marketing - Costs. I. Title.
HF5415 .D458 1987

DERAP publications .
(no. A 322) Jerve, Alf Morten. From research to implementation . Fantoft-Bergen, Norway [1984] 23 leaves ; LC Card 86-228812 DDC 386/.068 19
HE691.6 .J47 1984

(no. 141) Kristiansen, Stein. U-hjelp og handel . Bergen [1982] iv, 325 p. : LC Card 83-139901
HC60 .K76 1982

(no. 149) Norsk industris internasjonalisering, rettet mot utviklingslandene . Bergen [1982] vi, 57 p. ; LC Card 83-139811
HD2932 .N67 1982

DERAP working papers .
(A 363) Haaland, Gunnar. Evolution of socio-economic dualism in the Maldives /. Bergen [1987] 30 leaves ; LC Card 87-130051 DDC 330.9549/5 19
HC596 .H33 1987

Derecho (Universidad de Extemadura (Cáceres, Spain). Servicio de Publicaciones)
Soto Carniago, Juan José de. Sociedades cooperativas, plan de cuentas . Cáceres , 1984. xv, 150 p. ; ISBN 84-600-3441-0 LC Card 84-221264
HF5686.C67 S67 1984

The deregulated society /. Gerston, Larry N. Pacific Grove, Calif. , c1988. xvii, 244 p. : ISBN 0-534-08208-4 (pbk.) : LC Card 87-5116 DDC 338.973 19
HD3616.U47 G47 1988

Deregulating financial services : public policy in flux / editors, George G. Kaufman, Roger C. Kormendi. Cambridge, Mass. : Ballinger Pub. Co., 1986. xiii, 223 p. ; 24 cm. "A Mid America Institute for Public Policy Research Book" Includes bibliographies and index. ISBN 0-88730-111-8 LC Card 86-3355 DDC 332.1/0973 19
1. Banks and banking - United States. 2. Banks and banking - United States - State supervision. I. Kaufman, George G. II. Kormendi, Roger C.
HG2491 .R42 1986 ***NYPL [JLE 86-3307]***

Deregulation : increased competition is making airlines more efficient and responsive to consumers : a report / by the U. S. General Accounting Office. Washington, D.C. : The Office, [1985] vi, 86 p. : ill. ; 28 cm. Cover title. "November 6, 1985." Bibliography: p. 58-59. "GAO/RCED-86-26." LC Card 86-602035 DDC 387.7/1 19
1. Airlines - United States - Deregulation. 2. Aeronautics, Commercial - United States - Deregulation. I. United States. General Accounting Office.
HE9803.A3 D47 1985

Deregulation and the future of intercity passenger travel /. Meyer, John Robert. Cambridge, Mass. , c1987. xviii, 294 p. : ISBN 0-262-13225-7 LC Card 86-27308 DDC 387.7/42/0973 19
HE9803.A35 M49 1987

DEREGULATION - GERMANY (WEST)
Soltwedel, Rüdiger. Deregulierungspotentiale in der Bundesrepublik /. Tübingen , c1986. xi, 326 p. ; ISBN 3-16-345145-4 (Deut. Bibl. : pbk.) LC Card 87-408380 DDC 338.6/048 19
HD3616.G4 S665 1986

The deregulation of bus services /. Savage, Ian, 1960- Aldershot, Hampshire, England , Brookfield, Vt., U. S.A. , c1985. xx, 267 p. : ISBN 0-566-05051-X : LC Card 85-17650 DDC 388.3/22 19
HE5663.A6 S33 1985 ***NYPL [JLD 87-123]***

Deregulation of the radio spectrum in the UK /. CSP International (Firm) London , 1987. vi, 182, [30] p. : ISBN 0-11-513979-6 (pbk.) : LC Card 87-170465 DDC 384.54/52 19
HE8689.9.G7 C76 1987

DEREGULATION - QUÉBEC (PROVINCE)
Québec (Province). Groupe de travail sur la déréglementation. Réglementer moins et mieux . [Quebec] [1986] 2 v. ; ISBN 2-551-08729-5 (v. 1) LC Card 86-206349
HD3616.C24 Q47 1986

DEREGULATION - UNITED STATES.
Gerston, Larry N. The deregulated society /. Pacific Grove, Calif. , c1988. xvii, 244 p. : ISBN 0-534-08208-4 (pbk.) : LC Card 87-5116 DDC 338.973 19
HD3616.U47 G47 1988

Deregulierung im Luftverkehr . Knieps, Günter. Tübingen , c1987. 69 p. ; ISBN 3-16-345148-9 LC Card 87-121052 DDC 387.7/1 19
HE9776 .K6 1987

Deregulierungspotentiale in der Bundesrepublik /. Soltwedel, Rüdiger. Tübingen , c1986. xi, 326 p. ; ISBN 3-16-345145-4 (Deut. Bibl. : pbk.) LC Card 87-408380 DDC 338.6/048 19
HD3616.G4 S665 1986

Derev′i͡ankin, T. I. (Tymofiĭ Ivanovych)
Stanovlenie i razvitie sovetskoĭ ėkonomicheskoĭ nauki na Ukraine . Kiev , 1983. 285, [2] p. ; LC Card 84-120015 DDC 330/.072/04771 19
HB74.9.S65 S72 1983 ***NYPL [*QGA 87-275]***

Dergachev, A. F. Raschet zatrat i opredelenie ėkonomicheskoĭ ėffektivnosti avtomatizirovannykh sistem operativno-proizvodstvennogo planirovanii͡a na avtoremontnykh predprii͡atii͡akh : referativnai͡a informatsii͡a. Moskva : T͡SBNTI Minavtotransa RSFSR, 1978. 35 p. ; 20 cm. (Serii͡a "Ėkonomika, upravlenie i organizatsii͡a proizvodstva na avtomobil′nom transporte" . vyp. 2) By A.F. Dergachev, E.P. Shirmanov, and V.S. Savin. At head of title: Ministerstvo avtomobil′nogo transporta R.S.F.S.R. T͡Sentral′noe bi͡uro nauchno-tekhnicheskoĭ informat͡sii. LC Card 81-173259
1. Automobile industry and trade - Management - Data processing. I. Shirmanov, E. P. II. Savin, V. S. III. Title. IV. Series.
HD9710.A2 D47 1978

Deri͡abin, Anatoliĭ Aleksandrovich.
Kirillov, S. R. (Sergeĭ Rufovich) Soizmerenie zatrat i rezul′tatov v teorii planovogo tsenoobrazovanii͡a /. Moskva , 1987. 188 p. ; LC Card 87-157208
HB235.S73 K57 1987

T͡Sena i khozraschet /. Moskva , 1986. 144 p. ; LC Card 87-163568
HB235.S73 T72 1986

Derix, Hans-Heribert. Säkulare Inflation, kompetitive Geldordnung und "unbeschränkte Demokratie" : zu Bedeutung und Problematik der politischen Theorie der Inflation F.A. von Hayeks / von Hans-Heribert Derix. Stuttgart ; New York : G. Fischer, 1985. xiv, 630 p. : 4 ill. ; 23 cm. (Schriften zum Vergleich von Wirtschaftsordnungen, 0582-0243 . Heft 35) Bibliography: p. 574-[603] Includes indexes. ISBN 3-437-50284-0 LC Card 86-110730
1. Inflation (Finance). 2. Monetary policy. 3. Economic stabilization. 4. Democracy. 5. Hayek, Friedrich A. von (Friedrich August), 1899-. I. Title. II. Series.
HG229 .D46 1985

Dermer, Jerry. Competitiveness through technology . Lexington, Mass. , c1986. xix, 215 p. : ISBN 0-669-11604-1 (alk. paper) LC Card 85-45379 DDC 338.97306 19
T185 .C67 1986 ***NYPL [JLE 86-1968]***

DERNE (DORTMUND, GERMANY) - SOCIAL CONDITIONS - EXHIBITIONS.
Leben mit Gneisenau, hundert Jahre-- . Dortmund , Essen [1986?] 317 p. : ISBN 3-88474-323-6 LC Card 87-408388 DDC 331.7/622334/094355 19
HD8039.M62 G335 1986

Derr, C. Brooklyn (Clyde Brooklyn) Managing the new careerists / C. Brooklyn Derr. 1st ed. San Francisco : Jossey-Bass, 1986. xxii, 288 p. ; 24 cm. (Jossey-Bass management series) Jossey-Bass social and behavioral science series "The diverse career success orientations of today's workers."--Half title page. Includes index. Bibliography: p. 277-282. ISBN 0-87589-677-4 LC Card 85-45901 DDC 658.3/02 19
1. Supervision of employees - United States. 2. Personnel management - United States. I. Title. II. Title: Career success. III. Title: Careerists. IV. Series.
HF5549.2.U5 D47 1986
NYPL [JLE 86-2427]

Derrida, Jacques. Les Sauvages dans la cité . Seyssel , c1985. 229 p. ; ISBN 2-903528-53-5
NYPL [JLD 86-1133]

La derrota de Lechín . Calla, Ricardo. La Paz, Bolivia , 1986. 79 p. : LC Card 87-105127
HD6609.M62 F433 1986

Derrotemos al hambre . Roca, José Luis, 1935- La Paz, Bolivia , 1985. 157, [16] leaves of plates : LC Card 85-241330 DDC 363.8/56/0984 19
HD9014.B62 R63 1985 ***NYPL [JLD 87-385]***

Derthick, Martha. Nonprofit organizations, a government management tool /. New York , 1980. xxi, 173 p. ; ISBN 0-03-053966-8 : LC Card 79-23632 DDC 350 19
JK468.R45 N66 ***NYPL [JLE 80-1874]***

Des Moines. Des Moines : Des Moines Industrial Committee, [1929?] [16] p. : ill. ; 28 cm. Cover title. LC Card 85-666467
1. Des Moines (Iowa) - Economic conditions. I. Des Moines Industrial Committee.
HC108.D47 D47x 1929

Des Moines Industrial Committee. Des Moines. Des Moines [1929?] [16] p. : LC Card 85-666467
HC108.D47 D47x 1929

DES MOINES (IOWA) - ECONOMIC CONDITIONS.
Des Moines. Des Moines [1929?] [16] p. : LC Card 85-666467
HC108.D47 D47x 1929

Des réformes à opérer dans l'exploitation des chemins de fer. Proudhon, P.-J. (Pierre Joseph), 1809-1865. Paris, 1855. 2 p.l., 392 p. LC Card 05-35562
HE1031 .P92

Des sous et des hommes . Albertini, Jean Marie. Paris , c1985. 285 p. ; ISBN 2-02-008947-5 LC Card 86-124575 DDC 330 19
HB173 .A32 1985

Desabastecimiento de alimentos y alternativas de solución en las minas : los centros mineros de Catavi y Siglo XX. [1a ed.]. La Paz [Bolivia] :

Unión Nacional de Instituciones para el Trabajo de Acción Social : Programa de Asesoramiento Minero, 1986. 128 : ill. ; 21 cm. (Serie Programa de Asesoramiento Minero . 1) Includes bibliographical references. LC Card 87-401454 DDC 331.7/6223453/098413 19
1. Tin miners - Bolivia - Bustillo. 2. Empresa Minera Catavi. I. Unión Nacional de Instituciones para el Trabajo de Acción Social (Bolivia). II. Programa de Asesoramiento Minero (Bolivia). III. Series.
HD8039.M72 B624 1986

Desafio energético /. Dé Carli, Gileno. Recife , 1981 (Recife : Companhia Editora de Pernambuco) 309 p. ; LC Card 86-129710
HD9502.B72 D4 1981

Desai, A. R. see **Desai, Akshayakumar Ramanlal.**

Desai, Akshayakumar Ramanlal. Agrarian struggles in India after independence /. Delhi , 1986. xxvi, 666 p. : ***NYPL [JLD 86-3896]***

Desai, Padma. The Soviet economy : problems and prospects / Padma Desai. Oxford, OX, UK : Blackwell, 1987. viii, 281 p. : ill. ; 24 cm. Includes bibliographies and index. ISBN 0-631-15227-X : LC Card 86-28326 DDC 330.947/0853 19
1. Soviet Union - Economic conditions - 1976-. 2. Soviet Union - Economic policy - 1981-. I. Title.
HC336.25 .D47 1987

Desai, Vasant, 1933- Indian industry : profile & related issues / Vasant Desai.1st ed. Bombay : Himalaya Pub. House, 1987. xiii, 816 p. : ill. ; 23 cm. LC Card 87-901051 DDC 338.0954 19
1. India - Industries. I. Title.
HC435.2 .D45 1987

La desamortización de Mendizábal en Granada /. Gómez Oliver, Miguel. Granada [1983] 226 p. : LC Card 85-135214
HD479.G73 G65 1983

La desamortización de Mendizábal y Espartero en España /. Rueda Hernanz, Germán. Madrid , c1986. 200 p. ; ISBN 84-376-0592-X LC Card 86-216590
HD774 .R84 1986

La desamortización de Pascual Madoz en la ciudad de Logroño y su partido judicial (1855-1856) . Bilbao Díez, Juan Carlos. Logroño , 1983. 303 p. : ISBN 84-85379-12-8 LC Card 86-215897
HD780.L64 B55 1983

Desamortización, deuda pública y crecimiento económico, Andalucía, 1820/1823 /. González do Molina Navarro, Manuel. Granada , Córdoba :bFundación Paco Natera [1985?] 443 p. : ISBN 84-505-1053-8 LC Card 86-210676
HD779.A4 G66 1985

Desaraḍā, Eca. Ema. Śetī, udyoga, āṇi śikshaṇa : eka māgovā / Eca. Ema. Desaraḍā. Auraṅgābāda : Sāhityasevā Prakāśana, 1986. 18, 148 p. ; 23 cm. In Marathi. Articles on farming, industry, and education in Maharashtra. LC Card 87-900720
1. Maharashtra (India) - Industries. 2. Agriculture - India - Maharashtra. 3. Education - India - Maharashtra. I. Title.
HC437.M32 D47 1986

DeSario, Jack. Citizen participation in public decision making /. Westport, Conn. , 1987. xii, 237 p. ; ISBN 0-313-25478-8 (lib. bdg. : alk. paper) : LC Card 86-7571 DDC 323/.042/0973 19
JK1764 .C525 1987 ***NYPL [JLD 87-932]***

Desarrollo agroindustrial en Venezuela durante los próximos 10 años. Foro . San Felipe, Venezuela , 1984. ii, 92 p. ; LC Card 85-132901 DDC 338.1/0987 19
HD1912 .F67 1984 ***NYPL [JLD 86-424]***

El desarrollo costarricense y la fecundidad del hombre /. Sandoval Aguilar, Guillermo. Heredia , 1985. 233 p. ; LC Card 86-117576
HB947 .S26 1985

Desarrollo, crisis, deuda y política económica en Panamá . Gómez Pérez, José Antonio, 1950- Panamá , 1985. vii, 168 p. : LC Card 86-122320 DDC 338.97287 19
HC147 .G66 1985 ***NYPL [JLD 86-2899]***

Desarrollo, crisis e ideología en la formación del capitalismo . Cazadero, Manuel. México , 1986. 153 p. ; ISBN 968-16-2280-4 LC Card 87-403551 DDC 330.12/2 19
HB501 .C33 1986

Desarrollo de la formación profesional rural . International Labour Organisation. Ginebra , 1982. ii, 30 p. : ISBN 92-2-303048-X LC Card 84-113985
HD5715.5.H8 I58 1982

El desarrollo de la ganadería en Colombia, 1950-1972 . Kalmanovitz, Salomón. [Bogotá, Colombia] [1978] p. 195-238 : LC Card 86-157918
HD9433.C62 K35 1978

El desarrollo del capital en la industria de Costa Rica, 1950-1970 /. Esquivel, Francisco. Heredia, Costa Rica , 1985. 197 p. : ISBN 997-7650-16-0 LC Card 86-210026
HC143 .E83 1985

Desarrollo del subdesarrollo en el Perú. Humala Tasso, Ulises. Subdesarrollo o camino al colapso . [S.l. , 1987?] (Lima, Perú : Graphos 100 Editores) 175 p. ; LC Card 87-403093 DDC 330.985/0633 19
HC227 .H86 1987

Desarrollo demográfico, migraciones y urbanización en América Latina . Fachtagung "Bevölkerungsentwicklung, Bevölkerungswanderung und Urbanisierung in Lateinamerika" (1984 : Eichstätt, Germany) Regensburg , c1986. 432 p. : LC Card 86-181152
HB3530.5.A3 F33 1984

Desarrollo desigual y absorción de empleo . Tokman, Víctor E. [Santiago, Chile] , 1982. 34 p. ; LC Card 87-403246 DDC 330.98/0038 19
HC125 .T57 1982

Desarrollo desigual y política regional en Europa del Sur. Ungleiche Entwicklung und Regionalpolitik in Südeuropa . Bochum , 1985. 282 p. : ISBN 3-88339-441-6 : LC Card 85-205651
HC244.5 .U48 1985

El Desarrollo económico de Honduras : análisis del sector agropecuario : anexos / Consejo Nacional de Economía. Tegucigalpa, D.C. : El Consejo, 1959. [56] leaves : ill. ; 28 cm. Chiefly tables. LC Card 86-173618
1. Farm produce - Honduras - Statistics. 2. Forest products industry - Honduras - Statistics. I. Honduras. Consejo Nacional de Economía.
HD9014.H82 D47 1959

El desarrollo económico y social de Costa Rica . Acuña Ortega, Víctor H. [San José, Costa Rica] , 1986. vi, 135 p. ; ISBN 997-7440-08-5 LC Card 87-100815
HC143 .A54 1986

El desarrollo frutícola y forestal en Chile y sus derivaciones sociales. García Elizalde, Pedro. Santiago de Chile , 1986. 234 p. : ISBN 92-1-321204-6 LC Card 86-175421
HD9254.C52 G37 1986

Desarrollo regional del Sur del Ecuador, El Oro, Loja, Zamora, 1980-1983. Informe cuatrianual, 1980-1983 /. Cuenca, Ecuador [1983] 222 p. : LC Card 86-206868
HC203.O76 I53 1983

Desarrollo regional, incentivos fiscales y localización industrial /. Boneo, Horacio. Buenos Aires, Argentina [1985] 160 p. : ISBN 950-95720-8-X ***NYPL [JLD 86-4218]***

Desarrollo socio-económico de la Octava Región de Chile /. Ramírez C., Valeria (Ramírez Ceballos) Santiago, Chile , 1985. i, 45 leaves ; LC Card 86-115542
HC193.B5 R35 1985

Desatnick, Robert L. Managing to keep the customer : how to achieve and maintain superior customer service throughout the organization / Robert L. Desatnick.1st ed. San Francisco : Jossey-Bass, 1987. xvi, 163 p. ; 24 cm. (The Jossey-Bass management series) Bibliography: p. 155-158. Includes index. ISBN 1-555-42027-3 (alk. paper) LC Card 86-21399 DDC 658.8/12 19
1. Customer service. 2. Customer relations. I. Title. II. Series.
HF5415.5 .D47 1987

Descamps, Bernard, 1958- Descamps, Eugène, 1922- Les sociétés multinationales . Lyon [1985] 164 p. : ISBN 2-85008-062-4 : LC Card 86-168493
HD2755.5 .D47 1985

Descamps, Eugène, 1922- Les sociétés multinationales : pouvoirs et contre-pouvoirs / Eugène Descamps, Bernard Descamps. Lyon : Chronique sociale, [1985] 164 p. : ill. ; 22 cm. (Collection "Synthèse", 0183-682X) Bibliography: p. 161. ISBN 2-85008-062-4 : LC Card 86-168493
1. International business enterprises. I. Descamps, Bernard, 1958-. II. Title.
HD2755.5 .D47 1985

DESCENT AND DISTRIBUTION. see **INHERITANCE AND SUCCESSION.**

DESCENTS. see **INHERITANCE AND SUCCESSION.**

Deschamps, Benoit. Chief financial officer : strategy formulation and implementation / Benoit Deschamps, Dileep Mehta. New York : Wiley, c1988. xxvii, 582, [165] p. ; 25 cm. "Software to accompany CFO" in pockets. Includes indexes. ISBN 0-471-84892-1 LC Card 87-21656 DDC 658.1/5 19
1. Corporations - Finance. 2. Chief financial officers. 3. Management games. I. Mehta, Dileep R., 1932-. II. Title.
HG4026 .D48 1988

Descrição da área e caracterização do projeto /. Projeto de Desenvolvimento Integrado da Bacia do Araguaia-Tocantins. Brasília , 1983. 129 p. : LC Card 87-130908 DDC 338.981/73 19
HC188.A73 P76 1983

Description of Ural and Siberian factories in 1735 /. De-Gennin, Vil'gel'm, 1676-1750. [Opisanie ural'skikh i sibirskikh zavodov 1735. English.] [Washington, D.C.] , 1987. p. cm. LC Card 87-600052 DDC 338.0947/87 19
HC337.R852 U733613 1987

Descubro y acuso /. Bayo, Eliseo. Esplugues de Llobregat, Barcelona , 1985,c1984. 287 p. ; ISBN 84-01-33258-3 ***NYPL [JFD 86-7111]***

Desdobramentos inflacionários. Bulhões, Octávio Gouveia de. [Salvador] [1984] 43 p. : LC Card 86-861354 DDC 332.4/1/0981 19
HG835 .B85 1984

O desempenho dos mercados a termo . Tsunechiro, Alfredo. São Paulo , 1986. xi, 123 p. : LC Card 87-404554 DDC 332.64/4 19
HG6046 .T75 1986

Desempenho programático do DEPEA em 1984 . Brazil. Comissão Executiva do Plano da Lavoura Cacaueira. Departamento Especial da Amazônia. Belém/Pará [Brazil] , 1985. 76 p. : LC Card 87-404555 DDC 338.981/1 19
HD1875.A347 B68 1985

Desenbanco. see **Banco de Desenvolvimento do Estado da Bahia.**

Desenvolvimento com equilíbrio social . Martins Filho, Oséas de Souza. São Luís, Ma. , 1985 (São Luís, MA : Serviço de Impr. e Obras Gráficas do Estado) 314 p. ; LC Card 86-229862
HC187 .M33 1985

O desenvolvimento do porto de Vitória, 1870-1940 /. Siqueira, Penha. Vitória-ES , 1984. 162 p. : LC Card 85-144275
HE556.V5 S56 1984

Desenvolvimento econômico e urbanização . Rizzieri, Juarez Alexandre Baldini. São Paulo , 1982. 219 p. : LC Card 83-150574 DDC 330.9173/2 19
HT321 .R59 1982 ***NYPL [JLD 86-3817]***

Desenvolvimento industrial e rendimento da terra . Avila, Luiz Gonçalves. Rio de Janeiro, RJ , 1985. 111 p. : LC Card 86-233493
HD1875.S26 A95 1985

Desequilíbrio externo e reorientação do crescimento e dos investimentos . Werneck, Rogério L. Furquim. Rio de Janeiro-RJ [1983?] 130 p. ; LC Card 87-403024 DDC 338.981 19
HC187 .W47 1983

Desertification . Ahmad, Yusuf J. West Hartford, CT. , 1987. xviii, 187 p. : ISBN 0-931816-99-8 (pbk.) : LC Card 87-3650 DDC 333.73 19
HD111 .A44 1987

DESERTIFICATION - CONTROL - FINANCE.
Ahmad, Yusuf J. Desertification . West Hartford, CT. , 1987. xviii, 187 p. : ISBN 0-931816-99-8 (pbk.) : LC Card 87-3650 DDC 333.73 19
HD111 .A44 1987

Desezonizacija jugoslovenskih vremenskih serija 1971-1980 =. Nikolić, Miodrag M. Beograd , 1982. 287 p. : LC Card 85-157587
HA37.Y8 A37 no. 109 HC407

Desgualdo Netto, Domingos. Aspectos agroeconômicos da soja / Domingos Desgualdo Netto, Flávio Condé de Carvalho. São Paulo : Governo do Estado de São Paulo, Secretaria de Agricultura e Abastecimento, Instituto de Economia Agrícola, 1985. 139 p. ; 23 cm. (Relatório de pesquisa, 0101-5109 . 9/85) Summary in English. Bibliography: p. 134-138. LC Card 86-158570
1. Soyabean industry - Brazil. I. Carvalho, Flávio Condé de. II. Series: Relatório de pesquisa (São Paulo (Brazil : State). Instituto de Economia Agrícola) , no. 85/9. III. Title.
HD9235.S62 B74 1985

Desharnais, Marcel, 1924- Guyenne : vingt ans de colonisation sous le régime coopératif, et après ... / Marcel Desharnais. Montréal, Québec : Editions coopératives Albert Saint-Martin, c1983. 182 p. : ill. ; 23 cm. (Collection Recherches et documents) Title on spine: Guyenne ... et après ... ISBN 2-89035-062-2 LC Card 84-127460
1. Cooperation - Québec (Province) - Guyenne - History. 2. Guyenne (Québec) - Colonization - History. I. Title. II. Title: 20 ans de colonisation sous le régime coopératif, et après-- . III. Title: Guyenne-- et après-- . IV. Title: Vingt ans de colonisation sous le régime coopératif, et après-- .
HD3450.G89 D47 1983

DESHMUKH, CHINTAMAN DWARKANATH, 1896-
Narayan Prasad, P. S. C.D. Deshmukh, his contribution to monetary and economic policy /. New Delhi , c1985. xiv, 54 p., [1] leaf of plates : LC Card 85-905075 DDC 338.954 19
HC432.5.D47 N37 1985
NYPL [JLD 86-3239]

Deshmukh, P. D. Dhongade, M. P. Farmers' attitude survey in the Mula Command Area, Maharashtra /. Rahuri, Maharashtra, India , 1986. vi, 69 p. ; LC Card 86-903408 DDC 338.1/0954/792 19
HD8039.F32 I44 1986

Deshpande, V. D. (Vasant Dattatraya), 1930- The Mhaisal untouchables / Vasant Deshpande. 1st ed. Pune : Dastane Ramchandra & Co., 1983. xi, 168 p. ; 22 cm. (Struggle of the deprived for development . 1) LC Card 83-906084 DDC 338.954/792 19
1. Economic development projects - India - Mhaisal. 2. Volunteer workers in social service - India - Mhaisal. 3. Mhaisal (India) - Economic conditions. I. Title.
HC438.M45 D48 1983
NYPL [JLD 87-1139]

DESIGN COORDINATION, INDUSTRIAL. see **INDUSTRIAL DESIGN COORDINATION.**

Design for diversification / edited by Bruce Judd, John Dean and David Brown. Canberra : RAIA, Education Division ; Portland, OR. : Exclusive distributor ISBS, [1985] 57 p. : ill. ; 30 cm. (Housing issues . 1) Includes bibliographies and index. ISBN 0-909724-68-7 (pbk.) LC Card 86-222390 DDC 363.5/0994 19
1. Housing - Australia. I. Judd, Bruce. II. Dean, John, B. App. Sc. III. Brown, David. IV. Series.
HD7379.A3 D47 1985

DESIGN, INDUSTRIAL - PHILOSOPHY.
Zellinger, Alfred, 1945- Die Sinnlichkeit der Theorie . Wien , c1983. 173 p. : ISBN 3-85439-005-X LC Card 84-196565
HF1040.7 .Z45 1983

Design, innovation, and long cycles in economic development / edited by Christopher Freeman. London : Pinter, 1986. 248 p. : ill. ; 24 cm. Includes bibliographies. ISBN 0-86187-616-4
1. Long waves (Economics) - Addresses, essays, lectures. 2. Technological innovations - Addresses, essays, lectures. 3. Economic development - Addresses, essays, lectures. I. Freeman, Christopher.
NYPL [JLE 86-3312]

DESIGN - JAPAN - AWARDS.
The Best of Japan. Tokyo , New York, N.Y., U. S.A. , 1987. 288, xiv p. : ISBN 0-87011-801-3 (U. S. : pbk.) : LC Card 86-40432 DDC 338.4/7/000952 19
HF5415.153 .B47 1987

Design of adaptive organizations . Takahashi, Nobuo, 1957- Berlin , New York , c1987. vi, 140 p. : ISBN 0-387-17834-1 (U. S.) : LC Card 87-9834 DDC 658.4/06 19
HD58.8 .T35 1987

The Design of alternative development strategies / edited by Irma Adelman and J. Edward Taylor. Rohtak, India : Jan Tinbergen Institute of Development Planning, 1986. xiv, 330 p. : ill. ; 25 cm. "The volume grew out of the first joint United States-China Conference on Alternative Development Strategies for Economic Development ... Racine Wisconsin on November 20-24, 1980"--P. [xiii] Includes bibliographies. LC Card 86-901301 DDC 338.9 19
1. Economic development - Congresses. 2. Economic policy - Congresses. 3. Developing countries - Economic policy - Congresses. I. Adelman, Irmn. II. Taylor, J. Edward.
HD82 .D383 1986 *NYPL [JLE 86-4232]*

Design of office information systems /. Ellis, Clarence Arthur, 1943- Berlin , New York , c1987. vi, 248 p. : ISBN 0-387-17810-4 (U. S.) : LC Card 87-9582 DDC 651.8 19
HF5548.2 .E445 1987

DESIGN OF WORK SYSTEMS. see **WORK DESIGN.**

Designing for reliability and safety control /. Henley, Ernest J. Englewood Cliffs, N.J. , c1985. xvi, 527 p. : ISBN 0-13-201229-4 LC Card 84-17892 DDC 620/.00452 19
TA169 .H46 1985 *NYPL [JSE 86-2491]*

Designing jobs for handicapped workers . Joint Seminar on Designing Jobs for Handicapped Workers (1985 : Chicago, Ill.) Hot Springs, Ark. (P.O. Box 1358, Hot Spring 71902) [1986] 66 p. : LC Card 86-622317 DDC 658.3/045 19
HD7256.U5 J65 1985

Designing regulatory policy with limited information /. Besanko, David, 1955- Chur, Switzerland , New York , c1987. viii, 80 p. : ISBN 3-7186-0385-3 (pbk.) LC Card 87-277 DDC 351.82/6 19
HD3612 .B47 1987

DESIGNS (INDUSTRIAL PUBLICITY) see **INDUSTRIAL DESIGN COORDINATION.**

Desinga Raj, N. Development programmes in agriculture and the weaker sections / N. Desinga Raj. Allahabad, India : Chugh Publications, 1987. xvi, 217 p. : maps ; 23 cm. Study on the working of the Small Farmers Development Agency program in India. Bibliography: p. [203]-212. Includes index. ISBN 81-85076-16-2 : LC Card 87-900702 DDC 338.1/854 19
1. Farms, Small - Government policy - India. I. Title.
HD1476.I4 D47 1987

Desinvesititionen . Jansen, Ansgar, 1954- Frankfurt am Main , New York , c1986. 514 p. : ISBN 3-8204-9630-0 LC Card 86-205563
HG4515 .J36 1986

Desjardins, André. Lewis, Normande. Le travail à temps partiel, le partage du travail comme mesure de sécurité d'emploi et la sous-traitance . [Quebec] , c1985. 90 p. ; ISBN 2-551-08998-0 LC Card 85-213545
HD5110.2.C22 Q45 1985

The desk guide to training and work advisement /. Kuenstler, Gail Baugher. Springfield, Ill., U. S.A. , c1988. p. cm. ISBN 0-398-05414-2 LC Card 87-25626 DDC 331.7/02/0973 19
HF5382.5.U5 K84 1988

Desk-top encyclopedia of corporate finance & accounting. Woelfel, Charles J. The desktop encyclopedia of corporate finance & accounting /. Chicago, Ill. , c1987. viii, 518 p. : ISBN 0-917253-65-5 : LC Card 87-2302 DDC 658.1/5 19
HG4027.3 .W64 1987

The desktop encyclopedia of corporate finance & accounting /. Woelfel, Charles J. Chicago, Ill. , c1987. viii, 518 p. : ISBN 0-917253-65-5 : LC Card 87-2302 DDC 658.1/5 19
HG4027.3 .W64 1987

Desmond, Glenn M. Handbook of small business valuation formulas / by Glenn Desmond and John Marcello. Los Angeles : Valuation Press, c1987. 139 p. ; 27 cm. Includes bibliographies. ISBN 0-930458-04-4 LC Card 87-402145 DDC 658.1/522 19
1. Small business - United States - Valuation. I. Marcello, John. II. Title.
HG4028.V3 D478 1987

Desormeaux J., Jorge. Determinación de precios del sector exportador chileno, 1978-1982 / Jorge Desormeaux J. Santiago, Chile : Pontificia Universidad Católica de Chile, Instituto de Economía, Oficina de Publicaciones, 1983. 88 p. : ill. ; 27 cm. (Documento de trabajo . no. 89) Bibliography: p. 87-88. LC Card 87-403699 DDC 338.5/2/0983 19
1. Prices - Chile. 2. Chile - Commerce. I. Series: Documento de trabajo (Universidad Católica de Chile. Instituto de Economía) , no. 89. II. Title.
HB235.C57 D47 1983

Despesa da administração pública estadual (1965-1969) / Instituto de Pesquisas Econômico-Sociais e Informática--IPEI, Coordenadoria Técnica--COTEC, Assessoria Técnica. São Luís : A Assessoria Técnica, 1975. 37 p. : ill. ; 31 cm. LC Card 84-209699
1. Maranhão (Brazil) - Appropriations and expenditures. I. Maranhão (Brazil). Instituto de Pesquisas Econômico-Sociais e Informática. Assessoria Técnica.
HJ2080 .D47 1975

DESPOTISM - HISTORY - 17TH CENTURY.
Collins, James B. Fiscal limits of absolutism . Berkeley , c1987. p. cm. ISBN 0-520-05911-5 (alk. paper) LC Card 87-19090 DDC 336.2/00944 19
HJ2648 .C65 1987

DESQ (COMPUTER PROGRAM)
Seybold, Patricia B. Integrated desk-top environments . New York , c1985. ix, 181 p. : ISBN 0-07-056324-1 (pbk.) : LC Card 84-27841 DDC 650/.028/5425 19
HF5548.4.S95 S49 1985
NYPL [JSE 86-2011]

Dessler, Gary, 1942- Personnel management / Gary Dessler. 4th ed. Englewood Cliffs, N.J. : Prentice-Hall, c1988. viii, 727 p. : ill. (some col.) ; 25 cm. Includes bibliographies and indexes. ISBN 0-13-658543-4 : LC Card 87-21000 DDC 658.3 19
1. Personnel management. I. Title.
HF5549 .D4379 1988

Destination des expéditions des manufacturiers exportateurs du Québec, 1976-1980 / Bureau de la statistique du Québec, Direction des statistiques économiques, Service des entreprises. Québec, Québec : Centre d'information et de documentation, Bureau de la statistique du Québec, [1983] ix, 249 p. : ill. ; 28 cm. LC Card 85-115007
1. Québec (Province) - Commerce - Statistics. I. Bureau de la statistique du Québec. Service des entreprises. II. Bureau de la statistique du Québec. Centre d'information et de documentation.
HF3229.Q4 D47 1983

La destinazione dell'utile nelle società per azioni . Ecchia, Stefano. Padova , 1985. 133 p. : LC Card 86-214308
HG4028.P7 E23 1985

A destiny in diamonds /. Joris, Albert, 1915- Spring, Hill, Brisbane, Qld. , Portland, OR , 1986. vi, 113 p. : ISBN 0-86439-011-4 LC Card 87-161024 DDC 338.2/782/0924 B 19
HD9677.A82 J675 1986

DESTITUTION. see **POVERTY.**

Destler, I. M.
American trade politics : system under stress / I.M. Destler. Washington, DC : Institute for International Economics ; New York, NY : Twentieth Century Fund, 1986. xiii, 366 p. : ill. ; 23 cm. Includes bibliographical references and index. ISBN 0-88132-058-7 : LC Card 86-27168 DDC 380.1/3/0973 19
1. United States - Commercial policy. I. Institute for International Economics (U. S.). II. Twentieth Century Fund. III. Title.
HF1455 .D48 1986

Anti-protection : changing forces in United States trade politics / I.M. Destler, John S. Odell ; assisted by Kimberly Ann Elliott. Washington, DC : Institute for International Economics, c1987. xii, 204 p. ; 23 cm. (Policy analyses in international economics . 21) "September 1987." Includes bibliographical references. ISBN 0-88132-065-X (pbk.) LC Card 87-22545 DDC 382/.3/0973 19
1. United States - Commercial policy. 2. Free trade and protection. I. Odell, John S., 1945-. II. Elliott, Kimberly Ann, 1960-. III. Title. IV. Series.
HF1455 .D482 1987

DESTRUCTION OF THE JEWS (1939-1945) see **HOLOCAUST, JEWISH (1939-1945)**

Det Norske nasjonalregnskapet. Dokumentasjonsnotat .
(nr. 14) Røgeberg, Svein Lasse. Sektorberegninger for fiske og fangst /. Oslo , 1979. 34 p. ; ISBN 82-537-0977-3 LC Card 86-460230
HD9465.N62 R64 1979
(nr. 7) Jean-Hansen, Viggo. Sektorberegninger for samferdselssektorene og reparasjon av kjøretøyer m.v. /. Oslo , 1979. 56 p. ; ISBN 82-537-0968-4 LC Card 86-460231
HE259 .J4 1979

Detection of changes in the properties of random processes. Obnaruzhenie izmeneniĭ svoĭstv sluchaĭnykh protsessov . Vil'nius , 1984. 243 p. : LC Card 84-168819
HD38 .S715 vyp. 65 QA274.A1

DETENTE.
Wettig, Gerhard. Konflikt und Kooperation zwischen Ost und West . Bonn , c1981. 217 p. ; ISBN 3-7894-0082-3 LC Card 82-225671 DDC 327.1/7 19
D849 .W47 1981 ***NYPL [JLE 86-4503]***

DETERGENTS, SYNTHETIC - MARKETING.
Promotion strategies for household cleaning products. New York, N.Y. , c1983. 2 v. (xx, 635 p.) ; LC Card 87-142358 DDC 381/.456671/0973 19
HD9999.C4863 U56 1983

Deterioro de los términos de intercambio, migración eventual y pobreza campesina en el departamento del Cusco /. Díaz Gómez, Jorge. [Cuzco, Peru] , 1986. 17, 3 leaves, 2 leaves of plates : LC Card 86-200938
HD1531.P4 D52 1986

Determinação de itinerários de um sistema de transporte coletivo através de ônibus . Soares, Nilton de Brito. Brasília, DF , 1985. 98 p. : LC Card 87-113226 DDC 388.3/22/0981 19
HE5653.A6 S63 1985

Determinación de necesidades de formación profesional . Retuerto, Enrique. Montevideo , 1983. 110 p. ; LC Card 86-149551
HD5715 .R47 1983

Determinación de precios del sector exportador chileno, 1978-1982 /. Desormeaux J., Jorge. Santiago, Chile , 1983. 88 p. : LC Card 87-403699 DDC 338.5/2/0983 19
HB235.C57 D47 1983

Determinanten der Eigenkapitalbildung und Konsequenzen für die Wettbewerbsfähigkeit deutscher Grossunternehmen und Mittelbetriebe /. Schoppe, Siegfried, 1944- Hamburg , 1986. 24 p. : LC Card 86-185861
HG4156 .S36 1986

Determinanten der Eingliederung von Arbeitsmigranten /. Hill, Paul Bernhard, 1953- Königstein/Ts. , c1984. 228 p. : ISBN 3-7756-6939-6 LC Card 84-219137 DDC 331.6/2/0943 19
HD8458.A2 H55 1984
NYPL [JLD 86-2467]

Determinants of family size in rural Sudan /. Saghayroun, Atif A. Rahman. Khartoum, Sudan [1984] 36 leaves ; LC Card 87-119805 DDC 304.6/32/09624 19
HB1071.8.A3 S22 1984

Determinants of fertility in some African and Asian countries. Cairo : Cairo Demographic Centre, 1982. 698 p. : ill. ; 24 cm. (Research monograph series / Cairo Demographic Centre . no. 10) Spine title: Determinants of fertility. Papers presented at the 13th annual seminar of the Cairo Demographic Centre held in Dec. 1981. Includes bibliographies. LC Card 84-960893 DDC 304.6/32 19
1. Fertility, Human - Africa - Congresses. 2. Fertility, Human - Egypt - Congresses. 3. Fertility, Human - Asia - Congresses. 4. Fertility, Human - China - Congresses. I. al-Markaz al-Dīmūghrāfī bi-al-Qāhirah. Seminar (13th : 1981 : Cairo, Egypt). II. Series: al-Markaz al-Dīmūghrāfī bi-al-Qāhirah. Research monograph series, no. 10.
HB1071.7.A3 D48 1982
NYPL [JLL 73-297 no.10]

Determinants of import prices in Mauritius /. Pochun, Malati J. Réduit, Mauritius , 1981. 15 p. ; LC Card 82-980680
HB235.M38 P63 1981

The determinants of innovation in large and small firms /. Ács, Zoltán J. Berlin [1986] 39 p. ; LC Card 87-156684 DDC 338.6/4 19
HC110.T4 A59 1986

The Determinants of negotiated wage settlements in Canada (1966-1975) : a microeconometric analysis / by D. A. L. Auld ... [et al.]. [Ottawa] : Anti-inflation Board ; Hull, Quebec : available from Canadian Gov't. Pub. Centre, Supply and Services Canada, c1979. x, 256 p. : graphs ; 23 cm. "Catalogue no. F96-1/4-1979" Bibliography: p. 245-253. ISBN 0-660-10162-9 : LC Card 79-313202 DDC 331.2/971
1. Wages - Canada. 2. Phillips curve. 3. Inflation (Finance) and unemployment - Canada. I. Auld, Douglas Allen Lauriston. II. Canada. Anti-inflation Board.
HD4979 .D44 ***NYPL [JLE 80-447]***

Determinants of sectoral annual real wages in a developing economy /. Coeymans, Juan Eduardo. Santiago , 1986. 32, [4] leaves : LC Card 87-404007 DDC 331.12/5/0983 19
HD5006 .C64 1986

Determinanty polityki kadrowej w przedsiębiorstwie : prace Instytutu Polityki Społecznej / [redaktor naukowy Józef Orczyk].Wyd. 1. Poznań : Wydawn. Akademii Ekonomicznej w Poznaniu, 1984. 142 p. : ill. ; 24 cm. (Zeszyty naukowe / Akademia Ekonomiczna w Poznaniu. Seria I . zesz. 129) Summary in English and Russian. Includes bibliographical references. LC Card 86-194984
1. Personnel management - Poland. I. Orczyk, Józef. II. Instytut Polityki Społecznej (Akademia Ekonomiczna w Poznaniu). III. Series: Zeszyty naukowe / Akademia Ekonomiczna w Poznaniu. Seria I , zesz. nr. 129.
HB54 .P6 nr. 129 HF5549.2.P6

Determinatsionnyĭ analiz sotsial'no-ėkonomicheskikh dannykh /. Chesnokov, S. V. (Sergeĭ Valerianovich) Moskva , 1982. 167, [1] p. : LC Card 83-173210
HA29.5.R9 C52 1982

Detjen, Günther, 1930- Betriebswirtschaftslehre des Post- und Fernmeldewesens / bearbeitet von Günther Detjen, unter Mitarbeit von Karl Heinrich Hartmann ... [et al.]. Gelsenkirchen-Buer : Damm-Verlag, c1984-c1985. 2 v. : ill. ; 21 cm. (Fachbuchreihe für den Post- und Fernmeldedienst. Bd. 73-74) Bibliography: v. 1, p. 187-192; v. 2, p. 271-275. Includes index. ISBN 3-87333-070-9 (Bd. 1) LC Card 87-104294 DDC 383/.4943 19
1. Postal service - Germany (West) - Management. 2. Telecommunication - Germany (West) - Management. I. Title.
HE6995 .D37 1984

Detneva, Ėmma Vasil'evna. Voprosy postroeniia sistemy modeleĭ finansovogo aspekta vosproizvodstva /. Moskva , 1984. 154 p. : LC Card 86-144339
HG186.S55 V67 1984

Detnost' semi'i--vchera, segodnia, zavtra / [redaktsionnaia kollegiia, L.L. Rybakovskiĭ (predsedatel') ... et al.]. Moskva : "Mysl'", 1986. 205 p. : charts ; 20 cm. (Demografiia--problemy i perspektivy) Includes bibliographical references. Summaries in English. LC Card 87-109456 DDC 304.6/32/0947 19
1. Fertility, Human - Soviet Union. 2. Family size - Soviet Union. 3. Soviet Union - Population. I. Series.
HB1017 .D47 1986

Detroy, Erich-Norbert, 1945- Wie man mit Brief, Telefon und Erstbesuch neue Kunden systematisch und dauerhaft gewinnt / Erich-Norbert Detroy. Zürich : Moderne Industrie, c1982. 216 p. : ill. ; 22 cm. Includes index. ISBN 3-478-23510-3 : LC Card 82-242870
1. Canvassing. 2. Sales letters. 3. Telephone selling. 4. Direct selling. I. Title.
HF5446 .D47 1982

Dettmering, Joanne. Schultz, Gordon F. Cruise ship employment directory /. Centralia, Wash. (131 Elma Dr., Centralia 98531) , c1987. 102 p. ; LC Card 87-166826 DDC 385/.22/02373 19
HE566.E9 S38 1987

Deuda-- crisis cambiaria . Echevarría Salvat, Oscar A., 1935- Caracas , 1986. xx, 248 p. : ISBN 980-265-224-5 LC Card 87-400245 DDC 336.3/4/0987 19
HG3883.V4 E28 1986

La Deuda externa : informe de la situación chilena y latinoamericana. [Santiago, Chile] : Economic & Financial Survey, 1985. 105 leaves : ill. ; 28 cm. (Informe económico . no. 8) Bibliography: leaves 83-84. LC Card 86-171251
1. Debts, External - Latin America. 2. Debts, External - Chile. I. Economic & Financial Survey (Firm). II. Series: Informe económico (Economic & Financial Survey (Firm)) , no. 8.
HJ8514.5 .D47 1985

Deuda externa . Rebolledo Soberón, Luis. [Lima] , c1985. 58 p. : LC Card 86-120059
HJ8514.5 .R43 1985

La deuda externa de América Latina . Gavagnin Taffarel, Osvaldo. Lima, Perú , 1986. 157 p. : LC Card 86-235251
HJ8514.5 .G37 1986

Deuda externa latinoamericana /. Vela, Gil. Ecuador , 1984. 180 p. ; LC Card 85-180466 DDC 336.3/435/098 19
HJ8514.5 .V45 1984 ***NYPL [JLD 86-308]***

Deuda externa latinoamericana y proceso de ajuste : experiencias y perspectivas / editor, Edgar Revéiz. Bogotá, Colombia : Universidad de los Andes, Facultad de Economía, Centro de Estudios sobre Desarrollo Económico, 1985. 335 p. : ill. ; 24 cm. (Colección Debates-CEDE . no. 5) Includes bibliographical references. LC Card 86-164491
1. Debts, External - Latin America. 2. Debts, External - Latin America - Case studies. 3. Debt relief - Latin America. 4. Economic stabilization - Latin America. 5. Latin America - Economic policy. I. Revéiz, Edgar. II. Series.
HJ8514.5 .D484 1985

Deuda externa y reforma del sistema monetario internacional : resultados del II seminario internacional / organizado por Prodemocracia y la Fundación Friedrich Naumann de la República Federal de Alemania, Bogotá, noviembre 13-15 de 1985. Bogotá, D.E., Colombia : Prodemocracia, 1986. 235 p. ; 21 cm. Includes bibliographical references. ISBN 958-608-037-4 LC Card 87-400468 DDC 336.3/435/098 19
1. Debts, External - Latin America - Congresses. 2. Debts, External - Developing countries - Congresses. 3. International finance - Congresses. I. Prodemocracia (Organization). II. Friedrich Naumann Stiftung.
HJ8514.5 .D487 1986

Deuda o desarrollo . Alva Castro, Luis. Lima, Perú , 1987. 127 p. : LC Card 87-403115 DDC 336.3/4/0985 19
HJ8604 .A75 1987

Deutsch-englische Komödie der Irrungen um Südwestafrika . Phillips, John A. S. Pfaffenhofen, West Germany , 1986. 184 p., [12] p. of plates : ISBN 3-87010-105-9 LC Card 87-146587 DDC 338.4/76686366/09688 19
HD9484.G9 N366 1986

Die deutsch-englische Wirtschaftsrivalität . Banze, Angelika. Vaduz , 1965. 105 p. ; LC Card 85-243022 DDC 337.43041 19
HF1546.15.G7 B36 1965

Deutsch-englisches, englisch-deutsches Wörterbuch. Betteridge, Harold T. Cassell's German-English, English-German dictionary =. New York , 1978. xx, 1580 p. ; ISBN 0-02-522920-6 (standard) LC Card 77-18452 DDC 433/.21 19
PF3640 .B453 1978
NYPL [*P-Desk 86-5858]

Deutsch-Französisches Arbeitstreffen auf dem Gebiet der Demographie (1985 : Dijon, France) Referate zum Deutsch-Französischen Arbeitstreffen auf dem Gebiet der Demographie vom 30. September bis 3. Oktober 1985 in Dijon. Wiesbaden : Bundesinstitut für Bevölkerungsforschung, 1986. 134 p. : ill. ; 30 cm. (Materialien zur Bevölkerungswissenschaft, 0178-918X . Bd. 49) In English. LC Card 87-409287 DDC 304.6/0943 19
1. Germany, West - Population - Congresses. 2. France - Population - Congresses. I. Bundesinstitut zur Bevölkerungswissenschaft (Germany). II. Title. III. Series.
HB3595 .D45 1985

Deutsch, Robert. The food revolution in the Soviet Union and Eastern Europe / Robert

Deutsch. Boulder : Westview Press, 1986. xxii, 256 p. : ill. ; 23 cm. (Westview special studies on the Soviet Union and Eastern Europe) Includes indexes. Bibliography: p. 149-241. ISBN 0-8133-7161-9 (pbk.) : LC Card 85-26625 DDC 338.1/9/47 19
1. Sovet ėkonomicheskoĭ vzaimopomoshchi. 2. Food supply - Russia. 3. Produce trade - Russia. 4. Agriculture and state - Russia. 5. Food supply - Europe Eastern. 6. Produce trade - Europe, Eastern. 7. Agriculture and state - Europe, Eastern. I. Title.
HD9015.S652 D47 1986
NYPL [JLE 86-1588]

Deutsche Akademie für Staats- und Rechtswissenschaft "Walter Ulbricht." Institut für Internationale Beziehungen. Stimme und Aktion der Völker gegen das Wettrüsten . Berlin , 1985. 421 p. ;
NYPL [JLD 86-4257]

Die deutsche Arbeiterbewegung in Bielitz und Biala /. Wurbs, Gerhard. Stuttgart , 1983. 133 p. : LC Card 84-194473
HD8539.5.B542 W87 1983

DEUTSCHE ARBEITSFRONT.
Germanskiĭ trudovoĭ front . Berlin , 1943. 69 leaves : LC Card 85-204295
HD8443.D43 G47 1943

Smelser, Ronald, 1942- Robert Ley, Hitler's labor leader /. New York , 1988. p. cm. ISBN 0-85496-161-5 : LC Card 87-20960 DDC 331/.092/4 B 19
HD8453.L49 S64 1988

Deutsche Arbeitsfront. Arbeitswissenschaftliches Institut.
Germanskiĭ trudovoĭ front . Berlin , 1943. 69 leaves : LC Card 85-204295
HD8443.D43 G47 1943

Wirtschaftskarten von Österreich /. Berlin , 1938. 38 p. : LC Card 86-179061
HC265 .W554 1938

Deutsche Bank (1957-). Zentrale Internationale Abteilung. Aussenwirtschafts-Alphabet . Frankfurt am Main , c1986. 396 p. ; LC Card 87-401369 DDC 382/.03/31 19
HF1001 .A86 1986

DEUTSCHE BUNDESBAHN.
Krummheuer, Eberhard. Intercity experimental ICE, der neue Zug der neuen Bahn . München , c1986. 200 p. : ISBN 3-923967-25-X : LC Card 86-220676
HE3080.D37 K78 1986

DEUTSCHE BUNDESBAHN - FINANCE.
Michelbach, Roger. Probleme der Sanierung der Deutschen Bundesbahn durch die Änderung institutioneller Rahmenbedingungen /. Thun , c1984. xi, 450 p. : ISBN 3-87144-865-6 LC Card 85-137676
HE3080.D4 M53 1984

DEUTSCHE BUNDESBAHN - HISTORY.
Offizieller Jubiläumsband der Deutschen Bundesbahn . München , 1985. 239 p. : ISBN 3-923967-03-9 LC Card 86-168073
HE3078 .O44 1985b

DEUTSCHE BUNDESBANK.
Eschenbaum, Gerhard. Krisenbevorratung von Rohstoffen unter spezieller Berücksichtigung einer Finanzierung aus Währungsreserven der Deutschen Bundesbank /. Bochum , 1983. xix, 464 p. : ISBN 3-88339-314-2 : LC Card 83-218426
HF1054.G4 E83 1983

Langmár, Andrásné. A Német Szövetségi Köztársaság bankrendszere /. Budapest [1987] 71 p. : ISBN 963-7103-59-7 LC Card 87-409642
HG3048 .L47 1987

Seja, Jürgen, 1953- Selektive Effekte der global orientierten Geldpolitik der Deutschen Bundesbank auf die Marktstruktur im Bankensektor /. Frankfurt am Main , New York , c1983. xiii, 370 p. ; ISBN 3-8204-5282-6 LC Card 86-119382
HG3055 .S5 1983

Die Deutsche Bundespost . Herrmann, Ernst. Baden-Baden , 1986. 261 p. ; ISBN 3-7890-1323-4 LC Card 87-116897 DDC 383/.4943 19
HE6995 .H44 1986

DEUTSCHE BUNDESPOST.
Die Gebührenpolitik der Deutschen Bundespost im Kleingut- und Fernmeldebereich . [Mainz] [1984?] xi, 300 p. ; LC Card 87-407592 DDC 383/.23/0943 19
HE6998 .G42 1984

Germany (West). Monopolkommission. Die Rolle der Deutschen Bundespost im Fernmeldewesen /. Baden-Baden , 1981. 110 p. ; ISBN 3-7890-0675-0(pbk.) LC Card 81-130348 DDC 383/.4943 19
HE8155 .R64 1981 ***NYPL [JLE 87-312]***

DEUTSCHE BUNDESPOST - COMMUNICATION SYSTEMS.
Herrmann, Ernst. Die Deutsche Bundespost . Baden-Baden , 1986. 261 p. ; ISBN 3-7890-1323-4 LC Card 87-116897 DDC 383/.4943 19
HE6995 .H44 1986

Der deutsche Export nach Grossbritannien von 1923 bis 1933 . Ohlsen, Ralph-Rainer, 1955- Bergisch Gladbach , c1986. ii, 256 p. : ISBN 3-89012-043-1 LC Card 86-160346
HF1546.5.G7 O37 1986

Deutsche Forschungsgemeinschaft.
Borrmann, Axel. Die Wettbewerbsposition natürlicher Rohstoffe . Hamburg , 1984. 226 p. : ISBN 3-87895-250-3 LC Card 84-222130
HF1054.G4 B67 1984

Marr, Rainer, 1942- Flexibilisierung von Arbeitszeitstrukturen . [Neubiberg? , 1986] 111 leaves : LC Card 87-409556
HD5109.2.G3 M37 1986

Marstedt, Gerd. Psychische Belastungen in der Arbeitswelt . Opladen , c1986. vii, 366 p. : ISBN 3-531-11757-2 LC Card 87-135624
HF5548.8 .M373 1986

Deutsche Friedensgesellschaft--Vereinigte Kriegsdienstgegner. Wer fürchtet sich vor'm schwarzen Mann? niemand! und wenn er kommt? dann lesen wir . Velbert , c1985. 95 p. : ISBN 3-922319-08-4 : LC Card 86-206116 DDC 355.2/2363/0943 19
HD4870.G3 W47 1985

Deutsche Gartenbau-Gesellschaft. Bürger, es geht um Deine Gemeinde . [S.l. , 1983] ([Bonn] : Bundesdruckerei) 7 p. ; LC Card 84-198296
HD7339.A3 B97 1983

Das deutsche Genossenschaftswesen . Aschhoff, Gunther, 1934- Frankfurt am Main , 1985. 167 p. : ISBN 3-7819-0345-1 LC Card 86-145522
HD3038 .A77 1985

Deutsche Geschäftskorrespondenz . Roessler, Helmut R. Lanham, MD , c1987. xii, 218 p. : ISBN 0-8191-6277-9 (alk. paper) : LC Card 87-6086 DDC 658.4/53 19
HF5728.G3 R64 1987

Deutsche Gesellschaft für Friedens- und Konfliktforschung. Auf dem Weg zu einer neuen Weltwirtschaftsordnung? . Baden-Baden , 1983. 478 p. ; ISBN 3-7890-0919-9
NYPL [JLD 87-919]

Deutsche Gesellschaft für Natur- und Völkerkunde Ostasiens. Barth, Johannes, 1891- Als deutscher Kaufmann in Fernost . Berlin , c1984. 206 p. : ISBN 3-503-02366-6 LC Card 84-143117
HC289.B7 B373 1984

Deutsche Gesellschaft für Osteuropakunde.
Sibirien, ein russisches und sowjetisches Entwicklungsproblem /. Berlin , c1986. 274 p. : ISBN 3-87061-260-6 LC Card 86-229174
HC336.9.S53 S53 1986

Deutsche Gesellschaft für Soziologie. Sektion Soziale Indikatoren. Arbeitsmoral und Technikfeindlichkeit . Frankfurt , New York , c1986. 274 p. : ISBN 3-593-33757-6 LC Card 86-212283
HD8444 .A73 1986

Deutsche Gesellschaft für Technische Zusammenarbeit. Hinzen, Eckhard. Pre-feasibility study of the integrated Ras Hafun project in north east Somalia . Kronberg [West Germany] [1981] xii, 186 leaves : LC Card 85-980733
HC850.Z9 E444 1981

Deutsche Industrie, deutsche Kultur / unter Mitwirkung von Flodoard Freiherr v. Biedermann ... [et al.] ; mit Illustrationen von Hermann Angermeyer ... [et al.] ; herausgegeben von Julius Eckstein und J.J. Landau. Berlin : S.A. Fischer, 1900-1902. xvi, 388 p. : ill. ; 42 cm. Includes index. LC Card 85-666344
1. Germany - Industries. I. Biedermann, Flodoard, Freiherr v., b. 1858. II. Eckstein, Julius. III. Landau, J. J.
HC283 .D48x 1900

Das Deutsche Institut für Wirtschaftsforschung (Institut für Konjunkturforschung), 1925-1979 /. Krengel, Rolf. Berlin , c1986. xi, 229 p. ; ISBN 3-428-06074-1 LC Card 87-112851 DDC 330/.0943 19
HB74.9.G3 K74 1986

Der deutsche Maschinenbau im Wandel der industriellen Output-Struktur . Baumann, Hans, 1931- München , 1978. vi, 196 p. : LC Card 84-126586
HD9705.G4 B26 1978

Deutsche Orient-Stiftung. Zweite wissenschaftliche Regionaltagung über Nah- und Mittelost . Berlin , 1963. vi, 177 p. ; LC Card 85-167419
HC59.7 .D385 no. 62/93 HC415.15

Der Deutsche Osthandel 1982 / [herausgegeben vom Bundesministerium für Wirtschaft, Referat VB1/VB2]. Bonn : Das Ministerium, [1982] 87 p. : ill. ; 29 cm. (BMWI Studien-Reihe, 0170-0049 . 37) LC Card 86-212991
1. Germany, West - Commerce - Europe, Eastern. 2. Europe, Eastern - Commerce - Germany, West. I. Germany (West). Bundesministerium für Wirtschaft. Referat V B 1. II. Germany (West). Bundesministerium für Wirtschaft. Referat V B 2. III. Series.
HF3568.E35 D463 1982

Deutsche Polytechnische Gesellschaft e.V.
Uhlands Internationales Technisches Branchen-Adressbuch =. Leipzig , 1926. 22, 767 p. ; LC Card 85-666352
HC282.2 .U45x 1926

Deutsche Richterakademie. Wirtschaft und Umweltschutz /. Heidelberg , 1986. vii, 147 p. : ISBN 3-8114-2786-5 LC Card 87-134163 DDC 363.7/058/0943 19
HC290.5.E5 W57 1986

Deutsche Seeversicherung, 1958-1980 . Sasse, Jürgen. Karlsruhe , 1982. 331 p. ; ISBN 3-88487-030-0 LC Card 83-190184
HE964.5.G7 S27 1982

Der deutsche Software-Markt und die internationale Wettbewerbsfähigkeit deutscher Anbieter /. Maenner, Ulrike. Hamburg , 1986. 94 p. : ISBN 3-87895-320-8 LC Card 87-407404 DDC 338.4/70053/0943 19
HD9696.C63 G446 1986

Die deutsche Sparkassenwerbung, 1750-1981 /. Emmerich, Norbert-Christian. Stuttgart , 1983. 344 p. : LC Card 84-119079
HF6161.B2 E64 1983

DEUTSCHE STEUER-GEWERKSCHAFT - HISTORY.
Fredersdorf, Hermann, 1924- Der Steuerrebell und seine Gewerkschaft . Wiesbaden , c1982. 156 p., [3] folded leaves of plates : ISBN 3-922114-02-4 LC Card 83-102197
HJ2690 .F78 1982

Deutsche Stiftung für Entwicklungsländer.
Seminar "Planung des Berufsausbildungswesens in Entwicklungsländern" (1965 : Berlin, Germany) Seminar "Planung des Berufsausbildungswesens in Entwicklungsländern" vom 22. Juli bis 17. August 1965 /. Berlin-Tegel [1965?] 1 portfolio ; LC Card 87-407604
HD5715.5.D44 S46 1965

Zweite wissenschaftliche Regionaltagung über Nah- und Mittelost . Berlin , 1963. vi, 177 p. ; LC Card 85-167419
HC59.7 .D385 no. 62/93 HC415.15

Deutsche Stiftung für Umweltpolitik.
Umweltpolitisches Gespräch (1983 : Bad Godesberg, Bonn, Germany) Ökonomische Instrumente der Umweltpolitik . Berlin , c1984. 108 p. ; ISBN 3-503-02401-8 LC Card 86-152141
HC290.5.E5 U625 1983

Deutsche und englische Gewerkschaften . Eisenberg, Christiane, 1956- Göttingen , c1986. 391 p. ; ISBN 3-525-35733-8 LC Card 87-127078 DDC 331.88/0941 19
HD6694 .E27 1986

Deutsche Vereinigung für Parlamentsfragen. Die Deutschen Länder und die Europäischen Gemeinschaften . Baden-Baden , 1986. 294 p. ;

ISBN 3-7890-1350-1 LC Card 87-141896 DDC 341.24/22 19
HC241.25.G3 D48 1986

Die deutsche Versicherungswirtschaft . Farny, Dieter. Karlsruhe [c1983] xiv, 189 p. ; ISBN 3-88487-054-8 LC Card 84-205736
HG8618 .F37 1983

Die Deutschen Länder und die Europäischen Gemeinschaften : Referate und Diskussionsbeiträge eines Symposiums der Deutschen Vereinigung für Parlamentsfragen am 20./21. Juni 1986 in Stuttgart mit Dokumenten-Anhang / Rudolf Hrbek, Uwe Thaysen (Hrsg.).1. Aufl. Baden-Baden : Nomos, 1986. 294 p. ; 23 cm. Bibliography: p. 213-214. ISBN 3-7890-1350-1 LC Card 87-141896 DDC 341.24/22 19
1. European Economic Community - Germany, West - Congresses. 2. Federal government - Germany (West) - Congresses. I. Hrbek, R. (Rudolf). II. Thaysen, Uwe, 1940-. III. Deutsche Vereinigung für Parlamentsfragen.
HC241.25.G3 D48 1986

Die Deutschen werden ärmer . Merklein, Renate. Reinbek bei Hamburg , 1982. 189 p. : ISBN 3-499-33018-0 : LC Card 83-137339
HC286.7 .M475 1982

Deutscher Geographentag (42nd : 1979 : Göttingen, Germany) Periphere Räume . Paderborn , 1979. 183 p. : ISBN 3-506-73204-8 LC Card 85-209554
HC240 .P38 1979

Deutscher Gewerkschaftsbund. (Old Catalog form: Deutscher Gewerkschaftsbund (f. 1949))

DEUTSCHER GEWERKSCHAFTSBUND - HISTORY.
Roder, Hartmut, 1951- Der christlich-nationale Deutsche Gewerkschaftsbund (DGB) im politisch-ökonomischen Kräftefeld der Weimarer Republik . Frankfurt am Main , New York , c1986. 804 p. : ISBN 3-8204-9325-5 LC Card 86-194815
HD8443.D457 R63 1986

Deutscher Gewerkschaftsbund. Wirtschafts- und Sozialwissenschaftliches Institut.
Perspektiven der Vollbeschäftigung . Köln , c1987. vi, 263 p. : ISBN 3-7663-3033-0 LC Card 87-135012 DDC 339.5 19
HD5701.3 .P47 1987

Deutscher Historikertag (34th : 1982 : Münster in Westfalen, Germany) Vereinswesen und bürgerliche Gesellschaft in Deutschland /. München , 1984. 180 p. ; ISBN 3-486-52081-4 LC Card 84-205111
HD2429.G3 V46 1984

Deutscher Industrie- und Handelstag.
DIHT-Kongress (1983 : Frankfurt am Main, Germany) Kapital, Zins, Währung . Bonn , 1984. 68 p. : LC Card 84-212399
HC290.5.C3 D53 1983

DIHT-Meinung, 1982 / [Herausgeber, Deutscher Industrie- und Handelstag]. Bonn : Der Handelstag, 1982. 104 p. ; 21 cm. (DIHT . 206) Includes bibliographical references and index. LC Card 83-206569
1. Deutscher Industrie- und Handelstag. 2. Germany, West - Economic policy - 1974-. I. Title. II. Title: D.I.H.T.-Meinung, 1982.
HC286.7 .D47 1982

Klause, Dieter. Wegweiser zur Weiterbildung . Bonn , 1982. 101 p. ; LC Card 83-206662
HF5549.5.T7 K58 1982

Praxisleitfaden Privatisierung /. Bonn , 1984. 202 p. : LC Card 84-194479
HD4175 .P73 1984

Reininghaus, Wilfried. Quellen zur Geschichte des Deutschen Industrie- und Handelstages in Kammerarchiven, 1861 bis 1918 /. Bonn , 1986. 158 p. : ISBN 3-925925-01-5 LC Card 87-408272 DDC 354.430082/09 19
HF308 .R343 1986

Vom Gleis abgekommen . Bonn , 1977. 60 p. ; LC Card 86-176591
HE2445 .V65 1977

Votum für die Marktwirtschaft . Bonn , c1976. 26 p. ; LC Card 85-172115
HC286.7 .V69 1976

Zeugnisse der Zeit . Bonn , 1986. 113 p. : LC Card 87-408186
HD2429.G3 Z48 1986

DEUTSCHER INDUSTRIE- UND HANDELSTAG.
Deutscher Industrie- und Handelstag. DIHT-Meinung, 1982 /. Bonn , 1982. 104 p. ; LC Card 83-206569
HC286.7 .D47 1982

DEUTSCHER INDUSTRIE- UND HANDELSTAG - EXHIBITIONS.
Zeugnisse der Zeit . Bonn , 1986. 113 p. : LC Card 87-408186
HD2429.G3 Z48 1986

DEUTSCHER INDUSTRIE- UND HANDELSTAG - HISTORY - SOURCES.
Reininghaus, Wilfried. Quellen zur Geschichte des Deutschen Industrie- und Handelstages in Kammerarchiven, 1861 bis 1918 /. Bonn , 1986. 158 p. : ISBN 3-925925-01-5 LC Card 87-408272 DDC 354.430082/09 19
HF308 .R343 1986

Deutscher Sparkassen- und Giroverband.
Standortbestimmung . Stuttgart , c1984. 447 p. ; ISBN 3-09-311000-9 LC Card 85-150165
HG1939.G3 S73 1984

Deutscher Strassenkongress, Mannheim, 1984 /. Deutscher Strassenkongress (1984 : Mannheim, Germany) Köln [1985?] 255 p. : LC Card 87-408263 DDC 388.1/0943 19
HE363.G3 D48 1984

Deutscher Strassenkongress (1984 : Mannheim, Germany) Deutscher Strassenkongress, Mannheim, 1984 / [Veranstalter, Forschungsgesellschaft für Strassen- und Verkehrswesen]. Köln : Die Gesellschaft, [1985?] 255 p. : ill. ; 30 cm. Cover title: Verkehrswege für die mobile Gesellschaft. Includes bibliographies. LC Card 87-408263 DDC 388.1/0943 19
1. Roads - Germany (West) - Congresses. 2. Road construction - Germany (West) - Congresses. 3. Highway planning - Germany, West - Congresses. I. Forschungsgesellschaft für Strassen- und Verkehrswesen (Germany). II. Title. III. Title: Verkehrswege für die mobile Gesellschaft.
HE363.G3 D48 1984

DEUTSCHER ZOLLVEREIN - HISTORY.
Hahn, Hans-Werner. Geschichte des Deutschen Zollvereins /. Göttingen , c1984. 214 p. ; ISBN 3-525-33500-8 LC Card 85-129823
HF2106 .H27 1984

Deutsches Atomforum. Technik auf dem Prüfstand . Essen , Gräfelfing [1982] 183 p. : ISBN 3-7736-0340-1 LC Card 83-187518
HD9698.G42 T43 1982

Deutsches Institut für Entwicklungspolitik. Occasional papers. see **Deutsches Institut für Entwicklungspolitik. Schriften.**

Schriften.
(Bd. 70) Brandt, Hartmut. Projektplanung in der kleinbäuerlichen Produktion /. Berlin , 1982. xv, 208 p. : LC Card 83-193407
HD1476.G3 B73 1982 ***NYPL [JLE 87-2903]***

Deutsches Institut für Urbanistik.
Echter, Claus-Peter. Konzepte städtischer Wohnungspolitik . Berlin , 1985. 97 p. : ISBN 3-88118-123-7 LC Card 86-145702
HD7288.78.G3 E265 1985

Kempf, Thomas. Umsetzung organisatorischer Neuerungen . Berlin , 1986. 237 p. : ISBN 3-88118-133-4 LC Card 87-114986
HD58.8 .K46 1986

Reidenbach, Michael. Verfällt die öffentliche Infrastruktur? . Berlin , 1986. 212 p. : ISBN 3-88118-125-3 LC Card 86-233141
HC290.5.C3 R45 1986

Deutsches Institut für Wirtschaftsforschung, Berlin. see **Berlin. Deutsches Institut für Wirtschaftsforschung.**

Deutsches Institut für Luftverkehrsstatistik. Die Struktur des von der Bundesrepublik Deutschland ausgehenden Nordatlantik-Personen-Luftverkehrs . [Frankfurt am Main] [1963] 165 p. : LC Card 85-126310
HE9787.5.G4 S77 1963

Deutsches Institut für Wirtschaftsforschung.
Erhöhter Handlungsbedarf im Strukturwandel . Berlin [1984] xxix, 229 p. : ISBN 3-428-05565-9 LC Card 86-137115 DDC 330 s 330.943/0878 19
HC281 .B33 Heft 79 HC286.7

Regionale Struktur des Personenverkehrs in der Bundesrepublik Deutschland im Jahre 1980 /. Berlin , 1985. ix, 320 p. : ISBN 3-428-05961-1 LC Card 86-165242
HC281 .B33 Heft 88 HE249

DEUTSCHES INSTITUT FÜR WIRTSCHAFTSFORSCHUNG - HISTORY.
Krengel, Rolf. Das Deutsche Institut für Wirtschaftsforschung (Institut für Konjunkturforschung), 1925-1979 /. Berlin , c1986. xi, 229 p. ; ISBN 3-428-06074-1 LC Card 87-112851 DDC 330/.0943 19
HB74.9.G3 K74 1986

Deutschland, Heinz. Geschichte des FDGB . Berlin , c1985. 364 p. ; LC Card 86-124681 DDC 331.88/0943 19
HD8460.5.A5 F7326 1985

Dévai, Katalin. A nagyvállalatok helyzetéről / Dévai Katalin. [Budapest] : Művelődési Minisztérium Marxizmus-Leninizmus Oktatási Főosztálya, 1984. 68 p. ; 24 cm. (Politikai gazdaságtan füzetek, 0324-6396 . 46) Summary in Russian. Includes bibliographical references. ISBN 963-673-293-0 LC Card 85-175237
1. Industrial concentration - Hungary. 2. Industries, Size of - Hungary. 3. Industrial organization - Hungary. 4. New business enterprises - Hungary. I. Title. II. Series.
HD2852.5 .D48 1984

DEVALUATION OF CURRENCY - GHANA.
Denoon, David B. H. Devaluation under pressure . Cambridge, Mass. , c1986. xi, 260 p.; ISBN 0-262-04083-2 LC Card 85-15314 DDC 332.4/14 19
HG1235 .D37 1985 ***NYPL [JLE 86-2836]***

DEVALUATION OF CURRENCY - INDIA.
Denoon, David B. H. Devaluation under pressure . Cambridge, Mass. , c1986. xi, 260 p.; ISBN 0-262-04083-2 LC Card 85-15314 DDC 332.4/14 19
HG1235 .D37 1985 ***NYPL [JLE 86-2836]***

DEVALUATION OF CURRENCY - INDONESIA.
Denoon, David B. H. Devaluation under pressure . Cambridge, Mass. , c1986. xi, 260 p.; ISBN 0-262-04083-2 LC Card 85-15314 DDC 332.4/14 19
HG1235 .D37 1985 ***NYPL [JLE 86-2836]***

DEVALUATION OF CURRENCY - MEXICO.
De Murguía, Valdemar. Capital flight and economic crisis . La Jolla, Calif. , 1986. 27 p. ; LC Card 87-621351 DDC 332/.042 19
HG3916 .D4 1986

DEVALUATION OF CURRENCY - PERU.
Herrera, César. Inflación, política devaluatoria y apertura externa en el Perú, 1978-1984 /. Lima, Perú , 1985. 55 p. : LC Card 87-104441
HG895 .H47 1985

DEVALUATION OF CURRENCY - PHILIPPINES.
Navarro, Susan S. Dynamic effects of exchange rate changes in the Philippines in 1970-1980 /. [Quezon] [1986] 25 p. ; LC Card 87-120911 DDC 332.4/5609599 19
HG1265 .N38 1986

DEVALUATION OF CURRENCY - UNITED STATES - HISTORY.
Pick, Franz. The U. S. dollar . Bethel, CT , c1986. xvi, 103 p., [1] folded leaf of plates : ISBN 0-916373-04-5 (pbk.): LC Card 86-210094 DDC 332.4/973 19
HG539 .P5 1986

Devaluation under pressure . Denoon, David B. H. Cambridge, Mass. , c1986. xi, 260 p.; ISBN 0-262-04083-2 LC Card 85-15314 DDC 332.4/14 19
HG1235 .D37 1985 ***NYPL [JLE 86-2836]***

Developing a basic loan training program /. Pace, Edmond E. Philadelphia, Pa. , c1987. 108 p. ; ISBN 0-936742-41-0 (pbk.) : LC Card 87-7936 DDC 332.1/753/0683 19
HG1642.U5 P33 1987

Developing a winning marketing plan /. Cohen, William A., 1937- New York , c1987. ix, 324 p. : ISBN 0-471-84529-9 LC Card 86-32402 DDC 658.8/02 19
HF5415 .C54247 1987

Developing America's northern frontier / edited by Theodore Lane. Lanham, MD : University Press of America, c1987. xx, 250 p. ; 25 cm.

Includes bibliographies. ISBN 0-8191-6081-4 (alk. paper) : LC Card 86-28233 DDC 338.9719 19
1. Canada, Northern - Economic policy. 2. Canada, Northern - Economic conditions. 3. Alaska - Economic policy. 4. Alaska - Economic conditions. I. Lane, Theodore.
HC117.N48 D48 1987

Developing and using microcomputer business systems /. Huff, Kathryn. St. Paul , c1987. xvi, 224, [29] p. : ISBN 0-314-34730-5 (pbk.) LC Card 87-2184 DDC 658/.05416 19
HF5548.2 .H785 1987

Developing and using office applications with AppleWorks . Varnon, M. S. St. Paul , c1987. xi, 366 p. : ISBN 0-314-34129-3 (pbk.) : LC Card 86-24696 DDC 651.8/5369 19
HF5548.4.A68 V37 1987

Developing business systems in SQL . Gane, Chris, 1938- New York, NY , 1986. 1 v. (various pagings) : ISBN 0-914751-02-6 (pbk.) LC Card 87-107881 DDC 650/.028/557565 19
HF5548.5.S65 G36 1986

DEVELOPING COUNTRIES.

Az Elmélet és a fegyverek kritikája . Budapest [1981] xxv, 509 p. ; ISBN 963-461-775-1 (Magy. nemz. bibl.) LC Card 85-139263
HC59.7 .E45 1981

Latouche, Serge, 1940- Faut-il refuser le développement? . Paris , c1986. 216 p. ; ISBN 2-13-039202-4 : LC Card 86-160202
HD83 .L324 1986

Mortimer, Rex, 1926-1979. Stubborn survivors . [Clayton, Vic.] , 1984. xvii, 180 p. : ISBN 0-86746-299-X (pbk.) LC Card 87-672646
HC59.7 .M593x 1984

Nweihed, Kaldone G., 1929- Bolívar y el Tercer Mundo . Caracas, Venezuela , c1984. 400 p. : ISBN 84-499-7056-3 LC Card 85-136718
F2235.3 .N98 1984 ***NYPL [JFE 86-1176]***

Rangel Guevara, Carlos. [Tercermundismo. English.] Third world ideology and Western reality . New Brunswick , c1986. xiii, 180 p. ; ISBN 0-88738-601-6 (pbk.) LC Card 85-24486 DDC 330.9172/4 19
HC59.7 .R26513 1985 ***NYPL [JLE 86-3009]***

Third world development /. London , New York , 1985. 3 v. : ISBN 0-946027-65-X (v. 1)
NYPL [JLF 86-626]

DEVELOPING COUNTRIES - CIVILIZATION - OCCIDENTAL INFLUENCES.

Dahmani, Mohamed. L'occidentalisation des pays du Tiers Monde . Paris , Alger , c1983. 217 p. ; ISBN 2-7178-0623-7 : LC Card 83-162697 DDC 909/.09724082 19
HC59.7 .D273 1983 ***NYPL [JLE 86-566]***

DEVELOPING COUNTRIES - COMMERCE.

Exports of developing countries . Washington, D.C. , c1987. viii, 168 p. : ISBN 0-8213-0870-X (pbk.) : LC Card 87-15991 DDC 382/.6/091724 19
HF4055 .E96 1987

Habermayer, Wolfgang, 1959- Internationale Rohstoffabkommen als Beispiel des Nord-Süd Dialoges /. Frankfurt am Main , New York , c1985. xxxiii, 264 p. : ISBN 3-8204-8896-0 LC Card 86-111744
HF1054.D44 H33 1985

Hermann, Christian, 1954- Auswirkungen industrieller Exportproduktion im Rahmen der internationalen Arbeitsteilung auf die Einkommensverteilung von Entwicklungsländern /. Frankfurt am Main , New York , c1984. viii, 393 p. ; ISBN 3-8204-7456-0 LC Card 85-191626
HF4055 .H47 1984

Hoda, Anwarul, 1938- Developing countries in the international trading system /. Ahmedabad , 1987. xii, 302 p. ; LC Card 87-902308 DDC 382/.091724 19
HF4055 .H64 1987

Illarionov, Sergeĭ Ivanovich. Osvobodivshiesi͡a strany . Moskva , 1987. 260, [4] p. ; LC Card 87-118170
HF1413 .I54 1987

Langhammer, Rolf J. Economic impact of generalized tariff preferences /. Aldershot, Hants, England , Brookfield, Vt. , 1988. p. cm. ISBN 0-566-05338-1 : LC Card 87-15045 DDC 382.7/53 19
HF1721 .L35 1988

Mannur, H. G. The terms of trade and Third World countries /. Pulau Pinang , 1978. ii, 35 p. ; LC Card 84-940687
HF4055 .M36 1978

Neundörfer, Konrad. Wir und die Dritte Welt . Köln , c1985. x, 214 p. ; ISBN 3-452-20304-2 LC Card 85-164555
HC59.7 .N375 1985

The New Communist Third World . London , c1982. 392 p. ; ISBN 0-7099-2709-6 LC Card 86-673518
HF1413 .N495x 1982b

Rana, Pradumna Bickram, 1947- The impact of the current exchange rate system on trade and inflation of selected developing member countries /. Manila, Philippines , c1983. iv, 78 p. : LC Card 87-105105 DDC 332.4/56 19
HG3877 .R36 1983

Surveys in development economics /. Oxford, UK , New York, NY, USA , 1987. 390 p. : ISBN 0-631-14713-6 : LC Card 87-5164 DDC 338.9/009172/4 19
HC59.7 .S882 1987

Transnationals and development. Manchester, England , 1984. i, 64 p. ;
NYPL [JLD 86-3224]

Tussie, Diana. The less developed countries and the world trading system . London , 1987. viii, 162 p. ; ISBN 0-86187-614-8
NYPL [JLE 87-1597]

DEVELOPING COUNTRIES - COMMERCE - AUSTRALIA.

Anderson, Kym. Australia's trade growth with developing countries /. Canberra, Australia , 1983. iv, 55 p. ; ISBN 0-86413-001-5 (pbk.) LC Card 86-673748
HF3948.D44 A52x 1983

DEVELOPING COUNTRIES - COMMERCE - CONGRESSES.

Welthandel morgen . Stuttgart , 1984. 275 p. : ISBN 3-87959-225-X LC Card 85-132786
HF4055 .W45 1984

DEVELOPING COUNTRIES - COMMERCE - ECONOMETRIC MODELS.

Hasse, Rolf. Ökonometrie als Instrument der Interessenpolitik . Köln , 1985. ii, 109 p. : ISBN 3-921471-52-4 : LC Card 85-216061
HF1733.D44 H37 1985

Mohs, Ralf-Matthias. Exporte, komparative Vorteile und wirtschaftliche Entwicklung in den Schwellenländern . Göttingen [1983] 236 p. : ISBN 3-509-01345-X LC Card 84-126961
HF4055 .M64 1983

DEVELOPING COUNTRIES - COMMERCE - EUROPEAN ECONOMIC COMMUNITY COUNTRIES.

Davenport, Michael, 1940- Trade policy, protectionism, and the Third World /. London , Dover, N.H. , c1986. 152 p. : ISBN 0-7099-4516-7 : LC Card 86-6192 DDC 382.7/53 19
HF2039.5.Z7 D38 1986
NYPL [JLD 86-2759]

Perspectives on industrial readjustment, the EEC and the developing countries /. Tilburg, Netherlands , 1978. ii, 98 p. ;
NYPL [JLF 86-1708]

DEVELOPING COUNTRIES - COMMERCE - GERMANY (WEST)

Beyfuss, Jörg. Aussenhandel mit Entwicklungsländern . Köln , c1978. 55 p. : ISBN 3-88054-145-0 LC Card 85-242489
HF3568.D44 B49 1978

Der Neue Protektionismus . Bonn , c1983. 195 p. : ISBN 3-87831-370-5 LC Card 83-198686
HF1756 .N58 1983

DEVELOPING COUNTRIES - COMMERCE - GERMANY (WEST) - BADEN-WÜRTTEMBERG.

Moosmann, Bernfried, 1957- Mittelbetriebe und Entwicklungsländer . Frankfurt am Main , New York , c1986. x, 290 p. ; ISBN 3-8204-9518-5 LC Card 86-232976
HF3569.B2 M66 1986

DEVELOPING COUNTRIES - COMMERCE - HUNGARY.

Hungary--a market for products from developing countries /. Geneva , 1985. xi, 129 p. : LC Card 87-118542 DDC 382/.09439/01724 19
HF3550.5.Z7 D44 1985

DEVELOPING COUNTRIES - COMMERCE - STATISTICS.

UNCTAD statistical pocketbook /. New York , 1984. xv, 96 p. : LC Card 86-200987 DDC 330.9172/4 19
HF4055 .U53 1984

DEVELOPING COUNTRIES - COMMERCE - UNITED STATES.

Der Neue Protektionismus . Bonn , c1983. 195 p. : ISBN 3-87831-370-5 LC Card 83-198686
HF1756 .N58 1983

U. S. agriculture & Third World development . Boulder , 1987. xi, 258 p. ; ISBN 1-555-87011-2 (lib. bdg.) : LC Card 86-29860 DDC 338.1/09172/4 19
HD1765 .U15 1987

DEVELOPING COUNTRIES - COMMERCIAL POLICY.

D'Angelo, Massimo. Criteri per una cooperazione industriale con i paesi in via di sviluppo /. Milano , c1981. 294 p. ; ISBN 88-20-42145-3 : LC Card 82-113466
HF1549 .D36 1981 ***NYPL [JLD 86-3318]***

Development strategies reconsidered /. New Brunswick, N.J., U. S.A. , c1986. viii, 190 p. ; ISBN 0-87855-991-4 (pbk.) : LC Card 85-24582 DDC 338.9/009172/4 19
HC59.7 .D482 1986 ***NYPL [JLE 86-2976]***

European trade policies and the developing world /. London , New York , c1988. x, 368 p. ; ISBN 0-7099-4672-4 LC Card 87-8969 DDC 382/.3/094 19
HF1492 .E87 1988

Hall, Kenneth O. The Group of 77 . Nyon, Switzerland , 1979. 48 p. ; LC Card 86-202645
HF1413 .H27 1979

DEVELOPING COUNTRIES - COMMERCIAL POLICY - CONGRESSES.

Economic liberalization in developing countries /. Oxford [Oxfordshire] , New York , 1986. vi, 278 p. : ISBN 0-631-15023-4 : LC Card 86-6153 DDC 338.9/009172/4 19
HC59.7 .E3116 1986 ***NYPL [JLE 86-4644]***

DEVELOPING COUNTRIES - CONGRESSES.

Disarmament and world development /. Oxford, England , New York , 1986. xiii, 306 p. ; ISBN 0-08-031309-4 : LC Card 85-19231 DDC 338.4/7355 19
JX1974 .D515 1985 ***NYPL [JLE 86-3211]***

DEVELOPING COUNTRIES - DEPENDENCY ON FOREIGN COUNTRIES.

Alarcón, Reynaldo. Psicología, pobreza y subdesarrollo /. Lima, Perú , 1986. 153 p. ; LC Card 87-126266 DDC 155.9/2 19
HC79.P6 A55 1986

Amin, Samir. La déconnexion, pour sortir du système mondial /. Paris , 1986, c1985. 333 p. : ISBN 2-7071-1588-6 : LC Card 86-219988
HF1413 .A45 1986

Corbridge, Stuart. Capitalist world development . London , 1986. xi, 295 p. : ISBN 0-333-32405-6 ***NYPL [JLD 86-2925]***

Décolonisations et nouvelles dépendances . [Lille] , c1986. 282 p. : ISBN 2-85939-287-4 : LC Card 87-104133
HC59.7 .D354 1986

Held, Karl, 1944- Krieg und Frieden . Frankfurt am Main , c1983. 324 p. ; ISBN 3-518-11149-3 : LC Card 83-228517
HC79.D4 H45 1983

Shitov, V. N. (Vladimir Nikolaevich) Tekhnologicheskiĭ neokolonializm . Moskva , 1985. 154 p. : LC Card 86-130530
HC59.72.T4 S525 1985

Türkiye Komünist Partisi/Marksist-Leninist. Kritik der "Drei Welten Theorie" durch die TKP/ML . Wien [1978] 1 v. (various pagings) ; LC Card 85-134265
HC59.7 .T867 1978

Urien, Julio César. Un aporte para la liberación /. Buenos Aires, Argentina , c1985. 51 p. ; ISBN 950-9235-13-X LC Card 85-201095
HC125 .U75 1985

Vojnović, Milan. Svetska dominacija krupnog

kapitala /. Beograd , 1981. 150 p. : LC Card 85-235805
HF1411 .V655 1981

DEVELOPING COUNTRIES - DEPENDENCY ON FOREIGN COUNTRIES - CONGRESSES.

Entwicklungstheorie, Entwicklungspraxis . Berlin , c1986. 316 p. ; ISBN 3-428-05973-5 LC Card 86-233851 DDC 338.9/009172/4 19
HC59.7 .E6473 1986

Unterdrückung, Hunger, Krieg . Göttingen [1985?] 73 p. : LC Card 86-152237
HC59.7 .U55 1985

DEVELOPING COUNTRIES - DEPENDENCY ON FOREIGN COUNTRIES - MATHEMATICAL MODELS.

Ziesemer, Thomas. Economic theory of underdevelopment /. Regensburg , c1987. vi, 171 p. : ISBN 3-924956-15-4 (pbk.) LC Card 87-169372 DDC 338.9/001 19
HD75.5 .Z54 1987

DEVELOPING COUNTRIES - ECONOMIC CONDITIONS.

Alarcón, Reynaldo. Psicología, pobreza y subdesarrollo /. Lima, Perú , 1986. 153 p. ; LC Card 87-126266 DDC 155.9/2 19
HC79.P6 A55 1986

Auf dem Weg zu einer neuen Weltwirtschaftsordnung? . Baden-Baden , 1983. 478 p. ; ISBN 3-7890-0919-9
NYPL [JLD 87-919]

Belal, Abdel Aziz. Développement et facteurs non-économiques /. Rabat , 1980. 100 p. ; LC Card 82-960502
HD83 .B388 1980

Brandt, Willy, 1913- [Organisierte Wahnsinn. English.] Arms and hunger /. Cambridge, Mass. , 1987, c1986. 208 p. ; ISBN 0-262-52127-X (pbk.) LC Card 87-4057 DDC 330.9172/4 19
HC59.7 .B67713 1987

Búfalo, Enzo del. El pensamiento crítico latinoamericano /. [México?] , 1979. 236 p. ; LC Card 79-120323
HC59.7 .B84 ***NYPL [JLC 80-383]***

Capitalism and equality in the Third World /. Lanham [New York] , c1987. 375 p. ; ISBN 0-8191-5574-8 (v. 2 : alk. paper) : LC Card 86-24749 DDC 330.12/2 19
HB501 .C24234 1987

Capitalismes fin de siècle /. Paris , c1986. 268 p. : ISBN 2-13-039425-6 : LC Card 86-231136
HC106.8 .C364 1986

Clés pour une stratégie nouvelle du développement /. Paris , c1984. 226 p. : ISBN 2-7082-2365-7 : LC Card 85-116966 DDC 338.9/[illegible]72/4 19
HC59.7 .C[illegible] 1984

Cole, J. P. (John Peter), 1928- Development and underdevelopment . London , New York , 1987. vi, 104 p. : ISBN 0-416-92080-2 (pbk.) LC Card 86-23758 DDC 338.9/009172/4 19
HC59.7 .C59 1987

Comprendre l'économie africaine /. Paris , c1985. 566 p. : ISBN 2-85802-566-2 LC Card 86-222248
HC800 .C654 1985

David, Wilfred L. Conflicting paradigms in the economics of developing nations /. New York , 1986. xix, 215 p. : ISBN 0-275-92108-5 (alk. paper) : LC Card 86-16906 DDC 330.9172/4 19
HC59.7 .D335 1986 ***NYPL [JLE 86-4423]***

Décolonisations et nouvelles dépendances . [Lille] , c1986. 282 p. : ISBN 2-85939-287-4 : LC Card 87-104133
HC59.7 .D354 1986

Die Peripherie in der Weltwirtschaftskrise, Afrika, Asien und Lateinamerika, 1929-1939 /. Paderborn , c1982. 295 p. : ISBN 3-506-77461-1 LC Card 83-167120 DDC 330.9172/4 19
HC59.7 .P457 1982 ***NYPL [JLE 87-1202]***

Dumont, René, 1904- Les raisons de la colère, ou, L'utopie et les Verts /. Paris , c1986. 137 p. ; ISBN 2-7266-0075-1 LC Card 86-158407
HC59.72.E5 D85 1986

ECDC handbook . [New Delhi] , 1983. vi, 679 p. ; LC Card 83-903543 DDC 337.1/1724 19
HC59.7 .E23 1983 ***NYPL [JLF 86-1755]***

The Economic demography of mass poverty. [Williamsburg, Va., U. S.A. , c1986] xiv, 142 p. : LC Card 85-73339 DDC 339.4/6/091724 19
HB884 .E36 1986

Ėkonomicheskie problemy razvitiia stran sotsialisticheskoĭ orientatsii /. Moskva , 1986. 239 p. ; LC Card 86-221922
HC59.7 .E355 1986

Forbes, Dean K. The geography of underdevelopment . London , 1986. 214 p. ; ISBN 0-7099-1012-6 ***NYPL [JLD 86-1233]***

Glinz, Ferdinand N. Entwicklungsförderung am Wendepunkt . Zürich , c1986. 320 p. ; ISBN 3-280-01676-2 LC Card 86-227950
HC59.7 .G55 1986

Griffin, Keith B. World hunger and the world economy . New York , 1987. xvi, 274 p. ; ISBN 0-8419-1128-2 LC Card 86-33626 DDC 330.9172/4 19
HC59.7 .G749 1987

Guiton, R. J. (Raymond J.), 1915- Der Aufbruch . Rheinfelden , c1984. 2 v. : ISBN 3-87718-746-3 (Bd. 1) LC Card 85-181833 DDC 325/.344/09 19
JV1818 .G85 1984 ***NYPL [JFK 86-364]***

Guzmán Ortega, Gonzalo. Superestructuras y subdesarrollo . Quito , 1985. 178 p. : LC Card 86-132144
HC59.7 .G86 1985

Harris, Nigel. The end of the Third World . New York , 1987, c1986. 231 p. : ISBN 0-941533-14-X : LC Card 87-12295 DDC 330.9172/4 19
HC59.7 .H3536 1987

Holzhausen, Walter, 1929- Vision creates hope . Dhaka, Bangladesh , 1986. viii, 118 p. ; LC Card 87-901565 DDC 330.9172/4 19
HC59.7 .H624 1986

Illarionov, Sergeĭ Ivanovich. Osvobodivshiesia strany . Moskva , 1987. 260, [4] p. ; LC Card 87-118170
HF1413 .I54 1987

L'Impasse Nord-Sud . Paris , c1984. 103 p. : ISBN 2-11-001207-2 : LC Card 84-163951
HC59 .I44 1984

Iriarte, Gregorio. Esquemas para la interpretación de la realidad /. La Paz, Bolivia , 1985. 10 v. : LC Card 87-112879
HC182 .I727 1985

Joshi, Navin Chandra. Third World economy . New Delhi , 1983. x, 134 p. ; LC Card 83-904473 DDC 330.9172/4 19
HC59.7 .J645 1983 ***NYPL [JLD 86-3794]***

Kannapin, Klaus. Imperialistische Strategie gegen die neue Internationale Wirtschaftsordnung /. Berlin , 1984. 180 p. : LC Card 85-147404
HD84 .K28 1984

Karagodin, N. A. Mezhdunarodnye korporatsii i sotsial'no-ėkonomicheskie problemy razvivaiushchikhsia stran /. Moskva , 1981. 196, [3] p. ; LC Card 82-162679
HC59.7 .K28 1981

Krämer, Georg. Pädagogische Aspekte entwicklungspolitischer Öffentlichkeitsarbeit /. Frankfurt/Main , 1980. 233 p. : ISBN 3-88129-332-9 LC Card 81-466304
HC59.7 .K687 ***NYPL [JLD 87-528]***

Kupriianov, A. B. (Alekseĭ Borisovich) Razvivaiushchiesia strany i mezhdunarodnoe sotrudnichestvo . Moskva , 1980. 262 p. ; LC Card 81-131557
HC59.7 .K863 1980

Lafontaine, Oskar, 1943- Der andere Fortschritt . Hamburg , c1985. 222 p. ; ISBN 3-455-08248-3 LC Card 85-146223
HC286.7 .L33 1985

Latouche, Serge, 1940- Faut-il refuser le développement? . Paris , c1986. 216 p. ; ISBN 2-13-039202-4 : LC Card 86-160202
HD83 .L324 1986

Laursen, Karsten. Udviklingslandenes økonomi /. Århus [1986] ii, 203 p. : LC Card 86-215996
HC59.7 .L3243 1986

Low income countries . New Delhi , 1987. x, 106 p. ; ISBN 81-7027-101-0 : LC Card 87-900104 DDC 330.9172/4 19
HF1413 .L68 1987

McCord, William Maxwell, 1930- Paths to progress . New York , c1986. 352 p. ; ISBN 0-393-02307-9 : LC Card 85-29809 DDC 330.9172/4 19
HC59.7 .M358 1986 ***NYPL [JLD 86-3487]***

Machinery and economic development /. Houndmills, Basingstoke, Hampshire , 1986. xvii, 274 p. : ISBN 0-333-36391-4
NYPL [JLD 86-4380]

McLin, Jon B. Social and economic effects of petroleum development in non-OPEC developing countries . Geneva , 1986. xiii, 104 p., [4] folded leaves of plates : ISBN 92-2-105505-1 (pbk.) : LC Card 87-123328 DDC 338.2/782/091724 19
HD9578.D44 M396 1986

Menon, M. S. N., 1924- No to exploitation . New Delhi , 1983. 163, xxxii p. ; LC Card 83-902131 DDC 337/.09172/4 19
HC59.7 .M445 1983 ***NYPL [JLE 86-4184]***

Mittelman, James H. Out from underdevelopment . New York , 1988. p. cm. ISBN 0-312-01188-1 : LC Card 87-22927 DDC 338.9/009172/4 19
HC59.7 .M5337 1988

Mounbaga, Emmanuel Seidou, 1957- Finanzpolitik und Wirtschaftsentwicklung in der Dritten Welt . München , c1986. 265 p. ; ISBN 3-8039-0341-6 LC Card 86-233152
HJ1620 .M68 1986

Neundörfer, Konrad. Wir und die Dritte Welt . Köln , c1985. x, 214 p. ; ISBN 3-452-20304-2 LC Card 85-164555
HC59.7 .N375 1985

Nossiter, Bernard D. The global struggle for more . New York , c1987. xvi, 254 p. ; ISBN 0-06-435851-8 : LC Card 86-45762 DDC 337/.09172/4 19
HC59.7 .N676 1987

Pernoud, Régine, 1909- Le Moyen Age pour quoi faire? /. [Paris] , c1986. 315 p. : ISBN 2-234-01940-0 : LC Card 86-189820
HC41 .P46 1986

The Political economy of development and underdevelopment /. New York , c1988. xi, 611 p. ; ISBN 0-394-37499-1 (pbk.) LC Card 87-9668 DDC 330.9172/4 19
HD82 .P546 1988

Population growth and economic development . Washington, D.C. , 1986. ix, 108 p. ; ISBN 0-309-03641-0 (pbk.) LC Card 86-862 DDC 304.6/09172/4 19
HB884 .P6655 1986 ***NYPL [JLE 86-3533]***

Power and poverty . Boulder , 1988. v, 186 p. ; ISBN 0-8133-7351-4 (pbk. : alk. paper) : LC Card 86-32578 DDC 338.9/009172/4 19
HC59.72.E44 P68 1988

Problema tempov ėkonomicheskogo rosta v sovremennom mire /. Moskva , 1986. 383 p. : LC Card 87-124359
HC244 .P747 1986

Problemy khoziaĭstvennogo razvitiia osvobodivshikhsia stran . Moskva , 1987. 2 v. (306 p.) ; LC Card 87-157281
HC59.7 .P7354 1987

Prosterman, Roy L. Land reform and democratic development /. Baltimore , c1987. xii, 313 p. ; ISBN 0-8018-3482-1 (alk. paper) LC Card 87-4188 DDC 333.3/1/1724 19
HD1333.5 .P76 1987

Radke, Detlef. Auflagenpolitik und Politik-Dialog in der entwicklungspolitischen Zusammenarbeit /. Berlin , 1985. xiii, 91 p. : ISBN 3-88985-036-7 LC Card 85-134788
HC60 .R183 1985

Razvivaiushchiesia strany . Moskva , 1982. 307 p. ; LC Card 85-115259
HC59.7 .R33858 1982

Riedel, James. Myths and reality of external constraints on development /. Aldershot, Hampshire, U.K. , Brookfield, Vt., USA , 1987. xvi, 111 p. : ISBN 0-566-05336-5 (pbk.) : LC Card 86-31801 DDC 330.9172/4 19
HC59.7 .R494 1987

Seitz, John L., 1931- The politics of

development . New York, NY, USA , 1988. xiii, 194 p. : ISBN 0-631-15801-4 (pbk.) LC Card 87-20825 DDC 338.9 19
HD82 .S399 1988

The Socialist Third World . Oxford, UK , New York, NY , 1987. vii, 333 p. : ISBN 0-631-13442-5 : LC Card 87-5165 DDC 338.9/009172/4 19
HC59.7 .S5857 1987

Stone, Carl. Understanding Third World politics and economics /. Brown's Town P. O., St. Ann, Jamaica , c1980. 105 p. ;
NYPL [JLD 87-364]

A Strategy for restoration of growth in middle-income countries that face debt-servicing difficulties. Washington, D.C., U. S.A. , 1986. 43 p. : ISBN 0-8213-0811-4 (pbk.) LC Card 86-214478 DDC 338.9/009172/4 19
HJ8899 .S77 1986

Tabutin, Dominique. Les transitions de mortalité dans le Tiersmonde . Louvain-la-Neuve, Belgique [1985] 33 p. : LC Card 86-178578
HB1528 .T33 1985

The Third World and the world economic system /. New Delhi , Atlantic Highlands, N.J. , 1986. viii, 309 p. ; ISBN 81-7027-092-8 : LC Card 86-900419 DDC 330.9172/4 19
HC59.7 .T744 1986 ***NYPL [JLD 86-3145]***

Third world development /. London , New York , 1985. 3 v. : ISBN 0-946027-65-X (v. 1)
NYPL [JLF 86-626]

Toward a political economy of development . Berkeley , c1988. p. cm. ISBN 0-520-06051-2 (alk. paper) LC Card 87-10870 DDC 338.9/009172/4 19
HC59.7 .T7376 1988

Trade unions and the economic crisis of the 1980s /. Aldershot, Hants, England , Brookfield, Vt., U. S.A. , c1987. x, 210 p. ; ISBN 0-566-05245-8 : LC Card 86-25641 DDC 331.88/094 19
HD6657 .T68 1987

Überlebenslesebuch . Reinbek bei Hamburg [1984], c1983. 316 p. : ISBN 3-499-17672-6 : LC Card 85-168871
HC79.D4 U24 1984

Uphoff, Norman Thomas. Local institutional development . West Hartford, CT , c1986. xv, 421 p. ; ISBN 0-931816-45-9 LC Card 86-15288 DDC 302.3/5 19
HC59.7 .U64 1986 ***NYPL [JLE 87-1200]***

World prices and development /. Aldershot, Hants, England , Brookfield, Vt., U. S.A. , c1985. xi, 377 p. : ISBN 0-566-00890-4 LC Card 86-134604 DDC 338.5/2/0971724 19
HC59.7 .W684 1985 ***NYPL [JLD 86-4068]***

DEVELOPING COUNTRIES - ECONOMIC CONDITIONS - ADDRESSES, ESSAYS, LECTURES.

Bhagwati, Jagdish N., 1934- Essays in development economics /. Oxford [Oxfordshire] , 1985. 2 v. ; ISBN 0-631-14178-2 (v. 1) ***NYPL [JLL 86-16]***

Stagflation, savings, and the state . New York , 1986. xii, 402 p. : ISBN 0-19-520496-4 LC Card 85-31981 DDC 330.9172/4 19
HG229 .S74 1986 ***NYPL [JLE 86-2621]***

Theory and reality in development . Basingstoke, Hampshire , 1986. xii, 291 p. : ISBN 0-333-39824-6 ***NYPL [JLD 86-1827]***

DEVELOPING COUNTRIES - ECONOMIC CONDITIONS - CASE STUDIES.

Indebtedness and growth in developing countries /. Hamburg , 1986. 344 p. ; ISBN 3-87895-300-3 (pbk.) LC Card 86-213057 DDC 336.3/435/091724 19
HJ8899 .I53 1986

DEVELOPING COUNTRIES - ECONOMIC CONDITIONS - CONGRESSES.

Castro, Fidel, 1927- [Crisis económica y social del mundo. English.] The world economic and social crisis . New Delhi , 1983. 224 p. : LC Card 83-908475 DDC 337/.097172/4 19
HC59.7 .C31472 1983 ***NYPL [JLD 87-486]***

Les Libéraux et le dialogue Nord-Sud . Bonn , c1982. 220 p. ; ISBN 3-920590-36-8 LC Card 84-204748
HC59.7 .L4177 1982

Le Tiers-mondisme en question /. Paris , c1986. 225 p. ; ISBN 2-85565-299-5 : LC Card 86-185503
HC60 .T518 1986

Unterdrückung, Hunger, Krieg . Göttingen [1985?] 73 p. : LC Card 86-152237
HC59.7 .U55 1985

DEVELOPING COUNTRIES - ECONOMIC CONDITIONS - DICTIONARIES.

Razvivashti se strani . Sofiia , 1986. 423 p. ; LC Card 86-231951
HC59.7 .R3395 1986

DEVELOPING COUNTRIES - ECONOMIC CONDITIONS - MATHEMATICAL MODELS.

Ziesemer, Thomas. Economic theory of underdevelopment /. Regensburg , c1987. vi, 171 p. : ISBN 3-924956-15-4 (pbk.) LC Card 87-169372 DDC 338.9/001 19
HD75.5 .Z54 1987

DEVELOPING COUNTRIES - ECONOMIC CONDITIONS - REGIONAL DISPARITIES.

Ethnic preference and public policy in developing states /. Boulder, Colo. , 1986. ix, 203 p. ; ISBN 0-931477-89-1 : LC Card 86-13505 DDC 323.1/09172/4 19
JF1063.D44 E87 1986 ***NYPL [JLE 86-4694]***

DEVELOPING COUNTRIES - ECONOMIC CONDITIONS - STATISTICS.

UNCTAD statistical pocketbook /. New York , 1984. xv, 96 p. : LC Card 86-200987 DDC 330.9172/4 19
HF4055 .U53 1984

DEVELOPING COUNTRIES - ECONOMIC INTEGRATION.

Current problems of economic integration . New York , 1986. viii, 115 p. ; ISBN 92-1-112216-3 (pbk.) LC Card 87-106405 DDC 337.1/1724 19
HC59.7 .C845 1986

Kraft, Alfred. Aspekte der Regionalen wirtschaftlichen Integration zwischen Entwicklungsländern . Wiesbaden , 1982. x, 298 p. : ISBN 3-515-03801-9 LC Card 85-136228
HC441 .K69 1982

Langhammer, Rolf J. Wirtschaftliche Zusammenarbeit zwischen den Entwicklungsländern . Tübingen , c1984. xi, 135 p. : ISBN 3-16-344889-5 : LC Card 85-143693
HF1413 .L363 1984

DEVELOPING COUNTRIES - ECONOMIC POLICY.

Arndt, H. W. (Heinz Wolfgang), 1915- Economic development . Chicago , 1987. viii, 217 p. ; ISBN 0-226-02720-1 : LC Card 86-25108 DDC 338.9 19
HD82 .A66 1987

Autoafirmación colectiva . México , 1983. 327 p. ; ISBN 968-16-1335-X LC Card 86-159023
HC59.7 .A92 1983

Bacha, Edmar Lisboa. El milagro y la crisis . México , 1986. 468 p. : ISBN 968-16-2152-2 LC Card 87-400019 DDC 338.981 19
HC187 .B128 1986

Bartelmus, Peter. Environment and development /. Boston , 1986. xxii, 96 p. ; ISBN 0-04-333026-6 (alk. paper) LC Card 85-22838 DDC 333.7/09172/4 19
HC59.72.E5 B37 1986 ***NYPL [JLD 86-2378]***

Bentabet, Mohamed. Auto économie . Casablanca [1985] 106 p. ; LC Card 86-198953
HC59.72.T4 B46 1985

Betancur, Belisario, 1923- Un semáforo en rojo . [Bogotá] [1984] 12, 12, 12 p. ; LC Card 87-125515 DDC 338.98 19
HC125 .B42 1984

Capitalismes fin de siècle /. Paris , c1986. 268 p. : ISBN 2-13-039425-6 : LC Card 86-231136
HC106.8 .C364 1986

Clés pour une stratégie nouvelle du développement /. Paris , c1984. 226 p. : ISBN 2-7082-2365-7 : LC Card 85-116966 DDC 338.9/009172/4 19
HC59.7 .C584 1984

Dahmani, Mohamed. L'occidentalisation des pays du Tiers Monde . Paris , Alger , c1983. 217 p. ; ISBN 2-7178-0623-7 : LC Card 83-162697 DDC 909/.09724082 19
HC59.7 .D273 1983 ***NYPL [JLE 86-566]***

Dauderstädt, Michael. Entwicklungspolitik, Politik ohne Entwicklung . Bonn [1984] 38 p. ; LC Card 85-136902
HC59.7 .D327 1984

Development strategies reconsidered /. New Brunswick, N.J., U. S.A. , c1986. viii, 190 p. ; ISBN 0-87855-991-4 (pbk.) : LC Card 85-24582 DDC 338.9/009172/4 19
HC59.7 .D482 1986 ***NYPL [JLE 86-2976]***

Economic development and international trade /. New York , 1988. xi, 211 p. ; ISBN 0-312-01588-7 : LC Card 87-25629 DDC 382 19
HF1379 .E27 1988

Economics of development /. New York , 1987. xv, 623 p. : ISBN 0-393-95548-6 LC Card 87-5701 DDC 338.9 19
HC59.7 .E314 1987

Fransman, Martin. Technology and economic development /. Brighton, Sussex , 1986. xi, 161 p. : ISBN 0-7450-0104-1 ***NYPL [JLD 87-320]***

Ghosh, B. N. Political economy of neocolonialism in Third World countries /. New Delhi , c1985. vii, 174 p. ; LC Card 85-903172 DDC 338.9/009172/4 19
HC59.7 .G485 1985 ***NYPL [JLD 87-1141]***

Glinz, Ferdinand N. Entwicklungsförderung am Wendepunkt . Zürich , c1986. 320 p. ; ISBN 3-280-01676-2 LC Card 86-227950
HC59.7 .G55 1986

Gylfason, Thorvaldur. Credit policy and economic activity in developing countries with IMF stabilization programs /. Princeton, N.J. , c1987. 44 p. ; ISBN 0-88165-232-6 (pbk.) : LC Card 87-3389 DDC 332.7/09172/4 19
HG3711.D48 G94 1987

Haq, Mahbub ul, 1934- The poverty curtain . Lahore , 1983. li, 247 p. ; LC Card 83-931275 DDC 338.9/009172/4 19
HC59.7 .H35 1983 ***NYPL [JLD 87-439]***

Harris, Nigel. The end of the Third World . New York , 1987, c1986. 231 p. : ISBN 0-941533-14-X : LC Card 87-12295 DDC 330.9172/4 19
HC59.7 .H3536 1987

IAshkin, V. A. (Vladimir Andreevich) Planirovanie ėkonomicheskogo rosta v razvivaiushchikhsia stranakh . Moskva , 1986. 120 p. ; LC Card 86-220878
HC59.7 .I13 1986

Joshi, Navin Chandra. Third World economy . New Delhi , 1983. x, 134 p. ; LC Card 83-904473 DDC 330.9172/4 19
HC59.7 .J645 1983 ***NYPL [JLD 86-3794]***

Kalmanovitz, Salomón. El desarrollo tardío del capitalismo . [Bogotá] , 1983. 285 p. ; LC Card 84-155755 DDC 338.9/009172/4 19
HC59.7 .K246 1983 ***NYPL [JLD 85-2613]***

Kapur, Basant. Studies in inflationary dynamics . Kent Ridge, Singapore , c1986. xviii, 146 p., [1] folded leaf of plates : ISBN 997-16-9099-3 (pbk.) LC Card 87-116919 DDC 332.4/1 19
HC59.7 .K276 1986

Kruijer, G. J. (Gerardus Johannes), 1919- Development through liberation . Atlantic Highlands, NJ , 1987. x, 257 p. ; ISBN 0-391-03538-X LC Card 87-3710 DDC 338.9/009172/4 19
HC59.72.P6 K78 1987

Kuře, Miroslav. Alternativní strategie rozvoje rozvojových zemí /. Praha , 1986. 94 p. ; LC Card 86-227984
HC59.7 .K866 1986

L'Hériteau, Marie France. Le Fonds monétaire international et les pays du Tiers-monde /. Paris , c1986. 277 p. : ISBN 2-13-039203-2 : LC Card 86-165389
HG3881.5.I58 L52 1986

MacBean, Alasdair I. Commodity policies . London , New York , c1987. 438 p. : ISBN 0-7099-1708-2 LC Card 87-9069 DDC 382/.3/091724 19
HF1428 .M29 1987

McCord, William Maxwell, 1930- Paths to progress . New York , c1986. 352 p. ; ISBN 0-393-02307-9 : LC Card 85-29809 DDC

330.9172/4 19
HC59.7 .M358 1986 ***NYPL [JLD 86-3487]***

Macesich, George, 1927- Economic nationalism and stability /. New York , 1985. x, 163 p. ; ISBN 0-03-005748-5 : LC Card 85-12342 DDC 338.9/009172/4 19
HC59.7 .M2112 1985 ***NYPL [JLE 86-908]***

Marxian theory and the third world /. New Delhi , Beverly Hills , 1985. 325 p. ; ISBN 0-8039-9489-3 LC Card 85-1863 DDC 335.43/09172/4 19
HX517.8 .M37 1985 ***NYPL [JLE 86-3088]***

Menon, M. S. N., 1924- No to exploitation . New Delhi , 1983. 163, xxxii p. ; LC Card 83-902131 DDC 337/.09172/4 19
HC59.7 .M445 1983 ***NYPL [JLE 86-4184]***

Mittelman, James H. Out from underdevelopment . New York , 1988. p. cm. ISBN 0-312-01188-1 : LC Card 87-22927 DDC 338.9/009172/4 19
HC59.7 .M5337 1988

Mounbaga, Emmanuel Seidou, 1957- Finanzpolitik und Wirtschaftsentwicklung in der Dritten Welt . München , c1986. 265 p. ; ISBN 3-8039-0341-6 LC Card 86-233152
HJ1620 .M68 1986

Neundörfer, Konrad. Wir und die Dritte Welt . Köln , c1985. x, 214 p. ; ISBN 3-452-20304-2 LC Card 85-164555
HC59.7 .N375 1985

Nossiter, Bernard D. The global struggle for more . New York , c1987. xvi, 254 p. ; ISBN 0-06-435851-8 : LC Card 86-45762 DDC 337/.09172/4 19
HC59.7 .N676 1987

Population and socioeconomic development /. Moscow , 1986. 186 p. ; LC Card 86-226273 DDC 304.6/09172/4 19
HB849.41 .P644 1986

Population growth and economic development . Madison, Wis. , 1987. xiii, 702 p. ; ISBN 0-299-11130-X : LC Card 86-40447 DDC 338.9/009172/4 19
HB884 .P66547 1987

La Presencia del tercer mundo /. San José, Costa Rica , 1982. 239 p., [1] leaf of plates : LC Card 83-161829
HC59.7 .P718 1982

Restoring growth in the debt-laden Third World . New York , 1987. x, 82 p. : ISBN 0-930503-02-3 : LC Card 87-23778 DDC 336.3/435/091724 19
HJ8899 .R47 1987

Riedel, James. Myths and reality of external constraints on development /. Aldershot, Hampshire, U.K. , Brookfield, Vt., USA , 1987. xvi, 111 p. : ISBN 0-566-05336-5 (pbk.) : LC Card 86-31801 DDC 330.9172/4 19
HC59.7 .R494 1987

Seitz, John L., 1931- The politics of development . New York, NY, USA , 1988. xiii, 194 p. : ISBN 0-631-15801-4 (pbk.) LC Card 87-20825 DDC 338.9 19
HD82 .S399 1988

Siddayao, Corazon M. Energy demand and economic growth . Boulder , 1986. xiv, 127 p. : ISBN 0-8133-7154-6 : LC Card 86-906 DDC 333.79/13/091724 19
HD9502.D442 S54 1986 ***NYPL [JLE 86-3295]***

Silverman, Jerry M. Action-planning workshops for development management . Washington, D.C., U. S.A. , 1986. ix, 74 p. : ISBN 0-8213-0864-5 (pbk.) LC Card 86-28215 DDC 338.9/0068 19
HC59.7 .S4656 1986

The Socialist Third World . Oxford, UK , New York, NY , 1987. vii, 333 p. : ISBN 0-631-13442-5 : LC Card 87-5165 DDC 338.9/009172/4 19
HC59.7 .S5857 1987

Surveys in development economics /. Oxford, UK , New York, NY, USA , 1987. 390 p. : ISBN 0-631-14713-6 : LC Card 87-5164 DDC 338.9/009172/4 19
HC59.7 .S882 1987

Toward a political economy of development . Berkeley , c1988. p. cm. ISBN 0-520-06051-2 (alk. paper) LC Card 87-10870 DDC 338.9/009172/4 19
HC59.7 .T7376 1988

Toye, J. F. J. Dilemmas of development . Oxford, [Oxfordshire], UK , New York, NY, USA , 1987. ix, 177 p. ; ISBN 0-631-14569-9 (U. S.) : LC Card 86-30955 DDC 338.9/009172/4 19
HD82 .T65 1987

Vohra, Dewan C. Economic relevance of non-alignment /. New Delhi , 1983. xv, 387 p. ; LC Card 83-901770 DDC 338.9/009172/4 19
HC59.7 .V63 1983 ***NYPL [JLD 86-3799]***

Watzal, Ludwig, 1950- Entwicklungspolitik zwischen Immanenz und Transzendenz . Frankfurt am Main , New York , c1986. 121 p. ; ISBN 3-8204-8785-9 LC Card 86-198339
HD75 .W36 1986

DEVELOPING COUNTRIES - ECONOMIC POLICY - ADDRESSES, ESSAYS, LECTURES.

Adjustment crisis in the Third World /. New Brunswick, USA , c1984. x, 186 p. ; ISBN 0-88738-040-9 LC Card 84-8690 DDC 337/.09172/4 19
HC59.7 .A733 1984 ***NYPL [JLE 86-2491]***

Misra, Rameshwar Prasad, 1930- Development issues of our time /. New Delhi , 1985. xi, 368 p. : LC Card 85-903754 DDC 338.9/009172/4 19
HC59.7 .M5334 1985 ***NYPL [JLE 86-1375]***

New international economic order /. Moscow , 1984. 196 p. ; LC Card 85-151148 DDC 337/.09/047 19
HF1411 .N398 1984 ***NYPL [JLD 86-2664]***

DEVELOPING COUNTRIES - ECONOMIC POLICY - CONGRESSES.

The Design of alternative development strategies /. Rohtak, India , 1986. xiv, 330 p. : LC Card 86-901301 DDC 338.9 19
HD82 .D383 1986 ***NYPL [JLE 86-4232]***

Dritte-Welt-Kongress (1985 : Hof (Hof, Germany)) Entwicklungspolitik im Wandel . Stuttgart , 1986. 256 p. ; ISBN 3-87959-271-3 LC Card 86-193768
HD73 .D75 1985

Economic liberalization in developing countries /. Oxford [Oxfordshire] , New York , 1986. vi, 278 p. : ISBN 0-631-15023-4 : LC Card 86-6153 DDC 338.9/009172/4 19
HC59.7 .E3116 1986 ***NYPL [JLE 86-4644]***

Entwicklungstheorie, Entwicklungspraxis . Berlin , c1986. 316 p. ; ISBN 3-428-05973-5 LC Card 86-233851 DDC 338.9/009172/4 19
HC59.7 .E6473 1986

Grundbedürfnisse als Gegenstand der Entwicklungspolitik . Wiesbaden , 1982. viii, 220 p. : ISBN 3-515-03838-8 (Deut. Bibl.) LC Card 85-134671
HC59.72.B38 G78 1982

Le Tiers-mondisme en question /. Paris , c1986. 225 p. ; ISBN 2-85565-299-5 : LC Card 86-185503
HC60 .T518 1986

DEVELOPING COUNTRIES - ECONOMIC POLICY - MATHEMATICAL MODELS.

Martens, André. La planification économique du développement . Montréal [1982] 2 v. : LC Card 83-178486
HC59.7 .M323 1982

DEVELOPING COUNTRIES - EMIGRATION AND IMMIGRATION.

Cohen, Robin. The new helots . Aldershot, Hants, England , Brookfield, Vt., USA , c1987. xiii, 290 p. : ISBN 0-566-00932-3 : LC Card 87-19807 DDC 331.6/2 19
HD6304 .C64 1987

DEVELOPING COUNTRIES - ETHNIC RELATIONS.

Ethnic preference and public policy in developing states /. Boulder, Colo. , 1986. ix, 203 p. ; ISBN 0-931477-89-1 : LC Card 86-13505 DDC 323.1/09172/4 19
JF1063.D44 E87 1986 ***NYPL [JLE 86-4694]***

DEVELOPING COUNTRIES - FOREIGN ECONOMIC RELATIONS.

Autoafirmación colectiva . México , 1983. 327 p. ; ISBN 968-16-1335-X LC Card 86-159023
HC59.7 .A92 1983

Berberoglu, Berch. The internationalization of capital . New York , 1987. xxi, 223 p. : ISBN 0-275-92169-7 (alk. paper) : LC Card 86-25259 DDC 337 19
HF1411 .B367 1987

Bra Kanon, Denis, 1936- Développement ou appauvrissement /. Paris , c1985. 188 p. : ISBN 2-7178-0962-7 : LC Card 86-177676
HF1413 .B72 1985

ECDC handbook . [New Delhi] , 1983. vi, 679 p. ; LC Card 83-903543 DDC 337.1/1724 19
HC59.7 .E23 1983 ***NYPL [JLF 86-1755]***

Fuchs, Nikolaus, 1955- Ursachen- und Krisenanalyse der Verschuldung von Entwicklungsländern . Berlin , c1986. 258 p. : ISBN 3-925410-05-8 LC Card 87-124994 DDC 336.3/435/091724 19
HJ8899 .F83 1986

García Bocanegra, Angela Victoria. Posición de los países en desarrollo frente a la crisis económica mundial /. Bogotá, D.E. , 1984. 146 p. ; LC Card 85-205412
HF1413 .G312 1984

Ghosh, B. N. Political economy of neocolonialism in Third World countries /. New Delhi , c1985. vii, 174 p. ; LC Card 85-903172 DDC 338.9/009172/4 19
HC59.7 .G485 1985 ***NYPL [JLD 87-1141]***

Illarionov, Sergeĭ Ivanovich. Osvobodivshiesi͡a strany . Moskva , 1987. 260, [4] p. ; LC Card 87-118170
HF1413 .I54 1987

Low income countries . New Delhi , 1987. x, 106 p. ; ISBN 81-7027-101-0 : LC Card 87-900104 DDC 330.9172/4 19
HF1413 .L68 1987

Machado, Vera Barrouin Crivano. O diálogo norte-sul /. Brasília, DF , 1983. 58 p. ; LC Card 86-171831
HF1412 .M33 1983

Moser, Beat. Konflikt und Kooperation der Dritten Welt mit Industrieländern /. Diessenhofen , c1985. xi, 352 p. : ISBN 3-7253-0236-7 : LC Card 85-139491
HF1413 .M66 1985

Nossiter, Bernard D. The global struggle for more . New York , c1987. xvi, 254 p. ; ISBN 0-06-435851-8 : LC Card 86-45762 DDC 337/.09172/4 19
HC59.7 .N676 1987

Nunnenkamp, Peter. The international debt crisis of the Third World . New York , 1986. xvi, 205 p. ; ISBN 0-312-42003-X : LC Card 85-2008 DDC 336.3/435/091724 19
HJ8899 .N86 1985 ***NYPL [JLD 86-2529]***

Pankova, E. A. (Evgenii͡a Afanas´evna) Vneshneėkonomicheskie svi͡azi razvivai͡ushchikhsi͡a stran . Moskva , 1985. 158 p. ; LC Card 86-130427
HF1413 .P36 1985

Razvivai͡ushchiesi͡a strany . Moskva , 1982. 307 p. ; LC Card 85-115259
HC59.7 .R33858 1982

South-South economic cooperation . New Delhi , 1987. xii, 262 p. ; ISBN 81-7027-102-9 : LC Card 86-903797 DDC 337/.09172/4 19
HF1413 .S617 1987

Strukturelemente der Weltgesellschaft . Frankfurt am Main , 1981. v, 356 p. : ISBN 3-7875-1727-8 LC Card 83-190809
HF1411 .S845 1981

Vierbuchen, Ruth, 1954- Die Entwicklungsländer im Welthandel . Spardorf , c1983. iii, 230 p. : ISBN 3-922919-11-1 LC Card 83-150529
HF1411 .V473 1983

Zevin, Leon Zalmanovich. Strany razlichnogo urovni͡a razviti͡a v mirovom khozi͡aĭstve . Moskva , 1985. 193, [4] p. ; LC Card 86-157482
HF1411 .Z43 1985

DEVELOPING COUNTRIES - FOREIGN ECONOMIC RELATIONS - ADDRESSES, ESSAYS, LECTURES.

Adjustment crisis in the Third World /. New Brunswick, USA , c1984. x, 186 p. ; ISBN 0-88738-040-9 LC Card 84-8690 DDC 337/.09172/4 19
HC59.7 .A733 1984 ***NYPL [JLE 86-2491]***

Problemas económicos del Tercer Mundo /. Buenos Aires, República Argentina , c1983. 210

p. : ISBN 950-577-070-7 LC Card 84-120737 DDC 337/.09172/4 19
HF1413 .P75 1983 ***NYPL [JLC 86-394]***

The Third world, premises of U. S. policy /. San Francisco , c1978. xv, 332 p. : ISBN 0-917616-30-8 : LC Card 78-67593 DDC 309.1/172/4
HC59.7 .T456 ***NYPL [JLD 81-653]***

DEVELOPING COUNTRIES - FOREIGN ECONOMIC RELATIONS - BULGARIA.
Kreditni otnoshenii͡a na Narodna republika Bŭlgarii͡a s razvivashtite se strani /. Sofii͡a , 1986. 78, [1] p. ; LC Card 86-152274
HF1578.15.D44 K74 1986

DEVELOPING COUNTRIES - FOREIGN ECONOMIC RELATIONS - CASE STUDIES.
Newly industrializing countries and the political economy of south-south relations /. New York , 1988. p. cm. ISBN 0-312-01180-6 : LC Card 87-23476 DDC 337/.09172/4 19
HF1413 .N497 1988

DEVELOPING COUNTRIES - FOREIGN ECONOMIC RELATIONS - COMMUNIST COUNTRIES.
Kupri͡anov, A. B. (Alekseĭ Borisovich) Razvivai͡ushchiesi͡a strany i mezhdunarodnoe sotrudnichestvo . Moskva , 1980. 262 p. ; LC Card 81-131557
HC59.7 .K863 1980

DEVELOPING COUNTRIES - FOREIGN ECONOMIC RELATIONS - CONGRESSES.
Entwicklungspolitik im Spannungsfeld von Solidarität und Eigeninteresse . Stuttgart , New York , 1986. 155 p. ; ISBN 3-437-50306-5 LC Card 87-408212 DDC 338.91/43/01724 19
HC60 .E527 1986

Internationale Wirtschaft und revolutionärer Weltprozess /. [Berlin] , 1983. 390 p. ; LC Card 84-167604
HF1410.5 .I592 1983

DEVELOPING COUNTRIES - FOREIGN ECONOMIC RELATIONS - EUROPE, EASTERN.
Machowski, Heinrich. RGW-Staaten und Dritte Welt . Bonn , 1981. iii, 84 p. ; ISBN 3-7713-0167-X LC Card 85-224767
HF1532.15.D44 M33 1981

DEVELOPING COUNTRIES - FOREIGN ECONOMIC RELATIONS - EUROPEAN ECONOMIC COMMUNITY COUNTRIES.
Die Bundesrepublik Deutschland und die Entwicklungspolitik der Europäischen Gemeinschaft, 1957-1983 /. Münster [1986] 111 p. ; ISBN 3-88660-214-1 LC Card 86-213020
HC241.25.G3 B87 1986

Howell, Thomas R., 1949- The EEC and the third Multifiber Arrangement . Washington, DC , 1986. [14], 126, [12] p. : LC Card 86-224652 DDC 382/.45677/0094 19
HD9865.E852 H68 1986

Wiemann, Jürgen. Selektiver Protektionismus und aktive Strukturanpassung . Berlin , 1983. vii, 348 p. : ISBN 3-88985-028-6 : LC Card 83-223964
HD9865.E852 W54 1983

DEVELOPING COUNTRIES - FOREIGN ECONOMIC RELATIONS - EUROPEAN ECONOMIC COMMUNITY COUNTRIES - CONGRESSES.
The Common agricultural policy and the Third World . London , 1986. 97 p. : ISBN 0-946848-79-3 (pbk.) : LC Card 87-150069 DDC 338.1/81/094 19
HD9015.E82 C665 1986

DEVELOPING COUNTRIES - FOREIGN ECONOMIC RELATIONS - GERMANY (WEST)
Havemann, Hans A., 1912- Industrialisierungspolitik für Entwicklungsländer . Aachen , 1982. 68 p. ; ISBN 3-922525-06-7 LC Card 83-203761
HC59.7 .H386 1982

Held, Karl, 1944- Krieg und Frieden . Frankfurt am Main , c1983. 324 p. ; ISBN 3-518-11149-3 : LC Card 83-228517
HC79.D4 H45 1983

DEVELOPING COUNTRIES - FOREIGN ECONOMIC RELATIONS - GERMANY (WEST) - CONGRESSES.
Unterdrückung, Hunger, Krieg . Göttingen [1985?] 73 p. : LC Card 86-152237
HC59.7 .U55 1985

DEVELOPING COUNTRIES - FOREIGN ECONOMIC RELATIONS - GERMANY (WEST) - LOWER SAXONY.
Menck, Karl Wolfgang. Mittelstand und Entwicklungsländer . Hamburg , 1986. 192 p. ; ISBN 3-87895-318-6 LC Card 87-407405 DDC 337.43/59/01724 19
HF1546.19.L68 M46 1986

DEVELOPING COUNTRIES - FOREIGN ECONOMIC RELATIONS - ITALY.
D'Angelo, Massimo. Criteri per una cooperazione industriale con i paesi in via di sviluppo /. Milano , c1981. 294 p. ; ISBN 88-20-42145-3 : LC Card 82-113466
HF1549 .D36 1981 ***NYPL [JLD 86-3318]***

DEVELOPING COUNTRIES - FOREIGN ECONOMIC RELATIONS - SOVIET UNION.
SSSR--razvivai͡ushchiesi͡a strany . Moskva , 1985. 237 p. ; LC Card 86-158191
HF1558.5.D44 S77 1985

DEVELOPING COUNTRIES - FOREIGN ECONOMIC RELATIONS - SWITZERLAND.
Mugglin, Markus. Exportrisikogarantie, internationale Verschuldung und schweizerische Entwicklungspolitik /. Adliswil , 1985. 56 p. : ISBN 3-7229-4036-X LC Card 85-148130
HF1574.5.D44 M84 1985

DEVELOPING COUNTRIES - FOREIGN ECONOMIC RELATIONS - UNITED STATES.
America's new competitors . Cambridge, Mass. , c1988. xiv, 290 p. ; ISBN 0-88730-135-5 LC Card 87-19295 DDC 337.730172/4 19
HF1456.5.D44 A44 1988

Godfried, Nathan. Bridging the gap between rich and poor . New York , 1987. xii, 225 p. ; ISBN 0-313-25648-9 (lib. bdg. : alk. paper) LC Card 87-8471 DDC 338.91/73/056 19
HC415.15 .G63 1987

May, Bernhard. Reagan und die Entwicklungsländer . München , 1987. xiv, 271 p. ; ISBN 3-486-53981-7 LC Card 87-139481 DDC 337.730172/4 19
HF1456.5.D44 M39 1987

Portilla, Belfor. Alimentos . México , 1983. 149, [53] p. : ISBN 968-429-384-4 LC Card 84-172348 DDC 338.1/9/1724 19
HD9018.D44 P67 1983
NYPL [JLD 86-1520]

DEVELOPING COUNTRIES - FOREIGN ECONOMIC RELATIONS - UNITED STATES - ADDRESSES, ESSAYS, LECTURES.
The Third world, premises of U. S. policy /. San Francisco , c1978. xv, 332 p. : ISBN 0-917616-30-8 : LC Card 78-67593 DDC 309.1/172/4
HC59.7 .T456 ***NYPL [JLD 81-653]***

DEVELOPING COUNTRIES - FOREIGN ECONOMIC RELATIONS - UNITED STATES - CONGRESSES.
U. S. agriculture and Third World economic development . Washington, D.C. , c1987. xv, 103 p. : ISBN 0-89068-086-8 (pbk.): LC Card 86-62757 DDC 338.9/009172/4 19
HD1755 .U173 1987

Developing countries in the international trading system /. Hoda, Anwarul, 1938- Ahmedabad , 1987. xii, 302 p. ; LC Card 87-902308 DDC 382/.091724 19
HF4055 .H64 1987

DEVELOPING COUNTRIES - INDUSTRIES.
Garnsey, Elizabeth. Industrial change and women's employment . Geneva , 1987. ix, 100, x p. : ISBN 92-9014-411-4 (pbk.) : LC Card 87-163195 DDC 331.4/09172/4 19
HD6223 .G37 1987

Harris, Nigel. The end of the Third World . London , 1986. 231 p. : ISBN 1-85043-031-4
NYPL [JLE 87-858]

Harris, Nigel. The end of the Third World . New York , 1987, c1986. 231 p. : ISBN 0-941533-14-X : LC Card 87-12295 DDC 330.9172/4 19
HC59.7 .H3536 1987

Havemann, Hans A., 1912- Industrialisierungspolitik für Entwicklungsländer . Aachen , 1982. 68 p. ; ISBN 3-922525-06-7 LC Card 83-203761
HC59.7 .H386 1982

Hermann, Christian, 1954- Auswirkungen industrieller Exportproduktion im Rahmen der internationalen Arbeitsteilung auf die Einkommensverteilung von Entwicklungsländern /. Frankfurt am Main , New York , c1984. viii, 393 p. ; ISBN 3-8204-7456-0 LC Card 85-191626
HF4055 .H47 1984

Industrialization in developing and peripheral regions /. London , Dover, N.H. , c1986. 363 p. ; ISBN 0-7099-3827-6 : LC Card 86-4159 DDC 338.09172/4 19
HD2329 .I54 1986 ***NYPL [JLD 86-2985]***

Machinery and economic development /. Houndmills, Basingstoke, Hampshire , 1986. xvii, 274 p. : ISBN 0-333-36391-4
NYPL [JLD 86-4380]

Perspectives on industrial readjustment, the EEC and the developing countries /. Tilburg, Netherlands , 1978. ii, 98 p. ;
NYPL [JLF 86-1708]

Surveys in development economics /. Oxford, UK , New York, NY, USA , 1987. 390 p. : ISBN 0-631-14713-6 : LC Card 87-5164 DDC 338.9/009172/4 19
HC59.7 .S882 1987

DEVELOPING COUNTRIES - INDUSTRIES - CONGRESSES.
Stratégies d'industrialisation et maîtrise du développement. Paris , c1984. 115, [3] p. : ISBN 2-86844-002-9 LC Card 84-248894
HC59.7 .S854 1984

DEVELOPING COUNTRIES - MANUFACTURES.
Little, Ian Malcolm David. Small manufacturing enterprises . New York , 1987. x, 362 p. : ISBN 0-19-520619-3 LC Card 87-12365 DDC 338.6/42/0954 19
HD9736.I52 L57 1987

DEVELOPING COUNTRIES - MILITARY POLICY - CONGRESSES.
World peace and the developing countries . Basingstoke, Hampshire , 1986. xix, 272 p. ; ISBN 0-333-43636-9 ***NYPL [JLD 87-1192]***

DEVELOPING COUNTRIES - NATIONAL SECURITY - ECONOMIC ASPECTS.
Defence, security, and development /. New York , 1987. xiii, 219 p. : ISBN 0-312-01243-8 : LC Card 87-12129 DDC 338.4/76234/091724 19
HC59.72.D4 D436 1987

DEVELOPING COUNTRIES - POLITICS AND GOVERNMENT.
Apter, David Ernest, 1924- Rethinking development . Newbury Park, Calif. , c1987. 326 p. : ISBN 0-8039-2971-4 LC Card 86-29642 DDC 338.9 19
HD82 .A657 1987

Dahmani, Mohamed. L'occidentalisation des pays du Tiers Monde . Paris , Alger , c1983. 217 p. ; ISBN 2-7178-0623-7 : LC Card 83-162697 DDC 909/.09724082 19
HC59.7 .D273 1983 ***NYPL [JLE 86-566]***

Décolonisations et nouvelles dépendances . [Lille] , c1986. 282 p. : ISBN 2-85939-287-4 : LC Card 87-104133
HC59.7 .D354 1986

Ethnic preference and public policy in developing states /. Boulder, Colo. , 1986. ix, 203 p. ; ISBN 0-931477-89-1 : LC Card 86-13505 DDC 323.1/09172/4 19
JF1063.D44 E87 1986 ***NYPL [JLE 86-4694]***

Guiton, R. J. (Raymond J.), 1915- Der Aufbruch . Rheinfelden , c1984. 2 v. : ISBN 3-87718-746-3 (Bd. 1) LC Card 85-181833 DDC 325/.344/09 19
JV1818 .G85 1984 ***NYPL [JFK 86-364]***

Kruijer, G. J. (Gerardus Johannes), 1919- Development through liberation . Atlantic Highlands, NJ , 1987. x, 257 p. ; ISBN 0-391-03538-X LC Card 87-3710 DDC

338.9/009172/4 19
HC59.72.P6 K78 1987

McCord, William Maxwell, 1930- Paths to progress . New York , c1986. 352 p. ; ISBN 0-393-02307-9 : LC Card 85-29809 DDC 330.9172/4 19
HC59.7 .M358 1986 ***NYPL [JLD 86-3487]***

Prosterman, Roy L. Land reform and democratic development /. Baltimore , c1987. xii, 313 p. ; ISBN 0-8018-3482-1 (alk. paper) LC Card 87-4188 DDC 333.3/1/1724 19
HD1333.5 .P76 1987

Román de Silgado, Manuel. Burocracia y cambio social /. [Lima] , 1975. 327 p. : LC Card 77-553812
JF1355 .R688 ***NYPL [JLC 77-327]***

Sidell, Scott R. The IMF and third-world political instability . New York , 1988. p. cm. ISBN 0-312-00755-8 : LC Card 87-9880 DDC 332.1/52 19
HG3881.5.I58 S53 1988

Stone, Carl. Understanding Third World politics and economics /. Brown's Town P. O., St. Ann, Jamaica , c1980. 105 p. ;
NYPL [JLD 87-364]

Toward a political economy of development . Berkeley , c1988. p. cm. ISBN 0-520-06051-2 (alk. paper) LC Card 87-10870 DDC 338.9/009172/4 19
HC59.7 .T7376 1988

Vohra, Dewan C. Economic relevance of non-alignment /. New Delhi , 1983. xv, 387 p. ; LC Card 83-901770 DDC 338.9/009172/4 19
HC59.7 .V63 1983 ***NYPL [JLD 86-3799]***

DEVELOPING COUNTRIES - POPULATION.

Findlay, Allan M. Population and development in the Third World /. London , New York , 1987. xii, 84 p. : ISBN 0-416-91950-2 (pbk.) : LC Card 86-31094 DDC 304.6/09172/4 19
HB884 .F56 1987

Ivanov, S. F. (Sergeĭ Feliksovich) Razvivaiushchiesia strany . Moskva , 1984. 63 p. : LC Card 85-125223
HB884 .I93 1984

McGraw, Eric. Population growth /. Vero Bleach, FL , 1987. 46 p. : ISBN 0-86592-276-4 LC Card 87-12729 DDC 304.6/2 19
HB871 .M325 1987

Population distribution and urbanization . Nairobi, Kenya , 1985. 95 p. ; LC Card 85-980971 DDC 304.6/1 19
HB2160 .P67 1985

Population growth and economic development . Washington, D.C. , 1986. ix, 108 p. ; ISBN 0-309-03641-0 (pbk.) LC Card 86-862 DDC 304.6/09172/4 19
HB884 .P6655 1986 ***NYPL [JLE 86-3533]***

Population growth and economic development . Madison, Wis. , 1987. xiii, 702 p. ; ISBN 0-299-11130-X : LC Card 86-40447 DDC 338.9/009172/4 19
HB884 .P66547 1987

DEVELOPING COUNTRIES - POPULATION DENSITY.

Population distribution and urbanization . Nairobi, Kenya , 1985. 95 p. ; LC Card 85-980971 DDC 304.6/1 19
HB2160 .P67 1985

DEVELOPING COUNTRIES - POPULATION - ECONOMIC ASPECTS.

The Economic demography of mass poverty. [Williamsburg, Va., U. S.A. , c1986] xiv, 142 p. : LC Card 85-73339 DDC 339.4/6/091724 19
HB884 .E36 1986

DEVELOPING COUNTRIES - POPULATION POLICY.

Acsádi, György. Policy relevance of findings of the world fertility survey for developing countries /. New York , 1986. vi, 160 p. ; LC Card 85-37681 DDC 304.6/32/091724 19
HB1108 .A28 1986

Cairncross, John. Population and agriculture in the developing countries /. Rome , 1980. ii, 52 p. ; ISBN 92-5-100885-X (pbk.) LC Card 81-198370 DDC 338.1/09172/4 19
HD1417 .C34 1980 ***NYPL [JLF 86-1573]***

Findlay, Allan M. Population and development in the Third World /. London , New York , 1987. xii, 84 p. : ISBN 0-416-91950-2 (pbk.) : LC Card 86-31094 DDC 304.6/09172/4 19
HB884 .F56 1987

Haq, Mahbub ul, 1934- The poverty curtain . Lahore , 1983. li, 247 p. ; LC Card 83-931275 DDC 338.9/009172/4 19
HC59.7 .H35 1983 ***NYPL [JLD 87-439]***

Population and socioeconomic development /. Moscow , 1986. 186 p. ; LC Card 86-226273 DDC 304.6/09172/4 19
HB849.41 .P644 1986

Population distribution and urbanization . Nairobi, Kenya , 1985. 95 p. ; LC Card 85-980971 DDC 304.6/1 19
HB2160 .P67 1985

Population policy briefs . New York , 1986. viii, 49 p. ; LC Card 87-117649 DDC 304.6/09172/4 19
HB884 .P66557 1986

Wereldbevolking groeiend ontwikkelingsprobleem. Den Haag [1975] 66 p. : LC Card 87-118557
HB883.5 .W47 1975

DEVELOPING COUNTRIES - POPULATION, RURAL - ADDRESSES, ESSAYS, LECTURES.

Rural development and human fertility /. New York, N.Y. , London , c1984. ix, 318 p. : ISBN 0-02-949680-2 : LC Card 83-26834 DDC 304.6/32/091734 19
HB1108 .R87 1984 ***NYPL [JLE 86-1084]***

The Developing countries, problems and perspectives .
(no. 4) New international economic order /. Moscow , 1984. 196 p. ; LC Card 85-151148 DDC 337/.09/047 19
HF1411 .N398 1984 ***NYPL [JLD 86-2664]***

DEVELOPING COUNTRIES - PUBLIC OPINION.

Krämer, Georg. Pädagogische Aspekte entwicklungspolitischer Offentlichkeitsarbeit /. Frankfurt/Main , 1980. 233 p. : ISBN 3-88129-332-9 LC Card 81-466304
HC59.7 .K687 ***NYPL [JLD 87-528]***

DEVELOPING COUNTRIES - RURAL CONDITIONS.

Ellis, Frank. Peasant economics . Cambridge [Cambridgeshire] , New York , 1988. p. cm. ISBN 0-521-32446-7 LC Card 87-14815 DDC 338.1/09172/4 19
HD1542 .E43 1988

DEVELOPING COUNTRIES - RURAL CONDITIONS - CASE STUDIES.

Agricultural household models . Baltimore, Md. , 1986. xi, 335 p. : ISBN 0-8018-3149-0 LC Card 85-45102 DDC 331.7/63/091724 19
HD1542 .A34 1986 ***NYPL [JLE 86-2440]***

Critchfield, Richard. The golden bowl be broken . Bloomington , 1988. p. cm. ISBN 0-253-32554-4 LC Card 87-3690 DDC 305.5/63 19
HD1542 .C75 1988

DEVELOPING COUNTRIES - SOCIAL CONDITIONS.

Alarcón, Reynaldo. Psicología, pobreza y subdesarrollo /. Lima, Perú , 1986. 153 p. ; LC Card 87-126266 DDC 155.9/2 19
HC79.P6 A55 1986

Belal, Abdel Aziz. Développement et facteurs non-économiques /. Rabat , 1980. 100 p. ; LC Card 82-960502
HD83 .B388 1980

Décolonisations et nouvelles dépendances . [Lille] , c1986. 282 p. : ISBN 2-85939-287-4 : LC Card 87-104133
HC59.7 .D354 1986

Griffin, Keith B. World hunger and the world economy . New York , 1987. xvi, 274 p. ; ISBN 0-8419-1128-2 LC Card 86-33626 DDC 330.9172/4 19
HC59.7 .G749 1987

Guzmán Ortega, Gonzalo. Superestructuras y subdesarrollo . Quito , 1985. 178 p. : LC Card 86-132144
HC59.7 .G86 1985

McLin, Jon B. Social and economic effects of petroleum development in non-OPEC developing countries . Geneva , 1986. xiii, 104 p., [4] folded leaves of plates : ISBN 92-2-105505-1 (pbk.) : LC Card 87-123328 DDC 338.2/782/091724 19
HD9578.D44 M396 1986

Prosterman, Roy L. Land reform and democratic development /. Baltimore , c1987. xii, 313 p. ; ISBN 0-8018-3482-1 (alk. paper) LC Card 87-4188 DDC 333.3/1/1724 19
HD1333.5 .P76 1987

DEVELOPING COUNTRIES - SOCIAL CONDITIONS - CONGRESSES.

Les Libéraux et le dialogue Nord-Sud . Bonn , c1982. 220 p. ; ISBN 3-920590-36-8 LC Card 84-204748
HC59.7 .L4177 1982

Unterdrückung, Hunger, Krieg . Göttingen [1985?] 73 p. : LC Card 86-152237
HC59.7 .U55 1985

DEVELOPING COUNTRIES - SOCIAL POLICY.

Jimenez, Emmanuel, 1952- Pricing policy in the social sectors . Baltimore , 1987. v, 170 p. ; ISBN 0-8018-3501-1 : LC Card 86-27590 DDC 338.4/33621/091724 19
HJ7469 .J56 1987

La Presencia del tercer mundo /. San José, Costa Rica , 1982. 239 p., [1] leaf of plates : LC Card 83-161829
HC59.7 .P718 1982

DEVELOPING COUNTRIES - STATISTICAL SERVICES.

Casley, D. J. Data collection in developing countries /. Oxford [Oxfordshire] , New York , 1987. p. cm. ISBN 0-19-442425-1 (pbk.) : LC Card 87-12574 DDC 001.4/222/091724 19
HA31.2 .C37 1987

DEVELOPING COUNTRIES - STATISTICS, VITAL.

Tabutin, Dominique. Les transitions de mortalité dans le Tiersmonde . Louvain-la-Neuve, Belgique [1985] 33 p. : LC Card 86-178578
HB1528 .T33 1985

Developing country debt : implementing the consensus. Washington, D.C. : World Bank, c1987. xliii, 29 p. : ill. ; 28 cm. "An abridged version of World debt tables, 1986-87 edition." Includes index. ISBN 0-8213-0889-0 LC Card 87-2074 DDC 336.3/435/091724021 19
1. Debts, External - Developing countries - Statistics. I. International Bank for Reconstruction and Development. II. World debt tables.
HJ8899 .D483 1987

Developing country debt . Holley, H. A., 1924- London : London ; 85 p. ; ISBN 0-7102-1211-9 (pbk.) : LC Card 86-29838 DDC 336.3/435/091724 19
HG3891.5 .H65 1987

The developing country debt crisis /. Lomax, David F. Basingstoke, Hampshire , 1986. xxiv, 317 p. : ISBN 0-333-38581-0 LC Card 86-674010
HJ8899 .L64x 1986b

The developing country debt crisis /. Lomax, David F. London , 1986. xxiv, 317 p. ; ISBN 0-333-38581-0 ***NYPL [JLD 86-3497]***

DEVELOPING COUNTRY SPECIALISTS - BRAZIL - BIOGRAPHY.

Semana Josué de Castro e a nova geografia da fome, Rio de Janeiro, 19-24 de setembro de 1983 . [S.l. , 1983] 90 leaves : LC Card 86-201115
HD9000.5 .S3968 1983

Developing effective telephone skills /. Lapp, Robert. Eau Claire, WI , c1987. 56 p. : ISBN 0-941161-20-X (pbk.) LC Card 87-403090 DDC 651.7/3 19
HF5541.T4 L36 1987

Developing global new products . Van Nest, Dean G. (Dean Gillette), 1923- Ann Arbor, Mich. , c1987. viii, 123 p. : ISBN 0-8357-1793-3 (alk. paper) LC Card 87-5844 DDC 658.5/75/0973 19
HD69.N4 V36 1987

The Developing global securities market / chairman and general editor, F.W. Neate. London ; Boston : Graham & Trotman ; viii, 192 p. ; 25 cm. "Proceedings of an international seminar (The developing global securities market) organised by the International Bar Association Section on Business Law and held in Paris, France, 4-5 May 1987." Errata slip inserted. ISBN 0-86010-979-8 LC

Card 87-19086 DDC 332.6/5 19
1. Securities - Congresses. 2. Banks and banking, International - Congresses. I. Neate, F. W. II. International Bar Association. Section on Business Law.
HG4508 .D48 1987

Developing local economic strategies : some issues and ideas / edited by Allan Cochrane. Milton Keynes [England] ; Philadelphia : Open University Press, 1987. p. cm. Four papers originally presented at Conference on Local Economic Strategies, Parsifal College, Open University, 12/17-18/86. CONTENTS. - Investing in the private sector / Alan Clarke & Allan Cochrane -- Equal opportunities / Doreen Massey -- Planning the public sector / Maureen Mackintosh -- Social investment in production / Keith Jefferis & Mike Robinson. ISBN 0-335-15522-7 LC Card 87-22681 DDC 338.941 19
1. Great Britain - Economic policy - 1945- - Congresses. 2. Local government - Great Britain - Congresses. 3. Regional planning - Great Britain - Congresses. I. Cochrane, Allan. II. Open University Press. III. Conference on Local Economic Strategies (1986 : Parsifal College).
HC256.6 .D48 1987

Developing managers in Asia / edited by You Poh Seng, Tan Jing Jee, Emily Ding. Singapore ; Reading, Mass. : Addison-Wesley, 1986. p. cm. Bibliography: p. ISBN 0-201-13653-8 : LC Card 86-28717 DDC 658/.007/15 19
1. Executives - Training of - Asia. 2. Management - Study and teaching - Asia. I. You, Poh Seng. II. Tan, Jing Jee. III. Ding, Emily.
HD38.25.A78 D48 1986

Developing microcomputer-based business systems /. Edwards, Chris, 1947- Englewood Cliffs, N.J. , 1983, c1982. x, 202 p. : ISBN 0-13-204545-1 (pbk.) LC Card 83-60581 DDC 658/.054 19
HF5548.2 .E293 1983 ***NYPL [JLE 87-1181]***

Developing negotiation skills in sales personnel . Stumm, David Arthur. New York , 1987. xiv, 148 p. ; ISBN 0-89930-279-3 (alk. paper) LC Card 87-11260 DDC 658.8/1/00683 19
HF5438.25 .S773 1987

Developing new banking products . Reidenbach, R. Eric. Englewood Cliffs, N.J. , c1987. xii, 206 p. : ISBN 0-13-204603-2 LC Card 86-22708 DDC 332.1/7/0685 19
HG1616.C87 R45 1987
NYPL [JLE 87-1141]

Developing the informal sector in Senegal . Dijk, Meine Pieter van. Dakar [1976] 47 leaves ; LC Card 84-232063
HD2346.S4 D55 1976

Developing with foreign investment / edited by Vincent Cable and Bishnodat Persaud. London ; New York : Croom Helm, c1987. viii, 327 p. ; 25 cm. Includes bibliographies and index. ISBN 0-7099-4825-5 LC Card 87-3603 DDC 332.6/73/091724 19
1. Investments, Foreign - Developing countries. 2. Investments, Foreign - Government policy - Developing countries. I. Cable, Vincent. II. Persaud, B. (Bishnodat).
HG5993 .D47 1987

Development administration and U. S. foreign aid policy /. Rondinelli, Dennis A. Boulder , 1987. xi, 188 p. ; ISBN 0-931477-97-2 (lib. bdg.) : LC Card 87-4555 DDC 338.9/0068 19
HC59.72.E44 R66 1987

Development administration in a changing society / edited by R.D. Sharma. New Delhi, India : National Book Organisation, 1987. xix, 214 p. ; 23 cm. On development in Himachal Pradesh; papers presented at a seminar organized by the Post Graduate Centre of Public Administration, Himachal Pradesh University, 1984. Includes bibliographies and index. ISBN 81-85135-18-5 : LC Card 87-900453 DDC 338.954/52 19
1. Himachal Pradesh (India) - Economic conditions - Congresses. 2. Himachal Pradesh (India) - Social conditions - Congresses. I. Sharma, R. D. (Ram Dutt), 1945-. II. Himachal Pradesh University. Post Graduate Centre of Public Administration.
HC437.H5 D48 1987

Development administration in Nigeria . Heinecke, P. [Nigeria , 1985?] 201 p. ; LC Card 86-207544 DDC 338.9669 19
HC1055 .H446 1985

Development administration in Turkey . Heper, Metin. Bebek, Istanbul [1980] vi, 116 p. ; LC Card 87-400032 DDC 338.9561 19
HC492 .H47 1980

Development Alternatives, inc. Agricultural sector assistance strategy for Upper Volta. Washington, D.C. [1982] 1 v. (various pagings) : LC Card 87-120355 DDC 338.1/8 19
HD2144 .A38 1982

Development and dignity . Breslin, Patrick, 1940- Rosslyn, Va. [1987] xiii, 128 p. : ISBN 0-8133-0632-9 (alk. paper) LC Card 87-3920 DDC 338.91/7308/0601 19
HC125 .B725 1987

Development and planning /. Sachs, Ignacy. [Développer les champs de planification. English.] Cambridge [Cambridgeshire] ; New York : ix, 134 p. ; ISBN 0-521-33454-3 LC Card 87-11780 DDC 338.9 19
HD82 .S23313 1987

The development and resettlement of oncho-freed zones in the Volta River Basin of West Africa . Ewusi, Kodwo. [Legon, Ghana] [1985] 89 p. ; LC Card 87-127503 DDC 333.3/1/667 19
HD1022.Z8 V654 1985

Development and social change in rural Egypt /. Adams, Richard H. Syracuse, N.Y. , 1986. xii, 231 p. : ISBN 0-8156-2362-3 (alk. paper) LC Card 85-30251 DDC 307.1/4/0962 19
HN786.Z9 C63 1986 ***NYPL [JLE 86-1999]***

Development and underdevelopment . Cole, J. P. (John Peter), 1928- London , New York , 1987. vi, 104 p. : ISBN 0-416-92080-2 (pbk.) LC Card 86-23758 DDC 338.9/009172/4 19
HC59.7 .C59 1987

Development Bank Associates. Ludlow, Nicholas H. The Development Bank highways market, 1987-1991 . Washington, D.C., USA (1735 Eye St., NW, Suite 710, Washington 20006) , c1987. 387, 2 p. : LC Card 87-71066 DDC 388.1/14 19
HG3881 .L737 1987

The Development Bank highways market, 1987-1991 . Ludlow, Nicholas H. Washington, D.C., USA (1735 Eye St., NW, Suite 710, Washington 20006) , c1987. 387, 2 p. : LC Card 87-71066 DDC 388.1/14 19
HG3881 .L737 1987

DEVELOPMENT BANK OF SOUTHERN AFRICA.
An Introduction to economic development in Southern Africa and the role of DBSA /. Sandton, Republic of South Africa [1985] 78 p. ; LC Card 87-127414 DDC 338.968 19
HG3401.A8 D485 1985

La Grange, A. B. DBSA in the southern African development framework /. Sandton, Republic of South Africa [1985] 36 p. : LC Card 87-150256 DDC 332.2 19
HC900 .L3 1985

Development banking in India /. Poonia, M. S. (Mohan Singh), 1955- Jaipur , 1987. 140, iii, [i] p. ; LC Card 87-901804 DDC 332.2 19
HG3284 .P66 1987

DEVELOPMENT BANKS.
Ludlow, Nicholas H. The Development Bank highways market, 1987-1991 . Washington, D.C., USA (1735 Eye St., NW, Suite 710, Washington 20006) , c1987. 387, 2 p. : LC Card 87-71066 DDC 388.1/14 19
HG3881 .L737 1987

DEVELOPMENT BANKS - BRAZIL.
Criação de empresas de alta tecnologia . São Paulo . 192, [1] p. ; LC Card 87-403991 DDC 338.4/362/000981 19
HC190.H53 C75 1987

DEVELOPMENT BANKS - BRAZIL, SOUTH.
Banco Regional de Desenvolvimento do Extremo sul. BRDE . [Curitiba] , 1984. 95 p., [8] : LC Card 86-143911
HG2889.S6 B36 1984

Campos, José Hypólito Machado de. BRDE, a ação governamental na promoção do desenvolvimento econômico e social da Região Sul /. Porto Alegre [between 1983 and 1985] 51 p. ; LC Card 86-143903
HG2889.S6 C36 1983

DEVELOPMENT BANKS - DEVELOPING COUNTRIES.
Current problems of economic integration . New York , 1986. viii, 115 p. ; ISBN 92-1-112216-3 (pbk.) LC Card 87-106405 DDC 337.1/1724 19
HC59.7 .C845 1986

DEVELOPMENT BANKS - INDIA.
Gupta, S. C., 1954- Institutional financing and industrial growth . Jaipur , 1987. xx, 316 p. (some folded) : LC Card 87-900864
HD9886.I42 G83 1987

Lakshmana Rao, V., 1940- Progress of development banking in India /. Allahabad, India , 1986. xvi, 139 p. ; ISBN 81-85076-07-3 : LC Card 86-902782 DDC 332.2 19
HG3284 .L35 1986

Nigam, Brij Mohan Lall, 1935- Banking and economic growth. Bombay [1967] xii, 207 p. LC Card SA68-4077 DDC 332.1/0954
HG3284 .N5 ***NYPL [JLD 74-2222]***

Poonia, M. S. (Mohan Singh), 1955- Development banking in India /. Jaipur , 1987. 140, iii, [i] p. ; LC Card 87-901804 DDC 332.2 19
HG3284 .P66 1987

Ramakrishna Sarma, K. Financial institutions and regional development in India /. Allahabad, India , 1986. xvii, 211 p. ; ISBN 81-85076-04-9 : LC Card 86-902692 DDC 332.2 19
HG3288 .R32 1986

DEVELOPMENT BANKS - INDIA - ANDHRA PRADESH.
Reddy, C. R. Cooperative long term finance . Delhi, India , 1987. ix, 128 p. : LC Card 87-900729 DDC 334/.2/095484 19
HG2051.I5 A652 1987

DEVELOPMENT BANKS - INDIA - CONGRESSES.
Bank finance and rural development /. Tirupati [1986] vi, 222 p. ; LC Card 86-903530 DDC 332.2 19
HG3284 .B265 1986

DEVELOPMENT BANKS - INDIA - UTTAR PRADESH.
Mishra, M. N. (Maha Narain), 1945- Appraisal of credit facilities provided by banking institutions in rural development /. Meerut, U.P., India [1987?] x, 251, ii p. ; LC Card 87-900918 DDC 332.2 19
HG3284 .M49 1987

DEVELOPMENT BANKS - MANAGEMENT.
Mould, Maurice C., 1925- Financial information for management of a development finance institution . Washington, D.C. [1987] 1 v. (various pagings) : ISBN 0-8213-0913-7 (pbk.) LC Card 87-15989 DDC 332.2 19
HG3726 .M68 1987

DEVELOPMENT BANKS - MEXICO - HISTORY.
Nacional Financiera, 1934-1984 . México, D.F. , 1985. 310 p. ; ISBN 968-665-107-1 LC Card 87-400288 DDC 332.2 19
HG2718.N33 N33 1985

Development bureaucracy /. Pai Panandiker, V. A., 1935- New Delhi , c1983. ix, 252 p. ; LC Card 83-902420 DDC 352.94/233/09542 19
HD2075.K359 P34 1983
NYPL [JLD 86-3762]

Development Centre papers.
Lecaillon, Jacques. Economic policies and agricultural performance . Paris , 1985. 158 p. ; LC Card 86-216027 DDC 338.1/86625 19
HD2144 .L42 1985

Lecaillon, Jacques. Economic policies and agricultural performance . Paris , 1986. 174 p. ; LC Card 87-158595 DDC 338.1/86623 19
HD2143.5.Z8 L43 1986

Mitsotaki, Alexandra Gourdain. Public development finance corporations . Paris , 1986. 40 p. ; LC Card 86-221546 DDC 332.6/734/01724 19
HG5993 .M57 1986

Svejnar, Jan. Economic policies and agricultural performance . Paris , 1986. 167 p. ; LC Card 87-120115 DDC 338.1/85496 19
HD2065.9.Z8 S84 1986

Development Committee.
Status report on concessional flows, April 1986. Washington, D.C., U. S. A. , 1986. 25 p. ; ISBN 0-8213-0789-4 (pbk.) LC Card 86-214496 DDC 336.3/435/091724
HG3891 .S7 1986

A Strategy for restoration of growth in middle-income countries that face debt-servicing difficulties. Washington, D.C., U. S.A. , 1986. 43 p. : ISBN 0-8213-0811-4 (pbk.) LC Card 86-214478 DDC 338.9/009172/4 19
HJ8899 .S77 1986

Development Committee (Series) .
(no. 10) A Strategy for restoration of growth in middle-income countries that face debt-servicing difficulties. Washington, D.C., U. S.A. , 1986. 43 p. : ISBN 0-8213-0811-4 (pbk.) LC Card 86-214478 DDC 338.9/009172/4 19
HJ8899 .S77 1986

(no. 9) Status report on concessional flows, April 1986. Washington, D.C., U. S.A. , 1986. 25 p. ; ISBN 0-8213-0789-4 (pbk.) LC Card 86-214496 DDC 336.3/435/091724
HG3891 .S7 1986

DEVELOPMENT CREDIT CORPORATIONS - GUADELOUPE.
Carnet d'adresses /. [Pointe-à-Pitre, Guadeloupe] [1986?] 64 p. : LC Card 87-152834
HG3729.G862 C37 1986

DEVELOPMENT CREDIT CORPORATIONS - GUYANA.
Carnet d'adresses /. [Pointe-à-Pitre, Guadeloupe] [1986?] 64 p. : LC Card 87-152834
HG3729.G862 C37 1986

DEVELOPMENT CREDIT CORPORATIONS - MANAGEMENT.
Mould, Maurice C., 1925- Financial information for management of a development finance institution . Washington, D.C. [1987] 1 v. (various pagings) : ISBN 0-8213-0913-7 (pbk.) LC Card 87-15989 DDC 332.2 19
HG3726 .M68 1987

DEVELOPMENT CREDIT CORPORATIONS - MARTINIQUE.
Carnet d'adresses /. [Pointe-à-Pitre, Guadeloupe] [1986?] 64 p. : LC Card 87-152834
HG3729.G862 C37 1986

Development finance and the development process . Hope, Kempe R. New York , 1987. 100 p. ; ISBN 0-313-25835-X (lib. bdg. : alk. paper) LC Card 86-29617 DDC 336.729 19
HJ844.3 .H67 1987

Development Group for Alternative Policies. Hellinger, Steve. Aid for just development . Washington, D.C. (1010 Vermont Ave., N.W., Suite 521, Washington 20005) , c1987. vii, 191 p. ; LC Card 87-404422 DDC 338.91/09172/4 19
HC60 .H38516 1987

Development in Malaysia . Mehmet, Ozay. London , Dover, N.H. , c1986. 183 p. ; ISBN 0-7099-3525-0 : LC Card 85-29079 DDC 338.9595 19
HC445.5.Z9 I51834 1986 ***NYPL [JLD 86-2389]***

Development is for people / edited by Jan K. Coetzee. 1st ed. Braamfontein, Johannesburg : Macmillan South Africa, 1986. 253 p. : ill. ; 22 cm. Bibliography: p. 241-250. Includes index. CONTENTS. - 1. Modernisation / Jan K. Coetzee -- 2. Imperialism and underdevelopment / Yvonne Muthien -- 3. Dependency / Jan H. Vorster -- 4. A microfoundation as alternative for development thought / Jan K. Coetzee -- 5. Development as process of human consciousness / Fritz Hölscher and Norma Romm -- 6. The basic needs approach to economic development / Gavin R. Keeton -- 7. Development profiles and existing strategies / Stef. F. Coetzee and André A. Ligthelm -- 8. The evolution of development theories and regional development theories / Stef. F. Coetzee and André A. Ligthelm -- 9. Strategy options / Stef. F. Coetzee and André A. Ligthelm -- 10. Research needs in respect of development in southern Africa / Elwil P. Beukes. ISBN 0-86954-274-5 (pbk.) : LC Card 86-200074 DDC 338.9 19
1. Economic development. 2. Economic development - Social aspects. I. Coetzee, Jan Karel.
HD75 .D488 1986

Development issues of our time /. Misra, Rameshwar Prasad, 1930- New Delhi , 1985. xi, 368 p. : LC Card 85-903754 DDC 338.9/009172/4 19
HC59.7 .M5334 1985 ***NYPL [JLE 86-1375]***

Development, manpower and migration in the Red Sea region . Pennisi, Giuseppe. Hamburg , c1981. xi, 264 p. : LC Card 82-109615 DDC 331.6/2/091824 19
HD8656 .P46 1981 ***NYPL [JLF 86-1602]***

Development of agricultural production in small-scale and large-scale farms and their system of connections in the industrializing agriculture. Magyar-Lengyel Agrárközgazdasági Konferencia (1984 : Gödöllő, Hungary) A nagyüzemek és a kisüzemek termelésének fejlődése, kapcsolatuk az iparosodó mezőgazdaságban =. Gödöllő , 1984. 174 p. ; LC Card 86-145249
HD1995.7 .M32 1984

Development of backward areas . Vyasulu, Vinod. New Delhi, India , 1987. xi, 188 p. : ISBN 81-85030-05-7 : LC Card 87-902689 DDC 332.6/42/0954 19
HD2346.I5 V93 1987

The development of economic policy in Mexico with special reference to economic doctrines, 1600-1958 /. Austin, Ruben Vargas, 1915- New York , 1987. 336 p. ; ISBN 0-8240-1354-9 (alk. paper) : LC Card 87-8569 DDC 338.972 19
HC135 .A84 1987

Development of handloom industry . Das, Nagen C., 1943- New Delhi , c1986. 264 p. : LC Card 86-903222 DDC 338.4/767702822/0954162 19
HD9866.I63 A874 1986

The Development of high technology industries : an international survey / edited by Michael J. Breheny and Ronald McQuaid. London ; New York : Croom Helm, c1987. 363 p. : ill. ; 23 cm. "Published in the USA by Croom Helm in association with Methuen, Inc."--T.p. verso. Includes bibliographies and index. ISBN 0-7099-3942-6 LC Card 87-9086 DDC 338.4/762 19
1. High technology industries. I. Breheny, M.J. (Michael J.). II. McQuaid, Ronald, 1955-.
HC79.H53 D48 1987

Development of human resources . Ghafoor, Abdul. Islamabad [1984] v, ii leaves, 99 p., v, ii leaves ; LC Card 85-932024 DDC 331.11/09549/1 19
HD5819 .G48 1984

Development of irrigation and Indian agriculture /. Poddar, B. N. New Delhi , c1987. 331 p. ; LC Card 87-901300 DDC 338.1/62 19
HD2075.B5 P63 1967

The development of small scale industry in Kaduna State . Jaworek, Rudolf. Zaria [1980] vii, 162, [44] p., [2] leaves of plates : LC Card 84-256006
HD2356.N62 K34 1980

The development of the accountancy profession in Britain to the early twentieth century /. Parker, R. H. (Robert Henry) [University, Ala.] , 1986. ix, 74 p. ; LC Card 86-226162 DDC 657/.09 19
HF5616.G7 P36 1986

Development of the community . Economic Community of West African States. Lagos , 1981. 51 leaves ; LC Card 87-403455 DDC 337.1/66 19
HC1000 .E23 1981

The development of the labour process in capitalist societies . Littler, Craig R. London , Exeter, N.H. , 1982. 226 p. : ISBN 0-435-82540-2 : LC Card 82-210245 DDC 306/.36 19
HD8390 .L48 1982 ***NYPL [JLD 87-1005]***

Development of the Mexican tuna industry, 1976-86 /. Hudgins, Linda Lucas, 1946- Honolulu, Hawaii , 1987. p. cm. ISBN 0-86638-091-4 LC Card 87-505 DDC 338.3/72758 19
HD9469.T83 M64 1987

The development of the shadow economies for Denmark, Norway, and Sweden . Schneider, Friedrich. Aarhus, Denmark [1986] 46 p. : LC Card 86-215193 DDC 381 19
HD2346.S29 S35 1986

The Development of the tuna industry in the Pacific islands region : an analysis of options / edited by David J. Doulman. [Honolulu, Hawaii] : East-West Center, c1987. xviii, 416 p. : ill. ; 23 cm. Bibliography: p. 395-414. ISBN 0-86638-096-5 (pbk.) LC Card 87-6818 DDC 338.3/72758 19
1. Tuna industry - Pacific Area. I. Doulman, David J., 1950-.
HD9469.T83 P163 1987

Development of weaker sections . Kabra, Govind Das, 1943- New Delhi , 1984, c1983. ix, 182 p. ; LC Card 84-900357 DDC 338.1/8544 19
HD1476.I42 R345 1984 ***NYPL [JLE 86-4597]***

Development opportunities for the 80's. A Transcription of key addresses at San Antonio's Bio-Medical Seminar /. San Antonio, TX (8961 Tesoro Dr., Suite 308, San Antonio 78217) , c1985. v, 104, [4] leaves of plates : LC Card 87-144092 DDC 338.4/7681761/09764351 19
HD9999.B443 U667 1985

Development options . Kibria, Ghulam. Karachi , 1984. xi, 267 p. ; LC Card 84-931764 DDC 338.9549/1 19
HC440.5 .K53 1984

Development plan for Malta, 1986-1988. Malta. Ministry of Trade and Economic Planning. Economic Division. [Valletta, Malta] [1986] 95 p. ; LC Card 86-228319
HC310.2 .M335 1986

Development planning . Chakravarty, Sukhamoy. Oxford [Oxfordshire] , New York , 1987. viii, 137 p. ; ISBN 0-19-828555-8 : LC Card 87-1554 DDC 338.954 19
HC435.2 .C467 1987

Development planning in Transkei . May, Julian. Durban , 1985. 35 p., [5] p. ; ISBN 0-86980-483-9 (pbk.) : LC Card 86-222656 DDC 338.9687/91 19
HC905.Z7 T7347 1985

Development policy, inflation, and politics in Chile, 1938-1958 . Pisciotta, John L. (John Lee) New York , 1987. v, 188 p. ; ISBN 0-8240-1367-0 (alk. paper) : LC Card 87-7617 DDC 338.983 19
HC192 .P625 1987

The development process and technology . Fadahunsi, Akin. Uppsala , 1986. 41 p. ; ISBN 91-7106-257-2 (pbk.) LC Card 87-119156 DDC 338.9669/07 19
HC1055.Z9 T43 1986

The Development process of the Indian economy / edited by P.R. Brahmananda, V.R. Panchamukhi. 1st ed. Bombay : Himalaya Pub. House, 1987. xxxxxxviii, 1219, 78 p. : ill. ; 23 cm. Bibliography: p. [1]-62 (2nd group) Includes index. LC Card 87-901099 DDC 338.954 19
1. India - Economic conditions - 1947- - Congresses. 2. India - Economic policy - 1980- - Congresses. I. Brahmananda, P. R. II. Panchamukhi, Vadiraj Raghawendracharya, 1936-.
HC435.2 .D476 1987

Development programme of the Kagera Basin : final report : executive summary. [Kigali] : Multidisciplinary-Multidonor Mission : Executive Secretariat of the KBO, [1982] viii, 73 leaves : maps ; 28 cm. At head of title: Kagera Basin Organization, KBO [and] United Nations Development Programme, UNDP. Cover title. "February 1982." LC Card 85-980886 DDC 338.967 19
1. Economic development projects - Kagera River Watershed. 2. Economic development projects - Burundi. 3. Economic development projects - Rwanda. 4. Economic development projects - Tanzania. 5. Economic development projects - Uganda. I. Multidisciplinary-Multidonor Mission (United Nations Development Programme). II. Kagera Basin Organization. Secretariat. III. Kagera Basin Organization. IV. United Nations. Development Programme.
HC860.Z9 E444 1982

Development programmes in agriculture and the weaker sections /. Desinga Raj, N. Allahabad, India , 1987. xvi, 217 p. : ISBN 81-85076-16-2 : LC Card 87-900702 DDC 338.1/854 19
HD1476.I4 D47 1987

DEVELOPMENT, REAL ESTATE. see **REAL ESTATE DEVELOPMENT.**

Development region D . Kruger, Gudrun. Port Elizabeth [1985] iv, 89 p. : ISBN 0-86988-274-0 (pbk.) LC Card 86-233113 DDC 304.6/09687/5 19
HA4701.Z9 C354 1985

DEVELOPMENT, RURAL. see **RURAL DEVELOPMENT.**

Development, socio-cultural dimensions / edited by S.L. Sharma. 1st ed. Jaipur : Rawat Publications, 1986. xxi, 264 p. ; 23 cm. Papers presented at the Seminar "Development: "Socio-cultural Dimensions" held at Dept. of Sociology, Panjab

University, Chandigarh, February 15-17, 1982. Includes bibliographies and index. ISBN 81-7033-020-3 : LC Card 86-902849 DDC 306/.0954 19
1. India - Economic conditions - 1947- - Congresses. 2. India - Social conditions - 1947- - Congresses. I. Sharma, S. L. II. Seminar "Development: Socio-cultural Dimensions" (1982 : Dept. of Sociology, Panjab University). III. Panjab University. Dept. of Sociology.
HC435.2 .D478 1986

Development strategies and planning for farmers' communities : Asian case studies. College, Laguna, Philippines : Southeast Asian Regional Center for Graduate Study and Research in Agriculture, 1983. vi, 242 p. : ill. ; 28 cm. LC Card 84-102916 DDC 338.1/859 19
1. Agricultural development projects - Asia, Southeastern - Case studies. 2. Rural development projects - Asia, Southeastern - Case studies. I. Southeast Asian Regional Centre for Graduate Study and Research in Agriculture.
HD2075.8 .D48 1983

Development strategies reconsidered / John P. Lewis and Valeriana Kallab, editors. New Brunswick, N.J., U. S.A. : Transaction Books, c1986. viii, 190 p. ; 23 cm. (U. S.-Third World policy perspectives . no. 5) Includes bibliographies. ISBN 0-87855-991-4 (pbk.) : LC Card 85-24582 DDC 338.9/009172/4 19
1. Industrial promotion - Developing countries. 2. Developing countries - Economic policy. 3. Developing countries - Commercial policy. I. Lewis, John Prior. II. Kallab, Valeriana. III. Series.
HC59.7 .D482 1986 ***NYPL [JLE 86-2976]***

Development studies and colonial policy / edited by Barbara Ingham and Colin Simmons. London ; Totowa, N.J. : F. Cass, 1987. 292 p. : ill. ; 24 cm. Includes bibliographies. ISBN 0-7146-3231-7 : LC Card 87-6562 DDC 338.9171/241 19
1. Economic development. 2. Great Britain - Colonies - Economic conditions. I. Ingham, Barbara. II. Simmons, Colin.
HD82 .D395 1987

Development studies and management secondment programme /. United Nations Institute for Namibia. Lusaka, Zambia , 1985. v, 26 p. ; LC Card 87-980229 DDC 338.9/007/15 19
HD77.5.N3 U55 1985

Development Studies Institute (Lahore, Pakistan) Ghafoor, Abdul. Development of human resources . Islamabad [1984] v, ii leaves, 99 p., v, ii leaves ; LC Card 85-932024 DDC 331.11/09549/1 19
HD5819 .G48 1984

Development through liberation . Kruijer, G. J. (Gerardus Johannes), 1919- Atlantic Highlands, NJ , 1987. x, 257 p. ; ISBN 0-391-03538-X LC Card 87-3710 DDC 338.9/009172/4 19
HC59.72.P6 K78 1987

The Development trends, 1986 / the Urban Land Institute. Washington, D.C. : ULI, c1986. 48 p. : ill. (some col.) ; 28 cm. ISBN 0-87420-657-X (pbk.) LC Card 86-227316 DDC 333.3/8/0973 19
1. Real estate development - United States. I. Urban Land Institute.
HD1390 .D485 1986

Developments of commercial activities in space. Gli Sviluppi delle attività commerciali nello spazio . [Trieste] [1985] 238 p. : LC Card 86-215421 DDC 338.0919 19
HD9711.75.A2 S95 1983

DEVELOPMENTS (REAL ESTATE) see **REAL ESTATE DEVELOPMENT.**

Le développement de l'élevage des équidés en France . France. Conseil économique et social. [Paris] [1986] 166 p. in various pagings : LC Card 86-133487
HD9434.F72 F73 1986

Développement et facteurs non-économiques /. Belal, Abdel Aziz. Rabat , 1980. 100 p. ; LC Card 82-960502
HD83 .B388 1980

Le développement international des banques canadiennes . Moreau, François. Montréal, Québec , c1985. 159 p. ; ISBN 2-89035-120-3 LC Card 86-186883
HG2704 .M67 1985

Développement ou appauvrissement /. Bra Kanon, Denis, 1936- Paris , c1985. 188 p. : ISBN 2-7178-0962-7 : LC Card 86-177676
HF1413 .B72 1985

Deverre, Christian. Reforma agraria como proceso social . Piura, Perú [1984] 163 p. : LC Card 84-232526 DDC 333.3/1/85 19
HD1333.P4 R44 1984 ***NYPL [JLD 86-2537]***

DeVille, Philippe, 1920- Burns, Tom R. Man, decisions, society . New York , c1985. xiv, 342 p. : ISBN 2-88124-004-6 (France) LC Card 84-10303 DDC 301 19
HM24 .B85 1985 ***NYPL [JLE 86-2963]***

Devino, Gary T. Agribusiness finance / Gary T. Devino. Danville, Ill. : Interstate Printers & Publishers, c1981. xii, 166 p. : ill. ; 24 cm. Includes bibliographies and index. ISBN 0-8134-2191-8 (pbk.) LC Card 81-80386 DDC 658.1/5 19
1. Agriculture - Finance. 2. Agriculture - Accounting. 3. Agricultural industries - Finance. 4. Agricultural industries - Accounting. I. Title.
HD1437 .D48 ***NYPL [JLE 86-4573]***

Devisenmärkte und Wechselkurse . Gaab, Werner. Berlin , New York , 1983. vii, 305 p. : ISBN 0-387-12615-5 (U. S.) : LC Card 83-222336
HG3851 .G25 1983

Devlet Planlama Teşkilatı (Turkey)
Dördüncü Beş Yıllık Kalkınma Planı, 1979-1983. Ankara : T.C., Başbakanlık, Devlet Planlama Teşkilâtı, [1979] xiv, 692 p. ; 24 cm. (Yayın . no. DPT 1664) Spine title: 4. Beş Yıllık Kalkınma Planı. "Nisan 1979"--T.p. verso. Includes bibliographical references. LC Card 83-228455
1. Turkey - Economic policy. 2. Turkey - Social policy. I. Title. II. Title: 4. Beş Yıllık Kalkınma Planı. III. Series: Yayın (Devlet Planlama Teşkilatı (Turkey)) , no. DPT 1664.
HC401 .A356 no. 1664 HC492

1983-1993 Ulaştırma Ana Planı. [Ankara] : Başbakanlık, Devlet Planlama Teşkilâtı, [1982] 1 v. (various pagings) : col. ill. ; 29 cm. LC Card 85-226492
1. Transportation and state - Turkey. I. Title.
HE268.25 .D48 1982

DEVLET PLANLAMA TEŞKILATI (TURKEY)
Planned development in Turkey and the State Planning Organization. [Ankara] [1986] 47 p. : LC Card 87-151757 DDC 338.9561 19
HC492 .P63 1986

Devlet Planlama Teşkilatı (Turkey). Yayin ve Temsil Dairesi Başkanliği. Planned development in Turkey and the State Planning Organization. [Ankara] [1986] 47 p. : LC Card 87-151757 DDC 338.9561 19
HC492 .P63 1986

Devlin, Robert. External debt in Bolivia / prepared by Robert Devlin and Michael Mortimore for the Economic Commission for Latin America and the Caribbean. Boulder, Colo. : Westview Press, 1987. p. cm. (Foreign relations of Latin America . no. 6) Bibliography: p. Includes index. ISBN 0-8133-7366-2 : LC Card 87-2088 DDC 336.3/4/0984 19
1. Debts, External - Bolivia. 2. Loans, Foreign - Bolivia. I. Mortimore, Michael. II. United Nations. Economic Commission for Latin America and the Caribbean. III. Title. IV. Series.
HJ8574 .D48 1987

DEVNĪA (BULGARIA) - BIOGRAPHY.
Biografiia ot mnogo imena . Sofiia , 1983. 232 p. : LC Card 84-163061
HD8627.A1 B56 1983

DeVol, Karen R., 1949- Income replacement for long term disability : the role of workers' compensation and SSDI / Karen R. DeVol. Cambridge, Mass. : Workers Compensation Research Institute, 1986. p. cm. Bibliography: p. "WC-86-2." ISBN 0-935149-04-X : LC Card 86-28264 DDC 368.4/1/00973 19
1. Workers' compensation - United States. 2. Insurance, Disability - United States. 3. Social security - United States. I. Workers Compensation Research Institute (Cambridge, Mass.). II. Title.
HD7103.65.U6 D484 1986

Devos, Wouter. see **De Vos, Wouter.**

Dewerpe, Alain. L'industrie aux champs : essai sur la proto-industrialisation en Italie du Nord (1800-1880) / Alain Dewerpe. Roma : Ecole française de Rome, 1985. xxxv, 543 p. : ill. ; 24 cm. (Collection de l'Ecole française de Rome, 0223-5099 . 85) Bibliography: p. 505-530. Includes index. ISBN 2-7283-0081-X LC Card 86-221375
1. Italy, Northern - Industries - History - 19th century. 2. Italy, Northern - Economic conditions. 3. Italy, Northern - Social conditions. I. Title. II. Series.
HC307.N58 D48 1985

Dewey, Ballantine, Bushby, Palmer & Wood. The Textile and apparel trade crisis . Washington, D.C. (1775 Pennsylvania Ave., N.W., Washington 20006) , c1985. vi, 200, [23] p. : LC Card 87-122082 DDC 382/.45677 19
HD9850.6 .T475 1985

Dewhurst, Jim. Small business in Europe /. Basingstoke, Hampshire , 1986. xx, 211 p. : ISBN 0-333-38405-9 : LC Card 86-673899
HD2346.E9 S62x 1986

DeWind, Josh. Peasants become miners : the evolution of industrial mining systems in Peru, 1902-1974 / Josh DeWind. New York : Garland Pub., 1987. vii, 421 p. : ill. ; 25 cm. (South American and Latin American economic history) Bibliography: p. 407-421. ISBN 0-8240-1358-1 (alk. paper) LC Card 87-8361 DDC 338.2/0985/23 19
1. Miners - Peru - Cerro de Pasco - History. 2. Mineral industries - Peru - Cerro de Pasco - History. 3. Cerro de Pasco Mining Company - History. I. Title. II. Series.
HD8039.M61 P44 1987

Dex, Shirley. British and American women at work : do equal opportunities policies matter? / Shirley Dex and Lois B. Shaw. Houndmills, Basingstoke, Hampshire : Macmillan, 1986. xii, 159 p. : ill. ; 23 cm. Includes index. Bibliography: p. 152-158. ISBN 0-333-40219-7
1. Women - Employment - Great Britain. 2. Women - Employment - United States. 3. Sex discrimination in employment - Great Britain. 4. Sex discrimination in employment - United States. 5. Affirmative action programs - Great Britain. 6. Affirmative action programs - United States. I. Shaw, Lois Banfill. II. Title.
NYPL [JLD 86-3608]

Dey, P. B. (Purnendu Bhusan), 1930- The jute industry of India : India's export trade in jute goods since the first development decade : a study of its problems and prospects, 1961-79 / P.B. Dey. Calcutta : P.B. Dey, 1984. 12, 304, iii p. ; 22 cm. Bibliography: p. [298]-304. Includes index. LC Card 86-903224 DDC 382/.4567713/0954 19
1. Jute industry - India - History. I. Title.
HD9156.J8 I325 1984

Deyo, Frederic C. The Political economy of the new Asian industrialism /. Ithaca, N.Y. , 1987. 252 p. ; ISBN 0-8014-1948-4 (alk. paper) LC Card 86-29103 DDC 338.95 19
HC460.5 .P65 1987

Dhanikagoshṭhīra luṭapāṭera kāhinī /. Rahamāna, Matiura, 1946- Ḍhākā , 1987. 136 p. : LC Card 87-902373
HG3290.6.A6 R35 1987

Dhar, D. P., 1918-1975. Enterpreneurship and development / D.P. Dhar. New Delhi : Punjab, Haryana & Delhi Chamber of Commerce and Industry, [pref. 1974] 23 p., [2] p. of plates : ill. ; 22 cm. (Shri Ram memorial lecture . 1974) Cover title. LC Card 80-908353 DDC 338.954 19
1. Entrepreneur. 2. India - Economic conditions. I. Title. II. Series.
HB615 .D49 1974

Dhawan, B. D. Irrigation in India's agricultural development : productivity, stability, equity / B.D. Dhawan. New Delhi ; Newbury Park [Calif.] : Sage Publications, 1987. p. cm. Bibliography: p. Includes index. ISBN 0-8039-9544-X LC Card 87-22521 DDC 338.1/62 19
1. Irrigation - Economic aspects - India. 2. Agriculture - Economic aspects - India. I. Title.
HD1741.I29 D47 1987

Dhawan, O. P. Non resident Indians : investments & facilities, with tax planning / O.P. Dhawan.3rd ed. New Delhi : Institute of Financial & Customs Studies : Vimal Publications, 1984. xvi, 428 p. ; 25 cm. "Updated with supplements"--Stamp on t.p. verso. Library has suppl. 1-3 (28 March, 1985) LC Card 85-900577 DDC 346.54/07 345.4067 19
1. Investments, Foreign - India. 2. East Indians - Foreign countries. 3. Taxation - India. I. Title.
HG5732 .D43 1984 ***NYPL [JLE 86-1363]***

Dhirendra Sharma. see **Sharma, Dhirendra.**

Dholakia, Bakul H. 1947- The economics of housing in India : research project = Bhārata meṃ āvāsiya artha-vyavasthā / carried out by Bakul H. Dholakia. Delhi : Controller of Publications, 1982. xviii, 274 p. ; 22 cm. Preface also in Hindi. "[Sponsored by] Government of India, National Buildings Organisation, and U.N. Regional Housing Centre, ESCAP"--Cover. "PNBO.41/1000-1982(DSK.II)"--P. [4] of cover. LC Card 83-905798 DDC 363.5/0954 19
1. Housing - India. 2. Housing - India - Finance. 3. Housing policy - India. I. India (Republic). National Buildings Organisation. II. United Nations Regional Housing Centre for the E.S.C.A.P. Region. III. Title. IV. Title: Bhārata meṃ āvāsiya artha-vyavasthā.
HD7361.A3 D47 1982 ***NYPL [JLD 85-2908]***

Dhongade, M. P. Farmers' attitude survey in the Mula Command Area, Maharashtra / M.P. Dhongade, S.D. Suryawanshi, P.D. Deshmukh. Rahuri, Maharashtra, India : Dept. of Agricultural Economics, Mahatma Phule Agricultural University, 1986. vi, 69 p. ; 26 cm. (Publication / Department of Agril. Economics, Mahatma Phule Agril. University . 9) Based on the survey conducted in 1984-85, by the Dept. of Agricultural Economics, Mahatma Phule Agricultural Economics. LC Card 86-903408 DDC 338.1/0954/792 19
1. Farmers - India - Maharashtra - Attitudes. 2. Agricultural surveys - India - Maharashtra. I. Suryawanshi, S. D. II. Deshmukh, P. D. III. Series: Publication (Mahatma Phule Krishi Vidyapeeth. Dept. of Agricultural Economics) , 9. IV. Title.
HD8039.F32 I44 1986

Di Bernardo, Barbara. Transizione tecnologica e strategie evolutive : l'impresa industriale verso l'automazione / Barbara Di Bernardo, Enzo Rullani. Padova : CEDAM, 1985. xiii, 432 p. : ill. ; 22 cm. (Collana "Ca' Bembo" . 7) Includes bibliographical references. LC Card 86-214184
1. Technological innovations. 2. Industrial management. 3. Automation. I. Rullani, Enzo. II. Title. III. Series.
HD45 .D47 1985

Di Biase, C. (Carolina) Riuso e riqualificazione edilizia negli anni '80 /. Milano [1981] 706 p. :ill. ; ISBN 88-20-42135-6 (pbk.) : LC Card 81-210070
HD7341.A3 R58 1981 ***NYPL [JSD 86-493]***

Di Cagno, Elisabetta. Lear, Robert W. How to turn your MBA into a CEO /. New York , London , c1987. xvii, 222 p. ; ISBN 0-02-569610-6 LC Card 86-28332 DDC 650/.07/1173 19
HF1131 .L39 1987

Di là dalle rovine . Acocella, Giovanni, 1932- Napoli , c1982. 172, [4] p. ; ISBN 88-7042-185-6 : LC Card 82-181323 DDC 363.3/495 19
HC307.S69 A36 1982 ***NYPL [JLD 86-485]***

Di Mare, Alberto.
Cespedes S., Víctor Hugo. Costa Rica . San José, Costa Rica , 1986. 208 p. : ISBN 997-7210-06-3 LC Card 87-404067 DDC 330.97286/053 19
HC143 .C483 1986

Cespedes S., Víctor Hugo. Costa Rica--recuperación sin reactivación . San José, Costa Rica , 1985. 238 p. : ISBN 997-7210-05-5 LC Card 86-208956
HC143 .C484 1985

Di Nardi, Giuseppe. L'economia a una svolta critica / Giuseppe Di Nardi. Milano : A. Giuffrè, 1984- v. ; 25 cm. (Studi di economia politica. 25) Includes bibliographical references. CONTENTS. - v. 4. Il dualismo nello sviluppo. LC Card 84-216905 DDC 330 19
1. Economics - Addresses, essays, lectures. 2. Economic policy - Addresses, essays, lectures. 3. Economics - History - Addresses, essays, lectures. 4. Economic policy - History - Addresses, essays, lectures. I. Title. II. Series.
HB177 .D48 1984 ***NYPL [JLL 73-173 v.25]***

Di Paula, Jorge. Tierras para asentamientos populares . Quito, Ecuador , 1985. 378 p. : LC Card 87-400165 DDC 333.77/13/0986613 19
HD530.Q58 T54 1985

Di Tella, Guido, 1931- The Political economy of Argentina, 1946-83 /. Pittsburgh, Pa. , 1988. p. cm. ISBN 0-8229-1148-5 LC Card 87-24412 DDC 338.982 19
HC175 .P623 1988

Dia, Mamadou.
[Nations africaines et solidarité mondiale. English]
The African nations and world solidarity / Mamadou Dia ; translated from the French by Mercer Cook. Westport, Conn. : Greenwood Press, 1987, c1961. xii, 145 p. ; 23 cm. Translation of: Nations africaines et solidarité mondiale. Reprint. Originally published: New York : F.A. Praeger, 1961. ISBN 0-313-24569-X (lib. bdg. : alk. paper) LC Card 86-25734 DDC 330.96/03 19
1. Africa - Economic conditions - 1918-1945. 2. Africa - Foreign economic relations. 3. Nationalism - Africa. 4. Mali - Economic conditions. 5. Mali - Foreign economic relations. I. Title.
HC800 .D5213 1987

Los diablos del petróleo /. Leduc, Renato. [Mexico City, Mexico] [1986] 131 p. ; LC Card 86-219535 DDC 338.2/7282/0972 19
HD9574.M62 P3745 1986

DIAGNOSIS - DATA PROCESSING.
George, J. John. Opportunities in computer-assisted medical diagnostics . Menlo Park, Calif. (333 Ravenswood Ave., Menlo Park 94025-3476) , c1985. 32 p. : LC Card 86-232002 DDC 381/.45681761 19
HD9995.D543 U63 1985

DIAGNOSIS, LABORATORY - EQUIPMENT AND SUPPLIES.
Specimen collection and transport market. Tustin, CA, U. S.A. (17722 Irvine Blvd., Tustin 92680) , c1987. 1 v. (various foliations) : LC Card 87-402105 DDC 380.1/45681761 19
HD9995.L32 S64 1987

DIAGNOSTIC EQUIPMENT INDUSTRY - UNITED STATES.
George, J. John. Opportunities in computer-assisted medical diagnostics . Menlo Park, Calif. (333 Ravenswood Ave., Menlo Park 94025-3476) , c1985. 32 p. : LC Card 86-232002 DDC 381/.45681761 19
HD9995.D543 U63 1985

Le diagnostic financier de l'entreprise . Glais, Michel. Paris , 1984. 256 p. : ISBN 2-7178-0787-X : LC Card 85-105905
HG4011 .G56 1984

The Diagnostic radiology market in the U. S. New York, N.Y. : Frost & Sullivan, c1983. xxxix, 261 p. : ill. ; 29 cm. "June, 1983." "#A1174." LC Card 87-143803 DDC 381/.45681761 19
1. Radioscopic diagnostic equipment industry - United States. 2. Market surveys - United States. I. Frost & Sullivan.
HD9995.R333 U53 1983

Diagnóstico del sector industrial forestal /. Flores Rodas, José G. (José Guillermo) San José, Costa Rica , 1985. 116 p. : ISBN 997-7642-33-8 LC Card 86-218084
HD9764.C82 F56 1985

Diagnóstico energético, 1978/1983 / Governo do Estado de Minas Gerais, CEMIG--Companhia Energética de Minas Gerais, Conselho Estadual de Energia, Secretaria de Estado de Minas e Energia. Belo Horizonte : CEMIG, 1985. 177 p. : ill. ; 30 cm. LC Card 87-121240 DDC 333.79/0981/51 19
1. Energy industries - Brazil - Minas Gerais. 2. Energy consumption - Brazil - Minas Gerais. I. Companhia Energética de Minas Gerais.
HD9502.B73 M563 1985

Diagnóstico general de la Corporación Minera de Bolivia, 1985 : propuesta de la Federación Sindical de Trabajadores Mineros de Bolivia. La Paz, Bolivia : La Federación, 1986. 2 v. ; 34 cm. Vol. 2 has title: Conclusiones y recomendaciones propuestas por la Federación Sindical de Trabajadores Mineros de Bolivia para aplicación : plan de emergencia, gestión 1986-1987 : COMIBOL. LC Card 87-401587 DDC 338.2/0984 19
1. Corporación Minera de Bolivia. 2. Mineral industries - Government policy - Bolivia. 3. Mineral industries - Government ownership - Bolivia. I. Federación Sindical de Trabajadores Mineros de Bolivia. II. Title: Conclusiones y recomendaciones propuestas por la Federación Sindical de Trabajadores Mineros de Bolivia para aplicación.
HD9506.B64 C646 1986

Diagnóstico situacional del movimiento cooperativo peruano /. Wester León, Humberto. [Lima] , 1981- v. : ***NYPL [JLL 86-146]***

Diagnóstico técnico-económico de la actividad agrícola de los principales valles de la costa peruana. La Agricultura en la costa del Perú, 1978-1984 /. Lima, Perú , 1985. ca. 150 leaves : LC Card 87-403706 DDC 338.1/0985 19
HD1905.P33 A38 1985

Diagnóstico y debate .
(20) Ponce Vega, Luis. El propietario ausente . Lima , 1986. 80 p. ; LC Card 86-221571
HD9524.P44 S565 1986

(22) Aste Daffos, Juan. Minería peruana . Lima , 1986. 102 p. ; LC Card 87-143088 DDC 338.2/0985 19
HD9506.P42 A827 1986

Dialéctica de la administración . Garciacastillo, Rafael. México , 1983. 117 p. ; ISBN 968-597-416-0 LC Card 85-215880
HD37.S66 G38 1983

DIALECTS. see **LANGUAGE AND LANGUAGES.**

Dialektika ob″ektivnogo i sub″ektivnogo v razvitii nauchno-tekhnicheskoĭ revoli͡utsii /. Ergashev, A. (Atakul) Tashkent , 1980. 185 p. ; LC Card 81-143159
HC337.U963 T44 1980

A dialética da atividade pesqueira no nordeste amazônico /. Penner, Maria Eunice Soares. Belém , 1984. 158 p. : ISBN 85-24-70006-8 LC Card 86-158128
HD9464.B73 N676 1984

DIALOG (INFORMATION RETRIEVAL SYSTEM) - HANDBOOKS, MANUALS, ETC.
Search ACT . Louisville, Ky. , c1986. 1 v. (various pagings) ; ISBN 0-914604-27-9 LC Card 86-215617 DDC 025/.06004 19
HD9696.C62 S43 1986

O diálogo norte-sul /. Machado, Vera Barrouin Crivano. Brasília, DF , 1983. 58 p. ; LC Card 86-171831
HF1412 .M33 1983

Dialogues on development . Roy, Ramashray. New Delhi , Beverly Hills , 1986. 245 p. ; ISBN 0-8039-9492-3 (U. S.) LC Card 85-8368 DDC 338.954/12 19
HD87 .R69 1986 ***NYPL [JLD 86-3196]***

DIAMOND INDUSTRY AND TRADE - AUSTRALIA - HISTORY.
Joris, Albert, 1915- A destiny in diamonds /. Spring, Hill, Brisbane, Qld. , Portland, OR , 1986. vi, 113 p. : ISBN 0-86439-011-4 LC Card 87-161024 DDC 338.2/782/0924 B 19
HD9677.A82 J675 1986

DIAMOND INDUSTRY AND TRADE - BRAZIL - HISTORY.
Ciclo da mineração /. Rio de Janeiro-RJ , 1984. 95 p. : LC Card 85-186500
HD9536.B82 C56 1984

DIAMOND INDUSTRY AND TRADE - SOUTH AFRICA - HISTORY - 19TH CENTURY.
Wheatcroft, Geoffrey. The Randlords /. New York , 1987, c1985. xix, 314 p. : ISBN 0-671-63993-5 (pbk.) : LC Card 87-4513 DDC 338.2/0968 19
HD9536.S62 W44 1985

DIAMOND INDUSTRY AND TRADE - SOUTH AFRICA - KIMBERLEY - HISTORY.
Turrell, Robert Vicat. Capital and labour on the Kimberley diamond fields, 1871-1890 /. Cambridge [Cambridgeshire] , New York , 1987. xviii, 297 p. : ISBN 0-521-33354-7 LC Card 86-32740 DDC 331.7/622382/0968711 19
HD9677.S63 K567 1987

DIAMOND INDUSTRY AND TRADE - SOUTH AFRICA - KIMBERLEY - HISTORY - 19TH CENTURY.
Worger, William H. South Africa's city of diamonds . New Haven , c1987. xvi, 330 p. : ISBN 0-300-03716-3 (alk. paper) LC Card 86-24724 DDC 331.7/622382/0968711 19
HD9677.S63 K568 1987

Diamond, Jay. Pintel, Gerald. Retailing /. Englewood Cliffs, N.J. , c1987. iv, 488 p. : ISBN 0-13-778549-6 LC Card 86-25397 DDC 658.8/7 19
HF5429 .P57 1987

Diamond jubilee conference on technology management '85. Technology management '85 . London , c1985. 160 p. : ISBN 0-903748-61-4
NYPL [JLG 87-124]

Diamond, Michael A. Flamholtz, Eric. Principles of accounting /. New York , London , c1987. xli, 1159, [90] p. : ISBN 0-02-338210-4 LC Card 86-31086 DDC 657 19
HF5635 .F5645 1987

DIAMOND MINERS - SOUTH AFRICA - KIMBERLEY - HISTORY.
Turrell, Robert Vicat. Capital and labour on the Kimberley diamond fields, 1871-1890 /. Cambridge [Cambridgeshire] , New York , 1987. xviii, 297 p. : ISBN 0-521-33354-7 LC Card 86-32740 DDC 331.7/622382/0968711 19
HD9677.S63 K567 1987

DIAMOND MINERS - SOUTH AFRICA - KIMBERLEY - HISTORY - 19TH CENTURY.
Worger, William H. South Africa's city of diamonds . New Haven , c1987. xvi, 330 p. : ISBN 0-300-03716-3 (alk. paper) LC Card 86-24724 DDC 331.7/622382/0968711 19
HD9677.S63 K568 1987

Diamond thin film : the threshold of commercialization. Norwalk, Conn. : International Resource Development, c1987. iv, 136 leaves : ill. ; 28 cm. (Report / International Resource Development . #733) "April 1987." Bibliography: leaves 124-133. LC Card 87-157102 DDC 380.1/4566029453 19
1. Diamond thin film industry. 2. Market surveys. I. International Resource Development, inc. II. Series: Report / International Resource Development , #733.
HD9999.T492 D52 1987

DIAMOND THIN FILM INDUSTRY.
Diamond thin film . Norwalk, Conn. , c1987. iv, 136 leaves : LC Card 87-157102 DDC 380.1/4566029453 19
HD9999.T492 D52 1987

DIAMOND TOOLS. see **DIAMONDS, INDUSTRIAL.**

DIAMONDS AS AN INVESTMENT.
Sterne, George F. Investment opportunities for the mid 1980's . San Diego, Calif. , c1985. 304 p. ; ISBN 0-940398-11-7 : LC Card 78-64396
NYPL [JLE 86-1720]

DIAMONDS, INDUSTRIAL - AUSTRALIA - HISTORY.
Joris, Albert, 1915- A destiny in diamonds /. Spring, Hill, Brisbane, Qld. , Portland, OR , 1986. vi, 113 p. : ISBN 0-86439-011-4 LC Card 87-161024 DDC 338.2/782/0924 B 19
HD9677.A82 J675 1986

DiAntonio, Angelo E. Spreadsheet applications in financial accounting / Angelo E. DiAntonio. Englewood Cliffs, N.J. : Prentice-Hall, c1986. xvii, 391 p. : ill. ; 24 cm. "A Reston book." Includes index. ISBN 0-8359-6945-2 (pbk.) : LC Card 85-14303 DDC 657/.028/553 19
1. Accounting - Data processing. 2. Electronic spreadsheets. I. Title.
HF5679 .D52 1986 *NYPL [JLE 86-3100]*

Diário da navegação de Macau, 1759-1761 : códice no. 183, do Arquivo Histórico do Ministério das Finanças. Lisboa : Agência-Geral do Ultramar, 1970. 274 p. ; 24 cm. Includes index. LC Card 86-201114
1. Companhia Geral do Grão Pará e Maranhão - History - 18th century. 2. Trading companies - Macao - History - 18th century. I. Portugal. Ministerio das Finanças. Arquivo Histórico.
HF1009.7.M25 D53 1970

Dias, Renato Rodrigues. Canais de distribuição na indústria do mobiliário do Rio Grande do Sul / Renato Rodrigues Dias. Santa Maria-RS [Brazil] : Edições UFSM, 1983. 171 p. : ill. ; 23 cm. Bibliography: p. 169-171. LC Card 86-135650
1. Furniture industry and trade - Brazil - Rio Grande do Sul. I. Title.
HD9773.B73 R563 1983

Dias, Victor Manuel Pina. Pereira, Francisco José Piteira. A cultura da vinha na região do Redondo /. [Lisbon] , 1983. 11, 4, 30, 21 leaves, [2] leaves of plates : LC Card 84-238378
HD9259.G7 P47 1983

DIASPORA. see **ISRAEL AND THE DIASPORA.**

DISASTERS - ECONOMIC ASPECTS - MEXICO - MEXICO CITY REGION.
Esto pasó en México /. México, D.F. [1985] 126 p. : ISBN 968-415-098-9 LC Card 87-403762 DDC 363.3/495/097253 19
HC138.M4 E84 1985

Díaz Alejandro, Carlos Federico. Trade, development and the world economy : selected essays of Carlos Díaz-Alejandro / edited by Andrés Velasco. Oxford, OX, UK ; New York, NY, USA : B. Blackwell, 1988. p. cm. Includes bibliographical references and index. ISBN 0-631-15687-9 : LC Card 87-20836 DDC 337.8 19
1. Latin America - Foreign economic relations. 2. Latin America - Economic conditions - 1945-. 3. Economic stabilization - Latin America. 4. Investments, Foreign - Latin America. I. Velasco, Andrés. II. Title.
HF1480.5 .D52 1988

Díaz Arenas, Pedro Agustín. Latinoamérica, hiel y miel / Pedro Agustín Díaz Arenas ; [ilustraciones Alberto Cárdenas Patiño]. Bogotá : Editorial El Buho, 1982. 120 p. : ill. ; 17 cm. LC Card 83-103872
1. Latin America - Economic conditions - 1945-. 2. Latin America - Social conditions - 1945-. 3. Latin America - Politics and government - 1948-. I. Title.
HC125 .D535 1982

Diaz-Briquets, Sergio. Conflict in Central America : the demographic dimension / by Sergio Diaz-Briquets. Washington, D.C. (777 14th St. NW, Washington 20005) : Population Reference Bureau, 1986. 16 p. : ill. ; 26 cm. (Population trends and public policy, 0736-7716 . no. 10 (Feb. 1986)) Cover title. Bibliography: p. 16. LC Card 87-401095 DDC 304.6/09728 19
1. Central America - Population. I. Series: Population trends and public policy , no. 10. II. Title.
HB3533 .D5 1986

Díaz, Carlos Federico. see **Díaz Alejandro, Carlos Federico.**

Díaz del Moral, Juan, 1870-1948. Las agitaciones campesinas del período bolchevista, 1918-1920 / Juan Díaz del Moral. Sevilla : Editoriales Andaluzas Unidas, [1985?] 230 p. ; 19 cm. (Biblioteca de la cultura andaluza . 23.) Includes bibliographical references. ISBN 84-7587-031-7 LC Card 86-181529
1. Agricultural laborers - Spain - Córdoba (Province) - History - 20th century. 2. Communism - Spain - Córdoba (Province) - History - 20th century. 3. Córdoba (Spain : Province) - Rural conditions. I. Series: Biblioteca de la culura andaluza , 23. II. Title.
HD1536.S7 D48 1985

Díaz Gómez, Jorge. Deterioro de los términos de intercambio, migración eventual y pobreza campesina en el departamento del Cusco / Jorge Díaz Gómez. [Cuzco, Peru] : Universidad Nacional San Antonio Abad del Cusco, Instituto de Investigación UNSAAC-NUFFIC, 1986. 17, 3 leaves, 2 leaves of plates : ill. ; 31 cm. (Serie Avances de investigación) "Convenio de cooperación inter universitaria peruano-holandés"--Cover. LC Card 86-200938
1. Peasantry - Peru - Cuzco (Dept.). 2. Cuzco (Peru : Dept.) - Population. 3. Labor supply - Peru - Cuzco (Dept.). I. Instituto de Investigación UNSAAC-NUFFIC. II. Series: Serie Avances de Investigación (Cuzco, Peru). III. Title.
HD1531.P4 D52 1986

Díaz, Jorge [i. e. Jorge Díaz Gómez] see **Díaz Gómez, Jorge.**

Diaz, Manuel Burga. see **Burga, Manuel.**

Díaz Martínez, Antonio, 1933- Ayacucho : hambre y esperanza / Antonio Díaz Martínez.2a ed. Lima : Mosca Azul Editores, 1985. xvi, 224 p. ; 21 cm. Bibliography: p. 219-222. LC Card 86-134530
1. Ayacucho, Peru (Dept.) - Economic conditions. 2. Ayacucho, Peru (Dept.) - Social conditions. 3. Poor - Peru - Ayacucho (Dept.). I. Title.
HC228.A9 D5 1985

Díaz O., Oswaldo A. Ecuador, estudios retrospectivos / Oswaldo A. Díaz O. 1a ed. Bogotá, Colombia : Ediciones Tercer Mundo, 1980. 120 p. ; 20 cm. Includes bibliographical references. CONTENTS. - El latifundio en el Ecuador -- El plan andino en el Ecuador -- La política agraria de Arosemena -- Notas sobre la clase media del Ecuador -- Cambios sociales de las clases dominantes del Ecuador -- Los partidos políticos del Ecuador -- Ecuador, entre la revolución y el miedo -- La crisis económica de las universidades ecuatorianas -- Anexos: Gran descubrimiento arqueológico en Ecuador. Ecuador's loss. Respuesta al Gramma. LC Card 83-147164
1. Ecuador - Economic conditions - 1918-. 2. Ecuador - Social conditions. 3. Ecuador - Politics and government - 1944-. I. Title.
HC202 .D48 1980

Díaz Ontiveros, Raúl. Ramírez L., Fernando (Ramírez López) Estado y crisis del desarrollo nacional . México, D.F. , 1983. 242 p. ; LC Card 86-220975
HC135 .R234 1983

Díaz, Regino.
DiBacco, Thomas V. Made in the U. S.A. : the history of American business / Thomas V. DiBacco.1st ed. New York : Harper & Row, c1987. xii, 290 p. ; 22 cm. Includes index. Bibliography: p. 277-278. ISBN 0-06-015624-4 : LC Card 86-45652 DDC 338.0973 19
1. Business enterprises - United States - History. 2. Capitalists and financiers - United States - History. 3. Entrepreneur - History. 4. United States - Industries - History. I. Title. II. Title: Made in the USA.
HC103 .D46 1987 *NYPL [JLD 87-1292]*

Dibattiti contemporanei.
Convegno nazionale "Qualche idea sui fiumi" (1983 : Iesi, Italy) Atti del Convegno nazionale "Qualche idea sui fiumi," Jesi, aprile 1983. Ancona , c1983-c1984. 2 v. ; ISBN 88-7663-030-9 (v. 1) : LC Card 84-119835
HD1697.I8 C62 1983 *NYPL [JLK 87-40]*

Dible, Donald M. Up your own organizaion! : a handbook for today's entrepreneur / by Donald M. Dible ; edited by Jeannine Marschner ; introduction by Robert Townsend.[Rev. ed.] Reston, Va. : Reston Pub. Co., c1986. xx, 423 p. ; 24 cm. Includes bibliographies and index. ISBN 0-8359-8086-3 (pbk.) : LC Card 85-8293 DDC 658/.022 19
1. Small business - Management. 2. Small business - Finance. I. Title.
HD62.7 .D53 1986 *NYPL [*R-Econ. 86-288]*

Diccionario de economía /. Zorrilla, Santiago. México, D.F. , c1986. 182 p. : ISBN 968-493-060-7 LC Card 87-401043 DDC 330/.03/61 19
HB61 .Z63 1986

Dichmann, Werner. Nationalökonomie und Realität : Grundzüge einer historistischen Theorie und Politik sozialen Handelns / von Werner Dichmann. Berlin : Duncker & Humblot, c1983. 488 p. ; 24 cm. (Volkswirtschaftliche Schriften. Heft 336) Originally presented as the author's thesis (doctoral)--Universität Freiburg/Br., 1981. Bibliography: p. [471]-488. ISBN 3-428-05517-9 LC Card 84-172295
1. Economics. I. Title. II. Series.
HB71 .D48 1983

Dichtl, Erwin.
Die Wirksamkeit staatlicher Mittelstandsförderung im Einzelhandel /. Berlin , c1981. 223 p. : ISBN 3-428-04919-5 LC Card 82-175986 DDC 658.8 s 338.6/42/0943 19
HF5415.A2 S37 Bd. 12 HD2346.G3
NYPL [JLE 86-3464]

Exporte als Herausforderung für die deutsche Wirtschaft /. Köln , c1984. 469 p. : ISBN 3-602-34842-3 LC Card 85-139543
HF3564 .E96 1984

Dicionário inglês-português de termos econômicos & comerciais /. Cavalcante, José Cândido Marques. [Fortaleza] , Petrópolis , 1979. 408 p. ; LC Card 80-113110
HB61 .C37 *NYPL [JLE 81-244]*

Dick, Walter, 1949- Die ökonomische Bedeutung der Qualität des Schienengüterverkehrs : eine Analyse am Beispiel des Landes Nordrhein-Westfalen / von Walter Dick. Berlin : Duncker & Humblot, c1980. xi, 331 p. : 10 ill. ; 24 cm. (Verkehrswissenschaftliche Forschungen. Bd. 41) Bibliography: p. 295-[309] Includes index. ISBN 3-428-04731-1 LC Card 84-130833
1. Railroads - Germany (West) - North Rhine-Westphalia - Freight - Case studies. 2. North Rhine-Westphalia (Germany) - Economic conditions - Case studies. I. Title. II. Series.
HE2446.N67 D52 1980

Dick Young Productions.
Going for it [motion picture] /. New York,

NY , 1987. 1 film reel (12 min.) : LC Card 87-705727 DDC 331.3 11
HD6275

Going for it [videorecording] /. New York, NY , 1987. 1 videocassette (12 min.) : LC Card 87-705728 DDC 331.3 11
HD6275

Dickason, Clifford. Sloggett, Gordon. Ground-water mining in the United States /. Washington, D.C , 1986. iv, 19 p. : LC Card 86-602788 DDC 338.1 s 338.1/4 19
HD1751 .A91854 no. 555 S616.U6

Dicke, Detlev Christian. Foreign debts in the present and a new international economic order /. Boulder , 1987, c1986. p. cm. ISBN 0-8133-0489-X : LC Card 87-2185 DDC 336.3/435 19
HG3891.5 .F67 1987

Dickens, Rodney. Overseas experience with "strict" monetary targetry and its implications for New Zealand / Rodney Dickens. Wellington : Reserve Bank of New Zealand, [1986] iii, 24 leaves ; 30 cm. (Discussion paper . no. G86/7) "November 1986." Bibliography: leaves 22-24. LC Card 87-137038 DDC 332.4/9931 19
1. Monetary policy. 2. Monetary policy - New Zealand. I. Series: Discussion paper (Reserve Bank of New Zealand. Economic Dept.) , no. G86/7. II. Title.
HG230.3 .D53 1986

Dickerman, C. Robert. Die Wirtschaft der Vereinigten Staaten und der Bundesrepublik Deutschland . Bonn , c1977. 106 p. ; ISBN 3-87198-079-X LC Card 86-104673
HC106.7 .W57 1977

Dickerson, Charles S.
Commercial lending by thrift institutions : a management perspective / Charles S. Dickerson.2nd ed. Philadelphia, Pa. : R. Morris Associates, c1987. 50 p. ; 28 cm. ISBN 0-936742-39-9 (pbk.) LC Card 87-161133 DDC 332.7 19
1. Credit. 2. Commercial loans. I. Title.
HG3751 .D53 1987

Current approaches to grading commercial loans / Charles S. Dickerson. Philadelphia, Pa. : R. Morris Associates, c1987. 42 p. ; 23 cm. ISBN 0-936742-43-7 (pbk.) LC Card 87-18458 DDC 332.1/753/0685 19
1. Bank loans - United States. 2. Commercial loans - United States. I. Title.
HG1642.U5 D53 1987

Dickerson, Dennis C., 1949- Out of the crucible : Black steelworkers in western Pennsylvania, 1875-1980 / Dennis C. Dickerson. Albany : State University of New York Press, c1986. xiv, 323 p. : ill. ; 24 cm. (SUNY series in Afro-American studies) Includes bibliographical references and index. ISBN 0-88706-305-5 LC Card 85-30450 DDC 331.6/3/960730748 19
1. Afro-American iron and steel workers - Pennsylvania - History. 2. Afro-Americans - Employment - Pennsylvania - History. 3. Discrimination in employment - Pennsylvania - History. I. Title. II. Series.
HD8039.I52 U535 1986
NYPL [JLE 86-4411]

Dickhut, Harold W., 1911- The executive résumé handbook / Harold W. Dickhut. 1st ed. New York : Prentice Hall, c1987. vii, 215 p. ; 28 cm. Bibliography: p. 212-213. Includes index. ISBN 0-13-294331-X (pbk.) : LC Card 86-22692 DDC 650.1/4/024658 19
1. Résumés (Employment). 2. Executives. 3. Professions. 4. Job hunting. I. Title.
HF5383 .D469 1987

Dickie, Robert B.
Corporations and the common good /. Notre Dame, Ind. [Boston] , c1986. xii, 147 p. ; ISBN 0-268-00754-3 : LC Card 85-40597 DDC 174/.4 19
HB501 .C7614 1986 NYPL [JLD 86-2145]

Foreign investment and government policy in the Third World / Robert B. Dickie, Thomas A. Layman. New York : St. Martin's Press, 1988. p. cm. Includes bibliographies and index. ISBN 0-312-00520-2 : LC Card 87-25076 DDC 332.6/7322598 19
1. Investments, Foreign - Government policy - Indonesia. 2. Stock-exchange - Indonesia. 3. Stocks - Indonesia. I. Layman, Thomas A. II. Title.
HG5752 .D53 1988

Dickinson, Richard L., 1938- West, Bill W. Street talk in real estate /. Alameda, Calif. [1987] vi, 216 p. : ISBN 0-934189-04-8 (pbk. : trade) : LC Card 86-50605 DDC 333.33/03/21 19
HD1365 .W47 1987

Dickman, Fred. Employee assistance programs . Springfield, Ill., U. S.A. , c1988. xxiv, 493 p. ; ISBN 0-398-05401-0 LC Card 87-21048 DDC 658.3/82 19
HF5549.5.E42 E47 1988

Dickson, P. G. M. (Peter George Muir) Finance and government under Maria Theresia, 1740-1780 / P.G.M. Dickson. Oxford [Oxfordshire] : Clarendon Press ; New York : Oxford University Press, 1987. 2 v. : ill. ; 23 cm. Includes indexes. Bibliography: v. 2, p. [429]-445. CONTENTS. - v. 1. Society and government -- v. 2. Finance and credit. ISBN 0-19-822570-9 (v. 1) : LC Card 87-1614 DDC 336.436 19
1. Finance, Public - Austria - History - 18th century. 2. Austria - Politics and government - 1740-1780. 3. Social structure - Austria - History - 18th century. I. Maria Theresa, Empress of Austria, 1717-1780. II. Title.
HJ1059 .D52 1987

Dictation Disc Company. Blanc, Iris. DDC spreadsheets. [New York, N.Y.] [c1986] 161 p. : LC Card 87-159255 DDC 005.3/07/1273 19
HF5548.2 .B527 1986

DICTATION (OFFICE PRACTICE)
Matthews, Anne L. Managerial dictation /. Cincinnati , c1987. 76 p. : ISBN 0-538-07950-9 (pbk.) LC Card 86-63922 DDC 651.7/4 19
HF5547.5 .M383 1987

DICTATORS - SPAIN - HISTORY - 20TH CENTURY.
Nieto de Alba, Ubaldo, 1931- De la dictadura al socialismo democrático . Madrid , c1984. 269 p. ; ISBN 84-7209-177-5 LC Card 86-146735 DDC 338.946 19
HC385 .N49 1984 NYPL [JLD 86-2390]

Dictionary al fareed in finance & economics, English - Arabic. Farīd, 'Abd Allāh Muḥammad. al-Qāmūs al-farīd fī al-māl wa-al-iqtiṣād, 'Arabī-Injilīzī /. [S.l.] 1985 (al-Qāhirah, Miṣr : Maṭābi' al-Ahrām al-Tijārīyah) 150, 264 p. ; LC Card 86-960655
HB61 .F36 1985

Dictionary of administration and management . Banki, Ivan S. Los Angeles, Calif., USA , c1986. iv, 1369 p. ; ISBN 0-912352-08-6 LC Card 85-63870 DDC 650/.03/21 19
HD30.15 .B36 1986

Dictionary of advertising. Koschnick, Wolfgang J., 1942- Standard-Wörterbuch für Werbung, Massenmedien und Marketing, Deutsch-Englisch /. Berlin , New York , 1987. 590 p. ; ISBN 0-89925-293-1 (U. S.) : LC Card 87-19928 DDC 659.1/03/21 19
HF5803 .K67 1987

Dictionary of advertising and direct mail terms /. Imber, Jane. New York , c1987. xi, 514 p. : ISBN 0-8120-3765-0 (pbk.) : LC Card 87-1197 DDC 659.1/03/21 19
HF5803 .I46 1987

Dictionary of banking and financial services /. Rosenberg, Jerry Martin. New York , c1985. xv, 708 p. ; ISBN 0-471-83088-7 LC Card 85-12461 DDC 332/.03/21 19
HG151 .R67 1985
*NYPL [*R-Econ. 86-3275]*

Dictionary of business biography : a biographical dictionary of business leaders active in Britain in the period 1860-1980 / edited by David J. Jeremy ; foreword by the Duke of Edinburgh. London : Butterworths, 1984. 5 v. : ill. ; 26 cm. 1 supplement (120 p. ; 25 cm.) Supplement includes indexes, contributors, errata. Includes bibliographies. Library wanting supplement. CONTENTS. - v. 1. A-C -- v. 2. D-G -- v. 3. H-L -- v. 4. Mc-R -- v. 5. S-Z. ISBN 0-406-27340-5 (set) LC Card 86-188034 DDC 338/.0092/2 B 19
1. Businessmen - Great Britain - Biography - Dictionaries. 2. Industrialists - Great Britain - Biography - Dictionaries. 3. Capitalists and financiers - Great Britain - Biography - Dictionaries. I. Jeremy, David J.
HC252.5.A2 D53 1984 NYPL [JLM 86-569]

A dictionary of business terms /. AHI's complete portfolio of modern business terms. New York , 1987, c1986. 438 p. ; ISBN 0-531-15518-8 LC Card 86-24560 DDC 650/.03/21 19
HF1001 .A34 1987

Dictionary of business terms /. Friedman, Jack P. New York , c1987. vi, 650 p. ; ISBN 0-8120-3775-8 (pbk.) : LC Card 87-12640 DDC 650/.03/21 19
HF1001 .F78 1987

A Dictionary of economics & commerce : English-Arabic / compiled and edited by the Dictionaries Department, Librairie du Liban. Beirut : Librairie du Liban, 1983. 383 p. ; 25 cm. Title on added t.p.: Qāmūs al-iqtiṣād wa-al-tijārah. LC Card 83-961782 DDC 330/.03/21 19
1. Economics - Dictionaries. 2. Commerce - Dictionaries. 3. English language - Dictionaries - Arabic. I. Librairie du Liban. Dictionaries Dept. II. Title: Dictionary of economics and commerce. III. Title: Qāmūs al-iqtiṣād wa-al-tijārah.
*HB61 .D4896 1983 NYPL [*OEO 87-1397]*

Dictionary of economics and commerce. A Dictionary of economics & commerce . Beirut , 1983. 383 p. ; LC Card 83-961782 DDC 330/.03/21 19
*HB61 .D4896 1983 NYPL [*OEO 87-1397]*

Dictionary of geography. Majma' al-Lughah al-'Arabīyah, Cairo. Lajnat al-Jughrāfīyā. al-Mu'jam al-jughrāfī /. [al-Qāhirah] , 1974. 9,185 p. ; LC Card 77-961221
*G63 .M34 1974 NYPL [*OEO 86-3694]*

Dictionary of Holland occupational codes /. Gottfredson, Gary D. Palo Alto, CA , c1982. xviii, 500 p. ; ISBN 0-89106-020-X
NYPL [JLE 86-3992]

Dictionary of insurance terms /. Rubin, Harvey W. New York , c1987. ix, 371 p. ; ISBN 0-8120-3772-3 (pbk.) : LC Card 87-12549 DDC 368/.003/21 19
HG8025 .R83 1987

A dictionary of international finance /. Walmsley, Julian. Westport, Conn. , 1979. 270 p. ; ISBN 0-313-20974-X LC Card 79-17753 DDC 332/.042/0321 19
HG151 .W34 NYPL [JLD 87-1082]

Dictionary of legal, commercial and political terms. Erdsiek, Gerhard. Wörterbuch für Recht, Wirtschaft und Politik. Bleckede bei Hamburg [1964-1968] 2 v. LC Card 65-42077
NYPL [JLE 85-408]

Dictionary of occupational titles / U. S. Department of Labor, Employment and Training Administration, U. S. Employment Service. 4th ed. [Washington] : The Administration : for sale by the Supt. of Docs., U. S. Govt. Print. Off., 1977. xli, 1371 p. ; 28 cm. Supplement (xiii, 36 p. ; 28 cm) published 1982. Includes indexes. LC Card 78-601723 DDC 331.7/003
1. Occupations - Dictionaries. 2. Occupations - Classification. 3. United States - Occupations.
HB2595 .U543 1977
*NYPL [*R-TMH 78-1740]*

Dictionary of occupational titles. Gottfredson, Gary D. Dictionary of Holland occupational codes /. Palo Alto, CA , c1982. xviii, 500 p. ; ISBN 0-89106-020-X *NYPL [JLE 86-3992]*

Dictionary of personnel management and labor relations. Shafritz, Jay M. The Facts on File dictionary of personnel management and labor relations /. New York, N.Y. , c1985. 534 p. : ISBN 0-8160-1234-2 LC Card 85-20823 DDC 658.3/003/21 19
HF5549.A23 S52 1985
NYPL [JLE 86-4748]

Dictionary of printed circuit technology . Böhss, Günther. Amsterdam , New York , 1985. 187 p. ; ISBN 0-444-99555-2 (U. S.) : LC Card 85-12955 DDC 621.381/74/0331 19
TK7868.P7 B65 1985 NYPL [JSD 86-621]

The Dictionary of real estate appraisal. Chicago, Ill. : American Institute of Real Estate Appraisers, c1984. ix, 368 p. ; 24 cm. Bibliography: p. 333-368. ISBN 0-911780-74-2 LC Card 84-16834 DDC 333.33/2/0321 19
1. Real property - Valuation - Dictionaries. 2. Real estate business - Dictionaries. 3. Real property - Dictionaries.
HD1387 .D435 1984 NYPL [JLE 86-2371]

Dictionary of real estate terms /. Friedman, Jack P. New York , c1987. v, 329 p. : ISBN 0-8120-3898-3 (pbk.) : LC Card 87-19869

DDC 333.33/03/21 19
HD1365 .F75 1987

Dictionary of road transport terminology in four languages, English, French, German, and Spanish / compiled by International Road Transport Union. Amsterdam ; New York : Elsevier, 1988. xxviii, 351 p. ; 25 cm. ISBN 0-444-42819-4 : LC Card 87-13397 DDC 388/.03 19
1. Transportation, Automotive - Dictionaries - Polyglot. 2. Dictionaries, Polyglot. I. International Road Transport Union.
HE5613 .D53 1988

Dictionary of shipping terms /. Brodie, Peter R., 1947- London , New York , 1985. 155 p. ; ISBN 1-85044-069-7 (pbk.) : LC Card 86-164175 DDC 387.5/03/21 19
HE567 .B68 1985

Dictionary of worker traits /. Kerns, Allen F. Philadelphia, PA , 1987- p. cm. ISBN 0-9618599-9-7 LC Card 87-12478 DDC 331.7/02/0973 19
HB2595 .K43 1987

Dictionary of Yugoslav political and economic terminology. Andrlić, Vlasta. Rječnik terminologije jugoslavenskog političko-ekonomskog sistema . Zagreb , 1985. viii, 135 p. ; LC Card 86-182784
HB61 .A55 1985 ***NYPL [*QKK 87-1803]***

Dictionary, welding, cutting and allied processes. Kleiber, Achim W. Fachwörterbuch, Schweissen, Schneiden und verwandte Verfahren /. Düsseldorf , 1986- , c1985- v. ; ISBN 3-87155-707-2 (Bd. 1) LC Card 86-149500 DDC 671.5/2/0331 19
TS227.5 .K54 1986 ***NYPL [JSK 86-83]***

Dictionnaire américain-anglais-français du management /. Tixier, Maud. Paris , 1985. 381 p. ; ISBN 2-247-00647-7 : LC Card 86-160705
HD30.15 .T59 1985 ***NYPL [JLD 86-3975]***

Dictionnaire biographique du mouvement ouvrier international. Maitron, Jean. Paris, 1971-<c1985. <1-2, 5 > ISBN 2-7082-1955-3 (v. 2) LC Card 72-333529
HD4851 .M34

Dictionnaire des termes de marine français-anglais & anglais-français. Witcomb, Henry, 1822- Paris, 1883. 2 v. LC Card 29-23644
V24 .W5 ***NYPL [JSE 86-1965]***

Dictionnaire du management. Tixier, Maud. Dictionnaire américain-anglais-français du management /. Paris , 1985. 381 p. ; ISBN 2-247-00647-7 : LC Card 86-160705
HD30.15 .T59 1985 ***NYPL [JLD 86-3975]***

Did British capitalism breed inequality? /. Williamson, Jeffrey G., 1935- Boston , 1985. ix, 270 p. : ISBN 0-04-942186-7 : LC Card 84-20413 DDC 339.2/2/0941 19
HC260.I5 W45 1985 ***NYPL [JLE 86-1361]***

Didier, Michel, 1940- Economie : les règles du jeu / Michel Didier. Paris : Economica, 1984. 243 p. : ill. ; 24 cm. Bibliography: p. 235-239. ISBN 2-7178-0710-1 : LC Card 84-166256
1. Economics. I. Title.
HB173 .D455 1984

Die. see **Deutsches Institut für Entwicklungspolitik.**

Die algerisch-französische Arbeitsmigration . Voss, Timm. Königstein/Ts. , 1981. xiii, 193 p. : ISBN 3-7756-6937-X : LC Card 81-176949 DDC 331.6/2/65044 19
HD8438.A4 V67 1981 ***NYPL [JLD 86-2466]***

Die Anfänge der Raiffeisenkassen in Oberösterreich (1889-1914) . Kreinecker, Günther. Linz , c1982. xvi, 276 p. : ISBN 3-85320-279-9 LC Card 83-224597
HG2051.A89 U64 1982
NYPL [JLE 87-2440]

Die Aussenwanderung jugoslawischer Arbeitskräfte . Künne, Wilfried. Königstein/Ts. , 1979. xii, 269 p. : ISBN 3-7756-6931-0 : LC Card 79-394439
HD8633.5 .K83 ***NYPL [JLD 87-1148]***

Die Bankgeschäfte.
Glogowski, Erhard. Neue Finanzdienstleistungen . Wiesbaden , c1986. 305 p. : ISBN 3-409-14101-4 LC Card 87-131647
DDC 332.1/0943 19
HG3048 .G57 1986

Die Bedeutung des Osthandels für mittelständische Unternehmen /. Weimer, Theodor. Stuttgart , c1985. 172, 7 p. : ISBN 3-7910-5006-0 LC Card 86-160626
HF3568.E35 W43 1985
NYPL [JLL 73-505 Nr.5]

Die Behandlung von Immobilienrechten Deutscher mit Wohnsitz in der Bundesrepublik Deutschland und Berlin (West), in der DDR und Berlin (Ost) /. Breitkopf, Stephan. Berlin , 1983. xii, 203 p. ; ISBN 3-921374-25-1 LC Card 84-167165 DDC 330 s 346.431/55043 19
HC244.A1 B4 Heft 129 KK1315
NYPL [STN+ (Berlin. Freie Universität. Osteuropa-Institut. Berichte. Heft 129)]

Die Bibliophilen Taschenbücher .
(Nr. 253) Maier, Lotte. Militärmarken /. Dortmund , 1981. 158 p. : ISBN 3-88379-253-5 (kart.) : LC Card 81-180793
HE6184.S42 M35 1981

(Nr. 328) Aufbruch zum Himmel . Dortmund , c1982. 99 p. : ISBN 3-88379-328-0 : LC Card 83-125566
HE6184.A4 A84 1982

(Nr. 336) Appuhn, Klaus D. Wohlfeil und köstlich . Dortmund , c1982. 148 p. : ISBN 3-88379-336-1 (pbk.) LC Card 87-672473
HF5470 .A66x 1982

Die Bundesrepublik Deutschland . Fuchs, Gerhard, 1939- Stuttgart , 1983. 296 p. : ISBN 3-12-922191-3 LC Card 83-166769 DDC 330.943/087 19
HD656 .F8 1983 ***NYPL [JLE 86-578]***

Die Chancen der Krise . Dahrendorf, Ralf. Stuttgart , c1983. 240 p. ; ISBN 3-421-06148-3
NYPL [JFD 87-2528]

Die DDR in der Welt des Sozialismus / Autorenkollektiv unter Leitung von Siegmar Quilitzsch. 1. Aufl. Berlin : Staatsverlag der Deutschen Demokratischen Republik, 1985. 237 p. ; 22 cm. Includes bibliographical references. LC Card 85-188821 DDC 335.43/09431 19
1. Communism - Germany, East. 2. Communist countries - Economic integration. 3. Communist countries - Foreign relations - Germany (East). 4. Germany (East) - Foreign relations - Communist countries. I. Quilitzsch, Siegmar.
HX280.5.A6 D38 1985
NYPL [JLD 87-1167]

Die deutsche Arbeiterbewegung . Klönne, Arno. Düsseldorf , Köln , 1980. 382 p. ; ISBN 3-424-00652-1 : LC Card 81-453558 DDC 322/.2/0943 19
HX276 .K547 ***NYPL [JLD 81-689]***

Die DM als internationale Reservewährung . Boeck, Klaus. Hamburg , 1974. 75 p. ; LC Card 75-550711 ***NYPL [JLE 80-744]***

Die Effekte der Preisstabilisierung auf internationalen Rohstoffmärkten auf Erlöshöhe und -stabilität /. Maennig, Wolfgang. Berlin , 1985. 168 p. : ISBN 3-428-05947-6
NYPL [JLE 86-1670]

Die Einheit der Gesellschaftswissenschaften, 0424-6985 .
(Bd. 39) Tietzel, Manfred. Wirtschaftstheorie und Unwissen . Tübingen , 1985. viii, 208 p. ; ISBN 3-16-944919-2 LC Card 86-147807
HB175 .T55 1985

(Bd. 47) Witt, Ulrich. Individualistische Grundlagen der evolutorischen Ökonomik /. Tübingen , c1987. xi, 209 p. ; ISBN 3-16-945063-8 LC Card 87-115946 DDC 330.15/5 19
HB98.2 .W57 1987

(Bd. 50) Pommerehne, Werner W. Präferenzen für öffentliche Güter . Tübingen , 1987. xv, 290 p. : ISBN 3-16-945040-9 LC Card 87-138780 DDC 363 19
HB846.5 .P66 1987

Die Entstehung industrialisierter Volkswirtschaften . Hesse, Günter, Dr. Tübingen , 1982. vi, 100 p. : ISBN 3-16-344559-4 : LC Card 83-153439 DDC 338.9 19
HD84 .H4718 1982 ***NYPL [JLE 87-1169]***

Die Entwicklung der peruanischen Agrarreform 1969-1979 und ihre Durchführung im Departement Puno [microform] /. Monheim, Felix. Wiesbaden , 1981. 37 p. ; ISBN 3-515-03629-6 : LC Card 82-113404 DDC 333.3/1/8536 19
HD1333.P42 P955 1981
NYPL [*ZT-1647 no.11]

Die Frau in der Gesellschaft.
Maindok, Herlinde, 1948- Frauenalltag in Männerberufen /. Frankfurt am Main , 1987. 173, [2] p. ; ISBN 3-596-23786-6 LC Card 87-164114 DDC 331.4/81 19
HD6060.6 .M35 1987

Die Geldwertberichtigung in Brasilien im Rechnungswesen der Unternehmung /. Issel, Catarina Irene. Hamburg , 1983. iii, 181 p. : LC Card 84-112596 DDC 332.6/73/098 s 657/.48 19
HG5160.5.A3 P7 Nr. 10 HF5658.5
NYPL [JLK 73-84 Nr.10]

Die Geschichte des Sozialismus in Einzeldarstellungen .
(Bd. 1 1) Kautsky, Karl, 1854-1938. Die Vorläufer des neueren Sozialismus /. Stuttgart , 1895. 2 v. ; ***NYPL [JLF 85-168]***

Die grenzüberschreitende regionale Zusammenarbeit auf dem Gebiet der Raumordnung . Arnold-Palussiére, Martine. Hannover , 1983. xvii, 393 p. ; ISBN 3-87870-869-6 : LC Card 83-239646 DDC 361.6/1/0943 19
HT395.G4 A76 1983
NYPL [JLL 72-326 Bd. 71]

Die Hessen-Bibliothek im Insel Verlag.
Wagner, Kurt. Leben auf dem Lande im Wandel des Industrialisierung . Frankfurt am Main , 1986. 558, [1] p. : ISBN 3-458-14329-7 LC Card 87-112493 DDC 330.943/41 19
HC289.K66 W34 1986

Die Kommunale Gebietsreform .
(Bd. III, 1) Finanzwirtschaftliche Folgen kommunaler Gebiets- und Funktionalreformen . Baden-Baden , 1986. 209 p. : ISBN 3-7890-1163-0 (Deut. Bibl.) LC Card 86-169111
HJ1121 .F55 1986

(Bd. III, 4) Rosenfeld, Martin. Ausgabeneffekte kommunaler Funktionalreformen . Baden-Baden , 1985. 395 p. : ISBN 3-7890-1077-4 LC Card 86-156503
HJ9493.5.L6 R67 1985

Die Konkursrechnungslegung . Veit, Klaus-Rüdiger. Köln , c1982. xiv, 221 p. ; ISBN 3-452-19273-3 LC Card 83-130656 DDC 346.43/078 344.30678 19
KK4290 .V44 1982 ***NYPL [JLE 87-1129]***

Die Menschheit an der Schwelle zum 21. Jahrhundert.
Stempell, Dieter. Weltbevölkerung 2000 . Leipzig , 1985. 200 p. : LC Card 86-166553
HB849.53 .S74 1985

Die Messung des Führungsverhaltens . Ficher, Michael. Bochum , 1981. v, 366 p. : ISBN 3-88339-193-X : LC Card 81-205568
HD57.7 .F65 1981 ***NYPL [JLD 86-2580]***

Die mitbestimmte selbständige Aktiengesellschaft /. Kroneberg, Jürgen. Göttingen , 1982. xii, 211 p. ; ISBN 3-88415-554-7 : LC Card 83-159183 DDC 346.43/0664 344.306664 19
KK3000 .K76 1982 ***NYPL [JLD 86-1552]***

Die Peripherie in der Weltwirtschaftskrise, Afrika, Asien und Lateinamerika, 1929-1939 / Dietmar Rothermund (Hrsg.). Paderborn : Schöningh, c1982. 295 p. : ill. ; 24 cm. (Sammlung Schöningh zur Geschichte und Gegenwart) Title on spine: Die Peripherie in der Weltwirtschaftskrise. Includes index. Bibliography: p. [285]-288. CONTENTS. - Einleitung, Weltgefälle und Wirtschaftskrise / Dietmar Rothermund -- Die koloniale Dauerkrise in Westafrika / Helmut Bley -- Die Entwicklung der kolonialen Zwangswirtschaft in Belgisch-Kongo / Albert Wirz -- Die Reaktion auf die Krise in Westasien und Nordafrika / Helmut Mejcher -- Die Interferenz von Agrarpreissturz und Freiheitskampf in Indien / Dietmar Rothermund -- Die indische Baumwolltextilindustrie, 1929-1939 / Horst-Joachim Leue -- Das restriktive Krisenmanagement der indischen Juteindustrie / Saugata Mukherji -- Wirtschaftliche Konzentration und soziale Konflikte in Japan / Bernd Martin -- Chinas verspätete Krise, 1933-1935 / Dietmar Rothermund -- Lateinamerika in der Krise /

Hans-Joachim König. ISBN 3-506-77461-1 LC Card 83-167120 DDC 330.9172/4 19
1. Colonies - Economic conditions. 2. Depressions - 1929 - Developing countries. 3. Developing countries - Economic conditions. I. Rothermund, Dietmar.
HC59.7 .P457 1982 ***NYPL [JLE 87-1202]***

Die Planungszelle und ihre Umwelt . Garbe, Detlef, 1949- Frankfurt a.M. ; Bern ; xiv, 339 p. ; ISBN 3-8204-6017-9 LC Card 81-464829
HC79.E5 G33 1980 ***NYPL [JLD 81-2376]***

Die Rationalisierungsdebatte 1908-1933 . Stollberg, Gunnar. Frankfurt/Main , New York , c1981. 214 p. ; ISBN 3-593-32938-7 : LC Card 81-177695 DDC 331.88/0943 19
HD70.G2 S666 1981 ***NYPL [JLD 86-1662]***

Die regionale Dynamik des Salzburger Arbeitsmarktes, 1971-1980 . Fink, Karl, Mag. Salzburg [1981?] 212 p. : LC Card 82-171635
HD5772.S24 F56 1981 ***NYPL [JLG 86-301]***

Die Rolle der Deutschen Bundespost im Fernmeldewesen /. Germany (West). Monopolkommission. Baden-Baden , 1981. 110 p. ; ISBN 3-7890-0675-0(pbk.) LC Card 81-130348 DDC 383/.4943 19
HE8155 .R64 1981 ***NYPL [JLE 87-312]***

Die schlaflosen Nächte des Eugen E. . Eberle, Eugen, 1908- Stuttgart , 1982. 281 p. : ISBN 3-922836-06-2 LC Card 83-173587 DDC 305.5/62/0924 B 19
HD8453.E2 A37 1982 ***NYPL [JFD 87-3745]***

Die Sozialverträglichkeit von Energiesystemen . (Bd. 8) Meyer-Abich, Klaus Michael, 1936- Die Grenzen der Atomwirtschaft . München , c1986. 230 p. : ISBN 3-406-31317-5 LC Card 86-192439
HD9698.A2 M49 1986

Die Stadt- und Landkreise Baden-Württembergs in Wort und Zahl . (Heft 23) Landkreis Waiblingen /. [Stuttgart] [1965?] 25 p. : LC Card 85-230943
HC288.W34 L36 1965

Die Unternehmung in der demokratischen Gesellschaft = The business corporation in the democratic society / herausgegeben von Wolfgang Dorow. Berlin ; New York : W. de Gruyter, 1987. xiii, 390 p. : ill. ; 24 cm. "Günter Dlugos zum 65. Geburtstagegewidmet." English and German. Includes bibliographies. ISBN 0-89925-295-8 (U. S.) : LC Card 86-32864 DDC 658.3/152 19
1. Management - Employee participation. 2. Democracy. 3. Representative government and representation. 4. Efficiency, Industrial. 5. Dlugos, Günter. I. Dorow, Wolfgang. II. Dlugos, Günter. III. Title: Business corporation in the democratic society.
HD5650 .U67 1987

Die verhaltenswissenschaftlichen Grundlagen der Führung des Mitarbeiters /. Lattmann, Charles. Bern , c1981. 565 p. : ISBN 3-258-03094-4 : LC Card 82-163528 DDC 658.3 19
HD58.7 .L36 1981 ***NYPL [JLE 86-1595]***

Die verkannte Revolution /. Miegel, Meinhard. Stuttgart , 1983- v. : ISBN 3-87959-196-2 (Bd. 1) LC Card 83-206487 DDC 330.943/087 19
HC286.7 .M53 1983 ***NYPL [JLK 86-154]***

Die Vorläufer des neueren Sozialismus /. Kautsky, Karl, 1854-1938. Stuttgart , 1895. 2 v. ; ***NYPL [JLF 85-168]***

Die Wirksamkeit staatlicher Mittelstandsförderung im Einzelhandel / von E. Dichtl ... [et al.]. Berlin : Duncker & Humblot, c1981. 223 p. : ill. ; 24 cm. (Schriften zum Marketing. Bd. 12) Bibliography: p. 184-188. ISBN 3-428-04919-5 LC Card 82-175986 DDC 658.8 s 338.6/42/0943 19
1. Small business - Germany, West. 2. Retail trade - Germany, West. I. Dichtl, Erwin.
HF5415.A2 S37 Bd. 12 HD2346.G3 ***NYPL [JLE 86-3464]***

Die Wirtschaftliche Entwicklung in den Arbeitsmarktregionen des Bergischen Landes : Ergebnisse und Vorträge im Rahmen eines Praktiker-Seminars 1979-80 / [Herausgeber], Paul Klemmer ; Kommunale Arbeitsgemeinschaft Bergisch Land e.V., Ruhr-Universität Bochum. Bochum : Brockmeyer, 1981. 401 p. : ill. ; 21 cm. (Beiträge zur Struktur- und Konjunkturforschung . Bd. 17) Papers presented at a seminar held by the Ruhr-Universität Bochum and the Kommunale Arbeitsgemeinschaft Bergisch Land, Wintersemester 1979-80. Includes bibliographical references. ISBN 3-88339-217-0 LC Card 82-164818 DDC 331/.0943/55 19
1. Labor and laboring classes - Germany (West) - Bergisches Land - Congresses. 2. Labor supply - Germany (West) - Bergisches Land - Congresses. 3. Labor mobility - Germany (West) - Bergisches Land - Congresses. 4. Wages - Germany (West) - Bergisches Land - Congresses. I. Klemmer, Paul. II. Kommunale Arbeitsgemeinschaft Bergisch Land. III. Series.
HD8459.N66 W57 1981 ***NYPL [JLD 86-1639]***

Die Wohnflächenbestände der Gemeinden der Vorderpfalz . König, Robert. Heidelberg , 1980. [14], 226 p. : ISBN 3-88570-068-9 LC Card 81-136631 DDC 333.73/13/0724 19
HD659.P34 K66 1980 ***NYPL [L-10 4979 Heft 68]***

Diebold, John, 1926- Heyel, Carl, 1908- John Diebold on management. Englewood Cliffs, N.J. [1972] ix, 282 p. ISBN 0-13-510214-6 LC Card 75-170643 DDC 658
HD45 .H42 ***NYPL [JLF 73-1242]***

Dieckhöner, Bruno. Rentabilitätsrisiken aus dem Hypothekargeschäft von Kreditinstituten in Zeiten der Geldentwertung / Bruno Dieckhöner. Wiesbaden : Gabler, c1984. xi, 395 p. : ill. ; 24 cm. (Schriftenreihe des Instituts für Kredit- und Finanzwirtschaft . Bd. 11) Originally presented as the author's thesis (doctoral)--Ruhr-Universität Bochum, Wintersemester 1982/83. Bibliography: p. [375]-395. ISBN 3-409-14002-6 : LC Card 85-119494
1. Mortgage banks - Germany, West. 2. Inflation (Finance) - Germany, West. 3. Risk. I. Title. II. Series.
HG2040.5.G4 D53 1984

Diederich, Helmut, 1928- Stöffler, Michael. Markttransparenz in der Lebensversicherung . [Mainz] [1982?] vi, 248 p. : LC Card 83-202502
HG9078.Z9 S76 1982

Diederichs, Urs J. (Urs Justus) Schleswig-Holsteins Weg ins Industriezeitalter /. Hamburg , c1986. 175 p. : ISBN 3-7672-0965-9 LC Card 87-127674 DDC 338.0943/512 19
HC287.S35 S395 1986

Diedrich, Wolfgang. Arbeitsbedingungen in der Schweizer Hotellerie : Zukunft ohne Chance? Change ohne Zukunft? / Wolfgang Diedrich, Peter Saxenhofer. Bern : P. Haupt, c1984. 185 p. : ill. ; 23 cm. Bibliography: p. 178-181. ISBN 3-258-03437-0 : LC Card 85-113566
1. Hotels, taverns, etc. - Switzerland - Employees. I. Saxenhofer, Peter. II. Title.
HD5718.H82 S953 1984

Diefenbacher, Hans. Mitbestimmung, Norm und Wirklichkeit . Frankfurt , New York , c1984. 369 p. ; ISBN 3-593-33325-2 LC Card 85-128882
HD5658.A82 G35 1984

Diéguez, Héctor L. Mercados de trabajo y distribución de ingresos en cuatro centros urbanos de Argentina, 1974-1981 / Héctor L. Diéguez, Alberto Petrecolla. Buenos Aires, Argentina : Instituto Torcuato Di Tella, Centro de Investigaciones Económicas, 1984. 49 p. ; 26 cm. (Serie Documentos de trabajo . 115) ISBN 950-621-013-6 LC Card 87-401771 DDC 331.12/982 19
1. Labor supply - Argentina - Case studies. 2. Income distribution - Argentina - Case studies. I. Petrecolla, Alberto. II. Series: Serie Documentos de trabajo (Centro de Investigaciones Económicas (Instituto Torcuato Di Tella)) , 115. III. Title.
HD5749 .D54 1984

Diehn, Gwen, 1943- Comeau, John, 1952- Communication on the job . Englewood Cliffs, N.J. , c1987. xxvi, 356 p. : ISBN 0-13-153685-0 (pbk.) : LC Card 86-30555 DDC 651.7 19
HD30.3 .C62 1987

Diekmann, Andreas. Einkommensunterschiede zwischen Frauen und Männern : theoretische Perspektiven und empirische Ergebnisse zur Einkommensdiskriminierung von Arbeitnehmerinnen / Andreas Diekmann. Wien : Institut für Höhere Studien, [1985] 2 v. (244, 4 p.) : ill. ; 30 cm. (Forschungsbericht / Institut für Höhere Studien, Wien = Research memorandum / Institute for Advanced Studies, Vienna . no. 212, 218) "März 1984" [i.e. 1985]--V. 1, t.p. "Juni 1985"--V. 2, t.p. Summary in English and German. Bibliography: v. 1, p. 129-135; v. 2, p. 237-244. LC Card 86-150241
1. Wages - Women. 2. Sex discrimination against women. 3. Women - Employment. 4. Sex discrimination in employment. 5. Equal pay for equal work. I. Series: Research memorandum (Institut für Höhere Studien, Wien) , no. 212, 218. II. Title.
HD6061 .D54 1985

Dieleman, F. M. Toekomstverkenning volkshuisvesting . Delft , 1985. 100 p. : ISBN 90-6275-193-8 : LC Card 86-157352
HD7288.78.N4 T64 1985

Dienel, Peter C. Zukünftige Energiepolitik . München , 1985. 189 p. : ISBN 3-89147-002-9 LC Card 87-104306
HD9698.G42 Z85 1985

Dienes, Leslie. Soviet Asia : economic development and national policy choices / Leslie Dienes. Boulder : Westview Press, 1987. xx, 289 p. ; 24 cm. (Westview special studies on the Soviet Union and Eastern Europe) Includes bibliographies and index. ISBN 0-8133-7437-5 (pbk.) LC Card 87-8331 DDC 338.957 19
1. Siberia (R.S.F.S.R.) - Economic policy. 2. Siberia (R.S.F.S.R.) - Economic conditions. 3. Regional planning - Siberia (R.S.F.S.R.). 4. Soviet Central Asia - Economic policy. 5. Soviet Central Asia - Economic conditions. 6. Regional planning - Soviet Central Asia. I. Title.
HC336.9.S53 D53 1987

Die Dienstleistungsmarke . Graumann, Jens. München , c1983. l, 197 p. : ISBN 3-88259-244-3 LC Card 83-180401
HD9984.5 .G7 1983

Dienstleistungsmetropole Hamburg : zur Struktur, Entwicklung und Bedeutung des tertiären Sektors. Hamburg : Hamburgische Landesbank, [1980] 27 p. ; 21 cm. (Wirtschaftsanalysen . 1/1980) Compiled by the Hamburgische Landesbank. LC Card 84-216975
1. Service industries - Germany (West) - Hamburg. I. Hamburgische Landesbank, Girozentrale. II. Series: Wirtschaftsanalysen , 1980/1.
HD9984.8.H3 D54 1980

Dienstleistungsproduktion . Gerhardt, Jürgen. Bergisch Gladbach , c1987. 251 p. ; ISBN 3-89012-075-X LC Card 87-141416 DDC 338.4/6 19
HD9980.5 .G46 1987

Dienstmädchen . Walser, Karin, 1950- Frankfurt , 1985. 195 p. ; ISBN 3-88704-079-1 LC Card 86-141363
HD6072.2.G4 W35 1985

Dienststellenverzeichnis Arbeitsschutz : Gewerbeaufsicht, Bergaufsicht, Träger der gesetzlichen Unfallversicherung, technische Überwachung : Anschriften, Zuständigkeitsbereiche und Mitarbeiter der Dienststellen / im Auftrage des Bundesministers für Arbeit und Sozialordnung herausgegeben von der Bundesanstalt für Arbeitsschutz und Unfallforschung.Ausg. 1983. Dortmund : Die Bundesanstalt ; Bremerhaven : Vertrieb, Wirtschaftsverlag NW, 1983. 217 p. ; 21 cm. (Nachschlagewerke Arbeitsschutz) Includes index. ISBN 3-88314-274-3 LC Card 83-196051
1. Industrial hygiene - Germany (West) - Directories. 2. Industrial safety - Germany (West) - Directories. I. Germany (West). Bundesministerium für Arbeit und Sozialordnung. II. Bundesanstalt für Arbeitsschutz und Unfallforschung. III. Series.
HD7708 .D55 1983

Dierkes, Meinolf. Wenig Arbeit--aber viel zu tun . Opladen , c1985. 195 p. : ISBN 3-531-11724-6 ***NYPL [JLE 86-1602]***

Dies ist das Land : Landschaft und Kolonisation in Erez Jisrael. [Sweden : s.n.], 1946 (Lund : Berlingska Boktryckeriet) 102, [1] p., [1] folded leaf of plates : ill., maps ; 22 cm. (Materialsammlung des Hechaluz in Schweden . Nr. 7) Bibliography: p. [103]. LC Card 86-225837
1. Land use - Israel - Planning - History. 2. Land settlement - Israel - History. I. Hechalutz (Organization). II. Series.
HD850 .D54 1946

DIESAT (Organization) De que adoecem e morrem os trabalhadores /. São Paulo , 1985. 236 p. ; LC Card 85-231487
HD7683 .D4 1985

DIESEL FUELS - INDIA.
Upadhyaya, P. K. (Pratap Krishna), 1916- Distribution and consumption of diesel oil in agriculture /. Delhi, India , 1985. xii, 150 p. :

LC Card 86-902439 DDC 333.79 19
HD9579.D53 I68 1985

DIESEL FUELS INDUSTRY - BRAZIL.
Substituição de óleo diesel . [Brasília, Brazil] [19]84. 84 p. : LC Card 87-404960 DDC 338.4/76553 19
HD9579.D53 B737 1984

DIESEL MOTOR INDUSTRY.
Kliachko, Valerie A. World diesel engine markets . Menlo Park, Calif. (333 Ravenswood Ave., Menlo Park 94025-3476) , c1985. 36 p. : LC Card 87-145492 DDC 338.4/7621436 19
HD9705.5.M672 K65 1985

DIESEL MOTOR INDUSTRY - SOVIET UNION - MANAGEMENT.
Akhrameev, V. N. (Vasiliĭ Nikiforovich) "ÍUzhdizel′mash"--podgotovka k ėkonomicheskomu ėksperimentu /. Moskva , 1984. 96 p. : LC Card 85-144706
HD9705.S595 A36 1984

DIET - BOLIVIA.
Roca, José Luis, 1935- Derrotemos al hambre . La Paz, Bolivia , 1985. 157, [16] leaves of plates : LC Card 85-241330 DDC 363.8/56/0984 19
HD9014.B62 R63 1985 ***NYPL [JLD 87-385]***

Diet foods : markets, developments, players / Sandra McGowan, project analyst. Stamford, Conn., U. S.A. : Business Communications Co., c1986. xv, 195 leaves : ill. ; 29 cm. (Business opportunity report . GA-058) ISBN 0-89336-487-8 (pbk.) LC Card 87-160485 DDC 381/.4166463/0973 19
1. Food industry and trade - United States. 2. Natural foods industry - United States. 3. Low-calorie diet. 4. Market surveys - United States. I. McGowan, Sandra. II. Business Communications Co. III. Series.
HD9005 .D53 1986

DIET, LOW-CALORIE. see **LOW-CALORIE DIET.**

DIET - UNITED STATES.
Fox, Michael W., 1937- Agricide . New York , 1986. xv, 194 p., [10] p. of plates : ISBN 0-8052-4013-6 LC Card 85-27690 DDC 338.1/6/0973 19
S441 .F69 1986 ***NYPL [JLD 86-2542]***

Dieterle, Robert. Kostenrechnung : der Zusammenhang zwischen Buchhaltung, Betriebsabrechnung, Kalkulation, Betriebsanalyse / von Robert Dieterle und Franz Abplanalp. Bern : P. Haupt, c1983. 258 p. : ill. ; 23 cm. ISBN 3-258-03210-6 : LC Card 83-185404
1. Cost accounting. 2. Cost accounting - Problems, exercises, etc. I. Abplanalp, Franz. II. Title.
HF5686.C8 D53 1983

Dieterle, W. (Willi) Organisationsänderung in Unternehmungen : traditionale und evolutionäre Ansätze : Anwendungsmöglichkeiten im Rahmen einer Fallstudie / von Willi K.M. Dieterle. Göttingen : O. Schwartz, 1986. iii, 169 p. : ill. ; 23 cm. Bibliography: p. 158-169. ISBN 3-509-01425-1 LC Card 87-131121 DDC 338/.06 19
1. Organizational change. 2. Organizational change - Germany (West) - Case studies. 3. Organizational effectiveness. I. Title.
HD58.8 .D54 1986

DIETETICS. see **NUTRITION.**

Hē diethnopoiēsē tou kephalaiou stēn Hellada, hē periptōsē tōn diylistēriōn . Kapetanakē-Sēphakē, Katerina. Athēna , 1985. 234 p. : LC Card 86-206498
HE595.P4 K36 1985

Dietl, Clara-Erika.
Commercial dictionary : dictionary of commercial, business, and legal terms : including the terminology of the European Communities / by Clara-Erika Dietl, in collaboration with Donald B. Leaver. Wiesbaden : Gabler, c1985-c1987. 2 v. ; 20 cm. Added t.p. in German: Wirtschaftswörterbuch. Vol. 2 originally issued under the title: Wörterbuch der Wirtschafts-, Rechts- und Handelssprache. CONTENTS. - Pt. 1. German-English -- Pt. 2. English-German. 2d rev. ed. ISBN 3-409-19900-4 (v. 1) LC Card 86-160868
1. Commerce - Dictionaries - German. 2. Commerce - Dictionaries. 3. Business - Dictionaries - German. 4. Business - Dictionaries. 5. German language - Dictionaries - English. 6. English language - Dictionaries - German. I. Leaver, Donald B. II. Dietl, Clara-Erika. Wörterbuch der Wirtschafts-, Rechts- und Handelssprache. III. Title. IV. Title: Wirtschaftswörterbuch.
HF1002 .D493 1985
NYPL [*R-Econ. 87-1271]

(joint author) Erdsiek, Gerhard. Wörterbuch für Recht, Wirtschaft und Politik. Bleckede bei Hamburg [1964-1968] 2 v. LC Card 65-42077
NYPL [JLE 85-408]

Wörterbuch der Wirtschafts-, Rechts- und Handelssprache. Dietl, Clara-Erika. Commercial dictionary : dictionary of commercial, business, and legal terms : including the terminology of the European Communities / by Clara-Erika Dietl, in collaboration with Donald B. Leaver. Wiesbaden , c1985-c1987. 2 v. ; ISBN 3-409-19900-4 (v. 1) LC Card 86-160868
HF1002 .D493 1985
NYPL [*R-Econ. 87-1271]

Dietl, Jerzy. Problemy rynku i handlu w Łodzi i regionie łódzkim /. [Łódź] , 1978. 193 p. : LC Card 80-129744
HD9986.P72 L636 1978

Dietl, Wilhelm. Waffen für die Welt : die Milliardengeschäfte der Rüstungsindustrie / Wilhelm Dietl. München : Droemer Knaur, c1986. 335 p. : ill. ; 21 cm. Bibliography: p. 331-332. Includes index. ISBN 3-426-26268-1 LC Card 86-226603
1. Munitions. I. Title.
HD9743.A2 D54 1986

Dietrich, Bernhard R. Inkasso Unternehmungen / Bernhard R. Dietrich. Neuried : Hieronymus, c1986. xxxv, 200 p. ; 21 cm. (Typoskript-Edition Hieronymus. Wirtschafts- und Sozialwissenschaften . Bd. 15) Originally presented as the author's thesis (doctoral)--Universität Erlangen-Nürnberg, 1986. Bibliography: p. vi-xxxv. ISBN 3-88893-050-2 LC Card 87-133343 DDC 658.8/8 19
1. Collection agencies. 2. Collection agencies - Law and legislation. 3. Collecting of accounts. 4. Collection laws. I. Title. II. Title: Inkassounternehmungen. III. Series.
HG3752.5 .D54 1986

Dietz, August, 1869-1963. Skinner, Hubert C. The new Dietz Confederate States catalog and handbook /. Miami, Fla. (1007 Kane Concourse, Bay Harbor Islands 33154) , 1986. viii, 270 p. : LC Card 86-206685 DDC 769.56975/075/0973 19
HE6500 .S58 1986

Dietz Confederate States catalog. Skinner, Hubert C. The new Dietz Confederate States catalog and handbook /. Miami, Fla. (1007 Kane Concourse, Bay Harbor Islands 33154) , 1986. viii, 270 p. : LC Card 86-206685 DDC 769.56975/075/0973 19
HE6500 .S58 1986

Dietz, Hans. Überlebenslesebuch . Reinbek bei Hamburg [1984], c1983. 316 p. : ISBN 3-499-17672-6 : LC Card 85-168871
HC79.D4 U24 1984

Dietz, James L., 1947-
Economic history of Puerto Rico : institutional change and capitalist development / James L. Dietz. Princeton : Princeton University Press, c1986. xxiii, 337 p., [11] p. of plates : ill. ; 25 cm. Includes index. Bibliography: p. [311]-326. ISBN 0-691-07716-9 (alk. paper) : LC Card 86-12313 DDC 330.97295 19
1. Investments - Puerto Rico - History. 2. Capitalism - Puerto Rico - History. 3. Puerto Rico - Economic conditions. 4. Puerto Rico - Commerce - History. 5. Puerto Rico - History. I. Title.
HC154.5 .D54 1986 ***NYPL [JLE 87-1592]***

Latin America's economic development . Boulder , 1987. xii, 304 p. ; ISBN 1-555-87067-8 (lib. bdg. : alk. paper) : LC Card 87-10046 DDC 338.98 19
HC125 .L3536 1987

Dietz, Thomas. The risk professionals / by Thomas Dietz and Robert W. Rycroft. New York : Russell Sage Foundation, c1987. p. cm. (Social research perspectives . 14) Bibliography: p. ISBN 0-87154-214-5 : LC Card 87-19992 DDC 363.7/056/0973 19
1. Environmental policy - United States. 2. Risk managers - United States. I. Rycroft, Robert W., 1945-. II. Title. III. Series.
HC110.E5 D54 1987

Diewert, W. E. (W. Erwin)
Diez años de la industria petrolera nacional. 1976-1985, diez años de la industria petrolera nacional. [Caracas] [1986- v. <1-2 > : ISBN 980-259-069-X (set) LC Card 87-403692 DDC 338.2/7282/0987 19
HD9574.V42 A56 1986

Diez años después de Estocolmo : desarrollo, medio ambiente y supervivencia / Héctor Echechuri ... [et al.]. Madrid : CIFCA, [1983?] 285 p. : ill. ; 24 cm. Includes bibliographies. ISBN 84-85633-26-3 LC Card 84-122682 DDC 304.2 19
1. United Nations Conference on the Human Environment, Stockholm, 1972 - Addresses, essays, lectures. 2. Human ecology - Addresses, essays, lectures. 3. Environmental policy - Addresses, essays, lectures. I. Echechuri, Héctor. II. Centro Internacional de Formación en Ciencias Ambientales.
GF49 .D54 1983 ***NYPL [JLE 86-1307]***

Diéz Espinosa, José Ramón. Rueda Hernanz, Germán. La desamortización de Mendizábal y Espartero en España /. Madrid , c1986. 200 p. ; ISBN 84-376-0592-X LC Card 86-216590
HD774 .R84 1986

Diez, Rafael. Final report of the consultancy of Rafael Diez from August 3, 1982 to August 3, 1983. La Paz : R. Diez, [1983] 1 v. (various foliations) ; 35 cm. "Adviser in the Rural Development Planning Project 511-0471, carried out jointly by the Ministry of Planning and Coordination and USAID/Bolivia"--P. 1. English and Spanish. "La Paz, July 26, 1983." LC Card 83-243264
1. Economic assistance, American - Bolivia. 2. Rural development projects - Bolivia. I. Bolivia. Ministerio de Planeamiento y Coordinación. II. USAID-Bolivia (Mission). III. Title.
HC182 .D49 1983

Los diezmos en Zamora (1500-1840) /. Alvarez Vázquez, J. A. (José Antonio) Salamanca, España [Zamora] , 1984. ii, 318 p. ; ISBN 84-7481-296-8 LC Card 85-123559
HJ2287.S74 A58 1984

DIFFERENTIAL DUTY. see **TARIFF PREFERENCES.**

Differenzierte Globalsteuerung . Schalk, Hans Joachim. Berlin , New York , c1985. ix, 319 p. : ISBN 0-387-16045-0 (U. S.) LC Card 86-141700
HB3732 .S32 1985

Differenzierte Preise . Vormbaum, Herbert. Köln , 1960. xi, 291 p. : LC Card 86-191408
HB235.G3 V67 1960

Differenzierung der Berufsausbildung . Weibel, Bernd, 1951- Heidelberg , 1984. iv, 326, 6 p. : ISBN 3-88326-138-6 LC Card 85-189624
HF5381 .W43 1984

I difficili inizi di Karl Marx . Porcaro, Mimmo, 1953- Bari , c1986. 112 p. ; ISBN 88-22-03815-0 : LC Card 86-195836
HB501.M37 P63 1986

DIFFUSION OF INNOVATIONS.
Stoneman, Paul. The economic analysis of technology policy /. Oxford [Oxfordshire] , New York , 1987. x, 224 p. : ISBN 0-19-877260-2 (pbk.) LC Card 87-20374 DDC 338.9/26 19
HD45 .S844 1987

DIFFUSION OF INNOVATIONS - KOREA (SOUTH) - CASE STUDIES.
Enos, John L. (John Lawrence), 1924- The adoption and diffusion of imported technology . New York , c1988. 272 p. : ISBN 0-7099-2030-X LC Card 87-19894 DDC 338.9519/506 19
HC470.T4 E56 1987

DiFilippo, Anthony, 1950- Military spending and industrial decline : a study of the American machine tool industry / Anthony DiFilippo. Westport, Conn. : Greenwood Press, c1986. x, 199 p. ; 22 cm. (Contributions in economics and economic history, 0084-9235 . no. 68) Includes index. Bibliography: p.185-191. ISBN 0-313-25179-7 (lib bdg. : alk. paper) LC Card 85-27144 DDC 338.4/7621902/0973 19
1. Machine-tool industry - Government policy - United States. 2. Armaments - Economic aspects - United States. 3. Industry and state - United States - Case studies. 4. Technology and state - United States - Case studies. I. Title. II. Series.
HD9703.U5 D54 1986
NYPL [JLD 86-2930]

Difrieri, Jorge A. (Jorge Alberto) Progresos de la administración del trabajo en las últimas décadas : contribución del CIAT / Jorge Alberto Difrieri.1a ed. Lima, Perú : Centro Interamericano de Administración del Trabajo, 1985. 19 p. ; 25 cm. Includes bibliographical references. LC Card 86-152814
1. Centro Interamericano de Administración del Trabajo. 2. Labor and laboring classes - Latin America. I. Title.
HD8110.5 .D54 1985

Difusión científica.
Arredondo Ramírez, Pablo. Comunicación social, poder y democracia en México /. Guadalajara, Jalisco, México , c1986. 214 p. : LC Card 86-227944
HE8689.9.M6 A77 1986

Digging deeper : issues in the miners' strike / edited by Huw Beynon. London : Verso, 1985. xiv, 252 p. : ill. ; 21 cm. Includes bibliographies. ISBN 0-86091-820-3 (pbk.) : LC Card 87-118973 DDC 331.89/2822334/0941 19
1. Coal Strike, Great Britain, 1984-1985. I. Beynon, Huw.
HD5365.M6152 1984 .D54 1985

Dight, Janet. Breaking the secretary barrier : how to get out from behind the typewriter and into a management job / Janet Dight. New York : McGraw-Hill, c1986. xv, 303 p. ; 24 cm. Includes index. ISBN 0-07-016905-5 LC Card 85-11360 DDC 658.4/09/024042 19
1. Secretaries. 2. Women executives. I. Title.
HF5547.5 .D54 1986 ***NYPL [JLE 86-1072]***

Digital C.M.O.S. circuit design. Annaratone, Marco. Digital CMOS circuit design /. Boston , c1986. xv, 344 p. : ISBN 0-89838-224-6 LC Card 86-10646 DDC 621.395 19
TK7871.99.M44 A56 1986
NYPL [JSE 87-634]

Digital CMOS circuit design /. Annaratone, Marco. Boston , c1986. xv, 344 p. : ISBN 0-89838-224-6 LC Card 86-10646 DDC 621.395 19
TK7871.99.M44 A56 1986
NYPL [JSE 87-634]

DIGITAL COMMUNICATIONS.
ISDN . Boston, MA (200 Portland St., Boston 02114) , c1987. iv, 118 p. : LC Card 87-159823 DDC 380.1/450046 19
HD9696.D382 I82 1987

DIGITAL COMPUTERS, ELECTRONIC. see **ELECTRONIC DIGITAL COMPUTERS.**

DIGITAL COUNTER INDUSTRY - UNITED STATES.
The Counting instrument market in the U. S. New York, N.Y. , c1983. v, 197 p. : LC Card 87-143757 DDC 381/.4568114 19
HD9696.D543 U63 1983

Digital methods and algorithms of signal processing. T͡Sifrovye metody i algoritmy obrabotki signalov . Vil'ni͡us , 1986. 120 p. : LC Card 86-232937
HD38 .S715 vyp. 73 TK5102.5

The Digital telecommunications market. New York, N.Y. : Frost & Sullivan, c1983. 2 v. (vii, 269 leaves) : ill. ; 29 cm. "October 1983." "#A1223." LC Card 87-143942 DDC 384 19
1. Telephone supplies industry - United States. 2. Telecommunication switching systems equipment industry - United States. 3. Market surveys - United States. I. Frost & Sullivan.
HD9697.T453 U525 1983

DIHT-Arbeitskreis Kammerarchive/Dokumentation. Reininghaus, Wilfried. Quellen zur Geschichte des Deutschen Industrie- und Handelstages in Kammerarchiven, 1861 bis 1918 /. Bonn , 1986. 158 p. : ISBN 3-925925-01-5 LC Card 87-408272 DDC 354.430082/09 19
HF308 .R343 1986

DIHT-Kongress (1976 : Bad Kissingen, Germany) Votum für die Marktwirtschaft . Bonn , c1976. 26 p. ; LC Card 85-172115
HC286.7 .V69 1976

DIHT-Kongress (1983 : Frankfurt am Main, Germany) Kapital, Zins, Währung : DIHT-Kongress in Frankfurt, 18. und 19. Oktober 1983 / Karl Otto Pöhl, Otto Wolff von Amerongen ... [et al.]. Bonn : Deutscher Industrie- und Handelstag, 1984. 68 p. : ill. ; 21 cm. (DIHT . 214) LC Card 84-212399
1. Capital - Germany, West - Congresses. 2. Corporations - Germany (West) - Finance - Congresses. I. Pöhl, Karl Otto, 1929-. II. Wolff von Amerongen, Otto, 1918-. III. Deutscher Industrie- und Handelstag. IV. Series: DIHT (Series) , 214. V. Title.
HC290.5.C3 D53 1983

DIHT-Materialien zur Geschichte.
Reininghaus, Wilfried. Quellen zur Geschichte des Deutschen Industrie- und Handelstages in Kammerarchiven, 1861 bis 1918 /. Bonn , 1986. 158 p. : ISBN 3-925925-01-5 LC Card 87-408272 DDC 354.430082/09 19
HF308 .R343 1986

Zeugnisse der Zeit . Bonn , 1986. 113 p. : LC Card 87-408186
HD2429.G3 Z48 1986

DIHT-Meinung, 1982 /. Deutscher Industrie- und Handelstag. Bonn , 1982. 104 p. ; LC Card 83-206569
HC286.7 .D47 1982

DIHT (Series) .
(157) Votum für die Marktwirtschaft . Bonn , c1976. 26 p. ; LC Card 85-172115
HC286.7 .V69 1976

(160) Wolff von Amerongen, Otto, 1918- Trendwende im Osthandel /. Bonn , 1977. 23 p. ; LC Card 85-141570
HF1411 .W583 1977

(162) Vom Gleis abgekommen . Bonn , 1977. 60 p. ; LC Card 86-176591
HE2445 .V65 1977

(213) Praxisleitfaden Privatisierung /. Bonn , 1984. 202 p. : LC Card 84-194479
HD4175 .P73 1984

(214) DIHT-Kongress (1983 : Frankfurt am Main, Germany) Kapital, Zins, Währung . Bonn , 1984. 68 p. : LC Card 84-212399
HC290.5.C3 D53 1983

(224) Berufs- und Weiterbildung 1984/85 . Bonn , 1985. 201 p. : LC Card 86-171726
HF5549.5.T7 B488 1985

Dijagnoza samoupravljanja 1974-1981 /. Jovanov, Neca. Zagreb , 1983. 365 p. ; LC Card 84-146844
HD5660.Y8 J68 1983

Dijk, Jouke van. Migratie en arbeidsmarkt / Jouke van Dijk. Assen : Van Gorcum, 1986. 239 p. : ill. ; 24 cm. (Serie Mens en ruimte . 20) Summary in English. Bibliography: p. 222-236. ISBN 90-232-2213-X : LC Card 86-215033
1. Migration, Internal - Netherlands. 2. Labor supply - Netherlands. I. Title. II. Series.
HB2065 .D54 1986

Dijk, Meine Pieter van.
Burkina-Faso : le secteur informel de Ouagadougou / Meine Pieter van Dijk. Paris : L'Harmattan, c1986. 203 p. ; 24 cm. (Villes et entreprises) At head of title: Tome I. Vol. 1 of a multipart item without collective title. Vol. 2 has title: Sénégal : le secteur informel de Dakar. Bibliography: p. 195-199. ISBN 2-85802-638-6 LC Card 86-221033
1. Informal sector (Economics) - Burkina-Faso - Ouagadougou. 2. Informal sector (Economics) - Burkina-Faso. I. Series: Collection "Villes et entreprises". II. Title.
HD2346.B822 O933 1986

Developing the informal sector in Senegal : a study of its context and potential / Meine Pieter van Dijk. Dakar : World Employment Programme, Jobs ans [i.e. and] Skills Programme for Africa, International Labour Office, [1976] 47 leaves ; 30 cm. "December 1976." Includes bibliographical references. LC Card 84-232063
1. Informal sector (Economics) - Senegal. I. Title.
HD2346.S4 D55 1976

Sénégal : le secteur informel de Dakar / Meine Pieter van Dijk. Paris : L'Harmattan, [1986] 164 p. ; 24 cm. (Villes et entreprises) At head of title: Tome II. Vol. 2 of a multipart item without collective title. Vol. 1 has title: Burkina-Faso : le secteur informel de Ouagadougou. Bibliography: p. 157-162. ISBN 2-85802-637-8 LC Card 86-221017
1. Informal sector (Economics) - Senegal - Dakar. 2. Informal sector (Economics) - Senegal. I. Series: Collection "Villes et entreprises". II. Title.
HD2346.S42 D343 1986

Dijkstra, Bram. Defoe and economics : the fortunes of Roxana in the history of interpretation / by Bram Dijkstra. New York : St. Martin's Press, 1987. xvi, 247 p. ; 23 cm. Bibliography: p. 228-240. Includes index. ISBN 0-312-00535-0 : LC Card 86-29691 DDC 330.1 19
1. Defoe, Daniel, 1661?-1731 - Views on Economics. I. Title.
HB103.D4 D56 1987

Dikova, Elena. Slivenski okrŭg '85 =. Sofii͡a , 1985. 134 p. : LC Card 86-196443
HF5221.S56 S56 1985

O dilema da Amazônia /. Miranda Neto, Manoel José de. Belém, Pará [1986] 154 p. ; LC Card 87-119394 DDC 330.981/1063 19
HC188.A5 M57 1986

The Dilema of farmworker housing : an issue of statewide concern in Oregon : final report. [Portland, Or.] : Oregon Bureau of Labor and Industries, [1986] 78, [112] p. : ill. ; 28 cm. "March 1986." LC Card 86-622584 DDC 363.5/9 19
1. Migrant agricultural laborers - Housing - Oregon. I. Oregon. Bureau of Labor Industries.
HD7289.U7 O73 1986

Dilemas de la seguridad social en el Perú /. Slodky, Javier. [Lima] , 1985. 134 p. ; LC Card 86-232616
HD7161 .S57 1985

The dilemma of development in the Arabian Peninsula /. Osama, Abdul Rahman, 1942- London , c1987. 203 p. ; ISBN 0-7099-4240-0 : LC Card 86-29149 DDC 338.953 19
HC415.3 .O83 1987

The dilemma of human identity /. Lichtenstein, Heinz, 1904- New York , c1983. xiv, 399 p. ; ISBN 0-87668-677-3 : LC Card 84-45086 DDC 155.2 19
BF697 .L52 1983 ***NYPL [JFE 86-2218]***

The dilemma of working women hostelers . Chauhan, Indira, 1949- Delhi , New Delhi , 1986. 70 p. : ISBN 81-7018-374-X : LC Card 86-902619 DDC 305.4/0954/792 19
HD6189 .C42 1986

Dilemmas of development . Toye, J. F. J. Oxford, [Oxfordshire], UK , New York, NY, USA , 1987. ix, 177 p. ; ISBN 0-631-14569-9 (U. S.) : LC Card 86-30955 DDC 338.9/009172/4 19
HD82 .T65 1987

Dilger, Robert Jay, 1954- The deductibility of state and local taxes : implications of proposed policy changes / Robert Jay Dilger. Washington, D.C. : National League of Cities, [1985] 1 v. (various pagings) ; 28 cm. (Policy working paper / National League of Cities) "March 1985." Includes bibliographies. ISBN 0-933729-02-2 (pbk.) : LC Card 85-155605 DDC 336.24/216 19
1. Income tax - United States - Deductions - Taxes. 2. Intergovernmental tax relations - United States. I. Title.
HJ4653.D4 D55 1985 ***NYPL [JLF 86-412]***

Dilip Mukerjee. see **Mukerjee, Dilip.**

Dillon, K. Burke. Recent experience with multilateral official debt rescheduling / K. Burke Dillon and Gumersindo Oliveros. Washington, D.C. : International Monetary Fund, c1987. v, 22 p. : ill. ; 28 cm. (World economic and financial surveys, 0258-7440) "February 1987." LC Card 87-2633 DDC 336.3/435 19
1. Loans, Foreign. 2. Debt relief. 3. Debts, External. 4. Loans, Foreign - Developing countries. 5. Debt relief - Developing countries. 6. Debts, External - Developing countries. I. Oliveros, Gumersindo. II. Title. III. Series.
HG3891.5 .D55 1987

Dillon, Ray D. Shuster, Harvey L. The financial manager's guide to microsoftware /. New York , 1988. p. cm. ISBN 0-471-81176-9 LC Card 87-21663 DDC 658.1/5/0285536 19
HG4012.5 .S47 1988

Dillon, Read & Company. Infrastructure financing [microform] . [New York] , c1983. 22, 7, 17 p. : ***NYPL [*ZT-1565 no.20]***

Dillon, William R. Marketing research in a marketing environment / William R. Dillon, Thomas J. Madden, Neil H. Firtle. St. Louis : Times Mirror/Mosby College Pub., 1987. xxviii, 742, 21, 15 p. : ill. ; 25 cm. Includes bibliographies and indexes. ISBN 0-8016-1303-5 : LC Card 86-23189 DDC 658.8/3 19
1. Marketing research. I. Madden, Thomas J. II. Firtle,

Neil H. III. Title.
HF5415.2 .D54 1987

Dimen, Muriel. Surviving sexual contradictions : a startling and different look at a day in the life of a contemporary professional woman / Muriel Dimen. New York : Macmillan, c1986. xxi, 257 p. ; 24 cm. Includes index. Bibliography: p. 216-249. ISBN 0-02-531620-6 LC Card 86-12600 DDC 305.4/2/0973 19
1. Sex discrimination against women - United States. 2. Sexism - United States. 3. Sex role - United States. 4. Feminism - United States. I. Title.
HQ1426 .D56 1986 ***NYPL [JLE 86-4385]***

La dimensión política de la crisis y renegociación de la deuda externa mexicana /. Aschentrupp Toledo, Hermann. México, D.F. [1985] 229 p. ; LC Card 87-401754 DDC 336.3/4/0972 19
HJ8519 .A8 1985

Dimensions of dialogue /. Mathew, Mohan, 1931- St. Louis, Mo. , c1984. 136 p. ; ISBN 0-918833-00-0 (pbk.) : LC Card 84-17009 DDC 302.5/44 19
HM291 .M392 1984 ***NYPL [JLD 86-4125]***

Dimensions of executive positions . Hemphill, John K. (John Knox), 1919- New York , 1987, c1960. xiv, 103 p. ; ISBN 0-8240-8209-5 (alk. paper) : LC Card 86-27078 DDC 658.4 19
HD38.2 .H46 1987

Dimensions of hazardous waste politics and policy / edited by Charles E. Davis and James P. Lester ; prepared under the auspices of the Policy Studies Organization. New York : Greenwood Press, c1988. p. cm. (Contributions in political science, 0147-1066 . no. 200) Bibliography: p. Includes index. ISBN 0-313-25989-5 (lib. bdg. : alk. paper) LC Card 87-17792 DDC 363.7/28 19
1. Hazardous wastes - Government policy - United States. 2. Hazardous waste sites - United States. 3. Environmental policy - United States. I. Davis, Charles E., 1947-. II. Lester, James P., 1944-. III. Series.
HC110.E5 D56 1988

Dimensões do planejamento estadual no Brasil . Haddad, Paulo Roberto. Rio de Janeiro , 1985. 188 p. : LC Card 86-195636
HC188.M6 H33 1985

DiMento, Joseph F. The Urban caldron /. Boston, Mass. , 1986. 152 p. ; ISBN 0-89946-207-3 LC Card 85-21641 DDC 333.73/0973 19
HD257 .U73 1986 ***NYPL [JLE 86-4372]***

Dimitrov, Boris.
Aktualni ikonomicheski problemi . Sofiia , 1985. 227 p. ; LC Card 86-205815
HC403 .A67 1985

Elitnite i͡adra na trudovite kolektivi / Boris Dimitrov. Sofii͡a : T͡Sentr. sŭvet po organizatsii͡a na tekhnicheskoto tvorchestvo, 1985. 80 p. ; 19 cm. Bibliography: p. 78-80. LC Card 86-140524
1. Work groups - Bulgaria. 2. Labor productivity - Bulgaria. I. Title.
HD8626.5 .D55 1985

Dimitrov, D. Slivenski okrŭg '85 =. Sofii͡a , 1985. 134 p. : LC Card 86-196443
HF5221.S56 S56 1985

Dimitrov, Dimitŭr. 75 godini borba i sŭzidanie . Sofii͡a , 1985. 144 p. ; LC Card 86-195265
HD6784.M62 P762 1985

Dimitrov's Union of People's Youth. see **Dimitrovski komunisticheski mladezhki sŭi͡uz.**

DIMITROVSKI KOMUNISTICHESKI MLADEZHKI SŬI͡UZ. (Old Catalog form: Dimitrovski sŭyuz na narodnata mladezh v Bŭlgariya)
Zadachite na DKMS vŭv VUZ za povishavane na ikonomicheskata podgotovka na studentite i mladite khora ot drugite otri͡adi na mladezhta . Svishtov , 1985. 91 p. ; LC Card 86-159994
HB74.9.B9 Z33 1985

Dimitrovski sŭi͡uz na narodnata mladezh v Bŭlgarii͡a. see **Dimitrovski komunisticheski mladezhki sŭi͡uz.**

Dimmer, Klaus. Die optimale Versicherungsentscheidung als risikopolitisches Problem : eine Analyse auf der Grundlage des erweiterten Modells der einzelwirtschaftlichen Versicherungsnachfrage / von Klaus Dimmer. Karlsruhe : Verlag Versicherungswirtschaft, c1986. xiv, 320 p. : ill. ; 21 cm. (Beiträge zu wirtschaftswissenschaftlichen Problemen der Versicherung, 0522-618X . Bd. 20) Bibliography: p. 300-320. LC Card 87-114755 DDC 368/.0072 19
1. Insurance - Mathematical models. 2. Risk management - Mathematical models. I. Title. II. Series.
HG8054.5 .D555 1986

Dimson, Elroy, 1947-
Cases in corporate finance / by Elroy Dimson and Paul Marsh. Chichester [West Sussex] ; New York : Wiley, c1988. xxiv, 412 p. : ill. ; 24 cm. Includes index. ISBN 0-471-91764-8 : LC Card 87-6299 DDC 658.1/5 19
1. Corporations - Finance - Case studies. I. Marsh, Paul (Paul R.). II. Title.
HG4015.5 .D56 1988

Stock market anomalies /. Cambridge [Cambridgeshire] , New York , 1988. p. cm. ISBN 0-521-34104-3 LC Card 87-6622 DDC 332.63/2 19
HG4551 .S82 1988

Din istoria legăturilor revoluționare româno-bulgare (1909-1916) [microform]. Bâldescu, Emil. [București, 1966] 181 p. LC Card 81-475045
HD8646 .B34 ***NYPL [*ZT-1732 no.1]***

Dinâmica da economia e absorção de mão-de-obra : anais do seminário-SUDENE/CNPq / SUDENE, Superintendência-Adjunta de Desenvolvimento Social e Infra-Estrutura, Coordenação de Emprego e Mão-de-Obra. Recife : Editora Massangana, 1984. 79 p. ; 23 cm. (Série População e emprego / SUDENE . 18) Série Cursos e conferências / FUNDAJ ; 15 Includes bibliographical references. ISBN 85-7019-063-8 LC Card 85-156612 DDC 338.981/3 19
1. Labor supply - Brazil, Northeast - Congresses. 2. Regional planning - Brazil, Northeast - Congresses. 3. Brazil, Northeast - Economic policy - Congresses. I. Brazil. Superintendência do Desenvolvimento do Nordeste. Coordenação de Emprego e Mão-de-Obra. II. Series: Série População e emprego , 18.
HD5755.N63 D56 1984
NYPL [JLE 86-3545]

Dinamica dei prezzi relativi nell'economia internazionale . Aquino, Antonio, 1946- Bologna , c1986. 225 p. : ISBN 88-15-00970-1 : LC Card 86-182318
HB221 .A65 1986

Dinâmica demográfica recente dos estados e microrregiões do Nordeste, 1960/1980 /. Moura, Hélio A. de (Hélio Augusto) Recife [Brazil] , 1986. 95 p., [6] folded p. of plates : LC Card 87-131106 DDC 304.6/0981/3 19
HB3564.N66 M68 1986

Dinámica y distribución recientes de la población andaluza /. Jordá Borrell, Rosa Ma. (Rosa Maria) [Sevilla] [1985?] 80 p. : ISBN 84-600-3827-0 LC Card 87-124031
HB3620.A5 J67 1985

Dinamika proizvodstvennykh ob"edinenii i modeli planirovanii͡a ikh dei͡atel'nosti /. Modin, Anatoliĭ Andreevich. Moskva , 1984. 231 p. : LC Card 84-195690
HD9705.S595 M62 1984

A dinamikus egyensúly néhány elméleti kérdése /. Szira, Tamás. Budapest , 1986. 433, [1] p. ; ISBN 963-05-3987-X : LC Card 86-187062
HB145 .S95 1986

Dinero, precios y política monetaria /. García, Valeriano F. Buenos Aires, Argentina [1985] 334, [12] p. : ISBN 950-53-7077-7 LC Card 85-215884
HG221 .G3193 1985

El dinero y el sector financiero a su alcance /. Villar Borrero, Eduardo. Bogotá, Colombia , c1984. 64 p. : ISBN 84-8276-321-0 LC Card 84-241500
HG855 .V54 1984

Ding, Emily. Developing managers in Asia /. Singapore , Reading, Mass. , 1986. p. cm. ISBN 0-201-13653-8 : LC Card 86-28717 DDC 658/.007/15 19
HD38.25.A78 D48 1986

Dinham, Barbara. Agribusiness in Africa / Barbara Dinham & Colin Hines. 1st American ed. Trenton, N.J. : Africa World Press of the Africa Research & Publications Project, 1984. 224 p. : ill. ; 23 cm. "An Earth Resources Research publication"--Cover. Includes indexes. Bibliography: p. 201-212. ISBN 0-86543-003-9 : LC Card 85-672721
1. Food industry and trade - Africa. 2. Agriculture - Economic aspects - Africa. 3. International business enterprises - Africa. I. Hines, Colin. II. Title.
HD9017.A2 D56x 1984
NYPL [Sc D 86-769]

Dinkel, Reiner. Die Auswirkungen eines Geburten- und Bevölkerungsrückgangs auf Entwicklung und Ausgestaltung von gesetzlicher Alterssicherung und Familienlastenausgleich / von Reiner Dinkel. Berlin : Duncker & Humblot, c1984. 344 p. : ill. ; 24 cm. (Sozialpolitische Schriften. Heft 49) The author's Habilitationsschrift, Ludwig-Maximilians-Universität zu München. Bibliography: p. [321]-344. ISBN 3-428-05546-2 LC Card 84-186733
1. Social security - Germany, West. 2. Germany, West - Population. 3. Fertility, Human - Germany (West). I. Series: Sozialpolitische Schriften (Duncker & Humblot) , Heft 49. II. Title.
HD7179 .D65 1984

DINPROA. see **Dinproa, Grupo de Consulta Industrial y Asesoría Jurídica y Económica.**

Dinproa, Grupo de Consulta Industrial y Asesoría Jurídica y Económica. Poveda Ramos, Gabriel. Nueva alternativa para el desarrollo . Bogotá , 1974. 249 p. : LC Card 78-345029
HD1883 1974 .P68 ***NYPL [JLE 80-482]***

DIODORUS, SICULUS - INFLUENCE.
Pappa, Hellē. Hoi archaioi Hellēnes syngrapheis sto "Kephalaio" tou Marx /. Athēna , 1983. 112 p. ; LC Card 84-128852
HB501 .P24 1983

Dioikētikē diairesis tēs Hellados kata nomous, eparchias, dēmous kai koinotētas . Greece. Dieuthynsis Topikēs Autodioikēseōs. Athēnai , 1965. 39 p. ; LC Card 86-235329
HA1351.5 1961

Diokno, Benjamin E. Revenue mobilization and responsiveness of Philippine income taxes : implications for fiscal policy / by Benjamin E. Diokno. [Quezon City, Philippines] : University of the Philippines, School of Economics, [1986] 26 p. : ill. ; 28 cm. (Discussion paper / University of the Philippines, School of Economics . no. 8605) "May 1986." Bibliography: p. 26. LC Card 87-120920 DDC 339.5/25/09599 19
1. Income tax - Philippines. 2. Revenue - Philippines. 3. Fiscal policy - Philippines. I. Series: Discussion paper / University of the Philippines, School of Economics , 8605. II. Title.
HJ4743 .D56 1986

Dionne, Georges. Boyer, Marcel. Riscophobie et étalement à moyenne constante . Montréal [1982] 32 p. : LC Card 85-160864
HB615 .B68 1982

Diop, Anta. see **Diop, Cheikh Anta.**

Diop, Cheikh Anta.
[Fondements économiques et culturels d'un état fédéral d'Afrique noire. English]
Black Africa : the economic and cultural basis for a federated state / Cheikh Anta Diop ; translated by Harold J. Salemson.New expanded ed. Westport, Conn. : L. Hill ; Trenton, N.J. : Africa World Press, 1987. 125 p. ; 21 cm. Translation of: Les fondements économiques et culturels d'un état fédéral d'Afrique noire. "Africa World Press edition." Bibliography: p. 90. ISBN 0-88208-223-X (pbk.) : LC Card 87-17704 DDC 330.967 19
1. Africa, Sub-Saharan - Economic conditions. 2. Africa, Sub-Saharan - Civilization. 3. Pan-Africanism. 4. Africa, Sub-Saharan - Politics and government. 5. Africa, Sub-Saharan - Industries. 6. Power resources - Africa, Sub-Saharan. I. Title.
HC800 .D5413 1987

DIPLOMACY.
R'emy, Ernst. La diplomatie . Port-au-Prince , 1983. 299 p. ; ***NYPL [Sc D 85-315]***

DIPLOMATS - BRAZIL - BIOGRAPHY.
Semana Josué de Castro e a nova geografia da fome, Rio de Janeiro, 19-24 de setembro de 1983 . [S.l. , 1983] 90 leaves : LC Card 86-201115
HD9000.5 .S3968 1983

DIPLOMATS - CHILE - BIOGRAPHY.
Bernstein Carabantes, Enrique. Recuerdos de un diplomático /. Santiago de Chile [1984- v. : LC Card 84-172336 DDC 327.83 19
F3099 .B43 1984 ***NYPL [JFL 84-297]***

Dippmann, Werner. Wissenschaftliche Konferenz "Wissenschaftlich-Technischer Fortschritt, Bedingungen, Anforderungen, Möglichkeiten der Persönlichkeitsentwicklung" (1985 : Karl-Marx-Stadt, Germany) Wissenschaftliche Konferenz "Wissenschaftlich-Technischer Fortschritt, Bedingungen, Anforderungen, Möglichkeiten der Persönlichkeitsentwicklung" am 8. und 9. Oktober 1985 in Karl-Marx-Stadt /. Karl-Marx-Stadt , 1986. 98 p. ; LC Card 87-407801 DDC 338/.06 19
HD45 .W55 1985

DiPrima-LeConche, Patricia, 1958- The National directory of product publicity sources /. Westbury, N.Y. , 1987. p. cm. ISBN 0-87280-157-8 : LC Card 87-17542 DDC 338.7/616592/025 19
HD59 .N245 1987

DiPrimio, Anthony. Quality assurance in service organizations / Anthony DiPrimio. Radnor, Pa. : Chilton Book Co., c1987. xiv, 210 p. : ill. ; 24 cm. Includes index. ISBN 0-8019-7730-4 : LC Card 86-47961 DDC 658.5/62 19
1. Service industries - Quality control. I. Title.
HD9980.5 .D52 1987

DIPSOMANIA. see **ALCOHOLISM.**

DIRECT ADVERTISING. see **ADVERTISING, DIRECT-MAIL.**

Direct attacks on rural poverty . Ghate, Prabhu, 1941- New Delhi , 1984. xvi, 597 p. : LC Card 84-902455 DDC 338.954/2 19
HC437.G48 G46 1984 ***NYPL [JLD 87-651]***

DIRECT BROADCAST SATELLITE TELEVISION.
Holmlöv, Per Gunnar, 1951- Reklam i satellit-tv . Stockholm [1984] 147 p. ; ISBN 91-7258-183-2 : LC Card 84-229824
HF6146.T42 H64 1984

Direct electric utility competition . Primeaux, Walter J. New York, NY, USA , 1986. xiii, 297 p. ; ISBN 0-03-004858-3 (alk. paper) : LC Card 85-20487 DDC 338.8/26136362/0973 19
HD9685.U5 P74 1985 ***NYPL [JLE 86-4075]***

Direct foreign investment : costs and benefits / edited by Richard D. Robinson. New York : Praeger, 1987. xvii, 227 p. ; 25 cm. Includes bibliographies and index. ISBN 0-275-92717-2 (alk. paper) : LC Card 87-17750 DDC 332.6732 19
1. Investments, Foreign - Government policy - Congresses. I. Robinson, Richard D., 1921-.
HG4538 .D557 1987

Direct foreign investment in the United States /. Poniachek, Harvey A. Lexington, Mass. , c1986. xiii, 256 p. : ISBN 0-669-11076-0 (alk. paper) LC Card 85-40457 DDC 332.6/73/0973 19
HG4910 .P66 1986 ***NYPL [JLE 86-4295]***

DIRECT-MAIL ADVERTISING. see **ADVERTISING, DIRECT-MAIL.**

Direct mail profits . Bly, Robert W. Westbury, N.Y. , c1987. x, 206 p. : ISBN 0-87280-153-5 : LC Card 87-18678 DDC 659.13/3 19
HF5466 .B59 1987

DIRECT MARKETING.
Bly, Robert W. Direct mail profits . Westbury, N.Y. , c1987. x, 206 p. : ISBN 0-87280-153-5 : LC Card 87-18678 DDC 659.13/3 19
HF5466 .B59 1987

Grossman, Ann. The marketer's guide to media vehicles, methods, and options . New York , 1987. xiv, 238 p. : ISBN 0-89930-266-1 (lib. bdg. : alk. paper) LC Card 87-2473 DDC 659.1 19
HF5826.5 .G76 1987

Lumley, James E. A. Sell it by mail . New York , c1986. xviii, 382 p. : ISBN 0-471-87908-8 : LC Card 85-16362 DDC 658.8/4 19
HF5466 .L85 1986 ***NYPL [JLE 86-3044]***

Robinson, Dean L. Network marketing /. Salt Lake City, Utah , c1983. 137 p. : LC Card 86-202974 DDC 658.8/4 19
HF5415.126 .R63 1983

DIRECT MARKETING - GERMANY (WEST)
Engelhardt, Werner Hans. Der Direktvertrieb im Konsumgüterbereich . Stuttgart , c1984. 158 p. : ISBN 3-17-008550-6 : LC Card 84-234886
HF5415.126 .E54 1984

DIRECT MARKETING - UNITED STATES.
Christen, François G. Buying by mail . Menlo Park, CA (333 Ravenswood Ave., Menlo Park 94025) , c1986. v, 2, 59, 6 leaves : LC Card 86-209563 DDC 658.8/4 19
HF5415.126 .C48 1986

DIRECT SELLING - FRANCE.
Grémillard, Roger. 75 moyens qui ont fait leurs preuves d'augmenter vos rendements et diminuer vos coûts en publicité et en V.P.C. /. Créteil , c1982. 158 p. ; LC Card 82-238594
HF5466 .G718 1982

DIRECT SELLING - UNITED STATES.
Sutton, Howard, 1930- Rethinking the company's selling and distribution channels /. New York, N.Y. , c1986. v, 26 p. : ISBN 0-8237-0328-2 (pbk.) LC Card 87-404502 DDC 658.8/4 19
HF5415.129 .S87 1986

DIRECT TAXATION. see **INCOME TAX; TAXATION.**

Directions for reform : the future of the international monetary and financial system : report / by a group of experts set up by the chairperson of the Non-aligned Movement. New Delhi : Vikas, [1984] x, 78 p. ; 23 cm. Report by a group of experts set up by the chairperson of the 7th Conference of Heads of State or Government of Non-aligned Countries, New Delhi, 1983. ISBN 0-7069-2692-7 : LC Card 84-903168 DDC 332/.042 19
1. International finance - Congresses. 2. Monetary policy - Congresses. 3. Monetary policy - Developing countries - Congresses. I. Conference of Heads of State or Government of Non-aligned Countries (7th : 1983 : New Delhi, India).
HG3881 .D57 1984 ***NYPL [JLD 86-4409]***

Directorio artesanal, 1978 / Dirección General de Estadística, Ministerio de Economía. Guatemala : La Dirección, 1981. 6 v. ; 20 x 27 cm. Cover title: I censo artesanal, 1978. LC Card 87-403025
1. Artisans - Guatemala - Directories. 2. Cottage industries - Guatemala - Directories. 3. Guatemala - Census, 1978. I. Guatemala. Dirección General de Estadística. II. Title: I censo artesanal, 1978. III. Title: 1er censo artesanal, 1978. IV. Title: Primer censo artesanal, 1978.
HD2346.G8 D57 1981

Directorio de instituciones financieras. Restrepo Correa, Alejandro. Manual de crédito industrial y agropecuario . [Bogotá, D.E. , 1985] 270, 30, 4 p. : LC Card 86-110073
HG3751.9.C7 R47 1985

Directorio del sector energía, minas e industria paraestatal, 1984. Mexico. Secretaría de Energía, Minas e Industria Paraestatal. [Mexico City] , 1984. 497 p. ; ISBN 968-86000-4-0 LC Card 87-404794 DDC 333.79/0972 19
HD9502.M62 M49 1984

Directorio nacional de pequeñas industrias : período 1965-1985. [Quito] : Ministerio de Industrias, Comercio e Integración, Dirección General de Fomento de la Pequeña Industria y Artesanía, 1985. 264 p. ; 21 x 32 cm. "Actualizado al 30 de junio de 1985"--P. 1. LC Card 86-192239
1. Ecuador - Commerce - Directories. 2. Commercial products - Ecuador - Directories. 3. Small business - Ecuador - Directories. I. Ecuador. Dirección General de Fomento de la Pequeña Industria y Artesanía.
HF3433 .D59 1985

Directors and officers liability : is it a viable insurance product?. Hartford, Conn. (101 Pearl St., Hartford 06103) : Conning, c1986. 53 p. ; 28 cm. "June 1986." LC Card 86-211342
1. Insurance, Executives' liability - United States. I. Conning & Company.
HG8053.8 .D57 1986

DIRECTORS OF CORPORATIONS - EUROPE.
Bacon, Jeremy. Board committees in European companies /. New York, N.Y. , c1986. vii, 16 p. ; ISBN 0-8237-0325-8 (pbk.) LC Card 86-207711 DDC 658.4/22/094 19
HD2745 .B14 1986

DIRECTORS OF CORPORATIONS - INIDA - CONGRESSES.
Seminar on Role of Board of Directors in Corporate Governance (1984 : Bombay, India) Seminar on Role of Board of Directors in Corporate Governance . New Delhi [1984] vii, 140 p., [6] p. of plates : LC Card 87-902533 DDC 658.4/22/0954 19
HD2745 .S45 1984

DIRECTORS OF CORPORATIONS - UNITED STATES.
Epstein, Edward Jay, 1935- Who owns the corporation? . New York , 1986. vi, 69 p. ; ISBN 0-87078-208-8 (pbk.) : LC Card 87-101003 DDC 338.7/4/0973 19
HD2743 .E67 1986

Vancil, Richard F. Passing the baton . Boston, Mass. , c1987. xxii, 318 p. : ISBN 0-87584-182-1 LC Card 87-11962 DDC 658.4 19
HD38.25.U6 V36 1987

Directory. Inventaire . Paris [Washington, D.C.] 1986. xxvii, 262 p. ; ISBN 92-64-02871-4 : LC Card 87-129509
HD77.5.A34 I58 1986

Directory "Companies in Flemish Brabant." Adresboek "Bedrijven in Vlaams-Brabant" =. Vilvoorde , 1985. lxi, 186, 62, 63 p. : LC Card 87-111619
HC317.B7 A37 1985

Directory for international investors /. Kehrer, Daniel M. New York, NY, U. S.A. , c1984. 130 p. in various pagings : ISBN 0-86604-175-3 (pbk.) LC Card 86-231996 DDC 332.6/73/025 19
HG4538 .K39 1984

Directory of African central banks /. Association of African Central Banks. Dakar, Senegal [1985 or 1986] ca. 150 leaves : LC Card 87-402547 DDC 332.1/1/02567 19
HG3376 .A87 1985

Directory of aid agencies. 3rd ed. Suva, Fiji : South Pacific Bureau for Economic Co-operation, 1985. iv, 147 p. ; 30 cm. LC Card 86-204497 DDC 338.91/025/9 19
1. Economic assistance - Islands of the Pacific - Directories. 2. Technical assistance - Islands of the Pacific - Directories. I. South Pacific Bureau for Economic Cooperation.
HC681 .D57 1985

Directory of business and industry for Western Area and multiunit firms. Freetown : Sierra Leone Government, Central Statistics Office, [1968] 67 p. ; 33 cm. Cover title. LC Card 87-112242
1. Sierra Leone - Industries - Directories. 2. Sierra Leone - Commerce - Directories. I. Sierra Leone. Central Statistics Office.
HC1065 .D57 1968

Directory of business undertakings, Brunei Darussalam. Buku panduan badan-badan perusahaan perniagaan Negara Brunei Darussalam =. Bandar Seri Begawan, Negara Brunei Darussalam [1985] vii, 89, [9] p. ; LC Card 86-945171 DDC 338.7/4/0255955 19
HF3800.68 .B84 1985

Directory of Cashew exporters from India. Directory of exporters of cashew from India. Cochin, India [1986?] 138 p. ; LC Card 87-901352 DDC 382/.414573/02554 19
HD9259.C33 I423 1986

Directory of cooperative societies, 1986. Srinagar : Issued by Cooperative Dept., Govt. of J & K, [1986] 131 p. ; 28 cm. Cover title: Directory of cooperative societies, Kashmir Province, 1986. LC Card 87-900324 DDC 334/.025/546 19
1. Cooperative societies - India - Jammu and Kashmir - Directories. I. Jammu and Kashmir (India). Co-operative Dept. Statistical Wing.
HD3540.A3 J353 1986

Directory of executive search firms. Lewis, William, 1946- The Prentice-Hall directory of executive search firms /. New York , c1986. v, 328 p. ; ISBN 0-671-55518-9 (pbk.) LC Card 85-30190 DDC 658.4/07111/02573 19
HD38.25.U6 L49 1986
NYPL [*R-Econ. 87-1586]

Directory of exporters of cashew from India. [6th ed.]. Cochin, India : Cashew Export Promotion Council, [1986?] 138 p. ; 23 cm. Cover title: Directory of cashew exporters from India. LC Card 87-901352 DDC 382/.414573/02554 19
1. Cashew nut industry - India - Directories. 2. Export trading companies - India - Directories. I. Cashew Export Promotion Council. II. Title: Directory of Cashew exporters from India.
HD9259.C33 I423 1986

Directory of federal & state business assistance :

a guide for new and growing companies / prepared by the Center for the Utilization of Federal Technology, National Technical Information Service, U. S. Department of Commerce. Springfield, VA : The Service, c1986. xii, 159 p. : 2 ill. ; 28 cm. Cover title: Directory of federal and state business assistance, 1986-1987. "Update and expansion of the Guide to innovation resources and planning for the smaller business, which was developed by the Office of Productivity, Technology, and Innovation of the U. S. Department of Commerce." "May 1986." Bibliography: p. x. Includes index. "NTIS order number PB86-100344"--T.p. verso. ISBN 0-934213-03-8 (pbk.) : LC Card 86-601675 DDC 353.0082/025 19
1. Industrial promotion - United States - Directories. 2. Industrial promotion - United States - States - Directories. I. Center for the Utilization of Federal Technology (U. S.). II. Title: Directory of federal and state business assistance, 1986-1987.
HC110.I53 D57 1986

Directory of federal and state business assistance, 1986-1987. Directory of federal & state business assistance . Springfield, VA , c1986. xii, 159 p. : ISBN 0-934213-03-8 (pbk.) : LC Card 86-601675 DDC 353.0082/025 19
HC110.I53 D57 1986

Directory of financial research, marketing surveys, and services. Financial Sourcebooks' sources . Naperville, Ill. , c1987. 454 p. ; ISBN 0-942061-00-4 (pbk.) : LC Card 87-8793 DDC 332/.025/73 19
HG173 .F517 1987

Directory of licensed insurers, licensed motor clubs, licensed health maintenance organizations, licensed rating organizations, registered advisory organizations : revised July 1, 1985 / Maryland Department of Licensing and Regulation, Insurance Division. [Baltimore, Md.] (501 St. Paul Pl., Baltimore 21202) : The Division, [1985] viii, 150 p. ; 28 cm. Cover title. LC Card 86-621407 DDC 368/.0025/752 19
1. Insurance - Maryland - Directories. 2. Automobiles - Maryland - Societies, etc. - Directories. 3. Health maintenance organizations - Maryland - Directories. I. Maryland. Insurance Division.
HG8526.M3 D59 1985

Directory of licensed occupations and apprenticeship programs in Texas. Mercer, Kent. [Austin, Tex.] [1985] iv, 102 p. ; LC Card 86-622006 DDC 331.7/02/09764 19
HF5382.5.U6 T45 1985

The directory of mail order catalogs /. Gottlieb, Richard. [New York, N.Y.] , Sharon, CT , c1987. xi, 385 p. ; ISBN 0-8160-1740-9 LC Card 86-31959 DDC 016.381/14/0973 19
HF5466 .G63 1987

Directory of no-load mutual funds. Boca Raton, FL (P.O. Box 3007, Boca Raton 33431-0907) : Newsletter Management Corp., c1986. 19 p. ; 28 cm. LC Card 86-231040 DDC 332.63/27 19
1. Mutual funds - United States - Directories. I. Newsletter Management Corporation.
HG4930 .D57 1986

Directory of online data bases. Online databases in the securities and financial markets. New York, N.Y. , c1987. xxii, 322 p. ; ISBN 0-444-01276-1 (pbk.) LC Card 87-19954 DDC 025/.0633/0025 19
HG174 .O44 1987

Directory of regional gardening resources / compiled by the Horticulture Committee, the Garden Club of America. New York, NY (598 Madison Ave., New York 10022) : The Committee, 1987. 172 p. : ill. ; 22 cm. "May 1987"--P. 2 of cover. Includes index. LC Card 87-402229 DDC 338.7/6359/02573 19
1. Horticultural products industry - United States - Directories. I. Garden Club of America. Horticulture Committee.
HD9003 .D66 1987

A Directory of rural and specialized transit operators / prepared by Rural America ; prepared for Office of Grants Management, Urban Mass Transportation Administration. Washington, D.C. : The Office : Distributed in cooperation with Technology Sharing Program, Office of the Secretary of Transportation, 1986- v. <1-3 > : maps ; 22 x 28 cm. Distributed to depository libraries in microfiche. "DOT-I-86-26"--Vol. 1. "June 1986." "DOT-I-86-27"--Vol. 2. "DOT-I-86-28"--Vol. 3. Item 982-I-15 (microfiche) CONTENTS. - v. 1. Eastern U. S. systems -- v. 2. Central U. S. systems -- v. 3. Western U. S. systems. LC Card 86-603414 DDC 388.3/22/0973 19
1. Rural transit - United States - Directories. 2. Paratransit services - United States - Directories. 3. Local transit - United States - Directories. I. Rural America, inc. II. United States. Urban Mass Transportation Administration. Office of Grants Management.
HE203 .D57 1986

Directory of software producers. Fairfax, Va. (3150 Spring St., Fairfax 22031-2399) : International Communications Industries Association, c1986. [28] p. ; 28 cm. Cover title. LC Card 87-109219 DDC 338.7/6137139445 19
1. Computer software industry - United States - Directories. I. International Communications Industries Association.
HD9696.C63 U515957 1986

Directory of Virginia housing resources. [Richmond] : Office of Housing Services of the Virginia Dept. of Housing and Community Development, [1986] iii, 153 p. : ill. ; 28 cm. "September 1986." LC Card 87-620669 DDC 350.86/5/025755 19
1. Housing - Virginia - Directories. 2. Virginia. Office of Housing Services.
HD7303.V8 D57 1986

Direk Tengčhamrūn.
Khant Salam : panhā læ næothāng kækhai / dōi M Krung Thēp , 2525 [1982] 16, 249 p. : LC Card 82-916400
HC445.Z7 B3678 1982

Direkte Steuern und intertemporale Allokation . Naust, Hermann. Köln , c1983. xiv, 374 p. : ISBN 3-452-19402-7 : LC Card 83-163600 DDC 336.2 19
HJ3851 .N38 1983

Der Direktvertrieb im Konsumgüterbereich . Engelhardt, Werner Hans. Stuttgart , c1984. 158 p. : ISBN 3-17-008550-6 : LC Card 84-234886
HF5415.126 .E54 1984

Diretrizes básicas do governo . Suruagy, Divaldo. Maceió, Alagoas , 1983. 84 p. ; LC Card 85-200794
HC188.A46 S87 1983

Diretrizes de planejamento . Fundação Projeto Rondon. [Brasília , 1982] [21] leaves ; LC Card 85-186578
HD4870.B6 F86 1982

Diretrizes e proposições do governo Iris Rezende, março/83-março/87. Goiás, Brazil (State) [Goiânia] [1983?] 189 p. : LC Card 86-152733
HC188.G6 G63 1983

Dirigir con inflación . Blanco Martínez, Adolfo. Bilbao [1983?] 239 p. : ISBN 84-234-0537-0 LC Card 85-124395
HD49.5 .B48 1983

Dirt rich, dirt poor : America's food and farm crisis / Joseph N. Belden .. [et al.]. New York : Routledge & Kegan Paul, 1986. xii, 188 p. ; 22 cm. (Alternative policies for America) "The Institute for Policy Studies--world hunger year." Includes index. Bibliography: p. 183-185. ISBN 0-7102-0378-0 LC Card 85-8274 DDC 338.1/9/73 19
1. Agriculture and state - United States. 2. Nutrition policy - United States. 3. Food relief - United States. I. Belden, Joseph N. II. Institute for Policy Studies. III. Series.
HD1761 .D55 1986 ***NYPL [JLD 87-821]***

Dış ticaret politikası. Karluk, S. Rıdvan. Türkiye'de ihracata yönelik dış ticaret politikası ve ihracatın yapısal analizi /. Eskişehir , 1981. xx, 454 p. ; LC Card 82-241650
HF1583.4 .K37 1981

Disability benefits : factors determining application and awards / edited by Han Emanuel, Eric H. de Gier, Peter A.B. Kalker Konijn. Greenwich, Conn. : JAI Press, c1987. xxii, 282 p. ; 24 cm. (Contemporary studies in economic and financial analysis. vol. 59) Proceedings of a conference held in Zoetermeer, The Netherlands, Nov. 16-17, 1982, sponsored by International Social Security Association. Includes bibliographies and index. ISBN 0-89232-824-X : LC Card 87-17056 DDC 368.3/86/009492 19
1. Insurance, Disability - Netherlands - Congresses. 2. Insurance, Disability - Great Britain - Congresses. 3. Insurance, Disability - Congresses. 4. Disability evaluation - Netherlands - Congresses. 5. Disability evaluation - Great Britain - Congresses. 6. Disability - Congresses. I. Emanuel, Han. II. Gier, Eric H. de. III. Konijn, Peter A. B. Kalker. IV. International Social Security Association. V. ISSA Expert Meeting on Disability Research (1982 : Zoetermeer, Netherlands). VI. Series: Contemporary studies in economic and financial analysis, v. 59.
HD7105.25.N4 D57 1987

DISABILITY - CONGRESSES.
Disability benefits . Greenwich, Conn. , c1987. xxii, 282 p. ; ISBN 0-89232-824-X : LC Card 87-17056 DDC 368.3/86/009492 19
HD7105.25.N4 D57 1987

DISABILITY EVALUATION - GREAT BRITAIN - CONGRESSES.
Disability benefits . Greenwich, Conn. , c1987. xxii, 282 p. ; ISBN 0-89232-824-X : LC Card 87-17056 DDC 368.3/86/009492 19
HD7105.25.N4 D57 1987

DISABILITY EVALUATION - NETHERLANDS - CONGRESSES.
Disability benefits . Greenwich, Conn. , c1987. xxii, 282 p. ; ISBN 0-89232-824-X : LC Card 87-17056 DDC 368.3/86/009492 19
HD7105.25.N4 D57 1987

DISABILITY EVALUATION - UNITED STATES - CASE STUDIES.
Kizorek, Bill. Disability or deception /. [Naperville, Ill., USA] (Suite 12, 6 S 235 Steeple Run Dr., Naperville 60540) [c1986] 140 p. : LC Card 86-206432 DDC 363.2/5 19
HD7105.25.U6 K59 1986

Disability insurance . Morris, William H., Jr. Lexington, Ky. (98 Dennis Dr., Lexington 40503) , c1986. x, 93 p. : LC Card 87-402218 DDC 368.3/86/00973 19
HD7105.25.U6 M67 1986

DISABILITY INSURANCE. see **INSURANCE, DISABILITY.**

Disability or deception /. Kizorek, Bill. [Naperville, Ill., USA] (Suite 12, 6 S 235 Steeple Run Dr., Naperville 60540) [c1986] 140 p. : LC Card 86-206432 DDC 363.2/5 19
HD7105.25.U6 K59 1986

DISABLED - REHABILITATION, ETC. see **VOCATIONAL REHABILITATION.**

Disadvantaged youth in an isolated region . Ladbrook, Denis A. [Pilbara, W.A.] [1985] ix, 125 p. : LC Card 87-121044 DDC 331.3/4/099413 19
HD6276.A83 P555 1985

Disaggregated farm income by type of farm, 1959-82 /. Somwaru, Agapi. Washington, D.C. , 1986. iii, 113 p. : LC Card 86-602571 DDC 338.1 s 338.1/3/0973021 19
HD1751 .A91854 no. 558 HD1769

DISARMAMENT AND ATOMIC WEAPONS. see **ATOMIC WEAPONS AND DISARMAMENT.**

Disarmament and world development / edited by Mac Graham, Richard Jolly, and Chris Smith. 2nd ed. Oxford, England ; New York : Pergamon Press, 1986. xiii, 306 p. ; 24 cm. Includes index. Bibliography: p. 283-299. ISBN 0-08-031309-4 : LC Card 85-19231 DDC 338.4/7355 19
1. Disarmament - Congresses. 2. Economic development - Congresses. 3. Armed Forces - Appropriations and expenditures - Congresses. 4. Sociology, Military - Congresses. 5. Developing countries - Congresses. I. Graham, Mac. II. Jolly, Richard. III. Smith, Chris.
JX1974 .D515 1985 ***NYPL [JLE 86-3211]***

DISARMAMENT - CONGRESSES.
Disarmament and world development /. Oxford, England , New York , 1986. xiii, 306 p. ; ISBN 0-08-031309-4 : LC Card 85-19231 DDC 338.4/7355 19
JX1974 .D515 1985 ***NYPL [JLE 86-3211]***

Stimme und Aktion der Völker gegen das Wettrüsten . Berlin , 1985. 421 p. ;
NYPL [JLD 86-4257]

World peace and the developing countries . Basingstoke, Hampshire , 1986. xix, 272 p. ; ISBN 0-333-43636-9 ***NYPL [JLD 87-1192]***

DISARMAMENT - ECONOMIC ASPECTS.
United Nations. Secretary-General. [Economic and social consequences of the arms race and

of military expenditures. French.] Conséquences économiques et sociales de la course aux armements /. Paris , 1983. 121 p. : ISBN 2-7178-0645-8 : LC Card 84-136625
HC79.D4 U52 1983

Wilke, Peter. Manpower conversion in defence related industry . Hamburg [1986] 62 p. : LC Card 86-212660 DDC 331.25/924 19
HC79.D4 W55 1986

DISARMAMENT - ECONOMIC ASPECTS - DEVELOPING COUNTRIES.
Defence, security, and development /. New York , 1987. xiii, 219 p. : ISBN 0-312-01243-8 : LC Card 87-12129 DDC 338.4/76234/091724 19
HC59.72.D4 D436 1987

DISARMAMENT - ECONOMIC ASPECTS - GERMANY, WEST.
Zivile Alternativen für die Rüstungsindustrie /. Baden-Baden , 1986. 174 p. ; ISBN 3-7890-1262-9 LC Card 87-108651 DDC 338.4/76234/0943 19
HD9743.G48 Z58 1986

DISARMAMENT - ECONOMIC ASPECTS - SWITZERLAND.
Spälti, P. Die Rüstungsreferendumsinitiative--schlecht getarnter Anschlag auf unsere Landesverteidigung /. Zürich , 1987. 20 p. ; LC Card 87-409331 DDC 330.9494 s 327.1/74/09494 19
HC395 .Z43 Nr. 131 HC400.D4

DISARMAMENT - ECONOMIC ASPECTS - UNITED STATES.
Coalition of Northeast Governors. Policy Research Center. A case of inequity [microform] . [New York] , 1977. 39 p. ; ***NYPL [*ZT-1564 no.21]***

Economic adjustment and conversion of defense industries /. Boulder , 1987. xiv, 312 p. : ISBN 0-8133-7396-4 (pbk. : alk. paper) LC Card 87-50495 DDC 338.4/36234/0973 19
HC110.D4 E36 1987

The Economic and social consequences of disarmament . Washington, D.C. [1961] ii leaves, 89 p. ; LC Card 85-115648
HC110.D4 E37 1961

Kappus, Wolfgang. Abrüstung und Wirtschaftswachstum . Frankfurt , New York , c1985. 329 p. : ISBN 3-593-33531-X LC Card 85-232235
HC110.D4 K37 1985

DISARMAMENT - SOCIAL ASPECTS - UNITED STATES.
The Economic and social consequences of disarmament . Washington, D.C. [1961] ii leaves, 89 p. ; LC Card 85-115648
HC110.D4 E37 1961

DISASTER RELIEF - ETHIOPIA.
Combatting the effects of cyclical drought in Ethiopia. Addis Ababa, Ethiopia [1985] 56 p. : LC Card 86-224201 DDC 363.8/83/0963 19
HC845.Z9 F332 1985

DISASTER RELIEF - ITALY, SOUTHERN.
Acocella, Giovanni, 1932- Di là dalle rovine . Napoli , c1982. 172, [4] p. ; ISBN 88-7042-185-6 : LC Card 82-181323 DDC 363.3/495 19
HC307.S69 A36 1982 ***NYPL [JLD 86-485]***

Mezzogiorno . [S.l. , 1980?] (København : Kunstakademiets trykkeri) 78 p. : LC Card 85-128057
HC307.S6 M49 1980

Terremoto e crisi urbana . Napoli , 1981. 207 p. ; ***NYPL [JLE 86-4532]***

DISASTERS.
Schabeck, Timothy A. Managing microcomputer security . Port Jefferson Station, N.Y. (492 Old Town Rd., Port Jefferson Station 11776) , c1986. 1 v. (various pagings) : LC Card 86-216667 DDC 658.4/78 19
HF5548.37 .S33 1986

DISASTERS - ECONOMIC ASPECTS.
Grases G., José. Pérdidas como consecuencia de terremotos . Caracas , 1986. 71 p. : ISBN 980-265-358-6 LC Card 87-403100 DDC 338.4/33633495 19
HC79.D45 G7 1986

DISASTERS - ECONOMIC ASPECTS - MEXICO - MEXICO CITY METROPOLITAN AREA.
El Terremoto del 19 de septiembre y los trabajadores mexicanos. [Mexico City, Mexico?] [1985] 114 p. ; LC Card 86-144990
HC138.M4 T47 1985 ***NYPL [JLC 87-130]***

Disbursement handbook. Washington, D.C., U.S.A. : World Bank, c1986. iv, 58 p. : ill. ; 28 cm. Includes index. ISBN 0-8213-0746-0 (pbk.) LC Card 86-210947 DDC 332.1/532/0685 19
1. World Bank. 2. Bank loans - Handbooks, manuals, etc. 3. Loans, Foreign - Developing countries - Handbooks, manuals, etc. I. International Bank for Reconstruction and Development.
HG3881.5.W57 D57 1986

DISCIPLINE, INDUSTRIAL. see **LABOR DISCIPLINE.**

DISCIPLINE, LABOR. see **LABOR DISCIPLINE.**

DISCIPLINE, MENTAL. see **MENTAL DISCIPLINE.**

Den disciplinerade arbetaren . Horgby, Björn. Stockholm [1986] 322 p. : ISBN 91-22-00804-7 LC Card 87-105821
HC378.N67 H67 1986

Disclosure checklists for banks : a financial reporting practice aid / edited by Richard Rikert, Jack Shohet.Fall 1986 ed. New York, N.Y. : American Institute of Certified Public Accountants, c1986. 64 p. ; 28 cm. LC Card 86-224924 DDC 657/.833 19
1. Banks and banking - United States - Accounting. 2. Financial statements - United States. 3. Disclosure in accounting. I. Rikert, Richard. II. Shohet, Jack. III. American Institute of Certified Public Accountants.
HG1708 .D57 1986

DISCLOSURE IN ACCOUNTING.
Disclosure checklists for banks . New York, N.Y. , c1986. 64 p. ; LC Card 86-224924 DDC 657/.833 19
HG1708 .D57 1986

Mangold, Nancy R. (Nancy Rueyhwa), 1949- Changing auditors and the effect on earnings, auditors' opinions, and stock prices /. Ann Arbor, Mich. , c1987. viii, 165 p. ; ISBN 0-8357-1786-0 (alk. paper) LC Card 87-19128 DDC 338.7/4/0973 19
HF5686.C7 M3295 1987

Prodhan, B. Multinational accounting . London , Dover, N.H. , c1986. xi, 399 p. : ISBN 0-7099-4010-6 : LC Card 86-4521 DDC 657/.95 19
HF5686.I56 P76 1986 ***NYPL [JLD 86-2595]***

Discontinuità e permanenza . Gario, Giuseppe. Milano, Italy , c1986. 262 p. : LC Card 87-149940
HC307.L8 G37 1986

DISCOUNT HOUSES (RETAIL TRADE) - DENMARK.
Discountbutikker i dagligvarehandelen . København , 1983. 175 p. : ISBN 87-88149-11-0 : LC Card 83-237411
HF5429.215.D4 D57 1983

DISCOUNT HOUSES (RETAIL TRADE) - DIRECTORIES.
Goldstein, Sue, 1941- The 2nd underground shopper . Kansas City , c1985. 470 p. : ISBN 0-8362-7956-5 (pbk.) : LC Card 85-620 DDC 381/.1 19
HF5466 .G6 1985 ***NYPL [JLD 86-3080]***

Goldstein, Sue, 1941- The 3rd underground shopper . Kansas City , 1986. x, 532 p. ; ISBN 0-8362-7937-9 (pbk.) : LC Card 86-28758 DDC 381/.1 19
HF5466 .G6 1986

DISCOUNT HOUSES (RETAIL TRADE) - UNITED STATES.
Dollars & cents of off-price shopping centers . Washington, D.C. , c1986. v, 78 p. : ISBN 0-87420-660-X (pbk.) LC Card 86-51102 DDC 381/.1 19
HF5430.3 .D65 1986

DISCOUNT HOUSES (RETAIL TRADE) - UNITED STATES - DIRECTORIES.
Goldstein, Sue, 1941- The 2nd underground shopper . Kansas City , c1985. 470 p. : ISBN 0-8362-7956-5 (pbk.) : LC Card 85-620 DDC 381/.1 19
HF5466 .G6 1985 ***NYPL [JLD 86-3080]***

Goldstein, Sue, 1941- The 3rd underground shopper . Kansas City , 1986. x, 532 p. ; ISBN 0-8362-7937-9 (pbk.) : LC Card 86-28758 DDC 381/.1 19
HF5466 .G6 1986

Discountbutikker i dagligvarehandelen : markedsstruktur og prisforhold. København : Monopoltilsynet, 1983. 175 p. : ill. ; 24 cm. (Redegørelse fra Monopoltilsynet) ISBN 87-88149-11-0 : LC Card 83-237411
1. Discount houses (Retail trade) - Denmark. 2. Prices - Denmark. I. Denmark. Monopoltilsynet. II. Series.
HF5429.215.D4 D57 1983

DISCOUNTED CASH FLOW.
Crowe, Robert M. Time and money . Homewood, Ill. , c1987. 1 v. (various pagings) : ISBN 1-556-23051-6 (pbk.) LC Card 87-70621 DDC 332.024 19
HG1621 .C76 1987

Discounted mortgages. Bel Air, Roger. Make a fortune buying discounted mortgages /. Garden City, N.Y. , 1987. 152 p. : ISBN 0-385-23924-6 : LC Card 86-23949 DDC 332.63/244 19
HG5095 .B38 1987

Discover the North West of Cameroon : economy-business-tourism-society = Découvres la Province du Nord-Ouest : economie-affaires-societe-tourisme. [Bamenda? : s.n., 1984] 197 p., [2] p. of plates : ill. ; 26 cm. "September 1984." English and French. LC Card 87-101117 DDC 330.967/11204 19
1. North-West Province (Cameroon) - Economic conditions. 2. North-West Province (Cameroon) - Commerce. 3. Industrial promotion - Cameroon - North-West Province. I. Title: Decouvrez la Province du Nord-Ouest.
HC995.Z7 N673 1984

DISCOVERIES (IN SCIENCE) see **INVENTIONS; SCIENCE.**

Discovering causal structure : artificial intelligence, philosophy of science, and statistical modeling / Clark Glymour ... [et al.]. Orlando : Academic Press, 1987. xvii, 394 p. : ill. ; 24 cm. + 1 computer disk (5 1/4 in.) System requirements for computer disk: IBM PC or IBM-compatible machines; 512K recommended; DOS 2.1. Computer disk contains one version of TETRAD program for use with an 8087 coprocessor chip and a second version for computers without this chip. Bibliography: p. 378-388. Includes index. ISBN 0-12-286962-1 (alk. paper) LC Card 87-1860 DDC 300/.1/51 19
1. Social sciences - Statistical methods. 2. Social sciences - Data processing. 3. Social sciences - Mathematical models. 4. Artificial intelligence. I. Glymour, Clark N. II. Title: Causal structure.
HA29 .D495 1987

Discovering stamps /. Buchan, Bryan, 1945- Richmond Hill, Ont. , New York [1977], c1973. 91 p. : LC Card 85-148831
HE6213 .B83 1977

Discrepancies between imports and exports in OECD foreign trade statistics /. Blades, Derek W. Paris, France , c1984. i, 42 p. ; LC Card 86-205155 DDC 382/.021 19
HF1016 .B569 1984

Discrete-events simulations models in PASCAL/MT+ on a microcomputer /. Jennergren, L. Peter (Lars Peter), 1944- Lund, Sweden , c1984. 135 p. ; ISBN 91-44-22221-1 (pbk.) : ***NYPL [JSD 86-366]***

DISCRIMINATING DUTY. see **TARIFF PREFERENCES.**

DISCRIMINATION AGAINST WOMEN. see **SEX DISCRIMINATION AGAINST WOMEN.**

DISCRIMINATION IN EDUCATION - UNITED STATES.
Fuchs, Lawrence H. When to count by race . New York, NY , c1986. 32 p. ; ISBN 0-87495-082-1 (pbk.) : LC Card 86-71979 DDC 658.3 19
HD4903.5.U58 F83 1986

DISCRIMINATION IN EMPLOYMENT - BRAZIL.
Oliveira, Lúcia Elena Garcia de. O lugar do negro na força de trabalho /. Rio de Janeiro , 1983. 86 p. ; ISBN 85-24-00024-4 LC Card 86-129924
HD8288.5.B55 O45 1983

Silva, Manuela. A igualdade de oportunidades de formação profissional para as mulheres /. Lisboa , 1983. 51, [1] p. : LC Card 84-238349
HD6179 .S56 1983

DISCRIMINATION IN EMPLOYMENT - CANADA.
Employment equity for crown corporations . Ottawa , 1986. 17, 18 p. ; ISBN 0-662-54400-5 (pbk.) LC Card 86-207179 DDC 354.71001/04 19
HD4903.5.C2 E47 1986

DISCRIMINATION IN EMPLOYMENT - EUROPEAN ECONOMIC COMMUNITY COUNTRIES.
Equal opportunity counsellors . Berlin , Washington, DC , 1986. 50 p. : ISBN 92-825-6559-9 : LC Card 87-136233 DDC 331.13/3/094 19
HD4903.5.E8 E79 1986

DISCRIMINATION IN EMPLOYMENT - GERMANY, WEST.
Dohse, Knuth, 1948- [Ausländerpolitik und betriebeliche Ausländerdiskriminierung. English.] Foreign workers in the Federal Republic of Germany . Berlin [1982] 80 p. : LC Card 86-214190 DDC 331.6/2/0943 19
HD8458.A2 D6213 1982

DISCRIMINATION IN EMPLOYMENT - GERMANY (WEST) - CASE STUDIES.
Gesinnungs überprüft! . Berlin [1978] 263 p. : LC Card 84-198533
HD4903.5.G4 G47 1978

DISCRIMINATION IN EMPLOYMENT - GOVERNMENT POLICY - CANADA.
Coates, Mary Lou. Employment equity . Kingston, Ont., Canada , 1986. 109 p. : ISBN 0-88886-131-1 (pbk.) LC Card 86-182985 DDC 331.13/3/0971 19
HD4903.5.C2 C6 1986

DISCRIMINATION IN EMPLOYMENT - GREAT BRITAIN.
Jenkins, Richard, 1952- Racism and recruitment . Cambridge [Cambridgeshire] , New York , 1986. xi, 281 p. ; ISBN 0-521-32028-3 LC Card 85-17483 DDC 331.13/3/0941 19
HG4903.5.G7 J46 1986
NYPL [JLE 86-3305]

Wrench, John. Unequal comrades . Coventry , 1986. 30 p. ; ISBN 0-948303-65-4 (pbk.) : LC Card 87-146518 DDC 331.6 19
HD6490.R22 G78 1986

DISCRIMINATION IN EMPLOYMENT - LAW AND LEGISLATION - UNITED STATES.
Arvey, Richard D. Fairness in selecting employees /. Reading, Mass. , c1988. x, 361 p. : ISBN 0-201-00078-4 (pbk.) : LC Card 87-22173 DDC 658.3/112 19
HF5549.5.S38 A78 1988

Cope, Thom K. Executive guide to employment practices . Lincoln, Neb. , c1984. vii, 163 p. : ISBN 0-939644-14-2 (pbk.) : LC Card 84-62043 DDC 344.73/01133 347.3041133 19
KF3464.Z9 C65 1984 ***NYPL [JLE 87-75]***

Kohn, Stephen M. (Stephen Martin) Protecting environmental & nuclear whistleblowers . Washington, D.C. , c1985. xiii, 346 p. : ISBN 0-9615323-0-0 (pbk.) LC Card 85-61844 DDC 342.73/0684 347.302684 19
KF5342 .K64 1985 ***NYPL [JLE 86-1787]***

DISCRIMINATION IN EMPLOYMENT - PENNSYLVANIA - HISTORY.
Dickerson, Dennis C., 1949- Out of the crucible . Albany , c1986. xiv, 323 p. : ISBN 0-88706-305-5 LC Card 85-30450 DDC 331.6/3/960730748 19
HD8039.I52 U535 1986
NYPL [JLE 86-4411]

DISCRIMINATION IN EMPLOYMENT - UNITED STATES.
Arvey, Richard D. Fairness in selecting employees /. Reading, Mass. , c1988. x, 361 p. : ISBN 0-201-00078-4 (pbk.) : LC Card 87-22173 DDC 658.3/112 19
HF5549.5.S38 A78 1988

Fernandez, John P., 1941- Survival in the corporate fishbowl . Lexington, Mass. , c1987. xiii, 314 p. : ISBN 0-669-10336-5 (alk. paper) LC Card 85-40021 DDC 302.3/5 19
HD6957.U6 F47 1987

Fuchs, Lawrence H. When to count by race . New York, NY , c1986. 32 p. ; ISBN 0-87495-082-1 (pbk.) : LC Card 86-71979 DDC 658.3 19
HD4903.5.U58 F83 1986

DISCRIMINATION IN EMPLOYMENT - UNITED STATES - CASE STUDIES.
Copeland, Vincent. The blast furnace brothers /. New York, N.Y. , 1973. iv, 33 p. : LC Card 87-125932 DDC 331.13/3 19
HD4903.3.B582 U63 1973

DISCRIMINATION IN EMPLOYMENT - UZBEK S.S.R.
Lubin, Nancy. Labour and nationality in Soviet Central Asia . London , 1984. xix, 305 p. : ISBN 0-333-36739-1 LC Card 87-672162
HD5797.U9 L83x 1984b

DISCRIMINATION IN HOUSING - COLOMBIA - VALLE DEL CAUCA.
Mosquera Torres, Gilma. Clases, segregación y barrios /. Cali, Colombia , 1984. 126 p. : LC Card 86-218143
HD7325.V35 M67 1984

DISCRIMINATION IN HOUSING - ENGLAND - BIRMINGHAM (WEST MIDLANDS)
Henderson, J. W. (Jeffrey William), 1947- Race, class, and state housing . Aldershot, Hants, England ;Brookfield, Vt. , c1987. xxiii, 331 p. : ISBN 0-566-00785-1 :
NYPL [JLD 87-1476]

DISCRIMINATION IN HOUSING - LAW AND LEGISLATION - UNITED STATES.
Issues in housing discrimination. Washington, D.C. , 1986- v. <1 > : LC Card 86-602528 DDC 363.5/1 19
HD7288.76.U5 I88 1986

Issues in housing discrimination . [Washington, D.C. , 1986- v. : ***NYPL [JLM 86-1332]***

DISCRIMINATION IN HOUSING - UNITED STATES.
The Fair Housing Assistance Program evaluation /. Washington, D.C. [1985] 1 v. (various pagings) : ***NYPL [JLF 87-17]***

Issues in housing discrimination. Washington, D.C. , 1986- v. <1 > : LC Card 86-602528 DDC 363.5/1 19
HD7288.76.U5 I88 1986

Issues in housing discrimination . [Washington, D.C. , 1986- v. : ***NYPL [JLM 86-1332]***

Race, ethnicity, and minority housing in the United States /. New York , 1986. xxv, 224 p. ; ISBN 0-313-24848-6 (lib. bdg. : alk. paper) LC Card 86-9971 DDC 363.5/9 19
HD7288.72.U5 R33 1986
NYPL [JLE 87-946]

DISCRIMINATION IN INSURANCE - UNITED STATES.
Keenan, Gerald M. Insurance redlining . Chicago, Ill. , c1979. 135 p. :
NYPL [JLF 86-1590]

Discrimination or development?. Colombo, Sri Lanka : Society for Ethnic Amity, [1985?] vii, 40 p. ; 29 cm. LC Card 85-904128 DDC 338.9549/3 19
1. Sri Lanka - Economic policy. 2. Sri Lanka - Economic conditions. 3. Sri Lanka - Social conditions. I. Society for Ethnic Amity (Sri Lanka).
HC424 .D53 1985

DISCRIMINATION, RACIAL. see **RACE DISCRIMINATION.**

DISCRIMINATION, SEXUAL. see **SEX DISCRIMINATION.**

DISCRIMINATION - UNITED STATES.
Helping the sexually oppressed /. Englewood Cliffs, N.J. , c1986. xix, 282 p. : ISBN 0-13-386129-5 : LC Card 85-16687 DDC 305.3 19
HN57 .H46 1986 ***NYPL [JLE 86-3217]***

Discurso sobre la utilidad de los conocimientos económico-políticos y la necesidad de su estudio metódico ; Proposiciones de economía civil y comercio ; Espíritu del señor Melón en su ensayo político sobre el comercio /. Normante y Carcavilla, Lorenzo. [Aragón] [1984?] 1 v. (various pagings) ; ISBN 84-505-0473-2 LC Card 87-104302
HC385 .N57 1984

Discurso sobre la utilidad de los conocimientos económico-políticos y la necesidad de su estudio metódico. Normante y Carcavilla, Lorenzo. Discurso sobre la utilidad de los conocimientos económico-políticos y la necesidad de su estudio metódico ; Proposiciones de economía civil y comercio ; Espíritu del señor Melón en su ensayo político sobre el comercio /. [Aragón] [1984?] 1 v. (various pagings) ; ISBN 84-505-0473-2 LC Card 87-104302
HC385 .N57 1984

Discussion document (Great Britain. Health and Safety Commission)
Great Britain. Health and Safety Commission. Proposal to review the minimum age at which children may drive or ride on agricultural machinery /. London [1982] 12 p. ; ISBN 0-11-883635-8 (pbk.) LC Card 82-214120 DDC 363.1/89 19
HD6247.A4 G74 1982

Discussion of the Nicaragua ship canal and the Tehuantepec ship railway schemes before the Committee on Foreign Affairs of the House of Representatives. United States. Congress. House. Committee on Foreign Affairs. [Washington] [1882?] 80 p. ; LC Card 82-602443
HE536 .U55 1882

Discussion paper (Australian National University. Centre for Economic Policy Research) .
(no. 127) Gruen, F. H. (Fred Henry), 1921- How bad is Australia's economic performance and why? . Canberra, Australia [1985] 61 p. ; ISBN 0-949293-38-5 (pbk.) LC Card 86-228640 DDC 338.994 19
HC605 .G78 1985

Discussion paper (Australian National University. Centre for Economic Research) .
(no. 133) Forsyth, P. (Peter) Can international comparisons of air fares be made? /. Canberra, Australia [1985] 35 p. ; ISBN 0-949293-46-6 (pbk.) LC Card 86-212326 DDC 387.7/12 19
HE9783 .F67 1985

Discussion paper (Canada. Industry, Trade and Commerce)
Manufacturing performance. [Canada] [1977?] 18 p. : LC Card 85-194098
HD9734.C25 M36 1977

Discussion paper (Economic Council of Canada) .
(no. 259) Eglington, Peter. An economic analysis of oilsands policy in Canada . Ottawa, Ont. [1984] 1 v. (various pagings) : LC Card 84-213823 DDC 333.8/232 19
HD9574.C23 W654 1984

Discussion paper (Manitoba. Manitoba Industry, Trade and Technology)
Barber, Clarence L., 1917- Manitoba's interest in and attitude towards a proposed Canada-United States free trade area . [Winnipeg , 1985] 35 leaves : LC Card 86-175828 DDC 382/.0971/073 19
HF1479 .B37 1985

Discussion paper (Murdoch University) .
(n. 86/5) Taylor, Neil. The security of energy supplies in Western Australia /. Murdoch, W.A. , 1986. 35 p. : ISBN 0-86905-099-0 (pbk.) : LC Card 87-118009 DDC 333.79/09941 19
HD9502.A873 W45673 1986

(85/1) Taylor, Neil. Collie, coal, and energy policy in Western Australia /. Murdoch, W.A. [1985] 56 p. : ISBN 0-86905-080-X (pbk.) LC Card 87-116549 DDC 333.8/22/099412 19
HD9558.A83 C657 1985

Discussion paper (Ōsaka Daigaku. Shakai Keizai Kenkyūjo) .
(no. 131) Sekiguchi, Sueo. Technology transfer through direct foreign investment /. Ibaraki, Osaka, Japan , 1985. 61 leaves : LC Card 86-209818 DDC 332.6/7352 19
HC60 .S416 1985

Discussion paper (Queen's University (Kingston, Ont.). Institute for Economic Research) .
(no. 669) Abbott, Michael G. Male and female earnings in Canadian manufacturing, 1931 /. Kingston, Ont., Canada [1986] 82 p. ; LC Card 87-145991 DDC 331.2/87/0971 19
HD4979 .A22 1986

(no. 670) Abbott, Michael G. Alternative estimates of union-nonunion and public-private wage differentials in Ontario, 1981 /. Kingston, Ont., Canada [1986] ii, 61 p. ; LC Card 87-146006 DDC 331.2/2/09713 19
HD4980.O5 A64 1986

Discussion paper (Reserve Bank of New Zealand. Economic Dept.) .
(no. G86/7) Dickens, Rodney. Overseas experience with "strict" monetary targetry and its implications for New Zealand /. Wellington [1986] iii, 24 leaves ; LC Card 87-137038 DDC 332.4/9931 19
HG230.3 .D53 1986

(G86/2) LLoyd, K. A. The term structure of interest rates in New Zealand, 1977-1985 /. Wellington, N.Z. [1986] 41, 3 p. : LC Card 86-212755 DDC 332.8/2/09931 19
HG1623.N48 L56 1986

(G86/4) Brooks, R. Inflation, tax rules, and housing in New Zealand /. Wellington, N.Z. [1986] 22, [22] p. : LC Card 87-132461 DDC 363.5/8 19
HD7387.5.A3 B76 1986

Discussion paper series (International Institute of Management) .
(77-63) Fleischer, Manfred. Organisationstheoretische Analyse von Marketing-Entscheidungsprozessen . Berlin [1977] 93 p. : LC Card 85-111320
HF5415.135 .F58 1977

(79-57) Matzner, Egon, 1938- Die Soziogenese des Staates nach Elias und Schumpeter . Berlin [1979] 30, [4] p. ; LC Card 85-135122
HJ105 .M37 1979

(85-4) Albrecht, Christoph, 1950- Beschäftigungsentwicklung und Qualifikationsstruktur in Berlin 1977-1983 . Berlin [1985] 2 v. : LC Card 86-204299
HD5780.B4 A43 1985

Discussion paper series (Universiti Sains Malaysia. Pusat Pengajian Ilmu Kemasyarakatan) .
(no. 4) Mannur, H. G. The terms of trade and Third World countries /. Pulau Pinang , 1978. ii, 35 p. ; LC Card 84-940687
HF4055 .M36 1978

Discussion paper (University of Ghana. Institute of Statistical, Social, and Economic Research) .
(no. 5) Nyanteng, V. K. Local food prices . [Ghana] , 1978. 37 p. : LC Card 87-403379 DDC 338.4/3664/009667 19
HD9017.G452 N92 1978

(no. 8) Nyanteng, V. K. Supplementary occupations and incomes of cocoa farmers in the Suhum agricultural district of Ghana /. Legon , 1979. 17 p. ; LC Card 87-402747 DDC 331.7/63374/09667 19
HD8039.C6362 G46 1979

Discussion paper (University of Sussex. Institute of Development Studies) .
(DP 215) Stevens, Christopher. Negotiating Lome III . Sussex [1986] 23 p. : LC Card 86-222421 DDC 337.406 19
HC241.25.D44 S74 1986

(DP 216) Green, Reginald Herbold. The IMF and stabilisation in sub-Saharan Africa . Brighton, England [1986] ii, 70 p. ; LC Card 86-208478 DDC 332.1/52 19
HC800 .G72 1986

Discussion papers (Australia. Dept. of the Parliamentary Library. Legislative Research Service) .
(1982, no. 1) Gannicott, K. G. (Ken G.) Australia's dependence on foreign technology /. [Canberra, Australia] [1982] 38 p. ; LC Card 84-197120 DDC 338.994/06 19
HC610.T4 G36 1982

Discussion papers in economics and banking .
(discussion paper no. 5) Brimmer, Andrew F. Monetary policy and the international diffusion of interest rates /. Miami, Fla. [1982] iii, 47 p. : LC Card 86-204514 DDC 332.4/973 19
HG540 .B75 1982

Discussion papers (International Institute of Management) .
(84-2) Schettkat, Ronald. Generelle Arbeitszeitverkürzung . Berlin , 1984. iii, 108 p. : LC Card 84-182608
HD5106 .S3 1984

Discussion papers (International Institute of Management. Industrial Policy) .
(IIM/IP 84-23) Weiss, Leonard W. The extent and permanence of market dominance /. Berlin [1984] 30, 7 p. ; LC Card 85-183107 DDC 338.8/2 19
HD2757.3 .W45 1984

(IIM/IP 85-12) Kleindorfer, Paul R. Optimal capacity planning under stagnating demand /. Berlin [1985] 18, 4 leaves : LC Card 86-205882
HD69.C3 K49 1985

(IIM/IP 85-18) Schlesinger, Harris. Extending Arrow-Pratt risk premiums /. Berlin [1985] 13, 4 leaves : LC Card 86-206602 DDC 368 19
HG8054.5 .S35 1985

(IIM/IP 85-19) Gahlen, Bernhard. Zur internationalen Wettbewerbsfähigkeit der deutschen Wirtschaft /. [Berlin] [1985] 41, 4 p. ; LC Card 86-204589
HC286.7 .G29 1985

(IIM/IP 85-22) Geroski, Paul. The persistence of profits . Berlin [1985] 35, 6 p. : LC Card 86-212315 DDC 338.5/16/0724 19
HG4028.P7 G47 1985

(IIM/IP 85-29) Geroski, Paul A. Do dominant firms decline? /. Berlin [1985] 23, [8] p. ; LC Card 86-213583 DDC 338.6/44 19
HD2757 .G47 1985

(IIM/IP 85-39) Kraft, Kornelius. Wettbewerbssituation und Marktzutrittsbarrieren bei spezifischen Qualifikationen /. Berlin [1985] 35, 6 p. : LC Card 86-211574
HD5707 .K73 1985

(IIM/IP 86-11) Breyer, Friedrich. Family structure and intergenerational transfers in social health insurance . Berlin [1986] 24 p. : LC Card 87-156738 DDC 368.4/2016/0724 19
HD7101 .B73 1986

(IIM/IP 86-13) Audretsch, David B. Industrial policy, R&D, and U. S.-Japanese trade /. Berlin [1986] 39 p. ; LC Card 87-156721 DDC 382/.0952/073 19
HF3127 .A93 1986

(IIM/IP 86-14) Yamawaki, Hideki. Industry competition and the formation of the European common market /. Berlin [1986] 34, 3 p. ; LC Card 87-156700 DDC 341.24/22 19
HD41 .Y35 1986

(IIM/IP 86-18) Ács, Zoltán J. The determinants of innovation in large and small firms /. Berlin [1986] 39 p. ; LC Card 87-156684 DDC 338.6/4 19
HC110.T4 A59 1986

(IIM/IP 86-3) Odagiri, Hiroyuki, 1946- A study of company profit-rate time series . Berlin [1986] 15, 5 p. ; LC Card 87-165037 DDC 338.7/4/0952 19
HG4028.P7 O33 1986

(IIM/P 85-28) Geroski, Paul A. Entrepreneurship and small firms /. Berlin [1985] 31, 2, 6 p. ; LC Card 86-213576 DDC 338.6/42 19
HD2346.E9 G47 1985

Discussion papers (International Institute of Management. Labor Market Policy) .
(IIM/LMP 86-13) Funke, Michael, 1956- Tobin's q and industry investment in West Germany /. Berlin [1986] 36 p. : LC Card 87-156645 DDC 332.63 19
HC290.5.C3 F86 1986

Discussion papers (International Institute of Management. Labour Market Policy) .
(IIM/LMP 84-1) Burian, Klaus. Betriebliche Erfahrungen mit neuen Arbeitszeitformen . Berlin [1984] iv, 162 p. ; LC Card 84-182592
HD5110.2.G3 B87 1984

(IIM/LMP 84-12) Schettkat, Ronald. Bevölkerungs- und Erwerbsverhaltensentwicklung in Österreich, Schweden und der Bundesrepublik Deutschland /. Berlin [1984] 48 p. ; LC Card 85-198691
HD5771 .S34 1984

(IIM/LMP 85-10) Auer, Peter. Industrial relations, work organisation and new technology . Berlin [1985] 17, [6] p. ; LC Card 86-205891 DDC 331/.04292/09481 19
HD9710.S84 V6413 1985

(IIM/LMP 85-11) Sawyer, Malcolm C. Finance, money, and unemployment /. Berlin [1985] 65 p. ; LC Card 86-205291 DDC 332 19
HG230.3 .S29 1985

(IIM/LMP 85-18) Rein, Martin. Women in the social welfare labor market /. Berlin [1985] 180 p. ; LC Card 86-213535 DDC 331.4/129136294 19
HD6134 .R45 1985

(IIM/LMP 85-5) Industrial relations and technical change in the British, Italian, and German automobile industry . Berlin [1985] 1 v. (various pagings) : LC Card 86-206613 DDC 338/.04292/094 19
HD6976.A82 G75 1985

(IIM/LMP 85-5) Hollingsworth, J. Rogers (Joseph Rogers), 1932- The governance of the American economy . Berlin [1985] 60 p. ; LC Card 86-205784 DDC 330.973 19
HC106.8 .H635 1985

(IIM/LMP 85-6a) Casey, Bernard. Early retirement schemes with a replacement condition . Berlin [1985] 44 p. ; LC Card 86-205942 DDC 331.25/2 19
HD7110.B4 C37 1985

(IIM/LMP 86-3) Maier, Hans E. Das Handwerk und die Berufseingliederung Jugendlicher in der Bundesrepublik Deutschland /. Berlin [1986] 68 p. : LC Card 86-230660
HD5715.5.G4 M35 1986

(IIM/LMP 86-7) Gensior, Sabine. Mikroelektronik-Anwendung und ihre Bedeutung für die Qualifikationen . Berlin , 1986. 39, 118 p. ; LC Card 87-409403 DDC 338/.06 19
HD6331.2.G27 G46 1986

Discutindo a história.
Singer, Paul Israel, 1932- A formação da classe operária /. Campinas-SP , São Paulo-SP [1986] 80 p. : LC Card 86-224636
HD4841 .S32 1986

DISEASES, OCCUPATIONAL. see **OCCUPATIONAL DISEASES.**

DISEASES OF OCCUPATIONS. see **OCCUPATIONAL DISEASES.**

Disequilibrium macroeconomic models . Lambert, Jean-Paul, 1952- Cambridge [Cambridgeshire] , New York , 1988. p. cm. ISBN 0-521-32209-X LC Card 86-24966 DDC 339.5/0724 19
HB145 .L36 1988

Disequilibrium trade theories /. Itō, Motoshige, 1951- Chur, Switzerland , New York , c1987. viii, 100 p. : ISBN 3-7186-0412-4 LC Card 87-11834 DDC 380.1 19
HF1008 .I855 1987

Disertaciones sobre economía mexicana /. Sacristán, Antonio. México, D.F. , 1982. 39 p. ; LC Card 87-123937 DDC 332.1/0972 19
HG2714 .S23 1982

DISHES. see **POTTERY.**

Disinger, John F. Sustainable resource development in the Third World /. Boulder , 1987. vi, 177 p. : ISBN 0-8133-7522-3 (alk. paper) LC Card 87-20137 DDC 333.7/15/091724 19
HC59.7 .S8826 1987

DISINVESTMENT - SOUTH AFRICA.
Fernández Tabío, Luis René. Apuntes sobre el capital financiero en Estados Unidos . La Habana , 1981 [i.e. 1982] ii, 74 p. : LC Card 87-401153
HG5851.A3 F47 1982

Hauck, David. What happens when U. S. companies sell their South African operations? /. Washington, D.C. (Suite 600, 1755 Massachusetts Ave., N.W., Washington 20036) , c1987. 16 p. ; LC Card 87-163729 DDC 338.8/8973/068 19
HG5851.A3 H392 1987

Jenkins, Carolyn M. (Carolyn Marion) The economic implications of disinvestment for South Africa /. [Braamfontain?] , 1986. v, 100 p. ; ISBN 0-908371-51-9 (pbk.) : LC Card 87-164832 DDC 332.6/73/0968 19
HG5851.A3 J46 1986

United States Catholic Conference. Administrative Board. Divestment, disinvestment, and South Africa . Washington, D.C. , c1986. 36 p. ; ISBN 1-555-86137-7 (pbk.)

LC Card 87-136857 DDC 332.6/7373/068 19
HG5851.A3 U55 1986

Disinvestment, the struggle, and the future . Orkin, Mark. Johannesburg , 1986. xii, 78 p. : ISBN 0-86975-305-3 (pbk.) LC Card 87-100474 DDC 332.6/73/0968 19
HG5851.A3 O47 1986

DISINVESTMENT - UNITED STATES.
Fernández Tabío, Luis René. Apuntes sobre el capital financiero en Estados Unidos . La Habana , 1981 [i.e. 1982] ii, 74 p. : LC Card 87-401153
HG5851.A3 F47 1982

DISINVESTMENTS.
Jansen, Ansgar, 1954- Desinvesititionen . Frankfurt am Main , New York , c1986. 514 p. : ISBN 3-8204-9630-0 LC Card 86-205563
HG4515 .J36 1986

DISINVESTMENTS - SOUTH AFRICA.
Orkin, Mark. Disinvestment, the struggle, and the future . Johannesburg , 1986. xii, 78 p. : ISBN 0-86975-305-3 (pbk.) LC Card 87-100474 DDC 332.6/73/0968 19
HG5851.A3 O47 1986

Voorhes, Meg. Black South African views on disinvestment /. Washington, D.C. (Suite 600, 1755 Massachusetts Ave., N.W., Washington 20036) [1986] 36 p. ; LC Card 86-209279 DDC 332.6/73/0968 19
HG5851.A3 V66 1986

DISINVESTMENTS - SOUTH AFRICA - PUBLIC OPINION.
Orkin, Mark. Disinvestment, the struggle, and the future . Johannesburg , 1986. xii, 78 p. : ISBN 0-86975-305-3 (pbk.) LC Card 87-100474 DDC 332.6/73/0968 19
HG5851.A3 O47 1986

Voorhes, Meg. Black South African views on disinvestment /. Washington, D.C. (Suite 600, 1755 Massachusetts Ave., N.W., Washington 20036) [1986] 36 p. ; LC Card 86-209279 DDC 332.6/73/0968 19
HG5851.A3 V66 1986

Diskontinuitätenmanagement : strategische Bewältigung von Strukturbrüchen bei internationaler Unternehmenstätigkeit / herausgegeben von Klaus Macharzina ; Kommission Internationales Management im Verband der Hochschullehrer für Betriebswirtschaft e.V. Berlin : E. Schmidt, c1984. x, 320 p. : ill. ; 24 cm. Includes bibliographies and index. ISBN 3-503-02446-8 LC Card 85-128271
1. International business enterprises - Management. 2. Economic history - 1971-. 3. Strategic planning. I. Macharzina, Klaus. II. Verband der Hochschullehrer für Betriebswirtschaft. Kommission Internationales Management.
HD62.4 .D57 1984

Diskussiestukken van de Vakgroep Sociale Geografie van Ontwikkelingslanden .
(nr. 33) Verbeek, Henk. Residentiële mobiliteit in Ciudad Chihuahua, Mexico /. Utrecht [1986] iii, 142 p. : LC Card 86-172646
HD7288.92.M62 C488 1986

Diskussionsbeiträge (Universität Göttingen. Ibero-Amerika Institut für Wirtschaftsforschung) .
(no. 40) Nowak, Felicitas. Financial liberalization revisited . Göttingen [1986] 49 p. : LC Card 87-121206 DDC 332/.0983 19
HG185.C5 N69 1986

(no. 41) Nowak, Felicitas. The allocation of bank credit and the efficiency of investment /. Göttingen, Rep. Fed. de Alemania [1986] 23 p. : LC Card 87-121215 DDC 332.7/0724 19
HG1641 .N68 1986

(Nr. 42) Schinke, Rolf. Ursachen der Verschuldungskrise . Göttingen [1987] 33 p. : LC Card 87-409568 DDC 336.3/435/098 19
HJ8514.5 .S34 1987

Diskussionspapier (Technische Universität Berlin. Wirtschaftswissenschaftliche Dokumentation) .
(63) Helberger, Christof. Beitragsäquivalenz oder interpersonelle Umverteilung in der gesetzlichen Rentenversicherung? . Berlin , 1981. 96 p. ; LC Card 81-201422 DDC 331.25/2/0943 19
HD7105.35.G3 H44 1981 ***NYPL [JLM 81-818 v.63]***

DISMISSAL OF EMPLOYEES. see **EMPLOYEES, DISMISSAL OF.**

Disoccupazione e nuove forme di accesso al lavoro nel mondo bancario / S. Ammannati ... [et al.] ; a cura di Giuseppe Pera. Milano, Italy : F. Angeli, c1986. 186 p. ; 22 cm. (Collana di diritto del lavoro. 36) Proceedings of a meeting held in Viareggio in 1985. Includes bibliographical references. LC Card 87-150276
1. Bank employees - Italy - Supply and demand - Congresses. 2. Part-time employment - Italy - Congresses. I. Ammannati, S. (Sergio). II. Pera, Giuseppe, 1928-.
HD5718.B262 I83 1986

DISPLAY FIGURES. see **MODELS, FASHION.**

DISPLAY OF MERCHANDISE.
International display and visual merchandising /. Glen Cove, N.Y. , 1987. p. cm. ISBN 0-86636-052-2 : LC Card 87-61166 DDC 659.1/5 19
HF5845 .I73 1987

Medla, Karsten, 1954- Shop-in-the-shop . München , c1987. xxxi, 207, 6 p. ; ISBN 3-88259-428-4 LC Card 87-141864 DDC 658.8/7 19
HF5429 .M36 1987

Müller, Heinz, Dipl.-Kfm. Dr. Die Warenplazierung als absatzpolitisches Instrument im Selbstbedienungseinzelhandel /. Göttingen , 1982. 479 p. : ISBN 3-509-01287-9 LC Card 84-174456
HF5845 .M964 1982

Disponibilidade de alimentos a nível regional no Estado de São Paulo, 1974-83 / José Luiz Teixeira M. Vieira ... [et al.]. São Paulo : Governo do Estado de São Paulo, Secretaria de Agricultura e Abastecimento, Instituto de Economia Agrícola, 1985. 75 p. ; 24 cm. (Relatório de pesquisa, 0101-5109 . 7/85) Bibliography: p. 58. LC Card 86-196482
1. Produce trade - Brazil - São Paulo (State). 2. Food industry and trade - Brazil - São Paulo (State). I. Vieira, José Luiz Teixeira M. (Jose Luiz Teixeira Marques). II. Series: Relatório de pesquisa (São Paulo (Brazil : State). Instituto de Economia Agrícola) , no. 85/7.
HD9014.B83 S433 1985

Disponibilität--Mobilität--Fluktuation /. Schaefer, Reinhard. Berlin , 1982. 70 p. : LC Card 83-225572
HD5717.5.G35 S3 1982

DISPOSABLE MEDICAL SUPPLIES INDUSTRY - QUÉBEC (PROVINCE)
L'Industrie québécoise du matériel médical jetable . Québec [1983] xv, 235 p. : LC Card 84-235956
HD9995.D563 C35 1983

DISPOSABLE MEDICAL SUPPLIES INDUSTRY - UNITED STATES.
Patient monitoring disposables and equipment for critical care. Tustin, CA (17722 Irvine Blvd., Tustin 92680) , c1986. 1 v. (various foliations) : LC Card 86-203049 DDC 381/.45681761 19
HD9995.M653 U657 1986

Prepackaged kits & trays markets in the U. S. New York, N.Y. , c1983. xxiii, 188 p. : LC Card 87-142284 DDC 381/.45681761 19
HD9995.D563 U665 1983

Disposable products market in Europe.
Consumer & catering disposable products market in Europe. New York, N.Y. , c1983. [29], 386 p. ; LC Card 87-142586 DDC 380.1/4568 19
HD9971.5.T323 E853 1983

DISPOSABLE TABLEWARE INDUSTRY - EUROPE.
Consumer & catering disposable products market in Europe. New York, N.Y. , c1983. [29], 386 p. ; LC Card 87-142586 DDC 380.1/4568 19
HD9971.5.T323 E853 1983

DISPOSAL OF REFUSE. see **REFUSE AND REFUSE DISPOSAL.**

The disposition and sentencing of operating while intoxicated (OWI) offenders in Iowa . Davis, Dan J. [Des Moines, Iowa] (523 E. 12th St., Des Moines 50319) [1986] 29 leaves : LC Card 86-621927 DDC 364.1/47 19
HE5620.D7 D37 1986

DISPUTES, LABOR. see **LABOR DISPUTES.**

DISSENTERS - POLAND.
Stelmach, Waldemar. Drugie oblicze "Solidarności" /. Warszawa , 1985. 222 p. : ISBN 83-202-0391-0 : LC Card 86-208212
HD8537.N783 S74 1985

Dissertationen der Johannes Kepler-Universität Linz .
(35) Schadenhofer, Leopold. Analyseinstrumente für die strategische Marketingplanung /. Wien , 1982. 222 p. : ISBN 3-85369-497-7 : LC Card 82-237712
HF5415 .S29 1982

(42) Pernsteiner, August W. Gestaltkonforme partnerschaftliche "Beteiligungs-" und "Kreditfinanzierung" von "Klein-" und "Mittelbetrieben" /. Wien , 1983. 355, xxx p. : ISBN 3-85369-536-1 LC Card 83-206156
HG4027.7 .P47 1983

Dissertationen der Wirtschaftsuniversität Wien, 0259-0719 .
(42) Böhm, Walter. Längsschnittanalyse des österreichischen Arbeitsmarktes . Wien , 1986. 138 p. : ISBN 3-85369-654-6 LC Card 87-142156 DDC 331.12/5/09436 19
HD5771 .B64 1986

Dissertations on man, philosophical, physiological, and political. Jarrold, T. (Thomas), 1770-1853. London, 1806. vi p., 1 l., [9]-367, [1] p. LC Card 05-22565
HB863 .J38

Il distaccamento italiano di Palestina, 1917-1921 /. Buzzetti, Luciano. Milano , c1976. 55 p. : LC Card 86-179004
HE6185.P13 B89 1976

DISTANCE GEOMETRY.
Kuiper, J. H. Distribution of distances in pregeographical space /. Brookfield, Vt. , 1986. viii, 296 p. : ISBN 0-566-05214-8 : LC Card 86-7673 DDC 910 19
HT391.3 .K85 1986 ***NYPL [JSD 86-605]***

DISTILLING INDUSTRIES - URUGUAY.
Uruguay. Asemblea General. Cámara de Representantes. Investigación en la Administración, Nacional de Combustibles, Alcohol y Portland /. [Montevideo] , 1935. 352 p. ; LC Card 85-105071
HD9574.U72 U78 1935

The distorted world of Soviet type economies /. Winiecki, Jan. Pittsburgh, Pa. , 1988. p. cm. ISBN 0-8229-1149-3 LC Card 87-25193 DDC 338.947 19
HC244 .W573 1988

Distribución del ingreso en el Uruguay /. Melgar, Alicia. Montevideo , 1981. 87 p. ; LC Card 86-160100
HC235.I5 M448 1981

Distribuição da produção dos principais produtos agropecuários do Estado de Alagoas. [S.l.] : Empresa de Assistência Técnica e Extensão Rural do Estado de Alagoas, [198-] [29] p. : col. maps ; 21 x 30 cm. Cover title. LC Card 86-179132
1. Produce trade - Brazil - Alagoas - Statistics. I. Empresa de Assistência Técnica e Extensão Rural do Estado de Alagoas.
HD9014.B83 A653 1980z

The Distributed digital process control systems market in the U. S. New York, N.Y. : Frost & Sullivan, c1983. 229 p. ; 29 cm. "March 1983." "(#A1049)." Bibliography: p. 205-229. LC Card 87-141853
1. Process control equipment industry - United States. 2. Market surveys - United States. I. Frost & Sullivan.
HD9696.P763 U527 1983

Distributed systems.
Market leaders . Boston, MA (200 Portland St., Boston 02114) , c1987. v, 123 p. : LC Card 87-402841 DDC 381/.4500416/0973 19
HD9696.C63 U52476 1987

Distributing risk . Abraham, Kenneth S., 1946- New Haven , c1986. x, 254 p. ; ISBN 0-300-03460-1 (alk. paper) LC Card 85-22459 DDC 346.73/086 347.30686 19
KF1164 .A72 1986 ***NYPL [JLE 86-4347]***

Distribution and consumption of diesel oil in agriculture /. Upadhyaya, P. K. (Pratap Krishna), 1916- Delhi, India , 1985. xii, 150 p. : LC Card 86-902439 DDC 333.79 19
HD9579.D53 I68 1985

DISTRIBUTION CHANNELS. see **MARKETING CHANNELS.**

DISTRIBUTION, COOPERATIVE. see **COOPERATION; COOPERATIVE SOCIETIES.**

DISTRIBUTION (ECONOMIC THEORY)
Hoek, M. P. van der. De praktijk van de inkomensverdeling /. Groningen , c1987. 183 p. : ISBN 90-01-39430-2 : LC Card 87-157808
HC329.5.I5 H634 1987

Issues in contemporary macroeconomics and distribution /. London , 1985. xxviii, 465 p. : ISBN 0-333-35483-4 : LC Card 86-673473
HB172.5 .I87x 1985b

Kriesler, Peter. Kalecki's microanalysis . Cambridge , New York , 1987. xii, 132 p. : ISBN 0-521-33145-5 LC Card 86-24414 DDC 338.5/21 19
HB238 .K75 1987

Odink, J. G. Inkomensherverdeling . Groningen , c1985. 254 p. : ISBN 90-01-66101-7 : LC Card 86-149572
HC329.5.I5 O35 1985

Pöschl, Josef. Die Preisbildung in der industrialisierten Marktwirtschaft . Hamburg , c1987. v, 149 p. : ISBN 3-925630-12-0 LC Card 87-146592 DDC 338.5/2 19
HB221 .P65 1987

DISTRIBUTION (ECONOMICS) see **COMMERCE; MARKETING.**

Distribution of distances in pregeographical space /. Kuiper, J. H. Brookfield, Vt. , 1986. viii, 296 p. : ISBN 0-566-05214-8 : LC Card 86-7673 DDC 910 19
HT391.3 .K85 1986 ***NYPL [JSD 86-605]***

DISTRIBUTION OF GOODS, PHYSICAL. see **PHYSICAL DISTRIBUTION OF GOODS.**

Distribution of household wealth. International comparisons of the distribution of household wealth /. Oxford , New York , 1987. xii, 283 p. : ISBN 0-19-828511-6 : LC Card 86-31241 DDC 339.2/2/094 19
HC240.9.I5 I56 1987

DISTRIBUTION OF INCOME. see **INCOME DISTRIBUTION.**

Distribution of local sales tax revenue . Baynes, Peter A. Albany, N.Y. (119 Washington Ave., Albany 12210) [1986] 13 p. : LC Card 87-106773 DDC 336.2/713/09747 19
HJ5715.U62 N72 1986

Distribution of refinery products in India /. Jayashankar, R., 1954- New Delhi , 1986, c1985. 152 p. ; LC Card 86-902972 DDC 381/.4566553/0954 19
HD9576.I42 J39 1986

Distribution of rural employment growth by race . Oliveira, Victor J. Washington, D.C. [1986] vii, 17 p. : LC Card 86-601118 DDC 331.6/09758 19
HD5725.G4 O56 1986

Distribution of saleyards in Victoria . Victoria. Saleyard Working Party. [Melbourne] , 1986. 69, 7, 7 p. : LC Card 87-159450 DDC 338.1/760831 19
HD9428.A83 V538 1986

DISTRIBUTION OF WEALTH. see **WEALTH.**

The Distributional impacts of public policies / edited by Sheldon H. Danziger and Kent E. Portney. New York : St. Martin's Press in association with the Policy Studies Organization, 1988. xvii, 257 p. ; 23 cm. (Policy Studies Organization series) Includes bibliographies and index. ISBN 0-312-00749-3 : LC Card 87-11877 DDC 339.2/0973 19
1. Income distribution - United States. 2. Transfer payments - United States. I. Danziger, Sheldon. II. Portney, Kent E. III. Series: Policy Studies Organization series (New York, N.Y.).
HC110.I5 D535 1988

Distributionsutredning. Stockholm : Statens industriverk, 1981. 2 v. : ill. ; 29 cm. (SIND PM, 0346-573X . 1981:19-20) CONTENTS. - d. 1. Konsumtion och distribution av textilvaror. Textilfackhandelns lönsamhet -- d. 2. Handelns inköp och leveransrelationer. ISBN 91-38-06684-X (v. 1) LC Card 82-234445
1. Textile industry - Sweden. 2. Textile industry - Sweden - Statistics. I. Sweden. Statens industriverk. II. Series.
HD9865.S86 D57 1981

DISTRIBUTIVE EDUCATION.
Marketing and distributive education [videorecording] /. Chicago, Ill. , 1986. 2 videocassettes (24 min. each) : LC Card 86-708241 DDC 658.8 11
HF5415

DISTRIBUTIVE JUSTICE.
Baumol, William J. Superfairness . Cambridge, Mass. , c1986. xi, 266 p. : ISBN 0-262-02234-6 LC Card 85-15127 DDC 305 19
HB72 .B356 1986 ***NYPL [JLE 86-2402]***

Datta, Bhabatosh, 1911- Social justice in a mixed economy /. Calcutta , 1982. ii, 64 p. ; LC Card 82-905698 DDC 338.954 19
HC435.2 .D353 1982 ***NYPL [JLD 86-3172]***

Justice . New York , c1986. xii, 283 p. ; ISBN 0-306-42256-5 LC Card 86-20503 DDC 320/.01/1 19
JC578 .J89 1986 ***NYPL [JLE 87-304]***

Neppl, Rainer. Zur Wahrnehmung und Bewertung der Gerechtigkeit der Einkommens-Verteilung /. Regensburg , 1986. 310 p. : ISBN 3-89073-362-X LC Card 87-121773 DDC 339.2 19
HB523 .N47 1986

Norden, Gilbert. Einkommensgerechtigkeit, was darunter verstanden wird . Wien , 1985. 304 p. : ISBN 3-205-06324-4 LC Card 86-196913
HB523 .N67 1985

Poverty amidst plenty . Boulder, Colo. , 1989. p. cm. ISBN 0-8133-0523-3 LC Card 87-12829 DDC 330.9/048 19
HC59 .P639 1989

Wenz, Peter S. Environmental justice /. Albany, N.Y. , c1987. p. cm. ISBN 0-88706-644-5 LC Card 87-13206 DDC 363.7/0525 19
HB523 .W46 1987

Wolff, Nancy, 1955- Income redistribution and the Social Security program /. Ann Arbor , c1987. vi, 181 p. : ISBN 0-8357-1807-7 LC Card 87-10791 DDC 368.4/3/00973 19
HD7105.35.U6 W65 1987

DISTRIBUTIVE JUSTICE - ADDRESSES, ESSAYS, LECTURES.
Social goals and social organization . Cambridge [Cambridgeshire] , New York , 1985. xii, 365 p. : ISBN 0-521-26204-6 LC Card 85-6668 DDC 330.15/5 19
HB846 .S65 1985 ***NYPL [JLE 86-3786]***

DISTRIBUTIVE JUSTICE - RELIGIOUS ASPECTS - CHRISTIANITY.
Raines, John C. Modern work and human meaning /. Philadelphia , c1986. 150 p. ; ISBN 0-664-24703-2 (pbk.) LC Card 85-26370 DDC 241/.64 19
BJ1498 .R335 1986 ***NYPL [JLD 86-2382]***

Distribuzione commerciale .
(1) L'Affiliazione commerciale . Milano , 1986. 100 p. : ***NYPL [JLD 87-531]***

(6) Industria e commercio . Milano, Italy , c1985. 194 p. : LC Card 86-112174 DDC 658.7/88/0945 19
HF5415.12.I8 I53 1985 ***NYPL [JLD 87-432]***

District census handbook, series 22, Uttar Pradesh, District Jhansi, primary census abstract. Jilā janagaṇanā hastapustikā . [Lakhanaū] [1983] xi, 174, ii p., [5] folded leaves of plates : LC Card 86-903117
HA4587.J48 J55 1983

DISTRICT HEATING. see **HEATING FROM CENTRAL STATIONS.**

District of Columbia. Dept. of Public Works. 1986 D.C. Core Cordon Count of vehicular and passenger volumes /. [Washington, D.C.] , c1986. iv, 34 p., [66] p. : LC Card 87-105302 DDC 388.4/13142/09753 19
HE372.W3 A15 1986

The district resource analysis as applied to Kakamega District /. Bradley, Phil. Nairobi [1984] 11 leaves : LC Card 87-112452 DDC 333.75 19
HD9769.F843 K425 1984

DISTRITO FEDERAL (BRAZIL) - ADMINISTRATIVE AND POLITICAL DIVISIONS - MAPS.
Souza Filho, José Ornellas de. Exposição do governador do Distrito Federal, José Ornellas de Souza Filho, na ADESG, em 02/09/83. [Brasília , 1983 or 1984] 40, [31 leaves] : LC Card 85-148272
HC188.D57 S68 1983

Distrito Federal (Brazil). Coordenação do Sistema de Planejamento. Região geo-econômica de Brasília : idéias e ação DF/SEG, COSPLAN ; [elaboração, Cláudio Alves de Souza ; colaboração, João Alcides Homar ... et al.]. [Brasília] : COSPLAN, [1980?] [28] leaves : maps ; 21 x 31 cm. Cover title. LC Card 86-204066
1. Brasília Region (Brazil) - Economic policy. 2. Regional planning - Brazil - Brasília Region. I. Souza, Cláudio Alves de. II. Title.
HC189.B7 D57 1980

DISTRITO FEDERAL (BRAZIL) - ECONOMIC POLICY.
Notícias publicadas, de março de 1977 a janeiro de 1979. [Brasília] [198-?] 116 leaves : LC Card 85-108219
HC189.B7 N68 1980z

Souza Filho, José Ornellas de. Exposição do governador do Distrito Federal, José Ornellas de Souza Filho, na ADESG, em 02/09/83. [Brasília , 1983 or 1984] 40, [31 leaves] : LC Card 85-148272
HC188.D57 S68 1983

DISTRITO FEDERAL (BRAZIL) - POPULATION - STATISTICS.
Caracterização da população do Distrito Federal . Brasília , 1984. 56, [1] p. : LC Card 86-130173 DDC 331.12/0981/74021 19
HA988.D5 C37 1984

Os Distritos em números / República Popular de Moçambique, Conselho Coordenador do Recenseamento. [Maputo?] : O Conselho, [1983-1985] 10 v. ; 30 cm. "1983, ano do IV Congresso." "500 ejemplares"--Vol. 4, t.p. verso. Vols. 1-3, 5-6, 8-9 have cover title. Chiefly tables. CONTENTS. - 1. Niassa -- 2. Cabo Delgado -- 3. Nampula -- 4. Província de Zambézia -- 5. Tete -- 6. Manica -- 7. Província de Sofala -- 8. Inhambane -- 9. Gaza -- 10. Província e Cidade de Maputo. LC Card 86-980977 DDC 330.67/905021 19
1. Mozambique - Economic conditions - 1975- - Statistics. 2. Mozambique - Social conditions - 1975- - Statistics. I. Conselho Coordenador de Recenseamento (Mozambique).
HC890 .D57 1983

Dist͡siplina truda. Danchenko, M. I. (Mykola Ivanovych) Dystsyplina pratsi /. Kyïv , 1983. 110 p. ; LC Card 83-215106
HF5549.5.L3 D34 1983

Dist͡siplina truda--delo kazhdogo / [avtorskiĭ kollektiv S.M. Belozerova ... et al. ; sostavitelʹ V.S. ÎAzykova]. Moskva : Profizdat, 1982. 77 p. ; 20 cm. Includes bibliographical references. LC Card 83-126613
1. Labor discipline - Soviet Union. I. Belozerova, S. M. II. ÎAzykova, Valentina Spiridonovna.
HF5549.5.L3 D57 1982

Ditchburn, Derrick. Postage stamps honoring animals [slide] /. Elmira, NY , 1984. 20 slides : LC Card 83-720055 DDC 769.56 11
HE6183.A5

Dittmann, Roswitha. Die Verantwortung der örtlichen Staatsorgane für die planmässige Entwicklung und die effektive Inanspruchnahme von Leistungen der technischen Infrastruktur /. Potsdam-Babelsberg , 1986. 57 p. ; LC Card 87-407347 DDC 363/.09431 19
HC290.795.C3 V47 1986

Ditz, Toby L., 1951- Property and kinship : inheritance in early Connecticut, 1750-1820 / Toby L. Ditz. Princeton, N.J. : Princeton University Press, c1986. xvi, 213 p. : map ; 25 cm. Includes index. Bibliography: p. [195]-205. ISBN 0-691-04735-9 (alk. paper) : LC Card 86-5051 DDC 333.33 19
1. Inheritance and succession - Connecticut - History. 2. Property - Connecticut - History. 3. Family - Connecticut - History. 4. Kinship - Connecticut - History. I. Title.
HB715 .D58 1986 ***NYPL [JLE 86-4624]***

Dīūmulen, I. I. (Ippolit Ippolitovich)
Sovremennyĭ tarifnyĭ i netarifnyĭ protektsionizm : gosudarstvenno-monopolisticheskie sredstva

regulirovaniia importa promyshlenno-razvitykh kapitalisticheskikh gosudarstv : uchebnoe posobie / I.I. Diumulen. Moskva : Moskovskiĭ gos. in-t mezhdunarodnykh otnosheniĭ, 1975. 277 p. ; 21 cm. Bibliography: p. 271-273. LC Card 82-191746
1. Free trade and protection. 2. Import quotas. 3. Tariff. 4. Government monopolies. 5. Capitalism. I. Title.
HF1713 .D62 1975

Divaris, Costa. Old Mutual income tax guide, 1986/87 / C. Divaris, M.L. Stein. [S.l. : s.n.], c1987 (Cape Town : Old Mutual Print. Works) xvi, 261 p. : ill. ; 23 cm. LC Card 87-152138 DDC 343.6805/2 346.80352 19
1. Income tax - South Africa - Handbooks, manuals, etc. 2. Income tax - Law and legislation - South Africa. I. Stein, M. L. II. Title.
HJ4790.4 .D58 1987

Diversification and integration in American industry /. Gort, Michael, 1923- Westport, Conn. , 1984, c1962. xxi, 238 p. ; ISBN 0-313-24423-5 (lib. bdg.) LC Card 84-10730 DDC 338.8/0973 19
HD2756.2.U5 G67 1984 *NYPL [JLE 86-4435]*

DIVERSIFICATION IN INDUSTRY.
Bagó, Eszter. Diverzifikáció az iparban /. Budapest , 1985. 251, [1] p. : ISBN 963-221-544-3 : LC Card 86-186848
HD2755.8 .B34 1985

Goold, Michael. Strategies and styles . Oxford, UK , New York, NY, USA , 1988, c1987. p. cm. ISBN 0-631-15829-4 : LC Card 87-12151 DDC 658/.046 19
HD2756 .G66 1988

Smith, Clayton G. Established companies diversifying into young industries . West Lafayette, Ind. [1986] 27, 15 p. ; LC Card 86-621740 DDC 658/.001/9 s 338.8/3 19
HD6483 .P8 no. 893 HD2755.8

DIVERSIFICATION IN INDUSTRY - BRAZIL.
Hollanda Filho, Sergio Buarque de. Estrutura industrial no Brasil . Rio de Janeiro , 1983. 275 p. : LC Card 87-119359 DDC 338.8/0981 19
HD2834 .H65 1983

DIVERSIFICATION IN INDUSTRY - CALIFORNIA.
Shapiro, Michael E. Utility diversification . Sacramento, CA [1986] 50 p. ; LC Card 86-621960 DDC 338.8/3613636/0973 19
HD2766 .S47 1986

DIVERSIFICATION IN INDUSTRY - GERMANY (WEST) - HISTORY.
Maisel, Helmut. Diversifikation und konglomerate Interdependenz . Frankfurt , c1984. 237 p. : ISBN 3-88323-518-0 LC Card 84-213494
HD2756.2.G3 M34 1984

DIVERSIFICATION IN INDUSTRY - HUNGARY.
Bagó, Eszter. Diverzifikáció az iparban /. Budapest , 1985. 251, [1] p. : ISBN 963-221-544-3 : LC Card 86-186848
HD2755.8 .B34 1985

DIVERSIFICATION IN INDUSTRY - UNITED STATES.
Gort, Michael, 1923- Diversification and integration in American industry /. Westport, Conn. , 1984, c1962. xxi, 238 p. ; ISBN 0-313-24423-5 (lib. bdg.) LC Card 84-10730 DDC 338.8/0973 19
HD2756.2.U5 G67 1984 *NYPL [JLE 86-4435]*

Shapiro, Michael E. Utility diversification . Sacramento, CA [1986] 50 p. ; LC Card 86-621960 DDC 338.8/3613636/0973 19
HD2766 .S47 1986

Strickland, Allyn D. Firm diversification, mutual forbearance behavior and price-cost margins /. New York , 1984. 155 p. ; ISBN 0-8240-4159-3 (alk. paper) LC Card 79-53209 DDC 338.8/3/0973
HD2756.U5 S76 1984 *NYPL [JLE 86-3907]*

Diversification strategies and security-of-supply . Braathu, Jan. Oslo [1984?] 74 p. ; LC Card 85-129223 DDC 382/.42285/094 19
HD9581.E8552 B7 1984 *NYPL [JLM 78-136 no.88]*

Diversifikation und konglomerate Interdependenz . Maisel, Helmut. Frankfurt , c1984. 237 p. : ISBN 3-88323-518-0 LC Card 84-213494
HD2756.2.G3 M34 1984

Diversity in development : U. S. voluntary assistance to Africa : summary of findings. New York, NY : InterAction, c1985. 49 p. : ill. ; 23 cm. ISBN 0-932140-06-8 (pbk.) LC Card 86-231753 DDC 361.7/096 19
1. Non-governmental organizations - Africa. 2. Economic development projects - Africa. 3. Technical assistance, American - Africa. I. InterAction (Organization : U. S.).
HC800.Z9 E444 1985

Diversity in development : U. S. voluntary assistance to Africa : project descriptions by country and sector. New York, NY : InterAction, c1986. xvii, 620 p. : ill. ; 23 cm. Companion volume to: Diversity in development : U. S. voluntary assistance to Africa ; summary of findings. Includes indexes. ISBN 0-932140-07-6 (pbk.) LC Card 86-231757 DDC 361.7/025/73 19
1. Economic development projects - Africa - Directories. 2. Economic assistance, American - Africa - Directories. 3. Technical assistance, American - Africa - Directories. 4. Non-governmental organizations - Africa - Directories. I. InterAction (Organization : U. S.).
HC800.Z9 E444 1986

Diversos documentos y datos relativos al proyectado ferrocarril de Chamela a Aguascalientes / introducción por José Rogelio Alvarez ; [coordinador de la edición, Fernando Martínez Réding]. Ed. facsimilar. Guadalajara, México : Enciclopedia de México, 1982. 24, iii, 98 p. : ill. ; 20 cm. Spine title: FC a Chamela, 1890. Reprint. Originally published: México : Tip. de El Nacional, 1890. LC Card 86-115748 DDC 385/.0972 19
1. Railroads - Mexico - History - Sources. 2. Railroad law - Mexico - History - Sources. 3. Concessions - Mexico - History - Sources. I. Alvarez Noguera, José Rogelio. II. Martínez Réding, Fernando. III. Title: FC a Chamela, 1890.
HE2818 .D58 1982

Diverzifikáció az iparban /. Bagó, Eszter. Budapest , 1985. 251, [1] p. : ISBN 963-221-544-3 : LC Card 86-186848
HD2755.8 .B34 1985

Divestiture in developing countries /. Berg, Elliot. Washington, D.C. , 1987. vii, 30 p. : ISBN 0-8213-0917-X (pbk.) LC Card 87-14235 DDC 338.9/009172/4 19
HD4420.8 .B45 1987

Divestment, disinvestment, and South Africa . United States Catholic Conference. Administrative Board. Washington, D.C. , c1986. 36 p. ; ISBN 1-555-86137-7 (pbk.) LC Card 87-136857 DDC 332.6/7373/068 19
HG5851.A3 U55 1986

Divided we stand . Form, William Humbert, 1917- Urbana , c1985. xviii, 306 p. ; ISBN 0-252-01168-6 (alk. paper) LC Card 85-16537 DDC 305.5/62/0973 19
HD8072.5 .F667 1985 *NYPL [JLE 86-1940]*

Dividendenpolitik bei asymmetrischer Informationsverteilung /. Hartmann-Wendels, Thomas. Wiesbaden , c1986. 299 p. : ISBN 3-409-13706-8 LC Card 86-165737
HG4028.D5 H33 1986

DIVIDENDS.
Alfano, Salvatore. Work of the dividend department /. New York, NY , c1987. xvi, 180 p. ; ISBN 0-13-965096-2 LC Card 87-7733 DDC 332.6/068/5 19
HG4028.D5 A43 1987

Grande Esteban, Ildefonso. Modelos de valoración de acciones y metodos de constrastación /. Bilbao [1985?] 319 p. : ISBN 84-7585-025-1 LC Card 87-111240
HG4636 .G88 1985

DIVIDENDS - ITALY - DECISION MAKING.
Ecchia, Stefano. La destinazione dell'utile nelle società per azioni . Padova , 1985. 133 p. : LC Card 86-214308
HG4028.P7 E23 1985

DIVIDENDS - MATHEMATICAL MODELS.
Hartmann-Wendels, Thomas. Dividendenpolitik bei asymmetrischer Informationsverteilung /. Wiesbaden , c1986. 299 p. : ISBN 3-409-13706-8 LC Card 86-165737
HG4028.D5 H33 1986

DIVIDENDS - SWITZERLAND.
Vieli, Mario. La décision du dividende en Suisse /. [Fribourg] , c1984. 187 p. : ISBN 2-8271-0282-X : LC Card 84-225559 DDC 658.1/55 19
HG4028.D5 V54 1984

DIVIDENDS - SWITZERLAND - STATISTICS.
Schweizerische Dividendenstatistik, 1929 bis 1932. [Bern] , 1934. 91 p. ; LC Card 86-198072
HA1593 .B45 Heft 2 HG4226

Division administrative de la Grèce par départements, provinces, municipalités et communes. Greece. Dieuthynsis Topikēs Autodioikēseōs. Dioikētikē diairesis tēs Hellados kata nomous, eparchias, dēmous kai koinotētas . Athēnai , 1965. 39 p. ; LC Card 86-235329
HA1351.5 1961

DIVISION OF POWERS. see **FEDERAL GOVERNMENT; SEPARATION OF POWERS.**

Divisionalisering och därefter . Edgren, Jan, 1940- Stockholm , c1983. 157 p. : ISBN 91-7722-013-7 : LC Card 83-186664
HD50 .E34 1983

Divisions of labour : skilled workers and technological change in nineteenth century England / edited by Royden Harrison and Jonathan Zeitlin. Sussex [Eng.] : Harvester Press ; Urbana : University of Illinois Press, 1985. ix, 254 p. ; 23 cm. Includes bibliographical references and index. ISBN 0-252-01189-9 LC Card 84-23988 DDC 331.7/94 19
1. Skilled labor - Great Britain - History - 19th century. 2. Technological innovations - Great Britain - History - 19th century. I. Harrison, Royden. II. Zeitlin, Jonathan.
HD8390 .D58 1985 *NYPL [JLD 87-93]*

DIVORCED PEOPLE - FINANCE, PERSONAL.
Lewin, Elizabeth. Financial fitness through divorce . New York, N.Y. , c1987. vii, 146 p. : ISBN 0-8160-1323-3 (pbk.) : LC Card 86-24383 DDC 332.024 19
HG179 .L477 1987

Divorcing a corporation . Plumez, Jacqueline Hornor. New York, N.Y. , 1985. xxiii, 198 p. : ISBN 0-394-54457-9 : LC Card 85-40183 DDC 650.1/4 19
HF5384 .P58 1986 *NYPL [JLE 86-2346]*

DIW Symposion. DIW-Symposion (1983 : Berlin, Germany) Strategien für mehr Arbeitsplätze in Berlin . Berlin , c1984. 209 p. : ISBN 3-87061-277-0 LC Card 84-202956
HD5780.B4 D58 1983

DIW-Symposion (1983 : Berlin, Germany) Strategien für mehr Arbeitsplätze in Berlin : DIW-Symposion / Deutsches Institut für Wirtschaftsforschung. Berlin : A. Spitz, c1984. 209 p. : ill. ; 21 cm. (Politische Dokumente. Bd. 8) Papers of a meeting held Apr. 14-15, 1983 in Berlin, sponsored by the Deutsches Institut für Wirtschaftsforschung. Includes bibliographies. ISBN 3-87061-277-0 LC Card 84-202956
1. Labor supply - Berlin (Germany) - Congresses. 2. Labor policy - Berlin (Germany) - Congresses. 3. Berlin (Germany) - Economic conditions - Congresses. I. Title. II. Title: DIW Symposion. III. Title: D.I.W.-Symposion.
HD5780.B4 D58 1983

Diwok, Fritz. Struktur des Bankwesens in Österreich / von Fritz Diwok. Frankfurt am Main : F. Knapp, c1982. 142 p. ; 21 cm. (Struktur ausländischer Bankensysteme. Heft 19) Bibliography: p. 135-139. Includes index. ISBN 3-7819-2771-7 LC Card 83-190921 DDC 332.1/09436 19
1. Banks and banking - Austria. I. Title. II. Series.
HG3008 .D59 1982

Dix années d'espaces-piétons : bilan et perspectives d'avenir : colloque international, Lyon, 21 et 22 mars 1984, Chambre de commerce et d'industrie de Lyon, Salle des cordeliers / organisé par le Centre d'étude du commerce et de la distribution-CECOD. Paris : Le Centre, [1984] 191 p. : ill. ; 30 cm. At head of title: Piétons 84 villes. ISBN 2-85723-124-5 LC Card 85-104132
1. Pedestrian areas - Congresses. I. Centre d'étude du commerce et de la distribution. II. Title: 10 années

d'espaces piétons. *III. Title: Colloque international.*
HE336.P43 D59 1984

Dix, Bernard. Serving the public, building the union : the history of the National Union of Public Employees / Bernard Dix and Stephen Williams. London : Lawrence & Wishart, 1987- v. <1 > : ill. ; 23 cm. Spine subtitle: The history of NUPE. Bibliography: v. 1, p. 229-231. Includes index. CONTENTS. - v. 1. The forerunners, 1889-1928 ISBN 0-85315-645-X (v. 1) : LC Card 87-169851 DDC 331.88/09421 19
1. NUPE (Organization) - History. I. Williams, Stephen, 1954-. II. Title. III. Title: History of NUPE.
HD8005.2.G7 D59 1987

Dix études de cas de fiscalité avec corrigés détaillés. Lamorlette, Corine. 10 études de cas de fiscalité avec corrigés détaillés . Paris , 1984. 95 p. : ISBN 2-7178-0802-7 : LC Card 85-129474
HF5681.T3 L28 1984

Dixit, Praveen M.
Gardiner, Walter H. Price elasticity of export demand . Washington, D.C. [1986] iv, 43 p. ; LC Card 86-602820 DDC 382/.41/0973 19
HD9004 .G37 1986

Grigsby, S. Elaine. Alternative export strategies and U. S. agricultural policies for grains and oilseeds, 1950-83 /. [Washington, D.C.] , 1986. v., 37 p. : LC Card 86-602816 DDC 382/.4131/0973 19
HD9036 .G83 1986

Dixit, R. K. (Ramesh Kumar), 1946- Behaviour of share prices and investment in India / R.K. Dixit. New Delhi : Deep & Deep Publications, c1986. 328 p. ; 22 cm. Bibliography: p. [323]-326. Includes index. LC Card 86-902907 DDC 332.63/222/0954 19
1. Stocks - Prices - India. 2. Investments - India. I. Title.
HG5733 .D59 1986

Dixon, John A., 1946-
Economic valuation techniques for the environment . Baltimore , c1986. xx, 203 p. : ISBN 0-8018-3352-3 (alk. paper) LC Card 86-2730 DDC 363.7/05/0681 19
HC79.E5 E274 1986 ***NYPL [JLE 87-677]***

Watershed resource management . Boulder , 1986. xx, 236 p. : ISBN 0-8133-7300-X (pbk. : alk. paper) : LC Card 86-18987 DDC 333.91/0095 19
HD1691 .W37 1986 ***NYPL [JLD 87-767]***

Dixon-Mueller, Ruth. Women's work in Third World agriculture : concepts and indicators / Ruth Dixon-Mueller. Geneva : International Labour Office, 1985. xi, 151 p. : ill. ; 24 cm. (Women, work, and development, 0253-2042 . 9) Includes index. Bibliography: p. 136-148. ISBN 92-2-105107-2 (pbk.) LC Card 86-673111
1. Women in agriculture - Developing countries. 2. Women in development. I. Title. II. Series.
HD6073.A292 D442x 1985
NYPL [JLE 86-3760]

Dizionario commerciale . Emolumento, Vincenzo. Milano , 1983. 1150 p. ; ISBN 88-7075-068-X : LC Card 84-151136 DDC 380.1/03/41 19
HF1002 .E57 1983 ***NYPL [JLD 86-1323]***

Dizionario commerciale, italiano-inglese e inglese-italiano . Spinelli, Nicola, 1881- Torino , 1957. 464, 683, 138 p. ;
NYPL [JLD 85-226]

Dizionario di management, matematica, statistica, R.O., logistica, produzione, personale, psicologia e sociologia del lavoro e delle organizzazioni / a cura di Luciano Ratto. Milano, Italy : F. Angeli, c1986. 779 p. : ill. ; 23 cm. (Enciclopedia di direzione ed organizzazione aziendale . v. 30.) LC Card 86-225959
1. Management - Dictionaries - Italian. 2. Management science - Dictionaries - Italian. I. Ratto, Luciano. II. Series: Enciclopedia di direzione ed organizzazione aziendale , v. 30.
HD30 .E5 vol. 30 HD30.15

Dizionario enciclopedico economico e commerciale inglese italiano, italiano inglese. Picchi, Fernando. Economics and business . Bologna , 1986. 1333 p. ; ISBN 88-08-04550-1 LC Card 86-201141 DDC 330/.03/51 19
HB61 .P49 1986

DJI Forschungsbericht.
Arbeitsmarkterfahrungen und Berufsorientierungen Jugendlicher . München , c1983. 177 p. : ISBN 3-87966-202-9 LC Card 84-170074
HD6276.G4 A73 1983

Feuerstein, Thomas. Humanisierung der Arbeit und Reform der beruflichen Bildung . München , c1983. 221 p. ; ISBN 3-87966-184-7 LC Card 83-222687
HD5715.5.G4 F48 1983

Sardei-Biermann, Sabine. Jugendliche zwischen Schule und Arbeitswelt . München , c1984. v, 318 p. ; ISBN 3-87966-219-3 LC Card 84-240405
HD5715.5.G4 S27 1984

DJI Materialien.
Workshop "Berufswege von Frauen" (1984 : Berlin, Germany) Berufsverläufe von Frauen . München , Weinheim , c1986. 291 p. : ISBN 3-87966-253-3 LC Card 87-407975 DDC 331.7/02/024042 19
HF5382.67.G3 W67 1984

DJIBOUTI - ECONOMIC CONDITIONS - CONGRESSES.
Djibouti, ville et pays en voie de développement . Djibouti [c1983] 2 v. : LC Card 87-131462
HC855.Z9 E443 1983

Djibouti. Ministère des affaires étrangères et de la coopération. Djibouti, ville et pays en voie de développement . Djibouti [c1983] 2 v. : LC Card 87-131462
HC855.Z9 E443 1983

Djibouti, ville et pays en voie de développement : rapport / préparé par un groupe de travail (Anis Abdallah ... [et al.]) sous l'autorité du ministre des Affaires étrangères et de la coopération ... ; ce groupe a bénéficié de la collaboration du PNUD, Michel van Hulten, consultant. Djibouti : Impr. administrative, [c1983] 2 v. : ill. ; 31 cm. "Rapport de synthèse préparé pour la Conférence des donateurs." "Novembre 1983"--V. 1, cover. CONTENTS. - 1. Rapport de snythèse -- 2. Programme d'investissements et recueil de projets. LC Card 87-131462
1. Economic development projects - Djibouti - Congresses. 2. Investments - Djibouti - Congresses. 3. Djibouti - Economic conditions - Congresses. I. Abdallah, Anis. II. Hulten, Michel van. III. Conférence des donateurs (1983 : Djibouti, Djibouti). IV. Djibouti. Ministère des affaires étrangères et de la coopération. V. United Nations. Development Programme.
HC855.Z9 E443 1983

Dlesk, Mihael. Jugoslovenska privreda između stagnacije i razvoja /. Beograd , 1986. viii, 298 p. : LC Card 87-151260
HC407 .J83 1986

Dli͡a vuzov.
Nauchnai͡a organizat͡sii͡a truda na mashinostroitel′nykh predprii͡atii͡akh /. Moskva , 1986. 240 p. : LC Card 86-214776
HD9703.S652 N38 1986

Dli͡a vyssheĭ shkoly.
Zalevskiĭ, A. A. (Andreĭ Andreevich) Ėkonomika khimicheskoĭ promyshlennosti /. Moskva , 1986. 189 p. ; LC Card 86-225661
HD9656.S55 Z36 1986

Dlin, Norman. Social atlas of Shreveport, Louisiana / Norman Dlin, Kenneth Hinze, Norman Dolch. Rev. ed. Shreveport : Dept. of Social Sciences, LSU-Shreveport. 1985. 1 atlas (vii, 43 p.) : ill. ; 28 cm. Includes bibliographies. LC Card 86-622543 DDC 304.6/09763/99 19
1. Shreveport Metropolitan Area (La.) - Statistics - Maps. 2. Shreveport Metropolitan Area (La.) - Census - Maps. I. Hinze, Kenneth. II. Dolch, Norman A. (Norman Allan). III. Title.
HA730.S615 D57 1985

Dlugos, Günter. Die Unternehmung in der demokratischen Gesellschaft =. Berlin , New York , 1987. xiii, 390 p. : ISBN 0-89925-295-8 (U. S.) : LC Card 86-32864 DDC 658.3/152 19
HD5650 .U67 1987

DLUGOS, GÜNTER.
Die Unternehmung in der demokratischen Gesellschaft =. Berlin , New York , 1987. xiii, 390 p. : ISBN 0-89925-295-8 (U. S.) : LC Card 86-32864 DDC 658.3/152 19
HD5650 .U67 1987

Dlugoss, Eileen Bechtold. Mazursky, Alan D., 1955- Lotus 1-2-3 . Chicago , c1988. 480 p. : ISBN 0-574-18645-X (pbk.) : LC Card 87-4675 DDC 005.36/9 19
HF5548.4.L67 M32 1988

Dmitrenko, Vladimir Petrovich. Economic policy during the construction of socialism in the USSR / Vladimir Dmitrenko ; [translated from the Russian by Alexander Parnakh]. Moscow : Progress Publishers, c1987. 156 p. ; 17 cm. (The Way socialism began) Title on verso of t.p.: Ėkonomicheskai͡a politika v period postroenii͡a sot͡sializma v SSSR. Includes bibliographical references. LC Card 86-201129 DDC 338.947 19
1. Soviet Union - Economic policy - 1917-1928. 2. Soviet Union - Economic policy - 1928-1932. I. Title. II. Title: Ėkonomicheskai͡a politika v period postroenii͡a sot͡sializma v SSSR. III. Series.
HC335.2 .D56 1987

Dmitrevskiĭ, I͡U. D. (I͡Uriĭ Dmitrievich) Vol′f, M. B. (Mark Borisovich) Geografii͡a mirovogo sel′skogo khozi͡aĭstva /. Moskva , 1981. 326 p. : LC Card 82-122609
HD1415 .V62 1981

Dmitriev, N. U. (Nikolaĭ Ustinovich) Artynov, Aleksandr Petrovich. Prigorodnye passazhirskie perevozki /. Moskva , 1985. 160 p. : LC Card 86-208093
HE4834 .A78 1985

Dmitriev, S. S. (Sergeĭ Sergeevich) Druzhinin, N. M. (Nikolaĭ Mikhaĭlovich)
Sotsial′no-ėkonomicheskai͡a istorii͡a Rossii . Moskva , 1987. 421 p., [1] leaf of plates : LC Card 87-164847
HC334.5 .D78 1987

Dmitriev, Vasiliĭ Afanas′evich. Ėkonomika promyshlennogo zheleznodorozhnogo transporta /. Moskva , 1981. 295 p. ; LC Card 82-124231
HE2457 .E38 1981

Dmowski, Zygmunt. Organizacja i technika handlu zagranicznego : zagadnienia wybrane / Zygmunt Dmowski, Zenon Kamiński, Maciej Rydel.Wyd. 1. Gdańsk : UG, 1979. 201 p. ; 24 cm. (Skrypty uczelniane / Uniwersytet Gdański) Includes bibliographies. LC Card 81-181043
1. Poland - Commercial policy. 2. Poland - Foreign economic relations. I. Kamiński, Zenon. II. Rydel, M. (Maciej). III. Series: Skrypty uczelniane / Uniwersytet Gdański. IV. Title.
HF1558.7 .D59 1979

Dnipropetrovs′kyĭ derz͡havnyĭ universytet imeni 300-richchi͡a vozz′i͡ednanni͡a Ukraïny z Rosii͡eiu. Vozdeĭstvie khozi͡aĭstvennogo mekhanizma na povyshenie ėffektivnosti obshchestvennogo proizvodstva . Dnepropetrovsk , 1984. 119 p. ; LC Card 86-181397
HC340.I52 V68 1984

Do dominant firms decline? /. Geroski, Paul A. Berlin [1985] 23, [8] p. ; LC Card 86-213583 DDC 338.6/44 19
HD2757 .G47 1985

The do-it-yourself direct mail handbook /. Raphel, Murray, 1928- Philadelphia, PA (402 Bethlehem Pike, Philadelphia 19118) , c1986. xix, 218 p. : LC Card 86-203353
HF5861 .R35 1986

The do-it-yourself investor /. Burgauer, James. Chicago, Ill. , c1987. xi, 335 p. : ISBN 0-917253-68-X : LC Card 87-7006 DDC 332.6/78 19
HG4527 .B689 1987

Do latifundismo à reforma agrária . Barros, Afonso de. Oeiras [Portugal] , 1986. 636 p. : LC Card 87-404938 DDC 333.3/1/46955 19
HD1333.P82 B353 1986

Do what you love, the money will follow . Sinetar, Marsha. New York , c1986. p. cm. ISBN 0-8091-2874-8 : LC Card 86-30390 DDC 650.1 19
HF5381.5 .S53 1986

Do you speak televisionese? /. Benigni, Glauco. Milano [1985] 141 p. : LC Card 85-241850
HE8700.6 .B46 1985

Dobberthien, Marliese. Frauen und neue Technologien /. Hannover , 1986. 112 p. ; LC Card 87-407392 DDC 331.4/0943 19
HD6059.G3 F74 1986

Dobbin, Christine E., 1941- Islamic revivalism in a changing peasant economy : central Sumatra, 1784-1847 / Christine Dobbin. London : Curzon Press, 1983. xii, 300 p. : ill. ; 23 cm. (Monograph series / Scandinavian Institute of Asian

Studies, 0069-1712 . no. 47) Includes index. Bibliography: p. 258-270. ISBN 0-7007-0155-9 (pbk.) : LC Card 83-127619 DDC 303.4/84 19
1. Peasantry - Indonesia - Sumatra - History. 2. Economics - Religious aspects - Islam - History. I. Title.
HD1537.I56 D63 1983
NYPL [JLD 87-1053]

Dobischat, Rolf, 1950- Berufliche Weiterbildung, Arbeitsmarkt und Region : empirische Untersuchungen in ausgewählten Teilräumen unter besonderer Berücksichtigung der Teilnehmer in AFG-geförderten Bildungsmassnahmen / Rolf Dobischat, Herbert Wassmann. Frankfurt am Main ; New York : P. Lang, c1985. 691 p. : ill. ; 21 cm. (Europäische Hochschulschriften. Reihe XXII, Soziologie, 0721-3379 . Bd. 106 = vol. 106 = vol. 106) Bibliography: p. 665-691. ISBN 3-8204-5673-2 LC Card 86-158931
1. Occupational training - Germany (West) - Hesse - Case studies. 2. Occupational training - Germany (West) - North Rhine-Westphalia - Case studies. 3. Continuing education - Germany (West) - Hesse - Case studies. 4. Continuing education - Germany (West) - North Rhine-Westphalia - Case studies. I. Wassmann, Herbert, 1947-. II. Title.
HD5715.5.G42 H473 1985

Dobos, Irma B. Berey, András. Vezetés a gyakorlatban /. Budapest , 1986. 313 p. : ISBN 963-221-903-1 : LC Card 87-138251
HD37.H82 B486 1986

Dobosy, László. Gömörszőlős : egy gömöri falu néprajzi monográfiája / Dobosy László. Miskolc : Borsod-Abaúj-Zemplén Megyei Múzeumigazgatóság, 1984. 82 p., [16] p. of plates : ill. ; 21 cm. (Borsodi kismonográfiák, 0324-4563 . 19) Summary in English and German. Bibliography: p. 77. ISBN 963-01-5552-4 LC Card 87-408021
1. Gömörszőlős (Hungary) - Economic conditions. 2. Gömörszőlős(Hungary) - History. I. Title. II. Series.
HC300.292.G65 D63 1984

Dobozi, István. Policy responses to the changing international environment . Budapest , 1981. 170 p. ; ISBN 963-301-077-2 (pbk.) LC Card 81-179118 DDC 337/.09/048 19
HC59 .P573 1981 ***NYPL [JLL 79-189 no.33]***

DOBREV, KRŬSTIU, 1903-1976.
Krŭstiu Dobrev . Sofiia , 1987. 80 p., [16] p. of plates : LC Card 87-170598
HB108.3.D63 K78 1987

Dobroe imia /. Orlova, Zhanna. Moskva , 1986. 124 p. ; LC Card 86-131980
HD8530.M62 O75 1986

Dobrossy, István. Termelés és életmód : tíz község termelőszövetkezete / Dobrossy István, Fügedi Márta. Debrecen : Kossuth Lajos Tudományegyetem Néprajzi Tanszékének Kiadványa, 1983. 282 p. : ill. ; 20 cm. (Studia folkloristica et ethnographica, 0138-9882 . 9) Summary in German and Slovak. Includes bibliographical references. ISBN 963-471-276-2 LC Card 86-100359
1. Collective farms - Hungary - Putnok Region. 2. Agriculture - Hungary - Putnok Region. 3. Putnok Region (Hungary) - Social conditions. I. Fügedi, Márta. II. Title. III. Series.
HD1492.H82 P873 1983

Dobrovolny, Jiri, 1943- Preis- und Lohndirigismen im Dienste der Stabilisierungspolitik : Kritik der Begründung und Durchführung am Beispiel Grossbritannien / Jiri Dobrovolny. Bern ; New York : Lang, c1985. xi, 433 p. : ill. ; 21 cm. (Europäische Hochschulschriften. Reihe V, Volks- und Betriebswirtschaft . Bd. 675 = vol. 675 = vol. 675) Originally presented as the author's thesis (doctoral)--Hochschule St. Gallen. Bibliography: p. 413-433. ISBN 3-261-03517-X LC Card 86-105626 DDC 338.5/2/0945 19
1. Prices - Great Britain. 2. Unemployment - Great Britain - Effect of inflation on. 3. Economic stabilization - Great Britain. I. Series: Europäische Hochschulschriften. Reihe V, Volks- und Betriebswirtschaft , Bd. 675. II. Title.
HB236.G7 D63 1985

Dobrovol'skiĭ, V. K. (Vladimir Konstantinovich) Problemy optimizatsii mezhotraslevykh sviazeĭ . Kiev , 1976. 135 p. : LC Card 87-100694
HD9015.S653 U4547 1976

DOBRYĬ, ABRAM IUR'EVICH, 1867-1936.
Pamiati Abrama IUr'evicha Dobrogo. Pamiati Abrama IUr'evicha Dobrago. Parizh , 1939. 101 p., [1] leaf of plates : LC Card 83-136332
HG185.S65 P36 1939

Dobson, John M. A history of American enterprise / John M. Dobson. Englewood Cliffs, N.J. : Prentice Hall, c1988. p. cm. Includes bibliographies and index. ISBN 0-13-389081-3 LC Card 87-18679 DDC 338.0973 19
1. United States - Commerce - History. 2. United States - Industries - History. 3. Business enterprises - United States - History. I. Title.
HF3021 .D6 1988

Dobson, Wendy.
Canadian-Japanese economic relations in a triangular perspective /. Toronto , Scarborough, Ont. [1987] vi, 54 p. : ISBN 0-88806-139-0 (pbk.) LC Card 87-169818 DDC 337.52071 19
HF1480.15.J3 C35 1987

Canadian perspective. 1987. Canadian-Japanese economic relations in a triangular perspective / edited by Wendy Dobson. Toronto , Scarborough, Ont. [1987] vi, 54 p. : ISBN 0-88806-139-0 (pbk.) LC Card 87-169818 DDC 337.52071 19
HF1480.15.J3 C35 1987

Doc (Deutsche Stiftung für Entwicklungsländer) .
(62/93) Zweite wissenschaftliche Regionaltagung über Nah- und Mittelost . Berlin , 1963. vi, 177 p. ; LC Card 85-167419
HC59.7 .D385 no. 62/93 HC415.15

Doc. (Facultad Latinoamericana de Ciencias Sociales. Sede Académica de México) .
(82/1) Cortés, Fernando, 1941- Análisis del cambio en la concentración a través del coeficiente de Gini /. México, D.F. [1982] 55 leaves : LC Card 83-111847
HB523 .C67 1982

Dr. Jansen, Stadt- und Regionalplanung. Jansen, Paul Günter. Arbeitsmarktatlas . [Düsseldorf] [1977] 206, A19 p. : LC Card 85-173256
HD5780.A76 J36 1977

Dr. John Matthai, 1886-1959 . Haridasan, V., 1937- Cranganore, Trichur Dist., Kerala , 1986. xi, 192 p., [2] p. of plates : LC Card 86-903052 DDC 330/.092/4 B 19
HB126.I43 M374 1986

Dr. S.D. Punekar memorial lecture. Ranadive, K. R. Accumulation, employment, and labour aristocracy . Bombay [1982] 55 p. ; LC Card 83-903051 DDC 305.5/62/0954 19
HD8686.5 .R325 1982 ***NYPL [JLF 87-500]***

La doctrine coopérative /. Métellus, Champagne. Port-au-Prince, Haïti [1984] (Port-au-Prince, Haïti : Impr. La Phalange) 94 p. : LC Card 85-168867 DDC 334 19
HD2971 .M47 1984

Document d'initiation à l'informatique des organisations /. Gahungu, Fidèle. [Bujumbura?] [1983- v. <1 > : LC Card 86-980527
HD30.2 .G34 1983

Documentación e Información Laboral (Buenos Aires, Argentina) Guía de organizaciones gremiales, 1984 /. Capital Federal, República Argentina [between 1984 and 1986] [12], 651 p. : LC Card 87-123823 DDC 331.88/025/82 19
HD6601.5 .G85 1984

Documentación relacionada con la Conferencia Económica Latino Americana, Quito, 9-13 enero, 1984. Conferencia Económica Latinoamericana (1984 : Quito, Ecuador) [Rome, Italy] , 1984. 62 p. ; LC Card 86-134389 DDC 338.98 19
HC125 .C6555 1984

DOCUMENTARY CREDIT.
Empel, G. van. Betaling, waardepapier en documentair krediet /. Deventer , 1985. viii, 84 p. ; ISBN 90-268-1565-4 : LC Card 85-214764
HG173.6.D8 E46 1985

A Documentary history of the Petroleum Reserves Corporation, 1943-1944 : prepared for the use of Subcommittee on Multinational Corporations of the Committee on Foreign Relations, United States Senate. Washington : U. S. Govt. Print. Off., 1974. v, 119 p. : ill. ; 23 cm. At head of title: 93d Congress, 2d session. Committee print. LC Card 74-602382
1. War Assets Corporation. 2. Petroleum industry and trade - United States. 3. Energy policy - United States. I. United States. Congress. Senate. Committee on Foreign Relations. Subcommittee on Multinational Corporations.
HD9566 .D6 ***NYPL [JLE 78-1181]***

DOCUMENTATION.
Mayntz, Renate. Dokumentation und Organisation . Bergisch Gladbach , 1984. 132 p. : ISBN 3-89012-008-3 : LC Card 85-131112
HD30.3 .M394 1984

Documentation Centre for Corporate & Business Policy Research (India)
Banking in India in the eighties . New Delhi , 1986. 533 p. in various pagings ; LC Card 86-903123 DDC 332.1/068 19
HG3284 .B267 1986

Towards a viable and vibrant public sector in India . New Delhi , 1986. xiii, 188, 163, 8, 103 p. ; LC Card 86-903205 DDC 338.6/2/0954
HD4293 .T667 1986

Documenti ISVET .
(75) Le Iniziative locali per l'occupazione . Milano, Italy , c1985. 244 p. : LC Card 85-221711 DDC 331 s 331.12/042 19
HD85.I7 I68 no. 75 HD5713.5
NYPL [JLD 87-446]

(76) Le Strategie di acquisto della grande impresa nell'evoluzione dei sistemi produttivi . Milano, Italy , c1985. 223 p. : LC Card 85-233748
HD85.I7 I68 no. 76 HD39.5
NYPL [JLD 87-426]

(77) Hegedüs, Zsuzsa. Il presente è l'avvenire . Milano, Italy , c1985. 126 p. : LC Card 85-215705
HD85.I7 I68 no. 77 HD6955
NYPL [JLD 87-427]

Documento (Centro de Asesoría Profesional (Santiago, Chile). Area Comunicaciones) .
(no. 1) Gonzales Torres, Rodrigo. Los paros nacionales en Chile, 1919-1973 /. Santiago [Chile] , 1984. 234 p. ; LC Card 86-200794
HD5356.A6 G66 1984

Documento de estudo (Conselho Nacional de Desenvolvimento Urbano) .
(1) Estudos e propostas para a organização territorial e desenvolvimento urbano do Brasil. Brasilia , 1981. 126 leaves, [7] folded leaves of plates : ***NYPL [JLG 86-151]***

Documento de trabajo (Centro de Investigación y Docencia Económicas)
(núm. 3) Aschentrupp Toledo, Hermann. La dimensión política de la crisis y renegociación de la deuda externa mexicana /. México, D.F. [1985] 229 p. ; LC Card 87-401754 DDC 336.3/4/0972 19
HJ8519 .A8 1985

Espinoza Jaramillo, Frida. El estado de la investigación nacional acerca de la frontera norte de México /. [México] , 1985. 47 leaves ; LC Card 87-402765 DDC 330.972/10834 19
HC137.M46 E76 1985

Documento de trabajo (Centro de Investigaciones Sociales (Instituto Torcuato Di Tella)) .
(no. 94) Cornblit, Oscar. Sindicatos obreros y asociaciones empresarias hasta la década del centenario /. Buenos Aires, Argentina , 1984. 109 p. ; LC Card 87-401262 DDC 331.88/0982 19
HD6602 .C665 1984

Documento de trabajo (Facultad Latinoamericana de Ciencias Sociales. Sede Académica de México)

Documento de trabajo (Junta de Andalucía. Grupo de Trabajo 14, Planificación Económica de las Corporaciones Locales y Comarcalización) .
(1) Junta de Andalucía. Grupo de Trabajo 14, Planificación Económica de las Corporaciones Locales y Comarcalización. Plan económico de Andalucía, 1984-1986 /. [Andalucía] , 1983. 133 p. ; ISBN 84-505-1243-3 LC Card 86-223752
HJ1249.A4 J86 1983

Documento de trabajo (Programa de Investigaciones Sociales sobre Problemas de Población Relevantes para Políticas de Población en América Latina. Unidad Central) .
(no. 14) Lira, Luis Felipe. Estructura agraria, crecimiento de la población y migraciones . Santiago, Chile , 1976. 90 p. ; LC Card 83-169710
HB2025 .L57 1976

Documento de trabajo (Regional Employment Program for Latin America and the Caribbean) .
(226) Honduras . [Santiago, Chile] , 1983. vii, 99 p. ; LC Card 84-225233
HD5736.A6 H66 1983

(227) Problemas metodológicos de una encuesta rural en Chile y estructura del empleo /. [Santiago, Chile] [c1983] ii, 27 leaves ; LC Card 84-225128
HD1531.C5 P76 1983

(238) Reactivación con transformación . [Santiago, Chile] [c1984] 29 leaves ; LC Card 85-156967
HD5708.47.C5 R43 1984

(239) Salarios e inflación, Argentina, 1970-1983 /. [Santiago, Chile] [c1984] iv, 116 p. : LC Card 85-156959
HC180.W24 S25 1984

Documento de trabajo (Universidad Católica de Chile. Instituto de Ciencia Política) .
(año 5, no. 8-9) Fuenzalida Faivovich, Edmundo. [América Latina y la concentración del poder en la arena política.] América Latina y la concentración del poder en la arena política ; El impacto social del cambio tecnológico actual en los países menos desarrollados /. [Santiago de Chile] [between 1974 and 1979] 24, 25 leaves ; LC Card 82-180082
HD2810.5 .F84 1974

Documento de trabajo (Universidad Católica de Chile. Instituto de Economía) .
(no. 101) Coloma C., Fernando. Algunas consideraciones sobre los efectos distributivos del proceso de liberalización comercial /. Santiago , 1982. 31 leaves ; LC Card 87-102072
HF1713 .C617 1982

(no. 102) Coloma C., Fernando. Credibilidad de la política comercial /. Santiago, Chile , 1986. 43 p. : LC Card 87-102077
HF1515 .C64 1986

(no. 103) Coloma C., Fernando. Endeudamiento externo y tasa de descuento social . Santiago, Chile , 1986. 66 leaves : LC Card 87-102066
HJ8083 .C65 1986

(no. 104) Lagos, Luis Felipe. El efecto de los shocks externos sobre el producto . Santiago, Chile , 1985. 15, [8] leaves : LC Card 87-404321 DDC 339.383 19
HC195.I5 L34 1985

(no. 106) Coeymans, Juan Eduardo. Determinants of sectoral annual real wages in a developing economy /. Santiago , 1986. 32, [4] leaves : LC Card 87-404007 DDC 331.12/5/0983 19
HD5006 .C64 1986

(no. 89) Desormeaux J., Jorge. Determinación de precios del sector exportador chileno, 1978-1982 /. Santiago, Chile , 1983. 88 p. : LC Card 87-403699 DDC 338.5/2/0983 19
HB235.C57 D47 1983

(no. 94) Aedo, Cristián. Protección efectiva en Chile, 1974-1979 /. Santiago [1984] 56 leaves ; LC Card 85-152465
HF1956 .A35 1984

(no. 96) Coloma C., Fernando. Los efectos de una desgravación arancelaria en el contexto de una economía con movilidad imperfecta de trabajo /. Santiago , 1985. 46 leaves : LC Card 85-203579
HF1713 .C618 1985

Documento de trabajo (Universidad Católica de Chile. Instituto de Planificación del Desarrollo Urbano) .
(no. 123) Matas, Jaime. Los problemas ambientales del sistema de transporte urbano /. Santiago de Chile , 1981. 30 leaves : LC Card 82-201768
HE234.Z7 S355 1981

Documento de trabalho (Banco de Portugal. Gabinete de Estudos) .
(no. 11) Girão, José António. Salários, inflação e moeda . Lisboa , 1984. 50 p. : LC Card 85-157764
HG1145 .G57 1984

Documento final /. Debate Nacional sobre Abastecimento Popular (1986) Brasília, DF , 1986. 51 leaves : LC Card 87-146594 DDC 363.8/0981 19
HD9014.B82 D43 1986

Documento final do Debate Nacional sobre Abastecimento Popular. Debate Nacional sobre Abastecimento Popular (1986) Documento final /. Brasília, DF , 1986. 51 leaves : LC Card 87-146594 DDC 363.8/0981 19
HD9014.B82 D43 1986

Documento Serie investigación .
(no. 66) Riveros C., Luis. Structural reforms and wage setting across sectors . Santiago , 1984. 37, [5], 13 p. ; ***NYPL [JLF 87-136]***

(no. 76) Pardo V., Lucía. La historia laboral de las mujeres y su efecto en la tasa de salario . Santiago , 1986. 44, 5 p. : LC Card 86-217486
HD6126 .P37 1986

Documento (Universidad de los Andes (Bogotá, Colombia). Centro de Estudios sobre Desarrollo Económico) .
(072) Pedraja Tomán, René de la. Los Llanos . Bogotá, Colombia , 1984. 101 p. : LC Card 84-221343
HC198.L56 P4 1984

(073) Leibovich, José. Comercio exterior y distribución de ingresos . Bogotá, Colombia , 1984. vii, 221 p. : LC Card 87-402975 DDC 382/.41373/09861 19
HD9199.C62 L45 1984

(078) Rodríguez, Luis Hernando. Análisis descriptivo de las exportaciones colombianas, 1950-1980 /. Bogotá, Colombia , 1985. 3, 169 p. : LC Card 87-402978 DDC 382/.6/09861 19
HF3426.5 .R63 1985

(079) Reproducción de fuerza de trabajo, educación y migración en el sector rural colombiano /. Bogotá, Colombia , 1985. 98, [52] p. : LC Card 87-402979 DDC 331.1/09861 19
HD5757.A6 R46 1985

(081) Flórez Nieto, Carmen Elisa. The existence of a Latin American mortality pattern . Bogotá, Colombia , 1985. 153 p. : LC Card 87-145922
HB1397 .F56 1985

(082) Jaramillo, Samuel. Análisis de las condiciones de vivienda de los hogares colombianos, a partir de los resultados de la encuesta nacional de hogares, etapa 33, 1981 /. Bogotá, Colombia , 1985. ii, 166 p. ; LC Card 87-403605 DDC 363.5/1/09861 19
HD7325.A3 J37 1985

Documentos CELAM (Spanish ed.) .
(no. 82) Encuentro Latinoamericano de Pastoral Social (1986 : Bogotá, Colombia) El mundo del trabajo . Bogotá , 1986. 92 p. ; ISBN 958-625-053-9 LC Card 87-400623 DDC 261.8/5 19
HD6338 .C277 1981 Suppl.

(86) Abreu, Antonio. Dependencia y brechas entre ricos y pobres /. Bogotá , 1987. 112 p. ; ISBN 958-625-058-X LC Card 87-403548 DDC 337.8 19
HC125 .A23 1987

Documentos (Centro de Estudios Cristianos y Capacitación Popular (Peru))
Pacheco S., Janette. Situación y posibilidades alimentarias de la población urbano marginal de Arequipa /. Arequipa, Perú [1986] 38 p., 8 folded leaves of plates : LC Card 86-232480
HD9014.P53 A746 1986

Documentos (Centro Nacional de Pesquisa de Uva e Vinho (Brazil)) .
(1) Vitivinicultura no Brasil . Bento Gonçalves, RS , 1986, c1985. 50 p. ; LC Card 87-403937 DDC 338.1/748/0981021 19
HD9384.B72 V58 1986

Documentos (Colombia. Departamento Administrativo Nacional de Estadística)
Metodología de la encuesta nacional de hogares. Bogotá, D.E., Colombia [1985] 64 p. : LC Card 85-240042
HB849.49 .M48 1985

Documentos de trabajo (Centro Peruano de Estudios Internacionales) .
(1) Kisic Wagner, Drago. Reflexiones en torno al proceso de coordinación latinoamericano sobre la deuda externa /. [Lima, Perú] [1985] 29 p. ; LC Card 87-403187 DDC 336.3/435/098 19
HJ8514.5 .K57 1985

(7) Mac Lean U., Roberto. La coerción económica internacional . [Lima, Perú] [1986] 28 p. ; LC Card 87-142994 DDC 337 19
HF1411 .M218 1986

Documentos de trabajo (Instituto de Estudios Peruanos) .
(no. 7) Herrera, César. Inflación, política devaluatoria y apertura externa en el Perú, 1978-1984 /. Lima, Perú , 1985. 55 p. : LC Card 87-104441
HG895 .H47 1985

Documentos de trabajo (Universidad de Costa Rica. Instituto de Investigaciones en Ciencias Económicas) .
(no. 25) Mulquin, Marie Eve. Empalme del índice de precios al consumidor . [San José] , 1981. 15 leaves ; LC Card 81-216387
HB221 .M774 1981

(no. 25) Mulquin, Marie Eve. Empalme del índice de precios al consumidor . [San José] , 1981. 15 leaves ; LC Card 81-216387
HB221 .M774 1981

(no. 26) Mulquin, Marie Eve. Las estadísticas del sector construcción en Costa Rica . [San José] , 1981. 39 p. ; LC Card 81-216965
HD9715.C82 M85 1981

(no. 71) Morales C., Pedro A. Política industrial y adquisición de tecnología en la actividad química en Costa Rica /. [San José, Costa Rica] [1984] ii, 55 p. ; LC Card 86-199221
HD9655.C82 M67 1984

(no. 77) Pacheco O., Amparo. Préstamo del BID al sector pesquero . [San José] , 1984. 50 p. : LC Card 86-185463
HD9464.A2 P33 1984

Documentos de trabajo (Universidad de Murcia. Departamento de Geografía Humana)
(1) Bel Adell, María del Carmen. Datos básicos para el estudio de la población en la región de Murcia /. [Murcia] , c1985. 223 p. ; ISBN 84-600-3907-2 LC Card 86-218876
HA1558.M8 B44 1985

Documentos (Empresa Brasileira de Pesquisa Agropecuária. Centro de Pesquisa Agropecuária dos Cerrados) .
(no. 17) Franz, Paulo Renato Ferreira. Região geoeconômica de Brasília . Planaltina-DF [Brazil] , 1985. 70 p. : LC Card 87-143606 DDC 338.1/3/098174 19
HD1875.B7 F7 1985

Documentos (Instituto Boliviano de Estudios Empresariales) .
(1) Bolivia frente a la crisis del estaño . La Paz, Bolivia [1986] 62 p. ; LC Card 86-189109
HD9539.T6 B646 1986 ***NYPL [JLC 87-146]***

Documentos sindicales .
(no. 4-7) Lucha y polémica sindical, 1968-1973. [Montevideo?] , 1985. 4 v. ; LC Card 86-107744 DDC 322/.2/09895 19
HD6647 .L83 1985 ***NYPL [JLC 86-368]***

Documentos y estudios .
(37) La Reconversión industrial, la crisis y reforma agraria. [Madrid] [1984] 148 p. : ISBN 84-398-1197-7 LC Card 86-216324
HC385 .R375 1984

Documents de l'Union syndicale suisse.
Sécurité et santé au travail . Berne [1984] 47 p. ; LC Card 85-176432 DDC 363.1/1/09494 19
HD7740 .S43 1984

Documents de recherche (Institut québécois de recherche sur la culture) .
(no 5) Fortin, Andrée. Le Rézo . Québec, Québec , 1985. 282 p. : ISBN 2-89224-052-2 LC Card 86-225353
HD3290.A3 Q435 1985

Documents de travail (European Institute of Public Administration)
Can the CAP be reformed? /. Maastricht, The Netherlands , c1985. xii, 127 p. ; ISBN 90-6779-013-3 (pbk.) LC Card 86-214732 DDC 338.1/84 19
HD1920.5 .C36 1985

Coming to grips with the internal market /. Maastricht, The Netherlands , c1986. viii, 136 p. ; ISBN 90-6779-019-2 (pbk.) LC Card 86-222624 DDC 337.1/42 19
HC241.2 .C5548 1986

Documents du Centre d'étude des revenus et des coûts, 0336-1470 .
(no 71) Constat de l'évolution récente des revenus en France . Paris [1984] 220 p. : LC Card 85-127672
HC280.I5 C67 1984

Documents économiques .
(24) Chardonnens, Jean-Pierre. Le financement de l'entreprise en période de récession économique /. [Fribourg] , c1984. 269 p. : ISBN 2-8271-0281-1 : LC Card 84-225557 DDC 658.1/5 19
HG4026 .C457 1984

(25) Vieli, Mario. La décision du dividende en Suisse /. [Fribourg] , c1984. 187 p. : ISBN 2-8271-0282-X : LC Card 84-225559 DDC 658.1/55 19
HG4028.D5 V54 1984

(28) Ngirabatware, Augustin. Les taux de change flottants et les pays souscapitalisés . Fribourg, Suisse , c1986. 340 p. : ISBN 2-8271-0330-3 : LC Card 86-170584
HG3877 .N48 1986

(30) Caille, Pierre. La théorie de l'échange international de produits différenciés /. Fribourg, Suisse , c1986. 267 p. : ISBN 2-8271-0337-0 LC Card 86-210742
HF1008 .C35 1986

Documents généraux du GRIDEQ .
(no 11) Les Structures productives d'une région périphérique . Rimouski , c1984. xi, 718 p. : ISBN 2-920270-27-3 LC Card 85-132709 DDC 330.9714/77 19
HC117.G37 S78 1984

Documents tarifaires Lamy.
Tarifs routiers de marchandises. Paris [1986] 201 p. ; ISBN 2-7212-0295-2 LC Card 87-123802
HE5668.A6 T37 1986

Tarifs routiers de marchandises. Paris [1986] 956 p. ; ISBN 2-7212-0297-9 LC Card 87-119821
HE5668.A6 T38 1986

Dodd, David L. (David Le Fevre), 1895- Graham, Benjamin, 1894- [Security analysis.] Graham and Dodd's security analysis. New York , c1988. xiii, 656 p. : ISBN 0-07-013235-6 : LC Card 87-19990 DDC 332.63/2 19
HG4529 .G7 1988

Dødelighed og førtidspensionering blandt ansatte på danske kraftværker /. Rønne, Henning. København , 1985. 73 p. : ISBN 87-7359-155-6 LC Card 85-228083
HD7262.5.D4 R66 1985

Dødelighet i yrker og sosioøkonomiske grupper 1970-1980 /. Borgan, Jens-Kristian. Oslo , 1986. 217 p. : ISBN 82-537-2339-3 : LC Card 86-231576
HB1445 .B66 1986

Dodge, H. Robert, 1929- A Collection of cases in marketing management /. St. Paul , c1987. xix, 344 p. ; ISBN 0-314-85313-8 (pbk.) LC Card 87-6072 DDC 658.8/00973 19
HF5415.13 .C64 1987

Doe. see **United States. Dept. of Energy.**

Doeleman, David. Real estate financial management / David Doeleman, Ronald C. Rogers. Chicago, Ill. : Real Estate Brokerage Council, [1987], c1986. 152 p. : ill. ; 28 cm. Includes index. ISBN 0-913652-61-X (pbk.) LC Card 86-62851 DDC 333.33/068/1 19
1. Real estate agents - United States. 2. Real estate business - United States - Finance. I. Rogers, Ronald C. (Ronald Clifton), 1946-. II. Title.
HD278 .D64 1987

Doellinger, Carlos von.
Reordenamento do setor público. 1986. Setor público, reordenamento e privatização / Paulo Rabello de Castro, Carlos von Doellinger. [Rio de Janeiro, RJ , 1986] 47 p. : LC Card 87-403308 DDC 338.981 19
HC187 .S436 1986

Döring, Ulrich. Kostensteuern, der Einfluss von Steuern auf kurzfristige Produktions- und Absatzentscheidungen / Ulrich Döring. Stuttgart : C.E. Poeschel, c1984. x, 228 p. ; 23 cm. (Betriebswirtschaftliche Abhandlungen . n.F., Bd. 60) The author's Habilitationsschrift--Universität des Saarlandes. Bibliography: p. 217-225. Includes index. ISBN 3-7910-0369-0 LC Card 86-134925
1. Corporations - Taxation - Germany, West. 2. Production planning - Decision-making. 3. Costs, Industrial - Germany, West. I. Title. II. Series.
HD2753.G3 D73 1984

Doeringer, Peter B. Invisible factors in local economic development / Peter B. Doeringer, David G. Terkla, Gregory Topakian. New York : Oxford University Press, 1987. vii, 144 p. : ill. ; 25 cm. Bibliography: p. [135]-140. Includes index. ISBN 0-19-504965-9 (alk. paper) LC Card 87-13550 DDC 338.9744/3 19
1. Worcester County (Mass.) - Industries. 2. Regional planning - Massachusetts - Worcester County. 3. Competition - Government policy - Massachusetts - Worcester County. 4. Industrial promotion - Massachusetts - Worcestor County. I. Terkla, David G. II. Topakian, Gregory. III. Title.
HC107.M42 W674 1987

Dörner, Dietrich. Normengeleitetes Verhalten in den Sozialwissenschaften /. Berlin , c1984. 199 p. ; ISBN 3-428-05622-1 LC Card 86-140299
HB74.P8 N67 1984

Does aid work? : report to an intergovernmental task force / Robert Cassen & Associates. Oxford [Oxfordshire] : Clarendon Press ; New York : Oxford University Press, 1986. xv, 381 p. ; 25 cm. Bibliography: p. [363]-381. ISBN 0-19-877250-5 : LC Card 86-12621 DDC 338.91/09172/4 19
1. Economic assistance - Developing countries. 2. Technical assistance - Developing countries. I. Robert Cassen & Associates.
HC60 .D53 1986 ***NYPL [JLE 86-4563]***

Dötsch, Jochen. EG und Arbeiterrechte : der Kampf um die sozialen Rechte der Werktätigen kapitalistischer Länder Westeuropas / Jochen Dötsch, Manfred Premssler.1. Aufl. Berlin : Staatsverlag der Deutschen Demokratischen Republik, 1981. 143 p. ; 21 cm. Includes bibliographical references. LC Card 81-145834 DDC 331.11/094 19
1. Labor policy - European Economic Community countries. 2. Industrial relations - European Economic Community countries. 3. European Economic Community countries - Social policy. I. Premssler, Manfred. II. Title. III. Title: E.G. und Arbeiterrechte.
HD8380.5 .D67 1981 ***NYPL [JLD 86-2739]***

Dofny, Jacques. Garon-Audy, Muriel. Mobilités professionnelles et géographiques au Québec, 1954-64-74 /. Montréal , 1980. 61 p. ; LC Card 81-105620 DDC 331.12/7971 19
HD5717.5.C22 Q44 1980
NYPL [JLM 79-970 no.22]

Dögl, Rudolf. Strategisches Qualitätsmanagement im Industriebetrieb : pragmatischer Ansatz zur Erklärung und methodischen Handhabung des Qualitätsphänomens / Rudolf Dögl. Göttingen : Vandenhoeck & Ruprecht, c1986. xv, 267 p. : 41 ill. ; 24 cm. (Innovative Unternehmensführung. Bd. 14) Bibliography: p. [248]-267. ISBN 3-525-12562-3 (Deut. Bibl.) LC Card 86-210486
1. Strategic planning. 2. Quality control. I. Title.
HD30.28 .D64 1986

Dogra, Bharat. Empty stomachs and packed godowns : aspects of the food system in India / by Bharat Dogra. New Delhi : Bharat Dogra, 1987. viii, 126 p. ; 23 cm. (Social change paper . 10) Bibliography: p. 126. LC Card 87-900472 DDC 338.1/9/54 19
1. Food supply - India. 2. Food consumption - India. 3. Nutrition policy - India. I. Title. II. Series.
HD9016.I42 D64 1987

Dogramaci, Ali. Measurement issues and behavior of productivity variables /. Boston , Hingham, MA, USA , c1986. ix, 262 p. : ISBN 0-89838-171-1 LC Card 85-8017 DDC 338/.06/0287 19
HD56.25 .M43 1986 ***NYPL [JLE 86-3414]***

Doh, Rainer. Bevölkerungsentwicklung, Wirtschaftsordnung und Industrialisierungsprozess in Südosteuropa : dargestellt am Beispiel der Länder Rumänien und Türkei / Rainer Doh, Wienfried Senker. Neuried : Hieronymus, c1985. [12], 486, 19 p. : ill. ; 21 cm. (Wirtschaft und Gesellschaft in Südosteuropa . Bd. 4) Bibliography: p. 1-19 (3rd group). ISBN 3-88893-045-6 LC Card 87-140271 DDC 304.6/09498 19
1. Romania - Population. 2. Turkey - Population. 3. Romania - Economic conditions. 4. Turkey - Economic conditions. I. Senker, Wienfried. II. Title. III. Series.
HB3631 .D64 1985

Döhl, Volker. Belastungsabbau unter Tage . Essen , 1982. 315 p. : ISBN 3-7739-0380-4 : LC Card 83-186893 DDC 363.1/1/0943 19
HD7708 .B45 1982

Döhne, Ulrich. Analyse der Ansiedlung von Einkaufszentren und Verbrauchermärkten in Nordrhein-Westfalen / Ulrich Döhne. Dortmund : Institut für Landes- und Stadtentwicklungsforschung des Landes Nordrhein-Westfalen (ILS) ; Essen : Vertrieb, Verlag für Wirtschaft und Verwaltung H. Wingen, 1977. 39 p. : col. maps ; 30 cm. (Kurzberichte zur Landes- und Stadtentwicklungsforschung) LC Card 86-181973
1. Retail trade - Germany (West) - North Rhine-Westphalia. 2. Consumers - Germany (West) - North Rhine-Westphalia. I. Title. II. Series.
HF5429.6.G42 D64 1977

Döhrn, Roland. Privater Verbrauch und Einzelhandel in der Bundesrepublik Deutschland : Ausgabearten und Lieferbereiche des Privaten Verbrauchs sowie Umsätze in den Wirtschaftsbereichen des institutionellen Einzelhandels, 1960-1979 / von Roland Döhrn. Essen : RWI Essen, 1981. 280 p. ; 30 cm. (RWI-Papiere . Nr. 11) Chiefly tables. Bibliography: p. 278-280. LC Card 87-408859 DDC 338.5/28/0943 19
1. Consumer price indexes - Germany (West) - Statistics. 2. Prices - Germany (West) - Statistics. 3. Retail trade - Germany (West) - Statistics. I. Title. II. Series.
HB235.G3 D57 1981

Dohse, Knuth, 1948-
[Ausländerpolitik und betriebeliche Ausländerdiskriminierung. English]
Foreign workers in the Federal Republic of Germany : governmental policy and discrimination in employment / Knuth Dohse. Berlin : International Institute for Comparative Social Research/Labor Policy, [1982] 80 p. : ill. ; 30 cm. (IIVG papers, 0724-5084 . IIVG/pre82-207) Translation of: Ausländerpolitik und betrieblich Ausländerdiskriminierung. "Juni 1982." Includes bibliographical references. LC Card 86-214190 DDC 331.6/2/0943 19
1. Alien labor - Government policy - Germany (West). 2. Discrimination in employment - Germany, West. I. Series: IIVG papers , 82-207. II. Title.
HD8458.A2 D6213 1982

Dohse, Peter. Ziefuss, Horst. Jugendliche in der gewerblich-technischen Ausbildung in Industrie und Handwerk . Kiel , c1986. 352 p. : ISBN 3-89088-011-8 LC Card 87-407898 DDC 331.3/42592/0943 19
HD5715.5.G4 Z54 1986

Doing a feasibility study : training activities for starting or reviewing a small business / editor, Suzanne Kindervatter ; contributors, Marcy Kelly ... [et al.] ; poster story illustrations, Malick Pouye. Washington, D.C. : OEF International, c1987. 173 p. : ill., forms ; 22 x 28 cm. (Appropriate business skills for Third World women) ISBN 0-912917-07-5 (pbk.) : LC Card 86-61951 DDC 658/.022/091724 19
1. New business enterprises - Developing countries - Handbooks, manuals, etc. 2. Women-owned business enterprises - Developing countries - Handbooks, manuals, etc. I. Kindervatter, Suzanne. II. OEF International. III. Series.
HD62.5 .D63 1987

Doing business abroad /. Kennedy, Gavin. New York , c1985. 268 p. ; ISBN 0-671-55484-0 : LC Card 85-14416 DDC 658.4 19
HD58.6 .K45 1985 ***NYPL [JLD 86-2339]***

Doing business in Korea / edited by Arthur M. Whitehill. London : Croom Helm ; New York : Nichols Pub. Co., 1987. xvi, 121 p. : ill. ; 23 cm. Includes index. ISBN 0-89397-276-2 (Nichols) : LC Card 87-5665 DDC 330.9519/5043 19
1. Korea (South) - Economic conditions - 1960-. 2. Korea (South) - Commerce. 3. Investments, Foreign - Korea (South). 4. Business etiquette - Korea (South). I. Whitehill, Arthur M. (Arthur Murray).
HC467 .D58 1987

Doing business in Maine. [Augusta, Me. : State Development Office, 1983] iii, 93 p. : forms ; 28 cm. Cover title. "April 1983"--P. iii. Bibliography: p. 89-93. LC Card 86-620779 DDC 346.741/07 347.41067 19
1. New business enterprises - Maine - Handbooks, manuals, etc. 2. Small business - Maine - Handbooks, manuals, etc. 3. Business law - Maine - Handbooks,

manuals, etc. I. Maine. State Development Office.
HD62.5 .D64 1983

Doing business in Texas. [Austin, Tex.] : Texas Economic Development Commission : Price Waterhouse, [1986], c1985. 52, [64] p. : ill. ; 28 cm. LC Card 87-621557 DDC 332.6/7322764 19
1. Texas - Economic conditions. 2. Texas - Economic policy. 3. Texas - Commerce. 4. New business enterprises - Texas. 5. Texas - Description and travel - 1981-. I. Texas Economic Development Commission. II. Price Waterhouse (Firm).
HC107.T4 D65 1986

Doing well by doing good . McAdam, Terry W. [Careers in the nonprofit sector.] New York, N.Y., U. S.A. , 1988, c1986. xxi, 201 p. : ISBN 0-14-046820-X (pbk.) LC Card 87-23602 DDC 650.1/4 19
HF5381 .M12 1988

Dokos, Kōnstantinos. Hē Sterea Hellas kata ton Henetotourkikon polemon, 1684-1699 kai ho Salōnōn Philotheos / Kōnstantinou Dokou. Athēnai : Hetaireia Stereoelladikōn Meletōn, 1985. 255 p. ; 26 cm. (Keimena kai meletai / Hetaireia Stereoelladikōn Meletōn . 1) Thesis (doctoral)--Philosophikēs Scholēs tou Ethnikou kai Kapodistriakou Panepistēmiou Athēnōn, 1974. Summary in English. Bibliography: p. 213-217. Includes index. LC Card 86-211599
1. Migration, Internal - Greece - History - 17th century. 2. Greece - Colonization - History - 17th century. 3. Greece - History - 1453-1821. 4. Venice - History - Turkish Wars, 17th century. 5. Philotheos, Bishop of Salona. I. Series: Keimena kai meletai , 1. II. Title.
HB2092.5.A3 D64 1985

Dokoumenta tou Hellēnikou proodeutikou kinēmatos .
(11) Hexē hapla mathēmata . Thessalonikē , 1945. 32, 16 p. ; LC Card 87-122267
HB501 .H475 1945

Dokumentation (Studienzentrum Weikersheim) .
(10) Umweltschutz . [Mainz] , c1984. 130 p. ; ISBN 3-7758-1086-2 LC Card 85-146233
HC290.5.E5 U64 1984

Dokumentation und Organisation . Mayntz, Renate. Bergisch Gladbach , 1984. 132 p. : ISBN 3-89012-008-3 : LC Card 85-131112
HD30.3 .M394 1984

Dokumente aus Hoechst-Archiven .
(48) US-Administration . Frankfurt (M) , 1976. 153 p. : LC Card 85-224662
HD9654.9.H64 U7 1976

Dolan, Edwin G. Campbell, Colin Dearborn, 1917- Money, banking, and monetary policy /. Chicago , c1988. xx, 617 p. : ISBN 0-03-009494-1 LC Card 87-6890 DDC 332.1 19
HG221 .C245 1988

Dolan, Shimon.
Canadian readings in personnel and human resource management /. St. Paul, MN , c1987. xi, 467 p. ; ISBN 0-314-32487-9 (pbk.) LC Card 87-2211 DDC 658.3/00971 19
HF5549.2.C3 C36 1987

Personnel and human resource management in Canada / Shimon L. Dolan, Randall S. Schuler. St. Paul, MN : West Pub. Co., c1987. xvii, 620 p. : ill. ; 26 cm. "Selected journals and associations in personnel and human resource management": p. [593]-596. Includes bibliographies and index. ISBN 0-314-32486-0 LC Card 87-2207 DDC 658.3/00971 19
1. Personnel management - Canada. I. Schuler, Randall S. II. Title.
HF5549.2.C3 D65 1987

Dolch, Norman A. (Norman Allan) Dlin, Norman. Social atlas of Shreveport, Louisiana /. Shreveport , 1985. 1 atlas (vii, 43 p.) : LC Card 86-622543 DDC 304.6/09763/99 19
HA730.S615 D57 1985

Dolgikh, N. S. Rabochiĭ klass i stroitel'stvo sotsializma v stranakh TSentral'noĭ i IUgo-Vostochnoĭ Evropy /. Moskva , 1977. 382 p. ; LC Card 81-174150
HD8376.5 .R33 1977

Dolgosrochnoe sotsial'no-ėkonomicheskoe planirovanie / pod redaktsieĭ N.A. Moiseenko, B.R. Riashchenko. Leningrad : Izd-vo Leningradskogo universiteta, 1986. 165 p. : ill. ; 22 cm. At head of title: Leningradskiĭ ordena Lenina i ordena Trudovogo Krasnogo Znameni gosudarstvennyĭ universitet imeni A.A. Zhdanova. Includes bibliographical references. LC Card 87-146872
1. Tikhvin Region (R.S.F.S.R.) - Economic policy. 2. Central planning - Russian S.F.S.R. - Tikhvin Region. I. Moiseenko, Nikolaĭ Andreevich. II. Riashchenko, B. R. III. Leningradskiĭ gosudarstvennyĭ universitet imeni A.A. Zhdanova.
HC338.T5 D65 1986

Dolgosrochnye narodnokhoziaĭstvennye programmy . Budaveĭ, Vsevolod IUr'evich. Moskva , 1980. 205 p. ; LC Card 81-143196
HD45 .B792 1980

Dolgovremennye tendentsii v kapitalisticheskom vosproizvodstve : referativnyĭ sbornik / [otvetstvennye redaktory i sostaviteli sbornika Entov R.M., Makasheva N.A.]. Moskva : Akademiia nauk SSSR, In-t nauch. informatsii po obshchestvennym naukam, 1985. 229 p. : ill. ; 20 cm. (Seriia Teoriia i praktika gosudarstvenno-monopolisticheskogo kapitalizma) Includes bibliographies. LC Card 86-187722
1. Business cycles. 2. Capitalism. I. Entov, R. M. (Revol'd Mikhaĭlovich). II. Makasheva, N. A. III. Series.
HB3711 .D62 1985

Dolgozatok a közgazdaságtudományok köréből, 0209-9187.
Mellár, Tamás. Az érték átalakulása termelési árrá, avagy, Az un. transzformációs probléma /. Pécs , 1982. 55 p. ; LC Card 83-179021
HB203 .M44 1982

Vörös, József. A kockázat, haszon és a termelési szerkezet összefüggése /. Pécs , 1983. 77 leaves : LC Card 85-111246
HD61 .V67 1983

Dolishniĭ, Mar'ian Ivanovich. Kachestvo trudovogo potentsiala . Kiev , 1986. 228 p. ; LC Card 87-161614
HD5797.U37 K34 1986

DOLL INDUSTRY - UNITED STATES.
Hoffman, William, 1937- Fantasy . Dallas, Tex. , c1984. 217 p. : ISBN 0-87833-386-X LC Card 84-8817 DDC 338.4/76887221/0973 19
HD9993.D653 U64 1984 ***NYPL [JLE 87-218]***

Doll, Martin. Röhm, Helmut. Der Förderungsauftrag im Zielsystem der Bankgenossenschaften . Stuttgart , c1983. 306 p. ; ISBN 3-8001-8187-8 LC Card 84-106807
HG2039.G4 R568 1983

DOLLAR, AMERICAN.
Haley, Stephen L. The value of the dollar and competitiveness of U. S. wheat exports /. [Washington, D.C.] [1986] iv, 28 p. : LC Card 86-602853 DDC 382/.41311/0973 19
HD9049.W5 U4288 1986

Martinengo, Giancarlo. Lo SME e il dollaro . [Napoli] , c1983. 84 p. ; LC Card 85-150597
HG930.5 .M27 1983

DOLLAR, AMERICAN - HISTORY.
Denizet, Jean. Le dollar . Paris , c1985. 259 p. ; ISBN 2-213-01626-7 : LC Card 86-148501 DDC 332.4/560973 19
HG3881 .D344 1985 ***NYPL [JLD 87-337]***

The dollar, debt, and the trade deficit /. Solomon, Anthony M. New York , 1987. 55 p. ; ISBN 0-8147-7863-1 : LC Card 86-23651 DDC 382.1/7/0973 19
HF3031 .S65 1987

Dollars & borders . Hawley, James P., 1944- Armonk, N.Y. , c1987. xi, 204 p. ; ISBN 0-87332-386-6 : LC Card 86-31395 DDC 332/.041 19
HG3891 .H38 1987

Dollars and borders. Hawley, James P., 1944- Dollars & borders . Armonk, N.Y. , c1987. xi, 204 p. ; ISBN 0-87332-386-6 : LC Card 86-31395 DDC 332/.041 19
HG3891 .H38 1987

Dollars & cents of off-price shopping centers : a special report / Frank H. Spink, Jr., project director ; Main Hurdman accountants for the study, Charles A. Hass, Sidney C. Hodges. Washington, D.C. : ULI--the Urban Land Institute, c1986. v, 78 p. : ill. ; 28 cm. Bibliography: p. 75. ISBN 0-87420-660-X (pbk.) LC Card 86-51102 DDC 381/.1 19
1. Shopping centers - United States. 2. Discount houses (Retail trade) - United States. 3. Outlet stores - United States. I. Spink, Frank H. II. Main Hurdman (Firm). III. Urban Land Institute. IV. Title: Dollars and cents of off-price shopping centers. V. Title: Off-price shopping centers.
HF5430.3 .D65 1986

Dollars and cents of off-price shopping centers. Dollars & cents of off-price shopping centers . Washington, D.C. , c1986. v, 78 p. : ISBN 0-87420-660-X (pbk.) LC Card 86-51102 DDC 381/.1 19
HF5430.3 .D65 1986

Dollars and dreams . Levy, Frank, 1941- New York , 1987. p. cm. ISBN 0-87154-523-3 : LC Card 86-42952 DDC 339.2/0973 19
HC110.I5 L47 1987

DOLLARS AND SENSE (COMPUTER PROGRAM)
Adams, Steve, 1948- Using Dollars and Sense on the IBM /. Indianapolis, Ind. , c1987. xviii, 439 p. : ISBN 0-88022-287-5 (pbk.) : LC Card 86-63981 DDC 332.024/0028/55369 19
HG179 .A34 1987

Rozells, Gia L. Making dollars and cents with dollars and sense /. Greensboro, N.C. , c1987. ix, 207 p. : ISBN 0-87455-101-3 (pbk.) : LC Card 87-160661 DDC 332.024/0028/55369 19
HG179 .R74 1987

Dollé, Anne. Ça va comme un lundi : la vie de bureau / Anne Dollé. [Paris] : Hachette littérature, c1984. 237 p. ; 21 cm. ISBN 2-01-010177-4 : LC Card 85-143058 DDC 650.1/3 19
1. Office politics. 2. Success in business. I. Title.
HF5386 .D63 1984

Dolve, Olav. (joint author) Killi, Egil. Transportproblemer, -politikk, -forskning og -undervisning i USA. Slemdal, 1968. 65, 3, 5 l. LC Card 75-408744
HE203 .K5 ***NYPL [JLF 86-617]***

Dolzhnost'--direktor / [sostavitel' N.I. Petrov]. Moskva : Moskovskiĭ rabochiĭ, 1985. 333 p. : ill., ports. ; 20 cm. LC Card 85-145325
1. Executives - Russian S.F.S.R. - Moscow - Biography. I. Petrov, Nikolaĭ Ivanovich.
HC332.5.A2 D64 1985

Dom Alvaro Pais e o pensamento económico em Portugal na Idade Média. Amzalak, Moses Bensabat, 1892- D. Alvaro Pais e o pensamento económico em Portugal na Idade Média /. Lisboa , 1954. 71 p. : LC Card 84-213332
HB79.P45 A49 1954

Dom za politicheska prosveta (Plovdiv, Bulgaria)
Masovo-politicheskata i organizatorska rabota v usloviiata na noviia ikonomicheski mekhanizŭm. Plovdiv , 1981. 42 p. ; LC Card 82-153766
HC403 .M376 1981

Dom za politicheska prosveta (Sliven, Bulgaria)
Ikonomicheskiiat podkhod i ikonomicheskoto vŭzpitanie na trudeshtite se. Sliven , 1984. 195 p. ; LC Card 86-102634
HB74.9.B9 I37 1984

Dom za politicheska prosveta (Varna, Bulgaria)
Nauchno-tekhnicheskiiat progress--delo na vsichki. Varna , 1985. 187 p. : LC Card 86-198872
HC403.Z9 T46 1985

Domanda di lavoro e produttività nell'industria italiana /. Palazzi, Paolo. Bologna , c1980. 177 p. ; LC Card 82-156294 DDC 331.13/7945 19
HD5784 .P28 1980 ***NYPL [JLD 86-2811]***

Domdey, Karl Heinz.
Weltenergie- und Weltrohstoffwirtschaft / Karl-Heinz Domdey. Berlin : Humboldt-Universität zu Berlin, 1981. 198 p. ; 21 cm. (Wissenschaftliche Schriftenreihe der Humboldt-Universität zu Berlin) Bibliography: p. 196-198. LC Card 85-132039
1. Energy industries. 2. Raw materials. 3. Mineral industries. 4. Geography, Economic. I. Title.
HD9502.A2 D65 1981

Weltwirtschaft und Weltwirtschaftslehre : ein Diskussionsbeitrag / Karl-Heinz Domdey. Berlin : Humboldt-Universität zu Berlin, 1984. 366 p. : ill. ; 21 cm. (Wissenschaftliche Schriftenreihe der Humboldt-Universität zu Berlin) Includes bibliographical references. LC Card 84-245611
1. Economic history - 20th century. 2. Capitalism. 3. Imperialism. 4. Communism. 5. Communist countries - Economic policy. 6. International economic relations. I.

Title.
HC54 .D65 1984

DÔMES MOUNTAINS (FRANCE) - RURAL CONDITIONS.
Système agraire et pratiques paysannes dans les monts Dômes /. Paris , 1983. xi, 318 p., [8] p. of plates : ISBN 2-85340-478-1 LC Card 84-216594
HD1950.D65 S97 1983

Domestic and international banking /. Lewis, Mervyn. Cambridge, Mass. , 1987. ix, 440 p. : ISBN 0-262-12126-3 LC Card 87-2962 DDC 332.1 19
HG1586 .L39 1987

Domestic & international banking. Lewis, Mervyn. Domestic and international banking /. Cambridge, Mass. , 1987. ix, 440 p. : ISBN 0-262-12126-3 LC Card 87-2962 DDC 332.1 19
HG1586 .L39 1987

DOMESTIC APPLIANCES. see **HOUSEHOLD APPLIANCES.**

DOMESTIC ARCHITECTURE. see **ARCHITECTURE, DOMESTIC.**

DOMESTIC ECONOMY. see **HOME ECONOMICS.**

DOMESTIC INTERNATIONAL SALES CORPORATIONS - TAXATION - UNITED STATES.
Lees, Francis A. Financing export sales /. New York, N.Y. (845 3rd Ave., New York 10022) , c1986. 12 p. : LC Card 86-212400 DDC 658.1/5 19
HF3031 .L36 1986

Domestic pottery of the northeastern United States, 1625-1850 / edited by Sarah Peabody Turnbaugh. Orlando : Academic Press, 1985. xxi, 319 p. : ill. ; 24 cm. (Studies in historical archaeology) Includes index. Bibliography: p. 285-305. ISBN 0-12-703870-1 (alk. paper) LC Card 85-9038 DDC 338.4/76663974 19
1. Pottery industry - Northeastern States - History. 2. Pottery - Northeastern States - History. 3. Northeastern States - Economic conditions. I. Turnbaugh, Sarah Peabody. II. Series. III. Series: Studies in historical archaeology (Orlando, Fla.).
HD9611.7.A115 D66 1985
NYPL [3-MPH 86-2845]

DOMESTIC SCIENCE. see **HOME ECONOMICS.**

Domestic servants and households in Rochdale, 1851-1871 /. Higgs, Edward, 1952- New York , 1986. 423 p. ; ISBN 0-8240-6682-0 : LC Card 84-46002 DDC 305.5/6 19
HD8039.D52 G7755 1986
NYPL [JLE 86-4591]

The Domestic U. S. oil industry and low oil prices : policy alternatives : an analysis prepared for the New York Mercantile Exchange. [Cambridge, Mass.] : Cambridge Energy Research Associates, c1987. v, 61 leaves : ill. ; 29 cm. "March 31, 1987." LC Card 87-402219 DDC 338.2/7282/0973 19
1. Petroleum industry and trade - United States. 2. Petroleum products - Prices - United States. I. New York Mercantile Exchange (U. S.). II. Cambridge Energy Research Associates. III. Title: Domestic US oil industry and low oil prices.
HD9574.U62 D66 1987

Domestic US oil industry and low oil prices. The Domestic U. S. oil industry and low oil prices . [Cambridge, Mass.] , c1987. v, 61 leaves : LC Card 87-402219 DDC 338.2/7282/0973 19
HD9574.U62 D66 1987

DOMESTICS - ARGENTINA.
Szretter, Héctor. La terciarización del empleo en la Argentina. Buenos Aires , 1985. iv, 82, 3 p. ; LC Card 87-122558 DDC 331.7/6164046/0982 19
HD8039.D52 A657 1985

DOMESTICS - ENGLAND - ROCHDALE (GREATER MANCHESTER) - HISTORY - 19TH CENTURY.
Higgs, Edward, 1952- Domestic servants and households in Rochdale, 1851-1871 /. New York , 1986. 423 p. ; ISBN 0-8240-6682-0 : LC Card 84-46002 DDC 305.5/6 19
HD8039.D52 G7755 1986
NYPL [JLE 86-4591]

DOMESTICS - ENGLAND - ROCHDALE (GREATER MANCHESTER) - SOCIAL CONDITIONS.
Higgs, Edward, 1952- Domestic servants and households in Rochdale, 1851-1871 /. New York , 1986. 423 p. ; ISBN 0-8240-6682-0 : LC Card 84-46002 DDC 305.5/6 19
HD8039.D52 G7755 1986
NYPL [JLE 86-4591]

Dominação e desigualdade . Singer, Paul Israel, 1932- Rio de Janeiro, RJ , 1981. 185 p. ; LC Card 82-148154
HC190.I5 S55 1981 ***NYPL [JLD 86-3364]***

DOMINANCE (PSYCHOLOGY)
Sayers, Janet. Sexual contradictions . London , New York, NY , 1986. x, 214 p. : ISBN 0-422-78780-9 LC Card 85-27948 DDC 155.3/3 19
BF692.2 .S29 1986 ***NYPL [JFD 86-5840]***

Dominant firm price leadership . Hwang, Hae-Shin. Toronto, Ont. [1986] 40 p. : ISBN 0-7729-2122-9 : LC Card 87-161006 DDC 338.2/3 19
HD9539.N5 H93 1986

Domínguez, Jaime de Jesús, 1947- Feudalismo, capitalismo mercantil y capitalismo industrial / Jaime de Jesús Domínguez. Santo Domingo, República Dominicana : Editora de la UASD, 1981. 229 p. ; 21 cm. (Publicaciones de la Universidad Autónoma de Santo Domingo . vol. 294. no. 43) Bibliography: p. 223-229. ISBN 84-89527-00-8 LC Card 82-200900
1. Economic history. 2. Feudalism - History. 3. Capitalism - History. I. Series: Publicaciones de la Universidad Autónoma de Santo Domingo , v. 294. II. Title.
HC21 .D66 1981

Domínguez, Javier. Organizaciones obreras cristianas en la oposición al franquismo (1951-1975) : con 65 documentos clandestinos e inéditos / Javier Domínguez. Bilbao : Mensajero, [1985?] 479 p. ; 23 cm. (Colección realizarse. Biblioteca Educación y acción social) ISBN 84-271-1431-1 LC Card 87-153234
1. Trade-unions, Catholic - Spain - Political activity - History. 2. Spain - History - 1939-1975. 3. Franco, Francisco, 1892-1975. I. Title. II. Series.
HD6481.2.S7 D65 1985

Domínguez Machuca, J. A. (José Antonio) Modelización de sistemas financieros mediante dinámica de sistemas : el caso español / José A. Domínguez Machuca. [Sevilla] : Secretariado de Publicaciones de la Universidad de Sevilla, 1983. 269 p. : ill. ; 24 cm. (Anales de la Universidad Hispalense. Serie Ciencias económicas y empresariales . núm. 19) Bibliography: p. 223-228. ISBN 84-500-3164-8 LC Card 85-138246
1. Finance - Spain - Econometric models. 2. System analysis. I. Series: Anales de la Universidad Hispalense. Serie Ciencias económicas y empresariales , no. 19. II. Title.
HG186.S6 D65 1983

Domínguez Torrejón, Ramón. Wester León, Humberto. Diagnóstico situacional del movimiento cooperativo peruano /. [Lima] , 1981- v. : ***NYPL [JLL 86-146]***

Dominiak, Geraldine F. Managerial accounting / Geraldine F. Dominiak, Joseph G. Louderback III. 5th ed. Boston : PWS-KENT Pub. Co., c1988. xxiv, 808 p. : col. ill. ; 25 cm. (The Kent series in accounting) Includes index. ISBN 0-534-07740-4 : LC Card 87-21472 DDC 658.1/5 19
1. Managerial accounting. I. Louderback, Joseph G. II. Title. III. Series.
HF5657.4 .D66 1988

DOMINICA - ECONOMIC CONDITIONS.
Trouillot, Michel-Rolph. Peasants and capital . Baltimore , c1988. xiv, 344 p. : ISBN 0-8018-3481-3 (alk. paper) LC Card 87-20018 DDC 305.5/63 19
HD1531.D58 T76 1988

DOMINICA - ECONOMIC CONDITIONS - STATISTICS.
Dominique, juin 1985 . [Paris] , c1985. 102 p. : LC Card 86-209026
HC156.5.Z7 D6626 1985

DOMINICA - POPULATION - STATISTICS.
Dominique, juin 1985 . [Paris] , c1985. 102 p. : LC Card 86-209026
HC156.5.Z7 D6626 1985

DOMINICA - STATISTICS, VITAL.
Ebanks, G. E. Mortality, fertility, and family planning . Santiago, Chile [1985] 123 p. ; LC Card 87-131697 DDC 304.6/2/09729841 19
HB1376.D65 E32 1985

DOMINICAN REPUBLIC - CENSUS, 1981.
Censo nacional de población y vivienda, 1981 . Santo Domingo, Distrito Nacional, República Dominicana , 1985- v. <1 > : LC Card 86-223758
HA886.5 1981c

Dominican Republic. Comisión Nacional de Política Energética. Gómez, Carmen. Población y energía en la República Dominicana, 1990-2000. Santo Domingo, República Dominicana [1985] vi, 86 p. : LC Card 86-176044
HD9502.D652 G65 1985

DOMINICAN REPUBLIC - COMMERCIAL POLICY.
Najri, José Antonio, 1948- Crisis, producción y desarrollo . Santo Domingo, Repúblic Dominicana , 1986 (Santo Domingo, República Dominicana : Editora Corripio) ix, 248 p. ; LC Card 87-102092
HF1502 .N34 1986

DOMINICAN REPUBLIC - ECONOMIC CONDITIONS.
Bosch, Juan, 1909- Capitalismo tardío en la República Dominicana /. Santo Domingo, República Dominicana , 1986. 238 p. : LC Card 87-401709 DDC 330.97293/054 19
HC153.5 .B665 1986

DOMINICAN REPUBLIC - ECONOMIC CONDITIONS - 1961-
Castro, Aníbal de. R.D., frente a su propia realidad . [Santo Domingo, Dominican Republic? , 1986] 450, [2] p. ; LC Card 87-115306 DDC 330.97293/054 19
HC153.5 .C383 1986

Collado, Faustino, 1954- Crisis y situación política en República Dominicana /. Santo Domingo, República Dominicana [1985] 69 p. ; LC Card 87-115929
HC153.5 .C65 1985

Hacia una reestructuración dirigida de la economía dominicana /. Santo Domingo, República Dominicana , c1986. 355 p. : LC Card 87-402158 DDC 338.97293 19
HC153.5 .H33 1986

Sang Ben, Miguel. Economía, política y sociedad . Santo Domingo, R.D. , 1986. 109 p. ; ISBN 84-89529-00-0 LC Card 87-100772
HC153.5 .S27 1986

DOMINICAN REPUBLIC - ECONOMIC CONDITIONS - 1961- - ADDRESSES, ESSAYS, LECTURES.
Salvador Ortíz, S., 1917-1983. Comentarios económicos /. Santo Domingo, República Dominicana , 1984- v. ; LC Card 85-118318 DDC 330.9 19
HC125 .S2615 1984 ***NYPL [JLK 85-83]***

DOMINICAN REPUBLIC - ECONOMIC CONDITIONS - 1961- - CONGRESSES.
Causas y manejo de la crisis económica dominicana, 1974-1984 /. Santo Domingo, República Dominicana , 1986. 184 p. : LC Card 86-208551
HC153.5 .C385 1986

Influencia del sector privado sobre la realidad nacional. [Santo Domingo] [1986] 180 p., [1] leaf of plates : LC Card 86-190331
HC153.5 .I53 1986

DOMINICAN REPUBLIC - ECONOMIC POLICY.
Análisis de la economía dominicana /. Santo Domingo, República Dominicana , 1985. 73 p. ; LC Card 86-186259
HG3926.5 .A53 1985

Hacia una reestructuración dirigida de la economía dominicana /. Santo Domingo, República Dominicana , c1986. 355 p. : LC Card 87-402158 DDC 338.97293 19
HC153.5 .H33 1986

Sang Ben, Miguel. Economía, política y sociedad . Santo Domingo, R.D. , 1986. 109 p. ; ISBN 84-89529-00-0 LC Card 87-100772
HC153.5 .S27 1986

DOMINICAN REPUBLIC - ECONOMIC POLICY - CONGRESSES.

Causas y manejo de la crisis económica dominicana, 1974-1984 /. Santo Domingo, República Dominicana , 1986. 184 p. : LC Card 86-208551
HC153.5 .C385 1986

La Situación cambiaria en la República Dominicana /. Santo Domingo, República Dominicana , 1984. 252 p. : LC Card 87-401265 DDC 338.97293 19
HC153.5 .S575 1984

Dominican Republic - Government. see **Dominican Republic - Politics and government.**

DOMINICAN REPUBLIC - INDUSTRIES.
Informe final "estudio de oferta exportable" /. Santo Domingo, República Dominicana [1985] 101, [57] p. ; LC Card 85-203743
HC153.5 .I54 1985

Najri, José Antonio, 1948- Crisis, producción y desarrollo . Santo Domingo, Repúblic Dominicana , 1986 (Santo Domingo, República Dominicana : Editora Corripio) ix, 248 p. ; LC Card 87-102092
HF1502 .N34 1986

DOMINICAN REPUBLIC - POLITICS AND GOVERNMENT - 1961-
Castro, Aníbal de. R.D., frente a su propia realidad . [Santo Domingo, Dominican Republic? , 1986] 450, [2] p. ; LC Card 87-115306 DDC 330.97293/054 19
HC153.5 .C383 1986

Collado, Faustino, 1954- Crisis y situación política en República Dominicana /. Santo Domingo, República Dominicana [1985] 69 p. ; LC Card 87-115929
HC153.5 .C65 1985

DOMINICAN REPUBLIC - POPULATION - STATISTICS.
Censo nacional de población y vivienda, 1981 . Santo Domingo, Distrito Nacional, República Dominicana , 1985- v. <1 > : LC Card 86-223758
HA886.5 1981c

DOMINICAN REPUBLIC - SOCIAL CONDITIONS.
Madruga, José Manuel. Azúcar y haitianos en la República Dominicana /. Santo Domingo , 1986. 202 p. : LC Card 87-125442 DDC 331.6/2/729407293 19
HD9114.D62 M33 1986

Dominican Republic. Subsecretaría Técnica de Planificación Sectorial Agropecuaria. Departamento Planes, Programas y Proyectos. Producción versus consumo de alimentos . [Santo Domingo, Dominican Republic] , 1981. 74 p. ; LC Card 82-207744
HD9014.D62 P76 1981

Dominion Association of Chartered Accountants. see **Canadian Institute of Chartered Accountants.**

Dominique, juin 1985 : situation économique, financière et sociale / République française, Ministère des relations extérieures, coopération et développement, Direction des politiques du développement [et] Caisse centrale de coopération économique. [Paris] : Le Ministère : L'Harmattan, distributor, c1985. 102 p. : ill. ; 30 cm. Cover title. Title on half t.p.: Ile de la Dominique. Distributor from label on half t.p. Bibliography: p. 102. LC Card 86-209026
1. Dominica - Economic conditions - Statistics. 2. Dominica - Population - Statistics. I. France. Ministère des relations extérieures, coopération et développement. Direction des politiques du développement. II. Caisse centrale de coopération économique (France). III. Title: Situation économique, financière et sociale. IV. Title: Ile de la Dominique.
HC156.5.Z7 D6626 1985

Domitra, Michael. Mexiko : Wirtschaftskrise und politische Stabilität / Michael Domitra. Bonn : Forschungsinstitut der Friedrich-Ebert-Stiftung, [1984] 24 p. ; 21 cm. (Internationale Politik, 0174-5204 . 27) LC Card 85-134274 DDC 330.972/0834 19
1. Mexico - Economic conditions - 1970-. 2. Mexico - Politics and government - 1970-. I. Series: Internationale Politik (Bonn, Germany) , 27. II. Title.
HC135 .D65 1984

Don Miguel, queremos hechos. Flores Domínguez, David. Queremos hechos /. México, D.F. , c1982. 154 p. ; ISBN 968-7163-01-1 LC Card 83-142817
HC135 .F54 1982

Don Nelson's Mining & mining equipment/service companies world wide : an annual directory, 1982-83. Barnet, Herts., U.K. : Don Nelson Publications, ltd., [1982] 562 p. ; 21 cm. Only one issue published. Spine title: Mining and mining equipment/service companies worldwide, 1982-83. Includes advertising. Includes indexes. ISBN 946-0-04005-X
1. Mining machinery industry - Directories. 2. Mineral industries - Directories. I. Nelson, Don. II. Title: Mining & mining equipment/service companies worldwide. III. Title: Mining and mining equipment/service companies worldwide, 1982-83.
NYPL [JSD 86-337]

Don Vicente Martinez Ybor, the man and his empire . Westfall, L. Glenn, 1943- New York , 1987. vii, 214 p. : ISBN 0-8240-1374-3 (alk. paper) : LC Card 87-8690 DDC 338.7/67972/0924 19
HD9149.C5 U777 1987

Donadío, Alberto, 1953- Por qué cayó Jaime Michelsen? / Alberto Donadío. 1a ed. Bogotá : El Ancora Editores, c1984. 142 p. : ill. ; 20 cm. (Colección Periodismo de hoy) Includes bibliographical references and index. ISBN 84-89209-42-1 LC Card 85-122262
1. Michelsen Uribe, Jaime. 2. Banco de Colombia. 3. Grupo Grancolombiano. 4. Banks and banking - Colombia - Corrupt practices - Case studies. I. Title. II. Series.
HG2908.C65 D66 1984

Donald Hagman Memorial Conference (2nd) The Urban caldron /. Boston, Mass. , 1986. 152 p. ; ISBN 0-89946-207-3 LC Card 85-21641 DDC 333.73/0973 19
HD257 .U73 1986 ***NYPL [JLE 86-4372]***

Donaldson, Lufkin & Jenrette, inc. Leibowitz, Dennis. The cellular communications industry /. New York, N.Y. (140 Broadway, New York 10005) , c1985. ii, 67 p. : LC Card 86-201572 DDC 384.5/33/0973 19
HD9696.R363 U65 1985

Donaldson, T. H. (Thomas Hay), 1936- International lending by commercial banks.
Donaldson, T. H. (Thomas Hay), 1936- Lending in international commercial banking / T.H. Donaldson ; foreword by Steven I. Davis. 2nd ed. New York , c1987. p. cm. ISBN 0-471-63597-9 LC Card 87-19841 DDC 332.1/5 19
HG3891.5 .D65 1987

Lending in international commercial banking / T.H. Donaldson ; foreword by Steven I. Davis. 2nd ed. New York : Wiley, c1987. p. cm. Rev. ed. of: International lending by commercial banks. 1979. "A Wiley-Interscience publication." Bibliography: p. Includes index. ISBN 0-471-63597-9 LC Card 87-19841 DDC 332.1/5 19
1. Loans, Foreign. 2. Bank loans. I. Donaldson, T. H. (Thomas Hay), 1936- International lending by commercial banks. II. Title.
HG3891.5 .D65 1987

Donders, Joseph G. Bread broken . Eldoret, Kenya [1984] vi, 56 p. : LC Card 85-980419 DDC 363.8/0967 19
HC800.Z9 F32 1984

Donev, Kaliu. Kotsev, Tsvetan. Formirane i izpolzvane na parichnite fondove v stopanskite organizatsii /. Varna , 1985. 117 p. ; LC Card 85-213610
HC403.Z9 C347 1985

Donius, James F. Marketplace measurement : tracking and testing advertising and other marketing effects / James F. Donius. New York, NY (155 E. 44th St., New York 11710) : Association of National Advertisers, c1986. xiii, 206 p. : ill. ; 26 cm. Spine title: Tracking and testing advertising and other marketing effects. Bibliography: p. 204-206. LC Card 87-120244 DDC 659.1/11 19
1. Advertising campaigns - Evaluation. 2. Market surveys - Evaluation. I. Association of National Advertisers. II. Title. III. Title: Tracking and testing advertising and other marketing effects.
HF5823 .D655 1986

Donn, Clifford B. Collective bargaining in American industry . Lexington, Mass. , c1987. ix, 351 p. ; ISBN 0-669-12594-6 (alk. paper) LC Card 85-45936 DDC 331.89/0973 19
HD6508 .C656 1987

Donnahoe, Alan S. Basic business statistics for managers / Alan S. Donnahoe. New York : Wiley, c1988. vii, 228 p. : ill. ; 23 cm. Includes index. ISBN 0-471-62940-5 (pbk.) : LC Card 87-24273 DDC 519.5/024658 19
1. Commercial statistics. 2. Statistics. I. Title.
HF1017 .D64 1988

Données sur l'industrie régionale. Robert, Jacqueline. 1977 à 1982 . [Lyon] [1985] 143 p. ; LC Card 86-187676
HC277.R58 R62 1985

Donnelly, James H.
Fundamentals of management / James H. Donnelly, Jr., James L. Gibson, John M. Ivancevich. 6th ed. Plano, Tex. : Business Publications, 1987. xxviii, 827 p. : ill. (some col.) ; 25 cm. Includes bibliographies and indexes. ISBN 0-256-03682-9 LC Card 86-71879 DDC 658 19
1. Management. I. Gibson, James L. II. Ivancevich, John M. III. Title. IV. Title: Management.
HD31 .D594 1987

Peter, J. Paul. A preface to marketing management /. Plano, Tex. , 1988. xii, 320 p. : ISBN 0-256-06078-9 (pbk.) LC Card 87-71348 DDC 658.8 19
HF5415.13 .P388 1988

Donnelly, William A. The econometrics of energy demand : a survey of applications / William A. Donnelly. New York : Praeger, 1987. xv, 309 p. : ill. ; 25 cm. Bibliography: p. 247-290. ISBN 0-275-92610-9 (alk. paper) : LC Card 86-25220 DDC 333.79/12 19
1. Energy consumption - Econometric models. I. Title.
HD9502.A2 D67 1987

Donner, Wolf. Thailand ohne Tempel : Lebensfragen eines Tropenlandes / Wolf Donner. Frankfurt [am Main] : R.G. Fischer, c1984. 202 p. : ill. ; 21 cm. "Quellenverzeichnis": p. 190-202. ISBN 3-88323-499-0 LC Card 85-157332
1. Thailand - Economic conditions. 2. Thailand - Economic policy. 3. Thailand - Social conditions. I. Title.
HC445 .D67 1984

Donolo, Carlo. Carrieri, Mimmo. Il mestiere politico del sindacato /. Roma , 1986. 218 p. ; ISBN 88-359-2930-X : LC Card 86-200898
HD8485 .C37 1986

Os donos do Brasil . Banas, Geraldo. São Paulo , 1984. 330 p. ; LC Card 87-673258
HD2834 .B34 1984

Donoso, Vicente.
Alonso, José Antonio. Efectos de la adhesión de España a la CEE sobre las exportaciones de Iberoamérica /. Madrid , 1983. 316 p. : ISBN 84-7232-299-8 LC Card 87-116624
HF3688.L3 A45 1983

Alonso, José Antonio. La empresa exportadora española frente a Iberoamérica y la CEE /. Madrid , 1985. xiii, 263 p. ; ISBN 84-7232-380-3 LC Card 86-199177
HF3688.L3 A46 1985 ***NYPL [JLE 87-56]***

Donovan, Graeme. Binswanger, Hans P. Agricultural mechanization . Washington, D.C., U. S.A. , c1987. vi, 85 p. : ISBN 0-8213-0903-X (pbk.) LC Card 87-14082 DDC 338.1/61/091724 19
HD1459 .B57 1987

Donovan, Robert J. The second victory : the Marshall Plan and the postwar revival of Europe / Robert J. Donovan ; foreword by Clark M. Clifford. New York : Madison Books, c1987. 128 p. : ill., maps ; 29 cm. Bibliography: p. 126. Includes index. ISBN 0-8191-6498-4 (alk. paper) : LC Card 87-24021 DDC 338.91/73/04 19
1. Marshall Plan. 2. Economic assistance, American - Europe. 3. Europe - Economic conditions - 1945-. I. Title.
HC240 .D65 1987

Don't sell stocks on Monday /. Hirsch, Yale. New York, N.Y., U. S.A. , 1987, c1986. viii, 232 p. : ISBN 0-14-010375-9 (pbk.) LC Card 87-8717 DDC 332.63/22 19
HG4661 .H57 1987

Donzelli, Franco. Il concetto di equilibrio nella teoria economica neoclassica / Franco Donzelli. 1a ed. Roma : Nuova Italia scientifica, 1986.

518 p. ; 23 cm. (Studi NIS economia . 10) Bibliography: p. [471]-489. Includes indexes. LC Card 86-192826
1. Equilibrium (Economics). 2. Neoclassical school of economics. I. Title. II. Series.
HB145 .D65 1986

Dooley, Stephen R. Woodman, Byron E. Personal financial planning /. Andover, Mass. , c1987. 151 p. ; ISBN 0-931790-77-8 : LC Card 87-13229 DDC 332.024 19
HG179 .W578 1987

Doolittle, Fred C. Nathan, Richard P. Reagan and the States /. Princeton, N.J. , c1987. xv, 375 p. : ISBN 0-691-07748-7 (alk. paper) : LC Card 87-45529 DDC 353.0072/5 19
HJ2051 .N167 1987

Doomsday or deterrence? . Fehér, Ferenc, 1933- Armonk, N.Y. , c1986. 154 p. ; ISBN 0-87332-368-8 : LC Card 86-10074 DDC 327.1/74 19
JX1974.7 .F38 1986 ***NYPL [JLE 86-4319]***

Dooner, Patricio. La Opción preferencial por los pobres . [Santiago] [1987] 360 p. : LC Card 87-403060 DDC 362.5/098 19
HC130.P6 O63 1987

DOOR-TO-DOOR SELLING. see **CANVASSING.**

Doorewaard, H. (Hans) Autonomie als arbeidssociologisch vraagstuk . Zeist , 1987. 237 p. : ISBN 90-6720-032-8 : LC Card 87-169950
HD5660.N4 A94 1987

Doornbos, Paul. Some aspects of smuggling between Chad and Sudan [microform] / by Paul Doornbos. Khartoum : Development Studies and Research Centre, Faculty of Economic and Social Studies, University of Khartoum, [1983] 19 leaves, [1] leaf of plates : map ; 33 cm. (DSRC seminar series. Discussion paper . no. 33 33) "7 September 1983." Includes bibliographical references. Microfilm. New York : New York Public Library, 1986. 1 microfilm reel ; 35 mm. (MN *ZZ-25,866) LC Card 84-980097 DDC 364.1/33 19
1. Smuggling - Sudan. 2. Smuggling - Chad. 3. Darfur - Commerce. I. Title. II. Series.
HF3887.Z8 D373 1983
NYPL [*ZT-1646 no.52]

Dopravní podniky hl. m. Prahy. 110 let městské hromadné dopravy v Praze /. [Prague] [1985] 52 p. : LC Card 86-201750
HE4759.3.Z8 P732 1985

Dorcey, Anthony H. J., 1944- Bargaining in the governance of Pacific coastal resources : research and reform / Anthony H.J. Dorcey. Vancouver, B.C. : Westwater Research Centre, Faculty of Graduate Studies, University of British Columbia, c1986. xvi, 219 p. : ill. ; 23 cm. Bibliography: p. [177]-191. ISBN 0-920146-34-1 (pbk.) LC Card 86-222720 DDC 333.91/7/09711 19
1. Natural resources - British Columbia - Management. 2. Natural resources - Research - British Columbia. 3. Coastal zone management - British Columbia. 4. Negotiation. I. Title.
HC117.B8 D67 1986

Dordick, Herbert S., 1925- Innovative management using telecommunications : a guide to opportunities, strategies, and applications / Herbert S. Dordick, Frederick Williams. New York : Wiley, c1986. x, 226 p. : ill. ; 25 cm. Includes index. Bibliography: p. 197-198. ISBN 0-471-81296-X : LC Card 86-7797 DDC 658.4/5 19
1. Industrial management - Communication systems. 2. Telephone in business. 3. Office practice - Automation. I. Williams, Frederick, 1933-. II. Title.
HF5541.T4 D67 1986 ***NYPL [JLE 86-4425]***

Dördüncü Beş Yıllık Kalkınma Planı, 1979-1983. Devlet Planlama Teşkilatı (Turkey) Ankara [1979] xiv, 692 p. ; LC Card 83-228455
HC401 .A356 no. 1664 HC492

Dore, Elizabeth. Acumulación y crisis en la minería peruana, 1900-1977 / Elizabeth Dore. [Lima] : Universidad Nacional Mayor de San Marcos : Instituto Cultural José María Arguedas, [1986] 168 p. : ill. ; 21 cm. Translation of the author's thesis (Ph. D.)--Columbia University, 1981, presented under title: Accumulation and crisis in the Peruvian mining industry, 1900-1977. Bibliography: p. 159-168. LC Card 86-235232
1. Mineral industries - Peru - History - 20th century. 2. Peru - Dependency on foreign countries - History - 20th century. I. Title.
HD9506.P42 D66 1986

Dore, Ian, 1941- Fresh seafood, the commercial buyer's guide : buying, choosing, handling, and using fresh fish and shellfish / Ian Dore. Huntington, N.Y. : Osprey Books, c1984. 375 p. : ill. ; 23 cm. (Osprey seafood handbooks) Includes indexes. Bibliography: p. 359-364. ISBN 0-943738-07-5 : LC Card 84-5174 DDC 641.3/92/0687 19
1. Sea food - Purchasing. 2. Fish trade. 3. Sea food. 4. Cookery (Sea food). I. Title.
HD9450.5 .D67 1984 ***NYPL [JSD 86-449]***

Dore, Ronald Philip. Flexible rigidities : industrial policy and structural adjustment in the Japanese economy, 1970-80 / Ronald Dore. London : Athlone Press, 1986. 278 p. ; 23 cm. Bibliography: p. [266]-271. Includes index. ISBN 0-485-11269-8 LC Card 87-672689
1. Japan - Economic policy - 1945-. 2. Japan - Industries - 1945-. 3. Industry and state - Japan. I. Title.
HC462.9 .D65 1986

Das Dorf Singen und seine Finanzwirtschaft . Gebhard, Alfred. Singen , 1985. 484 p. : ISBN 3-921413-23-0 LC Card 87-133391 DDC 336.43/46 19
HJ9494.S57 G4 1985

Dorfman, Mark S., 1945- Introduction to insurance / Mark S. Dorfman. 3rd ed. Englewood Cliffs, NJ : Prentice-Hall, c1987. xix, 501 p. : ill. ; 25 cm. (The Prentice-Hall series in security and insurance) Includes index. ISBN 0-13-484809-8 LC Card 86-30319 DDC 368 19
1. Insurance. I. Title. II. Series.
HG8051 .D65 1987

Dorfman, Robert. Linear programming and economic analysis / Robert Dorfman, Paul A. Samuelson, Robert M. Solow. New York : Dover Publications, 1987, c1986. p. cm. Reprint. Originally published: New York : McGraw Hill, 1958. Bibliography: p. Includes index. ISBN 0-486-65491-5 (pbk.) LC Card 87-24382 DDC 330/.0724 19
1. Economics - Mathematical models. 2. Linear programming. I. Samuelson, Paul Anthony 1915-. II. Solow, Robert M. III. Title.
HB135 .D67 1987

Doria, Manlio Rossi- see **Rossi-Doria, Manlio, 1905-**

Doria Medina, Samuel, 1958- Morales, Juan Antonio. Coyuntura económica /. La Paz , 1987. 99 p. : LC Card 87-403036 DDC 330.984/052 19
HC182 .M66 1987

Dorman, Hattie L. United States. Small Business Administration. Office of Procurement and Technical Assistance. Report to the Administrator on the analysis of the management and administration of the Procurement and Technical Assistance programs /. [Washington, D.C.] , 1984. 1 v. (various pagings) : ***NYPL [JLF 86-1066]***

Dorn, James A. The Search for stable money . Chicago , 1987. xvii, 408 p. ; ISBN 0-226-15829-2 LC Card 86-25654 DDC 332.4/973 19
HG540 .S38 1987

Dornbusch, Hans-Ludwig.
Entwicklung wesentlicher Daten der öffentlichen Finanzwirtschaft in der Bundesrepublik Deutschland von 1973-1983 / [Bearbeiter, Hans-Ludwig Dornbusch]. Bonn : Institut "Finanzen und Steuern", 1984. 32 leaves ; 30 cm. (Brief / Institut "Finanzen und Steuern" . Nr. 236) Cover title. LC Card 86-186300
1. Finance, Public - Germany (West) - Statistics. I. Institut "Finanzen und Steuern" (Germany). II. Series: Brief (Institut "Finanzen und Steuern" (Germany)) , Nr. 236. III. Title.
HJ1120 .B65 Nr. 236

Entwicklung wesentlicher Daten der öffentlichen Finanzwirtschaft in der Bundesrepublik Deutschland von 1974-1984 /. Bonn , 1985. 31 leaves ; LC Card 86-186363
HJ1120 .B65 Nr. 247

Entwicklung wesentlicher Daten der öffentlichen Finanzwirtschaft in der Bundesrepublik Deutschland von 1975-1985 / [Bearbeiter, Hans-Ludwig Dornbusch]. Bonn : Institut "Finanzen und Steuern", [1986] 31 leaves ; 30 cm. (Brief / Institut "Finanzen und Steuern" . Nr. 260) Cover title. "Sept. 1986." Includes bibliographical references. LC Card 87-408897 DDC 332 s 336.43 19
1. Finance, Public - Germany (West) - Statistical methods. 2. Germany (West) - Appropriations and expenditures - Statistical methods. I. Series: Brief (Institut "Finanzen und Steuern" (Germany)) , Nr. 260. II. Title.
HJ1120 .B65 Nr. 260

Dornbusch, Rudiger.
Fischer, Stanley. Economics /. New York , c1988. xliii, 813 p. : ISBN 0-07-017781-3 : LC Card 87-21333 DDC 330 19
HB171.5 .F458 1988

Macro-economics / Rudiger Dornbusch, Stanley Fischer. 4th ed. New York : McGraw-Hill, c1987. xiv, 798 p. : ill. ; 24 cm. Includes bibliographical references and index. ISBN 0-07-017776-7 : LC Card 86-21114 DDC 339 19
1. Macroeconomics. I. Fischer, Stanley. II. Title.
HB172.5 .D67 1987

Macroeconomics. 4th ed. Readings and cases in macroeconomics / [edited by] Ben Bernanke. New York , c1987. x, 485 p. : ISBN 0-07-017779-1 (pbk.) : LC Card 86-27423 DDC 339 19
HB172.5 .D67 1987 Suppl.

The Political economy of Argentina, 1946-83 /. Pittsburgh, Pa. , 1988. p. cm. ISBN 0-8229-1148-5 LC Card 87-24412 DDC 338.982 19
HC175 .P623 1988

Dorneich, Philipp Herder- see **Herder-Dorneich, Philipp, 1928-**

Dorner, Peter. Was ist bei der Teilzeitbeschäftigung zu beachten? /. Wien , 1985. 64 p. ; LC Card 86-210129
HD5110.2.A9 W37 1985

Dorosh, Ivan Ĭosypovych. Material′no-tekhnichna baza ahropromyslovoho kompleksu . Kyïv , 1985. 294 p. ; LC Card 87-109155
HD9015.S653 U453 1985

Dorosz, Andrzej. Białecki, Klemens. Słownik handlu zagranicznego /. Warszawa , 1986. 359 p. ; ISBN 83-208-0112-5 : LC Card 86-221378
HF1001 .B47 1986

Dorow, Wolfgang. Die Unternehmung in der demokratischen Gesellschaft =. Berlin , New York , 1987. xiii, 390 p. : ISBN 0-89925-295-8 (U. S.) : LC Card 86-32864 DDC 658.3/152 19
HD5650 .U67 1987

Dorrell, Jean, 1926- The answer book : a reference manual for office personnel / Jean Dorrell.1st ed. Los Angeles, CA : Roxbury Pub. Co., c1987. ix, 358 p. : ill. ; 23 cm. Includes bibliographical references and index. ISBN 0-935732-12-8 (pbk.) : LC Card 87-23408 DDC 651 19
1. Office practice - Handbooks, manuals, etc. 2. Business communication - Handbooks, manuals, etc. 3. English language - Business English - Handbooks, manuals, etc. I. Title.
HF5547.5 .D63 1987

Dortmund. Bundesanstalt für Arbeitschutz und Unfallforschung. see **Bundesanstalt für Arbeitsschutz und Unfallforschung.**

DORTMUND (GERMANY) - SOCIAL CONDITIONS - EXHIBITIONS.
Leben mit Gneisenau, hundert Jahre-- . Dortmund , Essen [1986?] 317 p. : ISBN 3-88474-323-6 LC Card 87-408388 DDC 331.7/622334/094355 19
HD8039.M62 G335 1986

DORTMUND METROPOLITAN AREA (GERMANY) - ECONOMIC CONDITIONS.
Clemens, Reinhard. Standortprobleme von Industrieunternehmen in Ballungsräumen . Göttingen , c1983. xviii, 257 p. : ISBN 3-509-01330-1 LC Card 83-198706
HC289.D6 C54 1983

DORTMUND METROPOLITAN AREA (GERMANY) - ECONOMIC POLICY.
Clemens, Reinhard. Standortprobleme von Industrieunternehmen in Ballungsräumen . Göttingen , c1983. xviii, 257 p. : ISBN

3-509-01330-1 LC Card 83-198706
HC289.D6 C54 1983

DORTMUND METROPOLITAN AREA (GERMANY) - INDUSTRIES.
Clemens, Reinhard. Standortprobleme von Industrieunternehmen in Ballungsräumen . Göttingen , c1983. xviii, 257 p. : ISBN 3-509-01330-1 LC Card 83-198706
HC289.D6 C54 1983

Dortmund. Sozialforschungsstelle. see **Sozialforschungsstelle Dortmund.**

DORTMUNDER STADTWERKE AG.
Meifort, J. (Joachim) Arbeitsbedingungen von Linienbus- und Strassenbahnfahrern der Dortmunder Stadtwerke Aktiengesellschaft /. Dortmund , 1983. 137 p. : ISBN 3-88314-249-2 LC Card 83-204902
HD8039.T72 G36 1983

Dos documentos de 1627 sobre la economía de España /. Ebersole, Alva Vernon. Valencia [1986?] 49 p. ; ISBN 84-7274-144-3 LC Card 87-107711
HG1133 .E24 1986

Dossier professionnel.
Les Professions de l'informatique . Paris [1986-1987] 2 v. : ISBN 2-11-001675-2 (v. 1) : LC Card 87-156366
HF5548.2 .P7925 1986

Dossiers de l'économie réunionnaise .
(no 2) Abramovici, G. Comptes économiques de la Réunion, série 1975-1980 . Ste Clotilde, [Réunion] [1983?] 133 p. ; LC Card 86-980541
HC598 .A37 1983

Les dossiers noirs de l'industrie française /. Dacier, Pierre. [Paris] , c1985. 414 p. ; ISBN 2-213-01659-3 : LC Card 86-178468
HC276.2 .D2 1985

Dossiers (Québec (Province). Ministère des affaires culturelles) .
(56) Caron, Diane. Les postes de traite de fourrure sur la Côte-Nord et dans l'Outaouais /. [Québec] [1984] xvi, 150 p. : ISBN 2-551-06277-2 LC Card 84-220957
HD9944.C22 C34 1984

Dostal, Werner. Bildung und Beschäftigung im technischen Wandel : bildungsökonomische und arbeitsmarktpolitische Rahmenbedingungen des technischen Wandels am Beispiel der elektronischen Datenverarbeitung und der Mikroelektronik / Werner Dostal. Nürnberg : Institut für Arbeitsmarkt- und Berufsforschung der Bundesanstalt für Arbeit, 1982. viii, 380, 6 p. : ill. ; 21 cm. (Beiträge zur Arbeitsmarkt- und Berufsforschung, 0173-6574 . 65) Originally presented as the author's thesis (doctoral--Technische Universität Berlin, 1981) Bibliography: p. 320-376. LC Card 82-205035 DDC 306/.46 19
1. Automation - Social aspects. 2. Electronic data processing - Social aspects. I. Title. II. Series.
HD6331 .D53 1982 ***NYPL [JLD 86-3011]***

Doswell, R. T. Word processing [microform] : security guidelines / R T Doswell. [Manchester, Greater Manchester] : NCC Publications, 1983. 30 p. ; 30 cm. Microfilm. New York : New York Public Library, 1985. 1 microfilm reel ; 35 mm. (MN *ZZ-24,952) ISBN 0-85012-361-5
1. Computers - Access control. 2. Word processing (Office practice). I. Title.
NYPL [*ZT-1554 no.46]

Dottridge, M. B. Aspects of social and economic development in southern Kura District before the implementation of the Kano River Project irrigation scheme / by M.B. Dottridge. Zaria, Nigeria : Centre for Social and Economic Research, Ahmadu Bello University, 1980. v, 47 p., [1] p. of plates : ill. ; 31 cm. (C.S.E.R. research paper . no. 7) Cover title: Aspects of social & economic development in southern Kura District before the implementation of the Kano River Project irrigation scheme. "April 1980." Bibliography: p. 41-47. LC Card 84-256142
1. Kura District (Nigeria) - Economic conditions - Case studies. 2. Kura District (Nigeria) - Social conditions - Case studies. 3. Kura District (Nigeria) - Politics and government - Case studies. I. Title. II. Title: Aspects of social & economic development in southern Kura District before the implementation of the Kano River Project irrigation scheme. III. Series: C.S.E.R. research paper , 7.
HC1055.Z7 K873 1980

Dottrina e giurisprudenza di diritto del lavoro. Diritto sindacale.
Balducci, Cataldo. Il sindacato /. Torino , c1984. 2 v. ; ISBN 88-02-03818-X (set) : LC Card 85-158972 DDC 344.45/0188 344.504188 19
LAW ***NYPL [JLE 86-3250]***

Dou, Alberto. Cambio cultural e imagen del hombre /. Bilbao, España , c1984. 248 p. ; ISBN 84-271-1384-6 LC Card 85-234026
CB245 .C29 1984 ***NYPL [JFD 86-6394]***

Double-breasted operations and prehire agreements in construction. Northrup, Herbert Roof, 1918- Doublebreasted operations and pre-hire agreements in construction . Philadelphia, Penn., USA , c1987. viii, 127 p. : ISBN 0-89546-067-X (pbk.) LC Card 87-81475 DDC 331.88/92 19
HD9715.U52 N67 1984 Suppl.

Double dependency and constraints on class formation in Bugisu, Uganda /. Bunker, Stephen G., 1944- Urbana, Ill. , 1983. v, 88 p. : LC Card 86-229748 DDC 303.3/09676/1 19
HD1538.U43 B86 1983

DOUBLE EMPLOYMENT. see **SUPPLEMENTARY EMPLOYMENT.**

DOUBLE ENTRY BOOKKEEPING. see **BOOKKEEPING.**

DOUBLE TAXATION. see **TAXATION, DOUBLE.**

Double your sales commission using a personal computer /. Collins, Rip, 1947- Dubuque, Iowa , c1986. ix, 155 p. ; ISBN 0-697-00802-9 (pbk.) : LC Card 85-71486 DDC 658.8/1/00285536 19
HF5438.35 .C65 1986 ***NYPL [JLE 86-1773]***

Doublebreasted operations and pre-hire agreements in construction . Northrup, Herbert Roof, 1918- Philadelphia, Penn., USA , c1987. viii, 127 p. : ISBN 0-89546-067-X (pbk.) LC Card 87-81475 DDC 331.88/92 19
HD9715.U52 N67 1984 Suppl.

Doubling development finance . United Nations. Economic and Social Council. Committee for Development Planning. New York , 1986. v, 47 p. ; ISBN 92-1-104185-6 (pbk.) LC Card 87-103015 DDC 338.91/09172/4 19
HG3881 .U646 1986

Douët-d'Arcq, L. (Louis), 1808-1882. (ed)
Comptes de l'hôtel des rois de France aux XIVe et XVe siècles, pub. pour la Société de l'histoire de France, par M. L. Douët-d'Arcq. Paris, Mme Ve J. Renouard, 1865. 3 p.l., xlii p., 1 l., 437 p., 1 l. 25 cm. (Société de l'histoire de France. Publications in octavo. 130) LC Card 05-5875
1. France - History - House of Valois, 1328-1589. 2. France - Court and courtiers. 3. France - History - Sources. 4. Prices - France - History. I. Series: Publications in octavo (Société de l'histoire de France) , 130. II. Title.
HJ1077 .D6

Dougherty, Karla. Plumez, Jacqueline Hornor. Divorcing a corporation . New York, N.Y. , 1985. xxiii, 198 p. : ISBN 0-394-54457-9 : LC Card 85-40183 DDC 650.1/4 19
HF5384 .P58 1986 ***NYPL [JLE 86-2346]***

Douglas College. Fraser Port . Victoria, B.C. , 1986. 131 p., [16] p. of plates : ISBN 0-919203-17-5 (pbk.) LC Card 87-106756
HE554.V3 F73 1986

Douglas, George H., 1934- The early days of radio broadcasting / by George H. Douglas. Jefferson, N.C. : McFarland, c1987. viii, 248 p. : ill. ; 24 cm. Bibliography: p. 211-233. Includes index. ISBN 0-89950-285-7 (lib. bdg. : alk. paper) : LC Card 86-43090 DDC 384.54/0973 19
1. Radio broadcasting - United States - History. 2. Radio programs - United States - History. 3. Radio supplies industry - United States - History. I. Title.
HE8698 .D68 1987

Douglas, Gordon W. Energy and regional investment in Canada / Gordon W. Douglas and Ellen F. Battle. Calgary, Alta. : Canadian Energy Research Institute, [1983] x, 114 p. : ill. ; 21 cm. (Study . no. 17) Includes bibliographical references. ISBN 0-920522-28-9 (pbk.) : LC Card 83-160268 DDC 332.6/722 19
1. Energy industries - Canada. 2. Petroleum industry and trade - Canada. 3. Gas industry - Canada. 4. Investments - Canada. 5. Canada - Economic conditions - 1945- - Regional disparities. I. Battle, Ellen F. II. Series: Study / Canadian Energy Research Institute , no. 17. III. Title.
HD9502.C32 D68 1983 ***NYPL [JLD 87-996]***

Douglas, Neil J., 1959- A welfare assessment of transport deregulation : the case of the express coach market in 1980 / Neil J. Douglas. Aldershot, Hampshire, England ; Brookfield, Vt., USA : Gower, c1987. xxiv, 349 p. : ill. ; 23 cm. (Institute for Transport Studies . 2) Bibliography: p. 335-349. ISBN 0-566-05350-0 : LC Card 86-25703 DDC 388.3/22/0941 19
1. Bus lines - Government policy - Great Britain. I. Series: Institute for Transport Studies (Series) , 2. II. Title.
HE5663.A6 D68 1987

Douglas, Susan J. (Susan Jeanne), 1950-
Inventing American broadcasting, 1899-1922 / Susan J. Douglas. Baltimore : Johns Hopkins University Press, c1987. xxix, 363 p. : ill. ; 25 cm. (Johns Hopkins studies in the history of technology) Bibliography: p. 323-354. Includes index. ISBN 0-8018-3387-6 (alk. paper) LC Card 87-3717 DDC 384.54/0973 19
1. Radio broadcasting - United States - History. 2. Radio - United States - History. I. Title.
HE8698 .D685 1987

Douglas, Susan P. 1987 AMA educators' proceedings /. Chicago, Ill. , 1987. xiv, 287 p. ; ISBN 0-87757-182-1 LC Card 87-18680 DDC 658.8 19
HF5411 .A156 1987

The Douglass series on women's lives and the meaning of gender.
Glazer, Penina Migdal. Unequal colleagues . New Brunswick, N.J. , c1987. xii, 295 p. : ISBN 0-8135-1187-9 (pbk.) : LC Card 86-6568 DDC 331.4/81/000973 19
HD6054.2.U6 G55 1986
NYPL [JLD 87-581]

Wiesner, Merry, 1952- Working women in Renaissance Germany /. New Brunswick, N.J. , c1986. xiii, 263 p. : ISBN 0-8135-1138-0 : LC Card 85-14451 DDC 305.4/3/00943 19
HQ1149.G3 W54 1986
NYPL [JLE 86-3515]

Women, households, and the economy /. New Brunswick, N.J. , c1987. p. cm. ISBN 0-8135-1263-8 : LC Card 87-4840 DDC 331.4/0973 19
HD6060.65.U5 W65 1987

Doulman, David J., 1950-
The Development of the tuna industry in the Pacific islands region . [Honolulu, Hawaii] , c1987. xviii, 416 p. : ISBN 0-86638-096-5 (pbk.) LC Card 87-6818 DDC 338.3/72758 19
HD9469.T83 P163 1987

Options for U. S. fisheries investment in the Pacific Islands region / by David J. Doulman. Honolulu, Hawaii, U. S.A. : Pacific Islands Development Program, East-West Center, 1987. vi, 30 p. ; 23 cm. (Research report series . no. 8) Bibliography: p. 29-30. ISBN 0-86638-097-3 (pbk.) LC Card 87-9198 DDC 338.3/72758 19
1. Tuna industry - Islands of the Pacific. 2. Tuna industry - Islands of the Pacific - Finance. 3. Investments, American - Islands of the Pacific. I. Title. II. Title: Options for US fisheries investment in the Pacific Islands region. III. Series: Research report series (Pacific Islands Development Program (East-West Center)) , no. 8.
HD9469.T83 I743 1987

Doumergue, Émile, 1844-1937. La paix par la vérité [microform]. Paris, Éditions de Foi et vie, 1922-1924. 2 v. 19 cm. Vol. 2 has imprint: Paris, Stock, 1924. At head of title: E. Doumergue. Microfilm. New York: New York Public Library, 1986. 1 microfilm reel; 35 mm. (MN *ZZ-26037)
CONTENTS. - t. 1. Avant.--t. 2. Pendant et après. LC Card 26-3809
1. World War, 1914-1918 - Causes. 2. World War, 1914-1918. I. Title.
D511 .D67 ***NYPL [*Z-4048 no. 1]***

Doupnik, Timothy S. Evans, Thomas G. Foreign exchange risk management under statement 52 /. Stamford, Conn. , c1986. ix, 133 p. : ISBN 0-910065-21-7 (pbk.) LC Card 86-91435 DDC 657/.48 19
HG3853.7 .E935 1986

Douze années de Cotontchad, 1971-1983 . Société cotonnière du Tchad. Direction générale. N'Djaména [1984] 30 leaves ; LC Card

86-980210
HD9087.C474 S637 1984

Dovi-Sodemekou, Folly B. (Folly Bebey) Emploi et éducation dans le 2e plan de développement économique et social du Togo / Folly B. Dovi-Sodemekou. Les migrations des expulsés du Nigéria : aspects démo-économiques : cas du Sud-est Togo / K. Ekouevi. Lomé, Togo : Université du Bénin, Unité de recherche démographiques, [1985] 89, 52, 9, 2 p. : ill. ; 30 cm. (Etudes togolaises de population . no 10) Cover title. Originally presented as the authors' theses (maîtrise en économie)--Ecole supérieure des techniques économiques et de gestion, Lomé, 1984. Includes bibliographies. LC Card 87-131183
1. Labor supply - Togo. 2. Togo - Economic policy. 3. Togo - Social policy. 4. Migrant labor - Togo. 5. Immigrants - Togo. 6. Nigerians - Togo. I. Ekouevi, Koffi A. Migrations des expulsés du Nigéria. 1985. II. Title. III. Title: Migrations des explusés du Nigéria. IV. Series.
HD5846.5.A6 D68 1985

Dovring, Folke. Productivity and value : the political economy of measuring progress / Folke Dovring. New York : Praeger, 1987. vii, 194 p. ; 25 cm. Bibliography: p. 181-189. Includes index. ISBN 0-275-92668-0 (alk. paper) : LC Card 87-2347 DDC 338/.06 19
1. Industrial productivity. I. Title.
HC79.I52 D68 1987

Dow, Geoff. Clegg, Stewart. Class, politics and the economy /. London , Boston , 1986. viii, 451 p. ; ISBN 0-7102-0452-3 : LC Card 85-8369 DDC 305.5 19
HT609 .C62 1986 ***NYPL [JLD 87-459]***

DOW JONES & CO.
Winans, R. Foster. Trading secrets /. New York , c1986. xiv, 320 p., [8] p. of plates : ISBN 0-312-81227-2 : LC Card 86-12700 DDC 364.1/68 19
HG4572 .W547 1986 ***NYPL [JLE 86-4323]***

Dow Jones-Irwin.
Lehmann, Michael B. The Dow Jones-Irwin guide to using the Wall Street journal /. Homewood, Ill. , c1987. xii, 282 p. : ISBN 0-87094-923-3 LC Card 86-71441 DDC 332/.05 19
HB3743 .L44 1987

Powell, James B. The Dow Jones-Irwin guide to high tech investing . Homewood, Ill. , c1986. xix, 356 p. : ISBN 0-87094-596-3 : LC Card 85-72178 DDC 332.6/7253 19
HG4521 .P63 1986 ***NYPL [JLE 86-2261]***

The Dow Jones-Irwin guide to bond and money market investments /. Stigum, Marcia L. Homewood, Ill. , c1987. xiii, 298 p. : ISBN 0-87094-892-X : LC Card 86-71921
NYPL [*R-Econ. 87-1260]

The Dow Jones-Irwin guide to high tech investing . Powell, James B. Homewood, Ill. , c1986. xix, 356 p. : ISBN 0-87094-596-3 : LC Card 85-72178 DDC 332.6/7253 19
HG4521 .P63 1986 ***NYPL [JLE 86-2261]***

The Dow Jones-Irwin guide to retirement planning /. Vicker, Ray. Homewood, Ill. , c1987. ix, 332 p. : ISBN 1-556-23005-2 LC Card 86-72973 DDC 332.024/01 19
HG179 .V54 1987

The Dow Jones-Irwin guide to using the Wall Street journal /. Lehmann, Michael B. Homewood, Ill. , c1987. xii, 282 p. : ISBN 0-87094-923-3 LC Card 86-71441 DDC 332/.05 19
HB3743 .L44 1987

Dowall, David E.
Back-offices and San Francisco's office development growth cap / David E. Dowall. [Berkeley] : Institute of Urban and Regional Development, University of California, Berkeley, [1986] 23 p. : ill. ; 28 cm. (Working paper . no. 448) "March 1986." Includes bibliographical references. LC Card 86-622513 DDC 333.77/17/0979461 19
1. Land use - California - San Francisco. 2. Office buildings - California - San Francisco. 3. Office buildings - California - San Francisco Bay Area - Location. I. Series: Working paper (University of California, Berkeley. Institute of Urban and Regional Development) , no. 448. II. Title.
HD268.S4 D68 1986

Office automation and the implications for office development / David E. Dowall and Marcia Salkin. [Berkeley] : Institute of Urban and Regional Development, University of California, Berkeley, [1986] 171 p. ; 28 cm. (Working paper / Institute of Urban and Regional Development, University of California, Berkeley . no. 447) "April 1986." Bibliography: p. 154-171. LC Card 86-622512 DDC 651.8 19
1. Office practice - Automation. 2. White collar workers - Effect of technological innovations on. 3. Office buildings. 4. Office layout. I. Salkin, Marcia. II. Series: Working paper (University of California, Berkeley. Institute of Urban & Regional Development , no. 447. III. Title.
HF5547.5 .D64 1986

Dowd, Merle E. A consumer's guide to financial planning : how to get the best plan for your money / Merle E. Dowd. New York : F. Watts, 1987. 296 p. : ill. ; 24 cm. Bibliography: p. 289-291. Includes index. ISBN 0-531-15517-X LC Card 86-32491 DDC 332.024 19
1. Finance, Personal. 2. Financial planners. I. Title.
HG179 .D68 1987

Dowden, C. James. Creating a community association : the developer's role in condominium and homeowner associations / C. James Dowden.2nd rev. ed. Washington, D.C. : Urban Land Institute ; Alexandria, Va. : Community Associations Institute, 1986. vii, 76 p. : ill. ; 28 cm. Rev. ed. of: Creating a community association / manuscript authored by the staff of the Community Associations Institute. 1977? Bibliography: p. 75-76. ISBN 0-87420-659-6 (pbk.) LC Card 86-50785 DDC 643/.2 19
1. Condominium associations - United States. 2. Homeowners' associations - United States. I. Urban Land Institute. II. Community Associations Institute. III. Creating a community association. IV. Title.
HD7287.67.U5 C73 1986

Dowden, Tony. Tymes, Elna. Lotus 1-2-3 financial models /. Indianapolis, Ind. , c1988. vi, 307 p. ; ISBN 0-672-48410-2 (pbk.) LC Card 87-72205 DDC 005.36/9 19
HF5548.4.L67 T95 1988

Dowling, Anne M. Two years of accident experience under STOP-DWI, December 1981-November 1983 / by Anne M. Dowling, Anne Taylor McCartt. [Albany] : Institute for Traffic Safety Management and Research, [1984] xiii, 67 p. : ill. ; 28 cm. "Interim report by the Institute for Traffic Safety Management and Research for the New York State Department of Motor Vehicles"--Cover. "April 1984." Includes bibliographical references. LC Card 86-622431 DDC 363.1/251 19
1. Drinking and traffic accidents - New York (State). 2. Traffic accidents - New York (State). I. McCartt, Anne Taylor. II. State University of New York. Research Foundation. Institute for Traffic Safety Management and Research. III. New York (State). Dept. of Motor Vehicles. IV. Title.
HE5620.D7 D68 1984

Down to business . Pearson, Charles S. Washington, DC (1735 New York Ave., NW, Washington, DC 20006) , c1985. vii, 107 p. ; ISBN 0-915825-04-X (pbk.) : LC Card 84-52795
HD69.P6 P42 1985 ***NYPL [JLE 86-3186]***

Downes, John. Barron's finance and investment handbook / John Downes, Jordan Elliot Goodman. Woodbury, N.Y. : Barron's, c1986. xiv, 994 p. : ill. ; 24 cm. Includes index. Bibliography: p. 967-972. ISBN 0-8120-5729-5 : LC Card 86-10906 DDC 332.6/78 19
1. Finance - Handbooks, manuals, etc. 2. Investments - Handbooks, manuals, etc. 3. Finance - Dictionaries. 4. Investments - Dictionaries. I. Goodman, Jordan Elliot. II. Barron's Educational Series, inc. III. Title. IV. Title: Finance and investment handbook.
HG173 .D65 1986
NYPL [*R-Econ. 86-5261]

Downsizing . Tomasko, Robert M. New York , c1987. p. cm. ISBN 0-8144-5907-2 LC Card 87-47709 DDC 338.6/4 19
HD69.S5 T59 1987

Downtown and regional shopping centre retailing in Winnipeg / by Arch H. Honigmam ... [et al.]. Winnipeg, Man., Canada : Institute of Urban Studies, 1985. x, 90, [8] p. : ill. ; 28 cm. (Report / Institute of Urban Studies . no. 7) Bibliography: p. [84]-90. ISBN 0-920213-22-7 (pbk.) LC Card 86-137592 DDC 381/.1/0971274 19
1. Retail trade - Manitoba - Winnipeg. 2. Shopping centers - Manitoba - Winnipeg. 3. Stores, Retail - Manitoba - Winnipeg. 4. Central business districts - Manitoba - Winnipeg. I. Honigmann, Arch H., 1960-. II. Series: Report (University of Winnipeg. Institute of Urban Studies) , no. 7.
HF5429.6.C3 D69 1985
NYPL [JLF 86-1331]

The downwave . Beckman, Robert C. Portsmouth, Hants , 1983. 216 p. : ISBN 0-903852-38-1
NYPL [JLE 86-3347]

Doyle, Mel. Burns, Patrick. Democracy at work /. London , 1981. 164 p. : ISBN 0-330-26478-8 (pbk.) LC Card 86-673620
HD6664 .B845x 1981

Doyle, Michael W. Escalation and intervention . Boulder, Colo. , 1986. x, 181 p. ; ISBN 0-8133-7200-3 : LC Card 86-4020 DDC 327.1/6 19
U104 .E83 1986 ***NYPL [JLE 86-4131]***

Doyle, Peter. Case studies in international marketing /. London , 1982. vii, 391 p. : ISBN 0-434-90370-1 : LC Card 82-241323 DDC 658.8/48 19
HF1009.5 .C34 1982 ***NYPL [JLE 87-1196]***

Doyle, William J., 1946- Using SuperCalc 4 : the new generation / William J. Doyle, Jr. New York : Wiley, c1987. xvi, 382 p. : ill. ; 25 cm. Includes index. ISBN 0-471-85992-3 : LC Card 87-13804 DDC 005.36/9 19
1. SuperCalc 4 (Computer program). 2. Business - Data processing. I. Title.
HF5548.4.S87 D69 1987

Doz, Yves L.
Prahalad, C. K. The multinational mission . New York , London , c1987. ix, 290 p. : ISBN 0-02-925050-1 LC Card 87-11970 DDC 658/.049 19
HD62.4 .P69 1987

Strategic management in multinational companies / by Yves Doz. 1st ed. Oxford [Oxfordshire] ; New York : Pergamon Press, 1986. xii, 243 p. : ill. ; 24 cm. Includes bibliographical references and index. ISBN 0-08-031808-8 : LC Card 85-9282 DDC 658.4/012 19
1. International business enterprises - Management. 2. International business enterprises - Planning. I. Title.
HD62.4 .D69 1986 ***NYPL [JLE 86-1955]***

Dozier, Jeff. Marsh, William M. Landscape planning . New York , 1986. p. cm. ISBN 0-471-85434-4 LC Card 86-28951 DDC 712 19
HD108.6 .M37 1986

Dräger, Heinrich, 1898- Zu wenig Arbeit für zu viele Menschen : Lösungsmöglichkeiten zum Beschäftigungsproblem / Heinrich Dräger.1. Aufl. Stuttgart : Bonn Aktuell, 1984. 125 p. : 26 ill. ; 21 cm. (Edition Dräger-Stiftung . Bd. 7) Includes bibliographical references. ISBN 3-87959-220-9 LC Card 84-198317
1. Labor supply - Germany, West. 2. Full employment policies. 3. Economic policy. I. Title. II. Series.
HD5779 .D68 1984

Draeger, Werner. Strassenverkehrszählung 1978 in der Bundesrepublik Deutschland . Köln , 1979. 96 p. : LC Card 87-408379 DDC 388/.0943 s 388.3/0943 19
HE5601 .S89 Heft 13 HE5669.A6

Draft regional plan for the South Coast. Natal (South Africa). South Coast Regional Planning Committee. Pietermaritzburg, Natal, South Africa , 1974. 144 p., [2] folded leaves of plates : ISBN 0-909232-03-2 (pbk.) LC Card 84-246771
HC517.N3 A44 vol. 29 HC905.Z7N37

Draft Seventh Five Year Plan 1985-90 and Annual Plan 1985-86. Gujarat (India). General Administration Dept. (Planning) [Gandhinagar] , 1985. iii, 629 p. : LC Card 87-900571 DDC 338.954/75 19
HC437.G85 G7 1985

Dräger-Stiftung. Welthandel morgen . Stuttgart , 1984. 275 p. : ISBN 3-87959-225-X LC Card 85-132786
HF4055 .W45 1984

Dragon, Alan. Burpee, C. Gaye. 1985 household survey of Grenada . Ann Arbor, Mich. , 1986. 168 p. : ISBN 0-87944-317-0 (pbk.) LC Card 86-217405 DDC 339.4/1/0723 19
HD7009.9.Z8 G843 1986

DRAINAGE - GOVERNMENT POLICY - GREAT BRITAIN.

Penning-Rowsell, Edmund. Floods and drainage . London , Boston , 1986. xx, 199 p. : ISBN 0-04-627001-9 (alk. paper) : LC Card 85-13383 DDC 363.3/4936/0941 19
HD1676.G7 P46 1985 ***NYPL [JLE 86-3996]***

DRAINAGE - ITALY - HISTORY - ADDRESSES, ESSAYS, LECTURES.
Le Bonifiche in Italia dal '700 a oggi /. Roma , 1984. viii, 437 p. : ISBN 88-420-2429-5 : LC Card 85-173148
HD1683.I8 B66 1984 ***NYPL [JSD 87-50]***

Drakakis-Smith, D. W. Urbanisation in the developing world /. London , Dover, N.H. , c1986. 265 p. ; ISBN 0-7099-0884-9 : LC Card 86-4551 DDC 307.7/6/091724 19
HT149.5 .U74 1986 ***NYPL [JLD 86-2402]***

El drama de Panamá . Zúñiga, Mauro. [Panama? , 1986] 44 p. ; LC Card 86-232667
HC147 .Z57 1986

El drama quijotesco de los oficios en la época cervantina /. Guerrina Soderini, Alfonso. Montevideo, Uruguay , 1980 (Montevideo : Talleres Don Bosco) 209 p., [7] : LC Card 84-132190
HD2346.S7 G84 1980

Dramais, André. Emerson, Michael. What model for Europe? /. Cambridge, Mass. , c1988. xi, 151 p. : ISBN 0-262-05036-6 LC Card 87-15151 DDC 331.11/094 19
HD8380.5 .E47 1988

Dramé, Mamadou. Une expérience de grande envergure : le projet de développement intégré des Kalounayes, département de Bignona / Mamadou Dramé. [Dakar] : République du Sénégal, Ministère de l'enseignement supérieur et de la recherche scientifique et technique, Ecole nationale d'administration et de magistrature, 1980-1981 [i.e., 1981] 32, [3] leaves, [1] folded leaf of plates : col. map ; 31 cm. "Mémoire de stage"--Added t.p. Bibliography: leaf [35] LC Card 85-218589
1. Agricultural development projects - Senegal - Bignona. 2. Agriculture - Economic aspects - Senegal - Bignona. I. Title.
HD2144.5.Z9 B543 1981

Dramowicz, Elżbieta. Przestrzenne zróżnicowanie państwowej gospodarki rolnej w Polsce / Elżbieta Dramowicz. Wyd. 1. Warszawa : Państwowe Wydawn. Naukowe, 1986. 125 p. ; 24 cm. (Studia, 0079-3507 . t. 84) At head of title: Polska Akademia Nauk, Komitet Przestrzennego Zagospodarowania Kraju. 20 maps in pocket. Summary in English and Russian. Bibliography: p. 114-[118] ISBN 83-01-05021-7 : LC Card 86-212594
1. Agricultural productivity - Poland - Regional disparities. 2. State farms - Poland. I. Series: Studia / Polska Akademia Nauk, Komitet Przestrzennego Zagospodarowania Kraju , t. 84. II. Title.
HD1995.7 .D73 1986

DRAMSHOPS. see **HOTELS, TAVERNS, ETC.**

Drancourt, Michel. La fin du travail / Michel Drancourt. Paris : Hachette, c1984. 329 p. : ill. ; 18 cm. (Collection Pluriel) Includes bibliographical references. ISBN 2-01-009476-X LC Card 84-222228 DDC 306/.36 19
1. Quality of work life - France. 2. Hours of labor - France. 3. Leisure - France. I. Title.
HD6957.F8 D7 1984 ***NYPL [JLC 86-444]***

Draper, Rosemary. Keidel, Albert. China's dairy and food processing industries . Washington, D.C. , c1986. ii, 65 leaves ; LC Card 86-233105 DDC 338.1/77/0951 19
HD9275.C62 K45 1986

Hē drastēriotēta tēs ETVA to etos 1985. Hellēnikē Trapeza Viomēchanikēs Anaptyxeōs (Greece) [Athēna] [1985] 43 p. ; LC Card 86-212959
HG3250.5.A8 H444 1985

DRAWBACKS - SPAIN.
El Tráfico de perfeccionamiento . Madrid, España , 1983. 96 p. : ISBN 84-500-9221-3 LC Card 85-193715
HF1717.S7 T73 1983

Drawing the line on natural gas regulation : the Harvard study on the future of natural gas / edited by Joseph P. Kalt and Frank C. Schuller ; contributors ; Colin C. Blaydon ... [et al.]. New York : Quorum Books, 1987. xiii, 267 p. : ill. ; 25 cm. "Prepared under the auspices of the Energy and Environmental Policy Center, Harvard University." Includes bibliographies and index. ISBN 0-89930-174-6 (lib. bdg. : alk. paper) LC Card 86-25769 DDC 338.2/7285/0973 19
1. Gas industry - Government policy - United States - Congresses. I. Kalt, Joseph P. II. Schuller, Frank C. III. Blaydon, Colin C. IV. John F. Kennedy School of Government. Energy and Environmental Policy Center.
HD9581.U5 D73 1987

Dreams betrayed . Rochell, Carlton C. Lexington, Mass. , c1987. 138 p. ; ISBN 0-669-11105-8 (alk. paper) LC Card 85-45019 DDC 331.25 19
HD6331.2.U5 R63 1987

DREDGING - ITALY - SOTTOMARINA REGION.
Un Mestiere e un paese . Venezia , 1986. 172 p. : ISBN 88-317-4893-9 LC Card 86-219883
HD8039.S252 I85 1986

Drees, W. Nederlandse overheidsuitgaven / W. Drees. 's-Gravenhage : VUGA, 1985. 270 p. ; 24 cm. Includes bibliographies and indexes. ISBN 90-6095-330-4 : LC Card 85-197601
1. Netherlands - Appropriations and expenditures. 2. Finance, Public - Netherlands. I. Title.
HJ1200 .D74 1985

Dreher, Erich. Risikovorsorge . Frankfurt am Main , c1985. 130 p. : ISBN 3-7819-0323-0 LC Card 85-217569
HG1615 .R57 1985

Drei Generationen Arbeiterleben . Deppe, Wilfried. Frankfurt/Main , New York , c1982. 419 p. ; ISBN 3-593-33018-0 LC Card 82-167833 DDC 305.5/62/0922 19
HD6957.G3 D38 1982
NYPL [JLD 86-2569]

Das Dreieck Europa-Amerika-Asien / Beiträge von Kurt Furgler ... [et al.]. [Diessenhofen] : Rüegger, 1986. 154 p. : ill. ; 21 cm. (Sozialwissenschaftliche Studien des Schweizerischen Instituts für Auslandforschung . Bd. 15 (n.F.)) German and English. Includes bibliographical references. CONTENTS. - The coming era of the Pacific / Victor Hao Li -- A troubled partnership / Robert O'Neill -- Der pazifische Wirtschaftsraum / Kurt Furgler -- Zum Wirtschaftspotential der asiatischen Pazifikanrainer / Erwin Schurtenberger -- The role of commercial banks in the debt strategy / Jacques de Larosière -- Chancen und Risiken der Reformpolitik Chinas / Willy Linder -- Die Schweiz vor der globalen wirtschaftlichen Herausforderung / Stephan Schmidheiny -- Renewal of West European civilization? / Bohdan Hawrylyshyn. ISBN 3-7253-0272-3 LC Card 86-231548
1. Asia - Economic conditions - 1945-. 2. Economic forecasting - Asia. 3. Pacific Area cooperation. 4. Europe - Foreign economic relations - Asia. 5. Asia - Foreign economic relations - Europe. 6. United States - Foreign economic relations - Asia. 7. Asia - Foreign economic relations - United States. I. Furgler, Kurt. II. Series: Sozialwissenschaftliche Studien des Schweizerischen Instituts für Auslandforschung , n.F., Bd. 15.
HC412 .D7 1986

Dreifuss, René Armand. A internacional capitalista : estratégia e táticas do empresariado transnacional (1918-1986) / René Armand Dreifuss. Rio de Janeiro : Editora Espaço e Tempo, 1986. 502, [40] p. : ill. ; 23 cm. Portuguese with some English. Bibliography: p. 289-298. LC Card 87-126893 DDC 322/.3 19
1. International business enterprises - Political activity. I. Title.
HD2755.5 .D74 1986

Dreissig Jahre D.D.R. und das Fiasko imperialistischer Prognosen, Pläne und Propheten. 30 Jahre DDR und das Fiasko imperialistischer Prognosen, Pläne und Propheten . [Berlin] , 1979. 40 p. ; LC Card 83-198579
HC290.78 .A14 1979

Drennan, Matthew P., 1937- Modeling metropolitan economies for forecasting and policy analysis / Matthew P. Drennan. New York : New York University Press, 1985. x, 242 p. ; 24 cm. Includes index. Bibliography: p. [235]-238. ISBN 0-8147-1781-0 (alk. paper) : LC Card 85-13784 DDC 330.9173/2 19
1. Employment forecasting - United States - Econometric models. 2. Urban policy - United States. 3. New York (City) - Economic conditions - Econometric models. 4. Baltimore - Economic conditions - Econometric models. I. Title.
HT321 .D74 1985 ***NYPL [JLE 86-1102]***

Drenth, Pieter J. D. (Pieter Johan Diederick) Advances in organizational psychology . Newbury Park , c1987. 314 p. ; ISBN 0-8039-2802-5 LC Card 87-9484 DDC 158.7 19
HF5548.8 .A58 1987

Drentse historische reeks.
Jong, H. J. de (Herman J.) Schoonebeek, olierijk in Zuidoost-Drenthe /. [Zuidwolde] , 1986. 232 p. : ISBN 90-6509-902-6 : LC Card 86-175279
HD9575.N43 N435 1986

DRESDNER BANK - HISTORY - 20TH CENTURY.
Ermittlungen gegen die Dresdner Bank, 1946 /. Nördlingen , 1986. cxxxiv, 353 p., [8] p. of plates : ISBN 3-89190-297-2 : LC Card 87-121689
HG3058.D7 E76 1986

Der Dressierte Arbeiter : Geschichte und Gegenwart der industriellen Arbeitswelt / herausgegeben von Walter Sauer. München : C.H. Beck, c1984. 211 p. : 11 ill. ; 18 cm. (Beck'sche schwarze Reihe. Bd. 286) Bibliography: p. 204-[210] CONTENTS. - Arbeit, Krise und Chance der modernen Gesellschaft / Walter Sauer -- Der dressierte Mensch / Josef Ehmer, Gerhard Meissl -- Fremde Arbeit, fremde Häuser / Walter Sauer -- Von der Handarbeit zur Mechanisierung / Sylvia Spirig-Lausecker -- Harte Zeiten / Gerhard Meissl -- Arbeitslohn und Arbeitsleistung / Gerhard Meissl -- Arbeitsprozess und Arbeitergesundheit / Andreas Baryli -- Der Betrieb, ein latentes Konfliktfeld / Josef Ehmer -- Die Herausforderungen der Automation / Franz Ofner. ISBN 3-406-09286-1 LC Card 84-181068 DDC 331.25 19
1. Labor supply - Germany (West) - Effect of technological innovations on - History. 2. Artisans - Germany (West) - History. 3. Factory system - Germany (West) - History. 4. Automation - Germany (West) - History. I. Sauer, Walter, 1951-.
HD6331.2.G28 D74 1984

Dressler, Fritz R. S. The entrepreneurial age : the 21st century renaissance of the individual / Fritz R.S. Dressler and John W. Seybold. Media, PA : Seybold Publications, c1985. ii, 228, 5 p. ; 23 cm. Includes index. Bibliography: p. 223-228. ISBN 0-918514-10-X (pbk.) LC Card 85-232719 DDC 338.04/0973 19
1. Computer industry - United States. 2. Technological innovations - United States. I. Seybold, John W. II. Title.
HB615 .D73 1985 ***NYPL [JLD 86-3104]***

DREW, DANIEL, 1797-1879.
Browder, Clifford, 1928- The money game in old New York . Lexington, KY , c1986. viii, 319 p., [8] p. of plates : ISBN 0-8131-1573-6 LC Card 85-17938 DDC 332/.092/4 B 19
HG172.D74 B76 1986 ***NYPL [JFE 86-1911]***

Drew, Dennis M. Nuclear winter and national security . Maxwell Air Force Base, Ala. , Washington, D.C. , 1986. xiii, 76 p. ; LC Card 86-7967 DDC 355/.0217 19
U263 .N845 1986 ***NYPL [JFE 87-751]***

Drew, Rodney. Microcomputers for financial planning / Rodney Drew and Geoff Smith. 2nd ed. Aldershot, Hampshire, England ; Brookfield, Vt., U. S.A. : Gower in association with 3i Consultants Limited, c1987. x, 105 p. : ill. ; 30 cm. Includes index. ISBN 0-566-02579-5 (pbk.) : LC Card 87-8405 DDC 658.1/5/0285416 19
1. Business enterprises - Finance - Data processing. 2. Corporations - Finance - Data processing. 3. Microcomputers. I. Smith, Geoff, 1926-. II. Title.
HG4012.5 .D73 1987

Drexel, Ingrid. Vocational training problems in small and medium-sized enterprises : seminar report : report / prepared by Ingrid Drexel. Luxembourg : Office for Official Publications of the European Communities ; Washington, DC : European Community Information Service [distributor], 1986. 279 p. : ill. ; 30 cm. Includes bibliographical references. ISBN 92-825-5707-3 (pbk.) LC Card 86-213476 DDC 331.25/92/094 19
1. Occupational training - European Economic Community countries - Congresses. 2. Small business - European Economic Community countries - Congresses. I. Title.
HD5715.5.E8 D74 1986

Dreyfus, François G. Réformisme et révisionnisme dans les socialismes allemand, autrichien et français /. Paris , c1984. 195 p. ; ISBN

2-7351-0053-7 : LC Card 85-105830
HX273 .R39 1984 **NYPL [JLE 86-4752]**

Dreyhaupt, Franz Joseph, 1925- Wirtschaft und Umweltschutz /. Heidelberg , 1986. vii, 147 p. : ISBN 3-8114-2786-5 LC Card 87-134163 DDC 363.7/058/0943 19
HC290.5.E5 W57 1986

DRI forest products special study series . (no. 9) Fuller, Bernard. Treated wood update . Lexington, Mass., USA (24 Hartwell Ave., Lexington 02173) , c1985. iii, 121 p. : LC Card 86-201219 DDC 381/.45674/0973 19
HD9754 .F85 1985

DRIED FRUIT INDUSTRY - UNITED STATES - STATISTICS.
Fresh trends, 1987 . [Lincolnshire, Ill.] (400 Knightsbridge Pkwy., Lincolnshire 60069) , c1987. 4 v. ; LC Card 87-162047 DDC 381/.415/0973 19
HD9244 .F73 1987

DRIED MILK INDUSTRY - POLITICAL ASPECTS.
Chetley, Andrew. The politics of baby foods . London , 1986. xv, 189 p. ; ISBN 0-86187-293-2
NYPL [JLE 86-2969]

DRIED MILK INDUSTRY - UNITED STATES - STATISTICS.
Census of 1985 dry milk distribution & production trends /. Chicago, Ill. (130 N. Franklin St., Chicago 60606) , c1986. 13 p. ; LC Card 86-208490 DDC 338.1/77143/0973021 19
HD9282.U4 C463 1986

DRILLING, GAS WELL. see **GAS WELL DRILLING.**

DRILLING, OIL WELL. see **OIL WELL DRILLING.**

DRINKING AND TRAFFIC ACCIDENTS - CONGRESSES.
Young drivers impaired by alcohol and other drugs /. London , New York, NY , c1987. p. cm. ISBN 0-905958-48-9 (pbk) : LC Card 87-20657 DDC 363.1/251 19
HE5620.D7 Y68 1987

DRINKING AND TRAFFIC ACCIDENTS - DENMARK.
Thorsen, Thorkil. Alkoholforbrug og trafikulykker . København , 1986. 69 p. : ISBN 87-88225-38-3 LC Card 86-209934
HE5620.D7 T49 1986

DRINKING AND TRAFFIC ACCIDENTS - GERMANY (WEST) - COLOGNE - CASE STUDIES.
Triebler, Stephan Ferdinand, 1950- Verkehrskriminalität und Alkohol in einer Grossstadt . [West Germany , 1983?] (Köln : Copy-Star) xv, 190 p. : LC Card 84-240261
HE5620.D7 T75 1983

DRINKING AND TRAFFIC ACCIDENTS - NEW YORK (STATE)
Dowling, Anne M. Two years of accident experience under STOP-DWI, December 1981-November 1983 /. [Albany] [1984] xiii, 67 p. : LC Card 86-622431 DDC 363.1/251 19
HE5620.D7 D68 1984

DRINKING AND TRAFFIC ACCIDENTS - RUSSIAN S.F.S.R.
Osnovnye prichiny i usloviia vozniknoveniia PTP s tiazhelymi posledstviiami, puti i metody ikh ustraneniia. Bulgarian. Osnovni prichini i usloviia za vŭznikvane na PTP s tezhki posledstviia, pŭtishta i metodi za tiakhnoto otstraniavane /. Sofiia , 1985. 95 p. : LC Card 87-101607
HF5614.5.S62 O7516 1985

DRINKING AND TRAFFIC ACCIDENTS - UNITED STATE.
DUII, the price is too high [videorecording] /. Van Nuys, CA , 1987. 1 videocassette (23 min.) : LC Card 87-706706 DDC 363.1 11
HE5620.D7

DRINKING AND TRAFFIC ACCIDENTS - UNITED STATES.
Drunk driving [videorecording] . Lincoln, NE , 1983. 1 videocassette (30 min.) : LC Card 87-706347 DDC 363.1 11
HE5620.D7

DUI arrest [videorecording] /. Lincoln, NE , 1983. 1 videocassette (30 min.) : LC Card 87-706343 DDC 343 11
HE5620.D7

DUII, the price is too high [motion picture] /. Van Nuys, CA , 1987. 1 film reel (23 min.) : LC Card 87-706705 DDC 363.1 11
HE5620.D7

Task force implementation guidelines for the development of state and community alcohol highway safety programs. [Washington, D.C.?] , 1983. 1 v. (various pagings) ;
NYPL [JLF 86-245]

Driscoll, Bárbara A. El programa de braceros ferroviarios / Bárbara Driscoll. 1a ed. Tijuana, Baja California : Centro de Estudios Fronterizos del Norte de México, 1985. 45 p. ; 23 cm. (Cuadernos CEFNOMEX) Bibliography: p. 45. ISBN 968-607-501-1 LC Card 86-188661
1. Railroads - United States - Employees - History - 20th century. 2. Railroads - Southwest, New - Employees - History - 20th century. 3. Contract labor - Southwest, New - History - 20th century. 4. Alien labor, Mexican - Southwest, New - History - 20th century. I. Title. II. Series.
HD8039.R432 U62 1985

Drits, V. I. (Valentin Ivanovich) Intensifikatsiia--opredeliaiushchee napravlenie sovremennogo ėkonomicheskogo razvitiia / V.I. Drits ; pod redaktsieĭ IA.A. Gol'bina. Minsk : "Nauka i tekhnika", 1986. 76, [4] p. ; 16 cm. At head of title: Akademiia nauk Belorusskoĭ SSR. Institut ėkonomiki. Bibliography: p. 76-[77]. LC Card 87-144484
1. Soviet Union - Economic policy - 1986-. 2. Byelorussian S.S.R. - Economic policy. I. Gol'bin, IAkov Abramovich. II. Title.
HC336.25 .D75 1985

Sotsial'no-ėkonomicheskaia ėffektivnost' obshchestvennogo proizvodstva--sushchnost', komponenty i voprosy ikh otsenki /. Minsk , 1983. 158 p. ; LC Card 83-206045
HC340.I52 S67 1983

Dritte Krise der Profitrate. Helmedag, Fritz, 1953- Die Technikwahl bei linearer Einzelproduktion, oder, Die dritte Krise der Profitrate /. Frankfurt am Main , New York , c1986. viii, 301 p. : ISBN 3-8204-9645-9 LC Card 86-219002
HB601 .H44 1986

Dritte-Welt-Kongress (1985 : Hof (Hof, Germany)) Entwicklungspolitik im Wandel : Dokumentation, Dritte-Welt-Kongress 1985 / Hanns-Seidel-Stiftung (Hrsg.) ; mit Beiträgen von Fritz Pirkl ... [et al.]. Stuttgart : Bonn Aktuell, 1986. 256 p. ; 21 cm. Papers previously presented at the conference sponsored by the Hanns-Seidel-Stiftung, and held in Hof (Saale) on June 15, 1985. ISBN 3-87959-271-3 LC Card 86-193768
1. Economic development - Congresses. 2. Developing countries - Economic policy - Congresses. I. Pirkl, Fritz, 1925-. II. Hanns-Seidel-Stiftung. III. Title.
HD73 .D75 1985

Drivenes, Einar-Arne. Fiskarbonde og gruveslusk / Einar-Arne Drivenes. Oslo : Universitetsforlaget, c1985. 161, [1] p. : ill. ; 22 cm. Bibliography: p. 154-[162] ISBN 82-00-07480-3 LC Card 86-204801
1. Mineral industries - Norway - History - 19th century. 2. Labor supply - Norway - History - 19th century. 3. Norway - Economic conditions. I. Title.
HD9506.N72 D75 1985

Driver, Ciaran. Towards full employment : a policy appraisal / Ciaran Driver. London ; New York : Routledge & Kegan Paul, 1987. xii, 238 p. : ill. ; 23 cm. Bibliography: p. 215-229. Includes indexes. ISBN 0-7102-0918-5 LC Card 87-9814 DDC 339.5 19
1. Employment stabilization. 2. Full employment policies. 3. Unemployment. I. Title.
HD5713.2 .D75 1987

DRIVING, AUTOMOBILE. see **AUTOMOBILE DRIVING.**

DRIVING UNDER THE INFLUENCE OF ALCOHOL. see **DRUNK DRIVING.**

Drobot, Eve. Amazing investigations : money / Eve Drobot ; illustrated by Joe Weissmann. New York : Prentice Hall Books for Young Readers, 1988. p. cm. Includes index. A history of money from the days of barter to computer shopping. Includes myths, superstitions, etc. ISBN 0-13-023714-0 LC Card 87-18661 DDC 332.4/9 19
1. Money - History - Juvenile literature. I. Weissmann, Joe, ill. II. Title.
HG173.8 .D76 1988

Die drohende Katastrophe . Bömer, Hermann. Frankfurt am Main , 1984. 257 p. : ISBN 3-88012-708-5 : LC Card 85-128942
HC59 .B5925 1984

Droit, Hubert. Balfet, Michel. Les 50 mots clefs de la consommation /. Toulouse , c1985. 310 p. : ISBN 2-7089-1969-5 : LC Card 86-140639 DDC 339.4/7 19
HB801 .B276 1985

Dronov, Fedor Amosovich. OĖkonomicheskie problemy razvitiia narodnogo khoziaĭstva i povyshenie ėffektivnosti obshchestvennogo proizvodstva /. Minsk , 1984. 148 p. : LC Card 85-147020
HC337.B93 E45 1984

Drought and aid in the Sahel . Somerville, Carolyn M. Boulder , 1986. xxii, 306 p. : ISBN 0-8133-7087-6 : LC Card 86-5635 DDC 338.966 19
HC1002 .S65 1986 **NYPL [JLD 86-4038]**

Drought Control in Sahel, Permanent Inter-State Committee for. see **Permanent Inter-State Committee for Drought Control in the Sahel.**

DROUGHT RELIEF - BRAZIL.
Brazil. Inspectoria Federal de Obras contra as Seccas. Relatorio dos trabalhos executados durante o anno de 1925 . Rio de Janeiro , 1926. xiv, 75 p. ; LC Card 85-186786
HD1696.B8 B73 1926

Drought situation in Ethiopia and assistance requirements 1984/85 / The Provisional Military Government of Socialist Ethiopia, Relief and Rehabilitation Commission. Addis Ababa : [The Commission, 1984] 55 leaves in various pagings : ill. ; 28 cm. "October 1984." Cover title. LC Card 85-980926
1. Famines - Ethiopia - Statistics. 2. Droughts - Ethiopia - Statistics. 3. Economic assistance - Ethiopia - Statistics. 4. Ethiopia - Economic conditions - 1974- - Statistics. I. Ethiopia. Relief and Rehabilitation Commission.
HC845.Z9 F32x 1984

DROUGHTS - BRAZIL, NORTHEAST.
Guerra, Paulo de Brito, 1914- A civilização da seca . Fortaleza , 1981. 324 p. : LC Card 82-231215 DDC 361.6/0981/3 19
HT395.B72 N63 1981 **NYPL [JLD 86-2873]**

Secas no Nordeste, 1979-1983 . Recife , 1983. 48 p. : LC Card 86-168746
HD1696.B84 N685 1983

DROUGHTS - CAPE VERDE - HISTORY - 20TH CENTURY.
Carreira, António. Cabo Verde . Lisboa [1984] 207 p., [16] p. of plates : LC Card 87-400337 DDC 363.8/0966/58 19
HC594.Z9 F33 1984

DROUGHTS - ECONOMIC ASPECTS - BRAZIL.
Brazil. Inspectoria Federal de Obras contra as Seccas. Relatorio dos trabalhos executados durante o anno de 1925 . Rio de Janeiro , 1926. xiv, 75 p. ; LC Card 85-186786
HD1696.B8 B73 1926

DROUGHTS - ETHIOPIA.
Combatting the effects of cyclical drought in Ethiopia. Addis Ababa, Ethiopia [1985] 56 p. : LC Card 86-224201 DDC 363.8/83/0963 19
HC845.Z9 F332 1985

Faces in a famine [motion picture] /. New York, N.Y. , 1985. 1 film reel (51 min.) : LC Card 85-702803 DDC 963 11
HC845.Z9F3

Faces in a famine [videorecording] /. New York, N.Y. , 1985. 1 videocassette (51 min.) : LC Card 85-703663 DDC 963 11
HC845.Z9F3

DROUGHTS - ETHIOPIA - STATISTICS.
Drought situation in Ethiopia and assistance requirements 1984/85 /. Addis Ababa [1984] 55 leaves in various pagings : LC Card 85-980926
HC845.Z9 F32x 1984

DROUGHTS - SAHEL.
Somerville, Carolyn M. Drought and aid in the Sahel . Boulder , 1986. xxii, 306 p. : ISBN 0-8133-7087-6 : LC Card 86-5635 DDC

338.966 19
HC1002 .S65 1986 *NYPL [JLD 86-4038]*

DROUGHTS - SOCIAL ASPECTS - BRAZIL, NORTHEAST.
Malvezzi, Roberto. Mil quatrocentos e sessenta dias no império do sol . São Paulo , 1985. 197 p. : ISBN 85-05-00296-2 : LC Card 85-200637
HC188.N6 M34 1985

Drouin, Marie Josée. Western European adjustment to structural economic problems / by Marie-Josée, Maurice Ernst, Jimmy W. Wheeler, with the assistance of Catherine Albrecht, Adrienne Kearney, John E. Tedstrom. Lanham, MD : University Press of America ; Indianapolis, IN : Hudson Institute, c1987. xxii, 259 p. : ill. ; 24 cm. Includes index. ISBN 0-8191-6527-1 (alk. paper) : LC Card 87-18909 DDC 330.94/0558 19
1. Europe - Economic conditions - 1945-. 2. Europe - Economic policy. 3. European Economic Community. I. Ernst, Maurice. II. Wheeler, Jimmy W. III. Title.
HC240 .D75 1987

Drounkas, V. T. Baltas, N. K. Empeirikē diereunēsē tēs apotamieutikēs sympēriphoras kai tēs zētēsēs katatheseōn apo tous idiōtes /. Athēna [1979] 128 p. ; LC Card 86-203196
HG3250.5.A6 B34 1979

Drover, Glenn, 1935- Kerans, Patrick. Welfare and worker participation . New York , 1987. p. cm. ISBN 0-312-00908-9 : LC Card 87-11878 DDC 362.8/5 19
HD7261 .K47 1987

Drozdowski, Marian Marek, 1932- Kwiatkowski, Eugeniusz. Pisma o rzeczypospolitej morskiej /. Szczecin , 1985. 277 p., [24] p. of plates : ISBN 83-7007-012-4 :
*NYPL [*QO 86-2539]*

Druck, Kalman B. New technology and public relations . New York, NY (310 Madison Ave., New York 10017) , c1986. xviii, 170 p. : LC Card 87-105313 DDC 659.2/028/5 19
HD59 .N44 1986

Drucker, Peter Ferdinand, 1909- The frontiers of management : where tomorrow's decisions are being shaped today / Peter F. Drucker.1st Perennial Library ed. New York : Perennial Library, 1987, c1986. p. cm. Reprint. Originally published: New York : Truman Talley Books, c1986. Includes index. ISBN 0-06-097111-8 (pbk.) : LC Card 87-45043 DDC 658 19
1. Management. 2. Industrial management. I. Title.
HD31 .D7713 1987

Drug abuse : the workplace issues. New York, N.Y. : AMA Membership Publications Division, American Management Association, c1987. 132 p. : ill. ; 22 cm. (An AMA research study) Includes bibliographical references. ISBN 0-8144-3511-4 (pbk.) LC Card 86-32254 DDC 658.3/822 19
1. Drugs and employment - United States. 2. Drugs - Analysis. 3. Urine - Analysis. I. American Management Association. AMA Membership Publications Division.
HF5549.5.D7 D7 1987

DRUG ABUSE AND EMPLOYMENT. see **DRUGS AND EMPLOYMENT.**

Drug abuse, drug trafficking, and organized crime. United States. President's Commission on Organized Crime. America's habit . Washington, D.C. , 1986. 486, [312] p. ;
NYPL [JLE 86-3348]

DRUG ABUSE - UNITED STATES.
United States. President's Commission on Organized Crime. America's habit . Washington, D.C. , 1986. 486, [312] p. ;
NYPL [JLE 86-3348]

DRUG ABUSE - UNITED STATES - PREVENTION.
Chilnick, Lawrence D. The complete guide to drug testing . New York, N.Y. , c1987. p. cm. ISBN 0-394-56058-2 : LC Card 87-9631 DDC 658.3/82 19
HF5549.5.D7 C46 1987

Corporate strategies for controlling substance abuse /. New York, N.Y. , c1986. xi, 50 p. ; ISBN 0-8237-0327-4 (pbk.) LC Card 86-207704 DDC 658.3/82 19
HF5549.5.E42 C66 1986

DRUG-ADDICTION. see **DRUG ABUSE.**

DRUG ADULTERATION - UNITED STATES.
United States. Congress. House. Committee on Energy and Commerce. Subcommittee on Oversight and Investigations. Dangerous medicine . Washington , 1986. v, 31 p. ; LC Card 86-602099 DDC 363.1/942/0973 19
HD9665.9.U6 U55 1986

Drug and alcohol abuse in the workplace . Lodge, Joseph H., 1942- New York , c1987. xi, 91 p. ; ISBN 0-8247-7769-7 LC Card 87-627 DDC 658.3/822 19
HF5549.5.D7 L63 1987

Drug and alcohol abuse in the workplace . Walsh, J. Michael (Joseph Michael), 1943- Washington, D.C. , 1987. xiv, 149 p. ; ISBN 0-916559-08-4 (pbk.) LC Card 87-60167 DDC 658.3/822 19
HF5549.5.E42 W35 1987

DRUG HABIT. see **DRUG ABUSE.**

DRUG INDUSTRY. see **DRUG TRADE.**

Drug industry and the Indian people . "All India Seminar on National Drug Policy" (1986 : New Delhi, India) New Delhi , Patna , 1986. 333 p. : LC Card 87-900874 DDC 338.4/76151/0954 19
HD9611.I52 A44 1986

DRUG PACKAGING INDUSTRY - EUROPE.
Medical products packaging market in Europe. New York, N.Y. , c1983. vi, x, xi, 220 p. : LC Card 87-141779 DDC 380.1/456151 19
HD9671.A2 M43 1983

DRUG TESTING - UNITED STATES.
Chilnick, Lawrence D. The complete guide to drug testing . New York, N.Y. , c1987. p. cm. ISBN 0-394-56058-2 : LC Card 87-9631 DDC 658.3/82 19
HF5549.5.D7 C46 1987

DRUG TRADE - BRAZIL - DIRECTORIES.
Brasil--guia dos produtores de insumos farmacêuticos /. Rio de Janeiro, Brasil , 1983. 71 p. ; LC Card 86-202196
HD9670.B82 B7 1983

DRUG TRADE - CANADA - LOCATION.
Martin, Fernand. La localisation de l'industrie pharmaceutique au Canada /. [Ottawa] , c1986. 48 p. ; ISBN 0-662-93544-6 LC Card 86-206756
HD9670.C22 M37 1986

DRUG TRADE - CORRUPT PRACTICES.
Uncertain returns . Washington , 1986. v, 210 p. ; LC Card 86-603379 DDC 364.1/42 19
HD9665.5 .U53 1986

DRUG TRADE - INDIA - CONGRESSES.
"All India Seminar on National Drug Policy" (1986 : New Delhi, India) Drug industry and the Indian people . New Delhi , Patna , 1986. 333 p. : LC Card 87-900874 DDC 338.4/76151/0954 19
HD9611.I52 A44 1986

DRUG TRADE - INDIA - TECHNOLOGICAL INNOVATIONS.
Johri, Lalit M. Business strategies of multinational corporations in India . New Delhi , 1983. v, 172 p. ; LC Card 83-906128 DDC 338.8/87 19
HD9672.I52 J63 1983 *NYPL [JLD 86-4081]*

DRUG TRADE - MANITOBA - WINNIPEG - HISTORY - 20TH CENTURY.
Wilder, Joseph E., 1896- Lotions, potions, and liniments pure . Winnipeg, Man. , c1982. 100 p. : ISBN 0-919576-34-6 (pbk.) : LC Card 83-121333 DDC 381/.456151/0971274 19
HD9670.C23 W568 1982
NYPL [JLE 87-1213]

DRUG TRADE - UNITED STATES.
Uncertain returns . Washington , 1986. v, 210 p. ; LC Card 86-603379 DDC 364.1/42 19
HD9665.5 .U53 1986

Drugie oblicze "Solidarności" /. Stelmach, Waldemar. Warszawa , 1985. 222 p. : ISBN 83-202-0391-0 : LC Card 86-208212
HD8537.N783 S74 1985

DRUGS - ADULTERATION. see **DRUG ADULTERATION.**

DRUGS - ANALYSIS.
Drug abuse . New York, N.Y. , c1987. 132 p. : ISBN 0-8144-3511-4 (pbk.) LC Card 86-32254 DDC 658.3/822 19
HF5549.5.D7 D7 1987

DRUGS AND EMPLOYMENT - UNITED STATES.
Alcohol & drugs in the workplace . Washington, D.C. , c1986. iii, 136 p. ; ISBN 0-87179-905-7 (pbk.) : LC Card 87-106610 DDC 331.25/5 19
HF5549.5.A4 A35 1986

Chilnick, Lawrence D. The complete guide to drug testing . New York, N.Y. , c1987. p. cm. ISBN 0-394-56058-2 : LC Card 87-9631 DDC 658.3/82 19
HF5549.5.D7 C46 1987

Corporate strategies for controlling substance abuse /. New York, N.Y. , c1986. xi, 50 p. ; ISBN 0-8237-0327-4 (pbk.) LC Card 86-207704 DDC 658.3/82 19
HF5549.5.E42 C66 1986

Denenberg, Tia Schneider. Alcohol and drugs . Washington, D.C. , c1983. xv, 201 p. : ISBN 0-87179-410-1 LC Card 83-7560 DDC 344.73/01255 347.3041255 19
KF3540 .D46 1983 *NYPL [JLE 86-2348]*

Drug abuse . New York, N.Y. , c1987. 132 p. : ISBN 0-8144-3511-4 (pbk.) LC Card 86-32254 DDC 658.3/822 19
HF5549.5.D7 D7 1987

Lodge, Joseph H., 1942- Drug and alcohol abuse in the workplace . New York , c1987. xi, 91 p. ; ISBN 0-8247-7769-7 LC Card 87-627 DDC 658.3/822 19
HF5549.5.D7 L63 1987

United States. Dept. of the Interior. Division of Medical and Health Services. Help for the troubled employee. Washington [1975?] 57 p. ;
NYPL [JLF 86-1309]

DRUGS AND EMPLOYMENT - UNITED STATES - CASE STUDIES.
Alcohol & drugs in the workplace . Washington, D.C. , c1986. iii, 136 p. ; ISBN 0-87179-905-7 (pbk.) : LC Card 87-106610 DDC 331.25/5 19
HF5549.5.A4 A35 1986

DRUGS - GENERIC SUBSTITUTION.
Generic drugs . Stamford, Conn., U. S.A. , c1986. xiii, 311 leaves : ISBN 0-89336-434-7 (soft) LC Card 87-167077 DDC 380.1/456151 19
HD9665.5 .G46 1986

DRUGS - MARKETING.
Strategic marketing of hospital pharmacy products. Tustin, CA, U. S.A. (17722 Irvine Blvd., Tustin 92680) , c1986. iii leaves, 2, 12, 134, 111 p. : LC Card 87-149442 DDC 380.1/456151 19
HD9665.5 .S77 1986

DRUGS - PRICES - EUROPEAN ECONOMIC COMMUNITY COUNTRIES.
Mestmäcker, Ernst Joachim. Vereinbarkeit von Preisregelungen auf dem Arzneimittelmarkt mit dem Recht der Europäischen Wirtschaftsgemeinschaft /. Baden-Baden , 1979. 83 p. ; ISBN 3-7890-0444-8 : LC Card 80-515375
KK6444.D78 M47 *NYPL [JLD 81-684]*

DRUGS - PRICES - GERMANY, WEST.
Mestmäcker, Ernst Joachim. Vereinbarkeit von Preisregelungen auf dem Arzneimittelmarkt mit dem Recht der Europäischen Wirtschaftsgemeinschaft /. Baden-Baden , 1979. 83 p. ; ISBN 3-7890-0444-8 : LC Card 80-515375
KK6444.D78 M47 *NYPL [JLD 81-684]*

DRUGS - TRADE AND STAT. see **DRUG TRADE.**

DRUGS - UNITED STATES - MARKETING.
Maximizing sales to hospital national accounts /. Tustin, CA, U. S.A. (17722 Irvine Blvd., Tustin 92680) , c1987. 524 p. in various pagings : LC Card 87-401688 DDC 681/.761/0688 19
HD9994.U52 M39 1987

DRUGSTORES - CANADA.
Maule, Christopher J., 1934- A survey of the economics of the retail pharmacy sector in Canada /. [Toronto, Ont.] , c1986. 42 p. ; ISBN 0-662-14496-1 (pbk.) LC Card 86-206188 DDC 338.4/76151/0971 19
HD9670.C22 M38 1986

DRUGSTORES - MANITOBA - WINNIPEG - HISTORY - 20TH CENTURY.
Wilder, Joseph E., 1896- Lotions, potions, and liniments pure . Winnipeg, Man. , c1982. 100 p. : ISBN 0-919576-34-6 (pbk.) : LC Card 83-121333 DDC 381/.456151/0971274 19
HD9670.C23 W568 1982
NYPL [JLE 87-1213]

Drukarczyk, Jochen.
Credit contracts, collateral-based security agreements, and bankruptcy / von Jochen Drukarczyk. Regensburg : Universität Regensburg, Wirtschaftswissenschaftliche Fakultät, [1983?] 25 leaves ; 30 cm. (Regensburger Diskussionsbeiträge zur Wirtschaftswissenschaft . Nr. 168) "Paper presented at the 2nd Summer Workshop on Risk and Capital at the University of Ulm, June 1983." Bibliography: leaves 23-25. LC Card 84-181506 DDC 332.7/5/0943 19
1. Bankruptcy - Germany, West. 2. Credit - Germany, West. 3. Credit - Law and legislation - Germany (West). 4. Consolidation and merger of corporations - Germany, West. I. Title. II. Series.
HG3769.G34 D78 1983

Zum Problem der Auslösung insolvenzrechtlicher Verfahren / von Jochen Drukarczyk. 1. Fassung. [Regensburg] : Universität Regensburg, Fachbereich Wirtschaftswissenschaft, [198-?] 30, iv leaves : ill. ; 30 cm. (Regensburger Diskussionsbeiträge zur Wirtschaftswissenschaft . Nr. 124) Includes bibliographical references. LC Card 84-181525
1. Bankruptcy - Mathematical models. I. Title. II. Series.
HG3761 .D79 1980z

Drummond, Gary. Garofalo, Gene. The sales professional's survival guide, or, Things your sales manager never told you /. Englewood Cliffs, NJ , c1987. p. cm. ISBN 0-13-788076-6 LC Card 86-25603 DDC 650.1/2/024381 19
HF5439.5 .G37 1987

The Drunk driver and jail / prepared in cooperation with the American Correctional Association. [Washington, D.C.?] : U. S. Dept. of Transportation, National Highway Traffic Safety Administration, 1987- v. : ill., maps ; 28 cm. Distributed to depository libraries in microfiche. "January 1986"--P. [4] of cover. Includes bibliographies. "DOT HS 806 761"--Vol. 1, p. [4] of cover. "DOT HS 806 762"--Vol. 2, p. [4] of cover. "DOT HS 806 763"--Vol. 3, p. [4] of cover. "DOT HS 806 764"--Vol. 4, p. [4] of cover. Item 982-D-1 (microfiche) CONTENTS. - v. 1. The drunk driver and the jail problem -- v. 2. Alternatives to jail -- v. 3. Options for expanding residential facilities -- v. 4. Step by step to a comprehensive DWI corrections program -- v. 5. Resource materials. LC Card 87-600837 DDC 363.1/255 19
1. Drunk driving - United States. 2. Prison sentences - United States. 3. Alcoholism - Treatment - United States. I. American Correctional Association. II. United States. National Highway Traffic Safety Administration.
HE5620.D7 D77 1987

DRUNK DRIVING - CONGRESSES.
Young drivers impaired by alcohol and other drugs /. London , New York, NY , c1987. p. cm. ISBN 0-905958-48-9 (pbk) : LC Card 87-20657 DDC 363.1/251 19
HE5620.D7 Y68 1987

DRUNK DRIVING - GERMANY (WEST) - COLOGNE - CASE STUDIES.
Triebler, Stephan Ferdinand, 1950- Verkehrskriminalität und Alkohol in einer Grossstadt . [West Germany , 1983?] (Köln : Copy-Star) xv, 190 p. : LC Card 84-240261
HE5620.D7 T75 1983

DRUNK DRIVING - IOWA - STATISTICS.
Davis, Dan J. The disposition and sentencing of operating while intoxicated (OWI) offenders in Iowa . [Des Moines, Iowa] (523 E. 12th St., Des Moines 50319) [1986] 29 leaves : LC Card 86-621927 DDC 364.1/47 19
HE5620.D7 D37 1986

DRUNK DRIVING - PREVENTION - SOCIETIES, ETC.
Contract for life, the S.A.D.D. story [motion picture] /. Los Angeles, CA , 1985. 1 film reel (31 min.) : LC Card 85-700743 DDC 363.1 11
HE5620.D7

Contract for life, the S.A.D.D story [videorecording] /. Los Angeles, CA , 1985. 1 videocassette (31 min.) : LC Card 85-700744 DDC 363.1 11
HE5620.D7

DRUNK DRIVING - UNITED STATES.
The Drunk driver and jail /. [Washington, D.C.?] , 1987- v. : LC Card 87-600837 DDC 363.1/255 19
HE5620.D7 D77 1987

Drunk driving [videorecording] . Lincoln, NE , 1983. 1 videocassette (30 min.) : LC Card 87-706347 DDC 363.1 11
HE5620.D7

DUI arrest [videorecording] /. Lincoln, NE , 1983. 1 videocassette (30 min.) : LC Card 87-706343 DDC 343 11
HE5620.D7

DUII, the price is too high [motion picture] /. Van Nuys, CA , 1987. 1 film reel (23 min.) : LC Card 87-706705 DDC 363.1 11
HE5620.D7

DUII, the price is too high [videorecording] /. Van Nuys, CA , 1987. 1 videocassette (23 min.) : LC Card 87-706706 DDC 363.1 11
HE5620.D7

Reducing highway crashes through administrative license revocation. [Washington, D.C.?] , 1986. 89 p. : ***NYPL [JLF 86-1382]***

Stop DWI . Lexington, Mass. , c1986. xv, 183 p. : ISBN 0-669-12157-6 (alk. paper) LC Card 85-45676 DDC 363.1/2558 19
HE5620.D7 S89 1986 ***NYPL [JLE 86-2813]***

DRUNK DRIVING - UNITED STATES - PREVENTION.
Stop DWI . Lexington, Mass. , c1986. xv, 183 p. : ISBN 0-669-12157-6 (alk. paper) LC Card 85-45676 DDC 363.1/2558 19
HE5620.D7 S89 1986 ***NYPL [JLE 86-2813]***

DRUNK DRIVING - UNITED STATES - PREVENTION - CITIZEN PARTICIPATION.
Stop DWI . Lexington, Mass. , c1986. xv, 183 p. : ISBN 0-669-12157-6 (alk. paper) LC Card 85-45676 DDC 363.1/2558 19
HE5620.D7 S89 1986 ***NYPL [JLE 86-2813]***

Drunk driving [videorecording] : whose responsibility? / WCVE. Lincoln, NE : Great Plains National Instructional Television Library, 1983. 1 videocassette (30 min.) : sd., col. (Behind the wheel . 2) Title from data sheet. High school driver education students. Issued as U-matic 3/4 in. or Beta 1/2 in. or VHS 1/2 in. Using examples, attempts to get students to realize that prevention of teenage drunk driving is in their own best interests, and is their responsibility as well. LC Card 87-706347 DDC 363.1 11
1. Drinking and traffic accidents - United States. 2. Drunk driving - United States. 3. Youth - United States - Alcohol use. I. WCVE-TV (Television station : Richmond, Va.). II. Great Plains National Instructional Television Library. III. Series.
HE5620.D7

DRUNKEN DRIVERS. see **DRINKING AND TRAFFIC ACCIDENTS; DRUNK DRIVING.**

DRUNKENNESS. see **ALCOHOLISM.**

DRUNKENNESS AND TRAFFIC ACCIDENTS. see **DRINKING AND TRAFFIC ACCIDENTS.**

Drury, Colin. Management and cost accounting / Colin Drury. Workingham, Berkshire, England : Van Nostrand Reinhold (UK), 1985 xv, 599 p. : ill. ; 25 cm. (The VNR series in accounting and finance) Includes bibliographies and index. ISBN 0-442-30637-7 (pbk.) LC Card 85-3266 DDC 658.1/511 19
1. Managerial accounting. 2. Cost accounting. I. Title. II. Series.
HF5635 .D798 1986

Društvena reprodukcija u djelu Vladimira Bakarića / [urednik Stipe Pojatina]. Zagreb : Centar CK SKH za idejno-teorijski rad "Vladimir Bakarić" u suradnji sa ČGP "Delo," OOUR Globus, 1985 printing. 204 p. ; 20 cm. (Biblioteka "Istraživanja i rasprave") Edicija "Misao i djelo Vladimira Bakarića" ; knj. 1 In Serbo-Croatian (roman). Includes bibliographical references. LC Card 86-233326
1. Management - Employee participation. 2. Management - Yugoslavia - Employee participation. 3. Bakarić, Vladimir. I. Pojatina, Stipe. II. Centar CK SKH za idejno-teorijski rad "Vladimir Bakarić.". III. Series.
HD5650 .D68 1985

Družba, znanost, tehnologija : zbornik razprav / [avtorji Samo Cejan ... et al. ; uredil uredniški odbor Gojko Stanič (predsednik) ... et al.]. Ljubljana : Delavska enotnost, 1982. 472 p. ; 20 cm. (Zbirka Družboslovje) LC Card 84-235191
1. Technological innovations - Economic aspects - Yugoslavia. 2. Yugoslavia - Economic policy - 1945-. I. Cejan, Samo, 1949-. II. Stanič, Gojko. III. Series.
HC407.Z9 T434 1982

Družbeno bogastvo SR Slovenije ob koncu 1980. leta /. Flajs, Andrej. Ljubljana , 1986. 75 p. ; ISBN 86-81141-04-X LC Card 86-216767
HA1634.S58 F54 1986

DRUZHBA (FACTORY : VARNA, BULGARIA) - HISTORY.
Khadzhiev, Stefan. Zavod "Druzhba" . Varna , 1985. 161 p., [3] leaves of plates : LC Card 86-140096
HD8039.C62 B95 1985

Druzhba i sotrudnichestvo / [sostavitel′ Ė. Lepisto]. Tallin : Izd-vo "Ėesti raamat", 1985. 85 p. : ill., ports. ; 20 cm. LC Card 86-108625
1. Socialist competition - Baltic States. 2. Socialist competition - Byelorussian S.S.R. 3. Baltic States - Economic integration. I. Lepisto, Ė. (Ėndel′).
HC243.Z9 S63 1985

Druzhinin, N. M. (Nikolaĭ Mikhaĭlovich)
Sot͡sial′no-ėkonomicheskai͡a istorii͡a Rossii : izbrannye trudy / N.M. Druzhinin ; otvetstvennyĭ redaktor S.S. Dmitriev. Moskva : "Nauka", 1987. 421 p., [1] leaf of plates : port. ; 25 cm. On leaf preceding t.p.: Akademii͡a nauk SSSR. Otdelenie istorii. Institut istorii SSSR. Includes bibliographies and index. LC Card 87-164847
1. Soviet Union - Economic conditions - 1861-1917 - Collected works. 2. Soviet Union - Economic conditions - To 1861 - Collected works. 3. Soviet Union - Social conditions - 1801-1917 - Collected works. 4. Capitalism - Soviet Union - History - 19th century - Collected works. 5. Feudalism - Soviet Union - History - 19th century - Collected works. I. Dmitriev, S. S. (Sergeĭ Sergeevich). II. Title.
HC334.5 .D78 1987

DRY FARMING - BRAZIL, NORTHEAST.
Simas, José Ribamar. Subsídios para uma proposta de ocupação racional de novas áreas com agricultura de sequeiro no Nordeste brasileiro /. Recife , 1985 [i.e. 1986] 28, [16] p. : LC Card 87-404827 DDC 338.1/8 19
HD499.N67 S56 1986

DRY FARMING - ECONOMIC ASPECTS - INDIA - AHMADNAGAR DISTRICT - CASE STUDIES.
Dangat, S. B., 1942- Farm income stabilization in dry farming areas /. Delhi, India , 1986. xi, 237 p. ; LC Card 86-903137 DDC 338.1/3/0954792 19
HD2075.A36 D35 1986

DRY FARMING - ECONOMIC ASPECTS - INDIA - CASE STUDIES.
Dangat, S. B., 1942- Farm income stabilization in dry farming areas /. Delhi, India , 1986. xi, 237 p. ; LC Card 86-903137 DDC 338.1/3/0954792 19
HD2075.A36 D35 1986

DRY-GOODS - BRAZIL.
Ribeiro, Lêda Cristina de O. Santana Cançado. Considerações sobre o mercado das indústrias de confecções brasileiras. Belo Horizonte [Brazil] , 1985. 66 leaves : LC Card 87-404932 DDC 338.4/7687/0981 19
HD9940.B82 R53 1985

DRY-GOODS - BRAZIL - MINAS GERAIS.
Ribeiro, Lêda Cristina de O. Santana Cançado. Considerações sobre o mercado das indústrias de confecções brasileiras. Belo Horizonte [Brazil] , 1985. 66 leaves : LC Card 87-404932 DDC 338.4/7687/0981 19
HD9940.B82 R53 1985

The Dryden Press series in accounting.
Davidson, Sidney, 1919- Financial accounting . Chicago , c1988. xvi, 800 p. ; ISBN 0-03-011522-1 LC Card 87-9135 DDC 657 19
HF5635 .D228 1988

The Dryden Press series in economics.
Dryden Press series in economics.
Campbell, Colin Dearborn, 1917- Money, banking, and monetary policy /. Chicago , c1988. xx, 617 p. : ISBN 0-03-009494-1 LC Card 87-6890 DDC 332.1 19
HG221 .C245 1988

Eckert, Ross D. The price system and resource allocation. Chicago , c1988. xviii, 648 p. : ISBN 0-03-012533-2 LC Card 87-5068 DDC 338.5/2 19
HB172 .L45 1988

Johnson, Ivan C. Money and banking .

Chicago , c1988. xix, 604 p. : ISBN 0-03-012518-9 LC Card 87-15002 DDC 332.1 19
HG221 .J667 1988

Puth, Robert Christian, 1936- American economic history /. Chicago , c1988. xv, 640 p. : ISBN 0-03-011892-1 LC Card 87-6782 DDC 330.973 19
HC103 .P9 1988

The Dryden Press series in finance.
Brigham, Eugene F., 1930- Financial management . Chicago , c1988. xx, 901 p. : ISBN 0-03-012543-X LC Card 87-15616 DDC 658.1/5 19
HG4026 .B669 1988

Martin, John D., 1945- The theory of finance . Chicago , c1988. xxvi, 709 p. : ISBN 0-03-063854-2 LC Card 87-496 DDC 332/.01 19
HG173 .M353 1988

Dryden Press series in management.
Vecchio, Robert P. Organizational behavior /. Chicago [1987], c1988. xv, 576 p. : ISBN 0-03-000853-0 LC Card 86-29262 DDC 658.3 19
HD58.7 .V43 1988

Dryden Press series in marketing.
Churchill, Gilbert A. Basic marketing research /. Chicago [1987], c1988. xvii, 765 p. : ISBN 0-03-007278-6 LC Card 87-5288 DDC 658.8/3 19
HF5415.2 .C49 1988

Drygala, Anke, 1950- Obdachlosenhilfe im Sozialstaat : eine Untersuchung über Kontaktstellen zur Verhinderung von Obdachlosigkeit / Anke Drygala. Weinheim : Beltz, 1986. 154 p. ; 21 cm. (Beltz Forschungsberichte) Bibliography: p. 145-154. ISBN 3-407-58292-7 LC Card 87-103682 DDC 362.5/83 19
1. Homeless persons - Housing - Germany (West). 2. Homelessness - Germany, West. I. Title.
HD7287.96.G3 D79 1986

Dryzek, John S., 1953- Rational ecology : environment and political economy / John S. Dryzek. Oxford, OX, UK ; New York, NY, USA : B. Blackwell, 1987. ix, 270 p. : ill. ; 24 cm. Bibliography: p. [248]-264. Includes index. ISBN 0-631-15574-0 : LC Card 87-6587 DDC 363.7/0561 19
1. Environmental policy - Decision making. 2. Social choice. I. Title.
HC79.E5 D79 1987

D'Silva, Brian. Sudan's irrigated subsector : issues for policy analysis / Brian C. D'Silva. Washington, D.C. : U. S. Dept. of Agriculture, Economic Research Service, International Economics Division, 1986. iv, 31 p. : ill., 1 map ; 26 cm. (ERS staff report . no. AGES 860811) Bibliography: p. 31. Item 42-W-1 (microfiche) LC Card 86-602812 DDC 333.91/3/09624 19
1. Irrigation farming - Economic aspects - Sudan. 2. Agriculture and state - Sudan. I. United States. Dept. of Agriculture. Economic Research Service. International Economic Division. II. Title.
HD1741.S85 D75 1986

DSIR resource paper .
(no. 11A) Kaiser, Martin. The New Zealand software industry . Wellington, N.Z. , c1986. 110 p. : ISBN 0-477-06781-6 (pbk.) LC Card 86-212814 DDC 338.4/70053/09931 19
HD9696.C63 N454 1986

(no. 11B) Kaiser, Martin. The New Zealand software industry . Wellington, N.Z. , c1986. 1 v. (various pagings) : ISBN 0-477-06783-2 (pbk.) LC Card 86-212843 DDC 381/.450053/09931 19
HD9696.C63 N455 1986

D'Souza, S. M. (Stanislaus Michael) Mortality case study, Matlab, Bangladesh / Stan D'Souza. Dhaka, Bangladesh : International Centre for Diarrhoeal Disease Research, Bangladesh, 1985. 80 p. : ill. ; 26 cm. (Special publication. no. 24) Bibliography: p. 54-60. "Paper is based on a manuscript 'prepared for the United Nations/World Health Organization Third Project Collaborators Meeting on Case Studies of Determinants of Mortality Change and Differentials - Geneva 14-17 December, 1982." LC Card 86-902788 DDC 304.6/4/0954923 19
1. Mortality - Bangladesh - Matlab Bāzār Thana - Case studies. 2. Matlab Bāzār Thana (Bangladesh) - Statistics, Vital - Case studies. 3. Mortality - Bangladesh - Case studies. 4. Bangladesh - Statistics, Vital - Case studies. I. World Health Organization. II. Series: Special publication (International Centre for Diarrhoeal Disease Research, Bangladesh) , no. 24. III. Title.
HB1470.6.M37 D76 1985

DSRC seminar .
(no. 42) Abdel-Rahman, Awad Ibrahim. Population, environment, and agricultural change . [Khartoum] [1984] iii, 37 leaves : LC Card 84-980808 DDC 338.1/8624 19
HD2123.5 .A64 1984

(no. 56) Elbadawi, Ibrahim. The Sudan demand for international reserve . [Khartoum] [1984] 40 leaves : LC Card 85-981026 DDC 332.4/5609624 19
HG3982.8 .E42 1984

DSRC seminar series. Discussion paper .
(no. 33 33) Doornbos, Paul. Some aspects of smuggling between Chad and Sudan [microform] /. Khartoum [1983] 19 leaves, [1] leaf of plates : LC Card 84-980097 DDC 364.1/33 19
HF3887.Z8 D373 1983
NYPL [*ZT-1646 no.52]

(no. 16) Kursany, Ibrahim. The dynamics and limits of capitalist development in Sudanese agriculture /. Khartoum , 1982- v. ; LC Card 83-980112 DDC 338.1/09624 19
HD2123.5 .K87 1982 ***NYPL [JLM 86-825]***

Du conflit à la motivation . Enrègle, Yves. Paris , 1985. 196 p. : ISBN 2-7081-0642-2 : LC Card 85-231586
HF5549.5.M63 E57 1985

DUAL CAREER FAMILIES - UNITED STATES.
The Politics of professionalism, opportunity, employment, and gender /. New York , c1987. xx, 110 p. ; ISBN 0-86656-626-0 LC Card 86-29491 DDC 331.4/81/000973 19
HD6054.2.U6 P64 1987

DUAL EMPLOYMENT. see **SUPPLEMENTARY EMPLOYMENT.**

Dualism in the Rhodesian colonial economy /. Ndlela, Daniel Boda. [Lund] [1981] vi, 241 p. : LC Card 86-673434
HC910 .N34x 1981

DUALITY THEORY (MATHEMATICS)
Sgro, Pasquale M. The theory of duality & international trade /. London , c1986. 307 p. : ISBN 0-7099-3307-X ***NYPL [JLD 86-3202]***

Duarte, Dioclécio D. A indústria extrativa do sal e a sua importância na economia do Brasil / Dioclécio D. Duarte. Rio de Janeiro, Brasil : Serviço de Informação Agrícola, Ministério da Agricultura, 1941 i.e. 1942. 218 p., [24] leaves of plates : ill. ; 23 cm. Includes legislation. LC Card 85-222223
1. Salt industry and trade - Brazil. 2. Salt industry and trade - Law and legislation - Brazil. I. Title.
HD9213.B72 D83 1942

Duarte, Isis. Trabajadores urbanos : ensayos sobre fuerza laboral en República Dominicana / Isis Duarte ; colaboración de Andre Corten y Francis Pou. Santo Domingo, República Dominicana : Editora Universitaria, UASD, c1986. 314 p. ; 21 cm. (Publicaciones de la Universidad Autónoma de Santo Domingo . vol. 519. no. 1) "Forman parte del informe final de la investigación Proletariado y semiproletariado urbanos en República Dominicana, dirigida por la autora y auspiciada por el Centro de Estudios de la Realidad Social Dominicana (CERESD) de la Universidad Autónoma de Santo Domingo (UASD)"--P. 7. Bibliography: p. 295-299. LC Card 87-402153 DDC 331/.097293 19
1. Labor and laboring classes - Dominican Republic. I. Corten, André. II. Pou, Francis. III. Universidad Autónoma de Santo Domingo. IV. Series: Publicaciones de la Universidad Autónoma de Santo Domingo , v. 519. V. Title.
HD8218.5 .D83 1986

Duarte, Laura Maria Goulart. Capitalismo & cooperativismo no R.G.S. / Laura Maria Goulart Duarte. Porto Alegre-RS : L&PM Editores : Associação Nacional de Pós-Graduação e Pesquisa em Ciências Sociais, c1986. 96 p. : ill. ; 21 cm. "Tese de conclusão dos cursos de pos-graduação em sociologia rural e economia rural, 1985." Bibliography: p. 91-93. ISBN 85-25-40088-2 : LC Card 86-150404
1. Agriculture, Cooperative - Brazil - Rio Grande do Sul. 2. Capitalism - Brazil - Rio Grande do Sul. 3. Farms, Large - Brazil - Rio Grande do Sul. I. Title. II. Title: Capitalismo e cooperativismo no R.G.S.
HD1491.B82 R563 1986

Duas décadas da produção e do produto da agropecuária RS, 1964-84 /. Cunha, Rafael Alves de. Porto Alegre , 1986- v. <1 > : LC Card 87-404979 DDC 338.1/0981/65 19
HD9014.B83 R5416 1986

Dubarle, Patrick. The space industry : trade related issues. Paris, France : Organisation for Economic Co-operation and Development ; [Washington, D.C. : OECD Publications and Information Center, distributor], c1985. 92 p. : ill. ; 23 cm. Written by Patrick Dubarle and Susan Becker. Bibliography: p. 59-64. ISBN 92-64-12772-0 : LC Card 86-210154 DDC 338.4/76291 19
1. Aerospace industries. I. Becker, Susan. II. Organisation for Economic Co-operation and Development. III. Title.
HD9711.5.A2 D83 1985

Dubet, François.
Touraine, Alain. Le mouvement ouvrier /. [Paris] , c1984. 438 p. : ISBN 2-213-01361-6 : LC Card 84-202370 DDC 322/.2/0944 19
HD6684 .T655 1984 ***NYPL [JLE 86-279]***

Touraine, Alain. [Mouvement ouvrier. English.] The workers' movement /. Cambridge [Cambridgeshire] ; New York : xx, 322 p. ; ISBN 0-521-30852-6 LC Card 87-8010 DDC 322/.2/0944 19
HD6684 .T65513 1987

Dubhashi, P. R. Essays in development administration / P.R. Dubhashi. New Delhi, India : Archives Publishers, Distributors, 1987. x, 391 p. ; 23 cm. Bibliography: p. 21-22. LC Card 87-901132 DDC 338.954 19
1. India - Economic policy - 1980-. 2. India - Politics and government - 1977-. 3. Rural development - India. I. Title.
HC435.2 .D833 1987

Dubin, Robert. The world of work : industrial society and human relations / Robert Dubin. New York : Garland Pub., 1987. xiii, 448 p. : ill. ; 27 cm. (Continuity in administrative science) Reprint. Originally published: Englewood Cliffs, N.J. : Prentice-Hall, 1958. (Prentice-Hall sociology series) Bibliography: p. 399-432. Includes index. ISBN 0-8240-8204-4 (alk. paper) : LC Card 86-25791 DDC 306/.36 19
1. Industrial sociology. 2. Industrial management. I. Title. II. Series.
HD6955 .D817 1987

Dubinin, S. K. (Sergeĭ Konstantinovich) Krizis bi͡udzhetno-finansovogo regulirovanii͡a ėkonomiki kapitalizma / S.K. Dubinin. Moskva : Izd-vo Moskovskogo universiteta, 1984. 100 p. ; 22 cm. Includes bibliographical references. LC Card 84-222701
1. Finance, Public. 2. Budget. 3. Money. 4. Capitalism. I. Title.
HJ236 .D82 1984

DUBLIN COUNCIL OF TRADE UNIONS - HISTORY.
Cody, Seamus. The Parliament of labour . Dublin, Ireland , 1986. 253 p. : LC Card 87-102467 DDC 331.88/09418/35 19
HD8400.3.A5 D833 1986

DUBLIN (COUNTY) - POPULATION.
Eastern Regional Development Organisation (Ireland) Eastern Region settlement strategy, 2011. Dublin [1985] xviii, 269 p. : LC Card 87-672656
HB3589 .E27x 1985

Eastern Regional Development Organisation (Ireland) Eastern Region settlement strategy, 2011. Dublin [1985] viii, 21 p. : LC Card 87-672678
HB3589 .E27x 1985a

Dublin, Jack. Mid-term evaluation of the Malawi Union of Savings and Credit Co-operatives Project (612-0205) / prepared by Jack Dublin, David P. Harmon, Jr., Mebratu Tsegaye. Lilongwe, Malawi : USAID/Malawi, 1983. x, 84, [29] leaves ; 28 cm. "28 October 1983." Bibliography: leaves [25]-[26] (2nd group) LC Card 85-981350 DDC 334/.22/096897 19
1. Malawi Union of Savings and Credit Co-operatives - Evaluation. 2. Credit unions - Malawi - Evaluation. I. Harmon, David P., 1937-. II. Tsegaye, Mebratu. III.

Title.
HG2039.M29 D83 1983

Dubly, Alain. La organización campesina : imagen y realidad / Alain Dubly. Quito, Ecuador : Fondo Ecuatoriano Populorum Progressio, 1985. 37 p. : ill. ; 22 cm. (Opciones y experiencias . no. 4) Includes bibliographical references. LC Card 87-404544 DDC 322/.2/09866 19
1. Peasantry - Ecuador - Political activity. 2. Agricultural laborers - Ecuador - Political activity. I. Title. II. Series.
HD1531.E2 D83 1985

Dubnov, A. P. (Aleksandr Pavlovich)
Khoziaĭstvennoe osvoenie novykh raĭonov i ėkonomicheskiĭ rost Sibiri . Novosibirsk , 1980. 173 p. : LC Card 83-182452
HC337.R852 S5247 1980

Dubofsky, Melvyn, 1934-
"Big Bill" Haywood / Melvyn Dubofsky. New York : St. Martin's Press, 1987. viii, 184 p. ; 21 cm. Bibliography: p. 171-179. Includes index. ISBN 0-312-01272-1 : LC Card 87-17355 DDC 331.88/6 B 19
1. Haywood, Big Bill, 1869-1928. 2. Trade-unions - United States - Officials and employees - Biography. 3. Labor and laboring classes - United States - Biography. 4. Industrial Workers of the World - History. I. Title.
HD6509.H3 D82 1987

We shall be all : a history of the Industrial Workers of the World / by Melvyn Dubofsky.2nd ed. Urbana : University of Illinois Press, c1988. xviii, 561 p. ; 24 cm. Bibliography: p. 485-529. Includes index. ISBN 0-252-01408-1 (alk. paper) LC Card 87-16725 DDC 331.88/6/0973 19
1. Industrial Workers of the World - History. I. Title.
HD8055.I4 D83 1988

Duboin, Marie-Louise. Les affranchis de l'an 2000 / Marie-Louise Duboin. Paris : Syros, c1984. 303 p. ; 22 cm. (Collection Histoire et théorie) Includes bibliographical references. ISBN 2-86738-026-X : LC Card 84-203792
1. Economic policy. 2. Social policy. I. Title. II. Series.
HD83 .D74 1984

DuBois, Marilyn M. Conference on Cable Television (1981 : Brooklyn College Student Union) Proceedings /. [Albany, N.Y.] (P.O. Box 167, Albany 12248) [1982] 77 p. ; LC Card 86-622177 DDC 384.55/47/09747 19
HE8700.72.U6 C66 1981

DuBois, Philip H. (Philip Hunter), 1903- Mayo, G. Douglas. The complete book of training . San Diego, Calif. , c1987. ix, 217 p. : ISBN 0-88390-208-7 : LC Card 87-14090 DDC 658.3/124 19
HF5549.5.T7 M369 1987

Dubois, R. (Raphaël) Benhaïm, J.-P. (Jean-Pierre) Les radios locales privées /. Paris , c1985. 153 p. : ISBN 2-7101-0528-4 : LC Card 85-205602
HE8697.P57 B45 1985

DuBose, Philip B., 1949- Readings in management /. Englewood Cliffs, NJ , c1988. viii, 343 p. : ISBN 0-13-755166-5 (pbk.) : LC Card 87-2301 DDC 658.4 19
HD31 .R4175 1988

DuBrin, Andrew J. The practice of supervision : achieving results through people / Andrew J. DuBrin.2nd ed. Plano, Tex. : Business Publications, 1987. xvi, 571 p. : ill. ; 24 cm. Includes bibliographies and indexes. ISBN 0-256-03685-3 (pbk.) LC Card 86-71880 DDC 658.3/02 19
1. Supervision of employees. I. Title.
HF5549 .D82 1987

Dubrulle, Louis. Comptabilité analytique de gestion : manuel pratique / Louis Dubrulle, Didier Jourdain. [Paris] : Dunod, c1985-c1987. 2 v. : ill. ; 24 cm. (Gestion "module") Includes bibliographies. Vol. 2, written by Louis Dubrulle and Roger Servan, has subtitle: manuel pratique de gestion par les coûts. CONTENTS. - 1. L'analyse et le contrôle des couts -- [2. without special title]. ISBN 2-04-015766-2 (v. 2) : LC Card 86-149033 DDC 668/.65/0681 19
1. Managerial accounting. 2. Pesticides industry - Accounting. I. Jourdain, Didier. II. Servan, Roger. III. Title. IV. Series.
HF5642 .D74 1985

Duca, Riccardo Guala. see **Guala Duca, Riccardo, 1935-**

Ducci, María Angélica. Formación profesional : vía de apertura / María Angélica Ducci. Montevideo : CINTERFOR/OIT, 1983. 102 p. ; 23 cm. (Estudios y monografías . no. 61) Bibliography: p. 91-100. LC Card 86-142632
1. Occupational training - Latin America. I. Series: Estudios y monografías (CINTERFOR (Organization)) , no. 61. II. Title.
HD5715.5.L29 D83 1983

Duchaine, Paul. Bâtiments préfabriqués résidentiels et industriels à ossature de bois : évolution de l'industrie en 1984 / [préparé par Paul Duchaine, Service des produits du bâtiment, Direction des biens de consommation]. [Québec] : Gouvernement du Québec, Ministère de l'industrie et du commerce, c1985. 36 p. : ill. ; 28 cm. ISBN 2-550-12116-3 LC Card 86-133426
1. Modular construction industry - Québec (Province). 2. Prefabricated houses - Québec (Province). 3. Buildings, Prefabricated - Québec (Province). 4. Forest products industry - Québec (Province). I. Québec (Province). Service des produits du bâtiment. II. Title.
HD9715.5.C23 Q43 1985

Duchêne, François.
The European Community and the Mediterranean / manuscript written by François Duchêne. Luxembourg : Office for Official Publications of the European Communities ; Washington, DC : European Communities, Information [distributor], 1985. 102 p. : ill. ; 23 cm. (European documentation. Periodical . 3-4/1985) Bibliography: p. 101-102. ISBN 92-825-5326-4 (pbk.) LC Card 87-119518 DDC 337.40182/2 19
1. European Economic Community - Mediterranean region. 2. Mediterranean region - Economic conditions. I. Commission of the European Communities. II. Series: European documentation. Periodical , 3-4. III. Title.
HC241.25.M4 D83 1985

Managing industrial change in Western Europe /. London , New York , 1987. xii, 247 p. ; ISBN 0-86187-281-9 : LC Card 87-21875 DDC 338.94 19
HD3616.E8 M36 1987

Due, Jesper. Hva' nu Larsen : en sociologisk diskussion om funktionærerne og deres organisationer / af Jesper Due og Jørgen Steen Madsen. [Copenhagen] : Jurist- og økonomforbundet, c1984. 152 p. ; 23 cm. Bibliography: p. 148-152. ISBN 87-574-4410-2 : LC Card 84-229467
1. Trade and professional associations - Denmark. I. Madsen, Jørgen Steen. II. Title.
HD2429.D4 D84 1984

Due, John Fitzgerald. Brazil and the Ivory Coast . Greenwich, Conn. , c1987. p. cm. ISBN 0-89232-819-3 : LC Card 87-3667 DDC 332/.042/0981 19
HG3891.5 .B72 1987

Dülfer, Eberhard. Projektmanagement, INTERNATIONAL /. Stuttgart , c1982. x, 244 p. : ISBN 3-7910-0339-9 LC Card 83-183718
HD69.P75 P764 1982

Dueñas de Anhalzer, Carmen. Historia económica y social de Manabí / Carmen Dueñas de Anhalzer. [Quito, Ecuador] : Abya Yala, 1986. 140 p., [4] leaves of plates : ill. ; 22 cm. Cover title: Historia económica y social del norte de Manabí. Bibliography: p. 131-138. LC Card 87-107503
1. Sucre (Ecuador : Canton) - Economic conditions. 2. Sucre (Ecuador : Canton) - Social conditions. I. Title. II. Title: Historia económica y social del norte de Manabí.
HC203.S83 D84 1986

Dürr, Ernst. La Economía social de mercado . Buenos Aires, República Argentina [1984], c1983. 109 p. ; ISBN 950-9431-00-1 LC Card 86-120441 DDC 338.9 19
HD85.S7 E36 1983

Duesenberry, James Stemble, 1918-
Mayer, Thomas. Money, banking, and the economy /. New York , c1984. xiv, 574 p. : ISBN 0-393-95313-0 LC Card 83-13498 DDC 332.1/0973 19
HG540 .M39 1984 ***NYPL [JLE 86-2193]***

Mayer, Thomas, 1927- Money, banking, and the economy /. New York , c1987. xiv, 488 p. : ISBN 0-393-95557-5 LC Card 86-33160 DDC 332.1/0973 19
HG540 .M39 1987

Düwel, Klaus. Der Handel des frühen Mittelalters . Göttingen , 1985. 510 p. : ISBN 3-525-82433-5 (Deut. Bibl.) LC Card 86-209040
HF3495 .U57 1985 t. 3

Duffus Commission of Enquiry, 1977-78, report. Barbados. Duffus Commission of Enquiry. Report /. [Bridgetown, Barbados] [1978] vi, 118, 270 p. : LC Card 82-243628 DDC 354.7298/10072 19
HJ2073.B37 B37 1978 ***NYPL [JLG 86-221]***

Dufils, Pierre. Raffegeau, Jean. Les comptes consolidés . Paris , c1984. 971 p. : ISBN 2-85115-064-2 : LC Card 84-245353 DDC 657/.3 19
HF5681.B2 R25 1984

Dufour, Denise. Programme d'aide aux médias communautaires, 1979-80 . [Québec] [1979] 97 leaves ; LC Card 83-200428
HE8689.9.C3 P755 1979

Dufour, Jean-Marie. Jobin, Jacques. Mesure et incidence des dépenses fiscales au Québec /. Montréal [1984] 27 p. ; LC Card 85-169988
HB3 .C3 vol. 8511 HJ4662.A45

DUHEM, PIERRE MAURICE MARIE, 1861-1916 - PHILOSOPHY.
Siemianowski, Andrzej. Fakty, prawa, decyzje . [Wrocław] , 1983. 103 p. ; LC Card 85-113022
HB9 .B7522 nr. 245 Q175

Duhnkrack, Thomas. Zielbildung und strategisches Zielsystem der internationalen Unternehmung / Thomas Duhnkrack. Göttingen : Vandenhoeck & Ruprecht, c1984. xii, 287 p. : 34 ill. ; 24 cm. (Schriftenreihe des Seminars für Allgemeine Betriebswirtschaftslehre der Universität Hamburg . Bd. 26) Originally presented as the author's thesis (doctoral)--Universität Hamburg, 1983. Bibliography: p. [269]-287. ISBN 3-525-12664-6 (Deut. Bibl.) LC Card 85-127165
1. International business enterprises - Management. I. Title. II. Series.
HD62.4 .D86 1984

DUI arrest [videorecording] / WCVE. Lincoln, NE : Great Plains National Instructional Television Library, 1983. 1 videocassette (30 min.) : sd., col. (Behind the wheel . 1) Title from data sheet. High school driver education students. Issued as U-matic 3/4 in. or Beta 1/2 in. or VHS 1/2 in. Follows the sequence of events when someone is arrested for drunk driving. Explains every step of the arrest procedure with a view to making students aware of the possible consequences of disregarding the rules of the road. LC Card 87-706343 DDC 343 11
1. Drinking and traffic accidents - United States. 2. Drunk driving - United States. I. WCVE-TV (Television station : Richmond, Va.). II. Great Plains National Instructional Television Library. III. Series.
HE5620.D7

DUII, the price is too high [motion picture] / AIMS Media ; producer, Brad Tetheaux ; director, Dan Sandler. Van Nuys, CA : AIMS Media, 1987. 1 film reel (23 min.) : sd., col. ; 16 mm. Title from data sheet. Ages 16 through adults. Issued also as videorecording. Shows vignettes of young adults arrested for driving under the influence of intoxicants (DUII). Scenes inside a police station, an attorney's office, the workplace, and at a court ordered drug and alcohol awareness program underscore the legal, economic, and social ramifications of drinking and driving. LC Card 87-706705 DDC 363.1 11
1. Drinking and traffic accidents - United States. 2. Drunk driving - United States. 3. Youth - United States - Alcohol use. I. AIMS Media.
HE5620.D7

DUII, the price is too high [videorecording] / AIMS Media ; producer, Brad Tetheaux ; director, Dan Sandler. Van Nuys, CA : AIMS Media, 1987. 1 videocassette (23 min.) : sd., col. Title from data sheet. Ages 16 through adults. Issued as U-matic 3/4 in. or Beta 1/2 in. or VHS 1/2 in. Issued also as motion picture. Shows vignettes of young adults arrested for driving under the influence of intoxicants (DUII). Scenes inside a police station, an attorney's office, the workplace, and at a court ordered drug and alcohol awareness program underscore the legal, economic, and social ramifications of drinking and driving. LC Card 87-706706 DDC 363.1 11
1. Drinking and traffic accidents - United State. 2. Drunk driving - United States. 3. Youth - United States - Alcohol use. I. AIMS Media.
HE5620.D7

DUISBURG REGION (NORTH RHINE-WESTPHALIA, GERMANY) -

ECONOMIC CONDITIONS.
Schanz, Hermann J. Der niederrheinische Wirtschaftsraum . Stuttgart , c1986. xxii, 466 p. ; ISBN 3-7910-5014-1 LC Card 87-135757 DDC 330.943/55 19
HC289.D755 S32 1986

Duke, Beth Whitley, 1954- Sitterly, Connie, 1953- A woman's place . Englewood Cliffs, N.J. , c1988. xvi, 365 p. : ISBN 0-13-961954-2 (pbk.) : LC Card 87-25746 DDC 658.4/09/024042 19
HD6054.3 .S67 1988

Duke Power Company. Industrial Dept.
Piedmont Carolinas, where wealth awaits you. Charlotte, N.C. [1930?] 47 p. : LC Card 85-666462
HC107.N8 P53x 1930

Duke Press policy studies.
Galster, George C., 1948- Homeowners and neighborhood reinvestment /. Durham , 1987. xii, 354 p. ; ISBN 0-8223-0725-1 LC Card 87-13448 DDC 307.3/36 19
HD1387 .G34 1987

Jancar, Barbara Wolfe, 1935- Environmental management in the Soviet Union and Yugoslavia . Durham , 1987. xi, 481 p. : ISBN 0-8223-0719-7 LC Card 87-5412 DDC 363.7/06/0947 19
HC340.E5 J35 1987

Strand, Paul J., 1949- Indochinese refugees in America . Durham, N.C. , 1985. x, 182 p. ; ISBN 0-8223-0629-8 LC Card 84-25888 DDC 362.8/49592 19
HV640.5.I5 S77 1985 ***NYPL [JLE 86-4772]***

Dukhovnaia, L. T. (Lidiia Timofeevna)
Burzhuaznoe gosudarstvo i rynok truda : problemy i protivorechiia / L.T. Dukhovnaia. Kiev : Gol. izd-vo izdatel'skogo ob"edineniia "Vyshcha shkola", 1985. 155, [3] p. ; 20 cm. Bibliography: p. 147-[156] LC Card 86-150676
1. Labor policy. 2. Manpower policy. 3. Industrial relations. I. Title.
HD5713 .D84 1985

Dukhovnyĭ mir sovetskogo cheloveka /. Akopov, Mykhaĭlo Arutiunovych. Kiev , 1985. 124, [3] p. ; LC Card 86-139846
JN6581 .A64 1985 ***NYPL [*QIK 87-3448]***

Dulon, Günter. Nicaragua . Hamburg [1986] 95 p. : ISBN 3-921620-32-5 LC Card 86-191836 DDC 330.97285/053 19
HC146 .N56 1986

DUMAINE (MARTINIQUE) - SOCIAL CONDITIONS.
Rosélie, Roland. L'habitation sucrière au Quartier La Dumaine, Le François /. [Fort-deFrance? , 1986] ([Fort-de-France] : Impr. Désormeaux) 59 p. : LC Card 86-203128
HD8039.S86 M327 1986

Dumairy, 1956- Kredit pedesaan di Indonesia /. Yogyakarta , 1986. xii, 160 p. ; LC Card 86-943011
HG2051.I65 K74 1986

Dumas, Lloyd J. The overburdened economy : uncovering the causes of chronic unemployment, inflation, and national decline / Lloyd J. Dumas. Berkeley : University of California Press, c1986. xiv, 297 p. ; 22 cm. Includes index. Bibliography: p. 273-287. ISBN 0-520-05686-8 (alk. paper) LC Card 85-20856 DDC 331.13/7973 19
1. Unemployment - United States. 2. Underemployment - United States. 3. Poor - United States. 4. United States - Economic conditions - 1981-. I. Title.
HD5724 .D775 1986 ***NYPL [JLD 86-2582]***

Dumas, Neil S. The decision maker's guide to applied planning, organization, administration, research, evaluation, information processing and analysis techniques [by] Neil S. Dumas. [Gainesville] University of Florida, Regional Rehabilitation Research Institute, 1970. 191 p. 28 cm. LC Card 75-633083 DDC 016.6584
1. Decision-making - Abstracts. I. Title.
HD69.D4 D78

Dumont, Raymond A. Business communications / Raymond A. Dumont, John M. Lannon. 2nd ed. Boston : Little, Brown, c1987. xxii, 602 p. : ill. (some col.) ; 24 cm. Includes bibliographies and index. ISBN 0-316-19536-7 LC Card 86-21125 DDC 808/.066651 19
1. Communication in management. I. Lannon, John M. II. Title.
HF5718 .D845 1987

Dumont, René, 1904-
Pour l'Afrique, j'accuse : le journal d'un agronome au Sahel en voie de destruction / par René Dumont, en collaboration avec Charlotte Paquet ; postface de Michel Rocard. [Paris] : Plon, c1986. 457 p., [48] p. of plates : ill. ; 21 cm. (Terre humaine : civilisations et sociétés, 0492-7915) Bibliography: p. 413-[419] Includes index. ISBN 2-259-01455-0 LC Card 86-220056
1. Sahel - Economic conditions. 2. Sahel - Social conditions. 3. Sahel - Politics and government. 4. Economic assistance - Sahel. I. Paquet, Charlotte. II. Series: Terre humaine. III. Title.
HC1002 .D85 1986

Les raisons de la colère, ou, L'utopie et les Verts / René Dumont, avec Charlotte Paquet. Paris : Editions Entente, c1986. 137 p. ; 20 cm. (Antidotes, 0336-5298) Bibliography: p. 135-137. ISBN 2-7266-0075-1 LC Card 86-158407
1. Environmental policy - Developing countries. 2. Developing countries - Economic conditions. I. Paquet, Charlotte. II. Title. III. Title: Utopie et les Verts.
HC59.72.E5 D85 1986

Dumpierre, Erasmo. La Esso en Cuba : monopolio y república burguesa / Erasmo Dumpierre. La Habana : Editorial de Ciencias Sociales, 1984. xiii, 148 p., [7] p. of plates : ill. ; 18 cm. (Historia de Cuba) Bibliography: p. 147-148. LC Card 86-177066
1. Esso Standard Oil Company (Cuba) - History. 2. Petroleum industry and trade - Government policy - Cuba - History. I. Title. II. Series.
HD9574.C84 E774 1984

Dumsday, Robert. Land degradation . Cambridge [Cambridgeshire] , New York , c1987. p. cm. ISBN 0-521-34079-9 LC Card 87-13170 DDC 333.73/16 19
HD1036 .L36 1987

Dunaev, Ėrnst Pavlovich. Sovershenstvovanie proizvodstvennykh otnosheniĭ sotsializma /. Moskva , 1986. 203 p. ;
NYPL [*QIP 87-2800]

Dunaeva, V. S. (Vera Sergeevna) Aktual'nye problemy planomernogo razvitiia narodnogo khoziaistva /. Moskva , 1980. 247 p. ; LC Card 81-131558
HC336.25 .A455 1980

Duncan, A. R. C. (Alastair Robert Campbell), 1915- The concept of leisure, by A.R.C. Duncan. Kingston, Ont., Industrial Relations Centre, Queen's University [1970?] 8 p. 26 cm. (Queen's University. Industrial Relations Centre. Reprint ser. no. 5) Cover title. LC Card 70-534907 DDC 331/.08 s
1. Leisure - Addresses, essays, lectures. I. Series: Reprint series (Queen's University (Kingston, Ont.). Industrial Relations Centre) , no. 5. II. Title.
HD8102 .K52 no. 5

Duncan, C. H. (Charles Howard), 1924- College keyboarding/typewriting . Cincinnati , c1985. 396, xvi p. : ISBN 0-538-20750-7 LC Card 84-50474 DDC 652.3 19
Z49 .C65 1985 ***NYPL [JSF 86-1142]***

Dunfee, Thomas W.
Integrating ethics into the MBA core curriculum / Thomas W. Dunfee, principal investigator ; sponsored by the Exxon Education Foundation. [Philadelphia] : Trustees of the University of Pennsylvania, c1986. 169 leaves : ill. ; 28 cm. Includes bibliographical references. LC Card 87-123702 DDC 174/.4/071173 19
1. Business ethics - Study and teaching (Graduate) - United States. 2. Business education - United States. 3. Master of business administration degree. I. Title.
HF5387 .D86 1986

Legal aspects of government regulation of business / Thomas W. Dunfee, Frank F. Gibson. 3rd ed. New York : Wiley, c1984. viii, 335 p. ; 23 cm. Includes index. ISBN 0-471-87029-3 (pbk.) : LC Card 83-21879 DDC 346.73/07 347.3067 19
1. Industrial laws and legislation - United States. 2. Trade regulation - United States. 3. Antitrust law - United States. I. Gibson, Frank F. II. Title.
KF1600 .D86 1984 ***NYPL [JLE 86-3511]***

Dunkel, Arthur, 1932- Trade policies for a better future . Dordrecht ; Boston : vii, 174 p. : ISBN 0-89838-925-9 LC Card 87-22126 DDC 382.9/2 19
HF1411 .T712 1987

DUNKERQUE (FRANCE) - COMMERCE - HISTORY - 17TH CENTURY.
Pfister-Langanay, Christian. Ports, navires et négociants à Dunkerque, 1662-1792 /. Dunkerque , 1985. 677 p. : LC Card 87-115474
HD558.D85 P45 1985

DUNKERQUE (FRANCE) - COMMERCE - HISTORY - 18TH CENTURY.
Pfister-Langanay, Christian. Ports, navires et négociants à Dunkerque, 1662-1792 /. Dunkerque , 1985. 677 p. : LC Card 87-115474
HD558.D85 P45 1985

Dunlop. John Thomas, 1914-
How labor markets work . Lexington, Mass. , c1988. viii, 256 p. : ISBN 0-669-15126-2 (alk. paper) LC Card 87-22718 DDC 331.12 19
HD5701.3 .H68 1988

DUNLOP, JOHN THOMAS, 1914- - CONGRESSES.
How labor markets work . Lexington, Mass. , c1988. viii, 256 p. : ISBN 0-669-15126-2 (alk. paper) LC Card 87-22718 DDC 331.12 19
HD5701.3 .H68 1988

Dunman, Jack. Co-ops--the future. London, Communist Party [1969] 20 p. 22 cm. Cover title. ISBN 0-900302-01-1 : LC Card 77-428347 DDC 334/.5/0942
1. Cooperation - Great Britain. I. Communist Party of Great Britain. II. Title.
HD3486 .D84

Dunn, Pat. Script for an employee flipchart presentation titled The 401(k) plan : a tax-deferred savings program / Pat Dunn. Chicago, Ill. : Farnsworth Pub. Co., c1986. [40] p. : ill. ; 28 cm. Errata slip inserted. ISBN 0-88462-610-5 (pbk.) LC Card 86-201609 DDC 331.25/5 19
1. Individual retirement accounts - United States. 2. Retirement income - United States. 3. Deferred compensation - United States. I. Title.
HG1660.U5 D86 1986

Dunn, Stephen. The closed shop in British industry / Stephen Dunn and John Gennard. London : Macmillan, 1984. xii, 181 p. ; 23 cm. Bibliography: p. 171-175. Includes index. ISBN 0-333-26202-6 LC Card 87-673181
1. Open and closed shop - Great Britain. I. Gennard, John. II. Title.
HD6488.2.G7 D86x 1984

Dunn, Thomas G. How to shake the new money tree : creative fund-raising for today's nonprofit organizations / Thomas G. Dunn. New York, N.Y., U. S.A. : Penguin, 1988. xviii, 185 p. : ill. ; 20 cm. ISBN 0-14-046811-0 (pbk.) : LC Card 87-8795 DDC 658.1/5224 19
1. Fund raising. 2. Corporations, Nonprofit. I. Title.
HG177 .D86 1988

Dunnan, Nancy.
How to invest in real estate with as little as $1,000 / Nancy Dunnan. 1st ed. New York : Harper & Row, c1987. p. cm. (Smart money series) ISBN 0-06-096042-6 (pbk.) : LC Card 86-45648 DDC 332.63/24 19
1. Real estate investment. I. Title.
HD1382.5 .D86 1987

How to invest $50-$5000 / Nancy Dunnan. Rev. and updated. New York : Perennial Library, 1987. 124 p. ; 21 cm. ISBN 0-06-096159-7 (pbk.) : LC Card 86-45862 DDC 332.6/78 19
1. Investments - Handbooks, manuals, etc. I. Title. II. Title: How to invest fifty to five thousand dollars.
HG4527 .D77 1987

Dunnen, Emile den. Instrumenten van het geld- en valutamarktbeleid in Nederland / Emile den Dunnen. Amsterdam : Nederlands Instituut voor het Bank- en Effectenbedrijf ; Deventer : Kluwer, 1985. 109 p. : ill. ; 22 cm. (Serie Bank- en effectenbedrijf. nr. 21) Includes bibliographical references. ISBN 90-267-0955-2 : LC Card 85-115663
1. Gold - Netherlands. 2. Foreign exchange - Netherlands. I. Title. II. Series.
HG295.N4 D86 1985 ***NYPL [JLD 86-91]***

Dunnette, Marvin D. Handbook of industrial and organizational psychology /. New York , c1983. xxvii, 1740 p. : ISBN 0-471-88642-4 LC Card

83-42702 DDC 158.7 19
HF5548.8 .H265 1983 ***NYPL [JLE 86-1120]***

Dunning, Anthony. Anderla, Georges. Computer strategies, 1990-9 . Chichester [West Sussex] , New York , c1987. xxi, 299 p. : ISBN 0-471-91585-8 : LC Card 87-8173 DDC 338.4/7004 19
HD9696.C62 A53 1987

Dunnington, Steve, 1950- Stamets, John, 1949- Portrait of a market . Seattle , 1987. 95 p. : ISBN 0-941104-17-6 (pbk.) : LC Card 87-4746 DDC 381/.18/0979777 19
HF5472.U7 S48 1987

Dunton, Loren.
The financial planner : a new professional--yesterday-today-tomorrow / Loren Dunton. Chicago : Longman Financial Services Pub., c1986. xi, 306 p. : ports. ; 25 cm. ISBN 0-88462-544-3 LC Card 85-23821 DDC 332.024/01 19
1. Financial planners - United States. 2. Investment advisers - United States. 3. Investment analysis - United States. I. Title.
HG179.5 .D85 1986 ***NYPL [JLE 86-4019]***

Financial planning can make you rich--and 33 case histories to prove it / by Loren Dunton. Englewood Cliffs, N.J. : Prentice-Hall, c1987. xii, 352 p. : ill. ; 25 cm. ISBN 0-13-316589-2 LC Card 86-25179 DDC 332.024 19
1. Finance, Personal. I. Title.
HG179 .D88 1987

Dupont, Elaine. Se lancer en affaires . [Quebec] , c1986. 450 p. : ISBN 2-551-09144-6 LC Card 86-138587 DDC 658.1/1 19
HD62.5 .S4 1986

Duport, Claude. France. Conseil économique et social. Le crédit-bail . [Paris] [1985] 90 p. in various pagings : LC Card 86-184049
HD39.4 .F73 1985

Dupraz, Gérard. Terres australes et antarctiques françaises . [France] , 1982. 216 p. : LC Card 82-171424
HE6185.F83 T477 1982

Dupree, Marguerite. Streat, Raymond, Sir. Lancashire and Whitehall . Manchester [Greater Manchester] , c1987. 2 v. : ISBN 0-7190-2390-4 (v. 1) LC Card 87-11026 DDC 338.7/67721/0924 B 19
HD9881.5.S77 A3 1987

DURABLE GOODS, CONSUMER - GERMANY (WEST) - MARKETING.
Engelhardt, Werner Hans. Der Direktvertrieb im Konsumgüterbereich . Stuttgart , c1984. 158 p. : ISBN 3-17-008550-6 : LC Card 84-234886
HF5415.126 .E54 1984

DURABLE GOODS, CONSUMER - LATVIA.
Ėkonomicheskie svi͡azi proizvodstva i potreblenii͡a pri sotsializme . Riga , 1978. 152 p. ; LC Card 81-168062
HF1040.9.S65 E36 1978

Khozi͡aĭstvennyĭ mekhanizm proizvodstva i obrashchenii͡a tovarov narodnogo potreblenii͡a /. Riga , 1985. 115 p. ; LC Card 86-177827
HF1040.9.L38 K47 1985

DURABLE GOODS, CONSUMER - SOVIET UNION.
Kostin, Leonid Alekseevich. Proizvodstvo tovarov narodnogo potreblenii͡a . Moskva , 1980. 212 p. ; LC Card 87-107901
HF1040.9.S65 K67 1980

DURABLE GOODS, CONSUMER - SOVIET UNITED STATES.
Levin, A. I. (Aleksandr Ivanovich) Tovarnoe obrashchenie . Moskva , 1980. 286 p. ; LC Card 81-141540
HF1040.9.S65 L48 1980

Durand, Claude, 1927- Travail et sa sociologie. English. Industrial sociology . London , Newbury Park, Calif. , 1987. xvi, 184 p. ; ISBN 0-8039-8053-1 LC Card 87-50308 DDC 306/.36/0944 19
HD6957.F8 T7313 1987

Durand, José Carlos Garcia. Pequena empresa . São Paulo-Brasil [Brasília] , 1985. 2 v. : LC Card 85-180776 DDC 338.6/42/0981 19
HD9710.3.B72 P46 1985
NYPL [JLD 86-1588]

Durand-Lasserve, Alain. L'exclusion des pauvres dans les villes du Tiers-Monde : accès au sol et au logement / Alain Durand-Lasserve. Paris : L'Harmattan, c1986. 198 p. : ill. ; 24 cm. (Collection "Villes et entreprises") Bibliography: p. 171-195. ISBN 2-85802-613-8 LC Card 87-111461
1. Urban poor - Housing - Developing countries. 2. Land use, Urban - Developing countries. I. Title. II. Series.
HD7391 .D79 1986

Durand Ponte, Víctor Manuel. Las Derrotas obreras, 1946-1952 /. México , 1984. 204 p. ; ISBN 968-580-647-0 LC Card 84-255708 DDC 331.88/0972 19
HD6532 .D36 1984 ***NYPL [JLE 86-4685]***

Duration analysis . Bierwag, Gerald O. Cambridge, Mass. , c1987. xvi, 341 p. : ISBN 0-88730-116-9 LC Card 86-28745 DDC 332.8/2 19
HG4515.3 .B54 1987

Durchlaufzeiten im Büro . Zangl, Hans. Berlin , c1985. xvii, 365 p. : ISBN 3-503-02458-1 LC Card 85-137750
HF5549.5.C6 Z33 1985

DURHAM (COUNTY) - SOCIAL CONDITIONS.
But the world goes on the same . Whitley Bay, Tyne & Wear , 1979. 106 p. : LC Card 81-107503
HD8399.D872 B87 1979

Durham, Eng. University. (Old Catalog form: Durham University.)
Symposium on the Energy Economy (1984 : Durham, Durham) Prospects for the world oil industry . London , Dover, N.H. , c1985. 131 p. : ISBN 0-7099-4104-8 : LC Card 85-4186 DDC 338.2/7282 19
HD9560.5 .S96 1985 ***NYPL [JLD 85-2430]***

DURHAM REGION (N.C.) - SOCIAL CONDITIONS.
Janiewski, Dolores E., 1948- Sisterhood denied . Philadelphia , 1985. xvii, 248 p. : ISBN 0-87722-361-0 : LC Card 84-2640 DDC 305.4/2/09756563 19
HD6073.T62 U65 1985
NYPL [Sc E 86-322]

Durham University. see **Durham, Eng. University.**

Dürholt, Eva. Qualitative Arbeitsanalyse . Frankfurt , New York , c1983. 352 p. ; ISBN 3-593-32721-X LC Card 83-161600 DDC 158.7 19
HD6955 .Q35 1983 ***NYPL [JLD 87-1014]***

During, W. E. Innovatieproblematiek in kleine industriële bedrijven / W.E. During. Assen : Van Gorcum, 1986. 242 p. : ill. ; 22 cm. Summary in English. Thesis (doctoral)--Enschede. Bibliography: p. [188]-194. Includes index. ISBN 90-232-2196-6 : LC Card 86-186964
1. Small business - Netherlands - Technological innovations. 2. Organizational change - Netherlands. I. Title.
HD2346.N4 D87 1986

Durix, Pierre. Les structures économiques et sociales dans le Brionnais oriental aux XVIIe et XVIIIe siècles / Pierre Durix. Dijon : P. Durix, [1983] xxxiii, 608 p. : ill. ; 30 cm. Spine title: Histoire du Brionnais aux XVIIe et XVIIIe siècles. Thesis (doctoral)--Université de Dijon, 1983. Five folded maps inserted. Includes bibliographies. LC Card 86-200732
1. Brionne (Eure, France) - Economic conditions. 2. Eure (France) - Economic conditions. 3. Brionne (Eure, France) - Social conditions. 4. Eure (France) - Social conditions. I. Title. II. Title: Histoire du Brionnais aux XVIIe et XVIIIe siècles.
HC277.B68 D87 1983

Durkacz, Victor Edward. Financial planning for new businesses / Victor Durkacz, Ian Currie, Anne Phillips. Chichester [West Sussex] ; New York : J. Wiley, c1985. 257 p. : ill. ; 23 cm. Includes index. ISBN 0-471-90843-6 (pbk.) : LC Card 85-17927 DDC 658.1/5 19
1. New business enterprises - Finance. 2. New business enterprises - Great Britain - Finance. 3. Tax planning - Great Britain. I. Currie, Ian. II. Phillips, Anne. III. Title.
HG4027.6 .D87 1985 ***NYPL [JLE 86-929]***

Durö, Robert. The basic principles of marketing warfare / by Robert Durö and Björn Sandström. English language ed. Chichester [West Sussex] ; New York : Wiley, c1987. xi, 164 p. : ill. ; 24 cm. Bibliography: p. 163-164. Includes index. ISBN 0-471-91545-9 : LC Card 87-8317 DDC 658.8 19
1. Marketing. I. Sandström, Björn. II. Title.
HF5415 .D87 1987

Durrant, Lawrence L. The seawatchers : the story of Australia's Coast Radio Service / Lawrence Durrant. North Ryde, NSW, Australia : Angus & Robertson, 1986. xii, 248 p. : ill. ; 27 cm. Bibliography: p. 241. Includes index. ISBN 0-207-15198-9 LC Card 86-228332 DDC 384.5/3 19
1. Australia. Overseas Telecommunications Commission. Coast Radio Service - History. 2. Radio in navigation - Australia - History. I. Title.
HE8683.A8 D87 1986

Dürsteler, Urs. Kantonale Verteilung der Bundesausgaben 1983 : eine empirische Untersuchung / von Urs Dürsteler. Bern : P. Haupt, c1986. 55 p. ; 23 cm. (Schriftenreihe Finanzwirtschaft und Finanzrecht. 45) Bibliography: p. 55. ISBN 3-258-03577-6 : LC Card 86-149603
1. Intergovernmental fiscal relations - Switzerland. I. Title. II. Series.
HJ1264.A2 D87 1986

Duryee, David A. Cranfill, Steven L. Small business banking . Washington, D.C. (1120 Connecticut Ave. N.W., Washington, D.C.) , c1987. ix, 78 p. : LC Card 87-135069 DDC 332.1/753 19
HG4027.7 .C7 1987

Dŭrzhavno-monopolisticheskо regulirane na mezhdunarodnite ikonomicheski otnoshenii͡a / [otgovoren redaktor Stoil Kodinov]. 1. izd. Sofii͡a : Partizdat, 1986. 273 p. ; 20 cm. At head of title: Ikonomicheski institut. Bŭlgarska akademii͡a na naukite. Summary in English and Russian. Includes bibliographical references. LC Card 86-195948
1. International economic relations. 2. Industry and state. I. Kodinov, Stoil. II. Ikonomicheski institut (Bŭlgarska akademii͡a na naukite).
HF1411 .D86 1986

Duseberg, Hans Martin. Gaulke, Klaus-Peter. Lehre und Berufsausübung . Berlin , 1986. 122 p. ; ISBN 3-428-06000-8 LC Card 86-166545
HC281 .B33 Heft 89 HD5715.5.G42B47

Duso, Anna, 1952- L'autocritica del keynesiano / Anna Duso. Bari : Dedalo, c1985. 99 p. ; 18 cm. (Piccola biblioteca Dedalo . 12) Bibliography: p. 95-98. ISBN 88-22-03812-6 : LC Card 86-130684
1. Keynesian economics. 2. Keynes, John Maynard, 1883-1946. I. Title.
HB99.7 .D87 1985

Dussauge, Pierre.
Anastassopoulos, J. P. [Multinationales publiques. English.] State-owned multinationals /. Chichester [England] , New York , c1987. xii, 200 p. : ISBN 0-471-91502-5 : LC Card 87-2033 DDC 338.8/8 19
HD2755.5 .A613 1987

L'industrie française de l'armement : intervention de l'Etat et stratégies des entreprises dans un secteur à technologie de pointe / Pierre Dussauge ; préface de Christian Schmidt. Paris : Economica, c1985. xi, 179 p. : ill. ; 24 cm. Bibliography: p. [175]-176. ISBN 2-7178-0999-6 : LC Card 86-216731
1. Munitions - France. 2. Munitions - France - Technological innovations. 3. Technology and state - France. I. Title.
HD9743.F82 D87 1985

Dussault, François. Les modèles scandinaves et la détermination des ententes salariales des industries manufacturières canadiennes : une analyse microéconomique / par François Dussault et Robert Lacroix. Montréal : Université de Montréal, [1982] 21, [11] p. ; 28 cm. (Cahier / Département de science économique et Centre de recherche en développement économique, 0709-9231 . 8209) Summary in English and French. Bibliography: p. [22] LC Card 82-196710
1. Wages - Canada - Econometric models. 2. Wages - Scandinavia - Econometric models. 3. Canada - Manufactures - Econometric models. 4. Scandinavia - Manufactures - Econometric models. I. Lacroix, Robert. II. Series: Cahier (Université de Montréal. Département de sciences économiques) , 8209. III. Title.
HD4979 .D875 1982

Düsseldorf (Germany)
Mehrjahresinvestitionsprogramm (MIP) der Landeshauptstadt Düsseldorf 1978-1982 /. [Düsseldorf] [1978?] 68, 141, 174, 5 p. ; LC

Card 85-141884
HJ9494.D87 M44 1978

DÜSSELDORF (GERMANY) - APPROPRIATIONS AND EXPENDITURES - STATISTICS.
Mehrjahresinvestitionsprogramm (MIP) der Landeshauptstadt Düsseldorf 1978-1982 /. [Düsseldorf] [1978?] 68, 141, 174, 5 p. ; LC Card 85-141884
HJ9494.D87 M44 1978

DÜSSELDORF (GERMANY) - ECONOMIC CONDITIONS.
Arbeitslosigkeit und Neue Armut in Düsseldorf . Bochum , c1986. 65 p. : ISBN 3-925222-03-0 LC Card 87-409036 DDC 331.13/794355 19
HD5780.D85 A73 1986

Düsseldorf (Germany). Rat.
Mehrjahresinvestitionsprogramm (MIP) der Landeshauptstadt Düsseldorf 1978-1982 /. [Düsseldorf] [1978?] 68, 141, 174, 5 p. ; LC Card 85-141884
HJ9494.D87 M44 1978

DÜSSELDORF-HOLTHAUSEN (DÜSSELDORF, GERMANY)
Schöne, Manfred, 1935- Stammwerk Henkel, 80 Jahre in Düsseldorf-Holthausen /. Düsseldorf , 1981. 148 p. : LC Card 86-216690
HD9654.9.H444 S36 1981

Düsseldorfer Schriften zur neueren Landesgeschichte und zur Geschichte Nordrhein-Westfalens .
(Bd. 12) Wirtschaftspolitik im britischen Besatzungsgebiet 1945-1949 /. Düsseldorf , 1984. 338 p. : ISBN 3-590-18124-9 LC Card 84-188669
HC286.5 .W5655 1984

Dutch East India Company. see **Nederlandsche Oost-Indische Compagnie.**

DUTCH LANGUAGE - USAGE.
Aerts, Christel. Advertenties en affiches . [Wilrijk, Belgium] , 1986. 165, [7] p. : LC Card 86-222214
HF5827 .A43 1986

DUTIES. see **TARIFF; TAXATION.**

Dutt, Romesh Chunder, 1848-1909. The economic history of India in the Victorian Age : from the accession of Queen Victoria in 1837 to the commencement of the twentieth century / by Romesh Dutt.6th ed. London : Kegan Paul, Trench, Trubner, [19--] xxii, 628 p. ; 21 cm. (Trübner's oriental series) Includes bibliographical references and index. LC Card 87-131511
1. India - Economic conditions. 2. India - Politics and government - 19th century. 3. Great Britain - Colonies - India - Economic conditions. I. Title.
HC435 .D975 1900z

Dutta, B. B. Land use pattern in north-east India /. Ludhiana , c1986. 167 p. : LC Card 86-903235 DDC 333.73/13/09541 19
HD879.I425 L36 1986

Duttle, Josef. Ökonomische Analyse dinglicher Sicherheiten : die Reform der Mobiliarsicherheiten und Probleme ihrer Behandlung in insolvenzrechtlichen Verfahren / Josef Duttle. Krefeld : Marchal und Matzenbacher, 1986. xvii, 417 p. : ill. ; 21 cm. Bibliography: p. 402-417. ISBN 3-88358-062-7 LC Card 87-104300
1. Credit - Germany, West. 2. Credit - Law and legislation - Germany (West). 3. Bankruptcy - Germany, West. I. Title.
HG3711.G3 D87 1986

DUTY-FREE IMPORTATION - LATIN AMERICA.
Exenciones arancelarias e integración /. [Buenos Aires] , 1986. 273 p. ; LC Card 87-400577 DDC 382.7/1/098 19
HF1733.L29 E96 1986

Duwal al-Khalij. Bazarian, Carl J. The Gulf States =. New York, N.Y. , c1980. 577 p. : ISBN 0-916006-07-7 LC Card 80-65496
HC415.3 .B39 1980

The Duxbury series in statistics and decision sciences.
Bond, Kenneth M. Essential business statistics . Boston , c1988. xiii, 332 p. : ISBN 0-534-91530-2 LC Card 87-25652 DDC 519.5/028/55369 19
HF1017 .B63 1988

Miller, Robert B. (Robert Burnham), 1942- Minitab handbook for business and economics /. Boston , c1988. x, 331 p. : ISBN 0-87150-092-2 (pbk.) LC Card 86-32830 DDC 519.5/02855369 19
HF1017 .M494 1988

Dvacet let Československé demografické společnosti při ČSAV. Československá demografická společnost. 20 let Československé demografické společnosti při ČSAV /. Praha , 1985. 198 p. : LC Card 86-208016
HB3592.3.A3 C47 1985

Dvadtsat′shestoĭ s″ezd KPSS i voprosy ėkonomiki narodnogo khozia͡ĭstva ASSR. XXVI s″ezd KPSS i voprosy ėkonomiki narodnogo khozia͡ĭstva Chuvashskoĭ ASSR. Cheboksary , 1982. 157 p. ; LC Card 83-128420
HC337.C46 A17 1982

DWELLINGS - BRAZIL - ENERGY CONSUMPTION.
O'Keefe, Hsu Yuet Heung. A crise do petróleo e a economia brasileira /. São Paulo , 1984. 137 p. : LC Card 85-143617 DDC 338.2/3 19
HD9574.B82 O43 1984 ***NYPL [JLD 86-2712]***

DWELLINGS - COSTA RICA - ENERGY CONSUMPTION.
Obando S., Marta. Encuesta residencial de consumo energético /. San José, Costa Rica , 1985. iv, 56, [71] p. : LC Card 86-219603
HD9502.C82 O23 1985

DWELLINGS - ENERGY CONSERVATION.
Lenchek, Tom. Superinsulated design and construction . New York , c1987. ix, 172 p. : ISBN 0-442-26051-2 : LC Card 86-7089 DDC 693.8/32 19
TJ163.5.D86 L46 1987 ***NYPL [JSF 87-235]***

DWELLINGS - ENERGY CONSERVATION - ECONOMETRIC MODELS.
Khazzoom, J. Daniel. An econometric model integrating conservation measures in the residential demand for electricity /. Greenwich, Conn. , c1986. xx, 305 p. : ISBN 0-89232-606-9 : LC Card 86-7173 DDC 333.79/3216/0724 19
HD9685.A2 K54 1986 ***NYPL [JLE 86-4174]***

DWELLINGS - ENERGY CONSERVATION - GOVERNMENT POLICY - ADDRESSES, ESSAYS, LECTURES.
Swedish national and local government programs for conservation of energy in buildings /. Gävle, Sweden [1982] 187 p. : ISBN 91-540-9134-9 (pbk.) LC Card 82-208802 DDC 333.79 19
HD9502.S82 S98 1982 ***NYPL [JLG 86-107]***

DWELLINGS - FRANCE - COSTS - STATISTICS.
Les Logements neufs en 1978 . Paris , 1982. 40 p. : LC Card 83-176727
HD7338.A4 L64 1982

DWELLINGS - FRANCE - HEATING AND VENTILATION - EQUIPMENT AND SUPPLIES - COSTS - STATISTICS.
Les Logements neufs en 1978 . Paris , 1982. 40 p. : LC Card 83-176727
HD7338.A4 L64 1982

DWELLINGS - FRANCE - INSULATION - COSTS - STATISTICS.
Les Logements neufs en 1978 . Paris , 1982. 40 p. : LC Card 83-176727
HD7338.A4 L64 1982

DWELLINGS - GERMANY (WEST) - DESIGNS AND PLANS.
Bürger, es geht um Deine Gemeinde . [S.l. , 1983] ([Bonn] : Bundesdruckerei) 7 p. ; LC Card 84-198296
HD7339.A3 B97 1983

DWELLINGS - GREAT BRITAIN - DESIGN AND CONSTRUCTION - HISTORY.
Gaskell, S. Martin. Model housing from the great exhibition to the festival of Britain /. London , New York , 1986. x, 180 p. : ISBN 0-7201-1834-4 : LC Card 86-23775 DDC 363.5/0941 19
HD7333.A3 G37 1986

DWELLINGS - GUATEMALA - GUATEMALA - COSTS.
Revisión del índice del costo de la construcción de vivienda en la Ciudad de Guatemala, años 1975-1979. Guatemala , 1979. 35 p. : LC Card 82-182718
HD9715.G983 G827 1979

DWELLINGS - INSPECTION.
Scaduto, Joseph V. What's it worth . Blue Ridge Summit, PA , c1985. x, 244 p. : ISBN 0-8306-0761-7 : LC Card 85-2801 DDC 333.33/2 19
HD1379 .S33 1985 ***NYPL [JSE 86-1407]***

DWELLINGS - INSULATION.
Lenchek, Tom. Superinsulated design and construction . New York , c1987. ix, 172 p. : ISBN 0-442-26051-2 : LC Card 86-7089 DDC 693.8/32 19
TJ163.5.D86 L46 1987 ***NYPL [JSF 87-235]***

DWELLINGS - ITALY - LOMBARDY - DESIGN AND CONSTRUCTION.
Bianchi, Roberto, 1954- Le tecniche esecutive nell'edilizia residenziale degli anni '80 . Milano, Italy , c1986. 144 p. : LC Card 87-126093
HD9715.5.I83 L653 1986

DWELLINGS - MAINTENANCE AND REPAIR - ECONOMIC ASPECTS.
Galster, George C., 1948- Homeowners and neighborhood reinvestment /. Durham , 1987. xii, 354 p. ; ISBN 0-8223-0725-1 LC Card 87-13448 DDC 307.3/36 19
HD1387 .G34 1987

DWELLINGS - PRICES - ONTARIO - TORONTO METROPOLITAN AREA - INFORMATION SERVICES - ONTARIO - TORONTO METROPOLITAN AREA.
Morrison, Philip S., 1947- Data sources on residential change and the housing market . [Toronto] [1977] 76 p. : LC Card 85-158244
HD7305.T68 M67 1977

DWELLINGS - PRICES - ONTARIO - TORONTO METROPOLITAN AREA - STATISTICAL METHODS.
Morrison, Philip S., 1947- Data sources on residential change and the housing market . [Toronto] [1977] 76 p. : LC Card 85-158244
HD7305.T68 M67 1977

DWELLINGS - PRICES - TEXAS.
Wright, A. L. (Arthur L.) The Texas housing affordability index /. College Station, TX [1986] 5, [17] p. : LC Card 86-622195 DDC 338.4/369083/09764021 19
HD7303.T4 W748 1986

DWELLINGS - VALUATION.
Galster, George C., 1948- Homeowners and neighborhood reinvestment /. Durham , 1987. xii, 354 p. ; ISBN 0-8223-0725-1 LC Card 87-13448 DDC 307.3/36 19
HD1387 .G34 1987

Kaufman, Wallace. Finding hidden values in your home /. New York , London , c1987. xi, 302 p. : ISBN 0-02-560720-0 LC Card 86-26909 DDC 333.33/2 19
HD1387 .K38 1987b

Miller, George H. California real estate appraisal . Englewood Cliffs, N.J. , c1987. xiv, 348 p. : ISBN 0-13-112558-3 : LC Card 87-6956 DDC 333.33/2/09794 19
HD1387 .M545 1987

Miller, George H. Residential real estate appraisal . Englewood Cliffs, N.J. , c1988. xiv, 336 p. : ISBN 0-13-762428-X (pbk.) : LC Card 87-6960 DDC 333.33/2 19
HD1387 .M547 1988

Scaduto, Joseph V. What's it worth . Blue Ridge Summit, PA , c1985. x, 244 p. : ISBN 0-8306-0761-7 : LC Card 85-2801 DDC 333.33/2 19
HD1379 .S33 1985 ***NYPL [JSE 86-1407]***

DWELLINGS - VALUATION - CALIFORNIA.
Miller, George H. California real estate appraisal . Englewood Cliffs, N.J. , c1987. xiv, 348 p. : ISBN 0-13-112558-3 : LC Card 87-6956 DDC 333.33/2/09794 19
HD1387 .M545 1987

Dwivedi, R. C. (Ramesh Chandra), 1928-
Glimpses of cooperatives through press . New Delhi , 1986- v. <1- > ; LC Card 87-900398 DDC 334/.0954 19
HD3538 .G55 1986

Dworak, Brigitte M. Das Länderrisiko als bankbetriebliches Problem / von Brigitte M. Dworak. Berlin : Duncker & Humblot, c1985. 168 p. : ill. ; 24 cm. (Schriften zu internationalen Wirtschaftsfragen. Bd. 7) Originally presented as the

author's thesis (doctoral)--Universität Wien, 1983. Bibliography: p. [141]-168. ISBN 3-428-05761-9 LC Card 85-213576
1. Investments, Foreign - Developing countries. 2. Country risk. 3. Debts, External - Developing countries. 4. Loans, Foreign - Developing countries. I. Title.
HG5993 .D86 1985

Dworak, Oliver M. Gergely, Stefan M. Wirtschaftswissenschaften /. Wien , 1985. 170 p. ; ISBN 3-205-06108-X LC Card 85-229521
HB74.9.A9 G47 1985

Dy, Fe Josefina F. Visual display units : job content and stress in office work : new technologies and the improvement of data-entry work / Fe Josefina F. Dy. Geneva : International Labour Office, 1985. ix, 138 p. : ill. ; 24 cm. Includes bibliographies. ISBN 92-2-105083-1 (pbk.) : LC Card 86-214267 DDC 651.8 19
1. Office practice - Automation - Psychological aspects. 2. Video display terminals - Health aspects. 3. Electronic data processing - Data entry. 4. Job stress. I. Title.
HF5547.5 .D9 1985

Dyck, John H. South Korea : an export market profile / John H. Dyck and Donald A. Sillers. Washington, D.C. : U. S. Dept. of Agriculture, Economic Research Service, in cooperation with the Foreign Agricultural Service : Purchased from the Supt. of Docs., U. S. G.P.O., [1986] v, 74 p. : ill. ; 28 cm. (Foreign agricultural economic report . no. 216) Cover title. "May 1986"--P. i. Bibliography: p. 72-74. LC Card 86-602006 DDC 338.1 s 382/.41/095195 19
1. Farm produce - United States. 2. Farm produce - Korea (South). 3. United States - Commerce - Korea (South). 4. Korea (South) - Commerce - United States. I. Sillers, Donald A. II. United States. Dept. of Agriculture. Economic Research Service. III. United States. Foreign Agricultural Service. IV. Title. V. Series.
HD1411 .F59 no. 216 HD9005

DYE INDUSTRY - DENMARK - HISTORY.
Andersen, Kirsten Gøgsig. Det skal stampes halv stamp presses og klædeskæres . København [1984] 179 columns : LC Card 85-242146
HD9999.C483 D43 1984

Dyer, Constance E. Kyanon no seisan kakushin. English. Canon production system . Stamford, Conn. , c1987. xxi, 230 p. : ISBN 0-915299-06-2 : LC Card 85-63498 DDC 681/.418/0683 19
HD9708.5.C354 K92513 1987

Dyer, Davis. Changing alliances / Davis Dyer, Malcolm S. Salter, and Alan M. Webber ; the Harvard Business School Project on the Auto Industry and the American Economy. Boston, Mass. : Harvard Business School Press, c1987. xvi, 333 p. ; 25 cm. Bibliography: p. 311-324. Includes index. ISBN 0-87584-175-9 LC Card 86-33619 DDC 338.4/76292/0973 19
1. Automobile industry and trade - United States. I. Salter, Malcolm S. II. Webber, Alan M., 1948-. III. Harvard Business School Project on the Auto Industry and the American Economy. IV. Title.
HD9710.U52 D94 1987

Dyer, W. Gibb, 1954-
Cultural change in family firms : anticipating and managing business and family transitions / W. Gibb Dyer, Jr.1st ed. San Francisco : Jossey-Bass, 1986. xxi, 179 p. ; 24 cm. (The Jossey-Bass management series) The Jossey-Bass social and behavioral science series Includes index. Bibliography: p. 167-171. ISBN 1-555-42007-9 (alk. paper) LC Card 86-10585 DDC 658/.045 19
1. Family corporations - Management. 2. Corporate culture. I. Title. II. Series.
HD62.25 .D94 1986 ***NYPL [JLE 87-1079]***

Meek, Christopher. Managing by the numbers . Reading, Mass. , c1988. ix, 293 p. : ISBN 0-201-16129-X : LC Card 87-16088 DDC 338.7/4/0973 19
HD70.U5 M413 1988

Dyker, David A. The Soviet Union under Gorbachev . London , New York , c1987. 227 p. : ISBN 0-7099-4519-1 LC Card 87-15432 DDC 338.947 19
HC336.25 .S685 1987

Dykstra, Dennis P. The Global forest sector . Chichester [West Sussex] , New York , c1987. xiii, 706 p. : ISBN 0-471-91735-4 : LC Card 87-19700 DDC 338.1/749 19
HD9750.5 .G56 1987

Dyllick, Thomas. Gesellschaftliche Instabilität und Unternehmungsführung : Ansätze zu einer gesellschaftsbezogenen Managementlehre / Thomas Dyllick. Bern : P. Haupt, c1982. xiv, 394 p. : ill. ; 23 cm. (Veröffentlichungen der Hochschule St. Gallen für Wirtschafts- und Sozialwissenschaften. Schriftenreihe Betriebswirtschaft . Bd 11) Bibliography: p. 375-394. ISBN 3-258-03212-2 LC Card 83-115754
1. Organizational behavior. 2. Industrial management. I. Title. II. Series.
HD58.7 .D94 1982

Dymally, Mervyn M., 1926- Castro, Fidel, 1927- [Nada podrá detener la marcha de la historia. Selections.] Si no hay solución a la crisis, habrá explosiones sociales generalizadas de carácter revolucionario. La Habana , 1985. 97 p. ; LC Card 87-115245 DDC 338.9 19
HC125 .C37825 1985

Dymowski, Maciej. Socjologia pracy . Wrocław , 1978. 201 p. : LC Card 81-180007
HD6955 .S66 1978

Dynamic economic analysis /. Harris, Milton. New York , 1987. x, 137 p. : ISBN 0-19-504406-1 (alk. paper) LC Card 86-23925 DDC 339.5 19
HB145 .H37 1987

Dynamic effects of exchange rate changes in the Philippines in 1970-1980 /. Navarro, Susan S. [Quezon] [1986] 25 p. ; LC Card 87-120911 DDC 332.4/5609599 19
HG1265 .N38 1986

Dynamic fiscal policy /. Auerbach, Alan J. Cambridge [Cambridgeshire] , New York , 1987. xv, 196 p. : ISBN 0-521-30041-X LC Card 86-24447 DDC 339.5/2 19
HJ131 .A94 1987

The Dynamic organization series.
Corporate social responsibility . Santa Barbara, Calif. , c1986. xv, 229 p. ; ISBN 0-87436-469-8 (alk. paper) : LC Card 86-3416 DDC 658.4/08 19
HD60 .C693 1986 ***NYPL [JLE 86-3089]***

DYNAMIC PROGRAMMING - CONGRESSES.
Razrabotka i issledovanie algoritmov dinamicheskoĭ klassifikatsii protsessov . Vil'nius , 1979. 93 p. : LC Card 82-150323
HD38 .S715 vyp. 37 T57.83

The dynamics and limits of capitalist development in Sudanese agriculture /. Kursany, Ibrahim. Khartoum , 1982- v. ; LC Card 83-980112 DDC 338.1/09624 19
HD2123.5 .K87 1982 ***NYPL [JLM 86-825]***

The dynamics of a capitalist economy /. Goodwin, Richard M. (Richard Murphey), 1913- Boulder , 1987. p. cm. ISBN 0-8133-0482-2 : LC Card 86-33965 DDC 330.12/2 19
HB501 .G622 1987

The dynamics of America's housing /. Hughes, James W. New Brunswick, N.J. , c1987. xiv, 224 p. ; ISBN 0-88285-122-5 : LC Card 87-4515 DDC 363.5/0973 19
HD7293 .H826 1987

The dynamics of birth spacing and marital fertility in Kenya /. Mosley, W. Henry (Wiley Henry), 1933- [Nairobi? , 1981] 63 leaves : LC Card 85-980189
HB1072.5.A3 M66 1981

The dynamics of inflation in Iran, 1960-1977 /. Ikani, Azizollah. Tilburg, Netherlands , 1987. xii, 395 p. ; ISBN 90-361-9761-9 (pbk.) : LC Card 87-132510 DDC 332.4/1/0955 19
HG1220.2 .I36 1987

Dynamics of MacIntosh Excel /. Adler, John R. Homewood, Ill. , c1987. xii, 164 p. : ISBN 0-87094-907-1 (pbk.) LC Card 86-72565 DDC 005.36/9 19
HF5548.4.E93 A35 1987

The dynamics of productive relationships . Robertson, A. F. Cambridge [Cambridgeshire] , New York , 1987. xix, 321 p. : ISBN 0-521-32834-9 LC Card 86-11801 DDC 333.33/5 19
HD1478.A35 R63 1987 ***NYPL [JLE 87-1299]***

The dynamics of taking charge /. Gabarro, John J. Boston, Mass. , c1987. x, 204 p. : ISBN 0-87584-137-6 (jkt.) LC Card 86-25624 DDC 658.4 19
HD38 .G225 1987

The dynamics of working-class politics . Savage, Michael. Cambridge [Cambridgeshire] , New York , 1987. xii, 280 p. : LC Card 87-14636 DDC 322/.2/0941 19
HD8397.P74 S28 1987

Dynamika národohospodářských struktur a mezinárodních ekonomických vztahů v podmínkách SEI /. Amort, Jiří. Praha , 1986. 211 p. ; LC Card 86-206744
HC244 .A626 1986

Dynamique de l'emploi dans un système sahélien, le Niger : rapport / présenté au Gouvernement de la République du Niger.1ère éd. Addis Abéba : Bureau international du travail, Programme des emplois et des compétences techniques pour l'Afrique, 1980. lxxii, 301 p. ; 24 cm. Includes bibliographical references. ISBN 92-2-202351-X : LC Card 82-980599
1. Labor supply - Niger. 2. Niger - Economic conditions - 1970-. 3. Niger - Economic policy. I. Niger. II. International Labour Office. III. Jobs and Skills Programme for Africa.
HD5846.7.A6 D95 1980

La dynamique du capitalisme /. Braudel, Fernand. Paris , c1985. 120 p. ; ISBN 2-7003-0501-9 : LC Card 86-130442
HC51 .B675 1985

Dynamique paysanne et développement rural au Congo /. N'Kaloulou, Bernard, 1952- Paris , c1984. 260 p. : ISBN 2-85802-416-X LC Card 84-246506 DDC 305.5/63 19
HD1006 .N57 1984 ***NYPL [JLD 87-304]***

Dynamische Investitionsplanung für den Erdgasmarkt . Fahrion, Roland. Gräfelfing/München , c1984. iv, 308 p. : ISBN 3-87806-075-0 LC Card 85-111076
HD9581.G43 B34 1984

Dynamische Preisbildungsprozesse in Monopol /. Thomée, Friedrich, 1920- Wiesbaden , c1983. 247 p. : ISBN 3-409-13035-7 : LC Card 84-116637
HB221 .T465 1983

Dynamische Wirtschaftstheorie, 0930-2174 . (Bd. 1) Franke, Reiner. Production prices and dynamical processes of the gravitation of market prices /. Frankfurt am Main , New York , c1987. 231 p. : ISBN 3-8204-9435-9 (pbk.) LC Card 87-170397 DDC 338/.01 19
HB171.S7253 F73 1987

Dynamiska processer på arbejdsmarkedet /. Pedersen, Peder J. Aarhus [Copenhagen] [1982] 33 p. : LC Card 84-125613
HD5701.6 .P43 1982

The dynamos . Kingstone, Brett. New York , c1987. xx, 256 p. : ISBN 0-471-85827-7 LC Card 87-1754 DDC 338/.04/0922 B 19
HC102.5.A2 K56 1987

Dystsyplina pratsi /. Danchenko, M. I. (Mykola Ivanovych) Kyïv , 1983. 110 p. ; LC Card 83-215106
HF5549.5.L3 D34 1983

Dyzet vjet Shqipëri socialiste. 40 vjet Shqipëri socialiste . Tiranë , 1984. 166 p. : LC Card 85-195974
HA1620.5 .A616 1984

Dzarasov, S. S. (Soltan Safarbievich)
Ėkonomicheskie problemy razvitiia stran sotsialisticheskoĭ orientatsii /. Moskva , 1986. 239 p. ; LC Card 86-221922
HC59.7 .E355 1986

Dzhunusov, M. (Maskhud) Nekotorye problemy internatsional'nogo vospitaniia v mnogonatsional'nom trudovom kollektive /. Moskva , 1985. 135 p. ; LC Card 86-233779
HD8526.5 .N45 1985

Dzhurelov, Ivan. Godini na vŭzkhod . IAmbol , 1986. 87 p., [40] p. of plates : LC Card 87-103737
HC403.Z7 I64 1986

Dzięcielska-Machnikowska, Stefania. Praca zawodowa a życie rodzinne kobiet /. [Łódź] , 1979. 120 p. ; LC Card 81-109965
HD6054.2.P72 L636 1979

Dziesięć wieków pieniądza polskiego 980-1980 /. Cywiński, Henryk. Warszawa , 1982. 243 p., [24] p. of plates : ISBN 83-205-3413-5 LC Card 83-119732
HG1087 .C98 1982

E. A. P. see **European Labor Party.**

"E & M," economia e management. Protagonisti. Turani, Giuseppe. Briganti e gentiluomini della finanza italiana /. [Milano] , c1987. 394 p. ; ISBN 88-20-00657-X : LC Card 87-168620
HG186.I8 T86 1987

"E & M," economia e management. Trend. Turani, Giuseppe. 1985-1995, il secondo miracolo economico italiano . Milano , c1986. 147 p. : ISBN 88-20-00586-7 : LC Card 86-202136
HC305 .T85 1986

E. & T. Fairbanks & Co. Fairbanks' scales, the world's standard . Chicago , 1893. 20 p. : LC Card 85-666379
HD9706.2.U54 E22x 1893

E. & T. FAIRBANKS & CO.
Fairbanks' scales, the world's standard . Chicago , 1893. 20 p. : LC Card 85-666379
HD9706.2.U54 E22x 1893

E. C. A. see **United Nations. Economic Commission for Africa.**

E.C.D.C. handbook. ECDC handbook . [New Delhi] , 1983. vi, 679 p. ; LC Card 83-903543 DDC 337.1/1724 19
HC59.7 .E23 1983 ***NYPL [JLF 86-1755]***

E. C. L. A. see **United Nations. Economic Commission for Latin America.**

E. C. M. R. A. see **European Chemical Marketing Research Association.**

E. E. C. see **European Economic Community.**

E. E. G. see **European Economic Community.**

E. F. T. A. see **European Free Trade Association.**

E.G. und Arbeiterrechte. Dötsch, Jochen. EG und Arbeiterrechte . Berlin , 1981. 143 p. ; LC Card 81-145834 DDC 331.11/094 19
HD8380.5 .D67 1981 ***NYPL [JLD 86-2739]***

E-GX.
Kautsky, Karl, 1854-1938. [Agrarfrage. English.] The agrarian question /. London , Atlantic Highlands, N.J. , 1988- p. cm. ISBN 1-85305-024-5 (v. 2) LC Card 87-20593 DDC 338.1 19
HD1306.G3 K315 1988

E. L. C. see **Environment Liaison Centre.**

E. M. C. T. see **European Conference of Ministers of Transport.**

E. N. I. see **Ente nazionale idrocarburi.**

E. S. C. A. P. see **United Nations. Economic and Social Commission for Asia and the Pacific.**

E. S. O. M. A. R. see **Esomar.**

E. T. U. C. see **European Trade Union Confederation.**

E. W. G. see **European Economic Community.**

Eades, J. S. (Jeremy Seymour), 1945- ASA Conference, Migrants, Workers, and the Social Order (1986 : University of Kent) Migrants, workers, and the social order /. London , New York , 1987. p. cm. ISBN 0-422-61680-X (pbk.) LC Card 87-10253
HD5856.D44 A72 1986

The EAP solution : current trends & future issues / Jerry Spicer, editor. Center City, MN : Hazelden, 1987. 219 p. : ill. ; 24 cm. Includes bibliographies. ISBN 0-89486-405-X (pbk.) LC Card 86-82533 DDC 658.3/82 19
1. Employee assistance programs. I. Spicer, Jerry.
HF5549.5.E42 E367 1987

EAPs and the information revolution : the dark side of megatrends / Keith McClellan and Richard E. Miller, editors. New York : Haworth Press, c1987. 106 p. ; 23 cm. "Has also been published as Employee assistance quarterly, volume 2, number 2, winter 1986"--Copr. p. Includes bibliographies. ISBN 0-86656-606-6 LC Card 86-33519 DDC 331.25 19
1. Employee assistance programs - United States. 2. Automation - Social aspects - United States. 3. Computers - Social aspects - United States. 4. Quality of work life - United States. I. McClellan, Keith. II. Miller, Richard Edgar, 1947-.
HF5549.5.E42 E37 1987

Earl, Peter E.
Lifestyle economics : consumer behaviour in a turbulent world / Peter Earl. Brighton, Sussex : Wheatsheaf Books, 1986. xiii, 314 p. : ill. ; 23 cm. Includes index. Bibliography: p. 287-305. ISBN 0-7450-0083-5
1. Consumers. 2. Life style. I. Title.
NYPL [JLD 86-3424]

Psychological economics . Boston , c1987. p. cm. ISBN 0-89838-234-3 LC Card 87-3050 DDC 330/.01/9 19
HB74.P8 P697 1987

Earle, Gary. How to sell apartment buildings : the big money in real estate / Gary Earle. [Chicago] : Longman Financial Services Publishing, [1987], c1988. xiv, 183 p. : ill. ; 24 cm. Includes index. ISBN 0-88462-716-0 LC Card 87-13964 DDC 333.33/8 19
1. Apartment houses. 2. Real estate business. I. Title.
HD1394 .E24 1988

The early birds . Mahoney, Lawrence. Miami, FL , 1987. xii, 112 p. : ISBN 0-940495-07-4 (pbk.) LC Card 87-21974 DDC 387.7/065/73 19
HE9803.P36 M35 1987

The early days of radio broadcasting /. Douglas, George H., 1934- Jefferson, N.C. , c1987. viii, 248 p. : ISBN 0-89950-285-7 (lib. bdg. : alk. paper) : LC Card 86-43090 DDC 384.54/0973 19
HE8698 .D68 1987

Early results of seat belt legislation in the United States of America /. Campbell, Bob J. Chapel Hill, N.C. [1986] 25 p. : LC Card 86-622836 DDC 363.1/2572/0973 19
HE5614.2 .C35 1986

EARLY RETIREMENT - BELGIUM.
Casey, Bernard. Early retirement schemes with a replacement condition . Berlin [1985] 44 p. ; LC Card 86-205942 DDC 331.25/2 19
HD7110.B4 C37 1985

EARLY RETIREMENT - FRANCE.
Casey, Bernard. Early retirement schemes with a replacement condition . Berlin [1985] 44 p. ; LC Card 86-205942 DDC 331.25/2 19
HD7110.B4 C37 1985

EARLY RETIREMENT - GERMANY (WEST)
Casey, Bernard. Early retirement schemes with a replacement condition . Berlin [1985] 44 p. ; LC Card 86-205942 DDC 331.25/2 19
HD7110.B4 C37 1985

EARLY RETIREMENT - GREAT BRITAIN.
Casey, Bernard. Early retirement schemes with a replacement condition . Berlin [1985] 44 p. ; LC Card 86-205942 DDC 331.25/2 19
HD7110.B4 C37 1985

Early retirement schemes with a replacement condition . Casey, Bernard. Berlin [1985] 44 p. ; LC Card 86-205942 DDC 331.25/2 19
HD7110.B4 C37 1985

Early warning system report.
Belg (small) crop season synoptic report. Addis Abeba, Ethiopia , 1985. 23 leaves : LC Card 86-980254 DDC 338.1/9/63 19
HD9017.E82 B44 1985

Earning megabucks the video way. Parrish, Vernon. Great American video retailing . Arlington, Va. [1983?] viii, 448 p. : ISBN 0-9615774-0-1 LC Card 85-90437 DDC 621.388/332/0688 19
HD9697.V543 U544 1983

Earnings sharing options for the social security system. [Washington, D.C.?] : Congress of the U. S., Congressional Budget Office, [1986] xxv, 137 p. : ill. ; 26 cm. (CBO study) Shipping list no.: 86-202-P. "January 1986"--Cover. Item 100-C HD 7123 Includes bibliographical referecnes. LC Card 86-601147 DDC 368.4/3015/0973 19
1. Social security beneficiaries - United States. 2. Retirement income - United States. I. Series.
HD7125 .E227 1986 ***NYPL [JLF 86-1058]***

Earnings surprise report, February 1987. New York, N.Y. (90 Broad St., New York 10004) : Abel/Noser Corp., c1987. 167 p. ; 28 cm. Chiefly tables. LC Card 87-401689 DDC 332.63/222/0973 19
1. Stocks - Prices - United States - Statistics. I. Abel/Noser Corp.
HG4915 .E275 1987

EARTHENWARE. see **POTTERY.**

Earthquake insurance : problems and options / printed at the direction of Hon. John C. Danforth, Chairman, for the use of the Committee on Commerce, Science, and Transportation, United States Senate. Washington : U. S. G.P.O., 1987. ix, 61 p. : ill., maps ; 24 cm. (S. prt. . 99-220) Cover title. At head of title: 99th Congress, 2d session. Committee print. Distributed to some depository libraries in microfiche. Shipping list no.: 87-199-P. "December 1986." Includes bibliographical references. Item 1041-A, 1041-B (microfiche) LC Card 87-601349 DDC 368.1/22 19
1. Insurance, Earthquake - United States. 2. Earthquakes - Economic aspects - United States. I. United States. Congress. Senate. Committee on Commerce, Science, and Transportation. II. Series.
HG9981 .E17 1987

EARTHQUAKE PREDICTION.
Grases G., José. Pérdidas como consecuencia de terremotos . Caracas , 1986. 71 p. : ISBN 980-265-358-6 LC Card 87-403100 DDC 338.4/33633495 19
HC79.D45 G7 1986

EARTHQUAKES - CALIFORNIA.
California earthquake zoning and probable maximum loss evaluation program . Los Angeles, Calif. (600 S. Commonwealth Ave., Los Angeles 90005) [1986] 44, 15 p. : LC Card 86-623193 DDC 368.1/22/09794 19
HG9981.35.C2 C35 1986

EARTHQUAKES - ECONOMIC ASPECTS.
Grases G., José. Pérdidas como consecuencia de terremotos . Caracas , 1986. 71 p. : ISBN 980-265-358-6 LC Card 87-403100 DDC 338.4/33633495 19
HC79.D45 G7 1986

EARTHQUAKES - ECONOMIC ASPECTS - EL SALVADOR - SAN SALVADOR.
Lungo, Mario. El terremoto de octubre de 1986 en San Salvador y la situación habitacional de los sectores populares /. Ciudad Universitaria Rodrigo Facio [Costa Rica] , 1987. 26 leaves ; LC Card 87-125001 DDC 363.3/495 19
HD7287.96.S22 S265 1987

EARTHQUAKES - ECONOMIC ASPECTS - ITALY, SOUTHERN.
Acocella, Giovanni, 1932- Di là dalle rovine . Napoli , c1982. 172, [4] p. ; ISBN 88-7042-185-6 : LC Card 82-181323 DDC 363.3/495 19
HC307.S69 A36 1982 ***NYPL [JLD 86-485]***

EARTHQUAKES - ECONOMIC ASPECTS - MEXICO - MEXICO CITY METROPOLITAN AREA.
El Terremoto del 19 de septiembre y los trabajadores mexicanos. [Mexico City, Mexico?] [1985] 114 p. ; LC Card 86-144990
HC138.M4 T47 1985 ***NYPL [JLC 87-130]***

EARTHQUAKES - ECONOMIC ASPECTS - MEXICO - MEXICO CITY REGION.
Aún tiembla . México , c1986. 332 p., [8] p. of plates : ISBN 968-419-620-2 LC Card 87-403523 DDC 363.3/495/097253 19
HC138.M43 A95 1986

Esto pasó en México /. México, D.F. [1985] 126 p. : ISBN 968-415-098-9 LC Card 87-403762 DDC 363.3/495/097253 19
HC138.M4 E84 1985

EARTHQUAKES - ECONOMIC ASPECTS - UNITED STATES.
Earthquake insurance . Washington , 1987. ix, 61 p. : LC Card 87-601349 DDC 368.1/22 19
HG9981 .E17 1987

EARTHQUAKES - ITALY, SOUTHERN.
Mezzogiorno . [S.l. , 1980?] (København : Kunstakademiets trykkeri) 78 p. : LC Card 85-128057
HC307.S6 M49 1980

Terremoto e crisi urbana . Napoli , 1981. 207 p. ; ***NYPL [JLE 86-4532]***

EARTHQUAKES - MEXICO - MEXICO CITY REGION.
Mexican topics . [México, D.F.] [1986] 2 portfolios : LC Card 86-221843 DDC 972.08/3 19
HC135 .M52554 1986

EARTHQUAKES - PREDICTION. see **EARTHQUAKE PREDICTION.**

EARTHQUAKES - SOCIAL ASPECTS - MEXICO - MEXICO CITY REGION.
Aún tiembla . México , c1986. 332 p., [8] p. of plates : ISBN 968-419-620-2 LC Card 87-403523 DDC 363.3/495/097253 19
HC138.M43 A95 1986

Earthscan. Harrison, Paul. The greening of Africa . New York, N.Y., U. S.A. , 1987. 380

p. : ISBN 0-14-010192-6 (pbk.) : LC Card 87-404277 DDC 338.1/9/6 19
HD2117 .H37 1987

Earthwatch (Organization : Ireland) Closing the door on a nuclear future . [Harbour View, Bantry, Co. Cork , 1986] [7] leaves : LC Card 87-111333 DDC 333.79/27/0941 19
HD9698.G72 C56 1986

EARTHWATCH (ORGANIZATION : IRELAND)
Closing the door on a nuclear future . [Harbour View, Bantry, Co. Cork , 1986] [7] leaves : LC Card 87-111333 DDC 333.79/27/0941 19
HD9698.G72 C56 1986

Eason, Ken. Bjørn-Andersen, Niels. Managing computer impact . Norwood, N.J. , c1986. viii, 248 p. : ISBN 0-89391-358-8 LC Card 85-30754 DDC 658/.05 19
HD30.2 .B55 1986 *NYPL [JLE 86-2806]*

East African lessons on economic liberalization / by David Bevan ... [et al.] for the Trade Policy Research Centre, London. Aldershot, Hampshire, U.K. ; Brookfield, Vt., U. S.A. : Gower Pub. ; xxi, 72 p. : ill. ; 22 cm. (Thames essays, 0306-6991 . no. 48) Bibliography: p. [67] ISBN 0-566-05337-3 (pbk.) : LC Card 86-29602 DDC 338.967 19
1. Kenya - Economic policy. 2. Tanzania - Economic policy. 3. Kenya - Commercial policy. 4. Tanzania - Commercial policy. I. Bevan, David. II. Trade Policy Research Centre. III. Series.
HC865 .E27 1987

East African studies (London, England)
Kanogo, Tabitha M. Squatters and the roots of Mau Mau, 1905-63 /. London , Athens , 1987. xviii, 206 p. : ISBN 0-8214-0873-9 (U.S) LC Card 87-11201 DDC 307.3/36 19
HD1538.K4 K36 1987

EAST ASIA - COMMERCE - CHINA.
Lardy, Nicholas R. China's entry into the world economy . Lanham, MD , New York, N.Y. , c1987. xviii, 57 p. : ISBN 0-8191-6371-6 (alk. paper) : LC Card 87-10625 DDC 382/.0951 19
HF3820.5 .L37 1987

EAST ASIA - COMMERCE - UNITED STATES.
U. S. trade relations in the Pacific Rim . Washington , 1987. v, 57 p. ; LC Card 87-601361 DDC 382/.0973/09 19
HF3126.5 .U17 1987

Unfair foreign trade practices . Washington , 1986. v, 27 p. ; LC Card 86-603374 DDC 382/.0973/05 19
HF3126.5 .U53 1986

EAST ASIA - ECONOMIC CONDITIONS.
Economic development in East and South-east Asia . Canberra , 1984. x, 237 p. : ISBN 0-644-02983-8 (pbk.) LC Card 86-673760
HC460.5 .E26x 1984

Hernádi, András. A távol-keleti kihívás . Budapest , 1985. 233 p. ; ISBN 963-221-545-1 : LC Card 86-186844
HC460.5 .H47 1985

King, Frank H. H. The Hongkong Bank in the period of imperialism and war, 1895-1918 . Cambridge [Cambridgeshire] , New York , 1988. p. cm. ISBN 0-521-32707-5 LC Card 87-6349 DDC 332.1/5/095125 s 332.1/5/095125 19
HG1571 .K56 vol. 2 HG3354.H65

EAST ASIA - ECONOMIC POLICY.
The Political economy of the new Asian industrialism /. Ithaca, N.Y. , 1987. 252 p. ; ISBN 0-8014-1948-4 (alk. paper) LC Card 86-29103 DDC 338.95 19
HC460.5 .P65 1987

EAST ASIA - ECONOMIC POLICY - CONGRESSES.
In search of an East Asian development model /. New Brunswick, N.J., USA , c1988. xi, 243 p. ; ISBN 0-88738-686-5 (pbk.) LC Card 87-19061 DDC 338.95 19
HC460.5 .I5 1988

EAST ASIA - FOREIGN ECONOMIC RELATIONS - HUNGARY.
Hernádi, András. A távol-keleti kihívás . Budapest , 1985. 233 p. ; ISBN 963-221-545-1 : LC Card 86-186844
HC460.5 .H47 1985

EAST ASIA - INDUSTRIES.
The Pacific challenge in international business /. Ann Arbor, Mich. , 1987. viii, 342 p. ; ISBN 0-8357-1620-1 (alk. paper) LC Card 87-5008 DDC 338.09182/3 19
HC460.5 .P32 1987

EAST ASIA - MANUFACTURES.
The Pacific challenge in international business /. Ann Arbor, Mich. , 1987. viii, 342 p. ; ISBN 0-8357-1620-1 (alk. paper) LC Card 87-5008 DDC 338.09182/3 19
HC460.5 .P32 1987

EAST ASIA - SOCIAL LIFE AND CUSTOMS - CONGRESSES.
In search of an East Asian development model /. New Brunswick, N.J., USA , c1988. xi, 243 p. ; ISBN 0-88738-686-5 (pbk.) LC Card 87-19061 DDC 338.95 19
HC460.5 .I5 1988

EAST ASIANS - SOUTH AFRICA - MIGRATIONS - STATISTICS.
Cilliers, S. P. Patterns of migration and settlement in rural South Africa /. [Stellenbosch] , 1986. 19, 13 leaves, 5 folded leaves of plates : ISBN 0-908422-81-4 (pbk.) : LC Card 87-126315 DDC 304.8/0968 19
HB2123.4.A3 C56 1986

East-Central State, Nigeria.
Government white paper on the report of the Administrative Board of Inquiry into the Nigeria Construction and Furniture Company Limited / East-Central State of Nigeria. [Enugu, Nigeria] : The State, [1976] 19 p. ; 25 cm. Cover title. LC Card 86-205140
1. Nigeria Construction and Furniture Company. 2. Government business enterprises - Nigeria - Corrupt practices. I. East-Central State (Nigeria). Administrative Board of Inquiry into the Nigeria Construction and Furniture Company Limited. II. Title.
HD9773.N54 N543 1976

East-Central State (Nigeria). Administrative Board of Inquiry into the Enugu Market Authority. Anambra State, Nigeria. Government white paper on the Report of the Administrative Board of Inquiry into the Enugu Market Authority /. Enugu , 1976. 25 p. ; LC Card 86-204970
HF5475.N52 E373 1976

East-Central State (Nigeria). Administrative Board of Inquiry into the Nigeria Construction and Furniture Company Limited. East-Central State, Nigeria. Government white paper on the report of the Administrative Board of Inquiry into the Nigeria Construction and Furniture Company Limited /. [Enugu, Nigeria] [1976] 19 p. ; LC Card 86-205140
HD9773.N54 N543 1976

East-Central State (Nigeria). Administrative Board of Inquiry on Ministry of Works. Anambra State, Nigeria. Government white paper on the report of the Administrative Board of Inquiry on Ministry of Works /. [Enugu, Nigeria] [1976?] 100 p. ; LC Card 86-205027 DDC 354.669/4 19
HD4365.5.Z8 E373 1976

EAST-CENTRAL STATE (NIGERIA). ENUGU MARKET AUTHORITY.
Anambra State, Nigeria. Government white paper on the Report of the Administrative Board of Inquiry into the Enugu Market Authority /. Enugu , 1976. 25 p. ; LC Card 86-204970
HF5475.N52 E373 1976

EAST-CENTRAL STATE (NIGERIA). MINISTRY OF WORKS AND HOUSING.
Anambra State, Nigeria. Government white paper on the report of the Administrative Board of Inquiry on Ministry of Works /. [Enugu, Nigeria] [1976?] 100 p. ; LC Card 86-205027 DDC 354.669/4 19
HD4365.5.Z8 E373 1976

East Europe. see **Europe, Eastern.**

East European area audience and opinion research.
The Political self-assessment of Bulgarian respondents in terms of a left-right continuum. [Munich?] [1986] 16 p. ; LC Card 87-142360 DDC 384.55/43 19
HE8697.A8 P67 1986

The East German economy / edited by Ian Jeffries and Manfred Melzer ; advisory editor, Eleonore Breuning ; translations [from the German] by Eleonore Breuning and Ian Jeffries. London ; New York : Croom Helm, c1987. 328 p. : ill. ; 23 cm. Bibliography: p. 314-322. Includes index. ISBN 0-7099-1469-5 LC Card 87-17163 DDC 338.9431 19
1. Germany, East - Economic policy. 2. Germany, East - Economic conditions. I. Jeffries, Ian. II. Melzer, Manfred.
HC290.78 .E23 1987

EAST GODAVĀRI (INDIA) - ECONOMIC CONDITIONS.
Subrahmanyam, S. Poverty, unemployment, and perspective of development /. Allahabad, India , 1987. xi, 311 p. : ISBN 81-85076-22-7 : LC Card 87-900803 DDC 330.954/84 19
HC440.P6 S9 1987

EAST INDIA COMPANY.
Mukhopadhyay, Subhas Chandra, 1938- The agrarian policy of the British in Bengal . Allahabad, India , 1987. xi, 195 p. ; ISBN 81-85076-11-1 : LC Card 87-900481 DDC 338.1/85414 19
HJ4392.I4 M85 1987

East India Company (Dutch) see **Nederlandsche Oost-Indische Compagnie.**

EAST INDIANS - FOREIGN COUNTRIES.
Dhawan, O. P. Non resident Indians . New Delhi , 1984. xvi, 428 p. ; LC Card 85-900577 DDC 346.54/07 345.4067 19
HG5732 .D43 1984 *NYPL [JLE 86-1363]*

Puri, Vijay Kumar. Nabhi's manual for Indian residents abroad, 1985 /. New Delhi , 1985. xv, 352 p., [1] leaf of plate : LC Card 86-901951 DDC 346.54/07 345.4067 19
HG5732 .P83 1985

EAST INDIANS - MAURITIUS.
Ly-Tio-Fane Pineo, Huguette. Lured away . Moka, Mauritius , 1984. 261 p. :
NYPL [JLD 87-587]

EAST INDIANS - SOUTH AFRICA - DURBAN - ECONOMIC CONDITIONS - STATISTICS.
Martins, J. H. Income and expenditure patterns of urban Indian multiple households in Durban, 1985 /. Pretoria , 1986. xi, 126 p. : ISBN 0-908408-54-4 (pbk.) LC Card 86-208481 DDC 658.8/3968 s 339.4/1/09684 19
HC517.S7 S48 no. 130, pt. 1 HD7064.4.Z8D8

EAST INDIANS - SOUTH AFRICA - PIETERMARITZBURG - ECONOMIC CONDITIONS - STATISTICS.
Martins, J. H. Income and expenditure patterns of urban Indian households in Pietermaritzburg, 1985 /. Pretoria , 1986. xi, 126 p. : ISBN 0-908408-60-9 (pbk.) LC Card 87-140863 DDC 658.8/3968 s 339.4/1/0968475 19
HC517.S7 S48 no. 130, pt. 5 HD7064.4.Z8P54

East Kalimantan Transmigration Area Development Project. Kebschull, Dietrich. Transmigration in Indonesia . Hamburg , 1984. xxiv, 134 p. ; LC Card 86-223779 DDC 304.8/09598 19
HB2107 .K4 1984

East Prairie Metis Settlement . McCully, Al. [Edmonton, Alta.] [1982] iii, 99 p. :Bill. ; LC Card 82-202474 DDC 333.76/17/097123 19
HD319.A4 M52 1982

East, Roger. Government economic agencies of the world . Detroit , c1985. x, 546 p. ; ISBN 0-8103-2104-1 (Gale) LC Card 84-26861 DDC 351.82/025 19
HD87.25 .G68 1985
*NYPL [*R-Econ 86-6573]*

East Timor develops. [Dili] : Regional Government of East Timor Province, [1984] 45 p. : col. ill., col. maps ; 25 cm. LC Card 85-942048 DDC 338.9598/6 19
1. Timor Timur (Indonesia) - Economic conditions. 2. Timor Timur, Indonesia - Description and travel. I. Timor Timur, Indonesia.
HC448.T513 E2 1984

East-West Center's 25th Anniversary Conference on ASEAN and the Pacific Basin (1985 : Honolulu, Hawaii) The ASEAN success story . Honolulu, Hawaii , 1987. xviii, 253 p. : ISBN 0-8248-1107-0 (pbk.) : LC Card 86-29373 DDC 337.1/59 19
HC441 .A864 1987

East-West commercial relations series. Special study .
(1) Tariff, legal, and credit constraints on East-West commercial relations /. Ottawa , 1975. 101 p. ; LC Card 76-379543 DDC 382.1
K3823.A55 T3 ***NYPL [JLD 86-1752]***

East-West Resource Systems Institute.
China Energy Workshop I: Petroleum Processing (1985 : Honolulu, Hawaii) China's petroleum industry in the international context . Boulder [Colo.] , 1986. xvii, 166 p. : ISBN 0-86638-072-8 (pbk.) LC Card 86-50695 DDC 338.2/7282/0951 19
HD9576.C52 C524 1985
NYPL [JLD 86-3885]

Energy conservation in the Asian region . Tokyo, Japan [Honolulu, Hawaii] , 1986. vi, 173 p. : ISBN 92-833-2038-1 LC Card 87-122915 DDC 333.79/16/095 19
HD9502.A782 E53 1986

East-West technology transfer. The trade and economic aspects /. Wienert, Helgard. Paris , c1986. 453 p. : ISBN 92-64-12817-4
NYPL [JLE 87-1561]

East-West trade in technology . Rosenblatt, Samuel M. Washington, D.C. , c1980. viii, 64 p. ; LC Card 80-81923 DDC 382/.4560973 19
HF1414.5 .R67 ***NYPL [JLD 81-233]***

East-West trade in the medieval Mediterranean /. Ashtor, Eliyahu, 1914- London , 1986. [344] p. ; ISBN 0-86078-193-3 LC Card 87-134358 DDC 382/.094/056 19
HF3756.Z7 E92 1986

EAST-WEST TRADE (1945-)
Biró, Gerd. A kelet-nyugati kereskedelem fejlődési tendenciái a 80-as években /. Budapest , 1986. 152 p. ; ISBN 963-221-582-6 : LC Card 87-138649
HF4050 .B57 1986

Hartmann, Wolf-Dietrich, 1946- Internationaler Technologieaustausch--Kooperation oder Konfrontation? . Frankfurt/Main , 1984. 153 p. ; ISBN 3-88012-633-X LC Card 85-155132 DDC 338.9/26 19
HC79.T4 H36 1984

Knight, Misha G. How to do business with Russians . New York , 1987. xxiv, 311 p. : ISBN 0-89930-211-4 (lib. bdg. : alk. paper) LC Card 86-30396 DDC 658.8/48/0947 19
HF1558.5.U6 K56 1987

Laurent, Eric. La corde pour les pendre-- . Paris , c1985. 304 p. ; ISBN 2-213-01550-3 : LC Card 85-231994
HF1411 .L3645 1985

Losoncz, Miklós. Erők és érdekek . Budapest , 1986. 191 p. : ISBN 963-326-966-0 : LC Card 87-148142
HF1414.5 .L67 1986

Osteuropa im Blickpunkt . Linz [1985?] 168 p. ; LC Card 87-142952 DDC 382/.091713/01717 19
HF1411 .O687 1985

Palánkai, Tibor. Gazdasági hadviselés a kölcsönös függés korszakában /. [Budapest] , 1985. 88 p. ; ISBN 963-09-2633-4 : LC Card 86-128423
HF1413.5 .P35 1985

Rosenblatt, Samuel M. East-West trade in technology . Washington, D.C. , c1980. viii, 64 p. ; LC Card 80-81923 DDC 382/.4560973 19
HF1414.5 .R67 ***NYPL [JLD 81-233]***

Selling the rope to hang capitalism? . Washington , 1987. viii, 246 p. ; ISBN 0-08-034959-5 : LC Card 86-30401 DDC 382/.091713/01717 19
HF1412 .S45 1987

Sokoloff, Georges. L'économie de la détente . Paris , c1983. 255 p. : ISBN 2-7246-0483-0 : LC Card 84-117643
HF3646.5 .S65 1983

Sokoloff, Georges. [Economie de la détente. English.] The economy of détente . Leamington Spa ; New York : p. cm. ISBN 0-907582-62-1 : LC Card 86-32627 DDC 382/.0947 19
HF3646.5 .S6513 1987

Stern, Jonathan P. Soviet oil and gas exports to the West . Aldershot, Hants, England , Brookfield, Vt., USA , c1987. xi, 123 p. : ISBN 0-566-05124-9 : LC Card 86-32772 DDC 382/.4228/0947 19
HD9575.S652 S74 1987

Wienert, Helgard. East-West technology transfer. The trade and economic aspects /. Paris , c1986. 453 p. : ISBN 92-64-12817-4
NYPL [JLE 87-1561]

Wirtschaftskrieg oder Entspannung? . Bonn , c1984. 328 p. ; ISBN 3-87831-392-6 LC Card 84-251713
HF4050 .W57 1984

Wolff von Amerongen, Otto, 1918- Trendwende im Osthandel /. Bonn , 1977. 23 p. ; LC Card 85-141570
HF1411 .W583 1977

EAST-WEST TRADE (1945-) - CONGRESSES.
Varna Forum II "Tŭrgoviíata Iztok--Zapad" . [Sofia] , 1985. 248 p. ; LC Card 86-196109
HF1411 .V37 1985

Varna Forum (2nd : 1985 : Varna, Bulgaria) Varna Forum II . [Varna?] [s.n.] [1985] 166 p. ; LC Card 86-220415 DDC 382/.091713/01717 19
HF1410.5 .V37 1985

EAST-WEST TRADE (1945-) - STATISTICS.
Oechsler, Ronald G. Statistical abstract of East-West trade and finance . Washington, D.C. [1986]. vi, 43 p. : LC Card 86-601999 DDC 382/.091713/01717021 19
HF1411 .O3455 1986

Easter, K. William.
Irrigation investment, technology, and management strategies for development /. Boulder , 1986. xxvii, 270 p. : ISBN 0-8133-7177-5 (pbk. : alk. paper) : LC Card 85-31523 DDC 338.4/762752/091724 19
HD1741.D44 I77 1986 ***NYPL [JLD 87-766]***

Watershed resource management . Boulder , 1986. xx, 236 p. : ISBN 0-8133-7300-X (pbk. : alk. paper) : LC Card 86-18987 DDC 333.91/0095 19
HD1691 .W37 1986 ***NYPL [JLD 87-767]***

Easter, Walter Ray. The ABC's of marketing a successful business : how to quit your job with confidence by creating your own / Walter Ray Easter, Marilyn Kay Brent-Easter. [United States] : W.R. Easter, c1986. 118 p. : ill. ; 22 cm. LC Card 86-91127 DDC 658.8 19
1. Marketing. 2. New business enterprises. I. Brent-Easter, Marilyn Kay. II. Title.
HF5415.122 .E27 1986

Easterlin, Richard A., 1926- Birth and fortune : the impact of numbers on personal welfare / Richard A. Easterlin.2nd ed. Chicago : University of Chicago Press, 1987. xii, 228 p. : ill. ; 22 cm. Bibliography: p. 203-219. Includes index. ISBN 0-226-18032-8 (pbk.) : LC Card 86-30724 DDC 304.6/0973 19
1. Fertility, Human - United States. 2. United States - Population. 3. United States - Economic conditions - 1945-. 4. United States - Social conditions - 1945-. I. Title.
HB3505 .E247 1987

Eastern African studies (London, England)
Throup, David. Economic & social origins of Mau Mau 1945-53 /. London , Athens , c1988. xvi, 304 p. : ISBN 0-8214-0883-6 LC Card 87-12387 DDC 307.3/36 19
HD2126.5 .T48 1988

Eastern Empire. see **Byzantine Empire.**

Eastern Province (Zambia). Provincial Planning Unit. Interim Planning Group. Lupande Development Workshop (1983 : Nyamaluma Wildlife Conservation Camp) Proceedings of the Lupande Development Workshop . Chipata, Zambia , 1984. x, 121 p. : LC Card 84-980605 DDC 333.73/17/096894 19
HD993.Z8 L835 1983 ***NYPL [JLG 87-67]***

Eastern Region settlement strategy, 2011.
Eastern Regional Development Organisation (Ireland) Dublin [1985] viii, 21 p. : LC Card 87-672678
HB3589 .E27x 1985a

Eastern Region settlement strategy, 2011.
Eastern Regional Development Organisation (Ireland) Dublin [1985] xviii, 269 p. : LC Card 87-672656
HB3589 .E27x 1985

Eastern Regional Development Organisation (Ireland)
Eastern Region settlement strategy, 2011. Summary report. Dublin : Eastern Regional Development Organisation, [1985] viii, 21 p. : ill., maps ; 29 cm. "March 1985." LC Card 87-672678
1. Ireland - Population policy. 2. Dublin (County) - Population. 3. Kildare (County) - Population. 4. Meath - Population. 5. Wicklow (County) - Population. I. Title.
HB3589 .E27x 1985a

Eastern Region settlement strategy, 2011. Main report. Dublin : Eastern Regional Development Organisation, [1985] xviii, 269 p. : ill., maps ; 29 cm. "March 1985." LC Card 87-672656
1. Ireland - Population policy. 2. Dublin (County) - Population. 3. Kildare (County) - Population. 4. Meath - Population. 5. Wicklow (County) - Population. I. Title.
HB3589 .E27x 1985

Eastman, Clyde, 1936- Community grazing : practice and potential in New Mexico / Clyde Eastman and James R. Gray.1st ed. Albuquerque : University of New Mexico, c1987. xiii, 176 p. : maps ; 24 cm. Bibliography: p. 161-167. Includes index. ISBN 0-8263-0936-4 LC Card 86-25058 DDC 333.74/09789 19
1. Grazing districts - New Mexico. I. Gray, James R. II. Title.
HD243.N74 E18 1987

Eastman, Jorge Mario.
Hacia un populismo petrolero? y otros temas / Jorge Mario Eastman ; prólogo, Alfonso López Michelsen. 1a ed. Bogotá, Colombia : Fundación Publicaciones "Consigna", 1986. viii, 145 p., [8] p. of plates : ill. ; 21 cm. (Colección Fundación Publicaciones Consigna) Chiefly author's articles which appeared in the Revista Consigna between June 1976-July 1986. Errata slip inserted. LC Card 86-227075
1. Petroleum industry and trade - Government policy - Colombia. 2. Colombia - Economic conditions - 1970-. 3. Latin America - Economic conditions - 1945-. I. Title.
HD9574.C52 E18 1986

López, Alejandro, 1876-1940. [Selections. 1983.] Obras selectas /. Bogotá, D.E. , 1983. xiii, 458 p. ; LC Card 86-233252
HC197 .L6172 1983

EASTON REGION (PA.) - HISTORY - 19TH CENTURY.
Metz, Lance E. Sherman's guide to Hugh Moore Park /. Easton, PA , 1988. p. cm. ISBN 0-930973-07-0 (pbk.) : LC Card 87-25622 DDC 338.09748/22 19
HE395 .P43 1988

EASTON REGION (PA.) - INDUSTRIES - HISTORY - 19TH CENTURY.
Metz, Lance E. Sherman's guide to Hugh Moore Park /. Easton, PA , 1988. p. cm. ISBN 0-930973-07-0 (pbk.) : LC Card 87-25622 DDC 338.09748/22 19
HE395 .P43 1988

Easton, Thomas A. Private means--public ends . New York , 1987. xiii, 187 p. ; ISBN 0-275-92429-7 (alk. paper) : LC Card 86-25251 DDC 361.6/1/0973 19
HN65 .P69 1987 ***NYPL [JLE 87-1390]***

Eaton, Buford Curtis, 1943- Microeconomics / B. Curtis Eaton, Diane F. Eaton. New York, N.Y. : W.H. Freeman, c1988. xv, 471 p. : ill. (some col.) ; 26 cm. Includes bibliographies and index. ISBN 0-7167-1818-9 LC Card 87-15034 DDC 338.5 19
1. Microeconomics. I. Eaton, Diane F. II. Title.
HB172 .E23 1988

Eaton, Diane F. Eaton, Buford Curtis, 1943- Microeconomics /. New York, N.Y. , c1988. xv, 471 p. : ISBN 0-7167-1818-9 LC Card 87-15034 DDC 338.5 19
HB172 .E23 1988

Eaton, Jack. The trade union directory : a guide to all TUC unions / Jack Eaton and Colin Gill. London : Pluto Press, 1981. xii, 323 p. ; 20 cm. (Pluto Press workers' handbooks) Trade union studies Includes bibliographies and index. ISBN 0-86104-350-2 (pbk.) LC Card 86-673635
1. Trades Union Congress - Directories. 2. Trade-unions - Great Britain - Directories. I. Gill, Colin. II. Title. III. Series.
HD6663 .E27x 1981

Eatwell, John. The New Palgrave . New York , c1987. p. cm. ISBN 0-935859-10-1 (set) : LC Card 87-1946 DDC 330/.03/21 19
HB61 .N49 1987

Ebanks, G. E. Mortality, fertility, and family planning : Dominica and St. Lucia / G. Edward Ebanks. Santiago, Chile : Centro Latinoamericano de Demografia, [1985] 123 p. ; 25 cm. (Series A . no. 171) Bibliography: p. 119-123. "Canadian International Development Agency, Centro Latinoamericano de Demografia"--Cover. "LC/DEM/G.35"--Verso t.p. LC Card 87-131697 DDC 304.6/2/09729841 19
1. Mortality - Dominica. 2. Mortality - Saint Lucia. 3. Dominica - Statistics, Vital. 4. Saint Lucia - Statistics, Vital. 5. Fertility, Human - Dominica. 6. Fertility, Human - Saint Lucia. 7. Birth control - Dominica. 8. Birth control - Saint Lucia. I. CELADE (Organization). II. Canadian International Development Agency. III. Series: Serie A (CELADE (Organization)) , no. 171. IV. Title.
HB1376.D65 E32 1985

Ebel, Friedhelm.
Landwirtschaft am Niederrhein : regionale und einzelbetriebliche Entwicklungsmöglichkeiten / [Bearbeitung, Referat 213 "Buchführung und Statistik" ; Referatsleiter, F. Ebel ; Mitarbeit, F. Wunram, H.J. Schurz]. Bonn : Abt. Betriebsführung, Gruppe Betriebswirtschaft und Wirtschaftsberatung, 1976. 223 p. : ill. ; 22 cm. (Schriften der Landwirtschaftskammer Rheinland . Heft 33) Includes bibliographical references. LC Card 87-408419
1. Agriculture - Economic aspects - Germany (West) - Rhineland. 2. Regional planning - Germany (West) - Rhineland. I. Wunram, Friedrich. II. Schurz, H. J. III. Title. IV. Series.
HD1407 .L3 Heft 33 HD1960.R48

Was sagt mir der Buchführungsabschluss? / [Autor, Friedhelm Ebel]. Bonn : Auswertungs- und Informationsdienst für Ernährung, Landwirtschaft und Forsten, 1980. 36 p. : ill. ; 30 cm. (AID . 33) LC Card 84-145622
1. Agriculture - Germany (West) - Accounting. I. Series: AID (Series) , 33. II. Title.
HF5686.A36 E24 1980

Ebel, Theo, 1942- Held, Karl, 1944- Krieg und Frieden . Frankfurt am Main , c1983. 324 p. ; ISBN 3-518-11149-3 : LC Card 83-228517
HC79.D4 H45 1983

Eberhard, Rudolf, 1914- Stationen . Darmstadt , 1984. ix, 228 p., [1] leaf of plates : ISBN 3-534-02410-9 LC Card 85-138779
HC286.5 .S825 1984

EBERHARD, RUDOLF, 1914-
Stationen . Darmstadt , 1984. ix, 228 p., [1] leaf of plates : ISBN 3-534-02410-9 LC Card 85-138779
HC286.5 .S825 1984

Eberl, Immo. 150 Jahre Promotion an der Wirtschaftswissenschaftlichen Fakultät der Universität Tübingen . Stuttgart , c1984. xxxvi, 809 p. : ISBN 3-8062-0409-8 LC Card 85-140557
HB74.9.G3 A15 1984 ***NYPL [JFE 87-1673]***

Eberle, Eugen, 1908- Die schlaflosen Nächte des Eugen E. : Erinnerungen eines neuen schwäbischen Jacobiners / Eugen Eberle, Peter Grohmann.Originalausg. Stuttgart : Edition Cordeliers, 1982. 281 p. : ill. ; 21 cm. Includes index. ISBN 3-922836-06-2 LC Card 83-173587 DDC 305.5/62/0924 B 19
1. Eberle, Eugen, 1908-. 2. Labor and laboring classes - Germany - Biography. 3. Labor and laboring classes - Germany - History - 20th century. I. Grohmann, Peter, 1937-. II. Title.
HD8453.E2 A37 1982 ***NYPL [JFD 87-3745]***

EBERLE, EUGEN, 1908-
Eberle, Eugen, 1908- Die schlaflosen Nächte des Eugen E. . Stuttgart , 1982. 281 p. : ISBN 3-922836-06-2 LC Card 83-173587 DDC 305.5/62/0924 B 19
HD8453.E2 A37 1982 ***NYPL [JFD 87-3745]***

Ebers, Mark. Organisationskultur, ein neues Forschungsprogramm? / Mark Ebers. Wiesbaden : Gabler, c1985. 223 p. ; 24 cm. (Neue betriebswirtschaftliche Forschung . 33) Bibliography: p. [207]-223. ISBN 3-409-13105-1 LC Card 86-135588
1. Corporate culture. 2. Organizational change. I. Title. II. Series.
HD58.8 .E24 1985

Ebersole, Alva Vernon. Dos documentos de 1627 sobre la economía de España / monografía preparada por Alva V. Ebersole. Valencia : Albatros Hispanófila, [1986?] 49 p. ; 24 cm. (Colección Monografías. 7) Includes bibliographical references. ISBN 84-7274-144-3 LC Card 87-107711
1. Monetary policy - Spain - History - 17th century - Sources. 2. Price regulation - Spain - History - 17th century - Sources. I. Title.
HG1133 .E24 1986

Eberstadt, Nick, 1955- The poverty of communism / Nick Eberstadt. New Brunswick, N.J., U. S.A. : Transaction Books, c1987. p. cm. Bibliography: p. Includes index. ISBN 0-88738-188-X : LC Card 87-19097 DDC 362.5/09171/7 19
1. Poor - Communist countries. 2. Communist countries - Economic conditions. 3. Communist countries - Social conditions. I. Title.
HC710.P6 E24 1987

Eberstein, Hans Hermann. Schmidt-Tiedemann, K. J. Planung und Nutzung des technischen Fortschritts /. [Dortmund?] , 1976. 37 p. : LC Card 86-123518
HD30 .A7 Heft 173 T177.G4

Ebert, Kurt, 1954- Warenwirtschaftssysteme und Warenwirtschafts-Controlling / Kurt Ebert. Frankfurt am Main ; New York : P. Lang, c1986. xvi, 353 p. : ill. ; 21 cm. (Schriften zu Distribution und Handel, 0179-3608 . Bd. 1) Bibliography: p. 336-353. ISBN 3-8204-9673-4 LC Card 86-218178
1. Product management. 2. Marketing - Germany (West) - Management. I. Title. II. Series.
HF5415.15 .E24 1986

EBRI-ERF Policy Forum (1986 : Washington, D. C.) America in transition : benefits for the future : an EBRI-ERF Policy Forum. Washington, D.C. : Employee Benefit Research Institute, c1987. xix, 269 p. : ill. ; 23 cm. Papers and proceedings of the meeting held Oct. 15, 1986 in Washington, D.C. Bibliography: p. 22-24. Includes index. ISBN 0-86643-057-1 (hard) : LC Card 87-13421 DDC 331.25/5/0973 19
1. Employee fringe benefits - United States. 2. Economic security - United States. I. Employee Benefit Research Institute (Washington, D.C.). Education and Research Fund. II. Title.
HD4928.N62 U628 1987

An EBRI-ERF policy study.
Andrews, Emily S. The changing profile of pensions in America /. Washington, DC , c1985. xxvii, 234 p. ; ISBN 0-86643-038-5 (pbk.) LC Card 85-25296 DDC 332.6/7254 19
HD7105.45.U6 A53 1985
NYPL [JLE 87-62]

Measuring and funding corporate liabilities for retiree health benefits. Washington, D.C. , c1987. xxxviii, 226 p. : ISBN 0-86643-054-7 (pbk.) LC Card 87-24534 DDC 657/.75 19
HG9396 .M4 1987

ECA/UNIDO Basic Metals and Engineering Industries Development Programme Mission. Rapport de la Mission sur le programme de développement des industries métallurgiques de base et mécaniques en République du Sénégal. [S.l.] : Commission économique pour l'Afrique, Division mixte CEA/ONUDI de l'industrie, [1979] 41, 3 p. (2 fold.) ; 28 cm. Cover title. "Document de travail, 13 juin 1979." "M79-3321." Includes bibliographical references. LC Card 80-981173
1. Metal trade - Senegal. 2. Iron industry and trade - Senegal. 3. Senegal - Economic conditions. 4. Senegal - Economic policy. 5. Senegal - Industries. I. Title.
HD9506.S42 E33 1979

Ecchia, Stefano. La destinazione dell'utile nelle società per azioni : problemi e nuove vie di soluzione / Stefano Ecchia. Padova : CEDAM, 1985. 133 p. : ill. ; 24 cm. Bibliography: p. [131]-133. LC Card 86-214308
1. Corporate profits - Italy. 2. Dividends - Italy - Decision making. 3. Capital investments - Italy - Decision making. 4. Corporation reserves - Italy - Decision making. I. Title.
HG4028.P7 E23 1985

ECDC handbook : documents of the movement of nonaligned countries and the group of 77. [New Delhi] : Ministry of External Affairs, 1983. vi, 679 p. ; 29 cm. At head of title: Non-aligned Summit, New Delhi. LC Card 83-903543 DDC 337.1/1724 19
1. Developing countries - Economic conditions. 2. Developing countries - Foreign economic relations. I. India. Ministry of External Affairs. II. Title: E.C.D.C. handbook.
HC59.7 .E23 1983 ***NYPL [JLF 86-1755]***

Échange et projets (Association) Le Temps des initiatives /. Paris , c1983. 187 p. ; ISBN 2-226-01647-3 : LC Card 83-212781
HD3616.F83 T46 1983

Echavarría, Hernán. see **Echavarría Olózaga, Hernán.**

Echavarría Olózaga, Hernán. El hueco negro : cómo caímos en él, cómo podemos salir, cómo podemos volver a caer / [Hernán Echavarría Olózaga]. [S.l. : s.n., 1986] (Bogotá, Colombia : Editorial Andes) 244 p., [7] p. of plates : ill. ; 19 cm. Includes bibliographical references. LC Card 86-209093
1. Colombia - Economic conditions - 1970-. 2. Colombia - Economic policy. 3. Coffee trade - Colombia. 4. Debts, External - Colombia. I. Title.
HC197 .E34 1986

Echavarría Vélez, Luis Fernando. Síntesis de la economía colombiana, 1959-1974 /. Bogotá, D.E. , 1974. vii, 90 leaves, [6] leaves of plates : LC Card 87-403567 DDC 330.9861/0632 19
HC197 .S56 1974

Echechuri, Héctor. Diez años después de Estocolmo . Madrid [1983?] 285 p. : ISBN 84-85633-26-3 LC Card 84-122682 DDC 304.2 19
GF49 .D54 1983 ***NYPL [JLE 86-1307]***

Echegaray, Alfredo. Evolución y perspectivas de la cooperación financiera en América Latina / Alfredo Echegaray Simonet. Buenos Aires : Instituto para la Integración de América Latina, Banco Interamericano de Desarrollo, 1982. 147 p. ; 23 cm. Bibliography: p. [135]-140. LC Card 86-198731
1. Finance - Latin America. 2. Monetary policy - Latin America. 3. Latin America - Economic integration. I. Title.
HG185.L3 E25 1982

Echevarría Salvat, Oscar A., 1935- Deuda-- crisis cambiaria : causas y correctivos / Oscar A. Echevarría ; prólogo del Dr. Felipe Pazos. Caracas : Universidad Católica Andrés Bello, 1986. xx, 248 p. : ill. ; 23 cm. Includes bibliographical references. ISBN 980-265-224-5 LC Card 87-400245 DDC 336.3/4/0987 19
1. Balance of payments - Venezuela. 2. Debts, External - Venezuela. I. Title.
HG3883.V4 E28 1986

Echeverri Perico, Rafael. Seminario Taller sobre el XV Censo Nacional de Población y IV de Vivienda, 1985 (1986 : Girardot, Colombia) Seminario Taller sobre el XV Censo Nacional de Población y IV de Vivienda, 1985 /. Girardot [Colombia] , 1986. 327 p. : ISBN 958-608-038-2 LC Card 87-403863 DDC 304.6/0723 19
HA1011.5 1985b

Echter, Claus-Peter. Konzepte städtischer Wohnungspolitik : Ergebnisse einer Umfrage / Claus-Peter Echter, Werner Heinz. Berlin : Deutsches Institut für Urbanistik, 1985. 97 p. : ill. ; 30 cm. At head of title: Deutsches Institut für Urbanistik. Bibliography: p. 97. ISBN 3-88118-123-7 LC Card 86-145702
1. Public housing - Germany, West. 2. Housing policy - Germany, West. I. Heinz, Werner, Dr. phil., Dipl.-Ing. II. Deutsches Institut für Urbanistik. III. Title.
HD7288.78.G3 E265 1985

Echterhoff, Wilfried. Einfluss von Verkehrssicherheitsinformationen auf unfallbeteiligte Kraftfahrer / Wilfried Echterhoff. Köln : Bundesanstalt für Strassenwesen, Bereich Unfallforschung, [1983], c1981. 112 p. : ill. ; 21 cm. (Forschungsberichte der Bundesanstalt für Strassenwesen, Bereich Unfallforschung, 0173-7066 . 88) "Mai 1983." Bibliography: p. 88-93. LC Card 84-147580
1. Traffic accidents - Germany (West) - Cologne Region. 2. Automobile driver education - Germany (West) - Cologne Region. I. Title. II. Series.
HE5614.5.G3 E34 1983

Eck, Hélène. La Guerre des ondes . Paris , Lausanne , c1985. 382 p. : ISBN 2-601-00475-4 (Payot) ***NYPL [MWGK (France) 87-550]***

Eckert, Ross D. The price system and resource allocation. 10th ed. / Ross D. Eckert, Richard

H. Leftwich. Chicago : Dryden Press, c1988. xviii, 648 p. : ill. (some col.) ; 25 cm. (The Dryden Press series in economics) Authors' names reversed on previous ed. Includes bibliographies and indexes. ISBN 0-03-012533-2 LC Card 87-5068 DDC 338.5/2 19
1. Microeconomics. I. Leftwich, Richard H. II. Title. III. Series.
HB172 .L45 1988

Eckstein, Julius. Deutsche Industrie, deutsche Kultur /. Berlin , 1900-1902. xvi, 388 p. : LC Card 85-666344
HC283 .D48x 1900

Eckstein, Werner E. Kooperative Systembildung in der Transportwirtschaft : Innovationschancen mittelständischer Betriebe / Werner E. Eckstein. Karlsruhe : Loeper, c1985. vii, 263 p. : ill. ; 25 cm. (Karlsruher Beiträge zur Wirtschaftspolitik und Wirtschaftsforschung. [Heft 11]) Series no. from Deut. Bibl. Bibliography: p. 222-231. ISBN 3-88652-028-5 LC Card 86-135639
1. Freight and freightage - Germany (West) - Cost control. 2. Small business - Germany, West. I. Title. II. Series.
HE199.G3 E28 1985

Eckstein, Zvi. Cotton and wheat production in the Egyptian agriculture : an econometric estimation and interpretation / by Zvi Eckstein. [Tel Aviv] : David Horowitz Institute for the Research of Developing Countries, Tel Aviv University, [1984] 40 leaves : ill. ; 27 cm. (Paper / The David Horowitz Institute for Research in Developing Countries . no. 3/84) Working paper ; no. 6-84 Revision of thesis (Ph. D.)--University of Minnesota, 1981. "April, 1984." Bibliography: leaves 29-30. LC Card 84-186315 DDC 338.1/711/0962 19
1. Cotton trade - Egypt - Econometric models. 2. Wheat trade - Egypt - Econometric models. I. Series: Paper (Mekhon Horovits le-ḥeḳer aratsot mitpatḥot) , no. 84/3. II. Title.
HD9087.E42 E35 1984

Ecole nationale d'administration et de magistrature (Senegal) Sourang, Abdou. Le rôle du mouvement coopératif dans le développement du Sénégal . [Dakar] [1981] 44 leaves : LC Card 85-207626
HD3567.7.A4 S67 1981

Ecole nationale supérieure du pétrole et des moteurs (France). Centre d'études supérieures d'économie pétrolière. Guyot, F. Eléments de microéconomie /. Paris , 1985. 310 p. : ISBN 2-7108-0479-4 LC Card 86-210675
HB173 .G88 1985

Ecole pratique des hautes études (France) Perspectivas de la economía mundial y colombiana /. Bogotá, Colombia , 1986. 106 p. ; ISBN 958-616-044-0 LC Card 87-115573 DDC 330.9861/0632 19
HC197 .P35 1986

Ecological economics . Martínez Alier, Juan. [Ecologisme i l'economia. English.] Oxford [Oxfordshire] , New York, NY, USA , 1987. ix, 286 p. ; ISBN 0-631-15739-5 : LC Card 87-14512 DDC 333.7 19
HD85.S7 M363513 1987

ECOLOGY - AFRICA.
Lewis, Lawrence. African environments and resources /. Boston , 1987. p. cm. ISBN 0-04-916010-9 (alk. paper) LC Card 87-16751 DDC 333.7/096 19
HC800 .L48 1987

ECOLOGY - DEVELOPING COUNTRIES.
Garcia, Xavier, 1950- Supervivència 2000 . Barcelona , 1983. 267 p. ; ISBN 84-7306-196-9 LC Card 83-225437
HC59.72.E5 G37 1983 ***NYPL [JLD 86-2462]***

ECOLOGY, HUMAN. see **HUMAN ECOLOGY.**

ECOLOGY - NETHERLANDS.
Florizoone, Patrick, 1958- De groenen . [Deurne] , c1985. x, 194 p. : ISBN 90-6716-272-8 LC Card 86-148321
HC329.5.E5 F56 1985

ECOLOGY, SOCIAL. see **HUMAN ECOLOGY.**

ECOLOGY - SPAIN - CATALONIA.
Vilanova, Santiago, 1947- L'econacionalisme . Barcelona , 1981. 142 p. ; ISBN 84-7031-281-2 LC Card 81-212886
HC387.C25 V527 1981

Ecology wars . Arnold, Ron. Bellevue, Wash. , c1987. 182 p. ; ISBN 0-939571-00-5 LC Card 87-17 DDC 363.7/00973 19
HC110.E5 A77 1987

L'econacionalisme . Vilanova, Santiago, 1947- Barcelona , 1981. 142 p. ; ISBN 84-7031-281-2 LC Card 81-212886
HC387.C25 V527 1981

An econometric analysis of the world wheat market and simulation of alternative policies, 1960-80 /. Schiff, Maurice W. Washington, DC [1985] iv, 70 p. : LC Card 85-603033 DDC 382/.41 19
HD9049.W4 S37 1985

An econometric approach to forecasting demand for electricity in Tanzania to the year 2000 A.D. /. Joseph, G. [Dar es Salaam] [between 1978 and 1984] 42, [44] p. ; LC Card 84-980076 DDC 333.7/09678 333.79/3213/09678 19
HD107 .D36 no. 38a HD9685.T352

An Econometric model for Turkey, 1965-1984. Istanbul, Turkey : Türk Sanayicileri ve İş Adamları Derneği, [1986] x, 84 p. : ill. ; 30 cm. "15 January 1986." LC Card 87-142603 DDC 330.9561/038/0151 19
1. Turkey - Economic conditions - 1960- - Econometric models. I. Türk Sanayicileri ve İş Adamları Derneği.
HC492 .E28 1986

An econometric model integrating conservation measures in the residential demand for electricity /. Khazzoom, J. Daniel. Greenwich, Conn. , c1986. xx, 305 p. : ISBN 0-89232-606-9 : LC Card 86-7173 DDC 333.79/3216/0724 19
HD9685.A2 K54 1986 ***NYPL [JLE 86-4174]***

ECONOMETRIC MODELS.
Anderka, Siegfried. Computerunterstützte ökonometrische Modellerstellung in Lehre und Forschung . Idstein , 1985. 407 p. : ISBN 3-925196-11-0 LC Card 85-237458
HB141 .A56 1985

Büttler, Hans-Jürgen. Estimation of disequilibrium models /. Berlin , New York , c1986. vi, 114 p. : ISBN 0-387-16817-6 (U. S.) : LC Card 86-22073 DDC 339.5 19
HB145 .B88 1986 ***NYPL [JLM 72-289 v.279]***

Buscher, Herbert S. Modelle der neuen klassischen Makroökonomie . München , c1986. iv, 312 p. : ISBN 3-88259-386-5 LC Card 86-230281
HB141 .B87 1986

Ekonometria . Warszawa , 1978. 371 p. : LC Card 81-212730
HB139 .E386 1978

Gallant, A. Ronald, 1942- A unified theory of estimation and inference for nonlinear dynamic models /. Oxford [Oxfordshire] , New York, NY, USA. , 1988. p. cm. ISBN 0-631-15765-4 : LC Card 87-25602 DDC 330/.028 19
HB141 .G33 1988

The Practice of econometrics . Dordrecht , Boston , 1987. xii, 273 p. : ISBN 90-247-3502-5 LC Card 87-4054 DDC 330/.028 19
HB139 .P7 1987

Voprosy stranovogo makromodelirovaniia͡ /. Moskva , 1984. 177 p. : LC Card 86-144302
HB141 .V665 1984

ECONOMETRIC MODELS - COLLECTED WORKS.
Johansen, Leif. [Essays. Selections.] Collected works of Leif Johansen /. Amsterdam ; New York : 2 v. (xiii, 974 p.) ; ISBN 0-444-87833-5 (set) LC Card 87-6814 DDC 330.1 19
HB171 .J59725 1987

ECONOMETRIC MODELS - EUROPE, EASTERN - CONGRESSES.
Macromodels and forecasts of national economy . Warszawa , 1986. 284 p. : ISBN 83-01-06464-1 (pbk.) : LC Card 86-226942 DDC 338.947 19
HC244 .M227 1986

Econometric Society. Advances in economic theory . Cambridge [Cambridgeshire] , New York , 1982. x, 285 p. : ISBN 0-521-24443-9 LC Card 81-38500 DDC 330/.028 19
HB21 .A33 1982 ***NYPL [JLE 85-2041]***

Econometric Society monographs .
(no. 12) Advances in economic theory . Cambridge [Cambridgeshire] , New York , 1987. vii, 428 p. ; ISBN 0-521-34044-6 LC Card 87-889 DDC 330.1 19
HB21 .A329 1987

Econometric Society monographs in quantitative economics .
(no. 1) Advances in economic theory . Cambridge [Cambridgeshire] , New York , 1982. x, 285 p. : ISBN 0-521-24443-9 LC Card 81-38500 DDC 330/.028 19
HB21 .A33 1982 ***NYPL [JLE 85-2041]***

Econometrics . Wallace, T. Dudley. Reading, Mass. , c1988. xviii, 440 p. : ISBN 0-201-09896-2 : LC Card 87-14492 DDC 330/.028 19
HB139 .W32 1988

ECONOMETRICS - ADDRESSES, ESSAYS, LECTURES.
An Executive's guide to econometric forecasting . Flushing, N.Y. , c1983. 74 p. : ISBN 0-932126-10-3 (pbk.) LC Card 82-90726 DDC 330/.028 19
HB3730 .E978 1983 ***NYPL [JLF 86-1166]***

ECONOMETRICS - CONGRESSES.
Advances in economic theory . Cambridge [Cambridgeshire] , New York , 1987. vii, 428 p. ; ISBN 0-521-34044-6 LC Card 87-889 DDC 330.1 19
HB21 .A329 1987

ECONOMETRICS - DATA PROCESSING.
The IAS-System data base . Wien, Austria [1982] ii, 151, 3 p. : ***NYPL [JSG 86-170]***

ECONOMETRICS - HISTORY.
Epstein, Roy J. (Roy Jacob), 1954- A history of econometrics /. Amsterdam ; New York : x, 254 p. ; ISBN 0-444-70267-9 LC Card 87-15308 DDC 330/.028 19
HB139 .E67 1987

The econometrics of energy demand . Donnelly, William A. New York , 1987. xv, 309 p. : ISBN 0-275-92610-9 (alk. paper) : LC Card 86-25220 DDC 333.79/12 19
HD9502.A2 D67 1987

Econometrics of planning and efficiency / edited by Jati K. Sengupta, Gopal K. Kadekodi. Dordrecht ; Boston : Kluwer Academic Publishers, 1988. vi, 193 p., [2] p. of plates : ill., port. ; 25 cm. (Advanced studies in theoretical and applied econometrics . v. 11) Includes bibliographies. ISBN 90-247-3602-1 LC Card 87-21305 DDC 330/.028 19
1. Econometrics. 2. Economic policy. 3. Efficiency, Industrial. I. Sengupta, Jatikumar. II. Kadekodi, Gopal K. III. Series.
HB139 .E32 1988

Economía argentina, bases y puntos para su recuperación. Conesa, Eduardo R. Bases y puntos de partida para la recuperación de la economía argentina . Buenos Aires, Argentina , c1986. 178 p. : ISBN 950-53-7109-8 LC Card 87-400257 DDC 338.982 19
HC175 .C6145 1986

La Economía china de la revolución a las cuatro modernizaciones / prólogo de Miguel Boyer. Madrid : Banco Exterior de España, Servicio de Estudios Económicos, [1986?] 181 p. : ill. ; 24 cm. Prepared by a working group directed by Gonzalo Sáenz de Buruaga. Bibliography: p. 173-177. LC Card 86-229994
1. China - Economic conditions - 1949-. 2. China - Economic policy - 1949-. 3. Spain - Commerce - China. 4. China - Commerce - Spain. I. Sáenz de Buruaga, Gonzalo. II. Banco Exterior de España. Servicio de Estudios Económicos.
HC427.9 .E319 1986

Economia da alimentação e nutrição . Campino, Antonio Carlos Coelho. São Paulo , 1985. 238 p. : LC Card 86-129956 DDC 338.1/9/81 19
HD9014.B82 C35 1985 ***NYPL [JLD 86-4118]***

Economía de la actividad forestal /. Serrano Gálvez, Enrique. México , 1983. 139 p. : LC Card 86-200927
HD9764.M62 S47 1983

Economía de mercado y economía dirigida . Ballivián Calderón, René. La Paz , 1979. xxii, 608 p. : LC Card 83-167133
HB75 .B144 1979

La economía del banano en Centroamérica /. López, José Roberto. San José, Costa Rica , c1986. 236 p. : ISBN 997-7904-31-6 LC Card

87-404078 DDC 338.1/74772/09728 19
HD9259.B3 C4554 1986

A economia e o estado capitalista /. Viotti, Eduardo Baumgratz. Petrópolis , 1986. 96 p. ; LC Card 87-137699 DDC 338.9 19
HD85.P65 V56 1986

Economia e politica /. Pesante, Maria Luisa. Milano, Italy , c1986. 94 p. ; LC Card 86-196256
HB75 .P465 1986

Economia e sociedade do Rio Grande do Sul . Santos, Corcino Medeiros dos. São Paulo, SP, Brasil , 1984. xxi, 216 p. : ISBN 85-04-00203-9 : LC Card 85-199838
HF3409.R56 S25 1984

Economia e società della montagna parmense : Bedonia, 19 dicembre 1981 : atti del convegno. [Italy : s.n., 1984?] (Parma : Officina grafica artigiana) 115 p. ; 25 cm. At head of title: Provincia di Parma, Assessorati alla montagna e alla programmazione; Comunità montane, Val Taro e Val Ceno, Appenino Parma Est. LC Card 85-156635
1. Parma (Italy : Province) - Economic conditions - Congresses. 2. Rural development - Italy - Parma (Province) - Congresses. 3. Parma (Italy : Province) - Rural conditions - Congresses. 4. Mountains - Italy - Parma (Province) - Congresses.
HC307.P33 E27 1984

Economia e società in Lombardia dall'età delle riforme alla grande crisi .
(1) Colombo, Giuseppe, 1836-1921. Industria e politica nella storia d'Italia . [Milano] , Roma , c1985. 497 p. : ISBN 88-420-2555-0 : LC Card 85-180231 DDC 338.945 19
HC310.I53 C65 1985 ***NYPL [JLE 86-2517]***

(2) Bressan, E. (Edoardo) Povertà e assistenza in Lombardia nell'età napoleonica /. [Milano] , Bari , c1985. viii, 339 p. : ISBN 88-420-2653-0 : LC Card 86-162978
HC307.L8 B74 1985

Economía (Ediciones de Cultura Popular)
Dávila Flores, Alejandro, 1956- La crisis financiera en México /. [Mexico City, Mexico] , 1986. 228 p. : LC Card 87-401258 DDC 330.972/0834 19
HG185.M6 D33 1986

Huerta González, Arturo. Economía mexicana . [Mexico City, Mexico] , 1986. 246 p. : LC Card 87-404065 DDC 330.972/0834 19
HC135 .H84 1986

Economía (Ediciones El Caballito (Mexico City, Mexico))
Bortz, Jeff. El salario en México /. México, D.F. , 1986. 198 p. : ISBN 968-612-519-1 LC Card 87-404064 DDC 331.2/972 19
HD4981 .B677 1986

La economia en la Andalucia del descubrimiento /. Mercado, Thomas de, d. 1575. [Tratos y contratos de mercaderes. Selections.] Sevilla [1985?] 276 p. ; ISBN 84-7587-047-3 LC Card 86-151225
HF1003 .M525 1985

Economía (Fundación IESA) .
(no 2) Dauderstädt, Michael. Las relaciones hispano-portuguesas y la integración europea /. Madrid [1987?] 36 p. ; ISBN 84-398-8593-8 LC Card 87-161277
HF1570.15.P8 D38 1987

Economía (Fundación Investigaciones Económicas y Sociales Aplicadas) .
(no. 1) Costa Morata, Pedro. Centrales nucleares en España . Madrid [1987?] 51 p. : ISBN 84-398-8834-1 LC Card 87-165955
HD9698.S72 C62 1987

Economía (H. Blume Ediciones)
Azqueta Oyarzun, Diego. Teoría económica de la acumulación socialista . Madrid , 1983. 224 p. ; ISBN 84-7214-279-5 LC Card 84-140278 DDC 332/.0415/091717 19
HC710.S3 A97 1983 ***NYPL [JLD 86-1859]***

Gimeno Ullastres, Juan Antonio. El nuevo Estado fiscal español . Madrid , 1981. xx, 315 p. : ISBN 84-7214-219-1 LC Card 85-176738
HJ1249.A1 G56 1981

L'Economia in cifre, 1971-1985 / Confindustria, centro studi. Roma : S.I.P.I., [1986] viii, 154 p. ; 21 x 29 cm. "Maggio 1986." Chiefly tables. "Supplemento al n. 2 - maggio 1986 - Anno I"--Cover. LC Card 86-233222
1. Italy - Economic conditions - 1976- - Statistics. I. Centro studi Confindustria. II. Rassegna congiunturale. N. 2 (Supplement).
HC305 .E246 1986

Economia informal, tecnologia apropriada e associativismo / Diva Benevides Pinho [organizadora]. São Paulo : Instituto de Pesquisas Econômicas, 1986. 176 p. : ill. ; 23 cm. (Série Relatórios de pesquisa . no. 33) Includes bibliographies. LC Card 86-233370
1. Poor - Brazil. 2. Informal sector (Economics) - Brazil. 3. Cooperative societies - Brazil. 4. Self-help housing - Brazil - Finance. 5. Appropriate technology - Brazil. I. Pinho, Diva Benevides. II. Series.
HC190.P6 E34 1986

Economía internacional / selección de René Villarreal. 1a ed. México : Fondo de Cultura Económica, 1979- v. in : ill. ; 21 cm. (Lecturas. 30) Includes bibliographical references and indexes. CONTENTS. - [v. 1, pt.] 2. Teorías de imperialismo, la dependencia y su evidencia histórica.
1. International economic relations - Addresses, essays, lectures. 2. Commerce - Addresses, essays, lectures. 3. International finance - Addresses, essays, lectures. I. Villarreal, René. II. Series: El Trimestre económico. 30.
NYPL [JLK 86-184]

Economia internacional /. Medeiros, Eduardo Raposo de. Lisboa , 1984. 416 p., [2] folded leaves of plates : LC Card 85-125328
HC59 .M425 1984

Economía internacional y régimen cambiario /. Lleras Restrepo, Carlos, Pres, 1908- [S.l. , 1981] (Bogotá, D.E. : Osprey Impresores) 298, [3] p. ; LC Card 81-204089 DDC 337/.09/048 19
HF1411 .L542 1981 ***NYPL [JLE 86-3889]***

Economía mexicana . Huerta González, Arturo. [Mexico City, Mexico] , 1986. 246 p. : LC Card 87-404065 DDC 330.972/0834 19
HC135 .H84 1986

Economia mineira e o financiamento do setor público : aspectos recentes da política tributária. Belo Horizonte : Secretaria de Estado da Fazenda : Fundação João Pinheiro, 1985. 126 p. : ill. ; 22 cm. "Trabalho elaborado de acordo com o convênio de cooperação técnica, celebrado entre a Fundação João Pinheiro e a Secretaria de Estado da Fazenda de Minas Gerais através da Assessoria Econômica e Tributária." Includes bibliographical references. LC Card 85-207952
1. Revenue - Brazil - Minas Gerais. 2. Tax administration and procedure - Brazil - Minas Gerais. 3. Sales tax - Brazil - Minas Gerais. 4. Mineral resources - Taxation - Brazil - Minas Gerais. I. Fundação João Pinheiro. II. Minas Gerais (Brazil). Secretaria de Estado da Fazenda. Assessoria Econômica e Tributária.
HJ2529.M5 E26 1985

L'economia monetaria /. Walras, Léon, 1834-1910. Roma [1985] 2 v. (949 p.) : LC Card 87-140163
HG221 .W219 1985

Economía nacional /. Frischknecht, Federico. Buenos Aires , c1986. xi, 214 p. : ISBN 950-0-23599-4 LC Card 86-207933
HB178.5 .F75 1986

La economía nacional y el costo de vida /. Flecha, Agustín Oscar. Asunción, Paraguay , 1986. 49 p. ; LC Card 87-122881 DDC 330.9892/073 19
HD7018 .F57 1986

Economía, organización y planificación de la producción industrial /. Pereira, Nilda. La Habana , 1984. 2 v. : LC Card 87-401248
HD2328 .P47 1984

Economia para los trabajadores .
(3) Solterer, Josef, 1897- Notas y material de estudio sobre el desarrollo y el sindicalismo realizado en el Instituto Americano para el Desarrollo del Sindicalismo Libre /. Lima, Perú [1986] xv, 76, [5] p. : LC Card 86-235556
HD85.S7 S65 1986

Economía paraguaya, 1985. 1a ed. Asunción, Paraguay : Centro Paraguayo de Estudio [sic] Sociológicos, Foro de Economía, 1986. 285 p. : ill. ; 24 cm. (Serie Anuarios) Includes bibliographical references. LC Card 86-182987
1. Paraguay - Economic conditions - 1954-. I. Centro Paraguayo de Estudios Sociológicos. Foro de Economía. II. Series.
HC222 .E27 1986

Economia politica del lavoro /. Tarantelli, Ezio. Torino , c1986. xxiv, 549 p. : ISBN 88-02-03977-1 LC Card 86-213541
HD4901 .T368 1986

Economia politica e processi di urbanizzazione /. Singer, Paul Israel, 1932- Venezia , 1978. xx, 132 p. ; ***NYPL [JLD 86-786]***

Economía, política y sociedad . Sang Ben, Miguel. Santo Domingo, R.D. , 1986. 109 p. ; ISBN 84-89529-00-0 LC Card 87-100772
HC153.5 .S27 1986

A economia portuguesa após o 25 de abril /. Melo, M. Teixeira de. Queluz [Portugal] [1978] 149 p. ; LC Card 79-104785
HC392 .M45 1978

La Economía social de mercado : un proyecto económico y político alternativo / Ernst Dürr ... [et al.]. Buenos Aires, República Argentina : Centro Interdisciplinario de Estudios sobre el Desarrollo Latinoamericano, [1984], c1983. 109 p. ; 29 cm. Includes bibliographies. ISBN 950-9431-00-1 LC Card 86-120441 DDC 338.9 19
1. Economic policy. I. Dürr, Ernst. II. Centro Interdisciplinario de Estudios sobre el Desarrollo Latinoamericano.
HD85.S7 E36 1983

A economia subterrânea /. Santos, J. Albano. Lisboa , 1983. 86 p. : LC Card 86-171907
HD2346.P8 S36 1983

L'Economia tedesca : la Germania federale verso l'egemonia economica in Europa / S. Alessandrini ... [et al.] ; a cura di Vittorio Valli.1a ed. Milano : Etas, c1981. 273 p. : ill. ; 21 cm. (Biblioteca di economia. 8) Bibliography: p. 267-273. CONTENTS. - La Germania federale verso l'egemonia economica in Europa / di Vittorio Valli -- Le politiche macroeconomiche nei paesi dell'Europa occidentale, 1973-77 / di Lucio Izzo e Luigi Spaventa -- La politica economica della Germania federale e i suoi riflessi internazionali, 1969-79 / di Pierluigi Ciocca e Orietta Vito Colonna -- Sviluppo senza occupazione in un paese importatore di forza lavoro / di Vittorio Valli -- Salari e profitti nell'economia della Germania federale nel dopo-guerra / di Carlo Frateschi -- Note sul commercio estero della Germania / di Sergio Alessandrini -- Investimenti all'estero e internazionalizzazione dell'economia tedesca negli anni '70 / di Giancarlo Capitani. LC Card 87-673286
1. Germany, West - Economic conditions. 2. Germany, West - Economic policy. 3. Germany, West - Foreign economic relations. I. Alessandrini, Sergio. II. Valli, Vittorio, 1941-. III. Series: Biblioteca di economia (Etas libri (Firm)) , 8.
HC286.7 .E29x 1981

Economia tra teoria e politica / F. Batistoni Ferrara ... [et al.] ; a cura di Gino Niccodemi e Giuliano Pizzanelli. Milano : F. Angeli, c1984. 295 p. ; 22 cm. (Collana Università . 15) Includes bibliographies. LC Card 84-171327 DDC 330/.09 19
1. Economics - History - Addresses, essays, lectures. 2. Economic policy - Addresses, essays, lectures. I. Batistoni Ferrara, F. (Franco). II. Niccodemi, Gino. III. Pizzanelli, Giuliano. IV. Series.
HB75 .E28 1984 ***NYPL [JLD 87-819]***

La economía venezolana . Aranda, Sergio. Caracas, Venezuela , c1984. 328 p. ; LC Card 87-400622 DDC 330.987/0633 19
HC237 .A68 1984

Economía y administración de empresas.
Maravall, Fernando. Economía y política industrial en España /. Madrid , 1987. 231 p. : ISBN 84-368-0340-X LC Card 87-121800
HC385 .M2574 1987

Economía y demografía (Mexico City, Mexico)
América Latina, Estados Unidos . México , 1986. 223 p. : ISBN 968-231-378-3 LC Card 87-128005 DDC 337.7308 19
HF1456.5.L3 A44 1986

El FMI, el Banco Mundial y la crisis latinoamericana /. México , 1986. 474 p. : ISBN 968-231-373-2 LC Card 87-127860 DDC 332.1/52 19
HG3881.5.I58 F56 1986

Los Factores del cambio demográfico en México /. México, D.F. , 1984. 422 p. : ISBN 968-231-281-7 LC Card 85-231767
HB1361 .F33 1984 ***NYPL [JLE 87-753]***

Problemas agrarios colombianos /. [Bogotá, Colombia] , México, D.F. , 1986. 467 p. :

ISBN 958-606-005-5 LC Card 86-221632
HD1882 .P75 1986

Rey Romay, Benito. La ofensiva empresarial contra la intervención del estado /. México , 1984. 160 p. ; ISBN 968-231-283-3 LC Card 86-151140
HD4013 .R49 1984

Economía y energía en Costa Rica . Cussianovich, Pedro. San José, Costa Rica , 1982. viii, 71, [10] leaves : LC Card 86-179795
HD9502.C82 C87 1982

Economía y frustración social . Casas Grieve, Luis Felipe de las. Lima, Perú [1982?] 128 p. : LC Card 83-104684
HC227 .C27 1982

Economía y petróleo durante la Guerra del Chaco . Seiferheld, Alfredo M., 1950- Asunción , 1983. 535 p. : LC Card 84-121699 DDC 330.9892/071 19
HC222 .S36 1983 ***NYPL [JLD 85-1032]***

Economía y política . Martínez Díaz, Nicasio. [Asunción] 1986 ([Asunción] : El Gráfico) 54 p. ; LC Card 87-400204 DDC 338.9892 19
HC222 .M38 1986

Economía y política industrial en España /. Maravall, Fernando. Madrid , 1987. 231 p. : ISBN 84-368-0340-X LC Card 87-121800
HC385 .M2574 1987

Economic adjustment and conversion of defense industries / edited by John E. Lynch. Boulder : Westview Press, 1987. xiv, 312 p. : ill. ; 23 cm. (Westview special studies in public policy and public systems management) Bibliography: p. 245-304. ISBN 0-8133-7396-4 (pbk. : alk. paper) LC Card 87-50495 DDC 338.4/36234/0973 19
1. Disarmament - Economic aspects - United States. I. Lynch, John E.
HC110.D4 E36 1987

Economic adjustment and worker dislocation in a competitive society . United States. Secretary of Labor's Task Force on Economic Adjustment and Worker Dislocation. Washington, D.C. [1986] 189 p. in various pagings : LC Card 87-601034 DDC 331.13/7973 19
HC106.8 .U545 1986

Economic analyses of the farmer cropping system under risks and uncertainties in Sierra Leone /. Kireta-Katewu, Patrick R., 1953- Hamburg , 1985. xviii, 245 p. : ISBN 3-87895-266-X (pbk.) LC Card 87-103068 DDC 338.1/62 19
HD2146.5 .K57 1985

The economic analysis of accounting profitability /. Edwards, J. S. S. (Jeremy S. S.) Oxford , New York , 1987. 133 p. : ISBN 0-19-877241-6 : LC Card 87-5575 DDC 657/.95 19
HF5686.C7 E34 1987

Economic analysis of information and contracts : essays in honor of John E. Butterworth / edited by Gerald A. Feltham, Amin H. Amershi, and William T. Ziemba. Boston : Kluwer Academic Publishers, c1988. p. cm. Bibliography: p. Includes index. ISBN 0-89838-252-1 : LC Card 87-22508 DDC 657 19
1. Accounting. 2. Information theory in economics. 3. Butterworth, John E. I. Butterworth, John E. II. Feltham, Gerald A., 1938-. III. Amershi, Amin H. IV. Ziemba, W. T.
HF5625 .E28 1988

An Economic analysis of natural gas resources and supply / Energy Information Administration, Office of Oil and Gas, U. S. Department of Energy. Washington, D.C. : The Department : Available from the Supt. of Docs., U. S. G.P.O., [1986] xx, 179 p. : ill. ; 28 cm. Prepared by Richard P. O'Neill ... [et al.]. Bibliography: p. 97-106. LC Card 86-603066 DDC 338.2/7285/0973 19
1. Gas industry - United States - Forecasting. 2. Gas, Natural - United States - Reserves. I. O'Neill, Richard P. II. United States. Energy Information Administration. Office of Oil and Gas.
HD9581.U5 E26 1986

An economic analysis of oilsands policy in Canada . Eglington, Peter. Ottawa, Ont. [1984] 1 v. (various pagings) : LC Card 84-213823 DDC 333.8/232 19
HD9574.C23 W654 1984

The economic analysis of technology policy /. Stoneman, Paul. Oxford [Oxfordshire] , New York , 1987. x, 224 p. : ISBN 0-19-877260-2 (pbk.) LC Card 87-20374 DDC 338.9/26 19
HD45 .S844 1987

Economic analysis of the cost structure of commercial sugar cane farms in Louisiana /. Shuker, Iain G. W. Baton Rouge, La. [1986] vi, 50 p. : LC Card 86-622542 DDC 338.1/09763 s 338.1/7361/09763021 19
HD1775.L8 L7 no. 651 HD9107.L8

An economic analysis of the importance of saltwater beaches in Florida /. Bell, Frederick W. Gainesville, FL [1986] xi, 166 p. : LC Card 86-622310 DDC 333.91/7/09759 19
HD266.F6 B45 1986

Economic & Financial Survey (Firm) La Deuda externa . [Santiago, Chile] , 1985. 105 leaves : LC Card 86-171251
HJ8514.5 .D47 1985

The economic and fiscal effects of a primary source law for California wine imports. Vasche, Jon David. Sacramento, Calif. (925 L St., Suite 650, Sacramento 95814) [1986] vi, 130 p. : LC Card 86-622342 DDC 338.4/36632/009794 19
HD9377.C2 V37 1986

Economic and fiscal review : Province of Ontario. Toronto, Ont. : Ministry of Treasury and Economics, [1986] i, 89 p. : ill. ; 30 cm. "November 1986." Includes bibliographical references. ISBN 0-7729-1950-X (pbk.) LC Card 87-169450 DDC 330.9713/04 19
1. Revenue - Ontario - Forecasting. 2. Economic forecasting - Ontario. 3. Ontario - Economic conditions. I. Ontario. Ministry of Treasury and Economics.
HJ2460.O5 E28 1986

Economic and Policy Analysis Program (Conference Board)
Basche, James R., 1926- Eliminating barriers to international trade and investment in services /. New York, N.Y. (845 Third Ave., New York 10022) , c1986. 15 p. ; LC Card 87-147770 DDC 382/.45 19
HD9980.6 .B37 1986

The 1986-87 outlook . New York, N.Y. (845 3rd Ave., New York 10022) , c1986. 18 p. : LC Card 86-212392 DDC 338.5/443/0973 19
HC106.8 .A14 1986

The economic and political roots of the new protectionism /. Lieberman, Sima, 1927- Totowa, N.J. , 1987. p. cm. ISBN 0-8476-7595-5 LC Card 87-23329 DDC 382.7/3/09048 19
HF1411 .L533 1987

Economic and regional development agreements : partnerships for growth. [Ottawa?] : Govt. of Canada, [1985] 11, 12, [8] p. : ill. ; 21 cm. English and French. Title on added t.p.: Les ententes de développement économique et régional. On cover: "Annual Conference of First Ministers, Halifax, Nova Scotia, November 28-29, 1985"--Cover. LC Card 86-214896 DDC 338.971 19
1. Canada - Economic policy. 2. Federal government - Canada. 3. Regional planning - Canada. 4. Regional economics. I. Conference of First Ministers (1985 : Halifax, N.S.). II. Title: Ententes de développement économique et régional.
HC113 .E26 1985

Economic and Scientific Research Foundation (India) Chitale, V. P. Capital output ratio in the Indian economy /. New Delhi , 1986. viii, 106 p. ; ISBN 81-7027-099-5 : LC Card 86-901894 DDC 338/.06/0954 19
HC435.2 .C4872 1986

Economic and Social Committee of the European Communities.
Demographic situation in the Community . Brussels , 1986. ii, 40 p. : LC Card 87-135237 DDC 304.6/094 19
HB3582.5 .D46 1986

The economic and social situation of the Community / [European Communities, Economic and Social Committee]. Brussels : The Committee ; [Washington, D.C. : European Community Information Service, distributor], 1985. iii, 134 p. : ill. ; 30 cm. At head of title: Economic and Social Consultative Assembly. Includes bibliographical references. "Catalogue no. ESC-84-015-EN"--Prelim. p. 2. "Catalogue no. EX-43-85-175-EN-C"-Verso of t.p. ISBN 92-830-0054-4 : LC Card 86-221563 DDC 330.94/0558 19
1. European Economic Community countries - Economic conditions. 2. European Economic Community countries - Social conditions. I. Title.
HC241.2 .E292 1985

EEC air transport policy . Brussels [1985] iv, 72 p., [1] leaf of plates : LC Card 86-215015 DDC 387.7/094 19
HE9842.8 .E42 1985

EEC maritime transport policy . Brussels [1986] 88 p., [2] leaves : LC Card 87-135615 DDC 387.5/094 19
HE822.5 .E38 1986

EG-Wörterverzeichnis . Luxembourg , 1984. 1 v. (various pagings) ; ISBN 92-824-0123-5 LC Card 85-131398
KJE926.5 .E35 1984 ***NYPL [JLF 86-1818]***

Producer consumer dialogue . Brussels [1984] ii, 55 p. ; LC Card 85-178866 DDC 381/.34/094 19
HC240.9.C63 P77 1984 ***NYPL [JLD 86-2369]***

Economic and Social Committee of the European Communities. Section for Transport. EEC air transport policy . Brussels [1985] iv, 72 p., [1] leaf of plates : LC Card 86-215015 DDC 387.7/094 19
HE9842.8 .E42 1985

Economic and Social Committee of the European Community. Relations between the European Community and the member states of the Association of South-East Asian Nations /. Brussels [1986] 55 p. : LC Card 87-135576 DDC 337.4059 19
HF1532.5 .R46 1986

The Economic and social consequences of disarmament : the United States of America reply to the inquiry of the Secretary General of the United Nations, September 22, 1961. Washington, D.C. : [s.n., 1961] ii leaves, 89 p. ; 32 cm. Cover title. Submitted by the U. S. Arms Control and Disarmament Agency. "December 1961." Includes bibliographical references. "File number EC 212(13)" LC Card 85-115648
1. Disarmament - Economic aspects - United States. 2. Disarmament - Social aspects - United States. I. United Nations. Secretary-General. II. United States. Arms Control and Disarmament Agency.
HC110.D4 E37 1961

An economic and social history of Europe from 1939 to the present /. Tipton, Frank B., 1943- Baltimore, Md. , 1987. vii, 297 p. : ISBN 0-8018-3538-0 LC Card 87-3870 DDC 330.94/055 19
HC240 .T563 1987

An economic and social history of Europe, 1890-1939 /. Tipton, Frank B., 1943- Baltimore , 1987. vii, 323 p. : ISBN 0-8018-3537-2 LC Card 87-3869 DDC 330.94/028 19
HC240 .T56 1987

An economic and social history of Zimbabwe, 1890-1948 . Phimister, I. R. (Ian R.) London , New York , 1987. p. cm. ISBN 0-582-64423-2 LC Card 87-12471 DDC 330.96891/02 19
HC910.Z9 S36 1987

Economic and social origins of Mau Mau.
Throup, David. Economic & social origins of Mau Mau 1945-53 /. London , Athens , c1988. xvi, 304 p. : ISBN 0-8214-0883-6 LC Card 87-12387 DDC 307.3/36 19
HD2126.5 .T48 1988

Economic & social origins of Mau Mau 1945-53 /. Throup, David. London , Athens , c1988. xvi, 304 p. : ISBN 0-8214-0883-6 LC Card 87-12387 DDC 307.3/36 19
HD2126.5 .T48 1988

Economic and Social Research Council. see **Majlis al-Abḥāth al-Iqtiṣādīyah wa-al-Ijtimāʻīyah.**

Economic and Social Research Council (Great Britain)
Europe and the rise of capitalism /. Oxford [Oxfordshire] , New York, NY, USA , 1987. p. cm. ISBN 0-631-15006-4 : LC Card 87-12293 DDC 330.94 19
HC240.9.C3 E97 1987

Finance. Oxford [Oxfordshire] , New York , 1987. xiii, 495 p. ; ISBN 0-08-034780-0 : LC Card 87-7247 DDC 332/.0941 19
HG186.G7 F53 1987

Water demand forecasting . Norwich, U.K. ,

c1986. 139 p. : ISBN 0-86094-214-7 : LC Card 87-127184 DDC 333.91/13 19
HD1690.5 .W383 1986

The economic and social situation of the Community /. Economic and Social Committee of the European Communities. Brussels [Washington, D.C.] 1985. iii, 134 p. : ISBN 92-830-0054-4 : LC Card 86-221563 DDC 330.94/0558 19
HC241.2 .E292 1985

An economic and technical assessment of the establishment of an Australian fat-tail sheep industry /. Fisher, Brian S. [Sydney], N.S.W. , c1986. vi, 52 p. ; LC Card 87-154531 DDC 338.1/76386 19
HD9436.A82 F57 1986

ECONOMIC AND TECHNICAL ASSISTANCE. see **ECONOMIC ASSISTANCE; TECHNICAL ASSISTANCE.**

ECONOMIC ANTHROPOLOGY - ADDRESSES, ESSAYS, LECTURES.
Entrepreneurship and social change /. Lanham, MD [S.l.] , c1986. 275 p. : ISBN 0-8191-5165-3 (alk. paper) : LC Card 85-26533 DDC 338/.04 19
HB615 .E629 1986 ***NYPL [JLD 86-3073]***

ECONOMIC ANTHROPOLOGY - CONGRESSES.
ASA Conference, Migrants, Workers, and the Social Order (1986 : University of Kent) Migrants, workers, and the social order /. London , New York , 1987. p. cm. ISBN 0-422-61680-X (pbk.) LC Card 87-10253
HD5856.D44 A72 1986

ECONOMIC ANTHROPOLOGY - INDONESIA - SAROAKO.
Robinson, Kathryn May, 1949- Stepchildren of progress . Albany, N.Y. , c1986. xvi, 315 p. : ISBN 0-88706-119-2 LC Card 86-5847 DDC 307.7/66/095984 19
HD9539.N52 I547 1986
NYPL [JLE 86-4126]

ECONOMIC ANTHROPOLOGY - SUDAN - DAR MASALIT.
Tully, Dennis. Culture and context in Sudan . Albany, N.Y. , c1988. p. cm. ISBN 0-88706-502-3 LC Card 86-23180 DDC 338.1/09627 19
HC835.Z7 D377 1988

Economic appraisal of transport projects . Adler, Hans A. Baltimore , 1987. xii, 235 p. : ISBN 0-8018-3411-2 : LC Card 86-21348 DDC 380.5/068/1 19
HE151 .A32 1987

Economic aspects of the Vikings in the West-the archaeological basis /. Wilson, David McKenzie. Göteborg , 1980. 36 p. ; ISBN 91-7360-075-X (pbk.) LC Card 81-154587 DDC 330.94 19
HC41 .W55 1980

ECONOMIC ASSISTANCE - AFRICA.
Economic development in Africa . London , 1987. x, 266 p. ; ISBN 0-86187-909-0 : LC Card 87-15296 DDC 338.98 19
HC800 .E275 1987

Proceedings of second (special) general conference . Accra, Ghana [1985?] 73 p. ; LC Card 86-220781 DDC 338.96 19
HC800 .P77 1985

ECONOMIC ASSISTANCE - AFRICA - CONGRESSES.
World recession and the food crisis in Africa /. London , 1986. 314 p. ; ISBN 0-85255-309-9 : LC Card 86-235333 DDC 363.8/526/096 19
HD9017.A2 W67 1986b

World recession and the food crisis in Africa /. Boulder , 1986. p. cm. ISBN 0-8133-0511-X : LC Card 86-28250 DDC 363.8/526/096 19
HD9017.A2 W67 1986

ECONOMIC ASSISTANCE - AFRICA, SOUTHERN.
La Grange, A. B. DBSA in the southern African development framework /. Sandton, Republic of South Africa [1985] 36 p. : LC Card 87-150256 DDC 332.2 19
HC900 .L3 1985

ECONOMIC ASSISTANCE, AMERICAN - AFRICA.
Bereuter, Douglas K. United States and European Community development assistance to Africa . [Washington, D.C.? , 1985?] 22, [2] leaves ; LC Card 87-108848 DDC 338.91/4/06 19
HC800 .B455 1985

ECONOMIC ASSISTANCE, AMERICAN - AFRICA - DIRECTORIES.
Diversity in development . New York, NY , c1986. xvii, 620 p. : ISBN 0-932140-07-6 (pbk.) LC Card 86-231757 DDC 361.7/025/73 19
HC800.Z9 E444 1986

ECONOMIC ASSISTANCE, AMERICAN - AFRICA, SUB-SAHARAN.
Committee on African Development Strategies (U. S.) Compact for African development . Berkeley, CA (2120 Berkeley Way, Berkeley 94720) [1985] 24 p. : LC Card 86-200473 DDC 338.967 19
HC800 .C645 1985

ECONOMIC ASSISTANCE, AMERICAN - BOLIVIA.
Diez, Rafael. Final report of the consultancy of Rafael Diez from August 3, 1982 to August 3, 1983. La Paz [1983] 1 v. (various foliations) ; LC Card 83-243264
HC182 .D49 1983

ECONOMIC ASSISTANCE, AMERICAN - CARIBBEAN AREA - CASE STUDIES.
Grassroots development in Latin America & the Caribbean . New York , 1985. vii, 197 p. : ISBN 0-03-001689-4 (alk. paper) : LC Card 84-18180 DDC 334/.098 19
HD3450.5.A4 G72 1985

ECONOMIC ASSISTANCE, AMERICAN - CENTRAL AMERICA.
Barry, Tom, 1950- The soft war . New York , 1988. xv, 304 p. ; ISBN 0-8021-0003-1 LC Card 87-13238 DDC 338.91/73/0728 19
HC141 .B375 1988

Leonard, H. Jeffrey. Natural resources and economic development in Central America . New Brunswick, N.J., U. S.A. , c1987. xxii, 279 p. : ISBN 0-88738-722-5 (pbk.) LC Card 87-10871 DDC 333.7/09728 19
HC141 .L44 1987

ECONOMIC ASSISTANCE, AMERICAN - DEVELOPING COUNTRIES.
Hough, Richard L. Economic assistance and security . Fort Lesley J. McNair, Washington, D.C. , 1982. xii, 139 p. : LC Card 82-600548 DDC 338.91/73/01724 19
HC60 .H675 1982

May, Bernhard. Reagan und die Entwicklungsländer . München , 1987. xiv, 271 p. ; ISBN 3-486-53981-7 LC Card 87-139481 DDC 337.730172/4 19
HF1456.5.D44 M39 1987

Protz, Michael. Administrative Zusammenarbeit in der Entwicklungspolitik . Speyer , 1982. ix, 382, 2 p. ; LC Card 86-218043
HC60 .P77 1982

Rondinelli, Dennis A. Development administration and U. S. foreign aid policy /. Boulder , 1987. xi, 188 p. ; ISBN 0-931477-97-2 (lib. bdg.) : LC Card 87-4555 DDC 338.9/0068 19
HC59.72.E44 R66 1987

Winiecki, Jan. Rola pomocy gospodarczej w polityce zagranicznej USA wobec krajów rozwijających się /. Warszawa , 1979. 310, [1] p. ; LC Card 81-205172
HC60 .W54 1979

ECONOMIC ASSISTANCE, AMERICAN - DEVELOPING COUNTRIES - HISTORY.
Alcalde Cardoza, Xavier. The idea of Third World development . Lanham, MD [Charlottesville, Va.] , c1987. xxii, 236 p. ; ISBN 0-8191-6303-1 (alk. paper) : LC Card 87-8154 DDC 338.91/009172/4 19
HC60 .A4595 1987

ECONOMIC ASSISTANCE, AMERICAN - EGYPT.
Prosterman, Roy L. Egyptian development and U. S. aid . [Seattle, Wash.?] , c1985. i, 32, A1-A10 p. ; LC Card 87-104139 DDC 338.91/73/062 19
HC830.Z9 E446 1985

ECONOMIC ASSISTANCE, AMERICAN - EUROPE.
Donovan, Robert J. The second victory . New York , c1987. 128 p. : ISBN 0-8191-6498-4 (alk. paper) : LC Card 87-24021 DDC 338.91/73/04 19
HC240 .D65 1987

Wood, Robert Everett, 1944- From Marshall Plan to debt crisis . Berkeley , c1986. xviii, 400 p. ; ISBN 0-520-05526-8 (alk. paper) LC Card 86-6934 DDC 338.9/009172/4 19
HC60 .W62 1986 ***NYPL [JLE 86-4443]***

ECONOMIC ASSISTANCE, AMERICAN - EUROPE - HISTORY.
Kindleberger, Charles Poor, 1910- Marshall Plan days /. Boston , 1987. x, 273 p., [1] leaf of plates : ISBN 0-04-332142-9 (alk. paper) LC Card 86-32163 DDC 338.91/73/04 19
HC240 .K454 1987

ECONOMIC ASSISTANCE, AMERICAN - GAZA STRIP.
Laufer, Leopold Yehuda. U. S. aid to the West Bank and Gaza . [Jerusalem] [1985] 54 p. ; LC Card 87-400340 DDC 338.91/73/056951 19
HC415.25.Z7 W4735 1985

ECONOMIC ASSISTANCE, AMERICAN - GERMANY (WEST) - BREMEN - HISTORY - PICTORIAL WORKS.
Hilfe in der Not . [Bremen] [1947] 74 p. : LC Card 87-408692 DDC 338.91/73/04352 19
HC286.5 .H545 1947

ECONOMIC ASSISTANCE, AMERICAN - ISRAEL - HISTORY.
Laufer, Leopold Yehuda. U. S. aid to Israel . [Jerusalem] [1983] 55 p. : LC Card 87-400279 DDC 338.91/73/05694 19
HC415.25 .L38 1983

ECONOMIC ASSISTANCE, AMERICAN - ITALY.
Harper, John Lamberton. America and the reconstruction of Italy, 1945-1948 /. Cambridge [Cambridgeshire] , New York , 1986. x, 213 p. ; ISBN 0-521-32518-8 LC Card 85-30915 DDC 338.91/73/045 19
HC305 .H36 1986 ***NYPL [JLE 86-3600]***

Ortona, Egidio. Anni d'America /. Bologna , c1984- v. ; ISBN 88-15-00531-5 (v. 1) : LC Card 84-240652 DDC 338.91/73/045 19
HC305 .O78 1984 ***NYPL [JLL 86-503]***

ECONOMIC ASSISTANCE, AMERICAN - LATIN AMERICA.
Herrera, Felipe, 1922- América Latina, desarrollo e integracíon /. [Santiago, Chile] [1986] 302 p., [11] p. of plates : LC Card 87-115159 DDC 337.1/8 19
HC125 .H466 1986

ECONOMIC ASSISTANCE, AMERICAN - LATIN AMERICA - CASE STUDIES.
Grassroots development in Latin America & the Caribbean . New York , 1985. vii, 197 p. : ISBN 0-03-001689-4 (alk. paper) : LC Card 84-18180 DDC 334/.098 19
HD3450.5.A4 G72 1985

ECONOMIC ASSISTANCE, AMERICAN - LATIN AMERICA - HISTORY.
Breslin, Patrick, 1940- Development and dignity . Rosslyn, Va. [1987] xiii, 128 p. : ISBN 0-8133-0632-9 (alk. paper) LC Card 87-3920 DDC 338.91/7308/0601 19
HC125 .B725 1987

ECONOMIC ASSISTANCE, AMERICAN - MIDDLE EAST.
Godfried, Nathan. Bridging the gap between rich and poor . New York , 1987. xii, 225 p. ; ISBN 0-313-25648-9 (lib. bdg. : alk. paper) LC Card 87-8471 DDC 338.91/73/056 19
HC415.15 .G63 1987

ECONOMIC ASSISTANCE, AMERICAN - POLITICAL ASPECTS - DEVELOPING COUNTRIES.
Guess, George M. The politics of United States foreign aid /. New York , 1987. 297 p. ; ISBN 0-312-00448-6 : LC Card 86-26301 DDC 338.91/09172/4 19
HC60 .G7383 1987

ECONOMIC ASSISTANCE, AMERICAN - SOUTH AFRICA.
Seidman, Ann Willcox, 1926- The roots of crisis in southern Africa /. Trenton, N.J. [1985] xvii, 209 p. : ISBN 0-86543-026-8 (pbk.) : LC Card 85-72995 DDC 968.06/3 19
E183.8.S6 S45 1985 ***NYPL [Sc E 86-368]***

ECONOMIC ASSISTANCE, AMERICAN - TANZANIA.

USAID/Tanzania. Program and background materials for Tanzania/USAID bilateral talks, November 30 and December 1, 1983. [Dar es Salaam, Tanzania] [1983?] 1 v. (various pagings) ; LC Card 86-980179 DDC 338.91/73/0678 19
HC885 .U8 1983

ECONOMIC ASSISTANCE, AMERICAN - WEST BANK.
Laufer, Leopold Yehuda. U. S. aid to the West Bank and Gaza . [Jerusalem] [1985] 54 p. ; LC Card 87-400340 DDC 338.91/73/056951 19
HC415.25.Z7 W4735 1985

ECONOMIC ASSISTANCE, AMERICAN - ZIMBABWE.
Wasserman, Gary, 1944- U. S. aid to Zimbabwe . [Washington, D.C.?] [1983] ix, 20, [71] p. ; LC Card 87-109216 DDC 338.91/73/06891 19
HC910 .W37 1983

Economic assistance and security . Hough, Richard L. Fort Lesley J. McNair, Washington, D.C. , 1982. xii, 139 p. : LC Card 82-600548 DDC 338.91/73/01724 19
HC60 .H675 1982

ECONOMIC ASSISTANCE - ASIA - HISTORY - 20TH CENTURY.
Lewis, John Prior. Asian development . Lanham, MD , New York , c1987. 49 p. ; ISBN 0-8191-6590-5 (pbk.) : LC Card 87-21599 DDC 338.91/095 19
HC412 .L45 1987

ECONOMIC ASSISTANCE, AUSTRIAN - DEVELOPING COUNTRIES.
Höll, Otmar. Österreichische Entwicklungshilfe, 1970-1983 . Wien , Laxenburg, Austria , c1986. 187 p. : ISBN 3-7003-0659-8 LC Card 86-192362
HC60 .H6643 1986

ECONOMIC ASSISTANCE, AUSTRIAN - DEVELOPING COUNTRIES - PUBLIC OPINION.
Jäggle, Martin. Öffentlichkeitsarbeit 3. Welt in Österreich /. Wien , 1975- v. <1 > ; LC Card 86-234031
HC60 .J344 1975

ECONOMIC ASSISTANCE - BANGLADESH.
Bangladesh . Fantoft, Norway , 1986. xxxiii, 353 p. : ISBN 82-905840-8-3 (pbk.) LC Card 87-128545 DDC 330.9549/205 19
HC440.8 .B352 1986

ECONOMIC ASSISTANCE, BRITISH - DEVELOPING COUNTRIES.
Biraud, Gérard. L'aide britannique au développement . Paris , 1978. 17 leaves : LC Card 84-102197
HC60 .B52 1978

Nuscheler, Franz. Die Entwicklungspolitik der Regierung Thatcher . [Bonn] [1986] 93 p. : LC Card 86-186261
HC60 .N87 1986

Protz, Michael. Administrative Zusammenarbeit in der Entwicklungspolitik . Speyer , 1982. ix, 382, 2 p. ; LC Card 86-218043
HC60 .P77 1982

ECONOMIC ASSISTANCE, BRITISH - DEVELOPING COUNTRIES - HISTORY.
Alcalde Cardoza, Xavier. The idea of Third World development . Lanham, MD [Charlottesville, Va.] , c1987. xxii, 236 p. ; ISBN 0-8191-6303-1 (alk. paper) : LC Card 87-8154 DDC 338.91/009172/4 19
HC60 .A4595 1987

ECONOMIC ASSISTANCE, BRITISH - NICARAGUA.
Melrose, Dianna. Nicaragua . Oxford, U.K. , Boston, MA , 1985. 68 p. : ISBN 0-85598-070-2 (pbk.) : LC Card 87-116239 DDC 338.91/41/07285 19
HC146 .M45 1985

ECONOMIC ASSISTANCE - CAMEROON.
Répertoire financier et fiscal du Cameroun . Le Vésinet, France [1987?] 147 p. ; LC Card 87-124445
HJ1489 .R46 1987

ECONOMIC ASSISTANCE, CANADIAN - DEVELOPING COUNTRIES.
Hoffman, Gerard H. Foreign aid? yes, but-- . Toronto, Ont. , 1981. vi, 55 p. : LC Card 81-182755 DDC 338.91/71/01724 19
HC60 .H63 1981 ***NYPL [JLD 86-3406]***

With our own hands . Ottawa, Canada , c1986. 206 p. : ISBN 0-88936-460-5 (pbk.) LC Card 86-212405 DDC 338.91/71/01724 19
HC59.72.F44 W58 1986

ECONOMIC ASSISTANCE - CARIBBEAN AREA - CONGRESSES.
Trade, aid, and democracy in the Caribbean . [S.l.] [1986] 68 p. : LC Card 87-400829 DDC 338.91/09729 19
HC151 .T73 1986

ECONOMIC ASSISTANCE, COMMUNIST - DEVELOPING COUNTRIES.
Machowski, Heinrich. RGW-Staaten und Dritte Welt . Bonn , 1981. iii, 84 p. ; ISBN 3-7713-0167-X LC Card 85-224767
HF1532.15.D44 M33 1981

ECONOMIC ASSISTANCE, COMMUNIST - GRENADA - HISTORY.
Pryor, Frederic L. Revolutionary Grenada . New York , 1986. xx, 395 p. : ISBN 0-275-92155-7 (alk. paper) : LC Card 86-8109 DDC 338.97298/45 19
HC156.5.Z7 G747 1986
NYPL [JLE 86-3969]

ECONOMIC ASSISTANCE, DANISH - DEVELOPING COUNTRIES.
Denmark. Udvalget vedrørende dansk bistandspolitik. Betænkning om principperne for den danske bistand til udviklingslandene /. København , 1982. 224 p. ; ISBN 87-503-4037-9 LC Card 84-103068
HC60 .D435 1982

ECONOMIC ASSISTANCE - DEVELOPING COUNTRIES.
Auf dem Weg zu einer neuen Weltwirtschaftsordnung? . Baden-Baden , 1983. 478 p. ; ISBN 3-7890-0919-9
NYPL [JLD 87-919]

Commission of the European Communities. Directorate-General of Information. A Community research policy for development. Brussels [1983] 21 p. ; LC Card 85-166173 DDC 338.91/4/01724 19
HC60 .C584 1983

Does aid work? . Oxford [Oxfordshire] , New York , 1986. xv, 381 p. ; ISBN 0-19-877250-5 : LC Card 86-12621 DDC 338.91/09172/4 19
HC60 .D53 1986 ***NYPL [JLE 86-4563]***

Hauser, Heinz-Michael. Reform der Entwicklungsfinanzierung durch "Automatisierung"? . Baden-Baden , 1986. vi, 531 p. ; ISBN 3-7890-1235-1 LC Card 87-407969 DDC 338.91/09172/4 19
HC60 .H329 1986

Hellinger, Steve. Aid for just development . Washington, D.C. (1010 Vermont Ave., N.W., Suite 521, Washington 20005) , c1987. vii, 191 p. ; LC Card 87-404422 DDC 338.91/09172/4 19
HC60 .H38516 1987

Hoffman, Gerard H. Foreign aid? yes, but-- . Toronto, Ont. , 1981. vi, 55 p. : LC Card 81-182755 DDC 338.91/71/01724 19
HC60 .H63 1981 ***NYPL [JLD 86-3406]***

Höll, Otmar. Österreichische Entwicklungshilfe, 1970-1983 . Wien , Laxenburg, Austria , c1986. 187 p. : ISBN 3-7003-0659-8 LC Card 86-192362
HC60 .H6643 1986

Kress, Roland, 1961- Die politischen Stiftungen in der Entwicklungspolitik . Bochum , 1985. iv, 224 p. ; ISBN 3-88339-426-2 : LC Card 85-175519
HC60 .K727 1985

Lappé, Frances Moore. Betraying the national interest /. New York , 1987, c1986. p. cm. ISBN 0-8021-0012-0 LC Card 87-12067 DDC 338.91 19
HC60 .L325 1987

Mosley, Paul. Foreign aid, its defense and reform /. Lexington, Ky. , c1987. xiv, 264 p. ; ISBN 0-8131-1608-2 : LC Card 86-23400 DDC 338.91/09172/4 19
HC60 .M67 1987

Neundörfer, Konrad. Wir und die Dritte Welt . Köln , c1985. x, 214 p. ; ISBN 3-452-20304-2 LC Card 85-164555
HC59.7 .N375 1985

Radke, Detlef. Auflagenpolitik und Politik-Dialog in der entwicklungspolitischen Zusammenarbeit /. Berlin , 1985. xiii, 91 p. : ISBN 3-88985-036-7 LC Card 85-134788
HC60 .R183 1985

Schneider, Bertrand. La révolution aux pieds nus . Paris , c1985. 344 p. ; ISBN 2-213-01684-4 : LC Card 86-179661
HC60 .S314 1985

Status report on concessional flows, April 1986. Washington, D.C., U. S. A. , 1986. 25 p. ; ISBN 0-8213-0789-4 (pbk.) LC Card 86-214496 DDC 336.3/435/091724
HG3891 .S7 1986

Stockhausen, Joachim von. Theorie und Politik der Entwicklungshilfe . München , c1986. viii, 324 p. ; ISBN 3-8039-0332-1 LC Card 86-225372
HC60 .S7977 1986

United Nations. Economic and Social Council. Committee for Development Planning. Doubling development finance . New York , 1986. v, 47 p. ; ISBN 92-1-104185-6 (pbk.) LC Card 87-103015 DDC 338.91/09172/4 19
HG3881 .U646 1986

Wood, Robert Everett, 1944- From Marshall Plan to debt crisis . Berkeley , c1986. xviii, 400 p. ; ISBN 0-520-05526-8 (alk. paper) LC Card 86-6934 DDC 338.9/009172/4 19
HC60 .W62 1986 ***NYPL [JLE 86-4443]***

ECONOMIC ASSISTANCE - DEVELOPING COUNTRIES - CONGRESSES.
OPEC aid and the challenge of development /. London , New York , c1987. x, 130 p. ; ISBN 0-7099-1969-7 LC Card 87-9160 DDC 338.91/09172/4 19
HC60 .O5754 1987

Le Tiers-mondisme en question /. Paris , c1986. 225 p. ; ISBN 2-85565-299-5 : LC Card 86-185503
HC60 .T518 1986

ECONOMIC ASSISTANCE, DOMESTIC - ASIA - CASE STUDIES.
The Poor in Asia . Kuala Lumpur, Malaysia , 1985- v. <1 > ; ISBN 967-99954-0-2 (v. 1) LC Card 86-944764 DDC 362.5/8/095 19
HC415.P6 P66 1985

ECONOMIC ASSISTANCE, DOMESTIC - AUSTRALIA.
Hollingworth, Peter John, 1935- Australians in poverty /. Melbourne, Vic. , 1985. x, 166 p. : ISBN 0-17-006741-6 (pbk.) : LC Card 87-108662 DDC 305.5/69/0994 19
HC610.P6 H62 1985

ECONOMIC ASSISTANCE, DOMESTIC - BANGLADESH - CONGRESSES.
Jerve, Alf Morten. From research to implementation . Fantoft-Bergen, Norway [1984] 23 leaves ; LC Card 86-228812 DDC 386/.068 19
HE691.6 .J47 1984

ECONOMIC ASSISTANCE, DOMESTIC - GREAT BRITAIN.
Redundancy and recession . Norwich, England , c1986. xii, 174 p. : ISBN 0-86094-201-5 : LC Card 86-218942 DDC 330.941/0858 19
HC256.6 .R44 1986

ECONOMIC ASSISTANCE, DOMESTIC - GREAT BRITAIN - CITIZEN PARTICIPATION.
Whiteley, Paul. Pressure for the poor . London , New York , 1987. 174 p. ; ISBN 0-416-36370-9 LC Card 87-11205 DDC 362.5/8/0941 19
HC260.P63 W47 1987

ECONOMIC ASSISTANCE, DOMESTIC - INDIA.
Gupta, Anand P. Fiscal policy and the poor /. New Delhi , c1984. 90 p. ; LC Card 84-900303 DDC 339.5/2/0954 19
HJ1331 .G87 1984 ***NYPL [JLD 87-778]***

Sudarsana Rao, R. (Rokkam) Grants-in-aid and economic development in India /. Allahabad, India , 1986. ix, 271 p. ; ISBN 81-85076-14-6 : LC Card 86-903200 DDC 338.954
HJ1338 .S83 1986

ECONOMIC ASSISTANCE, DOMESTIC - INDIA - GUJARAT - CASE STUDIES.
Pathy, Jaganath, 1948- Tribal peasantry dynamics of development /. New Delhi , 1984, c1983. xiii, 233 p. : LC Card 84-900095 DDC 330.954/75052 19
HD879.G8 P37 1984 ***NYPL [JLD 87-724]***

ECONOMIC ASSISTANCE, DOMESTIC - INDIA - JHĀBUA (DISTRICT)
Pais, H. Poverty alleviation programmes . New Delhi , 1986. xii, 48, [3] p. (some folded) : LC Card 86-903597 DDC 362.5/8/09543 19
HC437.J43 P35 1986

ECONOMIC ASSISTANCE, DOMESTIC - INDIA - MANIPUR.
Roy Burman, B. K. Towards poverty alleviation programmes in Nagaland and Manipur /. Delhi , 1984. xxxi, 123 p. ; LC Card 84-902780 DDC 338.954/165 19
HC437.N25 R69 1984 NYPL [JLD 87-903]

ECONOMIC ASSISTANCE, DOMESTIC - INDIA - NĀGĀLAND.
Roy Burman, B. K. Towards poverty alleviation programmes in Nagaland and Manipur /. Delhi , 1984. xxxi, 123 p. ; LC Card 84-902780 DDC 338.954/165 19
HC437.N25 R69 1984 NYPL [JLD 87-903]

ECONOMIC ASSISTANCE, DOMESTIC - INDIA - PUNJAB.
Punjab (India). Economic and Statistical Organisation. Report on the evaluation study of working of the Punjab Scheduled Castes Land Development and Finance Corporation. Chandigarh [pref. 1978] viii, 98 p. ; LC Card 79-903307
HC437.P8 P85 1978a

ECONOMIC ASSISTANCE, DOMESTIC - ITALY.
Intervento straordinario e amministrazione locale nel mezzogiorno /. Milano, Italy , c1985. 348 p. ; LC Card 86-144245
HC310.I53 I58 1985

Relazione programmatica delle partecipazioni statali per il 1984 . Roma , 1985. 563 p. ; LC Card 86-176014
HC310.I53 R45 1985

ECONOMIC ASSISTANCE, DOMESTIC - ITALY - CORRUPT PRACTICES.
Risanamento e riordino delle partecipazioni statali . Milano, Italy , c1986. 429 p. : LC Card 86-169331
HC310.I53 R57 1986

ECONOMIC ASSISTANCE, DOMESTIC - ITALY - LOMBARDY - HISTORY.
Bressan, E. (Edoardo) Povertà e assistenza in Lombardia nell'età napoleonica /. [Milano] , Bari , c1985. viii, 339 p. : ISBN 88-420-2653-0 : LC Card 86-162978
HC307.L8 B74 1985

ECONOMIC ASSISTANCE, DOMESTIC - MICHIGAN.
Michigan. Dept. of Labor. An assessment of the effectiveness of the Bureau of Community Services, Michigan Economic and Social Opportunity Commission, and community action agencies /. [Lansing, Mich.] [1986] 56 p. : LC Card 87-620767 DDC 362/.9774 19
HC107.M53 P6333 1986

ECONOMIC ASSISTANCE, DOMESTIC - MICHIGAN - HANDBOOKS, MANUALS, ETC.
Helping handbook /. Lansing, MI (300 N. Washington Square, Suite 401, Lansing 48933) , 1986. v, 101 p. ; LC Card 87-110874 DDC 361.6/025/774 19
HC107.M53 P633 1986

ECONOMIC ASSISTANCE, DOMESTIC - NEW YORK (STATE)
ECONOMIC ASSISTANCE, DOMESTIC - NEW YORK (STATE) - HANDBOOKS, MANUALS, ETC.
A Step-by-step guide to resources for economic development /. Albany, N.Y. [New York, N.Y.] , 1983, c1980. 195 p. : LC Card 85-621196 DDC 353.0082/09747 19
HC107.N73 P6353 1983
NYPL [JLF 86-638]

ECONOMIC ASSISTANCE, DOMESTIC - SAUDI ARABIA.
Shaykh, Riyāḍ 'Abd al-Ḥafīẓ. Niẓām al-i'ānah fī al-iqtiṣād al-Sa'ūdī /. al-Mamlakah al-'Arabīyah al-Su'ūdīyah , 1985. 77 p. : LC Card 86-208281
HC415.33.Z9 E447 1985

ECONOMIC ASSISTANCE DOMESTIC - UNITED STATES - CONGRESSES.
Fighting poverty . Cambridge, Mass. , 1986. viii, 418 p. : ISBN 0-674-30085-8 (alk. paper) LC Card 85-24848 DDC 362.5/8/0973 19
HC110.P63 F54 1986 NYPL [JLE 86-4089]

ECONOMIC ASSISTANCE, DOMESTIC - UNITED STATES - DIRECTORIES.
Lesko, Matthew. Getting yours . New York, N.Y., U. S.A. , 1987. x, 368 p. ; ISBN 0-14-046760-2 (pbk.) : LC Card 86-22688 DDC 658.1/5224 19
HC110.P63 L37 1987

ECONOMIC ASSISTANCE, DOMESTIC - UNITED STATES - HISTORY - 20TH CENTURY - SOURCES.
The War on poverty, 1964-1968 [microform] . Frederick, MD , c1986- microfilm reel ISBN 0-89093-495-9 (microfilm : set) : LC Card 87-10510 DDC 338.973 19
HC110 .P63

ECONOMIC ASSISTANCE, DOMESTIC - UNITED STATES - STATES.
Hackett, Judith C. Managing rural infrastructure . Lexington, Ky. , c1986. iii, 36 p. : ISBN 0-87292-070-4 (pbk.) : LC Card 87-404481 DDC 363/.0973 19
HD3888 .H27 1986

ECONOMIC ASSISTANCE, DOMESTIC - UNITED STATES - STATISTICS.
Barnes, William R. Employment problems and America's cities /. [Washington, D.C.] , 1984. xiii, 66, 33 p. ; *NYPL [JLF 86-1]*

ECONOMIC ASSISTANCE - ETHIOPIA - STATISTICS.
Drought situation in Ethiopia and assistance requirements 1984/85 /. Addis Ababa [1984] 55 leaves in various pagings : LC Card 85-980926
HC845.Z9 F32x 1984

ECONOMIC ASSISTANCE, EUROPEAN - AFRICA.
Bereuter, Douglas K. United States and European Community development assistance to Africa . [Washington, D.C.? , 1985?] 22, [2] leaves ; LC Card 87-108848 DDC 338.91/4/06 19
HC800 .B455 1985

ECONOMIC ASSISTANCE, FINNISH - DEVELOPING COUNTRIES.
Regeringens berättelse om utvecklingssamarbetet till riksdagen. Helsingfors , 1986. 30 p. : LC Card 86-224775
HC60 .R33 1986

ECONOMIC ASSISTANCE, FRENCH - AFRICA.
Guth, Suzie. Exil sous contrat . Paris , c1984. 479 p. : ISBN 2-903871-53-1 : LC Card 85-141675
HC800 .G88 1984

ECONOMIC ASSISTANCE, FRENCH - DEVELOPING COUNTRIES.
France. Mission "Recherche, technologie et progrès en coopération." Recherche et coopération avec le Tiers Monde . Paris , c1983. 120 p. ; ISBN 2-11-001071-1 : LC Card 83-196852
HC60 .F727 1983

L'Impasse Nord-Sud . Paris , c1984. 103 p. : ISBN 2-11-001207-2 : LC Card 84-163951
HC59 .I44 1984

Protz, Michael. Administrative Zusammenarbeit in der Entwicklungspolitik . Speyer , 1982. ix, 382, 2 p. ; LC Card 86-218043
HC60 .P77 1982

ECONOMIC ASSISTANCE - HAITI.
Ronceray, Hubert de. Notre projet de société pour Haïti /. [Port-au-Prince?] [1986?] 52 p. : LC Card 86-210570
HC153 .R66 1986

ECONOMIC ASSISTANCE IN UNDERDEVELOPED AREAS. see **ECONOMIC ASSISTANCE.**

ECONOMIC ASSISTANCE - ISLANDS OF THE PACIFIC - DIRECTORIES.
Directory of aid agencies. Suva, Fiji , 1985. iv, 147 p. ; LC Card 86-204497 DDC 338.91/025/9 19
HC681 .D57 1985

ECONOMIC ASSISTANCE, ITALIAN - DEVELOPING COUNTRIES.
Cooperazione italiana allo sviluppo . Roma [1984] 144 p. ; ISBN 88-7621-170-5 : LC Card 85-223760 DDC 338.91/45/01724 19
HC60 .C65757 1984

ECONOMIC ASSISTANCE, JAPANESE - CONGRESSES.
Round Table Discussions on Japan in the Global Community. Japan in the global community . [Tokyo] , c1986. 129, [38] p. : ISBN 4-13-057014-5 : LC Card 87-129161 DDC 337.52 19
HF1601 .R68 1986

ECONOMIC ASSISTANCE, JAPANESE - OCEANIA.
Edo, Junko, 1947- Japanese aid to the Pacific islands region /. Honolulu, Hawaii, USA , 1986. x, 94 p. ; ISBN 0-86638-090-6 (pbk.) LC Card 87-5293 DDC 338.91/52/09 19
HC681. E36 1986

ECONOMIC ASSISTANCE - LATIN AMERICA - CONGRESSES.
Mesa Redonda sobre la Carta de Punta del Este (1961 : Universidad Nacional Autónoma de México) Memoria del ciclo de conferencias de Mesa Redonda sobre la Carta de Punta del Este /. México , 1962. 224 p. : LC Card 85-105213
HC125 .M48 1961

ECONOMIC ASSISTANCE, NEW ZEALAND - DEVELOPING COUNTRIES.
New Zealand's overseas development assistance . Wellington [1985] 79 p. ; LC Card 86-210636 DDC 338.91/931/01724 19
HC60 .N478 1985

ECONOMIC ASSISTANCE - NICARAGUA.
Melrose, Dianna. Nicaragua . Oxford, U.K. , Boston, MA , 1985. 68 p. : ISBN 0-85598-070-2 (pbk.) : LC Card 87-116239 DDC 338.91/41/07285 19
HC146 .M45 1985

ECONOMIC ASSISTANCE, NORWEGIAN - BANGLADESH.
Bangladesh . Fantoft, Norway , 1986. xxxiii, 353 p. : ISBN 82-905840-8-3 (pbk.) LC Card 87-128545 DDC 330.9549/205 19
HC440.8 .B352 1986

Chowdhury, Ashraf U. Norway's commodity assistance and import support to Bangladesh . [Oslo, Norway] [1986] 83 p. : LC Card 87-150872 DDC 338.91/481/05492 19
HC440.8 .C48 1986

ECONOMIC ASSISTANCE, NORWEGIAN - DEVELOPING COUNTRIES.
Kristiansen, Stein. U-hjelp og handel . Bergen [1982] iv, 325 p. : LC Card 83-139901
HC60 .K76 1982

ECONOMIC ASSISTANCE, NORWEGIAN - DEVELOPING COUNTRIES - COST EFFECTIVENESS.
Sandanger, Runar. Prosjektevaluering i u-land . Oslo [1983] viii, 97 p. : LC Card 83-144428
HC60 .S156 1983

ECONOMIC ASSISTANCE, NORWEGIAN - DEVELOPING COUNTRIES - PUBLIC OPINION.
Attidues to Norwegian development assistance, 1974. Oslo , 1975. 57 p. ; LC Card 86-460167
HA1503 .A18 nr. 34 HC60

ECONOMIC ASSISTANCE, NORWEGIAN - PAKISTAN.
Pakistan . Fantoft, Norway [1985] xvii, 414 p. : ISBN 82-905840-4-0 (pbk.) LC Card 86-235254 DDC 338.91/481/05491 19
HC440.5 .P26 1985

ECONOMIC ASSISTANCE, NORWEGIAN - ZAMBIA.
Zambia, country study and Norwegian aid review. Fantoft, Norway , 1986. xxi, 202 p., [1] leaf of plates : ISBN 82-905840-6-7 (pbk.) LC Card 87-105777 DDC 338.91/481/06894 19
HC915 .Z36 1986

ECONOMIC ASSISTANCE - PAKISTAN.
Cooperation in development and humanitarian assistance. Islamabad, Pakistan [1985] 50 p. : LC Card 86-930251 DDC 338.91/09549/1 19
HC440.5 .C66 1985

Report on development cooperation with Pakistan. Islamabad, Pakistan [1985] xxxvi, 267 p. : LC Card 85-931852 DDC 338.91/09549/2 19
HC440.5.Z9 E447 1985

ECONOMIC ASSISTANCE - POLITICAL ASPECTS - AFRICA, SUB-SAHARAN.
Görgens, Egon, 1941- Entwicklungshilfe und Ordnungspolitik . Bern , c1983. 111 p. ; ISBN

3-258-03324-2 : LC Card 84-108530
HC800 .G67 1983

ECONOMIC ASSISTANCE, RUSSIAN - DEVELOPING COUNTRIES - STATISTICS.
Bach, Quintin. Soviet economic assistance to the less developed countries . Oxford [Oxfordshire] , New York , 1987. p. cm. ISBN 0-19-828572-8 : LC Card 87-20349 DDC 338.91/47/01724 19
HC60 .B23 1987

ECONOMIC ASSISTANCE - SAHEL.
Berg, Elliot. Absorptive capacity in the Sahel countries. [Paris] [Ouagadougou, Burkina Faso] [1983] xi, 133 p. ; LC Card 87-402541 DDC 338.91/0966 19
HC1002 .B47 1983

Dumont, René, 1904- Pour l'Afrique, j'accuse . [Paris] , c1986. 457 p., [48] p. of plates : ISBN 2-259-01455-0 LC Card 86-220056
HC1002 .D85 1986

Sall, Alioune. Ressources humaines pour le développement . [Dakar, Sénégal , 1984] 51 p. : LC Card 85-129264 DDC 338.91/09624 19
HC1002 .S25 1984

Somerville, Carolyn M. Drought and aid in the Sahel . Boulder , 1986. xxii, 306 p. : ISBN 0-8133-7087-6 : LC Card 86-5635 DDC 338.966 19
HC1002 .S65 1986 ***NYPL [JLD 86-4038]***

ECONOMIC ASSISTANCE - SAHEL - DIRECTORIES.
L'Aide publique au développement dans les pays membres du CILSS en 1983 =. Paris , Burkina Faso [1984], c1985. v, 347 p. : LC Card 86-180117
HC1000 .A64 1985

ECONOMIC ASSISTANCE, SWEDISH - KENYA.
Millwood, David. Good aid . Stockholm, Sweden , c1985. 246 p. : ISBN 91-586-7059-9 (pbk.) : LC Card 87-142767 DDC 338.91/485 19
HC425.Z9 E446 1985

ECONOMIC ASSISTANCE, SWEDISH - NEPAL.
Millwood, David. Good aid . Stockholm, Sweden , c1985. 246 p. : ISBN 91-586-7059-9 (pbk.) : LC Card 87-142767 DDC 338.91/485 19
HC425.Z9 E446 1985

ECONOMIC ASSISTANCE, SWEDISH - TANZANIA.
Utvecklingssamarbetet med Tanzania 1983/84-1984/85. Stockholm, Sweden [1983] ca. 200 p. ; LC Card 86-216305
HC885 .U87 1983

ECONOMIC ASSISTANCE, SWEDISH - TUNISIA.
Millwood, David. Good aid . Stockholm, Sweden , c1985. 246 p. : ISBN 91-586-7059-9 (pbk.) : LC Card 87-142767 DDC 338.91/485 19
HC425.Z9 E446 1985

ECONOMIC ASSISTANCE, SWISS - DEVELOPING COUNTRIES.
Glinz, Ferdinand N. Entwicklungsförderung am Wendepunkt . Zürich , c1986. 320 p. ; ISBN 3-280-01676-2 LC Card 86-227950
HC59.7 .G55 1986

ECONOMIC ASSISTANCE, WEST GERMAN - DEVELOPING COUNTRIES.
Bruchhaus, Eva-Maria. Frauen in Entwicklungsländern . Freiburg im Breisgau , 1979. iii, 182 p. ; LC Card 81-121677 DDC 305.4/09172/4 19
HQ1870.9 .B78 1979 ***NYPL [JLG 86-106]***

Entwicklungspolitik, Bilanz und Perspektiven . Bonn , 1986. 256 p. ; LC Card 87-409363 DDC 338.91/43/01724 19
HC60 .E523 1986

Kress, Roland, 1961- Die politischen Stiftungen in der Entwicklungspolitik . Bochum , 1985. iv, 224 p. ; ISBN 3-88339-426-2 : LC Card 85-175519
HC60 .K727 1985

Neundörfer, Konrad. Wir und die Dritte Welt . Köln , c1985. x, 214 p. ; ISBN 3-452-20304-2 LC Card 85-164555
HC59.7 .N375 1985

Die Notwendige Hilfe . Melle [1986] 207 p. : ISBN 3-88368-111-3 : LC Card 86-197696
HC60 .N69 1986

Protz, Michael. Administrative Zusammenarbeit in der Entwicklungspolitik . Speyer , 1982. ix, 382, 2 p. ; LC Card 86-218043
HC60 .P77 1982

Stockhausen, Joachim von. Theorie und Politik der Entwicklungshilfe . München , c1986. viii, 324 p. ; ISBN 3-8039-0332-1 LC Card 86-225372
HC60 .S7977 1986

Watzal, Ludwig, 1950- Entwicklungspolitik zwischen Immanenz und Transzendenz . Frankfurt am Main , New York , c1986. 121 p. ; ISBN 3-8204-8785-9 LC Card 86-198339
HD75 .W36 1986

ECONOMIC ASSISTANCE, WEST GERMAN - DEVELOPING COUNTRIES - CONGRESSES.
Entwicklungspolitik im Spannungsfeld von Solidarität und Eigeninteresse . Stuttgart , New York , 1986. 155 p. ; ISBN 3-437-50306-5 LC Card 87-408212 DDC 338.91/43/01724 19
HC60 .E527 1986

Germany (West). Bundestag. Ausschuss für Wirtschaftliche Zusammenheit. Entwicklungspolitik, Bilanz und Perspektiven . Bonn , 1986. 256 p. ; LC Card 87-409259 DDC 339.91/43/01724 19
HC60 .G467 1986

ECONOMIC ASSISTANCE - ZIMBABWE - CONGRESSES.
Zimbabwe Conference on Reconstruction and Development (1981 : Salisbury, Zimbabwe) Zimbabwe Conference on Reconstruction and Development, Salisbury, 23rd to 27th March 1981 . Causeway, Zimbabwe [1981?] vi, 194 p. : LC Card 86-980955 DDC 338.96891 19
HC910 .Z318 1981a

Economic associations in Hungary with foreign participation. Budapest : Hungarian Foreign Trade Bank, 1986. 24 p. ; 24 cm. LC Card 87-106055 DDC 346.439/068 344.390668 19
1. Joint ventures - Hungary. I. Magyar Külkereskedelmi Bank.
HD62.47 .E25 1986

Economic behaviour in adversity /. Hirshleifer, Jack. Chicago , 1987. ix, 310 p. ; ISBN 0-226-34282-4 : LC Card 87-19846 DDC 330.9 19
HC79.D45 H57 1987

Economic cancer /. Evans, David Michael, 1955- Saratoga, CA [1987], c1986. 119 p. ; ISBN 0-88247-764-1 (pbk.) : LC Card 86-62711 DDC 338.973 19
HC106.8 .E93 1987

Economic choice under uncertainty . Ford, J. L. New York , c1987. ix, 146 p. ; ISBN 0-312-01244-6 : LC Card 87-18806 DDC 330.1 19
HB615 .F674 1987

Economic choices : political decisions that affect you. Arlington, Va. : Close Up Foundation, c1987. 73 p. : ill. ; 23 cm. ISBN 0-932765-08-4 (pbk.) : LC Card 87-686 DDC 338.973 19
1. United States - Economic policy. 2. Monetary policy - United States. 3. United States - Commercial policy. I. Close Up Foundation.
HC106 .E24 1987

Economic choices 1987 / Henry J. Aaron ... [et al.]. Washington, D.C. : Brookings Institution, 1986. xii, 126 p. ; 23 cm. Includes bibliographical references. ISBN 0-8157-1040-2 LC Card 85-48278
1. Deficit financing - United States. 2. Interest rates - United States. 3. Government spending policy - United States. 4. United States - Economic policy - 1981-. I. Aaron, Henry J. ***NYPL [JLE 86-2737]***

Economic Commission for Africa. The Cement industry in the African region /. Addis Ababa , 1983. 36, [40] p. ; LC Card 86-201071 DDC 338.4/766694/096 19
HD9622.A42 C46 1983

Economic Community of West African States. A Critical appraisal of the economic and social conditions in the west African subregion /. [Lagos , 1979-1980] 10 v. : LC Card 87-159535 DDC 330.966 19
HC1000 .C75 1979

Development of the community : the first five years, 1977-1981. Lagos : Economic Community of West African States, 1981. 51 leaves ; 26 cm. "ECW/DEVE/C/7781." LC Card 87-403455 DDC 337.1/66 19
1. Economic Community of West African States - History. 2. Africa, West - Economic integration - History. I. Title.
HC1000 .E23 1981

ECONOMIC COMMUNITY OF WEST AFRICAN STATES.
West Africa--regional cooperation and development /. Boulder , 1988. p. cm. ISBN 0-8133-7354-9 : LC Card 87-9290 DDC 338.966 19
HC1000 .W47 1988

ECONOMIC COMMUNITY OF WEST AFRICAN STATES - CONGRESSES.
Towards an African economic community . [Ibadan, Nigeria] , 1986. 401 p. ; ISBN 978-18-1040-8 LC Card 87-143033 DDC 337.1/66 19
HC1000 .T69 1986

ECONOMIC COMMUNITY OF WEST AFRICAN STATES - HISTORY.
Economic Community of West African States. Development of the community . Lagos , 1981. 51 leaves ; LC Card 87-403455 DDC 337.1/66 19
HC1000 .E23 1981

Economic competitiveness promoting America's living standard / the Senate Democratic Working Group on Economic Competitiveness of the Democratic Policy Committee ; Senator Jeff Bingaman of New Mexico, Chairman ... (et al.]. Washington : U. S. G.P.O., 1986 [i.e. 1987] vii, 34 p. : ill. ; 24 cm. (S. prt. . 99-205) At head of title: 99th Congress, 2d session. Committee print. Shipping list no.: 87-76-P. "September 1986." Item 998-A-1 LC Card 87-601340 DDC 338.973 19
1. United States - Economic policy - 1981-. 2. Competition - United States. 3. Balance of trade - United States. 4. Cost and standard of living - United States. 5. United States - Commercial policy. 6. United States - Economic conditions - 1981-. I. Bingaman, Jeff. II. United States. Congress. Senate. Democratic Policy Committee. Democratic Working Group on Economic Competitiveness. III. Series.
HC106.8 .E2745 1987

ECONOMIC CONCENTRATION. see **BIG BUSINESS; INDUSTRIAL CONCENTRATION.**

Economic concepts . Bingham, Robert C. New York , c1987. xv, 444 p. ; ISBN 0-07-044963-5 (pbk.) LC Card 87-3351 DDC 330/.07/7 19
HB171.5 .B52 1987

ECONOMIC CONDITIONS. see **ECONOMIC HISTORY.**

Economic contribution and impacts of changes in Iowa's livestock and meat processing industries /. Otto, Daniel. Oakdale, Iowa [1984] xi, 95 p. : LC Card 85-621899 DDC 338.1/76/009777021 19
HD9417.I8 O88 1984 ***NYPL [JLF 86-592]***

Economic co-operation between Nigeria and the socialist countries of Eastern Europe / [edited by A.B. Akinyemi]. Lagos : Nigerian Institute of International Affairs : Macmillan Nigeria, 1986, c1984. 210 p. : ill. ; 23 cm. Cover title: Economic co-operation between Nigeria and Eastern Europe. Proceedings of a conference held in Lagos, Nigeria, in May 1980, sponsored by the United Nations Conference on Trade and Development (UNCTAD) and the Nigerian Institute of International Affairs (NIIA) Title page dated 1984. Bibliography: p. 204-210. ISBN 978-13-2828-2 (pbk.) LC Card 87-155295 DDC 337.669047 19
1. Nigeria - Foreign economic relations - Europe, Eastern - Congresses. 2. Europe, Eastern - Foreign economic relations - Nigeria - Congresses. I. Akinyemi, A. B. II. Nigerian Institute of International Affairs. III. United Nations. Conference on Trade and Development. IV. Title: Economic cooperation between Nigeria and the socialist countries of Eastern Europe.
HF1616.7.Z4 E8523 1986

Economic cooperation between Nigeria and the socialist countries of Eastern Europe.
Economic co-operation between Nigeria and the socialist countries of Eastern Europe /. Lagos , 1986, c1984. 210 p. : ISBN 978-13-2828-2 (pbk.) LC Card 87-155295 DDC 337.669047 19
HF1616.7.Z4 E8523 1986

The Economic crisis : policies for adjustment, stabilization, and growth. 1st ed. Santiago,

Chile : Economic Commission for Latin American [sic] and the Caribbean, United Nations ; New York, NY, USA : Can be ordered from United Nations Sales Section, 1986. 132 p. : ill. ; 23 cm. (Cuadernos de la CEPAL, 0252-2195 . 54) Bibliography: p. 81-87. "LC/G.1408/Rev. 2 October 1986"--T.p. verso. "United Nations publication. Sales no. E.86.II.G.12"--T.p. verso. ISBN 92-1-121132-8 (pbk.) LC Card 87-404540 DDC 338.98 19
1. Latin America - Economic policy. 2. Economic stabilization - Latin America. 3. Latin America - Economic conditions - 1945-. I. United Nations. Economic Commission for Latin America and the Caribbean. II. Series.
HC125 .E368 1986

Economic crisis, trade unions, and the state / edited by Otto Jacobi ... [et al.]. London : Dover, N.H. : Croom Helm, c1986. 295 p. ; 23 cm. Includes bibliographies and index. ISBN 0-7099-1447-4 : LC Card 85-28055 DDC 331/.094 19
1. Industrial relations - Great Britain - Addresses, essays, lectures. 2. Industrial relations - Italy - Addresses, essays, lectures. 3. Industrial relations - Germany, West - Addresses, essays, lectures. 4. Trade unions - Europe - Addresses, essays, lectures. 5. Europe - Economic conditions - 1945- - Addresses, essays, lectures. I. Jacobi, Otto.
HD8391 .E26 1986 ***NYPL [JLD 86-1301]***

ECONOMIC CYCLES. see **BUSINESS CYCLES.**

The Economic demography of mass poverty. [Williamsburg, Va., U. S.A. : Dept. of Anthropology, College of William and Mary, c1986] xiv, 142 p. : ill. ; 23 cm. (Studies in Third World Societies . publication no. 29) Cover title. Includes bibliographies. LC Card 85-73339 DDC 339.4/6/091724 19
1. Developing countries - Population - Economic aspects. 2. Poor - Developing countries. 3. Developing countries - Economic conditions. I. College of William and Mary. Dept. of Anthropology. II. Series.
HB884 .E36 1986

ECONOMIC DEPRESSIONS. see **DEPRESSIONS.**

Economic development . Arndt, H. W. (Heinz Wolfgang), 1915- Chicago , 1987. viii, 217 p. ; ISBN 0-226-02720-1 : LC Card 86-25108 DDC 338.9 19
HD82 .A66 1987

Economic development /. Hogendorn, Jan S. New York , c1987. xv, 508 p. : ISBN 0-06-042853-8 LC Card 86-27034 DDC 338.9 19
HD75 .H64 1987

ECONOMIC DEVELOPMENT - ADDRESSES, ESSAYS, LECTURES.

Bhagwati, Jagdish N., 1934- Essays in development economics /. Oxford [Oxfordshire] , 1985. 2 v. ; ISBN 0-631-14178-2 (v. 1) ***NYPL [JLL 86-16]***

Design, innovation, and long cycles in economic development /. London , 1986. 248 p. : ISBN 0-86187-616-4 ***NYPL [JLE 86-3312]***

International dimension of development problems . Amsterdam , New York , 1984. 103 p. ; ISBN 0-444-85621-8 (pbk.) LC Card 85-209291 DDC 338.9 19
HD75 .I59 1984 ***NYPL [JLE 86-1391]***

Misra, Rameshwar Prasad, 1930- Development issues of our time /. New Delhi , 1985. xi, 368 p. : LC Card 85-903754 DDC 338.9/009172/4 19
HC59.7 .M5334 1985 ***NYPL [JLE 86-1375]***

Patel, I. G. (Indraprasad Gordhanbhai), 1924- Essays in economic policy and economic growth /. Basingstoke, Hampshire , 1986. xii, 261 p. ; ISBN 0-333-39213-2 ***NYPL [JLD 86-4061]***

The Political economy of international technology transfer /. Westport, Conn. , c1986. viii, 267 p. : ISBN 0-89930-128-2 (lib. bdg. : alk. paper) LC Card 85-28128 DDC 338.9/26 19
HD45 .P574 1986 ***NYPL [JLE 86-3313]***

Theory and reality in development . Basingstoke, Hampshire , 1986. xii, 291 p. : ISBN 0-333-39824-6 ***NYPL [JLD 86-1827]***

Wachstumsverlangsamung und Konjunkturzyklen in unterschiedlichen Wirtschaftssystemen /. Berlin , c1984. 191 p. : ISBN 3-428-05626-4 ***NYPL [JLL 73-186 Bd. 142]***

Economic development and international trade / edited by David Greenaway. New York : St. Martin's Press, 1988. xi, 211 p. ; 25 cm. Bibliography: p. 195-205. Includes indexes. ISBN 0-312-01588-7 : LC Card 87-25629 DDC 382 19
1. International trade. 2. Economic development. 3. Developing countries - Economic policy. I. Greenaway, David.
HF1379 .E27 1988

Economic development and real estate financing / the National Development Council. N[ew] Y[ork], N.Y. (41 E. 42nd St., N[ew] Y[ork] 10017) : The Council, [c1985] iii, 203 p. : ill. ; 28 cm. Cover title. LC Card 86-221586 DDC 332.7/2/0973 19
1. Real estate development - United States - Finance. 2. Mortgages - United States. 3. Real estate investment - United States. I. National Development Council (U. S.).
HD255 .E26 1985

Economic development and the structure of the balance of payments . Maroulis, Dimitris. Athens , 1986. 267 p. : LC Card 87-170680 DDC 382.1/7/09495 19
HC295 .M32 1986

ECONOMIC DEVELOPMENT - CASE STUDIES.

Alschuler, Lawrence R., 1941- Multinationals and maldevelopment . New York , 1988. xii, 218 p. : ISBN 0-312-00531-8 : LC Card 87-4307 DDC 338.9 19
HD82 .A5493 1988

Cole, J. P. (John Peter), 1928- Development and underdevelopment . London , New York , 1987. vi, 104 p. : ISBN 0-416-92080-2 (pbk.) LC Card 86-23758 DDC 338.9/009172/4 19
HC59.7 .C59 1987

Energy and growth . London , Boston , 1986. xvii, 199 p. : ISBN 0-408-02560-3 : LC Card 85-31336 DDC 333.79/13 19
HD9502.A2 E542 1986 ***NYPL [JLE 86-2717]***

Roy, Ramashray. Dialogues on development . New Delhi , Beverly Hills , 1986. 245 p. ; ISBN 0-8039-9492-3 (U. S.) LC Card 85-8368 DDC 338.954/12 19
HD87 .R69 1986 ***NYPL [JLD 86-3196]***

ECONOMIC DEVELOPMENT - CONGRESSES.

Adjustment policies and development strategies in the Arab world /. Washington, D.C. , 1987. ix, 200 p. ; ISBN 0-939934-96-5 (pbk.) LC Card 87-21377 DDC 338.9/00917/4927 19
HC498 .A6395 1987

Club of Rome Conference (1984 : Helsinki, Finland) Managing global issues . [Lahti] [1985] 216 p. : ISBN 951-45-3807-2 (pbk.) LC Card 87-140928 DDC 909.82/8 19
HC13 .C56 1984

The Design of alternative development strategies /. Rohtak, India , 1986. xiv, 330 p. : LC Card 86-901301 DDC 338.9 19
HD82 .D383 1986 ***NYPL [JLE 86-4232]***

Disarmament and world development /. Oxford, England , New York , 1986. xiii, 306 p. ; ISBN 0-08-031309-4 : LC Card 85-19231 DDC 338.4/7355 19
JX1974 .D515 1985 ***NYPL [JLE 86-3211]***

Dritte-Welt-Kongress (1985 : Hof (Hof, Germany)) Entwicklungspolitik im Wandel . Stuttgart , 1986. 256 p. ; ISBN 3-87959-271-3 LC Card 86-193768
HD73 .D75 1985

Economic incentives . London , 1986. xiii, 497 p. ; ISBN 0-333-40473-4 ***NYPL [JLD 87-367]***

Employment and growth . Dordrecht , Boston , 1987. xii, 310 p. : ISBN 90-247-3514-9 LC Card 87-3184 DDC 331.11 19
HD73 .E46 1987

Entwicklungstheorie, Entwicklungspraxis . Berlin , c1986. 316 p. ; ISBN 3-428-05973-5 LC Card 86-233851 DDC 338.9/009172/4 19
HC59.7 .E6473 1986

Epargne et développement /. Paris , 1985. 410 p. : ISBN 2-7178-0855-8 : LC Card 86-149765
HC59.72.S3 E62 1985

Die Gegenwärtige Wachstumskrise . Regensburg , c1985. viii, 262 p. : ISBN 3-924956-08-1 LC Card 86-122363 DDC 338.9 19
HD73 .G43 1985

Global Meeting on Environment and Development for Non-governmental Organisations (1985 : Nairobi, Kenya) Sustainable development . [Nairobi, Kenya] [1985 or 1986] 109 p. : LC Card 86-981176 DDC 363.7/057 19
HC79.E5 G595 1985

International Industrial Conference, 1st, San Francisco, 1957. Private investment /. New York , 1980, c1958. xi, 282 p. ; ISBN 0-405-13355-3 LC Card 80-606 DDC 332.6/7314
HG4538 .I537 1957d ***NYPL [JLD 81-249]***

Population and Development Symposium (1985 : Cairo, Egypt) Population and development . Cairo , 1986. 616 p. : LC Card 86-969481 DDC 304.6 19
HB849 .P575 1986

Rembser, Josef. Die Förderung des wirtschaftlichen und sozialen Wandels durch die Forschungs- und Entwicklungspolitik als präventive Strukturpolitik /. Dortmund , 1977. 100 p. : LC Card 84-130876
HD30 .A7 Heft 184 HD6331.2.G28

Seminar "Planung des Berufsausbildungswesens in Entwicklungsländern" (1965 : Berlin, Germany) Seminar "Planung des Berufsausbildungswesens in Entwicklungsländern" vom 22. Juli bis 17. August 1965 /. Berlin-Tegel [1965?] 1 portfolio ; LC Card 87-407604
HD5715.5.D44 S46 1965

Tanmiyah al-ʻArabīyah wa-al-ʻalāqāt al-dawlīyah /. al-Kuwayt , 1983. 230, 96 p. ; LC Card 86-964623
HC498 .T349 1983

Urbanisation in the developing world /. London , Dover, N.H. , c1986. 265 p. ; ISBN 0-7099-0884-9 : LC Card 86-4551 DDC 307.7/6/091724 19
HT149.5 .U74 1986 ***NYPL [JLD 86-2402]***

ECONOMIC DEVELOPMENT - DATA PROCESSING.

Application of computer technology for development. Hungarian. A számítástechnika felhasználása a fejlődés előmozdítására . [Budapest] [1971] 95 p. : LC Card 85-178670
HD85.H88 A6615 1971

ECONOMIC DEVELOPMENT - DICTIONARIES - POLYGLOT.

Brodmeier, Beate. Entwicklungspolitische Fachausdrücke (Auswahl) . Baden-Baden , 1985. 48 p. ; ISBN 3-7890-1093-6 LC Card 85-186152
HD84 .B765 1985

Logie, Gordon. Glossary of planning and development . Amsterdam , New York , 1986. xxv, 254 p. ; ISBN 0-444-42608-6 (U. S.) : LC Card 86-521 DDC 338.9/003 19
HT391 .L64 1987 ***NYPL [JLE 86-4010]***

ECONOMIC DEVELOPMENT - DIRECTORIES.

Government economic agencies of the world . Detroit , c1985. x, 546 p. ; ISBN 0-8103-2104-1 (Gale) LC Card 84-26861 DDC 351.82/025 19
HD87.25 .G68 1985 ***NYPL [*R-Econ 86-6573]***

ECONOMIC DEVELOPMENT - ECONOMETRIC MODELS.

Gerhardt, Gisela, 1955- Konsumverhalten und wirtschaftliche Entwicklung . München , c1984. 224 p. : ISBN 3-88259-278-8 LC Card 84-220049
HC79.C6 G47 1984

Paldam, Martin. How much does one percent of growth change the unemployment? . Aarhus, Denmark [1986] 35 p. : LC Card 86-221448 DDC 331.13/7 19
HD5707.5 .P34 1986

Schalk, Hans Joachim. Differenzierte Globalsteuerung . Berlin , New York , c1985. ix, 319 p. : ISBN 0-387-16045-0 (U. S.) LC Card 86-141700
HB3732 .S32 1985

Solomou, Solomos. Phases of economic growth, 1850-1973 . Cambridge [Cambridgeshire] , New York , 1987. p. cm. ISBN 0-521-33457-8 LC

Card 86-34324 DDC 338.9 19
HB3729 .S65 1987

ECONOMIC DEVELOPMENT - EFFECT OF EDUCATION ON.
Psacharopoulos, George. Education for development . New York , 1985. ix, 337 p. : ISBN 0-19-520477-8 LC Card 85-13782 DDC 338.9 19
HD75.7 .P77 1985 ***NYPL [JLE 86-1073]***

ECONOMIC DEVELOPMENT - ENVIRONMENTAL ASPECTS.
Community management . West Hartford, Conn. , c1986. xxii, 328 p. : ISBN 0-931816-40-8 (pbk.) LC Card 86-27691 DDC 338.95 19
HD75.6 .C65 1986

Globalni problemi . Sofiīa , 1986. 268 p. : LC Card 86-231293
HD75 .G555 1986

Görög, Tibor. Ökopesszimizmus, technooptimizmus és korunk globális problémái /. [Budapest] , 1984. 85 p. : ISBN 963-673-290-6 LC Card 85-130717
HC59 .G6226 1984

Leipert, Christian. Folgekosten des Wachstums als Wachstumsstimulans . Berlin [1985?] 35 p. : LC Card 86-116361
HD75.6 .L45 1985

Lindner, Eberhard. Ausweg aus der Weltkrise . Karlsruhe , 1984. 319 p. : ISBN 3-921653-15-0 LC Card 85-104217 DDC 363.7 19
HD75.6 .L56 1984 ***NYPL [JLD 87-484]***

Makalová, Eva. Ekonomické aspekty globálních problémů lidstva /. Praha , 1984. 97 p. ; LC Card 86-207353
HB9 .P72a 1984, 4/20 HD75

Martínez Alier, Juan. [Ecologisme i l'economia. English.] Ecological economics . Oxford [Oxfordshire] , New York, NY, USA , 1987. ix, 286 p. ; ISBN 0-631-15739-5 : LC Card 87-14512 DDC 333.7 19
HD85.S7 M363513 1987

Ökologische Unternehmenspolitik /. Frankfurt , New York , c1986. 280 p. ; ISBN 3-593-33580-8 LC Card 87-407999 DDC 363.7 19
HD75.6 .O347 1986

Our common future /. Oxford , New York , 1987. xv, 383 p. ; ISBN 0-19-282080-X (pbk.) : LC Card 87-7853 DDC 363.7 19
HD75.6 .O97 1987

Perrings, Charles. Economy and environment . Cambridge [Cambridgeshire] , New York , 1987. xv, 179 p. ; ISBN 0-521-34081-0 LC Card 87-18329 DDC 333.7 19
HD75.6 .P47 1987

Pogorelova, O. A. (Oksana Afanas'evna) Ėkologicheskiĭ krizis v usloviīakh sovremennogo kapitalizma . Kiev , 1986. 110, [2] p. ; LC Card 86-233475
HD75.6 .P64 1986

Los Problemas del conocimiento y la perspectiva ambiental del desarrollo /. México, D.F. , 1986. 476 p., [1] folded leaf of plates : ISBN 968-231-372-4 LC Card 87-119336 DDC 363.7/0098 19
HD75.6 .P76 1986

Raiātskas, R. L. (Raĭmundas Leonovich), 1937- Okruzhaiūshchaīa sreda i problemy planirovaniīa /. Moskva , 1981. 272 p. ; LC Card 87-462039
HD75.6 .R35 1981

Redclift, M. R. Sustainable development . London , New York , 1987. 221 p. : ISBN 0-416-90240-5 LC Card 87-5710 DDC 363.7 19
HD75.6 .R43 1987

ECONOMIC DEVELOPMENT - ENVIRONMENTAL ASPECTS - ADDRESSES, ESSAYS, LECTURES.
Marktwirtschaft 2000 /. Krefeld , c1983. 137 p. : ISBN 3-88289-302-8 LC Card 84-229313 DDC 338.9 19
HD75.6 .M37 1983 ***NYPL [JLD 86-3124]***

ECONOMIC DEVELOPMENT - ENVIRONMENTAL ASPECTS - CONGRESSES.
Alternative Ökonomie? /. Köln , 1982. 244 p. ; ISBN 3-7616-0671-0 (pbk.) LC Card 84-109717 DDC 338.9 19
HD88 .A48 1982 ***NYPL [JLC 86-230]***

Symposium Umweltprobleme als Herausforderung der Marktwirtschaft, Neue Ideen jenseits des Dirigismus (1983 : Stuttgart, Germany) Symposium Umweltprobleme als Herausforderung der Marktwirtschaft, Neue Ideen jenseits des Dirigismus . [Köln] [Freiburg] , 1983. 300 p. ; ISBN 3-7616-0722-9 LC Card 84-152335 DDC 363.7/058 19
HC79.E5 S96 1983 ***NYPL [JLD 86-1631]***

ECONOMIC DEVELOPMENT - ENVIRONMENTAL ASPECTS - FLORIDA.
The Saddlebrook papers . [Fort Lauderdale] [Tallahassee] [1985] v leaves, 177 p. : LC Card 86-621089 DDC 338.9759 19
HC107.F63 E547 1985

ECONOMIC DEVELOPMENT - ENVIRONMENTAL ASPECTS - MATHEMATICAL MODELS.
Müller, Karl-Wilhelm, 1953- Die Theorie erschöpfbarer natürlicher Ressourcen bei wachsender Bevölkerung /. Frankfurt am Main , New York , c1984. 191 p. : ISBN 3-8204-5315-6 LC Card 85-197540
HD75.6 .M85 1984

ECONOMIC DEVELOPMENT - FINANCE.
Kitchen, Richard L. Finance for the developing countries /. Chichester [West Sussex] , New York , c1986. xvii, 365 p. ; ISBN 0-471-90945-9 : LC Card 85-32331 DDC 332/.09172/4 19
HG195 .K58 1986 ***NYPL [JLE 86-4165]***

ECONOMIC DEVELOPMENT - GOVERNMENT POLICY - UNITED STATES - STATES - DIRECTORIES.
Guide to state capital formation incentives and innovations /. [Washington, D.C. , 1983] vii, 154 p. ; LC Card 86-673432
HC110.I53 G84x 1983

ECONOMIC DEVELOPMENT - GRAPHIC METHODS.
Metodología de evaluación y programación de sistemas de producción y consumo, MEPS /. Lima, Perú [1985]- v. <1 > : LC Card 86-215609
HD75 .M48 1985

ECONOMIC DEVELOPMENT - HISTORY.
Morris, Cynthia Taft. Comparative patterns of economic development, 1850-1914 /. Baltimore , c1988. xi, 575 p. ; ISBN 0-8018-3507-0 (alk. paper) LC Card 87-45480 DDC 338.9/009 19
HC51 .M645 1988

Economic development in a conscious state . Robbins, Bradley. Tallahassee, Fla. [1984] viii, 41, [5] p. : LC Card 86-621090 DDC 338.9759 19
HC107.F6 R63 1984

Economic development in Africa : international efforts, issues, and prospects / edited by Olusola Akinrinade and J. Kurt Barling. London : Pinter, 1987. x, 266 p. ; 24 cm. Bibliography: p. [239]-249. Includes index. ISBN 0-86187-909-0 : LC Card 87-15296 DDC 338.98 19
1. Economic assistance - Africa. 2. Africa - Economic conditions - 1960-. I. Akinrinade, Olusola. II. Barling, J. Kurt.
HC800 .E275 1987

Economic development in Chile under two growth strategies, 1925-1968 /. Pitts, Mary Anne, 1927- New York , 1987. vii, 246 p. ; ISBN 0-8240-1368-9 (alk. paper) : LC Card 87-7618 DDC 338.983 19
HC192 .P627 1987

Economic development in East and South-east Asia : implications for Australian agriculture in the 1980s / [contributors, Mike Adams ... et al.]. Canberra : Australian Govt. Pub. Service, 1984. x, 237 p. : ill. ; 25 cm. At head of title: Bureau of Agricultural Economics, Canberra. Includes bibliographies. ISBN 0-644-02983-8 (pbk.) LC Card 86-673760
1. East Asia - Economic conditions. 2. Asia, Southeastern - Economic conditions. 3. Agriculture - Economic aspects - Australia. I. Adams, M. G. (Mike G.). II. Australia. Bureau of Agricultural Economics.
HC460.5 .E26x 1984

Economic development in provincial China . Vermeer, E. B. (Eduard B.) Cambridge [Cambridgeshire] , New York , 1988. p. cm. ISBN 0-521-34392-5 LC Card 87-22499 DDC 330.951/17058 19
HC428.S54 V47 1988

ECONOMIC DEVELOPMENT - INFORMATION SERVICES.
Intelligence for economic development . Leamington Spa, [Warwickshire] ; New York : xiii, 264 p. : ISBN 0-85496-520-3 : LC Card 86-32250 DDC 025/.063389 19
HD76.2 .I58 1987

Economic Development Institute (Washington, D. C.) Food policy . Baltimore , c1987. xiv, 567 p. : ISBN 0-8018-3500-3 (pbk.) : LC Card 86-27613 DDC 363.8/56/091724 19
HD9018.D44 F665 1987

ECONOMIC DEVELOPMENT - INTERNATIONAL COOPERATION - CONGRESSES.
Der Nord-Süd-Dialog zu Beginn der 80er Jahre =. Baden-Baden , 1982. 99 p. ; ISBN 3-7890-0774-9 ***NYPL [JLE 87-1282]***

ECONOMIC DEVELOPMENT - MATHEMATICAL MODELS.
Ball, Helmut. Zukunftsvorsorge und ökonomische Entwicklung . Frankfurt [am Main] , New York , c1984. 263 p. : ISBN 3-593-33318-X LC Card 84-175872
HD75.5 .B35 1984

Dadaīan, V. S. (Vladislav Surenovich), 1933- Global'nye ėkonomicheskie modeli /. Moskva , 1981. 214 p. : LC Card 82-117634
HD75.5 .D33 1981

The Globus model . Boulder , 1986. p. cm. ISBN 0-8133-0528-4 : LC Card 87-8281 DDC 338.9/00724 19
HC59 .G577 1986

Modele matematice și semiotice ale dezvoltării sociale /. București , 1986. 190 p. : LC Card 86-208152
HD75.5 .M615 1986

Nerlove, Marc, 1933- Population policy and individual choice . Washington, D.C., U. S.A. , 1987. 52 p. : ISBN 0-89629-062-X (pbk.) LC Card 87-16802 DDC 363.9 19
HB901 .N474 1987

Reetz, Norbert. Konjunktur und Wachstum . St. Gallen , 1983. viii, 121 p. : LC Card 83-141234
HD75.5 .R44 1983

Serra, Daniel. Monnaie, inflation et croissance /. Paris , 1982. xi, 306 p. : ISBN 2-7178-0478-1 : LC Card 82-153767 DDC 332.4/0724 19
HG221 .S485 1982 ***NYPL [JLE 86-1903]***

Shakhdzhakhan, Ali. Issledovanie odnoĭ matematicheskoĭ modeli ėkonomicheskogo rosta /. Moskva , 1983. 29, [2] p. : LC Card 83-176389
HD75.5 .S52 1983

Simon, Julian Lincoln, 1932- Theory of population and economic growth /. Oxford , 1986. xi, 232 p. : ISBN 0-631-14427-7 : LC Card 85-28574 DDC 338.9/00724 19
HB849.41 .S55 1986 ***NYPL [JLE 86-3702]***

Ströbele, Wolfgang. Wirtschaftswachstum bei begrenzten Energieressourcen /. Berlin , c1984. 173 p. : ISBN 3-428-05541-1 LC Card 84-176734
HD84 .S747 1984

Wagner, Helmut. Inflation und Wirtschaftswachstum . Berlin , c1983. 234 p. : ISBN 3-428-05319-2 LC Card 83-219188
HG229 .W237 1983

Wallenwein, Erich, 1951- Die Bedeutung der Kapitalintensitätshypothese im neoklassischen Zwei-Sektoren-Modell und ihre empirische Überprüfung /. Frankfurt am Main , New York , c1986. x, 354 p. : ISBN 3-8204-9618-1 LC Card 86-194355
HD75.5 .W33 1986

Ziesemer, Thomas. Economic theory of underdevelopment /. Regensburg , c1987. vi, 171 p. : ISBN 3-924956-15-4 (pbk.) LC Card 87-169372 DDC 338.9/001 19
HD75.5 .Z54 1987

ECONOMIC DEVELOPMENT - MORAL AND ETHICAL ASPECTS.
Watzal, Ludwig, 1950- Entwicklungspolitik zwischen Immanenz und Transzendenz . Frankfurt am Main , New York , c1986. 121 p. ; ISBN 3-8204-8785-9 LC Card 86-198339
HD75 .W36 1986

Watzal, Ludwig, 1950- Ethik, Kultur, Entwicklung . Göttingen , c1985. 131 p. ; ISBN 3-7881-1741-9 LC Card 86-122983 DDC 338.9 19
HD75 .W37 1985

ECONOMIC DEVELOPMENT - MORAL AND ETHICAL ASPECTS - CONGRESSES.
Alternative Ökonomie? /. Köln , 1982. 244 p. ; ISBN 3-7616-0671-0 (pbk.) LC Card 84-109717 DDC 338.9 19
HD88 .A48 1982 ***NYPL [JLC 86-230]***

Tokyo Forum: Ethics of Human Survival (1985) Proceedings of the Tokyo Forum: Ethics of Human Survival . Tokyo, Japan , c1986. v, 88 p. : ISBN 4-7955-1024-5 LC Card 87-142747
HD73 .T65 1985

The economic development of Japan . Minami, Ryōshin, 1933- [Nihon no keizai hatten. English.] Basingstoke, Hampshire , 1986. xxvi, 487 p. : ISBN 0-333-38582-9 LC Card 87-672411
HC462.7 .M47513x 1986b

The economic development of the Pacific Basin . Kraus, Willy. New York , London , 1986. x, 180 p., [1] leaf of plates : ISBN 0-312-00452-4 (alk. paper) : LC Card 86-26292 DDC 338.95 19
HF1591 .K73 1986

Economic development of tribal India /. Mahapatro, Prafulla Ch. New Delhi , 1987. xvi, 408 p. : ISBN 81-7024-077-8 : LC Card 87-900212 DDC 338.954/13 19
HC437.K63 M34 1987

Economic development on the island of Kauai : issues and options. [Honolulu] : Dept. of Planning and Economic Development, Kauai Inter-Division Committee, [1985] xxii, 84 p. : ill. ; 28 cm. "December 1985." Bibliography: p. 81-84. LC Card 86-622084 DDC 338.9969/41 19
1. Kauai (Hawaii) - Economic conditions. 2. Agriculture - Economic aspects - Hawaii - Kauai. I. Hawaii. Dept. of Planning and Economic Development. Kauai Inter-Division Committee.
HC107.H32 K383 1985

ECONOMIC DEVELOPMENT - POLITICAL ASPECTS.
Brett, E. A. The world economy since the war . Houndmills, Basingstoke, Hampshire , 1985. x, 318 p. : ISBN 0-333-37199-2 LC Card 87-673378
HC59 .B754x 1985

ECONOMIC DEVELOPMENT - POLITICAL ASPECTS - CONGRESSES.
Reassessing the role of government in the mixed economy /. Boulder , 1987. p. cm. ISBN 0-8133-0598-5 : LC Card 87-20142 DDC 338.9 19
HD73 .R43 1987

ECONOMIC DEVELOPMENT PROJECTS - ACCOUNTING.
ECONOMIC DEVELOPMENT PROJECTS - AFRICA.
Diversity in development . New York, NY , c1985. 49 p. : ISBN 0-932140-06-8 (pbk.) LC Card 86-231753 DDC 361.7/096 19
HC800.Z9 E444 1985

United Nations transport and communications decade in Africa (1978-1988) . [S.l.] [1983?] iii, 32 p. ; LC Card 87-115721 DDC 380.3/096 19
HE8465 .U55 1983

ECONOMIC DEVELOPMENT PROJECTS - AFRICA - ACCOUNTING.
Ghartey, J. B., 1944- Crisis accountability and development in the Third World . Aldershot, Hants, England , Brookfield, Vt., USA , c1987. x, 170 p. ; ISBN 0-566-05290-3 : LC Card 86-25777 DDC 338.91/096 19
HC800 .G52 1987

ECONOMIC DEVELOPMENT PROJECTS - AFRICA - ADDRESSES, ESSAYS, LECTURES.
Population and development projects in Africa /. Cambridge [Cambridgeshire] , New York , 1985. xvi, 329 p. : ISBN 0-521-30527-6 LC Card 84-29323 DDC 304.6/096 19
HB2121.A3 P67 1985 ***NYPL [JLF 86-186]***

ECONOMIC DEVELOPMENT-PROJECTS - AFRICA - CONGRESSES.
Séminaire de formation aux techniques d'élaboration de projets (1980 : Conakry, Guinea, etc.) Séminaire de formation aux techniques d'élaboration de projets . Addis-Abeba , 1982. vii, 36, [31] p. : LC Card 86-168821
HC800 .S444 1980

ECONOMIC DEVELOPMENT PROJECTS - AFRICA - DIRECTORIES.
Diversity in development . New York, NY , c1986. xvii, 620 p. : ISBN 0-932140-07-6 (pbk.) LC Card 86-231757 DDC 361.7/025/73 19
HC800.Z9 E444 1986

ECONOMIC DEVELOPMENT PROJECTS - AMAZON RIVER REGION.
Brazil. Ministério do Interior. Subsecretaria de Programas Regionais. Programas especiais . [Brasília] [1981] 1 v. (various foliations) ; LC Card 87-403680 DDC 338.981/1 19
HD1875.A347 B7 1981

ECONOMIC DEVELOPMENT PROJECTS - ANGUILLA.
Caribbean Development Bank. Economics and Programming Dept. Economic memorandum on Anguilla. [Kingston, Jamaica] [1985] 2, 55 p. : LC Card 86-204700 DDC 330.97297/3 19
HC156.Z7 A483 1985

ECONOMIC DEVELOPMENT PROJECTS - ARAB COUNTRIES - FINANCE.
Arab Fund for Economic and Social Development. Arab Fund for Economic and Social Development, 1985. Kuwait, State of Kuwait [1986?] 15 p. : LC Card 87-128750 DDC 332.1/53 19
HG3881.5.A74 A73 1986

ECONOMIC DEVELOPMENT PROJECTS - ASIA - CASE STUDIES.
Fertility in Asia . London , 1986. xix, 177 p. : ISBN 0-86187-667-9 DDC 304.6/32/095 19
HB1043.A3 F47 1986b ***NYPL [JLD 87-1268]***

ECONOMIC DEVELOPMENT PROJECTS - BANGLADESH.
List of aid worth projects, 1984. [Dhaka] [1984] 431 p. ; LC Card 85-904102 DDC 338.9549/2 19
HC440.8.Z9 E445 1984

ECONOMIC DEVELOPMENT PROJECTS - BOLIVIA - LA PAZ - EVALUATION.
Salmen, Lawrence F., 1942- Listen to the people . New York , c1987. x, 149 p. : ISBN 0-19-520545-6 : LC Card 86-23672 DDC 338.984/12 19
HC185.E44 S25 1987

ECONOMIC DEVELOPMENT PROJECTS - BRAZIL.
Brazil. Ministerio do Interior. Ação de desenvolvimento, 1979-1983 /. [Brasília] [1983?] 89 p. : LC Card 87-404839 DDC 338.981 19
HC187 .B862 1983

Metais de Minas Gerais, S.A. Programa pegmatitos. Belo Horizonte , 1981. 95 p. : LC Card 83-220720
HD9506.B72 M48 1981

ECONOMIC DEVELOPMENT PROJECTS - BRAZIL - ALAGOAS.
Alagoas (Brazil) Plano Operativo 1983, Governo Divaldo Suruagy. [Maceió] [1983?] 196 p. ; LC Card 85-200834
HC188.A46 A44 1983a

ECONOMIC DEVELOPMENT PROJECTS - BRAZIL - ARAGUAIA RIVER REGION - FINANCE.
Projeto de Desenvolvimento Integrado da Bacia do Araguaia-Tocantins. Fontes de financiamento para projetos de desenvolvimento /. Brasília , 1985. 450 p. : LC Card 86-195649
HC188.A7 P76 1985

ECONOMIC DEVELOPMENT PROJECTS - BRAZIL - ARAGUAIA RIVER WATERSHED.
Projeto de Desenvolvimento Integrado da Bacia do Araguaia-Tocantins. Descrição da área e caracterização do projeto /. Brasília , 1983. 129 p. : LC Card 87-130908 DDC 338.981/73 19
HC188.A73 P76 1983

ECONOMIC DEVELOPMENT PROJECTS - BRAZIL, NORTHEAST.
ECONOMIC DEVELOPMENT PROJECTS - BRAZIL - RIO GRANDE DO NORTE.
Paiva, Francisco Ismar Martins. Projeto Pesca Industrial à Vela. [Natal, Brazil] [1982 or 1983] 91 p. : LC Card 85-102872
HD9464.B73 R487 1982

ECONOMIC DEVELOPMENT PROJECTS - BRAZIL - TOCANTINS RIVER REGION - FINANCE.
Projeto de Desenvolvimento Integrado da Bacia do Araguaia-Tocantins. Fontes de financiamento para projetos de desenvolvimento /. Brasília , 1985. 450 p. : LC Card 86-195649
HC188.A7 P76 1985

ECONOMIC DEVELOPMENT PROJECTS - BRAZIL - TOCANTINS RIVER WATERSHED.
Projeto de Desenvolvimento Integrado da Bacia do Araguaia-Tocantins. Descrição da área e caracterização do projeto /. Brasília , 1983. 129 p. : LC Card 87-130908 DDC 338.981/73 19
HC188.A73 P76 1983

ECONOMIC DEVELOPMENT PROJECTS - BURUNDI.
Development programme of the Kagera Basin . [Kigali] [1982] viii, 73 leaves : LC Card 85-980886 DDC 338.967 19
HC860.Z9 E444 1982

ECONOMIC DEVELOPMENT PROJECTS - COLOMBIA - ANTIOQUIA (DEPT.)
Foro El Suroeste de Antioquia y el Chocó Norte (1984 : Urrao, Colombia) Foro El Suroeste de Antioquia y el Chocó Norte . [Medellín] [1985] 65 p. : LC Card 87-400457 DDC 338.9861/2 19
HC198.A5 F595 1984

ECONOMIC DEVELOPMENT PROJECTS - COLOMBIA - CHOCÓ.
Foro El Suroeste de Antioquia y el Chocó Norte (1984 : Urrao, Colombia) Foro El Suroeste de Antioquia y el Chocó Norte . [Medellín] [1985] 65 p. : LC Card 87-400457 DDC 338.9861/2 19
HC198.A5 F595 1984

ECONOMIC DEVELOPMENT PROJECTS - COLOMBIA - LA CHORRERA REGION (AMAZONAS)
Plan integral de desarrollo del predio Putumayo. Bogotá [1986] 29 p. : LC Card 87-401011 DDC 338.9861/7 19
HC198.C49 P55 1986

ECONOMIC DEVELOPMENT PROJECTS - COLOMBIA - URRAO REGION.
Foro El Suroeste de Antioquia y el Chocó Norte (1984 : Urrao, Colombia) Foro El Suroeste de Antioquia y el Chocó Norte . [Medellín] [1985] 65 p. : LC Card 87-400457 DDC 338.9861/2 19
HC198.A5 F595 1984

ECONOMIC DEVELOPMENT PROJECTS - CONGRESSES.
Bidding for projects financed by international lending agencies /. Aldershot, Hants. , c1982. vii, 345 p. : ISBN 0-566-03033-0 LC Card 82-210482 DDC 332.1/53 19
HD2365 .B52 1982 ***NYPL [JLG 85-120]***

ECONOMIC DEVELOPMENT PROJECTS - COST EFFECTIVENESS - ADDRESSES, ESSAYS, LECTURES.
Economic valuation techniques for the environment . Baltimore , c1986. xx, 203 p. : ISBN 0-8018-3352-3 (alk. paper) LC Card 86-2730 DDC 363.7/05/0681 19
HC79.E5 E274 1986 ***NYPL [JLE 87-677]***

ECONOMIC DEVELOPMENT PROJECTS - DEVELOPING COUNTRIES.
Beyond bureaucracy . West Hartford, Conn. , c1986. xii, 256 p. : ISBN 0-931816-44-0 LC Card 86-34420 DDC 338.9/0068 19
HC59.72.E44 B48 1986

Havemann, Hans A., 1912- Industrialisierungspolitik für Entwicklungsländer . Aachen , 1982. 68 p. ; ISBN 3-922525-06-7 LC Card 83-203761
HC59.7 .H386 1982

Heaver, Richard, 1952- Country commitment to development projects /. Washington, D.C., U. S.A. [1986] 32 p. ; ISBN 0-8213-0860-2 (pbk.) LC Card 86-28114 DDC 338.91 19
HC59.72.E44 H43 1986

Hellinger, Steve. Aid for just development . Washington, D.C. (1010 Vermont Ave., N.W., Suite 521, Washington 20005) , c1987. vii, 191

p. ; LC Card 87-404422 DDC 338.91/09172/4 19
HC60 .H38516 1987

Israel, Arturo. Institutional development . Baltimore , 1987. x, 214 p. : ISBN 0-8018-3554-2 : LC Card 87-45494 DDC 338.9/009172/4 19
HC59.72.E44 I77 1987

Leisinger, Klaus M. Studien zur Entwicklungsökonomie /. Bern , c1986. 130 p. : ISBN 3-258-03665-9 LC Card 87-124013 DDC 338.9/009172/7 19
HC59.72.E44 L45 1986

Participatie, toegang tot ontwikkeling . Leiden , 1982, c1983. 313 p. ; ISBN 90-6624-043-1 LC Card 87-158868
HC59.72.E44 P37 1983

Power and poverty . Boulder , 1988. v, 186 p. ; ISBN 0-8133-7351-4 (pbk. : alk. paper) : LC Card 86-32578 DDC 338.9/009172/4 19
HC59.72.E44 P68 1988

With our own hands . Ottawa, Canada , c1986. 206 p. : ISBN 0-88936-460-5 (pbk.) LC Card 86-212405 DDC 338.91/71/01724 19
HC59.72.F44 W58 1986

ECONOMIC DEVELOPMENT PROJECTS - DEVELOPING COUNTRIES - CASE STUDIES.

Power and poverty . Boulder , 1988. v, 186 p. ; ISBN 0-8133-7351-4 (pbk. : alk. paper) : LC Card 86-32578 DDC 338.9/009172/4 19
HC59.72.E44 P68 1988

ECONOMIC DEVELOPMENT PROJECTS - DEVELOPING COUNTRIES - CITIZEN PARTICIPATION.

Jedlicka, Allen D. Organizational change and the Third World . New York , 1987. xii, 141 p. ; ISBN 0-275-92317-7 (alk. paper) : LC Card 87-13252 DDC 658.4/06/091724 19
HC59.72.E44 J43 1987

Participatie, toegang tot ontwikkeling . Leiden , 1982, c1983. 313 p. ; ISBN 90-6624-043-1 LC Card 87-158868
HC59.72.E44 P37 1983

ECONOMIC DEVELOPMENT PROJECTS - DEVELOPING COUNTRIES - CITIZEN PARTICIPATION - CASE STUDIES.

Paul, Samuel, 1930- Community participation in development projects . Washington, D.C. [1987]. v, 37 p. : ISBN 0-8213-0886-6 (pbk.) LC Card 87-2183 DDC 338.9/009172/4 19
HD75.8 .P38 1987

ECONOMIC DEVELOPMENT PROJECTS - DEVELOPING COUNTRIES - COST EFFECTIVENESS.

Sandanger, Runar. Prosjektevaluering i u-land . Oslo [1983] viii, 97 p. : LC Card 83-144428
HC60 .S156 1983

ECONOMIC DEVELOPMENT PROJECTS - DEVELOPING COUNTRIES - EVALUATION.

Evaluation du développement rural /. [Paris] , c1982. 201 p. : ISBN 2-11-084484-1 LC Card 84-134740
HC59.72.E44 E93 1982

Salmen, Lawrence F., 1942- Listen to the people . New York , c1987. x, 149 p. : ISBN 0-19-520545-6 : LC Card 86-23672 DDC 338.984/12 19
HC185.E44 S25 1987

Sang, Heng-Kang. Project evaluation . New York, N.Y. , c1987. p. cm. ISBN 0-9617304-0-4 : LC Card 87-6074 DDC 338.9/0068 19
HD75.9 .S26 1987

ECONOMIC DEVELOPMENT PROJECTS - DEVELOPING COUNTRIES - MANAGEMENT.

Hage, Jerald, 1932- Organizational change as a development strategy . Boulder, Colo. , 1987. xvi, 293 p. ; ISBN 1-555-87012-0 (lib. bdg. : alk. paper) : LC Card 87-12730 DDC 338.9/0068 19
HC59.72.E44 H34 1987

Jedlicka, Allen D. Organizational change and the Third World . New York , 1987. xii, 141 p. ; ISBN 0-275-92317-7 (alk. paper) : LC Card 87-13252 DDC 658.4/06/091724 19
HC59.72.E44 J43 1987

Neun, Hansjörg, 1953- Projektübergabe bei der technischen Zusammenarbeit mit Entwicklungsländer /. Augsburg [1985] viii, 315 p. : ISBN 3-87512-135-X : LC Card 86-228570
HD84 .N43 1985

Rondinelli, Dennis A. Development administration and U. S. foreign aid policy /. Boulder , 1987. xi, 188 p. ; ISBN 0-931477-97-2 (lib. bdg.) : LC Card 87-4555 DDC 338.9/0068 19
HC59.72.E44 R66 1987

ECONOMIC DEVELOPMENT PROJECTS - DJIBOUTI - CONGRESSES.

Djibouti, ville et pays en voie de développement . Djibouti [c1983] 2 v. : LC Card 87-131462
HC855.Z9 E443 1983

ECONOMIC DEVELOPMENT PROJECTS - ECUADOR - GUAYAQUIL - EVALUATION.

Salmen, Lawrence F., 1942- Listen to the people . New York , c1987. x, 149 p. : ISBN 0-19-520545-6 : LC Card 86-23672 DDC 338.984/12 19
HC185.E44 S25 1987

ECONOMIC DEVELOPMENT PROJECTS - EGYPT.

Prosterman, Roy L. Egyptian development and U. S. aid . [Seattle, Wash.?] , c1985. i, 32, A1-A10 p. ; LC Card 87-104139 DDC 338.91/73/062 19
HC830.Z9 E446 1985

ECONOMIC DEVELOPMENT PROJECTS - EVALUATION.

Brinkerhoff, Derick W. La gestion efficace des projets de développement . West Hartford, Conn. , c1987. vi, 186 p. : ISBN 0-931816-06-8 (pbk.) LC Card 86-33733 DDC 338.9/0068 19
HD75.8 .B75 1987

Bruchhaus, Eva-Maria. Frauen in Entwicklungsländern . Freiburg im Breisgau , 1979. iii, 182 p. ; LC Card 81-121677 DDC 305.4/09172/4 19
HQ1870.9 .B78 1979 ***NYPL [JLG 86-106]***

Monitoring and evaluating small business projects . [New York, NY] , c1987. ix, 262 p. : LC Card 87-6945 DDC 361.7 19
HD2346.5 .M65 1987

Preparación y presentación de proyectos de inversión /. [Santiago] , 1985. v, 138 p. : LC Card 87-116769
HD39 .P72 1985

Sang, Heng-Kang. Project evaluation . New York, N.Y. , c1987. p. cm. ISBN 0-9617304-0-4 : LC Card 87-6074 DDC 338.9/0068 19
HD75.9 .S26 1987

Stermole, Franklin J. Economic evaluation and investment decision methods /. Golden, Colo. , c1987. vi, 479 p. : ISBN 0-9603282-8-9 LC Card 86-83278 DDC 332.63 19
HG4028.C4 S714 1987

ECONOMIC DEVELOPMENT PROJECTS - EVALUATION - FORMS.

Metodología de evaluación y programación de sistemas de producción y consumo, MEPS /. Lima, Perú [1985]- v. <1 > : LC Card 86-215609
HD75 .M48 1985

ECONOMIC DEVELOPMENT PROJECTS - GHANA - VOLTA REGION - CONGRESSES.

Seminar on Economic Development of the Volta Region (1983 : Ho, Ghana) The Volta Region . Accra , c1986. iii, 140 p., [13] leaves of plates : ISBN 996-497-032-3 LC Card 87-402835 DDC 338.9667 19
HC1060.Z7 V647 1983

ECONOMIC DEVELOPMENT PROJECTS - GREAT BRITAIN.

Assessment of the employment effects of economic development projects funded under the Urban Programme /. London , 1986. vi, 52 p. : ISBN 0-11-751859-X (pbk.) : LC Card 86-197217 DDC 331.12/0941 19
HD5765.A6 A87 1986

ECONOMIC DEVELOPMENT PROJECTS - HONDURAS - INTIBUCÁ (DEPT.)

Consejo Superior de Planificación Económica (Honduras). Secretaría Técnica. Proyecto de desarrollo local de La Paz, Intibucá /. [Tegucigalpa, Honduras] [1984- v. <1 > : LC Card 86-213886
HC145.Z9 E443 1984

ECONOMIC DEVELOPMENT PROJECTS - HONDURAS - LA PAZ (DEPT.)

Consejo Superior de Planificación Económica (Honduras). Secretaría Técnica. Proyecto de desarrollo local de La Paz, Intibucá /. [Tegucigalpa, Honduras] [1984- v. <1 > : LC Card 86-213886
HC145.Z9 E443 1984

ECONOMIC DEVELOPMENT PROJECTS - INDIA - CITIZEN PARTICIPATION.

Ramana, D. V. A monograph on access planning as an essay on explorations in alternatives /. Kuala Lumpur [1982] 86 p. : LC Card 84-940306 DDC 338.954 19
HD75 .R36 1982

ECONOMIC DEVELOPMENT PROJECTS - INDIA - JHĀBUA (DISTRICT)

Pais, H. Poverty alleviation programmes . New Delhi , 1986. xii, 48, [3] p. (some folded) : LC Card 86-903597 DDC 362.5/8/09543 19
HC437.J43 P35 1986

ECONOMIC DEVELOPMENT PROJECTS - INDIA - MHAISAL.

Deshpande, V. D. (Vasant Dattatraya), 1930- The Mhaisal untouchables /. Pune , 1983. xi, 168 p. ; LC Card 83-906084 DDC 338.954/792 19
HC438.M45 D48 1983 ***NYPL [JLD 87-1139]***

ECONOMIC DEVELOPMENT PROJECTS - INDONESIA - CASE STUDIES.

Scott-Stevens, Susan. Foreign consultants and counterparts . Boulder , 1987. xvii, 229 p. : ISBN 0-8133-7370-0 (pbk. : alk. paper) LC Card 87-50750 DDC 306/.46 19
HC79.T4 S36 1987

ECONOMIC DEVELOPMENT PROJECTS - ITALY.

Rapporto sulle partecipazioni statali /. Milano [1981] 1 v. (in various pagings) ; ISBN 88-20-42161-5 : LC Card 81-199972 DDC 338.945 19
HC310.I53 R35 ***NYPL [JLD 83-2970]***

ECONOMIC DEVELOPMENT PROJECTS - KAGERA RIVER WATERSHED.

Development programme of the Kagera Basin . [Kigali] [1982] viii, 73 leaves : LC Card 85-980886 DDC 338.967 19
HC860.Z9 E444 1982

ECONOMIC DEVELOPMENT PROJECTS - KENYA.

Millwood, David. Good aid . Stockholm, Sweden , c1985. 246 p. : ISBN 91-586-7059-9 (pbk.) : LC Card 87-142767 DDC 338.91/485 19
HC425.Z9 E446 1985

ECONOMIC DEVELOPMENT PROJECTS - KENYA - EVALUATION.

Bethke, Klaus W. Small projects for rural development . [Nairobi] [1983] 33, [34] leaves ; LC Card 86-981325 DDC 354.676/20082 19
HC865 .B48 1983

ECONOMIC DEVELOPMENT PROJECTS - KENYA - PLANNING.

Bethke, Klaus W. Small projects for rural development . [Nairobi] [1983] 33, [34] leaves ; LC Card 86-981325 DDC 354.676/20082 19
HC865 .B48 1983

ECONOMIC DEVELOPMENT PROJECTS - MADAGASCAR - CASE STUDIES.

Leisinger, Klaus M. Studien zur Entwicklungsökonomie /. Bern , c1986. 130 p. : ISBN 3-258-03665-9 LC Card 87-124013 DDC 338.9/009172/7 19
HC59.72.E44 L45 1986

ECONOMIC DEVELOPMENT PROJECTS - MANAGEMENT.

Brinkerhoff, Derick W. La gestion efficace des projets de développement . West Hartford, Conn. , c1987. vi, 186 p. : ISBN 0-931816-06-8 (pbk.) LC Card 86-33733 DDC 338.9/0068 19
HD75.8 .B75 1987

White, Louise G. Creating opportunities for change . Boulder, Colo. , 1987. xvii, 283 p. : ISBN 1-555-87031-7 (lib. bdg.) : LC Card 87-4557 DDC 338.9/0068 19
HD75.8 .W47 1987

ECONOMIC DEVELOPMENT PROJECTS - MANAGEMENT - ADDRESSES, ESSAYS, LECTURES.
Entwicklungsmanagement . Berlin , c1982. 192 p. : ISBN 3-428-05208-0 LC Card 83-150764 DDC 338.9/0068 19
HD84 .E56 1982 ***NYPL [JLE 87-1179]***

ECONOMIC DEVELOPMENT PROJECTS - MEXICO - FINANCE - HISTORY.
Nacional Financiera, 1934-1984 . México, D.F. , 1985. 310 p. ; ISBN 968-665-107-1 LC Card 87-400288 DDC 332.2 19
HG2718.N33 N33 1985

ECONOMIC DEVELOPMENT PROJECTS - NEPAL.
Millwood, David. Good aid . Stockholm, Sweden , c1985. 246 p. : ISBN 91-586-7059-9 (pbk.) : LC Card 87-142767 DDC 338.91/485 19
HC425.Z9 E446 1985

ECONOMIC DEVELOPMENT PROJECTS - PAKISTAN.
Report on development cooperation with Pakistan. Islamabad, Pakistan [1985] xxxvi, 267 p. : LC Card 85-931852 DDC 338.91/09549/2 19
HC440.5.Z9 E447 1985

ECONOMIC DEVELOPMENT PROJECTS - PORTUGAL - FINANCE - CONGRESSES.
Seminário sobre Crescimento Económico e Dívida Externa (1982) Seminário sobre Crescimento Económico e Dívida Externa, 18 e 19 de março de 1982 . Lisboa , 1983. 163 p. ; LC Card 85-175819 DDC 336.3/4/09469 19
HJ8744 .S46 1982 ***NYPL [JLG 86-189]***

ECONOMIC DEVELOPMENT PROJECTS - QATAR.
Ritter, Wigand. Qatar, ein arabisches Erdölemirat /. Nürnberg , 1985. 201 p. : LC Card 86-205396
HC415.37 .R58 1985

ECONOMIC DEVELOPMENT PROJECTS - RWANDA.
Development programme of the Kagera Basin . [Kigali] [1982] viii, 73 leaves : LC Card 85-980886 DDC 338.967 19
HC860.Z9 E444 1982

ECONOMIC DEVELOPMENT PROJECTS - SAHEL - DIRECTORIES.
L'Aide publique au développement dans les pays membres du CILSS en 1983 =. Paris , Burkina Faso [1984], c1985. v, 347 p. : LC Card 86-180117
HC1000 .A64 1985

ECONOMIC DEVELOPMENT PROJECTS - SOLOMON ISLANDS - RENNELL ISLAND.
Infrastructural survey report for the development of the alumina resources in Rennell Island, Solomon Islands. [S.l.] [1976] xv, 321 p. : LC Card 84-230135
HC684.Z7 R455 1976

ECONOMIC DEVELOPMENT PROJECTS - SOMALIA - CASE STUDIES.
Hinzen, Eckhard. Pre-feasibility study of the integrated Ras Hafun project in north east Somalia . Kronberg [West Germany] [1981] xii, 186 leaves : LC Card 85-980733
HC850.Z9 E444 1981

ECONOMIC DEVELOPMENT PROJECTS - SOVIET UNION.
Adresa svershenii͡ /] Moskva , 1980. 271 p., [16] p. of plates : LC Card 81-130832
HC336.25 .A35 1980

ECONOMIC DEVELOPMENT PROJECTS - SWEDEN.
Lindmark, Leif. Företagsstöd och kommunalt risktagande /. Stockholm [1984] iv, 49 p. : ISBN 91-38-08297-7 LC Card 85-106839
HD3646.S8 L55 1984

Olofsson, Christer. Kommunala bolag med industriutvecklings uppgifter . Stockholm [1984] 82 p. ; ISBN 91-38-08114-8 LC Card 85-106731
HD3616.S53 O46 1984

Olofsson, Christer. De regionala utvecklingsbolagen . Stockholm [1983] 118 p. ; ISBN 91-38-07479-6 LC Card 83-234309
HC380.I53 O46 1983

ECONOMIC DEVELOPMENT PROJECTS - TANZANIA.
Development programme of the Kagera Basin . [Kigali] [1982] viii, 73 leaves : LC Card 85-980886 DDC 338.967 19
HC860.Z9 E444 1982

ECONOMIC DEVELOPMENT PROJECTS - TUNISIA.
Millwood, David. Good aid . Stockholm, Sweden , c1985. 246 p. : ISBN 91-586-7059-9 (pbk.) : LC Card 87-142767 DDC 338.91/485 19
HC425.Z9 E446 1985

ECONOMIC DEVELOPMENT PROJECTS - UGANDA.
Development programme of the Kagera Basin . [Kigali] [1982] viii, 73 leaves : LC Card 85-980886 DDC 338.967 19
HC860.Z9 E444 1982

ECONOMIC DEVELOPMENT PROJECTS - ZAMBIA - EVALUATION - CONGRESSES.
National Workshop on Project Evaluation (1984 : National Institute for Public Administration, Lusaka, Zambia) Collected papers of the National Workshop on Project Evaluation, held at the National Institute for Public Administration, 10-14 December, 1984. [Lusaka] , 1985. 1 v. in various pagings ; LC Card 85-981123 DDC 338.96894/0068 19
HC915.Z9 E446 1984

ECONOMIC DEVELOPMENT PROJECTS - ZAMBIA - GWEMBE DISTRICT.
Scudder, Thayer. An evaluation of the Gwembe South Development Project, Zambia /. Binghamton, N.Y., USA [1982] 48 p. ; LC Card 87-119502 DDC 338.96894 19
HC915.Z7 G846 1982

ECONOMIC DEVELOPMENT PROJECTS - ZIMBABWE - EVALUATION - CASE STUDIES.
Else, John F. Planning income generating projects . Harare, Zimbabwe [1986?] 46 p. : LC Card 87-400416 DDC 338.96891/0068 19
HC910 .E43 1986

ECONOMIC DEVELOPMENT - PSYCHOLOGICAL ASPECTS.
Alarcón, Reynaldo. Psicología, pobreza y subdesarrollo /. Lima, Perú , 1986. 153 p. ; LC Card 87-126266 DDC 155.9/2 19
HC79.P6 A55 1986

Harrison, Lawrence E. Underdevelopment is a state of mind . [Cambridge, Mass.] , Lanham, MD , 1988, c1985. p. cm. ISBN 0-8191-6490-9 (pbk. : alk. paper) : LC Card 87-24678 DDC 330.98/0038 19
HC125 .H384 1988

ECONOMIC DEVELOPMENT - RELIGIOUS ASPECTS - ISLAM.
Etika pembangunan dalam pemikiran Islam di Indonesia /. Jakarta , 1986. xi, 270 p. ; ISBN 979-421-043-9 (pbk.) LC Card 86-946413
HC447 .E78 1986

Muslim world . Lanham, MD , c1987. viii, 190 p. : ISBN 0-8191-6558-1 (alk. paper) : LC Card 87-14087 DDC 330.917/671 19
HC499 .M875 1987

ECONOMIC DEVELOPMENT - RESEARCH.
Research and other activities of the Development Centre, 1983-1985. Paris, France , 1985. 50 p. ; LC Card 86-213499 DDC 338.9 19
HD77 .R47 1985

ECONOMIC DEVELOPMENT - RESEARCH - AFRICA - DIRECTORIES.
Inventaire . Paris [Washington, D.C.] 1986. xxvii, 262 p. ; ISBN 92-64-02871-4 : LC Card 87-129509
HD77.5.A34 I58 1986

Organisation for Economic Co-operation and Development. Development Centre. Répertoire . Paris , Washington, D.C. , 1986. xxiv, 523 p. ; ISBN 92-64-02872-2 : LC Card 87-146730
HD77.5.A34 O75 1986

ECONOMIC DEVELOPMENT - RESEARCH - VENEZUELA.
Losada Aldana, Ramón. Investigación universitaria contra subdesarrollo /. Caracas , 1984. 288 p. ; LC Card 87-115963 DDC 338.987/0072 19
HD77.5.V4 L67 1984

ECONOMIC DEVELOPMENT - SOCIAL ASPECTS.
Bruchhaus, Eva-Maria. Frauen in Entwicklungsländern . Freiburg im Breisgau , 1979. iii, 182 p. ; LC Card 81-121677 DDC 305.4/09172/4 19
HQ1870.9 .B78 1979 ***NYPL [JLG 86-106]***

Búfalo, Enzo del. El pensamiento crítico latinoamericano /. [México?] , 1979. 236 p. ; LC Card 79-120323
HC59.7 .B84 ***NYPL [JLC 80-383]***

Community management . West Hartford, Conn. , c1986. xxii, 328 p. : ISBN 0-931816-40-8 (pbk.) LC Card 86-27691 DDC 338.95 19
HD75.6 .C65 1986

Development is for people /. Braamfontein, Johannesburg , 1986. 253 p. : ISBN 0-86954-274-5 (pbk.) : LC Card 86-200074 DDC 338.9 19
HD75 .D488 1986

Estructura política y políticas de población /. [Santiago, Chile] [1977] 442 p. ; LC Card 83-168971
HB3530.5 .E88 1977

Forbes, Dean K. The geography of underdevelopment . London , 1986. 214 p. ; ISBN 0-7099-1012-6 ***NYPL [JLD 86-1233]***

Globalni problemi . Sofii͡a , 1986. 268 p. : LC Card 86-231293
HD75 .G555 1986

Harrison, Lawrence E. Underdevelopment is a state of mind . [Cambridge, Mass.] , Lanham, MD , 1988, c1985. p. cm. ISBN 0-8191-6490-9 (pbk. : alk. paper) : LC Card 87-24678 DDC 330.98/0038 19
HC125 .H384 1988

Makalová, Eva. Ekonomické aspekty globálních problémů lidstva /. Praha , 1984. 97 p. ; LC Card 86-207353
HB9 .P72a 1984, 4/20 HD75

Metodologicheskie problemy analiza dolgosrochnykh sotsial'no-ėkonomicheskikh protsessov /. Moskva , 1979. 116 p. : LC Card 87-462037
HD87 .M48 1979

Samoĭlov, L. N. (Leonid Nikolaevich) Global'nye problemy obshchestvennogo progressa . Moskva , 1985. 92 p. ; LC Card 85-170113
HD75 .S258 1985

ECONOMIC DEVELOPMENT - SOCIAL ASPECTS - CONGRESSES.
Alternative Ökonomie? /. Köln , 1982. 244 p. ; ISBN 3-7616-0671-0 (pbk.) LC Card 84-109717 DDC 338.9 19
HD88 .A48 1982 ***NYPL [JLC 86-230]***

ECONOMIC DEVELOPMENT - STUDY AND TEACHING - AFRICA - DIRECTORIES.
Inventaire . Paris [Washington, D.C.] 1986. xxvii, 262 p. ; ISBN 92-64-02871-4 : LC Card 87-129509
HD77.5.A34 I58 1986

ECONOMIC DEVELOPMENT - STUDY AND TEACHING - CONGRESSES.
Medios de comunicación, hegemonía y proyectos de desarrollo. [Mexico City] [between 1982 and 1987] 179 p. ; LC Card 87-127821 DDC 338.9/007/1 19
HD77 .M43 1982

ECONOMIC DEVELOPMENT - STUDY AND TEACHING - GERMANY (WEST)
Osmers, Dieter. Entwicklungspolitische Erwachsenenbildung in der Bundesrepublik mit Hilfe kommunaler Konfliktfelder /. Frankfurt am Main , c1983. 161 p., [2] folded leaves of plates : ISBN 3-88129-669-7 LC Card 84-135387
HD77.5.G3 O85 1983

ECONOMIC DEVELOPMENT - STUDY AND TEACHING (HIGHER) - NAMIBIA.
United Nations Institute for Namibia. Development studies and management secondment programme /. Lusaka, Zambia , 1985. v, 26 p. ; LC Card 87-980229 DDC 338.9/007/15 19
HD77.5.N3 U55 1985

ECONOMIC DEVELOPMENT - STUDY AND TEACHING - MEXICO - CONGRESSES.

Medios de comunicación, hegemonía y proyectos de desarrollo. [Mexico City] [between 1982 and 1987] 179 p. ; LC Card 87-127821 DDC 338.9/007/1 19
HD77 .M43 1982

Economic development, Taiwan, Republic of China. Taipei, Taiwan, Republic of China : Council for Economic Planning & Development, [1986] 46 p. : col. ill. ; 15 x 21 cm. Cover title. "April 1986." LC Card 87-119341 DDC 338.951/249 19
1. Taiwan - Economic conditions - 1975-. 2. Taiwan - Economic conditions - 1975- - Statistics. 3. Taiwan - Economic policy - 1975-. I. Hsing cheng yüan ching chi chien she wei yüan hui (China).
HC430.5 .E34 1986

Economic development within the Philadelphia metropolitan area /. Summers, Anita A. Philadelphia , c1987. xiv, 268 p. : ISBN 0-8122-1231-2 (pbk.) LC Card 86-25091 DDC 338.9748/11 19
HC108.P5 S85 1987

Economic-ecological modeling / editors, Leon C. Braat and Wal F.J. van Lierop. Amsterdam ; New York : North-Holland ; x, 329 p. : ill. ; 25 cm. (Studies in regional science and urban economics. v. 16) Bibliography: p. 301-329. Includes index. ISBN 0-444-70298-9 LC Card 87-20048 DDC 333.7/0724 19
1. Environmental policy - Mathematical models. 2. Natural resources - Management - Mathematical models. I. Braat, Leon C. II. Lierop, Wal F. J. van.
HC79.E5 E267 1987

The economic effects of airline deregulation /. Morrison, Steven A., 1951- Washington, D.C. , c1986. xi, 84 : ISBN 0-8157-5845-6 (pbk.) : LC Card 85-48202 DDC 387.7/1 19
HE9803.A4 M67 1986 ***NYPL [JLE 86-3309]***

Economic effects of sanctions on southern Africa /. Hayes, J. P. (John Philip), 1924- Aldershot, Hampshire, England , Brookfield, Vt., USA , 1987. xii, 100 p. : ISBN 0-566-05539-2 (pbk.) : LC Card 87-11674 DDC 337.68 19
HF1413.5 .H39 1987

The economic effects of the American Civil War /. O'Brien, Patrick Karl. Atlantic Highlands, NJ , 1988. p. cm. ISBN 0-391-03561-4 : LC Card 87-18631 DDC 330.973/07 19
HC105.6 .O27 1988

Economic effects of the government budget / edited by Elhanan Helpman, Assaf Razin, and Efraim Sadka. Cambridge, Mass. : MIT Press, c1988. p. cm. Proceedings of the Fourth Pinhas Sapir Conference on Development, held in Dec. 1986 and sponsored by the Pinhas Sapir Center for Development at Tel-Aviv University. Includes bibliographies and index. ISBN 0-262-08172-5 LC Card 87-26187 DDC 338.9 19
1. Budget deficits - Congresses. 2. Finance, Public - Congresses. 3. Economic policy - Congresses. 4. Economic stabilization - Congresses. I. Helpman, Elhanan. II. Razin, Assaf. III. Sadka, Efraim. IV. Pinhas Sapir Conference on Development (4th : 1986 : Tel-Aviv University). V. Merkaz le-fituaḥ 'al-shem P. Sapir.
HJ2005 .E25 1988

Economic efficiency in agricultural and food marketing / edited by Richard L. Kilmer and Walter J. Armbruster. 1st ed. Ames : Published for Farm Foundation and Institute of Food and Agricultural Sciences of the University of Florida by Iowa State University Press, 1987. xii, 315 p. ; 24 cm. Includes bibliographies. ISBN 0-8138-0533-3 LC Card 87-2821 DDC 381/.41/0973 19
1. Farm produce - Marketing - Congresses. 2. Food - Marketing - Congresses. 3. Produce trade - United States - Congresses. 4. Food industry and trade - United States - Congresses. 5. Agriculture - Economic aspects - United States - Congresses. I. Kilmer, Richard L. II. Armbruster, Walter J. III. Farm Foundation (Chicago, Ill.). IV. University of Florida. Institute of Food and Agricultural Sciences.
HD9000.5 .E26 1987

ECONOMIC EQUILIBRIUM. see **EQUILIBRIUM (ECONOMICS)**

Economic evaluation and investment decision methods /. Stermole, Franklin J. Golden, Colo. , c1987. vi, 479 p. : ISBN 0-9603282-8-9 LC Card 86-83278 DDC 332.63 19
HG4028.C4 S714 1987

An economic evaluation of alternative sources of funding for agricultural lending by commercial banks /. Carraro, Kenneth C. Ithaca, N.Y. [1985] 48 p. ; LC Card 86-622432 DDC 332.7/1/09747 19
HG2051.U6 N53 1985

The economic evaluation of low traffic roads . Shimeles Asfaw. [Nairobi? , 1980?] ii, 28, 13 leaves, [2] leaves of plates : LC Card 85-981138
HE367.K43 E374 1980

The economic evaluation of roads in Australia /. Abelson, P. W. Mosman, N.S.W. , 1986. xi, 144 p. : ISBN 0-949416-06-1 (pbk.) : LC Card 87-142110 DDC 388.1/0994 19
HE368.Z55 E33 1986

The economic factors affecting state output and employment /. Standish, Barry, 1954- Rondebosch [South Africa] [1986] 86 p. : ISBN 0-7992-1016-1 (pbk.) : LC Card 87-112894 DDC 339.2/3 19
HB846 .S73 1986

ECONOMIC FLUCTUATIONS. see **BUSINESS CYCLES.**

ECONOMIC FORECASTING - ADDRESSES, ESSAYS, LECTURES.
Marktwirtschaft 2000 /. Krefeld , c1983. 137 p. : ISBN 3-88289-302-8 LC Card 84-229313 DDC 338.9 19
HD75.6 .M37 1983 ***NYPL [JLD 86-3124]***

ECONOMIC FORECASTING - ASIA.
Das Dreieck Europa-Amerika-Asien /. [Diessenhofen] , 1986. 154 p. : ISBN 3-7253-0272-3 LC Card 86-231548
HC412 .D7 1986

ECONOMIC FORECASTING - BELGIUM.
L'Avenir économique de la Belgique . [Bruxelles , 1981] 155 p. ; LC Card 87-672443
HC315 .A93x 1981

ECONOMIC FORECASTING - BOLIVIA - CONGRESSES.
Bolivia en el año 2010. [La Paz, Bolivia?] , 1986. ii, 325 p. : LC Card 87-101220
HC182 .B564 1986

ECONOMIC FORECASTING - BRAZIL.
Cenários para a economia brasileira, 1984-1990. [Rio de Janeiro] , 1984. 81 p. : LC Card 85-209337
HC187 .C28 1984

Perspectivas de longo prazo da economia brasileira /. [Rio de Janeiro, RJ] , 1985. 363 p. : LC Card 86-164342
HC187 .P415 1985

ECONOMIC FORECASTING - CALIFORNIA.
California. Legislature. Senate. Select Committee on Long Range Policy Planning. California and the 21st century . Sacramento, CA [1986] 3 v. : LC Card 86-622352 DDC 338.5/443/09794 19
HC107.C2 C227 1986

ECONOMIC FORECASTING - CENTRAL AMERICA.
El Crecimiento desigual en Centroamérica, 1950-2000. [Buenos Aires, Argentina] [between 1982 and 1986] 133 leaves ; LC Card 86-200824
HC141 .C73 1982

Mayorga Quirós, Román. El crecimiento desigual en Centroamérica (1950-2000) /. México, D.F. , 1983. 125 p. : ISBN 968-12-0238-4 LC Card 85-242511
HC141 .M39 1983

ECONOMIC FORECASTING - CHILE.
Vega F., Humberto (Vega Fernández) Política económica y movimiento laboral . Santiago, Chile , 1986. 52 p. : LC Card 87-101128
HC192 .V355 1986

ECONOMIC FORECASTING - COMMUNIST COUNTRIES.
Crisis and reform in socialist economies /. Boulder , 1987. xi, 196 p. ; ISBN 0-8133-7332-8 (pbk. : alk. paper) : LC Card 86-32602 DDC 338.9/009171/7 19
HC704 .C75 1987

ECONOMIC FORECASTING - CONGRESSES.
Club of Rome Conference (1984 : Helsinki, Finland) Managing global issues . [Lahti] [1985] 216 p. : ISBN 951-45-3807-2 (pbk.) LC Card 87-140928 DDC 909.82/8 19
HC13 .C56 1984

Colloque d'étude des politiques économiques Récession et relance (1984 : Paris, France) Récession et relance /. Paris , 1984. 218 p. : ISBN 2-7178-0690-3 : LC Card 85-158199 DDC 338.5/42 19
HB3711 .C59 1984

Population and the world economy in the 21st century /. Oxford , 1982. viii, 264 p. : ISBN 0-631-12964-2 LC Card 86-673281
HC59 .P638x 1982b

ECONOMIC FORECASTING - DATA PROCESSING.
Adams, Francis Gerard, 1929- The business forecasting revolution . New York , 1986. xiii, 265 p. : ISBN 0-19-503700-6 LC Card 85-18943 DDC 338.5/442 19
HD30.27 .A33 1986 ***NYPL [JLD 86-2257]***

ECONOMIC FORECASTING - DENMARK.
Danish economic survey. [Copenhagen] [1984] 72 p. : LC Card 86-220598 DDC 330.9489/058 19
HC355 .D226 1984

ECONOMIC FORECASTING - ECUADOR.
Resultados y perspectivas de la economía ecuatoriana, 1984-1985. Quito, Ecuador [1985] 27, 7 p. ; LC Card 85-215488
HC202 .R47 1985

ECONOMIC FORECASTING - EUROPE.
La Conjoncture économique en Europe . Lisboa, Portugal [1982] 78 p. : LC Card 83-181663
HC240 .C588 1982

Reuter, Edzard, 1928- Vom Geist der Wirtschaft . Stuttgart , c1986. 288 p. ; ISBN 3-421-06311-7 LC Card 86-181795
HC240 .R44 1986

ECONOMIC FORECASTING - FINLAND - ECONOMETRIC MODELS.
The BOF3 quarterly model of the Finnish economy /. Helsinki , 1985. 465 p. : ISBN 951-686-108-3 (pbk.) LC Card 86-205002 DDC 330.94897/005 s 338.5/443/094897 19
HB30 .S95 no. 59 HC340.2

ECONOMIC FORECASTING - FRANCE.
Demain la France . Paris , c1986. 423 p., [32] p. of plates : ISBN 2-01-011955-X LC Card 86-174163
HC276.2 .D42 1986

ECONOMIC FORECASTING - GEORGIAN S.S.R.
Meskhiia͡, I͡A. E. (I͡Akov Egnatovich) Voprosy metodologii regional'nogo ėkonomicheskogo prognozirovaniia͡ /. Moskva , 1983. 183 p. : LC Card 84-141931
HC337.G38 M43 1983

ECONOMIC FORECASTING - GERMANY, WEST.
Chancen für einen langen Aufschwung /. Stuttgart , 1984. xvii, 350 p. : ISBN 3-17-003288-7 : LC Card 86-178498
HC286.7 .C48 1984

Leben im Jahr 2000 und danach . Berlin , c1984. 213 p. : ISBN 3-7605-8571-X LC Card 85-128359
HB3595 .L43 1984

ECONOMIC FORECASTING - GERMANY (WEST) - ECONOMETRIC MODELS.
Kudiss, Reinhard, 1952- Die Bestimmung des Produktionspotentials in Theorie und Empirie . Frankfurt am Main , New York , c1984. xvi, 198 p. : ISBN 3-8204-5579-5 LC Card 85-189908
HB3730 .K766 1984

ECONOMIC FORECASTING - GHANA - STATISTICS.
Ewusi, Kodwo. Economic trends in Ghana in 1984-85 and prospects for 1986 /. [Legon] [1986] 52 p. : LC Card 87-127410 DDC 330.9667/05 19
HC1060 .E975 1986

ECONOMIC FORECASTING - HAWAII - STATISTICS.
Population and economic projections for the State of Hawaii, 1980-2005 [microform]. [Honolulu, Hawaii] [1984] 22 p. ; LC Card 84-622934 DDC 304.6/2/09969021 19
HB3525.H3 P67 1984
NYPL [*ZT-1745 no.28]

ECONOMIC FORECASTING - HONDURAS.
Consejo Superior de Planificación Económica (Honduras) Situación actual y perspectivas económicas, 1972 . Tegucigalpa, D.C.,

Honduras, C.A. , 1972. 38, [18] leaves ; LC Card 86-158684
HC145 .C66 1972

ECONOMIC FORECASTING - HUNGARY - STATISTICAL METHODS.
Sipos, Béla. Vállalati árelőrejelzések . Budapest , 1985. 290, [1] p. : ISBN 963-221-515-X : LC Card 86-190915
HB3730 .S495 1985

ECONOMIC FORECASTING - INDIA.
Seth, Satish C. India, the next 7000 days /. New Delhi , c1985. xxiv, 312 p. [1] spolded Leaf of plates ; ISBN 0-85226-864-5 : LC Card 85-904799 DDC 338.5/443/0954 19
HC435.2 .S416 1985 ***NYPL [JLD 86-3377]***

ECONOMIC FORECASTING - ITALY.
Turani, Giuseppe. 1985-1995, il secondo miracolo economico italiano . Milano , c1986. 147 p. : ISBN 88-20-00586-7 : LC Card 86-202136
HC305 .T85 1986

ECONOMIC FORECASTING - LATVIA.
Metodicheskie polozhenii͡a po prognozirovanii͡u ėkonomicheskogo i sotsial'nogo razvitii͡a soi͡uznoĭ respubliki /. Riga , 1979. 275 p. : LC Card 81-215536
HC337.L3 M35 1979

ECONOMIC FORECASTING - LITHUANIA.
Regional'noe modelirovanie obshchestvennogo vosproizvodstva . Vil'ni͡us , 1980. 280 p. : LC Card 81-191307
HC337.L5 R44 1980

ECONOMIC FORECASTING - MANITOBA.
Barber, Clarence L., 1917- Manitoba's interest in and attitude towards a proposed Canada-United States free trade area . [Winnipeg , 1985] 35 leaves : LC Card 86-175828 DDC 382/.0971/073 19
HF1479 .B37 1985

ECONOMIC FORECASTING - MARYLAND - BALTIMORE.
Szanton, Peter L. Baltimore 2000 . [Baltimore, Md.] , c1986. v, 51 p. : LC Card 87-125975 DDC 330.9752/71043 19
HC108.B2 S9 1986

ECONOMIC FORECASTING - MATHEMATICAL MODELS.
Kudiss, Reinhard, 1952- Die Bestimmung des Produktionspotentials in Theorie und Empirie . Frankfurt am Main , New York , c1984. xvi, 198 p. : ISBN 3-8204-5579-5 LC Card 85-189908
HB3730 .K766 1984

ECONOMIC FORECASTING - MATHEMATICAL MODELS - ADDRESSES, ESSAYS, LECTURES.
An Executive's guide to econometric forecasting . Flushing, N.Y. , c1983. 74 p. : ISBN 0-932126-10-3 (pbk.) LC Card 82-90726 DDC 330/.028 19
HB3730 .E978 1983 ***NYPL [JLF 86-1166]***

ECONOMIC FORECASTING - MEXICAN-AMERICAN BORDER REGION.
The U. S.-Mexico border region . [El Paso] , 1984, c1982. viii, 446 p. : ISBN 0-87404-091-4 (pbk.) LC Card 87-401861 DDC 333.7/0972/1 19
HC137.M46 U17 1984

ECONOMIC FORECASTING - MICHIGAN.
Johnston, William B., 1945- Michigan beyond 2000 /. Lanham , Indianapolis, IN , c1987. xxv, 161 p. : ISBN 0-8191-6462-3 (alk. paper) LC Card 87-10725 DDC 338.9774 19
HC107.M5 J64 1987

ECONOMIC FORECASTING - MONTANA.
House, Verne W. Trends in the Montana economy and taxation /. Bozeman [1986] 19 p. : LC Card 87-620963 DDC 330.9786/033 19
HC107.M9 H68 1986

ECONOMIC FORECASTING - NEW YORK (STATE)
New York State in the year 2000 /. Albany, N.Y. , 1988. 572 p. : ISBN 0-88706-602-X LC Card 87-6486 DDC 338.5/443/09747 19
HC107.N7 N447 1988

ECONOMIC FORECASTING - NORWAY.
Bergan, Roar. MINK . Oslo , 1984. 71 p. : ISBN 82-537-2138-2 : LC Card 85-178061
HC365 .B388 1984

Ertresvåg, Per-Aslak, 1931- Ekko av fremtiden /. Oslo , c1986. 163 p. : ISBN 82-504-0815-2 LC Card 86-217931
HC365 .E77 1986

ECONOMIC FORECASTING - ONTARIO.
Economic and fiscal review . Toronto, Ont. [1986] i, 89 p. : ISBN 0-7729-1950-X (pbk.) LC Card 87-169450 DDC 330.9713/04 19
HJ2460.O5 E28 1986

ECONOMIC FORECASTING - PACIFIC AREA - CONGRESSES.
International Symposium on the Role of the Asia-Pacific Region in World Economic Development (1984 : Tokyo, Japan) Proceedings of the International Symposium on the Role of the Asia-Pacific Region in World Economic Development . Tokyo , c1985. iv, 325 p. : LC Card 87-108109 DDC 337.9 19
HC681 .I58 1984

ECONOMIC FORECASTING - PERSIAN GULF STATES.
Bazarian, Carl J. The Gulf States =. New York, N.Y. , c1980. 577 p. : ISBN 0-916006-07-7 LC Card 80-65496
HC415.3 .B39 1980

ECONOMIC FORECASTING - RUSSIAN S.F.S.R. - SOVIET FAR EAST.
Nikitin, V. S. (Vadim Semenovich) Prognozirovanie razvitii͡a regional'nogo gorno-promyshlennogo kompleksa /. Moskva , 1982. 141, [3] p. : LC Card 83-154711
HD9506.S7473 S656 1982

ECONOMIC FORECASTING - SOVIET UNION.
Modelirovanie mezhotraslevykh vzaimodeĭstviĭ /. Moskva , 1984. 277 p. : LC Card 84-175111
HC336.25 .M6314 1984

ECONOMIC FORECASTING - SPAIN.
Sánchez, Victorio, 1936- España 1992 . Esplugues de Llobregat, Barcelona , 1984. 208 p. ; ISBN 84-01-33260-5 LC Card 86-205726
HC385 .S26 1984

ECONOMIC FORECASTING - SRI LANKA.
Public investment, 1983-1987. Colombo , 1983. 232 p. ; LC Card 83-905444 DDC 332.6/7252/095493 19
HC424 .P82 1983 ***NYPL [JLF 87-290]***

ECONOMIC FORECASTING - STATISTICAL METHODS.
Lütkepohl, Helmut. Forecasting aggregated vector ARMA processes /. Berlin , New York , c1987. x, 323 p. : ISBN 0-387-17208-4 (U. S. : pbk.) : LC Card 86-31599 DDC 519.5/5 19
HA30.3 .L87 1987

Sipos, Béla. Vállalati árelőrejelzések . Budapest , 1985. 290, [1] p. : ISBN 963-221-515-X : LC Card 86-190915
HB3730 .S495 1985

ECONOMIC FORECASTING - SWEDEN.
Iger, Svante. Den svenska ekonomins intertnationalisering . Lund , Stockholm [1976] iv, 144 p. : ISBN 91-38-03072-1 LC Card 84-226057
HF3674 .I36 1976

Jobb i framtid? . Stockholm , c1983. 121 p. : ISBN 91-7410-270-2 : LC Card 84-103510
HC375 .J53 1983

Kommunerna och framtiden . [Stockholm] , 1984] 224 p. : ISBN 91-38-08484-8 : LC Card 85-107984
HC375 .K654 1984

Trender och prognoser inför 90-talet. Stockholm , Örebro , 1985. 147 p. : ISBN 91-618-0001-5 LC Card 86-115921
LB2833 .S9 1985:2 HC375 ***NYPL [JLG 86-230]***

ECONOMIC FORECASTING - UKRAINE.
Narodno-khozi͡aĭstvennye proportsii, ikh planirovanie i prognozirovanie /. Kiev , 1985. 318 p. : LC Card 86-210651
HC337.U5 P5 1985 t. 1

ECONOMIC FORECASTING - UNITED STATES.
Andrews, George H., 1932- Actuarial projections for the old-age, survivors, and disability insurance program of social security in the United States of America /. Itasca, Ill., U. S.A. , c1987. viii, 188 p. : LC Card 87-1101 DDC 368.4/301/0973 19
HC106.8 .A56 1987

Batra, Raveendra N. The great depression of 1990 /. Dallas, Tex. , c1985. xv, 175 p. : ISBN 0-939352-02-8 : LC Card 85-50275 DDC 338.5/42 19
HC106.8 .B39 1985 ***NYPL [JLD 86-4007]***

Batra, Raveendra N. The great depression of 1990 /. New York , c1987. 235 p. ; ISBN 0-671-64022-4 LC Card 87-4816 DDC 338.5/42 19
HC106.8 .B39 1987

Collins, Lora S. The U. S. economy to 1990 /. New York, N.Y. , c1985. 21 p. : ISBN 0-8237-0307-X (pbk.) LC Card 86-200284 DDC 338.5/443/0973 19
HC106.8 .C636 1985

Frumkin, Norman. Tracking America's economy /. Armonk, N.Y. , c1987. 250 p. : ISBN 0-87332-437-4 : LC Card 87-9694 DDC 338.5/44/0973 19
HC106.8 .F78 1987

Grayson, C. Jackson (Charles Jackson), 1923- American business, a two-minute warning . New York , London , c1988. xvii, 368 p. : ISBN 0-02-912680-0 LC Card 87-19391 DDC 658/.00973 19
HD70.U5 G69 1988

Hunt, Lacy H. A time to be rich . New York , c1987. xvi, 282 p. : ISBN 0-89256-325-7 : LC Card 87-9431 DDC 332.6/78 19
HG4910 .H86 1987

Kiplinger forecasts . Washington, DC , New York, NY , c1986. vi, 330 p. ; ISBN 0-938721-01-1 (pbk.) : LC Card 86-203273 DDC 338.5/443/0973 19
HC106.8 .K56 1986

Manchester, Paul B. Are we on the road to a balanced budget? . Washington , 1986. v, 18 p. : LC Card 86-603373 DDC 353.0072/2 19
HJ2052 .M365 1986

Profile of the '80's /. [Washington, D.C.?] , 1980. v, 77 p. : LC Card 81-600725 DDC 380.5/0973 19
HE206.2 .P765 ***NYPL [JLF 86-1445]***

Russell, Cheryl, 1953- 100 predictions for the baby boom . New York , c1987. 249 p. ; ISBN 0-306-42527-0 LC Card 87-2443 DDC 338.5/443/0973 19
HC106.8 .R87 1987

Shilling, A. Gary. The world has definitely changed . New York, NY (111 Broadway, Suite 1200, New York 10006) , 1986. xx, 179 p. : LC Card 86-82936 DDC 338.5/443/0973 19
HC106.8 .S49 1986

Special analysis and outlook for E.I. Du Pont De Nemours & Company (Inc.), Chemicals and Pigments Department. Boston, Mass. (7 Liberty Sq., Boston 02109) [1986] 17, [6] p. : LC Card 86-205857 DDC 338.4/766/00973 19
HD9660.P253 U672 1986

U. S. economic review . Bala Cynwyd, Pa., USA (150 Monument Rd., Bala Cynwyd 19004-1790) , c1985. 7, 28 p. : LC Card 87-145506 DDC 338.5/443/0973 19
HC106.8 .U18 1985

ECONOMIC FORECASTING - UNITED STATES - CONGRESSES.
The 1986-87 outlook . New York, N.Y. (845 3rd Ave., New York 10022) , c1986. 18 p. : LC Card 86-212392 DDC 338.5/443/0973 19
HC106.8 .A14 1986

ECONOMIC FORECASTING - UNITED STATES - HANDBOOKS, MANUALS, ETC.
Stoken, Dick A. Strategic investment timing . New York , London , c1984. x, 225 p. : ISBN 0-02-614810-2 LC Card 84-12576 DDC 332.6/78 19
HG4921 .S795 1984 ***NYPL [JLD 86-2041]***

ECONOMIC FORECASTING - VENEZUELA.
Venezuela, periodic economic report . Caracas, Venezuela [1987] [166] p. : LC Card 87-403325 DDC 330.987/0633 19
HC237 .V487 1987

ECONOMIC FORECASTING - VIRGINIA.
Virginia alternatives for the 1990s . Fairfax, Va. , Lanham, MD , 1987. 183 p. : ISBN 0-8026-0016-6 (alk. paper) : LC Card 87-22757 DDC 338.9755 19
HC107.V8 V435 1987

ECONOMIC FORECASTING - WASHINGTON (D.C.)
Grier, George W. Greater Washington at mid decade . Washington, DC (1717 Massachusetts Ave., N.W., Washington 20036-2076) , c1985- v. <1 > : LC Card 86-200647 DDC 338.5/443/09753 19
HC108.W3 G73 1985

ECONOMIC FORECASTING - YUGOSLAVIA.
Savić, Nebojša, 1951- The scenario for Yugoslav economic recovery . Belgrade , c1986. 38 p. ; LC Card 87-165987 DDC 338.9497 19
HC407 .S284 1986

ECONOMIC FORECASTING - YUGOSLAVIA - CROATIA.
Osnove dugoročnog razvoja SR Hrvatske--svodna studija /. Zagreb , 1984. 437 p. ; LC Card 87-151188
HC407.Z7 C7647 1984

Economic gains from agricultural trade . Coyle, Barry. Washington, D.C. [Springfield, VA , 1986] iii, 41 p. : LC Card 86-602417 DDC 382/.41/0973 19
HD9005 .C86 1986

Economic geography . Berry, Brian Joe Lobley, 1934- Englewood Cliffs, N.J. , c1987. xi, 447 p. : ISBN 0-13-231440-1 : LC Card 87-2250 DDC 330.9 19
HC59 .B52 1987

Economic geography /. Hartshorn, Truman A. Englewood Cliffs, N.J. , 1988. xiii, 385 p. : ISBN 0-13-225160-4 LC Card 87-17407 DDC 330.9 19
HF1025 .H296 1988

ECONOMIC GEOGRAPHY. see **GEOGRAPHY, ECONOMIC.**

ECONOMIC GROWTH. see **ECONOMIC DEVELOPMENT.**

Economic growth and the returns to investment /. Anderson, Dennis, 1937- Washington, D.C. [1987] 93 p. : ISBN 0-8213-0918-8 (pbk.) LC Card 87-14178 DDC 338.9 19
HD75 .A53 1987

ECONOMIC HISTORY - TO 500.
Heinsohn, Gunnar. Privateigentum, Patriarchat, Geldwirtschaft . Frankfurt am Main , 1984. 218 p. ; ISBN 3-518-28055-4 : LC Card 84-150578
HC31 .H45 1984

Herrmann, Joachim, 1932- Ökonomie und Gesellschaft an der Wende von der Antike zum Mittelalter . Berlin , 1979. 72 p. : LC Card 85-209249
HC31 .H47 1979

ECONOMIC HISTORY - MEDIEVAL, 500-1500.
Day, John, 1924- The medieval market economy /. Oxford, UK , New York, NY, USA , 1987. p. cm. ISBN 0-631-15479-5 : LC Card 86-26862 DDC 330.94/01 19
HC41 .D39 1987

Le Goff, Jacques, 1924- [Bourse et la vie. English.] Your money or your life . New York , Cambridge, Mass. , 1988. 116 p. ; ISBN 0-942299-14-0 (alk. paper) : LC Card 87-25248 DDC 330.94/01 19
HC41 .L43 1988

Lopez, Robert Sabatino. The shape of medieval monetary history /. London , 1986. 330 p. 1 v. (various pagings) : ISBN 0-86078-195-X LC Card 87-133292 DDC 332.4/94 19
HG243 .L67 1986

Pernoud, Régine, 1909- Le Moyen Age pour quoi faire? /. [Paris] , c1986. 315 p. : ISBN 2-234-01940-0 : LC Card 86-189820
HC41 .P46 1986

Wilson, David McKenzie. Economic aspects of the Vikings in the West-the archaeological basis /. Göteborg , 1980. 36 p. ; ISBN 91-7360-075-X (pbk.) LC Card 81-154587 DDC 330.94 19
HC41 .W55 1980

ECONOMIC HISTORY - 1750-1918.
Morris, Cynthia Taft. Comparative patterns of economic development, 1850-1914 /. Baltimore , c1988. xi, 575 p. ; ISBN 0-8018-3507-0 (alk. paper) LC Card 87-45480 DDC 338.9/009 19
HC51 .M645 1988

Verley, Patrick. La révolution industrielle /. Paris , c1985. 270 p. : ISBN 2-86676-194-4 LC Card 86-116016 DDC 338.09 19
HD2321 .V47 1985

ECONOMIC HISTORY - 1750-1918 - ADDRESSES, ESSAYS, LECTURES.
Couri, Sergio, 1948- Ensaios sobre a evolução dos sistemas econômicos /. Brasília-Distrito Federal [1983] 133 p. : LC Card 84-116306 DDC 330.1 19
HB97.5 .C68 1983 ***NYPL [JLE 86-3363]***

Lenin, Vladimir Il'ich, 1870-1924. [Imperializm kak Vysshaia stadiia kapitalizma. Azerbaijani.] Imperijalizm kapitalizmin ăn jeni devri gibi [microform] /. Baqï , 1927. 99 p. ;
NYPL [*ZO-247 no. 1]

ECONOMIC HISTORY - 1750-1918 - CONGRESSES.
Rethinking the nineteenth century . New York , c1988. p. cm. ISBN 0-313-25997-6 (lib. bdg. : alk. paper) LC Card 87-17791 DDC 330.9/034 19
HC53 .R48 1988

ECONOMIC HISTORY - 1750-1918 - STATISTICAL METHODS - STUDY AND TEACHING - CONGRESSES.
Beiträge zur quantitativen vergleichenden Unternehmensgeschichte /. Stuttgart , c1985. 206 p. : ISBN 3-608-91325-4 LC Card 85-233589
HD2734 .B32 1985

ECONOMIC HISTORY - 20TH CENTURY.
Domdey, Karl Heinz. Weltwirtschaft und Weltwirtschaftslehre . Berlin , 1984. 366 p. : LC Card 84-245611
HC54 .D65 1984

Ginzberg, Eli, 1911- The skeptical economist /. Boulder, Colo. , 1987. ix, 182 p. ; ISBN 0-8133-7372-7 LC Card 87-2165 DDC 330 19
HB71 .G53 1987

Guiba (Writer) Por qué nos confunden-- el comunismo, el capitalismo, los economistas, las elites? /. Montevideo , 1981. 211 p. ; LC Card 82-125535 DDC 330.9/04 19
HC54 .G79 1981 ***NYPL [JLC 86-320]***

Lieberman, Sima, 1927- The economic and political roots of the new protectionism /. Totowa, N.J. , 1987. p. cm. ISBN 0-8476-7595-5 LC Card 87-23329 DDC 382.7/3/09048 19
HF1411 .L533 1987

Rabochiĭ klass v proshlom i nastoiashchem . Moskva , 1984, c1983. 255 p. ; LC Card 84-169518
HD4854 .R273 1984

Roncolini, Giuliana, 1948- La crisi della legittimità borghese . Napoli , 1978. 115 p. ; ISBN 88-20-70809-4 : LC Card 79-368996
HC54 .R64 ***NYPL [JLD 81-254]***

ECONOMIC HISTORY - 20TH CENTURY - COLLECTED WORKS.
Lotta, Raymond. America in decline . Chicago , c1984- v. : ISBN 0-916650-12-X (v. 1) : LC Card 83-22294 DDC 330.973/0927 19
HC54 .L63 1984 ***NYPL [JLL 87-106]***

ECONOMIC HISTORY - 1918-
Ideas para la cultura europea . Barcelona [1980?] 64 p. : ISBN 84-300-3210-X LC Card 85-105410
HC57 .I24 1980

Stewart, Michael, 1933- Keynes and after /. Harmondsworth, Middlesex, England , New York, N.Y., U. S.A. , 1986. 230 p. ; ISBN 0-14-022646-X (pbk.) : LC Card 86-218640 DDC 330.15/6 19
HB99.7 .S7 1986

Stewart, Michael, 1933- Keynes and after /. Harmondsworth, England , 1986. 230 p. ; ISBN 0-14-022646-X ***NYPL [JLD 86-2148]***

ECONOMIC HISTORY - 1918- - ADDRESSES, ESSAYS, LECTURES.
Couri, Sergio, 1948- Ensaios sobre a evolução dos sistemas econômicos /. Brasília-Distrito Federal [1983] 133 p. : LC Card 84-116306 DDC 330.1 19
HB97.5 .C68 1983 ***NYPL [JLE 86-3363]***

ECONOMIC HISTORY - 1918-1945.
Garraty, John Arthur, 1920- The Great Depression . New York, N.Y. , 1987. x, 292 p. : ISBN 0-385-24085-6 (pbk.) : LC Card 87-5458 DDC 338.5/42 19
HB3717 1929 .G36 1987

Schmid, Hanspeter, 1951- Wirtschaft, Staat und Macht . Zürich [c1983] 432 p. : ISBN 3-85791-073-9 (Schw. Buch) LC Card 83-244266
HF1573 .S335 1983

ECONOMIC HISTORY - 1945-
America's changing role in the world-system /. New York , 1987. xi, 300 p. : ISBN 0-275-92417-3 (alk. paper) : LC Card 86-25245 DDC 337.73 19
HC106.8 .A455 1987

Baade, Fritz, 1893- [Wettlauf zum Jahre 2000. English.] The race to the year 2000, our future. Garden City, N.Y., 1962. xix, 246 p. LC Card 62-7600 DDC 330.9/04 19
HC59 .B2513 1962

Ballance, Robert H. International industry and business . London , Boston , 1987. xxi, 357 p. ; ISBN 0-04-339037-4 (alk. paper) LC Card 86-28793 DDC 338/.09/04048 19
HC59 .B3537 1987

Beiträge zur Multiplizität wirtschaftsgeographischer Forschung . Frankfurt am Main , c1986. 151 p. : ISBN 3-89228-046-0 LC Card 87-131124 DDC 330.9 19
HC59 .B464 1986

Brett, E. A. International money and capitalist crisis . London , Boulder, Colo. , 1983. viii, 271 p. ; ISBN 0-86531-575-2 (Westview) LC Card 82-51289 DDC 332/.042 19
HG3881 .B6738 1983 ***NYPL [JLD 87-1020]***

Brett, E. A. The world economy since the war . Houndmills, Basingstoke, Hampshire , 1985. x, 318 p. : ISBN 0-333-37199-2 LC Card 87-673378
HC59 .B754x 1985

International capitalism and industrial restructuring . Boston , 1987. p. cm. ISBN 0-04-338132-4 (alk. paper) LC Card 86-28870 DDC 338.7 19
HD2321 .I58 1987

Medeiros, Eduardo Raposo de. Economia internacional /. Lisboa , 1984. 416 p., [2] folded leaves of plates : LC Card 85-125328
HC59 .M425 1984

Politik gegen die Krise . Marburg , 1985. 157 p. : ISBN 3-924800-01-4 : LC Card 86-119259 DDC 338.9 19
HC59 .P584 1985

Poverty amidst plenty . Boulder, Colo. , 1989. p. cm. ISBN 0-8133-0523-3 LC Card 87-12829 DDC 330.9/048 19
HC59 .P639 1989

Przemiany we współczesnej gospodarce światowej . Gdańsk , 1978. 360 p. ; LC Card 81-200306
HC59 .P78 1978

Simon, György. Gazdasági növekedés a két világrendszerben /. [Budapest] , 1986. 257, [1] p. ; ISBN 963-09-2771-3 : LC Card 87-409656
HD85.H88 S498 1986

Wannenmacher, Walter. Irrwege der Freiheit . München , c1986. 322 p. ; ISBN 3-7766-1429-3 LC Card 87-130925 DDC 330.9/048 19
HC59 .W279 1986

ECONOMIC HISTORY - 1945- - CONGRESSES.
Futures for the welfare state /. Bloomington , c1986. vi, 444 p. : ISBN 0-253-32440-8 LC Card 85-45959 DDC 330.12/6 19
HB846 .F87 1986 ***NYPL [JLE 86-3761]***

ECONOMIC HISTORY - 1945-1971.
Le Capitalisme monopoliste d'État. Paris [1971] 2 v. LC Card 75-585406
HC59 .C26 ***NYPL [JLC 71-28]***

The Third World and the world economic system /. New Delhi , Atlantic Highlands, N.J. , 1986. viii, 309 p. ; ISBN 81-7027-092-8 : LC Card 86-900419 DDC 330.9172/4 19
HC59.7 .T744 1986 ***NYPL [JLD 86-3145]***

ECONOMIC HISTORY - 1945-1971 - ADDRESSES, ESSAYS, LECTURES.
Capitalismul contemporan şi teoria [microform] . Bucureşti , 1965. 440 p. ; LC Card 77-452767
HB179.R6 C34 ***NYPL [*ZT-1732 no.2]***

ECONOMIC HISTORY - 1971-
Alvarado U., Hernán (Alvarado Ugarte) Crisis económica mundial, 1974-1975 . Heredia, Costa Rica , 1980. 62 p. ; LC Card 87-402100 DDC

330.9/047 19
HC59 .A765 1980

Bayo, Eliseo. Descubro y acuso /. Esplugues de Llobregat, Barcelona , 1985,c1984. 287 p. ; ISBN 84-01-33258-3 ***NYPL [JFD 86-7111]***

Beckman, Robert C. The downwave . Portsmouth, Hants , 1983. 216 p. : ISBN 0-903852-38-1 ***NYPL [JLE 86-3347]***

Behrman, Jack N. The rise of the phoenix . Boulder , 1987. xiii, 104 p. ; ISBN 0-8133-7511-8 (pbk. : alk. paper) : LC Card 87-21689 DDC 338.973 19
HC106.8 .B43 1987

Brenner, Y. S. Capitalism, competition and economic crisis . Brighton, Sussex , Washington, D.C. , 1984. x, 262 p. ; ISBN 0-7108-0722-8 ***NYPL [JLD 86-2553]***

Carlson, Richard C. Managing the changing work force . Menlo Park, Calif. (333 Ravenswood Ave., Menlo Park 94025-3476) , c1984. 44 p. : LC Card 86-212936 DDC 658.3 19
HD5706 .C29 1984

Dahrendorf, Ralf. Die Chancen der Krise . Stuttgart , c1983. 240 p. ; ISBN 3-421-06148-3 ***NYPL [JFD 87-2528]***

De Vos, Wouter. Point de mire . Antwerpen, Belgiëlai 147 a , 1977. 125 p. : ISBN 90-02-01132-6 : LC Card 78-370280 DDC 309.1
HC59 .D464 ***NYPL [JLD 80-3135]***

Dehmel, Alexander. Die Struktur der internationalen Liquiditätskrise seit dem ersten Ölpreisschub, 1973/1974 . Frankfurt am Main , New York , c1985. x, 221 p. : ISBN 3-8204-8941-X LC Card 86-108628
HG178 .D44 1985

Diskontinuitätenmanagement . Berlin , c1984. x, 320 p. : ISBN 3-503-02446-8 LC Card 85-128271
HD62.4 .D57 1984

Economie mondiale 1980-1990, la fracture? . Paris , c1984. x, 406 p. : ISBN 2-7178-0803-5 : LC Card 85-105930
HC59 .E384 1984

Engels, Wolfram. Einseitige Betrachtungen . Düsseldorf , 1986. 240 p. ; LC Card 87-146603 DDC 338.943 19
HD84 .E53 1986

Faminskiĭ, Igor′ Pavlovich. Ėkonomika sovremennogo imperializma . Moskva , 1987. 175 p. ; LC Card 87-170222
HB501 .F275 1987

Görög, Tibor. Ökopesszimizmus, technooptimizmus és korunk globális problémái /. [Budapest] , 1984. 85 p. : ISBN 963-673-290-6 LC Card 85-130717
HC59 .G6226 1984

Gorz, André. [Chemins du paradis. English.] Paths to paradise . London , 1985. vii, 120 p. ; ISBN 0-86104-762-1 (pbk.) : ***NYPL [JLD 86-3006]***

Herbst, Erika. Alle suchen nach Lösungen . Feucht , Stuttgart , c1984. 151 p. ; ISBN 3-7724-0688-2 LC Card 85-146171
HC59 .H395 1984

Industry in the 1980s . New York , 1985. xii, 228 p. : ISBN 92-1-106207-1 (pbk.) LC Card 86-227928 DDC 338.09 19
HD9720.5 .I53 1985

Iriarte, Gregorio. Esquemas para la interpretación de la realidad /. La Paz, Bolivia , 1985. 10 v. : LC Card 87-112879
HC182 .I727 1985

Jungblut, Michael. Der Wohlstand entlässt seine Kinder . Stuttgart , c1983. 303 p. ; ISBN 3-421-06164-5 LC Card 83-232938
HC59 .J78 1983

The Limits to growth. New York [1972] 205 p. ISBN 0-87663-165-0 LC Card 73-187907 DDC 330.9/04
HC59 .L54 ***NYPL [JLD 75-167]***

Linden, Ronald Haly. Communist states and international change . Boston , c1987. xviii, 201 p. ; ISBN 0-04-497050-1 : LC Card 87-11389 DDC 337.497 19
HF1581 .L56 1987

Malloch, Theodore R. Issues in international trade and development policy /. New York , 1987. ix, 178 p. ; ISBN 0-275-92356-8 (alk. paper) : LC Card 87-11697 DDC 382/.3 19
HF1411 .M3325 1987

Marcy, Sam, 1911- Anatomy of the economic crisis /. Atlanta , 1982. viii, 120 p. ; ISBN 0-89567-077-1 (pbk.) LC Card 87-132534 DDC 330.9/048 19
HC59 .M258 1982

Martin, Paul C. (Paul Christoph), 1939- Die Pleite . München , c1984. 416 p. : ISBN 3-7844-7145-5 : LC Card 85-188703
HJ8011 .M36 1984

Mirovoe kapitalisticheskoe khozi͡aĭstvo v 80-e gody . Moskva , 1985. 220 p. ; LC Card 87-166175
HC59 .M549 1985

Problema tempov ėkonomicheskogo rosta v sovremennom mire /. Moskva , 1986. 383 p. : LC Card 87-124359
HC244 .P747 1986

Rattner, Henrique. Informática e sociedade /. São Paulo-SP , 1985. 219 p. : LC Card 85-221850
HC79.T4 R387 1985

Rymalov, V. V. (Viktor Vladimirovich) Podryv vekovykh ustoev . Moskva , 1984. 268, [3] p. : LC Card 85-112238
HC59 .R839 1984

Sacristán, Antonio. La situación económica mundial y México . México, D.F. [1980] 72 p. ; LC Card 87-400921 DDC 330.972/0834 19
HC59 .S3122 1980

Schiller, Herbert I., 1919- Information and the crisis economy /. New York , 1986. xv, 133 p. ; ISBN 0-19-520514-6 (pbk. : alk. paper) LC Card 86-2374 DDC 302.2/34 19
HE7651 .S34 1986 ***NYPL [JLD 86-3695]***

Simai, Mihály. Az emberi tényező szerepe a világgazdaságban az 1980-as években . Budapest , c1986. 41 p. ; ISBN 963-05-4342-7 : LC Card 87-407712
HD4904.7 .S446 1986

Simai, Mihály. Hatalom, technika, világgazdaság /. Budapest , 1985. 436 p. ; ISBN 963-221-548-6 : LC Card 86-187337
HC59 .S529 1985

Staff studies for the world economic outlook /. Washington, D.C. , c1986. xi, 195 p. : LC Card 86-202629 DDC 338.5/443 19
HC59 .S682 1986

Stoga, Alan. Breaking the economic impasse . Washington, D.C. , c1987. viii, 48 p. ; ISBN 0-89206-104-9 (pbk.) LC Card 87-14682 DDC 338.9 19
HC59 .B73 1987

Strukturnye sdvigi v mirovom kapitalisticheskom khozi͡aĭstve /. Kiev , 1985. 295 p. ; LC Card 86-105339
HC59 .S8345 1985 ***NYPL [*QIP 87-3473]***

Sutcliffe, Robert B. Hard times . London , 1983. 118 p. ; ISBN 0-86104-505-X (pbk.) : LC Card 83-126438 DDC 330.9/04 19
HC59 .S8873 1983 ***NYPL [JLD 86-4088]***

T͡Sygankov, P. A. (Pavel Afanas′evich) V bor′be protiv vsevlastii͡a kapitala /. Moskva , 1986. 139 p. ; LC Card 86-132423
HB501 .T78 1986

U. S. economic review . Bala Cynwyd, Pa., USA (150 Monument Rd., Bala Cynwyd 19004-1790) , c1985. 7, 28 p. : LC Card 87-145506 DDC 338.5/443/0973 19
HC106.8 .U18 1985

Vacca, Roberto, 1927- Rinascimento prossimo venturo /. Milano , 1986. 281 p. : LC Card 87-100469
HC59 .V24 1986

A Világgazdaság fejlődésének kérdései tanulmányozásához . [Budapest] , 1981/1982. 415 p. ; LC Card 85-138909
HC59 .V489 1981

World economic data . Santa Barbara, Calif. , c1987. x, 231 p. ; ISBN 0-87436-485-X (alk. paper) : LC Card 87-14508 DDC 330.9/04 19
HC59 .W643 1987

ECONOMIC HISTORY - 1971- - ADDRESSES, ESSAYS, LECTURES.

Mandel, Ernest. La crise 1974-1982 . Paris , c1985. 352 p. : ISBN 2-08-081151-7 ***NYPL [JLC 86-204]***

Marcy, Sam, 1911- Anatomy of the economic crisis /. Atlanta , c1982. viii, 120 p. : ISBN 0-89567-077-1 (pbk.) ***NYPL [JLD 86-1329]***

Marktwirtschaft 2000 /. Krefeld , c1983. 137 p. : ISBN 3-88289-302-8 LC Card 84-229313 DDC 338.9 19
HD75.6 .M37 1983 ***NYPL [JLD 86-3124]***

Production, work, territory . Boston , 1986. xix, 344 p. : ISBN 0-04-338126-X (alk. paper) LC Card 85-20006 DDC 330 19
HC59 .P682 1986 ***NYPL [JLE 86-1745]***

Salvador Ortíz, S., 1917-1983. Comentarios económicos /. Santo Domingo, República Dominicana , 1984- v. ; LC Card 85-118318 DDC 330.9 19
HC125 .S2615 1984 ***NYPL [JLK 85-83]***

Unemployment and growth in the Western economies /. New York, N.Y. , c1984. x, 142 p. ; ISBN 0-87609-001-3 (pbk.) : LC Card 84-9415 DDC 331.13/791812 19
HD5707.5 .U54 1984 ***NYPL [JLE 86-1564]***

ECONOMIC HISTORY - 1971- - CONGRESSES.

Club of Rome Conference (1984 : Helsinki, Finland) Managing global issues . [Lahti] [1985] 216 p. : ISBN 951-45-3807-2 (pbk.) LC Card 87-140928 DDC 909.82/8 19
HC13 .C56 1984

Die Internationale Finanzierungskrise /. Frankfurt am Main , c1985. 153 p. ; ISBN 3-7819-2536-6 LC Card 87-146671 DDC 336.3/435 19
HG3891.5 .I587 1985

Öffentliche Unternehmen in Rezession und Aufschwung . Berlin , 1977. 165 p. : LC Card 85-180964
HD3845 .G43 Heft 14 HD3842

Perspectivas de la economía mundial y colombiana /. Bogotá, Colombia , 1986. 106 p. ; ISBN 958-616-044-0 LC Card 87-115573 DDC 330.9861/0632 19
HC197 .P35 1986

Policy responses to the changing international environment . Budapest , 1981. 170 p. ; ISBN 963-301-077-2 (pbk.) LC Card 81-179118 DDC 337/.09/048 19
HC59 .P573 1981 ***NYPL [JLL 79-189 no.33]***

Population and the world economy in the 21st century /. Oxford , 1982. viii, 264 p. : ISBN 0-631-12964-2 LC Card 86-673281
HC59 .P638x 1982b

A 80-as évek kapitalizmusa . [Budapest] , 1985. 406 p. ; ISBN 963-09-2696-2 : LC Card 86-186468
HB501 .A14 1985

ECONOMIC HISTORY - 1971- - MATHEMATICAL MODELS.

The Globus model . Boulder , 1986. p. cm. ISBN 0-8133-0528-4 : LC Card 87-8281 DDC 338.9/00724 19
HC59 .G577 1986

ECONOMIC HISTORY - 1971- - STATISTICS.

Il Mondo oggi . Milano , <[1986]- >, <c1983-. v. <2 > : ISBN 0-330-28132-1 LC Card 87-103039
HC59 .M596 1986

ECONOMIC HISTORY - ADDRESSES, ESSAYS, LECTURES.

Court, W. H. B. (William Henry Bassano) Scarcity and choice in history. London, 1970. viii, 256 p. LC Card 79-488977 DDC 330.9
HC253 .C675

Economic history and the modern economist /. Oxford, UK , New York, NY, USA , 1986. xi, 105 p. ; ISBN 0-631-14799-3 : LC Card 85-28584 DDC 330/.09 19
HC26 .E26 1986 ***NYPL [JLD 86-2947]***

Economic history and the modern economist / edited by William N. Parker. Oxford, UK ; New York, NY, USA : B. Blackwell, 1986. xi, 105 p. ; 23 cm. Includes bibliographical references and index. ISBN 0-631-14799-3 : LC Card 85-28584 DDC 330/.09 19
1. Economic history - Addresses, essays, lectures. 2. Economics - Addresses, essays, lectures. I. Parker, William Nelson.
HC26 .E26 1986 ***NYPL [JLD 86-2947]***

Economic History Association. International Congress on Economic History (8th : 1982 : Budapest, Hungary) Münzprägung, Geldumlauf und Wechselkurse . Trier , 1984. 421 p. : ISBN 3-923087-06-3 (pbk.)
HG205 1982 .I53 ***NYPL [JLE 86-3176]***

ECONOMIC HISTORY - CONGRESSES.
Der Bauer im Wandel der Zeit /. Bonn , 1986. x, 340 p., [1] leaf of plates : ISBN 3-416-04010-4 LC Card 86-228506
HD1521 .B37 1986

The economic history of India in the Victorian Age . Dutt, Romesh Chunder, 1848-1909. London [19--] xxii, 628 p. ; LC Card 87-131511
HC435 .D975 1900z

Economic history of Puerto Rico . Dietz, James L., 1947- Princeton , c1986. xxiii, 337 p., [11] p. of plates : ISBN 0-691-07716-9 (alk. paper) : LC Card 86-12313 DDC 330.97295 19
HC154.5 .D54 1986 ***NYPL [JLE 87-1592]***

Economic History Society.
O'Brien, Patrick Karl. The economic effects of the American Civil War /. Atlantic Highlands, NJ , 1988. p. cm. ISBN 0-391-03561-4 : LC Card 87-18631 DDC 330.973/07 19
HC105.6 .O27 1988

Turner, Michael Edward. Enclosures in Britain, 1750-1830 /. London , 1984. 96 p. : ISBN 0-333-31682-7 (pbk.) LC Card 86-673799
HD594.6 .T84x 1984

ECONOMIC HISTORY - STUDY AND TEACHING - GREAT BRITAIN.
Coleman, D. C. (Donald Cuthbert), 1920- History and the economic past . Oxford , New York , 1987. 150 p.; ISBN 0-19-828305-9 LC Card 86-28543 DDC 330/.07/1041 19
HC28.5.G7 C65 1987

Economic ideas in ancient India before Kautilya /. Sharma, Bankey Lal. New Delhi , 1987. viii, 208 p. ; LC Card 86-903545 DDC 330/.0954 19
HB126.I4 S467 1987

Economic impact assessment of the South Jersey Port Corporation /. Levinson, Alfred Linden, 1933- Newark, N.J. (323 High St., Newark 07102) [1982] 31 leaves : LC Card 86-622073 DDC 387.1/09749/88 19
HE554.C18 L48 1982

The economic impact of coal mining in Montana /. Brower, John C. Missoula, Mont. [1985] 31 p. : LC Card 87-620608 DDC 338.2/724/09786 19
HD9547.M6 B76 1985

Economic impact of generalized tariff preferences /. Langhammer, Rolf J. Aldershot, Hants, England , Brookfield, Vt. , 1988. p. cm. ISBN 0-566-05338-1 : LC Card 87-15045 DDC 382.7/53 19
HF1721 .L35 1988

Economic impact of the Port of Québec. [Québec, Québec] : Québec Port Autority [i.e. Authority], [1974] [16], [18] leaves ; 28 cm. English and French. Cover title. Title on added t.p.: Impact économique du Port de Québec. "May 1974." LC Card 85-183731 DDC 386/.8/09714471 19
1. Harbors - Québec (Province) - Québec. I. Port of Québec (Canada). II. Title: Impact économique du Port de Québec.
HE554.Q4 E27 1974

Economic impact of the recreational boating industry in Texas /. Stoll, John R. College Station, TX [1985] xiv, 86 p. : LC Card 86-622008 DDC 330.9764/063 19
HD9993.B633 U58 1985

The economic implications of disinvestment for South Africa /. Jenkins, Carolyn M. (Carolyn Marion) [Braamfontain?] , 1986. v, 100 p. ; ISBN 0-908371-51-9 (pbk.) : LC Card 87-164832 DDC 332.6/73/0968 19
HG5851.A3 J46 1986

Economic implications of import barriers to protect the U. S. sugar industry with particular reference to Hawaii /. Leong, Jerrold K. (Jerrold Kim), 1947- Manoa , 1987. p. cm. LC Card 87-11855 DDC 382/.456641/09969 19
HD9107.H3 L46 1987

Economic incentives : proceedings of a conference held by the International Economic Association at Kiel, West Germany / edited by Bela A. Balassa and Herbert Giersch. London : Macmillan, 1986. xiii, 497 p. ; 23 cm. Includes bibliographical references and index. ISBN 0-333-40473-4
1. Economic development - Congresses. 2. Incentives in industry - Congresses. 3. Industry and state - Congresses. 4. Comparative economics - Congresses. I. Balassa, Bela A. II. Giersch, Herbert.
NYPL [JLD 87-367]

Economic incentives to arm? . Gleditsch, Nils Petter, 1942- Oslo [1986] 72 p. : ISBN 82-7288-134-9 LC Card 87-163647 DDC 338.4/36234 19
HC79.D4 G54 1986

ECONOMIC INDICATORS.
Essays on the performance of leading indicators based on qualitative data /. Munich , 1985. 148 p. : ISBN 3-88512-009-7 (pbk.) : LC Card 86-181861 DDC 330/.0724 19
HB3730 .E78 1985

The Geographical digest. London , c1986. 122 p. : ISBN 0-540-01104-5 LC Card 87-124717 DDC 330.9/04/021 19
HA155 .G46 1986

McGranahan, Donald V. Measurement and analysis of socioeconomic development . Geneva , 1985. xx, 504 p. :
NYPL [JLK 74-447 no.85.5]

World economic data . Santa Barbara, Calif. , c1987. x, 231 p. ; ISBN 0-87436-485-X (alk. paper) : LC Card 87-14508 DDC 330.9/04 19
HC59 .W643 1987

ECONOMIC INDICATORS - ANDES REGION.
Indicadores de los países del Grupo Andino. [Lima] [1985] 172 p. in various pagings : LC Card 86-137319 DDC 330.98/0038 19
HC167.A5 I52 1985

ECONOMIC INDICATORS - BRAZIL.
Penna, João Camilo de Oliveira. As empresas estatais na economia brasileira /. [Brasília] , 1983. 43 p. ; LC Card 86-229392
HD4093 .P46 1983

ECONOMIC INDICATORS - CANADA.
Morin, André, analyste en rémunération. Analyse de l'évolution des principaux indicateurs économiques au Québec, en Ontario, au Canada et aux Etats-Unis . [Québec] [1982] 209 p. ; ISBN 2-551-04641-6 LC Card 83-103355
HC117.Q4 M66 1982

ECONOMIC INDICATORS - CARIBBEAN AREA.
Caribbean labour and the economic environment. Bri[d]getown, Barbados [1985] i, 40 p. ; LC Card 86-127832 DDC 330.9729/052 19
HC151 .C32 1985

ECONOMIC INDICATORS - CENTRAL AMERICA.
Gallardo, María Eugenia. Centroamérica . San José, Costa Rica , 1986. 259 p. : ISBN 92-9039-110-3 LC Card 87-401731 DDC 330.9728/053 19
HC141 .G35 1986

ECONOMIC INDICATORS - CHILE.
Indicadores económicos y sociales, 1960-1985 /. Santiago, Chile , c1986. xvi, 415 p. : LC Card 87-120338
HC192 .I52 1986

Teitelboim G., Berta. Indicadores económicos y sociales . Santiago, Chile , 1985. 57 p. :
NYPL [JLD 86-2146]

Teitelboim G., Berta. Indicadores económicos y sociales [microform] . Santiago, Chile [1984] 41 p. : ***NYPL [*ZT-1711 no.26]***

ECONOMIC INDICATORS - ITALY.
Mediobanca. Indici e dati relativi ad investimenti in titoli quotati nelle borse italiane (1985) =. [Milano] [1985] v, 427 p. : LC Card 86-210524
HG5522 .M43 1985

ECONOMIC INDICATORS - KENYA.
Kenya report of the pilot study on socio-economic indicators, 1981. [Nairobi?] [1982?] 107 leaves : LC Card 87-120114 DDC 330.9676/204 19
HC865 .K486 1982

ECONOMIC INDICATORS - MADAGASCAR.
Madagascar . Paris , 1986, c1985. 184 p. : ISBN 2-905760-02-8 LC Card 87-123718
HC895 .M34 1986

ECONOMIC INDICATORS - ONTARIO.
Morin, André, analyste en rémunération. Analyse de l'évolution des principaux indicateurs économiques au Québec, en Ontario, au Canada et aux Etats-Unis . [Québec] [1982] 209 p. ; ISBN 2-551-04641-6 LC Card 83-103355
HC117.Q4 M66 1982

ECONOMIC INDICATORS - PORTUGAL.
Indicadores económicos e financeiros da Central de Balanços (1978-1980). [Porto] [1982] 204 p. : LC Card 85-166692
HC394.5.C7 I53 1982

Melo, M. Teixeira de. A economia portuguesa após o 25 de abril /. Queluz [Portugal] [1978] 149 p. ; LC Card 79-104785
HC392 .M45 1978

ECONOMIC INDICATORS - QUÉBEC (PROVINCE)
Morin, André, analyste en rémunération. Analyse de l'évolution des principaux indicateurs économiques au Québec, en Ontario, au Canada et aux Etats-Unis . [Québec] [1982] 209 p. ; ISBN 2-551-04641-6 LC Card 83-103355
HC117.Q4 M66 1982

ECONOMIC INDICATORS - SOUTH AFRICA - ELSIES RIVER.
Ellis, George Francis Rayner. A quality of life and basic needs measurement system with application to Elsies River /. Cape Town [1983] 101, [84] p. : ISBN 0-7992-0551-6 LC Card 84-146635 DDC 338.968/00723 19
HC905.Z7 E473 1983 ***NYPL [JLF 86-1126]***

ECONOMIC INDICATORS - SOUTH AMERICA.
Indicadores de los países del Grupo Andino. [Lima] [1985] 172 p. in various pagings : LC Card 86-137319 DDC 330.98/0038 19
HC167.A5 I52 1985

ECONOMIC INDICATORS - SOVIET UNION.
Ozerov, V. K. (Viktor Konstantinovich) Analiz dinamiki sotsialisticheskogo rasshirennogo vosproizvodstva /. Novosibirsk , 1984. 263 p. ; LC Card 85-151291
HC340.I52 O97 1984

ECONOMIC INDICATORS - UNITED STATES.
Conference Board briefing charts /. New York, N.Y. (845 3rd Ave., New York 10022) , c1986. 42, 8 leaves : LC Card 87-104050 DDC 330.973/0927 19
HC106.8 .C663 1986

Folbre, Nancy. A field guide to the U. S. economy /. New York , c1987. 1 v. (various pagings) : ISBN 0-394-75047-0 (pbk.) : LC Card 86-42974 DDC 330.973 19
HC103 .F59 1987

Frumkin, Norman. Tracking America's economy /. Armonk, N.Y. , c1987. 250 p. : ISBN 0-87332-437-4 : LC Card 87-9694 DDC 338.5/44/0973 19
HC106.8 .F78 1987

Lehmann, Michael B. The Dow Jones-Irwin guide to using the Wall Street journal /. Homewood, Ill. , c1987. xii, 282 p. : ISBN 0-87094-923-3 LC Card 86-71441 DDC 332/.05 19
HB3743 .L44 1987

Morin, André, analyste en rémunération. Analyse de l'évolution des principaux indicateurs économiques au Québec, en Ontario, au Canada et aux Etats-Unis . [Québec] [1982] 209 p. ; ISBN 2-551-04641-6 LC Card 83-103355
HC117.Q4 M66 1982

Nelson, Charles R. The investor's guide to economic indicators /. New York , c1987. viii, 193 p. : ISBN 0-471-85902-8 LC Card 87-2134 DDC 330.973/0927 19
HC106.8 .N38 1987

ECONOMIC INDICATORS - UNITED STATES - CHARTS, DIAGRAMS, ETC.
Fisher, Kenneth L. The Wall Street waltz . Chicago , c1987. xii, 210 p. : ISBN 0-8092-4797-6 : LC Card 87-5310 DDC 332.63/222/0973 19
HG4916 .F47 1987.

ECONOMIC INDICATORS - UNITED STATES - STATES.
Making the grade . Washington, D.C. , c1987. ii, 142 p. : ISBN 0-9605804-4-1 (pbk.) LC Card 87-70671 DDC 330.973/0927 19
HC106.8 .M318 1987

ECONOMIC INFRASTRUCTURE. see **INFRASTRUCTURE (ECONOMICS)**

The economic institutions of capitalism . Williamson, Oliver E. New York , London , 1987, c1985. xiv, 450 p. : ISBN 0-02-934821-8 (pbk.) LC Card 87-11901 DDC 338.7 19
HB99.5 .W55 1987

Economic integration and planning in Maoist China /. Lyons, Thomas P. New York , 1987. xiii, 376 p. ; ISBN 0-231-06542-6 LC Card 87-5414 DDC 338.951 19
HC427.9 .L96 1987

ECONOMIC INTEGRATION, INTERNATIONAL. see **INTERNATIONAL ECONOMIC INTEGRATION.**

The economic integration process of Latin America in the 1980's . Seminar on Economic Integration (1982 : Inter-American Development Bank) Washington, D.C. [1984] 318 p. : ISBN 0-940602-17-2 (pbk.) LC Card 87-159367
HC125 .S3973 1982

Economic issues for consumers /. Miller, Roger LeRoy. St. Paul , c1987. xxxv, 526 p. : ISBN 0-314-30391-X (alk. paper) LC Card 86-24722 DDC 332.024 19
HG179 .M48 1987

Economic liberalization in developing countries / edited by Armeane M. Choksi and Demetris Papageorgiou. Oxford [Oxfordshire] ; New York : Basil Blackwell, 1986. vi, 278 p. : ill. ; 24 cm. Papers originally presented to "Economic Liberalization: Adjustments during the Transition Period," Washington, DC, 1983. Includes bibliographies and index. ISBN 0-631-15023-4 : LC Card 86-6153 DDC 338.9/009172/4 19
1. Monetary policy - Developing countries - Congresses. 2. Economic stabilization - Developing countries - Congresses. 3. Developing countries - Economic policy - Congresses. 4. Developing countries - Commercial policy - Congresses. 5. Chile - Economic policy - Congresses. I. Choksi, Armeane M., 1944-. II. Papageorgiou, Demetris.
HC59.7 .E3116 1986 ***NYPL [JLE 86-4644]***

ECONOMIC LIFE (OF ECONOMIC GOODS)
Normen voor nieuwwaarde en afschrijving van slijtende duurzame produktiemiddelen in de fruitteelt alsmede voor de grondwaarde . Den Haag [1986] 67 p. ; LC Card 86-234475
HF5686.F7 N67 1986

Economic memorandum on Anguilla. Caribbean Development Bank. Economics and Programming Dept. [Kingston, Jamaica] [1985] 2, 55 p. : LC Card 86-204700 DDC 330.97297/3 19
HC156.Z7 A483 1985

The economic modernization of Spain, 1830-1930 /. Modernización económica de España, 1830-1930. English. New York , c1987. xv, 295 p. : ISBN 0-8147-7861-5 : LC Card 87-5535 DDC 330.946/07 19
HC385 .M62313 1987

ECONOMIC MULTIPLIER. see **MULTIPLIER (ECONOMICS)**

ECONOMIC NATIONALISM. see **ECONOMIC POLICY.**

Economic nationalism and stability /. Macesich, George, 1927- New York , 1985. x, 163 p. ; ISBN 0-03-005748-5 : LC Card 85-12342 DDC 338.9/009172/4 19
HC59.7 .M2112 1985 ***NYPL [JLE 86-908]***

The economic outlook for U. S. cotton . Horne, M. K. (McDonald Kelso), 1909- Memphis, Tenn. , 1962. 32 p. : LC Card 86-162675
HD9075 .H73 1962

Economic outlook for US cotton. Horne, M. K. (McDonald Kelso), 1909- The economic outlook for U. S. cotton . Memphis, Tenn. , 1962. 32 p. : LC Card 86-162675
HD9075 .H73 1962

Economic overview of fish and wildlife. Alaska habitat management guide. Juneau, Alaska , 1986- 2 v. (loose-leaf) : LC Card 86-623159 DDC 333.95/09798 19
HD9457.A4 A427 1986

Economic panorama of Latin America, 1986 : Argentina, Brazil, Colombia, Chile, Mexico, Peru, Uruguay, Venezuela / Economic Commission for Latin America and the Caribbean.1st ed. Santiago, Chile : United Nations, [1986] 82 p. : ill. ; 25 cm. "October 1986." "LC/G.1435"--T.p. verso. LC Card 87-107353 DDC 330.98/0038 19
1. Latin America - Economic conditions - 1945-. I. United Nations. Economic Commission for Latin America and the Caribbean.
HC125 .E373 1986

Economic performance of public enterprises : major issues and strategies for action / Department of Technical Co-operation for Development. New York : United Nations, 1986. vii, 264 p. : ill. ; 28 cm. "ST/TCD/SER.E/2." "United Nations publication sales no. E.85.II.H.4."--T.p. verso. Includes bibliographies. ISBN 92-1-123103-5 (pbk.) LC Card 87-108199 DDC 338.6/2/091724 19
1. Government business enterprises - Developing countries. I. United Nations. Dept. of Technical Cooperation for Development.
HD4420.8 .E28 1986

Economic philosophy of ancient India /. Das, Arjun, 1946- Delhi , 1986. vi, 224 p. : LC Card 86-903116 DDC 330/.0954 19
HB126.I4 D36 1986

ECONOMIC PLANNING. see **ECONOMIC POLICY.**

ECONOMIC POISONS. see **PESTICIDES.**

Economic policies and agricultural performance . Lecaillon, Jacques. Paris , 1985. 158 p. ; LC Card 86-216027 DDC 338.1/86625 19
HD2144 .L42 1985

Economic policies and agricultural performance . Lecaillon, Jacques. Paris , 1986. 174 p. ; LC Card 87-158595 DDC 338.1/86623 19
HD2143.5.Z8 L43 1986

Economic policies and agricultural performance . Svejnar, Jan. Paris , 1986. 167 p. ; LC Card 87-120115 DDC 338.1/85496 19
HD2065.9.Z8 S84 1986

ECONOMIC POLICY - ADDRESSES, ESSAYS, LECTURES.
The Debate over stabilization policy /. Cambridge [Cambridgeshire] , New York , 1986. xiv, 270 p. : ISBN 0-521-26790-0 LC Card 84-21366 DDC 338.9 19
HB3732 .D43 1986 ***NYPL [JLF 86-1945]***

Di Nardi, Giuseppe. L'economia a una svolta critica /. Milano , 1984- v. ; LC Card 84-216905 DDC 330 19
HB177 .D48 1984 ***NYPL [JLL 73-173 v.25]***

Economia tra teoria e politica /. Milano , c1984. 295 p. ; LC Card 84-171327 DDC 330/.09 19
HB75 .E28 1984 ***NYPL [JLD 87-819]***

The Future of private enterprise /. Atlanta, Ga. , 1984-1986. 3 v. ; ISBN 0-88406-164-7 (pbk. : v. 1) LC Card 83-25386 DDC 338.6/1 19
HB501 .F83 1984 ***NYPL [JLK 87-49]***

Harcourt, Geoffrey Colin. Controversies in political economy . New York , 1986. 293 p. ; ISBN 0-8147-3437-5 : LC Card 85-31055 DDC 330.1 19
HB75 .H33 1986 ***NYPL [JLD 86-3571]***

The Impact of world recession on children /. Oxford [Oxfordshire] , New York , 1984. xiv, 221 p. : ISBN 0-08-031329-9 : LC Card 84-14694 DDC 362.7/042 19
HV715 .I475 1984 ***NYPL [JLE 86-2315]***

Incentive-based incomes policies . Cambridge, Mass. , c1986. xxi, 263 p. : ISBN 0-88730-082-0 LC Card 85-20090 DDC 331.2/9 19
HC79.W24 I465 1986 ***NYPL [JLE 86-3724]***

Natural resource economics . Boston , c1986. xiv, 234 p. : ISBN 0-89838-203-3 LC Card 85-24215 DDC 333.7 19
HC59 .N318 1986 ***NYPL [JLE 86-3471]***

Patel, I. G. (Indraprasad Gordhanbhai), 1924- Essays in economic policy and economic growth /. Basingstoke, Hampshire , 1986. xii, 261 p. ; ISBN 0-333-39213-2
NYPL [JLD 86-4061]

Unemployment and growth in the Western economies /. New York, N.Y. , c1984. x, 142 p. ; ISBN 0-87609-001-3 (pbk.) : LC Card 84-9415 DDC 331.13/791812 19
HD5707.5 .U54 1984 ***NYPL [JLE 86-1564]***

Economic policy and the adjustment problem /. Banks, Gary. Aldershot, Hants., England , Brookfield, Vt. , 1986. x, 101 p. ; ISBN 0-566-05332-2 : LC Card 86-14934 DDC 338.9 19
HF1421 .B36 1987
NYPL [JLL 74-802 no.45]

ECONOMIC POLICY - CASE STUDIES.
Roy, Ramashray. Dialogues on development . New Delhi , Beverly Hills , 1986. 245 p. ; ISBN 0-8039-9492-3 (U. S.) LC Card 85-8368 DDC 338.954/12 19
HD87 .R69 1986 ***NYPL [JLD 86-3196]***

ECONOMIC POLICY - CITIZEN PARTICIPATION.
Teichmann, Ulrich, 1942- Der Entscheidungsprozess in der Wirtschaftspolitik /. Darmstadt , 1983. vi, 135 p. ; ISBN 3-534-08177-3 LC Card 83-206492
HD84 .T39 1983

ECONOMIC POLICY - COLLECTED WORKS.
Johansen, Leif. [Essays. Selections.] Collected works of Leif Johansen /. Amsterdam ; New York : 2 v. (xiii, 974 p.) ; ISBN 0-444-87833-5 (set) LC Card 87-6814 DDC 330.1 19
HB171 .J59725 1987

ECONOMIC POLICY - CONGRESSES.
Capitalismo riformato e sinistra . Milano , 1986. 125 p. ; ISBN 88-24-50380-2 : LC Card 86-229688
HB501 .C24265 1986

Daly, Herman E. Crescimento ou economia estacionária. [Salvador] [1983] 56 p. : LC Card 87-127979 DDC 338.9 19
HD85.S7 D35 1983

Dauderstädt, Michael. Wettbewerbsfähig durch soziale Disziplin? . Bonn [1981] 38 p. ; LC Card 85-137321
HD41 .D38 1981

The Design of alternative development strategies /. Rohtak, India , 1986. xiv, 330 p. : LC Card 86-901301 DDC 338.9 19
HD82 .D383 1986 ***NYPL [JLE 86-4232]***

Economic effects of the government budget /. Cambridge, Mass. , c1988. p. cm. ISBN 0-262-08172-5 LC Card 87-26187 DDC 338.9 19
HJ2005 .E25 1988

Employment and growth . Dordrecht , Boston , 1987. xii, 310 p. : ISBN 90-247-3514-9 LC Card 87-3184 DDC 331.11 19
HD73 .E46 1987

Global economic imbalances /. Washington, DC , 1985. x, 116 p. ; ISBN 0-88132-038-2 (pbk.) LC Card 85-8279 DDC 330.9/048 19
HD73 .G56 1985 ***NYPL [JLE 87-1314]***

Growth-oriented adjustment programs /. Washington, D.C. , 1987. xiii, 537 p. : ISBN 0-939934-92-2 (pbk.) LC Card 87-21361 DDC 338.9 19
HD73 .G76 1987

Issues of the eighties . Wien , 1983. 119 p. : LC Card 83-201354 DDC 338.9 19
HD73 .I86 1983

Keynes and public policy after fifty years /. New York , <c1988-. v. <2 > : ISBN 0-8147-3444-8 (v. 1) : LC Card 87-20368 DDC 330.15/6 19
HB99.7 .K3815 1988

Policy responses to the changing international environment . Budapest , 1981. 170 p. ; ISBN 963-301-077-2 (pbk.) LC Card 81-179118 DDC 337/.09/048 19
HC59 .P573 1981 ***NYPL [JLL 79-189 no.33]***

Probleme der staatsmonopolistischen Wirtschaftsregulierung . Rostock , 1981. 35 p. ; LC Card 86-211250
HB501 .P694 1981

Reassessing the role of government in the mixed economy /. Boulder , 1987. p. cm. ISBN 0-8133-0598-5 : LC Card 87-20142 DDC 338.9 19
HD73 .R43 1987

Staatsfinanzierung und Notenbank . Wien [1984?] 211 p. : LC Card 85-198128
HG1811 .S78 1984

Structural adjustment and growth . Colombo, Sri Lanka , 1986. 170 p. ; LC Card 86-903207

DDC 338.9549/3 19
HC424 .S77 1986

ECONOMIC POLICY - DECISION MAKING - CONGRESSES.
International macroeconomic modelling for policy decisions /. Dordrecht , Boston , c1986. viii, 269 p. : ISBN 90-247-3201-8 LC Card 85-13698 DDC 337/.0724 19
HF1410.5 .I577 1986 ***NYPL [JLE 86-3469]***

ECONOMIC POLICY - DICTIONARIES - POLYGLOT.
Logie, Gordon. Glossary of planning and development . Amsterdam , New York , 1986. xxv, 254 p. ; ISBN 0-444-42608-6 (U. S.) : LC Card 86-521 DDC 338.9/003 19
HT391 .L64 1987 ***NYPL [JLE 86-4010]***

ECONOMIC POLICY - DIRECTORIES.
Government economic agencies of the world . Detroit , c1985. x, 546 p. ; ISBN 0-8103-2104-1 (Gale) LC Card 84-26861 DDC 351.82/025 19
HD87.25 .G68 1985
NYPL [*R-Econ 86-6573]

Economic policy during the construction of socialism in the USSR /. Dmitrenko, Vladimir Petrovich. Moscow , c1987. 156 p. ; LC Card 86-201129 DDC 338.947 19
HC335.2 .D56 1987

ECONOMIC POLICY - ECONOMETRIC MODELS.
Adolph, Brigitte. Rationale Erwartungen, Arbeitsverträge und Wirtschaftspolitik /. München , c1986. ii, 127 p. : ISBN 3-88259-346-6 LC Card 87-104701 DDC 330/.01/9 19
HB175 .A26 1986

Schalk, Hans Joachim. Differenzierte Globalsteuerung . Berlin , New York , c1985. ix, 319 p. : ISBN 0-387-16045-0 (U. S.) LC Card 86-141700
HB3732 .S32 1985

ECONOMIC POLICY - ENVIRONMENTAL ASPECTS.
Leipert, Christian. Folgekosten des Wachstums als Wachstumsstimulans . Berlin [1985?] 35 p. : LC Card 86-116361
HD75.6 .L45 1985

ECONOMIC POLICY - EVALUATION - FORMS.
Metodología de evaluación y programación de sistemas de producción y consumo, MEPS /. Lima, Perú [1985]- v. <1 > : LC Card 86-215609
HD75 .M48 1985

ECONOMIC POLICY - EVALUATION - MATHEMATICAL MODELS - ADDRESSES, ESSAYS, LECTURES.
Microanalytic simulation models to support social and financial policy /. Amsterdam ; New York : xvii, 553 p. : ISBN 0-444-87876-9 (U. S.) LC Card 85-25231 DDC 361.6/0724 19
HD87 .M52 1986 ***NYPL [JLD 86-3485]***

ECONOMIC POLICY, FOREIGN. see **INTERNATIONAL ECONOMIC RELATIONS.**

ECONOMIC POLICY - GERMANY (EAST)
Bottesi, Valentin, 1933- Kombinatsplanung und Leistungssteigerung /. Berlin , 1984. 120 p. ; LC Card 84-217968
HC290.795.I52 B67 1984

ECONOMIC POLICY - GERMANY (EAST) - CONGRESSES.
Sozialistische Einheitspartei Deutschlands. Zentralkomitee. [Bericht des Zentralkomitees der Sozialistischen Einheitspartei Deutschlands an den XI. Parteitag der SED. English.] Report of the Central Committee of the Socialist Unity Party of Germany to the 11th Congress of the SED /. Dresden [1986] 109 p. : LC Card 86-220057 DDC 338.9431 19
HC290.78 .S66 1986

ECONOMIC POLICY - HISTORY.
Pesante, Maria Luisa. Economia e politica /. Milano, Italy , c1986. 94 p. ; LC Card 86-196256
HB75 .P465 1986

ECONOMIC POLICY - HISTORY - ADDRESSES, ESSAYS, LECTURES.
Di Nardi, Giuseppe. L'economia a una svolta critica /. Milano , 1984- v. ; LC Card 84-216905
DDC 330 19
HB177 .D48 1984 ***NYPL [JLL 73-173 v.25]***

Economic policy in Iraq, 1932-1950 /. Sassoon, Joseph. London, England , Totowa, N.J. , 1987. p. cm. ISBN 0-7146-3305-4 : LC Card 87-6577 DDC 338.9567 19
HC415.4 .S27 1987

Economic policy-making /. Levačić, Rosalind. Sussex , Totowa, N.J. , 1987. xii, 372 p. : ISBN 0-389-20741-1 (Barnes & Noble) LC Card 87-11543 DDC 338.941 19
HD75 .L48 1987

ECONOMIC POLICY - MATHEMATICAL MODELS.
Macroeconomics [i.e. Macroeconomic] impacts of energy shocks /. Amsterdam ; New York : xvi, 331 p. : ISBN 0-444-70247-4 (U. S.) LC Card 87-9035 DDC 338.4/36655/0724 19
HG229 .M315 1987

Modele matematice și semiotice ale dezvoltării sociale /. București , 1986. 190 p. : LC Card 86-208152
HD75.5 .M615 1986

Murata, Yasuo, 1931- Optimal control methods for linear discrete-time economic systems /. New York , c1982. x, 202 p. ; ISBN 0-387-90709-2 LC Card 82-19137 DDC 338.9/00724 19
HD75.5 .M87 1982 ***NYPL [JLE 87-95]***

Opyt razrabotki i realizat͡sii sistemy ukrupnennykh modeleĭ perspektivnogo planirovanii͡a /. Moskva , 1984. 216 p. : LC Card 85-199888
HD75.5 .O69 1984

Picard, Pierre. Théorie du déséquilibre et politique économique /. Paris , 1985. 253 p. : ISBN 2-7178-0877-9 : LC Card 86-109716 DDC 339.5 19
HB145 .P53 1985

Schouten, D. B. J. Het wankele evenwicht in de economie . Leiden , 1986. xiv, 189 p. ; ISBN 90-207-1436-8 : LC Card 86-167831
HD85.D8 S36 1986

Sengupta, Jatikumar. Optimal decisions under uncertainty . Berlin , New York , 1985. 286 p. ; ISBN 0-387-15032-3 (U. S.) LC Card 84-26683 DDC 658.4/033 19
HD30.23 .S46 1985 ***NYPL [JLE 86-4652]***

Silva, Adroaldo Moura da. Emprego e preços no curto prazo /. São Paulo, SP (C.P. 11474, 01000 São Paulo, SP) , 1983. 94 p. ;
NYPL [JLD 86-3819]

Valencia Roa, Carlos Alberto, 1944- Social investments and economic growth /. 1974. xiv, 199 leaves : ***NYPL [JLD 86-2961]***

Willner, Johan. Economic policy under imperfect competition /. Åbo [Finland] 1983. 34 p. ; ISBN 951-648-926-5 (pbk.) LC Card 84-137942 DDC 338.9/00724 19
HB238 .W539 1983
NYPL [JLL 77-251 no.187]

ECONOMIC POLICY - MORAL AND ETHICAL ASPECTS.
Marktwirtschaft und Gesellschaftsordnung . Berlin , c1983. 220 p., [1] leaf of plates : ISBN 3-428-05365-6 LC Card 83-191615
HB72 .M248 1983

ECONOMIC POLICY - MORAL AND ETHICAL ASPECTS - CONGRESSES.
Tokyo Forum: Ethics of Human Survival (1985) Proceedings of the Tokyo Forum: Ethics of Human Survival . Tokyo, Japan , c1986. v, 88 p. : ISBN 4-7955-1024-5 LC Card 87-142747
HD73 .T65 1985

ECONOMIC POLICY - STUDY AND TEACHING (HIGHER) - LATIN AMERICA.
Latin American Institute for Economic and Social Planning. Instituto Latinoamericano de Planificación Económica y Social (ILPES) . [Santiago, Chile] [1984] iii, 52 p. ; LC Card 84-202400
HD77.5.L29 L38 1984

Economic policy under imperfect competition /. Willner, Johan. Åbo [Finland] 1983. 34 p. ; ISBN 951-648-926-5 (pbk.) LC Card 84-137942 DDC 338.9/00724 19
HB238 .W539 1983
NYPL [JLL 77-251 no.187]

The economic position of the British labourer /. Fawcett, Henry, 1833-1884. New York , 1984. vii, 256 p. ; ISBN 0-8240-5706-6 (alk. paper) : LC Card 83-48478 DDC 331/.0941 19
HD8390 .F28 1984 ***NYPL [JLC 86-366]***

Economic priorities for a labour government /. Hattersley, Roy. New York , 1987. ix, 198 p. ; ISBN 0-312-00987-9 : LC Card 87-9576 DDC 338.941 19
HC256.6 .H385 1987

The economic pursuit of quality /. Power, Thomas M. Armonk, N.Y. , c1987. p. cm. ISBN 0-87332-436-6 LC Card 87-12128 DDC 330 19
HB171 .P697 1987

Economic recovery and long-run growth : agenda for reforms / Florian A. Alburo ... [et al.]. Makati, Metro Manila : Philippine Institute for Development Studies, [1986- v. <1 > ; 28 cm. "May 1, 1986." CONTENTS. - v. 1. Main report. LC Card 86-232161 DDC 338.9599 19
1. Philippines - Economic policy. 2. Philippines - Economic conditions - 1946-. I. Alburo, Florian A. II. Philippine Institute for Development Studies.
HC453 .E27 1986

Economic recovery program, 1986/87-1988/89. Monrovia, Liberia : Ministry of Planning and Economic Affairs, [1986] 76, a-n p. ; 28 cm. At head of title: Republic of Liberia. "September 1986." LC Card 87-104460 DDC 338.9666/2 19
1. Liberia - Economic policy. 2. Liberia - Economic conditions - 1980-. 3. Public investments - Liberia. I. Liberia. Ministry of Planning and Economic Affairs.
HC1075 .E25 1986

Economic reform and migration in Yugoslavia. Sapir, André. Ekonomska reforma i migracije u Jugoslaviji . Zagreb , 1983. 56 p. ; LC Card 86-183906
HC407 .S26 1983

Economic reform and political change in eastern Europe . Batt, Judy. New York , 1987. p. cm. ISBN 0-312-01196-2 : LC Card 87-24065 DDC 338.9437 19
HC270.28 .B37 1987

Economic reform and stabilization in Latin America / edited by Michael Connolly and Claudio Gonzalez-Vega. New York : Praeger, c1986. xxiii, 348 p. : ill. ; 24 cm. Includes index. ISBN 0-275-92307-X (alk. paper) : LC Card 86-9405 DDC 338.98 19
1. Economic stabilization - Latin America. 2. Monetary policy - Latin America. 3. Foreign exchange administration - Latin America. 4. Latin America - Commercial policy. 5. Latin America - Economic conditions - 1945-. I. Connolly, Michael B. (Michael Bahaamonde), 1941-. II. González Vega, Claudio.
HC125 .E374 1986 ***NYPL [JLE 87-1073]***

Economic regulation and the federal system /. Schultz, Richard, 1945- Toronto , Buffalo , c1985. xv, 187 p. : ISBN 0-8020-7287-9 (pbk.) LC Card 86-672574
HD3616.C23 S38x 1985
NYPL [JLD 86-2821]

ECONOMIC RELATIONS, FOREIGN. see **INTERNATIONAL ECONOMIC RELATIONS.**

Economic relations in connection with succession of generations in agriculture. Knapskog, Kåre. Økonomiske forhold ved generasjonsskifte i landbruket =. Oslo , 1986. 95 p. : ISBN 82-7077-032-9 LC Card 86-231818
HD2012 .K6 1986

ECONOMIC RELATIONS, INTERNATIONAL. see **INTERNATIONAL ECONOMIC RELATIONS.**

Economic relevance of non-alignment /. Vohra, Dewan C. New Delhi , 1983. xv, 387 p. ; LC Card 83-901770 DDC 338.9/009172/4 19
HC59.7 .V63 1983 ***NYPL [JLD 86-3799]***

Economic report of the people / Center for Popular Economics. 1st ed. Boston : South End Press, c1986. xvii, 260 p. : ill. ; 22 cm. The crossed out word "President" appears in the title before the word "people." Includes bibliographies and index. ISBN 0-89608-315-2 (pbk.) : LC Card 85-30342 DDC 330.973/0927 19
1. Supply-side economics - United States. 2. Debts, External - Developing countries. 3. United States - Economic conditions - 1981-. 4. United States -

Economic policy - 1981-. I. Center for Popular Economics (U. S.).
HC106.8 .E29 1986 *NYPL [JLD 87-301]*

Economic research series (Hitotsubashi Daigaku. Keizai Kenkyūjo) .
(no. 23) Fujino, Shozaburo, 1927- Money, employment, and interest . Tokyo, Japan , New York, NY [1987] xii, 220 p. : ISBN 4-314-00464-9 : LC Card 87-165395 DDC 330.15/6 19
HB99.7 .F85 1987

The Economic revival of modern Britain : the debate between left and right / edited by David Coates, John Hillard. Aldershot, Hants, England : E. Elgar, c1987. xv, 349 p. : ill. ; 24 cm. Bibliography: p. 341. Includes index. ISBN 1-85278-000-2 (pbk.) : LC Card 87-170031 DDC 338.941 19
1. Great Britain - Economic conditions - 1945-. 2. Great Britain - Economic policy - 1945-. I. Coates, David. II. Hillard, John.
HC256.6 .E227 1987

ECONOMIC SANCTIONS.
Palánkai, Tibor. Gazdasági hadviselés a kölcsönös függés korszakában /. [Budapest] , 1985. 88 p. ; ISBN 963-09-2633-4 : LC Card 86-128423
HF1413.5 .P35 1985

Wirtschaftssanktionen im Ost-West-Verhältnis . Baden-Baden , 1983. 234 p. : ISBN 3-7890-0963-6 LC Card 84-132150
HF1413.5 .W57 1983

ECONOMIC SANCTIONS, AMERICAN - SOUTH AFRICA.
Automating apartheid . Philadelphia , c19. ix, 107 p. : ISBN 0-910082-00-6 (pbk.) : LC Card 86-201384 DDC 382/.45004/0968 19
HD9696.C63 S62 1984

The South African quagmire . Cambridge, Mass. , c1987. xvi, 444 p. ; ISBN 0-88730-191-6 LC Card 86-28754 DDC 320.5/6 19
HF1613.4.Z4 U67 1987

United States Catholic Conference. Administrative Board. Divestment, disinvestment, and South Africa . Washington, D.C. , c1986. 36 p. ; ISBN 1-555-86137-7 (pbk.) LC Card 87-136857 DDC 332.6/7373/068 19
HG5851.A3 U55 1986

ECONOMIC SANCTIONS, AMERICAN - SOVIET UNION - ECONOMETRIC MODELS.
Lundborg, Per, 1950- The economics of export embargoes . New York, NY , c1987. xi, 127 p. : ISBN 0-7099-4151-X : LC Card 86-29370 DDC 382/.4131/0947 19
HD9035 .L86 1987

ECONOMIC SANCTIONS, ARAB COUNTRIES.

ECONOMIC SANCTIONS, ARAB COUNTRIES - ISRAEL.
Sarna, A. J. Boycott and blacklist . Totowa, N.J. , 1986. xiv, 270 p. : ISBN 0-8476-7489-4 : LC Card 86-1891 DDC 337.5694/0174927 19
HF1610.Z4 I87 1986
*NYPL [*PXLB 86-6444]*

ECONOMIC SANCTIONS - SOUTH AFRICA.
Hayes, J. P. (John Philip), 1924- Economic effects of sanctions on southern Africa /. Aldershot, Hampshire, England , Brookfield, Vt., USA , 1987. xii, 100 p. : ISBN 0-566-05539-2 (pbk.) : LC Card 87-11674 DDC 337.68 19
HF1413.5 .H39 1987

Hunter, Jane, 1943- Undercutting sanctions . Washington, DC (918 16th St. NW, Suite 501, Washington 20006) , c1987. iv, 71 p. ; LC Card 87-403525 DDC 337.68 19
HF1613.4 .H86 1987

Moorsom, Richard. The scope for sanctions . London , 1986. 102 p. ; ISBN 0-946848-66-1 (pbk.) : LC Card 86-226230 DDC 337.41068 19
HF1613.4 .M66 1986

The South African quagmire . Cambridge, Mass. , c1987. xvi, 444 p. ; ISBN 0-88730-191-6 LC Card 86-28754 DDC 320.5/6 19
HF1613.4.Z4 U67 1987

Turner, Terisa. Trade union action to stop oil to South Africa /. Port Harcourt , c1985. v, 35 p. ; LC Card 87-673464
HF1613.4 .T87x 1985

ECONOMIC SANCTIONS - ZIMBABWE.
Paul, Jan-Peter. Ekonomiska sanktioner . Helsingfors [1985] 46 p. ; ISBN 951-555-224-9 LC Card 85-212001
HF1613.5 .P38 1985

ECONOMIC SECURITY.
Tinbergen, Jan, 1903- Warfare and welfare . Brighton, Sussex , New York , 1987. xiv, 189 p. ; ISBN 0-312-00957-7 (St. Martin's) : LC Card 87-9625 DDC 361.6/1 19
HB846 .T55 1987

ECONOMIC SECURITY - CANADA - ADDRESSES, ESSAYS, LECTURES.
Income distribution and economic security in Canada /. Toronto , Buffalo , c1985. xv, 321 p. : ISBN 0-8020-7241-0 (pbk.) LC Card 85-227851 DDC 330.971/064 19
HC120.I5 I53 1985 *NYPL [JLE 86-1881]*

ECONOMIC SECURITY - ITALY, SOUTHERN.
Boccella, Nicola Maria, 1952- Il Mezzogiorno sussidiato . Milano, Italy , c1982. 264 p. : LC Card 85-163271
HD7185.S68 B62 1982

ECONOMIC SECURITY - UNITED STATES.
EBRI-ERF Policy Forum (1986 : Washington, D.C.) America in transition . Washington, D.C. , c1987. xix, 269 p. : ISBN 0-86643-057-1 (hard) : LC Card 87-13421 DDC 331.25/5/0973 19
HD4928.N62 U628 1987

ECONOMIC SELF-SUFFICIENCY. see **AUTARCHY.**

Economic shocks and structural adjustments .
Conway, Patrick J. Amsterdam ; New York : xiv, 219 p. : ISBN 0-444-70281-4 LC Card 87-15667 DDC 338.9561 19
HC492 .C65 1987

ECONOMIC STABILIZATION - ADDRESSES, ESSAYS, LECTURES.
The Debate over stabilization policy /. Cambridge [Cambridgeshire] , New York , 1986. xiv, 270 p. : ISBN 0-521-26790-0 LC Card 84-21366 DDC 338.9 19
HB3732 .D43 1986 *NYPL [JLF 86-1945]*

ECONOMIC STABILIZATION - AFRICA, SUB-SAHARAN.
Green, Reginald Herbold. The IMF and stabilisation in sub-Saharan Africa . Brighton, England [1986] ii, 70 p. ; LC Card 86-208478 DDC 332.1/52 19
HC800 .G72 1986

ECONOMIC STABILIZATION - ARGENTINA.
Conesa, Eduardo R. Bases y puntos de partida para la recuperación de la economía argentina . Buenos Aires, Argentina , c1986. 178 p. : ISBN 950-53-7109-8 LC Card 87-400257 DDC 338.982 19
HC175 .C6145 1986

ECONOMIC STABILIZATION - BOLIVIA.
Conferencias sobre desarrollo económico, presupuesto, estabilización y nacionalización de empresas económicas. La Paz, Bolivia , 1955. 180 p. : LC Card 86-167406
HC182 .C54 1955

ECONOMIC STABILIZATION - BRAZIL.
Calcagnotto, Gilberto. Brasilien 1974-1981 . Hamburg [1983] xi, 78 p. : LC Card 83-222930
HC187 .C143 1983

Política econômica da Nova República /. Rio de Janeiro, RJ [1986] 275 p. : LC Card 87-102398
HC187 .P67 1986

ECONOMIC STABILIZATION - BRAZIL - ECONOMETRIC MODELS.
Melo, Valdir Ramalho de. Seleção de agregados monetários /. [Brasília] [1981] 136 p. : LC Card 85-161532
HG835 .M45 1981

ECONOMIC STABILIZATION - CHILE.
Edwards, Sebastián. Monetarism and liberalization . Cambridge, MA , c1987. xxi, 233 p. : ISBN 0-88730-105-3 LC Card 86-25959 DDC 338.983 19
HC192 .E249 1987 *NYPL [JLE 87-1485]*

ECONOMIC STABILIZATION - CONGRESSES.
Economic effects of the government budget /. Cambridge, Mass. , c1988. p. cm. ISBN 0-262-08172-5 LC Card 87-26187 DDC 338.9 19
HJ2005 .E25 1988

Growth-oriented adjustment programs /. Washington, D.C. , 1987. xiii, 537 p. : ISBN 0-939934-92-2 (pbk.) LC Card 87-21361 DDC 338.9 19
HD73 .G76 1987

Öffentliche Unternehmen in Rezession und Aufschwung . Berlin , 1977. 165 p. : LC Card 85-180964
HD3845 .G43 Heft 14 HD3842

ECONOMIC STABILIZATION - COSTA RICA.
Delgado Q., Félix. Programas de estabilización y condicionalidad en Costa Rica /. San José, Costa Rica , 1986. 30, [6] leaves ; LC Card 87-404196 DDC 338.97286 19
HC143 .D45 1986

ECONOMIC STABILIZATION - DEVELOPING COUNTRIES.
Gylfason, Thorvaldur. Credit policy and economic activity in developing countries with IMF stabilization programs /. Princeton, N.J. , c1987. 44 p. ; ISBN 0-88165-232-6 (pbk.) : LC Card 87-3389 DDC 332.7/09172/4 19
HG3711.D48 G94 1987

Im Teufelskreis der Verschuldung . Hamburg , 1984. 261 p. : ISBN 3-88506-126-0 LC Card 85-131681
HG3881.5.I58 I37 1984

Kapur, Basant. Studies in inflationary dynamics . Kent Ridge, Singapore , c1986. xviii, 146 p., [1] folded leaf of plates : ISBN 997-16-9099-3 (pbk.) LC Card 87-116919 DDC 332.4/1 19
HC59.7 .K276 1986

Macesich, George, 1927- Economic nationalism and stability /. New York , 1985. x, 163 p. ; ISBN 0-03-005748-5 : LC Card 85-12342 DDC 338.9/009172/4 19
HC59.7 .M2112 1985 *NYPL [JLE 86-908]*

ECONOMIC STABILIZATION - DEVELOPING COUNTRIES - CONGRESSES.
Economic liberalization in developing countries /. Oxford [Oxfordshire] , New York , 1986. vi, 278 p. : ISBN 0-631-15023-4 : LC Card 86-6153 DDC 338.9/009172/4 19
HC59.7 .E3116 1986 *NYPL [JLE 86-4644]*

ECONOMIC STABILIZATION - DOMINICAN REPUBLIC - CONGRESSES.
La Situación cambiaria en la República Dominicana /. Santo Domingo, República Dominicana , 1984. 252 p. : LC Card 87-401265 DDC 338.97293 19
HC153.5 .S575 1984

ECONOMIC STABILIZATION - DOMINICAN REPUBLIC - MATHEMATICAL MODELS.
Dauhajre, Andrés. Reforma financiera en pequeñas economías abiertas /. Santo Domingo, República Dominicana , 1986. 97 p. : LC Card 87-402920 DDC 332.4/56097293 19
HG3926.5 .D38 1986

ECONOMIC STABILIZATION - ECONOMETRIC MODELS.
Kontrolltheoretische Ansätze in makroökonometrischen Modellen /. Frankfurt am Main , New York , c1985. 170 p. : ISBN 3-8204-8314-4 LC Card 86-156081
HB3732 .K68 1985

Schalk, Hans Joachim. Differenzierte Globalsteuerung . Berlin , New York , c1985. ix, 319 p. : ISBN 0-387-16045-0 (U. S.) LC Card 86-141700
HB3732 .S32 1985

ECONOMIC STABILIZATION - EUROPE - CONGRESSES.
Nationale Wege der Inflationsbekämpfung /. Berlin , c1986. 223 p. : ISBN 3-428-06077-6 LC Card 87-132310 DDC 332.4/1/094 19
HC240 .N315 1986

ECONOMIC STABILIZATION - FRANCE - ADDRESSES, ESSAYS, LECTURES.

Stabilization policy in France and the Federal Republic of Germany /. Amsterdam ; New York : xii, 379 p. : ISBN 0-444-87529-8 LC Card 84-28614 DDC 338.943 19
HC276.2 .S77 1985 ***NYPL [TB (Contributions to economic analysis. no.153)]***

ECONOMIC STABILIZATION - GERMANY (WEST)
Hahn, Jörg. Ökonomie, Politik und Krise . Würzburg , 1984. 137 p. ; ISBN 3-88479-183-4 LC Card 85-113948
HB3732 .H34 1984

Leibinger, Hans-Bodo. Fiskalpolitik unter veränderten Rahmenbedingungen . Berlin , c1985. 256 p. : ISBN 3-428-05862-3 LC Card 85-218522
HJ1120 .L45 1985

Die Zukunft der Globalsteuerung /. Bern , c1986. 268 p. ; ISBN 3-258-03573-3 : LC Card 86-182288
HC286.7 .Z82 1986

ECONOMIC STABILIZATION - GERMANY (WEST) - ADDRESSES, ESSAYS, LECTURES.
Stabilization policy in France and the Federal Republic of Germany /. Amsterdam ; New York : xii, 379 p. : ISBN 0-444-87529-8 LC Card 84-28614 DDC 338.943 19
HC276.2 .S77 1985 ***NYPL [TB (Contributions to economic analysis. no.153)]***

ECONOMIC STABILIZATION - GERMANY (WEST) - ECONOMETRIC MODELS.
Kontrolltheoretische Ansätze in makroökonometrischen Modellen /. Frankfurt am Main , New York , c1985. 170 p. : ISBN 3-8204-8314-4 LC Card 86-156081
HB3732 .K68 1985

Stahlecker, Peter. Konzentration und gesamtwirtschaftliche Stabilität . Frankfurt am Main , New York , c1984. v, 592 p. : ISBN 3-8204-5318-0 LC Card 85-192714
HD2757 .S78 1984

ECONOMIC STABILIZATION - GREAT BRITAIN.
Dobrovolny, Jiri, 1943- Preis- und Lohndirigismen im Dienste der Stabilisierungspolitik . Bern , New York , c1985. xi, 433 p. : ISBN 3-261-03517-X LC Card 86-105626 DDC 338.5/2/0945 19
HB236.G7 D63 1985

ECONOMIC STABILIZATION - ITALY.
Oltre la crisi . Bologna , c1986. x, 745 p. : ISBN 88-15-01249-4 : LC Card 87-149887
HC305 .O45 1986

ECONOMIC STABILIZATION - LATIN AMERICA.
Deuda externa latinoamericana y proceso de ajuste . Bogotá, Colombia , 1985. 335 p. : LC Card 86-164491
HJ8514.5 .D484 1985

Díaz Alejandro, Carlos Federico. Trade, development and the world economy . Oxford, OX, UK , New York, NY, USA , 1988. p. cm. ISBN 0-631-15687-9 : LC Card 87-20836 DDC 337.8 19
HF1480.5 .D52 1988

The Economic crisis . Santiago, Chile , New York, NY, USA , 1986. 132 p. : ISBN 92-1-121132-8 (pbk.) LC Card 87-404540 DDC 338.98 19
HC125 .E368 1986

Economic reform and stabilization in Latin America /. New York , c1986. xxiii, 348 p. : ISBN 0-275-92307-X (alk. paper) : LC Card 86-9405 DDC 338.98 19
HC125 .E374 1986 ***NYPL [JLE 87-1073]***

From crisis to equitable growth ; a new development agenda for Latin America /. Aldershot , Brookfield, USA , 1987. ix, 144 p. ; ISBN 0-566-05536-8 : LC Card 87-21135 DDC 338.98 19
HC130.B38 F76 1987

Pastor, Manuel. The International Monetary Fund and Latin America . Boulder, Colo. , 1987. xvi, 228 p. : ISBN 0-8133-7373-5 (pbk. : alk. paper) : LC Card 86-32575 DDC 332.4/98 19
HG660.5 .P33 1987

Políticas macro-económicas . Santiago de Chile [1986] 409 p. : LC Card 87-403669 DDC 338.98 19
HC125 .P657 1986

ECONOMIC STABILIZATION - LATIN AMERICA - CASE STUDIES.
Gómez de Reyes, María Teresa. Experiencias de políticas de estabilización . México, D.F. , 1985. iv, 66 leaves ; LC Card 87-122042 DDC 338.982 19
HC125 .G57 1985

ECONOMIC STABILIZATION - LATIN AMERICA - CONGRESSES.
Políticas de ajuste y grupos más vulnerables en América Latina . [Bogotá, Colombia] , 1987. 278 p. : ISBN 958-9093-01-9 LC Card 87-404285 DDC 338.98 19
HC125 .P647 1987

ECONOMIC STABILIZATION - LATIN AMERICA - HISTORY.
Cardoso, Eliana A. Inflation, growth and the real exchange rate . New York , 1987. 98 p. : ISBN 0-8240-1356-5 (alk. paper) : LC Card 87-8570 DDC 330.981 19
HC187 .C218 1987

ECONOMIC STABILIZATION - MATHEMATICAL MODELS.
Ghosh, S. Stabilizing speculative commodity markets /. Oxford [Oxfordshire] , New York , 1987. xiii, 437 p. : ISBN 0-19-828472-1 : LC Card 86-32654 DDC 332.64/4 19
HG6046 .G485 1987

Murata, Yasuo, 1931- Optimal control methods for linear discrete-time economic systems /. New York , c1982. x, 202 p. ; ISBN 0-387-90709-2 LC Card 82-19137 DDC 338.9/00724 19
HD75.5 .M87 1982 ***NYPL [JLE 87-95]***

Stahlecker, Peter. Konzentration und gesamtwirtschaftliche Stabilität . Frankfurt am Main , New York , c1984. v, 592 p. : ISBN 3-8204-5318-0 LC Card 85-192714
HD2757 .S78 1984

Weigert, Edmund. Defizitfinanzierte Fiskalpolitik in einer kleinen offenen Volkswirtschaft bei flexiblen Wechselkursen . Krefeld , 1987, c1986. iii, 211 p. ; ISBN 3-88358-071-6 LC Card 87-146660 DDC 339.5/2/0724 19
HJ161 .W44 1987

ECONOMIC STABILIZATION - PERU.
Scheetz, Thomas Edward. Peru and the International Monetary Fund /. Pittsburgh, PA , c1986. xi, 257 p. : ISBN 0-8229-3816-2 LC Card 85-40855 DDC 332.1/52 19
HG3881.5.I58 S34 1986 ***NYPL [JLD 86-2893]***

ECONOMIC STABILIZATION - QUÉBEC (PROVINCE)
Fortin, Pierre. [Unemployment, inflation, and economic stabilization in Quebec. French.] Chômage, inflation et régulation de la conjoncture au Québec /. Montréal, Québec [1980] viii, 144 p. : ISBN 0-88806-063-7 (pbk.) LC Card 87-673448
HC117.Q4 F63x 1980

ECONOMIC STABILIZATION - SWEDEN.
Södersten, Bo. Makroekonomi och stabiliseringspolitik /. [Malmö] , c1983. 363 p. : ISBN 91-40-05037-8 : LC Card 84-166176
HB179.S8 S63 1983

ECONOMIC STABILIZATION - SWITZERLAND.
Genberg, Hans. External influences on the Swiss economy under fixed and flexible exchange rates /. Grüsch , c1985. ii, 182 p. : ISBN 3-7253-0249-9 (pbk.) LC Card 86-156330
HG3963 .G45 1985 ***NYPL [JLD 87-539]***

Genberg, Hans. Influences externes sur l'économie suisse en changes fixes et flottants /. Genève , c1985. ii, 202 p. : ISBN 2-8257-0127-0 : LC Card 85-235579 DDC 332.4/5609494 19
HG3963 .G46 1985 ***NYPL [JLD 86-2381]***

ECONOMIC STABILIZATION - TANZANIA.
Green, Reginald Herbold. The IMF and stabilisation in sub-Saharan Africa . Brighton, England [1986] ii, 70 p. ; LC Card 86-208478 DDC 332.1/52 19
HC800 .G72 1986

ECONOMIC STABILIZATION - UNITED STATES.
Müller, Ronald E. National economic growth and stabilization policy in the age of multinational corporations . [Sydney] , 1979. vi, 45 p. : ISBN 0-908470-00-2 (pbk.) LC Card 87-672345
HC106.7 .M84x 1979

ECONOMIC STABILIZATION - YUGOSLAVIA.
Jugoslovenska privreda između stagnacije i razvoja /. Beograd , 1986. viii, 298 p. : LC Card 87-151260
HC407 .J83 1986

ECONOMIC STATISTICS. see **ECONOMETRICS; ECONOMIC HISTORY; ECONOMICS, MATHEMATICAL; STATISTICS.**

Economic statistics and econometrics /. Mirer, Thad W. New York , London , c1988. xvi, 400 p. : ISBN 0-02-381821-2 LC Card 87-24027 DDC 330/.028 19
HB137 .M57 1988

The economic status of male Hispanic migrants and natives in the U. S. [microform] . Borjas, George J. Santa Barbara, Calif. , 1981. vi, 95 p. ; ***NYPL [*XME-11,311]***

Economic status of Texas agriculture / Extension economists, marketing & policy. College Station, Tex. : Dept. of Agricultural Economics, Texas A&M University, [1985] ii, 30 leaves : 1 ill. ; 28 cm. (Faculty paper series . FP 85-7) "October 1985." LC Card 87-620640 DDC 338.1/09764 19
1. Agriculture - Economic aspects - Texas. I. Texas Agricultural Extension Service. II. Texas A & M University. Dept. of Agricultural Economics. III. Series.
HD1775.T4 E28 1985

Economic structure and demographic performance in Jamaica, 1891-1935 /. Lobdell, Richard A. New York , 1987. xii, 259 p. ; ISBN 0-8240-1365-4 (alk. paper) : LC Card 87-8345 DDC 304.6/097292 19
HB3553 .L63 1987

Economic structure and development of Burma /. Sell, Axel. Bremen [1985] 39 p. ; LC Card 86-228833 DDC 338.9591 19
HC422 .S45 1985

Economic study of the establishment of sorghum mill and dehuller in Ethiopia . Dejene Aredo. [Addis Ababa?] [1986] 37 leaves ; LC Card 87-980144 DDC 338.1/73174/0963 19
HD9049.S6 E83 1986

An economic study on guava cultivation in some selected areas of Bangladesh /. Ali, Md. Harun, 1944- Mymensingh , 1986. 38 p. ; LC Card 87-902187 DDC 338.1/74421/095492 19
HD9259.G83 B353 1986

An economic survey of intensive bush cider orchards, 1972-1981 . Rendell, John. [Reading, Berks.] [1984] 24 p. : ISBN 0-7049-0814-X (pbk.) : LC Card 85-111963 DDC 338.1/74117 19
HD9398.G83 E57 1984

Economic survey on Western Samoa. Huh, Ko Kwang. [Manila, Philippines] [1984] vii, 44 p. : LC Card 87-403365 DDC 330.996/14 19
HC687.5 .H84 1984

ECONOMIC SURVEYS - BOTSWANA.
Botswana. Central Statistics Office. Guideline for designing and executing small scale surveys in Botswana. [Gaborone] [1982] 53 p. in various pagings : LC Card 83-154943 DDC 304.6/0723 19
HB849.49 .B68 1982 ***NYPL [JLG 86-217]***

ECONOMIC SURVEYS - BRAZIL - RIO GRANDE DO SUL.
O Emprego no Rio Grande do Sul . Porto Alegre , 1985. 163 p. : LC Card 85-207909
HD5755.R54 E46 1985

ECONOMIC SURVEYS - DEVELOPING COUNTRIES.
Grootaert, Christiaan, 1950- Measuring and analyzing levels of living in developing countries . Washington, D.C., U. S.A. , c1986. x, 139 p. : ISBN 0-8213-0758-4 (pbk.) LC Card 86-5611 DDC 339.4/7/091724 19
HD7067 .G76 1986b

ECONOMIC SURVEYS - IVORY COAST.
Grootaert, Christiaan, 1950- Measuring and analyzing levels of living in developing

countries . Washington, D.C., U. S.A. , c1986. x, 139 p. : ISBN 0-8213-0758-4 (pbk.) LC Card 86-5611 DDC 339.4/7/091724 19
HD7067 .G76 1986b

ECONOMIC THEORY. see **ECONOMICS.**

Economic theory and international trade in natural exhaustible resources /. Withagen, Cees, 1950- Berlin , New York , 1985. vi, 172 p. : ISBN 0-387-15970-3 LC Card 85-22101 DDC 333.7 19
HC59 .W55 1985 ***NYPL [JLM 72-289 no.253]***

Economic theory and its applications /. Krishnan-Kutty, G. Delhi, India , 1987. viii, 131 p. ; LC Card 87-900548 DDC 330.1 19
HB71 .K68 1987

The economic theory and measurement of environmental benefits /. Johansson, Per-Olov, 1949- Cambridge [Cambridgeshire] , New York , 1987. x, 223 p. : ISBN 0-521-32877-2 LC Card 86-33364 DDC 339.4 19
HB825 .J64 1987

Economic theory and the antitrust dilemma /. Asch, Peter. Malabar, Fla. , 1984, c1970. x, 414 p. : ISBN 0-89874-699-X LC Card 83-19947 DDC 338.8/0973 19
HD2785 .A78 1984 ***NYPL [JLE 86-4132]***

Economic theory of underdevelopment /. Ziesemer, Thomas. Regensburg , c1987. vi, 171 p. : ISBN 3-924956-15-4 (pbk.) LC Card 87-169372 DDC 338.9/001 19
HD75.5 .Z54 1987

The economic thought of Karl Polanyi . Stanfield, J. Ron, 1945- Basingstoke, Hampshire , 1986. x, 162 p. ; ISBN 0-333-39629-4 LC Card 87-673390
HB102.P64 S73x 1986b

Economic transportation survey. [Paris] : BCEOM ; [Courbevoie, Seine] : SETEC, 1966. 3 v. : ill., maps (some col.) ; 31 cm. At head of title: Government of Israel, Ministry of Labour, Public Works Department. A survey prepared by the Bureau central d'études pour les équipements d'outre-mer and the Société d'études techniques et économiques for the Government of Israel. Vol. 3 comprises maps and other illustrations on 13 folded leaves in portfolio. CONTENTS. - 1. Report -- 2. Appendix -- 3. Maps. LC Card 87-125917
1. Traffic surveys - Israel. I. France. Bureau central d'études pour les équipements d'outre-mer. II. Société d'études techniques et économiques (France). III. Israel. Maḥleḳet 'avodot tsiburiyot.
HE373.I75 E36 1966

Economic trends in Ghana in 1984-85 and prospects for 1986 /. Ewusi, Kodwo. [Legon] [1986] 52 p. : LC Card 87-127410 DDC 330.9667/05 19
HC1060 .E975 1986

Economic trends in metropolitan Washington, 1980-1985 ; [author, Jay Langford, Vetoria S. Alston]. Langford, Jay. Washington, D.C. (1875 Eye St., NW., Suite 200, Washington 20006) , c1986. viii, 68 p. : LC Card 87-105032 DDC 330.9753/04 19
HC108.W3 L36 1986

ECONOMIC UNION. see **INTERNATIONAL ECONOMIC INTEGRATION.**

Economic valuation techniques for the environment : a case study workbook / edited by John A. Dixon and Maynard M. Hufschmidt. Baltimore : Johns Hopkins University Press, c1986. xx, 203 p. : ill. ; 24 cm. Includes bibliographies and index. CONTENTS. - The role of economics in valuing environmental effects of development projects / by John A. Dixon -- A hypothetical case study, the Lake Burley Fishery Project / by David E. James -- Time horizons, discounting, and computational aids / by John A. Dixon and Anton D. Meister -- Case studies from Asia -- Economic valuation of environmental quality aspects of upland agricultural projects in Korea / by Sung-Hoon Kim and John A. Dixon -- Tongonan Geothermal Power Plant Project in Leyte, Philippines / adapted by Somluckrat Grandstaff from materials prepared by Beta Balagot -- Valuation of losses of marine product resources caused by coastal development to Tokyo Bay / adapted by Maynard M. Hufschmidt and John A. Dixon from materials prepared by Yuzuru Hanayama and Ikuo Sano -- Evaluation of Lumpinee Public Park in Bangkok, Thailand / adapted by Somluckrat Grandstaff and John A. Dixon from materials prepared by Siriwut Eutrirak and Somluckrat Grandstaff -- The Nam Pong Water Resources Project in Thailand / adapted by Maynard M. Hufschmidt from a paper prepared by Ruangdej Srivardhana -- Selected policy options for fuelwood production and use in the Philippines / adapted by John A. Dixon from materials prepared by Eric L. Hyman -- Systematic analysis of water pollution control options in a suburban region of Beijing, China / adapted by Maynard M. Hufschmidt from a report prepared by Fu Guowei ... [et al.]. ISBN 0-8018-3352-3 (alk. paper) LC Card 86-2730 DDC 363.7/05/0681 19
1. Environmental policy - Cost effectiveness - Addresses, essays, lectures. 2. Economic development projects - Cost effectiveness - Addresses, essays, lectures. I. Dixon, John A., 1946-. II. Hufschmidt, Maynard M.
HC79.E5 E274 1986 ***NYPL [JLE 87-677]***

Economic viability of Conrail. Dayton, Mark R. Washington, D.C. [1986] xvii, 85 p. : LC Card 86-602852 DDC 385/.1 19
HE2791.C8994 D39 1986

The economic world of 1787 and the Constitution /. Alexander, Albert. New York (150 Nassau St., Rm. 1625, New York 10038) [1987] 18 p. ; LC Card 87-403433 DDC 330.973/0318 19
HC105.6 .A44 1987

ECONOMIC ZONING - CHINA.
Guide to China's foreign economic relations and trade. Cities newly opened to foreign investors /. Hong Kong , 1985. 385 p. : ISBN 962-7063-19-3 ***NYPL [*OVY 86-3400]***

Economical study of spare parts consumption in textile industry in Egypt. Cairo, Egypt : Foreign Relations Coordination Unit, Supreme Council of Universities, [1984?] 2 v. : ill. ; 27-29 cm. "Grant FRCU 842067." LC Card 86-960234 DDC 338.4/76817677/0962 19
1. Machine parts industry - Egypt. 2. Textile machinery industry - Egypt. I. Egypt. Majlis al-A'lá lil-Jāmi'āt. Waḥdat Tansīq al-'Alāqāt al-Khārijīyah.
HD9705.5.P373 E34 1984

Economically active population : estimates and projections, 1950-2025 = Evaluations et projections de la population active, 1950-2025 = Estimaciones y proyecciones de la población económicamente activa, 1950-2025. 3rd ed. Geneva : International Labour Office, 1986- v. ; 21 x 30 cm. First ed. has title: Labour force projections. Second ed. has title: Labour force estimates and projections. English, French, and Spanish. CONTENTS. - v. 1. Asia -- v. 2. Africa -- v. 3. Latin America -- v. 4. Northern America, Europe, Oceania, and USSR -- v. 5. World summary. ISBN 92-2-005345-4 (v. 1)
1. Labor supply - Statistics. 2. Employment forecasting - Statistics. I. International Labour Office. II. Labour force projections. III. Labour force estimates and projections. IV. Title: Evaluations et projections de la population active, 1950-2025. V. Title: Estimaciones y proyecciones de la población económicamente activa, 1950-2025. ***NYPL [JLM 87-113]***

Economically active population estimates and projections, 1950-2025 = Evaluations et projections de la population active, 1950-2025. [3rd ed.]. Geneva : International Labour Office, [1986]- v. <1-5 > ; 21 x 30 cm. Parts 1-5 in English, French, and Spanish. Rev. ed. of: Labour force estimates and projections, 1950-2000. 2nd. ed. 1977. CONTENTS. - v. 1. Asia -- v. 2. Africa -- v. 3. Latin America -- v. 4. North America, Europe, Oceania, and USSR -- v. 5. World summary. ISBN 92-2-005345-4 (pbk. : v. 1) : LC Card 86-223275 DDC 331.12/021 19
1. Labor supply - Statistics. 2. Employment forecasting - Statistics. I. International Labour Office. II. Labour force estimates and projections, 1950-2000. III. Title: Evaluations et projections de la population active, 1950-2025.
HD5712 .E26 1986

Economics . Amos, Orley M., 1954- Belmont, Calif. , c1987. xxiv, 786 p. : ISBN 0-534-06948-7 : LC Card 86-24569 DDC 330 19
HB171.5 .A48 1987

Economics . Bach, George Leland, 1915- Englewood Cliffs, N.J. , c1987. xv, 752 p. : ISBN 0-13-227240-7 LC Card 86-25576 DDC 330.1 19
HB171.5 .B13 1987

Economics . Davis, James E. (James Edwin), 1940- Santa Barbara, Calif. , c1988. xv, 354 p. : ISBN 0-87436-479-5 (alk. paper) LC Card 87-18670 DDC 330/.07/1273 19
HB74.5 .D39 1988

Economics /. Ekelund, Robert B. (Robert Burton), 1940- Glenview, Ill. , c1988. xl, 942, [33] p. : ISBN 0-673-39717-3 LC Card 87-23306 DDC 330 19
HB171.5 .E47 1988

Economics /. Fischer, Stanley. New York , c1988. xliii, 813 p. : ISBN 0-07-017781-3 : LC Card 87-21333 DDC 330 19
HB171.5 .F458 1988

Economics /. Lipsey, Richard G., 1928- New York , c1987. xxvii, 942 p. : ISBN 0-06-043917-3 LC Card 86-29422 DDC 330 19
HB171.5 .L733 1987

Economics . Starr, Philip C. Belmont, Calif. , c1988. xxii, 422 p. : ISBN 0-534-08496-6 (pbk.) : LC Card 87-22755 DDC 330 19
HB171.5 .S78 1988

Economics /. Thompson, Allen R. Reading, Mass. , c1988. xxxii, 888, [46] p. : ISBN 0-201-09682-X : LC Card 87-912 DDC 330 19
HB171.5 .T33 1988

Economics /. Truett, Lila J. (Lila Jane) St. Louis , 1987. xxviii, 859, [57] p. : ISBN 0-8016-5149-2 LC Card 86-23102 DDC 330 19
HB171.5 .T69 1987

Economics . Wolff, Richard D. Baltimore , c1987. xiv, 279 p. : ISBN 0-8018-3479-1 (alk. paper) LC Card 87-4131 DDC 330.1 19
HB90 .W65 1987

ECONOMICS. Here and with local subdivisions are entered works on the discipline of economics. Works on the economic conditions of particular countries, regions, cities, etc., are entered under the name of the place subdivided by: Economic conditions.

ECONOMICS - ADDRESSES, ESSAYS, LECTURES.

Barbara Wootton--social science and public policy . London , New York , 1986. xi, 291 p. ; ISBN 0-422-79690-5 LC Card 85-27650 DDC 330 19
HB171 .B248 1985 ***NYPL [JLE 86-1743]***

Baumol, William J. Microtheory . Brighton, Sussex , c1986. xxvii, 286 p. : ISBN 0-7450-0110-6 ***NYPL [JLF 86-1374]***

Capitalismul contemporan și teoria [microform] . București , 1965. 440 p. ; LC Card 77-452767
HB179.R6 C34 ***NYPL [*ZT-1732 no.2]***

Di Nardi, Giuseppe. L'economia a una svolta critica /. Milano , 1984- v. ; LC Card 84-216905 DDC 330 19
HB177 .D48 1984 ***NYPL [JLL 73-173 v.25]***

Economic history and the modern economist /. Oxford, UK , New York, NY, USA , 1986. xi, 105 p. ; ISBN 0-631-14799-3 : LC Card 85-28584 DDC 330/.09 19
HC26 .E26 1986 ***NYPL [JLD 86-2947]***

Eichner, Alfred S. Toward a new economics . Armonk, N.Y. , c1985. ix, 240 p. : ISBN 0-87332-326-2 LC Card 84-27724 DDC 330 19
HB171 .E35 1985 ***NYPL [JLE 86-1977]***

Kornai, János. [Ellentmondások és dilemmák. English.] Contradictions and dilemmas . Cambridge, Mass. , 1986, c1983. ix, 165 p. : ISBN 0-262-11107-1 LC Card 85-5168 DDC 330.9439/053 19
HC300.28 .K67213 1986 ***NYPL [JLC 86-254]***

Subjectivism, intelligibility, and economic understanding . Basingstoke, Hampshire , 1986. xi, 319 p. : ISBN 0-333-41788-7 ***NYPL [JLD 86-2215]***

Economics and artificial intelligence . IFAC/IFORS/IFIP/IASC/AFCET Conference on Economics and Artificial Intelligence (1986 : Aix-en-Provence, France) Oxford [Oxfordshire] , New York , 1987. xiii, 194 p. : ISBN 0-08-034350-3 (U. S.) : LC Card 87-6943 DDC 330/.028/563 19
HB143.5 .I44 1986

Economics and business . Picchi, Fernando. Bologna , 1986. 1333 p. ; ISBN 88-08-04550-1 LC Card 86-201141 DDC 330/.03/51 19
HB61 .P49 1986

Economics and ethics . Wogaman, J. Philip. Philadelphia , c1986. xiii, 145 p. ; ISBN 0-8006-1904-8 (pbk.) LC Card 85-45478 DDC 261.8/5 19
HB72 .W633 1986 ***NYPL [JLD 86-3984]***

Economics and federal antitrust law /. Hovenkamp, Herbert, 1948- St. Paul, Minn. , 1985. xxvii, 414 p. : ISBN 0-314-86196-3 LC Card 84-25783 DDC 343.73/072 347.30372 19
KF1649 .H67 1985 ***NYPL [JLF 86-1373]***

Economics and free enterprise. Hodgetts, Richard M. Addison-Wesley economics /. Menlo Park, Calif. , c1988. vi, T1-T266, 31, 548 p. : ISBN 0-201-22775-4 LC Card 87-147565 DDC 330 19
HB171.5 .H676 1988

Economics and philosophy / edited by Peter Koslowski. Tübingen : J.C.B. Mohr, 1985. ix, 284 p. : ill. ; 24 cm. (Series Civitas Resultate . vol. 7) "Proceedings of a conference held in Munich on Jul 22nd-25th, 1984, by Civitas Society for the Advancement of Science and Art Inc."--P. [v]-vi. Includes bibliographies and index. ISBN 3-16-244944-8 LC Card 85-236925 DDC 330 19
1. Economics - Congresses. 2. Philosophy - Congresses. I. Koslowski, Peter, 1952-. II. Civitas (Society). III. Series: Civitas Resultate , v. 7.
HB72 .E27 1985 ***NYPL [JFE 86-2159]***

Economics and politics of industrial policy : the United States and Western Europe / edited by Steven A. Shull and Jeffrey E. Cohen. Boulder : Westview Press, 1986. xi, 120 p. ; 23 cm. (Monographs in comparative public policy) Proceedings of the seventh biannual symposium sponsored by the Institute for the Comparative Study of Public Policy and organized by the University of New Orleans and the University of Innsbruck, held on Feb. 21-22, 1985, in New Orleans. Bibliography: p. 107-118. ISBN 0-8133-7140-6 (pbk. : alk. paper) : LC Card 85-26478 DDC 338.94 19
1. Industry and state - United States - Congresses. 2. Industry and state - Europe - Congresses. I. Shull, Steven A. II. Cohen, Jeffrey E. III. University of New Orleans. Institute for the Comparative Study of Public Policy. IV. Series.
HD3616.U47 E34 1986 ***NYPL [JLE 86-4353]***

Economics and technological change /. Coombs, Rod. Totowa, N.J. , 1987. xv, 296 p. : ISBN 0-8476-7545-9 : LC Card 86-28000 DDC 338/.06 19
HC79.T4 C67 1987

Economics and the economy /. Jeffreys, Daniel. Burnt Mill, Harlow, Essex, England , 1985. 317 p. : ISBN 0-582-35452-8 (pbk.) LC Card 87-152784 DDC 330 19
HB171.5 .J45 1985

ECONOMICS - BIO-BIBLIOGRAPHY.
Krŭstiū Dobrev . Sofiia , 1987. 80 p., [16] p. of plates : LC Card 87-170598
HB108.3.D63 K78 1987

ECONOMICS - COLLECTED WORKS.
Beiträge zur experimentellen Wirtschaftsforschung. Tübingen, 1967-<78. v. <1-2, 4-8 > LC Card 68-85600 DDC 330 19
HB41 .B29 1967

Johansen, Leif. [Essays. Selections.] Collected works of Leif Johansen /. Amsterdam ; New York : 2 v. (xiii, 974 p.) ; ISBN 0-444-87833-5 (set) LC Card 87-6814 DDC 330.1 19
HB171 .J59725 1987

Popov, IU. N. (IUriĭ Nikolaevich), 1931- Essays in political economy /. Moscow , c1984- v. ; LC Card 84-202086 DDC 335.43 19
HB53 .P64 1984 ***NYPL [JLK 86-18]***

Smith, Adam, 1723-1790. [Selections. 1986.] The essential Adam Smith /. Oxford [Oxfordshire] , New York , 1986. p. cm. ISBN 0-19-877270-X : LC Card 86-23856 DDC 330.15/3 19
HB161 .S6522 1986b

ECONOMICS - COLOMBIA - HISTORY.
Consuegra Higgins, José. El pensamiento económico colombiano /. Bogotá, Colombia , 1984. 216 p. ; LC Card 84-200191 DDC 330/.09861 19
HB123.C6 C662 1984 ***NYPL [JLC 87-88]***

ECONOMICS, COMPARATIVE. see **COMPARATIVE ECONOMICS.**

ECONOMICS - CONGRESSES.
Advances in economic theory . Cambridge [Cambridgeshire] , New York , 1982. x, 285 p. : ISBN 0-521-24443-9 LC Card 81-38500 DDC 330/.028 19
HB21 .A33 1982 ***NYPL [JLE 85-2041]***

Advances in economic theory . Cambridge [Cambridgeshire] , New York , 1987. vii, 428 p. ; ISBN 0-521-34044-6 LC Card 87-889 DDC 330.1 19
HB21 .A329 1987

Economics and philosophy /. Tübingen , 1985. ix, 284 p. : ISBN 3-16-244944-8 LC Card 85-236925 DDC 330 19
HB72 .E27 1985 ***NYPL [JFE 86-2159]***

Economische wetenschappen . Maastricht , Assen , 1985. 224 p. ; ISBN 90-232-2148-6 LC Card 86-111599
HB21 .E248 1985

Schattenwirtschaft und alternative Ökonomie . Regensburg , c1984. 268 p. : ISBN 3-924956-00-6 LC Card 86-224071
HD2341 .S337 1984

ECONOMICS - DATA BASES.
Popovich, Charles J. Business and economics databases online . Littleton, Colo. , 1987. xviii, 276 p. : ISBN 0-87287-454-0 (pbk. : alk. paper) : LC Card 87-2672 DDC 300/.28/5 19
HF5548.2 .P612 1987

ECONOMICS - DATA PROCESSING - CONGRESSES.
Artificial intelligence in economics and management /. Amsterdam ; New York : xv, 292 p. : ISBN 0-444-87961-7 LC Card 85-31139 DDC 330/.028/563 19
HB143.5 .A78 1986 ***NYPL [JLE 86-3612]***

IFAC/IFORS/IFIP/IASC/AFCET Conference on Economics and Artificial Intelligence (1986 : Aix-en-Provence, France) Economics and artificial intelligence . Oxford [Oxfordshire] , New York , 1987. xiii, 194 p. : ISBN 0-08-034350-3 (U. S.) : LC Card 87-6943 DDC 330/.028/563 19
HB143.5 .I44 1986

ECONOMICS - DENMARK.
Beskrivende økonomi /. [Copenhagen] , c1985-c1986. 2 v. (810 p.) : ISBN 87-574-4652-0 (set) LC Card 86-159064
HB179.D8 B47 1986

ECONOMICS - DICTIONARIES.
Andrlić, Vlasta. Rječnik terminologije jugoslavenskog političko-ekonomskog sistema . Zagreb , 1985. viii, 135 p. ; LC Card 86-182784
HB61 .A55 1985 ***NYPL [*QKK 87-1803]***

Cavalcante, José Cândido Marques. Dicionário inglês-português de termos econômicos & comerciais /. [Fortaleza] , Petrópolis , 1979. 408 p. ; LC Card 80-113110
HB61 .C37 ***NYPL [JLE 81-244]***

A Dictionary of economics & commerce . Beirut , 1983. 383 p. ; LC Card 83-961782 DDC 330/.03/21 19
HB61 .D4896 1983 ***NYPL [*OEO 87-1397]***

Eichborn, Reinhart von. Wirtschaftswörterbuch. Düsseldorf, Wien [1961-70] 2 v. LC Card 70-463836 ***NYPL [JLD 85-120]***

Farīd, 'Abd Allāh Muḥammad. al-Qāmūs al-farīd fī al-māl wa-al-iqtiṣād, 'Arabī-Injilīzī /. [S.l.] 1985 (al-Qāhirah, Miṣr : Maṭābi' al-Ahrām al-Tijārīyah) 150, 264 p. ; LC Card 86-960655
HB61 .F36 1985

Heinrich, Lutz J. (Lutz Jürgen) Wirtschaftsinformatik-Lexikon /. München , c1986. xxi, 539 p. : ISBN 3-486-20045-3 LC Card 87-122992 DDC 330/.03/31 19
HB61 .H365 1986

Kadieva, D. A. Chastotnyĭ anglo-russkiĭ slovar′. Leningrad , 1986. 126 p. ; LC Card 87-146427
HB61 .K23 1986

Lee, Susan, 1943- [ABZs of economics.] Susan Lee's ABZs of economics /. New York , c1987. 224 p. : ISBN 0-671-55711-4 LC Card 86-25481 DDC 330/.03 19
HB61 .L34 1987

Mikheev, S. Glossary of economic and social terminology in Eastern European socialist countries /. Geneva , 1986. 52, x p. ; ISBN 92-9014-413-0 : LC Card 86-214600 DDC 335.4/03/21 19
HB61 .M487 1986

The New Palgrave . New York , c1987. p. cm. ISBN 0-935859-10-1 (set) : LC Card 87-1946 DDC 330/.03/21 19
HB61 .N49 1987

Pennant-Rea, Rupert. The pocket economist /. Oxford, UK , New York, NY , 1987, c1983. p. cm. ISBN 0-631-14586-9 : LC Card 87-10361 DDC 330/.03/21 19
HB61 .P435 1987

Picchi, Fernando. Economics and business . Bologna , 1986. 1333 p. ; ISBN 88-08-04550-1 LC Card 86-201141 DDC 330/.03/51 19
HB61 .P49 1986

Schäfer, Wilhelm, Dr. Wirtschaftswörterbuch /. München , c1986- v. <1 > ; ISBN 3-8006-1100-7 (Bd. 1) LC Card 86-214220
HB61 .S3 1986

ECONOMICS - DICTIONARIES - ARABIC.
Farīd, 'Abd Allāh Muḥammad. al-Qāmūs al-farīd fī al-māl wa-al-iqtiṣād, 'Arabī-Injilīzī /. [S.l.] 1985 (al-Qāhirah, Miṣr : Maṭābi' al-Ahrām al-Tijārīyah) 150, 264 p. ; LC Card 86-960655
HB61 .F36 1985

ECONOMICS - DICTIONARIES - CZECH.
Cheshsko-russkiĭ ėkonomicheskiĭ slovar′ . Moskva , Praga , 1986. 300 p. ; LC Card 85-146401
HB61 .C453 1986 ***NYPL [*QAD 87-1680]***

ECONOMICS - DICTIONARIES - ENGLISH.
Gligorijević, Vera. Englesko-srpskohrvatski i srpskohrvatsko-engleski ekonomski rečnik =. Beograd , 1986. 549, [1] p. ; LC Card 86-196648
HB61 .G49 1986 ***NYPL [*QAD 87-1743]***

ECONOMICS - DICTIONARIES - ESTONIAN.
Majandusteaduse ABC . Tallinn , 1985. 511 p. : LC Card 85-195109
HB61 .M225 1985

ECONOMICS - DICTIONARIES - GERMAN.
Eichborn, Reinhart von. Wirtschaftswörterbuch. Düsseldorf, Wien [1961-70] 2 v. LC Card 70-463836 ***NYPL [JLD 85-120]***

Schäfer, Wilhelm, Dr. Wirtschaftswörterbuch /. München , c1986- v. <1 > ; ISBN 3-8006-1100-7 (Bd. 1) LC Card 86-214220
HB61 .S3 1986

Wirtschaftslexikon /. München , c1987. xv, 661 p. : ISBN 3-486-29691-4 LC Card 87-127454 DDC 330/.03/31 19
HB61 .W558 1987

ECONOMICS - DICTIONARIES - HEBREW.
Yaḳir, E. (Eli), 1929- Milon munaḥim be-khalkalah ṿe-nihul 'asaḳim /. Tel-Aviv , 1986. 414, 38 p. : LC Card 87-162041
HB61 .Y25 1986

ECONOMICS - DICTIONARIES - INDONESIAN.
Kamus istilah ekonomi /. Jakarta , 1984. v, 216 p. ; LC Card 85-941380
HB61 .K26 1984

ECONOMICS - DICTIONARIES - ITALIAN.
Picchi, Fernando. Economics and business . Bologna , 1986. 1333 p. ; ISBN 88-08-04550-1 LC Card 86-201141 DDC 330/.03/51 19
HB61 .P49 1986

ECONOMICS - DICTIONARIES - POLYGLOT.
Angliĭsko-nemsko-frensko-rusko-bŭlgarski rechnik po upravlenie i ikonomika na promishlenostta, stroitelstvoto i transporta /. Sofiia , 1982. 764 p. ; LC Card 83-128751
HD30.15 .A43 1982 ***NYPL [*QAD 86-4204]***

ECONOMICS - DICTIONARIES - RUSSIAN.
Moiseev, Anatoliĭ Vasil′evich. Ėkonomicheskiĭ slovar'-spravochnik . Moskva , 1978. 239 p. ; LC Card 81-165938
HB61 .M56 1978

Rumiantsev, Alekseĭ Matveevich. Instrumentariĭ ėkonomicheskoĭ nauki i praktiki . Moskva , 1985. 303 p. : LC Card 87-109217
HB61 .R86 1985

ECONOMICS - DICTIONARIES - SERBO-CROATIAN.
Andrlić, Vlasta. Rječnik terminologije jugoslavenskog političko-ekonomskog sistema .

Zagreb , 1985. viii, 135 p. ; LC Card 86-182784
HB61 .A55 1985 ***NYPL [*QKK 87-1803]***

Gligorijević, Vera. Englesko-srpskohrvatski i srpskohrvatsko-engleski ekonomski rečnik =. Beograd , 1986. 549, [1] p. ; LC Card 86-196648
HB61 .G49 1986 ***NYPL [*QAD 87-1743]***

ECONOMICS - DICTIONARIES - SPANISH.
Glosario de términos económicos. Lima, Perú , 1985. 129 p. ; LC Card 86-221450
HB61 .G498 1985

Zorrilla, Santiago. Diccionario de economía /. México, D.F. , c1986. 182 p. : ISBN 968-493-060-7 LC Card 87-401043 DDC 330/.03/61 19
HB61 .Z63 1986

ECONOMICS - DICTIONARIES - SWEDISH.
Edström, N. F. (Nils Fritiof), 1918- Ekonomiordbok . Stockholm , c1984. 145 p. : ISBN 91-1-847152-8 : LC Card 84-253890
HB61 .E29 1984 ***NYPL [JFD 87-1265]***

Economics discussion papers .
(86/6) Hossain, Md. Akhtar. The short-run demand for real money balances in the Bangladesh economy . Bundoora, Vic., Australia [1986] 90 p. ; ISBN 0-85816-784-0 (pbk.) LC Card 86-228714 DDC 332.4/14 19
HG1240.6 .H67 1986

ECONOMICS - ECUADOR.
Baez, René. Ciencia y transformación social . Quito, Ecuador , 1986. 141 p. ; LC Card 86-214736 DDC 330.9/0038 19
HC125 .B195 1986

ECONOMICS - EXAMINATIONS, QUESTIONS, ETC.
Sobgui, Gabriel Alexis. L'épreuve écrite à la capacité en droit et en économie /. Yaoundé, Cameroun , 1981. 113 p. ; LC Card 84-118988
HB74.6 .S65 1981

Starr, Philip C. Economics . Belmont, Calif. , c1988. xxii, 422 p. : ISBN 0-534-08496-6 (pbk.) : LC Card 87-22755 DDC 330 19
HB171.5 .S78 1988

ECONOMICS - EXPERIMENTS.
Laboratory experimentation in economics . Cambridge , New York , 1987. ix, 219 p. : ISBN 0-521-33392-X LC Card 87-10343 DDC 330/.0724 19
HB131 .L32 1987

Economics explained /. Heilbroner, Robert L. New York , 1987. 250 p. : ISBN 0-671-64556-0 (pbk.) LC Card 87-12807 DDC 330 19
HB171 .H479 1987

Economics for consumers /. Gordon, Leland James, 1897- New York , c1977. ix, 693 p. : ISBN 0-442-22242-4 LC Card 76-50515 DDC 381/.3/0973 19
HB801 .G6 1977 ***NYPL [JLE 86-1506]***

ECONOMICS - FRANCE - CONGRESSES.
La Nueva economía en Francia y en España /. Madrid , c1980. 197 p. : ISBN 84-85355-27-X : LC Card 83-105425 DDC 330.944/0838 19
HB105.A2 N83 1980 ***NYPL [JLD 86-3024]***

ECONOMICS - FRANCE - HISTORY - 18TH CENTURY.
Vaggi, Gianni. The economics of François Quesnay /. Durham , 1987. xv, 247 p. : ISBN 0-8223-0757-X LC Card 87-3549 DDC 330.15/2 19
HB105.Q5 V34 1987

ECONOMICS - GERMANY - HISTORY.
Krauth, Wolf-Hagen. Wirtschaftsstruktur und Semantik . Berlin , c1984. 278 p. ; ISBN 3-428-05728-7 LC Card 85-143046
HB107.A2 K69 1984

ECONOMICS - GERMANY - HISTORY - 20TH CENTURY.
Holzwarth, Fritz. Ordnung der Wirtschaft durch Wettbewerb . Freiburg im Breisgau , c1985. 217 p. ; ISBN 3-448-01510-5 LC Card 86-109043
HB95 .H65 1985

ECONOMICS - GERMANY (WEST) - HISTORY - 20TH CENTURY.
Holzwarth, Fritz. Ordnung der Wirtschaft durch Wettbewerb . Freiburg im Breisgau , c1985. 217 p. ; ISBN 3-448-01510-5 LC Card 86-109043
HB95 .H65 1985

ECONOMICS - GERMANY (WEST) - PUBLIC OPINION.
Gewandelte Werte, erstarrte Strukturen . Bonn , c1985. ix, 329 p. : ISBN 3-87831-423-X LC Card 86-117688 DDC 330/.0943 19
HD8451 .G54 1985

ECONOMICS - GERMANY (WEST) - TEXTBOOKS.
Nordmann-Werner, Karin, 1945- Kompetenzvermittlung durch Sachliteratur . Frankfurt am Main , New York , c1984. 391 p. ; ISBN 3-8204-5278-8 LC Card 85-193184
HB74.9.G3 N67 1984

ECONOMICS - GRAPHIC METHODS.
Metodología de evaluación y programación de sistemas de producción y consumo, MEPS /. Lima, Perú [1985]- v. <1 > : LC Card 86-215609
HD75 .M48 1985

ECONOMICS - GREAT BRITAIN - HISTORY.
Beveridge, William Henry Beveridge, Baron, 1879-1963. A Beveridge reader /. London , Boston , 1987. viii, 190 p. ; ISBN 0-04-361070-6 (alk. paper) LC Card 87-11819 DDC 338.941 19
HB103.A2 B48 1987

Koot, Gerard M. English historical economics, 1870-1926 . Cambridge [Cambridgeshire] , New York , 1987. viii, 277 p. ; ISBN 0-521-32854-3 LC Card 87-11592 DDC 330/.0941 19
HB103.A2 K65 1987

ECONOMICS - GREAT BRITAIN - HISTORY - 19TH CENTURY.
Hollander, Samuel. The economics of John Stuart Mill /. Oxford, U.K. , 1985. 2 v. (xx, 1037 p.) ; ISBN 0-631-14045-X (set) LC Card 86-673535
HB103.M7 H64x 1985 ***NYPL [JLE 87-951]***

Langer, Gary F. The coming of age of political economy, 1815-1825 /. New York , 1987. x, 224 p. : ISBN 0-313-25645-4 (lib. bdg. : alk. paper) LC Card 86-31802 DDC 330/.0941 19
HB103.A2 L36 1987

ECONOMICS - GREAT BRITAIN - RELIGIOUS ASPECTS.
Storkey, Alan. Transforming economics . London , 1986. xi, 212 p. : ISBN 0-281-04225-X (pbk.) : LC Card 87-108686 DDC 261.8/5 19
HD5765.A6 S76 1986

ECONOMICS - GREECE - HISTORY.
Klever, W. N. A. Archeologie van de economie . Nijmegen , 1986. 157 p. : ISBN 90-6772-005-4 : LC Card 86-165833
HB77 .K54 1986

Lowry, S. Todd. The archaeology of economic ideas . Durham , 1987. xviii, 366 p. ; ISBN 0-8223-0774-X LC Card 87-15507 DDC 330/.0938 19
HB108.A2 L68 1987

Reekmans, T. Inleiding tot de antieke economie /. Leuven , 1984. 129 leaves in various foliations ; ISBN 90-334-0834-1 : LC Card 86-203767
HB77 .R44 1984

Economics, growth, and sustainable environments : essays in memory of Richard Lecomber / edited by David Collard, David Pearce, David Ulph. New York : St. Martin's Press, 1988. viii, 205 p. : ill. ; 23 cm. Includes bibliographies and index. ISBN 0-312-01240-3 : LC Card 87-12520 DDC 363.7 19
1. Environmental policy. 2. Economic development. 3. Lecomber, Richard, 1937-. I. Lecomber, Richard, 1937-. II. Collard, David A. III. Pearce, David W. (David William). IV. Ulph, David, 1946-.
HC79.E5 E2774 1988

ECONOMICS - HISTORY. Here are entered works on the history of economics as a discipline. Works on economic history or conditions are entered under the heading: Economic history or the subdivision: Economic conditions under the names of countries, regions, cities, etc.
Ballivián Calderón, René. Economía de mercado y economía dirigida . La Paz , 1979. xxii, 608 p. : LC Card 83-167133
HB75 .B144 1979

Bergh, Trond, 1946- Vitenskap og politikk . Oslo , 1984. 269 p. : ISBN 82-03-11342-7 : LC Card 84-184253
HB116.3.A2 B47 1984

Brems, Hans. Pioneering economic theory, 1630-1980 . Baltimore , c1986. xv, 411 p. : ISBN 0-8018-2667-5 (alk. paper) LC Card 85-19819 DDC 330.1 19
HB75 .B7845 1986 ***NYPL [JLE 86-2408]***

Butler, Eamonn. Milton Friedman . Aldershot, Hants, England , c1985. 272 p. : ISBN 0-85117-261-X : ***NYPL [JLD 86-1090]***

Galbraith, John Kenneth, 1908- Economics in perspective . Boston , 1987. 324 p. ; ISBN 0-395-35572-9 : LC Card 87-3644 DDC 330/.09 19
HB75 .G274 1987

Górski, Janusz. Z historii myśli ekonomicznej . Łódź , 1986, c1985. 312 p. ; ISBN 83-218-0319-9 : LC Card 83-189161
HB114.A2 G67 1986

Jessua, Claude. Histoire de la pensée économique /. Paris , 1981. 494, viii p. : LC Card 87-672485
HB75 .J47x 1981

Manfra, Modestino R. Formazione ed evoluzione della scienza economica /. [Firenze] [1985] viii, 163 p. ; ISBN 88-00-86023-0 : LC Card 86-118265
HB75 .M247 1985

Mirowski, Philip, 1951- Against mechanism . Totowa, N.J. , 1987. p. cm. ISBN 0-8476-7436-3 : LC Card 87-21925 DDC 330/.09 19
HB71 .M635 1987

Pasinetti, Luigi L. La ricchezza della nazioni /. Napoli , c1985. 35 p. ; ISBN 88-7042-841-9 : LC Card 86-196264
HB75 .P27 1985

Pesante, Maria Luisa. Economia e politica /. Milano, Italy , c1986. 94 p. ; LC Card 86-196256
HB75 .P465 1986

Porta, Pier Luigi. Scuola classica e teoria economica /. Milano , 1984. xi, 145 p. ; ISBN 88-14-00004-2 : LC Card 84-177305 DDC 330.15/3 19
HB167 .P67 1984 ***NYPL [JLE 86-4055]***

Le Radici intellettuali del progresso economico moderno /. Milano, Italy , c1986. 327 p. ; LC Card 86-197444
HB75 .R13 1986

Winterberger, Gerhard. Über Schumpeters Geschichtsdeterminismus /. Tübingen , 1983. 42 p. ; ISBN 3-16-344644-2 LC Card 83-152280 DDC 330/.092/4 19
HB119.S35 W56 1983

ECONOMICS - HISTORY - TO 1800.
Langholm, Odd Inge, 1928- The Aristotelian analysis of usury /. Bergen [Norway] , New York, NY , c1984. 153 p. ; ISBN 82-00-07290-8 LC Card 85-167906 DDC 332.8/3/09 19
HB551 .L36 1984 ***NYPL [JLD 86-2545]***

ECONOMICS - HISTORY - 20TH CENTURY.
Sovremennyĭ konservatizm i krizis burzhuaznoĭ ėkonomicheskoĭ nauki . Moskva , 1986. 175 p. ; LC Card 87-165796
HB241 .S673 1986

Urien, Julio César. Un aporte para la liberación /. Buenos Aires, Argentina , c1985. 51 p. ; ISBN 950-9235-13-X LC Card 85-201095
HC125 .U75 1985

ECONOMICS - HISTORY - 20TH CENTURY - ADDRESSES, ESSAYS, LECTURES.
Post Keynesian economic theory . Sussex , Armonk, N.Y. , 1985. xii, 235 p. ; ISBN 0-87332-318-1 LC Card 84-23615 DDC 330/.09/04 19
HB87 .P62 1985 ***NYPL [JLD 87-1155]***

ECONOMICS - HISTORY - ADDRESSES, ESSAYS, LECTURES.
Di Nardi, Giuseppe. L'economia a una svolta critica /. Milano , 1984- v. ; LC Card 84-216905 DDC 330 19
HB177 .D48 1984 ***NYPL [JLL 73-173 v.25]***

Economia tra teoria e politica /. Milano , c1984. 295 p. ; LC Card 84-171327 DDC 330/.09 19
HB75 .E28 1984 ***NYPL [JLD 87-819]***

Harcourt, Geoffrey Colin. Controversies in political economy . New York , 1986. 293 p. ; ISBN 0-8147-3437-5 : LC Card 85-31055

DDC 330.1 19
HB75 .H33 1986 **NYPL** ***[JLD 86-3571]***

ECONOMICS - HISTORY - CONGRESSES.
Studien zur Entwicklung der ökonomischen Theorie /. Berlin , c1981- v. ; ISBN 3-428-04862-8 (v. 1) : LC Card 81-154218 DDC 330/.09 19
HB75 .S787 1981
NYPL ***[JLL 73-186 Bd.115]***

ECONOMICS IN LITERATURE.
Brera, Paolo. Denaro . [Brescia] [1984] 110 p. ; LC Card 86-102925
HB49 .B74 1984

Economics in perspective . Galbraith, John Kenneth, 1908- Boston , 1987. 324 p. ; ISBN 0-395-35572-9 : LC Card 87-3644 DDC 330/.09 19
HB75 .G274 1987

ECONOMICS - INDIA - HISTORY.
Das, Arjun, 1946- Economic philosophy of ancient India /. Delhi , 1986. vi, 224 p. : LC Card 86-903116 DDC 330/.0954 19
HB126.I4 D36 1986

Krishnan-Kutty, G. Economic theory and its applications /. Delhi, India , 1987. viii, 131 p. ; LC Card 87-900548 DDC 330.1 19
HB71 .K68 1987

Sharma, Bankey Lal. Economic ideas in ancient India before Kautilya /. New Delhi , 1987. viii, 208 p. ; LC Card 86-903545 DDC 330/.0954 19
HB126.I4 S467 1987

ECONOMICS, INTERNATIONAL. see **INTERNATIONAL ECONOMIC RELATIONS.**

ECONOMICS - ITALY - HISTORY.
Nuccio, Oscar. Il pensiero economico italiano /. [Sassari] , 1984-<1985. <v. 1, t. 1-2; in 2 > ; LC Card 87-110173
HB109.A2 N833 1984

ECONOMICS - ITALY - HISTORY - 16TH CENTURY.
Begert, Roland. Elemente einer politischen Ökonomie im Werke Machiavellis /. Bern , c1983. 224 p. : ISBN 3-258-03136-3 LC Card 83-204993
HB109.M3 B44 1983

ECONOMICS - ITALY - HISTORY - 18TH CENTURY.
De Franchis, Carlo. Giammaria Ortes . Napoli , 1930. 165 p. ; LC Card 87-139766
HB109.O68 D4 1930

ECONOMICS - LANGUAGE.
Richelle Giampiccoli, Emma. La langue de l'économie, de la technique à la banalisation /. Torino [1983] 114 p. ; LC Card 84-141597
HB62 .R53 1983

ECONOMICS - LATIN AMERICA.
Baez, René. Ciencia y transformación social . Quito, Ecuador , 1986. 141 p. ; LC Card 86-214736 DDC 330.9/0038 19
HC125 .B195 1986

García, Antonio, 1912- [Bases de la economía contemporánea.] Bases de economía política /. [Bogotá] , 1981. 283 p. ; LC Card 82-138900 DDC 330/.098 19
HB122 .G37 1981 **NYPL** ***[JLD 87-868]***

ECONOMICS - LATVIA - HISTORY.
Kirtovskiĭ, I. Kh. Ocherki istorii marksistsko-leninskoĭ ėkonomicheskoĭ mysli Latvii, 1920-1980 /. Riga , 1985. 199 p. ; LC Card 86-176265
HB97.5 .K542 1985

Economics learning resource .
(no. 8) Standish, Barry, 1954- The economic factors affecting state output and employment /. Rondebosch [South Africa] [1986] 86 p. : ISBN 0-7992-1016-1 (pbk.) : LC Card 87-112894 DDC 339.2/3 19
HB846 .S73 1986

ECONOMICS - LINEAR PROGRAMMING.
Programmnoe obespechenie ėkonomiko-matematicheskikh issledovaniĭ /. Moskva , 1982. 142 p. : LC Card 84-209065
HD30.25 .P76 1982

ECONOMICS, MATHEMATICAL - CONGRESSES.
Advances in economic theory . Cambridge [Cambridgeshire] , New York , 1982. x, 285 p. : ISBN 0-521-24443-9 LC Card 81-38500 DDC 330/.028 19
HB21 .A33 1982 **NYPL** ***[JLE 85-2041]***

Advances in economic theory . Cambridge [Cambridgeshire] , New York , 1987. vii, 428 p. ; ISBN 0-521-34044-6 LC Card 87-889 DDC 330.1 19
HB21 .A329 1987

Nekotorye voprosy matematicheskoĭ ėkonomiki . Vil'nius , 1982. 90 p. ; LC Card 83-169081
HB135 .N45 1982

ECONOMICS, MATHEMATICAL - DICTIONARIES - RUSSIAN.
Lopatnikov, L. I. (Leonid Isidorovich) Ėkonomiko-matematicheskiĭ slovar' /. Moskva , 1987. 509 p. : LC Card 87-164866
HB135 .L64 1987

ECONOMICS, MATHEMATICAL - ITALY - HISTORY - 18TH CENTURY.
De Franchis, Carlo. Giammaria Ortes . Napoli , 1930. 165 p. ; LC Card 87-139766
HB109.O68 D4 1930

ECONOMICS - MATHEMATICAL MODELS.
Biliarski, Dimitŭr. Logikata i ikonomiko-matematicheskoto modelirane /. Sofiia , 1985. 307 p., [1] folded leaf of plates : LC Card 85-213972
HB135 .B523 1985

Brems, Hans. Pioneering economic theory, 1630-1980 . Baltimore , c1986. xv, 411 p. : ISBN 0-8018-2667-5 (alk. paper) LC Card 85-19819 DDC 330.1 19
HB75 .B7845 1986 **NYPL** ***[JLE 86-2408]***

Dorfman, Robert. Linear programming and economic analysis /. New York , 1987, c1986. p. cm. ISBN 0-486-65491-5 (pbk.) LC Card 87-24382 DDC 330/.0724 19
HB135 .D67 1987

Meissner, Werner, 1937- Weiche Modelle und iterative Schätzung . Frankfurt , New York , c1982. 114 p. : ISBN 3-593-33105-5 : LC Card 83-126780
HB141 .M415 1982

Razumikhin, Boris Sergeevich. [Fizicheskie modeli i metody teorii ravnovesiia v programmirovanii i ėkonomike. English.] Physical models and equilibrium methods in programming and economics /. Dordrecht ; Boston : xv, 351 p. : ISBN 90-277-1644-7 LC Card 83-17791 DDC 330/.0724 19
HB135 .R3913 1984 **NYPL** ***[JSD 86-491]***

Röhling, Wolfgang. Ökonometrische Systeme mit variablen Strukturen . Freiburg im Breisgau , c1983. x, 263 p. : ISBN 3-448-01353-6 LC Card 84-132199
HB139 .R63 1983

Santacoloma, Juan Francisco. Modelos macroeconómicos en economías abiertas /. Bilbao , 1983. 3 v. : ISBN 84-7485-037-1 (set) LC Card 84-168556 DDC 339/.0724 19
HB141 .S28 1983 **NYPL** ***[JLL 86-351]***

Seierstad, Atle. Optimal control theory with economic applications /. Amsterdam ; New York : xvi, 445 p. : ISBN 0-444-87923-4 (Elsevier Science Pub. Co.) LC Card 86-16504 DDC 629.8/312 19
QA402.3 .S4 1986 **NYPL** ***[JLE 87-1123]***

Sørensen, Peter Birch. Økonomisk politik i en åben økonomi /. København , 1985. vi, 179 p. : LC Card 86-135751
HB135 .S575 1985

ECONOMICS - MATHEMATICAL MODELS - CONGRESSES.
Nonlinear economic dynamics /. Boston , c1987. xiii, 195 p. : ISBN 0-12-295140-9 (alk. paper) LC Card 86-32129 DDC 338.5/442/0151 19
HB3711 .N655 1987

ECONOMICS - MATHEMATICAL MODELS - DATA PROCESSING.
Instrumental'nye sistemy modelirovaniia /. Moskva , 1983. 97 p. : LC Card 84-210491
HB143.5 .I57 1983

ECONOMICS - MATHEMATICAL MODELS - EXAMINATIONS, QUESTIONS, ETC.
Santacoloma, Juan Francisco. Modelos macroeconómicos, ejercicios resueltos /. Bilbao , 1985. 209 p. : ISBN 84-7485-059-2 LC Card 86-201846
HB141 .S276 1985

ECONOMICS, MATHEMATICAL - RESEARCH - CONGRESSES.
Quantity and quality in economic research /. Lanham, MD , c1985- v. : ISBN 0-8191-5112-2 (v. 1 : alk. paper) : LC Card 85-26360 DDC 330/.072 19
HB135 .Q38 1985 **NYPL** ***[JLL 86-232]***

ECONOMICS - MATHEMATICS.
Sengupta, Jatikumar. Applied mathematics for economics /. Dordrecht ; Boston : ix, 250 p. ; ISBN 90-277-2588-8 LC Card 87-20544 DDC 330/.028 19
HB71 .S398 1987

ECONOMICS, MEDICAL. see **MEDICAL ECONOMICS.**

ECONOMICS - METHODOLOGY.
Beschäftigung, Verteilung und Konjunktur . Bremen , 1984. 276 p. : ISBN 3-88722-088-9 : LC Card 85-176579
HB175 .B49 1984

Buračas, A. (Antanas) Metaeconomic conceptualization and social criteria of development /. Vilnius , 1987 [i.e. 1986] 60, [4] p. ; LC Card 87-672211
HB131 .B87x 1986

Johnson, Glenn Leroy, 1918- Research methodology for economists . New York , London , c1986. xx, 252 p. ; ISBN 0-02-949840-6 LC Card 85-24240 DDC 300/.72 19
HB74.5 .J65 1986 **NYPL** ***[JLE 86-4300]***

ECONOMICS - MEXICO - HISTORY.
Austin, Ruben Vargas, 1915- The development of economic policy in Mexico with special reference to economic doctrines, 1600-1958 /. New York , 1987. 336 p. ; ISBN 0-8240-1354-9 (alk. paper) : LC Card 87-8569 DDC 338.972 19
HC135 .A84 1987

ECONOMICS - MORAL AND ETHICAL ASPECTS.
Griffiths, Brian. The creation of wealth . Downers Grove, Ill. , c1984. 160 p. : ISBN 0-87784-566-2 (pbk.) : LC Card 85-5210 DDC 330.12/2 19
HB72 .G74 1984 **NYPL** ***[JLD 86-3576]***

Hamlin, Alan P., 1951- Ethics, economics, and the state /. Brighton, Sussex , 1986. x, 198 p. ;
NYPL ***[JLD 86-3648]***

Israel Zipper, Ricardo. Democracia y liberalismo /. Santiago de Chile , 1984. 56 p. ; LC Card 85-197546
HB95 .I87 1984

McKenzie, Richard B. The fairness of markets . Lexington, Mass. , c1987. xiv, 235 p. : ISBN 0-669-14801-6 (alk. paper) LC Card 86-45958 DDC 330 19
HB72 .M35 1987

Marktwirtschaft und Gesellschaftsordnung . Berlin , c1983. 220 p., [1] leaf of plates : ISBN 3-428-05365-6 LC Card 83-191615
HB72 .M248 1983

Vanberg, Viktor. Morality and economics . New Brunswick [N.J.] , 1987. p. cm ISBN 0-912051-19-1 (pbk.) LC Card 87-19213 DDC 174/.26 19
HB72 .V268 1987

Walker, Graham. The ethics of F.A. Hayek /. Lanham, MD , c1986. vii, 135 p. ; ISBN 0-8191-5250-1 (alk. paper) : LC Card 86-1515 DDC 171/.7 19
HB101.H39 W35 1986
NYPL ***[JFD 86-9138]***

Wogaman, J. Philip. Economics and ethics . Philadelphia , c1986. xiii, 145 p. ; ISBN 0-8006-1904-8 (pbk.) LC Card 85-45478 DDC 261.8/5 19
HB72 .W633 1986 **NYPL** ***[JLD 86-3984]***

ECONOMICS - MORAL AND ETHICAL ASPECTS - ADDRESSES, ESSAYS, LECTURES.
Harcourt, Geoffrey Colin. Controversies in political economy . New York , 1986. 293 p. ; ISBN 0-8147-3437-5 : LC Card 85-31055 DDC 330.1 19
HB75 .H33 1986 **NYPL** ***[JLD 86-3571]***

ECONOMICS - MORAL AND ETHICAL ASPECTS - CONGRESSES.
Ethik und Wirtschaftswissenschaft /. Berlin , c1985. 276 p. : ISBN 3-428-05910-7 LC Card 86-132826
HB72 .E79 1985

ECONOMICS - NETHERLANDS.
Wildenberg, Ivo W. (Ivo Willibrord) Johan & Pieter de la Court, 1622-1660 & 1618-1685 . Amsterdam , 1986. xiii, 180 p., [21] p. of plates : ISBN 90-302-1162-8 : LC Card 87-141484
HC322.5.A2 W55 1986

The economics of agricultural policies /. Gardner, Bruce L. New York, NY , c1987. xi, 387 p. : ISBN 0-02-947760-3 LC Card 87-20367 DDC 338.1/8 19
HD1761 .G245 1987

The economics of Alfred Marshall /. Reisman, David A. New York , 1986. ix, 433 p. ; ISBN 0-312-23430-9 : LC Card 85-22321 DDC 330.15/5 19
HB98.2 .R45 1986

The economics of amenity . McNulty, Robert H., 1940- Washington, D.C. , c1985. xvi, 157 p. : ISBN 0-941182-15-0 (pbk.) LC Card 85-6545 DDC 307.7/6/0973 19
HT321 .M36 1985 ***NYPL [JLE 86-4519]***

The economics of business enterprise . Ricketts, Martin J. Brighton, Sussex , 1987. xii, 306 p. : ISBN 0-7108-0221-8 : LC Card 87-104594 DDC 338.5 19
HD2731 .R53 1987

Economics of changing age distributions in developed countries / edited by Ronald D. Lee, W. Brian Arthur, Gerry Rogers. Oxford [Oxfordshire] : Oxford University Press ; Topsfield, Mass. : Salem House, 1987. p. cm. Bibliography: p. Includes index. ISBN 0-19-829503-0 : LC Card 86-25098 DDC 304.6/2/091722 19
1. Age distribution (Demography). 2. Age distribution (Demography) - Great Britain. 3. Age distribution (Demography) - Israel. 4. Age distribution (Demography) - Japan. 5. Age distribution (Demography) - United States. I. Lee, Ronald Demos, 1941-. II. Arthur, W. Brian. III. Rogers, Gerry.
HB1531 .E28 1987

Economics of cotton handloom industry in India /. Mahapatro, P. C. (Poorna Chandra), 1944- New Delhi , 1986. xvi, 277 p. ; ISBN 81-7024-060-3 : LC Card 86-903087 DDC 338.4/774614/0954
HD9866.I63 O745 1986

Economics of development / Malcolm Gillis ... [et al.]. 2nd ed. New York : Norton, 1987. xv, 623 p. : ill. ; 24 cm. Bibliography: p. [587]-610. Includes index. ISBN 0-393-95548-6 LC Card 87-5701 DDC 338.9 19
1. Developing countries - Economic policy. 2. Economic development. I. Gillis, Malcolm.
HC59.7 .E314 1987

Economics of exchange rate management /. Singh, Devi, 1952- New Delhi , 1986. 204 p. ; LC Card 86-903032 DDC 332.4/560954 19
HG3971 .S56 1975

The economics of export embargoes . Lundborg, Per, 1950- New York, NY , c1987. xi, 127 p. : ISBN 0-7099-4151-X : LC Card 86-29370 DDC 382/.4131/0947 19
HD9035 .L86 1987

The economics of federal credit programs /. Bosworth, Barry, 1942- Washington, D.C. , c1987. xii, 214 p. : ISBN 0-8157-1038-0 : LC Card 85-48205 DDC 336.3/44/0973 19
HJ8119 .B67 1987

The Economics of firm size, market structure, and social performance : proceedings of a conference / sponsored by Bureau of Economics, Federal Trade Commission ; edited by John J. Siegfried. [Washington, D.C.?] : The Bureau : For sale by the Supt. of Docs., U. S. G.P.O., 1980. viii, 388 p. ; 28 cm. "July, 1980"--Cover. "This conference was held on January 17 and 18, 1980, at the Ramada Inn in Rosslyn, Virginia. This volume contains the research papers and commentaries presented at that conference"--P. viii. Includes bibliographical references. LC Card 81-600757 DDC 338.6/4/0973 19
1. Industry - Social aspects - United States - Congresses. 2. Industries, Size of - Congresses. 3. Industrial organization (Economic theory) - Congresses. I. Siegfried, John J.
HD60.5.U5 E26 ***NYPL [JLF 86-704]***

Economics of food processing in the United States / edited by Chester O. McCorkle, Jr. San Diego : Academic Press, c1988. xiii, 449 p. : ill. ; 24 cm. (Food science and technology) Includes bibliographies and index. ISBN 0-12-482185-5 (alk. paper) LC Card 87-1245 DDC 338.4/7664/00973 19
1. Food industry and trade - United States. I. McCorkle, Chester O.
HD9005 .E37 1988

The economics of François Quesnay /. Vaggi, Gianni. Durham , 1987. xv, 247 p. : ISBN 0-8223-0757-X LC Card 87-3549 DDC 330.15/2 19
HB105.Q5 V34 1987

The economics of housing in India . Dholakia, Bakul H. 1947- Delhi , 1982. xviii, 274 p. ; LC Card 83-905798 DDC 363.5/0954 19
HD7361.A3 D47 1982
NYPL [JLD 85-2908]

The economics of imperfect competition . Greenhut, Melvin L. Cambridge [Cambridgeshire] , New York , 1987. xix, 408 p. : ISBN 0-521-30552-7 LC Card 86-11707 DDC 338.6/048 19
HB238 .G74 1987 ***NYPL [JLE 87-1413]***

The Economics of insurance regulation : a cross-national study / edited by Jörg Finsinger and Mark V. Pauly. Houndmills, Basingstoke, Hampshire : Macmillan, 1986. xi, 300 p. : ill. ; 23 cm. (WZB-Publication) Includes bibliographies and index. ISBN 0-333-39684-7
1. Insurance - State supervision - Addresses, essays, lectures. 2. Insurance law - Economic aspects - Addresses, essays, lectures. I. Finsinger, Jörg. II. Pauly, Mark V., 1941-. III. Series.
NYPL [JLD 87-1100]

The economics of international integration /. Robson, Peter, 1926- London , Boston , 1987. 285 p. : ISBN 0-04-445005-2 (pbk. : alk. paper) LC Card 87-11472 DDC 337.1 19
HF1418.5 .R63 1987

The economics of John Stuart Mill /. Hollander, Samuel. Oxford, U.K. , 1985. 2 v. (xx, 1037 p.) ; ISBN 0-631-14045-X (set) LC Card 86-673535
HB103.M7 H64x 1985 ***NYPL [JLE 87-951]***

Economics of labor /. Reynolds, Lloyd George, 1910- Englewood Cliffs, NJ , c1987. x, 518 p. : ISBN 0-13-225772-6 LC Card 86-25149 DDC 331 19
HD4901 .R469 1987

The Economics of market dominance / edited by Donald Hay and John Vickers. Oxford, UK ; New York, NY, USA : B. Blackwell, 1987. p. cm. "This volume is the outcome of a conference on the economics of market dominance held at Nuffield College, Oxford, in September 1985"--Pref. Bibliography: p. Includes index. ISBN 0-631-14784-5 : LC Card 86-26416 DDC 338.8/2 19
1. Industrial organization (Economic theory) - Congresses. 2. Monopolies - Congresses. I. Hay, Donald A. II. Vickers, John, 1958-.
HD2326 .E24 1987

The economics of medical care . Newhouse, Joseph P. Reading, Mass. , c1978. x, 116 p. : ISBN 0-201-08369-8 LC Card 78-52498
RA410.53 .N5 ***NYPL [JLE 79-2561]***

The Economics of military expenditures : military expenditures, economic growth, and fluctuations / edited by Christian Schmidt. New York : St. Martin's Press, 1987. xxiii, 391 p. : ill. ; 23 cm. "Proceedings of a conference held by the International Economic Association in Paris, France." Includes bibliographies and indexes. ISBN 0-312-00421-4 : LC Card 86-27886 DDC 338.4/7355 19
1. Armaments - Economic aspects - Congresses. I. Schmidt, Christian. II. International Economic Association.
HC79.D4 E27 1987

The economics of personal tax escalation in Australia /. Norman, Neville R. [Sydney] : Sydney ; xii, 173 p. : ISBN 0-86861-652-4 (pbk.) LC Card 84-72057 DDC 336.24/2/0994 19
HJ4802 .N67 1985 ***NYPL [JLD 86-1906]***

Economics of price and income /. Ohlson, M. K. Dubuque, Iowa , c1986. vi, 126 p. : ISBN 0-8403-4173-3 (pbk.); 0-8403-4173-4 LC Card 86-82292 DDC 338.5/2 19
HB221 .O38 1986

Economics of public distribution system in food-grains /. Mishra, Bhagabat, 1940- New Delhi , 1985. xviii, 306 p. (some folded) ; LC Card 85-902748 DDC 381/.4131/095413 19
HD9066.I63 O756 1982
NYPL [JLD 86-1149]

The economics of public issues /. North, Douglass Cecil. New York , c1987. ix, 214 p. ; ISBN 0-06-044832-6 (pbk.) LC Card 86-33627 DDC 330.973/092 19
HB34 .N6 1987

Economics of shipping practice and management /. Branch, Alan E. London , New York , c1988. p. cm. ISBN 0-412-31030-9 (pbk.) LC Card 87-24233 DDC 387/.0068 19
HE571 .B669 1988

Economics of social issues /. Sharp, Ansel Miree, 1924- Plano, Tex. , 1988. xiii, 431 p. : ISBN 0-256-06173-4 (pbk.) LC Card 87-71674 DDC 330 19
HB171.5 .S5498 1988

The economics of Soviet bloc trade and finance /. Holzman, Franklyn D. Boulder , 1987. xi, 215 p. : ISBN 0-8133-7274-7 (alk. paper) : LC Card 86-32598 DDC 382/.0947 19
HF3496.5 .H62 1987

The Economics of technological change. Teubal, Morris. Innovation performance, learning, and government policy . Madison, Wis. , 1987. xvi, 308 p. : ISBN 0-299-10950-X : LC Card 86-40448 DDC 338/.06 19
HC79.T4 T485 1987

The economics of telecommunications . Wenders, John T. Cambridge, Mass. , c1987. x, 284 p. : ISBN 0-88730-119-3 LC Card 86-17280 DDC 384/.041/0973 19
HE7787 .W47 1986 ***NYPL [JLE 87-1593]***

Economics of the environment . Siebert, Horst, 1938- Berlin , New York , c1987. xiv, 273 p. : ISBN 0-387-17283-1 (U. S.) LC Card 87-4703 DDC 363.7 19
HC79.E5 S437 1987

The Economics of the firm / edited by Roger Clarke and Tony McGuinness. Oxford [Oxfordshire] ; New York, NY, USA : B. Blackwell, 1987. p. cm. Bibliography: p. Includes index. ISBN 0-631-14075-1 : LC Card 86-27057 DDC 338.6 19
1. Industrial organization (Economic theory). 2. Managerial economics. I. Clarke, Roger. II. McGuinness, Tony.
HD2326 .E243 1987

Economics of the public sector /. Stiglitz, Joseph E. New York , c1986. xxiii, 599 p. : ISBN 0-393-01808-3 LC Card 86-211407 DDC 336.73 19
HJ257.2 .S84 1986

Economics of the retail petroleum market : papers presented at an Energy Economics Group conference on 7th May, 1986 / editor P.J. Ellis Jones. London : Institute of Petroleum, c1986. i, 79 p. : ill. ; 30 cm. LC Card 87-134547 DDC 381/.4566553827/0941 19
1. Gasoline industry - Great Britain - Congresses. 2. Petroleum industry and trade - Great Britain - Congresses. 3. Retail trade - Great Britain - Congresses. I. Jones, P. Ellis. II. Institute of Petroleum (Great Britain). Energy Economics Group.
HD9579.G5 G63 1986

The economics of the welfare state /. Barr, Nicholas. Stanford, Calif. , 1987. xiv, 475 p. : ISBN 0-8047-1427-4 LC Card 87-60997 DDC 338.941 19
HB846 .B37 1987

The economics of tractors in South Asia . Binswanger, Hans P. New York , Hyderabad, India , 1978. 96 p. ; LC Card 81-908104
HD2065.3 .B56 1978

The economics of U. S. slave and southern white fertility /. Steckel, Richard H. (Richard Hall), 1944- New York , 1985. 253 p. ; ISBN 0-8240-6662-6 (alk. paper) : LC Card 84-48314 DDC 304.6/32/08996073075 19
HB921 .S74 1985 ***NYPL [JLE 86-2085]***

The economics of unemployment /. Hobson, J. A. (John Atkinson), 1858-1940. New York , 1985. 157 p. ; ISBN 0-8240-7615-X : LC Card 85-13053

DDC 331.13/7 19
HB822 .H63 1985 ***NYPL [JLC 86-452]***

ECONOMICS OF WAR. see **WAR, COST OF.**

The economics of women, men, and work /. Blau, Francine D. Englewood Cliffs, N.J. , c1986. xiv, 365 p. : ISBN 0-13-233719-3 LC Card 85-30746 DDC 305.3/0973 19
HQ1426 .B62 1986 ***NYPL [JLE 86-4254]***

The economics of work and pay /. Hamermesh, Daniel S. New York , c1988. xii, 452 p. : ISBN 0-06-045356-7 LC Card 87-18355 DDC 331 19
HD4901 .H18 1988

ECONOMICS - OUTLINES, SYLLABI, ETC.
Borcz, Leszek. Przewodnik metodyczny do ekonomii politycznej dla doktorantów nieekonomistów /. Gliwice , 1979. 79 p. ; LC Card 81-182800
HB74.5 .B67 1979

ECONOMICS - PHILOSOPHY.
Delalande, Philippe, 1937- Science économique et maîtrise de l'avenir /. Paris , 1984. 305 p. : ISBN 2-7178-0790-X : LC Card 85-104627
HB71 .D45 1984

Hamlin, Alan P., 1951- Ethics, economics, and the state /. Brighton, Sussex , 1986. x, 198 p. ;
NYPL [JLD 86-3648]

Johnson, Glenn Leroy, 1918- Research methodology for economists . New York , London , c1986. xx, 252 p. ; ISBN 0-02-949840-6 LC Card 85-24240 DDC 300/.72 19
HB74.5 .J65 1986 ***NYPL [JLE 86-4300]***

Klant, J. J. Filosofie van de economische wetenschappen /. Leiden , c1987. 87 p. ; ISBN 90-6890-105-2 : LC Card 87-169944
HB72 .K55 1987

Shackle, G. L. S. (George Lennox Sharman), 1903- [Selections. 1987.] Business, time, and thought . New York , 1988. p. cm. ISBN 0-8147-2586-4 : LC Card 87-5528 DDC 330.1 19
HB72 .S462 1988

ECONOMICS - POLAND - HISTORY.
Górski, Janusz. Z historii myśli ekonomicznej . Łódź , 1986, c1985. 312 p. ; ISBN 83-218-0319-9 : LC Card 83-189161
HB114.A2 G67 1986

ECONOMICS, PRIMITIVE. see **ECONOMIC ANTHROPOLOGY.**

Economics, principles of political economy /. Fusfeld, Daniel Roland, 1922- Glenview, Ill. , c1988. xxii, 858 p. : ISBN 0-673-18958-9 LC Card 87-23370 DDC 330 19
HB171.5 .F87 1988

ECONOMICS - PROBLEMS, EXERCISES, ETC.
Harbury, C. D. Workbook in introductory economics /. Oxford [Oxfordshire] , New York , 1987, c1982. xvii, 176 p. : ISBN 0-08-034790-8 (pbk.) : LC Card 87-19011 DDC 330/.076 19
HB74.6 .H37 1987

ECONOMICS - PROGRAMMED INSTRUCTION.
Bingham, Robert C. Economic concepts . New York , c1987. xv, 444 p. ; ISBN 0-07-044963-5 (pbk.) LC Card 87-3351 DDC 330/.07/7 19
HB171.5 .B52 1987

ECONOMICS - PSYCHOLOGICAL ASPECTS.
Bökenkamp, Joachim. Methodologische Betrachtungen der Annahmen zum menschlichen Verhalten aus der Sicht der Volkswirtschaftslehre . Göttingen , c1985. v, 446 p. ; ISBN 3-925391-01-0 LC Card 87-121278 DDC 330/.01/9 19
HB74.P8 B59 1985

Katona, George, 1901- [Aspirations and affluence. Dutch.] Het psychologisch klimaat van de economie in de Verenigde Staten en West-Europa /. Utrecht , 1974. 247 p. ; ISBN 90-274-5826-X ***NYPL [JLD 86-295]***

Kurthen, Hermann. Politische Ökonomie und Persönlichkeitstheorie . Köln , 1985. 245 p. ; ISBN 3-7609-5181-3 LC Card 85-155083
HB74.P8 K87 1985

Psychological economics . Boston , c1987. p. cm. ISBN 0-89838-234-3 LC Card 87-3050 DDC 330/.01/9 19
HB74.P8 P697 1987

ECONOMICS - PSYCHOLOGICAL ASPECTS - CONGRESSES.
Behavioral foundations of economic theory. Rational choice . Chicago , 1987. ix, 332 p. : ISBN 0-226-34857-1 (alk. paper) LC Card 86-27241 DDC 330/.01/9 19
HB74.P8 B44 1987

Ehrenpromotion von Prof. Dr. George Katona, Ann Arbor, Michigan am 15. Juni 1981 . Berlin [1982] 51 p. : LC Card 83-200933
HB74.P8 E35 1982

Normengeleitetes Verhalten in den Sozialwissenschaften /. Berlin , c1984. 199 p. ; ISBN 3-428-05622-1 LC Card 86-140299
HB74.P8 N67 1984

ECONOMICS - RELIGIOUS ASPECTS.
The Best of This world /. Lanham, MD , c1986. x, 405 p. ; ISBN 0-8191-5605-1 (alk. paper) : LC Card 86-22411 DDC 261.8 19
HB72 .B5 1987 ***NYPL [JFE 86-5571]***

ECONOMICS - RELIGIOUS ASPECTS - CHRISTIANITY.
Christian ethics and economics . Edinburgh , New York , c1980. xii, 114 p. ; ISBN 0-8164-2282-6 (Seabury Press : pbk.) LC Card 80-50892
HF1411 .C422 1980

Griffiths, Brian. The creation of wealth . Downers Grove, Ill. , c1984. 160 p. : ISBN 0-87784-566-2 (pbk.) : LC Card 85-5210 DDC 330.12/2 19
HB72 .G74 1984 ***NYPL [JLD 86-3576]***

Raines, John C. Modern work and human meaning /. Philadelphia , c1986. 150 p. ; ISBN 0-664-24703-2 (pbk.) LC Card 85-26370 DDC 241/.64 19
BJ1498 .R335 1986 ***NYPL [JLD 86-2382]***

Wogaman, J. Philip. Economics and ethics . Philadelphia , c1986. xiii, 145 p. ; ISBN 0-8006-1904-8 (pbk.) LC Card 85-45478 DDC 261.8/5 19
HB72 .W633 1986 ***NYPL [JLD 86-3984]***

ECONOMICS - RELIGIOUS ASPECTS - CONGRESSES.
Morality of the market . Vancouver, B.C., Canada , c1985. xxv, 601 p. ; ISBN 0-88975-074-2 (pbk.) : LC Card 86-158049 DDC 174/.4 19
HB72 .M56 1985

ECONOMICS - RELIGIOUS ASPECTS - ISLAM.
'Abd al-Laṭīf, Badawī, 1909- al-Niẓām al-mālī. [al-Qāhirah] 1962. 115 p. LC Card NE63-525
HJ233 .A25 ***NYPL [*OGO 82-3888]***

Choudhury, Masudul Alam, 1948- Contributions to Islamic economic theory . Houndmills, Basingstoke, Hampshire , 1986. xvii, 241 p. : ISBN 0-333-38507-1 ***NYPL [JLD 86-3601]***

Ṣiddīqī, Muḥammad Iqbal. Model of an Islamic bank /. Lahore, Pakistan , 1986. 90 p. ; LC Card 87-931018 DDC 332.1/0917/671 19
HG3368.A6 S54 1986

ECONOMICS - RELIGIOUS ASPECTS - ISLAM - HISTORY.
Dobbin, Christine E., 1941- Islamic revivalism in a changing peasant economy . London , 1983. xii, 300 p. : ISBN 0-7007-0155-9 (pbk.) : LC Card 83-127619 DDC 303.4/84 19
HD1537.I56 D63 1983
NYPL [JLD 87-1053]

ECONOMICS - RESEARCH.
Johnson, Glenn Leroy, 1918- Research methodology for economists . New York , London , c1986. xx, 252 p. ; ISBN 0-02-949840-6 LC Card 85-24240 DDC 300/.72 19
HB74.5 .J65 1986 ***NYPL [JLE 86-4300]***

ECONOMICS - RESEARCH - AUSTRIA - DIRECTORIES.
Gergely, Stefan M. Wirtschaftswissenschaften /. Wien , 1985. 170 p. ; ISBN 3-205-06108-X LC Card 85-229521
HB74.9.A9 G47 1985

ECONOMICS - RESEARCH - ESTONIA.
Issledovaniia Instituta ėkonomiki Akademii nauk Ėstonskoĭ SSR v X piatiletke . Tallin , 1983. 233 p. ; LC Card 86-181279
HB74.9.S65 I86 1983

ECONOMICS - RESEARCH - ESTONIA - BIBLIOGRAPHY.
Issledovaniia Instituta ėkonomiki Akademii nauk Ėstonskoĭ SSR v X piatiletke . Tallin , 1983. 233 p. ; LC Card 86-181279
HB74.9.S65 I86 1983

ECONOMICS - RESEARCH - GERMANY - HISTORY.
Krengel, Rolf. Das Deutsche Institut für Wirtschaftsforschung (Institut für Konjunkturforschung), 1925-1979 /. Berlin , c1986. xi, 229 p. ; ISBN 3-428-06074-1 LC Card 87-112851 DDC 330/.0943 19
HB74.9.G3 K74 1986

ECONOMICS - RESEARCH - GERMANY (WEST) - HISTORY.
Krengel, Rolf. Das Deutsche Institut für Wirtschaftsforschung (Institut für Konjunkturforschung), 1925-1979 /. Berlin , c1986. xi, 229 p. ; ISBN 3-428-06074-1 LC Card 87-112851 DDC 330/.0943 19
HB74.9.G3 K74 1986

ECONOMICS - RESEARCH - HUNGARY.
Magyar Tudományos Akadémia. Közgazdaságtudományi Intézet. Activities of the Institute and Summary of the 3rd yearbook, 1960-1961. Budapest , 1962. 61 p. ; LC Card 87-146537
HB74.9.H9 M35 1962

ECONOMICS - RESEARCH - UKRAINE.
Ėkonomizatsiia nauki . Kiev , 1986. 221 p. ; LC Card 87-102107
HC337.U53 R44 1986

ECONOMICS - RESEARCH - UKRAINE - HISTORY.
Stanovlenie i razvitie sovetskoĭ ėkonomicheskoĭ nauki na Ukraine . Kiev , 1983. 285, [2] p. ; LC Card 84-120015 DDC 330/.072/04771 19
HB74.9.S65 S72 1983 ***NYPL [*QGA 87-275]***

ECONOMICS - ROME - HISTORY.
Poliānskiĭ, F. IA. (Fedor IAkovlevich) Ėkonomicheskaia mysl′ Drevnego Rima . Moskva , 1978. 355 p. ; LC Card 81-167944
HC39 .P65 1978

Reekmans, T. Inleiding tot de antieke economie /. Leuven , 1984. 129 leaves in various foliations ; ISBN 90-334-0834-1 : LC Card 86-203767
HB77 .R44 1984

ECONOMICS - SOCIAL ASPECTS - CONGRESSES.
Trusteeship, the Gandhian alternative /. New Delhi , c1986. xiii, 238 p. ; LC Card 86-903783 DDC 330.1 19
HB199 .T76 1986

ECONOMICS - SOVIET UNION.
Khachaturov, T. S. (Tigran Sergeevich), 1906- Intensifikatsiia i ėffektivnost′ v usloviiākh razvitogo sotsializma /. Moskva , 1978. 350 p. ; LC Card 81-167321
HC336.25 .K445 1978

ECONOMICS - SPAIN - CONGRESSES.
La Nueva economía en Francia y en España /. Madrid , c1980. 197 p. : ISBN 84-85355-27-X : LC Card 83-105425 DDC 330.944/0838 19
HB105.A2 N83 1980 ***NYPL [JLD 86-3024]***

ECONOMICS - SPAIN - HISTORY - 18TH CENTURY.
Campomanes, Pedro Rodríguez, Conde de, 1723-1803. Bosquejo de política económica española . Madrid , c1984. 182 p. ; ISBN 84-276-0691-5 : LC Card 86-153508
HB117.A2 C34 1984

Normante y Carcavilla, Lorenzo. Discurso sobre la utilidad de los conocimientos económico-políticos y la necesidad de su estudio metódico ; Proposiciones de economía civil y comercio ; Espíritu del señor Melón en su ensayo político sobre el comercio /. [Aragón] [1984?] 1 v. (various pagings) ; ISBN 84-505-0473-2 LC Card 87-104302
HC385 .N57 1984

ECONOMICS - STATISTICAL METHODS.
Andersen, Erling B. Statistics for economics, business administration, and the social sciences /. Berlin , New York , c1987. xi, 439 p. : ISBN 0-387-17720-5 (pbk. : U. S.) LC Card

87-9423 DDC 519.5 19
HB137 .A525 1987

Anderson, David Ray, 1941- Statistics for business and economics /. St. Paul, MN , c1987. xxviii, 792 p. : ISBN 0-314-25873-6 : LC Card 86-24613 DDC 519.5 19
HF1017 .A6 1987

Hildebrand, David K., 1940- Statistical thinking for managers /. Boston, Mass. , c1987. xvii, 894 p. : ISBN 0-87150-036-1 LC Card 86-29222 DDC 519.5/024658 19
HD30.215 .H54 1987

Keller, Gerald. Statistics for management and economics . Belmont, Calif. , c1988. xix, 987 p. : ISBN 0-534-08622-5 LC Card 87-19845 DDC 658.4/033 19
HD30.215 .K45 1988

McClave, James T. Statistics for business and economics /. San Francisco , c1988. xxii, 1267 p. : ISBN 0-02-379020-2 LC Card 87-20195 DDC 519.5 19
HF1017 .M36 1988

Martínez Garza, Angel. Métodos econométricos . Chapingo, Edo. de Méx. , 1982. 225 p. ; LC Card 84-227751
HB139 .M385 1982

Mirer, Thad W. Economic statistics and econometrics /. New York , London , c1988. xvi, 400 p. : ISBN 0-02-381821-2 LC Card 87-24027 DDC 330/.028 19
HB137 .M57 1988

Modeli i metody reshenii͡a zadach vzaimodeĭstvii͡a ėkonomicheskikh sistem /. Novosibirsk , 1982. 160 p. : LC Card 83-164468
HB137 .M6 1982

National income and economic progress . New York , 1988. p. cm. ISBN 0-312-01566-6 : LC Card 87-24063 DDC 339.3 19
HB141.5 .N375 1988

Newbold, Paul. Statistics for business and economics /. Englewood Cliffs, N.J. , c1988. xiii, 866 p. : ISBN 0-13-845173-7 LC Card 87-14363 DDC 519.5 19
HF1017 .N48 1988

Struktur und Dynamik der Wirtschaft . Freiburg im Breisgau , c1983. 530 p. : ISBN 3-448-01348-X : LC Card 83-184564 DDC 330 19
HB44 .S77 1983

ECONOMICS - STATISTICAL METHODS - CONGRESSES.
Quantity and quality in economic research /. Lanham, MD , c1985- v. : ISBN 0-8191-5112-2 (v. 1 : alk. paper) : LC Card 85-26360 DDC 330/.072 19
HB135 .Q38 1985 *NYPL [JLL 86-232]*

ECONOMICS - STUDY AND TEACHING.
Great ideas for teaching economics /. Glenview, Ill. , c1987. xxiv, 400 p. : ISBN 0-673-17245-7 (pbk.) LC Card 87-159026 DDC 330/.07 19
HB74.5.G73 1987

Kritika antimarksistskikh ėkonomicheskikh teoriĭ v prepodavanii politicheskoĭ ėkonomii /. Moskva , 1981. 356 p. ; LC Card 82-107917
HB178 .K7 1981

ECONOMICS - STUDY AND TEACHING - AFRICA, SUB-SAHARAN.
Albagli, Claude. Les circuits économiques en Afrique noire /. Abidjan , c1983. 67 p. : ISBN 2-7236-0585-X LC Card 86-179144
HB74.9.A357 A43 1983

ECONOMICS - STUDY AND TEACHING - AFRICA, SUB-SAHARAN - AUDIO-VISUAL AIDS.
Albagli, Claude. Les circuits économiques en Afrique noire /. Abidjan , c1983. 67 p. : ISBN 2-7236-0585-X LC Card 86-179144
HB74.9.A357 A43 1983

ECONOMICS - STUDY AND TEACHING - BULGARIA.
Ikonomicheskii͡at podkhod i ikonomicheskoto vŭzpitanie na trudeshtite se. Sliven , 1984. 195 p. ; LC Card 86-102634
HB74.9.B9 I37 1984

ECONOMICS - STUDY AND TEACHING (CONTINUING EDUCATION) - CHILE.
Así aprendemos . Santiago de Chile [1986] 126 p. : LC Card 87-404640 DDC 330/.07/15 19
HB74.9.C5 A85 1986

ECONOMICS - STUDY AND TEACHING - GERMANY, WEST.
Nordmann-Werner, Karin, 1945- Kompetenzvermittlung durch Sachliteratur . Frankfurt am Main , New York , c1984. 391 p. ; ISBN 3-8204-5278-8 LC Card 85-193184
HB74.9.G3 N67 1984

ECONOMICS - STUDY AND TEACHING - GERMANY (WEST) - BADEN-WÜRTTEMBERG.
Zarth, Michael. Wirtschaftsunterricht an allgemeinbildenden Schulen in Baden-Württemberg . Tübingen , 1987. x, 241 p. ; ISBN 3-88573-028-6 : LC Card 87-419933 DDC 330/.07/104346 19
HB74.9.G3 Z36 1987

ECONOMICS - STUDY AND TEACHING (HIGHER) - BULGARIA.
Zadachite na DKMS vŭv VUZ za povishavane na ikonomicheskata podgotovka na studentite i mladite khora ot drugite otri͡adi na mladezhta . Svishtov , 1985. 91 p. ; LC Card 86-159994
HB74.9.B9 Z33 1985

ECONOMICS - STUDY AND TEACHING (HIGHER) - INDIA.
Issues in teaching of economics in Indian universities /. New Delhi , c1987. vii, 145 p. ; ISBN 81-204-0203-0 : LC Card 87-901784 DDC 330/.07/1154 19
HB74.9.I4 I88 1987

ECONOMICS - STUDY AND TEACHING (HIGHER) - POLAND - KATOWICE - HISTORY.
Akademia Ekonomiczna im. Karola Adamieckiego w Katowicach . Katowice , 1977. 194 p. : LC Card 82-104777
HB74.9.P7 A38 1977

ECONOMICS - STUDY AND TEACHING (HIGHER) - POLAND - WARSAW - HISTORY.
Wyższa Szkoła Handlowa, Szkoła Główna Handlowa, Miejska Szkoła Handlowa, 1906-1945 /. Warszawa , 1984. 180 p. : LC Card 85-241871
HB74.9.P7 W98 1984

ECONOMICS - STUDY AND TEACHING (HIGHER) - UNITED STATES - HISTORY - 19TH CENTURY.
Breaking the academic mould . Middletown, Conn. , 1988. p. cm. ISBN 0-8195-5176-7 : LC Card 87-21023 DDC 330/.07/1173 19
HB74.8 .B74 1988

ECONOMICS - STUDY AND TEACHING (SECONDARY)
Davis, James E. (James Edwin), 1940- Economics . Santa Barbara, Calif. , c1988. xv, 354 p. : ISBN 0-87436-479-5 (alk. paper) LC Card 87-18670 DDC 330/.07/1273 19
HB74.5 .D39 1988

ECONOMICS - STUDY AND TEACHING (SECONDARY) - GERMANY, WEST.
Bachmann, Gerhard, 1935- Praxisbezug im wirtschaftswissenschaftlichen Studium . Frankfurt am Main , New York , c1986. 277 p. : ISBN 3-8204-9052-3 LC Card 86-147278
HB74.9.G3 B33 1986

ECONOMICS - STUDY AND TEACHING (SECONDARY) - ITALY.
L'Insegnamento dell'economia politica nella scuola secondaria superiore . Milano, Italy , c1982. 261 p. ; LC Card 87-673404
HB74.9.I8 I57x 1982

ECONOMICS - STUDY AND TEACHING (SECONDARY) - SOVIET UNION.
Popov, V. D. (Vladimir Dmitrievich) Ėkonomika pli͡us pedagogika . Moskva , 1986. 288 p. ; LC Card 86-103180
HB74.9.S65 P66 1986

ECONOMICS - STUDY AND TEACHING - UNITED STATES - COMPUTER PROGRAMS - CATALOGS.
Walstad, William B. An annotated catalog of microcomputer software in economics /. New York, NY (2 Park Ave., New York 10016) , c1986. viii, 160 p. ; LC Card 86-210285 DDC 330/.028/5536 19
HB74.8 .W34 1986

ECONOMICS - SWEDEN - HISTORY - 18TH CENTURY.
Liedman, Sven-Eric, 1939- Den synliga handen . [Stockholm] [1986] 268 p. ; ISBN 91-7014-210-6 : LC Card 86-215138
HB116.5.B47 L54 1986

ECONOMICS - SWITZERLAND.
Merk, Gerhard, 1931- Ausgewählte Aufsätze zur Wirtschaftstheorie /. Zürich , 1986. 138 p. ; ISBN 3-9999462-1-1 LC Card 87-409558 DDC 330.9494/073 19
HB118.A2 M47 1986

ECONOMICS - TERMINOLOGY.
Lozano Irueste, José María, 1920- Glosario de términos de economía y hacienda /. [Madrid] [1986] 56 p. ; *NYPL [JLF 87-148]*

T͡Sagolova, R. S. (Rufʹ Sergeevna) Leksiko-semanticheskie osobennosti politiko-ėkonomicheskoĭ terminologii /. Moskva , 1985. 146 p. ; LC Card 86-106188
HB62 .T76 1985

Economics today /. Miller, Roger LeRoy. New York , c1988. xxix, 893, [50] p. : ISBN 0-06-044489-4 LC Card 87-18453 DDC 330 19
HB171.5 .M642 1988

Economics U$A. Lesson 5, Keynes, the Great Depression [videorecording] / Chicago, IL : Films Inc., 1986. 1 videocassette (28 min.) : sd., col. + 1 study guide. Title from data sheet. Hosted by David Schoumacher. College students and adults. Issued as U-matic 3/4 in. or Beta 1/2 in. or VHS 1/2 in. Using John Maynard Keynes's economic theories, analyzes the depression in terms of the interaction of consumption spending and investment spending, and shows how this analysis differs from classical theory. LC Card 86-708020 DDC 330.15 11
1. Keynesian economics. 2. Depressions - 1929 - United States. 3. Consumers - United States - History - 20th century. 4. Public investments - United States - History - 20th century. I. Schoumacher, David. II. Educational Film Center (Annandale, Va.). III. Wharton Econometric Forecasting Associates. IV. Films Incorporated. V. Title: Economics USA. VI. Title: Keynes, the Great Depression.
HB99.7

ECONOMICS - UKRAINE - GALICIA, EASTERN - HISTORY.
Vytanovych, Illi͡a. Sotsialʹno-ekonomichni ideï v zmahanni͡akh halytsʹkykh ukraïntsiv na perelomi XIX-XX vv. /. Mi͡unkhen , 1970. 74 p. ; LC Card 86-214348
HC337.U52 G358 1970

Economics USA. Economics U$A. Chicago, IL , 1986. 1 videocassette (28 min.) : LC Card 86-708020 DDC 330.15 11
HB99.7

Economics without equilibrium /. Kaldor, Nicholas, 1908-1986. Cardiff, U.K. , 1985. 79 p. ; ISBN 0-906449-87-1 LC Card 86-673866
HB71 .K273x 1985b

ECONOMICS - YUGOSLAVIA.
Socialismo autogestionario en marcha . Mérida, Venezuela , 1984. 377 p. ; LC Card 87-403553 DDC 335.43/09497 19
HB108.4.A2 S65 1984

Economie . Didier, Michel, 1940- Paris , 1984. 243 p. : ISBN 2-7178-0710-1 : LC Card 84-166256
HB173 .D455 1984

Economie agricole /. Roux, Pierre, docteur en sciences économiques. Paris , c1986- v. <1 > : ISBN 2-85206-353-0 (set) LC Card 87-106675
HD1415 .R62 1986

Economie bafouée. Degrotte, Jean-André, 1947- L'économie bafouée, ou, Les hommes politiques au créneau /. Paris , c1985. 130, [11] p. : ISBN 2-7266-0074-3 LC Card 85-230533
HD5106 .D42 1985

L'économie bafouée, ou, Les hommes politiques au créneau /. Degrotte, Jean-André, 1947- Paris , c1985. 130, [11] p. : ISBN 2-7266-0074-3 LC Card 85-230533
HD5106 .D42 1985

Economie budgétaire et fiscale /. Galavielle, Jean-Pierre. Paris , c1984-c1986. 2 v. : ISBN 2-254-84071-2 (v. 1) : LC Card 87-137252
HJ151 .G18 1984

Economie critique.
Les Economies non officielles /. Paris , 1984.

247 p. : ISBN 2-7071-1441-3 : LC Card 86-460169
HD2341 .E26 1984

La Flexibilité du travail en Europe . Paris , 1986. 330 p. : ISBN 2-7071-1598-3 : LC Card 86-173845
HD8376.5 .F57 1986

L'économie de la détente . Sokoloff, Georges. Paris , c1983. 255 p. : ISBN 2-7246-0483-0 : LC Card 84-117643
HF3646.5 .S65 1983

Economie des changements technologiques.
Boubekeur, Sid, 1952- L'habitat en Algérie . Lyon , c1986. 256 p. : ISBN 2-7297-0272-5 : LC Card 86-217640
HD7372.4.A3 B68 1986

Nouvelles technologies et enjeux sociaux . Lyon , c1986. 230 p. : ISBN 2-7297-0279-2 : LC Card 86-187357
HC79.T4 N68 1986

L'Economie des pays de l'Afrique de l'Ouest. Bruxelles : Information, promotion et coopération internationales, A.S.B.L., [1978] 1 v. (various pagings) : maps ; 24 cm. "Décembre 1978." Includes bibliography. LC Card 86-673818
1. Africa, West - Economic conditions - 1960-. I. Information, promotion et coopération internationales, A.S.B.L.
HC1000 .E36x 1978

Economie du populisme. Vega Tapia, Héctor. L'économie du populisme et le projet de passage au socialisme proposé par l'Unité populaire au Chili /. [Brussels] , 1984. 511 p. ; LC Card 85-146534 DDC 338.983 19
HC192 .V37 1984 ***NYPL [JLE 86-3663]***

Economie en liberté, 0768-0988.
Capitalismes fin de siècle /. Paris , c1986. 268 p. : ISBN 2-13-039425-6 : LC Card 86-231136
HC106.8 .C364 1986

Latouche, Serge, 1940- Faut-il refuser le développement? . Paris , c1986. 216 p. ; ISBN 2-13-039202-4 : LC Card 86-160202
HD83 .L324 1986

Michalet, Charles Albert. Le capitalisme mondial /. Paris [c1985], c1976. 368 p. : ISBN 2-13-039215-6 : LC Card 86-137294 DDC 338.8/8 19
HD2755.5 .M52 1985

Economie et droit du développement /. Gaillard, Claude, 1930- Alger , c1982. 439 p. ; LC Card 83-216670
HD75 .G34 1982

L'économie française face aux défis mondiaux . Brémond, Janine. Paris , c1985. 320 p. : ISBN 2-218-07456-7 LC Card 86-168427
HC276.2 .B657 1985

Een economie in spanning . Luwel, A. Leuven , 1985. 168 p. ; ISBN 90-334-1193-8 LC Card 86-123424
HB179.D8 L89 1985

Economie industrielle européenne . Jacquemin, Alex. [Paris] , c1979. xxii, 376 p. : ISBN 2-04-010465-8 LC Card 86-673881
HD70.E8 J3x 1979

Economie "module," 0338-6074.
Roux, Dominique. Analyse économique et gestion de l'entreprise /. Paris , c1986- v. <1 > : ISBN 2-04-016455-3 LC Card 87-114498
HD33 .R647 1986

Salles, Pierre, 1913- Problèmes économiques généraux /. Paris , 1984-19. 2 v. : ISBN 2-04-016910-5 (v. 1) LC Card 87-116907
HB173 .S355 1986

Economie mondiale 1980-1990, la fracture? : rapport du CEPII / préface de Michel Albert. Paris : Economica, c1984. x, 406 p. : ill. (some col.) ; 24 cm. Errata (1 leaf) inserted. Includes bibliographical references. ISBN 2-7178-0803-5 : LC Card 85-105930
1. Economic history - 1971-. 2. Economic forecasting. 3. International economic relations. I. Centre d'études prospectives et d'informations internationales (France).
HC59 .E384 1984

Economie mondialiste et mutations politiques . Silbert, Alfred. Paris , c1985. 212 p. ; ISBN 2-7157-1114-X : LC Card 85-221451 DDC 330.944/08 19
HC276 .S52 1985

Economie monétaire . Etienne, Eddy V., 1947- Port-au-Prince, Haïti [1986] 207 p. : LC Card 86-221340
HG221 .E92 1986

Economie monétaire internationale. Paris : Documentation française, [1982] 156 p. : ill. ; 24 cm. (Recherches économiques et sociales, 0396-3683 . nouv. sér., no 3) Cover title. Includes bibliographies. CONTENTS. - Information économique et sociale et concertation dans la planification / Robert Fraisse -- Développements récents en économie monétaire internationale / Charles Wyplosz -- Déséquilibres courants et instabilité des taux de change / André Cartapanis -- Intégration des marchés de marchandises et parité internationale des prix / Liliane Crouhy-Veyrac et Michel Crouhy -- Quelques éléments sur les liens entre les taux d'intérêt et le refinancement bancaire / Dominique Strauss-Kahn -- Structure du système bancaire français et maniement des taux d'intérêt / Sophie Thomas-Roubine -- Une révision des conditions de refinancement du système bancaire français est-elle souhaitable, est-elle possible? / Michel Castel. LC Card 85-131349 DDC 332/.042 19
1. International finance. 2. Foreign exchange. I. Fraisse, Robert. II. Series.
HG3881 .E27 1982

Economie politique contemporaine . Lorriaux, Jean-Pierre. Paris , c1985. iv, 565 p. : ISBN 2-7178-0937-6 : LC Card 86-116111 DDC 330 19
HB173 .L784 1985

Economie politique et politique économique de la Suisse /. Deiss, Joseph. Fribourg , c1979. 412 p. : LC Card 86-673870
HC397 .D387x 1979

Economie, population et politique démographique /. Loriaux, M. Louvain-la-Neuve [c1984] 169 p. : ISBN 2-87085-041-7 : LC Card 86-144677
HB883.5 .L67 1984

Economie sociale et cycle de vie des institutions / avec Michel Rocard ... [et al.]. Paris : Economica, 1983. 162 p. : ports. ; 24 cm. At head of title: Association des âges. Proceedings of a conference organized by the Association des âges, held in Paris, Oct. 19, 1982. Includes index. ISBN 2-7178-0631-8 : LC Card 83-174618 DDC 334/.0944 19
1. Cooperative societies - France - Congresses. 2. Friendly societies - France - Congresses. I. Rocard, Michel, 1930-. II. Association des âges.
HD3494 .E26 1983 ***NYPL [JLE 86-537]***

Economies et sociétés (Lille, France)
Décolonisations et nouvelles dépendances . [Lille] , c1986. 282 p. : ISBN 2-85939-287-4 : LC Card 87-104133
HC59.7 .D354 1986

Morineau, Michel. Pour une histoire économique vraie /. [Lille] , c1985. 512 p. : ISBN 2-85939-234-3 : LC Card 86-142388 DDC 330.9 19
HC51 .M64 1985

Les Economies non officielles / sous la direction de Edith Archambault et Xavier Greffe. Paris : La Découverte, 1984. 247 p. : ill. ; 25 cm. (Economie critique) Includes bibliographies. ISBN 2-7071-1441-3 : LC Card 86-460169
1. Informal sector (Economics). 2. Informal sector (Economics) - Europe, Eastern. 3. Informal sector (Economics) - Developing countries. I. Archambault, E. II. Greffe, Xavier. III. Series.
HD2341 .E26 1984

ECONOMIES OF SCALE.
Fanjul, Oscar. La eficiencia del sistema bancario español /. Madrid , c1985. 275 p. : ISBN 84-206-2439-X LC Card 87-111325
HG3184 .F36 1985

ECONOMIES OF SIZE. see **ECONOMIES OF SCALE.**

Economies of the United States and the Federal Republic of Germany. Die Wirtschaft der Vereinigten Staaten und der Bundesrepublik Deutschland . Bonn , c1977. 106 p. ; ISBN 3-87198-079-X LC Card 86-104673
HC106.7 .W57 1977

The economies of West Africa /. Rimmer, Douglas. London , c1984. xii, 308 p. : ISBN 0-297-78095-6 LC Card 87-673367
HC1000 .R56x 1984b

Economische monografieën/Universiteit van Amsterdam .
(4) Roobeek, Annemieke J. M., 1958- De rol van de technologie in de ekonomische theorievorming /. Amsterdam , c1987. 175 p. : ISBN 90-71302-06-7 : LC Card 87-132353
HC79.T4 R64 1987

Economische wetenschappen : eenheid in verscheidenheid? / auteurs, W. Albeda ... [et al.] ; discussianten, H. Booy ... [et al.] ; onder redactie van J. Muysken en H. Schreuder ; met een voorwoord van H.W. Lambers. Maastricht : Faculteit der Economische Wetenschappen, Rijksuniversiteit Limburg ; Assen : Van Gorcum, 1985. 224 p. ; 22 cm. Includes bibliographies. ISBN 90-232-2148-6 LC Card 86-111599
1. Economics - Congresses. 2. Industrial organization (Economic theory) - Congresses. 3. Labor economics - Congresses. I. Albeda, W. II. Muysken, J. III. Schreuder, H. IV. Rijksuniversiteit Limburg. Faculteit der Economische Wetenschappen.
HB21 .E248 1985

The Economist books.
Lewis, Colin David. Managing with micros . Oxford, England , 1984. 200 p. : LC Card 85-103102 DDC 658/.054 19
HF5548.2 .L425 1984 ***NYPL [JLE 86-2215]***

The Economist economics /. Pennant-Rea, Rupert. Harmondsworth, Middlesex, England , New York, U. S.A. , 1986. 197 p. : ISBN 0-14-022703-2 (pbk.) : LC Card 86-219602 DDC 330 19
HB171 .P458 1986

Economist (London, England) Targett, David. The Pocket guide to business numeracy /. Oxford, OX ; New York, NY, USA : x, 184 p. : ISBN 0-631-15124-9 : LC Card 86-31032 DDC 513/.93/0321 19
HF5695 .T34 1987

Economista paraguayo. Seminario Estrategia de Desarrollo en Condiciones de Oferta Abundante de Energía Eléctrica (1980 : Asunción, Paraguay) Memoria del Seminario Estrategia de Desarrollo en Condiciones de Oferta Abundante de Energía Eléctrica . Asunción, Paraguay [s.l.] , 1980. 165 p., [18] leaves of plates : LC Card 83-169471 DDC 363.6/2 19
HD9685.P32 S45 1980 ***NYPL [JLE 87-995]***

Les économistes distingués . Caro, Jean-Yves. Paris , c1983. 287 p. : ISBN 2-7246-0484-9 : LC Card 84-117472
HB71 .C28 1983

ECONOMISTS.
Hudson, William J. Business without economists . New York, N.Y. , c1987. 178 p. : ISBN 0-8144-5896-3 : LC Card 86-47812 DDC 658.4/0355 19
HB3730 .H83 1987

ECONOMISTS - ADDRESSES, ESSAYS, LECTURES.
Harcourt, Geoffrey Colin. Controversies in political economy . New York , 1986. 293 p. ; ISBN 0-8147-3437-5 : LC Card 85-31055 DDC 330.1 19
HB75 .H33 1986 ***NYPL [JLD 86-3571]***

ECONOMISTS - AUSTRIA - BIOGRAPHY.
Boos, Margarete. Die Wissenschaftstheorie Carl Mengers . Wien , 1986. xiii, 252 p. ; ISBN 3-205-05044-4 LC Card 86-209140
HB101.M5 B6 1986

Somary, Felix, 1881-1956. [Erinnerungen aus meinem Leben. English.] The raven of Zürich . London , New York , c1986. xii, 310 p. : ISBN 0-312-66407-9 LC Card 86-6662 DDC 330/.092/4 B 19
HB101.S6 A313 1986 ***NYPL [JFE 87-54]***

ECONOMISTS - BIOGRAPHY.
Lives of the laureates . Cambridge, Mass. , c1986. xii, 135 p. : ISBN 0-262-02255-9 LC Card 86-2919 DDC 330/.092/2 B 19
HB76 .L58 1986 ***NYPL [JFD 86-9827]***

ECONOMISTS - BRAZIL.
O Perfil do economista. [São Paulo, Brazil] [1984?] 60 p. : LC Card 87-402012 DDC 330/.092/2 19
HB123.B8 P47 1984

ECONOMISTS - BRAZIL - BIOGRAPHY.
Semana Josué de Castro e a nova geografia da fome, Rio de Janeiro, 19-24 de setembro de 1983 . [S.l. , 1983] 90 leaves : LC Card 86-201115
HD9000.5 .S3968 1983

ECONOMISTS - BULGARIA - BIOGRAPHY.
Krŭstiu Dobrev . Sofiia , 1987. 80 p., [16] p. of plates : LC Card 87-170598
HB108.3.D63 K78 1987

ECONOMISTS - GERMANY - BIOGRAPHY.
150 Jahre Promotion an der Wirtschaftswissenschaftlichen Fakultät der Universität Tübingen . Stuttgart , c1984. xxxvi, 809 p. : ISBN 3-8062-0409-8 LC Card 85-140557
HB74.9.G3 A15 1984 ***NYPL [JFE 87-1673]***

ECONOMISTS - GERMANY, WEST - BIOGRAPHY.
150 Jahre Promotion an der Wirtschaftswissenschaftlichen Fakultät der Universität Tübingen . Stuttgart , c1984. xxxvi, 809 p. : ISBN 3-8062-0409-8 LC Card 85-140557
HB74.9.G3 A15 1984 ***NYPL [JFE 87-1673]***

ECONOMISTS - GREAT BRITAIN - BIOGRAPHY.
Anikin, Andreĭ Vladimirovich. Uilʹiam Petti /. Moskva , 1986. 92, [3] p. ; LC Card 86-206468 DDC 330.15/3 19
HB103.P5 A83 1986

Skidelsky, Robert Jacob Alexander, 1939- John Maynard Keynes . London , 1983- v. <1 > ; ISBN 0-333-11599-6 (v. 1) : LC Card 86-217586 DDC 330.15/6 B 19
HB103.K47 S57 1983

Thirlwall, A. P. Nicholas Kaldor /. Washington Square, NY , 1987. xvii, 360 p., [8] pages of plates : ISBN 0-8147-8177-2 : LC Card 87-22065 DDC 330/.092/4 B 19
HB103.K36 T45 1987

Thomas Robert Malthus, critical assessments /. London , Dover, N.H. , c1986. 4 v. : ISBN 0-7099-3650-8 (set) : LC Card 85-22412 DDC 304.6/092/4 19
HB863 .T38 1986 ***NYPL [JFF 86-588]***

ECONOMISTS - HUNGARY.
Stanfield, J. Ron, 1945- The economic thought of Karl Polanyi . Basingstoke, Hampshire , 1986. x, 162 p. ; ISBN 0-333-39629-4 LC Card 87-673390
HB102.P64 S73x 1986b

ECONOMISTS - INDIA - BIOGRAPHY.
Haridasan, V., 1937- Dr. John Matthai, 1886-1959 . Cranganore, Trichur Dist., Kerala , 1986. xi, 192 p., [2] p. of plates : LC Card 86-903052 DDC 330/.092/4 B 19
HB126.I43 M374 1986

Narayan Prasad, P. S. C.D. Deshmukh, his contribution to monetary and economic policy /. New Delhi , c1985. xiv, 54 p., [1] leaf of plates : LC Card 85-905075 DDC 338.954 19
HC432.5.D47 N37 1985
NYPL [JLD 86-3239]

ECONOMISTS - ITALY - BIOGRAPHY.
Ahijado, Manuel. Piero Sraffa . Madrid , 1985. 90 p. ; ISBN 84-85942-31-0 LC Card 87-104173
HB109.S73 A35 1985

De Franchis, Carlo. Giammaria Ortes . Napoli , 1930. 165 p. ; LC Card 87-139766
HB109.O68 D4 1930

ECONOMISTS - MEXICO - BIOGRAPHY.
Flores, Edmundo, 1918- Historias de Edmundo Flores. México , 1983-<c1986. v. <1-2 > : ISBN 968-471-052-6 (v. 1) LC Card 83-199689
HB123.M43 F564 1983

López Aparicio, Alfonso. Alamán, primer economista de México /. México [1986] 118 p. ; ISBN 968-423-013-3 LC Card 87-403286 DDC 330/.092/4 B 19
HB123.M43 A435 1986

ECONOMISTS - MEXICO - POLITICAL ACTIVITY.
Cleaves, Peter S. Professions and the state . Tucson , c1987. xv, 147 p. : ISBN 0-8165-1016-4 (alk. paper) LC Card 87-5911 DDC 331.7/12/0972 19
HD8038.M6 C55 1987

ECONOMISTS - POLAND - BIOGRAPHY.
Z Husowa po berła rektorskie . Warszawa , 1986. 340 p., [25] p. of plates : ISBN 83-205-3745-2 : LC Card 85-126839
HB114.S79 Z2 1986

ECONOMISTS - SWEDEN - BIOGRAPHY.
Liedman, Sven-Eric, 1939- Den synliga handen . [Stockholm] [1986] 268 p. ; ISBN 91-7014-210-6 : LC Card 86-215138
HB116.5.B47 L54 1986

ECONOMISTS - UNITED STATES - BIOGRAPHY.
Neikirk, William. Volcker, portrait of the money man /. New York , Chicago, Ill. , c1987. xvi, 222 p. ; ISBN 0-86553-178-1 LC Card 87-19953 DDC 332.1/1/0924 B 19
HB119.V6 N45 1987

Powelson, John P., 1920- Facing social revolution . Boulder, Colo. , c1987. v, 146 p. ; ISBN 0-934449-03-1 : LC Card 86-32186 DDC 330/.092/4 B 19
HB119.P68 A3 1987

Ryan, Christopher K. (Christopher Keith) Harry Gunnison Brown, economist /. Boulder , 1987. xv, 179 p. ; ISBN 0-8133-7355-7 (pbk. : alk. paper) : LC Card 86-28994 DDC 330/.092/4 B 19
HB119.B65 R93 1987

ECONOMISTS - UNITED STATES - HISTORY - 19TH CENTURY.
Breaking the academic mould . Middletown, Conn. , 1988. p. cm. ISBN 0-8195-5176-7 : LC Card 87-21023 DDC 330/.07/1173 19
HB74.8 .B74 1988

Economy and environment . Perrings, Charles. Cambridge [Cambridgeshire] , New York , 1987. xv, 179 p. ; ISBN 0-521-34081-0 LC Card 87-18329 DDC 333.7 19
HD75.6 .P47 1987

Economy and food in ancient India /. Om Prakash, 1916- Delhi , 1987- v. <1- > ; ISBN 81-217-0027-2 : LC Card 87-902484 DDC 338.1/9/34 19
HC434 .O45 1987

Economy and people in the north / edited by P. Loveday and D. Wade-Marshall. Darwin : Australian National University, North Australia Research Unit, 1985. v, 294 p. : ill. ; 30 cm. (Monograph / Australian National University. North Australia Research Unit) Includes bibliographies. ISBN 0-86784-591-0 (pbk.) : LC Card 86-159263 DDC 330.9719/03 19
1. Northern Territory - Economic conditions - Congresses. 2. Northern Territory - Industries - Congresses. I. Loveday, Peter. II. Wade-Marshall, D. III. Series: Monograph / Australian National University. North Australia Research Unit.
HC607.N6 E27 1985

Economy and society in Hungary / editors, Rudolf Andorka and László Bertalan ; [translations, József Böröcz]. Budapest : Karl Marx University of Economic Sciences, Dept. of Sociology, 1986. 331 p. : ill. ; 21 cm. (Hungarian sociological studies . 3) The English version of the papers were prepared for distribution at the XI World Congress of Sociology. Includes bibliographies. LC Card 87-147704 DDC 330.9439/053 19
1. Hungary - Economic conditions - 1945-. 2. Hungary - Social conditions - 1945-. 3. Hungary - Politics and government - 1945-. I. Andorka, Rudolf. II. Bertalan, László. III. Series.
HC300.28 .E36 1986

Economy & society paperbacks.
The Value dimension . London , New York , 1986. 239 p. ; ISBN 0-7102-0766-2 (pbk.) : LC Card 87-109334 DDC 338.5/21 19
HB203 .V33 1986

The economy of Abu Dhabi . ʻUtaybah, Mānīʻ Saʻīd, 1946- [S.l. , 197-?] (Beirut, Lebanon : Commercial & Industrial Press) 247 p. ; LC Card 86-965159
HC415.36.Z7 A288 1970z

The economy of détente . Sokoloff, Georges. [Economie de la détente. English.] Leamington Spa ; New York : p. cm. ISBN 0-907582-62-1 : LC Card 86-32627 DDC 382/.0947 19
HF3646.5 .S6513 1987

The Economy of early America : the revolutionary period, 1763-1790 / edited by Ronald Hoffman ... [et al.]. Charlottesville : Published for the United States Capitol Historical Society by the University Press of Virginia, 1988. xvi, 334 p. : ill. ; 24 cm. (Perspectives on the American Revolution) Includes bibliographical references and index. ISBN 0-8139-1139-7 LC Card 87-6169 DDC 330.973/02 19
1. United States - Economic conditions - To 1865 - Regional disparities. 2. Great Britain - Colonies - America - Economic conditions - Regional disparities. I. Hoffman, Ronald, 1941-. II. Series.
HC104 .E26 1988

The economy of Himachal Pradesh . Sharma, L. R., 1934- Delhi, India , 1987. vii, 167 p. ; LC Card 86-903541 DDC 330.954/52 19
HC437.H5 S52 1987

The Economy of Latin America and the Caribbean : guidelines for a comprehensive approach to the foreign debt problem and possible action by the inter-American system : informative document / Organization of American States, Executive Secretariat for Economic and Social Affairs. Washington, D.C. : General Secretariat, Organization of American States, [1986] v, 30 p. ; 28 cm. "January 1986." ISBN 0-8270-2333-2 (pbk.) : LC Card 86-203268 DDC 336.3/435/09729 19
1. Debts, External - Latin America. 2. Loans, Foreign - Latin America. 3. Latin America - Economic policy. I. Organization of American States. Executive Secretariat for Economic and Social Affairs.
HJ8514.5 .E34 1986

The economy of the earth . Sagoff, Mark. Cambridge [Cambridgeshire] , New York , 1988. p. cm. ISBN 0-521-34113-2 LC Card 87-16091 DDC 363.7/056/0973 19
HC110.E5 S34 1988

The Economy, small business, and the federal budget : a report / prepared for the use of the Joint Economic Committee, Congress of the United States, by the Republican staff of the Joint Economic Committee. Washington : U. S. G.P.O. : For sale by the Supt. of Docs., Congressional Sales Office, U. S. G.P.O., 1986. v, 20 p. : ill. ; 24 cm. (S. prt. . 99-174) At head of title: 99th Congress, 2d session. Joint committee print. Distributed to some depository libraries in microfiche. Shipping list no.: 86-713-P. "August 15, 1986." Item 1000-B, 1000-C (microfiche) LC Card 86-603392 DDC 338.6/42/0973 19
1. United States - Economic conditions - 1981-. 2. Small business - United States. 3. Budget - United States. I. United States. Congress. Joint Economic Committee. II. Series.
HC106.8 .E35 1986

Ecrement, Marc. Stratégies d'industrialisation et maîtrise du développement. Paris , c1984. 115, [3] p. : ISBN 2-86844-002-9 LC Card 84-248894
HC59.7 .S854 1984

The ECU market : current developments and future prospects of the European currency unit / edited by Richard M. Levich, Andrea Sommariva. Lexington, Mass. : Lexington Books, c1987. xiii, 246 p. : ill. ; 24 cm. (Lexington Books/Salomon Brothers Center series on financial institutions and markets) Includes bibliographies and index. ISBN 0-669-13833-9 (alk. paper) LC Card 87-4185 DDC 332.4/56094 19
1. European currency unit. 2. Capital market - European Economic Community countries. I. Levich, Richard M. II. Sommariva, Andrea. III. Series.
HG930.5 .E27 1987

ECUADOR - APPROPRIATIONS AND EXPENDITURES.
Análisis del presupuesto general del estado de 1986. [Quito, Ecuador] [1986] ii, 2, 26, 8 p. ; LC Card 87-115859
HJ955 .A523 1986

ECUADOR - COMMERCE.
Coyuntura económica ecuatoriana, 1985-1986. [Quito, Ecuador] [1986] i, 39 p. ; LC Card 86-217289
HC202 .C73 1986

León, I. Josefina. El quantum de exportaciones del Ecuador (1970-1983) /. [Guayaquil] , 1985. 93 p. : LC Card 87-123381 DDC 382/.6/09866 19
HF3431.5 .L46 1985

ECUADOR - COMMERCE - ANDES REGION.
El Acuerdo de Cartagena y el trato preferencial en favor de Bolivia y Ecuador. [Buenos Aires, Argentina] [1982] 148 leaves ; LC Card 86-202605 DDC 337.1/8 19
HC167.A5 A285 1982

ECUADOR - COMMERCE - DIRECTORIES.
Directorio nacional de pequeñas industrias . [Quito] , 1985. 264 p. ; LC Card 86-192239
HF3433 .D59 1985

ECUADOR - DEPENDENCY ON FOREIGN COUNTRIES.

Ecuador, política económica--teoría y realidad. [Guayaquil] [1986- v. <1-3 > ; LC Card 87-105005
HF1519 .E3 1986

Ecuador. Dirección General de Fomento de la Pequeña Industria y Artesanía. Directorio nacional de pequeñas industrias . [Quito] , 1985. 264 p. ; LC Card 86-192239
HF3433 .D59 1985

Ecuador. Dirección Nacional de Personal. Gestión de empresas públicas en América Latina . Quito, Ecuador , c1986. 146 p. : LC Card 87-401599 DDC 350/.0092/098 19
HD4010.5 .G47 1986

ECUADOR - ECONOMIC CONDITIONS.
Ecuador, pasado y presente /. Quito, Ecuador , 1982. 273 p. ; LC Card 83-156158
HC202 .E28 1982

González S., Víctor A. Las tierras comunales en el Ecuador /. Guayaquil, Ecuador , 1982. 109 p. ; LC Card 87-672596
HD1289.E2 G66x 1982

ECUADOR - ECONOMIC CONDITIONS - 1918-
Díaz O., Oswaldo A. Ecuador, estudios retrospectivos /. Bogotá, Colombia , 1980. 120 p. ; LC Card 83-147164
HC202 .D48 1980

ECUADOR - ECONOMIC CONDITIONS - 1918-1972.
Ycaza, Patricio. Movimiento obrero, estado y modernización capitalista en el Ecuador, 1960-1983 /. Ecuador [1985 or 1986] 38 p. ; LC Card 86-171415
HC202 .Y35 1985

ECUADOR - ECONOMIC CONDITIONS - 1972-
Baez, René. Ciencia y transformación social . Quito, Ecuador , 1986. 141 p. ; LC Card 86-214736 DDC 330.9/0038 19
HC125 .B195 1986

Coyuntura económica ecuatoriana, 1985-1986. [Quito, Ecuador] [1986] i, 39 p. ; LC Card 86-217289
HC202 .C73 1986

El Ecuador en la encrucijada . Quito , 1986. 307 p. : LC Card 87-400394 DDC 331.12/09866 19
HD5758.A6 E28 1986

Pacheco, Lucas. La política económica en el Ecuador . Quito, Ecuador , 1985. 219 p. ; LC Card 87-400294 DDC 338.9866 19
HC202 .P26 1985

La Política económica del gobierno de Febres Cordero. Quito, Ecuador [1986] 84 p. : LC Card 87-403470
HC202 .P65 1986

Resultados y perspectivas de la economía ecuatoriana, 1984-1985. Quito, Ecuador [1985] 27, 7 p. ; LC Card 85-215488
HC202 .R47 1985

Ycaza, Patricio. Movimiento obrero, estado y modernización capitalista en el Ecuador, 1960-1983 /. Ecuador [1985 or 1986] 38 p. ; LC Card 86-171415
HC202 .Y35 1985

ECUADOR - ECONOMIC CONDITIONS - 1972- - CONGRESSES.
La Crisis de la economía ecuatoriana . Quito , 1986. 232 p. : LC Card 87-400395 DDC 330.9866/074 19
HC202 .C755 1986

ECUADOR - ECONOMIC POLICY.
Consejo Nacional de Desarrollo (Ecuador). Secretaría General de Planificación. Plan Nacional de Desarrollo, 1985-1988 /. [Quito, Ecuador] [1985] 3 leaves, iv, 218 p. : LC Card 86-146646 DDC 338.9866 19
HC202 .C675 1985b

Lineamientos generales para el Plan de Desarrollo, 1984-1988. Quito, Ecuador , 1985. ii, 42 leaves ; LC Card 86-149211
HC202 .L52 1985

Pacheco, Lucas. La política económica en el Ecuador . Quito, Ecuador , 1985. 219 p. ; LC Card 87-400294 DDC 338.9866 19
HC202 .P26 1985

La Política económica del gobierno de Febres Cordero. Quito, Ecuador [1986] 84 p. : LC Card 87-403470
HC202 .P65 1986

Resultados y perspectivas de la economía ecuatoriana, 1984-1985. Quito, Ecuador [1985] 27, 7 p. ; LC Card 85-215488
HC202 .R47 1985

El Ecuador en la encrucijada : crisis, empleo y desarrollo. Quito : Corporación Editora Nacional, 1986. 307 p. : ill. ; 21 cm. (Biblioteca de ciencias sociales. v. 11) On cover: Federación Nacional de Economistas del Ecuador. Includes bibliographical references. LC Card 87-400394 DDC 331.12/09866 19
1. Labor supply - Ecuador. 2. Unemployment, Structural - Ecuador. 3. Ecuador - Economic conditions - 1972-. I. Corporación Editora Nacional (Quito, Ecuador). II. Federación Nacional de Economistas del Ecuador. III. Series: Biblioteca de ciencias sociales (Quito, Ecuador) , v. 11.
HD5758.A6 E28 1986

Ecuador, estudios retrospectivos /. Díaz O., Oswaldo A. Bogotá, Colombia , 1980. 120 p. ; LC Card 83-147164
HC202 .D48 1980

ECUADOR - FOREIGN ECONOMIC RELATIONS.
Ecuador, política económica--teoría y realidad. [Guayaquil] [1986- v. <1-3 > ; LC Card 87-105005
HF1519 .E3 1986

ECUADOR - FOREIGN ECONOMIC RELATIONS - CONGRESSES.
Seminario de Operaciones Internacionales (1981 : Quito, Ecuador) Memorias del Seminario de Operaciones Internacionales /. Quito, Ecuador , 1981. 156 p., [2] p. of plates : LC Card 86-174597
HF1519 .S46 1981

ECUADOR - INDUSTRIES.
Abril-Ojeda, Galo. Política monetaria y desarrollo industrial en el Ecuador, 1970-1983 /. Quito , 1985. 118 p. : ISBN 91-85894-10-9 LC Card 86-103812
HG865 .A27 1985

ECUADOR - INDUSTRIES - HISTORY - 20TH CENTURY.
Puig Vilazar, Carlos. Sacrificio de un pueblo, 15 de noviembre de 1922 /. [Guayaquil, Ecuador] , 1983. 88 p. ; LC Card 86-115462
HD5358.A6 P85 1983

ECUADOR - MANUFACTURES.
Villalobos, Fabio. La industrialización ecuatoriana y la utilización de los recursos productivos, 1976-1983 /. Quito, Ecuador , 1987. 148 p. : LC Card 87-404654 DDC 338.09866 19
HC204.5.I52 V55 1987

Ecuador, pasado y presente / Leonardo Mejía ... [et al.]. Quito, Ecuador : Editorial A. Crespo Encalada, 1982. 273 p. ; 21 cm. "Instituto de Investigaciones Económicas." Includes bibliographical references. LC Card 83-156158
1. Ecuador - Economic conditions. I. Mejía, Leonardo. II. Universidad Central de Ecuador. Instituto de Investigaciones Económicas.
HC202 .E28 1982

Ecuador, Plan Nacional de Desarrollo, 1985-1988. Consejo Nacional de Desarrollo (Ecuador). Secretaría General de Planificación. Plan Nacional de Desarrollo, 1985-1988 /. [Quito, Ecuador] [1985] 3 leaves, iv, 218 p. : LC Card 86-146646 DDC 338.9866 19
HC202 .C675 1985b

Ecuador, política económica--teoría y realidad. [Guayaquil] : Frente Democrático de Economistas, [1986- v. <1-3 > ; 22 cm. (Serie de publicaciones del Frente Democrático de Economistas, F.D.E) Includes bibliographical references. CONTENTS. - 1. Sector externo, Fondo Monetario Internacional, integración y dependencia / G. Salgado ... [et al.] -- 2. Inflación, precios, salarios y teoría monetaria / Carlos León G., Jorge Fernández L. -- 3. Coyuntura económica, decretos-leyes de urgencia y plan de desarrollo / L. Vicuña I., L. Roldós A., J. Moncada S. LC Card 87-105005
1. Ecuador - Foreign economic relations. 2. Ecuador - Dependency on foreign countries. 3. Investments, Foreign - Ecuador. 4. Andes region - Economic integration. 5. International Monetary Fund - Ecuador. I. Salgado, Germánico. II. Frente Democrático de Economistas (Ecuador). III. Series.
HF1519 .E3 1986

ECUADOR - POLITICS AND GOVERNMENT - 1944-
Díaz O., Oswaldo A. Ecuador, estudios retrospectivos /. Bogotá, Colombia , 1980. 120 p. ; LC Card 83-147164
HC202 .D48 1980

ECUADOR - RURAL CONDITIONS.
Tenencia de la tierra y desarrollo socio-económico del sector agrícola. [Guayaquil] [1981] xxv, 539 p., [16] leaves of plates : LC Card 87-673171
HD526 .T46x 1981

ECUADOR - SOCIAL CONDITIONS.
Díaz O., Oswaldo A. Ecuador, estudios retrospectivos /. Bogotá, Colombia , 1980. 120 p. ; LC Card 83-147164
HC202 .D48 1980

ECUADOR - SOCIAL POLICY.
Lineamientos generales para el Plan de Desarrollo, 1984-1988. Quito, Ecuador , 1985. ii, 42 leaves ; LC Card 86-149211
HC202 .L52 1985

Ecuador, tenencia de la tierra y desarrollo socio-económico del sector agrícola. Tenencia de la tierra y desarrollo socio-económico del sector agrícola. [Guayaquil] [1981] xxv, 539 p., [16] leaves of plates : LC Card 87-673171
HD526 .T46x 1981

Ecuarunari (Organization) Luchando por nuestros derechos . Quito , 1984. 50 p. : LC Card 86-174980
HD1531.L3 L79 1984

Edding, Cornelia, 1943- Einbruch in den Herrenclub : von den Erfahrungen, die Frauen auf Männerposten machen / Cornelia Edding.Originalausg. Reinbek bei Hamburg : Rowohlt, 1983. 184 p. : ports. ; 20 cm. (Frauen aktuell) Rororo aktuell Bibliography: p. 184. ISBN 3-499-15251-7 (pbk.) LC Card 87-673369
1. Women in the professions - Germany (West) - Case studies. 2. Women executives - Germany (West) - Case studies. 3. Women - Employment - Germany (West) - Case studies. 4. Sex discrimination in employment - Germany (West) - Case studies. I. Title. II. Series.
HD6054.2.G3 E33x 1983

Edelson, Miriam. Challenging unions : feminist process and democracy in the labour movement / Miriam Edelson. Ottawa, Ont. : Canadian Research Institute for the Advancement of Women, 1987. 28 p. ; 29 cm. (Feminist perspectives . no. 8) Bibliography: p. 26. ISBN 0-919653-64-2 (pbk.) : LC Card 87-165425 DDC 331.88/088042 19
1. Women in trade-unions - Canada. I. Title. II. Series.
HD6079.2.C2 E34 1987

Edelstein, Joel C. Chilcote, Ronald H. Latin America . Boulder , 1986. xv, 175 p. ; ISBN 0-8133-0239-0 (pbk.) : LC Card 85-13899 DDC 338.98 19
HC125 .C487 1986 ***NYPL [JLE 86-4264]***

Edelston, Bruce S. Newman, Marie Mastin. The vital link . Washington, DC , c1986. vii, 48 p. : ISBN 0-931032-21-0 (pbk.) LC Card 86-200991 DDC 363.6/2/0973 19
HD9685.U5 N493 1986

Eden, M. J. (Michael John) Remote sensing and tropical land management /. [New York] , c1986. xii, 365 p., [16] p. of plates : ISBN 0-471-90889-4 : LC Card 85-17932 DDC 333.73/13/028 19
HD108.8 .R45 1986 ***NYPL [JLE 87-943]***

EDGAR (INFORMATION RETRIEVAL SYSTEM)
Shad, John S. R., 1923- Statement of John S.R. Shad, Chairman of the Securities and Exchange Commission, before the House Subcommittee on Oversight and Investigations of the Committee on Energy and Commerce, concerning EDGAR (Electronic Data Gathering, Analysis, and Retrieval System), March 14, 1985. [Washington, D.C. , 1985] 21, 5, 2, [12] p. : LC Card 85-148449 DDC 353.0082/58 19
HG4910 .S417 1985

Edgar M. Jopson memorial lectures. Synthesis, before and beyond February 1986 . [Philippines] , 1986. xiv, 114 p. : ISBN 971-91058-0-1 (pbk.) LC Card 87-112023

DDC 338.9599 19
HC452 .S96 1986

Edgcomb, Elaine. Monitoring and evaluating small business projects . [New York, NY] , c1987. ix, 262 p. : LC Card 87-6945 DDC 361.7 19
HD2346.5 .M65 1987

The edge . United States. President's Commission on Organized Crime. Washington, D.C. , 1985. 356 p. ; *NYPL [JLE 87-41]*

The edge . United States. President's Commission on Organized Crime. Washington, D.C. , 1986. xxii, 393 p. ; *NYPL [JLE 86-2671]*

Edgmand, Michael R. Macroeconomics : theory and policy / Michael R. Edgmand.3rd ed. Englewood Cliffs, N.J. : Prentice-Hall, c1987. xvi, 495 p. : ill. ; 25 cm. Includes bibliographies and index. ISBN 0-13-542952-8 LC Card 86-25360 DDC 339 19
1. Macroeconomics. I. Title.
HB172.5 .E36 1987

Edgren, Jan, 1940- Divisionalisering och därefter : erfarenheter av decentraliserad organisation i sju svenska företag / Jan Edgren, Eric Rhenman och Per-Hugo Skärvad. Stockholm : Management media, c1983. 157 p. : ill. ; 24 cm. Bibliography: p. [156]-157. ISBN 91-7722-013-7 : LC Card 83-186664
1. Decentralization in management - Sweden. 2. Corporations - Sweden. I. Rhenman, Eric. II. Skärvad, Per-Hugo. III. Title.
HD50 .E34 1983

EDI series in economic development.
Adler, Hans A. Economic appraisal of transport projects . Baltimore , 1987. xii, 235 p. : ISBN 0-8018-3411-2 : LC Card 86-21348 DDC 380.5/068/1 19
HE151 .A32 1987

Food policy . Baltimore , c1987. xiv, 567 p. : ISBN 0-8018-3500-3 (pbk.) : LC Card 86-27613 DDC 363.8/56/091724 19
HD9018.D44 F665 1987

Roth, Gabriel Joseph, 1926- The private provision of public services in developing countries /. New York , c1987. xv, 278 p. : ISBN 0-19-520544-8 : LC Card 86-23880 DDC 338.91/09172/4 19
HD4420.8 .R68 1987

Ediciones CEM.
Gálvez, Thelma. Yo trabajo así-- en casa particular /. Santiago, Chile , 1985. 113 p. : LC Card 86-208887
HD6072.2.C5 G35 1985

Ediciones del cincuentenario. Colección Enfoques.
García Molina, Carlos. Mortalidad infantil y clases sociales . [Medellín, Colombia] [1986] 103 p. : ISBN 958-9127-05-3 LC Card 87-400685 DDC 304.6/4/0880542 19
HB1323.I42 C74 1986

Ediciones del IDES .
(7) Monza, Alfredo. Sraffa y sus usos /. Buenos Aires , 1985. 102 p. : ISBN 950-43-0654-3 LC Card 86-172226
HB117.S73 M66 1985

Edificación, 1972-1984. Buenos Aires : República Argentina, Presidencia de la Nación, Secretaría de Planificación, Instituto Nacional de Estadística y Censos, 1986. 36 p. : ill. ; 30 cm. (Recopilaciones INDEC . 3) Chiefly tables. LC Card 87-404780 DDC 338.4/7624/0982021 19
1. Construction industry - Argentina - Statistics. 2. Building permits - Argentina - Statistics. I. Instituto Nacional de Estadística y Censos (Argentina). II. Series.
HD9715.A72 E35 1986

Edin, Per-Anders. Individuella sysselsättningskonsekvenser av nedläggningar / Per-Anders Edin. Helsingfors : Forskningsinstituitet [sic] vid Svenska handelshögskolan, [1984] 20 leaves ; 30 cm. (Meddelanden från Svenska handelshögskolan, 0357-4598 = Swedish School of Economics and Business Administration working papers . 119 (1984)) "Augusti 1984." Bibliography: leaf 20. ISBN 951-555-208-7 LC Card 85-151846
1. Unemployment - Sweden - Mathematical models. I. Series: Meddelanden fran Svenska handelshögskolan , 119. II. Title.
HD5803 .E33 1984

Edition Dräger-Stiftung .
(Bd. 7) Dräger, Heinrich, 1898- Zu wenig Arbeit für zu viele Menschen . Stuttgart , 1984. 125 p. : ISBN 3-87959-220-9 LC Card 84-198317
HD5779 .D68 1984

(Bd. 8) Welthandel morgen . Stuttgart , 1984. 275 p. : ISBN 3-87959-225-X LC Card 85-132786
HF4055 .W45 1984

Edition Philosophie und Sozialwissenschaften .
(6) Spurk, Jan. Soziologie der französischen Arbeiterbewegung /. Berlin , c1986. 317 p. ; ISBN 3-88619-606-2 LC Card 87-235004 DDC 331.88/0944 19
HD6684 .S68 1986

EDITM (Firm)
Répertoire financier et fiscal du Cameroun . Le Vésinet, France [1987?] 147 p. ; LC Card 87-124445
HJ1489 .R46 1987

Répertoire financier et monétaire du Sénégal, 1985. Le Vésinet, France [1985?] ii, 98 leaves ; LC Card 86-202435
HJ2184.5 .R46 1985

Editorial Integrity Project (U. S.) Statement of principles of editorial integrity in public broadcasting /. Columbia, S.C. (P.O. Box 5966, Columbia 29250) [1985] 21 p. : LC Card 87-126452 DDC 384.54/53 19
HE8689.8 .S72 1986

Editorial Porvenir. Historia gráfica de las luchas populares en Costa Rica, 1870-1930. San José, Costa Rica , 1986- v. <1 > : ISBN 997-7944-12-1 (v. 1) LC Card 87-158835 DDC 305.5/62/097286 19
HD8138 .H57 1986

Editorial research reports.
Beyond Reagan . Washington, D.C. , c1987. v, 209 p. : ISBN 0-87187-437-7 (pbk.) : LC Card 87-3057 DDC 338.973 19
HC106.8 .B47 1987

Editorial research reports on the American work ethic. Washington [1973] iii, 180 p. ISBN 0-87187-042-8 LC Card 72-94080 DDC 331.1/1/0973
HD8072 .E34 *NYPL [JLD 86-1374]*

Editorial research reports on the American work ethic. Washington, Congressional Quarterly [1973] iii, 180 p. illus. 23 cm. Originally published separately in Editorial Research reports. CONTENTS. - Gimlin, H. Foreword.--Deans, R. C. Productivity and the new work ethic.--Shaffer, H. B. Four-day week.--Shaffer, H. B. Blue-collar America.--Gerber, W. Changing corporate world.--Deans, R. C. Technology lag in America.--Costello, M. Education for jobs.--Deans, R. C. Unemployment in recessions.--Gerber, W. Jobs for the future.--Deans, R. C. Leisure business. ISBN 0-87187-042-8 LC Card 72-94080 DDC 331.1/1/0973
1. Labor and laboring classes - United States - 1970- - Addresses, essays, lectures. 2. Work ethic - United States - Addresses, essays, lectures. I. Congressional Quarterly, inc. II. Editorial research reports.
HD8072 .E34 *NYPL [JLD 86-1374]*

Edizioni del lavoro. Cos'e il sindacato. Roma , c1986. 76 p. : ISBN 88-7910-145-5 : LC Card 86-163777
HD6709 .C675 1986

Edme, Robin. Les Industries agro-alimentaires . Paris [1986], c1987. 164 p. : ISBN 2-11-001722-8 : LC Card 87-167615
HD9012.5 .I53 1987

Edmonson, James M. From Mecanicien to ingenieur : technical education and the machine building industry in nineteenth-century France / by James M. Edmonson. New York, NY : Garland, 1987. x, 631 p. ; 24 cm. (Modern European history) Thesis (Ph. D.)--University of Delaware, 1981. Bibliography: p. 599-631. ISBN 0-8240-8036-X (alk. paper) : LC Card 87-300 DDC 338.4/76218/0944 19
1. Machinery industry - France - History - 19th century. 2. Machinists - France - History - 19th century. 3. Technicians in industry - France - History - 19th century. 4. Technical education - France - History - 19th century. I. Title. II. Series.
HD9705.F7 E35 1987

Edo, Junko, 1947- Japanese aid to the Pacific islands region / by Junko Edo. Honolulu, Hawaii, USA : Pacific Islands Development Program, East-West Center, 1986. x, 94 p. ; 23 cm. (Research report series . 4) Originally presented as the author's thesis (M.A.--University of Hawaii, 1986?) Bibliography: p. 92-94. ISBN 0-86638-090-6 (pbk.) LC Card 87-5293 DDC 338.91/52/09 19
1. Economic assistance, Japanese - Oceania. I. Series: Research report series (Pacific Islands Development Program (East-West Center)) , no. 4. II. Title.
HC681. E36 1986

Edo no shokunin . Nakae, Katsumi, 1935- Tōkyō , 1986. 229 p. : ISBN 4-88470-522-X : LC Card 86-184888
HD2346.J3 N26 1986 <Orien Japan> *NYPL [*OSM 87-1217]*

EDP, controls and auditing /. Porter, W. Thomas. Boston, Mass. , c1987. xviii, 617 p. : ISBN 0-534-07092-2 : LC Card 86-27564 DDC 657/.45/0285 19
HF5548.35 .P67 1987

Edsforth, Ronald, 1948- Class conflict and cultural consensus : the making of a mass consumer society in Flint, Michigan / Ronald Edsforth. New Brunswick, N.J. : Rutgers University Press, c1987. xvi, 294 p. ; 23 cm. (Class and culture) Includes index. Bibliography: p. 279-287. ISBN 0-8135-1184-4 LC Card 86-7955 DDC 330.9774/37 19
1. Automobile industry and trade - Michigan - Flint. 2. Automobile industry workers - Michigan - Flint. 3. Flint (Mich.) - Economic conditions. 4. Flint (Mich.) - Social conditions. I. Title. II. Series.
HC108.F55 E37 1987 *NYPL [JLE 87-978]*

Edström, N. F. (Nils Fritiof), 1918- Ekonomiordbok : svensk-engelsk fackordbok för ekonomifunktionen med begreppsförklaringar / N.F. Edström, L.A. Samuelson, O.K. Böök.2. uppl. Stockholm : Norstedt, c1984. 145 p. : ill. ; 23 cm. Bibliography: p. 9-10. ISBN 91-1-847152-8 : LC Card 84-253890
1. Economics - Dictionaries - Swedish. 2. Swedish language - Dictionaries - English. I. Samuelson, Lars A. II. Böök, O. K. (Ole K.). III. Title.
HB61 .E29 1984 *NYPL [JFD 87-1265]*

Educação & produtividade /. Reis, Ulysses A. (Ulysses Alves) Salvador-BA [Rio de Janeiro] , 1984. 184 p. : ISBN 85-85023-05-8 LC Card 87-130042 DDC 331.11/8/0981 19
HC190.L3 R45 1984

Educação e produtividade. Reis, Ulysses A. (Ulysses Alves) Educação & produtividade /. Salvador-BA [Rio de Janeiro] , 1984. 184 p. : ISBN 85-85023-05-8 LC Card 87-130042 DDC 331.11/8/0981 19
HC190.L3 R45 1984

The educated woman and professionalization . Antler, Joyce. New York , 1987. x, 448 p. ; ISBN 0-8240-6839-4 (alk. paper) : LC Card 87-17604 DDC 331.4/11423 19
HD6054.2.U6 A57 1987

Educated women.
Antler, Joyce. The educated woman and professionalization . New York , 1987. x, 448 p. ; ISBN 0-8240-6839-4 (alk. paper) : LC Card 87-17604 DDC 331.4/11423 19
HD6054.2.U6 A57 1987

EDUCATION, ADULT. see **ADULT EDUCATION.**

EDUCATION - AIMS AND OBJECTIVES - CONGRESSES.
Education and the new international order /. New Delhi , 1983, c1982. xx, 147 p. ; LC Card 83-902560 DDC 370/.11/5 19
HF1411 .E28 1983 *NYPL [JLD 86-3707]*

Education and employment from world capitalism to the rural Thais . Thailand. Samnakngān Khana Kammakān Kansksā hæng Chāt. Bangkok, Thailand , 1985. 46 p. : LC Card 86-915875 DDC 331.13/79593 19
HD5822.55.A6 T47 1985

Education and employment in agriculture, India . Abraham, A. S. (Abraham Saktimangalam), 1944- New Delhi , 1985. vii, 111 p. ; LC Card 85-904717 DDC 331.12/93/0954 19
HD1537.I4 A587 1985
NYPL [JLD 86-2251]

EDUCATION AND STATE - GERMANY, WEST.
Pieper, Beate. Vom Lehrermangel zur Lehrerarbeitslosigkeit . Münster , 1984. ix, 265 p. : ISBN 3-923881-11-8 : LC Card 85-195712 DDC 331.12 19
LB2833.4.G4 P54 1984
NYPL [JLD 87-1161]

EDUCATION AND STATE - JAPAN.
Reed, Steven R., 1947- Japanese prefectures and policy making /. Pittsburgh, Pa. , 1986. ix, 197 p. ; ISBN 0-8229-3527-9 LC Card 85-22528 DDC 352/.00047 19
JS7373.A3 R44 1986 NYPL [JLE 86-3757]

EDUCATION AND STATE - KANSAS.
Kansas policy choices . Lawrence, Kan. , c1986. x, 210 p. : ISBN 0-7006-0302-6 (pbk.) LC Card 86-204211 DDC 338.9781 19
HC107.K2 K387 1986

EDUCATION AND STATE - KENYA.
Cheru, Fantu. Dependence, underdevelopment, and unemployment in Kenya . Lanham, MD , c1987. xvii, 198 p. : ISBN 0-8191-6539-5 (alk. paper) : LC Card 87-13710 DDC 331.13/77/096762 19
HD6276.K42 C46 1987

Keller, Edmond J. (Edmond Joseph), 1942- Education, manpower, and development . Nairobi , 1980. xi, 251 p. ; LC Card 81-980037 DDC 379.676/2 19
LC95.K4 K45 1980 NYPL [Sc D 86-948]

EDUCATION AND STATE - MATHEMATICAL MODELS.
Valencia Roa, Carlos Alberto, 1944- Social investments and economic growth /. 1974. xiv, 199 leaves : *NYPL [JLD 86-2961]*

EDUCATION AND STATE - MEXICO.
Mexican topics . [México, D.F.] [1986] 2 portfolios : LC Card 86-221843 DDC 972.08/3 19
HC135 .M52554 1986

EDUCATION AND STATE - PAKISTAN.
Ghafoor, Abdul. Development of human resources . Islamabad [1984] v, ii leaves, 99 p., v, ii leaves ; LC Card 85-932024 DDC 331.11/09549/1 19
HD5819 .G48 1984

Education and the new international order / edited by J. Veera Raghavan. New Delhi : National Institute of Educational Planning and Administration : Concept, 1983, c1982. xx, 147 p. ; 23 cm. Papers of a seminar organized jointly by the National Institute of Educational Planning and Administration and the International Institute for Educational Planning. Includes bibliographical references and index. LC Card 83-902560 DDC 370/.11/5 19
1. International economic relations - Congresses. 2. Education - Aims and objectives - Congresses. I. Veera Raghavan, J. II. National Institute of Educational Planning and Administration (India). III. International Institute for Educational Planning.
HF1411 .E28 1983 NYPL [JLD 86-3707]

Education and training for industrial development in Singapore and other ASEAN countries . Vente, Rolf E. Baden-Baden , Singapore , 1984. 175 p. : ISBN 3-7890-0941-5 LC Card 84-186381 DDC 331.25/92/0959 19
HD5715.5.S55 V46 1984
NYPL [JLD 86-2773]

Education and training for older persons : a program guide. [Washington, D.C.?] : Dept. of Education, Office of Vocational Adult Education : For sale by the Supt. of Docs., U. S. G.P.O., 1981. iii, 64 p. : ill. ; 28 cm. "January 1981." "Contract no. 300790706"--Verso of cover. Includes bibliographies.
1. Aged - Employment - United States. 2. Aged - Education - United States. 3. Occupational training - United States. I. United States. Office of Vocational and Adult Education. NYPL [JLF 86-1274]

EDUCATION - BRAZIL.
Schneider, José Odelso. Realidade brasileira . Porto Alegre-RS , c1986. 438 p. : LC Card 87-119174
HC187 .S393 1986

A Transição incompleta . Rio de Janeiro-RJ , 1986. 2 v. ; LC Card 86-224684
HC187 .T72 1986

EDUCATION - BRAZIL - GOIÁS (STATE)
O Estado de Goiás . Goiánia-GO , 1983. 406 p. : LC Card 86-224747
HC188.G6 E85 1983

EDUCATION - BRAZIL - HISTORY - 19TH CENTURY.
Década republicana /. Brasília, Distrito Federal , c1986. 2 v. ; ISBN 85-23-00062-3 (set) LC Card 86-211423
HJ923 .D38 1986

EDUCATION - BRAZIL - RIO GRANDE DO SUL.
Rio Grande do Sul (Brazil) Relatorios provinciaes. [1850-1859] 19 pamphlets in 1 v. ; LC Card 84-217966
HD4635.R54 R56 1850

EDUCATION, BUSINESS. see **BUSINESS EDUCATION.**

EDUCATION - COLOMBIA.
Reproducción de fuerza de trabajo, educación y migración en el sector rural colombiano /. Bogotá, Colombia , 1985. 98, [52] p. : LC Card 87-402979 DDC 331.1/09861 19
HD5757.A6 R46 1985

EDUCATION - CONGO (BRAZZAVILLE)
N'Dzaba, Tobi. L'enseignement technique et professionnel et la satisfaction des besoins en main-d'œuvre . Paris [1983] i, 139 p. : LC Card 85-189543
HD5845.A6 N38 1983

EDUCATION - COSTA RICA.
Costa Rica--respuesta al cuestionario del Banco Interamericano de Desarrollo /. [San José] [1962] 69 leaves (some folded) ; LC Card 85-117361
HC143 .C685 1962

EDUCATION - COSTA RICA - HISTORY - 20TH CENTURY.
Las Instituciones costarricenses del siglo XX /. [San José] , 1986. 376 p. ; ISBN 997-7232-96-5 LC Card 86-231789
HC143 .I54 1986

EDUCATION - DEVELOPING COUNTRIES - FINANCE.
Psacharopoulos, George. Education for development . New York , 1985. ix, 337 p. : ISBN 0-19-520477-8 LC Card 85-13782 DDC 338.9 19
HD75.7 .P77 1985 NYPL [JLE 86-1073]

Education Development Center. Cases in business decision making /. Chicago , c1987. ix, 102 p. : ISBN 0-03-009108-X (pbk.) LC Card 86-29131 DDC 658.4/033 19
HD30.23 .C375 1987

EDUCATION, DISTRIBUTIVE. see **DISTRIBUTIVE EDUCATION.**

EDUCATION - ECONOMIC ASPECTS - BRAZIL.
Reis, Ulysses A. (Ulysses Alves) Educação & produtividade /. Salvador-BA [Rio de Janeiro] , 1984. 184 p. : ISBN 85-85023-05-8 LC Card 87-130042 DDC 331.11/8/0981 19
HC190.L3 R45 1984

EDUCATION - ECONOMIC ASPECTS - DEVELOPING COUNTRIES.
Jimenez, Emmanuel, 1952- Pricing policy in the social sectors . Baltimore , 1987. v, 170 p. ; ISBN 0-8018-3501-1 : LC Card 86-27590 DDC 338.4/33621/091724 19
HJ7469 .J56 1987

EDUCATION - FINANCE.
Finanzsysteme, Ideal- und Realtypen . Berlin , c1983. 278 p. : ISBN 3-428-05419-9 LC Card 83-240120
HJ161 .F575 1983

Education for development . Psacharopoulos, George. New York , 1985. ix, 337 p. : ISBN 0-19-520477-8 LC Card 85-13782 DDC 338.9 19
HD75.7 .P77 1985 NYPL [JLE 86-1073]

EDUCATION - GERMANY (WEST) - CONGRESSES.
Arbeitsmarkterfahrungen und Berufsorientierungen Jugendlicher . München , c1983. 177 p. : ISBN 3-87966-202-9 LC Card 84-170074
HD6276.G4 A73 1983

EDUCATION - GREAT BRITAIN - HISTORY - 20TH CENTURY.
Barnett, Correlli. The pride and the fall . New York , 1987, c1986. xii, 359 p. ; ISBN 0-02-901851-X LC Card 86-25701 DDC 330.941/0854 19
HC256.4 .B28 1987

EDUCATION, HIGHER - ECONOMIC ASPECTS - SWITZERLAND - BASELLAND.
Frey, René Leo. Die regionale Ausstrahlung der Universität Basel /. Basel , c1984. 73 p. : LC Card 84-166545 DDC 378/.103 19
HC395 .A75 no. 8 LC238.4.S92B37

EDUCATION, HIGHER - INDIA - WEST BENGAL.
Bose, P. K. Graduate employment and higher education in West Bengal /. Paris , New Delhi , 1983. vi, 288, [1] p. : ISBN 0-85226-078-4 (pbk.) LC Card 83-163900 DDC 331.11/423 19
HD6278.I52 W473 1983
NYPL [JLD 86-2269]

EDUCATION - HONDURAS.
Honduras, informe general de la situación socioeconómica. Tegucigalpa, D.C., Honduras, C.A. , 1971. 2, 6, 155 leaves ; LC Card 86-120957
HC145 .H665 1971

EDUCATION - HUNGARY - PÉCS.
Pécs a szocialista fejlődés útján . Pécs [1984] 127 p. : ISBN 963-00-0782-7 (Magy. nemz. bibl.) LC Card 85-178275
HC300.292.P4 P43 1984

EDUCATION - INDIA - MAHARASHTRA.
Desaraḍā, Eca. Ema. Śetī, udyoga, āṇi śikshaṇa . Auraṅgābāda , 1986. 18, 148 p. ; LC Card 87-900720
HC437.M32 D47 1986

EDUCATION, INDUSTRIAL. see **TECHNICAL EDUCATION.**

EDUCATION - IVORY COAST.
Ahonzo, Etienne. Population de la Côte d'Ivoire . Abidjan , 1984. ix, 324 p. : LC Card 86-110796 DDC 304.6/09666/8 19
HB3666.A3 A46 1984 NYPL [JLF 86-1466]

Education, manpower, and development . Keller, Edmond J. (Edmond Joseph), 1942- Nairobi , 1980. xi, 251 p. ; LC Card 81-980037 DDC 379.676/2 19
LC95.K4 K45 1980 NYPL [Sc D 86-948]

Education, manpower, and development in Singapore /. Pang, Eng Fong. Kent Ridge, Singapore , c1982. 242 p. : ISBN 997-16-9053-5 (bound) LC Card 83-941002 DDC 331.11/09595/7 19
HD5823.A6 P35 1982 NYPL [JLD 86-2364]

EDUCATION - NIGERIA.
Nigeria . Hyattsville, Md. , 1975. iii, 35 p. ; LC Card 85-114200
HC1055 .N533 1975

EDUCATION - OBJECTIVES. see **EDUCATION - AIMS AND OBJECTIVES.**

EDUCATION OF ADULTS. see **ADULT EDUCATION.**

EDUCATION OF WOMEN - AUSTRALIA.
O'Donnell, Carol. The basis of the bargain . Sydney , Boston , 1984. 186 p. ; ISBN 0-86861-497-1 LC Card 84-70146 DDC 331.4/133/0994 19
HD6060.5.A8 O36 1984
NYPL [JLD 86-2017]

EDUCATION - PERU - ORIENTE.
Peru, Kolonisation und Abhängigkeit . Saarbrücken , Fort Lauderdale , 1981. 192 p. : ISBN 3-88156-165-X : LC Card 82-104103
HD1905.O75 P47 1981

Education policy & development.
Bank investments and funds management. Washington, D.C. (1120 Connecticut Ave., N.W., Washington 20036) , c1987. vii, 357 p. : LC Card 87-405100 DDC 332.1/068/1 19
HG1615.25 .B36 1987

Ruth, George E. Commercial lending /. Washington, D.C. (1120 Connecticut Ave., N.W., Washington 20036) , c1987. vi, 427 p. : LC Card 87-405117 DDC 332.1/753/0685 19
HG1642.U5 R88 1987

EDUCATION, PROFESSIONAL. see **PROFESSIONAL EDUCATION.**

EDUCATION, RURAL - SENEGAL.
International Labour Organisation. Formation professionnelle rurale, SEN/71/526 . Genève , 1976. ii, 69 p. : ISBN 92-2-201512-6 LC Card 84-125056
HD5716.A292 S385 1976

EDUCATION, SECONDARY - CURRICULA.
Williams, Sonja, 1953- Exploding the hunger myths . San Francisco , c1987. xv, 173 p. : ISBN 0-935028-23-4 (pbk.) : LC Card 87-3360

DDC 363.8/07/1273 19
HD9000.5 .W476 1987

EDUCATION, SEX DISCRIMINATION IN. see **SEX DISCRIMINATION IN EDUCATION.**

EDUCATION - SOCIAL AND ECONOMIC ASPECTS. see **EDUCATION - ECONOMIC ASPECTS.**

EDUCATION - SPAIN - JAÉN (PROVINCE)
Ortega Campos, Pedro. Una década de la economía jiennense, 1969-1979 /. [Jaén] [1984] 122 leaves : ISBN 84-505-0662-X LC Card 86-187312
HC387.J3 O76 1984

EDUCATION - SWEDEN - FORECASTING.
Trender och prognoser inför 90-talet. Stockholm , Örebro , 1985. 147 p. : ISBN 91-618-0001-5 LC Card 86-115921
LB2833 .S9 1985:2 HC375
NYPL [JLG 86-230]

EDUCATION, TECHNICAL. see **TECHNICAL EDUCATION.**

EDUCATION - URUGUAY.
Argenti, Gisela. Cambio técnico, trabajo y educación . Montevideo , 1985. 91, 70 leaves : LC Card 87-124118
HC235.T4 A74 1985

EDUCATION - VENEZUELA - STATISTICS.
Estadísticas sociales . Caracas, Venezuela , 1983. 2 v. ; LC Card 84-183391 DDC 312/.0987 19
HA1095 .E88 1983 ***NYPL [JLM 85-550]***

EDUCATION - VIRGINIA.
Virginia alternatives for the 1990s . Fairfax, Va. , Lanham, MD , 1987. 183 p. : ISBN 0-8026-0016-6 (alk. paper) : LC Card 87-22757 DDC 338.9755 19
HC107.V8 V435 1987

EDUCATIONAL AIMS AND OBJECTIVES. see **EDUCATION - AIMS AND OBJECTIVES.**

EDUCATIONAL ASSISTANCE.
Landrum, Roger L. The role of the Peace Corps in education in developing countries . Washington, D.C. [1984] iv, 258 p. ; LC Card 86-601664 DDC 371.2/07 19
HC60.5 .L27 1984

Educational Film Center (Annandale, Va.) Economics U$A. Chicago, IL , 1986. 1 videocassette (28 min.) : LC Card 86-708020 DDC 330.15 11
HB99.7

Educational Images (Firm) Postage stamps honoring animals [slide] /. Elmira, NY , 1984. 20 slides : LC Card 83-720055 DDC 769.56 11
HE6183.A5

EDUCATIONAL LEAVE - GERMANY, WEST.
Angsturlaub statt Bildungsurlaub . Frankfurt am Main , c1979. 179 p. : ISBN 3-88203-044-5 LC Card 85-167471
HD5257.2.G3 A54 1979

EDUCATIONAL PLANNING - DEVELOPING COUNTRIES.
Landrum, Roger L. The role of the Peace Corps in education in developing countries . Washington, D.C. [1984] iv, 258 p. ; LC Card 86-601664 DDC 371.2/07 19
HC60.5 .L27 1984

EDUCATIONAL PLANNING - INDIA.
Seth, Satish C. India, the next 7000 days /. New Delhi , c1985. xxiv, 312 p. [1] spolded Leaf of plates ; ISBN 0-85226-864-5 : LC Card 85-904799 DDC 338.5/443/0954 19
HC435.2 .S416 1985 ***NYPL [JLD 86-3377]***

EDUCATIONAL POLICY. see **EDUCATION AND STATE.**

EDUCATIONAL TECHNOLOGY INDUSTRIES.
Industrial training products & services markets. Norwalk, Conn., U. S.A. (6 Prowitt St., Norwalk 06855) , c1987. vi, 174 leaves ; LC Card 87-153554 DDC 381/.45658312404 19
HD9811.A2 I53 1987

EDUCATIONAL TECHNOLOGY INDUSTRIES - IRELAND.
Ireland. Courseware Committee. Report of the Courseware Committee . Dublin [1986] vii, 79 p. ; LC Card 86-226148 DDC 338.4/70053 19
HD9811.I732 I74 1986

Educational Testing Service. The Official guide for GMAT review /. Princeton, N.J. , c1986. 372 p. : ISBN 0-446-38435-6 (pbk.) : LC Card 86-229958 DDC 650/.076 19
HF1118 .O33 1986

Die EDV als Wettbewerbsinstrument des Handels /. Opitz, Otto. Augsburg [1986] 37 leaves : LC Card 87-407366 DDC 650/.028/5416 19
HF5548.2 .O656 1986

Edward Shann memorial lecture in economics. Gruen, F. H. (Fred Henry), 1921- How bad is Australia's economic performance and why? . Canberra, Australia [1985] 61 p. ; ISBN 0-949293-38-5 (pbk.) LC Card 86-228640 DDC 338.994 19
HC605 .G78 1985

Edwardes, Michael, 1930- Back from the brink : an apocalyptic experience / Michael Edwardes. London : Collins, 1983. 301 p. : ill. ; 23 cm. Includes index. ISBN 0-00-217098-1; 0-00-217089-1 LC Card 83-127870 DDC 338.7/6292/0941 19
1. Edwardes, Michael, 1930-. 2. BL Public Limited Company. 3. Automobile industry and trade - Great Britain - Management. 4. Automobile industry and trade - Government policy - Great Britain. I. Title.
HD9710.G74 B573 1983
NYPL [JLD 86-3553]

EDWARDES, MICHAEL, 1930-
Edwardes, Michael, 1930- Back from the brink . London , 1983. 301 p. : ISBN 0-00-217098-1; 0-00-217089-1 LC Card 83-127870 DDC 338.7/6292/0941 19
HD9710.G74 B573 1983
NYPL [JLD 86-3553]

Edwards, Alejandra Cox, 1954- Edwards, Sebastián. Monetarism and liberalization . Cambridge, MA , c1987. xxi, 233 p. : ISBN 0-88730-105-3 LC Card 86-25959 DDC 338.983 19
HC192 .E249 1987 ***NYPL [JLE 87-1485]***

Edwards, Chris, 1947- Developing microcomputer-based business systems / Chris Edwards. Alternate ed. Englewood Cliffs, N.J. : Prentice-Hall, 1983, c1982. x, 202 p. : ill. ; 23 cm. Includes index. Bibliography: p. 197. ISBN 0-13-204545-1 (pbk.) LC Card 83-60581 DDC 658/.054 19
1. Business - Data processing. 2. Microcomputers - Programming. I. Title.
HF5548.2 .E293 1983 ***NYPL [JLE 87-1181]***

Edwards, Christopher G. Johnston, Robert F. Entrepreneurial science . New York , 1987. 157 p. ; ISBN 0-89930-260-2 (lib. bdg. : alk. paper) LC Card 87-2518 DDC 338/.06 19
HC110.H53 J65 1987

Edwards, D. A. Gunner, T. J. Gunner and Edwards on the carriage of crude oil by sea /. London , New York , 1986. xii, 137 p. : ISBN 1-85044-073-5 (pbk.) : LC Card 86-224898 DDC 387.5/448 19
HE595.P4 G86 1986

Edwards, E. W. British diplomacy and finance in China, 1895-1914 / E.W. Edwards. Oxford [Oxfordshire] : Clarendon Press ; New York : Oxford University Press, 1987. 212 p. : map ; 23 cm. Bibliography: p. [202]-208. Includes index. ISBN 0-19-822916-X : LC Card 86-28567 DDC 337.41051 19
1. Great Britain - Foreign economic relations - China. 2. China - Foreign economic relations - Great Britain. 3. Great Britain - Foreign relations - China. 4. China - Foreign relations - Great Britain. 5. Investments, British - China - History. I. Title.
HF1534.5.C5 E39 1987

Edwards, J. S. S. (Jeremy S. S.) The economic analysis of accounting profitability / Jeremy Edwards, John Kay, Colin Mayer. Oxford : Clarendon Press ; New York : Oxford University Press, 1987. 133 p. : ill. ; 23 cm. Bibliography: p. [127]-130. Includes index. ISBN 0-19-877241-6 : LC Card 87-5575 DDC 657/.95 19
1. Corporations - Accounting. 2. Accounting - Effect of inflation on. 3. Deferred tax. I. Kay, J. A. (John Anderson). II. Mayer, C. P. (Colin P.). III. Title.
HF5686.C7 E34 1987

Edwards, Kenneth W., 1928- Your successful real estate career / Kenneth W. Edwards. New York, NY : American Management Association, c1987. vii, 184 p. ; 23 cm. Bibliography: p. 176-177. Includes index. ISBN 0-8144-7675-9 (pbk.) : LC Card 86-47810 DDC 333.33/023/73 19
1. Real estate business - Vocational guidance. I. Title.
HD1375 .E33 1987

Edwards, Paul. Working from home : everything you need to know about living and working under the same roof / Paul and Sarah Edwards.1st rev. ed. Los Angeles : J.P. Tarcher ; New York : Distributed by St. Martin's Press, c1987. xii, 436 p. : ill. ; 23 cm. Bibliography: p. 421-430. Includes index. ISBN 0-87477-457-8 (pbk.) LC Card 87-10188 DDC 658/.041 19
1. Home-based businesses. 2. Self-employed. I. Edwards, Sarah (Sarah A.). II. Title.
HD62.5 .E39 1987

Edwards, Peter, 1956- Waterfront warlord : the life and violent times of Hal C. Banks / Peter Edwards. Toronto, Ont., Canada : Key Porter Books, c1987. ix, 213 p. : ill. ; 24 cm. Includes index. ISBN 1-550-13013-7 : LC Card 87-150705 DDC 331.88/113875/0924 B 19
1. Banks, Hal, 1909-. 2. Seafarers' International Union of Canada - Biography. 3. Trade-unions - Canada - Officials and employees - Biography. 4. Crime and criminals - Canada - Biography. 5. Trade-unions - Canada - Corrupt practices. I. Title.
HD6525.B36 E39 1987

Edwards, Peter (Peter Roger) The horse trade of Tudor and Stuart England / Peter Edwards. Cambridge [Cambridgeshire] ; New York : Cambridge University Press, 1988. p. cm. Bibliography: p. Includes index. ISBN 0-521-35058-1 LC Card 87-24243 DDC 338.1/761/00942 19
1. Horse industry - England - History. I. Title.
HD9434.G73 E654 1988

Edwards, Richard, 1944- Unions in crisis and beyond . Dover, Mass. , c1986. xii, 340 p. : ISBN 0-86569-127-4 : LC Card 85-26646 DDC 331.88 19
HD6508 .U45 1986 ***NYPL [JLE 86-1936]***

Edwards, Sarah (Sarah A.) Edwards, Paul. Working from home . Los Angeles , New York , c1987. xii, 436 p. : ISBN 0-87477-457-8 (pbk.) LC Card 87-10188 DDC 658/.041 19
HD62.5 .E39 1987

Edwards, Sebastián. Monetarism and liberalization : the Chilean experiment / Sebastian Edwards and Alejandra Cox Edwards. Cambridge, MA : Ballinger Pub. Co., c1987. xxi, 233 p. : ill. ; 24 cm. Includes index. Bibliography: p. 211-226. ISBN 0-88730-105-3 LC Card 86-25959 DDC 338.983 19
1. Monetary policy - Chile. 2. Economic stabilization - Chile. 3. Chile - Economic policy. 4. Chile - Economic conditions - 1970-. I. Edwards, Alejandra Cox, 1954-. II. Title.
HC192 .E249 1987 ***NYPL [JLE 87-1485]***

Edye, Dave, 1953- Immigrant labour and government policy : the cases of the Federal Republic of Germany and France / Dave Edye. Aldershot, Hants, England ; Brookfield, Vt., U. S.A. : Gower, c1987. vi, 157 p. ; 23 cm. Bibliography: p. 147-157. ISBN 0-566-05361-6 : LC Card 86-25704 DDC 331.6/2/0943 19
1. Alien labor - Government policy - Germany (West). 2. Alien labor - Government policy - France. I. Title.
HD8458.A2 E26 1987

EEC air transport policy : opinion of the Economic and Social Committee [and] report of the Section for Transport [on] Civil aviation memorandum no. 2, Progress towards the development of a community air transport policy. Brussels : The Committee, [1985] iv, 72 p., [1] leaf of plates : ill. ; 30 cm. "Brussels, October 1985." Includes bibliographical references. LC Card 86-215015 DDC 387.7/094 19
1. Aeronautics, Commercial - Government policy - European Economic Community countries. I. Economic and Social Committee of the European Communities. II. Economic and Social Committee of the European Communities. Section for Transport.
HE9842.8 .E42 1985

The EEC and the third Multifiber Arrangement . Howell, Thomas R., 1949- Washington, DC , 1986. [14], 126, [12] p. : LC Card 86-224652 DDC 382/.45677/0094 19
HD9865.E852 H68 1986

EEC maritime transport policy : progress towards a common transport policy : communication and proposals / by the Commission to the Council. Brussels : European Communities, Economic and Social Committee, [1986] 88 p., [2] leaves : ill. ; 30 cm. LC Card 87-135615 DDC 387.5/094 19

1. Shipping - Government policy - European Economic Community countries. 2. Shipping - European Economic Community countries. I. Economic and Social Committee of the European Communities.
HE822.5 .E38 1986

Eekels, J. Ondernemen en vernieuwen . Delft, Netherlands , 1985. 240 p. : ISBN 90-6275-189-X LC Card 86-113900
HD2346.N4 O53 1985

Eerste en tweede verslae van die Gekose Komitee oor die Rekenings van die Suid-Afrikaanse Vervoerdienste. South Africa. Parliament. House of Assembly. Select Committee on the Accounts of the South African Transport Services. First and second reports of the Select Committee on the Accounts of the South African Transport Services . Pretoria [1983] vii, 74, 7 p. ; ISBN 0-06-210896-5 (pbk.) : LC Card 84-168506 DDC 354.680087/5 19
HE284.4 .S68 1983

Eesti ala mõisate nimestik / koostanud V. Naaber ; toimetanud S. Vahtre. Tallinn : "Eesti Raamat", 1981. 191 p. ; 22 cm. At head of title: Eesti NSV Ministrite Nõukogu i.a. Arhiivide Peavalitsus. Essti NSV Riiklik Ajaloo Keskarhiiv. Tartu Riiklik Ülikool. Bibliography: p. 187-191. LC Card 82-143283

1. Manors - Estonia - Names - Registers. 2. House names - Estonia - Registers. I. Naaber, V. II. Vahtre, S.
HD1329.E75 E37 1981
NYPL [JFD 86-6806]

Eesti NSV, teatmik /. Vanatoa, Ė. Kh. Tallinn , 1985. 33 p. ; LC Card 86-131324
HA1448.E8 V36 1985

El efecto de los shocks externos sobre el producto . Lagos, Luis Felipe. Santiago, Chile , 1985. 15, [8] leaves : LC Card 87-404321 DDC 339.383 19
HC195.I5 L34 1985

El Efecto que tendrían los aumentos de los peajes del Canal de Panamá sobre países seleccionados de América Latina y el Caribe : XVII Reunión Anual a Nivel Ministerial, 19-22 de octubre de 1982, Washington, D.C. Washington, D.C. : Secretaría General de la Organización de los Estados Americanos, [1982] iii, 76 p. ; 28 cm. "OEA/Ser. H/X.40 CIES/3712 12 octubre 1982. Original: español." LC Card 85-176637

1. Panama Canal (Panama) - Rates and tolls. 2. Latin America - Commerce - Case studies. 3. Caribbean Area - Commerce - Case studies.
HE538.R3 E34 1982

Efectos de la adhesión de España a la CEE sobre las exportaciones de Iberoamérica /. Alonso, José Antonio. Madrid , 1983. 316 p. : ISBN 84-7232-299-8 LC Card 87-116624
HF3688.L3 A45 1983

Efectos de la política económica en el mercado de leche fluida /. Forteza, Alvaro. Montevideo, Uruguay [1986] 126 p. : LC Card 87-121158
HD9282.U72 F67 1986

Los efectos de una desgravación arancelaria en el contexto de una economía con movilidad imperfecta de trabajo /. Coloma C., Fernando. Santiago , 1985. 46 leaves : LC Card 85-203579
HF1713 .C618 1985

Efeitos sociais de grandes projetos hidrelétricos . Sigaud, Lygia. [Rio de Janeiro] , 1986. 116 p. ; LC Card 87-120281 DDC 333.91/4 19
HD1696.B84 S346 1986

Efektivnost ot teritorialnata organizat͡sii͡a na proizvodstvoto v usloviiata na noviia ikonomicheski mekhanizŭm : nauchno-prakticheska konferent͡sii͡a, gr. Tŭrgovishte, 29-30.X.1982. Tŭrgovishte : [s.n.], 1982. 215 p. ; 20 cm. At head of title: T͡Sentralno rŭkovodstvo na Sŭi͡uza po ikonomika ... Includes bibliographical references. LC Card 84-115638

1. Bulgaria - Industries - Location - Congresses. I. Sŭi͡uz po ikonomika (Bulgaria). T͡Sentralno rŭkovodstvo.
HC403.Z9 D516 1982

The effect of leader behavior on worker job satisfaction and job performance in Ethiopian textile factories . Regessa Kebede. [Turku] , c1987. 138 p. : LC Card 87-170154 DDC 677/.0068 19
HD5658.T42 E87 1987

The effect of state income tax policy on the development of marginal oil fields . Livey, Jay. [Juneau] [1986] vii leaves, 52 p., [17] leaves : LC Card 86-622190 DDC 333.8/232/09798 19
HD9560.8.U53 A445 1986

The effect of tax exempt forestland on town property tax revenues . Wise, Gregory J. Madison [1986] 40 leaves : LC Card 86-623093 DDC 336.22/09775 19
HJ4284.A3 W59 1986

The effect of the western accord and recent provincial royalty changes on petroleum industry capital expenditures /. Pasay, Janice L. Calgary, Alta. , 1986. iv, 27, 4 leaves ; LC Card 86-203742 DDC 338.2/3 19
HD9574.C22 P37 1986

The Effect of tire pressures on flexible pavements / by Freddy L. Roberts ... [et al.] ; conducted for State Department of Highways and Public Transportation in cooperation with the U. S. Department of Transportation, Federal Highway Administration, by the Texas Transportation Institute, Texas A&M University. Prelim. review copy. College Station, Tex. : The Institute ; Springfield, Va. : Available through the National Technical Information Service, 1985. viii, 235 p. : ill. ; 28 cm. (Research report . 372-1F) Errata Slip inserted. Bibliography: p. 199-202. "TTI-2-8-83-372-1F"--Cover. LC Card 86-622241 DDC 380.5 s 625.8 19

1. Pavements, Flexible - Live loads. 2. Tires, Rubber. I. Roberts, Freddy L. II. Texas Transportation Institute. III. Series: Research report (Texas Transportation Institute) , 372-1F.
HE203 .T43 no. 372-1F TE270

Effective behavior in organizations : learning from the interplay of cases, concepts, and student experiences / Allan R. Cohen ... [et al.].4th ed. Homewood, Ill. : Irwin, 1988. xxvi, 959 p. : ill. (some col.) ; 25 cm. (The Irwin series in management and the behavioral sciences) Includes bibliographies and index. ISBN 0-256-05967-5 LC Card 87-82176 DDC 658.4 19

1. Organizational behavior. I. Cohen, Allen R.
HD58.7 .E35 1988

Effective business communications /. Murphy, Herta A. New York , c1988. xx, 730 p. : ISBN 0-07-044094-8 LC Card 87-17330 DDC 651.7 19
HF5721 .M85 1988

Effective cash flow management. New York, N.Y., U. S.A. : Alexander Hamilton Institute, c1985. x, 223 p. : ill. ; 28 cm. (Modern business reports) ISBN 0-86604-176-1 (pbk.) LC Card 86-205438 DDC 658.1/5244 19

1. Cash management. 2. Cash flow. I. Alexander Hamilton Institute (U. S.). II. Series.
HG4028.C45 E34 1985

Effective communications and advertising for financial institutions /. Burns, Thomas J., 1942- Englewood Cliffs, N.J. , c1986. xvi, 299 p. : ISBN 0-8359-1556-5 LC Card 85-25641 DDC 659.1/93321 19
HG1616.M3 B87 1986 ***NYPL [JLE 86-1689]***

Effective corporate relations : applying public relations in business and industry / edited by Norman A. Hart. London ; New York : McGraw-Hill, c1987. xii, 207 p. : ill. ; 23 cm. Includes bibliographies and index. ISBN 0-07-084940-4 (pbk.) : LC Card 87-21520 DDC 659.2/85 19

1. Public relations - Corporations. 2. Public relations. I. Hart, Norman A.
HD59 .E33 1987

Effective credit management in the equipment leasing and finance industry /. Haley, Stephen W. Arlington, VA , c1986. ix, 121 p. : ISBN 0-912413-01-8 (pbk.) LC Card 87-105306 DDC 658.1/5242 19
HD39.4 .H35 1986

Effective delegation /. Goodworth, Clive T. London , Brookfield, Vt., USA , 1985. 148 p. : ISBN 0-09-161781-2 (pbk.) : LC Card 86-204300 DDC 658.4/02 19
HD50 .G66 1985

Effective group problem solving . Fox, William M. San Francisco , 1987. xvii, 204 p. : ISBN 1-555-42033-8 (alk. paper) LC Card 86-33742 DDC 658.4/036 19
HD30.29 .F69 1987

Effective listening . Murphy, Kevin J., 1950- Toronto , New York , 1987. ix, 179 p. ; ISBN 0-553-05212-8 LC Card 86-47893 DDC 658.4/52 19
HD30.3 .M87 1987

The effective management of technology . Bhalla, Sushil K. Columbus [Ohio] , Reading, Mass. , c1987. xiii, 205 p. : ISBN 0-201-10929-8 : LC Card 86-25847 DDC 658.5 19
HD45 .B47 1987

Effective management techniques . Mattar, Edward Paul. Worcester, MA , 1987. p. cm. LC Card 87-15556 DDC 658.4 19
HD62.7 .M38 1987

Effective meetings for busy people . Carnes, William T. New York , c1987. xvi, 348 p. ; ISBN 0-87942-211-4 LC Card 86-27719 DDC 658.4/563 19
HD2743 .C37 1987

Effective project planning and management . Randolph, W. Alan. Englewood Cliffs, N.J. [1987], c1988. x, 163 p. : ISBN 0-13-244815-7 LC Card 87-11399 DDC 658.4/04 19
HD69.P75 R36 1988

Effective real estate sales and marketing /. Rosenauer, Johnnie L. Chicago, Ill. , c1988. xiv, 258 p. : ISBN 0-88462-599-0 (pbk.) LC Card 87-9544 DDC 333.33/068/8 19
HD1375 .R597 1988

Effective selling and sales management /. Scott, Gini Graham. Andover, Mass. , c1988. p. cm. ISBN 0-931790-76-X : LC Card 87-13829 DDC 658.8/1 19
HF5438.25 .S35 1988

Effective strategic management . Hatten, Kenneth J. Englewood Cliffs, N.J. , c1988. xiv, 338 p. : ISBN 0-13-245200-6 (pbk.) LC Card 87-20589 DDC 658.4/012 19
HD30.28 .H383 1988

Effectiveness of road safety education programmes : report / prepared by an OECD Scientific Expert Group. Paris : Organisation for Economic Co-operation and Development ; [Washington, D.C. : OECD Publications and Information Centre, distributor], 1986. 134 p. : ill. ; 27 cm. (Road transport research) Bibliography: p. 120-127. ISBN 92-64-12881-6 : LC Card 87-119891 DDC 363.1/2575/07 19

1. Traffic safety - Study and teaching - Evaluation. I. Organisation for Economic Co-operation and Development. II. Series.
HE5613.5 .E33 1986

The effectiveness of town planning in Natal . Stretch, C. Pietermaritzburg, Natal, South Africa , 1986. 35 p. ; LC Card 86-159747 DDC 361.2/5/09684 s 307.1/2/096845 19
HC517.N3 A44 vol. 64 HT169.S62P56

Effectiviteit in de reclame : een beschrijving van marketing-praktijkgevallen die bekroond werden met de VEA-Effie 1983/1984. Alphen aan den Rijn : Samsom, 1986. 125 p. : ill. ; 23 cm. "Deze uitgave staat onder auspiciën van de Nederlandse Vereniging van Erkende Adviesbureaux." ISBN 90-14-03587-X : LC Card 86-205967

1. Advertising - Netherlands. 2. Advertising - Netherlands - Awards. I. Nederlandse Vereniging van Erkende Reclame Adviesbureaux.
HF5813.N4 E35 1986

The effects of capital taxation . Agell, Jonas. Uppsala , Stockholm, Sweden , 1986. 123 p. : ISBN 91-554-1938-0 (pbk.) LC Card 87-100538 DDC 330 s 336.2/009481 19
HB51 .S7 no. 9 HJ2838

Effects of deregulation on motor carriers /. Glaskowsky, Nicholas A. Westport, Conn. (P.O. Box 2055, Westport 06880) , 1986. viii, 86 p. : LC Card 86-80416 DDC 388.3/24/0973 19
HE5623 .G55 1986

Effects of neo-protectionism on the Korean exports /. Kim, Chungsoo. [Seoul] , 1986. 203 p. : LC Card 86-234427 DDC 382/.095195/073 19
HF3830.5.Z7 U54 1986

The effects of new technological change on shift work in the brewing industry /. Ghobadian, Abby, 1951- Aldershot, Hants, England , Brookfield, Vt. , c1986. xiv, 192 p. : ISBN 0-566-05132-X : LC Card 86-17536 DDC

331.25/72 19
HD8039.L62 G74 1986
NYPL [JLD 86-3864]

The effects of redundancy . Wooden, Mark. [Bedford Park, S. Aust.] [1987] 52 p. : LC Card 87-170621 DDC 331.13/7994 19
HD5708.55.A8 W66 1987

The effects of rice based cropping system research on women in Bangladesh /. Halim, Abdul, 1945- Mymensingh , 1986. 2, 30 leaves ; LC Card 86-901954 DDC 331.4/8318/095492 19
HD1537.B3 H35 1986

The Effects of semifinished steel imports on the U. S. iron and steel scrap industry : report to the Subcommittee on Trade, Committee on Ways and Means, on investigation no. 332-195 under section 332 of the Tariff Act of 1930. Washington, D.C. : U. S. International Trade Commission, [1985] xv, 137 p. : ill. ; 28 cm. (USITC publication. 1692) Cover title. Distributed to depository libraries in microfiche. "May 1985." Includes bibliographical references. Item 980-E (microfiche) LC Card 86-603428
1. Iron industry and trade - United States. 2. Steel industry and trade - United States. I. United States. International Trade Commission.
HD9515 .E33 1985

Effects of state income tax policy on the development of marginal oil fields. Livey, Jay. The effect of state income tax policy on the development of marginal oil fields . [Juneau] [1986] vii leaves, 52 p., [17] leaves : LC Card 86-622190 DDC 333.8/232/09798 19
HD9560.8.U53 A445 1986

The Effects of taxation on capital accumulation / edited by Martin Feldstein. Chicago : University of Chicago Press, 1987. ix, 490 p. : ill. ; 24 cm. (A National Bureau of Economic Research project report) Includes bibliographies and indexes. ISBN 0-226-24088-6 : LC Card 86-25025 DDC 332/.0415 19
1. Taxation. 2. Saving and investment. I. Feldstein, Martin S. II. Series.
HJ2305 .E29 1987

The effects of trade and exchange rate policies on agriculture in Nigeria /. Oyejide, T. Ademola. Washington, D.C., USA , c1986. 61 p. : ISBN 0-89629-056-5 (pbk.) LC Card 86-21309 DDC 338.1/09669 19
HD2145.5 .O94 1986

The effects of trade and exchange rate policies on agriculture in Zaire /. Tshibaka, Tshikala B., 1949- Washington, D.C., USA , 1986. 65 p. : ISBN 0-89629-057-3 LC Card 86-27449 DDC 338.1/09675/1 19
HD2135.5 .T75 1986

Effekter av TV-reklam . Sweden. TV-reklameffektutredningen. [Stockholm] [1986] 467 p. : ISBN 91-38-09425-8 LC Card 86-233988
HF6146.T42 S94 1986

Effektivität und Reproduktion : Bedingungen, Faktoren, Zusammenhänge / Autorenkollektiv, Gerhard Richter. Berlin : Verlag Die Wirtschaft, c1985. 148 p. ; 19 cm. Prepared in conjunction with the Forschungsgruppe "Effektivität" of the Zentralinstitut für Wirtschaftswissenschaften of the Akademie der Wissenschaften der DDR. Includes bibliographical references. LC Card 86-166628
1. Germany, East - Economic policy. 2. Germany, East - Economic conditions. I. Richter, Gerhard, 1920-. II. Akademie der Wissenschaften der DDR. Zentralinstitut für Wirtschaftswissenschaften. Forschungsgruppe "Effektivität.".
HC290.78 .E365 1985

Ėffektivnoe ispol´zovanie kapital´nykh vlozheniĭ v sel´skom stroitel´stve /. IAkovlev, IU. P. (IUriĭ Prokof´evich) Kiev , 1985. 104 p. : LC Card 86-214694
HD9715.S73 U383 1985

Ėffektivnoe ispol´zovanie vychislitel´noĭ tekhniki /. Vanags, I. IA. (Ilmar IAnovich) Moskva , 1982. 142, [2] p. : LC Card 83-165693
HF5548.2 .V345 1982

Ėffektivnost´ i intensifikatsiia : izmerenie i planirovanie / [otvetstvennyĭ redaktor Rybin V.I.; redaktory Kapitonov B.V., Spirina N.I.]. Moskva : Akademiia nauk SSSR, In-t ėkonomiki, 1986. 161 p. ; 21 cm. Includes bibliographical references. LC Card 87-163443
1. Industrial productivity - Soviet Union. I. Rybin, V. I. (Valeriĭ Ivanovich). II. Kapitonov, B. V. III. Spirina, N. I. IV. Institut ėkonomiki (Akademiia nauk SSSR).
HC340.I52 E33 1986

Ėffektivnost´ i optimal´nost´ kapital´nykh vlozheniĭ /. Cherniavskiĭ, V. O. (Vasiliĭ Osipovich) Leningrad , 1986. 68, [4] p. ; LC Card 85-179296
HC340.C3 C4 1986

Ėffektivnost´ kapital´nogo stroitel´stva v torgovle /. Androsov, V. I. (Vasiliĭ Ivanovich) Moskva , 1980. 213 p. ; LC Card 81-132839
HC340.C3 A65 1980

Ėffektivnost´ kapital´nykh vlozheniĭ i bankovskaia deiatel´nost´ /. Braginskiĭ, L. V. (Lev Vol´fovich) Moskva , 1981. 186 p. ; LC Card 82-144216
HG186.S55 B72 1981

Ėffektivnost´ kapital´nykh vlozheniĭ i novoĭ tekhniki v narodnom khoziaĭstve IAkutskoĭ ASSR : sbornik nauchnykh trudov / [otvetstvennyĭ redaktor E.G. Egorov]. IAkutsk : IAkutskiĭ filial SO AN SSSR, 1981. 91 p. ; 20 cm. At head of title: Akademiia nauk SSSR. Sibirskoe otdelenie. IAkutskiĭ filial. Otdel ėkonomiki. Includes bibliographical references. LC Card 82-217455
1. Capital productivity - Russian S.F.S.R. - IAkutskaia A.S.S.R. 2. Technological innovations - Russian S.F.S.R. - IAkutskaia A.S.S.R. 3. IAkutskaia A.S.S.R. (R.S.F.S.R.) - Economic conditions. I. Egorov, Egor Grigor´evich. II. Akademiia nauk SSSR. IAkutskiĭ filial. Otdel ėkonomiki.
HC337.I23 C34 1981

Ėffektivnost´ kapital´nykh vlozheniĭ v promyshlennosti Kirgizii /. Abdurakhmanov, I. (Ibraim) Frunze , 1981. 174 p. ; LC Card 82-160618
HC337.K5453 C32 1981

Ėffektivnost´ NTP : izmerenie i planirovanie na predpriiatii / pod redaktsieĭ A.A. Rumiantseva. Leningrad : Izd-vo "Nauka," Leningradskoe otd-nie, 1985. 215 p., [1] folded leaf of plates : ill. ; 20 cm. At head of title: Akademiia nauk SSSR. Institut sotsial´no-ėkonomicheskikh problem. Includes bibliographical references. LC Card 86-129301
1. Technological innovations - Europe, Eastern. I. Rumiantsev, A. A. II. Institut sotsial´no-ėkonomicheskikh problem (Akademiia nauk SSSR).
HC244.Z9 T435 1985

Ėffektivnost´ obshchestvennogo truda v usloviiakh razvitogo sotsializma . Bohynia, D. P. Kiev , 1982. 316 p. ; LC Card 82-200989
HC340.L3 B56 1982

Ėffektivnost´ proizvodstva v agropromyshlennom komplekse Chuvashskoĭ ASSR / [redaktory M.N. Ergachev, N.P. Gerasimova]. Cheboksary : Nauchno-issl. in-t iazyka, lit-ry, istorii i ėkonomiki pri Sovete Ministrov Chuvashskoĭ ASSR, 1985. 198 p. ; 21 cm. Includes bibliographies. LC Card 86-203897
1. Agricultural industries - Russian S.F.S.R. - Chuvashskaia A.S.S.R. 2. Agricultural productivity - Russian S.F.S.R. - Chuvashskaia A.S.S.R. I. Ergachev, M. N. II. Gerasimova, N. P. III. Chuvashskaia A.S.S.R. (R.S.F.S.R.). Nauchno-issledovatel´skiĭ institut iazyka, literatury, istorii i ėkonomiki.
HD9015.S653 C483 1985

Ėffektivnost´ proizvodstva v evropeĭskikh stranakh SEV /. Tromlakova, E. M. (Elena Mikhaĭlovna) Moskva , 1986. 157 p. ; LC Card 86-233225
HC244.Z9 I5188 1986

Ėffektivnost´ territorial´noĭ organizatsii promyshlennogo proizvodstva v Kazakhstane / [otvetstvennye redaktory, M.G. Isaeva, A.I. Chekeres]. Alma-Ata : Izd-vo "Nauka" Kazakhskoĭ SSR, 1980. 190 p. ; 20 cm. At head of title: Akademiia nauk Kazakhskoĭ SSR. Institut ėkonomiki. Includes bibliographical references. LC Card 82-164638
1. Kazakh S.S.R. - Industries - Location. 2. Territorial production complexes - Kazakh S.S.R. I. Isaeva, M. G. (Muza Gavrilovna). II. Chekeres, A. I. (Aleksandr Ivanovich). III. Institut ėkonomiki (Qazaq SSR ghylym akademiiasy).
HC337.K33 D53 1980

Les effets de la crise mondiale actuelle sur l'économie et la population gabonaises /. Mamder, Josué Sandjiman. Addis Abéba , c1984. 34 p. ; ISBN 92-2-203795-2 LC Card 86-215256
HC975 .M36 1984

Effets de la récession sur l'économie togolaise . Gozo, K. M. Addis Abéba , 1985. 50, 24 p. ; ISBN 92-2-205044-4 LC Card 86-159834 DDC 330.966/8104 19
HC1015 .G69 1985

Les Effets des conditions de travail sur la santé des travailleuses : actes du colloque / [organisé par le Comité de condition féminine de la CSN et parrainé par le Bureau international du travail (BIT) du 15 au 21 mai 1983 à l'Université du Québec à Montréal ; responsable de la publication, Jean-Anne Bouchard ; traduction, Eileen Shea, Hélène Laplante, Denise Sanche]. [Montréal] : CSN, [1984] 230 p., [5] p. of plates : ill. ; 23 cm. ISBN 2-920658-00-X : LC Card 86-158040
1. Women - Employment - Congresses. 2. Women - Health and hygiene - Congresses. 3. Industrial hygiene - Congresses. I. Bouchard, Jean-Anne. II. Confédération des syndicats nationaux. Comité de la condition féminine. III. International Labour Office.
HD6067 .E34 1984

Effets externes . Catin, Maurice. Paris , c1985. 455 p. : ISBN 2-254-85071-2 : LC Card 86-186253
HB846.3 .C37 1985

Gli effetti delle integrazioni salariali sulla mobilità del lavoro /. Seravalli, Gilberto, 1946- Milano, Italy , c1986. 119 p. : LC Card 86-222523
HD5717.5.I8 S47 1986

EFFICIENCY ENGINEERS. see **BUSINESS CONSULTANTS.**

EFFICIENCY, INDUSTRIAL - ADDRESSES, ESSAYS, LECTURES.
The Uneasy alliance . Boston, Mass. , c1985. x, 485 p. : ISBN 0-87584-172-4 LC Card 85-8709 DDC 658.5 19
HD56 .U53 1985 *NYPL [JLE 86-2361]*

EFFICIENCY, INDUSTRIAL - COMMUNIST COUNTRIES.
Utkin, Ė. A. (Ėduard Andreevich) Chemu uchit opyt druzeĭ /. Moskva , 1987. 141 p. ; LC Card 87-120824 DDC 658/.009171/7 19
HD70.C725 U85 1987

EFFICIENCY, INDUSTRIAL - ECUADOR.
Villalobos, Fabio. La industrialización ecuatoriana y la utilización de los recursos productivos, 1976-1983 /. Quito, Ecuador , 1987. 148 p. : LC Card 87-404654 DDC 338.09866 19
HC204.5.I52 V55 1987

EFFICIENCY, INDUSTRIAL - GERMANY.
Schalldach, Elisabeth, 1904- Rationalisierungsmassnahmen der Nachinflationszeit im Urteil der deutschen freien Gewerkschaften. Jena, 1930. ix, [1], 186 p. LC Card AC34-383
HD70.G2 S26 1930

EFFICIENCY, INDUSTRIAL - GERMANY (EAST)
Brandt, Horst. Kostensenkung und Gewinn /. Berlin , 1985. 100 p. ; LC Card 87-144350 DDC 338.5/1/09431 19
HC290.795.C7 B7 1985

EFFICIENCY, INDUSTRIAL - GREAT BRITAIN.
Willman, Paul. Technological change, collective bargaining, and industrial efficiency /. Oxford , New York , c1986. xvi, 282 p. : ISBN 0-19-827262-6 : LC Card 86-5104 DDC 331.88/0941 19
HD6664 .W56 1986 *NYPL [JLD 87-994]*

EFFICIENCY, INDUSTRIAL - ROMANIA.
Eficienţa economico-socială /. Craiova , 1983. 392 p. ; LC Card 84-152996
HC405.Z9 I523 1983

EFFICIENCY, INDUSTRIAL - RUSSIAN S.F. S.R. - DAGESTANSKAIA A.S.S.R.
Sovershenstvovanie khoziaĭstvennogo mekhanizma i ratsional´noe ispol´zovanie resursov . Makhachkala , 1985. 190 p. : LC Card 87-136485
HC337.D3 S655 1985

EFFICIENCY, INDUSTRIAL - RUSSIAN S.F. S.R. - MAGNITOGORSK.
Zubets, V. M. (Vasiliĭ Mikhaĭlovich) Rezervy povysheniia ėffektivnosti proizvodstva na magnitogorskom metallurgicheskom kombinate

/. Cheli͡abinsk , 1975. 183 p. ; LC Card 81-170397
HD9525.S653 M39 1975

EFFICIENCY, INDUSTRIAL - SOVIET UNION.
Chebanenko, Vladimir Mikhaĭlovich. Sistema planirovanii͡a tekhnicheskogo urovni͡a otrasli /. Moskva , 1985. 118, [7] p. : LC Card 85-241451
HD70.S63 C45 1985

Narodnokhozi͡aĭstvennai͡a ėffektivnost′--pokazateli, metody ot͡senki /. Moskva , 1984. 247 p. : LC Card 84-188306
HC336.25 .N3515 1984

Sot͡sial′no-ėkonomicheskie problemy intensifikat͡sii obshchestvennogo proizvodstva /. Moskva , 1983. 91 p. : LC Card 84-114234
HD56 .S688 1983

EFFICIENCY, INDUSTRIAL - SOVIET UNION - STATISTICAL METHODS.
Krylov, V. F. (Vladimir Fedorovich) Sravnitel′nyĭ analiz dei͡atel′nosti predprii͡atiĭ /. Moskva , 1981. 69 p. ; LC Card 82-112692
HC340.L3 K75 1981

EFFICIENCY, INDUSTRIAL - UNITED STATES.
Adams, Walter, 1922 (Aug. 27)- The bigness complex . New York , 1986. xiii, 426 p. ; ISBN 0-394-54721-7 : LC Card 86-42624 DDC 338.6/44/0973 19
HD2785 .A68 1986 *NYPL [JLE 87-1432]*

Willman, Paul. Technological change, collective bargaining, and industrial efficiency /. Oxford , New York , c1986. xvi, 282 p. : ISBN 0-19-827262-6 : LC Card 86-5104 DDC 331.88/0941 19
HD6664 .W56 1986 *NYPL [JLD 87-994]*

EFFICIENCY, INDUSTRIAL - UNITED STATES - CASE STUDIES.
Paul, Ronald N. The 101 best performing companies in America /. Chicago, Ill. , c1986. vii, 382 p. ; ISBN 0-917253-39-6 : LC Card 86-4947 DDC 338.7/4/0973 19
HD2785 .P38 1986 *NYPL [JLE 86-3151]*

EFFICIENCY, PERSONAL. see **SUCCESS.**

EFFICIENCY RATING. see **EMPLOYEES, RATING OF; EXECUTIVES, RATING OF.**

EFFICIENT MARKET THEORY.
Heri, Erwin W. Bestimmungsgründe kurzfristiger Wechselkursfluktuationen . Hamburg , 1982. v, 312 p. : ISBN 3-87895-225-2 LC Card 83-200160 DDC 332.4/5 19
HG3852 .H47 1982

Schleis, Konrad, 1935- Börsengewinne dank besserer Aktienkurs-Prognose /. Niederglatt , c1984. 257 p. : ISBN 3-85684-030-3 : LC Card 84-119396
HG5492 .S345 1984

EFFICIENT MARKET THEORY - MATHEMATICAL MODELS.
Capital market equilibria /. Berlin , New York , c1986. x, 228 p. : ISBN 0-387-16248-8 (U. S.) LC Card 86-10104 DDC 332.6/0724 19
HG4523 .C33 1986 *NYPL [JLE 86-4309]*

Die Effizienz der Finanzierungshilfen an Klein- und Mittelbetriebe im Berggebiet /. Burkhalter, Rudolf. Bern [1985] (Aarau : Cooperative Drucki) 216 p. : LC Card 86-115683
HG4027.7 .B86 1985

Effizienz- und Verteilungswirkungen des Steuersystems /. Kitterer, Wolfgang. Frankfurt am Main , New York , c1986. 197 p. ; ISBN 3-8204-8528-7 LC Card 86-194183
HJ2321 .K52 1986

Effizienzkontrolle von Umweltpolitik . Schulz, Bernhard. Frankfurt am Main , c1983. xv, 230 p. : ISBN 3-88129-744-8 LC Card 85-103230
HC290.5.E5 S38 1983

L'Effort économique de défense : exemples de la France et du Royaume-Uni / [les auteurs suivants ont participé ... Jacques Aben ... et al.] ; Jacques Fontanel, Ron Smith, éd. [Grenoble] : Arès, défense et sécurité, 1985. 235 p. : ill. ; 21 cm. "ARES reçoit dans ce troisième supplément le fruit d'une recherche menée en collaboration entre le Centre d'études de défense et de sécurité internationale (CEDSI) de l'Université des sciences sociales de Grenoble et le Birkbeck College de l'Université de Londres, sous les auspices du CNRS et du SSRC britannique"--p. 13. Includes bibliographies. LC Card 86-199399
1. France - Defenses - Economic aspects. 2. Great Britain - Defenses - Economic aspects. 3. France - Armed Forces - Appropriations and expenditures. 4. Great Britain - Armed Forces - Appropriations and expenditures. I. Aben, Jacques. II. Fontanel, Jacques. III. Smith, Ron, Ph. D. IV. CEDSI (Center). V. Birkbeck College. VI. Series: Supplément ... à l'Annuaire Arès, défense et sécurité , no 3.
HC280.D4 E38 1985

Efibanca/studi creditizi .
(2) Bagella, Michele. Gli istituti di credito speciale e il mercato finanziario, 1947-1962 /. Milano, Italy , c1986. 289 p. ; LC Card 86-232526
HG3729.I7 B34 1986

La eficiencia del sistema bancario español /. Fanjul, Oscar. Madrid , c1985. 275 p. : ISBN 84-206-2439-X LC Card 87-111325
HG3184 .F36 1985

Eficienţa economico-socială / coordonator, Ion Trăistaru. Craiova : Scrisul Românesc, 1983. 392 p. ; 21 cm. At head of title: Sistemul economic socialist. Table of contents in English, French, Romanian, and Russian. Includes bibliographical references. LC Card 84-152996
1. Industrial productivity - Romania. 2. Efficiency, Industrial - Romania. 3. Romania - Economic conditions - 1945-. I. Trăistaru, Ion. II. Title: Sistemul economic socialist.
HC405.Z9 I523 1983

Efimov, A. N. (Anatoliĭ Nikolaevich) Problemy obosnovanii͡a gosudarstvennogo plana / A.N. Efimov. Moskva : Ėkonomika, 1980. 197, [3] p. ; 21 cm. Bibliography: p. 197-[198] LC Card 81-135658
1. Central planning - Soviet Union. 2. Soviet Union - Economic policy - 1976-1980. I. Title.
HC336.25 .E346 1980

Efimov, V. I. Agrarnai͡a revoli͡ut͡sii͡a i sot͡sialisticheskie preobrazovanii͡a v sovetskoĭ derevne . Gor′kiĭ , 1980. 84 p. ; LC Card 82-141565
HD1995.R8 A68 1980

Efn-rapport, 0281-0301 .
(nr 19) Skogsbränsle . Stockholm [1986] 159 p. : ISBN 91-38-09241-7 LC Card 86-201607
HD9769.F842 S57 1986

(nr 4) Ny teknik för elproduktion, elanvändning . Stockholm [1983] 172 p. : LC Card 84-108404
HD9685.S852 N9 1983

EFT . Schmitzer, Iana L. Westport, CT (P.O. Box 431, Westport 06881) , c1986. vi leaves, 180 p. : LC Card 87-143208 DDC 332.1/028 19
HG1710 .S364 1986

EFTA. see **European Free Trade Association.**

EG und Arbeiterrechte . Dötsch, Jochen. Berlin , 1981. 143 p. ; LC Card 81-145834 DDC 331.11/094 19
HD8380.5 .D67 1981 *NYPL [JLD 86-2739]*

EG-Wörterverzeichnis : Französisch-Deutsch / Redaktion, Wirtschafts- und Sozialausschuss ; Rat der Europäischen Gemeinschaften, Generalsekretariat, Terminologiedienst = Glossaire des Communautés européennes : français-allemand / rédaction, Comité économique et social ; Conseil des communautés européennes, Secretariat général, Service de terminologie.3. Aufl. Luxembourg : Office des publications officielles des Communautés européennes, 1984. 1 v. (various pagings) ; 26 cm. Includes bibliographical references and index. ISBN 92-824-0123-5 LC Card 85-131398
1. European communities - Dictionaries - French. 2. French language - Dictionaries - German. 3. European communities - Dictionaries - German. 4. German language - Dictionaries - French. I. Economic and Social Committee of the European Communities. II. Council of the European Communities. Terminology Dept. III. Title: Glossaire des Communautés européennes.
KJE926.5 .E35 1984 *NYPL [JLF 86-1818]*

Egan, Gerard. Change agent skills in helping and human service settings / Gerard Egan. Monterey, Calif. : Brooks/Cole Pub. Co., c1985. xi, 306 p. : ill. ; 25 cm. Includes indexes. Bibliography: p. 289-300. ISBN 0-534-03624-4 : LC Card 84-7804 DDC 361.3/07 19
1. Social work education - United States. 2. Social service - United States - Case studies. 3. Public relations - Social service - Case studies. 4. Bureaucracy - United States - Case studies. 5. Organizational behavior - Case studies. 6. Communication in social work - United States - Case studies. 7. Social work administration - United States - Case studies. I. Title.
HV11 .E43 1985 *NYPL [JLE 86-1963]*

Egea Bruno, Pedro María. La minería cartagenera en torno a la primera guerra mundial, 1909-1923 / Pedro Ma. Egea Bruno. [Murcia] : Secretariado de Publicaciones, Universidad de Murcia, 1983. 76 p. : ill. ; 24 cm. "Resumen de tesis doctoral ... Facultad de Letras, Universidad de Murcia ... 1982"--P. opp. t.p. At head of title: Facultad de Letras. Includes bibliographical references. ISBN 84-86031-30-3 LC Card 85-199662
1. Mineral industries - Spain - Cartagena City Region - History - 20th century. 2. Shipping - Spain - Cartagena - History - 20th century. 3. Mineral industries - Europe - History - 20th century. 4. World War, 1914-1918 - Influence. I. Universidad de Murcia. Facultad de Filosofía y Letras. II. Title.
HD9506.S762 C374 1983

Egemo, Jerry, 1931- Kreativ personalplanering : hur tillvarata kapacitetsöverskott? / Jerry Egemo.Uppl. 1. Malmö : LiberFörlag, c1984. 99 p. ; 25 cm. Includes index. ISBN 91-38-61248-8 : LC Card 84-188831
1. Personnel management. 2. Personnel management - Sweden. I. Title.
HF5549 .E425 1984

Egengel′dyev, Ė. (Ėsengel′dy) Teoreticheskie issledovanii͡a regional′nykh faktorov razmeshchenii͡a khozi͡aĭstva / Ė. Egengel′dyev ; otvetstvennyĭ redaktor Dzh.B. Baĭramov. Ashkabad : Ylym, 1985. 227 p. : ill. ; 21 cm. At head of title: Akademii͡a nauk Turkmenskoĭ SSR. Turkmenskiĭ ordena Trudovogo Krasnogo Znameni gosudarstvennyĭ universitet im. A.M. Gor′kogo. Bibliography: p. 190-[201] LC Card 86-172008
1. Turkmen S.S.R. - Industries - Location. 2. Regional planning - Turkmen S.S.R. I. Baĭramov, Dzhuma. II. Title.
HC337.T853 D53 1985

EGG TRADE - SAUDI ARABIA.
Analytical study for the market of white meat and eggs /. Jeddah [1985?] 159 p. : LC Card 85-964046 DDC 381/.4566493/09538 19
HD9437.S332 A53 1985

Egger, Emil. Management Accounting in öffentlichen nichtgewinnorientierten Organisationen : dargestellt am Beispiel der Zentralbibliothek Zürich / von Emil Egger. Zürich : Schulthess Polygraphischer Verlag, c1985. xii, 220 p. : ill. ; 23 cm. (Mitteilungen aus dem Handelswissenschaftlichen Seminar der Universität Zürich . Heft 163) Originally presented as the author's thesis (doctoral)--Universität Zürich. Bibliography: p. 202-218. ISBN 3-7255-2410-6 LC Card 85-132536
1. Corporations, Nonprofit - Switzerland - Accounting - Case studies. 2. Managerial accounting - Case studies. 3. Zentralbibliothek Zürich - Accounting - Case studies. I. Title. II. Series.
HF5686.N56 E33 1985

Eggerstedt, Harald.
Politik gegen die Krise . Marburg , 1985. 157 p. : ISBN 3-924800-01-4 : LC Card 86-119259 DDC 338.9 19
HC59 .P584 1985

Produktwettbewerb und Dienstleistungsfreiheit auf Versicherungsmärkten / von Harald Eggerstedt. Berlin : Duncker & Humblot, c1987. 320 p. : ill. ; 21 cm. (Veröffentlichungen des Forschungsinstituts für Wirtschaftspolitik an der Universität Mainz . Bd. 48) Bibliography: p. [304]-317. Includes index. ISBN 3-428-06167-5 LC Card 87-143175 DDC 368/.94 19
1. Insurance - European Economic Community countries - State supervision. I. Title. II. Series.
HG8593.5.Z75 E34 1987

Eggert, Jim, 1943- What is economics? / Jim Eggert. Rev. ed. Los Altos, Calif. : W. Kaufmann, c1987. vii, 205 p. : ill. ; 23 cm. Bibliography: p. [195]-198. Includes index. ISBN 0-86576-104-3 (pbk.) LC Card 86-27297 DDC 330 19
1. Economics. I. Title.
HB171.5 .E464 1987

EGGS - TRADE AND STATISTICS. see **EGG TRADE.**

Az EGK szőlő- és borgazdaságának szabályozórendszere /. Harza, Lajos. Budapest ,

1985. 70 p. : ISBN 963-491-210-9 LC Card 86-196818
HD9259.G7 E864 1985

Eglajs, Gustav. Ridgely, Beverly S. Supplement to Birds of the world in philately /. Johnstown, PA , c1986. 62 p., [3] p. of plates : ISBN 0-935991-00-X (pbk.): LC Card 86-217462 DDC 769.56/4/075 769.56/432 19
HE6187 .A635 no. 106-1 HE6183.B53

Egli, Walter, 1945- San Pedro Amuzgos, ein mexikanisches Dorf kämpft um sein Land : Agrargeschichte der Costa Oaxaca von der Kolonialzeit bis zur Gegenwart / Walter Egli. Zürich : Limmat, c1982. 406 p. : ill. ; 21 cm. (Reihe W) Bibliography: p. 393-403. ISBN 3-85791-059-3 LC Card 83-139253
1. Land reform - Mexico - San Pedro Amuzgos - History. I. Title. II. Title: San Pedro Amuzgos.
HD1333.M62 S264 1982

Eglington, Peter. An economic analysis of oilsands policy in Canada : the case of Alsands and Wolf Lake / by Peter Eglington and Maris Uffelmann. Ottawa, Ont. : Economic Council of Canada, [1984] 1 v. (various pagings) : ill. ; 28 cm. (Discussion paper, 0225-8013 . no. 259) Summary in French. "A paper prepared for the Economic Council of Canada"--Cover. "May 1984." Includes bibliographical references. LC Card 84-213823 DDC 333.8/232 19
1. Oil sands industry - Government policy - Alberta - Wolf Lake Region. 2. Oil sands industry - Government policy - Canada. 3. Alsands Project. I. Uffelmann, Maris. II. Economic Council of Canada. III. Series: Discussion paper (Economic Council of Canada) , no. 259. IV. Title.
HD9574.C23 W654 1984

Egner, Erich, 1901- Hauswirtschaft und Lebenshaltung : eine qualitative Untersuchung ihres Zusammenhanges unter bes. Berücks. lateinamerikan. Entwicklungsländer / von Erich Egner. Berlin : Duncker und Humblot, 1974. 249 p. ; 24 cm. (Beiträge zur Ökonomie von Haushalt und Verbrauch. Heft 9) Includes bibliographical references and index. ISBN 3-428-03093-1 : LC Card 76-511945
1. Cost and standard of living - Latin America. 2. Indians of South America - Economic conditions. 3. Latin America - Social conditions - 1945-. I. Title.
TX7 .B4 Heft 9 HD6995.5
NYPL [JLE 86-3436]

Egorov, A. D. (Aleksandr Dmitrievich) Khoziaĭstvennyĭ mekhanizm uskoreniia nauchno-tekhnicheskogo progressa : voprosy i otvety / A.D. Egorov. Minsk : "Vysheĭshaia shkola", 1986. 61, [3] p. ; 17 cm. Bibliography: p. 61-[62]. LC Card 87-144749
1. Technological innovations - Economic aspects - Soviet Union. 2. Soviet Union - Economic policy - 1986-. I. Title.
HC340.Z9 T44 1986

Egorov, Egor Grigor′evich.
Ėffektivnost′ kapital′nykh vlozheniĭ i novoĭ tekhniki v narodnom khoziaĭstve IAkutskoĭ ASSR . IAkutsk , 1981. 91 p. ; LC Card 82-217455
HC337.I23 C34 1981

Intensifikatsiia i povyshenie ėffektivnosti promyshlennogo proizvodstva v usloviiakh Severa . IAkutsk , 1986. 109 p. ; LC Card 87-159706
HC337.I23 I5214 1986

Egorov, Nikolaĭ Egorovich. Voprosy istorii sotsialisticheskogo preobrazovaniia i razvitiia sel′skogo khoziaĭstva Chuvashskoĭ ASSR /. Cheboksary , 1985. 176 p. ; LC Card 86-100164
HD1492.5.S65 C488 1985

Eguilaz, Higinio París. see **París Eguilaz, Higinio.**

Egyesült Allamok. see **United States.**

EGYPT - COMMERCE - HISTORY.
Höltz, Joachim. Kritik der Geldentstehungstheorien . Berlin , c1984. ii, 401 p. ; ISBN 3-496-00796-6 LC Card 85-147094
HG237 .H64 1984

EGYPT - ECONOMIC CONDITIONS - TO 332 B.C.
Stuchevskiĭ, I. A. (Iosif Aleksandrovich) Zemledel′tsy gosudarstvennogo khoziaĭstva drevnego Egipta ėpokhi Ramessidov /. Moskva , 1982. 254, [2] p. ; LC Card 82-186646
HD2123 .S78 1982

EGYPT - ECONOMIC CONDITIONS - 1952-
Prosterman, Roy L. Egyptian development and U. S. aid . [Seattle, Wash.?] , c1985. i, 32, A1-A10 p. ; LC Card 87-104139 DDC 338.91/73/062 19
HC830.Z9 E446 1985

EGYPT - EMIGRATION AND IMMIGRATION.
Feiler, Gil. The number of Egyptian workers in the Arab oil countries, 1974-1983 . Tel Aviv , c1986. i, 30 leaves ; LC Card 87-404430 DDC 331.6/2/620536 19
HD8662 .F45 1986

EGYPT - FOREIGN ECONOMIC RELATIONS.
Caselli, Clara. L'internationalisation bancaire en Egypte /. Milano [1982] 223 p. ; LC Card 83-132087 DDC 332.1/5/0962 19
HG3386.A6 C37 1982 ***NYPL [JLE 86-1969]***

EGYPT - FOREIGN ECONOMIC RELATIONS - SOVIET UNION - HISTORY.
Makeev, D. A. Vneshnetorgovye sviazi SSSR so stranami Arabskogo Vostoka v 1922-1939 gg. /. Moskva , 1983. 112 p. ; LC Card 84-189987
HF1558.15.A65 M34 1983

Egypt - Government. see **Egypt - Politics and government.**

Egypt. Hay'ah al-'Āmmah lil-Isti'lāmāt.
Petroleum in the Arab Republic of Egypt. Cairo , 1983. 19 p. ; LC Card 84-960509 DDC 338.2/7282/0962 19
HD9577.E32 P48 1983

EGYPT - HISTORY - 1919-
Beinin, Joel, 1948- Workers on the Nile . Princeton, N.J. , c1987. xix, 488 p. : ISBN 0-691-05506-8 (alk. paper) : LC Card 87-45510 DDC 305.5/62/0962 19
HD8786 .B45 1987

Egypt. Majlis al-A'lá lil-Jāmi'āt. Waḥdat Tansīq al-'Alāqāt al-Khārijīyah. Economical study of spare parts consumption in textile industry in Egypt. Cairo, Egypt [1984?] 2 v. : LC Card 86-960234 DDC 338.4/76817677/0962 19
HD9705.5.P373 E34 1984

EGYPT - POLITICS AND GOVERNMENT - 1882-1952.
Beinin, Joel, 1948- Workers on the Nile . Princeton, N.J. , c1987. xix, 488 p. : ISBN 0-691-05506-8 (alk. paper) : LC Card 87-45510 DDC 305.5/62/0962 19
HD8786 .B45 1987

EGYPT - RURAL CONDITIONS.
Raḍwān, Samīr Muḥammad. Agrarian change in Egypt . London , Dover, N.H. , c1986. xii, 167 p. : ISBN 0-7099-4214-1 : LC Card 85-11356 DDC 305.5/69/0962 19
HN786.A8 R33 1985 ***NYPL [JLD 86-1045]***

Egyptian Businessmen Association : membership directory, 1985-1986. Guiza : the Association, [1986] ca. 150 p. : ports. ; 20 cm. LC Card 86-961030 DDC 338/.0025/62 19
1. Businessmen - Egypt - Directories. 2. Egyptian Businessmen Association - Directories. I. Egyptian Businessmen Association.
HC830 .E395 1986

Egyptian Businessmen Association.
Egyptian Businessmen Association . Guiza [1986] ca. 150 p. : LC Card 86-961030 DDC 338/.0025/62 19
HC830 .E395 1986

EGYPTIAN BUSINESSMEN ASSOCIATION - DIRECTORIES.
Egyptian Businessmen Association . Guiza [1986] ca. 150 p. : LC Card 86-961030 DDC 338/.0025/62 19
HC830 .E395 1986

Egyptian development and U. S. aid .
Prosterman, Roy L. [Seattle, Wash.?] , c1985. i, 32, A1-A10 p. ; LC Card 87-104139 DDC 338.91/73/062 19
HC830.Z9 E446 1985

Egységes szülészeti adatszolgáltatási rendszer : a szülések adatai, 1980-1983 / [készült a KSH Népesedésstatisztikai Főosztály Népesedésstatisztikai Osztályán]. Budapest : Központi Statisztikai Hivatal, 1986. 102 p. ; 29 cm. Tables. LC Card 86-233497
1. Childbirth - Hungary - Statistics. I. Hungary. Központi Statisztikai Hivatal. Népesedésstatisztikai Osztály.
HB1002.5.A3 E39 1986

Ehinger, Jürgen. Erfahrungen mit der Mitbestimmung in kommunalen Unternehmen : eine empirische Analyse aus betriebswirtschaftlicher Sicht / Jürgen Ehinger und Wolfgang Niopek.1. Aufl. Baden-Baden : Nomos, 1986. 147 p. ; 23 cm. (Schriften zur öffentlichen Verwaltung und öffentlichen Wirtschaft. Bd. 103) Summary in German and English. Bibliography: p. 139-144. Includes indexes. ISBN 3-7890-1289-0 LC Card 87-118963 DDC 350.87/00943 19
1. Public utilities - Germany (West) - Management - Employee participation. 2. Transportation - Germany (West) - Management - Employee participation. I. Niopek, Wolfgang. II. Title.
HD2768.G44 E38 1986

Ehmcke, Alex. Renckstorf, Karsten.
Landesprogramme von Hörfunk und Fernsehen in Hamburg . Hamburg , c1985. xlvii, vi, 388 p. : ISBN 3-87296-067-9 (pbk.) LC Card 86-109817 DDC 384.54/43/0943515 19
HE8700.9.G4 R45 1985 ***NYPL [MWGK (Germany, West) 86-4239]***

Ehn, Pelle, 1948- Computers and democracy . Aldershot [Hants, England] , Brookfield [Vt.], USA , c1987. x, 434 p. : ISBN 0-566-05476-0 : LC Card 87-8398 DDC 338/.06 19
HD5650 .C65 1987

Ehrenberg, Ronald G. Modern labor economics : theory and public policy / Ronald G. Ehrenberg, Robert S. Smith.3rd ed. Glenview, Ill. : Scott, Foresman, [1987], c1988. 721 p. : ill. ; 24 cm. Includes bibliographies and indexes. ISBN 0-673-18964-3 LC Card 87-9789 DDC 331 19
1. Labor economics. I. Smith, Robert Stewart. II. Title.
HD4901 .E34 1988

Ehrenhaft, Peter D. Countertrade and trading companies . New York, N.Y. , c1984. iv, 283 p. : LC Card 84-196766 DDC 343.73/0878 347.303878 19
KF1976 .C68 1984 ***NYPL [JLD 86-4098]***

Ehrenpromotion von Prof. Dr. George Katona, Ann Arbor, Michigan am 15. Juni 1981 : Gedenkschrift / Fachbereich Wirtschaftswissenschaft der Freien Universität Berlin. Berlin : Presse- und Informationsstelle der Freien Universität Berlin, [1982] 51 p. : port. ; 21 cm. (Informationen aus Lehre und Forschung . 1/1982) English and German. "Auflage 500"--Verso t.p. Bibliography: p. 49-50. LC Card 83-200933
1. Economics - Psychological aspects - Congresses. 2. Katona, George, 1901-. I. Katona, George, 1901-. II. Freie Universität Berlin. Fachbereich 10--Wirtschaftswissenschaft. III. Series: Informationen aus Lehre und Forschung , 1982/1.
HB74.P8 E35 1982

Ehrlicher, Werner.
Geld- und Währungsordnung /. Berlin , c1983. 249 p. : ISBN 3-428-05530-6 LC Card 84-141547
HG999.5 .G4556 1983

Öffentliche Finanzen, Kredit und Kapital . Berlin , c1985. xvi, 618 p., [1] leaf of plates : ISBN 3-428-05737-6 LC Card 85-164173
HJ161 .O33 1985

Steuerpolitik für die soziale Marktwirtschaft . Stuttgart , New York , 1986. 85 p. ; ISBN 3-437-50311-1 LC Card 87-122642 DDC 336.2/00943 19
HJ2687 .S73 1986

EHRLICHER, WERNER.
Öffentliche Finanzen, Kredit und Kapital . Berlin , c1985. xvi, 618 p., [1] leaf of plates : ISBN 3-428-05737-6 LC Card 85-164173
HJ161 .O33 1985

Ehrmann, Michael. United States. Office of Urban Rehabilitation and Community Reinvestment. FHA Title I property improvement loan insurance [microform] . Washington , 1978. 19 p. ;
NYPL [*ZT-1564 no.11]

E.I. du Pont de Nemours & Company. Chemicals and Pigments Dept. Special analysis and outlook for E.I. Du Pont De Nemours & Company (Inc.), Chemicals and Pigments Department. Boston, Mass. (7 Liberty Sq., Boston 02109) [1986] 17, [6] p. : LC Card

86-205857 DDC 338.4/766/00973 19
HD9660.P253 U672 1986

Eichberger, Jürgen, 1952- Geld und Kredit in einer Okonomie mit festen Preisen : ein mikroökonomischer Beitrag zur keynesianischen Unterbeschäftigungstheorie / Jürgen Eichberger. Frankfurt am Main ; New York : P. Lang, c1984. 152 p. : ill. ; 21 cm. (Europäische Hochschulschriften. Reihe V, Volks- und Betriebswirtschaft, 0531-7339 . Bd. 499 = vol. 499 = vol. 499) Bibliography: p. 147-152. ISBN 3-8204-5441-1 LC Card 85-191492
1. Monetary policy - Mathematical models. 2. Credit control - Mathematical models. 3. Underemployment - Mathematical models. 4. Keynesian economics. I. Series: Europäische Hochschulschriften. Reihe V, Volks- und Betriebswirtschaft , Bd. 499. II. Title.
HG230.3 .E53 1984

Eichborn, Ludwig Herman Heinrich Reinhart von. see **Eichborn, Reinhart von.**

Eichborn, Reinhart von. Wirtschaftswörterbuch. 3., völlig neu bearb. Aufl. Düsseldorf, Wien, Econ-Verl. [1961-70] 2 v. 23 cm. "Das vorliegende Werk ist in völliger Neubearbeitung eines erstmalig im Jahre 1947 veröffentlichten Wortschatzes der Wirtschaft entstanden." Prefaces in English and German. CONTENTS. - 1. Englisch-Deutsch. - 2. Deutsch-Englisch. LC Card 70-463836
1. Economics - Dictionaries - German. 2. Economics - Dictionaries. 3. German language - Dictionaries - English. 4. English language - Dictionaries - German.
NYPL [JLD 85-120]

Eichenhöfer, Claudia. Reidenbach, Michael. Verfällt die öffentliche Infrastruktur? . Berlin , 1986. 212 p. : ISBN 3-88118-125-3 LC Card 86-233141
HC290.5.C3 R45 1986

Eichholtz, Dietrich. Geschichte der deutschen Kriegswirtschaft 1939-1945. Berlin, Akademie-Verlag, 1969-<1985 > v. <1-2 > 25 cm. (Forschungen zur Wirtschaftsgeschichte. Bd. 1) One folded leaf in pocket of v. 2. Includes bibliographies and indexes. CONTENTS. - Bd. 1. 1939-1941.--Bd. 2. 1941-1943. LC Card 70-444798
1. World War, 1939-1945 - Economic aspects - Germany. I. Title.
HC286.4 .E34

Eichhorn, Peter, 1939-
Betriebswirtschaftliche Erkenntnisse für Regierung, Verwaltung und öffentliche Unternehmen . Baden-Baden , 1985. 266 p. : ISBN 3-7890-1104-5 LC Card 85-213984
HJ9705 .B48 1985

Erfolgskontrolle bei der Verausgabung öffentlicher Mittel /. Baden-Baden , 1986. 133 p. : ISBN 3-7890-1208-4 LC Card 86-164102
HJ7793 .E73 1986

Eichler, L. Zimmermann, Horst, 1934- Ökonomische Anreizinstrumente in einer auflagenorientierten Umweltpolitik . Stuttgart , 1983. 59 p. ; ISBN 3-17-003279-8 : LC Card 84-148886
HC110.A4 Z55 1983

Eichner, Alfred S.
The macrodynamics of advanced market economies / Alfred S. Eichner. Armonk, N.Y. : M.E. Sharpe, c1987. x, 945 p. : ill. ; 23 cm. Includes bibliographies. ISBN 0-87332-439-0 (pbk.) LC Card 87-9693 DDC 330.12/2 19
1. Capitalism. I. Title.
HB501 .E4 1987

Toward a new economics : essays in post-Keynesian and institutionalist theory / by Alfred S. Eichner. Armonk, N.Y. : M.E. Sharpe, c1985. ix, 240 p. : ill. ; 24 cm. Includes index. Bibliography: p. 219-229. ISBN 0-87332-326-2 LC Card 84-27724 DDC 330 19
1. Economics - Addresses, essays, lectures. 2. Keynesian economics - Addresses, essays, lectures. 3. Institutional economics - Addresses, essays, lectures. I. Title.
HB171 .E35 1985 ***NYPL [JLE 86-1977]***

Eichstätter Beiträge .
(Bd. 17) Fachtagung "Bevölkerungsentwicklung, Bevölkerungswanderung und Urbanisierung in Lateinamerika" (1984 : Eichstätt, Germany) Desarrollo demográfico, migraciones y urbanización en América Latina . Regensburg , c1986. 432 p. : LC Card 86-181152
HB3530.5.A3 F33 1984

EID report (New Mexico. Environmental Improvement Division) .
(no. EID/OHS/85-3) Characteristics of occupational injuries and illnesses in New Mexico, 1982 /. Santa Fe, N.M. [1983?] 43 p. : LC Card 86-621034 DDC 363.1/12/09789021 19
HD7262.5.U62 N625 1983

EIDELSTEDT (HAMBURG, GERMANY)
Pohle, Michael. Industriebrachen und extensiv genutzte Flächen in innenstadtnahen Gewerbegebieten . Paderborn , 1985. viii, 121 p. : ISBN 3-506-73577-2 : LC Card 86-183775
HC289.H2 P64 1985

EIDELSTEDT (HAMBURG, GERMANY) - INDUSTRIES - LOCATION.
Pohle, Michael. Industriebrachen und extensiv genutzte Flächen in innenstadtnahen Gewerbegebieten . Paderborn , 1985. viii, 121 p. : ISBN 3-506-73577-2 : LC Card 86-183775
HC289.H2 P64 1985

Eidem, Rolf, 1943- Ekonomisk demokrati . Stockholm [1984] ii, 169 p. : LC Card 85-108590
HD5660.S9 E38 1984

Eidgenössische Betriebszählung 1985.
Forstbetriebe nach Kantonen = Recensement fédéral des entreprises 1985. Entreprises forestières par cantons. Bern : Bundesamt für Forstwesen und Landschaftsschutz : Bundesamt für Statistik, Schweiz, 1986. 108 p. ; 30 cm. (Amtliche Statistik der Schweiz . Nr. 090 = no 090) Statistische Resultate. 7, Land- und Forstwirtschaft ; Bd. 7 = Données statistiques. 7, Agriculture et sylviculture ; Chiefly tables. Text in French and German. ISBN 3-303-07007-5 LC Card 87-407623 DDC 338.1/7498/09494021 19
1. Forest products industry - Switzerland - Cantons - Statistics. 2. Lumber trade - Switzerland - Cantons - Statistics. I. Switzerland. Bundesamt für Forstwesen und Landschaftsschutz. II. Switzerland. Bundesamt für Statistik. III. Title: Forstbetriebe nach Kantonen. IV. Title: Recensement fédéral des entreprises 1985. V. Series: Amtliche Statistik der Schweiz , Nr. 090.
HD9765.S92 E37 1986

Eidikes ekdoseis.
Hodēgos exagōgikōn diadikasiōn /. [Athēna] [1983] 184 p. : LC Card 86-170148
HF1009.7.E86 H63 1983

Eidikes epistēmonikes meletes .
(1) Sapounas, Giōrgos S. Epharmosmenē analysē tēs zētēsēs . Athēna , 1985. 483 p. : LC Card 86-212306
HD9000.5 .S29 1985

(3) Gkekos, Giōrgos. Polyethnikes hetairies dēmētriakōn kai hē diamorphōsē timōn /. Athēna , 1985. 292 p. : LC Card 86-212325
HD9030.5 .G58 1985

Eidman, Vernon R., 1936- Decision models for California turkey growers / Vernon R. Eidman, Harold O. Carter, and Gerald W. Dean. Berkeley, Calif. : University of California Division of Agricultural Sciences, Giannini Foundation of Agricultural Economics, California Agricultural Experiment Station, [1968] ii, 80 p. : ill. ; 26 cm. (Giannini Foundation monograph . no. 21) Cover title. "July 1968." Bibliography: p. 79-80. LC Card 87-401009 DDC 338.1/09794 s 636.5/92/0068 19
1. Turkey industry - California - Econometric models. I. Carter, Harold O. II. Dean, Gerald W. III. Title. IV. Series.
HD1407 .C27 no. 21 HD9437.U63C3

Eigenfertigung und Fremdbezug. Männel, Wolfgang. Die Wahl zwischen Eigenfertigung und Fremdbezug . Stuttgart , c1981. xvi, 406 p. : ISBN 3-7910-0270-8 LC Card 83-167804
HD2381 .M32 1981

Eigenfertigung und Fremdbezug unter finanzwirtschaftlichen Aspekten /. Kremeyer, Heinz. Wiesbaden , c1982. 330 p. : ISBN 3-409-37340-3 LC Card 83-148058
HD2748 .K74 1982

Eigenimporte der deutschen Industrie /. Jungnickel, Rolf. Hamburg , 1984. 392 p. : ISBN 3-87895-256-2 LC Card 84-247605
HF3566.5 .J86 1984

EIGHT-HOUR MOVEMENT - HISTORY.
Acuña Ortega, Víctor H. Los orígenes de la clase obrera en Costa Rica . San José [1986] 85 p. : LC Card 87-402904 DDC 331/.097286 19
HD8136 .A28 1986

Steinisch, Irmgard. Arbeitszeitverkürzung und sozialer Wandel . Berlin , New York , 1986. xiv, 640 p. : ISBN 3-11-010483-0 LC Card 87-110005 DDC 331.25/7/0973 19
HD5119.I52 U67 1986

Eignungsorientierte Personaleinsatzplanung . Meiritz, Wolfram. Frankfurt am Main , New York , c1984. xv, 304 p. : ISBN 3-8204-5164-1 LC Card 85-198624
HF5549 .M343 1984

Eijken, Anne. Bovenkerk, Frank. Italiaans ijs . Meppel [1983?] 203 p. : ISBN 90-6009-551-0 LC Card 83-179690
HD9281.N42 B68 1983

Eimicke, Victor W. Managing human resources : documenting the personnel function / by Victor W. Eimicke and Laura E. Klimley.1st ed. Oxford [Oxfordshire] ; New York : Pergammon Press, 1987. x, 211 p. : ill. ; 32 cm. ISBN 0-08-034768-1 (U. S.) : LC Card 86-25273 DDC 658.3 19
1. Personnel management. 2. Personnel records. 3. Personnel procedure manuals. I. Klimley, Laura E. II. Title.
HF5549 .E44 1987

Einbruch in den Herrenclub . Edding, Cornelia, 1943- Reinbek bei Hamburg , 1983. 184 p. : ISBN 3-499-15251-7 (pbk.) LC Card 87-673369
HD6054.2.G3 E33x 1983

Der Einfluss der Geldpolitik auf die Kapitalmarktentwicklung /. Jander, Sigurd. Berlin , c1986. 176 p. : ISBN 3-428-06122-5 LC Card 87-134174 DDC 332.63/2 19
HG4523 .J36 1986

Der Einfluss der Steuern auf die Investitionsentscheidungen der Unternehmen . Wittmann, Franz, 1933- Frankfurt , New York , c1986. 405 p. ; ISBN 3-593-33642-1 LC Card 86-173001
HG4028.C4 W585 1986

Der Einfluss des Staates auf den Wettbewerb / herausgegeben von Burkhardt Röper. Berlin : Duncker & Humblot, c1986. 101 p. ; 24 cm. (Schriften des Vereins für Socialpolitik, Gesellschaft für Wirtschafts- und Sozialwissenschaften . n.F., Bd. 158) Includes bibliographical references. CONTENTS. - Wettbewerbsbeeinträchtigungen als Folge der Kooperation von Staat und Wirtschaft / von Hellmuth St. Seidenfus -- Der Einfluss des Staates auf den Wettbewerb aus der Sicht der Monopolkommission / von Erhard Kantzenbach -- Der Einfluss des Staates auf den Wettbewerb aus der Sicht des Bundesministeriums für Wirtschaft / von Hans Tietmeyer -- Der Einfluss der Forschungs- und Entwicklungspolitik auf den Wettbewerb / von Josef Rembser -- Der Einfluss der öffentlichen Hand auf das Innovationsverhalten von Unternehmen, das Beispiel der Informationstechnologie / von Helmut Rausch. ISBN 3-428-06084-9 LC Card 87-132303 DDC 338.943 19
1. Industry and state - Germany, West. 2. Competition - Germany, West. I. Röper, Burkhardt. II. Series.
HD3616.G35 E38 1986

Der Einfluss staatlicher Budgetdefizite auf die Zinsentwicklung in der Bundesrepublik Deutschland und den Vereinigten Staaten . Sherman, Heidemarie C. München , c1986. xxiii, 190 p. : ISBN 3-88512-019-4 LC Card 86-192070
HJ2110 .S53 1986

Der Einfluss verschiedener Preisbildungsmechanismen auf die gesamtwirtschfliche Beschäftigung /. Borgmeier, Bernd, 1955- Frankfurt am Main , New York , c1984. 362 p. : ISBN 3-8204-5601-5 : LC Card 85-198888
HB221 .B592 1984

Einfluss von Verkehrssicherheitsinformationen auf unfallbeteiligte Kraftfahrer /. Echterhoff, Wilfried. Köln [1983], c1981. 112 p. : LC Card 84-147580
HE5614.5.G3 E34 1983

Einführung in die Ökonometrie /. Heil, Johann. München , c1984. 320 p. : ISBN 3-486-28801-6 (pbk.) LC Card 87-672731
HB139 .H44x 1984

Einführung in die Volkswirtschaft /. Ziegler, Wilhelm, 1891- Berlin , 1925. 94, [1] p. ; LC Card 83-234150
HB175 .Z515 1925

Einführung in die Volkswirtschaftslehre /. Borner, Silvio. Diessenhofen , c1983. 105 p. : ISBN 3-7253-0164-6 : LC Card 83-184501
HB175 .B7315 1983

Einführung in die Wirtschaftsinformatik /. Stahlknecht, Peter. Berlin , New York , c1985. xiv, 396 p. : ISBN 0-387-15466-3 (U. S.) LC Card 86-219262
HF5548.2 .S7725 1985

Eingangspostbearbeitung in Bürokommunikationssystemen . Schumann, Matthias. Berlin , New York , c1987. xi, 156 p. ; ISBN 0-387-17369-2 (U. S.) LC Card 87-133887 DDC 651.7/59 19
HF5547 .S457 1987

Einhundertfünfzig Jahre Ruhrgebiet. Schlieper, Andreas. 150 Jahre Ruhrgebiet . Düsseldorf , 1986. 224 p. : ISBN 3-590-18150-8 LC Card 86-231681
HC288.R8 S34 1986

Einige Aspekte moderner Normung unter Berücksichtigung der Produktnormung /. Hens, Albert T. Dortmund , 1977. 38 p. ; LC Card 84-121721
HD30 .A7 Heft 183 HD62

Einige reale Aspekte der Aussenhandelsliberalisierung in Entwicklungsländern /. Sánchez Holguín, Carlos Gerardo, 1952- München , c1986. 152 p. : ISBN 3-88259-368-7 LC Card 86-156293
HF2580.9 .S25 1986

Einkommensgerechtigkeit, was darunter verstanden wird . Norden, Gilbert. Wien , 1985. 304 p. : ISBN 3-205-06324-4 LC Card 86-196913
HB523 .N67 1985

Einkommensquellen und Lebenschancen . Krause, Detlef. Berlin , c1986. 189 p. : ISBN 3-428-06114-4 LC Card 87-130932 DDC 339.2/2/0943 19
HC290.5.I5 K7 1986

Einkommensunterschiede zwischen Frauen und Männern . Diekmann, Andreas. Wien [1985] 2 v. (244, 4 p.) : LC Card 86-150241
HD6061 .D54 1985

Einkommensverteilung und Qualifikation . Clement, Werner. Wien , 1984. vi, 201 p. : ISBN 3-85436-020-7 LC Card 84-191161
HC270.I5 C56 1984

Einsatz von Aggregaten, Modellierung und Planung /. Roski, Reinhold. Berlin , c1986. xi, 321 p. : ISBN 3-428-06038-5 LC Card 86-188767
HB241 .R67 1986

Einseitige Betrachtungen . Engels, Wolfram. Düsseldorf , 1986. 240 p. ; LC Card 87-146603 DDC 338.943 19
HD84 .E53 1986

Einstein, Gilles O., 1950- Learning to use SPSSx / Gilles O. Einstein, Elaine C. Nocks. Englewood Cliffs, N.J. : Prentice-Hall, c1987. viii, 183 p. : ill. ; 23 cm. On t.p. "x" is superscript. Includes index. ISBN 0-13-528050-8 (pbk.) LC Card 86-30263 DDC 005.3/29 19
1. SPSS X (Computer system). 2. Social sciences - Data processing. I. Nocks, Elaine C., 1945-. II. Title.
HA32 .E45 1987

Einwendungen bei Eurocheque und Kreditkarte /. Beck, Peter. [S.l. , 1986] (Köln : Druck und Verarbeitung, Druck- + Verlagshaus Wienand) xv, 146, 31 p. ; LC Card 86-233484
HG3756.G3 B43 1986

Einwitschläger, Arno. Amerikanische Wirtschaftspolitik in Österreich, 1945-1949 / Arno Einwitschläger. Wien : Böhlau, 1986. 206 p. : ill. ; 24 cm. (Böhlaus zeitgeschichtliche Bibliothek. Bd. 6) Bibliography: p. [193]-198. Includes indexes. ISBN 3-205-08814-X LC Card 87-112406
1. United States - Foreign economic relations - Austria. 2. Austria - Foreign economic relations - United States. I. Title.
HF1456.5.A9 E39 1986

Einzelschriften zur Statistik des Saarlandes, 0558-0838 .
(Nr. 67) Kommunal- und Europawahl am 17. Juni 1984. Saarbrücken , 1984. 115 p. : ISBN 3-88718-020-8 : LC Card 85-130989
HA1320 .S244 Nr. 67 JN4945.S265

Eisenbahn und Autowahn . Wolf, Winfried. Hamburg , c1987. 565 p. : ISBN 3-89136-105-X LC Card 87-167400 DDC 388/.09 19
HE151 .W58 1987

Die Eisenbahnen Österreich-Ungarns, 1822-1867 /. Kupka, P. F. (Peter Friedrich), 1846- Leipzig , 1888. x, 386 p. : LC Card 83-217358
HE3058 .K86 1888

Der Eisenbahnkönig, oder, Rumänien lag in Linden . Voigt, Wolfgang. München , 1982. 142 p. : ISBN 3-923126-15-8 (pbk.) LC Card 87-672921
HD7289.5.R1 V64x 1982

Eisenberg, Christiane, 1956- Deutsche und englische Gewerkschaften : Entstehung und Entwicklung bis 1878 im Vergleich / von Christiane Eisenberg. Göttingen : Vandenhoeck & Ruprecht, c1986. 391 p. ; 24 cm. (Kritische Studien zur Geschichtswissenschaft. Bd. 72) Originally presented as the author's thesis (doctoral)--Universität Bielefeld, Wintersemester 1985/86. Bibliography: p. 344-381. Includes index. ISBN 3-525-35733-8 LC Card 87-127078 DDC 331.88/0941 19
1. Trade-unions - Germany - History - 19th century. 2. Trade-unions - GreatBritain - History - 19th century. I. Title.
HD6694 .E27 1986

Eisenberg, Richard, 1956- How to avoid a mid-life financial crisis / Richard Eisenberg. Glenview, Ill. : Scott, Foresman, c1987. xxi, 426 p. : ill. ; 25 cm. Includes index. ISBN 0-673-18727-6 : LC Card 86-31647 DDC 332.024 19
1. Finance, Personal - United States. I. Title.
HG179 .E39 1987

Eisendrath, Joseph L.
Harmer, C. H. C. (Cyril Henry Carrington) Newfoundland air mails . Cinnaminson, N.J., U. S.A. , 1984. x, 181 p. : LC Card 87-147693 DDC 383/.144/09718 19
HE6185.C23 N475 1984

Kronstein, Max. Rocket mail flights of the world to 1986 /. Cinnaminson, N.J. , 1986. 191 p. : LC Card 87-400297 DDC 383/.144 19
HE6239.R6 K76 1986

Los ejidos de Yucatán y el henequén . Cárdenas, Lázaro, 1895-1970. [Mexico City, Mexico] , c1984. 79 p. : LC Card 87-403579 DDC 333.3/1/7265 19
HD1333.M62 Y823 1984

EJIDOS - MEXICO - LAGUNA REGION.
Rello, Fernando. Estado y ejidos en México . Ginebra , 1986. xxvi, 122 p. : LC Card 86-210274
HG2051.M62 L37 1986

EJIDOS - MEXICO - YAUTEPEC (MORELOS) - HISTORY.
Rounds, Christopher R., 1945- From hacienda to ejido . New York , 1987. viii, 268 p. ; ISBN 0-8240-1369-7 (alk. paper) : LC Card 87-8526 DDC 333.3/1/7249 19
HD1333.M62 Y387 1987

EJIDOS - MEXICO - YUCATÁN (STATE) - HISTORY.
Cárdenas, Lázaro, 1895-1970. Los ejidos de Yucatán y el henequén . [Mexico City, Mexico] , c1984. 79 p. : LC Card 87-403579 DDC 333.3/1/7265 19
HD1333.M62 Y823 1984

Ekaizer, Ernesto, 1949- José María Ruiz Mateos, el ultimo magnate / Ernesto Ekaizer. 2a ed. Esplugues de Llobregat, Barcelona : Plaza & Janes, 1985. 833 p., [16] p. of plates : ill., ports. ; 22 cm. (Epoca) Includes index. Bibliography: p. 827-[834] ISBN 84-01-33291-5 LC Card 86-122394 DDC 332.1/6 B 19
1. Ruiz Mateos, José María. 2. Businessmen - Spain - Biography. 3. Holding companies - Spain. 4. Bank holding companies - Spain. 5. Government ownship - Spain. I. Title.
HG4216.R85 E38 1985 ***NYPL [JFD 86-6856]***

Ekanam, N. F. (Nkanta F.) Transportation in Nigerian national development . Ibadan , c1981. xi, 602 p. : ISBN 978-18-1010-6 (pbk.) LC Card 82-196087 DDC 380.5/09669 19
HE287.7 .T72 1981 ***NYPL [Sc E 86-178]***

Ekelund, Robert B. (Robert Burton), 1940-
Economics / Robert B. Ekelund, Jr., Robert D. Tollison. 2nd ed. Glenview, Ill. : Scott, Foresman, c1988. xl, 942, [33] p. : ill. (some col.) ; 26 cm. Includes bibliographical references and index. ISBN 0-673-39717-3 LC Card 87-23306 DDC 330 19
1. Economics. I. Tollison, Robert D. II. Title.
HB171.5 .E47 1988

Macroeconomics. 2nd ed. / Robert B. Ekelund, Jr., Charles D. DeLorme, Jr. Plano, Tex. : Business Publications, 1987. xvi, 536 p. : col. ill. ; 24 cm. DeLorme's name appears first on the earlier ed. Includes bibliographies and index. ISBN 0-256-03678-0 LC Card 86-71959 DDC 339 19
1. Macroeconomics. I. DeLorme, Charles D. II. Title.
HB172.5 .D44 1987

Macroeconomics / Robert B. Ekelund, Jr., Robert D. Tollison. 2nd ed. Glenview, Ill. : Scott, Foresman, c1988. xxix, 592 p. : ill. (some col.) ; 26 cm. Includes index. ISBN 0-673-39768-8 (pbk.) LC Card 87-23513 DDC 339 19
1. Macroeconomics. I. Tollison, Robert D. II. Title.
HB172.5 .E42 1988

Microeconomics / Robert B. Ekelund, Jr., Robert D. Tollison. 2nd ed. Glenview, Ill. : Scott, Foresman, c1988. xxx, 619 p. : ill. ; 26 cm. Includes index. ISBN 0-673-39769-6 (pbk.) LC Card 87-23514 DDC 338.5 19
1. Microeconomics. I. Tollison, Robert D. II. Title.
HB172 .E39 1988

Ekenhill, Jan-Erik. Jobb i framtid? . Stockholm , c1983. 121 p. : ISBN 91-7410-270-2 : LC Card 84-103510
HC375 .J53 1983

Ekereke, Edet M.
Nigerian investment in education. 1975.
Nigeria : economic, education, and health themes / by HEERN Consultants Inc. Hyattsville, Md. , 1975. iii, 35 p. ; LC Card 85-114200
HC1055 .N533 1975

Ekholm, Bo-Göran. Skattetryckets fördelning inom finländska industriföretag / Bo-Göran Ekholm & Carl-Henrik Frejborg. Helsingfors : Svenska handelshögskolan, [1985] 39 p. ; 30 cm. (Meddelanden från Svenska handelshögskolan, 0357-4598 = Swedish School of Economics and Business Administration working papers . 131 (1985)) Bibliography: leaf 39. ISBN 951-555-222-2 LC Card 85-214497
1. Corporations - Taxation - Finland. I. Frejborg, Carl-Henrik. II. Series: Meddelanden fran Svenska handelshögskolan , 131. III. Title.
HD2753.F5 E38 1985

'Ekkasān kh
(B-SY ch. 69-no. 14) Samut sathiti rāi pī, 2509 . [Bangkok] [19]69. 35 p., [1] leaf of plates : LC Card 83-921129
HA4600.55.Z9 N3737 1969

(S-SIS ch. 71-no. 7) Sathiti thī samkhan, 2512. [Bangkok] [19]71. [11], 34 p., [1] leaf of plates : LC Card 83-921120 DDC 315.93 19
HA4600.55.Z9 P428 1971

(S-SIS ch. 71-no. 8) Sathiti thī samkhan, 2512, Changwat Krabī =. [Bangkok] [19]71. [8], 36 leaves, [1] leaf of plates : LC Card 83-921122
HA4600.55 .S275 1971

'Ekkasān (Thailand. Krom Rængngān) .
(māilēk 12) Saphāp læ 'ōkāt nai kānthamngān nai kitčhakān m [Bangkok] [2509 i.e. 1966] 2, 35 p., [5] leaves of plates : LC Card 80-911179
HD8039.M72 T527 1966

Ekko av fremtiden /. Ertresvåg, Per-Aslak, 1931- Oslo , c1986. 163 p. : ISBN 82-504-0815-2 LC Card 86-217931
HC365 .E77 1986

Ėkologicheskiĭ krizis v uslovii͡akh sovremennogo kapitalizma . Pogorelova, O. A. (Oksana Afanas'evna) Kiev , 1986. 110, [2] p. ; LC Card 86-233475
HD75.6 .P64 1986

Ėkologo-ėkonomicheskai͡a ėffektivnost' prirodopol'zovanii͡a /. Tupytsi͡a, I͡Uriĭ I͡Ur'evich. Moskva , 1980. 165 p. ; LC Card 81-146449
HC333.5 .T86 1980

Ekonometria : praca zbiorowa / pod redakcją naukową Mirosława Krzysztofiaka.Wyd. 1. Warszawa : Państwowe Wydawn. Ekonomiczne, 1978. 371 p. : ill. ; 25 cm. Bibliography: p. [362]-367. Includes index. LC Card 81-212730
1. Econometrics. 2. Econometric models. I. Krzysztofiak, Mirosław.
HB139 .E386 1978

Ekonometria /. Pawłowski, Zbigniew. Warszawa , 1978. 495 p. : LC Card 81-211573
HB139 .P375 1978

Ekonomi & pembangunan . Sastraatmaja, Entang. Bandung , c1986. viii, 284 p. : LC Card 86-944011
HC447 .S363 1986

Ekonomi dan pembangunan. Sastraatmaja, Entang. Ekonomi & pembangunan . Bandung , c1986. viii, 284 p. : LC Card 86-944011
HC447 .S363 1986

Ekonomi och kriminalitet . Schuller, Bernd-Joachim. [Göteborg , 1986] ix, 250 p. : LC Card 86-212186
HB54 .G65 no. 17 HV6171

Ekonomi och samhälle (Svenska handelshögskolan (Helsinki, Finland)) .
(nr. 31) Vetenskap och företagsledning . Helsingfors , 1982. 461 p. : ISBN 951-555-158-7 LC Card 82-239854
HB71 .V45 1982

(nr. 32) Lindqvist, Lars-Johan. Marknadsföring till handeln . Helsingfors , 1983. 309 p. : ISBN 951-555-183-8 LC Card 84-103976
HF5421.5.F5 L56 1983

(nr. 37) Berglund, Tom. Anomalies in stock returns on a thin security market /. Helsingfors , 1986. vi, 191 p. : ISBN 951-555-239-7 (pbk.) LC Card 86-224629 DDC 332.63/222 19
HG4636 .B47 1986

Ekonomi pembangunan. Sastraatmaja, Entang. Ekonomi & pembangunan . Bandung , c1986. viii, 284 p. : LC Card 86-944011
HC447 .S363 1986

Ekonomi politik kebutuhan pokok . Sjahrir, 1945- [Political economy of basic needs in Indonesia. Indonesian.] Jakarta , 1986. xxiii, 280 p. : ISBN 979-8015-02-9 (pbk.) LC Card 86-943050
HC450.B38 S5216 1986

Ekonomi styrning av projekt /. Magnusson, Åke, 1943- Stockholm [1984] 66 p., [3] folded leaves of plates : ISBN 91-524-0729-2 LC Card 85-149256
HD69.P75 M34 1984

Ekonomia e Shqipërisë në vitet e para të ndërtimit socialist, 1944-1948 /. Fishta, Iljaz. Tiranë , 1984. 489 p. ; LC Card 85-163026
HC402 .F55 1984

Ekonomia polityczna kapitalizmu : praca zbiorowa / pod redakcją Henryka Maciejewskiego.Wyd. 1. Poznań : Politechnika Poznańska, 1978. 240 p. : ill. ; 24 cm. Includes bibliographical references. LC Card 81-172481
1. Economics. I. Maciejewski, Henryk. II. Politechnika Poznańska.
HB179.P7 E37 1978

Ėkonomicheskaia ėffektivnost′ rekonstruktsii deĭstvuiushchikh predpriiatiĭ / [otvetstvennyĭ redaktor M.A. Sergeev]. Sverdlovsk : Akademiia nauk SSSR, Ural′skiĭ nauch. tsentr, 1981. 171 p. ; 20 cm. Includes bibliographical references. LC Card 83-192125
1. Industrial equipment - Russian S.F.S.R. - Ural Mountains Region. 2. Capital investments - Russian S.F.S.R. - Ural Mountains Region. 3. Replacement of industrial equipment. I. Sergeev, Mikhail Aleksandrovich. II. Akademiia nauk SSSR. Ural′skiĭ nauchnyĭ tsentr.
HD39.3 .E37 1981

Ėkonomicheskaia ėffektivnost′ zhivotnovodstva v sisteme APK /. Rukosuev, P. N. (Platon Nikolaevich) Moskva , 1985. 127 p. ; LC Card 86-133226
HD9425.S652 R86 1985

Ėkonomicheskaia ėkspansiia SShA. US economic expansion . Moscow , 1986. 216 p. ; LC Card 87-112029 DDC 337.7308 19
HF1456.5.L3 U8 1986

Ėkonomicheskaia ėkspansiia SShA. US economic expansion . Moscow , 1986. 172 p. ; LC Card 86-204071 DDC 337.7304 19
HF3092 .U8 1986

Ėkonomicheskaia i sotsial′naia geografiia : problemy i perspektivy : sbornik nauchnykh trudov / [otvetstvennyĭ redaktor O.P. Litovka]. Leningrad : Geogr. ob-vo SSSR, 1984. 149 p. : ports. ; 23 cm. At head of title: Akademiia nauk SSSR. Geograficheskoe obshchestvo SSSR. Includes bibliographies. LC Card 85-191961
1. Soviet Union - Economic conditions - 1976-. 2. Geography, Economic. I. Litovka, Oleg Petrovich. II. Geograficheskoe obshchestvo SSSR.
HC336.25 .E3812 1984

Ėkonomicheskaia mysl′ Drevnego Rima . Polianskiĭ, F. IA. (Fedor IAkovlevich) Moskva , 1978. 355 p. ; LC Card 81-167944
HC39 .P65 1978

Ėkonomicheskaia otsenka i prognozirovanie ispol′zovaniia prirodnykh resursov Kazakhstana / [otvetstvennyĭ redaktor M.G. Isaeva]. Alma-Ata : Izd-vo "Nauka" Kazakhskoĭ SSR, 1980. 161 p. ; 20 cm. At head of title: Akademiia nauk Kazakhskoĭ SSR. Institut ėkonomiki. Includes bibliographical references. LC Card 82-106708
1. Natural resources - Kazakh S.S.R. 2. Raw materials - Kazakh S.S.R. I. Isaeva, M. G. (Muza Gavrilovna). II. Institut ėkonomiki (Qazaq SSR ghylym akademiiasy).
HC337.K3 E34 1980

Ėkonomicheskaia politika v period postroeniia sotsializma v SSSR. Dmitrenko, Vladimir Petrovich. Economic policy during the construction of socialism in the USSR /. Moscow , c1987. 156 p. ; LC Card 86-201129 DDC 338.947 19
HC335.2 .D56 1987

Ėkonomicheskaia teoriia i khoziaĭstvennaia praktika (Moscow, R.S.F.S.R. : 1981)
Budaveĭ, Vsevolod IUr′evich. Dolgosrochnye narodnokhoziaĭstvennye programmy . Moskva , 1980. 205 p. ; LC Card 81-143196
HD45 .B792 1980

Ėkonomicheskaia zhizn′ strany.
Ėkonomicheskie problemy transporta SSSR /. Moskva , 1985. 181, [3] p. ; LC Card 86-100790
HE255.A2 E38 1985

Sovershenstvovanie khoziaĭstvennogo mekhanizma v stroitel′stve /. Minsk , 1984. 111 p. : LC Card 86-220340
HD9715.S73 B947 1984

Ėkonomicheskaia zhizn′ strany (Minsk, Byelorussian S.S.R.)
Sovershenstvovanie khoziaĭstvennogo mekhanizma v stroitel′stve /. Minsk , 1984. 111 p. : LC Card 86-220340
HD9715.S73 B947 1984

Ėkonomicheskiia teoriia i khoziaĭstvennaia praktika (Moscow, R.S.F.S.R. : 1981)
Chernoivanov, G. E. (Gennadiĭ Efimovich) Fondoėmkost′ produktsii i ėffektivnost′ sotsialisticheskogo proizvodstva /. Moskva , 1980. 156 p. ; LC Card 81-134415
HC340.C3 C54 1980

Ėkonomicheskie aspekty integratsii nauki i proizvodstva / pod redaktsieĭ S.G. Galuzy. Minsk : "Nauka i tekhnika", 1986. 204, [4] p. ; 21 cm. At head of title: Akademiia nauk Belorusskoĭ SSR. Institut ėkonomiki. Bibliography: p. 200-[205]. LC Card 87-106384
1. Research - Economic aspects - Byelorussian S.S.R. 2. Research, Industrial - Byelorussian S.S.R. I. Galuza, Stanislav Grigor′evich. II. Instytut ėkanomiki (Akadėmiia navuk Belaruskaĭ SSR).
HC337.B933 R43 1986

Ėkonomicheskie aspekty ratsional′nogo ispol′zovaniia resursov okeana i okhrany morskoĭ sredy : sbornik nauchnykh trudov / [redkollegiia, M.I. Kraeva (otvetstvennyĭ redaktor) ... et al.]. Vladivostok : DVNTS AN SSSR, 1984. 124 p. : ill. ; 20 cm. At head of title: Akademiia nauk SSSR. Dal′nevostochnyĭ nauchnyĭ tsentr. Institut ėkonomiki okeana. Includes bibliographies. LC Card 85-234774
1. Marine resources. 2. Marine resources conservation. I. Kraeva, M. I. II. Institut ėkonomiki okeana (Akademiia nauk SSSR).
HC92 .E37 1984

Ėkonomicheskie besedy. Ėkonomicheskiia besiedy. Moskva : Izd. Knizhnago magazina A. Lang, 1888. 79 p. ; 23 cm. LC Card 86-222027
1. Economics. I. Title.
HB178 .E38 1888

Ėkonomicheskie funktsii upravleniia proizvoditel′nym trudom / [Anatoliĭ Nikitovich Zhurlov ... et al. ; redaktor S.V. Pirogova]. Kiev : Gol. izd-vo ob″edineniia "Vyshcha shkola", 1986. 167 p. ; 20 cm. Bibliography: p. 163-[166]. LC Card 87-152432
1. Machinery industry - Soviet Union - Labor productivity. 2. Jewelry trade - Soviet Union - Labor productivity. 3. Labor productivity - Soviet Union - Measurement - Data processing. I. Zhurlov, Anatoliĭ Nikitovich. II. Pirogova, S. V.
HD9705.S595 E37 1986

Ėkonomicheskie interesy i stimuly pri sotsializme /. Ageev, V. M. (Valentin Mikhaĭlovich) Moskva , 1984. 190 p. ; LC Card 85-108645
HC336.25 .A375 1984

Ėkonomicheskie interesy i uskorenie nauchno-tekhnicheskogo progressa : mezhvuzovskiĭ sbornik nauchnykh trudov / [otvetstvennyĭ redaktor B.I. Tabachnikas ; redaktsionnaia kollegiia V.V. Karpov, I.V. Mikhaĭlov]. Leningrad : Leningradskiĭ gos. pedagog. in-t im. A.I. Gertsena, 1984. 157 p. ; 22 cm. At head of title: Ministerstvo prosveshcheniia RSFSR. Includes bibliographical references. LC Card 86-186728
1. Technological innovations - Soviet Union - Finance. I. Tabachnikas, B. I. II. Karpov, V. V. III. Mikhaĭlov, I. V. (Ivan Vasil′evich). IV. Leningradskiĭ gosudarstvennyĭ pedagogicheskiĭ institut imeni A.I. Gertsena.
HC340.T4 E36 1984

Ėkonomicheskie osnovy industrializatsii sel′skogo khoziaĭstva Severa /. Mal′tsev, V. I. (Valer′ian Ivanovich) Moskva , 1985. 142 p. ; LC Card 86-165352
HD1995.N55 M34 1985

Ėkonomicheskie osnovy intensifikatsii lesnogo khoziaĭstva Karel′skoĭ ASSR /. Valentik, I. IA. (Ivan IAkovlevich) Leningrad , 1986. 135, [1] p. : LC Card 87-125199
HD9765.S653 K378 1986

Ėkonomicheskie otnosheniia KNR so stranami IUgo-Vostochnoĭ Azii /. Manezhev, S. A. (Sergeĭ Aleksandrovich) Moskva , 1980. 191 p. ; LC Card 81-130904
HF1604.Z4 A7856 1980

Ėkonomicheskie problemy novogo ėtapa osushchestvleniia Leninskogo kooperativnogo plana / [otvetstvennyĭ redaktor E.S. Karnaukhova]. Moskva : Izd-vo "Nauka", 1979. 365 p. ; 21 cm. (Problemy sovetskoĭ ėkonomiki) At head of title: Akademiia nauk SSSR. Institut ėkonomiki. Includes bibliographical references. LC Card 81-165451
1. Agriculture - Economic aspects - Soviet Union. 2. Agricultural industries - Soviet Union. 3. Agricultural productivity - Soviet Union. I. Karnaukhova, E. S. (Evfraziia Stepanovna).
HD1992 .E3593 1979

Ėkonomicheskie problemy osvoeniia Ural′skogo Severa / [otvetstvennye redaktory O.V. Tiutkov, N.I. Chesnokov]. Sverdlovsk : Akademiia nauk SSSR, Ural′skiĭ nauch. tsentr, 1982. 69 p. : ill. ; 22 cm. Includes bibliographical references. LC Card 83-188353
1. Soviet Union, Northern - Economic conditions. 2. Ural Mountains Region (R.S.F.S.R.) - Economic conditions. I. Tiutkov, O. V. II. Chesnokov, N. I. (Nikolaĭ Ivanovich). III. Akademiia nauk SSSR. Ural′skiĭ nauchnyĭ tsentr.
HC336.9.N65 E37 1982

Ėkonomicheskie problemy perekhoda k sotsializmu stran s nerazvitoĭ ėkonomikoĭ . Sovetsko-v′etnamskiĭ simpozium na temu "Ėkonomicheskie problemy perekhoda k sotsializmu" (1984 : Moscow, R.S.F.S.R.) [Moskva , 1986. 254 p. ; LC Card 87-108102
HC444 .S69 1984

Ėkonomicheskie problemy povysheniia proizvoditel′nosti truda v stroitel′stve /. Borisov, IU. D. (IUriĭ Dmitrievich) Moskva , 1985. 183 p. ; LC Card 86-208622
HD9715.S72 B67 1985

Ėkonomicheskie problemy prirodopol′zovaniia / otvetstvennye redaktory K.G. Gofman, G.A. Motkin. Moskva : "Nauka", 1985. 137 p. : ill. ; 22 cm. At head of title: Akademiia nauk SSSR. TSentral′nyĭ ėkonomiko-matematicheskiĭ institut. Includes bibliographies. LC Card 86-119089
1. Environmental policy - Soviet Union. 2. Natural resources - Soviet Union. I. Gofman, K. G. (Konstantin Georgievich). II. Motkin, G. A. III. TSentral′nyĭ ėkonomiko-matematicheskiĭ institut (Akademiia nauk SSSR).
HC340.E5 E395 1985

Ėkonomicheskie problemy razvitiia promyshlennogo proizvodstva potrebitel′skoĭ kooperatsii . Istamov, D. I. (Damir Istamovich)

Tashkent , 1982. 126 p. ; LC Card 82-200979
HD3517.A3 C475 1982

Ėkonomicheskie problemy razvitiia stran sotsialisticheskoĭ orientatsii / [otvetstvennye redaktory S.S. Dzarasov, V.F. Stanis]. Moskva : Izd-vo "Nauka," Glav. red. vostochnoĭ lit-ry, 1986. 239 p. ; 23 cm. At head of title: Ordena Druzhby Narodov Universitet druzhby narodov imeni Patrisa Lumumby. Bibliography: p. 232-[238]. LC Card 86-221922
1. Developing countries - Economic conditions. 2. Socialism - Developing countries. I. Dzarasov, S. S. (Soltan Safarbievich). II. Stanis, V. F. (Vladimir Frantsevich). III. Universitet druzhby narodov imeni Patrisa Lumumby.
HC59.7 .E355 1986

Ėkonomicheskie problemy sovershenstvovaniia torgovli na osnove kompleksnoĭ ratsionalizatsii /. Gadzhiev, B. U. (Bagautdin Ustaevich) Makhachkala , 1984. 282 p. ; LC Card 86-213223
HF3629.D34 G33 1984

Ėkonomicheskie problemy transporta SSSR / S.P. Arsen´ev ... [et al.]. Moskva : "Transport", 1985. 181, [3] p. ; 20 cm. (Ėkonomicheskaia zhizn´ strany) Bibliography: p. 179-[182] LC Card 86-100790
1. Transportation - Soviet Union. I. Arsen´ev, S. P. (Sergeĭ Pavlovich). II. Series.
HE255.A2 E38 1985

Ėkonomicheskie problemy upravleniia stroitel´nym proizvodstvom na Severe /. Kaplan, L. M. (Lev Moiseevich) Leningrad , 1983. 167 p. : LC Card 84-113191
HD9715.S73 N675 1983

Ėkonomicheskie sviazi i sovershenstvovanie khoziaĭstvennogo mekhanizma : mezhvuzovskiĭ sbornik nauchnykh trudov / [redaktsionnaia kollegiia V.P. Mosin (otv. redaktor), V.P. Bardovskiĭ, Loskutov V.B.]. Kursk : Kurskiĭ gos. pedagog. in-t, 1985. 107 p. ; 20 cm. At head of title: Ministerstvo prosveshcheniia RSFSR. Kurskiĭ ordena "Znak Pocheta" gosudarstvennyĭ pedagogicheskiĭ institut. Includes bibliographical references. LC Card 86-235039
1. Input-output analysis - Soviet Union. 2. Central planning - Soviet Union. 3. Soviet Union - Economic policy - 1981-. I. Mosin, V. P. II. Bardovskiĭ, V. P. III. Luskutov, V. B. IV. Kurskiĭ gosudarstvennyĭ pedagogicheskiĭ institut.
HC340.I57 E37 1985

Ėkonomicheskie sviazi proizvodstva i potrebleniia pri sotsializme : mezhvuzovskiĭ sbornik nauchnykh trudov / [redaktsionnaia kollegiia, V.R. Praude (otvetstvennyĭ redaktor), L.S. Krylov, V.M. Pormale]. Riga : Latviĭskiĭ gos. universitet im. P. Stuchki, 1978. 152 p. ; 21 cm. At head of title: Ministerstvo vysshego i srednego spetsial´nogo obrazovaniia Latviĭskoĭ SSR. Latviĭskiĭ ordena Trudovogo Krasnogo Znameni gosudarstvennyĭ universitet imeni Petra Stuchki. Kafedra politicheskoĭ ėkonomiki. Includes bibliographical references. LC Card 81-168062
1. Durable goods, Consumer - Latvia. 2. Consumption (Economics) - Latvia. I. Praude, V. R. (Valeriĭ Robertovich). II. Krylov, L. S. III. Pormale, V. M. IV. Pētera Stučkas Latvijas Valsts universitāte. Republikas augstskolu politiskās ekonomijas bāzes katedra.
HF1040.9.S65 E36 1978

Ėkonomicheskie zakony i ėkonomicheskaia politika KPSS /. Palkin, IUriĭ Ivanovich. Kiev , 1985. 245 p. ; LC Card 87-104961
HC336.25 .P35 1985

Ėkonomicheskie znaniia--stroiteliu, srednee zveno.
Osnovy ėkonomiki i upravleniia stroitel´nym proizvodstvom /. Moskva , 1978. 285 p. ; LC Card 81-171493
HD9715.S72 O86 1978

Ėkonomicheskiĭ analiz deiatel´nosti proizvodstvennogo ob˝edineniia po dobyche uglia /. Shvarts, M. A. (Mikhail Aleksandrovich) Moskva , 1986. 222 p. ; LC Card 85-236907
HF5686.M6 S48 1986

Ėkonomicheskiĭ analiz khoziaĭstvennoĭ deiatel´nosti predpriiatiĭ i ob˝edineniĭ / pod redaktsieĭ S.B. Barngol´ts i G.M. Tatsiia. 3-e izd., perer. i dop. Moskva : "Finansy i statistika", 1986. 406 p. : ill. ; 24 cm. Authorized for instructional purposes. Includes bibliographical references. LC Card 86-227621
1. Soviet Union - Industries - 1957- - Auditing. 2. Accounting - Soviet Union. I. Barngol´ts, S. B. (Sarra Bentsionovna). II. Tatsiĭ, G. M. (Grigoriĭ Mikhaĭlovich).
HC340.A8 E417 1986

Ėkonomicheskiĭ analiz raboty predpriiatiĭ legkoĭ promyshlennosti /. Nogaĭ, A. I. (Anatoliĭ Il´ich) Moskva , 1982. 175 p. : LC Card 83-142136
HD9865.S652 N64 1982

Ėkonomicheskiĭ analiz v stroitel´stve /. Taganskiĭ, B. M. (Boris Mikhaĭlovich) Moskva , 1986. 148, [4] p. : LC Card 86-227177
HD9715.S72 T35 1986

Ėkonomicheskiĭ ėksperiment v ėlektrotekhnicheskoĭ promyshlennosti /. Astaf´ev, Vladimir Egorovich. Moskva , 1984. 108, [3] p. ; LC Card 85-125403
HD9697.A3 A77 1984

Ėkonomicheskiĭ mekhanizm ėksperimenta / P.G. Tkachenko ... [et al.]. Kiev : "Tekhnika", 1985. 166 p. : ill. ; 20 cm. LC Card 86-220234
1. Industrial productivity - Ukraine. 2. Industrial management - Ukraine. I. Tkachenko, P. G. (Pavel Grigor´evich).
HC337.U53 I524 1985

Ėkonomicheskiĭ rost Kirgizskoĭ SSR v usloviiakh intensifikatsii obshchestvennogo proizvodstva : regional´nye problemy ėkonomicheskogo i sotsial´nogo razvitiia Kirgizskoĭ SSR / [otvetstvennye redaktory Dzh.S. Laĭliev, T.K. Koĭchuev]. Frunze : Izd-vo "Ilim", 1984. 210 p. ; 21 cm. At head of title: Akademiia nauk Kirgizskoĭ SSR. Institut ėkonomiki. Includes bibliographical references. LC Card 85-131511
1. Kirghiz S.S.R. - Economic conditions. 2. Kirghiz S.S.R. - Economic policy. I. Laĭliev, Dzh. S. II. Koĭchuev, T. K. (Turar Koĭchuevich). III. Institut ėkonomiki (Kyrgyz SSR ilimder akademiiasy).
HC337.K545 E37 1984 ***NYPL [*QIP 87-105]***

Ėkonomicheskiĭ slovar'-spravochnik . Moiseev, Anatoliĭ Vasil´evich. Moskva , 1978. 239 p. ; LC Card 81-165938
HB61 .M56 1978

Ėkonomicheskiia besiedy. Ėkonomicheskie besedy. Moskva , 1888. 79 p. ; LC Card 86-222027
HB178 .E38 1888

Ėkonomicheskoe bremia militarizma /. Vlas´evich, IU. E. (IUriĭ Evlampievich) Moskva , 1980. 181 p. ; LC Card 81-134793
HC79.D4 V58 1980

Ėkonomicheskoe i sotsial´noe razvitie Sovetskogo Azerbaĭdzhana v desiatoĭ piatiletke.
Sămădzadă, Z. (Ziiad) Onunju beshillikdă Sovet Azărbaĭjanynyn igtisadi vă sosial inkishafy /. Baky , 1981. 237 p. ; LC Card 82-153126
HC337.A9 S32 1981

Ėkonomicheskoe izmerenie i otsenka ėffektivnosti nauchno-tekhnicheskogo progressa / [otvetstvennyĭ redaktor Petrakov Nikolaĭ IAkovlevich]. Moskva : Akademiia nauk SSSR, TSentr. ėkonomiko-matematicheskiĭ in-t, 1982. 172 p. ; 21 cm. Includes bibliographies. LC Card 84-209110
1. Technological innovations - Soviet Union - Evaluation - Mathematical models. I. Petrakov, Nikolaĭ IAkovlevich. II. TSentral´nyĭ ėkonomiko-matematicheskiĭ institut (Akademiia nauk SSSR).
HC79.T4 E55 1982

Ėkonomicheskoe razvitie Sibiri i Dal´nego Vostoka / pod redaktsieĭ V.P. Mozhina. Moskva : "Mysl´", 1980. 263 p. ; 21 cm. Bibliography: p. 260-262. LC Card 81-143669
1. Siberia (R.S.F.S.R.) - Economic conditions. 2. Soviet Far East (R.S.F.S.R.) - Economic conditions. I. Mozhin, V. P.
HC337.R852 S5242 1980

Ėkonomicheskoe soupravlenie . Uvarov, V. P. (Vladimir Pavlovich) Minsk , 1985. 159 p. ; LC Card 85-217045
HD5660.G4 U93 1985

Ėkonomicheskoe stimulirovanie povysheniia ėffektivnosti intensifikatsii sovkhoznogo proizvodstva /. Ivanov, V. A. (Valentin Aleksandrovich) Moskva , 1980. 248 p. ; LC Card 81-134017
HD1493.S652 N65 1980

Ėkonomicheskoe stimulirovanie truda v usloviiakh sotsializma : sbornik obzorov / [redkollegiia V.P. Kazakevich, M.E. Tovmosian ; otvetstvennyĭ redaktor M.E. Tovmosian]. Moskva : Akademiia nauk SSSR, In-t nauch. informatsii po obshchestvennym naukam, 1986. 179 p. ; 20 cm. (Seriia Aktual´nye problemy sovershenstvovaniia sotsializma) Includes bibliographies. LC Card 87-166364
1. Wages - Soviet Union. 2. Incentives in industry - Soviet Union. 3. Consumption (Economics) - Soviet Union. I. Kazakevich, V. P. II. Tovmosian, M. E. III. Series.
HD5046 .E47 1986

Ekonomické aspekty globálních problémů lidstva /. Makalová, Eva. Praha , 1984. 97 p. ; LC Card 86-207353
HB9 .P72a 1984, 4/20 HD75

Ekonomický rast a štrukturálne zmeny v socialistickej ekonomike /. Melišek, František. Bratislava , 1980. 175 p. : LC Card 82-464724 DDC 338.9 19
HD84.5 .M379 1980 ***NYPL [*QT 87-1737]***

Ekonomiczne i prawne problemy przedsiębiorstwa uspołecznionego / [redakcja naukowa Zdzisław Kołaczyk, Wojciech Siuda]. Wyd. 1. Poznań : Wydawn. Akademii Ekonomicznej, 1981. 137 p. ; 24 cm. (Zeszyty naukowe / Akademia Ekonomiczna w Poznaniu. Seria 1. . zesz. nr. 101) Includes bibliographical references. LC Card 83-167540
1. Corporations, Government - Poland - Addresses, essays, lectures. I. Kołaczyk, Zdzisław. II. Siuda, Wojciech. III. Akademia Ekonomiczna w Poznaniu. IV. Series: Zeszyty naukowe / Akademia Ekonomiczna w Poznaniu. Seria I , zesz. nr. 101.
HB54 .P6 nr. 101 HD4215.7

Ekonomiczne konsekwencje samorządności pracowniczej /. Dąbrowski, Marek. Wrocław , 1986. 140 p. ; ISBN 83-04-02213-3 : LC Card 86-199502
HD5660.P6 D33 1986

Ėkonomiia topliva i ėlektroėnergii (Ėnergoatomizdat (Firm))
Mikhaĭlov, V. V. (Vram Vagramovich) Tarify i rezhimy ėlektropotrebleniia /. Moskva , 1986. 214 p. : LC Card 86-108009
HD9685.S762 M55 1986

Ėkonomika i okruzhaiushchaia sreda /. Kneese, Allen V. [Economics and the environment. Russian.] Moskva , 1981. 189 p. : LC Card 82-187223
HC79.E5 K57517 1981

Ekonomika i programowanie rozwoju przemysłu / Bronisław Byrski ... [et al.] ; pod redakcją Józefa Gajdy. Kraków : Akademia Ekonomiczna w Krakowie, 1978. 378 p. : ill. ; 24 cm. Includes bibliographies. LC Card 81-172485
1. Industrial organization - Poland. I. Byrski, Bronisław. II. Gajda, Józef. III. Akademia Ekonomiczna w Krakowie.
HD70.P6 E38 1978

Ėkonomika i upravlenie.
Narodnokhoziaĭstvennaia ėffektivnost´--pokazateli, metody otsenki /. Moskva , 1984. 247 p. : LC Card 84-188306
HC336.25 .N3515 1984

Ėkonomika i upravlenie torgovleĭ v razvitom sotsialisticheskom obshchestve : mezhvuzovskiĭ sbornik nauchnykh trudov / pod red. R.IA. Garlei. Riga : Latviĭskiĭ gos. universitet im. P. Stuchki, 1980. 123 p. : ill. ; 20 cm. At head of title: Ministerstvo vysshego i srednego spetsial´nogo obrazovaniia Latviĭskoĭ SSR. Latviĭskiĭ ordena Trudovogo Krasnogo Znameni gosudarstvennyĭ universitet imeni Petra Stuchki. Kafedra ėkonomiki torgovli. Includes bibliographical references. LC Card 82-102627
1. Latvia - Commerce. 2. Latvia - Commercial policy. I. Garleĭa, R. IA. II. Pētera Stučkas Latvijas Valsts universitāte. Kafedra ėkonomiki torgovli.
HF3629.L37 E38 1980

Ėkonomika ispol´zovaniia vodnykh resursov / [IU.P. Lebedinskiĭ, S.M. Perekhrest, I.F. Vovk ... et al. ; Otv. red. IU.P. Lebedinskiĭ]. Kiev : "Nauk. dumka," 1980. 185 p. ; 20 cm. At head of title: Akademiia nauk Ukrainskoĭ SSR. Sovet po izucheniiu proizvoditel´nykh sil USSR. Includes bibliographical references. LC Card 87-462040
1. Water resources development - Ukraine. 2. Environmental policy - Ukraine. I. Lebedinskiĭ, IUriĭ Petrovich. II. Akademiia nauk Ukraïns´koï RSR. Rada po vyvchenniu produktyvnykh syl URSR.
HD1697.S653 U374 1980

Ėkonomika kapitalizma segodnia. Ėpshteĭn, S. I. (Samuil Isaakovich) Burzhuaznaia nauka upravleniia i neupravliaemaia ėkonomika /. Moskva , 1986. 76 p. ; LC Card 86-201018 DDC 658/.00973 19
HD70.U5 E6 1986

Ershov, Stal' Aleksandrovich. Mezhdunarodnye monopolii . Moskva , 1980. 125 p. : LC Card 81-135534
HD2755.5 .E77 1980

Ėkonomika khimicheskoĭ promyshlennosti /. Zalevskiĭ, A. A. (Andreĭ Andreevich) Moskva , 1986. 189 p. ; LC Card 86-225661
HD9656.S55 Z36 1986

Ėkonomika metallurgicheskogo proizvodstva. Bakanov, K. P. (Konstantin Pavlovich) Sovershenstvovanie organizatsii truda na predpriiatiiakh chernoĭ metallurgii /. Moskva , 1981. 47 p. ; LC Card 82-104389
HD9525.S652 B355 1981

Ėkonomika na urovne molekul /. Avrekh, G. L. (Gennadiĭ Lipanovich) Moskva , 1986. 141 p. : LC Card 86-179247
HD9656.S55 A95 1986

Ėkonomika, organizatsiia i planirovanie ėnergeticheskogo proizvodstva /. Pruzner, S. L. (Saul L'vovich) Moskva , 1984. 334 p. : LC Card 84-214102
HD9685.S762 P78 1984

Ėkonomika, organizatsiia i planirovanie konservnogo proizvodstva /. Kharabuga, V. S. (Vasiliĭ Spiridonovich) Moskva , 1977. 349 p. : LC Card 82-122880
HD9326.S62 K42 1977

Ėkonomika, organizatsiia i planirovanie priborostroitel'nogo proizvodstva . Kiselev, A. A. (Anatoliĭ Alekseevich) Leningrad , 1985. 271 p. : LC Card 86-127609
HD9706.S652 K57 1985

Ėkonomika, organizatsiia i planirovanie proizvodstva v khimicheskoĭ promyshlennosti / [avtory A.P. Prokof'ev ... et al.]. Moskva : "Khimiia", 1986. 254 p. : ill. ; 23 cm. Authorized for instructional purposes. "Dlia tekhnikumov." Includes index. Bibliography: p. 251-[252] LC Card 86-227240
1. Chemical industry - Soviet Union - Management. I. Prokof'ev, A. P. (Aleksandr Pavlovich).
HD9656.S55 E38 1986

Ėkonomika, organizatsiia i planirovanie spirtovogo i likerno-vodochnogo proizvodstva /. Kochubeeva, M. T. (Mariia Tikhonovna) Moskva , 1977. 342 p. : LC Card 82-122783
HD9365.S652 K63 1977

Ėkonomika pliūs pedagogika . Popov, V. D. (Vladimir Dmitrievich) Moskva , 1986. 288 p. ; LC Card 86-103180
HB74.9.S65 P66 1986

Ėkonomika--poisk, ėksperiment /. Silin, V. A. (Vladimir Andreevich) Moskva , 1978. 109 p. ; LC Card 81-167075
HC336.25 .S557 1978

Ėkonomika promyshlennogo zheleznodorozhnogo transporta / V.A. Dmitriev ... [et al.] ; pod redaktsieĭ V.A. Dmitrieva. Moskva : "Transport", 1981. 295 p. ; 24 cm. Authorized for instructional purposes. Bibliography: p. 290-[291] LC Card 82-124231
1. Railroads - Soviet Union - Freight. I. Dmitriev, Vasiliĭ Afanas'evich.
HE2457 .E38 1981

Ėkonomika promyshlennosti stroitel'nykh materialov /. Razumovskiĭ, A. V. (Al'bert Vadimovich) Moskva , 1986. 350 p. : LC Card 86-204591
HD9715.8.S652 R39 1986

Ėkonomika razvitogo sotsializma . Konferentsiia molodykh uchenykh-ėkonomistov respublik Pribaltiki (1978 : Riga, Latvia) Riga , 1978. 110 p. ; LC Card 82-100692
HC243 .K66 1978

Ėkonomika razvitogo sotsializma. Alymov, Aleksandr Nikolaevich. Sbalansirovannost' narodnokhoziaĭstvennogo razvitiia . Kiev , 1986. 221, [3] p. ; LC Card 86-214583
HC337.U5 A793 1986

Bohyniā, D. P. Ėffektivnost' obshchestvennogo truda v usloviiakh razvitogo sotsializma . Kiev , 1982. 316 p. ; LC Card 82-200989
HC340.L3 B56 1982

Igumnov, IU. S. (IUriĭ Stepanovich) Sebestoimost' i puti ee snizheniia v promyshlennosti /. Kiev , 1986. 223 p. ; LC Card 87-126676
HC340.C7 I38 1986

Ėkonomika sovremennogo imperializma . Faminskiĭ, Igor' Pavlovich. Moskva , 1987. 175 p. ; LC Card 87-170222
HB501 .F275 1987

Ėkonomika SSSR--edinyĭ narodnokhoziaĭstvennyĭ kompleks / pod redaktsieĭ A.V. Orlova. Moskva : "Prosveshchenie", 1981. 143 p. : ill. ; 22 cm. (Posobie dlia uchiteleĭ) Bibliography: p. [142] LC Card 82-111112
1. Soviet Union - Economic conditions - 1976-. 2. Territorial production complexes - Soviet Union. I. Orlov, A. V. (Aleksandr Vasil'evich).
HC336.25 .E39 1981

Ėkonomika SSSR, 1981-1985. Smirnov, A. A. (Alekseĭ Alekseevich) Potrebitel'skaia kooperatsiia v odinnadtsatoĭ piatiletke /. Moskva , 1981. 88 p. : LC Card 82-106193
HD3355 .S65 1981

Ėkonomika trudovykh resursov / pod obshcheĭ redaktsieĭ V.D. Areshchenko. Minsk : "Vysheĭshaia shkola", 1985. 159 p. ; 21 cm. Authorized for instructional purposes. Bibliography: p. 157-[158]. LC Card 87-156829
1. Labor supply - Soviet Union. 2. Labor economics - Soviet Union. I. Areshchenko, V. D. (Vladimir Denisovich).
HD5796 .E35 1985

Ėkonomika Urala, Sibiri i Dal'nego vostoka v odinnadtsatoĭ piatiletke /. Tolmachev, V. P. (Vladimir Petrovich) Moskva , 1981. 39 p. ; LC Card 82-153584
HC337.R852 U7382 1981

Ekonomikas institūts (Latvijas PSR Zinātņu akadēmija)
Konferentsiia molodykh uchenykh-ėkonomistov respublik Pribaltiki (1978 : Riga, Latvia) Ėkonomika razvitogo sotsializma . Riga , 1978. 110 p. ; LC Card 82-100692
HC243 .K66 1978

Metodicheskie polozheniia po prognozirovaniiu ėkonomicheskogo i sotsial'nogo razvitiia soiuznoĭ respubliki /. Riga , 1979. 275 p. : LC Card 81-215536
HC337.L3 M35 1979

Ėkonomiko-matematicheskaia biblioteka. Pospelov, Germogen Sergeevich. Protsedury i algoritmy formirovaniia kompleksnykh programm /. Moskva , 1985. 422, [2] p. : LC Card 86-203758
HC336.25 .P567 1985

Ėkonomiko-matematicheskie metody i modeli vo vneshneėkonomicheskoĭ deiatel'nosti / [otvetstvennyĭ redaktor Shagalov Grigoriĭ Lazarevich]. Moskva : Akademiia nauk SSSR, TSentr. ėkonomiko-matematicheskiĭ in-t, 1980. 179 p. : ill. ; 21 cm. Includes bibliographies. LC Card 87-109621
1. Soviet Union - Commerce - Mathematical models. 2. Soviet Union - Commerce - Europe, Eastern - Mathematical models. 3. Europe, Eastern - Commerce - Soviet Union - Mathematical models. I. Shagalov, G. L. (Grigoriĭ Lazarevich). II. TSentral'nyĭ ėkonomiko-matematicheskiĭ institut (Akademiia nauk SSSR).
HF3626.5 .E45 1980

Ėkonomiko-matematicheskie metody planirovaniia na predpriiatiiakh pishchevoĭ promyshlennosti /. Voronin, V. G. (Valeriĭ Grigor'evich) Moskva , 1981. 270 p. : LC Card 82-103139
HD9015.S65 V67 1981

Ėkonomiko-matematicheskie metody v analize khoziaĭstvennoĭ deiatel'nosti predpriiatiĭ i ob"edineniĭ / [Butnik-Siverskiĭ, Aleksandr Borisovich ... et al.]. Moskva : Finansy i statistika, 1982. 194, [5] p. : ill. ; 21 cm. Bibliography: p. 188-[195] LC Card 83-161166
1. Industrial management - Soviet Union - Mathematical models. 2. Industrial organization - Soviet Union - Mathematical models. I. Butnik-Siverskiĭ, Aleksandr Borisovich.
HD30.25 .E394 1982

Ėkonomiko-matematicheskie modeli v upravlenii proizvodstvennymi ob"edineniiami / [otvetstvennyĭ redaktor Shubkina Irina Pavlovna]. Moskva : Akademiia nauk SSSR, TSentr. ėkonomiko-matematicheskiĭ in-t, 1983. 190 p. : ill. ; 21 cm. Includes bibliographies. LC Card 85-199430
1. Industrial management - Soviet Union - Mathematical models. I. Shubkina, I. P. II. TSentral'nyĭ ėkonomiko-matematicheskiĭ institut (Akademiia nauk SSSR).
HD30.25 .E397 1983

Ėkonomiko-matematicheskiĭ slovar' /. Lopatnikov, L. I. (Leonid Isidorovich) Moskva , 1987. 509 p. : LC Card 87-164866
HB135 .L64 1987

Ekonomiko-statystychne vyvchennia mizhhaluzevykh narodnohospodars'kykh kompleksiv : zbirnyk naukovykh prats' / [redaktsiĭna kolehiia V.V. Bondarenko (vidp. red.) ... et al.]. Kyïv : IE AN URSR, 1985. 95 p. ; 21 cm. At head of title: Akademiia nauk Ukraïns'koï RSR. Instytut ekonomiky. Includes bibliographical references. LC Card 86-194555
1. Input-output analysis - Ukraine. 2. Ukraine - Economic conditions - 1945-. I. Bondarenko, V. V. (Viktor Viktorovich). II. Instytut ekonomiky (Akademiia nauk Ukraïns'koï RSR).
HC337.U53 I573 1985

Ekonomikos institutas (Lietuvos TSR Mokslų akademija)
Matematicheskie metody v organizatsii sotsialisticheskogo sorevnovaniia . Vil'nius , 1986. 238 p. : LC Card 87-130668
HC337.L53 S65 1986

Regional'noe modelirovanie obshchestvennogo vosproizvodstva . Vil'nius , 1980. 280 p. : LC Card 81-191307
HC337.L5 R44 1980

Tendentsii razvitiia passazhirskikh perevozok v Litovskoĭ SSR . Vil'nius , 1985. 179 p. : LC Card 86-199868
HE255.Z7 L577 1985

Ekonomiordbok . Edström, N. F. (Nils Fritiof), 1918- Stockholm , c1984. 145 p. : ISBN 91-1-847152-8 : LC Card 84-253890
HB61 .E29 1984 ***NYPL [JFD 87-1265]***

Ekonomisk demokrati : löntagarinflytande och ekonomisk organisation : dokumentation från doktorandkursen våren 1983 / Rolf Eidem (red). Stockholm : Arbetslivscentrum, [1984] ii, 169 p. : ill. ; 21 cm. (Varia, 0280-8293 . nr. 31) Includes bibliographies. PARTIAL CONTENTS. - Transaktionskostnadsansatsen--mot en nationalekonomisk organisationsteori för företaget / av Kurt Lundgren -- Svart låda eller självklarhet / av Anders Persson -- Ekonomisk demokrati i Sverige / av Göran Brulin. LC Card 85-108590
1. Management - Sweden - Employee participation. 2. Industrial management - Sweden - Employee participation. 3. Industrial sociology - Sweden. I. Eidem, Rolf, 1943-. II. Arbetslivscentrum (Stockholm, Sweden).
HD5660.S9 E38 1984

Ekonomiska sanktioner . Paul, Jan-Peter. Helsingfors [1985] 46 p. ; ISBN 951-555-224-9 LC Card 85-212001
HF1613.5 .P38 1985

Ekonomiska studier utgivna av Nationalekonomiska institutionen vid Göteborgs universitet .
(17) Schuller, Bernd-Joachim. Ekonomi och kriminalitet . [Göteborg , 1986] ix, 250 p. : LC Card 86-212186
HB54 .G65 no. 17 HV6171

Ėkonomizatsiia nauki : koordinatsiia, planirovanie, organizatsiia / [avtory L.K. Beschastnyĭ ... et al. ; otvetstvennyĭ redaktor L.K. Beschastnyĭ]. Kiev : Nauk. dumka, 1986. 221 p. ; 21 cm. At head of title: Akademiia nauk Ukrainskoĭ SSR. Institut ėkonomiki. Includes bibliographical references. LC Card 87-102107
1. Research - Economic aspects - Ukraine. 2. Science and industry - Ukraine. 3. Economics - Research - Ukraine. I. Beschastnyĭ, L. K.
HC337.U53 R44 1986

Ekonomska reforma i migracije u Jugoslaviji . Sapir, André. Zagreb , 1983. 56 p. ; LC Card 86-183906
HC407 .S26 1983

Ekonomski efekti posrednih poreza /. Popović, Dejan. Beograd , 1983. 286 p. : LC Card

86-173775
HJ5156.5 P67 1983

Ekouevi, Koffi A.
Migrations des expulsés du Nigéria. 1985. Dovi-Sodemekou, Folly B. (Folly Bebey) Emploi et éducation dans le 2e plan de développement économique et social du Togo / Folly B. Dovi-Sodemekou. Les migrations des expulsés du Nigéria : aspects démo-économiques : cas du Sud-est Togo / K. Ekouevi. Lomé, Togo [1985] 89, 52, 9, 2 p. : LC Card 87-131183
HD5846.5.A6 D68 1985

Ėkspansii͡a mezhdunarodnykh monopoliĭ v razvivai͡ushchiesi͡a strany Azii /. Rogach, A. I. (Aleksandr Igorevich) Kiev , 1987. 236, [4] p. ; LC Card 86-234922
HD2932 .R65 1987

Ėkspedit͡sionno-vakhtovoe stroitel´stvo v Zapadnoĭ Sibiri /. Khaĭtun, A. D. (Alekseĭ Davydovich) Leningrad , 1982. 175, [1] p. : LC Card 83-165812
HD9715.S73 S565 1982

Ėksperimental´nai͡a razrabotka natural´no-stoimostnykh mezhotraslevykh balansov soi͡uznoĭ respubliki / [otvetstvennyĭ redaktor Nikitina Valentina Zakharovna]. Moskva : Akademii͡a nauk SSSR, T͡Sentr. ėkonomiko-matematicheskiĭ in-t, 1980. 137 p. : ill. ; 21 cm. Includes bibliographies. LC Card 85-199427
1. Material balances - Estonia - Mathematical models. 2. Material balances - Latvia - Mathematical models. I. Nikitina, V. Z. (Valentina Zakharovna). II. T͡Sentral´nyĭ ėkonomiko-matematicheskiĭ institut (Akademii͡a nauk SSSR).
HC337.E7 E49 1980

Eksport warunkiem importu /. Basiuk, Jerzy. Warszawa , 1978. 57 p. ; LC Card 81-192725
HF1558.7 .B32 1978

Eksportrådgivning i Danmark 1910-1921 . Eriksen, August Wiemann. [Copenhagen] , 1984. 198 p. : ISBN 87-7497-075-5 LC Card 84-231455
HF1561 .E75 1984

Ekthesis tōn pepragmemōn tou Dioikētikou Symvouliou . Henōsis Hellēnōn Ephoplistōn (Greece). Dioikētikon Symvoulion. Athēnai , 1957. 23 p. ; LC Card 86-235109
HE564.E3 G824 1957

Ekthesis tou dioikētou k-ou Dēmētriou E. Chelmē ex onomatos tou Dioikētikou Symvouliou tēs Trapezēs kata tēn genikēn syneleusin tōn metochōn tēs 25ēs Maiou 1964. Chelmēs, D. (Dēmētrios), 1894-1967. Athēnai , 1964. 55 p. ; LC Card 87-109901
HC295 .C45 1964

El Aljarafe durante el antiguo régimen /. Herrera García, Antonio. Sevilla , 1981. 147 p., [3] leaves of plates : ISBN 84-500-4850-8 LC Card 82-142028 DDC 333.3/0946/86 19
HD779.A39 H47 1981 ***NYPL [JLC 86-126]***

El Aljarafe sevillano durante el antiguo régimen . Herrera García, Antonio. [Sevilla] , 1980. 517 p., [9] leaves of plates : ISBN 84-500-4373-5 LC Card 81-173649 DDC 946/.86 19
HD779.A39 H475 1980 ***NYPL [JLF 86-928]***

El-Ashker, Ahmed Abdel-Fattah, 1943- The Islamic business enterprise / Ahmed Abdel-Fattah El-Ashker. London ; Wolfboro, N.H. : Croom Helm, c1987. xi, 242 p. : ill. ; 23 cm. Bibliography: p. 233-240. Includes index. ISBN 0-7099-0985-3 : LC Card 86-24271 DDC 332.1/0917/671 19
1. Banks and banking - Islamic countries - Case studies. 2. Business enterprises - Islamic countries - Case studies. 3. Banks and banking - Religious aspects - Islam. I. Title.
HG3368.A6 E4 1987

El café en Nicaragua . Gariazzo, Alicia. Managua, Nicaragua , 1984. 175 p. : LC Card 85-192390
HD9199.N52 G37 1984
NYPL [JLF 86-1521]

El Caribe mexicano . Dachary, Alfredo César. México, D.F. , 1985. 110 p. : ISBN 968-496-069-7 LC Card 86-118335 DDC 338.3/7270972 19
HD8039.F66 M426 1985
NYPL [JLD 87-1321]

El crédito, la banca y la moneda panameña /. Conte Porras, J. Panamá, Panamá , 1983. 204 p. : ***NYPL [JLE 86-3126]***

El desarrollo tardío del capitalismo . Kalmanovitz, Salomón. [Bogotá] , 1983. 285 p. ; LC Card 84-155755 DDC 338.9/009172/4 19
HC59.7 .K246 1983 ***NYPL [JLD 85-2613]***

El equilibrio de los sexos . Ocampo, Silvia. Buenos Aires , 1980 (Buenos Aires : Audivert) 302 p. ; ***NYPL [JLD 86-913]***

El ferrocarril . Ubach i Soler, Tomàs M., 1955- Barcelona , 1984. 232 p. : ISBN 84-85256-39-5 LC Card 84-254098
HE3199.C38 U23 1984 ***NYPL [JSD 86-434]***

El fin de la autosuficiencia alimentaria /. Barkin, David. México, D.F. , 1985. 249 p. : ISBN 968-493-091-7 LC Card 82-230750
NYPL [JLE 87-404]

El Ghonemy, Mohamad Riad, 1924- Studies on agrarian reform and rural poverty /. Rome , New York, N.Y. , 1984. vii, 104 p. : ISBN 92-5-101371-3 (pbk.) LC Card 85-183713 DDC 338.9/009172/4 19
HD1333.5 .S78 1984 ***NYPL [JLE 86-2720]***

El-Hodiri, Mohamed A. Ōtani, Yoshihiko, 1938- Microeconomic theory /. Berlin , New York , c1987. xiii, 274 p. : ISBN 0-387-17994-1 (U. S. : pbk.) LC Card 87-20628 DDC 338.5 19
HB172 .O83 1987

El Mallakh, Ragaei, 1925- Qatar, energy & development / Ragaei El Mallakh. London ; Dover, N.H. : Croom Helm, c1985. 184 p. ; 23 cm. "Some material in this book previously appeared in Qatar, development of an oil economy by Ragaei El Mallakh"--Verso t.p. Includes index. Bibliography: p. 173-177. ISBN 0-7099-0955-1 : LC Card 84-29317 DDC 330.953/63 19
1. Petroleum industry and trade - Qatar. 2. Gas industry - Qatar. 3. Qatar - Economic conditions. I. Title. II. Title: Qatar, energy and development.
HC415.37 .E4 1985 ***NYPL [JLD 85-1980]***

El mayorazgo Rincón Gallardo . Gómez Serrano, Jesús. [Aguascalientes] [1984] 156 p., [24] p. of plates : LC Card 84-175622
HD329.Z3 G65 1984 ***NYPL [JLD 87-138]***

El-Naggar, Sa'id, 1920- Adjustment policies and development strategies in the Arab world /. Washington, D.C. , 1987. ix, 200 p. ; ISBN 0-939934-96-5 (pbk.) LC Card 87-21377 DDC 338.9/00917/4927 19
HC498 .A6395 1987

El och olja . Sweden. Elanvändningskommittén till restriktioner, användning och hushållning. [Stockholm] [1980] 265 p. : ISBN 91-38-05865-0 LC Card 84-102448
HD9502.S82 S898 1980

EL ORO (ECUADOR : PROVINCE) - ECONOMIC POLICY.
Informe cuatrianual, 1980-1983 /. Cuenca, Ecuador [1983] 222 p. : LC Card 86-206868
HC203.O76 I53 1983

El paro en España /. Albentosa Puche, Luis. Madrid , c1983. 349 p. : ISBN 84-85719-34-4 LC Card 86-121124 DDC 331.11/0946 19
HD5807 .A44 1983 ***NYPL [JLC 87-37]***

EL PASO, TEX. - HISTORY.
Austerman, Wayne R. (Wayne Randolph), 1948- Sharps rifles and Spanish mules . College Station , c1985. x, 367 p., [8] p. of plates : ISBN 0-89096-220-0 : LC Card 84-40557 DDC 383/.49764 19
HE6376.A1 T417 1985
NYPL [JLE 85-3346]

El pensamiento crítico latinoamericano /. Búfalo, Enzo del. [México?] , 1979. 236 p. ; LC Card 79-120323
HC59.7 .B84 ***NYPL [JLC 80-383]***

El pensamiento económico colombiano /. Consuegra Higgins, José. Bogotá, Colombia , 1984. 216 p. ; LC Card 84-200191 DDC 330/.09861 19
HB123.C6 C662 1984 ***NYPL [JLC 87-88]***

El Perú frente al capital extranjero : deuda e inversión / obra editada bajo la dirección de Eduardo Ferrero Costa ; [trabajos de Raimundo Barros ... et al.].1a ed. Lima, Perú : Centro Peruano de Estudios Internacionales, [1985] xl, 399 p. : ill. ; 21 cm. (Serie Simposios y seminarios internacionales . no. 2) Bibliography: p. 342-343. LC Card 86-109611 DDC 332.6/73/0985 19
1. Investments, Foreign - Peru - Congresses. 2. Debts, External - Peru - Congresses. 3. Investments, Foreign - Latin America - Congresses. 4. Debts, External - Latin America - Congresses. I. Ferrero Costa, Eduardo. II. Barros, Raimundo. III. Series.
HG5392 .P47 1985 ***NYPL [JLD 87-384]***

El Primer batllismo : cinco enfoques polémicos / Jorge Balbis ... [et al.]. Montevideo : Centro Latinoamericano de Economía Humana : Ediciones de la Banda Oriental, [1985] 159 p. : ill. ; 19 cm. (Colección Argumentos. no. 2) Includes bibliographical references. LC Card 85-233561 DDC 338.9895 19
1. Batlle y Ordónez, José, Press Uruguay, 1856-1929 - Addresses, essays, lectures. 2. Agriculture and state - Uruguay - History - 20th century - Addresses, essays, lectures. 3. Labor and laboring classes - Uruguay - History - 20th century - Addresses, essays, lectures. 4. Populism - Uruguay - History - 20th century - Addresses, essays, lectures. 5. Uruguay - Economic policy - Addresses, essays, lectures. 6. Uruguay - Economic conditions - Addresses, essays, lectures. 7. Uruguay - Economic conditions - 1918- - Addresses, essays, lectures. 8. Uruguay - Politics and government - 1904-1973 - Addresses, essays, lectures. I. Balbis, Jorge. II. Series: Colección Argumentos (Montevideo, Uruguay) , no. 2.
HC232 .P75 1985 ***NYPL [JLC 86-259]***

El proceso de electrificación en los pueblos jóvenes . Espinoza, Néstor. Lima, Perú [1983] 77 p. : LC Card 84-149923 DDC 363.6/2/098525 19
HD9685.P47 L54 1983
NYPL [JLD 86-3894]

EL SALVADOR - ECONOMIC CONDITIONS.
Luna, David Alejandro. Manual de historia económica de El Salvador /. San Salvador, El Salvador , 1986. 230 p. : LC Card 87-127350 DDC 330.97284/053 19
HC148 .L85 1986

Molina Osegueda, Carlos Alberto. Acumulación agrícola y agroindustrial /. [San Salvador, El Salvador, C.A. , 1980] 187 p. : LC Card 86-174381
HD1827 .M65 1980

EL SALVADOR - ECONOMIC CONDITIONS - 1945-
Calderón Chacón, Godofredo. Monografía de la República de El Salvador /. San Salvador, El Salvador , 1986. iv, 132 p. : LC Card 87-401545 DDC 330.97284/052 19
HC148 .C35 1986

EL SALVADOR - FOREIGN ECONOMIC RELATIONS.
Benítez Bonilla, Alberto. El sector externo de la economía salvadoreña /. [San Salvador] , 1982. 21 p., [7] leaves (some folded) ; LC Card 83-154713
HF1494 .B45 1982

Características básicas y evolución reciente del sector externo de El Salvador. San Salvador, El Salvador , 1986. 47 p. : LC Card 87-403789 DDC 337.7284 19
HF1494 .C37 1986

El Sammani, Mohammed Osman.
Abu Sin, M. E. (Mohad E.) Socio-economic aspects of integrated resource management, with special reference to the forest resources of Kassala Province, Eastern Region . Khartoum , 1986. vi leaves, 109 p. : LC Card 87-980440 DDC 333.75/09629/2 19
HD9767.S843 K3724 1986

Mohamed, Yagoub Abdalla. The North Kordofan rural water supply baseline survey /. Khartoum , 1982. xv, 152 p. : LC Card 85-981166
HD1699.S82 K875 1982

El sector exterior en España /. Albentosa Puche, Luis. Madrid , c1984. 343 p. : ISBN 84-85719-40-9 LC Card 85-214668 DDC 336.3/4/0946 19
HG3883.S69 A45 1984 ***NYPL [JLC 86-251]***

El sector financiero de las Antillas Neerlandesas /. Beers, H. C. [Financial sector of the Netherlands Antilles. Spanish.] [Willemstad, Curaçao] , 1980. 72 p. : LC Card 83-238068 DDC 332.1/097298/6 19
HG2847.A6 B4318 1980
NYPL [JLG 85-297]

El sindicalismo chileno después del plan laboral /. Ruiz-Tagle P., Jaime. Santiago, Chile [1985?] 211 p. ; *NYPL [JLD 87-1182]*

El Terremoto del 19 de septiembre y los trabajadores mexicanos. [Mexico City, Mexico?] : Centro de Estudios del Trabajo, [1985] 114 p. ; 17 cm. Includes bibliographical references. LC Card 86-144990
1. Earthquakes - Economic aspects - Mexico - Mexico City Metropolitan Area. 2. Disasters - Economic aspects - Mexico - Mexico City Metropolitan Area. 3. Labor and laboring classes - Mexico - Mexico City Metropolitan Area. I. Centro de Estudios del Trabajo. II. Title: Terremoto del diecinueve de septiembre y los trabajadores mexicanos.
HC138.M4 T47 1985 *NYPL [JLC 87-130]*

El tributo indígena en las finanzas bolivianas del siglo XIX /. Ovando, Jorge. La Paz, Bolivia [1985] 565 p. : *NYPL [JLC 86-407]*

El Trimestre económico. Lecturas . (30) Economía internacional /. México , 1979- v. in : *NYPL [JLK 86-184]*

Elaboration and investigation of algorithms for dynamic classification of processes. Razrabotka i issledovanie algoritmov dinamicheskoĭ klassifikatsii protsessov . Vil'nius , 1979. 93 p. : LC Card 82-150323
HD38 .S715 vyp. 37 T57.83

Elahi, K. Maudood. Population redistribution and development in South Asia /. Dordrecht , Boston , 1985. 243 p. : ISBN 90-277-1938-1 : LC Card 84-26260 DDC 304.8/0959 19
HB2096.5 .P66 1985 *NYPL [JLE 86-3852]*

Elahi, Mahboob. Rural labour market, with special reference to hired labour in Pakistan's Punjab / by Mahboob Elahi, M. Jameel Khan, and Habibur Rahman. Lahore, Pakistan : Punjab Economic Research Institute, Lahore, [1983] ii, ix, 186 leaves ; 29 cm. (Publication / Punjab Economic Research Institute, Lahore . no. 208) September 1983." Bibliography: leaves 185-186. LC Card 86-930467
1. Agricultural laborers - Pakistan - Punjab. 2. Rural poor - Employment - Pakistan - Punjab. I. Khan, Muhammad Jameel. II. Rahman, Habibur. III. Series: Publication / Punjab Economic Research Institute, Lahore , no. 208. IV. Title.
HD1537.P2 E4 1983

ELASTICITY, COEFFICIENT OF. see **ELASTICITY (ECONOMICS)**

ELASTICITY (ECONOMICS) - ECONOMETRIC MODELS.
Santos, José Carlos de Souza. Demanda de fatores e ofertas na agricultura brasileira . Rio de Janeiro , 1983. 110 p. ; LC Card 87-403023 DDC 338.1/0981 19
HD1872 .S25 1983

Elbadawi, Ibrahim. The Sudan demand for international reserve : a case of a labor-exporting country / by Ibrahim Elbadawi. [Khartoum] : University of Khartoum, Development Studies and Research Centre, Faculty of Economic & Social Studies, [1984] 40 leaves : ill. ; 29 cm. (DSRC seminar . no. 56) "December 1984." Bibliography: leaves 38-40. LC Card 85-981026 DDC 332.4/5609624 19
1. Foreign exchange administration - Sudan - Econometric models. 2. Emigrant remittances - Sudan - Econometric models. I. Title. II. Series.
HG3982.8 .E42 1984

Elbaum, Bernard. The Decline of the British economy /. Oxford [Oxfordshire] , New York , 1987, c1986. vii, 310 p. ; ISBN 0-19-877281-5 (pbk.) : LC Card 87-5479 DDC 330.941/08 19
HC255 .D43 1987

Elbracht-Hülseweh, Bettina. Problemlösungsverhalten und Problemlösungsmethoden bei schlecht-strukturierten Problemen / Bettina Elbracht-Hülseweh. Bochum : N. Brockmeyer, 1985. vi, 220 p. : 18 ill. ; 21 cm. (Bochumer wirtschaftswissenschaftliche Studien. Nr. 105) Bibliography: p. 194-220. ISBN 3-88339-425-4 LC Card 85-170755
1. Problem solving. 2. Problem solving - Cross-cultural studies. I. Title.
HD30.29 .E42 1985

Elcock, H. J. (Howard James) Learning from local authority budgeting /. Aldershot [Hampshire] , Brookfield, Vt., USA , c1987. x, 258 p. ; ISBN 0-566-05384-5 : LC Card 87-12096 DDC 352.1/2/0941 19
HJ9423 .L43 1987

Elderly housing options /. Scott, Terrence J. Chicago , c1987. 235 p. : ISBN 0-931028-87-6 LC Card 86-63411 DDC 363.5/9 19
HD7287.92.U54 S38 1987

ELDERLY PERSONS. see **AGED.**

Eldred, Gary W. Real estate : analysis and strategy / Gary Eldred. New York : Harper & Row, c1987. xxii, 567 p. : ill. ; 25 cm. Includes index. ISBN 0-06-041893-1 LC Card 86-22936 DDC 333.33 19
1. Real estate business. I. Title.
HD1375 .E354 1987

Eldred, Michael. La Forma-valore . Manduria , 1984. 301 p. : LC Card 86-130626 DDC 335.4/12 19
HB206 .F67 1984

Las elecciones sindicales en Euskadi, representación de los trabajadores en la empresa e implantación de los sindicatos . Kaiero Uria, Andoni. Vitoria , 1985. 629 p. : ISBN 84-7542-199-7 LC Card 87-146467
HD6490.R42 S74 1985

ELECTION DISTRICTS - MARYLAND - STATISTICS.
Zoned employment and unemployment statistics . Baltimore, Md. (1100 N. Eutaw St., Baltimore 21201) [1986] [51] p. : LC Card 86-622109 DDC 331.12/5/09752021 19
HD5725.M35 Z67 1986

ELECTIONS - GERMANY (WEST) - BADEN-WÜRTTEMBERG - STATISTICS.
Gemeindestatistik 1976. Stuttgart , <1976-. v. <2 > : LC Card 86-222059
HA1320.B2 A32 Bd. 230, etc. JN4939.A15

ELECTIONS - GERMANY (WEST) - LONGITUDINAL STUDIES.
Schenkluhn, Brigitte, 1951- Konjunkturpolitik und Wahlen . Bergisch Gladbach , 1985. xi, 482 p. : ISBN 3-89012-017-2 LC Card 85-153982
HB3789 .S34 1985

ELECTIONS - GERMANY (WEST) - MATHEMATICAL MODELS.
Wirtschaftlicher Wandel, religiöser Wandel und Wertwandel . Berlin , c1985. 411 p. : ISBN 3-428-05784-8 LC Card 85-218417
HC286.7 .W58 1985

ELECTIONS - GERMANY (WEST) - RHINELAND-PALATINATE - STATISTICS.
Die Wahl zum 9. Landtag in Rheinland-Pfalz am 18. März 1979 /. Bad Ems , 1979. 153, [18], 23 p. : LC Card 86-128836
HA1320 .R453 Bd. 284 JN4945.R4565

ELECTIONS - GERMANY (WEST) - SAARLAND - STATISTICS.
Kommunal- und Europawahl am 17. Juni 1984. Saarbrücken , 1984. 115 p. : ISBN 3-88718-020-8 : LC Card 85-130989
HA1320 .S244 Nr. 67 JN4945.S265

ELECTIONS - MEXICO - ADDRESSES, ESSAYS, LECTURES.
Quantitative Latin American studies . Los Angeles , 1977. xiv, 91 p. : ISBN 0-87903-227-8 LC Card 77-620011 DDC 330.9/8/003
HD5731.A6 Q36 *NYPL [JLF 80-242]*

Elections prud'homales : comparaison 1979-1982. Rennes : Centre d'études économiques et sociales du pays de Rennes, [1983] 92 p. : ill., maps ; 30 cm. "Décembre 1983." LC Card 85-136661
1. France. Conseils de prud'hommes - Elections. I. Centre d'études économiques et sociales du pays de Rennes.
HD5554.A3 E44 1983

ELECTIONS - QUEBEC (PROVINCE)
Comportement électoral au Québec /. Chicoutimi, Québec, Canada , c1984. xv, 447 p. : ISBN 2-89105-063-0 LC Card 85-177886 DDC 324.9714 19
JL258 .C65 1984 *NYPL [JLD 87-1351]*

ELECTIONS - SPAIN - GARROTXA REGION.
La Garrotxa . [Barcelona , c1983. xv, 323 p. : ISBN 84-7231-912-1 LC Card 85-184803
HC387.G34 G37 1983

ELECTIONS - SPAIN - SORIA (PROVINCE) - HISTORY.
Romero, Carmelo, 1950- Historia contemporánea de Soria, 1860-1936 . [Soria] , 1982. 510 p. : ISBN 84-85792-02-5 LC Card 85-136084
HC387.S67 R66 1982

ELECTRIC BATTERY INDUSTRY. see **BATTERY INDUSTRY.**

ELECTRIC COMMUNICATION. see **TELECOMMUNICATION.**

ELECTRIC ENGINEERING - DICTIONARIES.
Erekutoronikusu pawā shōjiten /. Tōkyō , 1985. v, 618 p. : ISBN 4-320-08454-3 : LC Card 85-229520
TK7804 .E73 1985 <Orien Japan> *NYPL [*OSG 86-3267]*

ELECTRIC ENGINEERING - DICTIONARIES - JAPANESE.
Erekutoronikusu pawā shōjiten /. Tōkyō , 1985. v, 618 p. : ISBN 4-320-08454-3 : LC Card 85-229520
TK7804 .E73 1985 <Orien Japan> *NYPL [*OSG 86-3267]*

ELECTRIC GENERATOR INDUSTRY - UNITED STATES.
The Cogeneration equipment and services market in the U. S. New York, N.Y. , c1983. 2 v. (ix, 306 leaves) : LC Card 87-138703 DDC 381/.456213141 19
HD9695.U52 C64 1983

ELECTRIC HOUSEHOLD APPLIANCES INDUSTRY - UNITED STATES.
Portable kitchen appliance market. New York, N.Y. , c1983. 2 v. (x, 405 p.) : LC Card 87-143951 DDC 381/.4568383/0973 19
HD9971.5.K583 U656 1983

ELECTRIC INDUSTRIES - CHILE.
Errázuriz, Enrique. Industria eléctrica, 1960-1985 . [Santiago, Chile] [1986] 243 p. : LC Card 87-403870 DDC 338.4/762131/0983 19
HD9685.C52 E77 1986

ELECTRIC INDUSTRIES - GERMANY - HISTORY.
Goetzeler, Herbert. Wilhelm und Carl Friedrich von Siemens . Stuttgart , 1986. 131 p. : ISBN 3-515-04558-9 LC Card 86-141456
HD9695.G43 S514 1986

Peschke, Hans-Peter von, 1951- Elektroindustrie und Staatsverwaltung am Beispiel Siemens, 1847-1914 /. Frankfurt am Main , Bern , c1981. 393 p. : ISBN 3-8204-5902-2 LC Card 81-141438
HD9697.A3 G35 1981

ELECTRIC INDUSTRIES - GERMANY, WEST.
Berger, Manfred, 1921- Elektrotechnische Industrie . Berlin , c1984. 261 p. : ISBN 3-428-05674-4 LC Card 85-137543
HD9696.A3 G42 1984 ***NYPL [TB (Struktur und Wachstum. Reihe Industrie. Heft 38)]***

ELECTRIC INDUSTRIES - INDIA - MANAGEMENT.
Goel, Madan Mohan, 1930- Administration and management of electricity in India /. New Delhi [1986], c1987. 280 p. ; LC Card 87-900202 DDC 621.31/068 19
HD9697.A3 I43 1987

ELECTRIC INDUSTRIES - MOROCCO.
Les Industries mécaniques et électriques au Maroc . Casablanca [1984] 1 v. (various pagings) ; LC Card 85-206543
HD9705.M72 I53 1984

ELECTRIC INDUSTRIES - QUÉBEC (PROVINCE)
"L'Energie, levier de développement économique" . [Ottawa?] [1983] 30 leaves ; LC Card 85-128816
HD9685.C3 Q4425 1983

ELECTRIC INDUSTRIES - SOVIET UNION - FINANCE - MANAGEMENT.
Moskovskiĭ, I. D. (Igor' Dmitrievich) Finansy i khoziaĭstvennyĭ raschet v usloviiakh ėkonomicheskogo ėksperimenta /. Moskva , 1984. 60 p. ; LC Card 87-100142
HD9697.A3 S656 1984

ELECTRIC INDUSTRIES - SOVIET UNION - MANAGEMENT.
Astaf'ev, Vladimir Egorovich. Ėkonomicheskiĭ ėksperiment v ėlektrotekhnicheskoĭ promyshlennosti /. Moskva , 1984. 108, [3] p. ;

LC Card 85-125403
HD9697.A3 A77 1984

ELECTRIC LIGHTING - RATES. see **ELECTRIC UTILITIES - RATES.**

ELECTRIC MACHINERY INDUSTRY.
A Competitive assessment of the U. S. transformer industry /. Washington, D.C. [1986] xii, 82 p. : *NYPL [JSF 86-672]*

ELECTRIC MACHINERY INDUSTRY - GERMANY - HISTORY.
Peschke, Hans-Peter von, 1951- Elektroindustrie und Staatsverwaltung am Beispiel Siemens, 1847-1914 /. Frankfurt am Main , Bern , c1981. 393 p. : ISBN 3-8204-5902-2 LC Card 81-141438
HD9697.A3 G35 1981

ELECTRIC MACHINERY INDUSTRY - UNITED STATES.
A Competitive assessment of the U. S. transformer industry /. Washington, D.C. [1986] xii, 82 p. : *NYPL [JSF 86-672]*

Industrial power systems market in the U. S. New York, N.Y. , c1983. v, 312 p. ; LC Card 87-143811 DDC 381/.4562143/0973
HD9695.U52 I53 1983

The electric mailbox /. Davis, Steve, 1953- Dallas, Tex. , c1986. 286 p. ; ISBN 0-911061-14-2 (pbk.) LC Card 84-91756 DDC 384.3/4 19
HE6239.E54 D38 1986

ELECTRIC MOTOR INDUSTRY - UNITED STATES.
Integral HP electric motors and asociated [sic] controls. New York, N.Y. , c1983. xii, 280 leaves ; LC Card 87-143831
HD9697.M693 U55 1983

ELECTRIC PLANTS. see **ELECTRIC POWER-PLANTS.**

ELECTRIC POWER CONSERVATION EQUIPMENT INDUSTRY.
Worldwide remote power sites. New York, N.Y. , c1983. 2 v. (xx, xxvii, 500 p.) : LC Card 87-141748
HD9695.A2 W67 1983

ELECTRIC POWER CONSUMPTION - ARGENTINA.
Energía eléctrica /. [Buenos Aires] [1981] 27 p., [6] leaves of plates : LC Card 87-401272 DDC 333.79/3212/0982 19
HD9685.A72 E54 1981

ELECTRIC POWER CONSUMPTION - DELMARVA PENINSULA - FORECASTING.
Estomin, Steven. Updated load forecast of energy and peak demand on the Delmarva Peninsula /. Bethesda, Md. (4550 Montgomery Ave., Bethesda 20814) [1986] iv, 4, 53, [18] p. : LC Card 87-620907 DDC 333.79/3212/097521 19
HD9685.U6 A123 1986

ELECTRIC POWER CONSUMPTION - ECONOMETRIC MODELS.
Khazzoom, J. Daniel. An econometric model integrating conservation measures in the residential demand for electricity /. Greenwich, Conn. , c1986. xx, 305 p. : ISBN 0-89232-606-9 : LC Card 86-7173 DDC 333.79/3216/0724 19
HD9685.A2 K54 1986 NYPL [JLE 86-4174]

ELECTRIC POWER CONSUMPTION - NEW YORK (STATE) - FORECASTING.
New York (State). State Energy Office. Division of Policy Analysis and Planning. Meeting the challenge . [Albany] [1985] 290 p. : LC Card 86-622429 DDC 333.79/3211/09747 19
HD9685.U6 N614 1985

ELECTRIC POWER CONSUMPTION - QUÉBEC (PROVINCE) - FORECASTING.
Hydro-Québec. Hydro-Quebéc development plan, 1986-1988 . [Québec] Montréal, Quebec [1986] x, 143 p. : LC Card 86-201868 DDC 333.79/32/09714 19
HD9685.C4 H857 1986

ELECTRIC POWER CONSUMPTION - SWEDEN.
Ny teknik för elproduktion, elanvändning . Stockholm [1983] 172 p. : LC Card 84-108404
HD9685.S852 N9 1983

ELECTRIC POWER CONSUMPTION - TANZANIA - FORECASTING.
Joseph, G. An econometric approach to forecasting demand for electricity in Tanzania to the year 2000 A.D. /. [Dar es Salaam] [between 1978 and 1984] 42, [44] p. ; LC Card 84-980076 DDC 333.7/09678 333.79/3213/09678 19
HD107 .D36 no. 38a HD9685.T352

ELECTRIC POWER CONSUMPTION - TANZANIA - FORECASTING - ECONOMETRIC MODELS.
Joseph, G. An econometric approach to forecasting demand for electricity in Tanzania to the year 2000 A.D. /. [Dar es Salaam] [between 1978 and 1984] 42, [44] p. ; LC Card 84-980076 DDC 333.7/09678 333.79/3213/09678 19
HD107 .D36 no. 38a HD9685.T352

ELECTRIC POWER CONSUMPTION - WEST (U. S.)
Energy and water management in western irrigated agriculture /. Boulder, Colo. , 1986. xxiv, 415 p. : ISBN 0-8133-7086-8 (pbk. : alk. paper) LC Card 85-52184 DDC 333.91/3/0978 19
HD1735 .E54 1986 NYPL [JLD 87-829]

ELECTRIC POWER DISTRIBUTION - SOCIAL ASPECTS - INDIA.
Hans, Asha. The power sector in India /. New Delhi , c1986. vi, 149 p. ; LC Card 86-901959 DDC 333.79/32/0954 19
HD9502.I42 H36 1986

ELECTRIC POWER PLANT EQUIPMENT INDUSTRY.
Worldwide remote power sites. New York, N.Y. , c1983. 2 v. (xx, xxvii, 500 p.) : LC Card 87-141748
HD9695.A2 W67 1983

ELECTRIC POWER PLANT EQUIPMENT INDUSTRY - EUROPE.
Surrey, John. The European power plant industry . [Brighton, Sussex] , c1981. viii, 90 p. ; ISBN 0-903422-31-X (pbk.) : LC Card 83-130609 DDC 338.4/76213121/094 19
HD9695.E92 S87 1981
NYPL [JLD 86-4078]

ELECTRIC POWER PLANT EQUIPMENT INDUSTRY - UNITED STATES.
Industrial power systems market in the U. S. New York, N.Y. , c1983. v, 312 p. ; LC Card 87-143811 DDC 381/.4562143/0973
HD9695.U52 I53 1983

ELECTRIC POWER-PLANTS - DEVELOPING COUNTRIES - DESIGN AND CONSTRUCTION.
Surrey, John. The European power plant industry . [Brighton, Sussex] , c1981. viii, 90 p. ; ISBN 0-903422-31-X (pbk.) : LC Card 83-130609 DDC 338.4/76213121/094 19
HD9695.E92 S87 1981
NYPL [JLD 86-4078]

ELECTRIC POWER-PLANTS - ILLINOIS - EAST PEORIA - REMODELING FOR OTHER USE.
Urban Land Institute. R.S. Wallace Station, East Peoria, Illinois . Washington, D.C. (1090 Vermont Ave., N.W., Washington 20005) , c1986. 36 p. : LC Card 86-216045 DDC 333.77/17/0977352 19
HD268.E26 U73 1986

ELECTRIC POWER PRODUCTION.
Wodopia, Franz-Josef. Intertemporale Produktionsentscheidungen . Frankfurt am Main , c1986. xx, 262 p. : ISBN 3-445-02403-0 LC Card 86-222211
HB241 .W63 1986

ELECTRIC POWER PRODUCTION - BRAZIL - CONGRESSES.
Lopes, Marcos José. Atendimento ao mercado de energia elétrica do Nordeste /. Recife, PE [1984] 2 v. in 4 : LC Card 86-166126
HD9685.B83 N675 1984

ELECTRIC POWER PRODUCTION - BRAZIL - SÃO FRANCISCO RIVER REGION.
Sigaud, Lygia. Efeitos sociais de grandes projetos hidrelétricos . [Rio de Janeiro] , 1986. 116 p. ; LC Card 87-120281 DDC 333.91/4 19
HD1696.B84 S346 1986

ELECTRIC POWER PRODUCTION - SOCIAL ASPECTS - INDIA.
Hans, Asha. The power sector in India /. New Delhi , c1986. vi, 149 p. ; LC Card 86-901959 DDC 333.79/32/0954 19
HD9502.I42 H36 1986

ELECTRIC POWER PRODUCTION - URUGUAY RIVER REGION.
Sigaud, Lygia. Efeitos sociais de grandes projetos hidrelétricos . [Rio de Janeiro] , 1986. 116 p. ; LC Card 87-120281 DDC 333.91/4 19
HD1696.B84 S346 1986

ELECTRIC POWER PRODUCTION - WEST (U. S.)
Energy and water management in western irrigated agriculture /. Boulder, Colo. , 1986. xxiv, 415 p. : ISBN 0-8133-7086-8 (pbk. : alk. paper) LC Card 85-52184 DDC 333.91/3/0978 19
HD1735 .E54 1986 NYPL [JLD 87-829]

ELECTRIC POWER - RATES. see **ELECTRIC UTILITIES - RATES.**

Electric Power Research Institute. Demand and Conservation Program. Models for investment and disinvestment decision making under uncertainty [microform] /. East Lansing , 1982. 173 p. : *NYPL [*XME-11,286]*

ELECTRIC POWER - SOVIET UNION - HISTORY.
Steklov, Vladimir I͡Ur'evich. V.I. Lenin i ėlektrifikat͡sii͡a /. Moskva , 1982. 511 p., [1] leaf of plates : LC Card 83-133950
HD9685.S762 S84 1982

ELECTRIC POWER - SWEDEN - CONSERVATION.
Ny teknik för elproduktion, elanvändning . Stockholm [1983] 172 p. : LC Card 84-108404
HD9685.S852 N9 1983

ELECTRIC POWER SYSTEMS - UNITED STATES.
Industrial power systems market in the U. S. New York, N.Y. , c1983. v, 312 p. ; LC Card 87-143811 DDC 381/.4562143/0973
HD9695.U52 I53 1983

ELECTRIC POWER SYSTEMS - UNITED STATES - LOAD DISPATCHING.
Load management /. New York , c1987. vii, 207 p. : ISBN 0-87942-214-9 LC Card 86-33824 DDC 363.6/2 19
HD9685.U5 L58 1987

ELECTRIC STREET-RAILROADS. see **STREET-RAILROADS.**

ELECTRIC TELEGRAPH. see **TELEGRAPH.**

ELECTRIC TRANSFORMERS - ECONOMIC ASPECTS.
A Competitive assessment of the U. S. transformer industry /. Washington, D.C. [1986] xii, 82 p. : *NYPL [JSF 86-672]*

ELECTRIC TRANSFORMERS - ECONOMIC ASPECTS - UNITED STATES.
A Competitive assessment of the U. S. transformer industry /. Washington, D.C. [1986] xii, 82 p. : *NYPL [JSF 86-672]*

ELECTRIC UTILITIES - ALGERIA - STATISTICS.
L'Energie électrique au Sahara. [Paris] [196-?] 19 p. : LC Card 83-123000
HD9685.A52 E54 1960z

ELECTRIC UTILITIES - ARGENTINA.
Energía eléctrica /. [Buenos Aires] [1981] 27 p., [6] leaves of plates : LC Card 87-401272 DDC 333.79/3212/0982 19
HD9685.A72 E54 1981

ELECTRIC UTILITIES - AUSTRIA - UPPER AUSTRIA - HISTORY.
Weigl, Franz, 1948- Die Entwicklung der oberösterreichischen Elektrizitätswirtschaft von den Anfängen bis zum Jahre 1938 /. Linz [1980] 210, xi p. : ISBN 3-85320-232-2 : LC Card 81-137632
HD9685.A93 U669 1980

ELECTRIC UTILITIES - AUSTRIA - UPPER AUSTRIA - HISTORY - 20TH CENTURY.
Hinterbuchner, Christian. Die Entwicklung der oberösterreichischen Elektrizitätswirtschaft in den Jahren 1938-1980 /. Linz , c1986. 344 p. : ISBN 3-85320-370-1 : LC Card 86-225017
HD9685.A93 U664 1986

ELECTRIC UTILITIES - BRAZIL.
Eletrobrás. Situação econômica-financeira das concessionárias de energia elétrica . [Rio de Janeiro] , 1979. 64 p. ; LC Card 84-256157
HD9685.B8 E47 1979

ELECTRIC UTILITIES - BRAZIL - COSTS.
Custos e tarifas de energia elétrica . [Rio de Janeiro] , 1982. 40 p. ; LC Card 86-146330
HD9685.B8 C87 1982

ELECTRIC UTILITIES - BRAZIL - FINANCE.
Eletrobrás. Situação econômica-financeira das concessionárias de energia elétrica . [Rio de Janeiro] , 1979. 64 p. ; LC Card 84-256157
HD9685.B8 E47 1979

ELECTRIC UTILITIES - BRAZIL, NORTHEAST - CONGRESSES.
Lopes, Marcos José. Atendimento ao mercado de energia elétrica do Nordeste /. Recife, PE [1984] 2 v. in 4 : LC Card 86-166126
HD9685.B83 N675 1984

ELECTRIC UTILITIES - BRAZIL - RATES.
Custos e tarifas de energia elétrica . [Rio de Janeiro] , 1982. 40 p. ; LC Card 86-146330
HD9685.B8 C87 1982

ELECTRIC UTILITIES - BRAZIL - RIO CLARO (SÃO PAULO) - HISTORY.
Marsiglia, Cecília. S/A Central Elétrica Rio Claro /. São Paulo , 1986. 105 p. : LC Card 87-404945 DDC 363.6/2/098161 19
HD9685.B83 C4886 1986

ELECTRIC UTILITIES - COLOMBIA - CÚCUTA.
Buenahora Febres-Cordero, Norma. Cúcuta y sus servicios públicos básicos /. Bogotá, D.E. , 1984. 136 p. ; LC Card 85-205425
HD4637.A5 B84 1984

ELECTRIC UTILITIES - DELMARVA PENINSULA - RATES - PEAK-LOAD PRICING.
Estomin, Steven. Updated load forecast of energy and peak demand on the Delmarva Peninsula /. Bethesda, Md. (4550 Montgomery Ave., Bethesda 20814) [1986] iv, 4, 53, [18] p. : LC Card 87-620907 DDC 333.79/3212/097521 19
HD9685.U6 A123 1986

ELECTRIC UTILITIES - ENVIRONMENTAL ASPECTS - QUÉBEC (PROVINCE)
Poste Des Cantons, lignes Nicolet-Des Cantons et Des Cantons-Nouvelle-Angleterre /. [Sainte-Foy, Qc] [1983] 1 v. (various pagings) ; ISBN 2-550-10466-8 LC Card 85-121505
HD9685.C3 Q455 1983

ELECTRIC UTILITIES - GERMANY, WEST.
Schröter, Klaus, 1953- Die wettbewerbspolitische Behandlung der leitungsgebundenen Energiewirtschaft . Frankfurt am Main , New York , c1986. viii, 300 p. ; ISBN 3-8204-9551-7 LC Card 87-407422 DDC 363.6/2/0943 19
HD9685.G3 S375 1986

ELECTRIC UTILITIES - GERMANY, WEST - RATES.
Wagner, Gerhard. Abbau regionaler Strompreisdisparitäten durch raumwirksame Massnahmen und Planungen /. Bonn , 1985. xv, 356 p. : ISBN 3-87994-415-6 LC Card 87-408008 DDC 338.4/336362/0943 19
HD9685.G3 W34 1985

ELECTRIC UTILITIES - GHANA.
Essays from the Ghana-Valco renegotiations, 1982-85 /. [Accra, Ghana] 1986 (Accra : Printed by the Ghana Pub. Corp.) viii, 163 p. ; ISBN 996-490-120-8 (pbk.) LC Card 87-127499 DDC 338.8/87 19
HD9539.A63 G44 1986

ELECTRIC UTILITIES - GOVERNMENT OWNERSHIP - UNITED STATES - HISTORY.
Schap, David. Municipal ownership in the electric utility industry . New York , 1986. xiii, 128 p. ; ISBN 0-03-006347-7 : LC Card 85-19418 DDC 363.6/2/0973 19
HD9685.U5 S3 1986 ***NYPL [JLE 86-3180]***

ELECTRIC UTILITIES - GOVERNMENT POLICY - CALIFORNIA.
Commission on California State Government Organization and Economy. A study of the organization and coordination of electric energy planning and electric utility regulation in California . [Sacramento] (11th & L Bldg., Suite 550, Sacramento 95814) [1984] 3, x leaves, 54 p. ; LC Card 85-623154 DDC 333.79/32/09794 19
HD9685.U6 C325 1984

ELECTRIC UTILITIES - GOVERNMENT POLICY - GERMANY (WEST) - CASE STUDIES.
Vogelsang, Ingo. Anreizmechanismen zur Regulierung der Elektrizitätswirtschaft . Tübingen , 1982. xii, 173 p. : ISBN 3-16-344549-7 : LC Card 83-153444
HD9685.G3 V64 1982

ELECTRIC UTILITIES - GOVERNMENT POLICY - ILLINOIS.
Illinois. Commerce Commission. Independent power production in Illinois /. Springfield, Ill. (P.O. Box 4905, Springfield 62708) [1986- v. <1 > : LC Card 86-622355 DDC 338.4/762131/09773 19
HD9685.U6 I263 1986

ELECTRIC UTILITIES - GOVERNMENT POLICY - ITALY.
Tronconi, Pier Attilio. Settore termoelettromeccanico . Roma , c1986. 729 p. : ISBN 88-7910-149-8 : LC Card 86-211311
HD9685.I82 T76 1986

ELECTRIC UTILITIES - GOVERNMENT POLICY - UNITED STATES.
Illinois. Commerce Commission. Independent power production in Illinois /. Springfield, Ill. (P.O. Box 4905, Springfield 62708) [1986- v. <1 > : LC Card 86-622355 DDC 338.4/762131/09773 19
HD9685.U6 I263 1986

Newman, Marie Mastin. The vital link . Washington, DC , c1986. vii, 48 p. : ISBN 0-931032-21-0 (pbk.) LC Card 86-200991 DDC 363.6/2/0973 19
HD9685.U5 N493 1986

ELECTRIC UTILITIES - INDIA - HARYANA - STATISTICS.
HSEB statistics, 1983-84. [Chandigarh] [1984] iii, 105 p., [7] p. of plates : LC Card 87-901651 DDC 363.6/2/0954558021 19
HD9696.A3 I5535 1984

ELECTRIC UTILITIES - ITALY - HISTORY.
Energia e sviluppo . Torino , c1986. xii, 346 p., [16] p. of plates : ISBN 88-06-59444-3 : LC Card 86-214309
HD9685.I84 S574 1986

ELECTRIC UTILITIES - IVORY COAST.
Énergie électrique de la Côte d'Ivoire (Company) L'Energie électrique de la Côte d'Ivoire . Abidjan, Côte d'Ivoire [1962] 23 p. : LC Card 83-120031 DDC 363.6/2/096668 19
HD9685.I94 E53 1962

ELECTRIC UTILITIES - LAW AND LEGISLATION - ILLINOIS.
Illinois. Commerce Commission. Independent power production in Illinois /. Springfield, Ill. (P.O. Box 4905, Springfield 62708) [1986- v. <1 > : LC Card 86-622355 DDC 338.4/762131/09773 19
HD9685.U6 I263 1986

ELECTRIC UTILITIES - LAW AND LEGISLATION - UNITED STATES.
Financial condition of the U. S. electric utility industry. [Washington] [1986] xviii, 82 p. :
NYPL [JLF 86-1386]

Illinois. Commerce Commission. Independent power production in Illinois /. Springfield, Ill. (P.O. Box 4905, Springfield 62708) [1986- v. <1 > : LC Card 86-622355 DDC 338.4/762131/09773 19
HD9685.U6 I263 1986

ELECTRIC UTILITIES - MANAGEMENT.
Gellings, Clark W. Demand-side management . Lilburn, GA , c1988. xi, 465 p. : ISBN 0-88173-027-0 : LC Card 86-46131 DDC 363.6/2/068 19
HD9685.A2 G45 1988

Wodopia, Franz-Josef. Intertemporale Produktionsentscheidungen . Frankfurt am Main , c1986. xx, 262 p. : ISBN 3-445-02403-0 LC Card 86-222211
HB241 .W63 1986

ELECTRIC UTILITIES - MICHIGAN.
Michigan. Legislature. House of Representatives. Special House Committee to Study Consumers Power Company. Report of the Special House Committee to Study Consumers Power Company . Lansing, Mich. (The Capitol, Lansing 48909) [1985] iv leaves, 57 p. ; LC Card 86-622638 DDC 338.7/6136362/09774 19
HD9685.U7 C785 1985

ELECTRIC UTILITIES - NEW YORK (STATE) - PLANNING.
New York (State). State Energy Office. Division of Policy Analysis and Planning. Meeting the challenge . [Albany] [1985] 290 p. : LC Card 86-622429 DDC 333.79/3211/09747 19
HD9685.U6 N614 1985

ELECTRIC UTILITIES - NORTHWEST, PACIFIC - HISTORY.
A Century of service . Bellevue, Wash. , c1987. 178 p. : ISBN 0-9619061-0-3 (pbk.) : LC Card 87-16582 DDC 338.7/6136362/097977 19
HD9685.U7 P923 1987

ELECTRIC UTILITIES - PARAGUAY - CONGRESSES.
Seminario Estrategia de Desarrollo en Condiciones de Oferta Abundante de Energía Eléctrica (1980 : Asunción, Paraguay) Memoria del Seminario Estrategia de Desarrollo en Condiciones de Oferta Abundante de Energía Eléctrica . Asunción, Paraguay [s.l.] , 1980. 165 p., [18] leaves of plates : LC Card 83-169471 DDC 363.6/2 19
HD9685.P32 S45 1980 ***NYPL [JLE 87-995]***

ELECTRIC UTILITIES - PERU - LIMA METROPOLITAN AREA.
Espinoza, Néstor. El proceso de electrificación en los pueblos jóvenes . Lima, Perú [1983] 77 p. : LC Card 84-149923 DDC 363.6/2/098525 19
HD9685.P47 L54 1983
NYPL [JLD 86-3894]

ELECTRIC UTILITIES - QUÉBEC (PROVINCE)
"L'Energie, levier de développement économique" . [Ottawa?] [1983] 30 leaves ; LC Card 85-128816
HD9685.C3 Q4425 1983

ELECTRIC UTILITIES - QUÉBEC (PROVINCE) - PLANNING.
Hydro-Québec. Hydro-Québec development plan, 1986-1988 . [Québec] Montréal, Quebec [1986] x, 143 p. : LC Card 86-201868 DDC 333.79/32/09714 19
HD9685.C4 H857 1986

ELECTRIC UTILITIES - QUÉBEC (PROVINCE) - PORTNEUF (COUNTY)
Le Projet Delaney . [St-Raymond, Québec] [1983] 76 leaves in various foliations : LC Card 84-224364
HD9685.C3 Q456 1983

ELECTRIC UTILITIES - RATES.
Stromerzeugungskosten im internationalen Vergleich /. München , 1986. ca. 450 p. : ISBN 3-486-26246-7 LC Card 87-135285 DDC 338.4/336362 19
HD9685.A2 S76 1986

ELECTRIC UTILITIES - SAHARA - STATISTICS.
L'Energie électrique au Sahara. [Paris] [196-?] 19 p. : LC Card 83-123000
HD9685.A52 E54 1960z

ELECTRIC UTILITIES - SOCIAL ASPECTS - INDIA - BIHAR.
Sachchidananda, 1926- Electricity and social change /. Patna , 1983. xii, 264 p. ; LC Card 83-902678 DDC 303.4/83 19
HD9685.I43 B547 1983
NYPL [JLD 86-4263]

ELECTRIC UTILITIES - SOUTH AFRICA - HISTORY.
Christie, Renfrew. Electricity, industry, and class in South Africa /. London , 1984. xiii, 241 p. : ISBN 0-333-36288-8 LC Card 87-673182
HD9685.S582 C47x 1984b

ELECTRIC UTILITIES - SOVIET UNION.
Pruzner, S. L. (Saul L'vovich) Ėkonomika, organizatsiía i planirovanie ėnergeticheskogo proizvodstva /. Moskva , 1984. 334 p. : LC Card 84-214102
HD9685.S762 P78 1984

ELECTRIC UTILITIES - SOVIET UNION - RATES.

Mikhaĭlov, V. V. (Vram Vagramovich) Tarify i rezhimy ėlektropotreblenii͡a /. Moskva , 1986. 214 p. : LC Card 86-108009
HD9685.S762 M55 1986

ELECTRIC UTILITIES - SPAIN.
Costa Morata, Pedro. Centrales nucleares en España . Madrid [1987?] 51 p. : ISBN 84-398-8834-1 LC Card 87-165955
HD9698.S72 C62 1987

ELECTRIC UTILITIES - SWEDEN.
Ny teknik för elproduktion, elanvändning . Stockholm [1983] 172 p. : LC Card 84-108404
HD9685.S852 N9 1983

Personligt präglat. [Stockholm] [1985] 107 p. : LC Card 85-191053
HD9685.S854 S945 1985

ELECTRIC UTILITIES - SWITZERLAND - RATES.
Meier, Kurt, Dr. Spitzenlasttarifierung, oekonomische Effizienz und Erhaltung der Eigenwirtschaftlichkeit . Bern , c1983. viii, 202 p. : ISBN 3-258-03322-6 : LC Card 84-108545
HD9685.S92 M45 1983

ELECTRIC UTILITIES - TENNESSEE RIVER VALLEY.
Van Fleet, Alanson A. The Tennessee Valley Authority /. New York , c1987. 92 p. : ISBN 1-555-46123-9 : LC Card 86-31738 DDC 353.0082/3/09768 19
HD9685.U7 T385 1987

ELECTRIC UTILITIES - UNITED STATES.
Load management /. New York , c1987. vii, 207 p. : ISBN 0-87942-214-9 LC Card 86-33824 DDC 363.6/2 19
HD9685.U5 L58 1987

Primeaux, Walter J. Direct electric utility competition . New York, NY, USA , 1986. xiii, 297 p. ; ISBN 0-03-004858-3 (alk. paper) : LC Card 85-20487 DDC 338.8/26136362/0973 19
HD9685.U5 P74 1985 ***NYPL [JLE 86-4075]***

ELECTRIC UTILITIES - UNITED STATES - ENERGY CONSERVATION.
Cogan, Douglas. Generating energy alternatives . Washington, D.C. , c1987. xi, 358 p. : ISBN 0-931035-16-3 (pbk.) LC Card 87-403993 DDC 333.79 19
HD9685.U5 C588 1987

ELECTRIC UTILITIES - UNITED STATES - FINANCE.
Financial condition of the U. S. electric utility industry. [Washington] [1986] xviii, 82 p. :
NYPL [JLF 86-1386]

Power investing . Alexandria, VA (P.O. Box 1467, Alexandria 22313) , c1987. vi, 42 leaves : LC Card 87-403629 DDC 332.63/22 19
HG4915 .P65 1987

ELECTRIC UTILITIES - UNITED STATES - RATES - TIME-OF-USE PRICING.
Load management /. New York , c1987. vii, 207 p. : ISBN 0-87942-214-9 LC Card 86-33824 DDC 363.6/2 19
HD9685.U5 L58 1987

ELECTRIC UTILITIES - WASHINGTON (STATE) - HISTORY.
Kramer, Arthur, 1908- Among the livewires . [Edmonds, Wash. , c1986] 141 p. : ISBN 0-939116-14-6 (pbk.) LC Card 86-91152 DDC 338.7/6136362/09797 19
HD9685.U7 P925 1986

ELECTRIC UTILITIES - WEST (U. S.) - HISTORY.
Frisbee, Don C. The PacifiCorp story . New Ycrk , 1985. 27 p. : LC Card 85-60699 DDC 338.7/6136362/09787 19
HD9685.U7 P344 1985

ELECTRIC UTILITIES - WYOMING - HISTORY.
Frisbee, Don C. The PacifiCorp story . New York , 1985. 27 p. : LC Card 85-60699 DDC 338.7/6136362/09787 19
HD9685.U7 P344 1985

Electrical and Electronic Manufacturers Association of Canada. "L'Energie, levier de développement économique" . [Ottawa?] [1983] 30 leaves ; LC Card 85-128816
HD9685.C3 Q4425 1983

Electricity and social change /. Sachchidananda, 1926- Patna , 1983. xii, 264 p. ; LC Card 83-902678 DDC 303.4/83 19
HD9685.I43 B547 1983
NYPL [JLD 86-4263]

ELECTRICITY - DISTRIBUTION. see **ELECTRIC POWER DISTRIBUTION.**

Electricity, industry, and class in South Africa /. Christie, Renfrew. London , 1984. xiii, 241 p. : ISBN 0-333-36288-8 LC Card 87-673182
HD9685.S582 C47x 1984b

ELECTRICITY - TRANSMISSION. see **ELECTRIC ENGINEERING.**

ELECTRIFICATION - ECONOMIC ASPECTS - SOVIET UNION - HISTORY.
Steklov, Vladimir I͡Ur'evich. V.I. Lenin i ėlektrifikat͡sii͡a /. Moskva , 1982. 511 p., [1] leaf of plates : LC Card 83-133950
HD9685.S762 S84 1982

ELECTRIFICATION - SOUTH AFRICA - HISTORY.
Christie, Renfrew. Electricity, industry, and class in South Africa /. London , 1984. xiii, 241 p. : ISBN 0-333-36288-8 LC Card 87-673182
HD9685.S582 C47x 1984b

ELECTROCHEMICAL INDUSTRY - UNITED STATES.
Electrochemistry . Stamford, Conn., U. S.A. , c1986. 231 leaves : ISBN 0-89336-483-5 (pbk.) LC Card 87-403910 DDC 380.1/45660297/0973 19
HD9660.E433 U544 1986

ELECTROCHEMICAL INDUSTRY - UNITED STATES - FORECASTING.
Electrochemistry . Stamford, Conn., U. S.A. , c1986. 231 leaves : ISBN 0-89336-483-5 (pbk.) LC Card 87-403910 DDC 380.1/45660297/0973 19
HD9660.E433 U544 1986

Electrochemistry : commercial developments and trends / Donald Saxman, project analyst. Stamford, Conn., U. S.A. : Business Communications Co., c1986. 231 leaves : ill. ; 29 cm. (Business opportunity report . C-044) "January 1986"--T.p. verso. Bibliography: leaves 226-229. ISBN 0-89336-483-5 (pbk.) LC Card 87-403910 DDC 380.1/45660297/0973 19
1. Electrochemical industry - United States. 2. Electrochemical industry - United States - Forecasting. I. Saxman, Donald. II. Business Communications Co. III. Series.
HD9660.E433 U544 1986

ELECTROMAGNETIC INTERFERENCE.
Mooney, Peter. Plastics EMI shielding . Stamford, Conn., U. S.A. , c1985. xxii, 297 leaves : ISBN 0-89336-409-6 (soft) LC Card 87-168832 DDC 338.4/76684 19
HD9661.U62 M654 1985

ELECTROMAGNETIC SCREENS. see **SHIELDING (ELECTRICITY)**

ELECTROMAGNETIC SHIELDS. see **SHIELDING (ELECTRICITY)**

ELECTRONIC APPARATUS AND APPLIANCES - TESTING - EQUIPMENT AND SUPPLIES.
The Microwave test equipment market in the U. S. New York, N.Y. , c1983. iii, 223 p. ; LC Card 87-143814
HD9696.M533 U56 1983

Electronic banking abroad.
Moore, L. K. S. (Linda K. S.) Videotext and home banking services in France. New York, NY (654 Madison Ave., New York 10021) , c1986. 59, 3 leaves : LC Card 86-203144 DDC 332.1/028 19
HG1711 .M66 1986

ELECTRONIC BRAINS. see **ARTIFICIAL INTELLIGENCE; COMPUTERS.**

The electronic business information sourcebook /. Wasik, John F. New York , c1987. xvi, 208 p. ; ISBN 0-471-62464-0 : LC Card 87-8289 DDC 026/.65 19
HF5548.2 .W324 1987

ELECTRONIC CHECK CLEARING. see **ELECTRONIC FUNDS TRANSFERS.**

ELECTRONIC COMPUTERS. see **COMPUTERS.**

Electronic copy boards--local & remote. Norwalk, Conn., U. S.A. (6 Prowitt St., Norwalk 06855) : International Resource Development, Inc., c1986. iii, 101 leaves : ill. ; 28 cm. (Report / International Resource Development Inc. . #706) "August 1986." LC Card 86-224860 DDC 381/.45621380414 19
1. Copying machine industry. 2. Data transmission equipment industry. 3. Facsimile transmission - Equipment and supplies. 4. Market surveys. I. International Resource Development, inc. II. Title: Electronic copy boards--local and remote. III. Series: Report / International Resource Development Inc. , #706.
HD9802.3.A2 E45 1986

Electronic copy boards--local and remote.
Electronic copy boards--local & remote. Norwalk, Conn., U. S.A. (6 Prowitt St., Norwalk 06855) , c1986. iii, 101 leaves : LC Card 86-224860 DDC 381/.45621380414 19
HD9802.3.A2 E45 1986

ELECTRONIC DATA PROCESSING - CONGRESSES.
Symposium on Logic in Computer Science (1986 : Cambridge, Mass.) Proceedings, Symposium on Logic in Computer Science, Cambridge, Massachusetts, June 16-18, 1986 /. Washington, D.C. , Los Angeles, CA , 1986. xi, 383 p. : ISBN 0-8186-0720-3 (pbk.) LC Card 86-81090 DDC 004 19
QA75.5 .S9813 1986 ***NYPL [JSF 86-1041]***

ELECTRONIC DATA PROCESSING - DATA ENTRY.
Dy, Fe Josefina F. Visual display units . Geneva , 1985. ix, 138 p. : ISBN 92-2-105083-1 (pbk.) : LC Card 86-214267 DDC 651.8 19
HF5547.5 .D9 1985

ELECTRONIC DATA PROCESSING DEPARTMENTS - ACCOUNTING.
McGee, Robert W. Accounting for data processing costs /. New York , c1988. p. cm. ISBN 0-89930-214-9 (lib. bdg. : alk. paper) LC Card 87-24933 DDC 657/.7 19
HF5548.35 .M38 1988

Porter, James. Integrating the computer with your business . London , 1980. 308 p. ; ISBN 0-372-30032-4 ***NYPL [JLD 86-2442]***

ELECTRONIC DATA PROCESSING DEPARTMENTS - AUDITING.
Porter, W. Thomas. EDP, controls and auditing /. Boston, Mass. , c1987. xviii, 617 p. : ISBN 0-534-07092-2 : LC Card 86-27564 DDC 657/.45/0285 19
HF5548.35 .P67 1987

ELECTRONIC DATA PROCESSING DEPARTMENTS - COSTS.
McGee, Robert W. Accounting for data processing costs /. New York , c1988. p. cm. ISBN 0-89930-214-9 (lib. bdg. : alk. paper) LC Card 87-24933 DDC 657/.7 19
HF5548.35 .M38 1988

Porter, James. Integrating the computer with your business . London , 1980. 308 p. ; ISBN 0-372-30032-4 ***NYPL [JLD 86-2442]***

ELECTRONIC DATA PROCESSING DEPARTMENTS - MANAGEMENT.
Head, Robert V. Planning and implementing information resource centers for end-user computing /. Wellesley, MA , c1985. viii, 186 p. : ISBN 0-89435-123-0 : LC Card 84-61536
NYPL [JLE 86-2117]

Managing corporate data centers . Boston, MA (200 Portland St., Boston 02114) , c1987. ii, 34 p. : LC Card 87-148811 DDC 658/.055133 19
HF5548.2 .M2955 1987

Schabeck, Timothy A. Managing microcomputer security . Port Jefferson Station, N.Y. (492 Old Town Rd., Port Jefferson Station 11776) , c1986. 1 v. (various pagings) : LC Card 86-216667 DDC 658.4/78 19
HF5548.37 .S33 1986

ELECTRONIC DATA PROCESSING DEPARTMENTS - SECURITY MEASURES - EQUIPMENT AND SUPPLIES.
Computer security markets. Norwalk, Conn., U. S.A. (6 Prowitt St., Norwalk 06855) , c1987. vii, 163 leaves ; LC Card 87-151110 DDC 380.1/450058 19
HD9696.C62 C6436 1987

ELECTRONIC DATA PROCESSING - DEVELOPING COUNTRIES.
Rada, Juan F. La microelectrónica, la tecnología

de la información y sus efectos en los países en vía de desarrollo /. México, D.F. , c1983. 158 p. ; ISBN 968-12-0214-7 LC Card 85-243097
HD9696.A3 D447 1983

ELECTRONIC DATA PROCESSING - GOVERNMENT POLICY.
Jussawalla, Meheroo, 1923- The calculus of international communications . Littleton, Colo. , 1987. xiv, 159 p. ; ISBN 0-87287-503-2 : LC Card 87-2640 DDC 384/.068 19
HE7645 .J87 1987

ELECTRONIC DATA PROCESSING - GOVERNMENT POLICY - BRAZIL.
Paim, Gilberto. Computador faz política /. Rio de Janeiro, RJ-Brasil [1985] 164 p. ; LC Card 86-128056
HD9696.C63 B75 1985

ELECTRONIC DATA PROCESSING IN PROGRAMMED INSTRUCTION. see **COMPUTER-ASSISTED INSTRUCTION.**

ELECTRONIC DATA PROCESSING - INFORMATION SERVICES - UNITED STATES - DIRECTORIES.
How to find information about companies in the telecommunications, data processing, and office automation industries /. Washington, DC , c1987. ii, 130 p. ; ISBN 0-934940-48-7 (pbk.) LC Card 86-51630 DDC 338.7/61004/072073 19
HD9696.A3 U559 1987

ELECTRONIC DATA PROCESSING - KEYBOARDING.
College keyboarding/typewriting . Cincinnati , c1985. 396, xvi p. : ISBN 0-538-20750-7 LC Card 84-50474 DDC 652.3 19
Z49 .C65 1985 ***NYPL [JSF 86-1142]***

ELECTRONIC DATA PROCESSING - LATIN AMERICA.
Sauvant, Karl P. Trade and foreign direct investment in data services /. Boulder Colo. , 1986. xv, 223 p. : ISBN 0-8133-7085-X : LC Card 85-22701 DDC 332.6/712 19
HD9696.C63 L387 1986
NYPL [JLD 86-3043]

ELECTRONIC DATA PROCESSING PERSONNEL - FRANCE - SUPPLY AND DEMAND.
France. Conseil économique et social. Informatique et emploi . [Paris] [1984] 24, 4 p., 8 leaves, 187, 13 p. : LC Card 84-218059
HD6331.2.F8 F73 1984

ELECTRONIC DATA PROCESSING PERSONNEL - JOB DESCRIPTIONS.
Berufe der Wirtschaftsinformatik in der Schweiz /. Zürich , Stuttgart , 1986. 83 p. : ISBN 3-7281-1499-5 : LC Card 86-182797
HD8039.D372 S953 1986

ELECTRONIC DATA PROCESSING PERSONNEL - SWITZERLAND - JOB DESCRIPTIONS.
Berufe der Wirtschaftsinformatik in der Schweiz /. Zürich , Stuttgart , 1986. 83 p. : ISBN 3-7281-1499-5 : LC Card 86-182797
HD8039.D372 S953 1986

ELECTRONIC DATA PROCESSING SERVICE CENTERS. see **DATA PROCESSING SERVICE CENTERS.**

ELECTRONIC DATA PROCESSING - SOCIAL ASPECTS.
Dostal, Werner. Bildung und Beschäftigung im technischen Wandel . Nürnberg , 1982. viii, 380, 6 p. : LC Card 82-205035 DDC 306/.46 19
HD6331 .D53 1982 ***NYPL [JLD 86-3011]***

ELECTRONIC DATA PROCESSING - SOCIAL ASPECTS - ITALY.
Pacifici, Giorgio. Il futuro presente . Milano, Italy , c1985. 201 p. ; LC Card 86-127322 DDC 384/.0945 19
HE8174 .P33 1985

ELECTRONIC DATA PROCESSING - SOVIET UNION.
Vanags, I. ÍA. (Ilmar ÍAnovich) Ėffektivnoe ispolʹzovanie vychislitelʹnoĭ tekhniki /. Moskva , 1982. 142, [2] p. : LC Card 83-165693
HF5548.2 .V345 1982

ELECTRONIC DATA PROCESSING - UNITED STATES - DISTRIBUTED PROCESSING.
Communications/Information Systems Planning Service . Boston, MA (89 Broad St., Boston 02110) , c1986. ii, 78 p. ; LC Card 86-225335 DDC 381/.45651853 19
HD9696.C63 U51492 1986

ELECTRONIC DATA PROCESSING - VOCATIONAL GUIDANCE.
Les Professions de l'informatique . Paris [1986-1987] 2 v. : ISBN 2-11-001675-2 (v. 1) : LC Card 87-156366
HF5548.2 .P7925 1986

ELECTRONIC DIGITAL COMPUTERS - PROGRAMMING.
(1984) Freedman, Roy S. Programming with APSE software tools /. Princeton, N.J. , c1984. viii, 253 p. : ISBN 0-89433-220-1 LC Card 84-20739 DDC 001.64/24 19
QA76.73.A35 F74 1984
NYPL [JSE 86-1512]

(1984) O'Dell, Jerry W. BASIC statistics, an introduction to problem solving with your personal computer /. Blue Ridge Summit, PA , c1984. vii, 452 p. : ISBN 0-8306-0759-5 : LC Card 84-8804 DDC 519.5/028/542 19
QA276.4 .O34 1984 ***NYPL [JSD 86-378]***

ELECTRONIC DIGITAL COMPUTERS - PROGRAMMING - CONGRESSES.
Symposium on Logic in Computer Science (1986 : Cambridge, Mass.) Proceedings, Symposium on Logic in Computer Science, Cambridge, Massachusetts, June 16-18, 1986 /. Washington, D.C. , Los Angeles, CA , 1986. xi, 383 p. : ISBN 0-8186-0720-3 (pbk.) LC Card 86-81090 DDC 004 19
QA75.5 .S9813 1986 ***NYPL [JSF 86-1041]***

ELECTRONIC DIGITAL COMPUTERS - PURCHASING.
Tampoe, M. Successful business computing /. London , 1982. 124 p. :
NYPL [JLD 86-2491]

Electronic document interchange markets : U. S. & international. Norwalk, Conn., U. S.A. (6 Prowitt St., Norwalk 06855) : International Resource Development Inc., c1987. v, 192 leaves : ill. ; 28 cm. (Report / International Resource Development Inc. . #732 (Apr. 1987)) LC Card 87-403217 DDC 384.3/1 19
1. Data transmission equipment industry. 2. Market surveys. I. International Resource Development, inc. II. Series: Report / International Resource Development Inc. , #732.
HD9696.D382 E44 1987

ELECTRONIC FILING SYSTEMS.
Parikh, Girish, 1934- The one minute organizing secret . Chicago, IL , c1986. 60, 2 p. ; ISBN 0-932888-37-2 (pbk.) : LC Card 85-62926 DDC 650.1 19
HF5736 .P34 1986

ELECTRONIC FUNDS TRANSFER - LAW AND LEGISLATION - UNITED STATES - COMPLIANCE COSTS.
Schroeder, Frederick J. Compliance costs and consumer benefits of the Electronic Fund Transfer Act . Washington, D.C. , 1985. 23 p. : LC Card 86-603417 DDC 332.1/028 19
HG1710 .S38 1985

Electronic funds transfer systems . Kirkman, Patrick R. A. Oxford, UK , New York, NY , 1987. x, 231 p. ; ISBN 0-631-15317-9 : LC Card 86-26410 DDC 332.1/028 19
HG1710 .K57 1987

ELECTRONIC FUNDS TRANSFER - UNITED STATES.
ACH marketing handbook. [Washington, DC] (1901 L St., NW, Suite 640, Washington 20036) [c1987] 123, [24] p. ; LC Card 87-130512 DDC 332.1/028 19
HG4028.C45 A28 1987

Schroeder, Frederick J. Compliance costs and consumer benefits of the Electronic Fund Transfer Act . Washington, D.C. , 1985. 23 p. : LC Card 86-603417 DDC 332.1/028 19
HG1710 .S38 1985

ELECTRONIC FUNDS TRANSFERS.
ACH receivers handbook. Washington, D.C. (1901 L St., N.W., Suite 640, Washington 20036) , c1986. 104 p. : LC Card 87-112783 DDC 332.1/028 19
HG2306 .A25 1986

Kirkman, Patrick R. A. Electronic funds transfer systems . Oxford, UK , New York, NY , 1987. x, 231 p. ; ISBN 0-631-15317-9 : LC Card 86-26410 DDC 332.1/028 19
HG1710 .K57 1987

Schmitzer, Iana L. EFT . Westport, CT (P.O. Box 431, Westport 06881) , c1986. vi leaves, 180 p. : LC Card 87-143208 DDC 332.1/028 19
HG1710 .S364 1986

ELECTRONIC FUNDS TRANSFERS - ECONOMIC ASPECTS.
Schmitzer, Iana L. EFT . Westport, CT (P.O. Box 431, Westport 06881) , c1986. vi leaves, 180 p. : LC Card 87-143208 DDC 332.1/028 19
HG1710 .S364 1986

ELECTRONIC FUNDS TRANSFERS - GERMANY (WEST)
Christians, Volker C. Neue Zahlungsverkehrsinstrumente . Frankfurt am Main , 1985. 216 p. ; ISBN 3-922182-17-8 : LC Card 86-100407
HG1710 .C48 1985

ELECTRONIC FUNDS TRANSFERS - GREAT BRITAIN.
Frazer, P. A. T. Plastic and electronic money . Cambridge [Cambridgeshire] , Dover, NH. USA , 1985. x, 294 p. ; ISBN 0-85941-290-3 : LC Card 85-22552 DDC 332.1/028 19
HG1710 .F73 1985 ***NYPL [JLE 86-1401]***

ELECTRONIC FUNDS TRANSFERS - UNITED STATES.
American Bankers Association. Retail Payments Task Force. Ad Hoc Committee. Implementation guidelines for online debit card systems at the point of sale /. [Washington, D.C.] , c1986. 1 v. (various pagings) : LC Card 86-224882 DDC 332.1/028 19
HG1710.5 .A47 1986

Friedman, David H., 1942- Deposit operations /. Washington, D.C. (1120 Connecticut Ave., N.W., Washington 20036) , c1987. xii, 354 p. : LC Card 87-165558 DDC 332.1/752 19
HG1660.U5 F75 1987

Introduction to ACH corporate payments /. Washington, D.C. (1901 L St., N.W., Suite 640, Washington 20036) [c1986] 90 p. : LC Card 86-222675 DDC 332.1/028 19
HG1710 .I58 1986

ELECTRONIC FUNDS TRANSFERS - UNITED STATES - DIRECTORIES.
Contacts . San Rafael, CA (1724 Lincoln Ave., San Rafael 94901) [c1986] 252 p. ; LC Card 86-217208 DDC 332.1/028 19
HG1710 .C66 1986

ELECTRONIC GAMES INDUSTRY - UNITED STATES.
The Electronic games market in the U. S. New York, N.Y. , c1983. vii, 291 p. : LC Card 87-142142 DDC 381/.45688728 19
HD9993.E453 U622 1983

The Electronic games market in the U. S. New York, N.Y. : Frost & Sullivan, c1983. vii, 291 p. : ill. ; 29 cm. "February 1983." "#A1153." LC Card 87-142142 DDC 381/.45688728 19
1. Electronic games industry - United States. 2. Market surveys - United States. I. Frost & Sullivan.
HD9993.E453 U622 1983

ELECTRONIC INDUSTRIES.
Information activities, electronics, and telecommunications technologies . Paris , Washington, D.C.] 1981- v. : ISBN 92-64-12241-9 (pbk. : v. 1) LC Card 81-211344 DDC 338.4/700151 19
HD9696.C62 I53 ***NYPL [JLL 86-393]***

Electronic Industries Association. Marketing Services. Sources . Washington, D.C. (2001 Eye St., N.W., Washington 20006) , c1987. vi, 147 p. ; LC Card 87-165452 DDC 016.3384/7621381 19
HD9696.A2 S594 1987

ELECTRONIC INDUSTRIES - DEVELOPING COUNTRIES.
Rada, Juan F. La microelectrónica, la tecnología de la información y sus efectos en los países en vía de desarrollo /. México, D.F. , c1983. 158 p. ; ISBN 968-12-0214-7 LC Card 85-243097
HD9696.A3 D447 1983

ELECTRONIC INDUSTRIES - GERMANY, WEST.
Berger, Manfred, 1921- Elektrotechnische Industrie . Berlin , c1984. 261 p. : ISBN

3-428-05674-4 LC Card 85-137543
HD9696.A3 G42 1984 ***NYPL [TB (Struktur und Wachstum. Reihe Industrie. Heft 38)]***

ELECTRONIC INDUSTRIES - GREAT BRITAIN.
U.K. consumer electronics. Norwalk, Conn., U. S.A. (6 Prowitt St., Norwalk 06855) , c1986. vi, 198 leaves ; LC Card 86-228422 DDC 381/.45621381/0941 19
HD9696.A3 G785 1986

ELECTRONIC INDUSTRIES - INFORMATION SERVICES - DIRECTORIES.
Sources . Washington, D.C. (2001 Eye St., N.W., Washington 20006) , c1987. vi, 147 p. ; LC Card 87-165452 DDC 016.3384/7621381 19
HD9696.A2 S594 1987

ELECTRONIC INDUSTRIES - INFORMATION SERVICES - UNITED STATES - DIRECTORIES.
How to find information about companies in the telecommunications, data processing, and office automation industries /. Washington, DC , c1987. ii, 130 p. ; ISBN 0-934940-48-7 (pbk.) LC Card 86-51630 DDC 338.7/61004/072073 19
HD9696.A3 U559 1987

ELECTRONIC INDUSTRIES - ISRAEL.
Electronics-1985 . [Jerusalem , 1985] 128 p. : LC Card 86-213293 DDC 338.4/7621381/095694 19
HD9696.A3 I654 1985

ELECTRONIC INDUSTRIES - ITALY - CONGRESSES.
Convegno nazionale del PCI (1982 : Milan, Italy) Le nuove frontiere dello sviluppo . Milano, Italy , c1983. 368 p. ; LC Card 85-174697
HD9696.A3 I727 1982

ELECTRONIC INDUSTRIES - ITALY - MANAGEMENT - CASE STUDIES.
Eminente, Giorgio. Strategia aziendale e sviluppo tecnologico . Bologna , c1985. 253 p. : ISBN 88-15-00917-5 : LC Card 86-176732
HD9696.A3 I733 1985

ELECTRONIC INDUSTRIES - ITALY - TECHNOLOGICAL INNOVATIONS - CASE STUDIES.
Eminente, Giorgio. Strategia aziendale e sviluppo tecnologico . Bologna , c1985. 253 p. : ISBN 88-15-00917-5 : LC Card 86-176732
HD9696.A3 I733 1985

ELECTRONIC INDUSTRIES - JAPAN - HISTORY.
Morita, Akio, 1921- Made in Japan . New York , c1986. viii, 309 p., [8] p. of plates : ISBN 0-525-24465-4 : LC Card 86-11479 DDC 338.7/6213/0924 B 19
HD9696.A3 J3658 1986 ***NYPL [JFE 86-5112]***

ELECTRONIC INDUSTRIES - MEXICO.
Quibrera Matienzo, Enrique. La informática nacional . [Xochimilco, Mexico] , 1984. 133 p. ; LC Card 86-124964 DDC 338.4/7004/0972 19
HD9696.C63 M617 1984

ELECTRONIC INDUSTRIES - SOVIET UNION - PLANNING.
Stukolov, P. M. (Petr Mikhaĭlovich) Otraslevaia͡ sistema planirovanii͡a . Moskva , 1985. 71 p. : LC Card 85-196558
HD9696.A3 S697 1985

ELECTRONIC INDUSTRY WORKERS - CALIFORNIA.
Seider, Maynard, 1943- A year in the life of a factory /. San Pedro, Calif. , 1984. 152 p. ; ISBN 0-917300-16-5 (pbk.) : LC Card 83-50914 DDC 331.89/28621381/0979466 19
HD8039.E38 U67 1984 ***NYPL [JLD 86-4400]***

ELECTRONIC INDUSTRY WORKERS - CALIFORNIA - ATTITUDES.
Oren, Ditza L. Preventing dishonest behavior in the electronics industry . [United States , 1985] vii, 115 leaves : LC Card 86-224386 DDC 621.381/068/3 19
HD8039.E38 U65 1985

ELECTRONIC MAIL EQUIPMENT INDUSTRY - UNITED STATES.
Mandela, Audrey L. Electronic mail update . Boston, Mass. (200 Portland St., Boston 02114) , c1986. ii, 135 p. : LC Card 87-124538 DDC 384.3/4/0973 19
HD9696.M353 U56 1986

ELECTRONIC MAIL SYSTEMS.
Electronic mail . Norwalk, Conn., U. S.A. (6 Prowitt St., Norwalk 06855) , c1986. viii, 230 leaves ; LC Card 86-226979 DDC 384.3/4 19
HE6239.E54 E59 1986

Mayer, Ira. The electronic mailbox /. New York, 1987. p. cm. ISBN 0-471-62576-0 : LC Card 87-6250 DDC 384.3/4 19
HE6239.E54 M39 1987

Simon, Sam, 1945- Phonewriting . [Washington, D.C.] , c1986. iv, 92 p., [4] p. of plates : ISBN 0-943444-03-9 (pbk.) LC Card 86-214171 DDC 004.6 19
HE6239.E54 S56 1986

Vervest, Peter. Innovation in electronic mail . Amsterdam ; New York : xv, 212 p. : ISBN 0-444-70153-2 LC Card 87-11145 DDC 384.3/4 19
HE6239.E54 V47 1987

ELECTRONIC MAIL SYSTEMS - HANDBOOKS, MANUALS, ETC.
Davis, Steve, 1953- The electric mailbox /. Dallas, Tex. , c1986. 286 p. ; ISBN 0-911061-14-2 (pbk.) LC Card 84-91756 DDC 384.3/4 19
HE6239.E54 D38 1986

Electronic mail update . Mandela, Audrey L. Boston, Mass. (200 Portland St., Boston 02114) , c1986. ii, 135 p. : LC Card 87-124538 DDC 384.3/4/0973 19
HD9696.M353 U56 1986

The electronic mailbox /. Mayer, Ira. New York, 1987. p. cm. ISBN 0-471-62576-0 : LC Card 87-6250 DDC 384.3/4 19
HE6239.E54 M39 1987

Electronic media and research technologies-IV. Advertising Research Foundation Key Issues Workshop (1985 : New York, N.Y.) Transcript proceedings . New York, NY (3 E. 54th St., New York 10022-3180) , c1985. 174 p. : LC Card 86-214476 DDC 659.14/3/0973 19
HF6146.T42 A27 1985a

Electronic media and research technologies-V. Advertising Research Foundation Key Issues Workshop (1986 : New York, N.Y.) Transcript proceedings . New York, NY (3 E. 54th St., New York 10022-3180) , c1986. 214 p. : LC Card 87-404527 DDC 659.14/3/0973 19
HF6146.T42 A27 1986

ELECTRONIC MONEY SYSTEMS. see **ELECTRONIC FUNDS TRANSFERS.**

The electronic office /. Kupsh, Joyce. Mission Hills, Calif. , c1987. x, 307 p. : ISBN 0-02-803510-0 (pbk.) LC Card 87-402084 DDC 651.8 19
HF5548 .K85 1987

The electronic office in the smaller business /. Harvey, David. Aldershot, Hants, England , Brookfield, Vt., U. S.A. , c1986. vii, 214 p. : ISBN 0-566-02578-7 LC Card 86-225568 DDC 651.8/416 19
HF5547.5 .H365 1986

ELECTRONIC OFFICE MACHINE INDUSTRY.
Converging voice/data/video technologies at the workstation /. Stamford, Conn., U. S.A. , c1986. v, 119 leaves ; ISBN 0-89336-466-5 (pbk.) LC Card 87-168057 DDC 380.1/45004 19
HD9801.A2 C66 1986

Glücksmann, Riccardo. Telematica . Milano , 1982. xii, 273 p., [4] p. of plates : ISBN 88-7056-120-8 LC Card 84-184344
HD9696.D383 I84 1982

Plastics in business machines . Stamford, Conn. , c1986. vii, 215 leaves : ISBN 0-89336-433-6 (soft) : LC Card 87-165036 DDC 380.1/456684 19
HD9801.A2 P56 1986

ELECTRONIC OFFICE MACHINE INDUSTRY - ITALY.
Glücksmann, Riccardo. Telematica . Milano , 1982. xii, 273 p., [4] p. of plates : ISBN 88-7056-120-8 LC Card 84-184344
HD9696.D383 I84 1982

ELECTRONIC OFFICE MACHINE INDUSTRY - JAPAN.
Japanese penetration into the United States communications data processing and office equipment markets. New York, N.Y. , c1983. v, 308 p. ; LC Card 87-143908 DDC 381/.45004/0973 19
HD9696.D383 U635 1983

ELECTRONIC OFFICE MACHINE INDUSTRY - UNITED STATES.
Consolidated data base . San Jose, Calif. (1290 Ridder Park Dr., San Jose 95131-2398) , c1986. ii, 94 p. ; LC Card 87-108611 DDC 381/.45004/0973
HD9696.C63 U515626 1986

Japanese penetration into the United States communications data processing and office equipment markets. New York, N.Y. , c1983. v, 308 p. ; LC Card 87-143908 DDC 381/.45004/0973 19
HD9696.D383 U635 1983

New marketing strategies for office equipment. New York, N.Y. , c1983. vii, 307 p. ; LC Card 87-142201 DDC 381/.456816/0973 19
HD9801.U542 N48 1983

The Office automation market in the U. S. New York, N.Y. , <c1983-. v. <2 > : LC Card 87-166011 DDC 381/.456816/0973 19
HD9801.U542 O34 1983

The U. S. professional/executive workstations market. New York, N.Y. , c1983. vi, 284 p. : LC Card 87-142071 DDC 381/.4500416/0973 19
HD9801.U542 U18 1983

ELECTRONIC OFFICE MACHINES - MARKETING.
New marketing strategies for office equipment. New York, N.Y. , c1983. vii, 307 p. ; LC Card 87-142201 DDC 381/.456816/0973 19
HD9801.U542 N48 1983

ELECTRONIC OFFICE MACHINES - MARKETING - CASE STUDIES.
Rodgers, F. G. (Francis G.) The IBM way . New York , c1986. xiv, 235 p. ; ISBN 0-06-015522-1 : LC Card 85-45223 DDC 338.7/61004/0973 19
HD9696.C64 I4875 1986 ***NYPL [JLE 86-1374]***

ELECTRONIC OFFICE MACHINES - MATERIALS.
Plastics in business machines . Stamford, Conn. , c1986. vii, 215 leaves : ISBN 0-89336-433-6 (soft) : LC Card 87-165036 DDC 380.1/456684 19
HD9801.A2 P56 1986

ELECTRONIC PAYMENTS SYSTEMS. see **ELECTRONIC FUNDS TRANSFERS.**

ELECTRONIC PUBLISHING.
Cavuoto, James. LaserWrite it! . Reading, Mass. , 1986. viii, 198 p. : ISBN 0-201-11327-9 : LC Card 86-3406 DDC 070.5/028/5 19
Z286.E43 C38 1986 ***NYPL [JSE 86-1226]***

ELECTRONIC SPREADSHEETS.
Blanc, Iris. DDC spreadsheets. [New York, N.Y.] [c1986] 161 p. : LC Card 87-159255 DDC 005.3/07/1273 19
HF5548.2 .B527 1986

DiAntonio, Angelo E. Spreadsheet applications in financial accounting /. Englewood Cliffs, N.J. , c1986. xvii, 391 p. : ISBN 0-8359-6945-2 (pbk.) : LC Card 85-14303 DDC 657/.028/553 19
HF5679 .D52 1986 ***NYPL [JLE 86-3100]***

Jackson, Mary, 1936- Creative modelling with Lotus 1-2-3 /. Chichester , New York , c1985. ix, 169 p. : ISBN 0-471-90796-0 (pbk.) LC Card 86-228784 DDC 005.36/9 19
HF5548.4.L67 J33 1985b

Kiczek, Paul. Decision making for bankers . Washington, D.C. (1120 Connecticut Ave., NW, Washington 20036) , c1986. 89 p. : LC Card 87-115307 DDC 332.1/2/02855369 19
HG1709 .K53 1986

Moore, James M. (James Mendon), 1925- An engineers guide to spreadsheets, word processors & data base managers /. Norcross, GA , c1986. xi, 154 p. : ISBN 0-89806-081-8 (pbk.) LC Card 87-157586 DDC 620/.0028/553 19
HF5548 .M566 1986

Nevison, John M. The elements of spreadsheet

style /. New York , c1987. xiv, 197 p. : ISBN 0-13-080565-3 (pbk.) : LC Card 87-6922 DDC 005.3 19
HF5548.2 .N416 1987

Nguyen, Tim K. Applied 1-2-3 . New York, N.Y. , c1987. p. cm. ISBN 0-13-729542-1 : LC Card 87-11390 DDC 005.36/9 19
HF5548.4.L67 N48 1987

Ross, Steven S. SPREADSTAT . New York , c1988. p. cm. ISBN 0-07-053909-X : LC Card 87-22811 DDC 005.36/9 19
HF1017 .R67 1988

Willis, Jerry, 1942- Working with SuperCalc 4 /. Blue Ridge Summit, PA , c1987. x, 320 p. : ISBN 0-8306-0214-3 : LC Card 86-30124 DDC 005.36/9 19
HF5548.4.S87 W54 1987

Witkin, Ruth K. Managing your business with Multiplan . Redmond, Wash. , 1987. xv, 525 p. ; ISBN 0-914845-94-2 (pbk.) : LC Card 87-7773 DDC 005.36/9 19
HF5548.4.M74 W57 1987

Wolf, Douglas, 1948- Compute!'s quick & easy guide to learning Lotus 1-2-3 /. Greensboro, N.C. , c1987. vi, 139 p. : ISBN 0-87455-106-4 (pbk.) : LC Card 87-163385 DDC 005.36/9 19
HF5548.4.L67 W65 1987

ELECTRONIC SPREADSHEETS - JUVENILE LITERATURE.
Luehrmann, Arthur. AppleWorks spreadsheets . Gilroy, Calif. , c1987. viii, 152 p. ; ISBN 0-941681-05-X (pbk.) : LC Card 87-11745 DDC 005.36/9 19
HF5548.4.A68 L847 1987

ELECTRONICS - APPARATUS AND APPLIANCES. see **ELECTRONIC APPARATUS AND APPLIANCES.**

ELECTRONICS - APPARATUS AND SUPPLIES. see **ELECTRONIC APPARATUS AND APPLIANCES.**

ELECTRONICS - APPARATUS AND SUPPLIES, MINIATURE. see **MICROELECTRONICS.**

ELECTRONICS - DICTIONARIES.
(1985) Erekutoronikusu pawā shōjiten /. Tōkyō , 1985. v, 618 p. : ISBN 4-320-08454-3 : LC Card 85-229520
TK7804 .E73 1985 <Orien Japan>
NYPL [*OSG 86-3267]

ELECTRONICS - DICTIONARIES - JAPANESE.
Erekutoronikusu pawā shōjiten /. Tōkyō , 1985. v, 618 p. : ISBN 4-320-08454-3 : LC Card 85-229520
TK7804 .E73 1985 <Orien Japan>
NYPL [*OSG 86-3267]

Electronics-1985 : high technology and science based industries in Israel. [Jerusalem : Israel Economist Pub. Service, 1985] 128 p. : ill. (some col.) ; 27 cm. Includes index. LC Card 86-213293 DDC 338.4/7621381/095694 19
1. Electronic industries - Israel. 2. High technology industries - Israel. I. Israel Economist Publishing Service.
HD9696.A3 I654 1985

ELECTROTHERAPEUTIC EQUIPMENT INDUSTRY - UNITED STATES.
Nerve, muscle, bone stimulation, and augmentation. Tustin, CA, U. S.A. (17722 Irvine Blvd., Tustin 92680) , c1987. iv, 8, 144, [112] p. : LC Card 87-402023 DDC 338.4/7681761 19
HD9995.E43 U56 1987

Elekes, Magdolna. A Magyarországi településrendszer strukturális változása /. Budapest , 1984. 155 p., [1] folded leaf of plates : ISBN 963-03-2079-7 (Magy. nemz. bibl.) LC Card 85-231254
HD640.5 .M343 1984

Elektroindustrie und Staatsverwaltung am Beispiel Siemens, 1847-1914 /. Peschke, Hans-Peter von, 1951- Frankfurt am Main , Bern , c1981. 393 p. : ISBN 3-8204-5902-2 LC Card 81-141438
HD9697.A3 G35 1981

Elektrotechnische Industrie . Berger, Manfred, 1921- Berlin , c1987. 261 p. : ISBN 3-428-05674-4 LC Card 85-137543
HD9696.A3 G42 1984 ***NYPL [TB (Struktur und Wachstum. Reihe Industrie. Heft 38)]***

Az Élelmiszer-gazdaság távlati fejlesztése / szerkesztette, Zsuffa Ervin ; [írta, Csendes Béla ... et al.]. Budapest : Mezőgazdasági Kiadó, 1984. 163 p. ; 21 cm. Bibliography: p. 23-24. ISBN 963-231-717-3 : LC Card 85-194280
1. Agriculture and state - Hungary. 2. Agriculture - Economic aspects - Hungary. 3. Food industry and trade - Hungary. I. Zsuffa, Ervin. II. Csendes, Béla.
HD1940.5.Z8 E54 1984

Élelmiszer-gazdaságunk versenyképessége . Borszéki, Éva. Budapest , 1986. 284, [1] p. : ISBN 963-221-590-7 : LC Card 87-148751
HD1940.5 .B66 1986

Az élelmiszerfogyasztás várható tendenciái hosszabb távon /. Orbánné Nagy, Mária. Budapest , 1983. 98 p. ; ISBN 963-491-166-8 LC Card 85-219700
HD9015.H82 O73 1983

Élelmiszergazdaságunk versenyképessége . Borszéki, Éva. Budapest , 1985. 147 p. ; ISBN 963-491-213-3 LC Card 86-199073
HD1940.5 .B67 1985

Elementar .
(E 6) Randak, Harald, 1942- Die soziale Marktwirtschaft /. München , 1985. 143 p. : LC Card 85-216985
HC286.5 .R36 1985

Elementary business statistics . Freund, John E. Englewood Cliffs, N.J. , c1988. xiii, 738 p. : ISBN 0-13-253196-8 LC Card 87-20586 DDC 519.5/024658 19
HF1017 .F73 1988

Elemente de teorie a valorilor economice în societatea noastră /. Marian, Vasile. Cluj-Napoca , 1984. 249 p. ; LC Card 85-213867
HB201 .M312 1984

Elemente einer politischen Ökonomie im Werke Machiavellis /. Begert, Roland. Bern , c1983. 224 p. : ISBN 3-258-03136-3 LC Card 83-204993
HB109.M3 B44 1983

Elementos de economía para uso de no economistas /. Fernández Russo, Omar. Caracas , 1985. 226 p. : LC Card 85-240123
HB178.5 .F38 1985

Elementos de finanzas públicas en Colombia /. Alviar Ramírez, Oscar, d. 1984. Bogotá, Colombia , 1985. xx, 584 p. ; ISBN 958-604-045-3 (pbk.) LC Card 86-129809 DDC 336.861 19
HJ945 .A48 1985

Elementos para la programación del desarrollo de la industria de aceites y pastas vegetales en México. 1a ed. México : Nacional Financiera : Comisión Nacional de Alimentación, 1985. 306 p. : ill. ; 24 cm. (Ensayos e investigaciones sobre el desarrollo industrial de México) Includes bibliographical references. "Noviembre 1984." ISBN 968-665-105-5 LC Card 86-232449
1. Oil industries - Mexico. 2. Flour and feed trade - Mexico. I. Nacional Financiera, S. A., Mexico. II. Mexico. Comisión Nacional de Alimentación. III. Series.
HD9490.M62 E44 1985

Eléments d'analyse et de gestion financières de l'entreprise en déficit /. Wuillemin, Lucien. Genève , c1982. 191 p. : ISBN 2-8257-0090-8 : LC Card 82-228134 DDC 658.1/5 19
HD49 .W84 1982 ***NYPL [JLE 87-1142]***

Eléments de microéconomie /. Guyot, F. Paris , 1985. 310 p. : ISBN 2-7108-0479-4 LC Card 86-210675
HB173 .G88 1985

Eléments de politique économique . Maris, Bernard. Toulouse , c1985. 235 p. : ISBN 2-7089-7608-7 : LC Card 85-160415 DDC 338.944 19
HC276.2 .M355 1985 ***NYPL [JLE 87-642]***

Eléments d'histoire de la FTQ . Cyr, François, 1952- [Laval] [1981] 205 p. ; ISBN 2-89035-045-2 : LC Card 82-105783 DDC 331.88/09714 19
HD8102.F43 C97 1981

Eléments du rapport annuel de la zone de Yaoundé /. Bureau de zone UNICEF de Yaoundé. N'Djaména [1984] [43] leaves : LC Card 86-980240
HC990 .B87 1984

Elements of banking /. Hall, Peter (Peter J.), 1932- London , New York , 1987. xi, 236 p. : ISBN 0-582-29728-1 (pbk.) LC Card 86-21144 DDC 332.1 19
HG1601 .H25 1987

The elements of spreadsheet style /. Nevison, John M. New York , c1987. xiv, 197 p. : ISBN 0-13-080565-3 (pbk.) : LC Card 87-6922 DDC 005.3 19
HF5548.2 .N416 1987

Elements of statistics for the life and social sciences /. Alfred, Braxton M. New York , c1987. xiii, 190 p. : ISBN 0-387-96500-9 : LC Card 87-4964 DDC 300/.1/5195 19
HA29 .A53 1987

Eléments pour une stratégie d'emploi dans les zones rurales au Bénin . Jobs and Skills Programme for Africa. Addis Abeba [1980] xii, 70, 5 p. : LC Card 87-100360
HD5846.3.A6 J63 1980

Elementy polityki ekonomicznej : praca zbiorowa / pod redakcją Stanisława Wacławowicza.Wyd. 2. Kraków : Akademia Ekonomiczna w Krakowie, 1977. 306 p. ; 24 cm. Includes bibliographies. LC Card 81-173152
1. Poland - Economic policy - 1966-1980. I. Wacławowicz, Stanisław. II. Akademia Ekonomiczna w Krakowie.
HC340.3 .E515 1977

Ėlementy teorii upravleniia zapasami . Pervozvanskaia, T. N. (Tat'iana Nikolaevna) Leningrad , 1983. 108 p. : LC Card 84-217972
HD40 .P47 1983

Eletrificação rural. Brazil. Departamento Nacional de Aguas e Energia Elétrica. Pontos básicos para uma política de eletrificação rural . Brasília, D.F. , 1984. 190 p. : LC Card 86-158852
HD9688.B72 B73 1984

Eletrificação rural no Brasil /. Brazil. Grupo Executivo de Eletrificação Rural de Cooperativas. Brasília, DF [1984] 93 p. : LC Card 86-200328
HD9688.B72 B74 1984

Eletrobrás. Situação econômica-financeira das concessionárias de energia elétrica : participação da Eletrobrás. [Rio de Janeiro] : Eletrobrás, 1979. 64 p. ; 27 cm. (Série "Projetos especiais para apoio ao planejamento" . projeto 11) Errata slip inserted. LC Card 84-256157
1. Electric utilities - Brazil. 2. Electric utilities - Brazil - Finance. 3. Eletrobrás. I. Series: Série "Projetos especiais para apoio ao planejamento" , 11. II. Title.
HD9685.B8 E47 1979

ELETROBRÁS.
Eletrobrás. Situação econômica-financeira das concessionárias de energia elétrica . [Rio de Janeiro] , 1979. 64 p. ; LC Card 84-256157
HD9685.B8 E47 1979

Eletrobrás. Itaipu (Power plant) see Itaipu (Power plant)

Életszínvonal és közhangulat / [a kötetet szerkesztette, Fébó László és Radnóti Éva]. Budapest : MTA Közgazdaságtudományi Intézet, 1984. 69 p. ; 24 cm. (Tanulmányok a gazdaság irányításáról és szervezetéről . 2. sz.) CONTENTS. - Az életszínvonal és mérése / Zafír Mihály -- Lét és tudat az életszínvonalpolitikában / Hoch Róbert -- Értékeink, életszínvonal-politika, propaganda / Pirityi Ottó. LC Card 86-147705
1. Cost and standard of living - Hungary. I. Fébó, László. II. Radnóti, Éva. III. Zafír, Mihály. IV. Hoch, Róbert. V. Pirityi, Ottó. VI. Series.
HD7027.5 .E44 1984

Életszínvonal-füzetek .
(4. sz) A Lakosság jövedelme, társadalombiztosítás, családpolitika /. Budapest [1983] 82 p. : LC Card 83-206799
HC30.295.I5 L332 1983
NYPL [JLE 87-179]

Eletti e abbandonati . Regalia, Ida, 1946- Bologna , c1984. 355 p. : ISBN 88-15-00592-7 : LC Card 84-250543 DDC 331.87/33/0945 19
HD6490.O42 I87 1984 ***NYPL [JLD 86-211]***

ELETTRONICA SAN GIORGIO-ELSAG, S.P.A. (GENOA, ITALY)
Eminente, Giorgio. Strategia aziendale e sviluppo tecnologico . Bologna , c1985. 253 p. :

ISBN 88-15-00917-5 : LC Card 86-176732
HD9696.A3 I733 1985

Eleuthero Politiko Ergastēri (Athens, Greece) Hellēniko syndikalistiko kinēma . Athēna , 1984. 215 p. ; LC Card 86-193159
HD6795.5 .H44 1984

ELEVATORS, GRAIN. see **GRAIN ELEVATORS.**

Elgers, Pieter T.
Accounting theory and policy . San Diego , c1987. xi, 654 p. : ISBN 0-15-500478-6 (pbk.) LC Card 86-81620 DDC 657 19
HF5629 .A26 1987

Backer, Morton. Financial accounting . San Diego , c1988. xvi, 685 p. : ISBN 0-15-527371-X LC Card 87-81140 DDC 657 19
HF5635 .B139 1988

Éliás, András. Mezőgazdasági és élelmiszeripari termékeink a külpiaci versenyben / Éliás András. Budapest : Mezőgazdasági Kiadó, 1985. 197 p. ; 20 cm. Bibliography: p. 194-195. ISBN 963-232-064-6 : LC Card 86-185883
1. Agricultural industries - Hungary. 2. Food industry and trade - Hungary. 3. Export marketing - Hungary. 4. Produce trade - Hungary. I. Title.
HD9015.H82 E59 1985

Elias, Hermann-Josef, 1949- Gestaltung und Bewertung von Arbeitssystemen / Hermann-Josef Elias, Bernhard Gottschalk, Wolfgang H. Staehle. Frankfurt am Main ; New York : Campus, c1985. 281 p. : ill. ; 21 cm. (Campus Forschung. Bd. 422) Bibliography: p. 272-281. ISBN 3-593-33444-5 LC Card 85-143343
1. Job analysis. 2. Job evaluation. 3. Work environment. I. Gottschalk, Bernhard, 1944-. II. Staehle, Wolfgang H., 1938-.
HF5549.5.J6 E45 1985

ELIAS, NORBERT.
Matzner, Egon, 1938- Die Soziogenese des Staates nach Elias und Schumpeter . Berlin [1979] 30, [4] p. ; LC Card 85-135122
HJ105 .M37 1979

Eliason, Alan L. Program analysis and design : a software maintenance project / Alan L. Eliason and James D. Trumper. Chicago : Science Research Associates, c1987. ix, 134 p. : ill. ; 28 cm. ISBN 0-574-18660-3 (pbk.) LC Card 87-4521 DDC 658/.055265 19
1. Business - Data processing. 2. Software maintenance. 3. IBM Personal Computer - Programming. 4. Basic (Computer program language). I. Trumper, James D., 1958-. II. Title.
HF5548.2 .E4275 1987

Eliassen, Peter. Kongeåen, eller, Den gamle grænse / [af] P. Eliassen ; [litteraturliste ved Gunnar Jakobsen]. Fotografisk genoptryk. [København, Amaliegade 44, 1256 K] : Toldhistorisk selskab ; [Esbjerg] : Historisk samfund for Ribe amt, 1980. 357, [4] p. : ill. ; 22 cm. Reprint. Originally published in 2 v.: Kolding : K. Jørgensen, 1926. Bibliography: p. [359]-[361] ISBN 87-87796-02-3 : LC Card 81-107972
1. Customs administration - Denmark - History. 2. Tariff - Denmark - History. I. Title.
HJ6971 .E45 1980

Eliminating barriers to international trade and investment in services /. Basche, James R., 1926- New York, N.Y. (845 Third Ave., New York 10022) , c1986. 15 p. ; LC Card 87-147770 DDC 382/.45 19
HD9980.6 .B37 1986

ELITE (SOCIAL SCIENCES) - AFRICA.
Nafziger, E. Wayne. Inequality in Africa . Cambridge [Cambridgeshire] , New York , c1988. p. cm. ISBN 0-521-26881-8 LC Card 87-24263 DDC 339.2/096 19
HC800.Z9 I5136 1988

ELITE (SOCIAL SCIENCES) - BRAZIL - HISTORY.
Mueller, Charles Curt. Das oligarquias agrárias ao predomínio urbano-industrial . Rio de Janeiro , 1983. 363 p. ; LC Card 87-403875 DDC 305.5/232/0981 19
HC187 .M76 1983

ELITE (SOCIAL SCIENCES) - CANADA.
Carroll, William K. Corporate power and Canadian capitalism /. Vancouver , 1986. xvii, 284 p. : ISBN 0-7748-0246-4 LC Card 86-223683 DDC 338.8/0971 19
HC120.C3 C37 1986

ELITE (SOCIAL SCIENCES) - CENTRAL AMERICA.
Brockett, Charles D., 1946- Land, power, and poverty . Boston , c1988. p. cm. ISBN 0-04-497027-7 LC Card 87-22746 DDC 338.1/09728 19
HD1797 .B76 1988

ELITE (SOCIAL SCIENCES) - DEVELOPING COUNTRIES.
Postimperialism . Boulder , 1987. x, 252 p. : ISBN 1-555-87046-5 (lib. bdg. : alk. paper) : LC Card 87-4455 DDC 338.8/881724 19
HD2932 .P67 1987

ELITE (SOCIAL SCIENCES) - FRANCE - HISTORY - 17TH CENTURY.
Collins, James B. Fiscal limits of absolutism . Berkeley , c1987. p. cm. ISBN 0-520-05911-5 (alk. paper) LC Card 87-19090 DDC 336.2/00944 19
HJ2648 .C65 1987

ELITE (SOCIAL SCIENCES) - INDIA.
Singh, V. B., 1941- Profiles of political elites in India /. Delhi , 1984. xii, 178 p. : LC Card 84-900272 DDC 305.5/24/0954 19
JQ281 .S565 1984 ***NYPL [JLD 86-4319]***

ELITE (SOCIAL SCIENCES) - MALAYSIA.
Mehmet, Ozay. Development in Malaysia . London , Dover, N.H. , c1986. 183 p. ; ISBN 0-7099-3525-0 : LC Card 85-29079 DDC 338.9595 19
HC445.5.Z9 I51834 1986 ***NYPL [JLD 86-2389]***

ELITE (SOCIAL SCIENCES) - MEXICO - MEXICO CITY - HISTORY.
Kicza, John E., 1947- Colonial entrepreneurs, families and business in Bourbon Mexico City /. Albuquerque , c1983. 1 v. : ISBN 0-8263-0655-1 (v. 1) LC Card 82-21962 DDC 305.5/54/097253 19
HF3240.M5 K52 1983 ***NYPL [JLL 83-164]***

ELITE (SOCIAL SCIENCES) - MEXICO - MONTERREY - HISTORY.
Saragoza, Alex. The Monterrey elite and the Mexican State, 1880-1940 /. Austin , c1988. p. cm. ISBN 0-292-71113-1 LC Card 87-23779 DDC 305.5/234/097213 19
HG185.M6 S27 1988

ELITE (SOCIAL SCIENCES) - SWITZERLAND - BIOGRAPHY.
Michel-Alder, Elisabeth. Männer im Glashaus . Zürich , c1986. 238 p. : ISBN 3-280-01561-8 LC Card 86-180438
HD38.25.S9 M52 1986

ELITE (SOCIAL SCIENCES) - UNITED STATES.
Neuman, W. Russell. The paradox of mass politics . Cambridge, Mass. , 1986. 241 p. : ISBN 0-674-65455-2 (alk. paper) LC Card 86-288 DDC 324.973 19
JK1967 .N48 1986 ***NYPL [JLE 86-4140]***

ELITES (SOCIAL SCIENCES) see **ELITE (SOCIAL SCIENCES)**

Elitnite i͡adra na trudovite kolektivi /. Dimitrov, Boris. Sofii͡a , 1985. 80 p. ; LC Card 86-140524
HD8626.5 .D55 1985

Elitnite i͡adra v trudovite kolektivi : sŭshtnost, funktsii i faktori za formirane / [redaktsionna kolegii͡a Tasho Pachev ... et al.]. [Sofia] : Sofiĭski gradski kom-t na BKP, [1985] 105 p. ; 21 cm. Includes bibliographical references. LC Card 86-104039
1. Work groups - Bulgaria. I. Pachev, Tasho. II. Bŭlgarska komunisticheska partii͡a. Sofiĭski gradski komitet.
HD66 .E42 1985

Elizaga, Juan C. (Juan Carlos) Investigaciones sobre recursos humanos en América Latina : documento preparado para discusión en las sesiones de trabajo de la Comisión de Demografía del CLACSO, realizadas del 17 al 19 de octubre de 1968 / Juan C. Elizaga. Santiago de Chile : Centro Latinoamericano de Demografía, 1972. 16 p. ; 28 cm. (Serie A / Centro Latinoamericano de Demografía . no. 91) Bibliography: p. 9-16. LC Card 83-103424
1. Labor supply - Latin America. 2. Human capital - Latin America. I. Consejo Latinoamericano de Ciencias Sociales. Comisión de Demografía. II. Series: Serie A (CELADE (Organization)) , no. 91. III. Title.
HA755 .U5 no. 91 HD5730.5.A6

Elizur, Dov. Systematic job evaluation and comparable worth / Dov Elizur. Aldershot, Hants, England ; Brookfield, Vt., USA : Gower, c1987. xxiv, 290 p. : ill. ; 23 cm. Bibliography: p. [217]-244. Includes index. ISBN 0-566-05113-3 : LC Card 86-25702 DDC 658.3/06 19
1. Job evaluation - Handbooks, manuals, etc. I. Title.
HF5549.5.J62 E44 1987

Elkin, Randyl D. Moore, Gary A. Labor and the economy . Cincinnati , c1983. viii, 502 p. : ISBN 0-538-08750-1 LC Card 81-85863 DDC 331/.0973 19
HD4901 .M825 1983 ***NYPL [JLE 87-831]***

Elkman, Richard. Building better ads : real estate advertising problems, solutions, and results / [Richard Elkman]. Washington, D.C. : National Association of Home Builders of the United States, c1987. 86 p. : ill. ; 28 cm. ISBN 0-86718-290-3 (pbk.) LC Card 87-122135 DDC 659.1/933333 19
1. Advertising - Real estate business. I. Title.
HF6161.R3 E439 1987

Elle, Michael. Roesler, Jörg. Wirtschaftswachstum in der Industrie der DDR, 1945-1970 /. Berlin , 1986. 280 p. ; ISBN 3-05-000074-0 LC Card 86-196020
HC290.78 .R64 1986

Ellefson, Paul V. U. S. wood-based industry : industrial organization and performance / Paul V. Ellefson and Robert N. Stone. New York : Praeger, 1984. xxv, 479 p. : ill. ; 25 cm. Includes index. Bibliography: p. 427-451. ISBN 0-03-063698-1 (alk. paper) : LC Card 84-8278 DDC 338.1/7498/0973 19
1. Lumber trade - United States. 2. Forest products industry - United States. 3. Wood-using industries - United States. I. Stone, Robert N. II. Title. III. Title: US wood-based industry.
HD9755 .45 1984 ***NYPL [JLE 85-706]***

Ellemann-Jensen, Uffe, 1941- Da Danmark igen sagde ja til det fælles-- / Uffe Ellemann-Jensen. [Copenhagen] : Schultz, c1987. 157 p. : ill. ; 24 cm. ISBN 87-569-2234-5 : LC Card 87-163358
1. European Economic Community - Denmark. I. Title.
HC241.25.D4 E45 1987

Ellenberg, Heinz, 1913-
[Desarrollar sin destruir. German]
Entwicklung ohne Rückschläge : Antworten eines Ökologen auf 20 Fragen im Hinblick auf die ländliche Entwicklung in den Tropen und Subtropen / Heinz Ellenberg. Eschborn : Deutsche Gesellschaft für Technische Zusammenarbeit, 1984. 139 p. : ill. ; 21 cm. (Schriftenreihe der GTZ, 0723-9637 . Nr. 156) Translation of: Desarrollar sin destruir. With new material added. ISBN 3-88085-228-6 LC Card 86-168369
1. Land use, Rural - Environmental aspects - Developing countries. 2. Land use, Rural - Environmental aspects - Tropics. I. Series: Schriftenreihe der Deutschen Gesellschaft für Technische Zusammenarbeit , 156. II. Title.
HD1131 .E4515 1984

Ellermeyer, Jürgen. Stadt und Hafen . Hamburg , 1986. 209 p. : ISBN 3-7672-0951-9 LC Card 87-130912 DDC 387.1/0943/515 19
HE558.H3 S7 1986

Elliot Berg Associates.
Agricultural input supply in Cameroon . Alexandria, Va. [1983] 2 v. : LC Card 87-119188 DDC 338.1/0967/11 19
HD2139.5 .A68 1983

Joint program assessment of grain marketing in Niger . [Niamey, Niger] [1983] 2 v. : LC Card 87-114421 DDC 381/.4131/096626 19
HD9049.N552 J65 1983

Elliot, Iain F. Towle, Philip, 1945- Protest and perish . London , 1982. 121 p. ; ISBN 0-907967-02-7 (pbk.) : LC Card 83-198296 DDC 355/.0217/0941 19
UA647 .T69 1982 ***NYPL [JLD 86-1904]***

Elliot, Jeffrey M. Castro, Fidel, 1927- [Nada podrá detener la marcha de la historia. Selections.] Si no hay solución a la crisis, habrá explosiones sociales generalizadas de carácter revolucionario. La Habana , 1985. 97 p. ; LC Card 87-115245 DDC 338.9 19
HC125 .C37825 1985

Elliott . Denton, Peter, 1955- Bedford, U.K. , c1986. 266 p. : ISBN 0-949773-47-6 LC Card

87-100702 DDC 338/.04/0924 B 19
HC602.5.E45 D45 1986

ELLIOTT, JOHN D. (JOHN DORMAN), 1941-
Denton, Peter, 1955- Elliott . Bedford, U.K. , c1986. 266 p. : ISBN 0-949773-47-6 LC Card 87-100702 DDC 338/.04/0924 B 19
HC602.5.E45 D45 1986

Elliott, Kimberly Ann, 1960- Destler, I. M. Anti-protection . Washington, DC , c1987. xii, 204 p. ; ISBN 0-88132-065-X (pbk.) LC Card 87-22545 DDC 382/.3/0973 19
HF1455 .D482 1987

Elliott, P. A. (Peter A.), 1923- The bank manager's handbook : a guide to branch management / P.A. Elliott. Cambridge, England ; Wolfeboro, NH : Woodhead-Faulkner, 1987. p. cm. ISBN 0-85941-330-6 : LC Card 86-28293 DDC 332.1/6 19
1. Banks and banking - Branch banks. 2. Bank management. I. Title.
HG1616.B7 E45 1987

Ellis, Clarence Arthur, 1943- Design of office information systems / C.A. Ellis, N. Naffah. Berlin ; New York : Springer-Verlag, c1987. vi, 248 p. : ill. ; 25 cm. (Surveys in computer science) Bibliography: p. [221]-248. ISBN 0-387-17810-4 (U. S.) : LC Card 87-9582 DDC 651.8 19
1. Information storage and retrieval systems - Business. 2. Office practice - Automation. I. Naffah, Najah, 1945-. II. Title. III. Series.
HF5548.2 .E445 1987

Ellis, Frank. Peasant economics : farm households and agrarian development / Frank Ellis. Cambridge [Cambridgeshire] ; New York : Cambridge University Press, 1988. p. cm. (Cambridge studies in agricultural and rural development) Bibliography: p. Includes index. ISBN 0-521-32446-7 LC Card 87-14815 DDC 338.1/09172/4 19
1. Peasantry - Developing countries - Economic conditions. 2. Peasantry - Developing countries - Social conditions. 3. Quality of life - Developing countries. 4. Developing countries - Rural conditions. I. Title. II. Series.
HD1542 .E43 1988

Ellis, George Francis Rayner. A quality of life and basic needs measurement system with application to Elsies River / G.F.R. Ellis and D. Erlank. Cape Town : Southern Africa Labour and Development Research Unit, [1983] 101, [84] p. : ill. ; 30 cm. (Saldru working paper . no. 56) "September 1983." Includes bibliographical references. ISBN 0-7992-0551-6 LC Card 84-146635 DDC 338.968/00723 19
1. Economic indicators - South Africa - Elsies River. 2. Social indicators - South Africa - Elsies River. 3. Quality of life - South Africa - Elsies River. 4. Elsies River (South Africa) - Economic conditions. 5. Elsies River (South Africa) - Social conditions. I. Erlank, D. II. Title. III. Series.
HC905.Z7 E473 1983 ***NYPL [JLF 86-1126]***

Ellis Horwood series in mathematics and its applications. Statistics and operational research.
Kim, Ki Hang. Team theory /. Chichester , New York , 1987. viii, 246 p. ; ISBN 0-7458-0154-4 : LC Card 87-4137 DDC 658.4/036 19
HD30.23 .K396 1987

Ellis, Junius. Winning with mutual funds /. Birmingham, Ala. , c1987. 224 p. : ISBN 0-8487-0722-2 LC Card 87-61719 DDC 332.63/27 19
HG4930 .W56 1987

Ellis, R. Jeffery. Managing strategy in the real world : conclusions and frameworks from field studies of business practice / R. Jeffery Ellis ; foreword by Robert J. Allio. Lexington, Mass. : Lexington Books, c1988. xviii, 340 p. : ill. ; 24 cm. Includes bibliographies and indexes. ISBN 0-669-15898-4 (alk. paper) LC Card 87-4259 DDC 658.4/012 19
1. Strategic planning. 2. Decision-making. 3. Problem solving. I. Title.
HD30.28 .E45 1988

Ellis, William Donohue. With a name like-- / by William Donohue Ellis. Orrville, Ohio : J.M. Smucker Co., c1987. vii, 161 p. : ill. ; 25 cm. LC Card 87-169333 DDC 338.7/664152/0973 19
1. J.M. Smucker Company - History. 2. Jam industry - United States - History. I. Title.
HD9330.J34 J154 1987

Ellison, James, 1930- Templeton, John, 1912- The Templeton plan . San Francisco , c1987. x, 181, [1] p. ; ISBN 0-06-250286-7 LC Card 86-43022 DDC 174/.4 19
HF5387 .T46 1987

Ellmers, Detlev. Handel en wandel in de dertiende eeuw /. Amsterdam , c1986. 139 p. : ISBN 90-6707-112-9 LC Card 86-199144
HC324 .H36 1986

ElMahgary, Yehia.
Integrated rural energy planning /. Guildford , c1985. xii, 200 p. : ISBN 0-408-22166-6
NYPL [JLF 87-3]

Integrated rural energy planning /. Guildford, Surrey, England , 1985. xii, 200 p. : ISBN 0-408-22166-6 LC Card 87-160993 DDC 333.79/09172/4 19
HD9502.D442 I57 1985

Az Elmélet és a fegyverek kritikája : ideológusok és filozófusok a Harmadik Világról / [a kötet fordítói, Béládi László ... et al. ; a szövegeket válogatta, Marton Imre ; a szöveggyűjteményt szerkesztette, Béládi László, Miszlivetz Ferenc]. Budapest : Eötvös Loránd Tudományegyetem Állam- és Jogtudományi Karának Tudományos Szocializmus Tanszéke, [1981] xxv, 509 p. ; 24 cm. (Fejlődés-tanulmányok . 3) Includes bibliographical references. ISBN 963-461-775-1 (Magy. nemz. bibl.) LC Card 85-139263
1. Developing countries. 2. Communism - Developing countries. 3. National liberation movements. I. Marton, Imre. II. Béládi, László. III. Miszlivetz, Ferenc. IV. Series.
HC59.7 .E45 1981

Elmélet, módszer, gyakorlat, 0139-2875 .
(25) Beluszky, Pál. Magyarország falutipusai /. Budapest , 1982. 167 p. : ISBN 963-7321-96-9 LC Card 84-159502
HD640.5.Z7 B44 1982

ELMER, CHARLES WESLEY, 1872-1954.
Fahy, Thomas P. Richard Scott Perkin and the Perkin-Elmer Corporation /. [United States] c1987. xv, 271 p. : ISBN 0-9618075-0-4 LC Card 86-63869 DDC 338.7/666156/0973 19
HD9707.U62 P474 1987

Eloge de la pauvreté /. Anglade, Georges. Montréal, Québec, Canada , c1983. 63 p. ; ISBN 2-920418-04-1 LC Card 84-140110
HC153.Z9 P612 1983

Els models d'empresa . Marzal, Antonio, 1929- Barcelona , 1981. 241 p. : ISBN 84-7410-078-X LC Card 81-174362
HD2736.C37 M37 1981
NYPL [JLD 87-485]

Elsässer, Martin, 1957- Marknadsinvesteringar : två fallstudier av etablering på utländsk marknad / Martin Elsässer.Uppl. 1. Malmö : Liber, c1984. 168 p. : ill. ; 25 cm. (Företagsekonomisk forskning och utbildning) Bibliography: p. 166-168. ISBN 91-38-61298-4 : LC Card 84-200312
1. Export marketing - Sweden - Case studies. I. Title. II. Series.
HF1009.7.S94 E47 1984

Else, John F. Planning income generating projects : a training handbook for conducting feasibility studies / prepared by John F. Else. Harare, Zimbabwe : Voluntary Organisations in Community Enterprise, [1986?] 46 p. : forms ; 31 cm. Drawn from two workshops held in 1985. LC Card 87-400416 DDC 338.96891/0068 19
1. Economic development projects - Zimbabwe - Evaluation - Case studies. 2. Rural development projects - Zimbabwe - Evaluation - Case studies. 3. Small business - Zimbabwe - Evaluation - Case studies. I. Voluntary Organisations in Community Enterprise (Zimbabwe). II. Title.
HC910 .E43 1986

Elsenau, Detlef von. Arbeitnehmerorientierte Sozialforschung : Erkenntnistheoretische und erkenntnispraktische Aspekte empirischer Sozialforschung im Aktionsprogramm "Humanisierung des Arbeitslebens" : eine Bestandsaufnahme von Erfolgen und Problemen industrie- und betriebssoziologischer Humanisierungsforschung anhand ausgewählter Beispiele / Detlef von Elsenau. Münster : Lit, [1986] ii, 233 p. ; 21 cm. (Industriesoziologie . Bd. 4) Bibliography: p. 223-233. ISBN 3-88660-246-X LC Card 86-200305
1. Quality of work life - Germany (West). 2. Industrial sociology - Germany, West. 3. Aktionsprogramm "Humanisierung des Arbeitslebens". I. Title. II. Series.
HD6957.G3 E59 1986

Elsenhans, Hartmut, 1941- Politik gegen die Krise . Marburg , 1985. 157 p. : ISBN 3-924800-01-4 : LC Card 86-119259 DDC 338.9 19
HC59 .P584 1985

Elsevier series in office automation .
(1) Human aspects in office automation /. Amsterdam , New York , 1984. xv, 322 p. : ISBN 0-444-42327-3 : LC Card 84-5917 DDC 363.1/19651 19
HF5547.5 .H85 1984 ***NYPL [JLF 86-892]***

Elsevier's dictionary of the labour market in five languages, English, German, Swedish, Spanish, and French /. Kunhardt, Ulla von. Amsterdam , New York , 1988. p. cm. ISBN 0-444-42884-4 : LC Card 87-24529 DDC 331/.03 19
HD4839 .K86 1988

ELSIES RIVER (SOUTH AFRICA) - ECONOMIC CONDITIONS.
Ellis, George Francis Rayner. A quality of life and basic needs measurement system with application to Elsies River /. Cape Town [1983] 101, [84] p. : ISBN 0-7992-0551-6 LC Card 84-146635 DDC 338.968/00723 19
HC905.Z7 E473 1983 ***NYPL [JLF 86-1126]***

ELSIES RIVER (SOUTH AFRICA) - SOCIAL CONDITIONS.
Ellis, George Francis Rayner. A quality of life and basic needs measurement system with application to Elsies River /. Cape Town [1983] 101, [84] p. : ISBN 0-7992-0551-6 LC Card 84-146635 DDC 338.968/00723 19
HC905.Z7 E473 1983 ***NYPL [JLF 86-1126]***

Elsner, Wolfram. Ökonomische Institutionenanalyse : paradigmatische Entwicklung der ökonomischen Theorie und der Sinn eines Rückgriffs auf die ökonomische Klassik am Beispiel der Institutionenanalyse ("property rights") / Wolfram Elsner. Berlin : Duncker & Humblot, c1986. xv, 469 p. : ill. ; 24 cm. (Volkswirtschaftliche Schriften. Heft 367) Summary in English. Bibliography: p. [455]-469. ISBN 3-428-06035-0 LC Card 86-206447
1. Institutional economics. 2. Right of property. 3. Classical school of economics. 4. Smith, Adam, 1723-1790. I. Title. II. Series.
HB99.5 .E47 1986

Az első és a második gazdaság közötti bér-, illetve jövedelem-diszparitás /. Falusné Szikra, Katalin. Budapest , c1986. 31 p. ; ISBN 963-05-4343-5 : LC Card 87-407713
HC300.295.I5 F35 1986

Az első évtized . Békés, Sándor. Pécs , 1986. 221 p. : LC Card 87-148227
HE8700.9.H8 B45 1986

Elster, Hans-Joachim, 1908- Umweltschutz . [Mainz] , c1984. 130 p. ; ISBN 3-7758-1086-2 LC Card 85-146233
HC290.5.E5 U64 1984

Eltern und Kinder . Schneewind, Klaus A., 1939- Stuttgart , c1983. 229 p. : ISBN 3-17-007744-9 LC Card 83-150745 DDC 303.3/23/0943 19
HQ739 .S29 1983 ***NYPL [JLE 87-1168]***

Elwert, Georg.
Bauern und Staat in Westafrika : die Verflechtung sozioökonomischer Sektoren am Beispiel Bénin / Georg Elwert. Frankfurt ; New York : Campus Verlag, c1983. 383 p. : ill. ; 21 cm. (Campus Forschung. Bd. 332) The author's Habilitationsschrift, Universität Bielefeld, 1980. Bibliography: p. 376-383. ISBN 3-593-33206-X : LC Card 84-152007
1. Peasantry - Government policy - Benin. I. Title.
HD1538.B46 E49 1983

Busacker, Dietrich. Energies à la mesure des villages . Bielefeld, Federal Republic of Germany , 1985. 21 leaves ; LC Card 85-160345
HD9502.A4993 B87 1985

Elz, Dieter, 1927- Agricultural marketing strategy and pricing policy /. Washington, D.C. , c1987. xiii, 132 p. : ISBN 0-8213-0830-0 (pbk.) LC Card 86-33992 DDC 380.1/41 19
HD9018.D44 A365 1987

Elzinga, Kenneth G.
Breit, William. Antitrust penalty reform . Washington, D.C. , c1986. x, 83 p. : ISBN 0-8447-3600-7 (alk. paper) LC Card 86-3203 DDC 343.73/072/0269 347.303720269 19
KF1657.T7 B74 1986 NYPL [JLE 86-3948]
Morality of the market . Vancouver, B.C., Canada , c1985. xxv, 601 p. ; ISBN 0-88975-074-2 (pbk.) : LC Card 86-158049 DDC 174/.4 19
HB72 .M56 1985

Em busca da dialética . Lima, Rômulo de Araújo, 1949- Campina Grande-Paraíba , 1983. 102 p. ; LC Card 86-130003
HB97.5 .L464 1983

Emancipatie in internationaal perspectief . Niessen, Jan. Amsterdam , 1987. 282 p. ; ISBN 90-6256-460-7 : LC Card 87-158046
HD8518.5.M6 N54 1987

Emancipatieraad (Netherlands) Koopman, A. F. Vrouwen zelfstandig . Den Haag [1986] 70 p. ; ISBN 90-346-0762-3 LC Card 86-172683
HD2346.N4 K66 1986

EMANCIPATION OF WOMEN. see **WOMEN'S RIGHTS.**

Emanuel, Han. Disability benefits . Greenwich, Conn. , c1987. xxii, 282 p. ; ISBN 0-89232-824-X : LC Card 87-17056 DDC 368.3/86/009492 19
HD7105.25.N4 D57 1987

A embalagem do sistema . Arruda, Maria Arminda do Nascimento. São Paulo , 1985. 203 p. : LC Card 85-211063
HF5813.B8 A77 1985

EMBARGO.
Oil tankers to South Africa, 1980-1981. Amsterdam , c1982. vi, 99 p. : ISBN 90-70331-05-5 (pbk.) LC Card 86-213340 DDC 387.5/448 19
HE595.P4 O37 1982
Turner, Terisa. Trade union action to stop oil to South Africa /. Port Harcourt , c1985. v, 35 p. ; LC Card 87-673464
HF1613.4 .T87x 1985

EMBARGO - ECONOMIC ASPECTS - UNITED STATES.
Embargoes, surplus disposal, and U. S. agriculture . Washington, D.C. , 1986. vi, 34 p. ; LC Card 86-603452 DDC 338.1/8 19
HD1761 .E45 1986

EMBARGO - ECONOMIC ASPECTS - UNITED STATES - ECONOMETRIC MODELS.
Lundborg, Per, 1950- The economics of export embargoes . New York, NY , c1987. xi, 127 p. : ISBN 0-7099-4151-X : LC Card 86-29370 DDC 382/.4131/0947 19
HD9035 .L86 1987

Embargoes, surplus disposal, and U. S. agriculture : a summary. Washington, D.C. : Economic Research Service, U. S. Dept. of Agriculture, 1986. vi, 34 p. ; 22 cm. (Agriculture information bulletin . no. 503) "November 1986"--P. [2] of cover. Item 4 LC Card 86-603452 DDC 338.1/8 19
1. Agriculture - Economic aspects - United States. 2. Surplus agricultural commodities - United States. 3. Embargo - Economic aspects - United States. 4. Agriculture and state - United States. I. United States. Dept. of Agriculture. Economic Research Service. II. Title: Embargoes, surplus disposal, and US agriculture. III. Series.
HD1761 .E45 1986

Embargoes, surplus disposal, and US agriculture. Embargoes, surplus disposal, and U. S. agriculture . Washington, D.C. , 1986. vi, 34 p. ; LC Card 86-603452 DDC 338.1/8 19
HD1761 .E45 1986

Embassy Consulting (Firm : Salt Lake City, Utah) Robinson, Dean L. Network marketing /. Salt Lake City, Utah , c1983. 137 p. : LC Card 86-202974 DDC 658.8/4 19
HF5415.126 .R63 1983

The embattled fortress . Izzo, Joseph E., 1931- San Francisco , 1987. xxii, 155 p. : ISBN 1-555-42059-1 (alk. paper) LC Card 87-45429 DDC 658.4/038 19
HF5548.2 .I97 1987

Az emberi tényező szerepe a világgazdaságban az 1980-as években . Simai, Mihály. Budapest , c1986. 41 p. ; ISBN 963-05-4342-7 : LC Card 87-407712
HD4904.7 .S446 1986

EMBEZZLEMENT - PREVENTION.
Snyder, Stanley G. Embezzlers' dirty tricks (and how to spot them) . San Diego, CA , c1987. 336 p. : ISBN 0-937535-00-1 (pbk.) : LC Card 87-50037 DDC 658.4/73 19
HF5549.5.E43 S59 1987

Embezzlers' dirty tricks (and how to spot them) . Snyder, Stanley G. San Diego, CA , c1987. 336 p. : ISBN 0-937535-00-1 (pbk.) : LC Card 87-50037 DDC 658.4/73 19
HF5549.5.E43 S59 1987

Emel'ianov, Aleksandr Sergeevich.
Narodno-khoziaistvennye proportsii, ikh planirovanie i prognozirovanie /. Kiev , 1985. 318 p. : LC Card 86-210651
HC337.U5 P5 1985 t. 1

Emel'ianov, Alekseĭ Mikhaĭlovich. Agrarnaia politika sotsialisticheskikh stran na sovremennom ėtape /. Moskva , 1981. 366 p. ; LC Card 82-109367
HD1918 .A37 1981

The emergence of the Cotton Kingdom in the Old Southwest . Moore, John Hebron. Baton Rouge , c1988. xii, 323 p. : ISBN 0-8071-1404-9 (pbk.) LC Card 87-2803 DDC 330.9762 19
HC107.M7 M66 1988

EMERGENCIES. see **ACCIDENTS.**

EMERGENCIES, MEDICAL. see **ACCIDENTS.**

EMERGENCY COMMUNICATION SYSTEMS - NEW JERSEY.
New Jersey. Legislature. Emergency Response System Study Commission. Public hearing before Emergency Response System Study Commission on implementation of a statewide enhanced 911 service . [Trenton, N.J.] [1986] 49 p. ; LC Card 87-621252 DDC 384.6/42 19
HE8840.N5 N48 1986

EMERGENCY HOUSING - GOVERNMENT POLICY - URUGUAY - MONTEVIDEO.
Vicario, Luis B. Lineamientos básicos del Programa Habitacional de Emergencia, 1985-86 /. [Montevideo] , 1985. 25 p. : LC Card 87-122422 DDC 363.5/8 19
HD7287.96.U82 M668 1985

EMERGENCY RELIEF. see **DISASTER RELIEF.**

Emerging careers . Feingold, S. Norman, 1914- Garrett Park, Md. , c1983- v. ; ISBN 0-912048-32-8 (pbk.) : LC Card 83-80074 DDC 331.7/02 19
HF5382 .F44 1983 NYPL [JLL 86-205]

Emerging leadership vistas / edited by James Gerald Hunt ... [et al.]. Lexington, Mass. : Lexington Books, c1988. xv, 331 p. : ill. ; 24 cm. (International leadership symposia series . v. 8) Bibliography: p. [287]-311. Includes indexes. ISBN 0-669-15331-1 (alk. paper) LC Card 86-46310 DDC 658.4/092 19
1. Leadership. 2. Management. I. Hunt, James G., 1932-. II. Series.
HD57.7 .E44 1987

The Emerging service economy / edited by Orio Giarini for the Services World Forum, Geneva. 1st ed. Oxford [Oxfordshire] ; New York : Pergamon Press, 1987. xii, 298 p. : ill. ; 24 cm. "First issue of Services world economy series" -- Pref. "Bibliography related to services [by] Raymond Krommenacker and Jean Remy Roulet": p. 283-289. Includes bibliographical references and index. ISBN 0-08-034270-1 : LC Card 86-25265 DDC 338.4/6 19
1. Service industries. I. Giarini, Orio. II. Services World Forum (Association).
HD9980.5 .E46 1987

Emerging textile-exporting countries, 1984 : report on investigation no. 332-184 under section 332 of the Tariff Act of 1930. Washington, D.C. : U. S. International Trade Commission, [1985] vii, 520 p. ; 28 cm. (USITC publication. 1716) Cover title. Distributed to depository libraries in microfiche. "July 1985." Includes bibliographical references. Item 980-E (microfiche) LC Card 86-603429 DDC 382/.456770091724 19
1. Textile industry - Developing countries. 2. Textile industry - United States. 3. Textile industry. I. United States. International Trade Commission.
HD9868.D44 E54 1985

Emerson, James C. Careers in public accounting 1986/87- : a comprehensive comparison of the big eight firms / James C. Emerson. Seattle, Wash. (2824 Sahalee Dr. E., Redmond 98053) : Big Eight Review, c1986. 261 p. ; 28 cm. LC Card 87-71857 DDC 338.7/61657/0973 19
1. Accounting firms - United States. 2. Big business - United States. I. Title.
HF5616.U5 E46 1986

Emerson, Michael. What model for Europe? / Michael Emerson with André Dramais. Cambridge, Mass. : MIT Press, c1988. xi, 151 p. : ill. ; 22 cm. Bibliography: p. [141]-147. Includes index. ISBN 0-262-05036-6 LC Card 87-15151 DDC 331.11/094 19
1. Labor policy - European Economic Community countries. 2. European Economic Community countries - Social policy. 3. Industrial relations - European Economic Community countries. 4. Social security - European Economic Community countries. I. Dramais, André. II. Title.
HD8380.5 .E47 1988

Emery, James J. Technology trade with the Middle East / James J. Emery, Norman A. Graham, Michael F. Oppenheimer ; in association with Richard Ferguson and Dana Rashti. Boulder : Westview Press, 1986. xvii, 302 p. : ill. ; 23 cm. (Westview special studies in international economics and business) Bibliography: p. [299]-302. ISBN 0-8133-7043-4 : LC Card 85-3215 DDC 338.9/26 19
1. High technology industries - Near East. 2. High technology industries. 3. Technology transfer - Near East. 4. Near East - Commerce. I. Graham, Norman A. II. Oppenheimer, Michael F. III. Title.
HC415.15.Z9 H533 1986 NYPL [JLE 86-2460]

Emery, Mary Ann. Principles of accounting / Mary Ann Emery. 1st ed. San Diego : Harcourt Brace Jovanovich, <c1987- > v. <2- > : ill. ; 28 cm. (Harcourt Brace Jovanovich college outline series) Books for professionals Includes index. ISBN 0-15-600029-6 (pbk.) : LC Card 86-27103 DDC 657 19
1. Accounting. I. Title. II. Series.
HF5635 .E537 1987

Emery, R. C. The postal history of the Australian Imperial Forces during World War One, 1914-1918 / by R.C. Emery. Worthing, West Sussex, England : R.C. Emery, [1984] viii, 343 p. : ill. ; 26 cm. Includes index. Bibliography: p. 331-332. LC Card 85-123155 DDC 355.3/41 19
1. Postal service - Australia - History - 20th century. 2. World War, 1914-1918 - Postal service. 3. Australia - Armed Forces - Postal service - History. I. Title.
HE7395 .E47 1984 NYPL [JLF 86-1054]

Emigración y retorno : una perspectiva europea / edición a cargo de José Cazorla Pérez. [Madrid] : Instituto Español de Emigración, 1981. 325 p., [2] folded leaves of plates : ill., maps ; 24 cm. Includes bibliographies. ISBN 84-500-5097-9 LC Card 82-145134 DDC 325.46 19
1. Return migration - Spain. 2. Return migration - Portugal. 3. Migration, Internal - Spain. 4. Spain - Emigration and immigration. 5. Portugal - Emigration and immigration. 6. Europe - Emigration and immigration. I. Cazorla Pérez, José.
JV8251 .E49 1981 NYPL [JLE 86-3179]

EMIGRANT REMITTANCES - ASIA.
Migration of Asian workers to the Arab world /. Tokyo, Japan , c1986. v, 358 p. ; ISBN 92-808-0555-X (pbk.) LC Card 87-131112 DDC 331.6/2/50174927 19
HD8656 .M53 1986

EMIGRANT REMITTANCES - BOTSWANA - PSYCHOLOGICAL ASPECTS.
Lucas, Robert E. B. Motivations to remit . [Tel Aviv] [1985] 27 leaves ; LC Card 86-177234
HG3984.9 .L83 1985

EMIGRANT REMITTANCES - PORTUGAL.
Ferreira, Eduardo de Sousa, 1936- Reintegração dos emigrantes portugueses . [Lisbon] , 1984. xiv, 137 p. ; LC Card 86-132652
HD8380.5 .F47 1984

EMIGRANT REMITTANCES - SUDAN.
Abu Gabal, Sayed Ahmed. Migration of Sudanese . [Khartoum] , 1984. 18, [14] p. ; LC Card 86-980176 DDC 331.6/2/6240174927 19
HD8766 .A65 1984

EMIGRANT REMITTANCES - SUDAN - ECONOMETRIC MODELS.
Elbadawi, Ibrahim. The Sudan demand for international reserve . [Khartoum] [1984] 40 leaves : LC Card 85-981026 DDC 332.4/5609624 19
HG3982.8 .E42 1984

EMIGRATION AND IMMIGRATION - PSYCHOLOGICAL ASPECTS.
Hill, Paul Bernhard, 1953- Determinanten der Eingliederung von Arbeitsmigranten /. Königstein/Ts. , c1984. 228 p. : ISBN 3-7756-6939-6 LC Card 84-219137 DDC 331.6/2/0943 19
HD8458.A2 H55 1984
NYPL [JLD 86-2467]

EMILIA-ROMAGNA, ITALY - ECONOMIC CONDITIONS.
Cooperazione di credito e sviluppo sociale ed economico delle campagne in Emilia Romagna . Bologna , c1983. 173 p. : LC Card 85-156690
HG2051.I82 E433 1983

EMILIA-ROMAGNA (ITALY) - ECONOMIC CONDITIONS - STATISTICS.
I Conti finanziari dell'Emilia-Romagna /. [Bologna] , c1984. 157 p. : ISBN 88-15-00522-6 : LC Card 84-235593 DDC 332.1/0945/4 19
HG3089.E45 C66 1984
NYPL [JLE 86-3198]

EMILIA-ROMAGNA, ITALY - HISTORY.
Dean, Trevor. Land and power in late medieval Ferrara . Cambridge , New York , 1988. xiv, 212 p. : ISBN 0-521-33127-7 LC Card 87-6583 DDC 333.3/0945/45 19
HD679.F47 D43 1988

EMILIA-ROMAGNA (ITALY) - RURAL CONDITIONS.
Cooperazione di credito e sviluppo sociale ed economico delle campagne in Emilia Romagna . Bologna , c1983. 173 p. : LC Card 85-156690
HG2051.I82 E433 1983

EMINENT DOMAIN - BRAZIL - PASSO REAL.
Rio Grande do Sul (Brazil). Assembléia Legislativa. Comissão Especial dos Agricultores Desalojados do Passo Real. Afogados, até quando? . [Porto Alegre] [1984] 99 p. : LC Card 85-150200
HD500.P39 R56 1984

Eminente, Giorgio.
Manuale delle simulazioni di gestione . Milano, Italy , 1985. 335 p. : LC Card 86-187906
HD30.26 .M36 1985

Strategia aziendale e sviluppo tecnologico : l'esperienza Elsag / Giorgio Eminente, Bernardo Nicoletti. Bologna : Il Mulino, c1985. 253 p. : ill. ; 22 cm. (Studi e ricerche / IFAP) Bibliography: p. 251-253. ISBN 88-15-00917-5 : LC Card 86-176732
1. Elettronica San Giorgio-ELSAG, s.p.a. (Genoa, Italy). 2. Electronic industries - Italy - Management - Case studies. 3. Electronic industries - Italy - Technological innovations - Case studies. I. Nicoletti, Bernardo. II. Series: Studi e ricerche (Istituto per la formazione e l'aggiornamento professionale (Rome, Italy)). III. Title.
HD9696.A3 I733 1985

Emmanuel College (University of Cambridge)
Europe and the rise of capitalism /. Oxford [Oxfordshire] , New York, NY, USA , 1987. p. cm. ISBN 0-631-15006-4 : LC Card 87-12293 DDC 330.94 19
HC240.9.C3 E97 1987

Emmer, P. C. Colonialism and migration . Dordrecht , Higham, MA, USA , 1986. vi, 303 p. : ISBN 90-247-3253-0 LC Card 85-21809 DDC 331.11/73 19
HD4875.A837 C65 1986
NYPL [JLE 86-3920]

Emmerich, Norbert-Christian. Die deutsche Sparkassenwerbung, 1750-1981 / von Norbert-Christian Emmerich. Stuttgart : Deutscher Sparkassenverlag, 1983. 344 p. : ill. ; 21 cm. (Forschungsberichte . Bd. 15) Bibliography: p. 323-344. LC Card 84-119079
1. Advertising - Banks and banking - Germany (West) - History. 2. Advertising - Banks and banking - Germany - History. 3. Savings-banks - Germany, West - History. 4. Savings-banks - Germany - History. I. Series: Forschungsberichte / Gesellschaft zur Førderung der Wissenschaftlichen Forschung über das Spar- und Girowesen , Bd. 15. II. Title.
HF6161.B2 E64 1983

Emmott, Bill. Pennant-Rea, Rupert. The pocket economist /. Oxford, UK , New York, NY , 1987, c1983. p. cm. ISBN 0-631-14586-9 : LC Card 87-10361 DDC 330/.03/21 19
HB61 .P435 1987

Emolumento, Vincenzo. Dizionario commerciale : italiano-francese, francese-italiano / Vincenzo Emolumento.1a ed. Milano : A. Mondadori, 1983. 1150 p. ; 23 cm. ISBN 88-7075-068-X : LC Card 84-151136 DDC 380.1/03/41 19
1. Commerce - Dictionaries - Italian. 2. Italian language - Dictionaries - French. 3. Commerce - Dictionaries - French. 4. French language - Dictionaries - Italian. I. Title.
HF1002 .E57 1983 *NYPL [JLD 86-1323]*

Empalme del índice de precios al consumidor . Mulquin, Marie Eve. [San José] , 1981. 15 leaves ; LC Card 81-216387
HB221 .M774 1981

Empeirikē diereunēsē tēs apotamieutikēs symperiphoras kai tēs zētēsēs katatheseōn apo tous idiōtes /. Baltas, N. K. Athēna [1979] 128 p. ; LC Card 86-203196
HG3250.5.A6 B34 1979

Empel, G. van. Betaling, waardepapier en documentair krediet / door G. van Empel. Deventer : Kluwer, 1985. viii, 84 p. ; 25 cm. Includes index. ISBN 90-268-1565-4 : LC Card 85-214764
1. Payment. 2. Securities. 3. Documentary credit. I. Title.
HG173.6.D8 E46 1985

EMPHYTEUSIS - ITALY - VENICE REGION - HISTORY - 16TH CENTURY.
Corazzol, Gigi, 1945- Livelli stipulati a Venezia nel 1591 . Pisa , c1986. 167 p., [8] leaves of plates : LC Card 86-192693
HD680.V4 C67 1986

Empire . Paper, Lewis J. New York , 1987. x, 384 p., [16] p. of plates : ISBN 0-312-00591-1 : LC Card 87-4368 DDC 384.54/092/4 B 19
HE8689.8.P34 P36 1987

The empire builders . Mark, J. Paul. New York , c1987. 303 p. : ISBN 0-688-06962-2 LC Card 87-13064 DDC 650/.07/117444 19
HF1134.H4 M37 1987

Empire, Islamic. see **Islamic Empire.**

Empire State Postal History Society. Manuscript post offices of New York State /. [Richford, N.Y.?] , 1984. xii, 54 p., [12] p. of plates : LC Card 86-213682 DDC 383/.49747 19
HE6376.A1 N729 1984

Empirical approaches to consumer protection economics : proceedings of a conference / sponsored by the Bureau of Economics, Federal Trade Commission, April 26-27, 1984 ; Pauline M. Ippolito, David T. Scheffman, editors. Washington, D.C. : F.T.C., [1986] ii, 484 p. : ill. ; 23 cm. Spine title: Consumer protection economics. Shipping list no.: 86-541-P. "March 1986"--Cover. Includes bibliographies. Item 535 LC Card 86-602207 DDC 381/.34/0973 19
1. Consumer protection - United States - Congresses. 2. Quality of products - United States - Congresses. 3. Consumption (Economics) - United States - Congresses. I. Ippolito, Pauline M. II. Scheffman, David T., 1943-. III. United States. Federal Trade Commission. Bureau of Economics. IV. Title: Consumer protection economics.
HC110.C63 E46 1986

Empirical approaches to consumer protection economics : proceedings of a conference sponsored by the Bureau of Economics, Federal Trade Commission, April 26-27, 1984 / Pauline M. Ippolito, David T. Scheffman, editors. Washington, D.C. : U. S. F.T.C., [1986] ii, 484 p. : ill. ; 23 cm. Spine title: Consumer protection economics. "March 1986." Includes bibliographies.
1. Consumer protection - Congresses. 2. Consumption (Economics) - Congresses. 3. Quality of products - Congresses. I. Ippolito, Pauline M. II. Scheffman, David T., 1943-. III. Title: Consumer protection economics.
NYPL [JLE 86-3552]

The empirical evidence on the efficiency of forward and futures foreign exchange markets /. Hodrick, Robert J. Chur, Switzerland , New York , c1987. viii, 174 p. ; ISBN 3-7186-0415-9 (pbk.) LC Card 87-17790 DDC 332.4/5 19
HG3853 .H43 1987

Empirical methods for international trade / edited by Robert C. Feenstra. Cambridge, Mass. : MIT Press, c1988. xiv, 322 p. : ill. ; 24 cm. Bibliography: p. [299]-314. Includes indexes. ISBN 0-262-06108-2 LC Card 87-3023 DDC 382 19
1. Commerce. I. Feenstra, Robert C.
HF1008 .E47 1988

Die empirische Erhebung von Unternehmenserwartungen als Beitrag zur Konjunkturprognose /. Pilder, Christhard. Frankfurt am Main , c1984. vii, 185 p. : ISBN 3-88129-769-3 LC Card 84-173409
HB3730 .P53 1984

Empirische Studien zur Agrarökonomie, 0177-0675 .
(Bd. 5) Reessing, Ludwig. Analyse der Wettbewerbsfähigkeit von Extensivblattfrüchten in Niedersachsen unter ökonomischen und ökologischen Gesichtspunkten /. Kiel , 1986. xiv, 251 p. : ISBN 3-922553-81-8 LC Card 86-163003
HD1960.L69 R44 1986

Empirische Wirtschaftsforschung .
(Bd. 1) Hergeth, Helmut H. A., 1956- Investitionsstrategien für stagnierende Branchen . Münster [1986?] xii, 261 p. : ISBN 3-88660-338-5 LC Card 87-134812 DDC 338.4/3677/00943 19
HD9863.5 .H39 1986

El empleo agrícola en una estructra en transformación . Hintermeister, Alberto. [Santiago, Chile] , 1982. 27 p. ; LC Card 87-403249 DDC 331.7/63/097285 19
HD1531.N5 H56 1982

Empleo, salarios y distribución del ingreso : márgenes de política / Germán Alarco ... [et al.]. [Miraflores, Lima] : Fundación Friedrich Ebert, 1986. 186 p. : ill. ; 20 cm. (Taller de investigación . 7) Includes bibliographies. LC Card 87-403082 DDC 331.11/0985 19
1. Manpower policy - Peru. 2. Wages - Government policy - Peru. 3. Income distribution - Government policy - Peru. I. Alarco, Germán. II. Series.
HD5761.A6 E47 1986

Empleo y capacitación en los talleres informales de Santiago /. Corvalán Vásquez, Oscar E., 1947- Montevideo , 1984. 150 p. ; LC Card 86-127324
HD2346.C54 S263 1984

Empleo y estructura ocupacional en grandes establecimientos industriales / República Oriental del Uruguay, Ministerio de Trabajo y Seguridad Social, Dirección Nacional de Recursos Humanos. Montevideo : La Dirección, 1984. 51 leaves ; 27 cm. (Informe especial. no. 73) Chiefly tables. LC Card 86-174021
1. Uruguay - Occupations - Statistics. 2. Labor supply - Uruguay - Statistics. I. Uruguay. Dirección Nacional de Recursos Humanos. II. Series: Informe especial (Uruguay. Dirección Nacional de Recursos Humanos) , no. 73.
HB2667 .E46 1984

Emploi d'abord : éléments de stratégies pour la priorité à l'emploi au Bénin : rapport / d'une mission technique du PECTA présenté au Gouvernement de la République populaire du Bénin. Addis Abeba : Bureau international du travail, Programme des emplois et des compétences techniques pour l'Afrique, 1982. xxxviii, 499 p. ; 29 cm. LC Card 84-983423
1. Labor supply - Benin. 2. Manpower policy - Benin. 3. Benin - Economic conditions - 1960-. I. Benin. II. Jobs and Skills Programme for Africa.
hD5846.3.A6 E47 1982

L'Emploi des femmes ... / Bureau international du travail, Programme des emplois et des compétences techniques pour l'Afrique (PECTA). Addis-Abéba : PECTA, 1985. 7 v. : ill. ; 29 cm. At head of title: Organisation internationale du travail. Includes bibliographies. CONTENTS. - [1] Bénin -- [2] Cameroun -- [3] Côte d'Ivoire -- [4] Madagascar -- [5] Sénégal -- [6] Togo -- [7] Afrique : rapport de synthèse dans 6 pays francophones (Bénin, Cameroun, Côte d'Ivoire, Madagascar, Sénégal et Togo). ISBN 92-2-205192-0 (v. 1) LC Card 86-981198
1. Women - Employment - Africa, French-speaking West. I. Jobs and Skills Programme for Africa. II. International Labour Organisation. III. Title: Emploi des

femmes en ... IV. Title: Emploi des femmes au ...
HD6216 .E46 1985

Emploi des femmes au ... L'Emploi des femmes ... /. Addis-Abéba , 1985. 7 v. : ISBN 92-2-205192-0 (v. 1) LC Card 86-981198
HD6216 .E46 1985

Emploi des femmes en ... L'Emploi des femmes ... /. Addis-Abéba , 1985. 7 v. : ISBN 92-2-205192-0 (v. 1) LC Card 86-981198
HD6216 .E46 1985

L'emploi des jeunes =. Organisation for Economic Co-operation and Development. Library. [Paris] , 1980. [6], 119 p. ; LC Card 81-122004 DDC 016.3313/4 19
HD6270 .O72 1980

Emploi et éducation dans le 2e plan de développement économique et social du Togo /. Dovi-Sodemekou, Folly B. (Folly Bebey) Lomé, Togo [1985] 89, 52, 9, 2 p. : LC Card 87-131183
HD5846.5.A6 D68 1985

Emploi et formation en Haute-Volta : méthodes d'observation et de prévision : rapport soumis au gouvernement de la Haute-Volta par une mission d'assistance technique du PECTA. Addis-Abéba : Bureau international du travail, Programme des emplois et des compétences techniques pour l'Afrique, 1983. x, 142 p. : ill. ; 30 cm. At head of title: Organisation internationale du travail. Bibliography: p. 139-140. LC Card 85-981183
1. Labor supply - Burkina Faso. 2. Vocational education - Burkina Faso. I. Jobs and Skills Programme for Africa. II. International Labour Organisation.
HD5847.5.A6 E48 1983

Emploi et revenus dans le secteur agricole traditionnel au Bénin /. Keddeman, Willem. Addis Abéba , 1982. 64 p. ; LC Card 87-980402
HD2141 .K43 1982

Emploi, potentialités et priorités au Mali : rapport présenté au Gouvernement du Mali / par une mission d'emploi globale du PECTA.1re éd. Addi Abeba : Bureau international du travail, Programme des emplois et compétences techniques pour l'Afrique, c1984. xix, 266 p. : ill. ; 24 cm. At head of title: Organisation internationale du travail. "Mai 1984." Includes bibliographical references. ISBN 92-2-203954-8 : LC Card 85-980540
1. Labor supply - Mali. 2. Manpower policy - Mali. 3. Mali - Economic conditions. 4. Mali - Economic policy. I. Mali. II. Jobs and Skills Programme for Africa.
HD5847.3.A6 E47 1984
NYPL [JLE 86-484]

Emplois et qualifications dans le secteur métaux-mécanique-électricité en Côte d'Ivoire /. Gboizo, J. [Abidjan] , 1981. 93 leaves ; LC Card 83-234024
HD5846.9.A6 G36 1981

EMPLOYEE ABSENTEEISM. see **ABSENTEEISM (LABOR)**

Employee assistance programs : a basic text / edited by Fred Dickman ... [et al.]. Springfield, Ill., U. S.A. : C.C. Thomas, c1988. xxiv, 493 p. ; 27 cm. Bibliography: p. 465-476. Includes indexes. ISBN 0-398-05401-0 LC Card 87-21048 DDC 658.3/82 19
1. Employee assistance programs - United States. I. Dickman, Fred.
HF5549.5.E42 E47 1988

EMPLOYEE ASSISTANCE PROGRAMS - CONGRESSES.
Occupational stress and organizational effectiveness /. New York , c1987. xii, 285 p. : ISBN 0-275-92281-2 (alk. paper) : LC Card 86-25250 DDC 158.7 19
HF5548.85 .O24 1987

EMPLOYEE ASSISTANCE PROGRAMS - LAW AND LEGISLATION - UNITED STATES.
Denenberg, Tia Schneider. Alcohol and drugs . Washington, D.C. , c1983. xv, 201 p. : ISBN 0-87179-410-1 LC Card 83-7560 DDC 344.73/01255 347.3041255 19
KF3540 .D46 1983 ***NYPL [JLE 86-2348]***

EMPLOYEE ASSISTANCE PROGRAMS - UNITED STATES.
Corporate strategies for controlling substance abuse /. New York, N.Y. , c1986. xi, 50 p. ; ISBN 0-8237-0327-4 (pbk.) LC Card 86-207704 DDC 658.3/82 19
HF5549.5.E42 C66 1986

EAPs and the information revolution . New York , c1987. 106 p. ; ISBN 0-86656-606-6 LC Card 86-33519 DDC 331.25 19
HF5549.5.E42 E37 1987

Employee assistance programs . Springfield, Ill., U. S.A. , c1988. xxiv, 493 p. ; ISBN 0-398-05401-0 LC Card 87-21048 DDC 658.3/82 19
HF5549.5.E42 E47 1988

Googins, Bradley, 1944- Occupational social work . Silver Spring, MD , 1987. p. cm. ISBN 0-87101-151-4 LC Card 87-20414 DDC 362.8/5 19
HD7261 .G66 1987b

Googins, Bradley, 1944- Occupational social work /. Englewood Cliffs, N.J. , c1987. xii, 227 p. : ISBN 0-13-629445-6 : LC Card 86-25514 DDC 658.3/82 19
HD7261 .G66 1987

McGowan, Brenda G. Trends in employee counseling programs /. New York , c1984. 55 p. ; ISBN 0-08-032361-8 (pbk.) : LC Card 84-22820 DDC 658.3/82 19
HF5549.5.C8 M34 1984
NYPL [JLM 83-380 no.37]

Employee assistance programs within the context of personnel policies /. Coudroglou, Aliki. Brookfield, Wis. , c1986. 26 p. ; ISBN 0-89154-322-8 (pbk.) LC Card 87-158924 DDC 658.3/82 19
HF5549.5.E42 C676 1986

Employee attitude surveys . Kendall, Stephanie. New York, NY, U. S.A. , c1986. x, 199, [30] p. : ISBN 0-86604-209-1 (pbk.) LC Card 86-233239 DDC 658.3/14 19
HF5549.5.A83 K46 1986

EMPLOYEE ATTITUDE SURVEYS.
Appraising and exploring organizations /. London , New York , c1988. p. cm. ISBN 0-7099-4340-7 : LC Card 87-20063 DDC 658.3/14 19
HF5549.5.A83 A66 1988

Job attitudes . New York , 1987. xii, 279 p. ; ISBN 0-8240-8210-9 (alk. paper) : LC Card 86-26935 DDC 331.25 19
HF5549.5.J63 J57 1987

Kendall, Stephanie. Employee attitude surveys . New York, NY, U. S.A. , c1986. x, 199, [30] p. : ISBN 0-86604-209-1 (pbk.) LC Card 86-233239 DDC 658.3/14 19
HF5549.5.A83 K46 1986

Employee benefit plans : a glossary of terms / edited by June M. Lehman.6th ed. Brookfield, Wis. : International Foundation of Employee Benefit Plans, 1987. ix, 157 p. ; 28 cm. ISBN 0-89154-317-1 (pbk.) LC Card 87-150660 DDC 658.3/25/0321 19
1. Employee fringe benefits - Dictionaries. I. Lehman, June M. II. International Foundation of Employee Benefit Plans.
HD4928.N6 E46 1987

Employee Benefit Research Institute (Washington, D.C.)
Fundamentals of employee benefit programs. Washington, DC , c1987. xviii, 304 p. : ISBN 0-86643-051-2 (pbk.) LC Card 87-660 DDC 331.25/5/0973 19
HD4928.N62 U634 1987

Employee Benefit Research Institute (Washington, D.C.). Education and Research Fund.
EBRI-ERF Policy Forum (1986 : Washington, D.C.) America in transition . Washington, D.C. , c1987. xix, 269 p. : ISBN 0-86643-057-1 (hard) : LC Card 87-13421 DDC 331.25/5/0973 19
HD4928.N62 U628 1987

Measuring and funding corporate liabilities for retiree health benefits. Washington, D.C. , c1987. xxxviii, 226 p. : ISBN 0-86643-054-7 (pbk.) LC Card 87-24534 DDC 657/.75 19
HG9396 .M4 1987

Employee benefits and conditions of employment in Canada . Hanson, R. [Ottawa, Ont.] , c1977. iv, 111 p. : ISBN 0-662-00630-5 (pbk.) LC Card 82-136152
HD4928.N62 C225 1977

EMPLOYEE COMMUNICATION. see **COMMUNICATION IN MANAGEMENT; COMMUNICATION IN PERSONNEL MANAGEMENT.**

Employee consultation and information in multinational corporations / edited by Jacques Vandamme. London ; Dover, N.H. : Croom Helm, c1986. 265 p. ; 23 cm. Includes bibliographical references. ISBN 0-7099-2624-3 : LC Card 85-21264 DDC 331.25 19
1. International business enterprises - Europe - Employees - Addresses, essays, lectures. 2. Collective bargaining - International business enterprises - Europe - Addresses, essays, lectures. 3. International business enterprises - Employees - Legal status, laws, etc. - Europe - Addresses, essays, lectures. I. Vandamme, J. ***NYPL [JLD 86-1612]***

EMPLOYEE COUNSELING.
Franz, Michael. Die Personalberatung bei der Stellenbesetzung /. Frankfurt am Main , c1984. viii, 214 p. ; ISBN 3-88129-789-8 LC Card 85-186519
HF5549.5.C8 F7 1984

EMPLOYEE COUNSELING - ADDRESSES, ESSAYS, LECTURES.
Employee problem prevention and counseling . Westport, Conn. , 1985. xii, 338 p. ; ISBN 0-89930-084-7 (lib. bdg.) LC Card 84-26499 DDC 658.3/85 19
HF5549.5.C8 E47 1985
NYPL [JLE 86-1105]

EMPLOYEE COUNSELING - UNITED STATES.
McGowan, Brenda G. Trends in employee counseling programs /. New York , c1984. 55 p. ; ISBN 0-08-032361-8 (pbk.) : LC Card 84-22820 DDC 658.3/82 19
HF5549.5.C8 M34 1984
NYPL [JLM 83-380 no.37]

EMPLOYEE-EMPLOYER RELATIONS. see **INDUSTRIAL RELATIONS.**

EMPLOYEE FRINGE BENEFITS.
Kamerman, Sheila B. The responsive workplace . New York , 1987. xi, 329 p. ; ISBN 0-231-06480-2 LC Card 87-6636 DDC 658.3 19
HF5549 .K253 1987

Zoeteweij, H. Indirect remuneration . Geneva , 1986. viii, 82 p. ; ISBN 92-2-105360-1 (pbk.) : LC Card 86-213666 DDC 331.25/5 19
HD4928.N6 Z64 1986

EMPLOYEE FRINGE BENEFITS - CANADA.
Hanson, R. Employee benefits and conditions of employment in Canada . [Ottawa, Ont.] , c1977. iv, 111 p. : ISBN 0-662-00630-5 (pbk.) LC Card 82-136152
HD4928.N62 C225 1977

EMPLOYEE FRINGE BENEFITS - CONGRESSES.
International Benefits Seminar (1985 : Saint Thomas, V.I.) International benefits, 1985-1986 /. Brookfield, Wis. , 1986. xi, 130 p. : ISBN 0-89154-306-6 (pbk.) LC Card 86-224351 DDC 331.25/5 19
HD4928.N6 I57 1986

EMPLOYEE FRINGE BENEFITS - DICTIONARIES.
Employee benefit plans . Brookfield, Wis. , 1987. ix, 157 p. ; ISBN 0-89154-317-1 (pbk.) LC Card 87-150660 DDC 658.3/25/0321 19
HD4928.N6 E46 1987

EMPLOYEE FRINGE BENEFITS - GERMANY (WEST)
Entwicklung und Struktur der Personalnebenkosten /. Bonn [1985] 14, [9] p. : LC Card 86-154479
HD4928.N62 G34 1985

EMPLOYEE FRINGE BENEFITS - SOUTH AFRICA.
Schroeder, Ighsaan. Conditions of employment . Cape Town [1985]- 1 v. (loose-leaf) ; ISBN 0-7992-1002-1 (loose-leaf) LC Card 86-232933 DDC 331.2/0968 19
HD4927.S6 S37 1985

EMPLOYEE FRINGE BENEFITS - TAXATION - GREAT BRITAIN.
Blackstone, L. R. (Lance R.) UK tax savings for the higher paid (1979) /. London , c1979. 10 p. ; LC Card 81-112830
HJ4708.A7 B533 1979

EMPLOYEE FRINGE BENEFITS - UNITED STATES.
EBRI-ERF Policy Forum (1986 : Washington, D.C.) America in transition . Washington, D.C. , c1987. xix, 269 p. : ISBN 0-86643-057-1 (hard) : LC Card 87-13421 DDC 331.25/5/0973 19
HD4928.N62 U628 1987

Fundamentals of employee benefit programs. Washington, DC , c1987. xviii, 304 p. : ISBN 0-86643-051-2 (pbk.) LC Card 87-660 DDC 331.25/5/0973 19
HD4928.N62 U634 1987

Kamerman, Sheila B. Meeting family needs . New York , c1983. 45 p. ; ISBN 0-08-030965-8 (pbk.) : LC Card 83-27159 DDC 658.3/8 19
HD4928.N62 U6355 1983
NYPL [JLM 83-380 no.33]

Kozlowski, Joseph G. Complete guide to cost-effective employee benefit programs /. Englewood Cliffs, N.J. , c1987. xix, 276 p. : ISBN 0-13-160037-0 LC Card 87-11816 DDC 658.3/25 19
HD4928.N62 U636 1987

EMPLOYEE FRINGE BENEFITS - UNITED STATES - MANAGEMENT - CONGRESSES.
Corporate Benefits Management Conferences (1986 : Phoenix, Ariz., etc.) Managing corporate benefit plans, 1986 /. Brookfield, Wis. , 1986. x, 129 p. : ISBN 0-89154-318-X (pbk.) : LC Card 87-403111 DDC 332.6/7254 19
HD7105.45.U6 C67 1986

EMPLOYEE FRINGE BENEFITS - UNITED STATES - STATISTICS.
Compensation and benefits in research & development /. Crete, IL , c1987. 692 p. ; ISBN 0-916506-34-7 (pbk.) LC Card 87-403067 DDC 331.2/816584/00973021 19
HD4965.5.U6 C656 1987

Wage and benefit settlements in construction, 1986. Washington, D.C. (1101 15th St., N.W., Suite 1040, Washington 20005) , c1986. 10 p. : LC Card 87-139726 DDC 331.2/824/0973021 19
HD4966.B892 U685 1986

EMPLOYEE FRINGE BENEFITS - WASHINGTON (STATE)
Washington (State). Dept. of Personnel. Part-time employment study . Olympia, Wash. (600 S. Franklin, FE-11, Olympia 98504) [1984] xi, 82 p. : LC Card 85-621558 DDC 331.25/72 19
HD5110.2.U52 W29 1984
NYPL [JLF 86-517]

EMPLOYEE INCENTIVES. see **INCENTIVES IN INDUSTRY.**

EMPLOYEE-MANAGEMENT RELATIONS IN GOVERNMENT - INDIA - RAJASTHAN.
Saxena, Pradeep. Trade unionism in civil services . Jaipur , 1986. ii, 164 p. ; LC Card 86-903231 DDC 331.88/11354544 19
HD8005.2.I523 R347 1986

EMPLOYEE-MANAGEMENT RELATIONS IN GOVERNMENT - UNITED STATES.
Public sector labor relations . Lexington, Mass. , c1988. xi, 648 p. ; ISBN 0-669-12893-7 (alk. paper) LC Card 82-64038 DDC 331.89/041353 19
HD8005.6.U5 P83 1988

Reischl, Dennis K. Managing for Uncle Sam . Huntsville, Ala. , c1986. ix, 271 p. : ISBN 0-936295-01-5 (pbk.) : LC Card 87-115055 DDC 353.001/7 19
HD8005.2.U5 R45 1986

EMPLOYEE MORALE.
Katz, Daniel, 1903- Productivity, supervision, and morale in an office situation, part I /. New York , 1987, c1950. vii, 84 p. ; ISBN 0-8240-8211-7 (alk. paper) : LC Card 86-25804 DDC 658.3 19
HF5549 .K282 1987

EMPLOYEE MORALE - CALIFORNIA.
Oren, Ditza L. Preventing dishonest behavior in the electronics industry . [United States , 1985] vii, 115 leaves : LC Card 86-224386 DDC 621.381/068/3 19
HD8039.E38 U65 1985

EMPLOYEE MORALE - GERMANY (EAST)
Möbis, Harry. Ordnung, Disziplin, Sicherheit . Berlin , 1983. 95 p. ; LC Card 83-186990
HF5549.5.L3 M63 1983

Sozialistisches Arbeitsverhalten als Leistungsverhalten /. Berlin [1984] 77 p. ; LC Card 84-250357
HD8460.5 .S694 1984

EMPLOYEE MORALE - GERMANY (WEST)
Briam, Karl-Heinz. Arbeiten ohne Angst . Düsseldorf , 1986. 200 p. ; ISBN 3-430-11560-4 LC Card 86-159578
HF5549.2.G3 B75 1986

EMPLOYEE MORALE - SOVIET UNION.
Aitov, Nariman Abdrakhmanovich. Rabotniki khoroshie i plokhie /. Moskva , 1983. 134 p. ; LC Card 84-178331
HD6957.S65 A37 1983

EMPLOYEE MOTIVATION - BULGARIA - HANDBOOKS, MANUALS, ETC.
Narŭchnik na profsŭi͡uznii͡a aktivist po proizvodstveno-masovata rabota /. Sofii͡a , 1986. 200 p. ; LC Card 86-197739
HC403.Z9 S658 1986

EMPLOYEE MOTIVATION - EUROPE, EASTERN.
Stimulierung in Industriebetrieben und Kombinaten /. Berlin , c1982. 290 p. : LC Card 83-164671
HF5549.5.M63 S75 1982

EMPLOYEE MOTIVATION - GERMANY, WEST.
Briam, Karl-Heinz. Arbeiten ohne Angst . Düsseldorf , 1986. 200 p. ; ISBN 3-430-11560-4 LC Card 86-159578
HF5549.2.G3 B75 1986

Huellen, Karl Konrad. Die Motivation von Arbeitnehmern im Innen- und Aussendienst des Vertriebs . Münster [1986] iv, 245 p. : ISBN 3-88660-356-3 (Deut. Bibl.) LC Card 87-114821 DDC 658.3/14 19
HF5549.5.M63 H84 1986

EMPLOYEE MOTIVATION - GERMANY (WEST) - CONGRESSES.
Processi formativi e coscienza operaia . Pisa , c1983. 509 p. ; LC Card 86-136656 DDC 658.3/124/0945 19
HF5549.5.T7 P69 1983
NYPL [JLE 87-1466]

EMPLOYEE MOTIVATION - ITALY - CONGRESSES.
Processi formativi e coscienza operaia . Pisa , c1983. 509 p. ; LC Card 86-136656 DDC 658.3/124/0945 19
HF5549.5.T7 P69 1983
NYPL [JLE 87-1466]

EMPLOYEE MOTIVATION - RUSSIAN S.F.S. R. - IVANOVSKAI͡A OBLASTʹ - POSTERS.
Korchagina, A. (Aleksandra) Nagli͡adnai͡a agitatsii͡a i vstrechnye plany /. Moskva , 1978. 44 p., [16] p. of plates : LC Card 81-161419
HC340.L3 K56 1978

EMPLOYEE MOTIVATION - SOVIET UNION.
Turkin, V. G. (Vladimir Gavrilovich) Povyshatʹ ėffektivnostʹ partiĭnoĭ raboty /. Moskva , 1978. 63 p. ; LC Card 81-170148
HF5549.5.M63 T87 1978

EMPLOYEE MOTIVATION - SOVIET UNION - POSTERS - CASE STUDIES.
Korchagina, A. (Aleksandra) Nagli͡adnai͡a agitatsii͡a i vstrechnye plany /. Moskva , 1978. 44 p., [16] p. of plates : LC Card 81-161419
HC340.L3 K56 1978

EMPLOYEE MOTIVATION - UKRAINE.
Danchenko, M. I. (Mykola Ivanovych) Dystsyplina pratsi /. Kyïv , 1983. 110 p. ; LC Card 83-215106
HF5549.5.L3 D34 1983

EMPLOYEE MOTIVATION - YUGOSLAVIA.
Pavlović, Dragiša, 1943- Ko radnike povezuje lažnim koncima . Beograd , 1984. 414 p. ; LC Card 84-178578
HC407.Z9 L36 1984

EMPLOYEE OWNERSHIP - CHILE - SANTIAGO.
Winn, Peter. Weavers of revolution . New York , 1986. xiv, 328 p. : ISBN 0-19-503960-2 : LC Card 85-18832 DDC 338.7/67721/098331 19
HD8039.T42 C478 1986
NYPL [JLE 86-1973]

EMPLOYEE OWNERSHIP - GERMANY (WEST) - LOWER SAXONY.
Schanz, Günther, 1943- Mitarbeiter-Kapitalbeteiligung in der Wirtschaft Niedersachsens . Spardorf , c1984. 228 p. : ISBN 3-922919-26-X : LC Card 84-162288
HD5660.G412 L687 1984

EMPLOYEE OWNERSHIP - LATIN AMERICA - CONGRESSES.
Reforma agraria como proceso social . Piura, Perú [1984] 163 p. : LC Card 84-232526 DDC 333.3/1/85 19
HD1333.P4 R44 1984 ***NYPL [JLD 86-2537]***

EMPLOYEE OWNERSHIP - OHIO.
Logue, John, 1947- Buyout! . [Kent, Ohio] [1986] vi, 98 p. : ISBN 0-933522-15-0 (pbk.) LC Card 86-623028 DDC 658.1/6 19
HD2746.5 .L64 1986

EMPLOYEE OWNERSHIP - POLITICAL ASPECTS - SWEDEN.
Larsson, Janerik, 1944- Vändpunkten . [Stockholm] [1983] 125 p. : ISBN 91-7566-040-7 : LC Card 84-189468
HD5660.S9 L35 1983

Employee ownership through ESOPs . Blasi, Joseph R. New York , c1987. 126 p. ; ISBN 0-08-029520-7 (pbk.) : LC Card 86-30281 DDC 658.3/225 19
HD5660.U5 B57 1987

EMPLOYEE OWNERSHIP - UNITED STATES.
Blasi, Joseph R. Employee ownership through ESOPs . New York , c1987. 126 p. ; ISBN 0-08-029520-7 (pbk.) : LC Card 86-30281 DDC 658.3/225 19
HD5660.U5 B57 1987

Industrial democracy . Beverly Hills , c1985. 308 p. : ISBN 0-8039-2476-3 LC Card 85-11741 DDC 338.973/009173/2 19
HT321 .I53 1985 ***NYPL [JLD 86-3621]***

Kelso, Louis O. Democracy and economic power . Cambridge, Mass. , 1986. xii, 175 p. : ISBN 0-88730-115-0 : LC Card 86-14027 DDC 338.6 19
HD5660.U5 K45 1986 ***NYPL [JLE 86-4658]***

Marshall, F. Ray. Unheard voices . New York , c1987. xi, 339 p. : ISBN 0-465-08869-4 : LC Card 83-46084 DDC 338.6 19
HD5660.U5 M36 1987

Meek, Christopher. Managing by the numbers . Reading, Mass. , c1988. ix, 293 p. : ISBN 0-201-16129-X : LC Card 87-16088 DDC 338.7/4/0973 19
HD70.U5 M413 1988

Quarrey, Michael. Taking stock . Cambridge, Mass. , c1986. xxii, 176 p. ; ISBN 0-88730-131-2 LC Card 86-14045 DDC 338.7/4 19
HD5660.U5 Q37 1986 ***NYPL [JLE 87-49]***

Wilson, Bryan David, 1954- Ownership and participation . 1985. xi, 356 ;
NYPL [JLD 87-209]

EMPLOYEE PENSION TRUSTS. see **PENSION TRUSTS.**

Employee problem prevention and counseling : a guide for professionals / edited by Donald W. Myers. Westport, Conn. : Quorum Books, 1985. xii, 338 p. ; ill. ; 24 cm. Includes bibliographies and index. ISBN 0-89930-084-7 (lib. bdg.) LC Card 84-26499 DDC 658.3/85 19
1. Employee counseling - Addresses, essays, lectures. 2. Counseling - Addresses, essays, lectures. I. Myers, Donald W.
HF5549.5.C8 E47 1985
NYPL [JLE 86-1105]

EMPLOYEE RECREATION. see **INDUSTRIAL RECREATION.**

EMPLOYEE RIGHTS - ITALY.
La Tutela del lavoro in Italia. [Roma] [1976] 144 p. ; LC Card 86-233354
HD8481 .T85 1976

EMPLOYEE RULES - GERMANY (EAST)
Möbis, Harry. Ordnung, Disziplin, Sicherheit . Berlin , 1983. 95 p. ; LC Card 83-186990
HF5549.5.L3 M63 1983

EMPLOYEE SELECTION.
Aoiz Iriarte, María Rosario. Técnicas psicosociales en la administración pública . Alcalá de Henares, Madrid, España [1984] 238 p. : ISBN 84-7351-179-4 LC Card 85-189583
HF5549.5.S38 A57 1984

Baehr, Melany E. Experience and background inventory . [Park Ridge, Ill.] (1550 Northwest Highway, Park Ridge 60068) [c1986] 48 p. ; LC Card 87-404267 DDC 658.3/112 19
HF5549.5.S38 B34 1986

Bowes, Lee, 1951- No one need apply . Boston, Mass. , c1987. xiv, 268 p. ; ISBN 0-87584-149-X (alk. paper) LC Card 86-29512 DDC 658.3/11 19
HF5549.5.R44 B69 1987

Caruth, Donald L. Staffing the contemporary organization . New York , 1988. xii, 309 p. : ISBN 0-89930-236-X (lib. bdg. : alk. paper) LC Card 87-13092 DDC 658.3 19
HF5549 .C296 1988

Cook, Mark. Personnel selection and productivity /. Chichester [West Sussex] , New York , c1988. p. cm. ISBN 0-471-91148-8 : LC Card 87-21070 DDC 658.3/112 19
HF5549.5.S38 C66 1988

Franz, Michael. Die Personalberatung bei der Stellenbesetzung /. Frankfurt am Main , c1984. viii, 214 p. ; ISBN 3-88129-789-8 LC Card 85-186519
HF5549.5.C8 F7 1984

Sears, Victoria Loufakis. Staffing for optimum performance /. New York, N.Y. , c1986. iv, 191 p. : ISBN 0-88057-403-8 (pbk.) LC Card 85-80707 DDC 658.3/112 19
HF5549.5.S38 S4 1986

Structured hiring . New York, NY, U. S.A. , c1987. viii leaves, 144 p. : ISBN 0-86604-221-0 (pbk.) LC Card 87-156398 DDC 658.3/112 19
HF5549.5.R44 S83 1987

Venne, Rosemary Amelia, 1956- Psychological testing in personnel selection /. Kingston, Ont., Canada , 1987. 65 p. ; ISBN 0-88886-152-4 (pbk.) LC Card 87-163203 DDC 658.3/1125 19
HF5549.5.E5 V46 1987

EMPLOYEE SELECTION - GERMANY (WEST)
Windolf, Paul. Recruitment and selection in the labour market . Aldershot, Hants, England , Brookfield, Vt. , c1988. p. cm. ISBN 0-566-00937-4 : LC Card 87-19763 DDC 658.3/11/0941 19
HF5549.5.R44 W494 1988

EMPLOYEE SELECTION - GREAT BRITAIN.
Windolf, Paul. Recruitment and selection in the labour market . Aldershot, Hants, England , Brookfield, Vt. , c1988. p. cm. ISBN 0-566-00937-4 : LC Card 87-19763 DDC 658.3/11/0941 19
HF5549.5.R44 W494 1988

EMPLOYEE SELECTION - LAW AND LEGISLATION - UNITED STATES.
Arvey, Richard D. Fairness in selecting employees /. Reading, Mass. , c1988. x, 361 p. : ISBN 0-201-00078-4 (pbk.) : LC Card 87-22173 DDC 658.3/112 19
HF5549.5.S38 A78 1988

EMPLOYEE SELECTION - SPAIN - CASE STUDIES.
Aoiz Iriarte, María Rosario. Técnicas psicosociales en la administración pública . Alcalá de Henares, Madrid, España [1984] 238 p. : ISBN 84-7351-179-4 LC Card 85-189583
HF5549.5.S38 A57 1984

EMPLOYEE SELECTION - UNITED STATES.
Arvey, Richard D. Fairness in selecting employees /. Reading, Mass. , c1988. x, 361 p. : ISBN 0-201-00078-4 (pbk.) : LC Card 87-22173 DDC 658.3/112 19
HF5549.5.S38 A78 1988

Hiring costs and strategies . New York , c1986. v, 82 p. : ISBN 0-8144-3153-4
NYPL [JLF 86-960]

EMPLOYEE SELECTIONS.
Baehr, Melany E. Experience and background questionnaire . [Park Ridge, Ill.] (1550 Northwest Highway, Park Ridge 60068) , c1986. 20 p. ; LC Card 87-404268 DDC 658.3/1125 19
HF5381.7 .B327 1986

EMPLOYEE STOCK OPTIONS - UNITED STATES.
Quarrey, Michael. Taking stock . Cambridge, Mass. , c1986. xxii, 176 p. ; ISBN 0-88730-131-2 LC Card 86-14045 DDC 338.7/4 19
HD5660.U5 Q37 1986 ***NYPL [JLE 87-49]***

EMPLOYEE THEFT - CALIFORNIA.
Oren, Ditza L. Preventing dishonest behavior in the electronics industry . [United States , 1985] vii, 115 leaves : LC Card 86-224386 DDC 621.381/068/3 19
HD8039.E38 U65 1985

EMPLOYEE THEFT - GREAT BRITAIN - HISTORY - 20TH CENTURY.
Smithies, Edward. The black economy in England since 1914 /. London , Atlantic Highlands, N.J. , 1984. 165 p. ; ISBN 0-391-03114-7 LC Card 84-6516 DDC 364.1/33 19
HF5482.65.G7 S64 1984
NYPL [JLD 86-2509]

EMPLOYEE THEFT - PREVENTION.
Snyder, Stanley G. Embezzlers' dirty tricks (and how to spot them) . San Diego, CA , c1987. 336 p. : ISBN 0-937535-00-1 (pbk.) : LC Card 87-50037 DDC 658.4/73 19
HF5549.5.E43 S59 1987

EMPLOYEE TRAINING. see **EMPLOYEES, TRAINING OF.**

EMPLOYEE TURNOVER. see **LABOR TURNOVER.**

EMPLOYEES, DISMISSAL OF - GREAT BRITAIN.
Coyle, Angela. Redundant women /. London , 1984. 154 p. : ISBN 0-7043-3923-4 (pbk.) : LC Card 84-100906 DDC 331.4/137941 19
HD5708.55.G7 C68 1984
NYPL [JLD 86-3916]

EMPLOYEES, DISMISSAL OF - LAW AND LEGISLATION - PAKISTAN.
Industrial democracy in India . Saddar, Karachi, Pakistan [1985] 21 p. ; LC Card 86-222345 DDC 331/.01/12095491 19
HD7262.5.P18 I53 1985

EMPLOYEES, DISMISSAL OF - LAW AND LEGISLATION - UNITED STATES.
Brandt, Ed. Fifty and fired . Bedford, Mass. , c1987. xii, 242 p. ; ISBN 0-938179-07-1 : LC Card 87-12150 DDC 650.1/4/0240564 19
HD38.25.U6 B7 1987

EMPLOYEES, DISMISSAL OF - UNITED STATES - ADDRESSES, ESSAYS, LECTURES.
Job equity and other studies in industrial relations . Los Angeles , c1982. 274 p. : LC Card 82-621216 DDC 331/.0973 19
HD5708.45.U6 J6 1982 ***NYPL [JLD 87-273]***

EMPLOYEES, DISMISSAL OF - UNITED STATES - CASE STUDIES.
Berenbeim, Ronald. Company programs to ease the impact of shutdowns /. New York, N.Y. , c1986. ix, 57 p. : ISBN 0-8237-0320-7 (pbk.) LC Card 86-207794 DDC 331.25 19
HF5549.5.D55 B47 1986

Harrison, Clifford E., 1931- Managing staff reductions in corporations /. Ann Arbor, Mich. , c1986. vi, 138 p. : ISBN 0-8357-1758-5 (alk. paper) LC Card 86-11223 DDC 658.3/134 19
HF5549.5.D55 H37 1986
NYPL [JLE 86-3391]

EMPLOYEES, RATING OF - UNITED STATES.
Morrisey, George L. Performance appraisals in the public sector . Reading, Mass. , 1983. xiii, 172 p. ; ISBN 0-201-04847-7 (pbk.) : LC Card 83-6049 DDC 353.001/42 19
JK766.6 .M67 1983 ***NYPL [JLE 83-3164]***

EMPLOYEES, RECRUITING OF. see **RECRUITING OF EMPLOYEES.**

EMPLOYEES' REPRESENTATION IN MANAGEMENT - LAW AND LEGISLATION - GERMANY (WEST)
Werner, Horst S. Der aktienrechtliche Abhängigkeitstatbestand . Göttingen , 1979. xxxix, 214 p. ; ISBN 3-88415-560-1 : LC Card 80-452340 DDC 346.43/066
LAW ***NYPL [JLD 86-1592]***

EMPLOYEES, SUPERVISION OF. see **SUPERVISION OF EMPLOYEES.**

EMPLOYEES, TRAINING OF - AUDIO-VISUAL AIDS.
Kearsley, Greg, 1951- Training and technology . Reading, Ma. , c1984. vii, 198 p. : ISBN 0-201-10335-4 : LC Card 83-22336 DDC 658.3/12404 19
HF5549.5.T7 K343 1984
NYPL [JLE 86-2641]

EMPLOYEES, TRAINING OF - CASE STUDIES.
Caffarella, Rosemary S. (Rosemary Shelly), 1946- Program development and evaluation resource book for trainers /. New York , c1988. xxi, 266 p. : ISBN 0-471-84235-4 LC Card 87-15990 DDC 658.3/12404 19
HF5549.5.T7 C23 1988

EMPLOYEES, TRAINING OF - COMPUTER-ASSISTED INSTRUCTION.
Gery, Gloria, 1944- Making CBT happen . Boston , 1987. xiv, 225 p. : ISBN 0-9617968-0-4 (pbk.) : LC Card 86-51671 DDC 658.3/12404 19
HF5549.5.T7 G42 1987

Kearsley, Greg, 1951- Training and technology . Reading, Ma. , c1984. vii, 198 p. : ISBN 0-201-10335-4 : LC Card 83-22336 DDC 658.3/12404 19
HF5549.5.T7 K343 1984
NYPL [JLE 86-2641]

Technology-based training. Oxford , New York , c1986. ix, 357 p. : ISBN 0-08-034097-0 LC Card 87-160178 DDC 658.3/12404 19
HF5549.5.T7 T39 1986

EMPLOYEES, TRAINING OF - CONGRESSES.
Technology management '85 . London , c1985. 160 p. : ISBN 0-903748-61-4
NYPL [JLG 87-124]

EMPLOYEES, TRAINING OF - EQUIPMENT AND SUPPLIES.
Industrial training products & services markets. Norwalk, Conn., U. S.A. (6 Prowitt St., Norwalk 06855) , c1987. vi, 174 leaves ; LC Card 87-153554 DDC 381/.45658312404 19
HD9811.A2 I53 1987

EMPLOYEES, TRAINING OF - EVALUATION.
Brinkerhoff, Robert O. Achieving results from training . San Francisco , 1987. xx, 248 p. ; ISBN 1-555-42044-3 (alk. paper) LC Card 86-46331 DDC 658.3/12404 19
HF5549.5.T7 B65 1987

Evaluating business and industry training /. Boston , Norwell, MA , c1987. xv, 294 p. : ISBN 0-89838-197-5 LC Card 87-5771 DDC 658.3/12404 19
HF5549.5.T7 E88 1987

Goldstein, Irwin L., 1937- Training in organizations . Monterey, Calif. , c1986. xv, 315 p. : ISBN 0-534-05604-0 : LC Card 85-21348 DDC 658.3/12404 19
HF5549.5.T7 G543 1985
NYPL [JLE 86-1519]

Hawthorne, Elizabeth M. Evaluating employee training programs . New York , 1987. xiv, 196 p. : ISBN 0-89930-242-4 (lib. bdg. : alk. paper) LC Card 87-5984 DDC 658.3/12404 19
HF5549.5.T7 H36 1987

EMPLOYEES, TRAINING OF - EVALUATION - HANDBOOKS, MANUALS, ETC.
Caffarella, Rosemary S. (Rosemary Shelly), 1946- Program development and evaluation resource book for trainers /. New York , c1988. xxi, 266 p. : ISBN 0-471-84235-4 LC Card 87-15990 DDC 658.3/12404 19
HF5549.5.T7 C23 1988

EMPLOYEES, TRAINING OF - GERMANY - HISTORY - 19TH CENTURY.
Rinneberg, Karl-Jürgen. Das betriebliche Ausbildungswesen in der Zeit der industriellen Umgestaltung Deutschlands /. Köln , 1985. xvi, 481 p. : ISBN 3-412-02885-1 LC Card 86-121691
HF5549.5.T7 R486 1985

EMPLOYEES, TRAINING OF - GERMANY, WEST.
Berufs- und Weiterbildung 1984/85 . Bonn , 1985. 201 p. : LC Card 86-171726
HF5549.5.T7 B488 1985

Feuerstein, Thomas. Humanisierung der Arbeit

und Reform der beruflichen Bildung . München , c1983. 221 p. ; ISBN 3-87966-184-7 LC Card 83-222687
HD5715.5.G4 F48 1983

Kempf, Theo, 1955- Theorie und Empirie betrieblicher Ausbildungsplatzangebote /. Frankfurt am Main , New York , c1985. 305 p. : ISBN 3-8204-8358-6 LC Card 86-111326
HF5549.5.T7 K42 1985

Klause, Dieter. Wegweiser zur Weiterbildung . Bonn , 1982. 101 p. ; LC Card 83-206662
HF5549.5.T7 K58 1982

Processi formativi e coscienza operaia . Pisa , c1983. 509 p. ; LC Card 86-136656 DDC 658.3/124/0945 19
HF5549.5.T7 P69 1983 *NYPL [JLE 87-1466]*

Sardei-Biermann, Sabine. Jugendliche zwischen Schule und Arbeitswelt . München , c1984. v, 318 p. ; ISBN 3-87966-219-3 LC Card 84-240405
HD5715.5.G4 S27 1984

Weiterbildungsmodelle und Weiterbildungspraxis in Industrie, Handel, Banken, Versicherungen und Fremdenverkehr /. München , c1984. 169 p. : ISBN 3-19-007546-8 LC Card 85-147442
HF5549.5.T7 W394 1984

Ziefuss, Horst. Jugendliche in der gewerblich-technischen Ausbildung in Industrie und Handwerk . Kiel , c1986. 352 p. : ISBN 3-89088-011-8 LC Card 87-407898 DDC 331.3/42592/0943 19
HD5715.5.G4 Z54 1986

EMPLOYEES, TRAINING OF - GERMANY (WEST) - BAVARIA - CASE STUDIES.
Maier, Hans E. Das Handwerk und die Berufseingliederung Jugendlicher in der Bundesrepublik Deutschland /. Berlin [1986] 68 p. : LC Card 86-230660
HD5715.5.G4 M35 1986

EMPLOYEES, TRAINING OF - HAITI.
International Labour Organisation. Institut national de formation professionnelle (INFP) . Genève , 1982. ii, 69 p. : ISBN 92-2-203229-2 LC Card 83-234817
HD5715.5.H2 I57 1982

EMPLOYEES, TRAINING OF - HANDBOOKS, MANUALS, ETC.
Sredl, Henry J., 1935- The ASTD reference guide to professional training roles & competencies /. New York , c1987. 2 v. : ISBN 0-394-55915-0 (v. 1) LC Card 86-26006 DDC 658.3/124 19
HF5549.5.T7 S657 1987

EMPLOYEES, TRAINING OF - ITALY.
Processi formativi e coscienza operaia . Pisa , c1983. 509 p. ; LC Card 86-136656 DDC 658.3/124/0945 19
HF5549.5.T7 P69 1983 *NYPL [JLE 87-1466]*

EMPLOYEES, TRAINING OF - PHILIPPINES.
Andres, Tomas Quintin D., 1942- Human resource training & development /. Quezon City , c1980. viii, 134 p. : LC Card 82-102431 DDC 658.3/12404/09599 19
HF5549.5.T7 A64 1980 *NYPL [JLD 87-935]*

EMPLOYEES, TRAINING OF - POLAND.
Kowtun, Józef. Rola, funkcje i zadania mistrza w systemie dokształcania i wychowania robotników /. Warszawa , 1979. 151, [1] p. ; LC Card 81-180277
HF5549.5.T7 K687 1979

EMPLOYEES, TRAINING OF - PROBLEMS, EXERCISES, ETC.
Caffarella, Rosemary S. (Rosemary Shelly), 1946- Program development and evaluation resource book for trainers /. New York , c1988. xxi, 266 p. : ISBN 0-471-84235-4 LC Card 87-15990 DDC 658.3/12404 19
HF5549.5.T7 C23 1988

EMPLOYEES, TRAINING OF - SOUTH AFRICA.
Verslag van die Nasionale Mannekragkommissie oor indiensopleiding in die Republiek van Suid-Afrika, 1980/81 =. [Pretoria] [1984] 267 p. ; ISBN 0-621-08502-2 : LC Card 86-109914
HF5549.5.T7 V44 1984

EMPLOYEES, TRAINING OF - SOVIET UNION.
Syrovatko, V. G. (Vitaliĭ Grigor′evich) Industrializatsiia i kadry sel′skogo khoziaistva /. Moskva , 1986. 191 p. ; LC Card 86-229171
HD1536.S65 S97 1986

EMPLOYEES, TRAINING OF - UNITED STATES.
Bushnell, David S. Training for new technology /. New York , c1983. 41 p. ; ISBN 0-08-029508-8 : LC Card 83-17341 DDC 658.3/124 19
HD5715.2 .B87 1983 *NYPL [JLM 83-380 no.27]*

Lusterman, Seymour. Trends in corporate education and training /. New York, N.Y. , c1985. vii, 23 p. ; ISBN 0-8237-0311-8 (pbk.) LC Card 87-106076 DDC 331.25/92/0973 19
HF5549.5.T7 L86 1985

Phillips, Jack J., 1945- Recruiting, training, and retaining new employees . San Francisco , 1987. xxii, 324 p. ; ISBN 1-555-42042-7 (alk. paper) LC Card 86-46332 DDC 658.3/14 19
HF5549.5.R44 P49 1987

Winick, Bradley H. Making the link . [Washinton, D.C.] , c1986. i, 17 p. ; ISBN 0-88713-678-8 (pbk.) LC Card 87-106145 DDC 331.11/0973 19
HD5724 .W557 1986

EMPLOYEES, TRAINING OF - UNITED STATES - DIRECTORIES.
Bard, Ray. Breaking in . New York , 1985. 256 p. ; ISBN 0-688-05893-0 (pbk.) LC Card 85-6571 DDC 331.25/92/02573 19
HF5549.5.T7 B29 1985 *NYPL [*R-Econ. 86-248]*

EMPLOYEES, TRAINING OF - UZBEK S.S.R.
Shister, G. A. (Grigoriĭ Aronovich) Rukovodstvo kompartii Uzbekistana podgotovkoĭ rabochikh kadrov v usloviiakh razvitogo sotsializma /. Tashkent , 1981. 274, [2] p. ; LC Card 82-204041
HD5797.U9 S54 1981

Employer concerns regarding workers with disabilities /. Greenwood, Reed. Hot Springs, Ark. [1985] xii, 170 p. ; LC Card 87-620863 DDC 658.3/045 19
HD7256.U5 G74 1985

EMPLOYER-EMPLOYEE RELATIONS. see **INDUSTRIAL RELATIONS.**

Employer sanctions in Western Europe /. Miller, Mark J. Staten Island, N.Y. , 1987. viii, 67 p. ; ISBN 0-934733-20-1 (pbk.) : LC Card 86-31739 DDC 331.6/2/094 19
HD8378.5.A2 M5395 1987

EMPLOYER SPONSORED EDUCATION - SAUDI ARABIA.
Viola, Joy Winkie. Human resources development in Saudi Arabia . Boston , c1986. xxvi, 291 p. : ISBN 0-88746-070-4 (IHRDC) LC Card 85-19694 DDC 303.4/8273/0538 19
HD5812.35.A6 V56 1986 *NYPL [JLE 86-2188]*

EMPLOYER-SUPPORTED EDUCATION - UNITED STATES.
Lusterman, Seymour. Trends in corporate education and training /. New York, N.Y. , c1985. vii, 23 p. ; ISBN 0-8237-0311-8 (pbk.) LC Card 87-106076 DDC 331.25/92/0973 19
HF5549.5.T7 L86 1985

Workplace literacy /. New York , c1986. 74 p. : ISBN 0-8144-2325-6 LC Card 86-14013 DDC 331.25/92 19
HF5549.5.T7 W66 1986 *NYPL [JLE 86-3510]*

Employers and the environmental challenge / edited by Harry Z. Evan. Geneva : International Labour Office, 1986. vii, 101 p. ; 24 cm. At head of title: International Labour Organisation, United Nations Environment Programme. Includes bibliographies. ISBN 92-2-105647-3 (pbk.) : LC Card 87-123427 DDC 363.7/056 19
1. Pollution - Economic aspects. 2. Industrial management - Environmental aspects. 3. Work environment. I. Evan, Harry Z. II. International Labour Organisation. III. United Nations. Environment Programme.
HD69.P6 E46 1986

EMPLOYERS' ASSOCIATIONS - ARGENTINA - HISTORY.
Cornblit, Oscar. Sindicatos obreros y asociaciones empresarias hasta la década del centenario /. Buenos Aires, Argentina , 1984. 109 p. ; LC Card 87-401262 DDC 331.88/0982 19
HD6602 .C665 1984

EMPLOYERS' ASSOCIATIONS - AUSTRIA.
Morawetz, Inge, 1955- Die verborgene Macht . Frankfurt , New York , c1986. 200 p. : ISBN 3-593-33662-6 LC Card 86-223864
HG3008 .M67 1986

EMPLOYERS' ASSOCIATIONS - BELGIUM - LANGUAGE.
Hotterbeex, M. (Marcel) Les verbos de la F.E.B. en 1979 /. Liège , 1982. 20 leaves ; LC Card 83-221745
HD6948.B4 H67 1982

EMPLOYERS' ASSOCIATIONS - EUROPEAN ECONOMIC COMMUNITY COUNTRIES.
Platzer, Hans-Wolfgang. Unternehmensverbände in der EG, ihre nationale und transnationale Organisation und Politik . Kehl am Rhein , 1984. xi, 283 p. ; ISBN 3-88357-024-9 LC Card 85-131940
HD6948.G3 P58 1984

EMPLOYERS' ASSOCIATIONS - FRANCE.
Chotard, Yvon, 1921- Les patrons et le patronat /. [Paris] , c1986. 231 p. ; ISBN 2-7021-1538-1 : LC Card 87-167099
HD6948.F8 C46 1986

Helbert, Jean-Pierre, 1947- L'insurrection des patrons /. Châteaugiron , 1984. 165 p. ; ISBN 2-903414-33-5 LC Card 85-180275 DDC 658/.006/044 19
HD6948.F8 H45 1984 *NYPL [JLE 86-526]*

Weber, Henri. Le parti des patrons . Paris , c1986. 437 p. ; ISBN 2-02-009352-9 : LC Card 87-106644
HD6948.F8 W43 1986

EMPLOYERS ASSOCIATIONS - GERMANY, WEST.
Kontos, Maria. Verbandsstrategien zur Ausländerbeschäftigung in der Bundesrepublik . Königstein/Ts. , c1983. viii, 235 p. ; ISBN 3-7756-6938-8 LC Card 83-190064 DDC 331.6/2/0943 19
HD8458.A2 K598 1983 *NYPL [JLD 86-2465]*

Platzer, Hans-Wolfgang. Unternehmensverbände in der EG, ihre nationale und transnationale Organisation und Politik . Kehl am Rhein , 1984. xi, 283 p. ; ISBN 3-88357-024-9 LC Card 85-131940
HD6948.G3 P58 1984

EMPLOYESS, RATING OF.
Slater, John, 1936- The skills of appraisal /. Aldershot, Hants, England , Brookfield, Vt., U.S.A. , c1988. p. cm. ISBN 0-566-02729-1 LC Card 87-22388 DDC 658.3/125 19
HF5549.5.R3 S57 1988

Employment, adjustment, and industrialisation, 0257-3415 .
(3) Gray, H. Peter. International trade, employment, and structural adjustment . Geneva , 1986. x, 108 p. ; ISBN 92-2-105325-3 (pbk.) : LC Card 87-119470 DDC 331.12/0973 19
HD5710.75.U6 G73 1986

(8) Renshaw, Geoffrey. Adjustment and economic performance in industrialised countries . Geneva , 1986. xiv, 180 p. ; ISBN 92-2-105510-8 (pbk.) : LC Card 87-123435 DDC 338.9/009172/2 19
HC286.7 .R46 1986

EMPLOYMENT AGENCIES - BERLIN (GERMANY)
Albrecht, Christoph, 1950- Beschäftigungsentwicklung und Qualifikationsstruktur in Berlin 1977-1983 . Berlin [1985] 2 v. : LC Card 86-204299
HD5780.B4 A43 1985

EMPLOYMENT AGENCIES - FRANCE - ROMANS-SUR-ISÈRE - HISTORY.
Armand, Marcel. Histoire de la Bourse du travail de Romans et de ceux qui l'ont faite . [Romans-sur-Isère , 1982] 80 p. ; LC Card 83-143101
HD5926.R66 A76 1982

EMPLOYMENT AND AGE. see **AGE AND EMPLOYMENT.**

EMPLOYMENT AND ALCOHOLISM. see **ALCOHOLISM AND EMPLOYMENT.**

Employment and development in Lesotho : report of a national seminar / organized by the Government of Lesotho in collaboration with ILO's Jobs and Skills Programme for Africa (JASPA) and Southern African Team for Employment Promotion (SATEP), 24-27 May 1983. Addis Ababa : The Programme, 1983. ii, 229 p. ; 30 cm. "Based on the JASPA Employment Advisory Mission report entitled Options for a dependent economy: development, employment and equity problems in Lesotho"--Cover. Bibliography: p. 167-168. ISBN 92-2-103780-0 LC Card 84-980769 DDC 331.12/09681/6 19
1. Labor supply - Lesotho - Congresses. 2. Lesotho - Economic conditions - 1966- - Congresses. 3. Agriculture - Economic aspects - Lesotho - Congresses. 4. Lesotho - Colonial influence - Congresses. I. Lesotho. II. Jobs and Skills Programme for Africa. III. Southern African Team for Employment Promotion. IV. Jaspa Employment Advisory Mission. Options for a dependent economy.
HD5842.7.A6 E46 1983

Employment and earnings, 1980-1985 : statewide hours, wages. Montpelier, Vt. : Vermont Dept. of Employment and Training, [1986] ii, 79 leaves : ill. ; 22 x 28 cm. Chiefly tables. LC Card 86-622186 DDC 331.12/5/09743021 19
1. Labor supply - Vermont - Statistics. 2. Wages - Vermont - Statistics. 3. Hours of labor - Vermont - Statistics. I. Vermont. Dept. of Employment and Training.
HD5725.V5 E46 1986

EMPLOYMENT AND FOREIGN TRADE. see **FOREIGN TRADE AND EMPLOYMENT.**

Employment and gross earnings of California residents in Alaska's commercial fisheries, 1977-1982 /. Focht, Rick. Juneau, AK [1984] v, 53 p. : LC Card 86-622320 DDC 331.12/5392/09798021 19
HD4966.F652 U54 1984c

Employment and gross earnings of Oregon residents in Alaska's commercial fisheries, 1977-1982 /. Focht, Rick. Juneau, AK [1984] v, 69 p. : LC Card 86-622319 DDC 331.12/5392/09798021 19
HD4966.F652 U54 1984b

Employment and gross earnings of Washington residents in Alaska's commercial fisheries, 1977-1982 /. Focht, Rick. Juneau, AK [1984] v leaves, 126 p. ; LC Card 86-622318 DDC 331.2/8392/09797021 19
HD4966.F542 U554 1984

Employment and housing renovation in Europe / by Euro-Construct. Luxembourg : Commission of the European Communities ; Washington, DC : European Community Information Service [distributor], 1986. 89 p. : ill. ; 29 cm. ISBN 92-825-6422-3 : LC Card 87-136222 DDC 331.2/89/083094 19
1. Construction workers - European Economic Community countries - Supply and demand. 2. Housing - European Economic Community countries. 3. Housing rehabilitation - European Economic Community countries. I. Euro-Construct (Firm : Neuilly-sur-Seine, France). II. Commission of the European Communities.
HD5718.B92 E863 1986

Employment and labor force in Maryland : trends and projections, 1967-2005 / [prepared by Office of Planning Data]. Baltimore, Md. (301 W. Preston St., Baltimore) : Maryland Dept. of State Planning, [1986] xliv, 164, [51] p. : maps ; 28 cm. (Projection series) Department of State Planning publication ; 86-3 Chiefly tables. "January 1986." LC Card 86-622107 DDC 331.12/5/09752 19
1. Labor supply - Maryland - Statistics. 2. Employment forecasting - Maryland - Statistics. I. Maryland. Office of Planning Data. II. Series.
HD5725.M35 E43 1986

Employment and multinational enterprises in export processing zones . Botchie, George. Geneva , 1984. iv, 74 p. ; ISBN 92-2-103770-3 (pbk.) : LC Card 86-213592
HF1417 .B68 1984

Employment and parking in suburban business parks : a pilot study. Washington, D.C. : Urban Land Institute, c1986. iv, 31 p. : ill. ; 28 cm. ISBN 0-87420-662-6 (pbk.) LC Card 86-219885 DDC 338.6/042 19
1. Business parks - United States - Parking facilities. 2. Business parks - United States - Employees. I. Urban Land Institute.
HD255 .E45 1986

Employment and technological choice of multinational enterprises in developing countries . Marsh, Lawrence. Geneva , 1983. iii, 37 p. ; ISBN 92-2-103353-8 (pbk.) : LC Card 86-213692 DDC 338.8/8854 19
HD2932 .M35 1983

Employment and wage policies in Poland, Czechoslovakia, and Hungary since 1950 /. Adam, Jan, 1920- New York , 1984. xix, 251 p. ; ISBN 0-312-24457-6 : LC Card 83-40125 DDC 331.12/042/0943 19
HD5797.7.A6 A3 1984 *NYPL [JLD 86-4389]*

Employment, distribution, and basic needs in Pakistan : essays in honour of Jawaid Azfar / edited by Mahbub ul Haq, Moin Baqai.1st ed. Lahore : Progressive Publishers, 1986. xxxiv, 408 p., [1] leaf of plates : port. ; 22 cm. Includes bibliographies. LC Card 86-930280 DDC 330.9549/1 19
1. Labor supply - Pakistan. 2. Income distribution - Pakistan. 3. Rural poor - Pakistan. 4. Pakistan - Economic conditions. 5. Azfar, Jawaid, 1939-1983. I. Azfar, Jawaid, 1939-1983. II. Haq, Mahbub ul, 1934-. III. Baqai, Moin.
HD5820.5.A6 E47 1986

EMPLOYMENT (ECONOMIC THEORY)

Arndt, Helmut, 1911- Leistungswettbewerb und ruinöse Konkurrenz in ihrem Einfluss auf Wohlfahrt und Beschäftigung . Berlin , c1986. 147 p. ; ISBN 3-428-06078-4 LC Card 87-112253 DDC 338.9 19
HD41 .A755 1986

Cooper, Russell W., 1955- Wage and employment patterns in labor contracts . Chur, Switzerland , New York , c1987. viii, 80 p. : ISBN 3-7186-0378-0 (pbk.) LC Card 86-31947 DDC 331.12/5 19
HD4909 .C57 1987

Unemployment, hysteresis, and the natural rate hypothesis . Oxford, UK , New York, NY, USA , 1987. p. cm. ISBN 0-631-15688-7 : LC Card 87-14071 DDC 331.13/7 19
HD5707.5 .U555 1987

EMPLOYMENT (ECONOMIC THEORY) - CONGRESSES.

Staat und Beschäftigung . Nürnberg , 1985. 471 p. : LC Card 86-674027
HD5713 .S72x 1985

Unemployment . Berlin , New York , 1987. xx, 353 p. : ISBN 0-89925-277-X : LC Card 87-24369 DDC 331.13/7 19
HD5701.3 .U53 1987

EMPLOYMENT (ECONOMIC THEORY) - DATA PROCESSING.

Fiorito, Riccardo, 1947- Mercato del lavoro e politica economica . Venezia , 1984. 247 p. : ISBN 88-317-4733-9 : LC Card 86-163951
HD5701.6 .F56 1984

EMPLOYMENT (ECONOMIC THEORY) - ECONOMETRIC MODELS.

Fiorito, Riccardo, 1947- Mercato del lavoro e politica economica . Venezia , 1984. 247 p. : ISBN 88-317-4733-9 : LC Card 86-163951
HD5701.6 .F56 1984

EMPLOYMENT (ECONOMIC THEORY) - MATHEMATICAL MODELS.

Fiorito, Riccardo, 1947- Mercato del lavoro e politica economica . Venezia , 1984. 247 p. : ISBN 88-317-4733-9 : LC Card 86-163951
HD5701.6 .F56 1984

Silva, Adroaldo Moura da. Emprego e preços no curto prazo /. São Paulo, SP (C.P. 11474, 01000 São Paulo, SP) , 1983. 94 p. ; *NYPL [JLD 86-3819]*

Employment equity . Coates, Mary Lou. Kingston, Ont., Canada , 1986. 109 p. : ISBN 0-88886-131-1 (pbk.) LC Card 86-182985 DDC 331.13/3/0971 19
HD4903.5.C2 C6 1986

Employment equity for crown corporations : policy and reference guide / Treasury Board of Canada, Secretariat. Ottawa : Human Resources Division, Personnel Policy Branch, 1986. 17, 18 p. ; 28 cm. English and French. Title on added t.p.: L'équité en matière d'emploi dans les sociétés d'Etat. Includes bibliographies. ISBN 0-662-54400-5 (pbk.) LC Card 86-207179 DDC 354.71001/04 19
1. Discrimination in employment - Canada. 2. Corporations, Government - Canada - Personnel management. I. Canada. Treasury Board. II. Title: Equité en matière d'emploi dans les sociétés d'Etat.
HD4903.5.C2 E47 1986

Employment forecasting : the employment problem in industrialised countries / edited by M.J.D. Hopkins. London ; New York : Pinter Publishers, c1988. p. cm. "A study prepared for the International Labour Office within the framework of the World Employment Programme." Papers presented at a workshop held in Geneva in Sept. 1983. Includes bibliographies and index. ISBN 0-86187-938-4 : LC Card 87-21882 DDC 331.12/094 19
1. Employment forecasting - Europe - Congresses. 2. Unemployment - Europe - Congresses. I. Hopkins, Mike. II. International Labour Office. III. World Employment Programme.
HD5764 .E47 1988

EMPLOYMENT FORECASTING.

Baethge, Martin. Zukunft der Angestellten . Frankfurt , New York , c1986. 460 p. : ISBN 3-593-33368-6 (pbk.) LC Card 87-673317
HD5707 .B28x 1986

Forecasting skilled-manpower needs . Paris , 1985. 259 p. : ISBN 92-803-1122-3 (pbk.) LC Card 86-214025 DDC 331.12/3 19
HD5701.55 .F67 1985

Jobs for the '90s [videorecording] /. Pleasantville, NY , 1987. 1 videocassette (48 min.) : LC Card 87-705264 DDC 331.7 11
HF5382

Richter, Lothar. Training needs . Geneva , 1986. viii, 83 p. : ISBN 92-2-105458-6 (pbk.) : LC Card 86-222104 DDC 331.25/92 19
HD5715 .R53 1986

EMPLOYMENT FORECASTING - ALASKA - STATISTICS.

Alaska occupational information /. Juneau, Alaska , 1986. 126 p. : LC Card 86-623154 DDC 331.12/09798/021 19
HD5725.A4 A62 1986

EMPLOYMENT FORECASTING - ARKANSAS.

Occupational trends, 1982-1995. Little Rock, AR (P.O. Box 2981, Little Rock, AR 72203) [1986]- v. ; *NYPL [JLM 87-353]*

EMPLOYMENT FORECASTING - CHINA.

Taylor, Jeffrey R., 1954- Employment outlook for China to the year 2000 /. Washington, D.C. [1986] 43 leaves, 2 p. ; LC Card 87-601289 DDC 331.12/3/0951021 19
HD5830.A6 T375 1986

EMPLOYMENT FORECASTING - CONGRESSES.

Freedman, Audrey. Perspectives on employment /. New York, N.Y. (845 3rd Ave., New York 10022) , c1986. 15 p. : LC Card 86-212384 DDC 331.12 19
HD5701.3 .F74 1986

EMPLOYMENT FORECASTING - EUROPE - CONGRESSES.

Employment forecasting . London , New York , c1988. p. cm. ISBN 0-86187-938-4 : LC Card 87-21882 DDC 331.12/094 19
HD5764 .E47 1988

EMPLOYMENT FORECASTING - GERMANY, WEST.

Raumordnungsprognose 1990 . Bonn-Bad-Godesberg , 1977. 95 p. : LC Card 86-100310
HB3595 .R38 1977

EMPLOYMENT FORECASTING - GREAT BRITAIN.

UK occupation and employment trends to 1990 . London , Boston , 1986. xxiv, 249 p. : ISBN 0-408-02980-3 : LC Card 86-13617 DDC 331.12/0941 19
HD5765.A6 U38 1986 *NYPL [JLE 86-4156]*

EMPLOYMENT FORECASTING - ILLINOIS.

Illinois . [Springfield, Ill. , 1985] 155 p. : LC Card 85-622626 DDC 338.9773 19
HD5725.I3 I517 1985 *NYPL [JLF 87-787]*

EMPLOYMENT FORECASTING - IOWA - STATISTICS.

Industry projections, occupational projections, 1985-1988, State of Iowa. [Iowa City] [1986] [42] leaves ; LC Card 86-622540 DDC 331.12/09777/021 19
HD5725.I8 I53 1986

Labor market information for Iowa (Job Training Partnership Act), State of Iowa. Des Moines, Iowa (1000 E. Grand Ave., Des Moines 50319) [1986] 125 p. : LC Card 86-622289 DDC 331.1/09777 19
HD5725.I8 L34 1986

Occupational projections, 1984-1995 . [Des Moines?] [1985] 16 v. in 1 ; LC Card 86-621925 DDC 331.12/09777/021 19
HD5725.I8 O26 1985

EMPLOYMENT FORECASTING - MAINE - STATISTICS.
Maine occupational employment in 1984 and projected to 1995 /. Auqusta, Me. (20 Union St., Augusta 04330) [1986] 32 leaves ; LC Card 87-620754 DDC 331.12/09741/021 19
HD5725.M3 M386 1986

EMPLOYMENT FORECASTING - MARYLAND - STATISTICS.
Employment and labor force in Maryland . Baltimore, Md. (301 W. Preston St., Baltimore) [1986] xliv, 164, [51] p. : LC Card 86-622107 DDC 331.12/5/09752 19
HD5725.M35 E43 1986

EMPLOYMENT FORECASTING - MASSACHUSETTS.
Foley, Catherine. Massachusetts job outlook, occupational employment projected changes, 1984 to 1995 /. [Boston, MA] [1987] vi, 59 p. : LC Card 87-621850 DDC 331.12/5/09744021 19
HD5725.M4 F65 1987

EMPLOYMENT FORECASTING - MASSACHUSETTS - STATISTICS.
Foley, Catherine. Massachusetts industrial employment projected changes, 1984-1995 /. [Boston] [1986] vi leaves, 37 p. : LC Card 87-620528 DDC 331.12/5/09744 19
HD5725.M4 F64 1986

EMPLOYMENT FORECASTING - MONTANA - STATISTICS.
Montana industry and occupational employment outlook, 1984-1990 /. Helena, MT (P.O. Box 1728, Helena 59624) [1986] 100 p. : LC Card 86-622364 DDC 331.12/09786/021 19
HD5725.M9 M665 1986

EMPLOYMENT FORECASTING - NEBRASKA - STATISTICS.
Greater Nebraska job prospects, 1983-1988 /. [Lincoln, Neb.] [1985] ii, 54 p. : LC Card 86-622213 DDC 331.12/09781/021 19
HD5725.N2 G74 1985

[Nebraska job prospects] 1983-1988. [Lincoln, Neb. (550 South 16th St., Lincoln 68509) , <1985- >] v. <1, 5-9 > : LC Card 86-622062 DDC 331.12/09782/021 19
HD5725.N2 N474 1985

EMPLOYMENT FORECASTING - NETHERLANDS.
Enige aspecten van arbeid in de toekomst . 's-Gravenhage , 1986. 178 p. : ISBN 90-12-05246-7 LC Card 87-101491
HD5792 .E47 1986

EMPLOYMENT FORECASTING - NEVADA - STATISTICS.
Nevada occupational information system . [Carson City, Nev.] (505 E. King St., Carson City 89710) [1986] vii, 385 p. : LC Card 86-622271 DDC 331.12/09793/021 19
HD5725.N3 N45843 1986

EMPLOYMENT FORECASTING - NEW JERSEY - STATISTICS.
Sheppard, Thomas M. Occupational outlook for New Jersey and JTPA labor market areas, 1982-1990 [microform]. Trenton, N.J. [1984] ii leaves, 50 p. ; LC Card 84-623480 DDC 331.12/09749 19
HD5725.N5 S47 1984
NYPL [*ZT-1745 no.24]

EMPLOYMENT FORECASTING - NEW ZEALAND.
Towards forecasting manpower requirements. Wellington [N.Z.] [1977] 90 p. : LC Card 85-184797
HD5850.4.A6 T69 1977

EMPLOYMENT FORECASTING - NORWAY.
Schreiner, Alette. Virkninger av oljevirksomhet i Nord-Norge /. Oslo , 1984. 43 p. : ISBN 82-537-2118-8 : LC Card 85-146089
HD9575.N62 S37 1984

EMPLOYMENT FORECASTING - NORWAY - AUST-AGDER FYLKE.
Fylkesplan for Aust-Agder . [Norway] [1983] 125 p. : LC Card 84-146306
HD5800.A95 F95 1983

EMPLOYMENT FORECASTING - NORWAY - MØRE OG ROMSDAL FYLKE.
4-årige arbeidskraftprognoser, Møre og Romsdal 1983-1986(1987). [Molde] [1983?] 59 p. ; LC Card 84-146499
HD5800.M67 A14 1983

EMPLOYMENT FORECASTING - NORWAY - TELEMARK FYLKE.
4-årig arbeidskraftprognose for perioden 1983-1987, Telemark fylke. [Telemark] [1983] 154 leaves ; LC Card 84-145787
HD5800.T44 A14 1983

EMPLOYMENT FORECASTING - PENNSYLVANIA.
Pennsylvania occupational trends and outlook for total civilian employment, 1980 and projected 1990 /. Harrisburg, Pa. , 1984. ii, 98 p. : ***NYPL [JLF 87-706]***

EMPLOYMENT FORECASTING - QUÉBEC (PROVINCE)
Messier, Suzanne. Perspectives d'emploi pour les Québécoises dans la décennie 1980 . Québec [1983] vi, 73 p. ; ISBN 2-550-10439-0 LC Card 84-221697
HD6100.Q4 M47 1983

EMPLOYMENT FORECASTING - SOUTH CAROLINA.
Meeting labor needs in South Carolina . Columbia, S.C. (2221 Devine St., Suite 420, Columbia 29205) [1986] 52 leaves ; LC Card 86-623031 DDC 331.12/3/09757 19
HD5725.S6 M44 1986

EMPLOYMENT FORECASTING - SOUTHERN STATES - CONGRESSES.
Critical employment issues facing the Southeast /. Atlanta, Ga. , 1986. xv, 156 p. ; ISBN 0-88406-191-4 LC Card 85-31410 DDC 331.12/5/0975 19
HD5725.S85 C75 1986
NYPL [JLD 86-2441]

EMPLOYMENT FORECASTING - STATISTICS.
Economically active population . Geneva , 1986- v. ; ISBN 92-2-005345-4 (v. 1)
NYPL [JLM 87-113]

Economically active population estimates and projections, 1950-2025 =. Geneva [1986]- v. <1-5 > ; ISBN 92-2-005345-4 (pbk. : v. 1) : LC Card 86-223275 DDC 331.12/021 19
HD5712 .E26 1986

EMPLOYMENT FORECASTING - SWEDEN.
Sveriges arbetskraft . Stockholm , Örebro [1986] 62 p. : ISBN 91-618-0162-3 : LC Card 87-151800
HD5803 .S943 1986

Trender och prognoser inför 90-talet. Stockholm , Örebro , 1985. 147 p. : ISBN 91-618-0001-5 LC Card 86-115921
LB2833 .S9 1985:2 HC375
NYPL [JLG 86-230]

EMPLOYMENT FORECASTING - UNITED STATES.
Employment policies . Washington, D.C. , 1986. 16, [2] p. ; ISBN 0-88713-611-7 (pbk.) LC Card 87-127759 DDC 331.12/042/0973 19
HD5724 .E449 1986

Employment projections for 1995 . Washington, D.C. , 1986. v, 131 p. : LC Card 86-602460 DDC 331.12/0723 19
HD5724 .E47 1986

EMPLOYMENT FORECASTING - UNITED STATES - ECONOMETRIC MODELS.
Drennan, Matthew P., 1937- Modeling metropolitan economies for forecasting and policy analysis /. New York , 1985. x, 242 p. ; ISBN 0-8147-1781-0 (alk. paper) : LC Card 85-13784 DDC 330.9173/2 19
HT321 .D74 1985 ***NYPL [JLE 86-1102]***

EMPLOYMENT FORECASTING - WASHINGTON (STATE) - PUGET SOUND REGION - STATISTICS.
Pethick, Donald R. Population and employment forecasts and distribution for the central Puget Sound region, 1975-1990 /. Seattle, Wash. [1969] 26 p., [2] leaves of plates : LC Card 87-400702 DDC 304.6/2/097977021 19
HA697.P84 P47 1969

EMPLOYMENT FORECASTING - WEST VIRGINIA - STATISTICS.
State of West Virginia Job Training Partnership Act . Charleston, W.Va. (112 California Ave., Charleston 25305-0112) [1986] vi, 233 p. ; LC Card 86-622901 DDC 331.1/09754/021 19
HD5725.W4 S7 1986

EMPLOYMENT, FREE CHOICE OF. see **FREE CHOICE OF EMPLOYMENT.**

Employment implications of agricultural growth /. Namdar, Shamim A. Lahore , 1980. 82 leaves : LC Card 84-930891 DDC 331.12/93/0954914 19
HD1537.P2 N36 1980 ***NYPL [JLF 86-1956]***

Employment, income, and housing /. Mulkh Raj. New Delhi , 1987. viii, 130 p. : ISBN 81-7000-025-4 : LC Card 87-901029 DDC 331.12/5/0954 19
HD7361.A3 M85 1987

Employment, income distribution, and consumption patterns in Nepal : results of a survey conducted by the National Planning Commission, Nepal, March-July 1977. Kathmandu, Nepal : His Majesty's Govt., National Planning Commission Secretariat, 1983. xiv, 122 p. ; 30 cm. Cover title: A survey of employment, income distribution, and consumption patterns in Nepal. LC Card 84-901199 DDC 330.9549/6 19
1. Labor supply - Nepal. 2. Income distribution - Nepal. 3. Consumption (Economics) - Nepal. I. Title: Survey of employment, income distribution, and consumption patterns in Nepal.
HD5812.9.A6 E47 1983
NYPL [JLF 86-1993]

Employment information series .
(no. 16) Historical trends in job vacancies by major occupation groups . Toronto, Ont. [1976] 26 p. : LC Card 82-213963 DDC 331.2 s 331.12/4/09713021 19
HD5729.O6 E46 no. 16

Employment injuries and occupational illnesses : federal jurisdiction industries and the Federal Government, 1981-1984 = Les accidents du travail et les maladies professionnelles: les secteurs d'activité de ressort fédéral et le gouvernement fédéral, 1981-1984. [3rd ed.] Ottawa, Ont. : Labour Canada, c1986. 92 p. ; 29 cm. English and French. ISBN 0-662-54738-1 (pbk.) LC Card 87-147113 DDC 363.1/12/0971 19
1. Industrial accidents - Canada - Statistics. 2. Occupational diseases - Canada - Statistics. 3. Government business enterprises - Canada - Employees - Statistics. I. Canada. Labour Canada. II. Title: Accidents du travail et les maladies professionnelles.
HD7262.5.C3 E463 1986

EMPLOYMENT INTERVIEWING.
Bezanson, H. A. (Harold A.), 1935- How to successfully win job interviews . Blaine, WA , c1986. 106 leaves : ISBN 0-9691828-0-5 (pbk.) : LC Card 86-31689 DDC 650.1/4 19
HF5549.5.I6 B48 1986

Biegeleisen, J. I. (Jacob Israel), 1910- Make your job interview a success . New York , c1987. 222 p. : ISBN 0-13-545716-5 : LC Card 87-19294 DDC 650.1/4 19
HF5549.5.I6 B5 1987

Gerberg, Robert J. [Job changing system.] Robert Gerberg's job changing system . Kansas City , c1986. xxii, 265 p. : ISBN 0-8362-7932-8 : LC Card 86-17298 DDC 650.1/4 19
NYPL [JD 87-125]

Hodgson, Philip. Interviewing skills /. London , New York , c1987. p. cm. ISBN 0-07-084941-2 : LC Card 87-3658 DDC 658.3/1124 19
HF5549.5.I6 H58 1987

Kohlmann, James D. Make them choose you . Englewood Cliffs, N.J. , c1988. xiv, 178 p. ; ISBN 0-13-547878-2 LC Card 87-17435 DDC 650.1/4 19
HF5549.5.I6 K58 1988

Moffatt, Thomas L. Selection interviewing for managers /. Madison, Wis. , c1987. x, 196 : ISBN 0-910239-08-8 : LC Card 86-26313 DDC 658.3/112 19
HF5549.5.I6 M64 1987

Payne, Richard A. How to get a better job quicker /. New York , 1987. x, 242 p. ; ISBN 0-8008-3965-X : LC Card 86-23101 DDC 650.1/4 19
HF5383 .P36 1987

Rae, Leslie. The skills of interviewing /. New York, N.Y. , 1988. p. cm. ISBN 0-89397-293-2 : LC Card 87-25066 DDC 658.3/1124 19
HF5549.5.I6 R34 1988

Résumés that get interviews, interviews that get jobs [videorecording] /. Mt. Kisco, NY , 1986, c1987. 1 videocassette (42 min.) : LC Card 86-707973 DDC 650.1 11
HF5383

Structured hiring . New York, NY, U. S.A. , c1987. viii leaves, 144 p. : ISBN 0-86604-221-0 (pbk.) LC Card 87-156398 DDC 658.3/112 19
HF5549.5.R44 S83 1987

EMPLOYMENT INTERVIEWING - ANECDOTES, FACETIAE, SATIRE, ETC.
Real inside [motion picture] /. Deerfield, IL , 1985. 1 film reel (12 min.) : LC Card 87-705522 DDC 791.43 11
HF5549.5.I6

Real inside [videorecording] /. Deerfield, IL, 1985. 1 videocassette (12 min.) : LC Card 87-705515 DDC 791.43 11
HF5549.5.I6

EMPLOYMENT INTERVIEWING - UNITED STATES.
Lewis, Diane, 1936- The insider's guide to finding the right job /. Nashville , c1987. 190 p. ; ISBN 0-8407-3107-8 (pbk.) : LC Card 86-33305 DDC 650.1/4 19
HF5382.75.U6 L49 1987

Employment maintenance and unemployment protection for young workers. Jonshagen, I. [Geneva , 1980] 102, 69 p. : LC Card 86-219323 DDC 368.4/4 19
HD7095 .J66 1980

EMPLOYMENT MANAGEMENT. see **PERSONNEL MANAGEMENT.**

EMPLOYMENT MANAGEMENT - COUNSELING. see **EMPLOYEE COUNSELING.**

EMPLOYMENT - MATHEMATICAL MODELS.
Borgmeier, Bernd, 1955- Der Einfluss verschiedener Preisbildungsmechanismen auf die gesamtwirtschfliche Beschäftigung /. Frankfurt am Main , New York , c1984. 362 p. : ISBN 3-8204-5601-5 : LC Card 85-198888
HB221 .B592 1984

EMPLOYMENT OF CHILDREN. see **CHILDREN - EMPLOYMENT.**

EMPLOYMENT OF MEN - NETHERLANDS.
Boon, Irene. Mannen in een vrouwenberoep . Den Haag , 1984. 139 p. : ISBN 90-6252-426-5 : LC Card 84-243593
Z682.4.W65 B66 1984 ***NYPL [JLG 87-4]***

EMPLOYMENT OF MEN - UNITED STATES - LONGITUDINAL STUDIES.
The Changing labor market . Lexington, Mass. , c1986. x, 166 p. : ISBN 0-669-11943-1 (alk. paper) LC Card 85-45710 DDC 331.12/0973 19
HD6331.2.U5 C47 1986
NYPL [JLE 86-1069]

EMPLOYMENT OF WIVES. see **WIVES - EMPLOYMENT.**

EMPLOYMENT OF WOMEN. see **WOMEN - EMPLOYMENT.**

EMPLOYMENT OF YOUTH. see **YOUTH - EMPLOYMENT.**

EMPLOYMENT OPPORTUNITIES. see **JOB VACANCIES.**

Employment outlook for China to the year 2000 /. Taylor, Jeffrey R., 1954- Washington, D.C. [1986] 43 leaves, 2 p. ; LC Card 87-601289 DDC 331.12/3/0951021 19
HD5830.A6 T375 1986

EMPLOYMENT, PART-TIME. see **PART-TIME EMPLOYMENT.**

Employment policies : looking to the year 2000 / National Alliance of Business. Washington, D.C. : National Alliance of Business, 1986. 16, [2] p. ; 28 cm. Bibliography: p. 2 (2nd group) ISBN 0-88713-611-7 (pbk.) LC Card 87-127759 DDC 331.12/042/0973 19
1. Employment forecasting - United States. 2. Labor supply - United States. I. National Alliance of Business.
HD5724 .E449 1986

Employment policy . Tomlinson, Jim. Oxford [Oxfordshire] , New York , 1987. xi, 185 p. ; ISBN 0-19-828564-7 : LC Card 87-7837 DDC 339.5/0941 19
HC256.4 .T586 1987

Employment policy and job creation in and through the construction industry : Building, Civil Engineering, and Public Works Committee, eleventh session, Geneva, 1987. Geneva : International Labour Office, 1986. vi, 110 p. : ill. ; 30 cm. "This report has been prepared by the International Labour Office to serve as a basis for discussion by the Building, Civil Engineering, and Public Works Committee of the International Labour Organisation at its 11th Session in April 1987"--Introd. At head of title: International Labour Organisation, Sectoral Activities Programme. "Report II." Includes bibliographies. ISBN 92-2-105709-7 (pbk.) : LC Card 87-167960 DDC 331.12/924 19
1. Construction industry. 2. Construction workers - Supply and demand. I. International Labour Office. II. International Labour Organisation. Building, Civil Engineering, and Public Works Committee. III. International Labour Organisation. Sectoral Activities Programme.
HD9715.A2 E42 1986

Employment problems and America's cities /. Barnes, William R. [Washington, D.C.] , 1984. xiii, 66, 33 p. ; ***NYPL [JLF 86-1]***

Employment projections for 1995 : data and methods. Washington, D.C. : U. S. Dept. of Labor, Bureau of Labor Statistics : For sale by the Supt. of Docs., U. S. G.P.O., 1986. v, 131 p. : ill. ; 28 cm. (Bulletin . 2253) Shipping list no.: 86-432-P. "April 1986." Includes bibliographical references. S/N 029-001-02897-1 Item 768-A-1 LC Card 86-602460 DDC 331.12/0723 19
1. Employment forecasting - United States. 2. Labor supply - United States. I. United States. Bureau of Labor Statistics. II. Series: Bulletin (United States. Bureau of Labor Statistics) , 2253.
HD5724 .E47 1986

Employment promotion and social security : fourth item on the agenda, report IV,(1). Geneva : International Labour Office, 1986. iv, 156 p. ; 24 cm. At head of title: International Labour Conference, 73rd Session, 1987. ISBN 92-2-105574-4 (pbk.) : LC Card 86-234498 DDC 368.4/4 19
1. Insurance, Unemployment - Congresses. 2. Full employment policies - Congresses. I. International Labour Office. II. International Labour Conference (73rd : 1986 : Geneva, Switzerland).
HD7095 .E46 1986

Employment promotion in Tanzania : prospects in the rural and informal sectors. Addis Ababa : International Labour Organisation, Jobs and Skills Programme for Africa, 1986. ii leaves, 107 p. ; 30 cm. LC Card 87-980150 DDC 331.11/09678 19
1. Manpower policy - Tanzania. 2. Informal sector (Economics) - Tanzania. 3. Tanzania - Economic conditions - 1964-. 4. Rural development - Tanzania. I. Jobs and Skills Programme for Africa.
HD5841.3.A6 E46 1986

EMPLOYMENT STABILIZATION.
Driver, Ciaran. Towards full employment . London , New York , 1987. xii, 238 p. : ISBN 0-7102-0918-5 LC Card 87-9814 DDC 339.5 19
HD5713.2 .D75 1987

EMPLOYMENT SUBSIDIES - UNITED STATES.
Startzel, Donna C. The CETA arts and humanities experience [microform] CETA Ahead project (Arts and humanities employment analysis and documentation) /. Columbia, Md. , 1981. 197 p. ;
NYPL [*XME-11,320]

Startzel, Donna C. CETA (Comprehensive Employment and Training Act) and the arts and humanities [microform] . Columbia, Md. , 1981. 160 p. ; ***NYPL [*XME-11,328]***

EMPLOYMENT, SUPPLEMENTARY. see **SUPPLEMENTARY EMPLOYMENT.**

EMPLOYMENT TESTS.
Venne, Rosemary Amelia, 1956- Psychological testing in personnel selection /. Kingston, Ont., Canada , 1987. 65 p. ; ISBN 0-88886-152-4 (pbk.) LC Card 87-163203 DDC 658.3/1125 19
HF5549.5.E5 V46 1987

Employment, the community link /. Wiechec, Jane. Perth, W.A. [1986] 108 p. ; LC Card 87-158082 DDC 331.12/5/09941 19
HD5850.W4 W54 1986

EMPLOYMENT - WOMEN - EUROPEAN ECONOMIC COMMUNITY COUNTRIES.
The Viability of employment initiatives involving women . Luxembourg , Washington, DC , 1986. 1 v. (various pagings) ; ISBN 92-825-6088-0 (pbk.) : LC Card 87-137342 DDC 331.4/12/094 19
HD3423.5.E86 V5 1986

Emprego e preços no curto prazo /. Silva, Adroaldo Moura da. São Paulo, SP (C.P. 11474, 01000 São Paulo, SP) , 1983. 94 p. ; ***NYPL [JLD 86-3819]***

O Emprego no Rio Grande do Sul : RAIS, PNAD e PME / Beatriz Regina Zago de Azevedo, org. ... [et al.]. Porto Alegre : Secretaria de Coordenação e Planejamento, Fundação de Economia e Estatística, 1985. 163 p. : ill. ; 23 cm. Includes bibliographies. LC Card 85-207909
1. Labor supply - Brazil - Rio Grande do Sul. 2. Underemployment - Brazil - Rio Grande do Sul. 3. Manpower policy - Brazil - Rio Grande do Sul. 4. Household surveys - Brazil - Rio Grande do Sul. 5. Economic surveys - Brazil - Rio Grande do Sul. I. Azevedo, Beatriz Regina Zago de. II. Rio Grande do Sul (Brazil). Fundação de Economia e Estatística.
HD5755.R54 E46 1985

Emprego urgente / [Cláudio Salm ... et al.]. Curitiba : Fundação Edison Vieira, Instituto Paranaense de Desenvolvimento Econômico e Social, apoio, Secretaria de Estado do Planejamento, Conselho Estadual de Ciência e Tecnologia, 1984. vii, 75 p. ; 30 cm. Includes bibliographies. LC Card 86-177208
1. Manpower policy. 2. Labor supply. 3. Manpower policy - Brazil. 4. Labor supply - Brazil. I. Salm, Cláudio. II. Fundação Edison Vieira. III. Paraná (Brazil : State). Conselho Estadual de Ciência e Tecnologia.
HD5713 .E47 1984

La Empresa. Madrid : Instituto de Estudios Políticos, 1962. 348 p. : ill. ; 22 cm. (Colección Estudios de trabajo y prevision) Papers presented at the Ciclo de Conferencias sobre "La Empresa," held at the Instituto de Estudios Políticos, Nov. 1961-Feb. 1962. Includes bibliographical references. LC Card 85-108024
1. Business enterprises - Spain - Congresses. 2. Government business enterprises - Spain - Congresses. 3. Agricultural industries - Spain - Congresses. I. Instituto de Estudios Políticos (Spain). II. Ciclo de Conferencias sobre "La Empresa" (1961-1962 : Instituto de Estudios Políticos).
HD2326 .E47 1962

EMPRESA BRASILEIRA DE AERONÁUTICA.
Green, Ronald D. Brazilian government support for the aerospace industry /. [Washington, D.C.?] [1987] xi, 44 p. ; LC Card 87-601479 DDC 338.4/76291/0981 19
HD9711.B72 G74 1987

Empresa Brasileira de Planejamento de Transportes. Estudo sobre o transporte rodioviário de carga. [Brasília] , 1984- v. <1- > : LC Card 87-403695 DDC 388.3/24/0981021 19
HE5653.A6 E85 1984

Empresa Brasileira dos Transportes Urbanos. Daibert, José Ricardo Motta. Avaliação do desempenho de transporte coletivo por ônibus /. Brasília, DF , 1985. 73 p. : LC Card 87-113224 DDC 388.4/1322/0981 19
HE5653.A6 D35 1985

Empresa de Assistência Técnica e Extensão Rural do Estado de Alagoas. Distribuição da produção dos principais produtos agropecuários do Estado de Alagoas. [S.l.] [198-] [29] p. : LC Card 86-179132
HD9014.B83 A653 1980z

EMPRESA DE LOS FERROCARRILES DEL ESTADO (CHILE) - HISTORY.
Poblete, Martiniano O. Una jornada ferroviaria . Santiago de Chile , 1930. 2 v. : LC Card

87-162075 DDC 385/.0983 19
HE2940.F47 P63 1930

La empresa española ante el impuesto sobre el valor añadido, medidas de adaptación y ajuste /. Lampreave Pérez, José Luis. Madrid, España , 1985. 493 p. : ISBN 84-7196-571-2 : LC Card 86-208329
HJ5715.S7 L36 1985

Empresa forte, mais trabalho . Federação do Comércio Varejista do Estado do Paraná. [Curitiba] , 1983. 67 leaves : LC Card 83-225279
HF5429.6.B7 F44 1983

EMPRESA MINERA CATAVI.
Desabastecimiento de alimentos y alternativas de solución en las minas . La Paz [Bolivia] , 1986. 128 : LC Card 87-401454 DDC 331.7/6223453/098413 19
HD8039.M72 B624 1986

Empresas del sector social de la economía /. Burgos Flores, Sigfrido. [S.l.] 1986 ([S.l.] : Lithopress Industrial) 237 p. : LC Card 87-400831 DDC 334 19
HD2956 .B85 1986

Empresas estatais na Bahia. Salvador, Bahia, Brasil : Secretaria do Planejamento, Ciência e Tecnologia, Centro de Projetos e Estudos, 1986. 134 p. : ill. ; 21 cm. Prepared by Oswaldo Guerra and others. Includes bibliographies. LC Card 87-137490 DDC 338.6/2/098142 19
1. Government business enterprises - Brazil - Bahia (State). I. Guerra, Oswaldo. II. Centro de Projetos e Estudos (Bahia, Brazil).
HD4095.B33 E47 1986

As empresas estatais na economia brasileira /. Penna, João Camilo de Oliveira. [Brasília] , 1983. 43 p. ; LC Card 86-229392
HD4093 .P46 1983

Empresas multinacionales y división internacional del trabajo / Eugène Heymann ... [et al.]. Salamanca : Ediciones Sígueme, 1977. 158 p. : ill. ; 22 cm. (Tierra dos tercios . 2) Includes bibliographical references. ISBN 84-301-0465-8 LC Card 86-164261
1. International business enterprises. 2. International business enterprises - Developing countries. 3. International division of labor. I. Heymann, Eugène.
HD2755.5 .E49 1977

Las empresas públicas en Panamá . Mock Cedeño, Ariel. Panamá, Rep. de Panamá , 1986. vi, 89, [5] p. ; LC Card 87-400433 DDC 338.97287 19
HD4043 .M63 1986

Las Empresas transnacionales en el desarrollo colombiano. 1a ed. Santiago de Chile : Comisión Económica para América Latina y el Caribe, Naciones Unidas ; Nueva York, NY : [Distributed in the U. S. by] Publicaciones de las Naciones Unidas, Sección de Ventas, 1986. 218 p. : ill. ; 23 cm. (Estudios e informes de la CEPAL, 0256-9795 . 60) "Publicación de las Naciones Unidas, número de venta: S.86.II.G.14"--T.p. verso. Bibliography: p. 149-161. "LC/G.1432, septiembre de 1986"--T.p. verso. ISBN 92-1-321213-5 LC Card 87-402186 DDC 338.8/88861 19
1. International business enterprises - Colombia - History - 20th century. 2. Colombia - Economic conditions - 1918-. I. United Nations. Economic Commission for Latin America and the Caribbean. II. Series.
HD2837 .E47 1986

Las empresas transnacionales en la economía del Paraguay. Parquet, Reinerio. Santiago de Chile , 1987. 115 p. ; ISBN 92-1-321223-2 LC Card 87-404657 DDC 338.8/88892 19
HG5382 .P37 1987

Empty promises . Wells, Don, 1946- New York , c1987. xviii, 167 p. ; ISBN 0-85345-710-7 : LC Card 87-24687 DDC 331.25 19
HD6957.U6 W34 1987

Empty stomachs and packed godowns . Dogra, Bharat. New Delhi , 1987. viii, 126 p. ; LC Card 87-900472 DDC 338.1/9/54 19
HD9016.I42 D64 1987

En defensa de la empresa . Pascual, Julio, 1944- Madrid , c1984. 242 p. ; ISBN 84-7209-175-9 LC Card 85-215607
HD3616.S49 P34 1984
NYPL [JLD 87-1507]

En Espagne . Demanche, Georges, b. 1855. Paris , 1883. 40 p. ; LC Card 85-665876
HE3195 .D45x 1883

Enclavement et sous-développement au Burundi : actes du colloque tenu dans le cadre de la semaine de l'université du 4-10 avril 1981. Bujumbura, Burundi : Université du Burundi, Faculté des sciences économiques et administratives, [1983] xi, 448 p. : ill. ; 30 cm. "Février 1983." Bibliography: p. [405]-427. LC Card 85-980729 DDC 338.967/572 19
1. Transit, International - Burundi - Congresses. 2. Burundi - Commerce - Congresses. 3. Burundi - Economic policy. I. Université du Burundi. Faculté des sciences économiques et administratives.
HE283.8 .E53 1983

Enclosures in Britain, 1750-1830 /. Turner, Michael Edward. London , 1984. 96 p. : ISBN 0-333-31682-7 (pbk.) LC Card 86-673799
HD594.6 .T84x 1984

ENCOMIENDAS (LATIN AMERICA)
Ovando, Jorge. El tributo indígena en las finanzas bolivianas del siglo XIX /. La Paz, Bolivia [1985] 565 p. : ***NYPL [JLC 86-407]***

Encontro de Trabalho sobre Descentralização dos Serviços Municipais (1983 : Rio de Janeiro, Brazil) Relatório final / Encontro de Trabalho sobre Descentralização dos Serviços Municipais ; promovido pelo IBAM-Instituto Brasileiro de Administração Municipal, através do CDM-Centro de Desenvolvimento Cívico e Municipal, Rio de Janeiro, maio de 1983. [Rio de Janeiro] : IBAM, [1983] 60 leaves ; 30 cm. Includes bibliographical references. LC Card 84-160735
1. Municipal services - Brazil - Congresses. 2. Municipal government - Brazil - Congresses. 3. Decentralization in government - Brazil - Congresses. I. Instituto Brasileiro de Administração Municipal. II. Centro de Desenvolvimento Cívico e Municipal do IBAM. III. Title.
HD4634 .E53 1983

Encontro Estadual de Cooperativismo (1979 : Curitiba, Brazil) Anais / Encontro Estadual de Cooperativismo, Curitiba, 05 e 06/07/79. [Curitiba] : OCEPAR, [1979] 41 leaves : ill. ; 32 cm. Cover title. LC Card 84-223142
1. Cooperation - Brazil - Paraná (State) - Congresses. I. Organização das Cooperativas do Estado do Paraná. II. Title.
HD3475.A3 P364 1979

Encounter file series.
Nedlog, D'Lanor. Insider's guide to antique bazaars in Japan /. Tokyo, Japan , c1986. 124 p. : ISBN 4-906231-00-4 LC Card 87-123282 DDC 381/.18 19
HF5475.J3 N43 1986

Encouraging cooperation among competitors . Tye, William B. New York , 1987. xix, 202 p. : ISBN 0-89930-246-7 (lib. bdg. : alk. paper) LC Card 86-25554 DDC 388.3/24 19
HE5623 .T94 1987

Encuentro de Historia y Realidad Económica y Social del Ecuador (5th : 1986 : Cuenca, Ecuador) La Crisis de la economía ecuatoriana . Quito , 1986. 232 p. : LC Card 87-400395 DDC 330.9866/074 19
HC202 .C755 1986

Encuentro-Debate sobre las Investigaciones Agrarias en el Area Andina (1985 : Quito, Ecuador) Investigación agraria y crisis . Quito , 1986. 498 p. : LC Card 87-400125 DDC 338.1/098 19
HD1860.A53 I58 1986

Encuentro Latinoamericano de Pastoral Social (1986 : Bogotá, Colombia) El mundo del trabajo : esperanza y compromiso : América Latina escucha la "Laborem exercens" : Encuentro Latinoamericano de Pastoral Social y conmemoración del quinto aniversario de la Laborem exercens : homenaje filial del CELAM al santo padre Juan Pablo II. 1a ed. Bogotá : Consejo Episcopal Latinoamericano, 1986. 92 p. ; 21 cm. (Documentos CELAM . no. 82) CONTENTS. - Encuentro Latinoamericano de Pastoral Social (sesión inaugural) -- Acto conmemorativo del V aniversario de la "Laborem exercens". ISBN 958-625-053-9 LC Card 87-400623 DDC 261.8/5 19
1. Catholic Church. Pope (1978- : John Paul II) Laborem exercens - Congresses. 2. Church and labor - Latin America - Congresses. I. John Paul II, Pope, 1920-. II. Catholic Church. Consejo Episcopal Latinoamericano. III. Series: Documentos CELAM (Spanish ed.) , no. 82. IV. Title.
HD6338 .C277 1981 Suppl.

Encuesta de consumo energético en el sector transporte /. Hernández C., Alexandra. San José, Costa Rica , 1985. 68, [137] p. : LC Card 86-218227
HE5638 .H37 1985

Encuesta de consumo energético, sector transporte. Hernández C., Alexandra. Encuesta de consumo energético en el sector transporte /. San José, Costa Rica , 1985. 68, [137] p. : LC Card 86-218227
HE5638 .H37 1985

Encuesta de fecundidad y salud. Avance de resultados, encuesta de fecundidad y salud /. [San José] Costa Rica , 1986. [32] leaves : LC Card 87-400666 DDC 304.6/32/097286 19
HB947 .A96 1986

Encuesta de gastos e ingresos de los hogares, 1982-1983 : metodología, resultados de Montevideo e interior / Presidencia de la República Oriental del Uruguay, Dirección General de Estadística y Censos. [Montevideo] : La Dirección General, [1986] 76, 96, 120 p. : ill., forms ; 27 cm. Cover title. LC Card 87-403151 DDC 339.4/2/09895 19
1. Cost and standard of living - Uruguay - Statistics. 2. Households - Uruguay - Statistics. I. Uruguay. Dirección General de Estadística y Censos.
HD7020 .E53 1986

Encuesta nacional de hogares, empleo y desempleo : noviembre 1981 / Ministerio de Trabajo y Seguridad Social, Dirección General de Planificación del Trabajo y el Empleo [y] Ministerio de Economía, Industria y Comercio, Dirección General de Estadística y Censos. San José, Costa Rica : [Sección de Publicaciones DGEC], 1982. xi, xi, 86 p. ; 28 cm. Chiefly tables. LC Card 82-202317
1. Labor supply - Costa Rica - Statistics. 2. Unemployed - Costa Rica - Statistics. 3. Household surveys - Costa Rica. I. Costa Rica. Dirección General de Planificación del Trabajo y el Empleo. II. Costa Rica. Dirección General de Estadística y Censos.
HD5734.A6 E53 1982

Encuesta pecuaria en profundidad : prácticas de manejo en explotaciones de ganadería extensiva. Montevideo, Uruguay : Ministerio de Agricultura y Pesca, Dirección de Investigaciones Económicas Agropecuarias, [1977-1978] 2 v. ; 27 cm. (Boletín estadístico . no. 12, 14) Chiefly tables. "Segunda edición de 50 ejemplares"--V. 1-2, colophon. CONTENTS. - pt. 1. Vacunos -- pt. 2. Ovinos. LC Card 87-402173 DDC 338.1/762/009895021 19
1. Cattle trade - Uruguay - Statistics. 2. Sheep industry - Uruguay - Statistics. I. Uruguay. Dirección de Investigaciones Económicas Agropecuarias. II. Series: Boletín estadístico (Uruguay. Dirección de Investigaciones Económicas Agropecuarias) , no. 12, 14.
HD9433.U82 E53 1979

Encuesta residencial de consumo energético /. Obando S., Marta. San José, Costa Rica , 1985. iv, 56, [71] p. : LC Card 86-219603
HD9502.C82 O23 1985

Encyclopaedia Britannica Educational Corporation.

Change master companies [videorecording] . Chicago, IL , 1987. 1 videocassette (42 min.) : LC Card 87-705608 DDC 658.3 11
HD45

The Change masters [motion picture] . Chicago, Ill. , 1987. 1 film reel (29 min.) : LC Card 87-705269 DDC 658.3 11
HD45

The Change masters [videorecording] . Chicago, Ill. , 1987. 1 videocassette (29 min.) : LC Card 86-707881 DDC 658.3 11
HD45

People skills in action, for loan officers and processors. Chicago, Ill. , 1986. 1 videocassette (20 min.) : LC Card 86-707349 DDC 658.8 11
HG1641

Project management. Chicago, Ill. , 1987, c1985. 1 videocassette (30 min.) : LC Card 87-705140 DDC 658.4 11
HD69.P75

Roadmap for change. Chicago, Ill. , 1987. 1 film reel (28 min.) : LC Card 87-705133 DDC

658 11
HD9710

Encyclopaedia of South African post offices and postal agencies (including their forerunners in the Cape, Natal, Orange Free State, and Transvaal, Basutoland, Bechuanaland, and Swaziland, etc.) /. Putzel, Ralph F. Cape Town , 1986- v. <1 > : ISBN 0-620-09781-7 LC Card 87-143880 DDC 383/.4968 19
HE7351 .P88 1986

The Encyclopedia of careers and vocational guidance / William E. Hopke, editor-in-chief. 7th ed. Chicago, Ill. : J.G. Ferguson Pub. Co., 1987. 3 v. : ill. ; 29 cm. Includes indexes. CONTENTS. - v. 1. Reviewing career fields -- v. 2. Selecting a career -- v. 3. Selecting a technician's career. ISBN 0-89434-083-2 (set) : LC Card 87-19084 DDC 331.7/02 19
1. Vocational guidance. 2. Occupations. I. Hopke, William E.
HF5381 .E52 1987

Encyclopedia of geographic information sources, international volume : a bibliographic guide to approximately 13,000 citations for publications and organizations of interest to business personnel, covering more than 160 cities, countries, and regions / Jennifer Mossman, editor.4th ed. Detroit, Mich. : Gale Research Co., c1988. 479 p. ; 29 cm. Includes index. ISBN 0-8103-0410-4 : LC Card 87-23777 DDC 016.33 19
1. Business - Information services. - Directories. 2. Reference books - Business - Bibliography. 3. Business - Periodicals - Bibliography. I. Mossman, Jennifer.
HF5341 .E53 1988

Encyclopedia of Lotus one-two-three. Stark, Robin. Encyclopedia of Lotus 1-2-3 /. Blue Ridge Summit, PA , c1987. x, 484 p. : ISBN 0-8306-7891-3 : LC Card 87-19839 DDC 005.36/9 19
HF5548.4.L67 S675 1987

Encyclopedia of Lotus 1-2-3 /. Stark, Robin. Blue Ridge Summit, PA , c1987. x, 484 p. : ISBN 0-8306-7891-3 : LC Card 87-19839 DDC 005.36/9 19
HF5548.4.L67 S675 1987

The encyclopedia of pre-written employment ads . Wolff, Rick, 1951- Westbury, N.Y. , c1986. vi, 196 p. ; ISBN 0-87280-142-X (loose-leaf) : LC Card 86-26526 DDC 659.1/9331128 19
HF6125 .W65 1986

The end of organized capitalism /. Lash, Scott. Madison, Wis. , c1987. 383 p. : ISBN 0-299-11670-0 : LC Card 87-14248 DDC 330.12/2 19
HB501 .L278 1987

The end of the Third World . Harris, Nigel. London , 1986. 231 p. : ISBN 1-85043-031-4
NYPL [JLE 87-858]

The end of the Third World . Harris, Nigel. New York , 1987, c1986. 231 p. : ISBN 0-941533-14-X : LC Card 87-12295 DDC 330.9172/4 19
HC59.7 .H3536 1987

The end of the world that was . Goldman, Peter Louis, 1933- New York , c1986. xiv, 129 p., [8] p. of plates : ISBN 0-525-24428-X LC Card 85-31223 DDC 920/.073 19
CT220 .G6 1986 ***NYPL [JFD 86-6015]***

End-use market for 13 non-ferrous metals. The End-use markets for 13 nonferrous metals /. Washington, D.C. [1986] vii, 52 p. ; LC Card 86-602419 DDC 381/.45673/0973 19
HD9539.A3 U44 1986

End-use markets for thirteen non-ferrous metals. The End-use markets for 13 nonferrous metals /. Washington, D.C. [1986] vii, 52 p. ; LC Card 86-602419 DDC 381/.45673/0973 19
HD9539.A3 U44 1986

The End-use markets for 13 nonferrous metals / prepared by the Nonferrous Metals Division, Office of Metals, Minerals, and Commodities, Basic Industries Sector. Washington, D.C. : U. S. Dept. of Commerce, International Trade Administration : For sale by the Supt. of Docs., U. S. G.P.O., [1986] vii, 52 p. ; 28 cm. Cover title: The end-use market for 13 non-ferrous metals. Shipping list no.: 86-632-P. "June 1986." S/N 003-009-00479-9 Item 231-B-1 LC Card 86-602419 DDC 381/.45673/0973 19
1. Nonferrous metal industries - United States. I. United States. International Trade Administration. Nonferrous Metals Division. II. Title: End-use market for 13 non-ferrous metals. III. Title: End-use markets for thirteen non-ferrous metals.
HD9539.A3 U44 1986

Endaka to kigyō shūeki . Yoshida, Satoshi, 1948- [Higashimurayama-shi] , Tōkyō , 1986. 137 p. : ISBN 4-315-50263-4 : LC Card 86-205176
HC462.9 .Y638 1986 <Orien Japan>
NYPL [*OSM 87-2489]

Das Ende des Kapitalismus . Keller, Friedrich Jakob, 1893- Lyss [1981] 211 p. : LC Card 84-104878
HB95 .K33 1981

Enderle, Georges. Ethik und Wirtschaftswissenschaft /. Berlin , c1985. 276 p. : ISBN 3-428-05910-7 LC Card 86-132826
HB72 .E79 1985

Enders, Walter, 1948- International economics : theory and policy / Walter Enders, Harvey E. Lapan. Englewood Cliffs, N.J. : Prentice-Hall, c1987. xii, 542 p. : ill. ; 25 cm. Includes bibliographies and index. ISBN 0-13-472853-X : LC Card 86-30623 DDC 337 19
1. International economic relations. 2. International finance. 3. Commerce. I. Lapan, Harvey. II. Title.
HF1411 .E49 1987

Endeudamiento externo y tasa de descuento social . Coloma C., Fernando. Santiago, Chile , 1986. 66 leaves : LC Card 87-102066
HJ8083 .C65 1986

ENDICOTT JOHNSON CORPORATION - EMPLOYEES - HISTORY.
Zahavi, Gerald, 1951- Workers, managers, and welfare capitalism . Urbana , c1988. xiii, 261 p., [14] p. of plates : ISBN 0-252-01444-8 (alk. paper) LC Card 87-6035 DDC 331.2/0475/0973 19
HD9787.U6 E654 1988

ENDICOTT JOHNSON CORPORATION - PERSONNEL MANAGEMENT - HISTORY.
Zahavi, Gerald, 1951- Workers, managers, and welfare capitalism . Urbana , c1988. xiii, 261 p., [14] p. of plates : ISBN 0-252-01444-8 (alk. paper) LC Card 87-6035 DDC 331.2/0475/0973 19
HD9787.U6 E654 1988

Endo, Seiti Kaneko. Pesquisa de orçamentos familiares no município de São Paulo / Seiti Kaneko Endo, Heron Carlos Esvael do Carmo. São Paulo : IPE/USP ; [Rio de Janeiro] : BID, 1984. 131 p. : ill. ; 21 cm. (Série Relatórios de pesquisa . v. 20) Bibliography: p. 131. LC Card 85-136517
1. Consumer price indexes - Brazil - São Paulo. 2. Prices - Brazil - São Paulo. 3. Home economics - Brazil - São Paulo - Accounting. I. Carmo, Heron Carlos E. do (Heron Carlos Esvael). II. Series. III. Series: Série Relatórios de pesquisa , no. 20. IV. Title.
HB235.B8 E53 1984

ENDORSEMENTS IN ADVERTISING.
H.W. Johns Manufacturing Co. Structural decoration. [New York] c1882. 32 p. : LC Card 86-224190
HD9660.P254 H174 1882

ENDOWED CHARITIES. see **CHARITIES.**

ENDOWMENTS - UNITED STATES - DIRECTORIES.
Blum, Laurie. Free money for small businesses and entrepreneurs /. New York , c1988. ix, 229 p. ; ISBN 0-471-85803-X : LC Card 87-20978 DDC 658.1/5224 19
HG4027.7 .B58 1988

The Enemy within : pit villages and the miners' strike of 1984-5 / edited by Raphael Samuel, Barbara Bloomfield, Guy Boanas. London ; New York : Routledge & Kegan Paul, 1986. xxiii, 260 p. : ill. ; 22 cm. (History workshop series) Includes indexes. ISBN 0-7102-0888-X (pbk.) : LC Card 86-12192 DDC 331.89/2822334/0941 19
1. Coal Strike, Great Britain, 1984-1985. I. Samuel, Raphael. II. Bloomfield, Barbara. III. Boanas, Guy.
HD5365.M6152 1984 .E54 1986

Ėnergeticheskoe khozíāĭstvo stran SĖV . Kozlov, I. D. (Igor′ Dmitrievich) Moskva , 1980. 158 p. ; LC Card 87-107887
HD9502.E83 K686 1980

ENERGEX '84 (1984 : Regina, Sask.) Energy developments : new forms, renewables, conservation / edited by Fred A. Curtis.1st ed. Toronto ; New York : Pergamon Press, 1984. xxiv, 1026 p. : ill. ; 29 cm. "Proceedings of ENERGEX '84, the global energy forum, Regina, Saskatchewan, Canada, May 14-19, 1984"--p. i. Includes bibliographies and indexes. ISBN 0-08-025407-1 LC Card 85-122124 DDC 333.79 19
1. Energy development - Congresses. 2. Renewable energy sources - Congresses. 3. Energy conservation - Congresses. I. Curtis, Fred A. (Fred Allen), 1946-. II. Title.
TJ163.15 .E46 1984 ***NYPL [JSF 86-799]***

Energia e assentamentos humanos. Porto Alegre : CEDU : CENERGS, 1983. 40 p. : ill. ; 21 cm. LC Card 86-200513
1. Cities and towns - Energy consumption. 2. Cities and towns - Brazil - Energy consumption. I. CEDU (Organization : Rio Grande do Sul, Brazil). II. Rio Grande do Sul (Brazil). Comissão Estadual de Energia.
HD9502.A2 E513 1983

Energia e sviluppo : l'industria elettrica italiana e la Società Edison / a cura di Bruno Bezza. Torino : G. Einaudi, c1986. xii, 346 p., [16] p. of plates : ill. ; 22 cm. (Biblioteca di cultura storica. 156) Includes bibliographical references and indexes. ISBN 88-06-59444-3 : LC Card 86-214309
1. Società Edison. 2. Electric utilities - Italy - History. I. Bezza, Bruno.
HD9685.I84 S574 1986

Energía eléctrica / preparado por Departamento de Actividad Industrial. [Buenos Aires] : Banco Central de la República Argentina, Gerencia de Investigaciones y Estadísticas Económicas, [1981] 27 p., [6] leaves of plates : ill. ; 30 cm. (Serie de trabajos metodológicos y sectoriales . no. 16 (julio de 1981)) CONTENTS. - Demanda sectorial de energía / por Eduardo A. Zuccotti -- Estudios de la relación entre la evolución de la actividad industrial y del consumo de energía eléctrica / por Juan I. Basco. LC Card 87-401272 DDC 333.79/3212/0982 19
1. Electric utilities - Argentina. 2. Electric power consumption - Argentina. I. Zuccotti, Eduardo A. II. Basco, Juan Ignacio. III. Banco Central de la República Argentina. Departamento de Actividad Industrial. IV. Series. V. Series: Serie de trabajos metodológicos y sectoriales , no. 16.
HD9685.A72 E54 1981

Energía y petróleo : Argentina y el mundo. Capital Federal : Shell Cía. Argentina de Petróleo, Departamento de Asuntos Públicos, [1985 or 1986] 60 p. : col. ill. ; 30 cm. (Problemática energética . 1) LC Card 87-403778 DDC 338.2/7282 19
1. Petroleum industry and trade. 2. Petroleum industry and trade - Argentina. I. Shell Compañía Argentina de Petróleo. Departamento de Asuntos Públicos. II. Series.
HD9560.5 .E525 1985

Energiaottanta : crisi energetica e proposte per lo sviluppo / a cura di G. B. Zorzoli e F. Dalla Valle ; con un contributo di P. Veronesi.2 ed. aggiornata. Milano : F. Angeli, 1980. [xv] 284 p. ; 23 cm. (Collana del C.D.R.L. . 1) CDRL/Centro documentazione e richerche per la Lombardia ; 1 Includes bibliographical references.
1. Energy policy - Italy. 2. Energy consumption - Italy. 3. Energy policy - European Economic Community countries. 4. Energy consumption - European Economic Community countries. I. Zorzoli, Giovanni Battista. II. Dalla Valle, F. ***NYPL [JLD 86-3690]***

Az Energiatermelés és az energiafelhasználás szerkezete : népgazdasági energiamérlegek, 1964-1968 / [összeállította a KSH Iparstatisztikai Főosztályának Nehézipari Osztálya]. Budapest : Központi Statisztikai Hivatal, 1970. 44 p. ; 29 cm. (Statisztikai időszaki közlemények . 162. köt.) Chiefly tables. LC Card 86-189699
1. Power resources - Hungary - Statistics. 2. Energy industries - Hungary - Statistics. 3. Energy consumption - Hungary - Statistics. I. Hungary. Központi Statisztikai Hivatal. Nehézipari Osztály. II. Series.
HD9502.H92 E54 1970

L'énergie à revendre /. Gerondeau, Christian, 1938- [Paris] , c1984. 333 p. : LC Card 84-166266
HD9502.A2 G47 1984

L'Energie électrique au Sahara. [Paris] : Organisation commune des régions sahariennes, Bureau des études statistiques, économiques et sociales, [196-?] 19 p. : ill. ; 28 cm. Cover title.

LC Card 83-123000
1. Electric utilities - Algeria - Statistics. 2. Electric utilities - Sahara - Statistics. I. Organisation commune des régions sahariennes (France). Bureau des études statistiques, économiques et sociales.
HD9685.A52 E54 1960z

L'Energie électrique de la Côte d'Ivoire . Énergie électrique de la Côte d'Ivoire (Company) Abidjan, Côte d'Ivoire [1962] 23 p. : LC Card 83-120031 DDC 363.6/2/096668 19
HD9685.I94 E53 1962

Énergie électrique de la Côte d'Ivoire (Company) L'Energie électrique de la Côte d'Ivoire : [1952-1962]. Abidjan, Côte d'Ivoire : E.E.C.I., [1962] 23 p. : ill. (some col.) ; 28 cm. LC Card 83-120031 DDC 363.6/2/096668 19
1. Énergie électrique de la Côte d'Ivoire (Company). 2. Electric utilities - Ivory Coast. I. Title.
HD9685.I94 E53 1962

ÉNERGIE ÉLECTRIQUE DE LA CÔTE D'IVOIRE (COMPANY)
Énergie électrique de la Côte d'Ivoire (Company) L'Energie électrique de la Côte d'Ivoire . Abidjan, Côte d'Ivoire [1962] 23 p. : LC Card 83-120031 DDC 363.6/2/096668 19
HD9685.I94 E53 1962

Energie et décentralisation / textes réunis par Maurice Bourjol et Christian Le Lamer. Paris : Economica, 1984. 297 p. : ill. ; 24 cm. (Etudes de la Faculté de droit et des sciences économiques de Tours) Papers presented at a meeting held in Tours, on April 23-24, 1982, sponsored by the Faculté de droit et des sciences économiques de Tours. Includes bibliographies. ISBN 2-7178-0782-9 : LC Card 84-249613
1. Energy policy - France - Congresses. 2. Decentralization in government - France - Congresses. I. Bourjol, Maurice. II. Le Lamer, Christian. III. Faculté de droit et des sciences économiques de Tours. IV. Series.
HD9502.F72 E5334 1984

"Energie et société", 0338-6120.
Rente et structures des industries de l'énergie /. [Saint-Martin-d'Hères] , 1983. 268 p. : ISBN 2-7061-0217-9 : LC Card 84-173320
HD9502.A2 R45 1983 ***NYPL [JLE 87-1263]***

Energie für den Verkehr . Kortzfleisch, Gert von. Frankfurt am Main , c1984. 115 p. : LC Card 84-192683
HD9710.G4 V4 Nr. 42 HE5620.E53

Energie für die Armen? . Mayer, Hans, 1951- Saarbrücken , Fort Lauderdale , 1984. 195 p. : ISBN 3-88156-288-5 : LC Card 85-199309
HD9502.I42 M38 1984

"L'Energie, levier de développement économique" : mémoire / de l'Association des manufacturiers d'équipements électriques et électroniques du Canada (l'AMEEC), [à la] Commission parlementaire. [Ottawa?] : AMEEC, [1983] 30 leaves ; 29 cm. Half title: Mémoire de l'AMEEC à la Commission parlementaire sur l'énergie. "Mars 1983." Stamped on cover: 48M. LC Card 85-128816
1. Electric utilities - Québec (Province). 2. Electric industries - Québec (Province). 3. Energy policy - Québec (Province). I. Electrical and Electronic Manufacturers Association of Canada. II. Québec (Province). Assemblée nationale. Commission permanente de l'énergie et des ressources. III. Title: Mémoire de l'AMEEC à la Commission parlementaire sur l'énergie.
HD9685.C3 Q4425 1983

Energie und Gerechtigkeit / herausgegeben im Auftrag der Studiengruppe Entwicklungsprobleme der Industriegesellschaft (STEIG) e.V. [von] Reiner Kümmel, Monika Suhrcke. München : Minerva Publikation, c1984. xii, 254 p. : ill. ; 21 cm. (Politik, Recht, Gesellschaft . Bd. 6) Includes papers presented at the Tagung "Energie und Gerechtigkeit" held Oct. 14-17, 1982 on the occasion of the 400th anniversary of the Universität Würzburg. Includes bibliographies. ISBN 3-597-10259-X LC Card 84-175053
1. Energy policy - Social aspects - Congresses. I. Kümmel, Reiner, 1939-. II. Suhrcke, Monika. III. Studiengruppe Entwicklungsprobleme der Industriegesellschaft (Germany). IV. Tagung "Energie und Gerechtigkeit" (1982 : Universität Würzburg). V. Bayerische Julius-Maximilians-Universität Würzburg. VI. Series.
HD9502.A2 E5192 1984

Energie und Umwelt . Friedrich, R. (Rainer) Stuttgart [1985] 124 p. : LC Card 87-409533 DDC 333.79/0943/46 19
HD9502.G43 B3238 1985

Energie und Umwelt . Friedrich, R. (Rainer) Stuttgart [1985] 115 p. : LC Card 87-409534 DDC 333.79/0943/46 19
HD9502.G43 B324 1985

Energieforschung und Arbeitnehmerinteressen . Grumbach, Jürgen. Frankfurt , New York , c1986. 307 p. ; ISBN 3-593-33655-3 LC Card 87-127360 DDC 331.1/0943 19
HC290.5.E5 G74 1986

Energiekosten und Anpassungsverhalten der Wirtschaft /. Richter, Josef. Wien , 1985. iv, 184 p. : ISBN 3-85436-031-2 LC Card 86-154099
HD9502.A92 R53 1985

Energies à la mesure des villages . Busacker, Dietrich. Bielefeld, Federal Republic of Germany , 1985. 21 leaves ; LC Card 85-160345
HD9502.A4993 B87 1985

Die Energiewirtschaft der DDR und die Planung ihrer künftigen Entwicklung /. Knop, Hans, Prof. Dr. sc. Berlin , 1960. 239 p. : LC Card 87-407618 DDC 333.79/0943 19
HD9502.G452 K58 1960

Energiförbrukningen fram till år 2005 : svensk resumé. Helsingfors : Handels- och industriministeriet, Energiavdelningen : Statens tryckericentral [distributor], 1985. ii, 36 p. : ill. ; 26 cm. (Serie B, 0356-9284 . 47) ISBN 951-46-9116-4 LC Card 87-102957
1. Energy consumption - Finland - Statistics. 2. Energy consumption - Finland - Forecasting - Statistics. I. Finland. Kauppa- ja teollisuusministeriö. Energiaosasto.
HD9502.S82 E46 1985

Energihushållning och samhällsekonomi : expertbilaga 1 till SOU 1980:43 "Program för energihushållning i befintlig bebyggelse.". [Stockholm] : Bostadsdepartementet : LiberFörlag, [1980] 70, 39, 29, 58 p. : ill. ; 25 cm. "Ds Bo 1980:4." Includes bibliographical references. ISBN 91-38-05980-0 LC Card 84-122675
1. Energy policy - Sweden. 2. Buildings - Sweden - Energy conservation. I. Sweden. Bostadsdepartementet. II. Sweden. Energihushållningsdelegationen. Program för energihushållning i befintlig bebyggelse.
HD9502.S82 E48 1980

Energy alternatives for rural development / edited by Rakesh Hooja, Yogeshwar Sharma. 1st ed. Jaipur : Centre for Management Studies, HCM Rajasthan State Institute of Public Administration, 1985. vi, 303 p. : ill. ; 22 cm. Papers presented at a seminar organized by the Centre for Management Studies, HCM Rajasthan State Institute of Public Administration, Jaipur, 1983. Includes bibliographies. LC Card 86-902191 DDC 333.79/0954 19
1. Power resources - India - Congresses. 2. Energy development - India - Congresses. 3. Rural development - India - Energy consumption - Congresses. I. Hooja, Rakesh. II. Sharma, Yogeshwar, 1936-. III. HCM Rajasthan State Institute of Public Administration. Centre for Management Studies.
HD9556.I42 E54 1985

Energy and agriculture . United Nations University Symposium on Energy and Agriculture Futures--Policy Implications of Global Models (1982 : Paris, France) [Chur, Switzerland , New York] , c1984. xii, 370 p. : ISBN 3-7186-0187-7 LC Card 83-18363 DDC 333.79 19
HD1405 .E53 1983 ***NYPL [JLD 86-1837]***

Energy and cities / edited by John Byrne and Daniel Rich. New Brunswick, U. S.A. : Transaction Books, c1985. 173 p. : ill. ; 23 cm. (Energy policy studies . v. 2) Bibliography: p. 143-171. ISBN 0-87855-813-6 (pbk.) LC Card 84-24074 DDC 333.79/13/091732 19
1. Land use, Urban - Energy consumption. 2. Urban transportation - Energy consumption. 3. Space in economics. I. Byrne, John, 1949-. II. Rich, Daniel. III. Series.
HD108.2 .E525 1985 ***NYPL [JLE 86-4441]***

Energy and economic adjustment / Lars Bergman ... [et al.]. Stockholm : Industrial Institute for Economic and Social Research 1983. 247 p. : ill. ; 25 cm. (Energy and economic structure research report . 4) Includes bibliographies. CONTENTS. - Oil price uncertainty and national energy strategies / by Lars Bergman and Karl-Göran Maier -- Oil prices and economic stability-simulation experiments with a macroeconomic model / by Tomas Nordström and Bengt-Christer Ysander. ISBN 91-7204-186-2
1. Petroleum products - Prices - Sweden. 2. Petroleum industry and trade - Sweden. 3. Energy policy - Sweden. I. Bergman, Lars. ***NYPL [JLE 86-1351]***

Energy and economic development /. Guru, D. D. Delhi , c1987. xi, 257 p. : ISBN 81-85061-53-6 : LC Card 87-901433 DDC 333.79/0954 19
HD9502.I4 G87 1987

Energy & economic development. Guru, D. D. Energy and economic development /. Delhi , c1987. xi, 257 p. : ISBN 81-85061-53-6 : LC Card 87-901433 DDC 333.79/0954 19
HD9502.I4 G87 1987

Energy and environment : the unfinished business. Washington, D.C. : Congresssional Quarterly Inc., c1985. x, 190 p. : ill. ; 24 cm. Includes index. ISBN 0-87187-360-5 : LC Card 85-25471 DDC 333.79/0973 19
1. Energy policy - United States. 2. Environmental policy - United States. I. Congressional Quarterly, inc.
HD9502.U52 E4524 1985
NYPL [JLE 86-2859]

Energy and Environmental Analysis, inc.
Benefit/cost analyses of laws and regulations affecting coal : case studies on reclamation, air pollution, and health and safety laws and regulations : final report / prepared for Office of Minerals Policy and Research Analysis, Department of the Interior by Energy and Environmental Analysis, Inc. Washington : For sale by the Supt. of Docs., U. S. Govt. Print. Off., 1977. ca. 750 p. : ill. ; 28 cm. "Contract # 14-01-001-2115." Includes bibliography. LC Card 77-603790 DDC 363.6
1. Coal mines and mining - Environmental aspects - United States. 2. Environmental law - United States. I. Title.
TD195.C58 E53 1977 ***NYPL [JLF 81-219]***

Energy and growth : a comparison of 13 industrial and developing countries / by Gerald Leach ... [et al.]. London ; Boston : Butterworths, 1986. xvii, 199 p. : ill. ; 24 cm. Includes index. Bibliography: p. 183-184. ISBN 0-408-02560-3 : LC Card 85-31336 DDC 333.79/13 19
1. Energy consumption - Case studies. 2. Economic development - Case studies. I. Leach, Gerald.
HD9502.A2 E542 1986
NYPL [JLE 86-2717]

Energy and regional investment in Canada /. Douglas, Gordon W. Calgary, Alta. [1983] x, 114 p. : ISBN 0-920522-28-9 (pbk.) : LC Card 83-160268 DDC 332.6/722 19
HD9502.C32 D68 1983 ***NYPL [JLD 87-996]***

ENERGY AND STATE. see **ENERGY POLICY.**

Energy and the federal government . Clark, John Garretson, 1932- Urbana , c1987. xxiii, 511 p. : ISBN 0-252-01295-X LC Card 85-20505 DDC 333.8/2/0973 19
HD9502.U52 C57 1987 ***NYPL [JLE 87-736]***

Energy and U. S. agriculture . Sloggett, Gordon. Washington, D.C. , 1985] iii, 43 p. : LC Card 86-600880 DDC 338.1 s 338.1/3 19
HD1751 .A91854 no. 545 S619.E53

Energy and water management in western irrigated agriculture / edited by Norman K. Whittlesey. Boulder, Colo. : Westview Press, 1986. xxiv, 415 p. : ill. ; 23 cm. (Studies in water policy and management . no. 7) Includes bibliographies and index. ISBN 0-8133-7086-8 (pbk. : alk. paper) LC Card 85-52184 DDC 333.91/3/0978 19
1. Irrigation - West (U. S.) - Energy conservation. 2. Electric power consumption - West (U. S.). 3. Electric power production - West (U. S.). 4. Water conservation - West (U. S.). 5. Water resources development - Government policy - United States. I. Whittlesey, Norman K. II. Series.
HD1735 .E54 1986 ***NYPL [JLD 87-829]***

ENERGY, BIOMASS. see **BIOMASS ENERGY.**

Energy conservation : successes and failures / John C. Sawhill and Richard Cotton, editors. Washington, D.C. : The Brookings Institution, c1986. xii, 270 p. : ill. ; 24 cm. Includes bibliographical references and index. ISBN 0-8157-7716-7 : LC Card 85-26894 DDC 333.79/16/0973 19
1. Energy conservation - United States. 2. Energy

policy - United States. 3. Public utilities - United States - Energy conservation. 4. Petroleum industry and trade - Government policy - United States. I. Sawhill, John C., 1936-. II. Cotton, Richard, 1944-.
HD9502.U62 E478 1986
NYPL [JLE 86-4084]

ENERGY CONSERVATION - AFRICA, WEST.
Busacker, Dietrich. Energies à la mesure des villages . Bielefeld, Federal Republic of Germany , 1985. 21 leaves ; LC Card 85-160345
HD9502.A4993 B87 1985

ENERGY CONSERVATION - ASIA.
Energy conservation in the Asian region . Tokyo, Japan [Honolulu, Hawaii] , 1986. vi, 173 p. : ISBN 92-833-2038-1 LC Card 87-122915 DDC 333.79/16/095 19
HD9502.A782 E53 1986

ENERGY CONSERVATION - CANADA.
Reinsch, Anthony Ernest. Industrial cogeneration in Canada . Calgary, Alta. [1987] xviii, 137 p. : ISBN 0-920522-41-6 (pbk.) : LC Card 87-163062 DDC 333.79/3 19
HD9685.C2 R45 1987

ENERGY CONSERVATION - CASE STUDIES.
Public policies and private actions . Aldershot, Hants, England , Brookfield, Vt., U. S.A. , c1987. p. cm. ISBN 0-566-05436-1 : LC Card 87-14909 DDC 333.79/16 19
HD9502.A2 P82 1987

ENERGY CONSERVATION - CONGRESSES.
ENERGEX '84 (1984 : Regina, Sask.) Energy developments . Toronto , New York , 1984. xxiv, 1026 p. : ISBN 0-08-025407-1 LC Card 85-122124 DDC 333.79 19
TJ163.15 .E46 1984 ***NYPL [JSF 86-799]***

Innovation for energy efficiency . Oxford [Oxfordshire] , 1988. p. cm. ISBN 0-08-034798-3 : LC Card 87-19016 DDC 333.79/094 19
HD9502.E8 I55 1988

ENERGY CONSERVATION - EUROPE - CONGRESSES.
Innovation for energy efficiency . Oxford [Oxfordshire] , 1988. p. cm. ISBN 0-08-034798-3 : LC Card 87-19016 DDC 333.79/094 19
HD9502.E8 I55 1988

ENERGY CONSERVATION - GERMANY, WEST.
Ziesing, Hans-Joachim. Beurteilung der Wirtschaftlichkeitsschwelle und Analyse der Produktionskapazitäten bei neuen Technologien zur Energieeinsparung in mittel- bis längerfristiger Sicht . Berlin , 1983. 458 p. : ISBN 3-428-05497-0
NYPL [JLL 73-207 Bd. 139]

Energy conservation in the Asian region : report of the seminar held in Tokyo and Taipei in September 1985 / edited by William E. James. Tokyo, Japan : Asian Productivity Organization ; [Honolulu, Hawaii] : Resource Systems Institute, East-West Center, 1986. vi, 173 p. : ill. ; 26 cm. Includes bibliographical references. ISBN 92-833-2038-1 LC Card 87-122915 DDC 333.79/16/095 19
1. Energy conservation - Asia. 2. Energy industries - Asia. 3. Petroleum industry and trade - Asia. 4. Energy policy - Asia. I. James, William E. II. Asian Productivity Organization. III. East-West Resource Systems Institute.
HD9502.A782 E53 1986

ENERGY CONSERVATION - INDIA.
Mayer, Hans, 1951- Energie für die Armen? . Saarbrücken , Fort Lauderdale , 1984. 195 p. : ISBN 3-88156-288-5 : LC Card 85-199309
HD9502.I42 M38 1984

ENERGY CONSERVATION - PSYCHOLOGICAL ASPECTS.
Katzev, Richard D. Promoting energy conservation . Boulder , 1987. xvi, 218 p. : ISBN 0-8133-7337-9 (pbk.) : LC Card 86-32587 DDC 333.79/16 19
HD9502.A2 K38 1987

ENERGY CONSERVATION - SPAIN.
Comisión Energía y Recursos de AEPDEN-Amigos de la Tierra. Modelo energético de tránsito /. Madrid [1979?] 136 p. ; ISBN 84-85639-02-2 LC Card 79-126051
HD9502.S662 C66 1979 ***NYPL [JLC 87-71]***

ENERGY CONSERVATION - SWEDEN.
Sweden. Elanvändningskommittén till restriktioner, användning och hushållning. El och olja . [Stockholm] [1980] 265 p. : ISBN 91-38-05865-0 LC Card 84-102448
HD9502.S82 S898 1980

Sweden. Oljeersättningsdelegationen. Redovisning och analys av kommunernas oljereduktionsplaner /. Stockholm [1983] 59, [91] p. : ISBN 91-38-07458-3 LC Card 83-239703
HD9502.S82 S96 1983a

ENERGY CONSERVATION - UNITED STATES.
Energy conservation . Washington, D.C. , c1986. xii, 270 p. : ISBN 0-8157-7716-7 : LC Card 85-26894 DDC 333.79/16/0973 19
HD9502.U62 E478 1986
NYPL [JLE 86-4084]

Energy economics . Englewood Cliffs, N.J. , c1987. viii, 328 p. : ISBN 0-13-277245-0 : LC Card 86-25254 DDC 333.79/0973 19
HD9502.U52 E4874 1987

Energy efficiency . Washington, D.C. , 1987, c1986. 333 p. : ISBN 0-918249-05-8 (pbk.) LC Card 86-28817 DDC 333.79/16/0973 19
HD9502.U52 E4883 1987

Nivola, Pietro S. The politics of energy conservation /. Washington, D.C. , c1986. x, 294 p. ; ISBN 0-8157-6088-4 : LC Card 85-48265 DDC 333.79/16/0973 19
TJ163.4.U6 N58 1986 ***NYPL [JLE 86-2515]***

ENERGY CONSERVATION - UNITED STATES - CONGRESSES.
Community energy management as an economic development strategy . [Lincoln, Neb.] (Box 95085, Lincoln 68509-5085) [1984 or 1985] iv, 396 p. : LC Card 86-622211 DDC 333.79/0973 19
HD9502.U52 C656 1984

ENERGY CONSUMPTION.
Castanho Filho, Eduardo Pires. A questão energética /. São Paulo , 1984. 15 p. ; LC Card 86-159794
HD9502.A2 C385 1984

Energy for a sustainable world /. New York, N.Y. , 1987. p. cm. LC Card 87-23099 DDC 333.79 19
HD9502.A2 AZ 1987

ENERGY CONSUMPTION - ALASKA.
Historical and projected oil and gas consumption . [Juneau] [1986] 1 v. (in various pagings) : LC Card 86-622301 DDC 333.8/2313/09798 19
HD9502.U53 A4574 1986

Rainery, Richard. Alaska's public energy resources . [Juneau?] [1985] 8, 124, 3, 7 p. : LC Card 86-622191 DDC 333.79/09798 19
HD9502.U53 A473 1985

ENERGY CONSUMPTION - AUSTRIA - COSTS.
Richter, Josef. Energiekosten und Anpassungsverhalten der Wirtschaft /. Wien , 1985. iv, 184 p. : ISBN 3-85436-031-2 LC Card 86-154099
HD9502.A92 R53 1985

ENERGY CONSUMPTION - BRAZIL - MINAS GERAIS.
Diagnóstico energético, 1978/1983 /. Belo Horizonte , 1985. 177 p. : LC Card 87-121240 DDC 333.79/0981/51 19
HD9502.B73 M563 1985

Fluxo energético estadual, 1983 /. [Belo Horizonte, Brazil] , 1985. 105 p. : LC Card 87-404947 DDC 333.79/0981/51 19
HD9502.B73 M5646 1985

ENERGY CONSUMPTION - CASE STUDIES.
Energy and growth . London , Boston , 1986. xvii, 199 p. : ISBN 0-408-02560-3 : LC Card 85-31336 DDC 333.79/13 19
HD9502.A2 E542 1986
NYPL [JLE 86-2717]

ENERGY CONSUMPTION - CHILE - STATISTICS.
Balance de energía, 1965-1984 . Santiago, Chile [1985 or 1986] 191 p. : LC Card 87-401010 DDC 333.79/0983 19
HD9502.C52 B35 1985

ENERGY CONSUMPTION - CHINA.
Chêng, Chu-yüan. The demand and supply of primary energy in mainland China /. Taipei, Taiwan, Republic of China , Seattle , c1984. viii, 178 p. ; LC Card 84-231216 DDC 333.79/11/0951 19
HD9502.C62 C49 1984 ***NYPL [JLF 87-21]***

ENERGY CONSUMPTION - DEVELOPING COUNTRIES.
Energy requirements and utilization in rural and urban low-income settlements. Nairobi , 1984. iii, 76 p. : LC Card 86-980596 DDC 333.79/13/091724 19
HD9502.D442 E57 1984

Siddayao, Corazon M. Energy demand and economic growth . Boulder , 1986. xiv, 127 p. : ISBN 0-8133-7154-6 : LC Card 86-906 DDC 333.79/13/091724 19
HD9502.D442 S54 1986
NYPL [JLE 86-3295]

ENERGY CONSUMPTION - DEVELOPING COUNTRIES - MANAGEMENT - CONGRESSES.
Management Training Seminar (1982 : Joint Research Centre, Ispra, Italy) National energy planning and management in developing countries . Dordrecht, Holland , Hingham, MA , c1983. xiii, 442 p. ; ISBN 90-277-1589-0 LC Card 83-4407 DDC 333.79/09172/4 19
HD9502.A2 M343 1982
NYPL [JLE 87-302]

ENERGY CONSUMPTION - DEVELOPING COUNTRIES - PLANNING - CONGRESSES.
Management Training Seminar (1982 : Joint Research Centre, Ispra, Italy) National energy planning and management in developing countries . Dordrecht, Holland , Hingham, MA , c1983. xiii, 442 p. ; ISBN 90-277-1589-0 LC Card 83-4407 DDC 333.79/09172/4 19
HD9502.A2 M343 1982
NYPL [JLE 87-302]

ENERGY CONSUMPTION - DOMINICAN REPUBLIC.
Gómez, Carmen. Población y energía en la República Dominicana, 1990-2000. Santo Domingo, República Dominicana [1985] vi, 86 p. : LC Card 86-176044
HD9502.D652 G65 1985

ENERGY CONSUMPTION - ECONOMETRIC MODELS.
Donnelly, William A. The econometrics of energy demand . New York , 1987. xv, 309 p. : ISBN 0-275-92610-9 (alk. paper) : LC Card 86-25220 DDC 333.79/12 19
HD9502.A2 D67 1987

ENERGY CONSUMPTION - ECUADOR.
Kublank, Peter. Balances energéticos del Ecuador . Quito, Ecuador , 1983. 1 v. (various foliations) : LC Card 86-153116
HD9502.E22 K82 1983

ENERGY CONSUMPTION - EUROPEAN ECONOMIC COMMUNITY COUNTRIES.
Energiaottanta . Milano , 1980. [xv] 284 p. ;
NYPL [JLD 86-3690]

ENERGY CONSUMPTION - FINLAND - FORECASTING - STATISTICS.
Energiförbrukningen fram till år 2005 . Helsingfors , 1985. ii, 36 p. : ISBN 951-46-9116-4 LC Card 87-102957
HD9502.S82 E46 1985

ENERGY CONSUMPTION - FINLAND - STATISTICS.
Energiförbrukningen fram till år 2005 . Helsingfors , 1985. ii, 36 p. : ISBN 951-46-9116-4 LC Card 87-102957
HD9502.S82 E46 1985

ENERGY CONSUMPTION - FLORIDA.
Llewellyn, Ralph A. Patterns of energy consumption in Florida, 1970-1983 . Tallahassee, Fla. [1985] xiv, 147 p. : LC Card 86-622312 DDC 333.79/13/09759 19
HD9502.U53 F5846 1985

ENERGY CONSUMPTION - FORECASTING.
Chant, Verne G. Two global scenarios . Laxenburg, Austria , c1981. vi, 75 p. : ISBN 3-7045-0026-7 (pbk.) LC Card 83-130587 DDC 333.79/12 19
HD9502.A2 C45 1981 ***NYPL [JLE 86-595]***

Energy demand . New York , 1987. 176 p. : ISBN 0-312-01361-2 : LC Card 87-21477

DDC 333.79/12 19
HD9502.A2 E54373 1987

ENERGY CONSUMPTION - FRANCE.
Offant, Pierre. Adaptation structurelle de l'économie française à la limitation de la consommation d'énergie /. Dijon , c1984. 224, iii p. : ISBN 2-85975-026-6 LC Card 85-205959
HD9502.F72 O33 1984

ENERGY CONSUMPTION - GERMANY (EAST)
Kaufmann, Manfred. Die persönliche materielle Interessiertheit an der Material- und Energieökonomie /. Jena , 1984. 112 p. : LC Card 85-224317
HF1054.G42 K38 1984

ENERGY CONSUMPTION - HUNGARY - STATISTICS.
Az Energiatermelés és az energiafelhasználás szerkezete . Budapest , 1970. 44 p. ; LC Card 86-189699
HD9502.H92 E54 1970

ENERGY CONSUMPTION - INDIA - GUJARAT.
Energy use in rural Gujarat /. New Delhi , c1987. iv, 186 p. : ISBN 81-204-0216-2 : LC Card 87-901949 DDC 333.79/13/095475 19
HD9502.I43 G844 1987

ENERGY CONSUMPTION - ITALY.
Energiaottanta . Milano , 1980. [xv] 284 p. ;
NYPL [JLD 86-3690]

ENERGY CONSUMPTION - KENYA.
Hosier, Richard. Energy use in rural Kenya . Stockholm , Uppsala , c1985. xi, 177 p. : ISBN 91-7106-241-6 ***NYPL [JLD 86-2653]***

ENERGY CONSUMPTION - PAKISTAN.
Rashed, Saeed Ahmed. Pakistan's energy policy . Islamabad, Pakistan , 1983. iv, 102 p. : LC Card 83-930777 DDC 333.79/09549/1 19
HD9502.P272 R373 1983
NYPL [JLD 86-3857]

ENERGY CONSUMPTION - PSYCHOLOGICAL ASPECTS.
Katzev, Richard D. Promoting energy conservation . Boulder , 1987. xvi, 218 p. : ISBN 0-8133-7337-9 (pbk.) : LC Card 86-32587 DDC 333.79/16 19
HD9502.A2 K38 1987

ENERGY CONSUMPTION - SOUTH AFRICA - FORECASTING.
Kotzé, D. J. (David Jacobus) Energy projections for South Africa /. Johannesburg, Republic of South Africa , 1985. 125 p. : ISBN 0-86970-259-9 (pbk.) : LC Card 86-219416 DDC 333.79/13/0968 19
HD9502.S56 K68 1985

ENERGY CONSUMPTION - SOUTH ASIA.
Leach, Gerald. Household energy in South Asia /. London ; New York : xii, 111 p. : ISBN 1-85166-125-5 (pbk.) : LC Card 87-13177 DDC 333.79 19
HD9502.S613 H68 1987

ENERGY CONSUMPTION - SOVIET UNION.
Kononov, I͡U. D. Vliīanie ėnergeticheskikh strategiĭ na ėnergopotreblenie /. Irkutsk , 1985. 106 p. : LC Card 86-233835
HD9502.S652 K65 1985

ENERGY CONSUMPTION - STATISTICS.
Facts and figures . Vienna , 1984? 45 p. :
NYPL [JLD 86-2319]

ENERGY CONSUMPTION - UNITED STATES.
Energy economics . Englewood Cliffs, N.J. , c1987. viii, 328 p. : ISBN 0-13-277245-0 : LC Card 86-25254 DDC 333.79/0973 19
HD9502.U52 E4874 1987

Energy efficiency . Washington, D.C. , 1987, c1986. 333 p. : ISBN 0-918249-05-8 (pbk.) LC Card 86-28817 DDC 333.79/16/0973 19
HD9502.U52 E4883 1987

Halberstam, David. The reckoning /. New York , c1986. 752 p. ; ISBN 0-688-04838-2 LC Card 86-16427 DDC 338.4/76292/0973 19
HD9710.U52 H28 1986
NYPL [JLE 86-4151]

Models for investment and disinvestment decision making under uncertainty [microform] /. East Lansing , 1982. 173 p. :
NYPL [*XME-11,286]

ENERGY CONSUMPTION - UNITED STATES - FORECASTING.
United States. Dept. of Energy. Office of Policy, Planning, and Analysis. National energy policy plan projections to 2010 . Washington, D.C. [1985] 1 v. (various pagings) : LC Card 86-601637 DDC 333.79/0973 19
HD9502.U52 U5125 1985

ENERGY CONVERSION, MICROBIAL. see **BIOMASS ENERGY.**

The energy crisis /. Gibson, Michael, 1942- Vero Beach, FL , 1987. 46 p. : ISBN 0-86592-277-2 LC Card 87-12768 DDC 333.79 19
HD9502.A2 G525 1987

ENERGY CROPS - AUSTRIA.
Landwirtschaftliche Produktionsalternativen am Beispiel Ethanol, Ölsaaten und Eiweissfutterpflanzen /. Wien , 1985. 141 p. : LC Card 86-108149 DDC 338.1/09436 19
HD1935 .L33 1985

Energy demand : prospects and trends / edited by Paul Stevens. New York : St. Martin's Press, 1987. 176 p. : ill. ; 23 cm. Includes bibliographies. ISBN 0-312-01361-2 : LC Card 87-21477 DDC 333.79/12 19
1. Energy consumption - Forecasting. I. Stevens, Paul, 1947-.
HD9502.A2 E54373 1987

Energy demand and economic growth . Siddayao, Corazon M. Boulder , 1986. xiv, 127 p. : ISBN 0-8133-7154-6 : LC Card 86-906 DDC 333.79/13/091724 19
HD9502.D442 S54 1986
NYPL [JLE 86-3295]

ENERGY DEVELOPMENT - ASIA - STATISTICS.
Asian energy problems . New York, N.Y., U. S.A. , Singapore , 1982. xxxviii, 363 p. : ISBN 0-03-061566-6 (pbk.) LC Card 81-84610
HD9502.A782 A84x 1982

ENERGY DEVELOPMENT - CHINA.
Lieberthal, Kenneth. Bureaucratic politics and Chinese energy development /. [Washington, D.C.] [1986] xii, 405 p. ; LC Card 86-602422 DDC 333.79/0951 19
HD9502.C62 L54 1986

ENERGY DEVELOPMENT - CONGRESSES.
ENERGEX '84 (1984 : Regina, Sask.) Energy developments . Toronto , New York , 1984. xxiv, 1026 p. : ISBN 0-08-025407-1 LC Card 85-122124 DDC 333.79 19
TJ163.15 .E46 1984 ***NYPL [JSF 86-799]***

ENERGY DEVELOPMENT - DEVELOPING COUNTRIES.
Energy for a sustainable world /. New York, N.Y. , 1987. p. cm. LC Card 87-23099 DDC 333.79 19
HD9502.A2 AZ 1987

United States. Agency for International Development. Directorate for Energy and Natural Resources. Energy programs in the Agency for International Development. [Washington, D.C.] [1986] 38 p. ; LC Card 86-603136 DDC 333.79/15/091724 19
HD9502.D442 U55 1986

ENERGY DEVELOPMENT - DEVELOPING COUNTRIES - CONGRESSES.
Integrated rural energy planning /. Guildford, Surrey, England , 1985. xii, 200 p. : ISBN 0-408-22166-6 LC Card 87-160993 DDC 333.79/09172/4 19
HD9502.D442 I57 1985

ENERGY DEVELOPMENT - ENVIRONMENTAL ASPECTS - DEVELOPING COUNTRIES.
Integrated rural energy planning /. Guildford , c1985. xii, 200 p. : ISBN 0-408-22166-6
NYPL [JLF 87-3]

ENERGY DEVELOPMENT - ENVIRONMENTAL ASPECTS - EUROPE, EASTERN.
A Környezeti erőforrások gazdasági értékelésének módszertani kérdései /. Pécs [Budapest] , 1981. 78 leaves ; LC Card 82-202704
HD9502.E83 K68 1981 ***NYPL [JLE 87-219]***

ENERGY DEVELOPMENT - FORECASTING.
Chant, Verne G. Two global scenarios . Laxenburg, Austria , c1981. vi, 75 p. : ISBN 3-7045-0026-7 (pbk.) LC Card 83-130587 DDC 333.79/12 19
HD9502.A2 C45 1981 ***NYPL [JLE 86-595]***

ENERGY DEVELOPMENT - GERMANY (EAST)
Knop, Hans, Prof. Dr. sc. Die Energiewirtschaft der DDR und die Planung ihrer künftigen Entwicklung /. Berlin , 1960. 239 p. : LC Card 87-407618 DDC 333.79/0943 19
HD9502.G452 K58 1960

ENERGY DEVELOPMENT - GERMANY (WEST) - ECONOMETRIC MODELS.
Suding, Paul H. Ökonomische Ansätze zur Analyse des Energieverbrauchs der Haushalte für Rauwärmzwecke /. München , 1984. ix, 252, 10 p. : ISBN 3-486-28661-7 LC Card 84-209002
HD9502.G42 S8 1984

ENERGY DEVELOPMENT - INDIA.
Somasekhara, N. Rural energy . New Delhi , 1985. xii, 113 p. ; ISBN 81-207-0121-6 : LC Card 86-900467 DDC 333.79/0954 19
HD9502.I42 S66 1985 ***NYPL [JLD 86-3315]***

ENERGY DEVELOPMENT - INDIA - CONGRESSES.
Energy alternatives for rural development /. Jaipur , 1985. vi, 303 p. : LC Card 86-902191 DDC 333.79/0954 19
HD9556.I42 E54 1985

ENERGY DEVELOPMENT - SOCIAL ASPECTS.
Technik von gestern für die Ziele von morgen? . Opladen , c1986. 153 p. ; ISBN 3-531-11713-0 LC Card 86-230906
HD9502.A2 T43 1986

ENERGY DEVELOPMENT - SWEDEN.
Sweden. Oljeersättningsdelegationen. Uppföljning av oljeersättningsprogrammet . [Stockholm] [1982] 83, [74] p. : ISBN 91-38-07111-8 LC Card 83-217864
HD9502.S82 S96 1982

ENERGY DEVELOPMENT - UNITED STATES.
Handbook of alternative energy technology development and policy /. [Washington, D.C.] , 1983. xiv, 341 p. : ***NYPL [JLF 86-1486]***

ENERGY DEVELOPMENT - UNITED STATES - ADDRESSES, ESSAYS, LECTURES.
The Politics of energy research and development /. New Brunswick, U. S.A. , c1986. 181 p. : ISBN 0-88738-653-9 (pbk.) LC Card 86-1307 DDC 333.79/0973 19
HD9502.U52 P63 1986
NYPL [JLE 86-3577]

Energy developments . ENERGEX '84 (1984 : Regina, Sask.) Toronto , New York , 1984. xxiv, 1026 p. : ISBN 0-08-025407-1 LC Card 85-122124 DDC 333.79 19
TJ163.15 .E46 1984 ***NYPL [JSF 86-799]***

Energy economics : theory and policy / Robert L. Pirog and Stephen C. Stamos, Jr. ; with contributions by Steve Cohn, Robert H. Knapp, Richard M. Simon. Englewood Cliffs, N.J. : Prentice-Hall, c1987. viii, 328 p. : ill. ; 25 cm. Includes bibliographies and index. ISBN 0-13-277245-0 : LC Card 86-25254 DDC 333.79/0973 19
1. Energy industries - United States. 2. Energy consumption - United States. 3. Energy conservation - United States. 4. Renewable energy sources - United States. 5. Energy policy - United States. I. Pirog, Robert L. II. Stamos, Steve, 1947-. III. Cohn, Steven. IV. Knapp, Robert H., 1944-. V. Simon, Richard M.
HD9502.U52 E4874 1987

Energy efficiency : perspectives on individual behavior / editors, Willett Kempton, Max Neiman. Washington, D.C. : American Council for an Energy-Efficient Economy, in cooperation with Universitywide Energy Research Group, University of California, Family Energy Project, Institute for Family and Child Studies, Michigan State Univerity, 1987, c1986. 333 p. : ill. ; 23 cm. (American Council for an Energy-Efficient Economy Series on energy conservation and energy policy) Includes bibliographies and index. ISBN 0-918249-05-8 (pbk.) LC Card 86-28817 DDC 333.79/16/0973 19
1. Energy consumption - United States. 2. Energy conservation - United States. 3. Consumers - United States. 4. Energy policy - United States. I. Kempton, Willett, 1948-. II. Neiman, Max. III. Series: Series on

energy conservation and energy policy.
HD9502.U52 E4883 1987

Energy efficiency in Canada's pulp & paper industry /. Battle, Ellen F. Calgary, Alta. [1986] xviii, 131, 4 p. : ISBN 0-920522-38-6 (pbk.) : LC Card 87-124507 DDC 333.79 19
HD9834.C22 B37 1986

Energy, environment and development in Africa 0281-8515 .
(7) Hosier, Richard. Energy use in rural Kenya . Stockholm , Uppsala , c1985. xi, 177 p. : ISBN 91-7106-241-6
NYPL [JLD 86-2653]

Energy for a sustainable world / editors, Jose Goldemberg ... [et al.]. New York, N.Y. : Wiley, 1987. p. cm. LC Card 87-23099 DDC 333.79 19
1. Energy industries. 2. Power resources. 3. Energy consumption. 4. Energy policy. 5. Energy development - Developing countries. I. Goldemberg, José, 1928-.
HD9502.A2 AZ 1987

Energy future for Saint Lucia. Search Conference on Energy Futures for St. Lucia (1982 : Castries, Saint Lucia) The energy future for St. Lucia . Castries, St. Lucia [1982] 23 p. ; LC Card 87-400749 DDC 333.79/097298/43 19
HD9502.S0552 S4 1982

The energy future for St. Lucia . Search Conference on Energy Futures for St. Lucia (1982 : Castries, Saint Lucia) Castries, St. Lucia [1982] 23 p. ; LC Card 87-400749 DDC 333.79/097298/43 19
HD9502.S0552 S4 1982

Energy in China's modernization . Smil, Vaclav. Armonk, N.Y. , c1988. xiv, 250 p. : ISBN 0-87332-423-4 LC Card 87-12922 DDC 333.79/0951 19
HD9502.C62 S644 1988

Energy in Europe . Weyman-Jones, Thomas G., 1947- London , New York , 1986. xii, 176 p. : ISBN 0-416-36590-6 LC Card 86-18169 DDC 333.79/094 19
TJ163.25.E85 W48 1986
NYPL [JLD 87-1305]

Energy in Nigeria /. Synge, Richard. London [c1986] x, 145 p. : ISBN 0-946510-20-2 (pbk.) LC Card 86-215864 DDC 333.79/09669 19
HD9502.N552 S96 1986

ENERGY INDUSTRIES.
Böttges, Norbert. Rationalisierung im Energiebereich . Essen , Bielefeld , 1984. 159 p. : ISBN 3-7736-0106-9 LC Card 85-130852
HD9502.A2 B68 1984

Domdey, Karl Heinz. Weltenergie- und Weltrohstoffwirtschaft /. Berlin , 1981. 198 p. ; LC Card 85-132039
HD9502.A2 D65 1981

Energy for a sustainable world /. New York, N.Y. , 1987. p. cm. LC Card 87-23099 DDC 333.79 19
HD9502.A2 AZ 1987

Gerondeau, Christian, 1938- L'énergie à revendre /. [Paris] , c1984. 333 p. : LC Card 84-166266
HD9502.A2 G47 1984

Pachauri, R. K. The political economy of global energy /. Delhi , New York , 1985. xiii, 191 p. : LC Card 85-900034 DDC 333.79 19
HD9502.A2 P32 1985

Powell, James B. The Dow Jones-Irwin guide to high tech investing . Homewood, Ill. , c1986. xix, 356 p. : ISBN 0-87094-596-3 : LC Card 85-72178 DDC 332.6/7253 19
HG4521 .P63 1986 NYPL [JLE 86-2261]

ENERGY INDUSTRIES - ALASKA.
Rainery, Richard. Alaska's public energy resources . [Juneau?] [1985] 8, 124, 3, 7 p. : LC Card 86-622191 DDC 333.79/09798 19
HD9502.U53 A473 1985

ENERGY INDUSTRIES - ASIA.
Energy conservation in the Asian region . Tokyo, Japan [Honolulu, Hawaii] , 1986. vi, 173 p. : ISBN 92-833-2038-1 LC Card 87-122915 DDC 333.79/16/095 19
HD9502.A782 E53 1986

ENERGY INDUSTRIES - BRAZIL - MINAS GERAIS.
Diagnóstico energético, 1978/1983 /. Belo Horizonte , 1985. 177 p. : LC Card 87-121240 DDC 333.79/0981/51 19
HD9502.B73 M563 1985

Fluxo energético estadual, 1983 /. [Belo Horizonte, Brazil] , 1985. 105 p. : LC Card 87-404947 DDC 333.79/0981/51 19
HD9502.B73 M5646 1985

ENERGY INDUSTRIES - BULGARIA - EMPLOYEES - BIOGRAPHY.
Trudova slava /. Sofiîa , <1986-. v. <4 > : LC Card 86-228746
HD8039.M62 B88 1986

ENERGY INDUSTRIES - CANADA.
Douglas, Gordon W. Energy and regional investment in Canada /. Calgary, Alta. [1983] x, 114 p. : ISBN 0-920522-28-9 (pbk.) : LC Card 83-160268 DDC 332.6/722 19
HD9502.C32 D68 1983 NYPL [JLD 87-996]

ENERGY INDUSTRIES - CHILE - STATISTICS.
Balance de energía, 1965-1984 . Santiago, Chile [1985 or 1986] 191 p. : LC Card 87-401010 DDC 333.79/0983 19
HD9502.C52 B35 1985

ENERGY INDUSTRIES - CHINA.
Chêng, Chu-yüan. The demand and supply of primary energy in mainland China /. Taipei, Taiwan, Republic of China , Seattle , c1984. viii, 178 p. ; LC Card 84-231216 DDC 333.79/11/0951 19
HD9502.C62 C49 1984 NYPL [JLF 87-21]

Lieberthal, Kenneth. Bureaucratic politics and Chinese energy development /. [Washington, D.C.] [1986] xii, 405 p. ; LC Card 86-602422 DDC 333.79/0951 19
HD9502.C62 L54 1986

Smil, Vaclav. Energy in China's modernization . Armonk, N.Y. , c1988. xiv, 250 p. : ISBN 0-87332-423-4 LC Card 87-12922 DDC 333.79/0951 19
HD9502.C62 S644 1988

ENERGY INDUSTRIES - CONGRESSES.
Global energy interactions /. Ahmedabad , 1987. xxxi, 1290 p. : LC Card 87-902497 DDC 333.79 19
HD9502.A2 G545 1987b

ENERGY INDUSTRIES - COSTA RICA.
Cussianovich, Pedro. Economía y energía en Costa Rica . San José, Costa Rica , 1982. viii, 71, [10] leaves : LC Card 86-179795
HD9502.C82 C87 1982

ENERGY INDUSTRIES - EMPLOYEES - SUPPLY AND DEMAND.
Major stages and steps in energy manpower analysis . Geneva , 1986. viii, 80 p. : ISBN 92-2-105246-X (pbk.) : LC Card 86-222080 DDC 331.12/921042 19
HD5718.E47 M35 1986

ENERGY INDUSTRIES - EUROPE, EASTERN - INTERNATIONAL COOPERATION.
Kozlov, I. D. (Igor′ Dmitrievich) Ėnergeticheskoe khoziaĭstvo stran SĖV . Moskva , 1980. 158 p. ; LC Card 87-107887
HD9502.E83 K686 1980

ENERGY INDUSTRIES - FORECASTING.
Chant, Verne G. Two global scenarios . Laxenburg, Austria , c1981. vi, 75 p. : ISBN 3-7045-0026-7 (pbk.) LC Card 83-130587 DDC 333.79/12 19
HD9502.A2 C45 1981 NYPL [JLE 86-595]

Energy after the eighties . Amsterdam , New York , 1984. xxii, 298 p. : ISBN 0-444-42404-0 : LC Card 84-13742 DDC 333.79 19
HD9502.A2 E537 1984
NYPL [JLE 86-1572]

Energy markets after the collapse . Cambridge, MA (56 John F. Kennedy St., Suite 5, Cambridge 02138) , c1987. 164 p. : LC Card 87-142725 DDC 338.2/728 19
HD9560.5 .E54 1987

Perspective on world energy . Arlington, Va. (1911 Fort Myer Dr., Suite 403, Arlington 22209) , c1987. 3, iii, 27, [19] p. : LC Card 87-142737 DDC 333.79 19
HD9560.5 .P3847 1987

ENERGY INDUSTRIES - FORECASTING - CASE STUDIES.
The Politics of energy forecasting . Oxford [Oxfordshire] , New York , 1987. xiii, 314 p. : ISBN 0-19-828547-7 : LC Card 86-23885 DDC 333.79 19
HD9502.A2 P66 1987

ENERGY INDUSTRIES - FRANCE - STATISTICS.
Cauwet, Martine. Images économiques des entreprises . Paris [1986] 41 p. ; ISBN 2-11-064902-X : LC Card 86-229455
HD9502.F72 C38 1986

ENERGY INDUSTRIES - GERMANY, WEST.
Gesamtkonzeption nachwachsende Rohstoffe des Bundesministeriums für Ernährung, Landwirtschaft und Forsten . Münster-Hiltrup , 1983. vi, 196 p. : ISBN 3-7843-0202-5 : LC Card 84-126491
HD9502.G42 G47 1983

Ziesing, Hans-Joachim. Beurteilung der Wirtschaftlichkeitsschwelle und Analyse der Produktionskapazitäten bei neuen Technologien zur Energieeinsparung in mittel- bis längerfristiger Sicht . Berlin , 1983. 458 p. : ISBN 3-428-05497-0
NYPL [JLL 73-207 Bd. 139]

ENERGY INDUSTRIES - GREAT BRITAIN.
Britain's energy resources /. London , 1981. 27 p. : ISBN 0-11-701010-3 (pbk.) LC Card 81-165936 DDC 333.79/0941 19
HD9502.G72 B74 1981

ENERGY INDUSTRIES - GREAT BRITAIN - SAFETY MEASURES.
Fremlin, J. H. Power production . Bristol , Boston , c1985. x, 318 p. : ISBN 0-85274-479-X : LC Card 85-115642 DDC 363.1/19621042/0941 19
HD7269.E472 G744 1985
NYPL [JLE 86-3055]

Fremlin, J. H. Power production . Oxford [Oxfordshire] , New York , 1987. p. cm. ISBN 0-19-286078-X (pbk.) : LC Card 87-1564 DDC 363.1/9621042/0941 19
HD7269.E472 G744 1987

ENERGY INDUSTRIES - HUNGARY.
Márton, Géza. A hazai energiaszerkezet-változás fontosabb regionális kérdései /. Budapest , 1974. 271 p. : ISBN 963-05-0062-0 LC Card 86-187425
HD9502.H92 M37 1974

ENERGY INDUSTRIES - HUNGARY - STATISTICS.
Az Energiatermelés és az energiafelhasználás szerkezete . Budapest , 1970. 44 p. ; LC Card 86-189699
HD9502.H92 E54 1970

ENERGY INDUSTRIES - HYGIENIC ASPECTS - GREAT BRITAIN.
Fremlin, J. H. Power production . Bristol , Boston , c1985. x, 318 p. : ISBN 0-85274-479-X : LC Card 85-115642 DDC 363.1/19621042/0941 19
HD7269.E472 G744 1985
NYPL [JLE 86-3055]

Fremlin, J. H. Power production . Oxford [Oxfordshire] , New York , 1987. p. cm. ISBN 0-19-286078-X (pbk.) : LC Card 87-1564 DDC 363.1/9621042/0941 19
HD7269.E472 G744 1987

ENERGY INDUSTRIES - JAPAN.
Samuels, Richard J. The business of the Japanese state . Ithaca , 1987. xii, 359 p. : ISBN 0-8014-2022-9 (alk. paper) LC Card 87-5230 DDC 338.4/7621042/0952 19
HD9502.J32 S27 1987

ENERGY INDUSTRIES - JUVENILE LITERATURE.
Gibson, Michael, 1942- The energy crisis /. Vero Beach, FL , 1987. 46 p. : ISBN 0-86592-277-2 LC Card 87-12768 DDC 333.79 19
HD9502.A2 G525 1987

ENERGY INDUSTRIES - MEXICO - DIRECTORIES.
Mexico. Secretaría de Energía, Minas e Industria Paraestatal. Directorio del sector energía, minas e industria paraestatal, 1984. [Mexico City] , 1984. 497 p. ; ISBN 968-86000-4-0 LC Card 87-404794 DDC 333.79/0972 19
HD9502.M62 M49 1984

ENERGY INDUSTRIES - NIGERIA.
Synge, Richard. Energy in Nigeria /. London [c1986] x, 145 p. : ISBN 0-946510-20-2 (pbk.) LC Card 86-215864 DDC 333.79/09669 19
HD9502.N552 S96 1986

ENERGY INDUSTRIES - PLANNING.
Planning for changing energy conditions /. New Brunswick, N.J., U. S.A. , c1988. xiii, 300 p. : ISBN 0-88738-713-6 (pbk.) : LC Card 87-13977 DDC 333.79 19
HD9502.A2 P59 1988

ENERGY INDUSTRIES - RUSSIAN S.F.S.R. - IAKUTSKAIA A.S.S.R.
Razvitie ėnergetiki IAkutskoĭ ASSR v sviazi s sooruzheniem BAM . IAkutsk , 1985. 99, 3 p. : LC Card 86-233736
HD9502.S653 I237 1985

ENERGY INDUSTRIES - RUSSIAN S.F.S.R. - KANSK-ACHINSK BASIN.
Territorial'no-proizvodstvennyĭ kompleks . Moskva , 1982. 107 p. : LC Card 83-200414
HC337.R852 K3685 1982

ENERGY INDUSTRIES - SOUTH AFRICA - FORECASTING.
Kotzé, D. J. (David Jacobus) Energy projections for South Africa /. Johannesburg, Republic of South Africa , 1985. 125 p. : ISBN 0-86970-259-9 (pbk.) : LC Card 86-219416 DDC 333.79/13/0968 19
HD9502.S56 K68 1985

ENERGY INDUSTRIES - SOUTH ASIA - INTERNATIONAL COOPERATION - CONGRESSES.
South Asian cooperation in industry, energy, and technology /. New Delhi , Newbury Park, Calif. , 1987. p. cm. ISBN 0-8039-9538-5 (pbk.) LC Card 87-14994 DDC 337.1/54 19
HC430.6 .S675 1987

ENERGY INDUSTRIES - SOVIET UNION - LOCATION.
Sagers, Matthew J. The transportation of Soviet energy resources /. Totowa, N.J. , 1986. xvi, 177 p. : ISBN 0-8476-7504-1 : LC Card 86-15508 DDC 380.5/24 19
HD9502.S652 S24 1986 ***NYPL [JLE 87-38]***

ENERGY INDUSTRIES - SOVIET UNION - MANAGEMENT.
Decision-making in the Soviet energy industry . Falls Church, VA (7700 Leesburg Pike, #250, Falls Church 22043) , c1986. ix, 166 leaves ; LC Card 87-401592 DDC 333.79/0947 19
HD9502.S652 D43 1986

ENERGY INDUSTRIES - SWEDEN.
Sweden. Utredningen rörande export av teknik inom energisektorn. Ökad export av svensk energiteknik--ett handlingsprogram . [Stockholm] [1983] 171, [64] p. : ISBN 91-38-08037-0 LC Card 84-219591
HD9502.S82 S974 1983

ENERGY INDUSTRIES - TAXATION - SWEDEN.
Sweden. Skattekreditutredningen. Kortare kredittid för skatter på energi m.m. . [Stockholm] [1983] 109 p. ; ISBN 0-913807-27-9 LC Card 84-218594
HJ5715.S84 S87 1983

ENERGY INDUSTRIES - UNITED STATES.
Conant, Melvin. Critique of Energy security, a report to the President of the United States by the U. S. Department of Energy /. Washington, D.C., U. S.A. (1511 K St., NW, Suite #725, Washington 20005) , c1987. 23 leaves ; LC Card 87-401127 DDC 333.79/0973 19
HD9502.U52 C658 1987

Energy economics . Englewood Cliffs, N.J. , c1987. viii, 328 p. : ISBN 0-13-277245-0 : LC Card 86-25254 DDC 333.79/0973 19
HD9502.U52 E4874 1987

ENERGY INDUSTRIES - UNITED STATES - FORECASTING.
United States. Dept. of Energy. Office of Policy, Planning, and Analysis. National energy policy plan projections to 2010 . Washington, D.C. [1985] 1 v. (various pagings) : LC Card 86-601637 DDC 333.79/0973 19
HD9502.U52 U5125 1985

Energy markets after the collapse : the new competition / edited by Daniel Yergin, James Rosenfield. Cambridge, MA (56 John F. Kennedy St., Suite 5, Cambridge 02138) : Cambridge Energy Research Associates, c1987. 164 p. : ill. ; 28 cm. (Cambridge energy forum) Includes bibliographical references. LC Card 87-142725 DDC 338.2/728 19
1. Petroleum industry and trade - Forecasting. 2. Gas industry - Forecasting. 3. Energy industries - Forecasting. I. Yergin, Daniel. II. Rosenfield, James, 1957-. III. Cambridge Energy Research Associates. IV. Series.
HD9560.5 .E54 1987

ENERGY MINERALS - RUSSIAN S.F.S.R. - KANSK-ACHINSK BASIN.
KATĖK i razvitie otrasleĭ khoziaĭstva Sibiri /. Novosibirsk , 1984. 164 p. ; LC Card 84-167870
HC337.R852 S5246 1984

Energy papers .
(no. 21) Stern, Jonathan P. Soviet oil and gas exports to the West . Aldershot, Hants, England , Brookfield, Vt., USA , c1987. xi, 123 p. : ISBN 0-566-05124-9 : LC Card 86-32772 DDC 382/.4228/0947 19
HD9575.S652 S74 1987

Energy policy. Rashed, Saeed Ahmed. Pakistan's energy policy . Islamabad, Pakistan , 1983. iv, 102 p. : LC Card 83-930777 DDC 333.79/09549/1 19
HD9502.P272 R373 1983 ***NYPL [JLD 86-3857]***

ENERGY POLICY - AFRICA, WEST.
Busacker, Dietrich. Energies à la mesure des villages . Bielefeld, Federal Republic of Germany , 1985. 21 leaves ; LC Card 85-160345
HD9502.A4993 B87 1985

ENERGY POLICY - ASIA.
Energy conservation in the Asian region . Tokyo, Japan [Honolulu, Hawaii] , 1986. vi, 173 p. : ISBN 92-833-2038-1 LC Card 87-122915 DDC 333.79/16/095 19
HD9502.A782 E53 1986

ENERGY POLICY - AUSTRALIA - WESTERN AUSTRALIA.
Taylor, Neil. Collie, coal, and energy policy in Western Australia /. Murdoch, W.A. [1985] 56 p. : ISBN 0-86905-080-X (pbk.) LC Card 87-116549 DDC 333.8/22/099412 19
HD9558.A83 C657 1985

Taylor, Neil. The security of energy supplies in Western Australia /. Murdoch, W.A. , 1986. 35 p. : ISBN 0-86905-099-0 (pbk.) : LC Card 87-118009 DDC 333.79/09941 19
HD9502.A873 W45673 1986

ENERGY POLICY BRAZIL.
Dé Carli, Gileno. Desafio energético /. Recife , 1981 (Recife : Companhia Editora de Pernambuco) 309 p. ; LC Card 86-129710
HD9502.B72 D4 1981

ENERGY POLICY - BRAZIL, NORTHEAST - CONGRESSES.
Lopes, Marcos José. Atendimento ao mercado de energia elétrica do Nordeste /. Recife, PE [1984] 2 v. in 4 : LC Card 86-166126
HD9685.B83 N675 1984

ENERGY POLICY - CANADA.
Connections . [Ottawa] , Ottawa, Canada , 1985. x, 207 p. : ISBN 0-660-11743-6 (pbk.) : LC Card 85-136746 DDC 333.79/0971 19
TJ163.25.C2 C66 1985 ***NYPL [JLF 87-326]***

Hampson, Fen Osler. Forming economic policy . London , 1986. x, 161 p. : ISBN 0-86187-628-8 ***NYPL [JLE 86-3813]***

ENERGY POLICY - CASE STUDIES.
The Politics of energy forecasting . Oxford [Oxfordshire] , New York , 1987. xiii, 314 p. : ISBN 0-19-828547-7 : LC Card 86-23885 DDC 333.79 19
HD9502.A2 P66 1987

ENERGY POLICY - CHINA.
Lieberthal, Kenneth. Bureaucratic politics and Chinese energy development /. [Washington, D.C.] [1986] xii, 405 p. ; LC Card 86-602422 DDC 333.79/0951 19
HD9502.C62 L54 1986

Smil, Vaclav. Energy in China's modernization . Armonk, N.Y. , c1988. xiv, 250 p. : ISBN 0-87332-423-4 LC Card 87-12922 DDC 333.79/0951 19
HD9502.C62 S644 1988

ENERGY POLICY - CONGRESSES.
IASTED Symposia on Modelling, Policy and Economics of Energy and Power Systems, and Alternative Energy Sources and Technology (1981 : San Francisco, Calif.) Proceedings of the IASTED Energy Symposia : Modelling, Policy and Economics of Energy and Power Systems [and] Alternative Energy Sources and Technology, May 20-22, 1981, San Francisco, U. S.A. /. Anaheim, Calif. [1981?] 209 p. : ISBN 0-88986-027-0 ***NYPL [JSF 86-1103]***

Innovation for energy efficiency . Oxford [Oxfordshire] , 1988. p. cm. ISBN 0-08-034798-3 : LC Card 87-19016 DDC 333.79/094 19
HD9502.E8 I55 1988

International Scientific Forum on Changes in Energy (1981 : Mexico City, Mexico) Global energy assessment and outlook . Chur, Switzerland , New York, N.Y. , c1984. xxix, 580 p. : ISBN 3-7186-0224-5 LC Card 84-12959 DDC 333.79 19
TJ163.15 .I5678 1981 ***NYPL [JSE 86-509]***

New dimensions in foreign economic policy . Washington, DC , 1986. xiii, 118 p. ; LC Card 86-600514 DDC 337.73 19
HF1410.5 .N488 1986

United Nations University Symposium on Energy and Agriculture Futures--Policy Implications of Global Models (1982 : Paris, France) Energy and agriculture . [Chur, Switzerland , New York] , c1984. xii, 370 p. : ISBN 3-7186-0187-7 LC Card 83-18363 DDC 333.79 19
HD1405 .E53 1983 ***NYPL [JLD 86-1837]***

ENERGY POLICY - COSTA RICA.
Cussianovich, Pedro. Economía y energía en Costa Rica . San José, Costa Rica , 1982. viii, 71, [10] leaves : LC Card 86-179795
HD9502.C82 C87 1982

ENERGY POLICY - DEVELOPING COUNTRIES.
Siddayao, Corazon M. Energy demand and economic growth . Boulder , 1986. xiv, 127 p. : ISBN 0-8133-7154-6 : LC Card 86-906 DDC 333.79/13/091724 19
HD9502.D442 S54 1986 ***NYPL [JLE 86-3295]***

United States. Agency for International Development. Directorate for Energy and Natural Resources. Energy programs in the Agency for International Development. [Washington, D.C.] [1986] 38 p. ; LC Card 86-603136 DDC 333.79/15/091724 19
HD9502.D442 U55 1986

ENERGY POLICY - DEVELOPING COUNTRIES - CONGRESSES.
Energy Pricing Policy Workshop (1984 : Bangkok, Thailand) Criteria for energy pricing policy . London , Gaithersburg, MD, USA , 1985. 247 p. : ISBN 0-86010-618-1 : LC Card 86-147259 DDC 333.79/17 19
HD9502.D442 E56 1984

Management Training Seminar (1982 : Joint Research Centre, Ispra, Italy) National energy planning and management in developing countries . Dordrecht, Holland , Hingham, MA , c1983. xiii, 442 p. ; ISBN 90-277-1589-0 LC Card 83-4407 DDC 333.79/09172/4 19
HD9502.A2 M343 1982 ***NYPL [JLE 87-302]***

ENERGY POLICY - DOMINICAN REPUBLIC.
Gómez, Carmen. Población y energía en la República Dominicana, 1990-2000. Santo Domingo, República Dominicana [1985] vi, 86 p. : LC Card 86-176044
HD9502.D652 G65 1985

ENERGY POLICY - ECONOMIC ASPECTS - UNITED STATES.
Models for investment and disinvestment decision making under uncertainty [microform] /. East Lansing , 1982. 173 p. : ***NYPL [*XME-11,286]***

ENERGY POLICY - ENVIRONMENTAL ASPECTS - GERMANY (WEST) - BADEN-WÜRTTEMBERG.
Friedrich, R. (Rainer) Energie und Umwelt . Stuttgart [1985] 124 p. : LC Card 87-409533 DDC 333.79/0943/46 19
HD9502.G43 B3238 1985

Friedrich, R. (Rainer) Energie und Umwelt . Stuttgart [1985] 115 p. : LC Card 87-409534

DDC 333.79/0943/46 19
HD9502.G43 B324 1985

ENERGY POLICY - EUROPE.
Braathu, Jan. Diversification strategies and security-of-supply . Oslo [1984?] 74 p. ; LC Card 85-129223 DDC 382/.42285/094 19
HD9581.E8552 B7 1984
NYPL [JLM 78-136 no.88]

The future for European energy security /. London , 1985. 177 p. : ISBN 0-86187-573-7
NYPL [JLE 86-1018]

Hatch, Michael T., 1945- Politics and nuclear power . Lexington, KY , 1986. xi, 219 p. ; ISBN 0-8131-1583-3 : LC Card 85-29545 DDC 333.79/24/094 19
HD9698.E82 H38 1986
NYPL [JLD 86-2137]

Weyman-Jones, Thomas G., 1947- Energy in Europe . London , New York , 1986. xii, 176 p. : ISBN 0-416-36590-6 LC Card 86-18169 DDC 333.79/094 19
TJ163.25.E85 W48 1986
NYPL [JLD 87-1305]

ENERGY POLICY - EUROPE - CONGRESSES.
Innovation for energy efficiency . Oxford [Oxfordshire] , 1988. p. cm. ISBN 0-08-034798-3 : LC Card 87-19016 DDC 333.79/094 19
HD9502.E8 I55 1988

ENERGY POLICY - EUROPEAN ECONOMIC COMMUNITY COUNTRIES.
Energiaottanta . Milano , 1980. [xv] 284 p. ;
NYPL [JLD 86-3690]

ENERGY POLICY - FRANCE.
Offant, Pierre. Adaptation structurelle de l'économie française à la limitation de la consommation d'énergie /. Dijon , c1984. 224, iii p. : ISBN 2-85975-026-6 LC Card 85-205959
HD9502.F72 O33 1984

ENERGY POLICY - FRANCE - CONGRESSES.
Energie et décentralisation /. Paris , 1984. 297 p. : ISBN 2-7178-0782-9 : LC Card 84-249613
HD9502.F72 E5334 1984

ENERGY POLICY - GERMANY, EAST.
Knop, Hans, Prof. Dr. sc. Die Energiewirtschaft der DDR und die Planung ihrer künftigen Entwicklung /. Berlin , 1960. 239 p. : LC Card 87-407618 DDC 333.79/0943 19
HD9502.G452 K58 1960

ENERGY POLICY - GERMANY, WEST.
Erklärungen zur kommunalen Versorgungswirtschaft. Köln , 1985. 146 p. ; ISBN 3-87750-141-9
NYPL [K-10 8934 Heft 63]

Innenpolitische Leistungsbilanz 1982-1986 /. Bonn , 1986. 124 p. : LC Card 86-215949
HC286.7 .I55 1986

Köhler, Axel, 1938- Konturen bundesdeutscher Rohstoffpolitik /. Köln , c1983. 56 p. : ISBN 3-602-24713-9 LC Card 83-215016
HF1054.G4 K64 1983

Neu, Axel Dietmar, 1942- Entkoppelung von Wirtschaftswachstum und Energieverbrauch . Kiel [1978] 91 p. : LC Card 85-174721
HB44 .K45 no. 52 HD9502.G42

Rehfeld, Dieter, 1951- Bestimmungsfaktoren der Energiepolitik in der Bundesrepublik Deutschland . Frankfurt am Main , New York , c1986. vii, 287 p. ; ISBN 3-8204-9354-9 LC Card 86-194761
HD9502.G42 R44 1986

Ziesing, Hans-Joachim. Beurteilung der Wirtschaftlichkeitsschwelle und Analyse der Produktionskapazitäten bei neuen Technologien zur Energieeinsparung in mittel- bis längerfristiger Sicht . Berlin , 1983. 458 p. : ISBN 3-428-05497-0
NYPL [JLL 73-207 Bd. 139]

Zukünftige Energiepolitik . München , 1985. 189 p. : ISBN 3-89147-002-9 LC Card 87-104306
HD9698.G42 Z85 1985

ENERGY POLICY - INDIA.
Energy problem and world economic development . New Delhi , c1983. vi, 192 p. ; LC Card 83-906441 DDC 333.79/0954 19
HD9502.I42 E54 1983 ***NYPL [JLD 87-629]***

Guru, D. D. Energy and economic development /. Delhi , c1987. xi, 257 p. : ISBN 81-85061-53-6 : LC Card 87-901433 DDC 333.79/0954 19
HD9502.I4 G87 1987

National energy policy. New Delhi , 1986. v, 67 p. ; LC Card 87-900181
HD9502.I42 N36 1986

Somasekhara, N. Rural energy . New Delhi , 1985. xii, 113 p. ; ISBN 81-207-0121-6 : LC Card 86-900467 DDC 333.79/0954 19
HD9502.I42 S66 1985 ***NYPL [JLD 86-3315]***

ENERGY POLICY - INDIA - CONGRESSES.
All India Seminar on Renewable Sources of Energy (1982 : Allahabad, India) All India Seminar on Renewable Sources of Energy, Allahabad, 20th and 21st October '82 . Allahabad [1982] 1 v. (various pagings) : LC Card 84-911087 ***NYPL [JSF 86-685]***

Energy policy issues . New Delhi , c1987. 146 p. : LC Card 87-900625 DDC 333.79/0954 19
HD9502.I42 E536 1987

ENERGY POLICY - INFORMATION SERVICES - DEVELOPING COUNTRIES - CONGRESSES.
National energy data systems . New Delhi , 1984, c1983. xxvi, 511 p. ; LC Card 84-901310 DDC 333.79/09172/4 19
HD9502.D442 N37 1984
NYPL [JLD 86-4320]

ENERGY POLICY - INFORMATION SERVICES - UNITED STATES.
Bloch, Carolyn. Federal energy information sources and data bases /. Park Ridge, N.J. , 1979. x, 115 p. ; ISBN 0-8155-0764-X : LC Card 79-15543 DDC 016.33379/0973 19
HD9502.U52 B58 ***NYPL [JLE 86-4259]***

Energy policy issues : proceedings of a workshop, Jaipur, October 1985 / edited by R.K. Pachauri, Leena Srivastava. New Delhi : Wiley Eastern, c1987. 146 p. : ill., maps ; 25 cm. Proceedings of the Workshop on Energy Policy Issues, organized by the Tata Energy Research Institute, New Delhi. Includes bibliographical references. LC Card 87-900625 DDC 333.79/0954 19
1. Energy policy - India - Congresses. I. Pachauri, R. K. II. Srivastava, Leena. III. Workshop on Energy Policy Issues (1985 : Jaipur, India). IV. Tata Energy Research Institute.
HD9502.I42 E536 1987

ENERGY POLICY - ITALY.
Energiaottanta . Milano , 1980. [xv] 284 p. ;
NYPL [JLD 86-3690]

ENERGY POLICY - ITALY - CONGRESSES.
Conferenza nazionale sull'energia (1987 : Rome, Italy) Conferenza nazionale sull'energia . Roma [1987]- v. <1-2 > : LC Card 87-167955
HD9502.I82 C63 1987

ENERGY POLICY - JAPAN.
Suzuki, Shigeru, 1949- Nihon no enerugī kaihatsu seisaku /. Kyōto-shi , 1985. vii, 274 p. : ISBN 4-623-01582-3 : LC Card 85-221878
HD9502.J32 S89 1985 <Orien Japan>
NYPL [*OSM 86-3954]

ENERGY POLICY - JUVENILE LITERATURE.
Gibson, Michael, 1942- The energy crisis /. Vero Beach, FL , 1987. 46 p. : ISBN 0-86592-277-2 LC Card 87-12768 DDC 333.79 19
HD9502.A2 G525 1987

ENERGY POLICY - MEXICO.
Hampson, Fen Osler. Forming economic policy . London , 1986. x, 161 p. : ISBN 0-86187-628-8 ***NYPL [JLE 86-3813]***

ENERGY POLICY - NORWAY.
Schreiner, Alette. Virkninger av oljevirksomhet i Nord-Norge /. Oslo , 1984. 43 p. : ISBN 82-537-2118-8 : LC Card 85-146089
HD9575.N62 S37 1984

ENERGY POLICY - PAKISTAN.
Pakistan. Planning Commission. The Sixth Five Year National Energy Plan, 1983-88. [Islamabad] [1983 or 1984] 88 p. ; LC Card 84-932174 DDC 333.79/09549/1 19
HD9502.P272 P33 1983

Rashed, Saeed Ahmed. Pakistan's energy policy . Islamabad, Pakistan , 1983. iv, 102 p. : LC Card 83-930777 DDC 333.79/09549/1 19
HD9502.P272 R373 1983
NYPL [JLD 86-3857]

ENERGY POLICY - PHILIPPINES.
National energy program, 1986-1990. Metro Manila, Philippines [1986] 64 p. : LC Card 86-207642 DDC 333.79/09599 19
HD9502.P62 N373 1986

ENERGY POLICY - QUÉBEC (PROVINCE)
"L'Energie, levier de développement économique" . [Ottawa?] [1983] 30 leaves ; LC Card 85-128816
HD9685.C3 Q4425 1983

ENERGY POLICY - RWANDA.
Joint UNDP/World Bank Energy Sector Assessment Program. Rwanda . [Washington, D.C.?] [1982] ii, 68 p., [1] folded leaf : LC Card 87-136863 DDC 333.79/0967/571 19
HD9502.R932 J65 1982

ENERGY POLICY - SAINT LUCIA - CONGRESSES.
Search Conference on Energy Futures for St. Lucia (1982 : Castries, Saint Lucia) The energy future for St. Lucia . Castries, St. Lucia [1982] 23 p. ; LC Card 87-400749 DDC 333.79/097298/43 19
HD9502.S0552 S4 1982

ENERGY POLICY - SOCIAL ASPECTS - CONGRESSES.
Energie und Gerechtigkeit /. München , c1984. xii, 254 p. : ISBN 3-597-10259-X LC Card 84-175053
HD9502.A2 E5192 1984

ENERGY POLICY - SOCIAL ASPECTS - INDIA.
Hans, Asha. The power sector in India /. New Delhi , c1986. vi, 149 p. ; LC Card 86-901959 DDC 333.79/32/0954 19
HD9502.I42 H36 1986

ENERGY POLICY - SOVIET UNION.
Decision-making in the Soviet energy industry . Falls Church, VA (7700 Leesburg Pike, #250, Falls Church 22043) , c1986. ix, 166 leaves ; LC Card 87-401592 DDC 333.79/0947 19
HD9502.S652 D43 1986

Kononov, I͡U. D. Vlii͡anie ėnergeticheskikh strategiĭ na ėnergopotreblenie /. Irkutsk , 1985. 106 p. : LC Card 86-233835
HD9502.S652 K65 1985

ENERGY POLICY - SOVIET UNION - MATHEMATICAL MODELS.
Pospelov, Germogen Sergeevich. Prot͡sedury i algoritmy formirovanii͡a kompleksnykh programm /. Moskva , 1985. 422, [2] p. : LC Card 86-203758
HC336.25 .P567 1985

ENERGY POLICY - SPAIN.
Comisión Energía y Recursos de AEPDEN-Amigos de la Tierra. Modelo energético de tránsito /. Madrid [1979?] 136 p. ; ISBN 84-85639-02-2 LC Card 79-126051
HD9502.S662 C66 1979 ***NYPL [JLC 87-71]***

Costa Morata, Pedro. Centrales nucleares en España . Madrid [1987?] 51 p. : ISBN 84-398-8834-1 LC Card 87-165955
HD9698.S72 C62 1987

ENERGY POLICY - SPAIN - ANDALUSIA.
Plan económico para Andalucía, 1984-1986 /. Andalucía [1985?] 164 p. ; ISBN 84-505-0611-5 LC Card 86-205786
HD3616.S495 A536 1985

Energy policy studies .
(v. 2) Energy and cities /. New Brunswick, U. S.A. , c1985. 173 p. : ISBN 0-87855-813-6 (pbk.) LC Card 84-24074 DDC 333.79/13/091732 19
HD108.2 .E525 1985 ***NYPL [JLE 86-4441]***

Energy policy studies (Newark, Del.)
The Politics of energy research and development /. New Brunswick, U. S.A. , c1986. 181 p. : ISBN 0-88738-653-9 (pbk.) LC Card 86-1307 DDC 333.79/0973 19
HD9502.U52 P63 1986
NYPL [JLE 86-3577]

Energy policy studies, 0882-3537 .
(v. 3) The Politics of energy research and development /. New Brunswick, U. S.A. , c1986. 181 p. : ISBN 0-88738-653-9 (pbk.) LC Card 86-1307 DDC 333.79/0973 19
HD9502.U52 P63 1986
NYPL [JLE 86-3577]

(v. 4) Planning for changing energy conditions /. New Brunswick, N.J., U. S.A. , c1988. xiii, 300 p. : ISBN 0-88738-713-6 (pbk.) : LC Card 87-13977 DDC 333.79 19
HD9502.A2 P59 1988

ENERGY POLICY - SUDAN.
Sudan. National Energy Plan Committee. The national energy plan, 1985-2000 /. Khartoum, Sudan , 1985. iii, iii, 158 p. : LC Card 86-980496 DDC 333.79/09624 19
HD9502.S732 S83 1985a

ENERGY POLICY - SWEDEN.
Energihushållning och samhällsekonomi . [Stockholm] [1980] 70, 39, 29, 58 p. : ISBN 91-38-05980-0 LC Card 84-122675
HD9502.S82 E48 1980

Energy and economic adjustment /. Stockholm , 1983. 247 p. : ISBN 91-7204-186-2
NYPL [JLE 86-1351]

Försörjningstryggheten för olja, kol och uran . Stockholm [1982] 175 p. : ISBN 91-38-07030-8 LC Card 82-240448
HD9502.S82 F68 1983

Internationella förutsättningar för den svenska oljeförsörjningen under 1980-talet. Stockholm , 1981. 172 p. in various pagings : ISBN 91-38-06244-5 LC Card 82-241303
HD9575.S82 I57 1981

Ny teknik för elproduktion, elanvändning . Stockholm [1983] 172 p. : LC Card 84-108404
HD9685.S852 N9 1983

Oljeersättningsprogrammet i ett samhällsekonomiskt perspektiv. Stockholm , 1983. 39, 67, 54, 71 p. : ISBN 91-38-07618-7 LC Card 83-232276
HD9502.S82 O55 1983

Regionala effekter av en kärnkraftsavveckling . [Stockholm] [1979] 254 p. : ISBN 91-38-05243-1 LC Card 82-219566
HD9698.S82 O42 1979b Suppl.

Samhällsekonomiska effekter av en kärnkraftsavveckling . [Stockholm] [1979] 149 p. ; ISBN 91-38-05244-X LC Card 82-219542
HD9698.S82 O42 1979

Sweden. 1980 års oljelagringskommitté. Kol, uran och gas för kristid. [Stockholm] [1981] 192 p. : ISBN 91-38-06450-2 LC Card 83-107879
HD9502.S82 S88 1981

Sweden. Elanvändningskommittén till restriktioner, användning och hushållning. El och olja . [Stockholm] [1980] 265 p. : ISBN 91-38-05865-0 LC Card 84-102448
HD9502.S82 S898 1980

Sweden. Oljeersättningsdelegationen. Redovisning och analys av kommunernas oljereduktionsplaner /. Stockholm [1983] 59, [91] p. : ISBN 91-38-07458-3 LC Card 83-239703
HD9502.S82 S96 1983a

Sweden. Oljeersättningsdelegationen. Statligt stöd till oljeersättning . [Stockholm] [1983] 1 v. (various pagings) : ISBN 91-38-07657-8 LC Card 84-218524
HD9502.S82 S96 1983

Sweden. Oljeersättningsdelegationen. Uppföljning av oljeersättningsprogrammet . [Stockholm] [1982] 83, [74] p. : ISBN 91-38-07111-8 LC Card 83-217864
HD9502.S82 S96 1982

Sweden. Statens industriverk. Kommunal energiplanering . Stockholm , 1980. 51 p. ; ISBN 91-38-05802-2 LC Card 82-236900
HD9502.S82 S97 1980

Wittrock, Björn. De stora programmens tid . Stockholm , 1984. 186 p. ; ISBN 91-7410-200-1 : LC Card 84-189613
HD9502.S82 W58 1984

ENERGY POLICY - SWEDEN - ADDRESSES, ESSAYS, LECTURES.
Swedish national and local government programs for conservation of energy in buildings /. Gävle, Sweden [1982] 187 p. : ISBN 91-540-9134-9 (pbk.) LC Card 82-208802 DDC 333.79 19
HD9502.S82 S98 1982 NYPL [JLG 86-107]

ENERGY POLICY - UNITED STATES.
Analysis of the federal residential energy tax credits [microform] . Boston, Mass. , 1982. v, 102 p. : *NYPL [*XME-11,559]*

Chlumský, Jiří. Hospodářská politika USA v oblasti energetiky /. Praha , 1986. 134 p. ; LC Card 86-215183
HD9502.U52 C526 1986

Conant, Melvin. Critique of Energy security, a report to the President of the United States by the U. S. Department of Energy /. Washington, D.C., U. S.A. (1511 K St., NW, Suite #725, Washington 20005) , c1987. 23 leaves ; LC Card 87-401127 DDC 333.79/0973 19
HD9502.U52 C658 1987

A Documentary history of the Petroleum Reserves Corporation, 1943-1944 . Washington , 1974. v, 119 p. : LC Card 74-602382
HD9566 .D6 NYPL [JLE 78-1181]

Energy and environment . Washington, D.C. , c1985. x, 190 p. : ISBN 0-87187-360-5 : LC Card 85-25471 DDC 333.79/0973 19
HD9502.U52 E4524 1985
NYPL [JLE 86-2859]

Energy conservation . Washington, D.C. , c1986. xii, 270 p. : ISBN 0-8157-7716-7 : LC Card 85-26894 DDC 333.79/16/0973 19
HD9502.U62 E478 1986
NYPL [JLE 86-4084]

Energy economics . Englewood Cliffs, N.J. , c1987. viii, 328 p. : ISBN 0-13-277245-0 : LC Card 86-25254 DDC 333.79/0973 19
HD9502.U52 E4874 1987

Energy efficiency . Washington, D.C. , 1987, c1986. 333 p. : ISBN 0-918249-05-8 (pbk.) LC Card 86-28817 DDC 333.79/16/0973 19
HD9502.U52 E4883 1987

Handbook of alternative energy technology development and policy /. [Washington, D.C.] , 1983. xiv, 341 p. : *NYPL [JLF 86-1486]*

Hines, Lawrence Gregory. The market, energy, and the environment /. Boston , c1988. xii, 305 p. : ISBN 0-205-10568-8 : LC Card 87-1037 DDC 333.7/0973 19
HC110.E5 H57 1988

Nivola, Pietro S. The politics of energy conservation /. Washington, D.C. , c1986. x, 294 p. ; ISBN 0-8157-6088-4 : LC Card 85-48265 DDC 333.79/16/0973 19
TJ163.4.U6 N58 1986 NYPL [JLE 86-2515]

Paulson, S. Lawrence. Reagan on energy . New York, NY (850 3rd Ave., New York 10022) , 1981. 248 p. in various pagings ; LC Card 82-111477 DDC 333.79/0973 19
HD9502.U52 P38 NYPL [JLF 87-368]

Rosenbaum, Walter A. Energy, politics, and public policy /. Washington, D.C. , c1987. viii, 221 p. : ISBN 0-87187-412-1 (pbk.) : LC Card 87-5301 DDC 333.79/0973 19
HD9502.U52 R64 1987

ENERGY POLICY - UNITED STATES - ADDRESSES, ESSAYS, LECTURES.
The Politics of energy research and development /. New Brunswick, U. S.A. , c1986. 181 p. : ISBN 0-88738-653-9 (pbk.) LC Card 86-1307 DDC 333.79/0973 19
HD9502.U52 P63 1986
NYPL [JLE 86-3577]

ENERGY POLICY - UNITED STATES - CONGRESSES.
Community energy management as an economic development strategy . [Lincoln, Neb.] (Box 95085, Lincoln 68509-5085) [1984 or 1985] iv, 396 p. : LC Card 86-622211 DDC 333.79/0973 19
HD9502.U52 C656 1984

ENERGY POLICY - UNITED STATES - HISTORY - 20TH CENTURY.
Clark, John Garretson, 1932- Energy and the federal government . Urbana , c1987. xxiii, 511 p. : ISBN 0-252-01295-X LC Card 85-20505 DDC 333.8/2/0973 19
HD9502.U52 C57 1987 NYPL [JLE 87-736]

Energy, politics, and public policy /. Rosenbaum, Walter A. Washington, D.C. , c1987. viii, 221 p. : ISBN 0-87187-412-1 (pbk.) : LC Card 87-5301 DDC 333.79/0973 19
HD9502.U52 R64 1987

Energy Pricing Policy Workshop (1984 : Bangkok, Thailand) Criteria for energy pricing policy : a collection of papers commissioned for the Energy Pricing Policy Workshop / organised under the Regional Energy Development Programme (RAS/84/001), Bangkok, 8-11 May 1984 ; sponsored by the United Nations Development Programme (UNDP) ... [et al.] ; edited by Corazón Morales Siddayao. London ; Gaithersburg, MD, USA : Graham & Trotman, 1985. 247 p. : ill. ; 24 cm. Includes bibliographies and index. ISBN 0-86010-618-1 : LC Card 86-147259 DDC 333.79/17 19
1. Fuel - Prices - Developing countries - Congresses. 2. Energy policy - Developing countries - Congresses. I. Siddayao, Corazon M. II. Regional Energy Development Programme (United Nations). III. United Nations. Development Programme. IV. Title.
HD9502.D442 E56 1984

Energy problem and world economic development : with special reference to India / edited by K.N. Subrahmanya. New Delhi : Deep & Deep, c1983. vi, 192 p. ; 23 cm. Includes index. Bibliography: p. [189]-190. LC Card 83-906441 DDC 333.79/0954 19
1. Energy policy - India. 2. Power resources - India. I. Subrahmanya, K. N.
HD9502.I42 E54 1983 NYPL [JLD 87-629]

Energy programs in the Agency for International Development. United States. Agency for International Development. Directorate for Energy and Natural Resources. [Washington, D.C.] [1986] 38 p. ; LC Card 86-603136 DDC 333.79/15/091724 19
HD9502.D442 U55 1986

Energy projections for South Africa /. Kotzé, D. J. (David Jacobus) Johannesburg, Republic of South Africa , 1985. 125 p. : ISBN 0-86970-259-9 (pbk.) : LC Card 86-219416 DDC 333.79/13/0968 19
HD9502.S56 K68 1985

Energy requirements and utilization in rural and urban low-income settlements. Nairobi : United Nations Centre for Human Settlements (Habitat), 1984. iii, 76 p. : ill. ; 30 cm. Bibliography: p. 74-76. "HS/61/84"--T.p. verso. LC Card 86-980596 DDC 333.79/13/091724 19
1. Energy consumption - Developing countries. I. United Nations Centre for Human Settlements.
HD9502.D442 E57 1984

ENERGY RESEARCH. see **POWER RESOURCES - RESEARCH.**

ENERGY RESOURCES. see **POWER RESOURCES.**

ENERGY RESOURCES DEVELOPMENT. see **ENERGY DEVELOPMENT.**

ENERGY SOURCE DEVELOPMENT. see **ENERGY DEVELOPMENT.**

ENERGY TAX CREDITS - UNITED STATES.
Analysis of the federal residential energy tax credits [microform] . Boston, Mass. , 1982. v, 102 p. : *NYPL [*XME-11,559]*

Energy use in rural Gujarat / editor, Girja Sharan ; study teams: north Gujarat, Indian Institute of Management, Ahmedabad ; central and south Gujarat, Jyoti Consultants Limited, Baroda ; Saurashtra and Kutch, Bhavnagar University, Bhavnagar. New Delhi : Oxford & IBH, c1987. iv, 186 p. : map ; 23 cm. "Sponsored by the Gujarat Energy Development Agency, 1982." Bibliography: p. [129]-130. Includes index. ISBN 81-204-0216-2 : LC Card 87-901949 DDC 333.79/13/095475 19
1. Power resources - India - Gujarat. 2. Energy consumption - India - Gujarat. I. Sharan, Girja, 1944-. II. Indian Institute of Management, Ahmedabad. III. Jyoti Consultants Limited. IV. Bhavnagar University. V. Gujarat Energy Development Agency.
HD9502.I43 G844 1987

Energy use in rural Kenya . Hosier, Richard. Stockholm , Uppsala , c1985. xi, 177 p. : ISBN 91-7106-241-6 *NYPL [JLD 86-2653]*

Energy 2000 : a global strategy for sustainable development : a report for the World Commission on Environment and Development. London ; [Atlantic Highlands] N.J. : Zed Books, 1987. viii, 76 p. : ill. ; 20 cm. Bibliography: p. 69-71. ISBN 0-86232-710-5 : LC Card 87-13371 DDC 333.79 19
1. Energy policy. 2. Energy development. 3. Energy conservation. I. World Commission on Environment and Development.
HD9502.A2 E536 1987

Enfants, familles, migrations. Charbit, Yves. Enfants, familles, migrations dans le bassin méditerranéen /. [Paris] , 1985. viii, 195 p. ; ISBN 2-7332-0110-7 (pbk.)
HQ792.E8 C47 1985
NYPL [JLL 72-295 cahier no 110]

Enfants, familles, migrations dans le bassin méditerranéen /. Charbit, Yves. [Paris] , 1985. viii, 195 p. ; ISBN 2-7332-0110-7 (pbk.)
HQ792.E8 C47 1985
NYPL [JLL 72-295 cahier no 110]

Enfermedades de trabajo. 1a ed. México, D.F. : Instituto Mexicano del Seguro Social, Secretaría General, Jefatura de Servicios del Secretariado Técnico, Centro de Documentación, c1983. 403 p. : ill. ; 23 cm. (Lecturas en materia de seguridad social) Includes bibliographies. ISBN 968-8242-08-X LC Card 85-216152
1. Occupational diseases - Mexico. 2. Industrial hygiene - Mexico. 3. Workers' compensation - Mexico. I. Instituto Mexicano del Seguro Social. Centro de Documentación. II. Series.
HD7262.5.M6 E54 1983

Eng, Robert J. Promotional management . Englewood Cliffs, N.J. , c1988. xi, 305 p. : ISBN 0-13-731035-8 (pbk.) LC Card 87-12041 DDC 658.8 19
HF5415 .P727 1988

Engalichev, Nicolas. Nevel, Robert L. The timber industries of New Hampshire and Vermont . Broomall, Pa. , 1986. 56 p. : LC Card 86-601144 DDC 338.1/7498/09742 19
HD9757.N4 N48 1986

Engel, Gábor. A kereskedelmi tevékenység komplex finanszirozása / [készitették, Engel Gábor, Lovassné Szecső Judit]. Budapest : Belkereskedelmi Kutató Intézet, [1985] 68 p. ; 30 cm. (Tanulmány) "In 1985. március." ISBN 963-7202-58-7 LC Card 86-157419
1. Business enterprises - Finance. 2. Business enterprises - Hungary - Finance. I. Lovassné Szecső, Judit. II. Series: Tanulmńy (Budapest, Hungary). III. Title.
HG4026 .E517 1985

Engelhard, Rutger J. Chavangi, Noel A. Culture as the basis for implementing self-sustaining wood fuel development programmes /. Nairobi, Kenya [1985] 24 leaves ; LC Card 87-111963 DDC 333.75 19
HD9769.F843 K433 1985

Engelhardt, Gunther.
Finanzwirtschaftliche Folgen kommunaler Gebiets- und Funktionalreformen . Baden-Baden , 1986. 209 p. : ISBN 3-7890-1163-0 (Deut. Bibl.) LC Card 86-169111
HJ1121 .F55 1986

Haushalts- und mehrjährige Finanzplanung im Planspiel : Anliegen, Grundkonzeption und erste Ergebnisse einer Hamburger Projektstudieneinheit / Gunther Engelhardt und Mitautoren.1. Aufl. Baden-Baden : Nomos, 1984. 331 p. : ill. ; 23 cm. (Schriften zur öffentlichen Verwaltung und öffentlichen Wirtschaft. Bd. 77) Summary in English and German. Bibliography: p. 323-327. Includes indexes. ISBN 3-7890-0975-X LC Card 85-140583
1. Budget - Germany (West) - Decision making. 2. Budget - Germany (West) - Hamburg - Decision making. I. Title.
HJ2109 .E54 1984

Engelhardt, Hans Dieter von. Die Livländische Gemeinnützige und Ökonomische Sozietät (1792-1939) : ein Beitrag zur Agrargeschichte des Ostseeraums / von Hans Dieter von Engelhardt und Hubertus Neuschäffer. Köln : Böhlau, 1983. ix, 215 p., [3] leaves of plates : ill. ; 24 cm. (Quellen und Studien zur baltischen Geschichte. Bd. 5) Bibliography: p. 196-207. Includes index. ISBN 3-412-04282-X LC Card 84-117318
1. Livländische Gemeinnützige und Ökonomische Sozietät - History. 2. Agriculture - Economic aspects - Livonia (Estonia and Latvia) - Societies, etc. - History. I. Neuschäffer, Hubertus. II. Title. III. Series.
HD1486.S65 E54 1983

Engelhardt, Klaus. Die Rolle der Rüstung in der Wirtschaft des heutigen Kapitalismus /. Berlin [1984] 127 p. ; LC Card 85-135711
HC281 .B39 1984 Heft 4 HC79.D4

Engelhardt, Werner Hans. Der Direktvertrieb im Konsumgüterbereich : eine absatzwirtschaftliche Analyse / Engelhardt, Kleinaltenkamp, Rieger. Stuttgart : W. Kohlhammer, c1984. 158 p. : ill. ; 24 cm. Bibliography: p. 151-156. ISBN 3-17-008550-6 : LC Card 84-234886
1. Direct marketing - Germany (West). 2. Durable goods, Consumer - Germany (West) - Marketing. I. Kleinaltenkamp, Michael. II. Rieger, Sören. III. Title.
HF5415.126 .E54 1984

Engelmann, Bernt, 1921- Wir hab'n ja den Kopf noch fest auf dem Hals : die Deutschen zwischen Stunde Null und Wirtschaftswunder / Bernt Engelmann. Köln : Kiepenheuer & Witsch, c1987. 257 p. : ill. ; 22 cm. ISBN 3-462-01688-1 LC Card 87-146658
1. Germany, West - Economic policy. 2. Germany, West - Economic conditions. 3. Germany, West - Social conditions. 4. Reconstruction (1939-1951) - Germany (West). I. Title.
HC286.5 .E594 1987

Engelmeier, Philip. Auctioneering : a complete treatise on how to become an auctioneer, non-fiction / by Philip Engelmeier. San Francisco, CA : P.A. Engelmeier, 1980. iii, 39 p. : ill. ; 14 x 22 cm. ISBN 0-9605002-0-0 (pbk.) LC Card 86-213457
1. Auctions - Handbooks, manuals, etc. I. Title.
HF5476 .E55 1980

Engels, Wolfram.
Den Staat erneuern, den Markt retten / Wolfram Engels ; [Hrsg. Stiftung Gesellschaft und Unternehmen und Institut der Deutschen Wirtschaft]. Köln : Deutscher Instituts-Verlag, c1983. 228 p. ; 19 cm. (DIV-Sachbuchreihe. 32) Includes bibliographical references. ISBN 3-602-34836-9 LC Card 84-182378
1. Germany, West - Economic conditions. 2. Laissez-faire. 3. Economic policy. I. Stiftung Gesellschaft und Unternehmen. II. Institut der Deutschen Wirtschaft. III. Title.
HC286 .E54 1983

Einseitige Betrachtungen : Kommentare des Herausgebers / Wolfram Engels.1. Aufl. Düsseldorf : Wirtschaftswoche, 1986. 240 p. ; 21 cm. LC Card 87-146603 DDC 338.943 19
1. Economic policy. 2. Germany, West - Economic policy - 1974-. 3. Economic history - 1971-. 4. Germany, West - Economic conditions - 1974-. I. Title.
HD84 .E53 1986

Internationaler Kapitalverkehr und Devisenhandel /. Frankfurt am Main , c1986. 133 p. ; ISBN 3-7819-0347-8 LC Card 87-164156 DDC 332/.042 19
HG3891 .I58 1986

Engelsk-svensk ordbok : skolupplaga / av Karl Kärre ... [et al.]. ; under medverkan av Grenville Grove.3. omarb uppl. Stockholm : Laromedelsforlagen, 1970. 2 v. ; 22 cm. Vol. [1] has added t.p. in English. Vol. [2] has title: Svensk-engelsk ordbok.
1. English language - Dictionaries - Swedish. 2. Swedish language - Dictionaries - English. I. Kärre, Karl, 1885-. II. Grove, Grenville. III. Title: Svensk-engelsk ordbok. IV. Title: English Swedish dictionary.
NYPL [JFD 87-817]

Engelstad, Kirsten. Viten som verktøy : nye muligheter for små og mellomstore industribedrifter / ved Kirsten Engelstad. Oslo : Riksbibliotektjenesten, 1985. 80 p. ; 30 cm. (Skrifter fra Riksbibliotektjenesten, 0800-4129 . nr. 26) Includes bibliographical references. ISBN 82-7195-048-7 LC Card 86-175688
1. Small business - Information services - Norway. I. Title. II. Series.
HD2346.N6 E53 1985

Engfer, Anette. Schneewind, Klaus A., 1939- Eltern und Kinder . Stuttgart , c1983. 229 p. : ISBN 3-17-007744-9 LC Card 83-150745 DDC 303.3/23/0943 19
HQ739 .S29 1983 ***NYPL [JLE 87-1168]***

ENGINEERING, ARCHITECTURAL. see **BUILDING.**

ENGINEERING CYBERNETICS. see **AUTOMATION.**

ENGINEERING, ELECTRICAL. see **ELECTRIC ENGINEERING.**

ENGINEERING, IRRIGATION. see **IRRIGATION ENGINEERING.**

ENGINEERING - MANAGEMENT - CONGRESSES.
Specialty Conference on Engineering and Construction Projects (1982 : New Orleans, La.) Proceedings of the Specialty Conference on Engineering and Construction Projects . New York, N.Y. , c1982. vi, 329 p. : ISBN 0-87262-299-1 (pbk.) LC Card 82-70492 DDC 658.5 19
TA190 .S67 1982 ***NYPL [JLD 86-1905]***

Engineering Management Society. see **IEEE Engineering Management Society.**

ENGINEERING - NEW ZEALAND.
Gapes, R. F. (Robert Francis) The heavy engineering industry in New Zealand . [Wellington, N.Z. , 1976] 105 p. : LC Card 84-255451
HD9705.N44 G36 1976

ENGINEERING, NUCLEAR. see **NUCLEAR ENGINEERING.**

ENGINEERING, TRAFFIC. see **TRAFFIC ENGINEERING.**

ENGINEERING - UNITED STATES - DATA PROCESSING - EQUIPMENT AND SUPPLIES.
The Mini-microcomputer turnkey engineering systems market. New York, N.Y. , c1983. vi, 228 p. ; LC Card 87-142400 DDC 381/.4500416 19
HD9696.C63 U5262 1983

ENGINEERING, WATER-SUPPLY. see **WATER-SUPPLY ENGINEERING.**

An engineers guide to spreadsheets, word processors & data base managers /. Moore, James M. (James Mendon), 1925- Norcross, GA , c1986. xi, 154 p. : ISBN 0-89806-081-8 (pbk.) LC Card 87-157586 DDC 620/.0028/553 19
HF5548 .M566 1986

ENGINEERS - UNITED STATES - BIOGRAPHY.
Wells, Della Wager. George Waldo Woodruff . [Macon, Ga.] c1987. x, 167 p. : ISBN 0-86554-298-8 LC Card 87-24700 DDC 338/.04/0924 B 19
HC102.5.W66 W45 1987

ENGLAND - COMMERCE - EUROPE - HISTORY.
Fryde, E. B. Studies in medieval trade and finance /. London , 1983. 1 v. (various pagings) ; ISBN 0-907628-10-9 LC Card 83-168474 DDC 382/.0942/04 19
HF3518.E85 F79 1983 ***NYPL [JLE 86-2481]***

ENGLAND - DESCRIPTION AND TRAVEL - GUIDE-BOOKS.
Atterbury, Paul. English rivers and canals /. London , 1984. 152 p. : ISBN 0-297-78318-1
NYPL [JFF 87-598]

ENGLAND - ECONOMIC CONDITIONS.
Lachmann, Richard. From manor to market . Madison, Wis. , 1987. xiv, 166 p. : ISBN 0-299-11420-1 : LC Card 87-40146 DDC 330.942/05 19
HC254 .L33 1987

Levine, David, 1946- Reproducing families . Cambridge [Cambridgeshire] , New York , 1987. ix, 251 p. ; ISBN 0-521-33256-7 LC Card 86-26372 DDC 304.6/0942 19
HB3585 .L48 1987

Power, Eileen Edna, 1889-1940. The wool trade in English medieval history /. New York [1987], c1941. viii, 128 p. ; ISBN 0-313-25656-X (lib. bdg. : alk. paper) LC Card 86-29442 DDC 338.4/767731/0942 19
HD9901.7.E54 P68 1987

ENGLAND - FOREIGN POPULATION - STATISTICS.
Marmot, M. G. Immigrant mortality in England and Wales, 1970-78 . London , 1984. xii, 144 p. : ISBN 0-11-691094-1 (pbk.) : LC Card 84-222968 DDC 614.4/242 19
HB1415 .M37 1984 ***NYPL [JLG 87-55]***

England - History. see **Great Britain - History.**

ENGLAND - INDUSTRIES - HISTORY.
Kenwood, A. G. Capital formation in north east England, 1800-1913 /. New York , 1985. xv, 444 p. : ISBN 0-8240-6685-5 : LC Card 84-46005 DDC 332/.0415/09428 19
HC260.S3 K46 1985 ***NYPL [JLE 86-3900]***

ENGLAND, NORTHERN - SOCIAL CONDITIONS.
Colls, Robert. The pitmen of the northern coalfield . Manchester, UK , Wolfeboro, NH,

USA , c1987. xv, 386 p., [2] p. of plates : ISBN 0-7190-2202-9 (U. S.) : LC Card 87-11029 DDC 305/.9622/09427 19
HD8039.M62 G737 1987

England, Paula. Households, employment, and gender : a social, economic, and demographic view / Paula England and George Farkas. New York : Aldine Pub. Co., c1986. ix, 237 p. : ill. ; 24 cm. Includes indexes. Bibliography: p. 197-222. ISBN 0-202-30322-5 (lib. bdg.) LC Card 85-18628 DDC 304.6 19
1. Households - United States. 2. Cost and standard of living - United States. 3. Women - Employment - United States. 4. Sex discrimination in employment - United States. I. Farkas, George, 1946-. II. Title.
HQ536 .E54 1986 ***NYPL [JLE 86-2828]***

ENGLAND - POPULATION - HISTORY.
Levine, David, 1946- Reproducing families . Cambridge [Cambridgeshire] , New York , 1987. ix, 251 p. ; ISBN 0-521-33256-7 LC Card 86-26372 DDC 304.6/0942 19
HB3585 .L48 1987

ENGLAND - SOCIAL CONDITIONS.
Lachmann, Richard. From manor to market . Madison, Wis. , 1987. xiv, 166 p. : ISBN 0-299-11420-1 : LC Card 87-40146 DDC 330.942/05 19
HC254 .L33 1987

Levine, David, 1946- Reproducing families . Cambridge [Cambridgeshire] , New York , 1987. ix, 251 p. ; ISBN 0-521-33256-7 LC Card 86-26372 DDC 304.6/0942 19
HB3585 .L48 1987

ENGLAND - SOCIAL CONDITIONS - MEDIEVAL PERIOD, 1066-1485 - ADDRESSES, ESSAYS, LECTURES.
Hilton, R. H. (Rodney Howard), 1916- Class conflict and the crisis of feudalism . London , Ronceverte, W. Va. , 1985. 349 p. ; ISBN 0-907628-36-2 : LC Card 85-21855 DDC 305.5/0942 19
HD604 .H48 1985 ***NYPL [JFE 87-391]***

ENGLAND - STATISTICS, VITAL.
Marmot, M. G. Immigrant mortality in England and Wales, 1970-78 . London , 1984. xii, 144 p. : ISBN 0-11-691094-1 (pbk.) : LC Card 84-222968 DDC 614.4/242 19
HB1415 .M37 1984 ***NYPL [JLG 87-55]***

Engler, Calvin. Managerial accounting / Calvin Engler. Homewood, Ill. : Irwin, 1987. xvi, 926 p. : col. ill. ; 24 cm. (The Robert N. Anthony/Willard J. Graham series in accounting) Includes index. Bibliography: p. 401. ISBN 0-256-03318-8 LC Card 86-81610 DDC 658.1/511 19
1. Managerial accounting. I. Title. II. Series.
HF5657 .E54 1987

Engler, Matthias. Mühlfeld, Claus, 1940- Konflikt und Kooperation in Arbeitgeberverbänden /. Augsburg , 1985. 403 p. ; ISBN 3-87512-138-4 : LC Card 86-152717
HD2429.G3 M84 1985

Englesko-srpskohrvatski i srpskohrvatsko-engleski ekonomski rečnik =. Gligorijević, Vera. Beograd , 1986. 549, [1] p. ; LC Card 86-196648
HB61 .G49 1986 ***NYPL [*QAD 87-1743]***

English-Arabic business dictionary /. Abdel Haleem, M. A. London , 1984. xxxii, 263 p. ; ISBN 0-86010-448-6 : LC Card 83-228731 DDC 650/.03/21 19
HF1002 .A23 1984 ***NYPL [JLD 86-2048]***

The English-Arabic dictionary of professional business terms / Saba and Co. London : MEED Group Books ; Boulder, Colo. : Distrebuted in North America by L. Reinner Pubishers, c1987. 210 p. ; 22 cm. Arabic and English. Title on added t.p.: Qāmūs Inkilīzī-ʻArabī khāṣṣ bi-muṣṭalaḥāt idārat al-aʻmāl. ISBN 0-946510-33-4 : LC Card 87-163985 DDC 650/.03/21 19
1. Business - Dictionaries. 2. Finance - Dictionaries. 3. English language - Dictionaries - Arabic. 4. Saba and Co. I. Title: Qāmūs Inkilīzī-ʻArabī khāṣṣ bi-muṣṭalaḥāt idārat al-aʻmāl.
HF1002 .E583 1987

The English Atlantic, 1675-1740 . Steele, Ian Kenneth. New York , 1986. xii, 400 p. ISBN 0-19-503968-8 LC Card 85-25828 DDC 380.3/09171/241 19
HE202 .S74 1986 ***NYPL [JLE 86-4056]***

English-Chinese philatelic dictionary and identification key =. Yang, Jan-Syau. Winter Park, Fla. (340 Park Ave., N., Winter Park 32789) , c1986. [55] p. : LC Card 87-169624 DDC 769.56/014 19
HE6204.C6 Y36 1986

English historical economics, 1870-1926 . Koot, Gerard M. Cambridge [Cambridgeshire] , New York , 1987. viii, 277 p. ; ISBN 0-521-32854-3 LC Card 87-11592 DDC 330/.0941 19
HB103.A2 K65 1987

English, John, 1944- Public housing . London , Wolfeboro, N.H. , c1987. 174 p. : ISBN 0-7099-4826-3 : LC Card 86-24056 DDC 363.5/8 19
HD7288.78.G7 P83 1987

ENGLISH LANGUAGE - BUSINESS ENGLISH - DICTIONARIES - FRENCH.
Geoghegan, C., 1945- Handbook of commercial French /. London , New York , 1988. p. cm. ISBN 0-7102-0857-X LC Card 87-16320 DDC 448/.002465 19
HF5728.F8 G46 1988

ENGLISH LANGUAGE - BUSINESS ENGLISH - HANDBOOKS, MANUALS, ETC.
Dorrell, Jean, 1926- The answer book . Los Angeles, CA , c1987. ix, 358 p. : ISBN 0-935732-12-8 (pbk.) : LC Card 87-23408 DDC 651 19
HF5547.5 .D63 1987

ENGLISH LANGUAGE - DICTIONARIES - ARABIC.
Abdel Haleem, M. A. English-Arabic business dictionary /. London , 1984. xxxii, 263 p. ; ISBN 0-86010-448-6 : LC Card 83-228731 DDC 650/.03/21 19
HF1002 .A23 1984 ***NYPL [JLD 86-2048]***

A Dictionary of economics & commerce . Beirut , 1983. 383 p. ; LC Card 83-961782 DDC 330/.03/21 19
HB61 .D4896 1983 ***NYPL [*OEO 87-1397]***

The English-Arabic dictionary of professional business terms /. London , Boulder, Colo. , c1987. 210 p. ; ISBN 0-946510-33-4 : LC Card 87-163985 DDC 650/.03/21 19
HF1002 .E583 1987

Farīd, ʻAbd Allāh Muḥammad. al-Qāmūs al-farīd fī al-māl wa-al-iqtiṣād, ʻArabī-Injilīzī /. [S.l.] 1985 (al-Qāhirah, Miṣr : Maṭābiʻ al-Ahrām al-Tijārīyah) 150, 264 p. ; LC Card 86-960655
HB61 .F36 1985

Majmaʻ al-Lughah al-ʻArabīyah, Cairo. Lajnat al-Jughrāfiyā. al-Muʻjam al-jughrāfī /. [al-Qāhirah] , 1974. 9,185 p. ; LC Card 77-961221
G63 .M34 1974 ***NYPL [*OEO 86-3694]***

Watt, Alec. Illustrated dictionary of geology . Beirut [Harlow, Essex] , 1982. 329 p. :
NYPL [*OG 85-2903]

ENGLISH LANGUAGE - DICTIONARIES - FRENCH.
Arnould, Michel. Les termes pétroliers . Paris , c1981. xii, 267 p. ; ISBN 2-04-011414-9 LC Card 82-167169 DDC 665.5/03/21 19
TN865 .A66 1981 ***NYPL [JSE 84-171]***

European Communities glossary . Luxembourg , 1984. 1589 p. ; ISBN 92-824-0131-6 : LC Card 85-175527
KJE926.5 .E87 1984 ***NYPL [JLF 87-216]***

Glossaire des Communautés européennes . Luxembourg , 1987, c1986. 706 p. ; ISBN 92-824-0410-2 : ***NYPL [JLF 87-217]***

Glossary of terms . [Ottawa] [1981]-1984. 3 v. ; ISBN 0-662-52389-X (v. 2) LC Card 81-180363 DDC 350/.0003/41 19
JA61 .G55 ***NYPL [JLF 87-379]***

Harrap's new standard French and English dictionary /. London , 1980-1981. 4 v. ; ISBN 0-245-50972-0 (v.1)

Lebas, Michel. Glossary of accounting =. Paris , c1985. 124 p. ; ISBN 2-86644-065-X (pbk.) : LC Card 86-179932
HF5621 .L42 1985

Marks, Georgette A. Harrap's slang dictionary English-French/French-English /. London , 1984. 476 p. ; ISBN 0-245-54047-4
NYPL [JFC 86-640]

Organisation for European Economic Co-operation. Terminologie des échanges et paiements internationaux et de la comptabilité nationale. Paris [1958] 146, [6] p. LC Card 58-47135 DDC 382.03
HF1002 .O7 ***NYPL [JLF 87-128]***

Thody, Philip Malcolm Waller, 1928- Faux amis & key words . London , 1985. 224 p. ; ISBN 0-485-11243-4 : LC Card 84-108125 DDC 443/.21 19
PC2593 .T45 1985 ***NYPL [JFD 86-5704]***

Thody, Philip Malcolm Waller, 1928- Mistakable French . New York , 1985. 224 p. ; ISBN 0-684-18324-2 : LC Card 84-51853 DDC 443/.21 19
PC2593 .T46 1985 ***NYPL [JFD 86-5781]***

Tixier, Maud. Dictionnaire américain-anglais-français du management /. Paris , 1985. 381 p. ; ISBN 2-247-00647-7 : LC Card 86-160705
HD30.15 .T59 1985 ***NYPL [JLD 86-3975]***

Witcomb, Henry, 1822- Dictionnaire des termes de marine français-anglais & anglais-français. Paris, 1883. 2 v. LC Card 29-23644
V24 .W5 ***NYPL [JSE 86-1965]***

ENGLISH LANGUAGE - DICTIONARIES - GERMAN.
Betteridge, Harold T. Cassell's German-English, English-German dictionary =. New York , 1978. xx, 1580 p. ; ISBN 0-02-522920-6 (standard) LC Card 77-18452 DDC 433/.21 19
PF3640 .B453 1978
NYPL [*P-Desk 86-5858]

Böhss, Günther. Dictionary of printed circuit technology . Amsterdam , New York , 1985. 187 p. ; ISBN 0-444-99555-2 (U. S.) : LC Card 85-12955 DDC 621.381/74/0331 19
TK7868.P7 B65 1985 ***NYPL [JSD 86-621]***

Collins English-German dictionary =. London , Stuttgart , 1986, c1983. 2 v. (xviii, 1390, xxiii, 1380 p.) ; ISBN 3-12-517131-8 (v. 1)
NYPL [JFC 86-2613]

Dietl, Clara-Erika. Commercial dictionary . Wiesbaden , c1985-c1987. 2 v. ; ISBN 3-409-19900-4 (v. 1) LC Card 86-160868
HF1002 .D493 1985
NYPL [*R-Econ. 87-1271]

Eichborn, Reinhart von. Wirtschaftswörterbuch. Düsseldorf, Wien [1961-70] 2 v. LC Card 70-463836 ***NYPL [JLD 85-120]***

Erdsiek, Gerhard. Wörterbuch für Recht, Wirtschaft und Politik. Bleckede bei Hamburg [1964-1968] 2 v. LC Card 65-42077
NYPL [JLE 85-408]

Klatt, Edmund. Langenscheidt's standard German dictionary /. New York , 1983-1984. 1341 p. ; ***NYPL [JFC 86-781]***

Kleiber, Achim W. Fachwörterbuch, Schweissen, Schneiden und verwandte Verfahren /. Düsseldorf , 1986- , c1985- v. ; ISBN 3-87155-707-2 (Bd. 1) LC Card 86-149500 DDC 671.5/2/0331 19
TS227.5 .K54 1986 ***NYPL [JSK 86-83]***

Koschnick, Wolfgang J., 1942- Standard-Wörterbuch für Werbung, Massenmedien und Marketing, Deutsch-Englisch /. Berlin , New York , 1987. 590 p. ; ISBN 0-89925-293-1 (U. S.) : LC Card 87-19928 DDC 659.1/03/21 19
HF5803 .K67 1987

Schäfer, Wilhelm, Dr. Wirtschaftswörterbuch /. München , c1986- v. <1 > ; ISBN 3-8006-1100-7 (Bd. 1) LC Card 86-214220
HB61 .S3 1986

Strutz, Henry. Talking business in German . Woodbury, N.Y. , c1987. iv, 256 p. : ISBN 0-8120-3747-2 (pbk.) LC Card 86-22360 DDC 650/.03/31 19
HF1002 .S79 1987

ENGLISH LANGUAGE - DICTIONARIES - HINDI.
Raghu Vira. A comprehensive English-Hindi dictionary of governmental & educational words & phrases ... /. New Delhi , 1962. 189, 1572 p. ; ***NYPL [JLF 87-203]***

ENGLISH LANGUAGE - DICTIONARIES - ITALIAN.
Picchi, Fernando. Economics and business . Bologna , 1986. 1333 p. ; ISBN 88-08-04550-1

LC Card 86-201141 DDC 330/.03/51 19
HB61 .P49 1986

Reynolds, Barbara, 1914- [Cambridge Italian dictionary.] Cambridge dizionario italiano-inglese, inglese-italiano, Signorelli . Cambridge [Cambridgeshire] ; New York : 2276 p. ; ISBN 0-521-32702-4 LC Card 86-1898 DDC 453/.21 19
*PC1640 .R4 1986 NYPL [*R-REK 86-3799]*

Spinelli, Nicola, 1881- Dizionario commerciale, italiano-inglese e inglese-italiano . Torino , 1957. 464, 683, 138 p. ;
NYPL [JLD 85-226]

ENGLISH LANGUAGE - DICTIONARIES - JAPANESE.
Akiyama, Nobuo. Talking business in Japanese /. Hauppauge, N.Y. , c1987. p. cm. ISBN 0-8120-3848-7 LC Card 87-19601 DDC 650/.03/956 19
HF1002 .A34 1987

Erekutoronikusu pawā shōjiten /. Tōkyō , 1985. v, 618 p. : ISBN 4-320-08454-3 : LC Card 85-229520
TK7804 .E73 1985 <Orien Japan>
*NYPL [*OSG 86-3267]*

Takabe, Yoshinobu, 1907- Amerika shingo jiten = The Kenkyūsha dictionary of new English /. Tokyo , 1978. 717 p. ;
*NYPL [*OSG 87-2157]*

Takahashi, M. (Morio), 1892-1959. Romanized English-Japanese, Japanese-English dictionary /. [Tokyo] , 1958. 457, 1226 p. ;
*NYPL [*O-*OSG 87-870]*

ENGLISH LANGUAGE - DICTIONARIES - PORTUGUESE.
Cavalcante, José Cândido Marques. Dicionário inglês-português de termos econômicos & comerciais /. [Fortaleza] , Petrópolis , 1979. 408 p. ; LC Card 80-113110
HB61 .C37 NYPL [JLE 81-244]

ENGLISH LANGUAGE - DICTIONARIES - RUSSIAN.
Kadieva, D. A. Chastotnyĭ anglo-russkiĭ slovar′. Leningrad , 1986. 126 p. ; LC Card 87-146427
HB61 .K23 1986

Kotz, Samuel. Russian-English, English-Russian glossary of statistical terms. Edinburgh, 1971. vii, 87 p. ISBN 0-05-002446-9 LC Card 72-197391 DDC 519.5/01/4
HA17 .K62 NYPL [JLF 73-1241]

ENGLISH LANGUAGE - DICTIONARIES - SERBO-CROATIAN.
Andrlić, Vlasta. Rječnik terminologije jugoslavenskog političko-ekonomskog sistema . Zagreb , 1985. viii, 135 p. ; LC Card 86-182784
*HB61 .A55 1985 NYPL [*QKK 87-1803]*

Bogadek, F. A. (Francis Aloysius), 1882- [New English-Croatian and Croatian-English dictionary.] Cassell's New English-Croatian and Croatian-English dictionary /. New York [c1985] vii, 531, 497, 46, 7 p. ; ISBN 0-02-512140-5 LC Card 85-23140 DDC 491.8/2321 19
*PG1377 .B72 1985 NYPL [*QAD 87-600]*

Gligorijević, Vera. Englesko-srpskohrvatski i srpskohrvatsko-engleski ekonomski rečnik =. Beograd , 1986. 549, [1] p. ; LC Card 86-196648
*HB61 .G49 1986 NYPL [*QAD 87-1743]*

ENGLISH LANGUAGE - DICTIONARIES - SPANISH.
The American heritage Larousse Spanish dictionary . Boston , c1986. xxx, 532, xviii, 572 p. ; ISBN 0-395-32429-7 : LC Card 86-7202 DDC 463/.21 19
PC4640 .A54 1986
*NYPL [*R-RGK 86-5942]*

Glossary of the petroleum industry . Tulsa, Okla. , c1982. vi, 378 p. ; ISBN 0-87814-194-4 (pbk.) : LC Card 82-7622 DDC 665.5/03/61 19
TN865 .G63 1982 NYPL [JSD 86-496]

Guiliani Cury, Hugo. Glosario de terminos de renegociacíon de deuda externa =. Santo Domingo, República Dominicana , 1985. 68 p. ; LC Card 86-184550
HJ8046 .G85 1985

Vox Modern Spanish and English dictionary . Lincolnwood, Ill. , c1986. xxxiv, 487, 45, 484 p. : ISBN 0-8442-7990-0 LC Card 86-61160
*NYPL [*R-RGK 86-7059]*

Vox new college Spanish and English dictionary . Lincolnwood, Ill., U. S.A. , c1984. xix, 1456, 60 p. : ISBN 0-8442-7998-6 (plain-edge ed.) : LC Card 84-61106 DDC 463/.21 19
PC4640 .V696 1984
*NYPL [*R-RGK 85-1500]*

ENGLISH LANGUAGE - DICTIONARIES - SWEDISH.
Engelsk-svensk ordbok . Stockholm , 1970. 2 v. ; *NYPL [JFD 87-817]*

ENGLISH LANGUAGE - PARONYMS - DICTIONARIES.
Thody, Philip Malcolm Waller, 1928- Faux amis & key words . London , 1985. 224 p. ; ISBN 0-485-11243-4 : LC Card 84-108125 DDC 443/.21 19
PC2593 .T45 1985 NYPL [JFD 86-5704]

Thody, Philip Malcolm Waller, 1928- Mistakable French . New York , 1985. 224 p. ; ISBN 0-684-18324-2 : LC Card 84-51853 DDC 443/.21 19
PC2593 .T46 1985 NYPL [JFD 86-5781]

ENGLISH LANGUAGE - SLANG - DICTIONARIES.
Marks, Georgette A. Harrap's slang dictionary English-French/French-English /. London , 1984. 476 p. ; ISBN 0-245-54047-4
NYPL [JFC 86-640]

ENGLISH LANGUAGE - WORD FREQUENCY.
Kadieva, D. A. Chastotnyĭ anglo-russkiĭ slovar′. Leningrad , 1986. 126 p. ; LC Card 87-146427
HB61 .K23 1986

English laundresses . Malcolmson, Patricia E., 1944- Urbana , c1986. xv, 220 p. ; ISBN 0-252-01293-3 LC Card 85-24599 DDC 305.4/3648/0942 19
HD6073.L32 G75 1986
NYPL [JLE 86-4640]

English rivers and canals /. Atterbury, Paul. London , 1984. 152 p. : ISBN 0-297-78318-1
NYPL [JFF 87-598]

English-Serbocroatian and Serbocroatian-English economic dictionary. Gligorijević, Vera. Englesko-srpskohrvatski i srpskohrvatsko-engleski ekonomski rečnik =. Beograd , 1986. 549, [1] p. ; LC Card 86-196648
*HB61 .G49 1986 NYPL [*QAD 87-1743]*

English shipowning during the industrial revolution . Ville, Simon P. Manchester, UK , Wolfeboro, NH, USA , c1987. x, 192 p. : ISBN 0-7190-1714-9 LC Card 87-11043 DDC 387.5/065/41 19
HE945.M49 V55 1987

English Swedish dictionary. Engelsk-svensk ordbok . Stockholm , 1970. 2 v. ;
NYPL [JFD 87-817]

English workers and the coming of the welfare state, 1918-1945.
([15]) Hilton, John, 1880-1943. Rich man, poor man /. New York , 1985. 174 p. ; ISBN 0-8240-7614-1 (alk. paper) : LC Card 85-13078 DDC 339.2/2/0941 19
HC256.4 .H54 1985 NYPL [JLC 86-342]

Britain's industrial future . New York , 1985. xxiv, 503 p. ; ISBN 0-8240-7605-2 (alk. paper) : LC Card 85-13042 DDC 338.941 19
HC256.3 .B728 1985 NYPL [JLD 86-3461]

Cole, George Douglas Howard, 1889-1959. The next ten years in British social and economic policy /. New York , 1985. xxi, 459 p. ; ISBN 0-8240-7607-9 (alk. paper) : LC Card 85-13055 DDC 338.941 19
HC256.3 .C6 1985 NYPL [JLD 86-3300]

Hannington, Wal, 1895- The problem of the distressed areas /. New York , 1985. 286 p. : ISBN 0-8240-7613-3 : LC Card 85-14663 DDC 338.941 19
HC256.3 .H265 1985 NYPL [JLD 86-3420]

Hobson, J. A. (John Atkinson), 1858-1940. The economics of unemployment /. New York , 1985. 157 p. ; ISBN 0-8240-7615-X : LC Card 85-13053 DDC 331.13/7 19
HB822 .H63 1985 NYPL [JLC 86-452]

Men without work . New York , 1985. xii, 447 p. ; ISBN 0-8240-7619-2 (alk. paper) : LC Card 85-13069 DDC 331.13/7941 19
HD5765.A6 M46 1985
NYPL [JLD 87-1031]

Public enterprise . New York , 1985. 416 p. ; ISBN 0-8240-7626-5 (alk. paper) : LC Card 85-13105 DDC 354.4109/1 19
HD4147 .P83 1985 NYPL [JLD 86-3467]

English working class.
Rowntree, B. Seebohm (Benjamin Seebohm), 1871-1954. Poverty . New York , 1980. xxi, 426 p. : ISBN 0-8240-0120-6 (alk. paper) : LC Card 79-56969 DDC 305.5/6 19
HC258.Y6 R64 1980 NYPL [JLD 86-3436]

Engmann, E. V. T. Population of Ghana, 1850-1960 / E.V.T. Engmann. Accra, Ghana : Published for the University of Cape Coast by Ghana Universities Press, 1986. xvii, 300 p. : ill. ; 22 cm. Bibliography: p. 292-298. Includes index. ISBN 996-430-088-3 (pbk.) LC Card 87-127395 DDC 304.6/09669 19
1. Ghana - Population - History. I. Title.
HB3666.8.A3 E535 1986

Engrosomsetningsindeks /. Holm, Yngvar. Oslo , 1984. 18 leaves ; ISBN 82-537-2141-2 : LC Card 85-178075
HB235.N6 H65 1984

Engrosprisstatistikk : engrosprisindeks, produsentprisindeks. Oslo : Statistisk sentralbyrå : I kommisjon hos H. Aschehoug og Universitetsforlaget, 1982. 120 p. ; 29 cm. (Rapporter fra Statistisk sentralbyrå, 0332-8422 . 82/29) ISBN 82-537-1833-0 : LC Card 83-139816
1. Wholesale prices indexes - Norway. 2. Prices - Norway. I. Norway. Statistisk sentralbyrå. II. Series.
HB235.N6 E54 1982

ENGROSSING. see **MONOPOLIES.**

Engshuber, Wolfgang. Die Auflagenpolitik des Internationalen Währungsfonds : (rechtliche Würdigung) / von Wolfgang Engshuber. [München] : Hochschule der Bundeswehr München, Fachbereich Wirtschafts- und Organisationswissenschaften, [1985?] 32 leaves ; 30 cm. (Materialien aus dem Institut für Rechtswissenschaft) Bibliography: leaves 28-32. LC Card 85-166626
1. International Monetary Fund. 2. Monetary policy. I. Title. II. Series.
HG3881.5.I58 E54 1985

Engstrom, John H. Hay, Leon Edwards, 1923- Essentials of accounting for governmental and not-for-profit organizations /. Homewood, Ill. , 1987. x, 310 p. ; ISBN 0-256-03454-0 (pbk.) LC Card 86-82587 DDC 657/.98 19
HJ9801 .H39 1987

ENGVALL & AUG. FALK NYA CHARKUTERI (STOCKHOLM, SWEDEN)
Grenander-Nyberg, Gertrud, 1912- En charkuterifabrik med tradition . Stockholm , c1985. 207 p. : ISBN 91-38-09206-9 LC Card 86-159511
HD9145.S88 E544 1985

Engwall, Lars. Multinationella förtag . Lund , 1985. 196 p. ; ISBN 91-578-0210-6 : LC Card 86-216456
HD2755.5 .M864 1985

The Enhanced data network (van) market. New York, N.Y. : Frost & Sullivan, c1983. v, 258 p. : ill. ; 29 cm. "September 1983." "(#A1224)" LC Card 87-143825
1. Data transmission equipment industry - United States. 2. Telecommunication - United States. 3. Market surveys - United States. I. Frost & Sullivan.
HD9696.D383 U6344 1983

The Enhanced oil recovery market, 1980-1990. New York, N.Y. : Frost & Sullivan, c1983. vi, 203 leaves : ill. ; 29 cm. "July 1983." "(A1155)" LC Card 87-142370 DDC 381/.45617665/0973 19
1. Petroleum industry and trade - United States. 2. Secondary recovery of oil - United States. 3. Oil field equipment and supplies industry - United States. 4. Oil field chemicals industry - United States. 5. Market surveys - United States. I. Frost & Sullivan.
HD9565 .E53 1983

Enige aspecten van arbeid in de toekomst : een verkenning tot het begin van de jaren negentig / J.W. Becker ... [et al.]. 's-Gravenhage : Sociaal en Cultureel Planbureau : Staatsuitgeverij, 1986. 178 p. : ill. ; 27 cm. (Sociale en culturele studies . 7) Includes

bibliographical references. ISBN 90-12-05246-7 LC Card 87-101491
1. Labor supply - Netherlands. 2. Unemployment - Netherlands. 3. Employment forecasting - Netherlands. I. Becker, J. W. II. Series.
HD5792 .E47 1986

L'enjeu de la formation professionnelle /. Soisson, Jean Pierre, 1934- [Paris] , c1986. iv, 315 p. : ISBN 2-213-01752-2 : LC Card 86-194690
HD5715.5.F8 S65 1986

Les enjeux du changement technologique /. Salomon, Jean Jacques. Paris , c1986. 206 p. : ISBN 2-7178-1092-7 : LC Card 86-172778
HC79.T4 S286 1986

Enjeux fonciers en Afrique noire / études réunies et présentées par E. Le Bris, E. Le Roy et F. Leimdorfer, avec la participation de E. Grégoire. Bondy : ORSTOM ; Paris : Karthala, c1982. 425 p. ; 24 cm. (Hommes et sociétés, 0290-6600) Includes bibliographical references and indexes. ISBN 2-86537-057-7 : LC Card 83-130847 DDC 333.3/096 19
1. Land tenure - Africa, Sub-Saharan. 2. Land use - Africa, Sub-Saharan. I. Le Bris, Émile. II. Le Roy, E. (Etienne). III. Leimdorfer, F. (François). IV. Series.
HD966 .E54 1982 ***NYPL [JLE 87-950]***

Enjeux internationaux.
Mayer, Pierre. La métamorphose . Paris , 1983. 110 p. : ISBN 2-86592-014-3 : LC Card 84-118610
HF1411 .M374 1983

Enke, Harald.
Der Konsumeffekt der Investitionen : eine Wachstumschance? / Harald Enke. Tübingen : Institut für Angewandte Wirtschaftsforschung Tübingen, 1986. xii, 114 p. ; 21 cm. (Forschungsberichte / Institut für Angewandte Wirtschaftsforschung Tübingen. Serie A . Nr. 42) Bibliography: p. 105-114. ISBN 3-88573-026-X LC Card 87-407594 DDC 339.4/3 19
1. Investments. 2. Consumers. 3. Saving and investment. I. Series: Forschungsberichte / Institut für Angewandte Wirtschaftsforschung Tübingen. Serie A , Nr. 42. II. Title.
HG4521 .E63 1986

Konsumtive Arbeit : ein wirtschaftstheoretischer Beitrag zur Humanisierung der Arbeitswelt / Harald Enke. Freiburg im Breisgau : R. Haufe, c1983. 354 p. : ill. ; 21 cm. (Bd. 12 der Schriftenreihe des Instituts für Allgemeine Wirtschaftsforschung der Albert-Ludwigs-Universität Freiburg i. Br) Bibliography: p. 310-325. Includes indexes. ISBN 3-448-01239-4 LC Card 83-224110
1. Job satisfaction. 2. Quality of work life. 3. Consumption (Economics). I. Series: Schriftenreihe des Instituts für Allgemeine Wirtschaftsforschung der Albert-Ludwigs-Universität Freiburg i. Br. , Bd. 12. II. Title.
HF5549.5.J63 E54 1983

Struktur und Dynamik der Wirtschaft . Freiburg im Breisgau , c1983. 530 p. : ISBN 3-448-01348-X : LC Card 83-184564 DDC 330 19
HB44 .S77 1983

Eno Foundation for Transportation. Glaskowsky, Nicholas A. Effects of deregulation on motor carriers /. Westport, Conn. (P.O. Box 2055, Westport 06880) , 1986. viii, 86 p. : LC Card 86-80416 DDC 388.3/24/0973 19
HE5623 .G55 1986

Enos, John L. (John Lawrence), 1924- The adoption and diffusion of imported technology : the case of Korea / J.L. Enos, W.-H. Park. New York : Croom Helm in association with Methuen, c1988. 272 p. : ill. ; 23 cm. Bibliography: p. 258-261. Includes index. ISBN 0-7099-2030-X LC Card 87-19894 DDC 338.9519/506 19
1. Technological innovations - Economic aspects - Korea (South) - Case studies. 2. Technology transfer - Korea (South) - Case studies. 3. Korea (South) - Industries - 1960- - Case studies. 4. Diffusion of innovations - Korea (South) - Case studies. I. Pak, U-hŭi. II. Title.
HC470.T4 E56 1987

L'enquête de 1848 sur le travail en Isère /. Perrin, Jacqueline. Grenoble , 1985. 251 p., [1] leaf of plates : ISBN 2-904661-03-4 : LC Card 86-227898
HC277.I8 P47 1985

Enquête démographique à passages répétés, 1978-1979 : résultats définitifs : méthodologie, structure, mortalite, fécondité / République de Côte d'Ivoire, Ministère du plan et de l'industrie, Direction de la statistique. [Abidjan] : La Direction, [1980?] 270 p. : ill. ; 29 cm. Includes bibliographical references. LC Card 85-213692 DDC 304.6/09666/8 19
1. Mortality - Ivory Coast. 2. Fertility, Human - Ivory Coast. 3. Demographic surveys - Ivory Coast. 4. Ivory Coast - Population. I. Ivory Coast. Direction de la statistique.
HB3666.A3 E57 1980 ***NYPL [JLF 86-1023]***

Enquête ivoirienne sur la fécondité, 1980-81 . Sombo, N'Cho. Voorburg, Netherlands [1985] 63 p. : LC Card 87-132644
HB1076.A3 S65 1985

Enquête sur les transports routiers de marchandises 1984. Erhebung über die Gütertransporte auf der Strasse 1984 /. Bern , 1986. 103 p. : ISBN 3-303-11041-7 : LC Card 87-408470 DDC 388.3/24/09494/021 19
HE5683.A6 E74 1986

Enquête sur l'utilisation des véhicules utilitaires légers : camions et camionnettes de moins de 3 tonnes de charge utile et de moins de 15 ans d'âge : autobus et autocars de moins de 10 places assises et de tous âges / Ministère des transports, Direction des affaires économiques, financières et administratives, Département des statistiques des transports. Paris : Le Département, [1983] 58 p. : ill. ; 30 cm. "Septembre 1983." LC Card 84-191337
1. Trucks - France - Statistics. 2. Vans - France - Statistics. I. France. Département des statistiques des transports.
HE5668.A6 E56 1983

Enquêtes et les rapports sur les accidents. Accident investigation and reporting . [Ottawa] , c1986. 15, 16 p. : ISBN 0-662-54332-7 (pbk.) LC Card 86-201756
HD7262.25 .A28 1986

Enrègle, Yves. Du conflit à la motivation : la gestion sociale / Yves Enrègle. Paris : Editions d'Organisation, 1985. 196 p. : ill. ; 24 cm. (Collection Management 2000) Bibliography: p. [193]-196. Includes index. ISBN 2-7081-0642-2 : LC Card 85-231586
1. Employee motivation. 2. Personnel management. 3. Conflict management. I. Title. II. Series.
HF5549.5.M63 E57 1985

Enrico Mattei, 1945-1953 . Mattei, Enrico. [Matelica] [1982] 199 p. : LC Card 84-190191
HD9575.I84 E585 1982

Enríquez, Rodrigo Sánchez. see **Sánchez Enríquez, Rodrigo.**

Ensaio sôbre a problemática dos transportes /. Carvalho, Osvaldo Ferraro de. Rio de Janeiro , 1957. 324 p., [5] folded leaves of plates : LC Card 85-197985
HE233 .C345 1957

Ensaios econômicos (Escola de Pós-Graduação em Economia) .
(no. 66) Cysne, Rubens Penha. Breve retrospecto da economia brasileira entre 1979 e 1984 /. [Rio de Janeiro] [1985] 30 leaves ; LC Card 86-176751
HC187 .C98 1985

Ensaios econômicos (Universidade de São Paulo. Instituto de Pesquisas Econômicas) .
(03) Longo, Carlos Alberto. Ajustamentos de impostos na fronteira e a alocação de receitas tributárias . São Paulo , 1979. 208 p. ; LC Card 80-152384
HJ5715.B8 L6617 ***NYPL [JLD 86-3846]***

(18) Rizzieri, Juarez Alexandre Baldini. Desenvolvimento econômico e urbanização . São Paulo , 1982. 219 p. : LC Card 83-150574 DDC 330.9173/2 19
HT321 .R59 1982 ***NYPL [JLD 86-3817]***

(2) Silva, Adroaldo Moura da. Emprego e preços no curto prazo /. São Paulo, SP (C.P. 11474, 01000 São Paulo, SP) , 1983. 94 p. ;
NYPL [JLD 86-3819]

(31) Silva, Marcos Eugênio da. Inovação tecnológica . São Paulo , 1984. 103 p. : LC Card 85-136373
HD9703.B72 S55 1984

(32) O'Keefe, Hsu Yuet Heung. A crise do petróleo e a economia brasileira /. São Paulo , 1984. 137 p. : LC Card 85-143617 DDC 338.2/3 19
HD9574.B82 O43 1984
NYPL [JLD 86-2712]

(38) Vieira, Cláudio Afonso. Urbanização e custo de reprodução da força de trabalho /. São Paulo , 1984. 175 p., [5] folded leaves ; LC Card 85-136502
HD5755.S3 V54 1984

(38) Vieira, Cláudio Afonso. Urbanização e custo de reprodução da força de trabalho /. São Paulo , 1984. 175 p., [5] folded leaves of plates :

(42) Campino, Antonio Carlos Coelho. Economia da alimentação e nutrição . São Paulo , 1985. 238 p. : LC Card 86-129956 DDC 338.1/9/81 19
HD9014.B82 C35 1985
NYPL [JLD 86-4118]

(53) Garcia, Manuel Enriquez. Salários indexados, preços e emprego . São Paulo , 1986. 149 p. : LC Card 86-234254
HD5004 .G37 1986

(54) Manoel, Alvaro. Política agrícola, eficiência e concentração na agricultura brasileira . São Paulo , 1986. 180 p. : LC Card 86-234338
HD1873 .M35 1986

(55) Santos, José Carlos de Souza. Demanda de fatores, energia e substituição na indústria brasileira, 1970/79 /. São Paulo , 1986. 183 p. : LC Card 86-234783
HB241 .S26 1986

(56) Saes, Flávio Azevedo Marques de, 1948- Crédito e bancos no desenvolvimento da economia paulista, 1850-1930 /. São Paulo , 1986. 238 p. : LC Card 87-144659 DDC 332.1/0981/61 19
HG2889.S25 S24 1986

(57) Tadini, Venilton. O setor de bens de capital sob encomenda . São Paulo , 1986. 142 p. : LC Card 87-154239 DDC 332/.0414/0981 19
HC190.C3 T33 1986

(58) Azzoni, Carlos Roberto. Indústria e reversão da polarização no Brasil /. São Paulo , 1986. 176 p. : LC Card 87-138915 DDC 338.6/042/0981 19
HC190.D5 A99 1986

(59) Casimiro, Liana Maria Carleial de. Acumulação capitalista, emprego e crise . São Paulo , 1986. 216 p. : LC Card 87-152202 DDC 331.12/0981/31 19
HD5755.F6 C37 1986

(60) Gomes, Sebastião Teixeira. Condicionantes da modernização do pequeno agricultor /. São Paulo , 1986. 181 p. : LC Card 87-153609 DDC 338.1/0981/51 19
HD1875.M5 G65 1986

(61) Biava, Adriano Henrique Rebelo. Contribuição de melhoria . São Paulo-SP , 1987. 243 p. : LC Card 87-404978 DDC 339.5/2/0981 19
HJ2525 .B5 1987

Ensaios sobre a evolução dos sistemas econômicos /. Couri, Sergio, 1948- Brasília-Distrito Federal [1983] 133 p. : LC Card 84-116306 DDC 330.1 19
HB97.5 .C68 1983 ***NYPL [JLE 86-3363]***

Ensayo de categorización de los municipios de Córdoba /. León Almeida, Pedro. Córdoba, Argentina , 1984. 74 leaves : LC Card 87-403755 DDC 330.982/54062/021 19
HC177.C7 L46 1984

Ensayo e investigación .
(6) Romeo Mateo, María Cruz, 1960- Realengo y municipio . Alicante , 1986. 171 p. : ISBN 84-505-3131-4 LC Card 87-137181
HD780.A435 R66 1986

Ensayos (Azcapotzalco, Mexico) .
(11) Freyre Rubio, Javier. Las organizaciones sindicales, obreras y burocráticas contemporáneas en México /. Azcapotzalco [Mexico] , c1983. 265 p. : ISBN 968-597-500-0 LC Card 86-218318
HD6532 .F74 1983

Ensayos (Centro de Estudios Monetarios Latinoamericanos) .
(31) Coers, Hermann Max. El Banco Central Latinoamericano . México , 1972. xv, 78 p. ; LC Card 87-401518 DDC 332.1/1/098 19
HG2710.5.A7 C6 1972

Ensayos e investigaciones sobre el desarrollo industrial de México. Elementos para la programación del desarrollo de la industria de aceites y pastas vegetales en México. México , 1985. 306 p. : ISBN 968-665-105-5 LC Card 86-232449
HD9490.M62 E44 1985

L'enseignement technique et professionnel et la satisfaction des besoins en main-d'œuvre . N'Dzaba, Tobi. Paris [1983] i, 139 p. : LC Card 85-189543
HD5845.A6 N38 1983

La enseñanza del cooperativismo en la Universidad /. Bragulat, Jorge. Madrid [1982] 119 p. : LC Card 85-203554
HD2955 .B72 1982

Ensinck, Oscar Luis. De Marco, Miguel Ángel. 1884-1984, los cien años de la Bolsa de Comercio de Rosario /. [S.l. , 1984?] (Rosario : Escuela de Artes Gráficas del Colegio San José de Rosario) 167 p. : LC Card 87-115398 DDC 332.64/28224 19
HG5320.R67 D4 1984

ENTAIL - SPAIN - LOGROÑO - HISTORY - 19TH CENTURY.
Bilbao Díez, Juan Carlos. La desamortización de Pascual Madoz en la ciudad de Logroño y su partido judicial (1855-1856) . Logroño , 1983. 303 p. : ISBN 84-85379-12-8 LC Card 86-215897
HD780.L64 B55 1983

Ente autonomo Fiera di Milano. Conferenza internazionale sul tema Le zone franche industriali, nuove forme di investimento, l'America latina (1985 : Milan, Italy) Le zone franche industriali nei paesi emergenti . Milano, Italy , c1986. 207 p. ; LC Card 86-223193
HF1418 .C525 1985

ENTE NAZIONALE IDROCARBURI.
Mattei, Enrico. Enrico Mattei, 1945-1953 . [Matelica] [1982] 199 p. : LC Card 84-190191
HD9575.I84 E585 1982

Ente per gli studi monetari, bancari e finanziari Luigi Einaudi. Oltre la crisi . Bologna , c1986. x, 745 p. : ISBN 88-15-01249-4 : LC Card 87-149887
HC305 .O45 1986

Entelis, G. S. Agrarnaia politika KPSS v deĭstvii /. Kishinev , 1983. 202 p. ; LC Card 84-235869
HD1993 .A38 1983

Ententes de développement économique et régional. Economic and regional development agreements . [Ottawa?] [1985] 11, 12, [8] p. : LC Card 86-214896 DDC 338.971 19
HC113 .E26 1985

Enterpreneurship and development /. Dhar, D. P., 1918-1975. New Delhi [pref. 1974] 23 p., [2] p. of plates : LC Card 80-908353 DDC 338.954 19
HB615 .D49 1974

Enterprise (WGBH (Television station : Boston, Mass.))
Billion dollar day [videorecording] /. Deerfield, IL , 1986. 1 videocassette (30 min.) : LC Card 86-700167 DDC 332.4 11
HG3903

ENTERPRISE ZONES - GERMANY (WEST) - HAMBURG.
Pohle, Michael. Industriebrachen und extensiv genutzte Flächen in innenstadtnahen Gewerbegebieten . Paderborn , 1985. viii, 121 p. : ISBN 3-506-73577-2 : LC Card 86-183775
HC289.H2 P64 1985

ENTERPRISES. see **ENTREPRENEUR.**

Enterprising elite . Dalzell, Robert F. Cambridge, Mass. , 1987. xviii, 298 p., [11] p. of plates : ISBN 0-674-25765-0 (alk. paper) LC Card 86-33649 DDC 338.4/7677/0097444 19
HD9858.L9 D35 1987

Enterprising families, Ithaca, New York . Sisler, Carol U., 1929- Ithaca, N.Y. (5 Cornell Walk, Ithaca 14850) , 1986. 159 p. : LC Card 86-81672 DDC 338/.092/2 B 19
HC102.5.A2 S55 1986

Entfremdung und Selbstverwaltung . Neff, Werner, 1947- Zürich , c1983. 322 p. : ISBN 3-85791-066-6 LC Card 87-672017
HD5660.F7 N43x 1983

ENTIDAD BINACIONAL YACYRETÁ.
Obras hidroeléctricas binacionales en América Latina. [Buenos Aires, Argentina] , 1985. vii leaves, 385 p., 3 leaves of plates : LC Card 86-180644
HD1696.A7 O27 1985

Entidades estatais, Decreto 5,768. Alagoas (Brazil). Comissão de Controle das Entidades Estatais. Programa de dispêndios globais para 1986 . [Maceió, Brazil] , 1985. 76 p. : LC Card 87-404783 DDC 354.81/35092 19
HD4095.A4 A4 1985

Entkoppelung von Wirtschaftswachstum und Energieverbrauch . Neu, Axel Dietmar, 1942- Kiel [1978] 91 p. : LC Card 85-174721
HB44 .K45 no. 52 HD9502.G42

Entlassen ins Nichts : Reportagen über Arbeitslosigkeit, 1918 bis heute : ein Lesebuch / Friedrich G. Kürbisch (Hg.). Berlin : J.H.W. Dietz, c1983. 255 p. ; 21 cm. ISBN 3-8012-0089-2 (pbk.) LC Card 87-672743
1. Unemployment - Germany - History - 20th century - Sources. 2. Unemployment - Austria - History - 20th century - Sources. 3. Unemployed - Germany - Case studies. 4. Unemployed - Austria - Case studies. I. Kürbisch, Friedrich G.
HD5779 .E57x 1983

Ėntov, R. M. (Revol'd Mikhaĭlovich)
Dolgovremennye tendentsii v kapitalisticheskom vosproizvodstve . Moskva , 1985. 229 p. : LC Card 86-187722
HB3711 .D62 1985

Entre la crisis y la agresión . Wheelock, Jaime. Managua, Nicaragua [1985] 148 p. : LC Card 85-241401 DDC 333.3/1/7285 19
HD1333.N5 W48 1985 ***NYPL [JLC 86-312]***

Entre la fábrica y la ciudad /. Pérez Sáinz, Juan Pablo. Quito, Ecuador , 1986, c1985. 87, [6] p. ; LC Card 87-403298 DDC 331.7/677/00986613 19
HD8039.T42 E26 1986

Entre le marteau et l'enclume /. Le Gal, André, 1920- Paris , c1984. 448 p. ; ISBN 2-214-05783-8 : LC Card 85-118954 DDC 658.3/02/0924 B 19
HD8433.L4 A34 1984 ***NYPL [JLD 87-438]***

Entre o deus e a vasilha . Callado, Antônio. Rio de Janeiro , c1985. 67 p. : LC Card 85-218767
HD496 .C23 1985

ENTREPRENEUR - ADDRESSES, ESSAYS, LECTURES.
Entrepreneurship . Wien , New York , 1984, c1983. 218 p. ; ISBN 0-387-81830-8 (U. S.) LC Card 84-26677 DDC 338/.04 19
HB615 .E635 1984 ***NYPL [JLE 85-1253]***

Entrepreneurship and social change /. Lanham, MD [S.l.] , c1986. 275 p. : ISBN 0-8191-5165-3 (alk. paper) : LC Card 85-26533 DDC 338/.04 19
HB615 .E629 1986 ***NYPL [JLD 86-3073]***

Entrepreneurship, intrapreneurship, and venture capital . Lexington, Mass. , 1986. xiv, 144 p. : ISBN 0-669-11867-2 (alk. paper) LC Card 85-45519 DDC 338/.04 19
HB615 .E634 1986 ***NYPL [JLE 86-3000]***

ENTREPRENEUR - BIOGRAPHY.
Chavers-Wright, Madrue, 1916- The guarantee . New York , 1985. xix, 425 p. : ISBN 0-931505-02-X (pbk.) : LC Card 84-51854 DDC 338/.04/0924 B 19
HG2463.C48 C48 1985
NYPL [Sc D 86-412]

Fucini, Joseph J. Experience, Inc. . New York , London , c1987. xi, 244 p. : ISBN 0-02-910971-X LC Card 87-11984 DDC 338/.04/0922 B 19
HC29 .F834 1987

Kiam, Victor. Going for it! . New York , c1986. 260 p. ; ISBN 0-688-06060-9 : LC Card 85-61762 DDC 338/.04/0924 B 19
HC102.5.K53 A34 1986
NYPL [JLE 86-2954]

Kingstone, Brett. The dynamos . New York , c1987. xx, 256 p. : ISBN 0-471-85827-7 LC Card 87-1754 DDC 338/.04/0922 B 19
HC102.5.A2 K56 1987

ENTREPRENEUR - CASE STUDIES.
Smith, Geoffrey N. Sweat equity . New York , c1986. 254 p. : ISBN 0-671-55210-4 LC Card 86-6622 DDC 658/.022 19
HD62.5 .S625 1986 ***NYPL [JLD 86-3014]***

ENTREPRENEUR - HISTORY.
Dary, David. Entrepreneurs of the old West /. New York , c1986. xi, 368 p. : ISBN 0-394-52405-5 LC Card 85-45590 DDC 338/.04/0978 19
HC102.5.A2 D37 1986
NYPL [JLE 86-4063]

Dary, David. Entrepreneurs of the old West /. Lincoln [1987], c1986. xi, 368 p. : ISBN 0-8032-6572-7 (pbk.) LC Card 87-5892 DDC 338/.04/0978 19
HC102.5.A2 D37 1987

DiBacco, Thomas V. Made in the U. S.A. . New York , c1987. xii, 290 p. ; ISBN 0-06-015624-4 : LC Card 86-45652 DDC 338.0973 19
HC103 .D46 1987 ***NYPL [JLD 87-1292]***

Vérin, Hélène, 1940- Entrepreneurs, entreprise . Paris , c1982. 262 p. ; ISBN 2-13-037449-2 (pbk.) : LC Card 82-153537 DDC 338/.04/09 19
HB615 .V44 1982 ***NYPL [JLD 86-3019]***

ENTREPRENEUR - STUDY AND TEACHING - INDONESIA.
Pedoman pembinaan kewiraswastaan bagi siswa. Jakarta , 1985. 1 v. (various pagings) : LC Card 86-942929
HF1171.I5 P43 1985

ENTREPRENEUR - STUDY AND TEACHING - UNITED STATES.
National Center for Research in Vocational Education (U. S.) A National entrepreneurship education agenda for action /. Columbus, Ohio , 1984. xiv, 114 p. : LC Card 86-201272 DDC 658.4/2 19
HF1131 .N28 1984

The entrepreneurial age . Dressler, Fritz R. S. Media, PA , c1985. ii, 228, 5 p. ; ISBN 0-918514-10-X (pbk.) LC Card 85-232719 DDC 338.04/0973 19
HB615 .D73 1985 ***NYPL [JLD 86-3104]***

Entrepreneurial science . Johnston, Robert F. New York , 1987. 157 p. ; ISBN 0-89930-260-2 (lib. bdg. : alk. paper) LC Card 87-2518 DDC 338/.06 19
HC110.H53 J65 1987

Entrepreneurial women /. Perri, Colleen, 1936- Kenosha, WI , c1987. 140 p. : ISBN 0-941579-00-X (pbk.) LC Card 87-154216 DDC 338/.04/088042 19
HD2346.U52 K376 1987b

Entrepreneurial women. Perri, Colleen, 1936- Kenosha, WI , c1988. p. cm. ISBN 0-941579-02-6 LC Card 87-7370 DDC 338/.04/088042 19
HD2346.U5 P43 1988

Entrepreneurial women /. Perri, Colleen, 1936- Kenosha, WI , c1988. p. cm. ISBN 0-941579-28-X LC Card 87-7380 DDC 338/.04/088042 19
HD2346.U52 K376 1988

The entrepreneurial workbook . Taylor, Charlotte. New York, N.Y. , c1985. ix, 148 p. : ISBN 0-452-25660-7 : LC Card 84-29439 DDC 658/.022 19
HD62.5 .T39 1985 ***NYPL [JLF 86-795]***

Entrepreneurs and parasites . MacGaffey, Janet. Cambridge [Cambridgeshire] , New York , 1987. xiii, 241 p. : ISBN 0-521-33533-7 LC Card 87-13160 DDC 338.09675/1 19
HC955.Z7 K49956 1987

Entrepreneurs, entreprise . Vérin, Hélène, 1940- Paris , c1982. 262 p. ; ISBN 2-13-037449-2 (pbk.) : LC Card 82-153537 DDC 338/.04/09 19
HB615 .V44 1982 ***NYPL [JLD 86-3019]***

The entrepreneur's guide to starting a successful business /. Halloran, James W. Blue Ridge Summit, PA , c1987. ix, 243 p. : ISBN 0-8306-3049-X (pbk.) : LC Card 86-27410 DDC 658.1/141 19
HD62.5 .H35 1987

Entrepreneurs of the old West /. Dary, David. New York , c1986. xi, 368 p. : ISBN 0-394-52405-5 LC Card 85-45590 DDC

338/.04/0978 19
HC102.5.A2 D37 1986 ***NYPL [JLE 86-4063]***

Entrepreneurs of the old West /. Dary, David. Lincoln [1987], c1986. xi, 368 p. : ISBN 0-8032-6572-7 (pbk.) LC Card 87-5892 DDC 338/.04/0978 19
HC102.5.A2 D37 1987

The entrepreneur's resource handbook /. Price, Courtney H. Denver, Colo. , 1987. 178 p. : ISBN 0-944303-00-5 (pbk.) LC Card 87-62190
HD62.5 .P65 1987

Entrepreneurs versus the historians /. Folsom, Burton W. Washington, DC , New York, NY , c1987. p. cm. ISBN 0-89526-573-7 : LC Card 87-23390 DDC 338/.04/0973 19
HG181 .F647 1987

ENTREPRENEURSHIP.
Fallows, James M. Human capital . New York, N.Y. , 1988. p. cm. ISBN 0-394-56498-7 : LC Card 87-42659 DDC 306/.3 19
HC106.8 .F35 1988

Hamer, Eberhard. Die Unternehmerlücke /. Stuttgart , 1984. 238 p. ; ISBN 3-87959-223-3 LC Card 85-128353
HB615 .H235 1984

Hunsdiek, Detlef. Entwicklungslinien und Entwicklungsrisiken neugegründeter Unternehmen /. Stuttgart , c1986. x, 190 p. : ISBN 3-7910-5009-5 LC Card 87-211045
HD62.5 .H86 1986

Koch, Helmut, 1919- Unternehmenstheorie als Entscheidungshilfe /. Wiesbaden , c1987. 199 p. : ISBN 3-409-13908-7 LC Card 87-143813 DDC 658.4/2 19
HB615 .K63 1987

Mokry, Benjamin W. Entrepreneurship and public policy . New York , c1988. p. cm. ISBN 0-89930-239-4 (lib. bdg. : alk. paper) LC Card 87-24934 DDC 338.9 19
HB615 .M65 1988

New opportunities for entrepreneurship /. Boulder , 1987. p. cm. ISBN 0-8133-0597-7 LC Card 87-20143 DDC 338/.04 19
HD62.5 .N48 1987

Schöllhammer, Hans, 1933- Entrepreneurship and small business management /. Malabar, Fla. , 1988. xvi, 608 p. : ISBN 0-89464-235-9 LC Card 87-14818 DDC 658/.022 19
HD62.5 .S354 1988

Silver, A. David (Aaron David), 1941- The Silver prescription . New York , c1987. xiii, 202 p. ; ISBN 0-471-85637-1 LC Card 86-28135 DDC 658.1/1 19
HD62.5 .S557 1987

Wittmann, Waldemar. Der Unternehmer /. Stuttgart , 1986. 27 p. ; ISBN 3-515-04666-6 : LC Card 87-136715 DDC 338/.04 19
HB615 .W58 1986

Entrepreneurship and public policy . Mokry, Benjamin W. New York , c1988. p. cm. ISBN 0-89930-239-4 (lib. bdg. : alk. paper) LC Card 87-24934 DDC 338.9 19
HB615 .M65 1988

Entrepreneurship and small business management /. Schöllhammer, Hans, 1933- Malabar, Fla. , 1988. xvi, 608 p. : ISBN 0-89464-235-9 LC Card 87-14818 DDC 658/.022 19
HD62.5 .S354 1988

Entrepreneurship and small firms /. Geroski, Paul A. Berlin [1985] 31, 2, 6 p. ; LC Card 86-213576 DDC 338.6/42 19
HD2346.E9 G47 1985

Entrepreneurship and social change / edited by Sidney M. Greenfield, Arnold Strickon. Lanham, MD : University Press of America ; [S.l.] : Society for Economic Anthropology, c1986. 275 p. : ill. ; 23 cm. (Monographs in economic anthropology . no. 2) Includes bibliographies and index. ISBN 0-8191-5165-3 (alk. paper) : LC Card 85-26533 DDC 338/.04 19
1. Entrepreneur - Addresses, essays, lectures. 2. Social change - Addresses, essays, lectures. 3. Economic anthropology - Addresses, essays, lectures. I. Greenfield, Sidney M. II. Strickon, Arnold. III. Society for Economic Anthropology (U. S.). IV. Series.
HB615 .E629 1986 ***NYPL [JLD 86-3073]***

Entrepreneurship and the privatizing of government / edited by Calvin A. Kent. New York : Quorum Books, 1987. x, 216 p. ; 24 cm. Includes bibliographies and index. ISBN 0-89930-196-7 (lib. bdg. : alk. paper) LC Card 86-25555 DDC 338.9 19
1. Privatization. I. Kent, Calvin A.
HD3850 .E57 1987

ENTREPRENEURSHIP - CASE STUDIES.
Lessem, Ronnie. [Enterprise development.] Intrapreneurship . Aldershot, Hants, England , Brookfield, Vt. , c1987. p. cm. ISBN 0-7045-0577-0 (pbk.) : LC Card 87-21608 DDC 658/.00941 19
HD70.G7 L45 1987

Entrepreneurship development . Bhanushali, S. G., 1933- Bombay , 1987. xvi, 255 p. ; LC Card 86-903834 DDC 338/.04 19
HB615 .B46 1987

Entrepreneurship development in India and the South-East Asian countries in agricultural and industrial sectors /. Bhattacharya, Sib Nath, 1938- New Delhi , 1983. xix, 156 p. : LC Card 83-903206 DDC 338/.04/0954 19
HC440.I53 B48 1983 ***NYPL [JLD 86-3764]***

ENTREPRENEURSHIP - DICTIONARIES.
Price, Courtney H. The entrepreneur's resource handbook /. Denver, Colo. , 1987. 178 p. : ISBN 0-944303-00-5 (pbk.) LC Card 87-62190
HD62.5 .P65 1987

Entrepreneurship, equity, and economic development /. Nafziger, E. Wayne. Greenwich, Conn. , c1986. xxiii, 308 p. : ISBN 0-89232-711-1 : LC Card 86-20151 DDC 338/.04 19
HB615 .N34 1986 ***NYPL [JLE 87-1672]***

ENTREPRENEURSHIP - EUROPE.
Entrepreneurship in Europe . London , New York , c1987. 197 p. ; ISBN 0-7099-3849-7 LC Card 87-15425 DDC 338/.04/094 19
HD2346.E9 E57 1987

Geroski, Paul A. Entrepreneurship and small firms /. Berlin [1985] 31, 2, 6 p. ; LC Card 86-213576 DDC 338.6/42 19
HD2346.E9 G47 1985

ENTREPRENEURSHIP - FRANCE.
Musnik, Isabelle. Tapie, les secrets de sa réussite /. Paris , c1986. 261 p. : ISBN 2-259-01546-8 : LC Card 87-167974
HC272.5.T3 M87 1986

ENTREPRENEURSHIP - GREAT BRITAIN - CASE STUDIES.
Chisnall, Peter M. Small firms in action . London , New York , c1987. vii, 149 p. ; ISBN 0-07-084180-2 (pbk.) : LC Card 87-21518 DDC 658/.022 19
HD2346.G7 C55 1987

ENTREPRENEURSHIP - HISTORY.
Folsom, Burton W. Entrepreneurs versus the historians /. Washington, DC , New York, NY , c1987. p. cm. ISBN 0-89526-573-7 : LC Card 87-23390 DDC 338/.04/0973 19
HG181 .F647 1987

Entrepreneurship in Europe : the social processes / edited by Robert Goffee and Richard Scase. London ; New York : Croom Helm, c1987. 197 p. ; 23 cm. (Social analysis) Includes bibliographies and index. ISBN 0-7099-3849-7 LC Card 87-15425 DDC 338/.04/094 19
1. Small business - Europe. 2. Entrepreneurship - Europe. I. Goffee, Robert. II. Scase, Richard.
HD2346.E9 E57 1987

Entrepreneurship, intrapreneurship, and venture capital : the foundation of economic renaissance / edited by Robert D. Hisrich. Lexington, Mass. : Lexington Books, 1986. xiv, 144 p. : ill. ; 24 cm. Includes bibliographical references. CONTENTS. - Importance of entrepreneurship in economic development / Howard H. Stevenson and William A. Sahlman -- Role of entrepreneurship in economic development / Donald L. Sexton -- Building indigenous companies / Raymond W. Smilor -- Entrepreneurship and intrapreneurship / Robert D. Hisrich -- The role of venture capital in the economic renaissance of an area / Barry M. Davis -- Entrepreneurs, angels, and economic renaissance / William E. Wetzel, Jr. ISBN 0-669-11867-2 (alk. paper) LC Card 85-45519 DDC 338/.04 19
1. Entrepreneur - Addresses, essays, lectures. 2. Venture capital - United States - Addresses, essays, lectures. I. Hisrich, Robert D.
HB615 .E634 1986 ***NYPL [JLE 86-3000]***

ENTREPRENEURSHIP - JAPAN.
Geroski, Paul A. Entrepreneurship and small firms /. Berlin [1985] 31, 2, 6 p. ; LC Card 86-213576 DDC 338.6/42 19
HD2346.E9 G47 1985

ENTREPRENEURSHIP - JUVENILE LITERATURE.
Risks & rewards of entrepreneurship /. Saint Paul, Minn. , c1988. 123 p. : ISBN 0-8219-0323-3 (pbk.) LC Card 87-21787 DDC 338/.04 19
HB615 .R56 1988

ENTREPRENEURSHIP - STUDY AND TEACHING - UNITED STATES.
National Survey of entreprenuerial [sic] education /. [Washington, D.C.?] . v. : LC Card 86-603453 DDC 658/.022/071173 19
HF1131 .N325 1986

ENTREPRENEURSHIP - UNITED STATES.
Geroski, Paul A. Entrepreneurship and small firms /. Berlin [1985] 31, 2, 6 p. ; LC Card 86-213576 DDC 338.6/42 19
HD2346.E9 G47 1985

ENTREPRENEURSHIP - UNITED STATES - CASE STUDIES.
Risk to riche$. Washington, DC (600 Maryland Ave., S.W., Suite 700, Washington 20024) , c1986. vii, 204 p. : LC Card 87-158511 DDC 338/.04/088042 19
HD2346.U5 R57 1986

ENTREPRENEURSHIP - WEST (U. S.)
Business entrepreneurs in the West /. Manhattan, Kan. , c1986. 120 p. : ISBN 0-89745-088-4 (pbk.) LC Card 87-135380 DDC 338/.04/0922 B 19
HC102.5.A2 B78 1986

Entreprise en déficit. Wuillemin, Lucien. Eléments d'analyse et de gestion financières de l'entreprise en déficit /. Genève , c1982. 191 p. : ISBN 2-8257-0090-8 : LC Card 82-228134 DDC 658.1/5 19
HD49 .W84 1982 ***NYPL [JLE 87-1142]***

Entreprises allemandes et coopération industrielle à l'échelle européenne . Urban, Sabine M.-L. Paris , c1986. 162 p. : ISBN 2-11-001580-2 : LC Card 86-175800
HD2844 .U7 1986

Entropie, Umweltschutz und Rohstoffverbrauch . Faber, Malte Michael. Berlin , New York , 1983. ix, 181 p. : ISBN 0-387-12297-4 (U. S.) LC Card 83-193381
HC79.E5 F23 1983

Entropologische Jahrbücher 1982. Arbeit, Entropie, Apokalypse . Zürich , 1982. 134 p. : LC Card 83-128724
HC106.8 .A73 1982

ENTROPY (INFORMATION THEORY)
Thakur, Baleshwar. Urban settlements in eastern India . New Delhi , 1980. 222 p. : LC Card 80-900438 DDC 307.7/6/09541
HT147.I5 T53 1980 ***NYPL [JLD 80-3943]***

Die Entscheidung des Handels über die Aufnahme neuer Produkte . Bauer, Hans H. Berlin , c1980. xxiii, 479 p. ; ISBN 3-428-04702-8 LC Card 87-408771 DDC 658.8 s 658.8/343 19
HF5415.A2 S37 Bd. 10 HF5415.153

Entscheidung über die Betriebspacht beziehungsweise Betriebsverpachtung. Slotta, Gerd. Die Entscheidung über die Betriebspacht bzw. Betriebsverpachtung /. Hamburg , c1986. xi, 374 p. : ISBN 3-925630-00-7 LC Card 86-152904
HD39.4 .S56 1986

Die Entscheidung über die Betriebspacht bzw. Betriebsverpachtung /. Slotta, Gerd. Hamburg , c1986. xi, 374 p. : ISBN 3-925630-00-7 LC Card 86-152904
HD39.4 .S56 1986

Entscheidungsansätze zur Rechtsformwahl . Kastner, Friedrich, 1951- München , c1984. xviii, 631 p. : ISBN 3-87821-200-3 LC Card 87-136549 DDC 658.4/03/0943 19
HD2859 .K37 1984

Entscheidungshilfen für die Infrastrukturplanung : neuere Entwicklungen auf dem Gebiet der Analyse und Bewertung öffentlicher Projekte / Joachim Klaus (Hrsg.).1. Aufl. Baden-Baden : Nomos Verlagsgesellschaft, 1984. 512 p. : ill. ; 23 cm. (Schriften zur

öffentlichen Verwaltung und öffentlichen Wirtschaft. Bd. 75) English and German summary. Bibliography: p. 481-500. Includes indexes. ISBN 3-7890-0808-7 LC Card 84-188792
1. Infrastructure (Economics) - Germany (West). I. Klaus, Joachim.
HC290.5.C3 E58 1984

Entscheidungsorganisation . Oelkers, Claus, 1952- Frankfurt am Main , New York , c1986. 263 p. : ISBN 3-8204-9396-4 LC Card 86-221177
HD2326 .O35 1986

Der Entscheidungsprozess in der Wirtschaftspolitik /. Teichmann, Ulrich, 1942- Darmstadt , 1983. vi, 135 p. ; ISBN 3-534-08177-3 LC Card 83-206492
HD84 .T39 1983

Entscheidungsspiele in Politik, Verwaltung und Wirtschaft /. Wender, Astrid. Opladen , c1983. vii, 248 p. : ISBN 3-531-11669-X LC Card 84-109871
HD30.23 .W46 1983

Entscheidungsträgermodelle bei Planungstechniken /. Früh, Bernhard, 1953- Frankfurt am Main , New York , c1984. 268 p. : ISBN 3-8204-5499-3 LC Card 85-197372
HD30.23 .F78 1984

Entscheidungsverlauf und Entscheidungseffizienz . Greinke, Helmut, 1957- Krefeld , 1986. viii, 249 p. : ISBN 3-88358-057-0 LC Card 86-172311
HD30.23 .G74 1986

Die Entsorgungswirtschaft einer Wirtschaftsregion . Meyer, Rolf. Schwarzenbek , 1983. 400 p. : ISBN 3-921757-20-7 LC Card 84-103993
HD9975.G43 H355 1983

Entstaatlichung im Telekommunikationsbereich . Knieps, Günter. Tübingen , 1985. xi, 205 p. : ISBN 3-16-344955-7 LC Card 86-156485
HE8154 .K55 1985

Die Entstehung der Briefmarke und ihre weltweite Verbreitung /. Haefeli-Meylan, Traugott. Lausanne , c1985. 167 p. : LC Card 86-202635
HE6203 .H25 1985

Die Entwicklung der Beschäftigungslage in Kärnten seit 1960 / Landesarbeitsamt Kärnten. Klagenfurt : Das Amt, [1979] 23 leaves : ill. ; 30 cm. Cover title. Chiefly tables. Includes bibliographical references. LC Card 85-143747
1. Labor supply - Austria - Carinthia - Statistics. 2. Carinthia (Austria) - Occupations - Statistics. I. Landesarbeitsamt Kärnten.
HD5772.C37 E57 1979

Entwicklung der Geburtenhäufigkeit in der Schweiz nach Wochentag und Stunden / [Herausgeber, Bundesamt für Statistik] = Evolution de la répartition journalière et horaire des naissances en Suisse / [editeur, Office fédéral de la statistique]. Bern : Das Bundesamt, 1984. 40 p. : ill. ; 30 cm. (Beiträge zur schweizerischen Statistik . Heft 114 = 114e fasc.) German and French. Bibliography: p. 40. LC Card 85-163580
1. Childbirth - Switzerland. I. Switzerland. Bundesamt für Statistik. II. Title: Evolution de la répartition journalière et horaire des naissances en Suisse. III. Series: Beiträge zur schweizerischen Statistik , Heft 114.
HA1593 .B45 Heft 114 HB1033

Die Entwicklung der oberösterreichischen Elektrizitätswirtschaft in den Jahren 1938-1980 /. Hinterbuchner, Christian. Linz , c1986. 344 p. : ISBN 3-85320-370-1 : LC Card 86-225017
HD9685.A93 U664 1986

Die Entwicklung der oberösterreichischen Elektrizitätswirtschaft von den Anfängen bis zum Jahre 1938 /. Weigl, Franz, 1948- Linz [1980] 210, xi p. : ISBN 3-85320-232-2 : LC Card 81-137632
HD9685.A93 U669 1980

Die Entwicklung der Organisationswissenschaft im deutschsprachigen Raum . Meyer, Petra. München , c1985. 309 p. : ISBN 3-924361-10-X LC Card 87-114143
HD70.E8 M48 1985

Entwicklung der Realsteuerhebesätze der Gemeinden mit mehr als 50.000 Einwohnern 1984 gegenüber 1983 /. Jasper, Lothar Th. Bonn , 1984. 29 leaves ; LC Card 86-186306
HJ1120 .B65 nr. 238 HJ4125.G35

Die Entwicklung der sowjetischen Besteuerung unter besonderer Berücksichtigung der ordnungspolitischen Funktionen /. Menz, Gertraud. Berlin , 1960. 247 p. : LC Card 86-161289
HJ2802 .M46 1960

Die Entwicklung der Wohnungsbautätigkeit in Leverkusen /. Marx, G. Leverkusen [1984] 37 p., [1] folded leaf of plates : LC Card 84-183932
HD9715.G33 L575 1984

Die Entwicklung kommunaler Finanzsysteme am Beispiel Grossbritanniens, Frankreichs und Deutschlands, 1790-1980 /. Köster, Thomas. Berlin , c1984. 422 p. : ISBN 3-428-05677-9 LC Card 85-127874
HJ9422.A4 K67 1984

Entwicklung ohne Rückschläge . Ellenberg, Heinz, 1913- [Desarrollar sin destruir. German.] Eschborn , 1984. 139 p. : ISBN 3-88085-228-6 LC Card 86-168369
HD1131 .E4515 1984

Entwicklung und Beurteilung von Aggregationsstrategien für lineare Entscheidungsmodelle /. Bartels, Sibylle, 1955- Frankfurt am Main , New York , c1986. xv, 265 p. : ISBN 3-8204-9190-2 LC Card 86-146466
HD30.25 .B365 1986

Entwicklung und empirische Überprüfung eines konjunkturgerechten Erfolgsprognosemodells zur Unterstützung der Kreditwürdigkeitsprüfung . Christians, Uwe, 1957- München , c1986. xiv, 412 p. : ISBN 3-88259-430-6 (Deut. Bibl.) LC Card 87-409324 DDC 332.7/0943 19
HG3754.5.G3 C48 1986

Entwicklung und Funktion des britischen und deutschen Systems der Arbeitsvermittlungs- und Berufsberatungsdienste . Träger, Manfred Georg. Nürnberg , 1981. ii, 80, 48 p. ; LC Card 82-200262 DDC 331.11/0941 19
HD5765.A6 T72 1981 ***NYPL [JLD 87-905]***

Entwicklung und Rüstung : öffentliche Anhörung des Ausschusses für Wirtschaftliche Zusammenarbeit des Deutschen Bundestages / Uwe Holtz (Hrsg.).1. Aufl. Baden-Baden : Nomos, 1984. 303 p. ; 23 cm. (Militär, Rüstung, Sicherheit . Bd. 32) Bibliography: p. 293-303. ISBN 3-7890-1068-5 LC Card 85-175510
1. Armaments - Economic aspects. I. Holtz, Uwe, 1944-. II. Germany (West). Bundestag. Ausschuss für Wirtschaftliche Zusammenarbeit. III. Series.
HC79.D4 E58 1984

Entwicklung und sozio-ökonomische Bedeutung der holzverarbeitenden Industrien im Südosten der Vereinigten Staaten von Amerika /. Grupp, Monika. Berlin , 1981, c1982. xii, 187, [30] p., [5] folded leaves of plates : ISBN 3-496-00301-4 LC Card 86-217598
HD9757.A13 G78 1982

Entwicklung und sozioökonomische Bedeutung der holzverarbeitenden Industrien im Südosten der Vereinigten Staaten von Amerika. Grupp, Monika. Entwicklung und sozio-ökonomische Bedeutung der holzverarbeitenden Industrien im Südosten der Vereinigten Staaten von Amerika /. Berlin , 1981, c1982. xii, 187, [30] p., [5] folded leaves of plates : ISBN 3-496-00301-4 LC Card 86-217598
HD9757.A13 G78 1982

Entwicklung und Struktur der Personalnebenkosten / [herausgegeben vom Bundesministerium für Wirtschaft, Referat Öffentlichkeitsarbeit]. Bonn : Bundesminister für Wirtschaft LP, [1985] 14, [9] p. : ill. ; 29 cm. (BMWI Dokumentation, 0342-9288 . Nr. 270) Cover title. LC Card 86-154479
1. Employee fringe benefits - Germany (West). I. Germany (West). Bundesministerium für Wirtschaft. Referat Öffentlichkeitsarbeit. II. Series.
HD4928.N62 G34 1985

Entwicklung und Ursachen der Frauenlohndiskriminierung . Pohl, Sigrid, 1954- Frankfurt am Main , New York , c1984. x, 387 p. : ISBN 3-8204-8017-X LC Card 85-189325 DDC 331.13/3/0943 19
HD6060.5.G3 P64 1984

Entwicklung von branchen-spezifischen integrierten Bürokommunikationssystemen . Walbrück, Hans-Jürgen, 1956- Bergisch Gladbach , c1986. 368 p. : ISBN 3-89012-044-X : LC Card 86-174155
HF5547.5 .W345 1986

Entwicklung wesentlicher Daten der öffentlichen Finanzwirtschaft in der Bundesrepublik Deutschland von 1974-1984 / [Bearbeiter, Hans-Ludwig Dornbusch]. Bonn : Institut "Finanzen und Steuern", 1985. 31 leaves ; 29 cm. (Brief / Institut "Finanzen und Steuern" . Nr. 247) Cover title. LC Card 86-186363
1. Finance, Public - Germany (West) - Statistics. I. Dornbusch, Hans-Ludwig. II. Series: Brief (Institut "Finanzen und Steuern" (Germany)) , Nr. 247.
HJ1120 .B65 Nr. 247

Entwicklung wesentlicher Daten der öffentlichen Finanzwirtschaft in der Bundesrepublik Deutschland von 1973-1983 /. Dornbusch, Hans-Ludwig. Bonn , 1984. 32 leaves ; LC Card 86-186300
HJ1120 .B65 Nr. 236

Entwicklung wesentlicher Daten der öffentlichen Finanzwirtschaft in der Bundesrepublik Deutschland von 1975-1985 /. Dornbusch, Hans-Ludwig. Bonn [1986] 31 leaves ; LC Card 87-408897 DDC 332 s 336.43 19
HJ1120 .B65 Nr. 260

Entwicklungen in der chinesischen Agrarpolitik seit 1978 /. Weitz, Maria. Berlin , 1986. 110 p. ; ISBN 3-428-06036-9 LC Card 87-409465 DDC 338.1/851 19
HD2097 .W45 1986

Entwicklungen in der Umweltpolitik Südkoreas im Widerspruch zwischen Industrialisierung und Umweltschutz /. Lee, Mu-Choon. Offenbach/Main, West Germany [1984] 21 p. : LC Card 86-172511
HC79.P55 L44 1984

Entwicklungseffekte durch Verkehrserschliessung in der Arabischen Republik Jemen . Becker, Fritz, 1947- Bochum , 1984. 50 p. : LC Card 84-241945
HE268.7 .B4 1984 ***NYPL [JLH 86-2]***

Entwicklungsförderung am Wendepunkt . Glinz, Ferdinand N. Zürich , c1986. 320 p. ; ISBN 3-280-01676-2 LC Card 86-227950
HC59.7 .G55 1986

Entwicklungshilfe und Ordnungspolitik . Görgens, Egon, 1941- Bern , c1983. 111 p. ; ISBN 3-258-03324-2 : LC Card 84-108530
HC800 .G67 1983

Entwicklungsländer im internationalen Konjunkturzusammenhang . Matz, Viktor, 1947- Bergisch Gladbach , c1986. 199, lxxvi p. ; ISBN 3-89012-052-0 LC Card 86-227998
HF3408.U5 M37 1986

Die Entwicklungsländer im Welthandel . Vierbuchen, Ruth, 1954- Spardorf , c1983. iii, 230 p. : ISBN 3-922919-11-1 LC Card 83-150529
HF1411 .V473 1983

Entwicklungslinien der Kosten- und Erlösrechnung / herausgegeben von Klaus Chmielewicz ; Kommission Rechnungswesen im Verband der Hochschullehrer für Betriebswirtschaft e.V. Stuttgart : Poeschel, c1983. viii, 232 p. : ill. ; 24 cm. Papers presented at a meeting of the Kommission Rechnungswesen im Verband der Hochschullehrer für Betriebswirtschaft e.V. Includes bibliographies and indexes. CONTENTS. - Vollkostenrechnung / Menrad, Siegfried -- Thesen zur Einzelkosten- und Deckungsbeitragsrechnung / Riebel, Paul -- Grenzplankostenrechnung / Kilger, Wolfgang -- Betriebsmodelle / Lassmann, Gert -- Zur Gestaltung der Erlösrechnung / Männel, Wolfgang. ISBN 3-7910-0304-6 : LC Card 83-200474
1. Cost accounting. I. Chmielewicz, Klaus. II. Verband der Hochschullehrer für Betriebswirtschaft. Kommission Rechnungswesen.
HF5686.C8 E65 1983

Entwicklungslinien und Entwicklungsrisiken neugegründeter Unternehmen /. Hunsdiek, Detlef. Stuttgart , c1986. x, 190 p. : ISBN 3-7910-5009-5 LC Card 87-211045
HD62.5 .H86 1986

Entwicklungsmanagement : Beiträge zu einer neuen Dimension im internationalen Management / mit einem Vorwort von Bundeskanzler Bruno Kreisky ; herausgegeben von Michael Hofmann und Klaus Schedl ; mit Beiträgen von Johann Bauer ... [et al.]. Berlin : Duncker & Humblot, c1982. 192 p. : 1 port. ; 24 cm. Bibliography: p. [185]-187. CONTENTS. -

Aspekte der Entwicklungshilfepolitik / Johann Bauer -- Das Konzept der "Technischen Hilfe" / Hans S. Fahlström -- Management of international development / Janos Fath -- Das Management der Gewerbeentwicklung / Erwin Fröhlich -- Die Feasibility-Studie / Friedrich Giersig -- Investitionsentscheidungen / Peter Hawranek -- Entwicklungs-Management / Michael Hofmann -- Specific requirements of managers in developing countries / Klaus Schedl -- Perspektiven der Energiewirtschaft in den Entwicklungsländern / Friedrich Ullmann -- Die Problematik der Propagierung des Energiespargedankens in Entwicklungsländern / Baldur Urban -- Anthropologische Auswirkungen auf das Management im arabischen Raum / Hanno Zaki. ISBN 3-428-05208-0 LC Card 83-150764 DDC 338.9/0068 19

1. Economic development projects - Management - Addresses, essays, lectures. 2. Industrial management - Developing countries - Addresses, essays, lectures. I. Hofmann, Michael. II. Schedl, Klaus, 1949-. III. Bauer, Johann, Dkfm.

HD84 .E56 1982 ***NYPL [JLE 87-1179]***

Das Entwicklungsmodell der italienischen Wirtschaft . Bieling, Thomas, 1953- Berlin , 1982 (Berlin : Copy-Center in Dahlem) 372 p. ; LC Card 87-673359
HC305 .B46x 1982

Entwicklungsmöglichkeiten des deutsch-sowjetischen Handels in der zweiten Hälfte der 80er Jahre vor dem Hintergrund der sowjetischen Planung /. Clement, Hermann. München , 1986. 14 leaves ; LC Card 86-167481
HF3568.S66 C58 1986

Entwicklungsmöglichkeiten landwirtschaftlicher Übergangsbetriebe in Niedersachsen . Schumacher, Karl-Edzard. Göttingen , 1985. 234, vi p. : LC Card 86-186858
HD9013.7.L68 S38 1985

Entwicklungspolitik, Bilanz und Perspektiven : öffentliche Anhörung des Bundestagsausschusses für wirtschaftliche Zusammenarbeit am 17. März 1986 / [Herausgeber, Deutscher Bundestag, Presse- und Informationszentrum, Referat Öffentlichkeitsarbeit, Bonn]. Bonn : Das Presse- und Informationszentrum, 1986. 256 p. ; 21 cm. (Zur Sache. 2/86) LC Card 87-409363 DDC 338.91/43/01724 19

1. Economic assistance, West German - Developing countries. 2. Technical assistance, West German - Developing countries. I. Germany (West). Bundestag. Ausschuss für Wirtschaftliche Zusammenarbeit. II. Germany (West). Bundestag. Presse- und Informationszentrum. Referat Öffentlichkeitsarbeit. III. Series: Zur Sache (Bonn, Germany) , 86/2.
HC60 .E523 1986

Entwicklungspolitik, Bilanz und Perspektiven . Germany (West). Bundestag. Ausschuss für Wirtschaftliche Zusammenheit. Bonn , 1986. 256 p. ; LC Card 87-409259 DDC 339.91/43/01724 19
HC60 .G467 1986

Die Entwicklungspolitik der Regierung Thatcher . Nuscheler, Franz. [Bonn] [1986] 93 p. : LC Card 86-186261
HC60 .N87 1986

Entwicklungspolitik im Spannungsfeld von Solidarität und Eigeninteresse : [ein Symposion der Ludwig-Erhard-Stiftung Bonn am 11. September 1985 in Bonn] / mit Beiträgen von Hans-Dietmar Barbier ... [et al.] ; Redaktion, Hartmut Pick. Stuttgart ; New York : G. Fischer, 1986. 155 p. ; 24 cm. ([Symposion / Ludwig-Erhard-Stiftung e.V. Bonn], 0177-0659 . [18]) Includes bibliographical references and indexes. CONTENTS. - Wandel der Konzeption deutscher Entwicklungspolitik / El-Shagi El-Shagi -- Formen praktischer Hilfe / Helga Henselder-Barzel -- Die Entwicklungspolitik der Kirchen / Ludwig Watzal -- Unternehmensförderung in Entwicklungsländern / Hans-Gert Braun -- Ist die Verschuldungskrise zu meistern? / Juergen B. Donges -- Die Neuorientierung der deutschen Entwicklungspolitik / Jürgen Warnke. ISBN 3-437-50306-5 LC Card 87-408212 DDC 338.91/43/01724 19

1. Economic assistance, West German - Developing countries - Congresses. 2. Developing countries - Foreign economic relations - Congresses. I. Barbier, Hans-Dietmar. II. Pick, Hartmut. III. Ludwig Erhard-Stiftung. IV. Series: Symposion (Ludwig-Erhard-Stiftung) , 18.
HC60 .E527 1986

Entwicklungspolitik im Wandel . Dritte-Welt-Kongress (1985 : Hof (Hof, Germany)) Stuttgart , 1986. 256 p. ; ISBN 3-87959-271-3 LC Card 86-193768
HD73 .D75 1985

Entwicklungspolitik, Politik ohne Entwicklung . Dauderstädt, Michael. Bonn [1984] 38 p. ; LC Card 85-136902
HC59.7 .D327 1984

Entwicklungspolitik zwischen Immanenz und Transzendenz . Watzal, Ludwig, 1950- Frankfurt am Main , New York , c1986. 121 p. ; ISBN 3-8204-8785-9 LC Card 86-198339
HD75 .W36 1986

Entwicklungspolitische Diskussionsbeiträge . (20) Rehsche, Guntram. Brain Drain . Adliswil , 1981. 71 p. ; ISBN 3-7229-4019-2 LC Card 81-206028 DDC 331.12/79 19
HD8038.S85 R44 1981

(24) Bluntschli, Franz. Schweizer Aussenwirtschaft, Wohlstand und Entwicklungsländer /. Adliswil , c1983. 38 p. : ISBN 3-7229-4032-X : LC Card 83-226336
HF1574 .B58 1983

(26) Mugglin, Markus. Exportrisikogarantie, internationale Verschuldung und schweizerische Entwicklungspolitik /. Adliswil , 1985. 56 p. : ISBN 3-7229-4036-X LC Card 85-148130
HF1574.5.D44 M84 1985

Entwicklungspolitische Erwachsenenbildung in der Bundesrepublik mit Hilfe kommunaler Konfliktfelder /. Osmers, Dieter. Frankfurt am Main , c1983. 161 p., [2] folded leaves of plates : ISBN 3-88129-669-7 LC Card 84-135387
HD77.5.G3 O85 1983

Entwicklungspolitische Fachausdrücke (Auswahl) . Brodmeier, Beate. Baden-Baden , 1985. 48 p. ; ISBN 3-7890-1093-6 LC Card 85-186152
HD84 .B765 1985

Entwicklungspolitische Schriften des Instituts für Industrie- und Verkehrspolitik der Universität Bonn und der Gesellschaft für Wirtschafts- u. Verkehrswissenschaftliche Forschung.
Chung, Shin-Yung, d. 1962. Der Zwangssparprozess als Werkzeug der Entwicklungspolitik . Bonn , c1982. xiv, 204 p., [1] leaf of plates : LC Card 83-214728
HC470.S3 C48 1982

"Entwicklungspolitische Texte"
Les Libéraux et le dialogue Nord-Sud . Bonn , c1982. 220 p. ; ISBN 3-920590-36-8 LC Card 84-204748
HC59.7 .L4177 1982

Entwicklungstendenzen im Konsumgüterhandwerk /. Kornhardt, Ullrich. Göttingen , 1986. 385 p. : ISBN 3-509-01418-9 LC Card 86-197187
HD2341.A1 G6 Bd. 37 HD2346.G3

Entwicklungstheorie, Entwicklungspraxis : eine kritische Bilanzierung / von Michael Bohnet ... [et al.] ; herausgegeben von Udo Ernst Simonis. Berlin : Duncker & Humblot, c1986. 316 p. ; 24 cm. (Schriften des Vereins für Socialpolitik, Gesellschaft für Wirtschafts- und Sozialwissenschaften . n.F., Bd. 154) English and German. Summaries in English. Papers presented at the annual meeting of the Gesellschaft's Ausschuss Entwicklungsländer, held in Berlin in Dec. of 1984. Includes bibliographies. CONTENTS. - Changing emphases in development theory / by Paul B. Streeten -- Wechselnde Akzente der Entwicklungspraxis / von Michael Bohnet -- Development theory / by Johan Galtung -- Does development economics have a future? / by Göran Ohlin -- Ökologiedebatte und Entwicklungstheorie / von Hans-Jürgen Harborth -- Entwicklungstheorie und Praxis der Entwicklungsplanung / von Walter Güldner -- Abkommen der multilateralen Zusammenarbeit im Spannungsfeld von Theorie und Praxis / von Karl Wolfgang Menck -- Das Lomé-Abkommen in seiner praktischen Handhabung / von Dieter Frisch unter der Mitarbeit von Jürgen Köppen und Michaela Collins -- Zur Fruchtbarkeit des Dependencia-Ansatzes für die Analyse von Entwicklung und Unterentwicklung / von Manfred Nitsch -- Entwicklung durch Weltmarktassoziation / von Hermann Sauter. ISBN 3-428-05973-5 LC Card 86-233851 DDC 338.9/009172/4 19

1. Developing countries - Economic policy - Congresses. 2. Developing countries - Dependency on foreign countries - Congresses. 3. Economic development - Congresses. I. Bohnet, Michael. II. Simonis, Ernst Udo. III. Series.
HC59.7 .E6473 1986

Entwicklungszusammenarbeit mit Indonesien . Geinitz, Dedo. Bremen , 1985. viii, 72 p. : ISBN 3-88299-046-5 LC Card 86-204688
HD9161.I63 A244 1985

Entwurff und Beschreibung von der Papiermacherey, worinnen der Ursprung des Papiermachens, der Fortgang, wie heutiges Tages das Papier gemachet wird, wie solches viele Mühe und Arbeit hat, benebst denen bey den Papiermachern befindlichen Wörtern, denen Kayserlichen Verordnungen und andern dahin einschlagenden Dingen / zum Druck befördert von Frantz Henning Schaden. [Mainz : Forschungsstelle Papiergeschichte, 1962] (Darmstadt : E. Roether) 1 v. (various pagings) : ill. ; 19 cm. Reprint. Originally published: Erfurt : J.A. Becker, 1740. Includes Anhang by J.M. Becker. LC Card 87-107659

1. Paper industry - History. 2. Papermaking - History. 3. Paper - History. I. Schaden, Franz Henning. II. Becker, Johann Michael.
HD9820.5 .E57 1962

ENVIRONMENT. see **ADAPTATION (BIOLOGY); ANTHROPO-GEOGRAPHY; ECOLOGY; HUMAN ECOLOGY.**

Environment, agriculture, and society in the Malay world / edited by Tsuyoshi Kato, Muchtar Lutfi, and Narifumi Maeda. Kyoto, Japan : Center for Southeast Asian Studies, Kyoto University, 1986. ix, 177 p. : ill. ; 26 cm. (Interim reports of the project "Transformation of the agricultural landscape in tropical archipelagos" . v. 4) Includes bibliographies. LC Card 86-201590 DDC 338.1/09595 19

1. Agriculture - Economic aspects - Malaysia. 2. Inland water transportation - Malaysia. 3. Farm produce - Malaysia - Transportation. 4. Malaysia - Rural conditions. I. Kato, Tsuyoshi. II. Lutfi, Muchtar. III. Maeda, Narifumi, 1940-. IV. Kyōto Daigaku. Tōnan Ajia Kenkyū Sentā. V. Series.
HD2080.6 .E58 1986

Environment and development /. Bartelmus, Peter. Boston , 1986. xxii, 96 p. ; ISBN 0-04-333026-6 (alk. paper) LC Card 85-22838 DDC 333.7/09172/4 19
HC59.72.E5 B37 1986 ***NYPL [JLD 86-2378]***

Environment and resources in the Pacific / United Nations Environment Programme. Geneva, Switzerland : UNEP, 1985. iv, 294 p. : ill. ; 30 cm. (UNEP regional seas reports and studies . no. 69) At head of title: Regional seas. "... papers presented at the 15th Pacific Science Congress organized by the Pacific Science Association in Dunedin, New Zealand on 1-11 February 1983"--P. i. Includes bibliographies. LC Card 86-217776 DDC 333.7/2/099 19

1. Environmental policy - Oceania - Congresses. 2. Conservation of natural resources - Oceania - Congresses. 3. Environmental protection - Oceania - Congresses. 4. Environmental policy - Asia, Southeastern - Congresses. 5. Conservation of natural resources - Asia, Southeastern - Congresses. 6. Environmental protection - Asia, Southeastern - Congresses. I. United Nations. Environment Programme. II. Pacific Science Congress (15th : 1983 : Dunedin, N.Z.). III. Pacific Science Association. IV. Series.
HC681.3.E5 E58 1985

ENVIRONMENT AND STATE. see **ENVIRONMENTAL POLICY.**

ENVIRONMENT IMPACT ASSESSMENT. see **ENVIRONMENTAL IMPACT ANALYSIS.**

Environment Liaison Centre. Global Meeting on Environment and Development for Non-governmental Organisations (1985 : Nairobi, Kenya) Sustainable development . [Nairobi, Kenya] [1985 or 1986] 109 p. : LC Card 86-981176 DDC 363.7/057 19
HC79.E5 G595 1985

The Environment of the workplace and human values / editor, Sheldon W. Samuels. New York : Liss, c1986. vii, 118 p. ; 26 cm. Published also as the American journal of industrial medicine, v. 9, no. 1, 1986. Conference cosponsored by the Labor Policy Institute and the Marshall-Wythe School of Law at the College of William and Mary, May 20-22, 1982. Includes bibliographical references and index. ISBN 0-8451-4205-4 LC Card 85-23908 DDC 174/.4 19

1. Industrial hygiene - Moral and ethical aspects - Congresses. 2. Environmental health - Moral and ethical aspects - Congresses. I. Samuels, Sheldon W. II. Labor Policy Institute (AFL-CIO). III. Marshall-Wythe School of Law.
HD7260.5 .E58 1986 NYPL [JLF 87-151]

ENVIRONMENT, WORK. see **WORK ENVIRONMENT.**

An Environmental agenda for the future / John H. Adams ... [et al.]. Washington, D.C. : Island Press, c1985. viii, 155 p. ; 23 cm. Bibliography: p. [149]-155. ISBN 0-933280-29-7 (pbk.) : LC Card 85-19760 DDC 304.2 19
1. Environmental protection - United States. 2. Conservation of natural resources - United States. I. Adams, John H. (John Hamilton), 1936-. II. Title: Agenda for the future.
TD171 .E56 1985 NYPL [JLE 86-2773]

Environmental and natural resource economics /. Tietenberg, Thomas H. Glenview, Ill. , c1988. 559 p. : ISBN 0-673-18945-7 LC Card 87-23250 DDC 333.7 19
HC79.E5 T525 1988

ENVIRONMENTAL ASSESSMENT. see **ENVIRONMENTAL IMPACT ANALYSIS.**

ENVIRONMENTAL AUDITING - UNITED STATES.
Cahill, Lawrence B. Environmental audits /. Rockville, Md., U. S.A. , 1987. xi, 656 p. : ISBN 0-86587-720-3 (soft) LC Card 87-404450 DDC 658.4/08 19
HC110.E5 C26 1987

Environmental audits /. Cahill, Lawrence B. Rockville, Md., U. S.A. , 1987. xi, 656 p. : ISBN 0-86587-720-3 (soft) LC Card 87-404450 DDC 658.4/08 19
HC110.E5 C26 1987

Environmental concerns and strategies /. Khoshoo, T. N., 1927- New Delhi, India , 1984. xii, 296 p. ; LC Card 84-901589
HC440.E5 K48 1984 NYPL [JLE 87-1015]

ENVIRONMENTAL CONTROL. see **ENVIRONMENTAL LAW; ENVIRONMENTAL POLICY.**

Environmental economics and management . Førsund, Finn R. London , New York , c1988. 307 p. : ISBN 0-85664-900-7 LC Card 87-9179 DDC 363.7/0525 19
HC79.E5 F64 1988

ENVIRONMENTAL EVALUATION. see **ENVIRONMENTAL IMPACT ANALYSIS.**

ENVIRONMENTAL HEALTH - JAPAN.
Huddle, Norie, 1944- Island of dreams . Cambridge, Mass. , c1987. xxiii, 355 p. : ISBN 0-87047-027-2 : LC Card 86-33842 DDC 363.7/00952 19
HC465.E5 H82 1987

ENVIRONMENTAL HEALTH - MORAL AND ETHICAL ASPECTS - CONGRESSES.
The Environment of the workplace and human values /. New York , c1986. vii, 118 p. ; ISBN 0-8451-4205-4 LC Card 85-23908 DDC 174/.4 19
HD7260.5 .E58 1986 NYPL [JLF 87-151]

ENVIRONMENTAL IMPACT ANALYSIS - EUROPE, EASTERN.
A Környezeti erőforrások gazdasági értékelésének módszertani kérdései /. Pécs [Budapest] , 1981. 78 leaves ; LC Card 82-202704
HD9502.E83 K68 1981 NYPL [JLE 87-219]

Environmental justice /. Wenz, Peter S. Albany, N.Y. , c1987. p. cm. ISBN 0-88706-644-5 LC Card 87-13206 DDC 363.7/0525 19
HB523 .W46 1987

ENVIRONMENTAL LAW.
Wenz, Peter S. Environmental justice /. Albany, N.Y. , c1987. p. cm. ISBN 0-88706-644-5 LC Card 87-13206 DDC 363.7/0525 19
HB523 .W46 1987

ENVIRONMENTAL LAW - BELIZE.
Belize . Belize City, Belize , 1984. xvi, 151 p. : LC Card 86-136310 DDC 333.7/097282 19
HC142 .B447 1984 NYPL [JLF 87-170]

ENVIRONMENTAL LAW - CALIFORNIA.
Massa, Alison K. Housing and the environment /. Sacramento, CA (921 10th St., Sacramento 95814-2774) [1985?] 2 v. : LC Card 87-621018 DDC 363.7 19
HD266.C2 M37 1985

ENVIRONMENTAL LAW - GERMANY (WEST) - CONGRESSES.
Umweltschutz und Verwaltung . Bonn , c1986. 171 p. ; ISBN 3-87999-040-9 LC Card 87-136048 DDC 363.7/056/0943 19
HC290.5.E5 U645 1986

ENVIRONMENTAL LAW - SOVIET UNION.
Jancar, Barbara Wolfe, 1935- Environmental management in the Soviet Union and Yugoslavia . Durham , 1987. xi, 481 p. : ISBN 0-8223-0719-7 LC Card 87-5412 DDC 363.7/06/0947 19
HC340.E5 J35 1987

ENVIRONMENTAL LAW - SWITZERLAND.
Aeberhardt, Werner. Die Umweltpolitik im Spannungsfeld politischer und wirtschaftlicher Interessen /. Köln , 1985. 134, [9] p. : ISBN 3-921471-55-9 : LC Card 86-145456
HC400.E5 A33 1985

ENVIRONMENTAL LAW - UNITED STATES.
Cahill, Lawrence B. Environmental audits /. Rockville, Md., U. S.A. , 1987. xi, 656 p. : ISBN 0-86587-720-3 (soft) LC Card 87-404450 DDC 658.4/08 19
HC110.E5 C26 1987

Energy and Environmental Analysis, inc. Benefit/cost analyses of laws and regulations affecting coal . Washington , 1977. ca. 750 p. : LC Card 77-603790 DDC 363.6
TD195.C58 E53 1977 NYPL [JLF 81-219]

Kohn, Stephen M. (Stephen Martin) Protecting environmental & nuclear whistleblowers . Washington, D.C. , c1985. xiii, 346 p. : ISBN 0-9615323-0-0 (pbk.) LC Card 85-61844 DDC 342.73/0684 347.302684 19
KF5342 .K64 1985 NYPL [JLE 86-1787]

Sagoff, Mark. The economy of the earth . Cambridge [Cambridgeshire] , New York , 1988. p. cm. ISBN 0-521-34113-2 LC Card 87-16091 DDC 363.7/056/0973 19
HC110.E5 S34 1988

ENVIRONMENTAL LAW - UNITED STATES - ADDRESSES, ESSAYS, LECTURES.
United States. Library of Congress. Environment and Natural Resources Policy Division. Pollution taxes, effluent charges, and other alternatives for pollution control . Washington , 19. iv, 869 p. : LC Card 78-602626
HC110.E5 U58 1977a NYPL [JLE 79-2372]

ENVIRONMENTAL LAW - YUGOSLAVIA.
Jancar, Barbara Wolfe, 1935- Environmental management in the Soviet Union and Yugoslavia . Durham , 1987. xi, 481 p. : ISBN 0-8223-0719-7 LC Card 87-5412 DDC 363.7/06/0947 19
HC340.E5 J35 1987

ENVIRONMENTAL MANAGEMENT. see **ENVIRONMENTAL LAW; ENVIRONMENTAL POLICY.**

Environmental management in the Soviet Union and Yugoslavia . Jancar, Barbara Wolfe, 1935- Durham , 1987. xi, 481 p. : ISBN 0-8223-0719-7 LC Card 87-5412 DDC 363.7/06/0947 19
HC340.E5 J35 1987

Environmental Management in the Sudan (Program) Abdel Ati, Hassan A. Lower River Atbara area (Nile Province) . [Khartoum] Sudan [1985] vii, 166 p., [19] leaves of plates : LC Card 86-981108 DDC 333.91/3/09625 19
HD1741.S852 A832 1985

Environmental monograph series (Jāmi'at al-Kharṭūm. Ma'had al-Dirāsāt al-Bī'īyah) . (no. 4) Atta el Moula, Mutasim el Amin. On the problem of resource management in the Sudan /. [Khartoum] , 1985. 131 leaves : LC Card 86-980662 DDC 333.7/09624 19
HC835 .A85 1985

Environmental monograph series (Jāmi'at al-Kharṭūm. Ma'had al-Divāsāt al-Bī'īyah) . (no. 5) Amin, Nasr El Din Osman. Nomadism versus sedenterization . [Khartoum?] Sudan , 1986. 105 leaves : LC Card 86-981112
HD977 .A65 1986

Environmental monographs and symposia. Arnon, Itzhak, 1909- Modernization of agriculture in developing countries . Chichester [West Sussex] , New York , c1987. xxiii, 626 p. : ISBN 0-471-91586-6 : LC Card 87-6288 DDC 338.1/09172/4 19
HD1417 .A76 1987

Environmental policies in Finland : national report. 2nd rev. version. [Helsinki] : Ministry of the Environment, Environmental Protection and Nature Conservation Dept., [1986] 542 p. : ill. ; 30 cm. (Serial D, 0780-6825 . 19, 1986) ISBN 951-46-9823-1 LC Card 87-100734 DDC 363.7/056/094897 19
1. Environmental policy - Finland. 2. Natural resources - Finland - Management. I. Finland. Ympäristön- ja luonnonsuojeluosasto. II. Series: Ympäristön- ja luonnonsuojeluosaston julkaisu D , 19.
HC340.2.Z9 E52 1986

Environmental policies in Yugoslavia : a review / by the OECD and its Environment Committee undertaken in 1985 at the request of the Government of Yugoslavia. Paris : Organisation for Economic Co-operation and Development ; [Washington, D.C. : OECD Publications and Information Centre, distributor], c1986. 160 p., [2] p. of plates : ill. (some col.) ; 23 cm. Includes bibliographical references. ISBN 92-64-12866-2 (pbk.) : LC Card 87-120078 DDC 363.7/056/09497 19
1. Yugoslavia - Environmental policy. I. Organisation for Economic Co-operation and Development. Environment Committee.
HC407.Z9 E555 1986

ENVIRONMENTAL POLICY - ADDRESSES, ESSAYS, LECTURES.
Diez años después de Estocolmo . Madrid [1983?] 285 p. : ISBN 84-85633-26-3 LC Card 84-122682 DDC 304.2 19
GF49 .D54 1983 NYPL [JLE 86-1307]

ENVIRONMENTAL POLICY - AFRICA.
Lewis, Lawrence. African environments and resources /. Boston , 1987. p. cm. ISBN 0-04-916010-9 (alk. paper) LC Card 87-16751 DDC 333.7/096 19
HC800 .L48 1987

Timberlake, Lloyd. Africa in crisis . Philadelphia , 1986. 232 p. : ISBN 0-86571-082-1
NYPL [Sc D 87-100]

ENVIRONMENTAL POLICY - ALASKA.
Skilbred, Amy. The Watt/Clark record . Washington, D.C. (1901 Pennsylvania Ave., N.W., Washington 20006) , c1984. iii, 63, [18] p. : LC Card 86-206945 DDC 363.7/009798 19
HC107.A47 E57 1984

ENVIRONMENTAL POLICY - AMAZON RIVER REGION.
Fearnside, Philip M. (Philip Martin) Human carrying capacity of the Brazilian rain-forest /. New York , 1986. xii, 293 p. : ISBN 0-231-06104-8 (alk. paper) LC Card 85-6643 DDC 330.981/1063 19
HC188.A5 F42 1986 NYPL [JLE 86-4554]

ENVIRONMENTAL POLICY - ASIA, SOUTHEASTERN - CONGRESSES.
Environment and resources in the Pacific /. Geneva, Switzerland , 1985. iv, 294 p. : LC Card 86-217776 DDC 333.7/2/099 19
HC681.3.E5 E58 1985

ENVIRONMENTAL POLICY - BELGIUM.
Kock, Suzan de, 1949- Milieuvervuiling en milieubeleid economisch bekeken /. Antwerpen [1977] 140 p. ; ISBN 90-289-0313-1 : LC Card 78-384758
HC320.E5 K6 NYPL [JLD 80-3195]

ENVIRONMENTAL POLICY - BELIZE.
Belize . Belize City, Belize , 1984. xvi, 151 p. : LC Card 86-136310 DDC 333.7/097282 19
HC142 .B447 1984 NYPL [JLF 87-170]

ENVIRONMENTAL POLICY - CANADA.
Canada's environment . [Ottawa] , 1986. 20 p. : ISBN 0-662-14571-2 (pbk.) LC Card 86-222737 DDC 333.7/0971 19
HC120.E5 C345 1986

Environmental quality strategic review . [Ottawa, Canada , c1986. 170 p. ; ISBN 0-660-12148-4 (pbk.) : LC Card 86-217056 DDC 363.7/00971 19
HC120.E5 E59 1986

ENVIRONMENTAL POLICY - CITIZEN PARTICIPATION.
Garbe, Detlef, 1949- Die Planungszelle und ihre Umwelt . Frankfurt a.M. ; Bern ; xiv, 339 p. ; ISBN 3-8204-6017-9 LC Card 81-464829
HC79.E5 G33 1980 NYPL [JLD 81-2376]

ENVIRONMENTAL POLICY - CONGRESSES.
Global Meeting on Environment and Development for Non-governmental Organisations (1985 : Nairobi, Kenya) Sustainable development . [Nairobi, Kenya] [1985 or 1986] 109 p. : LC Card 86-981176 DDC 363.7/057 19
HC79.E5 G595 1985

Regional environmental policy . New York , c1979. xii, 290 p. : ISBN 0-8147-7805-4 : LC Card 79-2058 DDC 301.31
HC79.E5 R44 ***NYPL [JLE 80-1854]***

Symposion "Marktwirtschaft und Umwelt" (1980 : Walter Eucken Institut) Marktwirtschaft und Umwelt . Tübingen , 1981. ix, 303 p. : ISBN 3-16-343372-3 : LC Card 81-128698 DDC 363.7/0526 19
HC79.E5 S92 1980 ***NYPL [TB (Walter Eucken Institut. Wirtschaftswissenschaftliche und wirtschaftsrechtliche Untersuchungen. Bd. 17)]***

Symposium Umweltprobleme als Herausforderung der Marktwirtschaft, Neue Ideen jenseits des Dirigismus (1983 : Stuttgart, Germany) Symposium Umweltprobleme als Herausforderung der Marktwirtschaft, Neue Ideen jenseits des Dirigismus . [Köln] [Freiburg] , 1983. 300 p. ; ISBN 3-7616-0722-9 LC Card 84-152335 DDC 363.7/058 19
HC79.E5 S96 1983 ***NYPL [JLD 86-1631]***

Umweltschutz . [Mainz] , c1984. 130 p. ; ISBN 3-7758-1086-2 LC Card 85-146233
HC290.5.E5 U64 1984

ENVIRONMENTAL POLICY - COST EFFECTIVENESS - ADDRESSES, ESSAYS, LECTURES.
Economic valuation techniques for the environment . Baltimore , c1986. xx, 203 p. : ISBN 0-8018-3352-3 (alk. paper) LC Card 86-2730 DDC 363.7/05/0681 19
HC79.E5 E274 1986 ***NYPL [JLE 87-677]***

ENVIRONMENTAL POLICY - COSTA RICA.
Bonilla, Alexander. Situación ambiental de Costa Rica /. [San José] [1985] 271 p. : ISBN 997-7590-57-5 LC Card 86-156609
HC143.Z9 E52 1985

ENVIRONMENTAL POLICY - DECISION MAKING.
Dryzek, John S., 1953- Rational ecology . Oxford, OX, UK , New York, NY, USA , 1987. ix, 270 p. : ISBN 0-631-15574-0 : LC Card 87-6587 DDC 363.7/0561 19
HC79.E5 D79 1987

Faludi, Andreas. A decision-centred view of environmental planning /. Oxford [Oxfordshire] , New York , 1987. xiii, 240 p. ; ISBN 0-08-032698-6 : LC Card 87-10414 DDC 333.7 19
HC79.E5 F28 1987

ENVIRONMENTAL POLICY - DEVELOPING COUNTRIES.
Bartelmus, Peter. Environment and development /. Boston , 1986. xxii, 96 p. ; ISBN 0-04-333026-6 (alk. paper) LC Card 85-22838 DDC 333.7/09172/4 19
HC59.72.E5 B37 1986 ***NYPL [JLD 86-2378]***

Dumont, René, 1904- Les raisons de la colère, ou, L'utopie et les Verts /. Paris , c1986. 137 p. ; ISBN 2-7266-0075-1 LC Card 86-158407
HC59.72.E5 D85 1986

Garcia, Xavier, 1950- Supervivència 2000 . Barcelona , 1983. 267 p. ; ISBN 84-7306-196-9 LC Card 83-225437
HC59.72.E5 G37 1983 ***NYPL [JLD 86-2462]***

Integrated rural energy planning /. Guildford , c1985. xii, 200 p. : ISBN 0-408-22166-6 ***NYPL [JLF 87-3]***

Knödgen, Gabriele, 1949- Umweltschutz und industrielle Standortentscheidung /. Frankfurt/Main , New York , c1982. 219 p. : ISBN 3-593-33158-6 LC Card 83-110653
HC59.72.P55 K58 1982

Sustainable resource development in the Third World /. Boulder , 1987. vi, 177 p. : ISBN 0-8133-7522-3 (alk. paper) LC Card 87-20137 DDC 333.7/15/091724 19
HC59.7 .S8826 1987

ENVIRONMENTAL POLICY - DOMINICAN REPUBLIC.
La República Dominicana . McLean, Va. , 1981. xii, 134 p. : LC Card 86-218146
HC153.5 .R45 1981

ENVIRONMENTAL POLICY - ECONOMIC ASPECTS.
Bartov, Vladimir Fotievich. Kontseptsii vzaimodeĭstviia ėkonomiki i prirody /. Moskva , 1984. 157 p. ; LC Card 84-225876
HC79.E5 B369 1984

Siebert, Horst, 1938- Economics of the environment . Berlin , New York , c1987. xiv, 273 p. : ISBN 0-387-17283-1 (U. S.) LC Card 87-4703 DDC 363.7 19
HC79.E5 S437 1987

ENVIRONMENTAL POLICY - ECONOMIC ASPECTS - DEVELOPING COUNTRIES.
Myers, Norman. Not far afield . Washington, DC , c1987. vi, 73 p. : ISBN 0-915825-24-4 (pbk.): LC Card 87-50723 DDC 333.7/09172/4 19
HC59.72.E5 M93 1987

ENVIRONMENTAL POLICY - ECONOMIC ASPECTS - UNITED STATES.
Haveman, Robert H. Jobs and the environment /. Scarsdale, N.Y. , c1979. 32 p. ; LC Card 79-15418 DDC 301.31/0973
HC110.E5 H38 ***NYPL [JLM 83-380 no.10]***

Myers, Norman. Not far afield . Washington, DC , c1987. vi, 73 p. : ISBN 0-915825-24-4 (pbk.): LC Card 87-50723 DDC 333.7/09172/4 19
HC59.72.E5 M93 1987

ENVIRONMENTAL POLICY - EUROPE.
Florizoone, Patrick, 1958- De groenen . [Deurne] , c1985. x, 194 p. : ISBN 90-6716-272-8 LC Card 86-148321
HC329.5.E5 F56 1985

ENVIRONMENTAL POLICY - EUROPE, EASTERN.
Polityka ochrony środowiska w krajach socjalistycznych . Warszawa , 1980. 318 p. ; ISBN 83-208-0067-6 LC Card 81-101337
HC244.Z9 E56 1980

ENVIRONMENTAL POLICY - EUROPEAN ECONOMIC COMMUNITY COUNTRIES.
Producer consumer dialogue . Brussels [1984] ii, 55 p. ; LC Card 85-178866 DDC 381/.34/094 19
HC240.9.C63 P77 1984 ***NYPL [JLD 86-2369]***

ENVIRONMENTAL POLICY - FINLAND.
Environmental policies in Finland . [Helsinki] [1986] 542 p. : ISBN 951-46-9823-1 LC Card 87-100734 DDC 363.7/056/094897 19
HC340.2.Z9 E52 1986

Finland. Ympäristöministeriö. Ympäristöministeriön hallinnonalan toiminta- ja taloussuunnitelma vuosiksi 1987-1990 . Helsinki , 1985. 152 leaves : LC Card 86-224557
HC340.2.Z9 E5 1985

ENVIRONMENTAL POLICY - FLORIDA.
Robbins, Bradley. Economic development in a conscious state . Tallahassee, Fla. [1984] viii, 41, [5] p. : LC Card 86-621090 DDC 338.9759 19
HC107.F6 R63 1984

The Saddlebrook papers . [Fort Lauderdale] [Tallahassee] [1985] v leaves, 177 p. : LC Card 86-621089 DDC 338.9759 19
HC107.F63 E547 1985

ENVIRONMENTAL POLICY - FRANCE - BASSE-NORMANDIE.
Livre blanc de l'environnement . [S.l. , 1982] (Caen : Impr. P.A.C.) 1 portfolio (32 p.) : LC Card 83-209058
HC277.B28 L58 1982

ENVIRONMENTAL POLICY - GERMANY, EAST.
Ökten, Rita. Die Bedeutung des Umweltschutzes für die Wirtschaft der DDR /. Berlin , c1986. 87 p. : ISBN 3-87061-311-4 LC Card 86-194057
HC290.795.E5 O38 1986

Umweltprobleme und Umweltbewusstsein in der DDR /. Köln , c1985. 252 p. : ISBN 3-8046-8649-4 LC Card 86-119841
HC290.795.E5 U585 1985

Wensierski, Peter. Von oben nach unten wächts gar nichts . Frankfurt am Main , 1986. 206 p. : ISBN 3-596-24274-6 LC Card 87-115154 DDC 363.7/058/09431 19
HC290.795.E5 W46 1986

ENVIRONMENTAL POLICY - GERMANY (EAST) - CITIZEN PARTICIPATION.
Wensierski, Peter. Von oben nach unten wächts gar nichts . Frankfurt am Main , 1986. 206 p. : ISBN 3-596-24274-6 LC Card 87-115154 DDC 363.7/058/09431 19
HC290.795.E5 W46 1986

ENVIRONMENTAL POLICY - GERMANY - HISTORY.
Roloff, Otto, 1937- Umweltschutz in öffentlichen Budgets /. Regensburg , c1986. 278 p. : ISBN 3-924956-14-6 LC Card 87-129127 DDC 363.7/00943 19
HC290.5.E5 R65 1986

ENVIRONMENTAL POLICY - GERMANY, WEST.
Brunowsky, Ralf-Dieter, 1949- Der ÖKO-Plan . München , c1984. 236, [1] p. ; ISBN 3-492-02922-1 LC Card 84-251156
HC290.5.E5 B78 1984

Grumbach, Jürgen. Energieforschung und Arbeitnehmerinteressen . Frankfurt , New York , c1986. 307 p. ; ISBN 3-593-33655-3 LC Card 87-127360 DDC 331.1/0943 19
HC290.5.E5 G74 1986

Innenpolitische Leistungsbilanz 1982-1986 /. Bonn , 1986. 124 p. : LC Card 86-215949
HC286.7 .I55 1986

Leonhard, Martin. Umweltverbände . Opladen , c1986. xiii, 352 p. ; ISBN 3-531-11820-X LC Card 86-192568
HC290.5.E5 L46 1986

Ökologie und Sozialismus . Köln , c1986. 369 p. ; ISBN 3-7663-0983-8 LC Card 87-107373 DDC 363.7/056/0943 19
HC290.E5 O39 1986

Paul, Joachim, 1956- Zur politischen Durchsetzungsfähigkeit einer ökologisch orientierten Marktwirtschaft . Frankfurt am Main , New York , c1986. xvii, 569 p. ; ISBN 3-8204-9810-9 LC Card 87-407614 DDC 363.7/056/0943 19
HC290.5.E5 P38 1986

Perspektiven einer ökologischen Ökonomie /. Hann. [i.e. Hannoversch] Münden , c1983. 91 p. ; ISBN 3-87998-402-6 : LC Card 83-180506
HC290.5.E5 P47 1983

Posse, Achim Ulrich, 1960- Föderative Politikverflechtung in der Umweltpolitik /. München , c1986. xiv, 181 p. : ISBN 3-597-10526-2 LC Card 86-222201
HC290.5.E5 P67 1986

Schmidt, Peter M. Unweltthemen in der öffentlichen Diskussion /. Konstanz , 1985. ix, 296 p. : ISBN 3-89191-001-0 LC Card 86-155948
HC290.5.E5 S37 1985

Schulz, Bernhard. Effizienzkontrolle von Umweltpolitik . Frankfurt am Main , c1983. xv, 230 p. : ISBN 3-88129-744-8 LC Card 85-103230
HC290.5.E5 S38 1983

Wirtschaft und Umweltschutz /. Heidelberg , 1986. vii, 147 p. : ISBN 3-8114-2786-5 LC Card 87-134163 DDC 363.7/058/0943 19
HC290.5.E5 W57 1986

Zwei Jahre Politik der Erneuerung . Bonn [1984] 110 p. : LC Card 85-180111
HC286.7 .Z865 1984

ENVIRONMENTAL POLICY - GERMANY, WEST - BAVARIA.
Umweltpolitik in Bayern /. München [1986] 176 p. : LC Card 86-204249
HC287.B3 U48 1986

ENVIRONMENTAL POLICY - GERMANY (WEST) - CONGRESSES.
Umweltpolitisches Gespräch (1983 : Bad Godesberg, Bonn, Germany) Ökonomische Instrumente der Umweltpolitik . Berlin , c1984. 108 p. ; ISBN 3-503-02401-8 LC Card 86-152141
HC290.5.E5 U625 1983

Umweltschutz . [Mainz] , c1984. 130 p. ; ISBN 3-7758-1086-2 LC Card 85-146233
HC290.5.E5 U64 1984

Umweltschutz und Verwaltung . Bonn , c1986. 171 p. ; ISBN 3-87999-040-9 LC Card 87-136048

DDC 363.7/056/0943 19
HC290.5.E5 U645 1986

ENVIRONMENTAL POLICY - GERMANY (WEST) - HAMBURG.
Vollzug und Wirkungen regionaler Umweltpolitik . Opladen , 1984. 199 p. ; ISBN 3-8100-0392-1 LC Card 84-228636
HC290.5.E5 V65 1984

ENVIRONMENTAL POLICY - GERMANY (WEST) - NORDRHEIN-WESTFALEN.
Roloff, Otto, 1937- Umweltschutz in öffentlichen Budgets /. Regensburg , c1986. 278 p. : ISBN 3-924956-14-6 LC Card 87-129127 DDC 363.7/00943 19
HC290.5.E5 R65 1986

ENVIRONMENTAL POLICY - GERMANY (WEST) - NORTH RHINE-WESTPHALIA.
Weimar, Robert. Die Umweltvorsorge im Rahmen der Landesplanung Nordrhein-Westfalen . Frankfurt am Main , New York , c1983. xxiii, 313 p. : ISBN 3-8204-7669-5 LC Card 83-206670
HC287.N6 W44 1983

ENVIRONMENTAL POLICY - GERMANY (WEST) - RHINELAND-PALATINATE.
Scholz, Bernhard, 1948- Bodenschutz zwischen Datenschwemme und Informationsdefizit . Speyer [1986] iii leaves, 385, 4 p. : LC Card 87-126271 DDC 333.73/13/094343 19
HD659.R54 S36 1986

ENVIRONMENTAL POLICY - GREAT BRITAIN.
The Green alternative . London , 1987. xv, 368 p. : ISBN 0-413-60280-X : LC Card 87-143624 DDC 333.7/2 19
HC260.E5 G736 1987

Vogel, David, 1947- National styles of regulation . Ithaca, N.Y. , 1986. 325 p. ; ISBN 0-8014-1658-2 LC Card 85-21332 DDC 363.7/056/0941 19
HC260.E5 V64 1986 ***NYPL [JLE 86-2434]***

ENVIRONMENTAL POLICY - HUNGARY - CONGRESSES.
A Vállalati magatartást motiváló gazdasági és társadalmi tényezők című konferencia előadásai . Pécs , 1985. 2 v. : LC Card 87-408547
HD70.H8 V334 1985

ENVIRONMENTAL POLICY - INDIA - ADDRESSES, ESSAYS, LECTURES.
Khoshoo, T. N., 1927- Environmental concerns and strategies /. New Delhi, India , 1984. xii, 296 p. ; LC Card 84-901589
HC440.E5 K48 1984 ***NYPL [JLE 87-1015]***

ENVIRONMENTAL POLICY - INTERNATIONAL COOPERATION.
Boardman, Robert. Pesticides in world agriculture . Houndsmills, Basingstoke, Hampshire , c1986. x, 221 p. ; ISBN 0-333-37417-7 ***NYPL [JLD 86-2934]***

ENVIRONMENTAL POLICY - ITALY - MILAN REGION.
Metropoli e agricoltura /. Milano , c1982. 319 p. : LC Card 82-246692 DDC 333.76/13/094521 19
HD680.M54 M47 1982
NYPL [JLD 86-3678]

ENVIRONMENTAL POLICY - JAPAN.
Environmental protection in the industrial sector in Japan . Tokyo, Japan , c1983. 168 p. : LC Card 87-672736
HC465.P55 E58x 1983

Huddle, Norie, 1944- Island of dreams . Cambridge, Mass. , c1987. xxiii, 355 p. : ISBN 0-87047-027-2 : LC Card 86-33842 DDC 363.7/00952 19
HC465.E5 H82 1987

Reed, Steven R., 1947- Japanese prefectures and policy making /. Pittsburgh, Pa. , 1986. ix, 197 p. ; ISBN 0-8229-3527-9 LC Card 85-22528 DDC 352/.00047 19
JS7373.A3 R44 1986 ***NYPL [JLE 86-3757]***

ENVIRONMENTAL POLICY - LATIN AMERICA.
Bordering on trouble . Bethesda, Md. , 1986. xii, 448 p. : ISBN 0-917561-25-2 (pbk.) LC Card 86-7941 DDC 338.98 19
HC125 .B594 1986 ***NYPL [JLE 86-4501]***

Política ambiental y desarrollo . [Bogotá, Colombia] , 1986. 221 p. : LC Card 86-207035
HC130.E5 P65 1986

Los Problemas del conocimiento y la perspectiva ambiental del desarrollo /. México, D.F. , 1986. 476 p., [1] folded leaf of plates : ISBN 968-231-372-4 LC Card 87-119336 DDC 363.7/0098 19
HD75.6 .P76 1986

ENVIRONMENTAL POLICY - MATHEMATICAL MODELS.
Economic-ecological modeling /. Amsterdam ; New York : x, 329 p. : ISBN 0-444-70298-9 LC Card 87-20048 DDC 333.7/0724 19
HC79.E5 E267 1987

Schmidt, Helmut, Dr. rer. oec. Informationsinstrumente zur Umweltplanung . Frankfurt/Main , c1985. ix, 441 p. : ISBN 3-88129-947-5 LC Card 86-141873
HC79.E5 S285 1985

ENVIRONMENTAL POLICY - MEXICO.
Mexican topics . [México, D.F.] [1986] 2 portfolios : LC Card 86-221843 DDC 972.08/3 19
HC135 .M52554 1986

ENVIRONMENTAL POLICY - NETHERLANDS.
Florizoone, Patrick, 1958- De groenen . [Deurne] , c1985. x, 194 p. : ISBN 90-6716-272-8 LC Card 86-148321
HC329.5.E5 F56 1985

Kock, Suzan de, 1949- Milieuvervuiling en milieubeleid economisch bekeken /. Antwerpen [1977] 140 p. ; ISBN 90-289-0313-1 : LC Card 78-384758
HC320.E5 K6 ***NYPL [JLD 80-3195]***

ENVIRONMENTAL POLICY - NETHERLANDS - NORTH HOLLAND.
North Holland (Netherlands) Milieubeleidsplan Noord-Holland 1982-1988 . [Haarlem] [1987] 60 p. ; LC Card 87-159912
HC327.N6 N67 1987

ENVIRONMENTAL POLICY - NORWAY.
Naturressurser og miljø 1983 . Oslo , 1984. 100 p. : ISBN 82-537-1993-0 : LC Card 84-161695
HC363.5 .N38 1984

ENVIRONMENTAL POLICY - OCEANIA - CONGRESSES.
Environment and resources in the Pacific /. Geneva, Switzerland , 1985. iv, 294 p. : LC Card 86-217776 DDC 333.7/2/099 19
HC681.3.E5 E58 1985

ENVIRONMENTAL POLICY - RHINE RIVER VALLEY - CONGRESSES.
Interparlamentarische Konferenz über die Rheinverschmutzung (1977 : Den Haag, Netherlands) Interparlamentarische Konferenz über die Rheinverschmutzung . 's Gravenhage , 1977. 62 p. ; ISBN 90-12-01782-3 LC Card 86-149213
HC240.9.E5 I77 1977

ENVIRONMENTAL POLICY - SOVIET UNION.
Ėkonomicheskie problemy prirodopol′zovaniīa /. Moskva , 1985. 137 p. : LC Card 86-119089
HC340.E5 E395 1985

Jancar, Barbara Wolfe, 1935- Environmental management in the Soviet Union and Yugoslavia . Durham , 1987. xi, 481 p. : ISBN 0-8223-0719-7 LC Card 87-5412 DDC 363.7/06/0947 19
HC340.E5 J35 1987

Novikov, Ė. A. (Ėnergiī Alekseevich) Gorod i prirodopol′zovanie /. Leningrad , 1984. 143 p. ; LC Card 85-125032
HC333.5 .N68 1984

Polityka ochrony środowiska w krajach socjalistycznych . Warszawa , 1980. 318 p. ; ISBN 83-208-0067-6 LC Card 81-101337
HC244.Z9 E56 1980

ENVIRONMENTAL POLICY - SPAIN - CATALONIA.
Vilanova, Santiago, 1947- L'econacionalisme . Barcelona , 1981. 142 p. ; ISBN 84-7031-281-2 LC Card 81-212886
HC387.C25 V527 1981

ENVIRONMENTAL POLICY - STUDY AND TEACHING.
New ideas in environmental education /. London , New York , c1988. xiv, 219 p. ; ISBN 0-7099-5042-X LC Card 87-15696 DDC 363.7/007/1 19
HC79.E5 N45 1988

ENVIRONMENTAL POLICY - SUDAN.
Atta el Moula, Mutasim el Amin. On the problem of resource management in the Sudan /. [Khartoum] , 1985. 131 leaves : LC Card 86-980662 DDC 333.7/09624 19
HC835 .A85 1985

ENVIRONMENTAL POLICY - SWITZERLAND.
Aeberhardt, Werner. Die Umweltpolitik im Spannungsfeld politischer und wirtschaftlicher Interessen /. Köln , 1985. 134, [9] p. : ISBN 3-921471-55-9 : LC Card 86-145456
HC400.E5 A33 1985

ENVIRONMENTAL POLICY - UKRAINE.
Ėkonomika ispol′zovaniīa vodnykh resursov /. Kiev , 1980. 185 p. ; LC Card 87-462040
HD1697.S653 U374 1980

Kompleksnoe ispol′zovanie prirodnykh resursov . Kiev , 1985. 174 p. ; LC Card 86-175133
HC337.U5 K6372 1985

ENVIRONMENTAL POLICY - UNITED STATES.
Arnold, Ron. Ecology wars . Bellevue, Wash. , c1987. 182 p. ; ISBN 0-939571-00-5 LC Card 87-17 DDC 363.7/00973 19
HC110.E5 A77 1987

Cahill, Lawrence B. Environmental audits /. Rockville, Md., U. S.A. , 1987. xi, 656 p. : ISBN 0-86587-720-3 (soft) LC Card 87-404450 DDC 658.4/08 19
HC110.E5 C26 1987

Dietz, Thomas. The risk professionals /. New York , c1987. p. cm. ISBN 0-87154-214-5 : LC Card 87-19992 DDC 363.7/056/0973 19
HC110.E5 D54 1987

Dimensions of hazardous waste politics and policy /. New York , c1988. p. cm. ISBN 0-313-25989-5 (lib. bdg. : alk. paper) LC Card 87-17792 DDC 363.7/28 19
HC110.E5 D56 1988

Energy and environment . Washington, D.C. , c1985. x, 190 p. : ISBN 0-87187-360-5 : LC Card 85-25471 DDC 333.79/0973 19
HD9502.U52 E4524 1985
NYPL [JLE 86-2859]

Hines, Lawrence Gregory. The market, energy, and the environment /. Boston , c1988. xii, 305 p. : ISBN 0-205-10568-8 : LC Card 87-1037 DDC 333.7/0973 19
HC110.E5 H57 1988

Protecting the environment . Washington, D.C. , c1986. iii, 88 p. ; ISBN 0-89195-040-0 (pbk.) : LC Card 86-82962 DDC 363.7/056/0973 19
HC110.E5 P77 1986

Sagoff, Mark. The economy of the earth . Cambridge [Cambridgeshire] , New York , 1988. p. cm. ISBN 0-521-34113-2 LC Card 87-16091 DDC 363.7/056/0973 19
HC110.E5 S34 1988

State of the environment . Washington, D.C. , c1984. xxxiv, 586 p. : ISBN 0-89164-084-3 LC Card 84-12651 DDC 363.7/00973 19
TD171 .S74 1984 ***NYPL [JLD 86-3097]***

Vogel, David, 1947- National styles of regulation . Ithaca, N.Y. , 1986. 325 p. ; ISBN 0-8014-1658-2 LC Card 85-21332 DDC 363.7/056/0941 19
HC260.E5 V64 1986 ***NYPL [JLE 86-2434]***

Waterfield, Larry W. Conflict and crisis in rural America /. New York , 1986. iv, 235 p. : ISBN 0-03-006074-5 (alk. paper) : LC Card 85-19366 DDC 333.76/0973 19
HD256 .W35 1986 ***NYPL [JLE 86-2792]***

ENVIRONMENTAL POLICY - UNITED STATES - ADDRESSES, ESSAYS, LECTURES.
United States. Library of Congress. Environment and Natural Resources Policy Division. Pollution taxes, effluent charges, and other alternatives for pollution control . Washington , 19. iv, 869 p. : LC Card 78-602626
HC110.E5 U58 1977a ***NYPL [JLE 79-2372]***

ENVIRONMENTAL POLICY - UNITED STATES - CITIZEN PARTICIPATION.
Alternative environmental conflict management

approaches . [Ann Arbor, MI] (Dana Bldg., Ann Arbor 48109-1115) [1986] 252 p. : LC Card 86-225219 DDC 363.7/058/0973 19
HC110.E5 A643 1986

ENVIRONMENTAL POLICY - UNITED STATES - CONGRESSES.
Agriculture and the environment /. Washington, D.C. , c1986. xvii, 298 p. : ISBN 0-915707-33-0 (pbk.) : LC Card 87-43010 DDC 363.7/31 19
HD1755 .P47 1986

Population change, natural resources, and regionalism /. Milford, Pa. , c1986. viii, 104 p. : ISBN 0-938549-00-6 (pbk.) LC Card 86-25682 DDC 304.6/0973 19
HB3505 .P62 1986

ENVIRONMENTAL POLICY - VENEZUELA.
Gabaldón, Arnoldo. Política ambiental y sociedad /. Caracas, Venezuela , 1986. 225 p. : ISBN 980-01-0034-2 LC Card 87-115207 DDC 363.7/056/0987 19
HC239.5.E5 G32 1986

ENVIRONMENTAL POLICY - VIRGIN ISLANDS OF THE UNITED STATES.
Towle, Edward L. Final report . St. Thomas, U. S.V.I. [1982] 17, 15, 4 leaves : LC Card 86-185489 DDC 333.7/097297/22 19
HC155.Z9 E56 1982

ENVIRONMENTAL POLICY - YUGOSLAVIA.
Crnobrnja, Mihailo. Čovekova životna sredina i ekonomski razvoj /. Beograd [1984?] 206 p. : LC Card 86-184927
HC407.Z9 E55 1984

Jancar, Barbara Wolfe, 1935- Environmental management in the Soviet Union and Yugoslavia . Durham , 1987. xi, 481 p. : ISBN 0-8223-0719-7 LC Card 87-5412 DDC 363.7/06/0947 19
HC340.E5 J35 1987

ENVIRONMENTAL PROTECTION - ASIA, SOUTHEASTERN - CONGRESSES.
Environment and resources in the Pacific /. Geneva, Switzerland , 1985. iv, 294 p. : LC Card 86-217776 DDC 333.7/2/099 19
HC681.3.E5 E58 1985

ENVIRONMENTAL PROTECTION - BRAZIL - SÃO PAULO (STATE)
Mineração meio-ambiente e o planejamento municipal. São Paulo [1982] 24 leaves : LC Card 85-210329
HD9506.B73 S3664 1982

ENVIRONMENTAL PROTECTION - CONGRESSES.
Umweltschutz . [Mainz] , c1984. 130 p. ; ISBN 3-7758-1086-2 LC Card 85-146233
HC290.5.E5 U64 1984

ENVIRONMENTAL PROTECTION - COSTA RICA.
Bonilla, Alexander. Situación ambiental de Costa Rica /. [San José] [1985] 271 p. : ISBN 997-7590-57-5 LC Card 86-156609
HC143.Z9 E52 1985

ENVIRONMENTAL PROTECTION - DEVELOPING COUNTRIES.
Pearson, Charles S. Down to business . Washington, DC (1735 New York Ave., NW, Washington, DC 20006) , c1985. vii, 107 p. ; ISBN 0-915825-04-X (pbk.) : LC Card 84-52795
HD69.P6 P42 1985 ***NYPL [JLE 86-3186]***

ENVIRONMENTAL PROTECTION - ECONOMIC ASPECTS - GERMANY (WEST)
Brunowsky, Ralf-Dieter, 1949- Der ÖKO-Plan . München , c1984. 236, [1] p. ; ISBN 3-492-02922-1 LC Card 84-251156
HC290.5.E5 B78 1984

ENVIRONMENTAL PROTECTION - ECONOMIC ASPECTS - MATHEMATICAL MODELS.
Faber, Malte Michael. Entropie, Umweltschutz und Rohstoffverbrauch . Berlin , New York , 1983. ix, 181 p. : ISBN 0-387-12297-4 (U. S.) LC Card 83-193381
HC79.E5 F23 1983

ENVIRONMENTAL PROTECTION - EUROPE, EASTERN.
Polityka ochrony środowiska w krajach socjalistycznych . Warszawa , 1980. 318 p. ; ISBN 83-208-0067-6 LC Card 81-101337
HC244.Z9 E56 1980

ENVIRONMENTAL PROTECTION - GERMANY, EAST.
Ökten, Rita. Die Bedeutung des Umweltschutzes für die Wirtschaft der DDR /. Berlin , c1986. 87 p. : ISBN 3-87061-311-4 LC Card 86-194057
HC290.795.E5 O38 1986

Umweltprobleme und Umweltbewusstsein in der DDR /. Köln , c1985. 252 p. : ISBN 3-8046-8649-4 LC Card 86-119841
HC290.795.E5 U585 1985

ENVIRONMENTAL PROTECTION - GERMANY, WEST.
Leonhard, Martin. Umweltverbände . Opladen , c1986. xiii, 352 p. ; ISBN 3-531-11820-X LC Card 86-192568
HC290.5.E5 L46 1986

Schmidt, Peter M. Unweltthemen in der öffentlichen Diskussion /. Konstanz , 1985. ix, 296 p. : ISBN 3-89191-001-0 LC Card 86-155948
HC290.5.E5 S37 1985

ENVIRONMENTAL PROTECTION - GERMANY (WEST) - BAVARIA.
Umweltpolitik in Bayern /. München [1986] 176 p. : LC Card 86-204249
HC287.B3 U48 1986

ENVIRONMENTAL PROTECTION - GERMANY (WEST) - CONGRESSES.
Umweltpolitisches Gespräch (1983 : Bad Godesberg, Bonn, Germany) Ökonomische Instrumente der Umweltpolitik . Berlin , c1984. 108 p. ; ISBN 3-503-02401-8 LC Card 86-152141
HC290.5.E5 U625 1983

Umweltschutz . [Mainz] , c1984. 130 p. ; ISBN 3-7758-1086-2 LC Card 85-146233
HC290.5.E5 U64 1984

Umweltschutz und Verwaltung . Bonn , c1986. 171 p. ; ISBN 3-87999-040-9 LC Card 87-136048 DDC 363.7/056/0943 19
HC290.5.E5 U645 1986

ENVIRONMENTAL PROTECTION - GERMANY (WEST) - HAMBURG.
Vollzug und Wirkungen regionaler Umweltpolitik . Opladen , 1984. 199 p. ; ISBN 3-8100-0392-1 LC Card 84-228636
HC290.5.E5 V65 1984

ENVIRONMENTAL PROTECTION - GERMANY (WEST) - RHINELAND-PALATINATE.
Scholz, Bernhard, 1948- Bodenschutz zwischen Datenschwemme und Informationsdefizit . Speyer [1986] iii leaves, 385, 4 p. : LC Card 87-126271 DDC 333.73/13/094343 19
HD659.R54 S36 1986

ENVIRONMENTAL PROTECTION - GOVERNMENT POLICY - UNITED STATES.
Protecting the environment . Washington, D.C. , c1986. iii, 88 p. ; ISBN 0-89195-040-0 (pbk.) : LC Card 86-82962 DDC 363.7/056/0973 19
HC110.E5 P77 1986

ENVIRONMENTAL PROTECTION - GREAT BRITAIN.
The Green alternative . London , 1987. xv, 368 p. : ISBN 0-413-60280-X : LC Card 87-143624 DDC 333.7/2 19
HC260.E5 G736 1987

Environmental protection in the industrial sector in Japan : a survey of achievement. Tokyo, Japan : Industrial Pollution Control Association of Japan : [Distributed by Maruzen Co.], c1983. 168 p. : ill. ; 28 cm. Distributor statement from label on p. 4 of cover. Errata slip inserted. LC Card 87-672736
1. Japan - Industries - 1945- - Environmental aspects. 2. Environmental policy - Japan. 3. Pollution - Japan. I. Sangyō Kōgai Bōshi Kyōkai (Japan).
HC465.P55 E58x 1983

ENVIRONMENTAL PROTECTION - MOLDAVIAN S.S.R.
Todyka, IUriĭ Nikolaevich. Gosudarstvennyĭ apparat i problemy okhrany prirody v usloviiakh APK /. Kishinev , 1986. 179, [5] p. ; LC Card 86-141430
HD1995.M5 T63 1986

ENVIRONMENTAL PROTECTION - NETHERLANDS - NORTH HOLLAND.
North Holland (Netherlands) Milieubeleidsplan Noord-Holland 1982-1988 . [Haarlem] [1987] 60 p. ; LC Card 87-159912
HC327.N6 N67 1987

ENVIRONMENTAL PROTECTION - OCEANIA - CONGRESSES.
Environment and resources in the Pacific /. Geneva, Switzerland , 1985. iv, 294 p. : LC Card 86-217776 DDC 333.7/2/099 19
HC681.3.E5 E58 1985

ENVIRONMENTAL PROTECTION - SOVIET UNION.
Polityka ochrony środowiska w krajach socjalistycznych . Warszawa , 1980. 318 p. ; ISBN 83-208-0067-6 LC Card 81-101337
HC244.Z9 E56 1980

Tupytsia, IUriĭ IUr'evich. Ėkologo-ėkonomicheskaia ėffektivnost' prirodopol'zovaniia /. Moskva , 1980. 165 p. ; LC Card 81-146449
HC333.5 .T86 1980

ENVIRONMENTAL PROTECTION - STUDY AND TEACHING.
New ideas in environmental education /. London , New York , c1988. xiv, 219 p. ; ISBN 0-7099-5042-X LC Card 87-15696 DDC 363.7/007/1 19
HC79.E5 N45 1988

ENVIRONMENTAL PROTECTION - SWITZERLAND.
Aeberhardt, Werner. Die Umweltpolitik im Spannungsfeld politischer und wirtschaftlicher Interessen /. Köln , 1985. 134, [9] p. : ISBN 3-921471-55-9 : LC Card 86-145456
HC400.E5 A33 1985

ENVIRONMENTAL PROTECTION - UNITED STATES.
An Environmental agenda for the future /. Washington, D.C. , c1985. viii, 155 p. ; ISBN 0-933280-29-7 (pbk.) : LC Card 85-19760 DDC 304.2 19
TD171 .E56 1985 ***NYPL [JLE 86-2773]***

State of the environment . Washington, D.C. , c1984. xxxiv, 586 p. : ISBN 0-89164-084-3 LC Card 84-12651 DDC 363.7/00973 19
TD171 .S74 1984 ***NYPL [JLD 86-3097]***

Environmental quality strategic review : a follow-on report of the Task Force on Program Review, February 21, 1986. [Ottawa, Canada : Minister of Supply and Services Canada : Available from Canadian Govt. Pub. Centre, Supply and Services Canada], c1986. 170 p. ; 28 cm. Cover title: Improved program delivery. ISBN 0-660-12148-4 (pbk.) : LC Card 86-217056 DDC 363.7/00971 19
1. Environmental policy - Canada. I. Canada. Task Force on Program Review. II. Title: Improved program delivery.
HC120.E5 E59 1986

Environmental science . Chiras, Daniel D. Menlo Park, Calif. , c1988. xxiii, 531 p., [16] p. of plates : ISBN 0-8053-2257-4 LC Card 87-13906 DDC 363.7 19
HC79.E5 C485 1988

Environmental study series, MAB .

Environmentalists for Full Employment (Australia) Andrews, John. Solar jobs in Victoria . [Victoria] [1982] xxxix p. : LC Card 87-160366
HD9681.A83 V5326 1982

Envisionary management . Anthony, William P. New York , c1988. p. cm. ISBN 0-89930-257-2 (lib. bdg. : alk. paper) LC Card 87-7373 DDC 658.3 19
HD38 .A6256 1988

ENZYMES INDUSTRY.
Crull, Anna W. Commercial and industrial enzymes /. Stamford, Conn., U. S.A. , c1986. xiii, 160 leaves : ISBN 0-89336-492-4 (pbk.) LC Card 87-164403 DDC 380.1/4566063 19
HD9660.E582 C783 1986

Epargne et développement / Caisse des dépôts et consignations, Centre national des caisses d'épargne et de prévoyance, Swedish Savings Bank Association ; [édité par Denis Kessler et Pierre-Antoine Ullmo]. Paris : Economica, 1985. 410 p. : ill. ; 24 cm. "Actes d'un colloque tenu à Paris les 28, 29 et 30 mai 1984"--P. [3] Includes bibliographical references. ISBN 2-7178-0855-8 : LC Card 86-149765
1. Saving and investment - Developing countries - Congresses. 2. Economic development - Congresses. 3.

Financial institutions - Developing countries - Congresses. I. Kessler, Denis. II. Ullmo, Pierre-Antoine. III. Caisse des dépôts et consignations (France). IV. CENCEP (Center : France). V. Svenska sparbanksföreningen.
HC59.72.S3 E62 1985

Ependyseis kai trapezikes chorēgēseis se periodo krisēs . Epistēmoniko Diēmero (1984 : Athens, Greece) Athēna , 1984. 225 p. ; LC Card 86-193395
HG5700.5.A3 E85 1984

Epharmosmenē analysē tēs zētēsēs . Sapounas, Giōrgos S. Athēna , 1985. 483 p. : LC Card 86-212306
HD9000.5 .S29 1985

EPHMRA (Association) EPHMRA/ESOMAR Seminar (1985 : Lisbon, Portugal) Pharmaceutical competitor analysis . Brooklands, Sale, Cheshire, U.K. [1985] iv, 390 p. : ISBN 92-831-1103-6 (pbk.) : LC Card 86-202276 DDC 338.4/76151 19
HD9665.5 .E64 1985

EPHMRA/ESOMAR Seminar (1985 : Lisbon, Portugal) Pharmaceutical competitor analysis : a guide for marketing researchers / EPHMRA/ESOMAR Seminar, Lisbon, Portugal, 27th February-2nd March 1985. Brooklands, Sale, Cheshire, U.K. : E.Ph.M.R.A., [1985] iv, 390 p. : ill. ; 23 cm. Includes bibliographies. ISBN 92-831-1103-6 (pbk.) : LC Card 86-202276 DDC 338.4/76151 19
1. Pharmaceutical industry - Congresses. 2. Competition, International - Congresses. I. EPHMRA (Association). II. Esomar. III. Title.
HD9665.5 .E64 1985

Epicheirēsiakē psychologia . Phanariōtēs, P. Athēna , 1983. ix, 359, [3] p. : LC Card 84-134693
HF5548.8 .P45 1983

EPISTEMOLOGY. see **KNOWLEDGE, THEORY OF.**

Epistēmoniko Diēmero (1984 : Athens, Greece) Ependyseis kai trapezikes chorēgēseis se periodo krisēs : praktika Epistēmonikou Diēmerou. Athēna : Agrotikē Trapeza tēs Hellados, Dieuthynsē Meletōn kai programmatismou, 1984. 225 p. ; 28 cm. LC Card 86-193395
1. Investments - Greece - Congresses. 2. Bank loans - Greece - Congresses. I. Agrotikē Trapeza tēs Hellados. Dieuthynsē Meletōn & Programmatismou. II. Title.
HG5700.5.A3 E85 1984

EPP Group. Working towards European unification . [Luxembourg] , 1986. 60 p. ; LC Card 87-149629 DDC 338/.06 19
HC240.9.T4 W67 1986

Epp, H. Peden, D. G. The use of resource survey data in decision-making with special reference to Kitui District in Kenya /. Nairobi, Kenya , 1982. 12 leaves ; LC Card 85-980593 DDC 333.74/09676/24 19
HD983.Z8 K587 1982

Eppers, Jürgen. Zur Feinsteuerung ökonomischer Entscheidungsfolgen / Jürgen Eppers. Frankfurt am Main : Haag + Herchen, c1985. 87 p. : ill. ; 21 cm. (Schriften zur angewandten Ökonometrie . Heft 16) Bibliography: p. 83-87. ISBN 3-88129-950-5 : LC Card 86-149502
1. Decision-making - Econometric models. 2. Control theory. I. Title. II. Series.
HD30.23 .E66 1985

L'épreuve écrite à la capacité en droit et en économie /. Sobgui, Gabriel Alexis. Yaoundé, Cameroun , 1981. 113 p. ; LC Card 84-118988
HB74.6 .S65 1981

Epshteĭn, S. I. (Samuil Isaakovich) Burzhuaznaia nauka upravleniia i neupravliaemaia ėkonomika / S.I. Epshteĭn. Moskva : Izd-vo polit. lit-ry, 1986. 76 p. ; 16 cm. (Ėkonomika kapitalizma segodnia) Includes bibliographical references. LC Card 86-201018 DDC 658/.00973 19
1. Management - United States. 2. Industrial management - United States. I. Title. II. Series.
HD70.U5 E6 1986

Epstein, Edward Jay, 1935- Who owns the corporation? : management vs. shareholders / by Edward Jay Epstein. New York : Priority Press Publications, 1986. vi, 69 p. ; 22 cm. "A Twentieth Century Fund paper." Bibliography: p. 47-50. ISBN 0-87078-208-8 (pbk.) : LC Card 87-101003 DDC 338.7/4/0973 19
1. Corporate meetings - United States. 2. Stockholders' meetings - United States. 3. Directors of corporations - United States. I. Title.
HD2743 .E67 1986

Epstein, Rachel S.
Alternative investments / Rachel S. Epstein. New York : Chelsea House Publishers, c1988. 47 p. : ill. ; 21 cm. (The Basic investor's library) Bibliography: p. 45. Includes index. Explains such forms of investments as insurance, savings accounts, real estate, gold, and collectibles, addressing how to turn a personal interest into a profitable venture. ISBN 1-555-46633-8 LC Card 87-21766 DDC 332.6/78 19
1. Investments - Juvenile literature. 2. Real estate investment - Juvenile literature. 3. Collectibles as an investment - Juvenile literature. 4. Art as an investment - Juvenile literature. I. Title. II. Series.
HG4521 .E685 1988

Careers in the world of investments / Rachel S. Epstein ; Paul A. Samuelson, senior editorial consultant. New York : Chelsea House, c1988. 47 p. : ill. ; 21 cm. (The Basic investor's library) Bibliography: p. 46. Includes index. ISBN 1-555-46631-1 LC Card 87-13182 DDC 332.6/023 19
1. Investments - Vocational guidance. 2. Finance - Vocational guidance. I. Samuelson, Paul Anthony 1915-. II. Title. III. Series.
HG4528 .E67 1988

Investment banking / Rachel S. Epstein ; Paul A. Samuelson, senior editorial consultant. New York : Chelsea House, c1988. 48 p. : ill. ; 22 cm. (The Basic investor's library) Bibliography: p. 46. Includes index. One in a fourteen-volume series, this volume explains the role of investment banking in the business world, the concepts of underwriting and issuing stocks and bonds, and mergers. ISBN 1-555-46630-3 LC Card 87-18194 DDC 332.66 19
1. Investment banking - Juvenile literature. I. Samuelson, Paul Anthony 1915-. II. Title. III. Series.
HG4534 .E67 1988

Epstein, Roy J. (Roy Jacob), 1954- A history of econometrics / Roy J. Epstein. Amsterdam ; New York : North-Holland ; x, 254 p. ; 24 cm. (Contributions to economic analysis. 165) Bibliography: p. 229-247. Includes indexes. ISBN 0-444-70267-9 LC Card 87-15308 DDC 330/.028 19
1. Econometrics - History. I. Title. II. Series.
HB139 .E67 1987

Epstein, Stephan R., 1960- Alle origini della fattoria toscana : l'Ospedale della Scala di Siena e le sue terre (metà '200-metà '400) / Stephan R. Epstein. Firenze : Salimbeni, c1986. 315 p. : ill. ; 24 cm. + 1 folded map. (Quaderni di storia urbana e rurale . 7) Originally presented as the author's thesis (doctoral--Università di Siena, 1984) Bibliography: p. [293]-303. Includes indexes. LC Card 87-104355
1. Ospedale della Scala di Siena - History. 2. Farms - Italy - Siena Region - History. 3. Church lands - Italy - Siena Region - History. 4. Monasteries - Italy - Siena Region - History. 5. Hospitals - Italy - Siena Region - History. I. Title. II. Series.
HD1470.5.I82 S544 1986

Epstein, Trude Scarlett. Women, work, and family in Britain and Germany /. London , 1986. 216 p. : ISBN 0-7099-0976-4
NYPL [JLD 86-3391]

Equal opportunities and vocational training . Morgan-Gérard, Florence. Berlin [1982] 69 p. ; ISBN 92-825-2489-2 ***NYPL [JLD 87-1318]***

Equal opportunity / edited by Norman E. Bowie. Boulder : Westview Press, 1988. viii, 200 p. ; 23 cm. Includes bibliographies. ISBN 0-8133-0567-5 (pbk. : alk. paper) LC Card 87-7253 DDC 331.13/3/0973 19
1. Affirmative action programs - United States. I. Bowie, Norman E., 1942-.
HF5549.5.A34 E7 1988

Equal opportunity counsellors : professional training and profile : report of a seminar / organized by CEDEFOP on 30 and 31 October 1985 ; drafted by Françoise Bernard at the request of CEDEFOP.1st ed. Berlin : CEDEFOP--European Centre for the Development of Vocational Training ; Washington, DC : European Community Information Service [distributor], 1986. 50 p. : ill. ; 30 cm. (CEDEFOP document) ISBN 92-825-6559-9 : LC Card 87-136233 DDC 331.13/3/094 19
1. Discrimination in employment - European Economic Community countries. 2. Counselors - European Economic Community countries. I. Bernard, Françoise. II. European Centre for the Development of Vocational Training. III. Series.
HD4903.5.E8 E79 1986

Equal pay for comparable worth . Hutner, Frances Cornwall. New York , 1986. xiii, 227 p. ; ISBN 0-03-062873-3 (alk. paper) : LC Card 85-19427 DDC 331.4/21/0973 19
HD6061.2.U6 H86 1986
NYPL [JLE 86-2946]

EQUAL PAY FOR EQUAL WORK.
Diekmann, Andreas. Einkommensunterschiede zwischen Frauen und Männern . Wien [1985] 2 v. (244, 4 p.) : LC Card 86-150241
HD6061 .D54 1985

Hutner, Frances Cornwall. Equal pay for comparable worth . New York , 1986. xiii, 227 p. ; ISBN 0-03-062873-3 (alk. paper) : LC Card 85-19427 DDC 331.4/21/0973 19
HD6061.2.U6 H86 1986
NYPL [JLE 86-2946]

EQUAL PAY FOR EQUAL WORK - AUSTRALIA.
O'Donnell, Carol. Getting equal . Sidney , Boston , 1988. p. cm. ISBN 0-04-302005-4 LC Card 87-22302 DDC 331.2/1 19
HD6060.5.A8 O365 1988

EQUAL PAY FOR EQUAL WORK - GOVERNMENT POLICY - OREGON.
Oregon. Task Force on State Compensation and Classification Equity. Final report and recommendations of the Task Force on State Compensation and Classification Equity to the Sixty third Legislative Assembly. [Salem OR] (338 State Capitol, Salem 97310) [1985] 51 p. : LC Card 86-622414 DDC 331.2/1 19
HD6061.2.U62 O75 1985

EQUAL PAY FOR EQUAL WORK - GREAT BRITAIN.
Women and paid work . New York , 1988. p. cm. ISBN 0-312-01200-4 : LC Card 87-23477 DDC 331.2/1 19
HD6061.2.G7 W66 1988

EQUAL PAY FOR EQUAL WORK - LAW AND LEGISLATION - AUSTRALIA.
O'Donnell, Carol. Getting equal . Sidney , Boston , 1988. p. cm. ISBN 0-04-302005-4 LC Card 87-22302 DDC 331.2/1 19
HD6060.5.A8 O365 1988

EQUAL PAY FOR EQUAL WORK - LAW AND LEGISLATION - SWEDEN.
O'Donnell, Carol. Getting equal . Sidney , Boston , 1988. p. cm. ISBN 0-04-302005-4 LC Card 87-22302 DDC 331.2/1 19
HD6060.5.A8 O365 1988

EQUAL PAY FOR EQUAL WORK - LAW AND LEGISLATION - UNITED STATES.
Lorber, Lawrence Z. Sex and salary . Alexandria, Va. , 1985. v, 61 p. ;
NYPL [JLF 86-417]

O'Donnell, Carol. Getting equal . Sidney , Boston , 1988. p. cm. ISBN 0-04-302005-4 LC Card 87-22302 DDC 331.2/1 19
HD6060.5.A8 O365 1988

EQUAL PAY FOR EQUAL WORK - NETHERLANDS.
Vrouwen en economische zelfstandigheid /. Amsterdam , c1986. 199 p. : ISBN 90-6222-139-4 : LC Card 86-182832
HD6162 .V74 1986

EQUAL PAY FOR EQUAL WORK - ONTARIO.
Report of the Consultation Panel on Pay Equity. Toronto, Ont., Canada [1986] 123 p. ; ISBN 0-7729-1657-8 (pbk.) LC Card 87-117472 DDC 331.2/1 19
HD6061.2.C22 O577 1986

EQUAL PAY FOR EQUAL WORK - SWEDEN.
O'Donnell, Carol. Getting equal . Sidney , Boston , 1988. p. cm. ISBN 0-04-302005-4 LC Card 87-22302 DDC 331.2/1 19
HD6060.5.A8 O365 1988

EQUAL PAY FOR EQUAL WORK - UNITED STATES.
Berger, Gilda. Women, work, and wages /. New York , 1986. 122 p. : ISBN 0-531-10074-X

LC Card 85-15379 DDC 331.4/0973 19
HD6095 .B47 1986 *NYPL [JLE 86-4592]*

DeGooyer, Janice. Women's work, undervalued, underpaid . Washington, D.C. , 1984, c1982. 27, [4] leaves : *NYPL [*ZT-1708 no.39]*

Hutner, Frances Cornwall. Equal pay for comparable worth . New York , 1986. xiii, 227 p. ; ISBN 0-03-062873-3 (alk. paper) : LC Card 85-19427 DDC 331.4/21/0973 19
HD6061.2.U6 H86 1986
NYPL [JLE 86-2946]

Lorber, Lawrence Z. Sex and salary . Alexandria, Va. , 1985. v, 61 p. ;
NYPL [JLF 86-417]

O'Donnell, Carol. Getting equal . Sidney , Boston , 1988. p. cm. ISBN 0-04-302005-4 LC Card 87-22302 DDC 331.2/1 19
HD6060.5.A8 O365 1988

Women's work, men's work . Washington, D.C. , 1986. xii, 173 p. : ISBN 0-309-03429-9 (pbk.) LC Card 85-11541 DDC 331.1/33/0973 19
HD6060.5.U5 W66 1986
NYPL [JLF 86-1430]

EQUAL PAY FOR EQUAL WORK - UNITED STATES - CASE STUDIES.
Hutner, Frances Cornwall. Equal pay for comparable worth . New York , 1986. xiii, 227 p. ; ISBN 0-03-062873-3 (alk. paper) : LC Card 85-19427 DDC 331.4/21/0973 19
HD6061.2.U6 H86 1986
NYPL [JLE 86-2946]

Equal pay for work of equal value /. Marcotte, Marilee, 1960- Kingston, Ont., Canada , 1987. 101 p. : ISBN 0-88886-157-5 (pbk.) LC Card 87-163236 DDC 331.2/1 19
HD6061.2.C2 M37 1987

EQUAL RIGHTS AMENDMENTS - UNITED STATES.
Berry, Mary Frances. Why ERA failed . Bloomington , c1986. ix, 147 p. ; ISBN 0-253-36537-6 LC Card 85-45985 DDC 342.73/0878/02632 347.30287802632 19
KF4758 .B45 1986 *NYPL [JLE 86-3979]*

Mansbridge, Jane J. Why we lost the ERA /. Chicago, Ill. , c1986. xii, 327 p. ; ISBN 0-226-50358-5 (pbk.) LC Card 86-6954 DDC 305.4/2/0973 19
HQ1236.5.U6 M37 1986
NYPL [JLE 86-4474]

EQUALITY - BRAZIL.
Martins Filho, Oséas de Souza. Desenvolvimento com equilíbrio social . São Luís, Ma. , 1985 (São Luís, MA : Serviço de Impr. e Obras Gráficas do Estado) 314 p. ; LC Card 86-229862
HC187 .M33 1985

EQUALITY - DEVELOPING COUNTRIES.
Capitalism and equality in the Third World /. Lanham [New York] , c1987. 375 p. ; ISBN 0-8191-5574-8 (v. 2 : alk. paper) : LC Card 86-24749 DDC 330.12/2 19
HB501 .C24234 1987

EQUALITY - FRANCE - HISTORY.
Harouel, Jean Louis. Essai sur l'inégalité /. Paris , c1984. 287, [1] p. ; ISBN 2-13-038354-8 : LC Card 84-150958
HC280.I5 H35 1984

EQUALITY - UNITED STATES.
Capitalism and equality in America /. Lanham [New York] , c1987. ix, 306 p. : ISBN 0-8191-5572-1 (v. 1 : alk. paper) : LC Card 86-24739 DDC 330.12/2 19
HB501 .C2423 1987

EQUATEUR (ZAIRE) - ECONOMIC POLICY.
Fiche technique pour la région de l'Equateur . Mbandaka [1984] 172 leaves ; LC Card 86-201790
HC955.Z7 E6725 1985

EQUATEUR (ZAIRE) - SOCIAL POLICY.
Fiche technique pour la région de l'Equateur . Mbandaka [1984] 172 leaves ; LC Card 86-201790
HC955.Z7 E6725 1985

EQUATIONS, FUNCTIONAL. see **FUNCTIONAL EQUATIONS.**

Equatoria Region (Sudan). Ministry of Finance and Economic Affairs. Division of Statistics. Regional statistical abstract, 1972-1980 /. Juba [Sudan] , 1986. xiii, 113 leaves ; LC Card 86-981387 DDC 316.24 19
HA4687 .R45 1986

EQUATORIAL FOREST ECOLOGY. see **RAIN FOREST ECOLOGY.**

EQUILIBRIUM.
Razumikhin, Boris Sergeevich. [Fizicheskie modeli i metody teorii ravnovesii͡a v programmirovanii i ėkonomike. English.] Physical models and equilibrium methods in programming and economics /. Dordrecht ; Boston : xv, 351 p. : ISBN 90-277-1644-7 LC Card 83-17791 DDC 330/.0724 19
HB135 .R3913 1984 *NYPL [JSD 86-491]*

Equilibrium and macroeconomics /. Hahn, Frank. Oxford , 1984. vi, 397 p. : ISBN 0-631-13482-4 : LC Card 87-672165
HB171 .H23x 1984b

EQUILIBRIUM (ECONOMICS) - CONGRESSES.
Contractual arrangements for intertemporal trade /. Minneapolis, MN , c1987. p. cm. ISBN 0-8166-1533-0 : LC Card 86-24888 DDC 332.64/4/0724 19
HB801 .C629 1987

EQUILIBRIUM (ECONOMICS) - ECONOMETRIC MODELS.
Bauer, Gerhard. Schätzung von ökonometrischen Ungleichgewichtsmodellen . Idstein , 1985. iii, 350 p. : ISBN 3-925196-04-8 LC Card 86-226456
HB145 .B38 1985

Lambert, Jean-Paul, 1952- Disequilibrium macroeconomic models . Cambridge [Cambridgeshire] , New York , 1988. p. cm. ISBN 0-521-32209-X LC Card 86-24966 DDC 339.5/0724 19
HB145 .L36 1988

Rudebusch, Glenn D., 1959- The estimation of macroeconomic disequilibrium models with regime classification information /. Berlin , New York , c1987. 128 p. : ISBN 0-387-17757-4 (U. S. : pbk.) : LC Card 87-9583 DDC 339.5 19
HB145 .R82 1987b

Vilks, Arnis. Aggregation und Kausalität im Modell des allgemeinen Konkurrenzgleichgewichts . Göttingen , c1984. 141 p. ; ISBN 3-525-11287-4 (Deut. Bibl.) LC Card 84-225754
HB842 .V55 1984

EQUILIBRIUM (ECONOMICS) - MATHEMATICAL MODELS.
Auerbach, Alan J. Dynamic fiscal policy /. Cambridge [Cambridgeshire] , New York , 1987. xv, 196 p. : ISBN 0-521-30041-X LC Card 86-24447 DDC 339.5/2 19
HJ131 .A94 1987

Brems, Hans. Pioneering economic theory, 1630-1980 . Baltimore , c1986. xv, 411 p. : ISBN 0-8018-2667-5 (alk. paper) LC Card 85-19819 DDC 330.1 19
HB75 .B7845 1986 *NYPL [JLE 86-2408]*

Canto, Victor A. Currency substitution . Boston , c1987. viii, 196 p. ; ISBN 0-89838-195-9 LC Card 86-27747 DDC 332.4/56/098 19
HG3823 .C36 1987

Capital market equilibria /. Berlin , New York , c1986. x, 228 p. : ISBN 0-387-16248-8 (U. S.) LC Card 86-10104 DDC 332.6/0724 19
HG4523 .C33 1986 *NYPL [JLE 86-4309]*

Cresta, Jean-Paul. Théorie des marchés d'assurance /. Paris , 1984. vii, 231 p. : ISBN 2-7178-0696-2 : LC Card 84-235141
HG8054.5 .C74 1984

Cuddington, John T. Budget deficits and the current account in the presence of classical unemployment /. [Madrid] [1984] 47 p. : ISBN 84-505-0847-9 (pbk.) LC Card 86-215031 DDC 339.5/23/0724 19
HJ2005 .C83 1984

Le Vaillant de Folleville, Patrice, 1954- Nicht-sequentielle Suche, Preiswerbung und Marktgleichgewicht /. Frankfurt am Main , New York , c1986. 198 p. : ISBN 3-8204-9058-2 LC Card 86-153194
HB221 .L42 1986

Manuelli, Rodolfo E. Exercises in dynamic macroeconomic theory /. Cambridge, Mass. , 1987. xi, 223 p. ; ISBN 0-674-27476-8 (pbk. : alk. paper) LC Card 86-25767 DDC 339/.0729 19
HB172.5 .S27 1987 Suppl.

Withagen, Cees, 1950- Economic theory and international trade in natural exhaustible resources /. Berlin , New York , 1985. vi, 172 p. : ISBN 0-387-15970-3 LC Card 85-22101 DDC 333.7 19
HC59 .W55 1985
NYPL [JLM 72-289 no.253]

Ziesemer, Thomas. Economic theory of underdevelopment /. Regensburg , c1987. vi, 171 p. : ISBN 3-924956-15-4 (pbk.) LC Card 87-169372 DDC 338.9/001 19
HD75.5 .Z54 1987

EQUILIBRIUM (ECONOMICS) - MATHEMATICAL MODELS - CONGRESSES.
The Computation and modelling of economic equilibria /. Amsterdam ; New York : xiv, 229 p. : ISBN 0-444-70285-7 LC Card 87-15666 DDC 339/.0724 19
HB145 .C64 1987

General equilibrium trade policy modeling /. Cambridge, Mass. , c1986. vii, 360 p. : ISBN 0-262-19245-4 LC Card 85-19144 DDC 382/.3/0724 19
HF1410.5 .G46 1986 *NYPL [JLE 86-4456]*

EQUILIBRIUM (ECONOMICS) - MATHEMATICAL MODELS - PROBLEMS, EXERCISES, ETC.
Manuelli, Rodolfo E. Exercises in dynamic macroeconomic theory /. Cambridge, Mass. , 1987. xi, 223 p. ; ISBN 0-674-27476-8 (pbk. : alk. paper) LC Card 86-25767 DDC 339/.0729 19
HB172.5 .S27 1987 Suppl.

Equipe da FASE/São Paulo. Comissão de fábrica . Petrópolis , 1981. 60 p. ; LC Card 86-190732
HD5660.B7 C66 1981

EQUIPMENT, CAPITAL. see **INDUSTRIAL EQUIPMENT.**

EQUIPMENT, INDUSTRIAL. see **INDUSTRIAL EQUIPMENT.**

EQUIPMENT LEASING. see **INDUSTRIAL EQUIPMENT LEASES.**

Equipment leasing for commercial bankers /. Nevitt, Peter K. Philadelphia, Pa. , c1987. x, 123 p. ; ISBN 0-936742-37-2 (pbk.) : LC Card 87-5532 DDC 332.1/068/5 19
HD39.4 .N485 1987

Equité en matière d'emploi dans les sociétés d'Etat. Employment equity for crown corporations . Ottawa , 1986. 17, 18 p. ; ISBN 0-662-54400-5 (pbk.) LC Card 86-207179 DDC 354.71001/04 19
HD4903.5.C2 E47 1986

Equity markets . Schwartz, Robert A. (Robert Alan), 1937- New York , c1988. xvi, 544 p. : ISBN 0-06-041322-0 LC Card 87-23173 DDC 332.64/0973 19
HG4963 .S38 1988

Equity performance 1977-1986 : banks vs. other managers / prepared for the American Bankers Association, Trust Division [by] CDA Investment Technologies, Inc., Silver Spring, Maryland. Washington, D.C. : American Bankers Association, c1987. 28, [A-Q] p. : ill. ; 28 cm. LC Card 87-159010 DDC 332.1/754/0973 19
1. Bank investments - United States. 2. Institutional investments - United States. 3. Stocks - Prices - United States. I. American Bankers Association. II. CDA Investment Technologies, Inc.
HG1616.I5 E68 1987

Equity sharing /. Anderson, Georgia. Chicago , c1986. xiv, 136 p. : ISBN 0-8092-4836-0 (pbk.) : LC Card 86-24083 DDC 332.63/24 19
HD1382.5 .A54 1986

Era posible la gran Venezuela? /. Rodríguez, Gumersindo, 1933- Caracas , 1986. 215 p. : ISBN 980-255-004-3 LC Card 87-118414 DDC 338.987 19
HC237 .R617 1986

Erb, Bruce. Bush, Fredy. Your fortune in foreclosures . Tucson, Ariz. , c1987. ix, 221 p. : ISBN 0-89586-572-6 LC Card 86-33793 DDC

332.63/24 19
HD1382.5 .B87 1987

E.R.B. paper .
(82.3) Msambichaka, L. A. (Lucian A.) Food grain shortfalls in Tanzania, 1961-1981 . Dar es Salaam, Tanzania , c1982. 38 p. ; LC Card 85-980863 DDC 338.1/9/678 19
HD9047.T32 M726 1982

(83.4) Hyuha, Mukwanason. Financial structure and economic development in Africa . Dar-es-Salaam, Tanzania , c1983. 43 p. : LC Card 85-981441 DDC 332/.096 19
HG187.5.A2 H98 1983

Erbe, Michael. Historische Anthropologie . Göttingen , c1984. 166 p. ; ISBN 3-525-33497-4 LC Card 84-203590 DDC 306/.09 19
GN345.2 .H57 1984 ***NYPL [JFC 86-1764]***

Erbès-Seguin, Sabine. Syndicats et relations de travail dans la vie économique française / Sabine Erbès-Seguin. [Villeneuve d'Ascq] : Presses universitaires de Lille, [1985] 137 p. ; 24 cm. Bibliography: p. 135-137. ISBN 2-85939-262-9 : LC Card 85-226210 DDC 331/.0944 19
1. Trade-unions - France. 2. Industrial relations - France. I. Title.
HD6684 .E75 1985 ***NYPL [JLE 86-2222]***

Erdei, Ferenc. Erdei Ferenc agrárgazdasági és szövetkezetelméleti munkásságáról . Budapest [1986] 39 p. ; LC Card 87-408584
HD1940.5.E72 E73 1986

ERDEI, FERENC.
Erdei Ferenc agrárgazdasági és szövetkezetelméleti munkásságáról . Budapest [1986] 39 p. ; LC Card 87-408584
HD1940.5.E72 E73 1986

Erdei Ferenc agrárgazdasági és szövetkezetelméleti munkásságáról : emlékülés születésének 75. évfordulójára / [szerkesztette, Pál József]. Budapest : Szövetkezeti Kutató Intézet, [1986] 39 p. ; 29 cm. (Közlemények, 0133-4905 . 196) Includes bibliographical references. LC Card 87-408584
1. Erdei, Ferenc. 2. Agriculture - Economic aspects - Hungary. 3. Agriculture, Cooperative - Hungary. I. Erdei, Ferenc. II. Pál, József, Dr. III. Series: Közlemények / Szövetkezeti Kutató Intézet, 196.
HD1940.5.E72 E73 1986

Erdélyi bányák, kohók, emberek, századok . Vajda, Lajos. Bukarest , 1981. 544 p. : LC Card 83-124763
HD8039.M61 R68 1981

Erdilek, Asim. Multinationals as mutual invaders . London , c1985. 217 p. : ISBN 0-7099-0935-7 : LC Card 86-673843
HG4538 .M85x 1985b

Erdkundliches Wissen, 0425-1741 .
(Heft 78) Erdmann, Claudia. Aachen im Jahre 1812 . Stuttgart , 1986. 257 p., [15] folded leaves of plates : ISBN 3-515-04634-8 LC Card 86-142584 DDC 330.943/55 19
HC289.A23 E73 1986

Erdman, Ken. Raphel, Murray, 1928- The do-it-yourself direct mail handbook /. Philadelphia, PA (402 Bethlehem Pike, Philadelphia 19118) , c1986. xix, 218 p. : LC Card 86-203353
HF5861 .R35 1986

Erdmann, Claudia. Aachen im Jahre 1812 : wirtschafts- und sozialräumliche Differenzierung einer frühindustriellen Stadt / Claudia Erdmann. Stuttgart : Steiner Verlag Wiesbaden, 1986. 257 p., [15] folded leaves of plates : ill., maps ; 24 cm. (Erdkundliches Wissen, 0425-1741 . Heft 78) Bibliography: p. 235-257. ISBN 3-515-04634-8 LC Card 86-142584 DDC 330.943/55 19
1. Aachen (Germany) - Economic conditions. 2. Aachen (Germany) - Social conditions. 3. Aachen (Germany) - Industries - History. I. Title. II. Series.
HC289.A23 E73 1986

Erdölinduzierte sozioökonomische Entwicklung in den OAPEC-Staaten . Shamleh, Omar. Frankfurt am Main , New York , c1986. 410 p. ; ISBN 3-8204-9097-3 LC Card 86-157642
HC825 .S55 1986

Erdőérték- és eredményszámítás /. Márkus, László. Budapest , 1986. 207 p. : ISBN 963-232-225-2 : LC Card 87-408586
HF5686.F62 M37 1986

Erdsiek, Gerhard. Wörterbuch für Recht, Wirtschaft und Politik, mit erläuternden und rechtsvergleichenden Kommentaren. Englisch-Deutsch einschliesslich der Besonderheiten des amerikanischen Sprachgebrauchs [von] Gerhard Erdsiek [und] Clara-Erika Dietl, unter Mitarbeit von Frederick Weil und Anneliese Weil. Mit einem Geleitwort von Walter Strauss. Bleckede bei Hamburg, O. Meissner [1964-1968] 2 v. 25 cm. Added t.p.: Dictionary of legal, commercial and political terms. Vol. 2 by Gerhard Erdsiek, Clara-Erika Dietl,and Anneliese A. Weil, with the collaboration of Egon Lorenz and Wiebke Buxbaum. Bibliography: v. 1, p. x-xii. LC Card 65-42077
1. Law - Dictionaries. 2. Political science - Dictionaries. 3. Social sciences - Dictionaries. 4. English language - Dictionaries - German. I. Dietl, Clara-Erika, joint author. II. Weil, Anneliese A., joint author. III. Title. IV. Title: Dictionary of legal, commercial and political terms. ***NYPL [JLE 85-408]***

Erekutoronikusu pawā shōjiten / Kogō Hiroshi, Kawase Tarō, Ikeda Hiroaki hen. 880-02 Shohan, 1-han. Tōkyō : Kyōritsu Shuppan Kabushiki Kaisha, 1985. v, 618 p. : ill. ; 19 cm. Includes index. ISBN 4-320-08454-3 : LC Card 85-229520
1. Electronics - Dictionaries - Japanese. 2. Electric engineering - Dictionaries - Japanese. 3. Japanese language - Dictionaries - English. 4. Electronics - Dictionaries. 5. Electric engineering - Dictionaries. 6. English language - Dictionaries - Japanese. I. Kogō, Hiroshi, 1921-. II. Kawase, Tarō, 1935-. III. Ikeda, Hiroaki, 1942-.
TK7804 .E73 1985 <Orien Japan> ***NYPL [*OSG 86-3267]***

Eremin, A. M. (Al'bert Mikhaĭlovich) Metodologiia opredeleniia osnovnogo i iskhodnogo otnosheniĭ ėkonomiki sotsializma / A.M. Eremin. Kazan' : Izd-vo Kazanskogo universiteta, 1980. 157, [3] p. ; 20 cm. Bibliography: p. 157-[159] LC Card 81-134646
1. Marxian economics - Methodology. 2. Communist countries - Economic policy. I. Title.
HB97.5 .E665 1980

Uchastie trudiashchikhsia v upravlenii proizvodstvom . Moskva , 1985. 69, [2] p. ; LC Card 85-224379
HD5660.S65 U27 1985

Érettségizettek a munkaerőpiacon / [szerkesztette, W. Reisz Terézia]. Budapest : Oktatáskutató Intézet, 1985. 124 p. ; 29 cm. On cover: Iskolakutatási témacsoport. CONTENTS. - A fiatalok munkavállalásának néhány szociológiai problémája Magyarországon / Szalai Júlia -- Szakközépiskolák / Liskó Ilona -- Érettségi után tovább nem tanuló gimnázisták / W. Reisz Terézia. ISBN 963-404-026-8 LC Card 87-409614
1. High school graduates - Employment - Hungary. 2. Youth - Employment - Hungary. I. Reisz, Terézia W. II. Szalai, Júlia. III. Liskó, Ilona. IV. Iskolakutatási témacsoport.
HD6276.H82 E73 1985

Ereuna gia tis hellēnikes exagōges stēn EOK . (8) Hypodēmata. Athēna , 1985. 86 p. : LC Card 86-194391
HD9787.G62 H96 1985

Erfahrungen mit der Mitbestimmung in kommunalen Unternehmen . Ehinger, Jürgen. Baden-Baden , 1986. 147 p. ; ISBN 3-7890-1289-0 LC Card 87-118963 DDC 350.87/00943 19
HD2768.G44 E38 1986

Erfahrungen mit der Profit-Center-Organisation /. Wolf, Martin, 1954- Frankfurt am Main , New York , c1985. viii, 285 p. : ISBN 3-8204-8746-8 LC Card 85-243838
HD2756.2.G3 W65 1985

Erfassung des Wohnungsangebotes /. Czasny, Karl. Wien , 1985. 284 p. ; ISBN 3-900551-04-9 LC Card 87-103427 DDC 333.33/8 19
HD7337.V3 C93 1985

Die Erfassung von Carryover-Effekten im Marketing . Langkamp, Peter. Thun , c1984. 335 p. : ISBN 3-87144-844-3 : LC Card 85-113501
HF5415.3 .L36 1984

Der Erfolg von Unternehmenszusammenschlüssen . Möller, Wolf-Peter. München , c1983. 403 p. : ISBN 3-597-10456-8 LC Card 83-227517
HD2746.5 .M65 1983

Erfolgsindikatoren und Betriebsvergleich bei Kreditgenossenschaften /. Krauss, Hans-Ulrich. Gelsenkirchen , 1983. 217 p. : ISBN 3-88485-471-2 LC Card 84-153354
HG2039.G4 K73 1983

Erfolgskontrolle bei der Verausgabung öffentlicher Mittel / Peter Eichhorn und Gert von Kortzfleisch, Hrsg. 1. Aufl. Baden-Baden : Nomos, 1986. 133 p. : ill. ; 23 cm. (Schriften zur öffentlichen Verwaltung und öffentlichen Wirtschaft. Bd. 91) Summary in German and English. Bibliography: p. 125-130. Includes indexes. CONTENTS. - Erfolgskontrolle bei der Verausgabung öffentlicher Mittel / Peter Eichhorn -- Zur Evaluation staatlicher Programme / Klaus König -- Erfolgskontrolle der regionalen Wirtschaftsförderung / Klaus-Peter Fox -- Ansatzpunkte für die Beurteilung öffentlicher Massnahmen / Johann Eekhoff -- Erfolgskriterien für mischfinanzierte Projekte oder Kommunen? / Ernst Pappermann -- Staatliche Rechnungsprüfung und Erfolgskontrolle / Heinz-Günter Zavelberg. ISBN 3-7890-1208-4 LC Card 86-164102
1. Germany (West) - Appropriations and expenditures - Accounting. 2. Expenditures, Public - Evaluation. 3. Expenditures, Public - Cost effectiveness. I. Eichhorn, Peter, 1939-. II. Kortzfleisch, Gert von.
HJ7793 .E73 1986

Erfolgskontrolle der Industrieansiedlungspolitik . Hanser, Christian. Bern , New York , c1986. 375 p. ; ISBN 3-261-03610-9 LC Card 87-407957 DDC 338.6/042/09494 19
HD58 .H36 1986

Ergachev, M. N. Ėffektivnost' proizvodstva v agropromyshlennom komplekse Chuvashskoĭ ASSR /. Cheboksary , 1985. 198 p. ; LC Card 86-203897
HD9015.S653 C483 1985

Ėrgashev, A. (Atakul) Dialektika ob"ektivnogo i sub"ektivnogo v razvitii nauchno-tekhnicheskoĭ revoliutsii / A. Ėrgashev. Tashkent : "Uzbekistan", 1980. 185 p. ; 20 cm. Includes bibliographical references. LC Card 81-143159
1. Technological innovations - Uzbek S.S.R. 2. Uzbek S.S.R. - Economic conditions. I. Title.
HC337.U963 T44 1980

Ėrgashev, N. (Nazirzhon) Rukovodstvo Kompartii Uzbekistana osvoeniem tselinnykh zemel' / N. Ėrgashev. Tashkent : "Uzbekistan", 1985. 159 p. ; 20 cm. Bibliography: p. 149-[155] LC Card 86-231568
1. Irrigation - Uzbek S.S.R. 2. Reclamation of land - Uzbek S.S.R. 3. Water resources development - Uzbek S.S.R. I. Title.
HD1741.S782 U84 1985

Ergatikon Kentron Athēnōn (Athens, Greece) Klōnarēs, N. G. (Nikos G.) Ho syndikalismos kai to politiko mas provlēma /. Athēnai , 1973. 78 p. ; LC Card 86-234658
HD6795.5 .K57 1973

Die Ergebnisrechnung nach dem Bilanzrichtlinie-Gesetzentwurf im internationalen Vergleich (BRD, Japan, USA) /. Hanisch, Bärbel, 1957- Frankfurt am Main , New York , c1984. 286 p. : ISBN 3-8204-8559-7 : LC Card 85-164345
HF5616.G3 H35 1984

Ergebnisse der Frauenforschung .
(Bd. 1) Biermann, Ingrid, 1955- Leben mit kurzfristigem Denken . Weinheim , 1985. 224 p. ; ISBN 3-407-58260-9 LC Card 86-106693
HD6053.6.G3 B54 1985 ***NYPL [JLD 86-3122]***

Ergebnisse der Gebäude- und Wohnungszählung in Berlin (West) am 25. Oktober 1968 : (Kreisveröffentlichungsprogramm, Quellenband) / Herausgeber, Statistisches Landesamt Berlin. Berlin : Kulturbuch-Verlag, [1971] 52 p. ; 30 cm. (Berliner Statistik. Sonderhefte . Sonderheft 169 (Feb. 1971)) Chiefly tables. LC Card 85-171262
1. Housing - Berlin (Germany) - Statistics. I. Statistisches Landesamt Berlin. II. Series: Berliner Statistik. Sonderhefte , 169.
HA1330.B6 B45 Heft 169 HD7339.B4

Ergebnisse der Gewerbesteuerstatistik in Berlin (West) 1966 / Herausgeber, Statistisches Landesamt Berlin. Berlin : Kulturbuch-Verlag, [1972] 51 p. ; 29 cm. (Berliner Statistik. Sonderhefte . Sonderheft 200 (Juni 1972)) Chiefly tables. LC Card 85-171275
1. Business tax - Berlin (Germany) - Statistics. I. Statistisches Landesamt Berlin. II. Series: Berliner

Statistik. Sonderhefte , 200.
HA1330.B6 B45 Heft 200 HJ5627.G2

Ergebnisse der nichtlandwirtschaftlichen Betriebszählung vom 1. September 1954 / bearbeitet und herausgegeben vom Österreichischen Statistischen Zentralamt. Wien : Ueberreuter, 1958. 84 p. ; 30 cm. LC Card 84-252994
1. Labor supply - Austria - Statistics. 2. Business enterprises - Austria - Statistics. 3. Austria - Industries - Statistics. I. Österreichisches Statistisches Zentralamt.
HD5779 .E74 1958

Ergebnisse der Personalstrukturerhebung in Berlin (West) am 2. Oktober 1968 / Herausgeber, Statistisches Landesamt Berlin. Berlin : Kulturbuch-Verlag, [1971] 75 p. ; 30 cm. (Berliner Statistik. Sonderhefte . Sonderheft 174 (Juli 1971)) Chiefly tables. LC Card 85-171250
1. Occupational mobility - Berlin (Germany) - Statistics. I. Statistisches Landesamt Berlin. II. Series: Berliner Statistik. Sonderhefte , 174.
HA1330.B6 B45 Heft 174 HD5717.5.G32B47

Ergebnisse der Volks- und Berufszählung in Berlin (West) am 27. Mai 1970 : Repräsentativteil der Zählung / Statistisches Landesamt Berlin. Berlin : Kulturbuch-Verlag, [1976] 4 v. : ill. ; 29 cm. (Berliner Statistik. Sonderhefte . Sonderheft 254 (4/76), 255 (5/76), 256 (8/76), 257 (9/76)) Chiefly tables. CONTENTS. - Heft 1. Ausbildungsstand der Bevölkerung, Vertriebene und Deutsche aus der DDR oder aus Ost-Berlin, Ausländer -- Heft 2. Deutsche Erwerbstätige nach dem Nettoerwerbseinkommen sowie in sozio-ökonomischer Gliederung -- Heft 3. Deutsche Erwerbstätige nach der beruflichen Gliederung -- Heft 4. Haushalte und Familien, erwerbstätige Frauen und Mütter. LC Card 85-171340
1. Berlin (Germany) - Population - Statistics. 2. Berlin (Germany) - Occupations - Statistics. I. Statistisches Landesamt Berlin. II. Series: Berliner Statistik. Sonderhefte , 254-257.
HA1330.B6 B45 Heft 254-257 HA1249.B47

ERGONOMICS. see **HUMAN ENGINEERING.**

Erhard, Ludwig. Kohl, Helmut, 1930- Soziale Marktwirtschaft, Fundament für morgen . Bonn [1987] 39 p. : ISBN 3-88991-011-4 LC Card 87-409383 DDC 338.943 19
HC286.5 .K565 1987

ERHARD, LUDWIG.
Kohl, Helmut, 1930- Soziale Marktwirtschaft, Fundament für morgen . Bonn [1987] 39 p. : ISBN 3-88991-011-4 LC Card 87-409383 DDC 338.943 19
HC286.5 .K565 1987

Wünsche, Horst Friedrich. Ludwig Erhards Gesellschafts- und Wirtschaftskonzeption . Stuttgart , 1986. 239 p. ; ISBN 3-87959-263-2 LC Card 86-201702
HC286.5 .W85 1986

Erhebung über die Gütertransporte auf der Strasse 1984 / Bearbeitung und Vertrieb, Bundesamt für Statistik = Enquête sur les transports routiers de marchandises 1984 / realisation et diffusion, Office fédéral de la statistique. Bern : Das Bundesamt, 1986. 103 p. : ill. ; 30 cm. (Amtliche Statistik der Schweiz . Nr. 064 = no 064) Statistische Resultate. 11, Verkehr = Données statistiques. 11, Transports et communications French and German. Chiefly tables. ISBN 3-303-11041-7 : LC Card 87-408470 DDC 388.3/24/09494/021 19
1. Trucking - Switzerland - Statistics. 2. Transportation, Automotive - Switzerland - Statistics. I. Switzerland. Bundesamt für Statistik. II. Title: Enquête sur les transports routiers de marchandises 1984. III. Series: Amtliche Statistik der Schweiz , Nr. 064.
HE5683.A6 E74 1986

Erhöhter Handlungsbedarf im Strukturwandel : Analyse der strukturellen Entwicklung der deutschen Wirtschaft : Strukturberichterstattung 1983. Berlin : Duncker & Humblot, [1984] xxix, 229 p. : ill. ; 30 cm. (Beiträge zur Strukturforschung . Heft 79, 1984) At head of title: Deutsches Institut für Wirtschaftsforschung. Includes index. ISBN 3-428-05565-9 LC Card 86-137115 DDC 330 s 330.943/0878 19
1. Germany, West - Economic conditions - 1974-. 2. Germany, West - Economic policy - 1974-. I. Deutsches Institut für Wirtschaftsforschung. II. Series: Beiträge zur Strukturforschung , Heft 79.
HC281 .B33 Heft 79 HC286.7

Erhvervsøkonomiske rapporter . (nr. 5) Beskatningen af aktieafkast i Danmark og i det øvrige Vesteuropa /. København [1986] 23 p. ; ISBN 87-7353-047-6 LC Card 87-144435
HJ5913.D4 B47 1986

Eric Louis Kohler in the accounting profession /. Wagner, Nancy A. Atlanta, Ga. , 1987. vi, 210 p. ; ISBN 0-88406-196-5 (pbk.) : LC Card 86-25633 DDC 657/.092/4 19
HF5604.5.K64 W34 1987

Erickson, Jack. Star Spangled beer : a guide to America's new microbreweries and brewpubs / by Jack Erickson. Reston, Va. : RedBrick Press, 1987. v, 155 p. : ill. ; 24 cm. Bibliography: p. 143-148. Includes index. ISBN 0-941397-00-9 (pbk.) : LC Card 86-63993 DDC 338.7/66342/02573 19
1. Brewing industry - United States - Directories. 2. Breweries - United States - Directories. 3. Brewing industry - United States - History. 4. Breweries - United States - History. I. Title.
HD9397.U52 E75 1987

ERIE COUNTY (N.Y.) - POPULATION - HISTORY.
Stern, Mark J. Society and family strategy . Albany, N.Y. , c1987. xiv, 172 p. : ISBN 0-88706-495-7 LC Card 86-23121 DDC 304.6/34/0974796 19
HB935.N7 S74 1987

ERIE COUNTY (N.Y.) - SOCIAL CONDITIONS.
Stern, Mark J. Society and family strategy . Albany, N.Y. , c1987. xiv, 172 p. : ISBN 0-88706-495-7 LC Card 86-23121 DDC 304.6/34/0974796 19
HB935.N7 S74 1987

Eriksen, August Wiemann. Eksportrådgivning i Danmark 1910-1921 : privat eller statslig opgave? : striden i erhvervsorganisationer og centraladministration om oprettelse af et statsligt oplysningsorgan for eksporterhvervene / af August Wiemann Eriksen. [Copenhagen] : Rigsarkivet : Gad, 1984. 198 p. : ill. ; 24 cm. (Administrationshistoriske studier . bd. 9) Bibliography: p. 194-196. ISBN 87-7497-075-5 LC Card 84-231455
1. Denmark - Commercial policy - History. 2. Foreign trade promotion - Denmark - History. I. Title. II. Series.
HF1561 .E75 1984

Eriksson, Kjell E. Hetzler, Antoinette, 1943- Arbetsskadeförsäkringens tillämpning . Lund [1984] 176 p. : ISBN 91-970351-3-0 : LC Card 84-159654
HD7103.65.S8 H48 1984

Der Erklärungsgehalt der Exportbasistheorie /. Krietemeyer, Hartmut, 1955- Hamburg , 1983. 224 p. : ISBN 3-87895-240-6 : LC Card 84-147595
HC287.H4 K75 1983

Erklärung von Graz für Solidarische Entwicklung (Association) Armut in Österreich . Graz , c1977. 168 p. : ISBN 3-7011-7080-0 LC Card 86-176543
HC270.P6 A75 1977

Erklärungen zur kommunalen Versorgungswirtschaft. 2. aktualisierte Aufl. Köln : Sigillum-Verlag, 1985. 146 p. ; 21 cm. (Beiträge zur kommunalen Versorgungswirtschaft. Heft 63) ISBN 3-87750-141-9
1. Public utilities - Germany, West. 2. Energy policy - Germany, West. I. Verband Kommunaler Unternehmen. II. Series. ***NYPL [K-10 8934 Heft 63]***

Erlank, D. Ellis, George Francis Rayner. A quality of life and basic needs measurement system with application to Elsies River /. Cape Town [1983] 101, [84] p. : ISBN 0-7992-0551-6 LC Card 84-146635 DDC 338.968/00723 19
HC905.Z7 E473 1983 ***NYPL [JLF 86-1126]***

Erlicher, L. (Luisella) Le 150 ore e la formazione professionale in azienda . Milano, Italy , c1985. 178 p. : LC Card 86-141990
HD5716.T242 I82 1985
NYPL [JFD 87-3739]

Ermakov, V. I. (Vladimir Ivanovich) Solodkova, S. V. (Serafima Vasil'evna) Sotsialisticheskie proizvodstvennye otnosheniia . Moskva , 1984. 141 p. ; LC Card 84-223476
HC336.25 .S65 1984

Ermittlungen gegen die Dresdner Bank, 1946 / bearbeitet von der Hamburger Stiftung für Sozialgeschichte des 20. Jahrhunderts ; übersetzt von Ulrike Bischoff. Nördlingen : F. Greno, 1986. cxxxiv, 353 p., [8] p. of plates : ill. ; 22 cm. At head of title: O.M.G.U. S., Office of Military Government for Germany, United States, Finance Division, Financial Investigation Section; Militärregierung der Vereinigten Staaten für Deutschland, Finanzabteilung, Sektion für Finanzielle Nachforschungen. Preface signed by Karl Heinz Roth. "Die Andere Bibliothek, herausgegeben von Hans Magnus Enzensberger, Sonderband." Bibliography: p. 275-[342] Includes index. ISBN 3-89190-297-2 : LC Card 87-121689
1. Dresdner Bank - History - 20th century. 2. Banks and banking - Germany - History - 20th century. I. Roth, Karl Heinz. II. Germany (Territory under Allied occupation, 1945-1955 : U. S. Zone). Office of Military Government. Financial Investigation Section. III. Hamburger Stiftung für Sozialgeschichte des 20. Jahrhunderts. IV. Andere Bibliothek. Special number.
HG3058.D7 E76 1986

Ernährungs- und Landwirtschafts-Organisation der Vereinten Nationen. see **Food and Agriculture Organization of the United Nations.**

Ernenputsch, Margit A. Theoretische und empirische Untersuchungen zum Beschaffungsprozess von konsumtiven Dienstleistungen / Margit A. Ernenputsch. Bochum : N. Brockmeyer, 1986. xiii, 263 p. ; 21 cm. (Bochumer wirtschaftswissenschaftliche Studien. Nr. 114) Bibliography: p. 252-262. ISBN 3-88339-548-X LC Card 87-143249 DDC 658.8 19
1. Service industries - Marketing. I. Title.
HF5415.122 .E76 1986

Ernoult, Victor. Gruère, Jean-Pierre. Optimiser les ressources humaines dans l'entreprise . Paris , c1984. 69, 42 p. : ISBN 2-7101-0462-8 : LC Card 84-217427
HF5549.5.A78 G78 1984

Ernst, Mario, 1953- Demokratische Wirtschaftspolitik : ein kommunikationsorientierter Ansatz politischer Ökonomie / Mario Ernst. Bern ; New York : P. Lang, c1986. x, 178 p. : ill. ; 21 cm. (Europäische Hochschulschriften. Reihe V, Volks- und Betriebswirtschaft . Bd. 710 = vol. 710 = vol. 710) Bibliography: p. 173-178. ISBN 3-261-03571-4 LC Card 86-198029
1. Communication in economic development. 2. Democracy. I. Series: Europäische Hochschulschriften. Reihe V, Volks- und Betriebswirtschaft , Bd. 710. II. Title.
HD76 .E76 1986

Ernst, Maurice. Drouin, Marie Josée. Western European adjustment to structural economic problems /. Lanham, MD , Indianapolis, IN , c1987. xxii, 259 p. : ISBN 0-8191-6527-1 (alk. paper) : LC Card 87-18909 DDC 330.94/0558 19
HC240 .D75 1987

Ernst-Poerksen, Michael. Staatsgrenzen . Berlin , c1982. 183 p. ; ISBN 3-88619-089-7 LC Card 84-142799
HB90 .S75 1982

Ernst, Walter R., 1929- Okun, Daniel Alexander. Community piped water supply systems in developing countries . Washington, D.C. , 1987. xi, 249 p. : ISBN 0-8213-0896-3 (pbk.) LC Card 87-8161 DDC 363.6/1/091724 19
HD4465.D44 O38 1987

Erők és érdekek . Losoncz, Miklós. Budapest , 1986. 191 p. : ISBN 963-326-966-0 : LC Card 87-148142
HF1414.5 .L67 1986

EROSION CONTROL. see **SOIL CONSERVATION.**

EROSION - ECONOMIC ASPECTS - UNITED STATES.
Webb, Shwu-Eng. Idling erodible cropland . Washington, D.C. [1986] iii, 31 p. : LC Card 86-601632 DDC 338.1 s 338.1/62 19
HD1751 .A91854 no. 550 HD256

Errázuriz, Enrique. Industria eléctrica, 1960-1985 : expansión, crisis y efectos económico-sociales / Enrique Errázuriz, Alicia Leiva, Jorge Tagle. [Santiago, Chile] : Programa de Economía del Trabajo, Academia de Humanismo Cristiano, [1986] 243 p. : ill. ; 22 cm. (Colección Estudios sectoriales . no. 3)

Bibliography: p. 239-243. LC Card 87-403870 DDC 338.4/762131/0983 19
1. Electric industries - Chile. 2. Trade-unions - Electric industries workers - Chile. I. Leiva, Alicia. II. Tagle, Jorge. III. Programa de Economía del Trabajo (Academia de Humanismo Cristiano). IV. Title. V. Series.
HD9685.C52 E77 1986

ERROR ANALYSIS (MATHEMATICS)
Krug, Walter, Prof. Dr. Quantifizierung des systematischen Fehlers in wirtschafts- und sozialstatistischen Daten . Berlin , 1976. 109 p. : ISBN 3-428-03710-3 LC Card 76-487801
HD5711 .K78 ***NYPL [JLE 80-187]***

Statistics Canada. Statistical Services Field. A compendium of methods of error evaluation in censuses and surveys /. Ottawa , 1978. 25 p. ; LC Card 80-499370 DDC 001.4/225 19
HA31.2 .C36 1978 ***NYPL [JLF 81-125]***

Errors . Datz, Stephen R. Loveland, Colo. (P.O. Box 402, Loveland 80537) , 1986. vi, 100 p. : LC Card 87-128178 DDC 769.56973 19
HE6184.E7 D38 1986

ERSATZ. see **SUBSTITUTE PRODUCTS.**

Erschliessung des U. S.-Marktes durch Direktinvestitionen mittelständischer deutscher Unternehmungen des Investitionsgüterbereichs. Klose, Roland, 1954- Die Erschliessung des US-Marktes durch Direktinvestitionen mittelständischer deutscher Unternehmungen des Investitionsgüterbereichs /. [Würzburg? , 1983] (Würzburg : Dissertationsdruck, Schmitt & Meyer) v, 307 p. ; LC Card 84-195414
HG4910 .K56 1983

Die Erschliessung des US-Marktes durch Direktinvestitionen mittelständischer deutscher Unternehmungen des Investitionsgüterbereichs /. Klose, Roland, 1954- [Würzburg? , 1983] (Würzburg : Dissertationsdruck, Schmitt & Meyer) v, 307 p. ; LC Card 84-195414
HG4910 .K56 1983

Ersel, Hasan. Boratav, Korkut. Housing yearbook /. Ankara, Turkey , 1985. 32, [2] p. ; LC Card 87-403323 DDC 363.5/09561 19
HD7358.25.A3 B67 1985

Ershov, Ė. B. Programmnoe obespechenie ėkonomiko-matematicheskikh issledovaniĭ /. Moskva , 1982. 142 p. : LC Card 84-209065
HD30.25 .P76 1982

Ershov, Stal′ Aleksandrovich. Mezhdunarodnye monopolii : strategii͡a razboi͡a / S.A. Ershov. Moskva : Izd-vo polit. lit-ry, 1980. 125 p. : ill. ; 16 cm. (Ėkonomika kapitalizma segodni͡a) Includes bibliographical references. LC Card 81-135534
1. International business enterprises. I. Title. II. Series.
HD2755.5 .E77 1980

Az érték átalakulása termelési árrá, avagy, Az un. transzformációs probléma /. Mellár, Tamás. Pécs , 1982. 55 p. ; LC Card 83-179021
HB203 .M44 1982

Értékelemzés a termékfejlesztésben /. Hegedűs, József. Budapest , 1983. 215 p., [2] p. of plates : ISBN 963-10-5784-4 LC Card 85-110177
HD69.N4 H38 1983

Értekezések, emlékezések.
Értekezések, emlékezések, 0236-6258.
Falusné Szikra, Katalin. Az első és a második gazdaság közötti bér-, illetve jövedelem-diszparitás /. Budapest , c1986. 31 p. ; ISBN 963-05-4343-5 : LC Card 87-407713
HC300.295.I5 F35 1986

Hoch, Róbert. A gazdaság nyitottságáról . Budapest , c1987. 33 p. ; ISBN 963-05-4444-X : LC Card 87-425574
HF1542.5 .H63 1987

Láng, István, 1931- A biomassza hasznosításának távlatai . Budapest , c1986. 28 p. ; ISBN 963-05-4357-5 : LC Card 87-407709
HD9502.5.B543 H95 1986

Simai, Mihály. Az emberi tényező szerepe a világgazdaságban az 1980-as években . Budapest , c1986. 41 p. ; ISBN 963-05-4342-7 : LC Card 87-407712
HD4904.7 .S446 1986

Ertl, Josef, 1925- Agrarpolitik ohne Illusionen : politische und persönliche Erfahrungen / Josef Ertl. Frankfurt am Main : A. Strothe, c1985. 208 p. : 1 port. ; 22 cm. ISBN 3-87795-022-1 LC Card 86-119627 DDC 338.1/84 19
1. Agriculture and state - European Economic Community countries. I. Title.
HD1920.5.Z8 E78 1985

Erträge der Forschung, 0174-0695 .
(Bd. 205) Nienhaus, Volker. Kontroversen um Markt und Plan . Darmstadt , 1984. vi, 171 p. ; ISBN 3-534-08700-3 LC Card 84-181049
HB95 .N47 1984

Ertresvåg, Per-Aslak, 1931- Ekko av fremtiden / Per-Aslak Ertresvåg. Oslo : Grøndahl, c1986. 163 p. : ill. ; 21 cm. Bibliography: p. 161-162. ISBN 82-504-0815-2 LC Card 86-217931
1. Economic forecasting - Norway. 2. Norway - Economic conditions - 1945-. 3. Social prediction - Norway. 4. Norway - Social conditions - 1945-. I. Title.
HC365 .E77 1986

Erwee, Johannes Albertus.
Trends in the construction of dwelling units in the Port Elizabeth/Uitenhage and East London/King William's town regions, 1970-1984, including additions and alterations / by J.A. Erwee and M. Myrdal. Port Elizabeth [South Africa] : Institute for Planning Research, [1985] 44 leaves : ill. ; 30 cm. (Fact paper . no. 56) Rev. ed. of: Trends in the construction of dwelling units (whites) in the Port Elizabeth/Uitenhage and East London/King William's Town regions, 1970-1981, including additions and alterations. 1982. "April 1985." ISBN 0-86988-244-9 (pbk.) LC Card 86-229280 DDC 363.5/1/096875 19
1. Housing - South Africa - Port Elizabeth - Statistics. 2. Housing - South Africa - East London Region - Statistics. I. Myrdal, M. II. Erwee, Johannes Albertus. Trends in the construction of dwelling units (whites) in the Port Elizabeth/Uitenhage and East London/King William's Town regions, 1970-1981, including additions and alterations. III. Series: Fact paper (University of Port Elizabeth. Institute for Planning Research) , no. 56. IV. Title.
HD7374.4.P6 E735 1985

Trends in the construction of dwelling units (whites) in the Port Elizabeth/Uitenhage and East London/King William's Town regions, 1970-1981, including additions and alterations. Erwee, Johannes Albertus. Trends in the construction of dwelling units in the Port Elizabeth/Uitenhage and East London/King William's town regions, 1970-1984, including additions and alterations / by J.A. Erwee and M. Myrdal. Port Elizabeth [South Africa] [1985] 44 leaves : ISBN 0-86988-244-9 (pbk.) LC Card 86-229280 DDC 363.5/1/096875 19
HD7374.4.P6 E735 1985

Erwerb und Verwendung des Einkommens von Arbeitnehmerhaushalten mit erwerbstätiger Ehefrau /. Freitäger, Jürgen, 1959- Frankfurt am Main , New York , c1986. xix, 327 p. : ISBN 3-8204-9148-1 : LC Card 86-195223
HD9850.1 .M58 Bd. 37 HD6055.2.G3

Erziehungswissenschaft aktuell .
(Bd. 2) Arnold-Rösner, Regina. Berufliche Integration junger Türken . Hamburg , 1986. 122 p. : ISBN 3-925408-05-3 LC Card 86-223625
HD8458.T9 A76 1986

Escalante Herrera, Ana Cecilia. Achío Tacsan, Mayra. Azúcar y política en Costa Rica /. San José , c1985. 172 p. : ISBN 997-7231-67-2 LC Card 86-209103
HD9114.C82 A24 1985

Escalation and intervention : multilateral security and its alternatives / edited by Arthur R. Day and Michael W. Doyle. Boulder, Colo. : Westview Press, 1986. x, 181 p. ; 24 cm. (Westview special studies in international security) Includes bibliographical references and index. CONTENTS. - Conflict in Chad / I. William Zartman -- Civil conflict in Lebanon / Arthur R. Day -- The Iran-Iraq war / Barry Rubin -- Multilateral approaches to multidimensional conflict resolution / John W. Harbeson -- Afghanistan 1984 / Louis Dupree -- Grenada / Michael W. Doyle -- Conclusion : a mix of means / Arthur R. Day. ISBN 0-8133-7200-3 : LC Card 86-4020 DDC 327.1/6 19
1. Escalation (Military science). 2. Conflict management. 3. Military history, Modern - 20th century. 4. World politics - 1975-1985. I. Day, Arthur R. II. Doyle, Michael W. III. Series.
U104 .E83 1986 ***NYPL [JLE 86-4131]***

ESCALATION (MILITARY SCIENCE)
Escalation and intervention . Boulder, Colo. , 1986. x, 181 p. ; ISBN 0-8133-7200-3 : LC Card 86-4020 DDC 327.1/6 19
U104 .E83 1986 ***NYPL [JLE 86-4131]***

ESCAP. see **United Nations. Economic and Social Commission for Asia and the Pacific.**

ESCAP port development series, 0252-3396 .
(no. 7) Port development policy . Bangkok, Thailand , 1985. ix, 83 p. : LC Card 87-106926 DDC 387.1/0952 19
HE559.J3 P653 1985

Escarmelle, Jean-François. L'Etat industriel dans les politiques de sortie de crise : les expériences belge et française / Jean-François Escarmelle, avec la collaboration de Lionel Monnier. Louvain-la-Neuve : Cabay, 1986. 237 p. : ill. ; 24 cm. Bibliography: p. 228-233. ISBN 2-87077-301-3 : LC Card 86-229137
1. Industry and state - Belgium. 2. Industry and state - France. 3. Government business enterprises - Belgium. 4. Government business enterprises - France. I. Monnier, Lionel. II. Title.
HD3616.B43 E84 1986

Escenarios políticos y sociales del desarrollo latinoamericano / César A. Aguiar ... [et al.] ; compilador, Germán W. Rama. [S.l.] : Comisión Económica para América Latina y el Caribe ; [Buenos Aires] : Universidad de Buenos Aires, c1986. 231 p. ; 23 cm. Papers presented at the seminario "Los Escenarios políticos y sociales del desarrollo de América Latina" held Nov. 5-10, 1984, organized by the Universidad de Buenos Aires and the Comisión Económica Para América Latina y el Caribe. Includes bibliographies. ISBN 950-23-0274-5 LC Card 87-400175 DDC 338.98 19
1. Latin America - Economic policy - Congresses. 2. Latin America - Social policy - Congresses. 3. Latin America - Politics and government - 1948- - Congresses. I. Aguiar, César A., 1943-. II. Rama, Germán W. III. Universidad de Buenos Aires. IV. United Nations. Economic Commission for Latin America and the Caribbean.
HC125 .E82 1986

Eschbach, Thomas H., 1954- Der Ausgleich funktionaler Defizite des wirtschaftlichen Systems durch die Unternehmensberatung : eine soziologische Analyse / Thomas H. Eschbach. Frankfurt am Main ; New York : P. Lang, c1984. 152 p. ; 21 cm. (Europäische Hochschulschriften. Reihe XXII, Soziologie, 0721-3379 . Bd. 85 = vol. 85 = vol. 85) Bibliography: p. 143-147. ISBN 3-8204-5127-7 LC Card 85-191647
1. Business consultants - Germany (West). 2. Business consultants - United States. 3. Business enterprises - Germany, West - Finance. 4. Business enterprises - United States - Finance. I. Title.
HD69.C6 E76 1984

Eschenbaum, Gerhard. Krisenbevorratung von Rohstoffen unter spezieller Berücksichtigung einer Finanzierung aus Währungsreserven der Deutschen Bundesbank / Gerhard Eschenbaum. Bochum : N. Brockmeyer, 1983. xix, 464 p. : ill. ; 21 cm. (Bochumer wirtschaftswissenschaftliche Studien. Nr. 93) Bibliography: p. 414-464. ISBN 3-88339-314-2 : LC Card 83-218426
1. Raw materials - Germany, West. 2. Foreign exchange administration - Germany, West. 3. Deutsche Bundesbank. 4. Monetary policy - Germany, West. I. Title.
HF1054.G4 E83 1983

Escóbar, Filemón, 1936- La mina vista desde el guardatojo : testimonio de Filemón Escóbar. La Paz, Bolivia : CIPCA, 1986. 77 p. ; 22 cm. (Cuaderno de investigación CIPCA . no. 27) LC Card 87-118481 DDC 331.7/622/0984 19
1. Miners - Bolivia. I. Series: Cuadernos de investigación (Centro de Investigación y Promoción del Campesinado) , no. 27. II. Title.
HD8039.M61 B57 1986

Escobar Latapí, Agustín.
Cambio regional, mercado de trabajo y vida obrera en Jalisco /. Guadalajara, Jalisco, México , 1986. 363 p. ; ISBN 968-614-201-0 LC Card 86-218238
HD5731.J35 C36 1986

Con el sudor de tu frente : mercado de trabajo y clase obrera en Guadalajara / Agustín Escobar Latapí ; traducción al castellano, Pastora Rodríguez Aviñoá ; corregida por el autor.1a ed. Guadalajara, Jalisco, México :

Colegio de Jalisco, c1986. 312 p. ; 21 cm. (Colección Estudios sociales. 2) Bibliography: p. 305-312. ISBN 968-614-200-2 LC Card 86-209222
1. Labor supply - Mexico - Guadalajara. I. Series: Colección Estudios sociales (Guadalajara, Mexico) , 2. II. Title.
HD5731.G84 E83 1986

Escobari de Querejazu, Laura. Producción y comercio en el espacio sur andino en el siglo XVII : Cuzco-Potosí, 1650-1700 / Laura Escobari de Querejazu.1a ed. La Paz : Publicación Auspiciada por la Embajada de España en Bolivia, 1985. 218 p., [12] p. of plates : ill. ; 24 cm. (Colección Arzans y Vela) Originally presented as the author's thesis (licenciatura en historia--Universidad Mayor de San Andrés) under title: Tráfico comercial a través de Charcas, 1650-1700. Bibliography: p. 211-218. LC Card 86-174929
1. Andes region - Economic conditions. 2. Agriculture - Economic aspects - Peru - History - 17th century. 3. Peru - Commerce - History - 17th century. 4. Agriculture - Economic aspects - Bolivia - History - 17th century. 5. Bolivia - Commerce - History - 17th century. I. Title. II. Series.
HC167.A5 E83 1985

Escola Interamericana de Administração Pública. Seminario Interamericano Conmemorativo de los 25 Años del BID (1985 : Rio de Janeiro, Brazil) Informe del Seminario Interamericano Conmemorativo de los 25 Años del BID /. Rio de Janeiro, RJ , 1986. 65 p. : LC Card 87-403948 DDC 332.1/538 19
HG3881.5.I44 S46 1985

Escola Superior de Guerra (Brazil). Associação dos Diplomados. Souza Filho, José Ornellas de. Exposição do governador do Distrito Federal, José Ornellas de Souza Filho, na ADESG, em 02/09/83. [Brasília , 1983 or 1984] 40, [31 leaves] : LC Card 85-148272
HC188.D57 S68 1983

Escolano Utrilla, Severino.

Escóssia Neto, Lauro da. O sistema financeiro nacional : um enfoque no Estado do Rio Grande do Norte / Lauro da Escóssia Neto. [Natal] : Universidade Federal do Rio Grande do Norte, 1985. 46, [1] p. : ill., forms ; 22 cm. (Coleção mossoroense. Série C . v. 303) Bibliography: p. [47] LC Card 86-158741
1. Financial institutions - Brazil - Rio Grande do Norte. 2. Banco do Estado do Rio Grande do Norte (Brazil). I. Series: Coleção mossoroense, v. 303. II. Title.
HG185.B7 E83 1985

Escritos económicos /. Murillo Toro, Manuel, 1816-1880. Bogotá, Colombia , 1985. 120 p. ; LC Card 86-165762
HJ943 .M87 1985

Escritos, 1978-1985. Acosta M., Amylkar (Acosta Medina), 1950- [Selections. 1986.] Escritos, 1978-1986 /. Medellín, Colombia , 1986. 201 p. ; LC Card 87-404338 DDC 330.9861/0632 19
HC197 .A5562 1986

Escritos, 1978-1986 /. Acosta M., Amylkar (Acosta Medina), 1950- [Selections. 1986.] Medellín, Colombia , 1986. 201 p. ; LC Card 87-404338 DDC 330.9861/0632 19
HC197 .A5562 1986

Escuela de Administración de Negocios para Graduados. Instituto de Desarrollo Económico. Situación petrolera peruana . [Lima, Perú] [1985] iii, 102 leaves : LC Card 86-193466
HD9574.P52 S58 1985

ESCUELA TÉCNICA SAN ALONSO (SANTA CRUZ, BOLIVIA)
Alaix, Ramón. Experiencias de educación y producción de fe y alegría en Oruro y Santa Cruz . La Paz, Bolivia , 1986. 191 p. ; LC Card 86-208411 DDC 331.25/92/098413 19
HD5715.5.B52 S262 1986

Eshchenko, P. S. (Petr Stepanovich) Palkin, I͡Uriĭ Ivanovich. Ėkonomicheskie zakony i ėkonomicheskai͡a politika KPSS /. Kiev , 1985. 245 p. ; LC Card 87-104961
HC336.25 .P35 1985

Esin, Pars. Türkiye'de işveren sendikacılığı / Pars Esin. Ankara : Ankara Üniversitesi, Siyasal Bilgiler Fakültesi, 1974. xii, 288 p. ; 24 cm. (Ankara Üniversitesi Siyasal Bilgiler Fakültesi yayınları. no. 373) Bibliography: p. 277-288. LC Card 83-103059
1. Trade-unions - Turkey. I. Title.
HD6796.7 .E85 1974

Esi͡utin, A. A. (Anatoliĭ Aleksandrovich) Lebedev, I. P. (Igor′ Pavlovich) Proizvodstvennye resursy predprii͡atii͡a . Moskva , 1984. 198 p. : LC Card 85-138003
HC340.I52 L42 1984

Eskişehir İktisadi ve Ticari İlimler Akademisi yayınları .
(no. 131/153) Ataç, Beyhan. Kuramda ve Türkiye'de istikrar politikası açısından parasal ve mali işlemler /. Eskişehir [1979?] iv, 173 p. ; LC Card 82-245649
HG1206.5 .A79 1979

(no. 237/158) Karluk, S. Rıdvan. Türkiye'de ihracata yönelik dış ticaret politikası ve ihracatın yapısal analizi /. Eskişehir , 1981. xx, 454 p. ; LC Card 82-241650
HF1583.4 .K37 1981

Eskridge, William N. A Dance along the precipice . Lexington, Mass. , c1985. xxxii, 283 p. : ISBN 0-669-10899-5 (alk. paper) LC Card 85-5789 DDC 336.3/435/091724 19
HJ8899 .D36 1985 ***NYPL [JLE 86-2308]***

ESMERALDAS (ECUADOR : PROVINCE) - ECONOMIC CONDITIONS - CASE STUDIES.
Campesinado y organización en Esmeraldas /. [Quito, Ecuador?] [1986] 213 p. : LC Card 86-171561
HD1531.E2 C36 1986

Esomar.
EPHMRA/ESOMAR Seminar (1985 : Lisbon, Portugal) Pharmaceutical competitor analysis . Brooklands, Sale, Cheshire, U.K. [1985] iv, 390 p. : ISBN 92-831-1103-6 (pbk.) : LC Card 86-202276 DDC 338.4/76151 19
HD9665.5 .E64 1985

Seminar on Problem Solving in Industrial Marketing (1986 : Lucerne, Switzerland) Seminar on Problem Solving in Idustrial Marketing, Lucerne (Switzerland) 26th-28th February 1986. Amsterdam, Netherlands [1986] iv, 179 p. : ISBN 92-831-1111-7 (pbk.) : LC Card 86-213119 DDC 658.8 19
HF5415 .S3687 1986

Seminar on Retail Strategies for Profit and Growth (1986 : Brussels, Belgium) Seminar on Retail Strategies for Profit and Growth . Amsterdam, Netherlands [1986] vi, 324 p. : ISBN 92-831-1113-3 (pbk.) : LC Card 86-218316 DDC 658.8/7/0094 19
HF5429.6.E9 S45 1986

Espace et liberté, 0222-3376.
Reichman, Shalom, 1935- Les transports, servitude ou liberté? /. Paris , c1983. 197 p. ; ISBN 2-13-037934-6 : LC Card 83-230014
HE151 .R44 1983

Espace et temps du travail domestique /. Chabaud-Rychter, Danielle. Paris , 1985. 156 p. ; ISBN 2-86563-127-3 LC Card 86-165713
HD6055 .C45 1985

Espace rural et pauvreté au nord-est du Brésil /. Pessoa, Dirceu Murilo. Paris , 1981. xvii, 288 leaves : LC Card 86-208627
HC188.N6 P47 1981

Espaces disputés en Afrique noire : pratiques foncières locales / études réunies et présentées par Bernard Crousse, Emile Le Bris et Etienne Le Roy, dans le cadre du Réseau international de chercheurs sur la question foncière, avec le concours de Gerti Hesseling ... [et al.]. Paris : Karthala, c1986. 426 p., [8] p. of plates : ill. ; 24 cm. (Hommes et sociétés, 0290-6600) Includes bibliographical references, indexes, and appendices. ISBN 2-86537-146-8 LC Card 86-210958
1. Land use - Africa. 2. Land reform - Africa. 3. Land tenure - Africa. I. Crousse, Bernard. II. Le Bris, Émile. III. Le Roy, E. (Etienne). IV. Series.
HD965 .E86 1986

Espaço e sociedade . Santos, Milton. Petrópolis [Brazil] , 1979. 152 p. : LC Card 80-109991
HT151 .S238 ***NYPL [JLD 81-405]***

Espaços de socialização e exploração do menor assalariado . Spindel, Cheywa R. São Paulo, SP , 1986. 254 p. ; LC Card 87-405001 DDC 331.3/1/0981 19
HD6276.B72 S67 1986

Espagne, Jean-Pierre. Quand les Pyrénéens parcouraient le monde : autobiographie et aventures d'un colporteur, orpailleur, sous le Second Empire / Jean-Pierre Espagne. Saint-Gaudens [France] : L'Adret, c1985. 224 p., [12] leaves of plates : ill. ; 27 cm. ISBN 2-904458-07-7 : LC Card 86-139944 DDC 381/.18 B 19
1. Espagne, Jean-Pierre. 2. Peddlers and peddling - France - Biography. I. Title.
HF5459.F8 E844 1985

ESPAGNE, JEAN-PIERRE.
Espagne, Jean-Pierre. Quand les Pyrénéens parcouraient le monde . Saint-Gaudens [France] , c1985. 224 p., [12] leaves of plates : ISBN 2-904458-07-7 : LC Card 86-139944 DDC 381/.18 B 19
HF5459.F8 E844 1985

España. see **Spain.**

España en el socialismo actual /. París Eguilaz, Higinio. Madrid [1984?] 234 p. ; ISBN 84-398-2401-7 LC Card 87-120643
HC385 .P313 1984

La España impertinente /. Punset, Eduard, 1936- Madrid , c1986. 188 p. ; ISBN 84-239-2420-3 LC Card 87-136770
HF1569 .P86 1986

España, Waldo Alvarez. see **Alvarez España, Waldo.**

España y la CEE . Fernández Ordóñez, Francisco. Madrid, España , 1985. 74 p. ; ISBN 84-505-4317-0 LC Card 86-151137
HG2980.5.A6 F47 1985

España y la Comunidad Económica Europea . Herrero de Miñón, Miguel, 1940- Barcelona, España , 1986. 225 p. ; ISBN 84-320-0661-0 LC Card 87-100785
HC241.25.S6 H47 1986

España y las inversiones extranjeras /. Cordón Munilla, Publio, 1935- Zaragoza [1968?] 79 p. ; LC Card 86-144082 DDC 332.6/73/0946 19
HG5632 .C66 1968

España 1992 . Sánchez, Victorio, 1936- Esplugues de Llobregat, Barcelona , 1984. 208 p. ; ISBN 84-01-33260-5 LC Card 86-205726
HC385 .S26 1984

ESPARTERO, BALDOMERO, 1793-1879.
Rueda Hernanz, Germán. La desamortización de Mendizábal y Espartero en España /. Madrid , c1986. 200 p. ; ISBN 84-376-0592-X LC Card 86-216590
HD774 .R84 1986

Esparza Cervera, José Ramón. Impuesto sobre la renta : supuestos prácticos / planteados y resueltos por José Ramón Esparza Cervera ; concordados y anotados por Emilio Salcedo Martín. Valencia : Ediciones Siete, [1982?] 1 v. (various pagings) ; 22 cm. (Cuadernos de formación tributaria) Cover title. Errata slip inserted. ISBN 84-85672-11-9 LC Card 83-134521
1. Income tax - Spain - Problems, exercises, etc. I. Salcedo Martín, Emilio. II. Title. III. Series.
HJ4744 .E86 1982

Esparza Oteo T., Luis. La política cultural del estado mexicano y el desarrollo de la T.V. / Luis Esparza O. México, D.F. : Universidad Autónoma Metropolitana-Xochimilco, División de Ciencias Sociales y Humanidades, Departamento de Educación y Comunicación, Taller de Investigación para la Comunicación Masiva, 1984. 116 p. ; 27 cm. (Cuadernos del TICOM . no. 35) Includes bibliographical references. LC Card 87-404017 DDC 384.55/4/0972 19
1. Television broadcasting - Mexico. 2. Mexico - Cultural policy. 3. Television - Law and legislation - Mexico. I. Title. II. Series.
HE8700.9.M6 E84 1984

Espasa universitaria. Historia .

Espenshade, Thomas J.
Muller, Thomas, 1933- The fourth wave . Washington , c1985. xvii, 217 p. ; ISBN 0-87766-349-1 LC Card 85-22646 DDC 331.6/2/720794 19
HD8081.M6 M85 1985
NYPL [JLE 86-3014]

Technological prospects and population trends /. Boulder, Colo. , 1987. xxiii, 211 p. ; ISBN 0-8133-7470-7 : LC Card 87-50897 DDC 304.6 19
HB871 .T3 1987

Esperança e mundança. [Brasília] : PMDB/Fundação Pedroso Horta, 1981. 95 p. ;

23 cm. (Col. Alberto Pasqualini . vol. 21) "Proposta à nação e aos companheiros do PMDB." LC Card 86-202933
1. Brazil - Economic policy. 2. Brazil - Social policy. 3. Partido do Movimento Democrático Brasileiro. I. Fundação Pedroso Horta. II. Series: Coleção Alberto Pasqualini , v. 21.
HC187 .E83 1981

Espinosa Reyes, Róger. Las Leyes de estabilidad laboral y sus efectos económicos /. Lima, Perú [1986?] 67 p. : LC Card 87-403254 DDC 331.11/0985 19
HD8344 .L49 1986

Espinoza C., Jorge. Reforma agraria en Bolivia / Jorge Espinoza C. Cochabamba, Bolivia : UMSS, Editorial Universitaria, 1984. 78 p. ; 20 cm. Includes texts by Ricardo Anaya. Bibliography: p. 44-45. LC Card 86-166584
1. Land reform - Bolivia - History. I. Anaya, Ricardo. II. Title.
HD1333.B5 E87 1984

Espinoza Claudio, César.
Alcabalas y protesta popular : Cerro de Pasco, 1780 / César Espinoza Claudio, José Boza Monteverde ; prólogo de Wilfredo Kapsoli. Lima, Perú : Universidad Nacional Mayor de San Marcos, Programa Académico de Ciencias Sociales, 1981. iii, 111 p., [1] leaf of plates : ill. ; 30 cm. Bibliography: p. 61-62. LC Card 82-146025
1. Sales tax - Peru - Cerro de Pasco - History - 18th century. 2. Social conflict - Peru - Cerro de Pasco - History - 18th century. I. Boza Monteverde, José. II. Title.
HJ5715.P4 E86 1981

Terratenientes y campesinos en Piura, ss. XVI-XIX : (comunidades de Colán y Amotape) / César Espinoza Claudio ; prólogo de Manuel Burga. Lima, Perú : Universidad Nacional Mayor de San Marcos, Programa Académico de Ciencias Sociales, 1981. xxviii, 123 p., [6] leaves of plates : ill. ; 30 cm. Includes bibliographical references. LC Card 82-146131
1. Land tenure - Peru - Piura (Dept.) - History. 2. Agriculture - Economic aspects - Peru - Piura (Dept.) - History. 3. Tallán Indians - Agriculture - History. 4. Tallán Indians - Land tenure - History. 5. Indians of South America - Peru - Piura (Dept.) - Agriculture. 6. Indians of South America - Peru - Piura (Dept.) - Land tenure. I. Title.
HD559.P5 E87 1981

Espinoza Jaramillo, Frida. El estado de la investigación nacional acerca de la frontera norte de México / Frida Espinoza y Jesús Tamayo. [México] : Centro de Investigación y Docencia Económicas, 1985. 47 leaves ; 28 cm. (Documentos de trabajo. Serie Programa de estudios regionales) Includes bibliographical references. LC Card 87-402765 DDC 330.972/10834 19
1. Mexican-American Border Region - Economic conditions - Research. 2. Mexico - Economic conditions - 1970- - Research. I. Tamayo, Jesús. II. Series: Documento de trabajo (Centro de Investigación y Docencia Económicas). III. Title.
HC137.M46 E76 1985

Espinoza, Néstor. El proceso de electrificación en los pueblos jóvenes : guía para las organizaciones vecinales / Néstor Espinoza. Lima, Perú : CIDAP, [1983] 77 p. : ill. ; 22 cm. (Serie Manuales. no 2) "Mayo 1983"--T.p. verso. LC Card 84-149923 DDC 363.6/2/098525 19
1. Electric utilities - Peru - Lima Metropolitan Area. 2. Squatter settlements - Peru - Lima metropolitan area. I. Title.
HD9685.P47 L54 1983 *NYPL [JLD 86-3894]*

ESPÍRITO SANTO (BRAZIL : STATE) - INDUSTRIES.
Setor de informações técnicas /. [Vitória] , 1983. 54 p. ; LC Card 85-202308
HC188.E7 S47 1983

Espírito Santo (Brazil : State). Secreria de Estado da Indústria e do Comércio. Setor de informações técnicas /. [Vitória] , 1983. 54 p. ; LC Card 85-202308
HC188.E7 S47 1983

ESPÍRITO SANTO, BRAZIL (STATE) - ECONOMIC CONDITIONS.
Setor de informações técnicas /. [Vitória] , 1983. 54 p. ; LC Card 85-202308
HC188.E7 S47 1983

Espíritu del señor Melón en su ensayo político sobre el comercio. Normante y Carcavilla, Lorenzo. Discurso sobre la utilidad de los conocimientos económico-políticos y la necesidad de su estudio metódico ; Proposiciones de economía civil y comercio ; Espíritu del señor Melón en su ensayo político sobre el comercio /. [Aragón] [1984?] 1 v. (various pagings) ; ISBN 84-505-0473-2 LC Card 87-104302
HC385 .N57 1984

Esposito, Gennaro, 1956- Decentramento produttivo, lavoro a domicilio e sindacato / Gennaro Esposito. Milano : Italia letteraria, [1983] 109 p. ; 21 cm. Includes bibliographical references. LC Card 85-150186
1. Home labor - Italy. 2. Cottage industries - Italy. 3. Industrial productivity - Italy. 4. Division of labor. 5. Trade-unions - Italy. I. Title.
HD2336.I8 E86 1983

Espy, Siri N. Handbook of strategic planning for nonprofit organizations / Siri N. Espy. New York : Praeger, 1986. ix, 131 p. ; 25 cm. Includes index. Bibliography: p. [127]-128 ISBN 0-275-92342-8 (alk. paper) LC Card 86-21192 DDC 658.1/148 19
1. Corporations, Nonprofit - Planning. 2. Corporations, Nonprofit - Management. 3. Strategic planning. I. Title.
HD62.6 .E86 1986 *NYPL [JLE 87-874]*

Esquema de ordenamiento territorial de la faja petrolífera del Orinoco : síntesis general / Ministerio del Ambiente y de los Recursos Naturales Renovables, Dirección General de Planificación y Ordenación del Ambiente. Caracas : El Ministero, 1982. 46 p. : ill. (some col.) ; 21 x 30 cm. (Serie de informes técnicos . DGSPOA/IT/109) LC Card 86-162734
1. Orinoco River Region (Venezuela) - Economic conditions. 2. Orinoco River Region (Venezuela) - Social conditions. 3. Petroleum industry and trade - Venezuela - Orinoco River Region. 4. Orinoco River Region (Venezuela) - Administrative and political divisions. I. Venezuela. Dirección General de Planificación y Ordenación del Ambiente. II. Series.
HC238.O75 E87 1982

Esquemas para la interpretación de la realidad /. Iriarte, Gregorio. La Paz, Bolivia , 1985. 10 v. : LC Card 87-112879
HC182 .I727 1985

Esquivel, Francisco. El desarrollo del capital en la industria de Costa Rica, 1950-1970 / Francisco Esquivel. 1a ed. Heredia, Costa Rica : Editorial de la Universidad Nacional, 1985. 197 p. : ill. ; 22 cm. (Colección Barva. Serie Pensamiento. Subserie Ensayo) Bibliography: p. 151-156. ISBN 997-7650-16-0 LC Card 86-210026
1. Costa Rica - Industries - History. 2. Capitalism - Costa Rica - History. 3. Saving and investment - Costa Rica - History. I. Title. II. Series.
HC143 .E83 1985

E.S.R.C. Economic Theory Study Group.
Oligopoly, competition, and welfare /. Oxford, OX, UK , New York, NY, USA , 1985. 191 p. : ISBN 0-631-14479-X (pbk.) LC Card 85-11200 DDC 338.8/2 19
HD2757.3 .O44 1985 *NYPL [JLE 86-1961]*

ESRC Environment and Planning Committee.
Global restructuring local response . London , Merstham, Redhill, Surrey , c1986. 308 p. : ISBN 0-86226-174-0 (pbk.) LC Card 86-197207 DDC 331.12/0941 19
HD6331.2.G7 G57 1986

E.S.R.C. Industrial Economics Study Group.
Oligopoly, competition, and welfare /. Oxford, OX, UK , New York, NY, USA , 1985. 191 p. : ISBN 0-631-14479-X (pbk.) LC Card 85-11200 DDC 338.8/2 19
HD2757.3 .O44 1985 *NYPL [JLE 86-1961]*

Essai sur l'économie ricardienne /. Schmidt, Christian, 1950- Paris , 1984. 168 p. ; ISBN 2-7178-0693-8 : LC Card 84-218068
HB103.R5 S25 1984

Essai sur les arts at les manufactures de l'empire d'Autriche /. Serres, Marcel de, 1783-1862. Paris , 1814-1815. 3 v. : LC Card 85-666370
HC263 .S47x 1814

Essai sur l'inégalité /. Harouel, Jean Louis. Paris , c1984. 287, [1] p. ; ISBN 2-13-038354-8 : LC Card 84-150958
HC280.I5 H35 1984

ESSAOUIRA (MOROCCO) - ECONOMIC CONDITIONS.
Schroeter, Daniel J. Merchants of Essaouira . Cambridge , New York , 1988. p. cm. ISBN 0-521-32455-6 LC Card 87-15163 DDC 330.964/6 19
HC810.Z7 E857 1988

An essay on the importance of being nonlinear /. West, Bruce J. Berlin , New York , c1985. viii, 204 p. : ISBN 0-387-16038-8 (U. S.)
NYPL [JSK 75-186 v.62]

An essay on the principle of population . Malthus, T. R. (Thomas Robert, 1766-1834. London , 1986. 2 v. (18, xv, 711 p.) : ISBN 1-85196-102-X (v. 1) LC Card 87-672118
HB861 .A2x 1986 vol. 2-3

An essay on the principle of population . Malthus, T. R. (Thomas Robert, 1766-1834. London , 1986. 139 p. : ISBN 1-85196-101-1 LC Card 87-672117
HB861 .A2x 1986 vol. 1

An essay on the principle of population, or, a view of its past and present effects on human happiness . Malthus, T. R. (Thomas Robert, 1766-1834. Cambridge [Cambridgeshire] , New York , 1988. p. cm. ISBN 0-521-24775-6 LC Card 87-9372 DDC 304.6 19
HB861 .E7 1988

Essays from the Ghana-Valco renegotiations, 1982-85 / edited by Fui S. Tsikata. [Accra, Ghana : Volta River Authority], 1986 (Accra : Printed by the Ghana Pub. Corp.) viii, 163 p. ; 25 cm. "This collection of essays is the product of informal discussions began [sic] among members of the Ghana negotiating team in July 1984 upon the conclusion of broad agreement with the Volta Aluminium Company Limited (Valco)"--P. [v]. Includes bibliographies and index. ISBN 996-490-120-8 (pbk.) LC Card 87-127499 DDC 338.8/87 19
1. Volta Aluminium Company. 2. Aluminum industry and trade - Ghana. 3. Volta River Authority. 4. Electric utilities - Ghana. 5. Negotiation in business - Ghana. 6. Transfer pricing - Developing countries. I. Tsikata, Fui S. II. Volta River Authority. III. Title: Ghana-Valco renegotiations, 1982-85.
HD9539.A63 G44 1986

Essays in development administration /. Dubhashi, P. R. New Delhi, India , 1987. x, 391 p. ; LC Card 87-901132 DDC 338.954 19
HC435.2 .D833 1987

Essays in development economics /. Bhagwati, Jagdish N., 1934- Oxford [Oxfordshire] , 1985. 2 v. ; ISBN 0-631-14178-2 (v. 1)
NYPL [JLL 86-16]

Essays in economic policy and economic growth /. Patel, I. G. (Indraprasad Gordhanbhai), 1924- Basingstoke, Hampshire , 1986. xii, 261 p. ; ISBN 0-333-39213-2
NYPL [JLD 86-4061]

Essays in economics . Tobin, James, 1918- Cambridge, Mass. , 1987. xvi, 526 p. : ISBN 0-262-20062-7 LC Card 86-21157 DDC 339 19
HB34 .T622 1987

Essays in economics. Tobin, James, 1918- Cambridge, Mass. , 1987. vii, 492 p. : ISBN 0-262-20064-3 LC Card 87-3913 DDC 330/.028 19
HB801 .T6 1987

Essays in economics and management in honour of Lars Wahlbeck. Vetenskap och företagsledning . Helsingfors , 1982. 461 p. : ISBN 951-555-158-7 LC Card 82-239854
HB71 .V45 1982

Essays in honor of Kenneth J. Arrow .
(v. 1) Social choice and public decision making /. Cambridge [Cambridgeshire] , New York , 1986. xix, 215 p. : ISBN 0-521-30454-7 LC Card 86-8580 DDC 339 19
HB846.8 .S59 1986 *NYPL [JLE 86-4189]*

Essays in international economics, 0826-4384. Daly, D. J. (Donald James), 1922- Canadian manufactured exports . Montreal, Quebec , c1986. xxviii, 180 p. ; ISBN 0-88645-025-X (pbk.) : LC Card 87-142389 DDC 382/.4567/0971 19
HF3226.5 .D26 1986

Essays in international finance .
(no. 166) Spraos, John. IMF conditionality . Princeton, N.J. , c1986. 34 p. ; ISBN

0-88165-073-0 (pbk.) : LC Card 86-33805 DDC 332/.042 s 332.1/52 19
HG136 .P7 no. 166 HG3881.5.I58

Essays in international finance, 0071-142X . (no. 166 (Dec. 1986)) Spraos, John. IMF conditionality . Princeton, N.J. , c1986. 34 p. ; ISBN 0-88165-073-0 (pbk.) : LC Card 86-33805 DDC 332/.042 s 332.1/52 19
HG136 .P7 no. 166 HG3881.5.I58

(no. 167) Masera, R. S. An increasing role for the ECU . Princeton, N.J. , 1987. vi, 50 p. ; ISBN 0-88165-074-9 (pbk.) : LC Card 87-3747 DDC 332/.042 s 332.4/56094 19
HG136 .P7 no. 167 HG930.5

Essays in political economics . Lowe, Adolph, 1893- New York , 1987. 257 p. ; ISBN 0-8147-6168-2 LC Card 87-11219 DDC 338.9 19
HD82 .L693 1987

Essays in political economy /. Popov, ÎU. N. (ÎUriĭ Nikolaevich), 1931- Moscow , c1984- v. ; LC Card 84-202086 DDC 335.43 19
HB53 .P64 1984 ***NYPL [JLK 86-18]***

Essays in social value theory . Tool, Marc R. Armonk, N.Y. , c1986. xviii, 203 p. ; ISBN 0-87332-382-3 : LC Card 86-10163 DDC 306 19
HB99.5 .T66 1986 ***NYPL [JLE 86-3931]***

Essays on banking and development /. Taheruddin, M. Dhaka , 1986. 145 p. ; LC Card 87-900643 DDC 332.1/09549/2 19
HG3290.6.A6 T35 1986

Essays on ethics in business and the professions /. Behrman, Jack N. Englewood Cliffs, N.J. , c1988. x, 358 p. ; ISBN 0-13-283623-8 (pbk.) LC Card 87-13697 DDC 174/.4 19
HF5387 .B44 1988

Essays on inflation /. Humphrey, Thomas M. Richmond, Va. , 1986. vii, 323 p. : LC Card 86-205422 DDC 332.4/1 19
HG229 .H884 1986

Essays on political economy /. Malthus, T. R. (Thomas Robert, 1766-1834. London , 1986. 327 p. : ISBN 1-85196-107-0 LC Card 87-672114
HB861 .A2x 1986 vol. 7

Essays on population /. Malthus, T. R. (Thomas Robert, 1766-1834. London , 1986. 246 p. : ISBN 1-85196-104-6 LC Card 87-672116
HB861 .A2x 1986 vol. 4

Essays on the performance of leading indicators based on qualitative data / contributions by W.H. Strigel ... [et al.]. Munich : Centre for International Research on Economic Tendency Surveys, 1985. 148 p. : ill. ; 21 cm. (CIRET-Studien, 0170-5679 . 36) Includes bibliographies. ISBN 3-88512-009-7 (pbk.) : LC Card 86-181861 DDC 330/.0724 19
1. Economic forecasting. 2. Economic indicators. 3. Business cycles. I. Strigel, Werner H. II. Series.
HB3730 .E78 1985

Essays on the political economy of rural Africa /. Bates, Robert H. Berkeley , 1987, c1983. p. cm. ISBN 0-520-06014-8 (pbk. : alk. paper) LC Card 86-25120 DDC 330.96/0328/091734 19
HD2117 .B37 1987

Essen. Universität. see Universität Essen.

The essence of corporate strategy /. Pümpin, Cuno Beat. Aldershot, Hants, England , Brookfield, Vt., U. S.A. , c1987. xi, 183 p. : ISBN 0-566-02565-5 : LC Card 87-14907 DDC 658.4/012 19
HD30.28 .P85 1987

The essence of Friedman /. Friedman, Milton, 1912- Stanford, Calif. , c1987. xxxiv, 566 p., [1] p. of plates : ISBN 0-8179-8661-8 LC Card 87-4003 DDC 330.1 19
HB171 .F774 1987

The essence of strategic decision making /. Schwenk, Charles R. Lexington, Mass. , c1988. xii, 138 p. : ISBN 0-669-13023-0 (alk. paper) LC Card 86-80040 DDC 658.4/03 19
HD30.23 .S39 1988

ESSENCES AND ESSENTIAL OILS INDUSTRY - EUROPE.
Flavors and fragrances market in Europe. New York, N.Y. , c1983. 5, 17, 8, 279 p. ; LC Card 87-141830 DDC 380.1/456645 19
HD9212.E852 F53 1983

Essener geographische Arbeiten . (Bd. 9) Wehling, Hans-Werner, 1949- Wohnstandorte und Wohnumfeldprobleme in der Kernzone des Ruhrgebietes /. Paderborn , 1984. ix, 285 p. : ISBN 3-506-72309-X LC Card 85-121205
HD7339.R79 W44 1984

The essential Adam Smith /. Smith, Adam, 1723-1790. [Selections. 1986.] Oxford [Oxfordshire] , New York , 1986. p. cm. ISBN 0-19-877270-X : LC Card 86-23856 DDC 330.15/3 19
HB161 .S6522 1986b

Essential business statistics . Bond, Kenneth M. Boston , c1988. xiii, 332 p. : ISBN 0-534-91530-2 LC Card 87-25652 DDC 519.5/028/55369 19
HF1017 .B63 1988

The essential guide to effective corporate board committees /. Braiotta, Louis, 1943- Englewood Cliffs, N.J. , c1987. xiii, 178 p. ; ISBN 0-13-286139-9 LC Card 87-2265 DDC 658.4/22 19
HD2745 .B63 1987

Essentials of accounting /. Anthony, Robert Newton, 1916- Reading, Mass. , 1988. p. cm. ISBN 0-201-00017-2 : LC Card 87-21944 DDC 657/.07/7 19
HF5635 .A6879 1988

Essentials of accounting for governmental and not-for-profit organizations /. Hay, Leon Edwards, 1923- Homewood, Ill. , 1987. x, 310 p. ; ISBN 0-256-03454-0 (pbk.) LC Card 86-82587 DDC 657/.98 19
HJ9801 .H39 1987

Essentials of business statistics /. Daniel, Wayne W., 1929- Boston , c1988. xvi, 426, 99, 4 p. : ISBN 0-395-35650-4 LC Card 87-80109 DDC 519.5/024658 19
HF1017 .D28 1988

Essentials of corporate finance /. Ben-Horim, Moshe. Boston , c1987. xviii, 712 p. : ISBN 0-205-08847-3 : LC Card 86-25882 DDC 658.1/5 19
HG4026 .B388 1987

Essentials of economics and free enterprise /. Hodgetts, Richard M. Menlo Park, Calif. , c1987. 437 p. : ISBN 0-201-20719-2 LC Card 86-207031 DDC 330 19
HB171.5 .H677 1987

Essentials of management series (New York, N. Y.)
What every manager needs to know about manufacturing /. New York, NY [1987], c1983. 181 p. : ISBN 0-8144-7686-4 (pbk.) LC Card 87-47714 DDC 658 19
HD9720.5 .W38 1987

Essentials of managerial finance /. Pringle, John J. Glenview, Ill. , c1987. xxxi, 811, [98] p. : ISBN 0-673-18331-9 : LC Card 86-31333 DDC 658.1/5 19
HG4026 .P73 1987

Essentials of media planning . Barban, Arnold M. Lincolnwood, Ill., U. S.A. , c1987. xii, 160 p. : ISBN 0-8442-3018-9 (pbk.) : LC Card 86-51055 DDC 659.1/11 19
HF5826.5 .B37 1987

Essentials of organizational behavior /. Robbins, Stephen P., 1943- Englewood Cliffs, N.J. , c1988. p. cm. ISBN 0-13-286485-1 LC Card 87-19876 DDC 658.3 19
HD58.7 .R6 1988

Essentials of real estate investment /. Sirota, David. Chicago , 1988. xiii, 254 p. ; ISBN 0-88462-667-9 (p. 4 of cover) LC Card 87-23222 DDC 332.63/24 19
HD1382.5 .S52 1988

Essentials of risk control / edited by George L. Head. 1st ed. Malvern, Pa. : Insurance Institute of America, 1986. 2 v. : ill. ; 23 cm. Includes bibliographies and indexes. ISBN 0-89462-033-9 (pbk.) LC Card 86-82833 DDC 368 19
1. Risk management. I. Head, George L., 1941-. II. Insurance Institute of America.
HD61 .E84 1986

Esser, Carsten, 1960- Das Fremdkapital im Unternehmen als Insolvenzursache und die Möglichkeiten rechtlicher Steuerung der Finanzierungsgrundlagen / Carsten Esser. Frankfurt am Main ; New York : P. Lang, c1986. xvi, 131 p. (1 folded) ; 21 cm. (Wirtschaftsrecht und Wirtschaftsverfassung, 0721-4316 . Bd. 11 = vol. 11 = vol. 11) "Als wissenschaftliche Abschlussarbeit aus dem Projekt 'Unternehmenssanierung' im Studiengang Juristenausbildung der Universität Bremen hervorgegangen"--7th prelim. page. Bibliography: p. iv-xiii. ISBN 3-8204-9398-0 LC Card 86-229108
1. Investments, Foreign - Germany, West. 2. Bankruptcy - Germany, West. 3. Corporations - Taxation - Germany, West. 4. Corporations - Taxation - Law and legislation - Germany (West). I. Series: Wirtschaftsrecht und Wirtschaftsverfassung , Bd. 11. II. Title.
HG5501 .E85 1986

Esser, Klaus. Zentralamerika, USA, EG und Bundesrepublik Deutschland / Klaus Esser. Berlin : Deutsches Institut für Entwicklungspolitik, 1987. xi, 137 p. : 1 map ; 24 cm. (Schriften des Deutschen Instituts für Entwicklungspolitik, DIE . Bd. 86) Bibliography: p. 129-137. ISBN 3-88985-043-X LC Card 87-401334 DDC 337.1/728 19
1. Central America - Economic integration. 2. Central America - Foreign relations - 1979-. 3. Central America - Politics and government - 1979-. 4. Geopolitics - Central America. I. Title. II. Series.
HC141 .E86 1987

La Esso en Cuba . Dumpierre, Erasmo. La Habana , 1984. xiii, 148 p., [7] p. of plates : LC Card 86-177066
HD9574.C84 E774 1984

Esso Petroleum Canada (Firm) Mémoire présenté à la Commission élue permanente de l'énergie et des ressources de l'Assemblée nationale du Québec / par Pétroles ESSO Canada, une division de la Compagnie pétrolière impériale Ltée. Québec : Pétroles Esso Canada, [1983] 44 leaves : ill. ; 29 cm. Cover title. "Mars 1983." LC Card 85-143347 DDC 338.2/7282/09714 19
1. Petroleum industry and trade - Quebec (Province). 2. Petroleum industry and trade - Canada, Eastern. I. Québec (Province). Assemblée nationale. Commission permanente de l'énergie et des ressources. II. Title.
HD9574.C23 Q43 1983

ESSO STANDARD OIL COMPANY (CUBA) - HISTORY.
Dumpierre, Erasmo. La Esso en Cuba . La Habana , 1984. xiii, 148 p., [7] p. of plates : LC Card 86-177066
HD9574.C84 E774 1984

Estaba, Rosa M. Geografía de los paisajes urbanos e industriales de Venezuela / Rosa M. Estaba, Ivonne Alvarado. Caracas : Editorial Ariel-Seix Barral Venezolana, c1985. 291 p., [4] folded leaves : ill. ; 21 cm. (Colección Geografía de Venezuela nueva . 5) Bibliography: p. [271]-281. ISBN 980-271-006-7 LC Card 86-148810 DDC 307.7/6/0987 19
1. Cities and towns - Venezuela - History. 2. Urbanization - Venezuela - History. 3. Petroleum industry and trade - Venezuela - History. 4. Coffee trade - Venezuela - History. 5. Venezuela - Economic conditions. I. Alvarado, Ivonne. II. Title.
HC237 .E766 1985 ***NYPL [JLD 86-2340]***

Established companies diversifying into young industries . Smith, Clayton G. West Lafayette, Ind. [1986] 27, 15 p. ; LC Card 86-621740 DDC 658/.001/9 s 338.8/3 19
HD6483 .P8 no. 893 HD2755.8

Establishment of oil refinery in Nigeria. Lagos : Federal Government Printer, 1960. 6 p. ; 25 cm. (Sessional paper / Federation of Nigeria . no. 5 of 1960) LC Card 87-401860
1. Petroleum industry and trade - Government policy - Nigeria. 2. Petroleum refineries - Government policy - Nigeria. I. Series: Sessional paper (Nigeria) , 1960, no. 5.
HD9577.N52 E84 1960

Estadística fiscal, años 1944-45 a 1953-54 / República de Venezuela, Ministerio de Hacienda, Dirección General del Presupuesto. Caracas : Editorial Sucre, 1955. 125 p. : ill. ; 29 cm. Chiefly tables. LC Card 85-128776
1. Finance, Public - Venezuela - Statistics. 2. Finance, Public - Venezuela - Accounting - Statistics. I. Venezuela. Direccion General del Presupuesto.
HJ990 .E86 1955

Estadística fiscal de Bogotá, D.E., 1970-1976. [Bogotá, Colombia] : Contraloría del Distrito Especial de Bogotá, División de Planeamiento y Análisis Financiero, [1977] 100 p. : col. ill. ; 24

x 28 cm. Cover title: Estadísticas fiscales, 1976. LC Card 87-128439 DDC 336.84/14 19
1. Finance, Public - Colombia - Bogotá - Statistics. I. Bogotá (Colombia). División de Planeamiento y Análisis Financiero. II. Title: Estadísticas fiscales, 1976.
HJ9394.B6 E847 1977

Estadística fiscal de Bogotá, D.E., 1971-1977. [Bogotá, Colombia] : Contraloría del Distrito Especial de Bogotá, División de Planeamiento y Análisis Financiero, [1979] 139 p. : col. ill. ; 23 x 28 cm. Cover title: Estadísticas fiscales de la Contraloría del Distrito Especial de Bogotá, 1977. Chiefly tables. LC Card 87-125994 DDC 336.861/4 19
1. Finance, Public - Colombia - Bogotá - Statistics - History - 20th century. I. Bogotá (Colombia). División de Planeamiento y Análisis Financiero. II. Title: Estadísticas fiscales de la Contraloría del Distrito Especial de Bogotá, 1977.
HJ9394.B6 E85 1979

Estadística fiscal del estado : año de 1977 / elaborada por Aníbal Martínez Zuleta [para la] Contraloría General de la República. [Bogotá] : Contraloría General de la República de Colombia, Dirección de Análisis Financiero y Estadística, 1978. 2 v. : ill. (some col.) ; 25 cm. Cover title.
1. Budget - Colombia. 2. Finance, Public - Colombia - Statistics. I. Martínez Zuleta, Aníbal.
NYPL [JLE 80-831]

Estadísticas agropecuarias. Montevideo, República Oriental del Uruguay : Comcorde, Secretaría Técnica, 1979. [79] p. ; 27 cm. Chiefly tables. "24 mayo 1979." "E.ST-1/979." LC Card 82-209370
1. Produce trade - Uruguay - Statistics. 2. Agriculture - Economic aspects - Uruguay - Statistics. I. Comcorde. Secretaría Técnica.
HD9014.U82 E78 1979

Estadísticas bancarias . Ramírez Bautista, Elia. México, D.F. , 1985. 10, ca. 200 p. ; ISBN 968-603-813-2 LC Card 87-401719 DDC 332.1/0972/021 19
HG2714 .R36 1985

Las estadísticas del sector construcción en Costa Rica . Mulquin, Marie Eve. [San José] , 1981. 39 p. ; LC Card 81-216965
HD9715.C82 M85 1981

Estadísticas e indicadores de los bancos y corporaciones financieras, 1970-1985 : evolución y desempeño del sistema bancario, evolución y desempeño de las corporaciones financieras privadas, estadísticas monetarias y financieras, análisis de los recursos de crédito / Asociación Bancaria de Colombia. [Bogotá, Colombia] : La Asociación, [1986] 64 p. : col. ill. ; 24 x 32 cm. Chiefly tables. LC Card 86-167798
1. Banks and banking - Colombia - Statistics. 2. Financial institutions - Colombia - Statistics. I. Asociación Bancaria de Colombia.
HG2904 .E77 1986

Estadísticas financieras del sector público ecuatoriano, años 1975-1981 / Dirección Coordinación y Política Fiscal, División Programación y Política Fiscal, Sección Programación del Sector Público. [Quito] : Secretaría General de Planificación del CONADE, [1983] 316 p. ; 21 x 30 cm. Chiefly tables. "500 ejemplares"--Colophon. LC Card 86-179747
1. Finance, Public - Ecuador - Statistics. I. Consejo Nacional de Desarrollo (Ecuador). Sección Programación del Sector Público.
HJ955 .E792 1983

Estadísticas fiscales de la Contraloría del Distrito Especial de Bogotá, 1977. Estadística fiscal de Bogotá, D.E., 1971-1977. [Bogotá, Colombia] [1979] 139 p. : LC Card 87-125994 DDC 336.861/4 19
HJ9394.B6 E85 1979

Estadísticas fiscales, 1976. Estadística fiscal de Bogotá, D.E., 1970-1976. [Bogotá, Colombia] [1977] 100 p. : LC Card 87-128439 DDC 336.84/14 19
HJ9394.B6 E847 1977

Estadísticas mineras de México en el siglo XIX /. Flores Clair, Eduardo. México, D.F. , 1985. 181 p. ; LC Card 87-401718 DDC 338.2/0972 19
HD9506.M62 F57 1985

Estadísticas sociales : información comparativa / investigadores, Lucía Pinedo Brigé, Norma González de Piñango, Rosalind Greaves de Pulido ; asistentes, Jesús Ramírez Chacín, Mery Broitman. Caracas, Venezuela : Despacho de la Ministro de Estado para la Participación de la Mujer en el Desarrollo, 1983. 2 v. ; 28 cm. Vol. 1 lacks volume number. Vol. 2 has author statement: coordinación, Lucía Pinedo Brigé; procesamiento y revisión, Rafael Barreto, Jesús Ramírez Chacín. Chiefly tables. Bibliography: v. 1, p. [8] LC Card 84-183391 DDC 312/.0987 19
1. Labor supply - Venezuela - Statistics. 2. Public health - Venezuela - Statistics. 3. Trade-unions - Venezuela - Statistics. 4. Education - Venezuela - Statistics. 5. Venezuela - Population - Statistics. I. Pinedo Brigé, Lucía. II. González de Piñango, Norma. III. Greaves de Pulido, Rosalind. IV. Venezuela. Despacho de la Ministro de Estado para la Participación de la Mujer en el Desarrollo.
HA1095 .E88 1983 ***NYPL [JLM 85-550]***

Estadísticas, 1950-1985. San José, Costa Rica : Banco Central de Costa Rica, División Económica, 1986. 221 p. ; 28 cm. LC Card 87-404209 DDC 332/.097286/021 19
1. Finance - Costa Rica - Statistics. 2. Costa Rica - Economic conditions - 1948- - Statistics. I. Banco Central de Costa Rica. División Económica.
HG185.C7 E84 1986

Estado capitalista e burocracia no Brasil pós-64 /. Martins, Luciano, 1934- Rio de Janeiro, RJ , 1985. 265 p. ; LC Card 85-232969 DDC 338.981 19
HC187 .M2947 1985 ***NYPL [JLD 86-1691]***

O Estado de Goiás : estudo. Goiânia-GO : Estado de Goiás, Secretaria da Indústria e Comércio, Divisão Informações Técnicas e Estatísticas, 1983. 406 p. : ill. ; 34 cm. LC Card 86-224747
1. Goiás, Brazil (State) - Economic conditions. 2. Goiás, Brazil (State) - Social conditions. 3. Public health - Brazil - Goiás (State). 4. Education - Brazil - Goiás (State). 5. Goiás (Brazil : State) - Industries. 6. Goiás, Brazil (State) - Commerce. I. Goiás (Brazil : State). Secretaria da Indústria e Comércio. Divisão de Informações Técnicas e Estatísticas.
HC188.G6 E85 1983

El estado de la investigación nacional acerca de la frontera norte de México /. Espinoza Jaramillo, Frida. [México] , 1985. 47 leaves ; LC Card 87-402765 DDC 330.972/10834 19
HC137.M46 E76 1985

Estado e controle sindical no Brasil . Costa, Sérgio Amad, 1958- São Paulo , 1986. xiv, 192 p. : ISBN 85-85008-48-2 : LC Card 87-154269 DDC 331.88/0981 19
HD6612 .C67 1986

Estado e economia no Brasil . Mendonça, Sonia Regina de. Rio de Janeiro-RJ, Brasil , 1986. 106 p. ; LC Card 86-197575
HC187 .M469 1986

Estado, economia e liberdade /. Poletti, Ronaldo. Brasília, DF [1986] 11 p. ; LC Card 87-403230 DDC 330 19
HB179.P75 P65 1986

Estado liberal y desarrollo capitalista en Honduras /. Molina Chocano, Guillermo. Tegucigalpa, Honduras , 1985. 136 p. : LC Card 86-233622
HG5202 .M65 1985

El estado mexicano entre la inversión extranjera directa y los grupos privados de empresarios /. Medina Cervantes, José Ramón. México, D.F. , 1984. 268 p. : ISBN 968-434-358-2 LC Card 86-222537
HG5162 .M43 1984

Estado tributario y librecambio en Potosí (siglo XIX) . Platt, Tristan. [La Paz?] , c1986. 73 p. ; LC Card 87-401159 DDC 330.984/1404 19
HC183.P67 P55 1986

Estado y agro en el Ecuador, 1960-1980 /. Cosse, Gustavo. Quito , 1984. 112 p. : LC Card 85-119842 DDC 338.1/8866 19
HD1888 .C67 1984 ***NYPL [JLD 86-2738]***

Estado y crisis del desarrollo nacional . Ramírez L., Fernando (Ramírez López) México, D.F. , 1983. 242 p. ; LC Card 86-220975
HC135 .R234 1983

Estado y ejidos en México . Rello, Fernando. Ginebra , 1986. xxvi, 122 p. : LC Card 86-210274
HG2051.M62 L37 1986

Estado y gasto público en Venezuela, 1936-1980 /. Kornblith, Miriam. Caracas , 1985. 287, [10] p. : LC Card 86-172043
HJ2093 .K67 1985

Estados Unidos de Colombia. see Colombia.

Estados Unidos y América Latina . Hernández, Rafael. La Habana , 1982. 209 p. : LC Card 87-403785 DDC 333.8/232/0973 19
HD9574.L3 H47 1982

ESTANCIA POZO DE CORREA - HISTORY.
Tagle Frías de Cuenca, Matilde. Historia de la Estancia "Pozo de Correa" /. [Córdoba, Argentina] , 1984. 88 p. : LC Card 86-157022
HD1471.A72 C677 1984

Estat autonòmic i finances públiques . Bricall, Josep Maria, 1936- [Barcelona] , 1984. 358 p. : ISBN 84-500-9868-8 LC Card 85-106586
HJ1000 .B75 1984 ***NYPL [JLE 86-3989]***

Estat d'execució dels programes d'actuació i pressupostos d'inversió de l'Ajuntament de Barcelona durant 1982. Barcelona (Spain). Ayuntamiento. Departament d'Estudis i Programació. [Barcelona] [1983] 126 leaves ; LC Card 84-249883
HC388.B3 B36 1983

ESTATE PLANNING.
Ivers, James F. Financial planning applications /. Bryn Mawr, Pa. , c1987. 2 v. : ISBN 0-943590-13-2 (pbk. : v. 1) LC Card 87-71366 DDC 332.024 19
HG179 .C326 1987

ESTATES (SOCIAL ORDER) - GERMANY (WEST) - JÜLICH-BERG - HISTORY - 16TH CENTURY.
Walz, Rainer. Stände und frühmoderner Staat . Neustadt an der Aisch , 1982. 257 p., [1] leaf of plates : ISBN 3-87707-040-9 LC Card 83-215104
HJ2675 .W35 1982

ESTATES (SOCIAL ORDER) - GERMANY (WEST) - JÜLICH-BERG - HISTORY - 17TH CENTURY.
Walz, Rainer. Stände und frühmoderner Staat . Neustadt an der Aisch , 1982. 257 p., [1] leaf of plates : ISBN 3-87707-040-9 LC Card 83-215104
HJ2675 .W35 1982

Estatísticas básicas do setor agrícola no Brasil /. Lima, José Luiz. São Paulo , 1983- v. : LC Card 83-219032 DDC 338.1/0981 19
HD9014.B82 L55 1983 ***NYPL [JLL 86-432]***

Estatísticas cadastrais : recadastramento-1978 / Ministério da Reforma e do Desenvolvimento Agrário--MIRAD, Instituto Nacional de Colonização e Reforma Agrária--INCRA, Diretoria de Cadastro e Tributação--DC. Brasília : INCRA, 1985- <v. 1-2; in 2 > : ill. ; 30 cm. At head of title: Sistema nacional de cadastro rural. Cover title: Estatísticas cadastrais, 1978. Spine title: Estatísticas cadastrais/78. CONTENTS. - v. 1. Brasil e grandes regiões -- v. 2, t. 3. Regiões Sudeste e Sul a nível de UF. LC Card 87-117732
1. Land tenure - Brazil - Statistics. 2. Land use, Rural - Brazil - Statistics. 3. Agriculture - Brazil - Statistics. I. Instituto Nacional de Colonização e Reforma Agrária. Diretoria de Cadastro e Tributação. II. Title: Sistema nacional de cadastro rural. III. Title: Estatísticas cadastrais, 1978. IV. Title: Estatísticas cadastrais/78.
HD498 .E77 1985

Estatísticas cadastrais, 1978. Estatísticas cadastrais . Brasília , 1985- <v. 1-2; in 2 > : LC Card 87-117732
HD498 .E77 1985

Estatísticas cadastrais/78. Estatísticas cadastrais . Brasília , 1985- <v. 1-2; in 2 > : LC Card 87-117732
HD498 .E77 1985

ESTE FAMILY.
Dean, Trevor. Land and power in late medieval Ferrara . Cambridge , New York , 1988. xiv, 212 p. : ISBN 0-521-33127-7 LC Card 87-6583 DDC 333.3/0945/45 19
HD679.F47 D43 1988

Esterhuyse, W. P. Anton Rupert : advocate of hope / W.P. Esterhuyse ; [translated by E.P. Hees].1st ed. Cape Town : Tafelberg, c1986. 150 p. ; 22 cm. ISBN 0-624-02429-6 LC Card 87-122279 DDC 361.7/4/0924 B 19
1. Rupert, Anton. 2. Industrialists - South Africa - Biography. 3. Rupert, Anton - View on social ethics. 4.

Social ethics. I. Title.
HC905.R87 E88 1986

Esteva, Gustavo. Por una nueva política alimentaria /. [México, D.F.] , 1984. 114 p. ; LC Card 85-131176 DDC 338.1/9/72 19
HD9014.M62 P67 1984 NYPL [JLC 86-348]

Estevez, Jaime, 1946- Vargas, Ines. The NIEO and the situatuon of workers . Oslo [1985] xiv, 290 p. ; ISBN 82-7288-121-7 (pbk.) LC Card 86-205407 DDC 331/.098 19
HD6530.5 .V36 1985

Estey, Willard Z. Report of the inquiry into the collapse of the CCB and Northland Bank / by Willard Z. Estey. Ottawa, Canada : Minister of Supply and Services Canada, c1986. xiii, 641 p. : ill. ; 25 cm. "August 1986." ISBN 0-660-12171-9 (pbk.) : LC Card 87-134617 DDC 332.1/2/0971 19
1. Canadian Commercial Bank. 2. Northland Bank. 3. Bank failures - Canada. 4. Banks and banking - Canada - State supervision. I. Title.
HG2708.C36 E89 1986

Estimación de la población potencialmente votante al 1o de julio de 1985 según departamentos, provincias, ciudades capital y cantones / Departamento de Estadísticas Sociales, División de Población y Vivienda. La Paz, Bolivia : La División, 1985. 58 p. : maps ; 22 cm. Limited edition of 400 copies. LC Card 87-400543 DDC 304.6/0984/021 19
1. Bolivia - Population - Statistics. 2. Voting research - Bolivia. I. Instituto Nacional de Estadística (Bolivia). División de Población y Vivienda.
HA965 .E85 1985

Estimación de las necesidades de formación profesional en el Uruguay : Programa de Naciones Unidas para el Desarrollo, Proyecto URU/79/001, "desarrollo de los recursos humanos" / República Oriental del Uruguay, Ministerio de Trabajo y Seguridad Social, Dirección Nacional de Recursos Humanos. Montevideo : La Dirección, 1981. 98 leaves ; 27 cm. Bibliography: leaves [81]-83. LC Card 86-174016
1. Occupational training - Uruguay. I. Uruguay. Dirección Nacional de Recursos Humanos.
HD5715.5.U8 E86 1981

Estimación de tasas de mortalidad infantil a partir de información de sobrevivencia de hijos clasificados por edad de la madre /. Feeney, Griffith. [Estimating infant mortality rates from child survivorship data by age of mother. Spanish.] Santiago de Chile , 1977. 19 p. : LC Card 83-176243
HB1323.I42 T87418 1977

Estimaciones y proyecciones de la población económicamente activa, 1950-2025. Economically active population . Geneva , 1986- v. ; ISBN 92-2-005345-4 (v. 1)
NYPL [JLM 87-113]

Estimaciones y proyecciones de población, 1950-2025 / República de Venezuela, Presidencia de la República, Oficina Central de Estadística e Informática. [Caracas] : La Oficina, 1985-[1987] 2 v. : ill. (some col.) ; 31 cm. Chiefly tables. Vol. 2 has title: Proyecciones de población, 1980-2000. Vol. 2: 2a ed. "Participación del Centro Latinoamericano de Demografía de las Naciones Unidas (CELADE)"--Pref. Bibliography: v. 1, p. xxxi. ISBN 980-280-006-6 (set) LC Card 87-123959 DDC 304.6/2/0987021 19
1. Venezuela - Population - Statistics. 2. Population forecasting - Venezuela - Statistics. I. Venezuela. Oficina Central de Estadística e Informática. II. CELADE (Organization). III. Title: Proyecciones de población, 1980-2000.
HA1095 .E885 1985

Estimate of the cost of completing the national system of interstate and defense highways in the Commonwealth of Virginia. 1987 estimate of the cost of completing the national system of interstate and defense highways in the Commonwealth of Virginia . [Richmond, Va.] [1986] 169 p. : LC Card 86-622650 DDC 388.1/12/09755 19
HE356.V8 A14 1986

Estimate of the expenditure ... of the United States, for the year 1789. United States. Dept. of the Treasury. New York [1789] 26, [2] p. (the last 2 pages blank) ; LC Card 87-109324 DDC n-us 19
HJ2050 .U55 1789

Estimates of national income at constant prices in the Gambia. [Banjul] : Central Statistics Dept., Ministry of Economic Planning and Industrial Development, [1985] 49 leaves ; 30 cm. Cover title. "July 1985." LC Card 87-120773 DDC 339.366/51 19
1. National income - Gambia - Statistics. I. Gambia. Central Statistics Dept.
HC1070.Z9 I54 1985

Estimates of poverty, including the value of noncash benefits, 1985. Washington, D.C. : U. S. Dept. of Commerce, Bureau of the Census : For sale by the Supt. of Docs., U. S. G.P.O., [1986] v, 86 p. ; 29 cm. (Technical paper . 56) "Issued September 1986." LC Card 86-603442 DDC 362.5/8/0973 19
1. Economic assistance, Domestic - United States. 2. Poor - United States. I. United States. Bureau of the Census. II. Series: Technical paper (United States. Bureau of the Census) , 56.
HC110.P63 E783 1986

Estimation of disequilibrium models /. Büttler, Hans-Jürgen. Berlin , New York , c1986. vi, 114 p. : ISBN 0-387-16817-6 (U. S.) : LC Card 86-22073 DDC 339.5 19
HB145 .B88 1986
NYPL [JLM 72-289 v.279]

The estimation of macroeconomic disequilibrium models with regime classification information /. Rudebusch, Glenn D., 1959- Berlin , New York , c1987. 128 p. : ISBN 0-387-17757-4 (U. S. : pbk.) : LC Card 87-9583 DDC 339.5 19
HB145 .R82 1987b

Estimations annuelles révisées de la population des divisions de recensement, 1971-1975. Revised annual estimates of population for census divisions, 1971-1976 /. Ottawa , c1979. 21 p. ; LC Card 82-216681
HA745 .R473 1979

Esto pasó en México / Enrique de la Garza ... [et al.]. México, D.F. : Editorial Extemporáneos, [1985] 126 p. : ill. ; 33 cm. (Documentos extemporáneos . 7) "7:19 a.m., 19 de septiembre, 1985"--Cover. ISBN 968-415-098-9 LC Card 87-403762 DDC 363.3/495/097253 19
1. Earthquakes - Economic aspects - Mexico - Mexico City Region. 2. Diasters - Economic aspects - Mexico - Mexico City Region. I. Garza, Enrique de la.
HC138.M4 E84 1985

Estomin, Steven. Updated load forecast of energy and peak demand on the Delmarva Peninsula / prepared by Steven L. Estomin and Matthew I. Kahal. Bethesda, Md. (4550 Montgomery Ave., Bethesda 20814) : Exeter Associates, [1986] iv, 4, 53, [18] p. : ill. ; 28 cm. "Prepared for Diane Brown, administrator, the Maryland Power Plant Siting Program." "May 1986." "PPES-86-2"--Cover. Includes bibliographical references. LC Card 87-620907 DDC 333.79/3212/097521 19
1. Electric power consumption - Delmarva Peninsula - Forecasting. 2. Electric utilities - Delmarva Peninsula - Rates - Peak-load pricing. I. Kahal, Matthew I. II. Maryland. Power Plant Siting Program. III. Title.
HD9685.U6 A123 1986

ESTONIA - ECONOMIC CONDITIONS - 1944- - ABSTRACTS.
Uspekhi ėkonomicheskogo i kul´turnogo razvitii͡a Ėstonskoĭ SSR za gody sovetskoĭ vlasti . Tallin , 1980. 222 p. ; LC Card 81-198881
HC337.E7 U86 1980

ESTONIA - OCCUPATIONS.
Osobennosti popolnenii͡a osnovnykh otri͡adov intelligentsii /. Tallin , 1981. 131 p. : LC Card 82-125732
HD8038.S652 E775 1981

ESTONIA - SOCIAL CONDITIONS - ABSTRACTS.
Uspekhi ėkonomicheskogo i kul´turnogo razvitii͡a Ėstonskoĭ SSR za gody sovetskoĭ vlasti . Tallin , 1980. 222 p. ; LC Card 81-198881
HC337.E7 U86 1980

ESTONIA - STATISTICS.
Vanatoa, Ė. Kh. Eesti NSV, teatmik /. Tallinn , 1985. 33 p. ; LC Card 86-131324
HA1448.E8 V36 1985

Ėstonskai͡a SSR, spravochnik. Vanatoa, Ė. Kh. Eesti NSV, teatmik /. Tallinn , 1985. 33 p. ; LC Card 86-131324
HA1448.E8 V36 1985

ESTRANGEMENT (SOCIAL PSYCHOLOGY) see **ALIENATION (SOCIAL PSYCHOLOGY)**

Estrategias competitivas para la banca . Ballarín, Eduard. Barcelona , 1985. 277 p. : ISBN 84-344-1040-0 LC Card 85-241009
HG1607.S7 B35 1985

Estrategias de desarrollo e integración en el Grupo Andino : del seminario realizado en Lima en agosto de 1984 / [Pedro Carmona et al.]. Lima, Perú : Instituto para la Integración de América Latina : Junta del Acuerdo de Cartagena, 1985. 414 p. : ill. ; 23 cm. Papers and debates presented at Seminario sobre Estrategias de Desarrollo e Integración en el Grupo Andino, sponsored by Junta del Acuerdo de Cartagena and INTAL, Lima, Peru, Aug. 22-24, 1984. Includes bibliographies. LC Card 87-125026 DDC 337.1/8 19
1. Andes Region - Economic policy - Congresses. 2. Andes region - Economic integration - Congresses. I. Carmona, Pedro, (Carmona Estanga). II. Institute for Latin American Integration. III. Board of the Cartagena Agreement. IV. Seminario sobre Estrategias de Desarrollo e Integración en el Grupo Andino (1984 : Lima, Peru).
HC167.A5 E87 1985

Estrategias para el desarrollo de la Sierra / [Alvaro Ortiz ... et al]. Cusco : Universidad Nacional Agraria "La Molina" : Centro de Estudios Rurales Andinos "Bartolomé de las Casas", c1986. 418 p. : ill. ; 24 cm. Includes bibliographies. LC Card 86-199393
1. Andes Region - Economic policy. 2. Andes region - Economic conditions. 3. Peru - Economic policy. 4. Peru - Economic conditions - 1968-. I. Ortíz Saravia, Alvaro. II. Universidad Nacional Agraria. III. Centro de Estudios Rurales Andinos Bartolomé de las Casas.
HC228.A54 E87 1986

Estrategias para la descentralización y el desarrollo regional /. Lizárraga Bobbio, Raúl. Lima, Perú , c1985. 356 p. : LC Card 86-146658
HT395.P4 L59 1985 NYPL [JLD 87-1315]

ESTREMADURA, SPAIN - ECONOMIC CONDITIONS.
Camacho Cabello, José. La Siberia extremeña . [Badajoz] , 1985. 201 p. : ISBN 84-505-1266-2 LC Card 86-200856
HB3620.E85 C35 1985

Gurría Gascón, José Luis. El paisaje de montaña en Extremadura . Cáceres [1985?] 273 p. : ISBN 84-600-3949-8 LC Card 87-111451
HC387.E7 G87 1985

ESTREMADURA (SPAIN) - POPULATION.
Gurría Gascón, José Luis. El paisaje de montaña en Extremadura . Cáceres [1985?] 273 p. : ISBN 84-600-3949-8 LC Card 87-111451
HC387.E7 G87 1985

ESTREMADURA (SPAIN) - POPULATION - HISTORY.
Camacho Cabello, José. La Siberia extremeña . [Badajoz] , 1985. 201 p. : ISBN 84-505-1266-2 LC Card 86-200856
HB3620.E85 C35 1985

ESTREMADURA, SPAIN - SOCIAL CONDITIONS.
Camacho Cabello, José. La Siberia extremeña . [Badajoz] , 1985. 201 p. : ISBN 84-505-1266-2 LC Card 86-200856
HB3620.E85 C35 1985

Estructura agraria, crecimiento de la población y migraciones . Lira, Luis Felipe. Santiago, Chile , 1976. 90 p. ; LC Card 83-169710
HB2025 .L57 1976

Estructura agraria y desarrollo agrícola en México : estudio sobre las relaciones entre la tenencia y uso de la tierra y el desarrollo agrícola de México / Sergio Reyes Osorio ... [et al.], con la colaboración de Iván Restrepo ... [et al.].1a ed. México : Fondo de Cultura Económica, 1974 (1979 printing) xvi, 1174 p. : ill. ; 24 cm. At head of title: Centro de Investigaciones Agrarias. Includes bibliographical references. LC Card 81-126616 DDC 338.1/0972 19
1. Agriculture - Economic aspects - Mexico. 2. Land reform - Mexico. 3. Agriculture and state - Mexico. I. Reyes Osorio, Sergio. II. Centro de Investigaciones Agrarias (Mexico City, Mexico).
HD1792 .E85 1974 NYPL [JLE 81-372]

La estructura de salarios en México /. Bortz, Jeff. Azcapotzalco, México, D.F. , 1985. 371

p. : ISBN 968-8402-76-1 LC Card 87-104886
HD4981 .B67 1985

La estructura del sindicalismo en Jalisco /. Tamayo Rodríguez, Jaime E. Guadalajara, Jalisco, México [1985] 224 p. ; ISBN 968-570-147-4 LC Card 86-208258
HD6535.J35 T36 1985

Estructura económica del Estado de [name of state] : sistema de cuentas nacionales de México : estructura económica regional, producto interno bruto por entidad federativa, 1970, 1975, 1980. México, D.F. : Instituto Nacional de Estadística, Geografía e Informática ; [s.l.] : Programa de las Naciones Unidas para el Desarrollo, c1985-<c1987 > v. <[1-7] > : ill. (some col.), col. maps ; 28 cm. Chiefly tables. CONTENTS. - [v. 1] Oaxaca -- [v. 2] Aguascalientes -- [v. 3] Sinaloa -- [v. 4] San Luis Potosí -- [v. 5] Michoacán -- [v. 6] Mexico -- [v. 7] Baja California Sur. ISBN 968-89202-6-6 (v. [1]) LC Card 86-229829
1. National income - Mexico - Accounting - Statistics - States. I. Instituto Nacional de Estadística, Geografía e Informática (Mexico). II. United Nations. Development Programme.
HC140.I5 E88 1985

Estructura financiera y actividad inversora de las administraciones públicas en Castilla y León /. García Villarejo, Avelino. Valladolid , 1984. 431 p. : ISBN 84-505-0331-0 LC Card 87-108720
HJ1249.C29 G37 1984

Estructura política y políticas de población / Raúl Atria ... [et al.]. [Santiago, Chile] : Consejo Latinoamericano de Ciencias Sociales, Comisión de Población y Desarrollo, [1977] 442 p. ; 21 cm. At head of title: Programa de Investigaciones Sociales sobre Problemas de Población Relevantes para Políticas de Población en América Latina, PISPAL, seminario organizado por Centro Latinoamericano de Demografía, Santiago de Chile, mayo, 1975. Includes bibliographical references. LC Card 83-168971
1. Latin America - Population policy. 2. Economic development - Social aspects. 3. Latin America - Emigration and immigration. I. Atria B., Raúl. II. Programa de Investigaciones Sociales sobre Problemas de Población Relevantes para Políticas de Población en América Latina.
HB3530.5 .E88 1977

Estructura social de la comarca "El Camp de Morvedre" / Institut Valencià d'Investigació Social (I.V.I.S.). Sagunt, Valencià : Obra Social de la Caixa d'Estalvis i Socors de Sagunt ; [Madrid] : Confederación Española de Cajas de Ahorros, 1982. 2 v. (1133 p.) : ill. ; 31 cm. (Publicaciones de la Caja de Ahorros y Socorros de Sagunto) CONTENTS. - t. 1. Demografía, estructura laboral, estructura de clases, economía, proceso de urbanización -- t. 2. Familia, vivienda, comunicación social, lengua, socio-ideología y socio-política, educación, sanidad, marginación social. ISBN 84-7231-763-3 (set) LC Card 85-188040
1. Sagunto (Spain) - Population. 2. Social structure - Spain - Sagunto. 3. Sagunto (Spain) - Social conditions. I. Institut Valencià d'Investigació Social. II. Series: Publicacions de la Caixa d'Estalvis i Socors de Sagunt.
HB3620.S24 E87 1982

Estructura social, estado democrático y cambio político /. Rubinstein, Juan Carlos, 1928- [Buenos Aires] , c1986. 159 p. : ISBN 950-23-0292-3 LC Card 87-114981 DDC 330.982/064 19
HC175 .R783 1986

Estructura y posibilidad de desarrollo del Campo de Gibraltar. Colaboración sindical al estudio sobre la estructura y posibilidad de desarrollo del Campo de Gibraltar, encomendado por la comisión interministerial designada al efecto /. Cádiz , 1965. 89 p. : LC Card 85-104938
HC390.6 .C65 1965

Estrutura e funcionamento do comércio exterior brasileiro / Banco do Brasil S.A., Carteira de Comércio Exterior-CACEX. Rio de Janeiro, RJ : CACEX, 1980. v, 98 p. : ill. ; 27 cm. LC Card 84-121064
1. Brazil - Commercial policy - History. 2. Foreign trade promotion - Brazil - History. I. Banco do Brasil. Carteira de Comércio Exterior.
HF1513 .E85 1980

Estrutura industrial no Brasil . Hollanda Filho, Sergio Buarque de. Rio de Janeiro , 1983. 275 p. : LC Card 87-119359 DDC 338.8/0981 19
HD2834 .H65 1983

ESTUARINE AREA CONSERVATION - SOUTH AFRICA - GREAT BRAK RIVER. Stauth, Roy. A methodology for determining the socially optimum uses of estuarine resources . Rondebosch, South Africa [1982] v, 119 leaves : LC Card 86-210152
HC905.Z7 G87 1982

Estudi de comunicació per a la campanya publicitària del foment de l'ús del transport col·lectiu. 1982. Estudi motivacional i d'opinió sobre els transports públics a la conurbació barcelonina ; Estudi de comunicació per a la campanya publicitària del foment de l'ús del transport col·lectiu /. [Barcelona] [1982?] 80 p. : ISBN 84-393-0087-5 LC Card 86-209206
HE4899.B43 E87 1982

Estudi motivacional i d'opinió sobre els transports públics a la conurbació barcelonina ; Estudi de comunicació per a la campanya publicitària del foment de l'ús del transport col·lectiu / Direcció General de Transports, Departament de Política Territorial i Obres Públiques, Generalitat de Catalunya. [Barcelona] : La Direcció, [1982?] 80 p. : ill. ; 30 cm. Cover title. ISBN 84-393-0087-5 LC Card 86-209206
1. Local transit - Spain - Barcelona Region - Public opinion. 2. Local transit - Spain - Barcelona Region - Management - Public opinion. I. Catalonia (Spain). Direcció General de Transports. II. Title: Estudi de comunicació per a la campanya publicitària del foment de l'ús del transport col·lectiu. 1982.
HE4899.B43 E87 1982

Estudio cultural socio económico, Mojocoya y Redención Pampa. Estudio cultural y socio económico de Mojocoya--Redención Pampa. Sucre, Bolivia , 1979. 266 p. : LC Card 83-204567
HC183.M65 E77 1979

Estudio cultural y socio económico de Mojocoya--Redención Pampa. Estudio cultural socio económico, Mojocoya y Redención Pampa. 2a ed. Sucre, Bolivia : Acción Cultural Loyola, 1979. 266 p. : ill. ; 28 cm. Cover title. Includes bibliographical references. LC Card 83-204567
1. Mojocoya (Bolivia) - Economic conditions. 2. Mojocoya (Bolivia) - Social conditions. 3. Redención Pampa (Bolivia) - Economic conditions. 4. Rendención Pampa (Bolivia) - Social conditions. 5. Social surveys - Bolivia - Mojocoya. 6. Social surveys - Bolivia - Rendención Pampa. I. ACLO (Organization). II. Title. III. Title: Mojocoya y Redención Pampa.
HC183.M65 E77 1979

Estudio de diagnóstico de la población de los barrios--Chamelecón, Suyapa, Fe y Esperanza, San Antonio, San José y San Miguel / MSPS/AID ; Nora de Martínez .. [et al.]. Tegucigalpa, D.C. : Asesores para el Desarrollo, [1984] 1 v. (various foliations) : forms ; 28 cm. Cover title: Estudio de diagnóstico de la población de los barrios--Chamelecón, Suyapa, Fe y Esperanza, San Antonio, San José y San Miguel, y, Estudios de pre-factibilidad para la expansión o instalación de industrias de barrios. Bibliography: last leaf. LC Card 85-205996
1. Poor - Honduras - Tegucigalpa. 2. Poor - Honduras - San Pedro Sula. 3. Slums - Honduras - Tegucigalpa. 4. Slums - Honduras - San Pedro Sula. 5. Small business - Honduras - Tegucigalpa. 6. Small business - Honduras - San Pedro Sula. I. Martínez, Nora de. II. Asesores para el Desarrollo (Tegucigalpa, Honduras). III. United States. Agency for International Development. IV. Title: Estudios de pre-factibilidad para la expansión o instalación de industrias de barrios.
HC145.Z7 T434 1984

Estudio de factibilidad para una cadena de silos intercomunales de papa : Chuquisaca-Potosí-Tarija. [Sucre, Bolivia : ACLO], 1982. 178 p., [2] leaves of plates : ill. ; 26 cm. Spine title: Cadena de silos. LC Card 83-202593 DDC 338.1/6 19
1. Potatoes - Bolivia - Chuquisaca - Storage. 2. Potatoes - Bolivia - Potosí (Dept.) - Storage. 3. Potatoes - Bolivia - Tarija (Dept.) - Storage. 4. Silos - Bolivia - Planning - Case studies. I. ACLO (Organization). II. Title: Cadena de silos.
HD9235.P82 B525 1982
NYPL [JLF 87-711]

Estudio de las comarcas Campiña Alta y Penibética de Córdoba . Barroso Rodríguez, Antonio. Córdoba , 1984. 268 p. : ISBN 84-505-0166-0 LC Card 85-182568
HC387.C58 B37 1984

Estudio de oferta exportable. Informe final "estudio de oferta exportable" /. Santo Domingo, República Dominicana [1985] 101, [57] p. ; LC Card 85-203743
HC153.5 .I54 1985

"Estudio de participación campesina en la estructura y acción de ACLO" . ACLO (Organization) [Sucre, Bolivia] , 1980. 94 leaves ; LC Card 83-203590
HD1531.B6 A24 1980

Estudio de transportes en la Región Amazónica y en el Alto Paraguay. Buenos Aires : Banco Interamericano de Desarrollo, Instituto para la Integración de América Latina, [1983- v. <1 > : ill. ; 29 cm. "Convenio ATN/SF-2084-RE." Includes bibliographical references. CONTENTS. - 1a pte. Región Amazónica LC Card 87-400601 DDC 380.5/0981/1 19
1. Transportation - Amazon River Region. 2. Transportation - Paraguay. I. Institute for Latin American Integration.
HE230 .E85 1983

Estudio del Plan de desarrollo carbonífero de la zona de Valle del Cauca en la República de Colombia. Tokio, Japon : Japan International Cooperation Agency, 1977. v, 149 leaves : ill. (some col.) ; 31 cm. Folded plans and maps inserted in 5 plastic pockets. LC Card 84-244429
1. Coal trade - Colombia - Valle del Cauca. 2. Coal - Geology - Colombia - Valle del Cauca - Maps. 3. Coal mines and mining - Colombia - Valle del Cauca - Maps. I. Kokusai Kyōryoku Jigyōdan.
HD9554.C63 V34 1977

Estudio económico de América Latina, 1981. [Santiago, Chile?] : Naciones Unidas, Consejo Económico y Social, Comisión Económica para América Latina, [1982- v. <1-9 > : ill. ; 25 cm. Cover title. "Distr. limitada." "Original: español." Includes bibliographical references. "E/CEPAL/L.268/Add. <10, 17, 20-22, 25, 28, 30-31 >, noviembre de 1982." "82-4-828." LC Card 86-202465
1. Latin America - Economic conditions - 1945- - Collected works. I. United Nations. Economic Commission for Latin America.
HC125 .E89 1982

Estudio (Instituto de Estudios de Población y Desarrollo (ADPBF)) . (no. 4) Gómez, Carmen. Población y energía en la República Dominicana, 1990-2000. Santo Domingo, República Dominicana [1985] vi, 86 p. : LC Card 86-176044
HD9502.D652 G65 1985

Estudio (Instituto de Estudios de Población y Desarrollo (ADPBF (Organization)) . (no. 3) Gómez, Carmen. Población y vivienda en la República Dominicana . Santo Domingo, República Dominicana , 1984. 116 p. : LC Card 85-154466
HD7316.5.A3 G65 1984
NYPL [JLF 86-1146]

Estudio integral de la Sierra de Segura . Ruiz Avilés, Pedro. [Jaén] [1985] 130 leaves : ISBN 84-505-1249-2 LC Card 86-187282
HC387.S438 R85 1985

Estudio oferta exportable, 1984. Informe final "estudio de oferta exportable" /. Santo Domingo, República Dominicana [1985] 101, [57] p. ; LC Card 85-203743
HC153.5 .I54 1985

Estudio para el desarrollo de las zonas económicas de la Provincia de Teruel / Consejo Económico Sindical Provincial. [Teruel] : El Consejo, 1965. 75, 61, 63, 65, 74, 61 p. ; 29 cm. Cover title. LC Card 85-110389
1. Teruel (Spain : Province) - Economic conditions. 2. Teruel, Spain (Province) - Economic policy. I. Consejo Económico Sindical Provincial (Teruel, Spain).
HC387.T4 E886 1965

Estudio sobre la sociedad soriana en el siglo XVIII . Pérez de Guinea, María del Carmen. [Spain] [1982?] 296 p. ; LC Card 85-136714
HA1559.S65 P47 1982

Estudios CEDES.
(v. 2, no. 3) Frenkel, Roberto. Decisiones de precio en alta inflación /. Buenos Aires, Argentina , 1979. 58 p. ; LC Card 80-125798 DDC 332.4/15 19
HF5416.5 .F73 ***NYPL [JLD 86-2701]***

(vol. 4, no. 3) Frenkel, Roberto. Mercado financiero, expectativas cambiarias y movimientos de capital /. Buenos Aires, Argentina [1981] 46 p. : LC Card 82-236987 DDC 332/.0724 19
HG173.6.S62 F73 1981 ***NYPL [JLD 86-2636]***

Boneo, Horacio. Desarrollo regional, incentivos fiscales y localización industrial /. Buenos Aires, Argentina [1985] 160 p. : ISBN 950-95720-8-X ***NYPL [JLD 86-4218]***

Feijoó, María del Carmen. Buscando un techo . Buenos Aires, Argentina [1984] 90, [5] p. : LC Card 85-214586
HD7321.B9 F45 1984

Estudios CEDES, 0326-1646 .
(v. 4, no. 7) Canitrot, Adolfo. Orden social y monetarismo /. Buenos Aires, Argentina [1982 or 1983] 50 p. ; LC Card 83-213595
HC173 .C35 1982

Estudios (Centro de Estudios Monetarios Latinoamericanos)
Brovedani, Bruno. Un modelo de análisis monetario y de programación financiera /. [Mexico City, Mexico] , 1984. ii, 203 p. : LC Card 86-158393
HG660.5 .B7 1984

Lejavitzer, Moisés. Los efectos del neoproteccionismo en América Latina /. México, D.F. , 1983. i, 231 p. ; LC Card 85-149154 DDC 382.7/3/098 19
HF3230.5.Z5 L45 1983 ***NYPL [JLD 86-434]***

Márquez, Javier, 1909- La banca mexicana . [Mexico City, Mexico] , 1987. xi, 299 p., [3] folded leaves of plates : ISBN 968-615-402-7 LC Card 87-404865 DDC 332.1/0972 19
HG2714 .M27 1987

Estudios (Centro de Investigaciones Económicas (Uruguay)) .
(no. 5) Barbato de Silva, Celia. La ganadería vacuna uruguaya . Montevideo, Uruguay [1980] 77 leaves ; ***NYPL [JLF 86-1101]***

Estudios córdobeses .
(34) Barroso Rodríguez, Antonio. Estudio de las comarcas Campiña Alta y Penibética de Córdoba . Córdoba , 1984. 268 p. : ISBN 84-505-0166-0 LC Card 85-182568
HC387.C58 B37 1984

Estudios de historia económica .
(no. 10-) Gómez Mendoza, Antonio. Ferrocarril y mercado interior en España, 1874-1913 /. Madrid , 1984- v. : ISBN 84-500-9728-2 (v. 1) LC Card 85-215275 DDC 385/.24/0946 19
HE2469 .G66 1984 ***NYPL [JLL 86-176]***

(no. 10, etc) Gómez Mendoza, Antonio. Ferrocarril y mercado interior en España, 1874-1913 /. Madrid , 1984- v. : ISBN 84-500-9728-2 (v. 1) LC Card 85-215275 DDC 385/.24/0946 19
HE2469 .G66 1984 ***NYPL [JLL 86-176]***

(no. 11) Robledo Hernández, Ricardo. La renta de la tierra en Castilla la Vieja y León (1836-1913) /. [Madrid] [1984?] 245 p. : ISBN 84-505-0885-1 LC Card 87-104999
HJ4375.C27 R63 1984

Estudios de pre-factibilidad para la expansión o instalación de industrias de barrios. Estudio de diagnóstico de la población de los barrios--Chamelecón, Suyapa, Fe y Esperanza, San Antonio, San José y San Miguel /. Tegucigalpa, D.C. [1984] 1 v. (various foliations) : LC Card 85-205996
HC145.Z7 T434 1984

Estudios e informes de la CEPAL, 0256-9795 .
(50) América Latina y la economía mundial del algodón. Santiago de Chile , 1985. 128 p. : ISBN 92-1-321189-9 LC Card 85-230001 DDC 338.1/7351/098 19
HD9884.L3 A46 1985 ***NYPL [JLE 86-3341]***

(57) García Elizalde, Pedro. El desarrollo frutícola y forestal en Chile y sus derivaciones sociales. Santiago de Chile , 1986. 234 p. : ISBN 92-1-321204-6 LC Card 86-175421
HD9254.C52 G37 1986

(58) Palau, Tomás. El cultivo del algodón y la soya en el Paraguay y sus derivaciones sociales. Santiago de Chile , 1986. 148 p. ; ISBN 92-1-321207-0 LC Card 87-400251 DDC 338.1/7351/09892 19
HD9084.P25 P35 1986

(59) Barbosa, Túlio. Expansión del cultivo de la caña de azúcar y de la ganadería en el Nordeste del Brasil . Santiago de Chile , Nueva York, NY, Estados Unidos de América , 1986. 170 p. : ISBN 92-1-321209-7 LC Card 87-400309 DDC 338.1/7361/09813 19
HD9114.B7 N67943 1986

(60) Las Empresas transnacionales en el desarrollo colombiano. Santiago de Chile , Nueva York, NY , 1986. 218 p. : ISBN 92-1-321213-5 LC Card 87-402186 DDC 338.8/88861 19
HD2837 .E47 1986

(61) Parquet, Reinerio. Las empresas transnacionales en la economía del Paraguay. Santiago de Chile , 1987. 115 p. ; ISBN 92-1-321223-2 LC Card 87-404657 DDC 338.8/88892 19
HG5382 .P37 1987

Estudios económicos (Banco de España. Servicio de Estudios) .
(no. 37) Gil, Gonzalo. Aspectos financieros y monetarios de la integración española en la Comunidad Económica Europea /. [Madrid] [1985] 187 p. : ISBN 84-505-2233-1 LC Card 87-101729
HC241.25.S6 G55 1985

Estudios históricos sobre estructuras agrarias andinas .
(nr 1) Mörner, Magnus. Compraventas de tierras en el Cuzco, 1825-1869 /. Estocolmo , 1984. 66 p. : LC Card 87-403757 DDC 333.3/0985/37 19
HD559.C87 M67 1984

Estudios INDEC .
(6o v) Exportaciones industriales . Buenos Aires, República Argentina [1987] 231 p. ; LC Card 87-405033 DDC 338.4/767/0982 19
HD9734.A7 E96 1987

Estudios (Peru. Oficina Nacional de Evaluación de Recursos Naturales) .
(50) Inventario, evaluación e integración de los recursos naturales de la zona Esperanza-Chandles-Yaco /. Lima, Perú , 1980. v, xi, 229, 24, [12] p. of plates : LC Card 84-155289
HC228.E86 I58 1980

Estudios sobre integración económica y cooperación regional en el Cono Sur : obra / editada bajo la dirección de Raymundo Barros Charlín. Santiago de Chile : Instituto de Estudios Internacionales, Universidad de Chile, c1985. 283 p. ; 23 cm. (Estudios internacionales) Spanish and Portuguese. Includes bibliographical references. LC Card 86-174604
1. Southern Cone of South America - Economic integration. 2. Agriculture - Economic aspects - Southern Cone of South America. 3. Transportation - Southern Cone of South America. 4. Colleges and universities - Southern Cone of South America. 5. International cooperation. I. Barros Charlín, Raymundo. II. Series: Colección Estudios internacionales (Universidad de Chile. Instituto de Estudios Internacionales).
HC167.S67 E78 1985

Estudios sobre la sociedad uruguaya .
(no. 5) Fortuna, Juan Carlos. Las bases de un desarrollo social diferente . Montevideo [1985] 117 p. ; LC Card 86-131906
HC232 .F76 1985

Estudios universitarios (Institución Alfonso el Magnánimo) .
(11) Lluch, Ernest, 1937- Agronomía y fisiocracia en España, 1750-1820 /. Valencia [1985?] lxi, 215 p. ; ISBN 84-00-05965-4 LC Card 85-240630
HD2022 .L58 1985

(15) Franch Benavent, Ricardo, 1956- Crecimiento comercial y enriquecimiento burgués en la Valencia del siglo XVIII /. Valencia [1986?] 340 p. : ISBN 84-505-4154-9 LC Card 87-110614
HF3690.V3 F7 1986

Estudios y documentos de trabajo sobre empleo, remuneraciones y recursos humanos.
Bour, Juan Luis. La terciarización del empleo en la Argentina. El sector de servicios a las empresas /. Buenos Aires , 1985. 117 p. ; LC Card 87-123717 DDC 338.4/6/0982 19
HD9985.A72 B68 1985

Cimillo, Elsa. La terciarización del empleo en la Argentina. [Buenos Aires] [1985] 23, [41], 3 p. ; LC Card 87-123708 DDC 381/.1/0982 19
HF5429.6.A7 C56 1985

Lindenboim, Javier. La terciarización del empleo en la Argentina. Buenos Aires , 1985. vi, 59, 50, 3 p. ; LC Card 87-122527 DDC 381 19
HD2346.A73 L56 1985

Szretter, Héctor. La terciarización del empleo en la Argentina. Buenos Aires , 1985. iv, 82, 3 p. ; LC Card 87-122558 DDC 331.7/6164046/0982 19
HD8039.D52 A657 1985

Estudios y monografías (CINTERFOR (Organization)) .
(no. 21) Novaes, Paulo, 1913- Organización y recursos humanos /. Montevideo , 1976, 1977 printing. 122 p. : LC Card 86-139048
HD5713 .N68 1977

(no. 37) Alcántara, Alcides de. Métodos para la aplicación de las series metódicas ocupacionales /. Montevideo , 1978. 73 p. : LC Card 86-142696
HD5715 .A44 1978

(no. 38) Maslankowski, Willi, 1936- Nachweis beruflicher Qualifikationen /. Montevideo , 1979. 102 p., [2] folded leaf of plates : LC Card 86-148766
HD5715.5.L3 M37 1979

(no. 43) Maslankowski, Willi, 1936- [Nachweis beruflicher Qualifikationen. Spanish. Selections.] Calificación ocupacional en la República Federal de Alemania /. Montevideo , 1979. 38 p. : LC Card 86-143001
HD5715.5.G4 M372518 1979

(no. 59) Agudelo Mejía, Santiago. Lineamientos para la implantación de un servicio de certificación ocupacional /. Montevideo , 1983. 67 p. : LC Card 86-142627
HD5715.5.L3 A348 1983

(no. 60) Retuerto, Enrique. Determinación de necesidades de formación profesional . Montevideo , 1983. 110 p. ; LC Card 86-149551
HD5715 .R47 1983

(no. 61) Ducci, María Angélica. Formación profesional . Montevideo , 1983. 102 p. ; LC Card 86-142632
HD5715.5.L29 D83 1983

(no. 67) Corvalán Vásquez, Oscar E., 1947- Empleo y capacitación en los talleres informales de Santiago /. Montevideo , 1984. 150 p. ; LC Card 86-127324
HD2346.C54 S263 1984

Estudo de custos do transporte nos rios Araguaia e Tocantins / Serviço Público Federal, M.T., Superintendência Nacional da Marinha Mercante. [Rio de Janeiro] : M.T., Superintendência Nacional da Marinha Mercante, Diretoria de Navegação Interior, Divisão de Navegação Fluvial e Lacustre, Seção de Estudos e Registros, 1985. 95 leaves : ill. ; 30 cm. LC Card 87-403933 DDC 386/.3/098173 19
1. Shipping - Brazil - Araguaia River - Costs. 2. Shipping - Brazil - Tocantins River - Costs. I. Brazil. Superintendência Nacional da Marinha Mercante.
HE424.A7 E84 1985

Estudo do mercado de carne bovina / Projeto de Desenvolvimento Integrado da Bacia do Araguaia-Tocantins. Brasília : PRODIAT, 1985. 89 p. : ill. ; 22 cm. (Série Estudos e pesquisas. no. 10) At head of title: Ministério do Interior, Organização dos Estados Americanos, Governo do Estado de Goiás, Governo do Estado do Maranhão, Governo do Estado do Pará, Governo do Estado de Mato Grosso. Bibliography: p. 67-68. LC Card 86-197081
1. Beef industry - Brazil - Araguaia River Region. 2. Beef industry - Brazil - Tocantins River Region. I. Projeto de Desenvolvimento Integrado da Bacia do Araguaia-Tocantins. II. Series: Série Estudos e pesquisas (Projeto de Desenvolvimento Integrado da Bacia do Araguaia-Tocantins) , no. 10.
HD9433.B82 A74 1985

Estudo especial : cooperativismo, desnivelamento e reprodução do campesinato : PDRI-Região Fumageira/Alagoas / [Fundação Estadual de Planejamento Agrícola de Alagoas, CEPA/AL.]. Maceió, AL. : A Fundação, 1983. 174 leaves : ill. ; 30 cm. Bibliography: leaves 165-170. LC Card

86-167829
1. Arapiraca Region (Brazil) - Economic conditions. 2. Credit - Brazil - Arapiraca Region. 3. Labor supply - Brazil - Arapiraca Region. 4. Capital - Brazil - Arapiraca Region. 5. Income - Brazil - Arapiraca Region. I. Fundação Estadual de Planejamento Agrícola de Alagoas. II. Title: Cooperativismo, desnivelamento e reprodução do campesinato.
HC189.A69 E88 1983

Estudo preliminar para o establecimento de prioridades no financiamento para construção de embarcações para a navegação interior / Serviço Público Federal, M.T.-Superintendência Nacional da Marinha Mercante. [Rio de Janeiro] : M.T., Superintendência Nacional da Marinha Mercante, Diretoria de Navegação Interior, 1985. [84] leaves : ill. ; 30 cm. LC Card 87-403936 DDC 386/.0981 19
1. Inland water transportation - Brazil. 2. Coastwise shipping - Brazil. 3. Shipbuilding - Brazil - Finance. I. Brazil. Superintendência Nacional da Marinha Mercante. II. Brazil. Diretoria de Navegação Interior.
HE653 .E88 1985

Estudo sobre a adequação floresta-indústria no Estado do Paraná / Secretaria de Estado da Indústria e do Comércio, Coordenadoria de Desenvolvimento Industrial. [Curitiba] : A Coordenadoria, [1982] vi, 106, [4] leaves ; 31 cm. Bibliography: leaves [107]-[109] LC Card 86-197076
1. Forest products industry - Brazil - Paraná (State). I. Paraná (Brazil : State). Coordenadoria de Desenvolvimento Industrial.
HD9764.B73 P32 1982

Estudo sobre a soja / Secretaria de Estado da Indústria e do Comércio do Paraná, Coordenadoria de Desenvolvimento Industrial. Curitiba : A Coordenadoria, 1980. 61 leaves : ill. ; 31 cm. Bibliography: leaves 59-60. LC Card 86-197070
1. Soybean industry - Brazil - Paraná (State). 2. Soybean products - Brazil - Paraná (State). I. Paraná (Brazil : State). Coordenadoria de Desenvolvimento Industrial.
HD9235.S62 B744 1980

Estudo sobre o setor de laticínios no Estado do Paraná / Secretaria de Estado da Indústria e do Comércio, Coordenadoria de Desenvolvimento Industrial. Curitiba : A Coordenadoria, 1980. iii, 47 leaves : ill. ; 30 cm. Bibliography: leaves 43-45. LC Card 86-201233
1. Dairy products industry - Brazil - Paraná (State). I. Paraná (Brazil : State). Coordenadoria de Desenvolvimento Industrial.
HD9275.B73 P34 1980

Estudo sobre o transporte rodioviário de carga. Anexo. [Brasília] : Ministério dos Transportes, Empresa Brasileira de Planejamento de Transportes, 1984- v. <1- > : ill. ; 30 x 42 cm. Chiefly tables. CONTENTS. - 1. Estatísticas por amostra LC Card 87-403695 DDC 388.3/24/0981021 19
1. Trucking - Brazil - Statistics. I. Empresa Brasileira de Planejamento de Transportes.
HE5653.A6 E85 1984

Estudos (Banco de Fomento Nacional) .
(13) Almeida, João Carreira. Fabricação de materiais de barro para construção . Lisboa , 1978. 186 p., [3] leaves of plates (one folded) : LC Card 82-112167 DDC 338.4/36914/09469 19
HD9596.P82 A85 1978
(24) Rendeiro, João Oliveira. Progresso técnico e evolução estratégica na indústria de máquinas-ferramentas . Lisboa , 1985. 111 p. : LC Card 86-189891
HD9703.E92 R45 1985
(24) Rendeiro, João Oliveira. Progresso técnico e evolução estratégica na indústria de máquinas-ferramentas . Lisboa , 1985. 111 p. : LC Card 86-189891
HD9703.E92 R45 1985

Estudos CEBRAP .
(no. 27) A Renda da terra . [São Paulo, Brazil] , Petrópolis , c1980. 152 p. : LC Card 81-214665
HC186 .C36a no. 27 HB401

Estudos de viabilidade técnica da implantação e plano diretor do distrito industrial de Mossoró : relatório final / Geotécnica S.A. [Natal] : Secretaria de Indústria e Comércio do Rio Grande do Norte, 1979. ca. 250 leaves, 8 folded leaves of plates : ill. ; 30 cm. "C-PR-120005/78." LC Card 84-256137
1. Industrial districts - Brazil - Mossoró - Planning. I. Geotécnica S.A. II. Rio Grande do Norte (Brazil). Secretaria da Indústria e Comércio.
HC189.M6 E86 1979

Estudos e documentos de trabalho.
Girão, José António. Salários, inflação e moeda . Lisboa , 1984. 50 p. : LC Card 85-157764
HG1145 .G57 1984

Estudos e propostas para a organização territorial e desenvolvimento urbano do Brasil. Brasilia : Ministério do Interior, Conselho Nacional de Desenvolvimento Urbano, 1981. 126 leaves, [7] folded leaves of plates : col. maps ; 30 cm. (Documento de estudo . 1) Bibliography: p. 125-126.
1. Cities and towns - Brazil - Growth. 2. Urbanization - Brazil. 3. Regional planning - Brazil. 4. Brazil - Surveys. I. Conselho Nacional de Desenvolvimento Urbano (Brazil). II. Series: Documento de estudo (Conselho Nacional de Desenvolvimento Urbano) , 1.
NYPL [JLG 86-151]

Estudos e seminários.
Cavaco Silva, Aníbal A. (Aníbal António), 1939- O mercado financeiro português em 1966 /. Lisboa , 1968. xiv, 104 p. : LC Card 85-133959
HG186.P8 C38 1968

Estudos e trabalhos mimeografados .
(no. 32) Michel, Nelson Emílio. Evolução dos índices do número e do valor de cheques compensados no Rio Grande do Sul, período de 1960-7, e sua análise estatística /. Porto Alegre , 1976. 79 leaves : LC Card 82-159893
HG1692 .M53 1976

Estudos económicos (Fundação Instituto de Pesquisas Econômicas (São Paulo, Brazil)
Kirsten, José Tiacci. Custo de vida . São Paulo , 1985. xi, 158 p. : LC Card 86-143942
HB235.B8 K57 1985

Estudos econômics (Fundação Instituto de Pesquisas Econômicas (São Paulo, Brazil))
Homem de Melo, Fernando Bento, 1942- Prioridade agrícola . São Paulo , 1985. xiii, 200 p. : LC Card 86-126447 DDC 338.1/881 19
HD1872 .H66 1985 ***NYPL [JLD 86-3809]***

Estudos especiais (Brasília, Brazil) .
(v. 19) Coelho, Carlos Nayro de Azevedo. Opções de política econômica /. Brasília , 1986. 137 p. ; LC Card 87-403318 DDC 338.981 19
HC187 .C565 1986

Estudos fundamentais : subsídios para uma política de artesanato no Estado do Ceará / Governo do Estado do Ceará, Secretaria de Planejamento e Coordenação--SEPLAN, Fundação Instituto de Planejamento do Ceará--IPLANCE. Fortaleza : IPLANCE, 1986. 120 p. : ill., maps ; 22 cm. Bibliography: p. 119-120. LC Card 87-120224
1. Handicraft - Government policy - Brazil - Ceará (State). 2. Cottage industries - Government policy - Brazil - Ceará (State). 3. Artisans - Brazil - Ceara (State). I. Fundação Instituto de Planejamento do Ceará.
HD2346.B72 C44 1986

Estudos (Instituto Gulbenkian de Ciência. Centro e Estudos e Economia Agrária)
Pereira, Mário. Alguns elementos para a caracterização da assimetria regional agrária portuguesa /. Oeiras [Portugal] , 1974. 59 p. : LC Card 85-133550
HD2027 .P388 1974

Estudos (Instituto Nacional de Estatística (Portugal)) .
(33) Inquérito às rendas e a outras características das habitações arrendadas na cidade de Evora em 1955-56 /. Lisboa [1958] 26 p. : LC Card 85-185037
HA1571 .A32 no. 33 HD7288.85.P82E93

Estudos para o planeamento regional e urbano .
(no. 20) Madeira em mapas e em números. [Lisboa] , 1984. iii, 61 leaves : LC Card 85-144457
HA2285 .M33 1984

Estudos para o planejamento. see Serie Estudos para o planejamento.

Estudos rurais.
Beskow, Paulo Roberto. O arrendamento capitalista na agricultura . São Paulo , Brasília , 1986. 219 p. : LC Card 86-229665
HD9066.B83 R463 1986

Estudos tributários /. Silva, Gerson Augusto da. Brasília, DF , 1983. 139 p. : LC Card 84-127110
HJ2525 .S49 1983

Észak-Magyarország hírközlésének története /. Kamody, Miklós. Miskolc , 1985. 153 p., [3] leaves of plates : ISBN 963-01-6902-9 : LC Card 87-408020
HE6980.5 .K36 1985

L'Etat anthropophage /. Peffer, Michel, 1948- Bruxelles , c1982. 279 p. ; ISBN 2-87005-164-5 LC Card 84-139080
HJ1197 .P44 1982

Etat breton aux quatorzième et quinzième siècles. Kerhervé, Jean. L'Etat breton aux 14e et 15e siècles . Paris , c1987. 2 v. (xii, x, 1078 p.) : ISBN 2-224-01703-0 (t. 1) LC Card 87-160693
HJ1078.B75 K47 1987

L'Etat breton aux 14e et 15e siècles . Kerhervé, Jean. Paris , c1987. 2 v. (xii, x, 1078 p.) : ISBN 2-224-01703-0 (t. 1) LC Card 87-160693
HJ1078.B75 K47 1987

Etat de besoin, besoin d'Etat . Schoonbroodt, Jos., 1936- Bruxelles , c1985. 272 p. : ISBN 2-87003-196-3 LC Card 86-146944 DDC 338.9493 19
HC315 .S17 1985

L'Etat industriel dans les politiques de sortie de crise . Escarmelle, Jean-François. Louvain-la-Neuve , 1986. 237 p. : ISBN 2-87077-301-3 : LC Card 86-229137
HD3616.B43 E84 1986

L'Etat-pieuvre /. Vedie, Henri-Louis, 1943- Paris , c1986. 172 p. : LC Card 86-219134
HD4165 .V38 1986

L'Etat providence /. Ewald, François. Paris , c1986. 608 p. ; ISBN 2-246-30731-7 : LC Card 86-160935
HD7175 .E93 1986

L'Etat solide . Brunelle, Dorval. Montréal, Québec , 1982. 174 p. : ISBN 2-89132-677-6 (pbk.) LC Card 87-672120
HC115 .B773x 1982

Etats régionaux de l'environnement. Livre blanc de l'environnement . [S.l. , 1982] (Caen : Impr. P.A.C.) 1 portfolio (32 p.) : LC Card 83-209058
HC277.B28 L58 1982

Les Etats-Unis à l'horizon de la troisième révolution industrielle /. Rivière, Jean, professeur. Nancy , c1986. 207 p. : ISBN 2-86480-174-4 LC Card 86-202607
HC106.8 .R57 1986

ETCO (Firm : Iran) Sāzmān-i Barnāmah (Iran) Feeder Road Programme . Tehran [1961?] ii, 117, 9 leaves, [59] leaves of plates (some folded) : LC Card 85-211363
HE365.I73 R857 1961

Ethanol, employment, and development . Pereira, A. (Armand) Geneva , 1986. xiv, 195 p. : ISBN 92-2-105380-6 (pbk.) : LC Card 87-107819 DDC 338.4/7662669 19
HD9502.5.A433 B646 1986

Etheridge, Elizabeth W. Head, Sylvia. The neighborhood mint . Macon, Ga. , c1986. xviii, 206 p. : ISBN 0-86554-240-6 (alk. paper) : LC Card 86-23500 DDC 737.49758/273 19
HG461.D342 H4 1986

Ethical dilemmas in the modern corporation /. Cavanagh, Gerald F. Englewood Cliffs, NJ , c1988. x, 198 p. : ISBN 0-13-290058-0 (pbk.) LC Card 87-25726 DDC 174/.4 19
HF5387 .C38 1988

ETHICS - ADDRESSES, ESSAYS, LECTURES.
Tarkunde, V. M. For freedom /. New Delhi , 1984. xii, 199 p. ; LC Card 84-902126 DDC 144 19
B821 .T285 1984 ***NYPL [JFD 87-1740]***

Ethics and morals in business /. Natale, Samuel M. Birmingham, Ala. , c1987. 209 p. ; ISBN 0-89135-036-5 LC Card 87-9424 DDC 174/.4 19
HF5387 .N36 1987

Ethics and Public Policy Center (Washington, D. C.) Sincere, Richard E. The politics of sentiment . Washington, D.C. : Lanham, MD ; xiv, 164 p. : ISBN 0-89633-116-4 (alk. paper) : LC Card 87-13441 DDC 332.6/73/0968 19
HG5851.A3 S56 1987

ETHICS, COMMERCIAL. see **BUSINESS ETHICS.**

Ethics, economics, and the state /. Hamlin, Alan P., 1951- Brighton, Sussex , 1986. x, 198 p. ; ***NYPL [JLD 86-3648]***

ETHICS - HISTORY.
Sichirollo, Livio. Morale e morali /. Roma , 1985. 179 p. ; ISBN 88-359-2798-6 : LC Card 85-233121 DDC 170/.9 19
BJ74 .S53 1985 ***NYPL [JFD 87-941]***

Ethics in management /. Goodpaster, Kenneth E., 1944- Boston , c1984. 154 p. : ISBN 0-87584-165-1 (course module : pbk.) LC Card 84-12847 DDC 174/.4 19
HF5387 .G66 1984

ETHICS, MODERN - 18TH CENTURY.
Markt, Staat und Solidarität bei Adam Smith /. Frankfurt , New York , c1984. 238 p. ; ISBN 3-593-33338-4 LC Card 84-202891
HB103.S6 M27 1984

The ethics of F.A. Hayek /. Walker, Graham. Lanham, MD , c1986. vii, 135 p. ; ISBN 0-8191-5250-1 (alk. paper) : LC Card 86-1515 DDC 171/.7 19
HB101.H39 W35 1986
NYPL [JFD 86-9138]

The ethics of management /. Hosmer, LaRue T. Homewood, Ill. , 1987. xiii, 185 p. : ISBN 0-256-03480-X LC Card 86-81804 DDC 174/.4 19
HF5387 .H67 1987

ETHICS, PRACTICAL. see **ETHICS.**

ETHICS, SOCIAL. see **SOCIAL ETHICS.**

Ethier, Wilfred. Modern international economics / Wilfred J. Ethier. 2nd ed. New York : Norton, c1988. xx, 556, 62 p. : ill. ; 25 cm. Includes bibliographies and index. "Source material in international economics": p. 43-46 (second group)
ISBN 0-393-95556-7 LC Card 87-21762 DDC 337 19
1. International economic relations. I. Title.
HF1411 .E824 1988

Ethik, Kultur, Entwicklung . Watzal, Ludwig, 1950- Göttingen , c1985. 131 p. ; ISBN 3-7881-1741-9 LC Card 86-122983 DDC 338.9 19
HD75 .W37 1985

Ethik und Wirtschaftswissenschaft / von C. Richard Barrett ... [et al.] ; herausgegeben von Georges Enderle. Berlin : Duncker & Humblot, c1985. 276 p. : ill. ; 24 cm. (Schriften des Vereins für Socialpolitik, Gesellschaft für Wirtschafts- und Sozialwissenschaften . n.F., Bd. 147) Contributions in German; one contribution in English. Papers presented at the St. Galler Forschungsgespräch, held Sept. 10-12, 1984. Includes bibliographies. CONTENTS. - Wirtschaftsethik als wissenschaftliche Disziplin? / von Jürgen Mittelstrass -- Ökonomische Rationalität und praktische Vernunft / von Oswald Schwemmer -- Anthropologie und Sachgesetzlichkeit im Dialog zwischen Moraltheologie und Wirtschaftsethik / von Franz Böckle -- On vague preferences / by C. Richard Barrett and Prasanta K. Pattanaik -- Egoismus, Altruismus und ökonomische Effizienz / von Günter Gabisch -- Einige Theorien der Verteilungsgerechtigkeit im Vergleich / von Wulf Gaertner -- Ethik, Selbstinteresse und bonum commune / von Horst Claus Recktenwald -- Sicherung des Exixtenzminimums für alle Menschen / von Georges Enderle -- Vermögensmaximierung als ethisches Prinzip? / von Rupert Windisch -- Die ethische Problematik von Allokationsentscheidungen / von Gérard Gäfgen.
ISBN 3-428-05910-7 LC Card 86-132826
1. Economics - Moral and ethical aspects - Congresses. I. Barrett, C. Richard. II. Enderle, Georges. III. St. Galler Forschungsgespräch (1984). IV. Series.
HB72 .E79 1985

Ethiopia /. Payne, Eric. Hampstead Norreys, Newbury, Berkshire, England , 1981-1982. 8 v. in 1 : LC Card 87-166672
HE6185.E8 P39 1981

Ethiopia. Central Statistical Office.
Average producers' prices of agricultural commodities in rural area by region, Miazia 1973-Miazia 1974, (May 1981-April 1982) /. Addis Ababa , 1985. 14 leaves ; LC Card 85-981293 DDC 338.1/3/0963021 19
HD2124.5 .A93 1985

Population of weredas and towns, by sex and average household size, based on the preliminary census results, and population projections by age, sex groups, and rural-urban, for total country and regions, 1984-1995 /. Addis Ababa [1985] 370 p. ; LC Card 86-980450 DDC 304.6/0963/021 19
HA4689 .P67 1985

The Rural integrated household survey programme . Addis Abeba [1983] 52 leaves ; LC Card 86-980701 DDC 307.7/2/0723 19
HB2542.A3 R87 1983

Rural labour force survey, April 1981-April 1982 /. Addis Ababa , 1985. xii, 170 p. ; LC Card 86-981178 DDC 331.1/0963 19
HD5839.7.A6 R87 1985

Ethiopia. Community Forests and Soil Conservation Development Dept. Yeraswork Admassie. Food-for-work in Ethiopia . Addis Abeba , 1985. viii, 102, [58] leaves : LC Card 86-980537 DDC 339.5/0963 19
HD5839.7.A6 Y47 1985

Ethiopia, deportations and forced-labour camps . Niggli, Peter, 1950- [Äthiopien, Deportationen und Zwangsarbeitslager. English.] [Berlin , 1986] 86 p., [1] leaf of plates : LC Card 87-131977 DDC 333.3/1/63 19
HD979 .N3413 1986

Ethiopia. Early Warning and Planning Services.
Belg (small) crop season synoptic report. Addis Abeba, Ethiopia , 1985. 23 leaves : LC Card 86-980254 DDC 338.1/9/63 19
HD9017.E82 B44 1985

Belg synoptic report [microform] . Addis Abeba, Ethiopia [1981] iv, 21 leaves : LC Card 82-980790 DDC 363.8/0963 19
HD9017.E82 B45 1981
NYPL [*ZT-1708 no.19]

ETHIOPIA - ECONOMIC CONDITIONS - 1974- - STATISTICS.
Drought situation in Ethiopia and assistance requirements 1984/85 /. Addis Ababa [1984] 55 leaves in various pagings : LC Card 85-980926
HC845.Z9 F32x 1984

ETHIOPIA - FULL EMPLOYMENT POLICIES.
Yeraswork Admassie. Food-for-work in Ethiopia . Addis Abeba , 1985. viii, 102, [58] leaves : LC Card 86-980537 DDC 339.5/0963 19
HD5839.7.A6 Y47 1985

ETHIOPIA - POLITICS AND GOVERNMENT - 1974-
Clay, Jason W. Politics and the Ethiopian famine, 1984-1985 /. Cambridge, MA (11 Divinity Ave., Cambridge 02138) , 1985. xi, 250 p. : LC Card 86-153948 DDC 363.8/56/0963 19
HC845.Z9 F33 1985 ***NYPL [JLF 87-364]***

Harris, Myles F. Breakfast in hell . New York , c1987. 271 p. ; ISBN 0-671-63272-8 : LC Card 86-25504 DDC 363.8/83/0963 19
HC845.Z9 F345 1987

ETHIOPIA - POPULATION, RURAL.
The Rural integrated household survey programme . Addis Abeba [1983] 52 leaves ; LC Card 86-980701 DDC 307.7/2/0723 19
HB2542.A3 R87 1983

ETHIOPIA - POPULATION - STATISTICS.
Population of weredas and towns, by sex and average household size, based on the preliminary census results, and population projections by age, sex groups, and rural-urban, for total country and regions, 1984-1995 /. Addis Ababa [1985] 370 p. ; LC Card 86-980450 DDC 304.6/0963/021 19
HA4689 .P67 1985

ETHIOPIA - PUBLIC WORKS.
Yeraswork Admassie. Food-for-work in Ethiopia . Addis Abeba , 1985. viii, 102, [58] leaves : LC Card 86-980537 DDC 339.5/0963 19
HD5839.7.A6 Y47 1985

Ethiopia. Relief and Rehabilitation Commission.
Combatting the effects of cyclical drought in Ethiopia. Addis Ababa, Ethiopia [1985] 56 p. : LC Card 86-224201 DDC 363.8/83/0963 19
HC845.Z9 F332 1985

Drought situation in Ethiopia and assistance requirements 1984/85 /. Addis Ababa [1984] 55 leaves in various pagings : LC Card 85-980926
HC845.Z9 F32x 1984

ETHIOPIA - RURAL CONDITIONS.
The Rural integrated household survey programme . Addis Abeba [1983] 52 leaves ; LC Card 86-980701 DDC 307.7/2/0723 19
HB2542.A3 R87 1983

Ethiopia. State Forests Conservation and Development Dept. Yeraswork Admassie. Food-for-work in Ethiopia . Addis Abeba , 1985. viii, 102, [58] leaves : LC Card 86-980537 DDC 339.5/0963 19
HD5839.7.A6 Y47 1985

Ethiopia's bitter medicine, settling for disaster : an evaluation of the Ethiopian government's resettlement programme, a report from Survival International / with photographs by Mike Goldwater ; edited by Marcus Colchester and Virginia Luling. London : Survival International for the Rights of Threatened Tribal Peoples, 1986. 55 p. : ill. ; 21 cm. (Survival International documents . new ser., 3rd) Bibliography: p. 48-54.
ISBN 0-946592-01-2 (pbk.) LC Card 86-232852 DDC 333.3/1/63
1. Land settlement - Government policy - Ethiopia. 2. Refugees - Ethiopia. I. Goldwater, Mike. II. Colchester, Marcus. III. Luling, Virginia. IV. Survival International. V. Series.
HD979.Z63 E74 1986

Ethiopie, du bon usage de la famine /. Jean, François. Paris [1986] 102 p. : LC Card 87-131143
HC845.Z9 F347 1986

Ethiopie, la face cachée /. Franey, Jean-Pierre. Paris , c1986. 127 p. : ISBN 2-209-05848-1 : LC Card 87-113107
HC845.Z9 F34 1986

Ethnic business enterprise . Min, Pyong Gap, 1942- Staten Island, N.Y. , 1988. p. cm. ISBN 0-934733-15-5 : LC Card 86-33366 DDC 338.6/422/0899570758231 19
HD2346.U52 A845 1988

ETHNIC FOOD INDUSTRY.
The New ethnic food market . Norwalk, Conn., U. S.A. , c1986. xv, 142 leaves ; ISBN 0-89336-486-X (pbk.) LC Card 87-168111 DDC 381/.45641592/00973 19
HD9333.U62 N48 1986

ETHNIC FOOD INDUSTRY - UNITED STATES.
The New ethnic food market . Norwalk, Conn., U. S.A. , c1986. xv, 142 leaves ; ISBN 0-89336-486-X (pbk.) LC Card 87-168111 DDC 381/.45641592/00973 19
HD9333.U62 N48 1986

ETHNIC GROUPS - GOVERNMENT POLICY - DEVELOPING COUNTRIES.
Ethnic preference and public policy in developing states /. Boulder, Colo. , 1986. ix, 203 p. ; ISBN 0-931477-89-1 : LC Card 86-13505 DDC 323.1/09172/4 19
JF1063.D44 E87 1986 ***NYPL [JLE 86-4694]***

Ethnic preference and public policy in developing states / edited by Neil Nevitte and Charles H. Kennedy. Boulder, Colo. : Lynne Rienner Publishers, 1986. ix, 203 p. ; 24 cm. Includes bibliographies and index. ISBN 0-931477-89-1 : LC Card 86-13505 DDC 323.1/09172/4 19
1. Ethnic groups - Government policy - Developing countries. 2. Developing countries - Ethnic relations. 3. Developing countries - Politics and government. 4. Developing countries - Economic conditions - Regional disparities. I. Nevitte, Neil. II. Kennedy, Charles H.
JF1063.D44 E87 1986 ***NYPL [JLE 86-4694]***

Ethnicity and fertility in Thailand /. Suchart Prasithrathsint. Singapore , 1985. xviii, 270 p. : ISBN 997-19-8813-5 ***NYPL [JLE 86-3668]***

ETHNICITY - THAILAND.
Suchart Prasithrathsint. Ethnicity and fertility in Thailand /. Singapore , 1985. xviii, 270 p. : ISBN 997-19-8813-5 ***NYPL [JLE 86-3668]***

ETHNICITY - UKRAINE - ODESSA - HISTORY.
Weinberg, Robert. Social democracy and workers in Odessa . Pittsburgh, Pa. (4E23

Forbes Quad, Pittsburgh 15260) [1986] 34 p. ; LC Card 86-199472
HD8530.O32 W45 1986

Ethnikē Trapeza tēs Hellados.
Chelmēs, D. (Dēmētrios), 1894-1967. Ekthesis tou dioikētou k-ou Dēmētriou E. Chelmē ex onomatos tou Dioikētikou Symvouliou tēs Trapezēs kata tēn genikēn syneleusin tōn metochōn tēs 25ēs Maiou 1964. Athēnai , 1964. 55 p. ; LC Card 87-109901
HC295 .C45 1964

ETHNIKĒ TRAPEZA TĒS HELLADOS.
Chelmēs, D. (Dēmētrios), 1894-1967. Ekthesis tou dioikētou k-ou Dēmētriou E. Chelmē ex onomatos tou Dioikētikou Symvouliou tēs Trapezēs kata tēn genikēn syneleusin tōn metochōn tēs 25ēs Maiou 1964. Athēnai , 1964. 55 p. ; LC Card 87-109901
HC295 .C45 1964

Ethnikē Trapeza tēs Hellados. Dioikētikon Symvoulion. Chelmēs, D. (Dēmētrios), 1894-1967. Ekthesis tou dioikētou k-ou Dēmētriou E. Chelmē ex onomatos tou Dioikētikou Symvouliou tēs Trapezēs kata tēn genikēn syneleusin tōn metochōn tēs 25ēs Maiou 1964. Athēnai , 1964. 55 p. ; LC Card 87-109901
HC295 .C45 1964

ETHNIKĒ TRAPEZA TĒS HELLADOS - OFFICIALS AND EMPLOYEES - SALARIES, ALLOWANCES, ETC. - HISTORY.
Pizanias, Petros. Misthoi kai eisodēmata stēn Hellada, 1842-1923 . Athēna , 1985. 324 p., [20] p. of plates : LC Card 87-111106
HG3250.5.A7 P59 1985

Ethniko Kentro Koinōnikōn Ereunōn (Greece)
Phrankos, Dionysios M., 1926- Hoi makrochronies exelixeis tou oikonomika mē energou plēthysmou tēs Hellados /. Athēna , 1983. 148 p. : LC Card 85-152730
HD5811.83.A6 P47 1983

ETHNOLOGY - ADDRESSES, ESSAYS, LECTURES.
Historische Anthropologie . Göttingen , c1984. 166 p. ; ISBN 3-525-33497-4 LC Card 84-203590 DDC 306/.09 19
GN345.2 .H57 1984 ***NYPL [JFC 86-1764]***

ETHNOLOGY - ARGENTINA - CORRIENTES - CASE STUDIES.
Proyecto Paraná Medio . Buenos Aires , 1985. 44 leaves : LC Card 86-218225
HD8039.F66 A746 1985

ETHNOLOGY - ARGENTINA - ENTRE RÍOS - CASE STUDIES.
Proyecto Paraná Medio . Buenos Aires , 1985. 44 leaves : LC Card 86-218225
HD8039.F66 A746 1985

ETHNOLOGY - PARANÁ RIVER VALLEY (BRAZIL-ARGENTINA) - CASE STUDIES.
Proyecto Paraná Medio . Buenos Aires , 1985. 44 leaves : LC Card 86-218225
HD8039.F66 A746 1985

ETHNOLOGY - PENNSYLVANIA - SCRANTON REGION - HISTORY - ADDRESSES, ESSAYS, LECTURES.
Hard coal, hard times . Scranton , 1984, c1983. xv, 193 p. ; ISBN 0-917445-00-7 LC Card 85-156422 DDC 331.7/622335/0974837
HD8039.M62 U633 1984
NYPL [JLE 87-1218]

ETHNOLOGY - SOVIET UNION - HISTORY - MATHEMATICAL MODELS - ADDRESSES, ESSAYS, LECTURES.
Soviet quantitative history /. Beverly Hills , c1984. 216 p. : ISBN 0-8039-2082-2 LC Card 83-19196 DDC 306/.072047 19
HD715 .S5956 1984 ***NYPL [JLD 87-841]***

ETHNOLOGY - UNITED STATES - CONGRESSES.
Farm work and fieldwork . Ithaca , 1987. 293 p. : ISBN 0-8014-9446-X (pbk. : alk. paper) LC Card 86-19960 DDC 305.5/55/0973 19
HD8039.F32 U635 1987

ETHNOLOGY - UZBEK S.S.R.
Lubin, Nancy. Labour and nationality in Soviet Central Asia . London , 1984. xix, 305 p. : ISBN 0-333-36739-1 LC Card 87-672162
HD5797.U9 L83x 1984b

ETHNOLOGY - ZAIRE.
Sala-Diakanda, Mpembele. Approche ethnique des phénomènes démographiques . Louvain-la-Neuve , 1980. 433 p. : LC Card 84-118066
HB3664.5.A3 S23 1980

ETHOLOGY. see **ETHICS.**

Etienne, Eddy V., 1947- Economie monétaire : théorie et pratique / par Eddy V. Etienne. Port-au-Prince, Haïti : Editions Etienne, [1986] 207 p. : ill. ; 21 cm. Bibliography: p. [189]-194. Includes index. LC Card 86-221340
1. Money. 2. Monetary policy. 3. Finance. I. Title.
HG221 .E92 1986

Étienne, Gilbert. Food and poverty : India's half won battle / Gilbert Etienne. New Delhi ; Newbury Park, Calif. : Sage Publications, 1987. p. cm. Bibliography: p. Includes index. ISBN 0-8039-9540-7 LC Card 87-16992 DDC 338.1/0954 19
1. Rural poor - India. 2. Food supply - India. 3. India - Rural conditions. 4. Agriculture - Economic aspects - India. I. Title.
HC440.P6 E86 1987

Etika pembangunan dalam pemikiran Islam di Indonesia / Nourouzzaman Shiddiqi ... [et al.] ; penyunting Machnun Husein. Cet. 1. Jakarta : Rajawali, 1986. xi, 270 p. ; 21 cm. "Kumpulan makalah dan hasil diskusi dari Seminar Etika Pembangunan Dalam Pemikiran Islam yang berlangsung di Yogyakarta akhir Februari 1985"--Pref. "Diterbitkan dalam rangka kerja sama dengan IAIN Sunan Kalijaga, Yogyakarta." Includes bibliographies. ISBN 979-421-043-9 (pbk.) LC Card 86-946413
1. Islam - Economic aspects - Indonesia. 2. Indonesia - Economic policy. 3. Economic development - Religious aspects - Islam. I. Shiddiqi, Nourouzzaman. II. Husein, Machnun, 1941-. III. Seminar Etika Pembangunan Dalam Pemikiran Islam (1985 : Yogyakarta, Indonesia). IV. Institut Agama Islam Negeri Sunan Kalijaga.
HC447 .E78 1986

ETIQUETTE, BUSINESS. see **BUSINESS ETIQUETTE.**

ETIQUETTE, OFFICE. see **BUSINESS ETIQUETTE.**

ETIQUETTE, TELEPHONE. see **TELEPHONE ETIQUETTE.**

ETIQUETTES. see **LABELS.**

Ėtnicheskiĭ sostav i ėtnosot͡sial'nai͡a struktura naselenii͡a Peterburga . I͡Ukhneva, N. V. Leningrad , 1984. 220 p., [1] folded leaf of plates : LC Card 85-116858
HB3608.L4 I94 1984 ***NYPL [*QGK 87-925]***

Etō, Hajime, 1935- R & D management systems in Japanese industry /. Amsterdam ; New York : ix, 331 p. : ISBN 0-444-86808-9 (U. S.) LC Card 83-20489 DDC 658.5/7/0952 19
HD45 .R2 1984 ***NYPL [JLD 87-107]***

Etonokani, Jean-René. Genèse et évolution du mouvement syndical congolais / Jean-René Etonokani. [Brazzaville? : s.n., between 1982 and 1986] (Brazzaville : Service polycopie de la Conférence épiscopale du Congo) 180 p., [20] p. of plates : ill. ; 21 cm. Bibliography: p. 175-176. LC Card 86-179682
1. Trade-unions - Congo (Brazzaville) - History. I. Title.
HD6878 .E86 1982

Etre constructif dans les négociations et les discussions /. Bellenger, Lionel. Paris , c1984. 182 p. ; ISBN 2-7101-0477-6 : LC Card 84-255673
HD58.6 .B45 1984 ***NYPL [JLE 87-551]***

ETS (COMPUTER PROGRAM)
Boose, John H. Expertise transfer for expert system design /. Amsterdam , New York , 1986. viii, 312 p. : ISBN 0-444-42634-5 LC Card 86-9044 DDC 006.3/3 19
QA76.76.E95 B66 1986
NYPL [JSE 86-1840]

Ettema, Wim. Small-scale industry in Malawi : a report on the vocational training and small-scale enterprise survey / presented by Wim Ettema. Zomba : University of Malawi, Centre for Social Research, [1983] iv, 50, [9] leaves, 9 p. : forms ; 30 cm. Cover title. "October 1983." Bibliography: leaves 49-50. LC Card 84-980489 DDC 338.6/42/096897 19
1. Small business - Malawi. 2. Occupational training - Malawi. I. University of Malawi. Centre for Social Research. II. Title.
HD2356.M3 E88 1983

Etterspørsel etter arbeidskraft i norske industrinæringer /. Stølen, Nils Martin. Oslo , 1983. 66 p. : ISBN 82-537-2001-7 : LC Card 84-191739
HD5800.A6 S76 1983

Etude de factibilité routière, Bujumbura-Cibitoke . Groupement Berger-BCEOM. [[Bujumbura] [1977] 162 p. : LC Card 82-980356
HE367.B872 G76 1977a

Etude de référence.
Martin, Fernand. La localisation de l'industrie pharmaceutique au Canada /. [Ottawa] , c1986. 48 p. ; ISBN 0-662-93544-6 LC Card 86-206756
HD9670.C22 M37 1986

Etude socio-économique sur la culture du riz irrigué dans le périmètre de Mugerero (S.R.D. Imbo) /. Bergen, D. Bujumbura , 1985. 96 leaves : LC Card 86-980581
HD9066.B952 B47 1985

Etude sur la petite et moyenne industrie et l'artisanat / coordonnateurs, P. Rutake, B. Taillefer. [Bujumbara] : CURDES, [1984] 7 v. in 6 : ill. ; 30 cm. + synthesis. "Décembre 1984." CONTENTS. - Contents: Etude no 1. Boulangeries de Bujumbura / C. Ntagungira -- Etude no 2. Les menuiseries modernes de Bujumbara / B. Bushoki -- Etude no 3. Les menuiseries artisanales en milieu rural et urbain / B. Taillefer, H. Hakizimana -- Etude no 4. Moulins et boulangeries en milieu rural / D. Banderembako -- Etude no 5. Le travail des fibres au Burundi / P. Rutake, P. Kalisa -- Etude no 6. Demande en produits à base de fibres, produits de la boulangerie et produits de la menuiserie à Bujumbura / S.N.E.S. -- Etude no 7. Interventions de l'administration et des organisations internationales vis-à-vis de la petite et moyenne industrie et de l'artisanat / P. Rutake. LC Card 86-980948
1. Small business - Burundi. 2. Artisans - Burundi. 3. Burundi - Industries, Rural. I. Rutake, P. (Pascal). II. Taillefer, Bernard. III. Université du Burundi. Centre universitaire de recherche pour le développement économique et social.
HD2346.B94 E78 1984

Etudes de la Faculté de droit et des sciences économiques de Tours.
Energie et décentralisation /. Paris , 1984. 297 p. : ISBN 2-7178-0782-9 : LC Card 84-249613
HD9502.F72 E5334 1984

Etudes et consultations économiques sarl.
Lebanese economic report. Beirut [1986] 137 p. : LC Card 86-231596 DDC 330.95692/044 19
HC415.24 .L43 1986

Etudes et documents du Centre de diffusion libanais.
Mesropian, André. Les relations du Liban avec la Communauté économique européenne /. Beyrouth, Liban [between 1972 and 1984] 65 p. ; LC Card 84-196415
HF1583.9.Z4 E865 1972

Etudes et documents (France. Ministère de la Coopération. Service des études et des questions internationales) .
(no. 30) Biraud, Gérard. L'aide britannique au développement . Paris , 1978. 17 leaves : LC Card 84-102197
HC60 .B52 1978

Etudes et documents (INRS-Urbanisation) .
(36) Bussière, Yves. Vieillissement de la population et demande de transport dans la région de Montréal . Montréal, Québec [1983] 83 p. : ISBN 2-89228-036-2 LC Card 84-177163
HE4509.M68 B88 1983

Etudes et recherches (France. Commissariat général du plan) .
(no 2) Urban, Sabine M.-L. Entreprises allemandes et coopération industrielle à l'échelle européenne . Paris , c1986. 162 p. : ISBN 2-11-001580-2 : LC Card 86-175800
HD2844 .U7 1986

Etudes et recherches (Québec (Province). Centre de recherche et de statistiques sur le marché du travail)
Jean, Diane. Le travail à domicile dans le vêtement pour dames . [Montréal] [1982] xi, 146, [1] p. : ISBN 2-550-02847-3 LC Card 83-242834
HD6073.C62 C25 1982

Etudes et recherches (Université de Liège. Département de science politique) .
(no 24) Hotterbeex, M. (Marcel) Les verbos de

la F.E.B. en 1979 /. Liège , 1982. 20 leaves ; LC Card 83-221745
HD6948.B4 H67 1982

Études méditerranéennes.
(fasc. 7 (1984)) Marchands ambulants et commerçants étrangers en France et en Allemagne fédérale /. Poitiers , 1984. 148 p. : LC Card 87-147724
HF5459.F8 M37 1984

Etudes méditerranéennes (Poitiers, France) . (fasc. 7) Marchands ambulants et commerçants étrangers en France et en Allemagne fédérale /. Poitiers , 1984. 148 p. : LC Card 87-147724
HF5459.F8 M37 1984

Etudes sur le renouveau économique dans le centre et le sud de la Manche . Gibon, Comte de (Paul), 1863-1929. Caen , 1919. 176 p. ; LC Card 85-666346
HC277.M26 G52x 1919

Etudes togolaises de population .
(no 1) Locoh, Thérèse. Comprendre les problèmes de population . Lomé, Togo , 1984. 72, [3], 3 p. : LC Card 87-131146
HB871 .L57 1984

(no 10) Dovi-Sodemekou, Folly B. (Folly Bebey) Emploi et éducation dans le 2e plan de développement économique et social du Togo /. Lomé, Togo [1985] 89, 52, 9, 2 p. : LC Card 87-131183
HD5846.5.A6 D68 1985

(no 9) Locoh, Thérèse. La fécondité en Afrique noire /. Lomé [1985] 36, 22 leaves : LC Card 87-126644
HB1071 .L63 1985

Etzioni-Halevy, Eva. National broadcasting under siege : a comparative study of Australia, Britain, Israel, and West Germany / Eva Etzioni-Halevy. New York : St. Martin's Press, 1987. xii, 228 p. ; 23 cm. Bibliography: p. 213-218. Includes index. ISBN 0-312-00772-8 : LC Card 87-4702 DDC 384.54 19
1. Public broadcasting - Australia. 2. Public broadcasting - Great Britain. 3. Public broadcasting - Israel. 4. Public broadcasting - Germany (West). I. Title.
HE8689.6 .E89 1987

Eu não tenho onde morar . Blay, Eva Alterman. São Paulo, SP [1985] 332 p. : ISBN 85-21-30298-3 : LC Card 85-211285
HD7323.S28 B56 1985

Eu preciso trabalhar : subsídios para o encontro sobre geração de renda pro menores. Rio de Janeiro : Ministério da Previdência Social, Secretaria de Assistência Social, Fundação Nacional de Bem-Estar do Menor : UNICEF, [between 1983 and 1986] 85 p. ; 28 cm. "Projeto 'Alternativas de Atendimento aos Meninos de Rua.'" LC Card 86-150189
1. Youth - Employment - Government policy - Brazil. 2. Youth - Employment - Brazil. I. Fundação Nacional do Bem-Estar do Menor. II. UNICEF. III. Projeto "Alternativas de Atendimento aos Meninos de Rua" (Brazil).
HD6276.B72 E9 1983

Euangelatou-Notara, Phlōrentia.

Euchner, Walter. Wirtschaftspolitik im britischen Besatzungsgebiet 1945-1949 /. Düsseldorf , 1984. 338 p. : ISBN 3-590-18124-9 LC Card 84-188669
HC286.5 .W5655 1984

Eucken Institut. see Walter Eucken Institut.

Eucker-Herresthal, Waltraud. Staatliche Eingriffe in den Mietwohnungsmarkt, Erfolgskontrolle und Reformvorschläge / wissenschaftliche Leitung, W. Hamm ; Bearbeiter, W. Eucker-Herresthal. [Mainz] : Forschungsinstitut für Wirtschaftspolitik an der Universität Mainz, [1985?] v, 242 p. ; 21 cm. Bibliography: p. 232-242. LC Card 87-407601 DDC 363.5/8 19
1. Rental housing - Government policy - Germany (West). 2. Rent control - Germany (West). 3. Rent subsidies - Germany (West). 4. Housing policy - Germany, West. I. Hamm, Walter. II. Title.
HD7288.85.G3 E92 1985

EUCLID'S ALGORITHM. see ALGORITHMS.

Eugen Schmalenbach : der Mann, sein Werk, die Wirkung / herausgegeben von Walter Cordes im Auftrag der Schmalenbach-Stiftung ; Autoren, Max Kruk, Erich Potthoff, Günter Sieben ; unter Mitarbeit von Harald Lutz. Stuttgart : Fachverlag für Wirtschafts- und Steuerrecht Schäffer, 1984. xvii, 478 p. : ill. ; 25 cm. Bibliography of works by E. Schmalenbach: p. 443-455. Includes bibliographical references and indexes. ISBN 3-8202-0295-1 LC Card 84-215889
1. Accounting - Germany, West - History. 2. Managerial economics - History. 3. Schmalenbach, E. (Eugen), 1873-1955. I. Cordes, Walter, 1907-. II. Kruk, Max. III. Potthoff, Erich. IV. Sieben, Günter. V. Schmalenbach-Stiftung.
HF5616.G3 E93 1984

Euler, Manfred. Haushalte mit ausgewählten staatlichen Transferzahlungen . Stuttgart , c1983. 352 p. : ISBN 3-17-007631-0 LC Card 83-117808
HC290.5.I5 H37 1983

EURE (FRANCE) - ECONOMIC CONDITIONS.
Durix, Pierre. Les structures économiques et sociales dans le Brionnais oriental aux XVIIe et XVIIIe siècles /. Dijon [1983] xxxiii, 608 p. : LC Card 86-200732
HC277.B68 D87 1983

EURE (FRANCE) - SOCIAL CONDITIONS.
Durix, Pierre. Les structures économiques et sociales dans le Brionnais oriental aux XVIIe et XVIIIe siècles /. Dijon [1983] xxxiii, 608 p. : LC Card 86-200732
HC277.B68 D87 1983

EURO-BOND MARKET.
Grabbe, J. Orlin. International financial markets /. New York , c1986. xi, 347 p. : ISBN 0-444-01032-7 LC Card 85-32545 DDC 332.4/5 19
HG3851 .G64 1986 ***NYPL [JLF 87-82]***

Euro-Construct (Firm : Neuilly-sur-Seine, France) Employment and housing renovation in Europe /. Luxembourg , Washington, DC , 1986. 89 p. : ISBN 92-825-6422-3 : LC Card 87-136222 DDC 331.2/89/083094 19
HD5718.B92 E863 1986

EURO-DOLLAR MARKET.
Grabbe, J. Orlin. International financial markets /. New York , c1986. xi, 347 p. : ISBN 0-444-01032-7 LC Card 85-32545 DDC 332.4/5 19
HG3851 .G64 1986 ***NYPL [JLF 87-82]***

Käsmeier, Josef H. Euromärkte und nationale Finanzmärkte . Berlin , c1984. 179 p. : ISBN 3-428-05595-0 : LC Card 86-134582 DDC 332.4/5 19
HG3897 .K375 1984
NYPL [JLL 74-61 Bd.117]

Sarver, Eugene. The Eurocurrency market handbook . New York, N.Y. , c1988. xiii, 384 p. : ISBN 0-13-296161-X LC Card 87-7739 DDC 332.4/5 19
HG3897 .S27 1988

EURO-DOLLAR MARKET - CONGRESSES.
Eurodollars and international banking /. London [Miami] , 1985. xiii, 226 p. : ISBN 0-333-36553-4 ***NYPL [JLD 85-3068]***

EURO-DOLLAR MARKET - HISTORY - 20TH CENTURY.
Hawley, James P., 1944- Dollars & borders . Armonk, N.Y. , c1987. xi, 204 p. ; ISBN 0-87332-386-6 : LC Card 86-31395 DDC 332/.041 19
HG3891 .H38 1987

Eurocomunismo e socialismo sovietico . Salvadori, Massimo L., 1908- Torino , 1978. xxvii, 161 p. ; LC Card 80-497655 DDC 324.245075 19
JN5657.C63 S24 ***NYPL [JLC 81-75]***

Eurocooperazione : studi economici europei : Spagna e Portogallo nella CEE. [Roma] : Europartners, [1986] 104 p. : ill. ; 21 cm. LC Card 86-219598
1. European Economic Community - Spain. 2. European Economic Community - Portugal. 3. Europe - Economic integration.
HC241.25.S7 E87 1986

The Eurocurrency market handbook . Sarver, Eugene. New York, N.Y. , c1988. xiii, 384 p. : ISBN 0-13-296161-X LC Card 87-7739 DDC 332.4/5 19
HG3897 .S27 1988

Eurodollars and international banking / edited by Paolo Savona and George Sutija. London : Macmillan ; [Miami] : in association with International Banking Center Florida International University, 1985. xiii, 226 p. : ill. ; 23 cm. A conference on Eurodollars was held in Miami organized by the International Banking Centre at Florida International University. Includes bibliographical references and indexes. ISBN 0-333-36553-4
1. Euro-dollar market - Congresses. 2. Banks and banking, International - Congresses. I. Savona, Paolo, 1936-. II. Sutija, George, 1926-. III. Florida International University. Internaional Banking Center.
NYPL [JLD 85-3068]

Eurofi (UK) Limited. Investment incentives worldwide . London ; Boston : 518 p. : ISBN 0-408-00990-X : LC Card 87-24928 DDC 332.6/7322 19
HG4516 .I58 1987

Euromärkte und nationale Finanzmärkte . Käsmeier, Josef H. Berlin , c1984. 179 p. : ISBN 3-428-05595-0 : LC Card 86-134582 DDC 332.4/5 19
HG3897 .K375 1984
NYPL [JLL 74-61 Bd.117]

Euromercati e finanziamento delle esportazioni /. Majnoni, Giovanni. Roma , Bologna , c1981. 130 p. ; LC Card 83-110156
HG3754.E86 M35 1981

Euromonitor Publications Limited. Consumer markets in Southern Africa. London , 1986. 173 p., [1] p. of plates : ISBN 0-86338-095-6 LC Card 87-160745 DDC 330.968/063 19
HF3900 .C66 1986

Europa hacia el sur (al hilo de la adhesión española a la Comunidad europea) /. Illescas Ortiz, Rafael. [Jerez] [1985], 1986 printing. 152 p. ; ISBN 84-600-4184-0 LC Card 86-150722
HC241.25.S6 I47 1986

Europa im Umbruch : die europäische Integration und die Schweiz / herausgegeben von Hans Fehr ; unter Mitarbeit von Walter B. Bing ... [et al.].2., Aufl. [Basel] : Verlag der "Basler Nachrichten", 1963. 91 p. ; 21 cm. Originally published in "Basler Nachrichten" in July and August, 1962. LC Card 85-125335
1. Europe - Economic integration. 2. European Economic Community - Switzerland. I. Fehr, Hans. II. Basler Nachrichten.
HC241 .E772 1963

L'Europa sindacale agli inizi degli anni '80 : Francia, Germania, Gran Bretagna, Svezia, Belgio / a cura di Guido Baglioni e Ettore Santi. Bologna : Il Mulino, c1982. 385 p. : ill. ; 22 cm. (Studi e ricerche. 138) At head of title: CESOS, Centro di studi sociali e sindacali. Includes bibliographical references and index. LC Card 84-140478 DDC 331.88/094 19
1. Trade unions - Europe - Case studies. I. Baglioni, Guido. II. Santi, Ettore, 1948-. III. Centro di studi sociali e sindacali (Rome, Italy).
HD6657 .E89 1982

Europa Union Deutschland. Landesverband Schleswig-Holstein. Schleswig-Holstein in Europa /. [Kiel] [1984?] 44 p. : LC Card 84-239599
HC287.S35 S39 1984

Europäische Agrarpolitik : wohin führt der Weg? / mit Beiträgen von K.P. Bruns ... [et al.]. Göttingen : ASG, 1985. 82 p. ; 21 cm. (Schriftenreihe für ländliche Sozialfragen, 0080-7133 . Heft 95) Papers presented at the spring meeting of the Agrarsoziale Gesellschaft, held on June 6-8, 1985 in Flensburg. CONTENTS. - Europa braucht gemeinsame agrarpolitische Ziele / Klaus Peter Bruns -- Bäuerliche Familienbetriebe / Günter Flessner -- Agrarpolitik als Teil des europäischen Einigungsprozesses / Werner Ungerer -- Europäische Perspektiven der Agrarpolitik aus der Sicht der Kommission der EG / Helmut Freiherr von Verschuer -- Europäische Perspektiven der Agrarpolitik aus der Sicht Grossbritanniens / Michael Strauss -- Europäische Perspektiven der Agrarpolitik aus der Sicht Dänemarks / Paul Ottosen -- Europäische Perspektiven der Agrarpolitik aus der Sicht der Bundesrepublik Deutschland / Christian Hofmann -- Zur zukünftigen europäischen Agrarpolitik aus der Sicht der Europäischen Föderation der Agrarischen Gewerkschaften (EFA) / Willi Lojewski -- Revision oder Umgestaltung der Gemeinsamen Agrarpolitik? / Jan Hinnekens. LC Card 86-170925
1. Agriculture and state - European Economic Community countries - Congresses. 2. Agricultural laborers - Government policy - European Economic Community countries - Congresses. I. Bruns, Klaus Peter. II. Agrarsoziale Gesellschaft. III. Series.
HD1920.5.Z8 E97 1985

Europäische Arbeiterbewegungen im 19. Jahrhundert : Deutschland, Österreich, England und Frankreich im Vergleich / mit Beiträgen von John Breuilly ... [et al.] ; herausgegeben von Jürgen Kocka. Göttingen : Vandenhoeck & Ruprecht, c1983. 169 p. ; 19 cm. (Kleine Vandenhoeck-Reihe. 1494) Includes bibliographies. ISBN 3-525-33488-5 (pbk.) LC Card 87-672976
1. Labor and laboring classes - Europe - Political activity - History - 19th century. I. Breuilly, John, 1946-. II. Kocka, Jürgen.
HD8378 .E97x 1983

Europäische Arbeiterpartei. see **European Labor Party.**

Europäische Commerzreisen um die Mitte des 18. Jahrhunderts /. Prokopp, Ludwig Ferdinand. Linz , c1982. xiii, 446 p., [1] folded leaf of plates : ISBN 3-85320-296-1 LC Card 83-150921
HF3548.C36 P76 1982

Europäische Einigung . Strizek, Helmut. Bonn , c1984. 144 p. ; ISBN 3-87831-274-1 LC Card 84-173216
HC241 .S72 1984

Europäische Gesellschaft für Meinungs- und Marketingforschung. see **Esomar.**

Europäische Konferenz der Verkehrsminister. see **European Conference of Ministers of Transport.**

Europäische Verkehrsminister-Konferenz. see **European Conference of Ministers of Transport.**

Europäische Wirtschaftsgemeinschaft. see **European Economic Community.**

Europäisches Koordinationszentrum für Sozial-Wissenschaftliche Forschung und Dokumentation. see **European Centre for the Co-ordination of Research and Documentation in Social Sciences.**

Europäisches Parlament. see **European Parliament.**

Az európai tőkés országok gazdaságföldrajza . Probáld, Ferenc, 1941- Budapest , 1984. 361 p. : ISBN 963-17-7607-7 : LC Card 85-154701
HC240 .P738 1984

Europaïsche Zentrale der Öffentlichen Wirtschaft. see **Centre européen de l'entreprise publique.**

Europarådet. see **Council of Europe.**

Europarat. see **Council of Europe.**

Europe and the international order.
Hall, Peter A. Governing the economy . Cambridge, U.K. , Oxford, U.K. , 1986. 341 p. ; ISBN 0-7456-0227-4 : LC Card 87-672535
HC256.5 .H256x 1986b

Europe and the rise of capitalism / edited by Jean Baechler, John Hall, and Michael Mann. Oxford [Oxfordshire] ; New York, NY, USA : B. Blackwell, 1987. p. cm. Based on papers from a symposium organized in September 1985 at Emmanuel College, Cambridge, under the title of "The European miracle", sponsored by the Economic and Social Research Council in co-operation with the Centre national de la recherche scientifique, Paris. Includes bibliographies and index. ISBN 0-631-15006-4 : LC Card 87-12293 DDC 330.94 19
1. Capitalism - Europe - History - Congresses. 2. Capitalism - Asia - History - Congresses. 3. Europe - Economic conditions - Congresses. 4. Asia - Economic conditions - Congresses. I. Baechler, Jean. II. Hall, John A., 1949-. III. Mann, Michael, 1942-. IV. Emmanuel College (University of Cambridge). V. Economic and Social Research Council (Great Britain). VI. Centre national de la recherche scientifique (France).
HC240.9.C3 E97 1987

EUROPE - COLONIES - AFRICA - ECONOMIC POLICY.
Rodney, Walter. How Europe underdeveloped Africa /. Washington, D.C. , 1981, c1972. xxiv, 312 p. ; ISBN 0-88258-105-8 LC Card 87-142601
HC800 .R62 1981b

EUROPE - COMMERCE - AMERICA - HISTORY.
Attman, Artur, 1910- American bullion in the European world trade, 1600-1800 /. Göteborg , 1986. 115 p. ; ISBN 91-85252-38-7 (pbk.) LC Card 87-147250 DDC 382/.4242/0973 19
HG285.A45 A88 1986

EUROPE - COMMERCE - ENGLAND - HISTORY.
Fryde, E. B. Studies in medieval trade and finance /. London , 1983. 1 v. (various pagings) ; ISBN 0-907628-10-9 LC Card 83-168474 DDC 382/.0942/04 19
HF3518.E85 F79 1983 ***NYPL [JLE 86-2481]***

EUROPE - COMMERCE - HISTORY.
Fremdling, Rainer. Technologischer Wandel und internationaler Handel im 18. und 19. Jahrhundert . Berlin , c1986. 493 p. ; ISBN 3-428-06042-3 LC Card 87-127793 DDC 382/.456691/094 19
HD9525.A2 F74 1986

Kürtz, Hans Joachim. Zu Zeiten der Hanse . Lübeck , c1983. 128 p. : ISBN 3-87498-330-7 LC Card 87-672840
HF455 .K87x 1983

EUROPE - COMMERCE - MIDDLE EAST - HISTORY.
Ashtor, Eliyahu, 1914- East-West trade in the medieval Mediterranean /. London , 1986. [344] p. ; ISBN 0-86078-193-3 LC Card 87-134358 DDC 382/.094/056 19
HF3756.Z7 E92 1986

EUROPE - COMMERCE - PORTUGAL - HISTORY.
Portugal, 1386-1986 . London [c1987] 156 p. : ISBN 0-947991-01-8 (pbk.) LC Card 87-404164 DDC 382/.09469/04 19
HF3698.E8 P67 1987

EUROPE - COMMERCE - STATISTICS.
André, J. L. da Costa. Portugal na Associação Europeia de Comércio Livre /. Lisboa , 1960. 98 p. ; LC Card 85-216282
HC241.4 .A56 1960

EUROPE - DEFENSES.
Achminow, Herman F., 1921- Am grossen Krieg "vorbeischleichen"? . Bonn , c1983. 304 p. ; ISBN 3-923920-00-8 LC Card 84-150915 DDC 355/.03304 19
UA646 .A38 1983 ***NYPL [JFD 87-1743]***

L'Europe du sud au milieu du gué /. Courlet, Claude. Grenoble , 1984. 122 p. ; ISBN 2-7061-0243-8 : LC Card 85-116696
HC244.5 .C68 1984

EUROPE, EASTERN - COMMERCE.
Holzman, Franklyn D. The economics of Soviet bloc trade and finance /. Boulder , 1987. xi, 215 p. : ISBN 0-8133-7274-7 (alk. paper) : LC Card 86-32598 DDC 382/.0947 19
HF3496.5 .H62 1987

Ost-Wirtschaftsreport Digest . Düsseldorf , Genève , 1977. 119 p. ; LC Card 84-154293
HC244 .O726 1977

EUROPE, EASTERN - COMMERCE - BRAZIL.
Kállay, Georges Christophe de. L'importance des marchés de l'Europe de l'Est . Genève , 1986. 247 p. ; LC Card 86-179357
HF3408.Z7 E8525 1986

EUROPE, EASTERN - COMMERCE - CZECHOSLOVAKIA.
Altmann, Franz-Lothar. Die tschechoslowakische Volkswirtschaft und der Rat für gegenseitige Wirtschaftshilfe (RGW) /. München [1986] 31 leaves ; LC Card 86-203484
HF3550.3.Z7 E8523 1986

EUROPE, EASTERN - COMMERCE - GERMANY, WEST.
Der Deutsche Osthandel 1982 /. Bonn [1982] 87 p. : LC Card 86-212991
HF3568.E35 D463 1982

Weimer, Theodor. Die Bedeutung des Osthandels für mittelständische Unternehmen /. Stuttgart , c1985. 172, 7 p. : ISBN 3-7910-5006-0 LC Card 86-160626
HF3568.E35 W43 1985
NYPL [JLL 73-505 Nr.5]

EUROPE, EASTERN - COMMERCE - SOVIET UNION.
Vneshniaia torgovlia SSSR so stranami SĖV /. Moskva , 1986. 108, [3] p. ; LC Card 86-213259
HF3628.E9 V54 1986

EUROPE, EASTERN - COMMERCE - SOVIET UNION - MATHEMATICAL MODELS.
Ėkonomiko-matematicheskie metody i modeli vo vneshneėkonomicheskoĭ deiatel'nosti /. Moskva , 1980. 179 p. : LC Card 87-109621
HF3626.5 .E45 1980

EUROPE, EASTERN - COMMERCE - UNITED STATES.
Lardy, Nicholas R. China's entry into the world economy . Lanham, MD , New York, N.Y. , c1987. xviii, 57 p. : ISBN 0-8191-6371-6 (alk. paper) : LC Card 87-10625 DDC 382/.0951 19
HF3820.5 .L37 1987

EUROPE, EASTERN - COMMERCIAL POLICY.
Brabant, Jozef M. van. Adjustment, structural change, and economic efficiency . Cambridge [Cambridgeshire] , New York , 1987. xviii, 480 p. ; ISBN 0-521-33455-1 LC Card 87-785 DDC 332.4/947 19
HG186.E82 B7 1987

EUROPE, EASTERN - ECONOMIC CONDITIONS.
Ost-Wirtschaftsreport Digest . Düsseldorf , Genève , 1977. 119 p. ; LC Card 84-154293
HC244 .O726 1977

EUROPE, EASTERN - ECONOMIC CONDITIONS - 1945-
Amort, Jiří. Dynamika národohospodářských struktur a mezinárodních ekonomických vztahů v podmínkách SEI /. Praha , 1986. 211 p. ; LC Card 86-206744
HC244 .A626 1986

Bondarenko, E. L. (Evgeniia Lavrent'evna) Zakonomernosti razvitiia sotsialisticheskikh mezhdunarodnykh proizvodstvennykh otnosheniĭ /. Moskva , 1983. 127 p. ; LC Card 84-200940
HC244 .B694 1983

Osobennosti khoziaĭstvennogo mekhanizma v zarubezhnykh stranakh--chlenakh SĖV . Leningrad , 1984. 54 p. ; LC Card 85-153742
HC244 .O723 1984

Prace z zakresu planowania i ekonomiki regionu /. Kraków , 1980. 220 p. : LC Card 80-131017
HB9 .K53 nr. 116 HC340.3

Pressler, Larry, 1942- Trip report, a visit to Eastern Europe in the wake of the 27th Soviet Party Congress and the Chernobyl nuclear accident (Czechoslovakia, Hungary, Yugoslavia, and Romania) on June 28, 1986 . Washington , 1987. vi, 58 p. ; LC Card 87-601360 DDC 337.47 19
HC244 .P744 1987

Problema tempov ėkonomicheskogo rosta v sovremennom mire /. Moskva , 1986. 383 p. : LC Card 87-124359
HC244 .P747 1986

Rabochiĭ klass i stroitel'stvo sotsializma v stranakh TSentral'noĭ i IUgo-Vostochnoĭ Evropy /. Moskva , 1977. 382 p. ; LC Card 81-174150
HD8376.5 .R33 1977

Winiecki, Jan. The distorted world of Soviet type economies /. Pittsburgh, Pa. , 1988. p. cm. ISBN 0-8229-1149-3 LC Card 87-25193 DDC 338.947 19
HC244 .W573 1988

Die Wirtschaftliche Entwicklung in den sozialistischen Ländern Osteuropas zur Jahreswende 1985/86 /. Hamburg , 1986. 336 p. ; ISBN 3-87895-295-3 LC Card 86-185852
HC244 .W5776 1986

EUROPE, EASTERN - ECONOMIC CONDITIONS - ANECDOTES, FACETIAE, SATIRE, ETC.
Broer, Wolfgang, 1944- Das rote Chaos . München , c1982. 237 p. ; ISBN 3-7844-7100-55 LC Card 87-672594
HC244 .B76x 1982

EUROPE, EASTERN - ECONOMIC INTEGRATION.
Amort, Jiří. Dynamika národohospodářských struktur a mezinárodních ekonomických vztahů v podmínkách SEI /. Praha , 1986. 211 p. ; LC Card 86-206744
HC244 .A626 1986

Bondarenko, E. L. (Evgeniia Lavrent'eva) Lichnoe potreblenie v usloviiakh ėkonomicheskoĭ integratsii stran--chlenov SĖV /. Moskva , 1984. 110 p. ; LC Card 84-222687
HC244.Z9 C613 1984

Bondarenko, E. L. (Evgeniia Lavrent'evna)

Zakonomernosti razvitiia sotsialisticheskikh mezhdunarodnykh proizvodstvennykh otnosheniĭ /. Moskva , 1983. 127 p. ; LC Card 84-200940
HC244 .B694 1983

Brabant, Jozef M. van. Adjustment, structural change, and economic efficiency . Cambridge [Cambridgeshire] , New York , 1987. xviii, 480 p. ; ISBN 0-521-33455-1 LC Card 87-785 DDC 332.4/947 19
HG186.E82 B7 1987

Bykov, A. N. (Aleksandr Naumovich) Sotsialisticheskaia integratsiia i nauchno-tekhnicheskaia revoliutsiia /. Moskva , 1981. 343 p. ; LC Card 82-101911
HC244.Z9 T43 1981

Bykov, A. N. (Aleksandr Naumovich) Sozialistische ökonomische Integration . Berlin , 1976. 218 p. ; LC Card 87-108725
HC244 .B94 1976

Konstantinov, IU. A. (IUriĭ Anatol'evich) Mezhdunarodnaia valiutnaia sistema stran--chlenov SĖV /. Moskva , 1982. 231 p. ; LC Card 82-210094
HG3942 .K67 1982

Leznik, A. D. (Aleksandr Davidovich) Upravlenie mezhdunarodnoĭ spetsializatsieĭ proizvodstva stran SĖV /. Moskva , 1982. 143 p. ; LC Card 83-123508
HC244 .L466 1982

SĖV -- osnovnye napravleniia sotrudnichestva . Moskva , 1984. 203 p. ; LC Card 85-177814
HC243.5 .S48 1984

Soglasovanie ėkonomicheskoĭ politiki stran SĖV /. Moskva , 1986. 287 p. ; LC Card 87-120408
HC244 .S5925 1986

Die Sozialistische Gemeinschaft . Berlin , 1985. 238 p. ; LC Card 86-120025 DDC 337.1/1717 19
HC243.5 .S685 1985

Stránská, Ludmila. Organizačně institucionální soustava řízení MSEI /. Praha , 1985. 167 p. : LC Card 86-215270
HC243.5 .S88 1985

TSarevski, Nesho Vŭlev. The People's Republic of Bulgaria . Sofia , 1986. 102 p. ; LC Card 87-123346 DDC 337.1/4977 19
HC403 .T748 1986

Vneshneėkonomicheskie sviazi stran-chlenov SĖV v usloviiakh sotsialisticheskoĭ integratsii /. Kiev , 1983. 245 p. ; LC Card 83-189711
HC243.5 .V54 1983

Vŭlkovski, Georgi Danov. Mezhdunarodni ikonomicheski otnosheniia pri sottsializma . Sofiia , 1985 [i.e. 1986] 151 p. ; LC Card 87-134453
HC244 .V84 1986

Zhamin, V. A. (Vitaliĭ Alekseevich) Sotsialisticheskaia ėkonomicheskaia integratsiia--faktor povysheniia ėffektivnosti proizvodstva stran SĖV /. Moskva , Varna , 1978. 93 p. ; LC Card 81-149558
HC244 .Z46 1978

EUROPE, EASTERN - ECONOMIC INTEGRATION - HISTORY.
Ladygin, Boris Nikolaevich. Istoricheskiĭ opyt sotrudnichestva stran SĖV /. Moskva , 1980. 284 p. ; LC Card 81-130900
HC244 .L282 1980

EUROPE, EASTERN - ECONOMIC POLICY.
Nielsen, Margit, 1950- Udenrigsøkonomi i Østeuropa . Esbjerg , 1985. 99 p. ; ISBN 87-88521-19-2 LC Card 85-227937
HF1531 .N54 1985

Osobennosti khoziaĭstvennogo mekhanizma v zarubezhnykh stranakh--chlenakh SĖV . Leningrad , 1984. 54 p. ; LC Card 85-153742
HC244 .O723 1984

Soglasovanie ėkonomicheskoĭ politiki stran SĖV /. Moskva , 1986. 287 p. ; LC Card 87-120408
HC244 .S5925 1986

Sovershenstvovanie sistemy narodnokhoziaĭstvennogo upravleniia v sotsialisticheskikh stranakh . Moskva , 1986. 196 p. ; LC Card 87-163453
HC244 .S595115 1986

Winiecki, Jan. The distorted world of Soviet type economies /. Pittsburgh, Pa. , 1988. p. cm. ISBN 0-8229-1149-3 LC Card 87-25193 DDC 338.947 19
HC244 .W573 1988

EUROPE, EASTERN - ECONOMIC POLICY - 1945-
Khoziaĭstvennyĭ mekhanizm funktsionirovaniia sotsialisticheskoĭ ėkonomiki /. Moskva , 1982. 358 p. ; LC Card 83-134242
HC243.5 .K47 1982

EUROPE, EASTERN - ECONOMIC POLICY - CONGRESSES.
Die Leistungsbewertung in der Industrie . Jena , 1983. 241 p. ; LC Card 84-176546
HD56.25 .L45 1983

EUROPE, EASTERN - ECONOMIC POLICY - DICTIONARIES.
Mikheev, S. Glossary of economic and social terminology in Eastern European socialist countries /. Geneva , 1986. 52, x p. ; ISBN 92-9014-413-0 : LC Card 86-214600 DDC 335.4/03/21 19
HB61 .M487 1986

EUROPE, EASTERN - ECONOMIC POLICY - ECONOMETRIC MODELS - CONGRESSES.
Macromodels and forecasts of national economy . Warszawa , 1986. 284 p. : ISBN 83-01-06464-1 (pbk.) : LC Card 86-226942 DDC 338.947 19
HC244 .M227 1986

EUROPE, EASTERN - FOREIGN ECONOMIC RELATIONS.
Nielsen, Margit, 1950- Udenrigsøkonomi i Østeuropa . Esbjerg , 1985. 99 p. ; ISBN 87-88521-19-2 LC Card 85-227937
HF1531 .N54 1985

Ost-Wirtschaftsreport Digest . Düsseldorf , Genève , 1977. 119 p. ; LC Card 84-154293
HC244 .O726 1977

Osteuropa im Blickpunkt . Linz [1985?] 168 p. ; LC Card 87-142952 DDC 382/.091713/01717 19
HF1411 .O687 1985

Sinkovics, Alfréd. Nemzetközi tőkemozgások és a KGST /. Budapest , 1986, c1985. 336, [1] p. : ISBN 963-221-493-5 : LC Card 87-408509
HG3891 .S57 1986

Vneshneėkonomicheskie otnosheniia sotsialisticheskikh stran v usloviiakh NTR /. Moskva , 1985. 215 p. ; LC Card 84-219529
HF1531 .V62 1985 ***NYPL [*QIP 87-2072]***

Vneshneėkonomicheskie sviazi stran-chlenov SĖV v usloviiakh sotsialisticheskoĭ integratsii /. Kiev , 1983. 245 p. ; LC Card 83-189711
HC243.5 .V54 1983

Vŭlkovski, Georgi Danov. Mezhdunarodni ikonomicheski otnosheniia pri sottsializma . Sofiia , 1985 [i.e. 1986] 151 p. ; LC Card 87-134453
HC244 .V84 1986

EUROPE, EASTERN - FOREIGN ECONOMIC RELATIONS - CUBA.
Kuba v mezhdunarodnom sotsialisticheskom razdelenii truda /. Moskva , 1986. 146 p. : LC Card 86-232928
HF1500.5.E852 K83 1986

EUROPE, EASTERN - FOREIGN ECONOMIC RELATIONS - DEVELOPING COUNTRIES.
Machowski, Heinrich. RGW-Staaten und Dritte Welt . Bonn , 1981. iii, 84 p. ; ISBN 3-7713-0167-X LC Card 85-224767
HF1532.15.D44 M33 1981

EUROPE, EASTERN - FOREIGN ECONOMIC RELATIONS - INDIA.
Indo-CMEA economic relations /. New Delhi , 1987. xviii, 263 p. ; ISBN 81-7024-078-6 : LC Card 87-901620 DDC 337.54047 19
HC433 .I535 1987

EUROPE, EASTERN - FOREIGN ECONOMIC RELATIONS - NIGERIA - CONGRESSES.
Economic co-operation between Nigeria and the socialist countries of Eastern Europe /. Lagos , 1986, c1984. 210 p. : ISBN 978-13-2828-2 (pbk.) LC Card 87-155295 DDC 337.669047 19
HF1616.7.Z4 E8523 1986

EUROPE, EASTERN - FOREIGN RELATIONS - 1945-
Pressler, Larry, 1942- Trip report, a visit to Eastern Europe in the wake of the 27th Soviet Party Congress and the Chernobyl nuclear accident (Czechoslovakia, Hungary, Yugoslavia, and Romania) on June 28, 1986 . Washington , 1987. vi, 58 p. ; LC Card 87-601360 DDC 337.47 19
HC244 .P744 1987

Europe, Eastern - Government. see **Europe, Eastern - Politics and government.**

EUROPE, EASTERN - INDUSTRIES.
Leznik, A. D. (Aleksandr Davidovich) Upravlenie mezhdunarodnoĭ spetsializatsieĭ proizvodstva stran SĖV /. Moskva , 1982. 143 p. ; LC Card 83-123508
HC244 .L466 1982

Ost-Wirtschaftsreport Digest . Düsseldorf , Genève , 1977. 119 p. ; LC Card 84-154293
HC244 .O726 1977

EUROPE, EASTERN - INDUSTRIES - LOCATION.
Territorial'nye struktury promyshlennosti /. Moskva , 1978. 128 p. : LC Card 81-147566
HC340.D5 T464 1978

EUROPE, EASTERN - MANUFACTURES.
Poznański, Kazimierz. Technology, competition, & the Soviet bloc in the world market /. Berkeley , c1987. ix, 226 p. ; ISBN 0-87725-170-3 (pbk.) : LC Card 87-3505 DDC 338/.06 19
HC244.Z9 T4716 1987

EUROPE, EASTERN - POLITICS AND GOVERNMENT - ANECDOTES, FACETIAE, SATIRE, ETC.
Broer, Wolfgang, 1944- Das rote Chaos . München , c1982. 237 p. ; ISBN 3-7844-7100-55 LC Card 87-672594
HC244 .B76x 1982

EUROPE, EASTERN - POPULATION.
Demograficheskie protsessy v sotsialisticheskom obshchestve. Hungarian. Demográfiai folyamatok a szocialista társadalomban az európai KGST országok példáján /. Budapest , 1984. 136 p. ; LC Card 85-154859
HB3581 .D4515 1984

Migrace a osídlení v socialistických zemích =. Praha , 1984- v. <1 > : LC Card 87-160334
HB2041 .M526 1984

Rakovskiĭ, S. N. (Sergeĭ Nikolaevich) Migratsii naseleniia v zarubezhnykh sotsialisticheskikh stranakh Evropy . Moskva , 1983. 152 p. ; LC Card 85-181642
HB2041 .R35 1983

EUROPE, EASTERN - POPULATION POLICY.
Demograficheskaia politika . Moskva , 1983. 187 p. : LC Card 84-145010
HB3581 .D44 1983

EUROPE, EASTERN - RELIGION.
Pressler, Larry, 1942- Trip report, a visit to Eastern Europe in the wake of the 27th Soviet Party Congress and the Chernobyl nuclear accident (Czechoslovakia, Hungary, Yugoslavia, and Romania) on June 28, 1986 . Washington , 1987. vi, 58 p. ; LC Card 87-601360 DDC 337.47 19
HC244 .P744 1987

EUROPE, EASTERN - SOCIAL CONDITIONS - ANECDOTES, FACETIAE, SATIRE, ETC.
Broer, Wolfgang, 1944- Das rote Chaos . München , c1982. 237 p. ; ISBN 3-7844-7100-55 LC Card 87-672594
HC244 .B76x 1982

EUROPE - ECONOMIC CONDITIONS.
Jones, E. L. (Eric Lionel) The European miracle . Cambridge , New York , 1987. xxxiii, 279 p., [1] leaf of plates : ISBN 0-521-33449-7 LC Card 87-8092 DDC 330.94/02 19
HC240 .J57 1987

Morineau, Michel. Incroyables gazettes et fabuleux métaux . London ; New York : 687 p. : ISBN 0-521-25384-5 : LC Card 83-7177 DDC 330.94/022 19
HC240 .M73 1985 ***NYPL [JLE 85-1587]***

Probáld, Ferenc, 1941- Az európai tőkés országok gazdaságföldrajza . Budapest , 1984. 361 p. : ISBN 963-17-7607-7 : LC Card 85-154701
HC240 .P738 1984

Theorie und Empirie in Wirtschaftspolitik und

Wirtschaftsgeschichte . Göttingen , 1984. 245 p. : LC Card 85-111313
HC284 .T46 1984

Theorie und Empirie in Wirtschaftspolitik und Wirtschaftsgeschichte . Göttingen , 1984. 242 p. : ISBN 3-509-01366-2 : LC Card 85-120064
HC240 .T45 1984

EUROPE - ECONOMIC CONDITIONS - TO 1492.
Day, John, 1924- The medieval market economy /. Oxford, UK , New York, NY, USA , 1987. p. cm. ISBN 0-631-15479-5 : LC Card 86-26862 DDC 330.94/01 19
HC41 .D39 1987

Herrmann, Joachim, 1932- Ökonomie und Gesellschaft an der Wende von der Antike zum Mittelalter . Berlin , 1979. 72 p. : LC Card 85-209249
HC31 .H47 1979

Wilson, David McKenzie. Economic aspects of the Vikings in the West-the archaeological basis /. Göteborg , 1980. 36 p. ; ISBN 91-7360-075-X (pbk.) LC Card 81-154587 DDC 330.94 19
HC41 .W55 1980

EUROPE - ECONOMIC CONDITIONS - 19TH CENTURY.
Meyer, Jean, 1924- Le poids de l'Etat /. Paris , c1983. 304 p. : ISBN 2-13-037770-X : LC Card 83-175028
HC280.D4 M49 1983

Tipton, Frank B., 1943- An economic and social history of Europe, 1890-1939 /. Baltimore , 1987. vii, 323 p. : ISBN 0-8018-3537-2 LC Card 87-3869 DDC 330.94/028 19
HC240 .T56 1987

EUROPE - ECONOMIC CONDITIONS - 20TH CENTURY.
Lutz, Burkart, 1925- Der kurze Traum immerwährender Prosperität . Frankfurt/Main , New York , c1984. 272 p. ; ISBN 3-593-33418-6 LC Card 85-131822
HC240 .L88 1984

Maier, Charles S. In search of stability . Cambridge [Cambridgeshire] , New York , 1987. x, 291 p. ; ISBN 0-521-23001-2 LC Card 87-6383 DDC 338.94 19
HC240 .M17 1987

Meyer, Jean, 1924- Le poids de l'Etat /. Paris , c1983. 304 p. : ISBN 2-13-037770-X : LC Card 83-175028
HC280.D4 M49 1983

Tipton, Frank B., 1943- An economic and social history of Europe, 1890-1939 /. Baltimore , 1987. vii, 323 p. : ISBN 0-8018-3537-2 LC Card 87-3869 DDC 330.94/028 19
HC240 .T56 1987

Trade unions and the economic crisis of the 1980s /. Aldershot, Hants, England , Brookfield, Vt., U. S.A. , c1987. x, 210 p. ; ISBN 0-566-05245-8 : LC Card 86-25641 DDC 331.88/094 19
HD6657 .T68 1987

EUROPE - ECONOMIC CONDITIONS - 1918-1945.
Tipton, Frank B., 1943- An economic and social history of Europe from 1939 to the present /. Baltimore, Md. , 1987. vii, 297 p. : ISBN 0-8018-3538-0 LC Card 87-3870 DDC 330.94/055 19
HC240 .T563 1987

EUROPE - ECONOMIC CONDITIONS - 1945-
La Conjoncture économique en Europe . Lisboa, Portugal [1982] 78 p. : LC Card 83-181663
HC240 .C588 1982

Donovan, Robert J. The second victory . New York , c1987. 128 p. : ISBN 0-8191-6498-4 (alk. paper) : LC Card 87-24021 DDC 338.91/73/04 19
HC240 .D65 1987

Drouin, Marie Josée. Western European adjustment to structural economic problems /. Lanham, MD , Indianapolis, IN , c1987. xxii, 259 p. : ISBN 0-8191-6527-1 (alk. paper) : LC Card 87-18909 DDC 330.94/0558 19
HC240 .D75 1987

Europe in the contemporary world . New York , c1986. ix, 297 p. : ISBN 0-677-21520-7 (pbk.) LC Card 86-212695 DDC 330.94/0558 19
HC240 .E8176 1986

Giersch, Herbert. Gegen Europessimismus . Stuttgart , c1986. 318 p. ; ISBN 3-421-06334-6 LC Card 87-672572
HF1411 .G53x 1986

Kindleberger, Charles Poor, 1910- Marshall Plan days /. Boston , 1987. x, 273 p., [1] leaf of plates : ISBN 0-04-332142-9 (alk. paper) LC Card 86-32163 DDC 338.91/73/04 19
HC240 .K454 1987

Reuter, Edzard, 1928- Vom Geist der Wirtschaft . Stuttgart , c1986. 288 p. ; ISBN 3-421-06311-7 LC Card 86-181795
HC240 .R44 1986

Späth, Lothar, 1937- [Wende in die Zukunft. English.] Facing the future . Berlin , New York , c1986. xvi, 196 p. ; ISBN 0-387-17105-3 (U. S.) LC Card 86-25994 DDC 338.943 19
HC286.7 .S713 1986

Stålindustri, kriseregioner og fagbevægelse . [Copenhagen] , 1983. 217 p. : LC Card 84-169019
HD9525.E752 S73 1983

Tipton, Frank B., 1943- An economic and social history of Europe from 1939 to the present /. Baltimore, Md. , 1987. vii, 297 p. : ISBN 0-8018-3538-0 LC Card 87-3870 DDC 330.94/055 19
HC240 .T563 1987

EUROPE - ECONOMIC CONDITIONS - 1945- - ADDRESSES. ESSAYS, LECTURES.
Economic crisis, trade unions, and the state /. London , Dover, N.H. , c1986. 295 p. ; ISBN 0-7099-1447-4 : LC Card 85-28055 DDC 331/.094 19
HD8391 .E26 1986 ***NYPL [JLD 86-1301]***

EUROPE - ECONOMIC CONDITIONS - 1945- - CONGRESSES.
Nationale Wege der Inflationsbekämpfung /. Berlin , c1986. 223 p. : ISBN 3-428-06077-6 LC Card 87-132310 DDC 332.4/1/094 19
HC240 .N315 1986

EUROPE - ECONOMIC CONDITIONS - 1945- - REGIONAL DISPARITIES.
Gosudarstvenno-monopolisticheskiĭ kapitalizm i razmeshchenie proizvoditel'nykh sil /. Moskva , 1984. 182 p. ; LC Card 84-239188
HC240 .G565 1984

Runggaldier, Ulrich. Le politiche regionali del lavoro . Milano, Italy , c1986. 160 p. ; LC Card 86-169484
HD8376.5 .R93 1986

EUROPE - ECONOMIC CONDITIONS - 1945- - REGIONAL DISPARITIES - CONGRESSES.
Periphere Räume . Paderborn , 1979. 183 p. : ISBN 3-506-73204-8 LC Card 85-209554
HC240 .P38 1979

EUROPE - ECONOMIC CONDITIONS - CONGRESSES.
Europe and the rise of capitalism /. Oxford [Oxfordshire] , New York, NY, USA , 1987. p. cm. ISBN 0-631-15006-4 : LC Card 87-12293 DDC 330.94 19
HC240.9.C3 E97 1987

International Congress on Economic History (8th : 1982 : Budapest, Hungary) Münzprägung, Geldumlauf und Wechselkurse . Trier , 1984. 421 p. : ISBN 3-923087-06-3 (pbk.)
HG205 1982 .I53 ***NYPL [JLE 86-3176]***

EUROPE - ECONOMIC CONDITIONS - REGIONAL DISPARITIES.
Technologie nouvelle et ruptures régionales /. Paris , c1986. 216 p. : ISBN 2-7178-1133-8 : LC Card 86-224660
HC240.9.T4 T42 1986

EUROPE - ECONOMIC POLICY.
Drouin, Marie Josée. Western European adjustment to structural economic problems /. Lanham, MD , Indianapolis, IN , c1987. xxii, 259 p. : ISBN 0-8191-6527-1 (alk. paper) : LC Card 87-18909 DDC 330.94/0558 19
HC240 .D75 1987

Henning, C. Randall. Macroeconomic diplomacy in the 1980s . London , New York , c1987. x, 76 p. ; ISBN 0-7099-3794-6 (pbk.) LC Card 87-20041 DDC 337/.09171/3 19
HF1455 .H46 1987

Maier, Charles S. In search of stability . Cambridge [Cambridgeshire] , New York , 1987. x, 291 p. ; ISBN 0-521-23001-2 LC Card 87-6383 DDC 338.94 19
HC240 .M17 1987

Späth, Lothar, 1937- [Wende in die Zukunft. English.] Facing the future . Berlin , New York , c1986. xvi, 196 p. ; ISBN 0-387-17105-3 (U. S.) LC Card 86-25994 DDC 338.943 19
HC286.7 .S713 1986

EUROPE - ECONOMIC POLICY - CONGRESSES.
Nationale Wege der Inflationsbekämpfung /. Berlin , c1986. 223 p. : ISBN 3-428-06077-6 LC Card 87-132310 DDC 332.4/1/094 19
HC240 .N315 1986

EUROPE - EMIGRATION AND IMMIGRATION.
Emigración y retorno . [Madrid] , 1981. 325 p., [2] folded leaves of plates : ISBN 84-500-5097-9 LC Card 82-145134 DDC 325.46 19
JV8251 .E49 1981 ***NYPL [JLE 86-3179]***

Rymarczyk, Jan. Migracja siły roboczej do krajów EWG i jej konsekwencje społeczno-gospodarcze /. [Wrocław] , 1982. 239 p., [4] folded leaves ; LC Card 83-153742
HB9 .B7522 nr. 218 HD8378.5.A2

L'Europe et le transport aérien /. Naveau, Jacques, docteur en droit. Bruxelles , 1983. 346 p. ; ISBN 2-8027-0304-8 LC Card 85-114595
HE9842.A4 N38 1983

EUROPE - FOREIGN ECONOMIC RELATIONS.
Henning, C. Randall. Macroeconomic diplomacy in the 1980s . London , New York , c1987. x, 76 p. ; ISBN 0-7099-3794-6 (pbk.) LC Card 87-20041 DDC 337/.09171/3 19
HF1455 .H46 1987

EUROPE - FOREIGN ECONOMIC RELATIONS - AFRICA.
Rodney, Walter. How Europe underdeveloped Africa /. Washington, D.C. , 1981, c1972. xxiv, 312 p. ; ISBN 0-88258-105-8 LC Card 87-142601
HC800 .R62 1981b

EUROPE - FOREIGN ECONOMIC RELATIONS - ASIA.
Das Dreieck Europa-Amerika-Asien /. [Diessenhofen] , 1986. 154 p. : ISBN 3-7253-0272-3 LC Card 86-231548
HC412 .D7 1986

EUROPE - FOREIGN ECONOMIC RELATIONS - CARIBBEAN AREA.
The Caribbean Basin and the changing world economic structure /. Groningen , c1986. 194 p. ; ISBN 90-01-18630-0 (pbk.) : LC Card 87-117415 DDC 330.9729/052 19
HC151 .C26 1986

EUROPE - FOREIGN ECONOMIC RELATIONS - GREAT BRITAIN.
Hogan, Michael J., 1943- The Marshall Plan . Cambridge [Cambridgeshire] , New York , 1987. xiv, 482 p. ; ISBN 0-521-25140-0 LC Card 86-31773 DDC 338.91/73/04 19
HC240 .H614 1987

EUROPE - FOREIGN ECONOMIC RELATIONS - MIDDLE EAST.
Ashtor, Eliyahu, 1914- East-West trade in the medieval Mediterranean /. London , 1986. [344] p. ; ISBN 0-86078-193-3 LC Card 87-134358 DDC 382/.094/056 19
HF3756.Z7 E92 1986

EUROPE - FOREIGN ECONOMIC RELATIONS - SOVIET UNION.
Blinken, Antony J. Ally versus ally . New York , 1987. ix, 193 p. : ISBN 0-275-92410-6 (alk. paper) : LC Card 86-25222 DDC 388.5 19
HD9581.S652 B58 1987

EUROPE - FOREIGN ECONOMIC RELATIONS - UNITED STATES.
Hogan, Michael J., 1943- The Marshall Plan . Cambridge [Cambridgeshire] , New York , 1987. xiv, 482 p. ; ISBN 0-521-25140-0 LC Card 86-31773 DDC 338.91/73/04 19
HC240 .H614 1987

Pullen, William George. World War debts and United States foreign policy, 1919-1929 /. New

York , 1987. 157 p. ; ISBN 0-8240-8088-2 : LC Card 87-23789 DDC 337.7304 19
HF1456.5.E8 P84 1987

Sanford, William F. The American business community and the European Recovery Program, 1947-1952 /. New York , 1987. xiv, 366 p. ; ISBN 0-8240-8091-2 (alk. paper) LC Card 87-23765 DDC 338.91/73/04 19
HC240 .S259 1987

US economic expansion . Moscow , 1986. 172 p. ; LC Card 86-204071 DDC 337.7304 19
HF3092 .U8 1986

EUROPE - FOREIGN POPULATION.
Charbit, Yves. Enfants, familles, migrations dans le bassin méditerranéen /. [Paris] , 1985. viii, 195 p. ; ISBN 2-7332-0110-7 (pbk.)
HQ792.E8 C47 1985
NYPL [JLL 72-295 cahier no 110]

EUROPE - FOREIGN RELATIONS - NORWAY.
Jørgensen, Nils-Johan. Norge mot Europa? . København , 1982. 250 p. ; ISBN 87-87733-30-7 : LC Card 82-172919
HC241.25.N7 J67 1982

EUROPE - FOREIGN RELATIONS - UNITED STATES.
Blinken, Antony J. Ally versus ally . New York , 1987. ix, 193 p. : ISBN 0-275-92410-6 (alk. paper) : LC Card 86-25222 DDC 388.5 19
HD9581.S652 B58 1987

EUROPE - FULL EMPLOYMENT POLICIES.
D'Angelillo, Massimo, 1956- Job creation . Milano, Italy , c1985. 231 p. ; LC Card 86-156936
HD5764.A6 D418 1985
NYPL [JLD 86-3248]

EUROPE - FULL EMPLOYMENT POLICY.
The Fight against unemployment . Cambridge, Mass. , 1987. xii, 204 p. : ISBN 0-262-12122-0 LC Card 87-5356 DDC 339.5/094 19
HD5764.A6 F54 1987

EUROPE - HISTORY - 1492-
Schulz, Knut. Handwerksgesellen und Lohnarbeiter . Sigmaringen , 1985. vii, 477 p., [20] p. of plates : ISBN 3-7995-7026-8 LC Card 85-149930
HD4885.E8 S38 1985 ***NYPL [JLE 86-1598]***

EUROPE - HISTORY - 20TH CENTURY.
Brown, Brendan, 1951- Monetary chaos in Europe . London , New York , c1987. p. cm. ISBN 0-7099-5035-7 : LC Card 87-23059 DDC 332.4/5/094 19
HG186.A2 B76 1987

Europe in the contemporary world : a special issue of World futures / edited by Ervin Laszlo. New York : Gordon and Breach Science Publishers, c1986. ix, 297 p. : ill. ; 23 cm.
"Papers from a symposium held at the United Nations University, Budapest, November 1985"--Cover. "Also appeared in World futures, volume 22, numbers 1 through 4"--T.p. verso. Includes bibliographies. "Bibliographic and reference materials": p. 271-297. CONTENTS. - The political and social economy of European globalism / Louis Emmeri -- European economic development with particular reference to the European periphery / Stefan A. Musto -- The structure of the European economy with particular reference to East European countries and East-West relations / Pawel Bozyk -- Management in Europe : countries and corporations / Bohdan Hawrylyshyn -- The situation and future of technology in Europe / Umberto Colombo and Giuseppe Lanzavecchia -- The "Europa paradigm" : European culture--world culture / Ivan Vitányi -- Youth and culture in Europe / Donato Fabbri Montesano and Alberto Munari -- An inventory of European social projects for peace and development / Bjorn Hettne. ISBN 0-677-21520-7 (pbk.) LC Card 86-212695 DDC 330.94/0558 19
1. Europe - Economic conditions - 1945-. 2. Europe - Social conditions. 3. Europe - Economic integration. I. Laszlo, Ervin, 1932-. II. World futures. III. United Nations University.
HC240 .E8176 1986

EUROPE - INDUSTRIES.
Reuter, Edzard, 1928- Vom Geist der Wirtschaft . Stuttgart , c1986. 288 p. ; ISBN 3-421-06311-7 LC Card 86-181795
HC240 .R44 1986

EUROPE - INDUSTRIES - HISTORY.
Theorie und Empirie in Wirtschaftspolitik und Wirtschaftsgeschichte . Göttingen , 1984. 242 p. : ISBN 3-509-01366-2 : LC Card 85-120064
HC240 .T45 1984

EUROPE - INDUSTRIES - HISTORY - 20TH CENTURY.
Lutz, Burkart, 1925- Der kurze Traum immerwährender Prosperität . Frankfurt/Main , New York , c1984. 272 p. ; ISBN 3-593-33418-6 LC Card 85-131822
HC240 .L88 1984

EUROPE - INDUSTRIES - LOCATION.
Gosudarstvenno-monopolisticheskiĭ kapitalizm i razmeshchenie proizvoditel'nykh sil /. Moskva , 1984. 182 p. ; LC Card 84-239188
HC240 .G565 1984

EUROPE - INDUSTRIES - LOCATION - ADDRESSES, ESSAYS, LECTURES.
New firms and regional development in Europe /. London , Dover, N.H. , c1986. 322 p. : ISBN 0-7099-1577-2 : LC Card 85-28372 DDC 338.7/1/094 19
HD2346.E9 N48 1986 ***NYPL [JLD 86-1597]***

Europe information. Development.
Commission of the European Communities. Directorate-General of Information. A Community research policy for development. Brussels [1983] 21 p. ; LC Card 85-166173 DDC 338.91/4/01724 19
HC60 .C584 1983

EUROPE, NORTHERN - COMMERCE - HISTORY.
Gilde und Korporation in den nordeuropäischen Städten des späten Mittelalters /. Köln , 1984. 114 p. ; ISBN 3-412-06883-3 LC Card 84-194645
HD6473.E853 G55 1984

Der Handel des frühen Mittelalters . Göttingen , 1985. 510 p. : ISBN 3-525-82433-5 (Deut. Bibl.) LC Card 86-209040
HF3495 .U57 1985 t. 3

EUROPE, NORTHERN - INDUSTRIES - HISTORY.
Gilde und Korporation in den nordeuropäischen Städten des späten Mittelalters /. Köln , 1984. 114 p. ; ISBN 3-412-06883-3 LC Card 84-194645
HD6473.E853 G55 1984

EUROPE - OCCUPATIONS.
Poppe, Johann Heinrich Moritz von, 1776-1854. Ausführliche Volks-Gewerbslehre, oder, Allgemeine und besondere Technologie zur Belehrung und zum Nutzen für alle Stände /. Stuttgart , Wien , 1833- v. <1 > : LC Card 87-409525 DDC 331.7/02/024042 19
HF5382.5.E84 P66 1833

EUROPE - OCCUPATIONS - HISTORY - ADDRESSES, ESSAYS, LECTURES.
Women and work in preindustrial Europe /. Bloomington , c1986. xviii, 233 p. ; ISBN 0-253-36610-0 LC Card 85-42829 DDC 331.4/094 19
HD6059.5.E85 W65 1986
NYPL [JLE 86-3381]

EUROPE - POLITICS AND GOVERNMENT.
Strizek, Helmut. Europäische Einigung . Bonn , c1984. 144 p. ; ISBN 3-87831-274-1 LC Card 84-173216
HC241 .S72 1984

EUROPE - POLITICS AND GOVERNMENT - 1918-1945.
Haigh, R. H. Soviet foreign policy, the League of Nations and Europe, 1917-39 /. Aldershot, Hants , 1986. x, 138 p. ;
NYPL [JFD 86-5778]

EUROPE - POLITICS AND GOVERNMENT - 1945-
Political stability and neo-corporatism . London , Beverly Hills , 1987. x, 276 p. ; ISBN 0-8039-8028-0 LC Card 86-63492 DDC 321.9 19
HD3616.E8 P64 1987

Rabochee dvizhenie v razvitykh kapitalisticheskikh stranakh . Moskva , 1987. 268 p. ; LC Card 87-164460
HD8378 .R29 1987

Wilensky, Harold L. Democratic corporatism and policy linkages . Berkeley , c1987. ix, 97 p. ; ISBN 0-87725-169-X (pbk.) : LC Card 87-3525 DDC 338.9 19
HD3616.E8 W54 1987

EUROPE - POPULATION - HISTORY.
Russell, Josiah Cox, 1900- The control of late ancient and medieval population /. Philadelphia , 1985. xv, 272 p. ; ISBN 0-87169-160-4 LC Card 83-71298
NYPL [JLF 85-844]

EUROPE - SOCIAL CONDITIONS.
Europe in the contemporary world . New York , c1986. ix, 297 p. : ISBN 0-677-21520-7 (pbk.) LC Card 86-212695 DDC 330.94/0558 19
HC240 .E8176 1986

Theorie und Empirie in Wirtschaftspolitik und Wirtschaftsgeschichte . Göttingen , 1984. 242 p. : ISBN 3-509-01366-2 : LC Card 85-120064
HC240 .T45 1984

EUROPE - SOCIAL CONDITIONS - TO 1492.
Herrmann, Joachim, 1932- Ökonomie und Gesellschaft an der Wende von der Antike zum Mittelalter . Berlin , 1979. 72 p. : LC Card 85-209249
HC31 .H47 1979

EUROPE - SOCIAL CONDITIONS - 1789-1900.
Tipton, Frank B., 1943- An economic and social history of Europe, 1890-1939 /. Baltimore , 1987. vii, 323 p. : ISBN 0-8018-3537-2 LC Card 87-3869 DDC 330.94/028 19
HC240 .T56 1987

EUROPE - SOCIAL CONDITIONS - 20TH CENTURY.
Tipton, Frank B., 1943- An economic and social history of Europe from 1939 to the present /. Baltimore, Md. , 1987. vii, 297 p. : ISBN 0-8018-3538-0 LC Card 87-3870 DDC 330.94/055 19
HC240 .T563 1987

Tipton, Frank B., 1943- An economic and social history of Europe, 1890-1939 /. Baltimore , 1987. vii, 323 p. : ISBN 0-8018-3537-2 LC Card 87-3869 DDC 330.94/028 19
HC240 .T56 1987

EUROPE, SOUTHERN - ECONOMIC CONDITIONS.
Courlet, Claude. L'Europe du sud au milieu du gué /. Grenoble , 1984. 122 p. ; ISBN 2-7061-0243-8 : LC Card 85-116696
HC244.5 .C68 1984

EUROPE, SOUTHERN - ECONOMIC CONDITIONS - REGIONAL DISPARITIES - CONGRESSES.
Ungleiche Entwicklung und Regionalpolitik in Südeuropa . Bochum , 1985. 282 p. : ISBN 3-88339-441-6 : LC Card 85-205651
HC244.5 .U48 1985

EUROPE, SOUTHERN - ECONOMIC POLICY.
Courlet, Claude. L'Europe du sud au milieu du gué /. Grenoble , 1984. 122 p. ; ISBN 2-7061-0243-8 : LC Card 85-116696
HC244.5 .C68 1984

Hē Eurōpē tōn deka. Hē Eurōpē tōn 10. [Athenai] [1981] 37 p. : LC Card 86-184401
HC241.25.G8 H42 1981

Hē Eurōpē tōn 10. [Athenai] : Hellēnikē Trapeza Viomēchanikēs Anaptyxeōs, [1981] 37 p. : ill. ; 27 cm. LC Card 86-184401
1. European Economic Community - Greece. I. Hellēnikē Trapeza Viomēchanikēs Anaptyxeōs (Greece). II. Title: Hē Eurōpē tōn deka.
HC241.25.G8 H42 1981

Europe/America .
(2) Unemployment and growth in the Western economies /. New York, N.Y. , c1984. x, 142 p. ; ISBN 0-87609-001-3 (pbk.) : LC Card 84-9415 DDC 331.13/791812 19
HD5707.5 .U54 1984 ***NYPL [JLE 86-1564]***

(6) A High technology gap? . New York, N.Y. , c1987. xii, 114 p. : ISBN 0-87609-021-8 (pbk.) : LC Card 87-6713 DDC 338/.06 19
HC240.9.T4 H54 1987

EUROPEAN AGRICULTURAL GUIDANCE AND GUARANTEE FUND.
Cuenca García, Eduardo. Las intervenciones financieras comunitarias /. Madrid [1985?] 53 p. ; ISBN 84-7196-523-2 LC Card 85-200493
HJ2094.5 .C84 1985

European Association for Industrial Marketing Research. Chemical Division. see European Chemical Marketing Research Association.

European Association for Industrial Marketing Research. European Chemical Marketing Research Association. see **European Chemical Marketing Research Association.**

European Association for National Productivity Centres. A Guide to small firms assistance in Europe /. Aldershot, Hants, England , Brookfield, Vt., U. S.A. , c1986. vii, 263 p. ; ISBN 0-566-05082-X : LC Card 85-27307 DDC 338.6/42/094 19
HD2346.E9 G85 1986 ***NYPL [JLG 86-205]***

European Association for Theoretical Computer Science. Symposium on Logic in Computer Science (1986 : Cambridge, Mass.) Proceedings, Symposium on Logic in Computer Science, Cambridge, Massachusetts, June 16-18, 1986 /. Washington, D.C. , Los Angeles, CA , 1986. xi, 383 p. : ISBN 0-8186-0720-3 (pbk.) LC Card 86-81090 DDC 004 19
QA75.5 .S9813 1986 ***NYPL [JSF 86-1041]***

European bills of entry and marine lists . McCusker, John J. Cambridge, Mass. , 1985. 75 p. : LC Card 86-673685
HE565.A3 M32 1985

European Centre for the Co-ordination of Research and Documentation in Social Sciences.
Automation and industrial workers . Oxford [Oxfordshire] , New York , 1979- v. : ISBN 0-08-023339-2 (v. 1, pt. 1) : LC Card 79-40811 DDC 331
HD6331 .A93 1979 ***NYPL [JLM 82-242]***

Technology and work . London , Dover, N.H. , c1986. 304 p. : ISBN 0-7099-3801-2 : LC Card 86-4202 DDC 303.4/83 19
HC244.Z9 T475 1986 ***NYPL [JLD 86-2160]***

European Centre for the Development of Vocational Training.
Equal opportunity counsellors . Berlin , Washington, DC , 1986. 50 p. : ISBN 92-825-6559-9 : LC Card 87-136233 DDC 331.13/3/094 19
HD4903.5.E8 E79 1986

Gizard, Xavier. Regional development and vocational training analysis and discussion of the relationship development . Berlin , Washington, DC , 1986. 49 p. ; ISBN 92-825-5911-4 (pbk.) : LC Card 87-137374 DDC 331.25/92/094 19
HD5715.5.E8 G58 1986

Morgan-Gérard, Florence. Equal opportunities and vocational training . Berlin [1982] 69 p. ; ISBN 92-825-2489-2 ***NYPL [JLD 87-1318]***

Promotion of cooperation amongst research and development organizations in the field of vocational training . Berlin , Washington, DC , 1986. 111 p. ; ISBN 92-825-6570-X (pbk.) : LC Card 87-133749 DDC 331.25/92/094
HD5715.5.E78 P77 1986

Raimond, Jean-Marie. Vocational training of young migrants in France /. Berlin , 1986. x, 101 p. : ISBN 92-825-6118-6
NYPL [JLG 87-134]

European Centre for Work and Society.
Social security and employment /. Assen, The Netherlands , 1983. 116 p. : ISBN 90-232-2011-0 (pbk.) : LC Card 83-216203 DDC 331.12/094 19
HD7164 .S594 1983 ***NYPL [JLE 86-1107]***

Sullerot, Évelyne. L'âge de travailler /. [Paris] , c1986. 224 p. : ISBN 2-213-01597-X : LC Card 86-176051
HD6283.E86 S85 1986

European Centre of Public Enterprise. see **Centre européen de l'entreprise publique.**

European Chemical Marketing Research Association. World petrochemicals . [Staten Island, N.Y. (139 Chestnut Ave., Staten Island 10305)] , c1985. 279 p. : LC Card 85-71088 DDC 338.4/7661804 19
HD9579.C32 W68 1985
NYPL [JLD 86-2185]

EUROPEAN COMMON MARKET (1955-) see **EUROPEAN ECONOMIC COMMUNITY.**

European Communities. Commission. see **Commission of the European Communities.**

European Communities. Council. see **Council of the European Communities.**

EUROPEAN COMMUNITIES - DICTIONARIES.
European Communities glossary . Luxembourg , 1984. 1589 p. ; ISBN 92-824-0131-6 : LC Card 85-175527
KJE926.5 .E87 1984 ***NYPL [JLF 87-216]***

Glossaire des Communautés européennes . Luxembourg , 1987, c1986. 706 p. ; ISBN 92-824-0410-2 : ***NYPL [JLF 87-217]***

EUROPEAN COMMUNITIES - DICTIONARIES - FRENCH.
EG-Wörterverzeichnis . Luxembourg , 1984. 1 v. (various pagings) ; ISBN 92-824-0123-5 LC Card 85-131398
KJE926.5 .E35 1984 ***NYPL [JLF 86-1818]***

European Communities glossary . Luxembourg , 1984. 1589 p. ; ISBN 92-824-0131-6 : LC Card 85-175527
KJE926.5 .E87 1984 ***NYPL [JLF 87-216]***

Glossaire des Communautés européennes . Luxembourg , 1987, c1986. 706 p. ; ISBN 92-824-0410-2 : ***NYPL [JLF 87-217]***

EUROPEAN COMMUNITIES - DICTIONARIES - GERMAN.
EG-Wörterverzeichnis . Luxembourg , 1984. 1 v. (various pagings) ; ISBN 92-824-0123-5 LC Card 85-131398
KJE926.5 .E35 1984 ***NYPL [JLF 86-1818]***

European Communities glossary : French-English = Glossaire des communautés européennes : français-anglais. 8th ed. Luxembourg : Office des publications officielles des Communautés européennes, 1984. 1589 p. ; 26 cm. At head of title: Council of the European Communities, General Secretariat. Includes index. ISBN 92-824-0131-6 : LC Card 85-175527
1. French language - Dictionaries - English. 2. English language - Dictionaries - French. 3. European communities - Dictionaries - French. 4. European communities - Dictionaries. I. Title: Glossaire des communautés européennes.
KJE926.5 .E87 1984 ***NYPL [JLF 87-216]***

European Communities glossary. Glossaire des Communautés européennes . Luxembourg , 1987, c1986. 706 p. ; ISBN 92-824-0410-2 :
NYPL [JLF 87-217]

The European Community /. Barnes, Ian. London , New York , 1988. p. cm. ISBN 0-582-29716-8 LC Card 87-16765 DDC 337.1/42 19
HC241.2 .B293 1988

The European Community and the management of international cooperation /. Hurwitz, Leon. New York , 1987. xvii, 267 p. ; ISBN 0-313-25030-8 (lib. bdg. : alk. paper) LC Card 87-229 DDC 337.1/4 19
HC241.2 .H87 1987

The European Community and the Mediterranean /. Duchêne, François. Luxembourg , Washington, DC , 1985. 102 p. : ISBN 92-825-5326-4 (pbk.) LC Card 87-119518 DDC 337.40182/2 19
HC241.25.M4 D83 1985

The European Community's development policy : the strategies ahead : conference organized at the College of Europe (Bruges, 4-6 July 1985) = La politique communautaire de développement : quelles stratégies pour demain? / C. Cosgrove & J. Jamar, eds. Bruges : De Tempel, 1986 285 p. : ill. ; 24 cm. (Cahiers de Bruges. n.s. 44) English and French. Includes bibliographies. LC Card 87-135534 DDC 338.94 19
1. European Economic Community - Economic assistance. I. Cosgrove Twitchett, Carol. II. Jamar, Joseph. III. Title: Politique communautaire de développement. IV. Series. V. Series: Cahiers de Bruges, n.s., 44.
HC60 .E7626 1986

European Conference of Ministers of Transport. Economic Research Centre. Report of the international seminar held in Paris on 15th-16th-17th January 1986 on the following topic, European dimension and future prospects of the railways /. Paris, France [Washington, D.C.] c1986. 289 p. : ISBN 92-821-1109-1 (pbk.) : LC Card 86-215627 DDC 385/.094 19
HE3005 .R47 1986

European Conference of Ministers Responsible for Regional Planning. The Regionalisation of transport and regional planning in practice . Paris, France [Washington, D.C.] c1984. 199 p. : ISBN 92-821-1091-5 (pbk.) : LC Card 85-180250 DDC 380.5/068 19
HE242 .R44 1984 ***NYPL [JLG 86-138]***

European Consortium for Political Research. Petersen, Ib Damgaard. The political economy of long waves . København, Denmark [1986] 10, [1] p. : ISBN 87-7393-042-3 (pbk.) LC Card 86-214084 DDC 338.9 19
HB3729 .P47 1986

EUROPEAN COOPERATION. Here are entered works on cooperation in all fields of activity. Works on political cooperation are entered under the heading European federation.
Zapadnoevropeĭskaia integratsiia . Moskva , 1986. 205, [3] p. ; LC Card 86-219781 DDC 327.1/7/094 19
HC241 .Z365 1986

European Coordination Center for Research and Documentation in Social Sciences. see **European Centre for the Co-ordination of Research and Documentation in Social Sciences.**

EUROPEAN CURRENCY UNIT.
The ECU market . Lexington, Mass. , c1987. xiii, 246 p. : ISBN 0-669-13833-9 (alk. paper) LC Card 87-4185 DDC 332.4/56094 19
HG930.5 .E27 1987

Masera, R. S. An increasing role for the ECU . Princeton, N.J. , 1987. vi, 50 p. ; ISBN 0-88165-074-9 (pbk.) : LC Card 87-3747 DDC 332/.042 s 332.4/56094 19
HG136 .P7 no. 167 HG930.5

The Role of the SDR in the international monetary system . Washington, D.C. , 1987. vii, 62 p. : ISBN 0-939934-81-7 (pbk.) : LC Card 87-4184 DDC 332.4/5 19
HG3898 .R65 1987

European dimension and future prospects of the railways. Report of the international seminar held in Paris on 15th-16th-17th January 1986 on the following topic, European dimension and future prospects of the railways /. Paris, France [Washington, D.C.] c1986. 289 p. : ISBN 92-821-1109-1 (pbk.) : LC Card 86-215627 DDC 385/.094 19
HE3005 .R47 1986

EUROPEAN ECONOMIC COMMUNITY - CONGRESSES.
Sverige--EFTA--EG. Stockholm , 1984. 145 p. ; LC Card 85-114840
HC241.4 .S87 1984

Was trennt Europa? /. Baden-Baden , 1986. 147 p. ; ISBN 3-7890-1320-X LC Card 87-108024 DDC 337.1/42 19
HC241.2 .W394 1986

EUROPEAN ECONOMIC COMMUNITY COUNTRIES - COMMERCE - BRAZIL.
Protectionism in the European community against Brazilian exports . Brasília , 1985. 125 p. ; LC Card 86-119107 DDC 382.7/3/094 19
HF3499.5.Z7 B76 1985

EUROPEAN ECONOMIC COMMUNITY COUNTRIES - COMMERCE - DEVELOPING COUNTRIES.
Davenport, Michael, 1940- Trade policy, protectionism, and the Third World /. London , Dover, N.H. , c1986. 152 p. : ISBN 0-7099-4516-7 : LC Card 86-6192 DDC 382.7/53 19
HF2039.5.Z7 D38 1986
NYPL [JLD 86-2759]

Perspectives on industrial readjustment, the EEC and the developing countries /. Tilburg, Netherlands , 1978. ii, 98 p. ;
NYPL [JLF 86-1708]

EUROPEAN ECONOMIC COMMUNITY COUNTRIES - COMMERCE - LEBANON.
Mesropian, André. Les relations du Liban avec la Communauté économique européenne /. Beyrouth, Liban [between 1972 and 1984] 65 p. ; LC Card 84-196415
HF1583.9.Z4 E865 1972

EUROPEAN ECONOMIC COMMUNITY COUNTRIES - COMMERCE - MOROCCO.
Qarouach, Mostafa. L'agriculture marocaine face au deuxième élargissement de la CEE /. [S.l.] 1983 (Casablanca : Editions maghrébines)

117 p. ; LC Card 83-192279 DDC 382/.41/0964 19
HD9017.M82 Q37 1983
NYPL [JLD 86-4326]

EUROPEAN ECONOMIC COMMUNITY COUNTRIES - COMMERCE - SPAIN.
Alonso, José Antonio. La empresa exportadora española frente a Iberoamérica y la CEE /. Madrid , 1985. xiii, 263 p. ; ISBN 84-7232-380-3 LC Card 86-199177
HF3688.L3 A46 1985 ***NYPL [JLE 87-56]***

EUROPEAN ECONOMIC COMMUNITY COUNTRIES - COMMERCE - THAILAND.
Schneider, Karl Josef. Das Selbstbeschränkungsabkommen zwischen Thailand und der Europäischen Gemeinschaft . Kiel , 1986. x, 192, 30 p. ; ISBN 3-922553-82-6 LC Card 87-408324 DDC 382/.413682/09593 19
HF3800.55.Z7 E867 1986

EUROPEAN ECONOMIC COMMUNITY COUNTRIES - COMMERCE - TURKEY.
Hale, William M. Turkish agriculture and Community enlargement /. [Ankara] , 1984. 37 p. ; LC Card 87-113782 DDC 338.9561 s 338.1/09561 19
HC401 .A356 no. 1949 HD9016.T82

EUROPEAN ECONOMIC COMMUNITY COUNTRIES - COMMERCIAL POLICY.
European trade policies and the developing world /. London , New York , c1988. x, 368 p. ; ISBN 0-7099-4672-4 LC Card 87-8969 DDC 382/.3/094 19
HF1492 .E87 1988

La Politica industriale della CEE . Roma , 1983. 371 p. ; LC Card 86-104849 DDC 338.94 19
HD3616.E83 P65 1983
NYPL [JLD 87-1225]

Protectionism in the European community against Brazilian exports . Brasília , 1985. 125 p. ; LC Card 86-119107 DDC 382.7/3/094 19
HF3499.5.Z7 B76 1985

EUROPEAN ECONOMIC COMMUNITY COUNTRIES - ECONOMIC CONDITIONS.
Berg, Hermann von, 1933- Die Analyse . Köln , c1985. 240 p. : ISBN 3-7663-0942-0 LC Card 86-122582 DDC 341.24/22 19
HC241 .B47 1985

Economic and Social Committee of the European Communities. The economic and social situation of the Community /. Brussels [Washington, D.C.] 1985. iii, 134 p. : ISBN 92-830-0054-4 : LC Card 86-221563 DDC 330.94/0558 19
HC241.2 .E292 1985

Grauwe, Paul de. Exchange rates, money, and output . New York , 1985. xii, 240 p. : ISBN 0-312-27403-3 : LC Card 84-11692 DDC 339/.094 19
HC241.2 .G69 1985 ***NYPL [JLD 86-3007]***

EUROPEAN ECONOMIC COMMUNITY COUNTRIES - ECONOMIC CONDITIONS - REGIONAL DISPARITIES.
Sweeney, G. P. (Gerald Patrick), 1928- Innovation, entrepreneurs, and regional development /. London , 1987. xvi, 271 p. : ISBN 0-86187-647-4 ***NYPL [JLD 87-1403]***

Sweeney, G. P. (Gerald Patrick), 1928- Innovation, entrepreneurs, and regional development /. New York , c1987. xvi, 271 p. : ISBN 0-312-00489-3 : LC Card 86-27999 DDC 338/.06/094 19
HC240.9.T4 S94 1987

EUROPEAN ECONOMIC COMMUNITY COUNTRIES - ECONOMIC INTEGRATION.
Evropeĭskoe soobshchestvo . Moskva , 1986. 270 p. : LC Card 86-202812
HC241.2 .E867 1986

Urban, Sabine M.-L. Entreprises allemandes et coopération industrielle à l'échelle européenne . Paris , c1986. 162 p. : ISBN 2-11-001580-2 : LC Card 86-175800
HD2844 .U7 1986

EUROPEAN ECONOMIC COMMUNITY COUNTRIES - EMIGRATION AND IMMIGRATION - GOVERNMENT POLICY.
Ferreira, Eduardo de Sousa, 1936- Reintegração dos emigrantes portugueses . [Lisbon] , 1984. xiv, 137 p. ; LC Card 86-132652
HD8380.5 .F47 1984

EUROPEAN ECONOMIC COMMUNITY COUNTRIES - FOREIGN ECONOMIC RELATIONS.
Baranovskiĭ, V. G. (Vladimir Georgievich) Evropeĭskoe soobshchestvo v sisteme mezhdunarodnykh otnosheniĭ /. Moskva , 1986. 319 p. ; LC Card 86-201822
HF1532.92 .B37 1986

La Politica industriale della CEE . Roma , 1983. 371 p. ; LC Card 86-104849 DDC 338.94 19
HD3616.E83 P65 1983
NYPL [JLD 87-1225]

EUROPEAN ECONOMIC COMMUNITY COUNTRIES - FOREIGN ECONOMIC RELATIONS - ARAB COUNTRIES.
Lerche, Dietrich, 1943- Grundlagen und Perspektiven des Euro-Arabischen Dialogs /. Berlin , 1977. iii, 78 p. : LC Card 85-129693
HF1532.5.Z4 A735 1977

EUROPEAN ECONOMIC COMMUNITY COUNTRIES - FOREIGN ECONOMIC RELATIONS - ASIA, SOUTHEASTERN.
Relations between the European Community and the member states of the Association of South-East Asian Nations /. Brussels [1986] 55 p. : LC Card 87-135576 DDC 337.4059 19
HF1532.5 .R46 1986

EUROPEAN ECONOMIC COMMUNITY COUNTRIES - FOREIGN ECONOMIC RELATIONS - CHINA.
Wiesegart, Kurt. Wirtschaftskooperation mit China . Hamburg , 1984. 126 p. ; ISBN 3-87895-260-0 LC Card 85-146617
HF1604.Z4 E869 1984

EUROPEAN ECONOMIC COMMUNITY COUNTRIES - FOREIGN ECONOMIC RELATIONS - DEVELOPING COUNTRIES.
Die Bundesrepublik Deutschland und die Entwicklungspolitik der Europäischen Gemeinschaft, 1957-1983 /. Münster [1986] 111 p. ; ISBN 3-88660-214-1 LC Card 86-213020
HC241.25.G3 B87 1986

Howell, Thomas R., 1949- The EEC and the third Multifiber Arrangement . Washington, DC , 1986. [14], 126, [12] p. : LC Card 86-224652 DDC 382/.45677/0094 19
HD9865.E852 H68 1986

Wiemann, Jürgen. Selektiver Protektionismus und aktive Strukturanpassung . Berlin , 1983. vii, 348 p. : ISBN 3-88985-028-6 : LC Card 83-223964
HD9865.E852 W54 1983

EUROPEAN ECONOMIC COMMUNITY COUNTRIES - FOREIGN ECONOMIC RELATIONS - DEVELOPING COUNTRIES - CONGRESSES.
The Common agricultural policy and the Third World . London , 1986. 97 p. : ISBN 0-946848-79-3 (pbk.) : LC Card 87-150069 DDC 338.1/81/094 19
HD9015.E82 C665 1986

EUROPEAN ECONOMIC COMMUNITY COUNTRIES - FOREIGN ECONOMIC RELATIONS - ITALY - ADDRESSES, ESSAYS, LECTURES.
Il Mezzogiorno nelle politiche nazionali e comunitarie . Milano , 1982. 379 p. ; LC Card 82-230171 DDC 338.945/7 19
HC305 .M42156 1982 ***NYPL [JLE 86-1611]***

EUROPEAN ECONOMIC COMMUNITY COUNTRIES - FOREIGN ECONOMIC RELATIONS - JAPAN.
Korte, Karl-Rudolf. Nippons neue Vasallen? . Bonn , c1984. 103 p. : ISBN 3-7713-0216-1 LC Card 86-230930
HF1602.15.E92 K67 1984

EUROPEAN ECONOMIC COMMUNITY COUNTRIES - FOREIGN ECONOMIC RELATIONS - LEBANON.
Mesropian, André. Les relations du Liban avec la Communauté économique européenne /. Beyrouth, Liban [between 1972 and 1984] 65 p. ; LC Card 84-196415
HF1583.9.Z4 E865 1972

EUROPEAN ECONOMIC COMMUNITY COUNTRIES - FOREIGN ECONOMIC RELATIONS - UNITED STATES.
U. S.-EC relations . Washington , 1986. vii, 78 p. ; LC Card 86-603395 DDC 337.4073 19
HF1456.5.E825 U17 1986

EUROPEAN ECONOMIC COMMUNITY COUNTRIES - FOREIGN ECONOMIC RELATIONS - UNITED STATES - CONGRESSES.
Confrontation or negotiation . Millwood, N.Y. , 1985. xvi, 303 p. : ISBN 0-8046-9397-8 : LC Card 85-18667 DDC 382/.41/094 19
HD9015.E82 C67 1985
NYPL [JLE 86-4594]

EUROPEAN ECONOMIC COMMUNITY COUNTRIES - FOREIGN RELATIONS.
Baranovskiĭ, V. G. (Vladimir Georgievich) Evropeĭskoe soobshchestvo v sisteme mezhdunarodnykh otnosheniĭ /. Moskva , 1986. 319 p. ; LC Card 86-201822
HF1532.92 .B37 1986

EUROPEAN ECONOMIC COMMUNITY COUNTRIES - FULL EMPLOYMENT POLICIES.
Vollbeschäftigung, eine Utopie? /. Bern , c1986. 330 p. : ISBN 3-258-03567-9 LC Card 86-224133
HD5779 .V64 1986

EUROPEAN ECONOMIC COMMUNITY COUNTRIES - POPULATION.
Demographic situation in the Community . Brussels , 1986. ii, 40 p. : LC Card 87-135237 DDC 304.6/094 19
HB3582.5 .D46 1986

EUROPEAN ECONOMIC COMMUNITY COUNTRIES - SOCIAL CONDITIONS.
Economic and Social Committee of the European Communities. The economic and social situation of the Community /. Brussels [Washington, D.C.] 1985. iii, 134 p. : ISBN 92-830-0054-4 : LC Card 86-221563 DDC 330.94/0558 19
HC241.2 .E292 1985

EUROPEAN ECONOMIC COMMUNITY COUNTRIES - SOCIAL POLICY.
Dötsch, Jochen. EG und Arbeiterrechte . Berlin , 1981. 143 p. ; LC Card 81-145834 DDC 331.11/094 19
HD8380.5 .D67 1981 ***NYPL [JLD 86-2739]***

Emerson, Michael. What model for Europe? /. Cambridge, Mass. , c1988. xi, 151 p. : ISBN 0-262-05036-6 LC Card 87-15151 DDC 331.11/094 19
HD8380.5 .E47 1988

EUROPEAN ECONOMIC COMMUNITY - DENMARK.
Ellemann-Jensen, Uffe, 1941- Da Danmark igen sagde ja til det fælles-- /. [Copenhagen] , c1987. 157 p. : ISBN 87-569-2234-5 : LC Card 87-163358
HC241.25.D4 E45 1987

Iversen, John, 1954- Om EF . København , 1984. 143 p. : ISBN 87-412-3775-7 : LC Card 84-186203
HC241.2 .I84 1984

EUROPEAN ECONOMIC COMMUNITY - DENMARK - CONGRESSES.
Consular conference in Denmark, June 76. [Copenhagen] [1976] 47 p. : LC Card 85-189659
HF1561 .C66 1976

EUROPEAN ECONOMIC COMMUNITY - DEVELOPING COUNTRIES.
Stevens, Christopher. Negotiating Lome III . Sussex [1986] 23 p. : LC Card 86-222421 DDC 337.406 19
HC241.25.D44 S74 1986

EUROPEAN ECONOMIC COMMUNITY - ECONOMIC ASSISTANCE.
Commission of the European Communities. Directorate-General of Information. A Community research policy for development. Brussels [1983] 21 p. ; LC Card 85-166173 DDC 338.91/4/01724 19
HC60 .C584 1983

The European Community's development policy . Bruges , 19. 285 p. : LC Card 87-135534 DDC 338.94 19
HC60 .E7626 1986

EUROPEAN ECONOMIC COMMUNITY - EUROPE, EASTERN.
Inotai, András. Válaszúton az Európai Gazdasági Közösség /. [Budapest] , 1985. 369 p. ; ISBN 963-09-2587-7 : LC Card 86-228244
HC241.2 .I583 1985

EUROPEAN ECONOMIC COMMUNITY - EUROPE, SOUTHERN - CONGRESSES.
Prospective evolution of EEC common agricultural policy . Lisboa , Oeiras , 1985. 122 p. : LC Card 86-221785
HD1920.5.Z8 P77 1985

Southern Europe and the enlargement of the EEC . Lisboa, Portugal , 1982. 324 p. : LC Card 86-201274 DDC 341.24/22 19
HC241.25.E85 S68 1982

EUROPEAN ECONOMIC COMMUNITY - FINANCE.
Cuenca García, Eduardo. Las intervenciones financieras comunitarias /. Madrid [1985?] 53 p. ; ISBN 84-7196-523-2 LC Card 85-200493
HJ2094.5 .C84 1985

EUROPEAN ECONOMIC COMMUNITY - GERMANY, WEST.
Bulmer, Simon. The Federal Republic of Germany and The European community /. London , Boston , 1987. p. cm. ISBN 0-04-382045-X (alk. paper) LC Card 86-25909 DDC 341.24/22 19
HC241.25.G3 B86 1987

Die Bundesrepublik Deutschland und die Entwicklungspolitik der Europäischen Gemeinschaft, 1957-1983 /. Münster [1986] 111 p. ; ISBN 3-88660-214-1 LC Card 86-213020
HC241.25.G3 B87 1986

Western Europe in transition . Baden-Baden , 1986. 223 p. : ISBN 3-7890-1220-3 LC Card 87-136015 DDC 341.24/22 19
HC241.25.G3 W47 1986

EUROPEAN ECONOMIC COMMUNITY - GERMANY, WEST - CONGRESSES.
Die Deutschen Länder und die Europäischen Gemeinschaften . Baden-Baden , 1986. 294 p. ; ISBN 3-7890-1350-1 LC Card 87-141896 DDC 341.24/22 19
HC241.25.G3 D48 1986

EUROPEAN ECONOMIC COMMUNITY - GREAT BRITAIN.
La Serre, Françoise de. La Grande-Bretagne et la Communauté européenne /. Paris , c1987. 223, [1] p. : ISBN 2-13-040114-7 : LC Card 87-165122
HC241.25.G7 L118 1987

Newton Dunn, Bill. Greater in Europe /. London , c1985. 85 p. ; ISBN 0-7212-0731-6 (pbk.) : LC Card 87-146946 DDC 341.24/22 19
HC241.25.G7 N48 1985

EUROPEAN ECONOMIC COMMUNITY - GREECE.
Hē Eurōpē tōn 10. [Athenai] [1981] 37 p. : LC Card 86-184401
HC241.25.G8 H42 1981

Hē Hellada stēn Eurōpaikē Koinotēta . Athēna , 1987. 14, 565 p. ; LC Card 87-169443
HC241.25.G8 H43 1987

Kontogeōrgēs, Geōrgios L. Hē Hellada stēn Eurōpē . [Athens] [1985] 311 p. : LC Card 86-206722
HC241.25.G8 K65 1985

Sarlēs, Dēmētrēs. Hoi politikes pleures tēs entaxēs tēs Helladas stēn EOK . Athēna , 1981. 212 p. ; LC Card 83-170595
HC241.25.G8 S27 1981

EUROPEAN ECONOMIC COMMUNITY - GREECE - CONGRESSES.
Southern Europe and the enlargement of the EEC . Lisboa, Portugal , 1982. 324 p. : LC Card 86-201274 DDC 341.24/22 19
HC241.25.E85 S68 1982

EUROPEAN ECONOMIC COMMUNITY - ITALY - ADDRESSES, ESSAYS, LECTURES.
Il Mezzogiorno nelle politiche nazionali e comunitarie . Milano , 1982. 379 p. ; LC Card 82-230171 DDC 338.945/7 19
HC305 .M42156 1982 ***NYPL [JLE 86-1611]***

EUROPEAN ECONOMIC COMMUNITY - MEDITERRANEAN REGION.
Arampatzēs, E. Hē mesogeiakē politikē tēs EOK . Thessalonikē , 1983. 268 p. ; LC Card 84-185339
HC241.25.M4 A73 1983

Duchêne, François. The European Community and the Mediterranean /. Luxembourg , Washington, DC , 1985. 102 p. : ISBN 92-825-5326-4 (pbk.) LC Card 87-119518 DDC 337.40182/2 19
HC241.25.M4 D83 1985

EUROPEAN ECONOMIC COMMUNITY - NORWAY.
Bjørklund, Tor, 1947- Mot strømmen . Oslo , c1982. 396 p. : ISBN 82-00-06338-0 : LC Card 83-134961
HC241.25.N7 B56 1982

Jørgensen, Nils-Johan. Norge mot Europa? . København , 1982. 250 p. ; ISBN 87-87733-30-7 : LC Card 82-172919
HC241.25.N7 J67 1982

Norge--EF, økonomisk samarbeid. [Oslo] [1981] 45 p. ; ISBN 82-7177-111-6 LC Card 84-167865
HC241.25.N7 N55 1981

EUROPEAN ECONOMIC COMMUNITY - PERIODICALS - BIBLIOGRAPHY.
Bibliographie der EG-Zeitschriften 1952-1980 . Kiel , 1981. ix, 280 p. ; LC Card 81-122713
HB41 .K55 Bd. 22 Z7165.E8 HC241.2

EUROPEAN ECONOMIC COMMUNITY - PORTUGAL.
Álvares, Pedro. Portugal na CEE . [Lisbon] , 1986. 543 p. ; LC Card 87-403268 DDC 341.24/22 19
HC241.25.P6 A48 1986

Azevedo, J. Cândido de. Portugal, Europa face ao Mercado Comum . Amadora , c1978. 300 p. ; LC Card 80-121153
HC241.25.P6 A94 1978

Carvalho, José António Segueira. A adesão de Portugal à C.E.E. . [Lisbon, Portugal] , 1985. 97 p. : LC Card 86-150962
HC241.25.P6 C38 1985

Dauderstädt, Michael. Las relaciones hispano-portuguesas y la integración europea /. Madrid [1987?] 36 p. ; ISBN 84-398-8593-8 LC Card 87-161277
HF1570.15.P8 D38 1987

Eurocooperazione . [Roma] [1986] 104 p. : LC Card 86-219598
HC241.25.S7 E87 1986

Reizinho, Eduardo J. Costa (Eduardo José Costa) A adesão portuguesa à CEE . Mem Martins, Portugal , c1985. 396 p. ; LC Card 86-205515
HC241.25.P6 R45 1985

Sousa, Fernando Freire de. A adesão de Portugal à CEE . [Porto] [1985] 96 p. ; LC Card 86-174408
HF2236 .S68 1985

EUROPEAN ECONOMIC COMMUNITY - PORTUGAL - CONGRESSES.
Custos certos, benefícios incertos . [Lisboa] [1986] 307 p. : LC Card 87-127179 DDC 341.24/22 19
HC241.25.P6 C87 1986

Southern Europe and the enlargement of the EEC . Lisboa, Portugal , 1982. 324 p. : LC Card 86-201274 DDC 341.24/22 19
HC241.25.E85 S68 1982

EUROPEAN ECONOMIC COMMUNITY - SPAIN.
Alonso, José Antonio. Efectos de la adhesión de España a la CEE sobre las exportaciones de Iberoamérica /. Madrid , 1983. 316 p. : ISBN 84-7232-299-8 LC Card 87-116624
HF3688.L3 A45 1983

Capdevila Batlles, José. Agricultura e industria española frente a la CEE . Barcelona [1985?] 252 p. : ISBN 84-7003-282-8 LC Card 86-171577
HC385 .C358 1985

Dauderstädt, Michael. Las relaciones hispano-portuguesas y la integración europea /. Madrid [1987?] 36 p. ; ISBN 84-398-8593-8 LC Card 87-161277
HF1570.15.P8 D38 1987

Eurocooperazione . [Roma] [1986] 104 p. : LC Card 86-219598
HC241.25.S7 E87 1986

Fernández Alvarez, Antonio. El impacto de la política agrícola común en la integración española /. Madrid [1986?] 48 p. ; ISBN 84-7075-333-9 LC Card 87-111468
HC241.25.S6 F47 1986

Fernández Ordóñez, Francisco. España y la CEE . Madrid, España , 1985. 74 p. ; ISBN 84-505-4317-0 LC Card 86-151137
HG2980.5.A6 F47 1985

Gil, Gonzalo. Aspectos financieros y monetarios de la integración española en la Comunidad Económica Europea /. [Madrid] [1985] 187 p. : ISBN 84-505-2233-1 LC Card 87-101729
HC241.25.S6 G55 1985

Gómez Fuentes, Angel, 1950- Así cambiará España . Esplugues de Llobregat, Barcelona , 1986. 333 p. ; ISBN 84-01-33317-2 LC Card 87-100798
HC241.25.S6 G65 1986

Herrero de Miñón, Miguel, 1940- España y la Comunidad Económica Europea . Barcelona, España , 1986. 225 p. ; ISBN 84-320-0661-0 LC Card 87-100785
HC241.25.S6 H47 1986

Illescas Ortiz, Rafael. Europa hacia el sur (al hilo de la adhesión española a la Comunidad europea) /. [Jerez] [1985], 1986 printing. 152 p. ; ISBN 84-600-4184-0 LC Card 86-150722
HC241.25.S6 I47 1986

Implicaciones para el sector comercio de la integración de España en el Mercado Común . [Madrid] [1979?] 106 p. ; LC Card 81-116650
HC241.25.S6 I48 1979

Loring, Jaime. Los sectores agrarios de Andalucía ante la integración en la C.E.E. /. Madrid , 1984. 303 p. : ISBN 84-7114-149-3 LC Card 86-152628
HD2025.A5 L67 1984

Maravall, Fernando. Economía y política industrial en España /. Madrid , 1987. 231 p. : ISBN 84-368-0340-X LC Card 87-121800
HC385 .M2574 1987

Möller, Ferdinand, 1955- Agrarstruktur und Agrarstrukturpolitik in Spanien, eine Analyse vor dem Hintergrund der Erweiterung der Europäischen Gemeinschaft /. Frankfurt am Main , New York , c1986. ix, 255 p. ; ISBN 3-8204-9529-0 LC Card 87-407540 DDC 338.1/846 19
HD2023 .M65 1986

Moreno Torregrosa, Pasqual. El Mercado Común frente a la agricultura española /. Madrid [1986?] 127 p. ; ISBN 84-86293-27-8 LC Card 86-202333
HD2022 .M67 1986

Seminario sobre Consequencias para las Entidades Oficiales de Crédito de la Entrada de España en las Comunidades Europeas (1984 : Madrid, Spain) Seminario sobre Consequencias para las Entidades Oficiales de Crédito de la Entrada de España en las Comunidades Europeas /. [Madrid] [1984?] 270 p. ; ISBN 84-505-0963-7 LC Card 85-186710
HG1642.E86 S46 1984

Tamames, Ramón, 1933- Guía del Mercado Común Europeo . Madrid , c1986. xii, 309 p. ; ISBN 84-206-9524-6 LC Card 86-150515
HC241.25.S6 T35 1986

Viernes europeos 81 . Madrid [1984?] 494 p. : LC Card 85-178055
HC241.25.S6 V48 1984

EUROPEAN ECONOMIC COMMUNITY - SPAIN - CATALONIA.
Clavera, Joan. La viticultura catalana davant la integració a la Comunitat Europea /. [Barcelona] [1986] 124 p. : ISBN 6-476-84021-8 LC Card 86-200618
HD9259.G7 S693 1986

EUROPEAN ECONOMIC COMMUNITY - SPAIN - CONGRESSES.
Southern Europe and the enlargement of the EEC . Lisboa, Portugal , 1982. 324 p. : LC Card 86-201274 DDC 341.24/22 19
HC241.25.E85 S68 1982

EUROPEAN ECONOMIC COMMUNITY - SPAIN - SEGURA MOUNTAINS REGION.

Ruiz Avilés, Pedro. Estudio integral de la Sierra de Segura . [Jaén] [1985] 130 leaves : ISBN 84-505-1249-2 LC Card 86-187282
HC387.S438 R85 1985

EUROPEAN ECONOMIC COMMUNITY - SWITZERLAND.
Europa im Umbruch . [Basel] , 1963. 91 p. ; LC Card 85-125335
HC241 .E772 1963

EUROPEAN ECONOMIC COMMUNITY - TECHNICAL ASSISTANCE.
Commission of the European Communities. Directorate-General of Information. A Community research policy for development. Brussels [1983] 21 p. ; LC Card 85-166173 DDC 338.91/4/01724 19
HC60 .C584 1983

EUROPEAN ECONOMIC COMMUNITY - TURKEY.
Hale, William M. Turkish agriculture and Community enlargement /. [Ankara] , 1984. 37 p. ; LC Card 87-113782 DDC 338.9561 s 338.1/09561 19
HC401 .A356 no. 1949 HD9016.T82

European equity markets : risk, return, and efficiency / edited by Gabriel A. Hawawini & Pierre A. Michel. New York : Garland Pub., 1984. 470 p. : ill. ; 24 cm. (Accounting history and the development of a profession) Includes bibliographies. ISBN 0-8240-6307-4 (alk. paper) : LC Card 83-49440 DDC 332.64/094
1. Stocks - Prices - European Economic Community countries - Addresses, essays, lectures. 2. Stock-exchange - European Economic Community countries - Addresses, essays, lectures. 3. Capital market - European Economic Community countries - Addresses, essays, lectures. I. Hawawini, Gabriel A. II. Michel, Pierre A. III. Series.
HG5430.5.A3 E84 1984
NYPL [JLE 86-4508]

EUROPEAN FEDERATION - ADDRESSES, ESSAYS, LECTURES.
Fred och säkerhet . [Stockholm] , c1983. 385 p. : ISBN 91-7410-249-4 : LC Card 83-229846
JX1963 .F817 1983 ***NYPL [JLD 84-2639]***

EUROPEAN FEDERATION - CONGRESSES.
Was trennt Europa? /. Baden-Baden , 1986. 147 p. ; ISBN 3-7890-1320-X LC Card 87-108024 DDC 337.1/42 19
HC241.2 .W394 1986

European Forestry Commission. Forestry and the forest industries . Dordrecht ; Boston : xi, 428 p. : ISBN 90-247-3592-0 LC Card 87-20400 DDC 338.1/749 19
HD9765.A2 F64 1987

European Foundation for Management Development. A Guide to small firms assistance in Europe /. Aldershot, Hants, England , Brookfield, Vt., U. S.A. , c1986. vii, 263 p. ; ISBN 0-566-05082-X : LC Card 85-27307 DDC 338.6/42/094 19
HD2346.E9 G85 1986 ***NYPL [JLG 86-205]***

European Foundation for the Improvement of Living and Working Conditions.
Copsey, S. M. Shiftwork review . Luxembourg , Washington, DC , 1986. xi, 122 p. : ISBN 92-825-6419-3 (pbk.) : LC Card 87-137298 DDC 331.25/72 19
HD5111.6.E86 C66 1986

Neue Arbeits- und Tätigkeitsformen . Dublin, Ireland [Washington, D.C.] c1986. xvi, 339 p. ; ISBN 92-825-6418-5 LC Card 87-408469 DDC 306/.36/094 19
HD6957.E86 N48 1986

Occupational accidents and diseases . Dublin, Ireland , Washington, DC , 1986. 116 p. ; ISBN 92-825-6426-6 LC Card 87-135635 DDC 363.1/1/094 19
HD7694.5 .O33 1986

EUROPEAN FREE TRADE ASSOCIATION - CONGRESSES.
Sverige--EFTA--EG. Stockholm , 1984. 145 p. ; LC Card 85-114840
HC241.4 .S87 1984

EUROPEAN FREE TRADE ASSOCIATION - PORTUGAL.
André, J. L. da Costa. Portugal na Associação Europeia de Comércio Livre /. Lisboa , 1960. 98 p. ; LC Card 85-216282
HC241.4 .A56 1960

European Institute of Printed Circuits.
Symposium on Management Data Processing for PCB Manufacturing (1982 : Luxembourg, Luxembourg) Symposium on Management Data Processing for PCB Manufacturing . Lugano [1982?] 1 v. (various pagings) : LC Card 84-211066 DDC 621.381/74/0685 19
HD9696.P742 S96 1982
NYPL [JSG 86-145]

European Institute of Public Administration.
Coming to grips with the internal market /. Maastricht, The Netherlands , c1986. viii, 136 p. ; ISBN 90-6779-019-2 (pbk.) LC Card 86-222624 DDC 337.1/42 19
HC241.2 .C5548 1986

EUROPEAN INTEGRATION.
Barnouin, Barbara. The European labour movement and European integration /. London , Wolfeboro, N.H. , 1986. viii, 172 p. ; ISBN 0-86187-650-4 : LC Card 86-5901 DDC 331.88/091 19
HD8372.E86 B37 1986
NYPL [JLE 86-4058]

European Labor Committees. Wer steuert die "Anti-Kernkraft-Bewegung"-- und mit welchem Ziel? /. Wiesbaden [1977] 38 p. : LC Card 86-140106 DDC 333.79/24 19
HD9698.A2 W44 1977

European Labor Party. Wer steuert die "Anti-Kernkraft-Bewegung"-- und mit welchem Ziel? /. Wiesbaden [1977] 38 p. : LC Card 86-140106 DDC 333.79/24 19
HD9698.A2 W44 1977

The European labour movement and European integration /. Barnouin, Barbara. London , Wolfeboro, N.H. , 1986. viii, 172 p. ; ISBN 0-86187-650-4 : LC Card 86-5901 DDC 331.88/091 19
HD8372.E86 B37 1986
NYPL [JLE 86-4058]

The European miracle . Jones, E. L. (Eric Lionel) Cambridge , New York , 1987. xxxiii, 279 p., [1] leaf of plates : ISBN 0-521-33449-7 LC Card 87-8092 DDC 330.94/02 19
HC240 .J57 1987

The European monetary system : recent developments / by Horst Ungerer ... [et al.]. Washington, D.C. : International Monetary Fund, c1986. vii, 75 p. : col. ill. ; 28 cm. (Occasional paper (International Monetary Fund) . no. 48) "December 1986." Bibliography: p. 74-75. ISBN 0-939934-79-5 (pbk.) : LC Card 86-21432 DDC 332.4/5/094 19
1. Money - European Economic Community countries. I. Ungerer, Horst. II. International Monetary Fund. III. Series. IV. Series: Occasional paper (International Monetary Fund) , no. 48.
HG930.5 .E86863 1986

EUROPEAN MONETARY SYSTEM (ORGANIZATION)
Martinengo, Giancarlo. Lo SME e il dollaro . [Napoli] , c1983. 84 p. ; LC Card 85-150597
HG930.5 .M27 1983

Masera, R. S. L'unificazione monetaria e lo SME /. Bologna , c1980. 220 p. ; LC Card 82-150717 DDC 332.4/566/094 19
HG930.5.Z8 M37 1980 ***NYPL [JLD 87-902]***

EUROPEAN MONETARY SYSTEM (ORGANIZATION) - CONGRESSES.
International monetary and financial integration . Dordrecht , Boston , c1988. xii, 403 p. : ISBN 90-247-3563-7 LC Card 87-3622 DDC 332.4/94 19
HG930.5 .I586 1988

The European monetary system--past, present, and future /. Coffey, Peter. Dordrecht ; Boston : p. cm. ISBN 90-247-3446-0 LC Card 86-23833 DDC 332.4/5/094 19
HG930.5 .C63 1987

EUROPEAN PARLIAMENT - ELECTIONS - STATISTICS.
Kommunal- und Europawahl am 17. Juni 1984. Saarbrücken , 1984. 115 p. : ISBN 3-88718-020-8 : LC Card 85-130989
HA1320 .S244 Nr. 67 JN4945.S265

European Parliamentary Assembly. see **European Parliament.**

European philately .
(11) Barefoot, John. Georgia /. York, England , c1983. 66 p. : ISBN 0-906845-19-X (pbk.) LC Card 87-100272 DDC 769.5694795 19
HE6185.S653 G463 1983

(13) Tuffs, V. Norway number one . York, England , c1983. 52 p. : ISBN 0-906845-26-2 (pbk.) LC Card 87-100273 DDC 769.569481 19
HE6183.K56 T83 1983

(9) Hall, Andrew. Baltic states revenues /. York, England , c1983. 40 p. : ISBN 0-906845-14-9 (pbk.) LC Card 87-100278 DDC 769.5/7 19
HJ5429.B34 H34 1983

The European potential for a venture capital industry /. Vlitos, Irene. Menlo Park, CA (333 Ravenswood Ave., Menlo Park 94025) , c1986. 13 leaves : LC Card 86-220533 DDC 332.6/6 19
HG5428 .V56 1986

The European power plant industry . Surrey, John. [Brighton, Sussex] , c1981. viii, 90 p. ; ISBN 0-903422-31-X (pbk.) : LC Card 83-130609 DDC 338.4/76213121/094 19
HD9695.E92 S87 1981
NYPL [JLD 86-4078]

European Production Study Group. Industrial investment in Europe . Dordrecht ; Boston : 389 p. ; ISBN 90-247-3270-0 LC Card 85-26036 DDC 332.6/7253 19
HG5430.5.A3 I54 1985
NYPL [JLE 86-2366]

EUROPEAN REGIONAL DEVELOPMENT FUND.
Cuenca García, Eduardo. Las intervenciones financieras comunitarias /. Madrid [1985?] 53 p. ; ISBN 84-7196-523-2 LC Card 85-200493
HJ2094.5 .C84 1985

European Science Foundation.
Multinationals--theory and history /. Aldershot, Hants, England , Brookfield, Vt., USA , c1986. vii, 200 p. : ISBN 0-566-05078-1 : LC Card 85-24955 DDC 338.8/8 19
HD2755.5 .M86 1986 ***NYPL [JLD 86-1575]***

European Society for Opinion Surveys and Market Research. see **Esomar.**

European trade policies and the developing world / edited by L.B.M. Mennes and Jacob Kol. London ; New York : Croom Helm, c1988. x, 368 p. ; 23 cm. "Published in the USA ... in association with Methuen, Inc." Includes bibliographies and indexes. ISBN 0-7099-4672-4 LC Card 87-8969 DDC 382/.3/094 19
1. European Economic Community countries - Commercial policy. 2. Developing countries - Commercial policy. I. Mennes, L. B. M. II. Kol, J.
HF1492 .E87 1988

EUROPEAN TRADE UNION CONFEDERATION - HISTORY.
Barnouin, Barbara. The European labour movement and European integration /. London , Wolfeboro, N.H. , 1986. viii, 172 p. ; ISBN 0-86187-650-4 : LC Card 86-5901 DDC 331.88/091 19
HD8372.E86 B37 1986
NYPL [JLE 86-4058]

Debunne, Georges. Vakbonden en Europa . Leuven , c1987. 206 p. ; ISBN 90-6303-228-5 : LC Card 87-157537
HD8372.E86 D43 1987

European Trade Union Institute. Flexibility and jobs . Bruxelles [1985] 157, 5 p. : LC Card 87-111122 DDC 331.25 19
HD5764.A6 F44 1985

EUROPEAN UNION. see **EUROPEAN FEDERATION.**

EUROPEAN WAR, 1914-1918 - EMBARGOES. see **EMBARGO.**

EUROPEAN WAR, 1914-1918 - GERMAN PROPAGANDA. see **PROPAGANDA, GERMAN.**

EUROPEAN WAR, 1914-1918 - INVENTIONS. see **INVENTIONS.**

EUROPEAN WAR, 1939-1945. see **WORLD WAR, 1939-1945.**

Europees Centrum von Gemeenschapsbedrijven. see **Centre européen de l'entreprise publique.**

Europees Parlement. see **European Parliament.**

Europeo. N. 21 (Supplement) Il Mondo oggi . Milano , <[1986]- >, <c1983-. v. <2 > :

ISBN 0-330-28132-1 LC Card 87-103039
HC59 .M596 1986

Europese economische gemeenschap. see **European Economic Community.**

Europese economische integratie : problemen en perspectieven / [W.G.C.M. Haack (red.)].1e druk. Utrecht : Spectrum, 1986. 304 p. : ill. ; 21 cm. (Aula paperback. 138) Includes bibliographies and index. ISBN 90-274-0506-9 : LC Card 86-206597
1. European Economic Community. 2. Europe - Economic integration. I. Haack, W. G. C. M.
HC241.2 .E8655 1986

Eurosocial. Social concerns for the 1980s . Wien , c1984. 359 p. ; ISBN 3-900376-18-2 (pbk.)
NYPL [JLE 86-2856]

Eurostat. Methodologie der EG-Agrarpreisindizes (Output und Input) =. Luxembourg , Washington, DC , 1985. 228 p. ; ISBN 92-825-5463-5 : LC Card 87-107275 DDC 338.1/3/094021 19
HD1920.5 .M47 1985

Euverte, Emmanuel, 1948- Degrotte, Jean-André, 1947- L'économie bafouée, ou, Les hommes politiques au créneau /. Paris , c1985. 130, [11] p. : ISBN 2-7266-0074-3 LC Card 85-230533
HD5106 .D42 1985

Evaluación de los datos censales de 1980 . Corona V., Rodolfo. Tijuana, Baja California , 1986. 172 p. : ISBN 968-607-510-0 LC Card 87-117630 DDC 304.6/0723 19
HA767.B34 C67 1986

Evaluación económica, 1986 : informe confidencial. [La Paz, Bolivia] : Müller & Machicado Asociados, [1986] 278 p. ; 21 cm. Cover title. LC Card 87-403510 DDC 330.884/052 19
1. Bolivia - Economic conditions - 1982-. I. Muller y Machicado Asociados.
HC182 .E95 1986

Evaluación económico-política de la reforma agraria /. Antezana Ergueta, Luis. La Paz, Bolivia , 1986. 113 p. : LC Card 87-400948 DDC 333.3/1/84 19
HD1333.B5 A56 1986

Evaluatiemethoden, een introductie : rapport van de Afdeling Beleidsanalyse van het Ministerie van Financiën. 2e geheel herziene druk. 's-Gravenhage : Staatsuitgeverij, [1984] v, 188 p. : ill. ; 24 cm. Bibliography: p. 177-184. Includes index. ISBN 90-12-04825-7 LC Card 85-196500
1. Organizational effectiveness. 2. Organization - Evaluation. I. Netherlands. Ministerie van Financiën. Afdeling Beleidsanalyse.
HD58.9 .E93 1984

Evaluating business and industry training / edited by Leslie Steven May, Carol Ann Moore, Stephen J. Zammit. Boston : Kluwer Academic Publishers ; Norwell, MA : Distributors for the U. S. and Canada, Kluwer Academic Publishers, c1987. xv, 294 p. : ill. ; 24 cm. (Evaluation in education and human services) Includes bibliographies and index. ISBN 0-89838-197-5 LC Card 87-5771 DDC 658.3/12404 19
1. Employees, Training of - Evaluation. I. May, Leslie Steven. II. Moore, Carol Ann. III. Zammit, Stephen J. IV. Series.
HF5549.5.T7 E88 1987

Evaluating electrification experience : a guide to the social evaluation of small hydroelectric units in lesser developed countries / by AMARU IV Cooperative. Washington, D.C. : Small Decentralized Hydropower (SDH) Program, International Programs Division, National Rural Electric Cooperative Association, 1982- v. <1 > : ill. ; 28 cm. Bibliography: v. 1, p. 93-101. LC Card 86-176385 DDC 333.91/4 19
1. Rural electrification - Developing countries. 2. Hydroelectric power plants - Developing countries. I. AMARU IV Cooperative. II. National Rural Electric Cooperative Association. Small Decentralized Hydropower (SDH) Program.
HD9688.D44 E9 1982

Evaluating employee training programs . Hawthorne, Elizabeth M. New York , 1987. xiv, 196 p. : ISBN 0-89930-242-4 (lib. bdg. : alk. paper) LC Card 87-5984 DDC 658.3/12404 19
HF5549.5.T7 H36 1987

Evaluating the effectiveness of newspaper promotion / edited by Thomas J. Holbein. Reston, Va. (11600 Sunrise Valley Dr., Reston 22091) : International Newspaper Marketing Association, c1987. iii, 123 p. : ill. ; 28 cm. Bibliography: p. 61-63. LC Card 87-152731 DDC 659.13/2 19
1. Advertising - Newspapers. 2. Advertising - Newspapers - United States. I. Holbein, Thomas J. II. International Newspaper Marketing Association.
HF6161.N4 E93 1987

Evaluation and research reports. Census of population and housing (1980). Evaluation and research reports. Programs to improve coverage in the 1980 census. 1980 census of population and housing. Washington, D.C. [1987] 83 p. : LC Card 87-601259
HA201 1980aa

Evaluation de la planification décentralisée / Commissariat général du plan ; président, Alex Raymond ... [et al.]. Paris : Documentation française, c1986. 97 p. : ill. ; 24 cm. (Plan / Commissariat général du plan. 9) "Rapport du Groupe de travail 'Evaluation de la planification décentralisée'"--P. 3. "Septembre 1985." ISBN 2-11-001562-4 : LC Card 86-193163
1. France - Economic policy - 1945-. 2. Regionalism - France. I. Raymond, Alex. II. France. Groupe de travail "Evaluation de la planification décentralisée.". III. Series: Plan (France. Commissariat général du plan) 9.
HC276.2 .E89 1986

Evaluation der Berufsberatung der Bundesanstalt für Arbeit : die Orientierungsmassnahmen in der gymnasialen Oberstufe / Ursula Becher ... [et al.]. Nürnberg : Institut für Arbeitsmarkt- und Berufsforschung der Bundesanstalt für Arbeit, 1983. vii, 282 p. : ill. ; 21 cm. (Beiträge zur Arbeitsmarkt- und Berufsforschung, 0173-6574 . 79) Study was conducted with the Universität Bielefeld and the Fachhochschule Bielefeld. Bibliography: p. 216-217. LC Card 85-107586
1. Vocational guidance - Germany, West. 2. Bundesanstalt für Arbeit (Germany). I. Becher, Ursula A. J. II. Universität Bielefeld. III. Fachhochschule Bielefeld. IV. Institut für Arbeitsmarkt- und Berufsforschung. V. Series.
HF5382.5.G3 E9 1983

Evaluation du développement rural / [J.M. Danel, et al.]. 2e éd. / rev. et complétée par G. Ancey. [Paris] : Société d'études pour le développement économique et social, c1982. 201 p. : ill. ; 24 cm. (Méthodologie, 0335-8186 . 14) At head of title: République française, Ministère des relations extérieures, Coopération et développement. Rev. and completed ed. of: Guide d'évaluation a posteriori des opérations de développement rural. c1979. Includes bibliographical references. ISBN 2-11-084484-1 LC Card 84-134740
1. Economic development projects - Developing countries - Evaluation. 2. Rural development projects - Developing countries - Evaluation. I. Danel, J. M. II. Ancey, Gérard. III. Société d'études pour le développement économique et social (France). IV. France. Ministère de la coopération et du développement. V. Guide d'évaluation a posteriori des opérations de développement rural. VI. Series: Méthodologie de la planification, no 14.
HC59.72.E44 E93 1982

Evaluation in education and human services. Evaluating business and industry training /. Boston , Norwell, MA , c1987. xv, 294 p. : ISBN 0-89838-197-5 LC Card 87-5771 DDC 658.3/12404 19
HF5549.5.T7 E88 1987

EVALUATION, JOB. see **JOB EVALUATION.**

An evaluation of Cuba's post-revolutionary socioeconomic models /. Jorge, Antonio, 1931- Coral Gables, Fla. [1984?] 26 p. ; LC Card 87-124135 DDC 330.97291/064 19
HC152.5 .J66 1984

An evaluation of development activities within Sixth Plan period in Bajhang District /. Malla, B. C. Kathmandu , 1985 [i.e. 1986] 76, [3] p. : LC Card 86-903487 DDC 338.9549/6 19
HC425.Z7 B355 1986

An evaluation of industrial purchasing and distribution trends : a research investigation. Cleveland, Ohio (1230 Keith Bldg., Cleveland 44115) : American Supply and Machinery Manufacturers' Association, c1985. 173 p. : ill. ; 28 cm. Prepared by Technical Marketing Associates. LC Card 86-219582 DDC 658.7 19
1. Industrial procurement - United States. 2. Physical distribution of goods - United States. I. American Supply & Machinery Manufacturers' Association. II. Technical Marketing Associates.
HD39.5 .E93 1985

An Evaluation of ROCAP activities in marketing, 1965-71 / Robert R. Nathan Associates, Inc. Draft. Washington, D.C. (1200 18th St., N.W., Washington 20036) : RRNA, [1971] xvii, 82, 3 leaves, [1] leaf of plates : ill. ; 29 cm. "For the Agency for International Development under contract AID/1a-650 (regional)" "May 1971." Photocopy of typescript. Includes bibliographical references. LC Card 81-146599
1. Technical assistance, American - Central America. 2. Marketing - Study and teaching - Central America. I. United States. Agency for International Development. Regional Office for Central America and Panama Affairs. II. Robert R. Nathan Associates.
HC141 .E93 1971

An Evaluation of short-time compensation programs. Washington, D.C. (601 D St., N.W., Room 7422, Washington 20213) : U. S. Dept. of Labor, Employment and Training Administration, Unemployment Insurance Service, 1986. xxv, 222 p. ; 28 cm. (Occasional paper / Unemployment Insurance Service . 86-4) "This report was prepared by Stuart Kerachsky ... [et al.]." Bibliography: p. 221-222. LC Card 86-602784 DDC 368.4/4/00973 s 368.4/4/00973 19
1. Workers' compensation - Government policy - United States - Evaluation. I. Kerachsky, Stuart. II. Series: Unemployment insurance occasional paper , 86-4.
HD7096.U5 U637 no. 86-4 HD7103.65.U6

Evaluation of the Fifth Five Year Plan, 1978-83. Islamabad : Planning Commission, Govt. of Pakistan, [1983] 54 p. ; 27 cm. Chiefly statistical tables. "March 1983." LC Card 84-931227 DDC 338.9549/1 19
1. Pakistan - Economic policy. I. Pakistan. Planning Commission.
HC440.5 .E86 1983

An evaluation of the Gwembe South Development Project, Zambia /. Scudder, Thayer. Binghamton, N.Y., USA [1982] 48 p. ; LC Card 87-119502 DDC 338.96894 19
HC915.Z7 G846 1982

An evaluation of the Ontario Home Renewal Program . Peter Barnard Associates. [Toronto] , 1976. x, 43, [28] p. : LC Card 85-192287
HD7305.O6 P47 1976

An evaluation of the sales tax audit program of the New York State Department of Taxation and Finance. [Albany] : Legislative Commission on the Modernization and Simplification of Tax Administration and the Tax Law, [1985] 2, 75 p. : ill. ; 29 cm. "May 30, 1985." Includes bibliographical references. LC Card 86-621117 DDC 353.97470072/47 19
1. Sales tax - New York (State) - Auditing. 2. Use tax - New York (State) - Auditing. I. New York (State). Legislature. Legislative Commission on the Modernization and Simplification of Tax Administration and the Tax Law.
HJ5715.U6 E83 1985

Evaluation of the small cities community development block grant program--the role of the counties [microform] /. Ferguson, Gary D. Cambridge, Mass. , 1981. vii, vi, 186 p. ;
NYPL [*XME-11,283]

Evaluation of the small cities component of the community development block grant program [microform] . Newman & Hermanson Company. Cambridge, Mass. , 1981. viii, xvii, 147 p. ; ***NYPL [*XME-11,274]***

Evaluation of the small cities program--the role of the counties. Ferguson, Gary D. Evaluation of the small cities community development block grant program--the role of the counties [microform] /. Cambridge, Mass. , 1981. vii, vi, 186 p. ; ***NYPL [*XME-11,283]***

Evaluation of the 1984 selective speed enforcement projects in Virginia /. Sharkey, Stephen M. Charlottesville, Va. [1987] xii, 117, [34] p. : LC Card 87-621546 DDC 388.3/144/09755 19
HE5620.S6 S532 1987

Evaluation report on essential supplies programme. India. Planning Commission. Programme Evaluation Organisation. New

Delhi , 1985. vii, 121 p. ; LC Card 87-902422 DDC 381/.41/0954 19
HF1040.9.I4 I46 1985

Evaluation report (Oslo, Norway) .
(86.7) Chowdhury, Ashraf U. Norway's commodity assistance and import support to Bangladesh . [Oslo, Norway] [1986] 83 p. : LC Card 87-150872 DDC 338.91/481/05492 19
HC440.8 .C48 1986

EVALUATION RESEARCH (SOCIAL ACTION PROGRAMS) - ADDRESSES, ESSAYS, LECTURES.
Performance and credibility . Lexington, Mass. , c1986. x, 307 p. : ISBN 0-669-11037-X (alk. paper) LC Card 85-50707 DDC 658/.048 19
HD62.6 .P47 1986 ***NYPL [JLE 86-1159]***

Evaluation study (Andhra Pradesh (India). Finance and Planning (Planning Wing) Dept. Evaluation Wing) .
(no. 59) Andhra Pradesh (India). Finance and Planning (Planning Wing) Dept. Evaluation Wing. Evaluation study on the working of crash scheme for rural employment. Hyderabad , 1983. 89 p. : LC Card 86-144139 DDC 331.12/042/095484 19
HD5710.85.I42 A532 1983

Evaluation study on the working of crash scheme for rural employment. Andhra Pradesh (India). Finance and Planning (Planning Wing) Dept. Evaluation Wing. Hyderabad , 1983. 89 p. : LC Card 86-144139 DDC 331.12/042/095484 19
HD5710.85.I42 A532 1983

Evaluations et projections de la population active, 1950-2025. Economically active population . Geneva , 1986- v. ; ISBN 92-2-005345-4 (v. 1) ***NYPL [JLM 87-113]***

Evaluations et projections de la population active, 1950-2025. Economically active population estimates and projections, 1950-2025 =. Geneva [1986]- v. <1-5 > ; ISBN 92-2-005345-4 (pbk. : v. 1) : LC Card 86-223275 DDC 331.12/021 19
HD5712 .E26 1986

Evan, Harry Z. Employers and the environmental challenge /. Geneva , 1986. vii, 101 p. ; ISBN 92-2-105647-3 (pbk.) : LC Card 87-123427 DDC 363.7/056 19
HD69.P6 E46 1986

Evangelische Akademie (Tutzing, Germany)
Renten 2000 . München , c1985. 124 p. : ISBN 3-7892-7267-1 LC Card 87-118239 DDC 331.25/2/0943 19
HD7105.35.G3 R46 1985

Evangelisches Missionswerk im Bereich der Bundesrepublik Deutschland und Berlin West. Armut und Reichtum . Hamburg , Göttingen , 1981. 80 p. : ISBN 3-921620-14-7 LC Card 81-159683 DDC 305.5/6 19
HC79.P6 A75 ***NYPL [JLG 85-309]***

Evans, David Michael, 1955- Economic cancer / by David Michael Evans. Saratoga, CA : R&E Publishers, [1987], c1986. 119 p. ; 21 cm. Bibliography: p. 114-119. ISBN 0-88247-764-1 (pbk.) : LC Card 86-62711 DDC 338.973 19
1. United States - Economic conditions - 1981-. 2. United States - Economic policy - 1981-. I. Title.
HC106.8 .E93 1987

Evans, Fred J. Managing the media : proactive strategy for better business-press relations / Fred J. Evans. New York : Quorum Books, 1987. xvii, 172 p. : ill. ; 22 cm. Bibliography: p. [161]-166. Includes index. ISBN 0-89930-156-8 (lib. bdg. : alk. paper) : LC Card 86-25736 DDC 659.2 19
1. Public relations. 2. Press releases. 3. Journalism, Commercial. I. Title.
HD59 .E93 1987

Evans, H. David (Henry David) The political economy of trade and development / H. David Evans. New York : St. Martin's Press, 1988- p. cm. Includes bibliographies and index. CONTENTS. - v. 1. Comparative advantage and growth. ISBN 0-312-00955-0 (v. 1) : LC Card 87-16370 DDC 382 19
1. Commerce. 2. Economic development. 3. Comparative advantage (Commerce). I. Title.
HF1008 .E83 1988

Evans, Howard.
Thody, Philip Malcolm Waller, 1928- Faux amis & key words . London , 1985. 224 p. ; ISBN 0-485-11243-4 : LC Card 84-108125 DDC 443/.21 19
PC2593 .T45 1985 ***NYPL [JFD 86-5704]***

Thody, Philip Malcolm Waller, 1928- Mistakable French . New York , 1985. 224 p. ; ISBN 0-684-18324-2 : LC Card 84-51853 DDC 443/.21 19
PC2593 .T46 1985 ***NYPL [JFD 86-5781]***

Evans, Joel R.
Essentials of marketing. Evans, Joel R. Principles of marketing / Joel R. Evans, Barry Berman. 2nd ed. New York , London , c1988. xxiii, 528, 44, 22 p. : ISBN 0-02-334340-0 LC Card 87-15223 DDC 658.8 19
HF5415 .E865 1988

The Evolution of education in collegiate schools of business . Hempstead, N.Y. , c1987. vi, 237 p. : LC Card 87-80670 DDC 650/.07/1073 19
HF1131 .E94 1987

Principles of marketing / Joel R. Evans, Barry Berman. 2nd ed. New York : Macmillan ; London : Collier Macmillan, c1988. xxiii, 528, 44, 22 p. : ill. (some col.) ; 26 cm. Rev. ed. of: Essentials of marketing. 1984. Includes bibliographies and indexes. ISBN 0-02-334340-0 LC Card 87-15223 DDC 658.8 19
1. Marketing. I. Berman, Barry. II. Evans, Joel R. Essentials of marketing. III. Title.
HF5415 .E865 1988

Evans, Marvin P., 1953- Smith, Harold T., 1932- The Administrative manager . Chicago , c1987. xii, 548 p. : ISBN 0-574-20065-7 : LC Card 86-24881 DDC 651.8 19
HF5547 .S577 1987

Evans, Peter B., 1944- States versus markets in the world-system /. Beverly Hills, Calif. , c1985. 295 p. ; ISBN 0-8039-2510-7 LC Card 85-11716 DDC 338.9 19
HD3611 .S76 1985 ***NYPL [JLD 86-3227]***

Evans, Richard J. The German unemployed . Beckenham, Kent , 1987. xviii, 314 p. : ISBN 0-7099-0941-1 ***NYPL [JLD 87-801]***

Evans, Thomas G. Foreign exchange risk management under statement 52 / Thomas G. Evans and Timothy S. Doupnik. Stamford, Conn. : Financial Accounting Standards Board of the Financial Accounting Foundation, c1986. ix, 133 p. : ill. ; 23 cm. (Research report / Financial Accounting Standards Board) Bibliography: p. 129-133. ISBN 0-910065-21-7 (pbk.) LC Card 86-91435 DDC 657/.48 19
1. Foreign exchange - Accounting. 2. Corporations, American - Accounting. 3. Risk management. I. Doupnik, Timothy S. II. Series: Research report / Financial Accounting Standards Board. III. Title.
HG3853.7 .E935 1986

Evans, William D. Buchholz, Rogene A. Management response to public issues . Englewood Cliffs, N.J. , c1985. x, 389 p. : ISBN 0-13-549940-2 (pbk.) : LC Card 84-18355 DDC 658.4/08 19
HD60 .B83 1985 ***NYPL [JLE 85-1984]***

EVASION, FISCAL. see **TAX EVASION.**

Ėvel′son, Evgeniia. Sudebnye protsessy po ėkonomicheskim delam v SSSR : shetidesiatye gody / Evgeniia Ėvel′son. London : Overseas Publications Interchange Ltd., 1986. 370 p. ; 17 cm. Title in English on added t.p.: "Second economy" in the USSR (trials of the 1960s). Includes indexes. Bibliography: p. 365-370.
1. Informal sector (Economics) - Soviet Union. 2. Offenses against socialist property - Law and legislation - Soviet Union. 3. Black market - Soviet Union. I. Title. II. Title: "Second economy" in the USSR (trials of the 1960s).
NYPL [*QIX 87-4024]

Evenko, Leonid Ivanovich. Mil′ner, Bentsion Zakharovich. Sistemnyĭ podkhod k organizatsii upravleniia /. Moskva , 1983. 223 p. : LC Card 83-229946
HD70.S63 M54 1983

Eventyret Anders Jahre /. Jacobsen, Alf R., 1950- Oslo , c1982. 303 p., [16] p. of plates : ISBN 82-7094-311-8 : LC Card 83-168197
HE569.J34 J33 1982 ***NYPL [JFD 87-4754]***

Everest, Larry. Behind the poison cloud : Union Carbide's Bhopal massacre / by Larry Everest. Chicago : Banner Press, 1986. 192 p. : ill., map ; 22 cm. Bibliography: p. 159-192 ISBN 0-916650-26-X : LC Card 85-26863 DDC 363.1/79 19
1. Union Carbide Ltd. (India). 2. Union Carbide Corporation. 3. Bhopal Union Carbide Plant Disaster, Bhopal, India, 1984. 4. Industrial toxicology - India - Bhopal. 5. Pesticides industry - India - Bhopal - Accidents. 6. Methyl isocyanate - Enviromental aspects - India - Bhopal. I. Title.
HD7269.C452 I524 1986
NYPL [JSD 86-425]

Evers, Adalbert.
Wohnen . Hamburg , c1983. 230 p. : ISBN 3-7672-0808-3 LC Card 83-219819 DDC 363.5/0943 19
HD7339.A3 W616 1983
NYPL [JLE 86-3338]

Die Zweite Stadt . Opladen , c1986. 407 p. : ISBN 3-531-11764-5 LC Card 87-497505 DDC 331.11/0943 19
HD8451 .Z94 1986

Evers, Ben. Perspectives on industrial readjustment, the EEC and the developing countries /. Tilburg, Netherlands , 1978. ii, 98 p. ; ***NYPL [JLF 86-1708]***

Evers, Hans-Dieter.
Auf dem Weg zu einer neuen Weltwirtschaftsordnung? . Baden-Baden , 1983. 478 p. ; ISBN 3-7890-0919-9 LC Card 84-113581
HF1411 .A92 1983

Auf dem Weg zu einer neuen Weltwirtschaftsordnung? . Baden-Baden , 1983. 478 p. ; ISBN 3-7890-0919-9
NYPL [JLD 87-919]

Evers, Maica. Mach mich nicht an . Berlin , c1986. [48] p. : ISBN 3-88114-313-0 : LC Card 87-118837 DDC 331.4/133/0943 19
HD6060.5.G3 M33 1986

Evert Vermeer Stichting. Honger op ons bord . Amsterdam , 1986. 164 p. : ISBN 90-70985-05-5 : LC Card 86-166714
HD9000.5 .H655 1986

Every woman's guide to profitable investing /. Fowler, Elizabeth M. New York, NY , c1986. 260 p. : ISBN 0-8144-5823-8 LC Card 85-48222 DDC 332.6/78/024042 19
HG4921 .F636 1986 ***NYPL [JLE 86-3339]***

Everywoman.
Berry, Mary Frances. Why ERA failed . Bloomington , c1986. ix, 147 p. ; ISBN 0-253-36537-6 LC Card 85-45985 DDC 342.73/0878/02632 347.30287802632 19
KF4758 .B45 1986 ***NYPL [JLE 86-3979]***

Evgeniev, Georgi. Shopov, Dimitŭr. Kachestvoto na truda . Sofiia , 1984. 202 p. : LC Card 85-117683
HC403.Z9 L375 1984

EVICTION CONTROL. see **RENT CONTROL.**

EVICTION - IRELAND - HISTORY.
Parnell, Anna, 1852-1911. The tale of a great sham /. Dublin , Wick, Littlehampton, West Sussex , 1986. 205 p. ; ISBN 0-905223-93-4 LC Card 86-234070 DDC 333.33/5/09415 19
HD625 .P37 1986

EVICTION - SCOTLAND - HIGHLANDS - HISTORY.
Richards, Eric. A history of the Highland clearances /. London , c1982-1985. 2 v. : ISBN 0-85664-496-X : LC Card 81-208122 DDC 333.33/5 19
HD1511.G7 R53 1982 ***NYPL [JLL 82-171]***

Evinger, William R., 1943- Federal statistical directory : the guide to personnel and data sources / William R. Evinger.28th ed. Phoenix, Ariz. : Oryx Press, 1987. iv, 127 p. ; 28 cm. Rev. and updated ed. of: Federal statistical directory 1984 / Richard J. D'Aleo, William R. Evinger. 27th ed. 1984. Includes index. ISBN 0-89774-398-9 (pbk.) LC Card 87-12359 DDC 353.0081/9 19
1. United States - Statistical services - Directories. 2. Statisticians - United States - Directories. I. D'Aleo, Richard J., 1943- Federal statistical directory 1984. II. Title.
HA37.U55 E85 1987

Evolução da situação económica em 1983 / Ministério das Finanças e do Plano, Secretaria de Estado do Planeamento, Departamento Central de Planeamento. 1a. ed. Lisboa : Serviços de Informação para o Planeamento do Departamento Central de Planeamento, 1984.

ix, 149 p. : ill. ; 30 cm. LC Card 85-208352
1. Portugal - Economic conditions - 1974-. 2. Portugal - Economic policy. 3. Portugal - Commercial policy. I. Portugal. Serviços de Informação para o Planeamento.
HC392 .E963 1984

A evolução demográfica portuguesa . Arroteia, Jorge Carvalho, 1947- Lisboa , Amadora, Portugal , 1984 [i.e. 1985] 119 p. : LC Card 86-125507 DDC 304.6/09469 19
HB3621 .A77 1985

Evolução dos índices do número e do valor de cheques compensados no Rio Grande do Sul, período de 1960-7, e sua análise estatística /. Michel, Nelson Emílio. Porto Alegre , 1976. 79 leaves : LC Card 82-159893
HG1692 .M53 1976

A Evolução dos setores secundário e terciário da economia baiana na década de 70 / Secretaria do Planejamento, Ciência e Tecnologia, Centro de Projetos e Estudos-CENPES. Salvador : CENPES, 1985. 80 p. : ill. ; 21 cm. (Série Estudos e projetos . 2) Bibliography: p. 77-80. LC Card 87-124067 DDC 338.4/7/00098142 19
1. Bahia (Brazil : State) - Manufactures. 2. Service industries - Brazil - Bahia (State). I. Centro de Projetos e Estudos (Bahia, Brazil). II. Series: Série Estudos e projetos (Centro de Projetos e Estudos (Bahia, Brazil)) , 2.
HD9734.B73 B334 1985

Evolução e definição da moeda /. Harris, John Andrew de Oliveira. Rio de Janeiro, RJ , 1985. 90 p. : LC Card 87-135878 DDC 332.4/981 19
HG835 .H37 1985

Evolução histórica do salário mínimo no Brasil . Saboia, João, 1944- Rio de Janeiro , 1984. 106 p. ; LC Card 87-403844 DDC 331.2/3 19
HD4920.B8 S265 1984

Evolução sócio-econômica do Brasil /. Ohlweiler, Otto Alcides. Porto Alegre-RS, Brasil [1986?] 209 p. ; LC Card 86-229515
HC187 .O43 1986

Evolució del transport a Salt /. Torrent, Emili. [Salt, Spain] [1984] 32 p. : ISBN 84-85946-59-6 LC Card 87-161246
HE311.S72 S257 1984

Evolución de la economía agraria en el Paraguay . Ayala, Eligio. Asunción, Paraguay , 1986. 196 p. : LC Card 86-234615
HD1898 1986 .A92

Evolución de la fecundidad de la mujer cubana en el período 1959-1984. [Havana?] : República de Cuba, Comité Estatal de Estadísticas, Instituto de Investigaciónes Estadísticas, 1985. 110 p. : ill. ; 28 cm. Bibliography: p. 109. LC Card 87-404207 DDC 304.6/32/097291 19
1. Fertility, Human - Cuba. I. Instituto de Investigaciones Estadísticas (Cuba).
HB959 .E96 1985

Evolución de la industria manufacturera, 1982-1984. Buenos Aires, República Argentina : República Argentina, Presidencia de la Nación, Secretaría de Planificación, Instituto Nacional de Estadística y Censos, [1986] 115 p. : ill. ; 25 cm. (Recopilaciones INDEC . 2) Chiefly tables. LC Card 86-226786
1. Wages - Argentina - Statistics. 2. Hours of labor - Argentina - Statistics. 3. Argentina - Manufactures - Statistics. I. Instituto Nacional de Estadística y Censos (Argentina). II. Series.
HD4999 .E95 1986

La evolución de la minería no cuprífera en Chile /. Zúñiga R., Víctor H. Santiago, Chile , 1985. 61 leaves ; LC Card 86-115526
HD9506.C52 Z86 1985

La evolución de la política monetaria española (1940-1978) . Fanjul Martín, Enrique. [Madrid] , 1979. 164 p. ; LC Card 85-202991
HG1135 .F35 1979

Evolución, presente y futuro de la política común de transportes /. Izquierdo de Bartolomé, Rafael. Madrid [1985?] 56 p. ; ISBN 84-7075-325-8 LC Card 87-111657
HE242.8 .I97 1985

Evolución y perspectivas de la cooperación financiera en América Latina /. Echegaray, Alfredo. Buenos Aires , 1982. 147 p. ; LC Card 86-198731
HG185.L3 E25 1982

Evolution and spatial organization of clan settlements . Ansari, Saiyad Hasan, 1952- New Delhi , 1986. 212 p., [8] p. of plates : LC Card 86-900654
HD879.G45 A57 1986 ***NYPL [JLD 86-3220]***

Evolution de la répartition journalière et horaire des naissances en Suisse. Entwicklung der Geburtenhäufigkeit in der Schweiz nach Wochentag und Stunden /. Bern , 1984. 40 p. : LC Card 85-163580
HA1593 .B45 Heft 114 HB1033

L'évolution des transports urbains de voyageurs face aux nouvelles technologies . France. Conseil économique et social. [Paris] [1986] 184 p. in various pagings : LC Card 86-179126
HE4764 .F73 1986

Evolution du marché du travail pour les diplômés du postsecondaire. Picot, W. Garnett. The changing labour market for postsecondary graduates, 1975-1984 /. Ottawa , c1987. 86, 94 p. : ISBN 0-660-52896-7 (pbk.) : LC Card 87-169612 DDC 331.11/423 19
HD6278.C3 P52 1987

L'évolution du système postal . Pasquet, Sylvie. Paris , c1986. 290 p. : ISBN 2-85757-038-4 LC Card 87-164960
HE7286.Y8 P37 1986

The evolution of corporate financial reporting /. Lee, Thomas Alexander. New York , 1984. x, 307 p. ; ISBN 0-8240-6332-5 (alk. paper) : LC Card 83-49431 DDC 657/.3 19
HF5686.C7 L43 1984 ***NYPL [JLD 86-2835]***

The Evolution of education in collegiate schools of business : past, present, and future : conference proceedings, Hofstra University, School of Business, March 12-14, 1986 / Joel R. Evans, editor. Hempstead, N.Y. : The University, c1987. vi, 237 p. : ill. ; 28 cm. Includes bibliographies. LC Card 87-80670 DDC 650/.07/1073 19
1. Business education - United States - Congresses. 2. Business schools - United States - Congresses. I. Evans, Joel R. II. Hofstra University. School of Business.
HF1131 .E94 1987

The evolution of labor relations in Japan . Gordon, Andrew, 1952- Cambridge, Mass. , 1985. xvi, 524 p. : ISBN 0-674-27130-0 (Harvard Univ. Pr.) LC Card 85-3747 DDC 331/.0952 19
HD8726 .G67 1985 ***NYPL [M-11 435 v.117]***

The evolution of policy behind Taiwan's development success /. Li, Kuo-ting. New Haven , c1988. p. cm. ISBN 0-300-04080-6 LC Card 87-23035 DDC 338.951/249 19
HC430.5 .L4725 1988

Evolution of socio-economic dualism in the Maldives /. Haaland, Gunnar. Bergen [1987] 30 leaves ; LC Card 87-130051 DDC 330.9549/5 19
HC596 .H33 1987

Evoluzione del processo produttivo nelle construzioni . Seminario di aggiornamento per i quadri sindacali della categoria (1985 : Rome, Italy) Milano, Italy , c1986. 142 p. : LC Card 86-210757
HD9715.I82 S46 1985

Evropeĭskoe soobshchestvo : regulirovanie integratsionnykh protsessov / otvetstvennye redaktory M.M. Maksimova, IU.V. Shishkov, T. Palankai ; [avtorskiĭ kollektiv M.M. Maksimova ... et al.]. Moskva : "Nauka", 1986. 270 p. : ill. ; 23 cm. At head of title: Akademiia nauk SSSR. Ordena Trudovogo Krasnogo Znameni Institut mirovoĭ ėkonomiki i mezhdunarodnykh otnosheniĭ. Includes bibliographies. LC Card 86-202812
1. European Economic Community countries - Economic integration. I. Maksimova, M. M. (Margarita Matveevna). II. Shishkov, IUriĭ Vital'evich. III. Palánkai, Tibor. IV. Institut mirovoĭ ėkonomiki i mezhdunarodnykh otnosheniĭ (Akademiia nauk SSSR).
HC241.2 .E867 1986

Evropeĭskoe soobshchestvo v sisteme mezhdunarodnykh otnosheniĭ /. Baranovskiĭ, V. G. (Vladimir Georgievich) Moskva , 1986. 319 p. ; LC Card 86-201822
HF1532.92 .B37 1986

Evstigneev, Ruben Nikolaevich. Kuligin, Pavel Ivanovich. Kriterii ėffektivnosti raboty predpriiatiĭ . Moskva , 1986. 172 p. ; LC Card 86-211780
HD70.E7 K85 1986

Evstigneeva, Liudmila Petrovna. Perspektivnoe finansovoe planirovanie : politėkonomicheskiĭ aspekt / L.P. Evstigneeva. Moskva : Izd-vo "Nauka", 1982. 182 p. ; 20 cm. (Problemy sovetskoĭ ėkonomiki) At head of title: Akademiia nauk SSSR. Institut ėkonomiki. Includes bibliographical references. LC Card 83-124268
1. Finance - Soviet Union. I. Title.
HG186.S55 E97 1982

Evtukh, V. G. (Vladimir Gavrilovich) Sovershenstvovanie khoziaĭstvennogo mekhanizma v stroitel'stve /. Minsk , 1984. 111 p. : LC Card 86-220340
HD9715.S73 B947 1984

Evzerov, R. IA. Rabochee dvizhenie v razvitykh kapitalisticheskikh stranakh . Moskva , 1987. 268 p. ; LC Card 87-164460
HD8378 .R29 1987

Ewald, François. L'Etat providence / François Ewald. Paris : B. Grasset, c1986. 608 p. ; 24 cm. Includes bibliographies. ISBN 2-246-30731-7 : LC Card 86-160935
1. Social security - France - History. 2. Welfare state - History. 3. Insurance, Accident - France - History. I. Title.
HD7175 .E93 1986

Ewanchuk, Michael, 1908- Hawaiian ordeal : Ukrainian contract workers, 1897-1910 / Michael Ewanchuk. Winnipeg, Man. : M. Ewanchuk, c1986. xii, 180 p. : ill. ; 23 cm. Bibliography: p. 177-178. Includes index. ISBN 0-9690768-7-8 (pbk.) : LC Card 87-156576
1. Contract labor - Hawaii - History. 2. Sugar workers - Hawaii - History. 3. Ukrainians - Hawaii - History. I. Title.
HD4875.U5 E93x 1986

Eweka, J. A. (Julius A.)
Nigerian small farmers . Benin-City, Bendel State, Nigeria , 1980. xv, 315 p. ; LC Card 82-206979 DDC 338.1/6 19
HD1339.N5 N54 1980 ***NYPL [Sc D 86-883]***

Village development : food basket management strategy / by J.A. Eweka, V.E. Bello-Osagie, S.O. Olayide. Ibadan, Nigeria : Published by Centre for Agricultural and Rural Development, University of Ibadan for Benin-Owena River Basin Development Authority, 1979. xvi, 194 p. ; 24 cm. Includes bibliographical references and index. LC Card 86-172121 DDC 338.1/9/669 19
1. Agriculture - Economic aspects - Nigeria. 2. Food supply - Nigeria. 3. Food industry and trade - Nigeria. 4. Rural development projects - Nigeria - Management. 5. Agriculture and state - Nigeria. I. Bello-Osagie, V. E. II. Olayide, S. Olajuwon. III. University of Ibadan. Centre for Agricultural and Rural Development. IV. Benin-Owena River Basin Development Authority. V. Title.
HD2145.5 .E94 1979

Ewell, Peter T., 1947- Uxpanapa : resettlement and agricultural development in the Mexican tropics / Peter T. Ewell and Thomas T. Poleman. Ithaca, N.Y. : Dept. of Agricultural Economics, New York State College of Agriculture and Life Sciences, Cornell University, [1982] xiv, 218 p., [35] leaves of plates : ill. ; 28 cm. (Cornell/international agricultural economics study) A.E. research ; 82-7 "January 1982." Cover title. Bibliography: p. 181-195. LC Card 84-621492 DDC 338.1/0972/6 19
1. Agricultural development projects - Mexico - Papaloapan River Valley. 2. Land settlement - Mexico - Papaloapan River Valley. 3. Chinantec Indians. I. Poleman, Thomas T. II. Series. III. Series: A.E. Res. , 82-7. IV. Title.
HD1795.P3 E94 1982

Ewer, Peter. Unions and the future of Australian manufacturing / Peter Ewer, Winton Higgins, and Annette Stevens. Sydney ; Boston : Allen & Unwin, 1987. xi, 189 p. : ill. ; 22 cm. Bibliography: p. 157-186. Includes index. ISBN 0-04-330382-X (pbk.) LC Card 87-164410 DDC 338.4/767/0994 19
1. Australia - Manufactures. 2. Trade-unions - Australia. 3. Industry and state - Australia. I. Higgins, Winton. II. Stevens, Annette. III. Title.
HD9738.A82 E93 1987

Ewers, Hans-Jürgen. Probleme der Ordnungs- und Strukturpolitik . Göttingen , c1984. viii, 311 p., [1] leaf of plates : ISBN 3-525-85925-2

LC Card 84-203472
HE152.6 .P76 1984

Ewert, Ralf. Rechnungslegung, Gläubigerschutz und Agency-Probleme / Ralf Ewert. Wiesbaden : Gabler, c1986. 429 p. ; 25 cm. (Beiträge zur betriebswirtschaftlichen Forschung. Bd. 61) Originally presented as the author's thesis (doctoral)--Universität Passau, 1985. Bibliography: p. 412-429. ISBN 3-409-13710-6 LC Card 87-134169 DDC 657/.3 19
1. Financial statements. 2. Corporations - Finance. 3. Credit. I. Title. II. Series.
HG4028.B2 E92 1986

Ewusi, Kodwo.
The development and resettlement of oncho-freed zones in the Volta River Basin of West Africa : a report to the Food and Agricultural [sic] Organization / by Kodwo Ewusi, S.K. Dapaah, Clement Ahiadeke. [Legon, Ghana] : Institute of Statistical, Social, and Economic Research, University of Ghana, [1985] 89 p. ; 33 cm. (Technical publication . no. 49) "July 1985." Includes bibliographical references. LC Card 87-127503 DDC 333.3/1/667 19
1. Land settlement - Ghana - Volta River Region. 2. Onchocerciasis - Ghana - Volta River Region. 3. Land settlement - Benin - Case studies. 4. Onchoceriasis - Benin - Case studies. 5. Land settlement - Burkina Faso - Case studies. 6. Onchoceriasis - Burkina Faso - Case studies. I. Dapaah, S. K. II. Ahiadeke, Clement. III. Food and Agriculture Organization of the United Nations. IV. Series: Technical publication series (University of Ghana. Institute of Statistical, Social, and Economic Research) , no. 49. V. Title.
HD1022.Z8 V654 1985

Economic trends in Ghana in 1984-85 and prospects for 1986 / by Kodwo Ewusi. [Legon] : Institute of Statistical, Social, and Economic Research, University of Ghana, [1986] 52 p. : ill. ; 33 cm. "December 1986." LC Card 87-127410 DDC 330.9667/05 19
1. Ghana - Economic conditions - 1979- - Statistics. 2. Ghana - Economic policy - Statistics. 3. Economic forecasting - Ghana - Statistics. I. Title.
HC1060 .E975 1986

EX-CONVICTS - EMPLOYMENT - INFORMATION SERVICES - UNITED STATES.
Rugh, Jack Leighton, 1911- Channels to employment for the disabled and ex-offenders /. San Gabriel, Calif. (5555 N. Charlotte Ave., San Gabriel 91776) , c1987. 89 p. : LC Card 87-402897 DDC 362.4/0484/02573 19
HD7256.U5 R75 1987

An examination of issues related to multibank holding companies /. Hultman, Charles W. [Frankfort, Ky. , 1983] [8], 56 leaves ; LC Card 86-620545 DDC 332.1/6 19
HG2567 .H85 1983

EXAMINATIONS, MEDICAL. see **DIAGNOSIS.**

Excedentes financieros y sistema bancario, Uruguay, 1974-1982 /. Rocca, José. Montevideo, Uruguay , 1985. 39 p. : LC Card 85-213768
HC235.S3 R63 1985

The Excel advanced user's guide /. Loggins, Richard, 1949- Indianapolis, Ind., USA , c1987. x, 189 p. : ISBN 0-672-46626-0 (pbk.) : LC Card 87-60109 DDC 005.36/9 19
HF5548.4.E93 L64 1987

EXCEL (COMPUTER PROGRAM)
Benjamin, Louis. The complete book of Excel macros /. Berkeley, Calif. , c1986. xviii, 123 p. : ISBN 0-07-881214-3 (pbk.) LC Card 86-106041 DDC 650/.028/55369 19
HF5548.4.E93 B46 1986
NYPL [JSE 87-239]

Bolocan, David. Advanced Excel /. Blue Ridge Summit, PA , c1986. x, 246 p. : ISBN 0-8306-0368-9 : LC Card 86-5767 DDC 005.36/9 19
HF5548.4.E93 B65 1986
NYPL [JSE 87-561]

Hergert, Douglas. Microsoft Excel with macros . Redmond, Wash. [New York, N.Y.] , c1986. xii, 265 p. : ISBN 0-914845-76-4 (pbk.) : LC Card 86-211548 DDC 005.36/9 19
HF5548.4.E93 H474 1986

Loggins, Richard, 1949- The Excel advanced user's guide /. Indianapolis, Ind., USA , c1987. x, 189 p. : ISBN 0-672-46626-0 (pbk.) : LC Card 87-60109 DDC 005.36/9 19
HF5548.4.E93 L64 1987

Excel macros. Benjamin, Louis. The complete book of Excel macros /. Berkeley, Calif. , c1986. xviii, 123 p. : ISBN 0-07-881214-3 (pbk.) LC Card 86-106041 DDC 650/.028/55369 19
HF5548.4.E93 B46 1986
NYPL [JSE 87-239]

Excélsior (Mexico City, Mexico)
EXCHANGE, BILLS OF. see **BILLS OF EXCHANGE.**

EXCHANGE - CONGRESSES.
Contractual arrangements for intertemporal trade /. Minneapolis, MN , c1987. p. cm. ISBN 0-8166-1533-0 : LC Card 86-24888 DDC 332.64/4/0724 19
HB801 .C629 1987

EXCHANGE CONTROL. see **FOREIGN EXCHANGE - LAW AND LEGISLATION.**

EXCHANGE, FOREIGN. see **FOREIGN EXCHANGE.**

Exchange rate policy and economic distortions . Befekadu Degefe. [Addis Ababa?] 1985. 22 leaves ; LC Card 86-221527 DDC 332.4/560963 19
HG3983 .B43 1985

Exchange rate targets : desirable or disastrous? / edited by John H. Makin. Washington, D.C. : American Enterprise Institute for Public Policy Research, c1986. ix, 59 p. ; 23 cm. (AEI studies . 451) Papers presented at an AEI conference, held on Sept. 17, 1986. ISBN 0-8447-3615-5 (pbk. : alk. paper) : LC Card 86-72463 DDC 332.4/5 19
1. Foreign exchange - Congresses. I. Makin, John H. II. American Enterprise Institute for Public Policy Research. III. Series.
HG203 .E98 1986

Exchange rates and international macroeconomics / edited by Jacob A. Frenkel. Chicago : University of Chicago Press, 1983. x, 382 p. : ill. ; 24 cm. (A conference report / National Bureau of Economic Research) Papers and comments presented at a conference held in Cambridge, Mass., Nov. 20-21, 1981; sponsored by the National Bureau of Economic Research. Includes bibliographical references and indexes. ISBN 0-226-26249-9 LC Card 83-14524 DDC 332.4/56 19
1. Foreign exchange - Congresses. 2. International finance - Congresses. I. Frenkel, Jacob A. II. Series: Conference report (National Bureau of Economic Research).
HG205 1981c ***NYPL [JLE 86-3231]***

Exchange rates, money, and output . Grauwe, Paul de. New York , 1985. xii, 240 p. : ISBN 0-312-27403-3 : LC Card 84-11692 DDC 339/.094 19
HC241.2 .G69 1985 ***NYPL [JLD 86-3007]***

Exchange rates, trade, and the U. S. economy / editors, Sven W. Arndt, Richard J. Sweeney, Thomas D. Willett. Cambridge, Mass. : Ballinger, c1985. xxi, 296 p. : ill. ; 24 cm. Includes bibliographies and index. ISBN 0-88410-948-8 LC Card 84-28328 DDC 332.4/560973 19
1. Foreign exchange problem - Addresses, essays, lectures. 2. Foreign exchange problem - United States - Addresses, essays, lectures. I. Arndt, Sven W. II. Sweeney, Richard J. III. Willett, Thomas D.
HG3851 .E94 1985 ***NYPL [JLE 85-2269]***

EXCHANGES, COMMODITY. see **COMMODITY EXCHANGES.**

EXCHANGES, PRODUCE. see **COMMODITY EXCHANGES.**

EXCHANGES, STOCK. see **STOCK-EXCHANGE.**

EXCISE. see **TAXATION OF ARTICLES OF CONSUMPTION.**

EXCISE TAX - CANADA - HISTORY.
McIntosh, Dave. The collectors . Toronto, Ont., Canada , c1984. 414 p. : ISBN 0-920053-29-7 LC Card 85-162089 DDC 354.710072/46/09 19
HJ6751.A6 M35 1984 ***NYPL [JLE 86-2880]***

EXCISE TAX - YUGOSLAVIA - ECONOMETRIC MODELS.
Popović, Dejan. Ekonomski efekti posrednih poreza /. Beograd , 1983. 286 p. : LC Card 86-173775
HJ5156.5 P67 1983

L'exclusion des pauvres dans les villes du Tiers-Monde . Durand-Lasserve, Alain. Paris , c1986. 198 p. : ISBN 2-85802-613-8 LC Card 87-111461
HD7391 .D79 1986

EXCLUSIVE CONTRACTS - ECONOMIC ASPECTS - EUROPE.
Bürge, Alfons. Rechtsdogmatik und Wirtschaft . Berlin , c1987. 280 p. ; ISBN 3-428-06124-1 LC Card 87-134998 DDC 332.8/3/094 19
HB551 .B87 1987

EXECUTIES - TIME MANAGEMENT.
Hatékony vezetői időgazdálkodás . Budapest , 1984. 62 p. ; ISBN 963-7902-09-0 (Magy. nemz. bibl.) LC Card 85-177403
HD69.T54 H38 1984

EXECUTIVE ABILITY - EVALUATION.
Ficher, Michael. Die Messung des Führungsverhaltens . Bochum , 1981. v, 366 p. : ISBN 3-88339-193-X : LC Card 81-205568
HD57.7 .F65 1981 ***NYPL [JLD 86-2580]***

EXECUTIVE ABILITY - HANDBOOKS, MANUALS, ETC.
Lewis, Mike. 20 activities for developing managerial effectiveness . Aldershot, Hants, England , c1986. xii, 276 p. : ISBN 0-566-02515-9 LC Card 87-147860 DDC 658.4/07124 19
HD31 .L387 1986

The Executive bookshelf.
The Art of managing human resources /. New York , 1987. xii, 307 p. : ISBN 0-19-504882-2 (alk. paper) LC Card 86-31107 DDC 658.3/01 19
HF5549.5.M3 A78 1987

Generating technological innovation /. New York , 1987. xii, 299 p. : ISBN 0-19-505023-1 (alk. paper) LC Card 86-33119 DDC 658.5/14 19
HD45 .G39 1987

Planning strategies that work /. New York , 1987. xii, 287 p. : ISBN 0-19-504883-0 (alk. paper) LC Card 86-31117 DDC 658.4/012 19
HD30.28 .P555 1987

The Strategic use of information technology /. New York , 1987. xiii, 206 p. : ISBN 0-19-505048-7 (alk. paper) : LC Card 87-1606 DDC 658/.05 19
HD30.2 .S79 1987

Executive chess /. Bennett, Steven J. New York , c1987. xv, 256 p. ; ISBN 0-453-00550-0 LC Card 87-1723 DDC 658.4/03 19
HD30.29 .B46 1987

EXECUTIVE DEPARTMENTS. See administrative agencies and subdivision Executive departments under names of countries, cities, etc, e.g.: **UNITED STATES - EXECUTIVE DEPARTMENTS.**

The executive deskbook /. Uris, Auren. New York , c1988. xiv, 427 p. : ISBN 0-442-28790-9 (pbk.) LC Card 87-10597 DDC 658.4 19
HD31 .U66 1988

Executive guide to employment practices . Cope, Thom K. Lincoln, Neb. , c1984. vii, 163 p. : ISBN 0-939644-14-2 (pbk.) : LC Card 84-62043 DDC 344.73/01133 347.3041133 19
KF3464.Z9 C65 1984 ***NYPL [JLE 87-75]***

The executive guide to operational planning /. Morrisey, George L. San Francisco , 1988. xxvii, 130 p. : ISBN 1-555-42064-8 (alk. paper) LC Card 87-45508 DDC 658.4/012 19
HD30.28 .M65 1988

The executive guide to strategic planning /. Below, Patrick J. San Francisco, Calif. , c1987. xxiii, 136 p. : ISBN 1-555-42032-X (alk. paper) LC Card 86-27863 DDC 658.4/012 19
HD30.28 .B45 1987

EXECUTIVE INVESTIGATIONS. see **GOVERNMENTAL INVESTIGATIONS.**

Executive reports series.
The Executive reports series.
How to find information about executives /. Washington, DC , c1986. 72 p. ; ISBN 0-934940-44-4 (pbk.) : LC Card 86-51569 DDC 658.4/0072 19
HD38.25.U6 H69 1986

How to find information about foreign firms /. Washington, D.C. , c1987. 93 p. ; ISBN 0-934940-46-0 (pbk.) : LC Card 86-51568

DDC 016.3388/8873 19
HD2785 .H69 1987

Rosenberg, Gerald I. How to find information about acquisition candidates /. Washington, D.C. , c1987. 79 p. ; ISBN 0-934940-45-2 LC Card 86-51570 DDC 016.3387/4/0973 19
HD2785 .R58 1987

The executive résumé handbook /. Dickhut, Harold W., 1911- New York , c1987. vii, 215 p. ; ISBN 0-13-294331-X (pbk.) : LC Card 86-22692 DDC 650.1/4/024658 19
HF5383 .D469 1987

Executive retirement management . Leedy, Jack J., 1921- New York, N.Y. , c1987. xi, 260 p. ; ISBN 0-8160-1286-5 LC Card 86-24010 DDC 658.4/07132 19
HD7125 .L43 1987

Executive safety and international terrorism . Scotti, Anthony J. Englewood Cliffs, N.J. , c1986. xv, 220 p. ; ISBN 0-13-294380-8 : LC Card 86-15079 DDC 658.4/73 19
HF5549.5.E45 S36 1986
NYPL [JLE 87-393]

Executive skills program. Bittel, Lester R. [New York, N.Y., U. S.A.] (1633 Broadway, New York 10019) [c1986] 4 v. : LC Card 86-233068 DDC 658.4/09 19
HD38.2 .B569 1986

Executive talent : developing and keeping the best people / Eli Ginzberg, editor. New York : J. Wiley, c1988. vii, 184 p. ; 24 cm. Bibliography: p. 140-142. Includes index. CONTENTS. - The new world of work / Eli Ginzberg -- Human resources in the large corporation / George Vojta -- Human resources in strategic planning / Boris Yavitz -- The human resources function / Stephen Drotter -- Restructuring for productivity / Kirby Warren -- Managers through time / Douglas W. Bray -- Executives in four fields / John T. Dunlop -- Corporate leadership and the public weal / Mitchell Sviridoff and Renee Berger -- Tomorrow's executives: findings and directions for research / Eli Ginzberg. ISBN 0-471-63422-0 LC Card 87-24946 DDC 658.4/09 19
1. Executives. 2. Executive ability. I. Ginzberg, Eli, 1911-.
HD38.2 .E94 1988

EXECUTIVES - ADDRESSES, ESSAYS, LECTURES.
The Leader-manager /. New York , c1986. xi, 511 p. : ISBN 0-471-83693-1 : LC Card 86-1316 DDC 658.4/092 19
HD38.2 .L42 1986 ***NYPL [JLE 86-2930]***

EXECUTIVES - AFRICA - TRAINING OF.
Rwegasira, Kami S. P. Administering management development institutions in Africa /. Aldershot, England , Brookfield, Vt. , 1988. p. cm. ISBN 0-566-05501-5 : LC Card 87-17688 DDC 658.4/07124/096 19
HF5549.5.A78 R94 1988

EXECUTIVES, BLACK - SOUTH AFRICA - CASE STUDIES.
Charoux, J. A. E. (J. A. Eric) The integration of the Black manager into South African organizations /. Cape Town , 1986. xi, 178 p. : ISBN 0-7021-1706-4 (pbk.) LC Card 87-113544 DDC 331.6/3/968 19
HD38.25.S6 C53 1986

EXECUTIVES - CALIFORNIA - SANTA CLARA COUNTY - BIOGRAPHY.
Caddes, Carolyn, 1935- Portraits of success . Palo Alto, Calif. , 1986. viii, 138 p. : ISBN 0-935382-56-9 : LC Card 86-40032 DDC 338.4/7621/0979473 19
HD9696.A3 U53173 1986
NYPL [MFX (Caddes) 87-542]

EXECUTIVES - EMPLOYMENT - UNITED STATES.
Lewis, William, 1946- Fast-track careers . New York , c1987. x, 212 p. ; ISBN 0-471-83801-2 (pbk.) : LC Card 87-10045 DDC 331.7/02/0973 19
HF5382.5.U5 L45 1987

EXECUTIVES - FRANCE.
Le Guen, René. Oxygène pour tous les cerveaux /. Paris , c1985. 204 p. : ISBN 2-209-05743-4 : LC Card 86-117864 DDC 331.7/12/0944 19
HD8038.F7 L4 1985

EXECUTIVES - GERMANY (WEST) - INTERVIEWS.
Möller, Wolf-Peter. Der Erfolg von Unternehmenszusammenschlüssen . München , c1983. 403 p. : ISBN 3-597-10456-8 LC Card 83-227517
HD2746.5 .M65 1983

An Executive's guide to econometric forecasting : a book of readings / edited by A. Migliaro and C.L. Jain. Flushing, N.Y. : Graceway Pub. Co., c1983. 74 p. : ill. ; 28 cm. Cover title. Includes bibliographical references. ISBN 0-932126-10-3 (pbk.) LC Card 82-90726 DDC 330/.028 19
1. Economic forecasting - Mathematical models - Addresses, essays, lectures. 2. Econometrics - Addresses, essays, lectures. I. Migliaro, Al. II. Jain, Chaman L.
HB3730 .E978 1983 ***NYPL [JLF 86-1166]***

The executive's guide to management accounting and control systems /. Rotch, William. Houston, Tex. , 1987. ix, 225 p. : ISBN 0-87393-044-4 LC Card 87-163287 DDC 658.1/511 19
HF5635 .R829 1987

EXECUTIVES - HANDBOOKS, MANUALS, ETC.
Brownstone, David M. The manager's advisor /. New York , c1987. vii, 296 p. ; ISBN 0-8144-7682-1 (pbk.) : LC Card 87-47712 DDC 658.4 19
HD38.2 .B75 1987

EXECUTIVES - HUNGARY.
Héthy, Lajos. A vezetők részvétele a vezetésben /. Budapest , 1983. 87 p. : ISBN 963-608-057-7 LC Card 85-110905
HD38.25.H9 H47 1983

EXECUTIVES - HUNGARY - DIRECTORIES.
Magyar Kereskedelmi Kamara. Managers in Hungary . [Budapest?] , 1986. 368 p. ; ISBN 963-7073-09-4 (pbk.) LC Card 87-137498 DDC 658/.0025/439 19
HD38.25.H9 M34 1986

EXECUTIVES - HUNGARY - RATING OF.
Várkonyi, Margit. A vezetők véleményezése /. Budapest , 1984. 66 p. : ISBN 963-322-189-7 : LC Card 85-176949
HD70.H8 V38 1984

EXECUTIVES - INTERVIEWS.
Bennett, Steven J. Executive chess /. New York , c1987. xv, 256 p. ; ISBN 0-453-00550-0 LC Card 87-1723 DDC 658.4/03 19
HD30.29 .B46 1987

Kanchier, Carole. Questers . Saratoga, Calif. , c1987. xi, 225 p. ; ISBN 0-88247-767-6 (pbk.) : LC Card 87-60351 DDC 658.4/09 19
HF5384 .K36 1987

Laskin, David. Getting into advertising /. New York , 1986. xiii, 272 p. : ISBN 0-345-32598-2 (pbk.) LC Card 86-90721 DDC 659.1/023/73 19
HF5828.4 .L37 1986

EXECUTIVES - ITALY.
Guala Duca, Riccardo, 1935- I nuovi colletti bianchi . Milano, Italy , c1985. 164 p. : LC Card 86-128292 DDC 331.7/92/0945 19
HD8039.M4 I854 1985

EXECUTIVES - KENYA.
Gershenberg, Irving. Multinational enterprises, transfer of managerial know-how, technology choice and employment effects . Geneva , 1983. iii, 33 p. ; ISBN 92-2-103508-5 (pbk.) LC Card 86-213574 DDC 338.8/886762 19
HD2920.5 .G47 1983

EXECUTIVES, RATING OF.
Tanulmányok a vezetők minősítéséről és a személyi értékelés rendszeréről. Budapest , 1985. 211 p. ; ISBN 963-02-3494-7 (Magy. nemz. bibl.) LC Card 85-193396
HF5549.5.R3 T35 1985

EXECUTIVES - RECRUITING.
Friedman, Stewart D. Leadership succession systems and corporate performance /. New York, N.Y. (316 Uris Hall, New York 10027) , c1985. ix, 141 p. ; LC Card 86-162460 DDC 331.25/96 19
HD38.2 .F73 1985

Korn, Lester. The winning edge . New York , c1988. p. cm. ISBN 0-671-55263-5 LC Card 87-23249 DDC 658.4/09 19
HD38.2 .K67 1988

Structured hiring . New York, NY, U. S.A. , c1987. viii leaves, 144 p. : ISBN 0-86604-221-0 (pbk.) LC Card 87-156398 DDC 658.3/112 19
HF5549.5.R44 S83 1987

EXECUTIVES - RUSSIAN S.F.S.R. - MOSCOW - BIOGRAPHY.
Dolzhnost´--direktor /. Moskva , 1985. 333 p. : LC Card 85-145325
HC332.5.A2 D64 1985

EXECUTIVES - SALARIES, ETC. - UNITED STATES.
Butler, Stephen A. Management incentive compensation plans /. Montvale, N.J. , c1986. v, 55 p. ; ISBN 0-86641-140-2 (pbk.) LC Card 86-230062 DDC 658.4/07225 19
HD4965.5.U6 B86 1986

EXECUTIVES - SALARIES ,ETC. - UNITED STATES - STATISTICS.
Compensation and benefits in research & development /. Crete, IL , c1987. 692 p. ; ISBN 0-916506-34-7 (pbk.) LC Card 87-403067 DDC 331.2/816584/00973021 19
HD4965.5.U6 C656 1987

Hiring costs and strategies . New York, N.Y. , c1986. v, 82 p. : ISBN 0-8144-3153-4 (pbk.) LC Card 86-209862 DDC 658.4/07111/0973 19
HD38.25.U6 H57 1986

EXECUTIVES - SALARIES, PENSIONS, ETC. - CANADA.
Hanson, R. Employee benefits and conditions of employment in Canada . [Ottawa, Ont.] , c1977. iv, 111 p. : ISBN 0-662-00630-5 (pbk.) LC Card 82-136152
HD4928.N62 C225 1977

EXECUTIVES - SALARIES, PENSIONS, ETC. - UNITED STATES.
Nash, Allan N. Managerial compensation /. Scarsdale, N.Y. , c1980. 56 p. ; ISBN 0-89361-022-4 : LC Card 80-21044 DDC 658.4/072/0973 19
HD4965.5.U6 N22
NYPL [JLM 83-380 no.15]

EXECUTIVES - SELECTION AND APPOINTMENT.
Wareham, John. [Basic business types.] Wareham's basic business types . New York , 1987. ix, 260 p. ; ISBN 0-689-11756-6 : LC Card 86-47686 DDC 658.4/09 19
HD38.2 .W37 1987

EXECUTIVES - SEXUAL BEHAVIOR.
Westoff, Leslie Aldridge. Corporate romance . New York, NY , c1985. xiii, 246 p. ; ISBN 0-8129-1257-8 : LC Card 85-40284 DDC 658.4/095 19
HD6054.3 .W47 1985 ***NYPL [JLD 86-1042]***

EXECUTIVES - SOVIET UNION.
Deĭneko, O. A. (Oleg Aleksandrovich) Sovremennyĭ organizator proizvodstva /. Moskva , 1984. 172, [2] p. : LC Card 85-112451
HD38.25.S65 D45 1984

Martanus, R. V. (Rīurik Vital´evich) Sotsial´noe upravlenie . Moskva , 1986. 141 p. ; LC Card 87-156789
HD38.25.S65 M35 1986

Perestroĭka i rukovoditel´ /. Moskva , 1987. 143 p. ; LC Card 87-164793
HD38.25.S65 P47 1987

EXECUTIVES - SWITZERLAND - BIOGRAPHY.
Michel-Alder, Elisabeth. Männer im Glashaus . Zürich , c1986. 238 p. : ISBN 3-280-01561-8 LC Card 86-180438
HD38.25.S9 M52 1986

EXECUTIVES - TAXATION - GREAT BRITAIN.
Blackstone, L. R. (Lance R.) UK tax savings for the higher paid (1979) /. London , c1979. 10 p. ; LC Card 81-112830
HJ4708.A7 B533 1979

EXECUTIVES - TRAINING. see **EXECUTIVES, TRAINING OF.**

EXECUTIVES - TRAINING OF - ASIA.
Developing managers in Asia /. Singapore , Reading, Mass. , 1986. p. cm. ISBN 0-201-13653-8 : LC Card 86-28717 DDC 658/.007/15 19
HD38.25.A78 D48 1986

EXECUTIVES, TRAINING OF - GREAT BRITAIN.

Hussey, D. E. (David E.) Management training and corporate strategy . Oxford [Oxfordshire] , New York , 1988. x, 201 p. : ISBN 0-08-034036-9 : LC Card 87-22075 DDC 658.4/07124 19
HD30.42.G7 H87 1988

EXECUTIVES - TRAINING OF - HANDBOOKS, MANUALS, ETC.
Lewis, Mike. 20 activities for developing managerial effectiveness . Aldershot, Hants, England , c1986. xii, 276 p. : ISBN 0-566-02515-9 LC Card 87-147860 DDC 658.4/07124 19
HD31 .L387 1986

EXECUTIVES - TRAINING OF - JAPAN.
Nötzli, Irene M. A view of Japanese management, especially management development in large business enterprises /. Zürich , c1982. ix, 281 p. : ISBN 3-7255-2191-3 (pbk.) LC Card 82-237094 DDC 658.4/07124 19
HF5549.5.T7 N638 1982 ***NYPL [TB (Zürich. Universität. Handelwissenschaftiches Seminar. Mitteilungen. Heft 156)]***

EXECUTIVES - TRAINING OF - SOVIET UNION.
Martanus, R. V. (Rīurik Vital′evich) Sotsial′noe upravlenie . Moskva , 1986. 141 p. ; LC Card 87-156789
HD38.25.S65 M35 1986

Podgotovka upravlencheskikh kadrov--opyt, problemy, perspektivy (po zarubezhnym materialam) . Moskva , 1984. 188 p. ; LC Card 85-188986
HD30.4 .P6 1984

EXECUTIVES, TRAINING OF - UNITED STATES - DIRECTORIES.
Jones, Constance. Beat the MBAs to the top! . Reading, Mass. , c1987. vii, 360 p. ; ISBN 0-201-11310-4 (pbk.) : LC Card 87-11363 DDC 650/.07/15 19
HF1131 .J756 1987

EXECUTIVES - UKRAINE.
Sumenko, ÎE. I. Kerivnyk-orhanizator i vykhovatel′ /. Kyïv , 1985. 189 p. ; LC Card 87-109649
HD38.2 .S85 1985

EXECUTIVES - UNITED STATES.
Birsner, E. Patricia. The 40+ job-hunting guide . New York, NY , c1987. xx, 250 p. : ISBN 0-13-329152-9 (pbk.) : LC Card 87-2438 DDC 650.1/4/024658 19
HD38.25.U6 B53 1987

Fernandez, John P., 1941- Survival in the corporate fishbowl . Lexington, Mass. , c1987. xiii, 314 p. : ISBN 0-669-10336-5 (alk. paper) LC Card 85-40021 DDC 302.3/5 19
HD6957.U6 F47 1987

Friedman, Stewart D. Leadership succession systems and corporate performance /. New York, N.Y. (316 Uris Hall, New York, N.Y. 10027) , c1985. ix, 141 p. :
NYPL [JLF 87-255]

Groneman, Carol. [Corporate Ph. D.] Corporate PhD . New York, N.Y., U. S.A. , 1987, c1985. xx, 156 p. ; ISBN 0-14-010123-3 (pbk.) LC Card 86-30654 DDC 658.4/09 19
HD38.25.U6 G76 1987

EXECUTIVES - UNITED STATES - ATTITUDES.
The Corporate view . Washington, DC , c1982. vii, 92 p. ; ***NYPL [JLF 87-940]***

EXECUTIVES - UNITED STATES - CASE STUDIES.
Friedman, Thomas. Up the ladder . New York, NY , 1986. xi, 203 p. ; ISBN 0-446-51291-5 LC Card 85-40655 DDC 658.4/09/0973 19
HD38.25.U6 F75 1986 ***NYPL [JLE 86-2840]***

EXECUTIVES - UNITED STATES - DISMISSAL OF.
Hirsch, Paul Morris. Pack your own parachute . Reading, Mass. , c1987. xix, 197 p. ; ISBN 0-201-12205-7 (pbk.) : LC Card 87-14388 DDC 658.4/09 19
HD38.25.U6 H578 1987

EXECUTIVES - UNITED STATES - INFORMATION SERVICES - UNITED STATES.
How to find information about executives /. Washington, DC , c1986. 72 p. ; ISBN 0-934940-44-4 (pbk.) : LC Card 86-51569 DDC 658.4/0072 19
HD38.25.U6 H69 1986

EXECUTIVES - UNITED STATES - INTERVIEWS.
Winner take all /. New York, NY , c1987. x, 222 p. ; ISBN 0-8144-7689-9 (pbk.) : LC Card 87-47708 DDC 658.4/09 19
HD38.25.U6 W56 1987

EXECUTIVES - UNITED STATES - RECRUITING.
Hiring costs and strategies . New York , c1986. v, 82 p. : ISBN 0-8144-3153-4
NYPL [JLF 86-960]

Lewis, William, 1946- The Prentice-Hall directory of executive search firms /. New York , c1986. v, 328 p. ; ISBN 0-671-55518-9 (pbk.) LC Card 85-30190 DDC 658.4/07111/02573 19
HD38.25.U6 L49 1986
NYPL [*R-Econ. 87-1586]

Lucht, John, 1933- Rites of passage at $100,000+ . New York , c1988. ix, 547 p. ; ISBN 0-942785-07-X : LC Card 87-50459 DDC 658.4/09 19
HD38.25.U6 L83 1988

EXECUTIVES - UNITED STATES - RECRUITING - COSTS - STATISTICS.
Hiring costs and strategies . New York, N.Y. , c1986. v, 82 p. : ISBN 0-8144-3153-4 (pbk.) LC Card 86-209862 DDC 658.4/07111/0973 19
HD38.25.U6 H57 1986

EXECUTIVES - UNITED STATES - RECRUITING - DIRECTORIES.
Lewis, William, 1946- The Prentice-Hall directory of executive search firms /. New York , c1986. v, 328 p. ; ISBN 0-671-55518-9 (pbk.) LC Card 85-30190 DDC 658.4/07111/02573 19
HD38.25.U6 L49 1986
NYPL [*R-Econ. 87-1586]

EXECUTIVES - UNITED STATES - RETIREMENT - MANAGEMENT.
Leedy, Jack J., 1921- Executive retirement management . New York, N.Y. , c1987. xi, 260 p. ; ISBN 0-8160-1286-5 LC Card 86-24010 DDC 658.4/07132 19
HD7125 .L43 1987

EXECUTIVES - VOCATIONAL GUIDANCE - UNITED STATES.
Lear, Robert W. How to turn your MBA into a CEO /. New York , London , c1987. xvii, 222 p. ; ISBN 0-02-569610-6 LC Card 86-28332 DDC 650/.07/1173 19
HF1131 .L39 1987

Exenciones arancelarias e integración / José María Aragão ... [et al.]. [Buenos Aires] : Banco Interamericano de Desarrollo, Instituto para la Integración de América Latina, 1986. 273 p. ; 23 cm. (Cooperación empresarial--estudios) Includes bibliographical references. LC Card 87-400577 DDC 382.7/1/098 19
1. Duty-free importation - Latin America. 2. Latin America - Economic integration. 3. Tariff - Law and legislation - Latin America. I. Aragão, José María. II. Institute for Latin American Integration. III. Series.
HF1733.L29 E96 1986

Exercises in dynamic macroeconomic theory /. Manuelli, Rodolfo E. Cambridge, Mass. , 1987. xi, 223 p. ; ISBN 0-674-27476-8 (pbk. : alk. paper) LC Card 86-25767 DDC 339/.0729 19
HB172.5 .S27 1987 Suppl.

Exhausting the earth . Perdue, Peter C., 1949- Cambridge, Mass. , 1987. xvii, 331 p. : ISBN 0-674-27504-7 LC Card 87-5067 DDC 338.1/0951/215 19
HD2100.H86 P47 1987

Exhibit marketing . Chapman, Edward A. New York , c1987. x, 309 p. : ISBN 0-07-010669-X : LC Card 87-2621 DDC 659.1/52 19
HF5845 .C47 1987

EXHIBITIONS.
Chapman, Edward A. Exhibit marketing . New York , c1987. x, 309 p. : ISBN 0-07-010669-X : LC Card 87-2621 DDC 659.1/52 19
HF5845 .C47 1987

Mortsiefer, Joachim. Messen und Ausstellungen als Mittel der Absatzpolitik mittelständischer Herstellerbetriebe /. Göttingen , 1986. 534 p. : ISBN 3-509-01399-9 : LC Card 86-210320 DDC 381/.18 19
HF5470 .M583 1986

EXHIBITS. see **EXHIBITIONS.**

Exil sous contrat . Guth, Suzie. Paris , c1984. 479 p. : ISBN 2-903871-53-1 : LC Card 85-141675
HC800 .G88 1984

Existe otra Argentina posible /. Perdía, Roberto Cirilo. Buenos Aires , 1986. 276 p. : ISBN 950-97640-0-0 LC Card 87-139879 DDC 336.3/4/0982 19
HG3881.5.I58 P47 1986

The existence of a Latin American mortality pattern . Flórez Nieto, Carmen Elisa. Bogotá, Colombia , 1985. 153 p. : LC Card 87-145922
HB1397 .F56 1985

EXISTENTIAL PSYCHOLOGY.
Lichtenstein, Heinz, 1904- The dilemma of human identity /. New York , c1983. xiv, 399 p. ; ISBN 0-87668-677-3 : LC Card 84-45086 DDC 155.2 19
BF697 .L52 1983 ***NYPL [JFE 86-2218]***

O êxodo rural no município de Pirajuí /. Rocha, José Carlos Rodrigues. Bauru-SP , 1984. iv, 66 p. : LC Card 86-158771
HB2024.P57 R62 1984

To exōteriko emporio portokaliōn tēs Hellados /. Mēliakos, Dēm. Iōan. Athēna , 1984. 176 p. ; LC Card 86-201864
HD9259.O8 G85 1984

Expand your investment horizons and increase your stock market profits /. Perritt, Gerald W. Chicago, IL , c1987. viii, 288 p. : ISBN 0-930369-03-3 (pbk.) LC Card 87-401495 DDC 332.63/2 19
HG4527 .P39 1987

Expanding empire . Copeland, Vincent. New York, N.Y. , 1972. 62 p. ; LC Card 87-404126 DDC 338.8/8973 19
HG4538 .C668 1972

Expanding your business with other people's money /. Seltz, David D. New York, N.Y. , c1984. 2 v. in 1 : ISBN 0-932648-29-0 LC Card 83-12233 DDC 658.8/708 19
HF5429.235.U5 S442 1984
NYPL [JLF 86-664]

Expanding your consulting practice with seminars /. Holtz, Herman. New York , c1987. xvi, 240 p. : ISBN 0-471-85899-4 LC Card 87-14231 DDC 658.4/6 19
HD69.C6 H625 1987

Expansão da fronteira agrícola e meio-ambiente . Mueller, Charles Curt. [S.l. , between 1979 and 1985] 38, [4] leaves, [1] leaf of plates : LC Card 86-197353
HD499.C45 M83 1979

Expansión del cultivo de la caña de azúcar y de la ganadería en el Nordeste del Brasil . Barbosa, Túlio. Santiago de Chile , Nueva York, NY, Estados Unidos de América , 1986. 170 p. : ISBN 92-1-321209-7 LC Card 87-400309 DDC 338.1/7361/09813 19
HD9114.B7 N67943 1986

The expansion of cocoa production in Ghana . Arhin, Kwame. [Ghana] [1985] xiii, 137 p., [5] p. of plates : LC Card 86-222543 DDC 338.1/7374/09667 19
HD8039.C6362 G42 1985

EXPANSION (U. S. POLITICS) see **IMPERIALISM.**

EXPEDITIONS, ANTARCTIC. see **ANTARCTIC REGIONS.**

EXPENDITURES, PUBLIC - CONGRESSES.
Public expenditure . Dublin, Ireland , 1986. 138 p. ; ISBN 0-906980-56-9 (pbk.) : LC Card 86-143826 DDC 336.3/9 19
HJ7461 .P83 1986 ***NYPL [JLD 87-553]***

EXPENDITURES, PUBLIC - COST EFFECTIVENESS.
Erfolgskontrolle bei der Verausgabung öffentlicher Mittel /. Baden-Baden , 1986. 133 p. : ISBN 3-7890-1208-4 LC Card 86-164102
HJ7793 .E73 1986

EXPENDITURES, PUBLIC - DEVELOPING COUNTRIES.
Jimenez, Emmanuel, 1952- Pricing policy in the social sectors . Baltimore , 1987. v, 170 p. ; ISBN 0-8018-3501-1 : LC Card 86-27590

DDC 338.4/33621/091724 19
HJ7469 .J56 1987

EXPENDITURES, PUBLIC - EVALUATION.
Erfolgskontrolle bei der Verausgabung öffentlicher Mittel /. Baden-Baden , 1986. 133 p. : ISBN 3-7890-1208-4 LC Card 86-164102
HJ7793 .E73 1986

EXPENDITURES, PUBLIC - HISTORY.
Webber, Carolyn. A history of taxation and expenditure in the Western world /. New York , c1986. 734 p. ,[16] p. of plates : ISBN 0-671-54617-1 LC Card 86-3863 DDC 336.2/009 19
HJ2250 .W42 1986 ***NYPL [JLE 86-3474]***

EXPENDITURES, PUBLIC - MATHEMATICAL MODELS.
Altenburg, Lutz, 1943- Zur Einbeziehung öffentlicher Zwischenprodukte in Mehrsektorenmodelle /. Frankfurt am Main , New York , c1985. 315 p. : ISBN 3-8204-9046-9 LC Card 85-231430 DDC 338.4/3363/0724 19
HB846.5 .A47 1985

EXPENDITURES, PUBLIC - UNITED STATES.
Tax expenditures . Washington, D.C. [1983] xiv, 82 p. ; ***NYPL [JLF 84-401]***

Verdier, James M. Tax expenditures . Washington, D.C. , 1982. xx, 102 p. ; ***NYPL [JLF 83-663]***

Experience and background inventory . Baehr, Melany E. [Park Ridge, Ill.] (1550 Northwest Highway, Park Ridge 60068) [c1986] 48 p. ; LC Card 87-404267 DDC 658.3/112 19
HF5549.5.S38 B34 1986

Experience and background questionnaire . Baehr, Melany E. [Park Ridge, Ill.] (1550 Northwest Highway, Park Ridge 60068) , c1986. 20 p. ; LC Card 87-404268 DDC 658.3/1125 19
HF5381.7 .B327 1986

Une expérience de grande envergure . Dramé, Mamadou. [Dakar] , 1980-1981 [i.e., 1981] 32, [3] leaves, [1] folded leaf of plates : LC Card 85-218589
HD2144.5.Z9 B543 1981

Experience, Inc. . Fucini, Joseph J. New York , London , c1987. xi, 244 p. : ISBN 0-02-910971-X LC Card 87-11984 DDC 338/.04/0922 B 19
HC29 .F834 1987

L'expérience pénivauxoise, 1971-1982 . Camus, Michel. [Vaux-le-Pénil , 1982] 187 p., [8] p. of plates : LC Card 84-190663
HC277.V35 C36 1982

Experiences of agricultural and rural cooperatives in socialist countries in Africa /. Cliffe, Lionel. [S.l.] [1985?] 40 p. ; LC Card 87-104467 DDC 334/.683/096 19
HD1491.A48 C55 1985

Experiencias de educación y producción de fe y alegría en Oruro y Santa Cruz . Alaix, Ramón. La Paz, Bolivia , 1986. 191 p. ; LC Card 86-208411 DDC 331.25/92/098413 19
HD5715.5.B52 S262 1986

Experiencias de políticas de estabilización . Gómez de Reyes, María Teresa. México, D.F. , 1985. iv, 66 leaves ; LC Card 87-122042 DDC 338.982 19
HC125 .G57 1985

Experiencing management /. Sashkin, Marshall, 1944- Reading, Mass. , c1987. x, 234 p. : ISBN 0-201-11545-X (pbk.) : LC Card 86-28731 DDC 658.4/0352 19
HD30.26 .S27 1987

An experiential approach to organization development /. Harvey, Donald F. Englewood Cliffs, N.J. , c1988. p. cm. ISBN 0-13-295122-3 LC Card 87-26207 DDC 658.4/063 19
HD58.8 .H37 1988

Experimental failure prediction models for small companies /. Shailer, G. E. P. [Newcastle, Australia] [1986] 52 p. ; ISBN 0-7259-0555-7 (pbk.) LC Card 87-121092 DDC 338.6/42 19
HD2747 .S42 1986

Experimental social dilemmas / Henk A.M. Wilke, Dave M. Messick, Christel G. Rutte, eds. Frankfurt am Main ; New York : P. Lang, c1986. vi, 234 p. : ill. ; 21 cm. (Psychologie des Entscheidungsverhaltens und des Konfliktes = Psychology of decisions and conflict, 0721-2852 . Bd. 3) Papers were presented at a conference held at the University of Groningen in the spring of 1984. Includes bibliographies. ISBN 3-8204-8574-0 (pbk.) : LC Card 86-10307 DDC 302 19
1. Interpersonal conflict - Congresses. 2. Decision-making, Group - Congresses. 3. Social choice - Congresses. 4. Social perception - Congresses. I. Wilke, H. A. M. II. Messick, David M. III. Rutte, Christel G. IV. Series: Psychologie des Entscheidungsverhaltens und des Konfliktes , Bd. 3.
HM132 .E96 1986 ***NYPL [JLD 87-1177]***

Experiments on decisions under risk . Schoemaker, Paul J. H. Boston , c1980. xxii, 211 p. : ISBN 0-89838-035-9 LC Card 79-27948 DDC 658.4/03
HB615 .S36 ***NYPL [JLE 81-559]***

Expert advisor, one-two-three. Williams, Mark M., 1948- Expert advisor, 1-2-3 . Reading, Mass. , 1988. p. cm. ISBN 0-201-18238-6 (pbk.) : LC Card 87-19286 DDC 005.36/9 19
HF5548.4.L67 W536 1988

Expert advisor, 1-2-3 . Williams, Mark M., 1948- Reading, Mass. , 1988. p. cm. ISBN 0-201-18238-6 (pbk.) : LC Card 87-19286 DDC 005.36/9 19
HF5548.4.L67 W536 1988

The expert executive . Hertz, David Bendel, 1919- New York , c1988. xvi, 238 p. ; ISBN 0-471-89677-2 LC Card 87-21682 DDC 658/.05633 19
HF5548.2 .H455 1988

Expert Group Meeting on Fertility and Mortality Levels and Trends in Africa and Their Policy Implications (1979 : Monrovia, Liberia) Population dynamics : fertility and mortality in Africa : proceedings of the Expert Group Meeting on Fertility and Mortality Levels and Trends in Africa and Their Policy Implications, Monrovia, Liberia, 26 November-1 December 1979. [Addis Ababa] : United Nations Economic Commission for Africa, [1981] ix, 581 p. : ill. ; 27 cm. Includes bibliographical references. LC Card 82-980086 DDC 304.6/3/096 19
1. Fertility, Human - Africa - Congresses. 2. Mortality - Africa - Congresses. 3. Africa - Population - Congresses. 4. Africa - Statistics, Vital - Congresses. I. Title.
HB3661.A3 E9 1979 ***NYPL [JLF 83-591]***

Expert systems. Boston, Mass. (89 Broad St., 14th Floor, Boston 02110) : Yankee Group, c1985. 61 p. : ill. ; 28 cm. (Small systems . v. 8 (1985)) LC Card 87-400871 DDC 381/.4500633/0973 19
1. Computer software industry - United States. 2. Market surveys - United States. 3. Expert systems (Computer science). I. Yankee Group. II. Series: Small systems , v. 8.
HD9696.C63 U516435 1985

Expert systems . Harmon, Paul. New York , c1988. xii, 289 p. : ISBN 0-471-83950-7 (pbk.) LC Card 87-17608 DDC 650/.028/5633 19
HF5548.2 .H367 1988

EXPERT SYSTEMS (COMPUTER SCIENCE)
Boose, John H. Expertise transfer for expert system design /. Amsterdam , New York , 1986. viii, 312 p. : ISBN 0-444-42634-5 LC Card 86-9044 DDC 006.3/3 19
QA76.76.E95 B66 1986 ***NYPL [JSE 86-1840]***

Building expert systems /. Reading, Mass. , 1983. xvi, 444 p. : ISBN 0-201-10686-8 LC Card 82-24511 DDC 001.64/2 19
QA76.9.E96 B84 1983 ***NYPL [JSE 87-204]***

Chorafas, Dimitris N. Applying expert systems in business /. New York , c1987. xii, 232 p. : ISBN 0-07-010880-3 : LC Card 86-2794 DDC 658/.05633 19
HD30.2 .C475 1987 ***NYPL [JLE 86-3893]***

Expert systems. Boston, Mass. (89 Broad St., 14th Floor, Boston 02110) , c1985. 61 p. : LC Card 87-400871 DDC 381/.4500633/0973 19
HD9696.C63 U516435 1985

Frost, R. A. (Richard A.) Introduction to knowledge base systems /. London , 1986. xxi, 677 p. : ISBN 0-00-383114-0 ***NYPL [JFE 86-3366]***

Harmon, Paul. Expert systems . New York , c1988. xii, 289 p. : ISBN 0-471-83950-7 (pbk.) LC Card 87-17608 DDC 650/.028/5633 19
HF5548.2 .H367 1988

Hertz, David Bendel, 1919- The expert executive . New York , c1988. xvi, 238 p. ; ISBN 0-471-89677-2 LC Card 87-21682 DDC 658/.05633 19
HF5548.2 .H455 1988

Kowalski, Thaddeus J. An artificial intelligence approach to VLSI design /. Boston , c1985. x, 226 p. : ISBN 0-89838-169-X LC Card 85-7581 DDC 621.3819/5835 19
TK7874 .K675 1985 ***NYPL [JSE 86-1182]***

Management decision support systems using fuzzy sets and possibility theory /. Köln , c1985. xi, 350 p. : ISBN 3-88585-143-1 (pbk.) LC Card 85-217558 DDC 658.4/033 19
HD30.23 .M353 1985 ***NYPL [JLE 86-4562]***

Turban, Efraim. Decision support and expert systems . New York , London , c1988. xxi, 697 p. : ISBN 0-02-421650-X LC Card 87-23911 DDC 658.4/03 19
HD30.2 .T87 1988

EXPERT SYSTEMS (COMPUTER SCIENCE) - CONGRESSES.
Artificial intelligence and statistics /. Reading, Mass. , c1986. xiv, 418 p. : ISBN 0-201-11568-9 : LC Card 85-28631 DDC 006.3 19
Q334 .A764 1986 ***NYPL [JSE 87-399]***

Artificial intelligence in economics and management /. Amsterdam ; New York : xv, 292 p. : ISBN 0-444-87961-7 LC Card 85-31139 DDC 330/.028/563 19
HB143.5 .A78 1986 ***NYPL [JLE 86-3612]***

Expertise comptable.
Cozian, Maurice. Annales de fiscalité . Paris , 1981. 127 p. ; ISBN 2-7111-0289-0 : LC Card 81-150065
HJ2659 .C65 1981

Expertise transfer for expert system design /. Boose, John H. Amsterdam , New York , 1986. viii, 312 p. : ISBN 0-444-42634-5 LC Card 86-9044 DDC 006.3/3 19
QA76.76.E95 B66 1986 ***NYPL [JSE 86-1840]***

Explanation in social history /. Lloyd, Christopher, 1950- Oxford, UK , New York, NY, USA , 1986. xi, 375 p. : ISBN 0-631-13113-2 : LC Card 85-13359 DDC 301/.09 19
HN28 .L58 1986 ***NYPL [JLE 86-1677]***

Explanatory notes on current statistics. Supplement to the Reserve Bank of India bulletin. Bombay : The Bank, [1978] iii, 74 p. ; 24 cm. "October 1978." LC Card 85-229381
1. Finance - India. 2. Banks and banking - India. 3. Money - India. I. Reserve Bank of India.
HG187.I4 E98 1978

Exploding the hunger myths . Williams, Sonja, 1953- San Francisco , c1987. xv, 173 p. : ISBN 0-935028-23-4 (pbk.) : LC Card 87-3360 DDC 363.8/07/1273 19
HD9000.5 .W476 1987

L'exploitation agricole familiale en Afrique soudano-sahélienne /. Benoit-Cattin, Michel. Paris , c1982. 94 p. : ISBN 2-85319-106-0 LC Card 86-116718
HD1476.S382 S563 1982

Exploiting opportunities in the Pacific Basin . McLean, Robert J. [Melbourne] [1986] 56 p. : ISBN 0-85801-162-X (pbk.) LC Card 86-203142 DDC 337.9409 19
HF1626.5.P33 M35 1986

Exploración de la Guayana / [fotografías, Julio Serrano]. [Caracas] : Interalumina, [1983] 158 p., [20] p. of plates : ill. (some col.), maps ; 28 cm. Errata slip inserted. Includes bibliographical references and index. LC Card 85-178221 DDC 333.7/0988/1 19
1. Natural resources - Venezuela - Guayana Region - Addresses, essays, lectures. 2. Birds - Venezuela - Guayana Region - Identification - Addresses, essays, lectures. 3. Public health - Venezuela - Guayana Region - Addresses, essays, lectures. I. Serrano, Julio.
HC238.G8 E98 1983 ***NYPL [JSF 86-461]***

Exploring nontraditional jobs for women /. Neufeld, Rose. New York , c1987. x, 149 p. : ISBN 0-8239-0698-1 : LC Card 86-29827 DDC 331.7/02/024042 19
HF5382.65 .N48 1987

Exploring word processors . Townsend, Carl, 1938- Beaverton, Or. , c1984. viii, 239 p. : ISBN 0-88056-104-1 (pbk.) : LC Card 83-26259 DDC 652 19
Z52.5.C65 T68 1984 ***NYPL [JSD 86-495]***

Export agriculture and the crisis in Central America /. Williams, Robert G. (Robert Gregory), 1948- Chapel Hill , c1986. xvi, 257 p. : ISBN 0-8078-1693-0 LC Card 85-20978 DDC 382/.41/09728 19
HD9884.C352 W55 1986 ***NYPL [JLE 86-3412]***

EXPORT AND CREDIT INSURANCE. see **INSURANCE, EXPORT CREDIT.**

EXPORT AND IMPORT CONTROLS. see **FOREIGN TRADE REGULATION.**

EXPORT CONTROLS.
Losoncz, Miklós. Erők és érdekek . Budapest , 1986. 191 p. : ISBN 963-326-966-0 : LC Card 87-148142
HF1414.5 .L67 1986

EXPORT CONTROLS - JAPAN - HISTORY - 20TH CENTURY.
Bauge, Kenneth L. (Kenneth LeRoy) Voluntary export restriction as a foreign commercial policy with special reference to Japanese cotton textiles, 1930-1962 /. New York , 1987. 277 p. ; ISBN 0-8240-8072-6 LC Card 87-23717 DDC 382/.4567721/0952 19
HD9886.J3 B38 1987

EXPORT CONTROLS - UNITED STATES.
Committee on Science, Engineering, and Public Policy (U. S.). Panel on the Impact of National Security Controls on International Technology Transfer. Balancing the national interest . Washington, D.C. , 1987. xiii, 321 p. : ISBN 0-309-03738-7 LC Card 87-60020 DDC 337.73 19
HF1456 .C65 1987

International trade in textiles & apparel . [Washington, D.C.] , c1987. 1 v. (various foliations) : LC Card 87-404516 DDC 382/.45677/00973 19
HD9850.5 .I43 1987

Losoncz, Miklós. Erők és érdekek . Budapest , 1986. 191 p. : ISBN 963-326-966-0 : LC Card 87-148142
HF1414.5 .L67 1986

Rosenblatt, Samuel M. East-West trade in technology . Washington, D.C. , c1980. viii, 64 p. ; LC Card 80-81923 DDC 382/.4560973 19
HF1414.5 .R67 ***NYPL [JLD 81-233]***

EXPORT CREDIT - EUROPE.
Loubergé, Henri. Financement et assurance des crédits à l'exportation . Genève , 1985. 502 p. :
NYPL [JLD 86-2109]

The Export credit financing systems in OECD member countries. 3rd ed. Paris : Organisation for Economic Co-operation and Development ; Washington, D.C. : OECD Publications and Information Centre [distributor], 1987. 285 p. : ill. ; 23 cm. ISBN 92-64-12947-2 (pbk.) : LC Card 87-170161 DDC 351.82/76 19
1. Export credit. I. Organization for Economic Co-operation and Development.
HG3753 .E88 1987

EXPORT CREDIT GUARANTEES. see **INSURANCE, EXPORT CREDIT.**

EXPORT CREDIT - ILLINOIS.
Seger, Daniel J. Financing Illinois agricultural exports /. [Urbana?] [1985] 74 p. : LC Card 86-621070 DDC 382/.63 19
HD9007.I3 S44 1985

EXPORT CREDIT - NETHERLANDS.
Gijsman, D., 1955- Exportfinanciering /. Deventer , 's-Gravenhage , 1986. 118 p. : ISBN 90-200-0992-3 : LC Card 86-176172
HG3754.N4 G55 1986

EXPORT CREDIT - UNITED STATES.
The Export-Import Bank at fifty . Lexington, Mass. , c1987. xii, 206 p. : ISBN 0-669-14828-8 (alk. paper) LC Card 86-21521 DDC 332.1/54 19
HG3754.U5 E94 1987 ***NYPL [JLE 87-1153]***

Henry, Donald Putnam, 1957- The financial cost of export credit guarantee programs /. Santa Monica, CA , 1987. ix, 37 p. ; ISBN 0-8330-0794-7 (pbk.) LC Card 87-4630 DDC 382/.63 19
HG3754.5.U6 H46 1987

Lees, Francis A. Financing export sales /. New York, N.Y. (845 3rd Ave., New York 10022) , c1986. 12 p. : LC Card 86-212400 DDC 658.1/5 19
HF3031 .L36 1986

Venedikian, Harry M. Export-import financing /. New York , c1986. xvii, 456 p. : ISBN 0-471-82449-6 : LC Card 85-29566 DDC 332.7/42 19
HG3754.U5 V46 1986 ***NYPL [JLE 86-2998]***

The export cult . Rubner, Alex. Boulder , 1987, c1986. p. cm. ISBN 0-8133-0514-4 : LC Card 86-51219 DDC 382/.6 19
HF1417.5 .R82 1987

Export effort of India /. Modwel, Suman Kumar, 1936- New Delhi , 1986. ix, 83, [1] p. ; LC Card 86-903364 DDC 382/.6/0954 19
HF1589 .M63 1986

The Export-Import Bank at fifty : the international environment and the institution's role / edited by Rita M. Rodriguez. Lexington, Mass. : Lexington Books, c1987. xii, 206 p. : ill. ; 24 cm. Includes bibliographies and index. ISBN 0-669-14828-8 (alk. paper) LC Card 86-21521 DDC 332.1/54 19
1. Export credit - United States. I. Rodriguez, Rita M., 1944-.
HG3754.U5 E94 1987 ***NYPL [JLE 87-1153]***

Export-import financing /. Venedikian, Harry M. New York , c1986. xvii, 456 p. : ISBN 0-471-82449-6 : LC Card 85-29566 DDC 332.7/42 19
HG3754.U5 V46 1986 ***NYPL [JLE 86-2998]***

Export instability and growth . Athukoralge, Premachandra. London , Wolfeboro, N.H. , c1987. 244 p. : ISBN 0-7099-3739-3 : LC Card 86-32833 DDC 382/.6/095493 19
HF3770.8.Z5 A84 1987

EXPORT LICENSES. see **EXPORT CONTROLS.**

EXPORT MARKETING.
Cateora, Philip R. Marketing . Homewood, Ill. , 1987. xi, 172 p. : ISBN 0-256-05626-9 (pbk.) LC Card 86-83392 DDC 658.8/48 19
HF1009.5 .C37 1987

Czinkota, Michael R. International marketing /. Chicago , c1988. xxi, 649 p. : ISBN 0-03-070297-6 LC Card 86-32959 DDC 658.8/48 19
HF1009.5 .C95 1988

Gilligan, Colin. International marketing . London , Dover N.H. , c1986. 310 p. : ISBN 0-7099-3811-X : LC Card 86-9015 DDC 658.8/48 19
HF1009.5 .G55 1986 ***NYPL [JLD 86-4466]***

Managing export entry and expansion . New York , 1987. xx, 439 p. : ISBN 0-275-92361-4 (alk. paper) : LC Card 86-30330 DDC 658.8/48 19
HF1009.5 .M345 1987

Moser, Reinhard. Exportmarketing /. [Linz , 1979?] 120 leaves : LC Card 84-183280
HF1009.5 .M67 1979

Snowdon, Sondra. The global edge . New York , c1986. 431 p. ; ISBN 0-671-60122-9 : LC Card 86-3990 DDC 395/.22 19
HF5387 .S59 1986 ***NYPL [JLE 86-3489]***

Somogyi, Dorottya. A fejlett tőkés országok exportpolitikája /. Budapest , 1985. 277, [1] p. : ISBN 963-221-507-9 : LC Card 85-231848
HF1417.5 .S66 1985

Topritzhofer, Edgar, 1944- Das Exportgeschäft . Wien , 1984. 250 p. : ISBN 3-85428-025-4 LC Card 84-232997
HF1009.5 .T665 1984

Uhlig, Karl-Heinz. Internationales Konzernmarketing /. Berlin , c1986. 143 p. : ISBN 3-349-00001-0 LC Card 87-118692 DDC 658.8/48 19
HF1009.5 .U36 1986

Walker, A. G. (Alexander George) Export practice and documentation /. London , Boston , 1987. 279 p. : ISBN 0-408-02800-9 : LC Card 86-29945 DDC 658.8/48 19
HF1009.5 .W34 1987

Wiklund, Erik. International marketing strategies . New York , c1987. xi, 195 p. ; ISBN 0-07-070176-8 : LC Card 86-21437 DDC 658.8/48 19
HF1009.5 .W555 1987

Wild, Rolf H. Strategy for export . Asheville, NC , c1986. 121 p. ; ISBN 0-914291-02-5 (pbk.) : LC Card 86-51529 DDC 658.8/48 19
HF1009.5 .W56 1986

EXPORT MARKETING - ADDRESSES, ESSAYS, LECTURES.
Research in international marketing /. London , Dover, N.H. , c1986. 376 p. : ISBN 0-7099-4313-X : LC Card 85-29052 DDC 382/.6 19
HF1009.5 .R46 1986 ***NYPL [JLD 86-2264]***

EXPORT MARKETING - AFRICA, EASTERN.
Export promotion of furniture/joinery products from east/southern Africa. Addis Ababa [1983] 34 p. in various pagings : LC Card 86-981008
HD9773.A472 E96 1983

EXPORT MARKETING - BRAZIL.
Pinto, Maurício Barata de Paula. O potencial das exportações brasileiras de manufaturados /. Rio de Janeiro , 1983. 46 p. ; LC Card 87-403022 DDC 382/.4567/0981 19
HD9734.B72 P56 1983

EXPORT MARKETING - BRAZIL - HANDBOOKS, MANUALS, ETC.
Manual básico do exportador. [São Paulo] [1985] 270 p. : LC Card 86-200367
HF3407 .M35 1985

EXPORT MARKETING - BULGARIA.
Atanasov, Mikhail, k.i.n. Vŭshnotŭrgovski aspekti na selskostopanskite i khranitelno-vkusovite stoki i problemi pred bŭlgarskiia iznos /. Sofiia , 1984. 118 p. ; LC Card 85-163481
HD9015.B82 A86 1984

EXPORT MARKETING - CASE STUDIES.
Gilligan, Colin. International marketing . London , Dover N.H. , c1986. 310 p. : ISBN 0-7099-3811-X : LC Card 86-9015 DDC 658.8/48 19
HF1009.5 .G55 1986 ***NYPL [JLD 86-4466]***

EXPORT MARKETING - CONGRESSES.
1987 AMA educators' proceedings /. Chicago, Ill. , 1987. xiv, 287 p. ; ISBN 0-87757-182-1 LC Card 87-18680 DDC 658.8 19
HF5411 .A156 1987

EXPORT MARKETING - DEVELOPING COUNTRIES.
Junginger-Dittel, K.-O. Marketing Boards für Agrarexportgüter in Entwicklungsländern /. [Kiel] , 1980. iii, 48 leaves ; LC Card 85-160428
HD9018.D44 J86 1980

Ohlinger, Hans A., 1954- Die Relevanz nicht-tarifärer Handelshemmnisse im internationalen Handel und ihre Wirkungen auf die Integration der Entwicklungsländer in die Weltwirtschaft /. Frankfurt am Main , New York , c1986. iii, 400 p. : ISBN 3-8204-8344-6 LC Card 87-407585 DDC 382/.5/091724 19
HF1430 .O38 1986

Wells, Jeremy. The export marketing of technical consulting services from developing countries /. Geneva , 1986. vi, 127 p. : LC Card 87-168669 DDC 658.4/6/091724 19
HD9989.D44 W46 1986

EXPORT MARKETING - DEVELOPING COUNTRIES - FINANCE.
Majnoni, Giovanni. Euromercati e finanziamento delle esportazioni /. Roma , Bologna , c1981. 130 p. ; LC Card 83-110156
HG3754.E86 M35 1981

EXPORT MARKETING - EUROPE - CASE STUDIES.
Case studies in international marketing /. London , 1982. vii, 391 p. : ISBN 0-434-90370-1 : LC Card 82-241323 DDC 658.8/48 19
HF1009.5 .C34 1982 ***NYPL [JLE 87-1196]***

Strategies for international industrial marketing . London , Dover, N.H. , c1986. 310 p. : ISBN 0-7099-2494-1 : LC Card 85-29047 DDC 658.8/48 19
HF1009.7.E85 S77 1986
NYPL [JLD 86-1596]

EXPORT MARKETING - EUROPE, EASTERN.
Poznański, Kazimierz. Technology,

competition, & the Soviet bloc in the world market /. Berkeley , c1987. ix, 226 p. ; ISBN 0-87725-170-3 (pbk.) : LC Card 87-3505 DDC 338/.06 19
HC244.Z9 T4716 1987

EXPORT MARKETING - EUROPE - HISTORY.
Fremdling, Rainer. Technologischer Wandel und internationaler Handel im 18. und 19. Jahrhundert . Berlin , c1986. 493 p. ; ISBN 3-428-06042-3 LC Card 87-127793 DDC 382/.456691/094 19
HD9525.A2 F74 1986

EXPORT MARKETING - EUROPEAN ECONOMIC COMMUNITY COUNTRIES - FINANCE.
Majnoni, Giovanni. Euromercati e finanziamento delle esportazioni /. Roma , Bologna , c1981. 130 p. ; LC Card 83-110156
HG3754.E86 M35 1981

EXPORT MARKETING - EUROPEAN ECONOMIC COMMUNITY COUNTRIES - HANDBOOKS, MANUALS, ETC.
Hodēgos exagōgikōn diadikasiōn /. [Athēna] [1983] 184 p. : LC Card 86-170148
HF1009.7.E86 H63 1983

EXPORT MARKETING - FRANCE.
Pezet, P. (Pierre) Les opérateurs français du commerce international agro-alimentaire /. Paris , c1984. 85 p. : ISBN 2-279-52812-6 LC Card 85-136648 DDC 382/.456413/00944 19
HD9012.5 .P43 1984

EXPORT MARKETING - GERMANY (WEST)
Peters, Kathrin. Binnenwirtschaftlich orientierte Hypothesen zur Aussenwirtschaftsentwicklung und ihre Gültigkeit für die Bundesrepublik Deutschland 1969-1982 /. Hamburg , c1986. vii, 311 p. : ISBN 3-925630-02-3 : LC Card 86-226488
HD5710.75.G3 P48 1986

EXPORT MARKETING - GREAT BRITAIN - CASE STUDIES.
Case studies in international marketing /. London , 1982. vii, 391 p. : ISBN 0-434-90370-1 : LC Card 82-241323 DDC 658.8/48 19
HF1009.5 .C34 1982 ***NYPL [JLE 87-1196]***

EXPORT MARKETING - HUNGARY.
Éliás, András. Mezőgazdasági és élelmiszeripari termékeink a külpiaci versenyben /. Budapest , 1985. 197 p. ; ISBN 963-232-064-6 : LC Card 86-185883
HD9015.H82 E59 1985

EXPORT MARKETING - INDIA.
Kumar, Maneet, 1952- Export marketing of non-traditional items . Delhi , 1987. xv, 274 p. ; ISBN 81-202-0185-X : LC Card 87-900875 DDC 382/.6/0954 19
HF1009.7.I4 K86 1987

EXPORT MARKETING - ITALY.
Tre incognite per lo sviluppo . Milano, Italy , c1986. 383 p. : LC Card 86-198933
HC310.I53 T74 1986

EXPORT MARKETING - JAMAICA.
Lyn-Cook, Marlene. Marketing guidelines for Jamaica's non-traditional exports. [Miami, FL] [1986] 83 leaves : LC Card 87-156503 DDC 382/.097292/073 19
HF1009.7.J25 L96 1986

EXPORT MARKETING - LATIN AMERICA.
Instituto Latinoamericano del Fierro y el Acero. The urgent need of Latin America to export steel [microform]. Santiago, Chile [1983?] 20 p. : LC Card 84-244660 DDC 382/.45669142/098 19
HD9524.L32 I57 1983
NYPL [*ZT-1708 no.49]

EXPORT MARKETING - MANAGEMENT.
Connolly, Seamus G. Finding, entering, and succeeding in a foreign market /. Englewood Cliffs, N.J. , c1987. xiii, 274 p. : ISBN 0-13-316951-0 LC Card 86-25395 DDC 658.8/48 19
HF1009.5 .C59 1986 ***NYPL [JLE 87-1310]***

Jain, Subhash C., 1942- International marketing management /. Boston, Mass. , c1987. xiv, 737 p. : ISBN 0-534-07824-9 : LC Card 86-27761 DDC 658.8/48 19
HF1009.5 .J336 1987

Multinational marketing management . Reading, Mass. , c1988. x, 500 p. : ISBN 0-201-07996-8 (pbk.) : LC Card 87-12599 DDC 658.8/48 19
HF1009.5 .M85 1988

EXPORT MARKETING - MANAGEMENT - ADDRESSES, ESSAYS, LECTURES.
International marketing . Boston, Mass. , c1986. xii, 466 p. : ISBN 0-534-06270-9 (pbk.) : LC Card 85-19820 DDC 658.8/48 19
HF1009.5 .I545 1986 ***NYPL [JLE 86-3023]***

EXPORT MARKETING - NETHERLANDS.
Exportnota. [Hague , 1982] 60 p. ; ISBN 90-12-04106-6 LC Card 83-197657
HF3616.5 .E9 1982

Puyenbroek, R. (Rien) Exportgids Japan /. Amsterdam , 1985. 149 p. : ISBN 90-10-05277-X LC Card 85-236503
HF3618.J33 P89 1985

Puyenbroek, R. (Rien) Exportgids Verenigde Staten /. Amsterdam , 1985. 140 p. : ISBN 90-10-05276-1 LC Card 85-236520
HF3618.U6 P89 1985

Export marketing of non-traditional items . Kumar, Maneet, 1952- Delhi , 1987. xv, 274 p. ; ISBN 81-202-0185-X : LC Card 87-900875 DDC 382/.6/0954 19
HF1009.7.I4 K86 1987

The export marketing of technical consulting services from developing countries /. Wells, Jeremy. Geneva , 1986. vi, 127 p. : LC Card 87-168669 DDC 658.4/6/091724 19
HD9989.D44 W46 1986

EXPORT MARKETING - RESEARCH - ADDRESSES, ESSAYS, LECTURES.
Research in international marketing /. London , Dover, N.H. , c1986. 376 p. : ISBN 0-7099-4313-X : LC Card 85-29052 DDC 382/.6 19
HF1009.5 .R46 1986 ***NYPL [JLD 86-2264]***

EXPORT MARKETING - SPAIN.
Alonso, José Antonio. La empresa exportadora española frente a Iberoamérica y la CEE /. Madrid , 1985. xiii, 263 p. ; ISBN 84-7232-380-3 LC Card 86-199177
HF3688.L3 A46 1985 ***NYPL [JLE 87-56]***

EXPORT MARKETING - SRI LANKA - MATHEMATICAL MODELS.
Athukoralge, Premachandra. Export instability and growth . London , Wolfeboro, N.H. , c1987. 244 p. : ISBN 0-7099-3739-3 : LC Card 86-32833 DDC 382/.6/095493 19
HF3770.8.Z5 A84 1987

EXPORT MARKETING - SWEDEN.
Sweden. Exportstödsutredningen. Ökad trähusexport . [Stockholm] [1984] 51 p. ; ISBN 91-38-08165-2 LC Card 84-219457
HD9715.5.S82 S94 1984

EXPORT MARKETING - SWEDEN - CASE STUDIES.
Elsässer, Martin, 1957- Marknadsinvesteringar . Malmö , c1984. 168 p. : ISBN 91-38-61298-4 : LC Card 84-200312
HF1009.7.S94 E47 1984

EXPORT MARKETING - UNITED STATES.
Cateora, Philip R. Marketing . Homewood, Ill. , 1987. xi, 172 p. : ISBN 0-256-05626-9 (pbk.) LC Card 86-83392 DDC 658.8/48 19
HF1009.5 .C37 1987

Medvedkov, S. I͡U. (Sergeĭ I͡Ur'evich) Mezhdunarodnyĭ marketing amerikanskoĭ tekhnologii /. Moskva , 1985. 189 p. : LC Card 85-187077
HF1009.6 .M43 1985

EXPORT MARKETING - UNITED STATES - HANDBOOKS, MANUALS, ETC.
A Basic guide to exporting /. [Reno, Nev.] [198-] 68 leaves ; LC Card 86-622819
HF3035 .B37 1980z

A Basic guide to exporting. Washington, D.C. , 1981. vii, 133 p. : LC Card 82-601093 DDC 658.8/48 19
HF1009.5 .B344 1981 ***NYPL [JLF 87-351]***

A Basic guide to exporting. Washington, D.C. [1986] viii, 148 p. : ***NYPL [*R-Econ. 87-422]***

A Basic guide to exporting. Washington, D.C. [1986] viii, 148 p. : LC Card 86-603426 DDC 658.8/48 19
HF1009.6 .B38 1986

Jagoe, John R., 1936- Export sales and marketing manual /. Minneapolis, MN , c1987. 1 v. (loose-leaf) ; ISBN 0-943677-00-9 (loose-leaf) : LC Card 87-19952 DDC 658.8/48 19
HF3035 .J34 1987

Manring, A. B. (Alvin Benjamin), 1925- Exporting from the U. S.A. . Vancouver , Seattle , c1986. xi, 114 p. : ISBN 0-88908-919-1 (pbk.) : LC Card 86-225987 DDC 658.8/48/0973 19
HF1009.5 .M356 1986

EXPORT OF NUCLEAR MATERIALS. see **NUCLEAR NONPROLIFERATION.**

EXPORT OF NUCLEAR TECHNOLOGY. see **NUCLEAR NONPROLIFERATION.**

Export practice and documentation /. Walker, A. G. (Alexander George) London , Boston , 1987. 279 p. : ISBN 0-408-02800-9 : LC Card 86-29945 DDC 658.8/48 19
HF1009.5 .W34 1987

EXPORT PROCESSING ZONES - GHANA.
Botchie, George. Employment and multinational enterprises in export processing zones . Geneva , 1984. iv, 74 p. ; ISBN 92-2-103770-3 (pbk.) : LC Card 86-213592
HF1417 .B68 1984

EXPORT PROCESSING ZONES - LATIN AMERICA - CONGRESSES.
Conferenza internazionale sul tema Le zone franche industriali, nuove forme di investimento, l'America latina (1985 : Milan, Italy) Le zone franche industriali nei paesi emergenti . Milano, Italy , c1986. 207 p. ; LC Card 86-223193
HF1418 .C525 1985

EXPORT PROCESSING ZONES - LIBERIA.
Botchie, George. Employment and multinational enterprises in export processing zones . Geneva , 1984. iv, 74 p. ; ISBN 92-2-103770-3 (pbk.) : LC Card 86-213592
HF1417 .B68 1984

EXPORT PROMOTION. see **FOREIGN TRADE PROMOTION.**

Export promotion of furniture/joinery products from east/southern Africa. Addis Ababa : United Nations Economic Commission for Africa, [1983] 34 p. in various pagings : ill. ; 30 cm. Cover title. Issued with French text: Rapport intérimaire sur l'étude de marketing sur le potentiel d'exportation de mobilier et de produits de ménuiserie des pays du MULPOC de Lusaka vers les états du Golfe, l'Algérie et la Jamahiriya arabe libyenne, in portfolio labeled: Rapport intérimaire sur la promotion des exportations de produits de bois. "Octobre 1983." "FIAG/83/22." LC Card 86-981008
1. Furniture - Africa, Eastern - Marketing. 2. Prefabricated houses - Africa, Eastern - Marketing. 3. Boxes, Wooden - Africa, Eastern - Marketing. 4. Woodworking industries - Africa, Eastern. 5. Export marketing - Africa, Eastern. I. United Nations. Economic Commission for Africa. II. Rapport intérimaire sur l'étude de marketing sur le potentiel d'exportation de mobilier et de produits de ménuiserie des pays du MULPOC de Lusaka vers les états du Golfe, l'Algérie et la Jamahiriya arabe libyenne. 1983. III. Title: Rapport intérimaire sur la promotion des exportations de produits de bois.
HD9773.A472 E96 1983

Export promotion policies in Costa Rica . Hallauer, Robert. Austin , 1985. 17 p. ; LC Card 86-622254 DDC 382/.63/097286 19
HF1487 .H35 1985

Export sales and marketing manual /. Jagoe, John R., 1936- Minneapolis, MN , c1987. 1 v. (loose-leaf) ; ISBN 0-943677-00-9 (loose-leaf) : LC Card 87-19952 DDC 658.8/48 19
HF3035 .J34 1987

EXPORT SALES - BRAZIL - STATISTICS - HISTORY.
Lima, José Luiz. Estatísticas básicas do setor agrícola no Brasil /. São Paulo , 1983- v. : LC Card 83-219032 DDC 338.1/0981 19
HD9014.B82 L55 1983 ***NYPL [JLL 86-432]***

EXPORT SALES - COLOMBIA - MATHEMATICAL MODELS.
Mayer, Thomas, 1927- Instabile Exportmärkte und wirtschaftliche Entwicklung . Tübingen , c1983. vii, 181 p. : ISBN 3-16-344673-6 LC Card 83-218666
HF3426.5 .M39 1983

EXPORT SALES - DEVELOPING COUNTRIES.
Exports of developing countries . Washington, D.C. , c1987. viii, 168 p. : ISBN 0-8213-0870-X (pbk.) : LC Card 87-15991 DDC 382/.6/091724 19
HF4055 .E96 1987

EXPORT SALES - EUROPEAN ECONOMIC COMMUNITY COUNTRIES - FORMS.
Hodēgos exagōgikōn diadikasiōn /. [Athēna] [1983] 184 p. : LC Card 86-170148
HF1009.7.E86 H63 1983

EXPORT SALES - MATHEMATICAL MODELS.
Thompson, Robert L. A survey of recent U. S. developments in international agricultural trade models /. Washington, D.C. , 1981. v, 74 p. ; LC Card 81-603138 DDC 382/.41/0973 19
HD1433 .T48 ***NYPL [JLF 84-568]***

EXPORT SALES - SWEDEN.
Sveriges varuexport 1977-1983 . [Stockholm] [1979] 168 p. : ISBN 91-38-04928-7 LC Card 83-241226
HF3676.5 .S84 1979

EXPORT SALES - UNITED STATES.
Lees, Francis A. Financing export sales /. New York, N.Y. (845 3rd Ave., New York 10022) , c1986. 12 p. : LC Card 86-212400 DDC 658.1/5 19
HF3031 .L36 1986

Nadel, Jack. Cracking the global market . New York, NY , c1987. ix, 246 p. ; ISBN 0-8144-5911-0 LC Card 87-47703 DDC 658.8/48 19
HF1008 .N33 1987

Solomon, Anthony M. The dollar, debt, and the trade deficit /. New York , 1987. 55 p. ; ISBN 0-8147-7863-1 : LC Card 86-23651 DDC 382.1/7/0973 19
HF3031 .S65 1987

EXPORT SALES - UNITED STATES - HANDBOOKS, MANUALS, ETC.
A Basic guide to exporting. Washington, D.C. , 1981. vii, 133 p. : LC Card 82-601093 DDC 658.8/48 19
HF1009.5 .B344 1981 ***NYPL [JLF 87-351]***

A Basic guide to exporting. Washington, D.C. [1986] viii, 148 p. : LC Card 86-603426 DDC 658.8/48 19
HF1009.6 .B38 1986

A Basic guide to exporting. Washington, D.C. [1986] viii, 148 p. : ***NYPL [*R-Econ. 87-422]***

Manring, A. B. (Alvin Benjamin), 1925- Exporting from the U. S.A. . Vancouver , Seattle , c1986. xi, 114 p. : ISBN 0-88908-919-1 (pbk.) : LC Card 86-225987 DDC 658.8/48/0973 19
HF1009.5 .M356 1986

EXPORT TRADE PROMOTION. see **FOREIGN TRADE PROMOTION.**

EXPORT TRADING COMPANIES - BRAZIL.
As "Trading companies" no comércio exterior brasileiro. Rio de Janeiro-RJ , 1984. 148 p. : LC Card 85-208188
HF1009.7.B8 T73 1984

EXPORT TRADING COMPANIES - INDIA.
Nunnenkamp, Peter. Die Rolle öffentlicher Industrieunternehmen im Exportsektor Indiens /. Hamburg , 1985. xiv, 268 p. : ISBN 3-87895-285-6 : LC Card 87-111454
HD4293 .N85 1985

EXPORT TRADING COMPANIES - INDIA - DIRECTORIES.
Directory of exporters of cashew from India. Cochin, India [1986?] 138 p. ; LC Card 87-901352 DDC 382/.414573/02554 19
HD9259.C33 I423 1986

EXPORT TRADING COMPANIES - JAMAICA.
Jamaica National Export Corporation. Report 1969-1984 /. [Kingston, Jamaica] [1984] x, 62, 8 p. : LC Card 87-110047 DDC 354.72920082/76/06 19
HF1009.7.J25 J35 1984

EXPORT TRADING COMPANIES - LAW AND LEGISLATION.
Countertrade and trading companies . New York, N.Y. , c1984. iv, 283 p. : LC Card 84-196766 DDC 343.73/0878 347.303878 19
KF1976 .C68 1984 ***NYPL [JLD 86-4098]***

EXPORT TRADING COMPANIES - LAW AND LEGISLATION - UNITED STATES.
Countertrade and trading companies . New York, N.Y. , c1984. iv, 283 p. : LC Card 84-196766 DDC 343.73/0878 347.303878 19
KF1976 .C68 1984 ***NYPL [JLD 86-4098]***

The export woodchip industry of south east NSW . McCormick, William A. Barton, A.C.T. , 1986. 23 p. : LC Card 87-163674 DDC 333.75/09944 19
HD9769.W383 A85 1986

Exportaciones de tecnología de Brasil y Argentina /. Sercovich, Francisco Colman. [Buenos Aires, Argentina?] , 1986. 269 p. ; LC Card 87-404009 DDC 338.981/06 19
HC190.T4 S47 1986

Exportaciones industriales : perfil y comportamiento de las empresas exportadoras de manufacturas. Buenos Aires, República Argentina : República Argentina, Presidencia de la Nación, Secretaría de Planificación, Instituto Nacional de Estadística y Censos, [1987] 231 p. ; 24 cm. (Estudios INDEC, 0326-6249 . 6) LC Card 87-405033 DDC 338.4/767/0982 19
1. Argentina - Manufactures. 2. Argentina - Commerce. I. Instituto Nacional de Estadística y Censos (Argentina). II. Series: Estudios INDEC , 6o v.
HD9734.A7 E96 1987

Las Exportaciones y la incidencia del sector externo en el desarrollo económico. [San José] : Banco Central de Costa Rica, Sección de Cuentas Nacionales, 1984. 32, [8], [7], 4 leaves ; 28 cm. (Serie "Comentarios sobre asuntos económicos" . no. [53]) Cover title. LC Card 87-115490 DDC 338.1/097286 19
1. Agricultural industries - Costa Rica. 2. Offshore assembly industry - Costa Rica. 3. Costa Rica - Commerce. I. Series.
HD9014.C772 E95 1984

Exportações e crescimento industrial no Brasil /. Baumann Neves, Renato. Rio de Janeiro , 1985. 274 p. : LC Card 86-195612
HF1513 .B38 1985

Exporte als Herausforderung für die deutsche Wirtschaft / Erwin Dichtl, Otmar Issing (Hrsg.). Köln : Deutscher Instituts-Verlag, c1984. 469 p. : ill. ; 19 cm. (DIV-Sachbuchreihe. 38) Includes bibliographies and index. ISBN 3-602-34842-3 LC Card 85-139543
1. Germany, West - Commerce. 2. Germany, West - Commercial policy. I. Dichtl, Erwin. II. Issing, Otmar.
HF3564 .E96 1984

Exporte, komparative Vorteile und wirtschaftliche Entwicklung in den Schwellenländern . Mohs, Ralf-Matthias. Göttingen [1983] 236 p. : ISBN 3-509-01345-X LC Card 84-126961
HF4055 .M64 1983

Exportfinanciering /. Gijsman, D., 1955- Deventer , 's-Gravenhage , 1986. 118 p. : ISBN 90-200-0992-3 : LC Card 86-176172
HG3754.N4 G55 1986

Exportfrämjande stöd till mindre och medelstora företag . Sweden. Exportstödsutredningen. [Stockholm] [1983] 8, 143, 3 p. : ISBN 91-38-08059-1 LC Card 84-218418
HF1567 .S92 1983

Das Exportgeschäft . Topritzhofer, Edgar, 1944- Wien , 1984. 250 p. : ISBN 3-85428-025-4 LC Card 84-232997
HF1009.5 .T665 1984

Exportgewerbe und Aussenhandel vor der Industriellen Revolution. Festschrift für Univ.-Prof. Dr. Georg Zwanowetz anlässlich der Vollendung des 65. Lebensjahres /. [Innsbruck] , c1984. 332 p. : LC Card 84-183487
HC244 .F48 1984

Exportgids Japan /. Puyenbroek, R. (Rien) Amsterdam , 1985. 149 p. : ISBN 90-10-05277-X LC Card 85-236503
HF3618.J33 P89 1985

Exportgids Verenigde Staten /. Puyenbroek, R. (Rien) Amsterdam , 1985. 140 p. : ISBN 90-10-05276-1 LC Card 85-236520
HF3618.U6 P89 1985

Exporting from the U. S.A. . Manring, A. B. (Alvin Benjamin), 1925- Vancouver , Seattle , c1986. xi, 114 p. : ISBN 0-88908-919-1 (pbk.) : LC Card 86-225987 DDC 658.8/48/0973 19
HF1009.5 .M356 1986

Exporting from the USA. Manring, A. B. (Alvin Benjamin), 1925- Exporting from the U. S.A. . Vancouver , Seattle , c1986. xi, 114 p. : ISBN 0-88908-919-1 (pbk.) : LC Card 86-225987 DDC 658.8/48/0973 19
HF1009.5 .M356 1986

Exporting to the United States. Importing into the United States . Washington, D.C. [1985] 84 p. : LC Card 85-603032 DDC 343.73/087 347.30387 19
HF3035 .I46 1985

Exportmarketing /. Moser, Reinhard. [Linz , 1979?] 120 leaves : LC Card 84-183280
HF1009.5 .M67 1979

Exportnota. [Hague : Staatsuitgeverij, 1982] 60 p. ; 28 cm. Cover title. "Tweede Kamer, zitting 1981-1982, 17532, nrs. 1-2, brief van de Staatssecretaris van Economische Zaken"--P. 1. Includes bibliographical references. ISBN 90-12-04106-6 LC Card 83-197657
1. Netherlands - Commerce. 2. Netherlands - Commercial policy. 3. Export marketing - Netherlands. I. Netherlands. Ministerie van Economische Zaken.
HF3616.5 .E9 1982

Exportrisikogarantie, internationale Verschuldung und schweizerische Entwicklungspolitik /. Mugglin, Markus. Adliswil , 1985. 56 p. : ISBN 3-7229-4036-X LC Card 85-148130
HF1574.5.D44 M84 1985

EXPORTS.
Blades, Derek W. Discrepancies between imports and exports in OECD foreign trade statistics /. Paris, France , c1984. i, 42 p. ; LC Card 86-205155 DDC 382/.021 19
HF1016 .B569 1984

EXPORTS - AUSTRALIA - NEW SOUTH WALES.
McCormick, William A. The export woodchip industry of south east NSW . Barton, A.C.T. , 1986. 23 p. : LC Card 87-163674 DDC 333.75/09944 19
HD9769.W383 A85 1986

EXPORTS - BRAZIL.
Sanson, João Rogério. A política de transportes marítimos no Brasil . Rio de Janeiro , 1986. vii, 178, 5 p. : LC Card 87-403931 DDC 387.5/44/0981 19
HE597.B7 S26 1986

EXPORTS - BRAZIL - ECONOMETRIC MODELS.
Werneck, Rogério L. Furquim. Desequilíbrio externo e reorientação do crescimento e dos investimentos . Rio de Janeiro-RJ [1983?] 130 p. ; LC Card 87-403024 DDC 338.981 19
HC187 .W47 1983

EXPORTS - CANADA.
Daly, D. J. (Donald James), 1922- Canadian manufactured exports . Montreal, Quebec , c1986. xxviii, 180 p. ; ISBN 0-88645-025-X (pbk.) : LC Card 87-142389 DDC 382/.4567/0971 19
HF3226.5 .D26 1986

Exports of developing countries : how direction affects performance / edited by Oli Havrylyshyn. Washington, D.C. : World Bank, c1987. viii, 168 p. : ill. ; 28 cm. (A World Bank symposium) Proceedings of a World Bank conference held Feb. 28-Mar. 1, 1983 in Brussels. Includes bibliographies. ISBN 0-8213-0870-X (pbk.) : LC Card 87-15991 DDC 382/.6/091724 19
1. Developing countries - Commerce. 2. Export sales - Developing countries. I. Havrylyshyn, Oli. II. International Bank for Reconstruction and Development. III. Series.
HF4055 .E96 1987

EXPORTS - PRICES - LATIN AMERICA - ECONOMETRIC MODELS.
Lord, Montague J. Market price models for Latin America's major commodity exports /. Washington, D.C. [1986] vii, 219 p. : LC Card 87-115208 DDC 338.5/2/098 19
HD9014.A2 L67 1986

EXPORTS - TURKEY.
Hale, William M. Turkish agriculture and Community enlargement /. [Ankara] , 1984. 37 p. ; LC Card 87-113782 DDC 338.9561 s 338.1/09561 19
HC401 .A356 no. 1949 HD9016.T82

EXPORTS - UNITED STATES.
Gardiner, Walter H. Price elasticity of export demand . Washington, D.C. [1986] iv, 43 p. ; LC Card 86-602820 DDC 382/.41/0973 19
HD9004 .G37 1986

EXPORTS - UNITED STATES - CASE STUDIES.
Oppenheimer, Michael F. Nontariff barriers . Boulder , 1987. xiii, 203 p. ; ISBN 0-8133-7403-0 (pbk. : alk. paper) LC Card 87-50073 DDC 338.4/762/000973 19
HC110.H53 O66 1987

EXPORTS - UNITED STATES - HANDBOOKS, MANUALS, ETC.
A Basic guide to exporting /. [Reno, Nev.] [198-] 68 leaves ; LC Card 86-622819
HF3035 .B37 1980z

Jagoe, John R., 1936- Export sales and marketing manual /. Minneapolis, MN , c1987. 1 v. (loose-leaf) ; ISBN 0-943677-00-9 (loose-leaf) : LC Card 87-19952 DDC 658.8/48 19
HF3035 .J34 1987

Exportsamverkan : företagens erfarenheter : utredning från Statens industriverk. [Stockholm] : Liber, [1985] 261 p. : ill. ; 25 cm. (SIND, 0346-5748 . 1985:3) By Anne-Christine Strandell and others. Bibliography: p. 257-261. ISBN 91-38-08810-X LC Card 86-114126
1. Sweden - Commerce. 2. Sweden - Commercial policy. 3. Foreign trade promotion - Sweden. I. Strandell, Anne-Christine. II. Sweden. Statens industriverk. III. Series.
HF3676.5 .E96 1985

Exposição do governador do Distrito Federal, José Ornellas de Souza Filho, na ADESG, em 02/09/83. Souza Filho, José Ornellas de. [Brasília , 1983 or 1984] 40, [31 leaves] : LC Card 85-148272
HC188.D57 S68 1983

Exposición sobre el estado de la hacienda pública /. Büchi Buc, Hernán. [Santiago] , 1985. 92 p. ; LC Card 87-105088 DDC 338.983 19
HC192 .B83 1985

EXPOSITIONS. see **EXHIBITIONS.**

Exposure draft. Public record . Stamford, Conn. (P.O. Box 3821, Stamford 06905-0821) [1986] 424 p. ; LC Card 86-81700 DDC 657/.75 19
HF5686.O5 P83 1986

EXPRESS SERVICE - OREGON - HISTORY.
Forster, Dale E. Oregon express companies /. Eugene, Ore. , c1985. vi, 231 p. : LC Card 87-121202 DDC 383/.143/09795 19
HE6376.A1 O735 1985

EXPRESS SERVICE - UNITED STATES - HISTORY - JUVENILE LITERATURE.
Brandt, Betty. Special delivery /. Minneapolis, Minn. , c1988. 40 p. : ISBN 0-87614-312-5 (lib. bdg.) LC Card 87-15647 DDC 383/.4973 19
HE6371 .B77 1988

Expulsion. see **United States - Emigration and immigration.**

Extending Arrow-Pratt risk premiums /. Schlesinger, Harris. Berlin [1985] 13, 4 leaves : LC Card 86-206602 DDC 368 19
HG8054.5 .S35 1985

Extensão e características da pobreza no Brasil /. Calsing, Elizeu F. Brasília , 1983. 44, [1] p. : LC Card 86-178277
HC190.P6 C29 1983

EXTENSION WORK, AGRICULTURAL. see **AGRICULTURAL EXTENSION WORK.**

The extent and permanence of market dominance /. Weiss, Leonard W. Berlin [1984] 30, 7 p. ; LC Card 85-183107 DDC 338.8/2 19
HD2757.3 .W45 1984

EXTERMINATION, JEWISH (1939-1945) see **HOLOCAUST, JEWISH (1939-1945)**

External constraints on economic policy in Brazil, 1889-1930 /. Fritsch, Winston. Pittsburgh, PA , 1988. p. cm. ISBN 0-8229-1147-7 LC Card 87-19209 DDC 338.981 19
HC187 .F757 1988

External debt and debt servicing in Nepal /. Upadhyaya, Kamal Prasad. Kathmandu , 1985. ii, 67, [1] p. ; LC Card 86-902874 DDC 336.3/4/095496 19
HJ8777.9 .U62 1985

External debt in Bolivia /. Devlin, Robert. Boulder, Colo. , 1987. p. cm. ISBN 0-8133-7366-2 : LC Card 87-2088 DDC 336.3/4/0984 19
HJ8574 .D48 1987

External debt, savings, and growth in Latin America : papers presented at a seminar sponsored by the International Monetary Fund and the Instituto Torcuato di Tella, held in Buenos Aires on October 13-16, 1986 / edited by Ana María Martirena-Mantel. Washington, D.C. : The Fund ; Buenos Aires : El Instituto, 1987. xv, 207 p. ; 23 cm. Includes bibliographies. ISBN 0-939934-95-7 (pbk.) : LC Card 87-21422 DDC 336.3/435/098 19
1. Debts, External - Latin America - Congresses. 2. Saving and investment - Latin America - Congresses. 3. Latin America - Economic policy - Congresses. I. Martirena-Mantel, Ana María. II. International Monetary Fund. III. Instituto Torcuato di Tella.
HJ8514.5 .E984 1987

EXTERNAL DEBTS. see **DEBTS, EXTERNAL.**

EXTERNAL ECONOMIES AND DISECONOMIES. see **EXTERNALITIES (ECONOMICS)**

External influences on the Swiss economy under fixed and flexible exchange rates /. Genberg, Hans. Grüsch , c1985. ii, 182 p. : ISBN 3-7253-0249-9 (pbk.) LC Card 86-156330
HG3963 .G45 1985 ***NYPL [JLD 87-539]***

EXTERNALITIES (ECONOMICS) - ADDRESSES, ESSAYS, LECTURES.
Natural resource economics . Boston , c1986. xiv, 234 p. : ISBN 0-89838-203-3 LC Card 85-24215 DDC 333.7 19
HC59 .N318 1986 ***NYPL [JLE 86-3471]***

EXTERNALITIES (ECONOMICS) - CONGRESSES.
Symposion "Marktwirtschaft und Umwelt" (1980 : Walter Eucken Institut) Marktwirtschaft und Umwelt . Tübingen , 1981. ix, 303 p. : ISBN 3-16-343372-3 : LC Card 81-128698 DDC 363.7/0526 19
HC79.E5 S92 1980 ***NYPL [TB (Walter Eucken Institut. Wirtschaftswissenschaftliche und wirtschaftsrechtliche Untersuchungen. Bd. 17)]***

La extinción de la artesanía gremial /. Castro Gutiérrez, Felipe. México , 1986. 188 p. ; ISBN 968-8374-01-6 LC Card 87-104891
HD6473.M64 M483 1986

Extremadura . Alvarado Corrales, Eduardo J. Cáceres [1984?] 101 p. : ISBN 84-600-3663-4 LC Card 86-165503
HD1333.S712 E783 1984

Exxon Education Foundation series on rhetoric and political discourse .
(v. 8) Alcalde Cardoza, Xavier. The idea of Third World development . Lanham, MD [Charlottesville, Va.] , c1987. xxii, 236 p. ; ISBN 0-8191-6303-1 (alk. paper) : LC Card 87-8154 DDC 338.91/009172/4 19
HC60 .A4595 1987

Eyll, Klara van.
Reininghaus, Wilfried. Quellen zur Geschichte des Deutschen Industrie- und Handelstages in Kammerarchiven, 1861 bis 1918 /. Bonn , 1986. 158 p. : ISBN 3-925925-01-5 LC Card 87-408272 DDC 354.430082/09 19
HF308 .R343 1986

Zeugnisse der Zeit . Bonn , 1986. 113 p. : LC Card 87-408186
HD2429.G3 Z48 1986

Eyüpgiller, Saygın. Akdoğan, Abdurrahman. Açıklamalı maliye ve vergi sözlüğü /. [Ankara?] , Yenişehir, Ankara , 1986. 229 p. ; LC Card 87-968120
HJ129.T9 A43 1986

Ez az a munkásság-- / [sajtó alá rendezte, Benedek István Gábor, Maris János, Varga Zsuzsa ; szerkesztette Benedek István Gábor]. Budapest : Népszava, 1984. 225 p., [40] p. of plates : ill., ports. ; 19 cm. ISBN 963-322-103-X LC Card 85-184724
1. Trade-unions - Hungary - History. 2. Labor and laboring classes - Hungary - History. I. Benedek, István Gábor. II. Maris, János. III. Varga, Zsuzsa.
HD6680.5 .E95 1984

Ezekiel, Mordecai, 1899- Blau, Gerda. Food aid for development . Rome , Ann Arbor, MI , 1985. xi, 343 p. : ISBN 92-5-102180-5 (pbk.) LC Card 86-220906 DDC 363.8/83/091724 19
HD9018.D44 B57 1985

Ezorsky, Gertrude, 1926- Moral rights in the workplace /. Albany , c1987. xii, 312 p. ; ISBN 0-88706-362-4 LC Card 86-6949 DDC 331.25 19
HD6957.U6 M67 1987 ***NYPL [JLE 87-1197]***

F & E und Marketing . Benkenstein, Martin. Wiesbaden , c1987. xvii, 319 p. : ISBN 3-409-13327-5 LC Card 87-144515 DDC 658.8/3 19
HF5415.2 .B4563 1987

FAO. see **Food and Agriculture Organization of the United Nations.**

F.A.S.B. Miller, Paul B. W. The FASB . Homewood, Ill. , 1986. xvi, 145 p. : ISBN 0-256-03520-2 LC Card 85-82340 ***NYPL [JLE 87-872]***

F. A. S. B. see **Financial Accounting Standards Board.**

F. E. O. G. A. see **European Agricultural Guidance and Guarantee Fund.**

F. I. U. see **Florida International University.**

FNBEM. see **Fundação Nacional do Bem-Estar do Menor.**

F. T. Q. see **Fédération des travailleurs du Québec.**

F und E Marketing. Benkenstein, Martin. F & E und Marketing . Wiesbaden , c1987. xvii, 319 p. ; ISBN 3-409-13327-5 LC Card 87-144515 DDC 658.8/3 19
HF5415.2 .B4563 1987

F. W. H. A. see **United States. Federal Highway Administration.**

Faaborg, Barbara Laue. Job resources for Colorado women : where to find good advice cheap / Barbara Laue Faaborg, Susan Stetson Renault. Colorado Springs, CO : Subar Publications, c1986. 128 p. : ill. ; 22 cm. Bibliography: p. 128. Includes index. ISBN 0-939411-00-8 (pbk.) : LC Card 87-103489 DDC 650.1/4/024042 19
1. Vocational guidance for women - Colorado. 2. Vocational guidance for women - Colorado - Directories. I. Renault, Susan Stetson. II. Title.
HF5382.65 .F33 1986

Faal, A. A. Money and capital markets in the Gambia and United Kingdom, and the problem of economic management at central bank level : an individual project paper / by A.A. Faal. [S.l. : s.n., 198-] 27 leaves ; 30 cm. Bibliography: leaf 27. LC Card 87-400415 DDC 332.1/0966/51 19
1. Finance - Gambia. 2. Central Bank of the Gambia. 3. Finance - Great Britain. I. Title.
HG187.5.G25 F3 1980z

Faaland, Just. Population and the world economy in the 21st century /. Oxford , 1982. viii, 264 p. : ISBN 0-631-12964-2 LC Card 86-673281
HC59 .P638x 1982b

Faber, Malte Michael.
Studies in Austrian capital theory, investment, and time /. Berlin , New York , c1986. vi, 316 p. : ISBN 0-387-16804-4 (U. S. : pbk.) LC Card 86-223780 DDC 330.15/7 19
HB98 .S83 1986

Fabián, Miguel Angel. Monografía del café / [compilación, Rolando Francisco Cañas ; gráficas e ilustraciones, José Antonio Henríquez ; colaboración, Miguel Angel Fabián, Martha de Rodríguez, Lorena Pineda Siriany]. 2a ed. actualizada. [San Salvador] : INCAFE, [Biblioteca "Ing. Félix Choussy"], 1984. 39 leaves : ill. ; 22 x 28 cm. Rev. ed. of: Monografía del cafe. 1982? LC Card 86-177543
1. Coffee trade - El Salvador. 2. Coffee - El Salvador. I. Rodríguez, Martha de. II. Pineda Siriany, Lorena. III. Cañas, Rolando Francisco. IV. Monografía del café. V. Title.
HD9199.S142 F33 1984

FABIAN SOCIETY (GREAT BRITAIN) - HISTORY.
Marucco, Dora. Fabianesimo, ghildismo, forme di democrazia industriale /. Milano, Italy ,

c1986. 82 p. ; LC Card 86-194327
HD6479 .M37 1986

Fabianesimo, ghildismo, forme di democrazia industriale /. Marucco, Dora. Milano, Italy , c1986. 82 p. ; LC Card 86-194327
HD6479 .M37 1986

Fabiani, Guido. L'agricoltura italiana tra sviluppo e crisi, 1945-1985 / Guido Fabiani. Nuova ed. Bologna : Il Mulino, 1986, c1979. 411 p. ; 22 cm. (Studi e ricerche. 208) Includes bibliographical references. ISBN 88-15-00984-1 : LC Card 86-181021
1. Agriculture and state - Italy - History - 20th century. I. Title.
HD1972 .F3 1986

Fabozzi, Frank J.
Handbook of financial markets . Homewood, Ill. , c1986. xix, 785 p. : ISBN 0-87094-600-5 LC Card 85-71920 DDC 332.6/78 19
HG4527 .H25 1986
NYPL [*R-Econ 86-3815]

Handbook of financial markets--securities, options, futures /. Homewood, Ill. , c1981. xxiii, 794 p. : ISBN 0-87094-216-6 LC Card 80-70448 DDC 332.6/78 19
HG4527 .H25 ***NYPL [JLE 86-1500]***

The Handbook of fixed income securities /. Homewood, Ill. , 1987. xxx, 1376 p. : ISBN 0-87094-745-1 LC Card 86-50815
NYPL [JLE 87-939]

Mortgage-backed securities . Chicago, Ill. , c1987. xi, 474 p. : ISBN 0-917253-47-7 : LC Card 86-15087 DDC 332.63/232 19
HG4655 .M65 1987 ***NYPL [JLE 87-783]***

Nevitt, Peter K. Equipment leasing for commercial bankers /. Philadelphia, Pa. , c1987. x, 123 p. ; ISBN 0-936742-37-2 (pbk.) : LC Card 87-5532 DDC 332.1/068/5 19
HD39.4 .N485 1987

Stigum, Marcia L. The Dow Jones-Irwin guide to bond and money market investments /. Homewood, Ill. , c1987. xiii, 298 p. : ISBN 0-87094-892-X : LC Card 86-71921
NYPL [*R-Econ. 87-1260]

FÁBRICA MILITAR DE AVIONES - HISTORY.
Angueira, María del Carmen. Capitalismo de estado, 1927-1956 /. Buenos Aires , c1986. 116 p. : ISBN 950-25-1416-5 LC Card 87-100705
HD9711.A72 A54 1986

Fabricação de materiais de barro para construção . Almeida, João Carreira. Lisboa , 1978. 186 p., [3] leaves of plates (one folded) : LC Card 82-112167 DDC 338.4/36914/09469 19
HD9596.P82 A85 1978

FABRICS. see **TEXTILE FABRICS.**

Fabrics for use as bed sheeting, pillow casing, or bolster casing. Australia. Industries Assistance Commission. Interim report . Canberra , 1976. 36 p. ; ISBN 0-642-02317-4 (pbk.) LC Card 85-132707
HD9969.B433 A83 1976

Fabrikbesichtigungen / Reportagen von Monique Laederach ... [et al.] ; Fotos von Lisa Schäublin ... [et al.] ; Vorwort von Niklaus Meienberg. Zürich : Limmat Verlag Genossenschaft : WochenZeitung, c1986. 206 p. : ill. ; 24 cm. ISBN 3-85791-109-3 LC Card 87-129952 DDC 305.5/62/09494 19
1. Labor and laboring classes - Switzerland. 2. Industrial housing - Switzerland. 3. Alien labor - Switzerland. I. Laederach, Monique, 1938-. II. Schäublin, Lisa, 1952-.
HD8606.5 .F33 1986

Fabrizi, Pier Luigi. La politica degli investimenti in titoli nelle banche di deposito / Pier Luigi Fabrizi. [Milano] : Giuffrè, 1982. xii, 138 p. ; 24 cm. (Università "L. Bocconi," Dipartimento di economia aziendale . 38. 3.21) Bibliography: p. [131]-138. LC Card 82-165568
1. Bank investments - Italy. 2. Deposit banking - Italy. 3. Securities - Italy. 4. Banking law - Italy. I. Series: Università "L. Bocconi," Dipartimento di economia aziendale (Series) , 38. II. Title.
HG1616.I5 F33 1982

FAC report .
(#6) U. S. agriculture and Third World economic development . Washington, D.C. , c1987. xv, 103 p. : ISBN 0-89068-086-8 (pbk.): LC Card 86-62757 DDC 338.9/009172/4 19
HD1755 .U173 1987

Faces in a famine [motion picture] / Ithaca Filmworks ; producer, director, Robert Lieberman. New York, N.Y. : Filmakers Library, 1985. 1 film reel (51 min.) : sd., col. ; 16 mm. In English and Ethopic with English subtitles. Title from data sheet. Ages 15 through adult. Issued also as videorecording. Documents the Ethiopian drought through a visual survey of the main characters in the tragedy: starving citizens, relief workers, journalists, and preening disaster groupies. LC Card 85-702803 DDC 963 11
1. Famines - Ethiopia. 2. Victims of famine - Ethiopia. 3. Food relief - Ethiopia. 4. Droughts - Ethiopia. I. Ithaca Filmworks. II. Filmakers Library, inc.
HC845.Z9F3

Faces in a famine [videorecording] / Ithaca Filmworks ; producer, director, Robert Lieberman. New York, N.Y. : Filmakers Library, 1985. 1 videocassette (51 min.) : sd., col. In English and Ethopic with English subtitles. Title from data sheet. Ages 15 through adult. Issued as U-matic 3/4 in. or Beta 1/2 in. or VHS 1/2 in. Issued also as motion picture. Documents the Ethiopian drought through a survey of the main characters in the tragedy: starving citizens, relief workers, journalists, and preening disaster groupies. LC Card 85-703663 DDC 963 11
1. Famines - Ethiopia. 2. Victims of famine - Ethiopia. 3. Food relief - Ethiopia. 4. Droughts - Ethiopia. I. Ithaca Filmworks. II. Filmakers Library, inc.
HC845.Z9F3

Fachberichte Simulation .
(Bd. 6) Simulation als betriebliche Entscheidungshilfe . Berlin , New York , 1987. xi, 282 p. : ISBN 0-387-17353-6 LC Card 87-121884 DDC 658.4/0352 19
HD30.23 .S56 1987

Fachhochschule Bielefeld. Evaluation der Berufsberatung der Bundesanstalt für Arbeit . Nürnberg , 1983. vii, 282 p. : LC Card 85-107586
HF5382.5.G3 E9 1983

Fachinformationen.
Rösch, Willi. Das tägliche Duell zwischen Handel und Verbraucher . [München-Gräfelfing] , c1975. 110 p. : LC Card 84-121903
HF5429.6.G42 R67 1975

Fachinformationsführer .
(3) Gergely, Stefan M. Lebensmittel- und Agrarwissenschaften /. Wien , 1983. iii, 317 p. ; ISBN 3-205-06103-9 LC Card 87-407964 DDC 338.1/9/4360285 19
HD9015.A8 G47 1983

(8) Gergely, Stefan M. Wirtschaftswissenschaften /. Wien , 1985. 170 p. ; ISBN 3-205-06108-X LC Card 85-229521
HB74.9.A9 G47 1985

Fachserie Achtzehn. Revidierte Ergebnisse, 1960 bis 1984 /. Stuttgart , 1985. 468 p. ; LC Card 86-204499 DDC 339.343 19
HC290.5.I5 R48 1985

Fachserie 18. Revidierte Ergebnisse, 1960 bis 1984 /. Stuttgart , 1985. 468 p. ; LC Card 86-204499 DDC 339.343 19
HC290.5.I5 R48 1985

Fachserie 9. Index der Aktienkurse --lange Reihen. Wiesbaden , Stuttgart , 1985. 211 p. : LC Card 86-204529 DDC 332.63/222/0943 19
HG5494 .I53 1985

Fachtagung "Bevölkerungsentwicklung, Bevölkerungswanderung und Urbanisierung in Lateinamerika" (1984 : Eichstätt, Germany) Desarrollo demográfico, migraciones y urbanización en América Latina : [Akten der Fachtagung "Bevölkerungsentwicklung, Bevölkerungswanderung und Urbanisierung in Lateinamerika" der Arbeitsgemeinschaft Deutsche Lateinamerika-Forschung vom 25.-27. Oktober 1984] / D.W. Benecke ... [et al.], eds. Regensburg : Pustet, c1986. 432 p. : ill., maps ; 24 cm. (Eichstätter Beiträge, 0720-6798 . Bd. 17. 1 = vol. 17. 1) Veröffentlichungen des Zentralinstituts für Lateinamerika-Studien. Serie A, Kongressakten = Publicaciones del Centro de Estudios Latinoamericanos. Serie A, Actas Spanish and Portuguese. Includes bibliographies. LC Card 86-181152
1. Latin America - Population - Congresses. 2. Latin America - Population density - Congresses. 3. Migration, Internal - Latin America - Congresses. 4. Latin America - Emigration and immigration - Congresses. 5. Rura-urban migration - Latin America - Congresses. 6. Urbanization - Latin America - Congresses. I. Benecke, Dieter W. II. Arbeitsgemeinschaft Deutsche Lateinamerika-Forschung. III. Series: Eichstätter Beiträge , Bd. 17. IV. Title.
HB3530.5.A3 F33 1984

Fachwörterbuch. Schramm, Herbert F. W. Burghagen Fachwörterbuch . Hamburg , c1964. 160 p. ; LC Card 84-256680
HF5548 .S37 1964

Fachwörterbuch, Schweissen, Schneiden und verwandte Verfahren /. Kleiber, Achim W. Düsseldorf , 1986- , c1985- v. ; ISBN 3-87155-707-2 (Bd. 1) LC Card 86-149500 DDC 671.5/2/0331 19
TS227.5 .K54 1986 ***NYPL [JSK 86-83]***

Facilitating technological change . Flynn, Patricia M. Cambridge, Mass. , c1988. x, 233 p. : ISBN 0-88730-104-5 LC Card 87-17839 DDC 331.2 19
HD6331 .F56 1988

Facility location and land use : the urban/rural dilemma : proceedings of a session / sponsored by the Committees on Land Use and Community Development of the Urban Planning and Development Division of the American Society of Civil Engineers in conjunction with the ASCE Convention in Boston, Massachusetts, October 31, 1986 ; edited by Yupo Chan. New York, N.Y. : ASCE, c1986. vii, 40 p. : ill. ; 22 cm. Includes bibliographies and indexes. ISBN 0-87262-574-5 (pbk.) LC Card 86-25926 DDC 338.6/042 19
1. Land use - United States - Planning - Congresses. 2. Nuclear power plants - United States - Location - Planning - Congresses. 3. Radioactive waste sites - United States - Location - Planning - Congresses. 4. Recreation areas - United States - Location - Planning - Congresses. 5. Water resources development - United States - Planning - Congresses. I. Chan, Yupo. II. American Society of Civil Engineers. Urban Planning and Development Division. Land Use Committee. III. American Society of Civil Engineers. Committee on Community Development. IV. ASCE National Convention (1986 : Boston, Mass.).
HD171.A15 F33 1986

Facility planning technology / edited by McKinley Conway and Linda L. Liston. Norcross, Ga. : Conway Data, c1987. viii, 935 p. : ill. ; 29 cm. "A compendium of articles published in Industrial development and Site selection handbook"--P. iii. Includes indexes. ISBN 0-910436-26-6 LC Card 86-72097 DDC 658.2/1 19
1. Corporate planning. 2. Industrial management. 3. Industry - Location - Decision making. I. Conway, H. McKinley (Hobart McKinley), 1920-. II. Liston, Linda L.
HD30.28 .F33 1987

Facing social revolution . Powelson, John P., 1920- Boulder, Colo. , c1987. v, 146 p. ; ISBN 0-934449-03-1 : LC Card 86-32186 DDC 330/.092/4 B 19
HB119.P68 A3 1987

Facing technology. Twentieth joint conference . [Charlottetown, P.E.I. , 1986] 94 p. ; LC Card 87-147512 DDC 338/.06 19
HC120.T4 T84 1986

Facing the future . Späth, Lothar, 1937- [Wende in die Zukunft. English.] Berlin , New York , c1986. xvi, 196 p. ; ISBN 0-387-17105-3 (U. S.) LC Card 86-25994 DDC 338.943 19
HC286.7 .S713 1986

Facing the squatter crisis / City of Cape Town, City Engineer's Department. Cape Town : The Dept., 1977. 21 p. : ill. ; 30 cm. Cover title. LC Card 81-194960
1. Squatter settlements - South Africa - Cape Town Region. I. Cape Town (South Africa). City Engineer's Dept.
HD7374.4.C343 F33 1977

Facoltà di economia e commercio di Urbino (Series) .
(3) Il Finanziamento dell'innovazione nelle imprese industriali /. Milano, Italy , c1985. 271 p. : LC Card 86-157239
HC310.T4 F55 1985

Facq, Hans J. O. de. Formation des adultes . [Bujumbura] [1984- v. <1 > : LC Card 86-980941
HD5715.5.B94 F67 1984

FACSIMILE TRANSMISSION - EQUIPMENT AND SUPPLIES.
Electronic copy boards--local & remote. Norwalk, Conn., U. S.A. (6 Prowitt St., Norwalk 06855) , c1986. iii, 101 leaves : LC Card 86-224860 DDC 381/.45621380414 19
HD9802.3.A2 E45 1986

Fact paper (University of Port Elizabeth. Institute for Planning Research) .
(no. 56) Erwee, Johannes Albertus. Trends in the construction of dwelling units in the Port Elizabeth/Uitenhage and East London/King William's town regions, 1970-1984, including additions and alterations /. Port Elizabeth [South Africa] [1985] 44 leaves : ISBN 0-86988-244-9 (pbk.) LC Card 86-229280 DDC 363.5/1/096875 19
HD7374.4.P6 E735 1985

FACTOR PROPORTIONS - DEVELOPING COUNTRIES.
Mohs, Ralf-Matthias. Exporte, komparative Vorteile und wirtschaftliche Entwicklung in den Schwellenländern . Göttingen [1983] 236 p. : ISBN 3-509-01345-X LC Card 84-126961
HF4055 .M64 1983

FACTORIES - INSPECTION. see **FACTORY INSPECTION.**

FACTORIES - MAINTENANCE AND REPAIR. see **PLANT MAINTENANCE.**

FACTORIES - PURCHASING.
Kellogg, Douglas E. A primer for buying and selling small manufacturing companies /. New York , c1987. xiv, 225 p. : ISBN 0-471-85235-X LC Card 87-19017 DDC 658.1/6 19
HD2341 .K44 1987

FACTORIES - SOVIET UNION - ACCOUNTING.
Tishkov, I. E. (Ivan Efremovich) Uchet i kal'kulirovanie sebestoimosti produktsii vspomogatel'nykh proizvodstv /. Moskva , 1980. 110 p. ; LC Card 81-143226
HC340.C7 T57 1980

FACTORIES - WASTE PRODUCTS. see **FACTORY AND TRADE WASTE.**

FACTORING (FINANCE)
Crichton, Susan. Understanding factoring and trade credit /. London , 1986. xv, 199 p. : ISBN 0-08-039204-0 (pbk.) : LC Card 87-122377 DDC 658.8/8 19
HG3752.3 .C75 1986

FACTORING (FINANCE) - GREAT BRITAIN.
Crichton, Susan. Understanding factoring and trade credit /. London , 1986. xv, 199 p. : ISBN 0-08-039204-0 (pbk.) : LC Card 87-122377 DDC 658.8/8 19
HG3752.3 .C75 1986

FACTORING (FINANCE) - LAW AND LEGISLATION - GREAT BRITAIN.
Crichton, Susan. Understanding factoring and trade credit /. London , 1986. xv, 199 p. : ISBN 0-08-039204-0 (pbk.) : LC Card 87-122377 DDC 658.8/8 19
HG3752.3 .C75 1986

Factors affecting efficiency in the informal sector in Lusaka and Kitwe /. Kamya, Andrew, 1941- Lusaka , 1981. iii, 40 p. ; LC Card 87-980491
HD2346.Z292 L875 1981

Factors which hinder or help productivity improvement in the Asian region, a review and the prospect . Hirono, Ryōkichi. Tokyo, Japan , c1980. v, 111 p. ; ISBN 92-833-1470-0 LC Card 81-174179 DDC 338/.06/0952 19
HD56 .H57 1980 ***NYPL [JLD 86-2287]***

FACTORY AND TRADE WASTE - ENVIRONMENTAL ASPECTS.
Kneese, Allen V. [Economics and the environment. Russian.] Ėkonomika i okruzhaiushchaia sreda /. Moskva , 1981. 189 p. : LC Card 82-187223
HC79.E5 K57517 1981

FACTORY AND TRADE WASTE - ENVIRONMENTAL ASPECTS - DEVELOPING COUNTRIES.
Knödgen, Gabriele, 1949- Umweltschutz und industrielle Standortentscheidung /. Frankfurt/Main , New York , c1982. 219 p. : ISBN 3-593-33158-6 LC Card 83-110653
HC59.72.P55 K58 1982

FACTORY AND TRADE WASTE - ENVIRONMENTAL ASPECTS - GOVERNMENT POLICY - GERMANY (WEST)
Paul, Joachim, 1956- Zur politischen Durchsetzungsfähigkeit einer ökologisch orientierten Marktwirtschaft . Frankfurt am Main , New York , c1986. xvii, 569 p. ; ISBN 3-8204-9810-9 LC Card 87-407614 DDC 363.7/056/0943 19
HC290.5.E5 P38 1986

FACTORY AND TRADE WASTE - LAW AND LEGISLATION - UNITED STATES - COMPLIANCE COSTS.
Gray, Wayne B. (Wayne Burger), 1955- Productivity versus OSHA and EPA regulations /. Ann Arbor, Mich. , c1986. xii, p. : ISBN 0-8357-1721-6 (alk. paper) LC Card 85-28873 DDC 338/.06/0973 19
HC110.I52 G73 1986 ***NYPL [JLE 86-2375]***

FACTORY AND TRADE WASTE - LAW AND LEGISLATION - WASHINGTON (STATE) - PUGET SOUND REGION.
Industrial and municipal discharges. Seattle, Wash. (217 Pine St., Ste 1100, Seattle 98101) [1986] viii, 136, 14 p. : LC Card 86-622616 DDC 363.7/31 19
HC107.W22 P85 1986

The factory automation industry /. Delson, Erwin B. New York, N.Y. , c1985. 1 v. (various pagings) : ISBN 0-931634-16-4 (pbk.) LC Card 86-203033 DDC 338.4/76298/0973 19
HD9696.A963 U635 1985

FACTORY INSPECTION.
Labour inspection . Geneva , 1986. ix, 100 p. ; ISBN 92-2-105359-8 (pbk.) : LC Card 87-123437 DDC 331.25 19
HD3656 .L33 1986

FACTORY INSPECTION - CALIFORNIA.
Schaefer, Andrew. CAL-OSHA routine compliance inspections . [Sacramento, CA , 1986] 25 p. ; LC Card 86-622709 DDC 363.1/164/09796 19
HD7262.5.U62 C573 1986

FACTORY SANITATION - LAW AND LEGISLATION. see **INDUSTRIAL HYGIENE - LAW AND LEGISLATION.**

FACTORY SYSTEM - CASE STUDIES.
Work in market and industrial societies /. Albany , c1984. viii, 316 p. ; ISBN 0-87395-810-1 LC Card 83-9267 DDC 306/.36 19
HD4901 .A659 1984 ***NYPL [JLE 86-4483]***

FACTORY SYSTEM - CZECHOSLOVAKIA - LIBEREC - HISTORY.
Album der Industrie des Reichenberger Handelskammer-Bezirks. [Praha] , 1981. 2 v. in 1 : LC Card 84-190839
HC270.292.L52 A42 1981

FACTORY SYSTEM - GERMANY (WEST) - HISTORY.
Der Dressierte Arbeiter . München , c1984. 211 p. : ISBN 3-406-09286-1 LC Card 84-181068 DDC 331.25 19
HD6331.2.G28 D74 1984

FACTORY WASTE. see **FACTORY AND TRADE WASTE.**

Facts and figures : a comparative statistical analysis. Vienna : The Secretariat, Organization of the Petroleum Exporting Countries, 1984? 45 p. : col. ill. ; 18 X 21 cm. Includes "Sources."
1. Organization of Petroleum Exporting Countries - Statistics. 2. Energy consumption - Statistics. 3. Petroleum industry and trade - Statistics.
NYPL [JLD 86-2319]

Facts from your figures / [prepared by Press and Information Service, Central Statistical Office, and the Central Office of Information]. London : Government Statistical Service, 1977. 37 p. : ill. ; 20 x 22 cm. LC Card 85-160272
1. Great Britain - Statistical services. 2. Great Britain - Economic conditions - Statistical services. I. Great Britain. Central Statistical Office. Press and Information Service. II. Great Britain. Central Office of Information.
HA37.G7 F33 1977

The Facts on File dictionary of personnel management and labor relations /. Shafritz, Jay M. New York, N.Y. , c1985. 534 p. : ISBN 0-8160-1234-2 LC Card 85-20823 DDC 658.3/003/21 19
HF5549.A23 S52 1985
NYPL [JLE 86-4748]

Facts on File, Inc. Shafritz, Jay M. The Facts on File dictionary of personnel management and labor relations /. New York, N.Y. , c1985. 534 p. : ISBN 0-8160-1234-2 LC Card 85-20823 DDC 658.3/003/21 19
HF5549.A23 S52 1985
NYPL [JLE 86-4748]

Faculté de droit et des sciences économiques de Tours. Energie et décentralisation /. Paris , 1984. 297 p. : ISBN 2-7178-0782-9 : LC Card 84-249613
HD9502.F72 E5334 1984

Facultés universitaires Notre-Dame de la Paix, Namur.
International trade and exchange rates in the late eighties /. Amsterdam ; New York : xii, 418 p. : ISBN 0-444-87941-2 LC Card 86-223111 DDC 382.4/5 19
HG203 .I58 1985

Facultés universitaires Notre-Dame de la Paix, Namur. Faculté des sciences économiques et sociales. International trade and exchange rates in the late eighties /. Amsterdam ; New York : xii, 418 p. : ISBN 2-8004-0892-8
NYPL [JLE 87-120]

Faculty of Actuaries in Scotland. McCutcheon, J. J. (John J.) An introduction to the mathematics of finance /. London , 1986. x, 463 p. : ISBN 0-434-91224-7 (pbk.) : LC Card 86-219539 DDC 332/.01/51 19
HF5691 .M385 1986

Faculty paper series .
(FP 85-7) Economic status of Texas agriculture /. College Station, Tex. [1985] ii, 30 leaves : LC Card 87-620640 DDC 338.1/09764 19
HD1775.T4 E28 1985

(FP 86-12) Paggi, Mechel S. Impact of agricultural exports for Texas /. College Station, Tex. [1986] 20 leaves, [1] leaf of plates : LC Card 87-620821 DDC 382/.41/09764 19
HD1775.T4 P34 1986

Fadahunsi, Akin. The development process and technology : a case for a resources based development strategy in Nigeria / Akin Fadahunsi. Uppsala : the Scandinavian Institute of African Studies, 1986. 41 p. ; 25 cm. (Research report, 0080-6714 . no. 77) Includes bibliographies. ISBN 91-7106-257-2 (pbk.) LC Card 87-119156 DDC 338.9669/07 19
1. Technological innovations - Economic aspects - Nigeria. 2. Appropriate technology - Nigeria. 3. Nigeria - Economic policy. 4. Economic development. I. Series: Research report (Nordiska Afrikainstitutet) , no. 77. II. Title.
HC1055.Z9 T43 1986

Fadda, Sebastiano. Gizard, Xavier. Regional development and vocational training analysis and discussion of the relationship development . Berlin , Washington, DC , 1986. 49 p. ; ISBN 92-825-5911-4 (pbk.) : LC Card 87-137374 DDC 331.25/92/094 19
HD5715.5.E8 G58 1986

Fafchamps, Marcel. Keddeman, Willem. Emploi et revenus dans le secteur agricole traditionnel au Bénin /. Addis Abéba , 1982. 64 p. ; LC Card 87-980402
HD2141 .K43 1982

Fagen, Richard R. Transition and development . New York, NY [Berkeley, Calif.] , c1986. 352 p. ; ISBN 0-85345-705-0 (pbk.) : LC Card 86-12579 DDC 335.43/09172/4 19
HX517.8 .T73 1986 ***NYPL [JLD 86-3907]***

FAGOAGA FAMILY - PORTRAITS.
Cortina Portilla, Manuel. Algo sobre la plata en México en el siglo XVIII /. México , 1986. 48 p., [1] folded leaf of plates : LC Card 87-404604 DDC 332.4/042/097253 19
HG661 .C67 1986

FAGOAGA IRAGORRI, FRANCISCO, 1679-1736 - PORTRAITS.
Cortina Portilla, Manuel. Algo sobre la plata en México en el siglo XVIII /. México , 1986. 48 p., [1] folded leaf of plates : LC Card 87-404604 DDC 332.4/042/097253 19
HG661 .C67 1986

Fahmy, H. A. African population projection according to eight models, sex & age groups (1970-2000) / prepared by Fahmy, H.A. [Lusaka] : Republic of Zambia, Ministry of Local Government & Housing, Dept. of Town & Country Planning, Development Planning & Research Unit, [198-?] 34, 9, 62 leaves, [3] leaves of plates : ill. ; 28 x 39 cm. Cover title: African population projection, 1970-2000. LC Card 85-980559 DDC 304.6/2/096894021 19
1. Population forecasting - Zambia - Provinces - Statistics. 2. Zambia - Population - Statistics. I. Zambia. Dept. of Town and Country Planning. Development Planning & Research Unit. II. Title. III. Title: African population projection, 1970-2000.
HA4703 .F34 1980z

Fahrion, Roland. Dynamische Investitionsplanung für den Erdgasmarkt : unter Berücksichtigung der generellen Energiepreisentwicklung und der verstärkten Penetration in den Verbrauchssektor private Haushalte, dargestellt für das Bundesland Bayern mit Szenarien für den Planungszeitraum, 1980-1995 / Roland Fahrion. Gräfelfing/München : Resch-Verlag, c1984. iv, 308 p. : ill. ; 25 cm. Bibliography: p. 272-277. ISBN 3-87806-075-0 LC Card 85-111076
1. Gas industry - Germany (West) - Bavaria - Capital investments - Decision making. 2. Gas industry - Germany (West) - Bavaria - Forecasting. I. Title.
HD9581.G43 B34 1984

Fahrni, Oliver, 1955- Kalte Kommunikation . Basel , c1985. 256 p. : ISBN 3-85787-134-2 LC Card 85-232413
HD9696.T463 S95 1985

Fahrnschon, Helmut. Agrarmärkte & Agrarmarketing . Hamburg , 1983. 220 p. : ISBN 3-922528-45-7 LC Card 84-162297
HD1955 .A515 1983

Fahrradfreundliche Verkehrspolitik in Stadt und Land . Bauer, Helfried. Wien , 1984. 87 p. : LC Card 85-150945
HE5739.A9 B38 1984

Fahy, Thomas P. Richard Scott Perkin and the Perkin-Elmer Corporation / Thomas P. Fahy. [United States : Perkin-Elmer Print Shop], c1987. xv, 271 p. : ill. ; 24 cm. Pages 269-271 blank for "Notes." ISBN 0-9618075-0-4 LC Card 86-63869 DDC 338.7/666156/0973 19
1. Perkin, Richard Scott, 1906-1969. 2. Elmer, Charles Wesley, 1872-1954. 3. Perkin-Elmer Corporation - History. 4. Industrialists - United States - Biography. 5. Optical industry - United States - History. I. Title.
HD9707.U62 P474 1987

FAI Seminar, 1986. Growth and modernisation of fertiliser industry . New Delhi , 1987. 1 v. (various pagings) : LC Card 87-902183 DDC 338.4/766862/0954 19
HD9483.I42 G78 1987

Faîans, O. G. (Oleg Grigor′evich) Matematicheskie metody v upravlenii gorodskimi transportnymi sistemami /. Leningrad , 1979. 150 p. : LC Card 81-163008
HE311.S652 M675 1979

Faig i Aumallé, Miquel. La Garrotxa . [Barcelona , c1983. xv, 323 p. : ISBN 84-7231-912-1 LC Card 85-184803
HC387.G34 G37 1983

Failed transitions to modern industrial society : Renaissance Italy and seventeenth century Holland : first international colloquium, April 18-20, 1974 proceedings / edited by Frederick Krantz & Paul M. Hohenberg. Montreal : Interuniversity Centre for European Studies, c1975. vii, 105 p. : ill. ; 25 cm. Includes index. Bibliography: p. 91-101. ISBN 0-919958-00-1 LC Card 80-510009 DDC 303.4/094 19
1. Social change - Congresses. 2. Industrialization - Congresses. 3. Social history - Congresses. 4. Italy - Industries - Congresses. 5. Netherlands - Industries - Congresses. I. Krantz, Frederick. II. Hohenberg, Paul M.
HM101 .F26 NYPL [JLE 81-166]

FAILURE IN BUSINESS. see **BUSINESS MORTALITY.**

Fair, Donald E.
International monetary and financial integration . Dordrecht , Boston , c1988. xii, 403 p. : ISBN 90-247-3563-7 LC Card 87-3622 DDC 332.4/94 19
HG930.5 .I586 1988

Shifting frontiers in financial markets /. Dordrecht ; Boston : xii, 360 p. : ISBN 90-247-3225-5 LC Card 85-18821 DDC 332 19
HG4523 .S54 1986 NYPL [JLE 86-2694]

A Fair go for people with disabilities : a discussion paper / by the Working Party on Equal Opportunity Legislation for People with Disabilities. Perth, W.A : Govt. of Western Australia, [1986] xxxv, 162 p. ; 30 cm. "August 1986." Bibliography: p. 157-162. ISBN 0-7309-0332-X LC Card 87-158098 DDC 331.5/9/09941 19
1. Handicapped - Employment - Government policy - Australia - Western Australia. I. Western Australia. Working Party on Equal Opportunity Legislation for People with Disabilities.
HD7256.A762 W474 1986

The Fair Housing Assistance Program evaluation / prepared by ABT Associates ; prepared for U. S. Department of Housing and Urban Development, Office of Policy Development and Research. Washington, D.C. : The Department, [1985] 1 v. (various pagings) : ill., map. ; 28 cm. "June 1985." "HUD-995-PDR-October 1985." Includes bibliographical references.
1. Discrimination in housing - United States. 2. Minorities - Housing - United States. 3. Housing policy - United States. I. Wallace, James E. II. United States. United States Dept. of Housing and Urban Development. Office of Policy Development and Research. *NYPL [JLF 87-17]*

Fair play in the marketplace . Okun, Mitchell. Dekalb, Ill. , 1986. xii, 345 p. : ISBN 0-87580-115-3 LC Card 85-25921 DDC 363.1/926/0973 19
HD9000.9.U5 O39 1986
NYPL [JLD 86-2513]

FAIR TRADE. see **COMPETITION, UNFAIR.**

FAIR TRADE (TARIFF) see **FREE TRADE AND PROTECTION.**

Fairbanks' scales, the world's standard : manufactured by E. & T. Fairbanks & Co. Chicago : Rand McNally, 1893. 20 p. : ill. ; 18 cm. Cover title: Fairbanks' souvenir of the World's Columbian Exposition. LC Card 85-666379
1. E. & T. Fairbanks & Co. 2. Weighing equipment industry - United States - History. I. E. & T. Fairbanks & Co. II. Title: Fairbanks' souvenir of the World's Columbian Exposition.
HD9706.2.U54 E22x 1893

Fairbanks' souvenir of the World's Columbian Exposition. Fairbanks' scales, the world's standard . Chicago , 1893. 20 p. : LC Card 85-666379
HD9706.2.U54 E22x 1893

Fairchild, Byron. The Army and industrial manpower / by Byron Fairchild and Jonathan Grossman. Westport, Conn. : Greenwood Press, 1987. xiv, 291 p. : 1 ill. ; 23 cm. At head of title: The War Department. Reprint. Originally published: Washington, D.C. : Office of the Chief of Military History, Dept. of the Army, 1959. (United States Army in World War II. The History of the War Department). Bibliography: p. [261]-268. Includes index. ISBN 0-313-25480-X (lib. bdg. : alk. paper) LC Card 86-25738 DDC 331.11/0973 19
1. Labor supply - United States - History. 2. World War, 1939-1945 - Manpower - United Staes - History. 3. Labor policy - United States - History. I. Grossman, Jonathan, 1915-. II. United States. War Dept. III. Series: United States Army in World War II. History of the War Department. IV. Title.
HD5724 .F25 1987

Fairchild, Gary F. Florida citrus production trends 1986-87 through 1995-96. Gainesville, Fla. : Economic Research Dept., Florida Dept. of Citrus, University of Florida, [1985] iv, 35 p. : ill. ; 28 cm. Cover title. LC Card 86-622647 DDC 338.1/7435/09759 19
1. Citrus fruit industry - Florida - Forecasting. I. Title.
HD9259.C53 U553 1985

Faire l'histoire du monde du travail : guide pratique. [Seyssel] : Champ Vallon ; [Le Creusot] : Institut Jean-Baptiste Dumay ; 52 p. : ill. ; 21 cm. "Rédaction ... Christian Bobin" et al.--P. 1. Bibliography: p. 50-51. ISBN 2-903528-49-7 : LC Card 85-180268 DDC 305.5/62/072044 19
1. Labor and laboring classes - France - Information services - France. 2. Labor and laboring classes - France - Research - France. I. Bobin, Christian. II. Institut Jean-Baptiste Dumay.
HD8428 .F35 1985 NYPL [JLD 87-1157]

FAIRFAX COUNTY (VA.) - DIRECTORIES.
Lusk's Fairfax County, Virginia assessment directory . Washington, D.C. (1824 Jefferson Pl., NW, Washington 20036) , 1986. 1251, [81] p. ; LC Card 87-144674 DDC 333.33/2/09755291 19
HD266.V82 F24 1986

Fairfax County, Virginia assessment directory. Lusk's Fairfax County, Virginia assessment directory . Washington, D.C. (1824 Jefferson Pl., NW, Washington 20036) , 1986. 1251, [81] p. ; LC Card 87-144674 DDC 333.33/2/09755291 19
HD266.V82 F24 1986

Fairfax, Sally K. Federal lands : a guide to planning, management, and state revenues / Sally K. Fairfax, Carolyn E. Yale (Western Office, Council of State Governments). Washington, D.C. : Island Press, c1987. xviii, 252 p. : ill. ; 23 cm. Bibliography: p. 225-234. Includes index. ISBN 0-933280-33-5 (pbk.) :$ LC Card 86-27512 DDC 333.1/0978 19
1. West (U. S.) - Public lands. I. Yale, Carolyn E. II. Council of State Governments. Western Office. III. Title.
HD243.A17 F35 1987

Fairfax, Va. George Mason University. see **George Mason University.**

Fairfield on-scene study of collisions : first quarterly report, October to December, 1976 / edited by David C. Herbert, Christopher W. Corben. [Sydney?] : Traffic Accident Research Unit, Dept. of Motor Transport, New South Wales, [1977] 120 p. : ill. ; 30 cm. (Paper / Traffic Accident Research Unit, Department of Motor Transport, New South Wales, 0313-2854 . 3/77) "June, 1977." Bibliography: p. 30-32. Includes index. LC Card 85-170609
1. Traffic accidents - Australia - Fairfield (N.S.W.). I. Herbert, David C. II. Corben, Christopher W. III. Series: Paper (New South Wales. Traffic Accident Research Unit) , 77/3.
HE5614.5.A8 F37 1977

FAIRNESS DOCTRINE (BROADCASTING) - UNITED STATES.
Political broadcast catechism. Washington , c1984. 61 p. : *NYPL [MWGH 85-3267]*

Fairness in selecting employees /. Arvey, Richard D. Reading, Mass. , c1988. x, 361 p. : ISBN 0-201-00078-4 (pbk.) : LC Card 87-22173 DDC 658.3/112 19
HF5549.5.S38 A78 1988

The fairness of markets . McKenzie, Richard B. Lexington, Mass. , c1987. xiv, 235 p. : ISBN 0-669-14801-6 (alk. paper) LC Card 86-45958 DDC 330 19
HB72 .M35 1987

FAIRS.
Mortsiefer, Joachim. Messen und Ausstellungen als Mittel der Absatzpolitik mittelständischer Herstellerbetriebe /. Göttingen , 1986. 534 p. : ISBN 3-509-01399-9 : LC Card 86-210320 DDC 381/.18 19
HF5470 .M583 1986

Street fair manual . Chicago , 1907. 79 p. : LC Card 86-227641
HF5481 .S77 1907

FAIRS - JAPAN - DIRECTORIES.
Nedlog, D'Lanor. Insider's guide to antique bazaars in Japan /. Tokyo, Japan , c1986. 124 p. : ISBN 4-906231-00-4 LC Card 87-123282 DDC 381/.18 19
HF5475.J3 N43 1986

FAIRS - SWITZERLAND - BASEL.
Interferex 86 (Basel, Switzerland) Interferex 86, Intertable . Basel, Schweiz [1986] 284 p., [6] p. of plates : LC Card 87-409294 DDC 381/.18 19
HF5474.S92 B365 1986

Faist, Thomas, 1959- Soziale Schliessung in rassistisch gespaltenen Arbeitsmärkten : eine Fallstudie zum Solidarismus schwarzer Müllarbeiter in Memphis, Tennessee / Thomas Faist. Frankfurt am Main ; New York : P. Lang, c1986. 161 p. ; 21 cm. (Europäische Hochschulschriften. Reihe XXXI, Politikwissenschaft, 0721-3654 . Bd. 98 = vol. 98 = vol. 98) Bibliography: p. 153-161. ISBN 3-8204-9525-8 LC Card 87-407927 DDC 331.89/28136372/0976819 19

1. Sanitation Workers Strike, Memphis, Tenn., 1968. 2. Memphis (Tenn.) - Officials and employees. 3. Memphis (Tenn.) - Race relations. I. Series: Europäische Hochschulschriften. Reihe XXXI, Politikwissenschaft , Bd. 98. II. Title.
HD5325.S2572 1968 .M46 1986

Fait, Eduardo Lizano. see **Lizano Fait, Eduardo.**

Fajardo, Darío. see **Fajardo M., Darío.**

Fajardo M., Darío. Campesinado y capitalismo en Colombia /. Bogotá, Colombia , 1981. 233 p. ; LC Card 82-141108 DDC 338.1/09861 19
HD516 .C35 1981 NYPL [JLD 86-1342]

Fajth, Gáspár. A Lakosság jövedelme és fogyasztása, 1970-1985 /. Budapest , 1986. 97 p. ; ISBN 963-340-805-9 : LC Card 87-408026
HC300.295.I5 L3317 1986

Faktornyĭ analiz ėffektivnosti razmeshcheniia proizvodstva /. Novitskiĭ, N. A. (Nikolaĭ Aleksandrovich) Moskva , 1982. 126 p. : LC Card 83-193429
HC340.D5 N68 1982

Fakty, prawa, decyzje . Siemianowski, Andrzej. [Wrocław] , 1983. 103 p. ; LC Card 85-113022
HB9 .B7522 nr. 245 Q175

Falaleev, A. N. Formirovanie predpriiatiia kommunisticheskogo tipa / A.N. Falaleev. Moskva : "Mysl'", 1980. 126 p. ; 20 cm. Includes bibliographical references. LC Card 81-144517
1. Industry and state - Soviet Union. I. Title.
HD3616.S472 F35 1980

Falbe, Cecilia M. Business and society . Lexington, Mass. , c1987. xv, 654 p. : ISBN 0-669-13207-1 (pbk : alk. paper) LC Card 86-45548 DDC 658.4/08/0973 19
HD60.5.U5 B853 1987

Falciola, Kristine. Conditions of work and quality of working life . Geneva , 1986. xxi, 306 p. ; ISBN 92-2-105328-8 (pbk.) : LC Card 86-215659 DDC 306/.36/025 19
HD7260 .C64 1986

Falcón, Ricardo. El mundo del trabajo urbano, 1890-1914 / Ricardo Falcón. Buenos Aires : Centro Editor de América Latina, c1986. 141 p. ; 18 cm. (Biblioteca Política argentina . 153) Spine title: El mundo del trabajo urbano. Includes bibliographies. ISBN 950-25-1414-2 : LC Card 87-101423
1. Labor and laboring classes - Argentina - History. 2. Trade-unions - Argentina - History. I. Title. II. Title: Mundo del trabajo urbano. III. Series.
HD8266 .F35 1986

Faley, Robert H. Arvey, Richard D. Fairness in selecting employees /. Reading, Mass. , c1988. x, 361 p. : ISBN 0-201-00078-4 (pbk.) : LC Card 87-22173 DDC 658.3/112 19
HF5549.5.S38 A78 1988

Falik, Marilyn. Ideology and abortion policy politics / Marilyn Falik. New York, N.Y. : Praeger, 1983. 228 p. ; 25 cm. "Landmark Dissertations in Women's Studies Series. Annette Baxter, editor." Bibliography: p. 220-228. ISBN 0-03-062813-X LC Card 83-2402 DDC 363.4/6 19
1. Abortion - Political aspects - United States. 2. Family policy - Political aspects - United States. 3. Ideology - Political aspects. 4. Conservatism - United States. 5. Liberalism - United States. I. Title.
HQ767.5.U5 F34 1983 NYPL [JLE 85-1581]

Falk, Bernd R. Immobilien-Handbuch : Wirtschaft, Recht, Bewertung / Bernd Falk. Stuttgart : W. Kohlhammer, c1985. xlii, 972 p. : ill. ; 22 cm. Bibliography: p. 951-969. Includes indexes. ISBN 3-17-008062-8 LC Card 86-129985
1. Real estate business - Germany (West) - Handbooks, manuals, etc. 2. Real estate business - Law and legislation - Germany (West) - Handbooks, manuals, etc. 3. Real estate business - Handbooks, manuals, etc. 4. Real estate business - Law and legislation - Handbooks, manuals, etc. I. Title.
HD656 .F35 1985

Falk, Dieter. Nevermann, Helga. Venture Capital . Baden-Baden , 1986. 146 p. ; ISBN 3-7890-1263-7 LC Card 87-121846 DDC 332/.0415/0943 19
HG5492 .N48 1986

Falk, Haim. Butterworth, John E. Financial reporting . Hamilton, Ont. , 1986. viii, 250 p. : ISBN 0-920212-52-2 (pbk.) LC Card 87-101758 DDC 657/.86203 19
HF5686.P3 B87 1986

Falk, Jack L., 1950- Brown, Constance C., 1952- Preparing documents with UNIX /. Englewood Cliffs, N.J. , c1986. xv, 206 p. : ISBN 0-13-699976-X LC Card 85-17016 DDC 652/.5 19
Z52.5.U54 B76 1986 NYPL [JSE 86-1215]

Fall Industrial Relations Seminar (1985 : Industrial Relations Centre, Queen's University, Kingston, Ont.) Carter, D. D. The changing face of Canadian labour relations law /. Kingston, Ont., Canada , 1985. 15 p. ; ISBN 0-88886-126-5 (pbk.) LC Card 86-145328 DDC 331 s 344.71/01 331 s 347.1041 19
HD8102 .K52 no. 54 KE3009

The fall of the Bell system . Temin, Peter. Cambridge , New York , 1987. xviii, 378 p. : ISBN 0-521-34557-X LC Card 87-10293 DDC 384.6/065/73 19
HE8846.A55 T44 1987

Faller, Eberhard. Zur Problematik der Zulässigkeit des Abweichens vom Grundsatz der Einzelerfassung und Einzelbewertung im aktienrechtlichen Jahresabschluss : ein Beitrag zur Analyse pauschalierender Bewertungstechniken unter dem De-lege-lata-Aspekt / Eberhard Faller. Pfaffenweiler : Centaurus-Verlagsgesellschaft, 1985. xiv, 386 p. : ill. ; 21 cm. (Reihe Wirtschaftswissenschaften, 0177-283X . Bd. 22) Bibliography: p. 342-382. ISBN 3-89085-078-2 : LC Card 86-140803
1. Stock companies - Germany (West) - Accounting. 2. Stock companies - Germany (West) - Taxation. I. Series: Reihe Wirtschaftswissenschaften (Pfaffenweiler, Breisgau-Hochschwarzwald, Germany) , Bd. 22. II. Title.
HF5681.S8 F34 1985

Fallik, Fred. Managing organizational change : human factors and automation / Fred Fallik. Philadelphia : Taylor & Francis, 1988. p. cm. (Case studies in ergonomics practice . v. 3) Bibliography: p. Includes index. ISBN 0-85066-430-6 : LC Card 87-18027 DDC 658.3 19
1. Office practice - Automation - Psychological aspects - Case studies. I. Title. II. Series.
HF5548 .F274 1988

Fallis, George, 1947- Housing economics / George Fallis. Toronto [Ont.] ; Boston : Butterworths, c1985. 241 p. : ill. ; 24 cm. Includes index. Bibliography: p. [221]-231. ISBN 0-409-82940-4 LC Card 85-177894 DDC 333.33/8 19
1. Housing - Canada. 2. Housing policy - Canada. 3. Households - Canada. I. Title.
HD7305.A3 F35 1985 NYPL [JLE 87-2573]

Fallows, James M. Human capital : the cultural sources of America's economic decline--and rebirth / by James Fallows. New York, N.Y. : Random House, 1988. p. cm. Includes index. ISBN 0-394-56498-7 : LC Card 87-42659 DDC 306/.3 19
1. United States - Economic conditions - 1981-. 2. United States - Social conditions - 1980-. 3. Individualism. 4. Social classes - United States. 5. Entrepreneurship. I. Title.
HC106.8 .F35 1988

Fallstudie Haiger . Brauer, Karl M. Berlin , c1983. 55 p. ; ISBN 3-428-05403-2 LC Card 83-233201
HE199.G3 B73 1983

Falola, Toyin.
Britain and Nigeria . London ; Atlantic Highlands, New Jersey : vi, 250 p. ; ISBN 0-86232-303-7 : LC Card 86-232062 DDC 337.410669 19
HF1534.5.N6 B75 1987

Nigeria and the international capitalist system /. Boulder, Colo. , 1988. v, 154 p. ; ISBN 1-555-87087-2 (alk. paper) : LC Card 87-23183 DDC 337.669 19
HF1616.7 .N54 1988

Fal'tsman, Vladimir Konstantinovich. Metodologiia prognozirovaniia vosproizvodstva i ispol'zovaniia resursov v ėkonomike SSSR /. Moskva , 1984. 201 p. : LC Card 85-199435
HC340.I52 M485 1984

Faludi, Andreas. A decision-centred view of environmental planning / by Andreas Faludi. 1st ed. Oxford [Oxfordshire] ; New York : Pergamon Press, 1987. xiii, 240 p. ; 23 cm. (Urban and regional planning series. v. 38) Includes bibliographies and index. ISBN 0-08-032698-6 : LC Card 87-10414 DDC 333.7 19
1. Environmental policy - Decision making. I. Title.
HC79.E5 F28 1987

Falusné Szikra, Katalin. Az első és a második gazdaság közötti bér-, illetve jövedelem-diszparitás / Falusné Szikra Katalin. Budapest : Akadémiai Kiadó, c1986. 31 p. ; 20 cm. (Értekezések, emlékezések, 0236-6258) "Akadémiai székfoglaló, 1985. november 27". ISBN 963-05-4343-5 : LC Card 87-407713
1. Income distribution - Hungary. 2. Informal sector (Economics) - Hungary. 3. Small business - Hungary. I. Title. II. Series.
HC300.295.I5 F35 1986

Falvey, Jack, 1938- What's next? : career strategies after 35 / Jack Falvey. Charlotte, Vt. : Williamson Pub., c1987. 189 p. ; 23 cm. Includes index. ISBN 0-913589-26-8 : LC Card 87-10553 DDC 650.1/4 19
1. Career changes. I. Title.
HF5384 .F35 1987

Familiebudgetter : sammenlignelige tabeller : Nederlandene, Belgien, Irland, Danmark, Grækenland, Spanien = Family budgets : comparative tables : Netherlands, Belgium, Ireland, Denmark, Greece, Spain. Luxembourg : EUROSTAT ; Washington, D.C. : Sales and subscriptions, European Community Information Service, c1986. 279 p. ; 30 cm. Danish, Dutch, English, and French. ISBN 92-825-5583-6 : LC Card 86-213531
1. Cost and standard of living - Belgium - Statistics. 2. Cost and standard of living - Netherlands - Statistics. 3. Cost and standard of living - Ireland - Statistics. 4. Cost and standard of living - Denmark - Statistics. 5. Cost and standard of living - Greece - Statistics. 6. Cost and standard of living - Spain - Statistics. I. Statistical Office of the European Communities. II. Title: Family budgets.
HD7033 .F35 1986

Familien und Unternehmungen der Industriepioniere J.W. Jäckel & Co. in Wiesenthal a.N., Gebrüder Redlhammer in Gablonz a.N., Johann Schowanek in Georgenthal. John, Walter. Glasspinnerei im Isergebirge /. Schwäbisch-Gmünd , 1984, c1974. 78 p. : LC Card 85-135799
HD9623.I94 J64 1984

Families and work / edited by Naomi Gerstel and Harriet Engel Gross. Philadelphia : Temple University Press, 1987. viii, 539 p. ; 24 cm. (Women in the political economy) Includes bibliographies. ISBN 0-87722-467-6 (alk. paper) : LC Card 86-30151 DDC 306.8/5 19
1. Work and family. I. Gerstel, Naomi. II. Gross, Harriet. III. Series.
HD4904.25 .F35 1987

FAMILY.
Mousourou, Loukia M. Gynaikeia apascholēsē kai oikogeneia stēn Hellada kai allou /. Athēna , c1985. 220 p. : LC Card 86-205975
HD6181.83 .M68 1985

Thomas, Sue. Family finance . Cambridge [Cambridgeshire] , Wolfeboro, NH, U. S.A. , 1988. p. cm. ISBN 0-85941-420-5 (pbk.) : LC Card 87-17386 DDC 332.024 19
HG179 .T457 1988

Wright, H. Norman. The family that listens /. Wheaton, Ill. , c1978. 142 p. ; ISBN 0-88207-633-7 : LC Card 78-57370 DDC 301.42/7
HQ734 .W9487 NYPL [JLD 81-655]

FAMILY ALLOWANCES - AUSTRALIA.
Cass, Bettina. Income support for families with children /. Canberra [1986] xiii, 126 p. : ISBN 0-644-05378-X (pbk.) LC Card 87-103419 DDC 362.5/82 19
HD4925.5.A8 C37 1986

Whiteford, Peter. Issues in assistance for families . Woden, ACT [1986] iii, 56 p. ; ISBN 0-642-51604-9 (pbk.) LC Card 86-231139 DDC 362/.0425 19
HD4925.5.A8 W47 1986

FAMILY ALLOWANCES - QUÉBEC (PROVINCE)
La Compensation des charges familiales au Québec /. [Quebec] [1986] xxi, 197 p. ; ISBN 2-551-08707-4 LC Card 86-179318
HD4925.5.C2 C65 1986

FAMILY ALLOWANCES - SOVIET UNION, NORTHERN.
Khlystova, E. A. (Evgenii͡a Andreevna) Sever i Sibir′ zovut molodykh /. Moskva , 1985. 109 p. : LC Card 86-153085
HF5549.5.I5 K452 1985

FAMILY ALLOWANCES - SWEDEN.
Bostadsbidragen . [Stockholm] [1982] 207 p. : ISBN 91-38-72586-X LC Card 83-240044
HD7350.A3 B697 1982

Family and economy in modern society / edited by Paul Close and Rosemary Collins ; foreword by David Morgan. Basingstoke, Hampshire : Macmillan, 1985. xvi, 234 p. ; 23 cm.
Bibliography: p. 212-227. Includes index.
CONTENTS. - Family form and economic production / Paul Close -- The production of people and domestic labour revisited / Linda Murgatroyd -- 'Horses for courses' / Rosemary Collins -- Gender divisions and power relationships in the Australian family / Lois Bryson -- Household technology / Graham Thomas and Christine Zmroczek -- Placing children in the division of labour / Jens Qvortrup -- Paid work and unpaid caring / Clare Ungerson -- Returning to work / Judith Chaney -- Women, the family, and unemployment / Jennie Popay -- Do we really know what 'the family' is? / Jon Bernardes. ISBN 0-333-37437-1 LC Card 86-674026
1. Work and family. 2. Family - Economic aspects. I. Close, Paul. II. Collins, Rosemary.
HD4904.25 .F35x 1985

FAMILY - AUSTRALIA.
Burke, Terry, 1942- A roof over their heads . Melbourne , 1984. xiv, 178 p. : ISBN 0-642-87172-8 ***NYPL [JLD 86-2639]***

FAMILY - BELGIUM.
Coomans, Géry, 1949- La production sociale des femmes /. Bruxelles , c1983. 223 p. : ISBN 2-8004-0820-0 : LC Card 84-199167
HD6158 .C66 1983

FAMILY - BOLIVIA.
Cisneros C., Antonio. La mujer trabajadora . La Paz, Bolivia [1984] 131 leaves : LC Card 85-129000 DDC 331.4/0984 19
HD6121 .C58 1984 ***NYPL [JLF 86-1704]***

FAMILY - BOLIVIA - COCHABAMBA (DEPT.)
Calderón G., Fernando. Jatun Llajta . La Paz, Bolivia , 1982. v, 448 p., [8] leaves of plates : LC Card 83-111937 DDC 381/.1 19
HF5473.B62 C623 1982
NYPL [JLF 86-1794]

FAMILY - BOLIVIA - LA PAZ.
Sector formal de la ciudad de La Paz . La Paz, Bolivia , 1980. 77 leaves ; LC Card 81-212597 DDC 331.1/0984/12 19
HD5751.L36 S42 1980 ***NYPL [JLF 87-369]***

Family budgets. Familiebudgetter . Luxembourg , Washington, D.C. , c1986. 279 p. ; ISBN 92-825-5583-6 : LC Card 86-213531
HD7033 .F35 1986

FAMILY - CANADA.
Wilson, S. J. (Susannah Jane) Women, the family, and the economy /. Toronto , New York , c1982. 176 p. : ISBN 0-07-548028-X (pbk.) LC Card 82-123177 DDC 305.4/0971 19
HQ1457 .W53 1982 ***NYPL [JLE 86-1735]***

FAMILY - CANADA - FORECASTING - STATISTICS.
Interim household and family projections for Canada, provinces, and territories to 2006 =. [Ottawa] [1987] 67 p. ; LC Card 87-162270 DDC 304.6/2/0971021 19
HA745 .I62 1987

Family characteristics and labour force activity : annual averages, 1977-1984 = Caractéristiques familiales et activité sur le marché du travail : moyennes annuelles, 1977-1984. Ottawa : Statistics Canada, c1986. xxii, 131 p. ; 28 cm.
French and English. "Catalogue 71-5333 occasional"--Cover. Includes bibliographical references. ISBN 0-660-52240-3 (pbk.) : LC Card 86-206978
1. Labor supply - Canada - Statistics. 2. Households - Canada - Statistics. I. Statistics Canada. II. Title: Caractéristiques familiales et activité sur le marché du travail.
HD5728 .F36 1986

FAMILY - CONNECTICUT - HISTORY.
Ditz, Toby L., 1951- Property and kinship . Princeton, N.J. , c1986. xvi, 213 p. : ISBN 0-691-04735-9 (alk. paper) : LC Card 86-5051 DDC 333.33 19
HB715 .D58 1986 ***NYPL [JLE 86-4624]***

FAMILY CORPORATIONS.
Krupa, Arlene. Couplepower . New York , c1987. 227 p. ; ISBN 0-396-09029-X (pbk.) : LC Card 87-20065 DDC 658.4/09 19
HD62.25 .K78 1987

FAMILY CORPORATIONS - MANAGEMENT.
Dyer, W. Gibb, 1954- Cultural change in family firms . San Francisco , 1986. xxi, 179 p. ; ISBN 1-555-42007-9 (alk. paper) LC Card 86-10585 DDC 658/.045 19
HD62.25 .D94 1986 ***NYPL [JLE 87-1079]***

FAMILY CORPORATIONS - SOUTHERN STATES - HISTORY.
Mayor, Archer H. Southern timberman . Athens , c1988. p. cm. ISBN 0-8203-0999-0 (alk. paper) LC Card 87-22897 DDC 338.7/63498/0975 19
HD9760.B83 M39 1988

FAMILY CORPORATIONS - UNITED STATES - MANAGEMENT - CASE STUDIES.
Goldwasser, Thomas. Family pride . New York , c1986. 226 p. ; ISBN 0-396-08587-3 LC Card 86-4546 DDC 338.7/4/0973 19
HD62.25 .G64 1986 ***NYPL [JLD 87-159]***

FAMILY DEMOGRAPHY - ENGLAND.
Levine, David, 1946- Reproducing families . Cambridge [Cambridgeshire] , New York , 1987. ix, 251 p. ; ISBN 0-521-33256-7 LC Card 86-26372 DDC 304.6/0942 19
HB3585 .L48 1987

FAMILY - ECONOMIC ASPECTS.
Family and economy in modern society /. Basingstoke, Hampshire , 1985. xvi, 234 p. ; ISBN 0-333-37437-1 LC Card 86-674026
HD4904.25 .F35x 1985

FAMILY - ECONOMIC ASPECTS - ENGLAND - LONDON.
Wilson, Gail. Money in the family . Aldershot, Hants., England , Brookfield, USA , c1987. ix, 271 p. ; ISBN 0-566-05389-6 : LC Card 87-7402 DDC 339.2/2 19
HG179 .W53517 1987

FAMILY - ECONOMIC ASPECTS - GERMANY (WEST)
Demographische Probleme der Haushaltsökonomie /. Bochum , 1986. vii, 212 p. : ISBN 3-88339-534-X LC Card 87-137970 DDC 339.4/1/0943 19
HD7029 .D37 1986

FAMILY ENTERPRISES. see **FAMILY CORPORATIONS.**

Family farming in Europe and America / edited by Boguslaw Galeski and Eugene Wilkening. Boulder : Westview Press, 1987. viii, 312 p. ; 23 cm. (Rural studies series) Includes bibliographies. ISBN 0-8133-7340-9 (soft : alk. paper) : LC Card 87-2041 DDC 338.1/6 19
1. Family farms - Europe - Case studies. 2. Family farms - United States - Case studies. 3. Family farms - Canada - Case studies. I. Gałęski, Bogusław. II. Wilkening, Eugene A. III. Series: Rural studies series of the Rural Sociological Society.
HD1476.E85 F35 1987

FAMILY FARMS - AFRICA, SUB-SAHARAN - ADDRESSES, ESSAYS, LECTURES.
Understanding Africa's rural households and farming systems /. Boulder , 1986. xiv, 234 p. : ISBN 0-8133-7175-9 : LC Card 85-32318 DDC 338.1/0967 19
HD1476.A357 U53 1986
NYPL [JLE 86-4336]

FAMILY FARMS - CANADA - CASE STUDIES.
Family farming in Europe and America /. Boulder , 1987. viii, 312 p. ; ISBN 0-8133-7340-9 (soft : alk. paper) : LC Card 87-2041 DDC 338.1/6 19
HD1476.E85 F35 1987

FAMILY FARMS - EUROPE - CASE STUDIES.
Family farming in Europe and America /. Boulder , 1987. viii, 312 p. ; ISBN 0-8133-7340-9 (soft : alk. paper) : LC Card 87-2041 DDC 338.1/6 19
HD1476.E85 F35 1987

FAMILY FARMS - GOVERNMENT POLICY - UNITED STATES.
Is there a moral obligation to save the family farm? /. Ames , 1987. xxvii, 427 p. : ISBN 0-8138-1000-0 (pbk.) LC Card 87-13399 DDC 338.1/0973 19
HD1476.U5 I8 1987

FAMILY FARMS - HUNGARY - HISTORY.
Szabó, László. Munkaszervezet és termelékenység a magyar parasztságnál a XIX-XX. században /. Szolnok , 1968 (Debrecen : Szabadság Lapnyomda) 167 p. : LC Card 86-188720
HD1536.H9 S89 1968

FAMILY FARMS - LATIN AMERICA - CONGRESSES.
Taller "Perspectivas y Alternativas de la Agricultura Familiar" (1983 : Montevideo, Uruguay) Taller "Perspectivas y Alternativas de la Agricultura Familiar". Montevideo, Uruguay [1984] 1 v. (various pagings) : LC Card 85-203149 DDC 338.1/6 19
HD1476.L29 T35 1983 ***NYPL [JLF 86-884]***

FAMILY FARMS - MISSISSIPPI RIVER - DELTA - FINANCE.
Neill, Robert Hitt. How to lose your farm in ten easy lessons and cope with it /. Leland, Miss. , c1987. xi, 138 p. ; ISBN 0-9617591-1-9 (pbk.) : LC Card 87-14176 DDC 338.1/3/097624 19
HD1476.U6 A156 1987

FAMILY FARMS - SENEGAL - SINE-SALOUM.
Benoit-Cattin, Michel. L'exploitation agricole familiale en Afrique soudano-sahélienne /. Paris , c1982. 94 p. : ISBN 2-85319-106-0 LC Card 86-116718
HD1476.S382 S563 1982

FAMILY FARMS - TEXAS - FINANCE - CONGRESSES.
Farm Crisis Workers Conference (1986 : Arlington, Tex.) Farm Crisis Workers Conference . [Austin?] , 1986] 136 p. ; LC Card 87-620630 DDC 338.1/3/09764 19
HD1476.U6 T44 1986

FAMILY FARMS - UNITED STATES.
Ambur, Owen D. Selling out the family farm . Washington , 1986. v, 40 p. : LC Card 87-601379 DDC 338.1/6 19
HD1476.U5 A65 1986

The Farm financial crisis . Boulder , 1988. xvi, 205 p. : ISBN 0-8133-7186-4 (pbk. : alk. paper) : LC Card 86-32601 DDC 338.1/3/0973 19
HD1761 .F295 1988

Gorman, Carol. America's farm crisis /. New York , 1987. 125 p. : ISBN 0-531-10408-7 LC Card 87-2087 DDC 338.1/0973 19
HD1476.U5 G67 1987

Hope for the family farm . Newton, Kan. , c1987. viii, 231 p. : ISBN 0-87303-126-1 (pbk.) LC Card 87-81635 DDC 338.1/6 19
HD1476.U5 H67 1987

FAMILY FARMS - UNITED STATES - CASE STUDIES.
Family farming in Europe and America /. Boulder , 1987. viii, 312 p. ; ISBN 0-8133-7340-9 (soft : alk. paper) : LC Card 87-2041 DDC 338.1/6 19
HD1476.E85 F35 1987

FAMILY FARMS - URUGUAY - CONGRESSES.
Taller "Perspectivas y Alternativas de la Agricultura Familiar" (1983 : Montevideo, Uruguay) Taller "Perspectivas y Alternativas de la Agricultura Familiar". Montevideo, Uruguay [1984] 1 v. (various pagings) : LC Card 85-203149 DDC 338.1/6 19
HD1476.L29 T35 1983 ***NYPL [JLF 86-884]***

Family finance . Thomas, Sue. Cambridge [Cambridgeshire] , Wolfeboro, NH, U. S.A. , 1988. p. cm. ISBN 0-85941-420-5 (pbk.) : LC Card 87-17386 DDC 332.024 19
HG179 .T457 1988

FAMILY - GERMANY, WEST.
Leben im Jahr 2000 und danach . Berlin , c1984. 213 p. : ISBN 3-7605-8571-X LC Card 85-128359
HB3595 .L43 1984

Schneewind, Klaus A., 1939- Eltern und Kinder . Stuttgart , c1983. 229 p. : ISBN

3-17-007744-9 LC Card 83-150745 DDC 303.3/23/0943 19
HQ739 .S29 1983 **NYPL [JLE 87-1168]**

FAMILY - GERMANY (WEST) - STATISTICS.
Schweitzer, Walter. Heiratstafeln versus Familienstandstafeln . Wiesbaden , 1985. iii, 102 p. : LC Card 87-408703 DDC 306.8/1/0943021 19
HB1215 .S39 1985

FAMILY - GREECE.
Mousourou, Loukia M. Gynaikeia apascholēsē kai oikogeneia stēn Hellada kai allou /. Athēna , c1985. 220 p. : LC Card 86-205975
HD6181.83 .M68 1985

FAMILY - HUNGARY - STATISTICS.
Csernák, Józsefné. A családok és háztartások előreszámítása, 1981-2001 /. Budapest , 1985. 125 p. : LC Card 86-166603
HA1201 .A64 no. 59 HA1205

FAMILY LIFE SURVEYS - UNITED STATES.
Pleck, Joseph H. Working wives, working husbands /. Beverly Hills, Calif. , c1985. 167 p. ; ISBN 0-8039-2489-5 LC Card 85-11974 DDC 306.8/7 19
HQ536 .P59 1985 **NYPL [JLD 86-1130]**

The family money game . Steen, Robert. Longmont, Colo. , 1986. viii, 120 p. : ISBN 0-917665-03-1 (pbk.) LC Card 85-70449
HG179 .S815 1986

FAMILY - NEW YORK (STATE) - ERIE COUNTY - HISTORY - 19TH CENTURY.
Stern, Mark J. Society and family strategy . Albany, N.Y. , c1987. xiv, 172 p. : ISBN 0-88706-495-7 LC Card 86-23121 DDC 304.6/34/0974796 19
HB935.N7 S74 1987

FAMILY - NEW YORK (STATE) - ERIE COUNTY - HISTORY - 20TH CENTURY.
Stern, Mark J. Society and family strategy . Albany, N.Y. , c1987. xiv, 172 p. : ISBN 0-88706-495-7 LC Card 86-23121 DDC 304.6/34/0974796 19
HB935.N7 S74 1987

FAMILY, PATRIARCHAL. see **PATRIARCHY.**

FAMILY - PHILIPPINES - ILOCOS NORTE - CASE STUDIES.
Findley, Sally E. Rural development and migration . Boulder , 1987. xxiii, 308 p. : ISBN 0-8133-7326-3 (pbk. : alk. paper) : LC Card 86-33987 DDC 304.8/09599 19
HB2110.I43 F56 1987

FAMILY PLANNING. see **BIRTH CONTROL.**

Family Planning Association of Sri Lanka.
International Congress on New Dimensions in Population Planning and Development (1978 : Colombo, Sri Lanka) The International Congress on New Dimensions in Population Planning and Development, Bandaranaike Memorial International Conference Hall, Colombo, 26-28 March 1978 /. Colombo, Sri Lanka , 1978. 114 p., [5] leaves of plates : LC Card 84-902651 DDC 304.6/6/095493 19
HB883.5 .I57 1978 **NYPL [JLF 86-1970]**

FAMILY POLICY - HUNGARY.
A Lakosság jövedelme, társadalombiztosítás, családpolitika /. Budapest [1983] 82 p. : LC Card 83-206799
HC30.295.I5 L332 1983
NYPL [JLE 87-179]

FAMILY POLICY - NETHERLANDS.
Aalberts, Monique M. J. Gezinsvorming door jonge migranten . 's-Gravenhage , 1985. 93 p. : ISBN 90-12-04999-7 LC Card 85-235621
HD8518.5.A2 A24 1985

FAMILY POLICY - POLITICAL ASPECTS - UNITED STATES.
Falik, Marilyn. Ideology and abortion policy politics /. New York, N.Y. , 1983. 228 p. ; ISBN 0-03-062813-X LC Card 83-2402 DDC 363.4/6 19
HQ767.5.U5 F34 1983 **NYPL [JLE 85-1581]**

Family pride . Goldwasser, Thomas. New York , c1986. 226 p. ; ISBN 0-396-08587-3 LC Card 86-4546 DDC 338.7/4/0973 19
HD62.25 .G64 1986 **NYPL [JLD 87-159]**

Family Service America. The State of families. Milwaukee, Wis. , <c1987-. v. <2 > : ISBN 0-87304-226-3 (pbk. : v. 2) LC Card 87-24374 DDC 306.8/5/0973 19
HD4904.25 .S83 1987

FAMILY SIZE.
Linde, Hans. Theorie der säkularen Nachwuchsbeschränkung 1800 bis 2000 /. Frankfurt [am Main] , New York , c1984. 201 p. ; ISBN 3-593-33385-6 LC Card 85-131521
HB901 .L55 1984

FAMILY SIZE - HONDURAS.
Suazo, Margarita. Problación y desarrollo socioeconómico en Honduras /. Chicago, Ill., USA (1313 E. 60th St., Chicago 60637) , c1984. 90 p., [2] leaves of plates : LC Card 85-203746
HB3540.A3 S82 1984

FAMILY SIZE - HUNGARY - PUBLIC OPINION.
Pataki, Judit. Közvéleménykutatás népesedési kérdésekről /. Budapest , c1985. 75 p. ; LC Card 86-166976
HA1201 .A64 no. 60 HB3592.5.A3

FAMILY SIZE - NORWAY.
Jensen, An-Magritt. Flere i yrke--færre barn? . Oslo , 1983. 59 p. : ISBN 82-537-2007-6 : LC Card 84-163552
HA1503 .A45 nr. 147 HQ762.N8

FAMILY SIZE - SOVIET UNION.
Detnost′ semi′i--vchera, segodni͡a, zavtra /. Moskva , 1986. 205 p. : LC Card 87-109456 DDC 304.6/32/0947 19
HB1017 .D47 1986

FAMILY SIZE - SUDAN.
Saghayroun, Atif A. Rahman. Determinants of family size in rural Sudan /. Khartoum, Sudan [1984] 36 leaves ; LC Card 87-119805 DDC 304.6/32/09624 19
HB1071.8.A3 S22 1984

FAMILY - SOUTHERN STATES - HISTORY.
McHugh, Cathy. Mill family . New York , 1988. p. cm. ISBN 0-19-504299-9 LC Card 87-7832 DDC 331.7/67721/0975 19
HD8039.T42 U654 1988

Family structure and intergenerational transfers in social health insurance . Breyer, Friedrich. Berlin [1986] 24 p. : LC Card 87-156738 DDC 368.4/2016/0724 19
HD7101 .B73 1986

The family that listens /. Wright, H. Norman. Wheaton, Ill. , c1978. 142 p. ; ISBN 0-88207-633-7 : LC Card 78-57370 DDC 301.42/7
HQ734 .W9487 **NYPL [JLD 81-655]**

FAMILY - UNITED STATES.
Kamerman, Sheila B. Meeting family needs . New York , c1983. 45 p. ; ISBN 0-08-030965-8 (pbk.) : LC Card 83-27159 DDC 658.3/8 19
HD4928.N62 U6355 1983
NYPL [JLM 83-380 no.33]

Kamerman, Sheila B. A workplace for people . New York , 1987. p. cm. ISBN 0-231-06480-2 LC Card 87-18223 DDC 331.2/0973 19
HD60.5.U5 K36 1987

FAMILY - UNITED STATES - RELIGIOUS LIFE.
Hope for the family farm . Newton, Kan. , c1987. viii, 231 p. : ISBN 0-87303-126-1 (pbk.) LC Card 87-81635 DDC 338.1/6 19
HD1476.U5 H67 1987

Famine, a heritage of hunger . Golkin, Arline T. (Arline Tartus) Claremont, Calif. , c1987. xvi, 168 p. : ISBN 0-941690-21-0 : LC Card 86-26138 DDC 363.8 19
HC79.F3 B63 1986 **NYPL [JLD 87-878]**

Famine and food supply in the Graeco-Roman world . Garnsey, Peter. Cambridge [Cambridgeshire] , New York , 1988. xiv, 303 p., [4] p. of plates : ISBN 0-521-35198-7 LC Card 87-16737 DDC 338.1/9/38 19
HD9015.G82 G37 1988

Famine in Ukraine, 1932-1933 / edited by Roman Serbyn and Bohdan Krawchenko. Edmonton : Canadian Institute of Ukrainian Studies, University of Alberta ; Downsview, Ont., Canada : Distributed by the University of Toronto Press, 1986. 192 p. ; 24 cm. (The Canadian library in Ukrainian studies) Includes bibliographies. CONTENTS. - The man-made famine of 1933 in Soviet Ukraine / James E. Mace -- The man-made famine of 1932-1933 and collectivization in Soviet Ukraine / Bohdan Krawchenko -- Ukraine's demographic losses, 1927-1938 / M. Maksudov -- The famine of 1933 / James E. Mace -- Making the news fit to print / Marco Carynnyk -- Russian Mensheviks and the famine of 1933 / André Liebich -- Blind eye to murder / Marco Carynnyk -- The impact of the man-made famine on the structure of Ukrainian society / Wsewolod W. Isajiw -- The famine of 1921-1923 / Roman Serbyn -- Conceptualizations of genocide and ethnocide / Frank Chalk and Kurt Jonassohn. ISBN 0-09-286243-8 LC Card 87-148658 DDC 363.8/0947/71 19
1. Famines - Ukraine - Congresses. 2. Ukraine - History - 1921-1944 - Congresses. 3. Press and politics - Congreses. 4. Journalistic ethics - Congresses. I. Serbyn, Roman. II. Krawchenko, Bohdan, 1946-. III. Title. IV. Series.
HC337.U53 F314 1986

FAMINE - IRELAND - HISTORY - 19TH CENTURY.
Griffiths, A. R. G., 1940- The Irish Board of Works, 1831-1878 /. New York , 1987. iii, 214 p. ; ISBN 0-8240-7810-1 (alk. paper) : LC Card 87-24495 DDC 363/.09415 19
HD4150.3 .G75 1987

FAMINES.
Castro, Josué de, 1908-1973. Fome, um tema proibido . Petrópolis , 1983. 154 p. ; LC Card 83-224629
HD9000.5 .C28 1983

Golkin, Arline T. (Arline Tartus) Famine, a heritage of hunger . Claremont, Calif. , c1987. xvi, 168 p. : ISBN 0-941690-21-0 : LC Card 86-26138 DDC 363.8 19
HC79.F3 B63 1986 **NYPL [JLD 87-878]**

Pike, Clarence Edward, 1917- Chronicles of hunger /. Millwood, N.Y. , 1988. p. cm. ISBN 0-8046-9410-9 LC Card 87-12332 DDC 363.8 19
HD9000.5 .P55 1988

Ravallion, Martin. Markets and famines /. Oxford [Oxfordshire] , New York , 1987. viii, 203 p. : ISBN 0-19-828514-0 : LC Card 86-23724 DDC 381/.456413/0095492 19
HC79.F3 R38 1987

FAMINES - AFRICA.
Gibb, Christopher. Food or famine? /. Vero Beach, FL , 1987. 48 p. : ISBN 0-86592-279-9 LC Card 87-12741 DDC 363.8/096 19
HC800.Z9 F335 1987

Walker, Brian W. Authentic development in Africa /. New York, N.Y. , c1985. 70 p. : ISBN 0-87124-102-1 (pbk.) : LC Card 85-82567 DDC 081 s 338.96 19
E744 .H43 no. 274 HC800
NYPL [JLD 86-3400]

FAMINES - AFRICA, NORTHEAST.
King, Preston T., 1936- An African winter /. Harmondsworth, Middlesex, England , New York, N.Y., U. S.A. , 1986. 249 p. : ISBN 0-14-052365-0 (pbk.) : LC Card 87-103265 DDC 363.8/096 19
HC840.Z9 F34 1986

FAMINES - AFRICA, SUB-SAHARAN.
Bread broken . Eldoret, Kenya [1984] vi, 56 p. : LC Card 85-980419 DDC 363.8/0967 19
HC800.Z9 F32 1984

Twose, Nigel. Fighting the famine /. London , 1985. 96 p. : ISBN 0-7453-0131-2 (pbk.) : LC Card 86-135675 DDC 363.8/83/0966 19
HC800.Z9 F385 1985 **NYPL [JLD 87-768]**

FAMINES - AUSTRIA - HISTORY.
Loewenfeld-Russ, Hans, 1873-1945. Im Kampf gegen den Hunger . München , 1986. xxiv, 381 p., [1] leaf of plates : ISBN 3-486-52451-8 LC Card 86-224948
HC270.F3 L64 1986

FAMINES - BANGLADESH.
Ravallion, Martin. Markets and famines /. Oxford [Oxfordshire] , New York , 1987. viii, 203 p. : ISBN 0-19-828514-0 : LC Card 86-23724 DDC 381/.456413/0095492 19
HC79.F3 R38 1987

FAMINES - CAPE VERDE - HISTORY - 20TH CENTURY.
Carreira, António. Cabo Verde . Lisboa [1984] 207 p., [16] p. of plates : LC Card 87-400337 DDC 363.8/0966/58 19
HC594.Z9 F33 1984

FAMINES - CONGRESSES.
Honger op ons bord . Amsterdam , 1986. 164

p. : ISBN 90-70985-05-5 : LC Card 86-166714
HD9000.5 .H655 1986

FAMINES - DEVELOPING COUNTRIES.
Fryer, Jonathan. [Food for thought. French.] L'aide alimentaire, un marché de dupes /. Genève, Suisse . 91 p. ; LC Card 86-218069
HD9018.D44 F7914 1982

Global hunger . [Evansville, Ind.] , 1986. iv, 164 p. : ISBN 0-930982-08-8 (pbk.) LC Card 87-400224 DDC 363.8/8/091724 19
HD9018.D44 G57 1986

FAMINES - ETHIOPIA.
Clay, Jason W. Politics and the Ethiopian famine, 1984-1985 /. Cambridge, MA (11 Divinity Ave., Cambridge 02138) , 1985. xi, 250 p. : LC Card 86-153948 DDC 363.8/56/0963 19
HC845.Z9 F33 1985 ***NYPL [JLF 87-364]***

Combatting the effects of cyclical drought in Ethiopia. Addis Ababa, Ethiopia [1985] 56 p. : LC Card 86-224201 DDC 363.8/83/0963 19
HC845.Z9 F332 1985

Faces in a famine [motion picture] /. New York, N.Y. , 1985. 1 film reel (51 min.) : LC Card 85-702803 DDC 963 11
HC845.Z9F3

Faces in a famine [videorecording] /. New York, N.Y. , 1985. 1 videocassette (51 min.) : LC Card 85-703663 DDC 963 11
HC845.Z9F3

Franey, Jean-Pierre. Ethiopie, la face cachée /. Paris , c1986. 127 p. : ISBN 2-209-05848-1 : LC Card 87-113107
HC845.Z9 F34 1986

Harris, Myles F. Breakfast in hell . New York , c1987. 271 p. ; ISBN 0-671-63272-8 : LC Card 86-25504 DDC 363.8/83/0963 19
HC845.Z9 F345 1987

Jean, François. Ethiopie, du bon usage de la famine /. Paris [1986] 102 p. : LC Card 87-131143
HC845.Z9 F347 1986

Twose, Nigel. Fighting the famine /. London , 1985. 96 p. : ISBN 0-7453-0131-2 (pbk.) : LC Card 86-135675 DDC 363.8/83/0966 19
HC800.Z9 F385 1985 ***NYPL [JLD 87-768]***

FAMINES - ETHIOPIA - PICTORIAL WORKS.
Franey, Jean-Pierre. Ethiopie, la face cachée /. Paris , c1986. 127 p. : ISBN 2-209-05848-1 : LC Card 87-113107
HC845.Z9 F34 1986

FAMINES - ETHIOPIA - STATISTICS.
Drought situation in Ethiopia and assistance requirements 1984/85 /. Addis Ababa [1984] 55 leaves in various pagings : LC Card 85-980926
HC845.Z9 F32x 1984

FAMINES - GREAT BRITAIN - HISTORY.
Wells, Roger A. E. Wretched faces . New York , 1988. p. cm. ISBN 0-312-01248-9 : LC Card 87-22164 DDC 363.8/0942 19
HC260.F3 W45 1988

FAMINES - GREECE - ATHENS.
Maroudēs, Giōrgos. To hēmerologio tēs peinas /. [Athens] , 1976. 99 p., [6] leaves of plates ; LC Card 84-107778
HC300.F3 M37 1976

FAMINES - GREECE - HISTORY.
Garnsey, Peter. Famine and food supply in the Graeco-Roman world . Cambridge [Cambridgeshire] , New York , 1988. xiv, 303 p., [4] p. of plates : ISBN 0-521-35198-7 LC Card 87-16737 DDC 338.1/9/38 19
HD9015.G82 G37 1988

FAMINES - INDIA - BENGAL - HISTORY.
Nag Chowdhury-Zilly, Aditee. The vagrant peasant . Wiesbaden , 1982. xv, 196 p. : ISBN 3-515-03855-8 (pbk.) LC Card 86-214350
HD1537.I4 N327 1982

FAMINES - INDIA - RAJASTHAN - HISTORY.
Maloo, Kamala, 1948- The history of famines in Rajputana, 1858-1900 A.D. /. Udaipur , 1987. xii, 296 p. : ISBN 81-85167-00-1 : LC Card 87-901599 DDC 363.8/0954/4 19
HC437.R3 M28 1987

FAMINES - IRELAND - FERMOY - HISTORY - 19TH CENTURY.
Garner, Edward. To die by inches . Fermoy, Co. Cork, Ireland , c1986. 133 p. : ISBN 0-907568-03-3 (pbk.) : LC Card 87-111519 DDC 363.5/85/094195 19
HC260.5.Z7 F474 1986

FAMINES - ROME - HISTORY.
Garnsey, Peter. Famine and food supply in the Graeco-Roman world . Cambridge [Cambridgeshire] , New York , 1988. xiv, 303 p., [4] p. of plates : ISBN 0-521-35198-7 LC Card 87-16737 DDC 338.1/9/38 19
HD9015.G82 G37 1988

FAMINES - SAHEL.
Somerville, Carolyn M. Drought and aid in the Sahel . Boulder , 1986. xxii, 306 p. : ISBN 0-8133-7087-6 : LC Card 86-5635 DDC 338.966 19
HC1002 .S65 1986 ***NYPL [JLD 86-4038]***

Twose, Nigel. Fighting the famine /. London , 1985. 96 p. : ISBN 0-7453-0131-2 (pbk.) : LC Card 86-135675 DDC 363.8/83/0966 19
HC800.Z9 F385 1985 ***NYPL [JLD 87-768]***

FAMINES - SOVIET UNION - HISTORY.
FAMINES - SUDAN.
Cater, Nick. Sudan . Oxford , c1986. i, 36 p. : ISBN 0-85598-075-3 (pbk.) : LC Card 86-234718 DDC 363.8/09624 19
HC835.Z9 F33 1986

ILO Identification and Programming Mission to the Republic of the Sudan. After the famine . Geneva , 1986. xi, 309 p. : ISBN 92-2-105401-2 (pbk.) LC Card 86-226792 DDC 363.8/83/09624 19
HC835.Z9 F35 1985

FAMINES - UKRAINE - CONGRESSES.
Famine in Ukraine, 1932-1933 /. Edmonton , Downsview, Ont., Canada , 1986. 192 p. ; ISBN 0-09-286243-8 LC Card 87-148658 DDC 363.8/0947/71 19
HC337.U53 F314 1986

FAMINES - UKRAINE - HISTORY.
Faminskiĭ, Igor´ Pavlovich.
Ėkonomika sovremennogo imperializma : otvety na voprosy / I.P. Faminskiĭ. Moskva : Izd-vo polit. lit-ry, 1987. 175 p. ; 20 cm. Includes bibliographical references. LC Card 87-170222
1. Capitalism. 2. Industry and state. 3. Imperialism. 4. Economic history - 1971-. I. Title.
HB501 .F275 1987

Vneshneėkonomicheskie otnoshenii͡a sotsialisticheskikh stran v uslovii͡akh NTR /. Moskva , 1985. 215 p. ; LC Card 84-219529
HF1531 .V62 1985 ***NYPL [*QIP 87-2072]***

Fandel, G. (Günter), 1943-
Fandel, (Günter),. 1943- Large-scale modelling and interactive decision analysis . Berlin , New York , c1986. vii, 362 p. : ISBN 3-540-16785-4 : LC Card 86-20205 DDC 658.4/03 19
T57.6 .L34 1986
NYPL [JLM 72-289 v. 273]

Fangl, Hans. Zum Kostencharakter von Ertragsteuern / von Hans Fangl. Berlin : Duncker & Humblot, c1986. 208 p. : ill. ; 24 cm. (Betriebswirtschaftliche Schriften. Heft 122) Originally presented as the author's thesis (doctoral)--Wirtschaftsuniversität Wien, 1986. Bibliography: p. [196]-208. ISBN 3-428-06032-6 LC Card 86-219710 DDC 336.24/3/0943 19
1. Corporations - Taxation - Germany, West. 2. Business enterprises - Taxation - Germany, West. 3. Corporations - Germany, West - Accounting. I. Title.
HD2753.G3 F26 1986

Fanjul Martín, Enrique. La evolución de la política monetaria española (1940-1978) : una aproximación / por Enrique Fanjul Martín, Donato Fernandez Navarrete, Gonzalo Rodríguez Prada. [Madrid] : Instituto de Estudios Fiscales, 1979. 164 p. ; 29 cm. (Monografías. núm. 7) Bibliography: p. 157-164. LC Card 85-202991
1. Monetary policy - Spain - History - 20th century. I. Fernández Navarrete, Donato. II. Rodríguez Prada, Gonzalo. III. Series: Monografías (Instituto de Estudios Fiscales (Spain)) , núm. 7. IV. Title.
HG1135 .F35 1979

Fanjul, Oscar. La eficiencia del sistema bancario español / Oscar Fanjul y Fernando Maravall ; prólogo de Enrique Fuentes Quintana. Madrid : Alianza, c1985. 275 p. : ill. ; 20 cm. (Alianza Universidad. 439) Includes bibliographies and index. ISBN 84-206-2439-X LC Card 87-111325
1. Banks and banking - Spain. 2. Economies of scale. I. Maravall, Fernando. II. Title.
HG3184 .F36 1985

Fantasia, Rick. Cultures of solidarity : consciousness, action, and contemporary American workers / Rick Fantasia. Berkeley : University of California Press, c1988. p. cm. Bibliography: p. Includes index. ISBN 0-520-06053-9 (alk. paper) LC Card 87-16748 DDC 331.8/0973 19
1. Labor and laboring classes - United States - History - 20th century. 2. Trade-unions - United States - History - 20th century. 3. Labor disputes - United States - Case studies. 4. Class consciousness - United States - History - 20th century. I. Title.
HD8072.5 .F36 1988

Fantasy . Hoffman, William, 1937- Dallas, Tex. , c1984. 217 p. : ISBN 0-87833-386-X LC Card 84-8817 DDC 338.4/76887221/0973 19
HD9993.D653 U64 1984
NYPL [JLE 87-218]

Fantus Company. Assessing Illinois' strengths and weaknesses in a changing national economy /. Chicago, IL [1986] 117 p. : LC Card 87-620507 DDC 330.9773/043 19
HC107.I3 A75 1986

FAO agricultural services bulletin .
(65) Farm management input to rural financial systems development /. Rome , 1985. xii, 57 p. : ISBN 92-5-102191-0 (pbk.) LC Card 86-207967 DDC 332.7/1/091724 19
HD1440.D44 F37 1985

FAO agriculture series .
(no. 17) Multifarm use of agricultural machinery. Rome , Ann Arbor, MI , 1985. viii, 63 p. ; ISBN 92-5-101469-8 (pbk.) LC Card 86-217873 DDC 631.3/09172/4 19
HD1417 .M85 1985

FAO environment and energy paper .
(6) Natural resources and the human environment for food and agriculture in Africa. Rome , 1986. iv, 83 p. : ISBN 92-5-102354-9 (pbk.) LC Card 86-222103 DDC 338.1/096 19
HC800 .N34 1986

FAO fertilizer and plant nutrition bulletin .
(8) Manual on fertilizer distribution /. Rome , 1985. x, 114 p. : ISBN 92-5-101433-7 (pbk.) LC Card 86-221068 DDC 668/.62/0688 19
HD9483.A2 M36 1985

FAO food and nutrition paper .
(35) Review of food consumption surveys-1985 . Rome , 1986. xxiv, 212 p. ; ISBN 92-5-102375-1 (pbk.) LC Card 86-222995 DDC 339.4/8664 19
HD9000.4 .R483 1986

FAO/Finland Expert Consultation on Appropriate Forest Industries (1985 : Jakarta, Indonesia) Appropriate forest industries . Rome , 1986. vii, 426 p. ; ISBN 92-5-102389-1 (pbk.) LC Card 86-214549 DDC 338.1/7498/091724 19
HD9768.D44 A66 1986

Far East Broadcasting Association. Trends in Kenyan short wave listening . Nairobi, Kenya , c1979. vii, 87 [26] leaves : LC Card 85-980967 DDC 384.54/3 19
HE8697.A8 T74 1979

Farago, Peter.
Verbände als Träger öffentlicher Politik : Aufbau und Bedeutung privater Regierungen in der Schweiz / Peter Farago. Grüsch : Rüegger, c1987. xi, 185 p. : 3 ill. ; 21 cm. Originally presented as the author's thesis (doctoral)--Universität Zürich, 1987. Bibliography: p. 164-174. ISBN 3-7253-0290-1 LC Card 87-140606 DDC 322/.3/09494 19
1. Trade and professional associations - Switzerland - Political activity. 2. Pressure groups - Switzerland. 3. Business and politics - Switzerland. 4. Corporate state - Switzerland. 5. Switzerland - Politics and government - 1945-. I. Title.
HD2429.S92 F37 1987

Wirtschaftsverbände in der Schweiz . Grüsch , c1986. xv, 294 p. : ISBN 3-7253-0260-X : LC Card 86-136455 DDC 322/.3/09494 19
HD2429.S92 W57 1986
NYPL [JLD 86-2919]

Farah, Badie. Sharifi, Mohsen. Integrated case studies in accounting and information systems /. Englewood Cliffs, N.J. , c1987. ix, 229 p. : ISBN 0-13-469016-8 (pbk.) LC Card 86-30297 DDC 657/.028/5 19
HF5679 .S4754 1987

FARAH MANUFACTURING COMPANY STRIKE, 1972-1974.
Lapides, Kenneth. The battle of the boycott . New York, N.Y. , 1974. 22 p., [3] p. of plates : LC Card 87-125953 DDC 331.89/3 19
HD5325.C62 1972 .L36 1974

Farberov, N. P. Demokratie . Berlin , 1981. 188 p. ; LC Card 81-149074 DDC 320.5/315 19
HX73 .D45 1981 ***NYPL [JLD 86-3341]***

Fareed in finance & economics, English - Arabic. Farīd, ʻAbd Allāh Muḥammad. al-Qāmūs al-farīd fī al-māl wa-al-iqtiṣād, ʻArabī-Injilīzī /. [S.l.] 1985 (al-Qāhirah, Miṣr : Maṭābiʻ al-Ahrām al-Tijārīyah) 150, 264 p. ; LC Card 86-960655
HB61 .F36 1985

Fareed in finance and economics, English - Arabic. Farīd, ʻAbd Allāh Muḥammad. al-Qāmūs al-farīd fī al-māl wa-al-iqtiṣād, ʻArabī-Injilīzī /. [S.l.] 1985 (al-Qāhirah, Miṣr : Maṭābiʻ al-Ahrām al-Tijārīyah) 150, 264 p. ; LC Card 86-960655
HB61 .F36 1985

Fargnoli, Allison. Rainery, Richard. Alaska's public energy resources . [Juneau?] [1985] 8, 124, 3, 7 p. : LC Card 86-622191 DDC 333.79/09798 19
HD9502.U53 A473 1985

Faria, A. J. Johnson, H. Herbert Webster, 1906- How to use the business library . Cincinnati , c1984. iv, 267 p. : ISBN 0-538-05750-5 (pbk.) LC Card 83-60484 DDC 027.6/9 19
Z675.B8 J6 1984 ***NYPL [JLE 86-3971]***

Farīd, ʻAbd Allāh Muḥammad. al-Qāmūs al-farīd fī al-māl wa-al-iqtiṣād, ʻArabī-Injilīzī / iʻdād ʻAbd Allāh Muḥammad Farīd. 1st ed. [S.l. : s.n.], 1985 (al-Qāhirah, Miṣr : Maṭābiʻ al-Ahrām al-Tijārīyah) 150, 264 p. ; 25 cm. Title on added t.p.: Dictionary al fareed in finance & economics, English - Arabic. LC Card 86-960655
1. Economics - Dictionaries. 2. Finance - Dictionaries. 3. Economics - Dictionaries - Arabic. 4. Finance - Dictionaries - Arabic. 5. English language - Dictionaries - Arabic. 6. Arabic language - Dictionaries - English. I. Title. II. Title: Dictionary al fareed in finance & economics, English - Arabic. III. Title: Fareed in finance & economics, English - Arabic. IV. Title: Fareed in finance and economics, English - Arabic.
HB61 .F36 1985

Farkas, George, 1946- England, Paula. Households, employment, and gender . New York , c1986. ix, 237 p. : ISBN 0-202-30322-5 (lib. bdg.) LC Card 85-18628 DDC 304.6 19
HQ536 .E54 1986 ***NYPL [JLE 86-2828]***

Farkas, János. Az innováció társadalmi-gazdasági akadályai / Farkas János. Budapest : Közgazdasági és Jogi Könyvkiadó, 1984. 350 p. ; 18 cm. (Időszerű közgazdasági kérdések, 0324-3214) Bibliography: p. 341-349. ISBN 963-221-453-6 : LC Card 85-157214
1. Technological innovations - Economic aspects - Hungary. 2. Technological innovations - Social aspects - Hungary. I. Title. II. Series.
HC300.295.T4 F36 1984

Farkas, Miklós, Dr. Két évtized . Szeged , 1987. 116 p., [67] p. of plates : LC Card 87-407665
HD1492.H82 C765 1987

Farley, H. W. Cheaper transportation : paper / read by H.W. Farley of Oswego, Illinois, before the Civil Engineers' Club of the Northwest, explaining a system of transportation by horizontal conveyor, Chicago, October 12th, 1874. Yorkville, Ill. : J.R. Marshall, 1874. 10 p. ; 23 cm. Cover title. LC Card 85-665909
1. Freight and freightage - United States - Costs. 2. Transportation - United States. I. Title.
HE199.U6 F3x 1874

Farley, John U.
Capon, Noel. Corporate strategic planning /. New York , 1987. p. cm. ISBN 0-231-06380-6 LC Card 87-18239 DDC 658.4/012 19
HD30.28 .C375 1987

Carpenter, Gregory. Business strategy and the life cycle concept . Cambridge, Mass. (1000 Massachusetts Ave., Cambridge 02138) [1985] [19] leaves ; LC Card 87-108925 DDC 658.5/038 19
HF5415.155 .C37 1985

Farley, Pamela J. Private health insurance in the United States : data from the Health insurance/employer survey of the 1977 National medical care expenditure survey / Pamela J. Farley. Rockville, MD : U. S. Dept. of Health and Human Services, Public Health Service, Office of the Assistant Secretary for Health, National Center for Health Services Research and Health Care Technology Assessment ; Springfield, VA : Available from National Technical Information Service, [1986] 106 p. : ill. ; 28 cm. (Data preview . no. 23) DHHS publication ; no. (PHS) 86-3406 "September 1986." Item 491-B-16 Bibliography: p. 99-100. LC Card 86-23618 DDC 368.3/82/00973 19
1. Insurance, Health - United States. 2. Medical care surveys - United States. I. National Center for Health Services Research and Health Care Technology Assessment (U. S.). II. Series. III. Series: DHHS publication, (PHS) 86-3406. IV. Title.
HG9396 .F3 1986

FARM ACCOUNTING. see **AGRICULTURE - ACCOUNTING.**

FARM ANIMALS. see **LIVESTOCK.**

FARM CORPORATIONS - INDIA.
Corporate sector and agriculture . New Delhi [1985] 88 p. ; LC Card 87-902181 DDC 338.1/0954 19
HD2072 .C65 1985

The Farm credit crisis : policy options and consequences. College Station, Tex. : Texas Agricultural Extension Service, Texas A&M University System, [1986] ii, 57 p. : ill. ; 28 cm. Cover title. LC Card 86-622188 DDC 332.7/1/0973 19
1. Agricultural credit - United States. 2. Agriculture - United States - Finance. I. Texas Agricultural Extension Service.
HG2051.U5 F26 1986

The Farm credit crisis policy options and consequences / Paul W. Barkley ... [et al.]. Ithaca, N.Y. : Dept. of Agricultural Economics, New York State College of Agriculture and Life Sciences, Cornell University, [1986] ii, 57 p. : ill. ; 28 cm. (A.E. ext. . 86-3) Cover title. "January 1986." LC Card 86-621935 DDC 338.1 s 332.7/1/0973 19
1. Agricultural credit - United States. 2. Agriculture - United States - Finance. I. Barkley, Paul W. II. New York State College of Agriculture and Life Sciences. Dept. of Agricultural Economics. III. Series.
HD1775.N8 C6 no. 86-3 HG2051.U6

Farm Crisis Workers Conference . Farm Crisis Workers Conference (1986 : Arlington, Tex.) [Austin? , 1986] 136 p. ; LC Card 87-620630 DDC 338.1/3/09764 19
HD1476.U6 T44 1986

Farm Crisis Workers Conference (1986 : Arlington, Tex.) Farm Crisis Workers Conference : proceedings, June 19-20, Arlington, Texas / co-sponsored by Texas Department of Agriculture [and] FarmAid. [Austin? : Texas Dept. of Agriculture, 1986] 136 p. ; 28 cm. LC Card 87-620630 DDC 338.1/3/09764 19
1. Family farms - Texas - Finance - Congresses. 2. Bankruptcy - Texas - Psychological aspects - Congresses. 3. Farmers - Texas - Psychology - Congresses. 4. Rural families - Texas - Congresses. I. Texas. Dept. of Agriculture. II. FarmAid. III. Title.
HD1476.U6 T44 1986

The Farm financial crisis : socioeconomic demensions and implications for producers and rural areas / edited by Steven H. Murdock and F. Larry Leistritz. Boulder : Westview Press, 1988. xvi, 205 p. : ill. ; 23 cm. (Westview special studies in agricultural science and policy) Bibliography: p. 191-202. Includes index. ISBN 0-8133-7186-4 (pbk. : alk. paper) : LC Card 86-32601 DDC 338.1/3/0973 19
1. Agriculture - Economic aspects - United States. 2. Agriculture - United States - Finance. 3. Agricultural credit - United States. 4. Agriculture and state - United States. 5. Family farms - United States. I. Murdock, Steven H. II. Leistritz, F. Larry. III. Series.
HD1761 .F295 1988

Farm Forum of the Ninth Federal Reserve District . Ninth Federal Reserve District Farm Forum (1965 : Minneapolis, Minn.) Hopkins, Minn. [1965] 99 p. : LC Card 87-110732
HD9007.A14 N56 1965

Farm Foundation (Chicago, Ill.)
Economic efficiency in agricultural and food marketing /. Ames , 1987. xii, 315 p. ; ISBN 0-8138-0533-3 LC Card 87-2821 DDC 381/.41/0973 19
HD9000.5 .E26 1987

Food demand analysis . Blacksburg, Va. [1986] xii, 292 p. : LC Card 87-620670 DDC 339.4/86413 19
HD9000.5 .F5946 1986

FARM INCOME - BELGIUM.
Politique agricole commune . Bruxelles, Belgique , c1982. 126 p. ; ISBN 1-8004-0773-5 LC Card 87-672469
HD1803 .P64x 1982

FARM INCOME - BRAZIL - PARANÁ (STATE)
Avila, Luiz Gonçalves. Desenvolvimento industrial e rendimento da terra . Rio de Janeiro, RJ , 1985. 111 p. : LC Card 86-233493
HD1875.S26 A95 1985

FARM INCOME - BRAZIL - SANTA CATARINA (STATE)
Avila, Luiz Gonçalves. Desenvolvimento industrial e rendimento da terra . Rio de Janeiro, RJ , 1985. 111 p. : LC Card 86-233493
HD1875.S26 A95 1985

Farm income data . Lucier, Gary. Washington, DC [1986] iv, 311 p. : LC Card 86-602022 DDC 338.1/0973 s 338.1/3/0973021 19
HD1751 .A5 no. 740 HD1769

FARM INCOME - GERMANY, WEST.
Intrasektorale Einkommensstreuung in der Landwirtschaft /. Münster-Hiltrup , 1983. 177 p. : ISBN 3-7843-0281-5 : LC Card 83-236007
HD1955 .I57 1983

FARM INCOME - INDIA - AHMADNAGAR DISTRICT - CASE STUDIES.
Dangat, S. B., 1942- Farm income stabilization in dry farming areas /. Delhi, India , 1986. xi, 237 p. ; LC Card 86-903137 DDC 338.1/3/0954792 19
HD2075.A36 D35 1986

FARM INCOME - INDIA - CASE STUDIES.
Dangat, S. B., 1942- Farm income stabilization in dry farming areas /. Delhi, India , 1986. xi, 237 p. ; LC Card 86-903137 DDC 338.1/3/0954792 19
HD2075.A36 D35 1986

FARM INCOME - INDIA - PUNJAB.
Inder Pal Singh, 1959- Rural income distribution . Delhi , New Delhi, India , 1986. xvi, 123 p. : ISBN 81-7018-299-9 : LC Card 86-900514 DDC 339.2/3/0954552 19
HC440.I5 I46 1986 ***NYPL [JLD 86-3077]***

FARM INCOME - INDIA - TIRUCHCHIRĀPPALLI (DISTRICT) - MATHEMATICAL MODELS.
Stanislaus, M. Sebastian. New farm technology and income distribution /. New Delhi , c1984. viii, 76 p. : LC Card 84-902272 DDC 338.1/3/095482 19
HD2075.T57 S73 1984 ***NYPL [JLD 87-669]***

FARM INCOME - OKLAHOMA.
Plaxico, James Sam, 1924- Financial status of Oklahoma farmers and ranchers, 1985 . [Stillwater] [1986] 42 p. ; LC Card 86-622478 DDC 338.1/3/09766021 19
HD1775.O5 P57 1986

Farm income stabilization in dry farming areas /. Dangat, S. B., 1942- Delhi, India , 1986. xi, 237 p. ; LC Card 86-903137 DDC 338.1/3/0954792 19
HD2075.A36 D35 1986

FARM INCOME - TAXATION - BELGIUM.
Politique agricole commune . Bruxelles, Belgique , c1982. 126 p. ; ISBN 1-8004-0773-5 LC Card 87-672469
HD1803 .P64x 1982

FARM INCOME - UNITED STATES - STATISTICS.
Lucier, Gary. Farm income data . Washington, DC [1986] iv, 311 p. : LC Card 86-602022 DDC 338.1/0973 s 338.1/3/0973021 19
HD1751 .A5 no. 740 HD1769

Somwaru, Agapi. Disaggregated farm income by type of farm, 1959-82 /. Washington, D.C. , 1986. iii, 113 p. : LC Card 86-602571 DDC 338.1 s 338.1/3/0973021 19
HD1751 .A91854 no. 558 HD1769

FARM INCOME - ZAMBIA - CHIBALE (SERENJE DISTRICT)
Farming systems and family economy in Chibale, Serenje District. Mpika, Zambia [1985?] 74 p. : LC Card 86-981248 DDC 338.1/096894 19
HD1476.Z352 C454 1985

FARM INCOME - ZAMBIA - NDUNYA.
Farming system and family economy in Ndunya, Chinsali District. Mpika, Zambia [1985?] 45 leaves, [12] leaves of plates : LC Card 86-981252 DDC 338.1/096894 19
HD1476.Z352 N384 1985

FARM MANAGEMENT - DEVELOPING COUNTRIES.
Farm management input to rural financial systems development /. Rome , 1985. xii, 57 p. : ISBN 92-5-102191-0 (pbk.) LC Card 86-207967 DDC 332.7/1/091724 19
HD1440.D44 F37 1985

FARM MANAGEMENT - HUNGARY - HISTORY.
Szabó, László. Munkaszervezet és termelékenység a magyar parasztságnál a XIX-XX. században /. Szolnok , 1968 (Debrecen : Szabadság Lapnyomda) 167 p. : LC Card 86-188720
HD1536.H9 S89 1968

FARM MANAGEMENT - INDIA - PUNJAB.
Rachhpal Singh, 1944- Farm production in rainfed sub-mountainous Punjab /. Delhi , New Delhi , 1987. vi, 349 p. ; ISBN 81-7018-450-9 : LC Card 87-902161 DDC 338.1/0954/552 19
HD2075.P8 R33 1987

Farm management input to rural financial systems development / the loan predictor system for agricultural banks. Rome : FAO, 1985. xii, 57 p. : ill. ; 30 cm. (FAO agricultural services bulletin . 65) Includes bibliographical references. ISBN 92-5-102191-0 (pbk.) LC Card 86-207967 DDC 332.7/1/091724 19
1. Agricultural credit - Developing countries. 2. Agriculture - Developing countries - Finance. 3. Farm management - Developing countries. 4. Saving and investment - Developing countries. I. Food and Agriculture Organization of the United Nations. II. Series.
HD1440.D44 F37 1985

FARM MANAGEMENT - NEPAL.
Maharjan, Bekha L. (Bekha Lal), 1943- Small farm development problems and strategies /. [Kathmandu] , 1984. 114 p. ; LC Card 84-901301 DDC 338.1/6 19
HD1476.N35 M33 1984 *NYPL [JLD 86-4365]*

Farm mechanisation and social change /.
Chander Bhan, 1949- New Delhi , c1987. x, 125 p. ; ISBN 81-85119-24-4 : LC Card 87-902310 DDC 338.1/61/0954558 19
HD2075.B48 C42 1987

FARM MECHANIZATION - BRAZIL.
Müller, Geraldo. Alimentação e agricultura no Brasil . [São Paulo] , 1984. 64 p. : LC Card 86-132127
HD1872 .M85 1984

FARM MECHANIZATION, COOPERATIVE - DEVELOPING COUNTRIES.
Multifarm use of agricultural machinery. Rome , Ann Arbor, MI , 1985. viii, 63 p. ; ISBN 92-5-101469-8 (pbk.) LC Card 86-217873 DDC 631.3/09172/4 19
HD1417 .M85 1985

FARM MECHANIZATION - DEVELOPING COUNTRIES.
Burch, David, 1942 Jan. 16- Overseas aid and the transfer of technology . Aldershot, [Hants, England] , Brookfield [Vt.], USA , c1987. xiv, 370 p. ; ISBN 0-566-00480-1 : LC Card 87-237 DDC 338.1/81 19
HD1431 .B87 1987

Tschiersch, Joachim E. Appropriate mechanization for small farmers in developing countries /. Saarbrücken , 1978. iii, 106 p. ; ISBN 3-88156-112-9 LC Card 80-472522 DDC 338.1/61/091724
S675 .T72 *NYPL [JLE 80-1482]*

FARM MECHANIZATION - ECONOMIC ASPECTS - DEVELOPING COUNTRIES.
Binswanger, Hans P. Agricultural mechanization . Washington, D.C., U. S.A. , c1987. vi, 85 p. : ISBN 0-8213-0903-X (pbk.) LC Card 87-14082 DDC 338.1/61/091724 19
HD1459 .B57 1987

FARM MECHANIZATION - ECONOMIC ASPECTS - MOZAMBIQUE.
Wuyts, Marc. On the question of mechanisation of Mozambican agriculture today . [Maputo, Mozambique] , 1979. 22 p. : LC Card 83-207389
HD2129 .W893 1979

FARM MECHANIZATION - GERMANY (WEST)
Landhandwerk und Landwirtschaft /. Göttingen , 1964. 104 p. : LC Card 87-409231 DDC 338.1/61/0943 19
HD1955 .L17 1964

FARM MECHANIZATION - INDIA - BHIWANI (DISTRICT)
Chander Bhan, 1949- Farm mechanisation and social change /. New Delhi , c1987. x, 125 p. ; ISBN 81-85119-24-4 : LC Card 87-902310 DDC 338.1/61/0954558 19
HD2075.B48 C42 1987

FARM MECHANIZATION - INDIA - HISAR (DISTRICT)
Chander Bhan, 1949- Farm mechanisation and social change /. New Delhi , c1987. x, 125 p. ; ISBN 81-85119-24-4 : LC Card 87-902310 DDC 338.1/61/0954558 19
HD2075.B48 C42 1987

FARM MECHANIZATION - INDIA - KARNAL (DISTRICT)
Chander Bhan, 1949- Farm mechanisation and social change /. New Delhi , c1987. x, 125 p. ; ISBN 81-85119-24-4 : LC Card 87-902310 DDC 338.1/61/0954558 19
HD2075.B48 C42 1987

FARM MECHANIZATION - NORWAY.
Hegrenes, Agnar. Mekaniseringsøkonomi på enkeltbruk /. Oslo , 1985. 175 p. : ISBN 82-7077-028-0 LC Card 86-180961
HD2012 .H44 1985

FARM MECHANIZATION - SOUTH ASIA.
Binswanger, Hans P. The economics of tractors in South Asia . New York , Hyderabad, India , 1978. 96 p. ; LC Card 81-908104
HD2065.3 .B56 1978

FARM MECHANIZATION - SOVIET UNION.
Syrovatko, V. G. (Vitaliĭ Grigor′evich) Industrializatsiia i kadry sel′skogo khoziaĭstva /. Moskva , 1986. 191 p. ; LC Card 86-229171
HD1536.S65 S97 1986

FARM MECHANIZATION - SOVIET UNION, NORTHERN.
Mal′tsev, V. I. (Valer′ian Ivanovich) Ėkonomicheskie osnovy industrializatsii sel′skogo khoziaĭstva Severa /. Moskva , 1985. 142 p. ; LC Card 86-165352
HD1995.N55 M34 1985

FARM ORGANIZATION. see **FARM MANAGEMENT.**

FARM OWNERSHIP - INDIA - JAUNPUR (DISTRICT)
Shankar, Kripa. Pattern of land ownership and backwardness . New Delhi , 1986. x, 119 p. ; ISBN 81-7024-021-2 : LC Card 87-900130 DDC 333.3/23/09542 19
HD879.J37 S5 1986

Farm policy in Australia /. Hefford, Ron. St. Lucia [Brisbane] , New York , c1985. xviii, 415 p. : ISBN 0-7022-1698-4 LC Card 83-23457 DDC 338.1/894 19
HD2153 .H43 1984 *NYPL [JLD 87-867]*

FARM PRODUCE - BRAZIL - RIO GRANDE DO SUL.
Cunha, Rafael Alves de. Duas décadas da produção e do produto da agropecuária RS, 1964-84 /. Porto Alegre , 1986- v. <1 > : LC Card 87-404979 DDC 338.1/0981/65 19
HD9014.B83 R5416 1986

FARM PRODUCE - BRAZIL - STATISTICS.
Produção agrícola brasileira . [Rio de Janeiro] , 1986. 188 p. : LC Card 87-403944 DDC 338.1/0981/021 19
HD9014.B82 P765 1986

FARM PRODUCE - COLOMBIA - MARKETING.
Isaza Tobón, Gabriela. El IDEMA, hacia una pérdida de los objetivos sociales. [Colombia? , between 1984 and 1987] ([Colombia?] : Litoarte) 126 p., [1] leaf of plates : LC Card 87-404223 DDC 381/.41/09861 19
HD9014.C72 I8 1984

FARM PRODUCE - DEVELOPING COUNTRIES - MARKETING.
Abbott, John Cave, 1919- Agricultural marketing enterprises for the developing world . Cambridge [Cambridgeshire] , New York , 1987. xi, 217 p. : ISBN 0-521-32597-8 LC Card 86-24462 DDC 381/.41/091724 19
HD9018.D44 A228 1987

Junginger-Dittel, K.-O. Marketing Boards für Agrarexportgüter in Entwicklungsländern /. [Kiel] , 1980. iii, 48 leaves ; LC Card 85-160428
HD9018.D44 J86 1980

FARM PRODUCE - DEVELOPING COUNTRIES - MARKETING - CASE STUDIES.
Abbott, John Cave, 1919- Agricultural marketing enterprises for the developing world . Cambridge [Cambridgeshire] , New York , 1987. xi, 217 p. : ISBN 0-521-32597-8 LC Card 86-24462 DDC 381/.41/091724 19
HD9018.D44 A228 1987

FARM PRODUCE - GAMBIA - MARKETING - HISTORY.
Barrett, Hazel R., 1955- The marketing of foodstuffs in the Gambia, 1400-1980 . Aldershot, Hants., England , Brookfield, Vt., U. S.A. , 1988, c1987. p. cm. ISBN 0-566-05487-6 LC Card 87-23063 DDC 381/.41/096651 19
HD9017.G262 B37 1988

FARM PRODUCE - GERMANY (WEST) - TRANSPORTATION.
Schmelzeisen, Hans-Michael. Bedeutung, Einsatzmöglichkeiten und -probleme des kombinierten Güterverkehrs in der Ernährungswirtschaft /. Münster [1986] xii, 350 p. : ISBN 3-88660-357-1 (Deut. Bibl.) LC Card 87-121511 DDC 380.5/24 19
HE199.5.F6 S36 1986

FARM PRODUCE - GREECE - CRETE - TRANSPORTATION.
Kalitsounakēs, Dēmētrios E. Aristopoiēsis paragōgēs Krētēs eis to plaision tēs Eurōpaikēs Oik. Koinotētos /. Hērakleion Krētēs , 1963. p. 167-173 ; LC Card 86-235201
HE595.F3 K35 1963

FARM PRODUCE - HONDURAS - STATISTICS.
El Desarrollo económico de Honduras . Tegucigalpa, D.C. , 1959. [56] leaves : LC Card 86-173618
HD9014.H82 D47 1959

FARM PRODUCE - INDIA.
India. Planning Commission. Programme Evaluation Organisation. Evaluation report on essential supplies programme. New Delhi , 1985. vii, 121 p. ; LC Card 87-902422 DDC 381/.41/0954 19
HF1040.9.I4 I46 1985

FARM PRODUCE - INDIA - MARKETING - CASE STUDIES.
Agarwal, N. L. Agricultural prices and marketing in India . Delhi, India , 1986. xv, 243 p. ; LC Card 86-902258 DDC 338.1/3/09544 19
HD2075.R27 A36 1986

FARM PRODUCE - INDIA - RAJASTHAN - MARKETING - CASE STUDIES.
Agarwal, N. L. Agricultural prices and marketing in India . Delhi, India , 1986. xv, 243 p. ; LC Card 86-902258 DDC 338.1/3/09544 19
HD2075.R27 A36 1986

FARM PRODUCE - ITALY - MARKETING.
Foglio, Antonio, 1940- Il marketing agroalimentare . Milano, Italy , c1985. 370 p. : LC Card 86-114259
HD9015.I8 F64 1985

FARM PRODUCE - ITALY - MARKETING - INFORMATION SERVICES - ITALY.
Strategia dei servizi per l'agricoltura . [Roma] [1983] 158 p. : LC Card 85-155420
HD9475.I82 S77 1983

FARM PRODUCE - KOREA (SOUTH)
Dyck, John H. South Korea . Washington, D.C. [1986] v, 74 p. : LC Card 86-602006 DDC 338.1 s 382/.41/095195 19
HD1411 .F59 no. 216 HD9005

FARM PRODUCE - LATIN AMERICA - CONGRESSES.
Comercialización interna de los alimentos en América Latina . Ottawa, Canada , c1985. 253 p. : ISBN 0-88936-448-6 LC Card 87-118494 DDC 338.1/9/8 19
HD9014.L32 C66 1985

FARM PRODUCE - LATIN AMERICA - TRANSPORTATION - COSTS.
Basco, Carlos A. El comercio intrarregional de alimentos básicos. [S.l.] , 1986. xi, 558 p. : LC Card 87-404784 DDC 382/.41/098 19
HD9014.L32 B37 1986

FARM PRODUCE - MALAWI - TRANSPORTATION.
Ahmad, Nisar. Locational pattern of agricultural production/purchases . Lilongwe [Malawi] , 1984. ii, 33 leaves ; LC Card 86-980325 DDC 380.1/41/096897 19
HE199.5.F3 A38 1984

FARM PRODUCE - MALAYSIA - TRANSPORTATION.
Environment, agriculture, and society in the Malay world /. Kyoto, Japan , 1986. ix, 177 p. : LC Card 86-201590 DDC 338.1/09595 19
HD2080.6 .E58 1986

FARM PRODUCE - MARKETING - CASE STUDIES.
World food marketing systems /. London , Boston , 1986. xviii, 333 p. : ISBN 0-407-00358-4 : LC Card 85-28371 DDC 380.1/456413 19
HD9000.5 .W587 1986
NYPL [JLE 86-3213]

FARM PRODUCE - MARKETING - CONGRESSES.
Economic efficiency in agricultural and food marketing /. Ames , 1987. xii, 315 p. ; ISBN 0-8138-0533-3 LC Card 87-2821 DDC 381/.41/0973 19
HD9000.5 .E26 1987

FARM PRODUCE - MARKETING - GOVERNMENT POLICY - DEVELOPING COUNTRIES - CONGRESSES.
Agricultural marketing strategy and pricing policy /. Washington, D.C. , c1987. xiii, 132 p. : ISBN 0-8213-0830-0 (pbk.) LC Card 86-33992 DDC 380.1/41 19
HD9018.D44 A365 1987

FARM PRODUCE - MEXICO.
Fragoso Gutiérrez, Juan M. El mercado y los precios de los productos agropecuarios /. México , 1983. 486 p. : LC Card 84-236815
HD9014.M62 F72 1983

FARM PRODUCE - MIDDLE WEST - MARKETING - CONGRESSES.
Ninth Federal Reserve District Farm Forum (1965 : Minneapolis, Minn.) Farm Forum of the Ninth Federal Reserve District . Hopkins, Minn. [1965] 99 p. : LC Card 87-110732
HD9007.A14 N56 1965

FARM PRODUCE - PERU - CUZCO (DEPT.) - MARKETING.
Cori Castro, Wilfredo. Mercados y precios en la economía campesina . [Cuzco, Peru] , 1986. 29 p. : LC Card 86-200941
HC228.C8 C59 1986

FARM PRODUCE - PRICES - GOVERNMENT POLICY - EUROPEAN ECONOMIC COMMUNITY COUNTRIES.
Kirschke, Dieter, 1952- Agrarmarktpolitik bei Unsicherheit . Berlin , c1987. 225 p. : ISBN 3-428-06111-X LC Card 87-131255 DDC 338.1/8 19
HD1920.5 .K57 1987

FARM PRODUCE - PRICES - UNITED STATES.
Gardiner, Walter H. Price elasticity of export demand . Washington, D.C. [1986] iv, 43 p. ; LC Card 86-602820 DDC 382/.41/0973 19
HD9004 .G37 1986

FARM PRODUCE - SOUTH AFRICA - CONGRESSES.
1985-bedryfskongresse =. [South Africa] [1985?] 1 v. (various pagings) ; LC Card 85-206777
HD9017.S72 A14 1985

FARM PRODUCE - SPAIN - ALJARAFE - HISTORY.
Herrera García, Antonio. El Aljarafe durante el antiguo régimen /. Sevilla , 1981. 147 p., [3] leaves of plates : ISBN 84-500-4850-8 LC Card 82-142028 DDC 333.3/0946/86 19
HD779.A39 H47 1981 *NYPL [JLC 86-126]*

Herrera García, Antonio. El Aljarafe sevillano durante el antiguo régimen . [Sevilla] , 1980. 517 p., [9] leaves of plates : ISBN 84-500-4373-5 LC Card 81-173649 DDC 946/.86 19
HD779.A39 H475 1980 *NYPL [JLF 86-928]*

FARM PRODUCE - SURPLUSES. see **SURPLUS AGRICULTURAL COMMODITIES.**

FARM PRODUCE - TARIFF. see **TARIFF ON FARM PRODUCE.**

FARM PRODUCE - UNITED STATES.
Dyck, John H. South Korea . Washington, D.C. [1986] v, 74 p. : LC Card 86-602006 DDC 338.1 s 382/.41/095195 19
HD1411 .F59 no. 216 HD9005

FARM PRODUCE - UNITED STATES - MARKETING.
Federal marketing programs in agriculture . Danville, Ill. , c1983. x, 326 p. ; ISBN 0-8134-2292-2 : LC Card 83-80130
NYPL [JLE 86-4572]

Kohls, Richard L. Marketing of agricultural products /. New York , London , c1985. xi, 624 p. : ISBN 0-02-365670-0 LC Card 84-817 DDC 381/.41 19
HD9000.5 .K57 1985 *NYPL [JLE 86-4145]*

A Review of U. S. competitiveness in agricultural trade. Washington, D.C. [1986] ix, 101 p. : LC Card 86-600586 DDC 382/.41/0973 19
HD1761 .R48 1986

FARM PRODUCE - UNITED STATES - MARKETING - CONGRESSES.
Ninth Federal Reserve District Farm Forum (1965 : Minneapolis, Minn.) Farm Forum of the Ninth Federal Reserve District . Hopkins, Minn. [1965] 99 p. : LC Card 87-110732
HD9007.A14 N56 1965

FARM PRODUCE - ZAMBIA - MARKETING - CONGRESSES.
Strengthening women's participation in food and agricultural marketing . [Lusaka] [1984] 78 p. ; LC Card 86-980282 DDC 331.4/83/096894 19
HD6073.A292 Z3374 1984

FARM PRODUCE - ZAMBIA - MARKETING - RESEARCH - METHODOLOGY.
Harbans Singh, 1940- Conceptual and methodological issues on agricultural marketing research in Zambia /. [Lusaka, Zambia] [1979?] 19, [2] leaves ; LC Card 85-980091
HD9017.Z32 H37 1979

Farm production in rainfed sub-mountainous Punjab /. Rachhpal Singh, 1944- Delhi , New Delhi , 1987. vi, 349 p. ; ISBN 81-7018-450-9 : LC Card 87-902161 DDC 338.1/0954/552 19
HD2075.P8 R33 1987

FARM PRODUCTION QUOTAS - CHINA.
Liu, Yung-ch'eng. She hui chu i ching chi tse jen chih /. [Ch'ang-ch'un shih] , 1985. 5, 264 p. ; LC Card 86-179707 DDC 658/.00951 19
HD70.C5 L58 1985 <Orien China>
*NYPL [*OVY 86-4140]*

FARM RENTS - SPAIN - CASTILLA Y LEON - HISTORY.
Robledo Hernández, Ricardo. La renta de la tierra en Castilla la Vieja y León (1836-1913) /. [Madrid] [1984?] 245 p. : ISBN 84-505-0885-1 LC Card 87-104999
HJ4375.C27 R63 1984

FARM ROADS - IRAN - ĀZARBĀYJAN-I BAKHTARI.
Sāzmān-i Barnāmah (Iran) Feeder Road Programme . Tehran [1961?] ii, 117, 9 leaves, [59] leaves of plates (some folded) : LC Card 85-211363
HE365.I73 R857 1961

FARM ROADS - IRAN - ĀZARBĀYJAN-I KHĀVARĪ.
Sāzmān-i Barnāmah (Iran) Feeder Road Programme . Tehran [1961?] ii, 117, 9 leaves, [59] leaves of plates (some folded) : LC Card 85-211363
HE365.I73 R857 1961

Farm Sector Economics Associates. FmHA guaranteed lending manual /. Washington, D.C. (1120 Connecticut Ave., N.W., Washington 20036) , c1986. xi, 88, [59] p. : LC Card 86-226067 DDC 332.1/753 19
HG2051.U5 F55 1986

FARM SUPPLIES - CAMEROON.
Agricultural input supply in Cameroon . Alexandria, Va. [1983] 2 v. : LC Card 87-119188 DDC 338.1/0967/11 19
HD2139.5 .A68 1983

FARM SUPPLY INDUSTRIES - ITALY.
Strategia dei servizi per l'agricoltura . [Roma] [1983] 158 p. : LC Card 85-155420
HD9475.I82 S77 1983

FARM SUPPLY INDUSTRIES - UNITED STATES.
The Commercial greenhouses & associated equipment & agrochemicals market. New York, N.Y. , c1983. vii, 274 leaves : LC Card 87-143480
HD9475.U52 C66 1983

FARM SURPLUSES. see **SURPLUS AGRICULTURAL COMMODITIES.**

FARM TENANCY - AUSTRALIA - WESTERN AUSTRALIA.
Western Australia. Pastoral Tenure Study Group. Final report on pastoral land tenure. Perth, W.A. [1986] [28], 63, 4 p. ; LC Card 87-120095 DDC 333.3/09941 19
HD1641.A9 W47 1986

FARM TENANCY - BRAZIL - RIO GRANDE DO SUL - HISTORY.
Beskow, Paulo Roberto. O arrendamento capitalista na agricultura . São Paulo , Brasília , 1986. 219 p. : LC Card 86-229665
HD9066.B83 R463 1986

FARM TENANCY - BRAZIL - SÃO PAULO (STATE) - HISTORY - 19TH CENTURY - CASE STUDIES.
Witter, José Sebastião. A Revolta dos Parceiros /. São Paulo, SP , 1986. 77 p. : LC Card 87-102716
HD4875.B8 W58 1986

FARM TENANCY - ECONOMIC ASPECTS - SPAIN - CATALONIA - HISTORY.
Terra, treball i propietat . Barcelona , c1986. 346 p. ; ISBN 84-7423-287-2 LC Card 86-216973
HD2025.C35 T47 1986

FARM TENANCY - GERMANY - HISTORY - ADDRESSES, ESSAYS, LECTURES.
Peasants and lords in modern Germany . Boston , 1986. 267 p. ; ISBN 0-04-943037-8 (alk. paper) LC Card 85-6113 DDC 305.5/63 19
HD655 .P34 1986 *NYPL [JLE 86-1702]*

FARM TENANCY - PORTUGAL.
Almeida, João Ferreira de. Classes sociais nos campos . Lisboa [1986] 544 p. : LC Card 87-400121 DDC 305.5/63 19
HD1536.P77 A44 1986

FARM TENANCY - SCOTLAND - HIGHLANDS - HISTORY.
Richards, Eric. A history of the Highland clearances /. London , c1982-1985. 2 v. : ISBN 0-85664-496-X : LC Card 81-208122 DDC 333.33/5 19
HD1511.G7 R53 1982 *NYPL [JLL 82-171]*

FARM TENANCY - VANUATU - LONGANA.
Rodman, Margaret, 1947- Masters of tradition . Vancouver , 1987. 198 p. : ISBN 0-7748-0234-0 LC Card 87-158135 DDC 333.3/0993/4 19
HD1125.Z9 L657 1987

FARM TRACTORS - ECONOMIC ASPECTS - SOUTH ASIA.
Binswanger, Hans P. The economics of tractors in South Asia . New York , Hyderabad, India , 1978. 96 p. ; LC Card 81-908104
HD2065.3 .B56 1978

FARM WOMEN. see **WOMEN IN AGRICULTURE.**

Farm work and fieldwork : American agriculture in anthropological perspective / edited by Michael Chibnik. Ithaca : Cornell University Press, 1987. 293 p. : ill. ; 23 cm. (Anthropology of contemporary issues) Includes bibliographies and index. ISBN 0-8014-9446-X (pbk. : alk. paper) LC

Card 86-19960 DDC 305.5/55/0973 19
1. Farmers - United States - Congresses. 2. Agricultural laborers - United States - Congresses. 3. Agriculture - Social aspects - United States - Congresses. 4. Farms - United States - Congresses. 5. Ethnology - United States - Congresses. I. Chibnik, Michael, 1946-. II. Series.
HD8039.F32 U635 1987

FarmAid. Farm Crisis Workers Conference (1986 : Arlington, Tex.) Farm Crisis Workers Conference . [Austin? , 1986] 136 p. ; LC Card 87-620630 DDC 338.1/3/09764 19
HD1476.U6 T44 1986

Farmer, David H. Baily, Peter J. H. Purchasing principles and management /. London , Marshfield, Mass. , 1985. 324 p. : ISBN 0-273-02242-3 LC Card 85-16704 DDC 658.7/2 19
HF5437 .B3415 1985 NYPL [JLE 86-3321]

The Farmer is the man [sound recording]. Los Angeles, Calif. : Pacifica Radio Archive, p1983. 1 sound cassette (58 min.) : analog. (The Great Depression) Radio broadcast. Produced by the People's Media Collective of San Francisco. Issued also on reel. Tells how the farmer as conservative, rugged, individualist became a radicalized highwayman during the Great Depression. Also tells about the dust bowl and the caravans between Kansas and California and how those who reached the Golden State were often exploited and disillusioned. LC Card 87-751678
1. Farmers - United States - History - 20th century. 2. Depressions - 1929 - United States. I. Pacifica Radio Archive. II. People's Media Collective of San Francisco. III. Series.
HD8039.F3

Farmers' attitude survey in the Mula Command Area, Maharashtra /. Dhongade, M. P. Rahuri, Maharashtra, India , 1986. vi, 69 p. ; LC Card 86-903408 DDC 338.1/0954/792 19
HD8039.F32 I44 1986

FARMERS - DENMARK - POLITICAL ACTIVITY - HISTORY.
Noter over dansk landbrugshistorie. Greve Strand , 1982. 53 p. : ISBN 87-7470-314-5 : LC Card 83-170741
HD2002 .N67 1982

FARMERS - EDUCATION - CASE STUDIES.
Abraham, A. S. (Abraham Saktimangalam), 1944- Education and employment in agriculture, India . New Delhi , 1985. vii, 111 p. ; LC Card 85-904717 DDC 331.12/93/0954 19
HD1537.I4 A587 1985
NYPL [JLD 86-2251]

FARMERS - EDUCATION - INDIA - CASE STUDIES.
Abraham, A. S. (Abraham Saktimangalam), 1944- Education and employment in agriculture, India . New Delhi , 1985. vii, 111 p. ; LC Card 85-904717 DDC 331.12/93/0954 19
HD1537.I4 A587 1985
NYPL [JLD 86-2251]

FARMERS - EDUCATION - SOUTHERN STATES - HISTORY - 19TH CENTURY.
Mitchell, Theodore R. Political education in the Southern Farmers' Alliance, 1887-1900 /. Madison, Wis. , 1987. xiv, 242 p. : ISBN 0-299-11470-8 : LC Card 87-40141 DDC 338.1/06/075 19
HD1485.N35 M58 1987

FARMERS - EGYPT - HISTORY.
Stuchevskiĭ, I. A. (Iosif Aleksandrovich) Zemledel'tsy gosudarstvennogo khoziaĭstva drevnego Egipta ėpokhi Ramessidov /. Moskva , 1982. 254, [2] p. ; LC Card 82-186646
HD2123 .S78 1982

The farmers' frontier, 1865-1900 /. Fite, Gilbert Courtland, 1918- Norman [1987], c1966. xiv, 272 p. : ISBN 0-8061-2063-0 (pbk.) LC Card 86-40534 DDC 338.1/0977 19
HD8039.F3 U643 1987

FARMERS - GERMANY - POLITICAL ACTIVITY - HISTORY.
Sondermann, Klaus. Wirtschaftsentwicklung und landwirtschaftliche Verbandspolitik . Münster-Hiltrup , 1983. vi, 300 p. : ISBN 3-7843-0283-1 : LC Card 84-126226
HD1486.G3 S66 1983

FARMERS - GERMANY (WEST) - NORTH RHINE-WESTPHALIA - SUPPLEMENTARY EMPLOYMENT - STATISTICS.
Agrarberichterstattung Nordrhein-Westfalen 1981 . Düsseldorf [1983] 189 p. ; LC Card 87-407320 DDC 943/.55 s 338.1/0943/55021 19
HA1320.N6 A32 Heft 490 HD1960.N67

FARMERS - INDIA - MAHARASHTRA - ATTITUDES.
Dhongade, M. P. Farmers' attitude survey in the Mula Command Area, Maharashtra /. Rahuri, Maharashtra, India , 1986. vi, 69 p. ; LC Card 86-903408 DDC 338.1/0954/792 19
HD8039.F32 I44 1986

FARMERS - INDIA - SOCIETIES, ETC.
Seth, A. N., 1914- Peasant organizations in India /. Delhi , New Delhi, India , 1984. xxxxiv, 174 p. ; LC Card 84-902298 DDC 305.5/63 19
HD1339.I4 S48 1984 NYPL [JLD 87-644]

FARMERS - INDIA - VĀRĀNASI DISTRICT.
Banerjee, B. N. (Biswa Nath), 1945- Identification & economic analysis of small farmers /. Delhi, India , 1986. viii, 127 p. : LC Card 86-903139 DDC 338.1/6 19
HD1476.I42 V373 1986

FARMERS - ITALY - POLITICAL ACTIVITY - CONGRESSES.
L'Imprenditore coltivatore nella società che cambia . [Italy] [1983] (Roma : Arti grafiche Jasillo) 364 p. : LC Card 86-185731
HD1972 .I44 1983

FARMERS - ITALY - STATISTICS.
Barberis, Corrado. Agricoltura e strati sociali /. Milano, Italy , c1986. 269 p. ; LC Card 86-214233
HD1536.I8 B328 1986

FARMERS - MIDDLE WEST - HISTORY - 19TH CENTURY.
Fite, Gilbert Courtland, 1918- The farmers' frontier, 1865-1900 /. Norman [1987], c1966. xiv, 272 p. : ISBN 0-8061-2063-0 (pbk.) LC Card 86-40534 DDC 338.1/0977 19
HD8039.F3 U643 1987

FARMERS - NEW ZEALAND - ATTITUDES.
Pryde, J. G. Survey of New Zealand farmer intentions and opinions, November 1985-January 1986 /. Canterbury, N.Z. [1986] 133 p. ; LC Card 87-107903 DDC 338.1/09931 19
HD8039.F32 N486 1986

FARMERS - OKLAHOMA - ECONOMIC CONDITIONS.
Plaxico, James Sam, 1924- Financial status of Oklahoma farmers and ranchers, 1985 . [Stillwater] [1986] 42 p. ; LC Card 86-622478 DDC 338.1/3/09766021 19
HD1775.O5 P57 1986

FARMERS, PART-TIME - AUSTRIA.
Aistleitner, Josef. Formen und Auswirkungen des bäuerlichen Nebenerwerbs . [Innsbruck] , 1986. 174 p. : LC Card 87-408342 DDC 338.1/6 19
HD1935 .A66 1986

FARMERS, PART-TIME - GERMANY (WEST) - NORTH RHINE-WESTPHALIA.
Kreiten, Kurt. Gestalt und Wandel der nebenberuflichen Landwirtschaft in Nordrhein-Westfalen /. Bonn , 1985. xi, 225 p. : ISBN 3-88488-272-4 LC Card 86-205281
HD1960.N67 K74 1985

FARMERS, PART-TIME - ITALY.
Pieroni, Osvaldo. Agricolture a tempo parziale /. Bologna , c1983. 220 p. : ISBN 88-15-00024-0 LC Card 85-233534
HD1970 .P54 1983

FARMERS, PART-TIME - ITALY - STATISTICS.
Barberis, Corrado. Agricoltura e strati sociali /. Milano, Italy , c1986. 269 p. ; LC Card 86-214233
HD1536.I8 B328 1986

FARMERS, PART-TIME - MALAYSIA - KELANTAN.
Chew, T. A. The off-farm labour supply of padi farmers in Kelantan, Malaysia [microform] /. [Canberra] , c1984. 19 p. ; ISBN 0-86784-513-9 (pbk.) LC Card 85-670027 DDC 331.12/93318/095951 19
HD5854.55.M4 C47 1984
*NYPL [*ZF-1745 no.58]*

FARMERS - POLAND.
Klank, Leszek. Czynniki kształtujące poziom dochodów w gospodarstwach indywidualnych /. Warszawa , 1985. 176 p. ; ISBN 83-01-05449-2 :
*NYPL [*QO 86-2601]*

FARMERS - RUSSIAN S.F.S.R. - SAKHALINSKAIA OBLAST'.
Potentsial ėffektivnosti /. IUzhno-Sakhalinsk , 1985. 67 p. ; LC Card 87-100690
HD8039.F32 S656 1985

FARMERS - SOUTHERN STATES - POLITICAL ACTIVITY - HISTORY - 19TH CENTURY.
Mitchell, Theodore R. Political education in the Southern Farmers' Alliance, 1887-1900 /. Madison, Wis. , 1987. xiv, 242 p. : ISBN 0-299-11470-8 : LC Card 87-40141 DDC 338.1/06/075 19
HD1485.N35 M58 1987

FARMERS - SOVIET UNION.
Shinn, William T., 1936- The decline of the Russian peasant household /. New York , 1987. xvii, 122 p. ; ISBN 0-275-92767-9 (alk. paper) LC Card 87-2554 DDC 338.1/0947 19
HD1992 .S4735 1987

FARMERS - SOVIET UNION - BIOGRAPHY.
Vernulsia soldat k poliu, 1945-1985 /. Moskva , 1985. 429, [16] p. : LC Card 85-228297
HD1536.S65 V47 1985

FARMERS - SWAZILAND - ATTITUDES.
Guma, Xolile P. Small farmer credit and small farmer attitudes towards co-operatives /. [Kwaluseni, Swaziland] [1982] 94 p. : LC Card 86-101161 DDC 332.7/1/096813 19
HD1491.S855 G85 1982
NYPL [JLG 86-262]

FARMERS - TEXAS - PSYCHOLOGY - CONGRESSES.
Farm Crisis Workers Conference (1986 : Arlington, Tex.) Farm Crisis Workers Conference . [Austin? , 1986] 136 p. ; LC Card 87-620630 DDC 338.1/3/09764 19
HD1476.U6 T44 1986

FARMERS - TRAINING OF - GERMANY (WEST)
Kretschmann, Rolf. Möglichkeiten des Berufswechsels von Haupterwerbslandwirten unter besonderer Berücksichtigung von Agrarstruktur und Arbeitsmarkt /. Göttingen , 1986. xi, 109 p. : LC Card 87-408871 DDC 331.25/924 19
HD1536.G3 K746 1986

FARMERS - UNITED STATES.
Gorman, Carol. America's farm crisis /. New York , 1987. 125 p. : ISBN 0-531-10408-7 LC Card 87-2087 DDC 338.1/0973 19
HD1476.U5 G67 1987

FARMERS - UNITED STATES - ATTITUDES.
The American farmer book . [Smithshire, Ill.] (Box 181, Smithshire 61478) [c1986] 192 p. : LC Card 86-203314 DDC 338.1/0973 19
HD8039.F32 U614 1986

FARMERS - UNITED STATES - BIOGRAPHY.
Harris, Lement, 1904- My tale of two worlds . New York , 1986. 289 p. : ISBN 0-7178-0645-6 : LC Card 86-10671 DDC 338.1/092/4 B 19
S417.H35 A36 1986 NYPL [JLD 87-1376]

FARMERS - UNITED STATES - CONGRESSES.
Farm work and fieldwork . Ithaca , 1987. 293 p. : ISBN 0-8014-9446-X (pbk. : alk. paper) LC Card 86-19960 DDC 305.5/55/0973 19
HD8039.F32 U635 1987

FARMERS - UNITED STATES - HISTORY - 20TH CENTURY.
The Farmer is the man [sound recording]. Los Angeles, Calif. , p1983. 1 sound cassette (58 min.) : LC Card 87-751678
HD8039.F3

FARMERS - WEST (U. S.) - HISTORY - 19TH CENTURY.
Fite, Gilbert Courtland, 1918- The farmers' frontier, 1865-1900 /. Norman [1987], c1966. xiv, 272 p. : ISBN 0-8061-2063-0 (pbk.) LC Card 86-40534 DDC 338.1/0977 19
HD8039.F3 U643 1987

FARMERS' WIVES - LATIN AMERICA.
A Mulher rural e mudanças no processo de produção agrícola . [Brasília] [1984] i, 161 p. ; LC Card 86-150197
HD6073.A292 L295 1984

FARMERS' WIVES - PORTUGAL.
Cavaco, Carminda. A mulher na agricultura portuguesa . [Lisbon] , 1981. 34 leaves : LC Card 85-216534
HD6073.F32 P83 1981

FARMING. see **AGRICULTURE.**

Farming system and family economy in Ndunya, Chinsali District. Mpika, Zambia : Republic of Zambia, Integrated Rural Development Project, Serenje-Mpika-Chinsali, [1985?] 45 leaves, [12] leaves of plates : ill. ; 30 cm. (IRDP occasional paper . no. 10) LC Card 86-981252 DDC 338.1/096894 19
1. Farms, Small - Zambia - Ndunya. 2. Farm income - Zambia - Ndunya. 3. Households - Zambia - Ndunya. 4. Field crops - Zambia - Ndunya. I. Integrated Rural Development Project, Serenje-Mpika-Chinsali (Zambia). II. Series.
HD1476.Z352 N384 1985

Farming systems and family economy in Chibale, Serenje District. Mpika, Zambia : Republic of Zambia, Integrated Rural Development Project, Serenje-Mpika-Chinsali, [1985?] 74 p. : ill. ; 30 cm. (IRDP occasional paper . no. 5) LC Card 86-981248 DDC 338.1/096894 19
1. Farms, Small - Zambia - Chibale (Serenje District). 2. Farm income - Zambia - Chibale (Serenje District). 3. Households - Zambia - Chibale (Serenje District). 4. Field crops - Zambia - Chibale (Serenje District). I. Integrated Rural Development Project, Serenje-Mpika-Chinsali (Zambia). II. Series.
HD1476.Z352 C454 1985

FARMS - ACCOUNTING. see **AGRICULTURE - ACCOUNTING.**

FARMS - ALBERTA - RECREATIONAL USE.
Swinnerton, Guy S. Recreation on agricultural land in Alberta /. Edmonton, Alta. [1982] x, 211 p. : LC Card 83-149875 DDC 333.76/17/097123 19
HD319.A4 S94 1982 ***NYPL [JLF 86-851]***

FARMS - GERMANY (WEST) - LOWER SAXONY - STATISTICS.
Landwirtschaftszählung 1979, Gartenbauerhebung 1981/82 . Hannover , 1983. xv, 132 p. ; LC Card 85-117833
HD9013.7.L68 L37 1983

FARMS - GERMANY (WEST) - NORTH RHINE-WESTPHALIA - STATISTICS.
Agrarberichterstattung Nordrhein-Westfalen 1981 . Düsseldorf [1983] 189 p. ; LC Card 87-407320 DDC 943/.55 s 338.1/0943/55021 19
HA1320.N6 A32 Heft 490 HD1960.N67

Agrarberichterstattung Nordrhein-Westfalen 1981 . Düsseldorf [1983] 131, [5] p. ; LC Card 87-407319 DDC 943/.55 s 338.1/0943/55021 19
HA1320.N6 A32 Heft 489 HD9013.7.N6

Agrarberichterstattung Nordrhein-Westfalen 1983 . Düsseldorf [1985] 191 p. ; LC Card 87-407316 DDC 943/.55 s 338.1/0943/55021 19
HA1320.N6 A32 Heft 531 HD1960.N67

FARMS - GOVERNMENT POLICY - UNITED STATES.
McKinzie, Lance. A perspective on U. S. farm problems and agricultural policy /. Boulder , 1987. xvii, 189 p. : ISBN 0-8133-7376-X (pbk. : alk. paper) LC Card 86-51501 DDC 338.1/873 19
HD1470.5.U6 M35 1987

FARMS - ITALY - SIENA REGION - HISTORY.
Epstein, Stephan R., 1960- Alle origini della fattoria toscana . Firenze , c1986. 315 p. : LC Card 87-104355
HD1470.5.I82 S544 1986

FARMS, LARGE - BRAZIL - RIO GRANDE DO SUL.
Duarte, Laura Maria Goulart. Capitalismo & cooperativismo no R.G.S. /. Porto Alegre-RS , c1986. 96 p. : ISBN 85-25-40088-2 : LC Card 86-150404
HD1491.B82 R563 1986

FARMS, LARGE - TANZANIA.
Bantje, Han. Mechanised food production in Tanzania . [Dar es Salaam] [1984] 3 leaves, 73 p. : LC Card 86-980118 DDC 338.1/61/09678 19
HD1471.T34 B36 1984

FARMS - LOUISIANA - STATISTICS.
Shuker, Iain G. W. Economic analysis of the cost structure of commercial sugar cane farms in Louisiana /. Baton Rouge, La. [1986] vi, 50 p. : LC Card 86-622542 DDC 338.1/09763 s 338.1/7361/09763021 19
HD1775.L8 L7 no. 651 HD9107.L8

FARMS, SIZE OF - BRAZIL.
Manoel, Alvaro. Política agrícola, eficiência e concentração na agricultura brasileira . São Paulo , 1986. 180 p. : LC Card 86-234338
HD1873 .M35 1986

FARMS, SIZE OF - GOVERNMENT POLICY - UNITED STATES.
McKinzie, Lance. A perspective on U. S. farm problems and agricultural policy /. Boulder , 1987. xvii, 189 p. : ISBN 0-8133-7376-X (pbk. : alk. paper) LC Card 86-51501 DDC 338.1/873 19
HD1470.5.U6 M35 1987

FARMS, SIZE OF - JAMAICA - STATISTICS.
Census of agriculture, 1978-1979 . [Kingston] [1983] vi, ix, 167 p. : LC Card 83-242227 DDC 338.1/097292 19
HD1847 .C46 1983 ***NYPL [JLF 86-1028]***

FARMS, SMALL - ASIA - MANAGEMENT.
Gaikwad, V. R., 1933- Managing paddy-rice business of small farmers . Bombay , 1986. xxiii, 239 p. : ISBN 0-86132-129-4 : LC Card 86-903247 DDC 334/.68318/0954 19
HD9066.A7 G35 1986

FARMS, SMALL - BRAZIL - MINAS GERAIS - CASE STUDIES.
Gomes, Sebastião Teixeira. Condicionantes da modernização do pequeno agricultor /. São Paulo , 1986. 181 p. : LC Card 87-153609 DDC 338.1/0981/51 19
HD1875.M5 G65 1986

FARMS, SMALL - COLOMBIA - BARBOSA (ANTIOQUIA)
Informe general y proyecto de parcelación, Antioquia # 2 (Barbosa y Santo Domingo) /. Bogotá, D.E. , 1964. 2, 73, 16 leaves, [1] leaf of plates : LC Card 85-107102
HD1476.C72 B375 1964

FARMS, SMALL - COLOMBIA - SANTO DOMINGO (ANTIOQUIA)
Informe general y proyecto de parcelación, Antioquia # 2 (Barbosa y Santo Domingo) /. Bogotá, D.E. , 1964. 2, 73, 16 leaves, [1] leaf of plates : LC Card 85-107102
HD1476.C72 B375 1964

FARMS, SMALL - DEVELOPING COUNTRIES.
Bryant, Coralie. Managing rural development with small farmer participation /. West Hartford, CT. , c1984. xiii, 79 p. : ISBN 0-931816-52-1 (pbk.) LC Card 84-4445 DDC 307.7/2 19
HD1417 .B79 1984 ***NYPL [JLE 87-1352]***

Tschiersch, Joachim E. Appropriate mechanization for small farmers in developing countries /. Saarbrücken , 1978. iii, 106 p. ; ISBN 3-88156-112-9 LC Card 80-472522 DDC 338.1/61/091724
S675 .T72 ***NYPL [JLE 80-1482]***

FARMS, SMALL - GERMANY (WEST)
Brandt, Hartmut. Projektplanung in der kleinbäuerlichen Produktion /. Berlin , 1982. xv, 208 p. : LC Card 83-193407
HD1476.G3 B73 1982 ***NYPL [JLE 87-2903]***

FARMS, SMALL - GOVERNMENT POLICY - INDIA.
Desinga Raj, N. Development programmes in agriculture and the weaker sections /. Allahabad, India , 1987. xvi, 217 p. : ISBN 81-85076-16-2 : LC Card 87-900702 DDC 338.1/854 19
HD1476.I4 D47 1987

FARMS, SMALL - GOVERNMENT POLICY - ITALY - CONGRESSES.
L'Imprenditore coltivatore nella società che cambia . [Italy] [1983] (Roma : Arti grafiche Jasillo) 364 p. : LC Card 86-185731
HD1972 .I44 1983

FARMS, SMALL - GOVERNMENT POLICY - UNITED STATES.
McKinzie, Lance. A perspective on U. S. farm problems and agricultural policy /. Boulder , 1987. xvii, 189 p. : ISBN 0-8133-7376-X (pbk. : alk. paper) LC Card 86-51501 DDC 338.1/873 19
HD1470.5.U6 M35 1987

FARMS, SMALL - INDIA - RAJASTHAN.
Kabra, Govind Das, 1943- Development of weaker sections . New Delhi , 1984, c1983. ix, 182 p. ; LC Card 84-900357 DDC 338.1/8544 19
HD1476.I42 R345 1984 ***NYPL [JLE 86-4597]***

FARMS, SMALL - INDIA - VĀRĀNASI DISTRICT.
Banerjee, B. N. (Biswa Nath), 1945- Identification & economic analysis of small farmers /. Delhi, India , 1986. viii, 127 p. : LC Card 86-903139 DDC 338.1/6 19
HD1476.I42 V373 1986

FARMS, SMALL - INDONESIA - ABAISIAT.
Geinitz, Dedo. Entwicklungszusammenarbeit mit Indonesien . Bremen , 1985. viii, 72 p. : ISBN 3-88299-046-5 LC Card 86-204688
HD9161.I63 A244 1985

FARMS, SMALL - ITALY - CALABRIA.
Bonanno, Alessandro. Small farms . Boulder, Colo. , 1987. xvi, 228 p. : ISBN 0-8133-7341-7 (pbk. : alk. paper) LC Card 86-51502 DDC 338.1/6 19
HD1339.I8 B66 1987

FARMS, SMALL - ITALY - SICILY.
Bonanno, Alessandro. Small farms . Boulder, Colo. , 1987. xvi, 228 p. : ISBN 0-8133-7341-7 (pbk. : alk. paper) LC Card 86-51502 DDC 338.1/6 19
HD1339.I8 B66 1987

FARMS, SMALL - KENYA - STATISTICS.
Barnes, Carolyn. Kenyan smallholdings and the division of labour /. Nairobi , 1982. 39 leaves ; LC Card 87-156293
HD1476.K4 B37 1982

FARMS, SMALL - MALAWI.
Mills, J. C. (Joseph C.) Price responses of Malawi smallholder farmers--fast, slow or none? [microform] /. [Zomba] [1975] 42, [2] p. ; LC Card 80-980238 DDC 338.1/3/096897 19
HD1476.M33 M54 1975 ***NYPL [*ZT-1646 no.53]***

FARMS, SMALL - NEPAL.
Maharjan, Bekha L. (Bekha Lal), 1943- Small farm development problems and strategies /. [Kathmandu] , 1984. 114 p. ; LC Card 84-901301 DDC 338.1/6 19
HD1476.N35 M33 1984 ***NYPL [JLD 86-4365]***

FARMS, SMALL - NIGERIA - ADDRESSES, ESSAYS, LECTURES.
Nigerian small farmers . Benin-City, Bendel State, Nigeria , 1980. xv, 315 p. ; LC Card 82-206979 DDC 338.1/6 19
HD1339.N5 N54 1980 ***NYPL [Sc D 86-883]***

FARMS, SMALL - UNITED STATES.
Bonanno, Alessandro. Small farms . Boulder, Colo. , 1987. xvi, 228 p. : ISBN 0-8133-7341-7 (pbk. : alk. paper) LC Card 86-51502 DDC 338.1/6 19
HD1339.I8 B66 1987

FARMS, SMALL - UNITED STATES - STATISTICS.
Banks, Vera J. Black farmers and their farms /. Washington, D.C. , 1986. v, 27 p. : LC Card 86-602201
HD8039.F32 U616 1986

FARMS, SMALL - URUGUAY.
Martorelli, Horacio. Nuevo estilo de desarrollo para Uruguay . Montevideo, Uruguay , 1982. 2 v. : LC Card 85-167867 DDC 338.1/09895 19
HD1907 .M376 1982 ***NYPL [JLF 86-935]***

FARMS, SMALL - ZAMBIA - CHIBALE (SERENJE DISTRICT)
Farming systems and family economy in Chibale, Serenje District. Mpika, Zambia [1985?] 74 p. : LC Card 86-981248 DDC 338.1/096894 19
HD1476.Z352 C454 1985

FARMS, SMALL - ZAMBIA - CHINSALI DISTRICT.
A Survey of constraints facing small-scale farmers in Mpika and Chinsali Districts, Northern Province . [Mpika, Zambia?] [1985 or 1986] 8 p., [1] leaf of plates : LC Card 86-981416 DDC 338.1/6 19
HD1476.Z352 M657 1985

FARMS, SMALL - ZAMBIA - MPIKA DISTRICT.
A Survey of constraints facing small-scale

farmers in Mpika and Chinsali Districts, Northern Province . [Mpika, Zambia?] [1985 or 1986] 8 p., [1] leaf of plates : LC Card 86-981416 DDC 338.1/6 19
HD1476.Z352 M657 1985

FARMS, SMALL - ZAMBIA - NDUNYA.
Farming system and family economy in Ndunya, Chinsali District. Mpika, Zambia [1985?] 45 leaves, [12] leaves of plates : LC Card 86-981252 DDC 338.1/096894 19
HD1476.Z352 N384 1985

FARMS - SWEDEN - HISTORY - 17TH CENTURY.
Larsson, Lars-Olof, 1934- Bönder och gårdar i stormaktspolitikens skugga . Växjö , 1983. 260 p. : ISBN 91-7636-011-3 : LC Card 84-159659
HD763 .L37 1983

FARMS - SWEDEN - HISTORY - 18TH CENTURY.
Larsson, Lars-Olof, 1934- Bönder och gårdar i stormaktspolitikens skugga . Växjö , 1983. 260 p. : ISBN 91-7636-011-3 : LC Card 84-159659
HD763 .L37 1983

FARMS - UNITED STATES.
Planning and zoning for farmland protection . East Lansing, MI , c1987. 58 p. : LC Card 87-119320 DDC 333.76/17/0973 19
HD256 .P57 1987

FARMS - UNITED STATES - CONGRESSES.
Farm work and fieldwork . Ithaca , 1987. 293 p. : ISBN 0-8014-9446-X (pbk. : alk. paper) LC Card 86-19960 DDC 305.5/55/0973 19
HD8039.F32 U635 1987

FARMS - UNITED STATES - STATISTICS.
Lucier, Gary. Farm income data . Washington, DC [1986] iv, 311 p. : LC Card 86-602022 DDC 338.1/0973 s 338.1/3/0973021 19
HD1751 .A5 no. 740 HD1769

Somwaru, Agapi. Disaggregated farm income by type of farm, 1959-82 /. Washington, D.C. , 1986. iii, 113 p. : LC Card 86-602571 DDC 338.1 s 338.1/3/0973021 19
HD1751 .A91854 no. 558 HD1769

FARMS - VALUATION - HUNGARY.
Fórizs, Józsefné. Földértékelés, termőhelyi értékelés problémái . Budapest , 1985. 211 p., [4] folded leaves of plates : ISBN 963-491-204-4 LC Card 86-196842
HD1387 .F596 1985

Farny, Dieter. Die deutsche Versicherungswirtschaft : Markt, Wettbewerb, Konzentration / von Dieter Farny, unter Mitarbeit von Peter Ackermann, Rolf Ulrich, Norbert Vogel. Karlsruhe : VVW, [c1983] xiv, 189 p. ; 24 cm. "Die Untersuchung wurde im Auftrag der Kommission der Europäischen Gemeinschaften, Generaldirektion für Wettbewerb, innerhalb der Reihe 'Entwicklung von Konzentration und Wettbewerb' durchgeführt."--P. [ii] Bibliography: p. 187-189. ISBN 3-88487-054-8 LC Card 84-205736
1. Insurance - Germany, West. I. Title.
HG8618 .F37 1983

Farrell, Gilda. Tenencia de la tierra y movimiento campesino en el Ecuador / investigación, Gilda Farrell. Quito, Ecuador : Fondo Ecuatoriano Populorum Progressio, 1981. 158 p., [2] leaves of plates : ill. ; 28 cm. Includes bibliographical references. LC Card 86-174088
1. Land tenure - Ecuador - Cotopaxi. 2. Peasantry - Ecuador - Cotopaxi - Political activity. 3. Land tenure - Ecuador - Pichincha (Province). 4. Peasantry - Ecuador - Pichincha (Province) - Political activity. 5. Land tenure - Ecuador - Tungurahua. 6. Peasantry - Ecuador - Tungurahua - Political activity. I. Fondo Ecuatoriano Populorum Progressio. II. Title.
HD529.C67 F37 1981

Farrell, Michael D. Tax shelters : illusions, delusions, and economic reality / Michael D. Farrell, Gaylon E. Greer. Chicago, Ill. : Investment Information Services Press, c1985. x, 250 p. : ill. ; 24 cm. Includes index. ISBN 0-930369-04-1 : LC Card 85-207994 DDC 343.7305/23 347.303523 19
1. Tax shelters - Law and legislation - United States. 2. Tax shelters - United States. I. Greer, Gaylon E. II. Title.
KF6297.5 .F37 1985 ***NYPL [JLE 86-1019]***

Farrell, Peter. Heirs, Ben J. The professional decision-thinker . New York , c1987. xiv, 294 ; ISBN 0-396-09203-9 : LC Card 87-15575 DDC 658.4/03 19
HD30.23 .H445 1987

Farris, Paul.
Advertising & promotion management : a manager's guide to theory & practice / Paul W. Farris & John A. Quelch ; with contributions from F. Beaven Ennis, Hollace M. Pfau, Robert Turner.Reprint ed. with corrections. Malabar, Fla. : R.E. Krieger Pub. Co., 1987, c1983. x, 301 p. : ill. ; 23 cm. Reprint. Originally published: Radnor, Pa. : Chilton, c1983. "A Craig T. Norback book." Includes bibliographical references and index. ISBN 0-89464-261-8 (pbk.) LC Card 87-15902 DDC 659.1 19
1. Advertising. 2. Sales promotion. I. Quelch, John A. II. Title. III. Title: Advertising and promotion management.
HF5821 .F36 1987

Quelch, John A. Cases in advertising and promotion management /. Plano, Tex. , 1987. xv, 759 p. : ISBN 0-256-03713-2 LC Card 86-72244 DDC 659.1 19
HF5823 .Q44 1987

Farrow, Nigel. The Gower handbook of management /. Aldershot, Hants, England , Brookfield, Vt., U. S.A. , 1987. p. cm. ISBN 0-566-02662-7 : LC Card 87-144 DDC 658 19
HD31 .G684 1987

Farsy, Fouad, 1946- Saudi Arabia : a case study in development / Fouad Al-Farsy.Completely rev. and updated ed. London ; New York : KPI, 1986. 264 p., [8] p. of plates : ill. ; 24 cm. Bibliography: p. [242]-255. Includes index. ISBN 0-7103-0128-6 LC Card 86-220645 DDC 330.953/8053 19
1. Saudi Arabia - Economic conditions. 2. Saudi Arabia - Politics and government. I. Title.
HC415.33 .F37 1986

Farzin, Yeganeh Hossein, 1950- Competition and substitutes in the market for an exhaustible resource / by Y. Hoosein Farzin. Greenwich, Conn. : Jai Press, c1985. xvi, 209 : ill. ; 24 cm. (Contemporary studies in energy analysis and policy . v 6) Includes index. Bibliography: p. 193-198. ISBN 0-89232-604-2 : LC Card 85-23765 DDC 338.2/7282/0724 19
1. Petroleum industry and trade - Econometric models. 2. Competition. 3. Substitution (Economics). I. Title. II. Series.
HD9560.5 .F385 1985 ***NYPL [JLE 86-1585]***

Fasano-Filho, Ugo, 1956- Nunnenkamp, Peter. Manufactured export performance of Brazil . Kiel [1986] v, 114 p. : LC Card 87-101193 DDC 382/.4567/0981 19
HF1513 .N86 1986

The FASB . Miller, Paul B. W. Homewood, Ill. , 1986. xvi, 145 p. : ISBN 0-256-03520-2 LC Card 85-82340 ***NYPL [JLE 87-872]***

FASB technical bulletin no. 86-1. Public record, FASB technical bulletin no. 86-1, Accounting for certain effects of the Tax Reform Act of 1986. Stamford, Conn. (P.O. Box 3821, Stamford 06905-0821) [1987] 172 p. ; LC Card 87-80349 DDC 657/.46 19
HF5681.T3 P83 1987

Fascículos da história da energia elétrica de São Paulo .
(no. 1) Marsiglia, Cecília. S/A Central Elétrica Rio Claro /. São Paulo , 1986. 105 p. : LC Card 87-404945 DDC 363.6/2/098161 19
HD9685.B83 C4886 1986

FASCISM - EUROPE - HISTORY - 20TH CENTURY.
Maier, Charles S. In search of stability . Cambridge [Cambridgeshire] , New York , 1987. x, 291 p. ; ISBN 0-521-23001-2 LC Card 87-6383 DDC 338.94 19
HC240 .M17 1987

FASCISM - ITALY - LUNIGIANA - HISTORY - 20TH CENTURY.
Bianchi, Antonio. Lotte sociali e dittatura in Lunigiana storica e Versilia (1919-1930) /. [Firenze] , 1981. xii, 309 p. ; ISBN 88-22-23028-0 LC Card 82-125955
HD8489.L86 B5 1981

FASCISM - ITALY - PUGLIA - HISTORY - 20TH CENTURY.
Snowden, Frank M. (Frank Martin), 1946- Violence and great estates in the south of Italy . Cambridge [Cambridgeshire] , New York , 1986. x, 245 p. : ISBN 0-521-30731-7 LC Card 85-11675 DDC 322.4/4/094575 19
HD679.P83 S66 1986 ***NYPL [JLD 86-1627]***

FASCISM - ITALY - VERSILIA PLAIN - HISTORY - 20TH CENTURY.
Bianchi, Antonio. Lotte sociali e dittatura in Lunigiana storica e Versilia (1919-1930) /. [Firenze] , 1981. xii, 309 p. ; ISBN 88-22-23028-0 LC Card 82-125955
HD8489.L86 B5 1981

FASHION MERCHANDISING - CANADA - CASE STUDIES.
Frontrunners. Chapel Hill, NC , 1987. 1 videocassette (28 min., 50 sec.) : LC Card 87-706853 DDC 338.6 11
HD9940

FASHION MODELS. see **MODELS, FASHION.**

Fashoyin, Tayo. Contemporary problems in Nigerian industrial relations /. Lagos, Nigeria , 1986. xii, 150 p. ; ISBN 978-252-200-7 LC Card 87-139560 DDC 331/.09669 19
HD8831 .C65 1986

Fassil G. Kiros. Mobilizing the peasantry for rural development [microform] : the Ethiopian experiment in progress / by Fassil G. Kiros. [Addis Ababa : s.n., 1982] 20 leaves ; 33 cm. "Paper presented to the Seventh International Congress of Ethiopian Studies." "Lund, Sweden. April 26-29, 1982." Cover title. Includes bibliographical references. Microfilm. New York : New York Public Library, 1986. 1 microfilm reel ; 35 mm. (MN *ZZ-25,868) LC Card 82-980723 DDC 334/.683/0963 19
1. Peasantry - Government policy - Ethiopia - Addresses, essays, lectures. 2. Agriculture, Cooperative - Government policy - Ethiopia - Addresses, essays, lectures. 3. Rural development - Government policy - Ethiopia - Addresses, essays, lectures. I. International Conference on Ethiopian Studies (7th : 1982 : Lund, Sweden). II. Title.
HD1538.E7 F37 1982
NYPL [*Z-3952 no.39]

Fassin, Yves. Japan, management van de toekomst? / Yves Fassin. Antwerpen : Kluwer, 1985. 131 p. : ill. ; 25 cm. Bibliography: p. [127]-131. ISBN 90-6716-242-6 : LC Card 86-167503
1. Management - Japan. I. Title.
HD70.J3 F37 1985

Fassini, M. G. Symposium on Management Data Processing for PCB Manufacturing (1982 : Luxembourg, Luxembourg) Symposium on Management Data Processing for PCB Manufacturing . Lugano [1982?] 1 v. (various pagings) : LC Card 84-211066 DDC 621.381/74/0685 19
HD9696.P742 S96 1982
NYPL [JSG 86-145]

FAST FOOD RESTAURANTS - MANAGEMENT.
Food courts . New York , c1987. 70 p. : ISBN 0-913598-66-6 (pbk.) LC Card 87-604 DDC 647/.9573 19
HF5430 .F66 1987

Fast, Irene. Gender identity : a differentiation model / Irene Fast. Hillsdale, N.J. : Analytic Press, 1984. vii, 189 p. ; 24 cm. (Advances in psychoanalysis . v. 2.) Includes bibliographical references and index. ISBN 0-88163-014-4 LC Card 84-6366 DDC 155.3/3 19
1. Sex differences (Psychology). 2. Identity (Psychology). I. Title. II. Series.
BF692.2 .F36 1984 ***NYPL [JFE 86-4829]***

Fast-track careers . Lewis, William, 1946- New York , c1987. x, 212 p. ; ISBN 0-471-83801-2 (pbk.) : LC Card 87-10045 DDC 331.7/02/0973 19
HF5382.5.U5 L45 1987

FASTENERS INDUSTRY - UNITED STATES.
Industrial fasteners market in the U. S. New York, N.Y. , c1983. iv, 375 p. : LC Card 87-143818
HD9999.F33 U476 1983

FASTER READING. see **RAPID READING.**

FAT-TAILED SHEEP INDUSTRY - AUSTRALIA.
Fisher, Brian S. An economic and technical assessment of the establishment of an Australian fat-tail sheep industry /. [Sydney], N.S.W. , c1986. vi, 52 p. ; LC Card 87-154531

DDC 338.1/76386 19
HD9436.A82 F57 1986

Fatchett, D. J. (Derek John), 1945- Trade unions and politics in the 1980s : the 1984 act and political funds / Derek Fatchett. London ; New York : Croom Helm, c1987. p. cm. Bibliography: p. Includes index. ISBN 0-7099-4903-0 LC Card 87-14092 DDC 322/.2/0941 19
1. Trade-unions - Great Britain - Political activity. 2. Trade-unions - Great Britain - Finance. 3. Labour Party (Great Britain). 4. Great Britain - Politics and government - 1979-. I. Title.
HD6667 .F37 1987

Fattigdom, arbejdsløshed, marginalisering . (8) Fattigdom i England . København [1986] 24 columns : ISBN 87-7296-008-6 : LC Card 87-168467
HC260.P6 F37 1986

Fattigdom i England : indtryk fra en studierejse. [1. udg.]. København : Sociologisk institut, Københavns universitet, [1986] 24 columns : ill. ; 21 x 30 cm. (Fattigdom, arbejdsløshed, marginalisering = Unemployment, poverty, marginalization . 8) Arbejdspapir ; nr. 7/1986 Cover title. Bibliography: columns 18-24. ISBN 87-7296-008-6 : LC Card 87-168467
1. Poor - Great Britain. 2. Unemployment - Great Britain. I. Series: Fattigdom, arbejdsløshed, marginalisering , 8.
HC260.P6 F37 1986

Fattinnanzi, Enrico. La Riconversione produttiva nell'edilizia /. Milano , 1984, c1981. 319 p. :
NYPL [JLD 86-3381]

Fatton, Robert. Black consciousness in South Africa : the dialectics of ideological resistance to white supremacy / Robert Fatton, Jr. Albany : State University of New York Press, c1986. ix, 189 p. ; 24 cm. (SUNY series in African politics and society) Revision of the author's thesis (Ph.D.)--University of Notre Dame. Includes index. Bibliography: p. 171-185. ISBN 0-88706-127-3 LC Card 85-2855 DDC 305.8/00968 19
1. Blacks - South Africa - Politics and government. 2. Blacks - South Africa - Race identity. 3. Blacks - South Africa - Social conditions. 4. South Africa - Politics and government - 1961-1978. 5. South Africa - Politics and government - 1978-. 6. South Africa - Social conditions - 1961-. I. Title. II. Series.
DT763.6 .F37 1986 ***NYPL [JLE 86-2289]***

Fauerbach, Vivien E. Bazarian, Carl J. The Gulf States =. New York, N.Y. , c1980. 577 p. : ISBN 0-916006-07-7 LC Card 80-65496
HC415.3 .B39 1980

Faulhaber, Gerald R. Telecommunications in turmoil : technology and public policy / Gerald R. Faulhaber. Cambridge, Mass. : Ballinger Pub. Co., c1987. xviii, 186 p. ; 24 cm. Includes bibliographies and index. ISBN 0-88730-157-6 LC Card 87-1377 DDC 384/.068 19
1. American Telephone and Telegraph Company - Reorganization. 2. Telephone - United States. 3. Telecommunication - United States. I. Title.
HE8846.A55 F38 1987

Faulks, Rex William. Bus and coach operation / R.W. Faulks. 5th ed. London ; Boston : Butterworths, 1987. xi, 259 p. : ill. ; 24 cm. Rev. ed. of: Bus and coach operation / William Lambden. 4th ed. 1969. Bibliography: p. 250-252. Includes index. ISBN 0-408-02810-6 : LC Card 87-10966 DDC 388.3/22/068 19
1. Bus lines. 2. Bus lines - Management. 3. Bus lines - Great Britain. 4. Bus lines - Great Britain - Management. I. Lambden, William. Bus and coach operation. II. Title.
HE5613 .F38 1987

Faust, Konrad. Gerstenberger, Wolfgang. Strukturwandel unter verschlechterten Rahmenbedingungen . Berlin , c1984. 255 p. : ISBN 3-428-05567-5 LC Card 84-180150
HC286.7 .G46 1984

Faustini, Gino, 1930- L'obiettivo occupazione nell'esperienza italiana / Gino Faustini. Torino : Loescher, c1984. 265 p. ; 20 cm. (Loescher università. Monografie) Bibliography: p. [262]-265. LC Card 86-168096
1. Italy - Full employment policies. I. Title.
HD5784 .F38 1984

Faut-il refuser le développement? . Latouche, Serge, 1940- Paris , c1986. 216 p. ; ISBN 2-13-039202-4 : LC Card 86-160202
HD83 .L324 1986

Fauvet, Jean-Christian. La sociodynamique : un art de gouverner / Jean-Christian Fauvet, Xavier Stefani. Paris : Editions d'organisation, 1983. 210, [5] p. : ill. ; 24 cm. Bibliography: p. [211] ISBN 2-7081-0524-8 : LC Card 83-152909
1. Personnel management. 2. Labor disputes. 3. Social interaction. I. Stefani, Xavier. II. Title.
HF5549 .F34 1983

Faux amis & key words . Thody, Philip Malcolm Waller, 1928- London , 1985. 224 p. ; ISBN 0-485-11243-4 : LC Card 84-108125 DDC 443/.21 19
PC2593 .T45 1985 ***NYPL [JFD 86-5704]***

Faux amis and key words. Thody, Philip Malcolm Waller, 1928- Faux amis & key words . London , 1985. 224 p. ; ISBN 0-485-11243-4 : LC Card 84-108125 DDC 443/.21 19
PC2593 .T45 1985 ***NYPL [JFD 86-5704]***

Favaretto, Ilario, 1945- L'impresa artigiana tra economia e territorio : analisi e considerazioni in un'area e economia diffusa, l'Associazione intercomunale pesarese / di Ilario Favaretto e Antonio Mezzino. Milano, Italy : F. Angeli, c1986. 212 p. : ill. ; 22 cm. At head of title: Associazione intercomunale pesarese. Comuni di Colbordolo ... [et al.] Includes bibliographical references. LC Card 86-193238
1. Artisans - Italy - Pesaro Region. 2. Pesaro Region (Italy) - Industries. I. Mezzino, Antonio, 1950-. II. Title.
HD2346.I82 P464 1986

Favaro, Edgardo. Peirano, Ricardo. El rol del empresario privado en el desarrollo económico y social en democracia /. Montevideo, Uruguay , 1986. 79 leaves ; LC Card 87-404359 DDC 338.9895 19
HC232 .P45 1986

Fawcett, Henry, 1833-1884. The economic position of the British labourer / Henry Fawcett. New York : Garland, 1984. vii, 256 p. ; 19 cm. (The World of labour : English workers, 1850-1890) Reprint. Originally published: Cambridge : Macmillan, 1865. ISBN 0-8240-5706-6 (alk. paper) : LC Card 83-48478 DDC 331/.0941 19
1. Labor and laboring classes - Great Britain - Addresses, essays, lectures. 2. Industrial relations - Great Britain - Addresses, essays, lectures. I. Series: World of labour. II. Title.
HD8390 .F28 1984 ***NYPL [JLC 86-366]***

Fawcett, P. (Paul) Bell, G. J. (Graham J.) The business of transport /. Plymouth [Devon] , 1984. viii, 344 p. : ISBN 0-7121-2406-3 (pbk.) LC Card 84-170770 DDC 380.5 19
HE151 .B436 1984 ***NYPL [JLD 87-86]***

Fawcett, Richard G. Debating United States agricultural policy . Kansas City, Mo. (P.O. Box 20626, Kansas City 64195) , c1986. 111 p. ; LC Card 86-224267 DDC 338.1/873 19
HD1761 .D37 1986b

FAX. see **FACSIMILE TRANSMISSION.**

Faye, Jacques. Benoit-Cattin, Michel. L'exploitation agricole familiale en Afrique soudano-sahélienne /. Paris , c1982. 94 p. : ISBN 2-85319-106-0 LC Card 86-116718
HD1476.S382 S563 1982

FC a Chamela, 1890. Diversos documentos y datos relativos al proyectado ferrocarril de Chamela a Aguascalientes /. Guadalajara, México , 1982. 24, iii, 98 p. : LC Card 86-115748 DDC 385/.0972 19
HE2818 .D58 1982

Feagin, Joe R. Benokraitis, Nijole V. (Nijole Vaicaitis) Modern sexism . Englewood Cliffs , c1986. xiii, 187 p. ; ISBN 0-13-597634-0 LC Card 85-28256
HQ1426 .B428 1986 ***NYPL [JLE 86-4225]***

Fearnside, Philip M. (Philip Martin) Human carrying capacity of the Brazilian rain-forest / Philip M. Fearnside. New York : Columbia University Press, 1986. xii, 293 p. : ill. ; 23 cm. Includes index. Bibliography: p. [241]-280. ISBN 0-231-06104-8 (alk. paper) LC Card 85-6643 DDC 330.981/1063 19
1. Environmental policy - Amazon River Region. 2. Land capability for agriculture - Amazon River Region. 3. Rain forest ecology - Amazon River Region. 4. Amazon River Region - Population density. 5. Rodovia Transamazônica, Brazil. I. Title.
HC188.A5 F42 1986 ***NYPL [JLE 86-4554]***

Fearon, Peter. War, prosperity, and depression : the United States economy, 1917-1945 / by Peter Fearon. Lawrence, Kan. : University Press of Kansas, 1987. p. cm. Bibliography: p. Includes index. ISBN 0-7006-0348-4 : LC Card 87-21571 DDC 330.973/091 19
1. United States - Economic conditions - 1918-1945. I. Title.
HC106.2 .F42 1987

FEASIBILITY STUDIES.
Barrett, G. Vincent. How to conduct and analyze real estate market and feasibility studies /. New York , c1988. xvii, 366 p. : ISBN 0-442-21220-8 : LC Card 87-18861 DDC 332.63/24 19
HD1390 .B37 1988

A feasibility study on the ox-driven scotch cart project . Rajeswaran, K. Lusaka, Zambia [1985] vii leaves, 66 p., [3] leaves of plates : LC Card 87-980373 DDC 388.3/41/096894 19
HE153 .R35 1985

Fébó, László. Életszínvonal és közhangulat /. Budapest , 1984. 69 p. ; LC Card 86-147705
HD7027.5 .E44 1984

Fechtel, Hans-Walter. Flächenhafte Verkehrsberuhigung : Methodenstudie zur Gefahrenbewertung für verkehrsberuhigte Bereiche / Hans-Walter Fechtel, Wilfried Ruske ; Institut für Stadtbauwesen, Technische Universität Braunschweig. Bergisch Gladbach : Bundesanstalt für Strassenwesen, Bereich Unfallforschung, 1986. 282 p. : ill. ; 21 cm. (Forschungsberichte der Bundesanstalt für Strassenwesen, Bereich Unfallforschung, 0173-7066 . 135) "Bericht zum Forschungsproject 8019/5 der Bundesanstalt für Strassenwesen, Bereich Unfallforschung ... Mai 1986." Bibliography: p. 269-276. LC Card 87-408360 DDC 388.4/0943 19
1. Urban transportation - Germany, West. 2. Urban transportation policy - Germany, West. 3. Traffic safety - Germany, West. 4. Traffic noise - Germany (West). I. Ruske, Wilfried. II. Technische Universität Braunschweig. Institut für Stadtbauwesen. III. Title. IV. Series.
HE311.G3 F4 1986

La fécondité en Afrique noire /. Locoh, Thérèse. Lomé [1985] 36, 22 leaves : LC Card 87-126644
HB1071 .L63 1985

La fécondité en France . Challier, Marie-Christine. Paris , 1985. 196 p. : ISBN 2-222-03773-5 : LC Card 86-234728
HB1003 .C46 1985

Fecundabilidad y edad de la mujer en las áreas rurales y semi-urbanas de cuatro países latinoamericanos /. Pinto, Claudio. Santiago de Chile [1978] 21, [2] p. : LC Card 83-175823
HA755 .U5 no. 151 HB940.5

La fecundidad en Cuba /. Alvarez Vázquez, Luisa. La Habana , 1985. ix, 182 p. : LC Card 87-401045 DDC 304.6/32/097291 19
HB959 .A44 1985

Federação das Industrias do Estado da Bahia. Seminário sobre Política Industrial da Bahia (1986 : Salvador, Brazil) Síntese das exposições e dos debates /. [Salvador] [1986] 89 p. ; LC Card 87-403843 DDC 338.981/42 19
HD3616.B84 B37 1986

Federação das Indústrias do Estado de Pernambuco. Departamento de Economia. Jucá, Alvaro Ferraz. Gênero industrial--têxtil /. [Recife] [1985?] 34 leaves ; LC Card 86-204296
HD9864.B83 P475 1985

Federação das Indústrias do Estado do Ceará. Vianna, Pedro Jorge Ramos. Inflação vs. indexação, uma contribuição ao tema /. Fortaleza-Ceará [19]84. 121 p. : LC Card 86-130092
HG835 .V53 1984

Federação do Comércio Varejista do Estado do Paraná. Empresa forte, mais trabalho : linhas de ação / Federação do Comércio Varejista do Estado do Paraná. [Curitiba] : A Federação, 1983. 67 leaves : ill. ; 29 cm. Cover title. LC Card 83-225279
1. Retail trade - Government policy - Brazil - Paraná (State). 2. Retail trade - Employees - Training of - Brazil - Paraná (State). I. Title. II. Title: Linhas de ação.
HF5429.6.B7 F44 1983

Federación Interamericana de Filatelia. Central America postal history and a listing of prephilatelic postmarks =. New York [Yonkers, N.Y.?] , 1986. xiv, 142 p. : ISBN 0-912574-41-0 (pbk.) LC Card 87-402819 DDC 383/.49728 19
HE6674 .C46 1986

Federación Internacional de Carreteras. see **International Road Federation.**

Federación Nacional de Economistas del Ecuador. El Ecuador en la encrucijada . Quito , 1986. 307 p. : LC Card 87-400394 DDC 331.12/09866 19
HD5758.A6 E28 1986

Federación Nacional de Organizaciones Campesinos (Ecuador) Luchando por nuestros derechos . Quito , 1984. 50 p. : LC Card 86-174980
HD1531.L3 L79 1984

Federación Sindical de Trabajadores Mineros de Bolivia. Diagnóstico general de la Corporación Minera de Bolivia, 1985 . La Paz, Bolivia , 1986. 2 v. ; LC Card 87-401587 DDC 338.2/0984 19
HD9506.B64 C646 1986

FEDERACIÓN SINDICAL DE TRABAJADORES MINEROS DE BOLIVIA.
Calla, Ricardo. La derrota de Lechín . La Paz, Bolivia , 1986. 79 p. : LC Card 87-105127
HD6609.M62 F433 1986

FEDERACIÓN VENEZOLANA DE CÁMARAS Y ASOCIACIONES DE COMERCIO Y PRODUCCIÓN.
Celis, Adán. 5 momentos, 5 planteamientos . Puerto la Cruz [Venezuela] , 1985. 99 p. ; LC Card 87-401953 DDC 338.987 19
HC237 .C445 1985

Federal aid interstate routes, 1985. Log of the federal-aid interstate system comprising the Nevada primary state highway system, 1985 /. Carson City, Nev. [Washington] [1985] 41 leaves ; LC Card 86-622234 DDC 388.1/09793 19
HE356.N37 L632 1985

FEDERAL AID TO BUSINESS RESEARCH - UNITED STATES - DIRECTORIES.
Business and economics funding guide /. Washington, D.C. , c1987. 122 p. ; ISBN 0-88044-087-2 (alk. paper) : LC Card 87-17436 DDC 001.4/4 19
HF1131 .B78 1987

Federal aid to Chicago /. Orlebeke, Charles J. Washington, D.C. , c1983. xvii, 80 p. ; ISBN 0-8157-6649-1 (pbk.) LC Card 82-74097 DDC 336.1/85 19
HJ9229.C5 O74 1983 NYPL [JLE 86-4696]

FEDERAL AID TO COMMUNITY DEVELOPMENT - INDIA.
Sharda, N. K. State finances and regional development in India /. New Delhi , c1986. 248 p. ; LC Card 86-900599 DDC 336.54/52 19
HJ1339.H55 S54 1986 NYPL [JLD 86-3211]

FEDERAL AID TO COMMUNITY DEVELOPMENT - NEW YORK (STATE)
FEDERAL AID TO COMMUNITY DEVELOPMENT - UNITED STATES.
Ferguson, Gary D. Evaluation of the small cities community development block grant program--the role of the counties [microform] /. Cambridge, Mass. , 1981. vii, vi, 186 p. ;
*NYPL [*XME-11,283]*

Newman & Hermanson Company. Evaluation of the small cities component of the community development block grant program [microform] . Cambridge, Mass. , 1981. viii, xvii, 147 p. ;
*NYPL [*XME-11,274]*

FEDERAL AID TO COMMUNITY DEVELOPMENT - UNITED STATES - DIRECTORIES.
Blum, Laurie. Free money for small businesses and entrepreneurs /. New York , c1988. ix, 229 p. ; ISBN 0-471-85803-X : LC Card 87-20978 DDC 658.1/5224 19
HG4027.7 .B58 1988

Federal aid to St. Louis /. Schmandt, Henry J. Washington, D.C. , c1983. xvii, 67 p. ; ISBN 0-8157-7727-2 (pbk.) LC Card 82-74100 DDC 336.1/85 19
HJ9268.S3 S352 1983 NYPL [JLE 87-1]

FEDERAL AID TO TRANSPORTATION - NEVADA.
1985 log, federal-aid urban routes /. Carson City, Nev. [1984] iii leaves, 165 p. ; LC Card 86-622235 DDC 388.4/042 19
HE356.N37 A17 1984

FEDERAL AID TO TRANSPORTATION - NEW YORK (STATE)
New York (State). Legislature. Legislative Commission on Expenditure Review. Federal rural transportation assistance . Albany, N.Y. (111 Washington Ave., Albany 12210-2277) [1986] 5, ii, 64 p. : LC Card 86-622160 DDC 353.0087/5/009747 19
HE5633.N7 N53 1986

FEDERAL AID TO TRANSPORTATION - UNITED STATES.
Black, William Richard, 1942- Railroads for rent . Bloomington , c1986. x, 341 p. ; ISBN 0-253-34774-2 LC Card 84-48546 DDC 385/.1 19
HE1061 .B57 1986 NYPL [JLE 86-3354]

Bloch, Arnold J. Interstate highway trade-in process. Vol. 1. Assessment /. New York , 1982. [45] p. : *NYPL [*XME-11,324]*

Ferris, Sally A. Federal subsidies to rail passenger service . Washington, D.C. , Congress of the United States, Congressional Budget Office [1982] xxiii, 85, [1] p. : LC Card 82-602556 DDC 385/.1 19
HE1061 .F47 1982 NYPL [JLF 86-1384]

Federal aid urban system routes, 1985. 1985 log, federal-aid urban routes /. Carson City, Nev. [1984] iii leaves, 165 p. ; LC Card 86-622235 DDC 388.4/042 19
HE356.N37 A17 1984

FEDERAL-CITY RELATIONS - ILLINOIS - CHICAGO.
Orlebeke, Charles J. Federal aid to Chicago /. Washington, D.C. , c1983. xvii, 80 p. ; ISBN 0-8157-6649-1 (pbk.) LC Card 82-74097 DDC 336.1/85 19
HJ9229.C5 O74 1983 NYPL [JLE 86-4696]

FEDERAL-CITY RELATIONS - MISSOURI - SAINT LOUIS.
Schmandt, Henry J. Federal aid to St. Louis /. Washington, D.C. , c1983. xvii, 67 p. ; ISBN 0-8157-7727-2 (pbk.) LC Card 82-74100 DDC 336.1/85 19
HJ9268.S3 S352 1983 NYPL [JLE 87-1]

FEDERAL-CITY RELATIONS - UNITED STATES.
Changing the course . Washington , 1986. xvii, 142 p. : LC Card 86-603365 DDC 336.1/85 19
HJ275 .C455 1986

Frieden, Bernard J. The politics of neglect . Cambridge, Mass. [1975] x, 281 p. ; ISBN 0-262-06061-2 LC Card 75-6792 DDC 309.2/62/0973
HT167 .F74 NYPL [JLE 80-1135]

Intergovernmental relations and public policy /. New York , 1986. viii, 224 p. : ISBN 0-313-25443-5 (lib. bdg. : alk. paper) LC Card 86-3155 DDC 353.9/29 19
JK325 .I575 1986 NYPL [JLE 87-749]

Urban policy problems . New York , 1986. vi, 261 p. : ISBN 0-03-004218-6 (alk. paper) : LC Card 86-596 DDC 307.7/6/0973 19
HT123 .U7466 1986 NYPL [JLE 86-3613]

FEDERAL CORPORATION TAX. see **CORPORATIONS - TAXATION.**

Federal Council on Aging (U. S.) The Future is Now: A Home Equity Conversion Conference (1985 : Washington, D.C.) Proceedings from The Future is Now, A Home Equity Conversion Conference. Washington, D.C. [1985?] ix, 76 p. ; LC Card 86-601425 DDC 332.7/22 19
HG2040.45 .F87 1985

Federal energy information sources and data bases /. Bloch, Carolyn. Park Ridge, N.J. , 1979. x, 115 p. ; ISBN 0-8155-0764-X : LC Card 79-15543 DDC 016.33379/0973 19
HD9502.U52 B58 NYPL [JLE 86-4259]

Federal finance in comparative perspective /. Bird, Richard M., 1938- Toronto, Canada , c1986. x, 250 p. : ISBN 0-88808-024-7 (pbk.) LC Card 86-215918 DDC 336 19
HJ141 .B57 1986

FEDERAL GOVERNMENT - AUSTRALIA.
Warhurst, John. Central agencies, intergovernmental managers, and Australian federal-state relations /. Canberra , 1983. vi, 27 p. : ISBN 0-86784-318-7 (pbk.) LC Card 85-217351
JQ4020.S8 W28 1983
NYPL [JLL 82-87 no.29]

FEDERAL GOVERNMENT - CANADA.
Brunelle, Dorval. L'Etat solide . Montréal, Québec , 1982. 174 p. : ISBN 2-89132-677-6 (pbk.) LC Card 87-672120
HC115 .B773x 1982

The Canadian economy . Toronto , New York , c1986. 291 p. : ISBN 0-458-99950-4 (pbk.) : LC Card 86-218828 DDC 338.971 19
HC113 .C37 1986

Economic and regional development agreements . [Ottawa?] [1985] 11, 12, [8] p. : LC Card 86-214896 DDC 338.971 19
HC113 .E26 1985

Schultz, Richard, 1945- Economic regulation and the federal system /. Toronto , Buffalo , c1985. xv, 187 p. : ISBN 0-8020-7287-9 (pbk.) LC Card 86-672574
HD3616.C23 S38x 1985
NYPL [JLD 86-2821]

FEDERAL GOVERNMENT - GERMANY, WEST.
Posse, Achim Ulrich, 1960- Föderative Politikverflechtung in der Umweltpolitik /. München , c1986. xiv, 181 p. : ISBN 3-597-10526-2 LC Card 86-222201
HC290.5.E5 P67 1986

FEDERAL GOVERNMENT - GERMANY (WEST) - CONGRESSES.
Die Deutschen Länder und die Europäischen Gemeinschaften . Baden-Baden , 1986. 294 p. ; ISBN 3-7890-1350-1 LC Card 87-141896 DDC 341.24/22 19
HC241.25.G3 D48 1986

FEDERAL GOVERNMENT - UNITED STATES.
Bowman, Ann O'M., 1948- The resurgence of the states /. Englewood Cliffs, N.J. , c1986. x, 269 p. : ISBN 0-13-774969-4 (pbk.) LC Card 85-19213 DDC 353.9 19
JK2408 .B68 1986 NYPL [JLE 86-4496]

Federal-state-local fiscal relations . Washington, D.C. [1986] 2 v. (viii, 1118 p.) : LC Card 86-603179 DDC 336.73 19
HJ275 .F427 1986

Houseman, Gerald L. State and local government . Englewood Cliffs, N.J. , c1986. xvi, 272 p. : ISBN 0-13-843368-2 (pbk.) LC Card 85-16981 DDC 320.973 19
JK2408 .H79 1986 NYPL [JLE 86-2916]

Intergovernmental relations and public policy /. New York , 1986. viii, 224 p. : ISBN 0-313-25443-5 (lib. bdg. : alk. paper) LC Card 86-3155 DDC 353.9/29 19
JK325 .I575 1986 NYPL [JLE 87-749]

Project on the Federal Social Role (U. S.). Committee on Federalism and National Purpose. To form a more perfect union /. Washington, D.C. (1730 M St., Suite 911, Washington 20036) , c1985. xi, 52 p. ;
NYPL [JLE 86-1879]

FEDERAL GOVERNMENT - UNITED STATES - ADDRESSES, ESSAYS, LECTURES.
State politics and the new federalism . White Plains, N.Y. , c1986. xv, 544 p. : ISBN 0-582-28474-0 (pbk.) LC Card 85-15956 DDC 321.02/0973 19
JK325 .S77 1986 NYPL [JLD 86-2766]

FEDERAL GRANTS. see **GRANTS-IN-AID.**

Federal grants-in-aid funding, 1964-83. Changing the course . Washington , 1986. xvii, 142 p. : LC Card 86-603365 DDC 336.1/85 19
HJ275 .C455 1986

Federal Highway Administration. see **United States. Federal Highway Administration.**

Federal Home Loan Bank of San Francisco. Financial stability of the thrift industry . San Francisco, Calif. (P.O. Box 7948, San Francisco 94120) [1986?] 230 p. : LC Card 86-81012
NYPL [JLE 86-3398]

Federal income taxation of real estate . Robinson, Gerald J. Boston, Mass. , c1984. ca.

750 p. in various pagings ; ISBN 0-88712-081-4 LC Card 83-50925 DDC 343.7305/2 347.30352 19
KF6535 .R6 1984 ***NYPL [JLL 87-136]***

Federal income taxation of real estate . Robinson, Gerald J. Boston, Mass. , c1987. ca. 480 p. in various pagings ; ISBN 0-88712-743-6 LC Card 83-50925
NYPL [JLL 87-136 Suppl. 1987/1]

Federal income taxation of real estate : text, forms, and tax planning ideas : 4th ed. Cumulative supplement /. Robinson, Gerald J. Boston, Mass. , c1985- v. ISBN 0-88712-305-8 (pbk.) LC Card 83-50925
NYPL [*R-Econ. 85-1660 Suppl.]

Federal lands . Fairfax, Sally K. Washington, D.C. , c1987. xviii, 252 p. : ISBN 0-933280-33-5 (pbk.) :$ LC Card 86-27512 DDC 333.1/0978 19
HD243.A17 F35 1987

Federal longitudinal surveys / prepared by Subcommittee on Federal Longitudinal Surveys, Federal Committee on Statistical Methodology. [Washington, D.C.?] : Statistical Policy Office, Office of Information and Regulatory Affairs, Office of Management and Budget ; [Springfield, VA : NTIS Document Sales], 1986. v, 159 p. : ill. ; 28 cm. (Statistical policy working paper . 13) Cover title. Distributed to depository libraries in microfiche. "May 1986." Bibliography: p. 153-159. S/N PB86-139730 Item 126-D-7 (microfiche) LC Card 86-603413 DDC 001.4/33 19
1. Longitudital method. 2. Surveys - Longitudinal studies. 3. Social surveys - United States - Longitudinal studies. I. United States. Federal Committee on Statistical Methodology. Subcommittee on Federal Longitudinal Surveys. II. United States. Office of Management and Budget. Statistical Policy Office. III. Series.
HA31.2 .F43 1986

Federal marketing programs in agriculture : issues and options / editors, Walter J. Armbruster, Dennis R. Henderson, Ronald D. Knutson. Danville, Ill. : Interstate Printers & Publishers, c1983. x, 326 p. ; 24 cm. Includes bibliographies. ISBN 0-8134-2292-2 : LC Card 83-80130
1. Farm produce - United States - Marketing. 2. Agricultural administration - United States. 3. Produce trade - United States. 4. Agriculture - Economic aspects - United States - Government policy. I. Armbruster, Walter J. II. Henderson, Dennis R. III. Knutson, Ronald D. ***NYPL [JLE 86-4572]***

Federal milk marketing orders : a review of research on their economic consequences / by the American Agricultural Economics Association, Task Force on Dairy Marketing Orders. [Ames, Iowa] : The Task Force, [1986] 50 p. : ill. ; 28 cm. (Occasional paper / American Agricultural Economics Association, Task Force on Dairy Marketing Orders . no. 3) Cover title. "June 1986". Bibliography: p. 36-50. LC Card 86-229061 DDC 338.1/771/0973 19
1. Milk trade - Government policy - United States. I. American Agricultural Economics Association. Task Force on Dairy Marketing Orders. II. Series: Occasional paper / American Agricultural Economics Association, Task Force on Dairy Marketing Orders , no. 3.
HD9282.U4 F43 1986

Federal policies in water resources planning /. American Society of Civil Engineers. Task Committee on Federal Policies in Water Resources Planning. New York, N.Y. , c1985. 61 p. : ISBN 0-87262-465-X (pbk.) LC Card 85-71265 DDC 333.91/15/0973 19
HD1694.A5 A67 1985
NYPL [JLD 86-4066]

Federal Publications Inc.
Cost estimating for government contracts . [Washington, D.C.] (1120 20th St., NW, Washington 20036) , c1986. 1 v. (various pagings) : LC Card 87-100120 DDC 658.1/552 19
HD3860 .C67 1986

Investing in broadcast stations . [Washington, D.C.] (1120 20th St., NW, Washington 20036) , c1987. 318 p. in various pagings : LC Card 87-115340 DDC 384.54/3/0681 19
HE8689.8 .I58 1987

Levine, Stuart M. The construction manager . [Washington, D.C.] (1120 20th St., NW, Washington 20036) , c1986. ii, 218 p. : LC Card 87-109137 DDC 624/.068 19
HD9715.A2 L43 1986

Federal Republic of Cameroon. see **Cameroon.**

The Federal Republic of Germany and The European community /. Bulmer, Simon. London , Boston , 1987. p. cm. ISBN 0-04-382045-X (alk. paper) LC Card 86-25909 DDC 341.24/22 19
HC241.25.G3 B86 1987

Federal Republic of Nigeria. see **Nigeria.**

Federal Reserve Bank of St. Louis. The Monetary versus fiscal policy debate . Totowa, N.J. , 1986. 171 p. : ISBN 0-8476-7454-1 : LC Card 85-11912 DDC 339.5/2 19
HG230.3 .M64 1986 ***NYPL [JLE 86-4720]***

FEDERAL RESERVE BANKS.
Greider, William. Secrets of the temple . New York , c1987. 798 p. ; ISBN 0-671-47989-X : LC Card 87-16712 DDC 332.1/1/0973 19
HG2563 .G72 1987

Federal rural transportation assistance . New York (State). Legislature. Legislative Commission on Expenditure Review. Albany, N.Y. (111 Washington Ave., Albany 12210-2277) [1986] 5, ii, 64 p. : LC Card 86-622160 DDC 353.0087/5/009747 19
HE5633.N7 N53 1986

Federal, state, and local highway financing / prepared by North Dakota State Highway Department, Planning Division. Bismarck, N.D. : The Department, [1986] 33 leaves : ill. ; 28 cm. Cover title. "October 1, 1986." Bibliography: p. 33. LC Card 87-620924 DDC 388.1/14/09784 19
1. Roads - North Dakota - Finance. 2. Roads - United States - Finance. I. North Dakota. State Highway Dept. Planning Division.
HE356.N9 F42 1986

FEDERAL-STATE FISCAL RELATIONS. see **INTERGOVERNMENTAL FISCAL RELATIONS.**

Federal-state-local fiscal relations : technical papers / Office of State and Local Finance, Department of the Treasury. Washington, D.C. : The Department : For sale by the Supt. of Docs., U. S. G.P.O., [1986] 2 v. (viii, 1118 p.) : ill. ; 28 cm. "September 1986." Includes bibliographies. LC Card 86-603179 DDC 336.73 19
1. Intergovernmental fiscal relations - United States. 2. Federal government - United States. I. United States. Dept. of the Treasury. Office of State and Local Finance.
HJ275 .F427 1986

FEDERAL-STATE RELATIONS. see **FEDERAL GOVERNMENT.**

Federal statistical directory . Evinger, William R., 1943- Phoenix, Ariz. , 1987. iv, 127 p. ; ISBN 0-89774-398-9 (pbk.) LC Card 87-12359 DDC 353.0081/9 19
HA37.U55 E85 1987

Federal subsidies for rail passenger service. Ferris, Sally A. Federal subsidies to rail passenger service . Washington, D.C. , Congress of the United States, Congressional Budget Office [1982] xxiii, 85, [1] p. : LC Card 82-602556 DDC 385/.1 19
HE1061 .F47 1982 ***NYPL [JLF 86-1384]***

Federal subsidies to rail passenger service . Ferris, Sally A. Washington, D.C. , Congress of the United States, Congressional Budget Office [1982] xxiii, 85, [1] p. : LC Card 82-602556 DDC 385/.1 19
HE1061 .F47 1982 ***NYPL [JLF 86-1384]***

Federal tax policy /. Pechman, Joseph A., 1918- Washington, D.C. , c1987. xix, 430 p. : ISBN 0-8157-6962-8 : LC Card 87-13159 DDC 336.2/00973 19
HJ257.2 .P4 1987

Federal tax reform and the states : issues for the retail industry / prepared by Public Strategies for the American Retail Education Foundation. Washington, D.C. (1616 H St., N.W., Suite 600, Washington 20006) : The Foundation, c1987. 84 p. ; 28 cm. LC Card 87-404532 DDC 336.2/05/0973 19
1. Taxation - United States. 2. Revenue - United States - States. 3. Corporations - Taxation - United States. I. Public Strategies (Firm). II. American Retail Education Foundation.
HJ2381 .F37 1987

FEDERALISM. see **FEDERAL GOVERNMENT.**

Federalisme. Televisió, federalisme. Barcelona [1986] 209 p. ; LC Card 86-210066
HE8700.9.S63 T44 1986

FÉDÉRATION DES ENTREPRISES DE BELGIQUE - LANGUAGE.
Hotterbeex, M. (Marcel) Les verbos de la F.E.B. en 1979 /. Liège , 1982. 20 leaves ; LC Card 83-221745
HD6948.B4 H67 1982

FÉDÉRATION DES TRAVAILLEURS DU PAPIER ET DE LA FORÊT - HISTORY.
Vanasse, Gilbert, 1948- Histoire de la Fédération des travailleurs du papier et de la forêt /. Montréal, Québec , 1986- v. <1 > : ISBN 2-89035-122-X (t. 1) LC Card 86-231295
HD6528.P332 F438 1986

FÉDÉRATION DES TRAVAILLEURS DU QUÉBEC. (Old catalog form: Quebec Provincial Federation of Labor)
Cyr, François, 1952- Eléments d'histoire de la FTQ . [Laval] [1981] 205 p. ; ISBN 2-89035-045-2 : LC Card 82-105783 DDC 331.88/09714 19
HD8102.F43 C97 1981

Fédération internationale des piétons. see **International Federation of Pedestrians.**

Fédération nationale des employés et cadres des assurances, du crédit, de la sécurité sociale et divers (France) Symposium sur les conséquences des techniques nouvelles de l'informatique sur les conditions de vie, et de travail, sur l'emploi des travailleurs des banques et des assurances (1980 : Paris, France) Symposium sur les conséquences des techniques nouvelles de l'informatique sur les conditions de vie, et de travail, sur l'emploi des travailleurs des banques et des assurances /. Berlin [1983?] 96 p. : LC Card 84-185736
HD8039.B27 F77 1980

FEDERATION OF EUROPE. see **EUROPEAN FEDERATION.**

Federation of Jewish Philanthropies of New York. Neighborhood Preservation Program. The Housing handbook . New York, N.Y. (130 E. 59 St., New York 10022) , 1986. 150 p. ; LC Card 87-107431 DDC 363.5/8/0681 19
HD7304.N5 H68 1986

Federation of Medical Representatives Association of India. "All India Seminar on National Drug Policy" (1986 : New Delhi, India) Drug industry and the Indian people . New Delhi , Patna , 1986. 333 p. : LC Card 87-900874 DDC 338.4/76151/0954 19
HD9611.I52 A44 1986

Federation of Nigeria. see **Nigeria.**

Fédération routière internationale. see **International Road Federation.**

Federativna Narodna Republika Jugoslavije. see **Yugoslavia.**

Federazione delle casse rurali ed artigiane dell'Emilia-Romagna. Cooperazione di credito e sviluppo sociale ed economico delle campagne in Emilia Romagna . Bologna , c1983. 173 p. : LC Card 85-156690
HG2051.I82 E433 1983

Federazione italiana lavoratori del legno dell'edilizia e industria affini. Seminario di aggiornamento per i quadri sindacali della categoria (1985 : Rome, Italy) Evoluzione del processo produttivo nelle construzioni . Milano, Italy , c1986. 142 p. : LC Card 86-210757
HD9715.I82 S46 1985

Federazione italiana pallavolo. Gilardi, Mauro. Volley e bolli . Milano , c1985. 107 p. : LC Card 86-128270
HE6183.V64 G55 1985

Federer, Richard L. Haggai, Tom. How the best is won /. Nashville , c1987. 228 p. ; ISBN 0-8407-4221-5 LC Card 87-14996 DDC 658.4/09 19
HD38.2 .H34 1987

Federico Motta editore (Milan, Italy) I Giovani e il mondo del lavoro. Milano [1982] 241 p. : LC Card 84-230716
HD6276.I7 G499 1982

Federwisch, Jacques. Technologie nouvelle et ruptures régionales /. Paris , c1986. 216 p. : ISBN 2-7178-1133-8 : LC Card 86-224660
HC240.9.T4 T42 1986

Fedorenko, Nikolaĭ Prokofʹevich.
K͡hozi͡aĭstvennyĭ mekhanizm funkt͡sionirovanii͡a sot͡sialisticheskoĭ ėkonomiki /. Moskva , 1982. 358 p. ; LC Card 83-134242
HC243.5 .K47 1982

Khozi͡aĭstvennyĭ mekhanizm v sisteme optimalʹnogo funkt͡sionirovanii͡a sot͡sialisticheskoĭ ėkonomiki /. Moskva , 1985. 346 p. ; LC Card 86-114802
HC336.25 .K474 1985

Lopatnikov, L. I. (Leonid Isidorovich) Ėkonomiko-matematicheskiĭ slovarʹ /. Moskva , 1987. 509 p. : LC Card 87-164866
HB135 .L64 1987

Mezhotraslevye kompleksy v sisteme modeleĭ /. Moskva , 1983. 319 p. : LC Card 83-236937
HC336.25 .M49 1983

Programmno-t͡selevoĭ metod v planirovanii /. Moskva , 1982. 150 p. : LC Card 83-162853
HC336.25 .P6577 1982

Sistema ėkonomiko-matematicheskikh modeleĭ dli͡a analiza i prognoza urovni͡a zhizni /. Moskva , 1986. 262 p. : LC Card 86-232874
HD6978 .S56 1986

Sistema modeleĭ narodnokhozi͡aĭstvennogo planirovanii͡a /. Moskva , 1982. 375 p. ; LC Card 83-172876
HC336.25 .S564 1982

Fedorovich, V. A. (Vladimir Antonovich) Medvedkov, S. IU. (Sergeĭ IUrʹevich) Mezhdunarodnyĭ marketing amerikanskoĭ tekhnologii /. Moskva , 1985. 189 p. : LC Card 85-187077
HF1009.6 .M43 1985

Fedoseev, Petr Nikolaevich. Die Wirtschaftliche Expansion der USA . Moskau , 1986. 175 p. ; LC Card 87-408806 DDC 337.7305 19
HF1456.5.A64 W57 1986

Fedspeak . Penoyar, William F. Arnold, Md. , c1985. v, 178 p. : ISBN 0-9615112-2-2 (pbk.) : LC Card 85-90360 DDC 353.0071/2 19
JK1673 .P46 1985 ***NYPL [JLD 87-568]***

Feduniak, Robert B. Fink, Robert E. Futures trading . New York, N.Y. , c1988. xiv, 685 p. : ISBN 0-13-345745-1 : LC Card 87-24030 DDC 332.64/4 19
HG6046 .F56 1988

Fee, Derek. Oil & gas databook for developing countries : with special reference to the ACP countries / Derek Fee. London : Graham & Trotman, 1985. 215 p. : ill. ; 24 cm. Includes bibliographical references. ISBN 0-86010-617-9 : LC Card 85-208594 DDC 333.8/23/091724 19
1. Petroleum industry and trade - Developing countries - Statistics. 2. Gas industry - Developing countries - Statistics. 3. Petroleum - Developing countries - Reserves - Statistics. 4. Gas, Natural - Developing countries - Reserves Statistics. I. Title. II. Title: Oil and gas databook for developing countries.
HD9578.D44 F44 1985
NYPL [JLE 86-3684]

FEE SYSTEM (TAXATION) see TAXATION.

Feedback . Kendrick, David A. Dordrecht , Boston , 1988. vi, 147 p. : ISBN 90-247-3593-9 LC Card 87-20990 DDC 339.5 19
HB172.5 .K45 1988

Feedback from Jhabua. Pais, H. Poverty alleviation programmes . New Delhi , 1986. xii, 48, [3] p. (some folded) : LC Card 86-903597 DDC 362.5/8/09543 19
HC437.J43 P35 1986

Feeder Road Programme . Sāzmān-i Barnāmah (Iran) Tehran [1961?] ii, 117, 9 leaves, [59] leaves of plates (some folded) : LC Card 85-211363
HE365.I73 R857 1961

Feeding a billion : frontiers of Chinese agriculture / by Sylvan Wittwer ... [et al.]. East Lansing : Michigan State University Press, 1987. 462 p., [16] p. of plates : ill. (some col.) ; 26 cm. Map on lining papers. Includes bibliographies. ISBN 0-87013-246-6 (alk. paper) : LC Card 87-60024 DDC 338.1/9/51 19
1. Agriculture - Economic aspects - China. 2. Food supply - China. I. Wittwer, S. H. (Sylvan Harold), 1917-.
HD2098 .F45 1987

Feeding African cities : studies in regional social history : edited by Jane I. Guyer. Bloomington : Indiana University Press in association with the International African Institute, London, c1987. x, 249 p. ; 24 cm. (International African library) Includes bibliographies and index. CONTENTS. - Introduction / Jane I. Guyer -- Brittle trade : a political economy of food supply in Kano / Michael Watts -- Feeding Yaoundé, capital of Cameroon / Jane I. Guyer -- A century of food supply in Dar es Salaam / Deborah F. Bryceson -- The development of food supplies to Salisbury (Harare) / Paul Mosley -- Comparative epilogue / Jane I. Guyer. ISBN 0-253-32102-6 LC Card 86-46323 DDC 338.1/9/6 19
1. Food supply - Africa. 2. Cities and towns - Africa - Growth. 3. Households - Africa. I. Guyer, Jane I. II. Series.
HD9017.A2 F44 1987

Feeding the world's population : developments in the decade following the World Food Conference of 1974 : report / prepared for the Committee on Foreign Affairs, U. S. House of Representatives by the Foreign Affairs and National Defense Division, Congressional Research Service, the Library of Congress. Washington : U. S. G.P.O. : For sale by the Supt. of Docs., U. S. G.P.O., 1984. xii, 779 p. : ill. ; 24 cm. At head of title: 98th Congress, 2d session. Committee print. Distributed to some depository libraries in microfiche. "October 1984." Includes bibliographical references. S/N 052-070-05958-3 Item 1019-A, 1019-B (microfiche) LC Card 86-602524 DDC 363.8 19
1. Food supply. 2. Nutrition policy. 3. World health. 4. Agricultural innovations. 5. Food relief. 6. Surplus agricultural commodities. I. United States. Congress. House. Committee on Foreign Affairs. II. Library of Congress. Foreign Affairs and National Defense Division.
HD9000.5 .F35 1986

Feeney, Griffith.
[Estimating infant mortality rates from child survivorship data by age of mother. Spanish]
Estimación de tasas de mortalidad infantil a partir de información de sobrevivencia de hijos clasificados por edad de la madre / Griffith Feeney. Santiago de Chile : Centro Latinoamericana de Demografía, 1977. 19 p. : ill. ; 27 cm. (Serie D . no. 87) Translation of: Estimating infant mortality rates from child survivorship data by age of mother. Summary in English. Bibliography: p. 19. LC Card 83-176243
1. Infants - Tuvalu - Mortality. 2. Infants - Kiribati - Mortality. I. Series: Serie D (CELADE (Organization)) , no. 87. II. Title.
HB1323.I42 T87418 1977

Feeney, Joan. Carter, John Mack. Starting at the top . New York [1985] 252 p. ; ISBN 0-688-04520-0 LC Card 85-4826 DDC 338/.04/0922 B 19
HC102.5.A2 C37 1985
NYPL [JLD 87-1089]

Feenstra, Robert C. Empirical methods for international trade /. Cambridge, Mass. , c1988. xiv, 322 p. : ISBN 0-262-06108-2 LC Card 87-3023 DDC 382 19
HF1008 .E47 1988

FEES, ADMINISTRATIVE - NEVADA.
Nevada. Legislature. Legislative Commission. Study of the fees and taxes which produce revenue for the construction and maintenance of the highways. [Carson City, Nev.] [1986] viii, 74 p. ; LC Card 86-623141 DDC 388.1/14/09793 19
HE356.N37 N42 1986

Fees for services . Thomas, Dale F. Menomonie, WI [1986] v, 90 p. : LC Card 86-622897 DDC 338.4/33620425 19
HD7256.U5 T47 1986

Fehér, Ferenc, 1933- Doomsday or deterrence? : on the antinuclear issue / Ferenc Fehér and Agnes Heller. Armonk, N.Y. : M.E. Sharpe, Inc. c1986. 154 p. ; 24 cm. Includes bibliographical references. ISBN 0-87332-368-8 : LC Card 86-10074 DDC 327.1/74 19
1. Nuclear disarmament. 2. Antinuclear movement. I. Heller, Ágnes. II. Title.
JX1974.7 .F38 1986 ***NYPL [JLE 86-4319]***

Fehr, Hans. Europa im Umbruch . [Basel] , 1963. 91 p. ; LC Card 85-125335
HC241 .E772 1963

Fei, John C. H. Li, Kuo-ting. The evolution of policy behind Taiwan's development success /. New Haven , c1988. p. cm. ISBN 0-300-04080-6 LC Card 87-23035 DDC 338.951/249 19
HC430.5 .L4725 1988

Feibel, Charles. Gilbert, Gorman, 1943- The management and regulation of ground transportation at U. S. airports . Washington, D.C. [1986] 153 p. : LC Card 87-600652 DDC 387.7/362 19
HE9797.4.A2 G55 1986

Feider, Josef. Konsumentenreaktion auf Preise / Josef Feider. Göttingen : Vandenhoeck & Ruprecht, c1985. xii, 303 p. : ill. ; 23 cm. (Schriftenreihe des Seminars für Allgemeine Betriebswirtschaftslehre der Universität Hamburg . Bd. 29) Bibliography: p. [286]-303. ISBN 3-525-12667-0 LC Card 85-203330
1. Consumers' Research. 2. Prices. I. Title. II. Series.
HF5415.3 .F39 1985

Feigenbaum, Todd R. New York's highway system : a vital economic asset. Albany, N.Y. (150 State St., Albany 12207) : State of New York, Legislative Commission on State-Local Relations, [1986] 2, iv, 130 p. : ill. ; 23 cm. "Prepared by Todd R. Feigenbaum and Deborah L. Pierce"--fwd. Cover title. Bibliography: p. 121-130. LC Card 87-620939 DDC 388.1/09747 19
1. Roads - New York (State). 2. Roads - Government policy - New York (State). I. Pierce, Deborah L. II. New York (State). Legislature. Legislative Commission on State-Local Relations. III. Title.
HE356.N7 F45 1986

Feigenoff, Charles Samuel. Ghadar, Fariborz. U. S. industrial competitiveness . Lexington, Mass. , c1987. x, 114 p. : ISBN 0-669-15689-2 (alk. paper) LC Card 86-46341 DDC 338.4/7677/00973 19
HD9855 .G47 1987

Feigl, Helmuth. Die niederösterreichische Grundherrschaft : vom ausgehenden Mittelalter bis zu den theresianisch-josephinischen Reformen / Helmuth Feigl. [Wien] : Verein für Landeskunde von Niederösterreich und Wien, 1964. 379 p. ; 25 cm. (Forschungen zur Landeskunde von Niederösterreich. Bd. 16) Bibliography: p. 342-350. Includes indexes. LC Card 85-127367
1. Landowners - Austria - Lower Austria - History. 2. Land tenure - Austria - Lower Austria - History. 3. Lower Austria (Austria) - Genealogy. I. Title. II. Series.
HD639.L6 F45 1964

Feijoó, María del Carmen. Buscando un techo : familia y vivienda popular / María del Carmen Feijoó. Buenos Aires, Argentina : Centro de Estudios de Estado y Sociedad, [1984] 90, [5] p. : ill. ; 22 cm. (Estudios CEDES) "Reimpresión." Bibliography: p. 89-[91] LC Card 85-214586
1. Housing - Argentina - Buenos Aires Metropolitan Area. 2. Housing policy - Argentina - Buenos Aires Metropolitan Area. I. Title. II. Series.
HD7321.B9 F45 1984

Feiler, Gil. The number of Egyptian workers in the Arab oil countries, 1974-1983 : a critical discussion / Gil Feiler. Tel Aviv : Dayan Center for Middle Eastern and African Studies, Shiloah Institute, Tel Aviv University, c1986. i, 30 leaves ; 28 cm. (Occasional papers / the Dayan Center for Middle Eastern and African Studies, the Shiloah Institute, Tel Aviv University . 96) "October 1986." Based on sections of the author's thesis (M.A.--Haifa University, 1985) under title: The emigration from Egypt to the Arab oil economies, 1974-1983. Bibliography: leaves 24-30. LC Card 87-404430 DDC 331.6/2/620536 19
1. Alien labor, Egyptian - Persian Gulf Region. 2. Egypt - Emigration and immigration. 3. Persian Gulf Region - Emigration and immigration. I. Series: Occasional papers (Mekhon Shiloaḥ le-ḥeḳer) ha-Mizraḥ ha-tikhon ṿe-Afriḳah) , 96. II. Title.
HD8662 .F45 1986

Fein, Rashi. Medical care, medical costs : the search for a health insurance policy / Rashi Fein. Cambridge, Mass. : Harvard University Press, 1986. viii, 240 p. ; 25 cm. Includes bibliographical references and index. ISBN 0-674-56052-3 (alk. paper) LC Card 86-7623 DDC 368.3/82/00973 19
1. Insurance, Health - United States. 2. Medicaid -

United States. 3. Medicare - United States. 4. Medical care, Cost of - United States. I. Title.
HG9396 .F45 1986 NYPL [JLE 86-3975]

Feinberg, Richard E.
Adjustment crisis in the Third World /. New Brunswick, USA , c1984. x, 186 p. ; ISBN 0-88738-040-9 LC Card 84-8690 DDC 337/.09172/4 19
HC59.7 .A733 1984 NYPL [JLE 86-2491]

Uncertain future . New Brunswick, N.J. , c1984. x, 129 p. ; ISBN 0-88738-041-7 : LC Card 84-16240 DDC 332.1/5 19
HG3891.5 .U53 1984 NYPL [JLE 86-2494]

Feingold, S. Norman, 1914-
Emerging careers : new occupations for the year 2000 and beyond / by S. Norman Feingold and Norma Reno Miller. Garrett Park, Md. : Garrett Park Press, c1983- v. ; 23 cm. Includes index. Bibliography: v. 1, p. 145-146. CONTENTS. - v. 1. The newest of the new ISBN 0-912048-32-8 (pbk.) : LC Card 83-80074 DDC 331.7/02 19
1. Occupations - Collected works. 2. Vocational guidance - Collected works. I. Miller, Norma R. II. Title.
HF5382 .F44 1983 NYPL [JLL 86-205]

Making it on your own / by S. Norman Feingold and Leonard G. Perlman. Rev. ed. Washington, D.C. : Acropolis Books, c1985. 300 p. ; 23 cm. "Guide to financial success, what to know before you start your own business"--Cover. Includes index. Bibliography: p. 167-171. ISBN 0-87491-779-4 (pbk.) : LC Card 85-7560 DDC 658/.022 19
1. Small business - Management - Handbooks, manuals, etc. 2. Small business - Finance - Handbooks, manuals, etc. I. Perlman, Leonard G. II. Title.
HD62.7 .F44 1985
NYPL [*R-Econ. 85-4850]

Feinstein, C. H. Studies in capital formation in Great Britain . Oxford [Oxfordshire] , New York , c1988. p. cm. ISBN 0-19-828408-X : LC Card 87-15196 DDC 332/.0415/0941 19
HC260.S3 S78 1988

Feinstein, Charles, 1954- Privatization possibilities among Pacific island countries / by Charles Feinstein. Honolulu, Hawaii, USA : Pacific Islands Development Program, East-West Center, 1986. iv, 48 p. ; 23 cm. (Research report series . no. 2) Bibliography: p. 47-48. ISBN 0-86638-084-1 LC Card 86-24012 DDC 338.99 19
1. Privatization - Oceania. 2. Government ownership - Oceania. I. Series: Research report series (Pacific Islands Development Program (East-West Center)) , no. 2. II. Title.
HD4415.6 .F45 1986

Feinstein, Guy. Cabaud, Michel. 1900, la Française au quotidien /. Paris , c1985. 204 p. : ISBN 2-200-37097-0 LC Card 86-137649
HD6059.F8 C33 1985

A Feira hippie de Campinas : encruzilhadas do artesanato e da contracultura / Alba Maria Zaluar ... [et al.]. Campinas, SP, Brasil : UNICAMP, IFCH ; São Paulo, SP : Distribuição, Editora HUCITEC, 1986. 73 p. ; 28 cm. (Cadernos IFCH-UNICAMP . 18) Bibliography: p. 72-73. LC Card 87-404187 DDC 381/.18/098161 19
1. Markets - Brazil - Campinas (São Paulo). 2. Hippies - Brazil - Campinas (São Paulo). 3. Artisans - Brazil - Campinas (São Paulo). I. Zaluar, Alba. II. Series.
HF5473.B72 C364 1986

Feira Internacional de Lisboa (9th : 1968 : Lisbon, Portugal) Representação do produtos alimentares de Angola na IX Feira Internacional de Lisboa . Luanda [1968] 248 p. : LC Card 87-400609 DDC 338.7/6413/0025673 19
HD9017.A532 R46 1968

Feith, Herbert. Mortimer, Rex, 1926-1979. Stubborn survivors . [Clayton, Vic.] , 1984. xvii, 180 p. : ISBN 0-86746-299-X (pbk.) LC Card 87-672646
HC59.7 .M593x 1984

Feiwel, George R. Issues in contemporary macroeconomics and distribution /. London , 1985. xxviii, 465 p. : ISBN 0-333-35483-4 : LC Card 86-673473
HB172.5 .I87x 1985b

Fejezetek a szocialista népesedéselmélet történetéből /. Szabó, A. Ferenc. [Budapest] , 1985. 94 p. ; ISBN 963-673-318-X LC Card 86-187050
HB871 .S86 1985

A fejlett tőkés országok exportpolitikája /. Somogyi, Dorottya. Budapest , 1985. 277, [1] p. : ISBN 963-221-507-9 : LC Card 85-231848
HF1417.5 .S66 1985

Fejlődés-tanulmányok .
(3) Az Elmélet és a fegyverek kritikája . Budapest [1981] xxv, 509 p. ; ISBN 963-461-775-1 (Magy. nemz. bibl.) LC Card 85-139263
HC59.7 .E45 1981

Fekete, György, 1925- A Folyamatos árszinvonal-emelkedés társadalmi hatásai . Budapest [1985] 176 p. ; ISBN 963-608-087-9 LC Card 87-407751
HG970.5 .F65 1985

Fekete, Gyula, Dr. A Lakosság jövedelme, társadalombiztosítás, családpolitika /. Budapest [1983] 82 p. : LC Card 83-206799
HC30.295.I5 L332 1983
NYPL [JLE 87-179]

Fekete, Susan A. Crocker, Olga L. Incidents and cases in Canadian personnel administration /. Toronto , New York , c1986. 216 p. : ISBN 0-458-98690-9 (pbk.) : LC Card 86-218837 DDC 658.3/00971 19
HF5549.2.C3 C76 1986

Felbertauern . Forcher, Michael. Thaur/Tirol [1982] 152 p. : ISBN 3-85395-044-2 LC Card 86-166479
HE363.A94 F454 1982

FELBERTAUERNSTRASSE (AUSTRIA)
Forcher, Michael. Felbertauern . Thaur/Tirol [1982] 152 p. : ISBN 3-85395-044-2 LC Card 86-166479
HE363.A94 F454 1982

Feldberg, Roslyn. Hidden aspects of women's work /. New York , 1987. x, 380 p. ; ISBN 0-275-92415-7 (alk. paper) : LC Card 87-2449 DDC 331.4/133/0973 19
HD6060.5.U5 H53 1987

Felder, Stefan. Finsinger, Jörg. Der Submissionswettbewerb . Bern , c1986. 104 p. : ISBN 3-258-03617-9 : LC Card 86-224617
HD9715.S92 F56 1986

Felderer, B. (Bernhard) Beiträge zur Bevölkerungsökonomie /. Berlin , c1986. 238 p. : ISBN 3-428-05969-7 LC Card 86-172600
HB3595 .B39 1986

Feldman, Daniel C. Managing careers in organizations / Daniel C. Feldman. Glenview, Ill. : Scott, Foresman, c1988. 249 p. : ill. ; 23 cm. (Organizational behavior and psychology series) Bibliography: p. [211]-234. Includes indexes. ISBN 0-673-18562-1 (pbk.) : LC Card 87-16580 DDC 650.1/4 19
1. Personnel management. 2. Career development. I. Title. II. Series.
HF5549 .F386 1988

Feldman, Elliot J. Land rites and wrongs . Boston , 1988. p. cm. ISBN 0-89946-222-7 LC Card 87-12186 DDC 333.73/13/0971 19
HD171.A15 L28 1988

Feldman, Ernesto V. (Ernesto Víctor) Crisis financiera y endeudamiento externo en la Argentina / Ernesto Feldman, Juan Sommer. [Buenos Aires] : Centro Editor de América Latina : Centro de Economía Transnacional, c1986. 184 p. ; 22 cm. (Bibliotecas universitarias. Economía) Bibliography: p. 181-184. ISBN 950-25-1313-4 LC Card 86-182663
1. Finance - Argentina. 2. Argentina - Economic policy. 3. Debts, External - Argentina. I. Sommer, Juan. II. Centro de Economía Transnacional. III. Title. IV. Series.
HG185.A7 F45 1986

Feldman, Gerald D.
The Adaptation to inflation /. Berlin , New York , 1986. xvi, 512 p. : ISBN 0-89925-287-7 (U. S.) LC Card 86-29134 DDC 338.943 19
HC286.2 .A62 1986

Vom Weltkrieg zur Weltwirtschaftskrise : Studien zur deutschen Wirtschafts- und Sozialgeschichte, 1914-1932 / von Gerald D. Feldman. Göttingen : Vandenhoeck & Ruprecht, 1984. 272 p. ; 24 cm. (Kritische Studien zur Geschichtswissenschaft. Bd. 60) Includes bibliographical references and index. ISBN 3-525-35719-2 LC Card 85-165291
1. Germany - Economic conditions - 20th century. 2. Germany - Economic policy. 3. Germany - Industries - History - 20th century. 4. Business cycles - Germany - History - 20th century. 5. Germany - Social conditions. I. Title.
HC286.2 .F45 1984

Fel'dman, IA. I., kandidat ėkonomicheskikh nauk. Sovershenstvovanie khoziaistvennogo mekhanizma i ratsional'noe ispol'zovanie resursov . Makhachkala , 1985. 190 p. : LC Card 87-136485
HC337.D3 S655 1985

Feldmann, Berthold. Unternehmenskonzentration, Marktmacht und Lohnniveau : eine empirische Analyse für die Bundesrepublik Deutschland / Berthold Feldmann. Göttingen : Vandenhoeck & Ruprecht, c1984. xii, 260 p. : ill. ; 24 cm. (Wirtschaftspolitische Studien. 68) Originally presented as the author's thesis (doctoral)--Universität Hamburg, 1983. Bibliography: p. 240-257. Includes index. ISBN 3-525-12269-1 LC Card 85-162393
1. Consolidation and merger of corporations - Germany, West. 2. Labor supply - Germany, West. 3. Wages - Germany, West. I. Title. II. Series.
HD2746.5 .F45 1984

Feldstein, Martin S.
The Effects of taxation on capital accumulation /. Chicago , 1987. ix, 490 p. : ISBN 0-226-24088-6 : LC Card 86-25025 DDC 332/.0415 19
HJ2305 .E29 1987

Restoring growth in the debt-laden Third World . New York , 1987. x, 82 p. : ISBN 0-930503-02-3 : LC Card 87-23778 DDC 336.3/435/091724 19
HJ8899 .R47 1987

Taxes and capital formation /. Chicago , 1987. xii, 118 p. : ISBN 0-226-24079-7 LC Card 87-5898 DDC 336.2/00973 19
HJ2381 .T395 1987

Feldtheorie und Konsumverhalten /. Horn, Christel-Margret. Freiburg im Breisgau , c1983. 121 p. : ISBN 3-448-01293-9 LC Card 84-136042
HF5415.3 .H65 1983

Felici, Luigi. Immagini di industria in Italia . Roma , c1985. [128] p. : LC Card 86-145396
HC305 .I46 1985

Fels, Gerhard.
Im Wendekreis des Krebsens : Traktat über Politik und Wirtschaft / Gerhard Fels. Köln : Informedia, c1985. 91 p. ; 21 cm. ISBN 3-921349-44-3 LC Card 85-200560
1. Germany, West - Economic policy - 1974-. 2. Germany (West) - Politics and government - 1982-. I. Title.
HC286.7 .F46 1985

Mehr Flexibilität am Arbeitsmarkt / von Gerhard Fels. Kiel : Institut für Weltwirtschaft an der Universität Kiel, 1986. 21 p. ; 24 cm. (Kieler Vorträge, 0340-6970 . n.F., 110) Paper presented at the Institut für Weltwirtschaft of the Universität Kiel on Sept. 30, 1986. Bibliography: p. 21. ISBN 3-925357-37-8 LC Card 87-126264 DDC 331.25/72/0943 19
1. Hours of labor, Flexible - Germany (West). 2. Labor supply - Germany (West) - Effect of technological innovations on. I. Universität Kiel. Institut für Weltwirtschaft. II. Title. III. Series.
HD5109.2.G3 F4 1986

Methoden der Politikberatung im wirtschaftspolitischen Bereich /. Wien , 1984. 116 p. ; LC Card 84-222756
HC265 .M39 1984

Feltham, Gerald A., 1938- Economic analysis of information and contracts . Boston , c1988. p. cm. ISBN 0-89838-252-1 : LC Card 87-22508 DDC 657 19
HF5625 .E28 1988

Felügyelőbizottságok az ÁFÉSZ-ekben /. Mészáros, Sándor. [Budapest] [1976] 58 p. ; LC Card 86-187734
HD3332.5.A5 M47 1976

Fel'vintsi, T. Razvivaiushchiesia strany . Moskva , 1982. 307 p. ; LC Card 85-115259
HC59.7 .R33858 1982

FEMALE. see **WOMEN.**

The female stress syndrome . Witkin-Lanoil, Georgia. New York , c1984. xi, 211 p. ; ISBN 0-937858-33-1 LC Card 83-25038 DDC 155.6/33 19
BF575.S75 W58 1984 ***NYPL [JFD 86-10468]***

FEMININITY.
Westkott, Marcia, 1943- The feminist legacy of Karen Horney /. New Haven , c1986. viii, 242 p. ; ISBN 0-300-03706-6 (alk. paper) LC Card 86-9201 DDC 305.4/2 19
HQ1206 .W47 1986 ***NYPL [JFD 86-10266]***

FEMINISM - NORWAY.
Den Norske kvinnerevolusjonen . Oslo , c1986. 166 p. : ISBN 82-00-18318-1 LC Card 87-155462
HD6170 .N68 1986

Feminism on trial . Hawkes, Ellen. New York , c1986. 420 p. ; ISBN 0-688-04850-1 : LC Card 85-31968 DDC 305.4/2/0973 19
HQ1413.F63 H39 1986 ***NYPL [JLE 86-2863]***

FEMINISM - PHILOSOPHY.
Nicholson, Linda J. Gender and history . New York , 1986. x, 238 p. ; ISBN 0-231-06220-6 (alk. paper) LC Card 85-21281 DDC 323.3/4/01 19
HQ1206 .N7 1986 ***NYPL [JLE 86-1987]***

FEMINISM - UNITED STATES.
Astrachan, Anthony. How men feel . Garden City, N.Y. , 1986. x, 444 p. ; ISBN 0-385-23333-7 : LC Card 85-22944 DDC 305.3/1 19
HQ1090.3 .A88 1986 ***NYPL [JLE 86-3421]***

Beckwith, Karen, 1950- American women and political participation . New York , 1986. xiv, 185 p. ; ISBN 0-313-24507-X ***NYPL [JLD 87-36]***

Dimen, Muriel. Surviving sexual contradictions . New York , c1986. xxi, 257 p. ; ISBN 0-02-531620-6 LC Card 86-12600 DDC 305.4/2/0973 19
HQ1426 .D56 1986 ***NYPL [JLE 86-4385]***

Follis, Anne Bowen, 1947- I'm not a women's libber, but--and other confessions of a Christian feminist /. Nashville , c1981. 128 p. ; ISBN 0-687-18687-0 LC Card 81-1241
HQ1426 .F75 ***NYPL [JLD 85-1976]***

Hawkes, Ellen. Feminism on trial . New York , c1986. 420 p. ; ISBN 0-688-04850-1 : LC Card 85-31968 DDC 305.4/2/0973 19
HQ1413.F63 H39 1986 ***NYPL [JLE 86-2863]***

Hewlett, Sylvia Ann, 1946- A lesser life . New York, N.Y. , 1986. 461 p. : ISBN 0-688-04855-2 LC Card 85-21395 DDC 305.4/2/0973 19
HQ1426 .H457 1986 ***NYPL [JLE 86-1460]***

Mansbridge, Jane J. Why we lost the ERA /. Chicago, Ill. , c1986. xii, 327 p. ; ISBN 0-226-50358-5 (pbk.) LC Card 86-6954 DDC 305.4/2/0973 19
HQ1236.5.U6 M37 1986 ***NYPL [JLE 86-4474]***

Venkatesh, Alladi. The significance of the women's movement to marketing . New York , 1985. 209 p. ; ISBN 0-03-069588-0 (alk. paper) : LC Card 85-19106 DDC 658.8/348 19
HF5415.3 .V46 1985 ***NYPL [JLE 86-1081]***

FEMINISM - UNITED STATES - HISTORY.
Andolsen, Barbara Hilkert. "Daughters of Jefferson, daughters of bootblacks" . Macon, GA , c1986. xiv, 130 p. ; ISBN 0-86554-204-X : LC Card 86-816 DDC 305.4/2/0973 19
HQ1426 .A6827 1986 ***NYPL [JLE 86-3359]***

Balser, Diane. Sisterhood & solidarity . Boston, MA , c1987. vii, 247 p. ; ISBN 0-89608-278-4 : LC Card 87-4733 DDC 331.4 19
HD6079.2.U5 B34 1987

Lerner, Gerda, 1920- The majority finds its past . New York , 1979. xxxii, 217 p. ; ISBN 0-19-502597-0 LC Card 79-14048 DDC 301.41/2/0973
HQ1426 .L47 ***NYPL [JLD 86-3348]***

Nicholson, Linda J. Gender and history . New York , 1986. x, 238 p. ; ISBN 0-231-06220-6 (alk. paper) LC Card 85-21281 DDC 323.3/4/01 19
HQ1206 .N7 1986 ***NYPL [JLE 86-1987]***

Payne, Elizabeth Anne, 1943- Reform, labor, and feminism . Urbana , c1988. p. cm. ISBN 0-252-01445-6 (alk. paper) LC Card 87-10794 DDC 331.88/092/4 B 19
HD6079.2.U5 P38 1988

The feminist legacy of Karen Horney /. Westkott, Marcia, 1943- New Haven , c1986. viii, 242 p. ; ISBN 0-300-03706-6 (alk. paper) LC Card 86-9201 DDC 305.4/2 19
HQ1206 .W47 1986 ***NYPL [JFD 86-10266]***

Feminist perspectives .
(no. 8) Edelson, Miriam. Challenging unions . Ottawa, Ont. , 1987. 28 p. ; ISBN 0-919653-64-2 (pbk.) : LC Card 87-165425 DDC 331.88/088042 19
HD6079.2.C2 E34 1987

Beechey, Veronica. A matter of hours . Minneapolis, MN , c1987. 212 p. ; ISBN 0-8166-1641-8 : LC Card 87-12459 DDC 331.4/12/0942498 19
HD6136.Z6 C683 1987

Walby, Sylvia. Patriarchy at work . Cambridge [Cambrigeshire] , c1986. vii, 292 p. ; ISBN 0-7456-0157-X ***NYPL [JLD 87-941]***

Walby, Sylvia. Patriarchy at work . Minneapolis , c1986. vii, 292 p. ; ISBN 0-8166-1588-8 : LC Card 86-24912 DDC 331.4/133/0941 19
HD6060.65.G7 W35 1986

Feminist review. Waged work . London , 1986. vi, 291 p. : ISBN 0-86068-801-1 (pbk.) : LC Card 86-232209 DDC 331.4/0941 19
HD6061.2.G7 W35 1986

FEMINISTS - UNITED STATES - BIOGRAPHY.
Hawkes, Ellen. Feminism on trial . New York , c1986. 420 p. ; ISBN 0-688-04850-1 : LC Card 85-31968 DDC 305.4/2/0973 19
HQ1413.F63 H39 1986 ***NYPL [JLE 86-2863]***

Salmond, John A. Miss Lucy of the CIO . Athens , c1988. p. cm. ISBN 0-8203-0956-7 (alk. paper) LC Card 87-5822 DDC 331.88/33/0924 B 19
HD6509.M375 S25 1988

Femmes à l'usine . Fourcaut, Annie, 1950- Paris , 1982. 268 p. : ISBN 2-7071-1258-5 : LC Card 82-151587
HD6145 .F65 1982

Les Femmes au travail 1882-1982 / [organisé par le] Ministère des droits de la femme. Paris : Le Ministère, 1982. [70] leaves : ill. ; 21 cm. "Le catalogue de l'exposition 'Les femmes au travail 1882-1982' a été réalisé par Janine Niepce pour le Ministère des droits de la femme"--Colophon. Photocopy. [S.l. : s.n., 1986] 21 cm. LC Card 86-161448
1. Women - Employment - France - History - Exhibitions. 2. Working class women - France - History - Exhibitions. I. Niepce, Janine. II. France. Ministère des droits de la femme.
HD6145 .F44 1982

Femmes du tiers-monde . Bisilliat, Jeanne. Paris , c1983. 122 p. : ISBN 2-86262-201-X ***NYPL [JLD 87-456]***

Les femmes et l'emploi /. Rheault, Sylvie. [Québec] [1983] 64 p. ; ISBN 2-550-10471-4 LC Card 85-108850 DDC 331.4/09714 19
HD6100.Q4 R44 1983

Femmes et politiques alimentaires . Séminaire international sur la place des femmes dans l'autosuffisance et les stratégies alimentaires (1985 : Paris, France) Paris , 1985. 741 p. : ISBN 2-7099-0763-1 LC Card 86-205282
HD6073.A292 D4477 1985

Fencl, George. The central Florida career guide / by George Fencl, Jr. and Janie Pritchett. Altamonte Springs, FL. : Edge Pub., c1987. 56, 48 p. : ill., map ; 28 cm. ISBN 0-942827-00-7 (pbk.) : LC Card 87-402073 DDC 650.1/4/09759 19
1. Job hunting - Florida. 2. Professions - Florida. 3. Florida - Occupations. 4. Business enterprises - Florida - Directories. I. Pritchett, Janie. II. Title.
HF5382.75.U62 F64 1987

Fenn, Scott. Institutional investment in renewable energy technologies / [Scott Fenn]. Washington, D.C. : Investor Responsibility Research Center : Renewable Energy Institute, c1987. iii, 50 p. : ill. ; 28 cm. "Prepared by the Investor Responsibility Research Center for educational purposes under a subcontract with the Renewable Energy Institute for the Solar Energy Research Institute under SERI subcontract no. XK-5-05082-1"--P. 2 of cover. "February 1987." Bibliography: p. 49-50. ISBN 0-930135-17-1 (pbk.) LC Card 87-401940 DDC 332.6/722 19
1. Renewable energy sources - United States - Finance. 2. Renewable energy sources - Research - United States - Finance. 3. Institutional investments - United States. I. Investor Responsibility Research Center. II. Renewable Energy Institute. III. Solar Energy Research Institute. IV. Title.
HD9502.U52 F46 1987

Fennefoss, Arvid. Colbjørnsen, Tom. Så samles vi på valen--? . [Oslo?] [1985] 88 p. : ISBN 82-991187-5-1 LC Card 85-220350
HD6752 .C644 1985

El Fenómeno migratorio en el Paraguay / Conferencia Episcopal Paraguaya, Equipo Nacional de Pastoral Social. Asunción, Paraguay : El Equipo Nacional, [1985] 258 p. : ill. ; 21 cm. (Cuadernos de pastoral social . 5) Bibliography: p. 208-212. LC Card 86-100044
1. Migration, Internal - Paraguay. 2. Paraguay - Emigration and immigration. I. Catholic Church. Conferencia Episcopal Paraguaya. Equipo Nacional de Pastoral Social. II. Series.
HB2033 .F45 1985

Feodālisms Baltijas reģionā : zinātnisko rakstu krājums / [redkolēģija A. Rolova (atbildīgā redaktore) ... et al.]. Rīga : P. Stučkas Latvijas Valsts universitāte, 1985. 147 p. : ill. ; 21 cm. Latvian and Russian. Title on added t.p.: Feodalizm v Baltiĭskom regione. At head of title: Latvijas PSR Augstākās un vidējās speciālās izglītības ministrija, Ar Darba Sarkanā Karoga ordeni apbalvotā Pētera Stučkas Latvijas Valsts universitāte, Seno un viduslaiku vēstures katedra. Includes bibliographies. LC Card 86-177836
1. Baltic States - Economic conditions. 2. Baltic States - History. 3. Latvia - Economic conditions. 4. Latvia - History - 1562-1918. I. Rolova, Aleksandra, 1920-. II. Pētera Stučkas Latvijas Valsts universitāte. Seno un viduslaiku vēstures katedra. III. Title: Feodalizm v Baltiĭskom regione.
HC243 .F46 1985

Feodalizm v Baltiĭskom regione. Feodālisms Baltijas reģionā . Rīga , 1985. 147 p. : LC Card 86-177836
HC243 .F46 1985

Ferber, Marianne A., 1923- Blau, Francine D. The economics of women, men, and work /. Englewood Cliffs, N.J. , c1986. xiv, 365 p. : ISBN 0-13-233719-3 LC Card 85-30746 DDC 305.3/0973 19
HQ1426 .B62 1986 ***NYPL [JLE 86-4254]***

Ferdinand von Steinbeis . Müller, Fr. (Friedrich), Dr. Tübingen , 1907. vi, 215 p. : LC Card 85-666358
HC282.5.S67 M85x 1907

Fereidun Fesharaki. see **Fesharaki, Fereidun.**

Ferguson, Gary D. Evaluation of the small cities community development block grant program--the role of the counties [microform] / by Gary D. Ferguson, Brian O. Burwell with Maynard T. Robison, R. Kent Shaffer. Cambridge, Mass. : Urban Systems Research and Engineering, 1981. vii, vi, 186 p. ; 28 cm. "October, 1981." "Contract no. H-5075." Prepared for Department of Housing and Urban Development Office of Policy Development and Research. Cover title: An evaluation of the small cities program: the role of the counties Microfiche. Springfield, Va. : NTIS, 1983. 3 microfiches : negative ; 11 x 15 cm. (PB83-186015)
1. Federal aid to community development - United States. 2. Block grants - United States. 3. Community development, Urban - United States. I. Burwell, Brian O. II. Robison, Maynard T. III. Shaffer, R. Kent. IV. Urban Systems Research & Engineering. V. Title. VI. Title: Evaluation of the small cities program--the role of the counties. ***NYPL [*XME-11,283]***

Ferguson, Henry. Tomorrow's global executive / Henry Ferguson. Homewood, Ill. : Dow Jones-Irwin, c1988. xiii, 265 p. : ill. ; 24 cm. Bibliography: p. 237-248. Includes index. ISBN 1-15-562305-75 LC Card 87-71259 DDC 658/.049 19
1. International business enterprises - Management. I. Title.
HD62.4 .F47 1988

Ferguson, Jerry T., 1938- Managing real estate taxes / Jerry T. Ferguson and Edward C. Spede. Westport, Conn. : Quorum Books, 1986. x, 185 p. ; 25 cm. Includes index. Bibliography: p. [18] ISBN 0-89930-106-1 (lib. bdg. : alk. paper) LC

Card 85-6360 DDC 343.7305/46 347.303546 19
1. Real property and taxation - United States. 2. Tax planning - United States. I. Spede, Edward C. II. Title.
HJ4181 .F47 1986 ***NYPL [JLE 86-2439]***

Ferguson, Sherry. Organizational communication /. New Brunswick, N.J., U. S.A. , c1987. p. cm. ISBN 0-88738-164-2 : LC Card 87-13856 DDC 658.4/5 19
HD30.3 .O72 1987

Ferguson, Stewart. Organizational communication /. New Brunswick, N.J., U. S.A. , c1987. p. cm. ISBN 0-88738-164-2 : LC Card 87-13856 DDC 658.4/5 19
HD30.3 .O72 1987

Ferk, Hans S., 1945- Gemeinkosten abbauen durch Wertanalyse : was tun? / Hans S. Ferk. Zürich : Verlag Moderne Industrie, c1983. 128 p. : ill. ; 26 cm. (Praxisratgeber) Bibliography: p. 126. Includes index. ISBN 3-478-36120-6 : LC Card 84-108512
1. Value analysis (Cost control). I. Title. II. Series.
HD47.3 .F47 1983

FERMOY POOR LAW UNION (FERMOY, CORK) - HISTORY - 19TH CENTURY. Garner, Edward. To die by inches . Fermoy, Co. Cork, Ireland , c1986. 133 p. : ISBN 0-907568-03-3 (pbk.) : LC Card 87-111519 DDC 363.5/85/094195 19
HC260.5.Z7 F474 1986

Fernandes, Adelita Neto Carleial. Condições de vida nos bairros de Fortaleza, nov/84 a mar/85 : relatório de pesquisa. Fortaleza : Governo do Estado do Ceará, Secretaria de Planejamento e Coordenação, Fundação Instituto de Planejamento do Ceará, 1986. 92 p. : map ; 22 cm. Prepared by Adelita Neto Carleial Fernandes, Maria das Graças de Sousa, and Maria Neuman Ribeiro Moreira. LC Card 86-196902
1. Fortaleza (Brazil) - Economic conditions. 2. Fortaleza (Brazil) - Social conditions. 3. Cost and standard of living - Brazil - Fortaleza. 4. Community development, Urban - Brazil - Fortaleza. 5. Municipal services - Brazil - Fortaleza. I. Sousa, Maria das Graças de. II. Moreira, Maria Neuman Ribeiro. III. Fundação Instituto de Planejamento do Ceará. IV. Title.
HC189.F67 F47 1986

Fernandes, Antónia Maria de Araújo. Paiva, Francisco Ismar Martins. Projeto Pesca Industrial à Vela. [Natal, Brazil] [1982 or 1983] 91 p. : LC Card 85-102872
HD9464.B73 R487 1982

Fernandes, Fátima Sobral. Aspectos de transporte urbano na modificação dos horários de trabalho / Fátima Sobral Fernandes. Brasília, DF : EBTU, 1985. 105 p. : ill. ; 28 cm. (Série Teses / Empresa Brasileira dos Transportes Urbanos . 5) Summary also in English and French. Originally presented as the author's thesis (mestre em ciências de transporte)--Instituto Militar de Engenharia, 1982. Bibliography: p. 103-105. LC Card 87-404953 DDC 331.25/72 19
1. Hours of labor - Brazil. 2. Local transit - Brazil - Employees. 3. Local transit - Brazil. I. Series: Série Teses / Empresa Brasileira dos Transportes Urbanos , 5. II. Title.
HD5108.2.B6 F47 1985

Fernández Alvarez, Antonio. El impacto de la política agrícola común en la integración española / Antonio Fernández Alvarez. Madrid : Fundación Juan March, [1986?] 48 p. ; 21 cm. (Serie universitaria (Fundación Juan March) . 230) "Edición no venal de 300 ejemplares." Bibliography: p. 48. ISBN 84-7075-333-9 LC Card 87-111468
1. European Economic Community - Spain. 2. Agriculture and state - European Economic Community countries. I. Series. II. Series: Serie universitaria (Fundación Juan March) , 230. III. Title.
HC241.25.S6 F47 1986

Fernández, Arturo. Ideologías de los grupos dirigentes sindicales / Arturo Fernández. Buenos Aires : Centro Editor de América Latina, c1986. 2 v. ; 18 cm. (Biblioteca Política argentina . 142, 144) Bibliography: v. 2, p. 141-143. CONTENTS. - 1. [without special title] -- 2. 1966-1973. ISBN 950-25-1403-3 (v. 1) LC Card 86-205687
1. Trade-unions - Argentina - Officials and employees - Political activity - History. 2. Labor and laboring classes - Argentina - Political activity - History. 3. Peronism - History. I. Series. II. Series: Biblioteca Política argentina , 142, etc. III. Title.
HD6603.5 .F47 1986

Fernandez, John P., 1941- Survival in the corporate fishbowl : making it into upper and middle management / by John P. Fernandez. Lexington, Mass. : Lexington Books, c1987. xiii, 314 p. : ill. ; 24 cm. Bibliography: p. [297]-301. Includes index. ISBN 0-669-10336-5 (alk. paper) LC Card 85-40021 DDC 302.3/5 19
1. Industrial sociology - United States. 2. Discrimination in employment - United States. 3. Executives - United States. 4. Office politics - United States. 5. Quality of work life - United States. I. Title.
HD6957.U6 F47 1987

Fernández Navarrete, Donato. Fanjul Martín, Enrique. La evolución de la política monetaria española (1940-1978) . [Madrid] , 1979. 164 p. ; LC Card 85-202991
HG1135 .F35 1979

Fernández Ordóñez, Francisco. España y la CEE : movimiento de capitales y banca / ponencia presentada por D. Francisco Fernández Ordóñez. Madrid, España : Banco Exterior de España, Servicio de Estudios Económicos, 1985. 74 p. ; 23 cm. (Serie CEE) Includes bibliographical references. ISBN 84-505-4317-0 LC Card 86-151137
1. Banks and banking - European Economic Community countries. 2. Capital movements - European Economic Community countries. 3. European Economic Community - Spain. I. Title. II. Series.
HG2980.5.A6 F47 1985

Fernandez, Ray. Prakash, Arun J. Financial, commercial, and mortgage mathematics and their applications /. New York , 1987. x, 245 p. ; ISBN 0-275-92119-0 (alk. paper) : LC Card 86-30579 DDC 513/.93 19
HF5691 .P69 1987

Fernández, Rufino. Mock Cedeño, Ariel. Las empresas públicas en Panamá . Panamá, Rep. de Panamá , 1986. vi, 89, [5] p. ; LC Card 87-400433 DDC 338.97287 19
HD4043 .M63 1986

Fernández Russo, Omar. Elementos de economía para uso de no economistas / Omar Fernández Russo. Caracas : Fondo Editorial de Humanidades y Educación, Universidad Central Venezuela, 1985. 226 p. : ill. ; 22 cm. (Colección Estudio) Bibliography: p. 225-226. LC Card 85-240123
1. Economics. I. Series: Colección Estudio (Universidad Central de Venezuela. Fondo Editorial de Humanidades y Educación). II. Title.
HB178.5 .F38 1985

Fernández, Sonia. Análisis comparativo de la información sobre población ocupada : censos de población y agrícola / Sonia Fernández, José B. Morelos. México, D.F. : Centro Nacional de Información y Estadísticas del Trabajo, [1977] 28 p. ; 24 cm. (Serie Avances de investigación . 5) Includes bibliographical references. LC Card 84-227473
1. Labor supply - Mexico. 2. Agricultural laborers - Mexico. 3. Mexico - Census. I. Morelos, José B. II. Title.
HD5731.A6 F46 1977

Fernández Tabío, Luis René.
Apuntes sobre el capital financiero en Estados Unidos : la conexión sudafricana / Luis R. Fernández Tabío, Rafael Hernández. La Habana : Centro de Estudios sobre América, 1981 [i.e. 1982] ii, 74 p. : ill. ; 27 cm. (Avances de investigación . no. 11) Summary in English. Cover title: Apuntes sobre el capital financiero en los Estados Unidos. Includes bibliographical references. LC Card 87-401153
1. Investments, American - South Africa. 2. Disinvestment - United States. 3. Disinvestment - South Africa. I. Hernández, Rafael. II. Centro de Estudios sobre América. III. Series: Avances de investigación (Havana, Cuba) , no. 11. IV. Title.
HG5851.A3 F47 1982

Los intereses económicos en la producción militar de los Estados Unidos / Luis René Fernández Tabío. La Habana : Centro de Estudios sobre América, 1982. ii, 87 p. : ill. ; 27 cm. (Avances de investigación . no. 14) Bibliography: p. 82-87. LC Card 87-400639 DDC 338.4/76234/0973 19
1. Munitions - Economic aspects - United States. I. Centro de Estudios sobre América. II. Series: Avances de investigación (Havana, Cuba) , no. 14. III. Title.
HD9743.U6 F46 1982

Fernando, Vijita. Punchiwilaththawa, household study of a dry zone village / by Vijita Fernando. Colombo, Sri Lanka : NGO Water Supply & Sanitation Decade Service, 1986. 36 p. : maps ; 31 cm. (Case study series . no. 2) LC Card 86-902299 DDC 330.9549/3 19
1. Punchiwilaththawa (Sri Lanka) - Economic conditions. 2. Punchiwilaththawa (Sri Lanka) - Social conditions. I. Series: Case study series (NGO Water Supply & Sanitation Decade Service (Sri Lanka)) , no. 2. II. Title.
HC424.Z7 P864 1986

Fernseh-Export der Bundesrepublik Deutschland. Gebrewold, Kiflemariam. Fernsehexport der Bundesrepublik Deutschland . Bochum , 1983. xiv, 316 p. : ISBN 3-88339-317-7 LC Card 83-232957
HE8700.66.G3 G43 1983

Fernsehen der DDR. Abteilung Öffentlichkeitsarbeit. Katins, Sabine. All you need is freedom . Berlin [1977] 35 p. : LC Card 86-207107 DDC 968.91/05 19
HC910 .K37 1977

Fernsehexport der Bundesrepublik Deutschland . Gebrewold, Kiflemariam. Bochum , 1983. xiv, 316 p. : ISBN 3-88339-317-7 LC Card 83-232957
HE8700.66.G3 G43 1983

Ferragni, Fabrizio. Guida al primo lavoro / Fabrizio Ferragni, Raffaello Masci ; introduzione di Romano Prodi. 1a ed. Milano : Rizzoli, 1986. 271 p. : ill. ; 18 cm. (BUR. 617) Novità Manuali BUR ISBN 88-17-13617-4 : LC Card 86-193250
1. Youth - Employment - Italy. 2. Job hunting - Italy. I. Masci, Raffaello. II. Title.
HD6276.I7 F47 1986

Ferrante, Gianni. Il Futuro del sindacato /. Roma , c1986. xxvii, 347 p. ; LC Card 86-223517
HD6709 .F88 1986

FERRARA (ITALY : PROVINCE) - HISTORY. Dean, Trevor. Land and power in late medieval Ferrara . Cambridge , New York , 1988. xiv, 212 p. : ISBN 0-521-33127-7 LC Card 87-6583 DDC 333.3/0945/45 19
HD679.F47 D43 1988

Ferrari, Paul L. U. S. arms exports : policies and contractors / Paul L. Ferrari, Jeffrey W. Knopf, Raúl L. Madrid. Washington, DC : Investor Responsibility Research Center, c1987. xii, 342 p. : ill. ; 26 cm. Includes bibliographies. ISBN 0-931035-12-0 (pbk.) LC Card 87-80032 DDC 382/.456234/0971 19
1. Munitions - United States. 2. Munitions - Government policy - United States. 3. Military assistance, American. I. Knopf, Jeffrey W. II. Madrid, Raúl L. III. Investor Responsibility Research Center. IV. Title.
HD9743.U6 F47 1987

Ferreira, António Fonseca. A acumulação capitalista em Portugal : das origens da nacionalidade aos inícios do século XIX / António Fonseca Ferreira. Porto : Afrontamento, 1977. 156 p. ; 21 cm. Includes bibliographical references. LC Card 85-194898
1. Portugal - Commerce - History. 2. Nationalism - Portugal - History. 3. Saving and investment - Portugal - History. 4. Industry and state - Portugal - History. 5. Portugal - Social conditions. I. Title.
HF3696 .F47 1977

Ferreira, António Mega.

Ferreira, Assuéro. As pequenas e médias empresas na expansão industrial brasileira : com ênfase para o Estado do Ceará / Assuéro Ferreira. Fortaleza-Ceará : Federação das Indústrias do Estado do Ceará, Instituto Euvaldo Lodi-Núcleo Regional do Ceará, 1985. 68 p. ; 21 cm. Bibliography: p. 67-68. LC Card 87-102632 DDC 338.6/42/098131 19
1. Small business - Brazil - Ceará (State). I. Title.
HD2346.B72 C445 1985

Ferreira, Benedito, 1932- A questão fundiária / Benedito Ferreira. Brasília : Senado Federal, Centro Gráfico, 1986. 171 p. ; 23 cm. Cover title: A questão fundiária (ocupação das terras brasileiras) LC Card 86-229678
1. Land tenure - Brazil. 2. Brazil - Public lands. 3. Land reform - Brazil. I. Title. II. Title: Questão fundiária

(ocupação das terras brasileiras).
HD496 .F42 1986

Ferreira, Eduardo de Sousa, 1936- Reintegração dos emigrantes portugueses : integração na CEE e desenvolvimento económico / Eduardo de Sousa Ferreira. [Lisbon] : Associaçao de Estudantes do Instituto Superior de Economia, 1984. xiv, 137 p. ; 20 cm. At head of title: Centro de Estudos da Dependência, CEDEP. Bibliography: p. [115]-137. LC Card 86-132652
1. Alien labor, Portuguese - European Economic Community countries. 2. Return migration - Portugal. 3. Portugal - Emigration and immigration - Government policy. 4. European Economic Community countries - Emigration and immigration - Government policy. 5. Emigrant remittances - Portugal. I. Centro de Estudos da Dependência (Lisbon, Portugal). II. Title.
HD8380.5 .F47 1984

Ferreira Filho, Manoel Gonçalves, 1934- A Intervenção do estado na economia . Brasília, D.F. , c1985. 83 p. ; ISBN 85-23-00198-0 : LC Card 87-102646 DDC 338.1/7373/0981 19
HD9199.B7 I628 1985

Ferreira, Maria Emília Cordeiro. Reflexões sobre história e cultura portuguesa . Lisboa , 1985. 286 p. ; LC Card 86-135021 DDC 946.9 19
HC392 .R34 1985

Ferrell, O. C. Strategic marketing for nonprofit organizations . Englewood Cliffs, NJ , c1987. x, 386 p. : ISBN 0-13-851312-0 (pbk.) : LC Card 86-25262 DDC 658.8 19
HF5415 .C2854 1987

Ferrer, José Vallés. see **Vallés Ferrer, José.**

Ferrer Roselló, Clemente, 1938- Los profesionales : la publicidad en España / Clemente Ferrer Roselló. Madrid : Ibérico Europea de Ediciones, [1984?] 643 p. : ports. ; 24 cm. Cover title. Includes bibliographical references. ISBN 84-256-0424-9 LC Card 86-213550
1. Advertising - Spain. I. Title.
HF5813.S8 F47 1984

Ferrero Costa, Eduardo. El Perú frente al capital extranjero . Lima, Perú [1985] xl, 399 p. : LC Card 86-109611 DDC 332.6/73/0985 19
HG5392 .P47 1985 **NYPL [JLD 87-384]**

Ferrier, Charles W. Crichton, Susan. Understanding factoring and trade credit /. London , 1986. xv, 199 p. : ISBN 0-08-039204-0 (pbk.) : LC Card 87-122377 DDC 658.8/8 19
HG3752.3 .C75 1986

FERRIES - GREECE - CRETE.
Kalitsounakēs, Dēmētrios E. Aristopoiēsis paragōgēs Krētēs eis to plaision tēs Eurōpaikēs Oik. Koinotētos /. Hērakleion Krētēs , 1963. p. 167-173 ; LC Card 86-235201
HE595.F3 K35 1963

FERRIES - HUDSON RIVER (N.Y. AND N.J.) - HISTORY - 20TH CENTURY.
Baxter, Raymond J., 1928- Railroad ferries of the Hudson . Woodcliff Lake, NJ , 1987. viii, 254 p. : ISBN 0-910389-01-2 : LC Card 87-22782 DDC 386/.2234/097473 19
HE5774. B39 1987

FERRIES - NORTH AMERICA.
Murphy, Michael, 1927- Ferryliner vacations in North America . New York , c1988. ix, 277 p. : ISBN 0-525-48355-1 (pbk.) : LC Card 87-13640 DDC 910/.2/02 19
HE5772.A3 M87 1988

Ferries of America . Wright, Sarah Bird. Atlanta, Ga. , c1987. 547 p. : ISBN 0-934601-13-5 (pbk.) : LC Card 86-63530 DDC 387.2/34/0973 19
HE5773.A3 W75 1987

FERRIES - UNITED STATES - HANDBOOKS, MANUALS, ETC.
Wright, Sarah Bird. Ferries of America . Atlanta, Ga. , c1987. 547 p. : ISBN 0-934601-13-5 (pbk.) : LC Card 86-63530 DDC 387.2/34/0973 19
HE5773.A3 W75 1987

Ferris, Kenneth R.
Behavioral accounting research . Columbus, Ohio , c1988. ix, 368 p. : ISBN 0-939787-02-4 (pbk.) : LC Card 87-24980 DDC 657/.072 19
HF5630 .B43 1988

Financial accounting and corporate reporting : a casebook / Kenneth R. Ferris. Plano, Tex. : Business Publications, 1987. xi, 422 p. : ill. ; 25 cm. ISBN 0-256-03554-7 (pbk.) LC Card 86-71236 DDC 657/.3 19
1. Corporations - Accounting - Case studies. 2. Financial statements - Case studies. 3. Corporation reports - Case studies. 4. Accounting - Case studies. I. Title.
HF5686.C7 F455 1987

Management planning and control . Beavercreek, Ohio , c1987. xvii, 249 p. : ISBN 0-939787-00-8 (pbk.) : LC Card 86-24930 DDC 658.1/511 19
HF5635 .M236 1987

Ferris, Sally A. Federal subsidies to rail passenger service : an assessment of Amtrak. Washington, D.C. : Congress of the United States, Congressional Budget Office : For sale by the Supt. of Docs., U. S. G.P.O., [1982] xxiii, 85, [1] p. : ill., 1 map ; 26 cm. (A CBO study) "July 1982"--Cover. Cover title: Federal subsidies for rail passenger service. S/N 052-070-05747-5 Item 1005-C Includes bibliographical references. LC Card 82-602556 DDC 385/.1 19
1. Amtrak - Appropriations and expenditures. 2. Amtrak - Finance. 3. Railroads - United States - Passenger traffic. 4. Federal aid to transportation - United States. I. Title. II. Title: Federal subsidies for rail passenger service.
HE1061 .F47 1982 **NYPL [JLF 86-1384]**

FERROCARRIL MEXICANO - HISTORY.
Schmidt, Arthur, 1943- The social and economic effect of the railroad in Puebla and Veracruz, Mexico, 1867-1911 /. New York , 1987. 297 p. : ISBN 0-8240-1370-0 (alk. paper) : LC Card 87-8628 DDC 385/.0972/48 19
HE2819.P84 S35 1987

FERROCARRIL VERACRUZ AL PACÍFICO STRIKE, 1900.
Zilli Manica, José Benigno. Braceros italianos para México . Xalapa, México , 1986. 93 p., [6] p. of plates : ISBN 968-8340-45-6 LC Card 87-400059
HD8118.5.I83 Z55 1986

Ferrocarril y mercado interior en España, 1874-1913 /. Gómez Mendoza, Antonio. Madrid , 1984- v. : ISBN 84-500-9728-2 (v. 1) LC Card 85-215275 DDC 385/.24/0946 19
HE2469 .G66 1984 **NYPL [JLL 86-176]**

FERROUS METAL INDUSTRIES. see **STEEL INDUSTRY AND TRADE; IRON INDUSTRY AND TRADE.**

FERROVIA PARANAGUÁ-CURITIBA - HISTORY.
Trevisan, Edilberto. Ao apito do trem . [Curitiba] , 1985-1986 [i.e. 1986] 123 p. : LC Card 87-121016 DDC 385/.0981/62 19
HE2930.P34 T74 1986

Ferrucci, Ricardo Jorge. La promoción industrial en Argentina / Ricardo J. Ferrucci. [Buenos Aires] : Editorial Universitaria de Buenos Aires, c1986. 274 p. : ill. ; 23 cm. (Colección Temas) Bibliography: p. 267-270. ISBN 950-23-0307-5 LC Card 87-124151 DDC 338.982 19
1. Industry and state - Argentina. 2. Industrial promotion - Argentina. I. Series: Colección Temas (Editorial Universitaria de Buenos Aires). II. Title.
HD3616.A73 F47 1986

Ferryliner vacations in North America . Murphy, Michael, 1927- New York , c1988. ix, 277 p. : ISBN 0-525-48355-1 (pbk.) : LC Card 87-13640 DDC 910/.2/02 19
HE5772.A3 M87 1988

Fertig, Klaus.
Borrmann, Axel. Die Wettbewerbsposition natürlicher Rohstoffe . Hamburg , 1984. 226 p. : ISBN 3-87895-250-3 LC Card 84-222130
HF1054.G4 B67 1984

Ölangebotsmodelle : Entscheidungshilfen für die Wirtschaftspolitik? / Klaus Fertig. Hamburg : Verlag Weltarchiv, 1986. 236 p. : ill. ; 24 cm. (Veröffentlichungen des HWWA-Institut für Wirtschaftsforschung-Hamburg) Bibliography: p. 219-236. ISBN 3-87895-302-X LC Card 86-225350
1. Petroleum industry and trade - Econometric models. I. Title.
HD9502.A2 F46 1986

The Fertile Crescent, 1800-1914 : a documentary economic history / Charles Issawi [editor]. New York : Oxford University Press, 1987. p. cm. (Studies in Middle Eastern history) Bibliography: p. Includes index. ISBN 0-19-504951-9 LC Card 86-33275 DDC 330.956 19
1. Middle East - Economic conditions - 19th century. 2. Middle East - History - 1517-. I. Issawi, Charles Philip. II. Series: Studies in Middle Eastern history (New York, N.Y.).
HC415.15 .F47 1987

Fertiliser Association of India.
Growth and modernisation of fertiliser industry . New Delhi , 1987. 1 v. (various pagings) : LC Card 87-902183 DDC 338.4/766862/0954 19
HD9483.I42 G78 1987

Gupta, Uttam. Impact of credit on fertiliser consumption /. New Delhi [1986] 158 p. ; LC Card 87-900336 DDC 338.4/766862/0954 19
HD9483.I42 G86 1986

Fertility and mortality : theory, methodology and emperical issues / edited by K. Mahadevan with P.J. Reddy & D.A. Naidu. New Delhi ; Beverly Hills : Sage Publications, 1986. 351 p. ; 25 cm. Includes bibliographies. ISBN 0-8039-9497-4 LC Card 85-22287 DDC 304.6/3 19
1. Fertility, Human - Addresses, essays, lectures. 2. Fertility, Human - India - Case studies - Addresses, essays, lectures. 3. Mortality - Addresses, essays, lectures. I. Mahadevan, K., 1940-. II. Reddy, P. J. III. Naidu, D. A.
HB901 .F468 1986 **NYPL [JLE 86-4122]**

Fertility decline in a traditional society . Streatfield, K. [Canberra, ACT] , 1986. xvii, 177 p. : ISBN 0-86784-711-5 (pbk.) LC Card 86-213262 DDC 304.6/32/095986 19
HB1058.B34 S87 1986

FERTILITY, HUMAN.
Culture and reproduction . Boulder, Colo. , 1986. xix, 389 p. : ISBN 0-8133-7199-6 (pbk. : alk. paper) : LC Card 86-5671 DDC 304.6/32 19
HB887 .C85 1986 **NYPL [JLE 86-3842]**

Linde, Hans. Theorie der säkularen Nachwuchsbeschränkung 1800 bis 2000 /. Frankfurt [am Main] , New York , c1984. 201 p. ; ISBN 3-593-33385-6 LC Card 85-131521
HB901 .L55 1984

Nerlove, Marc, 1933- Household and economy . Boston , 1987. xiii, 155 p. : ISBN 0-12-515752-5 LC Card 86-10764 DDC 304.6/32 19
HB901 .N47 1987 **NYPL [JLE 87-1715]**

Population geography . London , Dover, N.H. , c1986. 322 p. : ISBN 0-7099-4045-9 : LC Card 86-6210 DDC 304.6 19
HB1951 .P653 1986 **NYPL [JLD 86-3692]**

World Fertility Survey . Oxford [Oxfordshire] , New York , 1986. p. cm. ISBN 0-19-828525-6 : LC Card 86-23483 DDC 304.6/32/0732 19
HB901 .H664 1986

FERTILITY, HUMAN - ADDRESSES, ESSAYS, LECTURES.
Fertility and mortality . New Delhi , Beverly Hills , 1986. 351 p. ; ISBN 0-8039-9497-4 LC Card 85-22287 DDC 304.6/3 19
HB901 .F468 1986 **NYPL [JLE 86-4122]**

FERTILITY, HUMAN - AFRICA - CONGRESSES.
Determinants of fertility in some African and Asian countries. Cairo , 1982. 698 p. : LC Card 84-960893 DDC 304.6/32 19
HB1071.7.A3 D48 1982
NYPL [JLL 73-297 no.10]

Expert Group Meeting on Fertility and Mortality Levels and Trends in Africa and Their Policy Implications (1979 : Monrovia, Liberia) Population dynamics . [Addis Ababa] [1981] ix, 581 p. : LC Card 82-980086 DDC 304.6/3/096 19
HB3661.A3 E9 1979 **NYPL [JLF 83-591]**

FERTILITY, HUMAN - AFRICA, SUB-SAHARAN.
Frank, Odile. The demand for fertility control in Sub-Saharan Africa /. New York, N.Y., U. S.A. (1 Dag Hammarskjold Plaza, New York 10017) [1985] 50 p. ; LC Card 86-204127 DDC 363.9/6/09624 19
HB1071.A3 F69 1985

Locoh, Thérèse. La fécondité en Afrique noire /. Lomé [1985] 36, 22 leaves : LC Card 87-126644
HB1071 .L63 1985

FERTILITY, HUMAN - ASIA - CASE STUDIES.
Fertility in Asia . London , 1986. xix, 177 p. :

ISBN 0-86187-667-9 DDC 304.6/32/095 19
HB1043.A3 F47 1986b
NYPL [JLD 87-1268]

FERTILITY, HUMAN - ASIA - CONGRESSES.
Determinants of fertility in some African and Asian countries. Cairo , 1982. 698 p. : LC Card 84-960893 DDC 304.6/32 19
HB1071.7.A3 D48 1982
NYPL [JLL 73-297 no.10]

FERTILITY, HUMAN - BANGLADESH.
Mabud, Mohammed A. (Mohammed Abdul) Women's development, income, and fertility /. Dhaka , 1985. xi, 180 p. ; LC Card 85-903972 DDC 305.4/09549/2 19
HQ1745.6 .M33 1985 ***NYPL [JLD 86-2067]***

Noman, Ayesha. Status of women and fertility in Bangladesh /. Dhaka, Bangladesh , c1983. xv, 91 p. ; LC Card 83-905271 DDC 305.4/2/095492 19
HB1050.6.A3 N65 1983
NYPL [JLD 86-2056]

FERTILITY, HUMAN - BERMUDA ISLANDS - STATISTICS.
A Review of birth statistics, Bermuda, 1971-1978 /. [Hamilton] [1980] 62 p. ; LC Card 85-189032 DDC 304.6/3/097299021 19
HB1078.A3 R48 1980 ***NYPL [JLF 85-3121]***

FERTILITY, HUMAN - CHINA.
Greenhalgh, Susan. Fertility policy in China . New York, N.Y. [1986] 31 p. ; LC Card 87-154581 DDC 304.6/6/0951 19
HB1064.A3 G74 1986

FERTILITY, HUMAN - CHINA - CONGRESSES.
Determinants of fertility in some African and Asian countries. Cairo , 1982. 698 p. : LC Card 84-960893 DDC 304.6/32 19
HB1071.7.A3 D48 1982
NYPL [JLL 73-297 no.10]

FERTILITY, HUMAN - CHINA - PROVINCES - HISTORY.
Coale, Ansley J. Basic data on fertility in the provinces of China, 1940-82 /. Honolulu, HI [1987] xvii, 366 p. : ISBN 0-86638-088-4 (pbk.) : LC Card 86-32765 DDC 304.6/32/0951 19
HB1064.A3 C63 1987

FERTILITY, HUMAN - COMMUNIST COUNTRIES - CASE STUDIES.
Working women in socialist countries . Geneva , 1985. xvi, 234 p. : ISBN 92-2-103910-2 (pbk.) : LC Card 85-181464 DDC 304.6/32/091717 19
HB901 .W657 1985 ***NYPL [JLE 86-1433]***

FERTILITY, HUMAN - CONGRESSES.
Below-replacement fertility in industrial societies . Cambridge [Cambridgeshire] , New York , c1987. x, 360 p. : ISBN 0-521-34324-0 LC Card 87-6371 DDC 304.6/32 19
HB901 .B45 1987b

Below-replacement fertility in industrial societies . New York, N.Y., USA , c1987. x, 360 p. : LC Card 87-2458 DDC 304.6/32 19
HB901 .B45 1987

FERTILITY, HUMAN - COSTA RICA.
Avance de resultados, encuesta de fecundidad y salud /. [San José] Costa Rica , 1986. [32] leaves : LC Card 87-400666 DDC 304.6/32/097286 19
HB947 .A96 1986

Denton L., Carlos F. Población, fecundidad y desarrollo en Costa Rica, 1950-1970 /. [Heredia, Costa Rica] , 1984. iv, 150 p. : LC Card 86-117583 DDC 304.6/097286 19
HB3531 .D44 1984 ***NYPL [JLF 87-144]***

Sandoval Aguilar, Guillermo. El desarrollo costarricense y la fecundidad del hombre /. Heredia , 1985. 233 p. ; LC Card 86-117576
HB947 .S26 1985

FERTILITY, HUMAN - CUBA.
Alvarez Vázquez, Luisa. La fecundidad en Cuba /. La Habana , 1985. ix, 182 p. : LC Card 87-401045 DDC 304.6/32/097291 19
HB959 .A44 1985

Evolución de la fecundidad de la mujer cubana en el período 1959-1984. [Havana?] , 1985. 110 p. : LC Card 87-404207 DDC 304.6/32/097291 19
HB959 .E96 1985

FERTILITY, HUMAN - DEVELOPING COUNTRIES.
Acsádi, György. Policy relevance of findings of the world fertility survey for developing countries /. New York , 1986. vi, 160 p. ; LC Card 85-37681 DDC 304.6/32/091724 19
HB1108 .A28 1986

Bongaarts, John, 1945- The transition in reproductive behavior in the third world /. New York, N.Y. [1986] 29 p. : LC Card 87-154566 DDC 304.6/32/091724 19
HB1108 .B65 1986

FERTILITY, HUMAN - DEVELOPING COUNTRIES - ADDRESSES, ESSAYS, LECTURES.
Rural development and human fertility /. New York, N.Y. , London , c1984. ix, 318 p. : ISBN 0-02-949680-2 : LC Card 83-26834 DDC 304.6/32/091734 19
HB1108 .R87 1984 ***NYPL [JLE 86-1084]***

FERTILITY, HUMAN - DOMINICA.
Ebanks, G. E. Mortality, fertility, and family planning . Santiago, Chile [1985] 123 p. ; LC Card 87-131697 DDC 304.6/2/09729841 19
HB1376.D65 E32 1985

FERTILITY, HUMAN - ECONOMIC ASPECTS - FRANCE.
Challier, Marie-Christine. La fécondité en France . Paris , 1985. 196 p. : ISBN 2-222-03773-5 : LC Card 86-234728
HB1003 .C46 1985

FERTILITY, HUMAN - EGYPT - CONGRESSES.
Determinants of fertility in some African and Asian countries. Cairo , 1982. 698 p. : LC Card 84-960893 DDC 304.6/32 19
HB1071.7.A3 D48 1982
NYPL [JLL 73-297 no.10]

FERTILITY, HUMAN - ENGLAND - HISTORY.
Levine, David, 1946- Reproducing families . Cambridge [Cambridgeshire] , New York , 1987. ix, 251 p. ; ISBN 0-521-33256-7 LC Card 86-26372 DDC 304.6/0942 19
HB3585 .L48 1987

FERTILITY, HUMAN - EUROPE.
Wattenberg, Ben J. The birth dearth /. New York, NY , 1987. viii, 182 p. : ISBN 0-88687-304-5 : LC Card 83-63759 DDC 304.6/32 19
HB915 .W29 1987

FERTILITY, HUMAN - GERMANY (WEST)
Dinkel, Reiner. Die Auswirkungen eines Geburten- und Bevölkerungsrückgangs auf Entwicklung und Ausgestaltung von gesetzlicher Alterssicherung und Familienlastenausgleich /. Berlin , c1984. 344 p. : ISBN 3-428-05546-2 LC Card 84-186733
HD7179 .D65 1984

FERTILITY, HUMAN - GUATEMALA - HISTORY.
Guatemala . [Guatemala] , San José, Costa Rica [1984] vii, 73 p. : LC Card 86-158744
HA755 .U5 no. 1045 HB949.A3

FERTILITY, HUMAN - HUNGARY - STATISTICS.
Az 1937-68 években született nők kohorsz-termékenysége /. Budapest [1986] 77 p. ; LC Card 87-407670
HB1002.5.A3 A15 1986

FERTILITY, HUMAN - INDIA - CASE STUDIES - ADDRESSES, ESSAYS, LECTURES.
Fertility and mortality . New Delhi , Beverly Hills , 1986. 351 p. ; ISBN 0-8039-9497-4 LC Card 85-22287 DDC 304.6/3 19
HB901 .F468 1986 ***NYPL [JLE 86-4122]***

FERTILITY, HUMAN - INDIA - JAMMU AND KASHMIR.
Sadhu, Kanan K. (Kanan Kusum) Bio-demographic study of Kashmiris /. Delhi, India , c1987. viii, 217 p. : ISBN 81-212-0072-5 : LC Card 87-900298 DDC 304.6/0954/6 19
HB3640.J36 S23 1987

FERTILITY, HUMAN - INDIA - KERALA.
Mahadevan, K., 1940- Social development, cultural change, and fertility decline . New Delhi , Newbury Park, Calif. , 1987. p. cm. ISBN 0-8039-9536-9 LC Card 87-15001 DDC 304.6/32/095483 19
HB1050.K47 M34 1987

FERTILITY, HUMAN - INDONESIA.
Recent trends in fertility and mortality in Indonesia /. Honolulu, Hawaii , 1987. xvi, 96 p. : ISBN 0-86638-092-2 (pbk.) : LC Card 87-11178 DDC 304.6/32/09598 19
HB1057 .R43 1987

FERTILITY, HUMAN - INDONESIA - BALI (PROVINCE)
Streatfield, K. Fertility decline in a traditional society . [Canberra, ACT] , 1986. xvii, 177 p. : ISBN 0-86784-711-5 (pbk.) LC Card 86-213262 DDC 304.6/32/095986 19
HB1058.B34 S87 1986

FERTILITY, HUMAN - INDONESIA - JAVA.
Ananta, Aris. Perilaku fertilitas di beberapa daerah di Jawa /. Jakarta , 1986. vi, 56, 26 p. ; LC Card 86-946460
HB1058.J38 A52 1986

FERTILITY, HUMAN - ITALY.
Contribution of Italian scholars to the IUSSP XX General Conference =. Roma [1985?] 320 p. : LC Card 87-169376 DDC 304.6/0945 19
HB3599 .C647 1985

FERTILITY, HUMAN - IVORY COAST.
Enquête démographique à passages répétés, 1978-1979 . [Abidjan] [1980?] 270 p. : LC Card 85-213692 DDC 304.6/09666/8 19
HB3666.A3 E57 1980 ***NYPL [JLF 86-1023]***

Sombo, N'Cho. Enquête ivoirienne sur la fécondité, 1980-81 . Voorburg, Netherlands [1985] 63 p. : LC Card 87-132644
HB1076.A3 S65 1985

FERTILITY, HUMAN - KENYA.
Mosley, W. Henry (Wiley Henry), 1933- The dynamics of birth spacing and marital fertility in Kenya /. [Nairobi? , 1981] 63 leaves : LC Card 85-980189
HB1072.5.A3 M66 1981

FERTILITY, HUMAN - LATIN AMERICA - CASE STUDIES.
Pinto, Claudio. Fecundabilidad y edad de la mujer en las áreas rurales y semi-urbanas de cuatro países latinoamericanos /. Santiago de Chile [1978] 21, [2] p. : LC Card 83-175823
HA755 .U5 no. 151 HB940.5

FERTILITY, HUMAN - LESOTHO.
Makatjane, Tiisetso. Internal migration and fertility in Lesotho /. [Roma, Lesotho] [1985] iii, 36 leaves ; LC Card 87-132347 DDC 304.6/32/096816 19
HB2123.7.A3 M35 1985

FERTILITY, HUMAN - MATHEMATICAL MODELS.
Nerlove, Marc, 1933- Population policy and individual choice . Washington, D.C., U. S.A. , 1987. 52 p. : ISBN 0-89629-062-X (pbk.) LC Card 87-16802 DDC 363.9 19
HB901 .N474 1987

FERTILITY, HUMAN - MEASUREMENT.
Henry, Louis, writer on demography. [Fécondité des marriages. English.] Fertility of marriage . New York , 1980. iv, 136 p. : LC Card 81-133059
HB901 .H4613 1980

FERTILITY, HUMAN - MEXICO.
Planeación familiar y cambio demográfico. México, D.F. [1983], c1982. 554 p. : ISBN 968-8241-63-6 LC Card 84-227488 DDC 304.6/0972 19
HB3531 .P57 1983 ***NYPL [JLE 86-3248]***

Trabajo familiar, conducta reproductiva y estratificación social . México, D.F. , 1986. 226 p. ; ISBN 968-8241-06-7 LC Card 87-400355 DDC 304.6/32/0972 19
HB941 .T7 1986

FERTILITY, HUMAN - MEXICO - ADDRESSES, ESSAYS, LECTURES.
Los Factores del cambio demográfico en México /. México, D.F. , 1984. 422 p. : ISBN 968-231-281-7 LC Card 85-231767
HB1361 .F33 1984 ***NYPL [JLE 87-753]***

FERTILITY, HUMAN - NEPAL - STATISTICS.
Nepal fertility survey, 1976. Kathmandu, Nepal [1977] xi, 347 p. : LC Card 87-915005
HB1046.9.A3 N464 1977

FERTILITY, HUMAN - NETHERLANDS - STATISTICS.
Netherlands (Kingdom, 1815-). Centraal Bureau voor de Statistiek. Hoofdafdeling Bevolkingsstatistieken. De gehuwde vrouw en haar kindertal anno 1975 /. 's-Gravenhage , 1980. 78 p. : LC Card 81-100844
HB1015 .N47 1980
NYPL [JLM 78-1515 nr.9]

Nouwt, P. Vruchtbaarheid van geboortegeneraties gebaseerd op waarnemingen over de periode 1950-1983 /. 's-Gravenhage , 1985. 95 p. ; ISBN 90-357-0197-6 : LC Card 86-218161
HB1015 .N68 1985

FERTILITY, HUMAN - NEW YORK (STATE) - ERIE COUNTY - HISTORY - 19TH CENTURY.
Stern, Mark J. Society and family strategy . Albany, N.Y. , c1987. xiv, 172 p. : ISBN 0-88706-495-7 LC Card 86-23121 DDC 304.6/34/0974796 19
HB935.N7 S74 1987

FERTILITY, HUMAN - NEW YORK (STATE) - ERIE COUNTY - HISTORY - 20TH CENTURY.
Stern, Mark J. Society and family strategy . Albany, N.Y. , c1987. xiv, 172 p. : ISBN 0-88706-495-7 LC Card 86-23121 DDC 304.6/34/0974796 19
HB935.N7 S74 1987

FERTILITY, HUMAN - NEW ZEALAND - STATISTICS.
Trends and patterns in New Zealand fertility, 1912-1983. Wellington, N.Z. , 1986. 77 p. : ISBN 0-477-06453-1 (pbk.) : LC Card 86-219193 DDC 304.6/32/09931021 19
HB1102.5.A3 T74 1986

FERTILITY, HUMAN - NORWAY.
Jensen, An-Magritt. Flere i yrke--færre barn? . Oslo , 1983. 59 p. : ISBN 82-537-2007-6 : LC Card 84-163552
HA1503 .A45 nr. 147 HQ762.N8

FERTILITY, HUMAN - NORWAY - STATISTICS.
Siring, Erling. To notater om sammenlikning av data fra fruktbarhetsundersøkelsen 1977 med data fra registre /. Oslo , 1983. 43 p. : ISBN 82-537-2006-8 : LC Card 84-161768
HB1025 .S57 1983

FERTILITY, HUMAN - PORTUGAL - LANHEZES - HISTORY.
Brettell, Caroline. Men who migrate, women who wait . Princeton , c1986. xv, 329 p., [8] p. of plates : ISBN 0-691-09424-1 (alk. paper) : LC Card 86-11270 DDC 304.6/09469/12 19
HB2082.L36 B74 1986 ***NYPL [JLE 87-1417]***

FERTILITY, HUMAN - SAINT LUCIA.
Ebanks, G. E. Mortality, fertility, and family planning . Santiago, Chile [1985] 123 p. ; LC Card 87-131697 DDC 304.6/2/09729841 19
HB1376.D65 E32 1985

FERTILITY, HUMAN - SOUTHERN STATES - HISTORY - 19TH CENTURY.
Steckel, Richard H. (Richard Hall), 1944- The economics of U. S. slave and southern white fertility /. New York , 1985. 253 p. ; ISBN 0-8240-6662-6 (alk. paper) : LC Card 84-48314 DDC 304.6/32/08996073075 19
HB921 .S74 1985 ***NYPL [JLE 86-2085]***

FERTILITY, HUMAN - SOVIET UNION.
Detnost′ semi′i--vchera, segodnia͡, zavtra /. Moskva , 1986. 205 p. : LC Card 87-109456 DDC 304.6/32/0947 19
HB1017 .D47 1986

FERTILITY, HUMAN - SUDAN.
Saghayroun, Atif A. Rahman. Determinants of family size in rural Sudan /. Khartoum, Sudan [1984] 36 leaves ; LC Card 87-119805 DDC 304.6/32/09624 19
HB1071.8.A3 S22 1984

FERTILITY, HUMAN - TANZANIA.
FERTILITY, HUMAN - THAILAND.
Hogan, Dennis P. Cultural and economic factors in the fertility of Thai women /. Honolulu, HI [1987] p. cm. ISBN 0-86638-103-1 : LC Card 87-21459 DDC 304.6/32/09593 19
HB1054.55.A3 H64 1987

Knodel, John E. Thailand's reproductive revolution . Madison, Wis. , c1987. xiii, 251 p. : ISBN 0-299-11050-8 LC Card 87-8172 DDC 304.6/32/09593 19
HB1054.55.A3 K576 1987

Suchart Prasithrathsint. Ethnicity and fertility in Thailand /. Singapore , 1985. xviii, 270 p. : ISBN 997-19-8813-5 ***NYPL [JLE 86-3668]***

FERTILITY, HUMAN - THAILAND - BANGKOK METROPOLITAN AREA.
Charoon Vitiprod. Rapid population growth, living conditions, and fertility reduction implication (Bangkok metropolis) /. [Singapore] 1979. ii, 41 leaves : LC Card 82-940038
HB3644.55.B36 C48 1979

FERTILITY, HUMAN - UNITED STATES.
Easterlin, Richard A., 1926- Birth and fortune . Chicago , 1987. xii, 228 p. : ISBN 0-226-18032-8 (pbk.) : LC Card 86-30724 DDC 304.6/0973 19
HB3505 .E247 1987

Wattenberg, Ben J. The birth dearth /. New York, NY , 1987. viii, 182 p. : ISBN 0-88687-304-5 : LC Card 83-63759 DDC 304.6/32 19
HB915 .W29 1987

FERTILITY, HUMAN - UNITED STATES - HISTORY - 19TH CENTURY.
Schapiro, Morton Owen. Filling up America . Greenwich, Conn. , c1986. xiii, 149 p. : ISBN 0-89232-675-1 : LC Card 86-2771 DDC 304.6/0973 19
HB3505 .S33 1986 ***NYPL [JLE 86-3386]***

FERTILITY, HUMAN - VERMONT.
Changing fertility patterns in Vermont. Burlington, Vt. (Box 70, 60 Main St., Burlington 05402) [1986] 18 p. : LC Card 86-622900 DDC 304.6/32/09743 19
HB935.V4 C46 1986

FERTILITY, HUMAN - ZAMBIA - KEEMBE (CENTRAL PROVINCE)
Interrelationships among infant and childhood mortality, socio-economic factors and fertility in Zambia . Lusaka , Addis Ababa [1984?] 300 p. : LC Card 87-105950 DDC 304.6/32/096894 19
HB1323.I42 Z335 1984

FERTILITY, HUMAN - ZAMBIA - LUSAKA.
Interrelationships among infant and childhood mortality, socio-economic factors and fertility in Zambia . Lusaka , Addis Ababa [1984?] 300 p. : LC Card 87-105950 DDC 304.6/32/096894 19
HB1323.I42 Z335 1984

Fertility in Asia : assessing the impact of development projects / edited by John Stoeckel and Anrudh K. Jain. London : Frances Pinter, 1986. xix, 177 p. : ill. ; 23 cm. Includes bibliographies and index. ISBN 0-86187-667-9 DDC 304.6/32/095 19
1. Fertility, Human - Asia - Case studies. 2. Economic development projects - Asia - Case studies. I. Stoeckel, John E.
HB1043.A3 F47 1986b
NYPL [JLD 87-1268]

Fertility of marriage . Henry, Louis, writer on demography. [Fécondité des marriages. English.] New York , 1980. iv, 136 p. : LC Card 81-133059
HB901 .H4613 1980

Fertility policy in China . Greenhalgh, Susan. New York, N.Y. [1986] 31 p. ; LC Card 87-154581 DDC 304.6/6/0951 19
HB1064.A3 G74 1986

FERTILIZER INDUSTRY - FORECASTING - ECONOMETRIC MODELS.
Mészáros, Sándor. A világ műtrágyatermelésének és -felhasználásának előrejelzése /. Budapest , 1985. 143 p. : ISBN 963-05-3670-6 : LC Card 86-136326
HD9483.A2 M47 1985

FERTILIZER INDUSTRY - GERMANY, WEST.
Weber, Norbert. Markttransparenz bei Pflanzenschutz- und Düngemitteln . Münster-Hiltrup , 1983. xi, 247 p. : ISBN 3-7843-0277-7 : LC Card 83-234135
HD9660.P33 G328 1983

FERTILIZER INDUSTRY - GOVERNMENT POLICY - DEVELOPING COUNTRIES.
Mudahar, Mohinder S. Fertilizer marketing systems and policies in the developing world /. Muscle Shoals, Ala. , 1987. 43 p. : ISBN 0-88090-059-8 (pbk.) LC Card 87-3152 DDC 381/.4566862/091724 19
HD9483.D44 K36 1987

FERTILIZER INDUSTRY - INDIA.
Gupta, Uttam. Impact of credit on fertiliser consumption /. New Delhi [1986] 158 p. ; LC Card 87-900336 DDC 338.4/766862/0954 19
HD9483.I42 G86 1986

Leela, Pillalamarri. Import substitution and economic efficiency . Bombay , 1984. xvi, 129 p. ; LC Card 84-900166 DDC 382/.45668624/0954 19
HD94484.N6 I544 1984
NYPL [JLD 86-3888]

FERTILIZER INDUSTRY - INDIA - CONGRESSES.
Growth and modernisation of fertiliser industry . New Delhi , 1987. 1 v. (various pagings) : LC Card 87-902183 DDC 338.4/766862/0954 19
HD9483.I42 G78 1987

FERTILIZER INDUSTRY - PAKISTAN.
Suleman, R. M. U. 1983-84 rabi (winter) season fertilizer review . Islamabad [1984] iv, 28 leaves : LC Card 85-930451 DDC 338.4/766862/095491 19
HD9483.P22 S844 1984

Fertilizer marketing systems and policies in the developing world /. Mudahar, Mohinder S. Muscle Shoals, Ala. , 1987. 43 p. : ISBN 0-88090-059-8 (pbk.) LC Card 87-3152 DDC 381/.4566862/091724 19
HD9483.D44 K36 1987

FERTILIZERS AND MANURES - INDUSTRY AND TRADE. see FERTILIZER INDUSTRY.

FERTILIZERS - DEVELOPING COUNTRIES - MARKETING.
Mudahar, Mohinder S. Fertilizer marketing systems and policies in the developing world /. Muscle Shoals, Ala. , 1987. 43 p. : ISBN 0-88090-059-8 (pbk.) LC Card 87-3152 DDC 381/.4566862/091724 19
HD9483.D44 K36 1987

FERTILIZERS - MARKETING.
Manual on fertilizer distribution /. Rome , 1985. x, 114 p. : ISBN 92-5-101433-7 (pbk.) LC Card 86-221068 DDC 668/.62/0688 19
HD9483.A2 M36 1985

FERTILIZERS - TRANSPORTATION.
Manual on fertilizer distribution /. Rome , 1985. x, 114 p. : ISBN 92-5-101433-7 (pbk.) LC Card 86-221068 DDC 668/.62/0688 19
HD9483.A2 M36 1985

Fesharaki, Fereidun. China Energy Workshop I: Petroleum Processing (1985 : Honolulu, Hawaii) China's petroleum industry in the international context . Boulder [Colo.] , 1986. xvii, 166 p. : ISBN 0-86638-072-8 (pbk.) LC Card 86-50695 DDC 338.2/7282/0951 19
HD9576.C52 C524 1985
NYPL [JLD 86-3885]

Fess, Philip E. Accounting principles / Philip E. Fess, Carl S. Warren. 15th ed. Cincinnati : South-Western Pub. Co., c1987. xxiii, 1291, [92] p. : ill. (some col.) ; 24 cm. Includes bibliographical references and index. ISBN 0-538-00300-6 LC Card 86-62984 DDC 657 19
1. Accounting. I. Warren, Carl S. II. Title.
HF5635 .F386 1987

Fesseln für den Leviathan . Reis, Karl Eugen. Pfaffenweiler , 1987. xi, 338 p. ; ISBN 3-89085-159-2 LC Card 87-134876 DDC 336.973 19
HJ2381 .R356 1987

El festín de los gemelos . Márquez, Pompeyo. [Caracas , 1983] ([Caracas] : Industrias Sorocaima) 134 p. ; LC Card 84-195527
HC237 .M338 1983

Festschrift für Univ.-Prof. Dr. Georg Zwanowetz anlässlich der Vollendung des 65. Lebensjahres / herausgegeben von Franz Mathis und Josef Riedmann. [Innsbruck] : Universität Innsbruck, c1984. 332 p. : ill. ; 24 cm. (Veröffentlichungen der Universität Innsbruck . 142) Cover title: Exportgewerbe und Aussenhandel vor der Industriellen Revolution. English and German. Bibliography of works by G. Zwanowetz: p. 315-317. Bibliography: p. 291-299.

Includes indexes. LC Card 84-183487
1. Central Europe - Economic conditions. 2. Alpine regions - Economic aspects. 3. Zwanowetz, Georg. I. Zwanowetz, Georg. II. Mathis, Franz. III. Riedmann, Josef. IV. Title: Exportgewerbe und Aussenhandel vor der Industriellen Revolution. V. Series.
HC244 .F48 1984

FETICIDE. see **ABORTION.**

Fetzer, Hubert. Intensivierung der Forschung . Berlin , 1984. 354 p. ; LC Card 84-195559
HD30.42.G4 I57 1984

Feucht, Martin. Theorie des Konkurrenzsozialismus : Beitrag zu einer Phänomenologie der Wirtschaftssysteme / von Martin Feucht. Stuttgart ; New York : G. Fischer, 1983. iv, 222 p. : ill. ; 23 cm. (Schriften zum Vergleich von Wirtschaftsordnungen. Heft 32) Bibliography: p. 202-222. ISBN 3-437-50273-5 LC Card 83-205881
1. Socialist competition. 2. Industrial productivity. 3. Macroeconomics. I. Title. II. Series.
HC79.S6 F48 1983

Feuchtinger, Max Erich. Planungsbeispiele für Knotenpunkte des Strassenverkehrs / von Max-Erich Feuchtinger. Bad Godesberg : Kirschbaum, [1960] 93 p., [2] folded leaves of plates : ill. ; 30 cm. (Forschungsarbeiten aus dem Strassenwesen . n.F., Heft 44) Includes bibliographies. LC Card 86-191612
1. Traffic engineering - Germany, West. 2. Traffic congestion - Germany (West). I. Series: Forschungsarbeiten aus dem Strassenwesen , Heft 44. II. Title.
HE363.G3 F48 1960

Feuchtwang, Stephan. The Chinese economy since 1978 /. Boulder , 1988. p. cm. ISBN 0-8133-0555-1 (v. 1) : LC Card 87-10631 DDC 330.951/058 19
HC427.92 .C4674 1988

FEUDAL TENURE. see **FEUDALISM; LAND TENURE.**

FEUDALISM - ENGLAND - HISTORY.
Lachmann, Richard. From manor to market . Madison, Wis. , 1987. xiv, 166 p. : ISBN 0-299-11420-1 : LC Card 87-40146 DDC 330.942/05 19
HC254 .L33 1987

FEUDALISM - ENGLAND - HISTORY - ADDRESSES, ESSAYS, LECTURES.
Hilton, R. H. (Rodney Howard), 1916- Class conflict and the crisis of feudalism . London , Ronceverte, W. Va. , 1985. 349 p. ; ISBN 0-907628-36-2 : LC Card 85-21855 DDC 305.5/0942 19
HD604 .H48 1985 ***NYPL [JFE 87-391]***

FEUDALISM - EUROPE - HISTORY.
Istoriia krest'ianstva v Evrope, Epokha feodalizma . Moskva , 1985- v. :
NYPL [*QGS 86-1566]

FEUDALISM - GERMANY (WEST) - JÜLICH-BERG - HISTORY - 16TH CENTURY.
Walz, Rainer. Stände und frühmoderner Staat . Neustadt an der Aisch , 1982. 257 p., [1] leaf of plates : ISBN 3-87707-040-9 LC Card 83-215104
HJ2675 .W35 1982

FEUDALISM - GERMANY (WEST) - JÜLICH-BERG - HISTORY - 17TH CENTURY.
Walz, Rainer. Stände und frühmoderner Staat . Neustadt an der Aisch , 1982. 257 p., [1] leaf of plates : ISBN 3-87707-040-9 LC Card 83-215104
HJ2675 .W35 1982

FEUDALISM - HISTORY.
Domínguez, Jaime de Jesús, 1947- Feudalismo, capitalismo mercantil y capitalismo industrial /. Santo Domingo, República Dominicana , 1981. 229 p. ; ISBN 84-89527-00-8 LC Card 82-200900
HC21 .D66 1981

FEUDALISM - ITALY - NAPLES (KINGDOM) - HISTORY - 18TH CENTURY.
Rao, Anna Maria, 1949- L'"Amaro della feudalità" . Napoli , c1984. 382 p. ; ISBN 88-7042-265-8 : LC Card 85-200705
HD1333.I82 N367 1984

FEUDALISM - KOREA.
Vanin, IUriĭ Vasil'evich. Agrarnyĭ stroĭ feodal'noĭ Korei XV-XVI vv. /. Moskva , 1981. 309 p. ; LC Card 83-462393
HD1331.K6 V36 1981 ***NYPL [*QI 86-3898]***

FEUDALISM - SOVIET UNION - HISTORY - 19TH CENTURY - COLLECTED WORKS.
Druzhinin, N. M. (Nikolaĭ Mikhaĭlovich) Sotsial'no-ėkonomicheskaia istoriia Rossii . Moskva , 1987. 421 p., [1] leaf of plates : LC Card 87-164847
HC334.5 .D78 1987

FEUDALISM - SPAIN - TIERRA DE CAMPOS REGION - HISTORY.
Martínez Sopena, Pascual. La Tierra de Campos occidental . [Valladolid] , 1985. 843 p. : ISBN 84-505-1390-1 LC Card 86-231937
HD779.T54 M37 1985

Feudalismo, capitalismo mercantil y capitalismo industrial /. Domínguez, Jaime de Jesús, 1947- Santo Domingo, República Dominicana , 1981. 229 p. ; ISBN 84-89527-00-8 LC Card 82-200900
HC21 .D66 1981

Feuer, Björn. Consideraciones aproximativas en torno a la investigación laboral en América Latina / Björn Feuer. Stockholm : Institute of Latin American Studies, [1985] 18 p. ; 30 cm. (Research paper series . paper no. 42) "Versión reelaborada a partir de un informe más amplio, presentado originalmente en sueco al 'Arbetslivscentrum', Centro Sueco para la Vida Laboral." Bibliography: p. 15-18. LC Card 85-205735
1. Labor and laboring classes - Study and teaching - Latin America. I. Series. II. Series: Research paper series (Latinamerika-institutet i Stockholm) , paper no. 42. III. Title.
HD4824.5.L29 F48 1985

Feuerstein, Thomas. Humanisierung der Arbeit und Reform der beruflichen Bildung : zur persönlichkeitsförderlichen Gestaltung von Lernzielen und Qualifikationsanforderungen / Thomas Feuerstein. München : Deutsches Jugendinstitut, c1983. 221 p. ; 21 cm. (DJI Forschungsbericht) Bibliography: p. 207-221. ISBN 3-87966-184-7 LC Card 83-222687
1. Occupational training - Germany, West. 2. Employees, Training of - Germany, West. 3. Vocational education - Germany, West. I. Title. II. Series.
HD5715.5.G4 F48 1983

Feyerabend, Joachim. Die leisen Milliarden : das Imperium des Friedrich Karl Flick / Joachim Feyerabend.1. Aufl. Düsseldorf : Econ, 1984. 187 p. : ill. ; 21 cm. ISBN 3-430-12729-7 LC Card 84-176048
1. Flick, Friedrich Karl, 1927-. 2. Businessmen - Germany, West - Biography. 3. Industrialists - Germany (West) - Biography. I. Title.
HC282.5.F54 F49 1984

Fforde, Adam. The limits of national liberation : problems of economic management in the Democratic Republic of Vietnam, with a statistical appendix / Adam Fforde and Suzanne H. Paine. London ; New York : Croom Helm, c1987. 246 p. ; 22 cm. "Published in the USA by Croom Helm in association with Methuen ... New York, NY"--T.p. verso. Bibliography: p. 237-246. ISBN 0-7099-1036-3 LC Card 87-8977 DDC 338.9597 19
1. Vietnam (Democratic Republic) - Economic policy. 2. Vietnam (Democratic Republic) - Economic conditions. I. Paine, Suzanne. II. Title.
HC444 .F46 1987

Ffrench-Davis, Ricardo. Origen y destino de las exportaciones chilenas, 1965-80 / Ricardo Ffrench-Davis. 2a ed., rev. Santiago, Chile : Corporación de Investigaciones Económicas para Latinoamérica, 1981. 22, 6, [27] leaves ; 27 cm. (Notas técnicas . no. 31) Bibliography: leaves [26]-[27] LC Card 83-182100
1. Chile - Commerce. 2. Commercial products - Chile. I. Title. II. Series.
HF3416.5 .F46 1981b

FGTS e a rotatividade /. Macedo, Roberto Brás Matos. São Paulo-SP , Brasília-DF , 1985. 231 p. : ISBN 85-21-30271-1 LC Card 85-187484
HD7096.B6 M33 1985

FHA Title I property improvement loan insurance [microform] . United States. Office of Urban Rehabilitation and Community Reinvestment. Washington , 1978. 19 p. ;
NYPL [*ZT-1564 no.11]

FIAT (FIRM) - HISTORY.
Camerana, Oddone. L'enigma del cavalier Agnelli e altri itinerari /. Milano , c1985. 117 p. ; LC Card 85-191746
HD9710.I82 A6615 1985
NYPL [JLC 87-25]

FIAT MONEY. see **CURRENCY QUESTION; PAPER MONEY.**

Fiber, Fabric and Apparel Coalition for Trade (U. S.)
Howell, Thomas R., 1949- The EEC and the third Multifiber Arrangement . Washington, DC , 1986. [14], 126, [12] p. : LC Card 86-224652 DDC 382/.45677/0094 19
HD9865.E852 H68 1986

The Textile and apparel trade crisis . Washington, D.C. (1775 Pennsylvania Ave., N.W., Washington 20006) , c1985. vi, 200, [23] p. : LC Card 87-122082 DDC 382/.45677 19
HD9850.6 .T475 1985

Fiber optic sensors. Norwalk, Conn., U. S.A. (6 Prowitt St., Norwald 06855) : International Resource Development, c1987. iv, 179 leaves ; 28 cm. (Report / International Resource Development Inc. . #722) "January 1987." LC Card 87-134996 DDC 380.1/456213692 19
1. Fiber optics industry. 2. Market surveys. I. International Resource Development, inc. II. Series: Report / International Resource Development Inc. , #722.
HD9696.F522 F496 1987

Fiber optic telecommunications opportunities. Norwalk, Conn., U. S.A. (6 Prowitt St., Norwalk 06855) : International Resource Development, c1986. viii, 205 leaves ; 28 cm. (Report / International Resource Development . #714) LC Card 87-129456 DDC 381/.456213692/0973 19
1. Fiber optics industry. 2. Telecommunication equipment industry. 3. Market surveys. I. Series: Report / International Resource Development Inc. , #714.
HD9696.F522 F5 1986

Fiber optics after long distance / Communications Systems & Services. Boston, Mass. (89 Broad St., Boston 02110) : Yankee Group, c1986. vii, 114 p. : ill. ; 28 cm. At head of title: Communications/Information Systems. "July 1986." LC Card 86-220473 DDC 381/.456213692/0973 19
1. Fiber optics industry - United States. 2. Market surveys - United States. 3. Telephone - Long distance - United States. I. Communications Systems & Services. II. Yankee Group.
HD9696.F523 U5429 1986

FIBER OPTICS INDUSTRY.
Fiber optic sensors. Norwalk, Conn., U. S.A. (6 Prowitt St., Norwald 06855) , c1987. iv, 179 leaves ; LC Card 87-134996 DDC 380.1/456213692 19
HD9696.F522 F496 1987

Fiber optic telecommunications opportunities. Norwalk, Conn., U. S.A. (6 Prowitt St., Norwalk 06855) , c1986. viii, 205 leaves ; LC Card 87-129456 DDC 381/.456213692/0973 19
HD9696.F522 F5 1986

Optical fiber in the local loop. Norwalk, Conn. (6 Prowitt St., Norwalk 06855) , c1986. iv, 208 leaves : LC Card 87-127281 DDC 381/.456213692/0973 19
HD9696.F522 O67 1986

FIBER OPTICS INDUSTRY - FRANCE.
L'Avenir national des capteurs à fibres optiques /. Paris , c1984. 42 p. : ISBN 2-11-001350-8 LC Card 85-232999
HD9696.F523 F82 1984

FIBER OPTICS INDUSTRY - UNITED STATES.
Fiber optics after long distance /. Boston, Mass. (89 Broad St., Boston 02110) , c1986. vii, 114 p. : LC Card 86-220473 DDC 381/.456213692/0973 19
HD9696.F523 U5429 1986

The U. S. non telecommunications fiber optic component market in the U. S. New York, N.Y. , c1982. vi, 255 leaves : LC Card 87-143641 DDC 381/.456213692/0973 19
HD9696.F523 U557 1982

FIBER REINFORCED CONCRETE. see **REINFORCED CONCRETE, FIBER.**

FIBER REINFORCED PLASTICS INDUSTRY - UNITED STATES.
Reinforced plastics . Stamford, Conn., U. S.A. , c1986. v, 136 leaves : ISBN 0-89336-478-9 (pbk.) LC Card 87-167989 DDC 381/.45668494/0973 19
HD9662.F523 U57 1986

FIBROUS CONCRETE. see **REINFORCED CONCRETE, FIBER.**

Ficción y realidad de la economía argentina (1976-1983) /. Cafasso, José. [Bahía Blanca, Argentina] [1983] 61 p. ; LC Card 87-400128 DDC 330.982/064 19
HC175 .C15 1983

Ficek, Edmund F. Real estate principles and practices / Edmund Ficek, Thomas P. Henderson, Ross H. Johnson. 3rd ed. Columbus : C.E. Merrill Pub. Co., c1983. viii, 550 p. : ill. ; 25 cm. Includes bibliographies and index. ISBN 0-675-20016-4 LC Card 82-73775 DDC 346.7304/37 347.306437 19
1. Real estate business - Law and legislation - United States. 2. Real property - United States. 3. Real estate business - United States. I. Henderson, Thomas P. II. Johnson, Ross H. III. Title.
KF2042.R4 F46 1983 ***NYPL [JLE 86-2010]***

Fiche technique pour la région de l'Equateur : profil socio-économique. Mbandaka : République du Zaïre, Mouvement populaire de la Révolution Parti-Etat, Division régionale du plan, Mbandaka, [1984] 172 leaves ; 36 cm. "Juillet 1984." LC Card 86-201790
1. Equateur (Zaire) - Economic policy. 2. Equateur (Zaire) - Social policy. I. Zaire. Division régionale du plan, Mbandaka.
HC955.Z7 E6725 1985

Ficher, Michael. Die Messung des Führungsverhaltens : eine kritische Würdigung verschiedener Ansätze unter Berücksichtigung ihrer Relevanz für die Unternehmenspraxis / Michael Ficher. Bochum : Brockmeyer, 1981. v, 366 p. : ill. ; 21 cm. (Bochumer wirtschaftswissenschaftliche Studien. Nr. 78) Bibliography: p. 347-366. ISBN 3-88339-193-X : LC Card 81-205568
1. Leadership - Evaluation. 2. Executive ability - Evaluation. I. Title.
HD57.7 .F65 1981 ***NYPL [JLD 86-2580]***

Fichera, Franco. La Politica di bilancio in condizioni di stress fiscale . Milano, Italy , c1986. 377 p. ; LC Card 87-134343
HJ2119 .P65 1986

Ficken, Robert E. The forested land : a history of lumbering in western Washington / Robert E. Ficken. Durham, N.C. : Forest History Society ; Seattle : University of Washington Press, c1987. xv, 324 p., [8] p. of plates : ill. ; 24 cm. Bibliography: p. 283-308. Includes index. ISBN 0-295-96416-2 LC Card 87-2214 DDC 338.4/7674/09797 19
1. Lumber trade - Washington (State) - History. 2. Lumbermen - Washington (State) - History. 3. Forests and forestry - Washington (State) - History. I. Title.
HD9757.W2 F53 1987

Ficzere, Lajos. A gazdaság irányításának jellege, az irányitás szervezete, eszközei és módszerei / Ficzere Lajos. Budapest : Akadémiai Kiadó és Nyomda, 1984. 112 p. ; 24 cm. "A Közigazgatás fejlesztésének komplex tudományos vizsgálata." Bibliography: p. 107-112. ISBN 963-02-3265-0 (Magy. nemz. bibl.) LC Card 85-130150
1. Central planning. 2. Public administration. I. Title.
HD87.5 .F53 1984

Fidel, Stanley Leo. Start up telemarketing : how to launch a profitable sales operation / Stanley Leo Fidel. New York : Wiley, c1987. xiv, 287 p. : ill. ; 24 cm. (Wiley series on business strategy) Includes index. ISBN 0-471-01064-2 LC Card 87-21610 DDC 658.8/5 19
1. Telemarketing. I. Title. II. Series.
HF5415.1265 .F53 1987

Fidel Velázquez /. Velasco, Carlos. [Mexico City, Mexico] , 1986. 150 p. : ISBN 968-85606-1-8 LC Card 87-403697 DDC 331.88/0972 19
HD8112.C563 V45 1986

Fieber, Joachim. Die effektivere Gestaltung des Personennahverkehrs im Kreis Sondershausen : Probleme, Ergebnisse, Erfahrungen / Fieber, Joachim, Gorges, Hans, Kern, Hans ; Akademie für Staats- und Rechtswissenschaft der DDR, Lehrstuhl Staatliche Leitung der Volkswirtschaft. Potsdam-Babelsberg : Die Akademie ; Leipzig : Buchexport [distributor], 1983. 75 p. : ill. ; 21 cm. (Aktuelle Beiträge der Staats- und Rechtswissenschaft, 0568-7551 . Heft 280) Cover title. Errata slip laid in. Includes bibliographical references. LC Card 83-241076
1. Transportation - Germany (East) - Sondershausen (Landkreis). I. Gorges, Hans. II. Kern, Hans. III. Akademie für Staats- und Rechtswissenschaft der DDR. Lehrstuhl Staatliche Leitung der Volkswirtschaft. IV. Series.
HE249.5.Z7 S664 1983

Fiedler, Dorothee. Structure et perspectives de l'artisanat et de la petite industrie du sud-ouest de la Haute-Volta . Berlin (West) [1978] xxvi, 253 p. : LC Card 85-118488
HD2346.B82 S77 1978

Fiedler, Ulrich. Der Bedeutungswandel der Hedschasbahn : eine historisch-geographische Untersuchung / Ulrich Fiedler. Berlin : K. Schwarz, 1984. ix, 338 p. : ill. ; 21 cm. (Islamkundliche Untersuchungen. Bd. 94) Originally presented as the author's thesis (doctoral--Universität Freiburg im Br., 1984) Bibliography: p. 304-321. Includes indexes. ISBN 3-922968-37-6 LC Card 86-135345
1. Railroads - Middle East - History. 2. Muslim pilgrims and pilgrimages - Saudi Arabia - Mecca. 3. Railroads - Saudi Arabia - History. I. Title.
HE3380.5.M53 F54 1984

FIELD CROPS - GERMANY (WEST) - LOWER SAXONY.
Reessing, Ludwig. Analyse der Wettbewerbsfähigkeit von Extensivblattfrüchten in Niedersachsen unter ökonomischen und ökologischen Gesichtspunkten /. Kiel , 1986. xiv, 251 p. : ISBN 3-922553-81-8 LC Card 86-163003
HD1960.L69 R44 1986

FIELD CROPS - ZAMBIA - CHIBALE (SERENJE DISTRICT)
Farming systems and family economy in Chibale, Serenje District. Mpika, Zambia [1985?] 74 p. : LC Card 86-981248 DDC 338.1/096894 19
HD1476.Z352 C454 1985

FIELD CROPS - ZAMBIA - NDUNYA.
Farming system and family economy in Ndunya, Chinsali District. Mpika, Zambia [1985?] 45 leaves, [12] leaves of plates : LC Card 86-981252 DDC 338.1/096894 19
HD1476.Z352 N384 1985

Field document .
(no. 13) Abu Sin, M. E. (Mohad E.) Socio-economic aspects of integrated resource management, with special reference to the forest resources of Kassala Province, Eastern Region . Khartoum , 1986. vi leaves, 109 p. : LC Card 87-980440 DDC 333.75/09629/2 19
HD9767.S843 K3724 1986

Field, Elizabeth, 1947- Sanders, Mary. R.P.M. realize your power to motivate /. Farmington Hills, Mich. , c1986. 153 p., [2] p. of plates : ISBN 0-9616833-0-9 (pbk.) LC Card 87-111586 DDC 658.3/14 19
HF5549.5.M63 S26 1986

A field guide to the U. S. economy /. Folbre, Nancy. New York , c1987. 1 v. (various pagings) : ISBN 0-394-75047-0 (pbk.) : LC Card 86-42974 DDC 330.973 19
HC103 .F59 1987

Field, Michael, 1949- The merchants : the big business families of Arabia / Michael Field. London : J. Murray, 1984. xii, 371 p., [16] p. of plates : ill., geneal. tables ; 24 cm. Includes bibliographical references and index. ISBN 0-7195-4104-2 LC Card 87-672963
1. Businessmen - Arabian Peninsula. 2. Arabian Peninsula - Social conditions. I. Title.
HC415.3 .F54x 1984

The field of social investment /. Bruyn, Severyn Ten Haut, 1927- Cambridge , New York , 1987. xi, 304 p. : ISBN 0-521-33292-3 LC Card 86-26393 DDC 332.6 19
HG4910 .B77 1987

FIELD SPORTS. see **HUNTING.**

FIELD THEORY (SOCIAL PSYCHOLOGY)
Horn, Christel-Margret. Feldtheorie und Konsumverhalten /. Freiburg im Breisgau , c1983. 121 p. : ISBN 3-448-01293-9 LC Card 84-136042
HF5415.3 .H65 1983

Fielder, Lonnie L. Agricultural statistics and prices for Louisiana, 1909-1985 / Lonnie L. Fielder, Jr. and Steve Kelly, Bergen A. Nelson. [Baton Rouge, LA] : Dept. of Agricultural Economics and Agribusiness, Louisiana Agricultural Experiment Station, Louisiana State University Agricultural Center, [1986] iv, [122] p. : ill. ; 28 cm. (D.A.E. research report . no. 659) "September 1986." LC Card 87-620749 DDC 338.1/09763 s 338.1/09763/021 19
1. Agriculture - Economic aspects - Louisiana - Statistics. 2. Agricultural prices - Louisiana - Statistics. I. Kelly, Steve S. II. Nelson, Bergen A. III. Title. IV. Series.
HD1775.L8 L7 no. 659

Fielding, Gordon J. Managing public transit strategically : a comprehensive approach to strengthening service and monitoring performance / Gordon J. Fielding.1st ed. San Francisco : Jossey-Bass Publishers, 1987. xxii, 270 p. : ill. ; 24 cm. (Jossey-Bass public administration series) Jossey-Bass management series Bibliography: p. 247-257. Includes index. ISBN 1-555-42068-0 (alk. paper) LC Card 87-45497 DDC 388.4/068 19
1. Local transit - Management. 2. Urban transportation - Management. I. Title. II. Series.
HE4301 .F54 1987

Fielding, Jane L. Fielding, Nigel. Linking data /. Beverly Hills , c1986. 96 p. ; ISBN 0-8039-2518-2 (pbk.) LC Card 85-62290 DDC 300/.72 19
H62 .F425 1986 ***NYPL [JLD 86-3863]***

Fielding, Nigel. Linking data / Nigel G. Fielding, Jane L. Fielding. Beverly Hills : Sage Publications, c1986. 96 p. ; 22 cm. (Qualitative research methods . v. 4) "A Sage university paper"--Cover. Bibliography: p. 92-95. ISBN 0-8039-2518-2 (pbk.) LC Card 85-62290 DDC 300/.72 19
1. Social sciences - Research. 2. Social sciences - Methodology. I. Fielding, Jane L. II. Title. III. Series.
H62 .F425 1986 ***NYPL [JLD 86-3863]***

Fields, Debbi. "One smart cookie" : how a housewife's chocolate chip recipe turned into a multimillion-dollar business--the story of Mrs. Fields cookies / by Debbi Fields and Alan Furst. New York : Simon and Schuster, c1987. 173 p., [16] p. of plates : ill. ; 23 cm. ISBN 0-671-61838-5 LC Card 87-15172 DDC 338.7/6647525/0924 B 19
1. Fields, Debbi. 2. Women in business - United States - Biography. 3. Mrs. Fields Cookies (Firm). 4. Cookie industry - United States. I. Furst, Alan. II. Title.
HD9058.C65 F544 1987

FIELDS, DEBBI.
Fields, Debbi. "One smart cookie" . New York , c1987. 173 p., [16] p. of plates : ISBN 0-671-61838-5 LC Card 87-15172 DDC 338.7/6647525/0924 B 19
HD9058.C65 F544 1987

Fiéloux, Michèle. Bisilliat, Jeanne. Femmes du tiers-monde . Paris , c1983. 122 p. : ISBN 2-86262-201-X ***NYPL [JLD 87-456]***

Fietz, Günter. Kurzfristige Finanzplanung und Grossprojektfertigung / Günter Fietz. Frankfurt am Main ; New York : P. Lang, c1986. iv, 269 p. : ill. ; 21 cm. (Europäische Hochschulschriften. Reihe V, Volks- und Betriebswirtschaft, 0531-7339 . Bd. 691 = vol. 691 = vol. 691) Bibliography: p. 197-206. ISBN 3-8204-9322-0 LC Card 86-156212
1. Business enterprises - Finance - Mathematical models. 2. Cash management - Mathematical models. I. Series: Europäische Hochschulschriften. Reihe V, Volks- und Betriebswirtschaft , Bd. 691. II. Title.
HG4012 .F53 1986

Fifteen second commercials, is less more? Advertising Research Foundation Key Issues Workshop (1985 : New York, N.Y.) Transcript proceedings . New York, NY (3 E. 54th St., New York 10022-3180) , c1985. 161 p. : LC Card 86-211136 DDC 659.14/3/0973 19
HF6146.T42 A27 1985

Fifth Malaysia Plan, 1986-1990. Malaysia. Kuala Lumpur , 1986. xxxiv, 567 p., [1] folded leaf of plates : LC Card 86-945646 DDC 338.9595 19
HC445.5 .M33 1986

Fifty activities for unblocking organizational communication. Francis, Dave. 50 activities for unblocking organizational communication /. Aldershot, Hants, England , Brookfield, Vt., U. S.A. , c1987. p. cm. ISBN 0-566-02571-X : LC Card 87-14079 DDC 658.4/5 19
HD30.3 .F7 1987

Fifty and fired . Brandt, Ed. Bedford, Mass. , c1987. xii, 242 p. ; ISBN 0-938179-07-1 : LC

Card 87-12150 DDC 650.1/4/0240564 19
HD38.25.U6 B7 1987

Fifty rules to keep a client happy. Poppe, Fred C. 50 rules to keep a client happy /. New York , c1987. 90 p. : ISBN 0-06-015779-8 : LC Card 87-45139 DDC 659.1/125 19
HF6178 .P66 1987

Fifty years of unemployment insurance--a legislative history, 1935-1985. Rosbrow, James M. Washington, D.C. , 1986. vii, 97 p. ; LC Card 87-601117 DDC 368.4/4/00973 s 344.73/024/0262 368.4/4/00973 s 347.304240262 19
HD7096.U5 U637 no. 86-5 KF3675

The Fight against unemployment : macroeconomic papers from the Centre for European [Policy] Studies / edited by Richard Layard and Lars Calmfors.1st MIT Press ed. Cambridge, Mass. : MIT Press, 1987. xii, 204 p. : ill. ; 24 cm. Includes bibliographies. ISBN 0-262-12122-0 LC Card 87-5356 DDC 339.5/094 19
1. Unemployment - Europe. 2. Europe - Full employment policy. I. Layard, P. R. G. (P. Richard G.). II. Calmfors, Lars, 1948-. III. Centre for European Policy Studies (Louvain-la-Neuve, Belgium).
HD5764.A6 F54 1987

Fight, flight, fraud . Adams, Charles, 1930- Curaçao , c1982. iv, 307 p. : LC Card 83-80155 DDC 336.2/009 19
HJ2250 .A32 1982 ***NYPL [JLG 86-104]***

FIGHTING. see **WAR.**

Fighting heritage : highlights of the 1930s struggle for jobs and militant unionism in British Columbia / edited by Sean Griffin. Vancouver : Tribune Pub., [1986?] 159 p., [32] p. of plates : ill., ports. ; 21 cm. Includes bibliographical references. ISBN 0-9692365-0-6 (pbk.) LC Card 86-231043 DDC 331.88/09711 19
1. Labor and laboring classes - British Columbia - History - 20th century. 2. Trade-unions - British Columbia - History - 20th century. 3. Strikes and lockouts - British Columbia - History - 20th century. I. Griffin, Sean.
HD8109.B72 F54 1986

Fighting poverty : what works and what doesn't / edited by Sheldon H. Danziger and Daniel H. Weinberg. Cambridge, Mass. : Harvard University Press, 1986. viii, 418 p. : ill. ; 25 cm. Revised versions of papers presented at a conference held in Williamsburg, Va., in Dec. 1984, sponsored by the University of Wisconsin--Madison's Institute for Research on Poverty and the U. S. Dept. of Health and Human Services. Includes index. Bibliography: p. [359]-387. ISBN 0-674-30085-8 (alk. paper) LC Card 85-24848 DDC 362.5/8/0973 19
1. Economic assistance Domestic - United States - Congresses. 2. Poor - United States - Congresses. 3. Public welfare - United States - Congresses. I. Danziger, Sheldon. II. Weinberg, Daniel H. III. University of Wisconsin--Madison. Institute for Research on Poverty.
HC110.P63 F54 1986 ***NYPL [JLE 86-4089]***

Fighting the famine /. Twose, Nigel. London , 1985. 96 p. : ISBN 0-7453-0131-2 (pbk.) : LC Card 86-135675 DDC 363.8/83/0966 19
HC800.Z9 F385 1985 ***NYPL [JLD 87-768]***

Figueira, Ricardo Rezende, 1952- A justiça do lobo : posseiros e padres do Araguaia / Ricardo Rezende Figueira. Petrópolis : Vozes, 1986. 115 p. ; 21 cm. Includes bibliographical references. LC Card 87-137552 DDC 305.5/63 19
1. Land tenure - Brazil - Conceição do Araguaia. 2. Catholic Church - Brazil - Conceição do Araguaia - Clergy - Political activity. 3. Peasantry - Brazil - Conceição do Araguaia - Political activity. 4. Peasantry - Brazil - Conceição do Araguaia - Crimes against. 5. Squatters - Brazil - Conceição do Araguaia. I. Title.
HD500.C74 F54 1986

Figueiredo, João Kubitschek de. A situação das indústrias de base, TT1-39-59 / João Kubitschek de Figueiredo. [S.l.] : Presidência da República, Estado Maior das Fôrças Armadas, Escola Superior de Guerra, [1960?] 75, [2] p. : ill. ; 26 cm. Bibliography: p. [77] LC Card 85-144484
1. Steel industry and trade - Brazil. 2. Chemical industry - Brazil. I. Title.
HD9524.B82 F54 1960

Figueiredo, Vilma. Cidadão, estado e políticas no Brasil contemporâneo /. Brasília-Distrito Federal , c1986. 290 p. : ISBN 85-23-00214-6 LC Card 87-405054 DDC 338.981 19
HD1873 .C53 1986

Figueroa, Federico Brito. see **Brito Figueroa, Federico.**

Figueroa, Oscar. Transports urbains et services en Amérique latine . Arcueil, France , Quito [1985- v. <1 > : ISBN 2-85782-137-9 (set) LC Card 87-153020
HE311.L29 T73 1985

Figuerola, Francisco José. Teoría de la democracia social : humanismo, ética, participación, solidarismo, planificación / Francisco José Figuerola ; prólogo del profesor Pablo A. Ramella. Buenos Aires : F.J. Figuerola : Distribuidor Ediciones Depalma, 1986. xxv, 492 p. ; 23 cm. ISBN 950-43-0832-5 LC Card 86-184525
1. Representative government and representation - Argentina. 2. Democracy. 3. Argentina - Politics and government - 1983-. I. Title.
HD2081 .F54 1986

Fiji, a transition to manufacturing. Washington, D.C., U. S.A. : World Bank, c1987. xvi, 107 p., [1] folded leaf of plates : ill., col. map ; 28 cm. (A World Bank country study) "Prepared by a mission that visited Fiji during early April 1986; mission members were Shahid Yusuf (mission chief), R. Kyle Peters, and Vladimir Konovalov"--P. iv. ISBN 0-8213-0962-5 LC Card 87-23067 DDC 338.4/767/099611 19
1. Fiji - Manufactures. I. Yusuf, Shahid, 1949-. II. Peters, R. Kyle, 1954-. III. Konovalov, Vladimir. IV. International Bank for Reconstruction and Development. V. Series.
HD9738.F55 F55 1987

FIJI - MANUFACTURES.
Fiji, a transition to manufacturing. Washington, D.C., U. S.A. , c1987. xvi, 107 p., [1] folded leaf of plates : ISBN 0-8213-0962-5 LC Card 87-23067 DDC 338.4/767/099611 19
HD9738.F55 F55 1987

"Filantropicheskie" fondy SShA v sisteme vlasti monopoliĭ /. Zhurikhin, Ė. A. (Ėduard Alekseevich) Moskva , 1978. 182, [2] p. ; LC Card 81-160810
HG4028.C6 Z48 1978

Filasṭīn fī ṭawābi' al-barīd (1865-1981). English. Palestine stamps (1865-1981) [Abdel-Wahab Elmessiri, Jean O'Hanlon, translation]. Beirut : Dar Al-Fata Al-Arabi ; Cairo : Arab Graphic Centre, 1981. [80] p. : ill. (some col.), maps, ports. ; 25 cm. (Philatelists library) Translation of: Filasṭīn fī ṭawābi' al-barīd (1865-1981) Bibliography: p. [80] Includes index. LC Card 84-960260
1. Postage-stamps - Palestine - Catalogs. I. Series: Maktabat huwāt ṭawābi' al-barīd. English.
HE6185.P14 F5513 1981

Filatelia . Tripcovici, Nicolae. București , 1985. 213 p., [16] p. of plates : LC Card 87-164874
HE6213 .T75 1985

Filatelisticheskaia geografiia . Vladinets, N. I. (Nikolaĭ Ivanovich) Moskva , 1981. 159 p. : LC Card 82-110957
HE6185.E84 V54 1981

Filatelisticheskaia geografiia . Vladinets, N. I. (Nikolaĭ Ivanovich) Moskva , 1984. 175 p. : LC Card 85-153635
HE6185.A7 V53 1984

Filatelisticheskaia Pushkiniana /. Gdalin, A. D. (Aleksandr Davidovich) Moskva , 1981. 124 p. : LC Card 86-174858
HE6183.P86 G43 1981

Filbert, Judith Ann. Homemaking skills go to the office : a woman's guide to an office career / by Judith Ann Filbert. Bozeman, Mont. (P.O. Box 6244, Bozeman 59771) : J.A. Filbert, c1986. 46 p. ; 29 cm. LC Card 86-218123 DDC 651.3/741/02373 19
1. Office practice - Vocational guidance. 2. Women - Employment. 3. Secretaries. 4. Women - Time management. I. Title.
HF5547.5 .F53 1986

Filgueira, Carlos H. Argenti, Gisela. Cambio técnico, trabajo y educación . Montevideo , 1985. 91, 70 leaves : LC Card 87-124118
HC235.T4 A74 1985

Filing dynamics . Barber, Donald T. Emeryville, Calif. , 1987. 92 p. : ISBN 0-941151-00-X LC Card 87-60316 DDC 651.5/3 19
HF5741 .B44 1987

FILING SYSTEMS.
Barber, Donald T. Filing dynamics . Emeryville, Calif. , 1987. 92 p. : ISBN 0-941151-00-X LC Card 87-60316 DDC 651.5/3 19
HF5741 .B44 1987

Parikh, Girish, 1934- The one minute organizing secret . Chicago, IL , c1986. 60, 2 p. ; ISBN 0-932888-37-2 (pbk.) : LC Card 85-62926 DDC 650.1 19
HF5736 .P34 1986

Taylor, Mary Sue, 1938- Clear & simple filing and records management /. New York, NY , c1987. 171 p. : ISBN 0-671-62397-4 (pbk.) : LC Card 86-28534 DDC 651.5 19
HF5736 .T388 1987

Filip, Detlef. Gaulke, Klaus-Peter. Lehre und Berufsausübung . Berlin , 1986. 122 p. ; ISBN 3-428-06000-8 LC Card 86-166545
HC281 .B33 Heft 89 HD5715.5.G42B47

Filipov, Volodymyr Ivanovych. Strukturnye sdvigi v mirovom kapitalisticheskom khoziaĭstve /. Kiev , 1985. 295 p. ; LC Card 86-105339
HC59 .S8345 1985 ***NYPL [*QIP 87-3473]***

Filipović, Radojko. Novi devizni i spoljnotrgovinski režim SFRJ. English. The New foreign exchange and foreign trade regime of Yugoslavia /. Belgrade , 1986. 217 p. ; ISBN 86-7145-007-4 LC Card 87-148102 DDC 332.4/5609497 19
HG3965.5 .N6813 1986

Filippelli, Ronald L. Labor in the USA : a history / Ronald L. Filippelli. New York : Knopf, c1984. xii, 315 p. ; 23 cm. Includes bibliographies and index. ISBN 0-394-34149-X LC Card 83-23458 DDC 331/.0973 19
1. Labor and laboring classes - United States - History. 2. Industry and state - United States - History. 3. Trade-unions - United States - History. 4. Industrial relations - United States - History. 5. Technological innovations - United States - History. I. Title. II. Title: Labor in the U. S.A.
HD8066 .F54 1984 ***NYPL [JFE 86-5130]***

Filippov, N. N. Smekalov, Pavel Vasil'evich. Sel'skie kadry nechernozem'ia /. Moskva , 1981. 190 p. ; LC Card 82-177714
HD1536.S65 S64 1981

Fillea-Cgil/materiali .
(1) Seminario di aggiornamento per i quadri sindacali della categoria (1985 : Rome, Italy) Evoluzione del processo produttivo nelle construzioni . Milano, Italy , c1986. 142 p. : LC Card 86-210757
HD9715.I82 S46 1985

Filling up America . Schapiro, Morton Owen. Greenwich, Conn. , c1986. xiii, 149 p. : ISBN 0-89232-675-1 : LC Card 86-2771 DDC 304.6/0973 19
HB3505 .S33 1986 ***NYPL [JLE 86-3386]***

Fillmore, Mary Dingee. Women MBAs : a foot in the door / Mary Dingee Fillmore. Boston, MA : G.K. Hall, 1987. xii, 233 p. ; 25 cm. (G.K. Hall women's studies publications) Bibliography: p. 217-230. ISBN 0-8161-8728-2 LC Card 86-32002 DDC 331.4/816584/00973 19
1. Women executives - United States. 2. Women in business - United States. 3. Sex discrimination in employment - United States. I. Title. II. Series.
HD6054.4.U6 F54 1987

Filmakers Library, inc.
Faces in a famine [motion picture] /. New York, N.Y. , 1985. 1 film reel (51 min.) : LC Card 85-702803 DDC 963 11
HC845.Z9F3

Faces in a famine [videorecording] /. New York, N.Y. , 1985. 1 videocassette (51 min.) : LC Card 85-703663 DDC 963 11
HC845.Z9F3

Films Incorporated. Economics U$A. Chicago, IL , 1986. 1 videocassette (28 min.) : LC Card 86-708020 DDC 330.15 11
HB99.7

Filosofie van de economische wetenschappen /. Klant, J. J. Leiden , c1987. 87 p. ; ISBN 90-6890-105-2 : LC Card 87-169944
HB72 .K55 1987

Filter, Wolfgang, 1952- Aufbau und Ergebnisse einer Gesamtrechnung für das land- und forstwirtschaftliche Bodenvermögen in der Bundesrepublik Deutschland / Wolfgang Filter. Frankfurt am Main ; New York : P. Lang, c1984. xiii, 288 p. : ill. ; 21 cm. (Europäische Hochschulschriften. Reihe V, Volks- und Betriebswirtschaft, 0531-7339 . Bd. 490 = vol. 490 = vol. 490) Bibliography: p. 240-253. ISBN 3-8204-5290-7 LC Card 85-198973
1. Land use, Rural - Germany (West) - Data processing. 2. Land use, Rural - Germany (West) - Planning. I. Series: Europäische Hochschulschriften. Reihe V, Volks- und Betriebswirtschaft , Bd. 490. II. Title.
HD658 .F55 1984

Filtering and control of macroeconomic systems . Manohar Rao, M. J. Amsterdam ; New York : xii, 279 p. : ISBN 0-444-70188-5 (Elsevier Science Pub. Co.) LC Card 86-32928 DDC 339.5/0954 19
HC435.2 .M34 1987

FILTERS (MATHEMATICS)
Manohar Rao, M. J. Filtering and control of macroeconomic systems . Amsterdam ; New York : xii, 279 p. : ISBN 0-444-70188-5 (Elsevier Science Pub. Co.) LC Card 86-32928 DDC 339.5/0954 19
HC435.2 .M34 1987

Fimmtán gírar áfram . Indriði G. Þorsteinsson, 1926- Reykjavík , 1981. 178 p., [16] p. of plates : LC Card 83-185502
HD8039.M7952 I25 1981

Fin de fiesta /. Rangel, Domingo Alberto. Valencia, Venezuela , 1982. 181 p. ; LC Card 83-200321
HC125 .R29 1982

El fin de la autosuficiencia alimentaria /. Barkin, David. México, D.F. , c1985. 249 p. : ISBN 968-493-091-7 LC Card 86-209699
HD1792 .B38 1985

El fin de la era del petróleo y su impacto sobre la economía mundial . Vidal, Máximo Luis. San Pedro de Macorís, R.D. , 1981. 103 p. : LC Card 82-202556
HD9502.5.A433 D658 1981

Final report /. California. Governor's Task Force on Toxics, Waste, and Technology. [Sacramento, CA] [1986] 2 v. : LC Card 86-622772 DDC 363.7/28 19
HC107.C23 P553 1986

Final report /. Louisiana. Legislature. Joint Legislative Committee on Economies in State Government. [Baton Rouge] [1986] 62, 74, 105, [40] p. ; LC Card 86-621905 DDC 353.97630072 19
HJ2053.L8 L66 1986

Final report /. New York (State). Lieutenant Governor's Task Force on Plant Closings. [Albany] [1985] 1 v. (various foliations) ; LC Card 86-622454 DDC 338.6/042 19
HD5708.55.U62 N76 1985

Final report /. Regional Workshop on the Role and Prospects of Copper and Aluminium in African Development (1985 : Lusaka, Zambia) [Addis Ababa] , 1985. 9 p. ; LC Card 86-980966 DDC 338.2/743/096 19
HD9539.C7 A427 1985

Final report . Towle, Edward L. St. Thomas, U. S.V.I. [1982] 17, 15, 4 leaves : LC Card 86-185489 DDC 333.7/097297/22 19
HC155.Z9 E56 1982

Final report and recommendations of the Task Force on State Compensation and Classification Equity to the Sixty third Legislative Assembly. Oregon. Task Force on State Compensation and Classification Equity. [Salem OR] (338 State Capitol, Salem 97310) [1985] 51 p. : LC Card 86-622414 DDC 331.2/1 19
HD6061.2.U62 O75 1985

Final report of the consultancy of Rafael Diez from August 3, 1982 to August 3, 1983. Diez, Rafael. La Paz [1983] 1 v. (various foliations) ; LC Card 83-243264
HC182 .D49 1983

Final report of the Kentucky Tobacco Task Force /. Kentucky. General Assembly. Tobacco Task Force. Frankfort, Ky. [1986] vii, 91 p. : LC Card 86-622267 DDC 338.1/7371/09769 19
HD9137.K4 K45 1986

Final report of the Local Government Finance Commission, September 1986 /. Saskatchewan Local Government Finance Commission. [Regina, Canada] [1986] xiii, 440 p. : LC Card 87-163885 DDC 336/.014/7124 19
HJ9352.S3 S37 1986

Final report of the Regional Workshop on the Role and Prospects of Copper and Aluminium in African Development. Regional Workshop on the Role and Prospects of Copper and Aluminium in African Development (1985 : Lusaka, Zambia) Final report /. [Addis Ababa] , 1985. 9 p. ; LC Card 86-980966 DDC 338.2/743/096 19
HD9539.C7 A427 1985

Final report on pastoral land tenure. Western Australia. Pastoral Tenure Study Group. Perth, W.A. [1986] [28], 63, 4 p. ; LC Card 87-120095 DDC 333.3/09941 19
HD1641.A9 W47 1986

Final report on the San Diego job search and work experience demonstration /. Goldman, Barbara. New York, N.Y. (3 Park Ave., New York 10016) , c1986. xliv, 269 p. : LC Card 87-118376 DDC 331.12/042/0979498 19
HD5713.6.U542 S395 1986

El Finançament autonòmic : contribucions a un debat / Ll. Armet ... [et al.] ; pròleg de Josep M. Bricall.1a ed. Barcelona : Edicions 62, 1985. 157 p. ; 18 cm. (L'Escorpí. 59) Includes bibliographical references. ISBN 84-297-2364-1 LC Card 86-145741
1. Finance, Public - Spain - Autonomous communities. I. Armet, Lluís.
HJ1249.A1 F56 1985

Finançament del l'accés a l'habitatge a Catalunya en els darrers anys /. Trilla i Bellart, Carme. [Barcelona] [1984] 58 p. : LC Card 86-160332
HD7351.C37 T75 1984

Finanças municipais no Estado de São Paulo . Nalin, Irineu. São Paulo , 1985. 88 p. : LC Card 86-233330
HJ9388.A2 S286 1985

Finanças públicas dos Estados de Goiás, Maranhão, Mato Grosso e Pará / PRODIAT, Projeto de Desenvolvimento Integrado da Bacia do Araguaia-Tocantins. Brasília : PRODIAT, 1985. 114, [34] p. ; 22 cm. (Série Estudos e pesquisas. no. 7) At head of title: Ministério do Interior; Organização dos Estados Americanos; Governo do Estado de Goiás, Governo do Estado do Maranhão, Governo do Estado do Pará, Governo do Estado de Mato Grosso. Bibliography: p. 113-114. LC Card 87-404251 DDC 336.81 19
1. Finance, Public - Brazil - Goiás (State). 2. Finance, Public - Brazil - Maranhão. 3. Finance, Public - Brazil - Mato Grosso (State). 4. Finance, Public - Brazil - Pará (State). I. Projeto de Desenvolvimento Integrado da Bacia do Araguaia-Tocantins. II. Series: Série Estudos e pesquisas (Projeto de Desenvolvimento Integrado da Bacia do Araguaia-Tocantins) , no. 7.
HJ929.G65 F56 1985

Finanças públicas municipais da região do PRODIAT / Projeto de Desenvolvimento Integrado da Bacia do Araguaia-Tocantins. Brasília : PRODIAT, 1985. 420 p. ; 22 cm. (Série Estudos e pesquisas. no. 15) Chiefly tables. At head of title: Ministério do Interior, Organização dos Estados Americanos; Governo do Estado de Goiás, Governo do Estado do Maranhão, Governo do Estado do Pará, Governo do Estado de Mato Grosso. LC Card 86-195656
1. Local finance - Brazil - Araguaia River Region - Statistics. 2. Local finance - Brazil - Tocantins River Region - Statistics. I. Projeto de Desenvolvimento Integrado da Bacia do Araguaia-Tocantins. II. Series: Série Estudos e pesquisas (Projeto de Desenvolvimento Integrado da Bacia do Araguaia-Tocantins) , no. 15.
HJ9388.A2 A734 1985

Finance. 1st ed. Oxford [Oxfordshire] ; New York : Published for the Royal Statistical Society and Economic and Social Research Council by Pergamon Press, 1987. xiii, 495 p. ; 26 cm. (Reviews of United Kingdom statistical sources . v. 21) Includes bibliographies and indexes. CONTENTS. - Financial data of banks and other institutions / by Kate Phylaktis -- Life assurance and pension funds / by Geraldine Kaye. ISBN 0-08-034780-0 : LC Card 87-7247 DDC 332/.0941 19
1. Finance - Great Britain - Statistical services. I. Phylaktis, Kate. II. Kaye, Geraldine. III. Royal Statistical Society (Great Britain). IV. Economic and Social Research Council (Great Britain). V. Series.
HG186.G7 F53 1987

Finance . Augros, Jean-Claude. Paris , c1985. 320 p. : ISBN 2-7178-0911-2 : LC Card 85-219227 DDC 332.64/52/0944 19
HG6042 .A94 1985 ***NYPL [JLE 87-295]***

Finance /. Wood, Frank. London , 1986. 410 p. : ISBN 0-273-02587-2 (pbk.) : LC Card 86-224835 DDC 332/.0941 19
HG186.G7 W66 1986

FINANCE - AFRICA.
Nezavisimye strany Afriki . Moskva , 1986. 276 p. ; LC Card 87-110032
HG187.5.A2 N49 1986

Seidman, Ann Willcox, 1926- Money, banking, and public finance in Africa /. London , Atlantic Highlands, N.J., USA , 1986. xv, 363 p. : ISBN 0-86232-429-7 LC Card 87-111822 DDC 332.1/096 19
HG187.5.A2 S45 1986

Finance and government under Maria Theresia, 1740-1780 /. Dickson, P. G. M. (Peter George Muir) Oxford [Oxfordshire] , New York , 1987. 2 v. : ISBN 0-19-822570-9 (v. 1) : LC Card 87-1614 DDC 336.436 19
HJ1059 .D52 1987

Finance and investment handbook. Downes, John. Barron's finance and investment handbook /. Woodbury, N.Y. , c1986. xiv, 994 p. : ISBN 0-8120-5729-5 : LC Card 86-10906 DDC 332.6/78 19
HG173 .D65 1986
NYPL [*R-Econ. 86-5261]

FINANCE - ANECDOTES, FACETIAE, SATIRE, ETC. - DICTIONARIES.
Joy, Maurice. Not heard on the street . Chicago, Ill. , c1986. viii, 133 p. ; ISBN 0-917253-40-X : LC Card 86-3213 DDC 332.6/0207 19
HG4513 .J69 1986 ***NYPL [JLD 86-2885]***

FINANCE - ARAB COUNTRIES.
"Problema neftedollarov" . Moskva , 1984. 231 p. ; LC Card 85-189000
HC498 .P75 1984

FINANCE - ARGENTINA.
Feldman, Ernesto V. (Ernesto Víctor) Crisis financiera y endeudamiento externo en la Argentina /. [Buenos Aires] , c1986. 184 p. ; ISBN 950-25-1313-4 LC Card 86-182663
HG185.A7 F45 1986

Tami, Felipe S. Study of the financial sector of Argentina . Washington, D.C. [1979] x, 146 p. : LC Card 86-673765
HG185.A7 T35x 1979

FINANCE - ASIA.
Improving domestic resource mobilization through financial development . Manila, Philippines , c1985. vii, 51 p. : LC Card 87-101640 DDC 332.6/72/091724 19
HC415.S3 I45 1985

FINANCE - ASIA, SOUTHEASTERN.
Skully, Michael T. Financing East Asia's success . New York , 1987. xiii, 242 p. ; ISBN 0-312-00536-9 : LC Card 86-31527 DDC 332/.0959 19
HG187.E37 S68 1987

Finance Authority of Maine. Colgan, Charles S. The natural resource industries of Maine . [Augusta, Me.] [1986] 135 p. : LC Card 87-620550 DDC 338.09741 19
HD9007.M2 C64 1986

FINANCE - BAHAMAS.
A General information guide on the economy of the Bahamas /. Nassau, Bahamas [1986] x, 60 p. ; LC Card 87-400226 DDC 330.97296 19
HC152 .G46 1986

FINANCE - BELGIUM.
Verheirstraeten, A. Geld, krediet en intrest in de Belgische financiële sector /. Leuven , 1977. xxii, 337 p. : LC Card 78-345984
HG1055 .V47 ***NYPL [JLM 86-1310 nr.23]***

FINANCE - BIBLIOGRAPHY.
Financial Sourcebooks' sources . Naperville, Ill. , c1987. 454 p. ; ISBN 0-942061-00-4 (pbk.) : LC Card 87-8793 DDC 332/.025/73 19
HG173 .F517 1987

FINANCE - BRAZIL.
Baer, Mônica. A internacionalização financeira no Brasil /. Petrópolis , 1986. 159 p. ; LC Card 86-200812
HG185.B7 B28 1986

Galvêas, Ernane. Sistema financeiro e mercado de capitais /. Rio de Janeiro , 1985. 171 p. : LC Card 85-208367
HG185.B7 G35 1985

Martone, Celso L. (Celso Luiz) Mercado financeiro e ajustamento macroeconômico brasileiro, 1978-1985 /. São Paulo , 1986. 82 p. : LC Card 87-120453 DDC 332.4/981 19
HG835 .M375 1986

FINANCE - BRAZIL - CONGRESSES.
Ciclo Integrado sobre Administração Financeira (1983 : Escola de Administração Fazendária) Ciclo Integrado sobre Administração Financeira /. Salvador, BA [1984] 53 p. : LC Card 86-157989
HG185.B7 C52 1983

FINANCE - BRAZIL - HISTORY.
Topik, Steven. The political economy of the Brazilian State, 1889-1930 /. Austin , 1987. xii, 241 p. : ISBN 0-292-76500-2 LC Card 87-5835 DDC 338.981 19
HC187 .T558 1987

FINANCE - CANADA.
Hunter, W. T. Canadian financial markets /. Peterborough, Canada , c1986. 193 p. : ISBN 0-921149-01-8 (pbk.) LC Card 86-206029 DDC 332.6/0973 19
HG185.C2 H86 1986

FINANCE - CARIBBEAN AREA - CASE STUDIES.
Hope, Kempe R. Development finance and the development process . New York , 1987. 100 p. ; ISBN 0-313-25835-X (lib. bdg. : alk. paper) LC Card 86-29617 DDC 336.729 19
HJ844.3 .H67 1987

FINANCE - CARIBBEAN AREA - CONGRESSES.
Current economic and financial issues of the North American and Caribbean countries /. Mexico, D.F. , 1983. 390 p. : LC Card 87-106905 DDC 330.97/00539 19
HC95 .C87 1983

FINANCE - CHILE.
Nowak, Felicitas. Financial liberalization revisited . Göttingen [1986] 49 p. : LC Card 87-121206 DDC 332/.0983 19
HG185.C5 N69 1986

FINANCE - CONGRESSES.
Financial innovation and monetary policy . [Tokyo] , c1986. ix, 339 p. : ISBN 4-13-047029-9 : LC Card 86-222823 DDC 332/.095 19
HG187.E37 F55 1986

Shifting frontiers in financial markets /. Dordrecht ; Boston : xii, 360 p. : ISBN 90-247-3225-5 LC Card 85-18821 DDC 332 19
HG4523 .S54 1986 ***NYPL [JLE 86-2694]***

FINANCE - COSTA RICA - STATISTICS.
Estadísticas, 1950-1985. San José, Costa Rica , 1986. 221 p. ; LC Card 87-404209 DDC 332/.097286/021 19
HG185.C7 E84 1986

FINANCE - DATA BASES - DIRECTORIES.
Online databases in the securities and financial markets. New York, N.Y. , c1987. xxii, 322 p. ; ISBN 0-444-01276-1 (pbk.) LC Card 87-19954 DDC 025/.0633/0025 19
HG174 .O44 1987

FINANCE - DEVELOPING COUNTRIES.
Jenkins, Rhys Owen, 1948- Transnational corporations and uneven development . London , New York , 1987. p. cm. ISBN 0-416-73340-9 LC Card 87-12351 DDC 338.8/83 19
HD2932 .J45 1987

Kitchen, Richard L. Finance for the developing countries /. Chichester [West Sussex] , New York , c1986. xvii, 365 p. ; ISBN 0-471-90945-9 : LC Card 85-32331 DDC 332/.09172/4 19
HG195 .K58 1986 ***NYPL [JLE 86-4165]***

L'Hériteau, Marie France. Le Fonds monétaire international et les pays du Tiers-monde /. Paris , c1986. 277 p. : ISBN 2-13-039203-2 : LC Card 86-165389
HG3881.5.I58 L52 1986

Nezavisimye strany Afriki . Moskva , 1986. 276 p. ; LC Card 87-110032
HG187.5.A2 N49 1986

FINANCE - DEVELOPING COUNTRIES - CONGRESSES.
KIET International Finance Conference (1985 : Seoul, Korea) International financial markets and the NICs. Seoul, Korea [1985?] viii, 144 p. : LC Card 87-129000 DDC 332/.042 19
HG205 .K54 1985

FINANCE - DICTIONARIES.
AHI's complete portfolio of modern business terms. A dictionary of business terms /. New York , 1987, c1986. 438 p. ; ISBN 0-531-15518-8 LC Card 86-24560 DDC 650/.03/21 19
HF1001 .A34 1987

Downes, John. Barron's finance and investment handbook /. Woodbury, N.Y. , c1986. xiv, 994 p. : ISBN 0-8120-5729-5 : LC Card 86-10906 DDC 332.6/78 19
HG173 .D65 1986
NYPL [*R-Econ. 86-5261]

The English-Arabic dictionary of professional business terms /. London , Boulder, Colo. , c1987. 210 p. ; ISBN 0-946510-33-4 : LC Card 87-163985 DDC 650/.03/21 19
HF1002 .E583 1987

Farid, ʻAbd Allāh Muḥammad. al-Qāmūs al-farīd fī al-māl wa-al-iqtiṣād, ʻArabī-Injilīzī /. [S.l.] 1985 (al-Qāhirah, Miṣr : Maṭābiʻ al-Ahrām al-Tijārīyah) 150, 264 p. ; LC Card 86-960655
HB61 .F36 1985

Friedman, Jack P. Dictionary of business terms /. New York , c1987. vi, 650 p. ; ISBN 0-8120-3775-8 (pbk.) : LC Card 87-12640 DDC 650/.03/21 19
HF1001 .F78 1987

Kay, William. A-Z guide to money /. London , 1986, c1983. 281 p. : ISBN 0-09-467160-5 : LC Card 86-224824 DDC 332/.03/21 19
HG216 .K39 1986

Pessin, Allan H. More words of Wall Street . Homewood, Ill. , 1986. v, 269 p. ; ISBN 0-87094-701-X LC Card 86-70777
NYPL [JLE 86-4060]

Rosenberg, Jerry Martin. Dictionary of banking and financial services /. New York , c1985. xv, 708 p. ; ISBN 0-471-83088-7 LC Card 85-12461 DDC 332/.03/21 19
HG151 .R67 1985
NYPL [*R-Econ. 86-3275]

Walmsley, Julian. A dictionary of international finance /. Westport, Conn. , 1979. 270 p. ; ISBN 0-313-20974-X LC Card 79-17753 DDC 332/.042/0321 19
HG151 .W34 ***NYPL [JLD 87-1082]***

Woelfel, Charles J. Budgeting, pricing, and cost controls . Chicago, Ill. , c1987. p. cm. ISBN 0-917253-91-4 : LC Card 87-17921 DDC 658.1/5/0321 19
HG151 .W63 1987

FINANCE - DICTIONARIES - ANECDOTES, FACETIAE, SATIRE, ETC.
Lansky, Bruce. Wall Street bull /. Deephaven, MN , New York , c1987. iii, 111 p. : ISBN 0-88166-100-7 (pbk.) : LC Card 87-16467 DDC 332.6/0207 19
HG4513 .L29 1987

FINANCE - DICTIONARIES - ARABIC.
Farid, ʻAbd Allāh Muḥammad. al-Qāmūs al-farīd fī al-māl wa-al-iqtiṣād, ʻArabī-Injilīzī /. [S.l.] 1985 (al-Qāhirah, Miṣr : Maṭābiʻ al-Ahrām al-Tijārīyah) 150, 264 p. ; LC Card 86-960655
HB61 .F36 1985

FINANCE - DICTIONARIES - RUSSIAN.
Finansovo-kreditnyĭ slovarʹ /. Moskva , 1984- v. ; LC Card 84-203984
HG151 .F53 1984 ***NYPL [*QAC 85-1247]***

FINANCE - DOMINICAN REPUBLIC.
González Vega, Claudio. Mercados financieros y desarrollo /. Santo Domingo, República Dominicana , 1986. 73 p. : LC Card 87-102022
HG2817 .G66 1986

FINANCE - DOMINICAN REPUBLIC - CONGRESSES.
La Situación y los problemas del sistema financiero nacional. Santo Domingo, República Dominicana , 1986. 152 p. ; LC Card 86-208560
HG2817 .S57 1986

FINANCE - DOMINICAN REPUBLIC - MATHEMATICAL MODELS.
Dauhajre, Andrés. Reforma financiera en pequeñas economías abiertas /. Santo Domingo, República Dominicana , 1986. 97 p. : LC Card 87-402920 DDC 332.4/56097293 19
HG3926.5 .D38 1986

FINANCE - EAST ASIA.
Skully, Michael T. Financing East Asia's success . New York , 1987. xiii, 242 p. ; ISBN 0-312-00536-9 : LC Card 86-31527 DDC 332/.0959 19
HG187.E37 S68 1987

FINANCE - EAST ASIA - CONGRESSES.
Financial innovation and monetary policy . [Tokyo] , c1986. ix, 339 p. : ISBN 4-13-047029-9 : LC Card 86-222823 DDC 332/.095 19
HG187.E37 F55 1986

FINANCE - ECUADOR.
Pensamiento monetario y financiero /. Quito, Ecuador , 1986. 2 v. : LC Card 87-150740 DDC 332.4/9866 19
HG862 .P46 1986

FINANCE - ENGLAND - HISTORY.
Fryde, E. B. Studies in medieval trade and finance /. London , 1983. 1 v. (various pagings) ; ISBN 0-907628-10-9 LC Card 83-168474 DDC 382/.0942/04 19
HF3518.E85 F79 1983 ***NYPL [JLE 86-2481]***

FINANCE - ENGLAND - LONDON.
Hall, Maximilian. The city revolution . New York , 1987. xiii, 147 p. ; ISBN 0-312-00986-0 : LC Card 87-9684 DDC 332.6/0941 19
HG186.G7 H35 1987

FINANCE - ETHIOPIA.
Mauri, Arnaldo. Moneta e banca in Etiopia /. Milano [1986] xi, 316 p. : ISBN 88-14-00769-1 LC Card 86-182310
HG3389.A6 M38 1986
NYPL [JLE 87-1721]

FINANCE - EUROPE, EASTERN.
Belichenko, A. N. (Alʹbert Nikolaevich) Kreditnye otnoshenii͡a mezhdu stranami-chlenami SĖV /. Moskva , 1983. 134 p. : LC Card 84-171632
HG3729.E932 B45 1983

Brabant, Jozef M. van. Adjustment, structural change, and economic efficiency . Cambridge [Cambridgeshire] , New York , 1987. xviii, 480 p. ; ISBN 0-521-33455-1 LC Card 87-785 DDC 332.4/947 19
HG186.E82 B7 1987

Holzman, Franklyn D. The economics of Soviet bloc trade and finance /. Boulder , 1987. xi, 215 p. : ISBN 0-8133-7274-7 (alk. paper) : LC Card 86-32598 DDC 382/.0947 19
HF3496.5 .H62 1987

Konstantinov, I͡U. A. (I͡Uriĭ Anatolʹevich) Mezhdunarodnai͡a valiutnai͡a sistema stran--chlenov SĖV /. Moskva , 1982. 231 p. ; LC Card 82-210094
HG3942 .K67 1982

FINANCE - EUROPE - HISTORY.
Fryde, E. B. Studies in medieval trade and finance /. London , 1983. 1 v. (various pagings) ; ISBN 0-907628-10-9 LC Card 83-168474 DDC 382/.0942/04 19
HF3518.E85 F79 1983 ***NYPL [JLE 86-2481]***

FINANCE - EUROPE - HISTORY - 20TH CENTURY.
Brown, Brendan, 1951- Monetary chaos in Europe . London , New York , c1987. p. cm. ISBN 0-7099-5035-7 : LC Card 87-23059 DDC 332.4/5/094 19
HG186.A2 B76 1987

FINANCE - EUROPEAN ECONOMIC COMMUNITY COUNTRIES.
Gil, Gonzalo. Aspectos financieros y monetarios de la integración española en la Comunidad Económica Europea /. [Madrid] [1985] 187 p. : ISBN 84-505-2233-1 LC Card 87-101729
HC241.25.S6 G55 1985

FINANCE - EUROPEAN ECONOMIC COMMUNITY COUNTRIES - CONGRESSES.
International monetary and financial integration . Dordrecht , Boston , c1988. xii, 403 p. : ISBN 90-247-3563-7 LC Card 87-3622 DDC 332.4/94 19
HG930.5 .I586 1988

Finance for the developing countries /. Kitchen, Richard L. Chichester [West Sussex] , New York , c1986. xvii, 365 p. ; ISBN 0-471-90945-9 : LC Card 85-32331 DDC 332/.09172/4 19
HG195 .K58 1986 *NYPL [JLE 86-4165]*

FINANCE - FRANCE - BRITTANY - HISTORY.
Kerhervé, Jean. L'Etat breton aux 14e et 15e siècles . Paris , c1987. 2 v. (xii, x, 1078 p.) : ISBN 2-224-01703-0 (t. 1) LC Card 87-160693
HJ1078.B75 K47 1987

FINANCE - FRANCE - HISTORY - 18TH CENTURY.
Bruguière, Michel. Gestionnaires et profiteurs de la Révolution . Paris , c1986. 339 p. : ISBN 2-85565-332-0 : LC Card 87-123230
HJ1083 .B78 1986

FINANCE - FRANCE - HISTORY - 20TH CENTURY.
Néré, Jacques. Le problème du mur d'argent . Paris , c1985. 159 p. ; ISBN 2-214-06264-5 : LC Card 86-149791
HG979 .N47 1985

FINANCE - GAMBIA.
Faal, A. A. Money and capital markets in the Gambia and United Kingdom, and the problem of economic management at central bank level . [S.l. , 198-] 27 leaves ; LC Card 87-400415 DDC 332.1/0966/51 19
HG187.5.G25 F3 1980z

FINANCE - GERMANY, WEST.
Banken . Frankfurt am Main , c1983. 216 p. ; ISBN 3-7819-0297-8 : LC Card 83-217788
HG3048 .B27 1983

FINANCE - GERMANY (WEST) - DICTIONARIES - GERMAN.
Lexikon Wirtschaftspolitik . München , c1986. 236 p. : ISBN 3-406-31302-7 LC Card 86-221788
HG151 .L45 1986

FINANCE - GREAT BRITAIN.
Faal, A. A. Money and capital markets in the Gambia and United Kingdom, and the problem of economic management at central bank level . [S.l. , 198-] 27 leaves ; LC Card 87-400415 DDC 332.1/0966/51 19
HG187.5.G25 F3 1980z

Goacher, D. J. (David J.) British non-bank financial intermediaries /. London , Boston , 1987. xxiv, 460 p. : ISBN 0-04-332109-7 (alk. paper) LC Card 86-32146 DDC 332.1/0941 19
HG186.G7 B73 1987

Hall, Maximilian. The city revolution . New York , 1987. xiii, 147 p. ; ISBN 0-312-00986-0 : LC Card 87-9684 DDC 332.6/0941 19
HG186.G7 H35 1987

Hall, Peter (Peter J.), 1932- Elements of banking /. London , New York , 1987. xi, 236 p. : ISBN 0-582-29728-1 (pbk.) LC Card 86-21144 DDC 332.1 19
HG1601 .H25 1987

New perspectives on the financial system /. London , New York , c1988. 410 p. : ISBN 0-7099-3741-5 LC Card 87-15723 DDC 332/.0941 19
HG186.G7 N44 1988

Personal financial markets . Deddington, Oxford , Atlantic Highlands, N.J. , 1986. viii, 279 p. : ISBN 0-86003-540-9 LC Card 86-235455 DDC 332.1/7 19
HG186.G7 P38 1986

Rowley, Eric E. The financial system today /. Manchester, UK , Wolfeboro, NH, USA , c1987. p. cm. ISBN 0-7190-1487-5 LC Card 87-7938 DDC 332/.0941 19
HG186.G7 R64 1987

Wood, Frank. Finance /. London , 1986. 410 p. : ISBN 0-273-02587-2 (pbk.) : LC Card 86-224835 DDC 332/.0941 19
HG186.G7 W66 1986

FINANCE - GREAT BRITAIN - DEREGULATION - CONGRESSES.
Financial deregulation . Cambridge , Wolfeboro, N.H., USA , 1986. xiii, 88 p. ; ISBN 0-85941-366-7 : LC Card 87-104563 DDC 332/.0941 19
HG186.G7 F546 1986

FINANCE - GREAT BRITAIN - STATISTICAL SERVICES.
Finance. Oxford [Oxfordshire] , New York , 1987. xiii, 495 p. ; ISBN 0-08-034780-0 : LC Card 87-7247 DDC 332/.0941 19
HG186.G7 F53 1987

FINANCE - HANDBOOKS, MANUALS, ETC.
Downes, John. Barron's finance and investment handbook /. Woodbury, N.Y. , c1986. xiv, 994 p. : ISBN 0-8120-5729-5 : LC Card 86-10906 DDC 332.6/78 19
HG173 .D65 1986
*NYPL [*R-Econ. 86-5261]*

FINANCE - HUNGARY.
Kiefer, Márta. Magyarország tőkés viszonylatu gazdasági és pénzügyi kapcsolatairól /. [Budapest] [1985] 115 p. ; ISBN 963-608-080-1 LC Card 86-228329
HF1542.5 .K54 1985

Szentiványi, Iván. Lakossági pénzügyek, pénzintézeti tevékenység /. Budapest , 1985. 563, [1] p. ; ISBN 963-221-602-4 : LC Card 86-186953
HG186.H8 S94 1985

FINANCE - INDIA.
Explanatory notes on current statistics. Bombay [1978] iii, 74 p. ; LC Card 85-229381
HG187.I4 E98 1978

Narayan Prasad, P. S. C.D. Deshmukh, his contribution to monetary and economic policy /. New Delhi , c1985. xiv, 54 p., [1] leaf of plates : LC Card 85-905075 DDC 338.954 19
HC432.5.D47 N37 1985
NYPL [JLD 86-3239]

FINANCE - INFORMATION SERVICES - DIRECTORIES.
Financial Sourcebooks' sources . Naperville, Ill. , c1987. 454 p. ; ISBN 0-942061-00-4 (pbk.) : LC Card 87-8793 DDC 332/.025/73 19
HG173 .F517 1987

FINANCE - INFORMATION SERVICES - EUROPE - CONGRESSES.
L'Information financière . Bruxelles , 1983. 220 p. ; ISBN 2-8027-0298-X LC Card 84-104169
HG151.5 .I56 1983

Finance, insurance, and real estate : second quarter, 1984 / prepared by Research and Statistics. Bismarck, N.D. (1000 E. Divide, Bismarck 58502) : Job Service North Dakota, [1986] 55 p. : ill. ; 28 cm. (North Dakota occupational profiles) "May 1986." "OES 4-3." LC Card 86-623003 DDC 332.12/51/0009784 19
1. Bank employees - North Dakota - Statistics. 2. Financial institutions - North Dakota - Employees - Statistics. 3. Insurance companies - North Dakota - Employees - Statistics. 4. Real estate business - North Dakota - Employees - Statistics. I. Job Service North Dakota. Research and Statistics Section. II. Series.
HD5718.B262 U64 1986

FINANCE, INTERNATIONAL. see **INTERNATIONAL FINANCE.**

FINANCE - ITALY.
Politica monetaria e politica dell'occupazione in Italia, in un contesto di innovazione finanziaria /. Milano , c1984. 166 p. ; LC Card 84-245111 DDC 332/.0945 19
HG1029.5 .P63 1984

Turani, Giuseppe. Briganti e gentiluomini della finanza italiana /. [Milano] , c1987. 394 p. ; ISBN 88-20-00657-X : LC Card 87-168620
HG186.I8 T86 1987

FINANCE - ITALY - HISTORY - 20TH CENTURY.
Ciocca, Pierluigi, 1941- Interesse e profitto . Bologna , c1982. 245 p. : LC Card 84-139966 DDC 332/.0945 19
HG186.I8 C56 1982

FINANCE - JAPAN.
Suzuki, Yoshio, 1931- [Nihon kin'yū keizairon. English.] Money, finance, and macroeconomic performance in Japan /. New Haven , c1986. xvii, 218, p. : ISBN 0-300-03387-7 LC Card 85-26375 DDC 332/.0952 19
HG187.J3 S96 1986 *NYPL [JLE 86-2788]*

Viner, Aron. Inside Japanese financial markets /. Homewood, Ill. , c1988. xvi, 364 p. : ISBN 1-556-23020-6 LC Card 87-71357 DDC 332/.0952 19
HG187.J3 V57 1988

FINANCE - KOREA (SOUTH)
Dee, Philippa S. Financial markets and economic development . Tübingen , c1986. ix, 131 p. ; ISBN 3-16-345086-5 LC Card 86-190926 DDC 338.9519/5 19
HC467 .D44 1986

FINANCE - LATIN AMERICA.
Echegaray, Alfredo. Evolución y perspectivas de la cooperación financiera en América Latina /. Buenos Aires , 1982. 147 p. ; LC Card 86-198731
HG185.L3 E25 1982

Herrera, Felipe, 1922- América Latina, desarrollo e integracíon /. [Santiago, Chile] [1986] 302 p., [11] p. of plates : LC Card 87-115159 DDC 337.1/8 19
HC125 .H466 1986

Latinskaia͡ Amerika . Moskva , 1978. 271 p. ; LC Card 81-159488
HG185.L3 L37 1978

Quijano, José Manuel. Finanzas, desarrollo económico y penetración extranjera /. Puebla, Pue. , 1985. 395 p. : LC Card 86-112589 DDC 332/.0972 19
HG185.M6 Q55 1985 *NYPL [JLD 86-2195]*

FINANCE - LAW AND LEGISLATION - HUNGARY.
Ábel, István. A vállalatok pénzügyi szabályozása . Budapest , 1984. 32, [1] p. ; LC Card 85-175023
HG4149.5 .A54 1984

FINANCE - LAW AND LEGISLATION - VENEZUELA.
Venezuela, periodic economic report . Caracas, Venezuela [1987] [166] p. : LC Card 87-403325 DDC 330.987/0633 19
HC237 .V487 1987

FINANCE, LOCAL. see **LOCAL FINANCE.**

FINANCE - MATHEMATICAL MODELS.
Frenkel, Roberto. Mercado financiero, expectativas cambiarias y movimientos de capital /. Buenos Aires, Argentina [1981] 46 p. : LC Card 82-236987 DDC 332/.0724 19
HG173.6.S62 F73 1981
NYPL [JLD 86-2636]

Ohlson, James A. The theory of financial markets and information /. New York , c1987. xiii, 181 p. ; ISBN 0-444-01161-7 LC Card 87-9100 DDC 332.6 19
HG173 .O34 1987

FINANCE - MATHEMATICS. see **BUSINESS MATHEMATICS.**

FINANCE - MEXICO.
Dávila Flores, Alejandro, 1956- La crisis financiera en México /. [Mexico City, Mexico] , 1986. 228 p. : LC Card 87-401258 DDC 330.972/0834 19
HG185.M6 D33 1986

FINANCE - MEXICO - HISTORY.
Quijano, José Manuel. Finanzas, desarrollo económico y penetración extranjera /. Puebla, Pue. , 1985. 395 p. : LC Card 86-112589 DDC 332/.0972 19
HG185.M6 Q55 1985 *NYPL [JLD 86-2195]*

FINANCE - MEXICO - STATISTICS.
El Sistema bancario y financiero en México, 1970-1984. México, D.F. , c1985. 260 p. ; ISBN 968-89204-0-1 LC Card 86-223773
HG2714 .S57 1985

FINANCE, MILITARY. see **WAR, COST OF.**

Finance, money, and unemployment /. Sawyer, Malcolm C. Berlin [1985] 65 p. ; LC Card 86-205291 DDC 332 19
HG230.3 .S29 1985

FINANCE, MUNICIPAL. see **MUNICIPAL FINANCE.**

FINANCE - NETHERLANDS - ROTTERDAM - HISTORY.
Mees en Chabot, twee kassiers te Rotterdam . Delft , c1986. 87 p. : ISBN 90-70879-40-9 : LC

Card 86-205783
HG3120.R62 M44 1986

FINANCE - NORTH AMERICA - CONGRESSES.
Current economic and financial issues of the North American and Caribbean countries /. Mexico, D.F. , 1983. 390 p. : LC Card 87-106905 DDC 330.97/00539 19
HC95 .C87 1983

FINANCE - OCEANIA - CASE STUDIES.
Skully, Michael T. Financial institutions and markets in the South Pacific . New York , 1987. xvi, 379 p., [1] leaf of plates : ISBN 0-312-00529-6 : LC Card 87-4506 DDC 332.1/099 19
HG190.A2 S58 1987

FINANCE, PERSONAL - ANECDOTES, FACETIAE, SATIRE, ETC.
Lowe, Mifflin. The cheapskate's handbook . Los Angeles , 1986. 104 p. : ISBN 0-8431-1246-8 (pbk.): LC Card 86-207189 DDC 332.024 19
HG7931 .L68 1986

FINANCE, PERSONAL - DATA PROCESSING.
Adams, Steve, 1948- Using Dollars and Sense on the IBM /. Indianapolis, Ind. , c1987. xviii, 439 p. : ISBN 0-88022-287-5 (pbk.) : LC Card 86-63981 DDC 332.024/0028/55369 19
HG179 .A34 1987

Rozells, Gia L. Making dollars and cents with dollars and sense /. Greensboro, N.C. , c1987. ix, 207 p. : ISBN 0-87455-101-3 (pbk.) : LC Card 87-160661 DDC 332.024/0028/55369 19
HG179 .R74 1987

Weinberg, Mark D. Using Managing Your Money /. Indianapolis, Ind. , c1987. xviii, 422 p. : ISBN 0-88022-277-8 (pbk.) : LC Card 86-62530 DDC 332.024/0028/55369 19
HG179 .W42 1987

Witkin, Ruth K. Personal money management with AppleWorks /. Hasbrouck Heights, N.J. [New York] , c1986. 418 p. : ISBN 0-471-62575-2 (Wiley : pbk.) : LC Card 87-110545 DDC 332.024/0028/55369 19
HG179 .W554 1986

Witkin, Ruth K. Personal money mangement with AppleWorks /. New York , c1987. p. cm. ISBN 0-471-62575-2 : LC Card 87-6294 DDC 332.024/0028/55369 19
HG179 .W554 1987

FINANCE, PERSONAL - GREAT BRITAIN.
Personal financial markets . Deddington, Oxford , Atlantic Highlands, N.J. , 1986. viii, 279 p. : ISBN 0-86003-540-9 LC Card 86-235455 DDC 332.1/7 19
HG186.G7 P38 1986

FINANCE, PERSONAL - HANDBOOKS, MANUALS, ETC.
Personal financial planning . New York, N.Y. (1211 Ave. of the Americas, New York 10036-8775) , c1987. viii, 131 p. ; LC Card 87-142958 DDC 332.024 19
HG179 .P387 1987

Personal financial planning manual . New York, NY , c1987. 1 v. (loose-leaf) : LC Card 87-404512 DDC 332.024 19
HG179 .P3865 1987

FINANCE, PERSONAL - HUNGARY.
Szentiványi, Iván. Lakossági pénzügyek, pénzintézeti tevékenység /. Budapest , 1985. 563, [1] p. ; ISBN 963-221-602-4 : LC Card 86-186953
HG186.H8 S94 1985

FINANCE, PERSONAL - JUVENILE LITERATURE.
Spiselman, David, 1947- A teenager's guide to money, banking, and finance /. New York , c1987. p. cm. ISBN 0-671-64345-2 LC Card 87-11059 DDC 332.024 19
HG179 .S5554 1987

FINANCE, PERSONAL - PSYCHOLOGICAL ASPECTS.
Forman, Norm. Mind over money . Toronto, Ont. , Garden City, N.Y. , 1987. xi, 248 p. ; ISBN 0-385-25104-1 LC Card 86-32814 DDC 332.024 19
HG222.3 .F67 1987

FINANCE, PERSONAL - STUDY AND TEACHING.
Nichols, Harwood, 1942- Money sense . Washington, DC , 1987. p. cm. ISBN 0-87491-871-5 (pbk.) : LC Card 87-24129 DDC 332.024/007 19
HG179 .N53 1987

FINANCE, PERSONAL - UNITED STATES.
Bertot, Cathey H. The new financial planner . Homewood, Ill. , c1986. xvi, 266 p. : ISBN 0-87094-587-4 LC Card 85-52442 DDC 332.024/01 19
HG179 .B458 1986 ***NYPL [JLE 87-537]***

Chase, C. David. Mugged on Wall Street . New York , c1987. 349 p. : ISBN 0-671-62706-6 LC Card 87-4707 DDC 332.6/78 19
HG4910 .C52 1987

Cheeks, James E. Keoghs . New York , c1986. xviii, 248 p. ; ISBN 0-531-15505-6 LC Card 85-31753 DDC 332.024/01 19
HG1660.U5 C48 1986 ***NYPL [JLD 86-3669]***

Eisenberg, Richard, 1956- How to avoid a mid-life financial crisis /. Glenview, Ill. , c1987. xxi, 426 p. : ISBN 0-673-18727-6 : LC Card 86-31647 DDC 332.024 19
HG179 .E39 1987

Klein, Robert J. The Money book of money . Boston , c1987. xvii, 522 p. ; ISBN 0-316-49840-8 : LC Card 86-33777 DDC 332.024 19
HG179 .K57 1987

Lerner, Joel J. Financial planning for the utterly confused /. New York , c1986. xi, 210 p. ; ISBN 0-07-037224-1 (pbk.) : LC Card 85-19823 DDC 332.024 19
HG179 .L45 1986 ***NYPL [JLD 86-2290]***

Passell, Peter. Where to put your money, 1987 /. New York, NY , c1987. 82 p. ; ISBN 0-446-38497-6 (pbk.) : LC Card 86-28917 DDC 332.6/78 19
HG179 .P27 1987

Personal financial markets . Deddington, Oxford , Atlantic Highlands, N.J. , 1986. viii, 279 p. : ISBN 0-86003-540-9 LC Card 86-235455 DDC 332.1/7 19
HG186.G7 P38 1986

Personal financial planning for local government employees /. Washington, D.C. , c1987. 203 p. : ISBN 0-87326-051-1 (pbk.) LC Card 87-2948 DDC 332.024/354 19
HG179 .P386 1987

Pritchard, Robert E., 1941- Be your own financial advisor /. Englewood Cliffs, N.J. , c1988. xiv, 187 p. ; ISBN 0-13-071242-6 LC Card 87-14366 DDC 332.024 19
HG179 .P737 1988

Sheen, Brian J., 1952- Nest egg investing . New York , c1987. 224 p. : ISBN 0-399-13185-X : LC Card 87-2268 DDC 332.6/78 19
HG179 .S455 1987

Stribling, Catherine. Growing up financially . New York , 1987, c1986. 311 p. ; ISBN 0-345-33098-6 (pbk.) : LC Card 86-90719 DDC 332.6/78 19
HG179 .S846 1987

Thomsett, Michael C. Homeowners money management . Emmaus, Pa. , c1987. xiii, 238 p. : ISBN 0-87857-673-8 (alk. paper) : LC Card 86-26096 DDC 332.024 19
HD7287.82.U6 T47 1987

FINANCE, PERSONAL - UNITED STATES - HANDBOOKS, MANUALS, ETC.
Seglin, Jeffrey L., 1956- Personal financial planning in banks . Boston , c1986. xvii, 205 p. ; ISBN 0-87267-059-7 LC Card 85-28738 DDC 332.1/7 19
HG1616.C87 S44 1986 ***NYPL [JLE 87-820]***

FINANCE - PERU.
Ahorro interno y el sistema financiero /. [Lima, Peru] , 1986. 70 p. : LC Card 87-127322 DDC 332/.0985 19
HC230.S3 A38 1986

FINANCE - PERU - CONGRESSES.
Susano Lucero, Aurelio Reynaldo. Liberalización financiera [microform] . Lima , c1982. [40] p. : LC Card 84-227503 DDC 332.1/0985 19
HG2944 .S93 1982 ***NYPL [*ZT-1745 no.6]***

FINANCE - PERU - DEPARTMENTS.
Panorama del Departamento ... /. [Lima?] , 1984-<1987. v. <1-8 > : LC Card 86-202585
HC227 .P354 1984

FINANCE, PRIVATE. see **FINANCE, PERSONAL.**

FINANCE, PUBLIC - ACCOUNTING.
Glynn, John J. Public sector financial control and accounting /. Oxford [Oxfordshire] , New York, N.Y., USA , 1987. x, 278 p. : ISBN 0-631-14686-5 : LC Card 86-31725 DDC 657/.835 19
HJ9733 .G58 1987

Henke, Emerson O. Introduction to nonprofit organization accounting /. Boston , c1988. xvi, 670 p. : ISBN 0-534-08322-6 LC Card 87-7330 DDC 657/.98 19
HF5686.N56 H45 1988

FINANCE, PUBLIC - ACCOUNTING - CONGRESSES.
Betriebswirtschaftliche Erkenntnisse für Regierung, Verwaltung und öffentliche Unternehmen . Baden-Baden , 1985. 266 p. : ISBN 3-7890-1104-5 LC Card 85-213984
HJ9705 .B48 1985

FINANCE, PUBLIC - ACCOUNTING - LAW AND LEGISLATION - GERMANY (WEST)
Sollmann, Axel, 1952- Die Massnahme-, Berichts- und Missbilligungsbeschlüsse des Parlaments im Entlastungsverfahren /. Frankfurt am Main , New York , c1986. 261 p. ; ISBN 3-8204-9778-1 LC Card 86-233741
HJ9925.G3 S65 1986

FINANCE, PUBLIC - ACCOUNTING - LAW AND LEGISLATION - GERMANY (WEST) - HAMBURG.
Gührs, Eckhard. Leitfaden für Kostenermittlung und Wirtschaftlichkeitsprüfung . Hamburg , 1983. iii, 92 p. ; LC Card 85-212548
HJ9925.G3 G84 1983

FINANCE, PUBLIC - AFRICA.
Seidman, Ann Willcox, 1926- Money, banking, and public finance in Africa /. London , Atlantic Highlands, N.J., USA , 1986. xv, 363 p. : ISBN 0-86232-429-7 LC Card 87-111822 DDC 332.1/096 19
HG187.5.A2 S45 1986

FINANCE, PUBLIC - AUDITING.
Glynn, John J. Public sector financial control and accounting /. Oxford [Oxfordshire] , New York, N.Y., USA , 1987. x, 278 p. : ISBN 0-631-14686-5 : LC Card 86-31725 DDC 657/.835 19
HJ9733 .G58 1987

Guidelines for auditing governmental subdivisions /. [New York, NY] [c1987] ii, 50 p. ; LC Card 87-121255 DDC 350.72/32 19
HJ9733 .G85 1987

FINANCE, PUBLIC - AUSTRALIA - ACCOUNTING - DATA PROCESSING.
Australia. Parliament. Joint Committee of Public Accounts. Proposed computer acquisition by the Australian Audit Office /. Canberra , 1986. xiii, 256 p. : ISBN 0-644-05079-9 (pbk.) LC Card 86-234536 DDC 354.940072/32 19
HJ9931 .A875 1986

FINANCE, PUBLIC - AUSTRIA - ACCOUNTING - HISTORY.
Gilles, Franz-O., 1944- Die verkannte Macht . Berlin , 1986. 398 p. ; ISBN 3-923024-07-X LC Card 87-127716 DDC 354.430072/31/09 19
HJ9925.G3 G55 1986

FINANCE, PUBLIC - AUSTRIA - CONGRESSES.
Staatsfinanzierung und Notenbank . Wien [1984?] 211 p. : LC Card 85-198128
HG1811 .S78 1984

FINANCE, PUBLIC - AUSTRIA - HISTORY - 18TH CENTURY.
Dickson, P. G. M. (Peter George Muir) Finance and government under Maria Theresia, 1740-1780 /. Oxford [Oxfordshire] , New York , 1987. 2 v. : ISBN 0-19-822570-9 (v. 1) : LC Card 87-1614 DDC 336.436 19
HJ1059 .D52 1987

FINANCE, PUBLIC - AUSTRIA - HISTORY - 19TH CENTURY.
Bericht der vereinigten Ausschüsse I und III samt Materialien zum Referate über die Steigerung der Kosten der staatlichen inneren Verwaltung in der Periode von 1890 bis 1911 und über vorläufige Reformvorschläge bezüglich der Zentralstellen und der politischen

Landesbehörden. [S.l. , 1912?] 1 v. in various pagings ; LC Card 87-409311 DDC 336.436 19
HJ1062 .B47 1912

Wagner, Adolph, 1835-1917. Die Ordnung des österreichischen Staatshaushaltes--1863 /. Wien , c1984. 308 p. ; ISBN 3-85447-086-X LC Card 85-223615
HJ1065 .W34 1984

FINANCE, PUBLIC - AUSTRIA - HISTORY - 20TH CENTURY.
Bericht der vereinigten Ausschüsse I und III samt Materialien zum Referate über die Steigerung der Kosten der staatlichen inneren Verwaltung in der Periode von 1890 bis 1911 und über vorläufige Reformvorschläge bezüglich der Zentralstellen und der politischen Landesbehörden. [S.l. , 1912?] 1 v. in various pagings ; LC Card 87-409311 DDC 336.436 19
HJ1062 .B47 1912

FINANCE, PUBLIC - BARBADOS - ACCOUNTING.
Barbados. Duffus Commission of Enquiry. Report /. [Bridgetown, Barbados] [1978] vi, 118, 270 p. : LC Card 82-243628 DDC 354.7298/10072 19
HJ2073.B37 B37 1978 ***NYPL [JLG 86-221]***

FINANCE, PUBLIC - BELGIUM.
Peffer, Michel, 1948- L'Etat anthropophage /. Bruxelles , c1982. 279 p. ; ISBN 2-87005-164-5 LC Card 84-139080
HJ1197 .P44 1982

FINANCE, PUBLIC - BRAZIL - ALAGOAS.
Alagoas (Brazil). Secretaria da Fazenda. Posicionamento das finanças de Alagoas na atual crise /. [Maceió] , 1983. 97 p. : LC Card 86-201070
HJ929.A52 A42 1983

FINANCE, PUBLIC - BRAZIL - DISTRITO FEDERAL.
Souza Filho, José Ornellas de. Exposição do governador do Distrito Federal, José Ornellas de Souza Filho, na ADESG, em 02/09/83. [Brasília , 1983 or 1984] 40, [31 leaves] : LC Card 85-148272
HC188.D57 S68 1983

FINANCE, PUBLIC - BRAZIL - GOIÁS (STATE)
Finanças públicas dos Estados de Goiás, Maranhão, Mato Grosso e Pará /. Brasília , 1985. 114, [34] p. ; LC Card 87-404251 DDC 336.81 19
HJ929.G65 F56 1985

FINANCE, PUBLIC - BRAZIL - HISTORY - 19TH CENTURY.
Década republicana /. Brasília, Distrito Federal , c1986. 2 v. ; ISBN 85-23-00062-3 (set) LC Card 86-211423
HJ923 .D38 1986

FINANCE, PUBLIC - BRAZIL - MARANHÃO.
Finanças públicas dos Estados de Goiás, Maranhão, Mato Grosso e Pará /. Brasília , 1985. 114, [34] p. ; LC Card 87-404251 DDC 336.81 19
HJ929.G65 F56 1985

FINANCE, PUBLIC - BRAZIL - MATO GROSSO (STATE)
Finanças públicas dos Estados de Goiás, Maranhão, Mato Grosso e Pará /. Brasília , 1985. 114, [34] p. ; LC Card 87-404251 DDC 336.81 19
HJ929.G65 F56 1985

FINANCE, PUBLIC - BRAZIL - MINAS GERAIS.
Minas Gerais (Brazil). Secretaria de Estado da Fazenda. Secretaria de Estado da Fazenda . Belo Horizonte [1983] 48 p. ; LC Card 85-207912
HJ929.M52 M55 1983

FINANCE, PUBLIC - BRAZIL - PARÁ (STATE)
Finanças públicas dos Estados de Goiás, Maranhão, Mato Grosso e Pará /. Brasília , 1985. 114, [34] p. ; LC Card 87-404251 DDC 336.81 19
HJ929.G65 F56 1985

FINANCE, PUBLIC - BRAZIL - PORTO ALEGRE.
Porto Alegre (Brazil). Mayor. Mensagem apresentada á Camara Municipal /. Pôrto Alegre , 1936. 686 p., [7] folded leaves of plates : LC Card 85-135614
HD4635.P6 P67 1936

FINANCE, PUBLIC - BRAZIL - RIO GRANDE DO SUL.
Rio Grande do Sul (Brazil) Relatorios provinciaes. [1850-1859] 19 pamphlets in 1 v. ; LC Card 84-217966
HD4635.R54 R56 1850

Silva, J. Resende. A fronteira do sul . Rio de Janeiro , 1922. 723 p., [1] leaf of plates : LC Card 85-223002
HF3409.R56 S55 1922

FINANCE, PUBLIC - CAMEROON.
Répertoire financier et fiscal du Cameroun . Le Vésinet, France [1987?] 147 p. ; LC Card 87-124445
HJ1489 .R46 1987

FINANCE, PUBLIC - CANADA.
Bird, Richard M., 1938- Federal finance in comparative perspective /. Toronto, Canada , c1986. x, 250 p. : ISBN 0-88808-024-7 (pbk.) LC Card 86-215918 DDC 336 19
HJ141 .B57 1986

Kitchen, Harry M. Local government finance in Canada /. [Toronto, Ont.] , c1984. xvii, 495 p. ; ISBN 0-88808-020-4
NYPL [JLL 80-129 no.5]

Securing economic renewal . [Ottawa] [1987] 147, 161 p. : LC Card 87-144360 DDC 336.71 19
HJ793 .S43 1987

FINANCE, PUBLIC - CANADA - CONGRESSES.
State and local finance . Madison, Wis. , 1983. x, 243 p. : ISBN 0-299-09340-9 : LC Card 83-47757 DDC 336.73 19
HJ275 .S675 1983 ***NYPL [JLE 86-4001]***

FINANCE, PUBLIC - CARIBBEAN AREA.
Jones-Hendrickson, S. B. (Simon B.) Public finance and monetary policy in open economies . [Kingston, Jamaica] , 19. 172 p. ;
NYPL [Sc D 86-830]

FINANCE, PUBLIC - CARIBBEAN AREA - CASE STUDIES.
Hope, Kempe R. Development finance and the development process . New York , 1987. 100 p. ; ISBN 0-313-25835-X (lib. bdg. : alk. paper) LC Card 86-29617 DDC 336.729 19
HJ844.3 .H67 1987

FINANCE, PUBLIC - CENTRAL EUROPE - HISTORY.
Wealth and taxation in Central Europe . Leamington Spa, UK ; New York, N.Y., USA : 162 p. ; ISBN 0-85496-523-8 : LC Card 86-24490 DDC 336.43 19
HJ1000 .W4 1987

FINANCE, PUBLIC - CHILE.
Büchi Buc, Hernán. Exposición sobre el estado de la hacienda pública /. [Santiago] , 1985. 92 p. ; LC Card 87-105088 DDC 338.983 19
HC192 .B83 1985

FINANCE, PUBLIC - CHILE - ACCOUNTING - HANDBOOKS, MANUALS, ETC.
Sánchez González, Leonardo. Fundamento operacional del sistema de contabilidad general de la nación /. Santiago, Chile [1986] 227 p. : LC Card 87-403116 DDC 354.830072/31 19
HJ9923.C3 S264 1986

FINANCE, PUBLIC - COLOMBIA.
Alviar Ramírez, Oscar, d. 1984. Elementos de finanzas públicas en Colombia /. Bogotá, Colombia , 1985. xx, 584 p. ; ISBN 958-604-045-3 (pbk.) LC Card 86-129809 DDC 336.861 19
HJ945 .A48 1985

Murillo Toro, Manuel, 1816-1880. Escritos económicos /. Bogotá, Colombia , 1985. 120 p. ; LC Card 86-165762
HJ943 .M87 1985

FINANCE, PUBLIC - COLOMBIA - BOGOTÁ - STATISTICS.
Estadística fiscal de Bogotá, D.E., 1970-1976. [Bogotá, Colombia] [1977] 100 p. : LC Card 87-128439 DDC 336.84/14 19
HJ9394.B6 E847 1977

FINANCE, PUBLIC - COLOMBIA - BOGOTÁ - STATISTICS - HISTORY - 20TH CENTURY.
Estadística fiscal de Bogotá, D.E., 1971-1977. [Bogotá, Colombia] [1979] 139 p. : LC Card 87-125994 DDC 336.861/4 19
HJ9394.B6 E85 1979

FINANCE, PUBLIC - COLOMBIA - STATISTICS.
Estadística fiscal del estado . [Bogotá] , 1978. 2 v. : ***NYPL [JLE 80-831]***

El Sector público colombiano, 1970-1981. Bogotá , 1984. 261 p. ; LC Card 87-121830 DDC 336.861 19
HJ945 .S43 1984

FINANCE, PUBLIC - CONGRESSES.
Economic effects of the government budget /. Cambridge, Mass. , c1988. p. cm. ISBN 0-262-08172-5 LC Card 87-26187 DDC 338.9 19
HJ2005 .E25 1988

Geyer, Herbert, 1927- Budgetpolitik im Wandel /. Berlin , c1986. 111 p. : ISBN 3-428-05922-0 LC Card 86-165210
HJ113 .G49 1986

Staatsfinanzierung im Wandel . Berlin , c1983. xi, 877 p. : ISBN 3-428-05420-2
NYPL [JLL 73-186 Bd. 134]

Staatsfinanzierung und Notenbank . Wien [1984?] 211 p. : LC Card 85-198128
HG1811 .S78 1984

FINANCE, PUBLIC - COSTA RICA.
Costa Rica--respuesta al cuestionario del Banco Interamericano de Desarrollo /. [San José] [1962] 69 leaves (some folded) ; LC Card 85-117361
HC143 .C685 1962

FINANCE, PUBLIC - DECISION MAKING.
Kleinmann, Klaus, 1956- Die langfristige Entwicklung von Kommunikation und Staatsausgaben /. Frankfurt am Main , New York , c1985. v, 194 p. : ISBN 3-8204-8873-1 LC Card 85-200073
HJ131 .K56 1985

FINANCE, PUBLIC - DEVELOPING COUNTRIES.
Mounbaga, Emmanuel Seidou, 1957- Finanzpolitik und Wirtschaftsentwicklung in der Dritten Welt . München , c1986. 265 p. ; ISBN 3-8039-0341-6 LC Card 86-233152
HJ1620 .M68 1986

FINANCE, PUBLIC - DICTIONARIES - TURKISH.
Akdoğan, Abdurrahman. Açıklamalı maliye ve vergi sözlüğü /. [Ankara?] , Yenişehir, Ankara , 1986. 229 p. ; LC Card 87-968120
HJ129.T9 A43 1986

FINANCE, PUBLIC - ECUADOR.
Coyuntura económica ecuatoriana, 1985-1986. [Quito, Ecuador] [1986] i, 39 p. ; LC Card 86-217289
HC202 .C73 1986

FINANCE, PUBLIC - ECUADOR - STATISTICS.
Estadísticas financieras del sector público ecuatoriano, años 1975-1981 /. [Quito] [1983] 316 p. ; LC Card 86-179747
HJ955 .E792 1983

FINANCE, PUBLIC - EUROPE - HISTORY - 18TH CENTURY.
Stolleis, Michael, 1941- Pecunia nervus rerum . Frankfurt am Main , c1983. 184 p. ; ISBN 3-465-01590-8 (Deut Bibl.) LC Card 83-183704
HJ1000 .S76 1983

FINANCE, PUBLIC - EUROPEAN ECONOMIC COMMUNITY COUNTRIES.
Hackenbroch, Inge. Zur Theorie und Politik eines supranationalen Finanzausgleichs . München , c1983. xvi, 350 p. ; ISBN 3-8039-0259-2 LC Card 83-167962
HJ1000.5 .H33 1983

FINANCE, PUBLIC - FRANCE - TO 1789.
Un citoyen aux Etats-Généraux. Paris [1976] (Milan : Graphica Sipiel) 46 p. ; LC Card 87-672450
HJ1082 .C57x 1976

FINANCE, PUBLIC - FRANCE - ACCOUNTING.
Sources et méthodes d'élaboration des comptes nationaux. [Paris] [1983] 481 p. ; LC Card 84-161813
HC271 .A218 no. 440-441 HJ9925.F8

FINANCE, PUBLIC - FRANCE - AUDITING - HISTORY - 19TH CENTURY.
Chadeau, Emmanuel, 1956- Les inspecteurs des finances au XIXe siècle (1850-1914) . Paris , c1986. iii, 184 p. : ISBN 2-7178-1175-3 : LC Card 87-131650
HJ9925.F8 C42 1986

FINANCE, PUBLIC - FRANCE - AUDITING - HISTORY - 20TH CENTURY.
Chadeau, Emmanuel, 1956- Les inspecteurs des finances au XIXe siècle (1850-1914) . Paris , c1986. iii, 184 p. : ISBN 2-7178-1175-3 : LC Card 87-131650
HJ9925.F8 C42 1986

FINANCE, PUBLIC - FRANCE - BRITTANY - HISTORY.
Kerhervé, Jean. L'Etat breton aux 14e et 15e siècles . Paris , c1987. 2 v. (xii, x, 1078 p.) : ISBN 2-224-01703-0 (t. 1) LC Card 87-160693
HJ1078.B75 K47 1987

FINANCE, PUBLIC - FRANCE - BURGUNDY - HISTORY.
Nieuwenhuysen, A. van (Andrée) Les finances du duc de Bourgogne, Philippe le Hardi (1384-1404) . Bruxelles, Belgique , 1984. 556 p. ; ISBN 2-8004-0838-3 : LC Card 85-160639
HJ1099.B85 N54 1984

FINANCE, PUBLIC - FRANCE - HISTORY - 18TH CENTURY.
Bruguière, Michel. Gestionnaires et profiteurs de la Révolution . Paris , c1986. 339 p. : ISBN 2-85565-332-0 : LC Card 87-123230
HJ1083 .B78 1986

Riley, James C. The Seven Years War and the old regime in France . Princeton, N.J. , 1986. xxii, 256 p. : ISBN 0-691-05488-6 (alk. paper) : LC Card 86-42847 DDC 330.944/034 19
HC275 .R54 1986 ***NYPL [JLE 87-932]***

FINANCE, PUBLIC - GERMANY - ACCOUNTING - HISTORY.
Gilles, Franz-O., 1944- Die verkannte Macht . Berlin , 1986. 398 p. ; ISBN 3-923024-07-X LC Card 87-127716 DDC 354.430072/31/09 19
HJ9925.G3 G55 1986

FINANCE, PUBLIC - GERMANY (EAST) - ACCOUNTING - HISTORY.
Gilles, Franz-O., 1944- Die verkannte Macht . Berlin , 1986. 398 p. ; ISBN 3-923024-07-X LC Card 87-127716 DDC 354.430072/31/09 19
HJ9925.G3 G55 1986

FINANCE, PUBLIC - GERMANY - HISTORY.
Wild, Werner. Steuern und Reichsherrschaft . Bremen , 1984. 326 p. ; ISBN 3-88948-030-6 LC Card 85-127825
HJ2675 .W55 1984

FINANCE, PUBLIC - GERMANY - HISTORY - 20TH CENTURY.
Heindl, Wolfgang, 1951- Die Haushalte von Reich, Ländern und Gemeinden in Deutschland von 1925 bis 1933 . Frankfurt am Main , New York , c1984. 419 p. : ISBN 3-8204-5474-8 LC Card 85-198505
HJ1119 .H36 1984

FINANCE, PUBLIC - GERMANY, WEST.
Gesamtwirtschaftliche und strukturelle Auswirkungen von Veränderungen der Struktur des öffentlichen Sektors . Berlin , 1984. x, 266 p. : ISBN 3-428-05739-2 LC Card 86-138980
HC281 .B33 Heft 81 HJ1120

Die Haushalte der Flächenländer unter Konsolidierungszwang /. Bonn , 1986. 159 p. ; LC Card 87-409459 DDC 332 s 336.43 19
HJ1120 .B65 Nr. 262

Länderhaushalte. Bonn [1964] 112 p. ; LC Card 85-185971
HJ1101 .B6 Heft 73 HJ1120

Öffentliche Finanzen, Kredit und Kapital . Berlin , c1985. xvi, 618 p., [1] leaf of plates : ISBN 3-428-05737-6 LC Card 85-164173
HJ161 .O33 1985

Runge, Harry. Haushaltsfinanzierung durch Notendruck /. Berlin , c1986. 69 p. ; ISBN 3-428-05984-0 LC Card 86-165742
HG1004 .R75 1986

Stoltenberg, Gerhard. Unsere Verantwortung für eine gute Zukunft . München , c1986. 191 p. ; ISBN 3-7892-7290-6 LC Card 87-130881 DDC 339.5/2/0943 19
HC286.7 .S767 1986

Zahn, Joachim, Professor Dr. Eine Finanzpolitik des langen Atems erforderlich /. Bonn [1984] 31 leaves ; LC Card 86-198580
HJ1120 .B65 Nr. 234

FINANCE, PUBLIC - GERMANY, WEST - ACCOUNTING.
Sollmann, Axel, 1952- Die Massnahme-, Berichts- und Missbilligungsbeschlüsse des Parlaments im Entlastungsverfahren /. Frankfurt am Main , New York , c1986. 261 p. ; ISBN 3-8204-9778-1 LC Card 86-233741
HJ9925.G3 S65 1986

FINANCE, PUBLIC - GERMANY (WEST) - ACCOUNTING - HISTORY.
Gilles, Franz-O., 1944- Die verkannte Macht . Berlin , 1986. 398 p. ; ISBN 3-923024-07-X LC Card 87-127716 DDC 354.430072/31/09 19
HJ9925.G3 G55 1986

FINANCE, PUBLIC - GERMANY (WEST) - BADEN - HISTORY.
Ullmann, Hans-Peter. Staatsschulden und Reformpolitik . Göttingen , c1986. 2 v. (842 p.) ; ISBN 3-525-35398-7 LC Card 86-210338
HJ8655.B38 U55 1986

FINANCE, PUBLIC - GERMANY, WEST - BAVARIA - HISTORY.
Ullmann, Hans-Peter. Staatsschulden und Reformpolitik . Göttingen , c1986. 2 v. (842 p.) ; ISBN 3-525-35398-7 LC Card 86-210338
HJ8655.B38 U55 1986

FINANCE, PUBLIC - GERMANY (WEST) - BAVARIA - HISTORY - 20TH CENTURY.
Pohl, Harald. Kommunale Wirtschafts- und Finanzpolitik in Bayern zur Zeit der Weimarer Republik . Regensburg , c1985. xiv, 312 p. : ISBN 3-924956-01-4 LC Card 86-230648
HJ9494.I53 P63 1985

FINANCE, PUBLIC - GERMANY, WEST - CONGRESSES.
Staatsfinanzierung im Wandel . Berlin , c1983. xi, 877 p. : ISBN 3-428-05420-2
NYPL [JLL 73-186 Bd. 134]

Staatsfinanzierung und Notenbank . Wien [1984?] 211 p. : LC Card 85-198128
HG1811 .S78 1984

FINANCE, PUBLIC - GERMANY (WEST) - DICTIONARIES - GERMAN.
Lexikon Wirtschaftspolitik . München , c1986. 236 p. : ISBN 3-406-31302-7 LC Card 86-221788
HG151 .L45 1986

FINANCE, PUBLIC - GERMANY (WEST) - HAMBURG - ACCOUNTING.
Gührs, Eckhard. Leitfaden für Kostenermittlung und Wirtschaftlichkeitsprüfung . Hamburg , 1983. iii, 92 p. ; LC Card 85-212548
HJ9925.G3 G84 1983

FINANCE, PUBLIC - GERMANY (WEST) - HISTORY.
Scherpenberg, Jens van. Öffentliche Finanzwirtschaft in Westdeutschland, 1944-1948 . Frankfurt am Main , c1984. 544 p. : ISBN 3-88323-502-4 LC Card 84-182435
HJ1120 .S317 1984

FINANCE, PUBLIC - GERMANY (WEST) - INGOLSTADT METROPOLITAN AREA - HISTORY - 20TH CENTURY.
Pohl, Harald. Kommunale Wirtschafts- und Finanzpolitik in Bayern zur Zeit der Weimarer Republik . Regensburg , c1985. xiv, 312 p. : ISBN 3-924956-01-4 LC Card 86-230648
HJ9494.I53 P63 1985

FINANCE, PUBLIC - GERMANY (WEST) - NORTH RHINE-WESTPHALIA.
North Rhine-Westphalia (Germany). Finanzministerium. Finanzplanung des Landes Nordrhein-Westfalen 1986 bis 1990. Düsseldorf [1986] iii, 27, [28] p. ; LC Card 86-233121
HJ1150.N62 N62 1986

FINANCE, PUBLIC - GERMANY (WEST) - SINGEN AM HOHENTWIEL.
Gebhard, Alfred. Das Dorf Singen und seine Finanzwirtschaft . Singen , 1985. 484 p. : ISBN 3-921413-23-0 LC Card 87-133391 DDC 336.43/46 19
HJ9494.S57 G4 1985

FINANCE, PUBLIC - GERMANY (WEST) - STATISTICAL METHODS.
Dornbusch, Hans-Ludwig. Entwicklung wesentlicher Daten der öffentlichen Finanzwirtschaft in der Bundesrepublik Deutschland von 1975-1985 /. Bonn [1986] 31 leaves ; LC Card 87-408897 DDC 332 s 336.43 19
HJ1120 .B65 Nr. 260

FINANCE, PUBLIC - GERMANY (WEST) - STATISTICS.
Dornbusch, Hans-Ludwig. Entwicklung wesentlicher Daten der öffentlichen Finanzwirtschaft in der Bundesrepublik Deutschland von 1973-1983 /. Bonn , 1984. 32 leaves ; LC Card 86-186300
HJ1120 .B65 Nr. 236

Entwicklung wesentlicher Daten der öffentlichen Finanzwirtschaft in der Bundesrepublik Deutschland von 1974-1984 /. Bonn , 1985. 31 leaves ; LC Card 86-186363
HJ1120 .B65 Nr. 247

FINANCE, PUBLIC - GREAT BRITAIN - TO 1688.
Cust, Richard. The forced loan and English politics, 1626-1628 /. Oxford [Oxfordshire] , New York , 1987. x, 358 p. ; ISBN 0-19-822951-8 : LC Card 87-7977 DDC 336.42 19
HJ1012 .C87 1987

FINANCE, PUBLIC - GREAT BRITAIN - ACCOUNTING.
Glynn, John J. Public sector financial control and accounting /. Oxford [Oxfordshire] , New York, N.Y., USA , 1987. x, 278 p. : ISBN 0-631-14686-5 : LC Card 86-31725 DDC 657/.835 19
HJ9733 .G58 1987

FINANCE, PUBLIC - GREAT BRITAIN - AUDITING.
Glynn, John J. Public sector financial control and accounting /. Oxford [Oxfordshire] , New York, N.Y., USA , 1987. x, 278 p. : ISBN 0-631-14686-5 : LC Card 86-31725 DDC 657/.835 19
HJ9733 .G58 1987

FINANCE, PUBLIC - GREAT BRITAIN - HISTORY - 19TH CENTURY.
Braun, Hans-Joachim. Wirtschafts- und finanzpolitische Entscheidungsprozesse in England in der ersten Hälfte des 19. Jahrhunderts /. Frankfurt am Main , New York , c1984. 236 p. : ISBN 3-8204-7702-0 LC Card 85-191319 DDC 338.941 19
HC255 .B77 1984

FINANCE, PUBLIC - HONDURAS.
Imagen de la estructura económica-social y explotación de los recursos naturales /. Tegucigalpa, D.C., Honduras, C.A. , 1973. viii, 334 p. : LC Card 86-177356
HC145 .I52 1973

FINANCE, PUBLIC - INDIA.
Agarwal, A. K. (Ashok Kumar), 1949- Problems of Indian fiscal structure /. Delhi, India , 1987. xii, 157 p. ; LC Card 86-903836 DDC 336.54 19
HJ1334. A38 1987

Gaur, Achal Kumar, 1959- Centre-state financial relations and finance commissions /. Allahabad, India , 1985. x, 364 p. ; LC Card 85-904373 DDC 336.54 19
HJ1334 .G38 1985

FINANCE, PUBLIC - INDIA - ACCOUNTING.
Seshadri, R. K. The Indian financial system . Madras , 1985. ii, 287, v, iii p. ; LC Card 85-904230 DDC 336.54 19
HD4293 .S45 1985 ***NYPL [JLD 86-2433]***

FINANCE, PUBLIC - INDIA - CASE STUDIES.
Govinda Rao, M. Political economy of tax and expenditure determination . New Delhi , 1981. vii, 212 p. ; LC Card 81-905062 DDC 336.54 19
HJ1337 .G68 1981 ***NYPL [JLD 86-2603]***

FINANCE, PUBLIC - INDIA - HIMACHAL PRADESH.
Sharda, N. K. State finances and regional development in India /. New Delhi , c1986. 248 p. ; LC Card 86-900599 DDC 336.54/52 19
HJ1339.H55 S54 1986 ***NYPL [JLD 86-3211]***

FINANCE, PUBLIC - INDIA - HISTORY.
Reddy, K. N. (Kaipa Narayana), 1936- Central government expenditure . New Delhi , 1984. xvi, 175 p. ; LC Card 84-901866 DDC 336.3/9/0954 19
HJ2157 .R43 1984 ***NYPL [JLD 87-66]***

FINANCE, PUBLIC - INDIA - TRAVANCORE AND COCHIN.
Travancore and Cochin (India) Five year plan . Trivandrum , 1954. iii, 45 p. ; LC Card 83-238882
HJ2158.T7 T73 1954

FINANCE, PUBLIC - ISLAMIC COUNTRIES.
Sa'dī, 'Abd Allāh Jam'ān Sa'īd, 1954- Siyāsat al-māl fī al-Islām fī 'ahd 'Umar ibn al-Khaṭṭāb wa-muqāranatuhā bi-al-anẓimah al-ḥadīthah /. al-Dawḥah, Qaṭar , 1983. 291 p. ; LC Card 86-965028
HJ1438 .S23 1983

FINANCE, PUBLIC - ISLAMIC EMPIRE.
Sa'dī, 'Abd Allāh Jam'ān Sa'īd, 1954- Siyāsat al-māl fī al-Islām fī 'ahd 'Umar ibn al-Khaṭṭāb wa-muqāranatuhā bi-al-anẓimah al-ḥadīthah /. al-Dawḥah, Qaṭar , 1983. 291 p. ; LC Card 86-965028
HJ1438 .S23 1983

FINANCE, PUBLIC - ITALY - FLORENCE - HISTORY.
Conti, Elio. L'imposta diretta a Firenze nel Quattrocento (1427-1494) /. Roma , 1984. 406 p. ; LC Card 86-171245
HJ9500.F562 C65 1984

FINANCE, PUBLIC - ITALY - LOMBARDY - ACCOUNTING.
Conto consolidato della spesa pubblica in Lombardia /. Milano, Italy , c1982. 234 p. ; LC Card 85-147746
HJ9925.I8 C63 1982

FINANCE, PUBLIC - ITALY - STATISTICS.
Ghessi, Giuseppe. La finanza pubblica in cifre, 1965-1983 /. Milano, Italy , c1985. 186 p. : LC Card 85-180958 DDC 336.45 19
HJ1185 .G43 1985 ***NYPL [JLF 87-249]***

FINANCE, PUBLIC - JAPAN.
Sano, Shin'ichi, 1947- Kanryō fuyu no jidai /. Tōkyō , 1985. 6, 255 p. ; ISBN 4-8334-1266-7 : LC Card 86-179753
HC462.9 .S2534 1985 <Orien Japan> ***NYPL [*OSM 87-1196]***

FINANCE, PUBLIC - KENYA - NAIROBI - AUDITING.
Kenya. Public Accounts Committee. Report of the Public Accounts Committee on the Special report of the Controller and Auditor-General on the City Council of Nairobi. Nairobi [1981] i, 23 p. ; LC Card 85-980597
HJ9620.5.Z9 N344 1981

FINANCE, PUBLIC - LATIN AMERICA.
Brovedani, Bruno. Un modelo de análisis monetario y de programación financiera /. [Mexico City, Mexico] , 1984. ii, 203 p. : LC Card 86-158393
HG660.5 .B7 1984

FINANCE, PUBLIC - LAW AND LEGISLATION - CAMEROON.
Répertoire financier et fiscal du Cameroun . Le Vésinet, France [1987?] 147 p. ; LC Card 87-124445
HJ1489 .R46 1987

FINANCE, PUBLIC - LAW AND LEGISLATION - SPAIN.
García Villarejo, Avelino. Manual de hacienda pública . Madrid , c1985. 686 p. : ISBN 84-309-1197-9 LC Card 87-105048
HJ1244 .G37 1985

Spain. Tribunal de Cuentas. Memoria relativa a las cuentas generales del estado, 1935-1960 /. Madrid , 1964. 221 p. ; LC Card 85-104523
HJ1244 .S72 1964

FINANCE, PUBLIC - LAW AND LEGISLATION - SWEDEN.
Lybeck, Johan A., 1944- Konstitutionella begränsningar i Riksdagens finansmakt . [Stockholm] [1984] 147 p. : ISBN 91-38-08365-5 (Sve. bok.) : LC Card 84-240503
HJ1238 .L92 1984

FINANCE, PUBLIC - MADEIRA ISLANDS - ACCOUNTING - HISTORY - 16TH CENTURY.
Livros de contas da ilha da Madeira, 1504-1537 /. Coimbra , 1985- v. <1 > ; LC Card 86-232733
HJ9930.3.M33 L58 1985

FINANCE, PUBLIC - MARYLAND.
Major fiscal issues at the 1983-1986 sessions of the General Assembly. Annapolis, Md. (90 State Cir., Annapolis 21401-1991) [1986] vi, 100 p. ; LC Card 86-622757 DDC 336.752 19
HJ485 .M15 1986

FINANCE, PUBLIC - MATHEMATICAL MODELS.
Auerbach, Alan J. Dynamic fiscal policy /. Cambridge [Cambridgeshire] , New York , 1987. xv, 196 p. : ISBN 0-521-30041-X LC Card 86-24447 DDC 339.5/2 19
HJ131 .A94 1987

FINANCE, PUBLIC - MEXICO.
García Alba Iduñate, Pascual, 1948- [Financial aspects of macroeconomic management in Mexico. Spanish.] Causas y efectos de la crisis económica en México /. México, D.F. , 1984. 124 p. : ISBN 968-12-0285-6 LC Card 86-138030
HC135 .G29818 1984

FINANCE, PUBLIC - MEXICO - HISTORY - 19TH CENTURY.
Tenenbaum, Barbara, 1946- The politics of penury . Albuquerque , c1986. xviii, 250 p. ; ISBN 0-8263-0890-2 : LC Card 86-16027 DDC 336.72 19
HJ802 .T46 1986 ***NYPL [JLE 87-482]***

FINANCE, PUBLIC - MEXICO - JALISCO - HISTORY.
Gutiérrez y Ulloa, Antonio. Libro de la razón general de hacienda nacional . Guadalajara, Jalisco, México , 1983. 222 p. ; ISBN 968-8320-48-X LC Card 87-401751 DDC 336.72/35 19
HJ805.J3 G87 1983

FINANCE, PUBLIC - MINNESOTA.
Minnesota. Dept. of Finance. Cash flow report. [St. Paul] [1986] 26, [4] leaves : LC Card 86-622795 DDC 336.776 19
HJ515 .M56 1986

FINANCE, PUBLIC - NETHERLANDS.
Drees, W. Nederlandse overheidsuitgaven /. 's-Gravenhage , 1985. 270 p. ; ISBN 90-6095-330-4 : LC Card 85-197601
HJ1200 .D74 1985

FINANCE, PUBLIC - NEW YORK (N.Y.)
Staff report on modification no. 86-13 to New York City's FYs 1986-1989 financial plan, February 1986 /. [Albany, N.Y.] [1986] 128 leaves ; LC Card 86-622416 DDC 352.1/09747/1 19
HJ9289.N4 S734 1986

Staff report on modification no. 86-8 to New York City's FYs 1986-1989 financial plan. [Albany] [1985] 92 leaves ; LC Card 86-622159 DDC 336.747/1 19
HJ9289.N4 S73 1985

FINANCE, PUBLIC - NIGERIA.

FINANCE, PUBLIC - NORTH CAROLINA - STATISTICS.
North Carolina. General Assembly. Fiscal Research Division. Fiscal facts /. [Raleigh] , 1986. 51 p. : LC Card 87-620951 DDC 336.756 19
HJ615 .N65 1986

FINANCE, PUBLIC - PANAMA.
Panama . Washington, D.C., U. S.A. , c1985. xxv, 307 p., [8] p., [1] leaf of plates : ISBN 0-8213-0580-8 LC Card 85-12420 DDC 338.97287 19
HC147 .P43 1985 ***NYPL [JLF 86-1919]***

FINANCE, PUBLIC - PANAMA - ACCOUNTING - STATISTICS.
Panama. Contraloría General de la República. Informe sobre la administración fiscal correspondiente a 1971 /. [Panama, Panama] , 1972. iii, 31 p. ; LC Card 83-183287
HJ9923.P28 P35 1972

FINANCE, PUBLIC - PENNSYLVANIA - HISTORY - 18TH CENTURY.
Schweitzer, Mary M. Custom and contract . New York , 1987. xii, 271 p. : ISBN 0-231-06288-5 LC Card 87-8003 DDC 338.9748 19
HC107.P4 S417 1987

FINANCE, PUBLIC - PENNSYLVANIA - PHILADELPHIA METROPOLITAN AREA.
Luce, Thomas F. Local fiscal issues in the Philadelphia metropolitan area /. Philadelphia , c1987. xii, 248 p., [2] p. of plates : ISBN 0-8122-1255-X (pbk.) LC Card 87-25486 DDC 336.748/11 19
HJ9307.P4 L83 1987

FINANCE, PUBLIC - PERU.
Ycaza Clerc, Mónica de. Política de endeudamiento público interno en el Perú . Lima, Perú , 1985. ii, 23, [39] p. : LC Card 86-223472
HJ8604 .Y33 1985

FINANCE, PUBLIC - PERU - CALLAO (PROVINCE)
Memoria que la Junta Departamental del Callao eleva al Congreso de 1887. Callao , 1887. 23 p. ; LC Card 83-191762
HJ979.C34 M45 1887

FINANCE, PUBLIC - POLAND.
Tegler, Eugeniusz. Polityka finansowa PRL . Szczecin , 1984. 128 p. ; LC Card 86-100923
HJ1213.Z6 T44 1984

FINANCE, PUBLIC - PORTUGAL.
Liberalismo, intervencionismo e o caso português . [Lisbon] [1982] 44 p. ; LC Card 86-132673
HJ1252 .L52 1982

FINANCE, PUBLIC - PORTUGAL - CONGRESSES.
Seminário sobre Política Fiscal (1984? : CGTP-IN) Contribuições para a reforma do sistema fiscal português . Lisboa , 1985. 226 p. : LC Card 87-107879 DDC 336.469 19
HJ1252 .S46 1984

FINANCE, PUBLIC - RESEARCH - HISTORY.
International Institute of Public Finance . Detroit , 1987. vi, 106 p. : ISBN 0-8143-1984-X LC Card 87-10724 DDC 336/.006/01 19
HJ203 .I57 1987

FINANCE, PUBLIC - SENEGAL.
Répertoire financier et monétaire du Sénégal, 1985. Le Vésinet, France [1985?] ii, 98 leaves ; LC Card 86-202435
HJ2184.5 .R46 1985

FINANCE, PUBLIC - SOVIET UNION.
Shirshov, V. O. (Viacheslav Osipovich) Problemy razvitiia sotsialisticheskikh finansov /. Moskva , 1984. 87 p. ; LC Card 85-131694
HG4186 .S47 1984

FINANCE, PUBLIC - SPAIN.
García Villarejo, Avelino. Manual de hacienda pública . Madrid , c1985. 686 p. : ISBN 84-309-1197-9 LC Card 87-105048
HJ1244 .G37 1985

FINANCE, PUBLIC - SPAIN - AMPURDÁN (REGION)
El Baix Empordà . Barcelona , c1984. xii, 303 p. : ISBN 84-505-0289-6 LC Card 85-186183
HC387.A636 B35 1984

FINANCE, PUBLIC - SPAIN - ANDALUSIA.
Junta de Andalucía. Grupo de Trabajo 14, Planificación Económica de las Corporaciones Locales y Comarcalización. Plan económico de Andalucía, 1984-1986 /. [Andalucía] , 1983. 133 p. ; ISBN 84-505-1243-3 LC Card 86-223752
HJ1249.A4 J86 1983

FINANCE, PUBLIC - SPAIN - ARAGON (KINGDOM) - HISTORY.
Küchler, Winfried, d. 1975. Die Finanzen der Krone Aragon während des 15. Jahrhunderts (Alfons V. und Johann II.) /. Münster, Westfalen , c1983. ix, 318 p. ; ISBN 3-402-05823-5 LC Card 85-113533
HJ1249.A7 K83 1983

FINANCE, PUBLIC - SPAIN - AUTONOMOUS COMMUNITIES.
El Finançament autonòmic . Barcelona , 1985. 157 p. ; ISBN 84-297-2364-1 LC Card 86-145741
HJ1249.A1 F56 1985

Gimeno Ullastres, Juan Antonio. El nuevo Estado fiscal español . Madrid , 1981. xx, 315 p. : ISBN 84-7214-219-1 LC Card 85-176738
HJ1249.A1 G56 1981

FINANCE, PUBLIC - SPAIN - CASTILLA Y LEÓN.
García Villarejo, Avelino. Estructura financiera y actividad inversora de las administraciones públicas en Castilla y León /. Valladolid , 1984. 431 p. : ISBN 84-505-0331-0 LC Card 87-108720
HJ1249.C29 G37 1984

FINANCE, PUBLIC - SPAIN - COLONIES - AMERICA - HISTORY - SOURCES.

Hacienda colonial venezolana /. Caracas , 1946. 170 p. ; LC Card 85-105445
HJ991 .H323 1946

FINANCE, PUBLIC - SPAIN - HISTORY.
Spain. Tribunal de Cuentas. Memoria relativa a las cuentas generales del estado, 1935-1960 /. Madrid , 1964. 221 p. ; LC Card 85-104523
HJ1244 .S72 1964

FINANCE, PUBLIC - SPAIN - MADRID.
Madrid (Spain). Alcaldía. Situación de crédito, hacienda y presupuesto del Municipio de Madrid en 1907 . Madrid , 1907. viii, 137 p. ; LC Card 85-131486
HJ9528.M38 M34 1907

FINANCE, PUBLIC - SWEDEN.
Lybeck, Johan A., 1944- Konstitutionella begränsningar i Riksdagens finansmakt . [Stockholm] [1984] 147 p. : ISBN 91-38-08365-5 (Sve. bok.) : LC Card 84-240503
HJ1238 .L92 1984

FINANCE, PUBLIC - SWITZERLAND - BASEL (CANTON) - HISTORY.
Vettori, Arthur. Finanzhaushalt und Wirtschaftsverwaltung Basels (1689-1798) . Basel , 1984. xv, 439 p. : ISBN 3-7190-0878-9 LC Card 85-132787
HJ1264.B3 V47 1984

FINANCE, PUBLIC - SWITZERLAND - BASEL-STADT - HISTORY.
Rosen, Josef. Verwaltung und Ungeld in Basel, 1360-1535 . Stuttgart , 1986. 231 p. ; ISBN 3-515-03348-3 : LC Card 86-184510
HG1160.B37 R67 1986

Vettori, Arthur. Finanzhaushalt und Wirtschaftsverwaltung Basels (1689-1798) . Basel , 1984. xv, 439 p. : ISBN 3-7190-0878-9 LC Card 85-132787
HJ1264.B3 V47 1984

FINANCE, PUBLIC - SWITZERLAND - HISTORY - 20TH CENTURY.
Tanner, Jakob. Bundeshaushalt, Währung und Kriegswirtschaft . Zürich , c1986. 438 p. : ISBN 3-85791-100-X : LC Card 86-199729
HJ1258 .T35 1986

FINANCE, PUBLIC - UNITED STATES.
Financing a common wealth . Washington, DC , 1985. xx, 304 p. : ISBN 0-89125-090-5 LC Card 84-81918
HD3888 .F5 1985 NYPL [JLE 86-2519]

Öffentliche Finanzen, Kredit und Kapital . Berlin , c1985. xvi, 618 p., [1] leaf of plates : ISBN 3-428-05737-6 LC Card 85-164173
HJ161 .O33 1985

The Politics of American economic policy making /. Armonk, N.Y. , c1987. 455 p. : ISBN 0-87332-406-4 : LC Card 87-12827 DDC 338.973 19
HJ257 .P59 1987

Stiglitz, Joseph E. Economics of the public sector /. New York , c1986. xxiii, 599 p. : ISBN 0-393-01808-3 LC Card 86-211407 DDC 336.73 19
HJ257.2 .S84 1986

Swain, David, 1942- Managing public money . Lanham, MD , c1987. x, 221 p. : ISBN 0-8191-6505-0 (alk. paper) : LC Card 87-14261 DDC 350.72 19
HJ141 .S93 1987

FINANCE, PUBLIC - UNITED STATES - 1933- - ECONOMETRIC MODELS.
Berry, William Dale. Understanding United States government growth . New York , 1987. xiv, 212 p. : ISBN 0-275-92509-9 (alk. paper) : LC Card 87-11818 DDC 336.73 19
HJ257.2 .B47 1987

FINANCE, PUBLIC - UNITED STATES - ACCOUNTING.
Fraud, waste, and abuse in government . Philadelphia , c1986. x, 159 p. ; ISBN 0-89727-058-4 LC Card 86-2967 DDC 336.73 19
HJ257.2 .F72 1986 NYPL [JLE 86-4153]

Hay, Leon Edwards, 1923- Essentials of accounting for governmental and not-for-profit organizations /. Homewood, Ill. , 1987. x, 310 p. ; ISBN 0-256-03454-0 (pbk.) LC Card 86-82587 DDC 657/.98 19
HJ9801 .H39 1987

Moore, Mark Harrison. Inspectors-general . New York , c1986. 120 p. ; ISBN 0-87154-605-1 : LC Card 86-6728 DDC 353.0072/32 19
HJ9801 .M66 1987 NYPL [JLE 87-1762]

FINANCE, PUBLIC - UNITED STATES - ACCOUNTING - HANDBOOKS, MANUALS, ETC.
Handbook of governmental accounting and finance /. New York , c1988. 1 v. (various pagings) ; ISBN 0-471-84741-0 LC Card 87-23092 DDC 350.72/31 19
HJ9801 .H36 1988

FINANCE, PUBLIC - UNITED STATES - AUDITING.
Task Force on the Quality of Audits of Governmental Units. Report of the Task Force on the Quality of Audits of Governmental Units . New York, N.Y. , c1987. viii, 71 p. : LC Card 87-149765 DDC 350.72/32 19
HJ9777.A3 T37 1987

FINANCE, PUBLIC - UNITED STATES - STATES.
FINANCE, PUBLIC - UNITED STATES - STATES - ACCOUNTING.
Van Daniker, Relmond P., 1942- Infrastructure assets . Stamford, Conn. (High Ridge Park, P.O. Box 3821, Stamford 06905-0821) , c1986. xii, 155 p. ; LC Card 86-90661 DDC 657/.835 19
HJ9816 .V35 1986

FINANCE, PUBLIC - UNITED STATES - STATES - CASE STUDIES.
Nathan, Richard P. Reagan and the States /. Princeton, N.J. , c1987. xv, 375 p. : ISBN 0-691-07748-7 (alk. paper) : LC Card 87-45529 DDC 353.0072/5 19
HJ2051 .N167 1987

FINANCE, PUBLIC - UNITED STATES - STATES - CONGRESSES.
State and local finance . Madison, Wis. , 1983. x, 243 p. : ISBN 0-299-09340-9 : LC Card 83-47757 DDC 336.73 19
HJ275 .S675 1983 NYPL [JLE 86-4001]

FINANCE, PUBLIC - VENEZUELA - ACCOUNTING - STATISTICS.
Estadística fiscal, años 1944-45 a 1953-54 /. Caracas , 1955. 125 p. : LC Card 85-128776
HJ990 .E86 1955

FINANCE, PUBLIC - VENEZUELA - HISTORY - SOURCES.
Hacienda colonial venezolana /. Caracas , 1946. 170 p. ; LC Card 85-105445
HJ991 .H323 1946

FINANCE, PUBLIC - VENEZUELA - STATISTICS.
Estadística fiscal, años 1944-45 a 1953-54 /. Caracas , 1955. 125 p. : LC Card 85-128776
HJ990 .E86 1955

FINANCE, PUBLIC - VIRGIN ISLANDS OF THE UNITED STATES - ACCOUNTING.
The Financial condition of the government of the Virgin Islands as of September 30, 1981 /. Washington, D.C. [1983] 129 p. ; LC Card 84-603162 DDC 354.7297/22007231 19
HJ9923.V6 F56 1983

FINANCE, PUBLIC - WASHINGTON (D.C.)
Changing the course . Washington , 1986. xvii, 142 p. : LC Card 86-603365 DDC 336.1/85 19
HJ275 .C455 1986

FINANCE, PUBLIC - WYOMING - STATISTICS.
Wyoming. Legislature. Legislative Service Office. Fiscal facts & figures . [Wyoming] [1987] 40 leaves ; LC Card 87-621012 DDC 336.787 19
HJ785 .W86 1987

FINANCE - SOVIET UNION.
Braginskiĭ, L. V. (Lev Vol′fovich) Ėffektivnost′ kapital′nykh vlozheniĭ i bankovskaia︡ deiatel′nost′ /. Moskva , 1981. 186 p. ; LC Card 82-144216
HG186.S55 B72 1981

Cheblokov, A. T. (Andreĭ Timofeevich) Finansovoe planirovanie v promyshlennosti /. Moskva , 1983. 133, [2] p. ; LC Card 84-134674
HC336.25 .C48 1983

Evstigneeva, Li︠u︡dmila Petrovna. Perspektivnoe finansovoe planirovanie . Moskva , 1982. 182 p. ; LC Card 83-124268
HG186.S55 E97 1982

Konnik, I. I. (Iosif Isaakovich) Denezhnoe obrashchenie v prot︠s︡esse rasshirennogo sotsialisticheskogo vosproizvodstva /. Moskva , 1982. 269 p. ; LC Card 83-165373
HG186.S55 K65 1982

Pavlov, V. S. (Valentin Sergeevich) Finansovye plany i balansy v sisteme ėkonomicheskogo planirovaniia︡ /. Moskva , 1978. 238 p. ; LC Card 81-160805
HG186.S55 P38 1978

Shirshov, V. O. (Vi︠a︡cheslav Osipovich) Problemy razvitii︠a︡ sotsialisticheskikh finansov /. Moskva , 1984. 87 p. ; LC Card 85-131694
HG4186 .S47 1984

FINANCE - SOVIET UNION - CONGRESSES.
Rol′ finansovo-kreditnogo mekhanizma v povyshenii ėffektivnosti obshchestvennykh zatrat . Moskva , 1984. 153 p. ; LC Card 86-113408
HG186.S55 R64 1984

Sbalansirovannost′ sot︠s︡ialisticheskoĭ ėkonomiki i finansovo-kreditnyĭ mekhanizm /. Moskva , 1984. 108 p. ; LC Card 85-240300
HG186.S55 S27 1984

FINANCE - SOVIET UNION - HISTORY.
Illarionov, Sergeĭ Ivanovich. Problema tovarnogo proizvodstva . Moskva , 1984. 109 p. ; LC Card 85-111933
HF3626 .I64 1984

FINANCE - SOVIET UNION - MATHEMATICAL MODELS.
Voprosy postroenii︠a︡ sistemy modeleĭ finansovogo aspekta vosproizvodstva /. Moskva , 1984. 154 p. : LC Card 86-144339
HG186.S55 V67 1984

FINANCE - SPAIN.
Cuervo García, Alvaro. Manual de sistema financiero . Barcelona , 1987. 427 p. : ISBN 84-344-2013-9 LC Card 87-135198
HG186.S6 C84 1987

FINANCE - SPAIN - ECONOMETRIC MODELS.
Domínguez Machuca, J. A. (José Antonio) Modelización de sistemas financieros mediante dinámica de sistemas . [Sevilla] , 1983. 269 p. : ISBN 84-500-3164-8 LC Card 85-138246
HG186.S6 D65 1983

FINANCE - STUDY AND TEACHING - DEVELOPING COUNTRIES.
International Monetary Fund. Technical assistance and training services of the International Monetary Fund. Washington, D.C. , 1985. iii, 31 p. : LC Card 86-202820 DDC 332.1/52 19
HG3881.5.I58 I568 1985

FINANCE - SWITZERLAND - CONGRESSES.
Internationale Wettbewerbsfähigkeit des Finanzplatzes Schweiz /. Bern , c1987. 131 p. : ISBN 3-258-03806-6 LC Card 87-114764 DDC 332.1 s 332.1/09494 19
HG1526 .B27 Bd. 101 HG3206

Finance theory /. Jarrow, Robert A. Englewood Cliffs, N.J. , c1988. xiv, 298 p. : ISBN 0-13-314865-3 LC Card 87-2359 DDC 332/.0724 19
HG173 .J34 1988

FINANCE - UNITED STATES.
Financial institutions and markets in a changing world /. Plano, Tex. , 1987. xiii, 697 p. : ISBN 0-256-03695-0 (pbk.) LC Card 86-61850 DDC 332.1/0973 19
HG181 .F633 1987

Henning, Charles N. Financial markets and the economy /. Englewood Cliffs, N.J. , c1988. xvi, 638 p. : ISBN 0-13-316894-8 LC Card 87-24413 DDC 332/.0973 19
HG181 .H37 1988

Horvitz, Paul M. Monetary policy and the financial system /. Englewood Cliffs, N.J. , c1987. xii, 532 p. : ISBN 0-13-599861-1 LC Card 86-25447 DDC 332.4/973 19
HG540 .H67 1987

Klein, John J., 1929- Money and the economy /. San Diego , c1986. xi, 560 p. : ISBN 0-15-564007-0 LC Card 85-80078 DDC 332.4/973 19
HG540 .K57 1986 NYPL [JLE 86-3392]

Multi-agency financial investigative task forces

[microform] Washington, D.C. [1983] 1 v. (various pagings) : *NYPL [*ZT-1708 no.61]*

Personal financial markets . Deddington, Oxford , Atlantic Highlands, N.J. , 1986. viii, 279 p. : ISBN 0-86003-540-9 LC Card 86-235455 DDC 332.1/7 19
HG186.G7 P38 1986

Streit, Joachim. Finanzinnovationen, Deregulierung und Geldmengensteuerung in den USA /. Tübingen , c1986. xi, 188 p. : ISBN 3-16-345156-X (pbk.) LC Card 87-408200 DDC 332/.0973 19
HG181 .S825 1986

Warfield, Gerald. How to read and understand the financial news /. New York , c1986. 214 p. ; ISBN 0-06-015647-3 : LC Card 86-45161 DDC 332.63/2042 19
PN4888.C59 W37 1986 *NYPL [JLE 87-1488]*

Watts, John M., 1933- The financial services shockwave . Englewood Cliffs, N.J. , c1987. viii, 181 p. : ISBN 0-13-316852-2 : LC Card 86-22510 DDC 332.1/0973 19
HG181 .W37 1987 *NYPL [JLE 87-612]*

FINANCE - UNITED STATES - DEREGULATION - CONGRESSES.
Financial deregulation . Cambridge , Wolfeboro, N.H., USA , 1986. xiii, 88 p. ; ISBN 0-85941-366-7 : LC Card 87-104563 DDC 332/.0941 19
HG186.G7 F546 1986

FINANCE - UNITED STATES - HISTORY.
Allen, Frederick Lewis, 1890-1954. The lords of creation. New York, London, 1935. xii, 483 p. LC Card 35-20649 DDC 332.0973
HG181 .A57 *NYPL [JLD 86-1097]*

Krooss, Herman Edward, 1912-1975. A history of financial intermediaries. New York [1971] xi, 254 p. ISBN 0-394-31001-2 LC Card 78-127552 DDC 332.1/0973
HG181 .K73 *NYPL [JLE 87-572]*

FINANCE - UNITED STATES - HISTORY - 20TH CENTURY.
Greider, William. Secrets of the temple . New York , c1987. 798 p. ; ISBN 0-671-47989-X : LC Card 87-16712 DDC 332.1/1/0973 19
HG2563 .G72 1987

FINANCE - UNITED STATES - STATISTICS.
Statistical information on the financial services industry. Washington, D.C. (1120 Connecticut Ave., N.W., Washington 20036) , c1984. xi, 272 p. : LC Card 84-253106 DDC 332.1/0973/021 19
HG181 .S795 1984 *NYPL [*R-Econ. 86-285]*

Statistical information on the financial services industry. Washington, D.C. (1120 Connecticut Ave., N.W., Washington 20036) , c1987. xi, 273 p. : LC Card 87-402171 DDC 332.1/0973/021 19
HG181 .S795 1987

FINANCE - VENEZUELA.
Martín-Guédez, Rafael, 1942- Vigencia de la multibanca . [Caracas? , 1982 or 1983] 122 p. ; LC Card 83-201555
HG2964 .M37 1982

FINANCE - VENEZUELA - CONGRESSES.
Situaciones y políticas para el financiamiento industrial . [Caracas, Venezuela] [1985?] 48 p. ; LC Card 86-205909
HG185.V4 S58 1985

FINANCE - VOCATIONAL GUIDANCE.
Epstein, Rachel S. Careers in the world of investments /. New York , c1988. 47 p. : ISBN 1-555-46631-1 LC Card 87-13182 DDC 332.6/023 19
HG4528 .E67 1988

FINANCE - ZIMBABWE.
Whitsun Foundation. Project 1.09 . Harare, Zimbabwe [1983?] ix, 260 p. : ISBN 0-7974-0607-7 (pbk.) LC Card 87-402552 DDC 332.1/096891 19
HG1352 .W48 1983

FINANCE--ISLAMIC COUNTRIES.
'Abd al-Laṭif, Badawī, 1909- al-Niẓām al-mālī. [al-Qāhirah] 1962. 115 p. LC Card NE63-525
HJ233 .A25 *NYPL [*OGO 82-3888]*

Le financement de l'entreprise en période de récession économique /. Chardonnens, Jean-Pierre. [Fribourg] , c1984. 269 p. : ISBN 2-8271-0281-1 : LC Card 84-225557 DDC 658.1/5 19
HG4026 .C457 1984

Le Financement des équipements publics de demain / sous la direction de Guy Terny et Rémy Prud'homme ; préface, Michel Giraud ; postface, Jean-Louis Giral. Paris : Economica, c1986. 432 p. : ill. ; 24 cm. Bibliography: p. 393-394. Includes index. ISBN 2-7178-1186-9 : LC Card 87-117264
1. Infrastructure (Economics) - France - Finance. 2. Infrastructure (Economics) - United States - Finance. I. Terny, Guy. II. Prud'homme, Rémy.
HC280.C3 F56 1986

Financement et assurance des crédits à l'exportation . Loubergé, Henri. Genève , 1985. 502 p. : *NYPL [JLD 86-2109]*

Les finances du duc de Bourgogne, Philippe le Hardi (1384-1404) . Nieuwenhuysen, A. van (Andrée) Bruxelles, Belgique , 1984. 556 p. ; ISBN 2-8004-0838-3 : LC Card 85-160639
HJ1099.B85 N54 1984

La financiación del acceso a la vivienda de España, 1976-1981 /. Trilla i Bellart, Carme. [Barcelona] [1984] 56 p. : LC Card 86-160004
HD7351.A4 T75 1984

Financiadora de Estudos e Projetos (Brazil)
Pesquisas sobre o problema fundiário urbano. [São Paulo] [Brasília?] , 1983. 6 v. in 8 ; LC Card 87-404400 DDC 333.77/13/0981 19
HD496 .P47 1983

Financial accounting . Backer, Morton. San Diego , c1988. xvi, 685 p. : ISBN 0-15-527371-X LC Card 87-81140 DDC 657 19
HF5635 .B139 1988

Financial accounting /. Benjamin, James J. Houston, Tex. , 1986. xii, 718 p. : ISBN 0-87393-039-8 LC Card 86-214139 DDC 657/.48 19
HF5635 .B419 1986

Financial accounting . Davidson, Sidney, 1919- Chicago , c1988. xvi, 800 p. ; ISBN 0-03-011522-1 LC Card 87-9135 DDC 657 19
HF5635 .D228 1988

Financial accounting /. Imdieke, Leroy F. New York , c1987. xxii, 770, [44] p. : ISBN 0-471-80829-6 LC Card 86-28158 DDC 657 19
HF5635 .I43 1987

Financial accounting /. Meigs, Walter B. New York , c1987. xx, 738 p. : ISBN 0-07-041834-9 LC Card 87-3324 DDC 657 19
HF5635 .M492 1987

Financial accounting /. Smith, Jack L. New York , c1988. xxii, 706 p. : ISBN 0-07-059002-8 : LC Card 87-17233 DDC 657 19
HF5635 .S6445 1988

FINANCIAL ACCOUNTING. see **ACCOUNTING.**

Financial accounting and corporate reporting . Ferris, Kenneth R. Plano, Tex. , 1987. xi, 422 p. : ISBN 0-256-03554-7 (pbk.) LC Card 86-71236 DDC 657/.3 19
HF5686.C7 F455 1987

Financial accounting cases /. Hoskin, Robert E. Chicago , c1988. 201 p. : ISBN 0-03-011778-X (pbk.) LC Card 87-22238 DDC 657 19
HF5635 .H817 1988

Financial Accounting Foundation.
A Study of the attitudes toward and an assessment of the Financial Accounting Standards Board /. Stamford, CT , 1985. x, 141 p. : LC Card 86-230871 DDC 657/.0218 19
HF5616.U5 S78 1985

Financial Accounting Foundation. Financial Accounting Standards Board. see **Financial Accounting Standards Board.**

Financial Accounting Foundation. Governmental Accounting Standards Board. Van Daniker, Relmond P., 1942- Infrastructure assets . Stamford, Conn. (High Ridge Park, P.O. Box 3821, Stamford 06905-0821) , c1986. xii, 155 p. ; LC Card 86-90661 DDC 657/.835 19
HJ9816 .V35 1986

Financial accounting standards . Jarnagin, Bill D. Chicago, Ill. (4025 W. Peterson Ave., Chicago 60646) , 1986. xv, 1253 p. : LC Card 87-116311 DDC 657/.0218 19
HF5616.U5 B66 1986

Financial Accounting Standards Board. Examples of the use of FASB Statement no. 33, Financial reporting and changing prices.

FINANCIAL ACCOUNTING STANDARDS BOARD - PUBLIC OPINION.
A Study of the attitudes toward and an assessment of the Financial Accounting Standards Board /. Stamford, CT , 1985. x, 141 p. : LC Card 86-230871 DDC 657/.0218 19
HF5616.U5 S78 1985

Financial administration : handbook for small Wisconsin towns and villages / Bureau of Local Government Services, Division of State/Local Finance, Wisconsin Department of Revenue in conjunction with Philip Rosenberg & Associates. Madison, WI : The Bureau, c1986. vi, 97 p. : ill. ; 28 cm. "July, 1986." LC Card 87-620662 DDC 352.1/09775 19
1. Local finance - Wisconsin - Handbooks, manuals, etc. I. Wisconsin. Bureau of Local Government Services. II. Philip Rosenberg & Associates.
HJ9338 .F56 1986

Financial Analysts Federation. Standards of practice handbook : the Code of ethics and the Standards of professional conduct, with commentary and interpretation / the Institute of Chartered Financial Analysts [and] the Financial Analysts Federation.3rd ed. Charlottesville, Va. : The Institute ; New York, N.Y. : The Federation, 1986. xii, 150 p. ; 25 cm. Includes bibliographies and index. ISBN 0-938367-03-X (pbk.) : LC Card 87-138043 DDC 174/.9332 19
1. Investment advisers - Professional ethics - United States - Handbooks, manuals, etc. 2. Investment analysis - Standards - United States - Handbooks, manuals, etc. I. Institute of Chartered Financial Analysts. II. Title.
HG4921 .F38 1986

Financial and compliance report on federally assisted programs for the year ended June 30, 1985 /. Minnesota. [Saint Paul, Minn.] [1986] x, 92 p. ; LC Card 87-620971 DDC 353.97760072/52 19
HJ515 .M55 1986

Financial and strategic management for nonprofit organizations /. Bryce, Herrington J. Englewood Cliffs, N.J. , c1987. xviii, 395 p. : ISBN 0-13-316597-3 LC Card 86-30454 DDC 658/.049 19
HG4027.65 .B78 1987

The financial aspects of insurance against employment accidents /. Brancoli, Mario. Geneva , 1974. 42 p. ; LC Card 84-247775
HD7260.5 .B73 1974

Financial chapters of the war [microform]. Noyes, Alexander Dana, 1862-1945. New York, 1916. xi, 255 p. LC Card 16-19959
D635 .N6 *NYPL [*ZT-1735 no.5]*

Financial, commercial, and mortgage mathematics and their applications /. Prakash, Arun J. New York , 1987. x, 245 p. ; ISBN 0-275-92119-0 (alk. paper) : LC Card 86-30579 DDC 513/.93 19
HF5691 .P69 1987

Financial comprehensive ARM payment tables / computed and published by Financial Publishing Company. Boston, Mass. : Financial Pub. Co. ; Philadelphia, PA : Running Press, c1985. 255 p. ; 18 cm. (Publication-Financial Publishing Company. no. 493 (May 1985)) ISBN 0-89471-379-5 (pbk.) : LC Card 85-206951 DDC 332.8/2/021 19
1. Interest - Tables. 2. Mortgage loans, Variable rate - Tables. I. Financial Publishing Company. II. Title: Comprehensive ARM payment tables. III. Series: Publication-Financial Publishing Company, no. 493.
HG1634 .F44 1985

The Financial condition of the government of the Virgin Islands as of September 30, 1981 / U. S. Department of the Interior, Office of Inspector General. Washington, D.C. : The Office, [1983] 129 p. ; 28 cm. Cover title. "October 1983." "V-TG-VIS-08-83." LC Card 84-603162 DDC 354.7297/22007231 19
1. Finance, Public - Virgin Islands of the United States - Accounting. I. United States. Dept. of the Interior. Office of Inspector General.
HJ9923.V6 F56 1983

Financial condition of the U. S. electric utility industry. [Washington] : Congress of the United States, Congressional Budget Office, [1986] xviii, 82 p. : ill. ; 26 cm. "Dan Carol and Thomas Lutton ... prepared the report" ... pref. "CBO study." "March 1986."--Cover. Includes bibliographical references.
1. Electric utilities - United States - Finance. 2. Electric utilities - Law and legislation - United States. I. Carol, Dan. II. Lutton, Thomas. III. Title.
NYPL [JLF 86-1386]

The financial cost of export credit guarantee programs /. Henry, Donald Putnam, 1957- Santa Monica, CA , 1987. ix, 37 p. ; ISBN 0-8330-0794-7 (pbk.) LC Card 87-4630 DDC 382/.63 19
HG3754.5.U6 H46 1987

Financial crises and the world banking system / edited by Forrest Capie and Geoffrey E. Wood. London : Macmillan in association with Centre for Banking and International Finance The City University, c1986. x, 270 p. : ill. ; 23 cm. Includes bibliographies and index. ISBN 0-333-35129-0
1. Depressions - History - Congresses. 2. Bank failures - History - Congresses. 3. Banks and banking - History - Congresses. 4. Bank failures - Great Britain - History - Congresses. 5. Banks and banking - Great Britain - History - Congresses. I. Capie, Forrest. II. Wood, Geoffrey Edward. *NYPL [JLD 86-2132]*

Financial deregulation : the proceedings of a conference held by the David Hume Institute in May 1986 / edited by Richard Dale. Cambridge ; Wolfeboro, N.H., USA : Woodhead-Faulkner, 1986. xiii, 88 p. ; 25 cm. Errata slip inserted. Includes bibliographical references. CONTENTS. - The regularities of regulation / George Stigler -- Financial deregulation / Andrew Buxton -- The Securities and Investments Board / Sir Kenneth Berrill -- Preparing for the Big Bang / Philip Wilkinson -- A supervisor's perspective on deregulation / Rodney Galpin -- The audit role in the context of financial deregulation / John Bullock -- A review of the legal problems / R.B. Jack -- The American experience / L. William Seidman. ISBN 0-85941-366-7 : LC Card 87-104563 DDC 332/.0941 19
1. Finance - Great Britain - Deregulation - Congresses. 2. Finance - United States - Deregulation - Congresses. I. Dale, Richard. II. David Hume Institute.
HG186.G7 F546 1986

Financial dimensions of marketing : a source book / compiled by Richard M. S. Wilson. London : Macmillan, published in association with the Institute of Cost and Management Accountants, 1981. 2 v. : ill. ; 24 cm. ISBN 0-333-25741-3
1. Marketing - Decision making. 2. Marketing - Finance. I. Wilson, Richard M. S.
NYPL [JLL 82-44]

Financial diplomacy . Bodayla, Stephen D. New York , 1987. x, 216 p. ; ISBN 0-8240-8074-2 (alk. paper) LC Card 87-23790 DDC 337.73072 19
HF1456.5.M6 B63 1987

FINANCIAL DISCLOSURE - LAW AND LEGISLATION - BELGIUM.
Hawawini, Gabriel A. Mandatory financial information and capital market equilibrium in Belgium /. New York , 1987. 271 p. : ISBN 0-8240-7852-7 (alk. paper) : LC Card 87-54 DDC 332.63/222/09493 19
HG5553 .H39 1987

Financial Executives Research Foundation. Cash management and the payments system . Morristown, N.J. , c1986. viii, 102 p. : ISBN 0-910586-62-4 (pbk.) LC Card 86-82305 DDC 658.1/5244 19
HG4028.C45 C359 1986

Financial fitness through divorce . Lewin, Elizabeth. New York, N.Y. , c1987. vii, 146 p. : ISBN 0-8160-1323-3 (pbk.) : LC Card 86-24383 DDC 332.024 19
HG179 .L477 1987

FINANCIAL FUTURES.
Andersen, Torben Juul. Currency and interest rate hedging . New York, N.Y. , c1987. viii, 272 p. : ISBN 0-13-195645-0 LC Card 87-7758 DDC 332.64/5 19
HG3853 .A53 1987

Bernstein, Jacob, 1946- Short-term trading in futures . Chicago, Ill. , c1987. vii, 320 p. : ISBN 0-917253-66-3 (loose-leaf) : LC Card 87-4940 DDC 332.64/4 19
HG6024.3 .B477 1987

Clasing, Henry K. The secrets of a professional futures trader /. Brightwaters, N.Y. , c1987. 231 p. : ISBN 0-930233-15-8 LC Card 87-166047 DDC 332.64/4 19
HG6024.A3 C58 1987

Cordero, Ricardo. Der Financial Futures Markt /. Bern , c1986. xii, 200 p. : ISBN 3-258-03638-1 LC Card 87-408496 DDC 332.1 s 332.64/4 19
HG1526 .B27 Bd. 97 HG6024.3

Fink, Robert E. Futures trading . New York, N.Y. , c1988. xiv, 685 p. : ISBN 0-13-345745-1 : LC Card 87-24030 DDC 332.64/4 19
HG6046 .F56 1988

Futures trading course. Washington, D.C. (1825 Eye St., N.W., Washington 20006) , c1986. 3 v. : LC Card 86-215844 DDC 332.64/4 19
HG6024.A3 F89 1986

Goldstone, Nancy Bazelon. Trading up /. New York , c1988. viii, 262 p. ; ISBN 0-525-24621-5 : LC Card 87-19975 DDC 332.4/5/0924 B 19
HG3853 .G65 1988

Koziol, Joseph D. A handbook for professional futures and options traders /. New York , c1987. xvi, 325 p. : ISBN 0-471-87423-X : LC Card 87-8180 DDC 332.64/4 19
HG6024.A3 K68 1987

Smith, Courtney. Option strategies . New York , c1987. viii, 256 p. : ISBN 0-471-84367-9 LC Card 87-6174 DDC 332.64/52 19
HG6024.3 .S55 1987

Steidlmayer, J. Peter. Markets and market logic /. Chicago , c1986. 161 p. ; ISBN 0-941275-00-0 LC Card 87-401422 DDC 332.64 19
HG6046 .S673 1986

Understanding the futures markets. New York, NY (100 Church St., Suite 1850 New York 10007) , c1987. 61 p. ; LC Card 87-129996 DDC 332.64/4 19
HG6024.A3 U64 1987

FINANCIAL FUTURES - GOVERNMENT POLICY - UNITED STATES.
Futures and options trading for commercial banks . Chicago, Ill. (30 S. Wacker Dr., Chicago 60606) , c1986. 14 p. : LC Card 87-131777 DDC 332.1/754 19
HG2491 .F87 1986

FINANCIAL FUTURES - GREAT BRITAIN - ACCOUNTING.
Tiner, John I. Accounting for treasury products . Cambridge, England , Wolfeboro, N.H., USA , 1988. p. cm. ISBN 0-85941-389-6 : LC Card 87-12531 DDC 657/.833 19
HG1708 .T56 1988

Der Financial Futures Markt /. Cordero, Ricardo. Bern , c1986. xii, 200 p. : ISBN 3-258-03638-1 LC Card 87-408496 DDC 332.1 s 332.64/4 19
HG1526 .B27 Bd. 97 HG6024.3

FINANCIAL FUTURES - TAXATION - GREAT BRITAIN.
Tiner, John I. Accounting for treasury products . Cambridge, England , Wolfeboro, N.H., USA , 1988. p. cm. ISBN 0-85941-389-6 : LC Card 87-12531 DDC 657/.833 19
HG1708 .T56 1988

FINANCIAL FUTURES - UNITED STATES.
Atchison, Michael D. New financial instruments . Charlottesville, Va. (P.O. Box 3665, Charlottesville 22903) , c1985. viii, 108 p. ; LC Card 85-195578 DDC 332.63 19
HG6024.3 .A83 1985
NYPL [JLL 81-133 no.21]

Futures markets . Washington, D.C. , c1985. xiii, 325 p. : ISBN 0-8447-3592-2 LC Card 85-26705 DDC 332.64/4 19
HG6049 .F86 1985 *NYPL [JLE 86-1532]*

Financial Industry Securities Council Same Day Funds Settlement Task Force. Same day funds settlement for securities transactions : a research report / prepared for the Financial Industry Securities Council Same Day Funds Settlement Task Force under the sponsorship of American Bankers Association, Securities Industry Association. [New York, N.Y.] : A. Young ; [S.l.] : Treasury Strategies, Inc., c1985. 61 leaves in various foliations : ill. ; 29 cm. Cover title. "July 1985." LC Card 85-193287 DDC 332.64 19
1. Clearing of securities - United States. 2. Stock transfer - United States. I. Securities Industry Association. II. Young (Arthur) and Company. III. Treasury Strategies, Inc. IV. Title.
HG4631 .F56 1985 *NYPL [JLF 86-919]*

Financial information for management of a development finance institution . Mould, Maurice C., 1925- Washington, D.C. [1987] 1 v. (various pagings) : ISBN 0-8213-0913-7 (pbk.) LC Card 87-15989 DDC 332.2 19
HG3726 .M68 1987

Financial innovation and monetary policy : Asia and the West : proceedings of the second international conference held by the Institute for Monetary and Economic Studies of the Bank of Japan / edited by Yoshio Suzuki and Hiroshi Yomo. [Tokyo] : University of Tokyo Press, c1986. ix, 339 p. : ill. ; 24 cm. Includes bibliographies and index. ISBN 4-13-047029-9 : LC Card 86-222823 DDC 332/.095 19
1. Finance - East Asia - Congresses. 2. Banks and banking - East Asia - State supervision - Congresses. 3. Monetary policy - East Asia - Congresses. 4. Finance - Congresses. 5. Banks and banking - State supervision - Congresses. 6. Monetary policy - Congresses. I. Suzuki, Yoshio, 1931-. II. Yomo, Hiroshi. III. Nihon Ginkō. Kin'yū Kenkyūjo.
HG187.E37 F55 1986

FINANCIAL INSTITUTIONS - ACCOUNTING.
Moebs, G. Michael. Pricing financial services /. Homewood, Ill. , c1986. xviii, 246 p. : ISBN 0-87094-594-7 LC Card 85-73688
NYPL [JLE 86-2817]

FINANCIAL INSTITUTIONS - AFRICA.
Hyuha, Mukwanason. Financial structure and economic development in Africa . Dar-es-Salaam, Tanzania , c1983. 43 p. : LC Card 85-981441 DDC 332/.096 19
HG187.5.A2 H98 1983

Financial institutions and markets in a changing world / edited by Donald R. Fraser, Peter S. Rose. 3rd ed. Plano, Tex. : Business Publications, 1987. xiii, 697 p. : ill. ; 25 cm. Includes bibliographies. ISBN 0-256-03695-0 (pbk.) LC Card 86-61850 DDC 332.1/0973 19
1. Financial institutions - United States. 2. Finance - United States. I. Fraser, Donald R. II. Rose, Peter S.
HG181 .F633 1987

Financial institutions and markets in the South Pacific . Skully, Michael T. New York , 1987. xvi, 379 p., [1] leaf of plates : ISBN 0-312-00529-6 : LC Card 87-4506 DDC 332.1/099 19
HG190.A2 S58 1987

Financial institutions and regional development in India /. Ramakrishna Sarma, K. Allahabad, India , 1986. xvii, 211 p. ; ISBN 81-85076-04-9 : LC Card 86-902692 DDC 332.2 19
HG3288 .R32 1986

FINANCIAL INSTITUTIONS - ARAB COUNTRIES - DIRECTORIES.
The APS who's who in Middle East banking & trade. Nicosia, Cyprus , c1984. 2 v. : LC Card 83-149147 *NYPL [JLF 86-983]*

FINANCIAL INSTITUTIONS - ARGENTINA.
Tami, Felipe S. Study of the financial sector of Argentina . Washington, D.C. [1979] x, 146 p. : LC Card 86-673765
HG185.A7 T35x 1979

FINANCIAL INSTITUTIONS - ASIA, SOUTHEASTERN.
Skully, Michael T. Financing East Asia's success . New York , 1987. xiii, 242 p. ; ISBN 0-312-00536-9 : LC Card 86-31527 DDC 332/.0959 19
HG187.E37 S68 1987

FINANCIAL INSTITUTIONS - BRAZIL.
Costa, Roberto Teixeira da. Brazil's experience in creating a capital market /. São Paulo [1985] 114 p. : LC Card 86-207924 DDC 332.6/0981 19
HG4523 .C67 1985

Galvêas, Ernane. Sistema financeiro e mercado de capitais /. Rio de Janeiro , 1985. 171 p. : LC Card 85-208367
HG185.B7 G35 1985

Mercado financeiro e de capitais . [Brasília? , 1978?] 118 leaves, [25] leaves of plates : LC

Card 84-184169
HG185.B7 M47 1978

FINANCIAL INSTITUTIONS - BRAZIL - RIO GRANDE DO NORTE.
Escóssia Neto, Lauro da. O sistema financeiro nacional . [Natal] , 1985. 46, [1] p. : LC Card 86-158741
HG185.B7 E83 1985

FINANCIAL INSTITUTIONS - BRAZIL - STATISTICS.
Inquéritos especiais /. Rio de Janeiro, Brasil , 1984. 4 v. in 5. ; *NYPL [JLF 86-202]*

FINANCIAL INSTITUTIONS - CANADA - STATE SUPERVISION.

FINANCIAL INSTITUTIONS - CARIBBEAN AREA - DIRECTORIES.
Mercados de capital en América Latina y el Caribe . Caracas, Venezuela [1986] 114 p. ; LC Card 87-103358
HG5160.5.A3 M47 1986

FINANCIAL INSTITUTIONS - CASE STUDIES.
Le Crisi finanziarie /. Bologna , c1985. 348 p. : ISBN 88-15-00807-1 : LC Card 85-201934 DDC 332.1 19
HG1591 .C75 1985

FINANCIAL INSTITUTIONS - COLOMBIA.
Villar Borrero, Eduardo. El dinero y el sector financiero a su alcance /. Bogotá, Colombia , c1984. 64 p. : ISBN 84-8276-321-0 LC Card 84-241500
HG855 .V54 1984

FINANCIAL INSTITUTIONS - COLOMBIA - STATISTICS.
Estadísticas e indicadores de los bancos y corporaciones financieras, 1970-1985 . [Bogotá, Colombia] [1986] 64 p. : LC Card 86-167798
HG2904 .E77 1986

FINANCIAL INSTITUTIONS - CONGRESSES.
Monetary theory and economic institutions . New York , 1987. ix, 349 p. : ISBN 0-312-00407-9 : LC Card 86-26069 DDC 332.4/01 19
HG203 .M68 1987

FINANCIAL INSTITUTIONS - DEVELOPING COUNTRIES.
Wellons, Philip A. Banks and specialised financial intermediaries in development /. Paris , Washington, D.C. , 1986. 150 p. : ISBN 92-64-12867-0 (pbk.) : LC Card 87-114506 DDC 332.1/09172/4 19
HG3550 .W45 1986

FINANCIAL INSTITUTIONS - DEVELOPING COUNTRIES - CONGRESSES.
Epargne et développement /. Paris , 1985. 410 p. : ISBN 2-7178-0855-8 : LC Card 86-149765
HC59.72.S3 E62 1985

FINANCIAL INSTITUTIONS - DOMINICAN REPUBLIC.
González Vega, Claudio. Mercados financieros y desarrollo /. Santo Domingo, República Dominicana , 1986. 73 p. : LC Card 87-102022
HG2817 .G66 1986

Mercados financieros y distribución del ingreso /. Santo Domingo, República Dominicana , 1986. 117 p. : LC Card 87-405027 DDC 332.1/097293 19
HG185.D65 M47 1986

FINANCIAL INSTITUTIONS - EAST ASIA.
Skully, Michael T. Financing East Asia's success . New York , 1987. xiii, 242 p. ; ISBN 0-312-00536-9 : LC Card 86-31527 DDC 332/.0959 19
HG187.E37 S68 1987

FINANCIAL INSTITUTIONS - ENGLAND - LONDON - CORRUPT PRACTICES.
Clarke, Michael, 1945- Regulating the city . Milton Keynes, Eng. , Philadelphia, Pa. , 1986. 194 p. ; ISBN 0-335-15381-X LC Card 85-29715 DDC 332.1/09421/2 19
HG186.G7 C53 1985 NYPL [JLE 86-3357]

FINANCIAL INSTITUTIONS - EUROPEAN ECONOMIC COMMUNITY COUNTRIES.
Seminario sobre Consequencias para las Entidades Oficiales de Crédito de la Entrada de España en las Comunidades Europeas (1984 : Madrid, Spain) Seminario sobre Consequencias para las Entidades Oficiales de Crédito de la Entrada de España en las Comunidades Europeas /. [Madrid] [1984?] 270 p. ; ISBN 84-505-0963-7 LC Card 85-186710
HG1642.E86 S46 1984

Die Währungspolitik in den Ländern der Europäischen Wirtschaftsgemeinschaft . Luxembourg , Washington, D.C. , 1972. 451 p. ; LC Card 85-116654
HG930.5 .W34 1972

FINANCIAL INSTITUTIONS - GERMANY, WEST.
Seja, Jürgen, 1953- Selektive Effekte der global orientierten Geldpolitik der Deutschen Bundesbank auf die Marktstruktur im Bankensektor /. Frankfurt am Main , New York , c1983. xiii, 370 p. ; ISBN 3-8204-5282-6 LC Card 86-119382
HG3055 .S5 1983

FINANCIAL INSTITUTIONS - GERMANY (WEST) - MANAGEMENT - CONGRESSES.
Tagung Strategische Bankplanung (1982 : Bonn, Germany) Strategische Bankplanung . Frankfurt am Main , c1983. 345 p. : ISBN 3-7819-0293-5 LC Card 83-233043
HG1615 .T34 1982

FINANCIAL INSTITUTIONS - GOVERNMENT POLICY - ENGLAND - LONDON.
Clarke, Michael, 1945- Regulating the city . Milton Keynes, Eng. , Philadelphia, Pa. , 1986. 194 p. ; ISBN 0-335-15381-X LC Card 85-29715 DDC 332.1/09421/2 19
HG186.G7 C53 1985 NYPL [JLE 86-3357]

FINANCIAL INSTITUTIONS - GREAT BRITAIN.
Boléat, Mark. The mortgage market /. London , Boston , 1987. x, 176 p. ; ISBN 0-04-334011-3 (alk. paper) LC Card 86-28875 DDC 332.7/22 19
HG2040.5.G7 B65 1987

Geisst, Charles R. A guide to financial institutions /. New York , 1988. p. cm. ISBN 0-312-01132-6 : LC Card 87-13047 DDC 332.1 19
HG185.U5 G45 1988

Goacher, D. J. (David J.) British non-bank financial intermediaries /. London , Boston , 1987. xxiv, 460 p. : ISBN 0-04-332109-7 (alk. paper) LC Card 86-32146 DDC 332.1/0941 19
HG186.G7 B73 1987

FINANCIAL INSTITUTIONS - HANDBOOKS, MANUALS, ETC.
Handbook of financial markets--securities, options, futures /. Homewood, Ill. , c1981. xxiii, 794 p. : ISBN 0-87094-216-6 LC Card 80-70448 DDC 332.6/78 19
HG4527 .H25 NYPL [JLE 86-1500]

FINANCIAL INSTITUTIONS - HUNGARY.
Szentiványi, Iván. Lakossági pénzügyek, pénzintézeti tevékenység /. Budapest , 1985. 563, [1] p. ; ISBN 963-221-602-4 : LC Card 86-186953
HG186.H8 S94 1985

FINANCIAL INSTITUTIONS, INTERNATIONAL.
Geisst, Charles R. A guide to financial institutions /. New York , 1988. p. cm. ISBN 0-312-01132-6 : LC Card 87-13047 DDC 332.1 19
HG185.U5 G45 1988

Sury, Paul de. Milano, centro finanziario internazionale /. [Milano] [1984] viii, 138 p. : ISBN 88-14-00312-2 : LC Card 86-114645
HG3090.M52 S87 1984

FINANCIAL INSTITUTIONS, INTERNATIONAL - CONGRESSES.
Bidding for projects financed by international lending agencies /. Aldershot, Hants. , c1982. vii, 345 p. : ISBN 0-566-03033-0 LC Card 82-210482 DDC 332.1/53 19
HD2365 .B52 1982 NYPL [JLG 85-120]

FINANCIAL INSTITUTIONS - ITALY.
Bagella, Michele. Gli istituti di credito speciale e il mercato finanziario, 1947-1962 /. Milano, Italy , c1986. 289 p. ; LC Card 86-232526
HG3729.I7 B34 1986

FINANCIAL INSTITUTIONS - ITALY - EMILIA-ROMAGNA - ACCOUNTING.
I Conti finanziari dell'Emilia-Romagna /. [Bologna] , c1984. 157 p. : ISBN 88-15-00522-6 : LC Card 84-235593 DDC 332.1/0945/4 19
HG3089.E45 C66 1984
NYPL [JLE 86-3198]

FINANCIAL INSTITUTIONS - ITALY - MILAN.
Sury, Paul de. Milano, centro finanziario internazionale /. [Milano] [1984] viii, 138 p. : ISBN 88-14-00312-2 : LC Card 86-114645
HG3090.M52 S87 1984

FINANCIAL INSTITUTIONS - KENTUCKY - EMPLOYEES - SUPPLY AND DEMAND - STATISTICS.
Kentucky occupational profiles, finance, insurance, and real estate /. [Frankfort, Ky.] [1985] v, 33 p. : LC Card 85-622996 DDC 331.12/51/0009769 19
HD5718.B262 U66 1985

FINANCIAL INSTITUTIONS - LATIN AMERICA - DIRECTORIES.
Mercados de capital en América Latina y el Caribe . Caracas, Venezuela [1986] 114 p. ; LC Card 87-103358
HG5160.5.A3 M47 1986

FINANCIAL INSTITUTIONS - MAINE.
The Status of Maine's financial institutions . [Augusta] [1986] 38 leaves ; LC Card 86-621913 DDC 332.1/09741 19
HG183.M2 S7 1986

FINANCIAL INSTITUTIONS - MAINE - STATISTICS.
The Status of Maine's financial institutions . [Augusta] [1986] 38 leaves ; LC Card 86-621913 DDC 332.1/09741 19
HG183.M2 S7 1986

FINANCIAL INSTITUTIONS - MANAGEMENT.
Gardner, Mona J. Managing financial institutions . Chicago , c1988. xii, 795 p. : ISBN 0-03-005479-6 LC Card 86-32805 DDC 332.1/068/1 19
HG1615.25 .G37 1988

FINANCIAL INSTITUTIONS - MARKETING.
Benn, Alec. Advertising financial products and services . Westport, Conn. , c1986. xii, 231 p. : ISBN 0-89930-103-7 (lib bdg. : alk. paper) LC Card 85-24406 DDC 659.1/93321 19
HG1616.M3 B43 1986 NYPL [JLE 86-4110]

FINANCIAL INSTITUTIONS - MOROCCO.
Barrādah, Muḥammad. Les techniques de banque et de crédit au Maroc /. Casablanca , 1985. 590 p. : LC Card 86-967115
HG3382.A6 B37 1985

FINANCIAL INSTITUTIONS - NIGERIA.
Osubor, John Uche. Business finance and banking in Nigeria /. Owerri, Imo State, Nigeria , 1984. vii, 209 p. : ISBN 978-235-700-13 (pbk.) LC Card 86-207599 DDC 332.1/09669 19
HG3431.A6 O85 1984

FINANCIAL INSTITUTIONS - NORTH DAKOTA - EMPLOYEES - STATISTICS.
Finance, insurance, and real estate . Bismarck, N.D. (1000 E. Divide, Bismarck 58502) [1986] 55 p. : LC Card 86-623003 DDC 332.12/51/0009784 19
HD5718.B262 U64 1986

FINANCIAL INSTITUTIONS - OCEANIA - CASE STUDIES.
Skully, Michael T. Financial institutions and markets in the South Pacific . New York , 1987. xvi, 379 p., [1] leaf of plates : ISBN 0-312-00529-6 : LC Card 87-4506 DDC 332.1/099 19
HG190.A2 S58 1987

FINANCIAL INSTITUTIONS - PORTUGAL.
Cavaco Silva, Aníbal A. (Aníbal António), 1939- O mercado financeiro português em 1966 /. Lisboa , 1968. xiv, 104 p. : LC Card 85-133959
HG186.P8 C38 1968

FINANCIAL INSTITUTIONS - SPAIN.
Cuervo García, Alvaro. Manual de sistema financiero . Barcelona , 1987. 427 p. : ISBN 84-344-2013-9 LC Card 87-135198
HG186.S6 C84 1987

FINANCIAL INSTITUTIONS - SRI LANKA.
Karunatilake, H. N. S. The banking and financial system of Sri Lanka /. Colombo , 1986. 320 p. ; LC Card 87-902032 DDC

332.1/09549/3 19
HG3270.8.A6 K37 1986

FINANCIAL INSTITUTIONS - UNITED STATES.
Financial institutions and markets in a changing world /. Plano, Tex. , 1987. xiii, 697 p. : ISBN 0-256-03695-0 (pbk.) LC Card 86-61850 DDC 332.1/0973 19
HG181 .F633 1987

Gart, Alan. Handbook of the money and capital markets /. New York , c1988. p. cm. ISBN 0-89930-270-X (lib. bdg. : alk. paper) LC Card 87-24938 DDC 332.63/2/0973 19
HG181 .G367 1988

Geisst, Charles R. A guide to financial institutions /. New York , 1988. p. cm. ISBN 0-312-01132-6 : LC Card 87-13047 DDC 332.1 19
HG185.U5 G45 1988

Gourgues, Harold W. Revolution in financial services /. Washington, D.C. , c1987. xiii, 248 p. : ISBN 0-87179-561-2 LC Card 87-18390 DDC 332.1/0973 19
HG2491 .G68 1987

Henning, Charles N. Financial markets and the economy /. Englewood Cliffs, N.J. , c1988. xvi, 638 p. : ISBN 0-13-316894-8 LC Card 87-24413 DDC 332/.0973 19
HG181 .H37 1988

Hessick, Michael H. Achieving quality in financial service organizations . New York , c1988. p. cm. ISBN 0-89930-231-9 (lib. bdg. : alk. paper) LC Card 87-24937 DDC 332.1/2/0688 19
HG181 .H44 1988

Hoffman, Naphtali. The bank book . San Diego , 1986. xiii, 222 p. ; ISBN 0-15-610676-0 (pbk.) : LC Card 85-27271 DDC 332.1/7/0973 19
HG1616.C87 H64 1986
NYPL [JLE 86-3189]

Moebs, G. Michael. Pricing financial services /. Homewood, Ill. , c1986. xviii, 246 p. : ISBN 0-87094-594-7 LC Card 85-73688
NYPL [JLE 86-2817]

Watts, John M., 1933- The financial services shockwave . Englewood Cliffs, N.J. , c1987. viii, 181 p. : ISBN 0-13-316852-2 : LC Card 86-22510 DDC 332.1/0973 19
HG181 .W37 1987 ***NYPL [JLE 87-612]***

FINANCIAL INSTITUTIONS - UNITED STATES - CONGRESSES.
Financial stability of the thrift industry . San Francisco, Calif. (P.O. Box 7948, San Francisco 94120) [1986?] 230 p. : LC Card 86-81012
NYPL [JLE 86-3398]

FINANCIAL INSTITUTIONS - UNITED STATES - EMPLOYEES - STATISTICS.
Occupational employment in mining, construction, finance, and services. Washington, D.C. [1986] vi, 141 p. ; LC Card 86-603149 DDC 331.12/51/000973021 19
HD9506.U62 O23 1986

FINANCIAL INSTITUTIONS - UNITED STATES - HISTORY.
Kross, Herman Edward, 1912-1975. A history of financial intermediaries. New York [1971] xi, 254 p. ISBN 0-394-31001-2 LC Card 78-127552 DDC 332.1/0973
HG181 .K73 ***NYPL [JLE 87-572]***

FINANCIAL INSTITUTIONS - UNITED STATES - MANAGEMENT.
Austin, Douglas V. Modern banking . Boston , c1985. x, 406 p. : ISBN 0-87267-053-8 LC Card 84-21754 DDC 332.1/068 19
HG1615 .A98 1985 ***NYPL [JLE 85-3956]***

FINANCIAL INSTITUTIONS - UNITED STATES - MARKETING.
Small business market factbook. Tampa, FL (P.O. Box 30168, Tampa 33630) , c1986. 106 leaves : LC Card 87-100402 DDC 338.6/42/0973 19
HG4027.7 .S64 1986

FINANCIAL INSTITUTIONS - UNITED STATES - STATISTICS.
Statistical information on the financial services industry. Washington, D.C. (1120 Connecticut Ave., N.W., Washington 20036) , c1984. xi, 272 p. : LC Card 84-253106 DDC 332.1/0973/021 19
HG181 .S795 1984 ***NYPL [*R-Econ. 86-285]***

Statistical information on the financial services industry. Washington, D.C. (1120 Connecticut Ave., N.W., Washington 20036) , c1987. xi, 273 p. : LC Card 87-402171 DDC 332.1/0973/021 19
HG181 .S795 1987

FINANCIAL INSTITUTIONS - VENEZUELA.
Martín-Guédez, Rafael, 1942- Sistema financiero . Caracas [1984] (Caracas : Editorial Arte) 309 p. : LC Card 85-177967
HG2156.V42 M37 1984

Martín-Guédez, Rafael, 1942- Vigencia de la multibanca . [Caracas? , 1982 or 1983] 122 p. ; LC Card 83-201555
HG2964 .M37 1982

Financial integration and interest rate linkages between North Atlantic and Caribbean economies, January 1968 to December 1976 /. Joefield-Napier, Wallace. St. Augustine, Trinidad [1980] vii, 82 p. : LC Card 81-132125 DDC 332.8/2/0724 19
HG1623.C27 J64 1980 ***NYPL [Sc E 86-329]***

FINANCIAL INTERMEDIARIES. see **FINANCIAL INSTITUTIONS.**

Financial investigative task forces. Multi-agency financial investigative task forces [microform] Washington, D.C. [1983] 1 v. (various pagings) : ***NYPL [*ZT-1708 no.61]***

FINANCIAL JOURNALISM. see **JOURNALISM, COMMERCIAL.**

Financial liberalization revisited . Nowak, Felicitas. Göttingen [1986] 49 p. : LC Card 87-121206 DDC 332/.0983 19
HG185.C5 N69 1986

Financial management . Brigham, Eugene F., 1930- Chicago , c1988. xx, 901 p. : ISBN 0-03-012543-X LC Card 87-15616 DDC 658.1/5 19
HG4026 .B669 1988

Financial management . Rao, Ramesh K. S. New York , London , c1987. xvii, 798 p. : ISBN 0-02-398210-1 LC Card 86-26406 DDC 658.1/5 19
HG4026 .R36 1987

Financial management for the multinational firm /. Abdullah, Fuad A. (Fuad Abdul-Kader), 1930- Englewood Cliffs, N.J. , c1987. xiii, 594 p. : ISBN 0-13-316340-7 LC Card 86-25226 DDC 658.1/599 19
HG4027.5 .A23 1987

Financial management handbook / edited by Philip A. Vale. 3rd ed. Aldershot, Hants, England ; Brookfield, Vt., U. S.A. : Gower, c1987. p. cm. Bibliography: p. Includes index. ISBN 0-566-02623-6 : LC Card 87-40 DDC 658.1/5 19
1. Corporations - Finance - Handbooks, manuals, etc. 2. Business enterprises - Finance - Handbooks, manuals, etc. I. Vale, Philip A., 1955-.
HG4027.3 .F53 1987

Financial management of public enterprises /. Sahay, S. N. (Surendra Nath) New Delhi , 1984. xiii, 216 p. ; LC Card 84-900657 DDC 354.54/12092/0681 19
HD4295.B5 S24 1984 ***NYPL [JLD 86-4430]***

The Financial management survey and synthesis series.
Bierman, Harold. Implementation of capital budgeting techniques . Tampa, FL , c1986. i, 69 p. : ISBN 0-936795-01-8 (pbk.) LC Card 86-231118 DDC 658.1/54 19
HG4028.C4 B544 1986

Shapiro, Alan C. International corporate finance . Tampa, FL , c1986. 79 p. : ISBN 0-936795-00-X (pbk.) LC Card 86-231054 DDC 658.1/599 19
HG4027.5 .S46 1986

The financial manager's guide to microsoftware /. Shuster, Harvey L. New York , 1988. p. cm. ISBN 0-471-81176-9 LC Card 87-21663 DDC 658.1/5/0285536 19
HG4012.5 .S47 1988

Financial markets and economic development . Dee, Philippa S. Tübingen , c1986. ix, 131 p. ; ISBN 3-16-345086-5 LC Card 86-190926 DDC 338.9519/5 19
HC467 .D44 1986

Financial markets and the economy /. Henning, Charles N. Englewood Cliffs, N.J. , c1988. xvi, 638 p. : ISBN 0-13-316894-8 LC Card 87-24413 DDC 332/.0973 19
HG181 .H37 1988

Financial modelling in corporate management / edited by James W. Bryant. 2nd ed. Chichester [West Sussex] ; New York : Wiley, c1987. xv, 404 p. : ill. ; 24 cm. Includes bibliographies and index. ISBN 0-471-91476-2 : LC Card 86-32446 DDC 658.1/5/0724 19
1. Corporations - Finance - Mathematical models. I. Bryant, James W., Ph. D.
HG4012 .F54 1987

FINANCIAL NEWS. see **JOURNALISM, COMMERCIAL.**

Financial performance of PICIC assisted companies ... [Karachi] : Economic & Research Dept., Pakistan Industrial Credit & Investment Corp., [198-?] v. <1 > ; 28 cm. CONTENTS. - [v. 1] 1976-80. LC Card 85-931756
1. Corporations - Pakistan - Finance - Statistics. I. Pakistan. Industrial Credit & Investment Corporation. Economics & Research Dept.
HG4244.5 .F56 1980z

The financial planner . Dunton, Loren. Chicago , c1986. xi, 306 p. : ISBN 0-88462-544-3 LC Card 85-23821 DDC 332.024/01 19
HG179.5 .D85 1986 ***NYPL [JLE 86-4019]***

FINANCIAL PLANNERS.
Clark-James, Suzanne. Providing personal financial planning services in your CPA practice /. New York, NY (11 Penn Plaza, New York 10001) , 1987. 1 v. (various pagings) : LC Card 87-61984 DDC 657/.068/5 19
HG179 .C59 1987

Dowd, Merle E. A consumer's guide to financial planning . New York , 1987. 296 p. : ISBN 0-531-15517-X LC Card 86-32491 DDC 332.024 19
HG179 .D68 1987

Person to person . Chicago, Ill. , c1986. 310 p. : ISBN 0-912857-33-1 (pbk.) LC Card 85-81996 DDC 332.1/068/8 19
HG179 .P368 1986 ***NYPL [JLE 86-3903]***

Pulvino, Charles J. Communicating with clients . Paramus, NJ , c1987. ix, 194 p. : ISBN 0-13-153578-1 (pbk.) LC Card 87-153498 DDC 332.1/068/8 19
HG179.5 .P86 1987

Financial planners and planning organizations directory : a reference guide to concerns and individuals engaged in advising and counseling on financial affairs / Steven Wasserman, Jacqueline Wasserman O'Brien, and Judy Popp, editors.1st ed. Detroit, Mich. : Gale Research Co., c1987. viii, 605 p. ; 29 cm. Includes indexes. ISBN 0-8103-4397-5 : LC Card 87-21259 DDC 332.6/2 19
1. Financial planners - United States - Directories. I. Wasserman, Steven R. II. O'Brien, Jacqueline Wasserman. III. Popp, Judy.
HG179.5 .F56 1987

FINANCIAL PLANNERS - UNITED STATES.
Dunton, Loren. The financial planner . Chicago , c1986. xi, 306 p. : ISBN 0-88462-544-3 LC Card 85-23821 DDC 332.024/01 19
HG179.5 .D85 1986 ***NYPL [JLE 86-4019]***

FINANCIAL PLANNERS - UNITED STATES - DIRECTORIES.
Financial planners and planning organizations directory . Detroit, Mich. , c1987. viii, 605 p. ; ISBN 0-8103-4397-5 : LC Card 87-21259 DDC 332.6/2 19
HG179.5 .F56 1987

FINANCIAL PLANNERS - UNITED STATES - MARKETING.
Jones, H. Stanley. Marketing your financial planning services . New York , c1988. xvi, 304 p. ; ISBN 0-471-85649-5 LC Card 87-26373 DDC 332.6/2 19
HG179.5 .J66 1988

Financial planning applications /. Ivers, James F. Bryn Mawr, Pa. , c1987. 2 v. : ISBN 0-943590-13-2 (pbk. : v. 1) LC Card 87-71366 DDC 332.024 19
HG179 .C326 1987

Financial planning can make you rich--and 33 case histories to prove it /. Dunton, Loren.

Englewood Cliffs, N.J. , c1987. xii, 352 p. : ISBN 0-13-316589-2 LC Card 86-25179 DDC 332.024 19
HG179 .D88 1987

Financial planning for new businesses /. Durkacz, Victor Edward. Chichester [West Sussex] , New York , c1985. 257 p. : ISBN 0-471-90843-6 (pbk.) : LC Card 85-17927 DDC 658.1/5 19
HG4027.6 .D87 1985 ***NYPL [JLE 86-929]***

Financial planning for the utterly confused /. Lerner, Joel J. New York , c1986. xi, 210 p. ; ISBN 0-07-037224-1 (pbk.) : LC Card 85-19823 DDC 332.024 19
HG179 .L45 1986 ***NYPL [JLD 86-2290]***

A Financial Post book.
Husack, Glen A. More profit from your retail business . [S.l.] , c1977. 84 p. : ISBN 0-88896-066-2 (pbk.) LC Card 85-174558
HF5429 .H85 1977

Financial profile of cooperatives handling grain . Yager, Francis P. [Washington, D.C.] [1986] vii, 24 p. : LC Card 86-601622 DDC 334/.6831/0973021 19
HD9034 .Y34 1986

Financial Publishing Company. Financial comprehensive ARM payment tables /. Boston, Mass. , Philadelphia, PA , c1985. 255 p. ; ISBN 0-89471-379-5 (pbk.) : LC Card 85-206951 DDC 332.8/2/021 19
HG1634 .F44 1985

Financial ratios and the prediction of corporate failure /. Yadav, R. A. (Ram Avtar), 1949- New Delhi , 1986. xvi, 196 p. ; LC Card 86-903341 DDC 338.7/4/0954 19
HF5681.R25 Y33 1986

Financial reporting . Butterworth, John E. Hamilton, Ont. , 1986. viii, 250 p. : ISBN 0-920212-52-2 (pbk.) LC Card 87-101758 DDC 657/.86203 19
HF5686.P3 B87 1986

Financial reporting practices of local governments /. Ingram, Robert W. Stamford, Conn. (P.O. Box 3821, Stamford 06905-0821) , c1987. viii, 93 p. : LC Card 87-80564 DDC 657/.835 19
HJ9777.A3 I55 1987

Financial resources for local and regional authorities /. Kelly, G. Strasbourg , 1985. 79 p. ; LC Card 86-206535 DDC 336/.014/4 19
HJ9420 .K45 1985

The financial services shockwave . Watts, John M., 1933- Englewood Cliffs, N.J. , c1987. viii, 181 p. : ISBN 0-13-316852-2 : LC Card 86-22510 DDC 332.1/0973 19
HG181 .W37 1987 ***NYPL [JLE 87-612]***

Financial Sourcebooks' sources : the directory of financial research, marketing surveys, and services. Naperville, Ill. : Financial Sourcebooks, c1987. 454 p. ; 23 cm. ISBN 0-942061-00-4 (pbk.) : LC Card 87-8793 DDC 332/.025/73 19
1. Finance - Information services - Directories. 2. Market surveys - Information services - Directories. 3. Business - Information services. - Directories. 4. Finance - Bibliography. 5. Market surveys - Bibliography. 6. Business - Bibliography. I. Title: Sources. II. Title: Directory of financial research, marketing surveys, and services.
HG173 .F517 1987

Financial stability of the thrift industry : proceedings of the Eleventh Annual Conference, December 12-13, 1985, San Francisco, California. San Francisco, Calif. (P.O. Box 7948, San Francisco 94120) : Federal Home Loan Bank of San Francisco, [1986?] 230 p. : ill., ports. ; 23 cm. Includes bibliographies. LC Card 86-81012
1. Building and loan associations - United States - Congresses. 2. Financial institutions - United States - Congresses. 3. Savings-banks - United States - Congresses. I. Federal Home Loan Bank of San Francisco. II. Title: Thrift industry.
NYPL [JLE 86-3398]

FINANCIAL STATEMENTS - CASE STUDIES.
Ferris, Kenneth R. Financial accounting and corporate reporting . Plano, Tex. , 1987. xi, 422 p. : ISBN 0-256-03554-7 (pbk.) LC Card 86-71236 DDC 657/.3 19
HF5686.C7 F455 1987

FINANCIAL STATEMENTS, CONSOLIDATED.
Consolidation policies in OECD countries . Paris , 1987. 60, 63 p. ; ISBN 92-64-02876-5 : LC Card 87-168671 DDC 657/.3 19
HF5681.B2 C593 1987

Goodman, Hortense. Illustrations of "push down" accounting /. New York, N.Y. (1211 Ave., of the Americas, New York 10036) , c1985. 52 p. ; LC Card 87-100703 DDC 657/.3 19
HF5681.B2 G663 1985

Raffegeau, Jean. Les comptes consolidés . Paris , c1984. 971 p. : ISBN 2-85115-064-2 : LC Card 84-245353 DDC 657/.3 19
HF5681.B2 R25 1984

FINANCIAL STATEMENTS, CONSOLIDATED - EUROPE.
L'Impact de la Septième directive . Paris , c1985. 119 p. : ISBN 2-86658-027-3 : LC Card 86-122475
HF5681.B2 I5516 1985

FINANCIAL STATEMENTS, CONSOLIDATED - ITALY - LOMBARDY.
Conto consolidato della spesa pubblica in Lombardia /. Milano, Italy , c1982. 234 p. ; LC Card 85-147746
HJ9925.I8 C63 1982

FINANCIAL STATEMENTS, CONSOLIDATED - STANDARDS.
Consolidation policies in OECD countries . Paris , 1987. 60, 63 p. ; ISBN 92-64-02876-5 : LC Card 87-168671 DDC 657/.3 19
HF5681.B2 C593 1987

FINANCIAL STATEMENTS - GERMANY, WEST.
Russ, Wolfgang, 1955- Der Anhang als dritter Teil des Jahresabschlusses . Bergisch Gladbach , 1984. xi, 332 p. : ISBN 3-89012-013-X : LC Card 85-195717
HF5681.B2 R817 1984

FINANCIAL STATEMENTS - HANDBOOKS, MANUALS, ETC.
Vickman, Thomas M. Handbook of model accounting reports and formats /. Englewood Cliffs, N.J. , c1987. xvii, 350 p. : ISBN 0-13-380338-4 : LC Card 86-15068 DDC 658.1/512 19
HF5635 .V53 1987 ***NYPL [JLF 87-214]***

FINANCIAL STATEMENTS - HISTORY - ADDRESSES, ESSAYS, LECTURES.
Lee, Thomas Alexander. The evolution of corporate financial reporting /. New York , 1984. x, 307 p. ; ISBN 0-8240-6332-5 (alk. paper) : LC Card 83-49431 DDC 657/.3 19
HF5686.C7 L43 1984 ***NYPL [JLD 86-2835]***

FINANCIAL STATEMENTS - INDIA.
Agarwal, N. P. (Narain Prashad) Analysis of financial statements /. New Delhi , 1981. xii, 363 p. : LC Card 81-904955 DDC 657/.33 19
HD9539.A63 I522 1981
NYPL [JLD 86-2568]

FINANCIAL STATEMENTS - JUVENILE LITERATURE.
Little, Jeffrey B. Understanding a company /. New York , c1988. 47 p. : ISBN 1-555-46622-2 LC Card 87-17654 DDC 657/.33 19
HG4028.B2 L57 1988

FINANCIAL STATEMENTS - LAW AND LEGISLATION - GERMANY (WEST)
Russ, Wolfgang, 1955- Der Anhang als dritter Teil des Jahresabschlusses . Bergisch Gladbach , 1984. xi, 332 p. : ISBN 3-89012-013-X : LC Card 85-195717
HF5681.B2 R817 1984

FINANCIAL STATEMENTS - STANDARDS - CANADA.
Vézina, Pierre, 1935- Foreign currency translation . Toronto, Canada , c1985. 94 p. ; ISBN 0-88800-133-9 LC Card 86-201703 DDC 657/.48 19
HG3853.7 .V49 1985

FINANCIAL STATEMENTS - STANDARDS - UNITED STATES.
Jarnagin, Bill D. Financial accounting standards . Chicago, Ill. (4025 W. Peterson Ave., Chicago 60646) , 1986. xv, 1253 p. : LC Card 87-116311 DDC 657/.0218 19
HF5616.U5 B66 1986

Pallais, Don. Guide to forecasts and projections /. Fort Worth, Tex. , 1986. 2 v. (loose-leaf) : LC Card 87-108778 DDC 657/.3 19
HF5681.B2 P15 1986

FINANCIAL STATEMENTS, UNAUDITED.
Afterman, Allan B. Compilation and review practice manual, 1987 /. Boston , c1986. 1 v. (various pagings) : ISBN 0-88712-706-1 (pbk.) LC Card 87-105236 DDC 657/.3 19
HF5681.B2 A5914 1986

Clay, John R. Advanced compilation and review . Fort Worth, Tex. , c1987. 1 v. (various pagings) : LC Card 87-160681 DDC 657/.3 19
HF5667.65 .M42 1986 Suppl.

Meals, Dennis R. Guide to compilation and review engagements /. Fort Worth, Tex. , c1986- 3 v. (loose-leaf) : LC Card 86-224183 DDC 657/.3 19
HF5667.65 .M42 1986

FINANCIAL STATEMENTS, UNAUDITED - FORMS.
Perry, Larry L. Compilation and review manual /. Englewood Cliffs, N.J. , c1987- 1 v. (loose-leaf) : ISBN 0-13-162934-4 (loose-leaf) LC Card 86-63240 DDC 657/.3 19
HF5681.B2 P42185 1987

FINANCIAL STATEMENTS, UNAUDITED - HANDBOOKS, MANUALS, ETC.
Perry, Larry L. Compilation and review manual /. Englewood Cliffs, N.J. , c1987- 1 v. (loose-leaf) : ISBN 0-13-162934-4 (loose-leaf) LC Card 86-63240 DDC 657/.3 19
HF5681.B2 P42185 1987

FINANCIAL STATEMENTS, UNAUDITED - PROBLEMS, EXERCISES, ETC.
Clay, John R. Advanced compilation and review . Fort Worth, Tex. , c1987. 1 v. (various pagings) : LC Card 87-160681 DDC 657/.3 19
HF5667.65 .M42 1986 Suppl.

FINANCIAL STATEMENTS - UNITED STATES.
Disclosure checklists for banks . New York, N.Y. , c1986. 64 p. ; LC Card 86-224924 DDC 657/.833 19
HG1708 .D57 1986

McNairn, William N. The smart attorney's guide to accounting documents for discovery and evidence /. Redondo Beach, Calif. , 1987. x, 123 p. : ISBN 0-932621-02-3 (pbk.) LC Card 86-62954 DDC 657/.024344 19
HF5616.U5 M346 1987

Financial status of Oklahoma farmers and ranchers, 1985 . Plaxico, James Sam, 1924- [Stillwater] [1986] 42 p. ; LC Card 86-622478 DDC 338.1/3/09766021 19
HD1775.O5 P57 1986

Financial structure and economic development in Africa . Hyuha, Mukwanason. Dar-es-Salaam, Tanzania , c1983. 43 p. : LC Card 85-981441 DDC 332/.096 19
HG187.5.A2 H98 1983

The financial system today /. Rowley, Eric E. Manchester, UK , Wolfeboro, NH, USA , c1987. p. cm. ISBN 0-7190-1487-5 LC Card 87-7938 DDC 332/.0941 19
HG186.G7 R64 1987

Financial theory and corporate policy /. Copeland, Thomas E., 1946- Reading, Mass. , c1988. xiv, 946 p. : ISBN 0-201-10648-5 : LC Card 87-12595 DDC 658.1/5 19
HG4011 .C833 1988

Financial working of foreign multinational banks in India /. Sharma, R. D. (Ramji Dass) Delhi, India , 1987. 244 p. ; LC Card 86-903591 DDC 332.1/5 19
HG3284 .S487 1987

Financiamento do desenvolvimento económico . Almeida, João António R. Simões de. Lisboa , 1961. 60 p. ; LC Card 85-220891
HC392 .A466 1961

Financiamiento agrícola. 1a ed. México, D.F. : Centro de Estudios Monetarios Latinoamericanos, 1985. i, 156 p. ; 21 cm. (Reuniones y seminarios) Papers presented at a seminar sponsored by CEMLA in Quito, Ecuador, Oct. 17-23, 1983. Edited by Manuel Aguilera. Bibliography: p. 151-156. LC Card 86-156375
1. Agricultural credit - Latin America - Congresses. 2. Agriculture - Latin America - Finance - Congresses. I. Aguilera Gómez, Manuel. II. Centro de Estudios

Monetarios Latinoamericanos. III. Series.
HG2051.L26 F55 1985

Financiamiento de la integración subregional en América Latina. Reunión Técnica sobre el Financiamiento de la Integración Subregional en América Latina (1985 : Buenos Aires, Argentina) Reunión Técnica sobre el Financiamiento de la Integración Subregional en América Latina . [Buenos Aires, Argentina] . 335 p. : LC Card 86-217551
HC125 .R479 1985

Financieël management van non-profit organisaties /. Groot, T. L. C. M. Groningen , c1985. 200 p. : ISBN 90-01-30316-1 : LC Card 85-214807
HG4027.65 .G76 1985

Financieel meerjarenplan, 1986-1989 / Provincie Friesland. [Leeuwarden] : De Provincie, [1985?] vii, 169 p. ; 21 x 30 cm. Cover title. LC Card 87-111957
1. Budget - Netherlands - Friesland - Statistics. 2. Friesland (Netherlands) - Appropriations and expenditures - Forecasting - Statistics. I. Friesland (Netherlands). Provinciale Staten. II. Title: Provincie Friesland financieel meerjarenplan, 1986-1989.
HJ2128.5.F75 F563 1985

FINANCIERS. see **CAPITALISTS AND FINANCIERS.**

Financing a common wealth : public/private partnerships / Barbara Weiss, editor. Washington, DC : Government Finance Research Center, Government Finance Officers Associaton, 1985. xx, 304 p. : ill. ; 23 cm. Bibliography: p. 275-300. ISBN 0-89125-090-5 LC Card 84-81918
1. Privatization - United States. 2. Government ownership - United States. 3. Finance, Public - United States. 4. Regional planning - United States. I. Weiss, Barbara. II. Government Finance Research Center, Washington, D. C.
HD3888 .F5 1985 ***NYPL [JLE 86-2519]***

The financing and regulatory capital needs of the securities industry / U. S. Securities and Exchange Commission, Directorate of Economic and Policy Analysis. [Washington, D.C.] : The Commission, [1985?] xiv, 69, [49] p ; 28 cm. "January 1985." Title from cover. Includes bibliographical references.
1. Securities - United States. 2. Brokers - United States. I. United States. Securities and Exchange Commission. Directorate of Economic and Policy Analysis.
NYPL [JLF 86-863]

Financing East Asia's success . Skully, Michael T. New York , 1987. xiii, 242 p. ; ISBN 0-312-00536-9 : LC Card 86-31527 DDC 332/.0959 19
HG187.E37 S68 1987

Financing export sales /. Lees, Francis A. New York, N.Y. (845 3rd Ave., New York 10022) , c1986. 12 p. : LC Card 86-212400 DDC 658.1/5 19
HF3031 .L36 1986

Financing foreign development of non-fuel mineral resources : an analysis of loan terms of international financial institutions vs. those of commercial banks : final report / prepared by Price Waterhouse for the U. S. Department of the Interior, Bureau of Mines. [Washington, D.C.] : The Bureau, [1986] 308 p. : ill. ; 28 cm. (Open file report . 52-86) "Contract no. JO 156023." "May 16, 1986." LC Card 86-602175 DDC 332.1/5 19
1. Nonfuel minerals industries - Developing countries - Finance. 2. Loans, Foreign - Developing countries. I. Price Waterhouse (Firm). II. United States. Bureau of Mines. III. Series: Open file report (United States. Bureau of Mines) , 86-52.
HD9506.D452 F56 1986

Financing Illinois agricultural exports /. Seger, Daniel J. [Urbana?] [1985] 74 p. : LC Card 86-621070 DDC 382/.63 19
HD9007.I3 S44 1985

Financing land acquisition and development / National Association of Home Builders. Washington, D.C. : The Association, c1987. 134 p. : ill. ; 28 cm. Includes bibliographies. ISBN 0-86718-281-4 (pbk.) LC Card 87-61069 DDC 332.7/2/0973 19
1. Real estate development - United States - Finance. 2. Mortgage loans - United States. I. National Association of Home Builders (U. S.).
HD1390 .F56 1987

Financing livestock services in some countries of east and southern Africa /. Addis Anteneh. Addis Ababa, Ethiopia [1985] 26 p. ; LC Card 86-980745 DDC 338.1/36/0096 19
HD9427.A2 A33 1985

Financing new technology : based on the seminar held at Christ's College, Cambridge 9-14 September 1984. London : Institute of Bankers, 1984. 124 p. : ill. ; 21 cm. At head of title: Cambridge seminar 1984. Bibliography: p. 113-114. ISBN 0-85297-126-5 (pbk.) LC Card 86-117401 DDC 338.6/041 19
1. New business enterprises - Finance - Congresses. 2. High technology industries - Finance - Congresses. 3. Corporations - Finance - Congresses. I. Institute of Bankers (Great Britain).
HG4027.6 .F55 1984 ***NYPL [JLD 87-1346]***

Financing of kapas-cloth system /. Gurdev Singh. New Delhi , c1987. xi, 59 p. ; ISBN 81-204-0217-0 : LC Card 87-902510 DDC 338.4/367721/0954 19
HD9886.I42 G87 1987

Financing of the urban poor & small borrowers by commercial banks . Agrawal, R. B. L. Baroda , 1983. 108 p. ; LC Card 83-906426 DDC 332.1/753/095475 19
HG1642.I5 A38 1983 ***NYPL [JLD 86-4318]***

Financing real estate with securities /. Hines, Mary Alice. New York , c1988. p. cm. ISBN 0-471-62813-1 LC Card 87-26336 DDC 332.7/2 19
HG4655 .H56 1988

Financing small businesses /. Lal, Mohan. Palmerston North, N.Z. [1977] 25, [2] p. ; LC Card 85-151230
HG4027.7 .L35 1977

Financing the agricultural sector : future challenges and policy alternatives / Dean W. Hughes ... [et al.]. Boulder, Colo. : Westview Press, 1986. xi, 256 p. : ill. ; 23 cm. (Westview special studies in agriculture science and policy) Includes bibliographies and index. ISBN 0-8133-0055-X (pbk. : alk. paper) LC Card 86-50152 DDC 338.1/3/0973 19
1. Agriculture - United States - Finance. 2. Agriculture and state - United States. 3. Agriculture credit - Government policy - United States. I. Hughes, Dean W. II. Series.
HD1761 .F5 1986 ***NYPL [JLE 86-2766]***

Financing under the second Lomé Convention. [Luxembourg] : European Investment Bank, 1980. 24 p. ; 21 cm. ISBN 92-861-0008-6 (pbk.) LC Card 81-121215
1. European Investment Bank. I. European Investment Bank. II. Title: Financing under the 2nd Lomé Convention.
HG3881.5.E87 F56 1980

Financing under the 2nd Lomé Convention. Financing under the second Lomé Convention. [Luxembourg] , 1980. 24 p. ; ISBN 92-861-0008-6 (pbk.) LC Card 81-121215
HG3881.5.E87 F56 1980

Finansirovanie i kreditovanie kapital´nogo stroitel´stva v usloviiakh ėkonomicheskogo ėksperimenta /. Muzhitskikh, V. V. (Viktor Vasil´evich) Moskva , 1985. 157 p. ; LC Card 86-169842
HD9715.S72 M894 1985

Finansovo-kreditnyĭ slovar´ / glavnyĭ redaktor V.F. Garbuzov. Moskva : Finansy i statistika, 1984- v. ; 27 cm. Each vol. includes index. CONTENTS. - t. 1. A-Ĭ. -- t. 2. K-P. LC Card 84-203984
1. Finance - Dictionaries - Russian. 2. Credit - Dictionaries - Russian. I. Garbuzov, V. F. (Vasiliĭ Fedorovich).
HG151 .F53 1984 ***NYPL [*QAC 85-1247]***

Finansovoe planirovanie v promyshlennosti /. Cheblokov, A. T. (Andreĭ Timofeevich) Moskva , 1983. 133, [2] p. ; LC Card 84-134674
HC336.25 .C48 1983

Finansovoe polozhenie russkoĭ zheleznodorozhnoĭ seti i glavneishiia prichiny ukhudsheniia ego v poslednie gody. Petrov, N. P. S.-Peterburg, 1909. 185, ii, 17 p. LC Card 75-564261
HE3131 .A33 vyp. 5 HE3136

Finansovye metody material´nogo stimulirovaniia proizvodstva /. Artemov, IU. M. (IUriĭ Mikhaĭlovich) Moskva , 1983. 126 p. ; LC Card 84-118738
HF5549.5.I5 A69 1983

Finansovye plany i balansy v sisteme ėkonomicheskogo planirovaniia /. Pavlov, V. S. (Valentin Sergeevich) Moskva , 1978. 238 p. ; LC Card 81-160805
HG186.S55 P38 1978

Finansovye rychagi i material´nye stimuly sovershenstvovaniia stroitel´nogo proizvodstva /. IArmolovich, M. V. (Mikhail Viktorovich) Moskva , 1982. 196 p. ; LC Card 83-167253
HD9715.S72 I27 1982

Finansy i khoziaistvennyĭ raschet v usloviiakh ėkonomicheskogo ėksperimenta /. Moskovskiĭ, I. D. (Igor´ Dmitrievich) Moskva , 1984. 60 p. ; LC Card 87-100142
HD9697.A3 S656 1984

Finanz- und bankwirtschaftliche Probleme bei internationaler Unternehmenstätigkeit / herausgegeben von Klaus Macharzina. Stuttgart : Poeschel, c1985. x, 267 p. : ill. ; 24 cm. Papers from a meeting held Jan. 27-28, 1984 in Luxemburg and sponsored by the Kommission Internationales Management, Verband der Hochschullehrer für Betriebswirtschaft. Includes bibliographies and index. ISBN 3-7910-0394-1 LC Card 86-121195 DDC 658.1/5 19
1. International business enterprises - Finance - Congresses. 2. Banks and banking, International - Congresses. 3. International finance - Congresses. I. Macharzina, Klaus. II. Verband der Hochschullehrer für Betriebswirtschaft. Kommission Internationales Management.
HG4027.5 .F56 1985

Finanzas, desarrollo económico y penetración extranjera /. Quijano, José Manuel. Puebla, Pue. , 1985. 395 p. : LC Card 86-112589 DDC 332/.0972 19
HG185.M6 Q55 1985 ***NYPL [JLD 86-2195]***

Las Finanzas municipales en el estado de las autonomías : estudios y propuestas / Josep M. Bricall ... [et al.].1a ed. [Barcelona] : Diputació de Barcelona, 1985. 178 p. ; 24 cm. (Biblioteca Prat de la Riba . 2) "Jornadas de estudio celebradas en el Palacio de Congresos de Barcelona los días 21 y 22 de mayo de 1984"--P. 3. Includes bibliographies. ISBN 84-505-1593-9 LC Card 85-240344
1. Local finance - Spain - Congresses. I. Bricall, Josep Maria, 1936-. II. Series: Col·lecció Prat de la Riba , 2.
HJ9525 .F55 1985

Finanzbuchhaltung /. Andres, Willy. Zürich , 1983. 179 p. : ISBN 3-286-50261-8 LC Card 83-225439
HF5645 .A64 1983

Die Finanzen der Krone Aragon während des 15. Jahrhunderts (Alfons V. und Johann II.) /. Küchler, Winfried, d. 1975. Münster, Westfalen , c1983. ix, 318 p. ; ISBN 3-402-05823-5 LC Card 85-113533
HJ1249.A7 K83 1983

Finanzhaushalt und Wirtschaftsverwaltung Basels (1689-1798) . Vettori, Arthur. Basel , 1984. xv, 439 p. : ISBN 3-7190-0878-9 LC Card 85-132787
HJ1264.B3 V47 1984

Il finanziamento delle imprese /. Fossati, Giorgio. Milano, Italy , 1984. 270 p. : LC Card 86-141137 DDC 658.1/5 19
HG4011 .F58 1984

Il Finanziamento dell'innovazione nelle imprese industriali / G. Bognetti ... [et al.] ; a cura di Isa Marchini. Milano, Italy : F. Angeli, c1985. 271 p. : ill. ; 22 cm. (Facoltà di economia e commercio di Urbino . 3) LC Card 86-157239
1. Technological innovations - Italy - Finance - Congresses. 2. Capital investments - Italy - Congresses. 3. Research, Industrial - Italy - Finance - Congresses. I. Bognetti, Giuseppe. II. Marchini, Isa. III. Series: Facoltà di economia e commercio di Urbino (Series) , 3.
HC310.T4 F55 1985

Die finanzielle Führung und Kontrolle von Auslandsgesellschaften /. Swinne, Axel Hilmar. Frankfurt am Main , c1983. 422 p. : ISBN 3-7875-4200-0 LC Card 84-148375
HG4027.5 .S95 1983

Finanzierung mit Risikokapital /. Albach, Horst. Stuttgart , c1986. 312 p. ; ISBN 3-7910-5015-X

LC Card 87-127700 DDC 332/.0415/0943 19
HG5492 .A797 1986

Finanzinnovationen, Deregulierung und Geldmengensteuerung in den USA /. Streit, Joachim. Tübingen , c1986. xi, 188 p. : ISBN 3-16-345156-X (pbk.) LC Card 87-408200 DDC 332/.0973 19
HG181 .S825 1986

Finanzkraft der Gemeinden und kommunaler Ausgleichsstock in NW /. Puls, Heinz. Dortmund [1977] [15] p. : LC Card 86-211554
HJ9493.5.N6 P85 1977

Finanzplanung des Landes Nordrhein-Westfalen 1986 bis 1990. North Rhine-Westphalia (Germany). Finanzministerium. Düsseldorf [1986] iii, 27, [28] p. ; LC Card 86-233121
HJ1150.N62 N62 1986

Eine Finanzpolitik des langen Atems erforderlich /. Zahn, Joachim, Professor Dr. Bonn [1984] 31 leaves ; LC Card 86-198580
HJ1120 .B65 Nr. 234

Finanzpolitik und Einkommensverteilung . Steden, Werner. Frankfurt am Main ; Bern ; 378 p. ; ISBN 3-261-01763-5 LC Card 80-459125
HJ1120 .S74 *NYPL [JLD 80-3205]*

Finanzpolitik und Wirtschaftsentwicklung in der Dritten Welt . Mounbaga, Emmanuel Seidou, 1957- München , c1986. 265 p. ; ISBN 3-8039-0341-6 LC Card 86-233152
HJ1620 .M68 1986

Finanzsysteme, Ideal- und Realtypen : Gesundheitswesen und Hochschulbildung / von Reinar Lüdeke, Hans Heinrich Nachtkamp, Martin Pfaff ; herausgegeben von Karl Häuser. Berlin : Duncker & Humblot, c1983. 278 p. : ill. ; 24 cm. (Schriften des Vereins für Socialpolitik, Gesellschaft für Wirtschafts- und Sozialwissenschaften . n.F., Bd. 135) Summaries in English. Includes bibliographies. CONTENTS. - Idealtypen von Fiskalsystemen / von Hans Heinrich Nachtkamp -- Finanzierungs- und Ausgabenströme im Gesundheitssektor / von Martin Pfaff -- Fiskalische Systeme bei der Hochschulausbildung / von Reinar Lüdeke. ISBN 3-428-05419-9 LC Card 83-240120
1. Finance, Public. 2. Public health - Finance. 3. Education - Finance. I. Häuser, Karl, 1920-. II. Lüdeke, Rainar. III. Nachtkamp, Hans Heinrich. IV. Pfaff, Martin. V. Series.
HJ161 .F575 1983

Finanztransaktionen und Aussenpolitik . Lemke, Heinz. Berlin , 1985. 215 p. ; LC Card 86-196601
HG3955 .L45 1985

Finanzwirtschaft in Singen 1850-1900. Gebhard, Alfred. Das Dorf Singen und seine Finanzwirtschaft . Singen , 1985. 484 p. : ISBN 3-921413-23-0 LC Card 87-133391 DDC 336.43/46 19
HJ9494.S57 G4 1985

Finanzwirtschaftliche Folgen kommunaler Gebiets- und Funktionalreformen : Problembereiche und Hypothesen im Überblick / Gunther Engelhardt ... [et al.].1. Aufl. Baden-Baden : Nomos Verlagsgesellschaft, 1986. 209 p. : ill. ; 23 cm. (Die Kommunale Gebietsreform . Bd. III, 1) Summary in German, English, and French. Bibliography: p. 201-209. ISBN 3-7890-1163-0 (Deut. Bibl.) LC Card 86-169111
1. Revenue sharing - Germany (West). 2. Local finance - Germany (West) - Lower Saxony. 3. Local government - Germany (West) - Lower Saxony. I. Engelhardt, Gunther. II. Series.
HJ1121 .F55 1986

Finanzwirtschaftliche Nebenrechnungen . Schneider, Pia, 1956- Frankfurt am Main , New York , c1985. xiii, 303 p. : ISBN 3-8204-8472-8 LC Card 85-190966
HF5686.C7 S354 1985

Finanzwissenschaftliche Schriften, 0170-8252 . (Bd. 27) Zeidler, Achim, 1952- Möglichkeiten zur Fortsetzung der Gemeindefinanzreform . Frankfurt am Main , New York , c1985. xx, 301 p. : ISBN 3-8204-8534-1 LC Card 86-125215 DDC 336/.014/43 19
HJ9473 .Z4 1985

(Bd. 30) Kitterer, Wolfgang. Effizienz- und Verteilungswirkungen des Steuersystems /. Frankfurt am Main , New York , c1986. 397 p. ; ISBN 3-8204-8528-7 LC Card 86-194183
HJ2321 .K52 1986

Finanzwissenschaftliche Schriften, 0170-8253 . (Bd. 22) Weck-Hannemann, Hannelore. Schattenwirtschaft . Frankfurt am Main , New York , c1983. 152 p. : ISBN 3-8204-7590-7 (pbk.) LC Card 87-672943
HD2341 .W37x 1983

Finberg, I. Lee. Hadady, R. Earl (Robert Earl), 1920- Winning with the insiders /. West Palm Beach, Fla. , c1987. vi, 115 p. : ISBN 0-9613048-8-X : LC Card 87-40003 DDC 332.64/4 19
HG4910 .H18 1987

Finding and buying your place in the country /. Scher, Les. New York , London , c1987. p. cm. ISBN 0-02-008400-5 LC Card 87-24246 DDC 643/.2 19
HD256 .S27 1987

Finding, entering, and succeeding in a foreign market /. Connolly, Seamus G. Englewood Cliffs, N.J. , c1987. xiii, 274 p. : ISBN 0-13-316951-0 LC Card 86-25395 DDC 658.8/48 19
HF1009.5 .C59 1986 *NYPL [JLE 87-1310]*

Finding hidden values in your home /. Kaufman, Wallace. New York , London , c1987. xi, 302 p. : ISBN 0-02-560720-0 LC Card 86-26909 DDC 333.33/2 19
HD1387 .K38 1987b

Finding money . Hellmuth, James G. New York, N.Y. , c1983. p. cm. ISBN 0-932648-79-7 LC Card 86-31053 DDC 658.1/5224 19
HG4027.7 .H44 1983b

Finding your best place to live in America /. Bowman, Thomas F. New York , c1981. xiii, 337 p. : ISBN 0-940162-00-8 (pbk.) : LC Card 81-51506 DDC 973.927 19
HT123 .B665 *NYPL [Pub. Cat. 86-574]*

Findlay, A. M. Findlay, Allan M. Population and development in the Third World /. London , New York , 1987. xii, 84 p. : ISBN 0-416-91950-2 (pbk.) : LC Card 86-31094 DDC 304.6/09172/4 19
HB884 .F56 1987

Findlay, Allan M. Population and development in the Third World / Allan Findlay and Anne Findlay. London ; New York : Methuen, 1987. xii, 84 p. : ill. ; 21 cm. (Methuen introductions to development) Bibliography: p. [78]-81. Includes index. ISBN 0-416-91950-2 (pbk.) : LC Card 86-31094 DDC 304.6/09172/4 19
1. Developing countries - Population. 2. Developing countries - Population policy. I. Findlay, A. M. II. Title. III. Series.
HB884 .F56 1987

Findlay, Christopher C. (Christopher Charles) The flying kangaroo, an endangered species? : an economic perspective of Australian international civil aviation policy / Christopher C. Findlay. Sydney ; Boston : Allen and Unwin, 1985. xii, 121 p. : ill. ; 22 cm. Bibliography: p. 115-118. Includes index. ISBN 0-86861-406-8 (pbk.) LC Card 85-71362 DDC 387.7/065/94 19
1. Aeronautics, Commercial - Australia - Deregulation. 2. Qantas Airways. 3. Airlines - Australia. I. Title.
HE9889.A4 F56 1985

Findley, Sally E. Rural development and migration : a study of family choices in the Philippines / Sally E. Findley. Boulder : Westview Press, 1987. xxiii, 308 p. : ill. ; 22 cm. (Brown University studies in population and development) Bibliography: P. 275-308. ISBN 0-8133-7326-3 (pbk. : alk. paper) : LC Card 86-33987 DDC 304.8/09599 19
1. Migration, Internal - Philippines - Ilocos Norte - Case studies. 2. Ilocos Norte (Philippines) - Rural conditions - Case studies. 3. Rural development - Philippines - Ilocos Norte - Case studies. 4. Family - Philippines - Ilocos Norte - Case studies. I. Title. II. Series.
HB2110.I43 F56 1987

Find/SVP (Firm)
The Affluent market. New York, N.Y. (500 5th Ave., New York 10110) [1984] 227 leaves : LC Card 86-201904 DDC 658.8/348 19
HC110.C6 A63 1984

Delson, Erwin B. The bar coding systems industry. New York, N.Y. , c1986. 1 v. (various pagings) : ISBN 0-931634-64-4 (pbk.) LC Card 87-156445 DDC 380.1/45621399 19
HD9801.6.P762 D45 1986

Delson, Erwin B. The factory automation industry /. New York, N.Y. , c1985. 1 v. (various pagings) : ISBN 0-931634-16-4 (pbk.) LC Card 86-203033 DDC 338.4/76298/0973 19
HD9696.A963 U635 1985

The Maturity market . New York, N.Y. , c1985. 1 v. (various pagings) : ISBN 0-931634-47-4 (pbk.) LC Card 86-203045 DDC 658.8/348 19
HC110.C6 M33 1985

The Semiconductor industry. New York, N.Y. (500 5th Ave., New York 10110) , c1984. 1 v. (various foliations) : LC Card 86-203040 DDC 338.4/762138152 19
HD9696.S42 S375 1984

Valencia, Humberto. The U. S. Hispanic market. New York, N.Y. [1984] 1 v. (various foliations) : ISBN 0-931634-48-2 (pbk.) LC Card 86-203027 DDC 658.8/348 19
HC110.C6 V35 1984

The World market for high technology industrial ceramics. New York, N.Y. [1985] 1 v. (various pagings) ; ISBN 0-931634-52-0 (pbk.) LC Card 86-201912 DDC 382/.45666 19
HD9590.5 .W67 1985

Fine, Ben. The Value dimension . London , New York , 1986. 239 p. ; ISBN 0-7102-0766-2 (pbk.) : LC Card 87-109334 DDC 338.5/21 19
HB203 .V33 1986

Fingard, Judith. Jack in port : sailortowns of eastern Canada / Judith Fingard. Toronto ; Buffalo : University of Toronto Press, c1982. 292 p., [12] p. of plates : ill. ; 24 cm. (Social history of Canada, 0085-6207 . 36) Includes index. Bibliography: p. [281]-283. ISBN 0-8020-2458-0 LC Card 82-216821 DDC 331.7/6138754044/09715 19
1. Merchant seamen - Nova Scotia - Halifax - History - 19th century. 2. Merchant seamen - New Brunswick - Saint John - History - 19th century. 3. Merchant seamen - Québec (Province) - Québec - History - 19th century. I. Title.
HD8039.S42 C3 1982 *NYPL [JLE 86-4038]*

Finger, Herbert. Stimulierung in Industriebetrieben und Kombinaten /. Berlin , c1982. 290 p. : LC Card 83-164671
HF5549.5.M63 S75 1982

Fingerland, Jaroslav. Mezinárodní socialistická ekonomická integrace a předmětné sféry specializace národohospodářského komplexu ČSSR / Jaroslav Fingerland. Praha : Ekonomický ústav ČSAV, 1985. 169 p. ; 20 cm. (Výzkum. publ. VP . č. 234) Summary in Russian. Bibliography: p. 145-147. LC Card 86-215200
1. Czechoslovakia - Foreign economic relations - Communist countries. 2. Communist countries - Foreign economic relations - Czechoslovakia. 3. Communist countries - Economic integration. I. Series: Výzk. publ. (Ekonomicko-matematická laboratoř (Ekonomický ústav ČSAV)) , č. 234. II. Title.
HF1542.3.Z4 C654 1985

Fink, Gerhard. Socialist economy and economic policy /. Wien , New York , 1985. 279 p. : ISBN 0-387-81903-7 (pbk.) LC Card 86-201536
HC704 .S557 1985

Fink, Karl, Mag. Die regionale Dynamik des Salzburger Arbeitsmarktes, 1971-1980 : eine Untersuchung der Kammer für Arbeiter und Angestellte für Salzburg / Verfasser, Karl Fink, Gerhard Schmidt. Salzburg : Die Kammer, [1981?] 212 p. : ill. ; 30 cm. LC Card 82-171635
1. Labor supply - Austria - Salzburg (Land) - Regional disparities - Statistics. 2. Women - Employment - Austria - Salzburg (Land) - Regional disparities - Statistics. 3. Shift-share analysis - Austria - Salzburg (Land) - Statistics. I. Schmidt, Gerhard, Mag. II. Kammer für Arbeiter und Angestellte für Salzburg. III. Title.
HD5772.S24 F56 1981 *NYPL [JLG 86-301]*

Fink, Paul. Geschichte der Basler Bandindustrie 1550-1800 / von Paul Fink. Basel : Helbing & Lichtenhahn, 1983. 216 p. : ill. ; 24 cm. (Basler Beiträge zur Geschichtswissenschaft. Bd. 147) Bibliography: p. 208-216. ISBN 3-7190-0836-3 LC Card 83-220231 DDC 338.4/767776 19
1. Ribbon industry - Switzerland - Basel - History. 2. Silk industry - Switzerland - Basel - History. I. Title. II. Series.
HD9929.R6 S94 1983 *NYPL [JLE 86-2781]*

Fink, Richard H. A Nation in debt . Frederick, Md. , c1987. p. cm. ISBN 0-89093-963-2 : LC

Card 86-28254 DDC 339.5/23/0973 19
HJ2052 .N36 1987

Fink, Robert E. Futures trading : concepts and strategies / Robert E. Fink, Robert B. Feduniak. New York, N.Y. : New York Institute of Finance, c1988. xiv, 685 p. : ill. ; 24 cm. Bibliography: p. 669-670. Includes index. ISBN 0-13-345745-1 : LC Card 87-24030 DDC 332.64/4 19
1. Commodity exchanges. 2. Financial futures. I. Feduniak, Robert B. II. Title.
HG6046 .F56 1988

Finke, B. (Barbara) Studien zur kommunalen Industrieförderung im 20. Jahrhundert : das Beispiel Regensburg von 1900 bis 1985 / B. Finke, H. Pohl. Regensburg : Transfer Verlag, c1986. 125, [45], xxv p. : ill. ; 21 cm. (Wirtschafts- und sozialwissenschaftliche Forschungsbeiträge . Bd. 2) Bibliography: p. i-xxv. ISBN 3-924956-19-7 : LC Card 87-129091 DDC 338.943/34 19
1. Industrial promotion - Germany (West) - Regensburg - History - 20th century. 2. Industry and state - Germany (West) - Regensburg - History - 20th century. I. Pohl, Harald. II. Title. III. Series.
HC289.R36 F56 1986

Finkel, Rachel. Schwartz, Moshe. Non-agricultural employment for moshav youth in the Galilee /. Rehovot, Israel , c1985. 36, [2] p. ; LC Card 86-115596 DDC 331.3/4/0956945 19
HD6276.I66 G347 1985

Finkin, Eugene F. Successful corporate turnarounds : a guide for board members, financial managers, financial institutions, and other creditors / Eugene F. Finkin. New York : Quorum Books, 1987. xviii, 211 p. : ill. ; 25 cm. Includes index. ISBN 0-89930-232-7 (lib. bdg. : alk. paper) : LC Card 86-25280 DDC 658.4/063 19
1. Organizational change. 2. Organizational effectiveness. I. Title.
HD58.8 .F52 1987

FINLAND - COMMERCE - ECONOMETRIC MODELS.
Menzler-Hokkanen, Ingeborg. Measuring changes in intra-industry competitiveness /. Helsingfors [1986] 39 p. ; ISBN 951-555-247-8 (pbk.) LC Card 87-170429 DDC 338.6/048 19
HC79.I52 M46 1986

FINLAND - COMMERCE - SOVIET UNION.
Neuvostoliiton-kauppa Suomen kansantaloudessa /. Helsinki , 1986. 220 p. : ISBN 951-9206-18-3 LC Card 87-127628
HF3633.S65 N48 1986

FINLAND - ECONOMIC CONDITIONS.
Mansner, Markku. Suomalaista yhteiskuntaa rakentamassa . Helsinki [1984] 552 p., [4] p. of plates : ISBN 951-9240-75-6 LC Card 85-130291
HD8533 .M345 1984

FINLAND - ECONOMIC CONDITIONS - 1918-
Pihkala, Erkki. Toisen maailmansodan aikaisesta huoltotasosta Suomessa ja analogioista 1980-luvun alun tilanteeseen /. [Helsinki] , 1986. 49 leaves ; ISBN 951-46-9497-X LC Card 86-221750
HC340.2 .P54 1986

FINLAND - ECONOMIC CONDITIONS - 1945-
Neuvostoliiton-kauppa Suomen kansantaloudessa /. Helsinki , 1986. 220 p. : ISBN 951-9206-18-3 LC Card 87-127628
HF3633.S65 N48 1986

Pihkala, Erkki. Toisen maailmansodan aikaisesta huoltotasosta Suomessa ja analogioista 1980-luvun alun tilanteeseen /. [Helsinki] , 1986. 49 leaves ; ISBN 951-46-9497-X LC Card 86-221750
HC340.2 .P54 1986

FINLAND - ECONOMIC CONDITIONS - 1945- - ECONOMETRIC MODELS.
Blomqvist, H. C. (Hans-Christer), 1947- Lönebildningsforskning i Finland /. [Helsinki] [1984] 23 leaves : ISBN 951-555-207-9 LC Card 85-137027
HD5047.3 .B57 1984

The BOF3 quarterly model of the Finnish economy /. Helsinki , 1985. 465 p. : ISBN 951-686-108-3 (pbk.) LC Card 86-205002 DDC 330.94897/005 s 338.5/443/094897 19
HB30 .S95 no. 59 HC340.2

FINLAND - ECONOMIC POLICY - ECONOMETRIC MODELS.
The BOF3 quarterly model of the Finnish economy /. Helsinki , 1985. 465 p. : ISBN 951-686-108-3 (pbk.) LC Card 86-205002 DDC 330.94897/005 s 338.5/443/094897 19
HB30 .S95 no. 59 HC340.2

Finland. Foreign Affairs, Ministry for. see **Finland. Ulkoasiainministeriö.**

FINLAND - HISTORY - 1523-1611.
Orrman, Eljas. Bebyggelsen i Pargas, S:t Mårtens och Vemo socknar i egentliga Finland under senmedeltiden och på 1500-talet /. Helsingfors , 1986. 293 p. : ISBN 951-9254-73-0 LC Card 86-199875
HD723 .O77 1986

Finland. Kauppa- ja teollisuusministeriö. Energiaosasto. Energiförbrukningen fram till år 2005 . Helsingfors , 1985. ii, 36 p. : ISBN 951-46-9116-4 LC Card 87-102957
HD9502.S82 E46 1985

Finland. Ministry for Foreign Affairs. see **Finland. Ulkoasiainministeriö.**

FINLAND - POPULATION.
Finnäs, Fjalar. Den finlandssvenska befolkningsutvecklingen 1950-1980 . Helsingfors [1986] 216 p. : ISBN 951-9018-20-4 LC Card 86-232091
HB3608.3.A3 F56 1986

FINLAND - STATISTICAL SERVICES.
FINLAND - STATISTICS, VITAL.
Finnäs, Fjalar. Den finlandssvenska befolkningsutvecklingen 1950-1980 . Helsingfors [1986] 216 p. : ISBN 951-9018-20-4 LC Card 86-232091
HB3608.3.A3 F56 1986

Finland. Ulkoasiainministeriö. Kehityhteistyöosasto. Appropriate forest industries . Rome , 1986. vii, 426 p. ; ISBN 92-5-102389-1 (pbk.) LC Card 86-214549 DDC 338.1/7498/091724 19
HD9768.D44 A66 1986

Finland - Vital statistics. see **Finland - Statistics, Vital.**

Finland. Ympäristöministeriö.
Ympäristöministeriön hallinnonalan toiminta- ja taloussuunnitelma vuosiksi 1987-1990 : tarkistettu 5.12.1985. Helsinki : Valtion painatuskeskus, 1985. 152 leaves : forms ; 30 cm. LC Card 86-224557
1. Environmental policy - Finland. 2. Finland. Ympäristöministeriö. I. Title.
HC340.2.Z9 E5 1985

FINLAND. YMPÄRISTÖMINISTERIÖ.
Finland. Ympäristöministeriö. Ympäristöministeriön hallinnonalan toiminta- ja taloussuunnitelma vuosiksi 1987-1990 . Helsinki , 1985. 152 leaves : LC Card 86-224557
HC340.2.Z9 E5 1985

Finland. Ympäristön- ja luonnonsuojeluosasto. Environmental policies in Finland . [Helsinki] [1986] 542 p. : ISBN 951-46-9823-1 LC Card 87-100734 DDC 363.7/056/094897 19
HC340.2.Z9 E52 1986

Finlande . Grosfils-Berger, P. Southfield, MI (15565 Northland Dr., Suite 605 W, Southfield 48075-5308) , 1947, i.e. [1986?] 320 p. : LC Card 86-206197 DDC 769.5694897 19
HE6185.F52 G76 1986

Den finlandssvenska befolkningsutvecklingen 1950-1980 . Finnäs, Fjalar. Helsingfors [1986] 216 p. : ISBN 951-9018-20-4 LC Card 86-232091
HB3608.3.A3 F56 1986

Finlay, William. Work on the waterfront : worker power and technological change in a west coast port / William Finlay. Philadelphia : Temple University Press, 1988. p. cm. (Labor and social change) Bibliography: p. Includes index. ISBN 0-87722-523-0 (alk. paper) : LC Card 87-17976 DDC 331.88/11387164/0973 19
1. Trade-unions - Stevedores - West (U. S.) - History. 2. International Longshoremen's and Warehousemen's Union - History. 3. Machinery in industry - West (U. S.). 4. Stevedores - West (U. S.) - Effect of technological innovations on - History. I. Title. II. Series.
HD6515.L82 W474 1988

Finley, M. I. (Moses I.), 1912- Studies in land and credit in ancient Athens, 500-200 B.C. : the horos inscriptions / Moses I. Finley ; with a new introduction by Paul Millett. New Brunswick, U. S.A. : Transaction Books, c1985. xli, 332 p. ; 24 cm. (Social science classics series) English and Greek. Includes indexes. Bibliography: p. 304-308. Reprint. Originally published: New Brunswick, N.J. : Rutgers University Press, 1951. ISBN 0-88738-066-2 : LC Card 85-14091 DDC 333.3/0938/5 19
1. Land tenure - Greece - Athens - History. 2. Real property - Greece - Athens - History. 3. Credit - Greece - Athens - History. I. Title. II. Series.
HD134 .F5 1985 ***NYPL [JLE 86-4293]***

FINNAIR - HISTORY.
Wegg, John. Bluebirds /. [Helsinki?] , c1985. 216 p. : ISBN 951-99691-4-4 LC Card 86-223952 DDC 387.7/065/4897 19
HE9855.3.F5 W4 1985

Finnäs, Fjalar. Den finlandssvenska befolkningsutvecklingen 1950-1980 : en analys av en språkgrupps demografiska utveckling och effekten av blandäktenskap / Fjalar Finnäs. Helsingfors : Svenska litteratursällskapet i Finland, [1986] 216 p. : ill. ; 21 cm. (Skrifter utgivna av Svenska litteratursällskapet i Finland, 0039-6842 . nr. 533) Thesis (doctoral)--Åbo akademi, 1986. Extra t.p. with thesis statement inserted. Summary in English. Bibliography: p. 190-194. ISBN 951-9018-20-4 LC Card 86-232091
1. Finland - Population. 2. Finland - Statistics, Vital. 3. Swedes - Finland - Statistics. 4. Marriage - Finland - Statistics. I. Title. II. Series.
HB3608.3.A3 F56 1986

Finnegan, Carolyn M. Successful investing . New York , 1987. 529 p. : ISBN 0-671-64762-8 (pbk.) : LC Card 87-19736 DDC 332.6/78 19
HG4521 .S823 1987

Finney, Kenneth V. In quest of El Dorado : precious metal mining and the modernization of Honduras, 1880-1900 / Kenenth V. Finney. New York : Garland Pub., 1987. xii, 454 p. ; 24 cm. (South American and Latin American economic history) Bibliography: p. 436-454. ISBN 0-8240-1359-X (alk. paper) : LC Card 87-8342 DDC 338.2/742/097283 19
1. Gold industry - Honduras - History - 19th century. 2. Gold mines and mining - Honduras - History - 19th century. 3. Silver industry - Honduras - History - 19th century. 4. Silver mines and mining - History - 19th century. I. Title. II. Series.
HD9536.H82 F56 1987

Finney, Louis D. Berkowitz, Stephen A. The investment performance of corporate pension plans . New York , 1988. xi, 132 p. ; ISBN 0-89930-224-6 (lib. bdg. : alk. paper) LC Card 87-19030 DDC 332.6/7154 19
HD7105.45.U6 B475 1988

Finnland . Gummesson, Rolf. [Sweden , 1964] ([Kristianstad] : Kristianstads Länstryckeri) 96 p. : LC Card 86-209484
HE6185.F5 G85 1964

FINNMARK FYLKE (NORWAY) - COMMERCE - HISTORY.
Tronstad, Roger, 1955- Finnmarkshandelen i 1680-åra /. [Oslo , 1981] ix, 244 p., [20] p. of plates : LC Card 83-152832
HF3669.F5 T76 1981

Finnmarkshandelen i 1680-åra /. Tronstad, Roger, 1955- [Oslo , 1981] ix, 244 p., [20] p. of plates : LC Card 83-152832
HF3669.F5 T76 1981

Finsiel. L'Informatica nella società italiana, 1984 . Milano [1984] 257 p. ; LC Card 84-249272 DDC 338.4/7004/0945 19
HD9696.C63 I85 1984
NYPL [JLD 86-3303]

Finsinger, Jörg.
The Economics of insurance regulation . Houndmills, Basingstoke, Hampshire , 1986. xi, 300 p. : ISBN 0-333-39684-7
NYPL [JLD 87-1100]

Der Submissionswettbewerb : neue theoretische Ansätze und eine empirische Untersuchung des Baumarktes / Jörg Finsinger, unter Mitarbeit von Stefan Felder. Bern : P. Haupt, c1986. 104 p. : ill. ; 23 cm. (Publikationen des Schweizerischen Nationalfonds aus den nationalen Forschungsprogrammen . Bd. 38) Bibliography: p. 103-104. ISBN 3-258-03617-9 : LC Card 86-224617
1. Construction industry - Switzerland. 2. Building - Contracts and specifications - Switzerland. 3. Contracts, Letting of - Switzerland. I. Felder, Stefan. II. Title. III.

Series.
HD9715.S92 F56 1986

Finsterbusch, Kurt, 1935- Hage, Jerald, 1932- Organizational change as a development strategy . Boulder, Colo. , 1987. xvi, 293 p. ; ISBN 1-555-87012-0 (lib. bdg. : alk. paper) : LC Card 87-12730 DDC 338.9/0068 19
HC59.72.E44 H34 1987

Fiom Milano. Centro ricerche e studi sindacali. Bezza, Bruno. Le lotte degli elettromeccanici /. Milano , c1981. 179 p. : ISBN 88-20-42149-6 : LC Card 81-200954 DDC 331.89/282131/0945 19
HD5384.E3 B49 1981 ***NYPL [JLD 86-2898]***

Fiorito, Riccardo, 1947- Mercato del lavoro e politica economica : il modello econometrico dell'Isel / Riccardo Fiorito.1a ed. Venezia : Marsilio, 1984. 247 p. : ill. ; 22 m. (Biblioteca di economia e relazioni industriali) Bibliography: p. 235-244. Includes index. ISBN 88-317-4733-9 : LC Card 86-163951
1. Labor supply - Mathematical models. 2. Employment (Economic theory) - Mathematical models. 3. Labor supply - Data processing. 4. Employment (Economic theory) - Data processing. 5. Labor supply - Econometric models. 6. Employment (Economic theory) - Econometric models. I. Title. II. Series.
HD5701.6 .F56 1984

Firat, A. Fuat. Philosophical and radical thought in marketing /. Lexington, Mass. , c1987. xxi, 392 p. : ISBN 0-669-14301-4 (alk. paper) LC Card 86-45791 DDC 658.8 19
HF5415 .P485 1987

Fire-årig arbeidskraftprognose for perioden 1983-1987, Telemark fylke. 4-årig arbeidskraftprognose for perioden 1983-1987, Telemark fylke. [Telemark] [1983] 154 leaves ; LC Card 84-145787
HD5800.T44 A14 1983

Fire-årige arbeidskraftprognoser, Møre og Romsdal 1983-1986(1987) 4-årige arbeidskraftprognoser, Møre og Romsdal 1983-1986(1987). [Molde] [1983?] 59 p. ; LC Card 84-146499
HD5800.M67 A14 1983

FIREPROOFING AGENT INDUSTRY - UNITED STATES.
Flame retardants chemicals market. New York, N.Y. , c1983. vii, 315 p. : LC Card 87-143411 DDC 381/.456289223/0973 19
HD9999.F553 U64 1983

FIRES - SOCIAL ASPECTS - CASE STUDIES.
Rosen, Christine Meisner, 1951- The limits of power . Cambridge [Cambridgeshire] , New York , 1986. xii, 395 p. : ISBN 0-521-30319-2 LC Card 85-7753 DDC 307.7/6/0973 19
HT371 .R67 1986 ***NYPL [JLE 86-2388]***

FIRING OF EMPLOYEES. see EMPLOYEES, DISMISSAL OF.

The firm and the market . Casson, Mark, 1945- Cambridge, Mass. , 1987. xii, 283 p. : ISBN 0-262-03129-9 LC Card 86-27199 DDC 658/.049 19
HD2755.5 .C392 1987

Firm diversification, mutual forbearance behavior and price-cost margins /. Strickland, Allyn D. New York , 1984. 155 p. ; ISBN 0-8240-4159-3 (alk. paper) LC Card 79-53209 DDC 338.8/3/0973
HD2756.U5 S76 1984 ***NYPL [JLE 86-3907]***

The firm, the market, and the law /. Coase, R. H. (Ronald Harry) Chicago , 1988. p. cm. ISBN 0-226-11100-8 LC Card 87-24193 DDC 338.5/142 19
HD2326 .C6 1988

Firmenkultur am Beispiel der Sarna /. Kurmann, Bernadette, 1950- Bern [1985] 119 p. ; ISBN 3-258-03560-1 : LC Card 86-123837 DDC 338.7/6684/09494 19
HD9661.S94 S275 1985
NYPL [JLD 86-4028]

Firms and markets : essays in honour of Basil Yamey / edited by K. Tucker and C. Baden Fuller. London : Croom Helm, c1986. xiii, 271 p. : ill., port. ; 23 cm. Includes bibliographies and index. Bibliography of B.S. Yaney: p. 257-265. ISBN 0-7099-2446-1
1. Yamey, Basil S. 2. Industrial organization (Economic and theory) - Addresses, essays, lectures. 3. Markets - Addresses, essays, lectures. 4. Commodity exchanges - Addresses, essays, lectures. 5. Monopolies - Addresses, essays, lectures. 6. Competition - Addresses, essays, lectures. I. Yamey, Basil S. II. Tucker, Ken. III. Baden Fuller, Charles, 1948-. ***NYPL [JLD 86-2134]***

First and second reports of the Select Committee on the Accounts of the South African Transport Services . South Africa. Parliament. House of Assembly. Select Committee on the Accounts of the South African Transport Services. Pretoria [1983] vii, 74, 7 p. ; ISBN 0-06-210896-5 (pbk.) : LC Card 84-168506 DDC 354.680087/5 19
HE284.4 .S68 1983

FIRST CHOICE (COMPUTER PROGRAM)
Tymes, Elna. Mastering First Choice /. Glenview, Ill. , c1987. ix, 301 p. : ISBN 0-673-18767-5 (pbk.) : LC Card 86-26098 DDC 650/.028/55369 19
HF5548.4.F57 T96 1987

FIRST COALITION, WAR OF THE, 1792-1797 - ECONOMIC ASPECTS - GREAT BRITAIN.
Hueckel, Glenn R. (Glenn Russell), 1945- The Napoleonic wars and their impact on factor returns and output growth in England, 1793-1815 /. New York , 1985. lvi, 212 p. ; ISBN 0-8240-6683-9 : LC Card 84-46003 DDC 330.941/073 19
HC254.5 .H78 1985 ***NYPL [JLE 86-4294]***

FIRST DAY COVERS (PHILATELY) - LIECHTENSTEIN.
Die Briefmarkenausgabe vom 12. März 1984 =. Vaduz [1984?] 41 p. : LC Card 84-248309
HE6184.F57 B75 1984

FIRST DAY COVERS (PHILATELY) - SOVIET UNION - CATALOGS.
Katalog konvertov pervogo dni͡a i kartmaksimumov, 1980-1983 /. Moskva , 1985. 221 p. : LC Card 86-102861
HE6184.F57 K38 1985

First five-year national development plan, 1986-1990 /. Zimbabwe. [Harare?] [1986- v. <1 > ; LC Card 86-981132 DDC 338.96891 19
HC910 .Z26 1986

FIRST INTERSTATE BANK OF MISSOULA (MONT.) - HISTORY.
Toole, John H. Men, money, and power . Missoula, Mont. , c1986. xiv, 97 p. : ISBN 0-87842-210-2 LC Card 86-23569 DDC 332.1/224/0978685 19
HG2613.M634 F5737 1986

First Ministers' Conference (1985 : Halifax, N. S.) [Proceedings of the annual conference of First Ministers, held in Halifax, N.S., November 28-29, 1985]. [Canada : s.n., 1986-] portfolios <1-4 > : ill. ; 31 cm. Cover title. English and French. CONTENTS. - [1] Agriculture in Canada, challenges and opportunities -- [2] Canada and international trade -- [3] Fisheries in Canada, challenges and opportunities -- [4] National economic development, the regional dimension. LC Card 86-201687 DDC 338.971 19
1. Canada - Economic conditions - 1945- - Congresses. 2. Canada - Economic policy - Congresses. I. Title.
HC115 .F485 1985

First one hundred years are the toughest. Hoge, Cecil C. The first 100 years are the toughest /. Berkeley, Calif. , 1987. p. cm. ISBN 0-89815-221-6 LC Card 87-7077 DDC 380.1/45000/6073 19
HF5467.S4 H64 1987

The first-time investor /. Madigan, Bob, 1949- New York , c1987. xxii, 276 p. : ISBN 0-13-942376-1 (pbk.) : LC Card 87-14399 DDC 332.6/78 19
HG4521 .M217 1987

First-time manager /. Iaconetti, Joan. New York , London , 1987, c1985. xii, 290 p. : ISBN 0-02-085730-6 (pbk.) : LC Card 86-24454 DDC 658.4 19
HD38.2 .I19 1987

The first 100 years are the toughest /. Hoge, Cecil C. Berkeley, Calif. , 1987. p. cm. ISBN 0-89815-221-6 LC Card 87-7077 DDC 380.1/45000/6073 19
HF5467.S4 H64 1987

Firtle, Neil H. Dillon, William R. Marketing research in a marketing environment /. St. Louis , 1987. xxviii, 742, 21, 15 p. : ISBN 0-8016-1303-5 : LC Card 86-23189 DDC 658.8/3 19
HF5415.2 .D54 1987

Fiscal and monetary policy / John Sargent, research coordinator. Toronto ; Buffalo : University of Toronto Press, c1986. xviii, 339 p. : ill. ; 23 cm. (The Collected research studies, 0829-2396 . vol. 21) Includes bibliographies. CONTENTS. - Fiscal policy in Canada / Douglas D. Purvis and Constance Smith -- Consequences of government budget deficits / Neil Bruce and Douglas D. Purvis -- Issues in the analysis of government deficits / John Bossons -- High real interest rates and fiscal policy / John Grant -- The theory and practice of monetary policy in Canada / Gordon R. Sparks -- Regional stabilization in Canada / Yves Rabeau -- Monetary control in Canada / Jean-Marie Dufour and Daniel Racette -- The government budget, the accumulation of capital, and long-run welfare / Robin W. Broadway and W. Steven Clark -- Keynesian theories of accumulation and their policy implications / A. Asimakopulos. ISBN 0-8020-7263-1 (pbk.) LC Card 86-672943 DDC 336.3/0971 19
1. Fiscal policy - Canada. 2. Monetary policy - Canada. I. Sargent, John. II. Series: Collected research studies , v. 21.
HJ793 .F55 1986 ***NYPL [JLE 87-511]***

FISCAL EVASION. see **TAX EVASION.**

Fiscal facts /. North Carolina. General Assembly. Fiscal Research Division. [Raleigh] , 1986. 51 p. : LC Card 87-620951 DDC 336.756 19
HJ615 .N65 1986

Fiscal facts & figures . Wyoming. Legislature. Legislative Service Office. [Wyoming] [1987] 40 leaves ; LC Card 87-621012 DDC 336.787 19
HJ785 .W86 1987

Fiscal facts and figures. Wyoming. Legislature. Legislative Service Office. Fiscal facts & figures . [Wyoming] [1987] 40 leaves ; LC Card 87-621012 DDC 336.787 19
HJ785 .W86 1987

Fiscal federalism / Mark Krasnick, research coordinator. Toronto ; Buffalo : University of Toronto Press, c1986. xvi, 211 p. ; 23 cm. (The Collected research studies, 0829-2396 . vol. 65) "Published by the University of Toronto Press in cooperation with the Royal Commission on the Economic Union and Development Prospects for Canada and the Canadian Government Publishing Centre, Supply and Services Canada." Includes bibliographies. CONTENTS. - Federal-provincial transfers in Canada / Robin Broadway -- Equitable fiscal federalism / Peter A. Cumming -- The harmonization of social policy / Claude E. Forget -- Taxation policy and the Canadian economic union / Anthony F. Sheppard. ISBN 0-8020-7312-3 (pbk.)
1. Intergovernmental fiscal relations - Canada. 2. Fiscal policy - Canada. 3. Canada - Social policy. I. Krasnick, Mark R. II. Royal Commission on the Economic Union and Development Prospects for Canada.
HJ793 .F59 1986 ***NYPL [JLE 86-3253]***

Fiscal limits of absolutism . Collins, James B. Berkeley , c1987. p. cm. ISBN 0-520-05911-5 (alk. paper) LC Card 87-19090 DDC 336.2/00944 19
HJ2648 .C65 1987

Fiscal policies and the world economy . Frenkel, Jacob A. Cambridge, Mass. , c1987. xix, 484 p. : ISBN 0-262-06109-0 LC Card 87-3276 DDC 339.5/2 19
HJ141 .F74 1987

FISCAL POLICY.
Chouraqui, Jean Claude. Public debt in a medium-term context and its implications for fiscal policy /. [Paris, France] , c1986. 67 p. : LC Card 86-218210 DDC 339.5 19
HJ8030 .C48 1986

Fisher, Douglas, 1934- Monetary and fiscal policy /. New York , c1987. p. cm. ISBN 0-8147-2587-2 : LC Card 87-5478 DDC 339.5/2 19
HB172.5 .F54 1987

Frenkel, Jacob A. Fiscal policies and the world economy . Cambridge, Mass. , c1987. xix, 484 p. : ISBN 0-262-06109-0 LC Card 87-3276 DDC 339.5/2 19
HJ141 .F74 1987

Runge, Harry. Haushaltsfinanzierung durch Notendruck /. Berlin , c1986. 69 p. ; ISBN 3-428-05984-0 ***NYPL [JLE 86-2839]***

Wenzel, Heinz-Dieter. Defizitfinanzierung als Instrument einer zielorientierten Finanzpolitik . Baden-Baden , 1983. 249 p. : ISBN 3-7890-0869-9 : LC Card 83-240582
HJ8019 .W45 1983

FISCAL POLICY - AFRICA, SOUTHERN.
La Grange, A. B. DBSA in the southern African development framework /. Sandton, Republic of South Africa [1985] 36 p. : LC Card 87-150256 DDC 332.2 19
HC900 .L3 1985

Fiscal policy and environment . Sairam, T. V. (Trimurti V.), 1946- Delhi , 1986. 135 p. ; LC Card 86-902779 DDC 336.2/7863498/0954 19
HD9766.I62 S35 1986

Fiscal policy and the poor /. Gupta, Anand P. New Delhi , c1984. 90 p. ; LC Card 84-900303 DDC 339.5/2/0954 19
HJ1331 .G87 1984 ***NYPL [JLD 87-778]***

FISCAL POLICY - ARGENTINA.
Conesa, Eduardo R. Bases y puntos de partida para la recuperación de la economía argentina . Buenos Aires, Argentina , c1986. 178 p. : ISBN 950-53-7109-8 LC Card 87-400257 DDC 338.982 19
HC175 .C6145 1986

FISCAL POLICY - AUSTRALIA.
Norman, Neville R. The economics of personal tax escalation in Australia /. [Sydney] : Sydney ; xii, 173 p. : ISBN 0-86861-652-4 (pbk.) LC Card 84-72057 DDC 336.24/2/0994 19
HJ4802 .N67 1985 ***NYPL [JLD 86-1906]***

FISCAL POLICY - BRAZIL.
Biava, Adriano Henrique Rebelo. Contribuição de melhoria . São Paulo-SP , 1987. 243 p. : LC Card 87-404978 DDC 339.5/2/0981 19
HJ2525 .B5 1987

Silva, Gerson Augusto da. Estudos tributários /. Brasília, DF , 1983. 139 p. : LC Card 84-127110
HJ2525 .S49 1983

FISCAL POLICY - BRAZIL - PERNAMBUCO - HISTORY.
Bezerra, Agostinho Fernandes. As tarifas internas na 1a. República /. Brasília, DF , 1986. xv, 140 p. : LC Card 87-404990 DDC 381/.5/098134 19
HJ5101.P47 B49 1986

FISCAL POLICY - CANADA.
Fiscal and monetary policy /. Toronto , Buffalo , c1986. xviii, 339 p. : ISBN 0-8020-7263-1 (pbk.) LC Card 86-672943 DDC 336.3/0971 19
HJ793 .F55 1986 ***NYPL [JLE 87-511]***

Fiscal federalism /. Toronto , Buffalo , c1986. xvi, 211 p. ; ISBN 0-8020-7312-3 (pbk.)
HJ793 .F59 1986 ***NYPL [JLE 86-3253]***

FISCAL POLICY - CARIBBEAN AREA - CASE STUDIES.
Hope, Kempe R. Development finance and the development process . New York , 1987. 100 p. ; ISBN 0-313-25835-X (lib. bdg. : alk. paper) LC Card 86-29617 DDC 336.729 19
HJ844.3 .H67 1987

FISCAL POLICY - CONGRESSES.
The Monetary versus fiscal policy debate . Totowa, N.J. , 1986. 171 p. : ISBN 0-8476-7454-1 : LC Card 85-11912 DDC 339.5/2 19
HG230.3 .M64 1986 ***NYPL [JLE 86-4720]***

FISCAL POLICY - DENMARK - HISTORY - 20TH CENTURY.
Topp, Niels-Henrik. Udviklingen i de finanspolitiske ideer i Danmark 1930-1945 /. [Copenhagen] [1987] 437 p. ; ISBN 87-574-5100-1 : LC Card 87-149164
HB51 .C63 nr. 30 HJ1222

FISCAL POLICY - GERMANY, WEST.
Fuest, Winfried, 1946- Irrtümer in der aktuellen Steuerdiskussion /. Köln , c1987. 54 p. : ISBN 3-602-24749-X LC Card 87-409547 DDC 336.2/00943 19
HJ2687 .F834 1987

Leibinger, Hans-Bodo. Fiskalpolitik unter veränderten Rahmenbedingungen . Berlin , c1985. 256 p. : ISBN 3-428-05862-3 LC Card 85-218522
HJ1120 .L45 1985

Probleme monetärer und finanzwirtschaftlicher Steuerung im Systemvergleich /. Duisburg , c1986. 175 p. : ISBN 3-921473-43-8 LC Card 86-211745
HC286.6 .P754 1986

Staat, Steuern und Finanzausgleich . Berlin , c1984. 452 p., [1] leaf of plates : ISBN 3-428-05513-6 LC Card 84-166906
HJ1120 .S73 1984

Zahn, Joachim, Professor Dr. Eine Finanzpolitik des langen Atems erforderlich /. Bonn [1984] 31 leaves ; LC Card 86-198580
HJ1120 .B65 Nr. 234

FISCAL POLICY - GERMANY (WEST) - ECONOMETRIC MODELS.
Francke, Hans-Hermann. Zinswirkungen der Staatsverschuldung . Berlin , c1984. 138 p. : ISBN 3-428-05727-9 LC Card 86-107232
HJ8654 .F73 1984

Hunger, Carola, 1956- Crowding-out in einem Modell mit Mengenrationierung . Idstein , 1985. x, 251 p. : ISBN 3-925196-06-4 LC Card 86-136872
HJ1120 .H85 1985

FISCAL POLICY - GERMANY (WEST) - HISTORY.
Muscheid, Jutta. Die Steuerpolitik in der Bundesrepublik Deutschland, 1949-1982 /. Berlin , c1986. 212 p. : ISBN 3-428-06004-0 LC Card 86-206446
HJ2687 .M84 1986

FISCAL POLICY - GERMANY, WEST - MATHEMATICAL MODELS.
Steden, Werner. Finanzpolitik und Einkommensverteilung . Frankfurt am Main ; Bern ; 378 p. ; ISBN 3-261-01763-5 LC Card 80-459125
HJ1120 .S74 ***NYPL [JLD 80-3205]***

FISCAL POLICY - GREAT BRITAIN.
Hattersley, Roy. Economic priorities for a labour government /. New York , 1987. ix, 198 p. ; ISBN 0-312-00987-9 : LC Card 87-9576 DDC 338.941 19
HC256.6 .H385 1987

FISCAL POLICY - GREAT BRITAIN - CONGRESSES.
London Conference on Taxes and Growth (1986) London Conference on Taxes and Growth . New York, NY [1986] 61 p. ; LC Card 87-404887 DDC 339.5/25 19
HJ2279 .L655 1986

New priorities in public spending /. Brookfield, VT , 1987. 129 p. ; ISBN 0-566-05386-1 : LC Card 86-22946 DDC 336.3/9/0941 19
HJ7764 .N49 1987

FISCAL POLICY - INDIA.
Agarwal, A. K. (Ashok Kumar), 1949- Problems of Indian fiscal structure /. Delhi, India , 1987. xii, 157 p. ; LC Card 86-903836 DDC 336.54 19
HJ1334. A38 1987

Agarwala, N. L. (Natwar Lal) Commodity taxation and India's fiscal policy /. New Delhi , c1985. 294 p. ; LC Card 85-904360 DDC 339.5/25/0954 19
HJ5715.I4 A73 1985 ***NYPL [JLD 87-610]***

Gupta, Anand P. Fiscal policy and the poor /. New Delhi , c1984. 90 p. ; LC Card 84-900303 DDC 339.5/2/0954 19
HJ1331 .G87 1984 ***NYPL [JLD 87-778]***

Thaker, B. C. Fiscal policy, monetary analysis, and debt management . New Delhi , 1985. xvi, 356 p. : LC Card 85-903636 DDC 339.5/2/0954 19
HG230.3 .T46 1985 ***NYPL [JLD 86-1324]***

FISCAL POLICY - INDIA - CONGRESSES.
Integrated fiscal policy . New Delhi [1985] viii, 101 p. : LC Card 87-902182 DDC 339.5/2/0954 19
HJ1331 .I58 1985

FISCAL POLICY - INDIA - HISTORY.
Tripāṭhi, Oṅkāranātha, 1934- Taxation and fiscal administration in ancient India . Lucknow, U.P. , 1985. xii, 152 p. ; LC Card 85-903145 DDC 336.34 19
HJ2932 .T75 1985 ***NYPL [JLD 86-1318]***

FISCAL POLICY - ITALY.
Il Consolidamento regionale della finanza locale /. Milano [1980] 332 p. : ISBN 88-20-41859-2 : LC Card 80-143023
HJ9497 .C63 ***NYPL [JLD 87-1397]***

FISCAL POLICY - ITALY - CONGRESSES.
La Politica di bilancio in condizioni di stress fiscale . Milano, Italy , c1986. 377 p. ; LC Card 87-134343
HJ2119 .P65 1986

FISCAL POLICY - ITALY - HISTORY - 20TH CENTURY.
Confalonieri, Antonio. La politica del debito pubblico in Italia, 1919-1943 /. Milano , Roma , c1986. 2 v. (536 p.) ; ISBN 88-420-2794-4 : LC Card 87-125992
HJ8678 .C64 1986

FISCAL POLICY - LATIN AMERICA.
Foxley, Alejandro. Las desigualdades económicas y la acción del estado . México , 1980. 271 p. ; ISBN 968-16-0365-6 LC Card 82-215955 DDC 339.2/098 19
HC130.I5 F69 1980 ***NYPL [JLD 86-2631]***

Políticas macro-económicas . Santiago de Chile [1986] 409 p. : LC Card 87-403669 DDC 338.98 19
HC125 .P657 1986

FISCAL POLICY - MATHEMATICAL MODELS.
Auerbach, Alan J. Dynamic fiscal policy /. Cambridge [Cambridgeshire] , New York , 1987. xv, 196 p. : ISBN 0-521-30041-X LC Card 86-24447 DDC 339.5/2 19
HJ131 .A94 1987

Steingräber, Carola, 1956- Geld- und Fiskalpolitik in Portfolio-orientierten Modellen kleiner offener Volkswirtschaften . Rheinfelden , c1986. ix, 219 p. : ISBN 3-87718-532-0 LC Card 86-182509
HG230.3 .S74 1986

Weigert, Edmund. Defizitfinanzierte Fiskalpolitik in einer kleinen offenen Volkswirtschaft bei flexiblen Wechselkursen . Krefeld , 1987, c1986. iii, 211 p. ; ISBN 3-88358-071-6 LC Card 87-146660 DDC 339.5/2/0724 19
HJ161 .W44 1987

Fiscal policy, monetary analysis, and debt management . Thaker, B. C. New Delhi , 1985. xvi, 356 p. : LC Card 85-903636 DDC 339.5/2/0954 19
HG230.3 .T46 1985 ***NYPL [JLD 86-1324]***

FISCAL POLICY - NEW YORK (STATE)
Altschuler, David M. New York nonprofit organizations . Washington, D.C. (2100 M St., N.W., Washington 20037) , c1987. vii, 43 p. : LC Card 87-159600 DDC 658.1/5 19
HD2769.2.U6 A48 1987

FISCAL POLICY - PHILIPPINES.
Diokno, Benjamin E. Revenue mobilization and responsiveness of Philippine income taxes . [Quezon City, Philippines] [1986] 26 p. : LC Card 87-120920 DDC 339.5/25/09599 19
HJ4743 .D56 1986

FISCAL POLICY - POLAND.
Probleme monetärer und finanzwirtschaftlicher Steuerung im Systemvergleich /. Duisburg , c1986. 175 p. : ISBN 3-921473-43-8 LC Card 86-211745
HC286.6 .P754 1986

FISCAL POLICY - PORTUGAL - CONGRESSES.
Seminário sobre Política Fiscal (1984? : CGTP-IN) Contribuições para a reforma do sistema fiscal português . Lisboa , 1985. 226 p. : LC Card 87-107879 DDC 336.469 19
HJ1252 .S46 1984

FISCAL POLICY - PUBLIC OPINION.
Rondorf, Dieter, 1955- Die Bewertung öffentlicher Leistungen durch die Bürger . Frankfurt am Main , New York , c1985. 231 p. : ISBN 3-8204-5652-X LC Card 85-229645
HB846.5 .R65 1985

FISCAL POLICY - SWITZERLAND.
Hablützel, Peter. Staatsverschuldung . Basel , c1984. 96 p. : ISBN 3-7190-0864-9 LC Card 84-159813
HJ8749 .H33 1984

FISCAL POLICY - TURKEY.
Ataç, Beyhan. Kuramda ve Türkiye'de istikrar politikası açısından parasal ve mali işlemler /. Eskişehir [1979?] iv, 173 p. ; LC Card 82-245649
HG1206.5 .A79 1979

Kopits, George. Structural reform, stabilization,

and growth in Turkey /. Washington, D.C. , c1987. v, 46 p. : ISBN 0-939934-84-1 (pbk.) : LC Card 87-3583 DDC 338.9561 19
HC492 .K67 1987

FISCAL POLICY - UNITED STATES.
Anderson, Hugold. Government without taxation /. Warwick, R.I. , c1987. 52 p. ; LC Card 87-133116 DDC 336.2/00973 19
HJ2381 .A76 1987

Cebula, Richard J. The deficit problem in perspective /. Lexington, Mass. , c1987. x, 106 p. : ISBN 0-669-14303-0 (pbk. : alk. paper) LC Card 86-45792 DDC 339.5/23/0973 19
HJ2052 .C42 1987

Neustadt, Richard E. Richard E. Neustadt lecture, May 13, 1986. Seattle, WA [1986] 35 p. : LC Card 87-402984 DDC 339.5/2/0973 19
HJ257.2 .N48 1986

Pechman, Joseph A., 1918- Federal tax policy /. Washington, D.C. , c1987. xix, 430 p. : ISBN 0-8157-6962-8 : LC Card 87-13159 DDC 336.2/00973 19
HJ257.2 .P4 1987

The Politics of American economic policy making /. Armonk, N.Y. , c1987. 455 p. : ISBN 0-87332-406-4 : LC Card 87-12827 DDC 338.973 19
HJ257 .P59 1987

Stiglitz, Joseph E. Economics of the public sector /. New York , c1986. xxiii, 599 p. : ISBN 0-393-01808-3 LC Card 86-211407 DDC 336.73 19
HJ257.2 .S84 1986

Taxation and the deficit economy . San Francisco, Calif. , c1986. xxvii, 554 p. : ISBN 0-936488-13-1 : LC Card 85-63549 DDC 339.5/2/0973 19
HJ257.2 .T385 1986 *NYPL [JLE 86-4136]*

FISCAL POLICY - UNITED STATES - CONGRESSES.
Conference on the Effects of Taxation on Capital Formation (1986 : Palm Beach, Fla.) Taxes and capital formation. Cambridge, Mass. (1050 Massachusetts Ave., Cambridge 02138) , 1986. 40 p. ; LC Card 87-101954 DDC 336.2/00973 19
HJ2381 .C6974 1986

London Conference on Taxes and Growth (1986) London Conference on Taxes and Growth . New York, NY [1986] 61 p. ; LC Card 87-404887 DDC 339.5/25 19
HJ2279 .L655 1986

FISCAL RELATIONS, INTERGOVERNMENTAL. see **INTERGOVERNMENTAL FISCAL RELATIONS.**

Fiscale en juridische documentatie voor internationaal zakendoen .
(15) Gijsman, D., 1955- Exportfinanciering /. Deventer , 's-Gravenhage , 1986. 118 p. : ISBN 90-200-0992-3 : LC Card 86-176172
HG3754.N4 G55 1986

La fiscalité face au développement économique et social du Maroc /. Zemrani, Anas Bensalah. Rabat , 1982. 395 p. ; LC Card 83-183254
HJ3032 .Z34 1982

Fischbach, Thomas. Occupational characteristics of disabled workers, 1975-1976 . Cincinnati, Ohio (4676 Columbia Pkwy., Cincinnati 45226) [1986] xix, 187 p. ; LC Card 86-602391 DDC 363.1/12/0973 19
HD7105.25.U6 O23 1986

Fischer, Barbara S. Office systems integration : a decision-maker's guide to systems planning and implementation / Barbara S. Fischer. New York : Quorum Books, 1987. xxi, 215 p. : ill. ; 24 cm. Includes bibliographies and index. ISBN 0-89930-109-6 (lib. bdg. : alk. paper) LC Card 87-2498 DDC 651.8 19
1. Office practice - Automation. 2. Business - Data processing. 3. Business - Communication systems. I. Title.
HF5547.5 .F56 1987

Fischer, Bernhard, fl. 1979- Brasilien ohne Inflation? : eine kritische Würdigung des Cruzado-Planes / von Bernhard Fischer. Kiel : Institut für Weltwirtschaft Kiel, [1986] 28 p. ; 30 cm. (Kieler Diskussionsbeiträge, 0455-0420 = Kiel discussion papers . 124) Cover title. Bibliography: p. 27-28. LC Card 87-120443 DDC 330 s 332.4/1/0981 19
1. Monetary policy - Brazil. 2. Inflation (Finance) - Brazil. 3. Brazil - Economic policy. I. Series: Kieler Diskussionsbeiträge , 124. II. Title.
HB44 .K45 no. 124 HG835

Fischer, Dietrich. Baumol, William J. Superfairness . Cambridge, Mass. , c1986. xi, 266 p. : ISBN 0-262-02234-6 LC Card 85-15127 DDC 305 19
HB72 .B356 1986 *NYPL [JLE 86-2402]*

Fischer, Dietrich, 1941- Tinbergen, Jan, 1903- Warfare and welfare . Brighton, Sussex , New York , 1987. xiv, 189 p. ; ISBN 0-312-00957-7 (St. Martin's) : LC Card 87-9625 DDC 361.6/1 19
HB846 .T55 1987

Fischer, Donald E. Security analysis and portfolio management / Donald E. Fischer, Ronald J. Jordan. 4th ed. Englewood Cliffs, N.J. : Prentice-Hall, c1987. xii, 708 p. : ill. ; 25 cm. Includes bibliographical references and index. ISBN 0-13-798901-6 LC Card 86-25484 DDC 332.6 19
1. Investment analysis. 2. Portfolio management. I. Jordan, Ronald J. II. Title.
HG4529 .F57 1987

Fischer, Franz. Gach, Christian. Wirtschaftlichkeitsanalyse von Banken . Wien , c1983. iv, 75, iii, 89 p. ; ISBN 3-85428-017-3 : LC Card 84-118578
HG3008 .G28 1983

Fischer, Joachim, 1948- Neue Leistungspolitik in der Bekleidungsindustrie : Arbeitsstrukturierung und Produktionsflexibilisierung / Joachim Fischer, Heiner Minssen. Frankfurt/Main ; New York : Campus, c1986. 264 p. : ill. ; 21 cm. (Forschungsberichte aus dem Landesinstitut Sozialforschungsstelle Dortmund) Bibliography: p. 255-264. ISBN 3-593-33635-9 LC Card 86-197222
1. Clothing trade - Germany (West) - Personnel management. 2. Clothing trade - Germany (West) - Labor productivity. I. Minssen, Heiner. II. Title.
HD9940.G32 F57 1986

Fischer, Joel. Helping the sexually oppressed /. Englewood Cliffs, N.J. , c1986. xix, 282 p. : ISBN 0-13-386129-5 : LC Card 85-16687 DDC 305.3 19
HN57 .H46 1986 *NYPL [JLE 86-3217]*

Fischer, Lutz. Unternehmung und Steuer . Wiesbaden , c1983. 395 p. ; ISBN 3-409-50005-7 LC Card 83-161883
HD2753.G3 U57 1983

Fischer, Manfred M. Regional labour markets . Amsterdam ; New York : xvii, 500 p. : ISBN 0-444-70323-3 LC Card 87-22200 DDC 331.12 19
HD5707 .R37 1987

Fischer, Stanley.
Dornbusch, Rudiger. Macro-economics /. New York , c1987. xiv, 798 p. : ISBN 0-07-017776-7 : LC Card 86-21114 DDC 339 19
HB172.5 .D67 1987

Economics / Stanley Fischer, Rudiger Dornbusch, Richard Schmalensee. 2nd ed. New York : McGraw-Hill, c1988. xliii, 813 p. : ill. (some col.) ; 25 cm. Includes bibliographical references and index. ISBN 0-07-017781-3 : LC Card 87-21333 DDC 330 19
1. Economics. I. Dornbusch, Rudiger. II. Schmalensee, Richard. III. Title.
HB171.5 .F458 1988

Fischer, Thomas. Kontrolltheoretische Entscheidungsmodelle : ein Beitrag zur Abstimmung von Produktion und Lagerhaltung auf unsichere Nachfrage / Thomas Fischer. Berlin : Duncker & Humblot, c1982. x, 343 p. : ill. ; 24 cm. (Wirtschaftskybernetik und Systemanalyse. Bd. 7) Slightly revised version of the author's thesis (Johann Wolfgang Goethe-Universität, Frankfurt am Main, 1980) under the title: Möglichkeiten und Grenzen des Einsatzes system- und kontrolltheoretischer Lösungsverfahren für mehrdimensionale, dynamische, stochastische Entscheidungsprobleme im Bereich von Produktion und Lagerhaltung der Unternehmung. Includes indexes. Bibliography: p. 318-333. ISBN 3-428-05111-4 :
1. Decision-making - Mathematical models. 2. Inventory control - Mathematical models. I. Title.
NYPL [JLE 86-3084]

Fischerei und Fischereiwirtschaft im nördlichen Ceylon . Gläser, Thomas. Wiesbaden , 1983. xv, 196 p. : ISBN 3-515-04054-4 LC Card 86-155838
HD9466.S722 G53 1983

Fish, food, and hunger . Kent, George, 1939- Boulder , 1987. ix, 201 p. ; ISBN 0-8133-7409-X (pbk.) : LC Card 87-6066 DDC 338.3/7194 19
HD9450.5 .K46 1987

FISH TRADE.
Dore, Ian, 1941- Fresh seafood, the commercial buyer's guide . Huntington, N.Y. , c1984. 375 p. : ISBN 0-943738-07-5 : LC Card 84-5174 DDC 641.3/92/0687 19
HD9450.5 .D67 1984 *NYPL [JSD 86-449]*

Kent, George, 1939- Fish, food, and hunger . Boulder , 1987. ix, 201 p. ; ISBN 0-8133-7409-X (pbk.) : LC Card 87-6066 DDC 338.3/7194 19
HD9450.5 .K46 1987

Problems of trade in fishery products. Paris, France , Washington, D.C. , c1985. 384 p. : ISBN 92-64-12775-5 (pbk.) : LC Card 86-203595 DDC 382/.437 19
HD9450.5 .P76 1985

Seafood processing & distribution market opportunities. Norwalk, Conn., U. S.A. (6 Prowitt St., Norwalk 06855) , c1986. vii, 244 leaves : LC Card 87-129495 DDC 381/.4566494/0973 19
HD9450.5 .S4 1986

FISH TRADE - ALASKA.
Alaska habitat management guide. Juneau, Alaska , 1986- 2 v. (loose-leaf) : LC Card 86-623159 DDC 333.95/09798 19
HD9457.A4 A427 1986

FISH TRADE - AMAZON RIVER ESTUARY.
Loureiro, Violeta Refkalefsky. Os parceiros do mar . [Brasília] [Belém] , 1985. 227 p. : LC Card 85-211634
HD9464.A4 L68 1985

FISH TRADE - AMAZON RIVER REGION.
Penner, Maria Eunice Soares. A dialética da atividade pesqueira no nordeste amazônico /. Belém , 1984. 158 p. : ISBN 85-24-70006-8 LC Card 86-158128
HD9464.B73 N676 1984

FISH TRADE - ARGENTINA - STATISTICS.
Agricultura, caza, silvicultura y pesca . [Buenos Aires] [1982] 57 p. : LC Card 87-401763 DDC 338.1/0982/021 19
HD1862 .A58 1982

FISH TRADE - BRAZIL.
Brazil. Congresso Nacional. Câmara dos Deputados. Comissão de Agricultura e Política Rural. Subcomissão de Pesca. Relatório final da Subcomissão de Pesca da Comissão de Agricultura e Política Rural, durante a sessão legislativa de 1984. Brasília , 1985. 66 p. ; LC Card 86-203945
HD9464.B72 B64 1985

FISH TRADE - BRAZIL, NORTHEAST.
Penner, Maria Eunice Soares. A dialética da atividade pesqueira no nordeste amazônico /. Belém , 1984. 158 p. : ISBN 85-24-70006-8 LC Card 86-158128
HD9464.B73 N676 1984

FISH TRADE - BRAZIL - RIO GRANDE DO NORTE.
Paiva, Francisco Ismar Martins. Projeto Pesca Industrial à Vela. [Natal, Brazil] [1982 or 1983] 91 p. : LC Card 85-102872
HD9464.B73 R487 1982

FISH TRADE - BRAZIL - VIGIA (PARÁ)
Loureiro, Violeta Refkalefsky. Os parceiros do mar . [Brasília] [Belém] , 1985. 227 p. : LC Card 85-211634
HD9464.A4 L68 1985

FISH TRADE - FRANCE.
Miller, Charlotte L. The French market for U. S. seafood products /. Terminal Island, CA , 1986. ii, 63 p. ; LC Card 86-602854 DDC 382/.4566494/0944 19
HD9462.5 .M54 1986

FISH TRADE - FRANCE - DIRECTORIES.
Miller, Charlotte L. The French market for U. S. seafood products /. Terminal Island, CA , 1986. ii, 63 p. ; LC Card 86-602854 DDC 382/.4566494/0944 19
HD9462.5 .M54 1986

FISH TRADE - GOVERNMENT POLICY - BRAZIL.
Brazil. Congresso Nacional. Câmara dos

Deputados. Comissão de Agricultura e Política Rural. Subcomissão de Pesca. Relatório final da Subcomissão de Pesca da Comissão de Agricultura e Política Rural, durante a sessão legislativa de 1984. Brasília , 1985. 66 p. ; LC Card 86-203945
HD9464.B72 B64 1985

FISH TRADE - GOVERNMENT POLICY - LATIN AMERICA.
Pacheco O., Amparo. Préstamo del BID al sector pesquero . [San José] , 1984. 50 p. : LC Card 86-185463
HD9464.A2 P33 1984

FISH TRADE - GOVERNMENT POLICY - SRI LANKA - HISTORY.
Bavinck, Maarten, 1954- Small fry . Amsterdam , 1984. xii, 151 p. ; ISBN 90-6256-374-0 (pbk.) LC Card 84-187330 DDC 338.3/72709549/3 19
HD9466.S723 K343 1984
NYPL [JLD 86-2668]

FISH TRADE - GREAT BRITAIN.
Miller, Charlotte L. The market for seafood in the United Kingdom /. Terminal Island, CA , 1986. ii, 73 p. : LC Card 87-601563 DDC 382.1/4370941 19
HD9461.5 .M55 1986

FISH TRADE - GREAT BRITAIN - DIRECTORIES.
Miller, Charlotte L. The market for seafood in the United Kingdom /. Terminal Island, CA , 1986. ii, 73 p. : LC Card 87-601563 DDC 382.1/4370941 19
HD9461.5 .M55 1986

FISH TRADE - INDIA.
Rao, P. S. Fishery economics and management in India /. Bombay, India , 1983. 356, [1] p. : LC Card 83-906523 DDC 338.3/714/0954 19
HD9466.I52 R36 1983 ***NYPL [JLE 86-290]***

FISH TRADE - MAINE.
Colgan, Charles S. The natural resource industries of Maine . [Augusta, Me.] [1986] 135 p. : LC Card 87-620550 DDC 338.09741 19
HD9007.M2 C64 1986

FISH TRADE - MAURITIUS.
Paul, E. C. (Erik Charles), 1937- Fisheries development and the food needs of Mauritius /. Rotterdam , Boston , 1987. vi, 216 p. : ISBN 90-6191-627-5 LC Card 87-170375 DDC 338.3/7270969/82 19
HD9468.M452 P38 1987

FISH TRADE - MEXICO.
Nociones básicas sobre cooperativismo pesquero. [Mexico City, Mexico] , 1985. 313 p. : ISBN 968-8170-25-9 LC Card 86-217319 DDC 334/.6892/0972 19
HD9464.B72 N63 1985

Ortiz de Montellano, Ana. Tecnologías pesqueras en el trópico húmedo de México /. México, D.F. , 1985. 146 p. : LC Card 86-208331
HD9464.M42 O77 1985

FISH TRADE - MEXICO - TECHNOLOGICAL INNOVATIONS.
Ortiz de Montellano, Ana. Tecnologías pesqueras en el trópico húmedo de México /. México, D.F. , 1985. 146 p. : LC Card 86-208331
HD9464.M42 O77 1985

FISH TRADE - NORWAY - FINANCE.
Røgeberg, Svein Lasse. Sektorberegninger for fiske og fangst /. Oslo , 1979. 34 p. ; ISBN 82-537-0977-3 LC Card 86-460230
HD9465.N62 R64 1979

FISH TRADE - NORWAY - STATISTICS.
Ressursregnskap for fisk. Oslo , 1982. 53 p. : ISBN 82-537-1765-2 : LC Card 82-229877
HD9465.N62 R47 1982

FISH TRADE - PHILIPPINES - BAYAWAN.
Socio-economic and marketing study of municipal fishing households, Bayawan, Negros Oriental, Philippines. Manila, Philippines [1983] vii, 94, 7 p. : LC Card 86-225887
HD8039.F652 P67 1983

FISH TRADE - SAUDI ARABIA.
Analytical study for the market of white meat and eggs /. Jeddah [1985?] 159 p. : LC Card 85-964046 DDC 381/.4566493/09538 19
HD9437.S332 A53 1985

FISH TRADE - SPAIN.
La Agricultura y la pesca españolas en 1981. Madrid [1982?] 299 p. : ISBN 84-7479-164-2 : LC Card 83-125330 DDC 338.1/0946 19
HD2022 .A657 1982 ***NYPL [JLF 87-236]***

FISH TRADE - SRI LANKA.
Gläser, Thomas. Fischerei und Fischereiwirtschaft im nördlichen Ceylon . Wiesbaden , 1983. xv, 196 p. : ISBN 3-515-04054-4 LC Card 86-155838
HD9466.S722 G53 1983

FISH TRADE - SRI LANKA - KADALUR.
Bavinck, Maarten, 1954- Small fry . Amsterdam , 1984. xii, 151 p. ; ISBN 90-6256-374-0 (pbk.) LC Card 84-187330 DDC 338.3/72709549/3 19
HD9466.S723 K343 1984
NYPL [JLD 86-2668]

FISH TRADE - TAXATION - SPAIN - CATALONIA.
L'IVA en els sectors agrari i pesquer catalans. [Barcelona] , 1985. 49 p. ; ISBN 84-393-0632-6 LC Card 86-165858
HJ5715.S7 L58 1985

FISH TRADE - UNITED STATES.
Miller, Charlotte L. The French market for U. S. seafood products /. Terminal Island, CA , 1986. ii, 63 p. ; LC Card 86-602854 DDC 382/.4566494/0944 19
HD9462.5 .M54 1986

Miller, Charlotte L. The market for seafood in the United Kingdom /. Terminal Island, CA , 1986. ii, 73 p. : LC Card 87-601563 DDC 382.1/4370941 19
HD9461.5 .M55 1986

FISH TRADE - VENEZUELA - SUCRE (STATE)
Lárez, Ronald. Análisis económico social de las comunidades pesqueras del Estado Sucre /. [Carúpano, Venezuela] , 1983. 217, 19, 8 p. : LC Card 87-115222 DDC 338.3/72/098753 19
HD8039.F652 V45 1983

Fishburn, Peter C. Interprofile conditions and impossibility / Peter C. Fishburn. Chur, Switzerland ; New York : Harwood Academic Publishers, c1987. viii, 93 p. ; 23 cm. (Fundamentals of pure and applied economics, 0191-1708 . 18.) Bibliography: p. 81-88. Includes index. ISBN 3-7186-0377-2 (pbk.) LC Card 86-31892 DDC 302/.13 19
1. Social choice. I. Series: Fundamentals of pure and applied economics , 18. II. Title.
HB846.8 .F67 1987

Fisher, Brian S. An economic and technical assessment of the establishment of an Australian fat-tail sheep industry / by Brian S. Fisher and James M. Gooden. [Sydney], N.S.W. : Dept. of Agricultural Economics, University of Sydney, c1986. vi, 52 p. ; 30 cm. (Research report / Department of Agricultural Economics, University of Sydney, 0817-8771 . no. 10) Bibliography: p. 50-52. LC Card 87-154531 DDC 338.1/76386 19
1. Fat-tailed sheep industry - Australia. I. Gooden, James M. II. Series: Research report (University of Sydney. Dept. of Agricultural Economics) , no. 10. III. Title.
HD9436.A82 F57 1986

Fisher, Douglas, 1934-
Macroeconomic theory, a survey. Fisher, Douglas, 1934- Monetary and fiscal policy / Douglas Fisher. New York , c1987. p. cm. ISBN 0-8147-2587-2 : LC Card 87-5478 DDC 339.5/2 19
HB172.5 .F54 1987

Monetary and fiscal policy / Douglas Fisher. New York : New York University Press, c1987. p. cm. Continues: Macroeconomic theory, a survey. 1983. Bibliography: p. Includes index. ISBN 0-8147-2587-2 : LC Card 87-5478 DDC 339.5/2 19
1. Macroeconomics. 2. Fiscal policy. 3. Monetary policy. I. Fisher, Douglas, 1934- Macroeconomic theory, a survey. II. Title.
HB172.5 .F54 1987

Fisher, Joseph L. Virginia alternatives for the 1990s . Fairfax, Va. , Lanham, MD , 1987. 183 p. : ISBN 0-8026-0016-6 (alk. paper) : LC Card 87-22757 DDC 338.9755 19
HC107.V8 V435 1987

Fisher, Kenneth L. The Wall Street waltz : 90 visual perspectives : illustrated lessons from financial cycles and trends / Kenneth L. Fisher. Chicago : Contemporary Books, c1987. xii, 210 p. : ill. (some col.) ; 22 x 28 cm. Includes index. ISBN 0-8092-4797-6 : LC Card 87-5310 DDC 332.63/222/0973 19
1. Stocks - United States - Charts, diagrams, etc. 2. Interest rates - United States - Charts, diagrams, etc. 3. Economic indicators - United States - Charts, diagrams, etc. I. Title.
HG4916 .F47 1987.

FISHERIES.
Kent, George, 1939- Fish, food, and hunger . Boulder , 1987. ix, 201 p. ; ISBN 0-8133-7409-X (pbk.) : LC Card 87-6066 DDC 338.3/7194 19
HD9450.5 .K46 1987

Problems of trade in fishery products. Paris, France , Washington, D.C. , c1985. 384 p. : ISBN 92-64-12775-5 (pbk.) : LC Card 86-203595 DDC 382/.437 19
HD9450.5 .P76 1985

FISHERIES, COOPERATIVE - BANGLADESH - MANAGEMENT.
Habibullah, M. Management constraints of co-operatives /. Dhaka , 1986. 92 p. ; LC Card 87-900945
HD1491.B3 H34 1986

FISHERIES, COOPERATIVE - MEXICO.
Nociones básicas sobre cooperativismo pesquero. [Mexico City, Mexico] , 1985. 313 p. : ISBN 968-8170-25-9 LC Card 86-217319 DDC 334/.6892/0972 19
HD9464.B72 N63 1985

Fisheries development and the food needs of Mauritius /. Paul, E. C. (Erik Charles), 1937- Rotterdam , Boston , 1987. vi, 216 p. : ISBN 90-6191-627-5 LC Card 87-170375 DDC 338.3/7270969/82 19
HD9468.M452 P38 1987

FISHERIES - ECONOMIC ASPECTS - INDIA.
Rao, P. S. Fishery economics and management in India /. Bombay, India , 1983. 356, [1] p. : LC Card 83-906523 DDC 338.3/714/0954 19
HD9466.I52 R36 1983 ***NYPL [JLE 86-290]***

FISHERIES - ECONOMIC ASPECTS - SPAIN.
La Agricultura y la pesca españolas en 1981. Madrid [1982?] 299 p. : ISBN 84-7479-164-2 : LC Card 83-125330 DDC 338.1/0946 19
HD2022 .A657 1982 ***NYPL [JLF 87-236]***

FISHERIES - MANITOBA.
Manitoba. Manitoba Natural Resources. Five year report to the legislature on fisheries, year ending 1983-84. [Winnipeg, Man.] [1984?] 57 p. : LC Card 87-164861 DDC 338.3/713/097127 19
HD9464.C22 M365 1984

FISHERIES - SRI LANKA.
Gläser, Thomas. Fischerei und Fischereiwirtschaft im nördlichen Ceylon . Wiesbaden , 1983. xv, 196 p. : ISBN 3-515-04054-4 LC Card 86-155838
HD9466.S722 G53 1983

FISHERS - ALASKA - SUPPLY AND DEMAND - STATISTICS.
Focht, Rick. Employment and gross earnings of California residents in Alaska's commercial fisheries, 1977-1982 /. Juneau, AK [1984] v, 53 p. : LC Card 86-622320 DDC 331.12/5392/09798021 19
HD4966.F652 U54 1984c

Focht, Rick. Employment and gross earnings of Oregon residents in Alaska's commercial fisheries, 1977-1982 /. Juneau, AK [1984] v, 69 p. : LC Card 86-622319 DDC 331.12/5392/09798021 19
HD4966.F652 U54 1984b

FISHERS - ARGENTINA - CORRIENTES - CASE STUDIES.
Proyecto Paraná Medio . Buenos Aires , 1985. 44 leaves : LC Card 86-218225
HD8039.F66 A746 1985

FISHERS - ARGENTINA - ENTRE RÍOS - CASE STUDIES.
Proyecto Paraná Medio . Buenos Aires , 1985. 44 leaves : LC Card 86-218225
HD8039.F66 A746 1985

FISHERS - BRAZIL - UBATUBA (SÃO PAULO)
Marcilio, Maria Luiza. Caiçara . São Paulo-SP (Brasil) , c1986. 244 p. : ISBN 85-05-00523-6 LC Card 87-404833 DDC 304.6/0981/61 19
HD1531.B7 M34 1986

FISHERS - HOUSING - MEXICO - TECOLUTLA.
Alcalá, Graciela. Los pescadores de Tecolutla . México, D.F. , 1985. 215 p. : ISBN 968-496-070-0 LC Card 86-191825
HD8039.F652 M62 1985

FISHERS - JUVENILE LITERATURE.
Klein, John F. (John Frederick), 1950- A day in the life of a commercial fisherman /. Mahwah, N.J. , c1988. 32 p. : ISBN 0-8167-1109-7 (lib. bdg.) : LC Card 87-10949 DDC 639/.2/02373 19
HD8039.F65 K57 1988

FISHERS - MEXICO.
Ortiz de Montellano, Ana. Tecnologías pesqueras en el trópico húmedo de México /. México, D.F. , 1985. 146 p. : LC Card 86-208331
HD9464.M42 O77 1985

FISHERS - MEXICO - QUINTANA ROO (STATE)
Dachary, Alfredo César. El Caribe mexicano . México, D.F. , 1985. 110 p. : ISBN 968-496-069-7 LC Card 86-118335 DDC 338.3/7270972 19
HD8039.F66 M426 1985
NYPL [JLD 87-1321]

FISHERS - MEXICO - TECOLUTLA.
Alcalá, Graciela. Los pescadores de Tecolutla . México, D.F. , 1985. 215 p. : ISBN 968-496-070-0 LC Card 86-191825
HD8039.F652 M62 1985

FISHERS - MEXICO - TECOLUTLA - DWELLINGS.
Alcalá, Graciela. Los pescadores de Tecolutla . México, D.F. , 1985. 215 p. : ISBN 968-496-070-0 LC Card 86-191825
HD8039.F652 M62 1985

FISHERS - NEW YORK (STATE) - LONG ISLAND - HISTORY.
Matthiessen, Peter. Men's lives /. New York , 1988, c1986. xvi, 335 p. ; ISBN 0-394-75560-X (pbk.) : LC Card 87-40095 DDC 338.3/72709747/21 19
HD8039.F66 U5 1988

FISHERS - OMAN - BĀṬINAH.
Asche, H. (Hartmut) Mobile Lebensformgruppen Südost-Arabiens im Wandel . Berlin , 1981, c1982. xii, 344 p. : ISBN 3-496-00302-2 LC Card 86-217612
HD8039.F652 O522 1982

FISHERS - PARANÁ RIVER VALLEY (BRAZIL-ARGENTINA) - CASE STUDIES.
Proyecto Paraná Medio . Buenos Aires , 1985. 44 leaves : LC Card 86-218225
HD8039.F66 A746 1985

FISHERS - PHILIPPINES - BAYAWAN.
Socio-economic and marketing study of municipal fishing households, Bayawan, Negros Oriental, Philippines. Manila, Philippines [1983] vii, 94, 7 p. : LC Card 86-225887
HD8039.F652 P67 1983

FISHERS - PORTUGAL - PÓVOA DE VARZIM - SOCIAL CONDITIONS.
Santos Graça, A. (António), 1882-1956. O poveiro /. Póvoa de Varzim , 1982. 238, xvi p., [29] p. of plates : LC Card 83-215678
HD8039.F66 P67 1982

FISHERS - SRI LANKA - KADALUR.
Bavinck, Maarten, 1954- Small fry . Amsterdam , 1984. xii, 151 p. ; ISBN 90-6256-374-0 (pbk.) LC Card 84-187330 DDC 338.3/72709549/3 19
HD9466.S723 K343 1984
NYPL [JLD 86-2668]

FISHERS - TRAINING OF - SENEGAL.
International Labour Organisation. Formation professionnelle rurale, SEN/71/526 . Genève , 1976. ii, 69 p. : ISBN 92-2-201512-6 LC Card 84-125056
HD5716.A292 S385 1976

FISHERS - VENEZUELA - SUCRE (STATE)
Lárez, Ronald. Análisis económico social de las comunidades pesqueras del Estado Sucre /. [Carúpano, Venezuela] , 1983. 217, 19, 8 p. : LC Card 87-115222 DDC 338.3/72/098753 19
HD8039.F652 V45 1983

Fishery economics and management in India /.
Rao, P. S. Bombay, India , 1983. 356, [1] p. : LC Card 83-906523 DDC 338.3/714/0954 19
HD9466.I52 R36 1983 *NYPL [JLE 86-290]*

FISHERY MANAGEMENT - ALASKA.
Alaska habitat management guide. Juneau, Alaska , 1986- 2 v. (loose-leaf) : LC Card 86-623159 DDC 333.95/09798 19
HD9457.A4 A427 1986

FISHERY MANAGEMENT - INDIA.
Rao, P. S. Fishery economics and management in India /. Bombay, India , 1983. 356, [1] p. : LC Card 83-906523 DDC 338.3/714/0954 19
HD9466.I52 R36 1983 *NYPL [JLE 86-290]*

FISHERY POLICY - ALASKA.
Alaska habitat management guide. Juneau, Alaska , 1986- 2 v. (loose-leaf) : LC Card 86-623159 DDC 333.95/09798 19
HD9457.A4 A427 1986

FISHERY POLICY - MANITOBA.
Manitoba. Manitoba Natural Resources. Five year report to the legislature on fisheries, year ending 1983-84. [Winnipeg, Man.] [1984?] 57 p. : LC Card 87-164861 DDC 338.3/713/097127 19
HD9464.C22 M365 1984

FISHERY POLICY - MAURITIUS.
Paul, E. C. (Erik Charles), 1937- Fisheries development and the food needs of Mauritius /. Rotterdam , Boston , 1987. vi, 216 p. : ISBN 90-6191-627-5 LC Card 87-170375 DDC 338.3/7270969/82 19
HD9468.M452 P38 1987

FISHERY PRODUCTS - PHILIPPINES - BAYAWAN - MARKETING.
Socio-economic and marketing study of municipal fishing households, Bayawan, Negros Oriental, Philippines. Manila, Philippines [1983] vii, 94, 7 p. : LC Card 86-225887
HD8039.F652 P67 1983

FISHES - ALASKA - HABITAT.
Alaska habitat management guide. Juneau, Alaska , 1986- 2 v. (loose-leaf) : LC Card 86-623159 DDC 333.95/09798 19
HD9457.A4 A427 1986

FISHING - ALASKA.
Alaska habitat management guide. Juneau, Alaska , 1986- 2 v. (loose-leaf) : LC Card 86-623159 DDC 333.95/09798 19
HD9457.A4 A427 1986

FISHING - MEXICO - QUINTANA ROO (STATE)
Dachary, Alfredo César. El Caribe mexicano . México, D.F. , 1985. 110 p. : ISBN 968-496-069-7 LC Card 86-118335 DDC 338.3/7270972 19
HD8039.F66 M426 1985
NYPL [JLD 87-1321]

FISHING VILLAGES - VENEZUELA - SUCRE (STATE)
Lárez, Ronald. Análisis económico social de las comunidades pesqueras del Estado Sucre /. [Carúpano, Venezuela] , 1983. 217, 19, 8 p. : LC Card 87-115222 DDC 338.3/72/098753 19
HD8039.F652 V45 1983

Fishta, Iljaz. Ekonomia e Shqipërisë në vitet e para të ndërtimit socialist, 1944-1948 / Iljaz Fishta, Veniamin Toçi. Tiranë : Akademia e Shkencave e RPS të Shqipërisë, Instituti i Historisë, 1984. 489 p. ; 22 cm. Summary in French. Bibliography: p. 469-474. Includes index. LC Card 85-163026
1. Albania - Economic policy. 2. Albania - Economic conditions. 3. Communism - Albania - History - 20th century. I. Toçi, V. II. Title.
HC402 .F55 1984

Fiskalpolitik unter veränderten Rahmenbedingungen . Leibinger, Hans-Bodo. Berlin , c1985. 256 p. : ISBN 3-428-05862-3 LC Card 85-218522
HJ1120 .L45 1985

Fiskarbonde og gruveslusk /. Drivenes, Einar-Arne. Oslo , c1985. 161, [1] p. : ISBN 82-00-07480-3 LC Card 86-204801
HD9506.N72 D75 1985

Fisseha, Yacob. Milimo, J. T. Rural small enterprises in Zambia . [Lusaka] [1985] 71 p. ; LC Card 87-980231 DDC 338.6/42/096894 19
HD2346.Z29 M55 1985

Fite, Gilbert Courtland, 1918- The farmers' frontier, 1865-1900 / Gilbert C. Fite ; foreword by Ray Allen Billington. Norman : University of Oklahoma Press, [1987], c1966. xiv, 272 p. : ill. ; 23 cm. "An essay on bibliography": p. 247-262. Includes index. ISBN 0-8061-2063-0 (pbk.) LC Card 86-40534 DDC 338.1/0977 19
1. Farmers - Middle West - History - 19th century. 2. Farmers - West (U. S.) - History - 19th century. 3. Agriculture - Economic aspects - Middle West - History - 19th century. 4. Agriculture - Economic aspects - West (U. S.) - History - 19th century. 5. Middle West - History. 6. West (U. S.) - History - 1848-1950. 7. Frontier and pioneer life - Middle West. 8. Frontier and pioneer life - West (U. S.). I. Title.
HD8039.F3 U643 1987

Fitoussi, Jean Paul. Monetary theory and economic institutions . New York , 1987. ix, 349 p. : ISBN 0-312-00407-9 : LC Card 86-26069 DDC 332.4/01 19
HG203 .M68 1987

Fitton, K. B. Seychelles . [[Newbury, Berkshire, UK] [1986] iii, 41 p. : LC Card 86-214104 DDC 383/.144/09696 19
HE7389.9.Z9 A47 1986

Fituni, L. L. (Leonid Leonidovich) Ravitie ėkonomiki nezavisimoĭ Angoly / L.L. Fituni. Moskva : Izd-vo "Nauka," Glav. red. vostochnoĭ lit-ry, 1981. 171, [3] p. ; 20 cm. At head of title: Akademii͡a nauk SSSR. Institut Afriki. Bibliography: p. 163-[172] LC Card 82-115411
1. Angola - Economic conditions - 1975-. 2. Angola - Foreign economic relations. I. Title.
HC950 .F57 1981

Fitz-Gerald, Christine Maloney. I can be a textile worker / by Christine Maloney Fitz-Gerald. Chicago : Children's Press, c1987. 29 p. : col. ill. ; 25 cm. Includes index. "Prepared under the direction of Robert Hillerich." Discusses the people who work with textiles and clothing, including designers, factory workers involved in weaving and spinning, dyers, and finishers. ISBN 0-516-01912-0 (lib bdg.) LC Card 87-10716 DDC 677/.0023/73 19
1. Clothing workers - Juvenile literature. 2. Textile workers - Juvenile literature. I. Hillerich, Robert L., 1927-. II. Title. III. Title: Textile worker.
HD8039.C6 F57 1987

FitzGerald, John D. The national debt and economic policy in the medium term / John D. FitzGerald. Dublin : Economic and Social Research Institute, c1986. 62 p. : ill. ; 21 cm. (Policy research series . no. 7) Bibliography: p. 49-50. ISBN 0-7070-0089-0 (pbk.) : LC Card 87-110464 DDC 336.3/4/09417 19
1. Debts, Public - Ireland. 2. Ireland - Economic policy. I. Series: Policy research series (Dublin, Dublin) , no. 7. II. Title.
HJ8630.A2 F58 1986

Fitzgerald, Merni Ingrassia. The Voice of America / Merni Ingrassia Fitzgerald. New York : Dodd, Mead, c1987. ix, 118 p. : ill., ports. ; 24 cm. Includes index. Describes the activities and purposes of Voice of America, the radio organization that broadcasts music, news, and special features to countries all over the world. ISBN 0-396-08937-2 : LC Card 87-5346 DDC 384.54/53 19
1. Voice of America (Organization) - Juvenile literature. 2. International broadcasting - United States - Juvenile literature. I. Title.
HE8698 .F5 1987

FitzRoy, Felix. Mitarbeiterbeteiligung und Mitbestimmung im Unternehmen /. Berlin , New York , 1987, c1986. ix, 351 p. : ISBN 3-11-010668-X LC Card 87-137953 DDC 658.3/152/0943 19
HD5660.G4 M53 1987

Fiur, Merton. New technology and public relations . New York, NY (310 Madison Ave., New York 10017) , c1986. xviii, 170 p. : LC Card 87-105313 DDC 659.2/028/5 19
HD59 .N44 1986

Five hundred people problems managers face and how to solve them. Quick, Thomas L. Quick solutions . New York , c1987. xi, 377 p. ; ISBN 0-471-85229-5 LC Card 87-10540 DDC 658.4/03 19
HD30.29 .Q53 1987

Five year macro-economic plan for Belize, 1985-1989. Belize. Ministry of Foreign Affairs and Economic Development. Belmopan [1984?] 48 p. ; LC Card 87-105155 DDC 338.97282 19
HC142 .B443 1984

Five year plan . Travancore and Cochin (India) Trivandrum , 1954. iii, 45 p. ; LC Card 83-238882
HJ2158.T7 T73 1954

FIVE-YEAR PLAN (RUSSIA) see **RUSSIA - ECONOMIC POLICY.**

Five year report to the legislature on fisheries, year ending 1983-84. Manitoba. Manitoba Natural Resources. [Winnipeg, Man.] [1984?] 57 p. : LC Card 87-164861 DDC 338.3/713/097127 19
HD9464.C22 M365 1984

FIW-Dokumentation, 0071-769X .
(Heft 6) US-Fusionsrichtlinien, 1984 /. Köln , c1985. 83 p. ; ISBN 3-452-20248-8 : LC Card 86-100251
HB41 .F63 Heft 6 KF1477

FIW-Schriftenreihe, 0429-9485 .
(H. 116) Wettbewerbsbeschränkung in der Nachfrage. Köln , 1985. vii, 145 p. ; ISBN 3-452-20479-0 ***NYPL [JLE 86-2774]***

(Heft 120) Neuorientierung des Wettbewerbsschutzes . Köln , 1986. viii, 231 p. ; ISBN 3-452-20666-1 : LC Card 87-138003
HB41 .F22 Heft 120 KK6456

Fixed income securities. The Handbook of fixed income securities /. Homewood, Ill. , 1987. xxx, 1376 p. : ISBN 0-87094-745-1 LC Card 86-50815 ***NYPL [JLE 87-939]***

Fixed income securities analysis. CFA readings in fixed income securities analysis /. Charlottesville, VA (P.O. Box 3668, Charlottesville, VA 22903) , c1985. v, 255 p. : ***NYPL [JLF 86-1994]***

FIXED POINT THEORY.
König, Heinz, 1927- Mathematische Wirtschaftstheorie . Königstein/Ts. , c1986. x, 239 p. : ISBN 3-445-02393-X : LC Card 86-188816
HB135 .K66 1986

Fixing farm trade . Paarlberg, Robert L. Cambridge, Mass. , c1988. xiv, 159 p. ; ISBN 0-88730-196-7 LC Card 87-24118 DDC 382/.41/0973 19
HD9006 .P27 1988

Fizikinių-techninių energetikos problemų institutas (Lietuvos TSR Mokslų akademija)
Razrabotka i issledovanie algoritmov dinamicheskoĭ klassifikatsii protsessov . Vil'nius , 1979. 93 p. : LC Card 82-150323
HD38 .S715 vyp. 37 T57.83

Shpilevskiĭ, Ė. Printsipy dinamicheskoĭ klassifikatsii stokhasticheskikh protsessov i sistem . Vil'nius , 1978. 138 p. ; LC Card 81-173567
HD38 .S715 vyp. 28 QA274

Sistema raspoznavaniia ritmogramm serdtsa . Vil'nius , 1980. 55 p. : LC Card 81-194159
HD38 .S715 vyp. 49 QP112.5.C3

TSifrovye metody i algoritmy obrabotki signalov . Vil'nius , 1986. 120 p. : LC Card 86-232937
HD38 .S715 vyp. 73 TK5102.5

Flächenhafte Verkehrsberuhigung . Fechtel, Hans-Walter. Bergisch Gladbach , 1986. 282 p. : LC Card 87-408360 DDC 388.4/0943 19
HE311.G3 F4 1986

FLAGLER, HENRY MORRISON, 1830-1913.
Akin, Edward N. Flagler, Rockefeller partner and Florida baron /. Kent, Ohio , c1988. xiii, 305 p. : ISBN 0-87338-348-6 (alk. paper) LC Card 87-2070 DDC 338/.04/0924 B 19
HC102.5.F55 A75 1988

Flagler, Rockefeller partner and Florida baron /. Akin, Edward N. Kent, Ohio , c1988. xiii, 305 p. : ISBN 0-87338-348-6 (alk. paper) LC Card 87-2070 DDC 338/.04/0924 B 19
HC102.5.F55 A75 1988

Flaherty, Richard E., 1944- Chasteen, Lanny G., 1942- Intermediate accounting /. New York , c1987. xxviii, 1328 p. : ISBN 0-394-35802-3 : LC Card 86-29865 DDC 657/.044 19
HF5635 .C474 1987

Flaig, Jürgen. Verteilungsschwankungen im Konjunkturverlauf : ein ökonometrisches Modell zur Erklärung der kurzfristigen Schwankungen der Verteilungsquoten in der Bundesrepublik Deutschland für den Zeitraum von 1966-1975 / Jürgen Flaig. Freiburg im Breisgau : R. Haufe, c1983. vi, 221 p. : ill. ; 21 cm. (Bd. 18 der Schriftenreihe des Instituts für Allgemeine Wirtschaftsforschung der Albert-Ludwigs-Universität Freiburg i. Br) Bibliography: p. 215-221. ISBN 3-448-01325-0 LC Card 83-155341
1. Income distribution - Germany, West. 2. Income - Germany, West. 3. Germany, West - Economic conditions. 4. Competition, International. I. Series: Schriftenreihe des Instituts für Allgemeine Wirtschaftsforschung der Albert-Ludwigs-Universität Freiburg i. Br. , Bd. 18. II. Title.
HC290.5.I5 F55 1983

Flajs, Andrej. Družbeno bogastvo SR Slovenije ob koncu 1980. leta / Andrej Flajs. Ljubljana : Zavod SR Slovenije za statistiko, 1986. 75 p. ; 28 cm. Bibliography: p. 75. ISBN 86-81141-04-X LC Card 86-216767
1. National income - Slovenia - Statistics. I. Zavod SR Slovenije za statistiko. II. Title.
HA1634.S58 F54 1986

Flame retardant chemicals in the U. S. Flame retardants chemicals market. New York, N.Y. , c1983. vii, 315 p. : LC Card 87-143411 DDC 381/.456289223/0973 19
HD9999.F553 U64 1983

Flame retardants chemicals market. New York, N.Y. : Frost & Sullivan, c1983. vii, 315 p. : ill. ; 29 cm. Spine title: Flame retardant chemicals in the U. S. "#A1117." "March 1983." LC Card 87-143411 DDC 381/.456289223/0973 19
1. Fireproofing agent industry - United States. 2. Market surveys - United States. I. Frost & Sullivan. II. Title: Flame retardant chemicals in the U. S.
HD9999.F553 U64 1983

Flamholtz, Diana Troik. Flamholtz, Eric. Principles of accounting /. New York , London , c1987. xli, 1159, [90] p. : ISBN 0-02-338210-4 LC Card 86-31086 DDC 657 19
HF5635 .F5645 1987

Flamholtz, Eric.
The Future directions of employee relations /. Los Angeles, Calif. , c1985. xiv, 418 p. : ISBN 0-89215-132-3 (pbk.) LC Card 86-622936 DDC 331/.0973 19
HD8072.5 .F87 1985

The Future directions of employee relations /. Los Angeles, Calif. , c1985. xiv, 418 p. ; ISBN 0-89215-132-3 ***NYPL [JLD 86-3596]***

The inner game of management : how to make the transition to a managerial role / Eric G. Flamholtz and Yvonne Randle. New York, NY : AMACOM, c1987. xiv, 225 p. ; 24 cm. Bibliography: p. 212-220. Includes index. ISBN 0-8144-5867-X LC Card 87-47705 DDC 658.4/09 19
1. Management. I. Randle, Yvonne. II. Title.
HD31 .F538 1987

Principles of accounting / Eric G. Flamholtz, Diana Troik Flamholtz, Michael A. Diamond. New York : Macmillan ; London : Collier Macmillan, c1987. xli, 1159, [90] p. : ill. ; 27 cm. Includes index. ISBN 0-02-338210-4 LC Card 86-31086 DDC 657 19
1. Accounting. I. Flamholtz, Diana Troik. II. Diamond, Michael A. III. Title.
HF5635 .F5645 1987

Flamm, Kenneth, 1951- Targeting the computer : government support and international competition / Kenneth Flamm. Washington, D.C. : Brookings Institution, c1987. xiii, 266 p. ; 24 cm. Includes index. ISBN 0-8157-2852-2 : LC Card 87-11706 DDC 338.4/7004/0973 19
1. Computer industry - Government policy - United States. 2. Computers - Research - Government policy - United States. 3. Computer industry - United States - Technological innovations. 4. Competition, International. I. Title.
HD9696.C63 U516466 1987

Flanagan, Robert J. Bach, George Leland, 1915- [Economics. Selections.] Macroeconomics . Englewood Cliffs, N.J. , c1987. xiii, 458 p. : ISBN 0-13-542887-4 (pbk.) LC Card 86-30264 DDC 339 19
HB172.5 .B33 1987

Flashner, Esther, 1925- Hoffman, Frank. Accounting fundamentals . New York , c1987. vi, 229 p. : ISBN 0-07-029210-8 (pbk.) : LC Card 86-27352 DDC 657 19
HF5635 .H678 1987

Flaskamp, Jürgen, 1958- Aufgaben und Wirkungen der Reichsbank in der Zeit des Dawes-Planes / Jürgen Flaskamp. Bergisch Gladbach : J. Eul, c1986. 210 p. : ill. ; 21 cm. Bibliography: p. 192-210. ISBN 3-89012-060-1 LC Card 87-108166 DDC 332.1/1/0943 19
1. Reichsbank (Germany) - History. 2. Germany - Economic policy - 1918-1933. 3. Germany - Economic conditions - 1918-1945. I. Title.
HG3054 .F58 1986

FLATS. see **APARTMENT HOUSES.**

Flaus, Pascal. Glück auf! . Paris [1986] 117 p. : ISBN 2-86738-115-0 : LC Card 86-178958
HD8039.M6152 F84 1986

FLAVORING ESSENCES INDUSTRY - EUROPE.
Flavors and fragrances market in Europe. New York, N.Y. , c1983. 5, 17, 8, 279 p. ; LC Card 87-141830 DDC 380.1/456645 19
HD9212.E852 F53 1983

Flavors and fragrances market in Europe. New York, N.Y. : Frost & Sullivan, c1983. 5, 17, 8, 279 p. ; 29 cm. Spine title: Flavors & fragrances market in Europe. "May 1983." "E621." LC Card 87-141830 DDC 380.1/456645 19
1. Flavoring essences industry - Europe. 2. Essences and essential oils industry - Europe. 3. Perfumes industry - Europe. 4. Market surveys - Europe. I. Frost & Sullivan. II. Title: Flavors & fragrances market in Europe.
HD9212.E852 F53 1983

Flavors & fragrances market in Europe. Flavors and fragrances market in Europe. New York, N.Y. , c1983. 5, 17, 8, 279 p. ; LC Card 87-141830 DDC 380.1/456645 19
HD9212.E852 F53 1983

The flea market entrepreneur /. Harmon, Charlotte. Babylon, N.Y. , c1987. 31 p. ; ISBN 0-87576-134-8 (pbk.) : LC Card 87-2223 DDC 658.8/4 19
HF5482 .H36 1987

Flea markets, antique fairs, and auctions of Britain. Manston, Peter B., 1951- [Flea markets, antique fairs, and auctions of Britain.] Manston's flea markets, antique fairs, and auctions of Britain . Sacramento, Calif., U. S.A. , New York, N.Y. , c1987. 277 p. : ISBN 0-931367-10-7 (pbk. : alk. paper) : LC Card 87-16221 DDC 381/.1 19
HF5482 .M3125 1987

Flea markets, antique fairs, and auctions of Germany. Manston, Peter B., 1951- [Flea markets, antique fairs, and auctions of Germany.] Manston's flea markets, antique fairs, and auctions of Germany . Sacramento, Calif., U. S.A. , New York, N.Y. , c1987. 297 p. : ISBN 0-931367-08-5 (pbk.) : LC Card 86-30908 DDC 381/.1 19
HF5482 .M3135 1987

Flea markets, antique shows, and auctions of France. Manston, Peter B., 1951- [Flea markets, antique shows, and auctions of France.] Manston's flea markets, antique shows, and auctions of France . Sacramento, Calif., U. S.A. , New York, N.Y. , c1987. 195 p. : ISBN 0-931367-06-9 (pbk.) : LC Card 86-30909 DDC 381/.1 19
HF5482 .M313 1987

FLEA MARKETS - FRANCE.
Manston, Peter B., 1951- [Flea markets, antique shows, and auctions of France.] Manston's flea markets, antique shows, and auctions of France . Sacramento, Calif., U. S.A. , New York, N.Y. , c1987. 195 p. : ISBN 0-931367-06-9 (pbk.) : LC Card 86-30909 DDC 381/.1 19
HF5482 .M313 1987

FLEA MARKETS - GERMANY (WEST)
Manston, Peter B., 1951- [Flea markets, antique fairs, and auctions of Germany.] Manston's flea markets, antique fairs, and auctions of Germany . Sacramento, Calif., U. S.A. , New York, N.Y. , c1987. 297 p. : ISBN

0-931367-08-5 (pbk.) : LC Card 86-30908 DDC 381/.1 19
HF5482 .M3135 1987

FLEA MARKETS - GREAT BRITAIN.
Manston, Peter B., 1951- [Flea markets, antique fairs, and auctions of Britain.] Manston's flea markets, antique fairs, and auctions of Britain . Sacramento, Calif., U. S.A. , New York, N.Y. , c1987. 277 p. : ISBN 0-931367-10-7 (pbk. : alk. paper) : LC Card 87-16221 DDC 381/.1 19
HF5482 .M3125 1987

FLEA MARKETS - MANAGEMENT.
Harmon, Charlotte. The flea market entrepreneur /. Babylon, N.Y. , c1987. 31 p. ; ISBN 0-87576-134-8 (pbk.) : LC Card 87-2223 DDC 658.8/4 19
HF5482 .H36 1987

Flecha, Agustín Oscar.
Crisis económica : deterioro del salario y de la calidad de vida / Agustín Oscar Flecha. [Asunción] : Asociaciones de Profesores de la Universidad Católica, [1987] 65 p. ; 22 cm. LC Card 87-404003 DDC 331.2/3/09892 19
1. Wages - Minimum wage - Paraguay - Congresses. 2. Cost and standard of living - Paraguay - Congresses. 3. Quality of life - Paraguay - Congresses. 4. Gross national product - Paraguay - Congresses. 5. Paraguay - Economic conditions - 1954- - Congresses. I. Title.
HD4920.P2 F57 1987

La economía nacional y el costo de vida / Agustín Oscar Flecha. Asunción, Paraguay : Universidad Católica "Nuestra Señora de la Asunción", 1986. 49 p. ; 27 cm. Cover title. Includes bibliographical references. LC Card 87-122881 DDC 330.9892/073 19
1. Cost and standard of living - Paraguay. 2. Wages - Minimum wage - Paraguay. 3. Paraguay - Economic conditions - 1954-. I. Title.
HD7018 .F57 1986

Flecha, Antonio Salum- see **Salum-Flecha, Antonio, 1927-**

Fleck, Florian H. Technologischer Wandel in Wirtschaft und Gesellschaft =. Freiburg, Schweiz , 1985. 316 p., [1] leaf of plates : ISBN 3-7278-0347-9 : LC Card 86-129382
HC79.T4 T436 1985

FLECK, FLORIAN H.
Technologischer Wandel in Wirtschaft und Gesellschaft =. Freiburg, Schweiz , 1985. 316 p., [1] leaf of plates : ISBN 3-7278-0347-9 : LC Card 86-129382
HC79.T4 T436 1985

Fleischer, Manfred. Organisationstheoretische Analyse von Marketing-Entscheidungsprozessen : Konzept und Ergebnisse einer explorativen empirischen Untersuchung / von Manfred Fleischer und Manfred Röber. Berlin : International Institute of Management, Wissenschaftszentrum Berlin, [1977] 93 p. : ill. ; 30 cm. (Discussion paper series / International Institute of Management, Wissenschaftszentrum Berlin . 77-63) Summary in English and German. Bibliography: p. 83-93. LC Card 85-111320
1. Marketing - Decision making. 2. Organization. I. Röber, Manfred, 1947-. II. International Institute of Management. III. Series: Discussion paper series (International Institute of Management) , 77-63. IV. Title.
HF5415.135 .F58 1977

Fleischer, Peter. Bestimmungsgründe von Zahlungsbilanz und Wechselkursen in der Bundesrepublik Deutschland / Peter Fleischer. Frankfurt am Main ; New York : P. Lang, c1986. iv, 181 p. : ill. ; 21 cm. (Europäische Hochschulschriften. Reihe V, Volks- und Betriebswirtschaft, 0531-7339 . Bd. 712 = vol. 712 = vol. 712) Bibliography: p. 167-181. ISBN 3-8204-9610-6 LC Card 86-232901
1. Balance of payments - Germany, West. 2. Foreign exchange problem - Germany, West. I. Series: Europäische Hochschulschriften. Reihe V, Volks- und Betriebswirtschaft , Bd. 712. II. Title.
HG3883.G3 F57 1986

Fleischman, Richard K. Conditions of life among the cotton workers of southeastern Lancashire, 1780-1850 / Richard K. Fleischman, Jr. New York : Garland Pub., 1985. 475 p. ; 24 cm. (British economic history) Thesis (doctoral)--State University of New York at Buffalo, 1973. Bibliography: p. 458-475. ISBN 0-8240-6681-2 (alk. paper) : LC Card 84-46001 DDC 305/.9677/094276 19
1. Textile workers - England - Lancashire - History. 2. Cotton textile industry - England - Lancashire - History. 3. Lancashire, Eng. - Social conditions. 4. Lancashire, Eng. - Economic conditions. I. Title. II. Series.
HD8039.T42 G74 1985 ***NYPL [JLE 86-3899]***

Fleisher, Belton M.
Principles of macroeconomics / Belton M. Fleisher, Edward J. Ray, Thomas J. Kniesner. Dubuque, Iowa : W.C. Brown, c1987. xix, 427 p. : ill. (some col.) ; 27 cm. Bibliography: p. 409-412. Includes index. ISBN 0-697-01035-X (pbk.) LC Card 86-72959 DDC 339 19
1. Macroeconomics. I. Ray, Edward J. (Edward John), 1944-. II. Kniesner, Thomas J. III. Title.
HB172.5 .F545 1987

Principles of microeconomics / Belton M. Fleisher, Edward J. Ray, Thomas J. Kniesner. Dubuque, Iowa : W.C. Brown Publishers, c1987. xxi, 458 p. : ill. (some col.) ; 26 cm. Bibliography: p. 439-443. Includes index. ISBN 0-697-01038-4 (pbk.) LC Card 86-72958 DDC 338.5 19
1. Microeconomics. I. Ray, Edward J. (Edward John), 1944-. II. Kniesner, Thomas J. III. Title.
HB172 .F54 1987

Fleissner, Peter K. Arbeiterklasse, gibt's die noch? /. Wien , c1985. 246 p. : ISBN 3-900351-46-5 LC Card 86-123225
HD8451 .A836 1985

Det fleksible køn . Markussen, Randi. [Copenhagen] , c1984. 163 p. ; ISBN 87-7445-159-6 : LC Card 84-187146
HD6169 .M37 1984

Flemig, Günter. Für einen anhaltenden Aufschwung . Kiel [1986] 29 p. : ISBN 3-925357-33-5 (Deut. Bibl.) : LC Card 86-234971
HB44 .K45 no. 123 HC286.7

Fleming, Maureen. Microcomputers and productivity : an analysis of microcomputer hardware and software usage in business / by Maureen Fleming and Jeffrey Silverstein. White Plains, NY : Knowledge Industry Publications, c1984. iii, 125 p. ; 28 cm. (K.I.P. studies) Includes bibliographical references and index. ISBN 0-86729-109-5 (pbk.) LC Card 84-164284 DDC 650/.028/54 19
1. Business - Data processing. 2. Microcomputers - Programming. I. Silverstein, Jeffrey. II. Title. III. Series.
HF5548.2 .F49 1984 ***NYPL [JLf 87-8]***

Fleming, William J.
Region vs nation : Cuyo in the crosscurrents of Argentine national development, 1861-1914 / by William J. Fleming. Tempe : Center for Latin American Studies, Arizona State University, c1986. 82 p. ; 24 cm. Bibliography: p. 73-82. ISBN 0-87918-066-8 LC Card 86-29919 DDC 330.982/64 19
1. Mendoza (Argentina : Province) - Economic conditions. 2. Cuyo (Argentina) - Economic conditions. I. Title. II. Title: Region versus nation.
HC177.M4 F55 1986

Regional development and transportation in Argentina : Mendoza and the Gran Oeste Argentino railroad, 1885-1914 / William J. Fleming. New York : Garland Pub., 1987. ii, 218 p. : ill., maps ; 24 cm. (South American and Latin American economic history) Bibliography: p. [205]-218. ISBN 0-8240-1360-3 (alk. paper) : LC Card 87-8401 DDC 385/.065/82 19
1. Gran Oeste Argentino (Railroad) - History. 2. Railroads - Argentina - Mendoza (Province) - History. 3. Railroads - Argentina - History. 4. Mendoza (Argentina : Province) - Economic conditions. I. Title. II. Series.
HE2910.G64 F54 1987

FLEMISH LANGUAGE. see **DUTCH LANGUAGE.**

Flentje, H. Edward. Kansas policy choices . Lawrence, Kan. , c1986. x, 210 p. : ISBN 0-7006-0302-6 (pbk.) LC Card 86-204211 DDC 338.9781 19
HC107.K2 K387 1986

Flere i yrke--færre barn? . Jensen, An-Magritt. Oslo , 1983. 59 p. : ISBN 82-537-2007-6 : LC Card 84-163552
HA1503 .A45 nr. 147 HQ762.N8

Flesher, Dale L. Gleim, Irvin N. CMA examination review /. Gainesville, Fla. , c1987. 2 v. : ISBN 0-917537-21-1 (pbk. : v. 1) LC Card 87-70930 DDC 658.1/511/076 19
HF5661 .G42 1987

Fleszar, Mieczysław. Geografia ekonomiczna świata / Mieczysław Fleszar. Wyd. 6. Warszawa : Państwowe Wydawn. Ekonomiczne, 1978. 519 p. : ill. ; 25 cm. Includes bibliographies and index. LC Card 81-212600
1. Geography, Economic. I. Title.
HC54 .F556 1978

Fletcher, Alan D. Fundamentals of advertising research / Alan D. Fletcher, Thomas A. Bowers. 3rd ed. Belmont, Calif. : Wadsworth Pub. Co., c1988. xiii, 322 p. : ill. ; 25 cm. Includes bibliographies and index. ISBN 0-534-08454-0 LC Card 87-23106 DDC 659.1/072 19
1. Advertising research. I. Bowers, Thomas A. II. Title.
HF5814 .F57 1988

Fletcher, Bill, 1957- Nelson, Kay Yarborough. Using Lotus Manuscript /. Berkeley, Calif. , c1987. xvii, 410 p. : ISBN 0-07-881003-5 (pbk.) : LC Card 87-401628 DDC 652/.5 19
HF5548.115 .N45 1987

Fletcher School of Law and Diplomacy. International Security Studies Program.
Selling the rope to hang capitalism? . Washington , 1987. viii, 246 p. ; ISBN 0-08-034959-5 : LC Card 86-30401 DDC 382/.091713/01717 19
HF1412 .S45 1987

Fleury, Maria Tereza Leme. A organização do trabalho na lavoura algodoeira paulista / Maria Tereza Leme Fleury. [São Paulo, Brasil : Centro de Estudos Rurais e Urbanos da Faculdade de Filosofia, Letras e Ciências Humanas da Universidade de São Paulo], 1984. 208 p. : ill. ; 23 cm. (Coleção Textos. 5) Bibliography: p. [195]-198. LC Card 85-145302 DDC 338.1/7351/098161 19
1. Cotton trade - Brazil - São Paulo (State). 2. Cotton picking - Brazil - São Paulo (State). 3. Land tenure - Brazil - São Paulo (State). I. Title.
HD9084.B62 S264 1984 ***NYPL [JLE 86-1740]***

FLEVOLAND (NETHERLANDS) - CENSUS.
Flevoland statistisch bezien . 's-Gravenhage , 1986. 50 p. : ISBN 90-357-0466-5 : LC Card 86-208188
HA1387.F48 F56 1986

FLEVOLAND (NETHERLANDS) - STATISTICS.
Flevoland statistisch bezien . 's-Gravenhage , 1986. 50 p. : ISBN 90-357-0466-5 : LC Card 86-208188
HA1387.F48 F56 1986

Flevoland statistisch bezien : uitgave ter gelegenheid van de instelling van de nieuwe provincie op 1 januari 1986 / Centraal Bureau voor de Statistiek, Hoofdafdeling Sociale Rekeningen. 's-Gravenhage : Staatsuitgeverij/CBS-publikaties, 1986. 50 p. : ill. ; 24 cm. ISBN 90-357-0466-5 : LC Card 86-208188
1. Flevoland (Netherlands) - Statistics. 2. Flevoland (Netherlands) - Census. I. Netherlands. Centraal Bureau voor de Statistiek. Hoofdafdeling Sociale Rekeningen.
HA1387.F48 F56 1986

Flexibilisierung der Arbeit und wirtschaftliche Instabilität . Gabriel, Jürgen. München , c1985. x, 316 p. ; ISBN 3-597-10540-8 LC Card 86-118217 DDC 331.25/72 19
HD5109 .G33 1985

Flexibilisierung der Beschäftigungsverhältnisse /. Gaugler, Eduard. Berlin , c1986. 85 p. ; ISBN 3-428-06070-9 LC Card 87-118519 DDC 331.25/72/0943 19
HD5109.2.G3 G38 1986

Flexibilisierung von Arbeitszeitstrukturen . Marr, Rainer, 1942- [Neubiberg? , 1986] 111 leaves : LC Card 87-409556
HD5109.2.G3 M37 1986

Flexibilität und Rigidität in der Preisbewegung . Gerster, Hans Joachim, 1946- Frankfurt am Main , New York , c1984. xii, 298, 69 p. : ISBN 3-8204-5109-9 LC Card 85-195018
HB235.G3 G48 1984

La Flexibilité du travail en Europe : une étude comparative des transformations du rapport salarial dans sept pays de 1973 à 1985 / sous la

direction de Robert Boyer. Paris : Editions La Découverte, 1986. 330 p. : ill. ; 24 cm. (Economie critique) Bibliography: p. 307-[319] ISBN 2-7071-1598-3 : LC Card 86-173845
1. Labor policy - Europe. 2. Wages - Europe. 3. Labor and laboring classes - Europe. 4. Industrial relations - Europe. 5. Industry and state - Europe. I. Boyer, Robert. II. Series.
HD8376.5 .F57 1986

Flexibility and jobs : myths and realities. Bruxelles : G. Köpke, [1985] 157, 5 p. : ill. ; 30 cm. "European Trade Union Institute"--Cover. Includes bibliographical references. LC Card 87-111122 DDC 331.25 19
1. Labor supply - Europe. 2. Wages - Europe. 3. Hours of labor - Europe. I. European Trade Union Institute.
HD5764.A6 F44 1985

Flexibility in the labour market : the current debate : a technical report. Paris : Organisation for Economic Co-operation and Development ; [Washington, D.C. : OECD Publications and Information Centre, distributor], 1986. 146 p. ; 23 cm. "Prepared by the Secretariat."--P. 3. Includes bibliographies. ISBN 92-64-12892-1 (pbk.) LC Card 87-123763 DDC 331.12 19
1. Labor supply. 2. Labor costs. 3. Labor mobility. 4. Manpower planning. 5. Quality of work life. I. Organisation for Economic Co-operation and Development. Secretariat.
HD5707 .F59 1986

Flexible Arbeitszeit gegen starre Sozialsysteme / Günter Buttler, Karl Oettle, Helmut Winterstein (Hrsg.). 1. Aufl. Baden-Baden : Nomos, 1986. 254 p. ; 23 cm. (Soziale Ordnungspolitik) Summaries in German and English. Includes bibliographies. CONTENTS. - Individuelle und soziale Ziele der Arbeitszeitgestaltung / Hans-Günther Schlotter -- Arbeitszeitflexibilisierung und Beschäftigung / Günter Buttler -- Arbeitszeitflexibilisierung in der Industrie / Friedrich Fürstenberg -- Arbeitszeitflexibilisierung im Dienstleistungssektor und im öffentlichen Dienst / Karl Oettle -- Arbeitszeitflexibilisierung aus Sicht der Gewerkschaften / Diana Winkler-Büttner -- Öffnungsklauseln für Arbeitszeitflexibilisierung in Gesetzen und Tarifverträgen / Wolfgang Gitter -- Arbeitszeitpräferenzen der Erwerbsbevölkerung / Margarete Landenberger -- Arbeitszeitflexibilisierung und Zeitverwendung in Arbeitnehmerhaushalten / Hermann Scherl -- Arbeitszeitflexibilisierung und Sozialversicherung / Helmut Winterstein -- Arbeitszeitflexibilisierung als ordnungspolitisches Problem / Philip Herder-Dorneich. ISBN 3-7890-1213-0 LC Card 87-101055 DDC 331.25/72/0943 19
1. Hours of labor, Flexible - Germany (West). I. Buttler, Günter. II. Oettle, Karl. III. Winterstein, Helmut. IV. Series.
HD5109.2.G3 F43 1986

Flexible Fertigung und Industriearbeit : die Einführung eines flexiblen Fertigungssystems in einem Maschinenbaubetrieb / Rainer Schultz-Wild ... [et al.]. Frankfurt Main ; New York : Campus, c1986. v, 577, iii p. : ill. ; 21 cm. (Forschungsberichte aus dem Institut für Sozialwissenschaftliche Forschung e.V., ISF München) Bibliography: p. 551-558. ISBN 3-593-33648-0 LC Card 86-197535
1. Hours of labor, Flexible - Germany (West) - Case studies. 2. Germany (West) - Manufactures - Case studies. 3. Labor supply - Germany (West) - Effect of technological innovations on - Case studies. 4. Machinery industry - Germany (West) - Case studies. I. Schultz-Wild, Rainer. II. Series: Forschungsberichte aus dem Institut für Sozialwissenschaftliche Forschung München.
HD5109.2.G3 F45 1986

FLEXIBLE HOURS OF LABOR. see **HOURS OF LABOR, FLEXIBLE.**

FLEXIBLE MANUFACTURING SYSTEMS.
Ranky, Paul G., 1951- Computer integrated manufacturing . Englewood Cliffs, N.J. , c1986. xiii, 513 p. : ISBN 0-13-165655-4 : LC Card 85-19199 DDC 670.42/7 19
TS155.6 .R36 1985 ***NYPL [JSE 87-587]***

FLEXIBLE MANUFACTURING SYSTEMS - JAPAN.
Chacko, George Kuttickal, 1930- Robotics/artificial intelligence/productivity . Princeton, N.J. , c1986. 2 v. in 1 (xvii, 335 p.) : ISBN 0-89433-228-7 LC Card 86-12177 DDC 658.5/14 19
HD9725 .C48 1986 ***NYPL [JLE 87-1001]***

FLEXIBLE MANUFACTURING SYSTEMS - UNITED STATES.
Chacko, George Kuttickal, 1930- Robotics/artificial intelligence/productivity . Princeton, N.J. , c1986. 2 v. in 1 (xvii, 335 p.) : ISBN 0-89433-228-7 LC Card 86-12177 DDC 658.5/14 19
HD9725 .C48 1986 ***NYPL [JLE 87-1001]***

Flexible rigidities . Dore, Ronald Philip. London , 1986. 278 p. ; ISBN 0-485-11269-8 LC Card 87-672689
HC462.9 .D65 1986

FLEXIBLE WORK HOURS. see **HOURS OF LABOR, FLEXIBLE.**

FLEXITIME. see **HOURS OF LABOR, FLEXIBLE.**

FLEXTIME. see **HOURS OF LABOR, FLEXIBLE.**

FLICK, FRIEDRICH, 1883-
Ohlsen, Manfred. Milliarden für den Geier, oder, Der Fall des Friedrich Flick /. Berlin , 1985. 458 p. : LC Card 86-149056
HC282.5.F54 O35 1985

FLICK, FRIEDRICH KARL, 1927-
Feyerabend, Joachim. Die leisen Milliarden . Düsseldorf , 1984. 187 p. : ISBN 3-430-12729-7 LC Card 84-176048
HC282.5.F54 F49 1984

Fliess, Hildegard. Pospelowa, Galina. Schlachttier- und Fleischproduktion in Osteuropa . Giessen , Berlin , 1981. 144 p. ; ISBN 3-428-04944-6 LC Card 82-167577
HD9425.B92 P67 1981

FLIGHT ATTENDANTS - UNITED STATES - HISTORY.
McLaughlin, Helen E. Walking on air . Denver, Colo. , c1986. vi, 210 p. : ISBN 0-930161-04-1 (pbk.) LC Card 87-115599 DDC 387.7/42/0973 19
HD8039.A432 U66 1986

FLIGHT CREWS - UNITED STATES.
Komons, Nick A. The third man . Washington, D.C. , 1987. iv, 162 p. : LC Card 87-21267 DDC 363.1/2475 19
HD8039.A42 U54 1987

The flight of international capital . Brown, Brendan, 1951- London , New York , c1987. xiv, 447 p. : ISBN 0-7099-5036-5 : LC Card 87-8988 DDC 332.4/5 19
HG3891 .B76 1987

Flight of the Iolar . Share, Bernard. Goldenbridge, Dublin , Dallas [Texas] , c1986. xii, 306 p. : ISBN 0-7171-1457-0 LC Card 86-223299
HE9846.A47 S42 1986

Flinn, Michael W., 1917- The history of the British coal industry. Oxford [Oxfordshire] , New York , c1983- v. : ISBN 0-19-828283-4 (v. 2) : LC Card 83-4194 DDC 338.2/724/0941 19
HD9551.5 .F58 1983 ***NYPL [JLL 84-138]***

FLINT (MICH.) - ECONOMIC CONDITIONS.
Edsforth, Ronald, 1948- Class conflict and cultural consensus . New Brunswick, N.J. , c1987. xvi, 294 p. ; ISBN 0-8135-1184-4 LC Card 86-7955 DDC 330.9774/37 19
HC108.F55 E37 1987 ***NYPL [JLE 87-978]***

FLINT (MICH.) - SOCIAL CONDITIONS.
Edsforth, Ronald, 1948- Class conflict and cultural consensus . New Brunswick, N.J. , c1987. xvi, 294 p. ; ISBN 0-8135-1184-4 LC Card 86-7955 DDC 330.9774/37 19
HC108.F55 E37 1987 ***NYPL [JLE 87-978]***

Floating exchange rates . MacDonald, Ronald. London , Boston , 1987. p. cm. ISBN 0-04-338134-0 (alk. paper) LC Card 87-9259 DDC 332.4/562 19
HG3852 .M33 1987

Floating exchange rates and the state of world trade payments / edited by David Bigman, Teizo Taya. Cambridge, Mass. : Ballinger, 1984. xxvi, 309 p. ; 23 cm. Includes bibliographical references and indexes. ISBN 0-88410-998-4 (pbk.) LC Card 84-2905 DDC 332.4/562 19
1. Foreign exchange problem - Addresses, essays, lectures. 2. International finance - Addresses, essays, lectures. 3. International economic relations - Addresses, essays, lectures. 4. Balance of payments - Addresses, essays, lectures. I. Bigman, David. II. Taya, Teizo.
HG3852 .F56 1984 ***NYPL [JLD 86-2709]***

Floating exchange rates in developing countries : experience with auction and interbank markets / by Peter J. Quirk ... [et al.]. Washington, D.C. : International Monetary Fund, 1987. v, 43 p. : col. ill. ; 28 cm. (Occasional paper, 0251-6365 . no. 53) ISBN 0-939934-89-2 (pbk.) : LC Card 87-3025 DDC 332.4/56/091724 19
1. Foreign exchange problem - Developing countries. I. Quirk, Peter J. II. Series: Occasional paper (International Monetary Fund) , no. 53.
HG3877 .F58 1987

Flohr, Bernd. Fungibilität und Elastizität von Personal / Bernd Flohr. Göttingen : Vandenhoeck & Ruprecht, c1984. xvi, 439 p. ; 24 cm. (Schriftenreihe des Seminars für Allgemeine Betriebswirtschaftslehre der Universität Hamburg . Bd. 27) Bibliography: p. [416]-439. ISBN 3-525-12665-4 LC Card 85-125026
1. Personnel management. 2. Organizational behavior. I. Title. II. Series.
HF5549 .F584 1984

FLOOD CONTROL - GOVERNMENT POLICY - GREAT BRITAIN.
Penning-Rowsell, Edmund. Floods and drainage . London , Boston , 1986. xx, 199 p. : ISBN 0-04-627001-9 (alk. paper) : LC Card 85-13383 DDC 363.3/4936/0941 19
HD1676.G7 P46 1985 ***NYPL [JLE 86-3996]***

FLOOD CONTROL - ITALY - CREMONA REGION - HISTORY.
Bellabarba, Marco. Seriolanti e arzenisti . Cremona , 1986- v. <1 > : LC Card 86-167180
HD1676.I82 C743 1986

FLOOD CONTROL - ITALY - PO RIVER PLAIN - HISTORY.
Bellabarba, Marco. Seriolanti e arzenisti . Cremona , 1986- v. <1 > : LC Card 86-167180
HD1676.I82 C743 1986

FLOOD DAMAGE - ECONOMIC ASPECTS - GREAT BRITAIN.
Parker, Dennis J. Urban flood protection benefits . Aldershot, Hants, England , Brookfield, Vt., U. S.A. , c1987. xvii, 284 p. : ISBN 0-291-39707-7 LC Card 87-147842 DDC 363.3/49372 19
HD1676.G7 P37 1987

FLOOD DAMAGE PREVENTION - GREAT BRITAIN - COST EFFECTIVENESS.
Parker, Dennis J. Urban flood protection benefits . Aldershot, Hants, England , Brookfield, Vt., U. S.A. , c1987. xvii, 284 p. : ISBN 0-291-39707-7 LC Card 87-147842 DDC 363.3/49372 19
HD1676.G7 P37 1987

FLOOD PREVENTION. see **FLOOD CONTROL.**

FLOOD PROOFING. see **FLOOD DAMAGE PREVENTION.**

FLOOD PROTECTION. see **FLOOD DAMAGE PREVENTION.**

Floods and drainage . Penning-Rowsell, Edmund. London , Boston , 1986. xx, 199 p. : ISBN 0-04-627001-9 (alk. paper) : LC Card 85-13383 DDC 363.3/4936/0941 19
HD1676.G7 P46 1985 ***NYPL [JLE 86-3996]***

FLOODS - PREVENTION. see **FLOOD CONTROL.**

FLOOR TRADERS (FINANCE) - NEW YORK (N.Y.) - BIOGRAPHY.
Goldstone, Nancy Bazelon. Trading up /. New York , c1988. viii, 262 p. ; ISBN 0-525-24621-5 : LC Card 87-19975 DDC 332.4/5/0924 B 19
HG3853 .G65 1988

Florath, Walter, 1925- Der Typ ist richtig : Intensivierung, Alltag und Zukunft / Walter Florath. Berlin : Neues Leben, c1986. 151 p. : ill. ; 22 cm. (NL konkret. 68) ISBN 3-355-00005-1 LC Card 86-230122
1. Germany, East - Economic policy. 2. Germany, East - Economic conditions. 3. Socialism - Germany (East). I. Title.
HC290.78 .F57 1986

"Floréal," 0293-7476.
Luxardo, Hervé. Rase campagne . Paris , c1984. 253 p. : ISBN 2-7007-0376-6 : LC Card 85-101431
HD1536.F8 L893 1984

Florence Heller Graduate School for Advanced Studies in Social Welfare. Center for Social Change Practice and Theory. The Future of work . Cambridge, Mass. , c1987. xv, 126 p. : ISBN 0-87047-030-2 : LC Card 86-33894 DDC 306/.36 19
HD4904 .F87 1987

FLORENCE (ITALY) - HISTORY - 1421-1737.
Begert, Roland. Elemente einer politischen Ökonomie im Werke Machiavellis /. Bern , c1983. 224 p. : ISBN 3-258-03136-3 LC Card 83-204993
HB109.M3 B44 1983

Conti, Elio. L'imposta diretta a Firenze nel Quattrocento (1427-1494) /. Roma , 1984. 406 p. ; LC Card 86-171245
HJ9500.F562 C65 1984

Florent´ev, L. ÎA. (Leonid ÎAkovlevich)
Prodovol´stvennaîa programma SSSR . Moskva , 1986. 285 p. ; LC Card 87-110478 DDC 338.1/9/47 19
HD9015.S652 P743 1986

Flores Clair, Eduardo. Estadísticas mineras de México en el siglo XIX / Eduardo Flores Clair, Cuauhtémoc Velasco Avila, Elia Ramírez Bautista. 1a ed. México, D.F. : Dirección de Estudios Históricos, Instituto Nacional de Antropología e Historia, 1985. 181 p. ; 27 cm. (Recopilación de estadísticas económicas del siglo XIX en México . v. 2) Cuaderno de trabajo / Instituto Nacional de Antropología e Historia ; 47 Chiefly tables. Includes bibliographies. LC Card 87-401718 DDC 338.2/0972 19
1. Mineral industries - Mexico - Statistics - History - 19th century. I. Velasco Avila, Cuauhtémoc. II. Ramírez Bautista, Elia. III. Series. IV. Series: Cuaderno de trabajo (Instituto Nacional de Antropología e Historia (Mexico). Dirección de Estudios Históricos) , no. 47. V. Title.
HD9506.M62 F57 1985

Flores Domínguez, David. Queremos hechos / David Flores Domínguez. México, D.F. : Publicaciones Progresa, c1982. 154 p. ; 21 cm. Cover title: Don Miguel, queremos hechos. ISBN 968-7163-01-1 LC Card 83-142817
1. Mexico - Economic policy 1970-. 2. Mexico - Social policy. 3. Mexico - Executive departments. 4. Administrative agencies - Mexico. I. Title. II. Title: Don Miguel, queremos hechos.
HC135 .F54 1982

Flores, Edmundo, 1918- Historias de Edmundo Flores. 1a ed. México : Martín Casillas Editores, 1983-<c1986 > v. <1-2 > : ill., ports. ; 21 cm. (v. 1: Serie La Invención) Vol. 2- cover title. Vol. 2- published by Editorial Posada. Includes indexes. CONTENTS. - [1]. Autobiografía, 1919-1950 -- v. 2. Antesalas del poder : autobiografía, 1950-1973 ISBN 968-471-052-6 (v. 1) LC Card 83-199689
1. Flores, Edmundo, 1918-. 2. Economists - Mexico - Biography. I. Series: Serie La Invención. II. Title.
HB123.M43 F564 1983

FLORES, EDMUNDO, 1918-
Flores, Edmundo, 1918- Historias de Edmundo Flores. México , 1983-<c1986. v. <1-2 > : ISBN 968-471-052-6 (v. 1) LC Card 83-199689
HB123.M43 F564 1983

Flores Rodas, José G. (José Guillermo)
Diagnóstico del sector industrial forestal / José G. Flores Rodas. 1a ed. San José, Costa Rica : Editorial Universidad Estatal a Distancia, 1985. 116 p. : ill. ; 27 cm. "Ministerio de Agricultura y Ganadería--MAG; Dirección General Forestal--MAG; Universidad Estatal a Distancia, Programa de Educación Ambiental; Fundación de Parques Nacionales; Fundación Tinker, Nueva York, E.U.A." Includes bibliographies. ISBN 997-7642-33-8 LC Card 86-218084
1. Forest products industry - Costa Rica. 2. Forest policy - Costa Rica. 3. Forests and forestry - Costa Rica. I. Title.
HD9764.C82 F56 1985

Flórez Nieto, Carmen Elisa.
The existence of a Latin American mortality pattern : an analysis of the Colombian and Venezuelan cases / por Carmen Elisa Florez, Argemiro Morales. Bogotá, Colombia : Universidad de los Andes, Facultad de Economía, Centro de Estudios sobre Desarrollo Económico, 1985. 153 p. : ill. ; 28 cm. (Documento CEDE . 081) Bibliography: p. 152-153. LC Card 87-145922
1. Mortality - Colombia. 2. Mortality - Venezuela. 3. Colombia - Statistics, Vital. 4. Venezuela - Statistics, Vital. I. Morales, Argemiro. II. Universidad de los Andes (Bogotá, Colombia). Centro de Estudios sobre Desarrollo Económico. III. Series: Documento (Universidad de los Andes (Bogotá, Colombia). Centro de Estudios sobre Desarrollo Económico) , 081. IV. Title.
HB1397 .F56 1985

Seminario Taller sobre el XV Censo Nacional de Población y IV de Vivienda, 1985 (1986 : Girardot, Colombia) Seminario Taller sobre el XV Censo Nacional de Población y IV de Vivienda, 1985 /. Girardot [Colombia] , 1986. 327 p. : ISBN 958-608-038-2 LC Card 87-403863 DDC 304.6/0723 19
HA1011.5 1985b

Flórez Nohesell, Miguel. Los puertos del Perú / Miguel Flórez Nohesell. Lima, Perú : Instituto de Estudios Histórico-Marítimos del Perú, 1986. 947 p. : ill. (some col.) ; 25 cm. (Historia marítima del Perú. Serie Monografías . t. 1) Bibliography: p. 911-912. Includes indexes. LC Card 86-210075
1. Harbors - Peru. I. Title. II. Series.
HE555.P5 F58 1986

Florida Advisory Council on Intergovernmental Relations. Sapolsky, Joann. Catalogue of state shared revenue sources distributed between 1973-1986. Tallahassee, Fla. (House Office Bldg., Tallahassee 32301) [1986] v, 76 leaves : LC Card 86-623224 DDC 336.1/85/09759 19
HJ375 .S26 1986

Florida and Mexico competition for the winter fresh vegetable market / Katharine C. Buckley ... [et al.]. Washington, D.C. : U. S. Dept. of Agriculture, Economic Research Service : Available from Supt. of Docs., U. S. G.P.O., [1986] v, 101 p. : ill. ; 28 cm. (Agricultural economic report . no. 556) Cover title. Bibliography: p. 81. LC Card 86-602381 DDC 338.1 s 381/.415/0973 19
1. Vegetable trade - Florida. 2. Vegetable trade - Mexico. 3. Vegetable trade - United States. 4. Competition - Florida. 5. Competition - Mexico. 6. Competition - United States. I. Buckley, Katharine C. II. United States. Dept. of Agriculture. Economic Research Service. III. Series.
HD1751 .A91854 no. 556 HD9225.U53F5

Florida Association of Life Underwriters. Florida life and health study manual . [Chicago] , c1987. x, 358 p. : ISBN 0-88462-727-6 (pbk.) LC Card 87-17254 DDC 368.3/009759 19
HG8961.F6 F56 1987

Florida. Bureau of Traffic Engineering. Speed zoning for highways, roads & streets in Florida . Tallahassee, Fla. [1985] i, 43, [1] p. : LC Card 86-621262 DDC 388.3/144/09759 19
HE5620.S6 S65 1985

Florida citrus production trends 1986-87 through 1995-96. Fairchild, Gary F. Gainesville, Fla. [1985] iv, 35 p. : LC Card 86-622647 DDC 338.1/7435/09759 19
HD9259.C53 U553 1985

Florida. Community Affairs, Dept. of. see **Florida. Dept. of Community Affairs.**

Florida. Dept. of Community Affairs. Division of Local Resource Management. Tax incentives for community revitalization in Florida /. Tallahassee, Fla. [1983] 45 p. ; LC Card 86-623222 DDC 343.75906/6 347.590366 19
HJ4655.F64 T39 1983

Florida. Dept. of Insurance. Florida life and health study manual . [Chicago] , c1987. x, 358 p. : ISBN 0-88462-727-6 (pbk.) LC Card 87-17254 DDC 368.3/009759 19
HG8961.F6 F56 1987

Florida. Division of Real Estate. Real estate appraisal, finance, investment, and business management . [Tallahassee] , c1986. ix, 441, iv, 86 p. : LC Card 87-159867 DDC 333.33 19
HD1375 .R375 1986

FLORIDA - ECONOMIC CONDITIONS.
Bell, Frederick W. An economic analysis of the importance of saltwater beaches in Florida /. Gainesville, FL [1986] xi, 166 p. : LC Card 86-622310 DDC 333.91/7/09759 19
HD266.F6 B45 1986

Robbins, Bradley. Economic development in a conscious state . Tallahassee, Fla. [1984] viii, 41, [5] p. : LC Card 86-621090 DDC 338.9759 19
HC107.F6 R63 1984

FLORIDA - ECONOMIC POLICY.
Robbins, Bradley. Economic development in a conscious state . Tallahassee, Fla. [1984] viii, 41, [5] p. : LC Card 86-621090 DDC 338.9759 19
HC107.F6 R63 1984

Florida. Governor's Energy Office. Llewellyn, Ralph A. Patterns of energy consumption in Florida, 1970-1983 . Tallahassee, Fla. [1985] xiv, 147 p. : LC Card 86-622312 DDC 333.79/13/09759 19
HD9502.U53 F5846 1985

FLORIDA - HISTORY - 1865-
Akin, Edward N. Flagler, Rockefeller partner and Florida baron /. Kent, Ohio , c1988. xiii, 305 p. : ISBN 0-87338-348-6 (alk. paper) LC Card 87-2070 DDC 338/.04/0924 B 19
HC102.5.F55 A75 1988

Florida. House of Representatives. see **Florida. Legislature. House of Representatives.**

Florida index of retail activity /. Lacrosse, James. [Tallahassee] [1983] [22] leaves : LC Card 86-621941 DDC 381/.1/09759021 19
HF5429.4.F6 L33 1983

FLORIDA - INDUSTRIES - ENERGY CONSUMPTION.
Llewellyn, Ralph A. Patterns of energy consumption in Florida, 1970-1983 . Tallahassee, Fla. [1985] xiv, 147 p. : LC Card 86-622312 DDC 333.79/13/09759 19
HD9502.U53 F5846 1985

Florida Institute of Certified Public Accountants. Committees & consultation . Tallahassee, Fla. (325 W. College Ave., Tallahassee 32314) , c1986. 76 p. : LC Card 87-109390 DDC 657/.025/759 19
HF5616.U6 F63 1986

FLORIDA INSTITUTE OF CERTIFIED PUBLIC ACCOUNTANTS - DIRECTORIES.
Committees & consultation . Tallahassee, Fla. (325 W. College Ave., Tallahassee 32314) , c1986. 76 p. : LC Card 87-109390 DDC 657/.025/759 19
HF5616.U6 F63 1986

Florida International University.
Foreign investment, debt, and economic growth in Latin America /. New York , 1988. xix, 250 p. : ISBN 0-312-00936-4 : LC Card 87-18808 DDC 332.6/73/098 19
HG5160.5.A3 F675 1988

Florida International University. Internaional Banking Center. Eurodollars and international banking /. London [Miami] , 1985. xiii, 226 p. : ISBN 0-333-36553-4
NYPL [JLD 85-3068]

Florida. Legislature. Assembly. see **Florida. Legislature. House of Representatives.**

Florida. Legislature. House of Representatives. (Old Catalog form: Florida. House of Representatives.)

Florida. Legislature. House of Representatives. Select Committee on Growth Management. Robbins, Bradley. Economic development in a conscious state . Tallahassee, Fla. [1984] viii, 41, [5] p. : LC Card 86-621090 DDC 338.9759 19
HC107.F6 R63 1984

The Saddlebrook papers . [Fort Lauderdale] [Tallahassee] [1985] v leaves, 177 p. : LC Card 86-621089 DDC 338.9759 19
HC107.F63 E547 1985

Florida. Legislature. Joint Legislative Management Committee. Division of Economic and Demographic Research. Lacrosse, James. Florida index of retail activity /. [Tallahassee] [1983] [22] leaves : LC Card 86-621941 DDC 381/.1/09759021 19
HF5429.4.F6 L33 1983

Florida. Legislature. Senate. Finance, Tax & Claims Committee. The homestead exemption : the fiscal impact of potential changes / prepared by Senate Committee on Finance, Taxation, and Claims ; Robert Crawford, chairman. [Tallahassee, Fla.] : The Committee, [1986] ii leaves, 104 p. ; 28 cm. "April 1, 1986." LC Card 86-623229 DDC 336.22 19

1. Real property tax - Florida. I. Title.
HJ4204.A27 F57 1986

Florida life and health insurance. Florida life and health study manual . [Chicago] , c1987. x, 358 p. : ISBN 0-88462-727-6 (pbk.) LC Card 87-17254 DDC 368.3/009759 19
HG8961.F6 F56 1987

Florida life and health study manual : a license preparation manual with questions and answers / prepared by the Florida Association of Life Underwriters ; approved by the Florida Department of Insurance ; edited by Marshall W. Reavis.3rd ed. [Chicago] : Longman Financial Services Pub., c1987. x, 358 p. : ill. ; 28 cm. Rev. ed. of: Florida life and health insurance. Includes index. ISBN 0-88462-727-6 (pbk.) LC Card 87-17254 DDC 368.3/009759 19
1. Insurance, Life - Florida - Examinations, questions, etc. 2. Insurance, Health - Florida - Examinations, questions, etc. 3. Insurance, Life - Law and legislation - Florida - Examinations, questions, etc. 4. Insurance, Health - Law and legislations - Florida - Examinations, questions, etc. I. Reavis, Marshall W. II. Florida Association of Life Underwriters. III. Florida. Dept. of Insurance. IV. Florida life and health insurance.
HG8961.F6 F56 1987

FLORIDA - OCCUPATIONS.
Fencl, George. The central Florida career guide /. Altamonte Springs, FL. , c1987. 56, 48 p. : ISBN 0-942827-00-7 (pbk.) : LC Card 87-402073 DDC 650.1/4/09759 19
HF5382.75.U62 F64 1987

Florida. Public Facilities Financing Commission. Florida 2000, meeting the challenge : planning and financing public facilities / Governor Bob Graham's Public Facilities Financing Commission. [Tallahassee] : The Commission, [1984] v, 44 p. ; 28 cm. Cover title. "April 12, 1984." LC Card 86-623234 DDC 363/.09759 19
1. Infrastructure (Economics) - Florida - Planning. 2. Municipal services - Florida - Planning. I. Title.
HC107.F63 C345 1984

Florida. Real Estate Commission. Real estate appraisal, finance, investment, and business management . [Tallahassee] , c1986. ix, 441, iv, 86 p. : LC Card 87-159867 DDC 333.33 19
HD1375 .R375 1986

Florida Sea Grant College. Bell, Frederick W. An economic analysis of the importance of saltwater beaches in Florida /. Gainesville, FL [1986] xi, 166 p. : LC Card 86-622310 DDC 333.91/7/09759 19
HD266.F6 B45 1986

Florida. State Dept. of Community Affairs. see **Florida. Dept. of Community Affairs.**

Florida 2000, meeting the challenge . Florida. Public Facilities Financing Commission. [Tallahassee] [1984] v, 44 p. ; LC Card 86-623234 DDC 363/.09759 19
HC107.F63 C345 1984

Florizoone, Patrick, 1958- De groenen : ideeën, bewegingen en partijen / Patrick Florizoone. [Deurne] : Kluwer, c1985. x, 194 p. : ill. ; 21 cm. (Politieke bibliotheek) Bibliography: p. 177-187. Includes index. ISBN 90-6716-272-8 LC Card 86-148321
1. Environmental policy - Netherlands. 2. Ecology - Netherlands. 3. Environmental policy - Europe. I. Title. II. Series.
HC329.5.E5 F56 1985

La flotación cambiaría . Protasi, Juan Carlos. Montevideo, Uruguay [1985] 33 leaves : LC Card 86-160085
HG3940 .P76 1985

FLOUR AND FEED TRADE - AUSTRIA.
Aistleitner, Josef. Formen und Auswirkungen des bäuerlichen Nebenerwerbs . [Innsbruck] , 1986. 174 p. : LC Card 87-408342 DDC 338.1/6 19
HD1935 .A66 1986

Landwirtschaftliche Produktionsalternativen am Beispiel Ethanol, Ölsaaten und Eiweissfutterpflanzen /. Wien , 1985. 141 p. : LC Card 86-108149 DDC 338.1/09436 19
HD1935 .L33 1985

FLOUR AND FEED TRADE - BRAZIL.
Campos Netto, José Candido de, 1880-1963. O cavvaliere Aristides Germani /. [Caxias do Sul, Brazil] [Porto Alegre] , 1978. 111 p. : LC Card 79-121861
HD9056.B62 C35 1978 ***NYPL [JLD 81-342]***

FLOUR AND FEED TRADE - DEVELOPING COUNTRIES - FORECASTING.
Sarma, J. S. Cereal feed use in the Third World . Washington, D.C. , c1986. 68 p. : ISBN 0-89629-058-1 (pbk.) LC Card 86-27355 DDC 338.1/7325/091724 19
HD9052.D44 S27 1986

FLOUR AND FEED TRADE - GREAT BRITAIN.
Great Britain. Price Commission. Prices, costs, and margins in the production and distribution of compound feeding stuff for cattle, pigs, and poultry . London [1978] v, 35 p. ; ISBN 0-10-233878-7 (pbk.) LC Card 85-146987
HD9056.G72 G76 1978

FLOUR AND FEED TRADE - MEXICO.
Elementos para la programación del desarrollo de la industria de aceites y pastas vegetales en México. México , 1985. 306 p. : ISBN 968-665-105-5 LC Card 86-232449
HD9490.M62 E44 1985

FLOUR AND FEED TRADE - NETHERLANDS - HISTORY.
Bläsing, J. F. E. (Joachim F. E.), 1940- Op het spoor van de Körver . Leiden , 1986. xvi, 396 p. : ISBN 90-247-8065-9 : LC Card 86-214829
HD9052.N44 H453 1986

FLOUR-MILLS - BRAZIL - MANAGEMENT.
Campos Netto, José Candido de, 1880-1963. O cavvaliere Aristides Germani /. [Caxias do Sul, Brazil] [Porto Alegre] , 1978. 111 p. : LC Card 79-121861
HD9056.B62 C35 1978 ***NYPL [JLD 81-342]***

FLOW OF FUNDS.
Cohen, Jacob, 1918- The flow of funds in theory and practice . Dordrecht , Boston , 1987. viii, 341 p. : ISBN 90-247-3601-3 LC Card 87-21316 DDC 332.4 19
HG221 .C678 1987

Flow of funds in the Sudan /. Salih, Mohamed Abdel Aal. Khartoum, Sudan [1984] 38 leaves ; LC Card 84-980837 DDC 339.2/6/09624 19
HC835 .S25 1984

The flow of funds in theory and practice . Cohen, Jacob, 1918- Dordrecht , Boston , 1987. viii, 341 p. : ISBN 90-247-3601-3 LC Card 87-21316 DDC 332.4 19
HG221 .C678 1987

FLOW OF FUNDS - SPAIN - ACCOUNTING.
Cuentas financieras de la economía española, 1972-1982 /. [Madrid] , 1984. 157 p. ; ISBN 84-500-9729-0 LC Card 86-205358
HC390.F55 C84 1984

FLOW OF FUNDS - SUDAN.
Salih, Mohamed Abdel Aal. Flow of funds in the Sudan /. Khartoum, Sudan [1984] 38 leaves ; LC Card 84-980837 DDC 339.2/6/09624 19
HC835 .S25 1984

Floyd, Charles F. Real estate principles / Charles F. Floyd. 2nd ed., rev. Chicago : Longman Financial Services Pub., c1987. xxix, 511 p. : ill. ; 25 cm. Includes bibliographies and index. ISBN 0-88462-672-5 LC Card 87-3391 DDC 333.33/0973 19
1. Real estate business - United States. I. Title.
HD255 .F57 1987

Floyd Wickman's successful strategies for real estate agents. Wickman, Floyd. Successful strategies for real estate agents . Dubuque, Iowa , c1987. xii, 226 p. ; ISBN 0-8403-4185-7 (pbk.) : LC Card 86-82782 DDC 333.33/068/8 19
HD1382 .W53 1987

Flückiger, Hans. Siedlungsstruktur : Voraussetzung und Ergebnis regionaler Entwicklung / Hans Flückiger, Christoph Muggli. Bern : P. Haupt, c1985. 118 p. : ill. ; 23 cm. (Publikationen des Schweizerischen Nationalfonds aus den nationalen Forschungsprogrammen . Bd. 34, 2) "Arbeit, die im Rahmen des Nationalen Forschungsprogrammes 'Regionalprobleme in der Schweiz' des Schweizerischen Nationalfonds zur Förderung der wissenschaftlichen Forschung durchgeführt worden ist (Projekt-Nr. 4.079-4.77.05)"--T.p. verso. Bibliography: p. 105-118. ISBN 3-258-03529-6 : LC Card 86-134805
1. Human settlements - Switzerland. 2. Regional planning - Switzerland. 3. Housing - Switzerland. 4. Land use - Switzerland. 5. Switzerland - Industries - Location. I. Muggli, Christoph. II. Title. III. Series.
HN603.5 .F58 1985 ***NYPL [JLE 86-3789]***

Fluder, Robert. Oberhänsli, Urs. Altersvorsorge, Kapitalschwemme oder Kapitalmangel? . Bern , c1986. xii, 222 p. : ISBN 3-258-03578-4 : LC Card 86-149614
HD7105.35.S9 O24 1986

Fluxo energético estadual, 1983 / Companhia Energética de Minas Gerais, Conselho Estadual de Energia, Secretaria de Estado de Minas e Energia. [Belo Horizonte, Brazil] : CEMIG, 1985. 105 p. : ill. (some col.) ; 28 cm. Cover title. At head of title: Governo do Estado de Minas Gerais. LC Card 87-404947 DDC 333.79/0981/51 19
1. Energy industries - Brazil - Minas Gerais. 2. Power resources - Brazil - Minas Gerais. 3. Energy consumption - Brazil - Minas Gerais. I. Companhia Energética de Minas Gerais.
HD9502.B73 M5646 1985

Fly there for less . Martin, Bob, 1939- Kissimmee, Fla. , c1988. 136 p. ; ISBN 0-937281-01-8 (pbk.) : LC Card 87-16166 DDC 387.7/12 19
HE9783.5 .M37 1988

Flying high . Barrett, Sean D. Aldershot , Brookfield, USA , c1987. 96 p. ; ISBN 0-566-05541-4 (pbk.) : LC Card 87-11992 DDC 387.7/1 19
HE9783.3.E85 B37 1987

The flying kangaroo, an endangered species? . Findlay, Christopher C. (Christopher Charles) Sydney , Boston , 1985. xii, 121 p. : ISBN 0-86861-406-8 (pbk.) LC Card 85-71362 DDC 387.7/065/94 19
HE9889.A4 F56 1985

Flying the mail /. Jackson, Donald Dale, 1935- Alexandria, Va. , c1982. 176 p. : ISBN 0-8094-3329-X LC Card 82-2020 DDC 383/.144/09 19
HE6496 .J3 1982 ***NYPL [JLF 87-386]***

Flynn, Patricia M. Facilitating technological change : the human resource challenge / Patricia M. Flynn. Cambridge, Mass. : Ballinger Pub. Co., c1988. x, 233 p. : ill. ; 24 cm. Includes bibliographies and index. ISBN 0-88730-104-5 LC Card 87-17839 DDC 331.2 19
1. Labor supply - Effect of technological innovations on. 2. Industry - Social aspects. 3. Technological innovations. I. Title.
HD6331 .F56 1988

Flynn, Teresa M.
How to find information about foreign firms /. Washington, D.C. , c1987. 93 p. ; ISBN 0-934940-46-0 (pbk.) : LC Card 86-51568 DDC 016.3388/8873 19
HD2785 .H69 1987

Rosenberg, Gerald I. How to find information about acquisition candidates /. Washington, D.C. , c1987. 79 p. ; ISBN 0-934940-45-2 LC Card 86-51570 DDC 016.3387/4/0973 19
HD2785 .R58 1987

Flynt, J. Wayne, 1940- Mine, mill & microchip : a chronicle of Alabama enterprise / by Wayne Flynt ; pictorial research and captions by Michael Thomason.1st ed. Northridge, Calif. : Windsor Publications, 1987. 376 p. : ill. (some col.), map, ports ; 32 cm. "Produced in cooperation with the Business Council of Alabama." "'Alabama's enterprises' by Peter Cobun, Betty Doyle, Melody Gilchrist, and Marlene Hunt Rikard." Bibliography: p. 371-372. Includes index. ISBN 0-89781-215-8 LC Card 87-9192 DDC 338.09761 19
1. Alabama - Industries - History. 2. Alabama - Manufactures - History. 3. Industry and state - Alabama - History. I. Thomason, Michael. II. Title. III. Title: Alabama enterprise. IV. Title: Mine, mill, and microchip.
HC107.A4 F57 1987

FmHA guaranteed lending manual / prepared for the American Bankers Association by Farm Sector Economics Associates. Washington, D.C. (1120 Connecticut Ave., N.W., Washington 20036) : American Bankers Association, c1986. xi, 88, [59] p. : ill. ; 28 cm. LC Card 86-226067 DDC 332.1/753 19
1. Agricultural credit - United States - Handbooks, manuals, etc. 2. Loans - Government guaranty - United

States - Handbooks, manuals, etc. 3. United States. Farmers Home Administration. I. Farm Sector Economics Associates. II. American Bankers Division.
HG2051.U5 F55 1986

El FMI, el Banco Mundial y la crisis latinoamericana / por SELA (Sistema Económico Latinamericano). 1a ed. México : Siglo Veintiuno Editores, 1986. 474 p. : ill. ; 21 cm. (Economía y demografía) Includes bibliographical references. ISBN 968-231-373-2 LC Card 87-127860 DDC 332.1/52 19
1. International Monetary Fund - Latin America. 2. World Bank - latin America. 3. Latin America - Economic conditions - 1945-. I. Sistema Económico Latinoamericano. II. Series: Economía y demografía (Mexico City, Mexico).
HG3881.5.I58 F56 1986

FOAT, GINNY.
Hawkes, Ellen. Feminism on trial . New York , c1986. 420 p. ; ISBN 0-688-04850-1 : LC Card 85-31968 DDC 305.4/2/0973 19
HQ1413.F63 H39 1986
NYPL [JLE 86-2863]

Focht, Rick.
Employment and gross earnings of California residents in Alaska's commercial fisheries, 1977-1982 / prepared by Rick Focht, Nasser Kamali, and Kurt Schelle. Juneau, AK : Commercial Fisheries Entry Commission, [1984] v, 53 p. : map ; 28 cm. (CFEC report . no. 84-15) "December 1984." Bibliography: p. 20. LC Card 86-622320 DDC 331.12/5392/09798021 19
1. Wages - Fishers - Alaska - Statistics. 2. Wages - Fishers - California - Statistics. 3. Fishers - Alaska - Supply and demand - Statistics. I. Kamali, Nasser. II. Schelle, Kurt. III. Alaska Commercial Fisheries Entry Commission. IV. Title. V. Series.
HD4966.F652 U54 1984c

Employment and gross earnings of Oregon residents in Alaska's commercial fisheries, 1977-1982 / prepared by Rick Focht, Nasser Kamali, and Kurt Schelle. Juneau, AK : Commercial Fisheries Entry Commission, [1984] v, 69 p. : ill. ; 28 cm. (CFEC report . no. 84-14) "December 1984." Bibliography: p. 20. LC Card 86-622319 DDC 331.12/5392/09798021 19
1. Wages - Fishers - Alaska - Statistics. 2. Wages - Fishers - Oregon - Statistics. 3. Fishers - Alaska - Supply and demand - Statistics. I. Kamali, Nasser. II. Schelle, Kurt. III. Alaska Commercial Fisheries Entry Commission. IV. Title. V. Series.
HD4966.F652 U54 1984b

Employment and gross earnings of Washington residents in Alaska's commercial fisheries, 1977-1982 / prepared by Rick Focht, Nasser Kamali, and Kurt Schelle. Juneau, AK : Commercial Fisheries Entry Commission, [1984] v leaves, 126 p. ; 28 cm. (CFEC report . no. 84-13) "December 1984." Bibliography: p. 20. LC Card 86-622318 DDC 331.2/8392/09797021 19
1. Wages - Fishers - Alaska - Statistics. 2. Wages - Fishers - Washington (State) - Statistics. I. Kamali, Nasser. II. Schelle, Kurt. III. Title. IV. Series.
HD4966.F542 U554 1984

Focus (Fraser Institute (Vancouver, B.C.)) . (18) Daly, D. J. (Donald James), 1922- On real wage unemployment /. Vancouver, B.C., Canada , 1986. vi, 117 p. : ISBN 0-88975-079-3 (pbk.) LC Card 87-142391 DDC 331.13/7971 19
HD4946.C3 D35 1986

Focus group research. Greenbaum, Thomas L. The practical handbook and guide to focus group research /. Lexington, Mass. , c1988. xii, 191 p. ; ISBN 0-669-14775-3 (alk. paper) LC Card 86-45946 DDC 658.8/3 19
HF5415.2 .G695 1988

Focus groups . Templeton, Jane Farley. Chicago, Ill. , c1987. xiii, 315 p. ; ISBN 0-917253-78-7 : LC Card 87-4977 DDC 658.8/3 19
HF5415.2 .T43 1987

Focus on the Gulf Co-operation Council (GCC) : proceedings of a one-day conference held on 1 December 1983 by the Arab-British Chamber of Commerce. London : The Chamber, c1984. 48 p. : ill. ; 30 cm. (Focus reports, 0260-700X) LC Card 85-211534 DDC 337.53/6/041 19
1. Persian Gulf States - Foreign economic relations - Great Britain - Congresses. 2. Great Britain - Foreign economic relations - Persian Gulf States - Congresses. 3. Persian Gulf States - Economic policy - Congresses. 4. Majlis al-Ta'āwun li-Duwal al-Khalīj al-'Arabīyah - Congresses. I. Majlis al-Ta'āwun li-Duwal al-Khalīj al-'Arabīyah. II. Arab-British Chamber of Commerce. III. Series.
HF1584.5 .F63 1984

Focus reports, 0260-700X.
Focus on the Gulf Co-operation Council (GCC) . London , c1984. 48 p. : LC Card 85-211534 DDC 337.53/6/041 19
HF1584.5 .F63 1984

Fodor, András. A magyar társadalombiztosítás az V. ötéves terv időszakában, 1976-1980 / Fodor András, Varga Gyula. Budapest : SZOT Társadalombiztosítási Főigazgatóság, 1983. 147 p. ; 20 cm. ISBN 963-321-977-9 LC Card 85-129731
1. Social security - Hungary - History. I. Varga, Gyula, 1938-. II. Title. III. Title: Magyar társadalombiztosítás az 5. ötéves terv időszakában, 1976-1980. IV. Title: Magyar társadalombiztosítás az ötödik ötéves terv időszakában, 1976-1980.
HD7172.5 .F62 1983

Fodor, István, 1938- A Környezeti erőforrások gazdasági értékelésének módszertani kérdései /. Pécs [Budapest] , 1981. 78 leaves ; LC Card 82-202704
HD9502.E83 K68 1981 *NYPL [JLE 87-219]*

Föderative Politikverflechtung in der Umweltpolitik /. Posse, Achim Ulrich, 1960- München , c1986. xiv, 181 p. : ISBN 3-597-10526-2 LC Card 86-222201
HC290.5.E5 P67 1986

Die Förderung des wirtschaftlichen und sozialen Wandels durch die Forschungs- und Entwicklungspolitik als präventive Strukturpolitik /. Rembser, Josef. Dortmund , 1977. 100 p. : LC Card 84-130876
HD30 .A7 Heft 184 HD6331.2.G28

Der Förderungsauftrag im Zielsystem der Bankgenossenschaften . Röhm, Helmut. Stuttgart , c1983. 306 p. ; ISBN 3-8001-8187-8 LC Card 84-106807
HG2039.G4 R568 1983

Först, Walter, 1920- Nach fünfundzwanzig Jahren . Köln , 1980. 399 p. : ISBN 3-7745-6465-5
NYPL [MWGK (Germany) 74-75 Bd.4]

Fogarasi, László. A Gazdaságirányítás és a szakszervezetek /. Budapest , 1985. 191 p. ; ISBN 963-322-253-2 : LC Card 86-104573
HC300.28 .G349 1985

Foged, Brita. Markussen, Randi. Det fleksible køn . [Copenhagen] , c1984. 163 p. ; ISBN 87-7445-159-6 : LC Card 84-187146
HD6169 .M37 1984

Fogel, Daniel S. Dailey, Robert C. Understanding people in organizations /. St. Paul, MN , c1988. xviii, 525 p. : ISBN 0-314-24254-6 LC Card 86-32460 DDC 658.4 19
HD58.7 .D34 1988

Fogel, Gerald I. The Psychology of men . New York , c1986. x, 310 p. ; ISBN 0-465-06718-2 LC Card 85-48022 DDC 155.3/32 19
BF692.5 .P78 1986 *NYPL [JFE 86-2975]*

Fogel, Ramón B. Movimientos campesinos en el Paraguay / Ramón B. Fogel. 1st ed. Asunción, Paraguay : Centro Paraguayo de Estudios Sociológicos, 1986. 230 p., [1] leaf of plates : ill. ; 20 cm. (Serie Estudios agrarios) Bibliography: p. 225-230. LC Card 86-189517
1. Peasantry - Paraguay. 2. Peasantry - Paraguay - Misiones. 3. Land settlement - Paraguay - Caaguazu (Dept.). 4. Agricultural colonies - Paraguay - Caaguazu (Dept.). 5. Agricultural colonies - Argentina. 6. Millennialism - Paraguay. 7. Millennialism - Argentina. I. Series: Serie Estudios agrarios (Asunción, Paraguay). II. Title.
HD1531.P3 F64 1986

Fogel, Steven Jay, 1942- The yes-I-can guide to mastering real estate : how to build your confidence and your wealth / Steven Jay Fogel with Mark Bruce Rosin.1st ed. New York : Times Books, c1987. xviii, 302 p. ; 25 cm. Includes index. ISBN 0-8129-1637-9 : LC Card 86-28503 DDC 332.63/24 19
1. Real estate investment. I. Rosin, Mark Bruce. II. Title.
HD1382.5 .F64 1987

Fogel, Walter A. Job equity and other studies in industrial relations . Los Angeles , c1982. 274 p. : LC Card 82-621216 DDC 331/.0973 19
HD5708.45.U6 J6 1982 *NYPL [JLD 87-273]*

Foggi, Franco. Il Pappagallo giallo . [Pisa] , Firenze , c1986. 194 p., [1] leaf of plates : LC Card 86-212573
HD9780.I82 P37 1986

Foglio, Antonio, 1940-
Il commercio estero delle tecnologie, dei progetti industriali e dei know how / Antonio Foglio. 2a ed. Milano, Italy : F. Angeli, 1984. 269 p. ; 22 cm. (Azienda moderna. 177) Bibliography: p. [265]-269. LC Card 86-102943
1. High technology industries. 2. Technology transfer. I. Title.
HC79.H53 F64 1984

Il marketing agroalimentare : mercato e strategie di commercializzazione / Antonio Foglio. Milano, Italy : F. Angeli, c1985. 370 p. : ill. ; 22 cm. (Azienda moderna. 184) Bibliography: p. [369]-370. LC Card 86-114259
1. Farm produce - Italy - Marketing. I. Title.
HD9015.I8 F64 1985

Fogyasztási Szövetkezetek Országos Tanácsa (Hungary) Gazdálkodási és jövedelmezőségi adatok, mutatószámok a szövetkezeti bolti kiskereskedelemben /. Budapest , 1984. 113 p. ; ISBN 963-7006-24-9 : LC Card 85-154737
HF5429.6.H8 G39 1984

Fohlen, Claude. Le Radici intellettuali del progresso economico moderno /. Milano, Italy , c1986. 327 p. ; LC Card 86-197444
HB75 .R13 1986

Fokkink, Manfred, 1955- Denk ja nicht, Du bist selber schuld : [Arbeitslosigkeit im Ruhrgebiet : Analysen, Erfahrungen, Aktionen / Manfred Fokkink, Wolf Haug, Werner Montel].1. Aufl. Gelsenkirchen-Buer : Farin & Zwingmann, 1980. 180 p. : ill. ; 24 cm. LC Card 82-114713
1. Youth - Employment - Germany (West) - Ruhr (Region). 2. Unemployment - Germany (West) - Ruhr (Region). 3. Unemployed - Germany (West) - Ruhr (Region). I. Haug, Wolf, 1953-. II. Montel, Werner, 1947-. III. Title.
HD6276.G4 F6 1980 *NYPL [JLE 86-1457]*

Folayan, Adekunle. Agriculture and economic development in Nigeria : a prescription for the Nigerian green revolution / by Adekunle Folayan.1st ed. New York : Vantage Press, c1983. x, 276 p. : ill. ; 24 cm. Includes index. Bibliography: p. 241-243. ISBN 0-533-05325-0 : LC Card 81-90817 DDC 338.1/09669 19
1. Agriculture - Economic aspects - Nigeria. 2. Green Revolution - Nigeria. 3. Agriculture and state - Nigeria. I. Title.
HD2145.5 .F64 1983 *NYPL [JLE 86-1080]*

Folbre, Nancy. A field guide to the U. S. economy / the Center for Popular Economics ; coordinated and written by Nancy Folbre. New York : Pantheon Books, c1987. 1 v. (various pagings) : ill. ; 14 x 21 cm. Bibliography: at end of text. ISBN 0-394-75047-0 (pbk.) : LC Card 86-42974 DDC 330.973 19
1. United States - Economic conditions. 2. Economic indicators - United States. I. Center for Popular Economics (U. S.). II. Title.
HC103 .F59 1987

A Föld és a népgazdaság / [a kötetet szerkesztette, Tanka Endre]. [Budapest] : Igazságügyi Minisztérium Tudományos és Tájékoztatási Főosztálya, 1985. 514 p. ; 24 cm. (Igazságügyi Minisztérium Tudományos és Tájékoztatási Főosztály kiadványai. Tanulmánykötet, 0236-5057 . 12) Includes bibliographies. ISBN 963-03-2232-3 LC Card 86-228739
1. Land use - Hungary. 2. Land use - Law and legislation - Hungary. 3. Land tenure - Hungary. 4. Land tenure - Law and legislation - Hungary. I. Tanka, Endre. II. Series.
HD640.5.Z63 F65 1985

Földértékelés, termőhelyi értékelés problémái . Fórizs, Józsefné. Budapest , 1985. 211 p., [4] folded leaves of plates : ISBN 963-491-204-4 LC Card 86-196842
HD1387 .F596 1985

A földmüvesszövetkezetek, fogyasztási szövetkezetek négy évtizede Szolnok megyében /. Urbán, László. Szolnok , 1985 ([Szolnok] : Készült a Damjanich János Múzeum Rota Gépén) 435 p. ; ISBN 963-01-6642-9 LC Card

87-407748
HD3332.5.A6 S98 1985

Földmüvesszövetkezetek, fogyasztási szövetkezetek 4 évtizede Szolnok megyében. Urbán, László. A földmüvesszövetkezetek, fogyasztási szövetkezetek négy évtizede Szolnok megyében /. Szolnok , 1985 ([Szolnok] : Készült a Damjanich János Múzeum Rota Gépén) 435 p. ; ISBN 963-01-6642-9 LC Card 87-407748
HD3332.5.A6 S98 1985

Foley, Catherine.
Massachusetts industrial employment projected changes, 1984-1995 / prepared by Catherine Foley. [Boston] : Massachusetts Division of Employment Security, Economic Research & Analysis Service, [1986] vi leaves, 37 p. : ill. ; 28 cm. "May 1986." LC Card 87-620528 DDC 331.12/5/09744 19
1. Employment forecasting - Massachusetts - Statistics. 2. Massachusetts - Economic conditions - Statistics. 3. Labor supply - Massachusetts - Statistics. I. Massachusetts. Division of Employment Security. Economic Research & Analysis Service. II. Title.
HD5725.M4 F64 1986

Massachusetts job outlook, occupational employment projected changes, 1984 to 1995 / prepared by Catherine Foley. [Boston, MA] : Massachusetts Division of Employment Security, Economic Research & Analysis Service, [1987] vi, 59 p. : ill. ; 28 cm. "January 1987." LC Card 87-621850 DDC 331.12/5/09744021 19
1. Employment forecasting - Massachusetts. 2. Massachusetts - Economic conditions. I. Massachusetts. Division of Employment Security. Economic Research & Analysis Service. II. Title.
HD5725.M4 F65 1987

Foley, Denis. Stop DWI . Lexington, Mass. , c1986. xv, 183 p. : ISBN 0-669-12157-6 (alk. paper) LC Card 85-45676 DDC 363.1/2558 19
HE5620.D7 S89 1986 NYPL [JLE 86-2813]

Foley, Duncan K. Understanding Capital : Marx's economic theory / Duncan K. Foley. Cambridge, Mass. : Harvard University Press, 1986. viii, 183 p. : ill. ; 24 cm. Includes index. Bibliography: p. [177]-180. ISBN 0-674-92087-2 (alk. paper) LC Card 86-4736 DDC 335.4/1 19
1. Marx, Karl, 1881-1883. Kapital. 2. Capital. 3. Marxian economics. I. Title.
HB501 .F644 1986 NYPL [JLE 86-4606]

Folgekosten der Besteuerung . Täuber, Gudrun. Spardorf , c1984. 204, xii p. : ISBN 3-922919-40-5 LC Card 85-128537
HJ2323.G3 T38 1984

Folgekosten des Wachstums als Wachstumsstimulans . Leipert, Christian. Berlin [1985?] 35 p. : LC Card 86-116361
HD75.6 .L45 1985

Follett, Mary Parker, 1868-1933. Freedom & co-ordination : lectures in business organization / Mary Parker Follett. New York : Garland Pub., 1987. xvii, 89 p. ; 19 cm. (Continuity in administrative science) Reprint. Originally published: London : Management Publications Trust, 1949. ISBN 0-8240-8229-X (alk. paper) : LC Card 86-27079 DDC 658.4/092 19
1. Leadership. 2. Management. I. Title. II. Title: Freedom and co-ordination. III. Series.
HD57.7 .F66 1987

Follis, Anne Bowen, 1947- I'm not a women's libber, but--and other confessions of a Christian feminist / Anne Bowen Follis. Nashville : Abingdon, c1981. 128 p. ; 21 cm. ISBN 0-687-18687-0 LC Card 81-1241
1. Feminism - United States. 2. Women's rights - United States. 3. Housewives - United States. 4. Christian life - 1960-. I. Title.
HQ1426 .F75 NYPL [JLD 85-1976]

Folom´ev, A. N. (Aleksandr Nikolaevich) Orudiia truda : problemy proportsional´nogo vosproizvodstva / A.N. Folom´ev. Moskva : "Mysl´", 1984. 107, [4] p. ; 20 cm. Bibliography: p. 103-[108] LC Card 85-138858
1. Soviet Union - Economic policy - 1981-. 2. Marxian economics. 3. Production (Economic theory). I. Title.
HC336.25 .F64 1984

Folsom, Burton W. Entrepreneurs versus the historians / by Burton W. Folsom. Washington, DC : Regnery Gateway ; New York, NY : Distributed by Kampmann, c1987. p. cm. Examines the impact of entrepreneurs on the history of the United States by analyzing the various industries, steamship, railroads, oil, and steel, that were developed in the nineteenth century. ISBN 0-89526-573-7 : LC Card 87-23390 DDC 338/.04/0973 19
1. Capitalists and financiers - United States - History. 2. Competition - United States - History. 3. Laissez-faire - History. 4. Steamboats - United States - History. 5. Entrepreneurship - History. I. Title.
HG181 .F647 1987

Foltyn, Ferenc. Inflációelméletek és az amerikai monetáris politika / Foltyn Ferenc. Budapest : Akadémiai Kiadó, 1985. 126 p. ; 19 cm. Includes bibliographical references. ISBN 963-05-3905-5 : LC Card 85-191099
1. Inflation (Finance). 2. Inflation (Finance) - United States. 3. Monetary policy - United States. I. Title.
HG229 .F642 1985

A Folyamatos árszinvonal-emelkedés társadalmi hatásai : összefoglaló tanulmány / [a tanulmányt összeállította, Fekete György és Sebők Éva]. Budapest : Szakszervezetek Elméleti Kutató Intézete, [1985] 176 p. ; 21 cm. "Budapest, 1985. június." "A kutatás lezárult részben 1983 júniusban, részben 1985 januárban"--T.p. verso. Bibliography: p. [i]. ISBN 963-608-087-9 LC Card 87-407751
1. Inflation (Finance) - Hungary. 2. Prices - Hungary. I. Fekete, György, 1925-. II. Sebők, Éva, Dr. III. Szakszervezetek Elméleti Kutató Intézete.
HG970.5 .F65 1985

Fome, agricultura e política no Brasil . Lima Sobrinho, Antonio Estevam de. Petrópolis , 1981. 120 p. ; LC Card 81-185801 DDC 338.1/0981 19
HD9014.B82 L56 1981
NYPL [JLD 86-3297]

Fome, um tema proibido . Castro, Josué de, 1908-1973. Petrópolis , 1983. 154 p. ; LC Card 83-224629
HD9000.5 .C28 1983

Fondation allemande pour les pays en voie de developpement. see **Deutsche Stiftung für Entwicklungsländer.**

Fondation industrie-université (Brussels, Belgium) Travail, loisirs, culture. [Bruxelles] [Zwevegem]] 1970. ix, 163 p. LC Card 71-856101
HD4904.7 .T7 1970

Fondation Liberté sans frontières. Le Tiers-mondisme en question /. Paris , c1986. 225 p. ; ISBN 2-85565-299-5 : LC Card 86-185503
HC60 .T518 1986

Fondation Roi Baudouin. L'Avenir économique de la Belgique . [Bruxelles , 1981] 155 p. ; LC Card 87-672443
HC315 .A93x 1981

Fondazione Giacomo Brodolini. Organizzazione del lavoro, mobilità e aspetti formativi nella contrattazione . Milano, Italy , c1982. 172 p. ; LC Card 83-106874
HD6709 .O73 1982

Fondements de l'analyse macroéconomique à court terme /. Laroque, Guy. Paris , 1986. 98 p. : ISBN 2-222-03757-3 : LC Card 87-103537
HB173 .L35 1986

I Fondi comuni di investimento : atti del convegno di Amalfi, 3-4 giugno, 1983 / a cura di Biagio Grasso. Napoli : Edizioni scientifiche italiane, c1985. 183 p. ; 25 cm. (Pubblicazioni dell'Università degli studi di Salerno. Sezione Atti, convegni, miscellanee . 12) Includes bibliographical references. LC Card 86-193326
1. Mutual funds - Italy - Congresses. I. Grasso, Biagio. II. Series.
HG5526 .F66 1985

Fondo de Crédito Industrial (Caracas, Venezuela) Situaciones y políticas para el financiamiento industrial . [Caracas, Venezuela] [1985?] 48 p. ; LC Card 86-205909
HG185.V4 S58 1985

FONDO DE CRÉDITO INDUSTRIAL (CARACAS, VENEZUELA) - CONGRESSES.
Situaciones y políticas para el financiamiento industrial . [Caracas, Venezuela] [1985?] 48 p. ; LC Card 86-205909
HG185.V4 S58 1985

El fondo de garantía salarial /. García Murcia, Joaquín. Madrid , 1983. 454 p. ; ISBN 84-7434-201-5 LC Card 85-194099
HD7096.S7 G37 1983

Fondo Ecuatoriano Populorum Progressio. Farrell, Gilda. Tenencia de la tierra y movimiento campesino en el Ecuador /. Quito, Ecuador , 1981. 158 p., [2] leaves of plates : LC Card 86-174088
HD529.C67 F37 1981

Fondo Monetario como actor político en la escena internacional /. Alcalde Cardoza, Xavier. Lima, Perú [1986] 54 p. ; LC Card 87-400166 DDC 332.1/52 19
HG3881.5.I58 A44 1986

Fondo Monetario Internacional y Banco Mundial . Lichtensztejn, Samuel, 1934- San José, Costa Rica , Buenos Aires, Argentina , 1986. 215 p. : LC Card 86-233561
HG3881.5.I58 L527 1986

Fondoëmkost´ produktsii i ėffektivnost´ sotsialisticheskogo proizvodstva /. Chernoivanov, G. E. (Gennadiĭ Efimovich) Moskva , 1980. 156 p. ; LC Card 81-134415
HC340.C3 C54 1980

Fondos de pensiones /. Soler Bordetas, Francisco Javier. Bilbao [1985?] 152 p. : ISBN 84-234-0575-3 LC Card 86-166028
HD7105.45.S7 S57 1985

Fonds européen d'orientation et de garantie agricole. see **European Agricultural Guidance and Guarantee Fund.**

Le Fonds monétaire international et les pays du Tiers-monde /. L'Hériteau, Marie France. Paris , c1986. 277 p. : ISBN 2-13-039203-2 : LC Card 86-165389
HG3881.5.I58 L52 1986

Fones-Sundell, Melinda. Implementing rural development in Botswana : organizational structures and management procedures / Melinda Fones-Sundell. Uppsala : Swedish University of Agricultural Sciences, International Rural Development Centre, 1983. 75 p. : ill. ; 30 cm. (Working paper / Swedish University of Agricultural Sciences, International Rural Development Centre, 0280-4301 = Arbetsrapport / U-landsavdelningen . 15) Bibliography: leaf 69-leaf 75. LC Card 86-215071 DDC 338.1/86811 19
1. Rural development - Botswana. 2. Rural development projects - Botswana. 3. Agricultural development projects - Botswana. I. Series: Arbetsrapport (Sveriges lantbruksuniversitet. U-landsavdelningen) , 15. II. Title.
HD2133 .F66 1983

Fonotov, A. G.
Programmno-tselevoĭ metod v planirovanii /. Moskva , 1982. 150 p. : LC Card 83-162853
HC336.25 .P6577 1982

TSelevye kompleksnye programmy . Moskva , 1984. 198 p. : LC Card 86-176369
HC336.25 .T74 1984

FONPLATA (Organization) Reunión Técnica sobre el Financiamiento de la Integración Subregional en América Latina (1985 : Buenos Aires, Argentina) Reunión Técnica sobre el Financiamiento de la Integración Subregional en América Latina . [Buenos Aires, Argentina] . 335 p. : LC Card 86-217551
HC125 .R479 1985

Fonseca, Aloysio de Salles. Reorientação da assistência à saúde no âmbito da previdência social : primeiro ano / documento apresentado pelo Prof. Aloysio de Salles Fonseca à Comissão Parlamentar de Inquériro do Senado sobre a Previdência Social. [Brasília] : Ministério da Previdência e Assistência Social, Instituto Nacional de Assistência Médica da Previdência Social, 1983. 67 p. ; 24 cm. Bibliography: p. 64-67. LC Card 86-171863
1. Insurance, Health - Brazil. 2. Social security - Brazil. I. Brazil. Congresso Nacional. Senado Federal. Comissão Parlamentar de Inquérito. II. Instituto Nacional de Assistência Médica da Previdência Social (Brazil). III. Title.
HD7102.B7 F66 1983

Fonseca Tortós, Eugenio. Algunos aspectos sociográficos del área metropolitana de San José, Costa Rica /. [Ciudad Universitaria "Rodrigo Facio"] , 1970. 105 p. : LC Card 82-196053
HC143.Z7 S3515 1970

Fonseca Zamora, Jorge. El consumidor como agente económico / Jorge Fonseca Zamora. 1a

ed. Cartago : Editorial Tecnológica de Costa Rica, Instituto Tecnológico de Costa Rica, 1985. 196 p. : ill. ; 21 cm. Bibliography: p. 195-196. ISBN 997-7660-05-0 LC Card 87-116492 DDC 339.4/7 19
1. Consumption (Economics). I. Title.
HB801 .F57 1985

Fontaine, André, 1921- L'Impasse Nord-Sud . Paris , c1984. 103 p. : ISBN 2-11-001207-2 : LC Card 84-163951
HC59 .I44 1984

Fontaine Talavera, Arturo. Pautas para la confección de una política económica : una visión pro economía social de mercado / Arturo Fontaine T., Francisco Pérez M. Santiago, Chile : Centro de Estudios del Desarrollo, 1984. 92 leaves : ill. ; 28 cm. (Material para discusión . no. 29) Includes bibliographical references. LC Card 86-177872
1. Chile - Economic policy. 2. Capitalism - Chile. 3. Chile - Economic conditions - 1970-. I. Pérez Mackenna, Francisco. II. Centro de Estudios del Desarrollo (Santiago, Chile). III. Title. IV. Series.
HC192 .F58 1984

Fontan, Pere. El civisme mundial i la pau / Pere Fontan ; presentació, Joan Gomis. Barcelona : Claret, 1986. 104 p. : ill. ; 19 cm. (Els Daus . 79) Bibliography: p. 91-94. ISBN 84-7263-417-5 LC Card 86-186325
1. International economic integration. 2. International cooperation. I. Title.
HF1411 .F592 1986

Fontana, Giovanni L. Convegno nazionale di studi storici (1979 : Schio, Italy) Schio e Alessandro Rossi . Roma , 1985-1986. 2 v. (1487 p., [1] folded leaf of plates) : LC Card 87-110167
HC302.5.R6 C66 1979

Fontanel, Jacques. L'Effort économique de défense . [Grenoble] , 1985. 235 p. : LC Card 86-199399
HC280.D4 E38 1985

Fontenilles, Alfred. Lebas, Michel. Glossary of accounting =. Paris , c1985. 124 p. ; ISBN 2-86644-065-X (pbk.) : LC Card 86-179932
HF5621 .L42 1985

Fontes de financiamento aos municípios. São Paulo : Governo Democrático de São Paulo, Secretaria de Economia e Planejamento, Coordenadoria de Ação Regional, 1984. 175 p. ; 23 cm. Includes bibliographical references and index. LC Card 85-221901
1. Grants-in-aid - Brazil - São Paulo (State). 2. Public investments - Brazil - São Paulo (State). 3. São Paulo (Brazil : State) - Public works - Finance. I. São Paulo, Brazil (State). Secretaria de Economia e Planejamento. Coordenadoria de Ação Regional.
HJ925 .F66 1984

Fontes de financiamento para projetos de desenvolvimento /. Projeto de Desenvolvimento Integrado da Bacia do Araguaia-Tocantins. Brasília , 1985. 450 p. : LC Card 86-195649
HC188.A7 P76 1985

Fontes, Lauro (Lauro Barreto) Formação profissional & produtividade no desempenho humano / Lauro Barreto Fontes. [Rio de Janeiro] : Departamento Nacional--ACS, 1985. 119, [2] p. ; 21 cm. "Obras do autor"--P. [121] Bibliography: p. 117-119. LC Card 85-221895
1. Occupational training - Brazil. 2. Vocational education - Brazil. I. Title. II. Title: Formação profissional e produtividade no desempenho humano.
HD5715.5.B68 F66 1985

Fonti (Padova, Italy) .
(vol. 1) Regesti marittimi croati /. Padova , 1985- v. <v. 1, pt. 1 > : LC Card 86-215640
HE565.Y8 R42 1985

FOOD ADULTERATION AND INSPECTION - GOVERNMENT POLICY - GERMANY (WEST)
Groebel, Wilhelm. Lebensmittelüberwachung . Dortmund , 1976. 84 p. : LC Card 86-170104
HD30 .A7 Heft 167 HD9000.9

Grünen (Political party) Grüne Agrarpolitik, Bilanz und Perspektiven . Bonn [1985?] 62 p. : LC Card 86-152151
HD1957 .G79 1985

FOOD ADULTERATION AND INSPECTION - LAW AND LEGISLATION - NEW YORK (STATE) - HISTORY - 19TH CENTURY.
Okun, Mitchell. Fair play in the marketplace . Dekalb, Ill. , 1986. xii, 345 p. : ISBN 0-87580-115-3 LC Card 85-25921 DDC 363.1/926/0973 19
HD9000.9.U5 O39 1986
NYPL [JLD 86-2513]

FOOD ADULTERATION AND INSPECTION - LAW AND LEGISLATION - UNITED STATES - HISTORY - 19TH CENTURY.
Okun, Mitchell. Fair play in the marketplace . Dekalb, Ill. , 1986. xii, 345 p. : ISBN 0-87580-115-3 LC Card 85-25921 DDC 363.1/926/0973 19
HD9000.9.U5 O39 1986
NYPL [JLD 86-2513]

FOOD ADULTERATION AND INSPECTION - NEW YORK (STATE) - HISTORY - 19TH CENTURY.
Okun, Mitchell. Fair play in the marketplace . Dekalb, Ill. , 1986. xii, 345 p. : ISBN 0-87580-115-3 LC Card 85-25921 DDC 363.1/926/0973 19
HD9000.9.U5 O39 1986
NYPL [JLD 86-2513]

FOOD ADULTERATION AND INSPECTION - UNITED STATES - HISTORY - 19TH CENTURY.
Okun, Mitchell. Fair play in the marketplace . Dekalb, Ill. , 1986. xii, 345 p. : ISBN 0-87580-115-3 LC Card 85-25921 DDC 363.1/926/0973 19
HD9000.9.U5 O39 1986
NYPL [JLD 86-2513]

Food aid for development . Blau, Gerda. Rome , Ann Arbor, MI , 1985. xi, 343 p. : ISBN 92-5-102180-5 (pbk.) LC Card 86-220906 DDC 363.8/83/091724 19
HD9018.D44 B57 1985

FOOD AID PROGRAMS. see **FOOD RELIEF.**

Food and agricultural policy in Peru, 1960-1977 [microform] /. Kennedy, Peter, 1954- Austin (Sid Richardson Hall 1.310, Austin 78712) , 1983. 22 p. ; LC Card 83-623239 DDC 338.1/885 19
HD1903 .K46 1983 ***NYPL [*ZT-1646 no.20]***

Food and Agriculture Organization of the United Nations. Commodities and Trade Division.
Rice, selected aspects of production, trade, and price policies /. Rome , 1985. ii, 83 p. : ISBN 92-5-102329-8 (pbk.) LC Card 86-213105 DDC 338.1/7318 19
HD9066.D44 R53 1985

Thigpen, M. Elton, 1932- World demand prospects for jute /. Washington, D.C. , Rome , 1987. vi, 178 p. ; ISBN 0-8213-0867-X (pbk.) LC Card 86-32522 DDC 338.4/767713 19
HD9156.J7 T46 1987

The World banana economy, 1970-1984 . Rome , 1986. vi, 83 p. ; ISBN 92-5-102376-X (pbk.) LC Card 86-217497 DDC 382/.414772 19
HD9259.B2 W66 1986

Food and Agriculture Organization of the United Nations. Fertilizer and Plant Nutrition Service. Manual on fertilizer distribution /. Rome , 1985. x, 114 p. : ISBN 92-5-101433-7 (pbk.) LC Card 86-221068 DDC 668/.62/0688 19
HD9483.A2 M36 1985

Food and Agriculture Organization of the United Nations. Information Division. Information note on the technical cooperation programme /. Rome [1985?] 29 p. : LC Card 87-122600 DDC 338.9/26/091724 19
HC60 .I477 1985

Food and Agriculture Organization of the United Nations. Nutrition Planning, Assessment, and Evaluation Service. Integrating nutrition into agricultural and rural development projects . Rome , 1984. ix, 132 p. : ISBN 92-5-102150-3 ***NYPL [JLG 86-181]***

Food and Agriculture Organization of the United Nations. Regional Office for Latin America. Programa de Cooperación Regional y Comercio Exterior. El Mercado regional de frutas . [Montevideo] , 1983. 63 p. ; LC Card 86-171763
HD9259.T753 L295 1983

Food and Agriculture Organization of the United Nations. Statistics Division.
A Comparative study of food consumption data from food balance sheets and household surveys [microform] /. Rome , 1983. 33 p. : ISBN 92-5-101426-4 (pbk.) LC Card 84-197331 DDC 339.4/8664/0091724 19
HD9000.4 .C62 1983
NYPL [*ZT-1708 no.44]

Guidelines for the computation of selected statistical indicators /. Rome , 1986. vii, 71 p. : ISBN 92-5-102367-0 (pbk.) LC Card 87-119289 DDC 338.1/072 19
HD1425 .G85 1986

Inter-country comparisons of agricultural production aggregates /. Rome , 1986. v, 59 p. ; ISBN 92-5-102381-6 (pbk.) LC Card 86-222114 DDC 338.1 19
HD1425 .I59 1986

Food and Agriculture Organization of the United Nations. World Food Programme. see **World Food Programme.**

Food and beverages from Switzerland.
Lebensmittel und Getränke aus der Schweiz =. Zürich , 1984. 113 p. : ISBN 0-390-92140-3
NYPL [JFE 86-3409]

Food and poverty . Étienne, Gilbert. New Delhi , Newbury Park, Calif. , 1987. p. cm. ISBN 0-8039-9540-7 LC Card 87-16992 DDC 338.1/0954 19
HC440.P6 E86 1987

FOOD - CONGRESSES.
The World Food Conference . Washington , 1974. xv, 377 p. : LC Card 74-603025
TX345 .W58 ***NYPL [JLF 78-685]***

FOOD CONSUMPTION - AFRICA, NORTH - CONGRESSES.
Les Modèles de consommation et les politiques alimentaires dans les pays du Maghreb . Alger [1985?] 401 p. : LC Card 87-132818
HD9017.A24 M63 1985

FOOD CONSUMPTION - BRAZIL.
Campino, Antonio Carlos Coelho. Economia da alimentação e nutrição . São Paulo , 1985. 238 p. : LC Card 86-129956 DDC 338.1/9/81 19
HD9014.B82 C35 1985
NYPL [JLD 86-4118]

FOOD CONSUMPTION - BRAZIL - STATISTICS.
Balanço e disponibilidade interna de gêneros alimentícios de origem vegetal, 1979 a 1983 /. Rio de Janeiro, Brasil , 1985. 67 p. ; LC Card 87-404963 DDC 339.4/86413/00981021 19
HD9014.B82 B345 1985

FOOD CONSUMPTION - CANADA - STATISTICS.
Hassan, Zuhair A. Handbook of food expenditures, prices, and consumption /. Ottawa , c1983. 270 p., [2] p. of plates : LC Card 86-228246 DDC 339.4/8664/00971 19
HD9014.C3 H29 1983

FOOD CONSUMPTION - DEVELOPING COUNTRIES - STATISTICS.
A Comparative study of food consumption data from food balance sheets and household surveys [microform] /. Rome , 1983. 33 p. : ISBN 92-5-101426-4 (pbk.) LC Card 84-197331 DDC 339.4/8664/0091724 19
HD9000.4 .C62 1983
NYPL [*ZT-1708 no.44]

FOOD CONSUMPTION - DOMINICAN REPUBLIC.
Producción versus consumo de alimentos . [Santo Domingo, Dominican Republic] , 1981. 74 p. ; LC Card 82-207744
HD9014.D62 P76 1981

FOOD CONSUMPTION - ECONOMETRIC MODELS.
Food demand analysis . Ames , 1987. xvi, 285 p. : ISBN 0-8138-1841-9 LC Card 86-30534 DDC 338.4/76413 19
HD9000.5 .F5947 1987

FOOD CONSUMPTION FORECASTING.
Orbánné Nagy, Mária. Az élelmiszerfogyasztás várható tendenciái hosszabb távon /. Budapest , 1983. 98 p. ; ISBN 963-491-166-8 LC Card 85-219700
HD9015.H82 O73 1983

FOOD CONSUMPTION - FORECASTING - CONGRESSES.
Food demand analysis . Blacksburg, Va. [1986] xii, 292 p. : LC Card 87-620670 DDC

339.4/86413 19
HD9000.5 .F5946 1986

FOOD CONSUMPTION - HUNGARY - FORECASTING.
Orbánné Nagy, Mária. Az élelmiszerfogyasztás várható tendenciái hosszabb távon /. Budapest , 1983. 98 p. ; ISBN 963-491-166-8 LC Card 85-219700
HD9015.H82 O73 1983

FOOD CONSUMPTION - INDIA.
Dogra, Bharat. Empty stomachs and packed godowns . New Delhi , 1987. viii, 126 p. ; LC Card 87-900472 DDC 338.1/9/54 19
HD9016.I42 D64 1987

FOOD CONSUMPTION - ITALY - PRATO REGION - HISTORY.
Nigro, Giampiero. Gli uomini dell'irco . Firenze , 1983. xxii, 184 p. : ISBN 88-00-86022-2 : LC Card 84-238769
HD9425.I83 P76 1983 ***NYPL [JLE 86-2127]***

FOOD CONSUMPTION - KENYA - MATHEMATICAL MODELS.
Greer, Joel William, 1948- Food poverty and consumption patterns in Kenya /. Geneva , 1986. xii, 170 p. : ISBN 92-2-105374-1 (pbk.) : LC Card 87-115091 DDC 338.1/9/6762 19
HD9017.K42 G74 1986

FOOD CONSUMPTION - LATIN AMERICA - CONGRESSES.
Comercialización interna de los alimentos en América Latina . Ottawa, Canada , c1985. 253 p. : ISBN 0-88936-448-6 LC Card 87-118494 DDC 338.1/9/8 19
HD9014.L32 C66 1985

FOOD CONSUMPTION - MEXICO - ADDRESSES, ESSAYS, LECTURES.
Por una nueva política alimentaria /. [México, D.F.] , 1984. 114 p. ; LC Card 85-131176 DDC 338.1/9/72 19
HD9014.M62 P67 1984 ***NYPL [JLC 86-348]***

FOOD CONSUMPTION - MEXICO - DISTRITO FEDERAL.
Restrepo, Iván. La basura . México, D.F. , 1985. 193 p. : LC Card 86-209151
HD9014.M63 M47 1985

FOOD CONSUMPTION - PERU - AREQUIPA.
Pacheco S., Janette. Situación y posibilidades alimentarias de la población urbano marginal de Arequipa /. Arequipa, Perú [1986] 38 p., 8 folded leaves of plates : LC Card 86-232480
HD9014.P53 A746 1986

FOOD CONSUMPTION - PERU - CONGRESSES.
Agricultura y alimentación . [Lima] , 1982. 536 p. : LC Card 83-174688 DDC 338.1/9/85 19
HD9014.P52 A57 1982 ***NYPL [JLD 86-268]***

FOOD CONSUMPTION - SIERRA LEONE - MATHEMATICAL MODELS.
Strauss, John, 1951- Socio-economic determinants of food consumption and production in rural Sierra Leone . East Lansing, Mich. , 1983. vi, 91 p. : LC Card 83-622388 DDC 339.4/8664/00724 19
HD9017.S52 S88 1983 ***NYPL [JLF 86-684]***

FOOD CONSUMPTION - SOVIET UNION.
Treml, Vladimir G. Soviet foreign trade in foodstuffs . Washington, D.C. [1986] viii, 69, 2 p. ; LC Card 87-601290 DDC 382/.45664/00947 19
HD9015.S65 T74 1986

FOOD CONSUMPTION - STATISTICS.
A Comparative study of food consumption data from food balance sheets and household surveys [microform] /. Rome , 1983. 33 p. : ISBN 92-5-101426-4 (pbk.) LC Card 84-197331 DDC 339.4/8664/0091724 19
HD9000.4 .C62 1983
NYPL [*ZT-1708 no.44]

Review of food consumption surveys-1985 . Rome , 1986. xxiv, 212 p. ; ISBN 92-5-102375-1 (pbk.) LC Card 86-222995 DDC 339.4/8664 19
HD9000.4 .R483 1986

FOOD CONTAINER INDUSTRY - UNITED STATES.
Cholmar, Sidney. New directions in microwave ovens . Stamford, Conn., U. S.A. , c1985. x, 119 leaves ; ISBN 0-89336-459-2 (pbk.) LC Card 87-163958 DDC 381/.4568388 19
HD9971.5.S763 U53 1985

Gipson, Beckilynn. Aseptic food processing and packaging . Stamford, Conn., U. S.A. , c1986. xiii, 164 leaves ; ISBN 0-89336-471-1 (pbk.) LC Card 87-405014 DDC 381/.45664028 19
HD9999.C743 U629 1986

FOOD CONTAMINATION - GOVERNMENT POLICY - UNITED STATES - CONGRESSES.
Agriculture and the environment /. Washington, D.C. , c1986. xvii, 298 p. : ISBN 0-915707-33-0 (pbk.) : LC Card 87-43010 DDC 363.7/31 19
HD1755 .P47 1986

FOOD CONTROL. see **FOOD SUPPLY.**

FOOD, COST OF. see **COST AND STANDARD OF LIVING.**

Food courts : how to develop a food court in your shopping center. New York : International Council of Shopping Centers, c1987. 70 p. : ill. ; 22 x 28 cm. ISBN 0-913598-66-6 (pbk.) LC Card 87-604 DDC 647/.9573 19
1. Shopping malls - Management. 2. Fast food restaurants - Management. 3. Restaurants, lunch rooms, etc. - Management. I. International Council of Shopping Centers.
HF5430 .F66 1987

Food crisis and government response in Nigeria . Bashir, Ibrahim Lawan, 1948- Boston, MA (270 Bay State Rd., Boston 02215) , 1986. 22 leaves ; LC Card 87-155111 DDC 363.8/09669 19
HD9017.N52 B37 1986

FOOD CROPS - ETHIOPIA.
Belg synoptic report [microform] . Addis Abeba, Ethiopia [1981] iv, 21 leaves : LC Card 82-980790 DDC 363.8/0963 19
HD9017.E82 B45 1981
NYPL [*ZT-1708 no.19]

FOOD CROPS - PERU - AREQUIPA.
Pacheco S., Janette. Situación y posibilidades alimentarias de la población urbano marginal de Arequipa /. Arequipa, Perú [1986] 38 p., 8 folded leaves of plates : LC Card 86-232480
HD9014.P53 A746 1986

Food demand analysis : implications for future consumption / edited by Oral Capps, Jr. and Benjamin Senauer ; sponsored by the S-165 Southern Regional Research Committee and the Farm Foundation. Blacksburg, Va. : Dept. of Agricultural Economics, Virginia Polytechnic Institute and State University, [1986] xii, 292 p. : ill. ; 23 cm. "August 1986." Includes bibliographies and index. LC Card 87-620670 DDC 339.4/86413 19
1. Food supply - Forecasting - Congresses. 2. Food consumption - Forecasting - Congresses. I. Capps, Oral. II. Senauer, Benjamin. III. S-165 Southern Regional Research Committee (U. S.). IV. Farm Foundation (Chicago, Ill.). V. Virginia Polytechnic Institute and State University. Dept. of Agricultural Economics.
HD9000.5 .F5946 1986

Food demand analysis : problems, issues, and empirical evidence / edited by Robert Raunikar and Chung-Liang Huang.1st ed. Ames : Iowa State University Press, 1987. xvi, 285 p. : ill. ; 24 cm. Includes bibliographies and index. ISBN 0-8138-1841-9 LC Card 86-30534 DDC 338.4/76413 19
1. Food consumption - Econometric models. I. Raunikar, Robert. II. Huang, Chung-liang, 1945-.
HD9000.5 .F5947 1987

Food first curriculum /. Rubin, Laurie, 1956- San Francisco, CA , c1984. viii, 146 p. : ISBN 0-935028-17-X : LC Card 84-8986 DDC 372.8/3 19
HD9000.5 .R73 1984 ***NYPL [JLF 86-1436]***

Food for thought . Leviste, Jose P., 1945- Los Baños, Laguna, Philippines , c1985. 150 p. : LC Card 86-193278 DDC 338.1/8599 19
HD2088 .L48 1985

Food-for-work in Ethiopia . Yeraswork Admassie. Addis Abeba , 1985. viii, 102, [58] leaves : LC Card 86-980537 DDC 339.5/0963 19
HD5839.7.A6 Y47 1985

Food grain shortfalls in Tanzania, 1961-1981 . Msambichaka, L. A. (Lucian A.) Dar es Salaam, Tanzania , c1982. 38 p. ; LC Card 85-980863 DDC 338.1/9/678 19
HD9047.T32 M726 1982

FOOD INDUSTRY AND TRADE - AFRICA.
Dinham, Barbara. Agribusiness in Africa /. Trenton, N.J. , 1984. 224 p. : ISBN 0-86543-003-9 : LC Card 85-672721
HD9017.A2 D56x 1984
NYPL [Sc D 86-769]

FOOD INDUSTRY AND TRADE - ANGOLA - DIRECTORIES.
Representação do produtos alimentares de Angola na IX Feira Internacional de Lisboa . Luanda [1968] 248 p. : LC Card 87-400609 DDC 338.7/6413/0025673 19
HD9017.A532 R46 1968

FOOD INDUSTRY AND TRADE - BRAZIL - FORTALEZA.
Reestudo da parte de cereais e estivas relacionado com a viabilidade técnico-econômico-financeira da Central de Abastecimento de Gêneros Alimentícios da Região Metropolitana de Fortaleza. [Fortaleza] , 1973. 72 leaves : LC Card 82-147387
HD9014.B83 F587 1973

FOOD INDUSTRY AND TRADE - BRAZIL, NORTH.
Comercialização de alimentos na região norte, 1985 /. Brasília, DF , 1985. 51 p. ; LC Card 86-129086
HD9014.B83 N673 1985

FOOD INDUSTRY AND TRADE - BRAZIL - PARANÁ (STATE)
Caracterização da indústria agroalimentar no Paraná /. Curitiba , 1985. x, 50 leaves : LC Card 86-202725
HD9014.B83 P3718 1985

FOOD INDUSTRY AND TRADE - BRAZIL - SÃO PAULO (STATE)
Disponibilidade de alimentos a nível regional no Estado de São Paulo, 1974-83 /. São Paulo , 1985. 75 p. ; LC Card 86-196482
HD9014.B83 S433 1985

FOOD INDUSTRY AND TRADE - BULGARIA.
Atanasov, Mikhail, k.i.n. Vŭshnotŭrgovski aspekti na selskostopanskite i khranitelno-vkusovite stoki i problemi pred bŭlgarskiia iznos /. Sofiia , 1984. 118 p. ; LC Card 85-163481
HD9015.B82 A86 1984

FOOD INDUSTRY AND TRADE - CENTRAL AMERICA.
Barry, Tom, 1950- Roots of rebellion . Boston , c1987. xii, 220 p. : ISBN 0-89608-288-1 : LC Card 87-4519 DDC 338.1/9/728 19
HD9014.C462 B37 1987

FOOD INDUSTRY AND TRADE - CHINA.
Keidel, Albert. China's dairy and food processing industries . Washington, D.C. , c1986. ii, 65 leaves ; LC Card 86-233105 DDC 338.1/77/0951 19
HD9275.C62 K45 1986

FOOD INDUSTRY AND TRADE - COLOMBIA.
Problemas agrarios colombianos /. [Bogotá, Colombia] , México, D.F. , 1986. 467 p. : ISBN 958-606-005-5 LC Card 86-221632
HD1882 .P75 1986

FOOD INDUSTRY AND TRADE - DEVELOPING COUNTRIES.
Transnationals and development. Manchester, England , 1984. i, 64 p. ;
NYPL [JLD 86-3224]

FOOD INDUSTRY AND TRADE - EMPLOYEES.
Problems of workers in the meat, dairy, edible oils, and fats industries . Sofia , 1986. 43 p. ; LC Card 86-222996 DDC 338.4/7664 19
HD8039.F7 P76 1986

FOOD INDUSTRY AND TRADE - FRANCE.
Pezet, P. (Pierre) Les opérateurs français du commerce international agro-alimentaire /. Paris , c1984. 85 p. : ISBN 2-279-52812-6 LC Card 85-136648 DDC 382/.456413/00944 19
HD9012.5 .P43 1984

FOOD INDUSTRY AND TRADE - FRANCE - FINANCE.
Guide pratique du financement des industries agroalimentaires /. Paris [1986] 351 p. : LC Card 86-186921
HD9012.5 .G86 1986

FOOD INDUSTRY AND TRADE - GERMANY, WEST.

Schmelzeisen, Hans-Michael. Bedeutung, Einsatzmöglichkeiten und -probleme des kombinierten Güterverkehrs in der Ernährungswirtschaft /. Münster [1986] xii, 350 p. : ISBN 3-88660-357-1 (Deut. Bibl.) LC Card 87-121511 DDC 380.5/24 19
HE199.5.F6 S36 1986

FOOD INDUSTRY AND TRADE - GOVERNMENT POLICY.

Bennett, Jon. The hunger machine . Oxford , New York , 1987. 232 p. : ISBN 0-7456-0444-7 : LC Card 87-724 DDC 363.8 19
HD9000.5 .B449 1987

FOOD INDUSTRY AND TRADE - GOVERNMENT POLICY - FRANCE.

Les Industries agro-alimentaires . Paris [1986], c1987. 164 p. : ISBN 2-11-001722-8 : LC Card 87-167615
HD9012.5 .I53 1987

FOOD INDUSTRY AND TRADE - GOVERNMENT POLICY - HUNGARY.

Javaslatok az élelmiszer-gazdaság fejlesztésére . Budapest , 1984. 279 p. : ISBN 963-221-500-1 LC Card 85-229874
HD9015.H82 J38 1984

Szénay, Lászlóné. A közgazdasági szabályozás és az élelmiszeripari szakágazatok gazdasági eredményeinek összefüggései és problémái az 1977-82 közötti években /. Budapest , 1984. 161 p. ; ISBN 963-491-196-X LC Card 86-199432
HD9015.H82 S935 1984

FOOD INDUSTRY AND TRADE - GOVERNMENT POLICY - JAPAN.

Hillman, Jimmye S., 1923- Agricultural trade and protection in Japan /. Aldershot, Hants, England , Brookfield, Vt. , 1988. p. cm. ISBN 0-566-05339-X : LC Card 87-15043 DDC 382.7/3/0952 19
HD9016.J42 H55 1988

FOOD INDUSTRY AND TRADE - GOVERNMENT POLICY - MEXICO - ADDRESSES, ESSAYS, LECTURES.

Por una nueva política alimentaria /. [México, D.F.] , 1984. 114 p. ; LC Card 85-131176 DDC 338.1/9/72 19
HD9014.M62 P67 1984 ***NYPL [JLC 86-348]***

FOOD INDUSTRY AND TRADE - GREECE - DIRECTORIES.

Hodēgos geōrgikōn viomēchaniōn. Athēna , 1985. 510 p. : LC Card 86-193419
HD9015.G82 H58 1985

Hodēgos synetairistikōn geōrgikōn viomēchaniōn . Athēna , 1985. 102 p. : LC Card 86-194038
HD9015.G82 H59 1985

FOOD INDUSTRY AND TRADE - HUNGARY.

Az Élelmiszer-gazdaság távlati fejlesztése /. Budapest , 1984. 163 p. ; ISBN 963-231-717-3 : LC Card 85-194280
HD1940.5.Z8 E54 1984

Éliás, András. Mezőgazdasági és élelmiszeripari termékeink a külpiaci versenyben /. Budapest , 1985. 197 p. ; ISBN 963-232-064-6 : LC Card 86-185883
HD9015.H82 E59 1985

Javaslatok az élelmiszer-gazdaság fejlesztésére . Budapest , 1984. 279 p. : ISBN 963-221-500-1 LC Card 85-229874
HD9015.H82 J38 1984

Réder, Gyula. Helyzetkép az élelmiszeripari müvezetőkről /. Budapest , 1985. 81 p. ; ISBN 963-491-205-2 LC Card 86-196825
HD9015.H82 R43 1985

Soós, Gábor, 1922- Mit kell tudni a magyar agrártermelésről? /. [Budapest] , 1984. 218 p. ; ISBN 963-09-2474-9 : LC Card 85-154641
HD1940.5 .S66 1984

Szénay, Lászlóné. A közgazdasági szabályozás és az élelmiszeripari szakágazatok gazdasági eredményeinek összefüggései és problémái az 1977-82 közötti években /. Budapest , 1984. 161 p. ; ISBN 963-491-196-X LC Card 86-199432
HD9015.H82 S935 1984

FOOD INDUSTRY AND TRADE - HUNGARY - CONGRESSES.

A Vállalati magatartást motiváló gazdasági és társadalmi tényezők című konferencia előadásai . Pécs , 1985. 2 v. : LC Card 87-408547
HD70.H8 V334 1985

FOOD INDUSTRY AND TRADE - HUNGARY - FINANCE.

Szénay, Lászlóné. A közgazdasági szabályozás és az élelmiszeripari szakágazatok gazdasági eredményeinek összefüggései és problémái az 1977-82 közötti években /. Budapest , 1984. 161 p. ; ISBN 963-491-196-X LC Card 86-199432
HD9015.H82 S935 1984

FOOD INDUSTRY AND TRADE - HUNGARY - MANAGEMENT.

A Mezőgazdasági és élelmiszeripari vállalatok gazdálkodása /. Budapest , 1984. 315, [1] p. : ISBN 963-231-968-0 : LC Card 85-230887
HD1493.H8 M48 1984

FOOD INDUSTRY AND TRADE - HUNGARY - QUALITY CONTROL.

Kopcsó, István. Minőségfejlesztés az élelmiszer-termelésben . Budapest , 1984. 253 p. : ISBN 963-231-707-6 : LC Card 85-183244
HD9000.5 .K644 1984

FOOD INDUSTRY AND TRADE - HUNGARY - STATISTICS.

Mezőgazdasági és élelmiszeripari adattár a felszabadulástól napjainkig /. Budapest , 1985. 152 p. ; ISBN 963-502-393-6 LC Card 86-202515
HD1940.5 .M497 1985

Mezőgazdasági és élelmiszeripari adattár a felszabadulástól napjainkig. English. Collection of data of agriculture and food industry from the liberation till now /. Budapest , 1985. 85 p. ; ISBN 963-502-393-6 LC Card 86-230345
HD1940.5 .M49713 1985

FOOD INDUSTRY AND TRADE - HUNGARY - TECHNOLOGICAL INNOVATIONS.

Kopcsó, István. Minőségfejlesztés az élelmiszer-termelésben . Budapest , 1984. 253 p. : ISBN 963-231-707-6 : LC Card 85-183244
HD9000.5 .K644 1984

FOOD INDUSTRY AND TRADE - KAZAKH S.S.R.

Abdil'din, S. A. (Serikbolsyn Abdil'daevich) Razvitie prodovol'stvennogo kompleksa Kazakhstana /. Alma-Ata , 1985. 158 p. ; LC Card 85-226938
HD9015.S653 K393 1985

FOOD INDUSTRY AND TRADE - LATIN AMERICA - CONGRESSES.

Comercialización interna de los alimentos en América Latina . Ottawa, Canada , c1985. 253 p. : ISBN 0-88936-448-6 LC Card 87-118494 DDC 338.1/9/8 19
HD9014.L32 C66 1985

FOOD INDUSTRY AND TRADE - LOCATION.

Vol'f, M. B. (Mark Borisovich) Geografiia mirovogo sel'skogo khoziaistva /. Moskva , 1981. 326 p. : LC Card 82-122609
HD1415 .V62 1981

FOOD INDUSTRY AND TRADE - MEXICO - STATISTICS.

El Sector alimentario en México. México, D.F. [1984] vii, 673 p. : ISBN 968-8099-93-7 LC Card 85-205385
HD9014.M62 S26 1984

FOOD INDUSTRY AND TRADE - MORAL AND ETHICAL ASPECTS.

Yates, Geoffrey. Food, need, greed & myopia . Ryton, Tyne and Wear , 1986. 96 p. : ISBN 0-907367-04-6 (pbk.) : LC Card 87-129951 DDC 338.1/9 19
HD9000.5 .Y38 1986

FOOD INDUSTRY AND TRADE - MOZAMBIQUE.

Caballero, Lorenzo. Mozambique, food and agriculture sector /. Uppsala , 1984. 223, [30] p. : ISBN 91-576-2129-2 (pbk.) LC Card 86-218958 DDC 338.1/0967/9 19
HD9017.M86 C33 1984

FOOD INDUSTRY AND TRADE - NETHERLANDS.

Plas, W. Inventaris van het archief van Regeringscommissariaat voor de Buitenlandse Agrarische Aangelegenheden (RECOBAA), 1946-1950 /. [Hague] [1985] 111 p. ; LC Card 87-101964
HD9015.N42 P55 1985

De Toekomst van onze voedingsmiddelenindustrie /. Amsterdam , 1985. 156 p. : ISBN 90-10-05574-4 : LC Card 86-116607
HD9015.N42 T64 1985

FOOD INDUSTRY AND TRADE - NIGERIA.

Eweka, J. A. (Julius A.) Village development . Ibadan, Nigeria , 1979. xvi, 194 p. ; LC Card 86-172121 DDC 338.1/9/669 19
HD2145.5 .E94 1979

FOOD INDUSTRY AND TRADE - PERSONNEL MANAGEMENT.

Gáti, Gábor. A munkahely-racionalizálás korszerű megközelítési módjai az élelmiszeriparban /. Budapest , 1986. 106 p. : ISBN 963-02-4171-4 LC Card 87-137979
HD9000.5 .G336 1986

FOOD INDUSTRY AND TRADE - PERU - CONGRESSES.

Agricultura y alimentación . [Lima] , 1982. 536 p. : LC Card 83-174688 DDC 338.1/9/85 19
HD9014.P52 A57 1982 ***NYPL [JLD 86-268]***

FOOD INDUSTRY AND TRADE - POLAND - CONGRESSES.

Przestrzenne aspekty gospodarki żywnościowej do 2000 r. . Warszawa , 1986. 166 p. : ISBN 83-208-0497-3 : LC Card 86-223691
HD9015.P72 P72 1986

FOOD INDUSTRY AND TRADE - POLITICAL ASPECTS - DEVELOPING COUNTRIES.

Food, the state, and international political economy . Lincoln , c1986. xxiii, 351 p. : ISBN 0-8032-4413-4 (alk. paper) LC Card 85-30893 DDC 338.1/9/1724 19
HD9018.D44 F67 1986 ***NYPL [JLD 86-3440]***

FOOD INDUSTRY AND TRADE - QUALITY CONTROL.

Kopcsó, István. Minőségfejlesztés az élelmiszer-termelésben . Budapest , 1984. 253 p. : ISBN 963-231-707-6 : LC Card 85-183244
HD9000.5 .K644 1984

FOOD INDUSTRY AND TRADE - SEASONAL VARIATIONS - CONGRESSES.

Tripartite Technical Meeting for the Food Products and Drink Industries, 2d, Geneva, 1978. Labour and social problems arising out of seasonal fluctuations of the food products and drink industries /. Geneva , 1978. ii, 51 p. ; ISBN 92-2-101879-2 (pbk.) : LC Card 80-477150 DDC 331.2/0464
HD9000.1 .T75 1978a ***NYPL [JLE 80-1039]***

FOOD INDUSTRY AND TRADE - SOCIETIES, ETC.

Business interests, organizational development, and private interest government . Berlin , New York , 1987. viii, 232 p. ; ISBN 0-89925-380-6 (U. S.) : LC Card 87-21403 DDC 338.4/7664 19
HD9000.5 .B87 1987

FOOD INDUSTRY AND TRADE - SOVIET UNION.

Korobkina, Z. V. (Zoiia Vasil'evna) Tovarovedenie vkusovykh tovarov /. Moskva , 1986. 207 p. ; LC Card 86-220308
HD9015.S652 K67 1986

Kostin, Leonid Alekseevich. Proizvodstvo tovarov narodnogo potrebleniia . Moskva , 1980. 212 p. ; LC Card 87-107901
HF1040.9.S65 K67 1980

Treml, Vladimir G. Soviet foreign trade in foodstuffs . Washington, D.C. [1986] viii, 69, 2 p. ; LC Card 87-601290 DDC 382/.45664/00947 19
HD9015.S65 T74 1986

FOOD INDUSTRY AND TRADE - SOVIET UNION - MANAGEMENT - MATHEMATICAL MODELS.

Voronin, V. G. (Valeriĭ Grigor'evich) Ėkonomiko-matematicheskie metody planirovaniia na predpriiatiiakh pishchevoĭ promyshlennosti /. Moskva , 1981. 270 p. : LC Card 82-103139
HD9015.S65 V67 1981

FOOD INDUSTRY AND TRADE - SOVIET UNION - MISCELLANEA.

Prodovol'stvennaia programma SSSR . Moskva , 1986. 285 p. ; LC Card 87-110478

DDC 338.1/9/47 19
HD9015.S652 P743 1986

FOOD INDUSTRY AND TRADE - STATISTICS.
Korb, Penelope. U. S. and world food, beverages, and tobacco expenditures, 1970-83 /. Washington, D.C. , 1986. iv, 84 p. : LC Card 86-603160 DDC 339.4/8664/0021 19
HD9000.4 .K67 1986

FOOD INDUSTRY AND TRADE - SWEDEN.
Sweden. 1983 års livsmedelskommitté. Expertgruppen för handels- och industrifrågor. 1983 års livsmedelskommitté . [Stockholm] [1984] 655 p. in various pagings : ISBN 91-38-08506-2 LC Card 86-110501
HD9015.S86 S88 1984

Sweden. 1983 års livsmedelskommitté. Expertgruppen för prisregleringsfrågor. Prisstöd och jordbruksprisreglering . Stockholm [1984] xvi, 260 p. ; ISBN 91-38-08461-9 LC Card 86-109988
HD9015.S86 S883 1984

De Transnationella företagens roll i världshandeln ; Gränsskydd i andra länder /. [Stockholm] [1984] 62, [36] p. ; ISBN 91-38-08406-6 LC Card 86-115056
HD9015.S86 T73 1984

Underbilaga till rapport från 1983 års livsmedelskommittés expertgrupp för prisregleringsfrågor . [Sweden , 1983] (Jönköping . 1 v. (various pagings) : LC Card 85-191640
HD9015.S86 U47 1983

1983 års livsmedelskommitté . [Stockholm] [1984] 255, 18 p. : ISBN 91-38-08481-3 LC Card 86-110260
HD9015.S86 A11 1984a

FOOD INDUSTRY AND TRADE - SWITZERLAND.
Lebensmittel und Getränke aus der Schweiz =. Zürich , 1984. 113 p. : ISBN 0-390-92140-3
NYPL [JFE 86-3409]

FOOD INDUSTRY AND TRADE - TECHNOLOGICAL INNOVATIONS.
Goodman, David, 1938- From farming to biotechnology . Oxford , New York, N.Y. , 1987. 214 p. : ISBN 0-631-14405-6 : LC Card 87-687 DDC 338.1/6 19
HD1433 .G66 1987

Kopcsó, István. Minőségfejlesztés az élelmiszer-termelésben . Budapest , 1984. 253 p. : ISBN 963-231-707-6 : LC Card 85-183244
HD9000.5 .K644 1984

FOOD INDUSTRY AND TRADE - UKRAINE.
Agropromyshlennyĭ kompleks i problemy obespecheniia naseleniia prodovol'stviem . Kiev , 1983. 190 p. : LC Card 86-139699
HD9015.S653 U4295 1983

Savenko, V. N. (Valentina Nikolaevna) Prodovol'stvennyĭ kompleks goroda . Kiev , 1986. 173, [3] p. : LC Card 87-161654
HD9015.S653 U473 1986

FOOD INDUSTRY AND TRADE - UKRAINE - KRYMSKAIA OBLAST'.
Shchedrost' zemli krymskoĭ . Simferopol' , 1985. 158 p. ; LC Card 86-128000
HD9015.S653 K797 1985

FOOD INDUSTRY AND TRADE - UKRAINE - LOCATION.
Territorial'naia organizatsiia prodovol'stvennogo kompleksa . Kiev , 1985. 163 p. ; LC Card 86-175134
HD9015.S653 U4755 1985

Territorial'nye osobennosti razmeshcheniia pishchevoĭ promyshlennosti USSR /. Kiev , 1982. 282 p. ; LC Card 83-197067
HD9015.S653 U476 1982

FOOD INDUSTRY AND TRADE - UNITED STATES.
Browne, William Paul, 1945- Private interests, public policy, and American agriculture /. Lawrence, Kan. , c1988. p. cm. ISBN 0-7006-0334-4 : LC Card 87-23131 DDC 338.1/873 19
HD1761 .B73 1988

Diet foods . Stamford, Conn., U. S.A. , c1986. xv, 195 leaves : ISBN 0-89336-487-8 (pbk.) LC Card 87-160485 DDC 381/.4166463/0973 19
HD9005 .D53 1986

Economics of food processing in the United States /. San Diego , c1988. xiii, 449 p. : ISBN 0-12-482185-5 (alk. paper) LC Card 87-1245 DDC 338.4/7664/00973 19
HD9005 .E37 1988

Fox, Michael W., 1937- Agricide . New York , 1986. xv, 194 p., [10] p. of plates : ISBN 0-8052-4013-6 LC Card 85-27690 DDC 338.1/6/0973 19
S441 .F69 1986 ***NYPL [JLD 86-2542]***

Portilla, Belfor. Alimentos . México , 1983. 149, [53] p. : ISBN 968-429-384-4 LC Card 84-172348 DDC 338.1/9/1724 19
HD9018.D44 P67 1983
NYPL [JLD 86-1520]

Wallace, Luther T. Agriculture's futures . New York , c1987. x, 93 p. : ISBN 0-387-96482-7 (pbk.) LC Card 86-31390 DDC 338.1/0973 19
HD1761 .W274 1987

FOOD INDUSTRY AND TRADE - UNITED STATES - CONGRESSES.
Economic efficiency in agricultural and food marketing /. Ames , 1987. xii, 315 p. ; ISBN 0-8138-0533-3 LC Card 87-2821 DDC 381/.41/0973 19
HD9000.5 .E26 1987

FOOD INDUSTRY AND TRADE - UNITED STATES - HISTORY.
Walsh, William I. The rise and decline of the Great Atlantic & Pacific Tea Company /. Secaucus, N.J. , c1986. 254 p., [24] p. of plates : ISBN 0-8184-0382-9 : LC Card 85-24987 DDC 381/.456413/006073 19
HD9321.9.G7 W35 1986
NYPL [JLE 86-1952]

FOOD INDUSTRY AND TRADE - UNITED STATES - HISTORY - JUVENILE LITERATURE.
Wade, Mary Dodson. Milk, meat biscuits, and the terraqueous machine . Austin, Tex. , c1987. 49 p. : ISBN 0-89015-605-0 : LC Card 87-6813 DDC 338.7/664/00924 B 92 19
HD9010.B65 W33 1987

FOOD INDUSTRY AND TRADE - UNITED STATES - STATISTICS.
Food retailing review . Fair Lawn, NJ , 1985. 178 p. : ***NYPL [JLF 86-868]***

Korb, Penelope. U. S. and world food, beverages, and tobacco expenditures, 1970-83 /. Washington, D.C. , 1986. iv, 84 p. : LC Card 86-603160 DDC 339.4/8664/0021 19
HD9000.4 .K67 1986

Food insecurity in the Muslim world /. Quazi, Mohammed Hanif. Jeddah, Saudi Arabia (P.O. Box 9833, Jeddah) , 1985. 21, [26] p. : LC Card 87-133798 DDC 338.1/9/17671 19
HD9018.I84 Q39 1985

FOOD - INSPECTION. see **FOOD ADULTERATION AND INSPECTION.**

Food Institute (U. S.) Food retailing review . Fair Lawn, NJ , 1985. 178 p. :
NYPL [JLF 86-868]

FOOD - MARKETING - CASE STUDIES.
World food marketing systems /. London , Boston , 1986. xviii, 333 p. : ISBN 0-407-00358-4 : LC Card 85-28371 DDC 380.1/456413 19
HD9000.5 .W587 1986
NYPL [JLE 86-3213]

FOOD - MARKETING - CONGRESSES.
Economic efficiency in agricultural and food marketing /. Ames , 1987. xii, 315 p. ; ISBN 0-8138-0533-3 LC Card 87-2821 DDC 381/.41/0973 19
HD9000.5 .E26 1987

Food Marketing Institute.
Retail produce operations, 1986 /. Washington, D.C. (1750 K. St., N.W. Washington 20006) , Newark, Del. [1986] viii, 20 p. ; LC Card 87-101803 DDC 381/.456648/00973 19
HD9321.4 .R47 1986

Food Marketing Institute. Research Dept.
Operating results of independent supermarkets, 1984. Washington, D.C. (1750 K St., N.W., Washington 20006) , c1985. 137 p. : LC Card 86-218675 DDC 381/.456413/00973 19
HF5469.23.U62 O643 1985

Operating results of independent supermarkets, 1985. Washington, D.C. (1750 K St., Washington 20006) , c1986. ix, 141 p. : LC Card 86-225218 DDC 381/.456413/00973021 19
HF5469.23.U62 O64 1986

Food Marketing Institute. Research Division.
Information systems study, 1986. Washington, D.C. (1750 K St. N.W., Washington 20006) , c1986. v, 39 p. : LC Card 86-220211 DDC 381/.456413/00285 19
HF5469.23.U62 I543 1986

Traffic and transportation report, 1986. Washington, D.C. (1750 K St., NW, Washington 20006) , c1986. vi, 25 p. : LC Card 86-232133 DDC 388.3/24 19
HE199.5.F6 T715 1986

FOOD, NATURAL.
Fortin, Andrée. Le Rézo . Québec, Québec , 1985. 282 p. : ISBN 2-89224-052-2 LC Card 86-225353
HD3290.A3 Q435 1985

Food, need, greed & myopia . Yates, Geoffrey. Ryton, Tyne and Wear , 1986. 96 p. : ISBN 0-907367-04-6 (pbk.) : LC Card 87-129951 DDC 338.1/9 19
HD9000.5 .Y38 1986

Food, need, greed, and myopia. Yates, Geoffrey. Food, need, greed & myopia . Ryton, Tyne and Wear , 1986. 96 p. : ISBN 0-907367-04-6 (pbk.) : LC Card 87-129951 DDC 338.1/9 19
HD9000.5 .Y38 1986

Food or famine? /. Gibb, Christopher. Vero Beach, FL , 1987. 48 p. : ISBN 0-86592-279-9 LC Card 87-12741 DDC 363.8/096 19
HC800.Z9 F335 1987

FOOD - PACKAGING.
(1986) Gipson, Beckilynn. Aseptic food processing and packaging . Stamford, Conn., U. S.A. , c1986. xiii, 164 leaves ; ISBN 0-89336-471-1 (pbk.) LC Card 87-405014 DDC 381/.45664028 19
HD9999.C743 U629 1986

Food policy : integrating supply, distribution, and consumption / edited by J. Price Gittinger, Joanne Leslie, Caroline Hoisington. Baltimore : Published for the World Bank [by] Johns Hopkins University Press, c1987. xiv, 567 p. : ill. ; 24 cm. (EDI series in economic development) Bibliography: p. 509-555. Includes index. ISBN 0-8018-3500-3 (pbk.) : LC Card 86-27613 DDC 363.8/56/091724 19
1. Food supply - Developing countries. 2. Nutrition policy - Developing countries. 3. Agriculture and state - Developing countries. I. Gittinger, J. Price (James Price), 1928-. II. Leslie, Joanne. III. Hoisington, Caroline. IV. Economic Development Institute (Washington, D.C.). V. Series.
HD9018.D44 F665 1987

FOOD POLICY. see **NUTRITION POLICY.**

Food poverty and consumption patterns in Kenya /. Greer, Joel William, 1948- Geneva , 1986. xii, 170 p. : ISBN 92-2-105374-1 (pbk.) : LC Card 87-115091 DDC 338.1/9/6762 19
HD9017.K42 G74 1986

FOOD PREFERENCES - UNITED STATES - STATISTICS.
Fresh trends, 1987 . [Lincolnshire, Ill.] (400 Knightsbridge Pkwy., Lincolnshire 60069) , c1987. 4 v. ; LC Card 87-162047 DDC 381/.415/0973 19
HD9244 .F73 1987

FOOD PRICES - BRAZIL.
Pereira, José Maria Dias. A participação da alimentação na inflação brasileira nos anos 70 . Porto Alegre, RS , 1984. 139 p. : LC Card 85-128694 DDC 338.4/36413/00981 19
HD9014.B82 P47 1984
NYPL [JLE 86-2264]

FOOD PRICES - CANADA - STATISTICS.
Hassan, Zuhair A. Handbook of food expenditures, prices, and consumption /. Ottawa , c1983. 270 p., [2] p. of plates : LC Card 86-228246 DDC 339.4/8664/00971 19
HD9014.C3 H29 1983

FOOD PRICES - GHANA.
Nyanteng, V. K. Local food prices . [Ghana] , 1978. 37 p. : LC Card 87-403379 DDC 338.4/3664/009667 19
HD9017.G452 N92 1978

FOOD PRICES - GOVERNMENT POLICY - DEVELOPING COUNTRIES.

Streeten, Paul. What price food? . New York , 1987. viii, 127 p. : ISBN 0-312-00739-6 : LC Card 87-9577 DDC 338.1/8 19
HD1417 .S73 1987

FOOD PRICES - GOVERNMENT POLICY - ITALY - LOMBARDY - HISTORY - 18TH CENTURY.
Grab, Alexander I., 1946- La politica del pane . Milano, Italy , c1986. 180 p. ; LC Card 86-168239
HD9015.I85 L664 1986

FOOD PRICES - GOVERNMENT POLICY - UNITED STATES.
Timmer, C. Peter. Getting prices right . Ithaca , 1986. 160 p. : ISBN 0-8014-9441-9 (pbk. : alk. paper) LC Card 86-47649 DDC 338.1/8 19
HD9006 .T58 1986 ***NYPL [JLE 86-4488]***

FOOD PRICES - LATIN AMERICA - ECONOMETRIC MODELS.
Lord, Montague J. Market price models for Latin America's major commodity exports /. Washington, D.C. [1986] vii, 219 p. : LC Card 87-115208 DDC 338.5/2/098 19
HD9014.A2 L67 1986

FOOD PRICES - MALAWI.
Mills, J. C. (Joseph C.) Price responses of Malawi smallholder farmers--fast, slow or none? [microform] /. [Zomba] [1975] 42, [2] p. ; LC Card 80-980238 DDC 338.1/3/096897 19
HD1476.M33 M54 1975
NYPL [*ZT-1646 no.53]

FOOD PRICES - SWEDEN.
Sweden. 1983 års livsmedelskommitté. Expertgruppen för prisregleringsfrågor. Prisstöd och jordbruksprisreglering . Stockholm [1984] xvi, 260 p. ; ISBN 91-38-08461-9 LC Card 86-109988
HD9015.S86 S883 1984

Underbilaga till rapport från 1983 års livsmedelskommittés expertgrupp för prisregleringsfrågor . [Sweden , 1983] (Jönköping . 1 v. (various pagings) : LC Card 85-191640
HD9015.S86 U47 1983

FOOD PRICES - UNITED STATES.
Samtur, Susan J. Cashing in at the checkout /. New York , c1979. 152 p. : ISBN 0-448-15704-7 : LC Card 79-51120 DDC 381/.1 19
HF6127 .S25 ***NYPL [JLD 81-566]***

FOOD PROCESSING WORKERS. see **FOOD INDUSTRY AND TRADE - EMPLOYEES.**

FOOD, PURE. see **FOOD ADULTERATION AND INSPECTION.**

FOOD RELIEF - AFRICA, SUB-SAHARAN.
Committee on African Development Strategies (U. S.) Compact for African development . Berkeley, CA (2120 Berkeley Way, Berkeley 94720) [1985] 24 p. : LC Card 86-200473 DDC 338.967 19
HC800 .C645 1985

FOOD RELIEF, AMERICAN.
Special report on applying United States food surpluses to the problems of hunger /. Washington , 1984. ii, iv, 54 p. ; LC Card 87-601529 DDC 363.8/83 19
HD9000.5 .S666 1984

Trends in foreign aid, 1977-86 . Washington , 1986. vii, 21 p. : LC Card 87-601358 DDC 338.91/73 19
HC60 .T69 1986

FOOD RELIEF, AMERICAN - DEVELOPING COUNTRIES.
Solving world hunger, the U. S. stake /. Cabin John, MD , 1986. ix, 102 p. : ISBN 0-932020-42-9 (pbk.) : LC Card 86-17665 DDC 363.8/526/0973 19
HV696.F6 S65 1986 ***NYPL [JLF 87-531]***

FOOD RELIEF - AUSTRIA - HISTORY.
Loewenfeld-Russ, Hans, 1873-1945. Im Kampf gegen den Hunger . München , 1986. xxiv, 381 p., [1] leaf of plates : ISBN 3-486-52451-8 LC Card 86-224948
HC270.F3 L64 1986

FOOD RELIEF - CHILE.
Hardy, Clarisa. Hambre + dignidad=ollas comunes /. [Santiago, Chile] , 1986. 282 p., [16] p. of plates : ***NYPL [JLD 87-334]***

FOOD RELIEF - CONGRESSES.
Honger op ons bord . Amsterdam , 1986. 164 p. : ISBN 90-70985-05-5 : LC Card 86-166714
HD9000.5 .H655 1986

FOOD RELIEF - DEVELOPING COUNTRIES.
Blau, Gerda. Food aid for development . Rome , Ann Arbor, MI , 1985. xi, 343 p. : ISBN 92-5-102180-5 (pbk.) LC Card 86-220906 DDC 363.8/83/091724 19
HD9018.D44 B57 1985

Fryer, Jonathan. [Food for thought. French.] L'aide alimentaire, un marché de dupes /. Genève, Suisse . 91 p. ; LC Card 86-218069
HD9018.D44 F7914 1982

Manifiesto contra el hambre en el mundo. Madrid , c1985. 95 p. ; ISBN 84-85436-23-7 (IEPALA) LC Card 86-165078
HD9018.D44 M35 1985
NYPL [JLD 87-1535]

Tangermann, Stefan. Welternährung und die Verantwortlichkeit der Industrieländer /. Kiel , 1986. 27 p. ; ISBN 3-925357-38-6 LC Card 87-126268 DDC 338.1/9/1724 19
HD9018.D44 T36 1986

FOOD RELIEF - ETHIOPIA.
Faces in a famine [motion picture] /. New York, N.Y. , 1985. 1 film reel (51 min.) : LC Card 85-702803 DDC 963 11
HC845.Z9F3

Faces in a famine [videorecording] /. New York, N.Y. , 1985. 1 videocassette (51 min.) : LC Card 85-703663 DDC 963 11
HC845.Z9F3

FOOD RELIEF - GOVERNMENT POLICY.
Stevens, Charles J. Confronting the world food crisis /. Muscatine, Iowa [1981] 24 p. : LC Card 82-127279 DDC 338.1/9 19
HD9000.6 .S73 ***NYPL [JLK 75-198 no. 27]***

FOOD RELIEF - SAHEL - CONGRESSES.
Politiques vivrières, dépendances alimentaires et développement /. [Paris] , c1984. iv, 129 p. : ISBN 2-86844-000-2 : LC Card 84-248912
HD9017.S152 P65 1984

FOOD RELIEF - UNITED STATES.
Dirt rich, dirt poor . New York , 1986. xii, 188 p. ; ISBN 0-7102-0378-0 LC Card 85-8274 DDC 338.1/9/73 19
HD1761 .D55 1986 ***NYPL [JLD 87-821]***

Obert, Jessie Craig, 1911- Community nutrition /. New York , c1986. xviii, 478 p. : ISBN 0-471-82187-X LC Card 85-16910 DDC 363.8/8/0973 19
HV696.F6 O23 1986 ***NYPL [JLE 86-1398]***

Special report on applying United States food surpluses to the problems of hunger /. Washington , 1984. ii, iv, 54 p. ; LC Card 87-601529 DDC 363.8/83 19
HD9000.5 .S666 1984

Food retailing review : survey of performance at U. S. food stores and eating & drinking places. Fair Lawn, NJ : Food Institute (American Institute of Food Distribution, Inc.), 1985. 178 p. : ill. ; 28 cm.
1. Food industry and trade - United States - Statistics. 2. Grocery trade - United States - Statistics. 3. Restaurants, lunch rooms, etc. - United States - Statistics. I. Food Institute (U. S.).
NYPL [JLF 86-868]

The food revolution in the Soviet Union and Eastern Europe /. Deutsch, Robert. Boulder , 1986. xxii, 256 p. : ISBN 0-8133-7161-9 (pbk.) : LC Card 85-26625 DDC 338.1/9/47 19
HD9015.S652 D47 1986
NYPL [JLE 86-1588]

Food security system of India . Acharya, K. C. S., 1930- New Delhi , 1983. xviii, 285 p. : LC Card 83-906857 DDC 338.1/9/54 19
HD9016.I42 A63 1983 ***NYPL [JLD 87-652]***

FOOD SERVICE - ACCOUNTING.
Coltman, Michael M., 1930- Hospitality management accounting /. New York , c1987. xi, 449 p. : ISBN 0-442-21777-3 : LC Card 86-28201 DDC 657/.837 19
HF5686.H75 C53 1987

Cote, Raymond. Understanding hospitality accounting I /. East Lansing, Mich. , c1987. p. cm. ISBN 0-86612-035-1 : LC Card 87-15724 DDC 657/.837 19
HF5686.H75 C63 1987

FOOD SERVICE - LITHUANIA - CONGRESSES.
Problemy razvitii͡a i sovershenstvovanii͡a material′no-tekhnicheskoĭ bazy torgovli i obshchestvennogo pitanii͡a v dvenadtsatoĭ pi͡atiletke . Vil′ni͡us , 1985. 169 p. ; LC Card 86-102743
HF3629.L5 P76 1985

FOOD STAMP PROGRAM - UNITED STATES.
DeMilner, Lawrence E. Indexing with the consumer price index . [Washington, D.C.] , 1981. xx, 123 p. : LC Card 81-602368 DDC 338.5/28/0973 19
HG229.5 .D45 ***NYPL [JLF 85-3118]***

FOOD SUPPLY - ADDRESSES, ESSAYS, LECTURES.
George, Susan. Ill fares the land . Washington, D.C. , c1984. xviii, 102 p. ; ISBN 0-89758-039-7 (pbk.) : LC Card 84-25124 DDC 363.8 19
HD9000.5 .G385 1984
NYPL [JLD 86-3899]

FOOD SUPPLY - AFRICA.
Feeding African cities . Bloomington , c1987. x, 249 p. ; ISBN 0-253-32102-6 LC Card 86-46323 DDC 338.1/9/6 19
HD9017.A2 F44 1987

Harrison, Paul. The greening of Africa . New York, N.Y., U. S.A. , 1987. 380 p. : ISBN 0-14-010192-6 (pbk.) : LC Card 87-404277 DDC 338.1/9/6 19
HD2117 .H37 1987

Natural resources and the human environment for food and agriculture in Africa. Rome , 1986. iv, 83 p. : ISBN 92-5-102354-9 (pbk.) LC Card 86-222103 DDC 338.1/096 19
HC800 .N34 1986

FOOD SUPPLY - AFRICA - CONGRESSES.
World recession and the food crisis in Africa /. London , 1986. 314 p. ; ISBN 0-85255-309-9 : LC Card 86-235333 DDC 363.8/526/096 19
HD9017.A2 W67 1986b

World recession and the food crisis in Africa /. Boulder , 1986. p. cm. ISBN 0-8133-0511-X : LC Card 86-28250 DDC 363.8/526/096 19
HD9017.A2 W67 1986

FOOD SUPPLY - AFRICA, NORTH - CONGRESSES.
Les Modèles de consommation et les politiques alimentaires dans les pays du Maghreb . Alger [1985?] 401 p. : LC Card 87-132818
HD9017.A24 M63 1985

FOOD SUPPLY - AFRICA, SUB-SAHARAN.
Bread broken . Eldoret, Kenya [1984] vi, 56 p. : LC Card 85-980419 DDC 363.8/0967 19
HC800.Z9 F32 1984

Nourrir les villes en Afrique sub-saharienne /. Paris , c1985. 421 p. : ISBN 2-85802-562-X LC Card 86-222243
HD9017.S82 N68 1985

FOOD SUPPLY - AFRICA, SUB-SAHARAN - CONGRESSES.
Accelerating food production in Sub-Saharan Africa /. Baltimore , c1987. xix, 417 p. ; ISBN 0-8018-3390-6 (alk. paper) LC Card 86-10684 DDC 338.1/9/67 19
HD2117 .A33 1987 ***NYPL [JLE 87-1366]***

FOOD SUPPLY - AFRICA, SUB-SAHARAN - MISCELLANEA.
Albagli, Claude. Le rôle économique et social du paysan africain et l'autosuffisance alimentaire /. Abidjan , c1984. 70 p. : ISBN 2-7236-0648-1 LC Card 85-179020
HD9017.S82 A43 1984

FOOD SUPPLY - ARAB COUNTRIES.
Qāsim, Ṣubḥī, 1934- Mulakhkhaṣ kitāb Naẓrah taḥlīlīyah fī mushkilat al-ghidhā' fī al-buldān al-'Arabīyah /. [Jordan?] , 1982. 103 p. ; LC Card 86-203782
HD9018.A55 Q269 1982

FOOD SUPPLY - ASIA - CONGRESSES.
An Integrated approach to population, food, and nutrition policies and programmes for national development . Bangkok, Thailand [1979 or 1980] 39 p. ; LC Card 82-169080
HA4553 .I58 1979

FOOD SUPPLY - BOLIVIA.
Proyecto harinas compuestas . La Paz, Bolivia , 1982. 272, [2], 3 p., [9] p. of plates : LC Card 83-195592
HD9044.B52 P76 1982

Roca, José Luis, 1935- Derrotemos al hambre . La Paz, Bolivia , 1985. 157, [16] leaves of plates : LC Card 85-241330 DDC 363.8/56/0984 19
HD9014.B62 R63 1985 ***NYPL [JLD 87-385]***

FOOD SUPPLY - BRAZIL.
Campino, Antonio Carlos Coelho. Economia da alimentação e nutrição . São Paulo , 1985. 238 p. : LC Card 86-129956 DDC 338.1/9/81 19
HD9014.B82 C35 1985 ***NYPL [JLD 86-4118]***

Homem de Melo, Fernando Bento, 1942- Prioridade agrícola . São Paulo , 1985. xiii, 200 p. : LC Card 86-126447 DDC 338.1/881 19
HD1872 .H66 1985 ***NYPL [JLD 86-3809]***

Lima Sobrinho, Antonio Estevam de. Fome, agricultura e política no Brasil . Petrópolis , 1981. 120 p. ; LC Card 81-185801 DDC 338.1/0981 19
HD9014.B82 L56 1981 ***NYPL [JLD 86-3297]***

Müller, Geraldo. Alimentação e agricultura no Brasil . [São Paulo] , 1984. 64 p. : LC Card 86-132127
HD1872 .M85 1984

FOOD SUPPLY - BRAZIL - CONGRESSES.
Debate Nacional sobre Abastecimento Popular (1986) Documento final /. Brasília, DF , 1986. 51 leaves : LC Card 87-146594 DDC 363.8/0981 19
HD9014.B82 D43 1986

FOOD SUPPLY - BRAZIL - SÃO PAULO (STATE) - CONGRESSES.
Seminário Nacional de Abastecimento Alimentar em Grandes Cidades--a Experiência de São Paulo (1984 : São Paulo, Brazil) Anais /. São Paulo, São Paulo, Brasil , 1984. xii, 421 p. : LC Card 87-404933 DDC 363.8/0981/61 19
HD9014.B83 S447 1984

FOOD SUPPLY - BRAZIL - STATISTICS.
Balanço e disponibilidade interna de gêneros alimentícios de origem vegetal 1975 a 1980 /. Rio de Janeiro, RJ, Brasil , 1983. 72 p. ;
NYPL [JLG 85-94]

FOOD SUPPLY - CANADA - STATISTICS.
Hassan, Zuhair A. Handbook of food expenditures, prices, and consumption /. Ottawa , c1983. 270 p., [2] p. of plates : LC Card 86-228246 DDC 339.4/8664/00971 19
HD9014.C3 H29 1983

FOOD SUPPLY - CENTRAL AMERICA.
Barry, Tom, 1950- Roots of rebellion . Boston , c1987. xii, 220 p. : ISBN 0-89608-288-1 : LC Card 87-4519 DDC 338.1/9/728 19
HD9014.C462 B37 1987

FOOD SUPPLY - CHINA.
Feeding a billion . East Lansing , 1987. 462 p., [16] p. of plates : ISBN 0-87013-246-6 (alk. paper) : LC Card 87-60024 DDC 338.1/9/51 19
HD2098 .F45 1987

FOOD SUPPLY - CONGRESSES.
Honger op ons bord . Amsterdam , 1986. 164 p. : ISBN 90-70985-05-5 : LC Card 86-166714
HD9000.5 .H655 1986

The World Food Conference . Washington , 1974. xv, 377 p. : LC Card 74-603025
TX345 .W58 ***NYPL [JLF 78-685]***

FOOD SUPPLY - DEVELOPING COUNTRIES.
Blau, Gerda. Food aid for development . Rome , Ann Arbor, MI , 1985. xi, 343 p. : ISBN 92-5-102180-5 (pbk.) LC Card 86-220906 DDC 363.8/83/091724 19
HD9018.D44 B57 1985

Food policy . Baltimore , c1987. xiv, 567 p. : ISBN 0-8018-3500-3 (pbk.) : LC Card 86-27613 DDC 363.8/56/091724 19
HD9018.D44 F665 1987

Food, the state, and international political economy . Lincoln , c1986. xxiii, 351 p. : ISBN 0-8032-4413-4 (alk. paper) LC Card 85-30893 DDC 338.1/9/1724 19
HD9018.D44 F67 1986 ***NYPL [JLD 86-3440]***

France. Conseil économique et social. Les surplus agricoles et la pénurie alimentaire . [Paris] [1986] 1 v. (various pagings) : LC Card 86-179100
HD1431 .F7 1986

Fryer, Jonathan. [Food for thought. French.] L'aide alimentaire, un marché de dupes /. Genève, Suisse . 91 p. ; LC Card 86-218069
HD9018.D44 F7914 1982

Global hunger . [Evansville, Ind.] , 1986. iv, 164 p. : ISBN 0-930982-08-8 (pbk.) LC Card 87-400224 DDC 363.8/8/091724 19
HD9018.D44 G57 1986

Manifiesto contra el hambre en el mundo. Madrid , c1985. 95 p. ; ISBN 84-85436-23-7 (IEPALA) LC Card 86-165078
HD9018.D44 M35 1985 ***NYPL [JLD 87-1535]***

Perspektivy reshenii͡a prodovol'stvennoĭ problemy v razvivai͡ushchikhsi͡a stranakh . Moskva , 1985. 142 p. ; LC Card 85-188217
HD9018.D44 P47 1985

Population growth and economic development . Madison, Wis. , 1987. xiii, 702 p. ; ISBN 0-299-11130-X : LC Card 86-40447 DDC 338.9/009172/4 19
HB884 .P66547 1987

Tangermann, Stefan. Welternährung und die Verantwortlichkeit der Industrieländer /. Kiel , 1986. 27 p. ; ISBN 3-925357-38-6 LC Card 87-126268 DDC 338.1/9/1724 19
HD9018.D44 T36 1986

Warnock, John W., 1933- The politics of hunger . Toronto , New York , c1987. xv, 334 p. ; ISBN 0-458-80630-7 (pbk.) : LC Card 87-1659 DDC 363.8/09172/4 19
HD9018.D44 W37 1987

Yates, Geoffrey. Food, need, greed & myopia . Ryton, Tyne and Wear , 1986. 96 p. : ISBN 0-907367-04-6 (pbk.) : LC Card 87-129951 DDC 338.1/9 19
HD9000.5 .Y38 1986

FOOD SUPPLY - DEVELOPING COUNTRIES - CONGRESSES.
Alexander von Humboldt Award Colloquium (1984) Technology, human capital, and the world food problem /. St. Paul, MN , 1986. x, 167 p. : LC Card 86-622216 DDC 338.1/9/1724 19
HD9018.D44 A44 1984

Honger op ons bord . Amsterdam , 1986. 164 p. : ISBN 90-70985-05-5 : LC Card 86-166714
HD9000.5 .H655 1986

Pursuing food security . Boulder , 1987. xv, 357 p. : ISBN 1-555-87032-5 (lib. bdg. : alk. paper) : LC Card 87-4524 DDC 337/.05 s 338.1/9/1724 19
HF1410 .I579 vol. 3 HD9018.D44

Séminaire international sur la place des femmes dans l'autosuffisance et les stratégies alimentaires (1985 : Paris, France) Femmes et politiques alimentaires . Paris , 1985. 741 p. : ISBN 2-7099-0763-1 LC Card 86-205282
HD6073.A292 D4477 1985

FOOD SUPPLY - DOMINICAN REPUBLIC.
Producción versus consumo de alimentos . [Santo Domingo, Dominican Republic] , 1981. 74 p. ; LC Card 82-207744
HD9014.D62 P76 1981

FOOD SUPPLY - ETHIOPIA.
Belg synoptic report [microform] . Addis Abeba, Ethiopia [1981] iv, 21 leaves : LC Card 82-980790 DDC 363.8/0963 19
HD9017.E82 B45 1981 ***NYPL [*ZT-1708 no.19]***

FOOD SUPPLY - ETHIOPIA - FORECASTING.
Belg (small) crop season synoptic report. Addis Abeba, Ethiopia , 1985. 23 leaves : LC Card 86-980254 DDC 338.1/9/63 19
HD9017.E82 B44 1985

FOOD SUPPLY - EUROPE EASTERN.
Deutsch, Robert. The food revolution in the Soviet Union and Eastern Europe /. Boulder , 1986. xxii, 256 p. : ISBN 0-8133-7161-9 (pbk.) : LC Card 85-26625 DDC 338.1/9/47 19
HD9015.S652 D47 1986 ***NYPL [JLE 86-1588]***

FOOD SUPPLY - FORECASTING - CONGRESSES.
Food demand analysis . Blacksburg, Va. [1986] xii, 292 p. : LC Card 87-620670 DDC 339.4/86413 19
HD9000.5 .F5946 1986

FOOD SUPPLY - GOVERNMENT POLICY.
Bennett, Jon. The hunger machine . Oxford , New York , 1987. 232 p. : ISBN 0-7456-0444-7 : LC Card 87-724 DDC 363.8 19
HD9000.5 .B449 1987

Stevens, Charles J. Confronting the world food crisis /. Muscatine, Iowa [1981] 24 p. : LC Card 82-127279 DDC 338.1/9 19
HD9000.6 .S73 ***NYPL [JLK 75-198 no. 27]***

World food, population, and development /. Totowa, N.J. , 1985. xvi, 346 p. : ISBN 0-8476-7455-X : LC Card 85-14398 DDC 338.1/9 19
HD9000.5 .W59 1985 ***NYPL [JLE 86-1741]***

FOOD SUPPLY - GOVERNMENT POLICY - ADDRESSES, ESSAYS, LECTURES.
George, Susan. Ill fares the land . Washington, D.C. , c1984. xviii, 102 p. ; ISBN 0-89758-039-7 (pbk.) : LC Card 84-25124 DDC 363.8 19
HD9000.5 .G385 1984 ***NYPL [JLD 86-3899]***

FOOD SUPPLY - GOVERNMENT POLICY - AUSTRIA - HISTORY.
Loewenfeld-Russ, Hans, 1873-1945. Im Kampf gegen den Hunger . München , 1986. xxiv, 381 p., [1] leaf of plates : ISBN 3-486-52451-8 LC Card 86-224948
HC270.F3 L64 1986

FOOD SUPPLY - GOVERNMENT POLICY - BOLIVIA.
Roca, José Luis, 1935- Derrotemos al hambre . La Paz, Bolivia , 1985. 157, [16] leaves of plates : LC Card 85-241330 DDC 363.8/56/0984 19
HD9014.B62 R63 1985 ***NYPL [JLD 87-385]***

FOOD SUPPLY - GOVERNMENT POLICY - BRAZIL.
Avaliação global do programa de nutrição Brasil-BIRD . [São Paulo, SP] [Brasília] , 1981- v. <1 > : LC Card 87-123819 DDC 363.8/56/0981 19
HD9014.B82 A82 1981

FOOD SUPPLY - GOVERNMENT POLICY - CONGRESSES.
United Nations University Symposium on Energy and Agriculture Futures--Policy Implications of Global Models (1982 : Paris, France) Energy and agriculture . [Chur, Switzerland , New York] , c1984. xii, 370 p. : ISBN 3-7186-0187-7 LC Card 83-18363 DDC 333.79 19
HD1405 .E53 1983 ***NYPL [JLD 86-1837]***

FOOD SUPPLY - GOVERNMENT POLICY - DEVELOPING COUNTRIES.
Cairncross, John. Population and agriculture in the developing countries /. Rome , 1980. ii, 52 p. ; ISBN 92-5-100885-X (pbk.) LC Card 81-198370 DDC 338.1/09172/4 19
HD1417 .C34 1980 ***NYPL [JLF 86-1573]***

Lenoir, René. Le Tiers Monde peut se nourrir . [Paris] , c1984. 210 p. : ISBN 2-213-01385-3 : LC Card 84-188021 DDC 338.1/8/091724 19
HD1417 .L46 1984 ***NYPL [JLD 85-1065]***

FOOD SUPPLY - GOVERNMENT POLICY - ETHIOPIA.
Yeraswork Admassie. Food-for-work in Ethiopia . Addis Abeba , 1985. viii, 102, [58] leaves : LC Card 86-980537 DDC 339.5/0963 19
HD5839.7.A6 Y47 1985

FOOD SUPPLY - GOVERNMENT POLICY - INDIA.
Ojha, Ghanshyam Das, 1947- Organisation & management of public distribution system /. Delhi, India , 1987. x, 235 p. ; LC Card 87-900491 DDC 381/.1/0954 19
HF5415.12.I5 O44 1987

FOOD SUPPLY - GOVERNMENT POLICY - INDIA - EVALUATION.
Acharya, K. C. S., 1930- Food security system of India . New Delhi , 1983. xviii, 285 p. : LC

Card 83-906857 DDC 338.1/9/54 19
HD9016.I42 A63 1983 ***NYPL [JLD 87-652]***

FOOD SUPPLY - GOVERNMENT POLICY - INDIA - HISTORY.
Acharya, K. C. S., 1930- Food security system of India . New Delhi , 1983. xviii, 285 p. : LC Card 83-906857 DDC 338.1/9/54 19
HD9016.I42 A63 1983 ***NYPL [JLD 87-652]***

FOOD SUPPLY - GOVERNMENT POLICY - INDIA - ORISSA.
Mishra, Bhagabat, 1940- Economics of public distribution system in food-grains /. New Delhi , 1985. xviii, 306 p. (some folded) ; LC Card 85-902748 DDC 381/.4131/095413 19
HD9066.I63 O756 1982
NYPL [JLD 86-1149]

FOOD SUPPLY - GOVERNMENT POLICY - ITALY - LOMBARDY - HISTORY - 18TH CENTURY.
Grab, Alexander I., 1946- La politica del pane . Milano, Italy , c1986. 180 p. ; LC Card 86-168239
HD9015.I85 L664 1986

FOOD SUPPLY - GOVERNMENT POLICY - MAURITIUS.
Paul, E. C. (Erik Charles), 1937- Fisheries development and the food needs of Mauritius /. Rotterdam , Boston , 1987. vi, 216 p. : ISBN 90-6191-627-5 LC Card 87-170375 DDC 338.3/7270969/82 19
HD9468.M452 P38 1987

FOOD SUPPLY - GOVERNMENT POLICY - MEXICO.
FOOD SUPPLY - GOVERNMENT POLICY - MEXICO - ADDRESSES, ESSAYS, LECTURES.
Por una nueva política alimentaria /. [México, D.F.] , 1984. 114 p. ; LC Card 85-131176 DDC 338.1/9/72 19
HD9014.M62 P67 1984 ***NYPL [JLC 86-348]***

FOOD SUPPLY - GOVERNMENT POLICY - PERU - HISTORY - 20TH CENTURY.
Kennedy, Peter, 1954- Food and agricultural policy in Peru, 1960-1977 [microform] /. Austin (Sid Richardson Hall 1.310, Austin 78712) , 1983. 22 p. ; LC Card 83-623239 DDC 338.1/885 19
HD1903 .K46 1983 ***NYPL [*ZT-1646 no.20]***

FOOD SUPPLY - GREECE - HISTORY.
Garnsey, Peter. Famine and food supply in the Graeco-Roman world . Cambridge [Cambridgeshire] , New York , 1988. xiv, 303 p., [4] p. of plates : ISBN 0-521-35198-7 LC Card 87-16737 DDC 338.1/9/38 19
HD9015.G82 G37 1988

FOOD SUPPLY - INDIA.
Dogra, Bharat. Empty stomachs and packed godowns . New Delhi , 1987. viii, 126 p. ; LC Card 87-900472 DDC 338.1/9/54 19
HD9016.I42 D64 1987

Étienne, Gilbert. Food and poverty . New Delhi , Newbury Park, Calif. , 1987. p. cm. ISBN 0-8039-9540-7 LC Card 87-16992 DDC 338.1/0954 19
HC440.P6 E86 1987

Spitz, P. (Pierre) Food systems and society in India . Geneva [1983] 2 v. (393 p.) : LC Card 87-100437
HD9016.I42 S62 1983

FOOD SUPPLY - INDIA - HISTORY.
Om Prakash, 1916- Economy and food in ancient India /. Delhi , 1987- v. <1- > ; ISBN 81-217-0027-2 : LC Card 87-902484 DDC 338.1/9/34 19
HC434 .O45 1987

FOOD SUPPLY - INFORMATION SERVICES - AUSTRIA - DIRECTORIES.
Gergely, Stefan M. Lebensmittel- und Agrarwissenschaften /. Wien , 1983. iii, 317 p. ; ISBN 3-205-06103-9 LC Card 87-407964 DDC 338.1/9/4360285 19
HD9015.A8 G47 1983

FOOD SUPPLY - ISLAMIC COUNTRIES.
Quazi, Mohammed Hanif. Food insecurity in the Muslim world /. Jeddah, Saudi Arabia (P.O. Box 9833, Jeddah) , 1985. 21, [26] p. : LC Card 87-133798 DDC 338.1/9/17671 19
HD9018.I84 Q39 1985

FOOD SUPPLY - ISLAMIC COUNTRIES - STATISTICS.
Quazi, Mohammed Hanif. Food insecurity in the Muslim world /. Jeddah, Saudi Arabia (P.O. Box 9833, Jeddah) , 1985. 21, [26] p. : LC Card 87-133798 DDC 338.1/9/17671 19
HD9018.I84 Q39 1985

FOOD SUPPLY - JORDAN.
Shestopalova, Zoi͡a Vladimirovna. Prodovol'stvennai͡a problema i perspektivy ee reshenii͡a v arabskikh stranakh . Moskva , 1985. 151, [4] p. : LC Card 86-130508
HD9016.S92 S44 1985
NYPL [*QIP 87-3413]

FOOD SUPPLY - KENYA - MATHEMATICAL MODELS.
Greer, Joel William, 1948- Food poverty and consumption patterns in Kenya /. Geneva , 1986. xii, 170 p. : ISBN 92-2-105374-1 (pbk.) : LC Card 87-115091 DDC 338.1/9/6762 19
HD9017.K42 G74 1986

FOOD SUPPLY - LATIN AMERICA.
Buscando la equidad. English. In search for equity . Aldershot, Hants, England , Brookfield, USA , c1987. xvi, 249 p. ; ISBN 0-566-05537-6 : LC Card 87-21225 DDC 338.98 19
HC130.B38 B8713 1987

Prodovol'stvennai͡a problema i sel'skoe khozi͡aĭstvo stran Latinskoĭ Ameriki /. Moskva , 1981. 311 p. ; LC Card 82-108167
HD9014.L32 P76 1981

FOOD SUPPLY - LEBANON.
Shestopalova, Zoi͡a Vladimirovna. Prodovol'stvennai͡a problema i perspektivy ee reshenii͡a v arabskikh stranakh . Moskva , 1985. 151, [4] p. : LC Card 86-130508
HD9016.S92 S44 1985
NYPL [*QIP 87-3413]

FOOD SUPPLY - MEXICO.
Barkin, David. El fin de la autosuficiencia alimentaria /. México, D.F. , c1985. 249 p. : ISBN 968-493-091-7 LC Card 86-209699
HD1792 .B38 1985

FOOD SUPPLY - NEPAL.
Gurung, Harka B. Food systems and society in Nepal . Kathmandu, Nepal , 1981. 53, iii p. : LC Card 83-901141 DDC 338.1/9/5496 19
HD9016.N42 G87 1981 ***NYPL [JLG 86-71]***

FOOD SUPPLY - NIGERIA.
Bashir, Ibrahim Lawan, 1948- Food crisis and government response in Nigeria . Boston, MA (270 Bay State Rd., Boston 02215) , 1986. 22 leaves ; LC Card 87-155111 DDC 363.8/09669 19
HD9017.N52 B37 1986

Eweka, J. A. (Julius A.) Village development . Ibadan, Nigeria , 1979. xvi, 194 p. ; LC Card 86-172121 DDC 338.1/9/669 19
HD2145.5 .E94 1979

Sano, Hans-Otto. The political economy of food in Nigeria 1960-1982 . Uppsala , 1983. 108 p. : ISBN 91-7106-210-6 ***NYPL [JLD 84-860]***

FOOD SUPPLY - NIGERIA - HISTORY - 20TH CENTURY.
Rural underdevelopment in Nigeria, 1900-1980. Zaria, Nigeria , 1985. iv, 102 p. ; LC Card 86-154806 DDC 338.1/8669 19
HD2145.5.Z8 R87 1985

FOOD SUPPLY - PERU.
Hurtado Miller, Juan Carlos. Por una causa agraria . Lima, Perú , 1986. 348 p. : LC Card 87-400122 DDC 338.1/885 19
HD1903 .H87 1986

FOOD SUPPLY - PLANNING.
Blanckenburg, Peter von. Welternährung . München , c1986. 347 p. : ISBN 3-406-31300-0 LC Card 86-196307
HD9000.5 .B49 1986

FOOD SUPPLY - POLAND - CONGRESSES.
Przestrzenne aspekty gospodarki żywnościowej do 2000 r. . Warszawa , 1986. 166 p. : ISBN 83-208-0497-3 : LC Card 86-223691
HD9015.P72 P72 1986

FOOD SUPPLY - POLITICAL ASPECTS - DEVELOPING COUNTRIES.
Portilla, Belfor. Alimentos . México , 1983. 149, [53] p. : ISBN 968-429-384-4 LC Card 84-172348 DDC 338.1/9/1724 19
HD9018.D44 P67 1983
NYPL [JLD 86-1520]

FOOD SUPPLY - ROME - HISTORY.
Garnsey, Peter. Famine and food supply in the Graeco-Roman world . Cambridge [Cambridgeshire] , New York , 1988. xiv, 303 p., [4] p. of plates : ISBN 0-521-35198-7 LC Card 87-16737 DDC 338.1/9/38 19
HD9015.G82 G37 1988

FOOD SUPPLY - RUSSIA.
Deutsch, Robert. The food revolution in the Soviet Union and Eastern Europe /. Boulder , 1986. xxii, 256 p. : ISBN 0-8133-7161-9 (pbk.) : LC Card 85-26625 DDC 338.1/9/47 19
HD9015.S652 D47 1986
NYPL [JLE 86-1588]

FOOD SUPPLY - RUSSIAN S.F.S.R. - NON-CHERNOZEM REGION - ABSTRACT.
Vklad severnogo krest'i͡anstva v material'nui͡u i dukhovnui͡u kul'turu i ego znachenie v reshenii problem agropromyshlennogo kompleksa nechernozemnoĭ zony RSFSR . Vologda , 1984. 93 p. ; LC Card 85-156518
HD9015.S652 V54 1984

FOOD SUPPLY - RWANDA.
Twiyongere twongera umusaruro. Kigali [1981] 27 p. ; LC Card 82-980614
HB3662.7.A3 T88 1981

FOOD SUPPLY - SAHEL - CONGRESSES.
Politiques vivrières, dépendances alimentaires et développement /. [Paris] , c1984. iv, 129 p. : ISBN 2-86844-000-2 : LC Card 84-248912
HD9017.S152 P65 1984

FOOD SUPPLY - SIERRA LEONE - MATHEMATICAL MODELS.
Strauss, John, 1951- Socio-economic determinants of food consumption and production in rural Sierra Leone . East Lansing, Mich. , 1983. vi, 91 p. : LC Card 83-622388 DDC 339.4/8664/00724 19
HD9017.S52 S88 1983 ***NYPL [JLF 86-684]***

FOOD SUPPLY - SOVIET UNION.
Agropromyshlennyĭ kompleks v uslovii͡akh razvitogo sotsializma . Moskva , 1986. 167 p. ; LC Card 87-166350
HD9015.S652 A38 1986

FOOD SUPPLY - STUDY AND TEACHING (ELEMENTARY)
Rubin, Laurie, 1956- Food first curriculum /. San Francisco, CA , c1984. viii, 146 p. : ISBN 0-935028-17-X : LC Card 84-8986 DDC 372.8/3 19
HD9000.5 .R73 1984 ***NYPL [JLF 86-1436]***

FOOD SUPPLY - STUDY AND TEACHING (SECONDARY)
Williams, Sonja, 1953- Exploding the hunger myths . San Francisco , c1987. xv, 173 p. : ISBN 0-935028-23-4 (pbk.) : LC Card 87-3360 DDC 363.8/07/1273 19
HD9000.5 .W476 1987

FOOD SUPPLY - SUDAN.
ILO Identification and Programming Mission to the Republic of the Sudan. After the famine . Geneva , 1986. xi, 309 p. : ISBN 92-2-105401-2 (pbk.) LC Card 86-226792 DDC 363.8/83/09624 19
HC835.Z9 F35 1985

FOOD SUPPLY - SYRIA.
Shestopalova, Zoi͡a Vladimirovna. Prodovol'stvennai͡a problema i perspektivy ee reshenii͡a v arabskikh stranakh . Moskva , 1985. 151, [4] p. : LC Card 86-130508
HD9016.S92 S44 1985
NYPL [*QIP 87-3413]

FOOD SUPPLY - TANZANIA.
Msambichaka, L. A. (Lucian A.) Food grain shortfalls in Tanzania, 1961-1981 . Dar es Salaam, Tanzania , c1982. 38 p. ; LC Card 85-980863 DDC 338.1/9/678 19
HD9047.T32 M726 1982

FOOD SUPPLY - UKRAINE.
Savenko, V. N. (Valentina Nikolaevna) Prodovol'stvennyĭ kompleks goroda . Kiev , 1986. 173, [3] p. : LC Card 87-161654
HD9015.S653 U473 1986

Food systems and society in India . Spitz, P. (Pierre) Geneva [1983] 2 v. (393 p.) : LC Card 87-100437
HD9016.I42 S62 1983

Food systems and society in Nepal . Gurung, Harka B. Kathmandu, Nepal , 1981. 53, iii p. : LC Card 83-901141 DDC 338.1/9/5496 19
HD9016.N42 G87 1981 ***NYPL [JLG 86-71]***

Food, the state, and international political economy : dilemmas of developing countries / F. LaMond Tullis and W. Ladd Hollist, editors. Lincoln : University of Nebraska Press, c1986. xxiii, 351 p. : ill. ; 23 cm. Includes indexes. Bibliography: p. [303]-335. ISBN 0-8032-4413-4 (alk. paper) LC Card 85-30893 DDC 338.1/9/1724 19
1. Food supply - Developing countries. 2. Agriculture and state - Developing countries. 3. Food industry and trade - Political aspects - Developing countries. I. Tullis, F. LaMond, 1935-. II. Hollist, W. Ladd, 1947-.
HD9018.D44 F67 1986 *NYPL [JLD 86-3440]*

FOOD TRADE. see **PRODUCE TRADE; FARM PRODUCE - MARKETING.**

FOOD - TRADE AND STATISTICS. see **FOOD INDUSTRY AND TRADE; FOOD SUPPLY.**

FOOD - TRANSPORTATION
(1986) Schmelzeisen, Hans-Michael. Bedeutung, Einsatzmöglichkeiten und -probleme des kombinierten Güterverkehrs in der Ernährungswirtschaft /. Münster [1986] xii, 350 p. : ISBN 3-88660-357-1 (Deut. Bibl.) LC Card 87-121511 DDC 380.5/24 19
HE199.5.F6 S36 1986

(1986) Traffic and transportation report, 1986. Washington, D.C. (1750 K St., NW, Washington 20006) , c1986. vi, 25 p. : LC Card 86-232133 DDC 388.3/24 19
HE199.5.F6 T715 1986

Foodland preservation . Ontario. Toronto, Ont. [1986?] 16 p. : LC Card 86-226909 DDC 333.76/16/09713 19
HD319.O5 O5 1986

FOODS, CONTAMINATED. see **FOOD CONTAMINATION.**

Foot, David H.S. A comparison of some land-use allocation/interaction models [microform] / David H.S. Foot. Reading [Berkshire] : Department of Geography, University of Reading, 1974. 36 p. : ill., map ; 21 cm. (Geographical papers . no. 31) Bibliography: p. 25-26. Microfilm. New York: New York Public Library, 1986. 1 microfilm reel; 35 mm. (MN *ZZ-26,234) ISBN 0-7049-0338-5
1. Land use - Mathematical models. 2. Regional planning - Mathematical models. 3. Population forecasting - Mathematical models. I. Series: Geographical papers. [Reading, Eng.] no. 31. II. Title.
*NYPL [*ZT-1712 no.13]*

Foot, David K. A challenge of the 1980s : unemployment and labour force growth in Canada and the provinces / by David K. Foot. [Toronto] : Institute for Policy Analysis and Department of Political Economy, University of Toronto, c1981. 99 p. in various pagings : ill. ; 28 cm. "March, 1981." "A report prepared for the House of Commons Parliamentary Task Force on Employment Opportunities in the 1980s." Bibliography: p. 65.
1. Unemployment - Canada. 2. Labor supply - Canada. I. University of Toronto. Institute for Policy Analysis. II. Title. *NYPL [JLF 86-1304]*

Foote, Cameron S. The fourth medium : how to use promotional literature to increase sales and profits / Cameron S. Foote. Homewood, Ill. : Dow Jones-Irwin, c1986. xxix, 226 p. : ill. ; 24 cm. Includes index. ISBN 0-87094-913-6 LC Card 86-70966 DDC 658.8/2 19
1. Sales promotion. 2. Business literature. 3. Communication in marketing. I. Title.
HF5438.5 .F66 1986 *NYPL [JLE 87-1433]*

FOOTWEAR INDUSTRY - EMPLOYEES.
Social and labour practices of multinational enterprises in the textiles, clothing, and footwear industries. Geneva , 1984. xii, 184 p. ; ISBN 92-2-103882-3 (pbk.) : LC Card 85-183200 DDC 331.7/677 19
HF5549 .S83473 1984 *NYPL [JLE 85-2322]*

FOOTWEAR INDUSTRY - GOVERNMENT POLICY - CANADA.
Canada. Tariff Board. Relating to the reinstatement of the general preferential tariff on imports of rubber footwear . Ottawa, Canada , c1985. vi, 88 p. ; ISBN 0-660-11961-7 (pbk.) : LC Card 87-109471 DDC 382/.0971 s 382/.4568531/00971 19
HF1762 .A3 no. 161, pt. 1 HF2651.F757C22

For crying out loud : women and poverty in the United States / edited by Rochelle Lefkowitz and Ann Withorn. New York : Pilgrim Press, c1986. ix, 397 p. ; 21 cm. Bibliography: p. 394-397. ISBN 0-8298-0581-8 (pbk.) : LC Card 86-9302 DDC 305.4/2/0973 19
1. Women - United States - Economic conditions. 2. Women, Poor - United States - Attitudes. 3. Sex discrimination against women - United States. 4. Public welfare - United States. I. Lefkowitz, Rochelle, 1951-. II. Withorn, Ann, 1947-.
HQ1426 .F757 1986 *NYPL [JLD 86-3989]*

For freedom /. Tarkunde, V. M. New Delhi , 1984. xii, 199 p. ; LC Card 84-902126 DDC 144 19
B821 .T285 1984 *NYPL [JFD 87-1740]*

For rent by owner /. Prosser, Larry. New York , 1987. xii, 217 p. : ISBN 0-531-15526-9 LC Card 87-16206 DDC 333.33/8 19
HD1394 .P77 1987

For survival, development, and prosperity . Parris, W. H. Georgetown, Guyana [1985] 28 p. : LC Card 87-400751 DDC 338.1/8881 19
HD1895.3.Z8 P37 1985

For women only . MacKenzie, Warren, 1927- Alexandria, Va. , c1986. xiii, 196 p. ; ISBN 0-938125-00-1 : LC Card 86-70681 DDC 332.024/042 19
HG179 .M244 1986

Forbedring og rationalisering af rutebilkørsel /. Hansen, Christian Overgård. Esbjerg , 1986. 259 p. : ISBN 87-88521-37-0 LC Card 86-205999
HE5677.A6 H36 1986

Forbes, D. K. (Dean K.) The Socialist Third World . Oxford, UK , New York, NY , 1987. vii, 333 p. : ISBN 0-631-13442-5 : LC Card 87-5165 DDC 338.9/009172/4 19
HC59.7 .S5857 1987

Forbes, Dean K. The geography of underdevelopment : a critical survey / D.K. Forbes. London : Croom Helm, 1986. 214 p. ; 23 cm. (Croom Helm series in geography and environment) Includes index. Bibliography: p. 184-208. ISBN 0-7099-1012-6
1. Economic development - Social aspects. 2. Anthropo-geography - Developing countries. 3. Developing countries - Economic conditions. I. Title.
NYPL [JLD 86-1233]

Forbes, J. D. (James D.), 1932- The consumer interest : dimensions and policy implications / J.D. Forbes. London ; New York : Croom Helm, c1987. 341 p. : ill. ; 23 cm. Bibliography: p. [312]-331. Includes indexes. ISBN 0-7099-1063-0 LC Card 87-12947 DDC 381/.34 19
1. Consumers. 2. Consumer protection. I. Title.
HF5415.3 .F598 1987

Forbes, Malcolm H. Global hunger . [Evansville, Ind.] , 1986. iv, 164 p. : ISBN 0-930982-08-8 (pbk.) LC Card 87-400224 DDC 363.8/8/091724 19
HD9018.D44 G57 1986

Forbes, Ronald W. Petersen, John E. Innovative capital financing /. Chicago, IL (1313 E. 60th St., Chicago 60637) , 1985. ii, 38 p. : LC Card 86-175368 DDC 336.73 19
HG4936 .P424 1985

Força de trabalho no Brasil : uma análise de mobilidade ocupacional / Secretaria de Planejamento da Presidência da República, Fundação Instituto Brasileiro de Geografia e Estatística, Diretoria Técnica. Rio de Janeiro : A Diretoria, 1982. 73 p. : ill. ; 27 cm. (Série Estudos e pesquisas. 8) Bibliography: p. 69-70. ISBN 85-24-00002-3 LC Card 87-403683 DDC 331.12/72/0981 19
1. Occupational mobility - Brazil. I. Fundação Instituto Brasileiro de Geografia e Historia. Diretoria Técnica. II. Series: Série Estudos e pesquisas (Fundação Instituto Brasileiro de Geografia e Estatística. Diretoria Técnica) , 8.
HD5717.5.B6 F67 1982

FORCE (POLITICAL AND SOCIAL SCIENCE, ETC.) see **POWER (SOCIAL SCIENCES)**

FORCED LABOR - DOMINICAN REPUBLIC.
Plant, Roger. Sugar and modern slavery . London , Atlantic Highlands, N.J. , 1987. xiv, 177 p. : ISBN 0-86232-572-2 : LC Card 87-13315 DDC 331.7/6361/097293 19
HD8039.S86 D652 1987

FORCED LABOR - GERMANY - HISTORY.
Herbert, Ulrich, 1951- Geschichte der Ausländer, Beschäftigung in Deutschland, 1880 bis 1980 . Berlin , c1986. 272 p. : ISBN 3-8012-3019-8 LC Card 87-113703 DDC 331.6/2/0943 19
HD8458.A2 H39 1986

Herrenmensch und Arbeitsvölker . Berlin , c1986. 189 p. : ISBN 3-88022-952-X (cover); 3-88022-925-X : LC Card 87-119712 DDC 331.11/732/0943 19
HD4875.G4 H47 1986

FORCED LABOR - GERMANY - HISTORY - 20TH CENTURY.
Siegfried, Klaus-Jörg, 1940- Rüstungsproduktion und Zwangsarbeit im Volkswagenwerk, 1939-1945 . Frankfurt , New York , c1986. 239 p. : ISBN 3-593-33765-7 LC Card 87-133375 DDC 338.4/76234/0943 19
HD9743.G48 S56 1986

FORCED LABOR - GERMANY (WEST) - MÜNSTER IN WESTFALEN - HISTORY.
Weidner, Marcus, 1964- Nur Gräber als Spuren . Münster , c1984. 134 p. : ISBN 3-924550-02-6 LC Card 86-116688 DDC 331.11/732/094355 19
HD4875.G4 W45 1984

FORCED LABOR - INDIA - UTTARKHAND REGION - HISTORY.
Pāṭhaka, Śekhara, 1951- Uttarākhaṇḍa meṃ kulī begāra prathā . Nayī Dillī , 1987, c1986. 339 p., [16] p. of plates : LC Card 87-902810
HD1537.I4 P38 1987

FORCED LABOR - RUSSIAN S.F.S.R.
Ters'kyĭ, Ĭon. Shcho take stalins'ke "tyloopolchenni͡a"? . Toronto , 1969. 95 p. ; LC Card 82-105191
HD4865.S65 T47 1969

FORCED LABOR - SOVIET UNION.
United States. Congress. Commission on Security and Cooperation in Europe. Implementation of the Helsinki accords . Washington , 1986. iii, 85 p. ; LC Card 86-601286 DDC 331.11/732/0947 19
HD4875.S59 U55 1986

FORCED LABOR - SPAIN - ALMADÉN REGION - HISTORY - 16TH CENTURY.
Bleiberg, Germán, 1915- El "informe secreto" de Mateo Alemán sobre el trabajo forzoso en las minas de Almadén /. London , c1985. 150 p. ; ISBN 0-7293-0200-8 LC Card 86-178917
HD4875.S6 B58 1985

FORCED LABOR - UKRAINE.
Ters'kyĭ, Ĭon. Shcho take stalins'ke "tyloopolchenni͡a"? . Toronto , 1969. 95 p. ; LC Card 82-105191
HD4865.S65 T47 1969

The forced loan and English politics, 1626-1628 /. Cust, Richard. Oxford [Oxfordshire] , New York , 1987. x, 358 p. ; ISBN 0-19-822951-8 : LC Card 87-7977 DDC 336.42 19
HJ1012 .C87 1987

Forced out . Brudney, Juliet F. New York , c1987. 208 p. ; ISBN 0-671-64411-4 (pbk.) : LC Card 87-14927 DDC 650.1/4/0240564 19
HD6280 .B78 1987

Forcher, Michael. Felbertauern : vom Saumpfad zur Panoramastrasse : das Porträt eines europäischen Verkehrsweges / Michael Forcher. Thaur/Tirol : Österreichischer Kulturverlag, [1982] 152 p. : 154 ill. ; 28 cm. Ill. on lining papers. ISBN 3-85395-044-2 LC Card 86-166479
1. Felbertauernstrasse (Austria). 2. Roads - Austria - Tyrol - History. I. Title.
HE363.A94 F454 1982

Ford, Brian R. Siegel, Eric S. The Arthur Young business plan guide /. New York , c1987. xii, 184 p. ; ISBN 0-471-85885-4 LC Card 86-32622 DDC 658.4/012 19
HD62.5 .S556 1987

Ford, Deborah Ann. Haight, G. Timothy. REITs . Chicago, Ill. , c1987. x, 227 p. : ISBN 0-917253-71-X : LC Card 87-2558 DDC 346.7304/37 347.306437 19
HG5095 .H33 1987

Ford Foundation. Southern Europe and the enlargement of the EEC . Lisboa, Portugal , 1982. 324 p. : LC Card 86-201274 DDC 341.24/22 19
HC241.25.E85 S68 1982

Ford, J. L. Economic choice under uncertainty : a perspective theory approach / J.L. Ford. New

York : St. Martin's Press, c1987. ix, 146 p. ; 24 cm. Bibliography: p. [138]-141. Includes index. ISBN 0-312-01244-6 : LC Card 87-18806 DDC 330.1 19
1. Risk. 2. Uncertainty. 3. Decision-making. I. Title.
HB615 .F674 1987

Ford lectures. For other vols. in this series, see Old Catalog.
(1939) Power, Eileen Edna, 1889-1940. The wool trade in English medieval history /. New York [1987], c1941. viii, 128 p. ; ISBN 0-313-25656-X (lib. bdg. : alk. paper) LC Card 86-29442 DDC 338.4/767731/0942 19
HD9901.7.E54 P68 1987

FORD MOTOR COMPANY - MANAGEMENT.
Weaver, Paul, 1942 Oct. 18- The suicidal corporation /. New York , c1988. p. cm. ISBN 0-671-52378-3 LC Card 87-23468 DDC 338.7/4/0973 19
HD2785 .W38 1988

FORD MOTOR COMPANY OF SOUTH AFRICA.
The Sullivan principles at Ford--audit a [microform] /. [s.l.] , 1981. 16 p. ;
NYPL [*ZT-1745 no.32]

Ford, Richard, 1923- Top 500 RDT&E companies /. Greenwich, CT, U. S.A. (100 Northfield St., Greenwich 06830) , c1986. 721, [50] p. : LC Card 87-120786 DDC 338.7/6234/02573 19
HD9743.U6 T66 1986

Ford, Robert Clayton, 1945- Organization theory : an integrative approach / Robert C. Ford, Barry R. Armandi, Cherrill P. Heaton. New York : Harper & Row, c1988. xxii, 482 p. : ill. ; 25 cm. Includes bibliographies and indexes. ISBN 0-06-042124-X LC Card 87-23796 DDC 302.3/5 19
1. Organization. 2. Management. I. Armandi, Barry R. II. Heaton, Cherrill P. III. Title.
HD31 .F5726 1988

Ford, Wayne, 1944- Telemarketing management for business / Wayne Ford. Walnut Creek, Calif. : Springwell Pub. Co., c1987. 125 p. ; 21 cm. Includes index. ISBN 0-943995-01-9 (pbk.) LC Card 87-18050 DDC 658.8/5 19
1. Telemarketing - Management. I. Title.
HF5415.1265 .F67 1987

Ford, William F. (William Frank), 1934- The public policy roots of recent thrift crises / William F. Ford. Washington, D.C. : American Enterprises Institute for Public Policy Research, c1986. 14 p. ; 23 cm. (The G. Warren Nutter lectures in political economy) ISBN 0-8447-1376-7 (pbk.) LC Card 87-164463 DDC 332.3/2/0973 19
1. Building and loan associations - Government policy - United States. I. Title. II. Series.
HG2152 .F67 1986

Forecasting aggregated vector ARMA processes /. Lütkepohl, Helmut. Berlin , New York , c1987. x, 323 p. : ISBN 0-387-17208-4 (U. S. : pbk.) : LC Card 86-31599 DDC 519.5/5 19
HA30.3 .L87 1987

FORECASTING, BUSINESS. see **BUSINESS FORECASTING.**

FORECASTING, ECONOMIC. see **ECONOMIC FORECASTING.**

FORECASTING, EMPLOYMENT. see **EMPLOYMENT FORECASTING.**

Forecasting interstate migration with limited data : a demographic-economic approach [microform] / Andrew M. Isserman ... [et al.]. Iowa City : Institute of Urban and Regional Research, University of Iowa, 1982. 37 p. : ill. ; 28 cm. (ASA/census working paper . 2 2) Bibliography: p. 34-37. Microfilm. New York : New York Public Library, 1985. 1 microfilm reel ; 35 mm. (MN *ZZ-25,047)
1. Population forecasting - United States. 2. Migration, Internal - United States. I. Isserman, Andrew M. II. Iowa. University. Institute of Urban and Regional Research. III. Series. ***NYPL [*ZT-1564 no.33]***

Forecasting natural gas demand in a changing world /. Rose, Adam Zachary. Greenwich, Conn. , c1987. xix, 152 p. : ISBN 0-89232-838-X : LC Card 87-21390 DDC 333.8/23312 19
HD9581.A2 R67 1987

FORECASTING, POPULATION. see **POPULATION FORECASTING.**

FORECASTING, SALES. see **SALES FORECASTING.**

Forecasting sales with the personal computer . Berry, Dick. New York , c1988. p. cm. ISBN 0-89930-329-3 (lib. bdg. : alk. paper) : LC Card 87-7284 DDC 658.8/18/0285416 19
HF5415.2 .B458 1988

Forecasting skilled-manpower needs : the experience of eleven countries / edited by R. Vesituluta Youdi, Keith Hinchliffe. Paris : Unesco : International Institute for Educational Planning, 1985. 259 p. : ill. ; 24 cm. Includes bibliographies. CONTENTS. - Forecasting the needs for qualified manpower / M. Debeauvais and G. Psacharopoulos -- Forecasting skilled-manpower needs in France / by J.J. Paul -- An evaluation of labour-market and educational forecasts in the Federal Republic of Germany / M. Tessaring -- Manpower forecasting and manpower-development planning in the United Kingdom / C.R.S. Dougherty -- Review of manpower forecasts and changes in occupational structure in the United States of America / J.E. Hight -- Manpower planning and education in Hungary / J. Timar -- Manpower and education planning and policy experience in Poland, 1960-80 / A. Josefowicz, J. Kluczynski, and T. Obrebski -- Skilled-manpower planning, forecasting, and training in the USSR / I.V. Ivanov -- Retrospective evaluation of forecasting methods for qualified-manpower needs for Egypt / Mamdouh Saleh -- Review of skilled manpower forecasts in India / M.C. Verma -- Forecasts of skilled-manpower needs in the Ivory Coast / F. Achio -- Manpower forecasting in the United Republic of Tanzania / J.A. Rugumyamheto. ISBN 92-803-1122-3 (pbk.) LC Card 86-214025 DDC 331.12/3 19
1. Employment forecasting. 2. Skilled labor - Supply and demand - Forecasting. I. Youdi, R. Vesituluta. II. Hinchliffe, Keith.
HD5701.55 .F67 1985

FORECASTING, STOCK PRICE. see **STOCK PRICE FORECASTING.**

FORECASTING, TECHNOLOGICAL. see **TECHNOLOGICAL FORECASTING.**

Forecasts for U. S. maritime industries in 1989 . Ullman, Harlan. Washington, D.C. , c1984. ix, 42 p. : ISBN 0-89206-069-7 (pbk.) LC Card 84-27501 DDC 338.4/76238/0973 19
VM299.6 .U45 1984 ***NYPL [JLD 87-155]***

FORECLOSURE.
Bush, Fredy. Your fortune in foreclosures . Tucson, Ariz. , c1987. ix, 221 p. : ISBN 0-89586-572-6 LC Card 86-33793 DDC 332.63/24 19
HD1382.5 .B87 1987

Cook, Wade B. How to pick up foreclosures . Tempe, AZ , New York , c1983. xviii, 130 p. : ISBN 0-910019-04-5 LC Card 86-218222 DDC 332.63/244 19
HD1382.5 .C6694 1983

Porter, Steven L., 1952- Save your home . Bellaire, Tex. , c1987. 167 p. : ISBN 0-941599-02-7 (pbk.) : LC Card 87-3916 DDC 332.7/22 19
HG2040.15 .P67 1987

FORECLOSURE SALES. see **FORECLOSURE.**

Foreign agricultural economic report .
(no. 216) Dyck, John H. South Korea . Washington, D.C. [1986] v, 74 p. : LC Card 86-602006 DDC 338.1 s 382/.41/095195 19
HD1411 .F59 no. 216 HD9005

(no. 218) Mabbs-Zeno, Carl. Nigeria . Washington, D.C. [1986] vi, 54 p. : LC Card 86-601597 DDC 382/.41/09669 19
HD9017.N52 M3 1986

(no. 223) Trueblood, Michael A. The Ivory Coast . Washington, DC , 1986. iv, 32 p. : LC Card 86-602806 DDC 338.1 s 382/.41/096668 19
HD1411 .F59 no. 223 HD9017.I912

Foreign aid, its defense and reform /. Mosley, Paul. Lexington, Ky. , c1987. xiv, 264 p. ; ISBN 0-8131-1608-2 : LC Card 86-23400 DDC 338.91/09172/4 19
HC60 .M67 1987

FOREIGN AID PROGRAM. see **ECONOMIC ASSISTANCE.**

Foreign aid reconsidered /. Riddell, Roger. Baltimore , 1987. x, 309 p. ; ISBN 0-8018-3546-1 LC Card 87-2949 DDC 338.91 19
HC60 .R49 1987

FOREIGN AID TO AGRICULTURE. see **AGRICULTURAL ASSISTANCE.**

FOREIGN AID TO EDUCATION. see **EDUCATIONAL ASSISTANCE.**

Foreign aid? yes, but-- . Hoffman, Gerard H. Toronto, Ont. , 1981. vi, 55 p. : LC Card 81-182755 DDC 338.91/71/01724 19
HC60 .H63 1981 ***NYPL [JLD 86-3406]***

FOREIGN ASSISTANCE. see **TECHNICAL ASSISTANCE.**

FOREIGN AUTOMOBILES. see **AUTOMOBILES, FOREIGN.**

FOREIGN BANKS AND BANKING. see **BANKS AND BANKING, FOREIGN.**

Foreign capital and technology in China / edited by Richard D. Robinson. New York : Praeger, 1987. xvii, 191 p. : ill. ; 25 cm. Includes bibliographies and index. ISBN 0-275-92716-4 (alk. paper) : LC Card 87-2450 DDC 332.6/7314/0951 19
1. Investments, Foreign - China - Congresses. 2. Corporations, Foreign - China - Congresses. 3. China - Commercial policy - Congresses. 4. China - Economic policy - 1976- - Congresses. 5. Capitalism - China - Congresses. I. Robinson, Richard D., 1921-.
HG5782 .F67 1987

FOREIGN CARS. see **AUTOMOBILES, FOREIGN.**

Foreign collaborations : policy and procedure. 1st ed. New Delhi : Directorate of Research, Institute of Company Secretaries of India, 1986. xii, 362 p. ; 24 cm. Includes bibliographical references and index. LC Card 86-903089 DDC 332.6/73/0954 19
1. Investments, Foreign - India. I. Institute of Company Secretaries of India. Directorate of Research.
HG5732 .F67 1986

Foreign consultants and counterparts . Scott-Stevens, Susan. Boulder , 1987. xvii, 229 p. : ISBN 0-8133-7370-0 (pbk. : alk. paper) LC Card 87-50750 DDC 306/.46 19
HC79.T4 S36 1987

FOREIGN CORPORATIONS. see **CORPORATIONS, FOREIGN.**

Foreign currency translation . Vézina, Pierre, 1935- Toronto, Canada , c1985. 94 p. ; ISBN 0-88800-133-9 LC Card 86-201703 DDC 657/.48 19
HG3853.7 .V49 1985

Foreign debts in the present and a new international economic order / edited by Detlev C. Dicke. Boulder : Westview Press, 1987, c1986. p. cm. Includes index. ISBN 0-8133-0489-X : LC Card 87-2185 DDC 336.3/435 19
1. Loans, Foreign. 2. Debts, External. 3. International economic relations. I. Dicke, Detlev Christian.
HG3891.5 .F67 1987

FOREIGN ECONOMIC POLICY. see **INTERNATIONAL ECONOMIC RELATIONS.**

Foreign economic policy of the United States.
Baldridge, Donald C. (Donald Carl) Mexican petroleum and United States-Mexican relations, 1919-1923 /. New York , 1987. 255 p. ; ISBN 0-8240-8070-X (alk. paper) LC Card 87-23817 DDC 338.2/7282/0972 19
HD9574.M6 B324 1987

Barrie, Robert W. Congress and the Executive . New York , 1987. 347 p. ; ISBN 0-8240-8071-8 (alk. paper) LC Card 87-23814 DDC 382/.3/0973 19
HF1455 .B317 1987

Bauge, Kenneth L. (Kenneth LeRoy) Voluntary export restriction as a foreign commercial policy with special reference to Japanese cotton textiles, 1930-1962 /. New York , 1987. 277 p. ; ISBN 0-8240-8072-6 LC Card 87-23717 DDC 382/.4567721/0952 19
HD9886.J3 B38 1987

Beelen, George D. Harding and Mexico . New York , 1987. xiii, 200 p., [16] p. of plates : ISBN 0-8240-8073-4 (alk. paper) LC Card

87-23724 DDC 337.72073 19
HF1456.5.M6 B44 1987

Bodayla, Stephen D. Financial diplomacy . New York , 1987. x, 216 p. ; ISBN 0-8240-8074-2 (alk. paper) LC Card 87-23790 DDC 337.73072 19
HF1456.5.M6 B63 1987

Boe, Jonathan E. (Jonathan Evers) American business . New York , 1987. p. cm. ISBN 0-8240-8075-0 LC Card 87-23693 DDC 337.73047 337.4 19
HF1456.5.S624 B64 1987

Cammarosano, Joseph R. The contributions of John Maynard Keynes to foreign trade theory and policy, 1909-1946 /. New York , 1987. 437 p. ; ISBN 0-8240-8076-9 (alk. paper) : LC Card 87-23775 DDC 382.1/04 19
HF1411 .C323 1987

Carreras, Charles. United States economic penetration of Venezuela and its effects on diplomacy, 1895-1906 /. New York , 1987. 252 p. : ISBN 0-8240-8077-7 (alk. paper) : LC Card 87-23723 DDC 332.6/7373/087 19
HG5412 .C45 1987

Casillas, Rex J. Oil and diplomacy . New York , 1987. p. cm. ISBN 0-8240-8078-5 : LC Card 87-23769 DDC 337.730538 19
HF1456.5.S33 C37 1987

Cosgrove, Julia Fukuda. United States foreign economic policy toward China, 1943-1946 . New York , 1987. 235 p. ; ISBN 0-8240-8079-3 (alk. paper) : LC Card 87-23791 DDC 337.73051 19
HF1456.5.C6 C67 1987

Giesecke, Leonard F. (Leonard Frederick) History of American economic policy in the Philippines during the American colonial period, 1900-1935 /. New York , 1987. 279 p. ; ISBN 0-8240-8082-3 (alk. paper) : LC Card 87-23786 DDC 337.730599 19
HF1456.5.P6 G53 1987

Gold, Kenneth A. (Kenneth Alan) United States foreign economic policy-making . New York , 1987. 349 p. ; ISBN 0-8240-8083-1 : LC Card 87-23785 DDC 382/.456413/00973 19
HD9006 .G64 1987

Heston, Thomas J. (Thomas Janney) Sweet subsidy . New York , 1987. 544 p. ; ISBN 0-8240-8084-X (alk. paper) : LC Card 87-23776 DDC 338.1/8 19
HD9105 .H47 1987

Hodin, Michael W. A national policy for organized free trade . New York , 1987. 481 p. ; ISBN 0-8240-8085-8 (alk. paper) : LC Card 87-23719 DDC 382/.45669142/0973 19
HD9515 .H59 1987

Kolarik, William F. A model for the study of international trade politics . New York , 1987. 613 p. : ISBN 0-8240-8086-6 (alk. paper) : LC Card 87-23788 DDC 382/.0947/0730724 19
HF3105 .K64 1987

Mayer, Robert Stanley. The influence of Frank A. Vanderlip and the National City Bank on American commerce and foreign policy, 1910-1920 /. New York , 1987. viii, 221 p. ; ISBN 0-8240-8087-4 : LC Card 87-23793 DDC 332.1/5/097471 19
HG2613.N54 N3555 1987

Pullen, William George. World War debts and United States foreign policy, 1919-1929 /. New York , 1987. 157 p. ; ISBN 0-8240-8088-2 : LC Card 87-23789 DDC 337.7304 19
HF1456.5.E8 P84 1987

Rosenberg, Emily S., 1944- World War I and the growth of United States predominance in Latin America /. New York , 1987. p. cm. ISBN 0-8240-8089-0 : LC Card 87-23683 DDC 337.7308 19
HF1456.5.L3 R67 1987

Rowland, Benjamin M. Commercial conflict and foreign policy . New York , 1987. 431 p. ; ISBN 0-8240-8090-4 (alk. paper) : LC Card 87-23787 DDC 337.73041 19
HF1456.5.G7 R68 1987

Sanford, William F. The American business community and the European Recovery Program, 1947-1952 /. New York , 1987. xiv, 366 p. ; ISBN 0-8240-8091-2 (alk. paper) LC Card 87-23765 DDC 338.91/73/04 19
HC240 .S259 1987

Shook, Dale N. William G. McAdoo and the development of national economic policy, 1913-1918 /. New York , 1987. 427 p. ; ISBN 0-8240-8092-0 (alk. paper) : LC Card 87-23766 DDC 338.973 19
HC106.2 .S55 1987

Short, Joseph N. American business and foreign policy . New York , 1987. 340 p. : ISBN 0-8240-8093-9 (alk. paper) : LC Card 87-23792 DDC 382/.41373/0973 19
HD9199.U48 S46 1987

FOREIGN ECONOMIC RELATIONS - LATIN AMERICA.
Sheahan, John, 1923- Patterns of development in Latin America . Princeton, N.J. , c1987. x, 399 p. : ISBN 0-691-07735-5 (alk. paper) : LC Card 87-2853 DDC 338.98 19
HC125 .S498 1987

FOREIGN EDUCATIONAL AID. see **EDUCATIONAL ASSISTANCE.**

Foreign employment : Sri Lanka experience / research team, R.B.M. Korale ... [et al.] of the Employment and Manpower Planning Division, Ministry of Plan Implementation. [Colombo] : The Division, [1985] x, 202 p. ; 30 cm. Study of its socioeconomic impact on the country; survey conducted during Jan.-Oct. 1984. LC Card 87-900211 DDC 331.6/2/5493 19
1. Sri Lankans - Employment - Foreign countries. 2. Labor supply - Sri Lanka. I. Korale, R. B. M. II. Sri Lanka. Sālasum Kriyātmaka Kirīmē Amātyāmśaya. Rākiraksā hā Minisbalaya Sālasum Amśaya.
HD8670.8 .F67 1985

FOREIGN EXCHANGE - ACCOUNTING.
Evans, Thomas G. Foreign exchange risk management under statement 52 /. Stamford, Conn. , c1986. ix, 133 p. : ISBN 0-910065-21-7 (pbk.) LC Card 86-91435 DDC 657/.48 19
HG3853.7 .E935 1986

Griffin, Paul A. Accounting for the translation of foreign currencies . Stamford, Conn. , c1987. viii, 112 p. : ISBN 0-910065-22-5 (pbk.) LC Card 86-81640 DDC 657/.48 19
HG3853.7 .G75 1987

Müller, Herbert, 1948- Die Umrechnung der Jahresabschlüsse ausländischer Konzernunternehmen und die Verrechnung der daraus resultierenden Umrechnungsdifferenzen . Bochum , 1986. x, 348 p. ; ISBN 3-88339-547-1 LC Card 87-143252 DDC 657/.48 19
HG3853.7 .M84 1986

FOREIGN EXCHANGE - ACCOUNTING - STANDARDS.
Westwick, C. A. Accounting for overseas operations /. Aldershot, Hants, England , Brookfield, Vt. , c1986. ix, 184 p. ; ISBN 0-566-02586-8 : LC Card 85-30582 DDC 657/.95 19
HF5686.I56 W47 1986 ***NYPL [JLG 86-202]***

FOREIGN EXCHANGE - ACCOUNTING - STANDARDS - CANADA.
Vézina, Pierre, 1935- Foreign currency translation . Toronto, Canada , c1985. 94 p. ; ISBN 0-88800-133-9 LC Card 86-201703 DDC 657/.48 19
HG3853.7 .V49 1985

FOREIGN EXCHANGE - ADDRESSES, ESSAYS, LECTURES.
Lleras Restrepo, Carlos, Pres, 1908- Economía internacional y régimen cambiario /. [S.l. , 1981] (Bogotá, D.E. : Osprey Impresores) 298, [3] p. ; LC Card 81-204089 DDC 337/.09/048 19
HF1411 .L542 1981 ***NYPL [JLE 86-3889]***

FOREIGN EXCHANGE ADMINISTRATION - CANADA - ECONOMETRIC MODELS.
Bischofberger, Karlheinz. Theorie und Empirie flexibler Wechselkurse . Berlin , c1986. 248 p. : ISBN 3-428-05988-3 LC Card 86-206335
HG3823 .B57 1986

FOREIGN EXCHANGE ADMINISTRATION - CHILE.
Toso C., Roberto. El tipo de cambio fijo en Chile . Santiago , 1983. 64 p. ; LC Card 83-192876
HG3934 .T67 1983

FOREIGN EXCHANGE ADMINISTRATION - DENMARK.
Heinrich, Hans, 1952- Optimale valutaområder /. [Odense] , 1984. 142 p. : ISBN 87-981541-2-5 : LC Card 85-129406
HG3957 .H45 1984

Kolte, Lars. Det danske valutamarked /. København , 1984, c1983. 215 p. : ISBN 87-17-03415-9 LC Card 85-127552
HG3957 .K64 1984

FOREIGN EXCHANGE ADMINISTRATION - DOMINICAN REPUBLIC.
Análisis de la economía dominicana /. Santo Domingo, República Dominicana , 1985. 73 p. ; LC Card 86-186259
HG3926.5 .A53 1985

FOREIGN EXCHANGE ADMINISTRATION - DOMINICAN REPUBLIC - MATHEMATICAL MODELS.
Dauhajre, Andrés. Reforma financiera en pequeñas economías abiertas /. Santo Domingo, República Dominicana , 1986. 97 p. : LC Card 87-402920 DDC 332.4/56097293 19
HG3926.5 .D38 1986

FOREIGN EXCHANGE ADMINISTRATION - EUROPE - ECONOMETRIC MODELS.
Bischofberger, Karlheinz. Theorie und Empirie flexibler Wechselkurse . Berlin , c1986. 248 p. : ISBN 3-428-05988-3 LC Card 86-206335
HG3823 .B57 1986

FOREIGN EXCHANGE ADMINISTRATION - GERMANY, WEST.
Eschenbaum, Gerhard. Krisenbevorratung von Rohstoffen unter spezieller Berücksichtigung einer Finanzierung aus Währungsreserven der Deutschen Bundesbank /. Bochum , 1983. xix, 464 p. : ISBN 3-88339-314-2 : LC Card 83-218426
HF1054.G4 E83 1983

FOREIGN EXCHANGE ADMINISTRATION - HUNGARY.
Böhm, Edward. Wechselkurspolitik in der Planwirtschaft . Hamburg , 1986. 139 p. : ISBN 3-87895-301-1 LC Card 86-210978
HG3947.5 .B64 1986

FOREIGN EXCHANGE ADMINISTRATION - JAPAN - ECONOMETRIC MODELS.
Bischofberger, Karlheinz. Theorie und Empirie flexibler Wechselkurse . Berlin , c1986. 248 p. : ISBN 3-428-05988-3 LC Card 86-206335
HG3823 .B57 1986

FOREIGN EXCHANGE ADMINISTRATION - LATIN AMERICA.
Economic reform and stabilization in Latin America /. New York , c1986. xxiii, 348 p. : ISBN 0-275-92307-X (alk. paper) : LC Card 86-9405 DDC 338.98 19
HC125 .E374 1986 ***NYPL [JLE 87-1073]***

FOREIGN EXCHANGE ADMINISTRATION - LATIN AMERICA - CASE STUDIES.
Cervantes Islas, Joel. La inflación en dos marcos cambiarios . México, D.F. , 1985. iv, 67 leaves ; LC Card 87-108752 DDC 332.4/1/098 19
HG660.5 .C43 1985

FOREIGN EXCHANGE ADMINISTRATION - NIGERIA.
Oyejide, T. Ademola. The effects of trade and exchange rate policies on agriculture in Nigeria /. Washington, D.C., USA , c1986. 61 p. : ISBN 0-89629-056-5 (pbk.) LC Card 86-21309 DDC 338.1/09669 19
HD2145.5 .O94 1986

FOREIGN EXCHANGE ADMINISTRATION - POLAND.
Böhm, Edward. Wechselkurspolitik in der Planwirtschaft . Hamburg , 1986. 139 p. : ISBN 3-87895-301-1 LC Card 86-210978
HG3947.5 .B64 1986

FOREIGN EXCHANGE ADMINISTRATION - SUDAN - ECONOMETRIC MODELS.
Elbadawi, Ibrahim. The Sudan demand for international reserve . [Khartoum] [1984] 40 leaves : LC Card 85-981026 DDC 332.4/5609624 19
HG3982.8 .E42 1984

FOREIGN EXCHANGE ADMINISTRATION - UNITED STATES - ECONOMETRIC MODELS.
Bischofberger, Karlheinz. Theorie und Empirie flexibler Wechselkurse . Berlin , c1986. 248 p. : ISBN 3-428-05988-3 LC Card 86-206335
HG3823 .B57 1986

FOREIGN EXCHANGE ADMINISTRATION - URUGUAY.
Protasi, Juan Carlos. La flotación cambiaría .

Montevideo, Uruguay [1985] 33 leaves : LC Card 86-160085
HG3940 .P76 1985

FOREIGN EXCHANGE ADMINISTRATION - YUGOSLAVIA.
Kovač, Josef. Neuerungen in den Aussenwirtschafts- und Devisenvorschriften Jugoslawiens /. Hamburg , c1985. 100 p. : ISBN 3-9800762-9-6 LC Card 86-160924
HG3965.5 .K68 1985

Novi devizni i spoljnotrgovinski režim SFRJ. English. The New foreign exchange and foreign trade regime of Yugoslavia /. Belgrade , 1986. 217 p. ; ISBN 86-7145-007-4 LC Card 87-148102 DDC 332.4/5609497 19
HG3965.5 .N6813 1986

FOREIGN EXCHANGE - BRAZIL - HISTORY.
Cardoso, Eliana A. Inflation, growth and the real exchange rate . New York , 1987. 98 p. : ISBN 0-8240-1356-5 (alk. paper) : LC Card 87-8570 DDC 330.981 19
HC187 .C218 1987

FOREIGN EXCHANGE BROKERS - ENGLAND - LONDON.
Billion dollar day [videorecording] /. Deerfield, IL , 1986. 1 videocassette (30 min.) : LC Card 86-700167 DDC 332.4 11
HG3903

FOREIGN EXCHANGE BROKERS - HONG KONG.
Billion dollar day [videorecording] /. Deerfield, IL , 1986. 1 videocassette (30 min.) : LC Card 86-700167 DDC 332.4 11
HG3903

FOREIGN EXCHANGE BROKERS - NEW YORK (N.Y.)
Billion dollar day [videorecording] /. Deerfield, IL , 1986. 1 videocassette (30 min.) : LC Card 86-700167 DDC 332.4 11
HG3903

FOREIGN EXCHANGE - CHILE.
Toso C., Roberto. El tipo de cambio fijo en Chile . Santiago , 1983. 64 p. ; LC Card 83-192876
HG3934 .T67 1983

FOREIGN EXCHANGE - CONGRESSES.
Exchange rate targets . Washington, D.C. , c1986. ix, 59 p. ; ISBN 0-8447-3615-5 (pbk. : alk. paper) : LC Card 86-72463 DDC 332.4/5 19
HG203 .E98 1986

Exchange rates and international macroeconomics /. Chicago , 1983. x, 382 p. : ISBN 0-226-26249-9 LC Card 83-14524 DDC 332.4/56 19
HG205 1981c ***NYPL [JLE 86-3231]***

International trade and exchange rates in the late eighties /. Amsterdam ; New York : xii, 418 p. : ISBN 2-8004-0892-8
NYPL [JLE 87-120]

International trade and exchange rates in the late eighties /. Amsterdam ; New York : xii, 418 p. : ISBN 0-444-87941-2 LC Card 86-223111 DDC 382.4/5 19
HG203 .I58 1985

Internationaler Kapitalverkehr und Devisenhandel /. Frankfurt am Main , c1986. 133 p. ; ISBN 3-7819-0347-8 LC Card 87-164156 DDC 332/.042 19
HG3891 .I58 1986

FOREIGN EXCHANGE - ECONOMETRIC MODELS.
Gross, Alexander, 1953- The role of the current account in asset market models of exchange rate determination /. Berlin , New York , 1987. xiii, 391 p. : ISBN 0-89925-373-3 (U. S.) : LC Card 87-8852 DDC 332.4/56 19
HG3882 .G75 1987

Heitger, Bernhard. Strukturwandel und realer Wechselkurs . Tübingen , c1983. vii, 115 p. : ISBN 3-16-344735-X : LC Card 84-125132
HG3823 .H43 1983

Heri, Erwin W. Bestimmungsgründe kurzfristiger Wechselkursfluktuationen . Hamburg , 1982. v, 312 p. : ISBN 3-87895-225-2 LC Card 83-200160 DDC 332.4/5 19
HG3852 .H47 1982

Rötheli, Tobias F. Das Volkseinkommen und die internationalen Kapitalbewegungen /. Bern , c1986. 128 p. ; ISBN 3-258-03669-1 LC Card 87-110633 DDC 332.4/5/0724 19
HG3891 .R67 1986

FOREIGN EXCHANGE - FORECASTING - MATHEMATICAL MODELS.
Hinder, Alex, 1954- Wechselkursprognosen . Bern , New York , c1983. xvii, 424 p. : ISBN 3-261-03345-2 LC Card 86-104957
HG3823 .H5 1983

FOREIGN EXCHANGE FUTURES. see **FORWARD EXCHANGE.**

FOREIGN EXCHANGE - GOVERNMENT POLICY - INDIA.
Singh, Devi, 1952- Economics of exchange rate management /. New Delhi , 1986. 204 p. ; LC Card 86-903032 DDC 332.4/560954 19
HG3971 .S56 1975

FOREIGN EXCHANGE - GOVERNMENT POLICY - PHILIPPINES.
Alburo, Florian A. Trade liberalization experience in the Philippines, 1960-84 /. Makati, Metro Manila [1985] 159 p. : LC Card 87-167251 DDC 382/.09599/0021 19
HF1599 .A43 1985

FOREIGN EXCHANGE - HISTORY.
Denizet, Jean. Le dollar . Paris , c1985. 259 p. ; ISBN 2-213-01626-7 : LC Card 86-148501 DDC 332.4/560973 19
HG3881 .D344 1985 ***NYPL [JLD 87-337]***

Spufford, Peter. Handbook of medieval exchange /. London : Woodbridge, Suffolk ; xcii, 376 p., [3] leaves of plates (1 folded) : ISBN 0-86193-105-X LC Card 86-673816
HG3942 .S68x 1986

Spufford, Peter. Handbook of medieval exchange /. London : Woodbridge, Suffolk ; xcii, 376, [3] p., [1] fold. leaf : ISBN 0-86193-105-X ***NYPL [JLE 86-4344]***

FOREIGN EXCHANGE - INDIA.
Puri, Vijay Kumar. Nabhi's manual for Indian residents abroad, 1985 /. New Delhi , 1985. xv, 352 p., [1] leaf of plate : LC Card 86-901951 DDC 346.54/07 345.4067 19
HG5732 .P83 1985

FOREIGN EXCHANGE - LAW AND LEGISLATION - YUGOSLAVIA.
Novi devizni i spoljnotrgovinski režim SFRJ. English. The New foreign exchange and foreign trade regime of Yugoslavia /. Belgrade , 1986. 217 p. ; ISBN 86-7145-007-4 LC Card 87-148102 DDC 332.4/5609497 19
HG3965.5 .N6813 1986

FOREIGN EXCHANGE - MATHEMATICAL MODELS.
Bischofberger, Karlheinz. Theorie und Empirie flexibler Wechselkurse . Berlin , c1986. 248 p. : ISBN 3-428-05988-3 LC Card 86-206335
HG3823 .B57 1986

Canto, Victor A. Currency substitution . Boston , c1987. viii, 196 p. ; ISBN 0-89838-195-9 LC Card 86-27747 DDC 332.4/56/098 19
HG3823 .C36 1987

Frenkel, Michael. Ausgewählte makroökonomische Modelle offener Volkswirtschaften /. St. Gallen , 1982. 183 p. : LC Card 83-112497
HG3823 .F74 1982

Frenkel, Roberto. Mercado financiero, expectativas cambiarias y movimientos de capital /. Buenos Aires, Argentina [1981] 46 p. : LC Card 82-236987 DDC 332/.0724 19
HG173.6.S62 F73 1981
NYPL [JLD 86-2636]

Grössl, Ingrid. Der Zusammenhang von finanz- und realwirtschaftlichem Sektor einer offenen, stationären Volkswirtschaft . Berlin , c1986. 162 p. : ISBN 3-428-05986-7 LC Card 86-206327
HG3882 .G76 1986

Herberg, Horst. Stagflation as a consequence of an expansionary monetary or fiscal policy under flexible exchange rates /. Stockholm, Sweden [1978] 34 leaves ; LC Card 81-116937
HD5710 .H47 1978

Kostiainen, Seppo. Capital controls under alternative exchange rate and monetary policy regimes /. Joensuu , 1986. 27 p. ; ISBN 951-696-619-5 (pbk.) LC Card 87-100851 DDC 332.4/5 19
HG3823 .K673 1986

Puumanen, Kari. Three essays on money, wealth, and the exchange rate /. Helsinki , 1986. 143 p. : ISBN 951-686-119-9 (pbk.) LC Card 86-235460 DDC 332.4/0724 19
HG221 .P97 1986

Schmidt, Martin, 1953- Wechselkursrisiko, Informationsverarbeitung und Devisenterminmarkt /. Frankfurt am Main , New York , c1985. 253 p. : ISBN 3-8204-8882-0 : LC Card 85-209898
HG3823 .S35 1985

Steingräber, Carola, 1956- Geld- und Fiskalpolitik in Portfolio-orientierten Modellen kleiner offener Volkswirtschaften . Rheinfelden , c1986. ix, 219 p. : ISBN 3-87718-532-0 LC Card 86-182509
HG230.3 .S74 1986

Weigert, Edmund. Defizitfinanzierte Fiskalpolitik in einer kleinen offenen Volkswirtschaft bei flexiblen Wechselkursen . Krefeld , 1987, c1986. iii, 211 p. ; ISBN 3-88358-071-6 LC Card 87-146660 DDC 339.5/2/0724 19
HJ161 .W44 1987

FOREIGN EXCHANGE - NETHERLANDS.
Dunnen, Emile den. Instrumenten van het geld- en valutamarktbeleid in Nederland /. Amsterdam , Deventer , 1985. 109 p. : ISBN 90-267-0955-2 : LC Card 85-115663
HG295.N4 D86 1985 ***NYPL [JLD 86-91]***

FOREIGN EXCHANGE PROBLEM.
Bourguinat, Henri. L'entreprise française face aux variations de change . Paris , c1985. vi, 123 p. : ISBN 2-7178-0899-X : LC Card 85-190582 DDC 332.4/5 19
HG3815 .B68 1985 ***NYPL [JLE 86-494]***

Crockett, Andrew. Strengthening the international monetary system . Washington, D.C. , c1987. vii, 84 p. ; LC Card 86-33750 DDC 332.4/5 19
HG3881 .C694 1987

MacDonald, Ronald. Floating exchange rates . London , Boston , 1987. p. cm. ISBN 0-04-338134-0 (alk. paper) LC Card 87-9259 DDC 332.4/562 19
HG3852 .M33 1987

Nestone, Alberto. Protektionismus . München , c1984. 76 p. : ISBN 3-89019-108-8 LC Card 85-127389
HF1713 .N38 1984

Pastuszek, Rainer. Leading und Lagging kurzfristig variierbarer gruppeninterner Geldflüsse im Währungsrisikomanagement einer internationalen Unternehmung /. Pfaffenweiler , 1986. xvi, 275 p. : ISBN 3-89085-122-3 LC Card 87-128258 DDC 658.1/55 19
HG3851 .P295 1986

FOREIGN EXCHANGE PROBLEM - ADDRESSES, ESSAYS, LECTURES.
Exchange rates, trade, and the U. S. economy /. Cambridge, Mass. , c1985. xxi, 296 p. : ISBN 0-88410-948-8 LC Card 84-28328 DDC 332.4/560973 19
HG3851 .E94 1985 ***NYPL [JLE 85-2269]***

Floating exchange rates and the state of world trade payments /. Cambridge, Mass. , 1984. xxvi, 309 p. ; ISBN 0-88410-998-4 (pbk.) LC Card 84-2905 DDC 332.4/562 19
HG3852 .F56 1984 ***NYPL [JLD 86-2709]***

International finance and trade /. Cambridge, Mass. , c1979. 2 v. : ISBN 0-88410-680-2 LC Card 79-11158 DDC 332.4/5 19
HG3881 .I57617 ***NYPL [JLL 80-187]***

FOREIGN EXCHANGE PROBLEM - BULGARIA.
Petrov, Milan, k.i.n. Mezhdunarodnite pŭtnicheski prevozi i tekhnite valutno-finansovi problemi /. Sofiia , 1984. 95, [1] p. ; LC Card 85-167160
HE265.A2 P48 1984

FOREIGN EXCHANGE PROBLEM - CHILE - ECONOMETRIC MODELS.
Lagos, Luis Felipe. El efecto de los shocks externos sobre el producto . Santiago, Chile , 1985. 15, [8] leaves : LC Card 87-404321 DDC 339.383 19
HC195.I5 L34 1985

Rosende Ramírez, Francisco. Tipo de cambio y salarios reales . Santiago , 1985. 28 p. : LC Card 86-106380 DDC 332.4/5/0983 19
HG3934 .R67 1985

FOREIGN EXCHANGE PROBLEM - CONGRESSES.
World monetary system in a time of change . Budapest [1987] 283 p. ; ISBN 963-01-7937-7 (pbk.) LC Card 87-169001 DDC 332.4/5 19
HG230.3 .W68 1987

FOREIGN EXCHANGE PROBLEM - DEVELOPING COUNTRIES.
Floating exchange rates in developing countries . Washington, D.C. , 1987. v, 43 p. : ISBN 0-939934-89-2 (pbk.) : LC Card 87-3025 DDC 332.4/56/091724 19
HG3877 .F58 1987

Ngirabatware, Augustin. Les taux de change flottants et les pays souscapitalisés . Fribourg, Suisse , c1986. 340 p. : ISBN 2-8271-0330-3 : LC Card 86-170584
HG3877 .N48 1986

Rana, Pradumna Bickram, 1947- The impact of the current exchange rate system on trade and inflation of selected developing member countries /. Manila, Philippines , c1983. iv, 78 p. : LC Card 87-105105 DDC 332.4/56 19
HG3877 .R36 1983

FOREIGN EXCHANGE PROBLEM - DOMINICAN REPUBLIC - CONGRESSES.
La Situación cambiaria en la República Dominicana /. Santo Domingo, República Dominicana , 1984. 252 p. : LC Card 87-401265 DDC 338.97293 19
HC153.5 .S575 1984

FOREIGN EXCHANGE PROBLEM - ETHIOPIA.
Befekadu Degefe. Exchange rate policy and economic distortions . [Addis Ababa?] 1985. 22 leaves ; LC Card 86-221527 DDC 332.4/560963 19
HG3983 .B43 1985

FOREIGN EXCHANGE PROBLEM - EUROPE, EASTERN.
Belichenko, A. N. (Al'bert Nikolaevich) Kreditnye otnosheniia mezhdu stranami-chlenami SEV /. Moskva , 1983. 134 p. : LC Card 84-171632
HG3729.E932 B45 1983

Konstantinov, IU. A. (IUriĭ Anatol'evich) Mezhdunarodnaia valiutnaia sistema stran--chlenov SEV /. Moskva , 1982. 231 p. ; LC Card 82-210094
HG3942 .K67 1982

Zloch-Christy, Iliana, 1953- The debt problems of Eastern Europe /. Cambridge [Cambridgeshire] , New York , 1987. xix, 220 p. ; ISBN 0-521-33542-6 LC Card 87-11634 DDC 336.3/435/0947 19
HJ8615 .Z57 1987

FOREIGN EXCHANGE PROBLEM - EUROPEAN ECONOMIC COMMUNITY COUNTRIES.
Grauwe, Paul de. Exchange rates, money, and output . New York , 1985. xii, 240 p. : ISBN 0-312-27403-3 : LC Card 84-11692 DDC 339/.094 19
HC241.2 .G69 1985 ***NYPL [JLD 86-3007]***

Masera, R. S. L'unificazione monetaria e lo SME /. Bologna , c1980. 220 p. ; LC Card 82-150717 DDC 332.4/566/094 19
HG930.5.Z8 M37 1980 ***NYPL [JLD 87-902]***

Murtazina, E. N. Problemy valiutnoĭ integratsii v Evropeĭskom soobshchestve . Moskva , 1985. 75 p. ; LC Card 85-224384
HG3942.8 .M87 1985

FOREIGN EXCHANGE PROBLEM - EUROPEAN ECONOMIC COMMUNITY COUNTRIES - CONGRESSES.
Problemy valiutnogo soiuza stran-chlenov Evropeĭskogo ėkonomicheskogo soobshchestva i razvitie mezhdunarodnoĭ valiutnoĭ sistemy kapitalizma . Sofiia , 1984. 151 p. ; LC Card 85-224144
HG3942.8 .P76 1984

FOREIGN EXCHANGE PROBLEM - FRANCE.
Bourguinat, Henri. L'entreprise française face aux variations de change . Paris , c1985. vi, 123 p. : ISBN 2-7178-0899-X : LC Card 85-190582 DDC 332.4/5 19
HG3815 .B68 1985 ***NYPL [JLE 86-494]***

FOREIGN EXCHANGE PROBLEM - FRANCE - ECONOMETRIC MODELS.
Gubitz, Andrea. Geldmärkte und Europäisches Währungssystem . Idstein , 1985. vii, 201 p. : ISBN 3-925196-00-5 LC Card 86-230130
HG3949 .G82 1985

FOREIGN EXCHANGE PROBLEM - GERMANY, WEST.
Fleischer, Peter. Bestimmungsgründe von Zahlungsbilanz und Wechselkursen in der Bundesrepublik Deutschland /. Frankfurt am Main , New York , c1986. iv, 181 p. : ISBN 3-8204-9610-6 LC Card 86-232901
HG3883.G3 F57 1986

FOREIGN EXCHANGE PROBLEM - GERMANY (WEST) - ECONOMETRIC MODELS.
Gubitz, Andrea. Geldmärkte und Europäisches Währungssystem . Idstein , 1985. vii, 201 p. : ISBN 3-925196-00-5 LC Card 86-230130
HG3949 .G82 1985

Heitger, Bernhard. Strukturwandel und realer Wechselkurs . Tübingen , c1983. vii, 115 p. : ISBN 3-16-344735-X : LC Card 84-125132
HG3823 .H43 1983

FOREIGN EXCHANGE PROBLEM - GREAT BRITAIN.
Ricardo, David, 1772-1823. Scritti monetari /. Roma [1985] 495 p. ; LC Card 86-207988
HG938 .R63 1985

FOREIGN EXCHANGE PROBLEM - HUNGARY.
Kiefer, Márta. Magyarország tőkés viszonylatu gazdasági és pénzügyi kapcsolatairól /. [Budapest] [1985] 115 p. ; ISBN 963-608-080-1 LC Card 86-228329
HF1542.5 .K54 1985

Szilvássy, Erika. A nemzetközi pénzügyek és a külkereskedelmi fizetések gyakorlata /. Budapest , 1985. 286 p. ; ISBN 963-221-529-X : LC Card 86-190902
HG3881 .S95 1985

FOREIGN EXCHANGE PROBLEM - INDIA.
Singh, Devi, 1952- Economics of exchange rate management /. New Delhi , 1986. 204 p. ; LC Card 86-903032 DDC 332.4/560954 19
HG3971 .S56 1975

FOREIGN EXCHANGE PROBLEM - INDIA - HISTORY.
Goswami, Prodyot Kumar, 1940- Indian currency and exchange, 1835-1940 /. New Delhi , 1983. viii, 134 p. ; LC Card 83-903565 DDC 332.4/560954 19
HG1234 .G67 1983 ***NYPL [JLD 87-673]***

FOREIGN EXCHANGE PROBLEM - ITALY.
Tasgian, Astrig. L'imposta e il deposito previo sugli acquisti di valuta e la crisi della lira del 1976 . Milano , c1983. 139 p. : LC Card 83-187693 DDC 332.4/945 19
HG1029.5 .T37 1983 ***NYPL [JLD 87-813]***

FOREIGN EXCHANGE PROBLEM - JAPAN.
Japan's response to crisis and change in the world economy /. Armonk, N.Y. , c1986. xiii, 309 p. : ISBN 0-87332-405-6 LC Card 86-21907 DDC 338.952 19
HC462.9 .J355 1986 ***NYPL [JLE 87-1199]***

Roosa, Robert V. The United States and Japan in the international monetary system, 1946-1985 /. New York , 1986. ii, 76 p. ; LC Card 86-230043 DDC 332.4/560952 19
HG3881 .R66 1986

Yoshida, Satoshi, 1948- Endaka to kigyō shūeki . [Higashimurayama-shi] , Tōkyō , 1986. 137 p. : ISBN 4-315-50263-4 : LC Card 86-205176
HC462.9 .Y638 1986 <Orien Japan> ***NYPL [*OSM 87-2489]***

FOREIGN EXCHANGE PROBLEM - JAPAN - CONGRESSES.
Japan and the United States today . New York , 1986, c1987. vii, 234 p. : ISBN 0-231-06575-2 LC Card 86-32640 DDC 332/.042/0952 19
HG3903 .J35 1987

FOREIGN EXCHANGE PROBLEM - MATHEMATICAL MODELS.
Nyberg, Peter. On the choice of optimal central bank currency baskets /. Åbo , 1982. 24 p. ;
NYPL [JLL 77-251 no. 181]

Ohr, Renate. Internationale Interdependenz nationaler Geld- und Gütermärkte bei flexiblen Wechselkursen /. Hamburg , 1980. 217 p. : ISBN 3-87895-194-9 LC Card 84-120800
HG3823 .O47 1980

FOREIGN EXCHANGE PROBLEM - MEXICO.
Bennett, Mark. Public policy and industrial development . Boulder, Colo. , 1986. xii, 134 p. : ISBN 0-86531-821-2 : LC Card 83-23456 DDC 338.4/76292/0972 19
HD9710.3.M42 B46 1986
NYPL [JLE 86-2581]

FOREIGN EXCHANGE PROBLEM - PAKISTAN.
Ahrens, Heinz-Dietmar. Towards reducing the dependence on capital imports . Wiesbaden , 1982. xvi, 337 p. : ISBN 3-515-03853-1 (pbk.) LC Card 86-214363 DDC 338.9549/1 19
HC440.5 .A726 1982

FOREIGN EXCHANGE PROBLEM - PHILIPPINES.
Navarro, Susan S. Dynamic effects of exchange rate changes in the Philippines in 1970-1980 /. [Quezon] [1986] 25 p. ; LC Card 87-120911 DDC 332.4/5609599 19
HG1265 .N38 1986

FOREIGN EXCHANGE PROBLEM - SOVIET UNION.
Neu, C. R. (Carl Richard), 1949- Toward a profile of Soviet behavior in international financial markets /. Santa Monica, CA [1987] xv, 58 p. : ISBN 0-8330-0865-X (pbk.) LC Card 87-13084 DDC 332/.042/0947 19
HG3955 .N48 1987

FOREIGN EXCHANGE PROBLEM - SPAIN.
Albentosa Puche, Luis. El sector exterior en España /. Madrid , c1984. 343 p. : ISBN 84-85719-40-9 LC Card 85-214668 DDC 336.3/4/0946 19
HG3883.S69 A45 1984 ***NYPL [JLC 86-251]***

FOREIGN EXCHANGE PROBLEM - SWITZERLAND.
Genberg, Hans. Influences externes sur l'économie suisse en changes fixes et flottants /. Genève , c1985. ii, 202 p. : ISBN 2-8257-0127-0 : LC Card 85-235579 DDC 332.4/5609494 19
HG3963 .G46 1985 ***NYPL [JLD 86-2381]***

Jacobi, Klaus, 1929- Der induzierte Kapitalexport /. Zürich , c1959. viii, 106 p. ; LC Card 87-408198 DDC 332.4/5609494 19
HG3891 .J33 1959

Zenger, Christoph. Kursschwankungen des Schweizerfrankens in ihren Auswirkungen auf Produktion, Export, Import und Fremdenverkehr . Bern , c1982. vi, 263 p. : ISBN 3-258-03172-X : LC Card 83-242397 DDC 332.4/9494 19
HG1155 .Z46 1982

FOREIGN EXCHANGE PROBLEM - UNITED STATES.
Arndt, Sven W. Competitiveness . Washington, D.C. , Lanham, MD , c1987. 120 p. : ISBN 0-8447-3625-2 (alk. paper) LC Card 87-1250 DDC 382/.0973 19
HF3031 .A83 1987

Roosa, Robert V. The United States and Japan in the international monetary system, 1946-1985 /. New York , 1986. ii, 76 p. ; LC Card 86-230043 DDC 332.4/560952 19
HG3881 .R66 1986

Solomon, Anthony M. The dollar, debt, and the trade deficit /. New York , 1987. 55 p. ; ISBN 0-8147-7863-1 : LC Card 86-23651 DDC 382.1/7/0973 19
HF3031 .S65 1987

FOREIGN EXCHANGE PROBLEM - UNITED STATES - ADDRESSES, ESSAYS, LECTURES.
Exchange rates, trade, and the U. S. economy /. Cambridge, Mass. , c1985. xxi, 296 p. : ISBN 0-88410-948-8 LC Card 84-28328 DDC 332.4/560973 19
HG3851 .E94 1985 ***NYPL [JLE 85-2269]***

FOREIGN EXCHANGE PROBLEM - UNITED STATES - CONGRESSES.

Japan and the United States today . New York , 1986, c1987. vii, 234 p. : ISBN 0-231-06575-2 LC Card 86-32640 DDC 332/.042/0952 19
HG3903 .J35 1987

FOREIGN EXCHANGE PROBLEM - URUGUAY - ECONOMETRIC MODELS.
Medina Spangenberg, Ernesto. "Algunas consideraciones sobre el tipo real de cambio en el Uruguay, período 1.78-12.82" /. Montevideo, Uruguay [1984] 39 p. : LC Card 84-253583
HG3940 .M43 1984

FOREIGN EXCHANGE PROBLEM - VENEZUELA - CONGRESSES.
Crisis y control de cambio /. Maracaibo, Venezuela , 1984. 101 p. ; LC Card 87-400572 DDC 332.4/560987 19
HG3941 .C74 1984

FOREIGN EXCHANGE PROBLEM - ZAIRE.
Tshibaka, Tshikala B., 1949- The effects of trade and exchange rate policies on agriculture in Zaire /. Washington, D.C., USA , 1986. 65 p. : ISBN 0-89629-057-3 LC Card 86-27449 DDC 338.1/09675/1 19
HD2135.5 .T75 1986

FOREIGN EXCHANGE PROBLEMS - SWITZERLAND.
Genberg, Hans. External influences on the Swiss economy under fixed and flexible exchange rates /. Grüsch , c1985. ii, 182 p. : ISBN 3-7253-0249-9 (pbk.) LC Card 86-156330
HG3963 .G45 1985 ***NYPL [JLD 87-539]***

Foreign exchange risk management under statement 52 /. Evans, Thomas G. Stamford, Conn. , c1986. ix, 133 p. : ISBN 0-910065-21-7 (pbk.) LC Card 86-91435 DDC 657/.48 19
HG3853.7 .E935 1986

FOREIGN EXCHANGE - STATISTICAL METHODS.
Voeller, Joachim, 1946- Purchasing power parities for international comparisons /. Königstein/Ts. , Cambridge, Mass. , c1981. 104 p. ; ISBN 3-445-02225-9 (pbk.) LC Card 81-84382
HG3821 .V63x 1981

Foreign indebtedness and basic human needs in four African countries : study / prepared in the Foreign Affairs and National Defense Division of the Congressional Research Service for the Select Committee on Hunger, U. S. House of Representatives. Washington : U. S. G.P.O. : For sale by the Supt. of Docs., Congressional Sales Office, U. S. G.P.O, 1986. ii, 54 p. : ill., maps ; 24 cm. At head of title: 99th Congress, 2d session. Committee print. Distributed to some depository libraries in microfiche. Shipping list no.: 86-742-P. "September 1986." Includes bibliographical references. Item 1009-B-11, 1009-C-11 (microfiche) LC Card 86-603396 DDC 336.3/435/0967
1. Africa, Sub-Saharan - Economic conditions - 1960- - Case studies. 2. Debts, Public - Africa, Sub-Saharan - Case studies. 3. Debt relief - Africa, Sub-Saharan - Case studies. 4. Basic needs - Africa, Sub-Saharan - Case studies. I. Library of Congress. Foreign Affairs and National Defense Division. II. United States. Congress. House. Select Committee on Hunger.
HC800 .F67 1986

Foreign investment and government policy in the Third World /. Dickie, Robert B. New York , 1988. p. cm. ISBN 0-312-00520-2 : LC Card 87-25076 DDC 332.6/7322598 19
HG5752 .D53 1988

Foreign investment, debt, and economic growth in Latin America / edited by Antonio Jorge and Jorge Salazar-Carrillo. New York : St. Martin's Press, 1988. xix, 250 p. : ill. ; 23 cm. Proceedings of the Fourth Annual Conference on Key Problems of Latin America, held Dec. 3-4, 1985 in Miami, Fla.; organized by Florida International University. Includes bibliographies and index. ISBN 0-312-00936-4 : LC Card 87-18808 DDC 332.6/73/098 19
1. Investments, Foreign - Latin America - Congresses. 2. Debts, External - Latin America - Congresses. 3. Latin America - Economic conditions - 1945- - Congresses. I. Jorge, Antonio, 1931-. II. Salazar-Carrillo, Jorge. III. Conference on Key Problems of Latin America (4th : 1985 : Miami, Fla.). IV. Florida International University.
HG5160.5.A3 F675 1988

Foreign investment in Papua New Guinea . Daniel, Philip. Canberra , 1986. x, 144 p. : ISBN 0-86784-761-1 (pbk.) LC Card 87-151193 DDC 332.6/7322953 19
HG5982.A3 D36 1986

Foreign investment in South Africa and Namibia . Newman, Anne, 1951- Washington, D.C. [1984] ii, 279 p. ; ISBN 0-931035-00-7 (pbk.) LC Card 85-130985 DDC 332.6/73/0968 19
HG5851.A3 N49 1984 ***NYPL [Sc F 85-173]***

FOREIGN INVESTMENTS. see **INVESTMENTS, FOREIGN.**

FOREIGN LABOR. see **ALIEN LABOR.**

FOREIGN LICENSING AGREEMENTS - HISTORY.
Sekiguchi, Sueo. Technology transfer through direct foreign investment /. Ibaraki, Osaka, Japan , 1985. 61 leaves : LC Card 86-209818 DDC 332.6/7352 19
HC60 .S416 1985

FOREIGN LOANS. see **LOANS, FOREIGN.**

Foreign opinion of the United States. see **United States - Foreign opinion.**

FOREIGN POPULATION. see **EMIGRATION AND IMMIGRATION.**

Foreign regulations affecting U. S. textile/apparel exports. [Washington, D.C.] : U. S. Dept. of Commerce, International Trade Administration, Office of Textiles and Apparel, [1986] 283 p. ; 28 cm. Cover title. "A special report prepared by the Market Expansion Division." "April 1986." LC Card 86-601588
1. Tariff on textile fabrics. 2. Tariff on clothing. 3. Textile industry - United States. 4. Clothing trade - United States. 5. United States - Foreign economic relations. 6. Import quotas. 7. Nontariff trade barriers. 8. Foreign trade regulation. 9. Free trade and protection. I. United States. International Trade Administration. Market Expansion Division.
HF2651.T42 F67 1986

Foreign relations of Latin America .
(no. 6) Devlin, Robert. External debt in Bolivia /. Boulder, Colo. , 1987. p. cm. ISBN 0-8133-7366-2 : LC Card 87-2088 DDC 336.3/4/0984 19
HJ8574 .D48 1987

FOREIGN SALES CORPORATIONS - TAXATION - UNITED STATES.
Lees, Francis A. Financing export sales /. New York, N.Y. (845 3rd Ave., New York 10022) , c1986. 12 p. : LC Card 86-212400 DDC 658.1/5 19
HF3031 .L36 1986

FOREIGN TAX CREDIT - UNITED STATES - STATISTICS.
Statistics of income . Washington, D.C. , 1985. iii, 516 p. : ***NYPL [JLF 86-833]***

Foreign trade. Role of foreign trade in Indian economy /. New Delhi , 1986. 216 p. ; ISBN 81-7062-001-5 : LC Card 86-902110 DDC 382/.0954 19
HF3782 .R65 1986

FOREIGN TRADE. see **COMMERCE.**

FOREIGN TRADE AND EMPLOYMENT.
Ohlinger, Hans A., 1954- Die Relevanz nicht-tarifärer Handelshemmnisse im internationalen Handel und ihre Wirkungen auf die Integration der Entwicklungsländer in die Weltwirtschaft /. Frankfurt am Main , New York , c1986. iii, 400 p. : ISBN 3-8204-8344-6 LC Card 87-407585 DDC 382/.5/091724 19
HF1430 .O38 1986

Welzk, Stefan. Boom ohne Arbeitsplätze /. Köln , c1986. 250 p. ; ISBN 3-462-01787-X LC Card 86-230211
HD5710.75.G3 W44 1986

FOREIGN TRADE AND EMPLOYMENT - AUSTRIA.
Hutter, Monika, 1950- Die Warenstruktur des Aussenhandels . Frankfurt am Main , New York , c1987. 216 p. ; ISBN 3-8204-8810-3 LC Card 87-407938 DDC 382/.09436 19
HF3546.5 .H87 1987

FOREIGN TRADE AND EMPLOYMENT - GERMANY (WEST)
Bernschneider, Wolfgang. Staat, Gewerkschaft und Arbeitsprozess . Opladen , c1986. viii, 291 p. : ISBN 3-531-11797-1 LC Card 86-222066
HD5710.75.G3 B47 1986

Peters, Kathrin. Binnenwirtschaftlich orientierte Hypothesen zur Aussenwirtschaftsentwicklung und ihre Gültigkeit für die Bundesrepublik Deutschland 1969-1982 /. Hamburg , c1986. vii, 311 p. : ISBN 3-925630-02-3 : LC Card 86-226488
HD5710.75.G3 P48 1986

Welzk, Stefan. Boom ohne Arbeitsplätze /. Köln , c1986. 250 p. ; ISBN 3-462-01787-X LC Card 86-230211
HD5710.75.G3 W44 1986

FOREIGN TRADE AND EMPLOYMENT - SOUTHERN STATES - CONGRESSES.
Critical employment issues facing the Southeast /. Atlanta, Ga. , 1986. xv, 156 p. ; ISBN 0-88406-191-4 LC Card 85-31410 DDC 331.12/5/0975 19
HD5725.S85 C75 1986
NYPL [JLD 86-2441]

FOREIGN TRADE AND EMPLOYMENT - UNITED STATES.
Davis, Lester A. Contribution of exports to U. S. employment . Washington, D.C. , 1986. 33 p. : LC Card 86-602848 DDC 331.12/0973 19
HD5710.75.U6 D38 1986

Gray, H. Peter. International trade, employment, and structural adjustment . Geneva , 1986. x, 108 p. ; ISBN 92-2-105325-3 (pbk.) : LC Card 87-119470 DDC 331.12/0973 19
HD5710.75.U6 G73 1986

FOREIGN TRADE AND EMPLOYMENT - UNITED STATES - HISTORY.
Olnek, Jay I. The invisible hand . Riverdale, N.Y. , c1984. 176 p. : ISBN 0-938538-01-2 LC Card 82-24634 DDC 382.7/1/0973 19
HF1455 .O49 1984 ***NYPL [JLE 87-21]***

Foreign trade and the national economy . Gomes, Leonard. New York , 1987. viii, 323 p. ; ISBN 0-312-00765-5 : LC Card 87-4674 DDC 382 19
HF1008 .G65 1987

FOREIGN TRADE CONTROL. see **FOREIGN TRADE REGULATION.**

FOREIGN TRADE POLICY. see **COMMERCIAL POLICY.**

FOREIGN TRADE PROMOTION.
Rubner, Alex. The export cult . Boulder , 1987, c1986. p. cm. ISBN 0-8133-0514-4 : LC Card 86-51219 DDC 382/.6 19
HF1417.5 .R82 1987

Somogyi, Dorottya. A fejlett tőkés országok exportpolitikája /. Budapest , 1985. 277, [1] p. : ISBN 963-221-507-9 : LC Card 85-231848
HF1417.5 .S66 1985

FOREIGN TRADE PROMOTION - ARGENTINA.
Lejavitzer, Moisés. Políticas de incentivos a la exportación de manufacturas en América Latina . México, D.F. , 1985. iv, 155 leaves ; LC Card 87-122013 DDC 382/.4567/098 19
HF1480.5 .L44 1985

FOREIGN TRADE PROMOTION - BRAZIL.
Baumann Neves, Renato. Exportações e crescimento industrial no Brasil /. Rio de Janeiro , 1985. 274 p. : LC Card 86-195612
HF1513 .B38 1985

Lejavitzer, Moisés. Políticas de incentivos a la exportación de manufacturas en América Latina . México, D.F. , 1985. iv, 155 leaves ; LC Card 87-122013 DDC 382/.4567/098 19
HF1480.5 .L44 1985

Moldau, Juan Hersztajn. Custo dos recursos domésticos /. Rio de Janeiro , 1985. 94, 4 p. ; LC Card 86-200395
HC190.C7 M64 1985

Nunnenkamp, Peter. Manufactured export performance of Brazil . Kiel [1986] v, 114 p. : LC Card 87-101193 DDC 382/.4567/0981 19
HF1513 .N86 1986

FOREIGN TRADE PROMOTION - BRAZIL - CONGRESSES.
Formas alternativas de negociação das exportações brasileiras . Belo Horizonte, MG , c1984. 122 p. ; LC Card 86-200391
HF1513 .F67 1984

FOREIGN TRADE PROMOTION - BRAZIL - HISTORY.
Estrutura e funcionamento do comércio exterior brasileiro /. Rio de Janeiro, RJ , 1980. v, 98

p. : LC Card 84-121064
HF1513 .E85 1980

FOREIGN TRADE PROMOTION - BRAZIL - PARAÍBA (STATE)
Setor exportador paraibano . João Pessoa , 1976. 72 leaves : LC Card 84-239455
HF3409.P32 S47 1976

FOREIGN TRADE PROMOTION - BULGARIA.
Atanasov, Mikhail, k.i.n. Vŭshnotŭrgovski aspekti na selskostopanskite i khranitelno-vkusovite stoki i problemi pred bŭlgarskiia iznos /. Sofiia , 1984. 118 p. ; LC Card 85-163481
HD9015.B82 A86 1984

FOREIGN TRADE PROMOTION - CHILE - HISTORY - 20TH CENTURY.
Pitts, Mary Anne, 1927- Economic development in Chile under two growth strategies, 1925-1968 /. New York , 1987. vii, 246 p. ; ISBN 0-8240-1368-9 (alk. paper) : LC Card 87-7618 DDC 338.983 19
HC192 .P627 1987

FOREIGN TRADE PROMOTION - COLOMBIA.
Lejavitzer, Moisés. Políticas de incentivos a la exportación de manufacturas en América Latina . México, D.F. , 1985. iv, 155 leaves ; LC Card 87-122013 DDC 382/.4567/098 19
HF1480.5 .L44 1985

Perfiles económicos del Valle del Cauca, Colombia. Cali, Colombia [1981?] 40 p. : LC Card 86-120381 DDC 330.9861/520632 19
HC198.V3 P47 1981

FOREIGN TRADE PROMOTION - COSTA RICA.
Hallauer, Robert. Export promotion policies in Costa Rica . Austin , 1985. 17 p. ; LC Card 86-622254 DDC 382/.63/097286 19
HF1487 .H35 1985

FOREIGN TRADE PROMOTION - CUBA.
Banco Nacional de Cuba (Founded 1948) Cuba's financial crisis . Washington, D.C. (1000 Thomas Jefferson St., N.W., Suite 601, Washington 20007) , 1985. vii, 64, [19] p. : LC Card 86-105593 DDC 330.97291/064 19
HC152.5 .B36 1985 ***NYPL [JLE 86-3732]***

FOREIGN TRADE PROMOTION - DENMARK - HISTORY.
Eriksen, August Wiemann. Eksportrådgivning i Danmark 1910-1921 . [Copenhagen] , 1984. 198 p. : ISBN 87-7497-075-5 LC Card 84-231455
HF1561 .E75 1984

FOREIGN TRADE PROMOTION - DEVELOPING COUNTRIES.
Nicanovich, Marta Beatriz. The role fulfilled by the International Trade Centre UNCTAD/GATT within the framework of the United Nations development policy /. Genève , 1986. xii, 248, 103, xix p. : LC Card 86-225702 DDC 382/.06/01 19
HF1417.5 .N52 1986

FOREIGN TRADE PROMOTION - DOMINICAN REPUBLIC.
Informe final "estudio de oferta exportable" /. Santo Domingo, República Dominicana [1985] 101, [57] p. ; LC Card 85-203743
HC153.5 .I54 1985

FOREIGN TRADE PROMOTION - GERMANY (WEST)
Peters, Kathrin. Binnenwirtschaftlich orientierte Hypothesen zur Aussenwirtschaftsentwicklung und ihre Gültigkeit für die Bundesrepublik Deutschland 1969-1982 /. Hamburg , c1986. vii, 311 p. : ISBN 3-925630-02-3 : LC Card 86-226488
HD5710.75.G3 P48 1986

FOREIGN TRADE PROMOTION - INDIA.
Nunnenkamp, Peter. Die Rolle öffentlicher Industrieunternehmen im Exportsektor Indiens /. Hamburg , 1985. xiv, 268 p. : ISBN 3-87895-285-6 : LC Card 87-111454
HD4293 .N85 1985

FOREIGN TRADE PROMOTION - KOREA (REPUBLIC)
Luedde-Neurath, Richard. Import controls and export-oriented development . Boulder , 1986. xiv, 249 p. ; ISBN 0-8133-7080-9 : LC Card 85-10459 DDC 382/.3/095195 19
HF1602.5 .L84 1985 ***NYPL [JLE 86-1557]***

FOREIGN TRADE PROMOTION - MALAYSIA - HANDBOOKS, MANUALS, ETC.
Sales & distribution guide to Malaysia /. Oxford , New York , 1988. p. cm. ISBN 0-08-034987-0 (U. S.) : LC Card 87-21043 DDC 382/.61/09595 19
HG5750.6.A3 S25 1988

FOREIGN TRADE PROMOTION - MEXICO.
Lejavitzer, Moisés. Políticas de incentivos a la exportación de manufacturas en América Latina . México, D.F. , 1985. iv, 155 leaves ; LC Card 87-122013 DDC 382/.4567/098 19
HF1480.5 .L44 1985

FOREIGN TRADE PROMOTION - PERU.
Promoción de las exportaciones no tradicionales . [Lima, Peru] . 145 p. ; LC Card 86-146920
HF1569 .P76 1985 ***NYPL [JLD 87-1165]***

FOREIGN TRADE PROMOTION - PHILIPPINES.
Snow, Robert T. The bourgeois opposition to export-oriented industrialization in the Philippines /. Diliman, Quezon City, Philippines [1983] 45 p. ; LC Card 85-196519 DDC 382/.3/09599 19
HC453 .S66 1983

FOREIGN TRADE PROMOTION - SPAIN.
Promoción de las exportaciones no tradicionales . [Lima, Peru] . 145 p. ; LC Card 86-146920
HF1569 .P76 1985 ***NYPL [JLD 87-1165]***

FOREIGN TRADE PROMOTION - SWEDEN.
Exportsamverkan . [Stockholm] [1985] 261 p. : ISBN 91-38-08810-X LC Card 86-114126
HF3676.5 .E96 1985

Sveriges exportråd. Svensk byggexport . [Stockholm] [1984] v, 107, [23] p. : ISBN 91-38-08107-5 LC Card 84-217971
HD9715.8.S82 S86 1984

Sweden. Exportstödsutredningen. Exportfrämjande stöd till mindre och medelstora företag . [Stockholm] [1983] 8, 143, 3 p. : ISBN 91-38-08059-1 LC Card 84-218418
HF1567 .S92 1983

Sweden. Utredningen rörande export av teknik inom energisektorn. Ökad export av svensk energiteknik--ett handlingsprogram . [Stockholm] [1983] 171, [64] p. : ISBN 91-38-08037-0 LC Card 84-219591
HD9502.S82 S974 1983

FOREIGN TRADE PROMOTION - UNITED STATES.
Venedikian, Harry M. Export-import financing /. New York , c1986. xvii, 456 p. : ISBN 0-471-82449-6 : LC Card 85-29566 DDC 332.7/42 19
HG3754.U5 V46 1986 ***NYPL [JLE 86-2998]***

FOREIGN TRADE PROMOTION - UNITED STATES - CONGRESSES.
The Role of embassies in promoting business . Lanham, MD , 1987, c1981. p. cm. ISBN 0-8191-5053-3 (pbk. : alk. paper) LC Card 87-14027 DDC 382/.3/0973 19
HF1417.5 .R64 1987

FOREIGN TRADE REGULATION - CONGRESSES.
International Law Symposium (1984 : Cambridge, Cambridgeshire) The United States, transnational business, and the law . New York , c1985. x, 132 p. ; ISBN 0-379-20783-4 LC Card 85-61594 DDC 346/.07 342.67 19
K1004.6 1984 ***NYPL [JLF 86-1046]***

FOREIGN TRADE REGULATION - EUROPEAN ECONOMIC COMMUNITY COUNTRIES.
Lasok, Dominik. The customs law of the European Economic Community /. Deventer, Netherlands , Boston , c1983. xxiii, 292 p. : ISBN 90-6544-077-1 (pbk.) : LC Card 84-148702 DDC 343.405/6 344.0356 19
LAW ***NYPL [JLE 86-2073]***

McGovern, Edmond. International trade regulation . Exeter [Devon] , 1986. xliv, 629 p. ; ISBN 0-9508463-4-1 DDC 341.7/54 19
K3943 .M4 1982 ***NYPL [JLE 86-3637]***

FOREIGN TRADE REGULATION - INDONESIA.
Ibrahim, Saaduddin. Aspek-aspek proteksi dalam industri dan perdagangan /. Jakarta , 1987. 251 p. : LC Card 87-941314
HD4304 .I27 1987

FOREIGN TRADE REGULATION - MEXICO.
Información básica sobre el GATT y el desarrollo industrial y comercial de México. México , c1985. 79, 62 p. ; LC Card 87-400559 DDC 338.0972 19
HC135 .I53 1985

FOREIGN TRADE REGULATION - UNITED STATES.
Hall, R. Duane. International purchasing . New York , c1987. p. cm. ISBN 0-394-55326-8 : LC Card 87-4926 DDC 658.7/2 19
HD39.5 .H34 1987

Issues in international telecommunications policy . Washington, D.C. , c1983. xviii, 260 p. ; ISBN 0-9612072-0-5 (pbk.) LC Card 83-82231 DDC 343.73/0994 347.303994 19
KF2765 .I85 1983 ***NYPL [JLF 86-1125]***

McGovern, Edmond. International trade regulation . Exeter [Devon] , 1986. xliv, 629 p. ; ISBN 0-9508463-4-1 DDC 341.7/54 19
K3943 .M4 1982 ***NYPL [JLE 86-3637]***

Short, Joseph N. American business and foreign policy . New York , 1987. 340 p. : ISBN 0-8240-8093-9 (alk. paper) : LC Card 87-23792 DDC 382/.41373/0973 19
HD9199.U48 S46 1987

United States. Congress. Commission on Security and Cooperation in Europe. Implementation of the Helsinki accords . Washington , 1986. iii, 85 p. ; LC Card 86-601286 DDC 331.11/732/0947 19
HD4875.S59 U55 1986

FOREIGN TRADE REGULATION - UNITED STATES - CONGRESSES.
International Law Symposium (1984 : Cambridge, Cambridgeshire) The United States, transnational business, and the law . New York , c1985. x, 132 p. ; ISBN 0-379-20783-4 LC Card 85-61594 DDC 346/.07 342.67 19
K1004.6 1984 ***NYPL [JLF 86-1046]***

Foreign trade with the USSR . Bubnov, Boris. Oxford , New York , c1987. p. cm. ISBN 0-08-035844-6 : LC Card 87-7167 DDC 382/.0947 19
HF1557 .B83 1987

FOREIGN WORKERS. see **ALIEN LABOR.**

Foreign workers in the Federal Republic of Germany . Dohse, Knuth, 1948- [Ausländerpolitik und betriebeliche Ausländerdiskriminierung. English.] Berlin [1982] 80 p. : LC Card 86-214190 DDC 331.6/2/0943 19
HD8458.A2 D6213 1982

Foreman, Susan. Striking a balance . London , 1986. 76 p. : ISBN 0-11-513848-X (pbk.) : LC Card 86-231618 DDC 380.1/06/041 19
HF73.G7 S77 1986

FOREMEN. see **SUPERVISORS, INDUSTRIAL.**

Föreningsdemokrati och företagsdemokrati . Dellenbrant, Jan Åke, 1946- [Stockholm] [1981] 85 p. ; ISBN 91-38-06488-X LC Card 83-245188
HD5660.S9 D44 1981

FORENSIC ACCOUNTING - UNITED STATES.
McNairn, William N. The smart attorney's guide to accounting documents for discovery and evidence /. Redondo Beach, Calif. , 1987. x, 123 p. : ISBN 0-932621-02-3 (pbk.) LC Card 86-62954 DDC 657/.024344 19
HF5616.U5 M346 1987

FORENSIC PHOTOGRAPHY. see **PHOTOGRAPHY, LEGAL.**

Forente stater. see **United States.**

Forest, Alain. Décolonisations et nouvelles dépendances . [Lille] , c1986. 282 p. : ISBN 2-85939-287-4 : LC Card 87-104133
HC59.7 .D354 1986

FOREST CONSERVATION - CANADA.
Gillis, R. Peter. Lost initiatives . New York , 1986. 326 p. : ISBN 0-313-25415-X (lib. bdg. : alk. paper) LC Card 86-3122 DDC 333.75/0971 19
HD9764.C3 G55 1986 ***NYPL [JLE 87-947]***

FOREST CONSERVATION - ECONOMIC ASPECTS - SUDAN - KASSALA

(PROVINCE)
Abu Sin, M. E. (Mohad E.) Socio-economic aspects of integrated resource management, with special reference to the forest resources of Kassala Province, Eastern Region . Khartoum , 1986. vi leaves, 109 p. : LC Card 87-980440 DDC 333.75/09629/2 19
HD9767.S843 K3724 1986

FOREST MANAGEMENT - UNITED STATES.
Forests in demand . Boston, Mass. , c1982. xv, 265 p. : ISBN 0-86569-106-1 : LC Card 81-12881 DDC 333.75/0973 19
SD565 .F58 *NYPL [JLE 86-4465]*

Forest, Mrs. Organisation for Economic Co-operation and Development. Library. L'emploi des jeunes =. [Paris] , 1980. [6], 119 p. ; LC Card 81-122004 DDC 016.3313/4 19
HD6270 .O72 1980

FOREST PLANTING. see **FORESTS AND FORESTRY.**

FOREST POLICY - CANADA.
Gillis, R. Peter. Lost initiatives . New York , 1986. 326 p. : ISBN 0-313-25415-X (lib. bdg. : alk. paper) LC Card 86-3122 DDC 333.75/0971 19
HD9764.C3 G55 1986 *NYPL [JLE 87-947]*

FOREST POLICY - COSTA RICA.
Flores Rodas, José G. (José Guillermo) Diagnóstico del sector industrial forestal /. San José, Costa Rica , 1985. 116 p. : ISBN 997-7642-33-8 LC Card 86-218084
HD9764.C82 F56 1985

FOREST POLICY - ECONOMIC ASPECTS - SUDAN - KASSALA (PROVINCE)
Abu Sin, M. E. (Mohad E.) Socio-economic aspects of integrated resource management, with special reference to the forest resources of Kassala Province, Eastern Region . Khartoum , 1986. vi leaves, 109 p. : LC Card 87-980440 DDC 333.75/09629/2 19
HD9767.S843 K3724 1986

FOREST POLICY - INDIA.
Sairam, T. V. (Trimurti V.), 1946- Fiscal policy and environment . Delhi , 1986. 135 p. ; LC Card 86-902779 DDC 336.2/7863498/0954 19
HD9766.I62 S35 1986

FOREST POLICY - UNITED STATES.
Forests in demand . Boston, Mass. , c1982. xv, 265 p. : ISBN 0-86569-106-1 : LC Card 81-12881 DDC 333.75/0973 19
SD565 .F58 *NYPL [JLE 86-4465]*

Morandi, Larry B. Renewing resources . Denver, Colo. , 1984. vii, 133 p. ;
NYPL [JSF 86-712]

FOREST PRICES - PRICES - HUNGARY - STATISTICAL SERVICES.
A Mezőgazdasági és az erdőgazdálkodási árstatisztika módszere /. Budapest , 1986. 81 p. ; LC Card 87-408580
HD9015.H82 M486 1986

FOREST PRODUCTIVITY - HONDURAS - INTIBUCÁ (DEPT.)
Consejo Superior de Planificación Económica (Honduras). Secretaría Técnica. Proyecto de desarrollo local de La Paz, Intibucá /. [Tegucigalpa, Honduras] [1984- v. <1 > : LC Card 86-213886
HC145.Z9 E443 1984

FOREST PRODUCTIVITY - HONDURAS - LA PAZ (DEPT.)
Consejo Superior de Planificación Económica (Honduras). Secretaría Técnica. Proyecto de desarrollo local de La Paz, Intibucá /. [Tegucigalpa, Honduras] [1984- v. <1 > : LC Card 86-213886
HC145.Z9 E443 1984

FOREST PRODUCTS INDUSTRY.
The Global forest sector . Chichester [West Sussex] , New York , c1987. xiii, 706 p. : ISBN 0-471-91735-4 : LC Card 87-19700 DDC 338.1/749 19
HD9750.5 .G56 1987

FOREST PRODUCTS INDUSTRY - ALASKA.
Pierce, Brad. The timber industry in interior Alaska . [Juneau] [1986] 65 p. ; LC Card 86-621755 DDC 338.1/7498/09798 19
HD9757.A7 P54 1986

Van Patten, Jo. Alaska's commercial forest resource /. Juneau, Alaska [1986] v, 29 p. : LC Card 86-622970 DDC 333.75/09798 19
HD9757.A7 V36 1986

FOREST PRODUCTS INDUSTRY - ARGENTINA - STATISTICS.
Agricultura, caza, silvicultura y pesca . [Buenos Aires] [1982] 57 p. : LC Card 87-401763 DDC 338.1/0982/021 19
HD1862 .A58 1982

FOREST PRODUCTS INDUSTRY - BRAZIL - PARANÁ (STATE)
Estudo sobre a adequação floresta-indústria no Estado do Paraná /. [Curitiba] [1982] vi, 106, [4] leaves ; LC Card 86-197076
HD9764.B73 P32 1982

FOREST PRODUCTS INDUSTRY - CANADA.
Gillis, R. Peter. Lost initiatives . New York , 1986. 326 p. : ISBN 0-313-25415-X (lib. bdg. : alk. paper) LC Card 86-3122 DDC 333.75/0971 19
HD9764.C3 G55 1986 *NYPL [JLE 87-947]*

FOREST PRODUCTS INDUSTRY - CHILE - CONGRESSES.
García Elizalde, Pedro. El desarrollo frutícola y forestal en Chile y sus derivaciones sociales. Santiago de Chile , 1986. 234 p. : ISBN 92-1-321204-6 LC Card 86-175421
HD9254.C52 G37 1986

FOREST PRODUCTS INDUSTRY - CONGRESSES.
World trade in forest products, 2 /. Seattle , c1986. xi, 362 p. : ISBN 0-295-96337-9 LC Card 86-234388 DDC 382/.41498 19
HD9750.5 .W67 1986

FOREST PRODUCTS INDUSTRY - COSTA RICA.
Flores Rodas, José G. (José Guillermo) Diagnóstico del sector industrial forestal /. San José, Costa Rica , 1985. 116 p. : ISBN 997-7642-33-8 LC Card 86-218084
HD9764.C82 F56 1985

FOREST PRODUCTS INDUSTRY - DELAWARE RIVER VALLEY (N.Y.-DEL. AND N.J.) - HISTORY.
Myers, Frank Daniel. The wood chemical industry in the Delaware Valley /. Middletown, N.Y. , 1986. [160] p. : LC Card 87-108267
HD9660.M573 U616 1986

FOREST PRODUCTS INDUSTRY - DENMARK.
Juncker, Flemming, 1904- Men morsomt har det været /. [Copenhagen] , c1983. 423 p., [8] p. of plates : ISBN 87-00-54643-7 : LC Card 84-109657
HD9765.D42 J85 1983

FOREST PRODUCTS INDUSTRY - DEVELOPING COUNTRIES - CONGRESSES.
Appropriate forest industries . Rome , 1986. vii, 426 p. ; ISBN 92-5-102389-1 (pbk.) LC Card 86-214549 DDC 338.1/7498/091724 19
HD9768.D44 A66 1986

FOREST PRODUCTS INDUSTRY - EUROPE.
Forestry and the forest industries . Dordrecht ; Boston : xi, 428 p. : ISBN 90-247-3592-0 LC Card 87-20400 DDC 338.1/749 19
HD9765.A2 F64 1987

Major import markets for builders' woodwork /. Geneva , 1985. xiii, 180 p. : LC Card 87-118537 DDC 381/.45674/094 19
HD9765.A2 M29 1985

FOREST PRODUCTS INDUSTRY - GERMANY (WEST) - NORTH RHINE-WESTPHALIA - STATISTICS.
Agrarberichterstattung Nordrhein-Westfalen 1983 . Düsseldorf [1984] 263 p. ; LC Card 87-407317 DDC 943/.55 s 338.1/0943/55021 19
HA1320.N6 A32 Heft 532 HD1960.N67

FOREST PRODUCTS INDUSTRY - HONDURAS - STATISTICS.
El Desarrollo económico de Honduras . Tegucigalpa, D.C. , 1959. [56] leaves : LC Card 86-173618
HD9014.H82 D47 1959

FOREST PRODUCTS INDUSTRY - INDONESIA.
Profile of the primary commodity sector in Malaysia. [Kuala Lumpur] [1984] 77 p. : LC Card 86-945653 DDC 338.09595 19
HD9016.M32 P76 1984

FOREST PRODUCTS INDUSTRY - INDONESIA - KALIMANTAN TIMUR.
Monografi sumber daya ekonomi di bidang kehutanan Kalimantan Timur . Bogor , 1975. ix, 67 leaves : LC Card 80-941771
HD9766.I73 K356 1975

FOREST PRODUCTS INDUSTRY - MAINE.
Colgan, Charles S. The natural resource industries of Maine . [Augusta, Me.] [1986] 135 p. : LC Card 87-620550 DDC 338.09741 19
HD9007.M2 C64 1986

FOREST PRODUCTS INDUSTRY - MANAGEMENT.
Sierila, Pentti, 1934- Corporate planning and strategies in forest industries /. Atlanta, GA, USA , c1987. vii, 138 p. : ISBN 0-89852-441-5 (pbk.) LC Card 87-50439 DDC 634.9/8/068 19
HD9750.5 .S54 1987

FOREST PRODUCTS INDUSTRY - MEXICO.
Serrano Gálvez, Enrique. Economía de la actividad forestal /. México , 1983. 139 p. : LC Card 86-200927
HD9764.M62 S47 1983

FOREST PRODUCTS INDUSTRY - NETHERLANDS.
Meijenfeldt, C. F. W. M. von. Gebruik van en alternatieven voor tropisch hout. 's-Gravenhage , c1985. 207, [14] p. : ISBN 90-346-0647-3 : LC Card 86-231435
HD9750.8.T73 M45 1985

FOREST PRODUCTS INDUSTRY - NEW HAMPSHIRE.
Nevel, Robert L. The timber industries of New Hampshire and Vermont . Broomall, Pa. , 1986. 56 p. : LC Card 86-601144 DDC 338.1/7498/09742 19
HD9757.N4 N48 1986

FOREST PRODUCTS INDUSTRY - NEW ZEALAND - STATISTICS.

FOREST PRODUCTS INDUSTRY - NORTH AMERICA.
Forestry and the forest industries . Dordrecht ; Boston : xi, 428 p. : ISBN 90-247-3592-0 LC Card 87-20400 DDC 338.1/749 19
HD9765.A2 F64 1987

FOREST PRODUCTS INDUSTRY - OHIO - STATISTICS.
Widmann, Richard H. Ohio timber products output--1983 /. Broomall, PA [1986] 29 p. : LC Card 86-603412 DDC 338.1/7498/09771021 19
HD9757.O3 W53 1986

FOREST PRODUCTS INDUSTRY - PLANNING.
Sierila, Pentti, 1934- Corporate planning and strategies in forest industries /. Atlanta, GA, USA , c1987. vii, 138 p. : ISBN 0-89852-441-5 (pbk.) LC Card 87-50439 DDC 634.9/8/068 19
HD9750.5 .S54 1987

FOREST PRODUCTS INDUSTRY - QUÉBEC (PROVINCE)
Duchaine, Paul. Bâtiments préfabriqués résidentiels et industriels à ossature de bois . [Québec] , c1985. 36 p. : ISBN 2-550-12116-3 LC Card 86-133426
HD9715.5.C23 Q43 1985

FOREST PRODUCTS INDUSTRY - RUSSIAN S.F.S.R. - KAREL'SKAIA A.S.S.R.
Valentik, I. IA. (Ivan IAkovlevich) Ėkonomicheskie osnovy intensifikatsii lesnogo khoziaistva Karel'skoĭ ASSR /. Leningrad , 1986. 135, [1] p. : LC Card 87-125199
HD9765.S653 K378 1986

FOREST PRODUCTS INDUSTRY - RUSSIAN S.F.S.R. - KOMI A.S.S.R.
Kniazeva, G. A. (Galina Alekseevna) Kompleksnoe ispol'zovanie drevesiny v Komi ASSR /. Syktyvkar , 1986. 75 p. : LC Card 86-233834
HD9765.S653 K665 1986

FOREST PRODUCTS INDUSTRY - SOVIET UNION.
Forestry and the forest industries . Dordrecht ; Boston : xi, 428 p. : ISBN 90-247-3592-0 LC Card 87-20400 DDC 338.1/749 19
HD9765.A2 F64 1987

FOREST PRODUCTS INDUSTRY - SOVIET UNION - PLANNING - MATHEMATICAL MODELS.
Martynov, G. V. (Gennadiĭ Viktorovich) Mnogootraslevye kompleksy--problemy i metody optimizatsii /. Moskva , 1986. 229, [3]

p. : LC Card 86-232408
HC333 .M285 1986

FOREST PRODUCTS INDUSTRY - SPAIN - HUESCA (PROVINCE)
Cuevas, Enrique de las. Las industrias forestales en la Provincia de Huesca /. Huesca , 1919. 58 p. ; LC Card 84-100478
HD9765.S7 H833 1919

FOREST PRODUCTS INDUSTRY - SWEDEN.
Sweden. Statens industriverk. Ökad eldning med skogsråvara . Stockholm , 1980. 203 p. : ISBN 91-38-05361-6 LC Card 82-236954
HD9769.F843 S87 1980

FOREST PRODUCTS INDUSTRY - SWITZERLAND - CANTONS - STATISTICS.
Eidgenössische Betriebszählung 1985. Bern , 1986. 108 p. ; ISBN 3-303-07007-5 LC Card 87-407623 DDC 338.1/7498/09494021 19
HD9765.S92 E37 1986

FOREST PRODUCTS INDUSTRY - THAILAND.
Thailand. Krom Sētthakit Kānphānit. Rāingān phon kānsksā wičhai . [Krung Thēp Mahā Nakh 2521 [1978] 24, [7] folded p., [7] p. of plates : LC Card 81-183926
HD9766.T52 T47 1978

FOREST PRODUCTS INDUSTRY - TROPICS.
Meijenfeldt, C. F. W. M. von. Gebruik van en alternatieven voor tropisch hout. 's-Gravenhage , c1985. 207, [14] p. : ISBN 90-346-0647-3 : LC Card 86-231435
HD9750.8.T73 M45 1985

FOREST PRODUCTS INDUSTRY - UNITED STATES.
Ellefson, Paul V. U. S. wood-based industry . New York , 1984. xxv, 479 p. : ISBN 0-03-063698-1 (alk. paper) : LC Card 84-8278 DDC 338.1/7498/0973 19
HD9755 .45 1984 ***NYPL [JLE 85-706]***

Major import markets for builders' woodwork /. Geneva , 1985. xiii, 180 p. : LC Card 87-118537 DDC 381/.45674/094 19
HD9765.A2 M29 1985

FOREST PRODUCTS INDUSTRY - VERMONT.
Nevel, Robert L. The timber industries of New Hampshire and Vermont . Broomall, Pa. , 1986. 56 p. : LC Card 86-601144 DDC 338.1/7498/09742 19
HD9757.N4 N48 1986

FOREST PRODUCTS - TAXATION - INDIA.
Sairam, T. V. (Trimurti V.), 1946- Fiscal policy and environment . Delhi , 1986. 135 p. ; LC Card 86-902779 DDC 336.2/7863498/0954 19
HD9766.I62 S35 1986

FOREST RESERVES.
The Global forest sector . Chichester [West Sussex] , New York , c1987. xiii, 706 p. : ISBN 0-471-91735-4 : LC Card 87-19700 DDC 338.1/749 19
HD9750.5 .G56 1987

Forest resource, economy, and environment /. Singh, Anil K., 1953- New Delhi , 1987. xv, 124 p. : LC Card 87-901902 DDC 333.78/4 19
HD9766.I63 U887 1987

FORESTALLING. see **MONOPOLIES.**

FORESTATION. see **FORESTS AND FORESTRY.**

The forested land . Ficken, Robert E. Durham, N.C. , Seattle , c1987. xv, 324 p., [8] p. of plates : ISBN 0-295-96416-2 LC Card 87-2214 DDC 338.4/7674/09797 19
HD9757.W2 F53 1987

Forestry and the forest industries : past and future : major developments in the forest and forest industry sector since 1947 in Europe, the USSR, and North America / edited by E.G. Richards. Dordrecht ; Boston : M. Nijhoff for the United Nations, New York ; xi, 428 p. : ill. ; 25 cm. (Forestry sciences) English, French, Spanish, and Russian. "Prepared to mark the fortieth anniversary of the establishment of the Timber Committee of the United Nations Economic Commission for Europe (ECE) and the European Forestry Commission of the Food and Agriculture Organization of the United Nations (FAO)." ISBN 90-247-3592-0 LC Card 87-20400 DDC 338.1/749 19

1. Forests and forestry - Economic aspects - Europe. 2. Forests and forestry - Economic aspects - Soviet Union. 3. Forests and forestry - Economic aspects - North America. 4. Forest products industry - Europe. 5. Forest products industry - Soviet Union. 6. Forest products industry - North America. I. Richards, E. G. (Edward Graham). II. United Nations. Economic Commission for Europe. Timber Committee. III. European Forestry Commission. IV. Series.
HD9765.A2 F64 1987

Forestry sciences.
Forestry and the forest industries . Dordrecht ; Boston : xi, 428 p. : ISBN 90-247-3592-0 LC Card 87-20400 DDC 338.1/749 19
HD9765.A2 F64 1987

FORESTS AND FORESTRY - ACCOUNTING.
Márkus, László. Erdőérték- és eredményszámítás /. Budapest , 1986. 207 p. : ISBN 963-232-225-2 : LC Card 87-408586
HF5686.F62 M37 1986

FORESTS AND FORESTRY, COOPERATIVE - UNITED STATES - HISTORY.
Hartzell, Hal, 1946- Birth of a cooperative . Eugene, Or. , 1987. 351 p. : ISBN 0-938493-09-4 (pbk.) : LC Card 87-2656 DDC 334/.6834956/09795 19
HD9759.H64 H37 1987

FORESTS AND FORESTRY - COSTA RICA.
Flores Rodas, José G. (José Guillermo) Diagnóstico del sector industrial forestal /. San José, Costa Rica , 1985. 116 p. : ISBN 997-7642-33-8 LC Card 86-218084
HD9764.C82 F56 1985

FORESTS AND FORESTRY - ECONOMIC ASPECTS - ALASKA.
Van Patten, Jo. Alaska's commercial forest resource /. Juneau, Alaska [1986] v, 29 p. : LC Card 86-622970 DDC 333.75/09798 19
HD9757.A7 V36 1986

FORESTS AND FORESTRY - ECONOMIC ASPECTS - EUROPE.
Forestry and the forest industries . Dordrecht ; Boston : xi, 428 p. : ISBN 90-247-3592-0 LC Card 87-20400 DDC 338.1/749 19
HD9765.A2 F64 1987

FORESTS AND FORESTRY - ECONOMIC ASPECTS - GREAT BRITAIN.
Countryside conflicts . Aldershot, Hants, England , Brookfield, Vt., U. S.A. , c1986. vi, 378 p. [4] leaves of plates : ISBN 0-566-05088-9 : LC Card 85-24603 DDC 333.76/17/0941 19
HD596 .C675 1986 ***NYPL [JLD 86-2487]***

FORESTS AND FORESTRY - ECONOMIC ASPECTS - INDIA - UTTAR PRADESH.
Singh, Anil K., 1953- Forest resource, economy, and environment /. New Delhi , 1987. xv, 124 p. : LC Card 87-901902 DDC 333.78/4 19
HD9766.I63 U887 1987

FORESTS AND FORESTRY - ECONOMIC ASPECTS - NORTH AMERICA.
Forestry and the forest industries . Dordrecht ; Boston : xi, 428 p. : ISBN 90-247-3592-0 LC Card 87-20400 DDC 338.1/749 19
HD9765.A2 F64 1987

FORESTS AND FORESTRY - ECONOMIC ASPECTS - SOUTHERN STATES.
Healy, Robert G. Competition for land in the American South . Washington, D.C. , c1985. xxxii, 333 p. : ISBN 0-89164-094-0 (pbk.) LC Card 85-25459 DDC 333.76/13/0975 19
HD266.A13 H43 1985 ***NYPL [JLE 86-2724]***

FORESTS AND FORESTRY - ECONOMIC ASPECTS - SOVIET UNION.
Forestry and the forest industries . Dordrecht ; Boston : xi, 428 p. : ISBN 90-247-3592-0 LC Card 87-20400 DDC 338.1/749 19
HD9765.A2 F64 1987

FORESTS AND FORESTRY - ENVIRONMENTAL ASPECTS - INDIA - UTTAR PRADESH.
Singh, Anil K., 1953- Forest resource, economy, and environment /. New Delhi , 1987. xv, 124 p. : LC Card 87-901902 DDC 333.78/4 19
HD9766.I63 U887 1987

FORESTS AND FORESTRY - FINLAND - ACCIDENTS.
Metsä- ja uittotöiden työtapaturmat vuonna 1982 =. Tampere , Helsinki , 1984. 50 p. : ISBN 951-46-7685-8 LC Card 85-149625
HD7269.F7262 F56 1984

FORESTS AND FORESTRY - HUNGARY.
Soós, Gábor, 1922- Mit kell tudni a magyar agrártermelésről? /. [Budapest] , 1984. 218 p. ; ISBN 963-09-2474-9 : LC Card 85-154641
HD1940.5 .S66 1984

FORESTS AND FORESTRY - KENYA - KAKAMEGA DISTRICT.
Bradley, Phil. The district resource analysis as applied to Kakamega District /. Nairobi [1984] 11 leaves : LC Card 87-112452 DDC 333.75 19
HD9769.F843 K425 1984

FORESTS AND FORESTRY - NEW ZEALAND - STATISTICS.

FORESTS AND FORESTRY - SAHEL.
Kapp, Gerald B., 1956- Agroforstliche Landnutzung in der Sahel-Sudanzone . München , c1987. xii, 397 p. : ISBN 3-8039-0347-5 LC Card 87-419915 DDC 333.76/13/0966 19
HD1010.5.Z63 K37 1987

FORESTS AND FORESTRY - SUDAN.
Kapp, Gerald B., 1956- Agroforstliche Landnutzung in der Sahel-Sudanzone . München , c1987. xii, 397 p. : ISBN 3-8039-0347-5 LC Card 87-419915 DDC 333.76/13/0966 19
HD1010.5.Z63 K37 1987

FORESTS AND FORESTRY - TAXATION - WISCONSIN.
Wise, Gregory J. The effect of tax exempt forestland on town property tax revenues . Madison [1986] 40 leaves : LC Card 86-623093 DDC 336.22/09775 19
HJ4284.A3 W59 1986

FORESTS AND FORESTRY - UNITED STATES - MULTIPLE USE.
Forests in demand . Boston, Mass. , c1982. xv, 265 p. : ISBN 0-86569-106-1 : LC Card 81-12881 DDC 333.75/0973 19
SD565 .F58 ***NYPL [JLE 86-4465]***

FORESTS AND FORESTRY - VALUATION.
Márkus, László. Erdőérték- és eredményszámítás /. Budapest , 1986. 207 p. : ISBN 963-232-225-2 : LC Card 87-408586
HF5686.F62 M37 1986

FORESTS AND FORESTRY - WASHINGTON (STATE) - HISTORY.
Ficken, Robert E. The forested land . Durham, N.C. , Seattle , c1987. xv, 324 p., [8] p. of plates : ISBN 0-295-96416-2 LC Card 87-2214 DDC 338.4/7674/09797 19
HD9757.W2 F53 1987

Forests in demand : conflicts and solutions / edited by Charles E. Hewett, Thomas E. Hamilton, with Ina C. Anderson. Boston, Mass. : Auburn House Pub. Co., c1982. xv, 265 p. : ill. ; 24 cm. Includes bibliographical references and index. ISBN 0-86569-106-1 : LC Card 81-12881 DDC 333.75/0973 19

1. Forest policy - United States. 2. Forest management - United States. 3. Forests and forestry - United States - Multiple use. I. Hewett, Charles E., 1950-. II. Hamilton, Thomas E. III. Anderson, Ina C.
SD565 .F58 ***NYPL [JLE 86-4465]***

FORESTS, NATIONAL. see **FOREST RESERVES.**

Företagsekonomisk forskning och utbildning.
Elsässer, Martin, 1957- Marknadsinvesteringar . Malmö , c1984. 168 p. : ISBN 91-38-61298-4 : LC Card 84-200312
HF1009.7.S94 E47 1984

Företagsstöd och kommunalt risktagande /. Lindmark, Leif. Stockholm [1984] iv, 49 p. : ISBN 91-38-08297-7 LC Card 85-106839
HD3646.S8 L55 1984

Forgács, Katalin. A zöldség-gyümölcs szindróma : a megoldás útja a zöldség-gyümölcs termelésben és forgalmazásban / Forgács Katalin. Budapest : Közgazdasági és Jogi Könyvkiadó, 1986. 134, [1] p. ; 20 cm. (Versenyképes mezőgazdaság, 0237-5001) Bibliography: p. 133-[135]. ISBN 963-221-901-5 : LC Card 87-148760

1. Vegetable trade - Hungary. 2. Fruit trade - Hungary. 3. Produce trade - Hungary. I. Title. II. Series.
HD9220.H82 F67 1986

Forgács, Pál. A szakszervezetek változó szerepe a gazdaság szabályozásában az európai fejlett tőkésországokban / [írta, Forgács Pál].

Budapest : Szakszervezetek Elméleti Kutató Intézete, 1985. 118 p. ; 21 cm. Bibliography: p. 116-118. ISBN 963-608-079-8 LC Card 86-228056
1. Industrial management - Europe - Employee participation. 2. Trade-unions - Europe. I. Title.
HD5660.E9 F67 1985

Forgalomtechnika és közlekedéstervezés /. Koller, Sándor. Budapest , 1986. 291 p. : ISBN 963-10-6412-3 : LC Card 87-148352
HE333 .K575 1986

FORGERY.
Tazwīr al-mustanadāt wa-tazyīf al-ʻumlāt wa-al-asālīb al-ʻilmīyah lil-kashf ʻanhā. [Cairo] [1978] 296 p., [1] leaf of plates : ISBN 977-7049-73-0 LC Card 79-961630
HG335 .T3 1978

Forging a union of steel : Philip Murray, SWOC, and the United Steelworkers / Paul F. Clark, Peter Gottlieb, and Donald Kennedy, editors. Ithaca, N.Y. : ILR Press, New York State School of Industrial and Labor Relations, Cornell University, c1987. vii, 153 p. : ill. ; 22 cm. Based on papers presented at a symposium held on Nov. 13-14, 1986 and sponsored by the Dept. of Labor Studies at Penn State University and others. Bibliography: p. 131-137. Includes index. CONTENTS. - The history is missing / Ronald L. Filippelli -- The origins of modern steel unionism / David Brody -- Labor's odd couple / Melvyn Dubofsky -- Consolidating industrial citizenship / Mark McColloch -- Battling over government's role / Ronald W. Schatz -- Comments / I.W. Abel ... [et al.]. ISBN 0-87546-135-2 (pbk.) LC Card 87-21508 DDC 331.88/169142/0973 19
1. United Steelworkers of America - History - Congresses. 2. Steel Workers Organizing Committee (U. S.) - History - Congresses. 3. Murray, Philip, 1886-1952 - Congresses. 4. Trade-unions - Iron and steel workers - United States - History - Congresses. I. Clark, Paul F., 1954-. II. Gottlieb, Peter, 1949-. III. Kennedy, Donald. IV. Pennsylvania State University. Dept. of Labor Studies.
HD6515.I5 F58 1987

Forging accounting principles in five countries . Zeff, Stephen A. Champaign, Ill. , 1971, c1972. xvii, 332 p. ; LC Card 86-226472
HF5605 .Z44 1972

FORGING INDUSTRY - AUSTRALIA - WESTERN AUSTRALIA.
A Study of the Western Australian casting and forging industry. [Perth] [1984?]-[1985] 2 v. ; LC Card 86-207984 DDC 388.4/7671/09941 19
HD9506.A8 W385 1984

Forging new relationships among business, labor, and government / edited by Robert J. Thornton, J. Richard Aronson. Greenwich, Conn. : JAI Press, c1986. xiii, 210 p. ; 24 cm. (Contemporary studies in economic and financial analysis. v. 56) Includes index. Includes bibliographical references. ISBN 0-89232-656-5 : LC Card 86-2839 DDC 338.973 19
1. Industry and state - United States. 2. Industrial relations - United States. I. Thornton, Robert J. II. Aronson, Jay Richard.
HD3616.U47 F583 1986 ***NYPL [JLE 86-3452]***

A forgóeszköz finanszirozás elvei és gyakorlata /. Szabó, Sándor. [Budapest] , 1986. 67, [26] p. ; LC Card 87-150669
HG4028.W65 S93 1986

Forgóeszköz-gazdálkodás a mezőgazdaságban /. Reke, Barnabás. Budapest , 1986. 175 p. ; ISBN 963-232-219-3 : LC Card 87-408500
HD1440.H9 R45 1986

The forgotten deficit . Danielian, Ronald L. Boulder , 1987. xii, 84 p. ; ISBN 0-8133-7450-2 (pbk. : alk. paper) LC Card 87-50654 DDC 332.6/7373 19
HG3883.U7 D36 1987

Förhandla mer räkna mindre /. Holmquist, Carin, 1948- Stockholm [1984] 124 p. : ISBN 91-38-90409-8 : LC Card 84-241380
HD30.22 .H65 1984

Føringaredskaper i Aker fogderi . Winge, Harald. Oslo , 1976. 105 p. : LC Card 86-460271
HE259.Z7 A48 1976

Fórizs, Józsefné. Földértékelés, termőhelyi értékelés problémái : javaslat a termőhely korszerű értékelésére / Fórizs Józsefné. Budapest : Agrárgazdasági Kutató Intézet, 1985. 211 p., [4] folded leaves of plates : ill. ; 29 cm. (Agrárgazdasági Kutató Intézet, 0209-5696 . 1985/3) Bibliography: p. 99-105. ISBN 963-491-204-4 LC Card 86-196842
1. Real property - Valuation - Hungary. 2. Farms - Valuation - Hungary. I. Series: Agrárgazdasági Kutató Intézet (Series) , 1985/3. II. Title.
HD1387 .F596 1985

FORM LETTERS.
Hakoun, Mitchell. Accountant's complete model letter book /. Englewood Cliffs, N.J. , c1987. xxi, 424 p. : ISBN 0-13-001199-1 : LC Card 87-11548 DDC 657 19
HF5726 .H3257 1987

Tax letters . Calabasas, CA (5115 Douglas Fir, Suite H, Calabasas 91302) , c1986. 1 v. (various pagings) : LC Card 87-132645 DDC 651.7/52 19
HJ4652 .T374 1986

Form, William Humbert, 1917- Divided we stand : working-class stratification in America / William Form. Urbana : University of Illinois Press, c1985. xviii, 306 p. ; 24 cm. Includes indexes. Bibliography: p. 269-296. ISBN 0-252-01168-6 (alk. paper) LC Card 85-16537 DDC 305.5/62/0973 19
1. Labor and laboring classes - United States - History. 2. Social classes - United States - History. I. Title.
HD8072.5 .F667 1985 ***NYPL [JLE 86-1940]***

La Forma-valore : progetto di ricostruzione e completamento del frammento di sistema di Marx / Michael Eldred ... [et al.] / a cura e con introduzione di Emilio Agazzi. Manduria : Lacaita, 1984. 301 p. : ill. ; 23 cm. (Biblioteca di studi moderni. 19) Bibliography: p. 291-300. LC Card 86-130626 DDC 335.4/12 19
1. Labor theory of value. 2. Marxian economics. I. Eldred, Michael. II. Agazzi, Emilio.
HB206 .F67 1984

A formação da classe operária /. Singer, Paul Israel, 1932- Campinas-SP , São Paulo-SP [1986] 80 p. : LC Card 86-224636
HD4841 .S32 1986

Formação profissional & produtividade no desempenho humano /. Fontes, Lauro (Lauro Barreto) [Rio de Janeiro] , 1985. 119, [2] p. ; LC Card 85-221895
HD5715.5.B68 F66 1985

Formação profissional e produtividade no desempenho humano. Fontes, Lauro (Lauro Barreto) Formação profissional & produtividade no desempenho humano /. [Rio de Janeiro] , 1985. 119, [2] p. ; LC Card 85-221895
HD5715.5.B68 F66 1985

Formación profesional . Ducci, María Angélica. Montevideo , 1983. 102 p. ; LC Card 86-142632
HD5715.5.L29 D83 1983

La Formación profesional ante las exigencias del desarrollo. 1a ed. Montevideo : CINTERFOR/OIT, 1980. 98 p. ; 23 cm. (Informes / CINTERFOR/OIT . no. 103) "Proyecto 126." LC Card 86-139077
1. Occupational training - Latin America - Congresses. I. CINTERFOR (Organization). II. Series: Informed (CINTERFOR (Organization)) , no. 103.
HD5715.5.L3 F664 1980

Forman, Cynthia E. Pulvino, Charles J. Communicating with clients . Paramus, NJ , c1987. ix, 194 p. : ISBN 0-13-153578-1 (pbk.) LC Card 87-153498 DDC 332.1/068/8 19
HG179.5 .P86 1987

Forman, Dorchen. Rocks in her head /. Lake Dallas, Tex. (221 Wild Oak, Lake Dallas 75065) , c1987. vii, 97 p. : LC Card 87-151452
HD8039.P42 U676 1987

Forman, Norm. Mind over money : how to banish your financial headaches and achieve moneysanity / Norm Forman.1st ed. Toronto, Ont. : Doubleday Canada ; Garden City, N.Y. : Doubleday, 1987. xi, 248 p. ; 23 cm. Bibliography: p. 243-244. Includes index. ISBN 0-385-25104-1 LC Card 86-32814 DDC 332.024 19
1. Money - Psychological aspects. 2. Finance, Personal - Psychological aspects. 3. Personality assessment. I. Title.
HG222.3 .F67 1987

Formánek, Miloslav. Buržoazní sociálně politické teorie úlohy vědeckotechnického rozvoje / Miloslav Formánek. Vyd. 1. Praha : Academia, 1980. 350 p. ; 21 cm. Summary in Russian. Bibliography: p. 335-348.
1. Science - Social aspects. 2. Technology - Social aspects. I. Title. ***NYPL [*QT 87-1720]***

Formas alternativas de negociação das exportações brasileiras : seminário nacional, Belo Horizonte, 09 e 10 de novembro de 1983 : anais. Belo Horizonte, MG : Fundação Dom Cabral/CEDEX, c1984. 122 p. ; 26 cm. (Boletim CEDEX. Estudos especiais . no. 3) Bibliography: p. 122. LC Card 86-200391
1. Foreign trade promotion - Brazil - Congresses. I. Fundação Dom Cabral. II. CEDEX (Organization). III. Series.
HF1513 .F67 1984

Formation des adultes : méthodes actives et participatives / rédaction, Hans J.O. de Facq. [Bujumbura] : République du Burundi, Ministère de la fonction publique, Centre de perfectionnement et de formation en cours d'emploi : Programme des Nations Unies pour le développement, [1984- v. <1 > : ill. ; 30 cm. "Août 1984." Bibliography: v. 1, p. 153. LC Card 86-980941
1. Occupational training - Burundi. 2. Continuing education - Burundi. I. Facq, Hans J. O. de.
HD5715.5.B94 F67 1984

Formation des cadres supérieurs féminins /. Centre de perfectionnement et de formation en cours d'emploi (Bujumbura, Burundi) [Bujumbura?] , 1983. 2 v. : LC Card 87-104998
HD6054.4.B94 C46 1983

La Formation des syndicalistes aux nouvelles technologies de l'information et à leur introduction dans les entreprises : rapport final / par BRAEC, Bureau de recherches d'analyses et d'études coordonnées. Luxembourg : Office des publications officielles des communautés européennes ; Washington, D.C. : European Community Information Service, 1986. 52, 13, 7 p. : ill. ; 29 cm. At head of title: Commission des Communautés européennes. ISBN 92-825-5881-9 : LC Card 86-179989
1. Labor supply - European Economic Community countries - Effect of technological innovations on. 2. Occupational retraining - European Economic Community countries. 3. Trade-unions - European Economic Community countries. I. Commission of the European Communities. Bureau de recherches d'analyses et d'études coordonnées.
HD6331.2.E86 F67 1986

La formation du prix du logement /. Vincent, Maurice, 1955 or 6- Paris , c1986. v, 221 p. : ISBN 2-7178-1082-X : LC Card 86-190085
HD7338.A3 V55 1986

Formation et rôle des taux d'intérêt / Christian de Boissieu ... [et al.]. Paris : Economica, c1982. 204 p. : ill. ; 24 cm. (Recherches Panthéon-Sorbonne, Université de Paris I. Série Sciences économiques, 0338-8719) Includes bibliographical references. ISBN 2-7178-0562-1 : LC Card 83-103493
1. Interest. 2. Interest rates. I. Boissieu, Christian de. II. Series.
HB539 .F63 1982

Formation professionnelle rurale, SEN/71/526 . International Labour Organisation. Genève , 1976. ii, 69 p. : ISBN 92-2-201512-6 LC Card 84-125056
HD5716.A292 S385 1976

Formazione ed evoluzione della scienza economica /. Manfra, Modestino R. [Firenze] [1985] viii, 163 p. ; ISBN 88-00-86023-0 : LC Card 86-118265
HB75 .M247 1985

Forme della politica e teoria del cambiamento. Badaloni, Nicola. Forme della politica e teorie del cambiamento . Pisa , c1983. xxii, 264 p. ; LC Card 85-163265 DDC 306/.2 19
JA76 .B23 1983 ***NYPL [JLD 86-3306]***

Forme della politica e teorie del cambiamento . Badaloni, Nicola. Pisa , c1983. xxii, 264 p. ; LC Card 85-163265 DDC 306/.2 19
JA76 .B23 1983 ***NYPL [JLD 86-3306]***

Formen der Aufbauorganisation des betrieblichen Bildungswesens in industriellen Grossbetrieben . Rahn, Horst-J. Berlin , c1984. 99 p. : ISBN 3-428-05503-9 LC Card 84-147527
HF5549.5.T7 R254 1984

Formen und Auswirkungen des bäuerlichen Nebenerwerbs . Aistleitner, Josef. [Innsbruck] , 1986. 174 p. : LC Card 87-408342 DDC 338.1/6

19
HD1935 .A66 1986

Die Formierung der rohstoffpolitischen Forderungen der Entwicklungsländer auf der Ebene der Vereinten Nationen bis zur ersten Konferenz für Handel und Entwicklung (UNCTAD 1) 1946 /. Hagemann, Hermann. Münster , 1983. xix, 384, [14], 42 p. : ISBN 3-923676-11-5 LC Card 84-172079
HC59.7 .H27 1983

Formiga, Marcone. Personagens da crise / Marcone Formiga. Brasília : Dom Quixote Editora e Distribuidora, 1984. 160 p. : ports. ; 23 cm. (Coleção Hipólito José da Costa . v. 10) LC Card 86-157831
1. Brazil - Economic policy - Public opinion. 2. Brazil - Economic conditions - 1964-1985 - Public opinion. 3. Public opinion - Brazil. I. Title. II. Series.
HC187 .F636 1984

Forming economic policy . Hampson, Fen Osler. London , 1986. x, 161 p. : ISBN 0-86187-628-8
NYPL [JLE 86-3813]

Formirane i izpolzvane na parichnite fondove v stopanskite organizat͡sii /. Kotsev, Tsvetan. Varna , 1985. 117 p. ; LC Card 85-213610
HC403.Z9 C347 1985

Formirovanie i izmerenie rezervov proizvodstva /. I͡Akovleva, O. P. (Olimpiada Pavlovna) Leningrad , 1985. 86 p. : LC Card 86-168063
HC336.25 .I25 1985

Formirovanie i razvitie rabochego klassa i promyshlennosti Urala v period stroitel'stva sotsializma, 1917-1937 : informat͡sionnye materialy / [otv. redaktor V.G. Granin]. Sverdlovsk : UNT͡S AN SSSR, 1982. 138 p. ; 20 cm. At head of title: Akademii͡a nauk SSSR. Ural'skiĭ nauchnyĭ t͡sentr. Institut ėkonomiki. Includes bibliographical references. LC Card 84-211723
1. Labor and laboring classes - Russian S.F.S.R. - Ural Mountains Region - History. 2. Ural Mountains Region (R.S.F.S.R.) - Industries - History. I. Granin, V. G. II. Institut ėkonomiki (Akademii͡a nauk SSSR. Ural'skiĭ nauchnyĭ t͡sentr).
HD8529.U7 F67 1982

Formirovanie i razvitie rabochego klassa Sovetskoĭ Armenii (1920-1940) Karapetian, H. S. (Hovhannes Smbati) Sovetakan Hayastani banvor dasakargi dzevavorumĕ ev zargats'umĕ (1920-1940) /. Erevan , 1980. 272 p., [1] leaf of plates : LC Card 83-129694
HD8529.A692 K37 1980

Formirovanie predprii͡atii͡a kommunisticheskogo tipa /. Falaleev, A. N. Moskva , 1980. 126 p. ; LC Card 81-144517
HD3616.S472 F35 1980

Formsmark II. Formsmark II, the short-run forms market /. Arlington, VA (1730 N. Lynn St., Arlington 22209) , c1986. 107 leaves : LC Card 87-146216 DDC 381/.4565129 19
HD9800.7.A2 F67 1986

Formsmark II, the short-run forms market / prepared for International Business Forms Industries ; prepared by CAP International, Inc. Arlington, VA (1730 N. Lynn St., Arlington 22209) : International Business Form Industries, c1986. 107 leaves : ill. ; 30 cm. "August 1986." LC Card 87-146216 DDC 381/.4565129 19
1. Manifold business forms industry. 2. Market surveys. I. International Business Forms Industries. II. CAP International. III. Title: Formsmark II.
HD9800.7.A2 F67 1986

FormsMark III : the impact of the intelligent copier/printer on the continuous forms market / prepared for International Business Forms Industries ; prepared by CAP International, Inc. Arlington, VA (1730 N. Lynn St., Arlington 22209) : IBFI, c1986. 154 p. : ill. ; 30 cm. "December 1986." Loose-leaf format. LC Card 87-401995 DDC 381/.4565129 19
1. Copying machine industry. 2. Copying machine equipment industry. I. International Business Forms Industries. II. CAP Jnternational. III. Title: FormsMark 3. IV. Title: FormsMark Three.
HD9802.3.A2 F67 1986

FormsMark Three. FormsMark III . Arlington, VA (1730 N. Lynn St., Arlington 22209) , c1986. 154 p. : LC Card 87-401995 DDC 381/.4565129 19
HD9802.3.A2 F67 1986

FormsMark 3. FormsMark III . Arlington, VA (1730 N. Lynn St., Arlington 22209) , c1986. 154 p. : LC Card 87-401995 DDC 381/.4565129 19
HD9802.3.A2 F67 1986

The formulation of monetary policy . Atkinson, Paul. [Paris, France] [1986, c1985] 41 p. : LC Card 86-212837 DDC 332.4/6 19
HG230.3 .A75 1986

Formy i metody upravlenii͡a NTP / otvetstvennyĭ redaktor P.A. Sedlov. Moskva : "Nauka", 1987. 151 p. ; 20 cm. At head of title: Akademii͡a nauk SSSR. Ordena Trudovogo Krasnogo Znameni Institut ėkonomiki. Includes bibliographical references. LC Card 87-143073
1. Technological innovations - Soviet Union - Management. 2. Technological innovations - Economic aspects - Soviet Union - Forecasting. 3. Technological innovations - Czechoslovakia - Management. 4. Technological innovations - Economic aspects - Czechoslovakia - Forecasting. I. Sedlov, Pavel Alekseevich. II. Institut ėkonomiki (Akademii͡a nauk SSSR).
HC340.T4 F67 1987

Formy i metody vzaimodeĭstvii͡a nauki i proizvodstva /. Simpozium "Nauchno-tekhnicheskiĭ progress i intensifikat͡sii͡a obshchestvennogo proizvodstva" (1984 : Podol'sk, Moscow, R.S.F.S.R.) Moskva , 1984. 237 p. ; LC Card 85-240380
HC340.T4 S48 1984

Fornallaz, Pierre. Die ökologische Wirtschaft : auf dem Weg zu einer verantworteten Wirtschaftsweise / Pierre Fornallaz. Aarau : AT Verlag, c1986. 128 p. : ill. ; 21 cm. Bibliography: p. 127-128. ISBN 3-85502-252-6 : LC Card 86-180445
1. Environmental policy. 2. Human ecology. I. Title.
HC79.E5 F62 1986

Foro : el desarrollo agroindustrial en Venezuela durante los próximos 10 años / Gustavo Pinto Cohen ... [et al.].1a ed. San Felipe, Venezuela : Ediciones CIEPE, 1984. ii, 92 p. ; 22 cm. (Serie Eventos técnicos . no. 2) "Julio 1984." LC Card 85-132901 DDC 338.1/0987 19
1. Agriculture - Economic aspects - Venezuela - Addresses, essays, lectures. 2. Agricultural industries - Venezuela - Addresses, essays, lectures. I. Pinto Cohén, Gustavo. II. Title: Desarrollo agroindustrial en Venezuela durante los próximos 10 años. III. Series.
HD1912 .F67 1984 ***NYPL [JLD 86-424]***

Foro de la Esperanza . Foro de la Esperanza (1985 : Ibagué, Colombia) [Bogotá?] [1985] 154 p. ; LC Card 87-401285 DDC 338.9861 19
HC197 .F59 1985

Foro de la Esperanza (1985 : Ibagué, Colombia) Foro de la Esperanza : Ibagué, Tolima, diciembre 11 de 1985 / Consejo de Ministros, Consejo Nacional de Política Económica y Social (Conpes), Junta Directiva de Resurgir. [Bogotá?] : Presidencia de la República de Colombia, Secretaría de Información y Prensa, [1985] 154 p. ; 24 cm. (Cultura tairona) At head of title: Presidencia de la República. Cover title. LC Card 87-401285 DDC 338.9861 19
1. Colombia - Economic policy - Congresses. I. Colombia. Consejo de Ministros. II. Consejo Nacional de Política Económica y Social (Colombia). III. Resurgir (Agency : Colombia). Junta Directiva. IV. Title. V. Series.
HC197 .F59 1985

Foro de Proyectos de Inversión Colombo-Venezolanos (1986 : Cúcuta, Colombia) La frontera colombo-venezolana, una región donde invertir / Foro de Proyectos de Inversión Colombo-Venezolanos, Cúcuta, julio de 1986. Bogotá, D.E. : Departamento Nacional de Planeación, [1986] 96 p. ; 23 cm. LC Card 87-403851 DDC 332.6/09861 19
1. Investments - Colombia. 2. Investments - Venezuela. 3. Colombia - Boundaries - Venezuela. 4. Venezuela - Boundaries - Colombia. I. Colombia. Departamento Nacional de Planeación. II. Title.
HG5352 .F67 1986

Foro El Suroeste de Antioquia y el Chocó Norte . Foro El Suroeste de Antioquia y el Chocó Norte (1984 : Urrao, Colombia) [Medellín] [1985] 65 p. : LC Card 87-400457 DDC 338.9861/2 19
HC198.A5 F595 1984

Foro El Suroeste de Antioquia y el Chocó Norte (1984 : Urrao, Colombia) Foro El Suroeste de Antioquia y el Chocó Norte : Urrao, diciembre 7-8 y 9 de 1984 / recopilado por Jorge Restrepo Uribe. [Medellín]: Asamblea Departamental de Antioquia, [1985] 65 p. : maps ; 21 cm. LC Card 87-400457 DDC 338.9861/2 19
1. Economic development projects - Colombia - Antioquia (Dept.). 2. Economic development projects - Colombia - Chocó. 3. Economic development projects - Colombia - Urrao Region. 4. Canals, Interoceanic. I. Restrepo Uribe, Jorge. II. Antioquia (Colombia : Dept.). Asamblea Departamental. III. Title.
HC198.A5 F595 1984

Foro Nacional sobre Círculos de Participación (1st : 1983 : Bucaramanga, Colombia) Productividad y participación . [Bucaramanga, Colombia] , c1985. 165 p. : ISBN 958-9302-15-6 LC Card 86-166141
HD5660.C7 P76 1985

Foro políticas de fomento industrial en el Ecuador / redacción Felipe Burbano. [Quito, Ecuador] : ILDIS, [c1985] 58 p. : ill. ; 20 cm. Cover title. Includes bibliographical references. LC Card 86-134947 DDC 658/.009866 19
1. Industrial management - Ecuador. 2. Industrial management - Law and legislation - Ecuador. I. Burbano, Felipe. II. Instituto Latinoamericano de Investigaciones Sociales.
HD70.E25 F67 1985

Forschung für die Praxis .
(Bd. 9) Hemmers, K. (Karlheinz) Planung des Personalbedarfs in indirekten Bereichen /. Berlin , New York , 1986. viii, 141 p. : ISBN 0-387-16702-1 (U. S.) : LC Card 86-200805
HF5549.5.M3 H46 1986

Forschung Stadtverkehr. Reihe Auswertungen .
(Heft A2) Aufbereitung von Ergebnissen der Stadtverkehrsforschung . Hof/Saale , 1986. 2 v. : LC Card 87-408335 DDC 388.4/0943 19
HE4774 .A94 1986

Forschung und Entwicklung, eine Chance für die Wirtschaft /. Pieper, Antje, 1943- Köln , c1984. 56 p. : ISBN 3-602-24853-4 LC Card 85-217568
HC290.5.T4 P54 1984

Forschungen zur Landeskunde von Niederösterreich. For other vols. in this series, see Old Catalog.
(Bd. 16) Feigl, Helmuth. Die niederösterreichische Grundherrschaft . [Wien] , 1964. 379 p. ; LC Card 85-127367
HD639.L6 F45 1964

Forschungen zur Raumentwicklung, 0341-244X .
(Bd. 15) Wagner, Gerhard. Abbau regionaler Strompreisdisparitäten durch raumwirksame Massnahmen und Planungen /. Bonn , 1985. xv, 356 p. : ISBN 3-87994-415-6 LC Card 87-408008 DDC 338.4/336362/0943 19
HD9685.G3 W34 1985

Forschungen zur Wirtschaftsgeschichte, 0138-5100 .
(Bd. 23) Roesler, Jörg. Wirtschaftswachstum in der Industrie der DDR, 1945-1970 /. Berlin , 1986. 280 p. ; ISBN 3-05-000074-0 LC Card 86-196020
HC290.78 .R64 1986

Forschungs- und Entwicklungsplanung . Künzli, Ernst. Bern , c1984. 292 p. : ISBN 3-258-03351-X : LC Card 84-178059
HD30.4 .K86 1984

Forschungsbericht (Germany (West). Bundesministerium für Arbeit und Sozialordnung) .
(101) Der Ausbau von Fernwärmenetzen und seine Wirkungen auf Arbeitsmarkt und Beschäftigung, dargestellt am Beispiel der Freien und Hansestadt Hamburg . Bonn [1983] xiv, 172 p. : LC Card 85-107700
HD5780.H34 A87 1983

(103) Infratest Sozialforschung. Datenlage zur Alterssicherung . Bonn , 1984. 330 p. : LC Card 86-132439 DDC 331.25/2/0943 19
HD7105.35.G3 I54 1984

(117) Brandt, Franz. Ursachen für die Schwierigkeiten bei der Eingliederung von Schwerbehinderten auf dem allgemeinen Arbeitsmarkt /. Bonn [1984] 410 p. ; LC Card 87-408829 DDC 331.5/9/0943 19
HD7256.G3 B7 1984

(119) Zur Problematik der Abbrecher der beruflichen Rehabilitation /. Bonn [1985?] 118,

[29] p. ; LC Card 86-190824
HD7256.G3 Z87 1985

Forschungsbericht (Institut für Höhere Studien, Vienna, Austria) .
(no. 179) The IAS-System data base . Wien, Austria [1982] ii, 151, 3 p. :
NYPL [JSG 86-170]

Forschungsbericht (Konrad-Adenauer-Stiftung) .
(48) Die Notwendige Hilfe . Melle [1986] 207 p. : ISBN 3-88368-111-3 : LC Card 86-197696
HC60 .N69 1986

(48) Die Notwendige Hilfe . Melle [1986] 207 p. : ISBN 3-88368-111-3 : LC Card 86-197696
HC60 .N69 1986

Forschungsberichte (Akademie der Wissenschaften der DDR. Zentralinstitut für Wirtschaftswissenschaften) .
(Nr. 38) Schaefer, Reinhard. Disponibilität--Mobilität--Fluktuation /. Berlin , 1982. 70 p. : LC Card 83-225572
HD5717.5.G35 S3 1982

Forschungsberichte aus dem Institut für Sozialwissenschaftliche Forschung München. Flexible Fertigung und Industriearbeit . Frankfurt Main , New York , c1986. v, 577, iii p. : ISBN 3-593-33648-0 LC Card 86-197535
HD5109.2.G3 F45 1986

Forschungsberichte Betriebswirtschaftslehre .
(Bd. 1) Fuchs, Nikolaus, 1955- Ursachen- und Krisenanalyse der Verschuldung von Entwicklungsländern . Berlin , c1986. 258 p. : ISBN 3-925410-05-8 LC Card 87-124994 DDC 336.3/435/091724 19
HJ8899 .F83 1986

Forschungsberichte der Bundesanstalt für Strassenwesen, Bereich Unfallforschung, 0173-7066 .
(135) Fechtel, Hans-Walter. Flächenhafte Verkehrsberuhigung . Bergisch Gladbach , 1986. 282 p. : LC Card 87-408360 DDC 388.4/0943 19
HE311.G3 F4 1986

(67) Marburger, Ernst-Albrecht. Internationale Erfahrungen mit der Gurtanlegepflicht =. Köln , 1982. 29, 29 p. : LC Card 83-200842
HE5614 .M288 1982

(69) Methoden und Kriterien zur Überprüfung des Erfolgs von Aufklärungskampagnen . Köln , 1982. 99, [93] p. : LC Card 83-178796
HE5614.5.G3 M37 1982

(81) Rüter, Gert. Sicherheitsorientierte Ausbildung von Berufskraftfahren /. Köln [1983] vii, 91 p. : LC Card 83-235527
HD5716.M7952 G327 1983

(85) Haas, Ingrid. Funktion und Wirkung von Aufklebern an Personenkraftwagen /. Köln [1983] 101, [13] p. : LC Card 84-147451
HE5614.5.G3 H28 1983

(87) Grosse-Berndt, Gisela. Wirksamkeitsuntersuchung zum ADAC-Motorrad-Sicherheitstraining. Köln [1983] iii, 160, ii, 112, 27 p. : LC Card 84-147564
HE5614.5.G3 G75 1983

(88) Echterhoff, Wilfried. Einfluss von Verkehrssicherheitsinformationen auf unfallbeteiligte Kraftfahrer /. Köln [1983], c1981. 112 p. : LC Card 84-147580
HE5614.5.G3 E34 1983

(90) Kockelke, Wilhelm. Untersuchung der Vorfahrtregelung "Rechts vor Links" unter dem Aspekt der Verkehrssicherheit /. Bergisch Gladbach [1983] 63, 3 p. : LC Card 84-147884
HE363.G32 U744 1983

Forschungsberichte des Bundesministeriums für Wirtschaftliche Zusammenarbeit .
(Bd. 47) Agroforstliche Landnutzung im Einzugsbereich zentraler Orte im Sahel . Köln , 1983. ix, 374 p. : ISBN 3-8039-0276-2 LC Card 87-102956 DDC 333.73/13/09663 19
HD1019.Z63 A38 1983

Forschungsberichte des Instituts für Bevölkerungsforschung und Sozialpolitik (IBS), Universität Bielefeld .
(Bd. 8) Linde, Hans. Theorie der säkularen Nachwuchsbeschränkung 1800 bis 2000 /. Frankfurt [am Main] , New York , c1984. 201 p. ; ISBN 3-593-33385-6 LC Card 85-131521
HB901 .L55 1984

Forschungsberichte und Materialien .
(Bd. 7) Renckstorf, Karsten. Landesprogramme von Hörfunk und Fernsehen in Hamburg . Hamburg , c1985. xlvii, vi, 388 p. : ISBN 3-87296-067-9 (pbk.) LC Card 86-109817 DDC 384.54/43/0943515 19
HE8700.9.G4 R45 1985 *NYPL [MWGK (Germany, West) 86-4239]*

Forschungsberichte (Universität Hamburg. Institut für Aussenhandel und Überseewirtschaft) .
(Nr. 42) Schoppe, Siegfried, 1944- Determinanten der Eigenkapitalbildung und Konsequenzen für die Wettbewerbsfähigkeit deutscher Grossunternehmen und Mittelbetriebe /. Hamburg , 1986. 24 p. : LC Card 86-185861
HG4156 .S36 1986

Forschungsberichte (Wiener Institut für Internationale Wirtschaftsvergleiche) .
(Nr. 53) Boguszewski, Jan. Wachstum und Produktivität in der Industrie und ihren Hauptbereichen in der BRD, Österreich, Polen und Ungarn im Zeitraum, 1960-1972 /. Wien [1979] 71 p. : LC Card 84-119739
HC290.5.I52 B64 1979

Forschungsgemeinschaft Bauen und Wohnen. Standorte von Büros im Urteil der Beschäftigten und sonstiger Nutzer /. Stuttgart , 1983. 140 p. : LC Card 83-220559
HF5547.25 .S74 1983

Forschungsgesellschaft für Strassen- und Verkehrswesen. Aufbereitung von Ergebnissen der Stadtverkehrsforschung . Hof/Saale , 1986. 2 v. : LC Card 87-408335 DDC 388.4/0943 19
HE4774 .A94 1986

Forschungsgesellschaft für Strassen- und Verkehrswesen (Germany) Deutscher Strassenkongress (1984 : Mannheim, Germany) Deutscher Strassenkongress, Mannheim, 1984 /. Köln [1985?] 255 p. : LC Card 87-408263 DDC 388.1/0943 19
HE363.G3 D48 1984

Forschungsgruppe Analyse der Sektoralen Wirtschaftsstruktur (HWWA-Institut für Wirtschaftsforschung-Hamburg)
Zwischenbericht, Analyse der strukturellen Entwicklung der deutschen Wirtschaft . Hamburg , 1979. viii, 142, 49 leaves : LC Card 83-132166
HC286.7 .Z88 1979

Forschungsgruppe "Wissenschaftlich-Technischer und Sozialer Fortschritt" des Instituts für Soziologie und Sozialpolitik der AdW der DDR. Soziale Aspekte der Mikroelektronik /. Berlin , 1985. 122 p. ; LC Card 87-409418 DDC 306/.46 19
HD6331 .S683 1985

Forschungsinstitut für Wirtschaftsverfassung und Wettbewerb (Cologne, Germany)
Neuorientierung des Wettbewerbsschutzes . Köln , 1986. viii, 231 p. ; ISBN 3-452-20666-1 : LC Card 87-138003
HB41 .F22 Heft 120 KK6456

US-Fusionsrichtlinien, 1984 /. Köln , c1985. 83 p. ; ISBN 3-452-20248-8 : LC Card 86-100251
HB41 .F63 Heft 6 KF1477

Forschungsstelle für den Handel (Germany)
Handelsforschung heute . Berlin , c1979. 230 p. : ISBN 3-428-04408-8 LC Card 87-408239 DDC 380.1 s 380.1/06/04355 19
HF345 .F66 Folge 3, Nr. 7 HF308

FORSCHUNGSSTELLE FÜR DEN HANDEL (GERMANY) - HISTORY.
Handelsforschung heute . Berlin , c1979. 230 p. : ISBN 3-428-04408-8 LC Card 87-408239 DDC 380.1 s 380.1/06/04355 19
HF345 .F66 Folge 3, Nr. 7 HF308

Forschungstexte Wirtschafts- und Sozialwissenschaften .
(Bd. 20) Rosen, Rita. --Muss kommen, aber nix von Herzen . Opladen , 1986. 262 p. : ISBN 3-8100-0572-X LC Card 87-112784
HD6149 .R67 1986

(11) Vollzug und Wirkungen regionaler Umweltpolitik . Opladen , 1984. 199 p. ; ISBN 3-8100-0392-1 LC Card 84-228636
HC290.5.E5 V65 1984

Forschungsverbund "Empirische Verbraucherforschung" (Germany)
Schatz, Heribert. Verbraucherinteressen im politischen Entscheidungsprozess /. Frankfurt/Main , New York , c1984. 275 p. ; ISBN 3-593-33293-0 LC Card 84-212024
HC290.5.C63 S33 1984

Warentest und Konsument . Frankfurt/Main , New York , c1984. 268 p. : ISBN 3-593-33295-7 LC Card 84-150919
HF1040.9.G3 W37 1984

Forschungsvereinigung Automobiltechnik (Germany) Kortzfleisch, Gert von. Energie für den Verkehr . Frankfurt am Main , c1984. 115 p. : LC Card 84-192683
HD9710.G4 V4 Nr. 42 HE5620.E53

Forsikring i Norge / fra et utvalg oppnevnt ved kongelig resolusjon 22. desember 1978. Oslo : Universitetsforlaget, [1983] 226 p. ; 28 cm. (Norges offentlige utredninger . 1983:52) "Utredningen avgitt i desember 1983." ISBN 82-00-70870-5 LC Card 84-158459
1. Insurance - Norway. 2. Insurance law - Norway. I. Series.
HG8668.5 .F67 1983

Forskningens frontlinjer.
Holmquist, Carin, 1948- Förhandla mer räkna mindre /. Stockholm [1984] 124 p. : ISBN 91-38-90409-8 : LC Card 84-241380
HD30.22 .H65 1984

Forslin, Jan, 1939- Automation and industrial workers . Oxford [Oxfordshire] , New York , 1979- v. : ISBN 0-08-023339-2 (v. 1, pt. 1) : LC Card 79-40811 DDC 331
HD6331 .A93 1979 *NYPL [JLM 82-242]*

Försörjningstryggheten för olja, kol och uran : en metodstudie / Statens industriverk. Stockholm : LiberFörlag, [1982] 175 p. : ill. ; 25 cm. (SIND, 0346-5748 . 1982:8) Bibliography: p. 125. ISBN 91-38-07030-8 LC Card 82-240448
1. Energy policy - Sweden. 2. Power resources - Sweden. I. Sweden. Statens industriverk. II. Series.
HD9502.S82 F68 1983

Forst, Brian. Power in numbers : how to manage for profit / Brian Forst. New York : Wiley, c1987. xiv, 257 p. ; 24 cm. Includes index. ISBN 0-471-62809-3 LC Card 87-21555 DDC 658.1/51 19
1. Financial statements. 2. Corporations - Finance. I. Title.
HG4028.B2 F58 1987

Forstbetriebe nach Kantonen. Eidgenössische Betriebszählung 1985. Bern , 1986. 108 p. ; ISBN 3-303-07007-5 LC Card 87-407623 DDC 338.1/7498/09494021 19
HD9765.S92 E37 1986

Forster, Dale E. Oregon express companies / by Dale E. Forster. Eugene, Ore. : D.E. Forster, c1985. vi, 231 p. : ill. ; 27 cm. "Edition limited to five hundred copies." Bibliography: p. 225-226. Includes index. LC Card 87-121202 DDC 383/.143/09795 19
1. Postal service - Oregon - History. 2. Express service - Oregon - History. 3. Pony express - History. I. Title.
HE6376.A1 O735 1985

Forster, Edgar. Ökonomische Sicherungspolitik / Edgar Forster. Berlin : Duncker & Humblot, c1983. 280 p. : ill. ; 24 cm. (Volkswirtschaftliche Schriften. Heft 330) Bibliography: p. [251]-280. ISBN 3-428-05366-4 LC Card 83-220475
1. Insurance, Health. 2. Social security. 3. Risk (Insurance). I. Title. II. Series.
HD7101 .F67 1983

Forster, Jakob Johann Benjamin. A conjunction of interests : business, politics, and tariffs, 1825-1879 / Ben Forster. Toronto ; Buffalo : University of Toronto Press, c1986. vi, 288 p. ; 24 cm. (The State and economic life. 8) Bibliography: p. [259]-276. Includes index. ISBN 0-8020-5680-6 (alk. paper) LC Card 87-108915 DDC 382.7/0971 19
1. Tariff - Canada - History - 19th century. 2. Canada - Commercial policy - History - 19th century. 3. Industry and state - Canada - History - 19th century. 4. Free trade and protection - History - 19th century. I. Title. II. Series.
HF1765 .F67 1986

Forster, Karl Heinz. Beiträge zur Bankaufsicht, Bankbilanz und Bankprüfung . Düsseldorf , 1985. 226 p. : ISBN 3-8021-0267-3 LC Card 85-208772
HG1605 .B44 1985

Förster, Walter, 1914- Das Haus am Wall : aus Bremens Geldgeschichte / Walter Förster. Bremen : H.M. Hauschild, c1983. 159 p. : ill. ; 22 cm. Bibliography: p. 151-154. Includes indexes. ISBN 3-920699-45-9 LC Card 84-155521
1. Money - Germany (West) - Bremen - History. 2. Banks and banking - Germany (West) - Bremen - History. I. Title.
HG1010.B7 F67 1983

Førsund, Finn R.
Environmental economics and management : pollution and natural resources / Finn R. Førsund and Steinar Strøm. London ; New York : Croom Helm, c1988. 307 p. : ill. ; 23 cm. Includes bibliographies and indexes. "Published in the USA by Croom Helm in association with Methuen."--T.p. verso. ISBN 0-85664-900-7 LC Card 87-9179 DDC 363.7/0525 19
1. Environmental policy. 2. Pollution - Environmental aspects. 3. Natural resources. 4. Human ecology. I. Strøm, Steinar. II. Title.
HC79.E5 F64 1988

Johansen, Leif. [Essays. Selections.] Collected works of Leif Johansen /. Amsterdam ; New York : 2 v. (xiii, 974 p.) ; ISBN 0-444-87833-5 (set) LC Card 87-6814 DDC 330.1 19
HB171 .J59725 1987

Forsyth, P. (Peter) Can international comparisons of air fares be made? / Peter J. Forsyth. Canberra, Australia : Australian National University, Centre for Economic Research, [1985] 35 p. ; 21 cm. (Discussion papers, 0725-430X . no. 133) "December 1985"--Cover. Bibliography: p. 28-29. ISBN 0-949293-46-6 (pbk.) LC Card 86-212326 DDC 387.7/12 19
1. Airlines - Rates. I. Series: Discussion paper (Australian National University. Centre for Economic Research) , no. 133. II. Title.
HE9783 .F67 1985

Forsyth, Patrick. Sales management handbook /. Aldershot, Hants, England , Brookfield, Vt., U. S.A. , c1987. p. cm. ISBN 0-566-02585-X : LC Card 87-8619 DDC 658.8/1 19
HF5438.4 .S228 1987

FORT WORTH (TEX.) - INDUSTRIES - DIRECTORIES.
Camden, Thomas M., 1938- How to get a job in Dallas, Fort Worth . Chicago, IL , c1987. viii, 490 p. : ISBN 0-9609516-9-5 (pbk.) : LC Card 86-30123 DDC 650.1/4/097642812 19
HF5382.75.U6 C353 1987

Fortalecimiento del sistema de formación profesional . International Labour Organisation. Ginebra , 1982. 47 p. ; ISBN 92-2-303194-X LC Card 84-113933
HD5715.5.P3 I57 1982

FORTALEZA (BRAZIL) - ECONOMIC CONDITIONS.
Casimiro, Liana Maria Carleial de. Acumulação capitalista, emprego e crise . São Paulo , 1986. 216 p. : LC Card 87-152202 DDC 331.12/0981/31 19
HD5755.F6 C37 1986

Fernandes, Adelita Neto Carleial. Condições de vida nos bairros de Fortaleza, nov/84 a mar/85 . Fortaleza , 1986. 92 p. : LC Card 86-196902
HC189.F67 F47 1986

FORTALEZA (BRAZIL) - SOCIAL CONDITIONS.
Fernandes, Adelita Neto Carleial. Condições de vida nos bairros de Fortaleza, nov/84 a mar/85 . Fortaleza , 1986. 92 p. : LC Card 86-196902
HC189.F67 F47 1986

Forte, Francesco, 1929- Il bilancio nell'economia pubblica / F. Forte. Milano : Giuffrè, [1985] 2 v. ; 25 cm. (Trattato di economia pubblica . 4) Includes bibliographies. CONTENTS. - t. 1. Teoria generale del bilancio pubblico -- t. 2. Stato, Parastato, Enti pubblici, Enti locali, Regioni, CEE. ISBN 88-14-00636-9 : LC Card 86-151358 DDC 350.72/2 19
1. Budget. 2. Local budgets. 3. Budget - Italy. 4. Local budgets - Italy. 5. Budget - European Economic Community countries. 6. Local budgets - European Economic Community countries. I. Title. II. Series.
HJ2005 .F67 1985 ***NYPL [JLE 86-2653]***

Forteza, Alvaro. Efectos de la política económica en el mercado de leche fluida / Alvaro Forteza. Montevideo, Uruguay : Centro de Investigaciones Económicas, [1986] 126 p. : ill. ; 28 cm. (III. Serie Estudios . no. 27) "El presente trabajo se llevó a cabo en CINVE como parte de la investigación 'El productor lechero de la cuenca de Montevideo: determinantes de su comportamiento tecnológico en un proceso de adopción generalizado'"--P. [3]. Includes bibliographical references. LC Card 87-121158
1. Milk trade - Government policy - Uruguay. I. Centro de Investigaciones Económicas (Uruguay). II. Series: III. Serie, Estudios (Centro de Investigaciones Económicas (Uruguay)) , no. 27. III. Title.
HD9282.U72 F67 1986

Fortin, Andrée. Le Rézo : essai sur les coopératives d'alimentation saine au Québec / Andrée Fortin. Québec, Québec : Institut québécois de recherche sur la culture, 1985. 282 p. : ill. ; 22 cm. (Documents de recherche . no 5) Bibliography: p. 267-272. ISBN 2-89224-052-2 LC Card 86-225353
1. Consumer cooperatives - Québec (Province). 2. Food, Natural. 3. Natural foods industry - Québec (Province). I. Series: Documents de recherche (Institut québécois de recherche sur la culture) , no 5. II. Title.
HD3290.A3 Q435 1985

Fortin, Pierre.
[Unemployment, inflation, and economic stabilization in Quebec. French]
Chômage, inflation et régulation de la conjoncture au Québec / Pierre Fortin. Montréal, Québec : L'Institut de recherches C.D. Howe, [1980] viii, 144 p. : ill. ; 22 cm. (Accent Québec) Issued also in English under title: Unemployment, inflation, and economic stabilization in Quebec. Includes bibliographical references. ISBN 0-88806-063-7 (pbk.) LC Card 87-673448
1. Quebec (Province) - Economic conditions. 2. Unemployment - Québec (Province). 3. Inflation (Finance) - Quebec (Province). 4. Economic stabilization - Québec (Province). I. Series: Accent Québec. French. II. Title.
HC117.Q4 F63x 1980

Fortuna, Juan Carlos. Las bases de un desarrollo social diferente : estructura productiva y trabajo / Juan Carlos Fortuna. Montevideo : Centro de Informaciones y Estudios del Uruguay : Ediciones de la Banda Oriental, [1985] 117 p. ; 19 cm. (Colección Estudios sobre la sociedad uruguaya . no. 5) Originally presented as the author's thesis (maestría)-- Facultad Latinoamericana de Ciencias Sociales. Bibliography: p. [113]-117. LC Card 86-131906
1. Uruguay - Industries. 2. Labor supply - Uruguay. 3. Uruguay - Economic conditions - 1945-. I. Series: Estudios sobre la sociedad uruguaya , no. 5. II. Title.
HC232 .F76 1985

FORTUNES. see **INCOME; WEALTH.**

Forty-plus job-hunting guide. Birsner, E. Patricia. The 40+ job-hunting guide . New York, NY , c1987. xx, 250 p. : ISBN 0-13-329152-9 (pbk.) : LC Card 87-2438 DDC 650.1/4/024658 19
HD38.25.U6 B53 1987

Forty years on . Blythe, Ian. Aldershot, Hants., England , Brookfield, Vt., USA , c1987. p. cm. ISBN 0-566-05005-6 : LC Card 87-8653 DDC 658.8/3/06041 19
HF5410 .B58 1987

Fórum (Budapest, Hungary)
Szathmári, Gábor. Kinek lehet igaza? . Budapest , 1985. 118 p. ; ISBN 963-322-273-7 : LC Card 86-156416
HD6955 .S975 1985

FORUM (Debating society)
Causas y manejo de la crisis económica dominicana, 1974-1984 /. Santo Domingo, República Dominicana , 1986. 184 p. : LC Card 86-208551
HC153.5 .C385 1986

Condiciones socioeconómicas de la mujer trabajadora en la República Dominicana /. Santo Domingo, República Dominicana , 1986. 150 p. ; LC Card 86-208584
HD6112.5 .C65 1986

Los Problemas de la inflación en la República Dominicana /. Santo Domingo, República Dominicana , 1986. 111 p. : LC Card 86-208576
HG767 .P76 1986

La Situación cambiaria en la República Dominicana /. Santo Domingo, República Dominicana , 1984. 252 p. : LC Card 87-401265 DDC 338.97293 19
HC153.5 .S575 1984

La Situación y los problemas del sistema financiero nacional. Santo Domingo, República Dominicana , 1986. 152 p. ; LC Card 86-208560
HG2817 .S57 1986

Forum der Bundesstatistik .
(Bd. 2) Reich, Utz-Peter. Darstellungskonzepte der Input-Output-Rechnung /. Stuttgart , 1984. 185 p. : ISBN 3-17-003301-8
NYPL [JLE 86-1264]

Forum (Kiel, Germany) .
(no. 4) Herrmann, Roland. The compensatory financing system of the International Monetary Fund . Kiel, West-Germany , 1983. iii, 85 p. ; ISBN 3-922553-18-4 (pbk.) LC Card 83-227524 DDC 332.1/52 19
HG3881.5.I58 H47 1983 ***NYPL [JLD 97-7]***

FORUM (Series : Santo Domingo, Dominican Republic) .
(13) La Situación cambiaria en la República Dominicana /. Santo Domingo, República Dominicana , 1984. 252 p. : LC Card 87-401265 DDC 338.97293 19
HC153.5 .S575 1984

(18) Causas y manejo de la crisis económica dominicana, 1974-1984 /. Santo Domingo, República Dominicana , 1986. 184 p. : LC Card 86-208551
HC153.5 .C385 1986

(20) Los Problemas de la inflación en la República Dominicana /. Santo Domingo, República Dominicana , 1986. 111 p. : LC Card 86-208576
HG767 .P76 1986

(21) Condiciones socioeconómicas de la mujer trabajadora en la República Dominicana /. Santo Domingo, República Dominicana , 1986. 150 p. ; LC Card 86-208584
HD6112.5 .C65 1986

(24) La Situación y los problemas del sistema financiero nacional. Santo Domingo, República Dominicana , 1986. 152 p. ; LC Card 86-208560
HG2817 .S57 1986

Forum wohnen / Renate Petzinger, Detlev Ipsen, Gerd Köhler (Hg.). 1. Aufl. Freiburg i. Br. : Dreisam-Verlag ; Giessen : Vertrieb, Prolit-Buchvertrieb, 1986. 158 p. : ill. ; 21 cm. (GEW Forum) Bibliography: p. 157-158. ISBN 3-89125-009-6 LC Card 86-169106
1. Housing - Germany, West - Congresses. I. Petzinger, Renate, 1943-. II. Ipsen, Detlev. III. Köhler, Gerd, 1944-. IV. Series.
HD7339.A3 F68 1986

FORWARD EXCHANGE.
Andersen, Torben Juul. Currency and interest rate hedging . New York, N.Y. , c1987. viii, 272 p. : ISBN 0-13-195645-0 LC Card 87-7758 DDC 332.64/5 19
HG3853 .A53 1987

Hodrick, Robert J. The empirical evidence on the efficiency of forward and futures foreign exchange markets /. Chur, Switzerland , New York , c1987. viii, 174 p. ; ISBN 3-7186-0415-9 (pbk.) LC Card 87-17790 DDC 332.4/5 19
HG3853 .H43 1987

Jones, Eric T. (Eric Thomas) Hedging foreign exchange . New York , c1987. xiv, 239 p. : ISBN 0-471-84986-3 LC Card 86-26639 DDC 332.4/5 19
HG3853 .J66 1987

Quick, Rolf H. Informationsprozesse auf spekulativen Märkten . Thun , c1984. vii, 291 p. : ISBN 3-87144-790-0 : LC Card 84-159793
HG3853 .Q53 1984

Understanding the futures markets. New York, NY (100 Church St., Suite 1850 New York 10007) , c1987. 61 p. ; LC Card 87-129996 DDC 332.64/4 19
HG6024.A3 U64 1987

FORWARD EXCHANGE - BELGIUM.
Mercier, Paul. Le marché du call money garanti /. Bruxelles [1983] 64 p. : LC Card 84-210204
HG1055 .M47 1983

Forward thinking . Gilbreath, Robert D. (Robert Dean), 1949- New York , c1987. xvi, 184 p. ; ISBN 0-07-023262-8 : LC Card 86-27732 DDC 658.4 19
HD31 .G496 1987

Forward's Color Productions. Barlow, Raymond E. The glass industry in Sandwich /. Windham, N.H. , c1983- v. : ISBN 0-9610166-0-4 (v. 4) LC Card 82-73582 DDC 338.4/76661/0974492 19
HD9623.U46 S263 1983
NYPL [3-MPW+ 84-1016]

Fosler, R. Scott. The New economic role of American states . New York , 1988. x, 370 p. ; ISBN 0-19-505003-7 LC Card 87-12499 DDC 338.973 19
HC106.8 .N495 1988

Fossati, Giorgio. Il finanziamento delle imprese / Giorgio Fossati. Nuova ed. riv. e aggiornata, 3a ed. Milano, Italy : F. Angeli, 1984. 270 p. : ill. ; 22 cm. (Azienda moderna. 113) Bibliography: p. [251]-261. Includes index. LC Card 86-141137 DDC 658.1/5 19
1. Corporations - Finance. 2. Business enterprises - Finance. I. Title.
HG4011 .F58 1984

FOSSIL FUELS - GOVERNMENT POLICY - UNITED STATES - HISTORY - 20TH CENTURY.
Clark, John Garretson, 1932- Energy and the federal government . Urbana , c1987. xxiii, 511 p. : ISBN 0-252-01295-X LC Card 85-20505 DDC 333.8/2/0973 19
HD9502.U52 C57 1987 ***NYPL [JLE 87-736]***

Fossorier, Jean-Marc. Camus, Michel. L'expérience pénivauxoise, 1971-1982 . [Vaux-le-Pénil , 1982] 187 p., [8] p. of plates : LC Card 84-190663
HC277.V35 C36 1982

Föste, Wolfgang. Verkaufte Träume : Kinderarbeit und Kinderprostitution in Thailand / Wolfgang Föste. München : Simon & Magiera, c1982. 53 p. : ill., map ; 21 cm. (Thailand Correspondenz . 9) Politische Bilderbücher zum Fernen Osten. Thailand ISBN 3-88676-011-1 (pbk.) LC Card 87-672593
1. Children - Employment - Thailand. 2. Prostitution, Juvenile - Thailand. I. Title. II. Series.
HD6250.T52 F67x 1982

FOSTER BROTHERS - MANAGEMENT.
Johnson, Gerry. Strategic change and the management process /. Oxford, OX, UK , New York, NY, USA , 1987. xv, 319 p. : ISBN 0-631-14717-9 : LC Card 87-5152 DDC 658.4/012 19
HD30.28 .J65 1987

FOSTER DAY CARE. see **DAY CARE CENTERS.**

Foster, Dennis L.
The complete franchise book : what you must know (and are rarely told) about buying or starting your own franchise / Dennis L. Foster. Rocklin, Calif. : Prima Pub. and Communications, c1988. 249 p. ; 24 cm. Bibliography: p. 239. Includes index. ISBN 0-914629-24-7 : LC Card 87-2471 DDC 658.8/708 19
1. Franchises (Retail trade). I. Title.
HF5429.23 .F67 1988

Franchising for free : owning your own business without investing your own cash / Dennis L. Foster. New York : J. Wiley & Sons, c1988. x, 229 p. : ill. ; 23 cm. Bibliography: p. 197-198. Includes index. ISBN 0-471-62555-8 (pbk.) : LC Card 87-13379 DDC 658.8/708 19
1. Franchises (Retail trade) - United States. I. Title.
HF5429.235.U5 F67 1988

Foster, J. Rhoads. Regulatory reform . Washington, D.C. , c1984. ii, 267 p. : ISBN 0-913097-02-0 (pbk.) LC Card 84-80846 DDC 363.6/0973 19
HD2766 .R357 1984

Foster, John. The politics of the UCS work-in : class alliances and the right to work / John Foster and Charles Woolfson ; foreword by Tony Benn. London : Lawrence and Wishart ; Atlantic Highlands, N.J. : Distributed in the U. S.A. and Canada by Humanities Press, 1986. 446 p. : ill. ; 22 cm. Distributor from label on t.p. Includes bibliographies. ISBN 0-85315-663-8 (pbk.) : LC Card 86-235159 DDC 331.89/282383/094141 19
1. Labor disputes - Scotland - Case studies. 2. Upper Clyde Shipbuilders - Employees. 3. Right to labor - Scotland - Case studies. I. Woolfson, Charles, 1946-. II. Title.
HD5365.S512 1971 .C584 1986

Foster, John Bellamy. The theory of monopoly capitalism : an elaboration of Marxian political economy / John Bellamy Foster. New York : Monthly Review Press, 1986. 280 p. ; 22 cm. Includes index. ISBN 0-85345-688-7 : LC Card 85-32097 DDC 330.12/2 19
1. Capitalism. 2. Marxian economics. I. Title.
HB501 .F66 1986 ***NYPL [JLD 86-2415]***

Foster, Lawrence G., 1925- A company that cares : one hundred year illustrated history of Johnson & Johnson / by Lawrence G. Foster. New Brunswick, N.J. : Johnson & Johnson, c1986. 175 p. : ill. (some col.) ; 29 cm. Bibliography: p. 174. ISBN 0-9617676-1-8 LC Card 86-27478 DDC 338.7/616151/0973 19
1. Johnson and Johnson, inc. - History. 2. Pharmaceutical industry - United States - History. I. Johnson and Johnson, inc. II. Title.
HD9666.9.J6 F67 1986

Foster, Richard N. Innovation : the attacker's advantage / Richard N. Foster. New York : Summit Books, c1986. 316 p. : ill. ; 25 cm. Includes index. Bibliography: p. 287-299 ISBN 0-671-62250-1 : LC Card 86-1945 DDC 658.4/062 19
1. Technological innovations - Management. 2. Research, Industrial - Management. I. Title.
HD45 .F67 1986 ***NYPL [JLE 86-1899]***

Foster, William S. Management of local public works /. Washington, D.C. , c1986. xvii, 402 p. : ISBN 0-87326-048-1 : LC Card 86-125 DDC 363/.068 19
HD4431 .M35 1986 ***NYPL [JLF 86-1543]***

Fostering the capital-goods sector in LDCS . Pack, Howard. Washington, D.C. (1818 H St., N.W., Washington 20433) [1980] v, 59. 2 leaves ; LC Card 80-121299
HD9680.D44 P33 1980

Fothergill, Steve. Property and industrial development / Stephen Fothergill, Sarah Monk, Martin Perry. London : Hutchinson ; Wolfeboro, N.H. : Longwood, 1987. 187 p. : ill. ; 24 cm. (The Built environment series) Bibliography: p. [177]-180. Includes index. ISBN 0-09-170741-2 (pbk.) : LC Card 87-2627 DDC 333.3/8/0941 19
1. Industrial sites - Great Britain. 2. Great Britain - Industries - Location. 3. Real estate development - Great Britain. 4. Real property - Great Britain. 5. Land use - Great Britain. I. Monk, Sarah. II. Perry, Martin, 1956-. III. Title.
HD598 .F68 1987

Fouad, Mahmoud H. Introduction to economic issues /. Dubuque, Iowa , c1987. i, 220 p. : ISBN 0-8403-4366-3 (pbk.) LC Card 87-80994 DDC 330 19
HB171 .I58 1987

Fougeyrollas-Schwebel, Dominique.
Chabaud-Rychter, Danielle. Espace et temps du travail domestique /. Paris , 1985. 156 p. ; ISBN 2-86563-127-3 LC Card 86-165713
HD6055 .C45 1985

Foulhouze, I. Berger, Alain. Les récoltants vendeurs au kilo champenois face au contrat interprofessionnel /. Paris , Epernay [1984] 45, 63 p. : ISBN 2-85340-534-6 LC Card 85-111856
HD9382.7.C5 B47 1984

Foundation for Advanced Information and Research (Japan) Japan and the United States today . New York , 1986, c1987. vii, 234 p. : ISBN 0-231-06575-2 LC Card 86-32640 DDC 332/.042/0952 19
HG3903 .J35 1987

Foundation for Public Relations Research and Education (U. S.) New technology and public relations . New York, NY (310 Madison Ave., New York 10017) , c1986. xviii, 170 p. : LC Card 87-105313 DDC 659.2/028/5 19
HD59 .N44 1986

Foundation for Research on Human Behavior. Modern organization theory . New York , 1987, c1959. x, 324 p. : ISBN 0-8240-8208-7 (alk. paper) : LC Card 86-27072 DDC 658 19
HD31 .M614 1987

Foundation of the American Society of Association Executives. The Corporate view . Washington, DC , c1982. vii, 92 p. ;
NYPL [JLF 87-940]

Foundations of business telecommunications management /. Grover, Kenneth C. New York , c1986. xvi, 196 p. ; ISBN 0-306-42249-2 (pbk.) LC Card 86-5063 DDC 384 19
HF5541.T4 G76 1986 ***NYPL [JLE 86-3270]***

The Foundations of Keynesian analysis : proceedings of a conference held at the University of Paris I-Panthéon-Sorbonne / edited by Alain Barrère. New York : St. Martin's Press, 1988. xlvi, 267 p. ; 23 cm. Essays presented at a conference held to commemorate the centenary of John Maynard Keynes 12-15 September, 1983; organized by the University of Paris I-Panthéon-Sorbonne and the CNRS-Centre national de la recherche scientifique. Includes bibliographies and index. ISBN 0-312-00985-2 : LC Card 87-13048 DDC 330.15/6 19
1. Keynesian economics - Congresses. I. Barrère, Alain. II. Keynes, John Maynard, 1883-1946. III. Université de Paris I: Panthéon-Sorbonne. IV. Centre national de la recherche scientifique (France).
HB99.7 .F68 1988

The foundations of Paul Samuelson's revealed preference theory . Wong, Stanley. London , Boston , 1978. x, 148 p. : ISBN 0-7100-8643-1 : LC Card 78-40600 DDC 339.4/7
HB801 .W594 ***NYPL [JLD 87-1092]***

Foundations of radical political economy /. Sherman, Howard J. Armonk, N.Y. , c1987. xi, 425 p. ; ISBN 0-87332-416-1 : LC Card 86-33849 DDC 330.1 19
HB97.5 .S5117 1987

Foundations of real estate financing . Hamilton, S. W. (Stanley William), 1939- Vancouver , c1982. xv, 319 p. : ISBN 0-409-98843-X LC Card 87-143264
HF5695.5.R3 H36 1982

Foundations of the theory of general equilibrium /. Balasko, Yves. Orlando, Fla. , c1988. p. cm. ISBN 0-12-076975-1 (alk. paper) LC Card 87-68 DDC 339.5 19
HB145 .B32 1988

Foundations of the vocational rehabilitation process /. Rubin, Stanford E. Austin, Tex. , c1987. xiii, 400 p. : ISBN 0-89079-147-3 (pbk.) LC Card 86-30600 DDC 362/.0425 19
HD7255.5 .R823 1987

The founding fortunes . Allen, Michael Patrick. New York , c1987. p. cm. LC Card 87-9912 DDC 332/.0973 19
HC110.W4 A44 1987

FOUNDRIES - SWEDEN - STATISTICS.
Svensk gjuteriindustri . Stockholm , 1982. 62 p. : ISBN 91-38-07151-7 LC Card 83-220920
HD9506.S82 S92 1982

FOUNDRYMEN - SOUTH AFRICA.
Webster, Eddie. Cast in a racial mould . Johannesburg , 1985. xv, 299 p., [8] p. of plates : ISBN 0-86975-285-5
NYPL [JLD 87-780]

FOUNDRYMEN - SOUTH AFRICA - HISTORY.
Webster, Eddie. Cast in a racial mould . Johannesburg , 1985. xv, 299 p., [6] p. of plates : ISBN 0-86975-285-5 (pbk.) : LC Card 86-213551 DDC 331.88/1712/0968 19
HD6870.5.Z7 F758 1985

Four thousand years of urban growth . Chandler, Tertius. Lewiston, N.Y., U. S.A. , c1987. xiii, 656 p. : ISBN 0-88946-207-0 (alk. paper) LC Card 86-31122 DDC 307.1/4 19
HB2161 .C46 1987

Fourçans, André. La Rupture . Paris , c1986. 156 p. ; ISBN 2-7178-1134-6 : LC Card 87-117285
HC276.3 .R86 1986

Fourcaut, Annie, 1950- Femmes à l'usine : ouvrières et surintendantes dans les entreprises françaises de l'entre-deux-guerres / Annie Fourcaut. Paris : F. Maspero, 1982. 268 p. : ill. ; 22 cm. (Collection du Centre de recherches d'histoire des mouvements sociaux et du syndicalisme) Bibliography: p. 255-[259] Includes index. ISBN 2-7071-1258-5 : LC Card 82-151587
1. Women - Employment - France - History - 20th century. 2. Reconstruction (1914-1939) - France. I. Title. II. Series.
HD6145 .F65 1982

Fournier, Rick. How to use the HP-18C in real estate / Rick Fournier. Chicago, Ill. : Real Estate Education Co., c1987. xv, 173 p. : ill. ; 28 cm. ISBN 0-88462-592-3 (pbk.) LC Card 87-2079 DDC 333.33/028/54165 19

1. Business mathematics - Real estate business. 2. HP-18C (Calculator). I. Title.
HF5716.R4 F68 1987

Fournies, Ferdinand F. Coaching for improved work performance / Ferdinand F. Fournies. Blue Ridge Summit, PA : Liberty House, c1987. x, 214 p. : ill. ; 23 cm. Reprint. Originally published: New York : Von Nostrand Reinhold, c1978. Bibliography: p. 209-211. Includes index. ISBN 0-8306-3054-6 (pbk.) : LC Card 86-23098 DDC 658.3/14 19
1. Personnel management. 2. Achievement motivation. 3. Performance. I. Title.
HF5549 .F65 1987

Fourteen steps in managing an aging work force / [edited by] Helen Dennis. Lexington, Mass. : Lexington Books, c1988. xi, [247] p. : ill. ; 24 cm. Includes bibliographies and index. ISBN 0-669-13206-3 (alk. paper) LC Card 87-3322 DDC 658.3/042 19
1. Aged - Employment. 2. Personnel management. I. Dennis, Helen.
HF5549.5.O44 F68 1988

The Fourth company accounts directive of 1978 and the accounting systems of the Federal Republic of Germany, France, Italy, the United Kingdom, the United States, and Japan. Luxembourg : Office for Official Publications of the European Communities ; Washington, DC : European Community Information Service, 1986. 164, [47] p. ; 29 cm. (Document / Commission of the European Communities) At head of title: Commission of the European Communities. Bibliography: p. 163-164. ISBN 92-825-6454-1 (pbk.) : LC Card 87-134287 DDC 657 19
1. Comparative accounting. 2. Accounting - European Economic Community countries. 3. Accounting - United States. 4. Accounting - Japan. I. Commission of the European Communities. II. Series: Document / Commission of the European Communities.
HF5611 .F686 1986

Fourth Development Plan, 1405-1410 A.H. (1985-1990 A.D.) Saudi Arabia. Wizārat al-Tahkṭīṭ. [Khuṭṭat al-Tanmiyah al-Rābi'ah, 1405-1410 H. English.] [Riyadh] [1985?] xxxix, 435 p. : LC Card 86-202075 DDC 338.953/8 19
HC415.33 .S22 1985

Fourth general economic census 1978. Vierde algemene bedrijfstelling 1978 /. 's-Gravenhage , 1985-<1986. <3 v.; in 11 > ; ISBN 90-357-0319-7 (d. 2, A) : LC Card 86-202940
HC323 .V54 1985

The Fourth Malaysia Plan, 1981-1985 and a decade of progress, 1971-1980 in brief. Malaysia. Kuala Lumpur [1981?] 50 p. : LC Card 84-942047
HC445.5 .M33 1981a

The fourth medium . Foote, Cameron S. Homewood, Ill. , c1986. xxix, 226 p. : ISBN 0-87094-913-6 LC Card 86-70966 DDC 658.8/2 19
HF5438.5 .F66 1986 ***NYPL [JLE 87-1433]***

The fourth wave . Muller, Thomas, 1933- Washington , c1985. xvii, 217 p. ; ISBN 0-87766-349-1 LC Card 85-22646 DDC 331.6/2/720794 19
HD8081.M6 M85 1985
NYPL [JLE 86-3014]

Foust, Linda, 1950- Husch, Tony, 1943- That's a great idea /. Berkeley, Calif. , 1987, c1986. p. cm. ISBN 0-89815-218-6 LC Card 87-13891 DDC 658.5/75 19
HD69.N4 H87 1987

Fővárosi Közlekedésbiztonsági Tanács (Budapest, Hungary) Budapesti pedagógusok közlekedési oktatási és nevelési konferenciája . [Budapest , 1978] ([Budapest] :fKészült az MTI Sokszorosító Üzemében) 100 p. ; LC Card 82-204792
HE5614 .B78 1978

Fowler, Elizabeth M.
Every woman's guide to profitable investing / Elizabeth M. Fowler. New York, NY : American Management Association, c1986. 260 p. : charts ; 24 cm. Includes index. ISBN 0-8144-5823-8 LC Card 85-48222 DDC 332.6/78/024042 19
1. Investments - United States - Handbooks, manuals, etc. 2. Securities - United States - Handbooks, manuals, etc. I. Title.
HG4921 .F636 1986 ***NYPL [JLE 86-3339]***

The New York times career planner / Elizabeth M. Fowler. New York : Times Books, 1987. p. cm. Includes index. ISBN 0-8129-1212-8 : LC Card 87-9964 DDC 650.1/4 19
1. Job hunting - United States. 2. Vocational guidance - United States. I. New York times. II. Title.
HF5382.75.U6 F68 1987

Fowler, Gene, 1950- Border radio : quacks, yodelers, pitchmen, psychics & other amazing broadcasters of the American airwaves / by Gene Fowler and Bill Crawford ; foreword by Wolfman Jack. Austin, Tex. : Texas Monthly Press, c1987. p. cm. Bibliography: p. Includes index. ISBN 0-87719-066-6 : LC Card 87-17975 DDC 384.54/53/09721 19
1. Radio broadcasting - Mexican-American Border Region. 2. Radio stations - Mexican-American Border Region. I. Crawford, Bill, 1955-. II. Title.
HE8699.M4 F68 1987

Fowler, Ron. Washington sodas : the illustrated history of Washington's soft drink industry / by Ron Fowler. Seattle : Dolphin Point Writing Works, c1986. iv, 380 p. : ill. ; 29 cm. Bibliography: p. 360-361. Includes index. LC Card 86-219084 DDC 338.4/766362/09797 19
1. Soft drink industry - Washington (State) - History. I. Title.
HD9349.S633 U635 1986

Fox, Karl August, 1917- Systems economics . Ames , 1987. xvii, 252 p. : ISBN 0-8138-1738-2 LC Card 86-27586 DDC 330 19
HB171 .S99 1987

Fox, Marianne B. Metzelaar, Lawrence C. Learning to use Lotus 1-2-3 /. Menlo Park, Calif. , c1987. xi, 286 p. : ISBN 0-8053-6736-5 (pbk.) LC Card 86-214400 DDC 005.36/9 19
HF5548.4.L67 M47 1987

Fox, Michael W., 1937- Agricide : the hidden crisis that affects us all / Michael W. Fox. New York : Schocken Books, 1986. xv, 194 p., [10] p. of plates : ill. ; 22 cm. Includes index. Bibliography: p. 185-189. ISBN 0-8052-4013-6 LC Card 85-27690 DDC 338.1/6/0973 19
1. Agriculture - United States. 2. Agricultural industries - United States. 3. Agricultural ecology - United States. 4. Agricultural pollution - United States. 5. Livestock factories - United States. 6. Food industry and trade - United States. 7. Diet - United States. I. Title.
S441 .F69 1986 ***NYPL [JLD 86-2542]***

Fox, William M. Effective group problem solving : how to broaden participation, improve decision making, and increase commitment to action / William M. Fox.1st ed. San Francisco : Jossey-Bass, 1987. xvii, 204 p. : ill. ; 24 cm. (A joint publication in the Jossey-Bass management series and the Jossey-Bass social and behavioral science series) Bibliography: p. 181-192. Includes index. ISBN 1-555-42033-8 (alk. paper) LC Card 86-33742 DDC 658.4/036 19
1. Problem solving, Group. I. Series: Jossey-Bass management series. II. Title.
HD30.29 .F69 1987

Foxley, Alejandro. Las desigualdades económicas y la acción del estado : estudio preparado para el Programa Mundial del Empleo de la Organización Internacional del Trabajo / Alejandro Foxley, Eduardo Aninat, José Pablo Arellano.1a ed. México : Fondo de Cultura Económica, 1980. 271 p. ; 21 cm. (Sección de obras de economía) Includes bibliographical references. ISBN 968-16-0365-6 LC Card 82-215955 DDC 339.2/098 19
1. Income distribution - Latin America. 2. Fiscal policy - Latin America. 3. Latin America - Economic policy. I. Aninat, Eduardo. II. Arellano, José Pablo. III. International Labor Organisation. World Employment Programme. IV. Title.
HC130.15 F69 1980 ***NYPL [JLD 86-2631]***

Foyers des jeunes travailleurs. Galland, Olivier. Jeunes en transit . Paris , c1984. 236 p. ; ISBN 2-7082-2405-0 : LC Card 85-102779 DDC 367/.94486 19
HD6276.F72 G35 1984

Fra brygger til storhavn . Grude, Egil Harald, 1944- Stavanger , c1985. 167 p. : ISBN 82-00-07235-5 : LC Card 86-148407
HE558.S67 G78 1985

Fra dampmaskin til jetfly . Bjørnland, Dag, 1935- [Oslo] , c1982. 104 p. : ISBN 82-508-0180-6 : LC Card 83-134968
HE259 .B5 1982

O fracasso dos governos de direita em Portugal (1978 a 1981) . Rosa, Eugénio. [Lisbon?] [1982] 351 p. ; LC Card 85-228499
HC392 .R592 1982

The fragile bridge . Golin, Steve. Philadelphia , 1988. p. cm. ISBN 0-87722-534-6 (alk. paper) : LC Card 87-24356 DDC 331.89/287739/0974924 19
HD5325.T42 1913 .P383 1988

Fragoso Gutiérrez, Juan M. El mercado y los precios de los productos agropecuarios / Juan M. Fragoso Gutiérrez, Javier Sánchez Alvarez. México : Centro Nacional de Investigaciones Agrarias, 1983. 486 p. : ill. ; 23 cm. Cover title: Mercado y precios de productos agropecuarios. Bibliography: p. 469-473. LC Card 84-236815
1. Farm produce - Mexico. 2. Agricultural prices - Mexico. I. Sánchez Alvarez, Javier. II. Title. III. Title: Mercado y precios de productos agropecuarios.
HD9014.M62 F72 1983

Frahm, Herbert Ernst Karl. See his later name: **Brandt, Willy, 1913-**

Frahm, Karl. See his later name: **Brandt, Willy, 1913-**

Fraisse, Robert. Economie monétaire internationale. Paris [1982] 156 p. : LC Card 85-131349 DDC 332/.042 19
HG3881 .E27 1982

Fraleigh, Cynthia, 1957- Gerston, Larry N. The deregulated society /. Pacific Grove, Calif. , c1988. xvii, 244 p. : ISBN 0-534-08208-4 (pbk.) : LC Card 87-5116 DDC 338.973 19
HD3616.U47 G47 1988

Fram, Eugene H. Policy vs. paper clips : selling the corporate model to your nonprofit board / Eugene H. Fram, with Vicki Brown. Milwaukee, Wis. : Family Service America, 1988. p. cm. ISBN 0-87304-227-1 LC Card 87-24377 DDC 658/.048 19
1. Corporations, Nonprofit - Management. I. Brown, Vicki. II. Title.
HD62.6 .F73 1988

Frame, J. Davidson. Managing projects in organizations : how to make the best use of time, techniques, and people / J. Davidson Frame.1st ed. San Francisco : Jossey-Bass, 1987. xvii, 240 p. : ill. ; 24 cm. (The Jossey-Bass management series) Bibliography: p. 231-234. Includes index. ISBN 1-555-42031-1 (alk. paper) LC Card 86-33707 DDC 658.4/04 19
1. Industrial project management. I. Title. II. Series.
HD69.P75 F72 1987

Framework applications /. Baker, Richard H. Blue Ridge Summit, PA , c1985. x, 259 p. : ISBN 0-8306-0908-3 : LC Card 85-9826 DDC 650/.028/5425 19
HF5548.4.F7 B35 1985 ***NYPL [JSE 86-803]***

FRAMEWORK (COMPUTER PROGRAM)
Baker, Richard H. Framework applications /. Blue Ridge Summit, PA , c1985. x, 259 p. : ISBN 0-8306-0908-3 : LC Card 85-9826 DDC 650/.028/5425 19
HF5548.4.F7 B35 1985 ***NYPL [JSE 86-803]***

Baker, Richard H. Framework II applications /. Blue Ridge Summit, PA , c1987. xi, 320 p. ; ISBN 0-8306-2198-9 : LC Card 86-23104 DDC 650/.028/55369 19
HF5548.4.F7 B35 1987

Hoenig, Alan. Framework with applications for the IBM PC /. Dubuque, Iowa , c1985. xiii, 213 p. : ISBN 0-697-00725-1 (pbk.) : LC Card 85-60013 DDC 005.3/69 19
HF5548.4.F7 H64 1985
NYPL [JSE 86-2110]

Seybold, Patricia B. Integrated desk-top environments . New York , c1985. ix, 181 p. : ISBN 0-07-056324-1 (pbk.) : LC Card 84-27841 DDC 650/.028/5425 19
HF5548.4.S95 S49 1985
NYPL [JSE 86-2011]

Framework II applications /. Baker, Richard H. Blue Ridge Summit, PA , c1987. xi, 320 p. ; ISBN 0-8306-2198-9 : LC Card 86-23104 DDC 650/.028/55369 19
HF5548.4.F7 B35 1987

FRAMEWORK II (COMPUTER PROGRAM)
Hergert, Douglas. Mastering Framework II /. Berkeley , c1987. xvii, 509 p. : ISBN 0-89588-390-2 (pbk.) : LC Card 86-62808 DDC 650/.028/55369 19
HF5548.4.F72 H47 1987

The Framework of the impact study to monitor and evaluate rural access roads in Kenya. Nairobi : Chief Engineer (Roads and Aerodromes), Ministry of Transport and Communications, 1981. ii, 97, [97] leaves ; 30 cm. On cover: Republic of Kenya. Ministry of Transport and Communications, Roads and Aerodromes Department. LC Card 85-981022
1. Kenya Rural Access Roads Programme. 2. Rural roads - Kenya. I. Kenya. Roads and Aerodromes Dept.
HE367.K43 R8538 1981

Framework two applications. Baker, Richard H. Framework II applications /. Blue Ridge Summit, PA , c1987. xi, 320 p. ; ISBN 0-8306-2198-9 : LC Card 86-23104 DDC 650/.028/55369 19
HF5548.4.F7 B35 1987

Framework with applications for the IBM PC /. Hoenig, Alan. Dubuque, Iowa , c1985. xiii, 213 p. : ISBN 0-697-00725-1 (pbk.) : LC Card 85-60013 DDC 005.3/69 19
HF5548.4.F7 H64 1985 *NYPL [JSE 86-2110]*

Framework 2 applications. Baker, Richard H. Framework II applications /. Blue Ridge Summit, PA , c1987. xi, 320 p. ; ISBN 0-8306-2198-9 : LC Card 86-23104 DDC 650/.028/55369 19
HF5548.4.F7 B35 1987

Framtid i malmfälten . Sweden. Malmfältsutredningen. [Stockholm] [1984] 155, 5 p. : ISBN 91-38-08283-7 LC Card 86-111519
HD9506.S82 S94 1984

Framtidsstaden . Schunnesson, Torgny. [Stockholm] , c1985. 166 p. : ISBN 91-7054-498-0 LC Card 86-105915
HC378.L35 S38 1985

Framtidsstudien Sveriges internationella villkor . (rapport nr 206) Iger, Svante. Den svenska ekonomins intertnationalisering . Lund , Stockholm [1976] iv, 144 p. : ISBN 91-38-03072-1 LC Card 84-226057
HF3674 .I36 1976

Les Français à la corbeille /. Sassier, Philippe. Paris , c1985. 268 p. ; ISBN 2-221-04729-X : LC Card 86-126750 DDC 332.64/244 19
HG4583 .S27 1985

France. Administration et de la fonction publique, Direction générale de l'. see France. Direction générale de l'administration et de la fonction publique.

France. Agence de l'informatique. Les Professions de l'informatique . Paris [1986-1987] 2 v. : ISBN 2-11-001675-2 (v. 1) : LC Card 87-156366
HF5548.2 .P7925 1986

France. Ambassade (Spain) La Nueva economía en Francia y en España /. Madrid , c1980. 197 p. : ISBN 84-85355-27-X : LC Card 83-105425 DDC 330.944/0838 19
HB105.A2 N83 1980 *NYPL [JLD 86-3024]*

France. Aménagement du territoire et à l'action regionale, Délégation à l'. see France. Délégation à l'aménagement du territoire et à l'action régionale.

FRANCE - APPROPRIATIONS AND EXPENDITURES.
Baslé, Maurice. Le budget de l'Etat /. Paris , 1985. 127 p. : ISBN 2-7071-1534-7 LC Card 86-161271
HJ2106 .B37 1985

FRANCE - ARMED FORCES - APPROPRIATIONS AND EXPENDITURES.
L'Effort économique de défense . [Grenoble] , 1985. 235 p. : LC Card 86-199399
HC280.D4 E38 1985

France. Bureau central d'études pour les équipements d'outre-mer. Economic transportation survey. [Paris] [Courbevoie, Seine] , 1966. 3 v. : LC Card 87-125917
HE373.I75 E36 1966

FRANCE - CENSUS, 1982.
Kerromes, Armelle. Tableaux normalisés simplifiés par région et département . Paris [1984] 273 p. ; ISBN 2-11-064692-6 : LC Card 86-176720
HA1214 1982p

France. Centre d'étude du commerce et de la distribution. see Centre d'étude du commerce et de la distribution.

Actions thématiques programmées. A. T. P.: Sciences humaines. see Actions thématiques programmées. A. T. P.: Sciences humaines.

France. Collectivités locales, Direction générale des. see France. Direction générale des collectivités locales.

FRANCE - COLONIES - ECONOMIC CONDITIONS.
Guiton, R. J. (Raymond J.), 1915- Der Aufbruch . Rheinfelden , c1984. 2 v. : ISBN 3-87718-746-3 (Bd. 1) LC Card 85-181833 DDC 325/.344/09 19
JV1818 .G85 1984 *NYPL [JFK 86-364]*

FRANCE - COLONIES - HISTORY - 20TH CENTURY.
Guiton, R. J. (Raymond J.), 1915- Der Aufbruch . Rheinfelden , c1984. 2 v. : ISBN 3-87718-746-3 (Bd. 1) LC Card 85-181833 DDC 325/.344/09 19
JV1818 .G85 1984 *NYPL [JFK 86-364]*

France. Comité d'histoire de la sécurité sociale. Colloque sur l'histoire de la sécurité sociale (1980 : Caen, France) Colloque sur l'histoire de la sécurité sociale . Paris , 1981. 263 p. ; LC Card 81-201274
HD7175 .C58 1980

FRANCE - COMMERCE - GERMANY (EAST)
Marwege, Ulf, 1954- Neuorientierung im Westhandel der DDR? . Bonn , c1984. iv, 122 p. : ISBN 3-7713-0221-8 : LC Card 84-196602
HF3570.5.Z7 G75 1984

FRANCE - COMMERCE - SPAIN - HISTORY - CONGRESSES.
Les Communications dans la péninsule Ibérique au Moyen-Age . Paris , 1981. 208 p. : ISBN 2-222-02922-8 : LC Card 81-213698 DDC 380.5/0946 19
HE261.A5 C65 1981 *NYPL [JLG 86-113]*

France. Commissariat général du plan.
Les Industries agro-alimentaires . Paris [1986], c1987. 164 p. : ISBN 2-11-001722-8 : LC Card 87-167615
HD9012.5 .I53 1987

Legay, Marie-Agnès. Réduction de la durée du travail et changement des modes de vie . Aix-en-Provence [1984] ix, 366 p. : LC Card 86-185902
HD6066.F8 L44 1984

Rapport d'exécution du plan intérimaire, 1982-1983 /. Paris , c1984. 146 p. : ISBN 2-11-001229-3 : LC Card 85-121410
HC276.2 .R32 1984

Le Renouvellement du tissu industriel . Paris [1986] 130 p. ; ISBN 2-11-001568-3 : LC Card 86-191910
HD3616.F83 R46 1986

France. Commission centrale des marchés. Secrétariat général. Recensement des marchés et commandes des entreprises publiques et sociétés d'économie mixte . Paris [1984] 71 p. : LC Card 85-133146
HD4163 .R43 1984

France. Commission industrie-administration pour la mesure. L'Avenir national des capteurs à fibres optiques /. Paris , c1984. 42 p. : ISBN 2-11-001350-8 LC Card 85-232999
HD9696.F523 F82 1984

France. Comptabilité publique, Direction de la. see France. Direction de la comptabilité publique.

France. Conseil économique et social.
Le crédit-bail : avis / adopté par le Conseil économique et social au cours de sa séance du 12 juin 1985, sur le rapport de Claude Duport. [Paris] : Le Conseil, [1985] 90 p. in various pagings : ill. ; 29 cm. Cover title. "Juin 1985"--Spine. Includes bibliographical references. CONTENTS. - Le crédit-bail -- Avis adopté par le Conseil économique et social au cours de sa séance du 12 juin 1985 -- Annexe à l'avis (scrutin) -- Declarations des groupes -- Rapport / présenté par Claude Duport. LC Card 86-184049
1. Leases - France. 2. Industrial equipment leases - France. I. Duport, Claude. II. Title.
HD39.4 .F73 1985

Le développement de l'élevage des équidés en France : avis / adopté par le Conseil économique et social au cours de sa séance du 22 avril 1986 sur le rapport de Elisée Munet. [Paris] : Le Conseil, [1986] 166 p. in various pagings : ill. ; 30 cm. Cover title. CONTENTS. - Avis / adopté par le Conseil économique et social au cours de sa séance du 22 avril 1986 -- Annexe à l'avis (scrutin) -- Déclarations des groupes -- Rapport / présenté par Elisée Munet -- Annexe au rapport. LC Card 86-133487
1. Horse industry - France. I. Munet, Elisée. II. Title.
HD9434.F72 F73 1986

L'évolution des transports urbains de voyageurs face aux nouvelles technologies : avis / adopté par le Conseil économique et social au cours de sa séance du 15 janvier 1986 sur le rapport de Claude Quin. [Paris] : Le Conseil, [1986] 184 p. in various pagings : ill. ; 29 cm. Cover title. "Janvier 1986"--Spine. Includes bibliographical references. CONTENTS. - L'évolution des transports urbains de voyageurs face aux nouvelles technologies : avis adopté par le Conseil économique et social au cours de sa séance du 15 janvier 1986 -- Annexe à l'avis (scrutin) -- Déclarations des groupes -- Rapport / présenté par Claude Quin -- Annexes au rapport. LC Card 86-179126
1. Local transit - France - Technological innovations. I. Quin, Claude. II. Title.
HE4764 .F73 1986

Informatique et emploi : avis / adopté par le Conseil économique et social au cours de sa séance du 29 février 1984 sur le rapport de Bernard Boisson. [Paris] : Le Conseil, [1984] 24, 4 p., 8 leaves, 187, 13 p. : ill. ; 30 cm. Cover title. Includes bibliographical references. CONTENTS. - Avis / adopté par le Conseil économique et social au cours de sa séance du 29 février 1984 -- Annexe à l'Avis (scrutin) -- Déclaration des groupes -- Rapport / présenté par Bernard Boisson -- Annexes au rapport. LC Card 84-218059
1. Labor supply - France - Effect of technological innovations on. 2. Unemployment, Technological - France. 3. Electronic data processing personnel - France - Supply and demand. I. Boisson, Bernard. II. Title.
HD6331.2.F8 F73 1984

Les ports maritimes : avis / adopté par le Conseil économique et social au cours de sa séance du 15 juin 1983 sur le rapport de Bernard Maurize. Paris : Le Conseil, [1983] 1 v. (various pagings) : ill. ; 30 cm. Cover title. LC Card 83-186600
1. Harbors - Government policy - France. I. Maurize, Bernard. II. Title.
HE557.F8 F67 1983

Les surplus agricoles et la pénurie alimentaire : avis / adopté par le Conseil économique et social au cours de sa séance du 15 janvier 1986 sur le rapport de René Raimbault. [Paris] : Le Conseil, [1986] 1 v. (various pagings) : ill. ; 29 cm. Cover title. "Janvier 1986"--Spine. CONTENTS. - Avis / adopté par le Conseil économique et social au cours de sa séance du 15 janvier 1986 -- Annexe à l'avis (scrutins) -- Déclarations des groupes -- Rapport / présenté par René Raimbault -- Annexes au rapport. LC Card 86-179100
1. Surplus agricultural commodities, French - Developing countries. 2. Agricultural assistance, French - Developing countries. 3. Food supply - Developing countries. I. Raimbault, René. II. Title.
HD1431 .F7 1986

FRANCE. CONSEILS DE PRUD'HOMMES - ELECTIONS.
Elections prud'homales . Rennes [1983] 92 p. : LC Card 85-136661
HD5554.A3 E44 1983

FRANCE. CONSEILS DE PRUD'HOMMES - ELECTIONS - STATISTICS.
Bon, Frédéric, 1943- Résultats des élections aux conseils de prud'hommes par département . St. Martin d'Hères [France] [1982] 303 p. ; LC Card 84-152037
HD5555 .B65 1982

FRANCE - COURT AND COURTIERS.
Douët-d'Arcq, L. (Louis), 1808-1882. (ed) Comptes de l'hôtel des rois de France aux XIVe et XVe siècles. Paris, 1865. 3 p.l., xlii p., 1 l., 437 p., 1 l. LC Card 05-5875
HJ1077 .D6

La France dans la bataille des technologies de l'intelligence /. Baquiast, Jean-Paul. Paris , c1985. 221 p. ; ISBN 2-11-001440-7 : LC Card 86-126853 DDC 338.4/7004/094 19
HD9696.C63 F72 1985

FRANCE - DEFENSES - ECONOMIC ASPECTS.
L'Effort économique de défense . [Grenoble] , 1985. 235 p. : LC Card 86-199399
HC280.D4 E38 1985

FRANCE. DÉLÉGATION À L'AMÉNAGEMENT DU TERRITOIRE ET À L'ACTION RÉGIONALE.
Laborie, Jean Paul. La politique française d'amenagement du territoire de 1950 à 1985 /. Paris , 1985. 176 p., [8] p. of plates : ISBN 2-11-001488-1(pbk.) : ***NYPL [JLG 87-38]***

France. Département des statistiques des transports.
Enquête sur l'utilisation des véhicules utilitaires légers . Paris [1983] 58 p. : LC Card 84-191337
HE5668.A6 E56 1983

Les Transports routiers de marchandises effectués sur le territoire français par des véhicules étrangers /. Paris [1983] 26 p. ; LC Card 83-214677
HE5668.A6 T74 1983

France. Direction de la comptabilité publique. (Old Catalog form: France. Comptabilité publique, Direction de la.)
Sources et méthodes d'élaboration des comptes nationaux. [Paris] [1983] 481 p. ; LC Card 84-161813
HC271 .A218 no. 440-441 HJ9925.F8

France. Direction des transports terrestres. TGV atlantique . Paris [1984] 410 p., [8] folded leaves of plates : ISBN 2-11-001253-6 : LC Card 85-103473 DDC 385/.22 19
HE3065 .T34 1984

France. Direction du trésor. (Old Catalog form: France. Trésor, Direction du.)
Pastré, Olivier. La modernisation des banques françaises . Paris [1985] 234 p. : ISBN 2-11-001537-3 : LC Card 86-179536
HG3026 .P37 1985

France. Direction générale de l'administration et de la fonction publique. Quarré, Dominique. Les agents de l'Etat au 31 décembre 1980 /. Paris [1985] 305 p. ; ISBN 2-11-064767-1 : LC Card 86-162558
HD8013.F6 Q373 1985

France. Direction générale des collectivités locales. (Old Catalog form: France. Collectivités locales, Direction générale des.)
Instruction aux maires relative aux bulletins statistiques de l'état civil : métropole. [Paris] : République française, Ministère de l'intérieur et de la décentralisation, Direction générale des collectivités locales : Ministère de l'économie et des finances, Institut national de la statistique et des études économiques, [1983] 50 p. : forms ; 30 cm. Cover title. Errata slip and sample forms (12 leaves) inserted. Includes index. LC Card 84-112361
1. France - Statistical services. 2. Registers of births, etc. - France. I. Institut national de la statistique et des études économiques (France). II. Title.
HA37.F8 F73 1983

France. Division centrale des enquêtes et études statistiques. see France. Service central des enquêtes et études statistiques.

France. Division des enquêtes sur le marcheé du bâtiment. Les Logements neufs en 1978 . Paris , 1982. 40 p. : LC Card 83-176727
HD7338.A4 L64 1982

FRANCE - ECONOMIC CONDITIONS.
Mélanges Robert Laurent . Montpellier , 1980. xxi, 296 p. : LC Card 83-151672
HC273 .M43 1980

Riley, James C. The Seven Years War and the old regime in France . Princeton, N.J. , 1986. xxii, 256 p. : ISBN 0-691-05488-6 (alk. paper) : LC Card 86-42847 DDC 330.944/034 19
HC275 .R54 1986 ***NYPL [JLE 87-932]***

FRANCE - ECONOMIC CONDITIONS - 19TH CENTURY.
Beck, Thomas D. French notables . New York , c1987. 254 p. : ISBN 0-8204-0393-8 : LC Card 87-12156 DDC 338.0944 19
HC275 .B37 1987

Le Bas, Christian. Histoire sociale des faits économiques . Lyon , c1984. 242 p. : ISBN 2-7297-0221-0 : LC Card 85-152656
HC275 .L45 1984

Meyer, Jean, 1924- Le poids de l'Etat /. Paris , c1983. 304 p. : ISBN 2-13-037770-X : LC Card 83-175028
HC280.D4 M49 1983

FRANCE - ECONOMIC CONDITIONS - 20TH CENTURY.
Godfrey, John F. Capitalism at war . Leamington Spa, UK ; New York : xiv, 313 p. ; ISBN 0-85496-519-X : LC Card 86-32708 DDC 338.944 19
HD3616.F82 G63 1987

Meyer, Jean, 1924- Le poids de l'Etat /. Paris , c1983. 304 p. : ISBN 2-13-037770-X : LC Card 83-175028
HC280.D4 M49 1983

Minc, Alain. L'avenir en face /. Paris , c1984. 255 p. ; ISBN 2-02-006828-1 : LC Card 84-218171
HC276 .M6126 1984 ***NYPL [JLE 87-2165]***

Silbert, Alfred. Economie mondialiste et mutations politiques . Paris , c1985. 212 p. ; ISBN 2-7157-1114-X : LC Card 85-221451 DDC 330.944/08 19
HC276 .S52 1985

FRANCE - ECONOMIC CONDITIONS - 1918-
Rabochiĭ klass v proshlom i nastoi͡ashchem . Moskva , 1984, c1983. 255 p. ; LC Card 84-169518
HD4854 .R273 1984

FRANCE - ECONOMIC CONDITIONS - 1918-1945.
Néré, Jacques. Le problème du mur d'argent . Paris , c1985. 159 p. ; ISBN 2-214-06264-5 : LC Card 86-149791
HG979 .N47 1985

FRANCE - ECONOMIC CONDITIONS - 1945-
Brémond, Janine. L'économie française face aux défis mondiaux . Paris , c1985. 320 p. : ISBN 2-218-07456-7 LC Card 86-168427
HC276.2 .B657 1985

Briançon, Pierre. A droite en sortant de la gauche? /. Paris , c1986. 270 p. ; ISBN 2-246-34901-X : LC Card 86-159681
HC276.2 .B66 1986

Capitalismes fin de siècle /. Paris , c1986. 268 p. : ISBN 2-13-039425-6 : LC Card 86-231136
HC106.8 .C364 1986

Chalandon, Albin. Quitte ou double /. Paris , c1986. 317 p. ; ISBN 2-246-37401-4 : LC Card 86-170477
HD4165 .C47 1986

Dacier, Pierre. Les dossiers noirs de l'industrie française /. [Paris] , c1985. 414 p. ; ISBN 2-213-01659-3 : LC Card 86-178468
HC276.2 .D2 1985

Demain la France . Paris , c1986. 423 p., [32] p. of plates : ISBN 2-01-011955-X LC Card 86-174163
HC276.2 .D42 1986

Kolomiĭtsev, Valentin Fedorovich. Rabochiĭ klass i profsoi͡uzy Frantsii v bor´ybe protiv monopoliĭ, 1968-1981 gody /. Moskva , 1981. 173 p. ; LC Card 82-134380
HD8435 .K65 1981

Lorriaux, Jean-Pierre. Economie politique contemporaine . Paris , c1985. iv, 565 p. : ISBN 2-7178-0937-6 : LC Card 86-116111 DDC 330 19
HB173 .L784 1985

Naville, Pierre. La maîtrise du salariat /. Paris , c1984. 153 p. ; ISBN 2-7157-1099-2 : LC Card 85-100916
HD6957.F8 N38 1984 ***NYPL [JLD 87-333]***

Pébereau, Michel. La politique économique de la France. Paris , c1985. 319 p. : ISBN 2-200-31217-2 LC Card 86-179163 DDC 338.944 19
HC276.2 .P42 1985

Saint-Etienne, Christian, 1951- The Mitterrand and Reagan economic experiments . [Stanford, Calif.] , c1986. 36 p ; ISBN 0-8179-5082-6 (pbk.) LC Card 86-27776 DDC 338.944 19
HC276.2 .S24 1986

Vedie, Henri-Louis, 1943- L'Etat-pieuvre /. Paris , c1986. 172 p. : LC Card 86-219134
HD4165 .V38 1986

FRANCE - ECONOMIC CONDITIONS - 1945- - MAPS.
Savy, Michel. Atlas des Français /. Paris , c1985. 331 p. : ISBN 2-01-011512-0 LC Card 86-178635
HC276.2 .S325 1985

FRANCE - ECONOMIC CONDITIONS - 1945- - REGIONAL DISPARITIES.
Francéco 1986. [Paris] [1986] 383 p. : ISBN 2-7144-1910-0 : LC Card 87-148071
HC276.2 .F68596 1986

FRANCE - ECONOMIC CONDITIONS - 1945- - REGIONAL DISPARITIES - MAPS.
Savy, Michel. Atlas des Français /. Paris , c1985. 331 p. : ISBN 2-01-011512-0 LC Card 86-178635
HC276.2 .S325 1985

FRANCE - ECONOMIC CONDITIONS - 1981-
Tuppen, John N. France under recession, 1981-1986 /. Albany , c1988. p. cm. ISBN 0-88706-580-5 LC Card 87-1980 DDC 338.944 19
HC276.3 .T86 1988

FRANCE - ECONOMIC CONDITIONS - 1981- - STATISTICS.
Tout sur la France en 100 graphiques /. Paris , c1986. 113 p. : ISBN 2-86260-154-3 : LC Card 87-106635
HA1224 .T68 1986

FRANCE - ECONOMIC POLICY.
Administration et contrôle de l'économie, 1800-1914 /. Genève , Paris , 1985. 167 p. : LC Card 86-128349 DDC 338.944 19
HD3616.F82 A66 1985

Briançon, Pierre. A droite en sortant de la gauche? /. Paris , c1986. 270 p. ; ISBN 2-246-34901-X : LC Card 86-159681
HC276.2 .B66 1986

Hall, Peter A. Governing the economy . Cambridge, U.K. , Oxford, U.K. , 1986. 341 p. ; ISBN 0-7456-0227-4 : LC Card 87-672535
HC256.5 .H256x 1986b

Johanet, Gilles. Contes et mécomptes de la protection sociale /. Paris , c1986. 175 p. : ISBN 2-86702-024-4 : LC Card 86-179065
HD7175 .J64 1986

Lebovics, Herman. The alliance of iron and wheat in the Third French Republic, 1860-1914 . Baton Rouge , c1988. p. cm. ISBN 0-8071-1350-6 LC Card 87-21386 DDC 338.944 19
HC276 .L354 1988

FRANCE - ECONOMIC POLICY - 20TH CENTURY.
Bloch-Lainé, François. La France restaurée, 1944-1954 . Paris , c1986. 338 p. ; ISBN 2-213-01803-0 : LC Card 86-215777
HC276.2 .B58 1986

Minc, Alain. L'avenir en face /. Paris , c1984. 255 p. ; ISBN 2-02-006828-1 : LC Card 84-218171
HC276 .M6126 1984 ***NYPL [JLE 87-2165]***

FRANCE - ECONOMIC POLICY - 1945-
Bauchet, Pierre. Le plan dans l'économie française /. Paris , c1986. 246 p. : ISBN 2-7246-0532-2 : LC Card 86-223474
HC276.2 .B292 1986

Capitalismes fin de siècle /. Paris , c1986. 268 p. : ISBN 2-13-039425-6 : LC Card 86-231136
HC106.8 .C364 1986

Un Chemin pour sortir de la crise /. Paris , c1985. 249 p. ; ISBN 2-209-05753-1 LC Card 86-154397
HC276.2 .C517 1985

Demain la France . Paris , c1986. 423 p., [32] p. of plates : ISBN 2-01-011955-X LC Card 86-174163
HC276.2 .D42 1986

Evaluation de la planification décentralisée /. Paris , c1986. 97 p. : ISBN 2-11-001562-4 : LC Card 86-193163
HC276.2 .E89 1986

France. Groupe de stratégie industrielle no 8. Sous-groupe Travaux publics. La branche des travaux publics en France et sur les marchés extérieurs /. Paris , c1985. 202 p. : ISBN

2-11-001524-1 : LC Card 86-183130
HD4168 .F69 1985

The French socialists in power, 1981-1986 /. New York , c1987. xii, 212 p. ; ISBN 0-313-25407-9 (lib. bdg. : alk. paper) LC Card 86-33569 DDC 338.944 19
HC276.2 .F699 1987

Guilhaume, Philippe. Une volonté d'espérance . Paris , c1984. 218 p. ; ISBN 2-86418-178-9 : LC Card 84-163185
HC276.2 .G785 1984

Hayward, Jack Ernest Shalom. The state and the market economy . Brighton, Sussex , 1986. xv, 267 p. : ISBN 0-7450-0012-6 LC Card 87-672693
HC276.2 .H35x 1986b

Maris, Bernard. Eléments de politique économique . Toulouse , c1985. 235 p. : ISBN 2-7089-7608-7 : LC Card 85-160415 DDC 338.944 19
HC276.2 .M355 1985 ***NYPL [JLE 87-642]***

Noir, Michel, 1944- 1988 . [Paris] , c1984. 263 p. : LC Card 84-169744
HC280.H53 N65 1984 ***NYPL [JLE 87-2052]***

Pébereau, Michel. La politique économique de la France. Paris , c1985. 319 p. : ISBN 2-200-31217-2 LC Card 86-179163 DDC 338.944 19
HC276.2 .P42 1985

Poncins, Michel de. Tous capitalistes, ou, La réponse au socialisme /. Vouillé [France] , c1983. 164 p. ; LC Card 83-244442 DDC 338.944 19
HC276.2 .P63 1983 ***NYPL [JLD 86-427]***

Projet pour la France . Paris , c1983. 196 p. ; ISBN 2-7340-0032-6 : LC Card 83-196098
HC276.2 .P767 1983

Rapport d'exécution du plan intérimaire, 1982-1983 /. Paris , c1984. 146 p. : ISBN 2-11-001229-3 : LC Card 85-121410
HC276.2 .R32 1984

Saint-Etienne, Christian, 1951- The Mitterrand and Reagan economic experiments . [Stanford, Calif.] , c1986. 36 p ; ISBN 0-8179-5082-6 (pbk.) LC Card 86-27776 DDC 338.944 19
HC276.2 .S24 1986

Le Temps des initiatives /. Paris , c1983. 187 p. ; ISBN 2-226-01647-3 : LC Card 83-212781
HD3616.F83 T46 1983

Véron, Emile. Pour en sortir-- /. Paris , c1984. 185 p. : ISBN 2-226-02060-8 : LC Card 84-197071
HC276.2 .V465 1984

FRANCE - ECONOMIC POLICY - 1945- - ADDRESSES, ESSAYS, LECTURES.
Stabilization policy in France and the Federal Republic of Germany /. Amsterdam ; New York : xii, 379 p. : ISBN 0-444-87529-8 LC Card 84-28614 DDC 338.943 19
HC276.2 .S77 1985 ***NYPL [TB (Contributions to economic analysis. no.153)]***

FRANCE - ECONOMIC POLICY - 1981-
Boyer, Robert. La théorie de la régulation . Paris , 1986. 142 p. : ISBN 2-7071-1628-9 : LC Card 87-108410
HC276.3.B69 1986

Herzog, Philippe. La France peut se ressaisir /. Paris , c1987. 416 p. : ISBN 2-209-05941-0 : LC Card 87-169995
HC276.3 .H47 1987

Offant, Pierre. Adaptation structurelle de l'économie française à la limitation de la consommation d'énergie /. Dijon , c1984. 224, iii p. : ISBN 2-85975-026-6 LC Card 85-205959
HD9502.F72 O33 1984

La Rupture . Paris , c1986. 156 p. ; ISBN 2-7178-1134-6 : LC Card 87-117285
HC276.3 .R86 1986

Salomon, Jean Jacques. Le gaulois, le cow-boy, et le samouraï . Paris , c1986. 209 p. : ISBN 2-7178-1139-7 : LC Card 87-120178
HC280.T4 S25 1986

Tuppen, John N. France under recession, 1981-1986 /. Albany , c1988. p. cm. ISBN 0-88706-580-5 LC Card 87-1980 DDC 338.944 19
HC276.3 .T86 1988

Villette, Jean. Transports, décentralisation 9o plan /. Paris , c1986. 161 p. : ISBN 2-11-001549-7 : LC Card 86-181094
HE248.A2 V55 1986

France - Economic relations with foreign countries. see France - Foreign economic relations.

France - Employees. see France - Officials and employees.

France. Enquêtes et études statistiques, Service central des. see France. Service central des enquêtes et études statistiques.

France. Finances, Ministère des. see France. Ministère des finances.

France. Fonction publique, Direction de la. see France. Direction générale de l'administration et de la fonction publique.

FRANCE - FOREIGN ECONOMIC RELATIONS - AFRICA.
Guth, Suzie. Exil sous contrat . Paris , c1984. 479 p. : ISBN 2-903871-53-1 : LC Card 85-141675
HC800 .G88 1984

FRANCE - FOREIGN ECONOMIC RELATIONS - CAMEROON.
Ntumazah, Ndeh. France's satrapy in Kamerun is safe /. [London, England , 1985] 22 leaves ; LC Card 87-138988 DDC 337.6711044 19
HC995 .N78 1985

FRANCE - FOREIGN ECONOMIC RELATIONS - CZECHOSLOVAKIA.
Segal, Paul Harold, 1946- The French state and French private investment in Czechoslovakia, 1918-1938 . New York , 1987. vi, 379 p. ; ISBN 0-8240-8041-6 (alk. paper) : LC Card 87-252 DDC 332.6/7344/0437 19
HG5470.3.A3 S44 1987

FRANCE - FULL EMPLOYMENT POLICIES.
Vasseur, Philippe. Le chômage, c'est les autres /. Paris , c1985. 224 p. ; ISBN 2-7144-1867-8 : LC Card 86-120821 DDC 331.13/7944 19
HD5775 .V37 1985

France - Government. see France - Politics and government.

France - Government employees. see France - Officials and employees.

France. Groupe de politique des transports. Rapport du Groupe de politique des transports. Paris : La Documentation française, c1984. 246 p. : ill. ; 24 cm. (Préparation du IXe plan, 1984-1988) At head of title: Premier Ministre, Secrétariat d'Etat, Commissariat général du plan. ISBN 2-11-001216-1 : LC Card 84-163968
1. Transportation and state - France. I. Title. II. Title: Politique des transports. III. Series.
HE248 .F716 1984

France. Groupe de recherche et d'échanges technologiques. Cellule Industrie. Promotion de la petite industrie dans les pays en développement /. Paris , c1985. 103 p. : ISBN 2-86844-008-8 LC Card 85-242526 DDC 338.6/42/0943 19
HD2346.5 .P76 1985 ***NYPL [JLD 86-3171]***

France. Groupe de stratégie industrielle no 11. Le Renouvellement du tissu industriel . Paris [1986] 130 p. ; ISBN 2-11-001568-3 : LC Card 86-191910
HD3616.F83 R46 1986

France. Groupe de stratégie industrielle no 6. Les Industries agro-alimentaires . Paris [1986], c1987. 164 p. : ISBN 2-11-001722-8 : LC Card 87-167615
HD9012.5 .I53 1987

France. Groupe de stratégie industrielle no 8. Sous-groupe Travaux publics. La branche des travaux publics en France et sur les marchés extérieurs / Commissariat général du plan, Groupe de stratégie industrielle no 8, rapport du Sous-groupe Travaux publics. Paris : Documentation française, c1985. 202 p. : ill. ; 30 cm. (Plan / Commissariat général du plan. 8) "Octobre 1985." ISBN 2-11-001524-1 : LC Card 86-183130
1. France - Public works. 2. Industry and state - France. 3. Industrial promotion - France. 4. France - Economic policy - 1945-. I. Series: Plan (France. Commissariat général du plan) 8. II. Title.
HD4168 .F69 1985

France. Groupe de travail "Calcul économique." Calcul économique et résorption des déséquilibres : rapport du Groupe de travail "Calcul économique.". Paris : La Documentation française, c1984. 149 p. ; 24 cm. (Préparation du IXe plan, 1984-1988) Includes bibliographies. ISBN 2-11-001233-1 : LC Card 84-227039
1. Economics, Mathematical. I. Title. II. Series.
HB135 .F72 1984

France. Groupe de travail "Evaluation de la planification décentralisée." Evaluation de la planification décentralisée /. Paris , c1986. 97 p. : ISBN 2-11-001562-4 : LC Card 86-193163
HC276.2 .E89 1986

France. Groupe de travail sur la prospective des échanges mondiaux agricoles. Pour un rôle actif de la Communauté économique européenne sur la scène agricole internationale . Paris , c1986. 184 p. ; ISBN 2-11-001582-9 : LC Card 86-174918
HD1431 .P68 1986

France. Groupe long terme "Stratégie internationale de la France". Groupe de travail Nord-Sud. L'Impasse Nord-Sud . Paris , c1984. 103 p. : ISBN 2-11-001207-2 : LC Card 84-163951
HC59 .I44 1984

France. Haut conseil du secteur public. La Démocratisation du secteur public . Paris [1984] 87 p. ; LC Card 84-233767
HD4165 .D46 1984

FRANCE - HISTORY - HOUSE OF VALOIS, 1328-1589.
Douët-d'Arcq, L. (Louis), 1808-1882. (ed) Comptes de l'hôtel des rois de France aux XIVe et XVe siècles. Paris, 1865. 3 p.l., xlii p., 1 l., 437 p., 1 l. LC Card 05-5875
HJ1077 .D6

FRANCE - HISTORY - REVOLUTION, 1789-1799 - CONFISCATIONS AND CONTRIBUTIONS.
Arsac, Pierre. La vente des biens de la Grande Chartreuse sous la Révolution /. Grenoble , 1984. 104 p. : ISBN 2-904661-02-6 LC Card 86-118639
HD643 .A77 1984

FRANCE - HISTORY - REVOLUTION, 1789-1799 - ECONOMIC ASPECTS.
Arsac, Pierre. La vente des biens de la Grande Chartreuse sous la Révolution /. Grenoble , 1984. 104 p. : ISBN 2-904661-02-6 LC Card 86-118639
HD643 .A77 1984

FRANCE - HISTORY - REVOLUTION, 1789.
Beck, Thomas D. French notables . New York , c1987. 254 p. : ISBN 0-8204-0393-8 : LC Card 87-12156 DDC 338.0944 19
HC275 .B37 1987

FRANCE - HISTORY - SECOND EMPIRE, 1852-1870 - PUBLIC OPINION.
Simon, Dan, 1937- Das Frankreichbild der deutschen Arbeiterbewegung 1859-1865 /. [Gerlingen] , 1984. 334 p. ; ISBN 3-88350-451-3 LC Card 84-173175
HD8450 .S56 1984 ***NYPL [JLD 86-2711]***

FRANCE - HISTORY - THIRD REPUBLIC, 1870-1940.
Lebovics, Herman. The alliance of iron and wheat in the Third French Republic, 1860-1914 . Baton Rouge , c1988. p. cm. ISBN 0-8071-1350-6 LC Card 87-21386 DDC 338.944 19
HC276 .L354 1988

FRANCE - HISTORY - GERMAN OCCUPATION, 1940-1945.
Les Surcharges "France libre" dans les Etablissements français en Inde, 1941-1945 /. Orléans [1984] 19 p., [4] p. of plates : ISBN 2-9500569-0-3 : LC Card 86-122498
HE6185.F8 S87 1984

FRANCE - HISTORY - SOURCES.
Douët-d'Arcq, L. (Louis), 1808-1882. (ed) Comptes de l'hôtel des rois de France aux XIVe et XVe siècles. Paris, 1865. 3 p.l., xlii p., 1 l., 437 p., 1 l. LC Card 05-5875
HJ1077 .D6

FRANCE - INDUSTRIES.
Brémond, Janine. L'économie française face aux défis mondiaux . Paris , c1985. 320 p. : ISBN 2-218-07456-7 LC Card 86-168427
HC276.2 .B657 1985

Dacier, Pierre. Les dossiers noirs de l'industrie

française /. [Paris] , c1985. 414 p. ; ISBN 2-213-01659-3 : LC Card 86-178468
HC276.2 .D2 1985

Le Temps des initiatives /. Paris , c1983. 187 p. ; ISBN 2-226-01647-3 : LC Card 83-212781
HD3616.F83 T46 1983

FRANCE - INDUSTRIES - HISTORY - 19TH CENTURY.
Beck, Thomas D. French notables . New York , c1987. 254 p. : ISBN 0-8204-0393-8 : LC Card 87-12156 DDC 338.0944 19
HC275 .B37 1987

France. Institut national d'études démographiques.
Travaux et documents.
(cahier no 110) Charbit, Yves. Enfants, familles, migrations dans le bassin méditerranéen /. [Paris] , 1985. viii, 195 p. ; ISBN 2-7332-0110-7 (pbk.)
HQ792.E8 C47 1985
NYPL [JLL 72-295 cahier no 110]

FRANCE - INTELLECTUAL LIFE.
Harouel, Jean Louis. Essai sur l'inégalité /. Paris , c1984. 287, [1] p. ; ISBN 2-13-038354-8 : LC Card 84-150958
HC280.I5 H35 1984

France-Japon . Callies, Albane. Paris , 1986. 208 p. ; ISBN 2-86563-129-X LC Card 86-165719
HD8431 .C35 1986

France. Ministère de finances. Direction de la comptabilité publique. see **France. Direction de la comptabilité publique.**

France. Ministère de la coopération et du développement. Evaluation du développement rural /. [Paris] , c1982. 201 p. : ISBN 2-11-084484-1 LC Card 84-134740
HC59.72.E44 E93 1982

France. Ministère de la recherche et de l'industrie.
France. Mission "Recherche, technologie et progrès en coopération." Recherche et coopération avec le Tiers Monde . Paris , c1983. 120 p. ; ISBN 2-11-001071-1 : LC Card 83-196852
HC60 .F727 1983

Germon, Claude. La normalisation, clé d'un nouvel essor . Paris , c1983. 156 p. ; ISBN 2-11-001026-6 : LC Card 83-217768
HD3616.F83 G47 1983

France. Ministère de la recherche et de l'industrie. Commission de réflexion.
Germon, Claude. La normalisation, clé d'un nouvel essor . Paris , c1983. 156 p. ; ISBN 2-11-001026-6 : LC Card 83-217768
HD3616.F83 G47 1983

France. Ministère de l'agriculture. Service central des enqêtes et études statistiques. see **France. Service central des enquêtes et études statistiques.**

France. Ministère de l'amenagement du territoire, de l'équipement, du logement et du tourisme. Service des affaires économiques et internationales. Département des statistiques des transports. see **France. Département des statistiques des transports.**

France. Ministère de l'économie, des finances et du budget. Pastré, Olivier. La modernisation des banques françaises . Paris [1985] 234 p. : ISBN 2-11-001537-3 : LC Card 86-179536
HG3026 .P37 1985

France. Ministère de l'économie et des finances. Direction de la comptabilité publique. see **France. Direction de la comptabilité publique.**

France. Ministère de l'économie et des finances. Direction du trésor. see **France. Direction du trésor.**

France. Ministère de l'équipement et du logement. Service des affaires économiques et internationales. Département des statistiques des transports. see **France. Département des statistiques des transports.**

France. Ministère de l'équipement. Service d'analyse économique et financière. Département des statistiques des transports. see **France. Département des statistiques des transports.**

France. Ministère de l'équipement. Service des affaires économiques et internationales. Département des statistiques des transports. see **France. Département des statistiques des transports.**

France. Ministère de l'intérieur. Direction générale des collectivités locales. see **France. Direction générale des collectivités locales.**

France. Ministère des droits de la femme. Les Femmes au travail 1882-1982 /. Paris , 1982. [70] leaves : LC Card 86-161448
HD6145 .F44 1982

France. Ministère des finances. (Old Catalog form: France. Finances, Ministère des) Taxation in developed countries . Paris , Washington, D.C. , 1987. 99 p. ; ISBN 92-64-12929-4 (pbk.) : LC Card 87-163512 DDC 336.24 19
HJ4621 .T28 1987

France. Ministère des finances, des affaires économiques et du plan. see **France. Ministère des finances.**

France. Ministère des finances. Direction du trésor. see **France. Direction du trésor.**

France. Ministère des finances et des affaires économiques. see **France. Ministère des finances.**

France. Ministère des relations extérieures, coopération et développement. Direction des politiques du développement.
Dominique, juin 1985 . [Paris] , c1985. 102 p. : LC Card 86-209026
HC156.5.Z7 D6626 1985

Grenade, juin 1985 . [Paris] , 1985] 124 p. : LC Card 86-209038
HC156.5.Z7 G7465 1985

Sainte-Lucie, juin 1985 . [Paris] , 1985] 120 p. : LC Card 86-209048
HC155.5.Z7 S257 1985

France. Ministère des relations extérieurs, coopération et développement. Direction des politiques du développement. St.-Vincent et les Grenadines, juin 1985 . Paris , 1985] 85 p. : LC Card 86-209310
HC156.5 .S72 1985

France. Ministère des transports. (Old Catalog form: France. Transports, Ministère des) Le Transport fluvial . Paris , c1983. 108 p. : ISBN 2-11-001087-8 : LC Card 83-170808
HE668 .T73 1983

France. Ministère des transports. Service d'analyse économique. Département des statistiques des transports. see **France. Département des statistiques des transports.**

France. Ministère d'État chargé de la réforme administrative. Direction génerale de l'administration et de la fonction publique. see **France. Direction générale de l'administration et de la fonction publique.**

France. Ministère du plan et de l'aménagement du territoire. Le Transport fluvial . Paris , c1983. 108 p. : ISBN 2-11-001087-8 : LC Card 83-170808
HE668 .T73 1983

France. Ministre délégué auprès du ministre des affaires sociales et de la solidarité nationale, chargé de l'emploi. Comptes de l'emploi . Paris , c1984. 219 p. : ISBN 2-11-001264-1 : LC Card 85-132416
HD5775 .C5344 1984

France. Mission "Recherche, technologie et progrès en coopération." Recherche et coopération avec le Tiers Monde : rapport / remis à Jean-Pierre Chevènement, ministre d'Etat, ministre de la recherche et de l'industrie [par la] Mission "Recherche, technologie et progrès en coopération," placée sous la présidence de Jacques Berque. Paris : La Documentation française, c1983. 120 p. ; 24 cm. (Collection des rapports officiels) "Décembre 1982." ISBN 2-11-001071-1 : LC Card 83-196852
1. Economic assistance, French - Developing countries. 2. Technical assistance, French - Developing countries. I. Chevènement, Jean-Pierre. II. Berque, Jacques. III. France. Ministère de la recherche et de l'industrie. IV. Title. V. Series.
HC60 .F727 1983

FRANCE - OCCUPATIONS - HISTORY - 19TH CENTURY.
Cabaud, Michel. 1900, la Française au quotidien /. Paris , c1985. 204 p. : ISBN 2-200-37097-0 LC Card 86-137649
HD6059.F8 C33 1985

FRANCE - OCCUPATIONS - HISTORY - 19TH CENTURY - PICTORIAL WORKS.
Cabaud, Michel. 1900, la Française au quotidien /. Paris , c1985. 204 p. : ISBN 2-200-37097-0 LC Card 86-137649
HD6059.F8 C33 1985

FRANCE - OCCUPATIONS - PICTORIAL WORKS.
Kollar, François, 1904- La France travaille /. Paris , c1986. 238 p. : ISBN 2-85108-435-6 LC Card 87-108516
HD8430 .K65 1986

FRANCE - OFFICIALS AND EMPLOYEES - STATISTICS.
Quarré, Dominique. Les agents de l'Etat au 31 décembre 1980 /. Paris [1985] 305 p. ; ISBN 2-11-064767-1 : LC Card 86-162558
HD8013.F6 Q373 1985

France. Parlement (1946-)
Taxe professionelle . [Paris] [1983] v, 80, [23] p. ; LC Card 85-129298
HJ5412 .T39 1983

FRANCE. PARLEMENT (1946-) - ELECTIONS, 1986.
The French socialists in power, 1981-1986 /. New York , c1987. xii, 212 p. ; ISBN 0-313-25407-9 (lib. bdg. : alk. paper) LC Card 86-33569 DDC 338.944 19
HC276.2 .F699 1987

La France peut se ressaisir /. Herzog, Philippe. Paris , c1987. 416 p. : ISBN 2-209-05941-0 : LC Card 87-169995
HC276.3 .H47 1987

FRANCE - POLITICS AND GOVERNMENT - 17TH CENTURY.
Collins, James B. Fiscal limits of absolutism . Berkeley , c1987. p. cm. ISBN 0-520-05911-5 (alk. paper) LC Card 87-19090 DDC 336.2/00944 19
HJ2648 .C65 1987

FRANCE - POLITICS AND GOVERNMENT - 1852-1870.
Lebovics, Herman. The alliance of iron and wheat in the Third French Republic, 1860-1914 . Baton Rouge , c1988. p. cm. ISBN 0-8071-1350-6 LC Card 87-21386 DDC 338.944 19
HC276 .L354 1988

FRANCE - POLITICS AND GOVERNMENT - 1870-1940.
Lebovics, Herman. The alliance of iron and wheat in the Third French Republic, 1860-1914 . Baton Rouge , c1988. p. cm. ISBN 0-8071-1350-6 LC Card 87-21386 DDC 338.944 19
HC276 .L354 1988

FRANCE - POLITICS AND GOVERNMENT - 20TH CENTURY.
Silbert, Alfred. Economie mondialiste et mutations politiques . Paris , c1985. 212 p. ; ISBN 2-7157-1114-X : LC Card 85-221451 DDC 330.944/08 19
HC276 .S52 1985

FRANCE - POLITICS AND GOVERNMENT - 1914-1940.
Godfrey, John F. Capitalism at war . Leamington Spa, UK ; New York : xiv, 313 p. ; ISBN 0-85496-519-X : LC Card 86-32708 DDC 338.944 19
HD3616.F82 G63 1987

FRANCE - POLITICS AND GOVERNMENT - 1945-1958.
Rice-Maximin, Edward Francis, 1941- Accomodation and resistance . New York , 1986. xi, 175 p. ; ISBN 0-313-25355-2 (lib. bdg. : alk. paper) LC Card 86-4624 DDC 959.704/1 19
DS553.1 .R53 1986 ***NYPL [JFE 87-1024]***

FRANCE - POLITICS AND GOVERNMENT - 1969-
Kolomiĭtsev, Valentin Fedorovich. Rabochiĭ klass i profsoiuzy Frantsii v bor'ybe protiv monopoliĭ, 1968-1981 gody /. Moskva , 1981. 173 p. ; LC Card 82-134380
HD8435 .K65 1981

FRANCE - POLITICS AND GOVERNMENT - 1981-
Chotard, Yvon, 1921- Les patrons et le patronat /. [Paris] , c1986. 231 p. ; ISBN 2-7021-1538-1 : LC Card 87-167099
HD6948.F8 C46 1986

The French socialists in power, 1981-1986 /. New York , c1987. xii, 212 p. ; ISBN 0-313-25407-9 (lib. bdg. : alk. paper) LC Card 86-33569 DDC 338.944 19
HC276.2 .F699 1987

Herzog, Philippe. La France peut se ressaisir /. Paris , c1987. 416 p. : ISBN 2-209-05941-0 : LC Card 87-169995
HC276.3 .H47 1987

Noir, Michel, 1944- 1988 . [Paris] , c1984. 263 p. : LC Card 84-169744
HC280.H53 N65 1984 NYPL [JLE 87-2052]

Pébereau, Michel. La politique économique de la France. Paris , c1985. 319 p. : ISBN 2-200-31217-2 LC Card 86-179163 DDC 338.944 19
HC276.2 .P42 1985

Poncins, Michel de. Tous capitalistes, ou, La réponse au socialisme /. Vouillé [France] , c1983. 164 p. ; LC Card 83-244442 DDC 338.944 19
HC276.2 .P63 1983 NYPL [JLD 86-427]

La Rupture . Paris , c1986. 156 p. ; ISBN 2-7178-1134-6 : LC Card 87-117285
HC276.3 .R86 1986

Séguin, Philippe, 1943- Réussir l'alternance . Paris , c1985. 220 p. ; ISBN 2-221-04633-1 : LC Card 85-187945 DDC 944.083/8 19
JN2594.2 .S37 1985 NYPL [JLC 87-46]

Tuppen, John N. France under recession, 1981-1986 /. Albany , c1988. p. cm. ISBN 0-88706-580-5 LC Card 87-1980 DDC 338.944 19
HC276.3 .T86 1988

FRANCE - POPULATION.
Challier, Marie-Christine. La fécondité en France . Paris , 1985. 196 p. : ISBN 2-222-03773-5 : LC Card 86-234728
HB1003 .C46 1985

FRANCE - POPULATION - CONGRESSES.
Deutsch-Französisches Arbeitstreffen auf dem Gebiet der Demographie (1985 : Dijon, France) Referate zum Deutsch-Französischen Arbeitstreffen auf dem Gebiet der Demographie vom 30. September bis 3. Oktober 1985 in Dijon. Wiesbaden , 1986. 134 p. : LC Card 87-409287 DDC 304.6/0943 19
HB3595 .D45 1985

FRANCE - POPULATION - STATISTICS.
Kerromes, Armelle. Tableaux normalisés simplifiés par région et département . Paris [1984] 273 p. ; ISBN 2-11-064692-6 : LC Card 86-176720
HA1214 1982p

Tout sur la France en 100 graphiques /. Paris , c1986. 113 p. : ISBN 2-86260-154-3 : LC Card 87-106635
HA1224 .T68 1986

FRANCE - PUBLIC WORKS.
France. Groupe de stratégie industrielle no 8. Sous-groupe Travaux publics. La branche des travaux publics en France et sur les marchés extérieurs /. Paris , c1985. 202 p. : ISBN 2-11-001524-1 : LC Card 86-183130
HD4168 .F69 1985

France. Recherche Scientifique Outre-Mer, Office de la.
Travaux et documents de l'O.R.S.T.O.M. . (no. 170) Barbier, J. C. Migrations et développement . Paris , 1983, c1984. 372 p. : ISBN 2-7099-0711-7
NYPL [M-11 4991 no.170]

La France restaurée, 1944-1954 . Bloch-Lainé, François. Paris , c1986. 338 p. ; ISBN 2-213-01803-0 : LC Card 86-215777
HC276.2 .B58 1986

FRANCE - RURAL CONDITIONS.
Luxardo, Hervé. Rase campagne . Paris , c1984. 253 p. : ISBN 2-7007-0376-6 : LC Card 85-101431
HD1536.F8 L893 1984

Mélanges Robert Laurent . Montpellier , 1980. xxi, 296 p. : LC Card 83-151672
HC273 .M43 1980

Trunskiĭ, IU. G. Frantsuzskaia derevnia v XIX-XX vekakh . Moskva , 1986. 283 p. ; LC Card 86-201573
HD1945 .T78 1986

France. Service central des enquêtes et études statistiques. Recettes, dépenses et revenus des exploitations agricoles en 1983 /. Paris [1986] 138 p. : LC Card 86-187878
HD1945 .R374 1986

France. Service de la législation fiscale.
Taxe d'habitation : rapport au parlement : application de l'article 22 de la loi no 82-540 du 28 juin 1982 / Ministère de l'économie, des finances et du budget, Direction général des impôts, Service de la législation fiscale. [Paris] : Le Service, [1984] 192 p. in various pagings ; 30 cm. "Mai 1984." LC Card 85-103723
1. Real property tax - France - Statistics. I. Title.
HJ4346 .F73 1984

Taxe professionelle . [Paris] [1983] v, 80, [23] p. ; LC Card 85-129298
HJ5412 .T39 1983

France. Service des transports urbains régionaux et départementaux. Cent un réseaux urbains de transports collectifs . [Paris] [1982] 48 p. : LC Card 83-227229
HE4764 .C45 1982

FRANCE - SOCIAL CONDITIONS.
Luxardo, Hervé. Rase campagne . Paris , c1984. 253 p. : ISBN 2-7007-0376-6 : LC Card 85-101431
HD1536.F8 L893 1984

FRANCE - SOCIAL CONDITIONS - 18TH CENTURY.
Ménétra, Jacques-Louis, b. 1738. Journal de ma vie . Paris , c1982. 431 p. : ISBN 2-85870-022-2 : LC Card 82-166496 DDC 666/.1/0924 B 19
HD8039.G52 F73 1982
NYPL [JFD 86-6795]

Ménétra, Jacques-Louis, b. 1738. [Journal de ma vie. English.] Journal of my life /. New York , 1986. xviii, 368 p., [1] leaf of plate : ISBN 0-231-06128-5 LC Card 85-28068 DDC 666/.1/0924 B 19
HD8039.G52 F7313 1986
NYPL [JFE 86-2978]

FRANCE - SOCIAL CONDITIONS - 19TH CENTURY.
Beck, Thomas D. French notables . New York , c1987. 254 p. : ISBN 0-8204-0393-8 : LC Card 87-12156 DDC 338.0944 19
HC275 .B37 1987

Stein, Margot B. (Margot Ballou), 1945- The social origins of a labor elite . New York , 1987. xxiv, 515 p. : ISBN 0-8240-8043-2 (alk. paper) : LC Card 87-6913 DDC 305/.9385 19
HD8039.R322 F88 1987

FRANCE - SOCIAL CONDITIONS - 1945-
Tozzi, Michel. Militer autrement /. Bruxelles, Belgique , Lyon, France [1985] 162 p. ; ISBN 2-85008-067-5 : LC Card 86-178750
HD6684 .T66 1985

Tuppen, John N. France under recession, 1981-1986 /. Albany , c1988. p. cm. ISBN 0-88706-580-5 LC Card 87-1980 DDC 338.944 19
HC276.3 .T86 1988

FRANCE - SOCIAL CONDITIONS - 1945- - MAPS.
Savy, Michel. Atlas des Français /. Paris , c1985. 331 p. : ISBN 2-01-011512-0 LC Card 86-178635
HC276.2 .S325 1985

FRANCE - SOCIAL POLICY.
Guilhaume, Philippe. Une volonté d'espérance . Paris , c1984. 218 p. ; ISBN 2-86418-178-9 : LC Card 84-163185
HC276.2 .G785 1984

Johanet, Gilles. Contes et mécomptes de la protection sociale /. Paris , c1986. 175 p. : ISBN 2-86702-024-4 : LC Card 86-179065
HD7175 .J64 1986

Lebovics, Herman. The alliance of iron and wheat in the Third French Republic, 1860-1914 . Baton Rouge , c1988. p. cm. ISBN 0-8071-1350-6 LC Card 87-21386 DDC 338.944 19
HC276 .L354 1988

Poncins, Michel de. Tous capitalistes, ou, La réponse au socialisme /. Vouillé [France] , c1983. 164 p. ; LC Card 83-244442 DDC 338.944 19
HC276.2 .P63 1983 NYPL [JLD 86-427]

Rapport d'exécution du plan intérimaire, 1982-1983 /. Paris , c1984. 146 p. : ISBN 2-11-001229-3 : LC Card 85-121410
HC276.2 .R32 1984

FRANCE - SOCIAL POLICY - 1945-
The French socialists in power, 1981-1986 /. New York , c1987. xii, 212 p. ; ISBN 0-313-25407-9 (lib. bdg. : alk. paper) LC Card 86-33569 DDC 338.944 19
HC276.2 .F699 1987

Projet pour la France . Paris , c1983. 196 p. ; ISBN 2-7340-0032-6 : LC Card 83-196098
HC276.2 .P767 1983

FRANCE - STATISTICAL SERVICES.
France. Direction générale des collectivités locales. Instruction aux maires relative aux bulletins statistiques de l'état civil . [Paris] [1983] 50 p. : LC Card 84-112361
HA37.F8 F73 1983

Litz, Hans Peter. Amtliche Statistik in marktwirtschaftlich organisierten Industriegesellschaften . Frankfurt , New York , c1986. xii, 312 p. : ISBN 3-593-33752-5 LC Card 87-108767 DDC 350.81/9 19
HA37.G3 L58 1986

Recensement des marchés et commandes des entreprises publiques et sociétés d'économie mixte . Paris [1984] 71 p. : LC Card 85-133146
HD4163 .R43 1984

FRANCE - STATISTICAL SERVICES - HISTORY.
La Statistique en France . Bruxelles [1980] 194 p. ; LC Card 84-147748
HA19 .S73 1980

FRANCE - STATISTICS.
Tout sur la France en 100 graphiques /. Paris , c1986. 113 p. : ISBN 2-86260-154-3 : LC Card 87-106635
HA1224 .T68 1986

FRANCE - STATISTICS - MAPS.
Savy, Michel. Atlas des Français /. Paris , c1985. 331 p. : ISBN 2-01-011512-0 LC Card 86-178635
HC276.2 .S325 1985

FRANCE - STATISTICS, VITAL.
Statistique du mouvement de la population dans les D.O.M. . Paris [1985] 104 p. : ISBN 2-11-064898-8 : LC Card 86-216599
HB1003 .S73 1985

France. Statistiques des transports, Département des. see **France. Département des statistiques des transports.**

France. Territoire et à l'action régionale, Délégation à l'aménagement du. see **France. Délégation à l'aménagement du territoire et à l'action régionale.**

France. Transports, Ministère des. see **France. Ministère des transports.**

La France travaille /. Kollar, François, 1904- Paris , c1986. 238 p. : ISBN 2-85108-435-6 LC Card 87-108516
HD8430 .K65 1986

France. Trésor, Direction du. see **France. Direction du trésor.**

France under recession, 1981-1986 /. Tuppen, John N. Albany , c1988. p. cm. ISBN 0-88706-580-5 LC Card 87-1980 DDC 338.944 19
HC276.3 .T86 1988

Francéco. Francéco 1986. [Paris] [1986] 383 p. : ISBN 2-7144-1910-0 : LC Card 87-148071
HC276.2 .F68596 1986

Francéco, la vie économique des 22 régions françaises. Francéco 1986. [Paris] [1986] 383 p. : ISBN 2-7144-1910-0 : LC Card 87-148071
HC276.2 .F68596 1986

Francéco 1986. [Paris] : Le Pré aux Clercs, [1986] 383 p. : ill., maps ; 20 cm. Cover title: Francéco, la vie économique des 22 régions françaises. ISBN 2-7144-1910-0 : LC Card 87-148071
1. France - Economic conditions - 1945- - Regional disparities. I. Title: Francéco. II. Title: Francéco, la vie économique des 22 régions françaises.
HC276.2 .F68596 1986

France's satrapy in Kamerun is safe /. Ntumazah, Ndeh. [London, England , 1985] 22 leaves ; LC Card 87-138988 DDC 337.6711044 19
HC995 .N78 1985

Franch Benavent, Ricardo, 1956- Crecimiento comercial y enriquecimiento burgués en la Valencia del siglo XVIII / Ricardo Franch Benavent. Valencia : Institució Alfons el Magnànim, Institució Valenciana d'Estudis i Investigació, [1986?] 340 p. : ill. ; 21 cm. (Estudios universitarios. 15) Includes bibliographical references. ISBN 84-505-4154-9 LC Card 87-110614
1. Valencia (Spain) - Commerce - History - 18th century. 2. Businessmen - Spain - Valencia - History - 18th century. 3. Middle classes - Spain - Valencia - History - 18th century. I. Series: Estudios universitarios (Institución Alfonso el Magnánimo) , 15. II. Title.
HF3690.V3 F7 1986

Franchini, Augusto. Le aziende di credito : istituzioni tecnico-economiche / Augusto Franchini, Anna M. Lammioni, Antonio Ottavi ; coordinamento a cura di A. Ottavi. Bologna : Clueb, <1986- > v. <2 > ; 24 cm. CONTENTS. - -- v. 2. Le operazioni. LC Card 87-170318
1. Credit management. I. Ottavi, Antonio. II. Lammioni Vezzadini, Anna Maria. III. Title.
HG3751 .F73 1986

FRANCHISE. see **ELECTIONS.**

The franchise affair . Briggs, Asa, 1921- London , 1986. 226 p. ; ISBN 0-7126-1201-7 : LC Card 86-190561 DDC 384.55/453/0941 19
HE8700.9.G7 B72 1986

Franchise selection . Munna, Raymond J., 1941- Kenner, La. , c1987. 215 p. ; ISBN 0-935669-12-4 (pbk.) : LC Card 87-25039 DDC 658.8/708 19
HF5429.235.U5 M86 1987

FRANCHISES, RETAIL. see **FRANCHISES (RETAIL TRADE)**

FRANCHISES (RETAIL TRADE) - ITALY.
L'Affiliazione commerciale . Milano , 1986. 100 p. : ***NYPL [JLD 87-531]***

FRANCHISES (RETAIL TRADE) - LAW AND LEGISLATION - UNITED STATES.
Raab, Steven S., 1949- The blueprint for franchising a business /. New York , c1987. ix, 244 p. : ISBN 0-471-85617-7 LC Card 87-15932 DDC 658.8/7 19
HF5429.235.U5 R32 1987

Seltz, David D. Expanding your business with other people's money /. New York, N.Y. , c1984. 2 v. in 1 : ISBN 0-932648-29-0 LC Card 83-12233 DDC 658.8/708 19
HF5429.235.U5 S442 1984 ***NYPL [JLF 86-664]***

FRANCHISES (RETAIL TRADE) - UNITED STATES.
Bard, Ray. Own your own franchise . Reading, Mass. , 1987. vii, 455 p. ; ISBN 0-201-11439-9 (pbk.) : LC Card 87-14389 DDC 658.8/708 19
HF5429.235.U5 B37 1987

Foster, Dennis L. Franchising for free . New York , c1988. x, 229 p. : ISBN 0-471-62555-8 (pbk.) : LC Card 87-13379 DDC 658.8/708 19
HF5429.235.U5 F67 1988

Jones, Constance. The 220 best franchises to buy . Toronto , New York , 1987. xi, 459 p. ; ISBN 0-553-34385-8 (pbk.) : LC Card 86-47887 DDC 658.8/708 19
HF5429.235.U5 J66 1987

Munna, Raymond J., 1941- Franchise selection . Kenner, La. , c1987. 215 p. ; ISBN 0-935669-12-4 (pbk.) : LC Card 87-25039 DDC 658.8/708 19
HF5429.235.U5 M86 1987

Raab, Steven S., 1949- The blueprint for franchising a business /. New York , c1987. ix, 244 p. : ISBN 0-471-85617-7 LC Card 87-15932 DDC 658.8/7 19
HF5429.235.U5 R32 1987

Seltz, David D. Expanding your business with other people's money /. New York, N.Y. , c1984. 2 v. in 1 : ISBN 0-932648-29-0 LC Card 83-12233 DDC 658.8/708 19
HF5429.235.U5 S442 1984 ***NYPL [JLF 86-664]***

FRANCHISES - TAXATION. see **CORPORATIONS - TAXATION.**

Franchising for free . Foster, Dennis L. New York , c1988. x, 229 p. : ISBN 0-471-62555-8 (pbk.) : LC Card 87-13379 DDC 658.8/708 19
HF5429.235.U5 F67 1988

Francia, Arthur J.
Benjamin, James J. Financial accounting /. Houston, Tex. , 1986. xii, 718 p. : ISBN 0-87393-039-8 LC Card 86-214139 DDC 657/.48 19
HF5635 .B419 1986

Managerial accounting / Arthur J. Francia, Mattie C. Porter, Robert H. Strawser. 5th ed. Houston, Tex. : Dame Publications, 1984. xiv, 651 p. : ill. ; 24 cm. Includes index. ISBN 0-931920-70-1 LC Card 83-72203 DDC 658.1/511 19
1. Managerial accounting. I. Porter, Mattie C. II. Strawser, Robert H. III. Title.
HF5657.4 .F72 1984

Franciaország és Magyarország mezőgazdasága / [készült a Központi Statisztikai Hivatal Mezőgazdasági Statisztikai Főosztályának Módszertani és Elemzési Osztályán]. Budapest : Központi Statisztikai Hivatal, 1986. 43 p. : ill. ; 24 cm. ISBN 963-340-783-4 : LC Card 86-189634
1. Agriculture - Economic aspects - France - Statistics. 2. Agriculture - Economic aspects - Hungary - Statistics. I. Hungary. Központi Statisztikai Hivatal. Mezőgazdasági Statisztikai Főosztály. Módszertani és Elemzési Osztály.
HD1945 .F74 1986

Franciosi, Franco B. Professionalità e formazione nel settore delle costruzioni : i quadri intermedi / Franco B. Franciosi, Carlo Rossi.1a ed. Venezia : Marsilio, 1985. 178 p. ; 22 cm. (Quaderni della Fondazione Giacomo Brodolini) Bibliography: p. 175-178. ISBN 88-317-4781-9 : LC Card 86-234138
1. Construction workers - Training of - Italy. I. Rossi, Carlo. II. Title. III. Series.
HD5716.B92 I724 1985

Francis, Arthur. New technology at work / Arthur Francis. Oxford [Oxfordshire] : Clarendon Press ; New York : Oxford University Press, 1986. vi, 216 p. ; 23 cm. ISBN 0-19-878016-8 : LC Card 86-12705 DDC 338/.06 19
1. Labor supply - Effect of technological innovations on. 2. Technological innovations - Social aspects. 3. Quality of work life. I. Title.
HD6331 .F66 1987 ***NYPL [JLD 87-912]***

Francis, Clark. see **Francis, Jack Clark.**

Francis, Dave.
Unblocking organizational communication : a companion volume to 50 activities for unblocking organizational communication / Dave Francis. Aldershot, Hants, England ; Brookfield, Vt. : Gower, c1987. xiv, 185 p. ; 23 cm. Includes index. ISBN 0-566-02572-8 : LC Card 87-14836 DDC 658.4/5 19
1. Communication in organizations. I. Title.
HD30.3 .F73 1987

50 activities for unblocking organizational communication / Dave Francis. Aldershot, Hants, England ; Brookfield, Vt., U. S.A. : Gower Pub. Co., c1987. p. cm. Includes index. ISBN 0-566-02571-X : LC Card 87-14079 DDC 658.4/5 19
1. Communication in organizations. 2. Organizational change. 3. Work groups. I. Title. II. Title: Fifty activities for unblocking organizational communication.
HD30.3 .F7 1987

Francis, Devon. Power to fly : a history of the oil and aviation partnership / by Devon Francis. [Fallbrook, CA] : Aero Publishers USA, 1986. 97 p. : ill. (some col.) ; 24 x 33 cm. ISBN 0-8168-7632-0 : LC Card 85-20045 DDC 338.4/76655825/0973 19
1. Aeronautics - United States - History. 2. Petroleum industry and trade - United States - History. I. Title.
TL521 .F63 1986 ***NYPL [JSG 86-235]***

Francis, Diane. Controlling interest : who owns Canada? / Diane Francis. Toronto, Ont., Canada : Macmillan of Canada, c1986. 352 p. ; 24 cm. Includes index. ISBN 0-7715-9744-4 LC Card 86-218086 DDC 338.8/0971 19
1. Industrial concentration - Canada. 2. Millionaires - Canada. 3. Capitalists and financiers - Canada. I. Title.
HD2809 .F73 1986

Francis, Dick. The countertrade handbook / Dick Francis. New York : Quorum Books, 1987. ix, 270 p. : ill. ; 25 cm. Includes index. Bibliography: p. 262-263. ISBN 0-89930-320-X (lib. bdg. : alk. paper) LC Card 87-11867 DDC 382 19
1. Countertrade. I. Title.
HF1414.3 .F72 1987

Francis, Jack Clark.
Portfolio analysis. Alexander, Gordon J., 1947- Portfolio analysis / Gordon J. Alexander, Jack Clark Francis. 3rd ed. Englewood Cliffs, N.J. , c1986. xiv, 306 p. : ISBN 0-13-686825-8 : LC Card 85-28317 DDC 332.6 19
HG4521 .A42 1986 ***NYPL [JLE 86-4286]***

Francisco, Albert K.
Accounting theory and practice / Albert K. Francisco, Kenneth A. Smith. 1988-1989 ed. Belmont, CA : Professional Publications, c1987. 1 v. (various pagings) : ill. ; 28 cm. (CPA examination review series) Rev. ed. of: CPA review of theory and practice. 1983-1984 ed. c1984. Includes index. ISBN 0-932276-74-1 (pbk.) LC Card 87-62077 DDC 657/.076 19
1. Accounting - Examinations, questions, etc. I. Smith, Kenneth A. II. Francisco, Albert K. CPA review of theory and practice. III. Series: Francisco, Albert K. CPA examination review series. IV. Title.
HF5661 .F68 1987

Auditing / Albert K. Francisco, Kenneth A. Smith. 1988-1989 ed. Belmont, CA : Professional Publications, c1987. 1 v. (various pagings) : ill. ; 28 cm. (CPA examination review series) Rev. ed. of: CPA review of auditing. 1983-1984 ed. c1984. Includes index. ISBN 0-932276-76-8 (pbk.) LC Card 87-62076 DDC 657/.45/076 19
1. Auditing - Examinations, questions, etc. I. Smith, Kenneth A. II. Francisco, Albert K. CPA review of auditing. III. Series: Francisco, Albert K. CPA examination review series. IV. Title.
HF5667 .F68 1987

CPA exam questions on accounting practice / Albert K. Francisco, Kenneth A. Smith. 1988-1989 ed. Belmont, CA : Professional Publications, c1987. 1 v. (various pagings) ; 28 cm. (CPA examination review series) Includes index. ISBN 0-932276-80-6 (pbk.) LC Card 87-62331 DDC 657/.076 19
1. Accounting - Examinations, questions, etc. I. Smith, Kenneth A. II. Series: Francisco, Albert K. CPA examination review series. III. Title.
HF5661 .F67 1987

CPA exam questions on accounting theory / Albert K. Francisco, Kenneth A. Smith. 1988-1989 ed. Belmont, CA. : Professional Publications, c1987. 1 v. (various pagings) ; 28 cm. (CPA examination review series) Includes index. ISBN 0-932276-79-2 (pbk.) LC Card 87-62332 DDC 657/.076 19
1. Accounting - Examinations, questions, etc. I. Smith, Kenneth A. II. Series: Francisco, Albert K. CPA examination review series. III. Title.
HF5661 .F675 1987

CPA examination review series.
Francisco, Albert K. Accounting theory and practice /. Belmont, CA , c1987. 1 v. (various pagings) : ISBN 0-932276-74-1 (pbk.) LC Card 87-62077 DDC 657/.076 19
HF5661 .F68 1987

Francisco, Albert K. Auditing /. Belmont, CA , c1987. 1 v. (various pagings) : ISBN 0-932276-76-8 (pbk.) LC Card 87-62076 DDC 657/.45/076 19
HF5667 .F68 1987

Francisco, Albert K. CPA exam questions on accounting practice /. Belmont, CA , c1987. 1 v. (various pagings) ; ISBN 0-932276-80-6 (pbk.) LC Card 87-62331 DDC 657/.076 19
HF5661 .F67 1987

Francisco, Albert K. CPA exam questions on accounting theory /. Belmont, CA. , c1987. 1 v. (various pagings) ; ISBN 0-932276-79-2 (pbk.) LC Card 87-62332 DDC 657/.076 19
HF5661 .F675 1987

CPA review of auditing. Francisco, Albert K. Auditing / Albert K. Francisco, Kenneth A. Smith. 1988-1989 ed. Belmont, CA , c1987. 1 v. (various pagings) : ISBN 0-932276-76-8 (pbk.) LC Card 87-62076 DDC 657/.45/076 19
HF5667 .F68 1987

CPA review of theory and practice. Francisco, Albert K. Accounting theory and practice /

Albert K. Francisco, Kenneth A. Smith. 1988-1989 ed. Belmont, CA , c1987. 1 v. (various pagings) : ISBN 0-932276-74-1 (pbk.) LC Card 87-62077 DDC 657/.076 19
HF5661 .F68 1987

Francisque, Édouard. La structure économique et sociale d'Haïti / Edouard Francisque. [Port-au-Prince, Haïti] : Impr. H. Deschamps, [1986] 255 p. ; 21 cm. Bibliography: p. [247]-252. LC Card 87-113952
1. Haiti - Economic conditions - 1971-. 2. Haiti - Social conditions - 1971-. 3. Haiti - Population. I. Title.
HC153 .F72 1986

Franck, Irene M.
The AMA handbook of key management forms /. New York, NY , c1987. 732 p. : ISBN 0-8144-1144-4 LC Card 86-25955 DDC 651/.29 19
HD38 .A44 1987

Brownstone, David M. The manager's advisor /. New York , c1987. vii, 296 p. ; ISBN 0-8144-7682-1 (pbk.) : LC Card 87-47712 DDC 658.4 19
HD38.2 .B75 1987

Brownstone, David M. The sales professional's advisor /. New York , c1987. 298 p. ; ISBN 0-8144-7683-X (pbk.) : LC Card 87-47713 DDC 658.8/5 19
HF5438.25 .B747 1987

Helpers and aides / by Irene M. Franck and David M. Brownstone. New York, N.Y. : Facts on File, c1987. x, 182 p. : ill. ; 25 cm. (Work throughout history) "Hudson Group book." Bibliography: p. 173-177. Includes index. Explores the role throughout history of helping professions, including drivers, exterminators, firefighters, social workers, and others. ISBN 0-8160-1445-0 LC Card 86-24370 DDC 331.7 19
1. Occupations - History - Juvenile literature. 2. Service industries - History - Juvenile literature. I. Brownstone, David M. II. Title. III. Series.
HF5381.2 .F68 1987

Francke, Hans-Hermann.
Möglichkeiten einer binnenwirtschaftlich orientierten Geldpolitik bei weltweit hohen Zinsen /. Berlin , c1985. 240 p. : ISBN 3-428-05806-2 LC Card 85-199321
HG230.3 .M63 1985

Sparverhalten bei Unterbeschäftigung, stagnierendem oder sinkendem Realeinkommen / von Hans-Hermann Francke und Dieter Friedrich. Stuttgart : Deutscher Sparkassenverlag, [1985] 142 p. : ill. ; 21 cm. (Forschungsberichte / Gesellschaft zur Førderung der Wissenschaftlichen Forschung über das Spar- und Girowesen . Bd. 19) "Ergebnisse eines Forschungsprojekts im Auftrag der Gesellschaft zur Förderung der Wissenschaftlichen Forschung über das Spar- und Girowesen e.V. Bonn." Includes bibliographical references. LC Card 86-153649
1. Saving and investment - Germany, West. 2. Unemployment - Germany (West) - Effect of inflation on. 3. Income - Germany, West. I. Friedrich, Dieter. II. Series: Forschungsberichte / Gesellschaft zur Førderung der Wissenschaftlichen Forschung über das Spar- und Girowesen , Bd. 19. III. Title.
HC290.5.S3 F69 1985

Francke, Petra. Frauen und neue Technologien /. Hannover , 1986. 112 p. ; LC Card 87-407392 DDC 331.4/0943 19
HD6059.G3 F74 1986

Franco, Ernesto A. Pinoy management / Ernesto A. Franco. Metro Manila, Philippines : National Book Store, 1986. 230 p. : ill. ; 22 cm. Bibliography: p. 223-225. Includes index. ISBN 971-08-2961-0 (pbk.) LC Card 86-217631 DDC 658/.009599 19
1. Industrial management - Philippines. I. Title.
HD70.P5 F73 1986

FRANCO, FRANCISCO, 1892-1975.
Domínguez, Javier. Organizaciones obreras cristianas en la oposición al franquismo (1951-1975) . Bilbao [1985?] 479 p. ; ISBN 84-271-1431-1 LC Card 87-153234
HD6481.2.S7 D65 1985

Franco, José Ronaldo de Mello. O movimento sindical metalúrgico em Santa Luzia / José Ronaldo de Mello Franco. [Santa Luzia, Minas Gerais, Brazil? : s.n.], 1985. 111 p. ; 21 cm. Cover title. Bibliography: p. 111. LC Card 87-404244 DDC 331.88/171/098151 19
1. Trade-unions - Metal-workers - Brazil - Santa Luzia (Minas Gerais). I. Title.
HD6614.M5 F73 1985

Franco, Joseph. Hoffa's man : the rise and fall of Jimmy Hoffa as witnessed by his strongest arm / Joseph Franco with Richard Hammer.1st ed. New York : Prentice Hall Press, c1987. xv, 332 p., [8] p. of plates : ill. ; 25 cm. Includes index. ISBN 0-13-517764-2 : LC Card 87-42675 DDC 331.88/11388324/0924 B 19
1. Franco, Joseph. 2. Hoffa, James R. (James Riddle), 1913-. 3. Trade-unions - United States - Officials and employees - Biography. 4. International Brotherhood of Teamsters, Chauffeurs, Warehousemen and Helpers of America. I. Hammer, Richard, 1928-. II. Title.
HD6509.F69 A3 1987

FRANCO, JOSEPH.
Franco, Joseph. Hoffa's man . New York , c1987. xv, 332 p., [8] p. of plates : ISBN 0-13-517764-2 : LC Card 87-42675 DDC 331.88/11388324/0924 B 19
HD6509.F69 A3 1987

Franco, Luiz L. O Brasil que temos, o país que queremos / Luiz L. Franco. Guarulhos, S.P. [Brazil] : Editora Parma, c1985. 87 p. ; 21 cm. LC Card 86-223053
1. Brazil - Economic conditions - 1964-1985. 2. Inflation (Finance) - Brazil. 3. Capitalism - Brazil. 4. Taxation - Brazil. 5. Liberty. I. Title.
HC187 .F7315 1985

Franda, Marcus F. Voluntary associations and local development in India : the Janata phase / Marcus Franda. New Delhi : Young Asia Publications, 1983. vi, 356 p. ; 22 cm. Imprint date from label on t.p. verso. Includes bibliographical references and indexes. LC Card 83-900993 DDC 307/.14/0954 19
1. Rural development - India - Addresses, essays, lectures. 2. Voluntarism - India - Societies, etc. - Addresses, essays, lectures. 3. Agriculture and state - India - Addresses, essays, lectures. I. Title.
HN690.Z9 C6513 1983 ***NYPL [JLD 86-3866]***

Franey, Jean-Pierre. Ethiopie, la face cachée / texte, Jean-Pierre Franey ; photos, Lily Franey. Paris : Messidor, c1986. 127 p. : ill. (some col.) ; 29 cm. ISBN 2-209-05848-1 : LC Card 87-113107
1. Famines - Ethiopia. 2. Famines - Ethiopia - Pictorial works. I. Franey, Lily. II. Title.
HC845.Z9 F34 1986

Franey, Lily. Franey, Jean-Pierre. Ethiopie, la face cachée /. Paris , c1986. 127 p. : ISBN 2-209-05848-1 : LC Card 87-113107
HC845.Z9 F34 1986

Frank, Hermann. Project Financing : ein Verfahren zur finanziellen Absicherung des Unternehmenswachstums / Hermann Frank. Wien : Service, c1986. xii, 313 p. : ill. ; 21 cm. (Schriftenreihe der Abteilung für Gewerbe, Klein- und Mittelbetriebe an der Wirtschaftsuniversität Wien . Bd. 6) Bibliography: p. 292-313. ISBN 3-85428-066-1 LC Card 86-225790
1. Capital investments. 2. Corporations - Finance. I. Title.
HG4028.C4 F76 1986

Frank, Jeff. The new Keynesian economics : unemployment, search and contracting / Jeff Frank. Brighton : Wheatsheaf Books, 1986. xvii, 283 p. : ill. ; 23 cm. Includes index. Bibliography: p. 273-278. ISBN 0-7108-0239-0
1. Keynesian economics. 2. Macroeconomics. I. Title.
NYPL [JLD 86-2534]

Frank, Karl Heinz. Giersch, Herbert. Gegen Europessimismus . Stuttgart , c1986. 318 p. ; ISBN 3-421-06334-6 LC Card 87-672572
HF1411 .G53x 1986

Frank, Max, 1913- Politique agricole commune . Bruxelles, Belgique , c1982. 126 p. ; ISBN 1-8004-0773-5 LC Card 87-672469
HD1803 .P64x 1982

Frank, Meryl. The Parental leave crisis . New Haven , c1988. p. cm. ISBN 0-300-03984-0 (alk. paper) LC Card 87-10729 DDC 331.25/76 19
HD6065 .P37 1988

Frank, Odile. The demand for fertility control in Sub-Saharan Africa / Odile Frank. New York, N.Y., U. S.A. (1 Dag Hammarskjold Plaza, New York 10017) : Population Council, [1985] 50 p. ; 23 cm. (Center for policy studies working papers . no. 117 (November 1985)) Cover title. Bibliography: p. 46-50. LC Card 86-204127 DDC 363.9/6/09624 19
1. Fertility, Human - Africa, Sub-Saharan. 2. Birth control - Africa, Sub-Saharan. I. Series: Working papers (Population Council. Center for Policy Studies) , no. 117. II. Title.
HB1071.A3 F69 1985

Frank, Peter. Business opportunities for broadcasters in MDS pay television / by Peter Frank, John Shackelford. Washington, DC : National Association of Broadcasters, [c1982] 29 p. ; 28 cm. (Com/tech report . vol. 1, no. 2) Bibliography: p. 29. LC Card 86-201299
1. Subscription television - United States. I. Shackelford, John. II. National Association of Broadcasters. III. Series: Com/tech report series , vol. 1, no. 2. IV. Title.
HE8700.72.U6 F73 1982

Franke, Reiner. Production prices and dynamical processes of the gravitation of market prices / Reiner Franke. Frankfurt am Main ; New York : P. Lang, c1987. 231 p. : ill. ; 21 cm. (Dynamische Wirtschaftstheorie, 0930-2174 . Bd. 1) Bibliography: p. 227-231. ISBN 3-8204-9435-9 (pbk.) LC Card 87-170397 DDC 338/.01 19
1. Sraffa, Piero. Production of commodities by means of commodities. 2. Prices. I. Title. II. Series.
HB171.S7253 F73 1987

Frankel, Barbara, 1950- O'Connell, Julie, 1951- Medicaid reform . [Albany, N.Y.] [1983] 26 p. ; LC Card 86-620741 DDC 362.1/04252/09747 19
HD7102.U5 N668 1983

Frankel, Delma. Survey of income and program participation and related longitudinal surveys, 1984 . [Washington, D.C.] , 1985. ix, 201 p. : LC Card 85-601676 DDC 339.2/3/0973 19
HC110.I5 S89 1985 ***NYPL [JLF 86-1641]***

Frankel, Ernst G.
Port planning and development / Ernst G. Frankel. New York : Wiley, c1987. xxiv, 795 p. : ill. ; 25 cm. "A Wiley-Interscience publication." Bibliography: p. 727-777. Includes index. ISBN 0-471-83708-3 LC Card 86-24747 DDC 387.1/068 19
1. Harbors. 2. Harbors - Planning. I. Title.
HE551 .F7 1987

The world shipping industry / Ernst Gabriel Frankel. London ; New York : Croom Helm, c1987. xix, 261 p. : ill. ; 22 cm. Bibliography: p. 249-258. Includes index. ISBN 0-7099-1087-8 LC Card 87-3608 DDC 387.5 19
1. Shipping. 2. Shipping - United States. I. Title.
HE571 .F7 1987

Frankel, Harold H. Cash, R. Patrick. Improving apparel shop profits] [New York, N.Y.] [c1986] 285 p. : ISBN 0-87102-131-5 LC Card 86-61313 DDC 687/.068/8 19
HD9940.A2 C37 1986

Frankfurt am Main. Universität. Wissenschaftliche Gesellschaft. see **Wissenschaftliche Gesellschaft an der Johann Wolfgang Goethe-Universität Frankfurt am Main.**

Frankfurter wirtschafts- und sozialgeographische Schriften. For additional listing of contents, see Old Catalog.
(Heft 44) Jörs, Bernd. Die Bedeutung der Buntmetallhütten des mitteleuropäischen Raumes im Rahmen der Versorgung der Bundesrepublik Deutschland . Frankfurt/Main , 1983. 579 p. in various pagings : LC Card 83-226662
HD9539.Z6 C365 1983

Frankis, G. Anderson, Roy Claude. History of Royal Blue Express Services /. Newton Abbot , North Pomfret, Vt. , 1985. 216 p. : ISBN 0-7153-8654-9 : LC Card 86-136155 DDC 388.3/22/09423 19
HE5664.Z7 R63 1985

FRANKLIN NATIONAL BANK.
Ross, Walter Sanford, 1916- People's banker . New Canaan, Conn. , c1987. viii, 288 p. ; ISBN 0-87983-429-3 LC Card 87-4066 DDC 332.1/223/0924 B 19
HG2463.R68 R67 1987

Franks, D. S. (David S.) Blackstone, L. R. (Lance R.) UK tax savings for the higher paid (1979) /. London , c1979. 10 p. ; LC Card 81-112830
HJ4708.A7 B533 1979

Fransman, Martin.
Machinery and economic development /. Houndmills, Basingstoke, Hampshire , 1986. xvii, 274 p. : ISBN 0-333-36391-4
NYPL [JLD 86-4380]

Technology and economic development / Martin Fransman. Brighton, Sussex : Wheatsheaf Books, 1986. xi, 161 p. : ill. ; 23 cm. Includes index. Bibliography: p. 139-157. ISBN 0-7450-0104-1
1. Technological innovations - Developing countries. 2. Developing countries - Economic policy. I. Title.
NYPL [JLD 87-320]

Frantsuzskaia derevnia v deviatnadtsatom-dvadtsatom vekakh. Trunskiĭ, IU. G. Frantsuzskaia derevnia v XIX-XX vekakh . Moskva , 1986. 283 p. ; LC Card 86-201573
HD1945 .T78 1986

Frantsuzskaia derevnia v XIX-XX vekakh . Trunskiĭ, IU. G. Moskva , 1986. 283 p. ; LC Card 86-201573
HD1945 .T78 1986

Frantsuzskaia derevnia v 19-om-20-om vekakh. Trunskiĭ, IU. G. Frantsuzskaia derevnia v XIX-XX vekakh . Moskva , 1986. 283 p. ; LC Card 86-201573
HD1945 .T78 1986

Frantsuzskaia Kommunisticheskaia Partiia Cachin, Marcel. see **Parti communiste français.**

Frantz, Douglas. Levine & Co. : Wall Street's insider trading scandal / Douglas Frantz.1st ed. New York : Holt, c1987. x, 370 p. : ill. ; 24 cm. "Author's notes": p. 353-359. Includes index. ISBN 0-8050-0457-2 LC Card 87-8521 DDC 364.1/68 19
1. Levine, Dennis, 1952-. 2. Bankers - United States - Biography. 3. Insider trading in securities - United States. 4. Investment banking - United States - Corrupt practices. I. Title. II. Title: Levine and Co.
HG2463.L48 F72 1987

Frantz, Roger S. X-efficiency : theory, evidence, and applications / Roger S. Frantz. Boston : Kluwer Academic Publishers, c1988. xviii, 227 p. : ill. ; 24 cm. (Topics in regulatory economics and policy series) Bibliography: p. 211-219. Includes index. ISBN 0-89838-242-4 LC Card 87-17071 DDC 338/.06 19
1. Efficiency, Industrial. 2. Industrial productivity. 3. Industry and state. I. Title. II. Series.
HD56 .F725 1988

Frantziskakis, Fr. The Greek presence /. Athens , 1969. [32] p. : LC Card 87-101996
HC295 .G7545 1969

Franz, Herbert, 1908- Alpine Areas Workshop (1974 : Schloss Laxenburg) Alpine Areas Workshop, May 13-17, 1974 /. Laxenburg [1974] 80 p. : LC Card 82-212849
HC268.O25 A46 1974

Franz, Lothar. Verkehrsberuhigung in Städten und Gemeinden / Lothar Franz, Ludwig Blumentrath, Peter Isnenghi. Grafenau : Expert Verlag, c1982. 134 p. : ill. ; 21 cm. (Kontakt & Studium. Bd. 80.) Includes bibliographical references. ISBN 3-88508-780-4 : LC Card 82-204794
1. Urban transportation - Germany, West. 2. Urban transportation policy - Germany, West. 3. Traffic noise - Germany (West). I. Blumentrath, L. (Ludwig). II. Isnenghi, Peter. III. Series. IV. Series: Kontakt & Studium, Bd. 80. V. Title.
HE311.G3 F73 1982

Franz, Michael. Die Personalberatung bei der Stellenbesetzung / Michael Franz. Frankfurt am Main : Haag + Herchen, c1984. viii, 214 p. ; 21 cm. Bibliography: p. 202-214. ISBN 3-88129-789-8 LC Card 85-186519
1. Employee counseling. 2. Employee selection. I. Title.
HF5549.5.C8 F7 1984

Franz, Paulo Renato Ferreira. Região geoeconômica de Brasília : caracterização do setor agropecuário / Paulo Renato Ferreira Franz, Juan Carlos Torchelli. Planaltina-DF [Brazil] : EMBRAPA, Centro de Pesquisa Agropecuária dos Cerrados, 1985. 70 p. : forms, maps ; 29 cm. (Documentos / EMBRAPA-CPAC, 0102-0021 . no. 17) Bibliography: p. 43-44. LC Card 87-143606 DDC 338.1/3/098174 19
1. Agriculture - Economic aspects - Brazil - Brasília Region. 2. Natural resources - Brazil - Brasília Region. I. Torchelli, Juan Carlos. II. Series: Documentos (Empresa Brasileira de Pesquisa Agropecuária. Centro de Pesquisa Agropecuária dos Cerrados) , no. 17. III. Title.
HD1875.B7 F7 1985

Franzmeyer, Fritz. Industriepolitik im westlichen Ausland . Berlin , 1987. 2 v. ; ISBN 3-428-06143-8 (set) LC Card 87-133587 DDC 330 s 338.9 19
HC281 .B33 Heft 92 HD3611

Französische Kommunistische Partei. see **Parti communiste français.**

Frascona, Oliver E., 1947- The paper trail : the real estate professional's guide to documented liability protection and marketing success / Oliver E. Frascona. Boulder, Colo. : Denver Carrington Pub. Co., c1987. ix, 185 p. ; 26 cm. (Real law books series) ISBN 0-941937-00-3 (pbk.) LC Card 87-8904 DDC 333.33/068 19
1. Real estate business - Records and correspondence. 2. Real estate agents - Malpractice. 3. Real estate business - Law and legislation. I. Title. II. Series.
HD1386.5 .F7 1987

Fraser & Neave Ltd.
1883-1983, the great years. [Singapore] , 1983. 46 p. : LC Card 84-840800 DDC 338.7/663/095957 19
HD9348.S554 F715 1983

FRASER & NEAVE LTD. - HISTORY.
1883-1983, the great years. [Singapore] , 1983. 46 p. : LC Card 84-840800 DDC 338.7/663/095957 19
HD9348.S554 F715 1983

Fraser, Bryna Shore. Goldstein, Harold. Training for work in the computer age . Washington, D.C. , 1986. iv, 109 p. ; LC Card 86-601422 DDC 331.25/92 19
HD5715.2 .G63 1986

Fraser, Donald R. Financial institutions and markets in a changing world /. Plano, Tex. , 1987. xiii, 697 p. : ISBN 0-256-03695-0 (pbk.) LC Card 86-61850 DDC 332.1/0973 19
HG181 .F633 1987

Fraser, Edie. Risk to riche$. Washington, DC (600 Maryland Ave., S.W., Suite 700, Washington 20024) , c1986. vii, 204 p. : LC Card 87-158511 DDC 338/.04/088042 19
HD2346.U5 R57 1986

Fraser Institute (Vancouver, B.C.)
Martin, Peter, 1942- Inside the Bank of Canada's Weekly financial statistics . Vancouver, B. C. , 1985. xix, 201 p. : ISBN 0-88975-082-3 *NYPL [JLF 87-456]*

Morality of the market . Vancouver, B.C., Canada , c1985. xxv, 601 p. ; ISBN 0-88975-074-2 (pbk.) : LC Card 86-158049 DDC 174/.4 19
HB72 .M56 1985

Fraser Port : freightway to the Pacific, 1858-1985 / compiled by students at Douglas and Kwantlen colleges in British Columbia and edited by Jacqueline Gresko and Richard Howard. Victoria, B.C. : Sono Nis Press, 1986. 131 p., [16] p. of plates : ill. ; 23 cm. Bibliography: p. 115-125. ISBN 0-919203-17-5 (pbk.) LC Card 87-106756
1. Harbors - British Columbia - Vancouver Metropolitan Area - History. 2. Fraser River Region (B.C.) - History. I. Gresko, Jacqueline, 1947-. II. Howard, Richard, 1940-. III. Douglas College. IV. Kwantlen College.
HE554.V3 F73 1986

FRASER RIVER REGION (B.C.) - HISTORY.
Fraser Port . Victoria, B.C. , 1986. 131 p., [16] p. of plates : ISBN 0-919203-17-5 (pbk.) LC Card 87-106756
HE554.V3 F73 1986

Frater, Alexander, 1937- Beyond the blue horizon : on the track of Imperial Airways / Alexander Frater.1st American ed. New York : Scribner, 1987, c1986. xviii, 430 p. : maps ; 25 cm. ISBN 0-684-18837-6 LC Card 87-9426 DDC 387.7/065/73 19
1. Air travel - History. 2. Aeronautics, Commercial - Passenger traffic - History. 3. Imperial Airways - History. I. Title.
HE9787 .F7 1987

Fratev, D. Manolov, Manol Dimitrov. Narodnaia Respublika Bolgariia--40 let po puti sotsialisticheskogo voskhoda /. [Bulgaria? , 1983?] [48] p. : LC Card 85-133679
HC403 .M36 1983

Fratianni, Michele. Grauwe, Paul de. Exchange rates, money, and output . New York , 1985. xii, 240 p. : ISBN 0-312-27403-3 : LC Card 84-11692 DDC 339/.094 19
HC241.2 .G69 1985 NYPL [JLD 86-3007]

Frattini, Giovanni. Contabilità e bilancio : logica delle rilevazioni e delle determinazioni di esercizio / Giovanni Frattini. Milano : Giuffrè, [1986] xiii, 317 p. : ill. ; 24 cm. (Università "L. Bocconi," Dipartimento di economia aziendale . 97. 8.11) Bibliography: p. [315]-317. ISBN 88-14-00831-0 : LC Card 86-182373
1. Comparative accounting. 2. Accounting. 3. Budget in business. I. Series: Università "L. Bocconi," Dipartimento di economia aziendale (Series) , 97. II. Title.
HF5625 .F73 1986

FRAUD - GREAT BRITAIN - CASE STUDIES.
Sherrard, Michael. London Capital Group Limited (formerly British Bangladesh Trust Limited) . London , 1977. vi, 376 p. : ISBN 0-11-512127-7 (pbk.) LC Card 85-164377
HG4135 .S46 1977

FRAUD INVESTIGATION.
Comer, Michael J. Corporate fraud /. London , New York , 1985. xvi, 453 p. : ISBN 0-07-084791-6 : LC Card 85-11686 DDC 364.1/63 19
HV6768 .C65 1985 NYPL [JLE 86-909]

FRAUD INVESTIGATION - UNITED STATES - CASE STUDIES.
Kizorek, Bill. Disability or deception /. [Naperville, Ill., USA] (Suite 12, 6 S 235 Steeple Run Dr., Naperville 60540) [c1986] 140 p. : LC Card 86-206432 DDC 363.2/5 19
HD7105.25.U6 K59 1986

FRAUD - NETHERLANDS.
Fraudenota. [Hague , 1982] 42 p. ; ISBN 90-12-04091-4 LC Card 83-197641
HJ2348.5 .F72 1982

Fraud, waste, and abuse in government : causes, consequences, and cures / edited by Jerome B. McKinney and Michael Johnston. Philadelphia : Institute for the Study of Human Issues, c1986. x, 159 p. ; 25 cm. Includes bibliographical references and index. ISBN 0-89727-058-4 LC Card 86-2967 DDC 336.73 19
1. Waste in government spending - United States. 2. Corruption (in politics) - United States. 3. Finance, Public - United States - Accounting. 4. Civil service reform - United States. I. McKinney, Jerome B. II. Johnston, Michael, 1949-.
HJ257.2 .F72 1986 NYPL [JLE 86-4153]

Fraudebestrijding in de directe belastingen en de omzetbelasting. Fraudenota. [Hague , 1982] 42 p. ; ISBN 90-12-04091-4 LC Card 83-197641
HJ2348.5 .F72 1982

Fraudenota. [Hague : Staatsuitgeverij, 1982] 42 p. ; 28 cm. Cover title. Caption title: Fraudebestrijding in de directe belastingen en de omzetbelasting. "Tweede Kamer, zitting 1981-1982, 17522, nrs. 1-2, brief van de Minister van Financiën"--P. 1. ISBN 90-12-04091-4 LC Card 83-197641
1. Tax evasion - Netherlands. 2. Fraud - Netherlands. I. Netherlands. Ministerie van Financiën. II. Title: Fraudebestrijding in de directe belastingen en de omzetbelasting.
HJ2348.5 .F72 1982

Fraudulent and questionable financial reporting . Merchant, Kenneth A. Morristown, N.J. , c1987. iv, 48, [36] p. ; ISBN 0-910586-64-0 (pbk.) LC Card 87-80813 DDC 657/.3 19
HF5686.C7 M44 1987

Frauen aktuell.
Edding, Cornelia, 1943- Einbruch in den Herrenclub . Reinbek bei Hamburg , 1983. 184 p. : ISBN 3-499-15251-7 (pbk.) LC Card 87-673369
HD6054.2.G3 E33x 1983

Plogstedt, Sibylle. Übergriffe . Reinbek bei Hamburg , 1984. 157 p. ; ISBN 3-499-15353-X (pbk.) LC Card 87-672604
HD6060.3 .P56x 1984

Frauen in Entwicklungsländern . Bruchhaus, Eva-Maria. Freiburg im Breisgau , 1979. iii, 182 p. ; LC Card 81-121677 DDC 305.4/09172/4 19
HQ1870.9 .B78 1979 NYPL [JLG 86-106]

Frauen und Beruf, zwischen Wunsch und Realität : Beiträge aus Wissenschaft und Praxis zur Aus- und Weiterbildung von Frauen /

herausgegeben vom Bundesminister für Bildung und Wissenschaft. Bonn : Der Bundesminister ; Bad Honnef : Vertrieb, K.H. Bock, 1986. 142 p. ; 21 cm. (Schriftenreihe Studien zu Bildung und Wissenschaft, 0175-8055 . 41) Revised papers of a meeting sponsored by the Bundesministerium für Bildung und Wissenschaft, held Jan. 27-28, 1986 in Bonn, and edited by Ursula Rimele-Petzold. Bibliography: p. 141-142. ISBN 3-87066-629-3 : LC Card 87-409372 DDC 331.4/0943 19
1. Women - Employment - Germany, West. 2. Occupational training for women - Germany (West). 3. Vocational education - Germany, West. 4. Sexual division of labor - Germany (West). 5. Automation - Economic aspects - Germany, West. I. Rimele-Petzold, Ursula. II. Germany (West). Bundesministerium für Bildung und Wissenschaft. III. Series.
HD6149 .F719 1986

Frauen und neue Technologien / Marliese Dobberthien ... [et al. ; Redaktion, Hansgeorg Loebel und Petra Francke]. Hannover : Niedersächsische Landeszentrale für Politische Bildung, 1986. 112 p. ; 21 cm. Includes bibliographies. CONTENTS. - Die neuen Technologien, eine Herausforderung für die Frauen / Rita Süssmuth -- Ingenieurinnen, Amazonen der Technik? / Hedwig Rudolph -- Neue Techniken, Risiken oder neue Chancen für die Frauen in der Arbeitswelt? / Helga Herrmann -- Förderung der Frauen im Berufsleben / Ina Schmid-Jörg -- Neue Techniken und Arbeitsbedingungen / Marliese Dobberthien -- Neue Techniken, neue Arbeitsplätze / Eva Fasching. LC Card 87-407392 DDC 331.4/0943 19
1. Women - Employment - Germany (West) - Effect of technological innovations on. 2. Women white collar workers - Germany (West) - Effect of technological innovations on. 3. Automation - Social aspects - Germany, West. I. Dobberthien, Marliese. II. Loebel, Hansgeorg. III. Francke, Petra. IV. Niedersächsische Landeszentrale für Politische Bildung.
HD6059.G3 F74 1986

Frauenalltag in Männerberufen /. Maindok, Herlinde, 1948- Frankfurt am Main , 1987. 173, [2] p. ; ISBN 3-596-23786-6 LC Card 87-164114 DDC 331.4/81 19
HD6060.6 .M35 1987

Frauenarbeit in der Industrie . Hallensleben, Ruth. Berlin-Kreuzberg , c1985. 157 p. : ISBN 3-88940-602-5 : LC Card 86-201457
HD6149 .H27 1985

Fraumeni, Barbara M., 1949- Jorgenson, Dale Weldeau, 1933- Productivity and U. S. economic growth /. Cambridge, Mass. , 1987. 567 p. : ISBN 0-674-71175-0 (alk. paper) LC Card 87-12098 DDC 338/.06/0973 19
HC110.I52 J67 1987

Fraunhofer-Institut für Produktionstechnik und Automatisierung. Bendeich, E. (Eugen), 1945- Wirtschaftliche Datenerfassung in Klein- und Mittelbetrieben . München , c1979. 211 p. : ISBN 3-478-41740-6 LC Card 85-171162
HD62.7 .B4 1979

Frazer, Charles F. Patti, Charles H. Advertising . Chicago , c1988. xxxi, 590 p. : ISBN 0-03-071687-X LC Card 87-6898 DDC 659.1/11 19
HF5821 .P27 1988

Frazer, P. A. T. Plastic and electronic money : new payment systems and their implications / Patrick Frazer. Cambridge [Cambridgeshire] ; Dover, NH. USA : Woodhead-Faulkner, 1985. x, 294 p. ; 24 cm. Includes index. Bibliography: p. [283]-285. ISBN 0-85941-290-3 : LC Card 85-22552 DDC 332.1/028 19
1. Electronic funds transfers - Great Britain. 2. Credit cards - Great Britain. 3. Banks and banking - Great Britain. 4. Payment - Great Britain. I. Title.
HG1710 .F73 1985 ***NYPL [JLE 86-1401]***

Frazier, Gary L. Contemporary views on marketing practice /. Lexington, Mass. , c1987. vi, 282 p. : ISBN 0-669-15120-3 (alk. paper) LC Card 86-46218 DDC 658.8 19
HF5411 .C66 1987

FREC brokers course. Real estate appraisal, finance, investment, and business management . [Tallahassee] , c1986. ix, 441, iv, 86 p. : LC Card 87-159867 DDC 333.33 19
HD1375 .R375 1986

Freches, José. La guerre des images / José Frèches. Paris : Denoël, c1986. 173 p. : ill. ; 23 cm. Includes bibliographical references. ISBN 2-207-23215-8 : LC Card 86-141723
1. Television industry - France. 2. Television broadcasting - France. I. Title.
HE8700.9.F7 F77 1986

Fred och säkerhet : debatt och analys 1982-83 / Bo Huldt och Erik Holm (red). [Stockholm] : Akademilitteratur : Utrikespolitiska institutet, c1983. 385 p. : ill. ; 22 cm. Includes bibliographical references. ISBN 91-7410-249-4 : LC Card 83-229846
1. Peace - Addresses, essays, lectures. 2. Security, International - Addresses, essays, lectures. 3. International relations - Addresses, essays, lectures. 4. European federation - Addresses, essays, lectures. I. Huldt, Bo, 1941-. II. Holm, Erik, 1919-.
JX1963 .F817 1983 ***NYPL [JLD 84-2639]***

Frederick Billings, Vermonter, pioneer lawyer, business man, conservationist . Curtis, Jane, 1918- Woodstock, VT , c1986. 135 p. : ISBN 0-930985-04-4 (pbk.) : LC Card 86-28103 DDC 385/.092/4 B 19
HE2754.B5 C87 1986

Frederick, William Crittenden, 1925- Business and society : corporate strategy, public policy, ethics. 6th ed. / William C. Frederick, Keith Davis, James E. Post. New York : McGraw-Hill, c1988. xxvii, 626 p. : ill. ; 24 cm. (McGraw-Hill series in management) Davis's name appears first on the earlier editions. Bibliography: p. [608]-611. Includes indexes. ISBN 0-07-015561-5 : LC Card 87-21436 DDC 658.4/08 19
1. Industry - Social aspects. I. Davis, Keith, 1918-. II. Post, James E. III. Title.
HD60 .F72 1988

Fredersdorf, Hermann, 1924- Der Steuerrebell und seine Gewerkschaft : 30 Jahre Deutsche Steuer-Gewerkschaft, 1949-1979 / Hermann Fredersdorf. Wiesbaden : Wirtschaftsverlag, c1982. 156 p., [3] folded leaves of plates : ill. ; 21 cm. (Schriftenreihe Verbände der Bundesrepublik Deutschland) ISBN 3-922114-02-4 LC Card 83-102197
1. Deutsche Steuer-Gewerkschaft - History. 2. Taxation - Germany, West - History. I. Title. II. Series.
HJ2690 .F78 1982

Frediani, Ramón O. El rol del empresario mediano en el desarrollo argentino : un caso particular, la pequeña y mediana industria / por Ramón Osvaldo Frediani. Buenos Aires, República Argentina : Centro Interdisciplinario de Estudios sobre el Desarrollo Latinoamericano, c1985. 123 p. : ill. ; 25 cm. (Serie Investigaciones externas) Bibliography: p. 117-123. LC Card 87-101993
1. Small business - Argentina. 2. Industrial promotion - Argentina. I. Title. II. Series.
HD2346.A73 F73 1985

Fredriksson, Carl, 1947- Kooperationens industrisektor i 1980-talets industri-Sverige : en analys av historisk utveckling, nuläge och framtidsutsikter / av Carl Fredriksson och Sten Ljunggren, för Kooperationsutredningen. [Stockholm] : Industridepartementet : LiberFörlag, [1981] iv, 196, 24, 11 p. : ill. ; 21 cm. "Ds I 1981:12." ISBN 91-38-06535-5 LC Card 83-147552
1. Cooperation - Sweden. 2. Cooperative societies - Sweden. I. Ljunggren, Sten. II. Sweden. Kooperationsutredningen.
HD3522 .F74 1981

Free airline tickets-- worldwide!! . Ross, H. Edward. St. Paul, Minn., U. S.A. , c1986. 154 p. ; ISBN 0-9616129-0-8 (pbk.) LC Card 87-117304 DDC 387.7/1 19
HE9783.5 .R67 1986

Free banking: Money supply under competitive note issue. Selgin, George A., 1957- The theory of free banking . Totowa, N.J. , c1987. p. cm. ISBN 0-8476-7578-5 : LC Card 87-20012 DDC 332.4 19
HG1586 .S38 1987

FREE CHOICE OF EMPLOYMENT - GERMANY, WEST.
Mueller, H. Dieter (Heinz Dieter), 1952- Berufswahlfreiheit und Kultur . München , c1986. 276, [46] p. ; ISBN 3-89019-166-5 LC Card 87-124783 DDC 331.11/72/0943 19
HD4903.5.G4 M84 1986

FREE COINAGE. see **CURRENCY QUESTION.**

FREE ENTERPRISE. see **LAISSEZ-FAIRE.**

Free Europe Committee. Radio Free Europe. see **Radio Free Europe.**

Free Europe Committee. Szabad Európa Rádió. see **Radio Free Europe.**

Free money for small businesses and entrepreneurs /. Blum, Laurie. New York , c1988. ix, 229 p. ; ISBN 0-471-85803-X : LC Card 87-20978 DDC 658.1/5224 19
HG4027.7 .B58 1988

FREE PORTS AND ZONES - CHILE - IQUIQUE.
González M., Sergio (González Miranda) ZOFRI, un enclave comercial /. Iquique, Chile [1985] 38, [2] p. ; LC Card 86-167491
HF1418 .G66 1985

FREE PORTS AND ZONES - CHINA.
Guide to China's foreign economic relations and trade. Cities newly opened to foreign investors /. Hong Kong , 1985. 385 p. : ISBN 962-7063-19-3 ***NYPL [*OVY 86-3400]***

Oborne, Michael West. China's special economic zones /. Paris [Washington, D.C.] 1986. 185 p. : ISBN 92-64-12801-8 (pbk.) : LC Card 86-217671 DDC 338.6/042/0951 19
HC427.92 .O27 1986

FREE PORTS AND ZONES - COLOMBIA - CONGRESSES.
Régimen de zonas francas en Colombia. Bogotá , 1984. 157 leaves ; LC Card 86-185156
HF1418 .R44 1984

FREE PORTS AND ZONES - LATIN AMERICA - CONGRESSES.
Conferenza internazionale sul tema Le zone franche industriali, nuove forme di investimento, l'America latina (1985 : Milan, Italy) Le zone franche industriali nei paesi emergenti . Milano, Italy , c1986. 207 p. ; LC Card 86-223193
HF1418 .C525 1985

FREE PORTS AND ZONES - LAW AND LEGISLATION - COLOMBIA.
Régimen de zonas francas en Colombia. Bogotá , 1984. 157 leaves ; LC Card 86-185156
HF1418 .R44 1984

Free State Agricultural Union (South Africa) 1985-bedryfskongresse =. [South Africa] [1985?] 1 v. (various pagings) ; LC Card 85-206777
HD9017.S72 A14 1985

Free to lose . Roemer, John E. Cambridge, Mass. , 1988. p. cm. ISBN 0-674-31875-7 (alk. paper) LC Card 87-12121 DDC 335.4/12 19
HB97.5 .R6167 1988

FREE TRADE AND PROTECTION - CONGRESSES.
Confrontation or negotiation . Millwood, N.Y. , 1985. xvi, 303 p. : ISBN 0-8046-9397-8 : LC Card 85-18667 DDC 382/.41/094 19
HD9015.E82 C67 1985
NYPL [JLE 86-4594]

Free trade in the world economy . Boulder , 1987. p. cm. ISBN 0-8133-0596-9 LC Card 87-20148 DDC 382.7/1 19
HF1703 .F74 1987

Der Neue Protektionismus /. Hamburg , 1984. 149 p. ; ISBN 3-87895-251-1 LC Card 84-222112
HF1703 .N48 1984

FREE TRADE AND PROTECTION - EUROPEAN ECONOMIC COMMUNITY COUNTRIES - CONGRESSES.
Protektionismus in der Weltwirtschaft . Hamburg , 1984. viii, 147 p. ; ISBN 3-87895-253-8 LC Card 84-233895
HF1703 .P77 1984

FREE TRADE AND PROTECTION - FREE TRADE.
Barber, Clarence L., 1917- Manitoba's interest in and attitude towards a proposed Canada-United States free trade area . [Winnipeg , 1985] 35 leaves : LC Card 86-175828 DDC 382/.0971/073 19
HF1479 .B37 1985

Delfim Netto, Antônio. Só o político pode salvar o economista /. Rio de Janeiro , 1986. xvii, 146 p. ; LC Card 87-137681 DDC 338.981 19
HC187 .D565 1986

Dell, Edmund. The politics of economic interdependence /. New York , 1987. x, 268

p. ; ISBN 0-312-00526-1 : LC Card 86-31345 DDC 337 19
HF1411 .D332 1987

The Free trade papers /. Toronto , 1986. 1 [i.e. 50], 227 p. : ISBN 0-88862-972-9 LC Card 87-109310 DDC 382.7/1/0971 19
HF1479 .F74 1986

ÎUdanov, A. ÎU. (Andreĭ ÎUr′evich) Teorii "otkrytoĭ ėkonomiki," doktriny i deĭstvitel′nost′ /. Moskva , 1983. 190 p. ; LC Card 83-209639
HF1713 .I93 1983

Lawrence, Robert Z., 1949- Saving free trade . Washington, D.C. , c1986. xii, 132 p. ; ISBN 0-8157-5178-8 LC Card 86-14705 DDC 382.7/1/0973 19
HF1455 .L39 1986 ***NYPL [JLE 86-4368]***

FREE TRADE AND PROTECTION - FREE TRADE - CASE STUDIES.
Kaplan, Daniel P. Has trade protection revitalized domestic industries? Washington, D.C. [1986] xvi, 111 p. : LC Card 86-603423 DDC 382.7/3/0973 19
HF1421 .K36 1986

FREE TRADE AND PROTECTION - FREE TRADE - CONGRESSES.
Building a Canadian-American free trade area /. Washington, D.C. , c1987. xii, 217 p. ; ISBN 0-8157-2973-1 (pbk.) LC Card 87-71507 DDC 382/.0971/073 19
HF1480.15.U5 B85 1987

FREE TRADE AND PROTECTION - FREE TRADE - ECONOMETRIC MODELS.
Coloma C., Fernando. Algunas consideraciones sobre los efectos distributivos del proceso de liberalización comercial /. Santiago , 1982. 31 leaves ; LC Card 87-102072
HF1713 .C617 1982

FREE TRADE AND PROTECTION - FREE TRADE - MATHEMATICAL MODELS.
Sánchez Holguín, Carlos Gerardo, 1952- Einige reale Aspekte der Aussenhandelsliberalisierung in Entwicklungsländern /. München , c1986. 152 p. : ISBN 3-88259-368-7 LC Card 86-156293
HF2580.9 .S25 1986

FREE TRADE AND PROTECTION - HISTORY - 19TH CENTURY.
Forster, Jakob Johann Benjamin. A conjunction of interests . Toronto , Buffalo , c1986. vi, 288 p. ; ISBN 0-8020-5680-6 (alk. paper) LC Card 87-108915 DDC 382.7/0971 19
HF1765 .F67 1986

FREE TRADE AND PROTECTION - PROTECTION.
Anderson, Kym. Australian protectionism . Sydney , Boston , 1987. xii, 160 p. : ISBN 0-04-330383-8 (pbk.) LC Card 86-47990 DDC 382.7/3/0994 19
HF1625 .A53 1987

Banks, Gary. Economic policy and the adjustment problem /. Aldershot, Hants., England , Brookfield, Vt. , 1986. x, 101 p. ; ISBN 0-566-05332-2 : LC Card 86-14934 DDC 338.9 19
HF1421 .B36 1987
NYPL [JLL 74-802 no.45]

Hodin, Michael W. A national policy for organized free trade . New York , 1987. 481 p. ; ISBN 0-8240-8085-8 (alk. paper) : LC Card 87-23719 DDC 382/.45669142/0973 19
HD9515 .H59 1987

Jaeschke, Hans-Dieter. Nicht-tarifäre Instrumente der Agrarhandelspolitik . Münster-Hiltrup , 1986. 187 p. ; ISBN 3-7843-0326-9 LC Card 87-408954 DDC 382/.3 19
HD9000.5 .J33 1986

Kate, Adriaan ten. La política de protección en el desarrollo económico de México /. México , 1979. 376 p. ; ISBN 968-16-0352-4 LC Card 87-672671
HF1775 .K37x 1979

Lejavitzer, Moisés. Los efectos del neoproteccionismo en América Latina /. México, D.F. , 1983. i, 231 p. ; LC Card 85-149154 DDC 382.7/3/098 19
HF3230.5.Z5 L45 1983 ***NYPL [JLD 86-434]***

Luedde-Neurath, Richard. Import controls and export-oriented development . Boulder , 1986. xiv, 249 p. ; ISBN 0-8133-7080-9 : LC Card 85-10459 DDC 382/.3/095195 19
HF1602.5 .L84 1985 ***NYPL [JLE 86-1557]***

Nestone, Alberto. Protektionismus . München , c1984. 76 p. : ISBN 3-89019-108-8 LC Card 85-127389
HF1713 .N38 1984

Der Neue Protektionismus . Bonn , c1983. 195 p. : ISBN 3-87831-370-5 LC Card 83-198686
HF1756 .N58 1983

Protectionism in the European community against Brazilian exports . Brasília , 1985. 125 p. ; LC Card 86-119107 DDC 382.7/3/094 19
HF3499.5.Z7 B76 1985

Putting America first . Washington, D.C. , c1987. 87 p. ; ISBN 0-944468-00-4 (pbk.) : LC Card 87-50998 DDC 382/.3/0973 19
HF1455 .P87 1987

Vargish, George. What's made in the U. S.A.? /. New Brunswick, U. S.A. , c1988. 160 p. : ISBN 0-88738-187-1 LC Card 87-19164 DDC 382/.3/0973 19
HF1716 .V37 1988

FREE TRADE AND PROTECTION - PROTECTION - CONGRESSES.
Protektionismus in der Weltwirtschaft . Hamburg , 1984. viii, 147 p. ; ISBN 3-87895-253-8 LC Card 84-233895
HF1703 .P77 1984

FREE TRADE AND PROTECTION - PROTECTION - ECONOMETRIC MODELS.
The Protectionist threat . Philadelphia, PA (3624 Science Center, Philadelphia 19104) , c1985. 85 p. : LC Card 87-106782 DDC 382.7/3/0973 19
HF1716 .P76 1985

FREE TRADE AND PROTECTION - PROTECTION - HISTORY.
Olnek, Jay I. The invisible hand . Riverdale, N.Y. , c1984. 176 p. : ISBN 0-938538-01-2 LC Card 82-24634 DDC 382.7/1/0973 19
HF1455 .O49 1984 ***NYPL [JLE 87-21]***

FREE TRADE AND PROTECTION - PROTECTION - HISTORY - 20TH CENTURY.
Lieberman, Sima, 1927- The economic and political roots of the new protectionism /. Totowa, N.J. , 1987. p. cm. ISBN 0-8476-7595-5 LC Card 87-23329 DDC 382.7/3/09048 19
HF1411 .L533 1987

FREE TRADE AND PROTECTION - PROTECTION - MATHEMATICAL MODELS.
Aedo, Cristián. Protección efectiva en Chile, 1974-1979 /. Santiago [1984] 56 leaves ; LC Card 85-152465
HF1956 .A35 1984

FREE TRADE AREAS. see **CUSTOMS UNIONS.**

Free trade in the world economy : towards an opening of markets / edited by Herbert Giersch. Boulder : Westview Press, 1987. p. cm. (Publications of the Institute of World Economics, University of Kiel) Papers presented at an international symposium sponsored by the Kiel Institute of World Economics. ISBN 0-8133-0596-9 LC Card 87-20148 DDC 382.7/1 19
1. Free trade and protection - Congresses. 2. Commercial policy - Congresses. I. Giersch, Herbert. II. Universität Kiel. Institut für Weltwirtschaft. III. Series.
HF1703 .F74 1987

The Free trade papers / edited by Duncan Cameron. Toronto : J. Lorimer, 1986. 1 [i.e. 50], 227 p. : ill. ; 24 cm. Bibliography: p. [218] Includes index. ISBN 0-88862-972-9 LC Card 87-109310 DDC 382.7/1/0971 19
1. Canada - Commercial policy. 2. United States - Commercial policy. 3. Tariff - Canada. 4. Tariff - United States. 5. Free trade and protection - Free trade. I. Cameron, Duncan, 1944-.
HF1479 .F74 1986

Freedman, Audrey. Perspectives on employment / by Audrey Freedman. New York, N.Y. (845 3rd Ave., New York 10022) : Conference Board, c1986. 15 p. : ill. ; 28 cm. (Research bulletin / The Conference Board . no. 194) "Human Resources Program." A shorter, English version of a paper delivered at the International Seminar on Employment held in Paris, Oct. 23, 1985. Includes bibliographical references. LC Card 86-212384 DDC 331.12 19
1. Employment forecasting - Congresses. 2. Labor supply - Effect of technological innovations on - Congresses. I. Human Resources Program (Conference Board). II. Series: Research bulletin (Conference Board) , no. 194. III. Title.
HD5701.3 .F74 1986

Freedman, Charles. Monetary aggregates as targets : some theoretical aspects / by Charles Freedman. [Ottawa] : Bank of Canada, 1981. vii, 49 p. ; 28 cm. (Technical reports / Bank of Canada = Rapports techniques / Banque du Canada . 27) Caption title. Summary in English and French. Bibliography: p. 45-49. LC Card 81-198954 DDC 332.4/6/0724 19
1. Monetary policy - Mathematical models. 2. Money supply - Mathematical models. I. Series: Bank of Canada. Technical reports , 27. II. Title.
HG230.3 .F74 1981
NYPL [JLM 75-1420 no.27]

Freedman, Roy S. Programming with APSE software tools / Roy S. Freedman. Princeton, N.J. : Petrocelli Books, c1984. viii, 253 p. : ill. ; 24 cm. Includes index. Bibliography: p. 223-227. ISBN 0-89433-220-1 LC Card 84-20739 DDC 001.64/24 19
1. Ada (Computer program language). 2. Electronic digital computers - Programming. I. Title. II. Title: Programming with A.P.S.E. software tools.
QA76.73.A35 F74 1984
NYPL [JSE 86-1512]

FREEDOM. see **LIBERTY.**

Freedom and control in a democratic society / edited by Howard R. Bowen. New York : American Council of Life Insurance, c1976. 107 p. ; 23 cm. Report of a conference held at Harriman, N. Y., June 2-4, 1976, ... sponsored by the Graduate School of Business, Columbia University and the American Council of Life Insurance.
1. Liberty - Congresses. 2. Democracy - Congresses. I. Bowen, Howard Rothmann, 1908-.
NYPL [JLD 80-3590]

Freedom & co-ordination . Follett, Mary Parker, 1868-1933. New York , 1987. xvii, 89 p. ; ISBN 0-8240-8229-X (alk. paper) : LC Card 86-27079 DDC 658.4/092 19
HD57.7 .F66 1987

Freedom and co-ordination. Follett, Mary Parker, 1868-1933. Freedom & co-ordination . New York , 1987. xvii, 89 p. ; ISBN 0-8240-8229-X (alk. paper) : LC Card 86-27079 DDC 658.4/092 19
HD57.7 .F66 1987

Freedom and fairness : empowering people at work / edited by Ken Coates ; with contributions from Stephen Bodington ... [et al] ; foreword by John Prescott. Nottingham, England : Spokesman, for the Institute for Workers' Control ; Atlantic Highlands, N.J. : Distributed in the U. S.A. and Canada by Humanities Press, 1986. 157 p. ; 23 cm. Distributor from label on t.p. ISBN 0-85124-440-8 LC Card 86-28038 DDC 331.88/0942 19
1. Trade-unions - Great Britain. 2. Industrial relations - Great Britain. I. Coates, Ken.
HD6664 .F763 1986

Freedom in the grave . Heinecke, P. [Zaria, Nigeria] [1985] 178 p. ; LC Card 86-153310 DDC 337.66906 19
HC1055 .H45 1985

FREEDOM OF EMPLOYMENT. see **FREE CHOICE OF EMPLOYMENT.**

FREEDOM OF INFORMATION - UNITED STATES.
O'Reilly, James T., 1947- Unions' rights to company information /. Philadelphia, Pa. , c1987. xiii, 312 p. ; ISBN 0-89546-060-2 LC Card 85-82257 ***NYPL [JLL 74-174 no.21]***

FREEDOM OF OCCUPATION. see **FREE CHOICE OF EMPLOYMENT.**

FREEDOM OF THE PRESS - BRAZIL - HISTORY - 19TH CENTURY.
Década republicana /. Brasília, Distrito Federal , c1986. 2 v. ; ISBN 85-23-00062-3 (set) LC Card 86-211423
HJ923 .D38 1986

FREEDOM OF THE SEAS.
Sea lane security studies . Taipei, Taiwan, Republic of China , 1986. 100 p. ; LC Card

87-133640 DDC 359/.03 19
HE327 .S435 1986

FREEHOLD. see **REAL PROPERTY; LAND TENURE.**

Freeman, Anthony G. Black labor unions in South Africa . Washington, D.C. , 1987. vi, 63 p. ; LC Card 86-600599 DDC 331.6/9/968 19
HD6870.5 .B53 1987

Freeman, Christopher.
Design, innovation, and long cycles in economic development /. London , 1986. 248 p. : ISBN 0-86187-616-4
NYPL [JLE 86-3312]

Technical change and full employment /. Oxford, UK , New York, NY, USA , 1987. vii, 279 p. : ISBN 0-631-14099-9 : LC Card 87-6637 DDC 331.12/5/0941 19
HD6331.2.G7 T39 1987

Technology, policy, and economic performance : lessons from Japan / Christopher Freeman. London ; New York : Pinter Publishers, 1987. 155 p. : ill. ; 23 cm. Bibliography: p. 139-149. Includes index. ISBN 0-86187-928-7 : LC Card 87-18553 DDC 338.952 19
1. Technological innovations - Economic aspects - Japan. 2. Technology and state - Japan. 3. Japan - Economic conditions - 1945-. I. Title.
HC465.T4 F74 1987

Freeman, Elaine T. Taylor, John A. (John Alvin), 1930- U. S. imports of textile and apparel products under the multifiber arrangement, 1981-84 /. Washington, D.C. [1985] v, 136 p. ; LC Card 86-601665 DDC 382/.45677/00973021 19
HD9940.U4 T38 1985

Freeman, Richard Barry, 1943- The Black youth employment crisis /. Chicago , 1986. viii, 469 p. : ISBN 0-226-26164-6 LC Card 85-20989 DDC 331.3/46396073 19
HD6273 .B57 1986 *NYPL [JLE 86-3726]*

Freemantle, Brian. The steal : counterfeiting and industrial espionage / Brian Freemantle. London : M. Joseph, 1986. xi, 244 p. ; 23 cm. Bibliography: p. 235-236. Includes index. ISBN 0-7181-2584-3 : LC Card 87-105381 DDC 364.1/63 19
1. Product counterfeiting. 2. Business intelligence. I. Title.
HD38.7 .F74 1986

Freemantle, David. Superboss : the A-Z of managing people successfully / David Freemantle. Brookfield, Vt. : Wildwood House : Gower, 1987, c1985. p. cm. ISBN 0-7045-0551-7 (pbk.) : LC Card 87-19089 DDC 658.3 19
1. Personnel management. I. Title.
HF5549 .F697 1987

Frei, Gertrud, 1952- Büttler, Hans-Jürgen. Estimation of disequilibrium models /. Berlin , New York , c1986. vi, 114 p. : ISBN 0-387-16817-6 (U. S.) : LC Card 86-22073 DDC 339.5 19
HB145 .B88 1986
NYPL [JLM 72-289 v.279]

Freiberg, Robert. Taetzsch, Lyn. Taking charge on the job . New York , c1978. 144 p. ; ISBN 0-917386-22-1 : LC Card 78-111025 DDC 658.4
HD38 .T17 *NYPL [JLE 80-1910]*

Freiburg i. B. Arnold-Bergstraesser-Institut für kulturwissenschaftliche Forschung. (Old Catalog form: Arnold-Bergstraesser-Institut für Kulturwissenschaftliche Forschung, Freiburg im Breisgau, Germany.)
Bruchhaus, Eva-Maria. Frauen in Entwicklungsländern . Freiburg im Breisgau , 1979. iii, 182 p. ; LC Card 81-121677 DDC 305.4/09172/4 19
HQ1870.9 .B78 1979 *NYPL [JLG 86-106]*

Freiburg i. B. Universität. Institut für Allgemeine Wirtschaftsforschung. Schriftenreihe.
(Bd. 16) Sell, Friedrich L. Der Konsumcharakter der Einkommensentstehung . Freiburg im Breisgau , c1982. 221 p. : ISBN 3-448-01269-6 LC Card 82-233541 DDC 339.4/7/0724 19
HB820 .S44 1982 *NYPL [JLD 87-1580]*

Freiburg i. B. Walter Eucken Institut. see **Walter Eucken Institut.**

FREIBURG IM BREISGAU (GERMANY) - ECONOMIC CONDITIONS - SOURCES.
Die Freiburger Enquete von 1476 . Freiburg im Breisgau , c1986. xxxiv, 102 p. : ISBN 3-923272-20-2 LC Card 87-409559 DDC 330.943/46 19
HC289.F855 F74 1986

FREIBURG IM BREISGAU (GERMANY) - POLITICS AND GOVERNMENT - SOURCES.
Die Freiburger Enquete von 1476 . Freiburg im Breisgau , c1986. xxxiv, 102 p. : ISBN 3-923272-20-2 LC Card 87-409559 DDC 330.943/46 19
HC289.F855 F74 1986

Die Freiburger Enquete von 1476 : Quellen zur Wirtschafts- und Verwaltungsgeschichte der Stadt Freiburg im Breisgau im fünfzehnten Jahrhundert / bearbeitet von Tom Scott. Freiburg im Breisgau : Verlag Stadtarchiv Freiburg im Breisgau, c1986. xxxiv, 102 p. : ill. (one col.), facsims. ; 23 cm. (Veröffentlichungen aus dem Archiv der Stadt Freiburg im Breisgau . 20) Contains report by Johannes Gottschalk, city scribe of Freiburg im Breisgau, and related documents in Middle High German. Bibliography: p. 96-100. Includes index. ISBN 3-923272-20-2 LC Card 87-409559 DDC 330.943/46 19
1. Freiburg im Breisgau (Germany) - Economic conditions - Sources. 2. Freiburg im Breisgau (Germany) - Politics and government - Sources. I. Scott, Tom, 1947-. II. Gottschalk, Johannes. III. Series.
HC289.F855 F74 1986

Freiburger Studien zur Verteilung von Einkommen und Vermögen .
(Bd. 2) Lüthi, Ambros, 1938- Die wirtschaftliche Ungleichheit im Rentenalter in der Schweiz /. Freiburg/Schweiz , 1983. 229 p. : ISBN 3-7278-0282-0 : LC Card 83-163287
HD7105.35.S9 L87 1983

(Bd. 3) Meier, Christoph. Lebenszyklus und ökonomische Ungleichheit . Freiburg, Schweiz , 1983. 235 p. : ISBN 3-7278-0298-7 : LC Card 83-244050
HB601 .M389 1983

Freie Universität Berlin. Fachbereich 10--Wirtschaftswissenschaft. Ehrenpromotion von Prof. Dr. George Katona, Ann Arbor, Michigan am 15. Juni 1981 . Berlin [1982] 51 p. : LC Card 83-200933
HB74.P8 E35 1982

Freier Deutscher Gewerkschaftsbund. Gewerkschaftshochschule "Fritz Heckert." see **Gewerkschaftshochschule "Fritz Heckert. "**

FREIER DEUTSCHER GEWERKSCHAFTSBUND - HISTORY - CHRONOLOGY.
Geschichte des FDGB . Berlin , c1985. 364 p. ; LC Card 86-124681 DDC 331.88/0943 19
HD8460.5.A5 F7326 1985

FREIGHT, AIR. see **AERONAUTICS, COMMERCIAL - FREIGHT.**

FREIGHT AND FREIGHTAGE.
Koch, Hasso B. Funktions- und Sozialstrukturen auf Containerschiffen /. Frankfurt am Main , New York , c1986. vi, 542 p. : ISBN 3-8204-9334-4 LC Card 86-194048
HE566.C6 K63 1986

FREIGHT AND FREIGHTAGE - BRAZIL - RATES.
Sanson, João Rogério. A política de transportes marítimos no Brasil . Rio de Janeiro , 1986. vii, 178, 5 p. : LC Card 87-403931 DDC 387.5/44/0981 19
HE597.B7 S26 1986

FREIGHT AND FREIGHTAGE - CANADA.
Brouillette, Benoît, 1904-1979. [Perspectives de changements dans la manutention des marchandises aux ports canadiens. English.] Prospective changes for handling of commodities in Canadian ports. Montréal, Québec, Canada [1974] iv, 93, [3] p. ; LC Card 82-219246
HE553 .B7613 1974

FREIGHT AND FREIGHTAGE - DEVELOPING COUNTRIES - CONGRESSES.
Il Sistema dei trasporti nello sviluppo della cooperazione economica internazionale . Milano, Italy , c1985. 341 p. ; LC Card 85-218403
HE2449 .S57 1985

FREIGHT AND FREIGHTAGE - EUROPE - CONGRESSES.
International traffic and infrastructural needs. Paris, France [Washington, D.C.] c1986. 92 p. : ISBN 92-821-1111-3 (pbk.) : LC Card 87-167959 DDC 380.5/24/094 19
HE199.E85 I58 1986

FREIGHT AND FREIGHTAGE - EUROPEAN ECONOMIC COMMUNITY COUNTRIES - CONGRESSES.
Il Sistema dei trasporti nello sviluppo della cooperazione economica internazionale . Milano, Italy , c1985. 341 p. ; LC Card 85-218403
HE2449 .S57 1985

FREIGHT AND FREIGHTAGE - GERMANY (WEST) - COST CONTROL.
Eckstein, Werner E. Kooperative Systembildung in der Transportwirtschaft . Karlsruhe , c1985. vii, 263 p. : ISBN 3-88652-028-5 LC Card 86-135639
HE199.G3 E28 1985

FREIGHT AND FREIGHTAGE - GERMANY (WEST) - HAIGER - COSTS - CASE STUDIES.
Brauer, Karl M. Fallstudie Haiger . Berlin , c1983. 55 p. ; ISBN 3-428-05403-2 LC Card 83-233201
HE199.G3 B73 1983

FREIGHT AND FREIGHTAGE - GOVERNMENT POLICY - EUROPE - CONGRESSES.
International traffic and infrastructural needs. Paris, France [Washington, D.C.] c1986. 92 p. : ISBN 92-821-1111-3 (pbk.) : LC Card 87-167959 DDC 380.5/24/094 19
HE199.E85 I58 1986

FREIGHT AND FREIGHTAGE - GOVERNMENT POLICY - EUROPEAN ECONOMIC COMMUNITY COUNTRIES.
Mackie, Peter J., 1947- The British transport industry and the European Community . Aldershot, Hampshire, England , Brookfield, Vt., U. S.A. , c1987. xvi, 184 p. : ISBN 0-566-05368-3 : LC Card 86-24186 DDC 380.5/24/0941 19
HE199.G5 M33 1987

FREIGHT AND FREIGHTAGE - GOVERNMENT POLICY - GREAT BRITAIN.
Mackie, Peter J., 1947- The British transport industry and the European Community . Aldershot, Hampshire, England , Brookfield, Vt., U. S.A. , c1987. xvi, 184 p. : ISBN 0-566-05368-3 : LC Card 86-24186 DDC 380.5/24/0941 19
HE199.G5 M33 1987

FREIGHT AND FREIGHTAGE - GREAT BRITAIN.
Mackie, Peter J., 1947- The British transport industry and the European Community . Aldershot, Hampshire, England , Brookfield, Vt., U. S.A. , c1987. xvi, 184 p. : ISBN 0-566-05368-3 : LC Card 86-24186 DDC 380.5/24/0941 19
HE199.G5 M33 1987

FREIGHT AND FREIGHTAGE - ITALY - CONGRESSES.
Il Sistema dei trasporti nello sviluppo della cooperazione economica internazionale . Milano, Italy , c1985. 341 p. ; LC Card 85-218403
HE2449 .S57 1985

FREIGHT AND FREIGHTAGE - ITALY - LIGURIA.
Vallega, Adalberto. Dai porti al sistema portuale . Savona , 1985. 320 p. : LC Card 87-139096
HE558.L44 V35 1985

FREIGHT AND FREIGHTAGE - LINEAR PROGRAMMING - DATA PROCESSING.
Nakhla, Afaf Fouad. Update the transportation problem /. Cairo [1985- v. <1 > ; LC Card 87-401510 DDC 361.6/0962 s 380.5/24 19
HD82 .C23 no. 1415 HE199.A2

FREIGHT AND FREIGHTAGE - MANAGEMENT.
Bayliss, Brian T. The measurement of supply and demand in freight transport /. Aldershot,

Hants, England , Brookfield, USA , 1988. p. cm. ISBN 0-566-05526-0 : LC Card 87-19817 DDC 380.5/9 19
HE199.A2 B395 1988

FREIGHT AND FREIGHTAGE - MANAGEMENT - DATA PROCESSING.
Barrett, Colin. The practical handbook of computerization for distribution managers /. Washington , c1987. xvi, 317 p. ; ISBN 0-87408-040-1 LC Card 86-51299 DDC 658.7/8/0285 19
HF5415.7 .B36 1987

FREIGHT AND FREIGHTAGE - MATHEMATICAL MODELS.
Nakhla, Afaf Fouad. Update the transportation problem /. Cairo [1985- v. <1 > ; LC Card 87-401510 DDC 361.6/0962 s 380.5/24 19
HD82 .C23 no. 1415 HE199.A2

FREIGHT AND FREIGHTAGE - NIGERIA - KADUNA STATE.
Ogwude, Innocent C. (Innocent Chuka) Industrial demand for freight transport in Kaduna State /. Zaria [Nigeria] [1984] 101 p. : LC Card 86-152627 DDC 380.5/24/096695 19
HE287.7.Z7 K336 1984

FREIGHT AND FREIGHTAGE - POLAND.
Blotko, Kazimierz. Racjonalny podział przewozów ładunków między gałęzie transportu /. Warszawa , 1978. 126 p. ; LC Card 81-206824
HF5780.P7 B57 1978

FREIGHT AND FREIGHTAGE - SOVIET UNION.
Galaburda, V. G. Optimal′noe planirovanie gruzopotokov /. Moskva , 1985. 255 p. : LC Card 85-243810
HE2457 .G35 1985

Rakhovetskiĭ, A. N. (Anatoliĭ Nikolaevich) Operativnaia frakhtovaia deiatel′nost′ na morskom transporte /. Moskva , 1986. 159 p. : LC Card 86-115637
HE597.S615 R36 1986

FREIGHT AND FREIGHTAGE - SWEDEN.
Sverige och den internationella transportmarknaden . Stockholm [1983] 87 p. : ISBN 91-85402-64-8 : LC Card 83-223136
HE199.S77 S84 1983

FREIGHT AND FREIGHTAGE - UNITED STATES.
Barrett, Colin. Practical handbook of transportation contracting and rate negotiations /. Washington , c1987. ix, 269 p. ; ISBN 0-87408-037-1 LC Card 86-50988 DDC 380.5/24/068 19
HE199.U5 B37 1987

FREIGHT AND FREIGHTAGE - UNITED STATES - COSTS.
Farley, H. W. Cheaper transportation . Yorkville, Ill. , 1874. 10 p. ; LC Card 85-665909
HE199.U6 F3x 1874

FREIGHT AND FREIGHTAGE - UNITED STATES - RATES.
NASSTRAC's 1986 small shipments and parcels guidelines to the cost-effective selection of UPS/USPS/LTL domestic ground services (and other services). Washington, D.C. (1750 Pa. Ave., NW, Suite 1105, Washington 20006-4502) , 1986. 82 p. : LC Card 87-127320 DDC 380.5/24/0973 19
HE597.U6 N37 1986

FREIGHT FORWARDERS - GERMANY, WEST.
Seiffert, Bernd. Zahlungsmittelbewirtschaftung im Verkehrsbetrieb /. Berlin , c1986. 187 p. : ISBN 3-428-06094-6 : LC Card 87-143799 DDC 380.5/24/0943 19
HE5999.Z7 G374 1986

FREIGHT FORWARDERS - GERMANY (WEST) - RUHR RIVER.
Tress, Roland. Das Güterverkehrszentrum als infrastrukturelle Schnittstelle des Güterverkehrs /. Düsseldorf , 1984. xv, 288 p. : LC Card 86-140143
HE5 .C6 Nr. 45 HE5999.Z7G2

FREIGHT FORWARDERS - POLAND.
Marciniak-Neider, Danuta. Spedycja lądowa /. Gdańsk , 1979- v. <1 > ; LC Card 81-181249
HF5780.P7 M37 1979

FREIGHT FORWARDERS - RHINE RIVER.
Tress, Roland. Das Güterverkehrszentrum als infrastrukturelle Schnittstelle des Güterverkehrs /. Düsseldorf , 1984. xv, 288 p. : LC Card 86-140143
HE5 .C6 Nr. 45 HE5999.Z7G2

FREIGHT HANDLING. see **FREIGHT AND FREIGHTAGE.**

The freight rate structure on Soviet railroads /. Sagers, Matthew J. Washington, D.C. [1985] vii, 28 p. : LC Card 87-601285 DDC 385/.12/0947 19
HE1895 .S25 1985

FREIGHT RATES. see **FREIGHT AND FREIGHTAGE.**

Freitäger, Jürgen, 1959- Erwerb und Verwendung des Einkommens von Arbeitnehmerhaushalten mit erwerbstätiger Ehefrau / Jürgen Freitäger. Frankfurt am Main ; New York : P. Lang, c1986. xix, 327 p. : ill. ; 21 cm. (Schriften zur Textilwirtschaft, 0463-7585 . Bd. 37) Bibliography: p. 322-327. ISBN 3-8204-9148-1 : LC Card 86-195223
1. Married women - Employment - Germany (West). 2. Work and family - Germany (West). 3. Income - Germany, West. I. Title. II. Series.
HD9850.1 .M58 Bd. 37 HD6055.2.G3

Freitas, Benedicto. Santa Cruz : fazenda jesuítica, real, imperial / Benedicto Freitas. Rio de Janeiro : [s.n.], 1985-1987. 3 v. : ill ; 21 cm. Bibliography: v. 3, p. 643-645. CONTENTS. - v. 1. Era jesuítica, 1567-1759 -- v. 2. Vice reino e reinado, 1760-1821 -- v. 3. Império, 1822-1889. LC Card 86-225964
1. Santa Cruz Fazenda (Brazil) - History. 2. Jesuits - Missions - Brazil - Rio de Janeiro - History. I. Title.
HD1471.B72 R564 1985

Freizeit als Gegenstand der Politik . Mikolaschek, Cornelia. Frankfurt [am Main] , New York , c1984. 202 p. : ISBN 3-593-33346-5 LC Card 84-175844
HD7395.R4 M55 1984

Freizeitraum Oberstaufen . Maier, Jörg. München , 1976. xii, 92 p. : ISBN 3-920397-13-4 LC Card 87-408421 DDC 330.94 380.1/45914337 19
HC281 .M84 Heft 13 G155.G3

Frejborg, Carl-Henrik. Ekholm, Bo-Göran. Skattetryckets fördelning inom finländska industriföretag /. Helsingfors [1985] 39 p. ; ISBN 951-555-222-2 LC Card 85-214497
HD2753.F5 E38 1985

Fremdarbeiterpolitik des Imperialismus . (Heft 8) Zur Haltung der herrschenden Klasse und der Arbeiterbewegung zur Beschäftigung ausländischer Arbeiter. [Rostock] , 1980. 64 p. ; LC Card 82-209919 DDC 331.6/2/0943 19
HD8458.A2 Z87 1980 ***NYPL [JLD 87-143]***

Fremdarbeiterpolitik des Imperialismus, 0138-3396 . (Heft 10-13) Arbeiterwanderungen, Ausländerbeschäftigung und Ausländerpolitik in kapitalistischen Ländern Europas im 20. Jahrhundert. Rostock , 1981-1982. 4 v. ; LC Card 82-193086 DDC 331.6/2/094 19
HD8438.A2 A75 1982 ***NYPL [JLK 84-95]***

Der Fremde bin ich selber . Schmidt, Aurel, 1935- Basel , c1982. 261 p. : ISBN 3-85787-103-2 : LC Card 83-109021
HC79.E5 S284 1982

Das Fremdkapital im Unternehmen als Insolvenzursache und die Möglichkeiten rechtlicher Steuerung der Finanzierungsgrundlagen /. Esser, Carsten, 1960- Frankfurt am Main , New York , c1986. xvi, 131 p. (1 folded) ; ISBN 3-8204-9398-0 LC Card 86-229108
HG5501 .E85 1986

Fremdling, Rainer. Technologischer Wandel und internationaler Handel im 18. und 19. Jahrhundert : die Eisenindustrien in Grossbritannien, Belgien, Frankreich und Deutschland / von Rainer Fremdling. Berlin : Duncker & Humblot, c1986. 493 p. ; 24 cm. (Schriften zur Wirtschafts- und Sozialgeschichte. Bd. 35) A revision of the author's Habilitationsschrift (Universität Münster, 1982) originally submitted under the title: Technologietransfer in der Eisenindustrie. Bibliography: p. [456]-485. Includes index. ISBN 3-428-06042-3 LC Card 87-127793 DDC 382/.456691/094 19
1. Iron industry and trade - Europe - History. 2. Iron industry and trade - Technological innovations - Europe - History. 3. Europe - Commerce - History. 4. Export marketing - Europe - History. I. Title.
HD9525.A2 F74 1986

Fremer, Miloslav. Hospodářský mechanismus fungování socialistické ekonomiky /. Praha , 1985. 238 p. ; LC Card 86-203712
HC704 .H65 1985

Fremlin, J. H.
Power production : what are the risks? / J.H. Fremlin. Bristol ; Boston : A. Hilger, c1985. x, 318 p. : ill. ; 24 cm. Includes index. Bibliography: p. 303-307. ISBN 0-85274-479-X : LC Card 85-115642 DDC 363.1/19621042/0941 19
1. Energy industries - Hygienic aspects - Great Britain. 2. Energy industries - Great Britain - Safety measures. I. Title.
HD7269.E472 G744 1985 ***NYPL [JLE 86-3055]***

Power production : what are the risks? / J.H. Fremlin. Oxford [Oxfordshire] ; New York : Oxford University Press, 1987. p. cm. Bibliography: p. Includes index. ISBN 0-19-286078-X (pbk.) : LC Card 87-1564 DDC 363.1/9621042/0941 19
1. Energy industries - Hygienic aspects - Great Britain. 2. Energy industries - Great Britain - Safety measures. I. Title.
HD7269.E472 G744 1987

French, Alexander. Traffic data collection and analysis : methods and procedures / Alexander French and David Solomon. Washington, D.C. : Transportation Research Board, National Research Council, [1986] 58 p. : ill. ; 28 cm. (Synthesis of highway practice, 0547-5570 . 130) "Research sponsored by the American Association of State Highway and Transportation Officials in cooperation with the Federal Highway Administration." "December 1986." Bibliography: p. 43-45. ISBN 0-309-04406-5 (pbk.) : LC Card 86-51174 DDC 388.3/14/072 19
1. Traffic surveys - Data processing. 2. Traffic surveys - Equipment and supplies. I. Solomon, David. II. American Association of State Highway and Transportation Officials. III. United States. Federal Highway Administration. IV. Title. V. Series.
HE369 .F68 1986

FRENCH-CANADIANS - QUÉBEC (PROVINCE) - ETHNIC IDENTITY - CASE STUDIES.
Caron, André H. Les télévisions étrangères . [Montréal] , 1983. ix, 166 p., 12 leaves : ISBN 2-920396-86-2 : LC Card 83-157210 DDC 302.2/345/09714 19
HE8700.9.C2 C37 1983
NYPL [MWGS 86-2473]

French Communist Party. see **Parti communiste français.**

French Industrial Development Agency. see **France. Délégation à l'aménagement du territoire et à l'action régionale.**

French industrial policy / William James Adams, Christian Stoffaës, editors. Washington, D.C. : Brookings Institution, c1986. xii, 228 p. : ill. ; 24 cm. Includes bibliographical references and index. ISBN 0-8157-0098-9 : LC Card 85-48203 DDC 338.944 19
1. Industry and state - France. 2. Industry and state - United States. I. Adams, William James, 1947-. II. Stoffaës, Christian, 1947-.
HD3616.F82 F74 1986 ***NYPL [JLE 87-211]***

FRENCH LANGUAGE - BUSINESS FRENCH - DICTIONARIES - ENGLISH.
Geoghegan, C., 1945- Handbook of commercial French /. London , New York , 1988. p. cm. ISBN 0-7102-0857-X LC Card 87-16320 DDC 448/.002465 19
HF5728.F8 G46 1988

FRENCH LANGUAGE - DICTIONARIES - ENGLISH.
European Communities glossary . Luxembourg , 1984. 1589 p. ; ISBN 92-824-0131-6 : LC Card 85-175527
KJE926.5 .E87 1984 ***NYPL [JLF 87-216]***

Glossary of terms . [Ottawa] [1981]-1984. 3 v. ; ISBN 0-662-52389-X (v. 2) LC Card 81-180363 DDC 350/.0003/41 19
JA61 .G55 ***NYPL [JLF 87-379]***

Harrap's new standard French and English dictionary /. London , 1980-1981. 4 v. ; ISBN 0-245-50972-0 (v.1)

Lebas, Michel. Glossary of accounting =.

Paris , c1985. 124 p. ; ISBN 2-86644-065-X (pbk.) : LC Card 86-179932
HF5621 .L42 1985

Marks, Georgette A. Harrap's slang dictionary English-French/French-English /. London , 1984. 476 p. ; ISBN 0-245-54047-4
NYPL [JFC 86-640]

Organisation for European Economic Co-operation. Terminologie des échanges et paiements internationaux et de la comptabilité nationale. Paris [1958] 146, [6] p. LC Card 58-47135 DDC 382.03
HF1002 .O7 ***NYPL [JLF 87-128]***

Thody, Philip Malcolm Waller, 1928- Faux amis & key words . London , 1985. 224 p. ; ISBN 0-485-11243-4 : LC Card 84-108125 DDC 443/.21 19
PC2593 .T45 1985 ***NYPL [JFD 86-5704]***

Thody, Philip Malcolm Waller, 1928- Mistakable French . New York , 1985. 224 p. ; ISBN 0-684-18324-2 : LC Card 84-51853 DDC 443/.21 19
PC2593 .T46 1985 ***NYPL [JFD 86-5781]***

Tixier, Maud. Dictionnaire américain-anglais-français du management /. Paris , 1985. 381 p. ; ISBN 2-247-00647-7 : LC Card 86-160705
HD30.15 .T59 1985 ***NYPL [JLD 86-3975]***

Witcomb, Henry, 1822- Dictionnaire des termes de marine français-anglais & anglais-français. Paris, 1883. 2 v. LC Card 29-23644
V24 .W5 ***NYPL [JSE 86-1965]***

FRENCH LANGUAGE - DICTIONARIES - GERMAN.
EG-Wörterverzeichnis . Luxembourg , 1984. 1 v. (various pagings) ; ISBN 92-824-0123-5 LC Card 85-131398
KJE926.5 .E35 1984 ***NYPL [JLF 86-1818]***

FRENCH LANGUAGE - DICTIONARIES - ITALIAN.
Emolumento, Vincenzo. Dizionario commerciale . Milano , 1983. 1150 p. ; ISBN 88-7075-068-X : LC Card 84-151136 DDC 380.1/03/41 19
HF1002 .E57 1983 ***NYPL [JLD 86-1323]***

FRENCH LANGUAGE - ERRORS OF USAGE.
Thody, Philip Malcolm Waller, 1928- Faux amis & key words . London , 1985. 224 p. ; ISBN 0-485-11243-4 : LC Card 84-108125 DDC 443/.21 19
PC2593 .T45 1985 ***NYPL [JFD 86-5704]***

Thody, Philip Malcolm Waller, 1928- Mistakable French . New York , 1985. 224 p. ; ISBN 0-684-18324-2 : LC Card 84-51853 DDC 443/.21 19
PC2593 .T46 1985 ***NYPL [JFD 86-5781]***

FRENCH LANGUAGE - PARONYMS - DICTIONARIES.
Thody, Philip Malcolm Waller, 1928- Faux amis & key words . London , 1985. 224 p. ; ISBN 0-485-11243-4 : LC Card 84-108125 DDC 443/.21 19
PC2593 .T45 1985 ***NYPL [JFD 86-5704]***

Thody, Philip Malcolm Waller, 1928- Mistakable French . New York , 1985. 224 p. ; ISBN 0-684-18324-2 : LC Card 84-51853 DDC 443/.21 19
PC2593 .T46 1985 ***NYPL [JFD 86-5781]***

FRENCH LANGUAGE - SEMANTICS.
Richelle Giampiccoli, Emma. La langue de l'économie, de la technique à la banalisation /. Torino [1983] 114 p. ; LC Card 84-141597
HB62 .R53 1983

FRENCH LANGUAGE - SLANG - DICTIONARIES.
Marks, Georgette A. Harrap's slang dictionary English-French/French-English /. London , 1984. 476 p. ; ISBN 0-245-54047-4
NYPL [JFC 86-640]

FRENCH LANGUAGE - SYNONYMS AND ANTONYMS - DICTIONARIES.
Thody, Philip Malcolm Waller, 1928- Faux amis & key words . London , 1985. 224 p. ; ISBN 0-485-11243-4 : LC Card 84-108125 DDC 443/.21 19
PC2593 .T45 1985 ***NYPL [JFD 86-5704]***

Thody, Philip Malcolm Waller, 1928- Mistakable French . New York , 1985. 224 p. ; ISBN 0-684-18324-2 : LC Card 84-51853 DDC 443/.21 19
PC2593 .T46 1985 ***NYPL [JFD 86-5781]***

The French market for U. S. seafood products /. Miller, Charlotte L. Terminal Island, CA , 1986. ii, 63 p. ; LC Card 86-602854 DDC 382/.4566494/0944 19
HD9462.5 .M54 1986

French notables . Beck, Thomas D. New York , c1987. 254 p. : ISBN 0-8204-0393-8 : LC Card 87-12156 DDC 338.0944 19
HC275 .B37 1987

FRENCH REVOLUTION. see **FRANCE - HISTORY - REVOLUTION, 1789-1799.**

The French socialists in power, 1981-1986 / edited by Patrick McCarthy with essays by D.S. Bell ... [et al.]. New York : Greenwood Press, c1987. xii, 212 p. ; 25 cm. (Contributions in political science, 0147-1066 . no. 174) Bibliography: p. [199]-204. Includes index. ISBN 0-313-25407-9 (lib. bdg. : alk. paper) LC Card 86-33569 DDC 338.944 19
1. France - Economic policy - 1945-. 2. France - Social policy - 1945-. 3. France - Politics and government - 1981-. 4. France. Parlement (1946-) - Elections, 1986. 5. Socialism - France. I. McCarthy, Patrick, 1941-. II. Series.
HC276.2 .F699 1987

French solo /. Castellani, Maurice. Paris , c1985. 262 p. ; ISBN 2-86477-063-6 : LC Card 85-205040
HF5482.65.F7 C373 1985

French-speaking Equatorial Africa. see **Africa, French-speaking Equatorial.**

The French state and French private investment in Czechoslovakia, 1918-1938 . Segal, Paul Harold, 1946- New York , 1987. vi, 379 p. ; ISBN 0-8240-8041-6 (alk. paper) : LC Card 87-252 DDC 332.6/7344/0437 19
HG5470.3.A3 S44 1987

French, Wendell L., 1923- The personnel management process : human resources administration and development / Wendell L. French.6th ed. Boston : Houghton Mifflin Co., c1987. xxiv, 685 p. : ill. ; 25 cm. Includes bibliographies and indexes. ISBN 0-395-35661-X LC Card 86-81308 DDC 658.3 19
1. Personnel management. I. Title.
HF5549 .F73 1987

French, William B.
Guide to real estate licensing examinations for salespersons and brokers / William B. French, Stephen J. Martin, Thomas E. Battle, III. 4th ed. New York : Wiley, c1986. ix, 367 p. : ill. ; 29 cm. Rev. ed. of Real estate review's guide to real estate licensing examinations for salespersons and brokers. 2nd ed. c1981. Includes bibliographies and index. ISBN 0-471-87754-9 : LC Card 83-23484 DDC 333.33/0973 19
1. Real estate business - United States. 2. Real estate business - United States - Examinations, questions, etc. 3. Real estate agents - Licenses - United States. I. Martin, Stephen John, 1948-. II. Battle, Thomas E. III. French, William B. Real estate review's guide to real estate licensing examinations for salespersons and brokers. IV. Title.
HD1375 .F74 1984
NYPL [*R-Econ. 86-3475]

Real estate review's guide to real estate licensing examinations for salespersons and brokers. French, William B. Guide to real estate licensing examinations for salespersons and brokers / William B. French, Stephen J. Martin, Thomas E. Battle, III. 4th ed. New York , c1986. ix, 367 p. : ISBN 0-471-87754-9 : LC Card 83-23484 DDC 333.33/0973 19
HD1375 .F74 1984
NYPL [*R-Econ. 86-3475]

Frenkel, Jacob A.
Exchange rates and international macroeconomics /. Chicago , 1983. x, 382 p. : ISBN 0-226-26249-9 LC Card 83-14524 DDC 332.4/56 19
HG205 1981c ***NYPL [JLE 86-3231]***

Fiscal policies and the world economy : an intertemporal approach / Jacob A. Frenkel and Assaf Razin. Cambridge, Mass. : MIT Press, c1987. xix, 484 p. : ill. ; 24 cm. Bibliography: p. 455-466. Includes index. ISBN 0-262-06109-0 LC Card 87-3276 DDC 339.5/2 19
1. Fiscal policy. 2. International economic relations. I. Razin, Assaf. II. Title.
HJ141 .F74 1987

International banking and global financing . New York, NY , c1983. xiv, 257 p. : ISBN 0-88239-015-5 (pbk.) : LC Card 84-60076 DDC 332.1/5 19
HG205 .I54 1983

Frenkel, Michael. Ausgewählte makroökonomische Modelle offener Volkswirtschaften / Michael Frenkel. St. Gallen : W. Surbir, 1982. 183 p. : ill. ; 21 cm. Bibliography: p. 180-183. LC Card 83-112497
1. Foreign exchange - Mathematical models. 2. Macroeconomics - Mathematical models. I. Title.
HG3823 .F74 1982

Frenkel, Roberto.
Decisiones de precio en alta inflación / Roberto Frenkel. Buenos Aires, Argentina : Centro de Estudios de Estado y Sociedad, 1979. 58 p. ; 22 cm. (Estudios CEDES. v. 2, no. 3) Bibliography: p. 57-58. LC Card 80-125798 DDC 332.4/15 19
1. Price policy - Mathematical models. 2. Inflation (Finance) - Mathematical models. I. Title. II. Series.
HF5416.5 .F73 ***NYPL [JLD 86-2701]***

Mercado financiero, expectativas cambiarias y movimientos de capital / Roberto Frenkel. Buenos Aires, Argentina : Centro de Estudios de Estado y Sociedad, [1981] 46 p. : ill. ; 21 cm. (Estudios CEDES. vol. 4, no. 3) Bibliography: p. 46. LC Card 82-236987 DDC 332/.0724 19
1. Finance - Mathematical models. 2. Capital movements - Mathematical models. 3. Foreign exchange - Mathematical models. I. Title. II. Series.
HG173.6.S62 F73 1981
NYPL [JLD 86-2636]

Frenkel, Stephen. Australian industrial relations . London [1986] 24 p. ; ISBN 0-902499-56-4 (pbk.) : LC Card 86-233230 DDC 331/.0994 19
HD8846.5 .A96 1986

Frente Democrático de Economistas (Ecuador)
Ecuador, política económica--teoría y realidad. [Guayaquil] [1986- v. <1-3 > ; LC Card 87-105005
HF1519 .E3 1986

FREQUENT FLYER PROGRAMS - UNITED STATES.
Michaels, Susan. Points, a guide to frequent flyer bonus programs /. New York , c1987. 161 p. : ISBN 0-87052-375-9 (pbk.) : LC Card 87-8681 DDC 387.7/1 19
HF6161.A38 M53 1987

Frese, Dirk. Japan, Markt für deutsche Konsumgüter / Dirk Frese. Düsseldorf : Deutsch-Japanisches Wirtschaftsförderungsbüro, [1978?] 32 p. : ill. ; 15 x 21 cm. (Reihe Japanwirtschaft . Heft 3) LC Card 85-242493
1. Germany (West) - Commerce - Japan. 2. Japan - Commerce - Germany (West). I. Title. II. Series.
HF3568.J3 F74 1978

Fresh seafood, the commercial buyer's guide . Dore, Ian, 1941- Huntington, N.Y. , c1984. 375 p. : ISBN 0-943738-07-5 : LC Card 84-5174 DDC 641.3/92/0687 19
HD9450.5 .D67 1984 ***NYPL [JSD 86-449]***

Fresh trends, 1987 : a profile of fresh produce consumers / conducted for the Packer by Market Facts Inc. and Vance Research Services. [Lincolnshire, Ill.] (400 Knightsbridge Pkwy., Lincolnshire 60069) : [Vance Pub. Corp.], c1987. 4 v. ; 22 x 30 cm. Cover title. CONTENTS. - rept. 1. Fresh fruits/specialty fruits/dried fruits -- rept. 2. Fresh vegetables/specialty vegetables/herbs -- rept. 3. Shopping for fresh produce--preferences, influences, and attitudes -- rept. 4. Nutrition concerns and industry issues. LC Card 87-162047 DDC 381/.415/0973 19
1. Fruit trade - United States - Statistics. 2. Dried fruit industry - United States - Statistics. 3. Food preferences - United States - Statistics. 4. Consumers' preferences - United States - Statistics. 5. Market surveys - United States. I. Market Facts, Inc. II. Vance Research Services. III. Packer.
HD9244 .F73 1987

Freund, Alison. Walsh, Brendan P., 1955- On-line information . Oxford, [Oxfordshire] , New York, NY, USA , 1987. xli, 327 p. : ISBN 0-631-15543-0 : LC Card 87-13154 DDC 025/.04/02465 19
HF5548.2 .W294 1987

Freund, John E. Elementary business statistics : the modern approach / John E. Freund, Frank J. Williams, Benjamin M. Perles.5th ed. Englewood Cliffs, N.J. : Prentice Hall, c1988. xiii, 738 p. : ill. ; 25 cm. Includes index. ISBN 0-13-253196-8 LC Card 87-20586 DDC 519.5/024658 19
1. Commercial statistics. 2. Statistics. I. Williams, Frank Jefferson. II. Perles, Benjamin M., 1922-. III. Title.
HF1017 .F73 1988

Frey, Bruno S. Weck-Hannemann, Hannelore. Die heimliche Wirtschaft . Bern , c1986. 112 p. : ISBN 3-258-03541-5 LC Card 86-159961
HD2346.S9 W43 1986

Frey, Dianne. Survey of sole parent pensioners' workforce barriers / Dianne Frey. Woden, ACT : Social Security Review, Dept. of Social Security, [1986] 40 p. : ill. ; 30 cm. (Background/discussion paper . no. 12) Includes bibliographical references. ISBN 0-642-51708-8 LC Card 87-154429 DDC 331.4/4 19
1. Mothers - Employment - Australia. 2. Single parents - Employment - Australia. 3. Single parents - Government policy - Australia. I. Title. II. Series.
HD6220 .F74 1986

Frey, Luigi.
Albertini, Sergio. Il consolidamento strutturale dell'occupazione in specifiche aree con particolare riguardo alla provincia di Gorizia /. Milano , c1984. 184 p. ; LC Card 84-234951 DDC 331.12/0945/392 19
HD5785.G67 A42 1984

Politica monetaria e politica dell'occupazione in Italia, in un contesto di innovazione finanziaria /. Milano , c1984. 166 p. ; LC Card 84-245111 DDC 332/.0945 19
HG1029.5 .P63 1984

Frey, René Leo. Die regionale Ausstrahlung der Universität Basel / René L. Frey, unter Mitarbeit von Marcel Kaufmann. Basel : Regio Basiliensis, c1984. 73 p. : ill. ; 25 cm. (Schriften der Regio . 8) LC Card 84-166545 DDC 378/.103 19
1. Community and college - Switzerland - Baselland. 2. Education, Higher - Economic aspects - Switzerland - Baselland. 3. Universität Basel - Finance. 4. Universität Basel - Public relations. I. Kaufmann, Marcel. II. Title. III. Series.
HC395 .A75 no. 8 LC238.4.S92B37

FREYCINET, CHARLES LOUIS DE SAULSES DE 1828-1923.
Beck, Robert, 1953- Der Plan Freycinet und die Provinzen . Frankfurt am Main , New York , c1986. 354 p. : ISBN 3-8204-9791-9 LC Card 87-408148 DDC 385/.068 19
HE3067 .B43 1986

Freymond, Joël. Guide du spéculateur : méthodes et secrets des professionnels de la bourse / Joël Freymond. Paris : A. Michel, c1986. 175 p. : ill. ; 23 cm. Bibliography: p. [161]-[167]. ISBN 2-226-02463-8 : LC Card 87-166254
1. Speculation - France. 2. Stock-exchange - France. I. Title.
HG6041 .F82 1986

Freyre Rubio, Javier. Las organizaciones sindicales, obreras y burocráticas contemporáneas en México / [Javier Freyre Rubio]. Azcapotzalco [Mexico] : Universidad Autónoma Metropolitana, c1983. 265 p. : ill. ; 22 cm. (Ensayos. 11) Bibliography: p. 213-215. ISBN 968-597-500-0 LC Card 86-218318
1. Trade-unions - Mexico - History. 2. Syndicalism - Mexico - History. I. Series: Ensayos (Azcapotzalco, Mexico) , 11. II. Title.
HD6532 .F74 1983

Freyssinet, Jacques. Le chômage / Jacques Freyssinet. Paris : La Découverte, 1984. 128 p. : ill. ; 18 cm. (Collection Repères . 22) Repères. Série "Travail et emploi" Bibliography: p. 124-126. ISBN 2-7071-1478-2 LC Card 85-115448 DDC 331.13/7 19
1. Unemployment. 2. Full employment policies. I. Series: Collection Repères. Série "Travail et emploi.". II. Title.
HD5707.5 .F74 1984

Freytag, Lutz. Faber, Malte Michael. Entropie, Umweltschutz und Rohstoffverbrauch . Berlin , New York , 1983. ix, 181 p. : ISBN 0-387-12297-4 (U. S.) LC Card 83-193381
HC79.E5 F23 1983

Fria fackföreningsinternationalen. see **International Confederation of Free Trade Unions.**

Frías F., Patricio. Prácticas y orientaciones del movimiento sindical en la lucha por la democracia / Patricio Frías F. Santiago, Chile : Programa de Enconomía del Trabajo, Academia de Humanismo Cristiano, 1986. 57 p. ; 21 cm. "Trabajo preparado especialmente para el seminario 'El movimiento laboral y el retorno a la democracia,' organizado por el PET el 24 de mayo de 1986." Includes bibliographical references. LC Card 87-101389
1. Trade-unions - Chile - Political activity. I. Title.
HD6618.5 .F75 1986

FRIBOURG. UNIVERSITÉ. FACULTÉ DE DROIT ET DES SCIENCES ÉCONOMIQUES - ADDRESSES, ESSAYS, LECTURES.
Hundert Jahre Rechts- und Wirtschaftsgeschichte an der Rechts-, Wirtschafts- und Sozialwissenschaftlichen Fakultät der Universität Freiburg =. Freiburg, Schweiz , 1982. 96 p., [6] p. of plates : ISBN 3-7278-0277-4 : LC Card 83-108855 DDC 340 19
K296 .H86 1982 ***NYPL [JLD 86-676]***

Fricke, Gabriele. Rechnungslegung für Beteiligungen nach der Anschaffungskostenmethode und nach der Equity-Methode / Gabriele Fricke. Bochum : N. Brockmeyer, 1983. xv, 374 p. : ill. ; 21 cm. (Bochumer wirtschaftswissenschaftliche Studien. Nr. 91) Bibliography: p. 349-374. ISBN 3-88339-310-X : LC Card 83-218419
1. Investments - Accounting. I. Title.
HF5686.I6 F75 1983

Fricke, Werner. Beteiligung im Industriebetrieb : Probleme des mittleren Managements / Werner Fricke, Harald Wiedenhofer. Frankfurt/Main ; New York : Campus, c1985. 291 p. ; 21 cm. (Schriftenreihe "Humanisierung des Arbeitslebens" . Bd. 55) Bibliography: p. 288-290. ISBN 3-593-32735-X LC Card 85-202742
1. Industrial management - Germany (West) - Employee participation. 2. Middle managers - Germany (West). 3. Peiner Maschinen- und Schraubenwerke - Case studies. I. Wiedenhofer, Harald. II. Title. III. Series.
HD5660.G4 F73 1985

Fricke, Werner, 1927- Stand der grenzüberschreitenden Raumordnung am Oberrhein /. [Heidelberg] , 1981. 105 p. : ISBN 3-88570-071-9 LC Card 81-197772 DDC 361.6/0943/4 19
HT395.G4 S735 1981
NYPL [L-10 4979 Heft 71]

Friderichs, Hans. Lohndispersionen auf strukturierten Arbeitsmärkten : theoretische Erklärungsansätze und empirische Befunde für die Bundesrepublik Deutschland / Hans Friderichs. Pfaffenweiler : Centaurus-Verlagsgesellschaft, 1986. xvi, 404 p. : ill. ; 21 cm. (Reihe Wirtschaftswissenschaften, 0177-283X . Bd. 28) Bibliography: p. 377-404. ISBN 3-89085-133-9 LC Card 87-134875 DDC 331.2/943 19
1. Wages - Germany, West. 2. Labor supply - Germany, West. I. Series: Reihe Wirtschaftswissenschaften (Pfaffenweiler, Breisgau-Hochschwarzwald, Germany) , Bd. 28. II. Title.
HD5029 .F75 1986

Fridjhon, Michael. Conspiracy of giants : the South African liquor industry / by Michael Fridjhon, Andy Murray ; with chapters by David Rees, Jeremy Gordin. Johannesburg : D. Stein, c1986. xii, 419 p. : ill. ; 26 cm. ISBN 0-947012-34-6 LC Card 87-139111 DDC 338.4/76631/0968 19
1. Alcoholic beverage industry - South Africa - History. I. Murray, Andy. II. Title.
HD9367.S7 F75 1986

Fridley, David, 1956- China Energy Workshop I: Petroleum Processing (1985 : Honolulu, Hawaii) China's petroleum industry in the international context . Boulder [Colo.] , 1986. xvii, 166 p. : ISBN 0-86638-072-8 (pbk.) LC Card 86-50695 DDC 338.2/7282/0951 19
HD9576.C52 C524 1985
NYPL [JLD 86-3885]

Frie faglige internasjonale. see **International Confederation of Free Trade Unions.**

Fried, Edward R. Building a Canadian-American free trade area /. Washington, D.C. , c1987. xii, 217 p. ; ISBN 0-8157-2973-1 (pbk.) LC Card 87-71507 DDC 382/.0971/073 19
HF1480.15.U5 B85 1987

Friede, Christina. Albach, Horst. Kosten der Arbeit . Stuttgart , c1985. xi, 179 p. : ISBN 3-7910-5003-6 : LC Card 86-162885 DDC 658.3/00943 19
HD5029 .A43 1985
NYPL [JLL 73-505 Nr.2]

Friedeberg, R.
Parlamentarismus und Generalstreik. 1978. Wozu noch in die Parlamente? / [Zusammenstellung, Trotzdem-Kollektiv]. [1. Aufl.]. [Reutlingen] , 1978. 81 p. : LC Card 82-223081 DDC 322/.2/0943 19
HD6697 .W69 1978 ***NYPL [JLD 87-886]***

Frieden, Bernard J. The politics of neglect : urban aid from model cities to revenue sharing / Bernard J. Frieden and Marshall Kaplan. Cambridge, Mass. : MIT Press, [1975] x, 281 p. ; 23 cm. "A Publication of the Joint Center for Urban Studies." Includes bibliographical references and index. ISBN 0-262-06061-2 LC Card 75-6792 DDC 309.2/62/0973
1. City planning - United States. 2. Urban renewal - United States. 3. Federal-city relations - United States. I. Kaplan, Marshall, joint author. II. Title.
HT167 .F74 ***NYPL [JLE 80-1135]***

Frieden, Jeffry A. Banking on the world : the politics of American international finance / Jeffry A. Frieden.1st ed. New York : Harper & Row, c1987. 264 p. ; 22 cm. Bibliography: p. [247]-[254]. Includes index. ISBN 0-06-015822-0 : LC Card 87-45136 DDC 332.1/5/0973 19
1. International finance. 2. Banks and banking, International. 3. Banks and banking, American. I. Title.
HG3881 .F735 1987

Frieden und Friedenssicherung in Vergangenheit und Gegenwart : Symposium der Universitäten Tel Aviv und Mannheim 19.-21. Juni 1979 / mit Beiträgen von H. Chantraine ... [et al.] ; herausgegeben von Manfred Schlenke und Klaus-Jürgen Matz. München : Wilhelm Fink, 1984. 115 p. ; 24 cm. (Jahrbuch des Instituts für Deutsche Geschichte. Beiheft . 7) German, English, and French. Includes bibliographical footnotes. ISBN 3-7705-2147-1 (pbk.) :
1. Security, International - Congresses. 2. Peace - Congresses. I. Chantraine, Heinrich. II. Schlenke, Manfred. III. Matz, Klaus-Jürgen. IV. Series. V. Series: Tel-Aviv. University. Institute for German History. Jahrbuch Beiheft , 7. 7.
NYPL [JFL 76-295 Bd. 7]

Friedland, Klaus. Gilde und Korporation in den nordeuropäischen Städten des späten Mittelalters /. Köln , 1984. 114 p. ; ISBN 3-412-06883-3 LC Card 84-194645
HD6473.E853 G55 1984

Friedlander, Daniel. Goldman, Barbara. Final report on the San Diego job search and work experience demonstration /. New York, N.Y. (3 Park Ave., New York 10016) , c1986. xliv, 269 p. : LC Card 87-118376 DDC 331.12/042/0979498 19
HD5713.6.U542 S395 1986

Friedlander, Lee. Cray at Chippewa Falls / photographs by Lee Friedlander. Minneapolis, Minn. (608 2nd Ave., S., Minneapolis 55402) : Cray Research, 1987. 96 p. : chiefly ill. ; 30 x 31 cm. LC Card 86-73134
1. Cray Research, Inc. - Pictorial works. 2. Chippewa Falls (Wis.) - Description - Views. 3. Computer industry - Wisconsin - Chippewa Falls - Employees - Pictorial works. I. Cray Research, Inc. II. Title.
HD9696.C64 C734 1987

Friedman, David H., 1942- Deposit operations / David H. Friedman. 2nd ed. Washington, D.C. (1120 Connecticut Ave., N.W., Washington 20036) : Education Policy and Development, American Bankers Association, c1987. xii, 354 p. : ill. ; 25 cm. Includes index. LC Card 87-165558 DDC 332.1/752 19
1. Deposit banking - United States. 2. Electronic funds transfers - United States. I. Title.
HG1660.U5 F75 1987

Friedman, H. George. Schreiner, Axel T. Introduction to compiler construction with UNIX /. Englewood Cliffs , c1985. viii, 194 p. : ISBN 0-13-474396-2 LC Card 84-63039
NYPL [JSF 86-616]

Friedman, Jack P.
Adjustable rate mortgages / Jack P. Friedman, Jack C. Harris. New York : Barron's Educational Series, Inc., c1987. viii, 293 p. ; 18 cm. (Barron's financial guides) Barron's financial tables for better money management ISBN 0-8120-3764-2 (soft) : LC Card 86-28852 DDC 332.8/2 19
1. Interest - Tables. 2. Mortgage loans, Variable rate - Tables. I. Harris, Jack C., 1945-. II. Title. III. Series.
HG1634 .F75 1987

Dictionary of business terms / Jack P. Friedman ; contributing authors, Jeffrey Clark ... [et al.]. New York : Barron's, c1987. vi, 650 p. ; 16 cm. (Barron's business guides) ISBN 0-8120-3775-8 (pbk.) : LC Card 87-12640 DDC 650/.03/21 19
1. Business - Dictionaries. 2. Finance - Dictionaries. I. Title. II. Series.
HF1001 .F78 1987

Dictionary of real estate terms / Jack P. Friedman, Jack C. Harris, J. Bruce Lindeman. 2nd ed. New York : Barron's, c1987. v, 329 p. : ill. ; 18 cm. ISBN 0-8120-3898-3 (pbk.) : LC Card 87-19869 DDC 333.33/03/21 19
1. Real estate business - Dictionaries. 2. Real property - Dictionaries. I. Harris, Jack C., 1945-. II. Lindeman, J. Bruce (John Bruce). III. Title.
HD1365 .F75 1987

Friedman, Janet T. (Janet Teri), 1957-
Safecracking the mortgage secrets : the complete guide to home loans / by Janet T. Friedman ; edited by Marie-Louise Crozat. Houston, Tex. : Win Publishers, c1987. 141 p. : forms ; 28 cm. Includes index. ISBN 0-942037-00-6 (pbk.) : LC Card 87-13357 DDC 332.7/22/0973 19
1. Mortgage loans - United States - Handbooks, manuals, etc. I. Crozat, Marie-Louise. II. Title.
HG2040.5.U5 F75 1987

Friedman, Milton, 1912-
The essence of Friedman / edited by Kurt R. Leube ; foreword by W. Glenn Campbell ; introduction by Anna J. Schwartz. Stanford, Calif. : Hoover Institution Press, c1987. xxxiv, 566 p., [1] p. of plates : ill. ; 24 cm. (Hoover Press publication . 366) "Complete bibliography of Milton Friedman": p. [527]-551. Includes index. ISBN 0-8179-8661-8 LC Card 87-4003 DDC 330.1 19
1. Economics. 2. Monetary policy. I. Leube, Kurt R. II. Title.
HB171 .F774 1987

Politics and tyranny : lessons in the pursuit of freedom / Milton Friedman et al. ; edited with an introduction by David J. Theroux. San Francisco, Calif. : Pacific Institute for Public Policy Research, c1984. 68 p. ; 23 cm. (Pacific studies in public policy) "Assembles the proceedings of the Pacific Institute's National Dinner to honor Milton Friedman, held October 4, 1983, in San Francisco"--Cover p. 4. "Comprehensive bibliography, a chronological list of Milton Friedman's principal works from 1934 to present": p. 47-65. Includes bibliographical references. ISBN 0-936488-00-X (pbk.) : LC Card 84-61364 DDC 330 19
1. Friedman, Milton, 1912- - Congresses. 2. Friedman, Milton, 1912- - Bibliography - Congresses. 3. Chicago school of economics - Congresses. 4. Laissez-faire - Congresses. 5. Individualism - Congresses. 6. Liberty - Congresses. I. Theroux, David J. II. Pacific Institute for Public Policy Research. III. Title.
HB98.3 .F75 1984 ***NYPL [JLE 87-857]***

FRIEDMAN, MILTON, 1912-
Butler, Eamonn. Milton Friedman . Aldershot, Hants, England , c1985. 272 p. : ISBN 0-85117-261-X : ***NYPL [JLD 86-1090]***

FRIEDMAN, MILTON, 1912- - CONGRESSES.
Friedman, Milton, 1912- Politics and tyranny . San Francisco, Calif. , c1984. 68 p. ; ISBN 0-936488-00-X (pbk.) : LC Card 84-61364 DDC 330 19
HB98.3 .F75 1984 ***NYPL [JLE 87-857]***

FRIEDMAN, MILTON, 1912- - BIBLIOGRAPHY - CONGRESSES.
Friedman, Milton, 1912- Politics and tyranny . San Francisco, Calif. , c1984. 68 p. ; ISBN 0-936488-00-X (pbk.) : LC Card 84-61364 DDC 330 19
HB98.3 .F75 1984 ***NYPL [JLE 87-857]***

Friedman, Stewart D.
Leadership succession /. New Brunswick, [N.J.], U. S.A. , 1987. x, 157 p. : ISBN 0-88738-162-6 : LC Card 87-10947 DDC 658.4 19
HD38.25.U6 L43 1987

Leadership succession systems and corporate performance / Stewart D. Friedman. New York, N.Y. (316 Uris Hall, New York 10027) : Center for Career Research and Human Resource Management, Columbia Graduate School of Business, c1985. ix, 141 p. ; 28 cm. (Career Center research report) Revision of thesis (Ph. D.--University of Michigan) Bibliography: p. 135-141. LC Card 86-162460 DDC 331.25/96 19
1. Executives - Recruiting. 2. Organizational effectiveness. I. Title. II. Series.
HD38.2 .F73 1985

Leadership succession systems and corporate performance / Stewart D. Friedman. New York, N.Y. (316 Uris Hall, New York, N.Y. 10027) : Center for Career Research and Human Resource Management, Columbia Graduate School of Business, c1985. ix, 141 p. : ill. ; 28 cm. (Career Center research report) Based on author's thesis (Ph. D.)--University of Michigan. Bibliography: p. 135-141.
1. Executives - United States. 2. Corporate planning - United States. 3. Leadership. 4. Organizational effectiveness. I. Columbia University. Center for Career Research and Human Resource Management. II. Title. III. Title: Succession systems and corporate performance. IV. Series. ***NYPL [JLF 87-255]***

Friedman, Thomas. Up the ladder : coping with the corporate climb / Thomas Friedman. New York, NY : Warner Books, 1986. xi, 203 p. ; 24 cm. ISBN 0-446-51291-5 LC Card 85-40655 DDC 658.4/09/0973 19
1. Executives - United States - Case studies. 2. Success in business - United States - Case studies. I. Title.
HD38.25.U6 F75 1986 ***NYPL [JLE 86-2840]***

Friedmann, John. Planning in the public domain : from knowledge to action / John Friedmann. Princeton, N.J. : Princeton University Press, c1987. xii, 501 p. : ill. ; 25 cm. Bibliography: p. 449-487. Includes index. ISBN 0-691-07743-6 (alk. paper) : LC Card 87-3194 DDC 361.6 19
1. Planning - History. 2. Political planning - History. I. Title.
HD87.5 .F745 1987

Friedrich A. Sorge's labor movement in the United States . Sorge, Friedrich A. (Friedrich Adolf), 1828-1906. New York , c1987. xiii, 196 p. ; ISBN 0-313-25518-0 (lib. bdg. : alk. paper) LC Card 86-31792 DDC 331/.0973 19
HD8072 .S7175 1987

Friedrich, Alexander G. Der Nord-Süd-Dialog zu Beginn der 80er Jahre =. Baden-Baden , 1982. 99 p. ; ISBN 3-7890-0774-9
NYPL [JLE 87-1282]

Friedrich-Alexander-Universität Erlangen-Nürnberg. Institut für Freie Berufe. Gesellschaftliches Selbstverständnis und politische Orientierung der Freien Berufe . Nürnberg , 1978. 144 p. : LC Card 86-170378
HD8038.G32 B384 1978

Friedrich, Dieter.
Francke, Hans-Hermann. Sparverhalten bei Unterbeschäftigung, stagnierendem oder sinkendem Realeinkommen /. Stuttgart [1985] 142 p. : LC Card 86-153649
HC290.5.S3 F69 1985

Francke, Hans-Hermann. Zinswirkungen der Staatsverschuldung . Berlin , c1984. 138 p. : ISBN 3-428-05727-9 LC Card 86-107232
HJ8654 .F73 1984

Friedrich-Ebert Foundation. see **Friedrich-Ebert-Stiftung.**

Friedrich-Ebert-Stiftung. Forschungsinstitut. Probleme der Rohstoffsicherung =. Bonn [1981] 215 p. : LC Card 85-206699
HF1051 .P76 1980

Friedrich-Ebert-Stiftung. Forschungsstelle. see **Friedrich-Ebert-Stiftung. Forschungsinstitut.**

Friedrich-Ebert-Stiftung. Research institute. see **Friedrich-Ebert-Stiftung. Forschungsinstitut.**

Friedrich, Horst, 1935- Die Produktionsverhältnisse / Horst Friedrich ; herausgegeben im Auftrag des Wissenschaftlichen Rates für Marxistisch-Leninistische Philosophie der DDR von Wolfgang Eichhorn I, Erich Hahn, Frank Rupprecht. Berlin : Dietz, 1981. 228 p. ; 18 cm. (Grundfragen der marxistisch-leninistischen Philosophie) Includes bibliographical references. LC Card 81-175348
1. Industrial productivity. 2. Labor productivity. 3. Capital productivity. 4. Labor economics. 5. Marxian economics. 6. Marx, Karl, 1818-1883. I. Title.
HC79.I52 F75 1981

Friedrich, Karl. Das Süd-Nord-Gefälle . Stuttgart , 1986. 168 p. ; ISBN 3-87959-270-5 LC Card 87-103590 DDC 330.943/0878 19
HC286.7 .S9 1986

Friedrich List Gesellschaft. see **List-Gesellschaft.**

Friedrich, R. (Rainer)
Energie und Umwelt : Grundlagen zur Entwicklung örtlicher und regionaler Energieversorgungskonzepte : Regionalverband Schwarzwald-Baar-Heuberg / Rainer Friedrich, Thomas Müller, Rudi Wartmann ; [Auftragnehmer], IKE, Institut für Kernenergetik und Energiesysteme, Universität Stuttgart. Stuttgart : IRB Verlag, [1985] 115 p. : ill. ; 30 cm. (Veröffentlichung der Forschungsgemeinschaft Bauen und Wohnen, Stuttgart . Nr. 167/85) Forschungsbericht / IRB LC Card 87-409534 DDC 333.79/0943/46 19
1. Energy policy - Environmental aspects - Germany (West) - Baden-Württemberg. 2. Regional planning - Germany, West - Baden-Württemberg. I. Müller, Thomas. II. Wartmann, Rudi. III. Universität Stuttgart. Institut für Kernenergetik und Energiesysteme. IV. Series. V. Series: Veröffentlichung der Forschungsgemeinschaft Bauen und Wohnen, Stuttgart , Nr. 167. VI. Title.
HD9502.G43 B324 1985

Energie und Umwelt : Grundlagen zur Entwicklung örtlicher und regionaler Energieversorgungskonzepte : Regionalverband Franken / Rainer Friedrich, Thomas Müller, Rudi Wartmann ; [Auftragnehmer], IKE, Institut für Kernenergetik und Energiesysteme, Universität Stuttgart. Stuttgart : IRB Verlag, [1985] 124 p. : ill. ; 30 cm. (Veröffentlichung der Forschungsgemeinschaft Bauen und Wohnen, Stuttgart . Nr. 165/85) Forschungsbericht / IRB LC Card 87-409533 DDC 333.79/0943/46 19
1. Energy policy - Environmental aspects - Germany (West) - Baden-Württemberg. 2. Regional planning - Germany, West - Baden-Württemberg. I. Müller, Thomas. II. Wartmann, Rudi. III. Universität Stuttgart. Institut für Kernenergetik und Energiesysteme. IV. Series. V. Series: Veröffentlichung der Forschungsgemeinschaft Bauen und Wohnen, Stuttgart , Nr. 165. VI. Title.
HD9502.G43 B3238 1985

Friedrich-Schiller-Universität Jena.
Intensivierung des wissenschaftlich-technischen Arbeitsprozesses /. Jena , 1985. 200 p. : LC Card 86-132567 DDC 338/.06/09431 19
HC290.795.I52 I57 1985

Friedrich-Schiller-Universität Jena. Sektion Marxismus-Leninismus. Intensivierung des wissenschaftlich-technischen Arbeitsprozesses /. Jena , 1985. 200 p. : LC Card 86-132567 DDC 338/.06/09431 19
HC290.795.I52 I57 1985

Friedrich-Schiller-Universität Jena. Sektion Wirtschaftswissenschaften.
Die Leistungsbewertung in der Industrie . Jena , 1983. 241 p. ; LC Card 84-176546
HD56.25 .L45 1983

Produktion, Intensivierung, Effektivität /. Jena , 1978. 180 p. : LC Card 85-183724
HC290.795.I52 P75 1978

Friend, John. Planning under pressure : the strategic choice approach / by John Friend and Allen Hickling.1st ed. Oxford [Oxfordshire] ; New York : Pergamon Press, 1987. xix, 338 p. : ill. ; 24 cm. (Urban and regional planning series. 37) Bibliography: p. 317-322. Includes index. ISBN 0-08-018766-8 : LC Card 86-25219 DDC 658.4/012 19
1. Strategic planning. I. Hickling, Allen. II. Title.
HD30.28 .F75 1987

FRIENDLY SOCIETIES - BARBADOS - DIRECTORIES.
Blondel, Eaulin. Credit unions, co-operatives, trade unions, and friendly societies in Barbados . St. Augustine, Trinidad, Trinidad and Tobago [1986] v, 102 p. ; LC Card 87-403330 DDC 334/.025/72981 19
HD3464.9.A6 B353 1986

FRIENDLY SOCIETIES - FRANCE - CONGRESSES.
Economie sociale et cycle de vie des institutions /. Paris , 1983. 162 p. : ISBN 2-7178-0631-8 : LC Card 83-174618 DDC 334/.0944 19
HD3494 .E26 1983 *NYPL [JLE 86-537]*

Friends of Filipino Migrant Workers. Pinoy overseas handbook . [Manila, Philippines] , 1982. 88 p. : LC Card 83-207976
HD8656 .P56 1982

FRIESLAND (NETHERLANDS) - APPROPRIATIONS AND EXPENDITURES - FORECASTING - STATISTICS.
Financieel meerjarenplan, 1986-1989 /. [Leeuwarden] [1985?] vii, 169 p. ; LC Card 87-111957
HJ2128.5.F75 F563 1985

Friesland (Netherlands). Provinciale Staten. Financieel meerjarenplan, 1986-1989 /. [Leeuwarden] [1985?] vii, 169 p. ; LC Card 87-111957
HJ2128.5.F75 F563 1985

Frieswyk, Thomas S. Biomass statistics for Vermont : 1983 / Thomas S. Frieswyk, Anne M. Malley. [Broomall, Pa.] : U. S. Dept. of Agriculture, Forest Service, Northeastern Station, 1986. 105 p. : ill., map ; 28 cm. (Resource bulletin NE . 91) Distributed to depository libraries in microfiche. Item 83-B-5 (microfiche) LC Card 86-602390 DDC 333.79/38 19
I. Title. II. Series.
HD9502.5.B543 U635 1986

Frihetens idéer . Johansson, Mats, 1951- [Stockholm] , c1986. 224 p. : ISBN 91-7566-106-3 LC Card 86-226727
HC106.8 .J64 1986

Friman, Alfred, 1937- Ledning, produktion & marknadsföring av tjänster . Malmö , c1981. 318 p. : ISBN 91-40-54058-8 : LC Card 81-174255
HD9986.S82 L43 1981

Frisbee, Don C. The PacifiCorp story : 75 years of service and partnership / Don C. Frisbee. New York : Newcomen Society of the United States, 1985. 27 p. : ill. ; 23 cm. (Newcomen publication. no. 1232) Address delivered at a "1984 Wyoming Meeting" of the Newcomen Society of the United States held in Cheyenne on Nov. 9, 1984. LC Card 85-60699 DDC 338.7/6136362/09787 19
1. PacifiCorp - History. 2. Electric utilities - Wyoming - History. 3. Electric utilities - West (U. S.) - History. I. Title.
HD9685.U7 P344 1985

Frischknecht, Federico. Economía nacional / Federico Frischknecht. Buenos Aires : Librería "El Ateneo" Editorial, c1986. xi, 214 p. : ill. ; 23 cm. (Biblioteca de ciencias económicas. Serie economía) Bibliography: p. 193-200. Includes index. ISBN 950-0-23599-4 LC Card 86-207933
1. Economics. I. Title.
HB178.5 .F75 1986

Frischknecht, Jürg, 1947- Kalte Kommunikation . Basel , c1985. 256 p. : ISBN 3-85787-134-2 LC Card 85-232413
HD9696.T463 S95 1985

A friss és feldolgozott zöldségek, gyümölcsök bel- és külkereskedelmi forgalmazásának aktuális problémái /. Kartali, János. Budapest , 1985. 108 p. ; ISBN 963-491-203-6 LC Card 86-195487
HD9220.H82 K37 1985

Friss, István. Friss István emlékezete /. Budapest , 1984. 128 p. ; LC Card 86-145174
HC300.28 .F75 1984

FRISS, ISTVÁN.
Friss István emlékezete /. Budapest , 1984. 128 p. ; LC Card 86-145174
HC300.28 .F75 1984

Friss István emlékezete / [szerkesztette, Mérey Ildikó és Subáné Varga Judit]. Budapest : MTA Közgazdaságtudományi Intézet, 1984. 128 p. ; 24 cm. (A Magyar Tudományos Akadémia Közgazdaságtudományi Intézetének közleményei, 0460-5918 . új sorozat, 32) Summary in English and Russian. Bibliography of works by I. Friss: p. [102]-126. LC Card 86-145174
1. Hungary - Economic policy - 1968-. 2. Friss, István. I. Friss, István. II. Mérey, Ildikó. III. Subáné Varga, Judit. IV. Series.
HC300.28 .F75 1984

Fritsch, Bruno. Im Spannungsfeld von Wirtschaft, Technik und Politik . München , c1986. 570 p., [1] leaf of plates : ISBN 3-7892-7282-5 LC Card 87-112967
HF1411 .I353 1986

FRITSCH, BRUNO.
Im Spannungsfeld von Wirtschaft, Technik und Politik . München , c1986. 570 p., [1] leaf of plates : ISBN 3-7892-7282-5 LC Card 87-112967
HF1411 .I353 1986

Fritsch, Heinz. Intensivierung des wissenschaftlich-technischen Arbeitsprozesses /. Jena , 1985. 200 p. : LC Card 86-132567 DDC 338/.06/09431 19
HC290.795.I52 I57 1985

Fritsch, Winston. External constraints on economic policy in Brazil, 1889-1930 / Winston Fritsch. Pittsburgh, PA : University of Pittsburgh Press, 1988. p. cm. (Pitt Latin American series) Bibliography: p. Includes index. ISBN 0-8229-1147-7 LC Card 87-19209 DDC 338.981 19
1. Brazil - Economic policy. 2. Brazil - Commercial policy - History - 20th century. 3. Coffee trade - Government policy - Brazil - History - 20th century. I. Title.
HC187 .F757 1988

Fritz, Carl, b. 1890. München als Industriestadt / von Carl Fritz. Berlin : Puttkammer u. Mühlbrecht, 1913. 163 p. ; 24 cm. Includes bibliographical references. LC Card 85-666347
1. Munich (Germany) - Industries. I. Title.
HC289.M86 F74x 1913

Fritz-Krockow, Bernhard. Die Absorptionskapazität für Kapital : Determinanten und Indikatoren des entwicklungspolitischen Konzeptes / Bernhard Fritz-Krockow. Spardorf : R.F. Wilfer, c1986. 201 p. : ill. ; 21 cm. Originally presented as the author's thesis (doctoral)--Universität Münster, 1985. Bibliography: p. 187-201. ISBN 3-922919-78-2 LC Card 86-179843
1. Investments, Foreign. 2. Absorptive capacity (Economics). I. Title.
HG4538 .F75 1986

Fritz, Roger.
Personal performance contracts : the key to job success / Roger Fritz. Los Altos, Calif. : Crisp Publications, c1987. vi, 71 p. : ill. ; 26 cm. ISBN 0-931961-12-2 (pbk.) : LC Card 85-73466 DDC 658.3/142 19
1. Goal setting in personnel management. 2. Contracts. I. Title.
HF5549.5.G6 F75 1987

Rate your executive potential / Roger Fritz. New York : Wiley, c1988. xv, 239 p. : ill. ; 23 cm. Bibliography: p. 236. Includes index. ISBN 0-471-62598-1 (pbk.) : LC Card 87-13705 DDC 658.4/09 19
1. Executive ability. 2. Self-evaluation. 3. Management. I. Title.
HD38.2 .F74 1988

Fritz, Wolfgang, Dipl.-Kfm. Warentest und Konsumgüter-Marketing : Forschungskonzeption und Ergebnisse einer empirischen Untersuchung / Wolfgang Fritz. Wiesbaden : Gabler, c1984. 596 p. : ill. ; 24 cm. (Neue betriebswirtschaftliche Forschung . 27) Originally presented as the author's thesis (doctoral)--Universität Mannheim, 1983. Bibliography: p. 456-509. ISBN 3-409-13600-2 LC Card 84-207784
1. Marketing research. 2. Sales forecasting. 3. Consumers. 4. Commercial products - Testing. I. Title. II. Series.
HF5415.2 .F75 1984

Frjálshyggjan /. Birgir Björn Sigurjónsson, 1949- [Reykjavík] , 1981. 261 p. : LC Card 84-134561
HB95 .B55 1981

Fröhler, Ludwig. Linzer Kommunalwissenschaftliche Tagung (1978) Privatisierung kommunaler Aufgaben? . Linz , c1978. 62 p. ; ISBN 3-7141-7871-6 LC Card 85-185084
HD4651 .L56 1978

Froemel, Ernest C. Baehr, Melany E. Experience and background inventory . [Park Ridge, Ill.] (1550 Northwest Highway, Park Ridge 60068) [c1986] 48 p. ; LC Card 87-404267 DDC 658.3/112 19
HF5549.5.S38 B34 1986

Frohbieter-Mueller, Jo. Stay home and mind your own business : how to manage your time, space, personal obligations, money, business, and yourself while working at home / Jo Frohbieter-Mueller. White Hall, Va. : Betterway Publications, c1987. 280 p. : ill. ; 23 cm. Bibliography: p. 257-258. Includes index. ISBN 0-932620-83-3 (pbk.) : LC Card 87-15922 DDC 658/.041 19
1. Home-based businesses - Management. 2. Small business - Management. 3. New business enterprises. I. Title.
HD62.5 .F76 1987

Frohock, Fred M. Rational association / Fred M. Frohock. 1st ed. Syracuse, N.Y. : Syracuse University Press, 1987. xi, 201 p. ; 24 cm. Includes index. Bibliography: p. 185-189. ISBN 0-8156-2390-9 (alk. paper) LC Card 86-23026 DDC 302/.13 19
I. Title.
HB846.8 .F76 1987 *NYPL [JLE 87-1126]*

Frolova, L. Modelirovanie razvitiia mezhotraslevyh kompleksov Latviĭskoĭ SSR . Riga , 1985. 106 p. : LC Card 86-177817
HD9015.S653 L376 1985

From chartism to labourism /. Rothstein, Theodore. New York , 1984. vi, 365 p. ; ISBN 0-8240-5722-8 (alk. paper) : LC Card 83-48495 DDC 335/.1 19
HX249 .R68 1984 *NYPL [JLD 86-1828]*

From competition to rivalry. Von der Konkurrenz zur Rivalität . Stuttgart , 1986. 186 p. ; ISBN 3-515-04760-3 LC Card 87-134320 DDC 337/.09/04 19
HF1411 .V665 1986

From crisis to equitable growth ; a new development agenda for Latin America / [edited by] Rob Vos. Aldershot ; Brookfield, USA : Avebury, 1987. ix, 144 p. ; 23 cm. Includes bibliographies. ISBN 0-566-05536-8 : LC Card 87-21135 DDC 338.98 19
1. Basic needs - Government policy - Latin America. 2. Latin America - Economic policy. 3. Economic stabilization - Latin America. I. Vos, Rob, 1955-.
HC130.B38 F76 1987

From Eden to Eros . Roberts, Richard. San Anselmo, Ca. , 1985. 166 p. : ISBN 0-942380-05-3 (pbk.) LC Card 85-51722
NYPL [JLD 87-224]

From farming to biotechnology . Goodman, David, 1938- Oxford , New York, N.Y. , 1987. 214 p. : ISBN 0-631-14405-6 : LC Card 87-687 DDC 338.1/6 19
HD1433 .G66 1987

From fire to rust . Leary, Thomas E., 1946- Buffalo, N.Y. , c1987. 134 p. : ISBN 0-939032-00-7 (pbk.) LC Card 87-692 DDC 338.7/669142/0974796 19
HD9519.L2 L43 1987

From hacienda to ejido . Rounds, Christopher R., 1945- New York , 1987. viii, 268 p. ; ISBN 0-8240-1369-7 (alk. paper) : LC Card 87-8526 DDC 333.3/1/7249 19
HD1333.M62 Y387 1987

From losers to winners . Sherman, V. Clayton. New York, NY , c1987. xi, 188 p. : ISBN 0-8144-5918-8 LC Card 87-47710 DDC 658.3/045 19
HF5549.5.E42 S54 1987b

From losers to winners . Sherman, V. Clayton. New York, NY , c1987. 1 v. (various pagings) : ISBN 0-8144-1146-0 (loose-leaf) LC Card 86-47823 DDC 658.3/045 19
HF5549.5.E42 S54 1987

From manor to market . Lachmann, Richard. Madison, Wis. , 1987. xiv, 166 p. : ISBN 0-299-11420-1 : LC Card 87-40146 DDC 330.942/05 19
HC254 .L33 1987

From Marshall Plan to debt crisis . Wood, Robert Everett, 1944- Berkeley , c1986. xviii, 400 p. ; ISBN 0-520-05526-8 (alk. paper) LC Card 86-6934 DDC 338.9/009172/4 19
HC60 .W62 1986 *NYPL [JLE 86-4443]*

From Mecanicien to ingenieur . Edmonson, James M. New York, NY , 1987. x, 631 p. ; ISBN 0-8240-8036-X (alk. paper) : LC Card 87-300 DDC 338.4/76218/0944 19
HD9705.F7 E35 1987

From research to implementation . Jerve, Alf

Morten. Fantoft-Bergen, Norway [1984] 23 leaves ; LC Card 86-228812 DDC 386/.068 19
HE691.6 .J47 1984

From SGIO to Suncorp /. Thomis, Malcolm I. [Brisbane?] , 1986. xii, 272 p., [32] p. of plates : ISBN 0-7242-1698-7 LC Card 87-158138 DDC 368.4/009943 19
HG8220.A9 T56 1986

From syndicalism to trade unionism . Wortman, Roy T., 1940- New York , 1985. 217 p. : ISBN 0-8240-5675-2 (alk. paper) : LC Card 85-16249 DDC 331.88/6/09771 19
HD8055.I5 O38 1985 ***NYPL [JLE 86-4097]***

From trails to rails . Barklow, Irene. Enterprise, Or. , c1987. ix, 300 p. : ISBN 0-9618185-2-2 : LC Card 87-15709 DDC 383/.4979571 19
HE6376.A1 O727 1987

From working daughters to working mothers . Lamphere, Louise. Ithaca , 1987. xviii, 390 p. : ISBN 0-8014-9441-9 (pbk. : alk. paper) LC Card 86-32952 DDC 331.4/09745/1 19
HD6096.R4 L36 1987

Fronhoff, Bernd, 1956- Die Gestaltung von Marketingstrategien : ein konzeptioneller Planungsansatz im situativen Kontext der Unternehmung / Bernd Fronhoff. Bergisch Gladbach : J. Eul, 1986. ix, 369 p. : ill. ; 21 cm. (Reihe Planung, Information und Unternehmungsführung . Bd. 14) Bibliography: p. 332-369. ISBN 3-89012-067-9 LC Card 87-122913 DDC 658.8/02 19
1. Marketing - Decision making. 2. Strategic planning. 3. Competition. I. Title. II. Series.
HF5415.135 .F76 1986

Fronia, Joachim.
Auswirkungen von Umsatzsteuererhöhungen auf Preise, Produktion und Beschäftigung. 1982. Aktuelle Probleme der Wirtschaftspolitik : ökonometrische Untersuchungen anhand des F&T-Modells / von Joachim Fronia ; Wolfgang Röhling. Tübingen , 1982. vi, 69, vii, 62 p. : ISBN 3-16-344473-3 LC Card 84-125468
HJ5715.G3 A67 1982

FRONT POPULAIRE - HISTORY.
Validire, Jean-Louis. André Bergeron, une force ouvrière /. Paris , c1984. 244 p. ; ISBN 2-259-01206-X : LC Card 85-105625 DDC 331.88/0944 19
HD6684 .V35 1984

A fronteira do sul . Silva, J. Resende. Rio de Janeiro , 1922. 723 p., [1] leaf of plates : LC Card 85-223002
HF3409.R56 S55 1922

Frontera.
Carrillo V., Jorge (Carrillo Viveros) Mujeres fronterizas en la industria maquiladora /. [Mexico City] , Tijuana, B.C.N. , 1985. 216 p. : ISBN 968-290-389-0 LC Card 87-400964 DDC 331.4 19
HD6073.O332 M483 1985

La frontera colombo-venezolana, una región donde invertir /. Foro de Proyectos de Inversión Colombo-Venezolanos (1986 : Cúcuta, Colombia) Bogotá, D.E. [1986] 96 p. ; LC Card 87-403851 DDC 332.6/09861 19
HG5352 .F67 1986

La frontera de San Ysidro . Bilbao, Elena. Tijuana, Baja California , 1986. 27 p. ; ISBN 968-607-513-5 LC Card 87-125801 DDC 330.9794/98 19
HC108.S65 B55 1986

FRONTIER AND PIONEER LIFE - MIDDLE WEST.
Fite, Gilbert Courtland, 1918- The farmers' frontier, 1865-1900 /. Norman [1987], c1966. xiv, 272 p. : ISBN 0-8061-2063-0 (pbk.) LC Card 86-40534 DDC 338.1/0977 19
HD8039.F3 U643 1987

FRONTIER AND PIONEER LIFE - TROPICS.
Les Phénomènes de "frontière" dans les pays tropicaux . Paris , 1981. vii, 456 p. : LC Card 83-122397
HD1131 .P47 1981

FRONTIER AND PIONEER LIFE - WEST (U. S.)
Fite, Gilbert Courtland, 1918- The farmers' frontier, 1865-1900 /. Norman [1987], c1966. xiv, 272 p. : ISBN 0-8061-2063-0 (pbk.) LC Card 86-40534 DDC 338.1/0977 19
HD8039.F3 U643 1987

FRONTIER AND PIONEER LIFE - WEST (U. S.) - HISTORY.
Layton, Stanford J., 1941- To no privileged class . Provo, Utah , Salt Lake City, Utah , c1987. p. cm. ISBN 0-941214-59-1 : LC Card 87-14299 DDC 333.1/6/0978 19
HD1339.U5 L39 1987

Frontiers in creative and innovative management / edited by Robert Lawrence Kuhn. Cambridge, Mass. : Ballinger Pub. Co., 1985, c1986. xxv, 391 p. : ill. ; 24 cm. (Series on econometrics and management sciences . v. 4) "Papers presented at the Second International Conference on Creative and Innovative Management, held in Miami on 7-9 November 1984 ... sponsored by the RGK Foundation and the IC Institute at the University of Texas at Austin"--P. xv. Includes bibliographies and index. ISBN 0-88730-057-X LC Card 85-15125 DDC 658.4 19
1. Creative ability in business - Congresses. 2. Management - Congresses. 3. Organizational change - Congresses. I. Kuhn, Robert Lawrence. II. RGK Foundation. III. IC Institute. IV. International Conference on Creative and Innovative Management (2nd : 1984 : Miami, Fla.). V. Series.
HD53 .F76 1986 ***NYPL [JLE 86-3614]***

The frontiers of management . Drucker, Peter Ferdinand, 1909- New York , 1987, c1986. p. cm. ISBN 0-06-097111-8 (pbk.) : LC Card 87-45043 DDC 658 19
HD31 .D7713 1987

Frontline (Television program) Will there always be an England? [videorecording] /. Alexandria, VA , 1986. 1 videocassette (60 min.) : LC Card 86-707796 DDC 942.085 11
HC256.5

Frontori, Laura. Il mercato dei segni : consumi e comunicazione pubblicitaria / Laura Frontori. Milano : R. Cortina, c1986. xv, 186 p., [8] p. of plates : ill. ; 21 cm. (Collana di psicologia. 8) Includes bibliographical references. ISBN 88-7078-040-6 : LC Card 86-161029
1. Advertising - Psychological aspects. I. Series: Collana di psicologia (Raffaello Cortina editore) , 8. II. Title.
HF5822 .F74 1986

Frontrunners. Colours [videorecording] / TV Ontario ; producer, Caroline Gray ; director, Harvey Frost. Chapel Hill, NC : TV Ontario, 1987. 1 videocassette (28 min., 50 sec.) : sd., col. + 1 guide. Title from data sheet. A foreign videorecording (Canada) Ages 16 through adults. Issued as U-matic 3/4 in. or Beta 1/2 in. or VHS 1/2 in. Describes methods used by Brigette Manning in her fashion consultation business in Canada. Explains her development of products, services, franchises, and relationships with retailers. LC Card 87-706853 DDC 338.6 11
1. Fashion merchandising - Canada - Case studies. 2. Success in business - Canada - Case studies. I. Manning, Brigette. II. TV Ontario. III. Title: Colours.
HD9940

Frost & Sulivan. The Teleconferencing market. New York, N.Y. (106 Fulton St., New York 10038) , c1983. 288 p. : LC Card 87-143433
HD9696.T443 U574 1983

Frost & Sullivan.
Aliphatic solvents market. New York, N.Y. , c1983. viii, 181 leaves : LC Card 87-142189 DDC 381/.45661807 19
HD9660.S733 U525 1983

Analytical instruments markets in Europe. New York, N.Y. , c1983. xii, 253 p. ; LC Card 87-141819 DDC 380.1/45681754 19
HD9706.65.C573 E82 1983

Automotive aftermarket in the U. S. New York, N.Y. , c1983. 2 v. (xiii, 435 p.) ; LC Card 87-144460
HD9710.3.U52 A93 1983

The Automotive electronics market in the U. S. New York, N.Y. , c1983. vi, 262 p. : LC Card 87-142223 DDC 381/.456292549/0973 19
HD9710.3.U52 A943 1983

The Call accounting market in the United States. New York, N.Y. , c1983. x, 275 p. : LC Card 87-143500 DDC 381/.45621387 19
HD9697.T453 U522 1983

Cardiovascular surgery products markets in the U. S. New York, N.Y. , c1983. xxiii, 197 p. : LC Card 87-143453
HD9995.S93 U525 1983

Caulks & sealants market. New York, N.Y. , c1983. ix, 250 p. : LC Card 87-143824
HD9999.S44453 U53 1983

Coal bulk handling equipment market. New York, N.Y. , c1984. iv, 243 p. : LC Card 87-142522 DDC 380.1/45622334/028 19
HD9545 .C578 1984

The Cogeneration equipment and services market in the U. S. New York, N.Y. , c1983. 2 v. (ix, 306 leaves) : LC Card 87-138703 DDC 381/.456213141 19
HD9695.U52 C64 1983

The Commercial greenhouses & associated equipment & agrochemicals market. New York, N.Y. , c1983. vii, 274 leaves : LC Card 87-143480
HD9475.U52 C66 1983

Consumer & catering disposable products market in Europe. New York, N.Y. , c1983. [29], 386 p. ; LC Card 87-142586 DDC 380.1/4568 19
HD9971.5.T323 E853 1983

The Counting instrument market in the U. S. New York, N.Y. , c1983. v, 197 p. : LC Card 87-143757 DDC 381/.4568114 19
HD9696.D543 U63 1983

The Diagnostic radiology market in the U. S. New York, N.Y. , c1983. xxxix, 261 p. : LC Card 87-143803 DDC 381/.45681761 19
HD9995.R333 U53 1983

The Digital telecommunications market. New York, N.Y. , c1983. 2 v. (vii, 269 leaves) : LC Card 87-143942 DDC 384 19
HD9697.T453 U525 1983

The Distributed digital process control systems market in the U. S. New York, N.Y. , c1983. 229 p. ; LC Card 87-141853
HD9696.P763 U527 1983

The Electronic games market in the U. S. New York, N.Y. , c1983. vii, 291 p. : LC Card 87-142142 DDC 381/.45688728 19
HD9993.E453 U622 1983

The Enhanced data network (van) market. New York, N.Y. , c1983. v, 258 p. : LC Card 87-143825
HD9696.D383 U6344 1983

The Enhanced oil recovery market, 1980-1990. New York, N.Y. , c1983. vi, 203 leaves : LC Card 87-142370 DDC 381/.45617665/0973 19
HD9565 .E53 1983

Flame retardants chemicals market. New York, N.Y. , c1983. vii, 315 p. : LC Card 87-143411 DDC 381/.456289223/0973 19
HD9999.F553 U64 1983

Flavors and fragrances market in Europe. New York, N.Y. , c1983. 5, 17, 8, 279 p. ; LC Card 87-141830 DDC 380.1/456645 19
HD9212.E852 F53 1983

Frozen foods market in Europe. New York, N.Y. , c1983. 2 v. (vii, 438 p.) ; LC Card 87-142593 DDC 380.1/4566402853/094 19
HD9326.A2 F76 1983

Geriatrics OTC health aid and toiletries products market-U. S. New York, N.Y. , c1983. 2 v. (viii, 352 leaves) ; LC Card 87-144078 DDC 381/.456151/0973 19
HD9666.5 .G47 1983

The Home computer software market. New York, N.Y. , c1983. iv, 212 p. : LC Card 87-141858 DDC 381/.45004/0973 19
HD9696.C63 U5183245 1983

Home healthcare products and services markets in the U. S. New York, N.Y. , c1983. 2 v. (x, 368 leaves) ; LC Card 87-144925 DDC 381/.45681761 19
HD9995.H563 U5436 1983

The IBM market in Europe. New York, N.Y. , c1983. 2 v. (xv, 573, 9 p.) ; LC Card 87-146364 DDC 380.1/45004/094 19
HD9696.C64 I4846 1983

The Industrial display market in the U. S. New York, N.Y. , c1983. vi, 226 leaves ; LC Card 87-142373 DDC 381/.456213985/0973 19
HD9696.I533 U54 1983

Industrial fasteners market in the U. S. New

York, N.Y. , c1983. iv, 375 p. : LC Card 87-143818
HD9999.F33 U476 1983

Industrial hydraulics components market in Europe. New York, N.Y. , c1983. xxxvi, 338 p. ; LC Card 87-141832 DDC 381/.456212/094 19
HD9705.5.H933 E855 1983

Industrial power systems market in the U. S. New York, N.Y. , c1983. v, 312 p. ; LC Card 87-143811 DDC 381/.4562143/0973
HD9695.U52 I53 1983

Industrial robots market. New York, N.Y. , <c1983-. v. <2 > ; LC Card 87-166012 DDC 381/.45629892 19
HD9696.R623 U634 1983

Industrial robots market in Europe. New York, N.Y. , c1983. vi, 320 p. : LC Card 87-141842 DDC 380.1/45629892 19
HD9696.R623 E854 1983

The Industrial vision systems market in the U. S. New York, N.Y. , c1983. v, 246 p. : LC Card 87-143523
HD9696.I423 U5445 1983

Integral HP electric motors and asociated [sic] controls. New York, N.Y. , c1983. xii, 280 leaves ; LC Card 87-143831
HD9697.M693 U55 1983

Interactive videodisk software market. New York, N.Y. , c1983. iv, 228 leaves ; LC Card 87-143767
HD9696.C63 U518378 1983

Intravenous theraphy [sic] supplies and equipment market in Europe. New York, N.Y. , c1983. xix, 317 p. ; LC Card 87-141784 DDC 380.1/45681761 19
HD9995.I583 E854 1983

Japanese penetration into the United States communications data processing and office equipment markets. New York, N.Y. , c1983. v, 308 p. ; LC Card 87-143908 DDC 381/.45004/0973 19
HD9696.D383 U635 1983

The Market for advanced business communications in the United States. New York, N.Y. , c1983. 2 v. (x, 365 leaves) : LC Card 87-144924 DDC 384/.041 19
HD9696.T443 U5465 1983

Marketing strategies for selling cosmetics & toiletries in Europe. New York, N.Y. , c1983. 381 p. ; LC Card 87-141847 DDC 380.1/456685/094 19
HD9970.5.C673 E8555 1983

The Markets and competitive environment for portable computers. New York, N.Y. , c1983. xii, 356 p. : LC Card 87-143515 DDC 380.1/4500416 19
HD9696.C62 M369 1983

The Medical communications market. New York, N.Y. , c1972. vi, 163 leaves : LC Card 87-141851
HD9995.H63 U5454 1972

Medical products packaging market in Europe. New York, N.Y. , c1983. vi, x, xi, 220 p. : LC Card 87-141779 DDC 380.1/456151 19
HD9671.A2 M43 1983

Metal finishing machinery market. New York, N.Y. , c1983. vii, 220 p. ; LC Card 87-141856 DDC 381/.456817671/0973 19
HD9506.U62 M38 1983

Metal working plant market in Europe. New York, N.Y. , c1983. xvi, 262 p. ; LC Card 87-141761 DDC 380.1/456817671/094 19
HD9705.E72 M48 1983

The Microprocessor based measuring instrumentation market in West European manufacturing. New York, N.Y. , c1983. [22], 262, xi p. : LC Card 87-142563
HD9706.2.E8513 M53 1983

The Microprocessor development systems market in West Europe. New York, N.Y. (106 Fulton St., New York 10038) , c1983. 2 v. : LC Card 87-401674 DDC 380.1/4500416/094 19
HD9696.C63 E765 1983

The Microwave test equipment market in the U. S. New York, N.Y. , c1983. iii, 223 p. ; LC Card 87-143814
HD9696.M533 U56 1983

The Military tactical communications switching network market in West Europe. New York, N.Y. , c1983. xvi, 232 p. ; LC Card 87-141849
HD9744.C653 E854 1983

The Military test equipment market in the U. S. New York, N.Y. (106 Fulton St., New York 10038) , c1983. iv, 245 p. : LC Card 87-142060 DDC 381/.45621381/0287 19
HD9743.U6 M545 1983

The Mini-microcomputer turnkey engineering systems market. New York, N.Y. , c1983. vi, 228 p. ; LC Card 87-142400 DDC 381/.4500416 19
HD9696.C63 U5262 1983

Mining equipment market in Europe. New York, N.Y. , c1983. xxix, 294 p. ; LC Card 87-142591 DDC 380.1/4568176/094 19
HD9506.E85 M56 1983

The Mobile radio market in Western Europe. New York, N.Y. , c1982. x, 283 p. : LC Card 87-141850 DDC 380.1/45621384165/094 19
HD9696.R363 E855 1982

MSA, the software company. New York, N.Y. , c1982. v, 73 leaves : LC Card 87-143692 DDC 338.7/610053/0973 19
HD9696.C64 M355 1982

New marketing strategies for office equipment. New York, N.Y. , c1983. vii, 307 p. ; LC Card 87-142201 DDC 381/.456816/0973 19
HD9801.U542 N48 1983

Non-intelligent terminal market in the U. S. New York, N.Y. , c1983. vi, 197 p. : LC Card 87-143735 DDC 381/.456213985/0973 19
HD9696.C63 U52637 1983

The Office automation market in the U. S. New York, N.Y. , <c1983-. v. <2 > : LC Card 87-166011 DDC 381/.456816/0973 19
HD9801.U542 O34 1983

The Office systems software market in Europe. New York, N.Y. , c1983. xv, 256 p. : LC Card 87-144095 DDC 380.1/450053/094 19
HD9696.C63 E8555 1983

Oilfield machinery and equipment market in the U. S. New York, N.Y. , c1983. v, 213 leaves ; LC Card 87-142516 DDC 381/.4568176 19
HD9565 .O643 1983

The Optical memory media market in the U. S. New York, N.Y. , c1983. iv, 218 leaves : LC Card 87-143513 DDC 381/.4562139767/0973 19
HD9696.C63 U52734 1983

The OTC internal medications market. New York, N.Y. (106 Fulton St., New York 10038), c1983. a-d, iii, 279 p. ; LC Card 87-142032
HD9666.5 .O8 1983

The Personal computer hardware add-on device market. New York, N.Y. , c1983. viii, 2, 228 p. : LC Card 87-143524
HD9696.C63 U52783 1983

Petroleum products storage & distribution & information processing. New York, N.Y. , c1983. viii, 249 p. : LC Card 87-143725 DDC 381/.4566554/0973 19
HD9565 .P363 1983

The Portable compressor market. New York, N.Y. (106 Fulton St., New York 10038) , c1983. xi, 254 p. : LC Card 87-142051
HD9705.5.C643 U66 1983

Portable kitchen appliance market. New York, N.Y. , c1983. 2 v. (x, 405 p.) : LC Card 87-143951 DDC 381/.4568383/0973 19
HD9971.5.K583 U656 1983

Prepackaged kits & trays markets in the U. S. New York, N.Y. , c1983. xxiii, 188 p. : LC Card 87-142284 DDC 381/.45681761 19
HD9995.D563 U665 1983

Prepress graphic arts equipment and supplies market in Europe. New York, N.Y. , c1983. xxiii, 268 p. ; LC Card 87-141770 DDC 380.1/456816 19
HD9790.E85 P74 1983

The Process control equipment market (1982-1992). New York, N.Y. , c1983. vii, 241 leaves : LC Card 87-142195 DDC 380.1/456817 19
HD9696.A963 U66 1983

Process control instrumentation in Latin America. New York, N.Y. , c1983. vi, 404 p. ; LC Card 87-141802 DDC 380.1/456817 19
HD9696.P763 L296 1983

Promotion strategies for household cleaning products. New York, N.Y. , c1983. 2 v. (xx, 635 p.) ; LC Card 87-142358 DDC 381/.456671/0973 19
HD9999.C4863 U56 1983

Residential heating, ventilating & cooling systems market. New York, N.Y. , c1983. iv, 269 leaves : LC Card 87-138699 DDC 381/.45697/000973 19
HD9683.U52 R47 1983

The Rubber chemicals market in the EEC. New York, N.Y. , c1983. xxi, 303 p. ; LC Card 87-142579
HD9161.E8562 R83 1983

The Semiconductor assembly equipment market in the U. S. New York, N.Y. , c1983. viii, 326 p. ; LC Card 87-141854 DDC 381/.4562138152 19
HD9696.S43 U4955 1983

The Semiconductor market in the U. S. New York, N.Y. , c1983. v, 207 p. : LC Card 87-143827 DDC 381/.4562138152/0973 19
HD9696.S43 U496 1983

The Special surgery equipment and supplies market in the U. S. New York, N.Y. , c1983. xxiii, 332 p. : LC Card 87-142345 DDC 381/.45681761 19
HD9995.S93 U56 1983

Strategies for selling underground & surface mining equipment. New York, N.Y. , c1983. vii, 320 p. : LC Card 87-142333 DDC 381/.4568176/0973 19
HD9506.U62 S865 1983

Third party maintenance of computers and data terminals in the United States. New York, N.Y. , c1983. vi, 269 leaves ; LC Card 87-142515 DDC 381/.4562139/0973 19
HD9696.C63 U5874 1983

The U. S. market for hazardous duty liquid pumps and valves. New York, N.Y. , c1983. 2 v. (viii, 343 leaves) : LC Card 87-401677 DDC 381/.456216 19
HD9651.5 .U16 1983

The U. S. market for intelligent terminals. New York, N.Y. , c1983. vi, 195 p. : LC Card 87-143740 DDC 381/.456213985/0973 19
HD9696.C63 U5885 1983

The U. S. mobile radio communications equipment market. New York, N.Y. , c1983. viii, 253 p. : LC Card 87-142226 DDC 384.5/3 19
HD9696.R363 U684 1983

The U. S. non telecommunications fiber optic component market in the U. S. New York, N.Y. , c1982. vi, 255 leaves : LC Card 87-143641 DDC 381/.456213692/0973 19
HD9696.F523 U557 1982

The U. S. professional/executive workstations market. New York, N.Y. , c1983. vi, 284 p. : LC Card 87-142071 DDC 381/.4500416/0973 19
HD9801.U542 U18 1983

U. S. stationary compressors market. New York, N.Y. , c1983. xi, 271 p. : LC Card 87-143527 DDC 380.1/4562153/0973 19
HD9705.5.C643 U648 1983

Vinyl and acrylic latices markets in Europe. New York, N.Y. , c1983. 2 v. (xxxv, 328 leaves) : LC Card 87-143984 DDC 380.1/456684232/094 19
HD9661.E82 V55 1983

Welding equipment and supplies market. New York, N.Y. , c1983. 2 v. (v, 316 leaves) ; LC Card 87-143994
HD9697.W433 U548 1983

Worldwide remote power sites. New York, N.Y. , c1983. 2 v. (xx, xxvii, 500 p.) : LC Card 87-141748
HD9695.A2 W67 1983

The Worldwide solar electric generation market. New York, N.Y. , c1983. 2 v. (vii, 596 p.) : LC Card 87-401676 DDC 382/.4562131244 19
HD9681.A2 W67 1983

Frost, Floyd. Injury deaths in Washington State, 1968-1983 . Seattle, Wash. (1610 NE 150th, Seattle 98155) [1985] 49, [78] p. : LC Card

86-623057 DDC 363.1/02/09797021 19
HB1323.A22 U65 1985

Frost, Gerald. Towle, Philip, 1945- Protest and perish . London , 1982. 121 p. ; ISBN 0-907967-02-7 (pbk.) : LC Card 83-198296 DDC 355/.0217/0941 19
UA647 .T69 1982 ***NYPL [JLD 86-1904]***

Frost, R. A. (Richard A.) Introduction to knowledge base systems / Richard Frost. London : Collins, 1986. xxi, 677 p. : ill. ; 24 cm. Includes index. Bibliography: p. 633-653. ISBN 0-00-383114-0
1. Expert systems (Computer science). 2. Data base management. I. Title. ***NYPL [JFE 86-3366]***

Frowen, Stephen F. Shackle, G. L. S. (George Lennox Sharman), 1903- [Selections. 1987.] Business, time, and thought . New York , 1988. p. cm. ISBN 0-8147-2586-4 : LC Card 87-5528 DDC 330.1 19
HB72 .S462 1988

Frozen foods and associated equipment in Europe. Frozen foods market in Europe. New York, N.Y. , c1983. 2 v. (vii, 438 p.) ; LC Card 87-142593 DDC 380.1/4566402853/094 19
HD9326.A2 F76 1983

Frozen foods & associated equipment in Europe. Frozen foods market in Europe. New York, N.Y. , c1983. 2 v. (vii, 438 p.) ; LC Card 87-142593 DDC 380.1/4566402853/094 19
HD9326.A2 F76 1983

FROZEN FOODS INDUSTRY - EUROPE.
Frozen foods market in Europe. New York, N.Y. , c1983. 2 v. (vii, 438 p.) ; LC Card 87-142593 DDC 380.1/4566402853/094 19
HD9326.A2 F76 1983

Frozen foods market in Europe. New York, N.Y. : Frost & Sullivan, c1983. 2 v. (vii, 438 p.) ; 29 cm. Spine title: Frozen foods & associated equipment in Europe. "July 1983." "#E630." LC Card 87-142593 DDC 380.1/4566402853/094 19
1. Frozen foods industry - Europe. 2. Refrigerator industry - Europe. 3. Market surveys - Europe. I. Frost & Sullivan. II. Title: Frozen foods & associated equipment in Europe. III. Title: Frozen foods and associated equipment in Europe.
HD9326.A2 F76 1983

Frozen stakes . Mitchell, Barbara. London , Washington, D.C. , c1983. iii, 135 p. : ISBN 0-905347-45-5 (pbk.) : LC Card 84-173206 DDC 333.8/5/09989 19
HD9506.A585 M57 1983 ***NYPL [JLD 86-3548]***

Frude, Neil. A guide to SPSS/PC+ / Neil Frude. New York : Springer : Distributed in U. S. by Springer-Verlag NY, 1987. p. cm. Includes index. ISBN 0-387-91312-2 LC Card 87-16711 DDC 300/.285416 19
1. SPSS/PC+ (Computer system). 2. Social sciences - Data processing. I. Title.
HA32 .F78 1987

Früherkennung von Bankkrisen bei der Abschlussprüfung /. Holterhus, Gerhard. Frankfurt am Main , c1985. xvi, 360 p. : ISBN 3-7819-0348-6 LC Card 86-164226
HG1768.G3 H64 1985

Früh, Bernhard, 1953-
Entscheidungsträgermodelle bei Planungstechniken / Bernhard Früh. Frankfurt am Main ; New York : Lang, c1984. 268 p. : ill. ; 21 cm. (Schriften zur Unternehmensplanung, 0175-8985 . Bd. 1) Originally presented as the author's thesis (doctoral--Universität Hohenheim, 1984) under the title: Simulation als Planungstechnik. Bibliography: p. 253-268. ISBN 3-8204-5499-3 LC Card 85-197372
1. Industrial management - Decision making - Mathematical models. I. Title. II. Series.
HD30.23 .F78 1984

FRUIT - TRADE AND STATISTICS. see **FRUIT TRADE.**

FRUIT TRADE - ARGENTINA - RÍO NEGRO.
Lindenboim, Javier. Monetarismo y mercado de trabajo . Buenos Aires, Argentina , c1985. x, 471 p. : ISBN 950-9370-05-3 LC Card 87-122243 DDC 331.12/0982/73 19
HD5750.R56 L56 1985

FRUIT TRADE - CHILE - CONGRESSES.
García Elizalde, Pedro. El desarrollo frutícola y forestal en Chile y sus derivaciones sociales. Santiago de Chile , 1986. 234 p. : ISBN 92-1-321204-6 LC Card 86-175421
HD9254.C52 G37 1986

FRUIT TRADE - HUNGARY.
Forgács, Katalin. A zöldség-gyümölcs szindróma . Budapest , 1986. 134, [1] p. ; ISBN 963-221-901-5 : LC Card 87-148760
HD9220.H82 F67 1986

FRUIT TRADE - NETHERLANDS - ACCOUNTING.
Normen voor nieuwwaarde en afschrijving van slijtende duurzame produktiemiddelen in de fruitteelt alsmede voor de grondwaarde . Den Haag [1986] 67 p. ; LC Card 86-234475
HF5686.F7 N67 1986

FRUIT TRADE - PHILIPPINES.
Hawes, Gary, 1950- The Philippine State and the Marcos regime . Ithaca , 1987. 196 p. ; ISBN 0-8014-2012-1 (alk. paper) LC Card 86-29237 DDC 382/.41/09599 19
HD9016.P52 H38 1987

FRUIT TRADE - UNITED STATES - STATISTICS.
Fresh trends, 1987 . [Lincolnshire, Ill.] (400 Knightsbridge Pkwy., Lincolnshire 60069) , c1987. 4 v. ; LC Card 87-162047 DDC 381/.415/0973 19
HD9244 .F73 1987

FRUIT, TROPICAL. see **TROPICAL FRUIT.**

Frumento, Armando. Le repubbliche cisalpina e italiana : con particolare riguardo a siderurgia, armamenti, economia ed agli antichi luoghi lombardi del ferro, 1796-1805 / Armando Frumento. Milano : Banca commerciale italiana, 1985. xii, 608 p. ; 26 cm. (Studi e ricerche di storia economica italiana nell'età del Risorgimento) Bibliography: p. 571-587. Includes indexes. LC Card 86-215881
1. Iron industry and trade - Italy - History. 2. Munitions - Italy - History. 3. Italy - Economic conditions. 4. Iron foundries - Italy - Lombardy - History. I. Title.
HD9525.I82 F72 1985

Frumkin, Norman. Tracking America's economy / by Norman Frumkin. Armonk, N.Y. : M.E. Sharpe, c1987. 250 p. : ill. ; 24 cm. Includes bibliographies and index. ISBN 0-87332-437-4 : LC Card 87-9694 DDC 338.5/44/0973 19
1. Economic forecasting - United States. 2. United States - Economic policy - 1981-. 3. Economic indicators - United States. I. Title.
HC106.8 .F78 1987

Fruscio, Dario. Il sistema distributivo italiano : prospettive di sviluppo e piano triennale / Dario Fruscio ; prefazione di Giovanni Nasi. [Milano] : Giuffrè, 1983. vii, 184 p. ; 25 cm. (Collana di diritto ed economia . 3) At head of title: Università degli studi di Pavia, Dipartimento di ricerche aziendali. Includes bibliographical references. LC Card 83-233439 DDC 380.1/0945 19
1. Physical distribution of goods - Italy. 2. Marketing channels - Italy. I. Pavia. Università. Dipartimento di ricerche aziendali. II. Title. III. Series.
HF5415.6 .F78 1983 ***NYPL [JLE 86-3650]***

Fry, John, 1942- Towards a democratic rationality . Aldershot, Hants, England , Brookfield, Vt., USA , c1986. xi, 281 p. : ISBN 0-566-00761-4 : LC Card 86-14241 DDC 331/.09485 19
HD8576.5 .F79 1986 ***NYPL [JLD 86-3873]***

Fry, Robert A. Bennett, Peter D. Marketing /. New York , c1988. xxvii, 763 p. : ISBN 0-07-004721-9 : LC Card 87-17335 DDC 658.8 19
HF5415 .B4293 1988

Fry, Ronald. National Forum on Issues in Vocational Assessment (2nd : 1986 : Dallas, Tex.) Second National Forum on Issues in Vocational Assessment . Menomonie, Wis. , c1985. vii, 236 p. : ISBN 0-916671-71-2 (pbk.) LC Card 86-217148 DDC 362/.0425 19
HD7256.U5 N336 1986

Fryar, Maridell. Thomas, David Allen, 1939- Business communication today! /. Lincolnwood, Ill., U. S.A. , c1988. xi, 532 p. : ISBN 0-8442-5595-5 LC Card 87-60193 DDC 651.7 19
HF5718 .T46 1988

Fryde, E. B. Studies in medieval trade and finance / E.B. Fryde. London : Hambledon Press, 1983. 1 v. (various pagings) ; 24 cm. (History series . v. 13) Sixteen articles reprinted from various sources. "A select bibliography of publications by E.B. Fryde": p. ix-x. Includes bibliographical references and index. ISBN 0-907628-10-9 LC Card 83-168474 DDC 382/.0942/04 19
1. Finance - England - History. 2. Finance - Europe - History. 3. England - Commerce - Europe - History. 4. Europe - Commerce - England - History. I. Series: History series (London) , v. 13. II. Title.
HF3518.E85 F79 1983 ***NYPL [JLE 86-2481]***

Frydynskiĭ, A. I. (Aleksandr Ignat´evich)
Upravlenie trudovymi resursami . Kiev , 1986. 238 p. ; LC Card 86-233715
HD5797.U37 U67 1986

Fryer, David. Unemployed people . Milton Keynes, England , Philadelphia, PA, USA , 1987. 292 p. ; ISBN 0-335-15507-3 LC Card 87-5792 DDC 305/.90694 19
HD5708 .U57 1987

Fryer, Jonathan.
[Food for thought. French]
L'aide alimentaire, un marché de dupes / Jonathan Fryer. Genève, Suisse : Editions CETIM : [Distributor] ; 91 p. ; 18 cm. (PUBLICetim . 9) Bibliography: p. 87-91. Translation of: Food for thought, the use and abuse of food aide. LC Card 86-218069
1. Food supply - Developing countries. 2. Food relief - Developing countries. 3. Famines - Developing countries. I. Series: PUBLICetim , no. 9. II. Title.
HD9018.D44 F7914 1982

Fuchs, Gerhard, 1939- Die Bundesrepublik Deutschland : Neubearbeitung / Gerhard Fuchs.1. Aufl. Stuttgart : E. Klett, 1983. 296 p. : ill. (1 col.), maps ; 23 cm. (Länderprofile, geographische Strukturen, Daten, Entwicklungen) Two col. maps on folded leaf in pocket. Includes index. Bibliography: p. 282-292. ISBN 3-12-922191-3 LC Card 83-166769 DDC 330.943/087 19
1. Land use - Germany (West). 2. Migration, Internal - Germany (West). 3. Germany, West - Economic conditions. I. Title.
HD656 .F8 1983 ***NYPL [JLE 86-578]***

Fuchs, Hans-Jürgen, 1957- Das glückliche Bewusstsein und die Krise : Ausländerfeindlichkeit in der Bundesrepublik / Hans-Jürgen Fuchs. Frankfurt [am Main] : Brandes & Apsel, c1986. 133 p. ; 21 cm. (Wissen & Praxis . 5) Bibliography: 123-133. ISBN 3-925798-25-0 LC Card 87-112965
1. Alien labor - Germany, West. 2. Social integration - Germany (West). I. Title. II. Series.
HD8458.A2 F83 1986

Fuchs, Lawrence H. When to count by race : affirmative action, quotas, and equal opportunity / Lawrence H. Fuchs. New York, NY : American Jewish Committee, Institute of Human Relations, c1986. 32 p. ; 28 cm. Abridged and updated version of an address presented at a Conference on Black-Jewish Relations at the University of District of Columbia, Nov. 18-19, 1985. Bibliography: p. 28-32. ISBN 0-87495-082-1 (pbk.) : LC Card 86-71979 DDC 658.3 19
1. Discrimination in employment - United States. 2. Discrimination in education - United States. 3. Affirmative action programs - United States. I. Title.
HD4903.5.U58 F83 1986

Fuchs, Nikolaus, 1955- Ursachen- und Krisenanalyse der Verschuldung von Entwicklungsländern : unter besonderer Berücksichtigung betriebswirtschaftlicher Kriterien / Nikolaus Fuchs. Berlin : P. Oberhofer, c1986. 258 p. : ill. ; 21 cm. (Forschungsberichte Betriebswirtschaftslehre . Bd. 1) Bibliography: p. 237-258. ISBN 3-925410-05-8 LC Card 87-124994 DDC 336.3/435/091724 19
1. Debts, External - Developing countries. 2. Developing countries - Foreign economic relations. I. Title. II. Series.
HJ8899 .F83 1986

Fucini, Joseph J. Experience, Inc. : men and women who founded famous companies after the age of 40 / Joseph J. Fucini, Suzy Fucini. New York : Free Press ; London : Collier Macmillan, c1987. xi, 244 p. : ill. ; 25 cm. Bibliography: p. 228-236. Includes index. ISBN 0-02-910971-X LC Card 87-11984 DDC 338/.04/0922 B 19
1. Businessmen - Biography. 2. Entrepreneur - Biography. I. Fucini, Suzy. II. Title.
HC29 .F834 1987

Fucini, Suzy. Fucini, Joseph J. Experience, Inc. . New York , London , c1987. xi, 244 p. : ISBN 0-02-910971-X LC Card 87-11984 DDC 338/.04/0922 B 19
HC29 .F834 1987

FUEL - INDIA.
Mayer, Hans, 1951- Energie für die Armen? . Saarbrücken , Fort Lauderdale , 1984. 195 p. : ISBN 3-88156-288-5 : LC Card 85-199309
HD9502.I42 M38 1984

FUEL - PRICES - DEVELOPING COUNTRIES - CONGRESSES.
Energy Pricing Policy Workshop (1984 : Bangkok, Thailand) Criteria for energy pricing policy . London , Gaithersburg, MD, USA , 1985. 247 p. : ISBN 0-86010-618-1 : LC Card 86-147259 DDC 333.79/17 19
HD9502.D442 E56 1984

FUEL - PRICES - GERMANY (WEST) - ECONOMETRIC MODELS.
Borrmann, Axel. Die Wettbewerbsposition natürlicher Rohstoffe . Hamburg , 1984. 226 p. : ISBN 3-87895-250-3 LC Card 84-222130
HF1054.G4 B67 1984

FUEL - SWEDEN - STORAGE.
Sweden. 1980 års oljelagringskommitté. Kol, uran och gas för kristid. [Stockholm] [1981] 192 p. : ISBN 91-38-06450-2 LC Card 83-107879
HD9502.S82 S88 1981

FUEL TRADE - EUROPE, EASTERN - INTERNATIONAL COOPERATION.
Kozlov, I. D. (Igor′ Dmitrievich) Ėnergeticheskoe khoziaĭstvo stran SĖV . Moskva , 1980. 158 p. ; LC Card 87-107887
HD9502.E83 K686 1980

FUEL TRADE - GOVERNMENT POLICY - UNITED STATES - HISTORY - 20TH CENTURY.
Clark, John Garretson, 1932- Energy and the federal government . Urbana , c1987. xxiii, 511 p. : ISBN 0-252-01295-X LC Card 85-20505 DDC 333.8/2/0973 19
HD9502.U52 C57 1987 ***NYPL [JLE 87-736]***

FUEL TRADE - INDIA.
Mayer, Hans, 1951- Energie für die Armen? . Saarbrücken , Fort Lauderdale , 1984. 195 p. : ISBN 3-88156-288-5 : LC Card 85-199309
HD9502.I42 M38 1984

FUEL TRADE - SOUTH CAROLINA - HISTORY.
DeMontmollin, Richard Hall. The SCOJA story . [Columbia, S.C.] , c1986. xi, 191 p. : ISBN 0-9617613-0-X LC Card 86-62676 DDC 381/.456655/060757 19
HD9569.S663 D46 1986

FUELWOOD CONSUMPTION - AFRICA, EASTERN - CONGRESSES.
Regional Workshop on Wood Energy in East Africa (1982 : Nairobi, Kenya) Proceedings of the Regional Workshop on Wood Energy in East Africa . Ottawa, Canada [1983] 241 p. : LC Card 86-185703 DDC 333.75 19
HD9769.F843 A367 1982

FUELWOOD CONSUMPTION - SUDAN - KASSALĀ (PROVINCE)
Abu Sin, M. E. (Mohad E.) Socio-economic aspects of integrated resource management, with special reference to the forest resources of Kassala Province, Eastern Region . Khartoum , 1986. vi leaves, 109 p. : LC Card 87-980440 DDC 333.75/09629/2 19
HD9767.S843 K3724 1986

FUELWOOD INDUSTRY - AFRICA, EASTERN - CONGRESSES.
Regional Workshop on Wood Energy in East Africa (1982 : Nairobi, Kenya) Proceedings of the Regional Workshop on Wood Energy in East Africa . Ottawa, Canada [1983] 241 p. : LC Card 86-185703 DDC 333.75 19
HD9769.F843 A367 1982

FUELWOOD INDUSTRY - KENYA.
Chavangi, Noel A. Culture as the basis for implementing self-sustaining wood fuel development programmes /. Nairobi, Kenya [1985] 24 leaves ; LC Card 87-111963 DDC 333.75 19
HD9769.F843 K433 1985

FUELWOOD INDUSTRY - KENYA - KAKAMEGA DISTRICT.
Bradley, Phil. The district resource analysis as applied to Kakamega District /. Nairobi [1984] 11 leaves : LC Card 87-112452 DDC 333.75 19
HD9769.F843 K425 1984

Chavangi, Noel A. Cultural aspects of fuelwood procurement in Kakamega District /. Nairobi [1984] 13 leaves ; LC Card 87-112356 DDC 333.75 19
HD9769.F843 K43 1984

FUELWOOD INDUSTRY - SWEDEN.
Skogsbränsle . Stockholm [1986] 159 p. : ISBN 91-38-09241-7 LC Card 86-201607
HD9769.F842 S57 1986

Sweden. Statens industriverk. Ökad eldning med skogsråvara . Stockholm , 1980. 203 p. : ISBN 91-38-05361-6 LC Card 82-236954
HD9769.F843 S87 1980

FUELWOOD - RESEARCH - SWEDEN.
Skogsbränsle . Stockholm [1986] 159 p. : ISBN 91-38-09241-7 LC Card 86-201607
HD9769.F842 S57 1986

Fuenzalida Faivovich, Edmundo.
[América Latina y la concentración del poder en la arena política]
América Latina y la concentración del poder en la arena política ; El impacto social del cambio tecnológico actual en los países menos desarrollados / Edmundo Fuenzalida Faivovich. [Santiago de Chile] : Universidad Católica de Chile, Instituto de Ciencia Política, [between 1974 and 1979] 24, 25 leaves ; 26 cm. (Documento de trabajo . año 5, no. 8-9) Cover title. Includes bibliographies. LC Card 82-180082
1. International business enterprises - Latin America. 2. Latin America - Dependency on foreign countries. 3. Technological innovations - Economic aspects - Developing countries. I. Fuenzalida Faivovich, Edmundo. Impacto social del cambio tecnológico actual en los países menos desarrollados. 1974. II. Title: América Latina y la concentración del poder en la arena política. III. Title: Impacto social del cambio tecnológico actual en los países menos desarrollados. IV. Series: Documento de trabajo (Universidad Católica de Chile. Instituto de Ciencia Política) , año 5, no. 8-9.
HD2810.5 .F84 1974

Impacto social del cambio tecnológico actual en los países menos desarrollados. 1974.
Fuenzalida Faivovich, Edmundo. [América Latina y la concentración del poder en la arena política.] América Latina y la concentración del poder en la arena política ; El impacto social del cambio tecnológico actual en los países menos desarrollados / Edmundo Fuenzalida Faivovich. [Santiago de Chile] [between 1974 and 1979] 24, 25 leaves ; LC Card 82-180082
HD2810.5 .F84 1974

Fuenzalida, Valerio. Modelos de TV y radio y su influencia en la génesis cultural / Valerio Fuenzalida. [Santiago, Chile] : CENECA, 1980. 16 leaves ; 28 cm. (Serie Artículos) Photocopy. Bibliography: leaves 14-16. LC Card 85-209582
1. Broadcasting - Chile - Social aspects. I. Title. II. Title: Modelos de televisión y radio y su influencia en la génesis cultural. III. Series.
HE8689.9.C5 F84 1980

Für einen anhaltenden Aufschwung : was kann die Wirtschaftspolitik beitragen? : Thesen zum 34. Kieler Konjunkturgespräch. Kiel : Institut für Weltwirtschaft, [1986] 29 p. : ill. ; 30 cm. (Kieler Diskussionsbeiträge, 0455-0420 . 123 = 123) Cover title. Report prepared by G. Flemig and others. "September 1986." Includes bibliographical references. ISBN 3-925357-33-5 (Deut. Bibl.) : LC Card 86-234971
1. Germany, West - Economic policy - 1974-. 2. United States - Economic policy - 1981-. 3. Germany, West - Economic conditions - 1974-. 4. United States - Economic conditions - 1981-. I. Flemig, Günter. II. Kieler Konjunkturgespräch (34th : 1986?). III. Universität Kiel. Institut für Weltwirtschaft. IV. Series: Kieler Diskussionsbeiträge , 123.
HB44 .K45 no. 123 HC286.7

Fürstenberg, Friedrich. Arbeitsgestaltung in der Serienfertigung . Frankfurt [am Main] , New York , c1984. 315 p. : ISBN 3-593-32733-3 LC Card 84-230390
HD58.8 .A73 1984

FUERTE RIVER VALLEY (MEXICO) - ECONOMIC CONDITIONS.
Gill, Mario. La conquista del Valle del Fuerte /. Culiacán, Rosales, Sinaloa, México , c1983. 273 p., [4] folded leaves of plates : LC Card 86-121747
HC137.F84 G54 1983

Fuertes, Juan Velarde. see Velarde Fuertes, Juan.

La fuerza de trabajo en los países de la Cuenca del Plata según los censos de 1960 /. Chackiel, Juan. San José, Costa Rica , 1976. iv, 81 p. : LC Card 83-169596
HD5746.A6 C42 1976

Fues, Thomas. Crafts and small-scale industries in Lesotho . Berlin [1982] vi, 60, 16 p., [1] leaf of plates : LC Card 84-215894 DDC 338.6/42/096816 19
HD2346.L44 C73 1982 ***NYPL [Sc F 86-141]***

Fuest, Winfried, 1946-
Irrtümer in der aktuellen Steuerdiskussion / Winfried Fuest, Rolf Kroker. Köln : Deutscher Instituts-Verlag, c1987. 54 p. : 3 ill. ; 21 cm. (Beiträge zur Wirtschafts- und Sozialpolitik . 149 (2/1987)) Bibliography: p. 52-54. ISBN 3-602-24749-X LC Card 87-409547 DDC 336.2/00943 19
1. Taxation - Germany, West. 2. Fiscal policy - Germany, West. 3. Business enterprises - Taxation - Germany, West. I. Kroker, Rolf. II. Series: Beiträge zur Wirtschafts- und Sozialpolitik , 149. III. Title.
HJ2687 .F834 1987

Quantitative und qualitative Konsolidierung / Winfried Fuest, Rolf Kroker. Köln : Deutscher Instituts-Verlag, c1986. 44 p. : ill. ; 21 cm. (Beiträge zur Wirtschafts- und Sozialpolitik . 141 = 3/1986) Includes bibliographical references. ISBN 3-602-24741-4 LC Card 86-214118
1. Budget - Germany, West. I. Kroker, Rolf. II. Series: Beiträge zur Wirtschafts- und Sozialpolitik , 141. III. Title.
HJ2110 .F84 1986

Subventionen : Problematik und Begrenzungsmöglichkeiten / Winfried Fuest. Köln : Deutscher Instituts-Verlag, c1985. 40 p. : ill. ; 21 cm. (Beiträge zur Wirtschafts- und Sozialpolitik . 132, 3/1985) Includes bibliographical references. ISBN 3-602-24732-5 LC Card 85-200722
1. Subsidies - Germany, West. I. Series: Beiträge zur Wirtschafts- und Sozialpolitik , 132. II. Title.
HC290.5.S9 F84 1985

La fuga de capital en Centroamérica, 1977-1984 /. Glower, Carlos J., 1952- Tegucigalpa, D.C., Honduras, C.A. , 1986. 20 p. : LC Card 87-125008 DDC 332/.042 19
HG3917 .G56 1986

Fuga de capitales . Conesa, Eduardo R. Buenos Aires , 1986. 78 p. : LC Card 87-400256 DDC 332.4/5 19
HG3931 .C66 1986

Fügedi, Márta. Dobrossy, István. Termelés és életmód . Debrecen , 1983. 282 p. : ISBN 963-471-276-2 LC Card 86-100359
HD1492.H82 P873 1983

Fugmann, Friedrich. Working towards European unification . [Luxembourg] , 1986. 60 p. ; LC Card 87-149629 DDC 338/.06 19
HC240.9.T4 W67 1986

Fuhrich, Manfred, 1950-
Neue Heimat . Hamburg , 1983. 231 p. : ISBN 3-87975-238-9 LC Card 83-150360
HD7339.H3 N48 1983

Sicherung des Sozialmietwohnungsbestandes / Manfred Fuhrich. Frankfurt am Main : Haag + Herchen, c1986. xxiii, 180, 16 p. : ill. ; 21 cm. (Beiträge zur städtebaulichen Forschung . Bd. 1) Bibliography: p. 172-179. ISBN 3-88129-996-3 LC Card 86-223886
1. Public housing - Germany, West. 2. Public housing - Germany (West) - Finance. 3. Rent charges - Germany (West). I. Title. II. Series.
HD7288.78.G3 F84 1986

Führung : Festschrift zum 25jährigen Bestehen der Schweizerischen Kurse für Unternehmungsführung / hrsg. von der Vereinigung "Schweizerische Kurse für Unternehmungsführung". Zürich : Verlag Industrielle Organisation, cop. 1979. 189 p. : ill. ; 25 cm. Includes bibliographical references. CONTENTS. - Ist die Welt noch regierbar?, von C. Gasteyger.--Regieren oder "leiten"?, von P. Dürrenmatt.--Führung in Armee und Wirtschaft, von F. Seethaler.--Die Forschungspolitik als staatliche Führungsaufgabe, von A.P. Speiser.--Die Bedeutung der Persönlichkeit für die Führung einer Unternehmung,

von H. Biäsch.--Anforderungen an die Persönlichkeit des Führenden, von W. Hess.--Gedanken zum Wandel von Anforderungen und Weiterbildungszielen in der Unternehmungsführung, von E. Schmidt.--Zur Auswahl und Entwicklung der Führungskräfte, von H.B. Gamper.--Führungstechnik oder Führungskunst, von F. Muheim.--Systems Engineering als Führungsinstrument, von E. Brem.--Gedanken zum Krisenmanagement in der Unternehmung, von E. Rühli.--Führung und Verantwortung, von K. Schmid.--Führung? Ketzerische Gedanken eines alten, aber durchaus nicht frustrierten Praktikers, von M.E. Eisenring.--Verantwortung in der Unternehmensführung, von G. Huber.--Führung--wohin?, von H. Ulrich. ISBN 3-85743-841-X : LC Card 81-461814 DDC 658 19
1. Schweizerische Kurse für Unternehmungsführung. 2. Industrial management - Addresses, essays, lectures. 3. Management - Addresses, essays, lectures. I. Schweizerische Kurse für Unternehmungsführung.
HD35 .F8115 ***NYPL [JLE 82-593]***

Fujino, Shozaburo, 1927- Money, employment, and interest : towards a reconstruction of Keynesian economics / by Shozaburo Fujino. Tokyo, Japan : Kinokuniya ; New York, NY : Distributed by New York Kinokuniya Bookstores, [1987] xii, 220 p. : ill. ; 22 cm. (Economic research series / Institute of Economic Research, Hitotsubashi University . no. 23) Includes bibliographical references and indexes. ISBN 4-314-00464-9 : LC Card 87-165395 DDC 330.15/6 19
1. Keynesian economics - Mathematical models. I. Series: Economic research series (Hitotsubashi Daigaku. Keizai Kenkyūjo) , no. 23. II. Title.
HB99.7 .F85 1987

Fuld, Leonard M. Monitoring the competition : find out what's really going on over there / Leonard M. Fuld. New York, N.Y. : Wiley, c1988. xiii, 204 p. ; 24 cm. Bibliography: p. 168. Includes index. ISBN 0-471-85261-9 LC Card 87-21607 DDC 658.4/7 19
1. Business intelligence. 2. Competition, Unfair. I. Title.
HD38.7 .F86 1988

FULL EMPLOYMENT POLICIES.

Arndt, Helmut, 1911- Vollbeschäftigung . Berlin , c1984. 196 p. : ISBN 3-428-05602-7 LC Card 84-209024
HD5706 .A855 1984

Befreiung der Arbeit . Bonn , c1986. 197 p. : ISBN 3-87831-429-9 LC Card 86-194157
HD6955 .B389 1986

Dräger, Heinrich, 1898- Zu wenig Arbeit für zu viele Menschen . Stuttgart , 1984. 125 p. : ISBN 3-87959-220-9 LC Card 84-198317
HD5779 .D68 1984

Driver, Ciaran. Towards full employment . London , New York , 1987. xii, 238 p. : ISBN 0-7102-0918-5 LC Card 87-9814 DDC 339.5 19
HD5713.2 .D75 1987

Freyssinet, Jacques. Le chômage /. Paris , 1984. 128 p. : ISBN 2-7071-1478-2 LC Card 85-115448 DDC 331.13/7 19
HD5707.5 .F74 1984

Keane, John, 1949- After full employment /. London , Dover, N.H., USA , 1986. 198 p. ; ISBN 0-09-164091-1 (pbk.) : LC Card 86-213691 DDC 339.5/0941 19
HD5765.A6 K42 1986

Ravaioli, Carla. Tempo da vendere, tempo da usare . Milano, Italy , c1986. 142 p. ; LC Card 86-182560
HD5106 .R357 1986

Reineke, Ulrich, 1955- Segmentationstheorien des Arbeitsmarktes und Beschäftigungsniveau . Frankfurt am Main , New York , c1986. iv, 333 p. : ISBN 3-8204-9671-8 LC Card 87-407583 DDC 331.12/0943 19
HD5706 .R43 1986

Sawyer, Malcolm C. Finance, money, and unemployment /. Berlin [1985] 65 p. ; LC Card 86-205291 DDC 332 19
HG230.3 .S29 1985

FULL EMPLOYMENT POLICIES - ADDRESSES, ESSAYS, LECTURES.

Unemployment and growth in the Western economies /. New York, N.Y. , c1984. x, 142 p. ; ISBN 0-87609-001-3 (pbk.) : LC Card 84-9415 DDC 331.13/791812 19
HD5707.5 .U54 1984 ***NYPL [JLE 86-1564]***

FULL EMPLOYMENT POLICIES - CONGRESSES.

Employment promotion and social security . Geneva , 1986. iv, 156 p. ; ISBN 92-2-105574-4 (pbk.) : LC Card 86-234498 DDC 368.4/4 19
HD7095 .E46 1986

Le Iniziative locali per l'occupazione . Milano, Italy , c1985. 244 p. : LC Card 85-221711 DDC 331 s 331.12/042 19
HD85.I7 I68 no. 75 HD5713.5
NYPL [JLD 87-446]

Perspektiven der Vollbeschäftigung . Köln , c1987. vi, 263 p. : ISBN 3-7663-3033-0 LC Card 87-135012 DDC 339.5 19
HD5701.3 .P47 1987

Strukturpolitik als Dimension der Vollbeschäftigungspolitik /. Stuttgart , c1983. 103 p. : ISBN 3-437-50276-X : LC Card 83-233394
HD5706 .S82 1983

Full employment, uncertain futures /. International Conference on Employment and Training (1985 : Perth, W.A.) [Perth, W.A.] [1985] ix, 263 p. : LC Card 86-185208 DDC 339.5 19
HD5701.3 .I55 1985

Fullagar, Clive. Behaviour in organisations . Johannesburg , New York , 1986, c1983. 924 p. : ISBN 0-07-450690-0 (pbk.) : LC Card 87-113321 DDC 158.7/0968 19
HD58.7 .B426 1986

Fuller, Bernard. Treated wood update : the markets for treated lumber, timbers, and plywood through 2000. Lexington, Mass., USA (24 Hartwell Ave., Lexington 02173) : Data Resources, c1985. iii, 121 p. : ill. ; 28 cm. (DRI forest products special study series . no. 9) "July 1985." LC Card 86-201219 DDC 381/.45674/0973 19
1. Lumber trade - United States - Statistics. 2. Plywood industry - United States - Statistics. I. Title. II. Series.
HD9754 .F85 1985

Fuller, Ken. Radical aristocrats : London busworkers from the 1880s to the 1980s / Ken Fuller. London : Lawrence and Wishart ; Atlantic Highlands, N.J. : Distributed in the U. S.A. and Canada by Humanities Press, 1985. 256 p. : ill. ; 22 cm. Distributor from label on t.p. Includes bibliographies and index. ISBN 0-85315-649-2 (pbk.) : LC Card 86-214586 DDC 331.88/1138841322/09421 19
1. Bus lines - England - London - Employees - History. 2. Transport and General Workers' Union (Great Britain) - History. I. Title.
HD8039.M82 G74 1985

Fuller, Theodore, 1929- The Mid-Atlantic region in transition : employment trends, 1974-84 / Theodore E. Fuller. Washington, D.C. : U. S. Dept. of Agriculture, Economic Research Service, [1986] v, 13 p. : ill., col. maps ; 28 cm. (Rural development research report . no. 57) Cover title. Distributed to depository libraries in microfiche. "April 1986"--P. [iii] Bibliography: p. 12. Item 24-G-02 (microfiche) LC Card 86-602014 DDC 331.12/0974 19
1. Labor supply - Middle Atlantic States - Statistics. I. United States. Dept. of Agriculture. Economic Research Service. II. Title. III. Series.
HD5725.A12 F85 1986

Fullerton, Douglas H. Graham Towers and his times : a biography / by Douglas H. Fullerton. Toronto, Ont. : McClelland and Stewart, c1986. 348 p., [16] p. of plates : ill. ; 24 cm. Bibliography: p. 320-341. Includes index. ISBN 0-7710-3218-8 : LC Card 86-231010 DDC 332.1/1/092 B 19
1. Towers, Graham F., 1897-1975. 2. Bankers - Canada - Biography. 3. Bank of Canada - History. I. Title.
HG1552.T68 F85 1986

Fulpen, Hans van. Volkshuisvesting in demografisch en economisch perspectief / Hans van Fulpen. 's-Gravenhage : Sociaal en Cultureel Planbureau : Staatsuitgeverij, 1985. 354 p. : ill. ; 27 cm. (Sociale en culturele studies . 8) Summary in English. Bibliography: p. 323-349. ISBN 90-12-05159-2 LC Card 86-169936
1. Housing - Netherlands. 2. Housing - Netherlands - Finance. 3. Housing policy - Netherlands. 4. Netherlands - Population. I. Title. II. Series.
HD7344.A3 F85 1985

Fulton, Patsy J. General office procedures for colleges / Patsy J. Fulton. 9th ed. Cincinnati : South-Western Pub. Co., c1988. viii, 399 p. : ill. (some col.) ; 29 cm. "K73." Includes index. ISBN 0-538-11732-X (pbk.) LC Card 86-63580 DDC 651 19
1. Office practice. 2. Universities and colleges - Business management. I. Title. II. Title: Office practice.
HF5547.5 .F84 1988

Fumero Marta, Julio, 1934- Comercio exterior : organización y técnica / Julio Fumero Marta, Ramón Juliá Milanés. La Habana : Editorial de Ciencias Sociales, 1985. vii, 210 p. : ill. ; 21 cm. (Economía / Editorial de Ciencias Sociales) Bibliography: p. 207-208. LC Card 87-107270
1. Commerce. I. Juliá Milanés, Ramón, 1942-. II. Series: Economía / Editorial de Ciencias Sociales. III. Title.
HF1008 .F86 1985

La función gerencial en la empresa . Settembrino, Hugo O. Buenos Aires , c1985. viii, 127 p. : ISBN 950-0-23598-6 LC Card 85-201051
HD37.S66 S47 1985

Las funciones administrativas . Mendoza, José María. Barranquilla , c1985. xiv, 207 p. : ISBN 958-9105-00-9 LC Card 86-187780
HD37.S66 M46 1985

Funciones y servicios de competencia municipal / autores, Pedro León Almeida ... [et al.]. Córdoba, República Argentina : Centro de Investigación y Perfeccionamiento en Ciencias Económicas y Administración Pública, 1984. 94 leaves ; 29 cm. (Cuadernos de administración pública. no. 43) Includes bibliographical references. LC Card 87-121632 DDC 352.082 19
1. Municipal services - Argentina - Case studies. 2. Public schools - Argentina. 3. Public health - Argentina. 4. Housing - Argentina. 5. Water-supply - Argentina. I. León Almeida, Pedro. II. Series. III. Series: Cuadernos de administración pública (Universidad Católica de Córdoba. Centro de Investigación y Perfeccionamiento en Ciencias Económicas y Administración Pública) , 43.
HD4629 .F86 1984

Funck, Rolf H. Space-structure-economy . Karlsruhe [San Francisco, CA] c1986. vii, 311 p. : ISBN 3-88652-680-1 (pbk.) LC Card 87-129134 DDC 330.1 19
HB107.L66 S63 1986

FUNCTIONAL EQUATIONS.

Aczél, J. A short course on functional equations . Dordrecht, Holland ; Boston : vi, 169 p. : ISBN 90-277-2376-1 LC Card 86-26131 DDC 515/.25 19
HB135 .A28 1987

FUNCTIONS, DEMAND (ECONOMIC THEORY) see DEMAND FUNCTIONS (ECONOMIC THEORY)

FUNCTIONS, PRODUCTION (ECONOMIC THEORY) see PRODUCTION FUNCTIONS (ECONOMIC THEORY)

FUND RAISING - RESEARCH.

Bergan, Helen, 1937- Where the money is . Alexandria, Va. , c1985. 101 p. : ISBN 0-9615277-0-6 (pbk.) : LC Card 85-72141 DDC 361.7 19
HG177 .B48 1985 ***NYPL [JLD 87-844]***

FUND RAISING - UNITED STATES - BIBLIOGRAPHY.

Corporate support for community development. Washington, D.C. , c1984. 15 p. ; LC Card 87-100348 DDC 361.7/65/0973 19
HD60.5.U5 C689 1984

FUND RAISING - UNITED STATES - DIRECTORIES.

Capital campaign resource guide. San Francisco, Calif. , c1984. x, 1229 p. : LC Card 87-122608 DDC 658.1/5224 19
HG177.5.U6 C36 1984

FUND RAISING - UNITED STATES - HANDBOOKS, MANUALS, ETC.

Capital campaign resource guide. San Francisco, Calif. , c1984. x, 1229 p. : LC Card 87-122608 DDC 658.1/5224 19
HG177.5.U6 C36 1984

Fundação Bahiana para Estudos Econômicas e Sociais. Simonsen, Mário Henrique. A nova ordem econômica internacional e suas consequências no Brasil . Salvador , 1983. 60 p. ; LC Card 87-144638 DDC 337.81 19
HF1513 .S55 1983

Fundação Bahiana para Estudos Econômicos e Sociais.
Bulhões, Octávio Gouveia de. Desdobramentos inflacionários. [Salvador] [1984] 43 p. : LC Card 86-861354 DDC 332.4/1/0981 19
HG835 .B85 1984

Convivência do homem com a seca e irrigação no Nordeste /. [Salvador, Brazil] [1984] 76 p. : LC Card 87-130774 DDC 333.91/3/09813 19
HD1741.B82 N624 1984

Daly, Herman E. Crescimento ou economia estacionária. [Salvador] [1983] 56 p. : LC Card 87-127979 DDC 338.9 19
HD85.S7 D35 1983

Política demográfica /. Salvador [1983] 82 p. : LC Card 87-138903 DDC 304.6/0981 19
HB3563 .P65 1983

Fundação do Serviço Social do Distrito Federal. Coordenadoria de Planejamento e Controle. Sobrevivência, aspectos das condições de vida de menores trabalhadores de rua do Distrito Federal /. [Brasília] , 1983. 117 p. ; LC Card 86-197113
HD6276.B73 D577 1983

Fundação Dom Cabral. Formas alternativas de negociação das exportações brasileiras . Belo Horizonte, MG , c1984. 122 p. ; LC Card 86-200391
HF1513 .F67 1984

Fundação Edison Vieira.
Caracterização da indústria agroalimentar no Paraná /. Curitiba , 1985. x, 50 leaves : LC Card 86-202725
HD9014.B83 P3718 1985

Emprego urgente /. Curitiba , 1984. vii, 75 p. ; LC Card 86-177208
HD5713 .E47 1984

Produto interno bruto do Paraná, 1970-84 /. Curitiba , 1985. vi, 63 leaves : LC Card 87-403687 DDC 339.381/62 19
HC188.P35 P76 1985

Fundação Estadual de Planejamento Agrícola de Alagoas. Estudo especial . Maceió, AL. , 1983. 174 leaves : LC Card 86-167829
HC189.A69 E88 1983

Fundação Getúlio Vargas.
Produção agrícola brasileira . [Rio de Janeiro] , 1986. 188 p. : LC Card 87-403944 DDC 338.1/0981/021 19
HD9014.B82 P765 1986

Seminario Interamericano Conmemorativo de los 25 Años del BID (1985 : Rio de Janeiro, Brazil) Informe del Seminario Interamericano Conmemorativo de los 25 Años del BID /. Rio de Janeiro, RJ , 1986. 65 p. : LC Card 87-403948 DDC 332.1/538 19
HG3881.5.I44 S46 1985

Fundação IBGE. (Old Catalog form: Brazil. Fundação IBGE)
Inquéritos especiais /. Rio de Janeiro, Brasil , 1984. 4 v. in 5. ; ***NYPL [JLF 86-202]***

Fundação Instituto Brasileiro de Geografia e Estatística. Superintendência de Contas Nacionais e Agregados Macroeconômicos. Indices da produção industrial . Rio de Janeiro , 1986. 178 p. : ISBN 85-24-00246-8 LC Card 87-403858 DDC 338.0981/021 19
HC187 .I534 1986

Fundação Instituto Brasileiro de Geografia e Historia. Diretoria Técnica. Força de trabalho no Brasil . Rio de Janeiro , 1982. 73 p. : ISBN 85-24-00002-3 LC Card 87-403683 DDC 331.12/72/0981 19
HD5717.5.B6 F67 1982

Fundação Instituto de Pesquisas Econômicas (São Paulo, Brazil) Macedo, Roberto Brás Matos. FGTS e a rotatividade /. São Paulo-SP , Brasília-DF , 1985. 231 p. : ISBN 85-21-30271-1 LC Card 85-187484
HD7096.B6 M33 1985

Fundação Instituto de Planejamento da Paraíba. Santos, Madalena Herculano dos. Condições de vida nos municípios paraibanos /. João Pessoa (PB) : Brasília, DF : 103 p. : LC Card 87-403990 DDC 330.981/33063 19
HC188.P343 S26 1986

Fundação Instituto de Planejamento do Ceará. Estudos fundamentais . Fortaleza , 1986. 120 p. : LC Card 87-120224
HD2346.B72 C44 1986

Fernandes, Adelita Neto Carleial. Condições de vida nos bairros de Fortaleza, nov/84 a mar/85 . Fortaleza , 1986. 92 p. : LC Card 86-196902
HC189.F67 F47 1986

Fundação João Pinheiro. Economia mineira e o financiamento do setor público . Belo Horizonte , 1985. 126 p. : LC Card 85-207952
HJ2529.M5 E26 1985

Fundação Nacional do Bem-Estar do Menor. Eu preciso trabalhar . Rio de Janeiro [between 1983 and 1986] 85 p. ; LC Card 86-150189
HD6276.B72 E9 1983

Fundação para o Desenvolvimento da Região Metropolitana do Rio de Janeiro. Região metropolitana do Rio de Janeiro . [Rio de Janeiro, Brazil] [1984?] 242 p. : LC Card 87-404930 DDC 330.981/53 19
HC189.R45 R44 1984

Fundação Pedroso Horta. Esperança e mundança. [Brasília] , 1981. 95 p. ; LC Card 86-202933
HC187 .E83 1981

Fundação Prefeito Faria Lima. Superintendência de Desenvolvimento Urbano e Rural. Pesquisas sobre o problema fundiário urbano. [São Paulo] [Brasília?] , 1983. 6 v. in 8 ; LC Card 87-404400 DDC 333.77/13/0981 19
HD496 .P47 1983

Fundação Projeto Rondon. Diretrizes de planejamento : Projeto Rondon, 1983. [Brasília : Ministério do Interior, Fundação Projeto Rondon, 1982] [21] leaves ; 30 cm. LC Card 85-186578
1. Fundação Projeto Rondon. 2. National service - Brazil. 3. Volunteer workers in community development - Brazil. 4. College students - Brazil. I. Title.
HD4870.B6 F86 1982

FUNDAÇÃO PROJETO RONDON.
Fundação Projeto Rondon. Diretrizes de planejamento . [Brasília , 1982] [21] leaves ; LC Card 85-186578
HD4870.B6 F86 1982

Fundación AGAPE (Madrid, Spain) La Pobreza en España y sus causas /. Madrid , 1985. xx, 759 p. : ISBN 84-398-3252-4 : LC Card 86-230170
HC390.P6 P63 1985

Fundación de Investigaciones Económicas Latinoamericanas (Buenos Aires, Argentina) Gasto público : propuestas de reforma del sector público argentino. [Buenos Aires] : Fundación de Investigaciones Económicas Latinoamericanas, 1986. 6 v. in 8 : ill. ; 28 cm. + general introd. (xi leaves) "El trabajo fue dirigido por los economistas doctor Juan Carlos Iarezza y licenciado Enrique Szewach"--V. 1, prelim. leaf 3. Bibliography: v. 1, leaves 44-50 (2nd group) CONTENTS. - t. 1. Resumen general -- t. 2. Administración pública (3 v.) -- t. 3. Educación, salud y seguridad social -- t. 4. Sector energía -- t. 5. Sector transporte y comunicaciones -- t. 6. Empresas dependientes del Ministerio de Defensa. LC Card 87-403573 DDC 354.820072/252 19
1. Budget - Argentina. 2. Argentina - Economic policy. I. Iarezza, Juan Carlos. II. Szewach, Enrique. III. Title.
HJ2075 .F86 1986

Fundación Friedrich Ebert de Colombia. Política ambiental y desarrollo . [Bogotá, Colombia] , 1986. 221 p. : LC Card 86-207035
HC130.E5 P65 1986

Fundación para el Desarrollo Industrial (Cali, Colombia) Perfiles económicos del Valle del Cauca, Colombia. Cali, Colombia [1981?] 40 p. : LC Card 86-120381 DDC 330.9861/520632 19
HC198.V3 P47 1981

Fundación Salvadoreña para el Desarrollo Económico y Social. Departamento de Estudios Económicos y Sociales. Características básicas y evolución reciente del sector externo de El Salvador. San Salvador, El Salvador , 1986. 47 p. : LC Card 87-403789 DDC 337.7284 19
HF1494 .C37 1986

Fundación Universidad-Empresa (Madrid, Spain) La Nueva economía en Francia y en España /. Madrid , c1980. 197 p. : ISBN 84-85355-27-X : LC Card 83-105425 DDC 330.944/0838 19
HB105.A2 N83 1980 ***NYPL [JLD 86-3024]***

Fundación Universitaria de Jerez (Series) .
(4) Illescas Ortiz, Rafael. Europa hacia el sur (al hilo de la adhesión española a la Comunidad europea) /. [Jerez] [1985], 1986 printing. 152 p. ; ISBN 84-600-4184-0 LC Card 86-150722
HC241.25.S6 I47 1986

Fundamental accounting principles / Kermit D. Larson ... [et al.]. 5th Canadian ed. Homewood, Ill. : Irwin, 1987. xvii, 1230 p. : ill. ; 25 cm. Includes index. Rev. ed. of: Fundamental accounting principles / William W. Pyle, Kermit D. Larson, Michael Zin. 4th ed. 1984. ISBN 0-256-03601-2 LC Card 86-83105 DDC 657 19
1. Accounting. I. Larson, Kermit D. II. Pyle, William W. Fundamental accounting principles. III. Title.
HF5635 .P975 1987b

Fundamental accounting principles /. Larson, Kermit D. Homewood, Ill. , 1987. xxxi, 1076 p. : ISBN 0-256-03574-1 LC Card 86-81958 DDC 657 19
HF5635 .P975 1987

FUNDAMENTAL EDUCATION - BOLIVIA.
Segunda reforma agraria . La Paz, Bolivia [1987] 287 p. : LC Card 87-403057 DDC 333.3/1/84 19
HD1333.B5 S44 1987

FUNDAMENTAL EDUCATION (COMMUNITY DEVELOPMENT) see COMMUNITY DEVELOPMENT.

Fundamentals of accounting and finance . McGee, Robert W. Lanham, MD , c1987. p. cm. ISBN 0-8191-6289-2 (pbk. : alk. paper) LC Card 87-21581 DDC 657 19
HF5635 .M4883 1987

Fundamentals of advertising research /. Fletcher, Alan D. Belmont, Calif. , c1988. xiii, 322 p. : ISBN 0-534-08454-0 LC Card 87-23106 DDC 659.1/072 19
HF5814 .F57 1988

Fundamentals of behavioral statistics /. Runyon, Richard P. New York , c1988. p. cm. ISBN 0-394-36619-0 LC Card 87-23066 DDC 519.5 19
HA29 .R85 1988

Fundamentals of employee benefit programs. 3rd ed. Washington, DC : Employee Benefit Research Institute, c1987. xviii, 304 p. : ill. ; 23 cm. "An EBRI-ERF publication"--Spine. Includes bibliographies and index. ISBN 0-86643-051-2 (pbk.) LC Card 87-660 DDC 331.25/5/0973 19
1. Employee fringe benefits - United States. I. Employee Benefit Research Institute (Washington, D.C.).
HD4928.N62 U634 1987

Fundamentals of finance for equipment lessors . Johnson, James M., 1947- Arlington, Va. , c1986. xviii, 531 p. ; ISBN 0-912413-00-X LC Card 86-214227 DDC 658.1/5242 19
HD39.4 .J64 1986

Fundamentals of financial accounting /. Welsch, Glenn A. Homewood, Ill. , 1987. xviii, 958 p. : ISBN 0-256-03614-4 LC Card 86-82802 DDC 657 19
HF5635 .W458 1987b

Fundamentals of management /. Donnelly, James H. Plano, Tex. , 1987. xxviii, 827 p. : ISBN 0-256-03682-9 LC Card 86-71879 DDC 658 19
HD31 .D594 1987

Fundamentals of money, banking, and financial institutions /. Prager, Jonas. New York , c1987. xix, 783, 11 p. : ISBN 0-06-045253-6 LC Card 86-27023 DDC 332.1 19
HG221 .P9195 1987

Fundamentals of organizational communication . Shockley-Zalabak, Pamela. New York , c1988. xii, 445 p. : ISBN 0-582-28636-0 LC Card 87-3323 DDC 658.4/5 19
HD30.3 .S55 1988

Fundamentals of public economics /. Laffont, Jean-Jacques, 1947- [Fondements de l'économie publique. English.] Cambridge, Mass. , c1987. p. cm. ISBN 0-262-12127-1 LC Card 87-21895 DDC 338.5 19
HB173 .L23713 1987

Fundamentals of pure and applied economics . (v 20) Besanko, David, 1955- Designing regulatory policy with limited information /. Chur, Switzerland , New York , c1987. viii, 80 p. : ISBN 3-7186-0385-3 (pbk.) LC Card 87-277

DDC 351.82/6 19
HD3612 .B47 1987

(v. 11) Miyao, Takahiro. Urban dynamics and urban externalities /. Chur, Switzerland , New York , c1987. viii, 107 p. : ISBN 3-7186-0333-0 (pbk.) LC Card 86-25629 DDC 330.9173/2 19
HB2161 .M595 1987

(v. 17) Baldwin, William L., 1928- Market structure and technological change /. Chur, Switzerland , New York , c1987. viii, 170 p. ; ISBN 3-7186-0375-6 (pbk.) LC Card 86-25780 DDC 338/.06 19
HD2326 .B35 1987

(v. 17) Baldwin, William L., 1928- Market structure and technological change /. Chur, Switzerland , New York , c1987. viii, 170 p. ; ISBN 3-7186-0375-6 (pbk.) LC Card 86-25780 DDC 338/.06 19
HD2326 .B35 1987

(v. 19) Cooper, Russell W., 1955- Wage and employment patterns in labor contracts . Chur, Switzerland , New York , c1987. viii, 80 p. : ISBN 3-7186-0378-0 (pbk.) LC Card 86-31947 DDC 331.12/5 19
HD4909 .C57 1987

(v. 21) Thirtle, Colin G., 1944- The role of demand and supply in the generation and diffusion of technical change /. Chur, Switzerland , New York , c1987. viii, 173 p. : ISBN 3-7186-0384-5 (U. S. : pbk.) LC Card 87-138 DDC 338/.06 19
HC79.T4 T495 1987

(v. 23) Itō, Motoshige, 1951- Disequilibrium trade theories /. Chur, Switzerland , New York , c1987. viii, 100 p. : ISBN 3-7186-0412-4 LC Card 87-11834 DDC 380.1 19
HF1008 .I855 1987

(v. 24) Hodrick, Robert J. The empirical evidence on the efficiency of forward and futures foreign exchange markets /. Chur, Switzerland , New York , c1987. viii, 174 p. ; ISBN 3-7186-0415-9 (pbk.) LC Card 87-17790 DDC 332.4/5 19
HG3853 .H43 1987

(v. 25) Hanson, Philip. The comparative economics of research development in East and West . Chur, Switzerland , New York , c1987. viii, 101 ; ISBN 3-7186-0419-1 (pbk.) LC Card 87-23623 DDC 338/.06 19
HC79.T4 H355 1987

(v. 25) Hanson, Philip. The comparative economics of research development in East and West . Chur, Switzerland , New York , c1987. viii, 101 ; ISBN 3-7186-0419-1 (pbk.) LC Card 87-23623 DDC 338/.06 19
HC79.T4 H355 1987

(18) Fishburn, Peter C. Interprofile conditions and impossibility /. Chur, Switzerland , New York , c1987. viii, 93 p. ; ISBN 3-7186-0377-2 (pbk.) LC Card 86-31892 DDC 302/.13 19
HB846.8 .F67 1987

Fundamentals of real estate appraisal . Ventolo, William L. Chicago , c1987. 75 p. : ISBN 0-88462-571-0 (pbk.) LC Card 86-29715 DDC 333.33/2 19
HD1387 .V45 1987

Fundamento operacional del sistema de contabilidad general de la nación /. Sánchez González, Leonardo. Santiago, Chile [1986] 227 p. : LC Card 87-403116 DDC 354.830072/31 19
HJ9923.C3 S264 1986

Fundamentos de la ciencia económica /. Ballvé, Faustino. Guatemala, Guatemala , 1984. xii, 95 p. : LC Card 86-124459
HB178.5 .B325 1984

Fundamentos económicos del Imperio Español en América /. Arcila Farías, Eduardo, 1913- Caracas , 1985. 133 p. : LC Card 85-242008
HC389 .A73 1985

Funding and asset allocation decisions in corporate pension plans /. Joanette, Francois P. Brookfield, Wis. , c1986. 17 p. : ISBN 0-89154-304-X (pbk.) : LC Card 87-118785 DDC 658.2/253/0973 19
HD7105.45.U6 J6 1986

FUNDO DE INVESTIMENTOS DO NORDESTE.
Perfil de empresas. Fortaleza-CE [1984] 248 p. ; LC Card 85-191373
HG4111.5.N67 P47 1984

Fundo de Investimentos do Nordeste (Brazil)
Perfil de empresas. Fortaleza-CE [1984] 248 p. ; LC Card 85-191373
HG4111.5.N67 P47 1984

FUNDS. see **FINANCE.**

FUNDS, ELECTRONIC TRANSFERS OF. see **ELECTRONIC FUNDS TRANSFERS.**

Funds flow management . Allen, David. London , 1980. x, 84 p. : ***NYPL [JLD 86-2760]***

Funel, Jean Marie. Politiques d'aménagement hydro-agricole / J.-M. Funel, G. Laucoin. Paris : Presses universitaires de France, c1980. 212 p. : ill. ; 21 cm. (Techniques vivantes. Développement en zones arides) Bibliography: p. [201]-210. ISBN 2-85319-083-8 LC Card 86-112826
1. Water resources development - Senegal. 2. Water resources development - Niger. I. Laucoin, G. II. Title. III. Series.
HD1699.S37 F86 1980

Fünfundsiebzig Jahre Postauto. 75 Jahre Postauto . Bern [1981] 104 p. : LC Card 86-221362 DDC 388.3/22/09494 19
HE5683.A6 A14 1981

Fungibilität und Elastizität von Personal /. Flohr, Bernd. Göttingen , c1984. xvi, 439 p. ; ISBN 3-525-12665-4 LC Card 85-125026
HF5549 .F584 1984

Funk, Joachim. Langfristiges Anlagengeschäft, Risiko-Management und Controlling /. Düsseldorf , c1986. 148 p. : ISBN 3-7754-0016-8 LC Card 86-227044
HG4534 .L36 1986

Funkcjonowanie rynku usług w Polsce / pod redakcją Janusza Olearnika ;[autorzy Modesta Grad ... et al.]. Wrocław : Wydawn. Uczelniane Akademii Ekonomicznej we Wrocławiu, 1986. 176 p. ; 24 cm. (Prace naukowe Akademii Ekonomicznej imienia Oskara Langego we Wrocławiu, 0324-8445 . nr. 355. nr. 36) Bibliography: p. [175]-176. ISBN 83-7011-034-7 : LC Card 87-169457
1. Service industries - Poland. 2. Marketing - Poland. I. Olearnik, Janusz. II. Grad, Modesta. III. Series: Prace naukowe Akademii Ekonomicznej imienia Oskara Langego we Wrocławiu , nr. 355.
HB9 .B7522 nr. 355 HD9986.P7

Funke, Michael, 1956-
Tobin's q and industry investment in West Germany / Michael Funke. Berlin : Wissenschaftszentrum Berlin, [1986] 36 p. : ill. ; 30 cm. (Discussion papers, 0722-673X . IIM/LMP 86-13) "Oktober 1986." Bibliography: p. 34-36. LC Card 87-156645 DDC 332.63 19
1. Capital investments - Germany (West) - Econometric models. I. Series: Discussion papers (International Institute of Management. Labor Market Policy) , IIM/LMP 86-13. II. Title.
HC290.5.C3 F86 1986

Wachstumszyklen und funktionale Einkommensverteilung / Michael Funke. München : V. Florentz, c1985. iii, 244 p. : ill. ; 21 cm. (Volkswirtschaftliche Forschung und Entwicklung . Bd. 12) Bibliography: p. 231-244. Includes index. ISBN 3-88259-319-9 LC Card 85-175617
1. Business cycles - Econometric models. 2. Income distribution - Econometric models. I. Title. II. Series.
HB3711 .F896 1985

Funkhouser, G. Ray. The pursuit of growth : the challenges, opportunities, and dangers of managing and investing in today's economy / G. Ray Funkhouser, Robert R. Rothberg. Redmond, Wash. : Microsoft Press, c1987. 261 p. ; 24 cm. Bibliography: p. 251-254. Includes index. ISBN 1-556-15043-1 : LC Card 87-20230 DDC 658/.00973 19
1. Industrial management - United States. I. Rothberg, Robert R. II. Title.
HD70.U5 F86 1987

Funktion und Wirkung von Aufklebern an Personenkraftwagen /. Haas, Ingrid. Köln [1983] 101, [13] p. : LC Card 84-147451
HE5614.5.G3 H28 1983

Funktionäre . Schelsky, Helmut. Stuttgart-Degerloch , c1982. 310 p. ; ISBN 3-512-00652-3 : LC Card 83-124834
HD6694 .S2566 1982

Funktions- und Sozialstrukturen auf Containerschiffen /. Koch, Hasso B. Frankfurt am Main , New York , c1986. vi, 542 p. : ISBN 3-8204-9334-4 LC Card 86-194048
HE566.C6 K63 1986

Funktionsräumliche Arbeitsteilung. Hannover : C.R. Vincentz, <1986- > v. <3 > : maps ; 25 cm. (Veröffentlichungen der Akademie für Raumforschung und Landesplanung. Forschungs- und Sitzungsberichte, 0344-8940 . Bd. <167 >) Includes bibliographies. CONTENTS. - -- T. 3. Konzeption und Instrumente. ISBN 3-87870-770-3 (T. III) : LC Card 87-409060 DDC 361.6/0943 19
1. Division of labor. 2. Environmental policy. 3. Environmental protection. 4. Regional planning. 5. Regional planning - Germany, West - Case studies. I. Series.
HD51 .F86 1986

Funkt͡sional'no-stoimostnoĭ analiz v otraslevom upravlenii ėffektivnost'i͡u /. Karpunin, M. G. (Mikhail Grigor'evich) Moskva , 1983. 199 p. : LC Card 84-120682
HF5686.C8 K275 1983

Funzioni, strutture, strategie delle imprese commerciali complesse /. Cuomo, Gennaro. Padova , 1984. 236 p. : LC Card 86-214195
HD38.5 .C86 1984

FUR TRADE - CANADA - HISTORY.
Caron, Diane. Les postes de traite de fourrure sur la Côte-Nord et dans l'Outaouais /. [Québec] [1984] xvi, 150 p. : ISBN 2-551-06277-2 LC Card 84-220957
HD9944.C22 C34 1984

FUR TRADE - POLITICAL ASPECTS - SOVIET UNION - HISTORY.
Martin, Janet, 1945- Treasure of the land of darkness . Cambridge [Cambridgeshire] , New York , 1986. x, 277 p. : ISBN 0-521-32019-4 LC Card 86-6094 DDC 380.1/456753/0947 19
HD9944.S755 M37 1986
NYPL [JLE 87-1280]

FUR TRADE - SOVIET UNION - HISTORY.
Martin, Janet, 1945- Treasure of the land of darkness . Cambridge [Cambridgeshire] , New York , 1986. x, 277 p. : ISBN 0-521-32019-4 LC Card 86-6094 DDC 380.1/456753/0947 19
HD9944.S755 M37 1986
NYPL [JLE 87-1280]

Furgler, Kurt. Das Dreieck Europa-Amerika-Asien /. [Diessenhofen] , 1986. 154 p. : ISBN 3-7253-0272-3 LC Card 86-231548
HC412 .D7 1986

Furniss, Norman, 1944-
Futures for the welfare state /. Bloomington , c1986. vi, 444 p. : ISBN 0-253-32440-8 LC Card 85-45959 DDC 330.12/6 19
HB846 .F87 1986 ***NYPL [JLE 86-3761]***

Turkish workers in Europe . [Bloomington, Ind. (143 Goodbody Hall, Indiana University, Bloomington 47405) , c1985. 191 p. : LC Card 85-71750 DDC 331.6/2/56104 19
HD8378.5.T8 T87 1985
NYPL [JLE 86-2980]

FURNITURE - AFRICA, EASTERN - MARKETING.
Export promotion of furniture/joinery products from east/southern Africa. Addis Ababa [1983] 34 p. in various pagings : LC Card 86-981008
HD9773.A472 E96 1983

FURNITURE INDUSTRY AND TRADE - BRAZIL - RIO GRANDE DO SUL.
Dias, Renato Rodrigues. Canais de distribuição na indústria do mobiliário do Rio Grande do Sul /. Santa Maria-RS [Brazil] , 1983. 171 p. : LC Card 86-135650
HD9773.B73 R563 1983

FURNITURE INDUSTRY AND TRADE - GREAT BRITAIN - HISTORY.
Goodden, Susanna. A history of Heal's . [London] , Atlantic Highlands, N.J. , 1984. 137 p. : ISBN 0-85331-488-8 (pbk.) LC Card 86-221633 DDC 381/.456841/00941 19
HD9773.G74 H434 1984

FURNITURE INDUSTRY AND TRADE - QUÉBEC (PROVINCE)
Le Meuble . [Québec] [1983] xiii, 109 p. : ISBN 2-550-10196-0 LC Card 85-124226
HD9773.C23 Q425 1983

Furniture marketing . Bennington, Richard R. New York , c1985. x, 310 p. : ISBN 0-87005-491-0 LC Card 84-81057 DDC

684.1/068/8 19
HD9773.U5 B46 1985 ***NYPL [JLE 86-1997]***

FURNITURE - MARKETING.
Bennington, Richard R. Furniture marketing . New York , c1985. x, 310 p. : ISBN 0-87005-491-0 LC Card 84-81057 DDC 684.1/068/8 19
HD9773.U5 B46 1985 ***NYPL [JLE 86-1997]***

FURNITURE - UNITED STATES - MARKETING.
Bennington, Richard R. Furniture marketing . New York , c1985. x, 310 p. : ISBN 0-87005-491-0 LC Card 84-81057 DDC 684.1/068/8 19
HD9773.U5 B46 1985 ***NYPL [JLE 86-1997]***

Furst, Alan. Fields, Debbi. "One smart cookie" . New York , c1987. 173 p., [16] p. of plates : ISBN 0-671-61838-5 LC Card 87-15172 DDC 338.7/6647525/0924 B 19
HD9058.C65 F544 1987

Furtado, Alencar. Nery, Sebastiáo. Crime e castigo da dívida externa /. Brasília-Distrito Federal [1986] 170 p. ; LC Card 86-208917
HJ8579 .N47 1986

Fuseren in non-profit organisaties . Caris, J. Nijmegen , 1986. 107 p. : ISBN 90-255-0018-8 : LC Card 86-205531
HD2746.5 .C35 1986

Fusfeld, Daniel Roland, 1922- Economics, principles of political economy / Daniel R. Fusfeld. 3rd ed. Glenview, Ill. : Scott, Foresman and Co., c1988. xxii, 858 p. : ill. ; 24 cm. Includes bibliographical references and index. ISBN 0-673-18958-9 LC Card 87-23370 DDC 330 19
1. Economics. I. Title.
HB171.5 .F87 1988

Fusfeld, Herbert I. The technical enterprise : present and future patterns / Herbert I. Fusfeld. Cambridge, Mass. : Ballinger Pub. Co., 1986. xiii, 312 p. ; 24 cm. Includes bibliographical references and index. ISBN 0-88730-033-2 LC Card 86-3340 DDC 338/.06 19
1. Technological innovations - Economic aspects. 2. High technology industries. I. Title.
HC79.T4 F87 1986 ***NYPL [JLE 86-3344]***

FUSION OF CORPORATIONS. see **CONSOLIDATION AND MERGER OF CORPORATIONS.**

Fusko, Zoltán. Koncepcia ďalšieho rozvoja plánovitého riadenia efektívneho využívania pracovnej sily : (špev 904 113 105-CKŠ č. 4) / Zoltán Fusko. Bratislava : Československý výskumný ústav práce a sociálnych vecí, 1982. 62 p. ; 21 cm. (Výskumné práce / Československý výskumný ústav práce a sociálnych vecí . zv. 60. Rad A) Summary in English and Russian. LC Card 83-113861
1. Manpower policy - Czechoslovakia. 2. Central planning - Czechoslovakia. 3. Czechoslovakia - Economic policy - 1945-. I. Series: Výskumné práce / Československý výskumný ústav práce a sociálnych vecí , zv. 60. II. Title.
HD5772.3.A6 F87 1982

Futatsugi, Yūsaku, 1935-
[Gendai Nihon no kigyō shūdan. English] Japanese enterprise groups / Yusaku Futatsugi ; translated by Anthony Kaufmann. [Kobe] : School of Business Administration, Kobe University, 1986. 179 p. : ill. ; 21 cm. (Monograph . no. 4) Translation of: Gendai Nihon no kigyō shūdan. Bibliography: p. 175-179. LC Card 86-220427 DDC 338.8/0952 19
1. Conglomerate corporations - Japan. 2. Industrial concentration - Japan. 3. Big business - Japan. 4. Stockholders - Japan. I. Series: Monograph (Kōbe Daigaku. Keiei Gakubu) , no. 4. II. Title.
HD2756.2.J3 F8813 1986

Futrell, Charles. Sales management / Charles Futrell. 2nd ed. Chicago : Dryden Press, c1988. xxii, 789 p. : ill. ; 25 cm. Includes bibliographical references and indexes. ISBN 0-03-010963-9 LC Card 87-8976 DDC 658.8/1 19
1. Sales management. I. Title.
HF5438.4 .F87 1988

Futrell, Gene A., 1928- Otto, Daniel. Economic contribution and impacts of changes in Iowa's livestock and meat processing industries /. Oakdale, Iowa [1984] xi, 95 p. : LC Card 85-621899 DDC 338.1/76/009777021 19
HD9417.I8 O88 1984 ***NYPL [JLF 86-592]***

FUTUḤ. see **ISLAMIC EMPIRE.**

The Future directions of employee relations / edited by Eric G. Flamholtz with Felicitas Hinman. Los Angeles, Calif. : Center for Human Resource Management, Institute of Industrial Relations, University of California, Los Angeles, c1985. xiv, 418 p. ; 22 cm. (Monograph and research series . 45) Papers from a conference commissioned by IBM and organized by the Center for Human Resource Management of the Institute of Industrial Relations, UCLA, in June, 1984. Includes bibliographical references. ISBN 0-89215-132-3
1. Industrial relations - United States - Congresses. 2. Industrial relations - Congresses. I. Flamholtz, Eric. II. Hinman, Felicitas. III. California. University. University at Los Angeles. Institute of Industrial Relations. Center for Human Resource Management. IV. Series: Monograph and research series (University of California, Los Angeles. Institute of Industrial Relations) , 45. ***NYPL [JLD 86-3596]***

The Future directions of employee relations / edited by Eric G. Flamholtz with Felicitas Hinman. Los Angeles, Calif. : Center for Human Resource Management, Institute of Industrial Relations, University of California, Los Angeles, c1985. xiv, 418 p. : ill. ; 22 cm. (Monograph and research series . 45) Includes bibliographies. ISBN 0-89215-132-3 (pbk.) LC Card 86-622936 DDC 331/.0973 19
1. Industrial relations - United States. I. Flamholtz, Eric. II. Hinman, Felicitas. III. Series: Monograph and research series (University of California, Los Angeles. Institute of Industrial Relations) , 45.
HD8072.5 .F87 1985

Future employment & technological change /. Leach, Donald. London , 1986. 264 p. : ISBN 1-85091-017-0 (pbk.) : LC Card 86-180981 DDC 331.12/5 19
HD6331 .L34 1986

Future employment and technological change. Leach, Donald. Future employment & technological change /. London , 1986. 264 p. : ISBN 1-85091-017-0 (pbk.) : LC Card 86-180981 DDC 331.12/5 19
HD6331 .L34 1986

Future five hundred. Hickman, Craig R. The future 500 . New York, N.Y. , c1987. xiv, 274 p. ; ISBN 0-453-00544-6 LC Card 87-15204 DDC 658 19
HD31 .H4814 1987

The future for European energy security / edited by Curt Gasteyger. London : Frances Pinter, 1985. 177 p. : ill. ; 24 cm. Includes bibliographical references and index. ISBN 0-86187-573-7
1. Energy policy - Europe. 2. National security. ***NYPL [JLE 86-1018]***

The Future impact of technology on work and education / edited by Gerald Burke and Russell W. Rumberger. London ; New York : Falmer Press, 1987. p. cm. (The Stanford series on education and public policy . v. 5) Papers presented at the US-Australia Joint Seminar on the Future Impact of Technology on Work and Education, held in 1984 at Monash University, Melbourne, Australia. Bibliography: p. Includes index. ISBN 1-85000-083-2 : LC Card 87-13641 DDC 331.12/0994 19
1. Labor supply - Australia - Effect of technological innovations on - Congresses. 2. Labor supply - United States - Effect of technological innovations on - Congresses. 3. Career education - Australia - Congresses. 4. Career education - United States - Congresses. I. Burke, Gerald. II. Rumberger, Russell W. III. US-Australia Joint Seminar on the Future Impact of technology on Work and Education (1984 : Monash University). IV. Series.
HD6331.2.A8 F87 1987

The Future is now / prepared by the Food and Allied Service Trades Department, AFL-CIO. [Washington, D.C.] : The Department, [1985] 34, xxi, [ii], leaves ; 28 cm. "October 1985." Bibliography: leaves [xxii]-[xxiii] (2nd group) LC Card 86-211338 DDC 331.12/51/000973 19
1. Service industry workers - United States - Supply and demand. I. AFL-CIO. Food and Allied Service Trades Dept.
HD5718.S452 U535 1985

Future is Now, A Home Equity Conversion Conference. The Future is Now: A Home Equity Conversion Conference (1985 : Washington, D.C.) Proceedings from The Future is Now, A Home Equity Conversion Conference. Washington, D.C. [1985?] ix, 76 p. ; LC Card 86-601425 DDC 332.7/22 19
HG2040.45 .F87 1985

The Future of migration. Paris : Organisation for Economic Co-operation and Development ; Washington, D.C. : OECD Publications and Information Centre [distributor], 1987. 319 p. : ill. ; 23 cm. Includes bibliographical references. ISBN 92-64-12949-9 (pbk.) : LC Card 87-163484 DDC 304.8/094 19
1. Migration, Internal - Congresses. 2. Migration, Internal - Europe - Congresses. 3. Migration, Internal - Europe, Southern - Congresses. I. Conference of National Experts on the Future of Migration (1986 : Paris, France). II. Organisation for Economic Co-operation and Development.
HB1952 .F88 1987

The Future of pay determination : a discussion document. London : Confederation of British Industry, [1977] 56 p. ; 21 cm. "June 1977." LC Card 84-255776 DDC 331.2/15 19
1. Wage payment systems - Great Britain. 2. Wages and labor productivity - Great Britain. 3. Productivity bargaining - Great Britain. I. Confederation of British Industry.
HD5015 .F88 1977

The Future of private enterprise / edited by Craig E. Aronoff and John L. Ward. Atlanta, Ga. : Business Pub. Division, College of Business Administration, Georgia State University, 1984-1986. 3 v. ; 22 cm. "Sponsored by the Association of Private Enterprise Education." Vol. 2-3 edited by Craig E. Aronoff, Randall B. Goodwin, and John L. Ward. Includes bibliographical references. CONTENTS. - v. 1. Challenges and responses -- v. 2. Foundations, interpretations, and growth -- v. 3. Ideas for a changing world. ISBN 0-88406-164-7 (pbk. : v. 1) LC Card 83-25386 DDC 338.6/1 19
1. Capitalism - Addresses, essays, lectures. 2. Economic policy - Addresses, essays, lectures. 3. Industry and state - Addresses, essays, lectures. 4. Laissez-faire - Addresses, essays, lectures. I. Aronoff, Craig E. II. Ward, John (John L.). III. Goodwin, Randall B. IV. Association of Private Enterprise Education (U. S.).
HB501 .F83 1984 ***NYPL [JLK 87-49]***

The Future of the North American granary : politics, economics, and resource constraints in North American agriculture / edited by C. Ford Runge.1st ed. Ames, Iowa : Iowa State University Press, 1986. xx, 238 p. : ill. ; 23 cm. Includes bibliographies and index. ISBN 0-8138-0781-6 LC Card 85-23905 DDC 338.1/731/097 19
1. Grain trade - Government policy - United States - Congresses. 2. Grain trade - Government policy - Canada - Congresses. 3. Grain - United States - Congresses. 4. Grain - Canada - Congresses. I. Runge, C. Ford (Carlisle Ford).
HD9036 .F87 1986 ***NYPL [JLE 86-2437]***

The Future of the office products industry : complete report / prepared for NOPA by the Wharton Applied Research Center, the Wharton School, University of Pennsylvania. Alexandria, Va. (301 N. Fairfax St., Alexandria 22314) : National Office Products Association, c1985. viii, 212, 33 p. : ill. ; 28 cm. $1,200.00 (pbk.) ($300.00 to members) LC Card 86-200112 DDC 338.4/768 19
1. Office equipment and supplies industry - United States. 2. Market surveys - United States. I. National Office Products Association. II. Wharton Applied Research Center.
HD9800.U52 F86 1985

The Future of work : a conference of the Center for Social Change Practice and Theory, 1985 / edited by David G. Gil and Eva A. Gil. Cambridge, Mass. : Schenkman Books, c1987. xv, 126 p. : ill. ; 22 cm. Includes bibliographies. ISBN 0-87047-030-2 : LC Card 86-33894 DDC 306/.36 19
1. Work. I. Gil, David G. II. Gil, Eva A. III. Florence Heller Graduate School for Advanced Studies in Social Welfare. Center for Social Change Practice and Theory.
HD4904 .F87 1987

The future of world trade in textiles and apparel /. Cline, William R. Washington, DC , 1987. xiv, 325 p. : ISBN 0-88132-025-0 (pbk.) : LC Card 87-17068 DDC 382/.45677 19
HD9850.5 .C55 1987

Future perfect : a guide for professional development and competence / Kathleen E. Allen ... [et al.]. Columbia, S.C. (P.O. Box

6828, Columbia 29260) : NACA Educational Foundation, National Association for Campus Activities, c1987. x, 104 p. : ill. ; 23 cm. Bibliography: p. [71]-84. LC Card 87-143129 DDC 650.1 19
1. Career development. 2. Professions. I. Allen, Kathleen E. II. National Association for Campus Activities (U. S.).
HF5549.5.C35 F87 1987

Future perfect /. Davis, Stanley M. Reading, Mass. , c1987. 243 p. : ISBN 0-201-11513-1 : LC Card 87-18669 DDC 658 19
HD31 .D325 1987

The future 500 . Hickman, Craig R. New York, N.Y. , c1987. xiv, 274 p. ; ISBN 0-453-00544-6 LC Card 87-15204 DDC 658 19
HD31 .H4814 1987

FUTURES.
Kroll, Stanley. Kroll on futures trading strategy /. Homewood, Ill. , c1988. xvi, 203 p. : ISBN 1-556-23033-8 LC Card 87-71359 DDC 332.64/4 19
HG6024.A3 K76 1988

Futures and options trading for commercial banks : the regulatory environment : regulatory impact on futures trading program. Chicago, Ill. (30 S. Wacker Dr., Chicago 60606) : Chicago Mercantile Exchange, c1986. 14 p. : ill. ; 28 cm. (CME white paper series . no. 5) Cover title. Bibliography: p. 11. LC Card 87-131777 DDC 332.1/754 19
1. Banks and banking - United States - Deregulation. 2. Bank holding companies - United States - Deregulation. 3. Bank investments - Government policy - United States. 4. Financial futures - Government policy - United States. I. Chicago. Mercantile Exchange. II. Series.
HG2491 .F87 1986

FUTURES EXCHANGE. see **FORWARD EXCHANGE.**

Futures for the welfare state / edited by Norman Furniss. Bloomington : Indiana University Press, c1986. vi, 444 p. : ill. ; 25 cm. Bibliography: p. 404-423. ISBN 0-253-32440-8 LC Card 85-45959 DDC 330.12/6 19
1. Welfare state - Congresses. 2. Economic history - 1945- - Congresses. I. Furniss, Norman, 1944-.
HB846 .F87 1986 ***NYPL [JLE 86-3761]***

FUTURES INDUSTRY ASSOCIATION.
Futures trading course. Washington, D.C. (1825 Eye St., N.W., Washington 20006) , c1986. 3 v. : LC Card 86-215844 DDC 332.64/4 19
HG6024.A3 F89 1986

FUTURES, INTEREST RATE. see **INTEREST RATE FUTURES.**

FUTURES MARKET.
Goldstone, Nancy Bazelon. Trading up /. New York , c1988. viii, 262 p. ; ISBN 0-525-24621-5 : LC Card 87-19975 DDC 332.4/5/0924 B 19
HG3853 .G65 1988

Kroll, Stanley. Kroll on futures trading strategy /. Homewood, Ill. , c1988. xvi, 203 p. : ISBN 1-556-23033-8 LC Card 87-71359 DDC 332.64/4 19
HG6024.A3 K76 1988

Futures markets : their economic role / Anne E. Peck, editor ; Philip McBride Johnson ... [et al.]. Washington, D.C. : American Enterprise Institute for Public Policy Research, c1985. xiii, 325 p. : ill. ; 24 cm. (Studies in government regulation) AEI studies ; 434 Companion volume to Futures markets : regulatory issues. Includes bibliographies. CONTENTS. - The economic role of traditional commodity futures Markets / Anne E. Peck -- The economic role of financial futures / William L. Silber -- Futures markets and capital formation / Jerome L. Stein -- The new option markets / Hans R. Stoll and Robert E. Whaley -- Federal regulation in securities and futures markets / Philip McBride Johnson. ISBN 0-8447-3592-2 LC Card 85-26705 DDC 332.64/4 19
1. Commodity exchanges - United States. 2. Financial futures - United States. 3. Commodity exchanges - Law and legislation - United States. I. Peck, Anne E. II. Johnson, Philip McBride. III. Series: American Enterprise Institute for Public Policy Research. AEI studies, 434.
HG6049 .F86 1985 ***NYPL [JLE 86-1532]***

Futures trading . Fink, Robert E. New York, N.Y. , c1988. xiv, 685 p. : ISBN 0-13-345745-1 : LC Card 87-24030 DDC 332.64/4 19
HG6046 .F56 1988

Futures trading course. Washington, D.C. (1825 Eye St., N.W., Washington 20006) : Futures Industry Association, c1986. 3 v. : ill. ; 30 cm. Cover title. Includes bibliography and index. CONTENTS. - Bk. 1. Text -- bk. 2. Questions and answers. -- bk. 3. Fact sheet. LC Card 86-215844 DDC 332.64/4 19
1. Commodity exchanges. 2. Financial futures. 3. Futures Industry Association. I. Title.
HG6024.A3 F89 1986

Futures trading strategy. Kroll, Stanley. Kroll on futures trading strategy /. Homewood, Ill. , c1988. xvi, 203 p. : ISBN 1-556-23033-8 LC Card 87-71359 DDC 332.64/4 19
HG6024.A3 K76 1988

Il Futuro del sindacato / saggi di Accornero ... [et al.] ; prefazione di Bruno Trentin ; a cura di Gianni Ferrante. Roma : Ediesse, c1986. xxvii, 347 p. ; 19 cm. (Ragionamenti) Includes bibliographical references. LC Card 86-223517
1. Trade-unions - Italy. I. Accornero, Aris. II. Ferrante, Gianni.
HD6709 .F88 1986

Il futuro presente . Pacifici, Giorgio. Milano, Italy , c1985. 201 p. ; LC Card 86-127322 DDC 384/.0945 19
HE8174 .P33 1985

FUZZY SETS.
Management decision support systems using fuzzy sets and possibility theory /. Köln , c1985. xi, 350 p. : ISBN 3-88585-143-1 (pbk.) LC Card 85-217558 DDC 658.4/033 19
HD30.23 .M353 1985 ***NYPL [JLE 86-4562]***

FY 87 budget summary . Missouri. General Assembly. Senate. Appropriations Committee. [Jefferson City, Mo.] [1986] 66 leaves : LC Card 87-620981 DDC 353.97780072/253 19
HJ2053.M8 M57 1986

Fylkesarbeidskontoret i Aust-Agder. Fylkesplan for Aust-Agder . [Norway] [1983] 125 p. : LC Card 84-146306
HD5800.A95 F95 1983

Fylkesarbeidskontoret i Møre og Romsdal. 4-årige arbeidskraftprognoser, Møre og Romsdal 1983-1986(1987). [Molde] [1983?] 59 p. ; LC Card 84-146499
HD5800.M67 A14 1983

Fylkesarbeidskontoret i Telemark. 4-årig arbeidskraftprognose for perioden 1983-1987, Telemark fylke. [Telemark] [1983] 154 leaves ; LC Card 84-145787
HD5800.T44 A14 1983

Fylkesplan for Aust-Agder : sysselsettingsbudsjett for perioden 1982-1987. [Norway] : Fylkesarbeidskontoret i Aust-Agder, [1983] 125 p. : ill. ; 30 cm. Cover title. "Februar 1983." LC Card 84-146306
1. Labor supply - Norway - Aust-Agder fylke. 2. Employment forecasting - Norway - Aust-Agder fylke. I. Fylkesarbeidskontoret i Aust-Agder.
HD5800.A95 F95 1983

Fysisk planlægning og samfundsmæssige reproduktionsproblemer . Christoffersen, Mads. København , 1980, c1979. 317 p. ; ISBN 87-500-1922-8 ***NYPL [JLD 86-2303]***

ISSN 0360-2702

BIBLIOGRAPHIC GUIDE TO

BUSINESS AND ECONOMICS 1987

Volume 2
G—O

G.K. HALL & CO.
70 Lincoln Street, Boston, Massachusetts

Manufactured in the United States of America.
ISBN 0-8161-7086-X

G. E. I. P. O. T. see **Empresa Brasileira de Planejamento de Transportes.**

G. R. I. D. E. Q. see **Université du Québec à Rimouski. Groupe de recherche interdisciplinaire en développement de l'Est du Québec.**

The G. Warren Nutter lectures in political economy.
Ford, William F. (William Frank), 1934- The public policy roots of recent thrift crises /. Washington, D.C. , c1986. 14 p. ; ISBN 0-8447-1376-7 (pbk.) LC Card 87-164463 DDC 332.3/2/0973 19
HG2152 .F67 1986

Miller, James C., III. Spending and deficits /. Washington, D.C. , c1987. 18 p. ; ISBN 0-8447-1382-1 (pbk.) LC Card 87-134671 DDC 339.5/23/0973 19
HJ2052 .M54 1987

G-Yohannes, Arefaine. The professional's desktop guide to real estate finance / by Arefaine G-Yohannes. Chicago, Ill. : Probus Pub. Co., c1988. p. cm. Includes index. ISBN 0-917253-93-0 : LC Card 87-17918 DDC 332.7/2 19
1. Mortgage loans - United States. 2. Real estate development - United States - Finance. 3. Housing - United States - Finance. I. Title.
HG2040.5.U5 G125 1988

Gaab, Werner. Devisenmärkte und Wechselkurse : eine theoretische und empirische Analyse / Werner Gaab. Berlin ; New York : Springer, 1983. vii, 305 p. : ill. ; 25 cm. (Studies in contemporary economics . v. 3) Bibliography: p. [290]-305. ISBN 0-387-12615-5 (U. S.) : LC Card 83-222336
1. Foreign exchange. 2. Capital market. I. Title. II. Series.
HG3851 .G25 1983

Gab, V. I. (Valentin Ivanovich)
Tekhniko-ėkonomicheskie raschety na predprii͡atii /. Kiev , 1984. 126 p. : LC Card 84-234261
HD70.S63 T45 1984

Gabaldón, Arnoldo. Política ambiental y sociedad / Arnoldo José Gabaldón ; prólogo de Ernesto Mayz Vallenilla. 1a. ed. Caracas, Venezuela : Monte Avila Editores, 1986. 225 p. : ill. ; 22 cm. (Tiempo de Venezuela) Includes bibliographies. ISBN 980-01-0034-2 LC Card 87-115207 DDC 363.7/056/0987 19
1. Environmental policy - Venezuela. I. Title. II. Series.
HC239.5.E5 G32 1986

Gabarro, John J. The dynamics of taking charge / John J. Gabarro. Boston, Mass. : Harvard Business School Press, c1987. x, 204 p. : ill. ; 24 cm. Bibliography: p. 189-197. Includes index. ISBN 0-87584-137-6 (jkt.) LC Card 86-25624 DDC 658.4 19
1. Industrial management. 2. Corporate planning. 3. Executives. 4. Personnel management. I. Title.
HD38 .G225 1987

Gabel, H. Landis. Product standardization and competitive strategy /. Amsterdam ; New York : xii, 316 p. : ISBN 0-444-70232-6(U. S.) LC Card 87-8849 DDC 338/.02 19
HD62 .P75 1987

Gaber, Edwin, 1903- Kapitalbildung und Altersvorsorge . Köln , Bergisch Gladbach [1983?] 95 p. : LC Card 84-180205
HD7105.45.G3 K37 1983

GABER, ERWIN, 1903-
Kapitalbildung und Altersvorsorge . Köln , Bergisch Gladbach [1983?] 95 p. : LC Card 84-180205
HD7105.45.G3 K37 1983

Gabisch, Günter, 1943-

Gabler, Edwin, 1949- The American telegrapher : a social history, 1860-1900 / Edwin Gabler. New Brunswick, NJ : Rutgers University Press, c1988. p. cm. (Class and culture) Bibliography: p. Includes index. ISBN 0-8135-1284-0 : LC Card 87-19878 DDC 331.89/2813841/0973 19
1. Western Union Telegraph Company Strike, 1883. 2. Trade-unions - Telegraphers - United States - History - 19th century. 3. Telegraphers - United States - History - 19th century. I. Title. II. Series.
HD5325 .T252 1883

Gablers ökonomische Klassiker.
Justi, Johann Heinrich Gottlob von, d. 1771. Ausführliche Abhandlung von denen Steuern und Abgaben /. Wiesbaden , 1977. 202 p., [4] p. of plates : ISBN 3-409-50171-1 LC Card 84-235228
HJ2300 .J87 1977

GABON - ECONOMIC CONDITIONS - 1960-
Heldt, Sven. Die Wirtschaftsplanung Gabuns /. Kiel , 1978. 31 leaves ; LC Card 85-238709
HC975 .H45 1978

Mamder, Josué Sandjiman. Les effets de la crise mondiale actuelle sur l'économie et la population gabonaises /. Addis Abéba , c1984. 34 p. ; ISBN 92-2-203795-2 LC Card 86-215256
HC975 .M36 1984

GABON - ECONOMIC POLICY.
Heldt, Sven. Die Wirtschaftsplanung Gabuns /. Kiel , 1978. 31 leaves ; LC Card 85-238709
HC975 .H45 1978

Gabonese Republic. see **Gabon.**

Gábor, István. Az iparvállalatok könyvvitele, 1986 / Gábor István. Budapest : Közgazdasági és Jogi Könyvkiadó, 1986. 265 p. : ill. ; 20 cm. "A kézirat lezárva: 1985. december 31"--T.p. verso. ISBN 963-221-902-3 : LC Card 87-408573
1. Accounting - Standards - Hungary. I. Title.
HF5616.H9 G33 1986

Gabriel, Jürgen. Flexibilisierung der Arbeit und wirtschaftliche Instabilität : Überlegungen zur Theorie und Empirie des Beschäftigungsverhaltens von Unternehmen bei Unsicherheit / Jürgen Gabriel. München : Minerva Publikation, c1985. x, 316 p. ; 21 cm. (Beiträge zur Sozialökonomik der Arbeit . Bd. 10) Originally presented as the author's thesis (doctoral)--Freie Universität Berlin, 1984. Bibliography: p. 289-314. ISBN 3-597-10540-8 LC Card 86-118217 DDC 331.25/72 19
1. Hours of labor, Flexible. 2. Job satisfaction. I. Title. II. Series.
HD5109 .G33 1985

Gabriel-Lexikon. Schönen, Hans G. Christliche Motive auf Briefmarken . Rommerskirchen-Oekoven , 1984, c1983. xv, 830 p. ; ISBN 3-9800824-0-7 : LC Card 84-208011
HE6183.C47 S36 1984

Gabrisch, Hubert. Polen im RGW : Vor- und Nachteile der Integration Polens in den Rat für Gegenseitige Wirtschaftshilfe (RGW) in den 80er Jahren / Hubert Gabrisch. Hamburg : Verlag Weltarchiv, 1986. 308 p. ; 24 cm. (Veröffentlichungen des HWWA-Institut für Wirtschaftsforschung-Hamburg) Bibliography: p. 297-308. ISBN 3-87895-316-X LC Card 87-407406 DDC 330.9438/056 19
1. Poland - Economic conditions - 1945-. 2. Council for Mutual Economic Assistance. I. Title.
HC340.3 .G34 1986

Gabun. see **Gabon.**

Gach, Christian. Wirtschaftlichkeitsanalyse von Banken : Zweigstellenvergleich und Kennzahlenanalyse / Christian Gach, Franz Fischer. Wien : Service, Fachverlag an der Wirtschaftsuniversität Wien, c1983. iv, 75, iii, 89 p. ; 21 cm. (Schriftenreihe des Instituts für Kredit- u. Versicherungswirtschaft, Abteilung Bankbetriebslehre . Bd. 4) Includes bibliographies. ISBN 3-85428-017-3 : LC Card 84-118578
1. Banks and banking - Austria - Branch banks. I. Fischer, Franz. II. Title. III. Series.
HG3008 .G28 1983

Gadanecz, Béla. A vasutas munkásmozgalom története : a kezdetektől 1945-ig / Gadanecz Béla. Budapest : Magyar Államvasutak Vezérigazgatósága és a Vasutasok Szakszervezete, 1985. 351 p. ; 25 cm. Includes bibliographical references and index. ISBN 963-322-262-1 LC Card 86-227921
1. Railroads - Hungary - Employees - History. 2. Trade-unions - Railroads - Hungary - History. I. Vasutasok Szakszervezete. II. Title.
HD8039.R12 H93 1985

Gaddis, Edwin L. Hester, Edward J. Predicting which disabled employees will return to work . Topeka, Kan. (700 Jackson, 9th floor, Topeka 66603) , c1986. x, 86 p. : LC Card 86-231920 DDC 331.5/9 19
HD7256.U5 H43 1986

Gaddy, C. D. Applied behavioral science for plant managers /. Columbia, Md. , c1987. vii, 102 p. : ISBN 0-87683-830-1 (pbk.) LC Card 86-31926 DDC 658.3 19
HF5548.8 .A715 1987

Gadó, Ottó. Turnover tax-system in Hungary /. Budapest , 1985. 21 p. ; ISBN 963-621-208-2 (pbk.) : LC Card 86-202548 DDC 336.2/7 19
HJ5715.H9 T87 1985

Gadzhiev, B. U. (Bagautdin Ustaevich)
Ėkonomicheskie problemy sovershenstvovanii͡a torgovli na osnove kompleksnoĭ ratsionalizatsii / B.U. Gadzhiev. Makhachkala : Dagestanskoe knizhnoe izd-vo, 1984. 282 p. ; 22 cm. At head of title: Dagestanskiĭ filial AN SSSR. Includes bibliographical references. LC Card 86-213223
1. Dagestanskai͡a A.S.S.R. (R.S.F.S.R.) - Commerce. 2. Dagestanskai͡a A.S.S.R. (R.S.F.S.R.) - Commercial policy. I. Title.
HF3629.D34 G33 1984

Gaedeke, Ralph M. Cases and classics in marketing management /. San Diego , c1986. ix, 513 p. : ISBN 0-15-505775-8 LC Card 85-80071 DDC 658.8/00973 19
HF5415.13 .C28 1986 ***NYPL [JLE 86-3101]***

Gael, Sidney. The Job analysis handbook for business, industry, and government /. New York , c1988. 2 v. : ISBN 0-471-87237-7 (set) LC Card 87-8233 DDC 658.3/06 19
HF5549.5.J6 J63 1988

Gaertner, James F. Selected papers from the Charles Waldo Haskins accounting history seminars /. [University, Ala.] , 1983. iv, 172 p. ; LC Card 86-224698 DDC 657/.09 19
HF5611 .S45 1983

Gaffard, Jean Luc. Amendola, Mario. The innovative choice . Oxford [Oxfordshire] , New York, NY, USA , 1988. p. cm. ISBN 0-631-15791-3 : LC Card 87-25004 DDC 338/.06 19
HC79.T4 A46 1988

Gaft, L. Sh. (Leonid Shevelevich) Povyshenie ėffektivnosti ASUP . Kiev , 1985. 303 p. : LC Card 85-210269
HD30.2 .P68 1985 ***NYPL [*QIP 87-2760]***

Gagey, F.
Comprendre l'économie africaine /. Paris , c1985. 566 p. : ISBN 2-85802-566-2 LC Card 86-222248
HC800 .C654 1985

International macroeconomic modelling for policy decisions /. Dordrecht , Boston , c1986. viii, 269 p. : ISBN 90-247-3201-8 LC Card 85-13698 DDC 337/.0724 19
HF1410.5 .I577 1986 ***NYPL [JLE 86-3469]***

Gagnon, Alain. Le modèle centre-périphérique appliqué à l'est du Québec : contribution scientifique / Alain Gagnon. Rimouski : Groupe de recherche interdisciplinaire en développement de l'est du Québec, Université du Québec, c1979 ix, 154 p. ; 28 cm. (Cahiers du GRIDEQ. no 6) Thesis (M.A.)--Université Simon Fraser. Bibliography: p. [137]-154. LC Card 80-143484
1. Gaspé Peninsula (Québec) - Economic conditions. 2. Québec (Province) - Economic conditions - Regional disparities. I. Title.
HC117.G37 G33 1980

Gahlen, Bernhard.
Technologischer Wandel, Analyse und Fakten /. Tübingen , 1986. ix, 330 p. ; ISBN 3-16-345132-2 LC Card 87-109808 DDC 338/.06 19
HC79.T4 T4355 1986

Zur internationalen Wettbewerbsfähigkeit der deutschen Wirtschaft / von Bernhard Gahlen, Fritz Rahmeyer, Manfred Stadler. [Berlin] : Wissenschaftszentrum Berlin, [1985] 41, 4 p. ; 30 cm. (Discussion papers / IIMV/Strukturpolitik--IIM/Industrial Policy, Wissenschaftszentrum Berlin, 0722-6748 . IIM/IP 85-19) "September 1985." Summary in English and German. Bibliography: p. 38-41. LC Card 86-204589
1. Germany, West - Economic conditions - 1974-. 2. Germany, West - Foreign economic relations. 3. Competition, International. I. Rahmeyer, Fritz. II. Stadler, Manfred. III. Series: Discussion papers (International Institute of Management. Industrial Policy) , IIM/IP 85-19. IV. Title.
HC286.7 .G29 1985

Gahungu, Fidèle. Document d'initiation à l'informatique des organisations / par Fidèle Gahungu. [Bujumbura?] : Programme des

Nations Unies pour le développement, [1983- v. <1 > : ill. ; 30 cm. Cover title. At head of title: République du Burundi, Ministère de la fonction publique, C.P.F., Centre de perfectionnement et de formation en cours d'emploi. "Novembre 1983." Bibliography: v. 1, p. 53. LC Card 86-980527
1. Management - Data processing. I. Centre de perfectionnement et de formation en cours d'emploi (Bujumbura, Burundi). II. Title.
HD30.2 .G34 1983

Gaida, Kathleen A. Johnson, Eugene M. Profitable service marketing /. Homewood, Ill. , c1986. xiv, 303 p. : ISBN 0-87094-613-7 LC Card 86-70516 DDC 658.8 19
HF5415.122 .J64 1986 ***NYPL [JLE 87-666]***

Gaikwad, V. R., 1933- Managing paddy-rice business of small farmers : integrated co-operatives in Asia / V.R. Gaikwad, V.K. Gupta. Bombay : Popular Prakashan, 1986. xxiii, 239 p. : ill. ; 23 cm. (CMA monograph. no. 119) "This case book is the fourth in the series of collaborative research efforts between Food and Agriculture Organisation of the United Nations (FAO) and the Indian Institute of Management, Ahmedabad (IIMA), under the programme: Appropriate Management Systems for Agricultural Co-operatives (AMSAC) of FAO"--Pref. ISBN 0-86132-129-4 : LC Card 86-903247 DDC 334/.68318/0954 19
1. Rice - Asia - Cooperative marketing. 2. Agriculture, Cooperative - Asia. 3. Farms, Small - Asia - Management. I. Gupta, V. K. II. Indian Institute of Management, Ahmedabad. III. Food and Agriculture Organization of the United Nations. IV. Title.
HD9066.A7 G35 1986

Gaillard, Claude, 1930- Economie et droit du développement / par Claude Gaillard. Alger : Société nationale d'édition et de diffusion, c1982. 439 p. ; 24 cm. Bibliography: p. 437-439. LC Card 83-216670
1. Economic development. 2. International economic integration. 3. Capitalism. 4. Socialism. I. Title.
HD75 .G34 1982

Gaillard, Serge. Oberhänsli, Urs. Altersvorsorge, Kapitalschwemme oder Kapitalmangel? . Bern , c1986. xii, 222 p. : ISBN 3-258-03578-4 : LC Card 86-149614
HD7105.35.S9 O24 1986

GAIN SHARING - SWEDEN.
Trautwein, Hans-Michael, 1957- Arbeitnehmerfonds in Schweden, der dritte Weg? . Frankfurt am Main , New York , c1986. 353, 39, [116] p. : ISBN 3-8204-9336-0 LC Card 86-203867
HD4928.G342 S88 1986

Gainer, Kevin. The Japanese challenge . Stamford, Conn., U. S.A. , c1986. xii, 108 leaves : ISBN 0-89336-489-4 (pbk.) LC Card 87-404570 DDC 338/.06 19
HC465.T4 J365 1986

Gains from stock-market timing /. Chua, Jess H. New York, N.Y. (90 Trinity Pl., New York 10006) [c1986] 75 p. ; LC Card 87-129798 DDC 332.63/222 19
HG4637 .C48 1986

Gaitán García, Camilo. Productividad y participación . [Bucaramanga, Colombia] , c1985. 165 p. : ISBN 958-9302-15-6 LC Card 86-166141
HD5660.C7 P76 1985

Gajda, Józef. Ekonomika i programowanie rozwoju przemysłu /. Kraków , 1978. 378 p. : LC Card 81-172485
HD70.P6 E38 1978

Gajdosné Németh, Olga.
Mezőgazdasági és élelmiszeripari adattár a felszabadulástól napjainkig /. Budapest , 1985. 152 p. ; ISBN 963-502-393-6 LC Card 86-202515
HD1940.5 .M497 1985

Mezőgazdasági és élelmiszeripari adattár a felszabadulástól napjainkig. English. Collection of data of agriculture and food industry from the liberation till now /. Budapest , 1985. 85 p. ; ISBN 963-502-393-6 LC Card 86-230345
HD1940.5 .M49713 1985

Gakou, Mohamed Lamine.
[Crise de l'agriculture africaine. English]
The crisis in African agriculture / Mohamed Lamine Gakou ; [translated by A.M. Berrett]. London ; Atlantic Highlands, N.J., USA : Zed Books ; xii, 100 p. ; 23 cm. (Studies in African political economy) Translation of: La crise de l'agriculture africaine. Bibliography: p. 96-98. Includes index. ISBN 0-86232-732-6 : LC Card 87-13355 DDC 338.1/096 19
1. Agriculture - Economic aspects - Africa. I. Title. II. Series.
HD2117 .G3513 1987

Gal, Jan. Gál, Tomáš. Mathematik für Wirtschaftswissenschaftler. Berlin , New York , c1986. xi, 160 p. : ISBN 0-387-16381-6 (U. S.) LC Card 86-208763
HB135 .G35 1986

Gál, Tomáš.
Lehrbuch Mathematik für Wirtschaftswissenschaftler. Gál, Tomáš. Mathematik für Wirtschaftswissenschaftler. Aufgabensammlung / Tomas Gal, Jan Gal. Berlin , New York , c1986. xi, 160 p. : ISBN 0-387-16381-6 (U. S.) LC Card 86-208763
HB135 .G35 1986

Mathematik für Wirtschaftswissenschaftler. Aufgabensammlung / Tomas Gal, Jan Gal. Berlin ; New York : Springer, c1986. xi, 160 p. : ill. ; 25 cm. (Heidelberger Lehrtexte. Wirtschaftswissenschaften) "... Begleittext zu dem Lehrbuch Mathematik für Wirtschaftswissenschaftler ..."--P. 4 of cover. ISBN 0-387-16381-6 (U. S.) LC Card 86-208763
1. Economics, Mathematical. I. Gal, Jan. II. Gál, Tomáš. Lehrbuch Mathematik für Wirtschaftswissenschaftler. III. Title. IV. Series.
HB135 .G35 1986

Galaburda, V. G. Optimal'noe planirovanie gruzopotokov / V.G. Galaburda. Moskva : "Transport", 1985. 255 p. : ill. ; 21 cm. Bibliography: p. 247-251. Includes index. LC Card 85-243810
1. Railroads - Soviet Union - Freight. 2. Freight and freightage - Soviet Union. I. Title.
HE2457 .G35 1985

Galal, M. F. Pakistan : seed cotton and lint classification and grading / by M.F. Galal. Rome [i.e. Multan] : Food and Agriculture Organization of the United Nations, 1978. vii, 36 p. ; 27 cm. (Consultant report . 1) At head of title: Central Cotton Research Institute, Multan, Pakistan. "Ag: DP/PAK/73/026." LC Card 83-931176
1. Cotton - Pakistan - Grading. 2. Cotton - Prices - Pakistan. 3. Cotton - Pakistan - Marketing. 4. Cottonseed - Pakistan. I. Central Cotton Research Institute, Multan. II. Series: Consultant report (Food and Agriculture Organization of the United Nations) , 1. III. Title.
HD9086.P32 G35 1978

Galambos, Louis. Temin, Peter. The fall of the Bell system . Cambridge , New York , 1987. xviii, 378 p. : ISBN 0-521-34557-X LC Card 87-10293 DDC 384.6/065/73 19
HE8846.A55 T44 1987

Galambosi, László. Takarékszövetkezeti tisztségviselők kézikönyve / [írta Galambosi László]. Budapest : Szövetkezeti Gazdaságszervezési és Számítástechnikai Iroda, 1986. 135 p. ; 24 cm. ISBN 963-7006-73-7 LC Card 87-137992
1. Savings-banks - Hungary - Management - Handbooks, manuals, etc. 2. Banks and banking, Cooperative - Hungary - Management - Handbooks, manuals, etc. I. Title.
HG1939.H82 G35 1986

Galaty, John G. Power and poverty . Boulder , 1988. v, 186 p. ; ISBN 0-8133-7351-4 (pbk. : alk. paper) : LC Card 86-32578 DDC 338.9/009172/4 19
HC59.72.E44 P68 1988

Galavielle, Jean-Pierre. Economie budgétaire et fiscale / Jean-Pierre Galavielle ; préface de Pierre Uri. 1re éd. Paris : Cujas, c1984-c1986. 2 v. : ill. ; 27 cm. (Synthese) Includes bibliographies. Errata slip inserted in v. 1. CONTENTS. - [1. without special title -- 2] Recherches, documents et thèmes de réflexion / avec la participation de R. Puerto-Martínez ... [et al.]. ISBN 2-254-84071-2 (v. 1) : LC Card 87-137252
1. Finance, Public. I. Series: Collection Synthèse. II. Title.
HJ151 .G18 1984

Galbraith, John Kenneth, 1908- Economics in perspective : a critical history / John Kenneth Galbraith. Boston : Houghton Mifflin, 1987. 324 p. ; 24 cm. Includes bibliographical references and index. ISBN 0-395-35572-9 : LC Card 87-3644 DDC 330/.09 19
1. Economics - History. 2. Economic history. I. Title.
HB75 .G274 1987

Gałdzicki, Zygmunt. Socjologia pracy . Wrocław , 1978. 201 p. : LC Card 81-180007
HD6955 .S66 1978

Gale, Bradley T. Buzzell, Robert D. (Robert Dow), 1933- The PIMS principles . New York , London , c1987. xiii, 322 p. : ISBN 0-02-904430-8 LC Card 87-416 DDC 658.8/02 19
HF5415.13 .B893 1987

Gale, Dennis E. Black and white urban-to-suburban outmigrants : a comparative analysis, 1975-1980 / by Dennis E. Gale, George and Eunice Grier. Washington, D.C. : Center for Washington Area Studies, George Washington University, [1986] 46 p. : ill. ; 28 cm. (Occasional paper / Center for Washington Area Studies, George Washington University . no. 4) "May 1986." Bibliography: p. 41-45. LC Card 87-404424 DDC 307.2 19
1. Urban-rural migration - Washington Metropolitan Area. 2. Afro-Americans - Employment - Washington Metropolitan Area. 3. Residential mobility - Washington metropolitan area. I. Grier, George W. II. Grier, Eunice S. III. Series: Occasional paper (George Washington University. Center for Washington Area Studies) , no. 4. IV. Title.
HB1987.W34 G35 1986

Gale, Richard P. Social science in natural resource management systems /. Boulder , 1987. xii, 265 p. : ISBN 0-8133-7485-5 (pbk. : alk. paper) LC Card 87-23138 DDC 333.7/0973 19
HC103.7 .S62 1987

Gale, William A. Artificial intelligence and statistics /. Reading, Mass. , c1986. xiv, 418 p. : ISBN 0-201-11568-9 : LC Card 85-28631 DDC 006.3 19
Q334 .A764 1986 ***NYPL [JSE 87-399]***

GALES. see **STORMS.**

Gałęski, Bogusław. Family farming in Europe and America /. Boulder , 1987. viii, 312 p. ; ISBN 0-8133-7340-9 (soft : alk. paper) : LC Card 87-2041 DDC 338.1/6 19
HD1476.E85 F35 1987

GALICIA, EASTERN (UKRAINE) - ECONOMIC CONDITIONS.
Vytanovych, Illi͡a. Sotsial'no-ekonomichni ideï v zmahanni͡akh halyts'kykh ukraïntsiv na perelomi XIX-XX vv. /. Mi͡unkhen , 1970. 74 p. ; LC Card 86-214348
HC337.U52 G358 1970

GALICIA, EASTERN, UKRAINE - POLITICS AND GOVERNMENT.
Vytanovych, Illi͡a. Sotsial'no-ekonomichni ideï v zmahanni͡akh halyts'kykh ukraïntsiv na perelomi XIX-XX vv. /. Mi͡unkhen , 1970. 74 p. ; LC Card 86-214348
HC337.U52 G358 1970

GALICIA, EASTERN (UKRAINE) - SOCIAL CONDITIONS.
Vytanovych, Illi͡a. Sotsial'no-ekonomichni ideï v zmahanni͡akh halyts'kykh ukraïntsiv na perelomi XIX-XX vv. /. Mi͡unkhen , 1970. 74 p. ; LC Card 86-214348
HC337.U52 G358 1970

Galin, Pedro.
Asalariados y clases populares en Lima / Pedro Galin, Julio Carrión, Oscar Castillo. Lima : Instituto de Estudios Peruanos, [1986] 127 p. ; 21 cm. (Serie Urbanización, migraciones y cambios en la sociedad peruana . 6) Bibliography: p. [111]-127. LC Card 87-400199 DDC 331/.0985/25 19
1. Labor and laboring classes - Peru - Lima. I. Carrión, Julio. II. Castillo, Oscar. III. Series: Urbanización, migraciones y cambios en la sociedad peruana, 6. IV. Title.
HD8350.L562 G35 1986

Condiciones de trabajo y coordinación de las inspecciones / Pedro Galin. 1a ed. Lima, Perú : Centro Interamericano de Administración del Trabajo, 1986. 19 p. ; 25 cm. (Serie Inspección del trabajo . no. 24) Includes bibliographical references. LC Card 87-401748 DDC 331.25 19
1. Quality of work life - Latin America. 2. Labor inspection - Latin America. I. Title. II. Series.
HD6957.L29 G35 1986

Galindo, Daniel dos Santos. Comunicação mercadológica em tempo de incertezas / Daniel dos Santos Galindo. S. Paulo-SP : Icone

Editora, c1986. 167 p. : ill. ; 21 cm. Originally presented as the author's thesis (mestrado)--Instituto Metodista de Ensino Superior. Bibliography: p. 165-167. LC Card 86-224127
1. Marketing - Brazil. 2. Advertising - Brazil. I. Title.
HF5415.12.B7 G35 1986

Galjart, B. F. (Benno Franciscus) Participatie, toegang tot ontwikkeling . Leiden , 1982, c1983. 313 p. ; ISBN 90-6624-043-1 LC Card 87-158868
HC59.72.E44 P37 1983

Galkin, I. G. (Il'ia Grigor'evich)
Sovershenstvovanie planirovaniia stroitel'nogo proizvodstva / I.G. Galkin, Ė.I. Safonova, E.M. Shabalin ; pod redaktsieĭ I.G. Galkina. Moskva : Stroĭizdat, 1986. 167 p. : ill. ; 20 cm. Includes bibliographical references. LC Card 85-178938
1. Construction industry - Soviet Union - Finance. I. Safonova, Ė. I. (Ėleonora Ivanovna). II. Shabalin, Evgeniĭ Mikhaĭlovich. III. Title.
HD9715.S72 G35 1986

Gall, Norman. Brazil and Peru : social and economic effects of petroleum development / Norman Gall, Eleodoro Mayorga Alba. Geneva : International Labour Office, 1987. x, 123 p., [1] leaf of plates : ill. ; 30 cm. Includes bibliographies. ISBN 92-2-105506-X (pbk.) : LC Card 87-166425 DDC 338.2/7282/0981 19
1. Petroleum industry and trade - Brazil. 2. Petroleum industry and trade - Peru. 3. Brazil - Economic conditions - 1964-1985. 4. Peru - Economic conditions - 1968-. 5. Petróleo Brasileiro, S. A. 6. Petróleos del Perú. I. Mayorga Alba, Eleodoro. II. Title.
HD9574.B82 G34 1987

Galland, Olivier. Jeunes en transit : l'aventure ambiguë des foyers de jeunes travailleurs / Olivier Galland, Marie-Victoire Louis ; postface de Jean-Michel Belorgey. Paris : Economie et humanisme : Editions ouvrières, c1984. 236 p. ; 20 cm. (Collection Politique sociale, 0243-3265) Bibliography: p. [203]-212. ISBN 2-7082-2405-0 : LC Card 85-102779 DDC 367/.94486 19
1. Youth - Employment - France. 2. Youth centers - France. 3. Youth hostels - France. 4. Young adults - France - Housing. I. Louis, Marie Victoire. II. Title. III. Title: Foyers des jeunes travailleurs. IV. Series.
HD6276.F72 G35 1984

Gallant, A. Ronald, 1942- A unified theory of estimation and inference for nonlinear dynamic models / A. Ronald Gallant and Halbert White. Oxford [Oxfordshire] ; New York, NY, USA. : B. Blackwell, 1988. p. cm. Includes index. ISBN 0-631-15765-4 : LC Card 87-25602 DDC 330/.028 19
1. Econometric models. 2. Linear models (Statistics). I. White, Halbert. II. Title.
HB141 .G33 1988

Gallardo, María Eugenia. Centroamérica : la crisis en cifras / María Eugenia Gallardo, José Roberto López. San José, Costa Rica : Instituto Interamericano de Cooperación para la Agricultura : Facultad Latinoamericana de Ciencias Sociales, 1986. 259 p. : ill. ; 21 cm. Includes bibliographical references. ISBN 92-9039-110-3 LC Card 87-401731 DDC 330.9728/053 19
1. Economic indicators - Central America. 2. Social indicators - Central America. I. López, José Roberto. II. Title.
HC141 .G35 1986

Gallery, Shari Mendelson. Physical security . Boston , c1986. xii, 409 p. : ISBN 0-409-95105-6 (pbk.) LC Card 85-29083 DDC 658.4/73 19
HD38 .P49 1986 ***NYPL [JLE 86-3699]***

Gallessi, Roberto. Bezza, Bruno. Le lotte degli elettromeccanici /. Milano , c1981. 179 p. : ISBN 88-20-42149-6 : LC Card 81-200954 DDC 331.89/282131/0945 19
HD5384.E3 B49 1981 ***NYPL [JLD 86-2898]***

Galli, Rosemary. Guinea-Bissau : politics, economics, and society / Rosemary E. Galli and Jocelyn Jones. London : F. Pinter ; Boulder : L. Rienner, 1987. xvi, 217 p., [1] leaf of plates : ill. ; 23 cm. (Marxist regimes series) Bibliography: p. [197]-208. Includes index. ISBN 1-555-87025-2 (U. S. : lib. bdg.) : LC Card 86-28011 DDC 966/.5703 19
1. Guinea-Bissau - Economic conditions - To 1974. 2. Guinea-Bissau - Economic conditions - 1974-. 3. Guinea-Bissau - Politics and government - To 1974. 4. Guinea-Bissau - Politics and government - 1974-. 5. Guinea-Bissau - Social conditions. 6. Rural development - Guinea-Bissau. I. Jones, Jocelyn. II. Title. III. Series.
HC1080 .G35 1987

Gallissot, René. Les Aventures du marxisme /. Paris , c1984. 415 p. ; ISBN 2-86738-025-1 (pbk.)
NYPL [JLD 87-212]

Gallo, R. (Riccardo), 1943- Risanamento e riordino delle partecipazioni statali . Milano, Italy , c1986. 429 p. : LC Card 86-169331
HC310.I53 R57 1986

Gallón Giraldo, Gustavo. Concertación simple y concertación ampliada / Gustavo Gallón Giraldo. Bogotá, Colombia : Centro de Investigación y Educación Popular, [between 1982 and 1985] 62 p. ; 22 cm. (Serie Controversia . no. 105) Bibliography: p. 55-57. LC Card 85-147865
1. Colombia - Economic policy. 2. Colombia - Social policy. I. Title. II. Series.
HC197 .G25 1982

Gallup Organization.
The Corporate view . Washington, DC , c1982. vii, 92 p. ; ***NYPL [JLF 87-940]***

1986 air travel survey /. Princeton, N.J. (53 Bank St., Princeton 08542) , c1986. 77 leaves ; LC Card 86-225970 DDC 387.7/42/0973 19
HE9787.5.N7 A17 1986

Galper, Morton. Promotional management . Englewood Cliffs, N.J. , c1988. xi, 305 p. : ISBN 0-13-731035-8 (pbk.) LC Card 87-12041 DDC 658.8 19
HF5415 .P727 1988

Galster, George C., 1948- Homeowners and neighborhood reinvestment / George C. Galster. Durham : Duke University Press, 1987. xii, 354 p. ; 25 cm. (Duke Press policy studies) Bibliography: p. [335]-342. Includes index. ISBN 0-8223-0725-1 LC Card 87-13448 DDC 307.3/36 19
1. Dwellings - Valuation. 2. Dwellings - Maintenance and repair - Economic aspects. 3. Home ownership. 4. Neighborhood. I. Title. II. Series.
HD1387 .G34 1987

Galts, Helmut. Ungewissheit und Planungsmethodik : Probleme der Anwendung der Theorie des Gewinnvorbehalts / Helmut Galts. Münster : Lit, [1983] vi, 234 p. : ill. ; 21 cm. (Betriebswirtschaftliche Schriftenreihe . Bd. 11) Bibliography: p. 212-228. ISBN 3-88660-143-9 LC Card 84-178712
1. Uncertainty. 2. Risk. 3. Decision-making. I. Title. II. Series.
HB615 .G35 1983

Galuza, Stanislav Grigor'evich. Ėkonomicheskie aspekty integratsii nauki i proizvodstva /. Minsk , 1986. 204, [4] p. ; LC Card 87-106384
HC337.B933 R43 1986

Galvêas, Ernane. Sistema financeiro e mercado de capitais / Ernane Galvêas. Rio de Janeiro : Instituto Brasileiro de Mercado de Capitais, 1985. 171 p. : ill. ; 21 cm. LC Card 85-208367
1. Finance - Brazil. 2. Banks and banking - Brazil. 3. Banks and banking, Central - Brazil. 4. Financial institutions - Brazil. 5. Monetary policy - Brazil. 6. Inflation (Finance) - Brazil. I. Title.
HG185.B7 G35 1985

Gálvez, Thelma. Yo trabajo así-- en casa particular / Thelma Gálvez, Rosalba Todaro ; edición de entrevistas, Verónica Oxman ; [fotos, Patricia Mora]. Santiago, Chile : Centro de Estudios de la Mujer, 1985. 113 p. : ill. ; 18 cm. (Ediciones CEM) Interviews with four domestic workers. LC Card 86-208887
1. Women domestics - Chile - Interviews. I. Todaro C., Rosalba. II. Oxman V., Verónica. III. Title. IV. Series.
HD6072.2.C5 G35 1985

Gambaroff, Marina, 1943- Tschernobyl hat unser Leben verändert . Reinbek bei Hamburg , 1986. 203 p. : ISBN 3-499-15922-8 : LC Card 87-123041 DDC 363.1/79 19
HD9698.G42 T73 1986

Gambel, Edoardo L. La valutazione, simulazione e previsione nella gestione d'impresa : il programma "Gambel 1" su personal computer / Edoardo L. Gambel. Milano, Italy : F. Angeli, c1986. 190 p. : ill. ; 22 cm. (Azienda moderna. 187) Bibliography: p. [189]-190. LC Card 86-217652
1. Managerial accounting - Data processing. 2. Microcomputers - Programming. I. Title.
HF5679 .G36 1986

Gambia.
Preparation report, rural development programme, 1980-85 / The Republic of the Gambia. Banjul : Coordinator's Office, Rural Development Project, [1979- v. <1 > : ill. ; 30 cm. Cover title. "July 1979--Annex 1. CONTENTS. - Annex 1. Programme area. LC Card 86-203596
1. Agricultural development projects - Gambia. 2. Agriculture and state - Gambia. 3. Rural development projects - Gambia. 4. Rural development - Government policy - Gambia. I. Rural Development Project (Gambia). Coordinator's Office. II. Title. III. Title: Rural development programme, 1980-85.
HD2147 .G35 1980a

Gambia. Central Statistics Dept.
Estimates of national income at constant prices in the Gambia. [Banjul] [1985] 49 leaves ; LC Card 87-120773 DDC 339.366/51 19
HC1070.Z9 I54 1985

Sources and methods of estimation of national income at current prices in the Gambia. [Banjul, Gambia] [1985] vi, 151 p. ; LC Card 87-116289 DDC 339.366/51 19
HC1070.Z9 I57 1985

GAMBIA - ECONOMIC POLICY.
Sisay, S. S. Budget speech /. [Gambia] [1986] 60 leaves ; LC Card 87-403347 DDC 354.66/510072256 19
HJ2185 .S57 1986

GAMBIA - FOREIGN ECONOMIC RELATIONS.
Sisay, S. S. Budget speech /. [Gambia] [1986] 60 leaves ; LC Card 87-403347 DDC 354.66/510072256 19
HJ2185 .S57 1986

Gamble, Andrew. Britain in decline : economic policy, political strategy, and the British state / Andrew Gamble.2nd ed. Basingstoke, Hampshire : Macmillan, 1985. xxi, 261 p. ; 23 cm. Bibliography: p. [231]-256. Includes index. ISBN 0-333-39253-1 : LC Card 86-673896
1. Great Britain - Economic policy - 1945-. 2. Great Britain - Politics and government - 1945-. I. Title.
HC256.6 .G35x 1985

Gamboa Conejo, Rita Ma. (Rita María)
Resultados preliminares del análisis metodológico de los planes nacionales de desarrollo, 1974-1982 / Rita Ma. Gamboa Conejo, Jorge Vargas Cullell. Heredia : Universidad Nacional, Facultad de Ciencias Sociales, Escuela de Planificación y Promoción Social, 1985. 1 v. (various pagings) : ill. ; 28 cm. (Cuadernos de planificación y promoción social. Serie Avance de investigación . 2) At head of title: Proyecto: "Proyectos políticos y estrategias de planificación en los planes nacionales de desarrollo de Costa Rica: 1974-1982." Includes bibliographical references. LC Card 87-402159 DDC 338.97286 19
1. Costa Rica - Economic policy - Evaluation. I. Vargas Cullel, Jorge. II. Title. III. Title: Proyectos políticos y estrategias de planificación en los planes nacionales de desarrollo de Costa Rica: 1974-1982. IV. Series.
HC143 .G36 1985

Game plan. Peek, Stephen, 1947- Gameplan . White Hall, Va. , c1987. 135 p. ; ISBN 0-932620-85-X (pbk.) : LC Card 87-15921 DDC 794/.068 19
HD9993.G352 P44 1987

A game-theoretic approach to the design of an optimal sales policy /. Hu, Sheng C. West Lafayette, Ind. [1986] 30, 14 p. : LC Card 86-622755 DDC 658/.001/9 s 658.8/101 19
HD6483 .P8 no. 900 HF5438.25

GAME THEORY - DATA PROCESSING.
Löffler, Reiner, 1959- STRATEGOS . Mannheim , 1986 (Darmstadt : Copy Shop) 246, [49] p. : LC Card 87-408452 DDC 658.4/0353/0285 19
HD30.26 .L64 1986

Gameplan . Peek, Stephen, 1947- White Hall, Va. , c1987. 135 p. ; ISBN 0-932620-85-X (pbk.) : LC Card 87-15921 DDC 794/.068 19
HD9993.G352 P44 1987

GAMES, CHILDREN. see GAMES.

GAMES - MARKETING.
Peek, Stephen, 1947- Gameplan . White Hall, Va. , c1987. 135 p. ; ISBN 0-932620-85-X (pbk.) :

LC Card 87-15921 DDC 794/.068 19
HD9993.G352 P44 1987

GAMES, THEORY OF. see **GAME THEORY.**

Gamonalismo y lucha campesina . Sylva Charvet, Paola. [Quito] , 1986. 250 p., [3] leaves of plates : LC Card 87-101122
HD529.C47 S95 1986

Ganapini, Luigi. --Anche l'uomo doveva essere di ferro . Milano, Italy , c1986. 441 p. : LC Card 86-213675
HD8490.T742 A53 1986

Gandásegui, Marco A. La fuerza de trabajo en el agro : experiencia del desarrollo capitalista en Panamá / Marco A. Gandásegui, hijo. Panamá, R.P. : CELA, c1985. 404 p. : ill. ; 28 cm. Bibliography: p. [393]-404. ISBN 84-8385-002-X LC Card 86-111074 DDC 331.7/63/097287 19
1. Agriculture - Economic aspects - Panama. 2. Agricultural laborers - Panama. 3. Peasantry - Panama. 4. Labor supply - Panama. I. Title.
HD1822 .G36 1985 ***NYPL [JLF 86-1350]***

Gandhi Labour Institute, Ahmedabad. Migrant labour and related issues /. New Delhi , c1987. xii, 334 p. : ISBN 81-204-0199-9 : LC Card 87-901172
HD5856.I4 M54 1985

Gandhi Peace Foundation (New Delhi, India)
Trusteeship, the Gandhian alternative /. New Delhi , c1986. xiii, 238 p. ; LC Card 86-903783 DDC 330.1 19
HB199 .T76 1986

Gandolfo, Giancarlo.
International economics I : the pure theory of international trade / Giancarlo Gandolfo. Berlin ; New York : Springer-Verlag, c1987- p. cm. Bibliography: p. Includes indexes. ISBN 0-387-17971-2 (U. S.) LC Card 87-23367 DDC 337 19
1. International economic relations. 2. Commerce. 3. International finance. I. Title.
HF1411 .G33362 1987

International economics II : international monetary theory and open-economy macroeconomics / Giancarlo Gandolfo. Berlin ; New York : Springer-Verlag, c1987. p. cm. Includes bibliographies and index. ISBN 0-387-17978-X (U. S.) LC Card 87-16295 DDC 332.4/5 19
1. Interntional economic relations. 2. International finance. 3. Macroeconomics. I. Title.
HF1411 .G33363 1987

Gane, Chris, 1938- Developing business systems in SQL : using ORACLE on the IBM-PC / by Chris Gane.1st ed. New York, NY : Rapid System Development, 1986. 1 v. (various pagings) : ill. ; 28 cm. Includes index. ISBN 0-914751-02-6 (pbk.) LC Card 87-107881 DDC 650/.028/557565 19
1. SQL/ORACLE (Computer program language). 2. IBM Personal Computer - Programming. 3. Business - Data processing. I. Title.
HF5548.5.S65 G36 1986

Ganev, Ivan. Razvivashti se strani . Sofiia︡ , 1986. 423 p. ; LC Card 86-231951
HC59.7 .R3395 1986

Gangadhar Rakshit. see **Rakshit, Gangadhar, 1929-**

Gangadhara Rao, M. Human resources management in Indian railways / M. Gangadhara Rao and P. Subba Rao. 1st ed. Delhi : Manas Publications, 1986. xvi, 245 p. ; 25 cm. Includes index. Bibliography: p. [231]-238. ISBN 81-7049-004-9 : LC Card 86-900747 DDC 385/.068/3 19
1. Railroads - India - Employees. 2. Personnel management - India. 3. Manpower planning - India. I. Subba Rao, P. II. Title.
HD8039.R12 I437 1986
NYPL [JLE 86-4104]

GANGES RIVER (INDIA AND BANGLADESH) - WATER-RIGHTS.
Äbbāsa, Bi. Ema., 1911- The Ganges waters dispute /. New Delhi , c1982. xv, 157 p., 8 p. of plates : ISBN 0-7069-2080-5 : LC Card 83-900165 DDC 341.4/42 19
HD1698.G36 A23 1982

The Ganges waters dispute /. Äbbāsa, Bi. Ema., 1911- New Delhi , c1982. xv, 157 p., 8 p. of plates : ISBN 0-7069-2080-5 : LC Card 83-900165 DDC 341.4/42 19
HD1698.G36 A23 1982

Gangrade, K. D., 1926- Women and child workers in unorganised sector . New Delhi , 1983. xii, 104 p. ; LC Card 83-906999 DDC 331.3/1/0954 19
HD6189 .W64 1983 ***NYPL [JLD 87-730]***

O ganho médio do operário na indústria transformadora em Portugal e noutros países da OCDE de 1972 a 1982 /. Almedia, Maria Henriqueta de. Lisboa , 1985. 88 p. : LC Card 86-189354
HD5059 .A65 1985

Ganne, Roger. Baquiast, Jean-Paul. La France dans la bataille des technologies de l'intelligence /. Paris , c1985. 221 p. ; ISBN 2-11-001440-7 : LC Card 86-126853 DDC 338.4/7004/094 19
HD9696.C63 F72 1985

Gannicott, K. G. (Ken G.) Australia's dependence on foreign technology / K.G. Gannicott. [Canberra, Australia] : Parliament of the Commonwealth of Australia, Dept. of the Parliamentary Library, [1982] 38 p. ; 25 cm. (Discussion papers / Legislative Research Service . no. 1, 1982) "This discussion paper forms part of the occasional paper series of the Department of the Parliamentary Library"--P. [2] of cover. Includes bibliographical references. LC Card 84-197120 DDC 338.994/06 19
1. Technology transfer - Australia. 2. Australia - Dependency on foreign countries. I. Series: Discussion papers (Australia. Dept. of the Parliamentary Library. Legislative Research Service) , 1982, no. 1. II. Title.
HC610.T4 G36 1982

Ganster, Daniel C. Job stress . New York , c1987. 267 p. ; ISBN 0-86656-630-9 LC Card 87-8568 DDC 658.3/82 19
HF5548.85 .J65 1987

Gantman, Vladimir Izrail'evich. Baranovskiĭ, V. G. (Vladimir Georgievich) Evropeĭskoe soobshchestvo v sisteme mezhdunarodnykh otnosheniĭ /. Moskva , 1986. 319 p. ; LC Card 86-201822
HF1532.92 .B37 1986

Gantner, Manfried. Messprobleme öffentlicher Aktivitäten : Staatsquoten, Preissteigerungen, Outputkonzepte / Manfried Gantner.1. Aufl. Baden-Baden : Nomos Verlagsgesellschaft, 1984. 353 p. ; 23 cm. (Schriften zur monetären Ökonomie. Bd. 20) Bibliography: p. 335-353. ISBN 3-7890-0989-X : LC Card 84-252950
1. Expenditures, Public. I. Title.
HJ2005 .G35 1984

Gant︠s︡kiĭ, Vladimir Alekseevich.
Razvivai︠u︡shchiesi︠a︡ strany Azii v mirovom kapitalisticheskom syr'evom khozi︠a︡ĭstve / V.A. Gantskiĭ. Moskva : Izd-vo "Nauka," Glav. red. vostochnoĭ lit-ry, 1985. 204 p. ; 22 cm. At head of title: Akademii︠a︡ nauk SSSR. Ordena Trudovogo Krasnogo Znameni Institut vostokovedenii︠a︡. Summary in English. Bibliography: p. 196-[203] LC Card 86-154165
1. Raw materials - Asia. 2. Raw materials - Developing countries. I. Title.
HF1054.A8 G36 1985

Ganz, Carole, 1941- U. S.A.-Japan Conference on Manufacturing Research (1986 : Tokyo, Japan) Manufacturing research perspectives, U. S.A.-Japan . Amsterdam , New York , 1987. viii, 198 p. : ISBN 0-444-42868-2 LC Card 87-19851 DDC 338.4/767 19
HD9725 .U17 1986

Gapenski, Louis C. Brigham, Eugene F., 1930- Financial management . Chicago , c1988. xx, 901 p. : ISBN 0-03-012543-X LC Card 87-15616 DDC 658.1/5 19
HG4026 .B669 1988

Gapes, R. F. (Robert Francis) The heavy engineering industry in New Zealand : an industry study / prepared for the Advisory Committee on the Heavy Engineering Industry and the Minister of Trade and Industry, New Zealand [by] R.F. Gapes, W.D. Rose. [Wellington, N.Z. : Dept. of Trade and Industry, 1976] 105 p. : ill. ; 30 cm. LC Card 84-255451
1. Machinery industry - New Zealand. 2. New Zealand - Manufactures. 3. Engineering - New Zealand. I. Rose, W. D. (William Dennis). II. New Zealand. Advisory Committee on the Heavy Engineering Industry. III. New Zealand Dept. of Trade and Industry. IV. Title.
HD9705.N44 G36 1976

The garage sale book . Groberman, Jeff. Rocklin, CA , c1987. 90 p. : ISBN 0-914629-10-7 (pbk.) : LC Card 86-25388 DDC 658.8/7 19
HF5482.3 .G76 1987

GARAGE SALES.
Groberman, Jeff. The garage sale book . Rocklin, CA , c1987. 90 p. : ISBN 0-914629-10-7 (pbk.) : LC Card 86-25388 DDC 658.8/7 19
HF5482.3 .G76 1987

Garam, József.
Bagota, Béla. Mit kell tudni a hetedik ötéves tervről? /. [Budapest] , 1986. 238 p. ; ISBN 963-09-2815-9 : LC Card 86-210804
HC300.28 .B319 1986

Bagota, Béla. Mit kell tudni az 1987. évi népgazdasági tervről? /. [Budapest] , 1987. 239 p. ; ISBN 963-09-3110-9 : LC Card 87-151787
HC300.28 .B329 1987

Garamvölgyi, Judit. Betriebsräte und sozialer Wandel in Österreich 1919/1920 : Studien zur Konstituierungsphase der österreichischen Betriebsräte / Judit Garamvölgyi. München : Oldenbourg, c1983. 296 p. ; 24 cm. (Studien und Quellen zur österreichischen Zeitgeschichte . Bd. 5) Originally presented as the author's Habilitationsschrift. Includes bibliographical references and indexes. ISBN 3-486-51721-X LC Card 83-240283
1. Works councils - Austria - History - 20th century. 2. Trade-unions - Austria - History - 20th century. 3. Austria - Social conditions. I. Title. II. Series.
HD5660.A8 G37 1983

GARBAGE. see **REFUSE AND REFUSE DISPOSAL.**

Garbe, Detlef, 1949-
Bürgerbeteiligung in der Verbraucherinformationspolitik . Frankfurt , New York , c1986. 241 p. : ISBN 3-593-33681-2 LC Card 86-230016
HC290.5.C63 B87 1986

Die Planungszelle und ihre Umwelt : Analyse d. Beziehungsgefüges zwischen Verfahren, Teilnehmern u. Planern / Detlef Garbe. Frankfurt a.M. ; Bern ; xiv, 339 p. ; 21 cm. (Democratia experimentalis . Bd. 1) Originally presented as the author's thesis, Gesamthochschule, Wuppertal. Bibliography: p. 317-339. ISBN 3-8204-6017-9 LC Card 81-464829
1. Environmental policy - Citizen participation. 2. Planning - Citizen participation. I. Title.
HC79.E5 G33 1980 ***NYPL [JLD 81-2376]***

Zukünftige Energiepolitik . München , 1985. 189 p. : ISBN 3-89147-002-9 LC Card 87-104306
HD9698.G42 Z85 1985

Garbuzov, V. F. (Vasiliĭ Fedorovich)
Finansovo-kreditnyĭ slovar' /. Moskva , 1984- v. ; LC Card 84-203984
HG151 .F53 1984 ***NYPL [*QAC 85-1247]***

García Alba Iduñate, Pascual, 1948-
[Financial aspects of macroeconomic management in Mexico. Spanish]
Causas y efectos de la crisis económica en México / Pascual García Alba, Jaime Serra Puche. 1a ed. en español. México, D.F. : Centro de Estudios Económicos, Colegio de México, 1984. 124 p. : ill. ; 17 cm. (Jornadas. 104) Translation of: Financial aspects of macroeconomic management in Mexico. Bibliography: p. 123-124. ISBN 968-12-0285-6 LC Card 86-138030
1. Mexico - Economic policy. 2. Finance, Public - Mexico. 3. Inflation (Finance) - Mexico. I. Serra Puche, Jaime. II. Title. III. Series.
HC135 .G29818 1984

García, Antonio [i.e. Antonio García Ponce] see **García Ponce, Antonio, 1929-**

García, Antonio, 1912-
[Bases de la economía contemporánea]
Bases de economía política / Antonio García. 2a ed. [Bogotá] : Tiempo Americano Editores, 1981. 283 p. ; 21 cm. (Antología del pensamiento económico y social de América Latina . v. 4, t. 1) Includes bibliographical references. Reprint. Originally published: Bases de la economía contemporánea. Bogotá : Ediciones Revisoría Fiscal de Instituciones Oficiales de Crédito, 1948. LC Card 82-138900 DDC 330/.098 19
1. Economics - Latin America. 2. Capitalism. 3.

Marxian economics. I. Title. II. Series.
HB122 .G37 1981 *NYPL [JLD 87-868]*

Garcia, Avelino [i. e., Avelino Garcia Villarejo] see **García Villarejo, Avelino.**

García Bocanegra, Angela Victoria. Posición de los países en desarrollo frente a la crisis económica mundial / Angela Victoria García Bocanegra. Bogotá, D.E. : República de Colombia, Pontificia Universidad Javeriana, Facultad de Ciencias Jurídicas y Socioeconómicas, 1984. 146 p. ; 23 cm. Thesis (doctoral)--Pontificia Universidad Javeriana, Bogotá, 1984. Bibliography: p. 143-146. LC Card 85-205412
1. Developing countries - Foreign economic relations. 2. International economic relations. 3. Latin America - Foreign economic relations. I. Title.
HF1413 .G312 1984

García Cano, José Luis. Todo para la G.M. . Madrid [1981?] 174 p. : ISBN 84-85639-19-7 LC Card 82-134601 DDC 338.8/87 19
HD9710.S754 G467 1981
NYPL [JLC 86-300]

García Chuecos, Héctor. Hacienda colonial venezolana /. Caracas , 1946. 170 p. ; LC Card 85-105445
HJ991 .H323 1946

García Colmenares, Pablo. Rueda Hernanz, Germán. La desamortización de Mendizábal y Espartero en España /. Madrid , c1986. 200 p. ; ISBN 84-376-0592-X LC Card 86-216590
HD774 .R84 1986

Garcia Durand, José Carlos. see **Durand, José Carlos Garcia.**

García Elizalde, Pedro. El desarrollo frutícola y forestal en Chile y sus derivaciones sociales. 1a ed. Santiago de Chile : Naciones Unidas, 1986. 234 p. : ill. ; 23 cm. (Estudios e informes de la CEPAL, 0256-9795 . 57) Texts prepared by Pedro García Elizalde and José I. Leyton. "Los documentos incluidos en este número fueron presentados al Taller CEPAL/FAO sobre Política Agrícola y Desarrollo Rural (Santiago de Chile, 26 al 30 de agosto de 1985) que forma parte del proyecto conjunto del gobierno de los países bajos y la CEPAl relativo al mismo tema adscrito a la División Agrícolas Conjunta CEPAL/FAO"--T.p. verso. Includes bibliographies. "Publicación de las Naciones Unidas, número de venta S.86.II.G.7"--T.p. verso. "LC/G.1378, enero de 1986"--T.p. verso. ISBN 92-1-321204-6 LC Card 86-175421
1. Fruit trade - Chile - Congresses. 2. Forest products industry - Chile - Congresses. I. Leyton, José I. II. Title. III. Series.
HD9254.C52 G37 1986

García Euribe, Rafael. Ortiz, Rolando. CORDES . Lima, Perú , 1987. 96 p. ; LC Card 87-405059 DDC 338.985 19
HC227 .O73 1987

García Galló, Gaspar M. Jorge. General de las cañas / Gaspar Jorge García Galló. La Habana : Editora Política, 1983. 220 p., [18] p. of plates : ill., ports. ; 21 cm. LC Card 84-229562 DDC 331.88/13361/097291 19
1. Menéndez, Jesús, 1911-1948. 2. Sindicato Nacional de Trabajadores Azucareros (Cuba) - History. 3. Trade-unions - Cuba - Officials and employees - Biography. 4. Sugar workers - Cuba - History. I. Title.
HD6577.5.M46 G37 1983
NYPL [JFD 85-4783]

García, Héctor [i. e. Héctor García Chuecos] see **García Chuecos, Héctor.**

García, Jorge. Tierras para asentamientos populares . Quito, Ecuador , 1985. 378 p. : LC Card 87-400165 DDC 333.77/13/0986613 19
HD530.Q58 T54 1985

Garcia, José Manuel. Rau, Virginia. Sesmarias medievais portuguesas /. Lisboa [1982] 288 p. : LC Card 87-673341
HD784 .R3x 1982

García López, Lucía. Nahuatzen, agricultura y comercio en una comunidad serrana / Lucía García López. Zamora, Mich. : Colegio de Michoacán ; México, D.F. : Consejo Nacional de Ciencia Y Tecnología, c1984. 115 p. : maps ; 20 cm. Bibliography: p. 113-115. ISBN 968-7230-03-7 LC Card 85-154045 DDC 338.1/0972/37 19
1. Agriculture - Economic aspects - Mexico - Nahuatzen Region. 2. Hill farming - Mexico - Nahuatzen Region. 3. Cottage industries - Mexico - Nahuatzen Region. 4. Nahuatzen Region (Mexico) - Commerce. I. Title.
HD1795.N34 G37 1984 *NYPL [JLD 87-16]*

García Luna O., Margarita (García Luna Ortega) El movimiento obrero en el Estado de México : primeras fábricas, obreros y huelgas, 1830-1910 / Margarita García Luna.1a ed. Toluca, Estado de México : Universidad Autónoma del Estado de México, 1984. 302 p. : ill. ; 22 cm. (Colección Historia. 1) Bibliography: p. 283-296. ISBN 968-514-014-6 LC Card 86-173738
1. Mexico (Mexico) - Industries - History. 2. Labor and laboring classes - Mexico - Mexico - History. 3. Trade-unions - Mexico - Mexico - History. I. Series: Colección Historia (Toluca de Lerdo, Mexico) , 1. II. Title.
HC137.M473 G37 1984

Garcia, Manuel Enriquez. Salários indexados, preços e emprego : uma contribuição ao estudo da inflação brasileira / Manuel Enriquez Garcia. São Paulo : Instituto de Pesquisas Econômicas/USP, 1986. 149 p. : ill. ; 23 cm. (Série Ensaios econômicos . no. 53) Abstract in English. Originally presented as the author's thesis (doctorate)--Universidade de São Paulo, 1983. Bibliography: p. 143-149. LC Card 86-234254
1. Wages - Government policy - Brazil. 2. Indexation (Economics) - Brazil. 3. Inflation (Finance) - Brazil. 4. Unemployment - Brazil. I. Series: Ensaios econômicos (Universidade de São Paulo. Instituto de Pesquisas Econômicas) , 53. II. Title.
HD5004 .G37 1986

García, Miguel Angel. El nacimiento de América : la acumulación del capital como fundamento del orden colonial y de su crisis revolucionaria / Miguel Angel García.1a ed. en castellano. México, D.F. : Extemporáneos, 1984. 284 p. : ill. ; 20 cm. (Colección Latinoamérica. Serie Ensayo . 12) Bibliography: p. 273-284. ISBN 968-415-089-X LC Card 87-403199 DDC 332/.0415/091812 19
1. Saving and investment - America - History. 2. Capitalism - America - History. I. Title. II. Series.
HC94.Z9 S34 1984

García Molina, Carlos. Mortalidad infantil y clases sociales : el caso de Medellín en la década del 70 / Carlos García Molina. [Medellín, Colombia] : Universidad Pontificia Bolivariana, [1986] 103 p. : ill. ; 23 cm. (Ediciones del cincuentenario. Colección Enfoques) Includes bibliographical references. ISBN 958-9127-05-3 LC Card 87-400685 DDC 304.6/4/0880542 19
1. Infants - Colombia - Medellín - Mortality. 2. Social classes - Colombia - Medellín. I. Title. II. Series.
HB1323.I42 C74 1986

García Murcia, Joaquín. El fondo de garantía salarial / Joaquín García Murcia. 1a ed. Madrid : Instituto de Estudios Laborales y de la Seguridad Social : Servicio de Publicaciones, Ministerio de Trabajo y Seguridad Social, 1983. 454 p. ; 24 cm. (Colección Estudios e investigaciones) Originally presented as the author's thesis (doctoral--Universidad de Sevilla, 1982) Bibliography: p. [393]-405. ISBN 84-7434-201-5 LC Card 85-194099
1. Insurance, Unemployment - Spain. I. Title. II. Series.
HD7096.S7 G37 1983

García, Nora. Mántey de Anguiano, M. G. Análisis microeconómico de los factores que determinan el valor de mercado de las empresas industriales mexicanas y su tasa de expansión /. [Mexico City] [1986] iv, 63 leaves : LC Card 87-400949 DDC 658.1/5/0972 19
HG4092 .M36 1986

García, Norberto E.
Absorción creciente con subempleo persistente (América Latina, 1950-80) / Norberto E. García. [Santiago, Chile] : Organización Internacional del Trabajo, Programa Mundial del Empleo, Programa Regional del Empleo para América Latina y el Caribe, 1982. 35 p. ; 28 cm. (Trabajo ocasional . 48) "Original: español." Cover title. "Versión revisada de una parte del borrador de discusión interna del PREALC de noviembre de 1981, titulado 'Absorción suficiente o insuficiente?'" Bibliography: p. 29-35. LC Card 87-403250 DDC 331.12/098 19
1. Labor supply - Latin America. 2. Unemployment, Structural - Latin America. I. Regional Employment Program for Latin America and the Caribbean. II. Series: Occasional paper (Regional Employment Program for Latin America and the Caribbean) , 48. III. Title.
HD5730.5.A6 G355 1982

Industria manufacturera y empleo : América Latina 1950-1980 / Norberto E. García. [Santiago, Chile] : Organización Internacional del Trabajo, Programa Mundial del Empleo, Programa Regional del Empleo para América Latina y el Caribe, 1982. 51 p. ; 28 cm. (Trabajo ocasional . 49) "Original: español." Cover title. Bibliography: p. 47-51. LC Card 87-403251 DDC 338.4/767/098 19
1. Latin America - Manufactures - History - 20th century. 2. Labor and laboring classes - Latin America - History - 20th century. I. Series: Occasional paper (Regional Employment Program for Latin America and the Caribbean) , 49. II. Title.
HD9734.L32 G36 1982

García Ponce, Antonio, 1929- Crisis oligarquía y latifundio : Carora, 1929-1935 / Antonio García Ponce.1a ed. Barquisimeto, Venezuela : Fondo Editorial Buría, 1986. 104 p., [1] folded leaf of plates : ill. ; 22 cm. (Colección Claridad. 1) Bibliography: p. 61-62. ISBN 980-608-701-1 : LC Card 87-134729 DDC 338.1/762/0098725 19
1. Carora (Venezuela) - Commerce - History - 20th century. 2. Cattle trade - Venezuela - Carora - History - 20th century. 3. Agriculture - Economic aspects - Venezuela - Carora - History - 20th century. 4. Depressions - 1929 - Venezuela. I. Title.
HF3490.C375 G37 1986

García-Salve, Francisco. Con esta sangre obrera / Francisco García Salve. Madrid : Riego, D.L., 1980. 197 p., 1 leaf ; 18 cm. ISBN 84-85759-08-7 : LC Card 81-141428
1. Syndicalism. 2. Labor and laboring classes. 3. Communism. I. Title.
HD6477 .G37 1980

García Valcárcel, Jesús. La Pobreza en España y sus causas /. Madrid , 1985. xx, 759 p. : ISBN 84-398-3252-4 : LC Card 86-230170
HC390.P6 P63 1985

García, Valeriano F.
A critical inquiry into Argentine economic history, 1946-1970 / Valeriano F. García. New York : Garland Pub., 1987. vi, 127 p. : ill. ; 24 cm. (South American and Latin American economic history) Thesis (Ph. D.)--University of Chicago, 1973. Bibliography: p. 127. ISBN 0-8240-1361-1 (alk. paper) : LC Card 87-7620 DDC 330.982/062 19
1. Monetary policy - Argentina - History - 20th century. 2. Credit - Argentina - History - 20th century. 3. Argentina - Economic conditions - 1945-1983. 4. Argentina - Economic policy. 5. Quantity theory of money. I. Title. II. Series.
HG815 .G27 1987

Dinero, precios y política monetaria / Valeriano García, Alvaro Saieh. Buenos Aires, Argentina : Ediciones Macchi, [1985] 334, [12] p. : ill. ; 23 cm. Bibliography: p. [335]-[345] ISBN 950-53-7077-7 LC Card 85-215884
1. Money. 2. Prices. 3. Monetary policy. I. Saieh, Alvaro. II. Title.
HG221 .G3193 1985

García Villarejo, Avelino.
Estructura financiera y actividad inversora de las administraciones públicas en Castilla y León / Avelino García Villarejo, Javier Salinas Sánchez ; con la colaboración del equipo de trabajo del Departamento de Economía y Hacienda, Julio Valverde Travieso, Carlos Polo Benito, José María Martínez Sánchez. Valladolid : Junta de Castilla y León, 1984. 431 p. : ill., maps ; 24 cm. Includes bibliographical references. ISBN 84-505-0331-0 LC Card 87-108720
1. Finance, Public - Spain - Castilla y León. 2. Investment of public funds - Spain - Castilla y León. 3. Social security - Spain - Castilla y León. I. Salinas Sánchez, Javier. II. Castilla y León (Spain). Departamento de Economía y Hacienda. III. Title.
HJ1249.C29 G37 1984

Manual de hacienda pública : general y de España / Avelino García Villarejo, Javier Salinas Sánchez. Madrid : Tecnos, c1985. 686 p. : ill. ; 24 cm. (Biblioteca universitaria de Editorial Tecnos) Bibliography: p. [679]-686. ISBN 84-309-1197-9 LC Card 87-105048
1. Finance, Public - Spain. 2. Taxation - Spain. 3. Finance, Public - Law and legislation - Spain. 4. Taxation - Law and legislation - Spain. I. Salinas Sánchez, Javier. II. Title.
HJ1244 .G37 1985

Garcia, Xavier, 1950- Supervivència 2000 : accions mundials pel medi natural i humà / Xavier Garcia.1a ed. / [corregida per Joan Rossinyol]. Barcelona : Pòrtic, 1983. 267 p. ; 20 cm. (Col·lecció Portic 71. no. 28) 250 copies printed--T.p. verso. ISBN 84-7306-196-9 LC Card 83-225437
1. Environmental policy - Developing countries. 2. Ecology - Developing countries. I. Title.
HC59.72.E5 G37 1983
NYPL [JLD 86-2462]

Garciacastillo, Rafael. Dialéctica de la administración : la práctica de la administración en la producción, los negocios y el estado / Rafael Garciacastillo. México : R. Garciacastillo, 1983. 117 p. ; 22 cm. Bibliography: p. 103-117. ISBN 968-597-416-0 LC Card 85-215880
1. Industrial management. 2. Industry and state. 3. Industrial productivity. I. Title.
HD37.S66 G38 1983

Gárciga Marrero, Rogelio, 1941- Socialismo y la dirección de la producción / Rogelio Gárciga Marrero. La Habana : Editorial de Ciencias Sociales, 1986. 426 p. : ill. ; 23 cm. (Economía / Editorial de Ciencias Sociales) Bibliography: p. 423-426. LC Card 87-402070 DDC 658 19
1. Industrial management. 2. Industrial management - Communist countries. 3. Efficiency, Industrial. I. Series: Economía / Editorial de Ciencias Sociales. II. Title.
HD37.S66 G385 1986

Garczyński, Stefan. O dawaniu / Stefan Garczyński. Wyd. 1-e. Warszawa : Nasza Księgarnia, 1985. 172 p. ; 21 cm. Includes bibliographical references. ISBN 83-10-08676-8
1. Altruism. 2. Charity. I. Title.
NYPL [*QO 87-1235]

Gardelli, Raúl N. De Marco, Miguel Ángel. 1884-1984, los cien años de la Bolsa de Comercio de Rosario /. [S.l. , 1984?] (Rosario : Escuela de Artes Gráficas del Colegio San José de Rosario) 167 p. : LC Card 87-115398 DDC 332.64/28224 19
HG5320.R67 D4 1984

GARDEN ARCHITECTURE. see **ARCHITECTURE, DOMESTIC.**

Garden Club of America. Horticulture Committee. Directory of regional gardening resources /. New York, NY (598 Madison Ave., New York 10022) , 1987. 172 p. : LC Card 87-402229 DDC 338.7/6359/02573 19
HD9003 .D66 1987

Gardenswartz, Lee. What it takes : good news from 100 of America's top professional and business women / Lee Gardenswartz, Anita Rowe.1st ed. New York : Doubleday, 1987. ix, 205 p. ; 22 cm. "A Dolphin book." ISBN 0-385-23820-7 : LC Card 87-13657 DDC 650.1/024042 19
1. Success in business. 2. Personality and occupation. 3. Women in business - Interviews. 4. Women in the professions - Interviews. I. Rowe, Anita. II. Title.
HF5386 .G214 1987

Gardiner, Robert M. The Dean Witter guide for today's investor / by Robert M. Gardiner. New York, NY : New American Library, c1988. p. cm. "NAL books." Includes index. ISBN 0-453-00582-9 LC Card 87-24168 DDC 332.6/78 19
1. Investments - Handbooks, manuals, etc. I. Title.
HG4527 .G37 1988

Gardiner, V. Water demand forecasting . Norwich, U.K. , c1986. 139 p. : ISBN 0-86094-214-7 : LC Card 87-127184 DDC 333.91/13 19
HD1690.5 .W383 1986

Gardiner, Walter H. Price elasticity of export demand : concepts and estimates / Walter H. Gardiner, Praveen M. Dixit. Washington, D.C. : U. S. Dept. of Agriculture, Economic Research Service, International Economics Division, [1986] iv, 43 p. ; 28 cm. (ERS staff report . no. AGES 860408) "May 1986"--T.p. verso. Bibliography: p. 39-43. LC Card 86-602820 DDC 382/.41/0973 19
1. Farm produce - Prices - United States. 2. Elasticity (Economics). 3. Exports - United States. I. Dixit, Praveen M. II. Title.
HD9004 .G37 1986

Gardner, Bruce L. The economics of agricultural policies / Bruce L. Gardner. New York, NY : Macmillan, c1987. xi, 387 p. : ill. ; 25 cm. Bibliography: p. 377-384. Includes index. ISBN 0-02-947760-3 LC Card 87-20367 DDC 338.1/8 19
1. Agriculture - Economic aspects - United States. 2. Agriculture and state - United States. I. Title.
HD1761 .G245 1987

Gardner, James E. Choosing effective development programs : an appraisal guide for human resources and training managers / James E. Gardner. New York : Quorum Books, 1987. x, 194 p. ; 24 cm. Bibliography: p. [181]-188. Includes index. ISBN 0-89930-182-7 (lib. bdg. : alk. paper) LC Card 86-30604 DDC 658.4/071245 19
1. Supervisors - Training of. 2. Executives, Training of. I. Title.
HF5549.15 .G36 1987

Gardner, John A. Vocational rehabilitation outcomes : evidence from New York / John A. Gardner. Cambridge, Mass. : Workers Compensation Research Institute, c1986. xix, 48 p. : ill. ; 23 cm. "December 1986." Bibliography: p. 47-48. "WC-86-1." ISBN 0-935149-03-1 (pbk.) : LC Card 86-28144 DDC 362/.0425 19
1. Vocational rehabilitation - New York (State). I. Workers Compensation Research Institute (Cambridge, Mass.). II. Title.
HD7256.U6 N6926 1986

Gardner, John William, 1912- The nature of leadership : introductory considerations / by John W. Gardner. Washington, D.C. (1828 L St., N.W., Washington 20036) : Leadership Studies Program, Independent Sector, c1986. 20 p. ; 23 cm. (Leadership papers . 1) "January 1986." Bibliography: p. 20. LC Card 87-167132 DDC 303.3/4 19
1. Leadership. I. Leadership Studies Program (Independent Sector). II. Title. III. Series.
HD57.7 .G37 1986

Gardner, Mona J. Managing financial institutions : an asset/liability approach / Mona J. Gardner, Dixie L. Mills. Chicago : Dryden Press, c1988. xii, 795 p. : ill. ; 25 cm. Includes bibliographies and indexes. ISBN 0-03-005479-6 LC Card 86-32805 DDC 332.1/068/1 19
1. Asset-liability management (Banking). 2. Risk management. 3. Financial institutions - Management. I. Mills, Dixie L. II. Title.
HG1615.25 .G37 1988

Gardner, Nick. Decade of discontent : the changing British economy since 1973 / Nick Gardner. Oxford, OX, UK ; New York, NY, USA : B. Blackwell, 1987. 236 p. : ill. ; 24 cm. Includes bibliographies and index. ISBN 0-631-15307-1 : LC Card 86-30949 DDC 338.941 19
1. Great Britain - Economic policy - 1945-. 2. Great Britain - Economic conditions - 1945-. I. Title.
HC256.6 .G36 1987

Garfinkle, Adam M., 1951- The politics of the nuclear freeze / Adam M. Garfinkle. Philadelphia, Pa. : Foreign Policy Research Institute, 1984. xviii, 258 p. ; 23 cm. (Philadelphia policy papers) Includes bibliographical references and index. ISBN 0-910191-08-5 : LC Card 84-6030 DDC 327.1/74 19
1. Atomic weapons and disarmament. 2. Antinuclear movement - United States. I. Title.
JX1974.7 .G34 1984 ***NYPL [JLE 86-710]***

Gargar, Marcel. Guadeloupe. Conseil régional. Rapport aux assemblées régionales . [Basse-Terre] [1982] 62 p. ; LC Card 85-136896 DDC 338.97297/6 19
HC158.5 .G83 1982a

Gargiulo, Barbara.
Clay, John R. Accounting for S corporations and noncorporate entities . Fort Worth, Tex. , c1987. 1 v. (various pagings) ; LC Card 87-163295 DDC 657/.95/076 19
HF5686.C7 C58 1987

Clay, John R. Advanced compilation and review . Fort Worth, Tex. , c1987. 1 v. (various pagings) : LC Card 87-160681 DDC 657/.3 19
HF5667.65 .M42 1986 Suppl.

Gariazzo, Alicia. El café en Nicaragua : los pequeños productores de Matagalpa y Carazo / Alicia Gariazzo. Managua, Nicaragua : Instituto de Investigaciones Económicas y Sociales : Coordinadora Regional de Investigaciones Económicas y Sociales, 1984. 175 p. : map ; 27 cm. (Cuadernos de pensamiento propio. Serie Avances . 2) Bibliography: p. 173-175. LC Card 85-192390
1. Coffee trade - Nicaragua. 2. Coffee trade - Nicaragua - Matagalpa (Dept.). 3. Coffee trade - Nicaragua - Carazo. I. Instituto de Investigaciones Económicas y Sociales (Managua, Nicaragua). II. Coordinadora Regional de Investigaciones Económicas y Sociales. III. Title. IV. Series.
HD9199.N52 G37 1984
NYPL [JLF 86-1521]

Garibaldi, Annie. 150 meilleures entreprises françaises /. Paris , c1986. 313 p. ; ISBN 2-234-01894-3 : LC Card 87-107207
HF5382.75.F8 A13 1986

Garimpando reminiscências /. Loureiro, Orozimbo Roxo. São Paulo , 1976 (São Paulo : Grafikor) 317 p. ; LC Card 85-225740
HG5332 .L68 1976

Gario, Giuseppe. Discontinuità e permanenza : la funzione regionale di governo in un contesto innovativo / di Giuseppe Gario. Milano, Italy : F. Angeli, c1986. 262 p. : ill. ; 22 cm. (Collana IReR . 33) At head of title: IReR. Bibliography: p. [217]-262. LC Card 87-149940
1. Technological innovations - Economic aspects - Italy - Lombardy. 2. Lombardy (Italy) - Economic policy. I. Title. II. Series.
HC307.L8 G37 1986

Garlei͡a, R. I͡A. Ėkonomika i upravlenie torgovleĭ v razvitom sotsialisticheskom̆ obshchestve . Riga , 1980. 123 p. : LC Card 82-102627
HF3629.L37 E38 1980

Garlichs, Dietrich. Regionalisierte Arbeitsmarkt- und Beschäftigungspolitik /. Frankfurt/Main , New York , c1983. 322 p. : ISBN 3-593-33241-8 LC Card 84-106151
HC286.7 .R44 1983

Garlow, David Christopher. Sanson, João Rogério. A política de transportes marítimos no Brasil . Rio de Janeiro , 1986. vii, 178, 5 p. : LC Card 87-403931 DDC 387.5/44/0981 19
HE597.B7 S26 1986

Garmendia Larrañaga, Juan. Artesanos de la regata del Bidasoa : Sumbilla, Aranaz y Yanci / Juan Garmendia Larrañaga. San Sebastián : Txertoa, [1983] 123 p. : ill. ; 20 cm. (Colección Askatasun Haizea. 61) ISBN 84-7148-115-4 LC Card 84-140784 DDC 331.7/94 19
1. Artisans - Bidasoa River Valley (Spain and France). 2. Material culture - Bidasoa River Valley (Spain and France). 3. Bidasoa River Valley (Spain and France) - Social life and customs. I. Title.
HD2346.S72 B534 1983
NYPL [3-MNE 86-3657]

GARMENT WORKERS. see **CLOTHING WORKERS.**

Garnaut, Ross.
Anderson, Kym. Australian protectionism . Sydney , Boston , 1987. xii, 160 p. : ISBN 0-04-330383-8 (pbk.) LC Card 86-47990 DDC 382.7/3/0994 19
HF1625 .A53 1987

Anderson, Kym. Australia's trade growth with developing countries /. Canberra, Australia , 1983. iv, 55 p. ; ISBN 0-86413-001-5 (pbk.) LC Card 86-673748
HF3948.D44 A52x 1983

Garner, Daniel R. Owen, Robert R. (Robert Randolph) Arthur Young guide to financing for growth . New York , c1986. xiv, 298 p. ; ISBN 0-471-81946-8 : LC Card 86-1612 DDC 658.1/522 19
HG4027.7 .O94 1986 ***NYPL [JLE 86-2667]***

Garner, Edward. To die by inches : an account of the Fermoy Poor Law Union during the Great Famine, 1845-1850 / by Edward Garner. Fermoy, Co. Cork, Ireland : ÉIGSE BOOKS, c1986. 133 p. : ill. ; 21 cm. Bibliography: p. 132-133. ISBN 0-907568-03-3 (pbk.) : LC Card 87-111519 DDC 363.5/85/094195 19
1. Famines - Ireland - Fermoy - History - 19th century. 2. Fermoy Poor Law Union (Fermoy, Cork) - History - 19th century. I. Title.
HC260.5.Z7 F474 1986

Garner, J. Bradley, 1949- Mcloughlin, Caven S. Getting employed, staying employed . Baltimore , c1987. xvi, 239 p. ; ISBN 0-933716-70-2 (pbk.) : LC Card 87-13185 DDC 650.1/4/0240816 19
HD7255 .M395 1987

Garnier, Henry. Garnier, Pierre, 1899- Comptabilité des sociétés . [Paris] , c1985. xxiv, 344 p. : ISBN 2-04-015767-0 : LC Card 85-221781 DDC 657 19
HF5642 .G273 1985

Garnier, Pierre, 1899- Comptabilité des sociétés : plan comptable général révisé 1982 / Pierre Garnier, Henry Garnier.3e éd. [Paris] : Dunod, c1985. xxiv, 344 p. : ill. ; 24 cm. (Dunod entreprise, 0242-3804) ISBN 2-04-015767-0 : LC Card 85-221781 DDC 657 19
1. Accounting. I. Garnier, Henry. II. Title.
HF5642 .G273 1985

Garnsey, Elizabeth. Industrial change and women's employment : trends in the new international division of labour / Elizabeth Garnsey, Liba Paukert. Geneva : International Institute for Labour Studies, 1987. ix, 100, x p. : ill. ; 24 cm. (Women, work, and society) Research series ; no. 86 Bibliography: p. 94-100. ISBN 92-9014-411-4 (pbk.) : LC Card 87-163195 DDC 331.4/09172/4 19
1. Women - Employment - Developing countries. 2. Industrialization. 3. Developing countries - Industries. I. Paukert, Liba. II. Series. III. Series: Research series (International Institute for Labour Studies) , no. 86. IV. Title.
HD6223 .G37 1987

Garnsey, Peter. Famine and food supply in the Graeco-Roman world : responses to risk and crisis / Peter Garnsey. Cambridge [Cambridgeshire] ; New York : Cambridge University Press, 1988. xiv, 303 p., [4] p. of plates : maps ; 24 cm. Bibliography: p. 278-294. Includes index. ISBN 0-521-35198-7 LC Card 87-16737 DDC 338.1/9/38 19
1. Food supply - Greece - History. 2. Food supply - Rome - History. 3. Famines - Greece - History. 4. Famines - Rome - History. I. Title.
HD9015.G82 G37 1988

Garofalo, Gene. The sales professional's survival guide, or, Things your sales manager never told you / by Gene Garofalo and Gary Drummond. Englewood Cliffs, NJ : Prentice-Hall, c1987. p. cm. Includes index. ISBN 0-13-788076-6 LC Card 86-25603 DDC 650.1/2/024381 19
1. Sales personnel. 2. Employee rights. 3. Sales personnel - Salaries, etc. I. Drummond, Gary. II. Title. III. Title: Things your sales manager never told you.
HF5439.5 .G37 1987

Garon-Audy, Muriel. Mobilités professionnelles et géographiques au Québec, 1954-64-74 / par Muriel Garon-Audy, avec la collaboration de Jacques Dofny et Alberte Archambault. Montréal : Centre de recherche en développement économique, Université de Montréal, 1980. 61 p. ; 28 cm. (Cahier / Centre de recherche en développement économique . no 22) "Juin 1980." Bibliography: p. 50-54. LC Card 81-105620 DDC 331.12/7971 19
1. Occupational mobility - Québec (Province). 2. Social mobility - Quebec (Province). 3. Residental mobility - Québec (Province). I. Dofny, Jacques. II. Archambault, Alberte. III. Series: Université de Montréal. Centre de recherches en développement économique. Cahier , no 22. IV. Title.
HD5717.5.C22 Q44 1980 ***NYPL [JLM 79-970 no.22]***

Garon, Sheldon. The state and labor in modern Japan / Sheldon Garon. Berkeley : University of California Press, c1987. xvi, 326 p. ; 24 cm. Bibliography: p. 295-316. Includes index. ISBN 0-520-05983-2 (alk. paper) LC Card 86-30890 DDC 331/.0952 19
1. Industrial relations - Japan - History. 2. Industrial relations - Government policy - Japan - History. I. Title.
HD8726 .G37 1987

Garonna, P., 1948- Unions in crisis and beyond . Dover, Mass. , c1986. xii, 340 p. : ISBN 0-86569-127-4 : LC Card 85-26646 DDC 331.88 19
HD6508 .U45 1986 ***NYPL [JLE 86-1936]***

Garraty, John Arthur, 1920- The Great Depression : an inquiry into the causes, course, and consequences of the Worldwide depression of the nineteen-thirties, as seen by contemporaries and in the light of history / John A. Garraty. New York, N.Y. : Anchor Press/Doubleday, 1987. x, 292 p. : ill. ; 23 cm. Reprint. Originally published : San Diego : Harcourt Brace Jovanovich, c1986. Bibliography: p. 259-283. Includes index. ISBN 0-385-24085-6 (pbk.) : LC Card 87-5458 DDC 338.5/42 19
1. Depressions - 1929. 2. Economic history - 1918-1945. I. Title.
HB3717 1929 .G36 1987

Garrison, Dee. Vorse, Mary Heaton, 1874-1966. Rebel pen . New York , c1985. 345 p. : ISBN 0-85345-669-0 : LC Card 85-7130 DDC 331.4/0973 19
HD8072 .V755 1985 ***NYPL [JLD 86-2459]***

Garrison, G. H. Haley (George H. Haley) The insider's guide to antique securities / G.H. Haley Garrison, Jr. Limited ed. Williamsburg, Va. (P.O. Drawer JH, Williamsburg 23187) : G.H.H. Garrison, Jr., c1987. 1 v. (various pagings) : ill. ; 28 cm. Bibliography: p. 14.1.-14.4. Includes index. LC Card 87-149140 DDC 332.63/2/0750973 19
1. Stock certificates - Collectors and collecting. 2. Bonds - Collectors and collecting. I. Title.
HG4633 .G38 1987

La Garrotxa : medi natural, estructura econòmica i equipaments socials / [Miquel Faig i Aumallé ... [et al.]. Barcelona : Caixa d'Estalvis de Catalunya, c1983. xv, 323 p. : ill. (some col.) ; 24 cm. (Col·lecció Catalunya comarcal) Bibliography: p. 309-321. ISBN 84-7231-912-1 LC Card 85-184803
1. Garrotxa Region (Spain) - Economic conditions. 2. Garrotxa Region (Spain) - Population. 3. Agriculture - Economic aspects - Spain - Garrotxa Region. 4. Elections - Spain - Garrotxa Region. 5. Municipal services - Spain - Garrotxa Region. I. Faig i Aumallé, Miquel. II. Series.
HC387.G34 G37 1983

GARROTXA REGION (SPAIN) - ECONOMIC CONDITIONS.
La Garrotxa . [Barcelona , c1983. xv, 323 p. : ISBN 84-7231-912-1 LC Card 85-184803
HC387.G34 G37 1983

GARROTXA REGION (SPAIN) - POPULATION.
La Garrotxa . [Barcelona , c1983. xv, 323 p. : ISBN 84-7231-912-1 LC Card 85-184803
HC387.G34 G37 1983

Gart, Alan. Handbook of the money and capital markets / Alan Gart. New York : Quorum Books, c1988. p. cm. Includes index. ISBN 0-89930-270-X (lib. bdg. : alk. paper) LC Card 87-24938 DDC 332.63/2/0973 19
1. Money market - United States. 2. Capital market - United States. 3. Financial institutions - United States. I. Title.
HG181 .G367 1988

Garvin, David A.
Cases in business decision making /. Chicago , c1987. ix, 102 p. : ISBN 0-03-009108-X (pbk.) LC Card 86-29131 DDC 658.4/033 19
HD30.23 .C375 1987

Managing quality : the strategic and competitive edge / David A. Garvin. New York : Free Press ; London : Collier Macmillan, c1988. xiv, 319 p. ; 25 cm. Bibliography: p. 251-309. Includes index. ISBN 0-02-911380-6 LC Card 87-15145 DDC 658.5/62 19
1. Quality of products - United States - Management. 2. Quality assurance - United States - Management. 3. Quality of products - United States - Management - Case studies. 4. Quality assurance - United States - Management - Case studies. 5. Quality of products - Japan - Management. 6. Quality assurance - Japan - Management. 7. Quality of products - Japan - Management - Case studies. 8. Quality assurance - Japan - Management - Case studies. I. Title.
HF5415.157 .G37 1988

Gary Goodman's breakthroughs in telemarketing /. Goodman, Gary S. [Breakthroughs in telemarketing.] New York , c1987. ix, 148 p. ; ISBN 0-13-346891-7 (pbk.) : LC Card 86-43170 DDC 658.8/5 19
HF5415.1265 .G66 1987

Garza, Enrique de la. Esto pasó en México /. México, D.F. [1985] 126 p. : ISBN 968-415-098-9 LC Card 87-403762 DDC 363.3/495/097253 19
HC138.M4 E84 1985

GARZA-SADA FAMILY.
Saragoza, Alex. The Monterrey elite and the Mexican State, 1880-1940 /. Austin , c1988. p. cm. ISBN 0-292-71113-1 LC Card 87-23779 DDC 305.5/234/097213 19
HG185.M6 S27 1988

Garzón L., Isaías. Manual de cooperativismo estudiantil ecuatoriano / [Isaías Garzón L.]. 1a ed. Riobamba, Ecuador : Editorial Pedagógica Freire, [1983?] 244 p. : ill. ; 22 cm. Bibliography: p. 242. LC Card 86-134182
1. Cooperation. 2. Cooperative societies - Management. 3. Cooperation - Ecuador. 4. Cooperative societies - Ecuador - Management. I. Title.
HD2965 .G38 1983

GAS COMPANIES - ENGLAND - BOLTON (GREATER MANCHESTER)
Clegg, James. The Bolton Gas Company, 1818-1872 . Bolton , 1872. 46 p. ; LC Card 85-666285
HD9581.G74 B64x 1872

GAS COMPANIES - NEW YORK (N.Y.) - HISTORY.
Larson, Elwin S. Brooklyn Union Gas . New York , 1987. 23 p. : LC Card 87-60614 DDC 338.7/6657/0974723 19
HD9581.U53 B765 1987

GAS INDUSTRY.
Banks, Ferdinand E. The political economy of natural gas /. London , New York , c1987. 200 p. ; ISBN 0-7099-3940-X : LC Card 87-14098 DDC 338.2/7285 19
HD9581.A2 B36 1987

Natural gas markets and contracts /. Amsterdam ; New York : x, 320 p. : ISBN 0-444-70206-7 (U. S.) LC Card 87-5061 DDC 380.1/42285/094 19
HD9581.E82 N37 1987 ***NYPL [TB (Contributions to economic analysis. v.161)]***

Natural gas trade in transition /. Cambridge, MA , c1987. 91 p. ; ISBN 0-942781-00-7 (pbk.) LC Card 87-81051 DDC 338.2/7285 19
HD9581.A2 N38 1987

GAS INDUSTRY - ALASKA.
Historical and projected oil and gas consumption . [Juneau] [1986] 1 v. (in various pagings) : LC Card 86-622301 DDC 333.8/2313/09798 19
HD9502.U53 A4574 1986

GAS INDUSTRY - ARGENTINA - CONGRESSES.
El Gas y su contribución al desarrollo económico nacional. [Buenos Aires] [1983 or 1984] 316 p. : LC Card 84-222069
HD9581.A72 G37 1983

GAS INDUSTRY - CANADA.
Douglas, Gordon W. Energy and regional investment in Canada /. Calgary, Alta. [1983] x, 114 p. : ISBN 0-920522-28-9 (pbk.) : LC Card 83-160268 DDC 332.6/722 19
HD9502.C32 D68 1983 ***NYPL [JLD 87-996]***

Oil and natural gas industries in Canada, 1978. [Ottawa] , c1978. viii, 104 p. : LC Card 85-187299
HD9574.C22 O39 1978

GAS INDUSTRY - CANADA - ACCOUNTING.
Butterworth, John E. Financial reporting . Hamilton, Ont. , 1986. viii, 250 p. : ISBN 0-920212-52-2 (pbk.) LC Card 87-101758 DDC 657/.86203 19
HF5686.P3 B87 1986

GAS INDUSTRY - CONGRESSES.
Symposium on the Energy Economy (1984 : Durham, Durham) Prospects for the world oil industry . London , Dover, N.H. , c1985. 131 p. : ISBN 0-7099-4104-8 : LC Card 85-4186 DDC 338.2/7282 19
HD9560.5 .S96 1985 ***NYPL [JLD 85-2430]***

GAS INDUSTRY - DEVELOPING COUNTRIES - STATISTICS.
Fee, Derek. Oil & gas databook for developing countries . London , 1985. 215 p. : ISBN 0-86010-617-9 : LC Card 85-208594 DDC 333.8/23/091724 19
HD9578.D44 F44 1985 ***NYPL [JLE 86-3684]***

GAS INDUSTRY - EUROPE.
Braathu, Jan. Diversification strategies and security-of-supply . Oslo [1984?] 74 p. ; LC Card 85-129223 DDC 382/.42285/094 19
HD9581.E8552 B7 1984 ***NYPL [JLM 78-136 no.88]***

Natural gas markets and contracts /. Amsterdam ; New York : x, 320 p. : ISBN 0-444-70206-7 (U. S.) LC Card 87-5061 DDC

380.1/42285/094 19
HD9581.E82 N37 1987 ***NYPL [TB (Contributions to economic analysis. v.161)]***

GAS INDUSTRY - FORECASTING.
Energy markets after the collapse . Cambridge, MA (56 John F. Kennedy St., Suite 5, Cambridge 02138) , c1987. 164 p. : LC Card 87-142725 DDC 338.2/728 19
HD9560.5 .E54 1987

Perspective on world energy . Arlington, Va. (1911 Fort Myer Dr., Suite 403, Arlington 22209) , c1987. 3, iii, 27, [19] p. : LC Card 87-142737 DDC 333.79 19
HD9560.5 .P3847 1987

GAS INDUSTRY - FORECASTING - MATHEMATICAL MODELS.
Rose, Adam Zachary. Forecasting natural gas demand in a changing world /. Greenwich, Conn. , c1987. xix, 152 p. : ISBN 0-89232-838-X : LC Card 87-21390 DDC 333.8/23312 19
HD9581.A2 R67 1987

GAS INDUSTRY - GERMANY (WEST) - BAVARIA - CAPITAL INVESTMENTS - DECISION MAKING.
Fahrion, Roland. Dynamische Investitionsplanung für den Erdgasmarkt . Gräfelfing/München , c1984. iv, 308 p. : ISBN 3-87806-075-0 LC Card 85-111076
HD9581.G43 B34 1984

GAS INDUSTRY - GERMANY (WEST) - BAVARIA - FORECASTING.
Fahrion, Roland. Dynamische Investitionsplanung für den Erdgasmarkt . Gräfelfing/München , c1984. iv, 308 p. : ISBN 3-87806-075-0 LC Card 85-111076
HD9581.G43 B34 1984

GAS INDUSTRY - GOVERNMENT POLICY - UNITED STATES - CONGRESSES.
Drawing the line on natural gas regulation . New York , 1987. xiii, 267 p. : ISBN 0-89930-174-6 (lib. bdg. : alk. paper) LC Card 86-25769 DDC 338.2/7285/0973 19
HD9581.U5 D73 1987

GAS INDUSTRY - GREAT BRITAIN.
Britain's energy resources /. London , 1981. 27 p. : ISBN 0-11-701010-3 (pbk.) LC Card 81-165936 DDC 333.79/0941 19
HD9502.G72 B74 1981

GAS INDUSTRY - MICHIGAN.
Michigan. Legislature. House of Representatives. Special House Committee to Study Consumers Power Company. Report of the Special House Committee to Study Consumers Power Company . Lansing, Mich. (The Capitol, Lansing 48909) [1985] iv leaves, 57 p. ; LC Card 86-622638 DDC 338.7/6136362/09774 19
HD9685.U7 C785 1985

GAS INDUSTRY - NEW YORK (N.Y.) - HISTORY.
Larson, Elwin S. Brooklyn Union Gas . New York , 1987. 23 p. : LC Card 87-60614 DDC 338.7/6657/0974723 19
HD9581.U53 B765 1987

GAS INDUSTRY - NORWAY.
Braathu, Jan. Diversification strategies and security-of-supply . Oslo [1984?] 74 p. ; LC Card 85-129223 DDC 382/.42285/094 19
HD9581.E8552 B7 1984 ***NYPL [JLM 78-136 no.88]***

GAS INDUSTRY - OKLAHOMA - STATISTICS.
Oklahoma casinghead gas production report. [Denver, Colo.] (P.O. Box 2612, Denver 80201) , <[c1986-. v. <1-2 > ; LC Card 86-219814 DDC 338.2/7285/09766021 19
HD9581.U52 O56 1986

GAS INDUSTRY - POLITICAL ASPECTS - EUROPE.
Blinken, Antony J. Ally versus ally . New York , 1987. ix, 193 p. : ISBN 0-275-92410-6 (alk. paper) : LC Card 86-25222 DDC 388.5 19
HD9581.S652 B58 1987

GAS INDUSTRY - POLITICAL ASPECTS - SOVIET UNION.
Blinken, Antony J. Ally versus ally . New York , 1987. ix, 193 p. : ISBN 0-275-92410-6 (alk. paper) : LC Card 86-25222 DDC 388.5 19
HD9581.S652 B58 1987

Stern, Jonathan P. Soviet oil and gas exports to the West . Aldershot, Hants, England , Brookfield, Vt., USA , c1987. xi, 123 p. : ISBN 0-566-05124-9 : LC Card 86-32772 DDC 382/.4228/0947 19
HD9575.S652 S74 1987

GAS INDUSTRY - QATAR.
El Mallakh, Ragaei, 1925- Qatar, energy & development /. London , Dover, N.H. , c1985. 184 p. ; ISBN 0-7099-0955-1 : LC Card 84-29317 DDC 330.953/63 19
HC415.37 .E4 1985 ***NYPL [JLD 85-1980]***

GAS INDUSTRY - RUSSIAN S.F.S.R. - SIBERIA, WESTERN - MANAGEMENT.
Sovershenstvovanie planirovaniia i upravleniia neftegazovym kompleksom /. Novosibirsk , 1986. 208 p. : LC Card 87-124383
HD9575.S653 S577 1986

GAS INDUSTRY - RUSSIAN S.F.S.R. - SIBERIA, WESTERN - PLANNING.
Sovershenstvovanie planirovaniia i upravleniia neftegazovym kompleksom /. Novosibirsk , 1986. 208 p. : LC Card 87-124383
HD9575.S653 S577 1986

GAS INDUSTRY - SOVIET UNION.
Sagers, Matthew J. Natural gas liquids and the Soviet gas processing industry /. Washington, D.C. [1986] viii, 72, 2 p. : LC Card 87-601287 DDC 338.4/766573 19
HD9581.2.L573 S657 1986

GAS INDUSTRY - SOVIET UNION - COSTS - FORECASTING.
Tretyakova, Albina. Cost estimates for the Soviet gas industry, 1970 to 1990 /. Washington, D.C. [1986] vii, 116 p. ; LC Card 87-601292 DDC 338.2/3 19
HD9581.S652 T74 1986

GAS INDUSTRY - SOVIET UNION - COSTS - STATISTICS.
Tretyakova, Albina. Cost estimates for the Soviet gas industry, 1970 to 1990 /. Washington, D.C. [1986] vii, 116 p. ; LC Card 87-601292 DDC 338.2/3 19
HD9581.S652 T74 1986

GAS INDUSTRY - SWEDEN.
Introduktion av naturgas i Sverige . Stockholm , 1978. ii, 16, 13, 11 p. ; ISBN 91-38-04192-8 LC Card 83-238196
HD9581.S82 I58 1978

GAS INDUSTRY - UNITED STATES.
Gas rate fundamentals. Arlington, VA (1515 Wilson Blvd., Arlington 22209) , 1987. xxi, 311, [118] p. : LC Card 87-404451 DDC 353.0087/23044 19
HD9581.U5 G266 1987

Welker, Anthony J. The oil and gas Publishing /. Tulsa , c1985. xii, 258 p. : ISBN 0-87814-279-7 (pbk.) : LC Card 85-2096 DDC 338.2/728/0973 19
HD9565 .W46 1985 ***NYPL [JLD 86-4010]***

Williams, Anna Fay, 1935- New opportunities to purchase natural gas /. Lilburn, Ga. , c1988. xiv, 372 p. : ISBN 0-88173-034-3 : LC Card 86-46134 DDC 665.7/44/068 19
HD9581.U5 W54 1988

GAS INDUSTRY - UNITED STATES - DEREGULATION.
Gas rate fundamentals. Arlington, VA (1515 Wilson Blvd., Arlington 22209) , 1987. xxi, 311, [118] p. : LC Card 87-404451 DDC 353.0087/23044 19
HD9581.U5 G266 1987

GAS INDUSTRY - UNITED STATES - FINANCE.
Meurer, Heinrich W., 1950- Wirtschaftsgeologische Aspekte bei der privaten Investition in Öl- und Gasbohrvorhaben in den USA /. [Cologne? , 1982] (Aachen : Fotodruck J. Mainz) vi, 163 p., [3] folded leaves of plates : LC Card 84-200100
HD9565 .M48 1982

GAS INDUSTRY - UNITED STATES - FORECASTING.
An Economic analysis of natural gas resources and supply /. Washington, D.C. [1986] xx, 179 p. : LC Card 86-603066 DDC 338.2/7285/0973 19
HD9581.U5 E26 1986

The Outlook for gas demand in new markets, 1986-2010 . Arlington, Va. (1515 Wilson Blvd., Arlington 22209) , c1986. 54 p. : LC Card 87-403083 DDC 333.8/23312 19
HD9581.U5 O95 1986

GAS INDUSTRY - WYOMING - EMPLOYEES - STATISTICS.
Wessel, Louis. Wyoming oil and natural gas extraction industry . Cheyenne, Wyo. (Herschler Bldg., Cheyenne 82002) , 1986. 35 p. : LC Card 86-622902 DDC 331.12/522338/09787021 19
HD4966.P52 U5553 1986

GAS INDUSTRY - WYOMING - STATISTICS.
Wyoming oil and gas production by county /. Casper, Wyo. (P.O. Box 2640, Casper 82602) [1986] [40] p. : LC Card 86-622904 DDC 338.2/728/09787021 19
HD9567.W8 W94 1986

Wyoming oil and gas, 1985 /. Casper, Wyo. (P.O. Box 2640, Casper 82602) [1986?] 50 p. ; LC Card 86-622903 DDC 338.2/728/09787021 19
HD9567.W8 W96 1986

GAS, NATURAL - CONGRESSES.
Mercados mundiales de hidrocarburos . México, D.F. , 1983. 377 p. : ISBN 968-12-0231-7 LC Card 84-222729
HD9560.5 .M39 1983

GAS, NATURAL - DEVELOPING COUNTRIES - RESERVES STATISTICS.
Fee, Derek. Oil & gas databook for developing countries . London , 1985. 215 p. : ISBN 0-86010-617-9 : LC Card 85-208594 DDC 333.8/23/091724 19
HD9578.D44 F44 1985 ***NYPL [JLE 86-3684]***

GAS, NATURAL - EUROPE - PIPE LINES.
Blinken, Antony J. Ally versus ally . New York , 1987. ix, 193 p. : ISBN 0-275-92410-6 (alk. paper) : LC Card 86-25222 DDC 388.5 19
HD9581.S652 B58 1987

Gazovyĭ most . Sverdlovsk , 1985. 206 p. : LC Card 86-186324
HD9581.S653 S54 1985

GAS, NATURAL - GEOLOGY - UNITED STATES.
Meurer, Heinrich W., 1950- Wirtschaftsgeologische Aspekte bei der privaten Investition in Öl- und Gasbohrvorhaben in den USA /. [Cologne? , 1982] (Aachen : Fotodruck J. Mainz) vi, 163 p., [3] folded leaves of plates : LC Card 84-200100
HD9565 .M48 1982

GAS, NATURAL - LAW AND LEGISLATION - UNITED STATES.
Lowe, John S., 1941- Oil and gas in a nutshell /. St. Paul, Minn. , 1983. xlvii, 443 p. ; ISBN 0-314-73469-4 LC Card 83-6811 DDC 346.7304/6823 347.30646823 19
KF1850 .L68 1983 ***NYPL [JLC 86-226]***

Mogel, William A. Transportation and marketing of natural gas. New York, N.Y. , c1986. iii, 165 p. : ISBN 0-88057-466-6 (pbk.) LC Card 86-220986 DDC 388.5 19
HD9580.U5 M64 1985 Suppl.

GAS, NATURAL - PIPE LINES - ECONOMIC ASPECTS - UNITED STATES.
Williams, Anna Fay, 1935- New opportunities to purchase natural gas /. Lilburn, Ga. , c1988. xiv, 372 p. : ISBN 0-88173-034-3 : LC Card 86-46134 DDC 665.7/44/068 19
HD9581.U5 W54 1988

GAS, NATURAL - PIPE LINES - LAW AND LEGISLATION - UNITED STATES.
Mogel, William A. Transportation and marketing of natural gas. New York, N.Y. , c1986. iii, 165 p. : ISBN 0-88057-466-6 (pbk.) LC Card 86-220986 DDC 388.5 19
HD9580.U5 M64 1985 Suppl.

GAS, NATURAL - PRICES - LOUISIANA.
Lam, Manuel. Louisiana crude oil and natural gas report and severance and royalty sensitivity to price, second half 1985 /. Baton Rouge, La (P.O. Box 44156, Baton Rouge 70804-4156) [1986] iii, 31 p. : LC Card 86-621907 DDC 338.2/728/09763 19
HD9560.8.U53 L65 1986

GAS, NATURAL - RESERVES.

GAS, NATURAL - RUSSIAN S.F.S.R. - SIBERIA, WESTERN - PIPE LINES.
Gazovyĭ most . Sverdlovsk , 1985. 206 p. : LC Card 86-186324
HD9581.S653 S54 1985

GAS, NATURAL - SOVIET UNION.
Kozlov, P. T. (Petr Tikhonovich) Sovershenstvovanie khoziaĭstvennogo mekhanizma v neftianoĭ i gazovoĭ promyshlennosti /. Alma-Ata , 1983. 134 p. : LC Card 83-194289
HD9575.S652 K69 1983

GAS, NATURAL - SOVIET UNION - PIPE LINES.
Blinken, Antony J. Ally versus ally . New York , 1987. ix, 193 p. : ISBN 0-275-92410-6 (alk. paper) : LC Card 86-25222 DDC 388.5 19
HD9581.S652 B58 1987

Gazovyĭ most . Sverdlovsk , 1985. 206 p. : LC Card 86-186324
HD9581.S653 S54 1985

GAS, NATURAL - SWEDEN.
Introduktion av naturgas i Sverige . Stockholm , 1978. ii, 16, 13, 11 p. ; ISBN 91-38-04192-8 LC Card 83-238196
HD9581.S82 I58 1978

GAS, NATURAL - TAXATION - LOUISIANA.
Lam, Manuel. Louisiana crude oil and natural gas report and severance and royalty sensitivity to price, second half 1985 /. Baton Rouge, La (P.O. Box 44156, Baton Rouge 70804-4156) [1986] iii, 31 p. : LC Card 86-621907 DDC 338.2/728/09763 19
HD9560.8.U53 L65 1986

GAS, NATURAL - UNITED STATES - PURCHASING.
Williams, Anna Fay, 1935- New opportunities to purchase natural gas /. Lilburn, Ga. , c1988. xiv, 372 p. : ISBN 0-88173-034-3 : LC Card 86-46134 DDC 665.7/44/068 19
HD9581.U5 W54 1988

GAS, NATURAL - UNITED STATES - RATES.
Gas rate fundamentals. Arlington, VA (1515 Wilson Blvd., Arlington 22209) , 1987. xxi, 311, [118] p. : LC Card 87-404451 DDC 353.0087/23044 19
HD9581.U5 G266 1987

GAS, NATURAL - UNITED STATES - RESERVES.
An Economic analysis of natural gas resources and supply /. Washington, D.C. [1986] xx, 179 p. : LC Card 86-603066 DDC 338.2/7285/0973 19
HD9581.U5 E26 1986

GAS, NATURAL - WELL DRILLING. see **GAS WELL DRILLING.**

Gas rate fundamentals. 4th ed. Arlington, VA (1515 Wilson Blvd., Arlington 22209) : American Gas Association Rate Committee, 1987. xxi, 311, [118] p. : ill. ; 24 cm. Bibliography: p. 277-286. Includes index. LC Card 87-404451 DDC 353.0087/23044 19
1. Gas industry - United States. 2. Gas, Natural - United States - Rates. 3. Gas industry - United States - Deregulation. I. American Gas Association. Rate Committee.
HD9581.U5 G266 1987

GAS SEPARATION MEMBRANE INDUSTRY - UNITED STATES.
Crull, Anna W. New trends in gas separations . Stamford, Conn., U. S.A. , c1986. xvi, 222 leaves : ISBN 0-89336-422-3 (pbk.) LC Card 87-165549 DDC 660.2/842 19
HD9660.G372 C78 1986

GAS WELL DRILLING.
Orban, John. Money in the ground . Oklahoma City , 1985. xv, 216 p. : ISBN 0-9615776-0-6 (pbk.) : LC Card 86-120440 DDC 332.63 19
HG6047.P47 O73 1985

GAS WELLS - OKLAHOMA - STATISTICS.
Oklahoma casinghead gas production report. [Denver, Colo.] (P.O. Box 2612, Denver 80201) , <[c1986-. v. <1-2 > ; LC Card 86-219814 DDC 338.2/7285/09766021 19
HD9581.U52 O56 1986

GAS WELLS - WYOMING - STATISTICS.
Wyoming oil and gas production by county /. Casper, Wyo. (P.O. Box 2640, Casper 82602) [1986] [40] p. : LC Card 86-622904 DDC 338.2/728/09787021 19
HD9567.W8 W94 1986

Wyoming oil and gas, 1985 /. Casper, Wyo. (P.O. Box 2640, Casper 82602) [1986?] 50 p. ; LC Card 86-622903 DDC 338.2/728/09787021 19
HD9567.W8 W96 1986

El Gas y su contribución al desarrollo económico nacional. [Buenos Aires] : Ministerio de Obras y Servicios Públicos, Secretaría de Energía, [1983 or 1984] 316 p. : ill. ; 23 cm. Proceedings of a meeting held aboard the ship Ciudad de Paraná, Dec. 9-11, 1982. LC Card 84-222069
1. Gas industry - Argentina - Congresses. I. Argentina. Secretaría de Energía.
HD9581.A72 G37 1983

Gasca Allué, Carlos. González Blanch, Francisco. Implantación en España de un sistema de tarificación por el uso de la infraestructura viaria /. Madrid [1984?] 204 p. ; ISBN 84-7196-470-8 : LC Card 85-201965
HJ5956.E86 G66 1984

Gascón Bueno, Francisco. El Valle de Alcudia : un ejemplo típico de economía agropecuaria en la España del siglo XVIII / Francisco Gascón Bueno ; prólogo de Antonio Rumeu de Armas. Bilbao : [s.n.], 1978. xvi, 609 p., [10] folded leaves of plates : ill. (some col.) ; 25 cm. Cover title: El Valle de Alcudia durante el siglo XVIII. Originally presented as the author's thesis (doctoral--Universidad Complutense de Madrid, 1976) Bibliography: p. 19-30. ISBN 84-400-5486-6 LC Card 85-227628
1. Agriculture - Economic aspects - Spain - Ciudad Real (Province) - History - 18th century - Case studies. I. Title. II. Title: El Valle de Alcudia durante el siglo XVIII.
HD2025.C54 G37 1978

Gaskell, George. Public policies and private actions . Aldershot, Hants, England , Brookfield, Vt., U. S.A. , c1987. p. cm. ISBN 0-566-05436-1 : LC Card 87-14909 DDC 333.79/16 19
HD9502.A2 P82 1987

Gaskell, S. Martin. Model housing from the great exhibition to the festival of Britain / S. Martin Gaskell. London ; New York : Mansell, 1986. x, 180 p. : ill. ; 25 cm. (Studies in history, planning and the environment) "An Alexandrine Press book." Bibliography: p. 163-173. Includes index. ISBN 0-7201-1834-4 : LC Card 86-23775 DDC 363.5/0941 19
1. Housing - Great Britain - History. 2. Dwellings - Great Britain - Design and construction - History. 3. Architecture, Domestic - Great Britain - History. I. Title.
HD7333.A3 G37 1986

Gaskin, Carol. Klein, John F. (John Frederick), 1950- A day in the life of a commercial fisherman /. Mahwah, N.J. , c1988. 32 p. : ISBN 0-8167-1109-7 (lib. bdg.) : LC Card 87-10949 DDC 639/.2/02373 19
HD8039.F65 K57 1988

GASOLINE AUTOMOBILES. see **AUTOMOBILES.**

GASOLINE INDUSTRY - GERMANY (WEST)
Baum, Herbert, Dr. Wettbewerbspolitik auf dem Treibstoffmarkt /. Baden-Baden , c1983. 97 p. ; ISBN 3-7890-0881-8 LC Card 83-187053
HD9573.5 .B38 1983

GASOLINE INDUSTRY - GREAT BRITAIN - CONGRESSES.
Economics of the retail petroleum market . London , c1986. i, 79 p. : LC Card 87-134547 DDC 381/.4566553827/0941 19
HD9579.G5 G63 1986

GASOLINE INDUSTRY - SOUTH CAROLINA - HISTORY.
DeMontmollin, Richard Hall. The SCOJA story . [Columbia, S.C.] , c1986. xi, 191 p. : ISBN 0-9617613-0-X LC Card 86-62676 DDC 381/.456655/060757 19
HD9569.S663 D46 1986

GASOLINE - PRICES - GERMANY (WEST)
Baum, Herbert, Dr. Wettbewerbspolitik auf dem Treibstoffmarkt /. Baden-Baden , c1983. 97 p. ; ISBN 3-7890-0881-8 LC Card 83-187053
HD9573.5 .B38 1983

Gasoline tax advantages /. Oppenheimer, Ernest J., 1924- New York, N.Y. , c1987. 88 p. ; ISBN 0-9603982-5-2 (pbk.) : LC Card 86-862507 DDC 336.2/7866553827 19
HD9579.G5 U5732 1987

Gáspár, Sándor.
A munkásosztály szolgálatában / Gáspár Sándor. [Budapest] : Népszava, c1983. 326 p., [26] p. of plates : ill. ; 20 cm. ISBN 963-322-025-4 : LC Card 84-129952
1. Gáspár, Sándor - Interviews. 2. Trade-unions - Hungary - Officials and employees - Interviews. 3. Communists - Hungary - Interviews. 4. Statesmen - Hungary - Interviews. 5. Hungary - Politics and government - 1945-. I. Title.
HD6680.5.Z55 G375 1983

GÁSPÁR, SÁNDOR - INTERVIEWS.
Gáspár, Sándor. A munkásosztály szolgálatában /. [Budapest] , c1983. 326 p., [26] p. of plates : ISBN 963-322-025-4 : LC Card 84-129952
HD6680.5.Z55 G375 1983

Gasparini, Giovanni, 1940-
Il tempo e il lavoro / Giovanni Gasparini. Milano, Italy : F. Angeli, c1986. 178 p. ; 22 cm. (La Società. 112) Bibliography: p. [163]-173. Includes index. LC Card 86-180970
1. Hours of labor. 2. Leisure. 3. Quality of life. I. Title.
HD5106 .G37 1986

Teoria dell'organizzazione e realtà italiana . Milano [1980] 225 p. ; ISBN 88-20-41736-7 : LC Card 80-511472 DDC 302.3/5 19
HM131 .T4 ***NYPL [JLD 81-599]***

GASPÉ PENINSULA (QUÉBEC) - ECONOMIC CONDITIONS.
Gagnon, Alain. Le modèle centre-périphérique appliqué à l'est du Québec . Rimouski , c19. ix, 154 p. ; LC Card 80-143484
HC117.G37 G33 1980

Les Structures productives d'une région périphérique . Rimouski , c1984. xi, 718 p. : ISBN 2-920270-27-3 LC Card 85-132709 DDC 330.9714/77 19
HC117.G37 S78 1984

Gassner, Peter, 1941- Kollektivmacht und Individualschutz im amerikanischen Arbeitsrecht / Peter Gassner. Frankfurt am Main : P.D. Lang, c1981. 155 p. ; 21 cm. (Schriften zum Staats- und Völkerrecht . Bd. 13) Bibliography: p. 141-151. ISBN 3-8204-6119-1 : LC Card 82-164604 DDC 344.73/0189 347.304189 19
1. Collective labor agreements - United States. 2. Labor contract - United States. 3. Labor laws and legislation - United States. I. Title.
KF3408.Z94 G474 1981
NYPL [JLD 86-1212]

Gasson, Ruth M. Labour sharing in agriculture / Ruth Gasson. [London] : Wye College, [1979] 117 p. ; 30 cm. "Report prepared for the Agricultural Training Board, Central Council for Agricultural and Horticultural Cooperation, and the National Farmers' Union Development Trust." "April 1979." Bibliography: p. 112-117. ISBN 0-901859-82-6 (pbk.) LC Card 83-226074 DDC 331.25/72 19
1. Agricultural laborers - Great Britain. 2. Work sharing - Great Britain. I. Agricultural Training Board. II. Central Council for Agricultural and Horticultural Co-operation. III. National Farmers' Union Development Trust (Great Britain). IV. Title.
HD5119.A292 G744 1979

Gasto público . Fundación de Investigaciones Económicas Latinoamericanas (Buenos Aires, Argentina) [Buenos Aires] , 1986. 6 v. in 8 : LC Card 87-403573 DDC 354.820072/252 19
HJ2075 .F86 1986

Gatabaki-Kamau, Rose. Co-operative housing development in Kenya : a socio-economic appraisal / author, Rose Gatabaki-Kamau. Nairobi, Kenya : Housing Research and Development Unit, HRDU, [1985] vi leaves, 131 p. : ill. ; 30 cm. "June 1985." Errata slip inserted. Bibliography: p. 129-131. LC Card 86-980648 DDC 334/.1/096762 19
1. Housing, Cooperative - Kenya. 2. Housing, Cooperative - Kenya - Case studies. 3. Self-help housing - Kenya - Case studies. I. University of Nairobi. Housing Research and Development Unit. II. Title. III. Title: Cooperative housing development in Kenya.
HD7287.72.K4 G37 1985

Gates, Margaret Jane. Moore, Mark Harrison. Inspectors-general . New York , c1986. 120 p. ; ISBN 0-87154-605-1 : LC Card 86-6728 DDC

353.0072/32 19
HJ9801 .M66 1987 *NYPL [JLE 87-1762]*

Gathering rare ores . Helmreich, Jonathan E. Princeton, N.J. , c1986. xiv, 303 p. : ISBN 0-691-04738-3 (alk. paper) : LC Card 86-4862 DDC 327.1/11 19
HD9698.U52 H45 1986
NYPL [JLE 86-4584]

Gathia, J. A. (Joseph Anthony), 1946- Women and child workers in unorganised sector . New Delhi , 1983. xii, 104 p. ; LC Card 83-906999 DDC 331.3/1/0954 19
HD6189 .W64 1983 *NYPL [JLD 87-730]*

Gáti, Gábor. A munkahely-racionalizálás korszerű megközelítési módjai az élelmiszeriparban / szerző, Gáti Gábor ; közreműködött, Sebő Géza. Budapest : Mezőgazdasági és Élelmiszeripari Szervező Vállalat, 1986. 106 p. : ill. ; 29 cm. (Módszertani kiadványsorozat, 0230-7278 . 1986/2) Bibliography: p. 105-106. ISBN 963-02-4171-4 LC Card 87-137979
1. Food industry and trade - Personnel management. 2. Work design. I. Sebő, Géza. II. Title. III. Series.
HD9000.5 .G336 1986

Gatica, Jaime. Deindustrialization in Chile / by Jaime Gatica Barros. Boulder : Westview Press, 1988. p. cm. (Westview special studies on Latin America and the Caribbean) Bibliography: p. Includes index. ISBN 0-8133-7392-1 : LC Card 86-32513 DDC 338.983 19
1. Chile - Manufactures. 2. Chile - Industries. 3. Industry and state - Chile. 4. Monetary policy - Chile. 5. Chile - Economic policy. I. Title.
HD9734.C52 G37 1988

Gattermann, Hans H. Zahn, Joachim, Professor Dr. Eine Finanzpolitik des langen Atems erforderlich /. Bonn [1984] 31 leaves ; LC Card 86-198580
HJ1120 .B65 Nr. 234

Gatti, Ettore. Confalonieri, Antonio. La politica del debito pubblico in Italia, 1919-1943 /. Milano , Roma , c1986. 2 v. (536 p.) ; ISBN 88-420-2794-4 : LC Card 87-125992
HJ8678 .C64 1986

Gatti, M. (Mario) Servizi innovativi e professionalità : indagine sui sistemi professionali e i fabbisogni formativi del terziario avanzato nell'area produttiva barese / di M. Gatti e C. Tagliaferro. Roma : Istituto per lo sviluppo della formazione professionale dei lavoratori, [1985] 231 p. : ill. ; 24 cm. (Quaderni di formazione ISFOL, 0390-3532 . n. 1/85 (genn., febr. 1985)) Bibliography: p. 211-212. LC Card 85-237680
1. Service industries workers - Training of - Italy - Bari (Province). 2. Service industries - Italy - Bari (Province). I. Tagliaferro, C. (Claudio). II. Series: Quaderni di formazione ISFOL , n. 85/1. III. Title.
HD5716.S452 T84 1985

Gatto, Francisco. Sourrouille, Juan V. Inversiones extranjeras en América Latina . Buenos Aires [1984] viii, 142 p. : LC Card 86-183036
HG5160.5.A3 S64 1984

Gatton, T. Harry (Thomas Harry) Banking in North Carolina : a narrative history / by T. Harry Gatton.1st ed. Raleigh : North Carolina Bankers Association, 1987. xi, 155 p. : ill. (some col.) ; 27 cm. Includes index. ISBN 0-9617806-0-6 LC Card 86-63397 DDC 332.1/09756 19
1. Banks and banking - North Carolina - History. I. Title.
HG2611.N8 G38 1987

Gaudier, Maryse. Management, work, leisure . Geneva , c1986. viii, 154 p. : ISBN 92-9014-416-5 (pbk.) : LC Card 87-163300 DDC 306/.36/094 19
HD4904.6 .M35 1986

Gaugler, Eduard.
Ausländerintegration in deutschen Industriebetrieben /. Königstein/Ts. , c1985. viii, 273 p. : ISBN 3-7756-6935-3 LC Card 85-194662 DDC 305.8/00943 19
HD8458.A2 A9265 1985
NYPL [JLD 86-2193]

Flexibilisierung der Beschäftigungsverhältnisse / von Eduard Gaugler, Hans-Günter Krüsselberg. Berlin : Duncker & Humblot, c1986. 85 p. ; 21 cm. (Wirtschaftspolitische Kolloquien der Adolf-Weber-Stiftung) Papers presented at a meeting sponsored by the Adolf-Weber-Stiftung, Oct. 1985, Frankfurt am Main. Includes bibliographies. CONTENTS. - Flexibilisierung der Beschäftigungsverhältnisse : betriebswirtschaftliche Betrachtung / Eduard Gaugler -- Flexibilisierung der Beschäftigungsverhältnisse : volkswirtschaftliche Perspektiven / Hans-Günter Krüsselberg -- Zusammenfassung der Aussprache / [Eduard Gaugler, Hans-Günter Krüsselberg, Walter Leisner]. ISBN 3-428-06070-9 LC Card 87-118519 DDC 331.25/72/0943 19
1. Hours of labor, Flexible - Germany (West). I. Krüsselberg, Hans-Günter. II. Leisner, Walter, 1929-. III. Adolf-Weber-Stiftung. IV. Title.
HD5109.2.G3 G38 1986

Zukunftsaspekte der anwendungsorientierten Betriebswirtschaftslehre . Stuttgart , c1986. xii, 641 p. : ISBN 3-7910-0402-6 LC Card 86-202268
HD35 .Z84 1986

GAUL - COMMERCE - ROME - HISTORY.
Roman, Yves. De Narbonne à Bordeaux . Lyon , c1983. 333 p. : ISBN 2-7297-0200-8 : LC Card 84-179554
HF377 .R65 1983

Gaul, Dieter. Rechtsprobleme der Innovation : Wirtschaftsrecht, Gesellschaftsrecht, gewerblicher Rechtsschutz, Arbeitsrecht / Dieter Gaul. München : J. Schweitzer, 1984. xiv, 126 p. ; 21 cm. (Schriften zum gewerblichen Rechtsschutz, Urheber- und Medienrecht . Bd. 9) Includes index. Bibliography: p. [xi]-xiv. ISBN 3-88709-084-5
1. Technological innovations - Germany, West. 2. Industrial laws and legislation - Germany, West. I. Title. II. Series. *NYPL [JLD 85-2917]*

Gaulin, Huguette. Se lancer en affaires . [Quebec] , c1986. 450 p. : ISBN 2-551-09144-6 LC Card 86-138587 DDC 658.1/1 19
HD62.5 .S4 1986

Gaulke, Klaus-Peter. Lehre und Berufsausübung : eine Längsschnittuntersuchung für Berlin (West) / Klaus-Peter Gaulke und Detlef Filip, unter Mitarbeit von Hans M. Duseberg. Berlin : Duncker & Humblot, 1986. 122 p. ; 30 cm. (Beiträge zur Strukturforschung . Heft 89) Bibliography: p. 110. ISBN 3-428-06000-8 LC Card 86-166545
1. Occupational training - Berlin (Germany) - Statistics. 2. Occupational retraining - Berlin (Germany) - Statistics. I. Filip, Detlef. II. Duseberg, Hans Martin. III. Title.
HC281 .B33 Heft 89 HD5715.5.G42B47

Le gaulois, le cow-boy, et le samouraï . Salomon, Jean Jacques. Paris , c1986. 209 p. : ISBN 2-7178-1139-7 : LC Card 87-120178
HC280.T4 S25 1986

Gauny, Gabriel, 1806-1889.
[Selections. 1983]
Le philosophe plébéien / Gabriel Gauny ; textes présentés et rassemblés par Jacques Rancière. Paris : La Découverte/Maspero ; Saint-Denis : Presses universitaires de Vincennes, c1983. 205 p. ; 22 cm. (Actes et mémoires du peuple) Includes bibliographical references. ISBN 2-7071-1420-0 : LC Card 84-105473
1. Labor and laboring classes - Collected works. 2. Proletariat - Collected works. I. Rancière, Jacques. II. Title.
HD4853 .G382 1983

Gaur, Achal Kumar, 1959- Centre-state financial relations and finance commissions / by Achal Kumar Gaur. Allahabad, India : Chugh Publications, 1985. x, 364 p. ; 23 cm. Revision of the author's thesis (Ph. D.--Banaras Hindu University, 1984) with title: Federal transfers with special reference to Uttar Pradesh since planning in India. Bibliography: p. [348]-357. Includes index. LC Card 85-904373 DDC 336.54 19
1. Intergovernmental fiscal relations - India. 2. Finance, Public - India. I. Title.
HJ1334 .G38 1985

GAUTAMA BUDDHA - ART.
Songsan Ninkamhæng. Chotmāihēt kānsāng Phraphutthar̄up phra prathān Phutthamonthon /. Krung Thēp , 2525 [1982] 172 p. : ISBN 974-7921-05-7 LC Card 83-916060
HB1912.G38 S66 1982

Gavagnin Taffarel, Osvaldo. La deuda externa de América Latina : testimonio de la desigualdad mundial / Osvaldo Gavagnin Taffarel. Lima, Perú : CIEPSAL, 1986. 157 p. : ill. ; 21 cm. Bibliography: p. 155-157. LC Card 86-235251
1. Debts, External - Latin America. 2. Latin America - Economic conditions - 1945-. I. Title.
HJ8514.5 .G37 1986

Gavin, James. Organization development in the mining industry : theory and practice / James Gavin. New York : Praeger, 1986. viii, 247 p. : ill. ; 24 cm. Includes index. Bibliography: p. 241-244. ISBN 0-275-92061-5 (alk. paper) : LC Card 85-24400 DDC 622/.068 19
1. Mineral industries - United States - Management - Case studies. 2. Organizational change - United States - Case studies. I. Title.
HD9506.U62 G38 1986
NYPL [JLE 86-3024]

Gavrilets, ÎU. N. (ÎUriĭ Nikolaevich)
Modelirovanie sotsial′nykh faktorov v ėkonomiko-matematicheskikh issledovaniîakh /. Moskva , 1984. 148 p. : LC Card 87-125299
HC336.25. .M636 1984

Gavrilov, D. V. (Dmitriĭ Vasil′evich) Ural i problemy regional′noĭ istoriografii. Sverdlovsk , 1986. 83 p. ; LC Card 87-159699
HC337.R852 U73853 1986

Gazda, István. A Világ aluminiumipara . Budapest , 1985. 2 v. : LC Card 86-157446
HD9539.A62 V54 1985

Gazdálkodási és jövedelmezőségi adatok, mutatószámok a szövetkezeti bolti kiskereskedelemben / [összeállította, Karlik András, Kőrösy Gyula, Tóth Béláné]. Budapest : Fogyasztási Szövetkezetek Országos Tanácsa, 1984. 113 p. ; 29 cm. ISBN 963-7006-24-9 : LC Card 85-154737
1. Stores, Retail - Hungary - Statistics. 2. Consumer cooperatives - Hungary - Statistics. I. Karlik, András. II. Kőrösy, Gyula. III. Tóth, Béláné. IV. Fogyasztási Szövetkezetek Országos Tanácsa (Hungary).
HF5429.6.H8 G39 1984

Gazdaság és társadalom a nyolcvanas években Magyarországon / [összeállította és szerkesztette, Szpirulisz Ildikó és Lengyel Zsuzsa]. Budapest : MSZMP KB Társadalomtudományi Intézete, 1986- v. <1 > ; 20 cm. Summary in English and Russian. Includes bibliographies. CONTENTS. - 1. Emberi tényezők, termelési viszonyok. ISBN 963-7700-19-6 (set) LC Card 87-136629
1. Hungary - Economic conditions - 1968-. 2. Hungary - Social conditions - 1968-. 3. Hungary - Population. I. Szpirulisz, Ildikó. II. Lengyel, Zsuzsa. III. Magyar Szocialista Munkáspárt. Társadalomtudományi Intézet. IV. Title: Gazdaság és társadalom a 80-as években Magyarországon.
HC300.28 .G265 1986

Gazdaság és társadalom a 80-as években Magyarországon. Gazdaság és társadalom a nyolcvanas években Magyarországon /. Budapest , 1986- v. <1 > ; ISBN 963-7700-19-6 (set) LC Card 87-136629
HC300.28 .G265 1986

A Gazdaság és társadalom viszonya a szocializmus építésének jelenlegi időszakában : tudományos konferencia előadásai / [főszerkesztő, Nagy Lajos]. Szeged : József Attila Tudományegyetem Marxizmus-Leninizmus Központi Tanszékcsoport, 1985. 181 p. ; 24 cm. (Politikai gazdaságtan, 0563-0622) Conference organized by the József Attila Tudományegyetem Marxizmus-Leninizmus Központi Tanszékcsoport and the MSZMP Társadalomtudományi Intézete. Includes bibliographical references. LC Card 86-207975
1. Hungary - Economic conditions - 1968- - Congresses. 2. Hungary - Economic policy - 1968- - Congresses. 3. Hungary - Social conditions - 1945- - Congresses. 4. Hungary - Social policy - Congresses. I. Nagy, Lajos, 1926-. II. József Attila Tudományegyetem. Marxizmus-Leninizmus Központi Tanszékcsoport. III. Magyar Szocialista Munkáspárt. Társadalomtudományi Intézet. IV. Series: Politikai gazdaságtan (Szeged, Hungary).
HC300.28 .G27 1985

A gazdaság irányításának jellege, az irányítás szervezete, eszközei és módszerei /. Ficzere, Lajos. Budapest , 1984. 112 p. ; ISBN 963-02-3265-0 (Magy. nemz. bibl.) LC Card 85-130150
HD87.5 .F53 1984

A gazdaság nyitottságáról . Hoch, Róbert. Budapest , c1987. 33 p. ; ISBN 963-05-4444-X : LC Card 87-425574
HF1542.5 .H63 1987

Gazdasági fejlődésünk és a gazdaságirányítás továbbfejlesztése : országos elméleti tanácskozás, Veszprém, 1984. június 21-22. [Budapest] : Kossuth, 1984. 219 p. ; 22 cm. Meeting organized by the MSZMP KB Agitációs és Propaganda Osztálya, MSZMP KB Társadalomtudományi Intézete and the MSZMP Veszprém Megyei Bizottsága. ISBN 963-09-2571-0 : LC Card 85-186920
1. Hungary - Economic policy - 1968- - Congresses. I. Magyar Szocialista Munkáspárt. Agitációs és Propaganda Osztály. II. Magyar Szocialista Munkáspárt. Társadalomtudományi Intézet. III. Magyar Szocialista Munkáspárt. Veszprém Megyei Bizottság.
HC300.28 .G332 1984

Gazdasági hadviselés a kölcsönös függés korszakában /. Palánkai, Tibor. [Budapest] , 1985. 88 p. ; ISBN 963-09-2633-4 : LC Card 86-128423
HF1413.5 .P35 1985

A Gazdasági mérnök, 0324-4210.
Hegedűs, József. Értékelemzés a termékfejlesztésben /. Budapest , 1983. 215 p., [2] p. of plates : ISBN 963-10-5784-4 LC Card 85-110177
HD69.N4 H38 1983

Gazdasági növekedés a két világrendszerben /. Simon, György. [Budapest] , 1986. 257, [1] p. ; ISBN 963-09-2771-3 : LC Card 87-409656
HD85.H88 S498 1986

A Gazdaságirányítás és a szakszervezetek / [összeállították Fogarasi László ... et al. ; szerkesztette, Dankovits László]. Budapest : Népszava, 1985. 191 p. ; 21 cm. ISBN 963-322-253-2 : LC Card 86-104573
1. Hungary - Economic policy - 1968-. 2. Central planning - Hungary. 3. Industrial management - Hungary. 4. Trade-unions - Hungary. I. Fogarasi, László. II. Dankovits, László.
HC300.28 .G349 1985

Gazdaságirányítás, 1985 / szerkesztette, Pulai Miklós, Vissi Ferenc ; [a kötet szerzői, Balassa Ákos ... et al.]. Budapest : Közgazdasági és Jogi Könyvkiadó, 1984. 175 p. ; 24 cm. ISBN 963-221-540-0 : LC Card 85-229856
1. Hungary - Economic policy - 1968-. 2. Central planning - Hungary. I. Pulai, Miklós. II. Vissi, Ferenc. III. Balassa, Ákos.
HC300.28 .G338 1984

A gazdaságirányítási rendszer egyes kérdései, elmélettörténeti megközelítésben /. Vigvári, András. [Budapest] , 1985. 87 p. ; ISBN 963-673-302-3 LC Card 85-231820
HC300.28 .V53 1985

A Gazdaságirányítási rendszer továbbfejlesztése / [írták, Balogh Bálint ... et al. ; szerkesztette és lektorálta, Villányi Miklós]. Budapest : MÉM Mérnök- és Vezetőtovábbképző Intézet, 1984. 171 p. ; 29 cm. LC Card 86-145153
1. Hungary - Economic policy - 1968-. I. Balogh, Bálint. II. Villányi, Miklós.
HC300.28 .G339 1984

Gazdaságon innen és túl . Práger, László. Budapest , 1986. 194 p. : ISBN 963-05-4355-9 : LC Card 87-407707
HD70.H8 P7 1986

Gazdaságpolitika, elméletben és gyakorlatban . Pongrácz, Antal. [Budapest] , 1985. 73 p. ; ISBN 963-422-739-2 : LC Card 87-105897
HC300.28 .P66 1985

Gazdaságpolitika, szociálpolitika, 0231-0279.
Pongrácz, Antal. Gazdaságpolitika, elméletben és gyakorlatban . [Budapest] , 1985. 73 p. ; ISBN 963-422-739-2 : LC Card 87-105897
HC300.28 .P66 1985

Gazdaságpolitikai füzetek, 0230-3833.
Bontó, László. Iparfejlesztés a hetedik ötéves terv időszakában /. [Budapest] , 1986. 170, [4] p. : ISBN 963-09-3001-3 : LC Card 87-138631
HC300.28 .B659 1986

Papp, Sándor. A mezőgazdasági ipar, ellenfél vagy partner? /. [Budapest] , 1985. 154 p. : ISBN 963-09-2547-8 : LC Card 85-230966
HD9015.H82 P36 1985

Gazdaságpolitikai kézikönyv /. Sándorné Szennyessy, Judit. [Budapest] , 1985. 170 p. : LC Card 86-186314
HC300.28 .S26 1985

Gazdaságpolitikánk az élenjáró vállalatok gyakorlatában : országos elméleti tanácskozás, Győr, 1985. május 28-29. / [szerkesztette, Milei Lajos]. [Budapest] : Kossuth, 1985. 276 p. : ill. ; 22 cm. Meeting organized by the MSZMP KB Agitációs és Propaganda Osztálya, MSZMP KB Gazdaságpolitikai Osztálya and MSZMP Győr-Sopron Megyei Bizottsága. ISBN 963-09-2769-1 : LC Card 87-407761
1. Industrial management - Hungary - Congresses. 2. Business enterprises - Hungary - Congresses. I. Milei, Lajos. II. Magyar Szocialista Munkáspárt. Központi Bizottság. Agitációs és Propaganda Osztály. III. Magyar Szocialista Munkáspart. Gazdaságpolitikai Osztály. IV. Magyar Szocialista Munkáspárt. Győr-Sopron Megyei Bizottság.
HD70.H8 G39 1985

Gazdaságunk helye és rangja a világban . Illés, Iván. Budapest , 1985. 222 p. : ISBN 963-221-523-0 : LC Card 86-156571
HC300.28 .I45 1985

Gazdaságunk helyzetéről és fejlődésünk problémáiról. [Budapest] : Kossuth, 1985. 239 p. : ill. ; 20 cm. Published by the Magyar Tudományos Akadémia Közgazdaságtudományi Intézete. Includes bibliographies. ISBN 963-09-2681-4 : LC Card 86-202400
1. Hungary - Economic conditions - 1968-. 2. Hungary - Economic policy - 1968-. I. Magyar Tudományos Akadémia. Közgazdaságtudományi Intézet.
HC300.28 .G36 1985

Gazettes hollandaises. Morineau, Michel. Incroyables gazettes et fabuleux métaux . London ; New York : 687 p. : ISBN 0-521-25384-5 : LC Card 83-7177 DDC 330.94/022 19
HC240 .M73 1985 ***NYPL [JLE 85-1587]***

Gazovyĭ most : Zapadnaia Sibir'--Zapadnaia Evropa / [sostaviteli S.K. Babkin, L.G. Adamova, V.V. Mylov ; spetsial'naia fotos"emka A.G. Lobova]. Sverdlovsk : Sredne-Ural'skoe knizhnoe izd-vo, 1985. 206 p. : col. ill. ; 18 x 26 cm. (Vserossiĭskaia seriia "I vnov' prodolzhaetsia boĭ--") "K XXVII s"ezdu KPSS." LC Card 86-186324
1. Gas, Natural - Russian S.F.S.R. - Siberia, Western - Pipe lines. 2. Gas, Natural - Soviet Union - Pipe lines. 3. Gas, Natural - Europe - Pipe lines. I. Babkin, S. K. II. Adamova, L. G. III. Mylov, V. V. IV. Lobov, Aleksandr. V. Series.
HD9581.S653 S54 1985

GBC Golden Jubilee Publicity & Literature Subcommittee (Ghana) Golden jubilee, July 1935-1985 /. Accra [Ghana] [1985] 64 p. : LC Card 86-155961 DDC 384.54/06/0667 19
HE8689.9.G45 G65 1985

Gbenyon, Kuakuvi.
Locoh, Thérèse. Comprendre les problèmes de population . Lomé, Togo , 1984. 72, [3], 3 p. : LC Card 87-131146
HB871 .L57 1984

Pour une mesure indirecte de la mortalitè. 1985. Locoh, Thérèse. La fécondité en Afrique noire / Thérèse Locoh. Pour une mesure indirecte de la mortalité : la méthode de Courbage-Farques : adéquation ou inadéquation au cas du Togo en 1971? / Kuakuvi Gbenyon. Lomé [1985] 36, 22 leaves : LC Card 87-126644
HB1071 .L63 1985

Gboizo, J. Emplois et qualifications dans le secteur métaux-mécanique-électricité en Côte d'Ivoire / Republique de Côte d'Ivoire, Office national de formation professionnelle, Direction des études et recherches. [Abidjan] : Ministère de l'enseignement technique et de la formation professionnelle, 1981. 93 leaves ; 30 cm. "Réalisée par J. Gboizo avec la collaboration de P. Peguy, P. Akesse et J.K. Adou; rédaction ... par R. Anderson"--Prelim. p. [3] LC Card 83-234024
1. Labor supply - Ivory Coast. 2. Occupational training - Ivory Coast. I. Ivory Coast. Office national de formation professionnelle. Direction Etudes et recherches. II. Title.
HD5846.9.A6 G36 1981

Gdalin, A. D. (Aleksandr Davidovich)
Filatelisticheskaia Pushkiniana / A.D. Gdalin. Moskva : "Radio i sviaz'", 1981. 124 p. : ill. (some col.) ; 17 cm. (Biblioteka iunogo filatelista. vyp. 9) Bibliography: p. 120-121. Includes index. LC Card 86-174858
1. Postage-stamps - Topics - Pushkin, Aleksandr Sergeevich, 1799-1837. I. Title.
HE6183.P86 G43 1981

Geary, Dick. The German unemployed . Beckenham, Kent , 1987. xviii, 314 p. : ISBN 0-7099-0941-1 ***NYPL [JLD 87-801]***

Gebauer, Joachim. Die Kreisfreien Städte und Landkreise in Rheinland-Pfalz /. Bad Ems , 1977. 420 p. : LC Card 85-244499
HC287.R7 K74 1977

Gebhard, Alfred. Das Dorf Singen und seine Finanzwirtschaft : von 1850 bis zur Stadterhebung im Jahre 1899 / Alfred Gebhard. Singen : Stadtarchiv Singen, 1985. 484 p. : ill. ; 23 cm. (Beiträge zur Singener Geschichte. Bd. 7) Cover title: Finanzwirtschaft in Singen 1850-1900. Bibliography: p. 7. Includes index. ISBN 3-921413-23-0 LC Card 87-133391 DDC 336.43/46 19
1. Finance, Public - Germany (West) - Singen am Hohentwiel. 2. Singen am Hohentwiel (Germany) - Appropriations and expenditures. I. Title. II. Title: Finanzwirtschaft in Singen 1850-1900. III. Series.
HJ9494.S57 G4 1985

Gebhardt, Joan E. Townsend, Patrick L. Commit to quality /. New York , c1986. xvii, 189 p. : ISBN 0-471-83953-1 LC Card 85-29639 DDC 658.5/62 19
HD66 .T65 1986 ***NYPL [JLE 86-3004]***

Gebhardt, Peter. Der Markt gebrauchter Güter : theoretische Fundierung und empirische Analyse / Peter Gebhardt. Hamburg : Kovač, c1986. xxvii, 250, [69] p. : ill. ; 21 cm. Originally presented as the author's thesis (doctoral)--Universität Erlangen-Nürnberg. Bibliography: p. xi-xxvii. ISBN 3-925630-10-4 LC Card 87-127354 DDC 381/.1 19
1. Secondhand trade - Germany (West). 2. Marketing - Germany, West. I. Title.
HF5482 .G42 1986

Gebrewold, Kiflemariam. Fernsehexport der Bundesrepublik Deutschland : Studie zur Historie, Struktur und Funktion von TV-Transkriptionsdiensten / von Kiflemariam Gebrewold. Bochum : Studienverlag Brockmeyer, 1983. xiv, 316 p. : ill. ; 21 cm. (Bochumer Studien zur Publizistik- und Kommunikationswissenschaft . Bd. 37) Cover title: Fernseh-Export der Bundesrepublik Deutschland. "Die Studie wurde von der Fakultät der Abteilung für Philosophie, Pädagogik, Psychologie der Universität Bochum als Magister-Graduierungsarbeit angenommen"--Pref. Bibliography: p. 273-285. ISBN 3-88339-317-7 LC Card 83-232957
1. Television broadcasting - Germany, West. 2. Television adaptations. 3. Deutsche Welle. I. Title. II. Title: Fernseh-Export der Bundesrepublik Deutschland. III. Series.
HE8700.66.G3 G43 1983

GEBROEDERS CHABOT, FA. (ROTTERDAM, NETHERLANDS) - HISTORY.
Mees en Chabot, twee kassiers te Rotterdam . Delft , c1986. 87 p. : ISBN 90-70879-40-9 : LC Card 86-205783
HG3120.R62 M44 1986

Gebrüder Colsman (Essen, Germany) So schaffen wir! . [Germany , 193-?] (München : F. Bruckmann) [51] leaves : LC Card 86-213082
HD9539.C7 G57 1930z

GEBRÜDER COLSMAN (ESSEN, GERMANY)
So schaffen wir! . [Germany , 193-?] (München : F. Bruckmann) [51] leaves : LC Card 86-213082
HD9539.C7 G57 1930z

GEBRÜDER GIENANTH-EISENBERG - HISTORY.
Gienanth, Ulrich, Freiherr von, 1907- 250 Jahre Eisenwerk Eisenberg . Eisenberg/Pfalz [1986] 68 p. : LC Card 87-409570 DDC 338.7/6691/0943 19
HD9523.9.G4 G54 1986

Gebruik van en alternatieven voor tropisch hout. Meijenfeldt, C. F. W. M. von. 's-Gravenhage , c1985. 207, [14] p. : ISBN 90-346-0647-3 : LC Card 86-231435
HD9750.8.T73 M45 1985

Die Gebührenpolitik der Deutschen Bundespost im Kleingut- und Fernmeldebereich : Analyse und kritische Würdigung ihrer Marktgerechtigkeit / wissenschaftliche Leitung, W. Hamm ... [et al.] ; Bearbeiter, Jörg Rohde. [Mainz] : Forschungsinstitut für Wirtschaftspolitik an der Universität Mainz,

[1984?] xi, 300 p. ; 21 cm. Bibliography: p. 289-300. LC Card 87-407592 DDC 383/.23/0943 19
1. Postal service - Germany (West) - Rates. 2. Telecommunication - Germany (West) - Rates. 3. Deutsche Bundespost. I. Rohde, Jörg. II. Johannes Gutenberg-Universität. Forschungsinstitut für Wirtschatspolitik.
HE6998 .G42 1984

Gebührenpolitik im Privatgiroverkehr der Kreditinstitute /. Gladen, Werner. Berlin , c1985. 248 p. : ISBN 3-428-05820-8 LC Card 85-199227
HG1616.S4 G53 1985

Gebührenpolitik im Telekommunikationsbereich /. Neumann, Karl-Heinz. Baden-Baden , 1984. 348 p. : ISBN 3-7890-1049-9 : LC Card 86-166218
HE8157 .N48 1984

Gees, René. Schweiz UPU 1900 : die Ausgabe zum 25jährigen Jubiläum der Gründung des Weltpostvereins / René Gees. Bern : Kottelat, [1976?] 56 p. : ill. ; 25 cm. Reprint: Originally published: 1955? With new introd. in English. LC Card 86-170456
1. Universal Postal Union. 2. Commemorative postage stamps. I. Title.
HE6271 .G44 1976

Der geförderte Wohnungsbau in Mannheim 1850-1985 /. Hahn, Barbara. Mannheim , 1986. 236 p. : ISBN 3-87804-185-3 LC Card 87-121543 DDC 363.5/8/0943/46 19
HD7339.M35 H34 1986

Gegen Europessimismus . Giersch, Herbert. Stuttgart , c1986. 318 p. ; ISBN 3-421-06334-6 LC Card 87-672572
HF1411 .G53x 1986

Gegenkurs . Hankel, Wilhelm, 1929- Berlin , c1984. 261 p. : ISBN 3-88680-114-4 LC Card 84-174753
HB3723 .H26 1984

Die Gegenwärtige Wachstumskrise : theoretische und empirische Beiträge zu ihrer Erklärung / Rainer Künzel, Dirk Ipsen (Hrsg.). Regensburg : Transfer Verlag, c1985. viii, 262 p. : ill. ; 24 cm. Contributions presented at a meeting of the Arbeitskreis Politische Ökonomie held in Loccum, 1984. Includes one abridged contribution in English. Includes bibliographies. CONTENTS. - Wachstumskrise, soziale Probleme und Theoriebildung / R. Künzel, D. Ipsen, G. Rohwer -- Die Ursachen des Trendbruchs in den siebziger Jahren / J. Steindl -- Akkumulation und Wachstum in der Krise / H. Riese -- Die Konsumentwicklung im Zusammenhang mit Wachstumskrise und Beschäftigung / K.G. Zinn -- Das Wechselspiel von Profitratenfall, langen Wellen und Konjunkturen / G. Buchholz, E. Hödl -- Krisentendenzen und Stagnation in einem Akkumulationsmodell mit Marxschem Technischen Fortschritt / J. Glombowski, M. Krüger -- Periodization approaches of capitalist development / C. Pennavaja -- Zwei Anzätze zur Analyse institutioneller Grenzen des Wachstums / M. Buhbe -- De-Industrialisierung in Grossbritannien / M. Funke -- Die Wachstumskrise als Umweltkrise / H. Nutzinger -- Konjunktur und Massenphänomene / M. Kraft, P. Weise -- Ausgewählte Literatur zur Erklärung der gegenwärtigen Wachstumskrise / R. Künzel, D. Ipsen, G. Rohwer. ISBN 3-924956-08-1 LC Card 86-122363 DDC 338.9 19
1. Economic development - Congresses. I. Künzel, Rainer, 1942-. II. Ipsen, Dirk, 1939-. III. Arbeitskreis Politische Ökonomie (Germany).
HD73 .G43 1985

Gehalts- und Lohnstrukturerhebung 1978 : die Struktur der Arbeiter- und Angestelltenverdienste im Produzierenden Gewerbe, im Handel sowie in Kreditinstituten und im Versicherungsgewerbe / [herausgegeben vom Hessischen Statistischen Landesamt]. Wiesbaden : Das Landesamt, 1983. 285, [3] p. ; 30 cm. (Beiträge zur Statistik Hessens, 0440-7482 . n.F., Nr. 152) LC Card 84-217477
1. Wages - Germany (West) - Hesse - Statistics. 2. White collar workers - Salaries, etc. - Germany (West) - Hesse - Statistics. 3. Technicians in industry - Salaries, etc. - Germany (West) - Hesse - Statistics. I. Hessisches Statistisches Landesamt. II. Series.
HA1320 .H529 n.F., Nr. 152 HD5030.H47

Gehani, Narain, 1947-
Ada, an advanced introduction. Gehani, Narain, 1947- UNIX Ada programming / Narain Gehani. Englewood Cliffs, NJ , c1987. xix, 310 p. : ISBN 0-13-938325-5 LC Card 86-22547 DDC 005.4/465 19
QA76.73.A35 G437 1987
NYPL [JSE 87-568]

UNIX Ada programming / Narain Gehani. Englewood Cliffs, NJ : Prentice-Hall, c1987. xix, 310 p. : ill. ; 24 cm. At head of title: AT&T. On t.p. the registered trademark symbol "TM" is superscript following "UNIX" in the title. Modified ed. of: Ada, an advanced introduction. c1983. Includes index. Bibliography: p. 287-302. ISBN 0-13-938325-5 LC Card 86-22547 DDC 005.4/465 19
1. Ada (Computer program language). 2. UNIX (Computer operating system). I. Gehani, Narain, 1947- Ada, an advanced introduction. II. American Telephone and Telegraph Company. III. Title.
QA76.73.A35 G437 1987
NYPL [JSE 87-568]

Gehrmann, Dieter. (joint author) Boeck, Klaus. Die DM als internationale Reservewährung . Hamburg , 1974. 75 p. ; LC Card 75-550711
NYPL [JLE 80-744]

Gehrmann, Friedhelm. Ansprüche an die Arbeit . Frankfurt [am Main] , New York , c1984. 298 p. : ISBN 3-593-33390-2 LC Card 85-103333
HF5548.8 .A683 1984

Gehrmann, Friedhelm, 1939- Arbeitsmoral und Technikfeindlichkeit . Frankfurt , New York , c1986. 274 p. : ISBN 3-593-33757-6 LC Card 86-212283
HD8444 .A73 1986

Gehrmann, Rolf. Leezen 1720-1870 : ein historisch-demographischer Beitrag zur Sozialgeschichte des ländlichen Schleswig-Holstein / von Rolf Gehrmann. Neumünster : K. Wachholtz, 1984. 366 p. : ill. ; 24 cm. (Studien zur Wirtschafts- und Sozialgeschichte Schleswig-Holsteins, 0172-9152 . Bd. 7) Originally presented as the author's thesis (doctoral--Freie Universität Berlin) Summary in English and French. Bibliography: p. 329-360. ISBN 3-529-02907-6 : LC Card 85-217552
1. Leezen (Germany) - Population - History. I. Title. II. Series.
HB3596.L44 G44 1984

Geiger, Helmut, 1928- Bankinnovationen . Frankfurt am Main , c1986. 131 p. ; ISBN 3-7819-0363-X LC Card 87-120955 DDC 332.1/0943 19
HG3048 .B287 1986

Geiler, Nick. Wasser konkret : Schritte zur Neuorientierung hessischer Wasserpolitik / Nick Geiler, Reiner Hildebrandt. Wiesbaden : Die Grünen im Hessischen Landtag, [1985] 199 p. : ill. ; 21 cm. Bibliography: p. 182-189. LC Card 86-162674
1. Water resources development - Government policy - Germany (West) - Hesse. 2. Water quality management - Government policy - Germany (West) - Hesse. 3. Water conservation - Government policy - Germany (West) - Hesse. I. Hildebrandt, Reiner. II. Hesse (Germany). Landtag. Grünen. III. Title.
HD1697.G33 H474 1985

Geinitz, Dedo. Entwicklungszusammenarbeit mit Indonesien : kleinbäuerlicher Kautschukanbau in Abai Siat, West-Sumatra / Dedo Geinitz. Bremen : Übersee-Museum Bremen, 1985. viii, 72 p. : ill. ; 24 cm. (Veröffentlichungen aus dem Übersee-Museum Bremen. Reihe D, 0341-9274 . Bd. 14) "Publikation zur Indonesien-Abteilung des Übersee-Museums Bremen." Bibliography: p. 68-72. ISBN 3-88299-046-5 LC Card 86-204688
1. Rubber industry and trade - Indonesia - Abaisiat. 2. Agriculture, Cooperative - Indonesia - Abaisiat. 3. Farms, Small - Indonesia - Abaisiat. I. Übersee-Museum Bremen. Indonesien-Abteilung. II. Title.
HD9161.I63 A244 1985

Geipot. see **Empresa Brasileira de Planejamento de Transportes.**

Geis, George T. Micromanaging : transforming business leaders with personal computers / George T. Geis, Robert L. Kuhn. Englewood Cliffs, NJ : Prentice-Hall, c1987. xiv, 233 p. ; 24 cm. Disk in pocket. Includes bibliographies and index. ISBN 0-13-581901-6 (pbk.) LC Card 86-30470 DDC 658/.05416 19
1. Industrial management - Data processing. 2. Business - Data processing. 3. Microcomputers. I. Kuhn, Robert Lawrence. II. Title.
HD30.2 .G44 1987

Geiser, Josef. Wachstumshemmnisse mittelständischer Industriebetriebe / Josef Geiser. Göttingen : O. Schwartz, 1983. xi, 385 p. : ill. ; 24 cm. (Schriften zur Mittelstandsforschung . Nr. 90) Bibliography: p. 340-379. ISBN 3-509-01353-0 LC Card 84-221327
1. Small business - Germany, West. 2. Industries, Size of - Germany (West). 3. Organizational change - Germany (West). I. Title. II. Series.
HD2346.G3 G372 1983

Geiss, Imanuel. Gewerkschaften in Afrika / von Imanuel Geiss. Hannover : Verlag für Literatur und Zeitgeschehen, 1965. 233 p. : ill. ; 24 cm. (Schriftenreihe des Forschungsinstituts der Friedrich-Ebert-Stiftung. A. Sozialwissenschaftliche Schriften) Bibliography: p. 217-220. Includes indexes. LC Card 85-125305
1. Trade-unions - Africa. 2. Trade-unions, Black - Africa. 3. Pan-Africanism. I. Title.
HD6857 .G45 1965

Geiss, Wilfried. Betriebswirtschaftliche Kennzahlen : theoretische Grundlagen einer problemorientierten Kennzahlenanwendung / Wilfried Geiss. Frankfurt am Main ; New York : P. Lang, c1986. 405 p. : ill. ; 21 cm. (Schriften zum Controlling, 0178-9619 . Bd. 1) Bibliography: p. 377-405. Includes index. ISBN 3-8204-9629-7 LC Card 87-407301 DDC 657/.42 19
1. Cost accounting. I. Title. II. Series.
HF5686.C8 G384 1986

Geisst, Charles R. A guide to financial institutions / Charles R. Geisst. New York : St. Martin's Press, 1988. p. cm. "A companion volume to the same author's A guide to the financial markets"--Jacket. Includes bibliographies and index. ISBN 0-312-01132-6 : LC Card 87-13047 DDC 332.1 19
1. Financial institutions - United States. 2. Financial institutions - Great Britain. 3. Financial institutions, International. I. Title.
HG185.U5 G45 1988

Geivers, R. (joint author) De Vos, Wouter. Point de mire . Antwerpen, Belgiëlai 147 a , 1977. 125 p. : ISBN 90-02-01132-6 : LC Card 78-370280 DDC 309.1
HC59 .D464 ***NYPL [JLD 80-3135]***

Geld, krediet en intrest in de Belgische financiële sector /. Verheirstraeten, A. Leuven , 1977. xxii, 337 p. : LC Card 78-345984
HG1055 .V47 ***NYPL [JLM 86-1310 nr.23]***

Geld, Kredit und ökonomische Dynamik in marktvermittelten Ökonomien, die Vision einer Geldwirtschaft /. Herr, Hansjörg, 1951- München , c1986. ix, 240 p. ; ISBN 3-88259-396-2 LC Card 87-140289 DDC 332.4/6 19
HG230.3 .H47 1986

Geld oder Gott? . Wagner, Falk. Stuttgart , c1984. 162 p. ; ISBN 3-608-91389-0 LC Card 86-121379
HG221.3 .W255 1984

Geld ohne Mehrwert . Suhr, Dieter. Frankfurt am Main , c1983. 143 p. ; ISBN 3-7819-0302-8 LC Card 84-169137
HG221 .S8883 1983

Geld und asymmetrische Information /. Illing, Gerhard. Berlin , New York , 1985. vi, 148 p. : ISBN 0-387-13999-0 (U. S.) LC Card 85-142939
HG220.A2 I55 1985

Geld- und Fiskalpolitik in Portfolio-orientierten Modellen kleiner offener Volkswirtschaften . Steingräber, Carola, 1956- Rheinfelden , c1986. ix, 219 p. : ISBN 3-87718-532-0 LC Card 86-182509
HG230.3 .S74 1986

Geld und Kredit in einer Ökonomie mit festen Preisen . Eichberger, Jürgen, 1952- Frankfurt am Main , New York , c1984. 152 p. : ISBN 3-8204-5441-1 LC Card 85-191492
HG230.3 .E53 1984

Geld- und Währungsordnung / von Karl Brunner ... [et al.] ; herausgegeben von Werner Ehrlicher und Rudolf Richter. Berlin : Duncker & Humblot, c1983. 249 p. : ill. ; 24 cm. (Schriften des Vereins für Socialpolitik, Gesellschaft für Wirtschafts- und Sozialwissenschaften . n.F., Bd. 138) English and German. Includes bibliographies. CONTENTS. - Geldpolitische Instrumente und monetärer Transmissionsprozess im Bundesbankmodell / von Wilfried Jahnke --

Instrumente und quantitative Hilfsmittel der kurzfristigen Geldmengenkontrolle / von Hermann-Josef Dudler -- U. S. Monetary policy / von Henry C. Wallich -- The pragmatic and intellectual tradition of monetary policymaking and the international monetary order / von Karl Brunner -- Issues and results of the Gold Commission / von Jerry L. Jordan -- Das Europäische Währungssystem, ein Erfolg? / von Armin Gutowski und Hans-Eckart Scharrer -- Zur Beurteilung des europäischen Währungssystems / von Vincenz Timmermann -- The impact of the eurocurrency market on monetary policy / von Georg Rich -- Auf verlorenem Posten / von Helmut Mayer -- Goldpool und Reservepolitik aus der Sicht der Deutschen Bundesbank / von Otmar Emminger. ISBN 3-428-05530-6 LC Card 84-141547
1. Monetary policy - Germany, West. 2. Monetary policy - United States. 3. Monetary policy - Switzerland. 4. Monetary policy - Europe. I. Brunner, Karl, 1916-. II. Ehrlicher, Werner. III. Richter, Rudolf, 1926-. IV. Series.
HG999.5 .G4556 1983

Geldeinkommen in der DDR von 1955 bis zu Beginn der achtziger Jahre . Vortmann, Heinz. Berlin , 1985. 239 p. : ISBN 3-428-95952-2 LC Card 86-166538
HC281 .B33 Heft 85 HC290.795.I5

Gelderblom, D. Kok, P. C. Black migration to the PWV complex . Pretoria , 1985. viii, 79 p. : ISBN 0-7969-0313-1 (pbk.) : LC Card 86-232836 DDC 304.8/0968 19
HB2123.4.P68 K65 1985

Geldmärkte und Europäisches Währungssystem . Gubitz, Andrea. Idstein , 1985. vii, 201 p. : ISBN 3-925196-00-5 LC Card 86-230130
HG3949 .G82 1985

Geldmengenpolitik und Inflationskontrolle . Baltensperger, Ernst. Diessenhofen , c1984. 132 p. : ISBN 3-7253-0224-3 : LC Card 84-178054 DDC 332.4/9494 19
HG1155 .B345 1984 NYPL [JLD 87-168]

Die Geldnachfrage . Heri, Erwin W. Berlin , New York , c1986. 226 p. : ISBN 0-387-17157-6 (U. S.) LC Card 86-232268
HG226.5 .H47 1986

Geldner, Marian. Strategy of socio-economic development . Warsaw , 1980. 122 p. : LC Card 81-107307
HD75 .S8 1980

Geldwertstabilität und Wirtschaftswachstum : ein Seminar des Internationalen Währungsfonds und der Oesterreichischen Nationalbank, Baden bei Wien, 12.-14. Oktober 1983 / herausgegeben von Hans Seidel. Göttingen : Vandenhoeck & Ruprecht, c1984. xii, 230 p. : ill. ; 24 cm. Includes bibliographical references. ISBN 3-525-13169-0 LC Card 84-232466
1. International finance - Congresses. 2. Monetary policy - Congresses. I. Seidel, Hans. II. International Monetary Fund. III. Österreichische Nationalbank.
HG203 .G46 1984

Geleentheidstuk .
(no. 10) Cilliers, S. P. Patterns of migration and settlement in rural South Africa /. [Stellenbosch] , 1986. 19, 13 leaves, 5 folded leaves of plates : ISBN 0-908422-81-4 (pbk.) : LC Card 87-126315 DDC 304.8/0968 19
HB2123.4.A3 C56 1986

Gelfand, Lawrence Emerson, 1926- Agricultural distress in the Midwest, past & present /. Iowa City , 1986. ix, 111 p. : ISBN 0-87414-049-8 : LC Card 86-29932 DDC 338.1/0977 19
HD1773.A3 A37 1986

Gelfand, Mark I. The War on poverty, 1964-1968 [microform] . Frederick, MD , c1986- microfilm reel ISBN 0-89093-495-9 (microfilm : set) : LC Card 87-10510 DDC 338.973 19
HC110 .P63

Gellings, Clark W.
Demand-side management : concepts and methods / Clark W. Gellings, John H. Chamberlin. Lilburn, GA : Fairmont Press, c1988. xi, 465 p. : ill. ; 24 cm. Includes bibliographies and index. ISBN 0-88173-027-0 : LC Card 86-46131 DDC 363.6/2/068 19
1. Electric utilities - Management. I. Chamberlin, John H., 1950-. II. Title.
HD9685.A2 G45 1988

Load management /. New York , c1987. vii, 207 p. : ISBN 0-87942-214-9 LC Card 86-33824 DDC 363.6/2 19
HD9685.U5 L58 1987

Geltner, David, 1951- Moavenzadeh, Fred, 1935- Transportation, energy, and economic development . Amsterdam ; New York : viii, 529 p. : ISBN 0-444-42338-9 (U. S.) : LC Card 84-5954 DDC 333.79 19
HE148 .M6 1984 NYPL [JLE 86-1569]

Gematigd monetarisme . Zijlstra, J. Leiden , 1985. ix, 330 p. : ISBN 90-207-1382-5 : LC Card 85-201189
HG1065 .Z55 1985 NYPL [JLE 87-379]

Die Gemeindefinanzen im Ruhrgebiet . Zimmermann, Horst, 1934- Essen , 1983. xvi, 153 p. : ISBN 3-923494-28-9 LC Card 83-228289
HJ9493.5.R8 Z76 1983

Gemeindehaushalte zur Haushaltswirtschaft der Städte Hannover, Düsseldorf, Köln, Frankfurt, Stuttgart, München. Bonn am Rhein : Institut "Finanzen und Steuern" : Buchhändlerischer Vertrieb, W. Stollfuss, 1964. 148 p. ; 21 cm. (Institut "Finanzen und Steuern" . Heft 75) Includes bibliographical references. LC Card 87-408349 DDC 336/.014/43 19
1. Municipal budgets - Germany, West. 2. Municipal finance - Germany, West. I. Institut "Finanzen und Steuern" (Germany). II. Series: Schriftenreihe (Institut "Finanzen und Steuern" (Germany)) , Heft 75.
HJ9473 .G46 1964

Gemeindestatistik 1976. Stuttgart : Statistisches Landesamt Baden-Württemberg, <1976- > v. <2 > : ill. ; 30 cm. (Statistik von Baden-Württemberg . Bd. <230 >) CONTENTS. - -- Heft 2. Wahl zum Landtag von Baden-Württemberg am 4. April 1976. LC Card 86-222059
1. Elections - Germany (West) - Baden-Württemberg - Statistics. 2. Baden-Württemberg (Germany). Landtag - Elections, 1976. I. Statistisches Landesamt Baden-Württemberg. II. Series.
HA1320.B2 A32 Bd. 230, etc. JN4939.A15

Gemeindetypen der Pfalz . Hasenfratz, Eberhard. Mannheim , 1986. 197 p. : ISBN 3-923750-19-6 LC Card 86-185643
HB3596.R46 H37 1986

Gemeinkosten abbauen durch Wertanalyse . Ferk, Hans S., 1945- Zürich , c1983. 128 p. : ISBN 3-478-36120-6 : LC Card 84-108512
HD47.3 .F47 1983

Gemeinkosten-Management . Wegmann, 1951- München , c1982. 230, xliii p. : ISBN 3-88259-224-9 (Deut. Bibl.) LC Card 83-159003
HJ2033 .W43 1982

Gemeinkostenmanagement. Wegmann, 1951- Gemeinkosten-Management . München , c1982. 230, xliii p. : ISBN 3-88259-224-9 (Deut. Bibl.) LC Card 83-159003
HJ2033 .W43 1982

Gemeinwirtschaft im Sozialstaat . Hüttig, Christoph. Frankfurt am Main , c1986. vi, 355 p. : ISBN 3-88129-990-4 : LC Card 86-223747
HD4175 .H83 1986

Gemmell, Norman.
Iyare, S. International cost differences in developing countries . Durham, England [1983] 14, [9] leaves : LC Card 86-207078 DDC 338.4/367/09667 19
HD9737.G52 I97 1983

Surveys in development economics /. Oxford, UK , New York, NY, USA , 1987. 390 p. : ISBN 0-631-14713-6 : LC Card 87-5164 DDC 338.9/009172/4 19
HC59.7 .S882 1987

Gemper, Bodo B.
Industrial policy. Structural dynamics of industrial policy /. New Brunswick, N.J. (U. S.A.) , c1987. x, 208 p. : ISBN 0-88738-679-2 (pbk.) LC Card 87-5023 DDC 338.9 19
HD3611 .I385 1987

Protektionismus in der Weltwirtschaft . Hamburg , 1984. viii, 147 p. ; ISBN 3-87895-253-8 LC Card 84-233895
HF1703 .P77 1984

Genberg, Hans.
External influences on the Swiss economy under fixed and flexible exchange rates / Hans Genberg and Alexander K. Swoboda. Grüsch : Rüegger, c1985. ii, 182 p. : ill. ; 21 cm. (Schweizerisches Institut für Aussenwirtschafts-, Struktur- und Regionalforschung an der Hochschule St. Gallen . Bd. 10) Bibliography: p. 178-182. ISBN 3-7253-0249-9 (pbk.) LC Card 86-156330
1. Foreign exchange problems - Switzerland. 2. Monetary policy - Switzerland. 3. Economic stabilization - Switzerland. 4. Switzerland - Economic conditions - 1945-. I. Swoboda, Alexander K. II. Series: Schweizerisches Institut für Aussenwirtschafts-, Struktur- und Regionalforschung an der Hochschule St. Gallen (Series) , Bd. 10. III. Title.
HG3963 .G45 1985 NYPL [JLD 87-539]

Influences externes sur l'économie suisse en changes fixes et flottants / Hans Genberg et Alexander K. Swoboda. Genève : Georg, c1985. ii, 202 p. : ill. ; 21 cm. "Programme national de recherche no 9--Mécanismes et évolution de l'économie suisse"--Cover. Bibliography: p. 198-202. ISBN 2-8257-0127-0 : LC Card 85-235579 DDC 332.4/5609494 19
1. Foreign exchange problem - Switzerland. 2. Monetary policy - Switzerland. 3. Economic stabilization - Switzerland. 4. Switzerland - Economic conditions - 1945-. I. Swoboda, Alexander K. II. Nationales Forschungsprogramm Mechanismen und Entwicklung der Schweizerischen Wirtschaft. III. Title.
HG3963 .G46 1985 NYPL [JLD 86-2381]

GENDARMES. see **POLICE.**

Gender and education series.
Wickham, Ann. Women and training /. Milton Keynes, England , Philadelphia, PA, USA , c1986. x, 147 p. ; ISBN 0-335-15119-1 LC Card 86-5176 DDC 331.4/2592/0941 19
HD6059.6.G7 W52 1986
NYPL [JLD 86-3495]

Gender and history . Nicholson, Linda J. New York , 1986. x, 238 p. ; ISBN 0-231-06220-6 (alk. paper) LC Card 85-21281 DDC 323.3/4/01 19
HQ1206 .N7 1986 NYPL [JLE 86-1987]

Gender and stratification / edited by Rosemary Crompton and Michael Mann. Cambridge, CB, UK : Polity Press ; Oxford, OX, UK : In association with Blackwell, 1986. viii, 271 p. ; 24 cm. Includes index. Bibliography: p. [250]-263. ISBN 0-7456-0167-7 : LC Card 85-28342 DDC 305.3 19
1. Sex role - Addresses, essays, lectures. 2. Social status - Addresses, essays, lectures. 3. Social classes - Addresses, essays, lectures. I. Crompton, Rosemary. II. Mann, Michael.
HQ1075 .G46 1986 NYPL [JLE 86-2966]

Gender and the labour process / edited by David Knights, Hugh Willmott. Aldershot, Hampshire, Eng. ; Brookfield, Vt., U. S.A. : Gower, c1986. vii, 186 p. ; 23 cm. Includes bibliographies and index. ISBN 0-566-00999-4 : LC Card 85-21977 DDC 331.4 19
1. Sexual division of labor - Addresses, essays, lectures. 2. Women - Employment - Addresses, essays, lectures. I. Knights, David. II. Willmott, Hugh.
HD6060.6 .G45 1986 NYPL [JLD 86-3900]

Gender and work in the Third World . Humphrey, John, 1950- London , New York , 1987. p. cm. ISBN 0-422-61900-0 (cased) LC Card 87-12416 DDC 305.4/3/00981 19
HD6060.65.B6 H86 1987

Gender identification and working class solidarity among Maquila workers in Ciudad Juarez . Young, Gay. [East Lansing] , c1986. 24 p. ; LC Card 87-620601 DDC 331.4/87/097216 19
HD6073.O332 M4959 1986

Gender identity . Fast, Irene. Hillsdale, N.J. , 1984. vii, 189 p. ; ISBN 0-88163-014-4 LC Card 84-6366 DDC 155.3/3 19
BF692.2 .F36 1984 NYPL [JFE 86-4829]

Gender in the workplace / Clair Brown and Joseph A. Pechman, editors. Washington, D.C. : Brookings Institution, c1987. xiv, 316 p. ; 23 cm. Includes bibliographical references and index. ISBN 0-8157-1170-0 : LC Card 87-668 DDC 331.13/3 19
1. Sex discrimination in employment - United States. 2. Sex role in the work environment - United States. 3. Sex discrimination in employment. 4. Sex role in the work environment. I. Brown, Clair, 1946-. II. Pechman, Joseph A., 1918-. III. Brookings Institution.
HD6060.5.U5 G46 1987

Gender-related impacts and the work of the international agricultural research centers /. Jiggins, Janice. Washington, D.C. , c1986. x, 95 p. ; ISBN 0-8213-0840-8 (pbk.) LC Card 86-24709 DDC 331.4/83/091724 19
HD6073.A292 D444 1986

Gendreau, Francis. Barbier, J. C. Migrations et développement . Paris , 1983, c1984. 372 p. : ISBN 2-7099-0711-7
NYPL [M-11 4991 no.170]

Gene Kelly's catalog of the fiscal stamps of the Kantone and Gemeinden of Switzerland. Kelly, Gene. [Catalog of the fiscal stamps of the Kantone and Gemeinden of Switzerland.] [Diessenhofen, Switzerland] [1986- v. <1 > : LC Card 87-112466 DDC 769.5/7 19
HJ5437.Z7 K45 1986

Genealogica .
(Bd. 9) Hermesiade . Essen , c1986. 182 p. ; ISBN 3-89206-143-2 LC Card 86-226901 DDC 658.8/2 19
HF5438.5 .H47 1986

The general . Bilby, Kenneth. New York , c1986. 326 p. ; ISBN 0-06-015568-X : LC Card 85-45621 DDC 384.54/092/4 B 19
HE8689.8 B55 1985
NYPL [MWES (Sarnoff, D.) 86-4682]

GENERAL AGREEMENT ON TARIFFS AND TRADE (ORGANIZATION)
Agriculture in the GATT . Washington , 1986. v, 47 p. ; LC Card 86-603393 DDC 382/.41/0973 19
HD9006 .A77 1986

Hathaway, Dale E. Agriculture and the GATT . Washington, DC , c1987. xii, 157 p. : ISBN 0-88132-052-8 LC Card 87-21430 DDC 382/.41/0973 19
HD9006 .H28 1987

Información básica sobre el GATT y el desarrollo industrial y comercial de México. México , c1985. 79, 62 p. ; LC Card 87-400559 DDC 338.0972 19
HC135 .I53 1985

Mexico. Congreso. Cámara de Senadores. Consulta sobre el GATT . México , c1986. v, 540 p. ; LC Card 87-114865 DDC 382/.0972 19
HF1481 .M45 1986

Trade policies for a better future . Dordrecht ; Boston : vii, 174 p. : ISBN 0-89838-925-9 LC Card 87-22126 DDC 382.9/2 19
HF1411 .T712 1987

General Agreement on Tariffs and Trade (1947). Spanish. 1985. Información básica sobre el GATT y el desarrollo industrial y comercial de México. México , c1985. 79, 62 p. ; LC Card 87-400559 DDC 338.0972 19
HC135 .I53 1985

General aviation marketing /. Wells, Alexander T. Malabar, Fla. , 1987. viii, 268 p. : ISBN 0-89874-987-5 LC Card 86-21504 DDC 629.133/340422/0688 19
HD9711.A2 W45 1987

General de las cañas /. García Galló, Gaspar M. Jorge. La Habana , 1983. 220 p., [18] p. of plates : LC Card 84-229562 DDC 331.88/13361/097291 19
HD6577.5.M46 G37 1983
NYPL [JFD 85-4783]

GENERAL EQUILIBRIUM (ECONOMICS) see **EQUILIBRIUM (ECONOMICS)**

General equilibrium trade policy modeling / edited by T.N. Srinivasan and John Whalley. Cambridge, Mass. : MIT Press, c1986. vii, 360 p. : ill. ; 24 cm. Proceedings of a Conference on General Equilibrium Trade Policy Modeling, held at Columbia University in April 1984. Includes bibliographies and index. ISBN 0-262-19245-4 LC Card 85-19144 DDC 382/.3/0724 19
1. Commercial policy - Mathematical models - Congresses. 2. Equilibrium (Economics) - Mathematical models - Congresses. I. Srinivasan, T. N., 1933-. II. Whalley, John. III. Conference on General Equilibrium Trade Policy Modeling (1984 : Columbia University).
HF1410.5 .G46 1986 *NYPL [JLE 86-4456]*

General Export Association of Sweden. see **Sveriges allmänna exportförening.**

General government accounts and statistics, 1970-1981. Regnskaber og statistikker for den offentlige sektor 1970-1981 =. Luxembourg , Washington, DC , 1983. clxxii, 279 p. ; ISBN 92-825-4066-9 LC Card 84-174459
HC240.9.15 R45 1983

A General information guide on the economy of the Bahamas / prepared by the Economic Intelligence Department, Central Bank of the Bahamas. Nassau, Bahamas : The Bank, [1986] x, 60 p. ; 23 cm. "April 1986." LC Card 87-400226 DDC 330.97296 19
1. Bahamas - Economic conditions. 2. Finance - Bahamas. I. Central Bank of the Bahamas. Economic Intelligence Dept.
HC152 .G46 1986

General managers in action /. Aguilar, Francis J. (Francis Joseph) New York , 1988. viii, 498 p. : ISBN 0-19-504083-X (alk. paper) LC Card 87-12503 DDC 658.4 19
HD38.2 .A39 1987

GENERAL MOTORS CORPORATION.
Jones, Bryan D. The sustaining hand . Lawrence, Kan. , c1986. xii, 247 p. : ISBN 0-7006-0278-X : LC Card 85-24631 DDC 338.4/76292/09774 19
HD9710.U53 M433 1986
NYPL [JLE 86-2386]

Todo para la G.M. . Madrid [1981?] 174 p. : ISBN 84-85639-19-7 LC Card 82-134601 DDC 338.8/87 19
HD9710.S754 G467 1981
NYPL [JLC 86-300]

GENERAL MOTORS CORPORATION. PONTIAC MOTOR DIVISION.
Roadmap for change. Chicago, Ill. , 1987. 1 film reel (28 min.) : LC Card 87-705133 DDC 658 11
HD9710

General office procedures for colleges /. Fulton, Patsy J. Cincinnati , c1988. viii, 399 p. : ISBN 0-538-11732-X (pbk.) LC Card 86-63580 DDC 651 19
HF5547.5 .F84 1988

General plan for the development of the regional network in Africa. Plan général de développement du réseau régional en Afrique =. Genève , 1983. 134 p. : ISBN 92-71-02066-9 LC Card 85-146412
HE8465 .P54 1983

General recordkeeping /. Huffman, Harry. New York , c1988. x, 564 p. : ISBN 0-07-031054-8 LC Card 87-2982 DDC 657/.2 19
HF5635 .H8834 1988

General review / prepared by the FAO/ECE Agriculture and Timber Division of the Economic Commission for Europe, Geneva. New York : United Nations, 1986. iii, 81 p. ; 30 cm. (Agricultural review for Europe, 0501-3054 . no. 28, v. 1 (1984 and 1985) "ECE/AGRI/89(Vol. 1)"--Cover. "United Nations publication. Sales no. E.86.II.E.14"--T.p. verso. ISBN 92-1-116361-7 (pbk.) LC Card 87-120391 DDC 338.1/094 19
1. Agriculture - Economic aspects - Europe. I. United Nations. FAO/ECE Agriculture and Timber Division. II. Series: Agricultural review for Europe , no. 28, v. 1.
HD1917 .U5 no. 28, vol. 1

GENERAL STORES - UNITED STATES - HISTORY.
Beverley, Mary Frances. Cowbells and coffins . Austin, Tex. , c1987. xi, 63 p. : ISBN 0-89015-593-3 (pbk.) : LC Card 87-6711 DDC 381/.1 19
HF5429.3 .B49 1987

GENERAL STRIKE - ADDRESSES, ESSAYS, LECTURES.
Wozu noch in die Parlamente? /. [Reutlingen] , 1978. 81 p. : LC Card 82-223081 DDC 322/.2/0943 19
HD6697 .W69 1978 *NYPL [JLD 87-886]*

GENERAL STRIKE, BUENOS AIRES, ARGENTINA, 1919.

GENERAL STRIKE, ECUADOR, 1922.
Capelo C., J. Alejo (J. Alejo Capelo Cabello), d. 1973. El crimen del 15 de noviembre de 1922 /. [Guayaquil] , 1983. 10, 14, 19 p. : LC Card 86-114097
HD5358.A6 C36 1983

Puig Vilazar, Carlos. Sacrificio de un pueblo, 15 de noviembre de 1922 /. [Guayaquil, Ecuador] , 1983. 88 p. ; LC Card 86-115462
HD5358.A6 P85 1983

GENERAL STRIKE, GREAT BRITAIN, 1926 - HISTORY - SOURCES.
The Guardian book of the General Strike /. Aldershot, Hants, England , Brookfield, Vt. , 1987. p. cm. ISBN 0-7045-3081-3 : LC Card 87-25287 DDC 331.89/25/0941 19
HD5365.A6 G8 1987

GENERAL STRIKE, ROSARIO, ARGENTINA, 1969.
Balvé, Beba. De protesta a rebelión--la "subversión" (Rosario, mayo 1969) /. Buenos Aires, Argentina [1985] xvii, 123 p. ; LC Card 86-162379
HD5350.R67 B35 1985

Generale Nederlandsche Geoctroyeerde Oost-Indische Compagnie. see **Nederlandsche Oost-Indische Compagnie.**

GENERALS - GREECE - BIOGRAPHY.
Spēliōtakēs, K. K. Archeion Michaēl Iatrou, 1802-1893 /. Athēna , 1983. 189 p., [4] folded leaves of plates : LC Card 85-134031
HF3750.5.S64 A3 1983
NYPL [JFE 86-4131]

Generating energy alternatives . Cogan, Douglas. Washington, D.C. , c1987. xi, 358 p. : ISBN 0-931035-16-3 (pbk.) LC Card 87-403993 DDC 333.79 19
HD9685.U5 C588 1987

Generating technological innovation / edited by Edward B. Roberts. New York : Oxford University Press, 1987. xii, 299 p. : ill. ; 25 cm. (The Executive bookshelf) A selection of articles from the Sloan management review. Bibliography: p. 264-285. Includes index. ISBN 0-19-505023-1 (alk. paper) LC Card 86-33119 DDC 658.5/14 19
1. Technological innovations - Management. I. Roberts, Edward Baer. II. Sloan management review. III. Series.
HD45 .G39 1987

Generationen im Betrieb . Steinrücke, Margareta, 1953- Frankfurt , New York , c1986. 343 p. ; ISBN 3-593-33639-1 LC Card 87-137842 DDC 331.3/0943 19
HD6283.G4 S74 1986

Generelle Arbeitszeitverkürzung . Schettkat, Ronald. Berlin , 1984. iii, 108 p. : LC Card 84-182608
HD5106 .S3 1984

Generic drugs : markets, developments, opportunities / Cort Wrotnowski, project analyst. Stamford, Conn., U. S.A. : Business Communications Co., c1986. xiii, 311 leaves : ill. ; 29 cm. (Business opportunity report . C-058) "January 1986"--T.p. verso. ISBN 0-89336-434-7 (soft) LC Card 87-167077 DDC 380.1/456151 19
1. Pharmaceutical industry. 2. Drugs - Generic substitution. 3. Market surveys. I. Wrotnowski, Cort. II. Business Communications Co. III. Series.
HD9665.5 .G46 1986

Gênero industrial--têxtil /. Jucá, Alvaro Ferraz. [Recife] [1985?] 34 leaves ; LC Card 86-204296
HD9864.B83 P475 1985

Génese e estrutura da Guarda Fiscal . Santos, Pedro Ribeiro dos. [Lisbon] [1985] 193 p., [9] leaves of plates : LC Card 87-400399 DDC 354.4690072/46 19
HJ6996 .A25 1985

Genèse et évolution du mouvement syndical congolais /. Etonokani, Jean-René. [Brazzaville? , between 1982 and 1986] (Brazzaville : Service polycopie de la Conférence épiscopale du Congo) 180 p., [20] p. of plates : LC Card 86-179682
HD6878 .E86 1982

Génesis de la renta capitalista de la tierra y del arrendatario. Mendoza, Carlos. Teoría de la renta capitalista de la tierra ; y, Génesis de la renta capitalista de la tierra y del arrendatario /. Buenos Aires , 1985. 108 p. : ISBN 950-9478-11-3 LC Card 86-101927
HB401 .M38 1985

Genesis of Oklahoma oil banking /. McGuire, Paul F., 1907- Muskogee, Okla. , c1986. 160 p. : ISBN 0-86546-068-X (pbk.) LC Card 87-118559 DDC 332.1/223/0924 B 19
HG2463.M36 A3 1986

Genetic algorithms and their applications. Proceedings of an international conference on genetic algorithms and their applications . [S.l. , 1985] 225 p. : *NYPL [JSF 87-413]*

Geneva. Graduate Institute of International Studies. (Old Catalog form: Graduate institute of international studies, Geneva.)
Policy responses to the changing international environment . Budapest , 1981. 170 p. ; ISBN 963-301-077-2 (pbk.) LC Card 81-179118 DDC 337/.09/048 19
HC59 .P573 1981 *NYPL [JLL 79-189 no.33]*

Geneva. Institut universitaire de hautes études internationales. see **Geneva. Graduate Institute of International Studies.**

Geneva. International Institute for Labour Studies.
Research series.
(no. 83) Miernyk, William H. The coalmining industry in the United States /. Geneva , 1986. 53, ix p. : ISBN 92-9014-409-2 (pbk.)
NYPL [JLE 87-1534]

Série de recherche. see **Geneva. International Institute for Labour Studies. Research series.**

Geneva. International Labor Office. see **International Labor Office.**

Geneva. Postgraduate Institute of International Studies. see **Geneva. Graduate Institute of International Studies.**

Genezis teoriĭ monopolii v marksistsko-leninskoĭ i burzhuaznoĭ literature (1840-1930-e gody) /. Shishkin, M. V. (Mikhail Vladislavovich) Leningrad , 1985. 151 p. ; LC Card 86-140591
HD2757.2 .S49 1985

Geninet, Bernard. Mathématiques et statistiques générales appliquées au marketing : DEUG, DUT, BTS d'économie, de marketing et de gestion / Bernard Geninet. Paris : Economica, c1986. 198 p. : ill. ; 24 cm. ISBN 2-7178-1071-4 : LC Card 86-165417
1. Marketing - Mathematics. 2. Marketing - Statistical methods. I. Title.
HF5415 .G397 1986

Gennard, John. Dunn, Stephen. The closed shop in British industry /. London , 1984. xii, 181 p. ; ISBN 0-333-26202-6 LC Card 87-673181
HD6488.2.G7 D86x 1984

Genoa (Italy)
Convegno Genova nell'economia marittimo/portuale in Europa e nel mondo (1982 : Genoa, Italy) Atti del Convegno Genova nell'economia marittimo/portuale in Europa e nel mondo . Genova [1982?] 135 p. : LC Card 86-105783
HE558.G3 C66 1982

GENOA (ITALY) - COMMERCE - CONGRESSES.
Convegno Genova nell'economia marittimo/portuale in Europa e nel mondo (1982 : Genoa, Italy) Atti del Convegno Genova nell'economia marittimo/portuale in Europa e nel mondo . Genova [1982?] 135 p. : LC Card 86-105783
HE558.G3 C66 1982

Genosko, Joachim. Arbeitsangebot und Alterssicherung / Joachim Genosko. Regensburg : Transfer, c1985. vii, 287 p. : ill. ; 24 cm. (Volkswirtschaftliche Schriften der Universität Regensburg . Bd. 1) The author's Habilitationsschrift, Universität Regensburg. Bibliography: p. 273-287. ISBN 3-924956-05-7 LC Card 86-230675
1. Old age pensions - Germany, West. 2. Aged - Employment - Germany, West. I. Title.
HD7105.35.G3 G46 1985

Genossenschaften in Entwicklungsländern . Klöwer, Gerd Günter. Göttingen , 1981. 56 p. ; ISBN 3-509-01085-X LC Card 82-174706 DDC 334/.09172/4 19
HD3575 .K58 1981 *NYPL [JLE 86-3343]*

Genossenschafts-Bewegung . Novy, Klaus. Berlin , c1983. 176 p. : ISBN 3-88747-017-6 LC Card 84-190729
HD7287.72.G3 N68 1983

Gensewich, Irmtraud. Die Tabakarbeiterin in Baden, 1870-1914 / Irmtraud Gensewich. Mannheim : Institut für Landeskunde und Regionalforschung der Universität Mannheim, 1986. 496 p. : ill. ; 21 cm. (Südwestdeutsche Schriften . 2) Originally presented as the author's thesis (doctoral--Mannheim, 1985) under the title: Die badische Tabakarbeiterin im Kaiserreich, 1870-1914. "Quellen und Literatur": p. 418-446. ISBN 3-87804-183-7 LC Card 87-121532 DDC 331.4/8797/094346 19
1. Women tobacco workers - Germany (West) - Baden-Württemberg - History. 2. Baden-Württemberg (Germany) - Economic conditions. I. Title. II. Series.
HD6073.T62 G34 1986

Gensior, Sabine. Mikroelektronik-Anwendung und ihre Bedeutung für die Qualifikationen : ein Literaturbericht / Sabine Gensior. Berlin : Wissenschaftszentrum Berlin, 1986. 39, 118 p. ; 30 cm. (Discussion papers / International Institute of Management. Labour Market Policy, 0722-673X . IIM/LMP 86-7) Summary in English and German. Bibliography: p. 1-3 (2nd group) LC Card 87-409403 DDC 338/.06 19
1. Microelectronics - Social aspects - German-speaking countries. 2. Microelectronics - Information services - German-speaking countries. 3. Labor supply - German-speaking countries - Effect of technological innovations on. I. Series: Discussion papers (International Institute of Management. Labour Market Policy) , IIM/LMP 86-7. II. Title.
HD6331.2.G27 G46 1986

Gentner, R. Bendeich, E. (Eugen), 1945- Wirtschaftliche Datenerfassung in Klein- und Mittelbetrieben . München , c1979. 211 p. : ISBN 3-478-41740-6 LC Card 85-171162
HD62.7 .B4 1979

GENTRIFICATION - AUSTRALIA - MELBOURNE (VIC.)
Logan, William Stewart, 1942- The Gentrification of inner Melbourne . St. Lucia, Qld., Australia ; New York : xxxiii, 328 p. : ISBN 0-7022-1729-8 LC Card 84-17382 DDC 307/.2 19
HD7379.M45 L64 1985
NYPL [JLD 87-798]

The Gentrification of inner Melbourne . Logan, William Stewart, 1942- St. Lucia, Qld., Australia ; New York : xxxiii, 328 p. : ISBN 0-7022-1729-8 LC Card 84-17382 DDC 307/.2 19
HD7379.M45 L64 1985
NYPL [JLD 87-798]

Genzel, David. De la publicité à la communication / David Genzel ; [préface de Claude Chauvet]. Paris : Rochevignes, [1984?] 271 p. : ill. ; 22 cm. (Collection "Action et gestion") Errata slip inserted. Bibliography: p. 268. ISBN 2-86737-005-1 LC Card 84-175281
1. Advertising - France. 2. Advertising - France - Psychological aspects. I. Title. II. Series.
HF5813.F8 G46 1984

Geo. P. Rowell & Co. Newspaper Advertising Bureau. An advertising agency : a statement intended to make plain the nature and methods of the business, and the changes necesitated [sic] by the lapse of time and other circumstances. New York : Geo. P. Rowell & Co.'s Newspaper Advertising Bureau, [1878] 23 p. ; 14 cm. An advertisement. LC Card 87-158199
1. Advertising, Newspaper. 2. Advertising agencies. I. Title.
HF6107 .G45 1878

The geodesic network . Huber, Peter W. (Peter William), 1952- Washington, D.C. , 1987. 1 v. (various pagings) : LC Card 87-601031 DDC 384/.041 19
HE8819 .H76 1987

Geoghegan, C., 1945- Handbook of commercial French / C. Geoghegan and J. Gonthier Geoghegan. London ; New York : Routledge & Kegan Paul, 1988. p. cm. ISBN 0-7102-0857-X LC Card 87-16320 DDC 448/.002465 19
1. Commercial correspondence, French. 2. French language - Business French - Dictionaries - English. 3. English language - Business English - Dictionaries - French. I. Geoghegan, J. Gonthier, 1951-. II. Title.
HF5728.F8 G46 1988

Geoghegan, J. Gonthier, 1951- Geoghegan, C., 1945- Handbook of commercial French /. London , New York , 1988. p. cm. ISBN 0-7102-0857-X LC Card 87-16320 DDC 448/.002465 19
HF5728.F8 G46 1988

GEOGNOSY. see **GEOLOGY.**

Geografía de los paisajes urbanos e industriales de Venezuela /. Estaba, Rosa M. Caracas , c1985. 291 p., [4] folded leaves : ISBN 980-271-006-7 LC Card 86-148810 DDC 307.7/6/0987 19
HC237 .E766 1985 *NYPL [JLD 86-2340]*

Geografia ekonomiczna świata /. Fleszar, Mieczysław. Warszawa , 1978. 519 p. : LC Card 81-212600
HC54 .F556 1978

Geograficheskie osobennosti formirovaniia agrarno-promyshlennykh kompleksov v Predbaĭkal'e / [otvetstvennyĭ redaktor B.M. Ishmuratov]. Irkutsk : In-t geografii Sibiri i Dal'nego Vostoka, 1978. 145 p. : ill. ; 20 cm. At head of title: Akademiia nauk SSSR. Sibirskoe otdelenie. Institut geografii Sibiri i Dal'nego Vostoka. Includes bibliographies. LC Card 81-162870
1. Agricultural industries - Russian S.F.S.R. - Irkutskaia oblast'. I. Ishmuratov, Baĭron Mustafovich. II. Institut geografii Sibiri i Dal'nego Vostoka (Akademiia nauk SSSR).
HD9015.S653 I74 1978

Geograficheskie problemy razvitiia narodnogo khoziaistva Moskovskogo regiona / [redaktsionnaia E.M. Pospelov (predsedatel') ... et al. ; otvetstvennye redaktory V.G. Glushkova, N.P. Matveev]. Moskva : Akademiia nauk SSSR, Moskovskiĭ filial Geogr. ob-va SSSR, 1986. 104 p. : ill., maps ; 20 cm. Includes bibliographies. LC Card 87-135959
1. Moscow Region (R.S.F.S.R.) - Economic conditions. 2. City planning - Russian S.F.S.R. - Moscow Region. I. Pospelov, E. M. (Evgeniĭ Mikhaĭlovich). II. Glushkova, V. G. (Vera Georgievna). III. Matveev, N. P. (Nikolaĭ Petrovich). IV. Geograficheskoe obshchestvo SSSR. Moskovskiĭ filial.
HC338.M6 G46 1986

Geograficheskoe obshchestvo SSSR. (old Catalog form: Gosudarstennoye russkoye geograficheskoye obshchestvo)

Geograficheskoe obshchestvo SSSR. Moskovskiĭ filial.
Geograficheskie problemy razvitiia narodnogo khoziaistva Moskovskogo regiona /. Moskva , 1986. 104 p. : LC Card 87-135959
HC338.M6 G46 1986

Territorial'naia organizatsiia proizvoditel'nykh sil SSSR /. Moskva , 1978. 124 p. : LC Card 81-149822
HC340.D5 T44 1978

Territorial'nye struktury promyshlennosti /. Moskva , 1978. 128 p. : LC Card 81-147566
HC340.D5 T464 1978

Geografiia mirovogo sel'skogo khoziaistva /. Vol'f, M. B. (Mark Borisovich) Moskva , 1981. 326 p. : LC Card 82-122609
HD1415 .V62 1981

Geografiia promyshlennosti SSSR /. Khrushchev, A. T. ((Anatoliĭ Timofeevich)) Moskva , 1986. 415 p. : LC Card 87-117010
HC336.25 .K475 1986

The Geographical digest. 1st ed. London : G. Philip, c1986. 122 p. : ill. ; 29 cm. ISBN 0-540-01104-5 LC Card 87-124717 DDC 330.9/04/021 19
1. Economic indicators. I. George Philip & Son.
HA155 .G46 1986

GEOGRAPHICAL DISTRIBUTION OF MAN. see **ANTHROPO-GEOGRAPHY; ETHNOLOGY.**

Geographical economics /. O'Sullivan, Patrick. London , 1981. 199 p. : ISBN 0-333-31854-4 LC Card 86-673424
HF1025 .O86x 1981b

Geographical papers. [Reading, Eng.]
(no. 31) Foot, David H.S. A comparison of some land-use allocation/interaction models [microform] /. Reading [Berkshire] , 1974. 36 p. : ISBN 0-7049-0338-5
*NYPL [*ZT-1712 no.13]*

Géographie des transports /. Wolkowitsch, Maurice. Paris , 1982, c1973. 383 p. : ISBN 2-200-31188-5 LC Card 83-147243
HE151 .W63 1982

Géographie sociale, 0766-9267 .
(2) Colloque Les Périphéries urbaines (1984 : Angers, France) Actes du Colloque Les Périphéries urbaines . Caen , c1985. 270 p. : ISBN 2-905461-03-9 : LC Card 86-173712
HB2263 .C65 1984

Geographische Zeitschrift. Supplement.
Monheim, Felix. Die Entwicklung der peruanischen Agrarreform 1969-1979 und ihre Durchführung im Departement Puno [microform] /. Wiesbaden , 1981. 37 p. ; ISBN 3-515-03629-6 : LC Card 82-113404 DDC 333.3/1/8536 19
HD1333.P42 P955 1981
*NYPL [*ZT-1647 no.11]*

GEOGRAPHY, COMMERCIAL.
Wolkowitsch, Maurice. Géographie des transports /. Paris , 1982, c1973. 383 p. :

ISBN 2-200-31188-5 LC Card 83-147243
HE151 .W63 1982

GEOGRAPHY - DICTIONARIES.
Majma' al-Lughah al-'Arabiyah, Cairo. Lajnat al-Jughrāfīyā. al-Mu'jam al-jughrāfī /. [al-Qāhirah] , 1974. 9,185 p. ; LC Card 77-961221
G63 .M34 1974 ***NYPL [*OEO 86-3694]***

GEOGRAPHY - DICTIONARIES - ARABIC.
Majma' al-Lughah al-'Arabiyah, Cairo. Lajnat al-Jughrāfīyā. al-Mu'jam al-jughrāfī /. [al-Qāhirah] , 1974. 9,185 p. ; LC Card 77-961221
G63 .M34 1974 ***NYPL [*OEO 86-3694]***

GEOGRAPHY, ECONOMIC - CONGRESSES.
Seminario sobre Conceptos Teóricos de la Geografía Económica (1975 : Mexico City, Mexico?) Seminario sobre Conceptos Teóricos de la Geografía Económica . México , 1978. 78 p. ; LC Card 87-403767 DDC 330.9 19
HC13 .S46 1975

Sipozium "Geografiia v Kirgizii" (1980 : Frunze, Kirghiz S.S.R.) Sovremennye problemy geografii Kirgizii . Frunze , 1980. 167 p. : LC Card 82-121674
HC337.K545 S56 1980

Geography of multinationals. v. 2. Multinationals and the restructuring of the world economy /. London , Dover, N.H. , c1986- viii, 389 p. : ISBN 0-7099-2457-7 (v. 2) : LC Card 85-29081 DDC 338.8/81 19
HD2755.5 .M8442 1986
NYPL [JLD 86-2089]

GEOGRAPHY OF POPULATION. see **POPULATION GEOGRAPHY.**

Geography of the world-economy.
Agnew, John A. The United States in the world-economy . Cambridge , New York , 1987. xvii, 264 p. : ISBN 0-521-30410-5 LC Card 86-32743 DDC 337.73 19
HC103 .A37 1987

The geography of underdevelopment . Forbes, Dean K. London , 1986. 214 p. ; ISBN 0-7099-1012-6 ***NYPL [JLD 86-1233]***

GEOGRAPHY, PHYSICAL. see **PHYSICAL GEOGRAPHY.**

GEOGRAPHY, SOCIAL. see **ANTHROPO-GEOGRAPHY.**

GEOGRIDS.
Geotextiles, geomembranes, geomatrices . Stamford, Conn., U. S.A. , c1986. xii, 133 leaves : ISBN 0-89336-496-7 (pbk.) LC Card 87-403913 DDC 668.9 19
HD9869.I533 U64 1986

GeoJournal library.
The GeoJournal library.
Laulajainen, Risto. Spatial strategies in retailing /. Dordrecht ; Boston : xiii, 253 p. : ISBN 90-277-2595-0 LC Card 87-20803 DDC 658.8/7 19
HF5429.275 .L38 1987

Migration and settlement . Dordrecht ; Boston : xix, 496 p. ; ISBN 90-277-2119-X LC Card 85-25626 DDC 304.8 19
HB1952 .M539 1986 ***NYPL [JLE 86-4091]***

Geological Survey (U. S.) Resource studies of the Navajo Indian Reservation . [Denver? Colo.] , 1986. 187 p. in various pagings : LC Card 86-603130 DDC 333.7/09791/3 19
HC107.A165 R47 1986

GEOLOGISTS - BULGARIA - BIOGRAPHY.
Trudova slava /. Sofiia , <1986-. v. <4 > : LC Card 86-228746
HD8039.M62 B88 1986

GEOLOGY - DICTIONARIES.
Watt, Alec. Illustrated dictionary of geology . Beirut [Harlow, Essex] , 1982. 329 p. :
NYPL [*OG 85-2903]

GEOMEMBRANES.
Geotextiles, geomembranes, geomatrices . Stamford, Conn., U. S.A. , c1986. xii, 133 leaves : ISBN 0-89336-496-7 (pbk.) LC Card 87-403913 DDC 668.9 19
HD9869.I533 U64 1986

GEOPOLITICS - ARGENTINA - HISTORY.
Quadri Castillo, Mario. La Argentina descentralizada /. [Buenos Aires] , c1986. 236 p. : ISBN 950-23-0322-9 LC Card 87-402244 DDC 330.982/064 19
HC175 .Q33 1986

GEOPOLITICS - CENTRAL AMERICA.
Esser, Klaus. Zentralamerika, USA, EG und Bundesrepublik Deutschland /. Berlin , 1987. xi, 137 p. : ISBN 3-88985-043-X LC Card 87-401334 DDC 337.1/728 19
HC141 .E86 1987

Georg Michael Pfaff Gedächtnisstiftung. Mehr Technik, weniger Arbeit? . Karlsruhe , c1984. 228 p. : ISBN 3-7880-9697-7 LC Card 85-108996
HD6331 .M384 1984

George, Abraham M. International finance handbook /. New York , c1983. 2 v. : ISBN 0-471-09861-2 (set) : LC Card 82-23824 DDC 332/.042 19
HG3881 .I57633 1983 ***NYPL [JLE 86-1719]***

George, Henry, 1839-1897.
[Progress and poverty. Spanish]
Progreso y miseria / Henry George ; estudio preliminar por Ana María Martín Uriz. [Madrid : Ministerio de Agricultura, 1985?] cxv, 384 p. : ill., ports. ; 24 cm. (Clasicos agrarios) Cover title. Bibliography: p. [367]-384. Includes index. ISBN 84-7479-375-0 : LC Card 87-112201
1. Economics. 2. Single tax. I. Martín Uriz, Ana María. II. Title. III. Series.
HB171 .G276 1985

George, M. V. Interim household and family projections for Canada, provinces, and territories to 2006 =. [Ottawa] [1987] 67 p. ; LC Card 87-162270 DDC 304.6/2/0971021 19
HA745 .I62 1987

George Mason University. Dept. of Economics. Barth, James R. International debt . Fairfax, Va. , 1984. 36 p. ; ***NYPL [*ZT-1554 no.21]***

George Philip & Son. The Geographical digest. London , c1986. 122 p. : ISBN 0-540-01104-5 LC Card 87-124717 DDC 330.9/04/021 19
HA155 .G46 1986

George, Susan. Ill fares the land : essays on food, hunger, and power / Susan George.1st ed. Washington, D.C. : Institute for Policy Studies, c1984. xviii, 102 p. ; 22 cm. Includes bibliographical references. CONTENTS. - Overcoming hunger : strengthen the weak, weaken the strong -- Dangerous embrace : culture, economics, politics, and food systems -- Demeter's dilemma, decolonizing research -- Caveat emptor : the "transfer" of technology -- The SNOB theory of underdevelopment -- A knowledge of hunger. ISBN 0-89758-039-7 (pbk.) : LC Card 84-25124 DDC 363.8 19
1. Food supply - Addresses, essays, lectures. 2. Food supply - Government policy - Addresses, essays, lectures. 3. Agriculture and state - Addresses, essays, lectures. 4. Agricultural assistance - Addresses, essays, lectures. 5. Poverty - Addresses, essays, lectures. 6. Agriculture - Research - Developing countries - Addresses, essays, lectures. I. Title.
HD9000.5 .G385 1984
NYPL [JLD 86-3899]

George, Thomas F. Business algebra & mathematics / Thomas F. George. Englewood Cliffs, NJ : Prentice-Hall, c1987. xiv, 634 p. : ill. ; 25 cm. Includes index. ISBN 0-13-091562-9 LC Card 86-30333 DDC 512/.1 19
1. Business mathematics - Problems, exercises, etc. 2. Algebra - Problems, exercises, etc. 3. Business mathematics - Problems, exercises, etc. - Data processing. I. Title. II. Title: Business algebra and mathematics.
HF5694 .G46 1987

George Waldo Woodruff . Wells, Della Wager. [Macon, Ga.] c1987. x, 167 p. : ISBN 0-86554-298-8 LC Card 87-24700 DDC 338/.04/0924 B 19
HC102.5.W66 W45 1987

Georgetown University. Center for Strategic and International Studies. U. S. ASEAN relations . Washington, D.C. , 1987. xxii, 222 p. ; ISBN 0-943057-00-0 (pbk.) LC Card 87-50526 DDC 337.59073 19
HF1456.5.A7 U72 1987

Georgetown University. Continuing Legal Education Division. International trade in textiles & apparel . [Washington, D.C.] , c1987. 1 v. (various foliations) : LC Card 87-404516 DDC 382/.45677/00973 19
HD9850.5 .I43 1987

Georgetown University. Institute for the Study of Diplomacy. The Role of embassies in promoting business . Lanham, MD , 1987, c1981. p. cm. ISBN 0-8191-5053-3 (pbk. : alk. paper) LC Card 87-14027 DDC 382/.3/0973 19
HF1417.5 .R64 1987

Georgetown University, Washington, D.C. Dept. of Government. Order, freedom, and the polity . Lanham, MD [Bryn Mawr, Pa.] , c1986. x, 184 p. ; ISBN 0-8191-5155-6 (alk. paper) : LC Card 85-26438 DDC 323.44 19
JC571 .O77 1986 ***NYPL [JLE 86-3182]***

Georgi, Andreas A. Steuern in der Investitionsplanung : eine Analyse der Entscheidungsrelevanz von Ertrag- und Substanzsteuern / von Andreas A. Georgi. Hamburg : S + W Steuer- und Wirschaftsverlag, 1986. vii, 243, 16, xxviii p. : ill. ; 24 cm. (Schriften zum Steuer-, Rechnungs- und Prüfungswesen . Bd. 2) Originally presented as the author's thesis (doctoral--Technische Hochschule Darmstadt, 1985) under the title: Analyse der Entscheidungsrelevanz von Steuern in der Investitionsplanung. Bibliography: p. xi-xix. Includes index. ISBN 3-89161-702-X LC Card 86-227290
1. Capital investments - Germany (West) - Decision making - Econometric models. 2. Corporations - Taxation - Germany (West) - Econometric models. I. Title. II. Series.
HG4028.C4 G46 1986

Georgia /. Barefoot, John. York, England , c1983. 66 p. : ISBN 0-906845-19-X (pbk.) LC Card 87-100272 DDC 769.5694795 19
HE6185.S653 G463 1983

Georgia State University. Business Administration, College of. see **Georgia State University. College of Business Administration.**

Georgia State University. College of Business Administration. Critical employment issues facing the Southeast /. Atlanta, Ga. , 1986. xv, 156 p. ; ISBN 0-88406-191-4 LC Card 85-31410 DDC 331.12/5/0975 19
HD5725.S85 C75 1986
NYPL [JLD 86-2441]

GEORGIAN S.S.R. - COMMERCE - HISTORY - 19TH CENTURY.
Nac'vlišvili, N. Memamuluri meurneobis kapitalisturi evoluc'ia Aġmosavlet' Sak'art'veloši /. T'bilisi , 1971. 107 p. ; LC Card 86-168887
HC337.G38 N33 1971

Ordzhonikidze, Ė. A. (Ėteri Aleksandrovna) Vačroba da vačart'a p'ena rep'ormamdeli xanis Sak'art'veloši /. T'bilisi , 1974. 158 p. ; LC Card 86-168874
HF3629.G4 O73 1974

GEORGIAN S.S.R. - ECONOMIC CONDITIONS.
Nac'vlišvili, N. Memamuluri meurneobis kapitalisturi evoluc'ia Aġmosavlet' Sak'art'veloši /. T'bilisi , 1971. 107 p. ; LC Card 86-168887
HC337.G38 N33 1971

GEORGIAN S.S.R. - ECONOMIC CONDITIONS - ECONOMETRIC MODELS.
Meskhiia, IA. E. (IAkov Egnatovich) Voprosy metodologii regional'nogo ėkonomicheskogo prognozirovaniia /. Moskva , 1983. 183 p. : LC Card 84-141931
HC337.G38 M43 1983

Georgiev, Georgi Stoianov. Georgiev, IAncho. Strategiia na kachestveni promeni /. Sofiia , 1986- v. <1-2 > ; LC Card 86-232319
HC403 .G465 1986

Georgiev, IAncho. Strategiia na kachestveni promeni / IAncho Georgiev, Georgi Mateev, Georgi St. Georgiev. 1. izd. Sofiia : Partizdat, 1986- v. <1-2 > ; 20 cm. (Za partiinata prosveta) Vol. 2- by Marko Markov ... [et al.] "Trinadeseti kongres na BKP."--Cover. Includes bibliographies. LC Card 86-232319
1. Bulgaria - Economic policy - 1944-. 2. Socialism - Bulgaria. I. Mateev, Georgi. II. Georgiev, Georgi Stoianov. III. Markov, Marko. IV. Title. V. Series.
HC403 .G465 1986

Georgiev, Petŭr Borisov. Katalog na bŭlgarskite poshtenski marki 1979-1984 / [sŭstavitel Petŭr Borisov Georgiev]. 1. izd. Sofiia : Dŭrzhavno izd-vo "Tekhnika", 1985. 119 p. : ill. ; 20 cm. At head of title: Sŭiuz na bŭlgarskite filatelisti. LC

Card 86-112123
1. Postage-stamps - Bulgaria - Catalogs. I. Sŭi̇̂uz na bŭlgarskite filatelisti. II. Title.
HE6185.B82 G47 1985

Georgiev, Slavcho. Ikonomicheski otnosheniia ikonomicheska politika : teoretiko-metodologichni problemi / Slavcho Georgiev. Sofiia : Sofiiski gradski kom-t na Bŭlgarskata komunisticheska partiia : In-t za propaganda na marksizma-leninizma, 1986. 114 p. ; 22 cm. Includes bibliographical references. LC Card 86-209756
1. Bulgaria - Economic policy - 1944-. I. Title.
HC403 .G47 1986

GEOSCIENCE. see **GEOLOGY.**

Geotécnica S.A. Estudos de viabilidade técnica da implantação e plano diretor do distrito industrial de Mossoró . [Natal] , 1979. ca. 250 leaves, 8 folded leaves of plates : LC Card 84-256137
HC189.M6 E86 1979

GEOTEXTILES.
Geotextiles, geomembranes, geomatrices . Stamford, Conn., U. S.A. , c1986. xii, 133 leaves : ISBN 0-89336-496-7 (pbk.) LC Card 87-403913 DDC 668.9 19
HD9869.I533 U64 1986

Geotextiles, geomembranes, geomatrices : newmarkets [sic] and technologies / Anna W. Crull, project analyst. Stamford, Conn., U. S.A. : Business Communications Co., c1986. xii, 133 leaves : ill. ; 29 cm. (Business opportunity report . P-086) "June 1986"--T.p. verso. ISBN 0-89336-496-7 (pbk.) LC Card 87-403913 DDC 668.9 19
1. Industrial fabrics industry - United States. 2. Geotextiles. 3. Geomembranes. 4. Geogrids. I. Crull, Anna W. II. Business Communications Co. III. Series.
HD9869.I533 U64 1986

Geowissenschefter und Rohstoffe, Bundesanstalt für. see **Bundesanstalt für Geowissenschaften und Rohstoffe.**

Gepts, Stefaan J. Valuation and selection of convertible bonds : based on modern option theory / Stefaan J. Gepts. New York, NY : Praeger, 1987. xiii, 177 p. : ill. ; 22 cm. Bibliography: p. 171. Includes index. ISBN 0-275-92466-1 (alk. paper) : LC Card 87-14606 DDC 332.63/23 19
1. Convertible bonds. I. Title.
HG4651 .G46 1987

Gerardi, Ricardo E. El impacto de la crisis en los esquemas de integración / Ricardo E. Gerardi. [Buenos Aires, Argentina] : Banco Interamericano de Desarrollo, Instituto para la Integración de América Latina, 1985 [i.e. 1986] iii, 52, [26] leaves : ill. ; 29 cm. Includes bibliographical references. LC Card 87-125394 DDC 337.1/8 19
1. Latin America - Economic integration. 2. Latin America - Economic conditions - 1945-. I. Title.
HC125 .G465 1986

Gerashchenko, V. S. (Vladimir Sergeevich) Denezhnoe obrashchenie i kredit SSSR /. Moskva , 1986. 374 p. : LC Card 87-157773
HG3729.S632 D46 1986

Gerasimchuk, Nikolaĭ Semenovich. Rekomendatsii po ukrepleniiu trudovoĭ i proizvodstvennoĭ distsipliny /. Kiev , 1984. 41 p. ; LC Card 86-181301
HF5549.5.L3 R45 1984

Gerasimova, N. P. Ėffektivnost′ proizvodstva v agropromyshlennom komplekse Chuvashskoĭ ASSR /. Cheboksary , 1985. 198 p. ; LC Card 86-203897
HD9015.S653 C483 1985

Gerber, Quentin N., 1930- Wolk, Harry I. Management accounting . Boston, Mass. , c1988. xiii, 754 p. : ISBN 0-534-07050-7 : LC Card 87-7348 DDC 658.1/511 19
HF5657.4 .W64 1988

Gerberding, Axel. Jungnickel, Rolf. Investitionsbedingungen in der ASEAN-Region /. Hamburg , 1986. 346 p. : ISBN 3-87895-296-1 LC Card 86-192978
HG5740.8.A3 J85 1986

Gerberg, Robert J.
[Job changing system]
Robert Gerberg's job changing system : world's fastest way to get a better job / Robert J. Gerberg.14th ed. Kansas City : Andrews, McMeel & Parker, c1986. xxii, 265 p. : forms ; 22 cm. Rev. ed. of: The professional job changing system / by Robert J. Jameson. 4th ed. 1975. Includes index. ISBN 0-8362-7932-8 : LC Card 86-17298 DDC 650.1/4 19
1. Job hunting. 2. Employment interviewing. 3. Career changes. I. Jameson, Robert, 1938- Professional job changing system. II. Title. III. Title: Job changing system. ***NYPL [JD 87-125]***

Gerelli, Emilio. La Crisi delle partecipazioni statali, motivi e prospettive /. Milano , c1981. 240 p. ; ISBN 88-20-42148-8 : LC Card 81-200055
HC310.I53 C74 1981 ***NYPL [JLD 86-3503]***

Gerenstein, Grigori. Jones, Geoffrey. The history of the British Bank of the Middle East /. Cambridge [Cambridgeshire] , New York , 1986- v. : ISBN 0-521-32322-3 (v. 1) LC Card 85-31359 DDC 332.1/5/0955 19
HG3270.2.A8 B755 1986 ***NYPL [JLL 87-87]***

Gergely, Ernő. A Bányaipari Dolgozók Szakszervezetének története / Gergely Ernő. 2., bőv. kiad. [Budapest] : Bányaipari Dolgozók Szakszervezete, 1983. 218 p. ; 21 cm. Bibliography: p. 213-215. ISBN 963-00-0667-7 (Magy. nemz. bibl.) LC Card 85-109054
1. Bányaipari Dolgozók Szakszervezete - History. 2. Trade-unions - Miners - Hungary - History. I. Title.
HD6680.5.Z7 M6113 1983

Gergely, Stefan M.
Lebensmittel- und Agrarwissenschaften / von Stefan M. Gergely. Wien : H. Böhlau, 1983. iii, 317 p. ; 21 cm. (Fachinformationsführer . 3) Bibliography: p. 289-292. Includes index. ISBN 3-205-06103-9 LC Card 87-407964 DDC 338.1/9/4360285 19
1. Food supply - Information services - Austria - Directories. 2. Agriculture - Information services - Austria - Directories. I. Title. II. Series.
HD9015.A8 G47 1983

Wirtschaftswissenschaften / von Stefan M. Gergely, Herbert Pinzolits und Oliver M. Dworak. Wien : Böhlau, 1985. 170 p. ; 21 cm. (Fachinformationsführer . 8) At head of title: Bundesministerium für Wissenschaft und Forschung. Includes bibliographical references and index. ISBN 3-205-06108-X LC Card 85-229521
1. Economics - Research - Austria - Directories. I. Pinzolits, Herbert. II. Dworak, Oliver M. III. Austria. Bundesministerium für Wissenschaft und Forschung. IV. Title. V. Series.
HB74.9.A9 G47 1985

Gerhardt, Gisela, 1955- Konsumverhalten und wirtschaftliche Entwicklung : der Beitrag des Konzeptes der Anspruchsniveaus / Gisela Gerhardt. München : V. Florentz, c1984. 224 p. : 6 ill. ; 21 cm. (Volkswirtschaftliche Forschung und Entwicklung . Bd. 8) Bibliography: p. 212-221. Includes index. ISBN 3-88259-278-8 LC Card 84-220049
1. Consumers - Econometric models. 2. Economic development - Econometric models. I. Title. II. Series.
HC79.C6 G47 1984

Gerhardt, Jürgen. Dienstleistungsproduktion : eine produktionstheoretische Analyse der Dienstleistungsprozesse / Jürgen Gerhardt. Bergisch Gladbach : J. Eul, c1987. 251 p. ; 21 cm. Originally presented as the author's thesis (doctoral)--Universität-Gesamthochschule Siegen, 1986. Bibliography: p. 222-251. ISBN 3-89012-075-X LC Card 87-141416 DDC 338.4/6 19
1. Service industries. 2. Productivity accounting. I. Title.
HD9980.5 .G46 1987

Gerhart, Paul F. Saving plants and jobs : union-management negotiations in the context of threatened plant closing / by Paul F. Gerhart. Kalamazoo, MI : W.E. Upjohn Institute for Employment Research, 1987. vii, 109 p. ; 23 cm. Includes bibliographies. ISBN 0-88099-047-3 LC Card 87-10527 DDC 331.89/15 19
1. Plant shutdowns. I. Title.
HD5708.5 .G47 1987

GERIATRIC NURSING - UNITED STATES - EQUIPMENT AND SUPPLIES.
Geriatrics OTC health aid and toiletries products market-U. S. New York, N.Y. , c1983. 2 v. (viii, 352 leaves) ; LC Card 87-144078 DDC 381/.456151/0973 19
HD9666.5 .G47 1983

Geriatrics OTC health aid and toiletries products market-U. S. New York, N.Y. : Frost & Sullivan, c1983. 2 v. (viii, 352 leaves) ; 29 cm. "#A946." "October 1983." LC Card 87-144078 DDC 381/.456151/0973 19
1. Nonprescription drug industry - United States. 2. Toilet preparations industry - United States. 3. Geriatric nursing - United States - Equipment and supplies. 4. Market surveys - United States. I. Frost & Sullivan.
HD9666.5 .G47 1983

Geringer, G. F. Coetzee, S. F. Regional economic development in the Southern African development area /. Sandton, Republic of South Africa , 1985. xvi, 105 p. : LC Card 87-150264 DDC 338.968 19
HC905 .C64 1985

Gerke, Wolfgang. Mannheimer Bankenforum (1985) Risikokapital über die Börse . Berlin , New York , c1986. x, 190 p. ; ISBN 0-387-16671-8 (U. S.) LC Card 86-225903
HG5492 .M35 1985

Gerken, Egbert. Auf dem Wege zu einer Theorie der internationalen Koordination der Agrarpolitik / von Egbert Gerken. Kiel : Institut für Weltwirtschaft an der Universität Kiel, [1985] 29 p. : ill. ; 30 cm. (Kieler Arbeitspapiere, 0342-0787 = Kiel working papers . Arbeitspapier Nr. 229) "März 1985." Bibliography: p. 20-29. LC Card 85-203925
1. Agriculture and state - International cooperation. I. Series: Kieler Arbeitspapiere , Arbeitspapier Nr. 229. II. Title.
HD1415 .G395 1985

GERLOFF, WILHELM.
Höltz, Joachim. Kritik der Geldentstehungstheorien . Berlin , c1984. ii, 401 p. ; ISBN 3-496-00796-6 LC Card 85-147094
HG237 .H64 1984

GERMAN AMERICANS - EMPLOYMENT - ILLINOIS - CHICAGO - HISTORY - SOURCES.
German workers in Chicago . Urbana , c1988. p. cm. ISBN 0-252-01458-8 (alk. paper) LC Card 87-10780 DDC 331.6/2/43077311 19
HD8081.G4 G46 1988

GERMAN AMERICANS - HISTORY.
Rapone, Anita. The Guardian Life Insurance Company, 1860-1920 . New York , c1987. xiv, 209 p., [10] p. of plates : ISBN 0-8147-7401-6 : LC Card 87-7913 DDC 368.3/2/0068 19
HG8963.G942 R36 1987

GERMAN AMERICANS - ILLINOIS - CHICAGO - HISTORY - SOURCES.
German workers in Chicago . Urbana , c1988. p. cm. ISBN 0-252-01458-8 (alk. paper) LC Card 87-10780 DDC 331.6/2/43077311 19
HD8081.G4 G46 1988

GERMAN AMERICANS - ILLINOIS - CHICAGO - SOCIAL CONDITIONS - SOURCES.
German workers in Chicago . Urbana , c1988. p. cm. ISBN 0-252-01458-8 (alk. paper) LC Card 87-10780 DDC 331.6/2/43077311 19
HD8081.G4 G46 1988

GERMAN AMERICANS - ILLINOIS - CHICAGO - SOCIAL LIFE AND CUSTOMS - SOURCES.
German workers in Chicago . Urbana , c1988. p. cm. ISBN 0-252-01458-8 (alk. paper) LC Card 87-10780 DDC 331.6/2/43077311 19
HD8081.G4 G46 1988

GERMAN AMERICANS - UNITED STATES. see **GERMAN AMERICANS.**

German Development Institute. see **Deutsches Institut für Entwicklungspolitik.**

German Foundation for Developing Countries. see **Deutsche Stiftung für Entwicklungsländer.**

German Historical Institute in London. Publications. see **German Historical Institute in London. Veröffentlichungen.**

Veröffentlichungen.
(Bd. 17) Wengenroth, Ulrich. Unternehmensstrategien und technischer Fortschritt . Göttingen , c1986. 316 p. : ISBN 3-525-36302-8 ***NYPL [JLE 87-917]***

German historical perspectives .
(1) Population, labour, and migration in 19th- and 20th-century Germany /. Leamington Spa [UK] ; New York : xii, 200 p. : ISBN 0-85496-503-3 : LC Card 86-24470 DDC

331.6/2/0943 19
HD5856.G3 P66 1987

(2) Wealth and taxation in Central Europe . Leamington Spa, UK ; New York, N.Y., USA : 162 p. ; ISBN 0-85496-523-8 : LC Card 86-24490 DDC 336.43 19
HJ1000 .W4 1987

German Institute for Business Research, Berlin. see **Berlin. Deutsches Institut für Wirtschaftsforschung.**

GERMAN LANGUAGE - BUSINESS GERMAN - HANDBOOKS, MANUALS, ETC.

Roessler, Helmut R. Deutsche Geschäftskorrespondenz . Lanham, MD , c1987. xii, 218 p. : ISBN 0-8191-6277-9 (alk. paper) : LC Card 87-6086 DDC 658.4/53 19
HF5728.G3 R64 1987

GERMAN LANGUAGE - DICTIONARIES - ENGLISH.

Betteridge, Harold T. Cassell's German-English, English-German dictionary =. New York , 1978. xx, 1580 p. ; ISBN 0-02-522920-6 (standard) LC Card 77-18452 DDC 433/.21 19
PF3640 .B453 1978 ***NYPL [*P-Desk 86-5858]***

Böhss, Günther. Dictionary of printed circuit technology . Amsterdam , New York , 1985. 187 p. ; ISBN 0-444-99555-2 (U. S.) : LC Card 85-12955 DDC 621.381/74/0331 19
TK7868.P7 B65 1985 ***NYPL [JSD 86-621]***

Collins English-German dictionary =. London , Stuttgart , 1986, c1983. 2 v. (xviii, 1390, xxiii, 1380 p.) ; ISBN 3-12-517131-8 (v. 1) ***NYPL [JFC 86-2613]***

Dietl, Clara-Erika. Commercial dictionary . Wiesbaden , c1985-c1987. 2 v. ; ISBN 3-409-19900-4 (v. 1) LC Card 86-160868
HF1002 .D493 1985 ***NYPL [*R-Econ. 87-1271]***

Eichborn, Reinhart von. Wirtschaftswörterbuch. Düsseldorf, Wien [1961-70] 2 v. LC Card 70-463836 ***NYPL [JLD 85-120]***

Klatt, Edmund. Langenscheidt's standard German dictionary /. New York , 1983-1984. 1341 p. ; ***NYPL [JFC 86-781]***

Kleiber, Achim W. Fachwörterbuch, Schweissen, Schneiden und verwandte Verfahren /. Düsseldorf , 1986- , c1985- v. ; ISBN 3-87155-707-2 (Bd. 1) LC Card 86-149500 DDC 671.5/2/0331 19
TS227.5 .K54 1986 ***NYPL [JSK 86-83]***

Roessler, Helmut R. Deutsche Geschäftskorrespondenz . Lanham, MD , c1987. xii, 218 p. : ISBN 0-8191-6277-9 (alk. paper) : LC Card 87-6086 DDC 658.4/53 19
HF5728.G3 R64 1987

Schäfer, Wilhelm, Dr. Wirtschaftswörterbuch /. München , c1986- v. <1 > ; ISBN 3-8006-1100-7 (Bd. 1) LC Card 86-214220
HB61 .S3 1986

Strutz, Henry. Talking business in German . Woodbury, N.Y. , c1987. iv, 256 p. : ISBN 0-8120-3747-2 (pbk.) LC Card 86-22360 DDC 650/.03/31 19
HF1002 .S79 1987

GERMAN LANGUAGE - DICTIONARIES - FRENCH.

EG-Wörterverzeichnis . Luxembourg , 1984. 1 v. (various pagings) ; ISBN 92-824-0123-5 LC Card 85-131398
KJE926.5 .E35 1984 ***NYPL [JLF 86-1818]***

GERMAN LANGUAGE - DICTIONARIES - GREEK.

Siderēs, Euthymios G., 1957- Germanoellēniko lexiko horologias /. Athēna , 1984. 183 p. ; LC Card 86-180116
HD4839 .S56 1984

GERMAN LANGUAGE - DICTIONARIES - POLYGLOT.

Brodmeier, Beate. Entwicklungspolitische Fachausdrücke (Auswahl) . Baden-Baden , 1985. 48 p. ; ISBN 3-7890-1093-6 LC Card 85-186152
HD84 .B765 1985

Schramm, Herbert F. W. Burghagen Fachwörterbuch . Hamburg , c1964. 160 p. ; LC Card 84-256680
HF5548 .S37 1964

German Marshall Fund of the United States. Miller, Mark J. Employer sanctions in Western Europe /. Staten Island, N.Y. , 1987. viii, 67 p. ; ISBN 0-934733-20-1 (pbk.) : LC Card 86-31739 DDC 331.6/2/094 19
HD8378.5.A2 M5395 1987

GERMAN PROPAGANDA. see **PROPAGANDA, GERMAN.**

German, Rachel. DeGroh, Teresa. Standards for self-service storage facilities /. Chicago, IL (1313 E. 60th St., Chicago 60637) , c1986. 22 p. : LC Card 86-227124 DDC 658.7/85 19
HF5487 .D44 1986

GERMAN RESISTANCE MOVEMENT. see **ANTI-NAZI MOVEMENT.**

German Society for East European Affairs. see **Deutsche Gesellschaft für Osteuropakunde.**

German Southwest Africa. see **Namibia.**

The German unemployed : experiences and consequences of mass unemployment from the Weimar Republic to the Third Reich / edited by Richard J. Evans and Dick Geary. Beckenham, Kent : Croom Helm, 1987. xviii, 314 p. : ill. ; 23 cm. Includes bibliographical references and index. ISBN 0-7099-0941-1
1. Unemployed - Germany - History - 20th century. 2. Unemployment - Germany - History - 20th century. 3. Germany - Economic conditions - 1918-1945. I. Evans, Richard J. II. Geary, Dick. ***NYPL [JLD 87-801]***

German white-collar workers and the rise of Hitler /. Speier, Hans. New Haven , 1986. xv, 208 p. ; ISBN 0-300-03701-5 LC Card 86-9120 DDC 331.7/92/0943 19
HD8039.M4 G3639413 1986 ***NYPL [JLE 87-909]***

The German worker : working-class autobiographies from the age of industrialization / translated, edited, and with an introduction by Alfred Kelly. Berkeley : University of California Press, c1987. p. cm. Includes index. ISBN 0-520-05972-7 (alk. paper) LC Card 87-5076 DDC 305.5/62/0922 B 19
1. Labor and laboring classes - Germany - Biography. 2. Labor and laboring classes - Germany - History - 19th century. 3. Proletariat - History. 4. Germany - Economic conditions - 19th century. 5. Germany - Social conditions. I. Kelly, Alfred, 1947-.
HD8453.A1 G47 1987

German workers in Chicago : a documentary history of working class culture from 1850 to World War I / edited by Hartmut Keil and John B. Jentz with the assistance of Klaus Ensslen ... [et al] ; documents translated by Burt Weinshanker. Urbana : University of Illinois Press, c1988. p. cm. (The Working class in American history) "This anthology of documents ... resulting from the work of the Chicago Project on the social history of German workers from 1850 to 1910"--Pref. Bibliography: p. Includes index. ISBN 0-252-01458-8 (alk. paper) LC Card 87-10780 DDC 331.6/2/43077311 19
1. German Americans - Employment - Illinois - Chicago - History - Sources. 2. Labor and laboring classes - Illinois - Chicago - History - Sources. 3. German Americans - Illinois - Chicago - Social life and customs - Sources. 4. German Americans - Illinois - Chicago - Social conditions - Sources. 5. German Americans - Illinois - Chicago - History - Sources. I. Keil, Hartmut, 1942-. II. Jentz, John B., 1944-. III. Chicago Project (Universität München).
HD8081.G4 G46 1988

GERMANI, ARISTIDES, B. 1863.

Campos Netto, José Candido de, 1880-1963. O cavvaliere Aristides Germani /. [Caxias do Sul, Brazil] [Porto Alegre] , 1978. 111 p. : LC Card 79-121861
HD9056.B62 C35 1978 ***NYPL [JLD 81-342]***

GERMANIZATION.

Kremer, Manfred. Assimilation ausländischer Arbeitnehmer in der Bundesrepublik Deutschland . Königstein/Ts. , 1980. 203, 64 p. ; ISBN 3-7756-6934-5 LC Card 80-151671 DDC 303.4/8243 19
HD8458.A2 K73 1980 ***NYPL [JLD 86-2549]***

Germanoellēniko lexiko horologias /. Siderēs, Euthymios G., 1957- Athēna , 1984. 183 p. ; LC Card 86-180116
HD4839 .S56 1984

GERMANS - NAMIBIA - HISTORY - 19TH CENTURY.

Phillips, John A. S. Deutsch-englische Komödie der Irrungen um Südwestafrika . Pfaffenhofen, West Germany , 1986. 184 p., [12] p. of plates : ISBN 3-87010-105-9 LC Card 87-146587 DDC 338.4/76686366/09688 19
HD9484.G9 N366 1986

GERMANS - ROMANIA - HISTORY - 20TH CENTURY.

Kampf und Arbeit . Kronstadt , 1936. 102 p., [1] leaf of plates : LC Card 84-255742
HD7290 .K35 1936

Germanskiĭ trudovoĭ front : sushchnost'--tsel'-put'. Berlin : Izdatel' Nauch. in-t truda Germanskogo trudovogo fronta, 1943. 69 leaves : ill. ; 21 cm. LC Card 85-204295
1. Deutsche Arbeitsfront. 2. Labor and laboring classes - Germany. 3. Germany - Politics and government - 1933-1945. I. Deutsche Arbeitsfront. Arbeitswissenschaftliches Institut.
HD8443.D43 G47 1943

GERMANY - CENSUS, 1939.

Aly, Götz, 1947- Die restlose Erfassung . Berlin , c1984. 157 p. : ISBN 3-88022-282-7 : LC Card 84-206488
HA37.G3 A49 1984

GERMANY - COMMERCE - GREAT BRITAIN.

Ohlsen, Ralph-Rainer, 1955- Der deutsche Export nach Grossbritannien von 1923 bis 1933 . Bergisch Gladbach , c1986. ii, 256 p. : ISBN 3-89012-043-1 LC Card 86-160346
HF1546.5.G7 O37 1986

GERMANY - COMMERCE - HISTORY - CROATIA.

Sundhaussen, Holm. Wirtschaftsgeschichte Kroatiens im nationalsozialistischen Grossraum 1941-1945 . Stuttgart , 1983. 386 p. : ISBN 3-421-06150-5 LC Card 83-242921
HC407.Z7 C7678 1983

GERMANY - COMMERCE - JAPAN - HISTORY.

Barth, Johannes, 1891- Als deutscher Kaufmann in Fernost . Berlin , c1984. 206 p. : ISBN 3-503-02366-6 LC Card 84-143117
HC289.B7 B373 1984

GERMANY - COMMERCE - STATISTICS.

Rau, Heinrich. Vergleichende Statistik des Handels der deutschen Staaten /. Wien , 1863. vii, 183 p. ; LC Card 85-217948
HF3561.5 .R38 1863

GERMANY (EAST) - COMMERCE - AUSTRIA.

Marwege, Ulf, 1954- Neuorientierung im Westhandel der DDR? . Bonn , c1984. iv, 122 p. : ISBN 3-7713-0221-8 : LC Card 84-196602
HF3570.5.Z7 G75 1984

GERMANY (EAST) - COMMERCE - CONGRESSES.

Aussenwirtschaft der DDR und innerdeutsche Wirtschaftsbeziehungen . Berlin , c1986. 98 p. ; ISBN 3-428-06121-7 LC Card 87-137949 DDC 382/.0943/0431 19
HF3570.5.Z7 G352 1986

GERMANY (EAST) - COMMERCE - FRANCE.

Marwege, Ulf, 1954- Neuorientierung im Westhandel der DDR? . Bonn , c1984. iv, 122 p. : ISBN 3-7713-0221-8 : LC Card 84-196602
HF3570.5.Z7 G75 1984

GERMANY, EAST - COMMERCE - GERMANY, WEST.

Marwege, Ulf, 1954- Neuorientierung im Westhandel der DDR? . Bonn , c1984. iv, 122 p. : ISBN 3-7713-0221-8 : LC Card 84-196602
HF3570.5.Z7 G75 1984

GERMANY (EAST) - COMMERCE - GERMANY (WEST) - CONGRESSES.

Aussenwirtschaft der DDR und innerdeutsche Wirtschaftsbeziehungen . Berlin , c1986. 98 p. ; ISBN 3-428-06121-7 LC Card 87-137949 DDC 382/.0943/0431 19
HF3570.5.Z7 G352 1986

GERMANY (EAST) - COMMERCE - JAPAN.

Marwege, Ulf, 1954- Neuorientierung im Westhandel der DDR? . Bonn , c1984. iv, 122 p. : ISBN 3-7713-0221-8 : LC Card 84-196602
HF3570.5.Z7 G75 1984

GERMANY (EAST) - COMMERCIAL POLICY.

Bel'chikov, ÎA. M. Upravlenie sot͡sialisticheskoĭ torgovleĭ . Riga , 1978. 170, [2] p. ; LC Card

82-106625
HF2546.5 .B44 1978

GERMANY, EAST - ECONOMIC CONDITIONS.
Der Alltag in der DDR /. Bonn , c1984. 58 p. ; LC Card 86-170731
HC290.78 .A46 1984

The East German economy /. London , New York , c1987. 328 p. : ISBN 0-7099-1469-5 LC Card 87-17163 DDC 338.9431 19
HC290.78 .E23 1987

Effektivität und Reproduktion . Berlin , c1985. 148 p. ; LC Card 86-166628
HC290.78 .E365 1985

Florath, Walter, 1925- Der Typ ist richtig . Berlin , c1986. 151 p. : ISBN 3-355-00005-1 LC Card 86-230122
HC290.78 .F57 1986

Mitteilung der Staatlichen Zentralverwaltung für Statistik der DDR über die Durchführung des Volkswirtschaftsplanes 1982. Berlin , 1983. 46 p. ; LC Card 85-145182
HC290.78 .M58 1983

30 Jahre DDR und das Fiasko imperialistischer Prognosen, Pläne und Propheten . [Berlin] , 1979. 40 p. ; LC Card 83-198579
HC290.78 .A14 1979

GERMANY, EAST - ECONOMIC POLICY.
Auf sicherem Kurs . [Berlin] [1976] 80 leaves (some folded) : LC Card 85-190579
HC290.78 .A84 1976

The East German economy /. London , New York , c1987. 328 p. : ISBN 0-7099-1469-5 LC Card 87-17163 DDC 338.9431 19
HC290.78 .E23 1987

Effektivität und Reproduktion . Berlin , c1985. 148 p. ; LC Card 86-166628
HC290.78 .E365 1985

Florath, Walter, 1925- Der Typ ist richtig . Berlin , c1986. 151 p. : ISBN 3-355-00005-1 LC Card 86-230122
HC290.78 .F57 1986

Im Blickpunkt der Leistungsvergleich /. Berlin , 1985. 126 p. ; LC Card 85-155570
HC270.28 .I56 1985

Innovation und Wissenschaft . Berlin , 1985. 328 p. : LC Card 86-121669
HC290.795.T4 I56 1985

Koziolek, Helmut. Umfassende Intensivierung und Infrastruktur /. Berlin , 1986. 68 p. ; LC Card 86-169897
HC290.795.C3 K68 1986

Mit qualitativ neuen Schritten zu höchsten Leistungen . Berlin , 1986. 80 p. ; ISBN 3-320-00807-2 LC Card 87-144292 DDC 338.9431 19
HC290.78 .M567 1986

Mitteilung der Staatlichen Zentralverwaltung für Statistik der DDR über die Durchführung des Volkswirtschaftsplanes 1982. Berlin , 1983. 46 p. ; LC Card 85-145182
HC290.78 .M58 1983

Ökonomische Strategie und Vervollkommnung der staatlichen Leitung /. Potsdam-Babelsberg , 1983. 64 p. ; LC Card 84-180104
HC290.78 .O387 1983

Otto, Wolfgang, Diplom-Staatswissenschaftler. Ökonomische Strategie und volkswirtschaftliche Masseninitiative /. Berlin , 1984. 61 p. : LC Card 85-189271
HC290.78 .O88 1984

Produktion, Intensivierung, Effektivität /. Jena , 1978. 180 p. : LC Card 85-183724
HC290.795.I52 P75 1978

Reinhold, Otto. Mehr, besser, billiger, aber wie? /. Berlin , 1985. 80 p. : LC Card 86-179312
HD70.G22 R45 1985

Roesler, Jörg. Wirtschaftswachstum in der Industrie der DDR, 1945-1970 /. Berlin , 1986. 280 p. ; ISBN 3-05-000074-0 LC Card 86-196020
HC290.78 .R64 1986

Die Verantwortung der örtlichen Staatsorgane für die planmässige Entwicklung und die effektive Inanspruchnahme von Leistungen der technischen Infrastruktur /. Potsdam-Babelsberg , 1986. 57 p. ; LC Card 87-407347 DDC 363/.09431 19
HC290.795.C3 V47 1986

Waterkamp, Rainer. Das zentralstaatliche Planungssystem der DDR . Berlin , c1983. 194 p. : ISBN 3-428-05405-9 LC Card 83-217231
HC290.78 .W38 1983

GERMANY EAST - ECONOMIC POLICY - CONGRESSES.
Kolloquium 20 Jahre Weiterbildungs- und Forschungsarbeit (1987 : Leipzig, Germany) Kolloquium 20 Jahre Weiterbildungs- und Forschungsarbeit . [Leipzig] , 1986. 64 p. ; LC Card 87-408852 DDC 338.9431 19
HC290.78 .K64 1987

Ökonomische Strategie der 80er Jahre und Effektivität des Wirtschaftsrechts /. Berlin , 1984. 48 p. ; LC Card 84-159925
HC290.78 .O36 1984

Die Sozialistische Gemeinschaftsarbeit im Territorium . Potsdam-Babelsberg , 1986. 175 p. ; LC Card 86-212526
HD3616.G48 S68 1986

GERMANY (EAST) - ECONOMIC POLICY - ECONOMETRIC MODELS.
Collier, Irwin L., 1951- Connections, effective purchasing power, and real product in the German Democratic Republic /. Berlin , 1985. ix, 216 p. : ISBN 3-921374-34-0 (pbk.) LC Card 86-229298 DDC 330 s 338.9431/00724 19
HC244.A1 B4 Nr. 44 HC290.78

GERMANY (EAST) - FOREIGN RELATIONS - COMMUNIST COUNTRIES.
Die DDR in der Welt des Sozialismus /. Berlin , 1985. 237 p. ; LC Card 85-188821 DDC 335.43/09431 19
HX280.5.A6 D38 1985 ***NYPL [JLD 87-1167]***

GERMANY, EAST - INDUSTRIES.
Auf sicherem Kurs . [Berlin] [1976] 80 leaves (some folded) : LC Card 85-190579
HC290.78 .A84 1976

Mitteilung der Staatlichen Zentralverwaltung für Statistik der DDR über die Durchführung des Volkswirtschaftsplanes 1982. Berlin , 1983. 46 p. ; LC Card 85-145182
HC290.78 .M58 1983

Reinhold, Otto. Mehr, besser, billiger, aber wie? /. Berlin , 1985. 80 p. : LC Card 86-179312
HD70.G22 R45 1985

Volchenko, M. I͡A. (Maĭa I͡Akovlevna) Promyshlennostʹ GDR . Moskva , 1981. 179 p. ; LC Card 82-115880
HC290.74 .V63 1981

GERMANY (EAST) - INDUSTRIES - HISTORY.
Roesler, Jörg. Wirtschaftswachstum in der Industrie der DDR, 1945-1970 /. Berlin , 1986. 280 p. ; ISBN 3-05-000074-0 LC Card 86-196020
HC290.78 .R64 1986

GERMANY, EAST - POPULATION.
Koziolek, Helmut. Reproduktion und Infrastruktur /. Berlin , c1986. 224 p. : ISBN 3-349-00017-7 LC Card 87-130782 DDC 363/.09431 19
HC290.795.C3 K675 1986

GERMANY, EAST - SOCIAL CONDITIONS.
Der Alltag in der DDR /. Bonn , c1984. 58 p. ; LC Card 86-170731
HC290.78 .A46 1984

30 Jahre DDR und das Fiasko imperialistischer Prognosen, Pläne und Propheten . [Berlin] , 1979. 40 p. ; LC Card 83-198579
HC290.78 .A14 1979

Germany (East). Staatliche Zentralverwaltung für Statistik.
Mitteilung der Staatlichen Zentralverwaltung für Statistik der DDR über die Durchführung des Volkswirtschaftsplanes 1982. Berlin , 1983. 46 p. ; LC Card 85-145182
HC290.78 .M58 1983

Germany (East). Staatliche Zentralverwaltung für Statistik. Bezirksstelle Halle. Volks- und Berufszählung am 31. Dezember 1964 . [Halle] , 1966. 60 p. ; LC Card 85-123405
HA1347.H34 V64 1966

GERMANY - ECONOMIC CONDITIONS - 19TH CENTURY.
Born, Karl Erich. Wirtschafts- und Sozialgeschichte des Deutschen Kaiserreichs (1867/71-1914) /. Stuttgart , 1985. 175 p. ; ISBN 3-515-02419-0 LC Card 85-168335
HC285 .B66 1985

The German worker . Berkeley , c1987. p. cm. ISBN 0-520-05972-7 (alk. paper) LC Card 87-5076 DDC 305.5/62/0922 B 19
HD8453.A1 G47 1987

Kocka, Jürgen. Lohnarbeit und Klassenbildung . Berlin , c1983. 207 p. ; ISBN 3-8012-0088-4 LC Card 83-169041
HD8449 .K63 1983

Simon, Manfred. Handwerk in Krise und Umbruch . Köln , 1983. xvii, 652 p. : ISBN 3-412-02983-1 : LC Card 83-221725 DDC 322/.2/0943 19
HD2346.G3 S47 1983

Spilker, Ernst Moritz. Der Wirtschaftsraum zwischen den Wirtschaftsräumen . Köln , 1986. 223 p. : LC Card 87-408201 DDC 330.943/55 19
HC288.W46 S67 1986

GERMANY - ECONOMIC CONDITIONS - 1888-1918.
Born, Karl Erich. Wirtschafts- und Sozialgeschichte des Deutschen Kaiserreichs (1867/71-1914) /. Stuttgart , 1985. 175 p. ; ISBN 3-515-02419-0 LC Card 85-168335
HC285 .B66 1985

Horlacher, Michael. Der Wiederaufbau der deutschen Volkswirtschaft . Diessen vor München , 1919. 118 p. ; LC Card 87-409517 DDC 338.943 19
HC286.2 .H67 1919

GERMANY - ECONOMIC CONDITIONS - 20TH CENTURY.
Feldman, Gerald D. Vom Weltkrieg zur Weltwirtschaftskrise . Göttingen , 1984. 272 p. ; ISBN 3-525-35719-2 LC Card 85-165291
HC286.2 .F45 1984

GERMANY - ECONOMIC CONDITIONS - 1918-1945.
Ambrosius, Gerold. Die öffentliche Wirtschaft in der Weimarer Republik . Baden-Baden , 1984. 306 p. ; ISBN 3-7890-0912-1 LC Card 84-230508
HD4175 .A626 1984

Flaskamp, Jürgen, 1958- Aufgaben und Wirkungen der Reichsbank in der Zeit des Dawes-Planes /. Bergisch Gladbach , c1986. 210 p. : ISBN 3-89012-060-1 LC Card 87-108166 DDC 332.1/1/0943 19
HG3054 .F58 1986

The German unemployed . Beckenham, Kent , 1987. xviii, 314 p. : ISBN 0-7099-0941-1 ***NYPL [JLD 87-801]***

Lindenlaub, Dieter. Maschinenbauunternehmen in der Deutschen Inflation 1919-1923 . Berlin , New York , 1985. xiii, 262 p. ; ISBN 3-11-009934-9 LC Card 85-214738
HG999 .L75 1985

McNeil, William C. American money and the Weimar Republic . New York , 1986. x, 352 p. : ISBN 0-231-06236-2 LC Card 85-29962 DDC 336.3/4/0943 19
HG3949 .M38 1986 ***NYPL [JLE 86-3268]***

Die Weimarer Republik als Wohlfahrtsstaat . Stuttgart , 1987. 337 p. ; ISBN 3-515-04738-7 LC Card 87-131861 DDC 338.943 19
HC286.3 .W3546 1987

GERMANY - ECONOMIC CONDITIONS - 1945-
Wirtschaftspolitik im britischen Besatzungsgebiet 1945-1949 /. Düsseldorf , 1984. 338 p. : ISBN 3-590-18124-9 LC Card 84-188669
HC286.5 .W5655 1984

GERMANY - ECONOMIC CONDITIONS - EXHIBITIONS.
Zeugnisse der Zeit . Bonn , 1986. 113 p. : LC Card 87-408186
HD2429.G3 Z48 1986

GERMANY - ECONOMIC CONDITIONS - SOURCES.
Quellen zur deutschen Wirtschafts- und Sozialgeschichte von der Reichsgründung bis zum ersten Weltkrieg /. Darmstadt , 1985. xviii, 553 p. : ISBN 3-534-07561-7 LC Card 85-229315
HC285 .Q45 1985

GERMANY - ECONOMIC CONDITIONS - STATISTICAL METHODS - STUDY AND TEACHING - CONGRESSES.
Beiträge zur quantitativen vergleichenden Unternehmensgeschichte /. Stuttgart , c1985. 206 p. : ISBN 3-608-91325-4 LC Card 85-233589
HD2734 .B32 1985

GERMANY - ECONOMIC POLICY.
Feldman, Gerald D. Vom Weltkrieg zur Weltwirtschaftskrise . Göttingen , 1984. 272 p. ; ISBN 3-525-35719-2 LC Card 85-165291
HC286.2 .F45 1984

Sondermann, Klaus. Wirtschaftsentwicklung und landwirtschaftliche Verbandspolitik . Münster-Hiltrup , 1983. vi, 300 p. : ISBN 3-7843-0283-1 : LC Card 84-126226
HD1486.G3 S66 1983

GERMANY - ECONOMIC POLICY - 1888-1918.
The Adaptation to inflation /. Berlin , New York , 1986. xvi, 512 p. : ISBN 0-89925-287-7 (U. S.) LC Card 86-29134 DDC 338.943 19
HC286.2 .A62 1986

Horlacher, Michael. Der Wiederaufbau der deutschen Volkswirtschaft . Diessen vor München , 1919. 118 p. ; LC Card 87-409517 DDC 338.943 19
HC286.2 .H67 1919

GERMANY - ECONOMIC POLICY - 1918-1933.
The Adaptation to inflation /. Berlin , New York , 1986. xvi, 512 p. : ISBN 0-89925-287-7 (U. S.) LC Card 86-29134 DDC 338.943 19
HC286.2 .A62 1986

Ambrosius, Gerold. Die öffentliche Wirtschaft in der Weimarer Republik . Baden-Baden , 1984. 306 p. ; ISBN 3-7890-0912-1 LC Card 84-230508
HD4175 .A626 1984

Flaskamp, Jürgen, 1958- Aufgaben und Wirkungen der Reichsbank in der Zeit des Dawes-Planes /. Bergisch Gladbach , c1986. 210 p. : ISBN 3-89012-060-1 LC Card 87-108166 DDC 332.1/1/0943 19
HG3054 .F58 1986

Heindl, Wolfgang, 1951- Die Haushalte von Reich, Ländern und Gemeinden in Deutschland von 1925 bis 1933 . Frankfurt am Main , New York , c1984. 419 p. : ISBN 3-8204-5474-8 LC Card 85-198505
HJ1119 .H36 1984

Die Weimarer Republik als Wohlfahrtsstaat . Stuttgart , 1987. 337 p. ; ISBN 3-515-04738-7 LC Card 87-131861 DDC 338.943 19
HC286.3 .W3546 1987

GERMANY - ECONOMIC POLICY - 1933-1945.
Meyer, August. Das Syndikat . Braunschweig , c1986. 348 p. ; ISBN 3-925151-18-4 LC Card 87-129940 DDC 338.2/73/0943 19
HD9523.9.R45 M49 1986

Schlarp, Karl-Heinz. Wirtschaft und Besatzung in Serbien, 1941-1944 . Stuttgart , 1986. viii, 443 p., [6] p. of plates : ISBN 3-515-04401-9 LC Card 86-181062
HC407.Z7 S46676 1986

GERMANY - ECONOMIC POLICY - 1945-
Wirtschaftspolitik im britischen Besatzungsgebiet 1945-1949 /. Düsseldorf , 1984. 338 p. : ISBN 3-590-18124-9 LC Card 84-188669
HC286.5 .W5655 1984

Germany - Economic relations with foreign countries. see **Germany - Foreign economic relations.**

Germany (Federal Republic, 1949-) Bundesanstalt für Arbeitschutz und Unfallforschung. see **Bundesanstalt für Arbeitsschutz und Unfallforschung.**

Germany (Federal Republic, 1949-). Bundesanstalt für Geowissenschaften und Rohstoffe. see **Bundesanstalt für Geowissenschaften und Rohstoffe.**

Germany (Federal Republic, 1949-). Bundesversicherungsanstalt für Angestellte. see **Bundesversicherungsanstalt für Angestellte.**

Germany (Federal Republic, 1949-). Statistisches Bundesamt. Reich, Utz-Peter. Darstellungskonzepte der Input-Output-Rechnung /. Stuttgart , 1984. 185 p. : ISBN 3-17-003301-8
NYPL [JLE 86-1264]

GERMANY - FOREIGN ECONOMIC RELATIONS.
Von der Konkurrenz zur Rivalität . Stuttgart , 1986. 186 p. ; ISBN 3-515-04760-3 LC Card 87-134320 DDC 337/.09/04 19
HF1411 .V665 1986

GERMANY - FOREIGN ECONOMIC RELATIONS - AUSTRIA.
Otruba, Gustav. A. Hitler's "Tausend-Mark-Sperre" und die Folgen für Österreichs Fremdenverkehr (1933-1938) /. Linz , c1983. iii, 205 p. ; ISBN 3-85320-308-6 LC Card 84-213145
HG999 .O87 1983

GERMANY - FOREIGN ECONOMIC RELATIONS - GREAT BRITAIN.
Banze, Angelika. Die deutsch-englische Wirtschaftsrivalität . Vaduz , 1965. 105 p. ; LC Card 85-243022 DDC 337.43041 19
HF1546.15.G7 B36 1965

GERMANY - FOREIGN ECONOMIC RELATIONS - UNITED STATES.
McNeil, William C. American money and the Weimar Republic . New York , 1986. x, 352 p. : ISBN 0-231-06236-2 LC Card 85-29962 DDC 336.3/4/0943 19
HG3949 .M38 1986 *NYPL [JLE 86-3268]*

GERMANY - FOREIGN ECONOMIC RELATIONS - YUGOSLAVIA - SERBIA.
Schlarp, Karl-Heinz. Wirtschaft und Besatzung in Serbien, 1941-1944 . Stuttgart , 1986. viii, 443 p., [6] p. of plates : ISBN 3-515-04401-9 LC Card 86-181062
HC407.Z7 S46676 1986

GERMANY - FOREIGN RELATIONS - GREAT BRITAIN.
Wirtschaftspolitik im britischen Besatzungsgebiet 1945-1949 /. Düsseldorf , 1984. 338 p. : ISBN 3-590-18124-9 LC Card 84-188669
HC286.5 .W5655 1984

GERMANY - FOREIGN RELATIONS - SOVIET UNION.
Lemke, Heinz. Finanztransaktionen und Aussenpolitik . Berlin , 1985. 215 p. ; LC Card 86-196601
HG3955 .L45 1985

Germany - Government. see **Germany - Politics and government.**

GERMANY - HISTORY - ALLIED OCCUPATION, 1945-
Wirtschaftspolitik im britischen Besatzungsgebiet 1945-1949 /. Düsseldorf , 1984. 338 p. : ISBN 3-590-18124-9 LC Card 84-188669
HC286.5 .W5655 1984

Germany - History, Economic. see **Germany - Economic conditions.**

GERMANY - INDUSTRIES.
Deutsche Industrie, deutsche Kultur /. Berlin , 1900-1902. xvi, 388 p. : LC Card 85-666344
HC283 .D48x 1900

Weihe, Carl, b. 1872. Aus eigner Kraft . Leipzig , 1918. 139 p., X [i.e. 5] p. of plates : LC Card 85-666353
HC283 .W45x 1918

GERMANY - INDUSTRIES - DIRECTORIES.
Uhlands Internationales Technisches Branchen-Adressbuch =. Leipzig , 1926. 22, 767 p. ; LC Card 85-666352
HC282.2 .U45x 1926

GERMANY - INDUSTRIES - HISTORY.
Meyer, August. Das Syndikat . Braunschweig , c1986. 348 p. ; ISBN 3-925151-18-4 LC Card 87-129940 DDC 338.2/73/0943 19
HD9523.9.R45 M49 1986

Spilker, Ernst Moritz. Der Wirtschaftsraum zwischen den Wirtschaftsräumen . Köln , 1986. 223 p. : LC Card 87-408201 DDC 330.943/55 19
HC288.W46 S67 1986

GERMANY - INDUSTRIES - HISTORY - 19TH CENTURY.
Rinneberg, Karl-Jürgen. Das betriebliche Ausbildungswesen in der Zeit der industriellen Umgestaltung Deutschlands /. Köln , 1985. xvi, 481 p. : ISBN 3-412-02885-1 LC Card 86-121691
HF5549.5.T7 R486 1985

GERMANY - INDUSTRIES - HISTORY - 20TH CENTURY.
Feldman, Gerald D. Vom Weltkrieg zur Weltwirtschaftskrise . Göttingen , 1984. 272 p. ; ISBN 3-525-35719-2 LC Card 85-165291
HC286.2 .F45 1984

Ohlsen, Manfred. Milliarden für den Geier, oder, Der Fall des Friedrich Flick /. Berlin , 1985. 458 p. : LC Card 86-149056
HC282.5.F54 O35 1985

GERMANY - INDUSTRIES - HISTORY - SOURCES.
Quellen zur deutschen Wirtschafts- und Sozialgeschichte von der Reichsgründung bis zum ersten Weltkrieg /. Darmstadt , 1985. xviii, 553 p. : ISBN 3-534-07561-7 LC Card 85-229315
HC285 .Q45 1985

GERMANY, NORTHERN - ECONOMIC CONDITIONS - REGIONAL DISPARITIES.
Das Süd-Nord-Gefälle . Stuttgart , 1986. 168 p. ; ISBN 3-87959-270-5 LC Card 87-103590 DDC 330.943/0878 19
HC286.7 .S9 1986

GERMANY - POLITICS AND GOVERNMENT - 1871-
Sondermann, Klaus. Wirtschaftsentwicklung und landwirtschaftliche Verbandspolitik . Münster-Hiltrup , 1983. vi, 300 p. : ISBN 3-7843-0283-1 : LC Card 84-126226
HD1486.G3 S66 1983

GERMANY - POLITICS AND GOVERNMENT - 1918-1933.
Abraham, David, 1946- The collapse of the Weimar Republic . New York , 1986. liii, 352 p. ; ISBN 0-8419-1083-9 LC Card 86-27033 DDC 338.0943 19
HD3616.G35 A27 1986

Bierbach, Wolf. Rundfunk zwischen Kommerz und Politik . Frankfurt am Main , New York , c1986. 2 v. (595 p.) : ISBN 3-8204-9692-0 LC Card 86-233794
HE8699.G3 B54 1986

Die Weimarer Republik als Wohlfahrtsstaat . Stuttgart , 1987. 337 p. ; ISBN 3-515-04738-7 LC Card 87-131861 DDC 338.943 19
HC286.3 .W3546 1987

GERMANY - POLITICS AND GOVERNMENT - 1918-1933 - ADDRESSES, ESSAYS, LECTURES.
Solidargemeinschaft und Klassenkampf . Frankfurt am Main , 1986. 382 p. ; ISBN 3-518-11363-1 *NYPL [JLC 86-423]*

GERMANY - POLITICS AND GOVERNMENT - 1933-1945.
Germanskiĭ trudovoĭ front . Berlin , 1943. 69 leaves : LC Card 85-204295
HD8443.D43 G47 1943

Hayes, Peter, 1946- Industry and ideology . Cambridge [Cambridgeshire] , New York , 1987. xxviii, 411 p. : ISBN 0-521-32948-5 LC Card 86-28388 DDC 338.7/66/00943 19
HD9654.9.I5 H39 1987

GERMANY - POLITICS AND GOVERNMENT - 1933-1945 - ADDRESSES, ESSAYS, LECTURES.
Solidargemeinschaft und Klassenkampf . Frankfurt am Main , 1986. 382 p. ; ISBN 3-518-11363-1 *NYPL [JLC 86-423]*

GERMANY - POPULATION - HISTORY.
Population, labour, and migration in 19th- and 20th-century Germany /. Leamington Spa [UK] ; New York : xii, 200 p. : ISBN 0-85496-503-3 : LC Card 86-24470 DDC 331.6/2/0943 19
HD5856.G3 P66 1987

GERMANY - POPULATION - HISTORY - 18TH CENTURY.
Knodel, John E. Demographic behavior in the past . Cambridge [Cambridgeshire] , New York , 1988. p. cm. ISBN 0-521-32715-6 LC Card 87-20601 DDC 304.6/0943 19
HB3595 .K53 1988

GERMANY - POPULATION - HISTORY - 19TH CENTURY.

Knodel, John E. Demographic behavior in the past . Cambridge [Cambridgeshire] , New York , 1988. p. cm. ISBN 0-521-32715-6 LC Card 87-20601 DDC 304.6/0943 19
HB3595 .K53 1988

GERMANY - POPULATION, RURAL - HISTORY - 18TH CENTURY.
Knodel, John E. Demographic behavior in the past . Cambridge [Cambridgeshire] , New York , 1988. p. cm. ISBN 0-521-32715-6 LC Card 87-20601 DDC 304.6/0943 19
HB3595 .K53 1988

GERMANY - POPULATION, RURAL - HISTORY - 19TH CENTURY.
Knodel, John E. Demographic behavior in the past . Cambridge [Cambridgeshire] , New York , 1988. p. cm. ISBN 0-521-32715-6 LC Card 87-20601 DDC 304.6/0943 19
HB3595 .K53 1988

GERMANY - PUBLIC WORKS - HISTORY.
Peschke, Hans-Peter von, 1951- Elektroindustrie und Staatsverwaltung am Beispiel Siemens, 1847-1914 /. Frankfurt am Main , Bern , c1981. 393 p. : ISBN 3-8204-5902-2 LC Card 81-141438
HD9697.A3 G35 1981

GERMANY. REICHSARBEITSDIENST. ARBEITSGAU 28 (FRANKEN)
Schinnerer, Fritz. Unser Arbeitsgau 28 (Franken) . Würzburg , Nürnberg , 1935. 454 p. : LC Card 87-409298 DDC 331.3/41173/0943 19
HD4870.G3 S35 1935

GERMANY - RELATIONS (GENERAL) WITH GREAT BRITAIN.
Chesterton, Gilbert Keith, 1874-1936. [Crimes of England. French.] Les crimes de l'Angleterre [microform]. Paris, 1916. 273 p. LC Card 19-16286
DA47.2 .C55 ***NYPL [*Z-4049 no.7]***

GERMANY - SOCIAL CONDITIONS.
Born, Karl Erich. Wirtschafts- und Sozialgeschichte des Deutschen Kaiserreichs (1867/71-1914) /. Stuttgart , 1985. 175 p. ; ISBN 3-515-02419-0 LC Card 85-168335
HC285 .B66 1985

Feldman, Gerald D. Vom Weltkrieg zur Weltwirtschaftskrise . Göttingen , 1984. 272 p. ; ISBN 3-525-35719-2 LC Card 85-165291
HC286.2 .F45 1984

The German worker . Berkeley , c1987. p. cm. ISBN 0-520-05972-7 (alk. paper) LC Card 87-5076 DDC 305.5/62/0922 B 19
HD8453.A1 G47 1987

GERMANY - SOCIAL CONDITIONS - 1918-1933.
Die Weimarer Republik als Wohlfahrtsstaat . Stuttgart , 1987. 337 p. ; ISBN 3-515-04738-7 LC Card 87-131861 DDC 338.943 19
HC286.3 .W3546 1987

GERMANY - SOCIAL CONDITIONS - SOURCES.
Quellen zur deutschen Wirtschafts- und Sozialgeschichte von der Reichsgründung bis zum ersten Weltkrieg /. Darmstadt , 1985. xviii, 553 p. : ISBN 3-534-07561-7 LC Card 85-229315
HC285 .Q45 1985

GERMANY - SOCIAL POLICY.
Heindl, Wolfgang, 1951- Die Haushalte von Reich, Ländern und Gemeinden in Deutschland von 1925 bis 1933 . Frankfurt am Main , New York , c1984. 419 p. : ISBN 3-8204-5474-8 LC Card 85-198505
HJ1119 .H36 1984

Hennock, E. P., 1926- British social reform and German precedents . Oxford [Oxfordshire] , New York , 1987. vi, 243 p. ; ISBN 0-19-820127-3 : LC Card 87-11082 DDC 368.4/00941 19
HD7165 .H455 1987

GERMANY, SOUTHERN - ECONOMIC CONDITIONS - REGIONAL DISPARITIES.
Das Süd-Nord-Gefälle . Stuttgart , 1986. 168 p. ; ISBN 3-87959-270-5 LC Card 87-103590 DDC 330.943/0878 19
HC286.7 .S9 1986

GERMANY - STATISTICAL SERVICES - HISTORY - 20TH CENTURY.
Aly, Götz, 1947- Die restlose Erfassung . Berlin , c1984. 157 p. : ISBN 3-88022-282-7 : LC Card 84-206488
HA37.G3 A49 1984

GERMANY - STATISTICS, VITAL.
Rohde, Horst. Sterbetafeln für Personenkraftwagen und Kombinationskraftwagen . Essen , 1981. 64 p. ; LC Card 87-408032 DDC 363.1/252/0943021 19
HE5614.5.G3 R64 1981

Germany (Territory under Allied occupation, 1945-1955 : U. S. Zone). Office of Military Government. Financial Investigation Section.
Ermittlungen gegen die Dresdner Bank, 1946 /. Nördlingen , 1986. cxxxiv, 353 p., [8] p. of plates : ISBN 3-89190-297-2 : LC Card 87-121689
HG3058.D7 E76 1986

Germany (Territory under Allied Occupation, 1945-1955. U. S. Zone). Military Government Office. see Germany (Territory under Allied Occupation, 1945-1955. U. S. Zone). Office of Military Government.

Germany (Territory under Allied Occupation, 1945-1955. U. S. Zone). Office of Military Government. (Old Catalog form: Germany (Territory under Allied Occupation, 1945-1955. U. S. Zone) Military Government Office)

Germany, West. [Angestelltenversicherungsgesetz]
Angestelltenversicherungsgesetz mit Sozialgesetzbuch : Textausgabe mit den wichtigsten Nebengesetzen und Verordnungen : AVG/SGB. 21. Aufl. Berlin : Bundesversicherungsanstalt für Angestellte, Dezernat für Presse- und Öffentlichkeitsarbeit, [1985] 788 p. : ill. ; 21 cm. (Schriftenreihe / Bundesversicherungsanstalt für Angestellte . Nr. 18) Includes index. LC Card 86-145477
1. Social legislation - Germany, West. I. Germany (West). Sozialgesetzbuch. 1985. II. Series: Schriftenreihe der Bundesversicherungsanstalt für Angestellte , 18. III. Title.
HD7116.M42 G4334 Nr. 18, 1985 KK3270.5

Angestelltenversicherungsgesetz mit Sozialgesetzbuch : Textausgabe mit den wichtigsten Nebengesetzen und Verordnungen : AVG/SGB. Stand vom Mai 1986, 22. Aufl. Berlin : Bundesversicherungsanstalt für Angestellte, Dezernat für Presse- und Öffentlichkeitsarbeit, [1986] 792 p. ; 21 cm. (Schriftenreihe / Bundesversicherungsanstalt für Angestellte . Nr. 18) Includes the text of the Sozialgesetzbuch I, IV, and X. Includes index. LC Card 86-229132
1. Social legislation - Germany, West. I. Bundesversicherungsanstalt für Angestellte. Dezernat für Presse- und Öffentlichkeitsarbeit. II. Germany (West). Sozialgesetzbuch. Selections. 1986. III. Title. IV. Title: AVG/SGB. V. Series: Schriftenreihe der Bundesversicherungsanstalt für Angestellte , 18.
HD7116.M42 G4334 Nr. 18, 1986 KK3270.5

Sozialgesetzbuch. Selections. 1986. Germany (West) [Angestelltenversicherungsgesetz.] Angestelltenversicherungsgesetz mit Sozialgesetzbuch : Textausgabe mit den wichtigsten Nebengesetzen und Verordnungen : AVG/SGB. Stand vom Mai 1986, 22. Aufl. Berlin [1986] 792 p. ; LC Card 86-229132
HD7116.M42 G4334 Nr. 18, 1986 KK3270.5

Sozialgesetzbuch. 1985. Germany (West) [Angestelltenversicherungsgesetz.] Angestelltenversicherungsgesetz mit Sozialgesetzbuch : Textausgabe mit den wichtigsten Nebengesetzen und Verordnungen : AVG/SGB. 21. Aufl. Berlin [1985] 788 p. : LC Card 86-145477
HD7116.M42 G4334 Nr. 18, 1985 KK3270.5

GERMANY, WEST - APPROPRIATIONS AND EXPENDITURES.
Boss, Alfred. Ausgabenkürzungen im öffentlichen Sektor /. Tübingen , c1987. xiii, 220 p. : ISBN 3-16-345212-4 LC Card 87-408337 DDC 336.43 19
HJ2109 .B67 1987

Gesamtwirtschaftliche und strukturelle Auswirkungen von Veränderungen der Struktur des öffentlichen Sektors . Berlin , 1984. x, 266 p. : ISBN 3-428-05739-2 LC Card 86-138980
HC281 .B33 Heft 81 HJ1120

Langenbach, Peter. Wettbewerb und staatliche Sachausgaben /. Bochum , 1981. viii, 316 p. ; ISBN 3-88339-194-8 : LC Card 81-205020 DDC 336.3/9 19
HJ7461 .L36 1981 ***NYPL [JLD 86-2579]***

GERMANY (WEST) - APPROPRIATIONS AND EXPENDITURES - ACCOUNTING.
Erfolgskontrolle bei der Verausgabung öffentlicher Mittel /. Baden-Baden , 1986. 133 p. : ISBN 3-7890-1208-4 LC Card 86-164102
HJ7793 .E73 1986

GERMANY (WEST) - APPROPRIATIONS AND EXPENDITURES - STATISTICAL METHODS.
Dornbusch, Hans-Ludwig. Entwicklung wesentlicher Daten der öffentlichen Finanzwirtschaft in der Bundesrepublik Deutschland von 1975-1985 /. Bonn [1986] 31 leaves ; LC Card 87-408897 DDC 332 s 336.43 19
HJ1120 .B65 Nr. 260

Germany (West). Bundesministerium der Finanzen.
Rede zur Einbringung des Bundeshaushalts 1982 : mit Erläuterungen / Hans Matthöfer. Bonn : Bundesministerium der Finanzen, Referat Presse und Information, 1982. 56 p. : ill. ; 21 cm. (Reihe Berichte und Dokumentationen, 0172-7575) LC Card 82-221425
1. Budget - Germany, West. 2. Germany, West - Economic policy - 1974-. I. Matthöfer, Hans, 1925-. II. Germany (West). Bundesministerium der Finanzen. Referat Presse und Information. III. Series: Reihe Berichte und Dokumentationen (Bonn, Germany). IV. Title.
HJ2109 .G45 1982

Germany (West). Bundesministerium der Finanzen. Referat Presse und Information.
Germany (West). Bundesministerium der Finanzen. Rede zur Einbringung des Bundeshaushalts 1982 . Bonn , 1982. 56 p. : LC Card 82-221425
HJ2109 .G45 1982

Germany (West). Bundesministerium des Innern.
Innenpolitische Leistungsbilanz 1982-1986 /. Bonn , 1986. 124 p. : LC Card 86-215949
HC286.7 .I55 1986

Germany (West). Bundesministerium für Arbeit und Sozialordnung.
Arbeitssicherheit '86 . Bonn [1986] 47, 46, 22 p. : LC Card 87-409083 DDC 363.1/12/0943 19
HD7708 .A7 1986

Der Ausbau von Fernwärmenetzen und seine Wirkungen auf Arbeitsmarkt und Beschäftigung, dargestellt am Beispiel der Freien und Hansestadt Hamburg . Bonn [1983] xiv, 172 p. : LC Card 85-107700
HD5780.H34 A87 1983

Dienststellenverzeichnis Arbeitsschutz . Dortmund , Bremerhaven , 1983. 217 p. ; ISBN 3-88314-274-3 LC Card 83-196051
HD7708 .D55 1983

Infratest Sozialforschung. Datenlage zur Alterssicherung . Bonn , 1984. 330 p. : LC Card 86-132439 DDC 331.25/2/0943 19
HD7105.35.G3 I54 1984

Zur Problematik der Abbrecher der beruflichen Rehabilitation /. Bonn [1985?] 118, [29] p. ; LC Card 86-190824
HD7256.G3 Z87 1985

Germany (West). Bundesministerium für Bildung und Wissenschaft.
Abiturienten und Hochschulabsolventen beim Übergang vom Studium in den Beruf . Nürnberg , 1983. 407 p. : LC Card 84-140881
HD6278.G4 A25 1983

Frauen und Beruf, zwischen Wunsch und Realität . Bonn , Bad Honnef , 1986. 142 p. ; ISBN 3-87066-629-3 : LC Card 87-409372 DDC 331.4/0943 19
HD6149 .F719 1986

Hegelheimer, Armin. Gleichwertigkeit von allgemeiner und beruflicher Bildung /. Bonn , Bad Honnef , 1986. v, 74 p. ; ISBN 3-87066-628-5 : LC Card 87-409371 DDC 331.4/2592/0943 19
HD6059.6.G4 H42 1986

Mädchen und Berufswahl . Bonn , Bad Honnef , 1986. 96 p. : ISBN 3-87066-631-5 LC

Card 87-409396 DDC 331.4/2592/0943 19
HF5382.67.G3 M33 1986

Germany (West). Bundesministerium für Ernährung, Landwirtschaft und Forsten. Einkommenswirkungen von Getreidepreissenkungen /. Münster-Hiltrup , 1985. viii, 158 p. : ISBN 3-7843-0315-3 LC Card 87-408928 DDC 338.1/0943 s 338.1/331/094 19
HD1920.5 .E37 1985

Intrasektorale Einkommensstreuung in der Landwirtschaft /. Münster-Hiltrup , 1983. 177 p. : ISBN 3-7843-0281-5 : LC Card 83-236007
HD1955 .I57 1983

Germany (West). Bundesministerium für Ernährung, Landwirtschaft und Forsten. Abteilung 2--Referat "Energie und Rohstoffe, Landfristanalysen." Gesamtkonzeption nachwachsende Rohstoffe des Bundesministeriums für Ernährung, Landwirtschaft und Forsten . Münster-Hiltrup , 1983. vi, 196 p. : ISBN 3-7843-0202-5 : LC Card 84-126491
HD9502.G42 G47 1983

Germany (West). Bundesministerium für Ernährung, Landwirtschaft und Forsten. Wissenschaftlicher Beirat. Gutachten des Wissenschaftlichen Beirats beim Bundesministerium für Ernährung, Landwirtschaft und Forsten / bearbeitet und zusammengestellt von K. Petrich, in Zusammenarbeit mit den Mitgliedern des Wissenschaftlichen Beirats ; herausgegeben von F.W. Maier-Bode. Hiltrup bei Münster (Westf.) : Landwirtschaftsverlag, [1960?] 98 p. ; 21 cm. (Landwirtschaft--angewandte Wissenschaft) LC Card 86-185959
1. Agriculture and state - Germany, West. I. Petrich, K. II. Maier-Bode, F. W. III. Series.
HD1957 .G47 1960

Germany (West). Bundesministerium für Raumordnung, Bauwesen und Städtebau. Bürger, es geht um Deine Gemeinde . [S.l. , 1983] ([Bonn] : Bundesdruckerei) 7 p. ; LC Card 84-198296
HD7339.A3 B97 1983

Raumordnungsprognose 1990 . Bonn-Bad-Godesberg , 1977. 95 p. : LC Card 86-100310
HB3595 .R38 1977

Germany (West). Bundesministerium für Verkehr. Aufbereitung von Ergebnissen der Stadtverkehrsforschung . Hof/Saale , 1986. 2 v. : LC Card 87-408335 DDC 388.4/0943 19
HE4774 .A94 1986

Gscheidle, Kurt. Die Verkehrspolitik in der 8. Legislaturperiode /. Bonn-Bad Godesberg [1977] 29 p. : LC Card 86-173226
HE64 .A36 Heft 54 HE249

Strassenverkehrszählung 1978 in der Bundesrepublik Deutschland . Köln , 1979. 96 p. : LC Card 87-408379 DDC 388/.0943 s 388.3/0943 19
HE5601 .S89 Heft 13 HE5669.A6

Vorschläge für eine Neuordnung des organisatorischen Rahmens für den öffentlichen Personennahverkehr /. Bonn-Bad Godesberg [1977] 35 p. ; LC Card 86-173254
HE64 .A36 Heft 53 HE249

Germany (West). Bundesministerium für Wirtschaft. Aussagefähigkeit von Einkommensverteilungsrechnungen für die Bundesrepublik Deutschland . Tübingen , 1986. xxiv, 436 p. : ISBN 3-88573-027-8 LC Card 87-407588 DDC 339.2/0943 19
HC290.5.I5 A93 1986

Hochtechnologien und internationale Wettbewerbsfähigkeit der deutschen Wirtschaft /. Bonn [1984] 30 p. ; LC Card 85-184765
HF3564 .H63 1984

Hummel, Marlies. Subsidiaritätsprinzip als Leitlinie für einen Subventionsabbau . München , 1985. xiii, 306 p. ; ISBN 3-88512-003-8 : LC Card 86-125424
HC290.5.S9 H85 1985

Körber-Weik, Margot. Wirtschaftskraft und Wirtschaftsentwicklung in den Bundesländern seit 1970 . Tübingen , 1986. x, 271 p. ; ISBN 3-88573-303-X LC Card 87-401375 DDC 330.943/0878 19
HC286.6 .K67 1986

Sherman, Heidemarie C. Der Einfluss staatlicher Budgetdefizite auf die Zinsentwicklung in der Bundesrepublik Deutschland und den Vereinigten Staaten . München , c1986. xxiii, 190 p. : ISBN 3-88512-019-4 LC Card 86-192070
HJ2110 .S53 1986

Wechselwirkungen von Geldpolitik, Inflation und Strukturwandel . Hamburg , 1984. 179 p. : ISBN 3-87895-243-0 LC Card 84-221405
HB235.G3 W42 1984

Zwischenbericht, Analyse der strukturellen Entwicklung der deutschen Wirtschaft . Hamburg , 1979. viii, 142, 49 leaves : LC Card 83-132166
HC286.7 .Z88 1979

Germany (West). Bundesministerium für Wirtschaft. Referat Öffentlichkeitsarbeit. Entwicklung und Struktur der Personalnebenkosten /. Bonn [1985] 14, [9] p. : LC Card 86-154479
HD4928.N62 G34 1985

Technologische Entwicklung und Beschäftigung /. Bonn [1985] 10 p. ; LC Card 86-154491
HC290.5.T4 T44 1985

Germany (West). Bundesministerium für Wirtschaft. Referat V B 1. Der Deutsche Osthandel 1982 /. Bonn [1982] 87 p. : LC Card 86-212991
HF3568.E35 D463 1982

Germany (West). Bundesministerium für Wirtschaft. Referat V B 2. Der Deutsche Osthandel 1982 /. Bonn [1982] 87 p. : LC Card 86-212991
HF3568.E35 D463 1982

Germany (West). Bundesministerium für Wirtschaftliche Zusammenarbeit. Agroforstliche Landnutzung im Einzugsbereich zentraler Orte im Sahel . Köln , 1983. ix, 374 p. : ISBN 3-8039-0276-2 LC Card 87-102956 DDC 333.73/13/09663 19
HD1019.Z63 A38 1983

Germany (West). Bundesregierung. Germany (West). Bundestag. Haushaltsausschuss. Fragen der Subventionspolitik . Bonn , 1982. 222 p. ; LC Card 83-190544 DDC 338.943/02 19
HD3646.G4 G47 1982

Germany (West). Bundestag. Ausschuss für Wirtschaftliche Zusammenarbeit. Entwicklung und Rüstung . Baden-Baden , 1984. 303 p. ; ISBN 3-7890-1068-5 LC Card 85-175510
HC79.D4 E58 1984

Entwicklungspolitik, Bilanz und Perspektiven . Bonn , 1986. 256 p. ; LC Card 87-409363 DDC 338.91/43/01724 19
HC60 .E523 1986

Germany (West). Bundestag. Ausschuss für Wirtschaftliche Zusammenheit. Entwicklungspolitik, Bilanz und Perspektiven : öffentliche Anhörung des Bundestagsausschusses für Wirtschaftliche Zusammenarbeit am 17. März 1986. Bonn : Deutscher Bundestag, Presse- und Informationszentrum, Referat Öffentlichkeitsarbeit, 1986. 256 p. ; 21 cm. (Zur Sache. 2/86) Bibliography: p. 249-256. LC Card 87-409259 DDC 339.91/43/01724 19
1. Economic assistance, West German - Developing countries - Congresses. 2. Technical assistance, West German - Developing countries - Congresses. I. Series: Zur Sache (Bonn, Germany) , 86/2. II. Title.
HC60 .G467 1986

GERMANY (WEST). BUNDESTAG - ELECTIONS, 1976 - CONGRESSES. Votum für die Marktwirtschaft . Bonn , c1976. 26 p. ; LC Card 85-172115
HC286.7 .V69 1976

Germany (West). Bundestag. Grünen. Der Sofortige Ausstieg ist möglich . Bonn [1986] 35 cm : LC Card 87-409511 DDC 333.79/24/0943 19
HD9698.G42 S64 1986

Germany (West). Bundestag. Hauptabteilung Wissenschaftliche Dienste. Reform oder Revolution? . Bonn , 1987. vi, 241, A 140 p. : LC Card 87-409091 DDC 368.4/00943 19
HD7179 .R384 1987

Germany (West). Bundestag. Haushaltsausschuss. Fragen der Subventionspolitik : öffentliche Anhörung des Haushaltsausschusses des Deutschen Bundestages zum Achten Subventionsbericht der Bundesregierung. Bonn : Deutscher Bundestag, Presse- und Informationszentrum, Referat Öffentlichkeitsarbeit, 1982. 222 p. ; 22 cm. (Zur Sache. 0343-8899 . 3/82) Includes index. LC Card [illegible]90544 DDC 338.943/02 19
1. Subsidies - Germany, West. 2. Subsidies - Law and legislation - Germany (West). 3. Germany, West - Politics and government. I. Germany (West). Bundesregierung. II. Series: Zur Sache (Bonn, Germany) , 82/3.
HD3646.G4 G47 1982

Germany (West). Bundestag. Presse- und Informationszentrum. Referat Öffentlichkeitsarbeit. Entwicklungspolitik, Bilanz und Perspektiven . Bonn , 1986. 256 p. ; LC Card 87-409363 DDC 338.91/43/01724 19
HC60 .E523 1986

GERMANY (WEST) - CENSUS, 1983. Die Volkszählung /. Reinbek bei Hamburg , 1983. 284 p. : ISBN 3-499-15245-2 : LC Card 84-110844
HA1234 1983

GERMANY, WEST - CIVILIZATION. Wende wohin? . Köln , c1983. 139 p. ; ISBN 3-921349-34-6 LC Card 84-150290
HC286.7 .W4 1983 ***NYPL [JFC 87-1258]***

GERMANY, WEST - COMMERCE. Exporte als Herausforderung für die deutsche Wirtschaft /. Köln , c1984. 469 p. : ISBN 3-602-34842-3 LC Card 85-139543
HF3564 .E96 1984

Gerstenberger, Wolfgang. Strukturwandel unter verschlechterten Rahmenbedingungen . Berlin , c1984. 255 p. : ISBN 3-428-05567-5 LC Card 84-180150
HC286.7 .G46 1984

Gerster, Hans Joachim, 1946- Flexibilität und Rigidität in der Preisbewegung . Frankfurt am Main , New York , c1984. xii, 298, 69 p. : ISBN 3-8204-5109-9 LC Card 85-195018
HB235.G3 G48 1984

Hochtechnologien und internationale Wettbewerbsfähigkeit der deutschen Wirtschaft /. Bonn [1984] 30 p. ; LC Card 85-184765
HF3564 .H63 1984

Jungnickel, Rolf. Eigenimporte der deutschen Industrie /. Hamburg , 1984. 392 p. : ISBN 3-87895-256-2 LC Card 84-247605
HF3566.5 .J86 1984

Schenk, Hans-Otto. Die Konzentration im Handel . Berlin , c1984. 341 p. : ISBN 3-428-05618-3 LC Card 84-225438
HF345 .F66 Folge 3, Nr. 9 HF3566

Von der Bizonengründung zur ökonomisch-politischen Westintegration . Frankfurt am Main , c1984. v, 311 p. : ISBN 3-88129-640-9 LC Card 84-154481
HC286.5 .V64 1984

GERMANY (WEST) - COMMERCE - COMMUNIST COUNTRIES. Wolff von Amerongen, Otto, 1918- Trendwende im Osthandel /. Bonn , 1977. 23 p. ; LC Card 85-141570
HF1411 .W583 1977

GERMANY (WEST) - COMMERCE - DEVELOPING COUNTRIES. Beyfuss, Jörg. Aussenhandel mit Entwicklungsländern . Köln , c1978. 55 p. : ISBN 3-88054-145-0 LC Card 85-242489
HF3568.D44 B49 1978

Der Neue Protektionismus . Bonn , c1983. 195 p. : ISBN 3-87831-370-5 LC Card 83-198686
HF1756 .N58 1983

GERMANY (WEST) - COMMERCE - ECONOMETRIC MODELS. Scheiper, Ulrich. Die sektoralen Importe und Exporte der Bundesrepublik Deutschland . Frankfurt am Main , c1984. v, 203 p. : ISBN 3-88129-846-0 : LC Card 85-125395
HF3566.5 .S28 1984

GERMANY, WEST - COMMERCE - EUROPE, EASTERN. Der Deutsche Osthandel 1982 /. Bonn [1982] 87 p. : LC Card 86-212991
HF3568.E35 D463 1982

Weimer, Theodor. Die Bedeutung des Osthandels für mittelständische Unternehmen /. Stuttgart , c1985. 172, 7 p. : ISBN 3-7910-5006-0 LC Card 86-160626
HF3568.E35 W43 1985
NYPL [JLL 73-505 Nr.5]

GERMANY, WEST - COMMERCE - GERMANY, EAST.
Marwege, Ulf, 1954- Neuorientierung im Westhandel der DDR? . Bonn , c1984. iv, 122 p. : ISBN 3-7713-0221-8 : LC Card 84-196602
HF3570.5.Z7 G75 1984

GERMANY (WEST) - COMMERCE - GERMANY (EAST) - CONGRESSES.
Aussenwirtschaft der DDR und innerdeutsche Wirtschaftsbeziehungen . Berlin , c1986. 98 p. ; ISBN 3-428-06121-7 LC Card 87-137949 DDC 382/.0943/0431 19
HF3570.5.Z7 G352 1986

GERMANY, WEST - COMMERCE - INDIA.
Wiemann, Jürgen. India in transition . New Delhi , Berlin , 1986. xxi, 151 p. ; LC Card 87-900287 DDC 338.954 19
HD3616.I83 W54 1986

GERMANY (WEST) - COMMERCE - JAPAN.
Frese, Dirk. Japan, Markt für deutsche Konsumgüter /. Düsseldorf [1978?] 32 p. : LC Card 85-242493
HF3568.J3 F74 1978

GERMANY (WEST) - COMMERCE - SOVIET UNION - CONGRESSES.
Clement, Hermann. Entwicklungsmöglichkeiten des deutsch-sowjetischen Handels in der zweiten Hälfte der 80er Jahre vor dem Hintergrund der sowjetischen Planung /. München , 1986. 14 leaves ; LC Card 86-167481
HF3568.S66 C58 1986

GERMANY (WEST) - COMMERCE - STATISTICS.
Zahlenbild-Almanach 1972 . Berlin , c1972. 204 p. : ISBN 3-503-00861-6 LC Card 86-133643
HC286.5 .Z225 1972

GERMANY, WEST - COMMERCIAL POLICY.
Bundesverband des Deutschen Gross- und Aussenhandels. Vorschläge und Beiträge des Bundesverbandes des Deutschen Gross- und Aussenhandels e.V. für die X. Legislaturperiode des Deutschen Bundestages. Bonn [1983] 56 p. ; LC Card 83-243234
HF1545 .B83 1983

Exporte als Herausforderung für die deutsche Wirtschaft /. Köln , c1984. 469 p. : ISBN 3-602-34842-3 LC Card 85-139543
HF3564 .E96 1984

Der Neue Protektionismus . Bonn , c1983. 195 p. : ISBN 3-87831-370-5 LC Card 83-198686
HF1756 .N58 1983

GERMANY, WEST - ECONOMIC CONDITIONS.
Abelshauser, Werner. Wirtschaftsgeschichte der Bundesrepublik Deutschland (1945-1980) /. Frankfurt am Main , 1983. 186 p. : ISBN 3-518-11241-4 : LC Card 83-180531
HC286.7 .A26 1983

Das Politische System der BRD . Berlin , 1985. 479 p. ; LC Card 86-123928 DDC 320.943 19
JN3971.A2 P59 1985 ***NYPL [JLD 86-3144]***

L'Economia tedesca . Milano , c1981. 273 p. : LC Card 87-673286
HC286.7 .E29x 1981

Engelmann, Bernt, 1921- Wir hab'n ja den Kopf noch fest auf dem Hals . Köln , c1987. 257 p. : ISBN 3-462-01688-1 LC Card 87-146658
HC286.5 .E594 1987

Engels, Wolfram. Den Staat erneuern, den Markt retten /. Köln , c1983. 228 p. ; ISBN 3-602-34836-9 LC Card 84-182378
HC286 .E54 1983

Flaig, Jürgen. Verteilungsschwankungen im Konjunkturverlauf . Freiburg im Breisgau , c1983. vi, 221 p. : ISBN 3-448-01325-0 LC Card 83-155341
HC290.5.I5 F55 1983

Fuchs, Gerhard, 1939- Die Bundesrepublik Deutschland . Stuttgart , 1983. 296 p. : ISBN 3-12-922191-3 LC Card 83-166769 DDC 330.943/087 19
HD656 .F8 1983 ***NYPL [JLE 86-578]***

Gesamtwirtschaftliche und strukturelle Auswirkungen von Veränderungen der Struktur des öffentlichen Sektors . Berlin , 1984. x, 266 p. : ISBN 3-428-05739-2 LC Card 86-138980
HC281 .B33 Heft 81 HJ1120

Glismann, Hans H. Zur Natur der Wachstumsschwäche in der Bundesrepublik Deutschland . Kiel [1978] 32 p. : LC Card 85-166323
HB44 .K45 no. 55 HB3789

Leaman, Jeremy, 1947- The political economy of West Germany, 1945-85 . New York , 1988. xii, 287 p. : ISBN 0-312-00541-5 : LC Card 87-9458 DDC 338.943 19
HC286.5 .L4 1988

Panek, Hans-Thomas. Die Währungskrisen vom November 1968 bis Mai 1971 im politischen Prozess der Bundesrepublik Deutschland /. Köln , 1977. 293 p. ; ISBN 3-921471-29-X LC Card 86-184843
HG999.5 .P35 1977

Probleme monetärer und finanzwirtschaftlicher Steuerung im Systemvergleich /. Duisburg , c1986. 175 p. : ISBN 3-921473-43-8 LC Card 86-211745
HC286.6 .P754 1986

Randak, Harald, 1942- Die soziale Marktwirtschaft /. München , 1985. 143 p. : LC Card 85-216985
HC286.5 .R36 1985

Reese, Hartmut. Arbeiterbewegung in der Zusammenbruchsgesellschaft . Münster [1984?] 209 p. ; ISBN 3-88660-133-1 LC Card 85-128699
HD6694 .R35 1984

Schatz, Klaus-Werner. Die Bedeutung kleiner und mittlerer Unternehmen im Strukturwandel /. Kiel , 1984. 32 p. ; LC Card 85-136545
HB44 .K45 no. 103 HD2346.G3

Schmölders, Günter, 1903- Der Wohlfahrtsstaat am Ende . München , 1983. 283 p. ; ISBN 3-7844-7133-1 LC Card 84-138252
HC286.6 .S284 1983

Seifert, Hartmut, 1944- Öffentliche Arbeitsmarktpolitik in der Bundesrepublik Deutschland . Köln [1984] ix, 288 p. ; ISBN 3-7663-0857-2 LC Card 86-127331 DDC 331.11/0943 19
HD5779 .S34 1984

Stationen . Darmstadt , 1984. ix, 228 p., [1] leaf of plates : ISBN 3-534-02410-9 LC Card 85-138779
HC286.5 .S825 1984

Strasser, Johano. Grenzen des Sozialstaats? . Köln , 1983. 206 p. ; ISBN 3-7663-0800-9 LC Card 83-142735
HC286.6 .S73 1983

Timmer, Reinhard. Raumordnung und Industrialisierung /. Hannover , 1977. 103 p. : LC Card 84-150907
HC286.5 .T55 1977

Von der Bizonengründung zur ökonomisch-politischen Westintegration . Frankfurt am Main , c1984. v, 311 p. : ISBN 3-88129-640-9 LC Card 84-154481
HC286.5 .V64 1984

Die Wirtschaft heute /. Mannheim , 1980. 638 p. : ISBN 3-411-01793-7 LC Card 86-673960
HB175 .W5934x 1980

GERMANY, WEST - ECONOMIC CONDITIONS - 1974-
Abelshauser, Werner. Wirtschaftsgeschichte der Bundesrepublik Deutschland (1945-1980) /. Frankfurt am Main , 1983. 186 p. : ISBN 3-518-11241-4 : LC Card 83-180531
HC286.7 .A26 1983

Chancen für einen langen Aufschwung /. Stuttgart , 1984. xvii, 350 p. : ISBN 3-17-003288-7 : LC Card 86-178498
HC286.7 .C48 1984

Demontage des Sozialstaats . Köln , 1986. 177 p. ; ISBN 3-8161-0107-0 LC Card 87-104505 DDC 338.943 19
HC286.7 .D455 1986

Engels, Wolfram. Einseitige Betrachtungen . Düsseldorf , 1986. 240 p. ; LC Card 87-146603 DDC 338.943 19
HD84 .E53 1986

Erhöhter Handlungsbedarf im Strukturwandel . Berlin [1984] xxix, 229 p. : ISBN 3-428-05565-9 LC Card 86-137115 DDC 330 s 330.943/0878 19
HC281 .B33 Heft 79 HC286.7

Für einen anhaltenden Aufschwung . Kiel [1986] 29 p. : ISBN 3-925357-33-5 (Deut. Bibl.) : LC Card 86-234971
HB44 .K45 no. 123 HC286.7

Gahlen, Bernhard. Zur internationalen Wettbewerbsfähigkeit der deutschen Wirtschaft /. [Berlin] [1985] 41, 4 p. ; LC Card 86-204589
HC286.7 .G29 1985

Gerstenberger, Wolfgang. Strukturwandel unter verschlechterten Rahmenbedingungen . Berlin , c1984. 255 p. : ISBN 3-428-05567-5 LC Card 84-180150
HC286.7 .G46 1984

Grätz, Christian. Kommunale Wirtschaftsförderung, kritische Bestandsaufnahme ihrer Funktionen und Organisation /. Bochum , 1983. xiii, 263 p. : ISBN 3-88339-340-1 : LC Card 84-138569
HC290.5.D5 G74 1983

Herrschaft, Krise, Überleben . Münster , 1986. 396 p. : ISBN 3-924550-19-0 LC Card 86-229590
HC286.7 .H48 1986

Hübl, Lothar. Strukturwandel und Strukturpolitik . Hannover , 1983. 104 p. : LC Card 84-126938
HC286.7 .H83 1983

Inotai, András. Az NSZK a változó világgazdaságban /. Budapest , 1986, c1985. 259 p. : ISBN 963-221-584-2 : LC Card 87-136644
HC286.7 .I56 1986

Jungblut, Michael. Der Wohlstand entlässt seine Kinder . Stuttgart , c1983. 303 p. ; ISBN 3-421-06164-5 LC Card 83-232938
HC59 .J78 1983

Kampe, Dieter, 1953- Die Macher . Pfaffenweiler , 1986. 191 p. ; ISBN 3-89085-143-6 LC Card 87-133889 DDC 338.0943 19
HC286.7 .K36 1986

Krack, Jürgen. Lieber besser statt mehr? . Köln , c1985. 306, [2] p. : ISBN 3-7663-0569-7 LC Card 85-125869
HD5029 .K72 1985

Krisenverschärfung durch Angebotspolitik . Köln , c1984. 104 p. ; ISBN 3-7663-0877-7 LC Card 84-215633
HC286.7 .K75 1984

Lafontaine, Oskar, 1943- Der andere Fortschritt . Hamburg , c1985. 222 p. ; ISBN 3-455-08248-3 LC Card 85-146223
HC286.7 .L33 1985

Leben im Jahr 2000 und danach . Berlin , c1984. 213 p. : ISBN 3-7605-8571-X LC Card 85-128359
HB3595 .L43 1984

Merklein, Renate. Die Deutschen werden ärmer . Reinbek bei Hamburg , 1982. 189 p. : ISBN 3-499-33018-0 : LC Card 83-137339
HC286.7 .M475 1982

Miegel, Meinhard. Die verkannte Revolution /. Stuttgart , 1983- v. : ISBN 3-87959-196-2 (Bd. 1) LC Card 83-206487 DDC 330.943/087 19
HC286.7 .M53 1983 ***NYPL [JLK 86-154]***

Partnerschaft in der sozialen Marktwirtschaft . Bern , c1986. 367 p. ; ISBN 3-258-03604-7 LC Card 86-226613 DDC 330.943/087 19
HC286.7 .P37 1986

Piel, Manfred, 1945- [Staatsverschuldung, Schicksalsfrage der Nation?] Staatsverschuldung, Hintergründe und Probleme /. Stuttgart [1982] 128 p. ; LC Card 83-118137
HJ8654 .P52 1982

Schmidt, Klaus-Dieter. Im Anpassungsprozess zurückgeworfen . Tübingen , c1984. xx, 243 p. : ISBN 3-16-344755-4 LC Card 84-170512
HC286.7 .S352 1984

Späth, Lothar, 1937- [Wende in die Zukunft. English.] Facing the future . Berlin , New York , c1986. xvi, 196 p. ; ISBN 0-387-17105-3 (U. S.) LC Card 86-25994 DDC 338.943 19
HC286.7 .S713 1986

Wende wohin? . Köln , c1983. 139 p. ; ISBN 3-921349-34-6 LC Card 84-150290
HC286.7 .W4 1983 ***NYPL [JFC 87-1258]***

Die Zukunft der Globalsteuerung /. Bern , c1986. 268 p. ; ISBN 3-258-03573-3 : LC Card 86-182288
HC286.7 .Z82 1986

GERMANY, WEST - ECONOMIC CONDITIONS - 1974- - CONGRESSES.
Die Wirtschaft der Vereinigten Staaten und der Bundesrepublik Deutschland . Bonn , c1977. 106 p. ; ISBN 3-87198-079-X LC Card 86-104673
HC106.7 .W57 1977

GERMANY (WEST) - ECONOMIC CONDITIONS - 1974- - ECONOMETRIC MODELS.
Aktuelle Probleme der Wirtschaftspolitik . Tübingen , 1982. vi, 69, vii, 62 p. : ISBN 3-16-344473-3 LC Card 84-125468
HJ5715.G3 A67 1982

GERMANY (WEST) - ECONOMIC CONDITIONS - 1974- - MATHEMATICAL MODELS.
Wirtschaftlicher Wandel, religiöser Wandel und Wertwandel . Berlin , c1985. 411 p. : ISBN 3-428-05784-8 LC Card 85-218417
HC286.7 .W58 1985

GERMANY (WEST) - ECONOMIC CONDITIONS - 1974- - REGIONAL DISPARITIES.
Blum, Ulrich. Raumwirkungen des Budgets der gesetzlichen Rentenversicherung . Karlsruhe , c1986. xii, 184, 35 p. : ISBN 3-88652-029-3 LC Card 87-124826 DDC 368.4/00943 19
HD7179 .B57 1986

Klemmer, Paul. Abgrenzung von Fördergebieten /. Bochum , 1983. 206 p. : ISBN 3-88339-298-7 LC Card 83-183564
HC286.7 .K59 1983

Meyer, Willm Rolf. Ressourcenumverteilung zugunsten von Problemregionen . Frankfurt/Main , New York , c1982. 262 p. : ISBN 3-593-33036-9 LC Card 82-161064 DDC 336.1/85 19
HJ1121 .M49 1982 ***NYPL [JLD 86-3292]***

Struff, Richard. Räumliche Einkommens-, Preis- und Verbrauchsunterschiede in der Bundesrepublik Deutschland /. Bonn , 1983. xi, 258 p. : ISBN 3-88488-262-7 LC Card 84-196141
HC286.7 .S836 1983

Wilamowitz-Moellendorff, Ulrich von. Ansätze eines Konzepts zur Erfassung regionaler Lebensbedingungen in der Raumordnungspolitik /. Bonn , 1986. iv, 205 p. ; ISBN 3-88488-275-9 LC Card 87-407818 DDC 330.943/0878 19
HC286.7 .W54 1986

GERMANY (WEST) - ECONOMIC CONDITIONS - 1974- - REGIONAL DISPARITIES - CONGRESSES.
Regionalisierte Arbeitsmarkt- und Beschäftigungspolitik /. Frankfurt/Main , New York , c1983. 322 p. : ISBN 3-593-33241-8 LC Card 84-106151
HC286.7 .R44 1983

GERMANY (WEST) - ECONOMIC CONDITIONS - 1974- - REGIONAL DISPARITIES - ECONOMETRIC MODELS.
Müller, Jürgen, 1943- Sektorale Struktur und Entwicklung der industriellen Beschäftigung in den Regionen der Bundesrepublik Deutschland /. Berlin , c1983. xiii, 200 p. : ISBN 3-428-05449-0 LC Card 84-109872
HC286.7 .M8 1983

GERMANY (WEST) - ECONOMIC CONDITIONS - ARCHIVAL RESOURCES - GERMANY (WEST) - CONGRESSES.
Wirtschaftsarchive und Kammern--Aspekte wirtschaftlicher selbstverwaltung gestern und heute . Köln , 1982. 250 p. ; LC Card 86-198576
HC286 .W59 1982

GERMANY, WEST - ECONOMIC CONDITIONS - PUBLIC OPINION.
Gewandelte Werte, erstarrte Strukturen . Bonn , c1985. ix, 329 p. : ISBN 3-87831-423-X LC Card 86-117688 DDC 330/.0943 19
HD8451 .G54 1985

GERMANY (WEST) - ECONOMIC CONDITIONS - REGIONAL DISPARITIES.
Körber-Weik, Margot. Wirtschaftskraft und Wirtschaftsentwicklung in den Bundesländern seit 1970 . Tübingen , 1986. x, 271 p. ; ISBN 3-88573-303-X LC Card 87-401375 DDC 330.943/0878 19
HC286.6 .K67 1986

GERMANY, WEST - ECONOMIC CONDITIONS - STATISTICS.
Zahlenbild-Almanach 1972 . Berlin , c1972. 204 p. : ISBN 3-503-00861-6 LC Card 86-133643
HC286.5 .Z225 1972

GERMANY, WEST - ECONOMIC POLICY.
Die Bedingungen des Wirtschaftswachstums in Vergangenheit und Zukunft . Tübingen , 1984. viii, 321 p., [1] leaf of plates : ISBN 3-16-344727-9 LC Card 85-165269
HD84 .B415 1984

Berghahn, Volker Rolf. [Unternehmer und Politik in der Bundesrepublik. English.] The Americanisation of West German industry, 1945-1973 /. Leamington Spa , New York , c1986. viii, 344 p. : ISBN 0-907582-55-9 : LC Card 86-222514
HC286.5 .B37x 1986b

Biedenkopf, Kurt H. Die neue Sicht der Dinge . München , c1985. 458 p. ; ISBN 3-492-02813-6 LC Card 86-105815
HB95 .B53 1985

L'Economia tedesca . Milano , c1981. 273 p. : LC Card 87-673286
HC286.7 .E29x 1981

Engelmann, Bernt, 1921- Wir hab'n ja den Kopf noch fest auf dem Hals . Köln , c1987. 257 p. : ISBN 3-462-01688-1 LC Card 87-146658
HC286.5 .E594 1987

Gruhler, Wolfram. Die grosse Denkverbiegung . Köln , c1987. 159 p. ; ISBN 3-87427-657-0 LC Card 87-152206 DDC 338.943 19
HC286.5 .G715 1987

Internationale und nationale Problemfelder der Betriebswirtschaftslehre /. Berlin , c1984. 336 p., [1] leaf of plates : ISBN 3-428-05696-5 LC Card 85-141327
HD35 .I598 1984

Kohl, Helmut, 1930- Soziale Marktwirtschaft, Fundament für morgen . Bonn [1987] 39 p. : ISBN 3-88991-011-4 LC Card 87-409383 DDC 338.943 19
HC286.5 .K565 1987

Leaman, Jeremy, 1947- The political economy of West Germany, 1945-85 . New York , 1988. xii, 287 p. : ISBN 0-312-00541-5 : LC Card 87-9458 DDC 338.943 19
HC286.5 .L4 1988

Ludwig-Erhard-Preis für Wirtschaftspublizistik 1986 . Bonn [1986] 45 p. : ISBN 3-88991-009-2 LC Card 87-409497 DDC 338.943 19
HC286.5 .L825 1986

Nienhaus, Volker. Kontroversen um Markt und Plan . Darmstadt , 1984. vi, 171 p. ; ISBN 3-534-08700-3 LC Card 84-181049
HB95 .N47 1984

Probleme monetärer und finanzwirtschaftlicher Steuerung im Systemvergleich /. Duisburg , c1986. 175 p. : ISBN 3-921473-43-8 LC Card 86-211745
HC286.6 .P754 1986

Randak, Harald, 1942- Die soziale Marktwirtschaft /. München , 1985. 143 p. : LC Card 85-216985
HC286.5 .R36 1985

Schatz, Klaus-Werner. Die Bedeutung kleiner und mittlerer Unternehmen im Strukturwandel /. Kiel , 1984. 32 p. ; LC Card 85-136545
HB44 .K45 no. 103 HD2346.G3

Schlieper, Andreas. 150 Jahre Ruhrgebiet . Düsseldorf , 1986. 224 p. : ISBN 3-590-18150-8 LC Card 86-231681
HC288.R8 S34 1986

Staatsgrenzen . Berlin , c1982. 183 p. ; ISBN 3-88619-089-7 LC Card 84-142799
HB90 .S75 1982

Stationen . Darmstadt , 1984. ix, 228 p., [1] leaf of plates : ISBN 3-534-02410-9 LC Card 85-138779
HC286.5 .S825 1984

Von der Bizonengründung zur ökonomisch-politischen Westintegration . Frankfurt am Main , c1984. v, 311 p. : ISBN 3-88129-640-9 LC Card 84-154481
HC286.5 .V64 1984

Wünsche, Horst Friedrich. Ludwig Erhards Gesellschafts- und Wirtschaftskonzeption . Stuttgart , 1986. 239 p. ; ISBN 3-87959-263-2 LC Card 86-201702
HC286.5 .W85 1986

Zur Problematik von Subventionen als Instrument der Wirtschaftspolitik /. Bonn , 1986. 97 p. : LC Card 87-408486 DDC 336/.012/43 s 338.943 19
HJ1101 .B6 Heft 259 HD3646.G4

GERMANY, WEST - ECONOMIC POLICY - 1974-
Basler, Hans-Peter. Lohnentwicklung und Lohnpolitik als Bestimmungsgründe konjunktureller Verläufe und struktureller Verschiebungen . Berlin , 1981. 102 p. : ISBN 3-428-04970-5 LC Card 82-100546 DDC 330 s 331.2/943 19
HB41 .B4 Nr. 134 HD5029
NYPL [JLL 73-207 Heft 134]

Bundesverband des Deutschen Gross- und Aussenhandels. Vorschläge und Beiträge des Bundesverbandes des Deutschen Gross- und Aussenhandels e.V. für die X. Legislaturperiode des Deutschen Bundestages. Bonn [1983] 56 p. ; LC Card 83-243234
HF1545 .B83 1983

Chancen für einen langen Aufschwung /. Stuttgart , 1984. xvii, 350 p. : ISBN 3-17-003288-7 : LC Card 86-178498
HC286.7 .C48 1984

Demontage des Sozialstaats . Köln , 1986. 177 p. ; ISBN 3-8161-0107-0 LC Card 87-104505 DDC 338.943 19
HC286.7 .D455 1986

Deutscher Industrie- und Handelstag. DIHT-Meinung, 1982 /. Bonn , 1982. 104 p. ; LC Card 83-206569
HC286.7 .D47 1982

Engels, Wolfram. Einseitige Betrachtungen . Düsseldorf , 1986. 240 p. ; LC Card 87-146603 DDC 338.943 19
HD84 .E53 1986

Erhöhter Handlungsbedarf im Strukturwandel . Berlin [1984] xxix, 229 p. : ISBN 3-428-05565-9 LC Card 86-137115 DDC 330 s 330.943/0878 19
HC281 .B33 Heft 79 HC286.7

Fels, Gerhard. Im Wendekreis des Krebsens . Köln , c1985. 91 p. ; ISBN 3-921349-44-3 LC Card 85-200560
HC286.7 .F46 1985

Für einen anhaltenden Aufschwung . Kiel [1986] 29 p. : ISBN 3-925357-33-5 (Deut. Bibl.) : LC Card 86-234971
HB44 .K45 no. 123 HC286.7

Germany (West). Bundesministerium der Finanzen. Rede zur Einbringung des Bundeshaushalts 1982 . Bonn , 1982. 56 p. : LC Card 82-221425
HJ2109 .G45 1982

Gewerbeentwicklung und Gewerbepolitik in der Grossstadtregion /. Gerlingen , c1987. 390 p., [3] leaves of plates : ISBN 3-88350-596-X LC Card 87-146643 DDC 332.6/732243 19
HC290.5.I53 G4797 1987

Herrschaft, Krise, Überleben . Münster , 1986. 396 p. : ISBN 3-924550-19-0 LC Card 86-229590
HC286.7 .H48 1986

Hübl, Lothar. Strukturwandel und Strukturpolitik . Hannover , 1983. 104 p. : LC Card 84-126938
HC286.7 .H83 1983

Innenpolitische Leistungsbilanz 1982-1986 /. Bonn , 1986. 124 p. : LC Card 86-215949
HC286.7 .I55 1986

Inotai, András. Az NSZK a változó világgazdaságban /. Budapest , 1986, c1985. 259 p. ; ISBN 963-221-584-2 : LC Card 87-136644
HC286.7 .I56 1986

Jungblut, Michael. Der Wohlstand entlässt seine Kinder . Stuttgart , c1983. 303 p. ; ISBN 3-421-06164-5 LC Card 83-232938
HC59 .J78 1983

Lafontaine, Oskar, 1943- Der andere Fortschritt . Hamburg , c1985. 222 p. ; ISBN

3-455-08248-3 LC Card 85-146223
HC286.7 .L33 1985

Memorandum '84 . Köln , c1984. 475 p. : ISBN 3-7609-0883-7 : LC Card 85-128558
HC286.7 .M465 1984

Praxisleitfaden Privatisierung /. Bonn , 1984. 202 p. : LC Card 84-194479
HD4175 .P73 1984

Renshaw, Geoffrey. Adjustment and economic performance in industrialised countries . Geneva , 1986. xiv, 180 p. ; ISBN 92-2-105510-8 (pbk.) : LC Card 87-123435 DDC 338.9/009172/2 19
HC286.7 .R46 1986

Schmidt, Kurt, 1924- Der Sachverständigenrat zur Begutachtung der Gesamtwirtschaftlichen Entwicklung . Stuttgart , 1985. 24 p. ; ISBN 3-515-04462-0 (Deut. Bibl.) : LC Card 86-157934
HC286.7 .S353 1985

Späth, Lothar, 1937- [Wende in die Zukunft. English.] Facing the future . Berlin , New York , c1986. xvi, 196 p. ; ISBN 0-387-17105-3 (U. S.) LC Card 86-25994 DDC 338.943 19
HC286.7 .S713 1986

Stoltenberg, Gerhard. Unsere Verantwortung für eine gute Zukunft . München , c1986. 191 p. ; ISBN 3-7892-7290-6 LC Card 87-130881 DDC 339.5/2/0943 19
HC286.7 .S767 1986

Striner, Herbert E. Regaining the lead . Millwood, N.Y. , c1987. xvii, 205 p. ; ISBN 0-8046-9408-7 (pbk. : alk. paper) : LC Card 86-32218 DDC 338.973 19
HC106.8 .S77 1987

Wolfgart, Ludger. Die technische Entwicklung als Element des sozialen Wandels und ihre Auswirkungen auf den öffentlichen Sektor in der Bundesrepublik Deutschland /. Münster [1986] ii, 213 p. ; ISBN 3-88660-230-3 (cover); 3-88600-230-3 (Deut. Bibl.) LC Card 87-106473 DDC 338.943 19
HD4175 .W65 1986

Ziele und Möglichkeiten der Privatisierung in volkswirtschaftlicher Sicht . Bonn , 1985. 83 leaves ; LC Card 86-185728
HJ1120 .B65 Nr. 244 HD4178

Die Zukunft der Globalsteuerung /. Bern , c1986. 268 p. ; ISBN 3-258-03573-3 : LC Card 86-182288
HC286.7 .Z82 1986

Zwei Jahre Politik der Erneuerung . Bonn [1984] 110 p. : LC Card 85-180111
HC286.7 .Z865 1984

Zwischenbericht, Analyse der strukturellen Entwicklung der deutschen Wirtschaft . Hamburg , 1979. viii, 142, 49 leaves : LC Card 83-132166
HC286.7 .Z88 1979

GERMANY, WEST - ECONOMIC POLICY - 1974- - ADDRESSES, ESSAYS, LECTURES.

Stabilization policy in France and the Federal Republic of Germany /. Amsterdam ; New York : xii, 379 p. : ISBN 0-444-87529-8 LC Card 84-28614 DDC 338.943 19
HC276.2 .S77 1985 **NYPL [TB *(Contributions to economic analysis. no.153)*]**

GERMANY, WEST - ECONOMIC POLICY - 1974- - CONGRESSES.

Votum für die Marktwirtschaft . Bonn , c1976. 26 p. ; LC Card 85-172115
HC286.7 .V69 1976

Die Wirtschaft der Vereinigten Staaten und der Bundesrepublik Deutschland . Bonn , c1977. 106 p. ; ISBN 3-87198-079-X LC Card 86-104673
HC106.7 .W57 1977

GERMANY, WEST - ECONOMIC POLICY - CONGRESSES.

Kontinuität und Wandel in vier Jahrzehnten deutscher Wirtschaftspolitik /. Stuttgart , New York , 1986. 111 p. ; ISBN 3-437-50310-3 LC Card 87-116017 DDC 338.943 19
HC286.5 .K618 1986

Staatsfinanzierung und Notenbank . Wien [1984?] 211 p. : LC Card 85-198128
HG1811 .S78 1984

Wirtschaftspolitik und Arbeitnehmerinteressen . Pönitz , 1986. 198 p. ; ISBN 3-923826-06-0 LC Card 86-162801
HB99.7 .W57 1986

GERMANY (WEST) - ECONOMIC POLICY - ECONOMETRIC MODELS.

Kudiss, Reinhard, 1952- Die Bestimmung des Produktionspotentials in Theorie und Empirie . Frankfurt am Main , New York , c1984. xvi, 198 p. : ISBN 3-8204-5579-5 LC Card 85-189908
HB3730 .K766 1984

GERMANY (WEST) - ECONOMIC POLICY - LONGITUDINAL STUDIES.

Schenkluhn, Brigitte, 1951- Konjunkturpolitik und Wahlen . Bergisch Gladbach , 1985. xi, 482 p. : ISBN 3-89012-017-2 LC Card 85-153982
HB3789 .S34 1985

GERMANY (WEST) - ETHNIC RELATIONS - CONGRESSES.

Kongress "Ausländerpolitik und Menschenrechte" (1983 : Frankfurt am Main, Germany) Reader zum Kongress "Ausländerpolitik und Menschenrechte" /. Frankfurt , 1984. 60 p. ; LC Card 87-133583 DDC 331.6/2/0943 19
HD8458.A2 K594 1983

GERMANY, WEST - FOREIGN ECONOMIC RELATIONS.

L'Economia tedesca . Milano , c1981. 273 p. : LC Card 87-673286
HC286.7 .E29x 1981

Gahlen, Bernhard. Zur internationalen Wettbewerbsfähigkeit der deutschen Wirtschaft /. [Berlin] [1985] 41, 4 p. ; LC Card 86-204589
HC286.7 .G29 1985

Inotai, András. Az NSZK a változó világgazdaságban /. Budapest , 1986, c1985. 259 p. ; ISBN 963-221-584-2 : LC Card 87-136644
HC286.7 .I56 1986

GERMANY, WEST - FOREIGN ECONOMIC RELATIONS - AFRICA.

Batsa, Kofi, 1931- West German neo-colonialism and Africa . Accra, Ghana [1964] 98 p. ; LC Card 87-118442 DDC 337.4306 19
HF1546.15.A35 B37 1964

GERMANY, WEST - FOREIGN ECONOMIC RELATIONS - CHINA.

Wiesegart, Kurt. Wirtschaftskooperation mit China . Hamburg , 1984. 126 p. ; ISBN 3-87895-260-0 LC Card 85-146617
HF1604.Z4 E869 1984

GERMANY (WEST) - FOREIGN ECONOMIC RELATIONS - CHINA - CONGRESSES.

Wirtschaftsreformen und neue Entwicklungsstrategien in der Volksrepublik China /. Frankfurt am Main , New York , c1986. 185 p. ; ISBN 3-8204-9101-5 LC Card 86-220822
HC427.92 .W56 1986

GERMANY (WEST) - FOREIGN ECONOMIC RELATIONS - DEVELOPING COUNTRIES.

Havemann, Hans A., 1912- Industrialisierungspolitik für Entwicklungsländer . Aachen , 1982. 68 p. ; ISBN 3-922525-06-7 LC Card 83-203761
HC59.7 .H386 1982

Held, Karl, 1944- Krieg und Frieden . Frankfurt am Main , c1983. 324 p. ; ISBN 3-518-11149-3 : LC Card 83-228517
HC79.D4 H45 1983

GERMANY (WEST) - FOREIGN ECONOMIC RELATIONS - DEVELOPING COUNTRIES - CONGRESSES.

Unterdrückung, Hunger, Krieg . Göttingen [1985?] 73 p. : LC Card 86-152237
HC59.7 .U55 1985

GERMANY, WEST - FOREIGN ECONOMIC RELATIONS - LATIN AMERICA.

Wolffsohn, Michael. Politik als Investitionsmotor? . Frankfurt am Main , New York , c1985. 141 p. : ISBN 3-8204-7487-0 (pbk.) LC Card 87-672289
HD2810.5 W64x 1985

GERMANY, WEST - FOREIGN ECONOMIC RELATIONS - UNITED STATES.

Berghahn, Volker Rolf. [Unternehmer und Politik in der Bundesrepublik. English.] The Americanisation of West German industry, 1945-1973 /. Leamington Spa , New York , c1986. viii, 344 p. : ISBN 0-907582-55-9 : LC Card 86-222514
HC286.5 .B37x 1986b

GERMANY, WEST - FULL EMPLOYMENT POLICIES.

Hof, Bernd. Arbeitsmarktstrukturen im Wandel /. Köln , c1985. 56 p. : ISBN 3-602-24737-6 LC Card 86-119065 DDC 331.12/5/0943 19
HD5779 .H638 1985

Memorandum '84 . Köln , c1984. 475 p. : ISBN 3-7609-0883-7 : LC Card 85-128558
HC286.7 .M465 1984

Vollbeschäftigung, eine Utopie? /. Bern , c1986. 330 p. : ISBN 3-258-03567-9 LC Card 86-224133
HD5779 .V64 1986

GERMANY (WEST) - FULL EMPLOYMENT POLICIES - CONGRESSES.

Regionalisierte Arbeitsmarkt- und Beschäftigungspolitik /. Frankfurt/Main , New York , c1983. 322 p. : ISBN 3-593-33241-8 LC Card 84-106151
HC286.7 .R44 1983

GERMANY, WEST - INDUSTRIES.

Berghahn, Volker Rolf. Unternehmer und Politik in der Bundesrepublik /. Frankfurt am Main , 1985. 363 p. : ISBN 3-518-11265-1 LC Card 85-235608
HC286.5 .B37 1985

Berghahn, Volker Rolf. [Unternehmer und Politik in der Bundesrepublik. English.] The Americanisation of West German industry, 1945-1973 /. Leamington Spa , New York , c1986. viii, 344 p. : ISBN 0-907582-55-9 : LC Card 86-222514
HC286.5 .B37x 1986b

Grätz, Christian. Kommunale Wirtschaftsförderung, kritische Bestandsaufnahme ihrer Funktionen und Organisation /. Bochum , 1983. xiii, 263 p. : ISBN 3-88339-340-1 : LC Card 84-138569
HC290.5.D5 G74 1983

Die Hamburger Industrie im Anpassungsprozess. Hamburg , 1980. 31 p. : LC Card 84-216971
HC289.H2 H42 1980

Hemmers, K. (Karlheinz) Planung des Personalbedarfs in indirekten Bereichen /. Berlin , New York , 1986. viii, 141 p. : ISBN 0-387-16702-1 (U. S.) : LC Card 86-200805
HF5549.5.M3 H46 1986

Hornschild, Kurt. Präferenzregelung der Forschungs- und Entwicklungsförderung in Berlin /. Berlin , 1985. v, 55 p. ; ISBN 3-428-05800-3 LC Card 86-156799
HD30.42.G39 H67 1985

Jens, Uwe, 1935- Die weltwirtschaftliche Herausforderung . Baden-Baden , 1986. 182 p. : ISBN 3-7890-1335-8 (Deut. Bibl.) LC Card 87-146574
HD3616.G4 J46 1986

Jungnickel, Rolf. Eigenimporte der deutschen Industrie /. Hamburg , 1984. 392 p. : ISBN 3-87895-256-2 LC Card 84-247605
HF3566.5 .J86 1984

Kampe, Dieter, 1953- Die Macher . Pfaffenweiler , 1986. 191 p. ; ISBN 3-89085-143-6 LC Card 87-133889 DDC 338.0943 19
HC286.7 .K36 1986

Renshaw, Geoffrey. Adjustment and economic performance in industrialised countries . Geneva , 1986. xiv, 180 p. ; ISBN 92-2-105510-8 (pbk.) : LC Card 87-123435 DDC 338.9/009172/2 19
HC286.7 .R46 1986

Schmidt, Klaus-Dieter. Im Anpassungsprozess zurückgeworfen . Tübingen , c1984. xx, 243 p. : ISBN 3-16-344755-4 LC Card 84-170512
HC286.7 .S352 1984

GERMANY (WEST) - INDUSTRIES - ARCHIVAL RESOURCES - GERMANY (WEST) - CONGRESSES.

Wirtschaftsarchive und Kammern--Aspekte wirtschaftlicher selbstverwaltung gestern und heute . Köln , 1982. 250 p. ; LC Card 86-198576
HC286 .W59 1982

GERMANY (WEST) - INDUSTRIES - ENERGY CONSERVATION.

Neu, Axel Dietmar, 1942- Entkoppelung von Wirtschaftswachstum und Energieverbrauch . Kiel [1978] 91 p. : LC Card 85-174721
HB44 .K45 no. 52 HD9502.G42

GERMANY (WEST) - INDUSTRIES - ENVIRONMENTAL ASPECTS - GOVERNMENT POLICY.
Paul, Joachim, 1956- Zur politischen Durchsetzungsfähigkeit einer ökologisch orientierten Marktwirtschaft . Frankfurt am Main , New York , c1986. xvii, 569 p. ; ISBN 3-8204-9810-9 LC Card 87-407614 DDC 363.7/056/0943 19
HC290.5.E5 P38 1986

GERMANY (WEST) - INDUSTRIES - LOCATION - ECONOMETRIC MODELS.
Müller, Jürgen, 1943- Sektorale Struktur und Entwicklung der industriellen Beschäftigung in den Regionen der Bundesrepublik Deutschland /. Berlin , c1983. xiii, 200 p. : ISBN 3-428-05449-0 LC Card 84-109872
HC286.7 .M8 1983

GERMANY (WEST) - MANUFACTURES - CASE STUDIES.
Flexible Fertigung und Industriearbeit . Frankfurt Main , New York , c1986. v, 577, iii p. : ISBN 3-593-33648-0 LC Card 86-197535
HD5109.2.G3 F45 1986

Germany (West). Monopolkommission. Die Rolle der Deutschen Bundespost im Fernmeldewesen / Monopolkommission. 1. Aufl. Baden-Baden : Nomos-Verlagsgesellschaft, 1981. 110 p. ; 23 cm. (Sondergutachten der Monopolkommission . Bd. 9) ISBN 3-7890-0675-0(pbk.) LC Card 81-130348 DDC 383/.4943 19
1. Deutsche Bundespost. 2. Telecommunication - Germany, West. 3. Government monopolies - Germany (West) - Case studies. I. Title. II. Series.
HE8155 .R64 1981 ***NYPL [JLE 87-312]***

GERMANY, WEST - MORAL CONDITIONS.
Dachrodt, Heinz-G., 1944- Arbeit und Gesellschaft im Umbruch . Köln [1987], c1986. 128 p. : ISBN 3-7663-0961-7 LC Card 87-139264 DDC 331.12/0943 19
HD6331.2.G28 D33 1987

GERMANY, WEST - OCCUPATIONS.
Hemmers, K. (Karlheinz) Planung des Personalbedarfs in indirekten Bereichen /. Berlin , New York , 1986. viii, 141 p. : ISBN 0-387-16702-1 (U. S.) : LC Card 86-200805
HF5549.5.M3 H46 1986

GERMANY, WEST - POLITICS AND GOVERNMENT.
Berghahn, Volker Rolf. Unternehmer und Politik in der Bundesrepublik /. Frankfurt am Main , 1985. 363 p. : ISBN 3-518-11265-1 LC Card 85-235608
HC286.5 .B37 1985

Dahrendorf, Ralf. Die Chancen der Krise . Stuttgart , c1983. 240 p. ; ISBN 3-421-06148-3
NYPL [JFD 87-2528]

Das Politische System der BRD . Berlin , 1985. 479 p. ; LC Card 86-123928 DDC 320.943 19
JN3971.A2 P59 1985 ***NYPL [JLD 86-3144]***

Germany (West). Bundestag. Haushaltsausschuss. Fragen der Subventionspolitik . Bonn , 1982. 222 p. ; LC Card 83-190544 DDC 338.943/02 19
HD3646.G4 G47 1982

Hüttig, Christoph. Gemeinwirtschaft im Sozialstaat . Frankfurt am Main , c1986. vi, 355 p. : ISBN 3-88129-990-4 : LC Card 86-223747
HD4175 .H83 1986

Kempf, Thomas. Umsetzung organisatorischer Neuerungen . Berlin , 1986. 237 p. : ISBN 3-88118-133-4 LC Card 87-114986
HD58.8 .K46 1986

Panek, Hans-Thomas. Die Währungskrisen vom November 1968 bis Mai 1971 im politischen Prozess der Bundesrepublik Deutschland /. Köln , 1977. 293 p. ; ISBN 3-921471-29-X LC Card 86-184843
HG999.5 .P35 1977

Roth, Rainer A., 1942- Zur Problematik der politischen Kultur der Jungwähler in der Bundesrepublik Deutschland /. Passau , c1984. 516 p. : ISBN 3-922016-46-4
NYPL [JLE 87-703]

Stationen . Darmstadt , 1984. ix, 228 p., [1] leaf of plates : ISBN 3-534-02410-9 LC Card 85-138779
HC286.5 .S825 1984

GERMANY (WEST) - POLITICS AND GOVERNMENT - 1982-
Fels, Gerhard. Im Wendekreis des Krebsens . Köln , c1985. 91 p. ; ISBN 3-921349-44-3 LC Card 85-200560
HC286.7 .F46 1985

Herrschaft, Krise, Überleben . Münster , 1986. 396 p. : ISBN 3-924550-19-0 LC Card 86-229590
HC286.7 .H48 1986

Innenpolitische Leistungsbilanz 1982-1986 /. Bonn , 1986. 124 p. : LC Card 86-215949
HC286.7 .I55 1986

Lafontaine, Oskar, 1943- Der andere Fortschritt . Hamburg , c1985. 222 p. ; ISBN 3-455-08248-3 LC Card 85-146223
HC286.7 .L33 1985

Stoltenberg, Gerhard. Unsere Verantwortung für eine gute Zukunft . München , c1986. 191 p. ; ISBN 3-7892-7290-6 LC Card 87-130881 DDC 339.5/2/0943 19
HC286.7 .S767 1986

Wende wohin? . Köln , c1983. 139 p. ; ISBN 3-921349-34-6 LC Card 84-150290
HC286.7 .W4 1983 ***NYPL [JFC 87-1258]***

GERMANY (WEST) - POLITICS AND GOVERNMENT - DICTIONARIES - GERMAN.
Lexikon Wirtschaftspolitik . München , c1986. 236 p. : ISBN 3-406-31302-7 LC Card 86-221788
HG151 .L45 1986

GERMANY, WEST - POPULATION.
Dachrodt, Heinz-G., 1944- Arbeit und Gesellschaft im Umbruch . Köln [1987], c1986. 128 p. : ISBN 3-7663-0961-7 LC Card 87-139264 DDC 331.12/0943 19
HD6331.2.G28 D33 1987

Dinkel, Reiner. Die Auswirkungen eines Geburten- und Bevölkerungsrückgangs auf Entwicklung und Ausgestaltung von gesetzlicher Alterssicherung und Familienlastenausgleich /. Berlin , c1984. 344 p. : ISBN 3-428-05546-2 LC Card 84-186733
HD7179 .D65 1984

Leben im Jahr 2000 und danach . Berlin , c1984. 213 p. : ISBN 3-7605-8571-X LC Card 85-128359
HB3595 .L43 1984

Schettkat, Ronald. Bevölkerungs- und Erwerbsverhaltensentwicklung in Österreich, Schweden und der Bundesrepublik Deutschland /. Berlin [1984] 48 p. ; LC Card 85-198691
HD5771 .S34 1984

GERMANY, WEST - POPULATION - CONGRESSES.
Deutsch-Französisches Arbeitstreffen auf dem Gebiet der Demographie (1985 : Dijon, France) Referate zum Deutsch-Französischen Arbeitstreffen auf dem Gebiet der Demographie vom 30. September bis 3. Oktober 1985 in Dijon. Wiesbaden , 1986. 134 p. : LC Card 87-409287 DDC 304.6/0943 19
HB3595 .D45 1985

GERMANY (WEST) - POPULATION - ECONOMIC ASPECTS - CONGRESSES.
Beiträge zur Bevölkerungsökonomie /. Berlin , c1986. 238 p. : ISBN 3-428-05969-7 LC Card 86-172600
HB3595 .B39 1986

GERMANY (WEST) - POPULATION - STATISTICAL METHODS.
Schaefer, Felix, 1950- Muster-Stichproben-Pläne für Bevölkerungs-Stichproben in der Bundesrepublik Deutschland und West-Berlin /. München , c1979. 160 p. : ISBN 3-478-39760-X; 3-478-39760-1 LC Card 84-135457
HB3595 .S29 1979

GERMANY, WEST - POPULATION - STATISTICS.
Städte in Zahlen . Hamburg , 1985. 199 p. : ISBN 3-922421-11-3 LC Card 86-212560
HB2265 .S73 1985

Germany (West). Presse- und Informationsamt. Zwei Jahre Politik der Erneuerung . Bonn [1984] 110 p. : LC Card 85-180111
HC286.7 .Z865 1984

GERMANY (WEST) - RELATIONS.
Zwei Jahre Politik der Erneuerung . Bonn [1984] 110 p. : LC Card 85-180111
HC286.7 .Z865 1984

GERMANY, WEST - SOCIAL CONDITIONS.
Engelmann, Bernt, 1921- Wir hab'n ja den Kopf noch fest auf dem Hals . Köln , c1987. 257 p. : ISBN 3-462-01688-1 LC Card 87-146658
HC286.5 .E594 1987

Herrschaft, Krise, Überleben . Münster , 1986. 396 p. : ISBN 3-924550-19-0 LC Card 86-229590
HC286.7 .H48 1986

Jungblut, Michael. Der Wohlstand entlässt seine Kinder . Stuttgart , c1983. 303 p. ; ISBN 3-421-06164-5 LC Card 83-232938
HC59 .J78 1983

Schmidt, Klaus-Dieter. Im Anpassungsprozess zurückgeworfen . Tübingen , c1984. xx, 243 p. : ISBN 3-16-344755-4 LC Card 84-170512
HC286.7 .S352 1984

GERMANY, WEST - SOCIAL POLICY.
Arend, Brigitte, 1953- Vom Lohnarbeiter zum Klienten . Frankfurt am Main , c1986. 206 p. ; ISBN 3-445-02490-1 LC Card 86-231993
HD5708 .A74 1986

Biedenkopf, Kurt H. Die neue Sicht der Dinge . München , c1985. 458 p. ; ISBN 3-492-02813-6 LC Card 86-105815
HB95 .B53 1985

Böpple, Arthur. "Sozialstaat" im Abbruch . Frankfurt/Main , c1986. 277 p. : ISBN 3-88367-062-6 LC Card 87-104497
HD7179 .B624 1986

Demontage des Sozialstaats . Köln , 1986. 177 p. ; ISBN 3-8161-0107-0 LC Card 87-104505 DDC 338.943 19
HC286.7 .D455 1986

Gruhler, Wolfram. Die grosse Denkverbiegung . Köln , c1987. 159 p. ; ISBN 3-87427-657-0 LC Card 87-152206 DDC 338.943 19
HC286.5 .G715 1987

Herrschaft, Krise, Überleben . Münster , 1986. 396 p. : ISBN 3-924550-19-0 LC Card 86-229590
HC286.7 .H48 1986

Innenpolitische Leistungsbilanz 1982-1986 /. Bonn , 1986. 124 p. : LC Card 86-215949
HC286.7 .I55 1986

Jungblut, Michael. Der Wohlstand entlässt seine Kinder . Stuttgart , c1983. 303 p. ; ISBN 3-421-06164-5 LC Card 83-232938
HC59 .J78 1983

Politik der Armut und die Spaltung des Sozialstaats /. Frankfurt am Main , 1985. 474 p. : ISBN 3-518-11233-3 : LC Card 85-183026
HC290.5.P6 P65 1985

Scheer, Christian. Verteilungswirkungen der Einkommensteuer /. Göttingen , c1982. xii, 457 p. : ISBN 3-509-01260-7 : LC Card 83-150522
HJ4719 .S34 1982

Schmölders, Günter, 1903- Der Wohlfahrtsstaat am Ende . München , 1983. 283 p. ; ISBN 3-7844-7133-1 LC Card 84-138252
HC286.6 .S284 1983

Strasser, Johano. Grenzen des Sozialstaats? . Köln , 1983. 206 p. ; ISBN 3-7663-0800-9 LC Card 83-142735
HC286.6 .S73 1983

Zwei Jahre Politik der Erneuerung . Bonn [1984] 110 p. : LC Card 85-180111
HC286.7 .Z865 1984

Die Zweite Stadt . Opladen , c1986. 407 p. : ISBN 3-531-11764-5 LC Card 87-497505 DDC 331.11/0943 19
HD8451 .Z94 1986

GERMANY, WEST - SOCIAL POLICY - ADDRESSES, ESSAYS, LECTURES.
Verwaltung und Planung im Wandel /. Köln , 1979. 112 p. ; ISBN 3-7745-6438-8 : LC Card 81-473982
HT395.G4 V48 ***NYPL [JLE 86-2107]***

GERMANY, WEST - STATISTICAL SERVICES.
Litz, Hans Peter. Amtliche Statistik in marktwirtschaftlich organisierten Industriegesellschaften . Frankfurt , New York , c1986. xii, 312 p. : ISBN 3-593-33752-5 LC Card 87-108767 DDC 350.81/9 19
HA37.G3 L58 1986

GERMANY, WEST - STATISTICS.
Schweitzer, Walter. Heiratstafeln versus Familienstandstafeln . Wiesbaden , 1985. iii, 102 p. : LC Card 87-408703 DDC 306.8/1/0943021 19
HB1215 .S39 1985

Germany (West). Statistisches Bundesamt. Index der Aktienkurse --lange Reihen. Wiesbaden , Stuttgart , 1985. 211 p. : LC Card 86-204529 DDC 332.63/222/0943 19
HG5494 .I53 1985

Nutzung von anonymisierten Einzelangaben aus Daten der amtlichen Statistik . Stuttgart , 1987. 200 p. : ISBN 3-17-003338-7 LC Card 87-401358
HA29.5.G4 N88 1987

Revidierte Ergebnisse, 1960 bis 1984 /. Stuttgart , 1985. 468 p. ; LC Card 86-204499 DDC 339.343 19
HC290.5.I5 R48 1985

Zur Neuberechnung der Indizes des Auftragseingangs und des Auftragsbestands für das Verarbeitende Gewerbe und das Bauhauptgewerbe auf Basis 1976. English. Indices of orders received and unfilled orders /. Wiesbaden , Stuttgart , 1986. 16 p. ; LC Card 86-215307
HF5437 .Z8713 1976

Germany, Western. see **Germany, West.**

Germany. Zollverein. see **Zollverein.**

Germidis, Dimitri A. Wellons, Philip A. Banks and specialised financial intermediaries in development /. Paris , Washington, D.C. , 1986. 150 p. : ISBN 92-64-12867-0 (pbk.) : LC Card 87-114506 DDC 332.1/09172/4 19
HG3550 .W45 1986

Germon, Claude. La normalisation, clé d'un nouvel essor : rapport de la Commission de réflexion présidée par Claude Germon, député au ministre d'Etat, ministre de la Recherche et de l'industrie / Claude Germon, Philippe Marano ; préface de Jean-Pierre Chevènement. Paris : Documentation française, c1983. 156 p. ; 24 cm. (Collection des rapports officiels) "Rapport au ministre de la Recherche et de l'industrie"--Cover. "Juillet 1982." Includes legislation. ISBN 2-11-001026-6 : LC Card 83-217768
1. Industry and state - France. 2. Industrial laws and legislation - France. I. Marano, Philippe. II. France. Ministère de la recherche et de l'industrie. Commission de réflexion. III. France. Ministère de la recherche et de l'industrie. IV. Title. V. Series.
HD3616.F83 G47 1983

Geroi nashikh dneĭ.
Rasskazy o kalinint͡sakh. Moskva , 1978. 172 p. : LC Card 81-147895
HD8529.K3162 R37 1978

GERONA (SPAIN : PROVINCE) - ADMINISTRATIVE AND POLITICAL DIVISIONS.
Medir i Huerta, Rosa M. Les comarques gironines . Girona , 1986. 211 p. : ISBN 84-505-3103-9 LC Card 87-101047
HC387.G4 M43 1986

GERONA, SPAIN (PROVINCE) - ECONOMIC CONDITIONS.
Medir i Huerta, Rosa M. Les comarques gironines . Girona , 1986. 211 p. : ISBN 84-505-3103-9 LC Card 87-101047
HC387.G4 M43 1986

GERONA, SPAIN (PROVINCE) - POPULATION.
Medir i Huerta, Rosa M. Les comarques gironines . Girona , 1986. 211 p. : ISBN 84-505-3103-9 LC Card 87-101047
HC387.G4 M43 1986

Gerondeau, Christian, 1938- L'énergie à revendre / Christian Gerondeau. [Paris] : J.-C. Lattès, c1984. 333 p. : ill. ; 24 cm. Bibliography: p. 331-[332] LC Card 84-166266
1. Energy industries. 2. Surplus (Economics). I. Title.
HD9502.A2 G47 1984

Geroski, Paul.
Oligopoly, competition, and welfare /. Oxford, OX, UK , New York, NY, USA , 1985. 191 p. : ISBN 0-631-14479-X (pbk.) LC Card 85-11200 DDC 338.8/2 19
HD2757.3 .O44 1985 ***NYPL [JLE 86-1961]***

The persistence of profits : some methodological remarks on measurement and explanation / by Paul A. Geroski. Berlin : Wissenschaftszentrum Berlin, [1985] 35, 6 p. : ill. ; 30 cm. (Discussion papers / IIMV Strukturpolitik, 0722-6748 = IIM industrial policy . IIM/IP 85-22) Summary in German. Bibliography: p. 34-35. LC Card 86-212315 DDC 338.5/16/0724 19
1. Corporate profits - Mathematical models. I. Series: Discussion papers (International Institute of Management. Industrial Policy) , IIM/IP 85-22. II. Title.
HG4028.P7 G47 1985

Geroski, Paul A.
Do dominant firms decline? / by Paul A. Geroski. Berlin : Wissenschaftszentrum Berlin, [1985] 23, [8] p. ; 30 cm. (Discussion papers / IIM/Industrial Policy, 0722-6748 . IIM/IP 85-29) Bibliography: p. [6-8] (2nd sequence) LC Card 86-213583 DDC 338.6/44 19
1. Big business. 2. Industrial concentration. 3. Competition. I. Series: Discussion papers (International Institute of Management. Industrial Policy) , IIM/IP 85-29. II. Title.
HD2757 .G47 1985

Entrepreneurship and small firms / by Paul A. Geroski and Joachim Schwalbach. Berlin : Wissenschaftszentrum Berlin, [1985] 31, 2, 6 p. ; 30 cm. (Discussion papers / IIM/Industrial Policy, 0722-6748 . IIM/IP 85-28) "October 1985." Bibliography: p. [1]-2 (2nd set). Summary also in German. LC Card 86-213576 DDC 338.6/42 19
1. Small business - Europe. 2. Small business - United States. 3. Small business - Japan. 4. Entrepreneurship - Europe. 5. Entrepreneurship - United States. 6. Entrepreneurship - Japan. I. Schwalbach, Joachim. II. Series: Discussion papers (International Institute of Management. Industrial Policy) , IIM/P 85-28. III. Title.
HD2346.E9 G47 1985

Gerrichhauzen, J. (John) Selles, G. (Gert) Mid career crisis /. Deventer [1985?] 135 p. : ISBN 90-6001-934-2 LC Card 86-163138
HF5384 .S45 1985

Gershenberg, Irving.
Multinational enterprises, transfer of managerial know-how, technology choice and employment effects : a case study of Kenya / by Irving Gershenberg. Geneva : International Labour Office, 1983. iii, 33 p. ; 30 cm. (Working papers / Multinational Enterprises Programme . working paper no. 28) Bibliography: p. 29. ISBN 92-2-103508-5 (pbk.) LC Card 86-213574 DDC 338.8/886762 19
1. International business enterprises - Kenya. 2. Executives - Kenya. 3. Management - Study and teaching - Kenya. I. Series: Working papers / Multinational Enterprises Programme , working paper no. 28. II. Title.
HD2920.5 .G47 1983

Slack in Kenya's modern manufacturing sector / by Irving Gershenberg. Boston, MA (270 Bay State Rd., Boston 02215) : African Studies Center, Boston University, 1985. 15 leaves ; 28 cm. (Working papers / African Studies Center . no. 105) Bibliography: leaves 10-12. LC Card 87-404089 DDC 338.4/767/096762 19
1. Industrial management - Kenya. 2. Kenya - Manufactures - Labor productivity. 3. Kenya - Manufactures - Industrial capacity. I. Boston University. African Studies Center. II. Series: Working papers (Boston University. African Studies Center) , no. 105. III. Title.
HD70.K4 G47 1985

Gershkovich, B. I͡A. (Boris I͡Akovlevich)
Obobshchestvlenie i ėkonomicheskie interesy v sot͡sialisticheskom obshchestve /. Moskva , 1983. 127 p. ; LC Card 84-204638
HD3856.R9 O26 1983

Gersovitz, Mark. The Political economy of risk and choice in Senegal /. London, England , Totowa, N.J. , 1987. xv, 363 p. : ISBN 0-7146-3297-X : LC Card 86-26859 DDC 338.966/3 19
HC1045 .P65 1987

Gerstein, Arnold, 1940- Win-win approaches to conflict avoidance / by Arnold Gerstein and James Reagan ; foreword by Bryant Wedge, preface by James Forest. 1st ed. Salt Lake City, Utah : G.M. Smith, 1986. xvii, 110 p. : ill. ; 23 cm. Bibliography: p. 109-110. ISBN 0-87905-215-5 LC Card 85-26261 DDC 303.6 19
1. Conflict management. 2. Interpersonal conflict. I. Reagan, James, 1931-. II. Title.
HM136 .G46 1986 ***NYPL [JLD 86-2104]***

Gerstein, Marc Saul. The technology connection : strategy and change in the Information Age / Marc S. Gerstein. Reading, Mass. : Addison-Wesley, c1987. xiv, 194 p. : ill. ; 21 cm. (The Addison-Wesley OD series) Includes bibliographical references. ISBN 0-201-12188-3 (pbk.) : LC Card 86-22343 DDC 658.4/012 19
1. Corporate planning. 2. Management information systems. 3. Information technology. I. Series: Addison-Wesley series on organization development. II. Title.
HD30.28 .G47 1987

Gerstel, Naomi. Families and work /. Philadelphia , 1987. viii, 539 p. ; ISBN 0-87722-467-6 (alk. paper) : LC Card 86-30151 DDC 306.8/5 19
HD4904.25 .F35 1987

Gerstenberger, Wolfgang. Strukturwandel unter verschlechterten Rahmenbedingungen : Strukturberichterstattung 1983 / von Wolfgang Gerstenberger ; unter Mitarbeit von Konrad Faust ... [et al.]. Berlin : Duncker & Humblot, c1984. 255 p. : ill. ; 24 cm. (Schriftenreihe des IFO-Instituts für Wirtschaftsforschung . Nr. 114) Bibliography: p. 247-251. Includes indexes. ISBN 3-428-05567-5 LC Card 84-180150
1. Germany, West - Economic conditions - 1974-. 2. Industrial productivity - Germany, West. 3. Germany, West - Commerce. 4. Labor supply - Germany, West. I. Faust, Konrad. II. Title. III. Series.
HC286.7 .G46 1984

Gerstenfeld, Arthur, 1927- U. S.A.-Japan Conference on Manufacturing Research (1986 : Tokyo, Japan) Manufacturing research perspectives, U. S.A.-Japan . Amsterdam , New York , 1987. viii, 198 p. : ISBN 0-444-42868-2 LC Card 87-19851 DDC 338.4/767 19
HD9725 .U17 1986

Gerster, Hans Joachim, 1946- Flexibilität und Rigidität in der Preisbewegung : empirische Untersuchung zum pro- und kontrazyklischen Preisverhalten für die Bundesrepublik Deutschland im Zeitraum 1949-1978 an Hand der Grundstoffpreise, Erzeugerpreise, Grosshandels- und Einzelhandelspreise / Hans Joachim Gerster. Frankfurt am Main ; New York : P. Lang, c1984. xii, 298, 69 p. : ill. ; 21 cm. (Europäische Hochschulschriften. Reihe V, Volks- und Betriebswirtschaft, 0531-7339 . Bd. 489 = vol. 489 = vol. 489) Originally presented as the author's thesis (doctoral)--Technische Hochschule Aachen, 1984. Bibliography: p. 288-289. ISBN 3-8204-5109-9 LC Card 85-195018
1. Prices - Germany, West. 2. Prices - United States. 3. Germany, West - Commerce. 4. United States - Commerce. I. Series: Europäische Hochschulschriften. Reihe V, Volks- und Betriebswirtschaft , Bd. 489. II. Title.
HB235.G3 G48 1984

Gerston, Larry N. The deregulated society / Larry N. Gerston, Cynthia Fraleigh, Robert Schwab. Pacific Grove, Calif. : Brooks/Cole Pub. Co., c1988. xvii, 244 p. : ill. ; 23 cm. Includes bibliographies and index. ISBN 0-534-08208-4 (pbk.) : LC Card 87-5116 DDC 338.973 19
1. Deregulation - United States. I. Fraleigh, Cynthia, 1957-. II. Schwab, Robert, 1957-. III. Title.
HD3616.U47 G47 1988

Gertcher, Frank L. Weida, William J. The political economy of national defense /. Boulder , 1987. xvii, 230 p. ; ISBN 0-8133-0432-6 (alk. paper) : LC Card 86-19015 DDC 355.6/22/0973 19
UA23 .W3694 1987 ***NYPL [JLE 87-1043]***

Gertich, Werner. Stimulierung in Industriebetrieben und Kombinaten /. Berlin , c1982. 290 p. : LC Card 83-164671
HF5549.5.M63 S75 1982

GERVAIS, ROLAND, 1906- - INTERVIEWS.
Lemieux-Pépin, Madeleine. P'tit train va loin . Ottawa , 1985. vii, 191 p. ; LC Card 86-177382
HE2808.1 .L45 1985

Gery, Gloria, 1944- Making CBT happen : prescriptions for successful implementation of computer-based training in your organization / by Gloria Gery.1st ed. Boston : Weingarten Publications, 1987. xiv, 225 p. : ill. ; 23 cm. Includes bibliographies and index. ISBN 0-9617968-0-4 (pbk.) : LC Card 86-51671 DDC 658.3/12404 19
1. Employees, Training of - Computer-assisted

instruction. 2. Computer-assisted instruction. I. Title.
HF5549.5.T7 G42 1987

Gesamtkonzeption nachwachsende Rohstoffe des Bundesministeriums für Ernährung, Landwirtschaft und Forsten : Ergebnis einer ministeriellen Arbeitsgruppe unter Federführung der Abteilung 2. Referat "Energie und Rohstoffe, Langfristanalysen.". Münster-Hiltrup : Landwirtschaftsverlag, 1983. vi, 196 p. : ill. ; 21 cm. "Schriftenreihe des Bundesministers für Ernährung, Landwirtschaft und Forsten. Reihe A: Angewandte Wissenschaft, Sonderheft." Includes bibliographical references. "ISSN 0723-7847"--Verso t.p. ISBN 3-7843-0202-5 : LC Card 84-126491
1. Energy industries - Germany, West. 2. Power resources - Germany, West. 3. Natural resources - Germany (West). I. Germany (West). Bundesministerium für Ernährung, Landwirtschaft und Forsten. Abteilung 2--Referat "Energie und Rohstoffe, Landfristanalysen.". II. Schriftenreihe des Bundesministers für Ernährung, Landwirtschaft und Forsten. Reihe A, Angewandte Wissenschaft. Supplement.
HD9502.G42 G47 1983

GESAMTVERBAND DER CHRISTLICHEN GEWERKSCHAFTEN DEUTSCHLANDS - HISTORY.
Roder, Hartmut, 1951- Der christlich-nationale Deutsche Gewerkschaftsbund (DGB) im politisch-ökonomischen Kräftefeld der Weimarer Republik . Frankfurt am Main , New York , c1986. 804 p. : ISBN 3-8204-9325-5 LC Card 86-194815
HD8443.D457 R63 1986

Gesamtverband der Deutschen Versicherungswirtschaft (Germany) Sicherung der Altersvorsorge durch Aufgabenteilung zwischen Individualversicherung und gesetzlicher Rentenversicherung . München , 1986. xi, 242 p. : ISBN 3-88512-017-8 : LC Card 86-163171
HD7105.35.G3 S53 1986

Die gesamtwirtschaftliche Bedeutung der Agrar- und Ernährungswirtschaft . Heilig, Bernd. Kiel , 1986. 171 p. : ISBN 3-922553-80-X LC Card 86-177526
HD1955 .H38 1986

Gesamtwirtschaftliche und strukturelle Auswirkungen von Veränderungen der Struktur des öffentlichen Sektors : Schwerpunktthema im Rahmen der Strukturberichterstattung 1983 / von Bernd Bartholmai ... [et al.]. Berlin : Duncker & Humblot, 1984. x, 266 p. : ill. ; 30 cm. (Beiträge zur Strukturforschung . Heft 81, 1984) Includes bibliographical references and index. ISBN 3-428-05739-2 LC Card 86-138980
1. Finance, Public - Germany, West. 2. Germany, West - Appropriations and expenditures. 3. Germany, West - Economic conditions. I. Bartholmai, Bernd. II. Series: Beiträge zur Strukturforschung , Heft 81.
HC281 .B33 Heft 81 HJ1120

Geschäfte mit der Armut . Bühler, Marcel. Frankfurt/M. , c1982. 200 p. : ISBN 3-923363-02-8 (pbk.) LC Card 86-674004
HD9673.D44 B83x 1982

Geschichte der Ausländer, Beschäftigung in Deutschland, 1880 bis 1980 . Herbert, Ulrich, 1951- Berlin , c1986. 272 p. : ISBN 3-8012-3019-8 LC Card 87-113703 DDC 331.6/2/0943 19
HD8458.A2 H39 1986

Geschichte der Basler Bandindustrie 1550-1800 /. Fink, Paul. Basel , 1983. 216 p. : ISBN 3-7190-0836-3 LC Card 83-220231 DDC 338.4/767776 19
HD9929.R6 S94 1983 ***NYPL [JLE 86-2781]***

Geschichte der deutschen Kriegswirtschaft 1939-1945. Eichholtz, Dietrich. Berlin, 1969-<1985. v. <1-2 > LC Card 70-444798
HC286.4 .E34

Geschichte der internationalen Arbeiterbewegung in Daten / Institut für Marxismus-Leninismus beim ZK der SED ; [Autoren- und Redaktionskollektiv, Horst Schumacher (Leiter) ... et al. ; weitere Autoren, Lutz-Stephan Albrecht ... et al.]. Berlin : Dietz, 1986. 868 p. ; 23 cm. Includes indexes. ISBN 3-320-00635-5 LC Card 86-210352
1. International labor activities - History - Chronology. I. Schumacher, Horst, 1929-. II. Institut für Marxismus-Leninismus beim ZK der SED.
HD6475.A1 G47 1986

Geschichte der Jugend .
(Bd. 9) Hein, Peter Ulrich. Protestkultur und Jugend . Münster , 1984. iii, 151 p. ; ISBN 3-88660-109-9 ***NYPL [JLD 86-2444]***

Geschichte der Philatelie /. Brühl, Carlrichard, 1925- Hildesheim , New York , 1985-1986. 2 v. : ISBN 3-487-07619-5 (v. 1) LC Card 86-118167 DDC 769.569 19
HE6203 .B78 1985 ***NYPL [JFM 86-350]***

Geschichte der Unternehmungen in der deutschen Rheinschiffahrt /. Jolmes, Lothar L. V. Köln , 1960. 164 p. : LC Card 85-147446
HE5 .C6 Nr. 17 HE619.R48

Geschichte des deutschen Einzelhandels /. Berekoven, Ludwig. Frankfurt am Main , c1986. 175 p. : ISBN 3-87150-246-4 LC Card 87-121881
HF5429.6.G42 B46 1986

Geschichte des Deutschen Zollvereins /. Hahn, Hans-Werner. Göttingen , c1984. 214 p. ; ISBN 3-525-33500-8 LC Card 85-129823
HF2106 .H27 1984

Geschichte des FDGB : Chronik, 1945-1982 / [Autoren, H. Bednareck ... et al. ; Redaktionskollektiv, H. Deutschland ... et al. ; Herausgeber, Gewerkschaftshochschule "Fritz Heckert" beim Bundesvorstand des FDGB].2., unveränderte Aufl. Berlin : Tribüne, c1985. 364 p. ; 21 cm. Includes indexes. LC Card 86-124681 DDC 331.88/0943 19
1. Freier Deutscher Gewerkschaftsbund - History - Chronology. 2. Trade-unions - Germany (East) - History - Chronology. I. Bednareck, Horst. II. Deutschland, Heinz. III. Gewerkschaftshochschule "Fritz Heckert.".
HD8460.5.A5 F7326 1985

Die Geschichte des Suezkanals : nach bisher unveröffentlichten Dokumenten / [Herausgegeben von der Schriftleitung der "Rundschau für Technik und Wirtschaft"]. Prag : J.G. Calve, [1912?] 26 p. ; 23 cm. "Sonderabdruck aus der 'Rundschau für Technik und Wirtschaft' Jahrgang 1912." LC Card 86-209445
1. Suez Canal (Egypt). I. Rundschau für Technik und Wirtschaft.
HE543 .G47 1912

Die geschichtliche Umwandlung der ökonomischen Gesellschaftsformation der Türkei /. Ceylan, Sadi, 1951- Berlin , c1985. 270 p. ; ISBN 3-88548-482-X LC Card 86-221332
HC492 .C49 1985

Geschlecht und Berufswahl . Selk, Michael, 1943- Frankfurt am Main , New York , c1984. 289 p. : ISBN 3-8204-5375-X LC Card 85-193055
HD6059.6.G4 S45 1984

Der geschlossene Immobilienfonds . Bölter, Hendrick H., 1957- Frankfurt am Main , New York , c1986. xv, 290 p. : ISBN 3-8204-9460-X LC Card 86-195280
HG5502 .B65 1986

Gesellschaft für Strahlen- und Umweltforschung. Informationsseminar Alkohol am Arbeitsplatz (1985 : Obereifenberg, Schmitten, Germany) Informationsseminar Alkohol am Arbeitzplatz /. München [1985?] ii, 49 p. : LC Card 86-162315
HF5549.5.A4 I54 1985

Gesellschaft für Unternehmensgeschichte. Goetzeler, Herbert. Wilhelm und Carl Friedrich von Siemens . Stuttgart , 1986. 131 p. : ISBN 3-515-04558-9 LC Card 86-141456
HD9695.G43 S514 1986

Gesellschaft für Wirtschafts- und Sozialkybernetik. Kybernetik und Management . Berlin , c1983. viii, 131 p. : ISBN 3-428-05448-2 LC Card 84-109870
HD29 .K92 1983

Gesellschaft für Wirtschafts- und Sozialwissenschaften, Verein für Socialpolitik. (Old Catalog form: Verein für Sozialpolitik, Gesellschaft für Wirtschafts- und Sozialwissenschaften.)
Schriften.
(Bd. 134. 134) Staatsfinanzierung im Wandel . Berlin , c1983. xi, 877 p. : ISBN 3-428-05420-2
NYPL [JLL 73-186 Bd. 134]

Gesellschaft für Wirtschafts- und Sozialwissenschaften, Verein für Socialpolitik. Ausschuss zum Vergleich von Wirtschaftssystemen. China im Konflikt zwischen verschiedenen Ordnungskonzeptionen /. Berlin , c1985. 157 p. : ISBN 3-428-05923-9 LC Card 86-164406
HC427.9 .C56525 1985

Gesellschaft für Wirtschafts- und Sozialwissenschaften, Verein für Socialpolitik. Wirtschaftspolitischer Ausschuss. Arbeitsgruppe Wettbewerb. Strukturpolitische Probleme der Automobil-Industrie unter dem Aspekt des Wettbewerbs /. Berlin , c1985. 247 p. : ISBN 3-428-05924-7 LC Card 86-165212 DDC 338.4/76292/094 19
HD9710.E82 S77 1985

Gesellschaft für Deutsch-Chinesische Freundschaft. Wirtschaftsreformen und neue Entwicklungsstrategien in der Volksrepublik China /. Frankfurt am Main , New York , c1986. 185 p. ; ISBN 3-8204-9101-5 LC Card 86-220822
HC427.92 .W56 1986

Gesellschaft für Öffentliche Wirtschaft und Gemeinwirtschaft. Wissenschaftlicher Beirat. Zum Problem der Aufgabenverlagerung auf öffentliche Unternehmen : Gutachten des Wissenschaftlichen Beirats der Gesellschaft für Öffentliche Wirtschaft und Gemeinwirtschaft / Federführung, Paul Münch, Günter Püttner ; Herausgeber, Wissenschaftlicher Beirat der Gesellschaft für Öffentliche Wirtschaft und Gemeinwirtschaft.1. Aufl. Baden-Baden : Nomos, 1984. 73 p. ; 23 cm. (Schriftenreihe der Gesellschaft für Öffentliche Wirtschaft und Gemeinwirtschaft . Heft 27) Includes bibliographical references. ISBN 3-7890-1048-0 LC Card 85-143795
1. Government business enterprises - Germany, West. I. Münch, Paul, 1913-. II. Püttner, Günter. III. Title. IV. Series.
HD4177 .G47 1984

Gesellschaft für Ost- und Südostkunde (Linz, Austria) Osteuropa im Blickpunkt . Linz [1985?] 168 p. ; LC Card 87-142952 DDC 382/.091713/01717 19
HF1411 .O687 1985

Gesellschaft für Sozialwissenschaftliche und Ökologische Forschung (Germany) Bode, Peter M. Alptraum Auto . München , 1986. 237 p. : ISBN 3-922696-46-5 LC Card 87-107197 DDC 303.4/832 19
HE5613 .B63 1986

Gesellschaft für Versicherungswissenschaft und -gestaltung e.V. Köln.
Demographische Entwicklung und kapitalbildende Altersversorgungssysteme /. Bergisch Gladbach , 1984. iii, 67 p. ; LC Card 85-154174
HD7091 .D46 1984

Kapitalbildung und Altersvorsorge . Köln , Bergisch Gladbach [1983?] 95 p. : LC Card 84-180205
HD7105.45.G3 K37 1983

Gesellschaft für Westfälische Wirtschaftsgeschichte. Henning, Friedrich-Wilhelm. Vorindustrielles Gewerbe und wirtschaftlicher Wandel im Paderborner Land im 19. Jahrhundert /. Dortmund , 1983. 67 p. ; LC Card 83-198581
HC288.P27 H46 1983

Gesellschaft für Wirtschafts- und Sozialwissenschaft, Verein für Socialpolitik. Wirtschaftspolitischer Ausschuss. Nationale Wege der Inflationsbekämpfung /. Berlin , c1986. 223 p. : ISBN 3-428-06077-6 LC Card 87-132310 DDC 332.4/1/094 19
HC240 .N315 1986

Gesellschaft für Wirtschafts- und Sozialwissenschaften, Verein für Socialpolitik. Ausschuss für Sozialpolitik. Sozialpolitik in der Beschäftigungskrise /. Berlin , c1986. 2 v. : ISBN 3-428-05949-2 (Bd. I) : LC Card 87-119211 DDC 361.6/1 19
HD5710 .S67 1986

Gesellschaft für Wirtschafts- und Sozialwissenschaften, Verein für Socialpolitik. Sozialwissenschaftlicher Ausschuss. Normengeleitetes Verhalten in den Sozialwissenschaften /. Berlin , c1984. 199 p. ; ISBN 3-428-05622-1 LC Card 86-140299
HB74.P8 N67 1984

Wert- und Präferenzprobleme in den Sozialwissenschaften /. Berlin , c1981. 268 p. :

ISBN 3-428-05013-4 LC Card 86-230716
HF5415.3 .W47 1981

Gesellschaft für Wirtschafts- und Sozialwissenschaften, Verein für Sozialpolitik.
Schriften .
(n.F., Bd. 142) Wachstumsverlangsamung und Konjunkturzyklen in unterschiedlichen Wirtschaftssystemen /. Berlin , c1984. 191 p. : ISBN 3-428-05626-4
NYPL [JLL 73-186 Bd. 142]

Schriften. Neue Folge .
(Bd. 115) Studien zur Entwicklung der ökonomischen Theorie /. Berlin , c1981- v. ; ISBN 3-428-04862-8 (v. 1) : LC Card 81-154218 DDC 330/.09 19
HB75 .S787 1981
NYPL [JLL 73-186 Bd.115]

Gesellschaft Jesu. see **Jesuits.**

Gesellschaftliche Instabilität und Unternehmungsführung . Dyllick, Thomas. Bern , c1982. xiv, 394 p. : ISBN 3-258-03212-2 LC Card 83-115754
HD58.7 .D94 1982

Gesellschaftliches Selbstverständnis und politische Orientierung der Freien Berufe : Kurzfassung der Ergebnisse einer empirischen Untersuchung Freier Berufe in Bayern / Projektbearbeiter, Walter Lang, unter Mitarbeit von Manfred Koch. Nürnberg : Institut für Freie Berufe an der Friedrich-Alexander-Universität Erlangen-Nürnberg, 1978. 144 p. : ill. ; 23 cm. LC Card 86-170378
1. Professional employees - Germany (West) - Bavaria. 2. Party affiliation - Germany (West) - Bavaria. I. Lang, Walter. II. Koch, Manfred. III. Friedrich-Alexander-Universität Erlangen-Nürnberg. Institut für Freie Berufe.
HD8038.G32 B384 1978

Gesellschaftssteuerung zwischen Korporatismus und Subsidiarität / Manfred Glagow (Hg.) ; mit Beiträgen von M. Glagow ... [et al.]. Bielefeld : AJZ, 1984. 239 p. ; 21 cm. Includes bibliographies. CONTENTS. - Formen politischer Steuerung / Uwe Schimank, Manfred Glagow -- Gesellschaftssteuerung / Helmut Willke -- Neokorporatismus in steuerungstheoretischer Perspektive / Wilfried Gotsch -- Korporative Strategien und Strukturen in kapitalistischen Gesellschaften / Hans Kastendiek -- Zur Delegation staatlicher Aufgaben im Umweltschutz an Selbstverwaltungskörperschaften / Manfred Glagow -- Umweltschutz durch Wirtschaft[s]verbände? Josef Hilbert, Helmut Voelzkow -- Sozialpolitische Steuerung / Rolf G. Heinze, Thomas Olk -- Subsidiarität / Klaus Gretschmann -- "Alternative Politik" und Politikreform / Volker Ronge. ISBN 3-921680-46-8 LC Card 86-223831
1. Taxation. 2. Corporate state. I. Glagow, M.
HJ2309 .G47 1984

Gesellschaftswissenschaften (Berlin, Germany) .
(GW 41) Soziale Aspekte der Mikroelektronik /. Berlin , 1985. 122 p. ; LC Card 87-409418 DDC 306/.46 19
HD6331 .S683 1985

Geser, Hans. Strukturformen und Funktionsleistungen sozialer Systeme : ein soziologisches Paradigma / Hans Geser. Opladen : Westdeutscher Verlag, c1983. 275 p. : ill. ; 24 cm. Bibliography: p. 264-275. ISBN 3-531-11612-6 :
1. Sociology - Methodology. 2. Social systems. I. Title.
NYPL [JLE 87-1162]

Gesinnungs überprüft! : Gespräche mit Betroffenen / [herausgegeben vom Komitee zur Verteidigung Demokratischer Grundrechte und der Demokratischen Hochschule/Aktionskomitee gegen Berufsverbote an der Freien Universität Berlin]. Berlin : Das Komitee, [1978] 263 p. : ill. ; 21 cm. Cover title. Bibliography: p. 263. LC Card 84-198533
1. Right to labor - Germany (West) - Case studies. 2. Professions - Germany (West) - Case studies. 3. Discrimination in employment - Germany (West) - Case studies. I. Komitee zur Verteidigung Demokratischer Grundrechte (Berlin, Germany). II. Aktionskomitee gegen Berufsverbote (Berlin, Germany).
HD4903.5.G4 G47 1978

Gespräche der List Gesellschaft e.V. .
(n.F., Bd. 10) Was trennt Europa? /. Baden-Baden , 1986. 147 p. ; ISBN 3-7890-1320-X LC Card 87-108024 DDC 337.1/42 19
HC241.2 .W394 1986

Gessford, John Evans. Modern information systems : designed for decision support / John Evans Gessford. Reading, Mass. : Addison-Wesley Pub. Co., c1980. xii, 512 p. : ill. ; 25 cm. Includes bibliographies and index. ISBN 0-201-03099-3 : LC Card 78-74684 DDC 658/.05/4
1. Management information systems. 2. Decision support systems. I. Title.
HF5548.2 .G48 *NYPL [JLE 80-1913]*

Gessler, Joachim. Werbung der Banken / Joachim Gessler. [S.l. : s.n., 1983] (Köln : Druck- und Verlagshaus Wienand) xxvii, 200 p. ; 21 cm. (Bankrechtliche Sonderveröffentlichungen des Instituts für Bankwirtschaft und Bankrecht an der Universität zu Köln . 30. Bd.) Bibliography: p. xiii-xxvii. LC Card 83-214619
1. Advertising - Banks and banking - Germany (West). I. Title. II. Series.
HF6161.B2 G47 1983

Gessler, Joan E. Schabeck, Timothy A. Managing microcomputer security . Port Jefferson Station, N.Y. (492 Old Town Rd., Port Jefferson Station 11776) , c1986. 1 v. (various pagings) : LC Card 86-216667 DDC 658.4/78 19
HF5548.37 .S33 1986

Gesswein, Joachim P., 1955- Die Berücksichtigung des Geldes und der Banken als gesellschaftliche Institutionen in der Property Rights-Theorie / Joachim P. Gesswein. München : Florentz, c1986. vi, 309 p. ; 21 cm. (Volkswirtschaftliche Forschung und Entwicklung . Bd. 22) Originally presented as the author's thesis (doctoral--Universität Augsburg, 1985) under the title: Die Property Rights-Theorie als neue Gesellschaftstheorie und ihre Anwendung auf die qualitativ-statische Theorie des Geldes und das Wesen der monetären Unternehmung, insbesondere der Bank. Bibliography p. 274-306. Includes index. ISBN 3-88259-374-1 LC Card 86-172234
1. Right of property. 2. Money. 3. Banks and banking. I. Title. II. Series.
HB711 .G47 1986

Gestalt und Wandel der nebenberuflichen Landwirtschaft in Nordrhein-Westfalen /. Kreiten, Kurt. Bonn , 1985. xi, 225 p. : ISBN 3-88488-272-4 LC Card 86-205281
HD1960.N67 K74 1985

Gestaltkonforme partnerschaftliche "Beteiligungs-" und "Kreditfinanzierung" von "Klein-" und "Mittelbetrieben" /. Pernsteiner, August W. Wien , 1983. 355, xxx p. : ISBN 3-85369-536-1 LC Card 83-206156
HG4027.7 .P47 1983

Gestaltung künftiger Raumstrukturen durch veränderte Verkehrskonzepte : Referate und Diskussionsberichte anlässlich der wissenschaftlichen Plenarsitzung 1985 in Lübeck. Hannover : C.R. Vincentz, 1986. xii, 173 p. : 2 ill. ; 25 cm. (Veröffentlichungen der Akademie für Raumforschung und Landesplanung. Forschungs- und Sitzungsberichte, 0587-2642 . Bd. 164) 24. Wissenschaftliche Plenarsitzung Proceedings of the 24th meeting organized by the Akademie für Raumforschung und Landesplanung. Includes bibliographical references. ISBN 3-87870-767-3 LC Card 87-401351 DDC 380.5/0943/512 19
1. Transportation - Germany (West) - Schleswig-Holstein - Congresses. 2. Transportation and state - Germany (West) - Schleswig-Holstein - Congresses. 3. Regional planning - Germany (West) - Schleswig-Holstein - Congresses. I. Akademie für Raumforschung und Landesplanung (Germany). II. Series. III. Series: Wissenschaftliche Plenarsitzung , 24.
HE249.Z7 S343 1986

Die Gestaltung von Marketingstrategien . Fronhoff, Bernd, 1956- Bergisch Gladbach , 1986. ix, 369 p. : ISBN 3-89012-067-9 LC Card 87-122913 DDC 658.8/02 19
HF5415.135 .F76 1986

Gestaltungsspielräume der Arbeitsmarktpolitik auf regionalen Arbeitsmärkten : Vorträge anlässlich eines Workshops zum Thema Gestaltungsspielräume der Arbeitsmarktpolitik auf regionalen Arbeitsmärkten, der Stellenwert regionaler Arbeitsmarktuntersuchungen am 29. und 30. April 1981 in Augsburg / herausgegeben von Peter Hurler und Martin Pfaff. Berlin : Duncker & Humblot, c1984. 180 p. : ill. ; 24 cm. (Schriften des Internationalen Instituts für Empirische Sozialökonomie (INIFES) . Bd. 8) Workshop was sponsored by Amt für Wirtschaftförderung der Stadt Augsburg and INIFES. Bibliography: p. 83-84. CONTENTS. - Regionalisierung der Arbeitsmarktpolitik und ihre Bedeutung aus der Sicht der Raumordnung / Hans-Peter Gatzweiler -- Was sollte und was kann regionale Arbeitsmarktpolitik leisten? / Werner Tegtmeier -- Begrenzte Gestaltungsspielräume der lokalen Arbeitsverwaltung / Manfred Rademacher -- Regionalisierung der Arbeitsmarktpolitik / Dietrich Garlichs -- Möglichkeiten und Grenzen einer mittelfristigen Prognose der Arbeitskräftenachfrage nach Wirtschaftszweigen und Berufen im Wirtschaftsraum Augsburg / Peter Hurler -- Strukturierte Expertengespräche im Rahmen des Projekts "Regionaler Arbeitsmarkt Augsburg" / Martin Held -- Veränderungen der Produktions- und Arbeitsmarktstruktur in der Berliner Industrie / Harald Bremm, Dieter Isensee und Thomas Ranneberg -- Überlegungen zum Aufbau eines Arbeitsmarkt-Informationssystem in Hamburg / Jobst Fiedler. ISBN 3-428-05614-0 LC Card 84-218530
1. Labor policy - Germany, West - Congresses. 2. Unemployment - Germany (West) - Regional disparities - Congresses. I. Hurler, Peter. II. Pfaff, Martin. III. Augsburg (Germany). Amt für Wirtschaftsförderung. IV. Internationales Institut für Empirische Sozialökonomie. V. Series.
HD8444 .G47 1984

Gestion budgétaire /. Meyer, Jean, 1926- [Paris] , 1984. xvi, 283, 191 p. : ISBN 2-04-015608-9 : LC Card 85-166398 DDC 658.1/54 19
HG4026 .M49 1984

Gestión de empresas públicas en América Latina : memoria del seminario internacional. Quito, Ecuador : Dirección Nacional de Personal del Ecuador, c1986. 146 p. : ill. ; 21 cm. Proceedings of the Seminario Internacional sobre "Gestión de Empresas Públicas," held in Quito, Ecuador, Oct. 29-31, 1985, sponsored by the Dirección Nacional de Personal del Gobierno Ecuatoriano; co-sponsored by Consejo Nacional de Desarrollo, Instituto Latinoamericano de Investigaciones Sociales, and Sección Ecuatoriana de la Asociación Latinoamericana de Administración Pública. Includes bibliographical references. LC Card 87-401599 DDC 350/.0092/098 19
1. Government business enterprises - Latin America - Management - Congresses. I. Ecuador. Dirección Nacional de Personal. II. Seminario Internacional sobre "Gestión de Empresas Públicas" (1985 : Quito, Ecuador).
HD4010.5 .G47 1986

La gestion efficace des projets de développement . Brinkerhoff, Derick W. West Hartford, Conn. , c1987. vi, 186 p. : ISBN 0-931816-06-8 (pbk.) LC Card 86-33733 DDC 338.9/0068 19
HD75.8 .B75 1987

La Gestión en empresas cooperativas : análisis interdisciplinario de dieciocho organizaciones / Costa, Ricardo ... [et al.]. Buenos Aires, Argentina : INTERCOOP, Editora Cooperativa, [1985] 146 p. ; 22 cm. (Serie Documentos / Ediciones INTERCOOP, Argentina . no. 8) Includes bibliographical references. ISBN 950-0-01257-11 LC Card 87-115117 DDC 334/.0982/54 19
1. Cooperative societies - Argentina - Córdoba (Province) - Management - Case studies. I. Costa, Ricardo L. II. Series: Serie Documentos (INTERCOOP, Editora Cooperativa Ltda.) , no. 8.
HD3470.A3 C674 1985

Gestion et stratégie financières internationales /. Klein, Jean, docteur ès sciences économiques. Paris , c1985. v, 266 p. : ISBN 2-04-015504-X : LC Card 86-192918
HG4027.5 .K58 1985

Gestion internationale de l'entreprise / Henri de Bodinat ... [et al.]. 2e éd. Paris : Dalloz, 1984. 393 p. : ill. ; 23 cm. (Dalloz Gestion. Vie internationale de l'entreprise) Includes bibliographical references and index. ISBN 2-247-00496-2 : LC Card 85-114907
1. International business enterprises - Management. I. Bodinat, Henri de. II. Series.
HD62.4 .G47 1984

Gestion "module"
Dubrulle, Louis. Comptabilité analytique de gestion . [Paris] , c1985-c1987. 2 v. : ISBN 2-04-015766-2 (v. 2) : LC Card 86-149033

DDC 668/.65/0681 19
HF5642 .D74 1985

Meyer, Jean, 1926- Gestion budgétaire /. [Paris] , 1984. xvi, 283, 191 p. : ISBN 2-04-015608-9 : LC Card 85-166398 DDC 658.1/54 19
HG4026 .M49 1984

La gestion planifiée de l'entreprise commerciale de détail . Mwanza Mujila. Lubumbashi [Zaire] , 1984. 287 p. : LC Card 85-177323
HF5429 .M88 1984

Gestion, travail, loisirs. Management, work, leisure . Geneva , c1986. viii, 154 p. : ISBN 92-9014-416-5 (pbk.) : LC Card 87-163300 DDC 306/.36/094 19
HD4904.6 .M35 1986

La Gestione degli istituti di credito industriale / Paolo Mottura ... [et al.] ; a cura di Paolo Mottura. Milano : Giuffrè, [1985] xviii, 868 p. : ill. ; 24 cm. (Università "L. Bocconi," Dipartimento di economia aziendale . 96. 3.39) Includes bibliographies. ISBN 88-14-00665-2 : LC Card 86-170383
1. Credit management. 2. Bank management. I. Mottura, Paolo. II. Series: Università "L. Bocconi," Dipartimento di economia aziendale (Series) , 96.
HG3726 .G47 1985

La gestione dei rischi di azienda . Borghesi, Antonio. Padova , 1985. 299 p. : LC Card 86-214201
HD61 .B65 1985

Gestionnaires et profiteurs de la Révolution . Bruguière, Michel. Paris , c1986. 339 p. : ISBN 2-85565-332-0 : LC Card 87-123230
HJ1083 .B78 1986

Gesundheitssystemforschung.
Molinaro, Remo. Gesundheitswesen und Kostendämpfung in der Bundesrepublik . Berlin , New York , c1986. xvi, 108 p. ; ISBN 0-387-16648-3 (U. S.) LC Card 86-200720
HD7102.G3 M58 1986

Gesundheitswesen und Kostendämpfung in der Bundesrepublik . Molinaro, Remo. Berlin , New York , c1986. xvi, 108 p. ; ISBN 0-387-16648-3 (U. S.) LC Card 86-200720
HD7102.G3 M58 1986

Get that business loan . Rennhoff, Harley A. Gretna, La. , 1987. viii, 163 p. ; ISBN 0-88289-602-4 LC Card 87-2245 DDC 658.1/5224 19
HG4027.7 .R46 1987

Getting by in three economies . Rose, Richard, 1933- Glasgow , 1983. 40 p. ; LC Card 83-150133 DDC 330.941/0858 19
HC256.6 .R67 1983

Getting employed, staying employed . Mcloughlin, Caven S. Baltimore , c1987. xvi, 239 p. ; ISBN 0-933716-70-2 (pbk.) : LC Card 87-13185 DDC 650.1/4/0240816 19
HD7255 .M395 1987

Getting equal . O'Donnell, Carol. Sidney , Boston , 1988. p. cm. ISBN 0-04-302005-4 LC Card 87-22302 DDC 331.2/1 19
HD6060.5.A8 O365 1988

Getting into advertising /. Laskin, David. New York , 1986. xiii, 272 p. : ISBN 0-345-32598-2 (pbk.) LC Card 86-90721 DDC 659.1/023/73 19
HF5828.4 .L37 1986

Getting into life / edited by Halla Beloff ; afterword by David Hargreaves ; contributions from Michael Billig ... [et al.]. London ; New York : Methuen, c1986. xii, 157 p. ; 23 cm. Includes bibliographical references and index. ISBN 0-416-40850-8 LC Card 86-16186 DDC 305.2/35/0941 19
1. Youth - Great Britain. 2. Youth - Employment - Great Britain. 3. Youth - Great Britain - Psychology. 4. Great Britain - Social conditions - 1945-. I. Beloff, Halla. II. Billig, Michael.
HQ799.G7 G48 1986 ***NYPL [JLD 87-892]***

Getting it to the bottom line . Sloma, Richard S. New York , London , c1987. ix, 196 p. : ISBN 0-02-929540-8 LC Card 87-411 DDC 658.4/063 19
HD58.9 .S56 1987

Getting new clients /. Connor, Richard A. New York , c1987. xxiii, 305 p. : ISBN 0-471-62778-X LC Card 87-21657 DDC 658.8 19
HD8038.A1 C665 1987

Getting prices right . Timmer, C. Peter. Ithaca , 1986. 160 p. : ISBN 0-8014-9441-9 (pbk. : alk. paper) LC Card 86-47649 DDC 338.1/8 19
HD9006 .T58 1986 ***NYPL [JLE 86-4488]***

Getting the best out of yourself and others /. Rodgers, F. G. (Francis G.) New York , c1987. xi, 227 p. ; ISBN 0-06-015670-8 : LC Card 86-46125 DDC 658.3/4 19
HF5549.5.M63 R63 1987

Getting the most from social security : medicare and other government benefits / Consumer guide.New, rev. Skokie, IL (3841 W. Oakton St., Skokie 60076) : Publications International, c1986. 192 p. : ill. : 21 cm. (Consumer guide investment series . no. 3) "Volume 405." "WPS 37666"--Cover. LC Card 86-219986 DDC 344.73/023 347.30423 19
1. Social Security - United States - Handbooks, manuals, etc. 2. Medicare - Handbooks, manuals, etc. I. Consumer guide. II. Series.
HD7125 .G43 1986

Getting to the right job /. Cohen, Steve, 1950- New York , 1987. 288 p. ; ISBN 0-89480-040-X (pbk.) : LC Card 85-40899 DDC 650.1/4 19
HF5381 .C6814 1987

Getting yours . Lesko, Matthew. New York, N.Y., U. S.A. , 1987. x, 368 p. ; ISBN 0-14-046760-2 (pbk.) : LC Card 86-22688 DDC 658.1/5224 19
HC110.P63 L37 1987

GETTY FAMILY.
Coll, Steve. The taking of Getty Oil . New York , 1987. xiii, 528 p. ; ISBN 0-689-11860-0 LC Card 87-11467 DDC 338.8/3622338/0973 19
HD9569.G48 C65 1987

Miller, Russell. The house of Getty /. London , 19. 361 p., [32] p. of plates : ISBN 0-7181-2601-7 : LC Card 86-222703 DDC 332/.092/4 B 19
HD9570.G4 M55 1986b

Miller, Russell. The house of Getty /. South Yarmouth, Ma. [1987], c1985. 669 p. [16] p. of plates : ISBN 1-555-04230-9 LC Card 86-24259 DDC 332/.092/4 B 19
HD9570.G4 M55 1987

GETTY, J. PAUL (JEAN PAUL), 1892-1976.
Miller, Russell. The house of Getty /. London , 19. 361 p., [32] p. of plates : ISBN 0-7181-2601-7 : LC Card 86-222703 DDC 332/.092/4 B 19
HD9570.G4 M55 1986b

Miller, Russell. The house of Getty /. South Yarmouth, Ma. [1987], c1985. 669 p. [16] p. of plates : ISBN 1-555-04230-9 LC Card 86-24259 DDC 332/.092/4 B 19
HD9570.G4 M55 1987

GETTY OIL COMPANY.
Coll, Steve. The taking of Getty Oil . New York , 1987. xiii, 528 p. ; ISBN 0-689-11860-0 LC Card 87-11467 DDC 338.8/3622338/0973 19
HD9569.G48 C65 1987

Petzinger, Thomas. Oil & honor . New York , c1987. 495 p., [8] p. of plates : ISBN 0-399-13276-7 LC Card 87-2255 DDC 338.8/3622338/0973 19
HD9569.T4 P48 1987

GEW Forum.
Forum wohnen /. Freiburg i. Br. , Giessen , 1986. 158 p. : ISBN 3-89125-009-6 LC Card 86-169106
HD7339.A3 F68 1986

Gewandelte Werte, erstarrte Strukturen : wie die Bürger Wirtschaft und Arbeit erleben / Michael von Klipstein, Burkhard Strümpel (Hg.). Bonn : Verlag Neue Gesellschaft, c1985. ix, 329 p. : ill. ; 21 cm. (Reihe Wirtschaft und Beschäftigung . Bd. 3) Bibliography: p. 323-328. CONTENTS. - Wachstum im populären Wirtschaftsdenken / Michael von Klipstein -- Technikakzeptanz, oder, Das Dilemma zwischen Sachzwang und Menschlichkeit / Michael von Klipstein -- Arbeitslosigkeit im Meinungsbild der Bevölkerung / Karl Brenke, Michael Peter -- Wie stimmig ist das populäre Wirtschaftsdenken? / Joachim Scholz -- Arbeitsorientierungen zwischen neuen Ansprüchen und alten Strukturen / Peter Pawlowsky -- Mitbestimmung am Arbeitsplatz und ihr Einfluss auf die Arbeitsorientierung / Charlotta Flodell -- Arbeit und Gesundheit / Charlotta Flodell, Peter Pawlowsky -- Erwerbsarbeit von Frauen zwischen Lebensunterhalt und Lebensinhalt / Gerda Lischke -- Haben die Jugendlichen noch Lust zu arbeiten? / Karl Brenke, Michael von Klipstein -- Die Entmythologisierung der Produktion / Burkhard Strümpel, Michael von Klipstein -- Methodische Anmerkungen / Michael von Klipstein. ISBN 3-87831-423-X LC Card 86-117688 DDC 330/.0943 19
1. Work ethic - Germany (West) - Public opinion. 2. Economics - Germany (West) - Public opinion. 3. Labor and laboring classes - Germany, West - Attitudes. 4. Germany, West - Economic conditions - Public opinion. 5. Public opinion - Germany, West. I. Klipstein, Michael von. II. Strumpel, Burkhard. III. Series.
HD8451 .G54 1985

Gewerbeentwicklung und Gewerbepolitik in der Grossstadtregion / herausgegeben von Heik Afheldt, Walter Siebel, Thomas Sieverts ; mit Beiträgen von Dieter Bullinger ... [et al.]. Gerlingen : Bleicher, c1987. 390 p., [3] leaves of plates : ill., maps ; 24 cm. (Beiträge zur Stadtforschung. 4) Schriftenreihe der Robert Bosch Stiftung Bibliography: p. 369-374. Includes index. ISBN 3-88350-596-X LC Card 87-146643 DDC 332.6/732243 19
1. Industrial promotion - Germany, West. 2. Regional planning - Germany, West. 3. Germany, West - Economic policy - 1974-. I. Afheldt, Heik, 1937-. II. Siebel, Walter. III. Sieverts, Thomas. IV. Series. V. Series: Beiträge zur Stadtforschung (Gerlingen, Baden-Württemberg, Germany) , 4.
HC290.5.I53 G4797 1987

GEWERKSCHAFT DER BAU- UND HOLZARBEITER (AUSTRIA)
Czasny, Karl. Lehrjahre bei Bau-Holz . Wien , c1985. ix, 148 p. ; ISBN 3-900351-34-1 LC Card 86-227367 DDC 331.88/174/09436 19
HD6678.W62 G493 1985

Gewerkschaft Öffentliche Dienste, Transport und Verkehr. Bezirksfrauenausschuss der ÖTV Berlin. Mach mich nicht an . Berlin , c1986. [48] p. : ISBN 3-88114-313-0 : LC Card 87-118837 DDC 331.4/133/0943 19
HD6060.5.G3 M33 1986

Gewerkschaften in Afrika /. Geiss, Imanuel. Hannover , 1965. 233 p. : LC Card 85-125305
HD6857 .G45 1965

Gewerkschaften und Strukturwandel . Welsch, Johann. Köln , c1986. iii, 114 p. ; ISBN 3-7663-3011-X LC Card 86-223645 DDC 331.13/704 19
HD6694 .W37 1986

Die Gewerkschaften von der Stabilisierung bis zur Weltwirtschaftskrise, 1924-1930 / bearbeitet von Horst-A. Kukuck und Dieter Schiffmann. Köln : Bund-Verlag, c1986. 2 v. (1586 p.) ; 25 cm. (Quellen zur Geschichte der deutschen Gewerkschaftsbewegung im 20. Jahrhundert . Bd. 3) Bibliography: p. 1483-1488. Includes indexes. ISBN 3-7663-0902-1 (Bd. 1) LC Card 87-123987
1. Trade-unions - Germany - History - 20th century - Sources. I. Kukuck, Horst-Albert, 1939-. II. Schiffmann, Dieter. III. Series.
HD6694 .Q44 1985 Bd. 3

Gewerkschaftshochschule "Fritz Heckert."
Geschichte des FDGB . Berlin , c1985. 364 p. ; LC Card 86-124681 DDC 331.88/0943 19
HD8460.5.A5 F7326 1985

Gewestelijke Ontwikkelingsmaatschappij voor Vlaams-Brabant. Adresboek "Bedrijven in Vlaams-Brabant" =. Vilvoorde , 1985. lxi, 186, 62, 63 p. : LC Card 87-111619
HC317.B7 A37 1985

Gewinn- und Kapitalbeteiligung der Arbeitnehmer (Vermögensbildung) /. Schultz, Reinhard. München , c1987. 256 p. ; ISBN 3-597-10525-4 LC Card 87-127356 DDC 331.2/164 19
HD3038 .S365 1987

Gewinnung, Verarbeitung und Aufbereitung von Informationen für die Geschäftsfeldplanung . Krause, Hans-Ulrich. Giessen , c1984. xii,324 p. ; ISBN 3-922730-52-3 LC Card 85-150146
HD35 .K71215 1984

Gey, Peter. Crisis and reform in socialist economies /. Boulder , 1987. xi, 196 p. ; ISBN 0-8133-7332-8 (pbk. : alk. paper) : LC Card 86-32602 DDC 338.9/009171/7 19
HC704 .C75 1987

Geyer, Herbert, 1927- Budgetpolitik im Wandel / von Herbert Geyer, Karl-Heinrich Hansmeyer, Gerold Krause-Junk ; herausgegeben von Karl

Häuser. Berlin : Duncker & Humblot, c1986. 111 p. : ill. ; 24 cm. (Schriften des Vereins für Socialpolitik, Gesellschaft für Wirtschafts- und Sozialwissenschaften . n.F., Bd. 149) Originally presented as lectures at a session of the Ausschuss für Finanzwissenschaft, Zurich, 1984. Bibliography: p. 109-111. CONTENTS. - Ursachen des Wandels der Budgetpolitik / von Karl-Heinrich Hansmeyer -- Changes in budget-policy, goals and instruments / Herbert Geyer -- Automatismen versus Autonomie / von Gerold Krause-Junk. ISBN 3-428-05922-0 LC Card 86-165210
1. Budget - Congresses. 2. Finance, Public - Congresses. I. Hansmeyer, Karl-Heinrich. II. Krause-Junk, Gerold. III. Häuser, Karl, 1920-. IV. Title. V. Series.
HJ113 .G49 1986

Gezelius, Helena. Millwood, David. Good aid . Stockholm, Sweden , c1985. 246 p. : ISBN 91-586-7059-9 (pbk.) : LC Card 87-142767 DDC 338.91/485 19
HC425.Z9 E446 1985

Gezinsvorming door jonge migranten . Aalberts, Monique M. J. 's-Gravenhage , 1985. 93 p. : ISBN 90-12-04999-7 LC Card 85-235621
HD8518.5.A2 A24 1985

Ghadar, Fariborz. U. S. industrial competitiveness : the case of the textile and apparel industries / Fariborz Ghadar, William H. Davidson, Charles S. Feigenoff. Lexington, Mass. : Lexington Books, c1987. x, 114 p. : ill. ; 24 cm. Includes index. ISBN 0-669-15689-2 (alk. paper) LC Card 86-46341 DDC 338.4/7677/00973 19
1. Textile industry - United States. 2. Clothing trade - United States. 3. Competition, International. I. Davidson, William Harley, 1951-. II. Feigenoff, Charles Samuel. III. Title. IV. Title: US industrial competitiveness. V. Title: United States industrial competitiveness.
HD9855 .G47 1987

Ghadoliya, M. K. (Mahendra Kumar) Structure of employment, earnings, and assets in India : a case study / M.K. Ghadoliya. Delhi : Mittal Publications, 1986. xi, 248 p. : ill., map ; 22 cm. Based on the author's thesis (doctoral--Sukhadia University, Udaipur, 1984) Study, based on 1981-1982 data, with reference to selected villages in Udaipur District, Rajasthan. Bibliography: p. [233]-243. Includes index. LC Card 86-903221 DDC 331.12/5/09544 19
1. Labor supply - India - Udaipur (District) - Case studies. 2. Labor supply - India - Case studies. 3. Income - India - Udaipur (District) - Case studies. 4. Income - India - Case studies. 5. Personal property - India - Udaipur (District) - Case studies. 6. Personal property - India - Case studies. I. Title.
HD5820.U33 G47 1986

Ghafoor, Abdul. Development of human resources : population, manpower, and employment policies in Pakistan / by Abdul Ghafoor. Islamabad : Academy of Educational Planning and Management, [1984] v, ii leaves, 99 p., v, ii leaves ; 30 cm. "June 1984." "Paper prepared on behalf of the Development Studies Institute Ltd. Lahore Cantt for the Committee on Studies for Cooperation in Development in South Asia (CSCD)" Bibliography: leaves [i]-ii (last group) LC Card 85-932024 DDC 331.11/09549/1 19
1. Manpower policy - Pakistan. 2. Education and state - Pakistan. I. Development Studies Institute (Lahore, Pakistan). II. Committee on Studies for Cooperation in Development in South Asia. III. Academy of Educational Planning and Management (Pakistan). IV. Title.
HD5819 .G48 1984

GHANA BROADCASTING CORPORATION - HISTORY.
Golden jubilee, July 1935-1985 /. Accra [Ghana] [1985] 64 p. : LC Card 86-155961 DDC 384.54/06/0667 19
HE8689.9.G45 G65 1985

GHANA - ECONOMIC CONDITIONS - 1979- - STATISTICS.
Ewusi, Kodwo. Economic trends in Ghana in 1984-85 and prospects for 1986 /. [Legon] [1986] 52 p. : LC Card 87-127410 DDC 330.9667/05 19
HC1060 .E975 1986

GHANA - ECONOMIC POLICY - STATISTICS.
Ewusi, Kodwo. Economic trends in Ghana in 1984-85 and prospects for 1986 /. [Legon] [1986] 52 p. : LC Card 87-127410 DDC 330.9667/05 19
HC1060 .E975 1986

GHANA - MANUFACTURES - COSTS - ECONOMETRIC MODELS.
Iyare, S. International cost differences in developing countries . Durham, England [1983] 14, [9] leaves : LC Card 86-207078 DDC 338.4/367/09667 19
HD9737.G52 I97 1983

GHANA - POPULATION - HISTORY.
Engmann, E. V. T. Population of Ghana, 1850-1960 /. Accra, Ghana , 1986. xvii, 300 p. : ISBN 996-430-088-3 (pbk.) LC Card 87-127395 DDC 304.6/09669 19
HB3666.8.A3 E535 1986

GHANA - RURAL CONDITIONS.
Konings, Piet. The state and rural class formation in Ghana . London ; Boston : xvi, 391 p. : ISBN 0-7103-0117-0 LC Card 85-28109 DDC 305.5/09667 19
HN832.Z9 S65 1986 ***NYPL [Sc D 86-574]***

Ghana-Valco renegotiations, 1982-85. Essays from the Ghana-Valco renegotiations, 1982-85 /. [Accra, Ghana] 1986 (Accra : Printed by the Ghana Pub. Corp.) viii, 163 p. ; ISBN 996-490-120-8 (pbk.) LC Card 87-127499 DDC 338.8/87 19
HD9539.A63 G44 1986

Ghanem, Shukri Mohammed. OPEC, the rise and fall of an exclusive club / Shukri Ghanem. London ; New York : KPI ; x, 233 p. ; 23 cm. Includes bibliographies and index. ISBN 0-7103-0175-8 LC Card 87-131574 DDC 341.7/5472282 19
1. Organization of Petroleum Exporting Countries. 2. Petroleum industry and trade. 3. Cartels. I. Title.
HD9560.1.O66 G55 1986

Ghartey, J. B., 1944- Crisis accountability and development in the Third World : the case of Africa / J.B. Ghartey. Aldershot, Hants, England ; Brookfield, Vt., USA : Avebury, c1987. x, 170 p. ; 23 cm. Bibliography: p. 153-164. Includes index. ISBN 0-566-05290-3 : LC Card 86-25777 DDC 338.91/096 19
1. Economic development projects - Africa - Accounting. 2. Accounting - Africa. I. Title.
HC800 .G52 1987

Ghate, Prabhu, 1941- Direct attacks on rural poverty : policy, programmes, and implementation / Prabhu Ghate. New Delhi : Concept, 1984. xvi, 597 p. : maps ; 22 cm. Includes index. Bibliography: p. [577]-591. LC Card 84-902455 DDC 338.954/2 19
1. Ghazipur (India : District) - Economic policy. 2. Rural development - India - Ghazipur (District). 3. Poverty - Government policy - India - Ghazipur (District). I. Title.
HC437.G48 G46 1984 ***NYPL [JLD 87-651]***

GHAZIPUR (INDIA : DISTRICT) - ECONOMIC POLICY.
Ghate, Prabhu, 1941- Direct attacks on rural poverty . New Delhi , 1984. xvi, 597 p. : LC Card 84-902455 DDC 338.954/2 19
HC437.G48 G46 1984 ***NYPL [JLD 87-651]***

Ghelfi, Linda M. Poverty among black families in the nonmetro South / Linda M. Ghelfi. Washington, D.C. : U. S. Dept. of Agriculture, Economic Research Service : Supt. of Docs., U. S. G.P.O. [distributor, 1986] vii, 27 p. : ill., 1 map ; 28 cm. (Rural development research report . no. 62) Distributed to depository libraries in microfiche. "August 1986"--P. iii. Bibliography: p. 24-26. S/N 001-019-00454-1 Item 24-G-2 (microfiche) LC Card 86-602435 DDC 330.975/043/0899607301734 19
1. Rural poor - Southern States. 2. Afro-Americans - Southern States - Economic conditions. I. United States. Dept. of Agriculture. Economic Research Service. II. Title. III. Series.
HC107.A13 G48 1986

Ghersi, Enrique. Soto, Hernando de, 1941- El otro sendero . [Lima] , 1986. xxxvi, 317 p. : LC Card 87-400476 DDC 381 19
HD2346.P4 S67 1986

Ghertman, Michel. Decision-making in multinational enterprises : concepts and research approaches / by Michel Ghertman. Geneva : International Labour Office, 1984. v, 62 p. : ill. ; 30 cm. (Working papers / Multinational Enterprises Programme . working paper no. 31) Bibliography: p. 51-58. ISBN 92-2-103831-9 (pbk.) : LC Card 86-213603 DDC 658.4/03 19
1. International business enterprises - Decision making. I. Series: Working papers / Multinational Enterprises Programme , working paper no. 31. II. Title.
HD62.4 .G48 1984

Ghessi, Giuseppe. La finanza pubblica in cifre, 1965-1983 / Giuseppe Ghessi ; presentazione di Emilio Gerelli. Milano, Italy : F. Angeli, c1985. 186 p. : ill. ; 28 cm. (Collana dell'Istituto di finanza dell'Università di Pavia . 14) Includes index. LC Card 85-180958 DDC 336.45 19
1. Finance, Public - Italy - Statistics. 2. Revenue - Italy - Statistics. I. Series: Pavia. Università. Istituto di finanza. Collana, 14. II. Title.
HJ1185 .G43 1985 ***NYPL [JLF 87-249]***

Gheventer, Boris. Produção agrícola brasileira . [Rio de Janeiro] , 1986. 188 p. : LC Card 87-403944 DDC 338.1/0981/021 19
HD9014.B82 P765 1986

Gheysens, Lieven. International diversification through the government bond market : a risk-return analysis / Lieven Gheysens. [Leuven] : Katholieke Universiteit Leuven, Faculteit der Economische en Toegepaste Economische Wetenschappen, 1977. 188 leaves ; 30 cm. (Katholieke Universiteit Leuven, Faculteit der Economische en Toegepaste Economische Wetenschappen . nr. 24) Originally presented as the author's thesis (doctoral--Katholieke Universiteit Leuven) Bibliography: leaves 181-188. LC Card 85-186317 DDC 332.63/232 19
1. Government securities. 2. Rate of return. I. Series: Katholieke Universiteit te Leuven. Faculteit der Economische en Toegepaste Economische Wetenschappen. Reeks, nr.24. II. Title.
HG4715 .G44 1977
NYPL [JLM 86-1310 nr.24]

Ghias-ud-Din, Mian. Role of management, training & research in railroad operations / by Mian Ghias-ud-Din. [Pakistan : s.n., 1983?] (Lahore : Caxton Printing Press) 98 p., A-C folded leaves of plates : charts ; 28 cm. "Paper no. 450." Bibliography: p. 97-98. LC Card 86-903113 DDC 385/.068 19
1. Railroads - Pakistan - Management. 2. Railroads - Research - Pakistan. 3. Railroad engineers - Training of - Pakistan. I. Pakistan Engineering Congress. II. Title.
HE3300.5 .G48 1983

Ghibellini, Mario. Soto, Hernando de, 1941- El otro sendero . [Lima] , 1986. xxxvi, 317 p. : LC Card 87-400476 DDC 381 19
HD2346.P4 S67 1986

Ghobadian, Abby, 1951- The effects of new technological change on shift work in the brewing industry / Abby Ghobadian. Aldershot, Hants, England ; Brookfield, Vt. : Gower, c1986. xiv, 192 p. : ill. ; 24 cm. Bibliography: p. 177-179. ISBN 0-566-05132-X : LC Card 86-17536 DDC 331.25/72 19
1. Brewery workers - Great Britain - Effect of technological innovations on. 2. Shift systems - Great Britain. 3. Brewing industry - Great Britain - Automation. I. Title.
HD8039.L62 G74 1986
NYPL [JLD 86-3864]

Ghonemy, Mohamad Riad El. see **El Ghonemy, Mohamad Riad, 1924-**

Ghorpade, Jai, 1936- Job analysis : a handbook for the human resource director / Jai Ghorpade. Englewood Cliffs, N.J. : Prentice Hall, c1988. xix, 348 p. ; 29 cm. Bibliography: p. 333-340. Includes indexes. ISBN 0-13-510256-1 LC Card 87-14350 DDC 658.3/06 19
1. Job analysis. I. Title.
HF5549.5.J6 G48 1988

Ghosh, A., 1921-
Contribution to national and regional planning problems /. Calcutta , 1983. vii, 174 p., [2] leaves of plates (some folded) : LC Card 83-907550 DDC 338.954 19
HC435.2 .C63 1983 ***NYPL [JLD 86-3868]***

Income distribution and the structure of production / A. Ghosh, A.K. Sengupta. New Delhi : South Asian Publishers, c1984. ix, 186 p. ; 23 cm. (SCIMA special studies) Includes index. Bibliography: p. [179]-181. LC Card 83-907762 DDC 339.2/0724 19
1. Income distribution - Mathematical models. 2. Production functions (Economic theory) - Mathematical models. 3. Input-output analysis - Mathematical models.

I. Sengupta, A. K. II. Title. III. Series.
HB523 .G46 1984 **NYPL [JLD 86-4234]**

Ghosh, Avijit. Location strategies for retail and service firms / Avijit Ghosh, Sara L. McLafferty. Lexington, Mass. : Lexington Books, c1987. x, 212 p. : ill. ; 24 cm. Includes bibliographies and index. ISBN 0-669-12032-4 (alk. paper) LC Card 85-45583 DDC 658.1/1 19
1. Stores, Retail - Location. 2. Service industries - Location. I. McLafferty, Sara L. II. Title.
HF5429.275 .G47 1987

Ghosh, B. N. Political economy of neocolonialism in Third World countries / B.N. Ghosh. New Delhi : Sterling, c1985. vii, 174 p. ; 23 cm. Includes index. Bibliography: p. [157]-166. LC Card 85-903172 DDC 338.9/009172/4 19
1. Developing countries - Economic policy. 2. Developing countries - Foreign economic relations. 3. India - Economic policy - 1947-. 4. India - Foreign economic relations. I. Title.
HC59.7 .G485 1985 **NYPL [JLD 87-1141]**

Ghosh, S. Stabilizing speculative commodity markets / S. Ghosh, C.L. Gilbert, and A.J. Hughes Hallett. Oxford [Oxfordshire] : Clarendon Press ; New York : Oxford University Press, 1987. xiii, 437 p. : ill. ; 24 cm. Bibliography: p. [418]-430. Includes indexes. ISBN 0-19-828472-1 : LC Card 86-32654 DDC 332.64/4 19
1. Commodity exchanges - Mathematical models. 2. Speculation - Mathematical models. 3. Copper industry and trade - Mathematical models. 4. Economic stabilization - Mathematical models. I. Gilbert, C. L. II. Hughes Hallett, Andrew. III. Title.
HG6046 .G485 1987

Ghosh, S. N., 1943- Tables on houses and disabled population, series 23, West Bengal /. Delhi , 1986. v, 128 p. ; LC Card 87-900630
HA4587.W47 T33 1986

Ghosh, Tushar Kanti. Operation Barga and land reforms : an Indian experiment / Tushar Kanti Ghosh. Delhi : B.R. Pub. Corp. ; New Delhi, India : Distributed by D.K. Publishers' Distributors, 1986. vii, 200 p. ; 23 cm. Includes index. Bibliography: p. [151]-157. ISBN 81-7018-315-4 : LC Card 86-900505 DDC 333.3/1/54 19
1. Métayer system - India. 2. Land reform - India. I. Title.
HD1478.I5 G48 1986 **NYPL [JLD 86-4347]**

Ghosha, Madana. Bhūmibyabasthā, Kaṃgresa, o Kṛshakasabhā / Madana Ghosha. Bardhamāna : Natuna Ciṭhi Prakāśanā, [1986?] 100 p. ; 23 cm. In Bengali. Study on the land tenure system in India; in the context of peasant movements, and policies of the Indian National Congress, and Krishak Sabha, a leftist organization. LC Card 87-900325
1. Land tenure - India. 2. Indian National Congress. 3. Kṛshakasabhā (India). 4. Peasant uprisings - India. I. Title.
HD875 .G56 1986

Ghurfah al-Tijārīyah al-Ṣināʻīyah bi-Jiddah. Markaz al-Buḥūth. Analytical study for the market of white meat and eggs /. Jeddah [1985?] 159 p. : LC Card 85-964046 DDC 381/.4566493/09538 19
HD9437.S332 A53 1985

Ghurfat al-Tijārah wa-al-Ṣināʻah fī Bayrūt. The Tax system in Lebanon /. Beirut, Lebanon , 1983. 14 p. ; LC Card 87-402832 DDC 343.569204 345.692034 19
HJ2909 .T39 1983

Ghurfat Tijārat wa-Ṣināʻat Abū Ẓaby. Qism al-Dirāsāt wa-al-Buḥūth al-Iqtiṣādiyah. Dalīl rajul al-aʻmāl fī al-ṣināʻah wa-al-tijārah . [Abu Ẓaby] , 1984. 305 p. : LC Card 86-965166
HF5233.A56 D35 1984

Giammaria Ortes . De Franchis, Carlo. Napoli , 1930. 165 p. ; LC Card 87-139766
HB109.O68 D4 1930

Giannini Foundation monograph .
(no. 18) Dean, Gerald W. World trade in fresh oranges . Berkeley, Calif. [1967] 70 p. : LC Card 87-401008 DDC 338.1/09794 s 382/.41431 19
HD1407 .C27 no. 18 HD9259.O7

(no. 21) Eidman, Vernon R., 1936- Decision models for California turkey growers /. Berkeley, Calif. [1968] ii, 80 p. : LC Card 87-401009 DDC 338.1/09794 s 636.5/92/0068 19
HD1407 .C27 no. 21 HD9437.U63C3

Gianniōtēs, Alexandros. Oikonomikē politikē / Alexandrou Gianniōtē. Thessalonikē : Paratērētēs, [1984?] 298 p. : ill. ; 21 cm. Includes bibliographies. LC Card 86-184634
1. Economic policy. I. Title.
HD85.G7 G53 1984

Gianotten, Vera. Organización campesina : el objetivo político de la educación popular y la investigación participativa / Vera Gianotten y Ton de Wit. Amsterdam : CEDLA ; Cinnaminson, N.J. : Distribuido por Forbis Publications USA, c1985. ix, 531 p., [4] p. of plates : ill. ; 24 cm. (Latin America studies . 30) Bibliography: p. 491-531. ISBN 90-6765-162-1 LC Card 85-200688
1. Peasantry - Peru - Ayacucho (Dept.). 2. Rural development - Peru - Ayacucho (Dept.). 3. Adult education - Peru - Ayacucho (Dept.). I. Wit, Ton de. II. Title. III. Series.
HD1531.P4 G5 1985

Giarda, Piero D. Conto consolidato della spesa pubblica in Lombardia /. Milano, Italy , c1982. 234 p. ; LC Card 85-147746
HJ9925.I8 C63 1982

Giarini, Orio. The Emerging service economy /. Oxford [Oxfordshire] , New York , 1987. xii, 298 p. : ISBN 0-08-034270-1 : LC Card 86-25265 DDC 338.4/6 19
HD9980.5 .E46 1987

Gibb, Allan. A Guide to small firms assistance in Europe /. Aldershot, Hants, England , Brookfield, Vt., U. S.A. , c1986. vii, 263 p. ; ISBN 0-566-05082-X : LC Card 85-27307 DDC 338.6/42/094 19
HD2346.E9 G85 1986 **NYPL [JLG 86-205]**

Gibb, Christopher. Food or famine? / Christopher Gibb. Vero Beach, FL : Rourke Enterprises, 1987. 48 p. : ill. (some col.), col. maps ; 27 cm. (World issues) Bibliography: p. 47. Includes index. ISBN 0-86592-279-9 LC Card 87-12741 DDC 363.8/096 19
1. Famines - Africa. I. Series: World issues (Vero Beach, Fla.). II. Title.
HC800.Z9 F335 1987

Gibbon, Peter. Thurcroft, a village and the miners' strike . Nottingham [Nottinghamshire] , Atlantic Highlands, NJ , 1986. 276 p. : ISBN 0-85124-441-6 LC Card 86-21887 DDC 331.89/2822334/0942823 19
HD5346.M6152 1984 .T48 1987
NYPL [JLD 87-985]

Gibin, Cinzio. Un Mestiere e un paese . Venezia , 1986. 172 p. : ISBN 88-317-4893-9 LC Card 86-219883
HD8039.S252 I85 1986

Gibon, Comte de (Paul), 1863-1929. Etudes sur le renouveau économique dans le centre et le sud de la Manche : 1., industrie, II., commerce dans le passé, le présent et l'avenir / Vte de Gibon. Caen : L. Jouan, 1919. 176 p. ; 23 cm. Includes bibliographical references. LC Card 85-666346
1. Manche (France) - Economic conditions. 2. Manche (France) - Industries. 3. Manche (France) - Commerce. I. Title.
HC277.M26 G52x 1919

GIBRALTAR - ECONOMIC CONDITIONS. Colaboración sindical al estudio sobre la estructura y posibilidad de desarrollo del Campo de Gibraltar, encomendado por la comisión interministerial designada al efecto /. Cádiz , 1965. 89 p. : LC Card 85-104938
HC390.6 .C65 1965

GIBRALTAR - ECONOMIC POLICY. Colaboración sindical al estudio sobre la estructura y posibilidad de desarrollo del Campo de Gibraltar, encomendado por la comisión interministerial designada al efecto /. Cádiz , 1965. 89 p. : LC Card 85-104938
HC390.6 .C65 1965

Gibriel, Mohamed Farah. Groundnuts production and marketing in Sudan / by Mohamed Farah Gibriel. Khartoum, Sudan : Economic and Social Research Council, National Council for Research, 1984. 24 leaves : ill. ; 33 cm. (Bulletin . no. 119) "June, 1984." Includes bibliographical references. LC Card 85-981430 DDC 338.1/73368/09624 19
1. Peanut industry - Sudan. 2. Peanuts - Sudan - Marketing. I. Series: Bulletin (Majlis al-Abḥāth al-Iqtiṣādīyah wa-al-Ijtimāʻīyah) , no. 119. II. Title.
HD9235.P32 S734 1984

Gibson, Cyrus F. The information imperative : managing the impact of information technology on businesses and people / Cyrus F. Gibson and Barbara Bund Jackson ; with contributions by Thomas H. Davenport ... [et al.] ; foreword by F. Warren McFarlan. Lexington, Mass. : Lexington Books, c1987. xxii, 160 p. : ill. ; 24 cm. Includes bibliographies and index. ISBN 0-669-12338-2 (alk. paper) LC Card 85-45797 DDC 658/.05 19
1. Business - Data processing. 2. Business - Communication systems. 3. Information technology. I. Jackson, Barbara B. II. Title.
HF5548.2 .G496 1987

Gibson, Donald M. T. (Donald Morton Tait) Gilmour, Peter, 1942- Australian marketing casebook /. St. Lucia , c1988. p. cm. ISBN 0-7022-2091-4 (pbk.) LC Card 87-16220 DDC 658.8/00994 19
HF5415.12.A9 G54 1988

Gibson, Frank F. Dunfee, Thomas W. Legal aspects of government regulation of business /. New York , c1984. viii, 335 p. ; ISBN 0-471-87029-3 (pbk.) : LC Card 83-21879 DDC 346.73/07 347.3067 19
KF1600 .D86 1984 **NYPL [JLE 86-3511]**

Gibson, Jack P. McIntyre, William Stokes. 101 ways to cut your business insurance costs without sacrificing protection /. New York , c1988. viii, 190 p. : ISBN 0-07-045112-5 : LC Card 87-17255 DDC 368 19
HG8059 .M38 1988

Gibson, James L. Donnelly, James H. Fundamentals of management /. Plano, Tex. , 1987. xxviii, 827 p. : ISBN 0-256-03682-9 LC Card 86-71879 DDC 658 19
HD31 .D594 1987

Gibson, Michael, 1942- The energy crisis / Michael Gibson. Vero Beach, FL : Rourke Enterprises, 1987. 46 p. : col. ill. ; 27 cm. (World issues) Bibliography: p. 45. Includes index. Examines the inadequacy of America's supply of energy resources, the political and economic ratifications of a growing dependency on foreign countries for energy, and the problem of developing new sources of energy while protecting the environment. ISBN 0-86592-277-2 LC Card 87-12768 DDC 333.79 19
1. Energy policy - Juvenile literature. 2. Energy industries - Juvenile literature. 3. Power resources - Juvenile literature. 4. Renewable energy sources - Juvenile literature. I. Series: World issues (Vero Beach, Fla.). II. Title.
HD9502.A2 G525 1987

Giddy, Ian H. International finance handbook /. New York , c1983. 2 v. : ISBN 0-471-09861-2 (set) : LC Card 82-23824 DDC 332/.042 19
HG3881 .I57633 1983 **NYPL [JLE 86-1719]**

Gienanth, Ulrich, Freiherr von, 1907- 250 Jahre Eisenwerk Eisenberg : die Geschichte der Eisengiesser-Familie Gienanth / aufgezeichnet von Ulrich Freiherr von Gienanth. Eisenberg/Pfalz : Gebr. Gienanth, [1986] 68 p. : ill. (some col.) ; 22 x 30 cm. Bibliography: p. 68. LC Card 87-409570 DDC 338.7/6691/0943 19
1. Gebrüder Gienanth-Eisenberg - History. 2. Iron industry and trade - Germany (West) - History. I. Title. II. Title: Zweihundertfünfzig Jahre Eisenwerk Eisenberg.
HD9523.9.G4 G54 1986

Gier, Eric H. de. Disability benefits . Greenwich, Conn. , c1987. xxii, 282 p. ; ISBN 0-89232-824-X : LC Card 87-17056 DDC 368.3/86/009492 19
HD7105.25.N4 D57 1987

Gierman, D. M. Rural to urban land conversion = Urbanisation des terres rurales / by D.M. Gierman. [Ottawa] : Fisheries and Environment Canada, Lands Directorate ; Hull, Que. : available from Canadian Govt. Pub. Centre, c1977. xvii, 74 p. ; 28 cm. (Map folio . no. 5) Occasional paper - Lands Directorate ; no.16. English and French. Includes bibliographical references. ISBN 0-662-01301-8
1. Land use, Rural - Canada. 2. Urbanization - Canada. I. Title. II. Title: Urbanisation des terres rurales. III. Series: Canada. Lands Directorate. Occasional paper, no.16. **NYPL [JLM 80-106 no.16]**

Giersch, Herbert.
Economic incentives . London , 1986. xiii, 497 p. ; ISBN 0-333-40473-4 ***NYPL [JLD 87-367]***

Free trade in the world economy . Boulder , 1987. p. cm. ISBN 0-8133-0596-9 LC Card 87-20148 DDC 382.7/1 19
HF1703 .F74 1987

Gegen Europessimismus : kritische Beiträge 1977 bis 1985 / herausgegeben von Karl Heinz Frank. Stuttgart : Deutsche Verlags-Anstalt, c1986. 318 p. ; 21 cm. Bibliography: p. 310-[316]. ISBN 3-421-06334-6 LC Card 87-672572
1. International economic relations. 2. Europe - Economic conditions - 1945-. I. Frank, Karl Heinz. II. Title.
HF1411 .G53x 1986

The International debt problem . Tübingen , 1986. vi, 193 p. : ISBN 3-16-345084-9 (pbk.) LC Card 86-201893 DDC 336.3/435 19
HG3891.5 .I557 1986

The International debt problem . Boulder , 1987. p. cm. ISBN 0-8133-0595-0 LC Card 87-20149 DDC 336.3/435 19
HG3891.5 .I557 1987

New opportunities for entrepreneurship /. Boulder , 1987. p. cm. ISBN 0-8133-0597-7 LC Card 87-20143 DDC 338/.04 19
HD62.5 .N48 1987

Reassessing the role of government in the mixed economy /. Boulder , 1987. p. cm. ISBN 0-8133-0598-5 : LC Card 87-20142 DDC 338.9 19
HD73 .R43 1987

Gies, Christoph. Die Spielregeln für Kapitalanlagen in Mexiko : Hintergründe, Erfahrungen und Analysen / Christoph Gies. Frankfurt : R.G. Fischer, c1986. ix, 314 p. : ill. ; 21 cm. Bibliography: p. 291-314. ISBN 3-88323-603-9 LC Card 86-231145
1. Investments, Foreign - Mexico. 2. Investments, West German - Mexico. 3. Mexico - Economic policy. 4. Mexico - Industries. I. Title.
HG5162 .G48 1986

Giesecke, Leonard F. (Leonard Frederick)
History of American economic policy in the Philippines during the American colonial period, 1900-1935 / Leonard F. Giesecke. New York : Garland Pub., 1987. 279 p. ; 23 cm. (Foreign economic policy of the United States) Originally presented as the author's thesis (Ph. D.)--University of Texas at Austin, 1975. Bibliography: p. 271-279. ISBN 0-8240-8082-3 (alk. paper) : LC Card 87-23786 DDC 337.730599 19
1. United States - Foreign economic relations - Philippines. 2. Philippines - Foreign economic relations - United States. 3. Philippines - Economic policy. 4. Philippines - Politics and government - 1898-1935. 5. United States - Colonies - Asia - Economic policy. I. Title. II. Series.
HF1456.5.P6 G53 1987

Giesen, David. Contemporary business planning : a guide for savings institutions / David W. Giesen. Chicago, IL (111 E. Wacker Dr., Chicago 60601) : United States League of Savings Institutions, c1987. 128 p. : col. ill. ; 23 cm. Bibliography: p. 109-116. LC Card 87-401916 DDC 332.3/2/068 19
1. Bank investments - United States. 2. Savings-banks - United States. I. Title.
HG1897 .G54 1987

O gigante invisível : estudo sobre o mercado informal de trabalho na Região Metropolitana de Salvador. [Salvador] : Bahia, Governo Antônio Carlos Magalhães, Secretaria da Indústria e Comércio, [1983] 105 p. : ill., ports. ; 30 cm. Bibliography: p. 89-90. LC Card 84-181184
1. Informal sector (Economics) - Brazil - Salvador Metropolitan Area. 2. Labor supply - Brazil - Salvador Metropolitan Area. I. Bahia, Brazil (State). Secretaria da Indústria e Comércio.
HD2346.B72 S25 1983

Gigov, Todor. Trudova slava /. Sofiia , <1986-. v. <4 > : LC Card 86-228746
HD8039.M62 B88 1986

Gijsman, D., 1955- Exportfinanciering / D. Gijsman. Deventer : Kluwer ; 's-Gravenhage : Fenedex, 1986. 118 p. : ill. ; 25 cm. (Fiscale en juridische documentatie voor internationaal zakendoen . 15) ISBN 90-200-0992-3 : LC Card 86-176172
1. Export credit - Netherlands. I. Title. II. Series.
HG3754.N4 G55 1986

Gijutsu kakushin to joshi rōdō / Nakamura Masanori hen ; Hayashi Takeshi sōhenshū. 880-02 Shohan. Tōkyō : Kokusai Rengō Daigaku : hatsubaisho Tōkyō Daigaku Shuppankai, 1985. x, 219 p. : ill. ; 22 cm. (Kokuren Daigaku purojekuto "Nihon no keiken" shirīzu) In Japanese. Includes bibliographical references. ISBN 4-13-051068-1
1. Women - Employment - Japan - Addresses, essays, lectures. 2. Technological innovations - Japan. I. Nakamura, Masanori, 1935-. II. Hayashi, Takeshi, 1930-. ***NYPL [*OSL 87-1658]***

Gikis, I. Pervichnoe opisanie signalov rechi . Vil'nius , 1980. 67 p. : LC Card 82-107723
HD38 .S715 vyp. 42 TK7882.S65

Gil, David G. The Future of work . Cambridge, Mass. , c1987. xv, 126 p. : ISBN 0-87047-030-2 : LC Card 86-33894 DDC 306/.36 19
HD4904 .F87 1987

Gil-Díaz, Francisco, 1943- Rubio F., Luis. A Mexican response /. New York , 1987. vi, 72 p. ; ISBN 0-87078-215-0 (pbk.) LC Card 87-162458 DDC 336.3/4/0972 19
HJ8519 .R83 1987

Gil, Eva A. The Future of work . Cambridge, Mass. , c1987. xv, 126 p. : ISBN 0-87047-030-2 : LC Card 86-33894 DDC 306/.36 19
HD4904 .F87 1987

Gil, Gonzalo. Aspectos financieros y monetarios de la integración española en la Comunidad Económica Europea / Gonzalo Gil. [Madrid] : Banco de España, Servicio de Estudios, [1985] 187 p. : ill. ; 24 cm. (Estudios económicos . no. 37 (1985)) Includes bibliographical references. ISBN 84-505-2233-1 LC Card 87-101729
1. European Economic Community - Spain. 2. Monetary policy - European Economic Community countries. 3. Finance - European Economic Community countries. I. Series: Estudios económicos (Banco de España. Servicio de Estudios) , no. 37. II. Title.
HC241.25.S6 G55 1985

Gil Pacheco, Rufino. Ciento cinco años de vida bancaria en Costa Rica / Rufino Gil Pacheco. 4a. ed. San José : Editorial Costa Rica, 1982. 406 p. : ill. ; 21 cm. Includes bibliographical references. LC Card 83-228041 DDC 332.1/097286 19
1. Banks and banking - Costa Rica - History - 19th century. 2. Banks and banking - Costa Rica - History - 20th century. I. Title. II. Title: 105 años de vida bancaria en Costa Rica.
HG2734 .G55 1982 ***NYPL [JLD 86-3356]***

Gil, Rufino. see **Gil Pacheco, Rufino.**

Gilani, Ijaz. Citizens slaves, guest-workers : the dynamics of labour migration from South Asia / Ijaz Shafi Gilani with Jonathan S. Addelton. Islamabad, Pakistan : Institute of Policy Studies, c1985. 84 p. ; 22 cm. Bibliography: p. 76-83. LC Card 85-931825 DDC 331.6/2/54 19
1. Migrant labor - South Asia. I. Addelton, Jonathan S. II. Title.
HD5856.S64 G55 1985

Gilardi, Mauro. Volley e bolli : la pallavolo nella filatelia / Mauro Gilardi ; realizzato dalla FIPAV, Federazione italiana pallavolo in collaborazione con il Gruppo sport del C.I.F.T. Milano : Studio Erre, c1985. 107 p. : ill. (some col.) ; 28 cm. Includes indexes. LC Card 86-128270
1. Postage-stamps - Topics - Volleyball. I. Federazione italiana pallavolo. II. Gruppo sport del C.I.F.T. (Italy). III. Title.
HE6183.V64 G55 1985

Gilbeau, Kenneth W.
Miller, George H. California real estate appraisal . Englewood Cliffs, N.J. , c1987. xiv, 348 p. : ISBN 0-13-112558-3 : LC Card 87-6956 DDC 333.33/2/09794 19
HD1387 .M545 1987

Miller, George H. Residential real estate appraisal . Englewood Cliffs, N.J. , c1988. xiv, 336 p. : ISBN 0-13-762428-X (pbk.) : LC Card 87-6960 DDC 333.33/2 19
HD1387 .M547 1988

Gilbert, Alan, 1944- The political economy of land : urban development in an oil economy / Alan Gilbert, Patsy Healey. Aldershot, Hants ; Brookfield, Vt., U. S.A. : Gower, c1985. xv, 163 p. : ill. ; 23 cm. Bibliography: p. 150-163. ISBN 0-566-05007-2 : LC Card 85-17535 DDC 333.77/13/0987 19
1. Land use, Urban - Venezuela. 2. City planning - Venezuela. 3. Housing - Venezuela. 4. Petroleum industry and trade - Venezuela. I. Healey, Patsy. II. Title.
HD576 .G54 1985 ***NYPL [JLD 86-3632]***

Gilbert, C. L. Ghosh, S. Stabilizing speculative commodity markets /. Oxford [Oxfordshire] , New York , 1987. xiii, 437 p. : ISBN 0-19-828472-1 : LC Card 86-32654 DDC 332.64/4 19
HG6046 .G485 1987

Gilbert, Gorman, 1943- The management and regulation of ground transportation at U. S. airports : final report / prepared by Gorman Gilbert, Charles Feibel, and Thomas Wiley ; prepared for Office of Service and Management Demonstrations, Urban Mass Transportation Administration. Washington, D.C. : The Administration : Distributed in cooperation with Technology Sharing Program, Office of the Secretary of Transportation, [1986] 153 p. : ill. ; 28 cm. "January 1986." Bibliography: p. 153. "DOT-I-86-29." LC Card 87-600652 DDC 387.7/362 19
1. Access to airports - United States. 2. Access to airports - Government policy - United States. 3. Access to airports - United States - Case studies. I. Feibel, Charles. II. Wiley, Thomas, 1959-. III. United States. Urban Mass Transportation Administration. Office of Service and Management Demonstrations. IV. Technology Sharing Program (U. S.). V. Title.
HE9797.4.A2 G55 1986

Gilbreath, Robert D. (Robert Dean), 1949-
Forward thinking : the pragmatist's guide to today's business trends / Robert D. Gilbreath. New York : McGraw-Hill, c1987. xvi, 184 p. ; 24 cm. Bibliography: p. 177. Includes index. ISBN 0-07-023262-8 : LC Card 86-27732 DDC 658.4 19
1. Industrial management. 2. Organizational change. I. Title.
HD31 .G496 1987

Gilde und Korporation in den nordeuropäischen Städten des späten Mittelalters / herausgegeben von Klaus Friedland. Köln : Böhlau, 1984. 114 p. ; 24 cm. (Quellen und Darstellungen zur Hansischen Geschichte. n.F., Bd. 29) Includes bibliographical references. CONTENTS. - Der Ursprung der Gilden in Norwegen und ihre Entwicklung in den Städten während des Mittelalters / Grethe Authén Blom -- Gilden, Kalande, Bruderschaften, / Tore Nyberg -- Königlich-dänische Kaufleute / Kai Hørby -- Die Schleswiger Knutsgilde als mögliches Bindeglied zwischen westmitteleuropäischem und nordischem Gildewesen / Erich Hoffmann -- Personale und lokale Strukturen kaufmännischen Rechts als Vorformen genossenschaftlichen Stadtrechts / Gerhard Dilcher -- Die Körperschaften in den Niederlanden und Nordfrankreich / Jean-Pierre Sosson -- Die funktionale Gliederung des städtischen Raumes / Henryk Samsonowicz -- Forschungen zur Typenentwicklung des lübeckischen Kaufmannshauses / Wolfgang Erdmann. ISBN 3-412-06883-3 LC Card 84-194645
1. Guilds - Europe, Northern - History. 2. Corporations - Europe, Northern - History. 3. Europe, Northern - Commerce - History. 4. Europe, Northern - Industries - History. I. Friedland, Klaus. II. Series.
HD6473.E853 G55 1984

Gilder, Gilford C. Alabama municipal data book, 1985 / [compiled by Gilford C. Gilder]. Montgomery, Ala. (State Capitol, Montgomery 36130) : Alabama Dept. of Economic and Community Affairs, Office of State Planning and Federal Programs, [1986] 97 p. : ill. ; 22 cm. LC Card 86-622909 DDC 307.7/6/09761021 19
1. Alabama - Statistics. 2. Cities and towns - Alabama - Statistics. I. Alabama. Office of State Planning and Federal Programs. II. Title.
HA225 .G55 1986

Gilder, Jules H., 1947- Apple IIc and IIe assembly language / by Jules H. Gilder. New York : Chapman and Hall, 1986. 178 p. : ill. ; 24 cm. (Chapman and Hall computing) Includes indexes. ISBN 0-412-01121-2 (pbk.) : LC Card 86-2592 DDC 005.265 19
1. Apple IIc (Computer) - Programming. 2. Apple IIe (Computer) - Programming. I. Title. II. Title: Apple 2c and 2e assembly language. III. Title: Apple two c and

two e assembly language. IV. Series.
QA76.8.A66225 G55 1986
NYPL [JSE 87-575]

Gilderbloom, John Ingram. Rethinking rental housing / John I. Gilderbloom and Richard P. Appelbaum. Philadelphia : Temple University Press, 1987. p. cm. Bibliography: p. Includes index. ISBN 0-87722-498-6 (alk. paper) LC Card 87-1958 DDC 363.5/8 19
1. Rental housing - Government policy - United States. 2. Housing policy - United States. I. Appelbaum, Richard P. II. Title.
HD7288.85.U6 G55 1987

Gilhespy, Diana. Socialist enterprise . gottingham , Atlantic Highlands [1987] p. cm. ISBN 0-85124-460-2 LC Card 86-29699 DDC 338.941 19
HC256.6 .S629 1987

Gilkey, Duane C. Pace, Edmond E. Developing a basic loan training program /. Philadelphia, Pa. , c1987. 108 p. ; ISBN 0-936742-41-0 (pbk.) : LC Card 87-7936 DDC 332.1/753/0683 19
HG1642.U5 P33 1987

Gill, Colin. Eaton, Jack. The trade union directory . London , 1981. xii, 323 p. ; ISBN 0-86104-350-2 (pbk.) LC Card 86-673635
HD6663 .E27x 1981

Gill, Lesley. Peasants, entrepreneurs, and social change : frontier development in lowland Bolivia / Lesley Gill. Boulder : Westview Press, 1987. xiv, 246 p. : ill. ; 23 cm. (Westview special studies on Latin America and the Caribbean) Bibliography: p. 225-236. Includes index. ISBN 0-8133-7339-5 (pbk. : alk. paper) : LC Card 86-28207 DDC 303.4/0984/3 19
1. Agriculture - Economic aspects - Bolivia - Santa Cruz (Dept.). 2. Santa Cruz (Bolivia : Dept.) - Commerce. 3. Sugarcane industry - Bolivia - Santa Cruz (Dept.). 4. Land settlement - Bolivia - Santa Cruz (Dept.). 5. Peasantry - Bolivia - Santa Cruz (Dept.). 6. Agriculture, Cooperative - Bolivia - Santa Cruz (Dept.). 7. Social change - Bolivia - Santa Cruz (Dept.). I. Title.
HD1870.S25 G54 1987

Gill, Manohar Singh, 1936- Agriculture cooperatives : a case study of Punjab / Manohar Singh Gill. New Delhi : Vikas, c1983. viii, 560 p. ; 23 cm. Includes bibliographical references and index. ISBN 0-7069-2371-5 : LC Card 84-900335 DDC 334/.683/0954552 19
1. Agriculture, Cooperative - India - Punjab. 2. Agriculture, Cooperative - India - Case studies. 3. Agricultural credit - India - Punjab. 4. Agricultural credit - India - Case studies. I. Title.
HD1491.I392 P844 1983
NYPL [JLD 86-4240]

Gill, Mario. La conquista del Valle del Fuerte / Mario Gill. Culiacán, Rosales, Sinaloa, México : Universidad Autónoma de Sinaloa, Instituto de Investigaciones de Ciencias y Humanidades, c1983. 273 p., [4] folded leaves of plates : ill. ; 22 cm. (Colección Rescate. 19) Bibliography: p. [271]-273. LC Card 86-121747
1. Fuerte River Valley (Mexico) - Economic conditions. 2. Capitalism - Mexico - Fuerte River Valley - History. 3. Collective settlements - Mexico - Fuerte River Valley - History. 4. Agriculture - Economic aspects - Mexico - Fuerte River Valley - History. 5. Railroads - Mexico - Fuerte River Valley - History. I. Series: Colección Rescate (Culiacán, Mexico) , 19. II. Title.
HC137.F84 G54 1983

Gilles, Franz-O., 1944- Die verkannte Macht : Determinanten der Nachkriegsgeschichte der Institution Rechnungshof / Franz-O. Gilles.1. Aufl. Berlin : Schelzky & Jeep, 1986. 398 p. ; 22 cm. Bibliography: p. 349-398. ISBN 3-923024-07-X LC Card 87-127716 DDC 354.430072/31/09 19
1. Finance, Public - Germany (West) - Accounting - History. 2. Finance, Public - Germany - Accounting - History. 3. Finance, Public - Germany (East) - Accounting - History. 4. Finance, Public - Austria - Accounting - History. I. Title.
HJ9925.G3 G55 1986

Gilles, Martina, 1956- Die Standortfrage in der Versicherungswirtschaft : eine empirisch-historische Analyse der Standortwahl von Versicherungsunternehmen und der Standortentwicklung in der deutschen Versicherungswirtschaft seit 1914 / Martina Gilles. Köln : Müller Botermann, c1987. xv, 309 p., [4] folded leaves of plates : ill., maps ; 21 cm. (Reihe Wirtschafts- und Rechtsgeschichte . Bd. 4) Bibliography: p. 265-309. ISBN 3-924361-26-6 LC Card 87-144415 DDC 368/.006 19
1. Insurance companies - Germany - Location. 2. Insurance companies - Germany (West) - Location. I. Title. II. Series.
HG8618 .G55 1987

Gillett, Peter L. Hise, Richard T. Marketing . Houston, Tex. , 1986. xiv, 891 p. : ISBN 0-87393-038-X LC Card 83-72200 DDC 658.8 19
HF5415 .H543 1986

Gillick, John J. Schlesinger, Stephen E. Stop drinking and start living /. Blue Ridge Summit, PA , 1985. xx, 133 p. : ISBN 0-8306-1937-2 : LC Card 85-14885 DDC 362.2/92 19
HV5033 .S34 1985 ***NYPL [JLD 86-1606]***

Gilligan, Colin. International marketing : strategy and management / Colin Gilligan and Martin Hird. London ; Dover N.H. : Croom Helm, c1986. 310 p. : ill. ; 23 cm. Includes bibliographical references and index. ISBN 0-7099-3811-X : LC Card 86-9015 DDC 658.8/48 19
1. Export marketing. 2. Export marketing - Case studies. I. Hird, Martin. II. Title.
HF1009.5 .G55 1986 ***NYPL [JLD 86-4466]***

Gillis, Jack. Hoffman, Naphtali. The bank book . San Diego , 1986. xiii, 222 p. ; ISBN 0-15-610676-0 (pbk.) : LC Card 85-27271 DDC 332.1/7/0973 19
HG1616.C87 H64 1986
NYPL [JLE 86-3189]

Gillis, M. Arthur. In-house computer trends for community banks / M. Arthur Gillis. Rev. ed. New Orleans, LA (833 Howard Ave., Suite 501, New Orleans 70113) : Computer Based Solutions, 1987. 40, 18, [16] leaves : ill. ; 28 cm. LC Card 87-147932 DDC 332.1/028/5 19
1. Banks and banking - United States - Data processing. I. Title.
HG1709 .G525 1987

Gillis, Malcolm. Economics of development /. New York , 1987. xv, 623 p. : ISBN 0-393-95548-6 LC Card 87-5701 DDC 338.9 19
HC59.7 .E314 1987

Gillis, R. Peter. Lost initiatives : Canada's forest industries, forest policy and forest conservation / R. Peter Gillis and Thomas R. Roach. New York : Greenwood Press, 1986. 326 p. : map ; 25 cm. (Contributions in economics and economic history, 0084-9235 . no. 69) Includes index. Bibliography: p. [301]-314. ISBN 0-313-25415-X (lib. bdg. : alk. paper) LC Card 86-3122 DDC 333.75/0971 19
1. Forest policy - Canada. 2. Forest products industry - Canada. 3. Forest conservation - Canada. I. Roach, Thomas R. II. Title. III. Series.
HD9764.C3 G55 1986 ***NYPL [JLE 87-947]***

Gilmour, Peter, 1942- Australian marketing casebook / Peter Gilmour, David L. Rados, Donald M.T. Gibson. 2nd ed. St. Lucia : University of Queensland Press, c1988. p. cm. Rados' name appears 1st on the earlier ed. Includes bibliographical references. ISBN 0-7022-2091-4 (pbk.) LC Card 87-16220 DDC 658.8/00994 19
1. Marketing - Australia - Case studies. I. Rados, David L., 1933-. II. Gibson, Donald M. T. (Donald Morton Tait). III. Title.
HF5415.12.A9 G54 1988

Gilpin, Jean M. Gilpin, Robert. The political economy of international relations /. Princeton, N.J. , 1987. xvi, 449 p. ; ISBN 0-691-07732-0 (alk. paper) : LC Card 86-25562 DDC 337 19
HF1411 .G55 1987

Gilpin, Robert. The political economy of international relations / Robert Gilpin, with the assistance of Jean M. Gilpin. Princeton, N.J. : Princeton University Press, 1987. xvi, 449 p. ; 25 cm. Bibliography: p. 409-435. Includes index. ISBN 0-691-07732-0 (alk. paper) : LC Card 86-25562 DDC 337 19
1. International economic relations. 2. Commercial policy. 3. International finance. I. Gilpin, Jean M. II. Title.
HF1411 .G55 1987

Gilson, Christopher C. Berkman, Harold E. Advertising, concepts and strategies /. New York , c1987. xxiv, 614 p. : ISBN 0-394-36165-2 : LC Card 86-29790 DDC 659.1/11 19
HF5823 .B45 1987

Gimeno Ullastres, Juan Antonio.
Lampreave Pérez, José Luis. La empresa española ante el impuesto sobre el valor añadido, medidas de adaptación y ajuste /. Madrid, España , 1985. 493 p. : ISBN 84-7196-571-2 : LC Card 86-208329
HJ5715.S7 L36 1985

El nuevo Estado fiscal español : reforma fiscal y financiación de las autonomías / Juan A. Gimeno y Jesús R.-Huerta ; prólogo de José T. Raga Gil.1a ed. Madrid : H. Blume Ediciones, 1981. xx, 315 p. : ill. ; 21 cm. (Economía) Includes bibliographical references. ISBN 84-7214-219-1 LC Card 85-176738
1. Intergovernmental fiscal relations - Spain. 2. Intergovernmental tax relations - Spain. 3. Decentralization in government - Spain. 4. Finance, Public - Spain - Autonomous communities. 5. Taxation - Spain - Autonomous communities. I. Huerta, Jesús R.- (Jesús Ruíz). II. Series: Economía (H. Blume Ediciones). III. Title.
HJ1249.A1 G56 1981

Gimpel, Jean. Pernoud, Régine, 1909- Le Moyen Age pour quoi faire? /. [Paris] , c1986. 315 p. : ISBN 2-234-01940-0 : LC Card 86-189820
HC41 .P46 1986

Gindraux, Jim. (illus) Davis, Charlotte. Ports of California. Los Angeles [1970] 80 p. LC Card 79-114863 DDC 387.1/09794
HE554.C16 D3

Ginger, Ann Fagan. The Cold war against labor . Berkeley, CA , c1987. 2 v. (xxii, 915 p.) : ISBN 0-913876-19-4 (set); 0-913876-20-4 (set) : LC Card 87-18510 DDC 331.88/0973 19
HD6508 .C62 1987

GINI COEFFICIENT.
Cortés, Fernando, 1941- Análisis del cambio en la concentración a través del coeficiente de Gini /. México, D.F. [1982] 55 leaves : LC Card 83-111847
HB523 .C67 1982

Ginsberg, Ralph B. Lambert, Richard D. The transformation of an Indian labor market . Amsterdam , Philadelphia , 1986. ix, 249 p. ; ISBN 0-915027-63-1 (alk. paper) : LC Card 86-26900 DDC 331.11/0954/792 19
HD5820.P78 L36 1986

Ginsburg, Paul B. A private health plan option strategy for Medicare / Paul B. Ginsburg, Glenn M. Hackbarth. Santa Monica, CA : Rand, [1987] xvi, 116 p. ; 23 cm. "Prepared for the Health Care Financing Administration, U. S. Department of Health and Human Services." "R-3540-HCFA." "July 1987." Bibliography: p. 113-116. Includes index. ISBN 0-8330-0863-3 (pbk.) LC Card 87-17593 DDC 368.4/26/00973 19
1. Insurance, Health - United States. 2. Medicare - Claims administration. 3. Medical care, Cost of - United States. 4. Medicare policy - United States. I. Hackbarth, Glenn M. II. Rand Corporation. III. United States. Health Care Financing Administration. IV. Title.
HD7102.U4 G56 1987

Gintis, Herbert. Bowles, Samuel. Democracy and capitalism . New York , c1986. x, 244 p. ; ISBN 0-465-06052-8 : LC Card 85-47991 DDC 321.8 19
JC423 .B76 1986 ***NYPL [JLE 86-2928]***

Ginzberg, Eli, 1911-
Executive talent . New York , c1988. vii, 184 p. ; ISBN 0-471-63422-0 LC Card 87-24946 DDC 658.4/09 19
HD38.2 .E94 1988

Resizing for organizational effectiveness : a report of a workshop / Eli Ginzberg ; introduction, E. Kirby Warren. New York, N.Y. (316 Uris Hall, New York 10027) : Center for Career Research and Human Resource Management, Graduate School of Business, Columbia University, c1985. vii, 43 p. ; 28 cm. (Career Center research report) Report of the Workshop on Downsizing held at Arden House, Feb. 20-22, 1985. LC Card 86-162474 DDC 658.1/6 19
1. Organizational effectiveness - Congresses. 2. Industries, Size of - Congresses. 3. Corporate reorganizations - Congresses. I. Columbia University. Center for Career Research and Human Resource Management. II. Workshop on Downsizing (1985 : Arden House). III. Title. IV. Series.
HD58.9 .G56 1985

The skeptical economist / Eli Ginzberg. Boulder, Colo. : Westview Press, 1987. ix, 182

p. ; 24 cm. Bibliography: p. 173-175. Includes index. ISBN 0-8133-7372-7 LC Card 87-2165 DDC 330 19
1. Economics. 2. Economic history - 20th century. 3. Economic policy. I. Title.
HB71 .G53 1987

Gioia, Dennis A., 1947- Sims, Henry P., 1939- The thinking organization /. San Francisco , 1986. xxvii, 375 p. : ISBN 0-87589-690-1 LC Card 85-45913 DDC 302.3/5 19
HD58.7 .S584 1986 *NYPL [JLE 86-2921]*

I Giovani e il mondo del lavoro. 2a ed. Milano : F. Motta, [1982] 241 p. : ill. ; 24 cm. "Premio giornalistico Federico Motta editore"--T.p. verso. Includes indexes. LC Card 84-230716
1. Youth - Employment - Italy. I. Federico Motta editore (Milan, Italy).
HD6276.I7 G499 1982

Gipson, Beckilynn. Aseptic food processing and packaging : a technical/economic analysis / Becki Gipson. Stamford, Conn., U. S.A. : Business Communications Co., c1986. xiii, 164 leaves ; 29 cm. (Business opportunity report . GA-050R) Updated ed. of: Aseptic food packaging and processing / Bobbi Bernard. 1983. "May 1986"--T.p. verso. ISBN 0-89336-471-1 (pbk.) LC Card 87-405014 DDC 381/.45664028 19
1. Food container industry - United States. 2. Food - Packaging. 3. Market surveys - United States. I. Bernard, Bobbi. Aseptic food packaging and processing. II. Business Communications Co. III. Title. IV. Series.
HD9999.C743 U629 1986

Giraldo Valencia, Federico, 1950- Una crítica puntual : reflexiones económicas / Federico Giraldo Valencia.1a ed. Medellín : Editorial Etcétera, 1986. 204 p. ; 21 cm. LC Card 87-400327 DDC 338.9861 19
1. Colombia - Economic conditions - 1970-. 2. Colombia - Economic policy. I. Title.
HC197 .G52 1986

Giraldo Zuluaga, Luisa Fernanda, 1957- La colonización antioqueña y la fundación de Manizales / Luisa Fernanda Giraldo Zuluaga. Manizales, Colombia : Biblioteca de Escritores Caldenses, [1983] 217 p. : ill. ; 21 cm. (Biblioteca de escritores caldenses) Includes bibliographies. LC Card 84-107745
1. Land settlement - Colombia - Caldas (Dept.) - History. 2. Manizales, Colombia - Economic conditions. 3. Antioquia, Colombia (Dept.) - Economic conditions. 4. Manizales, Colombia - History. 5. Antioquia, Colombia (Dept.) - History. I. Title.
HD519.C35 G57 1983

Girão, José António.
Salários, inflação e moeda : a experiência portuguesa / José António Girão. Lisboa : Banco de Portugal, Gabinete de Estudos, 1984. 50 p. : ill. (some col.) ; 30 cm. (Estudos e documentos de trabalho) Documento de trabalho ; no. 11 Abstract in English. Bibliography: p. 45-47. LC Card 85-157764
1. Inflation (Finance) - Portugal. 2. Wages - Portugal. 3. Money - Portugal. I. Series. II. Series: Documento de trabalho (Banco de Portugal. Gabinete de Estudos) , no. 11. III. Title.
HG1145 .G57 1984

Southern Europe and the enlargement of the EEC . Lisboa, Portugal , 1982. 324 p. : LC Card 86-201274 DDC 341.24/22 19
HC241.25.E85 S68 1982

Girault, Christian A.
[Commerce du café en Haïti. Spanish]
El comercio del café en Haití : campesinos-cosecheros/habitants, intermediarios/speculateurs y exportadores / Christian A. Girault ; [traducido por Ana Maritza de la Mota]. Santo Domingo, República Dominicana : Taller, c1985. 426 p. : ill. ; 23 cm. (Biblioteca Taller. no. 220) Translation of: Commerce du café en Haïti. Bibliography: p. 402-408. Includes index. LC Card 86-200427
1. Coffee trade - Haiti. 2. Haiti - Dependency on foreign countries. I. Title.
HD9199.H22 G5518 1985

Girebulebit'i urt'iert'obani soc'ialistur ekonomikaši. Nanitashvili, B. Stoimostnye otnosheniia v sotsialisticheskoĭ ėkonomike /. Tbilisi , 1978. 182 p. ; LC Card 81-149294
HB201 .N293 1978

Giriappa, S. Income, saving and investment patterns in rural India / S. Giriappa. New Delhi : Ashish Publishing House, 1984. 82 p. ; 23 cm. Includes index.
1. Income - India. 2. Saving and investment - India. I. Title. *NYPL [JLD 86-4357]*

Girish Kumar Misra. see **Misra, Girish Kumar, 1941-**

GIRLS - EMPLOYMENT. see **YOUTH - EMPLOYMENT; CHILDREN - EMPLOYMENT.**

Girls, wives, factory lives /. Pollert, Anna. London, England , 1981. 251 p. ; ISBN 0-333-29177-8 *NYPL [JLD 83-884]*

GIRÓN DE LEÓN, ANDRÉS DE JESÚS, 1946-
Cambranes, J. C. Agrarismo en Guatemala /. Guatemala , 1986. 255 p. : LC Card 87-401042 DDC 322/.2/097281 19
HD1531.G9 C36 1986

Gisteren, Roland van, 1950- Branchenorientierte Bonitätsanalyse mit Früherkennungseigenschaften : dargestellt am Beispiel von Hochbauunternehmungen / Roland van Gisteren. München : Florentz, c1986. 2, xi, 393 p. : ill. ; 21 cm. (Hochschulschriften zur Betriebswirtschaftslehre . Bd. 35) Originally presented as the author's thesis (doctoral--Universität Dortmund, 1985/86) under the title: Informationsgrundlagen und Instrumente der Bonitätsanalyse von Hochbauunternehmungen unter Einbeziehung einer branchenumweltspezifischen Früherkennungskonzeption. Bibliography: p. 349-386. Includes index. ISBN 3-88259-370-9 LC Card 86-173025
1. Construction industry - Germany (West) - Finance. 2. Construction industry - Law and legislation - Germany, West. I. Title. II. Series.
HD9715.G32 G57 1986

Gitman, Lawrence J.
Basic managerial finance / Lawrence J. Gitman. New York : Harper & Row, c1987. xxxi, 653 p., [2] p. of plates : col. ill. ; 24 cm. Includes index. ISBN 0-06-042366-8 LC Card 86-25666 DDC 658.1/5 19
1. Business enterprises - Finance. 2. Corporations - Finance. I. Title.
HG4026 .G59 1987

Business world 2 / Lawrence J. Gitman, Carl McDaniel, Jr. New York : Wiley, c1987. xvii, 616, [70] p. : ill. (some col.) ; 28 cm. Accompanied by "Supplement sampler" (15, 12 p. ; 27 cm.) Includes indexes. ISBN 0-471-80596-3 LC Card 86-23441 DDC 658 19
1. Business. 2. Industrial management. I. McDaniel, Carl D. II. Title.
HF5351 .G5 1987

Gittell, Marilyn. State politics and the new federalism . White Plains, N.Y. , c1986. xv, 544 p. : ISBN 0-582-28474-0 (pbk.) LC Card 85-15956 DDC 321.02/0973 19
JK325 .S77 1986 *NYPL [JLD 86-2766]*

Gittinger, J. Price (James Price), 1928- Food policy . Baltimore , c1987. xiv, 567 p. : ISBN 0-8018-3500-3 (pbk.) : LC Card 86-27613 DDC 363.8/56/091724 19
HD9018.D44 F665 1987

Giua, Roberto. Pacifici, Giorgio. Il futuro presente . Milano, Italy , c1985. 201 p. ; LC Card 86-127322 DDC 384/.0945 19
HE8174 .P33 1985

Giuliani, George A., 1938- Bowman, Thomas F. Finding your best place to live in America /. New York , c1981. xiii, 337 p. : ISBN 0-940162-00-8 (pbk.) : LC Card 81-51506 DDC 973.927 19
HT123 .B665 *NYPL [Pub. Cat. 86-574]*

GIVING, CHRISTIAN. see **CHRISTIAN GIVING.**

Gizard, Xavier. Regional development and vocational training analysis and discussion of the relationship development : vocational training experience and perspectives : inter-regional forum of 24, 25, and 26 October, 1984, CEDEFOP, Berlin / [prepared by Xavier Gizard and Martine Bernard, Sebastiano Fadda]. Berlin : CEDEFOP, European Centre for the Development of Vocational Training ; Washington, DC : European Community Information Service [distributor], 1986. 49 p. ; 30 cm. ISBN 92-825-5911-4 (pbk.) : LC Card 87-137374 DDC 331.25/92/094 19
1. Occupational training - European Economic Community countries. 2. Manpower policy - European Economic Community countries. I. Bernard, Martine. II. Fadda, Sebastiano. III. European Centre for the Development of Vocational Training. IV. Title.
HD5715.5.E8 G58 1986

Gizatullin, Kh. N. Matematicheskie metody v prilozhenii k resheniiu ėkonomicheskikh zadach /. Sverdlovsk , 1985. 116 p. : LC Card 86-135187
HC337.R852 U7355 1985

G.K. Hall women's studies publications. Fillmore, Mary Dingee. Women MBAs . Boston, MA , 1987. xii, 233 p. ; ISBN 0-8161-8728-2 LC Card 86-32002 DDC 331.4/816584/00973 19
HD6054.4.U6 F54 1987

Gkekos, Giōrgos. Polyethnikes hetairies dēmētriakōn kai hē diamorphōsē timōn / Giōrgos Gkekos. Athēna : Agrotikē Trapeza Hellados, 1985. 292 p. : ill. ; 24 cm. (Eidikes epistēmonikes meletes . 3) Bibliography: p. 259-268. LC Card 86-212325
1. Grain trade. 2. Grain - Prices. 3. International business enterprises. I. Title. II. Series.
HD9030.5 .G58 1985

GLACIER METAL COMPANY - EMPLOYEES.
Jaques, Elliott. The changing culture of a factory /. New York , 1987. xvii, 341 p. ; ISBN 0-8240-8212-5 (alk. paper) : LC Card 86-25815 DDC 671/.068 19
HD8039.M5 J37 1987

Gladstone, David.
Venture capital handbook / David Gladstone. New and rev. Englewood Cliffs, N.J. : Prentice Hall, c1988. xv, 350 p. ; 23 cm. Includes index. ISBN 0-13-941501-7 (pbk.) LC Card 87-61607 DDC 658.1/5224 19
1. Venture capital - United States - Handbooks, manuals, etc. 2. Small business - United States - Finance - Handbooks, manuals, etc. I. Title.
HG4965 .G57 1988

Venture capital investing : the complete handbook for investing in small private businesses for outstanding profits / David Gladstone. Englewood Cliffs, N.J. : Prentice-Hall, c1988. xiii, 400 p. ; 24 cm. Includes index. ISBN 0-13-941428-2 LC Card 87-14414 DDC 332.6/722 19
1. Venture capital - United States - Handbooks, manuals, etc. 2. Small business - United States - Finance - Handbooks, manuals, etc. I. Title.
HG4965 .G575 1988

Gladyshevskiĭ, Alekseĭ Igorevich.
Metodologiia prognozirovaniia vosproizvodstva i ispolʹzovaniia resursov v ėkonomike SSSR /. Moskva , 1984. 201 p. : LC Card 85-199435
HC340.I52 M485 1984

Modelirovanie i prognozirovanie ėlementov uslovno-chistoĭ produktsii i finansovykh potokov /. Moskva , 1981. 180 p. : LC Card 83-171742
HD30.25 .M635 1981

Gładzicki, Zygmunt. Organizacja produkcji w przemyśle /. Wrocław , 1970. 64 p. : LC Card 87-137344
HD70.P6 O745 1970

Glaeser, Ernst, 1902-1963. Der Staat ohne Arbeitslose : drei Jahre "Fünfjahresplan" / Ernst Glaeser und F.C. Weiskopf ; mit einem Nachwort von Alfred Kurella. Berlin : G. Kiepenheuer, c1931. viii, 198 p. : 265 ill. ; 27 cm. German, English, and French. LC Card 87-409524 DDC 305.5/62/0947 19
1. Labor and laboring classes - Soviet Union - Pictorial works. I. Weiskopf, F. C. (Franz Carl), 1900-1955. II. Title.
HD8526 .G53 1931

Glässer, Ewald. Island / von Ewald Glässer und Achim Schnütgen. Darmstadt : Wissenschaftliche Buchgesellschaft, 1986. xii, 315 p., [20] p. of plates (4 folded) : ill., 3 col. maps ; 23 cm. (Wissenschaftliche Länderkunden, 0174-0725 . Bd. 28) Bibliography: p. [239]-305. Includes index. ISBN 3-534-01225-9 LC Card 87-101040
1. Iceland - Economic conditions - 1945-. 2. Iceland - Population. 3. Physical geography - Iceland. I. Schnütgen, Achim. II. Title. III. Series.
HC360.5 .G57 1986

Glagow, M. Gesellschaftssteuerung zwischen Korporatismus und Subsidiarität /. Bielefeld ,

1984. 239 p. ; ISBN 3-921680-46-8 LC Card 86-223831
HJ2309 .G47 1984

Glais, Michel. Le diagnostic financier de l'entreprise : avec cas corrigés / Michel Glais. Paris : Economica, 1984. 256 p. : ill. ; 24 cm. Includes bibliographical references. ISBN 2-7178-0787-X : LC Card 85-105905
1. Business enterprises - Finance. 2. Corporations - Finance. I. Title.
HG4011 .G56 1984

Glamann, Kristof. Studier i dansk merkantilisme : omkring tekster af Otto Thott / Kristof Glamann og Erik Oxenbøll. [Copenhagen] : Akademisk forlag, c1983. 243 p. ; 25 cm. (Publikation / Københavns universitet, Institut for økonomisk historie . nr. 20) Includes bibliographical references and index. CONTENTS. - Et kameralistisk programskrift, "Uforgribelige tanker om kommerciens tilstand og opkomst" / Kristof Glamann -- Manufakturer og fabrikker / Erik Oxenbøll -- Danske finansieringsproblemer, Otto Thotts rentebetænkning fra 1754 / Erik Oxenbøll -- Allerunderdanigste uforgribelige tanker om commerciens telstand og opkomst / Otto Thott -- Betænkning vedrørende rentefoden / Otto Thott. ISBN 87-500-2476-0 LC Card 85-125251
1. Mercantile system - Denmark - Historiography. 2. Mercantile system - Denmark - History - 18th century. 3. Denmark - Commerce - History. 4. Thott, Otto, 1703-1785. I. Thott, Otto, 1703-1785. II. Oxenbøll, Erik. III. Series: Publikation / Københavns universitet, Institut for økonomisk historie , nr. 20. IV. Title.
HB91 .G57 1983

GLARUS (CANTON : SWITZERLAND) - INDUSTRIES - HISTORY.
Siegenthaler, Jürg K., 1939- Konflikte der Industrialisierung . Bern , New York , c1985. 249 p. : ISBN 3-261-04012-2 LC Card 85-226977
HC398.G55 S54 1985

GLARUS (CANTON : SWITZERLAND) - SOCIAL CONDITIONS.
Siegenthaler, Jürg K., 1939- Konflikte der Industrialisierung . Bern , New York , c1985. 249 p. : ISBN 3-261-04012-2 LC Card 85-226977
HC398.G55 S54 1985

Glas, Miroslav, 1950- Delitev po delu v socialistični družbi / Miroslav Glas. 1. natis. Ljubljana : Delavska enotnost, 1986. 631 p. : ill. ; 20 cm. (Zbirka Družboslovje) Bibliography: p. 604-628. LC Card 87-147216
1. Income distribution - Yugoslavia. 2. Income distribution - Communist countries. I. Title. II. Series.
HC407.Z9 I51473 1986

Glasauer, Herbert. Ipsen, Detlev. Markt und Raum . Frankfurt , New York , c1986. 250 p. : ISBN 3-593-33685-5 LC Card 87-127593 DDC 363.5/8 19
HD7339.M35 I67 1986

Gläser, Thomas. Fischerei und Fischereiwirtschaft im nördlichen Ceylon : Standort und Lebensraum der Fischer im Norden der Tropeninsel / von Thomas Gläser. Wiesbaden : F. Steiner, 1983. xv, 196 p. : ill. ; 24 cm. (Beiträge zur Südasienforschung. Bd. 84) Summary in English. Bibliography: p. 162-176. ISBN 3-515-04054-4 LC Card 86-155838
1. Fish trade - Sri Lanka. 2. Fisheries - Sri Lanka. I. Title. II. Series.
HD9466.S722 G53 1983

GLASGOW (STRATHCLYDE) - ECONOMIC CONDITIONS.
The working class in Glasgow, 1750-1914 /. London , Wolfeboro, N.H. , c1987. xix, 203 p. ; ISBN 0-7099-3415-7 : LC Card 86-24059 DDC 305.5/62/0941443 19
HD8400.G57 W67 1987

Glaskowsky, Nicholas A. Effects of deregulation on motor carriers / by Nicholas A. Glaskowsky. Westport, Conn. (P.O. Box 2055, Westport 06880) : Eno Foundation for Transportation, 1986. viii, 86 p. : ill. ; 28 cm. Bibliography: p. 73-81. Includes index. LC Card 86-80416 DDC 388.3/24/0973 19
1. Trucking - United States - Deregulation. I. Eno Foundation for Transportation. II. Title.
HE5623 .G55 1986

Glass, Christian. Alheit, Peter. Beschädigtes Leben . Frankfurt[/Main] , New York , c1986. 361 p. ; ISBN 3-593-33606-5 LC Card 86-148737
HD6276.G4 A44 1986

Glass, Humphrey. Nattrass, Jill. Informal Black business in Durban . Pietermaritzburg, Natal, South Africa , 1986. xviii, 138 p. : ISBN 0-909232-58-X (pbk.) : LC Card 87-112836 DDC 381 19
HD2346.S632 D86 1986

GLASS INDUSTRY - ENERGY CONSERVATION.
Böttges, Norbert. Rationalisierung im Energiebereich . Essen , Bielefeld , 1984. 159 p. : ISBN 3-7736-0106-9 LC Card 85-130852
HD9502.A2 B68 1984

The glass industry in Sandwich /. Barlow, Raymond E. Windham, N.H. , c1983- v. : ISBN 0-9610166-0-4 (v. 4) LC Card 82-73582 DDC 338.4/76661/0974492 19
HD9623.U46 S263 1983
NYPL [3-MPW+ 84-1016]

GLASS MANUFACTURE - FRANCE - HISTORY.
La Verrerie champenoise, Charbonneaux-B.S.N. Reims, de 1870 à nos jours /. Die , c1984. 279 p. : ISBN 2-904638-12-1 : LC Card 84-247744
HD9623.F8 V47 1984

GLASS MANUFACTURE - MASSACHUSETTS - SANDWICH - HISTORY.
Barlow, Raymond E. The glass industry in Sandwich /. Windham, N.H. , c1983- v. : ISBN 0-9610166-0-4 (v. 4) LC Card 82-73582 DDC 338.4/76661/0974492 19
HD9623.U46 S263 1983
NYPL [3-MPW+ 84-1016]

GLASS TRADE - FRANCE - HISTORY.
La Verrerie champenoise, Charbonneaux-B.S.N. Reims, de 1870 à nos jours /. Die , c1984. 279 p. : ISBN 2-904638-12-1 : LC Card 84-247744
HD9623.F8 V47 1984

GLASS TRADE - GERMANY (WEST) - CASE STUDIES.
Offergeld, Johannes. Spezialisierung des Verkehrsangebotes und Strukturwandel in der verladenden Wirtschaft . Göttingen , 1984. 185 p. : ISBN 3-525-85690-3 (Deut. Bibl.) LC Card 84-197725
HE131 .M8 Heft 102 HE249

GLASS TRADE - IZERSKIE MOUNTAINS (POLAND AND CZECHOSLOVAKIA) - HISTORY.
John, Walter. Glasspinnerei im Isergebirge /. Schwäbisch-Gmünd , 1984, c1974. 78 p. : LC Card 85-135799
HD9623.I94 J64 1984

GLASS TRADE - MASSACHUSETTS - SANDWICH - HISTORY.
Barlow, Raymond E. The glass industry in Sandwich /. Windham, N.H. , c1983- v. : ISBN 0-9610166-0-4 (v. 4) LC Card 82-73582 DDC 338.4/76661/0974492 19
HD9623.U46 S263 1983
NYPL [3-MPW+ 84-1016]

GLASS TRADE - PORTUGAL - HISTORY.
Mónica, Maria Filomena, 1943- Artesãos e operários . Lisboa [1986] 228 p., [24] p. of plates : LC Card 86-229921
HD8596 .M65 1986

GLASS-WORKERS - FRANCE - BIOGRAPHY.
Ménétra, Jacques-Louis, b. 1738. Journal de ma vie . Paris , c1982. 431 p. : ISBN 2-85870-022-2 : LC Card 82-166496 DDC 666/.1/0924 B 19
HD8039.G52 F73 1982
NYPL [JFD 86-6795]

Ménétra, Jacques-Louis, b. 1738. [Journal de ma vie. English.] Journal of my life /. New York , 1986. xviii, 368 p., [1] leaf of plate : ISBN 0-231-06128-5 LC Card 85-28068 DDC 666/.1/0924 B 19
HD8039.G52 F7313 1986
NYPL [JFE 86-2978]

GLASS-WORKERS - FRANCE - HISTORY - 18TH CENTURY.
Ménétra, Jacques-Louis, b. 1738. Journal de ma vie . Paris , c1982. 431 p. : ISBN 2-85870-022-2 : LC Card 82-166496 DDC 666/.1/0924 B 19
HD8039.G52 F73 1982
NYPL [JFD 86-6795]

Ménétra, Jacques-Louis, b. 1738. [Journal de ma vie. English.] Journal of my life /. New York , 1986. xviii, 368 p., [1] leaf of plate : ISBN 0-231-06128-5 LC Card 85-28068 DDC 666/.1/0924 B 19
HD8039.G52 F7313 1986
NYPL [JFE 86-2978]

Glassner, Barry. Sylvan, David J., 1953- A rationalist methodology for the social sciences /. Oxford [Oxfordshire] , 1985. 188 p. : ISBN 0-631-13443-3 : LC Card 84-14480 DDC 300/.1/8 19
HM24 .S95 1985 ***NYPL [JLE 86-1125]***

Glasspinnerei im Isergebirge /. John, Walter. Schwäbisch-Gmünd , 1984, c1974. 78 p. : LC Card 85-135799
HD9623.I94 J64 1984

GLASSWARE - MASSACHUSETTS - SANDWICH - COLLECTORS AND COLLECTING.
Barlow, Raymond E. The glass industry in Sandwich /. Windham, N.H. , c1983- v. : ISBN 0-9610166-0-4 (v. 4) LC Card 82-73582 DDC 338.4/76661/0974492 19
HD9623.U46 S263 1983
NYPL [3-MPW+ 84-1016]

GLASSWARE - MASSACHUSETTS - SANDWICH - HISTORY.
Barlow, Raymond E. The glass industry in Sandwich /. Windham, N.H. , c1983- v. : ISBN 0-9610166-0-4 (v. 4) LC Card 82-73582 DDC 338.4/76661/0974492 19
HD9623.U46 S263 1983
NYPL [3-MPW+ 84-1016]

Glatt, Moisés. Daly, Herman E. Crescimento ou economia estacionária. [Salvador] [1983] 56 p. : LC Card 87-127979 DDC 338.9 19
HD85.S7 D35 1983

Glaubrecht, Helmut. Arbeitszeit im Wandel : neue Formen der Arbeitszeitgestaltung / von Helmut Glaubrecht, Dieter Wagner, Ernst Zander.2., überarbeitete und erw. Aufl. Freiburg im Breisgau : R. Haufe, 1985. 273 p. : ill. ; 21 cm. Bibliography: p. 260-269. Includes index. ISBN 3-448-01509-1 LC Card 85-216364 DDC 331.25/72 19
1. Hours of labor, Flexible. 2. Job sharing. I. Wagner, Dieter, 1947-. II. Zander, Ernst. III. Title.
HD5109 .G55 1985

Glavanis, Bianca. Wellons, Philip A. Banks and specialised financial intermediaries in development /. Paris , Washington, D.C. , 1986. 150 p. : ISBN 92-64-12867-0 (pbk.) : LC Card 87-114506 DDC 332.1/09172/4 19
HG3550 .W45 1986

Glave Testino, Manuel. Burga, Manuel. La historia agraria /. Chiclayo, Perú , 1986. 196 p. ; ***NYPL [JLD 87-1524]***

Glazer, Penina Migdal. Unequal colleagues : the entrance of women into the professions, 1890-1940 / Penina Migdal Glazer and Miriam Slater. New Brunswick, N.J. : Rutgers University Press, c1987. xii, 295 p. : ports. ; 21 cm. (The Douglass series on women's lives and the meaning of gender) Includes index. Bibliography: p. 247-285. ISBN 0-8135-1187-9 (pbk.) : LC Card 86-6568 DDC 331.4/81/000973 19
1. Women in the professions - United States - History - 20th century - Case studies. 2. Sex discrimination in employment - United States - History - 20th century - Case studies. I. Slater, Miriam, 1930-. II. Title. III. Series.
HD6054.2.U6 G55 1986
NYPL [JLD 87-581]

Glazunov, E. P. Preobrazovanie chastnoĭ promyshlennosti i torgovli vo V'etname / E.P. Glazunov. Moskva : Izd-vo "Nauka," Glav. red. vostochnoĭ lit-ry, 1981. 213, [1] p. ; 22 cm. Bibliography: p. 202-[214] LC Card 82-112489
1. Vietnam - Industries - History. 2. Government ownership - Vietnam - History. 3. Vietnam - Commerce - History. I. Title.
HC444 .G58 1981

GLC Housing Dept. The Relationship between the GLC Housing Department, its tenants, and the public /. London , c1977. iv, 107 p. ; ISBN 0-7168-0895-1 (pbk.) LC Card 87-107202
HD7288.78.G72 L68 1977

Gleditsch, Nils Petter, 1942- Economic incentives to arm? : effects of military spending on industrialized market economies / Nils Petter Gleditsch, Olav Bjerkholt, and Ådne Cappelen ; with an appendix by Nicole Ball. Oslo :

International Peace Research Institute, [1986] 72 p. : ill. ; 30 cm. Cover title. Includes bibliographies. ISBN 82-7288-134-9 LC Card 87-163647 DDC 338.4/36234 19
1. Armaments - Economic aspects. I. Bjerkholt, Olav, 1942-. II. Cappelen, Ådne, 1942-. III. Series: PRIO report , 86/21. IV. Title.
HC79.D4 G54 1986

Gleichwertigkeit von allgemeiner und beruflicher Bildung /. Hegelheimer, Armin. Bonn , Bad Honnef , 1986. v, 74 p. ; ISBN 3-87066-628-5 : LC Card 87-409371 DDC 331.4/2592/0943 19
HD6059.6.G4 H42 1986

Gleim, Irvin N. CMA examination review / by Irvin N. Gleim and Dale L. Flesher. 3rd ed. Gainesville, Fla. : Accounting Publications, c1987. 2 v. : ill. ; 28 cm. Bibliography: v. 1, p. 18-22. Includes index. CONTENTS. - v. 1. Outlines and study guides -- v. 2. Problems and solutions. ISBN 0-917537-21-1 (pbk. : v. 1) LC Card 87-70930 DDC 658.1/511/076 19
1. Managerial accounting - Examinations, questions, etc. I. Flesher, Dale L. II. Title.
HF5661 .G42 1987

Glembotzki, Jürgen. Landwirtschaftliche Entwicklung und Agrarreform in Nicaragua zwischen 1960 und 1982 : zu den wirtschaftlichen und politischen Voraussetzungen der sandinistischen Reformbestrebungen / Jürgen Glembotzki. Hamburg : Institut für Iberoamerika-Kunde im Verbund der Stiftung Deutsches Übersee-Institut, 1984. 80, xliv p. : ill., maps ; 30 cm. (Arbeitsunterlagen und Diskussionsbeiträge / Institut für Iberoamerika-Kunde . Nr. 21 =) Summary in Spanish. Bibliography: p. iii-ix. LC Card 84-208160 DDC 333.3/1/7285 19
1. Land reform - Nicaragua. 2. Agriculture and state - Nicaragua. I. Series: Institut für Iberoamerika-Kunde. Arbeitsunterlagen und Diskussionsbeiträge, Nr. 21. II. Title.
HD1333.N5 G57 1984
NYPL [JLM 75-816 Nr.21]

Glenn, Evelyn Nakano. Issei, Nisei, war bride : three generations of Japanese American women in domestic service / Evelyn Nakano Glenn. Philadelphia : Temple University Press, 1986. xviii, 290 p. ; 22 cm. Includes index. Bibliography: p. 251-276. ISBN 0-87722-412-9 LC Card 85-25107 DDC 331.4/8164046/0899560794 19
1. Women domestics - California - History. 2. Japanese Americans - California - Social conditions. I. Title.
HD6072.2.U52 C24 1986
NYPL [IEA 86-1929]

Glenn, Peggy. Word processing profits at home / by Peggy Glenn. Huntington Beach, CA : Aames-Allen Pub. Co., 1987, c1986. p. cm. Bibliography: p. Includes index. ISBN 0-936930-86-1 : LC Card 87-25188 DDC 652/.5 19
1. Word processing. 2. Home-based businesses. I. Title.
HF5548.115 .G56 1987

Gli uomini dell'irco . Nigro, Giampiero. Firenze , 1983. xxii, 184 p. : ISBN 88-00-86022-2 : LC Card 84-238769
HD9425.I83 P76 1983 ***NYPL [JLE 86-2127]***

Glider mail . Short, Simine, 1944- Cinnaminson, NJ , 1987. 261 p. : ISBN 0-939429-00-4 : LC Card 86-72751 DDC 383/.144 19
HE6239.G54 S56 1987

GLIDER POST - HANDBOOKS, MANUALS, ETC.
Short, Simine, 1944- Glider mail . Cinnaminson, NJ , 1987. 261 p. : ISBN 0-939429-00-4 : LC Card 86-72751 DDC 383/.144 19
HE6239.G54 S56 1987

Gligorijević, Vera. Englesko-srpskohrvatski i srpskohrvatsko-engleski ekonomski rečnik = English-Serbocroatian and Serbocroatian-English economic dictionary / Vera Gligorijević. Beograd : IŠKRO "Savremena administracija," OOUR "Savremena izdanja", 1986. 549, [1] p. ; 17 cm. In Serbo-Croatian (roman) Bibliography: p. 549-[550] LC Card 86-196648
1. Economics - Dictionaries - English. 2. English language - Dictionaries - Serbo-Croatian. 3. Economics - Dictionaries - Serbo-Croatian. 4. Serbo-Croatian language - Dictionaries - English. I. Title. II. Title: English-Serbocroatian and Serbocroatian-English economic dictionary.
HB61 .G49 1986 ***NYPL [*QAD 87-1743]***

Glimpses of cooperatives through press : compendium of 25 years press clippings / by R.C. Dwivedi. New Delhi : Coop Times, 1986- v. <1- > ; 29 cm. (Coop image series) Includes index. LC Card 87-900398 DDC 334/.0954 19
1. Cooperation - India. I. Dwivedi, R. C. (Ramesh Chandra), 1928-. II. Series.
HD3538 .G55 1986

Glimpses of Irish industries /. Daly, J. Bowles (John Bowles) London , 1889. xvi, 219, 16 p. ; LC Card 85-666357
HC260.5 .D35x 1889

Glinz, Ferdinand N. Entwicklungsförderung am Wendepunkt : Neuorientierung unter optimaler Wahrung der Menschenrechte / Ferdinand N. Glinz ; mit einem Geleitwort von Jean Pictet. Zürich : Orell Füssli, c1986. 320 p. ; 23 cm. Pref. in German and French. Bibliography: p. 313-319. ISBN 3-280-01676-2 LC Card 86-227950
1. Developing countries - Economic conditions. 2. Developing countries - Economic policy. 3. Human rights - Developing countries. 4. Economic assistance, Swiss - Developing countries. 5. Technical assistance, Swiss - Developing countries. I. Title.
HC59.7 .G55 1986

Glismann, Hans H. Zur Natur der Wachstumsschwäche in der Bundesrepublik Deutschland : eine empirische Analyse langer Zyklen wirtschaftlicher Entwicklung / von Hans H. Glismann, Horst Rodemer und Frank Wolter. Kiel : Institut für Weltwirtschaft Kiel, [1978] 32 p. : 8 ill. ; 30 cm. (Kieler Diskussionsbeiträge = Kiel discussion papers, 0455-0420 . 55) Cover title. "Juni 1978." Bibliography: p. 31-32. LC Card 85-166323
1. Business cycles - Germany (West). 2. Germany, West - Economic conditions. I. Rodemer, Horst. II. Wolter, Frank. III. Series: Kieler Diskussionsbeiträge , 55. IV. Title.
HB44 .K45 no. 55 HB3789

Glissmeyer, Hans. Transpress Lexikon Stadtverkehr /. Berlin , 1985. 487 p., 33 p. of plates : LC Card 86-166711
HE305 .T78 1985

The global copper industry . Mikesell, Raymond Frech. London , New York , c1988. p. cm. ISBN 0-7099-3508-0 LC Card 87-23073 DDC 338.2/743 19
HD9539.C6 M53 1988

Global defence . Williams, Geoffrey Lee. New Delhi , c1984. xlvi, 366 p. ; ISBN 0-7069-2478-9 : LC Card 84-900260 DDC 355/.0335 19
UA11 .W55 1984 ***NYPL [JLD 86-3709]***

Global denken, vor Ort handeln . Grün, Josef, 1951- Freiburg i. Br. , 1984. 373 p. : ISBN 3-921472-73-3 LC Card 84-246414
HC79.E5 G77 1984

Global economic imbalances / edited by C. Fred Bergsten. Washington, DC : Institute for International Economics, 1985. x, 116 p. ; 23 cm. (Special reports . 4) Papers presented at a conference held in Washington, D.C., Sept. 21-23, 1984. Includes bibliographical references. ISBN 0-88132-038-2 (pbk.) LC Card 85-8279 DDC 330.9/048 19
1. Economic policy - Congresses. 2. Commerce - Congresses. 3. Debts, External - Congresses. I. Bergsten, C. Fred, 1941-. II. Institute for International Economics (U. S.). III. Series: Special reports (Institute for International Economics (U. S.)) , 4.
HD73 .G56 1985 ***NYPL [JLE 87-1314]***

The global economy . Holland, Stuart. New York , 1987. xiv, 443 p. : ISBN 0-312-01323-X : LC Card 87-20566 DDC 339 19
HB172.5 .H655 1987

The global edge . Snowdon, Sondra. New York , c1986. 431 p. ; ISBN 0-671-60122-9 : LC Card 86-3990 DDC 395/.22 19
HF5387 .S59 1986 ***NYPL [JLE 86-3489]***

Global energy assessment and outlook . International Scientific Forum on Changes in Energy (1981 : Mexico City, Mexico) Chur, Switzerland , New York, N.Y. , c1984. xxix, 580 p. : ISBN 3-7186-0224-5 LC Card 84-12959 DDC 333.79 19
TJ163.15 .I5678 1981 ***NYPL [JSE 86-509]***

Global energy interactions / editor, R.K. Pachauri. Ahmedabad : Allied Publishers, 1987. xxxi, 1290 p. : ill. ; 24 cm. "Selected from contributions made at the Fifth International Conference of the International Association of Energy Economists (IAEE) at New Delhi in 1984"--Pref. Includes bibliographies and indexes. LC Card 87-902497 DDC 333.79 19
1. Energy industries - Congresses. 2. Petroleum industry and trade - Congresses. 3. International economic relations - Congresses. I. Pachauri, R. K. II. IAEE Conference (5th : 1984 : New Delhi, India).
HD9502.A2 G545 1987b

The Global forest sector : an analytical perspective / Markku Kallio, Dennis P. Dykstra, Clark S. Binkley, editors. Chichester [West Sussex] ; New York : Wiley, c1987. xiii, 706 p. : ill. ; 24 cm. "A Wiley-Interscience publication." "Final report of forest sector project at the International Institute for Applied Systems Analysis"--P. ix. Includes bibliographies and index. ISBN 0-471-91735-4 : LC Card 87-19700 DDC 338.1/749 19
1. Forest products industry. 2. Forest reserves. I. Kallio, Markku. II. Dykstra, Dennis P. III. Binkley, Clark Shepard. IV. International Institute for Applied Systems Analysis.
HD9750.5 .G56 1987

Global hunger : a look at the problem and potential solutions / Malcolm H. Forbes, Lois J. Merrill, co-editors. [Evansville, Ind.] : University of Evansville Press, 1986. iv, 164 p. : ill. ; 22 cm. Includes bibliographies. ISBN 0-930982-08-8 (pbk.) LC Card 87-400224 DDC 363.8/8/091724 19
1. Food supply - Developing countries. 2. Famines - Developing countries. I. Forbes, Malcolm H. II. Merrill, Lois J.
HD9018.D44 G57 1986

The global marketplace . Moskowitz, Milton. New York , c1987. xi, 708 p. : ISBN 0-02-587590-6 LC Card 87-15897 DDC 338.8/8 19
HD2755.5 .M675 1987

Global Meeting on Environment and Development for Non-governmental Organisations (1985 : Nairobi, Kenya)
Sustainable development : report of the proceedings of the Global Meeting on Environment and Development for Non-governmental Organisations, Nairobi, 4-8 February 1985. [Nairobi, Kenya] : Environment Liaison Centre, [1985 or 1986] 109 p. : ill. ; 30 cm. Cover title. Bibliography: p. 94. LC Card 86-981176 DDC 363.7/057 19
1. Environmental policy - Congresses. 2. Economic development - Congresses. 3. Non-governmental organizations - Congresses. I. Environment Liaison Centre. II. Title.
HC79.E5 G595 1985

Global modelling and applications, 0739-5671 . (v. 1) United Nations University Symposium on Energy and Agriculture Futures--Policy Implications of Global Models (1982 : Paris, France) Energy and agriculture . [Chur, Switzerland , New York] , c1984. xii, 370 p. : ISBN 3-7186-0187-7 LC Card 83-18363 DDC 333.79 19
HD1405 .E53 1983 ***NYPL [JLD 86-1837]***

Global problems and world order /. McKinlay, Robert D. Madison, Wis. , c1986. 292 p. ; ISBN 0-299-11384-1 (pbk.) : LC Card 86-40489 DDC 337 19
HF1411 .M376 1986

Global restructuring local response : a report commissioned by the Environment and Planning Committee of the ESRC / edited by Philip Cooke. London : Economic and Social Research Council ; Merstham, Redhill, Surrey : Available from the School Govt. Pub. Co., c1986. 308 p. : ill. ; 30 cm. Includes bibliographies. ISBN 0-86226-174-0 (pbk.) LC Card 86-197207 DDC 331.12/0941 19
1. Labor supply - Great Britain - Effect of technological innovations on. 2. Industrial organization - Great Britain. 3. Corporate reorganizations - Great Britain. I. Cooke, Philip. II. ESRC Environment and Planning Committee.
HD6331.2.G7 G57 1986

GLOBAL SATELLITE COMMUNICATIONS SYSTEMS. see **ARTIFICIAL SATELLITES IN TELECOMMUNICATION.**

Global stock market reforms /. Stonham, Paul. Aldershot, Hants, England , Brookfield, Vt., USA , c1987. x, 157 p. ; ISBN 0-566-00821-1 : LC Card 87-276 DDC 332.64/2 19
HG4551 .S83 1987

The global struggle for more . Nossiter, Bernard D. New York , c1987. xvi, 254 p. ; ISBN 0-06-435851-8 : LC Card 86-45762 DDC 337/.09172/4 19
HC59.7 .N676 1987

The global 2000 report to the President--entering the twenty-first century . Global 2000 Study (United States) Washington, D.C. , 1980-1981. 3 v. : LC Card 80-602859 DDC 333.7
HC79.E5 G59 1980b ***NYPL [JLF 87-206]***

Global 2000 Study (United States) The global 2000 report to the President--entering the twenty-first century : a report / prepared by the Council on Environmental Quality and the Department of State ; Gerald O. Barney, study director. Washington, D.C. : For sale by the Supt. of Docs., U. S. Govt. Print. Off., 1980-1981. 3 v. : ill. ; 27 cm. Vol. 2 has also special title: The technical report; v. 3, Documentation on the government's global sectoral models: the government's "global model". Includes bibliographies and index. LC Card 80-602859 DDC 333.7
1. Twenty-first century - Forecasts. 2. Twentieth century - Forecasts. I. Barney, Gerald O. II. United States. Council on Environmental Quality. III. Title.
HC79.E5 G59 1980b ***NYPL [JLF 87-206]***

Globalni problemi : bŭlgaro-sŭvetski sbornik / sŭstaviteli A. Polikarov ... [et al.].1. izd. Sofiia : Nauka i izkustvo, 1986. 268 p. : ill. ; 20 cm. Includes bibliographies. LC Card 86-231293
1. Economic development - Social aspects. 2. Economic development - Environmental aspects. I. Polikarov, Azariia Prizenti.
HD75 .G555 1986

Global'nye ėkonomicheskie modeli /. Dadaian, V. S. (Vladislav Surenovich), 1933- Moskva , 1981. 214 p. : LC Card 82-117634
HD75.5 .D33 1981

Global'nye problemy obshchestvennogo progressa . Samoĭlov, L. N. (Leonid Nikolaevich) Moskva , 1985. 92 p. ; LC Card 85-170113
HD75 .S258 1985

Globalsteuerung und gespaltene Konjunktur . Willke, Gerhard. Leyden ; Boston : xiii, 243 p. : ISBN 3-12-915020-X LC Card 84-181249
HD5779 .W55 1978

Globalwörterbuch Deutsch-Englisch. Collins English-German dictionary =. London , Stuttgart , 1986, c1983. 2 v. (xviii, 1390, xxiii, 1380 p.) ; ISBN 3-12-517131-8 (v. 1)
NYPL [JFC 86-2613]

Globalwörterbuch Englisch-Deutsch. Collins English-German dictionary =. London , Stuttgart , 1986, c1983. 2 v. (xviii, 1390, xxiii, 1380 p.) ; ISBN 3-12-517131-8 (v. 1)
NYPL [JFC 86-2613]

Globecon Group. Cash management and the payments system . Morristown, N.J. , c1986. viii, 102 p. : ISBN 0-910586-62-4 (pbk.) LC Card 86-82305 DDC 658.1/5244 19
HG4028.C45 C359 1986

The Globus model : computer simulation of worldwide political and economic developments / edited by Stuart A. Bremer. Boulder : Westview Press, 1986. p. cm. Bibliography: p. Includes index. ISBN 0-8133-0528-4 : LC Card 87-8281 DDC 338.9/00724 19
1. Economic history - 1971- - Mathematical models. 2. Economic development - Mathematical models. I. Bremer, Stuart A.
HC59 .G577 1986

Glochla, Erwin. Zukunftsaspekte der anwendungsorientierten Betriebswirtschaftslehre . Stuttgart , c1986. xii, 641 p. : ISBN 3-7910-0402-6 LC Card 86-202268
HD35 .Z84 1986

Glock, Werner. Strukturanalyse Ruhrgebiet . [Essen] [1983?] 185 p. : LC Card 86-218075
HD5760.R84 S77 1983

Glodeanu, Ion. Cazacu, Honorina. Democrația socialistă în acțiune . București , 1985. 192 p. : LC Card 86-216024
HD5660.R6 C39 1985

Glogowski, Erhard. Neue Finanzdienstleistungen : deutsche Bankenmärkte im Wandel / Erhard Glogowski, Manfred Münch. Wiesbaden : Gabler, c1986. 305 p. : ill. ; 25 cm. (Die Bankgeschäfte) Includes bibliographies and indexes. ISBN 3-409-14101-4 LC Card 87-131647 DDC 332.1/0943 19
1. Banks and banking - Germany, West. 2. Banks and banking - Germany (West) - Customer services. I. Münch, Manfred. II. Title. III. Series.
HG3048 .G57 1986

Glosario de la industria petrolera. Glossary of the petroleum industry . Tulsa, Okla. , c1982. vi, 378 p. ; ISBN 0-87814-194-4 (pbk.) : LC Card 82-7622 DDC 665.5/03/61 19
TN865 .G63 1982 ***NYPL [JSD 86-496]***

Glosario de términos de economía y hacienda /. Lozano Irueste, José María, 1920- [Madrid] [1986] 56 p. ; ***NYPL [JLF 87-148]***

Glosario de terminos de renegociacíon de deuda externa =. Guiliani Cury, Hugo. Santo Domingo, República Dominicana , 1985. 68 p. ; LC Card 86-184550
HJ8046 .G85 1985

Glosario de términos económicos. Lima, Perú : Banco Central de Reserva del Perú, Gerencia de Investigación Económica, Subgerencia de Investigación y Análisis Global, 1985. 129 p. ; 23 cm. LC Card 86-221450
1. Economics - Dictionaries - Spanish. I. Banco Central de Reserva del Perú. Gerencia de Investigación Económica. Subgerencia de Investigación y Análisis Global.
HB61 .G498 1985

Glossaire d'anglais comptable. Lebas, Michel. Glossary of accounting =. Paris , c1985. 124 p. ; ISBN 2-86644-065-X (pbk.) : LC Card 86-179932
HF5621 .L42 1985

Glossaire des Communautés européennes : anglais-français / Conseil des Communautés européennes, Secrétariat général = European Communities glossary : English-French / Council of the European Communities, General Secretariat.3e éd, rev. et corr. Luxembourg : Office des publications officielles des Communautés européennes, 1987, c1986. 706 p. ; 26 cm. "Cat.: BX-47-86-656-2A-C." ISBN 92-824-0410-2 :
1. Council of the European Communities - Dictionaries. 2. English language - Dictionaries - French. 3. European communities - Dictionaries. 4. European communities - Dictionaries - French. I. Council of the European Communities. General Secretariat. II. Title: European Communities glossary.
NYPL [JLF 87-217]

Glossaire des Communautés européennes. EG-Wörterverzeichnis . Luxembourg , 1984. 1 v. (various pagings) ; ISBN 92-824-0123-5 LC Card 85-131398
KJE926.5 .E35 1984 ***NYPL [JLF 86-1818]***

Glossaire des communautés européennes. European Communities glossary . Luxembourg , 1984. 1589 p. ; ISBN 92-824-0131-6 : LC Card 85-175527
KJE926.5 .E87 1984 ***NYPL [JLF 87-216]***

Glossary of accounting =. Lebas, Michel. Paris , c1985. 124 p. ; ISBN 2-86644-065-X (pbk.) : LC Card 86-179932
HF5621 .L42 1985

Glossary of economic and social terminology in Eastern European socialist countries /. Mikheev, S. Geneva , 1986. 52, x p. ; ISBN 92-9014-413-0 : LC Card 86-214600 DDC 335.4/03/21 19
HB61 .M487 1986

Glossary of external debt renegotiation. Guiliani Cury, Hugo. Glosario de terminos de renegociacíon de deuda externa =. Santo Domingo, República Dominicana , 1985. 68 p. ; LC Card 86-184550
HJ8046 .G85 1985

Glossary of planning and development . Logie, Gordon. Amsterdam , New York , 1986. xxv, 254 p. ; ISBN 0-444-42608-6 (U. S.) : LC Card 86-521 DDC 338.9/003 19
HT391 .L64 1987 ***NYPL [JLE 86-4010]***

Glossary of terms : English/French. [Ottawa] : Official Languages Directorate, [1981]-1984. 3 v. ; 28 cm. On cover: Employment and Immigration Canada. Added t.p.: Lexique des termes. English and French. Includes bibliographies. CONTENTS. - v. 1. Immigration -- v. 2. Employment -- v. 3. Unemployment insurance. ISBN 0-662-52389-X (v. 2) LC Card 81-180363 DDC 350/.0003/41 19
1. Public administration - Dictionaries. 2. English language - Dictionaries - French. 3. Public administration - Dictionaries - French. 4. French language - Dictionaries - English. I. Canada. Employment and Immigration Canada (Commission). II. Title: Lexique des termes.
JA61 .G55 ***NYPL [JLF 87-379]***

Glossary of the petroleum industry : English-Spanish, Spanish-English / compiled by the staff of Petróleo internacional.2nd ed. Tulsa, Okla. : PennWell Pub., c1982. vi, 378 p. ; 21 cm. Rev. ed. of: Glosario de la industria petrolera. [1973] Title on added t.p.: Glossario de la industria petrolera. "Contains more than 14,000 technical terms and idiomatic expressions commonly used in all phases of the oil and gas industry ..." ISBN 0-87814-194-4 (pbk.) : LC Card 82-7622 DDC 665.5/03/61 19
1. Petroleum engineering - Dictionaries. 2. English language - Dictionaries - Spanish. 3. Petroleum engineering - Dictionaries - Spanish. 4. Spanish language - Dictionaries - English. I. PennWell Publishing Company. II. Petróleo internacional. III. Title: Glosario de la industria petrolera.
TN865 .G63 1982 ***NYPL [JSD 86-496]***

Glotz, Peter, 1939- Manifest für eine Neue Europäische Linke / Peter Glotz. Berlin : Siedler, c1985. 112, [1] p. ; 21 cm. Bibliography: p. 105-[113] ISBN 3-88680-162-4 LC Card 86-100474 DDC 320.5/31/094 19
1. Socialism - Europe. 2. Radicalism - Europe. 3. Individualism. I. Title.
HX238.5 .G56 1985 ***NYPL [JLD 87-1162]***

Głowacki, Andrzej. Ruch robotniczy na Pomorzu Zachodnim do 1914 roku / Andrzej Gołowacki. Warszawa : Państwowe Wydawn. Nauk., 1979. 160 p. ; 24 cm. (Societas Scientiarum Stetinensis = Szczecińskie Towarzystwo Naukowe, Wydział Nauk Społecznych, 0082-1292 . t. 31) Errata slip inserted. Summary in German. Bibliography: p. [150]-156. ISBN 83-01-01306-0 LC Card 81-107475
1. Labor and laboring classes - Pomerania (Poland and Germany) - Political activity - History. 2. Sozialdemokratische Partei Deutschlands - History. I. Series: Szczecińskie Towarzystwo Naukowe, Wydział Nauk Społecznych (Series) , t. 31. II. Title.
HD8457.P66 G56 1979

Glower, Carlos J., 1952-
América Latina y el sistema monetario internacional / Carlos J. Glower y Joel Cervantes I. [Mexico City, Mexico] : Centro de Estudios Monetarios Latinoamericanos, Departamento de Investigaciones, [1986] iv, 28 leaves : ill. ; 28 cm. (Serie Cuadernos de investigación . núm. 9) Summary also in English, French, and Portuguese. Bibliography: leaves 27-28. LC Card 87-400944 DDC 332.4/56098 29
1. International finance. 2. Latin America - Foreign economic relations. I. Cervantes Islas, Joel. II. Series: Serie Cuadernos de investigación (Centro de Estudios Monetarios Latinoamericanos, Departamento de Investigaciones) , núm. 9. III. Title.
HG3881 .G577 1986

Cervantes Islas, Joel. La inflación en dos marcos cambiarios . México, D.F. , 1985. iv, 67 leaves ; LC Card 87-108752 DDC 332.4/1/098 19
HG660.5 .C43 1985

La fuga de capital en Centroamérica, 1977-1984 / por Carlos Glower. Tegucigalpa, D.C., Honduras, C.A. : Banco Centroamericano de Integración Económica, División de Planificación, 1986. 20 p. : ill. ; 28 cm. (Cuadernos de economía y finanzas . cuaderno no. 1) Bibliography: p. 20. LC Card 87-125008 DDC 332/.042 19
1. Capital movements - Central America. I. Title. II. Series.
HG3917 .G56 1986

Glück auf! : la vie quotidienne dans le bassin houiller lorrain / une réalisation de l'Action culturelle du bassin houiller lorrain ; [recherche photographique et légendes, Michel Sirey, Philippe Krucker, Pascal Flaus]. Nouvelle de R. Bichelberger / traduction allemande de Irmengard Peller-Séguy. Paris : Syros, [1986] 117 p. : ill. ; 25 cm. French and German. ISBN 2-86738-115-0 : LC Card 86-178958
1. Coal miners - France - Lorraine - History - Pictorial works. 2. Lorraine (France) - Social life and customs - Pictorial works. I. Sirey, Michel. II. Krucker, Philippe. III. Flaus, Pascal. IV. Bichelberger, Roger. Tiroir aux souvenirs. German & French. 1986. V. Action culturelle du bassin houiller lorrain (France).
HD8039.M6152 F84 1986

Gluck, Sherna Berger. Rosie the Riveter revisited : women, the war, and social change / Sherna Berger Gluck. Boston : Twayne Publishers, c1987. xiii, 282 p. : ports. ; 23 cm. Bibliography: p. 271-275. Includes index. ISBN 0-8057-9022-5 (alk. paper) LC Card 86-31852 DDC 331.4/0973 19
1. Women aircraft industry workers - California - Los Angeles - Interviews. 2. Aircraft industry - Social aspects - California - Los Angeles - History. 3. Women - Employment - California - Los Angeles - History. 4. World War, 1939-1945 - Women - California - Los Angeles. I. Title.
HD6073.A452 U64 1987

Glücksmann, Riccardo. Telematica : dal viewdata all'office automation : situazione e prospettive in Italia e nel mondo / di Riccardo Glücksmann.1a ed. Milano : Gruppo editoriale Jackson, 1982. xii, 273 p., [4] p. of plates : ill. (some col.&) ; 21 cm. On spine: 64. Bibliography: p. 263-269. Includes index. ISBN 88-7056-120-8 LC Card 84-184344
1. Data transmission equipment industry - Italy. 2. Computer industry - Italy. 3. Electronic office machine industry - Italy. 4. Data transmission equipment industry. 5. Computer industry. 6. Electronic office machine industry. 7. Market surveys - Italy. 8. Market surveys. I. Title.
HD9696.D383 I84 1982

Glueck, William F.
Jauch, Lawrence R. Business policy and strategic management /. New York , c1988. xix, 940 p. : ISBN 0-7032-2347-X : LC Card 87-16859 DDC 658.4/012 19
HD30.28 .J375 1988

Jauch, Lawrence R. Strategic management and business policy /. New York , c1988. xviii, 428 p. : ISBN 0-07-032339-9 (pbk.) : LC Card 87-7191 DDC 658.4/012 19
HD30.28 .J38 1988

Das glückliche Bewusstsein und die Krise . Fuchs, Hans-Jürgen, 1957- Frankfurt [am Main] , c1986. 133 p. ; ISBN 3-925798-25-0 LC Card 87-112965
HD8458.A2 F83 1986

Glushkova, V. G. (Vera Georgievna)
Geograficheskie problemy razvitii͡a narodnogo khozi͡aĭstva Moskovskogo regiona /. Moskva , 1986. 104 p. : LC Card 87-135959
HC338.M6 G46 1986

Glymour, Clark N. Discovering causal structure . Orlando , 1987. xvii, 394 p. : ISBN 0-12-286962-1 (alk. paper) LC Card 87-1860 DDC 300/.1/51 19
HA29 .D495 1987

Glynn, John J. Public sector financial control and accounting / John Glynn. Oxford [Oxfordshire] ; New York, N.Y., USA : B. Blackwell, 1987. x, 278 p. : ill. ; 24 cm. Bibliography: p. [266]-275. Includes index. ISBN 0-631-14686-5 : LC Card 86-31725 DDC 657/.835 19
1. Finance, Public - Accounting. 2. Finance, Public - Auditing. 3. Finance, Public - Great Britain - Accounting. 4. Finance, Public - Great Britain - Auditing. I. Title.
HJ9733 .G58 1987

GMAT review. The Official guide for GMAT review /. Princeton, N.J. , c1986. 372 p. : ISBN 0-446-38435-6 (pbk.) : LC Card 86-229958 DDC 650/.076 19
HF1118 .O33 1986

GNEISENAU MINE (GERMANY) - HISTORY - EXHIBITIONS.
Leben mit Gneisenau, hundert Jahre-- . Dortmund , Essen [1986?] 317 p. : ISBN 3-88474-323-6 LC Card 87-408388 DDC 331.7/622334/094355 19
HD8039.M62 G335 1986

Gniset, Jacques Aprile- see **Aprile-Gniset, Jacques.**

Gnoevoĭ, V. N. (Vladimir Nikolaevich)
Sovershenstvovanie metodologii ėkonomicheskogo analiza v nauchnykh uchrezhdenii͡akh i nauchno-tekhnicheskikh kompleksakh . Kiev , 1986. 116 p. ; LC Card 87-126466
HC340.R4 S68 1986

Go hire yourself an employer /. Irish, Richard K. New York , 1987. xxviii, 280 ; ISBN 0-385-23378-7 (pbk.) : LC Card 87-6896 DDC 650.1/4 19
HF5382.7 .I74 1987

GOA, DAMAN AND DIU (INDIA) - CENSUS, 1981.
Census of India, 1981. Delhi , <1983-[1985]. v. in : LC Card 87-915036 DDC 304.6/0954/799021 19
HA4587.W47 C46 1983

GOA, DAMAN AND DIU (INDIA) - ECONOMIC CONDITIONS.
Martinez, José Fernando Trindade. Recursos económicos do Ultramar Português, sua valorização e perspectivas futuras . Lisboa , 1960. 113 p. ; LC Card 86-169892
HC890 .M37 1960

Goacher, D. J. (David J.) British non-bank financial intermediaries / D.J. Goacher, P.J. Curwen with R. Apps ... [et al.]. London ; Boston : Allen & Unwin, 1987. xxiv, 460 p. : ill. ; 23 cm. Bibliography: p. 452-453. Includes index. ISBN 0-04-332109-7 (alk. paper) LC Card 86-32146 DDC 332.1/0941 19
1. Financial institutions - Great Britain. 2. Finance - Great Britain. I. Curwen, Peter J. II. Title.
HG186.G7 B73 1987

GOAL SETTING IN PERSONNEL MANAGEMENT.
Fritz, Roger. Personal performance contracts . Los Altos, Calif. , c1987. vi, 71 p. : ISBN 0-931961-12-2 (pbk.) : LC Card 85-73466 DDC 658.3/142 19
HF5549.5.G6 F75 1987

How to define goals and objectives [videorecording] /. Del Mar, CA , 1986. 1 videocassette (18 min.) : ISBN 0-07-109094-0 (3/4 in.) LC Card 86-700128 DDC 658.4 11
HF5549.5.G6

GOAT INDUSTRY - ASIA - CONGRESSES.
International Seminar on Recent Improvements in Goat Production in Asia (1984 : Los Baños, Laguna, Philippines) Goat production in Asia . Los Baños, Laguna, Philippines , Taipei, Taiwan, Republic of China , 1985. viii, 186 p. : LC Card 86-200478
HD9438.G632 A785 1984

GOAT INDUSTRY - ASIA - TECHNOLOGICAL INNOVATIONS - CONGRESSES.
International Seminar on Recent Improvements in Goat Production in Asia (1984 : Los Baños, Laguna, Philippines) Goat production in Asia . Los Baños, Laguna, Philippines , Taipei, Taiwan, Republic of China , 1985. viii, 186 p. : LC Card 86-200478
HD9438.G632 A785 1984

Goat production in Asia . International Seminar on Recent Improvements in Goat Production in Asia (1984 : Los Baños, Laguna, Philippines) Los Baños, Laguna, Philippines , Taipei, Taiwan, Republic of China , 1985. viii, 186 p. : LC Card 86-200478
HD9438.G632 A785 1984

Gobbo, Fabio, 1947- Per una ristrutturazione e riconversione dell'industria italiana /. Bologna , 1980. 244 p. ; LC Card 82-102594 DDC 338.945 19
HD3616.I83 P43 ***NYPL [JLD 86-599]***

Gobedzhishvili, Z. R. (Zakhariĭ Rubenovich)
Vanags, I. I͡A. (Ilmar I͡Anovich) Ėffektivnoe ispol′zovanie vychislitel′noĭ tekhniki /. Moskva , 1982. 142, [2] p. : LC Card 83-165693
HF5548.2 .V345 1982

Göbel, Dieter, 1949- Lebenseinkommen und Erwerbsbiographie : eine Längsschnittuntersuchung mit Daten der gesetzlichen Rentenversicherung / Dieter Göbel. Frankfurt/Main ; New York : Campus, c1983. xix, 364 p. : 22 ill. ; 21 cm. (Sonderforschungsbereich 3 der Universitäten Frankfurt und Mannheim "Mikroanalytische Grundlagen der Gesellschaftspolitik") Bibliography: p. 279-293. ISBN 3-593-33244-2 LC Card 84-132204
1. Income distribution - Germany (West) - Longitudinal studies. I. Series: Sonderforschungsbereich 3 der Universitäten Frankfurt und Mannheim "Mikroanalytische Grundlagen der Gesellschaftspolitik" (Series). II. Title.
HC290.5.I5 G63 1983

Gobierno Militar. Guatemala. Informe de la obra realizada por el Gobierno Militar, período del 8 de agosto 1983/31 de diciembre 1985. Guatemala [1986] 192 p., [17] p. of plates : LC Card 86-200374
HC144 .G76 1986

Gobotswang, Z. Pilot evaluation report on Mahalapye Development Trust / by Z. Gobotswang, K. Rakorong & M. Segale. Gaborone, Botswana : National Institute of Development & Cultural Research, Educational Research Programme, University College of Botswana, University of Botswana and Swaziland, [1982] v leaves, 61, 3 p. ; 30 cm. (NIR-research notes . no. 7) "February 1982." LC Card 87-122810
1. Mahalpye Development Trust. 2. Manpower policy, Rural - Botswana. 3. Rural development - Botswana. I. Rakorong, K. II. Segale, M. III. Series: Research notes (National Institute of Development and Cultural Research (Botswana)) , no. 7. IV. Title.
HD5710.85.B59 G63 1982

Gocheva, Rositsa. Krŭstiu Dobrev . Sofii͡a , 1987. 80 p., [16] p. of plates : LC Card 87-170598
HB108.3.D63 K78 1987

Gochros, Harvey L. Helping the sexually oppressed /. Englewood Cliffs, N.J. , c1986. xix, 282 p. : ISBN 0-13-386129-5 : LC Card 85-16687 DDC 305.3 19
HN57 .H46 1986 ***NYPL [JLE 86-3217]***

Gochros, Jean S. Helping the sexually oppressed /. Englewood Cliffs, N.J. , c1986. xix, 282 p. : ISBN 0-13-386129-5 : LC Card 85-16687 DDC 305.3 19
HN57 .H46 1986 ***NYPL [JLE 86-3217]***

Goddard, Walter E. Just-in-time : surviving by breaking tradition / Walter E. Goddard. Essex Junction, VT : O. Wight Ltd. Publications, c1986. x, 199 p. : ill. ; 24 cm. Bibliography: p. 191-193. Includes index. ISBN 0-939246-07-4 LC Card 86-61728 DDC 658.5 19
1. Industrial productivity. 2. Efficiency, Industrial. 3. Quality of products. I. Title.
HD56 .G62 1986

Godet, Michel.
[Prospective et planification stratégique. English]
Scenarios and strategic management / by Michel Godet ; translated from the French by David Green and Alan Rodney. London ; Boston : Butterworths, 1987. xviii, 210 p. : ill. ; 25 cm. Translation of: Prospective et planification stratégique. Bibliography: p. 207-210. Includes index. ISBN 0-408-02890-4 LC Card 87-15774 DDC 658.4/012 19
1. Strategic planning. 2. Forecasting. I. Title.
HD30.28 .G6313 1987

Godfrey, John F. Capitalism at war : industrial policy and bureaucracy in France, 1914-1918 / John F. Godfrey ; with a foreword by Jay Winter. Leamington Spa, UK ; New York : Berg ; xiv, 313 p. ; 23 cm. Bibliography: p. 301-309. Includes index. ISBN 0-85496-519-X : LC Card 86-32708 DDC 338.944 19
1. Industry and state - France - History. 2. Bureaucracy - France - History. 3. France - Economic conditions - 20th century. 4. France - Politics and government - 1914-1940. 5. Government business enterprises - France - History. I. Title.
HD3616.F82 G63 1987

Godfrey, Joline. Googins, Bradley, 1944- Occupational social work /. Englewood Cliffs, N.J. , c1987. xii, 227 p. : ISBN 0-13-629445-6 : LC Card 86-25514 DDC 658.3/82 19
HD7261 .G66 1987

Godfried, Nathan. Bridging the gap between rich and poor : American economic development policy toward the Arab East, 1942-1949 / Nathan Godfried. New York : Greenwood Press, 1987. xii, 225 p. ; 25 cm. (Contributions in economics and economic history, 0084-9235 . no. 75) Bibliography: p. [205]-215. Includes index. ISBN 0-313-25648-9 (lib. bdg. : alk. paper) LC Card 87-8471 DDC 338.91/73/056 19
1. Economic assistance, American - Middle East. 2. United States - Foreign economic relations - Middle East. 3. Middle East - Foreign economic relations - United States. 4. United States - Foreign economic relations - Developing countries. 5. Developing countries - Foreign economic relations - United States. I. Title. II. Series.
HC415.15 .G63 1987

Godin, Francine. Bénin, 1972-1982 : la logique de l'Etat africain / Francine Godin. Paris : L'Harmattan, c1986. 325 p. ; 22 cm. (Racines du

présent, 0757-6366) Bibliography: p. 303-321. ISBN 2-85802-609-X LC Card 87-112975
1. Benin - Economic conditions - 1960-. 2. Benin - Politics and government - 1960-. I. Title. II. Series.
HC1010 .G63 1986

Godin, Seth. Business rules of thumb / Seth Godin and Chip Conley. New York, NY : Warner Books, c1987. x, 165 p. ; 21 cm. ISBN 0-446-37026-6 (pbk.) LC Card 87-6262 DDC 650.1 19
1. Success in business. I. Conley, Chip. II. Title.
HF5386 .G55 1987

Godini na vŭzkhod : I͡Ambolskiĭ okrŭg 1981-1985 / [redaktor, urednik Ivan Dzhurelov]. I͡Ambol : [s.n.], 1986. 87 p., [40] p. of plates : ill. ; 20 cm. At head of title: Okrŭzhen komitet na BKP. Okrŭzhen naroden sŭvet. Okrŭzhen komitet na Otechestveniia front. LC Card 87-103737
1. I͡Ambolski okrŭg (Bulgaria) - Economic conditions. I. Dzhurelov, Ivan. II. Okrŭzhen komitet na BKP--I͡Ambol. III. Okrŭzhen naroden sŭvet--I͡Ambol. IV. Otechestven front. Okrŭzhen komitet (I͡Ambolski okrŭg, Bulgaria).
HC403.Z7 I64 1986

Godinot, Xavier, 1951- Les travailleurs sous-prolétaires face aux mutations de l'emploi / Xavier Godinot. Paris : Quart-Monde Science et service, [1985] 155 p. ; 21 cm. Includes bibliographical references. ISBN 2-904972-04-08 LC Card 86-166442
1. Unemployment - France. 2. Underemployment - France. 3. Poor - France. I. Title.
HD5775 .G63 1985

Godio, Julio.
Sindicalismo y política en América Latina / Julio Godio. Caracas, Venezuela : Instituto Latinoamericano de Investigaciones Sociales, [1983] 315 p. ; 22 cm. (Democracia económica) "El presente libro ... es el producto de una serie de temas expuestos por el autor en conferencias y foros sindicales como experto laboral del Instituto Latinoamericano de Investigaciones Sociales"--Prólogo. Includes bibliographical references. LC Card 83-157510 DDC 322/.2/098 19
1. Labor and laboring classes - Latin America - History. 2. Trade-unions - Latin America -History. 3. Populism - Latin America - History. 4. Socialism - Latin America - History. I. Title. II. Series.
HD8110.5 .G64 1983 *NYPL [JLD 86-1758]*

50 años de la C.T.V., 1936-1986 : historia, doctrina y acción / Julio Godio. Caracas, Venezuela : Instituto Lationamericano de Investigaciones Sociales : Distribuido por Editorial Nueva Sociedad, [1986] 149 p. ; 22 cm. ISBN 980-607-709-1 LC Card 87-401745 DDC 331.88/0987 19
1. Confederación de Trabajadores de Venezuela - History - 20th century. 2. Trade-unions - Venezuela - History - 20th century. I. Title. II. Title: Cincuenta años de la CTV, 1936-1986.
HD8362.C68 G63 1986

Gödöllői Agrártudományi Egyetem. Agrárgazdaságtani Tanszék. Magyar-Lengyel Agrárközgazdasági Konferencia (1984 : Gödöllő, Hungary) A nagyüzemek és a kisüzemek termelésének fejlődése, kapcsolatuk az iparosodó mezőgazdaságban =. Gödöllő , 1984. 174 p. ; LC Card 86-145249
HD1995.7 .M32 1984

Godoy López, Luis. Loring, Jaime. Los sectores agrarios de Andalucía ante la integración en la C.E.E. /. Madrid , 1984. 303 p. : ISBN 84-7114-149-3 LC Card 86-152628
HD2025.A5 L67 1984

Godschalk, Hugo T. C. Suhr, Dieter. Optimale Liquidität . Frankfurt am Main , c1986. 155 p. ; ISBN 3-7819-0349-4 LC Card 86-228333
HG178 .S84 1986

Godsejerrøster : landøkonomiske indberetninger fra Roskilde amt 1735-1770 / udgivet af Landbohistorisk selskab ved Margit Mogensen og Poul Erik Olsen, under tilsyn af Claus Bjørn og Erik Helmer Pedersen. København : Selskabet, 1984. 320 p. : ill. ; 22 cm. Includes index. ISBN 87-7526-018-2 : LC Card 84-224395
1. Land reform - Denmark - Roskilde amt - History - 18th century. 2. Roskilde amt (Denmark) - Economic conditions. I. Mogensen, Margit, 1946-. II. Olsen, Poul Erik, 1952-. III. Landbohistorisk selskab.
HD1333.D42 R674 1984

Goedecke, Wolfgang. Realkredit : Perspektiven und Probleme : ein letztes Kapitel / Wolfgang Goedecke. Frankfurt am Main : Knapp, c1982. 120 p. ; 22 cm. Includes bibliographical references. ISBN 3-7819-0275-7 LC Card 83-139826
1. Mortgage banks - Germany, West. I. Title.
HG2040.5.G4 G64 1982

Goedhart, C. (Cornelis) Zijlstra, J. Gematigd monetarisme . Leiden , 1985. ix, 330 p. : ISBN 90-207-1382-5 : LC Card 85-201189
HG1065 .Z55 1985 *NYPL [JLE 87-379]*

Goel, Brij Bhushan. Project management : a development perspective / B.B. Goel ; foreword, Iqbal Narain ; introduction, D.N. Davar. New Delhi : Deep & Deep Publications, c1987. 352 p. : ill. ; 22 cm. Indian context. Bibliography: p. [334]-345. Includes index. LC Card 87-900676 DDC 338.954/0068 19
1. Industrial project management. 2. India - Economic policy - 1947-. I. Title.
HD69.P75 G635 1987

Goel, Madan Mohan, 1930- Administration and management of electricity in India / Madan Mohan Goel ; foreword by S.S. Surjewala. New Delhi : Deep & Deep Publications, [1986], c1987. 280 p. ; 22 cm. Bibliography: p. [274]-278. Includes index. LC Card 87-900202 DDC 621.31/068 19
1. Electric industries - India - Management. I. Title.
HD9697.A3 I43 1987

Görgens, Egon, 1941- Entwicklungshilfe und Ordnungspolitik : eine theoretisch-empirische Wirkungsanalyse unter besonderer Berücksichtigung Schwarzafrikas / Egon Görgens. Bern : P. Haupt, c1983. 111 p. ; 25 cm. (Sozioökonomische Forschungen. Bd. 18) Bibliography: p. 105-111. ISBN 3-258-03324-2 : LC Card 84-108530
1. Economic assistance - Political aspects - Africa, Sub-Saharan. 2. Africa, Sub-Saharan - Social conditions - 1960-. 3. Communism - Africa, Sub-Saharan. 4. Africa, Sub-Saharan - Politics and government - 1960-. I. Title.
HC800 .G67 1983

Goetzeler, Herbert. Wilhelm und Carl Friedrich von Siemens : die zweite Unternehmergeneration / Herbert Goetzeler, Lothar Schoen ; [herausegeben von Wilhelm Treue und Hans Pohl im Auftrag der Gesellschaft für Unternehmensgeschichte (GUG)]. Stuttgart : Steiner Verlag Wiesbaden, 1986. 131 p. : ill. ; 25 cm. ISBN 3-515-04558-9 LC Card 86-141456
1. Electric industries - Germany - History. 2. Siemens & Halske - History. 3. Siemens, Wilhelm von, 1855-1919. 4. Siemens, Carl Friedrich, 1872-1941. 5. Industrialists - Germany - Biography. I. Schoen, Lothar. II. Treue, Wilhelm, 1909-. III. Pohl, Hans. IV. Gesellschaft für Unternehmensgeschichte. V. Title.
HD9695.G43 S514 1986

Goffee, Robert.
Entrepreneurship in Europe . London , New York , c1987. 197 p. ; ISBN 0-7099-3849-7 LC Card 87-15425 DDC 338/.04/094 19
HD2346.E9 E57 1987

Scase, Richard. The real world of the small business owner /. London , New York , c1987. 170 p. ; ISBN 0-7099-5416-6 (pbk.) LC Card 87-6756 DDC 338.6/42/0941 19
HD2346.G7 S28 1987

Gofman, K. G. (Konstantin Georgievich)
Ėkonomicheskie problemy prirodopol'zovaniia /. Moskva , 1985. 137 p. : LC Card 86-119089
HC340.E5 E395 1985

Gol'd, G. S. (Grigoriĭ Solomonovich) Optimizatsiia dolgosrochnogo planirovaniia razvitiia mineral'no-syr'evykh otrasleĭ /. Moskva , 1985. 148 p. : LC Card 86-118644
HD9506.S7472 G65 1985

Goggin, Malcolm L., 1938- Governing science and technology in a democracy /. Knoxville, TN , c1986. xviii, 314 p. ; ISBN 0-87049-506-2 (alk. paper) : LC Card 86-7074 DDC 338.9/26 19
Q125 .G68 1986 *NYPL [JLD 87-462]*

Gohibi, Bernard. Les incidences financières de l'assurance maritime sur l'économie ivoirienne / exposé de Bernard Gohibi, à l'occasion des Journées de réflexions ivoiro-britanniques sur "Le développement des liens financiers entre la Côte d'Ivoire et la Grande Bretagne.". Abidjan : République de Côte d'Ivoire, Ministère de la marine, Institut de documentation, de recherches et d'études maritimes, 1984. 24 leaves ; 28 cm. "24 janvier 1984." LC Card 86-111379 DDC 368.2/2/0096668 19
1. Insurance, Marine - Ivory Coast. 2. Shipping - Ivory Coast. 3. Ivory Coast - Commerce. I. Institut de documentation, de recherches et d'études maritimes (Ivory Coast). II. Title.
HE964.5.I94 G64 1984
NYPL [JLF 86-1484]

GOIÁS (BRAZIL : STATE) - INDUSTRIES.
O Estado de Goiás . Goiánia-GO , 1983. 406 p. : LC Card 86-224747
HC188.G6 E85 1983

Goiás (Brazil : State). Secretaria da Indústria e Comércio. Divisão de Informações Técnicas e Estatísticas.
O Estado de Goiás . Goiánia-GO , 1983. 406 p. : LC Card 86-224747
HC188.G6 E85 1983

Insumos estatísticos para o diagnóstico da pecuária no Estado de Goiás /. [Goiânia-Goiás] [19]84. 156 leaves : LC Card 86-178269
HD9424.B73 G655 1984

Goiás, Brazil (State)
Diretrizes e proposições do governo Iris Rezende, março/83-março/87. Versão 1. [Goiânia] : Governo de Goiás, [1983?] 189 p. : ill. (some col.), col. maps ; 30 cm. LC Card 86-152733
1. Goiás, Brazil (State) - Economic policy. 2. Goiás, Brazil (State) - Social policy. 3. Goiás, Brazil (State) - Politics and government. 4. Goiás, Brazil (State) - Economic conditions. 5. Goiás, Brazil (State) - Social conditions. I. Title.
HC188.G6 G63 1983

GOIÁS, BRAZIL (STATE) - COMMERCE.
O Estado de Goiás . Goiánia-GO , 1983. 406 p. : LC Card 86-224747
HC188.G6 E85 1983

GOIÁS, BRAZIL (STATE) - ECONOMIC CONDITIONS.
O Estado de Goiás . Goiánia-GO , 1983. 406 p. : LC Card 86-224747
HC188.G6 E85 1983

Goiás, Brazil (State) Diretrizes e proposições do governo Iris Rezende, março/83-março/87. [Goiânia] [1983?] 189 p. : LC Card 86-152733
HC188.G6 G63 1983

GOIÁS, BRAZIL (STATE) - ECONOMIC POLICY.
Goiás, Brazil (State) Diretrizes e proposições do governo Iris Rezende, março/83-março/87. [Goiânia] [1983?] 189 p. : LC Card 86-152733
HC188.G6 G63 1983

Goiás, Brazil (State) - Government. see **Goiás, Brazil (State) - Politics and government.**

GOIÁS, BRAZIL (STATE) - POLITICS AND GOVERNMENT.
Goiás, Brazil (State) Diretrizes e proposições do governo Iris Rezende, março/83-março/87. [Goiânia] [1983?] 189 p. : LC Card 86-152733
HC188.G6 G63 1983

GOIÁS, BRAZIL (STATE) - SOCIAL CONDITIONS.
O Estado de Goiás . Goiánia-GO , 1983. 406 p. : LC Card 86-224747
HC188.G6 E85 1983

Goiás, Brazil (State) Diretrizes e proposições do governo Iris Rezende, março/83-março/87. [Goiânia] [1983?] 189 p. : LC Card 86-152733
HC188.G6 G63 1983

GOIÁS, BRAZIL (STATE) - SOCIAL POLICY.
Goiás, Brazil (State) Diretrizes e proposições do governo Iris Rezende, março/83-março/87. [Goiânia] [1983?] 189 p. : LC Card 86-152733
HC188.G6 G63 1983

Goiaz, Brazil (State) see **Goiás, Brazil (State)**

Goicochea Luna, Augusto. see **Luna, Paco.**

Going for it! . Kiam, Victor. New York , c1986. 260 p. ; ISBN 0-688-06060-9 : LC Card 85-61762 DDC 338/.04/0924 B 19
HC102.5.K53 A34 1986
NYPL [JLE 86-2954]

Going for it [motion picture] / IBM Corporation, New York City Partnership, Inc. ; [produced by] Dick Young Productions, Ltd. ; producer, director, Dick Young ; screenwriter, Stephan Wilkinson. New York, NY : The Partnership, 1987. 1 film reel (12 min.) : sd., col. ; 16 mm.

Title from data sheet. Camera, Dick Young ; editors, Bill McNally, Stephen Mack ; narrator, Peter Thomas. Young adults and potential employers. Issued also as videorecording. Describes the Summer Jobs '87 program of New York City, a joint venture between government and business to provide summer jobs for inner-city young people. Explains the benefits of participation and encourages youths to apply for these jobs. LC Card 87-705727 DDC 331.3 11
1. Youth - Employment - New York (N.Y.). I. International Business Machines Corporation. II. New York City Partnership. III. Dick Young Productions.
HD6275

Going for it [videorecording] / IBM Corporation, New York City Partnership, Inc. ; [produced by] Dick Young Productions, Ltd. ; producer, director, Dick Young ; screenwriter, Stephan Wilkinson. New York, NY : The Partnership, 1987. 1 videocassette (12 min.) : sd., col. Title from data sheet. Camera, Dick Young ; editors, Bill McNally, Stephen Mack ; narrator, Peter Thomas. Young adults and potential employers. Issued as U-matic 3/4 in. or Beta 1/2 in. or VHS 1/2 in. Issued also as motion picture. Describes the Summer Jobs '87 program of New York City, a joint venture between government and business to provide summer jobs for inner-city young people. Explains the benefits of participation and encourages youths to apply for these jobs. LC Card 87-705728 DDC 331.3 11
1. Youth - Employment - New York (N.Y.). I. International Business Machines Corporation. II. New York City Partnership. III. Dick Young Productions.
HD6275

GOING PUBLIC (SECURITIES)
Altman, Richard M. Creating investor demand for company stock . New York , c1988. p. cm. ISBN 0-89930-173-8 (lib. bdg. : alk. paper) LC Card 86-25566 DDC 332.6/42 19
HG4661 .A57 1988

Goizueta-Mimó, Félix.
[Effects of sugar monoculture upon colonial Cuba]
Bitter Cuban sugar : monoculture and economic dependence from 1825-1899 / Félix Goizueta-Mimó. New York : Garland, 1987. xvii, 287 p. : ill. ; 24 cm. (South American and Latin American economic history) Reprint. Originally published: Effects of sugar monoculture upon colonial Cuba. [Philadelphia : s.n.], c1972. Revision of the author's thesis (Ph. D.--University of Pennsylvania, 1971) under the title: Effects of sugar monoculture upon colonial Cuba. Bibliography: p. 277-287. ISBN 0-8240-1362-X (alk. paper) : LC Card 87-8632 DDC 338.1/7361/097291 19
1. Sugar trade - Cuba - History. 2. Sugarcane industry - Cuba - History. 3. Cuba - Dependency on foreign countries - History. 4. Cuba - Economic conditions. 5. Cuba - Economic policy. I. Title. II. Series.
HD9114.C89 G6419 1987

Gokhshtand, A. D. (Abram Davidovich) Stukolov, P. M. (Petr Mikhaĭlovich) Otraslevaia sistema planirovaniia . Moskva , 1985. 71 p. : LC Card 85-196558
HD9696.A3 S697 1985

Gol'bin, IAkov Abramovich. Drits, V. I. (Valentin Ivanovich) Intensifikatsiia--opredeliaiushchee napravlenie sovremennogo ėkonomicheskogo razvitiia /. Minsk , 1986. 76, [4] p. ; LC Card 87-144484
HC336.25 .D75 1985

GOLD ARTICLES. see **GOLDWORK.**

GOLD-CURE. see **ALCOHOLISM - TREATMENT.**

GOLD EXCHANGE STANDARD. see **GOLD STANDARD.**

GOLD FIELDS OF SOUTH AFRICA LIMITED - HISTORY - 19TH CENTURY.
Macnab, Roy Martin, 1923- Gold their touchstone . Johannesburg , 1987. xii, 332 p., [16] p. of plates : ISBN 0-86850-140-9 LC Card 87-148896 DDC 338.7/6223422/09682 19
HD9536.S64 G656 1987

GOLD FIELDS OF SOUTH AFRICA LIMITED - HISTORY - 20TH CENTURY.
Macnab, Roy Martin, 1923- Gold their touchstone . Johannesburg , 1987. xii, 332 p., [16] p. of plates : ISBN 0-86850-140-9 LC Card 87-148896 DDC 338.7/6223422/09682 19
HD9536.S64 G656 1987

Gol'd, G. S. (Grigoriĭ Solomonovich)
Optimizatsiia dolgosrochnogo planirovaniia razvitiia mineral'no-syr'evykh otrasleĭ / G.S. Gol'd ; otvetstvennyĭ redaktor K.G. Gofman. Moskva : "Nauka", 1985. 148 p. : ill. ; 22 cm. (Problemy sovetskoĭ ėkonomiki) At head of title: Akademiia nauk SSSR. TSentral'nyĭ ėkonomiko-matematicheskiĭ institut. Nauchnyĭ sovet po kompleksnoĭ probleme "Optimal'noe planirovanie i upravlenie narodnym khoziaĭstvom." LC Card 86-118644
1. Mineral industries - Soviet Union - Planning. I. Gofman, K. G. (Konstantin Georgievich). II. Title.
HD9506.S7472 G65 1985

GOLD INDUSTRY - AUSTRALIA - COOLGARDIE REGION (W.A.) - HISTORY.
Wattone, Mike, 1939- Quest for gold /. Scarborough, W.A. , 1985. 103 p. : ISBN 0-949731-03-X (pbk.) LC Card 86-142484 DDC 338.2/741/09941 19
HD9536.A83 C669 1985
NYPL [JLE 87-662]

GOLD INDUSTRY - BRAZIL - MINAS GERAIS - HISTORY.
Dornas Filho, João. O ouro das Gerais e a civilização da Capitania /. São Paulo , 1957. 238 p., [8] leaves of plates : LC Card 84-215039
HC187 .D72 1957

GOLD INDUSTRY - FRANCE - TRÉVOUX - HISTORY - 18TH CENTURY.
Benoît, Bruno. L'or de la Dombes . Trévoux [1983] 120 p. : ISBN 2-85698-025-2 LC Card 83-229770
HD9536.F83 T743 1983

GOLD INDUSTRY - HONDURAS - HISTORY - 19TH CENTURY.
Finney, Kenneth V. In quest of El Dorado . New York , 1987. xii, 454 p. ; ISBN 0-8240-1359-X (alk. paper) : LC Card 87-8342 DDC 338.2/742/097283 19
HD9536.H82 F56 1987

GOLD INDUSTRY - SOUTH AFRICA.
Rosenthal, Daniel M. The case for South African gold mining stocks . Bethel, CT , c1987. vi, 57 p. : ISBN 0-938689-05-3 (pbk.) LC Card 87-160603 DDC 332.63/22 19
HG293 .R676 1987

GOLD INDUSTRY - SOUTH AFRICA - HISTORY.
Johnson, Paul (Paul A.) Consolidated Gold Fields . New York , 1987. p. cm. ISBN 0-312-00549-0 : LC Card 86-31307 DDC 338.7/6223422/0968 19
HD9536.S64 C665 1987

GOLD INDUSTRY - SOUTH AFRICA - HISTORY - 19TH CENTURY.
Macnab, Roy Martin, 1923- Gold their touchstone . Johannesburg , 1987. xii, 332 p., [16] p. of plates : ISBN 0-86850-140-9 LC Card 87-148896 DDC 338.7/6223422/09682 19
HD9536.S64 G656 1987

Wheatcroft, Geoffrey. The Randlords /. New York , 1987, c1985. xix, 314 p. : ISBN 0-671-63993-5 (pbk.) : LC Card 87-4513 DDC 338.2/0968 19
HD9536.S62 W44 1985

GOLD INDUSTRY - SOUTH AFRICA - HISTORY - 20TH CENTURY.
Macnab, Roy Martin, 1923- Gold their touchstone . Johannesburg , 1987. xii, 332 p., [16] p. of plates : ISBN 0-86850-140-9 LC Card 87-148896 DDC 338.7/6223422/09682 19
HD9536.S64 G656 1987

Gold, Kenneth A. (Kenneth Alan) United States foreign economic policy-making : an analysis of the use of food resources, 1972-1980 / Kenneth A. Gold. New York : Garland Pub., 1987. 349 p. ; 23 cm. (Foreign economic policy of the United States) Originally presented as the author's thesis (Ph. D.--Pennsylvania State University, 1982) Bibliography: p. 322-337. ISBN 0-8240-8083-1 : LC Card 87-23785 DDC 382/.456413/00973 19
1. Produce trade - Government policy - United States. 2. Agriculture and state - United States. 3. United States - Commercial policy. 4. United States - Foreign economic relations. I. Title. II. Series.
HD9006 .G64 1987

Gold, Margaret.
[Older American's guide to housing and living arrangements]
Guide to housing alternatives for older citizens / Margaret Gold. Mount Vernon, N.Y. : Consumer Reports Books, c1985. ix, 170 p. : ill. ; 23 cm. "Formerly published by the Institute for Consumer Policy Research as The older American's guide to housing and living arrangements"--Cover. Includes bibliographies and index. ISBN 0-89043-031-4 (pbk.) : LC Card 87-401956 DDC 646/.79 19
1. Aged - United States - Dwellings - Finance. 2. Aged - United States - Dwellings. I. Title.
HD7287.92.U54 G65 1985

Gold, Mark S. Stop drugs at work ; implementation manual / Mark S. Gold, Lawrence Chilnick & Associates, Inc. New York, N.Y. : Random House, c1986. p. cm. Bibliography: p. Includes index. ISBN 0-394-55091-9 LC Card 86-26168 DDC 658.3/822 19
1. Employee assistance programs. 2. Drugs and employment. 3. Alcoholism and employment. I. Lawrence Chilnick & Associates. II. Title.
HF5549.5.E42 G65 1986

GOLD MINERS - BRAZIL - NOVA LIMA.
Grossi, Yonne de Souza. Mina de Morro Velho . Rio de Janeiro, RJ , 1981. 265 p. : LC Card 81-216799 DDC 338.7/6223422/098151 19
HD8039.M74 B65 1981
NYPL [JLD 86-3591]

GOLD MINERS - BRAZIL - SERRA PELADA.
Kotscho, Ricardo. Serra Pelada . São Paulo , 1984. 106 p., [16] p. of plates : LC Card 84-206686
HD8039.M732 B75 1984

GOLD MINERS - RUSSIAN S.F.S.R. - SIBERIA, EASTERN.
Khatylaev, M. M. (Mikhail Mikhaĭlovich) Rabochie zolotodobyvaiushcheĭ promyshlennosti Vostochnoĭ Sibiri 1921--1937 gg. /. Novosibirsk , 1986. 171, [4] p. ; LC Card 86-231511
HD8039.M74 S545 1986

GOLD MINERS - SOUTH AFRICA.
Jeeves, Alan. Migrant labour in South Africa's mining economy . Kingston, Canada , 1985. xiv, 323 p. ; ISBN 0-7735-0420-6 DDC 331.7'6223422 ***NYPL [JLE 85-3148]***

GOLD MINES AND MINING - AUSTRALIA - COOLGARDIE REGION (W.A.) - HISTORY.
Wattone, Mike, 1939- Quest for gold /. Scarborough, W.A. , 1985. 103 p. : ISBN 0-949731-03-X (pbk.) LC Card 86-142484 DDC 338.2/741/09941 19
HD9536.A83 C669 1985
NYPL [JLE 87-662]

GOLD MINES AND MINING - BRAZIL - HISTORY.
Ciclo da mineração /. Rio de Janeiro-RJ , 1984. 95 p. : LC Card 85-186500
HD9536.B82 C56 1984

GOLD MINES AND MINING - BRAZIL - NOVA LIMA.
Grossi, Yonne de Souza. Mina de Morro Velho . Rio de Janeiro, RJ , 1981. 265 p. : LC Card 81-216799 DDC 338.7/6223422/098151 19
HD8039.M74 B65 1981
NYPL [JLD 86-3591]

GOLD MINES AND MINING - BRAZIL - SERRA PELADA.
Kotscho, Ricardo. Serra Pelada . São Paulo , 1984. 106 p., [16] p. of plates : LC Card 84-206686
HD8039.M732 B75 1984

GOLD MINES AND MINING - HISTORY.
Johnson, Paul (Paul A.) Consolidated Gold Fields . New York , 1987. p. cm. ISBN 0-312-00549-0 : LC Card 86-31307 DDC 338.7/6223422/0968 19
HD9536.S64 C665 1987

GOLD MINES AND MINING - HONDURAS - HISTORY - 19TH CENTURY.
Finney, Kenneth V. In quest of El Dorado . New York , 1987. xii, 454 p. ; ISBN 0-8240-1359-X (alk. paper) : LC Card 87-8342 DDC 338.2/742/097283 19
HD9536.H82 F56 1987

GOLD MINES AND MINING - RUSSIAN S.F.S.R. - SIBERIA, EASTERN - HISTORY.

Khatylaev, M. M. (Mikhail Mikhaĭlovich) Rabochie zolotodobyvaiushcheĭ promyshlennosti Vostochnoĭ Sibiri 1921--1937 gg. /. Novosibirsk , 1986. 171, [4] p. ; LC Card 86-231511
HD8039.M74 S545 1986

Pletnev, V. Lena . Moskva , 1925. 103 p., [4] leaves of plates : LC Card 85-217266
HD9536.S653 S536 1925

GOLD MINES AND MINING - SOUTH AFRICA - HISTORY - 19TH CENTURY.
Macnab, Roy Martin, 1923- Gold their touchstone . Johannesburg , 1987. xii, 332 p., [16] p. of plates : ISBN 0-86850-140-9 LC Card 87-148896 DDC 338.7/6223422/09682 19
HD9536.S64 G656 1987

GOLD MINES AND MINING - SOUTH AFRICA - HISTORY - 20TH CENTURY.
Macnab, Roy Martin, 1923- Gold their touchstone . Johannesburg , 1987. xii, 332 p., [16] p. of plates : ISBN 0-86850-140-9 LC Card 87-148896 DDC 338.7/6223422/09682 19
HD9536.S64 G656 1987

GOLD - NETHERLANDS.
Dunnen, Emile den. Instrumenten van het geld- en valutamarktbeleid in Nederland /. Amsterdam , Deventer , 1985. 109 p. : ISBN 90-267-0955-2 : LC Card 85-115663
HG295.N4 D86 1985 ***NYPL [JLD 86-91]***

Gold, Philip, 1948- Advertising, politics, and American culture : from salesmanship to therapy / Philip Gold. New York : Paragon House, c1987. xix, 217 p. ; 24 cm. Bibliography: p. 189-209. Includes index. ISBN 0-913729-35-3 LC Card 86-30291 DDC 659.1/0973 19
1. Advertising - United States. 2. Advertising - Social aspects - United States. 3. Advertising, Political - United States. 4. Advocacy advertising - United States. I. Title.
HF5813.U6 G58 1987

GOLD - PRICES.
Rosenthal, Daniel M. The case for South African gold mining stocks . Bethel, CT , c1987. vi, 57 p. : ISBN 0-938689-05-3 (pbk.) LC Card 87-160603 DDC 332.63/22 19
HG293 .R676 1987

GOLD - PRICES - SOUTH AFRICA.
Rosenthal, Daniel M. The case for South African gold mining stocks . Bethel, CT , c1987. vi, 57 p. : ISBN 0-938689-05-3 (pbk.) LC Card 87-160603 DDC 332.63/22 19
HG293 .R676 1987

GOLD - PURCHASING.
Löhr, Andreas F. W. Gold und Goldfutures . Berlin , c1986. 217 p. : ISBN 3-428-06029-6 LC Card 86-189745
HG295.U6 L64 1986

GOLD STANDARD - HISTORY.
Kunz, Diane B., 1952- The battle for Britain's gold standard in 1931 /. London , New York , c1987. viii, 207 p. ; ISBN 0-7099-3120-4 LC Card 87-9065 DDC 332.4/222/0941 19
HG939 .K85 1987

Schwartz, Anna Jacobson. Money in historical perspective /. Chicago , 1987. xvii, 442 p. : ISBN 0-226-74228-8 : LC Card 87-5973 DDC 332.4/9 19
HG538 .S354 1987

Gold their touchstone . Macnab, Roy Martin, 1923- Johannesburg , 1987. xii, 332 p., [16] p. of plates : ISBN 0-86850-140-9 LC Card 87-148896 DDC 338.7/6223422/09682 19
HD9536.S64 G656 1987

Gold und Goldfutures . Löhr, Andreas F. W. Berlin , c1986. 217 p. : ISBN 3-428-06029-6 LC Card 86-189745
HG295.U6 L64 1986

GOLD - UNITED STATES.
Rosenthal, Daniel M. The silver & gold investor's profit guide . Bethel, CT , c1986. viii, 90 leaves : ISBN 0-938689-02-9 (pbk.) : LC Card 86-232188 DDC 332.63 19
HG307.U5 R67 1986

GOLD - UNITED STATES - PURCHASING.
Löhr, Andreas F. W. Gold und Goldfutures . Berlin , c1986. 217 p. : ISBN 3-428-06029-6 LC Card 86-189745
HG295.U6 L64 1986

Rosenthal, Daniel M. A short course in gold investing . Bethel, CT , c1986. 90 leaves : ISBN 0-938689-00-2 (pbk.) : LC Card 86-207234 DDC 332.63 19
HG295.U6 R67 1986

Rosenthal, Daniel M. Which 3 silver and gold dealers give you the worst prices? . Lafayette, CA , c1986. 58 leaves : ISBN 0-9615814-3-3 (pbk.) : LC Card 86-209287 DDC 332.63 19
HG307.U5 R673 1986

GOLD WORK. see GOLDWORK.

Goldar, B. N. Productivity growth in Indian industry / B.N. Goldar. New Delhi : Allied Publishers, 1986, c1985. xvi, 206 p. ; 22 cm. (Studies in economic development and planning / Institute of Economic Growth . no. 39) Revision of the author's thesis (Ph. D.--University of Delhi, 1981) Bibliography: p. [191]-199. Includes index. ISBN 81-7023-062-4 : LC Card 86-902812 DDC 338/.06/0954 19
1. Industrial productivity - India. 2. India - Industries. I. Title. II. Series.
HC440.I52 G65 1986

Goldberg, Arthur Daniel. Stern, Richard Walter. Internationale Steuervorteile /. Zürich , 1977. 56 leaves : LC Card 85-173548
HJ2336 .S74 1977

Goldberg, Ellen S. On edge : international banking and country risk / Ellen S. Goldberg, Dan Haendel. New York : Praeger, 1987. ix, 116 p. ; 26 cm. Bibliography: p. 107-111. Includes index. ISBN 0-275-92604-4 (alk. paper) : LC Card 86-25324 DDC 332.1/5 19
1. Banks and banking, International. 2. Country risk. I. Haendel, Dan, 1950-. II. Title.
HG3881 .G6142 1987

Goldberg, Ellis. Tinker, tailor, and textile worker : class and politics in Egypt, 1930-1952 / Ellis Goldberg. Berkeley : University of California Press, 1986. xiii, 234 p. : maps ; 24 cm. Includes index. Bibliography: p. 221-228. ISBN 0-520-05353-2 (alk. paper) LC Card 85-16472 DDC 322.4/4/0962 19
1. Labor and laboring classes - Egypt - Political activity. 2. Textile workers - Egypt - Political activity. 3. Communism - Egypt. I. Title.
HD8786 .G65 1986 ***NYPL [JLE 87-500]***

Goldberg, Michael A. Land rites and wrongs . Boston , 1988. p. cm. ISBN 0-89946-222-7 LC Card 87-12186 DDC 333.73/13/0971 19
HD171.A15 L28 1988

Goldberg, Samuel. El stock de capital en la Argentina : medición y problemas conceptuales / Samuel Goldberg, Beatriz Ianchilovici. [Buenos Aires] : Presidencia de la Nación, Secretaría de Planificación, 1986. 28 leaves : ill. ; 31 cm. Bibliography: leaves 27-28. LC Card 87-403996 DDC 332/.0414 19
1. Capital - Argentina. 2. Industrial equipment - Argentina. I. Ianchilovici, Beatriz. II. Title.
HC180.C3 G65 1986

Goldberg, Walter, 1924- Ailing steel : the transoceanic quarrel / Walter H. Goldberg. Aldershot, England : Gower, c1986. xxiv, 535 p. : ill., maps ; 23 cm. Includes indexes. Bibliography: p. 517-527. ISBN 0-566-00733-9
1. Steel industry and trade - Europe - Addresses, essays, lectures. 2. Steel industry and trade - United States - Addresses, essays, lectures. 3. Steel industry and trade - Japan - Addresses, essays, lectures. I. Title.
NYPL [JLD 87-399]

Goldemberg, José, 1928- Energy for a sustainable world /. New York, N.Y. , 1987. p. cm. LC Card 87-23099 DDC 333.79 19
HD9502.A2 AZ 1987

The golden bowl be broken . Critchfield, Richard. Bloomington , 1988. p. cm. ISBN 0-253-32554-4 LC Card 87-3690 DDC 305.5/63 19
HD1542 .C75 1988

Golden, Gary. Survey research methods / Gary Golden, course designer. Chicago, IL : Association of College and Research Libraries : Copies from Continuing Education Syllabi, ACRL/ALA, c1982. 69 leaves : ill. ; 28 cm. "CE 503." Bibliography: leaves 51-69. ISBN 0-8389-6753-1 (pbk.) LC Card 87-107560 DDC 300/.723 19
1. Social surveys. 2. Sampling (Statistics). I. Association of College and Research Libraries. II. Title.
HA31.2 .G65 1982

Golden jubilee, July 1935-1985 / [editor, Ernest Asamoah ; compiled and published by the GBC Golden Jubilee Publicity & Literature Sub-committee]. Accra [Ghana] : The Sub-committee, [1985] 64 p. : ill. ; 21 x 27 cm. Cover title: 50 years of broadcasting in Ghana. LC Card 86-155961 DDC 384.54/06/0667 19
1. Ghana Broadcasting Corporation - History. 2. Radio broadcasting - Ghana. 3. Television broadcasting - Ghana. I. Asamoah, Ernest. II. GBC Golden Jubilee Publicity & Literature Sub-committee (Ghana). III. Title: 50 years of broadcasting in Ghana.
HE8689.9.G45 G65 1985

Golden, Peggy A. Smith, Jerald R. Airline . Englewood Cliffs, NJ , c1987. v, 115, [38] p. : ISBN 0-13-020801-9 (pbk.) LC Card 86-30488 DDC 387.7/068 19
HD30.28 .S57 1987

The golden sword . Neuschatz, Michael. New York , 1986. xii, 301 p. ; ISBN 0-313-25104-5 (lib. bdg. : alk. Paper) LC Card 85-27026 DDC 331.88/122334/09788 19
HD8039.M61 U48 1986
NYPL [JLE 87-766]

Golden tokens : subway treasure hunt & trivia game / illustrator, Michael Nelson ; prepared by the editorial staff of I Write Books. Roxbury, Conn. : I Write Books, c1987. p. cm. On t.p. the registered trademark symbol "TM" is superscript following "Token" in the title. ISBN 0-941067-00-9 LC Card 86-27826 DDC 388.4/28 19
1. Subways - Miscellanea. I. Nelson, Michael, 1966-. II. I Write Books (Firm).
HE4211 .G58 1987

Der Goldene Boden : Gedanken über das Handwerk / herausgegeben von Paul Schnitker. Stuttgart : Deutsche Verlags-Anstalt, c1987. 359 p. ; 21 cm. Includes bibliographies. ISBN 3-421-02885-0 LC Card 87-139261 DDC 331.7/94 19
1. Artisans - Germany (West) - History. 2. Artisans - Germany (West) - Economic conditions. I. Schnitker, Paul.
HD2346.G3 G55 1987

Goldfield, Michael. The decline of organized labor in the United States / Michael Goldfield. Chicago : University of Chicago Press, 1987. xv, 294 p. : ill. ; 24 cm. Bibliography: p. 261-285. Includes index. ISBN 0-226-30102-8 LC Card 86-24890 DDC 331.88/0973 19
1. Trade-unions - United States - History - 20th century. I. Title.
HD6508 .G683 1987

Goldfield, Randy J.
Office information technology : a decision-maker's guide to systems planning and implementation / Randy J. Goldfield. New York : Quorum Books, 1986. xiv, 226 p. : ill. ; 25 cm. Includes index. ISBN 0-89930-108-8 (lib. bdg. : alk. paper) LC Card 86-614 DDC 651.8 19
1. Office practice - Automation. 2. Business - Data processing. I. Title.
HF5547.5 .G65 1986 ***NYPL [JLE 87-1107]***

Training in the automated office : a decision-maker's guide to systems planning and implementation / Randy J. Goldfield. New York : Quorum Books, 1987. ix, 190 p. ; 25 cm. Includes index. ISBN 0-89930-112-6 (lib. bdg. : alk. paper) LC Card 86-30605 DDC 658.3/1245 19
1. Office practice - Automation - Study and teaching - United States. I. Title.
HF5547.5 .G655 1987

Goldfields-Esperance regional profile. Kalgoorlie, W.A. : Goldfields-Esperance Regional Development Advisory Committee ; Perth, W.A. : Dept. of Regional Development and the North West, [1986] 58 p. : ill. ; 30 cm. "May 1986." Bibliography: p. 57. LC Card 87-169717 DDC 330.9941/7 19
1. Western Australia - Economic conditions. 2. Western Australia - Social conditions. 3. Regional planning - Australia - Western Australia. 4. Industrial promotion - Australia - Western Australia. I. Western Australia. Goldfields-Esperance Regional Development Advisory Committee.
HC607.W47 G65 1986

Goldfischer, Morrie. Zweig, Martin E. [Winning with new IRAs.] Martin Zweig's winning with new IRAs /. New York, NY , c1987. xvi, 207 p. : ISBN 0-446-51276-1 LC Card 86-28203 DDC

332.024/01 19
HG1660.A3 Z94 1987

Goldhaber, Gerald M. Handbook of organizational communication /. Norwood, N.J. , c1988. 502 p. : ISBN 0-89391-446-0 LC Card 87-19380 DDC 658.4/5 19
HD30.3 .H357 1988

Goldin, Ian. The poverty of Coloured labour preference : economics and ideology in the Western Cape / Ian Goldin. Cape Town : Southern Africa Labour and Development Research Unit, [1984] ii, 97 p. : ill. ; 22 cm. (Saldu working paper . no. 59) "January 1984." Bibliography: p. 96-97. ISBN 0-7992-0570-2 (pbk.) LC Card 84-195453
1. Colored people (South Africa) - Employment - South Africa - Cape of Good Hope. 2. Labor policy - South Africa - Cape of Good Hope. 3. Labor and laboring classes - South Africa - Cape of Good Hope. 4. Labor supply - South Africa - Cape of Good Hope. I. Title. II. Series.
HD8801.Z8 C324 1984

Goldman, Barbara. Final report on the San Diego job search and work experience demonstration / Barbara Goldman, Daniel Friedlander, David Long with Marjorie Erickson, Judith Gueron. New York, N.Y. (3 Park Ave., New York 10016) : Manpower Demonstration Research Corp., c1986. xliv, 269 p. : ill. ; 28 cm. On cover: California, the demonstration of state work/welfare initiatives. On spine: California, final report on the San Diego demonstration. Bibliography: p. 265-267. LC Card 87-118376 DDC 331.12/042/0979498 19
1. Public service employment - California - San Diego County. 2. Manpower policy - California - San Diego County. 3. Occupational training - California - San Diego County. I. Friedlander, Daniel. II. Long, David. III. Title. IV. Title: California, the demonstration of state work/welfare initiatives. V. Title: California, final report on the San Diego demonstration.
HD5713.6.U542 S395 1986

Goldman, Benjamin A. Hazardous waste management : reducing the risk / Council on Economic Priorities ; foreword, Lee B. Thomas, Jr. ; project directors, Benjamin A. Goldman, James A. Hulme, Cameron Johnson ; research assistants, Alexander C. Stewart, Bridget Weighart ; editors, Alice Tepper Marlin, Steven S. Ross. Washington, D.C. : Island Press, c1986. xx, 316 p. : ill. ; 23 cm. Includes index. Bibliography: p. 285-304. ISBN 0-933280-30-0 : LC Card 86-2748 DDC 363.7/28 19
1. Hazardous waste management industry - United States. 2. Hazardous waste sites - United States. I. Hulme, James A. II. Johnson, Cameron. III. Marlin, Alice Tepper. IV. Ross, Steven S. V. Council on Economic Priorities. VI. Title.
HD9975.U52 G65 1986 ***NYPL [JLE 87-1159]***

Goldman, Marshall I. Gorbachev's challenge : economic reform in the age of high technology / Marshall I. Goldman.1st ed. New York : W.W. Norton, c1987. xvii, 296 p. : ill. ; 22 cm. Errata slip inserted. Bibliography: p. [266]-280. Includes index. ISBN 0-393-02454-7 LC Card 86-33187 DDC 338.947 19
1. Soviet Union - Economic policy - 1981-. 2. Soviet Union - Economic conditions - 1976-. 3. Technology transfer - Soviet Union. I. Title.
HC336.25 .G6365 1987

Goldman, Peter Louis, 1933- The end of the world that was : six lives in the atomic age / by Peter Goldman with Pamela Abramson ... [et al.].1st ed. New York : Dutton, c1986. xiv, 129 p., [8] p. of plates : ill. ; 23 cm. (A Newsweek book) Includes index. ISBN 0-525-24428-X LC Card 85-31223 DDC 920/.073 19
1. World War, 1939-1945 - Biography. 2. World War, 1939-1945 - Influence. 3. Atomic bomb - Japan. 4. Nuclear warfare. 5. United States - Biography. 6. Japan - Biography. I. Abramson, Pamela. II. Title.
CT220 .G6 1986 ***NYPL [JFD 86-6015]***

Goldschmidt, H. O. Omgeving, doelstellingen en organisatie . Assen , 1986. viii, 464 p. : ISBN 90-232-2208-3 : LC Card 86-182876
HG4181 .O44 1986

GOLDSCHMIDT, H. O.
Omgeving, doelstellingen en organisatie . Assen , 1986. viii, 464 p. : ISBN 90-232-2208-3 : LC Card 86-182876
HG4181 .O44 1986

Goldschmidt, Yaaqov. The impact of inflation on financial activity in business, with applications to the U. S. farming sector / Yaaqov Goldschmidt, Leon Shashua, Jimmye S. Hillman. Totowa, N.J. : Rowman & Littlefield, 1986. xvi, 181 p. ; 24 cm. Includes index. Bibliography: p. [175]-176. ISBN 0-8476-7427-4 : LC Card 85-14196 DDC 338.1/3/0973 19
1. Agriculture - Economic aspects - United States. 2. Inflation (Finance) - United States. I. Shashua, Leon. II. Hillman, Jimmye S., 1923-. III. Title.
HD1761 .G645 1986 ***NYPL [JLE 86-3484]***

Goldshmidt, Ya'akov. see **Goldschmidt, Yaaqov.**

Goldsmith, David, 1946- Safety management in construction and industry / David Goldsmith. New York : McGraw-Hill, c1987. viii, 120 p. : ill. ; 24 cm. Bibliography: p. 115. Includes index. ISBN 0-07-023677-1 LC Card 86-27733 DDC 363.1/19624 19
1. Industrial safety. 2. Construction industry - Safety measures. I. Title.
HD7262 .G58 1987

GOLDSMITH, JAMES, SIR, 1933-
Wansell, Geoffrey, 1945- Tycoon . New York , 1987. 396 p., [16] p. of plates : ISBN 0-689-11817-1 LC Card 87-11473 DDC 338/.04/0924 B 19
HC252.5.G64 W36 1987

Goldsmith, Oliver Scott. How state spending reductions affect economic activity / by Scott Goldsmith. Fairbanks : Institute of Social and Economic Research, University of Alaska, [1986] 40, 10 p. : ill. ; 28 cm. (ISER working paper . 86.2) "March 5, 1986." Includes bibliographical references. LC Card 86-622972 DDC 330.9798/05 19
1. Alaska - Appropriations and expenditures. 2. Government spending policy - Alaska. 3. Alaska - Economic conditions. I. Title. II. Series.
HJ7553 .G64 1986

The goldsmiths . Banerjee, Deb Kumar. Calcutta , 1983. ii, 56 p., [3] leaves of plates : LC Card 85-903366 DDC 331.7/67322/095414 19
HD8039.G72 I53 1983 ***NYPL [JLE 86-2038]***

GOLDSMITHS - INDIA - CALCUTTA.
Banerjee, Deb Kumar. The goldsmiths . Calcutta , 1983. ii, 56 p., [3] leaves of plates : LC Card 85-903366 DDC 331.7/67322/095414 19
HD8039.G72 I53 1983 ***NYPL [JLE 86-2038]***

Goldstein, Alice. (joint author) Goldstein, Sidney, 1927- Urban-rural migration differentials in Thailand /. [Bangkok] , 1974. 49 p. ; LC Card 78-301310 DDC 301.36/1
HB2104.55.A3 G64 ***NYPL [JLM 83-719 no.12]***

Goldstein, Bernard. Poppel, Harvey L. Information technology . New York , c1987. xx, 207 p. : ISBN 0-07-050511-X : LC Card 86-27782 DDC 338.4/7004/0973 19
HD9696.C62 P623 1987

Goldstein, Harold. Training for work in the computer age : how workers who use computers get their training / by Harold Goldstein and Bryna Shore Fraser. Washington, D.C. : National Commission for Employment Policy, 1986. iv, 109 p. ; 28 cm. (Research report series . RR-85-09) Shipping list no.: 86-269-P. "June 1985." Bibliography: p. 103-108. Item 1089-H LC Card 86-601422 DDC 331.25/92 19
1. Occupational retraining - United States. 2. Computer literacy - United States. I. Fraser, Bryna Shore. II. United States. National Commission for Employment Policy. III. Series: Research report series (United States. National Commission for Employment Policy) , RR-85-09. IV. Title.
HD5715.2 .G63 1986

Goldstein, Harvey A. The State and local industrial policy /. Chicago, Ill. , c1987. x, 195 p. : ISBN 0-918286-46-8 (pbk.) LC Card 86-72373 DDC 338.973 19
HD3616.U47 S68 1987

Goldstein, Harvey A. (Harvey Arthur), 1939- Up your cash flow : an easy-to-use business guide to immediately increase your profits and cash flow / Harvey A. Goldstein. Los Angeles, Calif. : Granville Publications, c1986. 174 p. : ill. ; 23 cm. Formerly "122 minutes a month a greater profits."--T.p. verso. Includes index. ISBN 0-931349-04-4 (pbk.) LC Card 86-213003 DDC 658.1/592 19
1. Small business - Management. 2. Small business - Finance. 3. Small business - Cash position. I. Title.
HD62.7 .G68 1986

Goldstein, Irwin L., 1937-
Training in organizations : needs assessment, development, and evaluation / Irwin L. Goldstein.2nd ed. Monterey, Calif. : Brooks/Cole Pub. Co., c1986. xv, 315 p. : ill. ; 23 cm. Rev. ed. of: Training. 1974. Includes index. Bibliography: p. 291-305. ISBN 0-534-05604-0 : LC Card 85-21348 DDC 658.3/12404 19
1. Employees, Training of - Evaluation. 2. Assessment centers (Personnel management procedure). I. Goldstein, Irwin L., 1937- Training. II. Title.
HF5549.5.T7 G543 1985 ***NYPL [JLE 86-1519]***

Training. Goldstein, Irwin L., 1937- Training in organizations : needs assessment, development, and evaluation / Irwin L. Goldstein.2nd ed. Monterey, Calif. , c1986. xv, 315 p. : ISBN 0-534-05604-0 : LC Card 85-21348 DDC 658.3/12404 19
HF5549.5.T7 G543 1985 ***NYPL [JLE 86-1519]***

Goldstein, Joshua S., 1952- Long cycles : prosperity and war in the modern age / Joshua S. Goldstein. New Haven : Yale University Press, c1988. p. cm. Revision of thesis (Ph. D.)--Massachusetts Institute of Technology. Bibliography: p. Includes index. ISBN 0-300-03994-8 (alk. paper) LC Card 87-10723 DDC 338.5/42 19
1. Long waves (Economics). 2. Business cycles. I. Title.
HB3729 .G64 1988

Goldstein, Ken. Collins, Lora S. The U. S. economy to 1990 /. New York, N.Y. , c1985. 21 p. : ISBN 0-8237-0307-X (pbk.) LC Card 86-200284 DDC 338.5/443/0973 19
HC106.8 .C636 1985

Goldstein, Morris, 1944-
Crockett, Andrew. Strengthening the international monetary system . Washington, D.C. , c1987. vii, 84 p. ; LC Card 86-33750 DDC 332.4/5 19
HG3881 .C694 1987

Growth-oriented adjustment programs /. Washington, D.C. , 1987. xiii, 537 p. : ISBN 0-939934-92-2 (pbk.) LC Card 87-21361 DDC 338.9 19
HD73 .G76 1987

Goldstein, Sidney, 1927- Urban-rural migration differentials in Thailand / by Sidney Goldstein, Visid Prachuabmoh, Alice Goldstein. [Bangkok] : Institute of Population Studies, Chulalongkorn University, 1974. 49 p. ; 26 cm. (Research report - Institute of Population Studies . no. 12) "February, 1974." Includes bibliographical references. LC Card 78-301310 DDC 301.36/1
1. Migration, Internal - Thailand. 2. Rural-urban migration - Thailand. I. Visid Prachuabmoh, joint author. II. Goldstein, Alice, joint author. III. Series: Research report (Sathāban Prachāk
HB2104.55.A3 G64 ***NYPL [JLM 83-719 no.12]***

Goldstein, Sue, 1941-
The 2nd underground shopper : new guide to discount mail-order shopping / Sue Goldstein. Kansas City : Andrews, McMeel & Parker, c1985. 470 p. : ill. ; 22 cm. Rev. ed. of: The underground shopper. 1983. Includes indexes. ISBN 0-8362-7956-5 (pbk.) : LC Card 85-620 DDC 381/.1 19
1. Mail-order business - United States - Directories. 2. Mail-order business - Directories. 3. Discount houses (Retail trade) - United States - Directories. 4. Discount houses (Retail trade) - Directories. I. Goldstein, Sue, 1941- Underground shopper. II. Title. III. Title: Second underground shopper.
HF5466 .G6 1985 ***NYPL [JLD 86-3080]***

The 3rd underground shopper : new guide to discount mail-order shopping / Sue Goldstein. Kansas City : Andrews, McMeel & Parker, 1986. x, 532 p. ; 22 cm. Includes indexes. ISBN 0-8362-7937-9 (pbk.) : LC Card 86-28758 DDC 381/.1 19
1. Mail-order business - United States - Directories. 2. Mail-order business - Directories. 3. Discount houses (Retail trade) - United States - Directories. 4. Discount houses (Retail trade) - Directories. I. Third

underground shopper. II. Title.
HF5466 .G6 1986

Underground shopper. Goldstein, Sue, 1941- The 2nd underground shopper : new guide to discount mail-order shopping / Sue Goldstein. Kansas City , c1985. 470 p. : ISBN 0-8362-7956-5 (pbk.) : LC Card 85-620 DDC 381/.1 19
HF5466 .G6 1985 NYPL [JLD 86-3080]

Goldstone, Nancy Bazelon. Trading up / Nancy Bazelon Goldstone. 1st ed. New York : Dutton, c1988. viii, 262 p. ; 22 cm. ISBN 0-525-24621-5 : LC Card 87-19975 DDC 332.4/5/0924 B 19
1. Goldstone, Nancy Bazelon. 2. Floor traders (Finance) - New York (N.Y.) - Biography. 3. Futures market. 4. Financial futures. I. Title.
HG3853 .G65 1988

GOLDSTONE, NANCY BAZELON.
Goldstone, Nancy Bazelon. Trading up /. New York , c1988. viii, 262 p. ; ISBN 0-525-24621-5 : LC Card 87-19975 DDC 332.4/5/0924 B 19
HG3853 .G65 1988

Goldwasser, Thomas. Family pride : profiles of five of America's best-run family businesses / Thomas Goldwasser.1st ed. New York : Dodd, Mead, c1986. 226 p. ; 22 cm. Includes index. ISBN 0-396-08587-3 LC Card 86-4546 DDC 338.7/4/0973 19
1. Family corporations - United States - Management - Case studies. 2. Success in business - United States - Case studies. I. Title.
HD62.25 .G64 1986 NYPL [JLD 87-159]

Goldwater, Mike.
Ethiopia's bitter medicine, settling for disaster . London , 1986. 55 p. : ISBN 0-946592-01-2 (pbk.) LC Card 86-232852 DDC 333.3/1/63
HD979.Z63 E74 1986

Twose, Nigel. Fighting the famine /. London , 1985. 96 p. : ISBN 0-7453-0131-2 (pbk.) : LC Card 86-135675 DDC 363.8/83/0966 19
HC800.Z9 F385 1985 NYPL [JLD 87-768]

GOLDWORK - INDIA - CALCUTTA.
Banerjee, Deb Kumar. The goldsmiths . Calcutta , 1983. ii, 56 p., [3] leaves of plates : LC Card 85-903366 DDC 331.7/67322/095414 19
HD8039.G72 I53 1983
NYPL [JLE 86-2038]

Gołębiowski, Jerzy. Sektor państwowy w gospodarce Polski międzywojennej / Jerzy Gołębiowski. Wyd. 1. Warszawa : Państwowe Wydawn. Nauk., 1985. 366 p. ; 24 cm. Bibliography: p. 336-[355] Includes index. ISBN 83-01-06292-4 : LC Card 86-108406
1. Government ownership - Poland. 2. Poland - Economic conditions - 1918-1945. I. Title.
HD4215.7 .G65 1985

Golin, Steve. The fragile bridge : Paterson Silk Strike, 1913 / Steve Golin. Philadelphia : Temple University Press, 1988. p. cm. Bibliography: p. Includes index. ISBN 0-87722-534-6 (alk. paper) : LC Card 87-24356 DDC 331.89/287739/0974924 19
1. Silk Workers' Strike, Paterson, N.J., 1913. 2. Industrial Workers of the World - History - 20th century. 3. Intellectuals - New York (N.Y.) - History - 20th century. 4. Socialism - United States - History - 20th century. I. Title.
HD5325.T42 1913 .P383 1988

Golkin, Arline T. (Arline Tartus) Famine, a heritage of hunger : a guide to issues and references / Arline T. Golkin. Claremont, Calif. : Regina Books, c1987. xvi, 168 p. : ill. ; 23 cm. (Guides to contemporary issues . 6) Includes index. Bibliography: p. [117]-161. ISBN 0-941690-21-0 : LC Card 86-26138 DDC 363.8 19
1. Famines. I. Title. II. Series.
HC79.F3 B63 1986 NYPL [JLD 87-878]

Gollop, Frank M. Jorgenson, Dale Weldeau, 1933- Productivity and U. S. economic growth /. Cambridge, Mass. , 1987. 567 p. : ISBN 0-674-71175-0 (alk. paper) LC Card 87-12098 DDC 338/.06/0973 19
HC110.I52 J67 1987

Gollub, James O. Business opportunities among the aging population : unexpected diversity in a growing market / James O. Gollub. Menlo Park, Calif. (333 Ravenswood Ave., Menlo Park 94025-3476) : SRI International, Business Intelligence Pregram, c1984. 36 p. : ill. (some col.) ; 28 cm. (Report / SRI International, Business Intelligence Program . no. 706 (summer 1984)) Cover title. LC Card 86-210219 DDC 658.8/348 19
1. Aged as consumers - United States. I. Series: Research report (Business Intelligence Program (SRI International)) , 706. II. Title.
HC110.C6 G62 1984

Golombek, Rolf, 1959- Natural gas markets and contracts /. Amsterdam ; New York : x, 320 p. : ISBN 0-444-70206-7 (U. S.) LC Card 87-5061 DDC 380.1/42285/094 19
HD9581.E82 N37 1987 NYPL [TB (Contributions to economic analysis. v.161)]

Golosov, V. V. Kritika antimarksistskikh ėkonomicheskikh teoriĭ v prepodavanii politicheskoĭ ėkonomii /. Moskva , 1981. 356 p. ; LC Card 82-107917
HB178 .K7 1981

Golovanov, A. N.
Agropromyshlennyĭ kompleks i problemy obespecheniia naseleniia prodovol´stviem . Kiev , 1983. 190 p. : LC Card 86-139699
HD9015.S653 U4295 1983

Material´no-tekhnichna baza ahropromyslovoho kompleksu . Kyïv , 1985. 294 p. ; LC Card 87-109155
HD9015.S653 U453 1985

Golovko, N. A. (Nikolaĭ Anatol´evich) Osnovnye neproizvodstvennye fondy kolkhozov /cN.A. Golovko ; nauchnyĭ redaktor F.S. Martinkevich. Minsk : "Nauka i tekhnika", 1984. 94, [2] p. ; 20 cm. At head of title: Akademiia nauk Belorusskoĭ SSR. Institut ėkonomiki. Bibliography: p. 92-[95] LC Card 84-177536
1. Collective farms - Byelorussian S.S.R. - Finance. 2. Collective farms - Byelorussian S.S.R. - Capital investments. I. Martinkevich, F. S. (Feliks Stanislavovich). II. Title.
HD1492.S652 B9237 1984

Gol´shteĭn, E. G. (Evgeniĭ Grigor´evich)
Sheviakov, Alekseĭ IUr´evich. Modelirovanie sbalansirovannosti i soglasovaniia planovykh resheniĭ v sfere narodnogo blagosostoianiia /. Moskva , 1986. 211 p. : LC Card 86-177908
HC336.25 .S525 1986

Golubev, V. A. (Vladimir Alekseevich)
Vneshneėkonomicheskie sviazi stran-chlenov SĖV v usloviiakh sotsialisticheskoĭ integratsii /. Kiev , 1983. 245 p. ; LC Card 83-189711
HC243.5 .V54 1983

Gomes, Leonard. Foreign trade and the national economy : mercantilist and classical perspectives / Leonard Gomes. New York : St. Martin's Press, 1987. viii, 323 p. ; 23 cm. Bibliography: p. 278-313. Includes index. ISBN 0-312-00765-5 : LC Card 87-4674 DDC 382 19
1. Commerce. 2. Mercantile system. 3. Classical school of economics. I. Title.
HF1008 .G65 1987

Gomes, Maria Lucília Traça. Ribeiro, Maria Eduarda. Aspectos analíticos da distribuição da massa salarial no período de 1972 a 1983 /. Lisboa , 1985. 58 p. : LC Card 86-132683
HC394.5.I5 R52 1985

Gomes, Sebastião Teixeira. Condicionantes da modernização do pequeno agricultor / autor, Sebastião Teixeira Gomes ; orientador, Fernando Bento Homem de Melo. São Paulo : Instituto de Pesquisas Econômicas, 1986. 181 p. : ill. ; 23 cm. (Série Ensaios econômicos . no. 60) At head of title: Universidade de São Pãulo, Faculdade de Economia e Administração, Departamento de Economia. Summary also in English. Thesis (doutor em economia)--Universidade de São Paulo, 1986. Bibliography: p. 171-181. LC Card 87-153609 DDC 338.1/0981/51 19
1. Agriculture - Economic aspects - Brazil - Minas Gerais - Case studies. 2. Agricultural credit - Brazil - Minas Gerais - Case studies. 3. Agricultural innovations - Brazil - Minas Gerais - Case studies. 4. Farms, Small - Brazil - Minas Gerais - Case studies. I. Series: Ensaios econômicos (Universidade de São Paulo. Instituto de Pesquisas Econômicas) , 60. II. Title.
HD1875.M5 G65 1986

Gomes, Zizeuda Souza. Paiva, Francisco Ismar Martins. Projeto Pesca Industrial à Vela. [Natal, Brazil] [1982 or 1983] 91 p. : LC Card 85-102872
HD9464.B73 R487 1982

Gómez Buendía, Hernando. Sindicalismo y política económica / Hernando Gómez Buendía, Rocío Londoño Botero, Guillermo Perry Rubio. 1a ed. Bogotá, Colombia : FEDESARROLLO : Fondo Editorial CEREC, 1986. 324 p. : ill. ; 21 cm. Includes bibliographical references. ISBN 958-9061-16-8 LC Card 87-401441 DDC 331.88/09861 19
1. Trade-unions - Colombia. 2. Colombia - Economic policy. 3. Trade-unions. 4. Economic policy. I. Londoño Botero, Rocío. II. Perry, Guillermo. III. Title.
HD6622 .G64 1986

Gómez, Carmen.
Población y energía en la República Dominicana, 1990-2000. Santo Domingo, República Dominicana : Instituto de Estudios de Población y Desarrollo, [1985] vi, 86 p. : ill. (some col.) : 27 cm. (Estudio. no. 4) "Este estudio fue realizado en colaboración con la Comisión Nacional de Política Energética (COENER). El equipo de investigadores lo integraron Carmen Gómez, Antonio Tatis (IEPD) y Elba Musalén (COENER)" Errata slip tipped in. Bibliography: p. 85-86. LC Card 86-176044
1. Energy consumption - Dominican Republic. 2. Energy policy - Dominican Republic. I. Tatis, Antonio. II. Musalén, Elba. III. Instituto de Estudios de Población y Desarrollo (ADPBF). IV. Dominican Republic. Comisión Nacional de Política Energética. V. Series: Estudio (Instituto de Estudios de Población y Desarrollo (ADPBF)) , no. 4. VI. Title.
HD9502.D652 G65 1985

Población y vivienda en la República Dominicana : diagnóstico del sector vivienda y proyección de oferta vs. necesidades en esta área, 1985-2000 / Carmen Gómez, Antonio Tatis, Nelson Ramírez. Santo Domingo, República Dominicana : Instituto de Estudios de Población y Desarrollo, 1984. 116 p. : ill. ; 27 cm. (Estudio. no. 3) "Auspicado por PROFAMILIA." Bibliography: p. 73-74. LC Card 85-154466
1. Housing - Dominican Republic - Statistics. 2. Housing forecasting - Dominican Republic - Statistics. 3. Labor and laboring classes - Dwellings - Dominican Republic - Statistics. I. Tatis, Antonio. II. Ramírez, Nelson. III. Series: Estudio (Instituto de Estudios de Población y Desarrollo (ADPBF (Organization)) , no. 3. IV. Title.
HD7316.5.A3 G65 1984
NYPL [JLF 86-1146]

Gómez de Reyes, María Teresa. Experiencias de políticas de estabilización : los casos de Argentina, Chile, México y Uruguay / María Teresa Gómez de Reyes. México, D.F. : Centro de Estudios Monetarios Latinoamericanos, Departamento de Investigaciones, 1985. iv, 66 leaves ; 28 cm. (Serie Cuadernos de investigación . núm. 3) Bibliography: leaves 65-66. LC Card 87-122042 DDC 338.982 19
1. Argentina - Economic policy. 2. Chile - Economic policy. 3. Mexico - Economic policy - 1971-. 4. Uruguay - Economic policy. 5. Economic stabilization - Latin America - Case studies. I. Series: Serie Cuadernos de investigación (Centro de Estudios Monetarios Latinamericanos. Departamento de Investigaciones) , núm. 3. II. Title.
HC125 .G57 1985

Gómez Díaz, José Emilio. Argos Villar, José Carlos. El movimiento obrero en Cantabria (1955-1977) /. [Santander?] [1982?] 227 p. ; ISBN 84-300-6979-8 LC Card 86-203186
HD8589.C3 A74 1982

GÓMEZ FARÍAS (MICHOACÁN DE OCAMPO, MEXICO) - ECONOMIC CONDITIONS.
López Castro, Gustavo. La casa dividida . Zamora, Mich. [i.e. Michoacán] [S.l.] , 1986. 169 p. : ISBN 968-7230-19-3 LC Card 87-400954 DDC 304.8/73/07237 19
HB3532.G66 L66 1986

GÓMEZ FARÍAS (MICHOACÁN DE OCAMPO, MEXICO) - POPULATION.
López Castro, Gustavo. La casa dividida . Zamora, Mich. [i.e. Michoacán] [S.l.] , 1986. 169 p. : ISBN 968-7230-19-3 LC Card 87-400954 DDC 304.8/73/07237 19
HB3532.G66 L66 1986

GÓMEZ FARÍAS (MICHOACÁN DE OCAMPO, MEXICO) - SOCIAL CONDITIONS.
López Castro, Gustavo. La casa dividida . Zamora, Mich. [i.e. Michoacán] [S.l.] , 1986. 169 p. : ISBN 968-7230-19-3 LC Card 87-400954

DDC 304.8/73/07237 19
HB3532.G66 L66 1986

Gómez Fuentes, Angel, 1950- Así cambiará España : la batalla del Mercado Común / Angel Gómez Fuentes.1a ed. Esplugues de Llobregat, Barcelona : Plaza & Janés, 1986. 333 p. ; 22 cm. (Política española) Epoca Bibliography: p. [332]-333. ISBN 84-01-33317-2 LC Card 87-100798
1. European Economic Community - Spain. 2. Spain - Economic conditions - 1975-. I. Title. II. Series.
HC241.25.S6 G65 1986

Gómez, Hernando [i.e. Hernando Gómez Buendía] see **Gómez Buendía, Hernando.**

Gómez, Jorge Díaz. see **Díaz Gómez, Jorge.**

Gomez-Mejia, Luis R. New perspectives on compensation /. Englewood Cliffs, N.J. , c1987. xviii, 363 p. : ISBN 0-13-615212-0 (pbk.) LC Card 86-25534 DDC 658.3/2 19
HF5549.5.C67 N49 1987

Gómez Mendoza, Antonio. Ferrocarril y mercado interior en España, 1874-1913 / Antonio Gómez Mendoza. Madrid : Banco de España, Servicio de Estudios, 1984- v. : ill. ; 24 cm. (Estudios de historia económica . no. 10-) Includes bibliographical references. CONTENTS. - v. 1. Cereales, harinas y vinos. ISBN 84-500-9728-2 (v. 1) LC Card 85-215275 DDC 385/.24/0946 19
1. Railroads - Spain - Freight - History. 2. Railroads - Spain - Traffic - History. 3. Spain - Commerce - History. I. Series. II. Series: Estudios de historia económica , no. 10, etc. III. Title.
HE2469 .G66 1984 ***NYPL [JLL 86-176]***

Gómez Oliver, Miguel. La desamortización de Mendizábal en Granada / Miguel Gómez Oliver. Granada : Excma. Diputación Provincial, Instituto de Promoción y Desarrollo, [1983] 226 p. : ill. ; 24 cm. Bibliography: p. 221-226. LC Card 85-135214
1. Church lands - Spain - Granada (Province) - History - 19th century. 2. Secularization - Spain - Granada (Province) - History - 19th century. 3. Land reform - Spain - Granada (Province) - History - 19th century. 4. Granada (Spain : Province) - History. I. Title.
HD479.G73 G65 1983

Gómez Pérez, José Antonio, 1950- Desarrollo, crisis, deuda y política económica en Panamá : aporte al debate nacional / Gómez Pérez, José Antonio [y] Hughes Ortega, William. Panamá : Universidad de Panamá, 1985. vii, 168 p. : ill. ; 21 cm. Bibliogrpahy: p. 165-168. LC Card 86-122320 DDC 338.97287 19
1. Debts, External - Panama. 2. Debts, External - Latin America. 3. Panama - Economic conditions - 1979-. 4. Panama - Economic policy. 5. Latin America - Economic conditions - 1945-. 6. Latin America - Economic policy. I. Hughes Ortega, William, 1953-. II. Title.
HC147 .G66 1985 ***NYPL [JLD 86-2899]***

Gómez-Samper, Henry. Los módulos de servicios : mecanismo administrativo para llevar los servicios públicos a los barrios / por Henry Gómez-Samper y Richard A. Myers, con la colaboración de Nelson Morales. Caracas : Ediciones IESA, c1984. 48, 3 [i.e. 4] leaves ; 29 cm. (Papeles de trabajo IESA . PTI-84-5) Includes bibliographical references. ISBN 980-217-005-4 LC Card 86-193565
1. Municipal services - Venezuela - Caracas - Case studies. I. Myers, Richard A. II. Morales, Nelson. III. Title. IV. Series.
HD4343 .G65 1984

Gómez Serrano, Jesús.
El mayorazgo Rincón Gallardo : disolución del vínculo y reparto de las haciendas / Jesús Gómez Serrano.1a ed. [Aguascalientes] : Centro de Investigaciónes Regionales de Aguascalientes, [1984] 156 p., [24] p. of plates : ill. ; 22 cm. (Paralelo . 2) Bibliography: p. [151]-152. LC Card 84-175622
1. Rincón Gallardo, José María, marqués de Guadalupe, b. 1802. 2. Latifundio - Mexico - Zacatecas (State) - Case studies. 3. Latifundio - Mexico - Jalisco - Case studies. I. Title. II. Series.
HD329.Z3 G65 1984 ***NYPL [JLD 87-138]***

Hacendados y campesinos en Aguascalientes / Jesús Gómez Serrano ; fotografías, Ernesto García Campos ; dibujos, Carolina Lomeli Beherendt. 1a ed. [Aguascalientes] : Centro de Investigaciones Regionales de Aguascalientes, 1985. 221 p., [20] p. of plates : ill. ; 21 cm. (Paralelo . 5) Bibliography: p. [213]-221. LC Card 86-217321
1. Haciendas - Mexico - Aguascalientes (State) - History - Case studies. 2. Peasantry - Mexico - Aguascalientes (State) - History - Case studies. 3. Agricultural laborers - Mexico - Aguascalientes (State) - History - Case studies. 4. Agriculture and state - Mexico - Aguascalientes (State) - History. I. Title. II. Series.
HD1471.M62 A384 1985

Gómez U., Carmen Lila. Las Instituciones costarricenses del siglo XX /. [San José] , 1986. 376 p. ; ISBN 997-7232-96-5 LC Card 86-231789
HC143 .I54 1986

Gömmel, Rainer. Vorindustrielle Bauwirtschaft in der Reichsstadt Nürnberg und ihrem Umland (16.-18. Jh.) / von Rainer Gömmel. [Stuttgart] : In Kommission bei F. Steiner Verlag Wiesbaden, 1985. xii, 300 p. : ill. ; 23 cm. (Beiträge zur Wirtschafts- und Sozialgeschichte, 0723-5453 . Bd. 30) The author's Habilitationsschrift--Universität Regensburg, 1984, presented under the title: Vorindustrielle Bauwirtschaft vom 16. bis zum 18. Jahrhundert in der Reichsstadt Nürnberg und ihrem Umland. Bibliography: p. 280-295. Includes index. ISBN 3-515-04481-7 LC Card 86-122013
1. Construction industry - Germany - Nuremberg - History. 2. Building trades - Germany - Nuremberg - History. 3. Construction workers - Germany - Nuremberg - History. I. Title.
HD9715.G33 N874 1985

Gömörszőlős . Dobosy, László. Miskolc , 1984. 82 p., [16] p. of plates : ISBN 963-01-5552-4 LC Card 87-408021
HC300.292.G65 D63 1984

GÖMÖRSZŐLŐS (HUNGARY) - ECONOMIC CONDITIONS.
Dobosy, László. Gömörszőlős . Miskolc , 1984. 82 p., [16] p. of plates : ISBN 963-01-5552-4 LC Card 87-408021
HC300.292.G65 D63 1984

GÖMÖRSZŐLŐS(HUNGARY) - HISTORY.
Dobosy, László. Gömörszőlős . Miskolc , 1984. 82 p., [16] p. of plates : ISBN 963-01-5552-4 LC Card 87-408021
HC300.292.G65 D63 1984

Gompers, Samuel, 1850-1924.
The Samuel Gompers papers /. Urbana , c1986- v. : ISBN 0-252-01138-4 (alk. paper : set) LC Card 84-2469 DDC 331.88/32/0924 19
HD6508 .S218 1986 ***NYPL [JLL 86-230]***

GOMPERS, SAMUEL, 1850-1924 - ARCHIVES.
The Samuel Gompers papers /. Urbana , c1986- v. : ISBN 0-252-01138-4 (alk. paper : set) LC Card 84-2469 DDC 331.88/32/0924 19
HD6508 .S218 1986 ***NYPL [JLL 86-230]***

Gonçalves, Sérgio Ricardo Vieira, 1940-
Rondônia--política, agrária e transformação : subsídios para uma nova visão desenvolvimentista / Sérgio Ricardo Vieira Gonçalves. Porto Velho : UBE-RO, 1982. 40 p. : port. ; 21 cm. (Caderno de cultura . 2 (ano 1, 1982)) LC Card 87-401465 DDC 338.981/75 19
1. Rondônia (Brazil : State) - Economic policy. 2. Agriculture and state - Brazil - Rondônia (State). I. Series: Caderno de cultura (Porto Velho, Rondônia, Brazil) , 2. II. Title.
HC188.R6 G66 1982

Goncharov, Leongard Vasil'evich.
Afrika v tsifrakh . Moskva , 1986. 421 p. ; LC Card 87-143124
HA4675 .A37 1986

Agrarnye preobrazovaniia v stranakh Afriki na sovremennom ėtape /. Moskva , 1982. 227 p. ; LC Card 83-143645
HD2117 .A347 1982

Goncharova, N. P. Printsipy ėkonomicheskogo upravleniia nauchno-tekhnicheskim progressom . Kiev , 1982. 122 p. ; LC Card 83-143870
HC340.T4 P67 1982

Gondra y Oraá, María Victoria de, 1929- El Bilbao de Julio Lazúrtegui : la acertada visión del futuro industrial y mercantil del País Vasco adelantada por un bilbaino del XIX / María Victoria de Gondra y Oraá ; presentación de Antón de Madariaga ; prólogo de José María de Areilza. Bilbao : Cámara Oficial de Comercio, Industria y Navegación de Bilbao, 1984. 472 p. : ill. ; 21 cm. Bibliography: p. 406-417. ISBN 84-505-0689-1 LC Card 87-125134
1. Lazúrtegui, Julio. 2. Industrialists - Spain - Bilbao - Biography. I. Title.
HC382.5.L39 G66 1984

Gonella, Guido, 1905- Contestazioni / Guido Gonella ; premessa di Gianni Letta ; a cura di Paola Gonella. 1a ed. Roma : Logos, 1983. 3 v. ; 23 cm. (Incidenza . 4-6) CONTENTS. - v. 1. Stato e democrazia -- v. 2. Politica interna ed estera -- v. 3. Diritto, morale, religione. LC Card 84-237282 DDC 945.092 19
1. Catholic Church - Addresses, essays, lectures. 2. World politics - 1945- - Addresses, essays, lectures. 3. Political science - Addresses, essays, lectures. 4. Social problems - Addresses, essays, lectures. 5. Italy - Politics and government - 1945- - Addresses, essays, lectures. 6. Italy - Foreign relations - 1976- - Addresses, essays, lectures. 7. Italy - Social conditions - 1976- - Addresses, essays, lectures. I. Gonella, Paola. II. Title.
JN5451 .G57 1983 ***NYPL [JFE 86-1367]***

Gonella, Paola. Gonella, Guido, 1905- Contestazioni /. Roma , 1983. 3 v. ; LC Card 84-237282 DDC 945.092 19
JN5451 .G57 1983 ***NYPL [JFE 86-1367]***

Gonick, Cy. The great economic debate : failed economics and a future for Canada / Cy Gonick. Toronto : J. Lorimer, 1987. xii, 425 p. : ill. ; 24 cm. Bibliography: p. [389]-409. Includes index. ISBN 0-88862-702-5 LC Card 87-144697 DDC 338.971 19
1. Canada - Economic conditions - 1945-. 2. Canada - Economic policy. I. Title.
HC115 .G576 1987

Gontard, Jean-Pierre. Sall, Alioune. Ressources humaines pour le développement . [Dakar, Sénégal , 1984] 51 p. : LC Card 85-129264 DDC 338.91/09624 19
HC1002 .S25 1984

Gonzales Torres, Rodrigo. Los paros nacionales en Chile, 1919-1973 / Rodrigo Gonzales Torres, Alonso Daire Tolmo. Santiago [Chile] : Centro de Asesoría Profesional, Area Comunicaciones, 1984. 234 p. ; 28 cm. (Documento / Centro de Asesoría Profesional, Area Comunicaciones . no. 1) Bibliography: p. [233]-234. LC Card 86-200794
1. Strikes and lockouts - Chile - History - 20th century. I. Daire Tolmo, Alonso. II. Series: Documento (Centro de Asesoría Profesional (Santiago, Chile). Area Comunicaciones) , no. 1. III. Title.
HD5356.A6 G66 1984

González-Aramayo Z., Vicente (González-Aramayo Zuleta) Breve historia de la industria orureña / Vicente González-Aramayo. Oruro, Bolivia : Cordeor, [1983] 199 p. ; 17 cm. Bibliography: p. 197-199. LC Card 85-144157
1. Oruro (Bolivia) - Industries - History. I. Title.
HC183.O7 G66 1983

González-Aréchiga, Bernardo. Vinculación fronteriza a Estados Unidos y su cambio con la crisis / Bernardo González-Aréchiga. 1a ed. Tijuana, Baja California : Centro de Estudios Fronterizos del Norte de México, 1985. 54 p. ; 23 cm. (Cuadernos CEFNOMEX) "500 ejemplares"--Colophon. Includes bibliographical references. ISBN 968-607-500-3 LC Card 86-187758
1. Mexican-American Border Region - Commerce. 2. Mexico - Foreign economic relations - United States. 3. United States - Foreign economic relations - Mexico. I. Title. II. Series.
HF3239.M49 G66 1985

González Blanch, Francisco. Implantación en España de un sistema de tarificación por el uso de la infraestructura viaria / Francisco González Blanch, Carlos Gasca Allué, Carlos Ibarz del Olmo ; presentación por Enrique Balaguer Camphuis. Madrid : Ministerio de Economía y Hacienda, Instituto de Estudios Fiscales, [1984?] 204 p. ; 29 cm. (Monografia. no. 30) Bibliography: p. 201-204. ISBN 84-7196-470-8 : LC Card 85-201965
1. Transportation, Automotive - Taxation - European Economic Community countries. 2. Transportation, Automotive - Taxation - Spain. I. Gasca Allué, Carlos. II. Ibarz del Olmo, Carlos. III. Series: Monografías (Instituto de Estudios Fiscales (Spain)) , no. 30. IV. Title.
HJ5956.E86 G66 1984

González Corugedo, Rosa. Argüelles, Alfonso. Los Oscos y la Cuenca del Eo . [Asturias] [1984?] ix, 317 p. : ISBN 84-505-0237-3 LC Card 86-174593
HC387.A7 A74 1984

González de Piñango, Norma. Estadísticas sociales . Caracas, Venezuela , 1983. 2 v. ; LC Card 84-183391 DDC 312/.0987 19
HA1095 .E88 1983 *NYPL [JLM 85-550]*

González do Molina Navarro, Manuel. Desamortización, deuda pública y crecimiento económico, Andalucía, 1820/1823 / Manuel González de Molina Navarro. Granada : Diputación Provincial de Granada ; Córdoba :bFundación Paco Natera, [1985?] 443 p. : ill. ; 20 cm. (Biblioteca de ensayo . 6) Bibliography: p. [419]-443. ISBN 84-505-1053-8 LC Card 86-210676
1. Church Lands - Spain - Andalusia - History - 19th century. 2. Land tenure - Spain - Andalusia - History - 19th century. 3. Secularization - Spain - Andalusia - History - 19th century. 4. Andalusia (Spain) - Economic conditions. 5. Debts, Public - Spain - Andalusia - History - 19th century. I. Title. II. Series.
HD779.A4 G66 1985

González G., Godofredo (González González) La revolución de Los Barrosos / Godofredo González. Caracas, Venezuela : Ediciones Centauro, [19]87. xii, 276 p. ; 22 cm. ISBN 980-263-047-0 LC Card 87-400058 DDC 338.2/7282/0987 19
1. Petroleum industry and trade - Venezuela - History - 20th century. 2. Investments, Foreign - Venezuela - History - 20th century. 3. Venezuela - Dependency on foreign countries - History - 20th century. I. Title.
HD9574.V42 G59 1987

Gonzalez, Jean, 1945-
Bergerud, Marly, 1942- Introduction to office systems . New York , c1987. xvi, 440 p., [12] p. of plates : ISBN 0-471-85532-4 (pbk.) LC Card 86-28188 DDC 652/.5 19
HF5548.115 .B462 1987

Bergerud, Marly, 1942- Word and information processing . New York , c1987. xvi, 578 p. : ISBN 0-471-84504-3 LC Card 86-24748 DDC 652/.5 19
HF5548.115 .B46 1987

Bergerud, Marly, 1942- Word processing . New York , c1988. xiv, 336 p., [12] p. of plates : ISBN 0-471-84503-5 (pbk.) LC Card 87-8181 DDC 652/.5/02373 19
HF5548.115 .B47 1988

Schick, P. Charlene, 1943- Accounting fundamentals /. Englewood Cliffs, N.J. , c1987. xviii, 509 p. : ISBN 0-13-001918-6 LC Card 86-23732 DDC 657 19
HF5635 .S3124 1987

González, José I. (José Iván), 1944- La segmentación del mercado del crédito y sus impactos sobre la distribución del ingreso / José I. González. Montevideo, Uruguay : Centro Interdisciplinario de Estudios sobre el Desarrollo, Uruguay, 1984. ii, 5, 123 p. : ill. ; 28 cm. (Serie Investigaciones. no. 18) Bibliography: p. 89-92 [i.e. 91]. LC Card 85-236586
1. Credit - Uruguay. 2. Income distribution - Uruguay. I. Series: Serie Investigaciones (Montevideo, Uruguay) , no. 18. II. Title.
HG3754.5.U8 G66 1984

González M., Sergio (González Miranda) ZOFRI, un enclave comercial / Sergio González M. Iquique, Chile : Centro de Investigación de la Realidad del Norte, [1985] 38, [2] p. ; 27 cm. (Cuadernos de investigación social. v. 1, no. 14) Cover title. Bibliography: p. [39]-[40] LC Card 86-167491
1. Free ports and zones - Chile - Iquique. I. Series: Cuadernos de investigación social (Iquique, Chile) , vol. 1, no. 14. II. Title.
HF1418 .G66 1985

González O., Alfonso. Sandoval Aguilar, Guillermo. El desarrollo costarricense y la fecundidad del hombre /. Heredia , 1985. 233 p. ; LC Card 86-117576
HB947 .S26 1985

González Podestá, Aquilino. Los tranvías de Buenos Aires / Aquilino González Podestá. Buenos Aires, República Argentina : Asociación Amigos del Tranvía, c1986. 95 p. : ill. (some col.) ; 17 cm. Bibliography: p. 93. ISBN 950-796-900-2 LC Card 87-400950 DDC 388.4/6/098211 19
1. Street-railroads - Argentina - Buenos Aires - History. I. Title.
HE4609.B82 G66 1986

González Rodríguez, Juan Jesús. La patronal agraria : estrategias de política agraria y de negociación colectiva / Juan Jesús González Rodríguez. Madrid : Fundación Juan March, [1986?] 46 p. ; 21 cm. (Serie universitaria (Fundación Juan March) . 232) "Edición no venal de 300 ejemplares." Includes bibliographical references. ISBN 84-7075-335-3 LC Card 87-111477
1. Collective bargaining - Agriculture - Spain. 2. Agriculture and state - Spain. 3. Agricultural wages - Spain. 4. Agricultural prices - Spain. I. Series. II. Series: Serie universitaria (Fundación Juan March) , 232. III. Title.
HD6976.A292 S74 1986

González, Rosa. [i. e., Rosa González Corugedo] see **González Corugedo, Rosa.**

González S., Pablo. Coloma C., Fernando. Credibilidad de la política comercial /. Santiago, Chile , 1986. 43 p. : LC Card 87-102077
HF1515 .C64 1986

González S., Víctor A. Las tierras comunales en el Ecuador / Víctor A. González S. Guayaquil, Ecuador : Casa de la Cultura Ecuatoriana, Núcleo del Guayas, 1982. 109 p. ; 17 cm. Bibliography: p. 107-109. LC Card 87-672596
1. Commons - Ecuador - History. 2. Collective settlements - Ecuador - History. 3. Ecuador - Economic conditions. 4. Village communities - Ecuador. I. Title.
HD1289.E2 G66x 1982

González Vega, Claudio.
Economic reform and stabilization in Latin America /. New York , c1986. xxiii, 348 p. : ISBN 0-275-92307-X (alk. paper) : LC Card 86-9405 DDC 338.98 19
HC125 .E374 1986 *NYPL [JLE 87-1073]*

Mercados financieros rurales en América Latina / Claudio González Vega. 1a ed. Santo Domingo, República Dominicana : Centro de Estudios Monetarios y Bancarios, 1986. 44 p. ; 21 cm. (Biblioteca Mercados financieros . 3) Serie Estudios A paper originally presented at the Tercer Taller del Proyecto Movilización de Ahorros Rurales en la República Dominicana, held in Puerto Plata, Sept. 19-21, 1985 under title: Hacia el fortalecimiento de los sistemas financieros rurales en América Latina y el Caribe. Includes bibliographical references. LC Card 87-400002 DDC 332.7/1/098 19
1. Agricultural credit - Latin America. 2. Agricultural cooperative credit associations - Latin America. 3. Agricultural credit corporations - Latin America. I. Series. II. Series: Serie Estudios (Centro de Estudios Monetarios y Bancarios (Santo Domingo, Dominican Republic)). III. Title.
HG2051.L26 G66 1986

Mercados financieros y desarrollo / Claudio González Vega. 1a ed. Santo Domingo, República Dominicana : Centro de Estudios Monetarios y Bancarios, 1986. 73 p. : ill. ; 21 cm. (Biblioteca Mercados financieros . 1) Serie Estudios Includes bibliographical references. CONTENTS. - Mercados financieros y desarrollo -- Crisis económica y sistema financiero -- Reforma financiera. LC Card 87-102022
1. Banks and banking - Dominican Republic. 2. Financial institutions - Dominican Republic. 3. Finance - Dominican Republic. I. Series. II. Series: Serie Estudios (Centro de Estudios Monetarios y Bancarios (Santo Domingo, Dominican Republic)). III. Title.
HG2817 .G66 1986

Mercados financieros y distribución del ingreso /. Santo Domingo, República Dominicana , 1986. 117 p. : LC Card 87-405027 DDC 332.1/097293 19
HG185.D65 M47 1986

González, Víctor A. see **González S., Víctor A.**

Goobey, Alastair Ross. The money moguls : the inside story of investment management / Alastair Ross Goobey. Cambridge [Cambridgeshire] ; Wolfeboro, N.H. : Woodhead-Faulkner, 1987. viii, 19 p. : ill. ; 24 cm. Includes index. ISBN 0-85941-391-8 (U. S.) : LC Card 86-26669 DDC 332.6 19
1. Investments. I. Title.
HG4521 .G5558 1986 *NYPL [JLE 87-826]*

Good aid . Millwood, David. Stockholm, Sweden , c1985. 246 p. : ISBN 91-586-7059-9 (pbk.) : LC Card 87-142767 DDC 338.91/485 19
HC425.Z9 E446 1985

Good faith and credit /. Hammer, Gottlieb, 1911- New York , c1985. 258 p., [12] p. of plates : ISBN 0-8453-4798-5 (alk. paper) LC Card 85-13962 DDC 956.94/001/0973 19
DS151.H34 A34 1985
*NYPL [*PWZ (Hammer, G.) 86-2026]*

GOOD-WILL (IN BUSINESS, ETC.)
Simon, Hermann. Goodwill und Marketingstrategie /. Wiesbaden , c1985. 250 p. : ISBN 3-409-13603-7 LC Card 85-232089 DDC 658.8/02 19
HF5415 .S4958 1985

Goodall, H. Lloyd. Wilson, Gerald L., 1943- Organizational communication /. New York , c1986. xiv, 322 p. : ISBN 0-06-042387-0 LC Card 85-8723 DDC 658.4/5 19
HD58.7 .W55 1986 *NYPL [JLE 86-2600]*

Goodden, Susanna. A history of Heal's : at the sign of the fourposter / by Susanna Goodden ; foreword by Sir Hugh Casson.1st ed. [London] : Heal & Son ; Atlantic Highlands, N.J. : Distributed in the U. S.A. and Canada by Humanities Press, 1984. 137 p. : ill. (some col.) ; 21 cm. Distributor from label on t.p. ISBN 0-85331-488-8 (pbk.) LC Card 86-221633 DDC 381/.456841/00941 19
1. Heal & Son - History. 2. Furniture industry and trade - Great Britain - History. I. Title.
HD9773.G74 H434 1984

Gooden, James M. Fisher, Brian S. An economic and technical assessment of the establishment of an Australian fat-tail sheep industry /. [Sydney], N.S.W. , c1986. vi, 52 p. ; LC Card 87-154531 DDC 338.1/76386 19
HD9436.A82 F57 1986

Goodkin, Debbie. Curwin, Jon. Business studies in context . London , New York , 1987. p. cm. ISBN 0-07-707034-8 : LC Card 87-22560 DDC 658.4/0352 19
HD30.25 .C87 1987

Goodkin, Sanford R. Higher density housing . Washington, D.C. , c1986. 155 p. : ISBN 0-86718-271-7 (pbk.) LC Card 86-63356 DDC 690/.83 19
HD1390.5 .H545 1986

Goodman, David, 1938- From farming to biotechnology : a theory of agro-industrial development / David Goodman, Bernardo Sorj, and John Wilkinson. Oxford ; New York, N.Y. : Basil Blackwell, 1987. 214 p. : ill. ; 24 cm. Bibliography: p. [190]-202. Includes index. ISBN 0-631-14405-6 : LC Card 87-687 DDC 338.1/6 19
1. Agriculture - Economic aspects. 2. Agricultural innovations. 3. Food industry and trade - Technological innovations. 4. Biotechnology. 5. Genetic engineering. I. Sorj, Bernardo. II. Wilkinson, John, 1946-. III. Title.
HD1433 .G66 1987

Goodman, Gary S.
[Breakthroughs in telemarketing]
Gary Goodman's breakthroughs in telemarketing / Gary S. Goodman. 1st ed. New York : Prentice Hall, c1987. ix, 148 p. ; 22 cm. Includes index. ISBN 0-13-346891-7 (pbk.) : LC Card 86-43170 DDC 658.8/5 19
1. Telemarketing. I. Title. II. Title: Breakthroughs in telemarketing.
HF5415.1265 .G66 1987

Goodman, Hortense. Illustrations of "push down" accounting / by Hortense Goodman and Leonard Lorensen. New York, N.Y. (1211 Ave., of the Americas, New York 10036) : American Institute of Certified Public Accountants, c1985. 52 p. ; 28 cm. (Financial report survey. 31) LC Card 87-100703 DDC 657/.3 19
1. Financial statements, Consolidated. 2. Subsidiary corporations - Accounting. 3. Holding companies - Accounting. I. Lorensen, Leonard. II. Title. III. Title: "Push down" accounting.
HF5681.B2 G663 1985

Goodman, Jordan Elliot. Downes, John. Barron's finance and investment handbook /. Woodbury, N.Y. , c1986. xiv, 994 p. : ISBN 0-8120-5729-5 : LC Card 86-10906 DDC 332.6/78 19
HG173 .D65 1986
*NYPL [*R-Econ. 86-5261]*

Goodman, Louis J. Project planning and management : an integrated system for improving productivity / Louis J. Goodman. New York : Van Nostrand Reinhold, 1988. ix, 302 p. : ill. ; 24 cm. (Van Nostrand Reinhold

environmental engineering series) Bibliography: p. 297-298. Includes index. ISBN 0-442-22762-0 LC Card 87-6192 DDC 658.4/04 19
1. Industrial project management. I. Title.
HD69.P75 G65 1988

Goodman, Louis Wolf. Small nations, giant firms / Louis W. Goodman. New York : Holmes & Meier, c1987. xiii, 181 p. : ill. ; 24 cm. Bibliography: p. 167-174. Includes index. ISBN 0-8419-0996-2 LC Card 87-42 DDC 338.8/888 19
1. International business enterprises. 2. International business enterprises - Latin America. 3. States, Small. I. Title.
HD2755.5 .G66 1987

Goodman, Marshall R. Managing regulatory reform : the Reagan strategy and its impact / Marshall R. Goodman, Margaret T. Wrightson. New York : Praeger, 1987. xvi, 236 p. : ill. ; 25 cm. Bibliography: p. [213]-226. Includes index. ISBN 0-275-92472-5 (alk. paper) : LC Card 87-2436 DDC 338.973 19
1. Trade regulation - United States. 2. United States - Politics and government - 1981-. I. Wrightson, Margaret Tucker, 1950-. II. Title.
HD3616.U47 G67 1987

Goodolphim, Costa, 1842-1910. A associação : história e desenvolvimento das associações portuguesas / Costa Goodolphim ; prefácio e notas de César Oliveira. Lisboa, Portugal : Seara Nova, 1974. 206 p. ; 21 cm. (Biblioteca socialista portuguesa. 1) Includes bibliographical references. LC Card 87-401116 DDC 334/.09494 19
1. Cooperative societies - Portugal - History. 2. Trade-unions - Portugal - History. 3. Associations, institutions, etc. - Portugal - History. I. Oliveira, César. II. Title.
HD3529.A4 G66 1974

Goodpaster, Kenneth E., 1944- Ethics in management / Kenneth E. Goodpaster. Boston : Division of Research, Harvard Business School, c1984. 154 p. : ill. ; 28 cm. (Course module series) "Supplementary materials" ([20] p.) inserted. Includes bibliographical references. ISBN 0-87584-165-1 (course module : pbk.) LC Card 84-12847 DDC 174/.4 19
1. Business ethics - Case studies. I. Harvard University. Graduate School of Business Administration. Division of Research. II. Title. III. Series.
HF5387 .G66 1984

GOODS, PUBLIC. see **PUBLIC GOODS.**

Goodwill und Marketingstrategie /. Simon, Hermann. Wiesbaden , c1985. 250 p. : ISBN 3-409-13603-7 LC Card 85-232089 DDC 658.8/02 19
HF5415 .S4958 1985

Goodwin, Randall B. The Future of private enterprise /. Atlanta, Ga. , 1984-1986. 3 v. ; ISBN 0-88406-164-7 (pbk. : v. 1) LC Card 83-25386 DDC 338.6/1 19
HB501 .F83 1984 ***NYPL [JLK 87-49]***

Goodwin, Richard M. (Richard Murphey), 1913- The dynamics of a capitalist economy / by Richard M. Goodwin and Lionello F. Punzo. Boulder : Westview Press, 1987. p. cm. ISBN 0-8133-0482-2 : LC Card 86-33965 DDC 330.12/2 19
1. Capitalism - Mathematical models. I. Punzo, Lionello F. II. Title.
HB501 .G622 1987

Goodworth, Clive T. Effective delegation / Clive T. Goodworth. London : Business Books ; Brookfield, Vt., USA : Brookfield Pub. Co., 1985. 148 p. : ill. ; 22 cm. (Better business guides) Bibliography: p. 145. Includes index. ISBN 0-09-161781-2 (pbk.) : LC Card 86-204300 DDC 658.4/02 19
1. Delegation of authority. I. Title. II. Series.
HD50 .G66 1985

Googie . Hess, Alan. San Francisco, CA [1986]. 144 p. : ISBN 0-87701-334-9 (pbk.) : LC Card 85-17089 DDC 725/.71/0973 19
NA7856 .H47 1986
NYPL [3-MQWO 86-2210]

Googins, Bradley, 1944-
Occupational social work : an annotated bibliography / prepared by Bradley Googins. Silver Spring, MD : National Association of Social Workers, Commission on Employment and Economic Support, 1987. p. cm. ISBN 0-87101-151-4 LC Card 87-20414 DDC 362.8/5 19
1. Welfare work in industry. 2. Welfare work in industry - United States. 3. Employee assistance programs. 4. Employee assistance programs - United States. I. Title.
HD7261 .G66 1987b

Occupational social work / Bradley Googins, Joline Godfrey. Englewood Cliffs, N.J. : Prentice-Hall, c1987. xii, 227 p. : ill. ; 24 cm. Bibliography: p. 211-215. Includes index. ISBN 0-13-629445-6 : LC Card 86-25514 DDC 658.3/82 19
1. Welfare work in industry. 2. Welfare work in industry - United States. 3. Employee assistance programs. 4. Employee assistance programs - United States. I. Godfrey, Joline. II. Title.
HD7261 .G66 1987

Goold, Michael. Strategies and styles : the role of the centre in managing diversified corporations / Michael Goold and Andrew Campbell. Oxford, UK ; New York, NY, USA : B. Blackwell, 1988, c1987. p. cm. Includes index. ISBN 0-631-15829-4 : LC Card 87-12151 DDC 658/.046 19
1. Conglomerate corporations. 2. Diversification in industry. I. Campbell, Andrew. II. Title.
HD2756 .G66 1988

Goonatilake, Susantha. In retrospect . Colombo , 1986. 149 p. ; LC Card 86-903248 DDC 334/.2/095493
HG2039.S65 I5 1986

Goosmann, Cornelia. Ein Jahrhundert Wasserglas von Henkel / Cornelia Goosmann. Düsseldorf : Henkel, c1985. 76 p. : ill. (some col.) ; 21 cm. (Schriften des Werkarchivs der Henkel KGaA Düsseldorf, 0724-2557 . 17) Bibliography: p. 75. ISBN 3-923324-67-8 LC Card 86-171258
1. Henkel KGaA - History. 2. Chemical industry - Germany (West) - History. 3. Silicate industry - Germany (West) - History. I. Title. II. Series.
HD9654.9.H444 G66 1985

Gopal, Krishna, 1937- Rationalism, humanism, and democracy . Meerut , 1985. xcii, 514 p., [2] p. of plates : LC Card 85-901252 DDC 144 19
B833 .R29 1985 ***NYPL [JFD 86-3589]***

Gopalakrishnan, N. K. National energy data systems . New Delhi , 1984, c1983. xxvi, 511 p. ; LC Card 84-901310 DDC 333.79/09172/4 19
HD9502.D442 N37 1984
NYPL [JLD 86-4320]

Goppel, Alfons, 1905- Votum für die Marktwirtschaft . Bonn , c1976. 26 p. ; LC Card 85-172115
HC286.7 .V69 1976

Gorazd, Antoni.
Przed kolejną reformą. 1981. Samecki, Wiesław. Czego można oczekiwać od ekonomii / Wiesław Samecki. Systemy ekonomiczne, gospodarka rynkowa, gospodarka planowa / Wiesław Samecki. Przed kolejną reformą / Antoni Gorazd. Wyd. 1. Warszawa , 1981. 35 p. ; ISBN 83-202-0150-0 LC Card 86-150577
HC340.3 .S24 1981

Gorbachev, Mikhail Sergeevich, 1931-
Aktivno deĭstvovat′, ne teri͡at′ vremeni : vystuplenie na vstreche s kollektivom Dnepropetrovskogo metallurgicheskogo zavoda i rech′ na sobranii aktiva respublikanskoĭ partiĭnoĭ organizatsii Ukrainy, 26, 27 i͡uni͡a 1985 goda. Moskva : Izd-vo polit. lit-ry, 1985. 45 p. ; 20 cm. LC Card 86-181428
1. Industrial productivity - Ukraine. 2. Ukraine - Economic conditions - 1945-. I. Title.
HC337.U53 I525 1985

[Perestroĭka--krovnoe delo naroda. English] Restructuring, a vital concern of the people : speech at the 18th Congress of the Trade Unions of the USSR, February 25, 1987 / Mikhail Gorbachev. Moscow : Novosti Press Agency Pub. House, 1987. 28 p. ; 20 cm. Translation of: Perestroĭka--krovnoe delo naroda. LC Card 87-165567 DDC 338.947 19
1. Soviet Union - Economic policy - 1986-. I. Title.
HC336.26 .G6713 1987

Gorbachev's challenge . Goldman, Marshall I. New York , c1987. xvii, 296 p. : ISBN 0-393-02454-7 LC Card 86-33187 DDC 338.947 19
HC336.25 .G6365 1987

Gorbatyĭ, M. M. (Mark Moiseevich) Teorii͡a i praktika optimizatsii proizvodstvennykh moshchnosteĭ morskikh portov / M.M. Gorbatyĭ. Moskva : "Transport", 1981. 167 p. : ill. ; 21 cm. Bibliography: p. 164-167. LC Card 82-162836
1. Harbors - Economic aspects. 2. Harbors - Mathematical models. I. Title.
HE551 .G625 1981

Gorbunov, V. K. (Vladimir Konstantinovich) Primenenie ėkonomiko-matematicheskikh metodov v sovershenstvovanii upravlenii͡a narodnym khozi͡aĭstvom /. Frunze , 1982. 225 p. : LC Card 83-193778
HD9115.S652 P75 1982

Gorbushin, Petr Borisovich. Osnovy ėkonomiki i upravlenii͡a stroitel′nym proizvodstvom /. Moskva , 1978. 285 p. ; LC Card 81-171493
HD9715.S72 O86 1978

Gordon, Andrew, 1952- The evolution of labor relations in Japan : heavy industry, 1853-1955 / Andrew Gordon. Cambridge, Mass. : Council on East Asian Studies, Harvard University : Distributed by Harvard University Press, 1985. xvi, 524 p. : ill. ; 24 cm. (Harvard East Asian monographs. 117.) Includes index. Bibliography: p. [487]-503. ISBN 0-674-27130-0 (Harvard Univ. Pr.) LC Card 85-3747 DDC 331/.0952 19
1. Industrial relations - Japan - History - 19th century. 2. Industrial relations - Japan - History - 20th century. 3. Labor policy - Japan - History - 20th century. I. Series. II. Series: Harvard East Asian monographs, 117. III. Title.
HD8726 .G67 1985 ***NYPL [M-11 435 v.117]***

Gordon, Leland James, 1897- Economics for consumers / Leland J. Gordon, Stewart M. Lee. 7th ed. New York : Van Nostrand, c1977. ix, 693 p. : ill. ; 25 cm. Includes bibliographical references and indexes. ISBN 0-442-22242-4 LC Card 76-50515 DDC 381/.3/0973 19
1. Consumption (Economics). 2. Consumers - United States. 3. Consumer protection - United States. I. Lee, Stewart Munro, joint author. II. Title.
HB801 .G6 1977 ***NYPL [JLE 86-1506]***

Gordon, Marilyn J. Warmbrod, Catharine P. Skills for the changing workplace . Columbus, Ohio (1960 Kenny Rd., Columbus 43210-1090) , 1985. ix, 86 p. ; LC Card 86-205842 DDC 658.8/007/15 19
HF5415 .W3155 1985

Gordon, Richard L., 1934- World coal : economics, policies, and prospects / Richard L. Gordon. Cambridge [Cambridgeshire] ; New York : Cambridge University Press, 1987. xvi, 145 p. : ill. ; 24 cm. (Cambridge energy studies) Bibliography: p. [132]-141. Includes index. ISBN 0-521-30827-5 LC Card 86-26349 DDC 338.2/724 19
1. Coal trade. I. Title. II. Series.
HD9540.5 .G64 1987

Gordon, Robert Aaron. Higher education for business / Robert Aaron Gordon, James Edwin Howell. New York : Garland Pub., 1987, c1959. xi, 491 p. ; 22 cm. (Continuity in administrative science) Reprint. Originally published: New York : Columbia University Press, 1959. "Literature on personal qualities contributing to business success": p. [453]-455. Includes bibliographical references and index. ISBN 0-8240-8207-9 (alk. paper) : LC Card 86-25813 DDC 650/.07/1173 19
1. Business education - United States. I. Howell, James Edwin. II. Title. III. Series.
HF1131 .G6 1987

Gordon, Robert B. (Robert Boyd), 1929- Toward a new Iron Age? . Cambridge, Mass. , 1987. vi, 173 p. : ISBN 0-674-89818-4 (alk. paper) LC Card 86-22923 DDC 333.8/5 19
HC59 .T63 1987

Gordon, Sanford D. Introductory economics / Sanford D. Gordon, George G. Dawson. 6th ed. Lexington, Mass. : D.C. Heath, c1987. xviii, 490 p. : ill. (some col.) ; 25 cm. Includes bibliographical references and index. ISBN 0-669-09119-7 LC Card 86-80503 DDC 330.973/092 19
1. Economics. 2. United States - Economic conditions - 1981-. I. Dawson, George Glenn, 1925-. II. Title.
HB171.5 .G648 1987

Goreham, Gary. South Dakotans on the move : characteristics of people leaving and entering the state, 1970 to 1980 / by Gary A. Goreham,

Sidney G. Goss, and Robert T. Wagner. Brookings, S.D. : Dept. of Rural Sociology, Agricultural Experiment Station, College of Agriculture and Biological Sciences, South Dakota State University, [1984] 24 p. : ill. ; 28 cm. (Update series C229 . no. 14) "October 1984"--Cover. Chiefly tables. LC Card 85-620511 DDC 304.8/09783/021 19
1. South Dakota - Population - Statistics. 2. Migration, Internal - United States - Statistics. I. Goss, Sidney G. II. Wagner, Robert T. III. Title. IV. Series.
HB1985.S8 G67 1984

Gorges, Hans. Fieber, Joachim. Die effektivere Gestaltung des Personennahverkehrs im Kreis Sondershausen . Potsdam-Babelsberg , Leipzig , 1983. 75 p. : LC Card 83-241076
HE249.5.Z7 S664 1983

Gorham, Kenneth D. Personal productivity with Lotus 1-2-3 / Kenneth D. Gorham. Dubuque, Iowa : W.C. Brown Publishers, c1987. x, 164 p. : ill. ; 28 cm. Includes index. ISBN 0-697-05227-3 (pbk.) LC Card 87-70158 DDC 005.36/9 19
1. Lotus 1-2-3 (Computer program). 2. Business - Data processing. I. Title.
HF5548.4 L67 G67 1987

Gorina, G. A. (Galina Anatol'evna) T͡Seny i tarify /. Moskva , 1983. 150 p. : LC Card 84-117348
HB235.S73 T735 1983

Gori͡uchee--frontu, 1941-1945 /. Nikitin, V. V. (Vasiliĭ Vasil'evich) Moskva , 1984. 203 p. : LC Card 85-152473
HD9575.S652 N55 1984

GORIZIA (ITALY : PROVINCE) - OCCUPATIONS.
Albertini, Sergio. Il consolidamento strutturale dell'occupazione in specifiche aree con particolare riguardo alla provincia di Gorizia /. Milano , c1984. 184 p. ; LC Card 84-234951 DDC 331.12/0945/392 19
HD5785.G67 A42 1984

Gorkin, Julián, 1901- Los problemas del socialismo en nuestra tiempo [microform]. México, 1944. 119 p. DDC 335.082
HX40 .P73 ***NYPL [*ZT-1711 no.21]***

Gor'kovskiĭ gosudarstvennyĭ universitet imeni N.I. Lobachevskogo. Agrarnai͡a revoli͡utsii͡a i sotsialisticheskie preobrazovanii͡a v sovetskoĭ derevne . Gor'kiĭ , 1980. 84 p. ; LC Card 82-141565
HD1995.R8 A68 1980

Gorlanov, I. A. Prodovol'stvennai͡a programma SSSR . Moskva , 1986. 285 p. ; LC Card 87-110478 DDC 338.1/9/47 19
HD9015.S652 P743 1986

Gorman, Carol. America's farm crisis / by Carol Gorman. New York : F. Watts, 1987. 125 p. : ill. ; 24 cm. (An Impact book) Bibliography: p. 121. Includes index. Surveys the history of American farming since the 1960s and examines the effects of the farm crisis on different segments of the population. ISBN 0-531-10408-7 LC Card 87-2087 DDC 338.1/0973 19
1. Family farms - United States. 2. Farmers - United States. 3. Agriculture - Economic aspects - United States. I. Title.
HD1476.U5 G67 1987

Gornas, Jürgen. Zur Berücksichtigung der finanziellen Leistungsfähigkeit in kommunalen Investitions- und Finanzplanungsmodellen / Jürgen Gornas. Hamburg : Hochschule der Bundeswehr Hamburg, Institut für Verwaltungswissenschaft, 1984. 40 p. ; 30 cm. (Beiträge zur Verwaltungswissenschaft, 0176-0890 . Nr. 2) Includes bibliographical references. LC Card 85-166310
1. Local finance - Germany, West. 2. Public investments - Germany (West). I. Title. II. Series.
HJ9473 .G67 1984

Gorod i prirodopol'zovanie /. Novikov, Ė. A. (Ėnergiĭ Alekseevich) Leningrad , 1984. 143 p. ; LC Card 85-125032
HC333.5 .N68 1984

Görög, Tibor. Ökopesszimizmus, technooptimizmus és korunk globális problémái / Görög Tibor, Darai L. Mihály. [Budapest] : Művelődési Minisztérium Marxizmus-Leninizmus Oktatási Főosztálya, 1984. 85 p. : ill. ; 24 cm. (Tudományos szocializmus füzetek, 0324-5683 . 76) Summary in Russian. Bibliography: p. 65-77. ISBN 963-673-290-6 LC Card 85-130717
1. Economic history - 1971-. 2. Technological innovations. 3. Economic development - Environmental aspects. 4. Twenty-first century - Forecasts. I. Darai, Lajos Mihály. II. Title. III. Series.
HC59 .G6226 1984

Gorokhov, B. A. Nauchno-tekhnicheskiĭ progress i strukturnye sdvigi v ėkonomike sovremennogo kapitalizma . Moskva , 1987. 168 p. ; LC Card 87-165811
HC240.9.T4 N38 1987

Górski, Janusz. Z historii myśli ekonomicznej : studia i materiały / Janusz Górski.Wyd. 1. Łódź : Wydawn. Łódzkie, 1986, c1985. 312 p. ; 19 cm. Includes bibliographical references and index. ISBN 83-218-0319-9 : LC Card 83-189161
1. Economics - Poland - History. 2. Economics - History. I. Title.
HB114.A2 G67 1986

Gort, Michael, 1923- Diversification and integration in American industry / by Michael Gort. Westport, Conn. : Greenwood Press, 1984, c1962. xxi, 238 p. ; 24 cm. Includes bibliographical references and index. Reprint. Originally published: Princeton, N.J. : Princeton University Press, 1962. ISBN 0-313-24423-5 (lib. bdg.) LC Card 84-10730 DDC 338.8/0973 19
1. Diversification in industry - United States. 2. Consolidation and merger of corporations - United States. 3. Conglomerate corporations - United States. 4. Industrial concentration - United States. I. Title.
HD2756.2.U5 G67 1984
NYPL [JLE 86-4435]

Görtz, Vera. Physische und psychische Erkrankungen bei Arbeitsmigranten in der BRD : ein soziologischer Erklärungsversuch / Vera Görtz. Gelsenkirchen : A. Müller, [1986?] 250 p. : ill. ; 21 cm. Originally presented as the author's thesis (doctoral--Ruhr-Universität Bochum) under the title: Physische und psychische Morbidität bei Arbeitsmigranten und ihren Familien in der BRD. Errata slip inserted. Bibliography: p. 237-250. ISBN 3-89049-007-7 LC Card 87-141880 DDC 331.6/2/0943 19
1. Alien labor - Germany (West) - Psychological aspects. I. Title.
HD8458.A2 G67 1986

Gorz, André.
[Chemins du paradis. English]
Paths to paradise : on the liberation from work / André Gorz ; translated by Malcolm Imrie. London : Pluto Press, 1985. vii, 120 p. ; 20 cm. Translation of: Les chemins du paradis. Includes bibliographical references. ISBN 0-86104-762-1 (pbk.) :
1. Economic history - 1971-. 2. Industry - Social aspects. 3. Technology - Social aspects. 4. Capitalism. I. Title. ***NYPL [JLD 86-3006]***

Goskomitet RSFSR po trudu i sot͡sial'nym voprosam. Kardinal'nyĭ rost ėffektivnosti zhivogo truda--glavnyĭ faktor uskorenii͡a sotsial'no-ėkonomicheskogo razvitii͡a . Sverdlovsk , 1986. 2 v. ; LC Card 87-136690
HC337.R853 L35 1986

Gosplan RSFSR. Metodicheskie ukazanii͡a k razrabotke planov ėkonomicheskogo i sotsial'nogo razvitii͡a RSFSR / Gosplan RSFSR ; [zav. red. G.L. Podvoĭskiĭ ; redaktory N.I. Balashova ... et al.]. Moskva : "Ėkonomika", 1985. 462 p. ; 23 cm. LC Card 85-232541
1. Russian S.F.S.R. - Economic policy. I. Podvoĭskiĭ, G. L. (Gleb L'vovich). II. Balashova, N. I. III. Title.
HC337.R85 G67 1985

Gospodăriile agricole de stat /. Şchiopu, Bucur. Bucureşti , 1966. 295 p. : LC Card 84-183905
HD1493.R6 S35 1966

Gospodarka inwestycyjna i remontowa w latach 1984-1985 /. Kapustka, Aleksander. Zielona Góra , 1984. 294 p. ; LC Card 86-670001
HC340.3.Z9 C35 1984

Gospodarka w procesie reformowania / praca zbiorowa pod redakcją naukową Józefa Pajestki. Wyd. 1. Warszawa : Państwowe Wydawn. Ekonomiczne, 1986. 423 p. : ill. ; 21 cm. At head of title: Polska Akademia Nauk. Instytut Nauk Ekonomicznych. Includes bibliographical references. ISBN 83-208-0514-7 : LC Card 87-102275
1. Poland - Economic policy - 1981-. I. Pajestka, Jozef. II. Instytut Nauk Ekonomicznych (Polska Akademia Nauk).
HC340.3 .G68 1986

Goss, De Vee E. South Dakota county and subcounty population estimates (1980, 1982, 1984) / De Vee E. Goss. Vermillion, S.D. : Business Research Bureau, University of South Dakota, [1985] 42 p. ; 28 cm. "Fall 1985 no. 85-101"--Cover. Chiefly tables. LC Card 87-620701 DDC 304.6/2/09783021 19
1. South Dakota - Population - Statistics. 2. Population forecasting - South Dakota - Statistics. 3. South Dakota - Census, 1980. I. Title.
HA635 .G67 1985

Goss, Sidney G. Goreham, Gary. South Dakotans on the move . Brookings, S.D. [1984] 24 p. : LC Card 85-620511 DDC 304.8/09783/021 19
HB1985.S8 G67 1984

GOSSELIN, JEAN, 1921- - INTERVIEWS.
Lemieux-Pépin, Madeleine. P'tit train va loin . Ottawa , 1985. vii, 191 p. ; LC Card 86-177382
HE2808.1 .L45 1985

Gosselin, J.-F. Statistics Canada. Statistical Services Field. A compendium of methods of error evaluation in censuses and surveys /. Ottawa , 1978. 25 p. ; LC Card 80-499370 DDC 001.4/225 19
HA31.2 .C36 1978 ***NYPL [JLF 81-125]***

Gostev, B. I. Sovetskai͡a ėkonomika na novom ėtape /. Moskva , 1981. 223 p. : LC Card 82-118778
HC336.25 .S677 1981

Gosudarstvenno-monopolisticheskiĭ kapitalizm i razmeshchenie proizvoditel'nykh sil / otvetstvennye redaktory, N.N. Nekrasov, V.P. Mozhin ; [avtorskiĭ kollektiv, A.D. Sapozhnikov ... et al.]. Moskva : Izd-vo "Nauka", 1984. 182 p. ; 22 cm. At head of title: Akademii͡a nauk SSSR. Sovet po izuchenii͡u proizvoditel'nykh sil pri Gosplane SSSR. Bibliography: p. 178-[181] LC Card 84-239188
1. Europe - Industries - Location. 2. Europe - Economic conditions - 1945- - Regional disparities. 3. Japan - Industries - Location. 4. Japan - Economic conditions - 1945- - Regional disparities. I. Nekrasov, Nikolai Nikolaevich. II. Mozhin, V. P. III. Sapozhnikov, A. D. IV. Sovet po izuchenii͡u proizvoditel'nykh sil (Soviet Union).
HC240 .G565 1984

Gosudarstvennoe upravlenie ispol'zovaniem i okhranoĭ vod /. Ataev, M. (Murruk) Ashkhabad , 1982. 175 p. ; LC Card 82-244366
HD1697.S653 T873 1982

Gosudarstvennoye russkoye geograficheskoye obshchestvo. see **Geograficheskoe obshchestvo SSSR.**

Gosudarstvennyĭ apparat i problemy okhrany prirody v uslovii͡akh APK /. Todyka, I͡Uriĭ Nikolaevich. Kishinev , 1986. 179, [5] p. ; LC Card 86-141430
HD1995.M5 T63 1986

GOSUDARSTVENNYĬ BANK SSSR.
Organizatsii͡a i planirovanie kredita i denezhnogo obrashchenii͡a /. Moskva , 1984. 350 p. ; LC Card 85-108172
HG3729.S632 O74 1984

Gosudarstvennyĭ komitet po trudu Ukrainskoĭ SSR. Rekomendatsii po ukreplenii͡u trudovoĭ i proizvodstvennoĭ distsipliny /. Kiev , 1984. 41 p. ; LC Card 86-181301
HF5549.5.L3 R45 1984

Gosudarstvennyĭ universitet, Kalinin, Russia. see **Kalininskiĭ gosudarstvennyĭ universitet.**

Gosudarstvo i agrarnai͡a ėvoli͡utsii͡a v razvivai͡ushchikhsi͡a stranakh Azii i Afriki / [redaktsionnai͡a kollegii͡a I͡U.G. Aleksandrov ... et al., V.G. Rastiannikov (otvetstvennyĭ redaktor i avtor predislovii͡a)]. Moskva : Izd-vo "Nauka", 1980. 227 p. ; 22 cm. At head of title: Akademii͡a nauk SSSR. Institut vostokovedenii͡a. LC Card 81-143353
1. Agriculture and state - Asia. 2. Agriculture and state - Africa. 3. Asia - Rural conditions. 4. Africa - Rural conditions. I. Aleksandrov, I͡U. G. (I͡Uriĭ Georgievich). II. Rastiannikov, V. G. (Viktor Georgievich). III. Institut vostokovedenii͡a (Akademii͡a nauk SSSR).
HD2056 .G67 1980

Goswami, Prodyot Kumar, 1940- Indian currency and exchange, 1835-1940 / Prodyot Kumar Goswami. New Delhi : Milind, 1983. viii, 134 p. ; 23 cm. Revision of the author's thesis (Ph. D.--Jadavpur University, 1975) Bibliography: p.

130-134. LC Card 83-903565 DDC 332.4/560954 19
1. Money - India - History. 2. Foreign exchange problem - India - History. 3. Balance of payments - India - History. I. Title.
HG1234 .G67 1983 ***NYPL [JLD 87-673]***

Goswami, Shrutidev, 1947- Aspects of revenue administration in Assam, 1826-1874 / Shrutidev Goswami. Delhi, India : Mittal Publications, 1987. xii, 184 p. ; 23 cm. Revision of the author's thesis (Ph. D.--University of Dibrugarh, 1981) Bibliography: p. [172]-179. Includes index. LC Card 87-900200 DDC 336.02/54162 19
1. Revenue - India - Assam - History. I. Title.
HJ2939.A87 G67 1987

Goswami, Surendra Kumar, 1929-1985. A history of revenue administration in Assam, 1228-1826 A.D. : a detailed history of the revenue system of the Ahom rulers / Surendra Kumar Goswami. Delhi : Spectrum Publications, 1986. xii, 321 p. : ill., folded map ; 23 cm. Revision of the author's thesis (Ph. D.--Dibrugarh University, 1982) under the title: Revenue administration in Assam during the Ahom period, 1228-1826 A.D. Bibliography: p. [311]-321. LC Card 86-903188 DDC 354.54/16200726/09 19
1. Revenue - India - Assam - History. 2. Assam (India) - History. I. Title.
HJ2939.Z9 A874 1986

Goswani, A., 1937- Land reforms and peasant movement . New Delhi , Guwahati , c1986. xix, 232 p. ; LC Card 86-902255 DDC 333.3/1/541 19
HD1333.I42 N65 1986

Gothe, Richard, 1928- Zusammenwirken von örtlichen Staatsorganen und Kombinaten / Richard Gothe ; [Mitautor, Karl Lerche]. 1. Aufl. Berlin : Staatsverlag der Deutschen Demokratischen Republik, 1983. 89 p. ; 22 cm. (Der Sozialistische Staat) Includes bibliographical references. LC Card 84-166789
1. Industry and state - Germany, East. 2. Local government - Germany, East. 3. Business enterprises - Germany, East. I. Lerche, Karl. II. Title.
HD3616.G48 G67 1983

Gottfredson, Gary D. Dictionary of Holland occupational codes / Gary D. Gottfredson, John L. Holland, Deborah Kimiko Ogawa. Palo Alto, CA : Consulting Psychologists Press, c1982. xviii, 500 p. ; 23 cm. "This volume is a translation of the Dictionary of occupational titles ... into the Holland ... classification system"--p. ix. Bibliography: p. 497-500. ISBN 0-89106-020-X
1. Occupations - Classification. 2. Occupations - Dictionaries. I. Holland, John L., 1919-. II. Ogawa, Deborah Kimiko. III. Dictionary of occupational titles. IV. Title. ***NYPL [JLE 86-3992]***

Gottifredi, Marcelo Antonio. Vela, Gil. Deuda externa latinoamericana /. Ecuador , 1984. 180 p. ; LC Card 85-180466 DDC 336.3/435/098 19
HJ8514.5 .V45 1984 ***NYPL [JLD 86-308]***

Göttinger Arbeitskreis Gegen Atomenergie. Unterdrückung, Hunger, Krieg . Göttingen [1985?] 73 p. : LC Card 86-152237
HC59.7 .U55 1985

Göttinger Beiträge zur Gesellschaftstheorie . (5) Stamatis, Georg. Sraffa und sein Verhältnis zu Ricardo und Marx /. Göttingen , Lollar , c1984. ix, 459 p. : ISBN 3-921701-04-X LC Card 84-213549
HB103.S7 S73 1984

Göttinger Hefte zur Bankbetriebslehre und Unternehmungsfinanzierung .
(Heft 10) Cordewener, Karl-Friedrich, 1951- Kundenbediente Datenstationen als marktpolitische Instrumente des Bankbetriebs /. Göttingen , 1982. 268 p. : ISBN 3-509-01312-3 LC Card 84-182492
HG3048 .C67 1982

(Heft 12) Zessin, Axel, 1953- Unternehmungsbewertung von Kreditinstituten /. Göttingen , 1982. 296 p. : ISBN 3-509-01313-1 LC Card 84-109138
HG4028.V3 Z47 1982

(Heft 3) Benner, Wolfgang, 1940- Betriebliche Finanzwirtschaft als monetäres System /. Göttingen , 1983. 486 p. : ISBN 3-509-01323-9 LC Card 83-240817
HG4011 .B433 1983

(Heft 9) Janssen, Friedrich, 1948- Bedeutung und Ausstattung von Wandel- und Optionsanleihen /. Göttingen , 1982. 279 p. : ISBN 3-509-01319-0 LC Card 83-240528
HG5501 .J35 1982

Gottlieb, Peter, 1949- Forging a union of steel . Ithaca, N.Y. , c1987. vii, 153 p. : ISBN 0-87546-135-2 (pbk.) LC Card 87-21508 DDC 331.88/169142/0973 19
HD6515.I5 F58 1987

Gottlieb, Richard. The directory of mail order catalogs / Richard Gottlieb, general editor. 3rd ed. [New York, N.Y.] : Facts on File ; Sharon, CT : Grey House Pub., c1987. xi, 385 p. ; 29 cm. Includes indexes. ISBN 0-8160-1740-9 LC Card 86-31959 DDC 016.381/14/0973 19
1. Mail-order business - United States - Directories. 2. Catalogs, Commercial - Directories. I. Title.
HF5466 .G63 1987

Gottman, John Mordechai. Bakeman, Roger. Observing interaction . Cambridge [Cambridgeshire] , New York , 1986. ix, 221 p. : ISBN 0-521-25632-1 LC Card 85-22362 DDC 300/.1/51954 19
H62 .B284 1986 ***NYPL [JLD 86-3069]***

Gottschalk, Bernhard, 1944- Elias, Hermann-Josef, 1949- Gestaltung und Bewertung von Arbeitssystemen /. Frankfurt am Main , New York , c1985. 281 p. : ISBN 3-593-33444-5 LC Card 85-143343
HF5549.5.J6 E45 1985

Gottschalk, Johannes. Die Freiburger Enquete von 1476 . Freiburg im Breisgau , c1986. xxxiv, 102 p. : ISBN 3-923272-20-2 LC Card 87-409559 DDC 330.943/46 19
HC289.F855 F74 1986

Götz, Gerd, 1956- Bildschirmtext : Bedeutung und Anwendung im Investitionsgütermarketing / Gerd Götz. Berlin : VDE-Verlag, c1985. xi, 285 p. : ill. ; 21 cm. Bibliography: p. 244-280. Includes index. ISBN 3-8007-1348-9 LC Card 87-125311 DDC 384.3/5/0943 19
1. Videotex systems - Germany (West). 2. Investments - Germany, West. I. Title.
HD9696.T463 G346 1985

Goudswaard, A. De ontwikkeling van de paprikateelt : bedrijfseconomische en marktkundige aspecten / A. Goudswaard. Den Haag : Landbouw-Economisch Instituut, Afd. Tuinbouw, [1986] 60 p. : ill. ; 24 cm. (Onderzoekverslag . no. 26) "Augustus 1986." LC Card 86-233094
1. Paprika industry - Netherlands. I. Series: Onderzoekverslag , 26. II. Title.
HD9211.P353 N424 1986

Gould, Bryan. Monetarism or prosperity? / Bryan Gould, John Mills, and Shaun Stewart ; foreword by Peter Shore. London : Macmillan, 1981. x, 222 p. : ill. ; 23 cm. Bibliography: p. [213]-217. Includes index. ISBN 0-333-30782-8 LC Card 86-673392
1. Monetary policy - Great Britain. 2. Foreign exchange. 3. Great Britain - Economic policy - 1945-. 4. Great Britain - Economic conditions - 1945-. I. Mills, John. II. Stewart, Shaun. III. Title.
HG939.5 .G65x 1981

Gould, J. Sutherland. Starting from scratch : 50 profitable business opportunities / Joe Sutherland Gould. New York : Wiley, c1987. xiii, 366 p. ; 24 cm. Includes index. ISBN 0-471-85024-1 LC Card 86-28136 DDC 658.1/1 19
1. New business enterprises. I. Title.
HD62.5 .G68 1987

GOULD, JAY, 1836-1892.
Klein, Maury, 1939- The life and legend of Jay Gould /. Baltimore , c1986. xvi, 595 p., [24] p. of plates : ISBN 0-8018-2880-5 (alk. paper) LC Card 85-24107 DDC 332/.092/4 B 19
HC102.5.G68 K55 1986 ***NYPL [JFE 86-2364]***

Gourgues, Harold W. Revolution in financial services / Harold W. Gourgues, Jr., Jeffrey R. Lauterbach. Washington, D.C. : Bureau of National Affairs, c1987. xiii, 248 p. : ill. ; 24 cm. Includes bibliographical references and index. ISBN 0-87179-561-2 LC Card 87-18390 DDC 332.1/0973 19
1. Financial institutions - United States. I. Lauterbach, Jeffrey R. II. Title.
HG2491 .G68 1987

Gourlay, Stephen, 1949- Batstone, Eric. Unions, unemployment and innovation /. Oxford [Oxfordshire] , New York, N.Y., USA , 1986. viii, 320 p. ; ISBN 0-631-14961-9 : LC Card 85-30679 DDC 331.88/0941 19
HD6664 .B335 1986 ***NYPL [JLE 86-4031]***

Gouws, P. A. (Pieter Andries), 1949- Arbeidsverhoudinge in Suid-Afrika / P.A. Gouws. 1ste uitgawe. Pretoria : J.L. van Schaik, 1986. 127 p. ; 22 cm. Bibliography: p. 122-123. Includes index. ISBN 0-627-01492-5 : LC Card 87-127172
1. Industrial relations - South Africa. 2. Labor and laboring classes - South Africa. I. Title.
HD8801 .G66 1986

Gove, William G. Nevel, Robert L. The timber industries of New Hampshire and Vermont . Broomall, Pa. , 1986. 56 p. : LC Card 86-601144 DDC 338.1/7498/09742 19
HD9757.N4 N48 1986

The governance of the American economy . Hollingsworth, J. Rogers (Joseph Rogers), 1932- Berlin [1985] 60 p. ; LC Card 86-205784 DDC 330.973 19
HC106.8 .H635 1985

Governing science and technology in a democracy / edited with an introduction by Malcolm L. Goggin ; William A. Blanpied ... [et al.]. 1st ed. Knoxville, TN : University of Tennessee Press, c1986. xviii, 314 p. ; 22 cm. Includes indexes. Bibliography: p. 279-296. ISBN 0-87049-506-2 (alk. paper) : LC Card 86-7074 DDC 338.9/26 19
1. Science - Social aspects. 2. Technology - Social aspects. I. Goggin, Malcolm L., 1938-. II. Blanpied, William A., 1933-.
Q125 .G68 1986 ***NYPL [JLD 87-462]***

Governing the economy . Hall, Peter A. Cambridge, U.K. , Oxford, U.K. , 1986. 341 p. ; ISBN 0-7456-0227-4 : LC Card 87-672535
HC256.5 .H256x 1986b

Governing the heartland . Stinson, Thomas F., 1942- Washington , 1986. xii, 159 p. : LC Card 86-603376 DDC 336/.014/77 19
HJ9181 .S75 1986

GOVERNMENT. see **POLITICAL SCIENCE.**

GOVERNMENT ACCOUNTING. see **FINANCE, PUBLIC - ACCOUNTING.**

Government and North Sea oil /. Hann, Danny. Basingstoke, Hampshire , c1986. ix, 175 p. : ISBN 0-333-39436-4 ***NYPL [JLD 86-2581]***

Government and peasant in Russia, 1861-1906 . Macey, David, A. J., 1942- Dekalb, Ill. , 1987. xviii, 380 p. ; ISBN 0-87580-122-6 LC Card 87-7684 DDC 338.1/847 19
HD1992 .M19 1987

Government and private sector in contemporary Mexico / edited by Sylvia Maxfield and Ricardo Anzaldúa M. [La Jolla, Calif.] : Center for U. S.-Mexican Studies, University of California, San Diego, 1987. iv, 146 p. ; 23 cm. (Monograph series / Center for U. S.-Mexican Studies, University of California, San Diego . 20) Includes bibliographical references. LC Card 87-622060 DDC 338.972 19
1. Industry and state - Mexico. 2. Business and politics - Mexico. 3. Businessmen - Mexico. I. Maxfield, Sylvia. II. Anzaldúa Montoya, Ricardo. III. Series: Monograph series (University of California, San Diego. Center for U. S.-Mexican Studies) , 20.
HD3616.M43 G68 1987

GOVERNMENT BUSINESS ENTERPRISES - ACCOUNTING - CONGRESSES.
Betriebswirtschaftliche Erkenntnisse für Regierung, Verwaltung und öffentliche Unternehmen . Baden-Baden , 1985. 266 p. : ISBN 3-7890-1104-5 LC Card 85-213984
HJ9705 .B48 1985

GOVERNMENT BUSINESS ENTERPRISES - AFRICA.
Mesfin Gabre Michael. Labour-management relations in public enterprises in Africa. Geneva, Switzerland , 1983. 84 p. ; ISBN 92-2-103009-1 (pbk.) LC Card 86-213649 DDC 658.3 s 331/.04135/000096 19
HD6961.A1 I73 no. 60 HD8776.5

GOVERNMENT BUSINESS ENTERPRISES - AFRICA, SUB-SAHARAN.
Nellis, John R. Public enterprises in Sub-Saharan Africa /. Washington, D.C., U. S.A. [1986] vii, 66 p. : ISBN 0-8213-0845-9 (pbk.) LC Card 86-24756 DDC 338.7/4/0967

19
HD4338 .N45 1986

GOVERNMENT BUSINESS ENTERPRISES - ALGERIA - MANAGEMENT.
Boutefnouchet, Mostefa. Le socialisme dans l'entreprise . Alger , c1978. 253 p. ; LC Card 84-207677
HD5660.A4 B68 1978

GOVERNMENT BUSINESS ENTERPRISES - ARGENTINA - HISTORY.
Angueira, María del Carmen. Capitalismo de estado, 1927-1956 /. Buenos Aires , c1986. 116 p. : ISBN 950-25-1416-5 LC Card 87-100705
HD9711.A72 A54 1986

GOVERNMENT BUSINESS ENTERPRISES - ASIA.
Natsionalizatsiia i gossektor v razvivaiushchikhsia stranakh . Moskva , 1986. 210 p. ; LC Card 87-165820
HD4276 .N38 1986

GOVERNMENT BUSINESS ENTERPRISES - AUSTRIA.
Tieber, Herbert. Verstaatliche Industrie . Wien , c1983. 91 p. : LC Card 84-169053
HD4155 .T54 1983

GOVERNMENT BUSINESS ENTERPRISES - BELGIUM.
Escarmelle, Jean-François. L'Etat industriel dans les politiques de sortie de crise . Louvain-la-Neuve , 1986. 237 p. : ISBN 2-87077-301-3 : LC Card 86-229137
HD3616.B43 E84 1986

GOVERNMENT BUSINESS ENTERPRISES - BOLIVIA.
Conferencias sobre desarrollo económico, presupuesto, estabilización y nacionalización de empresas económicas. La Paz, Bolivia , 1955. 180 p. : LC Card 86-167406
HC182 .C54 1955

GOVERNMENT BUSINESS ENTERPRISES - BRAZIL.
Castro, J. As instituições para-estatais no estado novo /. Rio de Janeiro, Brasil , 1939 (Rio [de Janeiro] : Companhia Carioca) 225 p., [2] leaves of plates : LC Card 85-222446
HD4094 .C35 1939

Martins, Luciano, 1934- Estado capitalista e burocracia no Brasil pós-64 /. Rio de Janeiro, RJ , 1985. 265 p. ; LC Card 85-232969 DDC 338.981 19
HC187 .M2947 1985 ***NYPL [JLD 86-1691]***

Penna, João Camilo de Oliveira. As empresas estatais na economia brasileira /. [Brasília] , 1983. 43 p. ; LC Card 86-229392
HD4093 .P46 1983

Setor público, reordenamento e privatização /. [Rio de Janeiro, RJ , 1986] 47 p. : LC Card 87-403308 DDC 338.981 19
HC187 .S436 1986

GOVERNMENT BUSINESS ENTERPRISES - BRAZIL - ALAGOAS - DIRECTORIES.
Cadastro de entidades estatais . [Maceió] , 1985. 77 p. ; LC Card 86-171884
HD4095.A4 C33 1985

GOVERNMENT BUSINESS ENTERPRISES - BRAZIL - ALAGOAS - FINANCE.
Alagoas (Brazil). Comissão de Controle das Entidades Estatais. Programa de dispêndios globais para 1986 . [Maceió, Brazil] , 1985. 76 p. : LC Card 87-404783 DDC 354.81/35092 19
HD4095.A4 A4 1985

GOVERNMENT BUSINESS ENTERPRISES - BRAZIL - BAHIA (STATE)
Empresas estatais na Bahia. Salvador, Bahia, Brasil , 1986. 134 p. : LC Card 87-137490 DDC 338.6/2/098142 19
HD4095.B33 E47 1986

GOVERNMENT BUSINESS ENTERPRISES - BRAZIL - FINANCE - CONGRESSES.
Ciclo Integrado sobre Administração Financeira (1983 : Escola de Administração Fazendária) Ciclo Integrado sobre Administração Financeira /. Salvador, BA [1984] 53 p. : LC Card 86-157989
HG185.B7 C52 1983

GOVERNMENT BUSINESS ENTERPRISES - BURUNDI.
Ndabahagamye, Illuminata. Inventaire du secteur parapublic au Burundi, 1960-1984 /. Bujumbura, Burundi , c1986. 211 p. : LC Card 86-981403
HD4348 .N3 1986

GOVERNMENT BUSINESS ENTERPRISES - CANADA.
Canadian industrial policy in action /. Toronto , Buffalo , c1985. xvii, 231 p. : ISBN 0-8020-7244-5 (pbk.) LC Card 86-672572
HD3616.C23 C36x 1985 ***NYPL [JLD 86-2871]***

Laux, Jeanne Kirk, 1942- State capitalism . Ithaca , 1988. ix, 250 p. ; ISBN 0-8014-2079-2 (alk. paper) LC Card 87-47600 DDC 338.6/2/0971 19
HD4005 .L38 1988

Minding the public's business. [Ottawa] , 1986. xii, 180 p. : ISBN 0-660-12217-0 (pbk.) : LC Card 87-127219 DDC 338.971 19
HD4005 .M53 1986

GOVERNMENT BUSINESS ENTERPRISES - CANADA - CASE STUDIES.
Borins, Sandford F., 1949- Investments in failure . Toronto , New York , c1986. x, 175 p. ; ISBN 0-458-80340-5 (pbk.) : LC Card 87-142330 DDC 354.7109/2 19
HD4005 .B67 1986

GOVERNMENT BUSINESS ENTERPRISES - CANADA - EMPLOYEES - STATISTICS.
Employment injuries and occupational illnesses . Ottawa, Ont. , c1986. 92 p. ; ISBN 0-662-54738-1 (pbk.) LC Card 87-147113 DDC 363.1/12/0971 19
HD7262.5.C3 E463 1986

GOVERNMENT BUSINESS ENTERPRISES - CHILE - ACCOUNTING - HANDBOOKS, MANUALS, ETC.
Sánchez González, Leonardo. Fundamento operacional del sistema de contabilidad general de la nación /. Santiago, Chile [1986] 227 p. : LC Card 87-403116 DDC 354.830072/31 19
HJ9923.C3 S264 1986

GOVERNMENT BUSINESS ENTERPRISES - CONGRESSES.
Öffentliche Unternehmen in Rezession und Aufschwung . Berlin , 1977. 165 p. : LC Card 85-180964
HD3845 .G43 Heft 14 HD3842

GOVERNMENT BUSINESS ENTERPRISES - DEVELOPING COUNTRIES.
Berg, Elliot. Divestiture in developing countries /. Washington, D.C. , 1987. vii, 30 p. : ISBN 0-8213-0917-X (pbk.) LC Card 87-14235 DDC 338.9/009172/4 19
HD4420.8 .B45 1987

Boneo, Horacio. Interlinkages, concept, characteristics, and determining factors /. Austin , 1986. 17 p. : LC Card 86-622253 DDC 338.7/4/091724 19
HD4420.8 .B67 1986

Economic performance of public enterprises . New York , 1986. vii, 264 p. : ISBN 92-1-123103-5 (pbk.) LC Card 87-108199 DDC 338.6/2/091724 19
HD4420.8 .E28 1986

Natsionalizatsiia i gossektor v razvivaiushchikhsia stranakh . Moskva , 1986. 210 p. ; LC Card 87-165820
HD4276 .N38 1986

Ramanadham, Venkata Vemuri, 1920- The Nature of public enterprise /. New York , 1984. 302 p. : ISBN 0-312-86778-6 : LC Card 83-40570 ***NYPL [JLD 86-1037]***

GOVERNMENT BUSINESS ENTERPRISES - DEVELOPING COUNTRIES - MANAGEMENT.
Powell, Victor. Improving public enterprise performance . Geneva , 1987. x, 226 p. : ISBN 92-2-105563-9 (pbk.) : LC Card 87-166309 DDC 350/.0092/091724 19
HD4420.8 .P68 1987

GOVERNMENT BUSINESS ENTERPRISES - EMPLOYEES - LEGAL STATUS, LAWS, ETC. - FRANCE.
La Démocratisation du secteur public . Paris [1984] 87 p. ; LC Card 84-233767
HD4165 .D46 1984

GOVERNMENT BUSINESS ENTERPRISES - EUROPE.
Parris, Henry. Public enterprise in Western Europe /. London , Wolfeboro, N.H. , c1987. viii, 197 p. : ISBN 0-7099-0548-3 : LC Card 86-24133 DDC 338.7/4/094 19
HD4138 .P37 1987 ***NYPL [JLD 87-757]***

Thürmer, Lothar. Bürokratie und Effizienz staatlichen Handelns . Berlin , c1984. 177 p. : ISBN 3-428-05543-8 LC Card 84-156948
HD38.4 .T47 1984

GOVERNMENT BUSINESS ENTERPRISES - FINANCE - CONGRESSES.
Pricing policy and investment criteria in public enterprises . Ljubljana, Yugoslavia , 1982. 297 p. : ISBN 92-9038-024-1 (pbk.) LC Card 85-242542 DDC 338.7/4 19
HD3842 .P75 1985 ***NYPL [JLE 87-547]***

GOVERNMENT BUSINESS ENTERPRISES - FRANCE.
Escarmelle, Jean-François. L'Etat industriel dans les politiques de sortie de crise . Louvain-la-Neuve , 1986. 237 p. : ISBN 2-87077-301-3 : LC Card 86-229137
HD3616.B43 E84 1986

Recensement des marchés et commandes des entreprises publiques et sociétés d'économie mixte . Paris [1984] 71 p. : LC Card 85-133146
HD4163 .R43 1984

GOVERNMENT BUSINESS ENTERPRISES - FRANCE - DIRECTORIES.
La Démocratisation du secteur public . Paris [1984] 87 p. ; LC Card 84-233767
HD4165 .D46 1984

GOVERNMENT BUSINESS ENTERPRISES - FRANCE - HISTORY.
Godfrey, John F. Capitalism at war . Leamington Spa, UK ; New York : xiv, 313 p. ; ISBN 0-85496-519-X : LC Card 86-32708 DDC 338.944 19
HD3616.F82 G63 1987

GOVERNMENT BUSINESS ENTERPRISES - FRANCE - MANAGEMENT - EMPLOYEE PARTICIPATION.
La Démocratisation du secteur public . Paris [1984] 87 p. ; LC Card 84-233767
HD4165 .D46 1984

GOVERNMENT BUSINESS ENTERPRISES - GERMANY - HISTORY.
Meyer, August. Das Syndikat . Braunschweig , c1986. 348 p. ; ISBN 3-925151-18-4 LC Card 87-129940 DDC 338.2/73/0943 19
HD9523.9.R45 M49 1986

GOVERNMENT BUSINESS ENTERPRISES - GERMANY, WEST.
Gesellschaft für Öffentliche Wirtschaft und Gemeinwirtschaft. Wissenschaftlicher Beirat. Zum Problem der Aufgabenverlagerung auf öffentliche Unternehmen . Baden-Baden , 1984. 73 p. ; ISBN 3-7890-1048-0 LC Card 85-143795
HD4177 .G47 1984

Hüttig, Christoph. Gemeinwirtschaft im Sozialstaat . Frankfurt am Main , c1986. vi, 355 p. : ISBN 3-88129-990-4 : LC Card 86-223747
HD4175 .H83 1986

Sander, Otfried. Kommunale Wirtschaftsunternehmen /. Köln , 1982. xiv, 144 p. : ISBN 3-555-00464-6 LC Card 81-192097
HD4659 .S26 1982

GOVERNMENT BUSINESS ENTERPRISES - GERMANY (WEST) - MANAGEMENT - EMPLOYEE PARTICIPATION.
Süllow, Bernd. Korporative Repräsentation der Gewerkschaften . Frankfurt , New York , c1982. 146 p. ; ISBN 3-593-33169-1 LC Card 83-153450
HD4177 .S85 1982

GOVERNMENT BUSINESS ENTERPRISES - GOVERNMENT POLICY.

GOVERNMENT BUSINESS ENTERPRISES - GREAT BRITAIN.
Curwen, Peter J. Public enterprise . Brighton, Sussex , 1986. xvii, 318 p. : ISBN 0-312-65435-9 : LC Card 85-26234 DDC 354.4109/2 19
HD4145 .C87 1986 ***NYPL [JLD 86-1636]***

Loebl, Herbert. Government factories and the origins of British regional policy, 1934-1948 . Aldershot, Hants, England , Brookfield, Vt., USA , c1987. p. cm. ISBN 0-566-05343-8 LC Card 87-23075 DDC 338.6/2/0941 19
HD4145 .L64 1987

GOVERNMENT BUSINESS ENTERPRISES - GREAT BRITAIN - ACCOUNTING.
Accounting for economic costs and changing

prices . London , 1986. 2 v. : ISBN 0-11-560004-3 (pbk. : v. 1) : LC Card 86-216162 DDC 657/.42 19
HF5658.5 .A22 1986

GOVERNMENT BUSINESS ENTERPRISES - GREAT BRITAIN - CASE STUDIES.
Public enterprise . New York , 1985. 416 p. ; ISBN 0-8240-7626-5 (alk. paper) : LC Card 85-13105 DDC 354.4109/1 19
HD4147 .P83 1985 ***NYPL [JLD 86-3467]***

GOVERNMENT BUSINESS ENTERPRISES - GREAT BRITAIN - CONGRESSES.
Public enterprise policy in India and U.K. in 1980s /. Bombay , 1987. xx, 286 p. ; LC Card 86-903771 DDC 338.6/2/0941 19
HD4293 .P775 1987

GOVERNMENT BUSINESS ENTERPRISES - HUNGARY.
Az Állami vállalatok szervezete, vezetése, működése és irányítása /. Budapest , 1985. 262 p. ; ISBN 963-322-140-4 : LC Card 86-202934
HD4160.5 .A78 1985

GOVERNMENT BUSINESS ENTERPRISES - INDIA.
India. Parliament. Committee on Public Undertakings. Tenth report on public undertakings, delays in commencement of production business, under utilisation of capacity and related matters, Ministry of Finance (Bureau of Public Enterprises) . New Delhi , c1981. vii, 50 p. ; LC Card 81-902947 DDC 354.5409/2 19
HD4293 .I515 1981

Nunnenkamp, Peter. Die Rolle öffentlicher Industrieunternehmen im Exportsektor Indiens /. Hamburg , 1985. xiv, 268 p. : ISBN 3-87895-285-6 : LC Card 87-111454
HD4293 .N85 1985

Public administration in India . Allahabad , 1983. xii, 308 p. ; LC Card 83-907416 DDC 354.54 19
JQ224 .P75 1983 ***NYPL [JLE 86-4197]***

Surya Prakash. Parliamentary control over public enterprises in India /. Allahabad, India , 1985. 293 p. ; LC Card 85-903454 DDC 354.5409/2 19
HD4293 .S87 1985 ***NYPL [JLD 87-325]***

Towards a viable and vibrant public sector in India . New Delhi , 1986. xiii, 188, 163, 8, 103 p. ; LC Card 86-903205 DDC 338.6/2/0954
HD4293 .T667 1986

GOVERNMENT BUSINESS ENTERPRISES - INDIA - ACCOUNTING.
Seshadri, R. K. The Indian financial system . Madras , 1985. ii, 287, v, iii p. ; LC Card 85-904230 DDC 336.54 19
HD4293 .S45 1985 ***NYPL [JLD 86-2433]***

GOVERNMENT BUSINESS ENTERPRISES - INDIA - ANDHRA PRADESH.
Public enterprises, a state level perspective /. Delhi , New Delhi , 1986. xix, 287 p. ; ISBN 81-7018-370-7 : LC Card 86-902715 DDC 338.6/2/095484 19
HD4295.A5 P8 1986

GOVERNMENT BUSINESS ENTERPRISES - INDIA - ANDHRA PRADESH - MANAGEMENT.
Venkatswamy, G. Management of state government enterprises /. New Delhi, India , 1987. viii, 362 p. : ISBN 81-7051-020-1 : LC Card 87-901167 DDC 354.54/84092 19
HD4295.A5 V45 1987

GOVERNMENT BUSINESS ENTERPRISES - INDIA - BIHAR - FINANCE.
Sahay, S. N. (Surendra Nath) Financial management of public enterprises /. New Delhi , 1984. xiii, 216 p. ; LC Card 84-900657 DDC 354.54/12092/0681 19
HD4295.B5 S24 1984 ***NYPL [JLD 86-4430]***

GOVERNMENT BUSINESS ENTERPRISES - INDIA - CASE STUDIES.
Hassan, Shabir. Public enterprises in economic development . Delhi , 1987. xiii, 230 p. ; LC Card 86-903835
HD2900.12.J35 H37 1987

GOVERNMENT BUSINESS ENTERPRISES - INDIA - CONGRESSES.
Government media and the public sector . New Delhi , 1983. 270 p. ; LC Card 83-907479 DDC 302.3/24/0954 19
HD59 .G62 1983 ***NYPL [JLD 86-3767]***

Public enterprise policy in India and U.K. in 1980s /. Bombay , 1987. xx, 286 p. ; LC Card 86-903771 DDC 338.6/2/0941 19
HD4293 .P775 1987

Public enterprises in India . Bombay , 1983. xxii, 524 p. ; LC Card 83-905617 DDC 354.5409/2 19
HD4293 .P793 1983 ***NYPL [JLD 87-723]***

GOVERNMENT BUSINESS ENTERPRISES - INDIA - EMPLOYEES.
Mathur, Reeta. Industrial relations in public enterprises /. Jaipur , 1986. vii, 226 p. ; LC Card 86-902265 DDC 331/.04135454 19
HD6976.I52 M37 1986

GOVERNMENT BUSINESS ENTERPRISES - INDIA - FINANCE - CASE STUDIES.
Sahay, S. N. (Surendra Nath) Financial management of public enterprises /. New Delhi , 1984. xiii, 216 p. ; LC Card 84-900657 DDC 354.54/12092/0681 19
HD4295.B5 S24 1984 ***NYPL [JLD 86-4430]***

GOVERNMENT BUSINESS ENTERPRISES - INDIA - JAMMU AND KASHMIR - CASE STUDIES.
Hassan, Shabir. Public enterprises in economic development . Delhi , 1987. xiii, 230 p. ; LC Card 86-903835
HD2900.12.J35 H37 1987

GOVERNMENT BUSINESS ENTERPRISES - INDIA - LOCATION.
Kundu, Amitabh, 1948- Location of public enterprises and regional development /. New Delhi , 1986. xv, 178 p. ; LC Card 86-903373 DDC 338.954 19
HD9697.A3 I45 1986

GOVERNMENT BUSINESS ENTERPRISES - INDIA - ORISSA - FINANCE.
Sahu, Promod K. (Promod Kumar), 1942- Industrial economy of Orissa /. Delhi , New Delhi , 1986. viii, 152 p. ; ISBN 81-7018-401-0 : LC Card 86-903551 DDC 338.0954/13 19
HC437.O7 S24 1986

GOVERNMENT BUSINESS ENTERPRISES - INDIA - PERSONNEL MANAGEMENT.
Management of human resources in public enterprises /. New Delhi, India , 1985. vi, 304 p. ; LC Card 87-402995 DDC 354.5409/2/0683 19
HD4293 .M355 1985

GOVERNMENT BUSINESS ENTERPRISES - JAPAN.
Nihon kōkigyō no saisei /. Kyōto-shi , 1986. 4, 8, 289 p. : ISBN 4-589-01273-1 : LC Card 86-216062
HD4313 .N46 1986 <Orien Japan> ***NYPL [*OSM 87-2537]***

GOVERNMENT BUSINESS ENTERPRISES - JAPAN - FINANCE.
Nihon kōkigyō no saisei /. Kyōto-shi , 1986. 4, 8, 289 p. : ISBN 4-589-01273-1 : LC Card 86-216062
HD4313 .N46 1986 <Orien Japan> ***NYPL [*OSM 87-2537]***

GOVERNMENT BUSINESS ENTERPRISES - KOREA (SOUTH)
Song, Dae-Hee. The performance evaluation of Korean public enterprises . Seoul, Korea [1986] 109 p. : LC Card 87-404432 DDC 354.519/5092 19
HD4315.5 .S65 1986

GOVERNMENT BUSINESS ENTERPRISES - KOREA (SOUTH) - EVALUATION.
Park, Yung Chul. A system for evaluating the performance of government-invested enterprises in Korea /. Washington, D.C. [1986] vi, 49 p. : ISBN 0-8213-0859-9 (pbk.) LC Card 86-28907 DDC 338.7/4/0723 19
HD4315.5 .P37 1986

GOVERNMENT BUSINESS ENTERPRISES - KOREA (SOUTH) - MANAGEMENT - EVALUATION.
Song, Dae-Hee. The performance evaluation of Korean public enterprises . Seoul, Korea [1986] 109 p. : LC Card 87-404432 DDC 354.519/5092 19
HD4315.5 .S65 1986

GOVERNMENT BUSINESS ENTERPRISES - LATIN AMERICA - MANAGEMENT - CONGRESSES.
Gestión de empresas públicas en América Latina . Quito, Ecuador , c1985. 146 p. : LC Card 87-401599 DDC 350/.0092/098 19
HD4010.5 .G47 1986

GOVERNMENT BUSINESS ENTERPRISES - LAW AND LEGISLATION - FRANCE.
La Démocratisation du secteur public . Paris [1984] 87 p. ; LC Card 84-233767
HD4165 .D46 1984

GOVERNMENT BUSINESS ENTERPRISES - LAW AND LEGISLATION - HUNGARY.
Az Állami vállalatok szervezete, vezetése, működése és irányítása /. Budapest , 1985. 262 p. ; ISBN 963-322-140-4 : LC Card 86-202934
HD4160.5 .A78 1985

GOVERNMENT BUSINESS ENTERPRISES - MANAGEMENT.
Ramanadham, Venkata Vemuri, 1920- The Nature of public enterprise /. New York , 1984. 302 p. : ISBN 0-312-86778-6 : LC Card 83-40570 ***NYPL [JLD 86-1037]***

GOVERNMENT BUSINESS ENTERPRISES - MANAGEMENT - EVALUATION.
Kelly de Escobar, Janet. Opciones para la evaluación de las empresas públicas /. Caracas , c1985. 36 p. ; ISBN 980-217-008-9 LC Card 86-201812
HD62.35 .K45 1985

GOVERNMENT BUSINESS ENTERPRISES - MANAGEMENT - EVALUATION - CONGRESSES.
Die Leistungsbewertung in der Industrie . Jena , 1983. 241 p. ; LC Card 84-176546
HD56.25 .L45 1983

GOVERNMENT BUSINESS ENTERPRISES - MEXICO.
Mexican topics . [México, D.F.] [1986] 2 portfolios : LC Card 86-221843 DDC 972.08/3 19
HC135 .M52554 1986

Rey Romay, Benito. La ofensiva empresarial contra la intervención del estado /. México , 1984. 160 p. ; ISBN 968-231-283-3 LC Card 86-151140
HD4013 .R49 1984

GOVERNMENT BUSINESS ENTERPRISES - MEXICO - DIRECTORIES.
Mexico. Secretaría de Energía, Minas e Industria Paraestatal. Directorio del sector energía, minas e industria paraestatal, 1984. [Mexico City] , 1984. 497 p. ; ISBN 968-86000-4-0 LC Card 87-404794 DDC 333.79/0972 19
HD9502.M62 M49 1984

GOVERNMENT BUSINESS ENTERPRISES - NIGERIA.
Mesfin Gabre Michael. Labour-management relations in public enterprises in Africa. Geneva, Switzerland , 1983. 84 p. ; ISBN 92-2-103009-1 (pbk.) LC Card 86-213649 DDC 658.3 s 331/.04135/000096 19
HD6961.A1 I73 no. 60 HD8776.5

GOVERNMENT BUSINESS ENTERPRISES - NIGERIA - CORRUPT PRACTICES.
East-Central State, Nigeria. Government white paper on the report of the Administrative Board of Inquiry into the Nigeria Construction and Furniture Company Limited /. [Enugu, Nigeria] [1976] 19 p. ; LC Card 86-205140
HD9773.N54 N543 1976

GOVERNMENT BUSINESS ENTERPRISES - PANAMA.
Mock Cedeño, Ariel. Las empresas públicas en Panamá . Panamá, Rep. de Panamá , 1986. vi, 89, [5] p. ; LC Card 87-400433 DDC 338.97287 19
HD4043 .M63 1986

GOVERNMENT BUSINESS ENTERPRISES - PERSONNEL MANAGEMENT.
Management of human resources in public enterprises /. New Delhi, India , 1985. vi, 304 p. ; LC Card 87-402995 DDC 354.5409/2/0683 19
HD4293 .M355 1985

GOVERNMENT BUSINESS ENTERPRISES - PERU - MANAGEMENT.
Saulniers, Alfred H., 1945- Beyond management control . Austin , 1985. 22 p. : LC Card 86-622251 DDC 354.8509/2 19
HD4124 .S28 1985

GOVERNMENT BUSINESS ENTERPRISES - PERU - MANAGEMENT - EVALUATION.

Ponce Vega, Luis. El propietario ausente . Lima , 1986. 80 p. ; LC Card 86-221571
HD9524.P44 S565 1986

GOVERNMENT BUSINESS ENTERPRISES - PLANNING.

GOVERNMENT BUSINESS ENTERPRISES - PORTUGAL - FINANCE.
Instituto de Gestão Financeira das Empresas Públicas (Portugal). Comissão Instaladora. Relatório da Comissão Instaladora do Instituto de Gestão Financeira das Empresas Públicas . Lisboa , 1984. 81 p. ; LC Card 84-240299
HD4248 .I57 1984

GOVERNMENT BUSINESS ENTERPRISES - PRICE POLICY - CONGRESSES.
Pricing policy and investment criteria in public enterprises . Ljubljana, Yugoslavia , 1982. 297 p. : ISBN 92-9038-024-1 (pbk.) LC Card 85-242542 DDC 338.7/4 19
HD3842 .P75 1985 *NYPL [JLE 87-547]*

GOVERNMENT BUSINESS ENTERPRISES - RESEARCH - INDIA - CONGRESSES.
Public enterprises in India . Bombay , 1983. xxii, 524 p. ; LC Card 83-905617 DDC 354.5409/2 19
HD4293 .P793 1983 *NYPL [JLD 87-723]*

GOVERNMENT BUSINESS ENTERPRISES - SOVIET UNION - ACCOUNTING.
Obukhov, V. N. (Valeriĭ Nikolaevich) Organizatsiia i provedenie vnutrivedomstvennykh reviziĭ na promyshlennykh predpriiatiiakh /. Moskva , 1978. 75 p. ; LC Card 81-153891
HD4213 .O28 1978

GOVERNMENT BUSINESS ENTERPRISES - SOVIET UNION - MANAGEMENT.
Obukhov, V. N. (Valeriĭ Nikolaevich) Organizatsiia i provedenie vnutrivedomstvennykh reviziĭ na promyshlennykh predpriiatiiakh /. Moskva , 1978. 75 p. ; LC Card 81-153891
HD4213 .O28 1978

GOVERNMENT BUSINESS ENTERPRISES - SPAIN - CONGRESSES.
La Empresa. Madrid , 1962. 348 p. : LC Card 85-108024
HD2326 .E47 1962

GOVERNMENT BUSINESS ENTERPRISES - TANZANIA - STATISTICS.
Analysis of accounts of parastatals, 1966-1977. Dar Es Salaam [1979] 43 p. ; LC Card 81-142522 DDC 354.67809/2 19
HD4348.5 .A52 1979

GOVERNMENT BUSINESS ENTERPRISES - TUNISIA.
Mesfin Gabre Michael. Labour-management relations in public enterprises in Africa. Geneva, Switzerland , 1983. 84 p. ; ISBN 92-2-103009-1 (pbk.) LC Card 86-213649 DDC 658.3 s 331/.04135/000096 19
HD6961.A1 I73 no. 60 HD8776.5

GOVERNMENT BUSINESS ENTERPRISES - YUGOSLAVIA.
Turk, Ivan. Iskazivanje i ocjenjivanje rezultata poslovanja organizacija udruženog rada /. Zagreb , 1982. x, 171 p. ; LC Card 83-110726
HD70.Y8 T87 1982

Government by proxy . Kettl, Donald F. Washington, D.C. , c1988. x, 170 p. ; ISBN 0-87187-429-6 (pbk.) : LC Card 87-13645 DDC 353.009 19
HD3861.U6 K47 1988

GOVERNMENT CENTRALIZATION. see **DECENTRALIZATION IN GOVERNMENT.**

GOVERNMENT, COMPARATIVE. see **COMPARATIVE GOVERNMENT.**

GOVERNMENT CONTRACTS. see **PUBLIC CONTRACTS.**

Government controls and industrial expansion in India /. Baig, Nafees, 1941- Aligarh , 1983. viii, 223 p. ; LC Card 83-907504 DDC 338.954 19
HD3616.I43 B35 1983
NYPL [JLD 86-4330]

GOVERNMENT CORPORATIONS. see **CORPORATIONS, GOVERNMENT.**

GOVERNMENT DECENTRALIZATION. see **DECENTRALIZATION IN GOVERNMENT.**

Government economic agencies of the world : an international directory of governmental organisations concerned with economic development and planning / edited by Alan J. Day ; contributors, Roger East ... [et al.]. Detroit : Gale Research Co., c1985. x, 546 p. ; 25 cm. (A Keesing's reference publication) Includes index. ISBN 0-8103-2104-1 (Gale) LC Card 84-26861 DDC 351.82/025 19
1. Economic development - Directories. 2. Economic policy - Directories. I. Day, Alan J. (Alan John). II. East, Roger. III. Series.
HD87.25 .G68 1985
*NYPL [*R-Econ 86-6573]*

GOVERNMENT ECONOMISTS - UNITED STATES - DIRECTORIES.
Who knows about industries and markets /. Washington, D.C. , c1986. 54 p. ; ISBN 0-934940-33-9 (pbk.) LC Card 86-217691 DDC 338/.06/072073 19
HC102.2 .W48 1986

GOVERNMENT EMPLOYEES. see **CIVIL SERVICE.**

GOVERNMENT EXECUTIVES - JAPAN.
Sano, Shin'ichi, 1947- Kanryō fuyu no jidai /. Tōkyō , 1985. 6, 255 p. ; ISBN 4-8334-1266-7 : LC Card 86-179753
HC462.9 .S2534 1985 <Orien Japan>
*NYPL [*OSM 87-1196]*

GOVERNMENT EXECUTIVES - TRAINING OF - DEVELOPING COUNTRIES.
Powell, Victor. Improving public enterprise performance . Geneva , 1987. x, 226 p. : ISBN 92-2-105563-9 (pbk.) : LC Card 87-166309 DDC 350/.0092/091724 19
HD4420.8 .P68 1987

GOVERNMENT EXPENDITURES. see **EXPENDITURES, PUBLIC.**

Government factories and the origins of British regional policy, 1934-1948 . Loebl, Herbert. Aldershot, Hants, England , Brookfield, Vt., USA , c1987. p. cm. ISBN 0-566-05343-8 LC Card 87-23075 DDC 338.6/2/0941 19
HD4145 .L64 1987

GOVERNMENT, FEDERAL. see **FEDERAL GOVERNMENT.**

Government Finance Research Center, Washington, D. C. Financing a common wealth . Washington, DC , 1985. xx, 304 p. : ISBN 0-89125-090-5 LC Card 84-81918
HD3888 .F5 1985 *NYPL [JLE 86-2519]*

GOVERNMENT FINANCIAL INSTITUTIONS - INDIA.
Ramakrishna Sarma, K. Financial institutions and regional development in India /. Allahabad, India , 1986. xvii, 211 p. ; ISBN 81-85076-04-9 : LC Card 86-902692 DDC 332.2 19
HG3288 .R32 1986

Government-industry relations.
Comparative government-industry relations . Oxford , New York , 1987. xiii, 321 p. ; ISBN 0-19-827493-9 : LC Card 86-28631 DDC 338.9 19
HD3611 .C63 1987

GOVERNMENT INFORMATION - UNITED STATES - HANDBOOKS, MANUALS, ETC.
How to find information about private companies /. Washington, DC , c1987. iii, 149 p. ; ISBN 0-934940-47-9 (pbk.) : LC Card 86-51566 DDC 016.3387/4/0973 19
HG4013.5 .H69 1987

Government Institutes. Cahill, Lawrence B. Environmental audits /. Rockville, Md., U. S.A. , 1987. xi, 656 p. : ISBN 0-86587-720-3 (soft) LC Card 87-404450 DDC 658.4/08 19
HC110.E5 C26 1987

GOVERNMENT INVESTIGATIONS. see **GOVERNMENTAL INVESTIGATIONS.**

GOVERNMENT LENDING - CANADA - CASE STUDIES.
Borins, Sandford F., 1949- Investments in failure . Toronto , New York , c1986. x, 175 p. ; ISBN 0-458-80340-5 (pbk.) : LC Card 87-142330 DDC 354.7109/2 19
HD4005 .B67 1986

GOVERNMENT LENDING - INDIA.

GOVERNMENT LENDING - UNITED STATES.
Bosworth, Barry, 1942- The economics of federal credit programs /. Washington, D.C. , c1987. xii, 214 p. : ISBN 0-8157-1038-0 : LC Card 85-48205 DDC 336.3/44/0973 19
HJ8119 .B67 1987

Kettl, Donald F. Government by proxy . Washington, D.C. , c1988. x, 170 p. ; ISBN 0-87187-429-6 (pbk.) : LC Card 87-13645 DDC 353.009 19
HD3861.U6 K47 1988

President's Private Sector Survey on Cost Control (U. S.) President's private sector survey on cost control . Washington, D.C. , 1983. viii, 320 p. ; *NYPL [JLF 86-727]*

GOVERNMENT, LOCAL. see **LOCAL GOVERNMENT.**

Government media and the public sector : based on seminar held under the auspices of Parliamentary Forum on Public Sector ... / edited by M.R. Virmani. New Delhi : Centre for Public Sector Studies, 1983. 270 p. ; 22 cm. "Seminar on 'Government Media and the Public Sector' held on March 24-25, 1983"--P. 19. Includes index. LC Card 83-907479 DDC 302.3/24/0954 19
1. Mass media and business - India - Congresses. 2. Government business enterprises - India - Congresses. I. Virmani, M. R. II. Centre for Public Sector Studies (India). III. Parliamentary Forum on Public Sector (India). IV. Seminar on "Government Media and the Public Sector" (1983 : New Delhi, India).
HD59 .G62 1983 *NYPL [JLD 86-3767]*

GOVERNMENT MONOPOLIES.
Diumulen, I. I. (Ippolit Ippolitovich) Sovremennyĭ tarifnyĭ i netarifnyĭ protektsionizm . Moskva , 1975. 277 p. ; LC Card 82-191746
HF1713 .D62 1975

GOVERNMENT MONOPOLIES - GERMANY (WEST) - CASE STUDIES.
Germany (West). Monopolkommission. Die Rolle der Deutschen Bundespost im Fernmeldewesen /. Baden-Baden , 1981. 110 p. ; ISBN 3-7890-0675-0(pbk.) LC Card 81-130348 DDC 383/.4943 19
HE8155 .R64 1981 *NYPL [JLE 87-312]*

GOVERNMENT, MUNICIPAL. see **MUNICIPAL GOVERNMENT.**

The government of business /. Thomas, R. E. (Raymond Elliott) Oxford, UK , Atlantic Highlands, NJ, USA , 1987. viii, 277 p. : ISBN 0-86003-548-4 LC Card 87-12647 DDC 338.0941 19
HD70.G7 T48 1987

GOVERNMENT-OWNED CORPORATIONS. see **CORPORATIONS, GOVERNMENT.**

GOVERNMENT OWNERSHIP - ADDRESSES, ESSAYS, LECTURES.
The Private exercise of public functions /. Port Washington, N.Y. , 1985. 251 p. ; ISBN 0-8046-9368-4 LC Card 84-9254 DDC 361.6/1 19
H97 .P76 1985 *NYPL [JLE 86-2611]*

GOVERNMENT OWNERSHIP - ASIA.
Natsionalizatsiia i gossektor v razvivaiushchikhsia stranakh . Moskva , 1986. 210 p. ; LC Card 87-165820
HD4276 .N38 1986

GOVERNMENT OWNERSHIP - AUSTRIA.
Tieber, Herbert. Verstaatliche Industrie . Wien , c1983. 91 p. : LC Card 84-169053
HD4155 .T54 1983

GOVERNMENT OWNERSHIP - BULGARIA.
Kostov, Ivan Dimitrov. Obshtestvenata sobstvenost pri sotsializma /. Sofiia , 1985. 111 p. ; LC Card 86-122395
HD4263 .K67 1985

GOVERNMENT OWNERSHIP - CZECHOSLOVAKIA - HISTORY.
Murashko, G. P. (Galina Pavlovna) Politicheskaia bor'ba v Chekhoslovakii v 1944-1948 gg. i natsionalizatsiia sredstv proizvodstva /. Moskva , 1986. 326, [2] p. ; LC Card 86-202951
HC270.28 .M87 1986

GOVERNMENT OWNERSHIP - DEVELOPING COUNTRIES.
Mattsson, Jan. Nationella övertaganden av

utländska dotterbolag . Stockholm [1982] 213 p. : ISBN 91-1-827592-3 LC Card 83-122459
HD2932 .M38 1982

Nat͡sionalizat͡sii͡a i gossektor v razvivai͡ushchikhsi͡a stranakh . Moskva , 1986. 210 p. ; LC Card 87-165820
HD4276 .N38 1986

Rodman, Kenneth Aaron. Sanctity versus sovereignty . New York , 1988. p. cm. ISBN 0-231-06448-9 LC Card 87-24970 DDC 332.6/7373/01724 19
HG5993 .R63 1988

GOVERNMENT OWNERSHIP - FRANCE.
Paillet, Marc. Le grand inventaire . Paris , c1985. 176 p. ; ISBN 2-207-23172-0 : LC Card 86-127029 DDC 338.944 19
HD4168 .P35 1985 ***NYPL [JLE 87-1232]***

GOVERNMENT OWNERSHIP - GERMANY - HISTORY - 20TH CENTURY.
Ambrosius, Gerold. Die öffentliche Wirtschaft in der Weimarer Republik . Baden-Baden , 1984. 306 p. ; ISBN 3-7890-0912-1 LC Card 84-230508
HD4175 .A626 1984

GOVERNMENT OWNERSHIP - GERMANY, WEST.
Wirtschaftsdemokratie gegen Wirtschaftskrise . Hamburg , 1986. 177 p. : ISBN 3-87975-310-5 LC Card 86-193914
HD4175 .W54 1986

GOVERNMENT OWNERSHIP - GREAT BRITAIN.
Curwen, Peter J. Public enterprise . Brighton, Sussex , 1986. xvii, 318 p. : ISBN 0-312-65435-9 : LC Card 85-26234 DDC 354.4109/2 19
HD4145 .C87 1986 ***NYPL [JLD 86-1636]***

GOVERNMENT OWNERSHIP - OCEANIA.
Feinstein, Charles, 1954- Privatization possibilities among Pacific island countries /. Honolulu, Hawaii, USA , 1986. iv, 48 p. ; ISBN 0-86638-084-1 LC Card 86-24012 DDC 338.99 19
HD4415.6 .F45 1986

GOVERNMENT OWNERSHIP - POLAND.
Gołębiowski, Jerzy. Sektor państwowy w gospodarce Polski międzywojennej /. Warszawa , 1985. 366 p. ; ISBN 83-01-06292-4 : LC Card 86-108406
HD4215.7 .G65 1985

GOVERNMENT OWNERSHIP - POLAND - WESTERN AND NORTHERN TERRITORIES - HISTORY.
Magierska, Anna. Przywrócić Polsce . Warszawa , 1986. 467 p. ; ISBN 83-01-06606-7 : LC Card 86-228089
HC340.3.Z7 W4765 1986

GOVERNMENT OWNERSHIP - SOVIET UNION.
Napravlenii͡a i formy realizat͡sii obshchenarodnoĭ sobstvennosti /. Moskva , 1986. 171 p. ; LC Card 87-163156
HD4213 .N36 1986

Obobshchestvlenie i ėkonomicheskie interesy v sotsialisticheskom obshchestve /. Moskva , 1983. 127 p. ; LC Card 84-204638
HD3856.R9 O26 1983

GOVERNMENT OWNERSHIP - SPAIN - CATALONIA.
Pérez Baró, Albert. Trenta mesos de col·lectivisme a Catalunya, cinquanta anys després /. Barcelona , 1986. 283 p. : ISBN 84-297-2412-5 LC Card 86-186185
HD4245.C3 P45 1986

GOVERNMENT OWNERSHIP - UNITED STATES.
Financing a common wealth . Washington, DC , 1985. xx, 304 p. : ISBN 0-89125-090-5 LC Card 84-81918
HD3888 .F5 1985 ***NYPL [JLE 86-2519]***

GOVERNMENT OWNERSHIP - VIETNAM - HISTORY.
Glazunov, E. P. Preobrazovanie chastnoĭ promyshlennosti i torgovli vo V'etname /. Moskva , 1981. 213, [1] p. ; LC Card 82-112489
HC444 .G58 1981

GOVERNMENT OWNSHIP - SPAIN.
Ekaizer, Ernesto, 1949- José María Ruiz Mateos, el ultimo magnate /. Esplugues de Llobregat, Barcelona , 1985. 833 p., [16] p. of plates : ISBN 84-01-33291-5 LC Card 86-122394 DDC 332.1/6 B 19
HG4216.R85 E38 1985
NYPL [JFD 86-6856]

Government policy towards FDI and the reaction of foreign investors in DCs /. Ahn, Doo-Soon. Bochum [1985] 23, 33 leaves ; LC Card 86-219920 DDC 332.6/73225195 19
HG5780.5.A3 A34 1985

GOVERNMENT PRODUCTIVITY - GREAT BRITAIN.
Levitt, M. S., 1938- The growth and efficiency of public spending /. Cambridge [Cambridgeshire] , New York , 1987. xiv, 201 p. : ISBN 0-521-34621-5 (U. S.) LC Card 87-11636 DDC 339.5/22/0941 19
HJ7764 .L475 1987

GOVERNMENT PRODUCTIVITY - UNITED STATES.
Silkman, Richard H. Subsidizing inefficiency . New York , 1985. xviii, 101 p.: ISBN 0-03-000662-7 (alk. paper) : LC Card 84-26628 DDC 336.1/85 19
HJ275 .S53 1985 ***NYPL [JLE 85-2261]***

GOVERNMENT PURCHASING - INDIA - GUJARAT - HISTORY.
Reddy, K. N. (Kaipa Narayana), 1936- Central government expenditure . New Delhi , 1984. xvi, 175 p. ; LC Card 84-901866 DDC 336.3/9/0954 19
HJ2157 .R43 1984 ***NYPL [JLD 87-66]***

GOVERNMENT PURCHASING OF REAL PROPERTY - DEVELOPING COUNTRIES.
Kitay, Michael G. Land acquisition in developing countries . Boston , c1985. xx, 199 p. ; ISBN 0-89946-192-1 LC Card 85-7225 DDC 333.1/3/091724 19
HD1131 .K58 1985 ***NYPL [JLE 86-3827]***

GOVERNMENT PURCHASING - UNITED STATES.
Penoyar, William F. Fedspeak . Arnold, Md. , c1985. v, 178 p. : ISBN 0-9615112-2-2 (pbk.) : LC Card 85-90360 DDC 353.0071/2 19
JK1673 .P46 1985 ***NYPL [JLD 87-568]***

GOVERNMENT PURCHASING - UNITED STATES - DIRECTORIES.
Minority business advisor. [Great Falls, Mont.] (1101 15th St. N., Great Falls 59401) [c1985- 1 v. (loose-leaf) : LC Card 86-200612 DDC 338.973 19
HD2346.U5 M55 1985

Government regulation of business . Chamber of Commerce of the United States of America. Council on Trends and Perspective. Washington, D.C. , c1979. x, 108 p. ; ISBN 0-89834-018-7(pbk.) : LC Card 79-91604 DDC 338.973
HD3616.U46 C44 1979
NYPL [JLE 80-2446]

GOVERNMENT REGULATION OF COMMERCE. see COMMERCIAL POLICY; INDUSTRIAL LAWS AND LEGISLATION; INDUSTRY AND STATE; INTERSTATE COMMERCE; TRADE REGULATION.

Government regulation of financial management of private corporate sector in India /. Kulshreshtha, V. D. (Visheshwar Dayal), 1922- Bombay , 1986. xxiv, 306 p. ; LC Card 87-902600
HG4241 .K85 1986

GOVERNMENT REGULATION OF RAILROADS. see INTERSTATE COMMERCE.

GOVERNMENT SECURITIES.
Gheysens, Lieven. International diversification through the government bond market . [Leuven] , 1977. 188 leaves ; LC Card 85-186317 DDC 332.63/232 19
HG4715 .G44 1977
NYPL [JLM 86-1310 nr.24]

GOVERNMENT SECURITIES - INDIA.
Structure and management of the gilt-edged securities market in India. New Delhi , 1983. v, 186 p. : LC Card 84-901424 DDC 332.63/2044 19
HG5735 .S77 1983 ***NYPL [JLD 87-871]***

GOVERNMENT SECURITIES - SPAIN.
Sala Garrido, Ramón. El mercado de deuda pública /. [Valencia] [1984] 163 p. : ISBN 84-505-0146-6 LC Card 86-213799
HJ8739 .S25 1984

GOVERNMENT SECURITIES - UNITED STATES - HANDBOOKS, MANUALS, ETC.
Stigum, Marcia L. After the trade . Homewood, Ill. , c1988. xvii, 303 p. : ISBN 0-87094-937-3 LC Card 87-50773 DDC 332.63/232/0973 19
HG4941 .S75 1988

Government spending and the nonprofit sector in [name of community]. Washington, D.C. : Urban Institute, <c1984-c1985 > v. <1-11 > ; 28 cm. (v. <2, 4, 5, 8, 9, 11 > : An Urban Institute research report) "An Urban Institute paperback"--V. <1, 3, 6, 10 > At head of title: The Nonprofit Sector Project. CONTENTS. - [v. 1] Atlanta/Fulton County -- [v. 2] Boise/Ada County, Idaho -- [v. 3] Cook County/Chicago -- [v. 4] Dallas -- [v. 5] Minneapolis/Hennepin County, Minnesota -- [v. 6] Pittsburgh/Allegheny County -- [v. 7] San Francisco -- [v. 8] St. Paul/Ramsey County, Minnesota -- [v. 9] Two Arizona communities: Phoenix/Maricopa County and Pinal County -- [v. 10] Two Michigan communities: Flint/Genesee County and Tuscola County -- [v. 11] Two Mississippi communities: Jackson/Hinds County and Vicksburg/Warren County. LC Card 87-168173 DDC 339.5/22/0973 19
1. Government spending policy - United States - Collected works. 2. Corporations, Nonprofit - United States - Finance - Collected works. 3. Social service - United States - Finance - Collected works. I. Urban Institute. II. Nonprofit Sector Project (Urban Institute). III. Series.
HJ2052 .G67 1984

GOVERNMENT SPENDING POLICY - ALASKA.
Goldsmith, Oliver Scott. How state spending reductions affect economic activity /. Fairbanks [1986] 40, 10 p. : LC Card 86-622972 DDC 330.9798/05 19
HJ7553 .G64 1986

GOVERNMENT SPENDING POLICY - BELGIUM.
Peffer, Michel, 1948- L'Etat anthropophage /. Bruxelles , c1982. 279 p. ; ISBN 2-87005-164-5 LC Card 84-139080
HJ1197 .P44 1982

GOVERNMENT SPENDING POLICY - CANADA.
Guide to the policy & expenditure management system. [Ottawa] , c1980. 33, 33 p. ; ISBN 0-662-51109-3 (pbk.) LC Card 81-116818
HJ7660 .G85 1980

GOVERNMENT SPENDING POLICY - DEVELOPING COUNTRIES.
Jimenez, Emmanuel, 1952- Pricing policy in the social sectors . Baltimore , 1987. v, 170 p. ; ISBN 0-8018-3501-1 : LC Card 86-27590 DDC 338.4/33621/091724 19
HJ7469 .J56 1987

GOVERNMENT SPENDING POLICY - ENGLAND - BRIGHTON (EAST SUSSEX)
Brighton on the rocks . Brighton [1983?] 192 p. : ISBN 0-904733-00-4 (pbk.) : LC Card 84-173777 DDC 336.3/9/0942256 19
HJ9438.B75 B75 1983 ***NYPL [JLD 87-104]***

GOVERNMENT SPENDING POLICY - EUROPE.
Meadows, W. J. The response of local authorities to central government incitement to reduce expenditure . Strasbourg , 1986. 33 p. ; LC Card 87-135687 DDC 336.3/9/094 19
HJ9415 .M43 1986

GOVERNMENT SPENDING POLICY - GERMANY (WEST) - ECONOMETRIC MODELS.
Busch, Wilfried, 1948- Staatsausgaben, Produktion und Beschäftigung . Frankfurt am Main , New York , c1984. viii, 304 p. : ISBN 3-8204-5352-0 LC Card 85-199154
HJ7792 .B87 1984

GOVERNMENT SPENDING POLICY - GREAT BRITAIN.
Levitt, M. S., 1938- The growth and efficiency of public spending /. Cambridge [Cambridgeshire] , New York , 1987. xiv, 201 p. : ISBN 0-521-34621-5 (U. S.) LC Card 87-11636 DDC 339.5/22/0941 19
HJ7764 .L475 1987

Mullard, Maurice, 1946- The politics of public

expenditure /. London , New York , c1987. 220 p. : ISBN 0-7099-4674-0 : LC Card 87-6777 DDC 336.3/9/0941 19
HJ7764 .M85 1987

GOVERNMENT SPENDING POLICY - GREAT BRITAIN - CONGRESSES.
New priorities in public spending /. Brookfield, VT , 1987. 129 p. ; ISBN 0-566-05386-1 : LC Card 86-22946 DDC 336.3/9/0941 19
HJ7764 .N49 1987

GOVERNMENT SPENDING POLICY - ITALY - CONGRESSES.
La Politica di bilancio in condizioni di stress fiscale . Milano, Italy , c1986. 377 p. ; LC Card 87-134343
HJ2119 .P65 1986

GOVERNMENT SPENDING POLICY - SWEDEN.
Hadenius, Axel, 1945- A crisis of the welfare state? . Stockholm, Sweden , c1986. 151 p. : ISBN 91-22-00821-7 (pbk.) : LC Card 87-127805 DDC 339.5/22/09485 19
HJ2837 .H34 1986

GOVERNMENT SPENDING POLICY - SWITZERLAND.
Grossen, Andreas. Bürger, Parlament und Steuern . Bern , c1986. vi, 134 p. : ISBN 3-7165-0510-2 LC Card 86-187534
HJ2145 .G76 1986

GOVERNMENT SPENDING POLICY - UNITED STATES.
Economic choices 1987 /. Washington, D.C. , 1986. xii, 126 p. ; ISBN 0-8157-1040-2 LC Card 85-48278 ***NYPL [JLE 86-2737]***

Manchester, Paul B. Are we on the road to a balanced budget? . Washington , 1986. v, 18 p. : LC Card 86-603373 DDC 353.0072/2 19
HJ2052 .M365 1986

Miller, James C., III. Spending and deficits /. Washington, D.C. , c1987. 18 p. ; ISBN 0-8447-1382-1 (pbk.) LC Card 87-134671 DDC 339.5/23/0973 19
HJ2052 .M54 1987

Reducing the federal deficit . Washington, D.C. , 1982. 1 v. (various pagings) : ***NYPL [JLF 86-1219]***

Stockman, David Alan, 1946- The triumph of politics . New York , c1986. 422 p. : ISBN 0-06-015560-4 : LC Card 85-45541 DDC 338.973 19
HC106.8 .S75 1986 ***NYPL [JLE 86-2647]***

Stockman, David Alan, 1946- The triumph of politics . Boston, Mass. , 1987, c1986. xxxiii, 654 p. (large print) ; ISBN 0-8161-4231-9 (lg. print) : LC Card 86-22950 DDC 338.973 19
HC106.8 .S75 1986b

Taxation and the deficit economy . San Francisco, Calif. , c1986. xxvii, 554 p. : ISBN 0-936488-13-1 : LC Card 85-63549 DDC 339.5/2/0973 19
HJ257.2 .T385 1986 ***NYPL [JLE 86-4136]***

GOVERNMENT SPENDING POLICY - UNITED STATES - COLLECTED WORKS.
Government spending and the nonprofit sector in [name of community]. Washington, D.C. , <c1984-c1985. v. <1-11 > ; LC Card 87-168173 DDC 339.5/22/0973 19
HJ2052 .G67 1984

GOVERNMENT SPENDING POLICY - UNITED STATES - ECONOMETRIC MODELS.
Berry, William Dale. Understanding United States government growth . New York , 1987. xiv, 212 p. : ISBN 0-275-92509-9 (alk. paper) : LC Card 87-11818 DDC 336.73 19
HJ257.2 .B47 1987

GOVERNMENT TRANSFER PAYMENTS. see **TRANSFER PAYMENTS.**

Government views and decisions on the Report of the Panel on the Allocation of Stalls in the Three Temporary Markets in Jos . Plateau State (Nigeria) Jos [Nigeria] [1976?] 9 p. ; LC Card 87-401792 DDC 381/.18/096695 19
HF5475.N52 J66 1976

Government white paper on the Report of the Administrative Board of Inquiry into the Enugu Market Authority /. Anambra State, Nigeria. Enugu , 1976. 25 p. ; LC Card 86-204970
HF5475.N52 E373 1976

Government white paper on the report of the Administrative Board of Inquiry into the Nigeria Construction and Furniture Company Limited /. East-Central State, Nigeria. [Enugu, Nigeria] [1976] 19 p. ; LC Card 86-205140
HD9773.N54 N543 1976

Government white paper on the report of the Administrative Board of Inquiry on Ministry of Works /. Anambra State, Nigeria. [Enugu, Nigeria] [1976?] 100 p. ; LC Card 86-205027 DDC 354.669/4 19
HD4365.5.Z8 E373 1976

Government without taxation /. Anderson, Hugold. Warwick, R.I. , c1987. 52 p. ; LC Card 87-133116 DDC 336.2/00973 19
HJ2381 .A76 1987

GOVERNMENTAL INVESTIGATIONS - BARBADOS.
Barbados. Duffus Commission of Enquiry. Report /. [Bridgetown, Barbados] [1978] vi, 118, 270 p. : LC Card 82-243628 DDC 354.7298/10072 19
HJ2073.B37 B37 1978 ***NYPL [JLG 86-221]***

GOVERNMENTAL INVESTIGATIONS - COLOMBIA.
Colombia. Congreso. Cámara de Representantes. Comisión Nombrada para Estudiar el Conflicto Surgido entre la United Fruit Company y la Cooperativa Bananera Colombiana. Informe de la Comisión Nombrada para Estudiar el Conflicto Surgido entre la United Fruit Company y la Cooperativa Bananera Colombiana. Bogotá , 1930. 32 p. ; LC Card 83-189629
HD9259.B3 C728 1930

GOVERNMENTAL INVESTIGATIONS - NIGERIA - EAST-CENTRAL STATE.
Anambra State, Nigeria. Government white paper on the Report of the Administrative Board of Inquiry into the Enugu Market Authority /. Enugu , 1976. 25 p. ; LC Card 86-204970
HF5475.N52 E373 1976

GOVERNMENTAL INVESTIGATIONS - URUGUAY.
Uruguay. Asemblea General. Cámara de Representantes. Investigación en la Administración, Nacional de Combustibles, Alcohol y Portland /. [Montevideo] , 1935. 352 p. ; LC Card 85-105071
HD9574.U72 U78 1935

Govil, Rishi Kumar, 1933- Agriculture planning and social justice in India / by R.K. Govil, B.B. Tripathi. 1st ed. Allahabad : Kitab Mahal : Selling agents, Kitab Mahal Agencies, 1986. vii, 214 p. ; 23 cm. Study based on 1951-1984 data. Bibliography: p. [213]-214. Includes index. LC Card 86-902616 DDC 338.1/854 19
1. Agriculture and state - India. 2. Social justice. I. Tripathi, B. B. II. Title.
HD2073 .G68 1986

Govinda Rao, M. Political economy of tax and expenditure determination : a case study of four Indian states / M. Govinda Rao. New Delhi : Allied, 1981. vii, 212 p. ; 22 cm. Revision of the author's thesis (Ph.D.--Sambalpur University, 1977) Includes index. Bibliography: p. [203]-208. LC Card 81-905062 DDC 336.54 19
1. Finance, Public - India - Case studies. 2. Intergovernmental fiscal relations - India - Case studies. I. Title.
HJ1337 .G68 1981 ***NYPL [JLD 86-2603]***

Govoni, Norman A. P. Promotional management . Englewood Cliffs, N.J. , c1988. xi, 305 p. : ISBN 0-13-731035-8 (pbk.) LC Card 87-12041 DDC 658.8 19
HF5415 .P727 1988

Gow, Kay F. Ricks, Betty R. Business communication . New York , c1987. xiii, 479 p. : ISBN 0-471-81824-0 LC Card 86-26747 DDC 651.7 19
HF5718 .R53 1987

Gower Conferences Ltd. Bidding for projects financed by international lending agencies /. Aldershot, Hants. , c1982. vii, 345 p. : ISBN 0-566-03033-0 LC Card 82-210482 DDC 332.1/53 19
HD2365 .B52 1982 ***NYPL [JLG 85-120]***

Gower executive report.
Hall, John, 1946- Reducing industrial oil costs /. Aldershot, Hants England , Brookfield, Vt., U. S.A. , c1987. xvii, 118 p. : ISBN 0-291-39740-9 (U. S.) : LC Card 86-29511 DDC 338.2/3 19
HD9560.4 .H35 1987

The Gower handbook of management / edited by Dennis Lock and Nigel Farrow. 2nd ed. Aldershot, Hants, England ; Brookfield, Vt., U. S.A. : Gower Pub. Co., 1987. p. cm. Includes index. ISBN 0-566-02662-7 : LC Card 87-144 DDC 658 19
1. Management. I. Lock, Dennis. II. Farrow, Nigel. III. Gower Publishing Company.
HD31 .G684 1987

Gower Publishing Company. The Gower handbook of management /. Aldershot, Hants, England , Brookfield, Vt., U. S.A. , 1987. p. cm. ISBN 0-566-02662-7 : LC Card 87-144 DDC 658 19
HD31 .G684 1987

Gower studies in finance and investment .
(4) Stonham, Paul. Global stock market reforms /. Aldershot, Hants, England , Brookfield, Vt., USA , c1987. x, 157 p. ; ISBN 0-566-00821-1 : LC Card 87-276 DDC 332.64/2 19
HG4551 .S83 1987

Goyaz, Brazil (State) see **Goiás, Brazil (State)**

Gozo, K. M.
Crise et pauvreté en Côte d'Ivoire : les effets de la récession actuelle sur les couches les plus défavorisés de la population / K.M. Gozo. Addis Abéba : Programme des emplois et des compétences techniques pour l'Afrique, c1983. iv, 84 p. ; 29 cm. (Crise et pauvreté en Afrique : les effets de la réccession [sic] sur les économies africaines) At head of title: Bureau international du travail. "Le cas de la Côte d'Ivoire"--Cover. Includes bibliographical references. ISBN 92-2-203648-4 LC Card 85-981192
1. Ivory Coast - Economic conditions - 1960-. 2. Labor supply - Ivory Coast. I. International Labour Office. II. Series: Crise et pauvreté en Afrique. III. Title.
HC1025 .G69 1983

Effets de la récession sur l'économie togolaise : évolution récente et perspectives de croissance économique et de l'emploi à moyen terme / K.M. Gozo. Addis Abéba : Bureau international du travail, Programme des emplois et des compétences techniques pour l'Afrique, 1985. 50, 24 p. ; 29 cm. (Crise et pauvreté en Afrique : les effets de la récession sur les écomonies africaines) "Contribution à une mission globale d'emploi du BIT/PECTA au Togo du 19 février au 17 mars 1984." At head of title: Organisation internationale du travail. "Le cas du Togo"--Cover. Includes bibliographical references. ISBN 92-2-205044-4 LC Card 86-159834 DDC 330.966/8104 19
1. Togo - Economic conditions. 2. Togo - Foreign economic relations. I. Series: Crise et pauvreté en Afrique. II. Title.
HC1015 .G69 1985

Le secteur non structuré d'Antananarivo : analyse typologique, facteurs de blocage et perspectives de promotion des activités du bois, construction métallique, garages et réparations / K.M. Gozo. Addis-Abéba : Bureau international du travail, Programme des emplois et des compétences techniques pour l'Afrique, c1985. vi, 175 p. : ill. ; 30 cm. "Rapport d'une enquête réalisée pour le compte du Gouvernement malgache." At head of title: Organisation internationale du travail. Bibliography: p. 155. LC Card 85-981181
1. Informal sector (Economics) - Madagascar - Antananarivo. 2. Small business - Madagascar - Antananarivo. I. Jobs and Skills Programme for Africa. II. Title.
HD2346.M282 A574 1985

Le secteur non structuré de Kinshasa : caractéristiques des entreprises et de la main d'oeuvre : potentialités d'emploi et de distribution de revenu / M.K. [i.e. K.M.] Gozo. Addis Abéba : Bureau international du travail, Programme des emplois et des compétences techniques pour l'Afrique, c1985. iii, 64, [8] p. : ill. ; 29 cm. "Contribution à une mission sectorielle d'emploi au Zaïre." At head of title: Organisation internationale du travail. Includes bibliographical references. ISBN 92-2-100538-0 LC Card 85-981182
1. Informal sector (Economics) - Zaire - Kinshasa. 2. Labor supply - Zaire - Kinshasa. 3. Income distribution - Zaire - Kinshasa. I. Jobs and Skills

Programme for Africa. II. Title.
HD2346.Z27 K54 1985

Grab, Alexander I., 1946- La politica del pane : le riforme annonarie in Lombardia nell'età teresiana e giuseppina / Alexander I. Grab. Milano, Italy : F. Angeli, c1986. 180 p. ; 22 cm. (Studi e ricerche storiche. 69) Includes bibliographical references. LC Card 86-168239
1. Food supply - Government policy - Italy - Lombardy - History - 18th century. 2. Food prices - Government policy - Italy - Lombardy - History - 18th century. 3. Lombardy (Italy) - History - Austrian rule, 1714-1796. I. Title.
HD9015.I85 L664 1986

Grabb, John R., 1915- A history of the Chillicothe and other Ross County, Ohio, post offices, 1799-1987 / by John R. Grabb. Chillicothe, Ohio (206 Caldwell St., Chillicothe 45601) : J.R. Grabb, c1987. iv, 76 p. : ill. ; 28 cm. Bibliography: p. 62. Includes index. LC Card 87-80919 DDC 383/.4977182 19
1. Postal service - Ohio - Chillicothe - History. 2. Postal service - Ohio - Ross County - History. I. Title.
HE6376.C45 G73 1987

Grabbe, J. Orlin. International financial markets / J. Orlin Grabbe. New York : Elsevier, c1986. xi, 347 p. : ill. ; 26 cm. Includes index. Bibliography: p. [335]-340. ISBN 0-444-01032-7 LC Card 85-32545 DDC 332.4/5 19
1. Euro-bond market. 2. Euro-dollar market. 3. Currency question - Europe. I. Title.
HG3851 .G64 1986 ***NYPL [JLF 87-82]***

Grabenhorst, Antje. Versicherungen in der Altbauerneuerung /. Berlin , c1985. 83 p. ; ISBN 3-433-02219-4 LC Card 86-104351
HG9986.4.G3 V47 1985

Grace . Clayton, Lawrence A. Ottawa, Ill. , c1985. xiii, 403 p., [32] p. of plates : ISBN 0-915463-25-3 LC Card 85-14856 DDC 338.8/8885 19
HD9505.P4 C43 1986 ***NYPL [JLE 86-3892]***

Grad, Modesta. Funkcjonowanie rynku usług w Polsce /. Wrocław , 1986. 176 p. ; ISBN 83-7011-034-7 : LC Card 87-169457
HB9 .B7522 nr. 355 HD9986.P7

GRADE LABELING. see **LABELS.**

GRADE SEPARATION (HIGHWAY ENGINEERING) see **ROADS - INTERCHANGES AND INTERSECTIONS.**

Gradin, Victor. Bulhões, Octávio Gouveia de. Desdobramentos inflacionários. [Salvador] [1984] 43 p. : LC Card 86-861354 DDC 332.4/1/0981 19
HG835 .B85 1984

Gradowski, Lech.
Ceny detaliczne 1971-1985 /. Warszawa , 1985. 160 p. ; LC Card 86-196060
HB235.P6 C45 1985

Spis ludności i mieszkań metodą reprezentacyjną z dnia 6 XII 1984 r. . Warszawa , 1985. xx, 93 p., [2] p. of plates : LC Card 86-176185
HD7345.7.A3 S65 1985

Graduate employment and higher education in West Bengal /. Bose, P. K. Paris , New Delhi , 1983. vi, 288, [1] p. : ISBN 0-85226-078-4 (pbk.) LC Card 83-163900 DDC 331.11/423 19
HD6278.I52 W473 1983
NYPL [JLD 86-2269]

Graduate Institute of International Studies, Geneva. see **Geneva. Graduate Institute of International Studies.**

Graduate Institute of International Studies (Geneva, Switzerland)
Pfeiffer, Gabrielle. Mountains of butter, lakes of milk . Genève , 1986. 78, [4] p. : LC Card 87-109400 DDC 382/.417 19
HD9275.A2 P48 1986

Yang, Yuming. L'industrie horlogère suisse et ses relations avec la Chine de 1949 à 1982 /. Geneve , 1984. 186 leaves : LC Card 85-104853
HD9999.C583 S99 1984

Graduate Management Admission Council.
The Official guide for GMAT review /. Princeton, N.J. , c1986. 372 p. : ISBN 0-446-38435-6 (pbk.) : LC Card 86-229958 DDC 650/.076 19
HF1118 .O33 1986

The Official guide to MBA programs /. [Los Angeles, Calif.] , Princeton, N.J. , c1986. 603 p. ; ISBN 0-446-38437-2 (pbk.) : LC Card 87-102516 DDC 658/.007/1173 19
HF1131 .O359 1986

GRADUATE MANAGEMENT ADMISSION TEST.
Jaffe, Eugene D. How to prepare for the graduate management admission test GMAT /. New York , c1987. x, 541 p. : ISBN 0-8120-3882-7 (pbk.) LC Card 87-18619 DDC 650/.076 19
HD30.413 .J33 1987

GRADUATE MANAGEMENT ADMISSION TEST - STUDY GUIDES.
The Official guide for GMAT review /. Princeton, N.J. , c1986. 372 p. : ISBN 0-446-38435-6 (pbk.) : LC Card 86-229958 DDC 650/.076 19
HF1118 .O33 1986

Graduate School, USDA. Neyman, Jerzy, 1894- Lectures and conferences on mathematical statistics and probability. Washington, 1952. vii, 274 p. LC Card Agr52-278 DDC 311.2
HA29 .N48 1952

GRADUATE STUDENTS - EMPLOYMENT - UNITED STATES.
Groneman, Carol. [Corporate Ph. D.] Corporate PhD . New York, N.Y., U. S.A. , 1987, c1985. xx, 156 p. ; ISBN 0-14-010123-3 (pbk.) LC Card 86-30654 DDC 658.4/09 19
HD38.25.U6 G76 1987

GRADUATE WORK. see **UNIVERSITIES AND COLLEGES - GRADUATE WORK.**

GRADUATION (STATISTICS)
London, Dick, 1943- Graduation, the revision of estimates /. Winsted, Conn. , c1985. viii, 183 p. : ISBN 0-936031-00-X (pbk.) : LC Card 85-23001 DDC 519.5 19
HG8782 .L56 1985 ***NYPL [JLE 86-3272]***

Graduation, the revision of estimates /. London, Dick, 1943- Winsted, Conn. , c1985. viii, 183 p. : ISBN 0-936031-00-X (pbk.) : LC Card 85-23001 DDC 519.5 19
HG8782 .L56 1985 ***NYPL [JLE 86-3272]***

Graf, Oskar. So schaffen wir! . [Germany , 193-?] (München : F. Bruckmann) [51] leaves : LC Card 86-213082
HD9539.C7 G57 1930z

Gräf, Peter. Zur Raumrelevanz infrastruktureller Massnahmen : kleinräumliche Struktur- und Prozessanalyse im Landkreis Miesbach : ein Beitrag zur sozialgeographischen Infrastrukturforschung / von Peter Gräf. Kallmünz/Regensburg : M. Lassleben, 1978. xxxvii, 259 p., [9] leaves of plates (7 folded) : ill., maps (some col.) ; 30 cm. (Münchner Studien zur Sozial- und Wirtschaftsgeographie. Bd. 18) Summary in English, French, German, and Russian. Bibliography: p. xi-xxix. ISBN 3-7847-6518-1 LC Card 85-205909
1. Infrastructure (Economics) - Germany (West) - Miesbach. 2. Central places - Germany (West) - Miesbach. 3. Miesbach (Germany : Landkreis) - Economic conditions. I. Title. II. Series.
HC281 .M8 Bd. 18 HC288.M53

Grafički zavod Hrvatske. Review of exporters and importers of Yugoslavia . Zagreb , 1965. ca. 650 p. : LC Card 84-149403
HF3732.3 .R46 1965

GRAFT (IN POLITICS) see **CORRUPTION (IN POLITICS)**

Graham and Dodd's security analysis. Graham, Benjamin, 1894- [Security analysis.] New York , c1988. xiii, 656 p. : ISBN 0-07-013235-6 : LC Card 87-19990 DDC 332.63/2 19
HG4529 .G7 1988

Graham, Benjamin, 1894-
[Security analysis]
Graham and Dodd's security analysis. 5th ed. / Sidney Cottle, Roger F. Murray, Frank E. Block ; with the collaboration of Martin L. Leibowitz. New York : McGraw-Hill, c1988. xiii, 656 p. : ill. ; 24 cm. Rev. ed. of: Security analysis. 4th ed. 1962. Includes bibliographical references and index. ISBN 0-07-013235-6 : LC Card 87-19990 DDC 332.63/2 19
1. Investment analysis. 2. Securities - United States. I. Dodd, David L. (David Le Fevre), 1895-. II. Cottle, Sidney. III. Murray, Roger F. IV. Block, Frank E. V. Title. VI. Title: Security analysis.
HG4529 .G7 1988

Graham, Lawrence. Youthtrends : capturing the $200 billion youth market / Lawrence Graham and Lawrence Hamdan.1st ed. New York : St. Martin's Press, c1987. xx, 282 p. ; 22 cm. On t.p. the registered trademark symbol "TM" is superscript following "Youthtrends" in the title. Includes index. ISBN 0-312-00704-3 : LC Card 87-4426 DDC 658.8/348 19
1. Youth as consumers - United States. I. Hamdan, Lawrence. II. Title. III. Title: Youth trends.
HC110.C6 G67 1987

Graham, Mac. Disarmament and world development /. Oxford, England , New York , 1986. xiii, 306 p. ; ISBN 0-08-031309-4 : LC Card 85-19231 DDC 338.4/7355 19
JX1974 .D515 1985 ***NYPL [JLE 86-3211]***

Graham, Norman A. Emery, James J. Technology trade with the Middle East /. Boulder , 1986. xvii, 302 p. : ISBN 0-8133-7043-4 : LC Card 85-3215 DDC 338.9/26 19
HC415.15.Z9 H533 1986
NYPL [JLE 86-2460]

Graham Towers and his times . Fullerton, Douglas H. Toronto, Ont. , c1986. 348 p., [16] p. of plates : ISBN 0-7710-3218-8 : LC Card 86-231010 DDC 332.1/1/092 B 19
HG1552.T68 F85 1986

GRAIN - ARGENTINA - TRANSPORTATION.
Argerich, Federico Raúl. Posibilidades de intercambio compensado entre Argentina y Chile y exportaciones graníferas al area del Pacífico, ambos por el paso de San Francisco /. Córdoba , 1985. 35 p. ; LC Card 87-402749 DDC 382/.0983/082 19
HF3418.A7 A8 1985

GRAIN - CANADA - CONGRESSES.
The Future of the North American granary . Ames, Iowa , 1986. xx, 238 p. : ISBN 0-8138-0781-6 LC Card 85-23905 DDC 338.1/731/097 19
HD9036 .F87 1986 ***NYPL [JLE 86-2437]***

GRAIN - CHILE - TRANSPORTATION.
Argerich, Federico Raúl. Posibilidades de intercambio compensado entre Argentina y Chile y exportaciones graníferas al area del Pacífico, ambos por el paso de San Francisco /. Córdoba , 1985. 35 p. ; LC Card 87-402749 DDC 382/.0983/082 19
HF3418.A7 A8 1985

GRAIN ELEVATORS, COOPERATIVE - UNITED STATES - FINANCE - STATISTICS.
Yager, Francis P. Financial profile of cooperatives handling grain . [Washington, D.C.] [1986] vii, 24 p. : LC Card 86-601622 DDC 334/.6831/0973021 19
HD9034 .Y34 1986

GRAIN ELEVATORS - ECONOMIC ASPECTS - LOUISIANA.
Traylor, Harlon D. An analysis of grain elevator bankruptcies in Louisiana /. [Baton Rouge?] [1986] iii, 77 p. ; LC Card 87-620885 DDC 338.1/09763 s 338.1/6 19
HD1775.L8 L7 no. 661 HD9037.L6

GRAIN - NIGER - MARKETING.
Joint program assessment of grain marketing in Niger . [Niamey, Niger] [1983] 2 v. : LC Card 87-114421 DDC 381/.4131/096626 19
HD9049.N552 J65 1983

GRAIN - PRICES.
Gkekos, Giōrgos. Polyethnikes hetairies dēmētriakōn kai hē diamorphōsē timōn /. Athēna , 1985. 292 p. : LC Card 86-212325
HD9030.5 .G58 1985

GRAIN - PRICES - EUROPEAN ECONOMIC COMMUNITY COUNTRIES - ECONOMETRIC MODELS.
Einkommenswirkungen von Getreidepreissenkungen /. Münster-Hiltrup , 1985. viii, 158 p. : ISBN 3-7843-0315-3 LC Card 87-408928 DDC 338.1/0943 s 338.1/331/094 19
HD1920.5 .E37 1985

GRAIN - PRICES - GERMANY (WEST) - LOWER SAXONY - HISTORY - SOURCES.
Beiträge zur niedersächsischen Preisgeschichte des 16. bis 19. Jahrhunderts /. Hildesheim , 1986. lxiii, 541 p. ; ISBN 3-7848-3874-X LC

Card 87-407399 DDC 338.1/331/094359 19
HD9043.4 .B45 1986

GRAIN - PRICES - GOVERNMENT POLICY - SOMALIA.
Report of the joint Somali government and World Bank study of agricultural incentives and grain marketing in Somalia /. [Alexandria, Va. , 1984] xviii, 170, 2 p. : LC Card 87-404086 DDC 338.1/8 19
HD9047.S582 R47 1984

GRAIN - SOMALIA - MARKETING.
Report of the joint Somali government and World Bank study of agricultural incentives and grain marketing in Somalia /. [Alexandria, Va. , 1984] xviii, 170, 2 p. : LC Card 87-404086 DDC 338.1/8 19
HD9047.S582 R47 1984

GRAIN - STORAGE - ECONOMIC ASPECTS - LOUISIANA.
Traylor, Harlon D. An analysis of grain elevator bankruptcies in Louisiana /. [Baton Rouge?] [1986] iii, 77 p. ; LC Card 87-620885 DDC 338.1/09763 s 338.1/6 19
HD1775.L8 L7 no. 661 HD9037.L6

GRAIN - TRADE AND STATISTICS. see **GRAIN TRADE.**

GRAIN TRADE - ANDES REGION.
Comercio de granos entre la Argentina y los países del Grupo Andino. [Buenos Aires, Argentina] , 1983. ii, 154 p. : LC Card 86-201891
HD9044.A8 C65 1983

GRAIN TRADE - ARGENTINA.
Comercio de granos entre la Argentina y los países del Grupo Andino. [Buenos Aires, Argentina] , 1983. ii, 154 p. : LC Card 86-201891
HD9044.A8 C65 1983

GRAIN TRADE - ARGENTINA - ROSARIO (SANTE FE) - HISTORY.
De Marco, Miguel Angel. 1884-1984, los cien años de la Bolsa de Comercio de Rosario /. [S.l. , 1984?] (Rosario : Escuela de Artes Gráficas del Colegio San José de Rosario) 167 p. : LC Card 87-115398 DDC 332.64/28224 19
HG5320.R67 D4 1984

GRAIN TRADE - AUSTRALIA.
Hussey, Denis D. Australian grain marketing . Perth, W.A. , 1986. 72 p. : ISBN 0-949186-11-2 (pbk.) : LC Card 86-213695 DDC 338.1/731/0994 19
HD9048.A82 H87 1986

GRAIN TRADE - BALTIC STATES - HISTORY - 17TH CENTURY.
Soom, Arnold. Der baltische Getreidehandel im 17. Jahrhundert /. Stockholm , 1961. 350 p. ; LC Card 85-122593 DDC 380.1/4131/09474 19
HD9045.S63 B37 1961

GRAIN TRADE - BOLIVIA.
Proyecto harinas compuestas . La Paz, Bolivia , 1982. 272, [2], 3 p., [9] p. of plates : LC Card 83-195592
HD9044.B52 P76 1982

GRAIN TRADE - BRAZIL.
Cerrado . [Rio de Janeiro] , 1984. 53 p., [2] leaves of plates : LC Card 87-132493 DDC 380.1/4131/0981 19
HD9044.B682 C47 1984

GRAIN TRADE - BRAZIL - TRANSPORTATION - COSTS.
Cerrado . [Rio de Janeiro] , 1984. 53 p., [2] leaves of plates : LC Card 87-132493 DDC 380.1/4131/0981 19
HD9044.B682 C47 1984

GRAIN TRADE - CANADA.
Stanton, B. F. (Bernard Freeland), 1925- The cereals dilemma . Ithaca, N.Y. [1986] 50 p. : LC Card 86-622419 DDC 338.1/731/094 19
HD9045.A2 S7 1986

GRAIN TRADE - DEVELOPING COUNTRIES - FORECASTING.
Sarma, J. S. Cereal feed use in the Third World . Washington, D.C. , c1986. 68 p. : ISBN 0-89629-058-1 (pbk.) LC Card 86-27355 DDC 338.1/7325/091724 19
HD9052.D44 S27 1986

GRAIN TRADE - EUROPE.
Stanton, B. F. (Bernard Freeland), 1925- The cereals dilemma . Ithaca, N.Y. [1986] 50 p. : LC Card 86-622419 DDC 338.1/731/094 19
HD9045.A2 S7 1986

GRAIN TRADE - FRANCE - BEAUCE.
Charvet, Jean-Paul. Les greniers du monde /. Paris , c1985. 368 p. : ISBN 2-7178-0925-2 : LC Card 85-191889 DDC 338.1/731 19
HD9030.5 .C47 1985 ***NYPL [JLE 86-488]***

GRAIN TRADE - GERMANY (WEST) - LOWER SAXONY - HISTORY - SOURCES.
Beiträge zur niedersächsischen Preisgeschichte des 16. bis 19. Jahrhunderts /. Hildesheim , 1986. lxiii, 541 p. ; ISBN 3-7848-3874-X LC Card 87-407399 DDC 338.1/331/094359 19
HD9043.4 .B45 1986

GRAIN TRADE - GOVERNMENT POLICY - BRAZIL.
Cerrado . [Rio de Janeiro] , 1984. 53 p., [2] leaves of plates : LC Card 87-132493 DDC 380.1/4131/0981 19
HD9044.B682 C47 1984

GRAIN TRADE - GOVERNMENT POLICY - CANADA - CONGRESSES.
The Future of the North American granary . Ames, Iowa , 1986. xx, 238 p. : ISBN 0-8138-0781-6 LC Card 85-23905 DDC 338.1/731/097 19
HD9036 .F87 1986 ***NYPL [JLE 86-2437]***

GRAIN TRADE - GOVERNMENT POLICY - INDIA - ORISSA.
Mishra, Bhagabat, 1940- Economics of public distribution system in food-grains /. New Delhi , 1985. xviii, 306 p. (some folded) ; LC Card 85-902748 DDC 381/.4131/095413 19
HD9066.I63 O756 1982
NYPL [JLD 86-1149]

GRAIN TRADE - GOVERNMENT POLICY - UNITED STATES.
Grigsby, S. Elaine. Alternative export strategies and U. S. agricultural policies for grains and oilseeds, 1950-83 /. [Washington, D.C.] , 1986. v., 37 p. : LC Card 86-602816 DDC 382/.4131/0973 19
HD9036 .G83 1986

GRAIN TRADE - GOVERNMENT POLICY - UNITED STATES - CONGRESSES.
The Future of the North American granary . Ames, Iowa , 1986. xx, 238 p. : ISBN 0-8138-0781-6 LC Card 85-23905 DDC 338.1/731/097 19
HD9036 .F87 1986 ***NYPL [JLE 86-2437]***

GRAIN TRADE - ILLINOIS.
Charvet, Jean-Paul. Les greniers du monde /. Paris , c1985. 368 p. : ISBN 2-7178-0925-2 : LC Card 85-191889 DDC 338.1/731 19
HD9030.5 .C47 1985 ***NYPL [JLE 86-488]***

GRAIN TRADE - INDIA.
Narayanan, S. Demand-supply gap and public distribution of foodgrains in India /. New Delhi , 1986. xii, 166 p. ; ISBN 81-85005-00-1 : LC Card 86-902667 DDC 338.1/731/0954 19
HD9046.I4 N28 1986

GRAIN TRADE - MEXICO.
Barkin, David. El fin de la autosuficiencia alimentaria /. México, D.F. , 1985. 249 p. : ISBN 968-493-091-7 LC Card 82-230750
NYPL [JLE 87-404]

Barkin, David. El fin de la autosuficiencia alimentaria /. México, D.F. , c1985. 249 p. : ISBN 968-493-091-7 LC Card 86-209699
HD1792 .B38 1985

GRAIN TRADE - NIGER.
Joint program assessment of grain marketing in Niger . [Niamey, Niger] [1983] 2 v. : LC Card 87-114421 DDC 381/.4131/096626 19
HD9049.N552 J65 1983

GRAIN TRADE - SOMALIA.
Report of the joint Somali government and World Bank study of agricultural incentives and grain marketing in Somalia /. [Alexandria, Va. , 1984] xviii, 170, 2 p. : LC Card 87-404086 DDC 338.1/8 19
HD9047.S582 R47 1984

GRAIN TRADE - SOVIET UNION - ECONOMETRIC MODELS.
Lundborg, Per, 1950- The economics of export embargoes . New York, NY , c1987. xi, 127 p. : ISBN 0-7099-4151-X : LC Card 86-29370 DDC 382/.4131/0947 19
HD9035 .L86 1987

GRAIN TRADE - TANZANIA.
Bantje, Han. Mechanised food production in Tanzania . [Dar es Salaam] [1984] 3 leaves, 73 p. : LC Card 86-980118 DDC 338.1/61/09678 19
HD1471.T34 B36 1984

Msambichaka, L. A. (Lucian A.) Food grain shortfalls in Tanzania, 1961-1981 . Dar es Salaam, Tanzania , c1982. 38 p. ; LC Card 85-980863 DDC 338.1/9/678 19
HD9047.T32 M726 1982

GRAIN TRADE - UNITED STATES.
Angell, George. Agricultural options . New York, NY , c1986. ix, 230 p. : ISBN 0-8144-5822-X LC Card 85-48215 DDC 332.64/25 19
HG6047.G8 A54 1986 ***NYPL [JLE 86-2854]***

Stanton, B. F. (Bernard Freeland), 1925- The cereals dilemma . Ithaca, N.Y. [1986] 50 p. : LC Card 86-622419 DDC 338.1/731/094 19
HD9045.A2 S7 1986

GRAIN TRADE - UNITED STATES - CONGRESSES.
Proceedings of a symposium on competitiveness of U. S. grains in international markets /. Fargo, N.D. [1986] ii leaves, 67 p. : LC Card 86-622839 DDC 382/.4131/0973 19
HD9035 .P76 1986

GRAIN TRADE - UNITED STATES - ECONOMETRIC MODELS.
Lundborg, Per, 1950- The economics of export embargoes . New York, NY , c1987. xi, 127 p. : ISBN 0-7099-4151-X : LC Card 86-29370 DDC 382/.4131/0947 19
HD9035 .L86 1987

GRAIN TRADE - UNITED STATES - FINANCE - STATISTICS.
Yager, Francis P. Financial profile of cooperatives handling grain . [Washington, D.C.] [1986] vii, 24 p. : LC Card 86-601622 DDC 334/.6831/0973021 19
HD9034 .Y34 1986

GRAIN - UNITED STATES - CONGRESSES.
The Future of the North American granary . Ames, Iowa , 1986. xx, 238 p. : ISBN 0-8138-0781-6 LC Card 85-23905 DDC 338.1/731/097 19
HD9036 .F87 1986 ***NYPL [JLE 86-2437]***

Grainger, D. H. Whitsun Foundation. Project 3,04(a), Peasant sector credit plan (revised) . Salisbury, Rhodesia [1978] ii, 18 leaves ; LC Card 86-981359
HG2051.Z55 W45 1978

Graĭvoronskiĭ, Vladimir Viktorovich.
Kooperirovannoe aratstvo MNR--izmeneniia v urovne zhizni, 1960-1980 / V.V. Graĭvoronskiĭ. Moskva : Izd-vo "Nauka," Glav. red. vostochnoĭ lit-ry, 1982. 213 p. : ill. ; 20 cm. At head of title: Akademiia nauk SSSR. Ordena Trudovogo Krasnogo Znameni Institut vostokovedeniia. Bibliography: p. 193-[209] Includes indexes. LC Card 82-213253
1. Agriculture, Cooperative - Mongolia. 2. Mongolia - Rural conditions. 3. Agriculture and state - Mongolia. I. Title. II. Title: Kooperirovannoe aratstvo M.N.R.--izmeneniia v urovne zhizni, 1960-1980.
HD1491.M55 G73 1982

Gramley, Lyle E. Real estate finance and housing : 1987 outlook and fact book. Washington, D.C. (1125 15th St., N.W., Washington 20005) : Mortgage Bankers Association of America, c1987. vii, 132 p. : ill. ; 23 cm. Written by Lyle E. Gramley, Richard W. Peach, and Edison R. Zayas; statistical tables prepared by Robert M. Rosenblatt and Carlos Davila. LC Card 87-124264 DDC 332.7/2/0973021 19
1. Mortgage loans - United States - Statistics. 2. Housing - United States - Finance - Statistics. 3. Housing - United States - Statistics. I. Peach, Richard Wilson, 1951-. II. Zayas, Edison R. III. Rosenblatt, Robert M. IV. Davila, Carlos. V. Title.
HG2040.5.U5 G73 1987

Gran Colombia. see **Colombia.**

GRAN OESTE ARGENTINO (RAILROAD) - HISTORY.
Fleming, William J. Regional development and transportation in Argentina . New York , 1987. ii, 218 p. : ISBN 0-8240-1360-3 (alk. paper) : LC Card 87-8401 DDC 385/.065/82 19
HE2910.G64 F54 1987

GRANADA (SPAIN : PROVINCE) - HISTORY.

Gómez Oliver, Miguel. La desamortización de Mendizábal en Granada /. Granada [1983] 226 p. : LC Card 85-135214
HD479.G73 G65 1983

Granadine Confederation. see **Colombia.**

Granado Cosio, Hugo del. Transnacionales y nación : el capital petrolero y la experiencia boliviana / Hugo del Granado Cosio.1a ed. [La Paz, Bolivia] : Centro de Documentación e Información, 1986. 24 p. ; 29 cm. (Informe especial) Includes bibliographical references. LC Card 87-115866 DDC 338.8/87 19
1. Petroleum industry and trade - Bolivia. 2. International business enterprises - Bolivia. I. Series: Informe especial (Centro de Documentación e Información--Bolivia). II. Title.
HD9574.B82 G73 1986

GRANARIES - PERU.
Hinojosa Tapia, Juan. La problemática de los almacenes generales de depósito como instituciones financieras no bancarias en el Perú (1970-1983) /. Lima, Perú , 1985. iii, 29, [43] p. : LC Card 86-218257
HG3751.9.P4 H56 1985

Granata, Ivano, 1949- Sindacato e crisi della democrazia : la Camera del lavoro di Milano dallo "splendore" del biennio rosso allo scioglimento (1919-1925) / Ivano Granata. Milano, Italy : F. Angeli, c1986. 224 p. ; 22 cm. (Il Sindacato in Lombardia. Storia . 1.2) Includes bibliographical references and index. LC Card 87-103965
1. Camera del lavoro di Milano - History - 20th century. 2. Trade-unions - Italy - Milan - History - 20th century. I. Title. II. Series.
HD6714.M54 G724 1986

Granath, Erna. Kvinnoplats : en arbetsstudie om kvinnors vardag på kontor / Erna Granath och Lena Larsson.Uppl. 1. Stockholm : Liber, c1985. 141 p. ; 25 cm. Bibliography: p. [140]-141. ISBN 91-38-90602-3 : LC Card 85-236327
1. Women white collar workers - Sweden. 2. Sex discrimination in employment - Sweden. I. Larsson, Lena. II. Title.
HD6073.M392 S84 1985
NYPL [JLE 86-3898]

Granberg, Aleksandr Grigor'evich.
Matematicheskie modeli sotsialisticheskoĭ ėkonomiki : obshchie printsipy modelirovaniia i staticheskie modeli narodnogo khoziaĭstva / A.G. Granberg. Moskva : "Ėkonomika", 1978. 350 p. : ill. ; 22 cm. Authorized for instructional purposes. Includes bibliographies and indexes. LC Card 81-160608
1. Soviet Union - Economic policy - 1976-1980 - Econometric models. 2. Soviet Union - Economic conditions - 1976- - Econometric models. I. Title.
HC336.25 .G697 1978

Mezhregional'nye mezhotraslevye balansy /. Novosibirsk , 1983. 220 p. : LC Card 84-172934
HF3626.5 .M49 1983

Grancelli, Bruno, 1943-
Le relazioni industriali di tipo sovietico : il modello ufficiale, la realtà operativa / Bruno Grancelli. Milano, Italy : F. Angeli, c1986. 337 p. ; 22 cm. (Sociologia del lavoro e delle organizzazioni. 26) Bibliography: p. [328]-337. LC Card 86-222589
1. Industrial relations - Soviet Union. I. Title.
HD8526.5 .G73 1986

Soviet management and labor relations / Bruno Grancelli. Boston : Allen & Unwin, c1988. xvi, 248 p. ; /23 cm. Bibliography: p. [225]-236. Includes index. ISBN 0-04-497040-4 : LC Card 87-11516 DDC 331/.0947 19
1. Industrial relations - Soviet Union. 2. Labor and laboring classes - Soviet Union. I. Title.
HD8526.5 .G74 1988

Grand illusions . Campbell, Robert Malcolm. Peterborough, Canada , Lewiston, N.Y. , c1987. 270 p. ; ISBN 0-921149-03-4 LC Card 87-147385 DDC 338.971 19
HC115 .C16 1987

Grand Metropolitan . Reader, W. J. (William Joseph), 1920- Oxford [Oxfordshire] , New York , 1988. p. cm. ISBN 0-19-822976-3 : LC Card 87-21942 DDC 338.8/8941 19
HD2845.Z75 G77 1988

GRAND METROPOLITAN (FIRM) - HISTORY.
Reader, W. J. (William Joseph), 1920- Grand Metropolitan . Oxford [Oxfordshire] , New York , 1988. p. cm. ISBN 0-19-822976-3 : LC Card 87-21942 DDC 338.8/8941 19
HD2845.Z75 G77 1988

Grand rendez-vous. Noir, Michel, 1944- 1988 . [Paris] , c1984. 263 p. : LC Card 84-169744
HC280.H53 N65 1984 ***NYPL [JLE 87-2052]***

La Grande-Bretagne et la Communauté européenne /. La Serre, Françoise de. Paris , c1987. 223, [1] p. : ISBN 2-13-040114-7 : LC Card 87-165122
HC241.25.G7 L118 1987

GRANDE CHARTREUSE - HISTORY - 18TH CENTURY.
Arsac, Pierre. La vente des biens de la Grande Chartreuse sous la Révolution /. Grenoble , 1984. 104 p. : ISBN 2-904661-02-6 LC Card 86-118639
HD643 .A77 1984

A grande crise . Loureiro, Antônio José Souto. Manaus, Amazonas, Brasil , 1986. 282 p. : LC Card 86-222988
HD9161.B8 L68 1986

Grande Esteban, Ildefonso. Modelos de valoración de acciones y metodos de constrastación / Ildefonso Grande Esteban. Bilbao : Servicio Editorial, Universidad del País Vasco, [1985?] 319 p. : ill. ; 23 cm. Bibliography: p. 299-319. ISBN 84-7585-025-1 LC Card 87-111240
1. Stocks - Prices. 2. Corporations - Valuation. 3. Dividends. I. Title.
HG4636 .G88 1985

Grandes maestros mexicanos .

Grandi, Roberto. Come parla la pubblicità : modelli comunicativi degli spot pubblicitari / Roberto Grandi.1a ed. Milano : Edizioni del sole 24 ore, 1987. 175 p. ; 24 cm. (Comunicazione e marketing) Bibliography: p. 175. LC Card 87-168680
1. Television advertising. 2. Television commercial films. I. Title. II. Series.
HF6146.T42 G7 1987

Grandinetti, Roberto, 1953- Sistema industriale e politiche regionali : analisi e proposte per il Friuli-Venezia Giulia / Roberto Grandinetti. Milano, Italy : F. Angeli, 1984. 234 p. : ill. ; 22 cm. Includes bibliographies. "GEG/ECN/PUB/6"--Cover p. [4] LC Card 85-176111 DDC 338.945/39 19
1. Industrial promotion - Italy - Friuli-Venezia Giulia. 2. Industry and state - Italy - Friuli-Venezia Giulia. I. Title.
HC307.F68 G73 1984

Grandmont, Jean-Michel.
Nonlinear economic dynamics /. Boston , c1987. xiii, 195 p. : ISBN 0-12-295140-9 (alk. paper) LC Card 86-32129 DDC 338.5/442/0151 19
HB3711 .N655 1987

Temporary equilibrium . Boston , c1987. p. cm. ISBN 0-12-295145-X (alk. paper) LC Card 87-1128 DDC 339.5 19
HB145 .T45 1987

Grandner, Margarete, 1953- Historische Wurzeln der Sozialpartnerschaft /. München , 1986. 368 p. ; ISBN 3-486-52971-4 LC Card 87-146580 DDC 306/.36/09436 19
HD6957.A9 H57 1986

Grandori, Anna.
Teorie dell'organizzazione : ecologia delle popolazioni, apprendimento adattivo, progettazione razionale / Anna Grandori. [Milano] : A. Giuffrè, 1984. xxiii, 213 p. : ill. ; 24 cm. (Università "L. Bocconi," Dipartimento di economia aziendale . 90. 7.9) Bibliography: p. [xi]-xxiii. ISBN 88-14-00411-0 : LC Card 85-162760
1. Organization. 2. Management. 3. Organizational behavior. 4. Organizational change. 5. Corporate planning. I. Series: Università "L. Bocconi," Dipartimento di economia aziendale (Series) , 90. II. Title.
HD37.I8 G73 1984

[Teorie dell'organizzazione. English]
Perspectives on organization theory / Anna Grandori. Cambridge, Mass. : Ballinger Pub. Co., c1987. xxvi, 199 p. : ill. ; 24 cm. Translation of: Teorie dell'organizzazione. Bibliography: p. 179-189. Includes indexes. ISBN 0-88730-214-9 LC Card 87-11359 DDC 302.3/5 19
1. Organization. 2. Management. 3. Organizational behavior. 4. Organizational change. 5. Corporate planning. I. Title.
HD37.I8 G7313 1987

Granger, Louis. Catalogue des vignettes françaises de Croix-Rouge / Louis Granger. [Aurillac] : Société L'Arc-en-Ciel, [1964] 117 p. ; 22 cm . Atlas has cover title: Photocopies des vignettes françaises de Croix-Rouge. LC Card 68-39071
1. Seals and labels (Philately) - Catalogs. 2. Croix-Rouge française - Miscellanea. I. Title. II. Title: Photocopies des vignettes françaises de Croix-Rouge.
HE6184.S42 G7 1964

Granick, David. Job rights in the Soviet Union : their consequences / David Granick. Cambridge ; New York : Cambridge University Press, 1987. ix, 344 p. ; 23 cm. (Soviet and East European studies) Bibliography: p. 316-325. Includes index. ISBN 0-521-33295-8 LC Card 86-26392 DDC 331.11/0947 19
1. Manpower policy - Soviet Union. 2. Labor supply - Soviet Union. 3. Central planning - Soviet Union. 4. Labor turnover - Soviet Union. I. Title.
HD5796 .G72 1987

Granin, V. G. Formirovanie i razvitie rabochego klassa i promyshlennosti Urala v period stroitel'stva sotsializma, 1917-1937 . Sverdlovsk , 1982. 138 p. ; LC Card 84-211723
HD8529.U7 F67 1982

GRANITE BUILDING (ROCHESTER, N.Y.) - ANECDOTES, FACETIAE, SATIRE, ETC.
Jackson, Mason, 1926- The building /. Interlaken, N.Y. , 1987. 128 p. : ISBN 0-932334-90-3 LC Card 86-24115 DDC 974.7/89043 19
HD8039.M4 U54 1987

Grant, Land. High-tech exporter's sourcebook : a guide to the essential resources for profitable exporting of high-technology products / by Land Grant.2nd print. 1987 rev. Brooklyn, N.Y. : LGC Pub., 1987. viii, 263 p. ; 23 cm. Includes index. LC Card 87-157599 DDC 382/.6/02573 19
1. Technology transfer - Economic aspects - Handbooks, manuals, etc. 2. High technology industries - Handbooks, manuals, etc. I. Title.
HC79.T4 G68 1987

Grant, Pamela, 1944- Youth employment and technological change : the educational and social implications / Pamela Grant. Aldershot, [England] ; Brookfield, USA : Avebury, c1987. xii, 393 p. : ill. ; 23 cm. Bibliography: p. 356-370. ISBN 0-566-05423-X : LC Card 86-33659 DDC 331.3/4125/0941 19
1. Youth - Employment - Great Britain. 2. Unemployment, Technological - Great Britain. 3. Technicians in industry - Great Britain. 4. Technical education - Great Britain. I. Title. II. Title: Youth employment and technological change.
HD6276.G7 G66 1987

Grant, Philip C. The performance management process : an integrative approach to human resource management / Philip C. Grant. Dubuque, Iowa : Kendall/Hunt, c1986. xvi, 333 p. : ill. ; 23 cm. Bibliography: p. 325-328. Includes index. ISBN 0-8403-4086-9 (pbk.) LC Card 86-81844 DDC 658.3 19
1. Personnel management. I. Title.
HF5549 .G6755 1986

Grant, Simon. Martin, James, 1933- The wired world . Carnforth, Lancashire, England , 1986. xiii, 140 p. : ISBN 0-906774-49-7 (pbk.) LC Card 87-157689 DDC 384 19
HE7631 .M373 1986

Grant-Sokolosky, Valerie. Corporate protocol : a brief case for business etiquette / by Valerie Grant-Sokolosky ; [cartoons by Richard Domingus]. Tulsa : Honor, c1986. 203 p. : ill. ; 22 cm. Bibliography: p. 203. Includes index. ISBN 0-89274-417-0 (pbk.): LC Card 86-205553 DDC 174/.4 19
1. Business etiquette. I. Title.
HF5387 .G7 1986

The grant system /. Kalas, John W. Albany , c1987. xii, 168 p. : ISBN 0-88706-583-X LC Card 87-6156 DDC 001.4/4 19
HJ275 .K34 1987

Grant, Wyn. Business interests, organizational development, and private interest government . Berlin , New York , 1987. viii, 232 p. ; ISBN 0-89925-380-6 (U. S.) : LC Card 87-21403

DDC 338.4/7664 19
HD9000.5 .B87 1987

Grants-in-aid and economic development in India /. Sudarsana Rao, R. (Rokkam) Allahabad, India , 1986. ix, 271 p. ; ISBN 81-85076-14-6 : LC Card 86-903200 DDC 338.954
HJ1338 .S83 1986

GRANTS-IN-AID - BRAZIL - SÃO PAULO (STATE)
Fontes de financiamento aos municípios. São Paulo , 1984. 175 p. ; LC Card 85-221901
HJ925 .F66 1984

GRANTS-IN-AID - EUROPE.
Policies with regard to grants to local authorities . Strasbourg , 1986. 35 p. : LC Card 86-218329 DDC 336.1/85 19
HJ1000 .P65 1986

GRANTS-IN-AID - GERMANY (WEST)
Massat, Dieter. Die ökonomische Problematik von Zuweisungen an Kommunen /. Thun , c1984. vii, 321 p. : ISBN 3-87144-792-7 LC Card 84-183709
HJ1121 .M37 1984

GRANTS-IN-AID - ILLINOIS - CHICAGO.
Orlebeke, Charles J. Federal aid to Chicago /. Washington, D.C. , c1983. xvii, 80 p. ; ISBN 0-8157-6649-1 (pbk.) LC Card 82-74097 DDC 336.1/85 19
HJ9229.C5 O74 1983 ***NYPL [JLE 86-4696]***

GRANTS-IN-AID - INDIA.
Sudarsana Rao, R. (Rokkam) Grants-in-aid and economic development in India /. Allahabad, India , 1986. ix, 271 p. ; ISBN 81-85076-14-6 : LC Card 86-903200 DDC 338.954
HJ1338 .S83 1986

GRANTS-IN-AID, INTERNATIONAL. see **ECONOMIC ASSISTANCE.**

GRANTS-IN-AID - ITALY - CORRUPT PRACTICES.
Risanamento e riordino delle partecipazioni statali . Milano, Italy , c1986. 429 p. : LC Card 86-169331
HC310.I53 R57 1986

GRANTS-IN-AID - MINNESOTA - ACCOUNTING.
Minnesota. Financial and compliance report on federally assisted programs for the year ended June 30, 1985 /. [Saint Paul, Minn.] [1986] x, 92 p. ; LC Card 87-620971 DDC 353.97760072/52 19
HJ515 .M55 1986

GRANTS-IN-AID - MISSOURI - SAINT LOUIS.
Schmandt, Henry J. Federal aid to St. Louis /. Washington, D.C. , c1983. xvii, 67 p. ; ISBN 0-8157-7727-2 (pbk.) LC Card 82-74100 DDC 336.1/85 19
HJ9268.S3 S352 1983 ***NYPL [JLE 87-1]***

GRANTS-IN-AID - UNITED STATES.
Changing the course . Washington , 1986. xvii, 142 p. : LC Card 86-603365 DDC 336.1/85 19
HJ275 .C455 1986

Kalas, John W. The grant system /. Albany , c1987. xii, 168 p. : ISBN 0-88706-583-X LC Card 87-6156 DDC 001.4/4 19
HJ275 .K34 1987

Kettl, Donald F. Government by proxy . Washington, D.C. , c1988. x, 170 p. ; ISBN 0-87187-429-6 (pbk.) : LC Card 87-13645 DDC 353.009 19
HD3861.U6 K47 1988

Nathan, Richard P. Reagan and the States /. Princeton, N.J. , c1987. xv, 375 p. : ISBN 0-691-07748-7 (alk. paper) : LC Card 87-45529 DDC 353.0072/5 19
HJ2051 .N167 1987

Pagano, Michael A. How the public works . Washington, D.C. , c1986. ix, 68, 6 p. : ISBN 0-933729-13-8 (pbk.) : LC Card 87-129719 DDC 338.4/3363/0973 19
HJ9145 .P343 1986

GRANTS-IN-AID - UNITED STATES - STATES.
Silkman, Richard H. Subsidizing inefficiency . New York , 1985. xviii, 101 p.: ISBN 0-03-000662-7 (alk. paper) : LC Card 84-26628 DDC 336.1/85 19
HJ275 .S53 1985 ***NYPL [JLE 85-2261]***

Granville, Joseph Ensign, 1923- The warning : the coming great crash in the stock market / Joseph Granville. New York : Freundlich Books, c1985. xvi, 397 p. ; 24 cm. Includes bibliographical references and index. ISBN 0-88191-034-1 : LC Card 85-13107 DDC 332.64/273 19
1. Stock-exchange - United States - History. 2. Depressions - 1929 - United States. 3. United States - Economic conditions - 1981-. I. Title.
HG4910 .G76 1985 ***NYPL [JLE 86-3122]***

Granziera, Rui Guilherme, 1942- Getúlio Vargas e a economia contemporânea /. Campinas , 1986. 179 p. ; ISBN 85-26-80033-7 LC Card 87-403048 DDC 330.981/063 19
HC187 .G45 1986

GRAPE CULTURE. see **VITICULTURE.**

GRAPE INDUSTRY - AUSTRALIA - WESTERN AUSTRALIA - CONGRESSES.
The Production, promotion, and marketing of Western Australian table grapes . Perth, WA [1985] viii, 180 p. : LC Card 87-120107 DDC 338.1/748/09941 19
HD9259.G7 A827 1985

GRAPE INDUSTRY - EUROPEAN ECONOMIC COMMUNITY COUNTRIES.
Harza, Lajos. Az EGK szőlő- és borgazdaságának szabályozórendszere /. Budapest , 1985. 70 p. : ISBN 963-491-210-9 LC Card 86-196818
HD9259.G7 E864 1985

GRAPE INDUSTRY - HUNGARY - STATISTICS - HISTORY.
Szőlőtermelés . Budapest , 1986. 519 p. ; ISBN 963-340-777-X : LC Card 86-196884
HD9385.H82 S95 1986

GRAPE INDUSTRY - PORTUGAL - REDONDO (EVORA)
Pereira, Francisco José Piteira. A cultura da vinha na região do Redondo /. [Lisbon] , 1983. 11, 4, 30, 21 leaves, [2] leaves of plates : LC Card 84-238378
HD9259.G7 P47 1983

GRAPE INDUSTRY - SPAIN - CATALONIA.
Clavera, Joan. La viticultura catalana davant la integració a la Comunitat Europea /. [Barcelona] [1986] 124 p. : ISBN 6-476-84021-8 LC Card 86-200618
HD9259.G7 S693 1986

GRAPHIC ARTS EQUIPMENT INDUSTRY - EUROPE.
Prepress graphic arts equipment and supplies market in Europe. New York, N.Y. , c1983. xxiii, 268 p. ; LC Card 87-141770 DDC 380.1/456816 19
HD9790.E85 P74 1983

Das Gras wuchs ja umsonst /. Baroth, Hans Dieter, 1937- Köln , c1983. 232 p. ; ISBN 3-462-01577-X LC Card 83-227195
HD8459.R82 B37 1983

Grasberger, Helmut, 1941- Die Untersuchung des Wohnwertes von Wohngebieten / Helmut Grasberger ; herausgegeben von der Österreichischen Gesellschaft für Raumforschung und Raumplanung. Wien ; New York : Springer-Verlag, 1983. 108 p., [15] folded leaves of plates : ill. ; 24 cm. (Schriftenreihe der Österreichischen Gesellschaft für Raumforschung und Raumplanung, 0078-3498 . Bd. 28) Includes bibliographical references. ISBN 0-387-81752-2 (U. S.) LC Card 84-142695
1. Housing - Austria - Location - Evaluation. 2. Housing - Location - Evaluation. I. Österreichische Gesellschaft für Raumforschung und Raumplanung. II. Title. III. Series.
HD7337.A3 G73 1983

Grases G., José. Pérdidas como consecuencia de terremotos : métodos para su estimación / por José Grases G. Caracas : Seguros Caracas, 1986. 71 p. : ill. ; 24 cm. Bibliography: p. 65-69. ISBN 980-265-358-6 LC Card 87-403100 DDC 338.4/33633495 19
1. Disasters - Economic aspects. 2. Earthquakes - Economic aspects. 3. Earthquake prediction. I. Title.
HC79.D45 G7 1986

Grashof, John F. Readings and cases in basic marketing /. Homewood, Ill. , 1987. ix, 365 p. : ISBN 0-256-05795-8 (pbk.) LC Card 86-83136 DDC 658.8 19
HF5415 .R334 1987

Grasing, Robert E. Hessick, Michael H. Achieving quality in financial service organizations . New York , c1988. p. cm. ISBN 0-89930-231-9 (lib. bdg. : alk. paper) LC Card 87-24937 DDC 332.1/2/0688 19
HG181 .H44 1988

Grasnick, Georg, 1927- Alter Kapitalismus, "neue Armut" / Georg Grasnick. Berlin : Dietz, 1985. 78 p. : ill. ; 19 cm. Includes bibliographical references. LC Card 86-132510 DDC 330.12/2 19
1. Capitalism. 2. Poor. I. Title.
HB501 .G64 1985

Grassi, Mercia. Rogers, Dorothy S., 1929- Retailing . Hinsdale, IL , 1987, c1988. p. cm. ISBN 0-03-001997-4 LC Card 87-5337 DDC 658.8/7 19
HF5429 .R5793 1988

Grasso, Biagio. I Fondi comuni di investimento . Napoli , c1985. 183 p. ; LC Card 86-193326
HG5526 .F66 1985

Grasso, Mario. Convegno nazionale del PCI (1982 : Milan, Italy) Le nuove frontiere dello sviluppo . Milano, Italy , c1983. 368 p. ; LC Card 85-174697
HD9696.A3 I727 1982

Grassroots, an agriculture retention and development program for New Jersey. New Jersey. Dept. of Agriculture. [Trenton, N.J.] [1980] 65 p. : LC Card 81-621630 DDC 333.76/17/09749 19
HD211.N5 N47 1980 ***NYPL [JLF 86-1575]***

Grassroots development in Latin America & the Caribbean : oral histories of social change / [edited by] Robert Wasserstrom. New York : Praeger, 1985. vii, 197 p. : ill. ; 25 cm. Includes index. Bibliography: p. 184-190. ISBN 0-03-001689-4 (alk. paper) : LC Card 84-18180 DDC 334/.098 19
1. Cooperative societies - Latin America - Case studies. 2. Industrial management - Latin America - Employee participation - Case studies. 3. Women in community development - Latin America - Case studies. 4. Rural development - Mexico - Jalisco - Case studies. 5. Economic assistance, American - Latin America - Case studies. 6. Economic assistance, American - Caribbean Area - Case studies. I. Wasserstrom, Robert.
HD3450.5.A4 G72 1985

Gratsershteĭn, I. M. (Izrailʹ Markovich) Ėkonomika, organizatsiia i planirovanie proizvodstva v tsvetnoĭ metallurgii.
Gratsershteĭn, I. M. (Izrailʹ Markovich) Organizatsiia, planirovanie i upravlenie na predpriiatiiakh tsvetnoĭ metallurgii / I.M. Gratsershteĭn, R.D. Malinova. Izd. 3-e, perer. i dop. Moskva , 1987. 415 p. : LC Card 87-156156
HD9539.A3 S5546 1987

Organizatsiia, planirovanie i upravlenie na predpriiatiiakh tsvetnoĭ metallurgii / I.M. Gratsershteĭn, R.D. Malinova. Izd. 3-e, perer. i dop. Moskva : "Metallurgiia", 1987. 415 p. : ill. ; 22 cm. Rev. and enl. ed. of: Ėkonomika, organizatsiia i planirovanie proizvodstva v tsvetnoĭ metallurgii. Izd. 2-e, perer. i dop. 1985. Authorized for instructional purposes. Includes index. LC Card 87-156156
1. Nonferrous metal industries - Soviet Union - Management. I. Malinova, R. D. (Revekka Davydovna). II. Gratsershteĭn, I. M. (Izrailʹ Markovich) Ėkonomika, organizatsiia i planirovanie proizvodstva v tsvetnoĭ metallurgii. III. Title.
HD9539.A3 S5546 1987

Grätz, Christian. Kommunale Wirtschaftsförderung, kritische Bestandsaufnahme ihrer Funktionen und Organisation / Christian Grätz. Bochum : Studienverlag N. Brockmeyer, 1983. xiii, 263 p. : ill. ; 21 cm. (Beiträge zur Struktur- und Konjunkturforschung . Bd. 22) Originally presented as the author's thesis (doctoral)--Ruhr-Universität Bochum, 1983. Bibliography: p. 249-263. ISBN 3-88339-340-1 : LC Card 84-138569
1. Germany, West - Industries. 2. Germany, West - Economic conditions - 1974-. I. Title. II. Series.
HC290.5.D5 G74 1983

Graumann, Jens. Die Dienstleistungsmarke : Charakterisierung und Bewertung eines neuen Markentypus aus absatzwirtschaftlicher Sicht / Jens Graumann. München : Florentz, c1983. l, 197 p. : ill. ; 21 cm. (Hochschulschriften zur Betriebswirtschaftslehre . Bd. 18) Bibliography: p. xxxviii-l. Includes index. ISBN 3-88259-244-3 LC

Card 83-180401
1. Service industries - Germany (West) - Management. I. Title. II. Series.
HD9984.5 .G7 1983

Grauwe, Paul de. Exchange rates, money, and output : the European experience / Paul De Grauwe, Michele Fratianni, Mustapha K. Nabli. New York : St. Martin's Press, 1985. xii, 240 p. : ill. ; 23 cm. Includes index. Bibliography: p. 230-236. ISBN 0-312-27403-3 : LC Card 84-11692 DDC 339/.094 19
1. Foreign exchange problem - European Economic Community countries. 2. Money - European Economic Community countries. 3. European Economic Community countries - Economic conditions. I. Fratianni, Michele. II. Nabli, Mustapha K. III. Title.
HC241.2 .G69 1985 ***NYPL [JLD 86-3007]***

GRAVEL, LUDGER, 1864-1933.
Richer, Laurette B. Ludger Gravel, 1864-1933 . [Montréal] , c1986. 170 p. : ISBN 2-9800028-1-X LC Card 87-115031
HC112.5.G73 R53 1986

Graves, Norman John. Land, water, and mineral resources in science education /. Oxford , New York , 1987. xii, 312 p. : ISBN 0-08-033915-8 : LC Card 86-30527 DDC 333.7/07/101724 19
HC28 .L27 1987

Graves, Stephen C. Balakrishnan, Anantaram. A composite algorithm for the concave-cost LTL consolidation problem /. West Lafayette, Ind. [1985] 43, 14 p. : LC Card 86-139493
HD6483 .P8 no. 877 T57.85

Gray, H. Peter. International trade, employment, and structural adjustment : the United States / H. Peter Gray, Thomas Pugel, and Ingo Walter. Geneva : International Labour Office, 1986. x, 108 p. ; 24 cm. (Employment, adjustment, and industrialisation, 0257-3415 . 3) Includes bibliographies. ISBN 92-2-105325-3 (pbk.) : LC Card 87-119470 DDC 331.12/0973 19
1. Foreign trade and employment - United States. 2. Trade adjustment assistance - United States. I. Pugel, Thomas A. II. Walter, Ingo. III. Title. IV. Series.
HD5710.75.U6 G73 1986

Gray, James R. Eastman, Clyde, 1936- Community grazing . Albuquerque , c1987. xiii, 176 p. : ISBN 0-8263-0936-4 LC Card 86-25058 DDC 333.74/09789 19
HD243.N74 E18 1987

Gray, Jeffrey. The Subject of a moment [motion picture] /. Provo, Utah , 1985. 1 film reel (ca. 27 min.) : LC Card 85-700877 DDC 362.7 11
HE5620.D7

Gray, Paul, 1930-
Guide to IFPS (Interactive Financial Planning System) / Paul Gray. 2nd ed. New York : McGraw-Hill, c1987. xii, 497 p. : ill. ; 28 cm. Rev. ed. of: Student guide to IFPS (Interactive Financial Planning System). c1983. Bibliography: p. 25. Includes index. ISBN 0-07-024394-8 (pbk.) : LC Card 86-21514 DDC 658.1/5/02855329 19
1. IFPS (Computer system). I. Gray, Paul, 1930- Student guide to IFPS (Interactive Financial Planning System). II. Title.
HG4012.5 .G7 1987

Student guide to IFPS (Interactive Financial Planning System) Gray, Paul, 1930- Guide to IFPS (Interactive Financial Planning System) / Paul Gray. 2nd ed. New York , c1987. xii, 497 p. : ISBN 0-07-024394-8 (pbk.) : LC Card 86-21514 DDC 658.1/5/02855329 19
HG4012.5 .G7 1987

Gray, Wayne B. (Wayne Burger), 1955-
Productivity versus OSHA and EPA regulations / by Wayne B. Gray. Ann Arbor, Mich. : UMI Research Press, c1986. xii, p. : ill. ; 24 cm. (Research for business decisions. no. 86) Revision of thesis (Ph. D.)--Harvard University, 1984. Includes index. Bibliography: p. [109]-113. ISBN 0-8357-1721-6 (alk. paper) LC Card 85-28873 DDC 338/.06/0973 19
1. Industrial productivity - United States. 2. Factory and trade waste - Law and legislation - United States - Compliance costs. 3. Industrial safety - Law and legislation - United States - Compliance costs. 4. United States - Manufactures. I. Title.
HC110.I52 G73 1986 ***NYPL [JLE 86-2375]***

Gray, William, Rev. The kanaka, or, How the Queensland planters get and treat their-- / by William Gray. Adelaide : E.S. Wigg, 1895. 40 p. ; 21 cm. LC Card 87-123897 DDC 331.6/2/960943 19
1. Alien labor, Polynesian - Australia - Queensland - History. 2. Kanaka (New Caledonian people). I. Title. II. Title: Kanaka. III. Title: How the Queensland planters get and treat their--.
HD8848.5.P75 G73 1895

Gray, William S. Broader perspectives on the interest of pension plan participants /. Charlottesville, Va. (P.O. Box 3665, Charlottesville 22903) , c1985. vii, 43 p. : LC Card 85-196669 DDC 332.6/7254 19
HD7105.45.U6 B76 1985
NYPL [JLL 81-133 no. 22]

Graymer, LeRoy, 1932- The Urban caldron /. Boston, Mass. , 1986. 152 p. ; ISBN 0-89946-207-3 LC Card 85-21641 DDC 333.73/0973 19
HD257 .U73 1986 ***NYPL [JLE 86-4372]***

GRAYS HARBOR, WASH. - HARBOR.
The Ports of Tacoma, Grays Harbor, and Olympia, Washington /. Washington, D.C. , Fort Belvoir, Va. , 1983. vi, 98 p. : LC Card 83-603527 DDC 387.1/09797/7 19
HE554.T2 P67 1983 ***NYPL [JLF 85-2000]***

Grayson, C. Jackson (Charles Jackson), 1923-
American business, a two-minute warning : ten changes managers must make to survive into the 21st century / C. Jackson Grayson, Jr., Carla O'Dell. New York : Free Press ; London : Collier Macmillan, c1988. xvii, 368 p. : ill. ; 25 cm. Bibliography: p. 343-360. Includes index. ISBN 0-02-912680-0 LC Card 87-19391 DDC 658/.00973 19
1. Industrial management - United States. 2. Industrial management - Japan. 3. Industrial productivity - United States. 4. Industrial productivity - Japan. 5. Economic forecasting - United States. 6. United States - Economic conditions - 1981-. I. O'Dell, Carla S., 1950-. II. Title.
HD70.U5 G69 1988

Graziano, Loretta. Interpreting the money supply : human and institutional factors / Loretta Graziano. New York : Quorum Books, 1987. xiii, 245 p. ; 25 cm. Bibliography: p. [235]-241. Includes index. ISBN 0-89930-151-7 (lib. bdg. : alk. paper) LC Card 87-2539 DDC 332.4/14 19
1. Money supply. I. Title.
HG226.3 .G72 1987

GRAZING DISTRICTS - BOTSWANA.
Wily, Liz. The TGLP and hunter-gatherers . Gaborone, Botswana , 1981. ii, 102 p. ; LC Card 82-207525
DT797 W55 1981 ***NYPL [JLG 87-6]***

GRAZING DISTRICTS - NEW MEXICO.
Eastman, Clyde, 1936- Community grazing . Albuquerque , c1987. xiii, 176 p. : ISBN 0-8263-0936-4 LC Card 86-25058 DDC 333.74/09789 19
HD243.N74 E18 1987

Great American video retailing . Parrish, Vernon. Arlington, Va. [1983?] viii, 448 p. : ISBN 0-9615774-0-1 LC Card 85-90437 DDC 621.388/332/0688 19
HD9697.V543 U544 1983

GREAT ATLANTIC AND PACIFIC TEA COMPANY - HISTORY.
Walsh, William I. The rise and decline of the Great Atlantic & Pacific Tea Company /. Secaucus, N.J. , c1986. 254 p., [24] p. of plates : ISBN 0-8184-0382-9 : LC Card 85-24987 DDC 381/.456413/006073 19
HD9321.9.G7 W35 1986
NYPL [JLE 86-1952]

GREAT BRAK RIVER ESTUARY (SOUTH AFRICA) - ECONOMIC CONDITIONS.
Stauth, Roy. A methodology for determining the socially optimum uses of estuarine resources . Rondebosch, South Africa [1982] v, 119 leaves : LC Card 86-210152
HC905.Z7 G87 1982

Great Britain. Advisory Council for Applied Research and Development. Software, a vital key to UK competitiveness / Cabinet Office, Advisory Council for Applied Research and Development. London : H.M.S.O., 1986. viii, 87 p. : ill. ; 21 cm. "An ACARD report." ISBN 0-11-630829-X (pbk.) : LC Card 86-209046 DDC 338.4/70053/0941 19
1. Computer software industry - Great Britain. 2. Competition, International. I. Title.
HD9696.C63 G74 1986

GREAT BRITAIN - APPROPRIATIONS AND EXPENDITURES.
Levitt, M. S., 1938- The growth and efficiency of public spending /. Cambridge [Cambridgeshire] , New York , 1987. xiv, 201 p. : ISBN 0-521-34621-5 (U. S.) LC Card 87-11636 DDC 339.5/22/0941 19
HJ7764 .L475 1987

Mullard, Maurice, 1946- The politics of public expenditure /. London , New York , c1987. 220 p. : ISBN 0-7099-4674-0 : LC Card 87-6777 DDC 336.3/9/0941 19
HJ7764 .M85 1987

GREAT BRITAIN - APPROPRIATIONS AND EXPENDITURES - CONGRESSES.
New priorities in public spending /. Brookfield, VT , 1987. 129 p. ; ISBN 0-566-05386-1 : LC Card 86-22946 DDC 336.3/9/0941 19
HJ7764 .N49 1987

GREAT BRITAIN - ARMED FORCES - APPROPRIATIONS AND EXPENDITURES.
L'Effort économique de défense . [Grenoble] , 1985. 235 p. : LC Card 86-199399
HC280.D4 E38 1985

GREAT BRITAIN. BOARD OF TRADE - HISTORY.
Striking a balance . London , 1986. 76 p. : ISBN 0-11-513848-X (pbk.) : LC Card 86-231618 DDC 380.1/06/041 19
HF73.G7 S77 1986

Great Britain. British Broadcasting Corporation. see **British Broadcasting Corporation.**

Great Britain. Central Juvenile Employment Executive. see **Great Britain. Central Youth Employment Executive.**

Great Britain. Central Office of Information.
(Old Catalog note: Great Britain. Information. Central Office of)
Facts from your figures /. London , 1977. 37 p. : LC Card 85-160272
HA37.G7 F33 1977

Great Britain. Central Office of Information. Reference Division. Housing and town and country planning in the United Kingdom dependencies. [London, 1960] 51 p. illus. 24 cm. LC Card 72-222605
1. Housing - Great Britain - Colonies. I. Title.
HD7333.A3 A54 1960b

Great Britain. Central Office of Information. Reference Services.
Britain's energy resources /. London , 1981. 27 p. : ISBN 0-11-701010-3 (pbk.) LC Card 81-165936 DDC 333.79/0941 19
HD9502.G72 B74 1981

Nuclear energy in Britain /. London , 1981. 31, [1] p. : ISBN 0-11-701011-1 (pbk.) LC Card 81-165924 DDC 333.79/24/0941 19
HD9698.G72 N83 1981

Great Britain. Central Statistical Office. Press and Information Service. Facts from your figures /. London , 1977. 37 p. : LC Card 85-160272
HA37.G7 F33 1977

Great Britain. Central Youth Employment Executive. Company secretary. [4th ed. London] H.M. Stationery Off. [1970] 15 p. 22 cm. (Choice of careers. 29) Cover title. ISBN 0-11-360036-4 : LC Card 72-534885 DDC 331.702 s
1. Corporation secretaries - Great Britain. I. Title. II. Series.
HF5381.A1 G73 no. 29, 1970

GREAT BRITAIN - COLONIES - AFRICA - ECONOMIC CONDITIONS.
Munro, J. Forbes. Britain in tropical Africa, 1880-1960 . London , 1984. 89 p. : ISBN 0-333-32330-0 LC Card 87-672364
HC800 .M86x 1984

GREAT BRITAIN - COLONIES - AFRICA - ECONOMIC POLICY.
Kanduza, Ackson M. The political economy of underdevelopment in Northern Rhodesia, 1918-1960 . Lanham, MD , c1986. x, 336 p. : ISBN 0-8191-5189-0 (alk. paper) : LC Card 85-29835 DDC 338.96894 19
HC915 .K36 1986 ***NYPL [JLD 86-2962]***

Munro, J. Forbes. Britain in tropical Africa, 1880-1960 . London , 1984. 89 p. : ISBN

0-333-32330-0 LC Card 87-672364
HC800 .M86x 1984

GREAT BRITAIN - COLONIES - AMERICA - COMMERCE.
Steele, Ian Kenneth. The English Atlantic, 1675-1740 . New York , 1986. xii, 400 p. ISBN 0-19-503968-8 LC Card 85-25828 DDC 380.3/09171/241 19
HE202 .S74 1986 ***NYPL [JLE 86-4056]***

GREAT BRITAIN - COLONIES - AMERICA - ECONOMIC CONDITIONS - REGIONAL DISPARITIES.
The Economy of early America . Charlottesville , 1988. xvi, 334 p. : ISBN 0-8139-1139-7 LC Card 87-6169 DDC 330.973/02 19
HC104 .E26 1988

GREAT BRITAIN - COLONIES - ECONOMIC CONDITIONS.
Development studies and colonial policy /. London , Totowa, N.J. , 1987. 292 p. : ISBN 0-7146-3231-7 : LC Card 87-6562 DDC 338.9171/241 19
HD82 .D395 1987

GREAT BRITAIN - COLONIES - ECONOMIC POLICY.
Ndlela, Daniel Boda. Dualism in the Rhodesian colonial economy /. [Lund] [1981] vi, 241 p. : LC Card 86-673434
HC910 .N34x 1981

GREAT BRITAIN - COLONIES - INDIA - ECONOMIC CONDITIONS.
Dutt, Romesh Chunder, 1848-1909. The economic history of India in the Victorian Age . London [19--] xxii, 628 p. ; LC Card 87-131511
HC435 .D975 1900z

Great Britain - Colonies - North America. see **Great Britain - Colonies - America.**

GREAT BRITAIN - COMMERCE.
Morgan, Ann D. British imports of consumer goods . Cambridge [Cambridgeshire] , New York , 1988. xi, 129 p. ; ISBN 0-521-35349-1 LC Card 87-25662 DDC 382/.5/0941 19
HF3506.5 .M67 1988

Rowthorn, Bob. De-industrialization and foreign trade /. Cambridge [Cambridgeshire] , New York , 1987. xi, 422 p. : ISBN 0-521-26360-3 LC Card 87-6331 DDC 338.0941 19
HC256.5 .R683 1987

GREAT BRITAIN - COMMERCE - BALKAN PENINSULA - HISTORY - 19TH CENTURY.
Cernovodeanu, Paul. Relaţiile comerciale româno-engleze în contextul politicii orientale a Marii Britanii . Cluj-Napoca , 1986. 404 p. ; LC Card 87-143711
HF3508.R6 C47 1986

GREAT BRITAIN - COMMERCE - GERMANY.
Ohlsen, Ralph-Rainer, 1955- Der deutsche Export nach Grossbritannien von 1923 bis 1933 . Bergisch Gladbach , c1986. ii, 256 p. : ISBN 3-89012-043-1 LC Card 86-160346
HF1546.5.G7 O37 1986

GREAT BRITAIN - COMMERCE - HISTORY.
Striking a balance . London , 1986. 76 p. : ISBN 0-11-513848-X (pbk.) : LC Card 86-231618 DDC 380.1/06/041 19
HF73.G7 S77 1986

GREAT BRITAIN - COMMERCE - HISTORY - 19TH CENTURY.
Braun, Hans-Joachim. Wirtschafts- und finanzpolitische Entscheidungsprozesse in England in der ersten Hälfte des 19. Jahrhunderts /. Frankfurt am Main , New York , c1984. 236 p. : ISBN 3-8204-7702-0 LC Card 85-191319 DDC 338.941 19
HC255 .B77 1984

GREAT BRITAIN - COMMERCE - INDIA.
Assocham Trade Mission to UK, 1984. Opportunities for Indo-British economic cooperation . New Delhi [1985] 43, xiii p., [4] p. of plates : LC Card 87-902558 DDC 337.54041 19
HF3788.G7 A87 1985

GREAT BRITAIN - COMMERCE - ROMANIA - HISTORY - 19TH CENTURY.
Cernovodeanu, Paul. Relaţiile comerciale româno-engleze în contextul politicii orientale a Marii Britanii . Cluj-Napoca , 1986. 404 p. ; LC Card 87-143711
HF3508.R6 C47 1986

GREAT BRITAIN - COMMERCE - UNITED STATES.
Sheffield, John Holroyd, Earl of, 1735-1821. Observations on the commerce of the American states. London, 1784. 2 p.l., xlvii, 345, [21] p., 1 l. LC Card 06-17319
HF3025 .S58

GREAT BRITAIN - COMMERCIAL POLICY - HISTORY - 16TH CENTURY.
Ide, Arthur Frederick. The mercantile policies of Henry VII /. Irving, Tex. , 1987. v, 78 p. : ISBN 0-938659-02-2 (pbk.) : LC Card 87-4316 DDC 382/.3/0942 19
HF1533 .I34 1987

Great Britain. Decimal Currency Board.
Conversion of accounting records. London, H.M.S.O., 1969. [1], 33 p. 21 cm. Cover title. Bibliography: p. 31-32. ISBN 0-11-700407-3 : LC Card 77-489376 DDC 657
1. Accounting. 2. Money - Great Britain. 3. Decimal system - Great Britain. I. Title.
HF5635 .G777

GREAT BRITAIN - DEFENSES - ECONOMIC ASPECTS.
L'Effort économique de défense . [Grenoble] , 1985. 235 p. : LC Card 86-199399
HC280.D4 E38 1985

Great Britain. Dept. of Employment. (Old Catalog form: Great Britain. Employment and Insurance department)
Inspecting industry . London , 1986. 110 p. ; ISBN 0-11-751910-3 (pbk.) : LC Card 87-164869 DDC 363.1/1/0941 19
HD7695 .I63 1986

Great Britain. Dept. of Energy. Coal industry examination . London [1974] 35 p. ; LC Card 85-192146 DDC 338.2/724/0941 19
HD9551.5 .C43 1974

Great Britain. Dept. of Industry and Trade. see **Great Britain. Dept. of Trade and Industry.**

Great Britain. Dept. of Trade and Industry. (Old Catalog form: Great Britain. Trade and industry, Dept. of)
Striking a balance . London , 1986. 76 p. : ISBN 0-11-513848-X (pbk.) : LC Card 86-231618 DDC 380.1/06/041 19
HF73.G7 S77 1986

GREAT BRITAIN. DEPT. OF TRADE AND INDUSTRY - HISTORY.
Striking a balance . London , 1986. 76 p. : ISBN 0-11-513848-X (pbk.) : LC Card 86-231618 DDC 380.1/06/041 19
HF73.G7 S77 1986

Great Britain. Dept. of Trade and Industry. Radiocommunications Division. CSP International (Firm) Deregulation of the radio spectrum in the UK /. London , 1987. vi, 182, [30] p. : ISBN 0-11-513979-6 (pbk.) : LC Card 87-170465 DDC 384.54/52 19
HE8689.9.G7 C76 1987

GREAT BRITAIN - ECONOMIC CONDITIONS - 18TH CENTURY.
Korzeniewicz, Richard. British economic and social history, 1700-1950 /. London , c1985. 261 p. : ISBN 0-7212-0711-1 : LC Card 87-144405 DDC 330.941 19
HC254.5 .K67 1985

GREAT BRITAIN - ECONOMIC CONDITIONS - 1760-1860.
Hueckel, Glenn R. (Glenn Russell), 1945- The Napoleonic wars and their impact on factor returns and output growth in England, 1793-1815 /. New York , 1985. lvi, 212 p. ; ISBN 0-8240-6683-9 : LC Card 84-46003 DDC 330.941/073 19
HC254.5 .H78 1985 ***NYPL [JLE 86-4294]***

Wells, Roger A. E. Wretched faces . New York , 1988. p. cm. ISBN 0-312-01248-9 : LC Card 87-22164 DDC 363.8/0942 19
HC260.F3 W45 1988

GREAT BRITAIN - ECONOMIC CONDITIONS - 19TH CENTURY.
The Decline of the British economy /. Oxford [Oxfordshire] , New York , 1987, c1986. vii, 310 p. ; ISBN 0-19-877281-5 (pbk.) : LC Card 87-5479 DDC 330.941/08 19
HC255 .D43 1987

Ingham, Geoffrey K. Capitalism divided? . Basingstoke, Hampshire , 1984. viii, 304 p. : ISBN 0-333-30116-1 LC Card 86-673507
HC255 .I495x 1984b

Kennedy, William P. (William Paca), 1944- Industrial structure, capital markets, and the origins of British economic decline /. Cambridge [Cambridgeshire] , New York , 1987. xii, 230 p. ; ISBN 0-521-23018-7 LC Card 86-24411 DDC 330.941 19
HC255 .K45 1987

Korzeniewicz, Richard. British economic and social history, 1700-1950 /. London , c1985. 261 p. : ISBN 0-7212-0711-1 : LC Card 87-144405 DDC 330.941 19
HC254.5 .K67 1985

GREAT BRITAIN - ECONOMIC CONDITIONS - 20TH CENTURY.
The Decline of the British economy /. Oxford [Oxfordshire] , New York , 1987, c1986. vii, 310 p. ; ISBN 0-19-877281-5 (pbk.) : LC Card 87-5479 DDC 330.941/08 19
HC255 .D43 1987

Ingham, Geoffrey K. Capitalism divided? . Basingstoke, Hampshire , 1984. viii, 304 p. : ISBN 0-333-30116-1 LC Card 86-673507
HC255 .I495x 1984b

Kennedy, William P. (William Paca), 1944- Industrial structure, capital markets, and the origins of British economic decline /. Cambridge [Cambridgeshire] , New York , 1987. xii, 230 p. ; ISBN 0-521-23018-7 LC Card 86-24411 DDC 330.941 19
HC255 .K45 1987

Korzeniewicz, Richard. British economic and social history, 1700-1950 /. London , c1985. 261 p. : ISBN 0-7212-0711-1 : LC Card 87-144405 DDC 330.941 19
HC254.5 .K67 1985

Perevozchikov, V. I. (Viktor Ivanovich) Stanovlenie i periody razvitiia gosudarstvenno-monopolisticheskogo kapitalizma v Anglii /. Kiev , 1982. 153 p. ; LC Card 83-102577
HC256 .P47 1982

GREAT BRITAIN - ECONOMIC CONDITIONS - 1918-1945.
Barnett, Correlli. The pride and the fall . New York , 1987, c1986. xii, 359 p. ; ISBN 0-02-901851-X LC Card 86-25701 DDC 330.941/0854 19
HC256.4 .B28 1987

Cole, George Douglas Howard, 1889-1959. The next ten years in British social and economic policy /. New York , 1985. xxi, 459 p. ; ISBN 0-8240-7607-9 (alk. paper) : LC Card 85-13055 DDC 338.941 19
HC256.3 .C6 1985 ***NYPL [JLD 86-3300]***

Hannington, Wal, 1895- The problem of the distressed areas /. New York , 1985. 286 p. : ISBN 0-8240-7613-3 : LC Card 85-14663 DDC 338.941 19
HC256.3 .H265 1985 ***NYPL [JLD 86-3420]***

Hilton, John, 1880-1943. Rich man, poor man /. New York , 1985. 174 p. ; ISBN 0-8240-7614-1 (alk. paper) : LC Card 85-13078 DDC 339.2/2/0941 19
HC256.4 .H54 1985 ***NYPL [JLC 86-342]***

The Worst of times . London , 1985. 201 p., [8] p. of plates : ISBN 0-7045-0513-4
NYPL [JLD 86-1799]

GREAT BRITAIN - ECONOMIC CONDITIONS - 1945-
Cairncross, Frances. Guide to the economy /. London , 1987. viii, 161 p. : ISBN 0-416-39600-3 (pbk.) : LC Card 87-138822 DDC 330.941/085 19
HC256.6 .C27 1987

The Changing experience of employment . Houndmills, Basingstoke, Hampshire , 1986. x, 230 p. ; ISBN 0-333-39695-2
NYPL [JLD 87-933]

Changing places . London , Baltimore, Md., USA , 1987. xv, 144 p. : ISBN 0-7131-6498-0 (pbk.) : LC Card 87-148942 DDC 331.12/5/0941 19
HD5765.A6 C49 1987

Current controversies in economics /. Oxford [Oxfordshire] UK , New York, NY, USA , 1987. xii, 319 p. : ISBN 0-631-15157-5 : LC Card 86-29928 DDC 338.941 19
HB171.5 .C975 1987

The Economic revival of modern Britain . Aldershot, Hants, England , c1987. xv, 349 p. : ISBN 1-85278-000-2 (pbk.) : LC Card 87-170031 DDC 338.941 19
HC256.6 .E227 1987

Gardner, Nick. Decade of discontent . Oxford, OX, UK , New York, NY, USA , 1987. 236 p. : ISBN 0-631-15307-1 : LC Card 86-30949 DDC 338.941 19
HC256.6 .G36 1987

Gould, Bryan. Monetarism or prosperity? /. London , 1981. x, 222 p. : ISBN 0-333-30782-8 LC Card 86-673392
HG939.5 .G65x 1981

Herington, John. The outer city /. London , New York , 1984. 205 p. : ISBN 0-06-318237-8
NYPL [JLE 86-1465]

Jeffreys, Daniel. Economics and the economy /. Burnt Mill, Harlow, Essex, England , 1985. 317 p. : ISBN 0-582-35452-8 (pbk.) LC Card 87-152784 DDC 330 19
HB171.5 .J45 1985

Jones, Aubrey, 1911- Britain's economy . Cambridge [Cambridgeshire] , New York , 1985. x, 158 p. : ISBN 0-521-30816-X LC Card 85-9649 DDC 330.941/0858 19
HC256.6 .J64 1985 ***NYPL [JLD 86-1581]***

MacInnes, John. Thatcherism at work . Milton Keynes, England , Philadelphia , 1987. p. cm. ISBN 0-335-15517-0 LC Card 87-24722 DDC 338.941 19
HD8391 .M26 1987

Marx, Roland. La vie quotidienne en Angleterre au temps de l'expérience socialiste . [Paris] , c1983. 323 p. ; ISBN 2-01-008679-1 : LC Card 83-220426
HC256.5 .M3955 1983

Nolan, Brian. Income distribution and the macroeconomy /. Cambridge [Cambridgeshire] , New York , 1987. xii, 208 p. : ISBN 0-521-32612-5 LC Card 87-6606 DDC 339.2/0941 19
HC260.I5 N65 1987

Political economy . Jackson , c1987. vii, 276 p. ; ISBN 0-87805-313-1 (alk. paper) LC Card 87-10425 DDC 361.6/1/0941 19
HC106 .P68 1987

Robertson, Alex. The bleak midwinter, 1947 /. Manchester, U.K. , Wolfeboro, N.H., U. S.A. , 1987. x, 207 p. : ISBN 0-7190-1902-8 : LC Card 87-11085 DDC 333.8/22/0941 19
HD9551.5 .R56 1987

Rose, Richard, 1933- Getting by in three economies . Glasgow , 1983. 40 p. ; LC Card 83-150133 DDC 330.941/0858 19
HC256.6 .R67 1983

Rowthorn, Bob. De-industrialization and foreign trade /. Cambridge [Cambridgeshire] , New York , 1987. xi, 422 p. : ISBN 0-521-26360-3 LC Card 87-6331 DDC 338.0941 19
HC256.5 .R683 1987

Short, John R. The urban arena . London , 1984. viii, 202 p. : ISBN 0-333-36139-3 LC Card 87-672913
HC256.6 .S49x 1984

GREAT BRITAIN - ECONOMIC CONDITIONS - 1945- - BIBLIOGRAPHY.

Shaw, Christine. The A-Z of UK marketing information sources /. London , 1984. 233 p. ; ISBN 0-86338-048-4 (pbk.) : LC Card 84-217782 DDC 330.941/0858 19
HC256.6 .S47 1984 ***NYPL [JLD 86-2248]***

GREAT BRITAIN - ECONOMIC CONDITIONS - 1945- - ECONOMETRIC MODELS.

The Cambridge multisectoral dynamic model of the British economy /. Cambridge [Cambridgeshire] , New York , 1988. p. cm. ISBN 0-521-33004-1 LC Card 86-33375 DDC 330.941/00724 19
HC256.6 .C29 1988

GREAT BRITAIN - ECONOMIC CONDITIONS - 1945- - INFORMATION SERVICES.

Shaw, Christine. The A-Z of UK marketing information sources /. London , 1984. 233 p. ; ISBN 0-86338-048-4 (pbk.) : LC Card 84-217782 DDC 330.941/0858 19
HC256.6 .S47 1984 ***NYPL [JLD 86-2248]***

GREAT BRITAIN - ECONOMIC CONDITIONS - 1945- - REGIONAL DISPARITIES.

Redundancy and recession . Norwich, England , c1986. xii, 174 p. : ISBN 0-86094-201-5 : LC Card 86-218942 DDC 330.941/0858 19
HC256.6 .R44 1986

Will there always be an England? [videorecording] /. Alexandria, VA , 1986. 1 videocassette (60 min.) : LC Card 86-707796 DDC 942.085 11
HC256.5

GREAT BRITAIN - ECONOMIC CONDITIONS - ADDRESSES, ESSAYS, LECTURES.

Court, W. H. B. (William Henry Bassano) Scarcity and choice in history. London, 1970. viii, 256 p. LC Card 79-488977 DDC 330.9
HC253 .C675

GREAT BRITAIN - ECONOMIC CONDITIONS - PROBLEMS, EXERCISES, ETC.

Harbury, C. D. Workbook in introductory economics /. Oxford [Oxfordshire] , New York , 1987, c1982. xvii, 176 p. : ISBN 0-08-034790-8 (pbk.) : LC Card 87-19011 DDC 330/.076 19
HB74.6 .H37 1987

GREAT BRITAIN - ECONOMIC CONDITIONS - STATISTICAL SERVICES.

Facts from your figures /. London , 1977. 37 p. : LC Card 85-160272
HA37.G7 F33 1977

GREAT BRITAIN - ECONOMIC POLICY.

Beveridge, William Henry Beveridge, Baron, 1879-1963. A Beveridge reader /. London , Boston , 1987. viii, 190 p. ; ISBN 0-04-361070-6 (alk. paper) LC Card 87-11819 DDC 338.941 19
HB103.A2 B48 1987

Braun, Hans-Joachim. Wirtschafts- und finanzpolitische Entscheidungsprozesse in England in der ersten Hälfte des 19. Jahrhunderts /. Frankfurt am Main , New York , c1984. 236 p. : ISBN 3-8204-7702-0 LC Card 85-191319 DDC 338.941 19
HC255 .B77 1984

The Decline of the British economy /. Oxford [Oxfordshire] , New York , 1987, c1986. vii, 310 p. ; ISBN 0-19-877281-5 (pbk.) : LC Card 87-5479 DDC 330.941/08 19
HC255 .D43 1987

Levačić, Rosalind. Economic policy-making /. Sussex , Totowa, N.J. , 1987. xii, 372 p. : ISBN 0-389-20741-1 (Barnes & Noble) LC Card 87-11543 DDC 338.941 19
HD75 .L48 1987

Slack, Paul. Poverty and policy in Tudor and Stuart England /. London , New York , 1988. p. cm. ISBN 0-582-48965-2 (alk. paper) LC Card 87-2657 DDC 362.5/561/0942 19
HC254.4 .S42 1988

GREAT BRITAIN - ECONOMIC POLICY - 1918-1945.

Britain's industrial future . New York , 1985. xxiv, 503 p. ; ISBN 0-8240-7605-2 (alk. paper) : LC Card 85-13042 DDC 338.941 19
HC256.3 .B728 1985 ***NYPL [JLD 86-3461]***

Cole, George Douglas Howard, 1889-1959. The next ten years in British social and economic policy /. New York , 1985. xxi, 459 p. ; ISBN 0-8240-7607-9 (alk. paper) : LC Card 85-13055 DDC 338.941 19
HC256.3 .C6 1985 ***NYPL [JLD 86-3300]***

Hannington, Wal, 1895- The problem of the distressed areas /. New York , 1985. 286 p. : ISBN 0-8240-7613-3 : LC Card 85-14663 DDC 338.941 19
HC256.3 .H265 1985 ***NYPL [JLD 86-3420]***

Tomlinson, Jim. Employment policy . Oxford [Oxfordshire] , New York , 1987. xi, 185 p. ; ISBN 0-19-828564-7 : LC Card 87-7837 DDC 339.5/0941 19
HC256.4 .T586 1987

GREAT BRITAIN - ECONOMIC POLICY - 1945-

Barr, Nicholas. The economics of the welfare state /. Stanford, Calif. , 1987. xiv, 475 p. : ISBN 0-8047-1427-4 LC Card 87-60997 DDC 338.941 19
HB846 .B37 1987

Current controversies in economics /. Oxford [Oxfordshire] UK , New York, NY, USA , 1987. xii, 319 p. : ISBN 0-631-15157-5 : LC Card 86-29928 DDC 338.941 19
HB171.5 .C975 1987

The Economic revival of modern Britain . Aldershot, Hants, England , c1987. xv, 349 p. : ISBN 1-85278-000-2 (pbk.) : LC Card 87-170031 DDC 338.941 19
HC256.6 .E227 1987

Gamble, Andrew. Britain in decline . Basingstoke, Hampshire , 1985. xxi, 261 p. ; ISBN 0-333-39253-1 : LC Card 86-673896
HC256.6 .G35x 1985

Gardner, Nick. Decade of discontent . Oxford, OX, UK , New York, NY, USA , 1987. 236 p. : ISBN 0-631-15307-1 : LC Card 86-30949 DDC 338.941 19
HC256.6 .G36 1987

Gould, Bryan. Monetarism or prosperity? /. London , 1981. x, 222 p. : ISBN 0-333-30782-8 LC Card 86-673392
HG939.5 .G65x 1981

Greenaway, David. Macroeconomics . Oxford, OX, UK , New York, NY, USA , 1987. p. cm. ISBN 0-631-15763-8 (pbk.) : LC Card 87-20831 DDC 339/.0941 19
HB172.5 .G75 1987

Hall, Peter A. Governing the economy . Cambridge, U.K. , Oxford, U.K. , 1986. 341 p. ; ISBN 0-7456-0227-4 : LC Card 87-672535
HC256.5 .H256x 1986b

Hattersley, Roy. Economic priorities for a labour government /. New York , 1987. ix, 198 p. ; ISBN 0-312-00987-9 : LC Card 87-9576 DDC 338.941 19
HC256.6 .H385 1987

Howell, David, 1936- Blind victory . London , 1986. xiv, 191 p. ; ISBN 0-241-11743-7 : LC Card 86-223521 DDC 338.941 19
HC256.6 .H639 1986

La Serre, Françoise de. La Grande-Bretagne et la Communauté européenne /. Paris , c1987. 223, [1] p. : ISBN 2-13-040114-7 : LC Card 87-165122
HC241.25.G7 L118 1987

MacInnes, John. Thatcherism at work . Milton Keynes, England , Philadelphia , 1987. p. cm. ISBN 0-335-15517-0 LC Card 87-24722 DDC 338.941 19
HD8391 .M26 1987

Managing the UK economy . Cambridge, UK , 1987. xxvii, 328 p. : ISBN 0-7456-0316-5 : LC Card 86-26860 DDC 338.941 19
HC256.5 .M392 1987

Nolan, Brian. Income distribution and the macroeconomy /. Cambridge [Cambridgeshire] , New York , 1987. xii, 208 p. : ISBN 0-521-32612-5 LC Card 87-6606 DDC 339.2/0941 19
HC260.I5 N65 1987

Nuscheler, Franz. Die Entwicklungspolitik der Regierung Thatcher . [Bonn] [1986] 93 p. : LC Card 86-186261
HC60 .N87 1986

Political economy . Jackson , c1987. vii, 276 p. ; ISBN 0-87805-313-1 (alk. paper) LC Card 87-10425 DDC 361.6/1/0941 19
HC106 .P68 1987

Renshaw, Geoffrey. Adjustment and economic performance in industrialised countries . Geneva , 1986. xiv, 180 p. ; ISBN 92-2-105510-8 (pbk.) : LC Card 87-123435 DDC 338.9/009172/2 19
HC286.7 .R46 1986

Short, John R. The urban arena . London , 1984. viii, 202 p. : ISBN 0-333-36139-3 LC Card 87-672913
HC256.6 .S49x 1984

Stewart, Michael, 1933- Keynes and after /. Harmondsworth, Middlesex, England , New

York, N.Y., U. S.A. , 1986. 230 p. ; ISBN 0-14-022646-X (pbk.) : LC Card 86-218640 DDC 330.15/6 19
HB99.7 .S7 1986

Tomlinson, Jim. Employment policy . Oxford [Oxfordshire] , New York , 1987. xi, 185 p. ; ISBN 0-19-828564-7 : LC Card 87-7837 DDC 339.5/0941 19
HC256.4 .T586 1987

GREAT BRITAIN - ECONOMIC POLICY - 1945- - CONGRESSES.
Developing local economic strategies . Milton Keynes [England] , Philadelphia , 1987. p. cm. ISBN 0-335-15522-7 LC Card 87-22681 DDC 338.941 19
HC256.6 .D48 1987

Public enterprise policy in India and U.K. in 1980s /. Bombay , 1987. xx, 286 p. ; LC Card 86-903771 DDC 338.6/2/0941 19
HD4293 .P775 1987

Great Britain. Employment, Dept. of. see **Great Britain. Dept. of Employment.**

Great Britain. Energy, Dept. of. see **Great Britain. Dept. of Energy.**

Great Britain. Equal Opportunities Commission.
Green paper : reform of social security : response of the Equal Opportunities Commission. Manchester : The Commission, [1985] 66 p. : ill. ; 31 cm. "August 1985." Includes bibliographical references. LC Card 87-124211 DDC 368.4/00941 19
1. Social security - Great Britain. I. Title.
HD7165 .G725 1985

GREAT BRITAIN - FOREIGN ECONOMIC RELATIONS.
Stopford, John M. Britain and the multinationals /. Chichester , New York , c1985. xiv, 282 p. : ISBN 0-471-90839-8 : LC Card 85-12352 DDC 338.8/8841 19
HD2845 .S76 1985 ***NYPL [JLE 86-924]***

Von der Konkurrenz zur Rivalität . Stuttgart , 1986. 186 p. ; ISBN 3-515-04760-3 LC Card 87-134320 DDC 337/.09/04 19
HF1411 .V665 1986

GREAT BRITAIN - FOREIGN ECONOMIC RELATIONS - CHILE.
Couyoumdjian, Juan Ricardo. Chile y Gran Bretaña . [Santiago] [1986] xvi, 340 p., [4] p. of plates : LC Card 86-222403
HF1516.5.G72 C68 1986

GREAT BRITAIN - FOREIGN ECONOMIC RELATIONS - CHINA.
Edwards, E. W. British diplomacy and finance in China, 1895-1914 /. Oxford [Oxfordshire] , New York , 1987. 212 p. : ISBN 0-19-822916-X : LC Card 86-28567 DDC 337.41051 19
HF1534.5.C5 E39 1987

GREAT BRITAIN - FOREIGN ECONOMIC RELATIONS - EUROPE.
Hogan, Michael J., 1943- The Marshall Plan . Cambridge [Cambridgeshire] , New York , 1987. xiv, 482 p. ; ISBN 0-521-25140-0 LC Card 86-31773 DDC 338.91/73/04 19
HC240 .H614 1987

GREAT BRITAIN - FOREIGN ECONOMIC RELATIONS - GERMANY.
Banze, Angelika. Die deutsch-englische Wirtschaftsrivalität . Vaduz , 1965. 105 p. ; LC Card 85-243022 DDC 337.43041 19
HF1546.15.G7 B36 1965

GREAT BRITAIN - FOREIGN ECONOMIC RELATIONS - INDIA.
Assocham Trade Mission to UK, 1984. Opportunities for Indo-British economic cooperation . New Delhi [1985] 43, xiii p., [4] p. of plates : LC Card 87-902558 DDC 337.54041 19
HF3788.G7 A87 1985

GREAT BRITAIN - FOREIGN ECONOMIC RELATIONS - NIGERIA.
Britain and Nigeria . London ; Atlantic Highlands, New Jersey : vi, 250 p. ; ISBN 0-86232-303-7 : LC Card 86-232062 DDC 337.410669 19
HF1534.5.N6 B75 1987

GREAT BRITAIN - FOREIGN ECONOMIC RELATIONS - PERSIAN GULF STATES - CONGRESSES.
Focus on the Gulf Co-operation Council (GCC) . London , c1984. 48 p. : LC Card 85-211534 DDC 337.53/6/041 19
HF1584.5 .F63 1984

GREAT BRITAIN - FOREIGN ECONOMIC RELATIONS - SOUTH AFRICA.
Moorsom, Richard. The scope for sanctions . London , 1986. 102 p. ; ISBN 0-946848-66-1 (pbk.) : LC Card 86-226230 DDC 337.41068 19
HF1613.4 .M66 1986

GREAT BRITAIN - FOREIGN ECONOMIC RELATIONS - SWEDEN.
Nilson, Bengt, 1952- Handelspolitik under skärpt konkurrens . Lund , c1983. 217 p. ; ISBN 91-40-04894-2 : LC Card 84-144528
HF1567 .N55 1983

GREAT BRITAIN - FOREIGN ECONOMIC RELATIONS - UNITED STATES.
Rowland, Benjamin M. Commercial conflict and foreign policy . New York , 1987. 431 p. ; ISBN 0-8240-8090-4 (alk. paper) : LC Card 87-23787 DDC 337.73041 19
HF1456.5.G7 R68 1987

GREAT BRITAIN - FOREIGN ECONOMIC RELATIONS - VENEZUELA.
Vetencourt Guerra, Lola. El Imperio Británico en la economía de Venezuela, 1830-1870 /. Caracas , 1981. 233 p. : LC Card 83-201772
HF1530.5.G7 V47 1981

GREAT BRITAIN - FOREIGN RELATIONS - 1910-1936.
Rowland, Benjamin M. Commercial conflict and foreign policy . New York , 1987. 431 p. ; ISBN 0-8240-8090-4 (alk. paper) : LC Card 87-23787 DDC 337.73041 19
HF1456.5.G7 R68 1987

GREAT BRITAIN - FOREIGN RELATIONS - 1936-1945.
Rowland, Benjamin M. Commercial conflict and foreign policy . New York , 1987. 431 p. ; ISBN 0-8240-8090-4 (alk. paper) : LC Card 87-23787 DDC 337.73041 19
HF1456.5.G7 R68 1987

GREAT BRITAIN - FOREIGN RELATIONS - CHINA.
Edwards, E. W. British diplomacy and finance in China, 1895-1914 /. Oxford [Oxfordshire] , New York , 1987. 212 p. : ISBN 0-19-822916-X : LC Card 86-28567 DDC 337.41051 19
HF1534.5.C5 E39 1987

GREAT BRITAIN - FOREIGN RELATIONS - GERMANY.
Wirtschaftspolitik im britischen Besatzungsgebiet 1945-1949 /. Düsseldorf , 1984. 338 p. : ISBN 3-590-18124-9 LC Card 84-188669
HC286.5 .W5655 1984

GREAT BRITAIN - FOREIGN RELATIONS - IRAQ.
Sassoon, Joseph. Economic policy in Iraq, 1932-1950 /. London, England , Totowa, N.J. , 1987. p. cm. ISBN 0-7146-3305-4 : LC Card 87-6577 DDC 338.9567 19
HC415.4 .S27 1987

GREAT BRITAIN - FOREIGN RELATIONS - UNITED STATES.
Helmreich, Jonathan E. Gathering rare ores . Princeton, N.J. , c1986. xiv, 303 p. : ISBN 0-691-04738-3 (alk. paper) : LC Card 86-4862 DDC 327.1/11 19
HD9698.U52 H45 1986
NYPL [JLE 86-4584]

GREAT BRITAIN - FULL EMPLOYMENT POLICIES.
Tomlinson, Jim. Employment policy . Oxford [Oxfordshire] , New York , 1987. xi, 185 p. ; ISBN 0-19-828564-7 : LC Card 87-7837 DDC 339.5/0941 19
HC256.4 .T586 1987

GREAT BRITAIN - FULL EMPLOYMENT POLICIES - HISTORY - 20TH CENTURY.
Jones, Russell, 1959- Wages and employment policy, 1936-1985 /. London , Boston , 1987. xvii, 175 p. ; ISBN 0-04-331110-5 (alk. paper) LC Card 86-14143 DDC 339.5/0941 19
HD5015 .J66 1987 ***NYPL [JLD 87-831]***

Great Britain - Government. see **Great Britain - Politics and government.**

Great Britain. Government Actuary. Variant population projections . London , 1986. 17 p. : ISBN 0-11-690777-0 (pbk.) : LC Card 86-234516 DDC 304.6/2/0941021 19
HB3583 .V368 1986

Great Britain. Health and Safety Commission.
Proposal to review the minimum age at which children may drive or ride on agricultural machinery / Health and Safety Commission. London : H.M.S.O., [1982] 12 p. ; 30 cm. (Discussion document / Health and Safety Commission) ISBN 0-11-883635-8 (pbk.) LC Card 82-214120 DDC 363.1/89 19
1. Children - Employment - Great Britain. 2. Agricultural laborers - Great Britain. 3. Agricultural machinery - Great Britain - Safety measures. I. Series: Discussion document (Great Britain. Health and Safety Commission). II. Title.
HD6247.A4 G74 1982

GREAT BRITAIN - HISTORY - MEDIEVAL PERIOD, 1066-1485.
Power, Eileen Edna, 1889-1940. The wool trade in English medieval history /. New York [1987], c1941. viii, 128 p. ; ISBN 0-313-25656-X (lib. bdg. : alk. paper) LC Card 86-29442 DDC 338.4/767731/0942 19
HD9901.7.E54 P68 1987

GREAT BRITAIN - HISTORY - HENRY VII, 1485-1509.
Ide, Arthur Frederick. The mercantile policies of Henry VII /. Irving, Tex. , 1987. v, 78 p. : ISBN 0-938659-02-2 (pbk.) : LC Card 87-4316 DDC 382/.3/0942 19
HF1533 .I34 1987

GREAT BRITAIN - HISTORY - GEORGE V, 1910-1936.
Couyoumdjian, Juan Ricardo. Chile y Gran Bretaña . [Santiago] [1986] xvi, 340 p., [4] p. of plates : LC Card 86-222403
HF1516.5.G72 C68 1986

Great Britain - History, Economic. see **Great Britain - Economic conditions.**

Great Britain - History, Political. see **Great Britain - Politics and government.**

Great Britain. Home Office.
Review of the ITV and ILR levy structures, 1984-85 . London , c1986. 44 p. ; ISBN 0-86252-236-6 (pbk.) LC Card 86-202703 DDC 384.54/3 19
HE8689.9.G7 R48 1986

Two studies concerning the British Broadcasting Corporation /. London , 1979. 48 p. : ISBN 0-11-340763-7 (pbk.) LC Card 83-221765
HE8689.9.G7 T85 1979

GREAT BRITAIN - INDUSTRIES.
The Challenge of new technology . Aldershot, Hants, England , Brookfield, Vt., U. S.A. , c1988. x, 155 p. : ISBN 0-566-05147-8 : LC Card 87-8592 DDC 338/.06 19
HC260.T4 C46 1988

Renshaw, Geoffrey. Adjustment and economic performance in industrialised countries . Geneva , 1986. xiv, 180 p. ; ISBN 92-2-105510-8 (pbk.) : LC Card 87-123435 DDC 338.9/009172/2 19
HC286.7 .R46 1986

Rowthorn, Bob. De-industrialization and foreign trade /. Cambridge [Cambridgeshire] , New York , 1987. xi, 422 p. : ISBN 0-521-26360-3 LC Card 87-6331 DDC 338.0941 19
HC256.5 .R683 1987

The Structure of British industry /. London , Boston , 1988. p. cm. ISBN 0-04-338146-4 (alk. paper) LC Card 87-18803 DDC 338.0941 19
HC256.6 .S76 1988

Wilkinson, Barry. The shopfloor politics of new technology /. London , 1983. 120 p. ; ISBN 0-435-82950-5 : LC Card 82-236198 DDC 338/.06 19
HC260.T4 W54 1983 ***NYPL [JLD 86-1322]***

GREAT BRITAIN - INDUSTRIES - HISTORY.
Blackford, Mansel G., 1944- The rise of modern business in Great Britain, the United States, and Japan /. Chapel Hill , c1988. xi, 176 p. : ISBN 0-8078-1760-0 (alk. paper) LC Card 87-10022 DDC 338.09 19
HC255 .B59 1988

Collar, George. An industrial and social history of England /. London , New York [1912] 283 p. : LC Card 85-666355
HC253 .C65x 1912

Hueckel, Glenn R. (Glenn Russell), 1945- The Napoleonic wars and their impact on factor returns and output growth in England, 1793-1815 /. New York , 1985. lvi, 212 p. ; ISBN 0-8240-6683-9 : LC Card 84-46003 DDC 330.941/073 19
HC254.5 .H78 1985 ***NYPL [JLE 86-4294]***

Kennedy, William P. (William Paca), 1944- Industrial structure, capital markets, and the origins of British economic decline /. Cambridge [Cambridgeshire] , New York , 1987. xii, 230 p. ; ISBN 0-521-23018-7 LC Card 86-24411 DDC 330.941 19
HC255 .K45 1987

Striking a balance . London , 1986. 76 p. : ISBN 0-11-513848-X (pbk.) : LC Card 86-231618 DDC 380.1/06/041 19
HF73.G7 S77 1986

Studies in capital formation in Great Britain . Oxford [Oxfordshire] , New York , c1988. p. cm. ISBN 0-19-828408-X : LC Card 87-15196 DDC 332/.0415/0941 19
HC260.S3 S78 1988

GREAT BRITAIN - INDUSTRIES - HISTORY - 20TH CENTURY.
Barnett, Correlli. The pride and the fall . New York , 1987, c1986. xii, 359 p. ; ISBN 0-02-901851-X LC Card 86-25701 DDC 330.941/0854 19
HC256.4 .B28 1987

GREAT BRITAIN - INDUSTRIES - LOCATION.
Fothergill, Steve. Property and industrial development /. London , Wolfeboro, N.H. , 1987. 187 p. : ISBN 0-09-170741-2 (pbk.) : LC Card 87-2627 DDC 333.3/8/0941 19
HD598 .F68 1987

Perry, Martin, 1956- Small factories and economic development /. Aldershot, Hants., England , Brookfield, VT, USA , c1986. xvi, 229 p. ; ISBN 0-566-05208-3 : LC Card 86-9904 DDC 338.6/42/0941 19
HC260.D5 P47 1986 ***NYPL [JLD 86-3993]***

Great Britain. Information, Central Office of. see **Great Britain. Central Office of Information.**

Great Britain. Inter-departmental Committee on Social Insurance and Allied Services. SOCIAL INSURANCE AND ALLIED SERVICES.
Costa, F. Ramos da. O Plano Beveridge criticado /. Lisboa , 1943. 75 p. ; LC Card 85-211958
HD7165.A72 C66 1943

GREAT BRITAIN - MILITARY POLICY.
Rumble, Greville. The politics of nuclear defence . Cambridge [Cambridgeshire] , 1985. xi, 285 p. ; ISBN 0-7456-0194-4 : LC Card 85-18643 DDC 355/.0217 19
U263 .R86 1985 ***NYPL [JLD 86-1092]***

Towle, Philip, 1945- Protest and perish . London , 1982. 121 p. ; ISBN 0-907967-02-7 (pbk.) : LC Card 83-198296 DDC 355/.0217/0941 19
UA647 .T69 1982 ***NYPL [JLD 86-1904]***

Great Britain. Ministry of Labour and National Service. Central Juvenile Employment Executive. see **Great Britain. Central Youth Employment Executive.**

Great Britain. Ministry of Labour and National Service. Central Youth Employment Executive. see **Great Britain. Central Youth Employment Executive.**

Great Britain. Ministry of Labour. Central Youth Employment Executive. see **Great Britain. Central Youth Employment Executive.**

GREAT BRITAIN. MINISTRY OF OVERSEAS DEVELOPMENT. (Old Catalog form: Great Britain. Overseas development, Dept. of)
Biraud, Gérard. L'aide britannique au développement . Paris , 1978. 17 leaves : LC Card 84-102197
HC60 .B52 1978

Great Britain. Ministry of Transport. (Old Catalog form: Great Britain. Transport ministry)
Railway accident . London , 1922-<1985. <74 > v. LC Card 47-22771
HE1783.G7 A52

Great Britain. National Economic Development Office. see **National Economic Development Office.**

GREAT BRITAIN - OCCUPATIONS - FORECASTING.
UK occupation and employment trends to 1990 . London , Boston , 1986. xxiv, 249 p. : ISBN 0-408-02980-3 : LC Card 86-13617 DDC 331.12/0941 19
HD5765.A6 U38 1986 ***NYPL [JLE 86-4156]***

Great Britain. Office of Population Censuses and Surveys. (Old Catalog form: Great Britain. Population Census and Surveys, Office of)

Great Britain. Office of Population Censuses and Surveys. Social Survey Division. Todd, Jean Elizabeth. Changing the definition of a household . London , 1986. viii, 43 p. : ISBN 0-11-691071-2 (pbk.) : LC Card 87-132272
HB849.49 .T63 1986

Great Britain. Overseas Development, Ministry of. see **Great Britain. Ministry of Overseas Development.**

GREAT BRITAIN - POLITICS AND GOVERNMENT - 1625-1649.
Cust, Richard. The forced loan and English politics, 1626-1628 /. Oxford [Oxfordshire] , New York , 1987. x, 358 p. ; ISBN 0-19-822951-8 : LC Card 87-7977 DDC 336.42 19
HJ1012 .C87 1987

GREAT BRITAIN - POLITICS AND GOVERNMENT - 18TH CENTURY.
Wright, D. G. Popular radicalism . London , New York , 1988. p. cm. ISBN 0-582-49440-0 LC Card 87-4093 DDC 322/.2/0942 19
HD8395 .W75 1988

GREAT BRITAIN - POLITICS AND GOVERNMENT - 19TH CENTURY.
Wright, D. G. Popular radicalism . London , New York , 1988. p. cm. ISBN 0-582-49440-0 LC Card 87-4093 DDC 322/.2/0942 19
HD8395 .W75 1988

GREAT BRITAIN - POLITICS AND GOVERNMENT - 1800-1837.
Braun, Hans-Joachim. Wirtschafts- und finanzpolitische Entscheidungsprozesse in England in der ersten Hälfte des 19. Jahrhunderts /. Frankfurt am Main , New York , c1984. 236 p. : ISBN 3-8204-7702-0 LC Card 85-191319 DDC 338.941 19
HC255 .B77 1984

GREAT BRITAIN - POLITICS AND GOVERNMENT - 1837-1901.
Chartism in Wales and Ireland. New York , 1986. 15, 32, 16, 18, 20 p. : ISBN 0-8240-5594-2 (alk. paper) : LC Card 86-25706 DDC 322/.2/0941 19
HD8396 .C494 1986

Saville, John. 1848 . Cambridge [Cambridgeshire] , New York , 1987. ix, 310 p. ; ISBN 0-521-33341-5 LC Card 86-29975 DDC 322/.2/0941 19
HD8396 .S28 1987

GREAT BRITAIN - POLITICS AND GOVERNMENT - 1936-1945.
Barnett, Correlli. The pride and the fall . New York , 1987, c1986. xii, 359 p. ; ISBN 0-02-901851-X LC Card 86-25701 DDC 330.941/0854 19
HC256.4 .B28 1987

GREAT BRITAIN - POLITICS AND GOVERNMENT - 1945-
Gamble, Andrew. Britain in decline . Basingstoke, Hampshire , 1985. xxi, 261 p. ; ISBN 0-333-39253-1 : LC Card 86-673896
HC256.6 .G35x 1985

La Serre, Françoise de. La Grande-Bretagne et la Communauté européenne /. Paris , c1987. 223, [1] p. : ISBN 2-13-040114-7 : LC Card 87-165122
HC241.25.G7 L118 1987

Sirs, Bill. Hard labour /. London , 1985. 151 p., [8] p. of plates : ISBN 0-283-99241-7 : LC Card 86-191030 DDC 331.88/1691/0924 B 19
HD6665.S57 A3 1985

GREAT BRITAIN - POLITICS AND GOVERNMENT - 1945-1964.
Marx, Roland. La vie quotidienne en Angleterre au temps de l'expérience socialiste . [Paris] , c1983. 323 p. ; ISBN 2-01-008679-1 : LC Card 83-220426
HC256.5 .M3955 1983

GREAT BRITAIN - POLITICS AND GOVERNMENT - 1979-
Fatchett, D. J. (Derek John), 1945- Trade unions and politics in the 1980s . London , New York , c1987. p. cm. ISBN 0-7099-4903-0 LC Card 87-14092 DDC 322/.2/0941 19
HD6667 .F37 1987

Whiteley, Paul. Pressure for the poor . London , New York , 1987. 174 p. ; ISBN 0-416-36370-9 LC Card 87-11205 DDC 362.5/8/0941 19
HC260.P63 W47 1987

GREAT BRITAIN - POPULATION.
Changing places . London , Baltimore, Md., USA , 1987. xv, 144 p. : ISBN 0-7131-6498-0 (pbk.) : LC Card 87-148942 DDC 331.12/5/0941 19
HD5765.A6 C49 1987

Variant population projections . London , 1986. 17 p. : ISBN 0-11-690777-0 (pbk.) : LC Card 86-234516 DDC 304.6/2/0941021 19
HB3583 .V368 1986

Great Britain. Population Censuses and Surveys, Office of. see **Great Britain. Office of Population Censuses and Surveys.**

GREAT BRITAIN - POPULATION - HISTORY - 20TH CENTURY.
Winter, J. M. The great war and the British people /. Basingstoke, Hampshire , 1986, c1985. xiv, 360 p. : ISBN 0-333-26582-3
NYPL [JLD 86-1426]

GREAT BRITAIN - POPULATION - STATISTICS.
Variant population projections . London , 1986. 17 p. : ISBN 0-11-690777-0 (pbk.) : LC Card 86-234516 DDC 304.6/2/0941021 19
HB3583 .V368 1986

GREAT BRITAIN. POST OFFICE - SECURITY MEASURES - HISTORY.
Dear cats . London , 1986. 128 p. : LC Card 87-126969 DDC 628.9/693 19
HE6939.S42 D42 1986

Great Britain. Price Commission. Prices, costs, and margins in the production and distribution of compound feeding stuff for cattle, pigs, and poultry : presented to Parliament in pursuance of Section 11(3) of the Price Commission Act 1977 / Price Commission. London : H.M.S.O., [1978] v, 35 p. ; 25 cm. ISBN 0-10-233878-7 (pbk.) LC Card 85-146987
1. Flour and feed trade - Great Britain. I. Title.
HD9056.G72 G76 1978

GREAT BRITAIN - RACE RELATIONS - HISTORY - 20TH CENTURY.
Sherwood, Marika. Many struggles . London , 1985, c1984. 138 p. : ISBN 0-946918-00-7 (pbk.) LC Card 86-110617 DDC 305.8/00941 19
HD8398.B55 S54 1985 ***NYPL [Sc D 86-815]***

GREAT BRITAIN - RELATIONS (GENERA) WITH GERMANY.
Chesterton, Gilbert Keith, 1874-1936. [Crimes of England. French.] Les crimes de l'Angleterre [microform]. Paris, 1916. 273 p. LC Card 19-16286
DA47.2 .C55 ***NYPL [*Z-4049 no.7]***

GREAT BRITAIN - RURAL CONDITIONS - CONGRESSES.
The Industrialization of the countryside /. Norwich [Norfolk] , c1985. xiv, 315 p. : ISBN 0-86094-202-3 LC Card 87-141251 DDC 338.9/009173/4 19
HC256.6 .I524 1985

GREAT BRITAIN - SOCIAL CONDITIONS.
Harrison, J. F. C. (John Fletcher Clews) The common people of Great Britain . Bloomington , 1985. 445 p. : ISBN 0-253-20357-0 (pbk.) LC Card 84-48820 DDC 305.5/62/0942 19
HD8388 .H36 1985 ***NYPL [JLD 86-3656]***

Slack, Paul. Poverty and policy in Tudor and Stuart England /. London , New York , 1988. p. cm. ISBN 0-582-48965-2 (alk. paper) LC Card 87-2657 DDC 362.5/561/0942 19
HC254.4 .S42 1988

GREAT BRITAIN - SOCIAL CONDITIONS - 18TH CENTURY.
Korzeniewicz, Richard. British economic and social history, 1700-1950 /. London , c1985.

261 p. : ISBN 0-7212-0711-1 : LC Card 87-144405 DDC 330.941 19
HC254.5 .K67 1985

GREAT BRITAIN - SOCIAL CONDITIONS - 19TH CENTURY.
Korzeniewicz, Richard. British economic and social history, 1700-1950 /. London , c1985. 261 p. : ISBN 0-7212-0711-1 : LC Card 87-144405 DDC 330.941 19
HC254.5 .K67 1985

GREAT BRITAIN - SOCIAL CONDITIONS - 20TH CENTURY.
Korzeniewicz, Richard. British economic and social history, 1700-1950 /. London , c1985. 261 p. : ISBN 0-7212-0711-1 : LC Card 87-144405 DDC 330.941 19
HC254.5 .K67 1985

Men without work . New York , 1985. xii, 447 p. ; ISBN 0-8240-7619-2 (alk. paper) : LC Card 85-13069 DDC 331.13/7941 19
HD5765.A6 M46 1985 ***NYPL [JLD 87-1031]***

Winter, J. M. The great war and the British people /. Basingstoke, Hampshire , 1986, c1985. xiv, 360 p. : ISBN 0-333-26582-3
NYPL [JLD 86-1426]

GREAT BRITAIN - SOCIAL CONDITIONS - 1945-
Changing places . London , Baltimore, Md., USA , 1987. xv, 144 p. : ISBN 0-7131-6498-0 (pbk.) : LC Card 87-148942 DDC 331.12/5/0941 19
HD5765.A6 C49 1987

Getting into life /. London , New York , c1986. xii, 157 p. ; ISBN 0-416-40850-8 LC Card 86-16186 DDC 305.2/35/0941 19
HQ799.G7 G48 1986 ***NYPL [JLD 87-892]***

Marx, Roland. La vie quotidienne en Angleterre au temps de l'expérience socialiste . [Paris] , c1983. 323 p. ; ISBN 2-01-008679-1 : LC Card 83-220426
HC256.5 .M3955 1983

Robertson, Alex. The bleak midwinter, 1947 /. Manchester, U.K. , Wolfeboro, N.H., U. S.A. , 1987. x, 207 p. : ISBN 0-7190-1902-8 : LC Card 87-11085 DDC 333.8/22/0941 19
HD9551.5 .R56 1987

GREAT BRITAIN - SOCIAL POLICY.
Alcock, Peter, 1951- Poverty and state support /. London , New York , 1987. xi, 215 p. : ISBN 0-582-29652-8 (pbk.) LC Card 86-27857 DDC 368.4/00941 19
HD7165 .A77 1987

Hennock, E. P., 1926- British social reform and German precedents . Oxford [Oxfordshire] , New York , 1987. vi, 243 p. ; ISBN 0-19-820127-3 : LC Card 87-11082 DDC 368.4/00941 19
HD7165 .H455 1987

Page, Robert M. Stigma /. London , Boston , 1984. xii, 207 p. ; ISBN 0-7100-9786-7 : LC Card 83-24638 DDC 302/.12 19
HM291 .P25 1984 ***NYPL [JLD 86-3113]***

Slack, Paul. Poverty and policy in Tudor and Stuart England /. London , New York , 1988. p. cm. ISBN 0-582-48965-2 (alk. paper) LC Card 87-2657 DDC 362.5/561/0942 19
HC254.4 .S42 1988

GREAT BRITAIN - STATISTICAL SERVICES.
Facts from your figures /. London , 1977. 37 p. : LC Card 85-160272
HA37.G7 F33 1977

GREAT BRITAIN - STATISTICS - HISTORY.
Mitchell, B. R. (Brian R.) British historical statistics /. Cambridge [Cambridgeshire] , New York , 1988. p. cm. ISBN 0-521-33008-4 LC Card 86-24513 DDC 314.1 19
HA1134 .M58 1988

Great Britain. Trade and Industry, Dept. of. see **Great Britain. Dept. of Trade and Industry.**

Great Britain. Trade Board. see **Great Britain. Board of Trade.**

Great Britain. Transport Ministry. see **Great Britain. Ministry of Transport.**

Great Britain. Treasury.
Accounting for economic costs and changing prices . London , 1986. 2 v. : ISBN 0-11-560004-3 (pbk. : v. 1) : LC Card 86-216162 DDC 657/.42 19
HF5658.5 .A22 1986

Review of the ITV and ILR levy structures, 1984-85 . London , c1986. 44 p. ; ISBN 0-86252-236-6 (pbk.) LC Card 86-202703 DDC 384.54/3 19
HE8689.9.G7 R48 1986

The Great Depression . Bernstein, Michael A. (Michael Alan), 1954- Cambridge [Cambridgeshire] , New York , 1987. xvii, 269 p. : ISBN 0-521-34048-9 LC Card 87-6403 DDC 338.5/42 19
HB3717 1929 .B37 1987

The Great Depression . Garraty, John Arthur, 1920- New York, N.Y. , 1987. x, 292 p. : ISBN 0-385-24085-6 (pbk.) : LC Card 87-5458 DDC 338.5/42 19
HB3717 1929 .G36 1987

The Great Depression.
The Farmer is the man [sound recording]. Los Angeles, Calif. , p1983. 1 sound cassette (58 min.) : LC Card 87-751678
HD8039.F3

The great depression and agrarian economy . Singh, Kanti. Delhi, India , 1987. xii, 206 p. ; LC Card 86-903533 DDC 338.1/0954/12 19
HC437.B47 S53 1987

The great depression of 1990 /. Batra, Raveendra N. Dallas, Tex. , c1985. xv, 175 p. : ISBN 0-939352-02-8 : LC Card 85-50275 DDC 338.5/42 19
HC106.8 .B39 1985 ***NYPL [JLD 86-4007]***

The great depression of 1990 /. Batra, Raveendra N. New York , c1987. 235 p. ; ISBN 0-671-64022-4 LC Card 87-4816 DDC 338.5/42 19
HC106.8 .B39 1987

The great economic debate . Gonick, Cy. Toronto , 1987. xii, 425 p. : ISBN 0-88862-702-5 LC Card 87-144697 DDC 338.971 19
HC115 .G576 1987

Great expectations . Bortz, Paul I. Washington, D.C. , c1986. vii, 137 p., [3] folded leaves : ISBN 0-89324-012-5 (pbk.) LC Card 87-401854 DDC 384.55/453/068 19
HE8700.8 .B66 1986

Great expectorations . Chapman, Simon. London , 1986. 158 p. : ISBN 0-906890-86-1 (pbk.) : LC Card 86-204305 DDC 659.1/96797 19
HF6161.T6 C48 1986

Great ideas for teaching economics / edited by Ralph T. Byrns, Gerald W. Stone. 3rd ed. Glenview, Ill. : Scott, Foresman, c1987. xxiv, 400 p. : ill. ; 23 cm. ISBN 0-673-17245-7 (pbk.) LC Card 87-159026 DDC 330/.07 19
1. Economics - Study and teaching. I. Byrns, Ralph T. II. Stone, Gerald W.
HB74.5.G73 1987

GREAT LAKES REGION - ECONOMIC CONDITIONS.
Heilmann, Ronald L. Great Lakes transportation in the eighties /. Madison, WI , c1986. 100 p. : ISBN 0-936287-00-4 (pbk.) : LC Card 86-622259 DDC 386/.544/0977 19
HE398 .H45 1986

Great Lakes transportation in the eighties /. Heilmann, Ronald L. Madison, WI , c1986. 100 p. : ISBN 0-936287-00-4 (pbk.) : LC Card 86-622259 DDC 386/.544/0977 19
HE398 .H45 1986

The Great Northern Railway : a history / Ralph W. Hidy ... [et al.] ; editorial assistance from Elizabeth A. Burnham. Boston, Mass. : Harvard Business School Press, c1988. xv, 360 p. : ill. ; 22 x 28 cm. Bibliography: p. 329-347. Includes index. ISBN 0-87584-185-6 LC Card 87-25040 DDC 385/.065/78 19
1. Great Northern Railway - History. I. Hidy, Ralph Willard, 1905-.
HE2791.G775 G73 1988

GREAT NORTHERN RAILWAY - HISTORY.
The Great Northern Railway . Boston, Mass. , c1988. xv, 360 p. : ISBN 0-87584-185-6 LC Card 87-25040 DDC 385/.065/78 19
HE2791.G775 G73 1988

Great Plains National Instructional Television Library.
Drunk driving [videorecording] . Lincoln, NE , 1983. 1 videocassette (30 min.) : LC Card 87-706347 DDC 363.1 11
HE5620.D7

DUI arrest [videorecording] /. Lincoln, NE , 1983. 1 videocassette (30 min.) : LC Card 87-706343 DDC 343 11
HE5620.D7

Science/earth science on stamps and banknotes [slide] /. Lincoln, Neb. , 1984. 30 slides : LC Card 85-702119 DDC 551 11
HE6183.S36

The great war and the British people /. Winter, J. M. Basingstoke, Hampshire , 1986, c1985. xiv, 360 p. : ISBN 0-333-26582-3
NYPL [JLD 86-1426]

The great war, its lessons and its warnings [microform]. Collings, Jesse, 1831-1920. London [1915] 113 p. LC Card 16-1094
HC256.2 .C55 ***NYPL [*Z-4053 no.6]***

The Great writings in management and organizational behavior / Louise E. Boone, Donald D. Bowen. 2nd ed. New York : Random House, c1987. p. cm. Bibliography: p. Includes indexes. ISBN 0-394-36099-0 LC Card 86-33900 DDC 658 19
1. Management. 2. Organizational behavior. 3. Industrial management. I. Boone, Louis E. II. Bowen, Donald D.
HD31 .G74 1987

Greater in Europe /. Newton Dunn, Bill. London , c1985. 85 p. ; ISBN 0-7212-0731-6 (pbk.) : LC Card 87-146946 DDC 341.24/22 19
HC241.25.G7 N48 1985

Greater London Council. Behavioural Science Unit. The Relationship between the GLC Housing Department, its tenants, and the public /. London , c1977. iv, 107 p. ; ISBN 0-7168-0895-1 (pbk.) LC Card 87-107202
HD7288.78.G72 L68 1977

Greater Nebraska job prospects, 1983-1988 / Nebraska Occupational Information Coordinating Committee. [Lincoln, Neb.] : The Committee, [1985] ii, 54 p. : ill. ; 22 x 28 cm. "August 1985." LC Card 86-622213 DDC 331.12/09781/021 19
1. Labor supply - Nebraska - Statistics. 2. Employment forecasting - Nebraska - Statistics. 3. Job vacancies - Nebraska - Statistics. I. Nebraska Occupational Information Coordinating Committee.
HD5725.N2 G74 1985

Greater Washington at mid decade . Grier, George W. Washington, DC (1717 Massachusetts Ave., N.W., Washington 20036-2076) , c1985- v. <1 > : LC Card 86-200647 DDC 338.5/443/09753 19
HC108.W3 G73 1985

The greatest bull market in history . Armstrong, Martin A. [Princeton?] , <c1986-. v. <2 > : LC Card 87-138809 DDC 332.64 19
HG4516 .A75 1986

Greaves de Pulido, Rosalind. Estadísticas sociales . Caracas, Venezuela , 1983. 2 v. ; LC Card 84-183391 DDC 312/.0987 19
HA1095 .E88 1983 ***NYPL [JLM 85-550]***

Grebennikov, Valeriĭ Grigor′evich.
Metodologicheskie problemy analiza dolgosrochnykh sotsial′no-ėkonomicheskikh protsessov /. Moskva , 1979. 116 p. : LC Card 87-462037
HD87 .M48 1979

Renta . Moskva , 1984. 95 p. : LC Card 85-192538
HB401 .R48 1984

Sotsial′no-ėkonomicheskie problemy intensifikatsii obshchestvennogo proizvodstva /. Moskva , 1983. 91 p. : LC Card 84-114234
HD56 .S688 1983

Grechishnikov, P. V. (Petr Vladimirovich)
Antanaĭtis, IU. A. (IUstinas Antanovich) Sotsialisticheskoe sorevnovanie i intensifikatsiia proizvodstva /. Moskva , 1987. 157 p. : LC Card 87-103350
HC337.L53 S63 1987

Greckol, Sonja Ruth, 1946- Armstrong, Pat, 1945- A working majority . Ottawa, Ont. , c1983. v, 280 p. : ISBN 0-660-11314-7 (pbk.) :

LC Card 83-158188 DDC 331.4/0971 19
HD6067.2.C2 A75 1983
NYPL [JLD 86-1585]

GRECO CNRS EFIQ (Group) La Crise de l'endettement international . Paris , c1986. 410 p. : ISBN 2-7178-1127-3 : LC Card 86-222862
HJ8017 .C74 1986

Greco, Eugenio. Storia demografica dei comuni siciliani dal 1832 al 1858 / Eugenio Greco ; presentazioni dei proff. Stefano Somogyi e Franco Vaccina. Palermo : Università di Palermo, Istituto di statistica sociale e scienze demografiche e biometriche, [1982] 60, [61] p. ; 25 cm. (Collana di studi demografici. 13) Includes bibliographical references. LC Card 85-103229
1. Sicily - Population - Statistics. 2. Cities and towns - Italy - Sicily - Statistics. I. Università di Palermo. Istituto di statistica sociale e scienze demografiche e biometriche. II. Title. III. Series.
HB2270.S5 G74 1982

GREECE - ADMINISTRATIVE AND POLITICAL DIVISIONS.
Greece. Dieuthynsis Topikēs Autodioikēseōs. Dioikētikē diairesis tēs Hellados kata nomous, eparchias, dēmous kai koinotētas . Athēnai , 1965. 39 p. ; LC Card 86-235329
HA1351.5 1961

GREECE - CENSUS, 1961.
Greece. Dieuthynsis Topikēs Autodioikēseōs. Dioikētikē diairesis tēs Hellados kata nomous, eparchias, dēmous kai koinotētas . Athēnai , 1965. 39 p. ; LC Card 86-235329
HA1351.5 1961

GREECE - COLONIZATION - HISTORY - 17TH CENTURY.
Dokos, Kōnstantinos. Hē Sterea Hellas kata ton Henetotourkikon polemon, 1684-1699 kai ho Salōnōn Philotheos /. Athēnai , 1985. 255 p. ; LC Card 86-211599
HB2092.5.A3 D64 1985

Greece. Dieuthynsis Topikēs Autodioikēseōs. Dioikētikē diairesis tēs Hellados kata nomous, eparchias, dēmous kai koinotētas : periechousa tas mechri tēs 31-12-1964 epelthousas dioikētikas metavolas / Vasileion tēs Hellados, Hypourgeion Esōterikōn, Dieuthynsis Topikēs Autodioikēseōs = Division administrative de la Grèce par départements, provinces, municipalités et communes : contenant les changement administratifs apportés jusqu'au 31 décembre 1964 / Royaume de Grèce, Ministère de l'intérieur, Direction de gouvernment. Athēnai : Ethnikon Typogr., 1965. 39 p. ; 31 cm. LC Card 86-235329
1. Greece - Population - Statistics. 2. Greece - Census, 1961. 3. Greece - Administrative and political divisions. I. Title. II. Title: Division administrative de la Grèce par départements, provinces, municipalités et communes.
HA1351.5 1961

GREECE - ECONOMIC CONDITIONS.
Kamouzēs, Kōn/nos Ch. (Kōnstantinos Ch.), 1946- Anatomia tēs Hellēnikēs oikonomias apo to 1953 mechri sēmera /. Thessalonikē , 1981. 197 p. : LC Card 84-140694
HC295 .K28 1981

GREECE - ECONOMIC CONDITIONS - TO 146 B.C.
Lowry, S. Todd. The archaeology of economic ideas . Durham , 1987. xviii, 366 p. ; ISBN 0-8223-0774-X LC Card 87-15507 DDC 330/.0938 19
HB108.A2 L68 1987

Polanyi, Karl, 1886-1964. [Livelihood of man. Hungarian. Selections.] Kereskedelem, piacok és pénz az ókori Görögországban /. Budapest , 1984. 327 p. ; ISBN 963-281-335-9 : LC Card 85-189578
HC37 .P65155 1984

Reekmans, T. Inleiding tot de antieke economie /. Leuven , 1984. 129 leaves in various foliations ; ISBN 90-334-0834-1 : LC Card 86-203767
HB77 .R44 1984

GREECE - ECONOMIC CONDITIONS - 1918-
Drakos, Geōrgios P. Apostagmata mias zōēs /. Athēna , c1985. 194 p. ; LC Card 86-175014
HC295 .D7 1985

GREECE - ECONOMIC CONDITIONS - 1918-1974.
Chelmēs, D. (Dēmētrios), 1894-1967. Ekthesis tou dioikētou k-ou Dēmētriou E. Chelmē ex onomatos tou Dioikētikou Symvouliou tēs Trapezēs kata tēn genikēn syneleusin tōn metochōn tēs 25ēs Maiou 1964. Athēnai , 1964. 55 p. ; LC Card 87-109901
HC295 .C45 1964

GREECE - ECONOMIC CONDITIONS - 1974-
The Greek presence /. Athens , 1969. [32] p. : LC Card 87-101996
HC295 .G7545 1969

Liverēs, Anastasēs I. Politikē oikonomia gia holous . Athēna , 1985. 424 p. ; LC Card 86-178760
HB97.5 .L555 1985

Maroulis, Dimitris. Economic development and the structure of the balance of payments . Athens , 1986. 267 p. : LC Card 87-170680 DDC 382.1/7/09495 19
HC295 .M32 1986

GREECE - ECONOMIC POLICY.
Kamouzēs, Kōn/nos Ch. (Kōnstantinos Ch.), 1946- Anatomia tēs Hellēnikēs oikonomias apo to 1953 mechri sēmera /. Thessalonikē , 1981. 197 p. : LC Card 84-140694
HC295 .K28 1981

Greece - Government. see **Greece - Politics and government.**

GREECE - HISTORY - 1453-1821.
Dokos, Kōnstantinos. Hē Sterea Hellas kata ton Henetotourkikon polemon, 1684-1699 kai ho Salōnōn Philotheos /. Athēnai , 1985. 255 p. ; LC Card 86-211599
HB2092.5.A3 D64 1985

GREECE - HISTORY - 19TH CENTURY - SOURCES.
Spēliōtakēs, K. K. Archeion Michaēl Iatrou, 1802-1893 /. Athēna , 1983. 189 p., [4] folded leaves of plates : LC Card 85-134031
HF3750.5.S64 A3 1983
NYPL [JFE 86-4131]

Greece. Hypourgeion Esōterikōn. Dieuthynsis Topikēs Autodioikēseōs. see **Greece. Dieuthynsis Topikēs Autodioikēseōs.**

Greece. Hypourgeion Politismou kai Epistēmōn.
Dēmographikē Hēmerida (1984 : Athens, Greece) Hē Dēmographikē krisē stēn Hellada . Athēna , 1985. 205 p. : LC Card 86-192606
HB3632.5.A3 D45 1984

Dēmographikē Hēmerida (1984 : Athens, Greece) Hē Dēmographikē krisē stēn Hellada . Athēna , 1986. 205 p. : LC Card 86-201713
HB3632.5.A3 D45 1986

Greece in the European Community. Hē Hellada stēn Eurōpaikē Koinotēta . Athēna , 1987. 14, 565 p. ; LC Card 87-169443
HC241.25.G8 H43 1987

GREECE - INDUSTRIES.
Kazēs, D. A. (Dēmētrēs A.) [Licensing kai viomēchanikē anaptyxē. English.] Licensing and industrial development . Athens , 1986. 208 p. : LC Card 87-170691 DDC 338.09495 19
HF1429 .K3813 1986

GREECE - INDUSTRIES - HISTORY.
Kintis, Andreas A. Anaptyxē tēs Hellēnikēs viomēchanias /. Athēna [1982] 180 p. ; LC Card 84-132514
HC295 .K515 1982

GREECE - INDUSTRIES - HISTORY - 19TH CENTURY.
Hē Hellēnikē viomēchania apo ton 19o ston 20o aiōna /. Athēna , 1985. 32 p., [22] p. of plates : LC Card 86-212947
HC295 .H373 1985

GREECE - INDUSTRIES - HISTORY - 20TH CENTURY.
Hē Hellēnikē viomēchania apo ton 19o ston 20o aiōna /. Athēna , 1985. 32 p., [22] p. of plates : LC Card 86-212947
HC295 .H373 1985

Greece. Periphereiakē Dioikēsis Anat. Makedonias-Thrakēs. VII Hypēresia Syntonismou Anaptyxeōs Periphereias. Grapheion Prōtogenous Paragōgēs.
Oikonomikē kai koinōnikē anaptyxis Anat. Makedonias kai Thrakēs . Kavalla [1973-] v. <1> : LC Card 87-125407
HD2055.5 .O54 1973

GREECE - POLITICS AND GOVERNMENT - 1967-1974.
Klōnarēs, N. G. (Nikos G.) Ho syndikalismos kai to politiko mas provlēma /. Athēnai , 1973. 78 p. ; LC Card 86-234658
HD6795.5 .K57 1973

GREECE - POLITICS AND GOVERNMENT - 1974-
Sarlēs, Dēmētrēs. Hoi politikes pleures tēs entaxēs tēs Helladas stēn EOK . Athēna , 1981. 212 p. ; LC Card 83-170595
HC241.25.G8 S27 1981

GREECE - POPULATION - CONGRESSES.
Dēmographikē Hēmerida (1984 : Athens, Greece) Hē Dēmographikē krisē stēn Hellada . Athēna , 1985. 205 p. : LC Card 86-192606
HB3632.5.A3 D45 1984

Dēmographikē Hēmerida (1984 : Athens, Greece) Hē Dēmographikē krisē stēn Hellada . Athēna , 1986. 205 p. : LC Card 86-201713
HB3632.5.A3 D45 1986

GREECE - POPULATION POLICY - CONGRESSES.
Dēmographikē Hēmerida (1984 : Athens, Greece) Hē Dēmographikē krisē stēn Hellada . Athēna , 1986. 205 p. : LC Card 86-201713
HB3632.5.A3 D45 1986

GREECE - POPULATION - STATISTICS.
Greece. Dieuthynsis Topikēs Autodioikēseōs. Dioikētikē diairesis tēs Hellados kata nomous, eparchias, dēmous kai koinotētas . Athēnai , 1965. 39 p. ; LC Card 86-235329
HA1351.5 1961

GREECE - RURAL CONDITIONS.
Vrachniarēs, Chrēstos. Anamesa se dyo exegerseis . Athēna , 1985. 139, [5] p. ; LC Card 86-206897
HD1536.G7 V73 1985

GREECE - SOCIAL CONDITIONS.
Drakos, Geōrgios P. Apostagmata mias zōēs /. Athēna , c1985. 194 p. ; LC Card 86-175014
HC295 .D7 1985

Greed and glory on Wall Street . Auletta, Ken. New York , c1986. xiii, 253 p., [16] p. of plates : ISBN 0-394-54410-2 : LC Card 85-10700 DDC 332.66/09747/1 19
HG5129.N5 A8 1986 *NYPL [JLE 86-856]*

Greed and glory on Wall Street . Auletta, Ken. Boston, Mass. , 1987, c1986. xii, 423 p. (large print) ; ISBN 0-8161-4189-4 (lg. print) : LC Card 86-26968 DDC 332.66/09747/1 19
HG5129.N5 A8 1987b

Greed and glory on Wall Street . Auletta, Ken. New York, N.Y. [1987], c1986. xi, 260 p., [16] p. of plates : ISBN 0-446-38406-2 (pbk.) LC Card 86-23416 DDC 332.66/09747/1 19
HG5129.N5 A8 1987

The Greek presence / [editor-in-chief Fr. Frantziskakis]. Athens : Ministry of Commerce, Directorate of Exhibitions, 1969. [32] p. : ill. ; 23 x 24 cm. LC Card 87-101996
1. Greece - Economic conditions - 1974-. I. Frantziskakis, Fr.
HC295 .G7545 1969

GREEKS - GERMANY (WEST) - CRIMES AGAINST.
Pitsela, Angelika. Straffälligkeit und Viktimisierung ausländischer Minderheiten in der Bundesrepublik Deutschland . Freiburg [i.B.] , 1986. xxvii, 479 p. ; ISBN 3-922498-16-7 LC Card 87-131111 DDC 331.6/2/495043 19
HD8458.G7 P57 1986

Greeley, Martin. Postharvest losses, technology, and employment : the case of rice in Bangladesh / Martin Greeley. Boulder, Colo. : Westview Press, 1987. xvii, 345 p. : ill. ; 23 cm. (Westview special studies in social, political and economic development) Bibliography: p. 310-328. Includes index. ISBN 0-8133-7371-9 (pbk. : alk. paper) : LC Card 87-10648 DDC 338.1/7318/095492 19
1. Rice trade - Bangladesh. 2. Rice - Bangladesh - Processing - Cost effectiveness. 3. Women rice workers - Bangladesh. I. Title. II. Title: Post-harvest losses, technology, and employment.
HD9066.B32 G73 1987

Greeley, Tamara. The Housing handbook . New York, N.Y. (130 E. 59 St., New York 10022) , 1986. 150 p. ; LC Card 87-107431 DDC 363.5/8/0681 19
HD7304.N5 H68 1986

The Green alternative : guide to good living /

edited by Peter Bunyard and Fern Morgan-Grenville ; with illustrations by Richard Willson. London : Methuen, 1987. xv, 368 p. : ill. ; 23 cm. Bibliography: p. 356-[363] Includes index. ISBN 0-413-60280-X : LC Card 87-143624 DDC 333.7/2 19
1. Environmental policy - Great Britain. 2. Environmental protection - Great Britain. 3. Environmental policy. 4. Environmental protection. I. Bunyard, Peter. II. Morgan-Grenville, Fern.
HC260.E5 G736 1987

Green, Anne Canevari. (ill) Davis, Bertha, 1910- The national debt /. New York , c1987. 112 p. ; ISBN 0-531-10415-X LC Card 87-10441 DDC 336.3/4/0973 19
HJ2052 .D38 1987

Green, Barbara K. Calder, Eugene B. Advising clients on real estate investments /. New York, NY (11 Penn Plaza, New York 10001) , 1987. 95 p. in various pagings : LC Card 87-61983 DDC 332.63/24 19
HD1382.5 .C34 1987

Green, Colin H. Parker, Dennis J. Urban flood protection benefits . Aldershot, Hants, England , Brookfield, Vt., U. S.A. , c1987. xvii, 284 p. : ISBN 0-291-39707-7 LC Card 87-147842 DDC 363.3/49372 19
HD1676.G7 P37 1987

Green, Cynthia B. Reducing New York State's deficit / Citizens Budget Commission. New York, N.Y. (110 E. 42nd St., New York 10017) : The Commission, [1986] ii leaves, 33 p. ; 28 cm. "January 1986, volume 53, no. 1." Bibliography: p. 33. LC Card 87-108691 DDC 336.747 19
1. Budget deficits - New York (State). I. Citizens Budget Commission (New York, N.Y.). II. Title.
HJ2053.N7 G74 1986

Green, Danny. Business guide to communications systems /. London , 1987. x, 230 p. : ISBN 0-273-02671-2 (pbk.) : LC Card 87-147021 DDC 651.7 19
HD30.335 .B85 1987

Green, Howard L. Wright, Giles R. Work /. Trenton , c1987. 82 p. : ISBN 0-89743-072-7 (pbk.) LC Card 87-1573 DDC 331.6/2/09749 19
HD8083.N4 W75 1987

Green, Jim. Against the tide : the story of the Canadian Seamen's Union / Jim Green. Toronto : Progress Books, 1986. xvii, 324 p., [16] p. of plates : ill. ; 21 cm. Bibliography: p. 297-316. Includes index. ISBN 0-919396-49-6 (pbk.) LC Card 87-127604 DDC 331.88/113875/0971 19
1. Canadian Seamen's Union - History. 2. Seafarers' International Union of Canada - History. I. Title.
HD6528.S4 G74 1986

Green machine. Marketing. Fountain Valley, CA , 1985. 1 videocassette (30 min.) : LC Card 87-705967 DDC 658.8 11
HF5415

Green, Milford B.
Sagers, Matthew J. The freight rate structure on Soviet railroads /. Washington, D.C. [1985] vii, 28 p. : LC Card 87-601285 DDC 385/.12/0947 19
HE1895 .S25 1985

Sagers, Matthew J. The transportation of Soviet energy resources /. Totowa, N.J. , 1986. xvi, 177 p. : ISBN 0-8476-7504-1 : LC Card 86-15508 DDC 380.5/24 19
HD9502.S652 S24 1986 ***NYPL [JLE 87-38]***

Green paper . Great Britain. Equal Opportunities Commission. Manchester [1985] 66 p. : LC Card 87-124211 DDC 368.4/00941 19
HD7165 .G725 1985

Green, Reginald Herbold. The IMF and stabilisation in sub-Saharan Africa : a critical review / by Reginald Herbold Green. Brighton, England : IDS Publications, [1986] ii, 70 p. ; 21 cm. (Discussion paper, 0308-5864 . DP 216 (June 1986)) Bibliography: p. 67-70. LC Card 86-208478 DDC 332.1/52 19
1. Economic stabilization - Africa, Sub-Saharan. 2. Debts, External - Africa, Sub-Saharan. 3. Monetary policy - Africa, Sub-Saharan. 4. Economic stabilization - Tanzania. 5. Debts, External - Tanzania. 6. Monetary policy - Tanzania. 7. International Monetary Fund - Africa, Sub-Saharan. 8. International Monetary Fund - Tanzania. I. Series: Discussion paper (University of Sussex. Institute of Development Studies) , DP 216. II. Title.
HC800 .G72 1986

GREEN REVOLUTION - CHINA.
On rolls the green revolution /. Beijing, China [1984] 142 p., [36] p. of plates : LC Card 86-115054 DDC 338.1/0951 19
HD2097 .O5 1984 ***NYPL [JLK 83-122 no.9]***

GREEN REVOLUTION - NIGERIA.
Folayan, Adekunle. Agriculture and economic development in Nigeria . New York , c1983. x, 276 p. : ISBN 0-533-05325-0 : LC Card 81-90817 DDC 338.1/09669 19
HD2145.5 .F64 1983 ***NYPL [JLE 86-1080]***

GREEN REVOLUTION - PAKISTAN - PUNJAB.
Namdar, Shamim A. Employment implications of agricultural growth /. Lahore , 1980. 82 leaves : LC Card 84-930891 DDC 331.12/93/0954914 19
HD1537.P2 N36 1980 ***NYPL [JLF 86-1956]***

Green, Ronald D. Brazilian government support for the aerospace industry / prepared by Ronald D. Green. [Washington, D.C.?] : U. S. Dept. of Commerce, International Trade Commission, [1987] xi, 44 p. ; 28 cm. Shipping list no.: 87-198-P. "March 1987." Bibliography: p. 40-44. Item 231-B-1 LC Card 87-601479 DDC 338.4/76291/0981 19
1. Aircraft industry - Brazil. 2. Aircraft industry - Government policy - Brazil. 3. Aerospace industries - Brazil. 4. Empresa Brasileira de Aeronáutica. 5. Nontariff trade barriers - Brazil. 6. Tariff - Brazil. 7. Aircraft industry - United States. I. United States. International Trade Administration. II. Title.
HD9711.B72 G74 1987

Green, Timothy, 1936- The prospect for gold : the view to the year 2000 / Timothy Green. New York, N.Y. : Walker, 1987. xi, 204 p. : ill. ; 24 cm. Bibliography: p. 195. Includes index. ISBN 0-8027-1002-6 LC Card 87-16046 DDC 338.2/741 19
1. Gold. I. Title.
HG289 .G7395 1987

Green, William C., 1941- The Unfulfilled promise of synthetic fuels . New York , 1987. xxii, 225 p. ; ISBN 0-313-25666-7 (lib. bdg. : alk. paper) LC Card 87-247 DDC 338.4/766266/0973 19
HD9502.5.S963 U5475 1987

Greenaway, David.
Economic development and international trade /. New York , 1988. xi, 211 p. ; ISBN 0-312-01588-7 : LC Card 87-25629 DDC 382 19
HF1379 .E27 1988

Macroeconomics : theory and policy in the UK / David Greenaway and G.K. Shaw.2nd ed. Oxford, OX, UK ; New York, NY, USA : B. Blackwell, 1987. p. cm. Bibliography: p. Includes index. ISBN 0-631-15763-8 (pbk.) : LC Card 87-20831 DDC 339/.0941 19
1. Macroeconomics. 2. Great Britain - Economic policy - 1945-. I. Shaw, G. K. (Graham Keith), 1938-. II. Title.
HB172.5 .G75 1987

Greenbaum, Thomas L. The practical handbook and guide to focus group research / Thomas L. Greenbaum. Lexington, Mass. : Lexington Books, c1988. xii, 191 p. ; 25 cm. Bibliography: p. [183]-186. Includes index. ISBN 0-669-14775-3 (alk. paper) LC Card 86-45946 DDC 658.8/3 19
1. Marketing research. I. Title. II. Title: Focus group research.
HF5415.2 .G695 1988

Greenberg, Edward S., 1942- Workplace democracy : the political effects of participation / Edward S. Greenberg. Ithaca : Cornell University Press, 1986. 257 p. ; 24 cm. Includes index. Bibliography: p. 243-253. ISBN 0-8014-1921-2 (alk. paper) LC Card 86-47641 DDC 674/.834/068 19
1. Plywood industry - Northwest, Pacific - Management - Employee participation - Case studies. 2. Producer cooperatives - Northwest, Pacific - Management - Employee participation - Case studies. 3. Industrial management - Northwest, Pacific - Employee participation - Case studies. I. Title.
HD5658.P622 U554 1986
NYPL [JLE 86-4586]

Greenberg, Eric Rolfe.
Greenberg, Eric Rolfe. The 1985 AMA report on information centers /. New York, N.Y. , c1985. vi, 121 p. ; ISBN 0-8144-3151-8 LC Card 85-7552 DDC 658.4/038 19
HF5321 .G665 1985 ***NYPL [JLF 86-1167]***

Hiring costs and strategies . New York , c1986. v, 82 p. : ISBN 0-8144-3153-4
NYPL [JLF 86-960]

The 1985 AMA report on information centers / Eric Rolfe Greenberg. New York, N.Y. : AMA Membership Publications Division, American Management Association, c1985. vi, 121 p. ; 28 cm. (AMACOM briefings and surveys) ISBN 0-8144-3151-8 LC Card 85-7552 DDC 658.4/038 19
1. Business - Information services. 2. Business - Data processing. I. Greenberg, Eric Rolfe. II. Title.
HF5321 .G665 1985 ***NYPL [JLF 86-1167]***

Greene, Kevin. The archaeology of the Roman economy / Kevin Greene. London : B.T. Batsford, 1986. 192 p. : ill. ; 26 cm. Bibliography: p. 172-188. Includes index. ISBN 0-7134-4593-9 : LC Card 86-226151 DDC 330.937/06 19
1. Rome - Economic conditions. 2. Money - Rome. 3. Rome - Antiquities. I. Title.
HC39 .G72 1986

Greene, Richard, 1953- 1,001 advertising cuts from the twenties and thirties /. New York , 1987. 103 p. : ISBN 0-486-25490-9 (pbk.) LC Card 87-15546 DDC 659.13/2/0973 19
HF5813.U6 A525 1987

Greenfield, Gerald Michael. Latin American labor organizations /. New York , 1987. xiv, 929 p. ; ISBN 0-313-22834-5 (lib. bdg. : alk. paper) LC Card 86-33613 DDC 331.88/098 19
HD6530.5 .L38 1987

Greenfield, Sidney M. Entrepreneurship and social change /. Lanham, MD [S.l.] , c1986. 275 p. : ISBN 0-8191-5165-3 (alk. paper) : LC Card 85-26533 DDC 338/.04 19
HB615 .E629 1986 ***NYPL [JLD 86-3073]***

Greenfield, W. M.
Accounting with 1-2-3 / W.M. Greenfield. Englewood Cliffs, N.J. : Prentice-Hall, 1987. p. cm. Includes index. ISBN 0-13-001686-1 LC Card 87-12485 DDC 657/.028/55369 19
1. Accounting - Data processing. 2. Lotus 1-2-3 (Computer program). I. Title. II. Title: Accounting with one-two-three.
HF5679 .G737 1987

Successful management consulting : building a practice with smaller company clients / W.M. Greenfield. Englewood Cliffs, N.J. : Prentice-Hall, c1987. xii, 192 p. ; 24 cm. Bibliography: p. 178-179. Includes index. ISBN 0-13-863143-3 : LC Card 86-30494 DDC 658.4/6 19
1. Business consultants. 2. Small business. I. Title.
HD69.C6 G72 1987

Greenhalgh, Susan.
Contending approaches to the political economy of Taiwan /. Armonk, N.Y. , c1988. p. cm. ISBN 0-87332-440-4 : LC Card 87-16413 DDC 338.951/249 19
HC430.5 .C75 1988

Fertility policy in China : future options / Susan Greenhalgh, John Bongaarts. New York, N.Y. : Population Council, [1986] 31 p. ; 23 cm. (Working papers / Center for Policy Studies . no. 127 (Oct. 1986)) Cover title. "An earlier version of this paper was presented at the 1986 Annual Meeting of the Population Association of America, held in San Francisco, California, 3-5 April."--T.p. verso. Bibliography: p. 26-28. LC Card 87-154581 DDC 304.6/6/0951 19
1. Fertility, Human - China. 2. China - Population policy. 3. Birth control - China. I. Bongaarts, John, 1945-. II. Series: Working papers (Population Council. Center for Policy Studies) , no. 127. III. Title.
HB1064.A3 G74 1986

Greenham women everywhere . Cook, Alice. Boston, Mass. , 1984, c1983. 127, [1] p. : ISBN 0-89608-199-0 ***NYPL [JLD 87-215]***

GREENHOUSE CLIMATE. see **GREENHOUSES.**

GREENHOUSES - GERMANY (WEST) - LOWER SAXONY - STATISTICS.
Landwirtschaftszählung 1979, Gartenbauerhebung 1981/82 . Hannover , 1983. xv, 132 p. ; LC Card 85-117833
HD9013.7.L68 L37 1983

Greenhut, Melvin L.
The economics of imperfect competition : a spatial approach / Melvin L. Greenhut, George Norman, Chao-shun Hung. Cambridge [Cambridgeshire] ; New York : Cambridge University Press, 1987. xix, 408 p. : ill. ; 24 cm. Includes indexes. Bibliography: p. 389-399. ISBN 0-521-30552-7 LC Card 86-11707 DDC 338.6/048 19
1. Competition, Imperfect. 2. Space in economics. I. Norman, George, 1946-. II. Hung, Chao-shun, 1942-. III. Title.
HB238 .G74 1987 ***NYPL [JLE 87-1413]***

Report on an income tax in Texas / by M.L. Greenhut. College Station, Tex. : Center for Education and Research in Free Enterprise, Texas A&M University, c1986. 40 p. : ill. ; 22 cm. (Series on public issues . no. 21) Includes bibliographical references. ISBN 0-86599-057-3 (pbk.) LC Card 86-622258 DDC 336.24/09764 19
1. Income tax - Texas. I. Title. II. Series.
HJ4655.T4 G74 1986

The greening of Africa . Harrison, Paul. New York, N.Y., U. S.A. , 1987. 380 p. : ISBN 0-14-010192-6 (pbk.) : LC Card 87-404277 DDC 338.1/9/6 19
HD2117 .H37 1987

Greenleigh Associates, inc. The Role of the sheltered workshops in the rehabilitation of the severely handicapped. New York , 1976. xxiv, 467 p. ; ***NYPL [JLF 86-1287]***

Greenwood, David. The SDI and Europe / by David Greenwood. Aberdeen, Scotland : Centre for Defence Studies, [1985] 64 p. ; 30 cm. (Aberdeen studies in defence economics . no. 26) Bibliography: p. 59-64. LC Card 86-150232 DDC 355/.07/094 19
1. Military research - Europe. 2. Munitions - Europe. 3. Strategic Defense Initiative. I. Title. II. Series.
U395.E85 G73 1985 ***NYPL [JFG 87-57]***

Greenwood, Reed.
Employer concerns regarding workers with disabilities / Reed Greenwood, Virginia Anne Johnson. Hot Springs, Ark. : Arkansas Research & Training Center in Vocational Rehabilitation : University of Arkansas, Arkansas Rehabilitation Services, [1985] xii, 170 p. ; 28 cm. "December 1985." At head of title: Arkansas Research and Training Center in Vocational Rehabilitation. Bibliography: p. 157-170. LC Card 87-620863 DDC 658.3/045 19
1. Vocational Rehabilitation - United States. 2. Handicapped - Employment - United States. 3. Selection of employees - United States. I. Johnson, Virginia Anne. II. Arkansas Research and Training Center in Vocational Rehabilitation. III. Title.
HD7256.U5 G74 1985

Joint Seminar on Designing Jobs for Handicapped Workers (1985 : Chicago, Ill.) Designing jobs for handicapped workers . Hot Springs, Ark. (P.O. Box 1358, Hot Spring 71902) [1986] 66 p. : LC Card 86-622317 DDC 658.3/045 19
HD7256.U5 J65 1985

Greer, Gaylon E. Farrell, Michael D. Tax shelters . Chicago, Ill. , c1985. x, 250 p. : ISBN 0-930369-04-1 : LC Card 85-207994 DDC 343.7305/23 347.303523 19
KF6297.5 .F37 1985 ***NYPL [JLE 86-1019]***

Greer, Joel William, 1948- Food poverty and consumption patterns in Kenya / Joel Greer and Erik Thorbecke. Geneva : International Labour Office, 1986. xii, 170 p. : ill. ; 24 cm. Bibliography: p. 167-170. ISBN 92-2-105374-1 (pbk.) : LC Card 87-115091 DDC 338.1/9/6762 19
1. Food supply - Kenya - Mathematical models. 2. Food consumption - Kenya - Mathematical models. 3. Poverty - Mathematical models. I. Thorbecke, Erik, 1929-. II. Title.
HD9017.K42 G74 1986

Greevey, Lucy E. Women farmers in Africa . Syracuse, N.Y. , 1986. xvi, 212 p. : ISBN 0-8156-2358-5 (alk. paper) LC Card 85-27771 DDC 331.4/83/096 19
HD6073.A292 A358 1986
NYPL [JLE 86-2556]

Grefenstette, John J. Proceedings of an international conference on genetic algorithms and their applications . [S.l. , 1985] 225 p. : ***NYPL [JSF 87-413]***

Grefermann, Klaus. Papier- und Pappeverarbeitung : Strukturwandlungen und Entwicklungsperspektiven / von Klaus Grefermann. Berlin : Duncker & Humblot, c1986. 209 p. : 10 ill. ; 24 cm. (Struktur und Wachstum: Reihe Industrie. Heft 41) Bibliography: p. [157]-160. ISBN 3-428-06050-4 LC Card 86-233133
1. Paper industry - Germany (West). 2. Wood-pulp industry - Germany (West). 3. Paper industry. 4. Wood-pulp industry. I. Title. II. Series.
HD9833.5 .G73 1986

Greffe, Xavier. Les Economies non officielles /. Paris , 1984. 247 p. : ISBN 2-7071-1441-3 : LC Card 86-460169
HD2341 .E26 1984

Grégoire, Roger, 1913- Le Transport fluvial . Paris , c1983. 108 p. : ISBN 2-11-001087-8 : LC Card 83-170808
HE668 .T73 1983

Gregory, P. World offshore markets : can Britain compete? / P. Gregory, I.H. McNicoll, L. Moar. London : Eastlords Pub., 1986. xiv, 215 p. ; 22 cm. Bibliography: p. 212-215. ISBN 0-946416-06-0 (pbk.) : LC Card 86-217327 DDC 338.2/7282/0941 19
1. Offshore oil industry - Great Britain. 2. Offshore oil industry. 3. Competition, International. I. McNicoll, Iain H. (Iain Hugh). II. Moar, L. III. Title.
HD9571.5 .G75 1986

Gregory, Paul R. Ruffin, Roy, 1938- Principles of economics /. Glenview, Ill. , c1988. xxxi, 918, [42] p. : ISBN 0-673-18871-X : LC Card 87-23369 DDC 330 19
HB171.5 .R82 1988

Gregory, Peter. The myth of market failure : employment and the labor market in Mexico / Peter Gregory. Baltimore : Johns Hopkins University Press, 1986. viii, 299 p. ; 25 cm. "Published for the World Bank." Includes index. Bibliography: p. 281-291. ISBN 0-8018-3343-4 : LC Card 85-45927 DDC 331.12/0972 19
1. Labor supply - Mexico. 2. Wages - Mexico. 3. Migration, Internal - Mexico. 4. Mexico - Emigration and immigration. I. Title.
HD5731.A6 G74 1986 ***NYPL [JLE 86-3065]***

Greider, William. Secrets of the temple : how the Federal Reserve runs the country / William Greider. New York : Simon and Schuster, c1987. 798 p. ; 24 cm. Bibliography: p. [733]-768. Includes index. ISBN 0-671-47989-X : LC Card 87-16712 DDC 332.1/1/0973 19
1. Board of Governors of the Federal Reserve System (U. S.). 2. Federal Reserve banks. 3. Monetary policy - United States - History - 20th century. 4. Banks and banking - United States - History - 20th century. 5. Finance - United States - History - 20th century. I. Title.
HG2563 .G72 1987

Greif, Helmut. Nuremberg thimblemakers / Helmut Greif ; English translation by Gertrude Kuebler. [Des Moines, Iowa] : Thimble Collectors International, c1986. 30 p. : ill. ; 28 cm. LC Card 86-209810 DDC 338.4/76878 19
1. Thimblemakers - Germany (West) - Nuremberg - History. I. Title.
HD8039.T522 G34 1986

Greif, Siegfried. Konzepte der Organisationspsychologie : eine Einführung in grundlegende theoretische Ansätze / Siegfried Greif ; mit einem Vorwort von Eberhard Ulich. Bern : H. Huber, c1983. 320 p. : ill. ; 23 cm. (Schriften zur Arbeitspsychologie. Nr. 38) Bibliography: p. 293-304. Includes indexes. ISBN 3-456-81262-0 LC Card 83-240680
1. Organizational behavior. 2. Psychology, Industrial. I. Title.
HD58.7 .G72 1983

Greinke, Helmut, 1957- Entscheidungsverlauf und Entscheidungseffizienz : eine Experimentaluntersuchung / Helmut Greinke. Krefeld : G. Marchal und H.-J. Matzenbacher Wissenschaftsverlag, 1986. viii, 249 p. : ill. ; 21 cm. Bibliography: p. 227-249. ISBN 3-88358-057-0 LC Card 86-172311
1. Decision-making. 2. Organizational effectiveness. I. Title.
HD30.23 .G74 1986

GREMI D'ESCULTORS DE BARCELONA (SPAIN) - HISTORY - 18TH CENTURY.
Martinell, César, 1888-1973. L'antic Gremi d'Escultors de Barcelona /. Valls , 1956. 68 p. ; LC Card 86-180958
HD6473.S73 B356 1956

Grémillard, Roger. 75 moyens qui ont fait leurs preuves d'augmenter vos rendements et diminuer vos coûts en publicité et en V.P.C. / Roger Grémillard. Créteil : R. Grémillard, c1982. 158 p. ; 22 cm. (Collection "Encyclopédie pratique complète de la V.P.C. et de la publicité directe" . 2) LC Card 82-238594
1. Mail-order business - France. 2. Direct selling - France. I. Title. II. Title: Soixante-quinze moyens qui ont fait leurs preuves d'augmenter vos rendements et diminuer vos coûts en publicité directe et en V.P.C. III. Series.
HF5466 .G718 1982

Gremillion, Lee L. (Lee Louis) Computers and information systems in business : an introduction / Lee L. Gremillion, Phillip J. Pyburn. New York : McGraw-Hill, c1988. xxi, 359 p., [16] p. of plates : ill. (some col.) ; 26 cm. Includes bibliographies and index. ISBN 0-07-051007-5 (pbk.) LC Card 87-20300 DDC 650/.028/5 19
1. Business - Data processing. 2. Information storage and retrieval systems - Business. I. Pyburn, Phillip J. II. Title.
HF5548.2 .G7196 1988

GRENADA - ECONOMIC CONDITIONS.
Pryor, Frederic L. Revolutionary Grenada . New York , 1986. xx, 395 p. : ISBN 0-275-92155-7 (alk. paper) : LC Card 86-8109 DDC 338.97298/45 19
HC156.5.Z7 G747 1986
NYPL [JLE 86-3969]

GRENADA - ECONOMIC CONDITIONS - STATISTICS.
Grenade, juin 1985 . [Paris] , 1985] 124 p. : LC Card 86-209038
HC156.5.Z7 G7465 1985

GRENADA - ECONOMIC POLICY.
Pryor, Frederic L. Revolutionary Grenada . New York , 1986. xx, 395 p. : ISBN 0-275-92155-7 (alk. paper) : LC Card 86-8109 DDC 338.97298/45 19
HC156.5.Z7 G747 1986
NYPL [JLE 86-3969]

GRENADA - HISTORY - AMERICAN INVASION, 1983.
Historia del contingente internacionalista de Granada. [Havana, Cuba] [1984] 157 p. : LC Card 85-213062
HC156.5.Z7 G844 1984

GRENADA - POLITICS AND GOVERNMENT - 1974-
Pryor, Frederic L. Revolutionary Grenada . New York , 1986. xx, 395 p. : ISBN 0-275-92155-7 (alk. paper) : LC Card 86-8109 DDC 338.97298/45 19
HC156.5.Z7 G747 1986
NYPL [JLE 86-3969]

GRENADA - POPULATION - STATISTICS.
Grenade, juin 1985 . [Paris] , 1985] 124 p. : LC Card 86-209038
HC156.5.Z7 G7465 1985

Grenade. Grenade, juin 1985 . [Paris] , 1985] 124 p. : LC Card 86-209038
HC156.5.Z7 G7465 1985

Grenade, juin 1985 : situation économique, financière et sociale / République française, Ministère des relations extérieures, coopération et développement, Direction des politiques du développement [et] Caisse centrale de coopération économique. [Paris] : La Direction : L'Harmattan, [distributor, 1985] 124 p. : ill. ; 30 cm. Cover title. Title on half t.p.: Grenade. Distributor from label on half t.p. Bibliography: p. 124. LC Card 86-209038
1. Grenada - Economic conditions - Statistics. 2. Grenada - Population - Statistics. I. France. Ministère des relations extérieures, coopération et développement. Direction des politiques du développement. II. Caisse centrale de coopération économique (France). III. Title: Situation économique, financière et sociale. IV. Title: Grenade.
HC156.5.Z7 G7465 1985

Grenander-Nyberg, Gertrud, 1912- En charkuterifabrik med tradition : folklivsskildring från 1950-talets Stockholm / Gertrud Grenander Nyberg.Uppl. 1:1. Stockholm : Liber, c1985. 207 p. : ill. ; 26 cm. (Stockholmsmonografier utgivna av Stockholms

kommun . 64) Bibliography: p. 191-192. ISBN 91-38-09206-9 LC Card 86-159511
1. Engvall & Aug. Falk nya charkuteri (Stockholm, Sweden). 2. Meat industry and trade - Sweden - Stockholm - Case studies. I. Series: Stockholmsmonografier , 64. II. Title.
HD9145.S88 E544 1985

Grenier, Guillermo J. Inhuman relations : quality circles and anti-unionism in American industry / Guillermo J. Grenier. Philadelphia : Temple University Press, 1988. xx, 232 p. ; 22 cm. (Labor and social change) Bibliography: p. 211-225. Includes index. ISBN 0-87722-502-8 (alk. paper) : LC Card 87-10116 DDC 331.25 19
1. Trade-unions - United States - Organizing - Case studies. 2. Quality circles - United States - Case studies. 3. Quality of work life - United States - Case studies. 4. Industrial relations - United States - Case studies. 5. Industrial management - United States - Employee participation - Case studies. I. Title. II. Series.
HD6490.Q72 U645 1988

GRENOBLE METROPOLITAN AREA (FRANCE) - INDUSTRIES - HISTORY.
Tiger, Henri. Restructuration industrielle et filières de main-d'œuvre . Paris , 1979. 389 p. : LC Card 85-126419
HD5776.G74 T54 1979

Grenoble. Université des sciences sociales. see **Université des sciences sociales de Grenoble.**

Grenville, William Wyndham Grenville, Baron, 1759-1834. Pullen, J. M. Lord Grenville's manuscript notes on Malthus /. [Newcastle] [1986] 94 p. ; ISBN 0-7259-0557-3 (pbk.) LC Card 87-150102 DDC 330.15/3 19
HB161.M28 P85 1986

Die Grenzen der Atomwirtschaft . Meyer-Abich, Klaus Michael, 1936- München , c1986. 230 p. : ISBN 3-406-31317-5 LC Card 86-192439
HD9698.A2 M49 1986

Grenzen der Frauenlohnarbeit : Frauenstrategien in Lohn- und Hausarbeit seit der Jahrhundertwende / Helgard Kramer ... [et al.]. Frankfurt/Main ; New York : Campus, c1986. 250 p. : ill. ; 21 cm. (Studienreihe des Instituts für Sozialforschung Frankfurt am Main) Results of a research project on women's labor conducted since 1978 at the Institut für Sozialforschung. Includes bibliographies. CONTENTS. - Dienstmädchen um 1900 / Karin Walser -- Die Interessen der Frauen in sozialen Berufen / Ilka Riemann -- Weibliche Büroangestellte während der Weltwirtschaftskrise / Helgard Kramer -- Halbtags durch das Wirtschaftswunder / Christel Eckart. ISBN 3-593-33628-6 LC Card 86-228323
1. Women domestics - Germany. 2. Women in charitable work. 3. Women white collar workers - Germany. 4. Part-time employment - Germany, West. I. Kramer, Helgard. II. Institut für Sozialforschung (Frankfurt am Main, Germany). III. Series: Studienreihe des Instituts für Sozialforschung Frankfurt am Main (Campus Verlag).
HD6072.2.G4 G74 1986

Grenzen des Sozialstaats? . Strasser, Johano. Köln , 1983. 206 p. ; ISBN 3-7663-0800-9 LC Card 83-142735
HC286.6 .S73 1983

Gresko, Jacqueline, 1947- Fraser Port . Victoria, B.C. , 1986. 131 p., [16] p. of plates : ISBN 0-919203-17-5 (pbk.) LC Card 87-106756
HE554.V3 F73 1986

Greussing, Kurt. Im Prinzip, Hoffnung . Bregenz , c1984. 368 p. : ISBN 3-900438-07-9 LC Card 86-120542 DDC 331.88/09436/45 19
HD6679.V67 I4 1984 ***NYPL [JLD 87-1568]***

Greve, fatos e significados /. Castro, Pedro. São Paulo , 1986. 72 p. ; ISBN 85-08-01170-9 : LC Card 86-230606
HD5353 .C37 1986

Greves de mil e novecentos e dezessete em São Paulo. Khoury, Yara Aun. As greves de 1917 em São Paulo e o processo de organização proletária /. São Paulo , 1981. 221 p. ; LC Card 81-210934 DDC 331.2/98161 19
HD5355.S26 K48 1981
NYPL [JLD 86-3514]

Grèves et lock-out au Canada, 1973. Strikes and lockouts in Canada, 1973 /. Ottawa , 1975. 88 p. : ISBN 2-7114-5902-3 (pbk.) LC Card 82-212112
HD5328 .S77 1975

Griaznov, Gennadiĭ Viktorovich. Opyt stroitel'stva sotsialisticheskoĭ ėkonomiki v stranakh Azii /. Moskva , 1986. 290 p. ; LC Card 87-126301
HC412 .O675 1986

Grideq. see **Université du Québec à Rimouski. Groupe de recherche interdisciplinaire en développement de l'Est du Québec.**

Grieb, William E. The small business computer today and tomorrow / William E. Grieb, Jr. New York, N.Y. : Baen Enterprises : Distributed by Simon & Schuster, c1984. 287 p. : ill. ; 21 cm. (A Pournelle users guide) ISBN 0-671-55907-9 (pbk.) : LC Card 86-207213 DDC 658/.05416 19
1. Small business - Data processing. 2. Microcomputers - Purchasing. I. Title. II. Series.
HF5548.2 .G733 1984

Grier, Eunice S.
Gale, Dennis E. Black and white urban-to-suburban outmigrants . Washington, D.C. [1986] 46 p. : LC Card 87-404424 DDC 307.2 19
HB1987.W34 G35 1986

Grier, George W. Greater Washington at mid decade . Washington, DC (1717 Massachusetts Ave., N.W., Washington 20036-2076) , c1985- v. <1 > : LC Card 86-200647 DDC 338.5/443/09753 19
HC108.W3 G73 1985

Grier, George W.
Gale, Dennis E. Black and white urban-to-suburban outmigrants . Washington, D.C. [1986] 46 p. : LC Card 87-404424 DDC 307.2 19
HB1987.W34 G35 1986

Greater Washington at mid decade : report / George and Eunice Grier. Washington, DC (1717 Massachusetts Ave., N.W., Washington 20036-2076) : Greater Washington Research Center, c1985- v. <1 > : ill. ; 23 cm. "December 1985." CONTENTS. - no. 1. Executive summary, shifting growth trends and their implications for the region's future. LC Card 86-200647 DDC 338.5/443/09753 19
1. Economic forecasting - Washington (D.C.). 2. Washington, D. C. - Economic conditions. 3. Population forecasting - Washington (D.C.). 4. Washington, D. C. - Population. I. Grier, Eunice S. II. Title.
HC108.W3 G73 1985

Grieser, Dietmar, 1934- Historische Strassen in Europa : von der Via Appia bis zur Avus / Dietmar Grieser. München : Keyser, c1983. 95 p. : 66 ill. (some col.) ; 24 cm. (Keysers kleine Kulturgeschichte) ISBN 3-87405-160-9 (pbk.) LC Card 87-672444
1. Streets - Europe. I. Title. II. Series.
HE361 .G74x 1983

Grieser, Rudolf, 1899- Schatz- und Zinsverzeichnisse des 15. Jahrhunderts aus dem Fürstentum Lüneburg . Hildesheim , 1942. 153 p. ; LC Card 87-409521 DDC 336.2/00943/59 19
HJ2110.5.L86 S3 1942

GRIEVANCE ARBITRATION - UNITED STATES - CASE STUDIES.
Beal, Edwin Fletcher. The practice of collective bargaining /. Homewood, Ill. , 1985. xvi, 560 p. : ISBN 0-256-03214-9 LC Card 84-82023 DDC 331.89 19
HD6508 .B375 1985
NYPL [*R-Econ. 86-3458]

Grievance guide / by the BNA editorial staff. 7th ed. Washington, D.C. : Bureau of National Affairs, c1987. ix, 400 p. ; 23 cm. ISBN 0-87179-554-X (pbk.) LC Card 87-24926 DDC 658.3/155 19
1. Grievance procedures - United States. I. Bureau of National Affairs, Washington, D. C.
HD6972.5 .G74 1987

GRIEVANCE PROCEDURES - UNITED STATES.
Grievance guide /. Washington, D.C. , c1987. ix, 400 p. ; ISBN 0-87179-554-X (pbk.) LC Card 87-24926 DDC 658.3/155 19
HD6972.5 .G74 1987

Grieves, Keith. The politics of manpower, 1914-1918 / Keith Grieves. New York, NY : St. Martin's Press, 1988. vii, 241 p. ; 22 cm. (War, armed forces, and society) Bibliography: p. [221]-234. Includes index. ISBN 0-312-01320-5 LC Card 87-20511 DDC 331.12/042/0941 19
1. Manpower policy - Great Britain - History - 20th century. 2. Military service, Compulsory - Great Britain - History - 20th century. 3. World War, 1914-1918 - Economic aspects - Great Britain. I. Title. II. Series.
HD5765.A6 G77 1988

Griffin, Keith B. World hunger and the world economy : and other essays in development economics / Keith Griffin. New York : Holmes & Meier, 1987. xvi, 274 p. ; 22 cm. Includes bibliographical references and index. ISBN 0-8419-1128-2 LC Card 86-33626 DDC 330.9172/4 19
1. Developing countries - Economic conditions. 2. Developing countries - Social conditions. 3. Hunger. 4. Debts, External - Developing countries. 5. Agriculture - Economic aspects - Developing countries. I. Title.
HC59.7 .G749 1987

Griffin, Paul A.
Accounting for the translation of foreign currencies : the effects of statement 52 on equity analysts / Paul A. Griffin and Richard P. Castanias II. Stamford, Conn. : Financial Accounting Standards Board of the Financial Accounting Foundation, c1987. viii, 112 p. : ill. ; 23 cm. (Research report / Financial Accounting Standards Board) Bibliography: p. 107-112. ISBN 0-910065-22-5 (pbk.) LC Card 86-81640 DDC 657/.48 19
1. Foreign exchange - Accounting. 2. Stock price forecasting. I. Castanias, Richard P. II. Series: Research report / Financial Accounting Standards Board. III. Title.
HG3853.7 .G75 1987

Usefulness to investors and creditors of information provided by financial reporting / Paul A. Griffin. 2nd ed. Stamford, Conn. : Financial Accounting Standards Board of the Financial Accounting Foundation, c1987. xii, 294 p. ; 23 cm. (Research report) Bibliography: p. 229-294. Includes index. ISBN 0-910065-24-1 (pbk.) LC Card 87-81637 DDC 657/.3 19
1. Financial statements. 2. Investments. 3. Credit management. I. Series: Research report / Financial Accounting Standards Board. II. Title.
HF5681.B2 G79 1987

Griffin, Ricky W.
Instructor's manual, Practicing management, second edition / Ricky W. Griffin, Thomas C. Head. Boston : Houghton Mifflin, c1987. xiii, 167 p. ; 24 cm. ISBN 0-395-42585-9 (pbk.) LC Card 87-400618 DDC 658 19
1. Management. 2. Management - Case studies. I. Head, Thomas C. II. Practicing management. III. Title.
HD31 .G7627 1987

Management. Griffin, Ricky W. Practicing management / Ricky W. Griffin, Thomas C. Head. 2nd ed. Boston , c1987. xii, 368 p. : ISBN 0-395-42584-0 (pbk.) LC Card 87-163492 DDC 658 19
HD31 .G7635 1987

Practicing management / Ricky W. Griffin, Thomas C. Head. 2nd ed. Boston : Houghton Mifflin Co., c1987. xii, 368 p. : ill. ; 24 cm. Companion volume to: Management. Includes bibliographies. ISBN 0-395-42584-0 (pbk.) LC Card 87-163492 DDC 658 19
1. Management. 2. Management - Case studies. I. Head, Thomas C. II. Griffin, Ricky W. Management. III. Title.
HD31 .G7635 1987

Griffin, Sean. Fighting heritage . Vancouver [1986?] 159 p., [32] p. of plates : ISBN 0-9692365-0-6 (pbk.) LC Card 86-231043 DDC 331.88/09711 19
HD8109.B72 F54 1986

Griffith, Barbara S. The crisis of American labor : Operation Dixie and the defeat of the CIO / Barbara S. Griffith. Philadelphia : Temple University Press, 1988. xvi, 239 p. : ill. ; 22 cm. Bibliography: p. 213-232. Includes index. ISBN 0-87722-503-6 (alk. paper) : LC Card 87-9998 DDC 331.88/33/0975 19
1. Congress of Industrial Organizations (U. S.) - History. 2. Trade-unions - Southern States - Organizing - History. I. Title.
HD8055.C75 G75 1988

Griffith-Jones, Stephany. World prices and development /. Aldershot, Hants, England , Brookfield, Vt., U. S.A. , c1985. xi, 377 p. : ISBN 0-566-00890-4 LC Card 86-134604 DDC 338.5/2/0971724 19
HC59.7 .W684 1985 ***NYPL [JLD 86-4068]***

Griffiths, A. R. G., 1940- The Irish Board of Works, 1831-1878 / A.R.G. Griffiths. New York : Garland Pub., 1987. iii, 214 p. ; 24 cm. (Modern European history) Bibliography: p. 175-208. Includes index. ISBN 0-8240-7810-1 (alk. paper) : LC Card 87-24495 DDC 363/.09415 19
1. Ireland. Board of Public Works - History - 19th century. 2. Infrastructure (Economics) - Ireland - History - 19th century. 3. Famine - Ireland - History - 19th century. I. Title. II. Series.
HD4150.3 .G75 1987

Griffiths, Brian. The creation of wealth : a Christian's case for capitalism / Brian Griffiths. Downers Grove, Ill. : InterVarsity Press, c1984. 160 p. : ill. ; 21 cm. Includes index. Bibliography: p. [124]-150. ISBN 0-87784-566-2 (pbk.) : LC Card 85-5210 DDC 330.12/2 19
1. Economics - Moral and ethical aspects. 2. Economics - Religious aspects - Christianity. 3. Capitalism - Religious aspects - Christianity. I. Title.
HB72 .G74 1984 ***NYPL [JLD 86-3576]***

Griffiths, David. Todd, Jean Elizabeth. Changing the definition of a household . London , 1986. viii, 43 p. : ISBN 0-11-691071-2 (pbk.) : LC Card 87-132272
HB849.49 .T63 1986

Grigsby, S. Elaine. Alternative export strategies and U. S. agricultural policies for grains and oilseeds, 1950-83 / S. Elaine Grigsby, Praveen M. Dixit. [Washington, D.C.] : U. S. Dept. of Agriculture, Economic Research Service, International Economics Division, 1986. v., 37 p. : ill., 28 cm. (ERS staff report . no. AGES 860616) Distributed to depository libraries in microfiche. "September 1986"--P. iii. Bibliography: p. 34-37. Item 42-W-1 (microfiche) LC Card 86-602816 DDC 382/.4131/0973 19
1. Grain trade - Government policy - United States. 2. Oil industries - Government policy - United States. I. Dixit, Praveen M. II. United States. Dept. of Agriculture. Economic Research Service. International Economics Division. III. Title. IV. Title: Alternative export strategies and US agricultural policies for grains and oilseeds, 1950-83.
HD9036 .G83 1986

Grimal͡iuk, V. A. (Viktor Andreevich) Neposredstvenno obobshchestvlennyĭ trud / V.A. Grimal͡iuk. Moskva : "Mysl′", 1985. 110, [2] p. ; 20 cm. Bibliography: p. 109-[111] LC Card 86-111859
1. Labor supply - Soviet Union. 2. Labor and laboring classes - Soviet Union. 3. Marxian economics. I. Title.
HD5796 .G75 1985

Grime, G. (Geoffrey) Handbook of road safety research / Geoffrey Grime. London ; Boston : Butterworths, 1987. ix, 149 p. : ill. ; 25 cm. Includes bibliographies and index. ISBN 0-408-02780-0 : LC Card 86-26427 DDC 363.1/25/0941 19
1. Traffic accidents - Great Britain. 2. Traffic safety - Great Britain. I. Title.
HE5614.5.G7 G77 1987

Grimm, Bernd Christian. Handbuch der Hausfinanzierung : alles über Finanzierungsmöglichkeiten und Steuerersparnisse beim Bauen und Kaufen / von Bernd Christian Grimm, Dieter Weber.10., neu bearbeitete Aufl. Mannheim : Akademische Arbeitsgemeinschaft Verlagsgesellschaft, 1985. 174, [318] p. ; 21 cm. LC Card 85-188627
1. Housing - Germany, West - Finance. I. Weber, Dieter, Dipl.-Kfm. Dr. II. Title.
HD7339.Z9 G75 1985

Grimm, Ulrich. Analyse strategischer Faktoren : ein Beitrag zur Theorie der strategischen Unternehmensplanung / Ulrich Grimm. Wiesbaden : T. Gabler, c1983. 294 p. : ill. ; 24 cm. (Beiträge zur betriebswirtschaftlichen Forschung. Bd. 56) Bibliography: p. 274-294. ISBN 3-409-18720-0 LC Card 84-173895
1. Strategic planning. I. Title. II. Series.
HD30.28 .G76 1983

Grinage, Kent M. Arctic Slope Consulting Engineers. Western Arctic Coal Development Project . Anchorage, Alaska [1986] 2 v. : LC Card 87-621058 DDC 333.8/22/09798 19
HD9547.A4 A85 1986

Grinder, Dale. United States. Women's Bureau. Records of the Women's Bureau of the Department of Labor, 1918-1965 [microform] /. Frederick, MD , 1987- microfilm reel ISBN 0-89093-870-9 (microfilm : pt. 1) : LC Card 87-6239 DDC 331.4/0973 19
HD6095

Grindle, Art, 1923- I want to sell you success / by Art Grindle. 1st ed. Charleston [S.C.] : Professional Research Pub. Co., c1987. p. cm. ISBN 0-931807-12-3 : LC Card 87-6962 DDC 650.1 19
1. Success in business. 2. Achievement motivation. 3. Finance, Personal. I. Title.
HF5386 .G776 1987

Grinnell, J. D., 1944- The national register of advertising slogans & headlines / compiled by J.D. Grinnell. Westbury, N.Y. : Asher-Gallant, 1987. p. cm. ISBN 0-87280-159-4 : LC Card 87-17577 DDC 659.13/22 19
1. Slogans. 2. Advertising. I. Title.
HF6135 .G74 1987

Grinspan, Mel G. News and views from National Public Radio /. Memphis, Tenn. , 1989. p. cm. LC Card 87-23331 DDC 384.54/06/073 19
HE8697.P6 N48 1989

The Grist guide . Grist, John. Amherst, MA, U. S.A. (P.O. Box 227, Amherst 01004) , c1984. ii, 48 p. ; LC Card 85-108426 DDC 382/.025/73 19
HF294 .G75 1984 ***NYPL [*R-Econ. 87-1266]***

Grist, John. The Grist guide : U. S.A. and international export/import guide / edited by John Grist.1984-1985ed. Amherst, MA, U. S.A (P.O. Box 227, Amherst 01004) : Grist, c1984. ii, 48 p. ; 29 cm. LC Card 85-108426 DDC 382/.025/73 19
1. Boards of trade - Directories. 2. Boards of trade - United States - Directories. 3. Commerce - Information services - Bibliography. I. Title.
HF294 .G75 1984 ***NYPL [*R-Econ. 87-1266]***

GRIST-MILLS. see **FLOUR-MILLS.**

Grjebine, Tovy. Colloque d'étude des politiques économiques Récession et relance (1984 : Paris, France) Récession et relance /. Paris , 1984. 218 p. : ISBN 2-7178-0690-3 : LC Card 85-158199 DDC 338.5/42 19
HB3711 .C59 1984

Grobar, Bonnie. Mercer, Kent. Directory of licensed occupations and apprenticeship programs in Texas. [Austin, Tex.] [1985] iv, 102 p. ; LC Card 86-622006 DDC 331.7/02/09764 19
HF5382.5.U6 T45 1985

Groberman, Jeff. The garage sale book : turn your trash into cash / Jeff Groberman and Colin Yardley. Rocklin, CA : Prima Pub. & Communications, c1987. 90 p. : ill. ; 21 cm. ISBN 0-914629-10-7 (pbk.) : LC Card 86-25388 DDC 658.8/7 19
1. Garage sales. I. Yardley, Colin. II. Title.
HF5482.3 .G76 1987

GROCERIES - TAXATION - ITALY.
Scanu, Salvatore. I costi dell'adempimento tributario in Italia . [Cagliari] , Milano, Italy , c1984. 153 p. ; LC Card 85-118845
HD9326.I82 S32 1984

GROCERS - LATIN AMERICA - HISTORY - CASE STUDIES.
Kinsbruner, Jay. Petty capitalism in Spanish America . Boulder, Colo. , 1987. xxii, 159 p. : ISBN 0-8133-7272-0 (pbk.) LC Card 86-51526 DDC 381/.456413/0098 19
HD9325.L29 K56 1987

GROCERY TRADE - ITALY - COSTS.
Scanu, Salvatore. I costi dell'adempimento tributario in Italia . [Cagliari] , Milano, Italy , c1984. 153 p. ; LC Card 85-118845
HD9326.I82 S32 1984

GROCERY TRADE - LATIN AMERICA - HISTORY - CASE STUDIES.
Kinsbruner, Jay. Petty capitalism in Spanish America . Boulder, Colo. , 1987. xxii, 159 p. : ISBN 0-8133-7272-0 (pbk.) LC Card 86-51526 DDC 381/.456413/0098 19
HD9325.L29 K56 1987

GROCERY TRADE - UNITED STATES.
New trends in food retailing /. Stamford, Conn., U. S.A. , c1985. xiii, 135 leaves : ISBN 0-89336-457-6 (soft) LC Card 87-165228 DDC 381/.45664/00973 19
HD9321.5 .N47 1985

GROCERY TRADE - UNITED STATES - DATA PROCESSING - COSTS - STATISTICS.
Information systems study, 1986. Washington, D.C. (1750 K St. N.W., Washington 20006) , c1986. v, 39 p. : LC Card 86-220211 DDC 381/.456413/00285 19
HF5469.23.U62 I543 1986

GROCERY TRADE - UNITED STATES - FINANCE - STATISTICS.
Operating results of independent supermarkets, 1984. Washington, D.C. (1750 K St., N.W., Washington 20006) , c1985. 137 p. : LC Card 86-218675 DDC 381/.456413/00973 19
HF5469.23.U62 O643 1985

GROCERY TRADE - UNITED STATES - HISTORY.
Walsh, William I. The rise and decline of the Great Atlantic & Pacific Tea Company /. Secaucus, N.J. , c1986. 254 p., [24] p. of plates : ISBN 0-8184-0382-9 : LC Card 85-24987 DDC 381/.456413/006073 19
HD9321.9.G7 W35 1986 ***NYPL [JLE 86-1952]***

GROCERY TRADE - UNITED STATES - STATISTICS.
Food retailing review . Fair Lawn, NJ , 1985. 178 p. : ***NYPL [JLF 86-868]***

Operating results of independent supermarkets, 1985. Washington, D.C. (1750 K St., Washington 20006) , c1986. ix, 141 p. : LC Card 86-225218 DDC 381/.456413/00973021 19
HF5469.23.U62 O64 1986

Retail produce operations, 1986 /. Washington, D.C. (1750 K. St., N.W. Washington 20006) , Newark, Del. [1986] viii, 20 p. ; LC Card 87-101803 DDC 381/.456648/00973 19
HD9321.4 .R47 1986

Grochla, Erwin. Stand und Entwicklung des Vorschlagswesens in Wirtschaft und Verwaltung /. Dortmund , 1978. 108 p. : ISBN 3-922104-00-2 LC Card 85-124069
HD30 .A7 Heft 193 HF5549.5.S8

GROCHLA, ERWIN.
Zukunftsaspekte der anwendungsorientierten Betriebswirtschaftslehre . Stuttgart , c1986. xii, 641 p. : ISBN 3-7910-0402-6 LC Card 86-202268
HD35 .Z84 1986

De groenen . Florizoone, Patrick, 1958- [Deurne] , c1985. x, 194 p. : ISBN 90-6716-272-8 LC Card 86-148321
HC329.5.E5 F56 1985

Die Grösse der Kleinen . Aiginger, Karl. Wien [between 1984 and 1987] 160, [1] p. : ISBN 3-85436-025-8 LC Card 87-141921 DDC 658.1/592 19
HG4027.7 .A38 1984

Groff, William H. Income variability in Connecticut, 1980 / by William H. Groff and Kenneth P. Hadden. Storrs, CT : Storrs Agricultural Experiment Station, College of Agriculture and Natural Resources, University of Connecticut, [1987] 32 p. : map ; 22 cm. (Bulletin (Storrs Agricultural Experiment Station) . 474 (Jan. 1987)) Cover title. Bibliography: p. 25. LC Card 87-621355 DDC 339.2/2/09746 19
1. Income distribution - Connecticut. I. Hadden, Kenneth. II. Storrs Agricultural Experiment Station. III. Series. IV. Series: Bulletin (Storrs Agricultural Experiment Station) , 474. V. Title.
HC107.C83 I5138 1987

Grohmann, Dieter. Arbeit, mehr als Kapital . Wuppertal , c1983. 191 p. ; ISBN 3-87294-224-7 LC Card 84-182379
HD6338 .A69 1983

Grohmann, Peter, 1937- Eberle, Eugen, 1908- Die schlaflosen Nächte des Eugen E. . Stuttgart , 1982. 281 p. : ISBN 3-922836-06-2 LC Card 83-173587 DDC 305.5/62/0924 B 19
HD8453.E2 A37 1982 ***NYPL [JFD 87-3745]***

Grolleau, Charles, 1867- (tr) Chesterton, Gilbert Keith, 1874-1936. [Crimes of England. French.] Les crimes de l'Angleterre [microform]. Paris, 1916. 273 p. LC Card 19-16286
DA47.2 .C55 ***NYPL [*Z-4049 no.7]***

Grompone, Romeo. Talleristas y vendedores ambulantes en Lima / Romeo Grompone. Lima : Desco, 1985. 319 p. : ill. ; 21 cm. Bibliography: p. 315-319. LC Card 85-243089

1. Informal sector (Economics) - Peru - Lima. 2. Merchants - Peru - Lima. 3. Peddlers and peddling - Peru - Lima. 4. Poor - Peru - Lima. I. Desco. II. Title.
HD2346.P42 L564 1985

Groneman, Carol.
[Corporate Ph. D]
Corporate PhD : making the grade in business / Carol Groneman and Robert N. Lear ; foreword by Roger B. Smith. New York, N.Y., U. S.A. : Penguin, 1987, c1985. xx, 156 p. ; 20 cm. Cover title: Corporate Ph. D. Reprint. Originally published: Corporate Ph. D. New York, N.Y. : Facts on File, c1985. "A book of the Institute for Research in History." Bibliography: p. 147-151. Includes index. ISBN 0-14-010123-3 (pbk.) LC Card 86-30654 DDC 658.4/09 19
1. Executives - United States. 2. Industrial management - United States. 3. Humanities - Study and teaching (Graduate) - United States. 4. Graduate students - Employment - United States. I. Lear, Robert N. II. Institute for Research in History (New York, N.Y.). III. Title. IV. Title: Corporate Ph. D.
HD38.25.U6 G76 1987

"To toil the livelong day" . Ithaca, N.Y. , 1987. xi, 312 p. ; ISBN 0-8014-1847-X (alk. paper) LC Card 86-47975 DDC 331.4/0973 19
HD6095 .T6 1987

Groot, T. L. C. M. Financieël management van non-profit organisaties / T.L.C.M. Groot, J.H.R. van de Poel. Groningen : Wolters-Noordhoff, c1985. 200 p. : ill. ; 24 cm. Bibliography: p. 190-194. Includes index. ISBN 90-01-30316-1 : LC Card 85-214807
1. Corporations, Nonprofit - Finance. I. Poel, J. H. R. van de. II. Title.
HG4027.65 .G76 1985

Grootaert, Christiaan, 1950- Measuring and analyzing levels of living in developing countries : an annotated questionnaire / Christiaan Grootaert. Washington, D.C., U. S.A. : World Bank, c1986. x, 139 p. : ill. ; 28 cm. (LSMS working papers, 0253-4517 . no. 24) Includes bibliographical references. ISBN 0-8213-0758-4 (pbk.) LC Card 86-5611 DDC 339.4/7/091724 19
1. Cost and standard of living - Ivory Coast. 2. Cost and standard of living - Developing countries. 3. Economic surveys - Ivory Coast. 4. Economic surveys - Developing countries. 5. Questionnaires. I. Series: LSMS working paper , no. 24. II. Title.
HD7067 .G76 1986b

Grootings, Peter, 1951- Technology and work . London , Dover, N.H. , c1986. 304 p. : ISBN 0-7099-3801-2 : LC Card 86-4202 DDC 303.4/83 19
HC244.Z9 T475 1986 ***NYPL [JLD 86-2160]***

Grose, Vernon L., 1928- Managing risk : systematic loss prevention for executives / Vernon L. Grose. Englewood Cliffs, N.J. : Prentice-Hall, c1987. xii, 404 p. : ill. ; 24 cm. Bibliography: p. 392-394. Includes index. ISBN 0-13-551110-0 : LC Card 87-12309 DDC 658 19
1. Risk management. I. Title.
HD61 .G76 1987

Grosfils-Berger, P. Finlande : les timbres des premières émissions de 1856 à 1889-95 / P. Grosfils-Berger. Southfield, MI (15565 Northland Dr., Suite 605 W, Southfield 48075-5308) : R. Koerber, 1947, i.e. [1986?] 320 p. : ill. ; 30 cm. (Postilion publications) LC Card 86-206197 DDC 769.5694897 19
1. Postage-stamps - Finland - Catalogs. 2. Postage-stamps - Finland - History - 19th century. 3. Postmarks - Finland - History - 19th century. I. Title. II. Series.
HE6185.F52 G76 1986

Gross, Alexander, 1953- The role of the current account in asset market models of exchange rate determination / by Alexander Gross. Berlin ; New York : W. de Gruyter, 1987. xiii, 391 p. : ill. ; 24 cm. (Series D--Economics = Economiques = Wirtschaft = Economia . 2) Based on the author's thesis (doctoral)--European University Institute, Florence, Italy. Bibliography: p. [373]-391. ISBN 0-89925-373-3 (U. S.) : LC Card 87-8852 DDC 332.4/56 19
1. Balance of payments - Econometric models. 2. Foreign exchange - Econometric models. I. Title. II. Title: Current account in asset market models of exchange rate determination. III. Series: Series D--Economics , 2.
HG3882 .G75 1987

Gross, Charles W. Marketing : concepts and decision making / Charles W. Gross, Robin T. Peterson. St. Paul : West Pub. Co., c1987. xxviii, 700 p. : ill. (some col.) ; 26 cm. Bibliography: p. 655-677. Includes indexes. ISBN 0-314-85242-5 : LC Card 86-26676 DDC 658.8/02 19
1. Marketing - Decision making. 2. Marketing management. I. Peterson, Robin. II. Title.
HF5415.135 .G76 1987

Gross, François. Weck, Philippe de, 1919- Un banquier suisse parle . Fribourg , c1983. 159 p. ; LC Card 84-119161
HG1552.W43 A3 1983

Gross, Harriet. Families and work /. Philadelphia , 1987. viii, 539 p. ; ISBN 0-87722-467-6 (alk. paper) : LC Card 86-30151 DDC 306.8/5 19
HD4904.25 .F35 1987

Gross, Jerome S.
Illustrated encyclopedic dictionary of real estate. Gross, Jerome S. Webster's new world illustrated encyclopedic dictionary of real estate / Jerome S. Gross. 3rd ed. New York , c1987. 418 p. : ISBN 0-13-947318-1 (pbk.) : LC Card 87-2360 DDC 333.33/03/21 19
HD1365 .G76 1987

Webster's new world illustrated encyclopedic dictionary of real estate / Jerome S. Gross. 3rd ed. New York : Prentice Hall, c1987. 418 p. : ill., forms ; 24 cm. Rev. ed. of: Illustrated encyclopedic dictionary of real estate. 2nd ed. 1978. ISBN 0-13-947318-1 (pbk.) : LC Card 87-2360 DDC 333.33/03/21 19
1. Real estate business - Dictionaries. I. Gross, Jerome S. Illustrated encyclopedic dictionary of real estate. II. Title.
HD1365 .G76 1987

Gross, Johannes, 1932- Ludwig-Erhard-Preis für Wirtschaftspublizistik 1986 . Bonn [1986] 45 p. : ISBN 3-88991-009-2 LC Card 87-409497 DDC 338.943 19
HC286.5 .L825 1986

Gross, LeRoy.
Phone power : telephone selling and prospecting / LeRoy Gross. New York, N.Y. : New York Institute of Finance, c1987. xiii, 208 p. : ill. ; 29 cm. Includes index. ISBN 0-13-664350-7 LC Card 87-7740 DDC 332.6/068/8 19
1. Brokers. 2. Telephone selling. I. Title.
HG4621 .G776 1987

The stockbroker's guide to put and call option strategies. [New York] New York Institute of Finance [1974] viii, 116 p. 24 cm. ISBN 0-13-846741-9 LC Card 74-166476 DDC 332.6/45
1. Put and call transactions - United States. 2. Over-the-counter markets - United States. I. Title.
HG6041 .G75 ***NYPL [JLE 87-573]***

GROSS NATIONAL PRODUCT - ARGENTINA - CÓRDOBA (PROVINCE) - STATISTICS.
Compendio estadístico /. Córdoba, República Argentina [1984] 110 leaves : LC Card 87-400414 DDC 304.6/0982/54021 19
HA958.C6 C64 1984

GROSS NATIONAL PRODUCT - ARGENTINA - RÍO NEGRO - STATISTICS.
Producto bruto geográfico . [Viedma, Argentina] , 1977. 153 p. ; LC Card 79-107106
HC177.R5 P76 1977

GROSS NATIONAL PRODUCT - BRAZIL - ECONOMETRIC MODELS.
Castro, Paulo Furtado de. Modelo estocástico para a estimação do produto potencial "IPEA/Depto. de Economia-UnB.". [Brasília, Brazil] [1981] 12, [16] : LC Card 85-210547
HC190.I5 C37 1981

GROSS NATIONAL PRODUCT - BRAZIL - PARANÁ (STATE)
Produto interno bruto do Paraná, 1970-84 /. Curitiba , 1985. vi, 63 leaves : LC Card 87-403687 DDC 339.381/62 19
HC188.P35 P76 1985

GROSS NATIONAL PRODUCT - BRAZIL - RIO GRANDE DO NORTE.
Agregados econômicos estaduais do Rio Grande do Norte, 1970-1982 /. Natal , 1985. 35 leaves : LC Card 86-158766
HC188.R38 A53 1985

GROSS NATIONAL PRODUCT - CHILE - ECONOMETRIC MODELS.
Lagos, Luis Felipe. El efecto de los shocks externos sobre el producto . Santiago, Chile , 1985. 15, [8] leaves : LC Card 87-404321 DDC 339.383 19
HC195.I5 L34 1985

GROSS NATIONAL PRODUCT - CUBA.
Pérez-López, Jorge F. Measuring Cuban economic performance /. Austin , 1987. xii, 202 p. : ISBN 0-292-75092-7 LC Card 86-24907 DDC 339.37291 19
HC152.5 .P47 1987

GROSS NATIONAL PRODUCT - ECUADOR.
Coyuntura económica ecuatoriana, 1985-1986. [Quito, Ecuador] [1986] i, 39 p. ; LC Card 86-217289
HC202 .C73 1986

Resultados y perspectivas de la economía ecuatoriana, 1984-1985. Quito, Ecuador [1985] 27, 7 p. ; LC Card 85-215488
HC202 .R47 1985

GROSS NATIONAL PRODUCT - GERMANY, WEST.
Müller, Frieder, 1944- Volkswirtschaftliche Gesamtrechnung und Preisveränderungen . Königstein/Ts. , 1984. xx, 414 p. : ISBN 3-445-02378-6 LC Card 85-142948 DDC 339.343 19
HC79.I5 M85 1984 ***NYPL [JLE 86-3225]***

GROSS NATIONAL PRODUCT - HUNGARY - STATISTICS.
A Nemzeti vagyon és az állóeszközállomány 1970-1978 /. [Budapest] [1979] 140 p. ; LC Card 82-193609
HC300.295.W4 N454 1979

GROSS NATIONAL PRODUCT - MEXICO - STATES - STATISTICS.
Sistema de cuentas nacionales de México . México, D.F. , 1985. xiii, 577 p. : ISBN 968-89200-8-8 LC Card 87-401458 DDC 339.372 19
HC140.I5 S5725 1985

GROSS NATIONAL PRODUCT - MEXICO - STATISTICS.
Producto interno bruto y gasto, cuaderno 1970-1979. [Mexico City] [1980] 123 p. ; LC Card 82-197714
HC140.I5 P76 1980

GROSS NATIONAL PRODUCT - PARAGUAY - CONGRESSES.
Flecha, Agustín Oscar. Crisis económica . [Asunción] [1987] 65 p. ; LC Card 87-404003 DDC 331.2/3/09892 19
HD4920.P2 F57 1987

Gross, Patricio. Matas, Jaime. Los problemas ambientales del sistema de transporte urbano /. Santiago de Chile , 1981. 30 leaves : LC Card 82-201768
HE234.Z7 S355 1981

Gross, Peter, Dr. Logistik einer Grossbank : am Beispiel der Schweizerischen Bankgesellschaft / von Peter Gross. Bern : P. Haupt, c1983. 52 p. : ill. ; 23 cm. (Bankwirtschaftliche Forschungen. Bd. 80) ISBN 3-258-03274-2 : LC Card 83-181853
1. Union de banques suisses. 2. Banks and banking - Switzerland. I. Title. II. Series.
HG1526 .B27 Bd. 80 HG3208.U54

Grosse-Berndt, Gisela. Wirksamkeitsuntersuchung zum ADAC-Motorrad-Sicherheitstraining. Köln : Bundesanstalt für Strassenwesen, Bereich Unfallforschung, [1983] iii, 160, ii, 112, 27 p. : ill. ; 21 cm. (Forschungsberichte der Bundesanstalt für Strassenwesen, Bereich Unfallforschung, 0173-7066 . 87) "Juli 1983." Includes bibliographies. CONTENTS. - T. 1. Instrumentenentwicklung / Gisela Grosse-Berndt -- T. 2. Ergebnisdiskussion / Katrin Niesen. LC Card 84-147564
1. Traffic safety - Germany, West. 2. Motorcycles - Germany (West) - Safety measures. 3. ADAC. I. Niesen, Katrin. II. Title. III. Title: Wirksamkeitsuntersuchung zum A.D.A.C.-Motorrad-Sicherheitstraining. IV. Series.
HE5614.5.G3 G75 1983

Grosse, Christine Uber. Case studies in international business / Christine Uber Grosse, Robert E. Grosse. Englewood Cliffs, N.J. : Prentice Hall, c1988. xv, 155 p. : ill. ; 23 cm.

Includes index. ISBN 0-13-119314-7 (pbk.) LC Card 87-22307 DDC 658/.049 19
1. International business enterprises - Management - Case studies. I. Grosse, Robert E. II. Title.
HD62.4 .G76 1988

Die grosse Denkverbiegung . Gruhler, Wolfram. Köln , c1987. 159 p. ; ISBN 3-87427-657-0 LC Card 87-152206 DDC 338.943 19
HC286.5 .G715 1987

Grosse, Robert E. Grosse, Christine Uber. Case studies in international business /. Englewood Cliffs, N.J. , c1988. xv, 155 p. : ISBN 0-13-119314-7 (pbk.) LC Card 87-22307 DDC 658/.049 19
HD62.4 .G76 1988

Grossen, Andreas. Bürger, Parlament und Steuern : Fallstudie über die Willensbildung von Parlament und Stimmbürgern beim Finanzpaket 1976/77 / Andreas Grossen. Bern : Benteli, c1986. vi, 134 p. : ill. ; 23 cm. (Helvetica politica. Series B . vol. 20) Bibliography: p. 115-117. ISBN 3-7165-0510-2 LC Card 86-187534
1. Budget - Switzerland. 2. Switzerland - Politics and government - 20th century. 3. Government spending policy - Switzerland. 4. Switzerland. Bundesversammlung. I. Series: Helvetica politica. Series B , v. 20. II. Title.
HJ2145 .G76 1986

GROSSENBURG IMPLEMENT, INC. - HISTORY.
Nelson, Selmer, 1917- Grossenburg's fifty years with John Deere /. Freeman, S.D. , c1987. viii, 167 p. : LC Card 87-80826 DDC 338.7/681763/0978361 19
HD9486.U6 G766 1987

Grossenburg's fifty years with John Deere /. Nelson, Selmer, 1917- Freeman, S.D. , c1987. viii, 167 p. : LC Card 87-80826 DDC 338.7/681763/0978361 19
HD9486.U6 G766 1987

Grossenburg's 50 years with John Deere. Nelson, Selmer, 1917- Grossenburg's fifty years with John Deere /. Freeman, S.D. , c1987. viii, 167 p. : LC Card 87-80826 DDC 338.7/681763/0978361 19
HD9486.U6 G766 1987

Grosser, Ilse. Die Wirtschaftliche Entwicklung in den sozialistischen Ländern Osteuropas zur Jahreswende 1985/86 /. Hamburg , 1986. 336 p. ; ISBN 3-87895-295-3 LC Card 86-185852
HC244 .W5776 1986

Grossi, Yonne de Souza. Mina de Morro Velho : a extração do homem : uma história de experiência operária / Yonne de Souza Grossi. Rio de Janeiro, RJ : Paz e Terra, 1981. 265 p. : ill. ; 21 cm. (Coleção Estudos brasileiros. vol. 55) Originally presented as the author's thesis (master's)-Universidade Federal de Minas Gerais), 1980. Bibliography: p. 261-265. LC Card 81-216799 DDC 338.7/6223422/098151 19
1. Gold miners - Brazil - Nova Lima. 2. Trade-unions - Miners - Brazil - Nova Lima. 3. Social classes - Brazil - Nova Lima. 4. Gold mines and mining - Brazil - Nova Lima. I. Title.
HD8039.M74 B65 1981 ***NYPL [JLD 86-3591]***

Die Grossindustrie Böhmens, 1848-1918 /. Brousek, Karl M. München , 1987. 223 p., 8 leaves of plates : ISBN 3-486-51871-2 LC Card 87-142819 DDC 338.6/44/094371 19
HD2356.C96 B643 1987

Grossiord, Sophie. Atget, Géniaux, Vert . Paris [1984] 63, [1] p. : ISBN 2-901414-09-5 : LC Card 86-137985
HF5459.F8 A87 1984 ***NYPL [MFW 87-159]***

Grössl, Ingrid. Der Zusammenhang von finanz- und realwirtschaftlichem Sektor einer offenen, stationären Volkswirtschaft : eine kritische Würdigung ausgewählter neoklassischer Ansätze / von Ingrid Grössl. Berlin : Duncker & Humblot, c1986. 162 p. : ill. ; 24 cm. (Volkswirtschaftliche Schriften. Heft 362) Bibliography: p. [155]-162. ISBN 3-428-05986-7 LC Card 86-206327
1. Balance of payments - Mathematical models. 2. Foreign exchange - Mathematical models. 3. Monetary policy - Mathematical models. 4. Neoclassical school of economics. I. Title. II. Series.
HG3882 .G76 1986

Grossman, Ann. The marketer's guide to media vehicles, methods, and options : a sourcebook in advertising and promotion / Ann Grossman. New York : Quorum Books, 1987. xiv, 238 p. : ill. ; 22 cm. Bibliography: p. [229]-232. Includes index. ISBN 0-89930-266-1 (lib. bdg. : alk. paper) LC Card 87-2473 DDC 659.1 19
1. Advertising media planning. 2. Sales promotion. 3. Direct marketing. 4. Telemarketing. I. Title.
HF5826.5 .G76 1987

Grossman, Gene M. Bhagwati, Jagdish N., 1934- Essays in development economics /. Oxford [Oxfordshire] , 1985. 2 v. ; ISBN 0-631-14178-2 (v. 1) ***NYPL [JLL 86-16]***

Grossman, Gregory. Treml, Vladimir G. Referent USSR economic and demographic statistics for normalization of Berkeley-Duke emigre questionnaire data /. [Durham, N.C. [1986] 1 v. (various pagings) ; LC Card 86-70618 DDC 304.6/0947/021 19
HB3607 .T74 1986

Grossman, Jonathan, 1915- Fairchild, Byron. The Army and industrial manpower /. Westport, Conn. , 1987. xiv, 291 p. : ISBN 0-313-25480-X (lib. bdg. : alk. paper) LC Card 86-25738 DDC 331.11/0973 19
HD5724 .F25 1987

Grossmann, Christa. Stimme und Aktion der Völker gegen das Wettrüsten . Berlin , 1985. 421 p. ; ***NYPL [JLD 86-4257]***

Grostein, Marta Dora. Sócrates, Jodete Rios. A cidade invade as águas . [São Paulo] , 1985. 296 p., [2] folded leaves of plates : LC Card 87-118596 DDC 333.91/00981/61 19
HD1696.B84 S427 1985

Grothe-Senf, Anja. Bürgerbeteiligung in der Verbraucherinformationspolitik . Frankfurt , New York , c1986. 241 p. : ISBN 3-593-33681-2 LC Card 86-230016
HC290.5.C63 B87 1986

Grotz, Reinhold. Industrialisierung und Stadtentwicklung im ländlichen Südost-Australien / Reinhold Grotz. Stuttgart : Geographisches Institut der Universität Stuttgart, 1982. 299 p. : ill. ; 24 cm. (Stuttgarter geographische Studien, 0343-7906 . Bd. 98) Habilitationsschrift--Universität Stuttgart, 1982. Summary in English. Bibliography: p. 255-268. ISBN 3-88028-098-3 : LC Card 83-215667
1. South Australia - Industries, Rural - History. 2. Rural development - Australia - South Australia - History. I. Title. II. Series.
HC607.S68 G76 1982

GROUND-RENT. see **RENT (ECONOMIC THEORY)**

GROUND WATER. see **WATER, UNDERGROUND.**

Ground-water mining in the United States /. Sloggett, Gordon. Washington, D.C , 1986. iv, 19 p. : LC Card 86-602788 DDC 338.1 s 338.1/4 19
HD1751 .A91854 no. 555 S616.U6

Groundnuts production and marketing in Sudan /. Gibriel, Mohamed Farah. Khartoum, Sudan , 1984. 24 leaves : LC Card 85-981430 DDC 338.1/73368/09624 19
HD9235.P32 S734 1984

GROUP DECISION-MAKING. see **DECISION MAKING, GROUP.**

Group decision making under multiple criteria . Hwang, C. L. (Ching-Lai), 1929- Berlin , New York , c1987. xi, 400 p. : ISBN 0-387-17177-0 (U. S. : pbk.) : LC Card 86-29729 DDC 658.4/036 19
HD30.23 .H87 1987

GROUP DYNAMICS. see **SOCIAL GROUPS.**

GROUP MEDICAL PRACTICE, PREPAID. see **HEALTH MAINTENANCE ORGANIZATIONS.**

Group of Twenty-four. The International monetary system and its reform . Amsterdam ; New York : 3 v. : ISBN 0-444-70227-X LC Card 87-6737 DDC 332.4/5 19
HG3881 .I57672 1987

The Group of 77 . Hall, Kenneth O. Nyon, Switzerland , 1979. 48 p. ; LC Card 86-202645
HF1413 .H27 1979

Group power . Daniels, William R. (William Roy), 1941- San Diego, Calif. , c1986. vi, 94 p. : ISBN 0-88390-204-4 (pbk.) : LC Card 86-24955 DDC 658.4/563 19
HD30.3 .D34 1986

Group problem solving . Brightman, Harvey J. Atlanta, Ga. , 1987. p. cm. ISBN 0-88406-201-5 : LC Card 87-21876 DDC 658.4/036 19
HD30.29 .B735 1987

GROUP PROBLEM SOLVING. see **PROBLEM SOLVING, GROUP.**

Groupe de recherche interdisciplinaire en développement de l'Est du Québec. see **Université du Québec à Rimouski. Groupe de recherche interdisciplinaire en développement de l'Est du Québec.**

Groupe d'études et de recherches permanent sur l'industrie et les salariés de l'automobile. Travail et automatisation dans l'industrie automobile /. [France] , Grenoble , 1986. 141 p. ; ISBN 2-86561-070-5 : LC Card 87-151670
HD9710.F72 T72 1986

Groupe d'études politiques européennes. L'Information et la consultation des travailleurs dans les entreprises multinationales /. [Paris] [Genève?] , 1984. 290 p. ; ISBN 2-13-038651-2 (pbk.)
HD62.4 .I53 1984 ***NYPL [JLD 87-60]***

Groupe liégeois d'information et d'action contre l'apartheid. L'Afrique du Sud et nous . [Liège, Belgium] [1984] [69] p. : LC Card 86-200334
HF1554.5.S6 A37 1984

Groupement Berger-BCEOM. Etude de factibilité routière, Bujumbura-Cibitoke : rapport final / [Louis Berger International, inc. et Bureau central d'études pour les équipements d'outre mer, Groupement BERGER-BCEOM. [Bujumbura] : Le Groupement, [1977] 162 p. : ill., maps ; 30 cm. At head of title: République du Burundi, Ministère des travaux publics, de l'équipement et du logement. "Février 1977." One folded map inserted. Includes bibliographical references. LC Card 82-980356
1. Roads - Burundi - Case studies. I. Burundi. Ministère des travaux publics, de l'équipement et du logement. II. Title.
HE367.B872 G76 1977a

Groups at work /. Mink, Oscar G. Englewood Cliffs, N.J. , c1987. xiii, 279 p. : ISBN 0-87778-196-6 LC Card 87-9081 DDC 658.4/036 19
HD66 .M55 1987

GROUPS, ETHNIC. see **ETHNIC GROUPS.**

GROUPS, SOCIAL. see **SOCIAL GROUPS.**

GROUPS, WORK. see **WORK GROUPS.**

Grout, Bill. Hewes, Jeremy Joan. Wordprocessing on IBM PCs /. New York , c1985. xiii, 178 p. : ISBN 0-471-88663-7 : LC Card 84-11966 DDC 652/.5 19
Z52.5.I27 H48 1985 ***NYPL [JSF 87-232]***

Grout, Gary. Business computing for small contractors / Gary Grout. Berkeley, Calif. : Osborne McGraw-Hill, c1986. xv, 314 p. : ill. ; 24 cm. Includes index. ISBN 0-07-881229-1 (pbk.) LC Card 86-206636 DDC 690/.8/0285536 19
1. Construction industry - Accounting - Data processing. 2. Construction industry - Data processing. I. Title.
HF5686.B7 G75 1986

Grove, Andrew S. One-on-one with Andy Grove : how to manage your boss, yourself, and your coworkers / Andrew S. Grove. New York : G.P. Putnam's Sons, c1987. 235 p. ; 24 cm. ISBN 0-399-13250-3 : LC Card 86-30483 DDC 650.1/3 19
1. Managing your boss. 2. Interpersonal relations. 3. Personnel management. I. Title. II. Title: How to manage your boss, yourself, and your coworkers.
HF5548.83 .G77 1987

Grove, Grenville. Engelsk-svensk ordbok . Stockholm , 1970. 2 v. ; ***NYPL [JFD 87-817]***

Grover, Kenneth C. Foundations of business telecommunications management / Kenneth C. Grover. New York : Plenum Press, c1986. xvi, 196 p. ; 23 cm. (Approaches to information technology) Includes index. ISBN 0-306-42249-2 (pbk.) LC Card 86-5063 DDC 384 19
1. Business - Communication systems. 2. Telecommunication systems. 3. Telephone in business. I. Title. II. Title: Business telecommunications

management.
HF5541.T4 G76 1986 ***NYPL [JLE 86-3270]***

Grover, Subhash C. (Shubash Chander), 1938- Paths to profits / by Shubhash C. Grover. Dallas : Monument Press, 1985. v, 142 p. ; 21 cm. ISBN 0-930383-04-4 (pbk.) : LC Card 84-25548 DDC 650.1 19
1. Small business. 2. Success in business. I. Title.
HD62.7 .G75 1985 ***NYPL [JLD 86-1907]***

Groves, F. P. Denton, A. S. Coventry transport . Birmingham [West Midlands, England] , c1985- v. <1 > : ISBN 0-905103-05-X (pbk.) : LC Card 86-224227 DDC 388.4/09424/98 19
HE4719.C68 D46 1985

Growing a business /. Hawken, Paul. New York , c1987. 251 p. ; ISBN 0-671-64457-2 LC Card 87-16431 DDC 658.1/141 19
HD62.5 .H38 1987

Growing up financially . Stribling, Catherine. New York , 1987, c1986. 311 p. ; ISBN 0-345-33098-6 (pbk.) : LC Card 86-90719 DDC 332.6/78 19
HG179 .S846 1987

Growing up poor /. Williams, Terry (Terry M.) Lexington, MA , c1985. xvi, 136 p. ; ISBN 0-669-09687-3 (alk. paper) LC Card 84-48564 DDC 362.7/044 19
HV1431 .W55 1985 ***NYPL [JLE 85-2236]***

Growing your business. Jones, Seymour, 1931- The Coopers & Lybrand guide to growing your business /. New York , c1988. xiii, 477 p. ; ISBN 0-471-85941-9 LC Card 87-21688 DDC 658 19
HD31 .J627 1988

The growth and efficiency of public spending /. Levitt, M. S., 1938- Cambridge [Cambridgeshire] , New York , 1987. xiv, 201 p. : ISBN 0-521-34621-5 (U. S.) LC Card 87-11636 DDC 339.5/22/0941 19
HJ7764 .L475 1987

Growth and equity . Datta, Anindya. Calcutta , New York , 1986. xii, 119 p. : ISBN 0-19-561882-3 : LC Card 87-900001 DDC 338.954 19
HD82 .D334 1986

Growth and income distribution in India . Sundrum, R. M. New Delhi , Beverly Hills , 1986. p. cm. ISBN 0-8039-9522-9 (U. S.) LC Card 86-26323 DDC 330.954/04 19
HC435.2 .S883 1986

Growth and modernisation of fertiliser industry : proceedings of the seminar held at New Delhi from December 15-17, 1986. New Delhi : Fertiliser Association of India, 1987. 1 v. (various pagings) : ill. (some col.) ; 29 cm. At head of title: FAI Seminar, 1986. Proceedings of the Seminar on "Growth and Modernisation of Fertiliser Industry", held at New Delhi, 1986. Includes bibliographies. LC Card 87-902183 DDC 338.4/766862/0954 19
1. Fertilizer industry - India - Congresses. I. Fertiliser Association of India. II. Seminar on "Growth and Modernisation of Fertiliser Industry" (1986 : New Delhi, India). III. Title: FAI Seminar, 1986.
HD9483.I42 G78 1987

Growth areas in dentistry : the burgeoning dental implants market. Tustin, CA (17722 Irvine Blvd., Tustin 92680) : Biomedical Business International, c1986. 1 v. (various foliations) : ill. ; 29 cm. (Report / Biomedical Business International . #7070) "August 1986." LC Card 86-212546 DDC 381/.45681761 19
1. Dental instruments and apparatus industry. 2. Implant dentures. 3. Market surveys. I. Biomedical Business International, Inc. II. Series: Report (Biomedical Business International, Inc.) , #7070.
HD9995.D42 G76 1986

Growth, equity, and self reliance : private enterprise and African economic development / edited by Ampah G. Johnson and Adeyemi O. Lawson. Boulder : Westview Press, 1987. xi, 162 p. ; 23 cm. (Westview special studies on Africa) Includes bibliographies and index. ISBN 0-8133-0486-5 (pbk.) : LC Card 87-14290 DDC 338.96 19
1. Industry and state - Africa. 2. Africa - Economic policy. 3. Laissez-faire. I. Johnson, Ampah G. II. Lawson, Adeyemi O.
HD3616.A36 G76 1987

Growth management : keeping on target? / Douglas R. Porter, editor. Washington, D.C. : ULI--the Urban Land Institute, in association with Lincoln Institute of Land Policy, c1986. iv, 218 p. : ill. ; 23 cm. (Lincoln Institute monograph. #86-1) Includes bibliographical references. ISBN 0-87420-655-3 (pbk.) LC Card 86-50332 DDC 307.1/4/0973 19
1. Land use - United States - Planning - Case studies. 2. Cities and towns - United States - Growth - Case studies. I. Porter, Douglas R. II. Series. III. Series: Lincoln Institute monograph, no. 86-1.
HD205 .G76 1986 ***NYPL [JLE 87-558]***

Growth market Southeast Asia. Wachstumsmarkt Südostasien . München , c1984. x, 807 p. : ISBN 3-8039-0292-4 : LC Card 84-249861
HF3790.8.Z5 W33 1984

Growth, migration, and the balance of payments in a small open economy, Portugal /. Barbosa, Manuel P. (Manuel Pinto), 1944- New York , 1984. xv, 212 p. : ISBN 0-8240-4169-0 : LC Card 79-53646 DDC 382.1/7/0724 19
HD5809.A6 B37 1984 ***NYPL [JLE 86-4171]***

Growth of agriculture and industry in India /. Mahajan, V. S., 1923- New Delhi , c1983. 176 p. ; LC Card 83-906175 DDC 338.0954 19
HD2072 .M23 1983 ***NYPL [JLD 87-671]***

Growth of agriculture and rural development in India / edited by S. Subrahmanya and I. Satya Sundaram. New Delhi : Deep & Deep Publications, c1987. xx, 496 p. ; 23 cm. Contributed articles. Bibliography: p. [488]-493. Includes index. LC Card 87-900250 DDC 338.1/0954 19
1. Agriculture - Economic aspects - India. 2. Agriculture and state - India. 3. Rural development - India. I. Subrahmanya, S. (Susheela). II. Satya Sundaram, I., 1947-.
HD2072 .G7 1987

Growth of capitalism in agriculture . Krishna Rao, Y. V. Vijayawada , 1984. x, 62 p. ; LC Card 84-900585 DDC 338.1/3/095484 19
HD2075.A5 K75 1984 ***NYPL [JLD 86-4256]***

Growth of Pakistani banking . Seminar on Growth of Pakistani Banking at Home & Abroad (1982 : Peshawar, Pakistan) Karachi , 1982. 26 p. ; LC Card 83-931177 DDC 332.1/09549/1 19
HG3290.5.A6 S46 1982
NYPL [JLE 86-4582]

Growth of R & D manpower and expenditure in Pakistan. Islamabad : Pakistan Council for Science and echnology, 1985. 66 p. ; 24 cm. Chiefly statistical tables. LC Card 85-932022 DDC 331.12/510014/095491021 19
1. Research - Economic aspects - Pakistan - Statistics. 2. Labor supply - Pakistan - Statistics. 3. Research - Pakistan - Finance - Statistics. I. Pakistan Council for Science and Technology.
HC440.5.Z9 R44 1985

Growth of road traffic densities in Malaŵi. Lilongwe : Transport Planning Unit, Economic Planning Division, Office of the President and Cabinet, 1985. 88 leaves ; 30 cm. Chiefly tables. LC Card 86-980330 DDC 388.3/142/096897 19
1. Transportation, Automotive - Malawi - Statistics. I. Malawi. Transport Planning Unit.
HE367.M32 G76 1985

Growth-oriented adjustment programs / edited by Vittorio Corbo, Morris Goldstein, Mohsin Khan. Washington, D.C. : International Monetary Fund : World Bank, 1987. xiii, 537 p. : ill. ; 23 cm. "Proceedings of a symposium held in Washington D.C., February 25-27, 1987." Includes bibliographies. ISBN 0-939934-92-2 (pbk.) LC Card 87-21361 DDC 338.9 19
1. Economic policy - Congresses. 2. Industry and state - Congresses. 3. Economic stabilization - Congresses. I. Corbo, Vittorio. II. Goldstein, Morris, 1944-. III. Khan, Mohsin S. IV. International Monetary Fund. V. World Bank.
HD73 .G76 1987

The growth revolt . Barbaria, Janet. Sacramento, Calif. [1980] 66 p. : LC Card 81-620644 DDC 336.794 19
HJ4191 .B37 1980 ***NYPL [JLF 86-369]***

Growth stocks /. Little, Jeffrey B. New York , c1988. p. cm. ISBN 1-555-46624-9 LC Card 87-24482 DDC 332.63/22 19
HG4661 .L57 1988

Growth-track business guidebooks, 0886-6732. National emerging industries site selection guide /. Minneapolis, MN , c1986. 124 p. ; LC Card 86-231272 DDC 338.6/042/02573 19
HC110.D5 N38 1986

Growth trends to the year 2010. Population forecasts for 183 COG analysis districts / [Department of Metropolitan Development and Information Resources]. Washington, D.C. : Metropolitan Washington Council of Governments : Order copies from COG Information Center, Metropolitan Washington Council of Governments, c1986. i, 9 p. : ill. ; 22 x 28 cm. "Metropolitan Washington region forecast data tables." LC Card 87-153125 DDC 304.6/2/09753021 19
1. Population forecasting - Washington Metropolitan Area - Statistics. 2. Washington Metropolitan Area - Population - Statistics. I. Metropolitan Washington Council of Governments. Dept. of Metropolitan Development and Information Resources.
HA305 .G77 1986

Growth trends to the year 2010. Household forecasts for 1,353 COG analysis zones. Washington, D.C. : Metropolitan Washington Council of Governments : Order copies from COG Information Center, Metropolitan Washington Council of Governments, c1986. i, 32 p. : ill. ; 22 x 28 cm. "Metropolitan Washington region forecast data tables." LC Card 87-129483 DDC 304.6/2/09753021 19
1. Population forecasting - Washington Metropolitan Area - Statistics. 2. Washington Metropolitan Area - Population - Statistics. 3. Households - Washington Metropolitan Area - Statistics. I. Metropolitan Washington Council of Governments.
HA305 .G76 1986

Grubbs, M. Ray. Reidenbach, R. Eric. Developing new banking products . Englewood Cliffs, N.J. , c1987. xii, 206 p. : ISBN 0-13-204603-2 LC Card 86-22708 DDC 332.1/7/0685 19
HG1616.C87 R45 1987
NYPL [JLE 87-1141]

Grubel, Herbert G. Multinational banking / by Herbert G. Grubel. Singapore : Institute of Southeast Asian studies, 1985. iii, 21 p. ; 23 cm. (Research notes and discussions paper / Institute of Southeast Asian Studies, ASEAN Economic Research Unit, 0129-8828 . no. 56) Bibliography: p. 21. ISBN 997-19-8817-8 (pbk.) LC Card 86-940563 DDC 332.1/6 19
1. Banks and banking, International. 2. Capital market. I. Series: Research notes and discussions paper , no. 56. II. Title.
HG3881 .G747 1985

Gruber, Edward C. Brennan, Lawrence D. (Lawrence David), 1915- Resumes for better jobs /. New York, NY , c1987. 202 p. ; ISBN 0-13-329152-9 : LC Card 87-2383 DDC 650.1/4 19
HF5383 .B68 1987

Gruchy, Allan Garfield, 1906- The reconstruction of economics : an analysis of the fundamentals of institutional economics / Allan G. Gruchy ; foreword by Donald R. Stabile and Norton T. Dodge. New York : Greenwood Press, 1987. xx, 173 p. ; 25 cm. (Contributions in economics and economic history, 0084-9235 . no. 71) Bibliography: p. [167]-168. Includes index. ISBN 0-313-25679-9 (lib. bdg. : alk. paper) LC Card 86-25721 DDC 330 19
1. Institutional economics. I. Title. II. Series.
HB99.5 .G79 1987

Grude, Egil Harald, 1944- Fra brygger til storhavn : Stavanger havn / Egil Harald Grude. Stavanger : Universitetsforlaget, c1985. 167 p. : ill. (some col.) ; 28 cm. Summary in English. Bibliography: p. 165-167. ISBN 82-00-07235-5 : LC Card 86-148407
1. Harbors - Norway - Stavanger - History - 19th century. 2. Harbors - Norway - Stavanger - History - 20th century. 3. Shipping - Norway - Stavanger - History - 19th century. 4. Shipping - Norway - Stavanger - History - 20th century. I. Title.
HE558.S67 G78 1985

Gruen, F. H. (Fred Henry), 1921- How bad is Australia's economic performance and why? : the twenty-fourth Edward Shann memorial lecture in economics, delivered at the University of Western Australia, 23 September 1985 / F.H. Gruen. Canberra, Australia : Australian National University, Centre for Economic Policy Research, [1985] 61 p. ; 21 cm. (Discussion paper, 0725-430X . no. 127) "September 1985"--Cover. Includes bibliography

references. ISBN 0-949293-38-5 (pbk.) LC Card 86-228640 DDC 338.994 19
1. Australia - Economic conditions - 1945-. 2. Australia - Economic policy. I. Title. II. Title: Edward Shann memorial lecture in economics. III. Series: Discussion paper (Australian National University. Centre for Economic Policy Research) , no. 127.
HC605 .G78 1985

Gründungsfinanzierung . Plaschka, Martina. Wien , c1986. vii, 159 p. : ISBN 3-85428-067-X LC Card 86-225844
HG4146 .P57 1986

Grüne Agrarpolitik, Bilanz und Perspektiven . Grünen (Political party) Bonn [1985?] 62 p. : LC Card 86-152151
HD1957 .G79 1985

Gruère, Jean-Pierre. Optimiser les ressources humaines dans l'entreprise : formation à la méthode du bilan comportemental (assessment center) : séminaire de Jean-Pierre Gruère, Fabienne Pezeu et Victor Ernoult. Paris : Editions ESF, c1984. 69, 42 p. : ill. ; 25 cm. (Formation permanente en sciences humaines. 53) Bibliography: p. 64-66. CONTENTS. - Connaissance du problème -- Applications pratiques. ISBN 2-7101-0462-8 : LC Card 84-217427
1. Assessment centers (Personnel management procedure). I. Pezeu, Fabienne. II. Ernoult, Victor. III. Title.
HF5549.5.A78 G78 1984

Grüttner, Michael. Arbeitswelt an der Wasserkante : Sozialgeschichte der Hamburger Hafenarbeiter, 1886-1914 / von Michael Grüttner. Göttingen : Vandenhoeck & Ruprecht, 1984. 331 p. ; 24 cm. (Kritische Studien zur Geschichtswissenschaft. Bd. 63) Originally presented as the author's thesis (doctoral)--Universität Hamburg, Wintersemester 1982/83. Bibliography: p. 314-327. Includes index. ISBN 3-525-35722-2 (Deut. Bibl.) LC Card 86-139479
1. Stevedores - Germany (West) - Hamburg. 2. Harbors - Germany (West) - Hamburg - History. 3. Trade-unions - Stevedores - Germany (West) - Hamburg - History. 4. Hamburg (Germany) - Social conditions. I. Title.
HD8039.L82 G4335 1984

Gruhl, Herbert, 1921- Der atomare Selbstmord / Herbert Gruhl. München : Herbig, c1986. 190 p. : ill. ; 21 cm. Bibliography: p. 189-190. ISBN 3-7766-1448-X LC Card 86-226120
1. Nuclear industry - Government policy. 2. Antinuclear movement. I. Title.
HD9698.A2 G74 1986

Gruhler, Wolfram.
Die grosse Denkverbiegung : Beobachtungen und Anmerkungen zur Missachtung wirtschaftlicher und sozialer Funktionszusammenhänge / Wolfram Gruhler. Köln : Kölner Universitätsverlag, c1987. 159 p. ; 21 cm. Bibliography: p. 151-159. ISBN 3-87427-657-0 LC Card 87-152206 DDC 338.943 19
1. Germany, West - Economic policy. 2. Germany, West - Social policy. 3. Technological innovations - Economic aspects - Germany, West. I. Title.
HC286.5 .G715 1987

Wirtschaftsfaktor Mittelstand : zu Wesen und Bedeutung kleiner und mittlerer Unternehmen in der Bundesrepublik Deutschland / Wolfram Gruhler. Köln : Deutscher Instituts-Verlag, c1984. 195 p. : ill. ; 19 cm. (DIV-Sachbuchreihe. 41) Bibliography: p. 182-189. Includes index. ISBN 3-602-34845-8 (pbk.) LC Card 87-672069
1. Small business - Germany, West. I. Title.
HD2346.G3 G78x 1984

Gruhn, Werner. Umweltprobleme und Umweltbewusstsein in der DDR /. Köln , c1985. 252 p. : ISBN 3-8046-8649-4 LC Card 86-119841
HC290.795.E5 U585 1985

Grumbach, Jürgen. Energieforschung und Arbeitnehmerinteressen : Zielfindungsprobleme gewerkschaftlicher Forschungs- und Technologiepolitik / Jürgen Grumbach. Frankfurt ; New York : Campus, c1986. 307 p. ; 21 cm. (Campus Forschung. Bd. 502) Bibliography: p. 292-307. ISBN 3-593-33655-3 LC Card 87-127360 DDC 331.1/0943 19
1. Environmental policy - Germany, West. 2. Labor supply - Germany (West) - Effect of technological innovations on. 3. Trade-unions - Germany, West. I. Title.
HC290.5.E5 G74 1986

Grumbkow, J. von. Werk en organisatie /. Lisse , 1986- v. <1 > ; ISBN 90-265-0755-0 (deel 1) : LC Card 86-221124
HF5549.2.N4 W47 1986

GRUMMAN AEROSPACE CORPORATION - HISTORY.
Gunston, Bill. The Grumman story /. New York , 1988, c1987. p. cm. ISBN 0-517-56796-2 : LC Card 87-21964 DDC 338.7/6291/0973 19
HD9711.5.U63 G784 1988

GRUMMAN AIRPLANES - HISTORY.
Gunston, Bill. The Grumman story /. New York , 1988, c1987. p. cm. ISBN 0-517-56796-2 : LC Card 87-21964 DDC 338.7/6291/0973 19
HD9711.5.U63 G784 1988

The Grumman story /. Gunston, Bill. New York , 1988, c1987. p. cm. ISBN 0-517-56796-2 : LC Card 87-21964 DDC 338.7/6291/0973 19
HD9711.5.U63 G784 1988

Grumptmann, J. (Jörg) Haas, Hans-Dieter. Karibische Klein- und Mikrostaaten . Tübingen , 1985. xvi, 200 p. : ISBN 3-921552-62-1 LC Card 86-155952
HC141 .H25 129693

Grün-Alternative Liste (Political party). Hamburg. Alternative Hafen- und Küstenpolitik /. Hamburg , 1985. 260 p. : ISBN 3-88876-034-8 LC Card 87-133678 DDC 387.1/094 19
HE557.G3 A55 1985

Grün, Josef, 1951- Global denken, vor Ort handeln : Weltmodelle von Global 2000 bis Herman Kahn : Kontroversen über unsere Zukunft / Josef Grün, Detlev Wiener.1. Aufl. Freiburg i. Br. : Dreisam-Verlag, 1984. 373 p. : ill. ; 21 cm. Bibliography: p. 353-366. Includes index. ISBN 3-921472-73-3 LC Card 84-246414
1. Environmental policy. 2. Natural resources. 3. Food supply. 4. Twenty-first century - Forecasts. 5. Twentieth century - Forecasts. 6. Economic forecasting. I. Wiener, Detlev, 1947-. II. Title.
HC79.E5 G77 1984

Grund, Jan. Velferdsstat i motvind / Jan Grund. 2. opplag Oslo : Universitetsforlaget, 1986, c1985. 139 p. : ill. ; 22 cm. Bibliography: p. 139. ISBN 82-00-07590-7 : LC Card 86-132818
1. Medical policy - Norway. 2. Privatization - Norway. 3. Norway - Economic policy. 4. Norway - Social policy. I. Title.
HC365 .G78 1985 ***NYPL [JLD 86-4433]***

Grundbedürfnisse als Gegenstand der Entwicklungspolitik : interdisziplinäre Aspekte der Grundbedarfsstrategie / Norbert Wagner und Hans Christoph Rieger (Hrsg.). Wiesbaden : F. Steiner, 1982. viii, 220 p. : ill. ; 24 cm. (Beiträge zur Südasienforschung. Bd. 70) Papers read at a seminar of the Südasien-Institut, Universität Heidelberg, summer 1980. English and German. Includes bibliographies. CONTENTS. - Zur Bestimmbarkeit des menschlichen Grundbedarfs / Martin Kaiser -- Ökonomische Implikationen des Grundbedarfskonzepts / Norbert Wagner -- Bedarf und Kultur / András Höfer -- "Wahre" und "falsche" Bedürfnisse / Karl Jettmar -- Das Menschenrecht auf Befriedigung des Grundbedarfs / Dieter Conrad -- "Grundbedürfnisstrategie" / Hans Jochen Diesfeld -- Grundbedarfsbefriedigung im Weltmassstab / Hans Christoph Rieger -- Die Dimensionen der Armut / Dietmar Rothermund -- Basic needs and Nepal / Govind Ram Agrawal -- Die Befriedigung der Grundbedürfnisse in der schweizerischen Entwicklungspolitik / Rudolf Högger. ISBN 3-515-03838-8 (Deut. Bibl.) LC Card 85-134671
1. Basic needs - Developing countries - Congresses. 2. Developing countries - Economic policy - Congresses. I. Wagner, Norbert. II. Rieger, Hans Christoph. III. Universität Heidelberg. Südasien-Institut. IV. Series.
HC59.72.B38 G78 1982

Der Grundeigentumswechsel im Kanton Zürich 1973-1980 : Entwicklung der Bodenpreise / [herausgegeben vom Statistischen Amt des Kantons Zürich]. [Zürich] : Das Amt, [1982] 74 p. : ill. ; 21 cm. (Statistische Mitteilungen des Kantons Zürich . Heft 107, 3. Folge) "Dezember 1982." LC Card 85-161363
1. Real property - Prices - Switzerland - Zurich (Canton) - Statistics. 2. Land tenure - Switzerland - Zurich (Canton) - Statistics. 3. Land use - Switzerland - Zurich (Canton) - Statistics. I. Statistisches Amt des Kantons Zürich. II. Series.
HA1608.Z6 A3 Heft 107, Folge 3 HD799.Z8

Grundeinkommen ohne Arbeit . Büchele, Herwig, 1935- Wien , c1985. 191 p. : ISBN 3-203-50898-2 LC Card 85-207929
HC79.I5 B83 1985

Grundfragen der Erfolgskontrolle /. Laux, Helmut. Berlin , New York , c1986. x, 161 p. : ISBN 0-387-17037-5 LC Card 86-232406
HD30.23 .L39 1986

Grundlagen der Bankenwerbung aus verhaltenswissenschaftlicher Sicht /. Wünsche, Gert. Wiesbaden , c1982. 304 p. : ISBN 3-409-47003-4 LC Card 83-151107
HF6161.B2 W86 1982

Grundlagen der Gestaltung aussenorganisationsbezogener Vertriebssteuerungssysteme in Versicherungsunternehmen /. Zietsch, Dietmar. Karlsruhe , c1985. xx, 308 p. : ISBN 3-88487-084-X LC Card 86-169097
HG8618 .Z53 1985

Grundlagen und Perspektiven des Euro-Arabischen Dialogs /. Lerche, Dietrich, 1943- Berlin , 1977. iii, 78 p. : LC Card 85-129693
HF1532.5.Z4 A735 1977

Grundlagen und Probleme der indikativen sektoralen Planung in marktwirtschaftlich orientierten Systemen /. Wolfertz, Dirk. Berlin , c1983. 165 p. ; ISBN 3-428-05379-6 LC Card 83-225373
HD84 .W59 1983

Grundsätze für die Bewertung von Kulturland bei Güterzusammenlegungen : Bonitierungsanleitung / Verfasser, Ernst Tanner ... [et al.]. [Bern? : s.n., 1973?] 1 v. (loose leaf) : ill., col. maps ; 31 cm. "Forschungsarbeit im Auftrage der Abteilung Landwirtschaft des Eidgenössischen Volkswirtschaftsdepartementes, Bern." One folded, col. map in pocket. Includes bibliography. LC Card 86-184960
1. Land capability for agriculture - Switzerland. I. Tanner, Ernst, Prof., Dipl. Kult.-Ing. II. Switzerland. Eidgenössisches Volkswirtschaftsdepartement. Abteilung für Landwirtschaft. III. Title: Bonitierungsanleitung.
HD798 .G78 1973

Grundsätze ordnungsmässiger EDV-Dokumentation . Rausch, Helmar. Schwarzenbek , 1985. vii, 323 p. : ISBN 3-921757-21-5 LC Card 86-227042
HF5667 .R335 1985

Grundwissen der Ökonomik. Volkswirtschaftslehre.
Siebert, Horst, 1938- Aussenwirtschaft /. Stuttgart , c1984. xi, 303 p. : ISBN 3-437-40149-1 (pbk.) LC Card 87-672497
HF1007 .S49x 1984

Grundzüge der Finanzanalyse /. Büchner, Robert. München , c1981. x, 426 p. : ISBN 3-8006-0885-5 LC Card 82-156543
HF5693.G47 B83 1981

Grundzüge der internationalen Unternehmenspolitik des Versicherungsunternehmens /. Reuter, Frank, Dr. Berlin , c1983. 178 p. : ISBN 3-428-05308-7 LC Card 83-161541
HG8018 .C6 n.F., Heft 39 HG8059

Grünen (Political party)
Grüne Agrarpolitik, Bilanz und Perspektiven : Materialien zur parlamentarischen Arbeit / Die Grünen. Bonn : Bundesgeschäftsstelle Die Grünen, [1985?] 62 p. : ill. ; 30 cm. Cover title. Bibliography: p. 62. LC Card 86-152151
1. Agriculture and state - Germany, West. 2. Agricultural conservation - Government policy - Germany (West). 3. Agricultural pollution - Government policy - Germany (West). 4. Food adulteration and inspection - Government policy - Germany (West). 5. Grünen (Political party). I. Title.
HD1957 .G79 1985

GRÜNEN (POLITICAL PARTY)
Grünen (Political party) Grüne Agrarpolitik, Bilanz und Perspektiven . Bonn [1985?] 62 p. : LC Card 86-152151
HD1957 .G79 1985

Ökologie und Sozialismus . Köln , c1986. 369 p. ; ISBN 3-7663-0983-8 LC Card 87-107373 DDC 363.7/056/0943 19
HC290.E5 O39 1986

Grünen (Political party). Hessen. Wie war denn das? . Frankfurt [1983?] 30 p., [1] leaf of plates : LC Card 84-158849
HC287.H4 W47 1983

Grünig, Rudolf. Verfahren zur Erarbeitung eines Grundsatzsystems für den Investitionsbereich / Rudolf Grünig. Bern : P. Haupt, c1984. 144 p. : ill. ; 23 cm. Bibliography: p. 138-144. ISBN 3-258-03442-7 : LC Card 85-139475
1. Capital investments - Decision-making. 2. Industrial management - Decision making. I. Title.
HG4028.C4 G75 1984

El Grupo Andino . Dávila Andrade, Oswaldo. [Lima? , 1985] ([Lima?] : Oficina de Publicaciones) 110 p. ; LC Card 86-158814
HC167.A5 D38 1985

GRUPO ANDINO.
Dávila Andrade, Oswaldo. El Grupo Andino . [Lima? , 1985] ([Lima?] : Oficina de Publicaciones) 110 p. ; LC Card 86-158814
HC167.A5 D38 1985

GRUPO COROA-BRASTEL.
Suplicy, Eduardo Matarazzo, 1941- Investigando o Caso Coroa-Brastel . Brasília , 1984. 215 p. ; LC Card 86-200269
HG4109 .S85 1984

A Verdade sobre o "Caso Coroa-Brastel.". Brasília, DF , 1984. 156 p. ; LC Card 85-207657
HG4109 .V47 1984

Grupo de Investigación Económica (Dominican Republic) Hacia una reestructuración dirigida de la economía dominicana /. Santo Domingo, República Dominicana , c1986. 355 p. : LC Card 87-402158 DDC 338.97293 19
HC153.5 .H33 1986

Grupo de Trabajo no. 3 sobre Industria, Energía y Minería (Andalusia, Spain) Plan económico para Andalucía, 1984-1986 /. Andalucía [1985?] 164 p. ; ISBN 84-505-0611-5 LC Card 86-205786
HD3616.S495 A536 1985

GRUPO GRANCOLOMBIANO.
Donadío, Alberto, 1953- Por qué cayó Jaime Michelsen? /. Bogotá , c1984. 142 p. : ISBN 84-89209-42-1 LC Card 85-122262
HG2908.C65 D66 1984

Grupos homogêneos no mercado de trabalho assalariado : um estudo sobre a formação dos salários, a partir dos dados da RAIS / Paulo Vieira da Cunha, coordenador ; Marco Antonio Sandoval de Vasconcellos ... [et al.]. Brasília : Ministério do Trabalho, Secretaria de Mão-de-Obra, Subsecretaria de Estudos, Análises e Metodologia, 1985. 56 p. : ill. ; 28 cm. Bibliography: p. 56. LC Card 85-231654
1. Wages - Brazil. 2. Wages - Brazil - São Paulo (State). 3. Wages - Brazil, Northeast. 4. Labor supply - Brazil. 5. Labor supply - Brazil - São Paulo (State). 6. Labor supply - Brazil, Northeast. I. Cunha, Paulo Vieira da. II. Vasconcellos, Marco Antonio Sandoval de. III. Brazil. Secretaria de Mão-de-Obra. Subsecretaria de Estudos, Análises e Metodologia.
HD5004 .G78 1985

Grupos monopólicos. Los Grupos monopólicos en el Ecuador . Quito, Ecuador , 1986. 208 p. : LC Card 87-404236 DDC 338.8/2/09866 19
HD2838 .G78 1986

Los Grupos monopólicos en el Ecuador : un ensayo de difusión popular. Quito, Ecuador : Centro de Estudios y Difusión Social, 1986. 208 p. : ill. ; 22 cm. (Serie La Economía ecuatoriana de los últimos años . no. 4) Cover title: Los grupos monopólicos. Bibliography: p. 197-200. LC Card 87-404236 DDC 338.8/2/09866 19
1. Monopolies - Ecuador. 2. Industry and state - Ecuador. 3. Capitalism - Ecuador. I. CEDIS (Organization). II. Title: Grupos monopólicos. III. Series.
HD2838 .G78 1986

Grupp, Monika. Entwicklung und sozio-ökonomische Bedeutung der holzverarbeitenden Industrien im Südosten der Vereinigten Staaten von Amerika / Monika Grupp. Berlin : D. Reimer, 1981, c1982. xii, 187, [30] p., [5] folded leaves of plates : ill., maps ; 30 cm. (Abhandlungen des Geographischen Instituts, Anthropogeographie . Bd. 30) Summary in English. Bibliography: p. 177-184. ISBN 3-496-00301-4 LC Card 86-217598
1. Lumber trade - Southern States. 2. Southern States - Economic conditions. I. Title. II. Title: Entwicklung und sozioökonomische Bedeutung der holzverarbeitenden Industrien im Südosten der Vereinigten Staaten von Amerika. III. Series.
HD9757.A13 G78 1982

Gruppendiskussion als Methode zur Rekonstruktion der Lebenswelt von Lehrlingen .
(Bd. 2) Behnken, Imbke, 1941- Jugendbiografie und Handlungsforschung /. Frankfurt [am Main] , c1984. xi, 239 p. ; ISBN 3-88704-402-9 LC Card 84-174719 DDC 331.3/425922/0943 19
HD4885.G3 B425 1984
NYPL [JLD 86-1892]

Gruppo sport del C.I.F.T. (Italy) Gilardi, Mauro. Volley e bolli . Milano , c1985. 107 p. : LC Card 86-128270
HE6183.V64 G55 1985

Grzelakowski, Andrzej. Organizacja i technika portów morskich /. Gdańsk , 1978. 292 p. : LC Card 81-200313
HE557.P58 O73 1978

Gsänger, Hans. Strengthening local linkages for socioeconomic development at regional level . Berlin [1986] 2 v. : LC Card 87-143388 DDC 338.96894 19
HC915.Z7 G847 1986

Gscheidle, Kurt. Die Verkehrspolitik in der 8. Legislaturperiode / Kurt Gscheidle ; herausgegeben vom Bundesminister für Verkehr. Bonn-Bad Godesberg : Der Bundesminister, [1977] 29 p. : ill. ; 30 cm. (Schriftenreihe . Heft 54, 1977) Speech given at the Verkehrspolitisches Jahresgespräch in Bonn, Feb. 15, 1977. Includes bibliographical references. LC Card 86-173226
1. Transportation and state - Germany, West. I. Germany (West). Bundesministerium für Verkehr. II. Series: Schriftenreihe (Germany (West). Bundesministerium für Verkehr) , Heft 54. III. Title.
HE64 .A36 Heft 54 HE249

Gschwandtner, Gerhard. Supersellers : portraits of success from Personal selling power / Gerhard Gschwandtner, Laura B. Gschwandtner. New York, N.Y. : Amacom, c1986. xi, 169 p. : ill. ; 25 cm. ISBN 0-8144-5883-1 LC Card 86-47586 DDC 658.8/5 19
1. Selling - Case studies. 2. Success in business - United States - Case studies. I. Gschwandtner, Laura B. II. Personal selling power. III. Title.
HF5438.25 .G785 1986
NYPL [JLE 87-1489]

Gschwandtner, Laura B. Gschwandtner, Gerhard. Supersellers . New York, N.Y. , c1986. xi, 169 p. : ISBN 0-8144-5883-1 LC Card 86-47586 DDC 658.8/5 19
HF5438.25 .G785 1986
NYPL [JLE 87-1489]

GSIS monograph series in world affairs.
Nigeria and the international capitalist system /. Boulder, Colo. , 1988. v, 154 p. ; ISBN 1-555-87087-2 (alk. paper) : LC Card 87-23183 DDC 337.669 19
HF1616.7 .N54 1988

G.T.I. pub. .
(no. 65) Halim, Abdul, 1945- The effects of rice based cropping system research on women in Bangladesh /. Mymensingh , 1986. 2, 30 leaves ; LC Card 86-901954 DDC 331.4/8318/095492 19
HD1537.B3 H35 1986

Gù-Konu, E. Y. Population et progrès socio-économique au Togo / E.Y. Gù-Konu. Lome : Université du Bénin, Ecole des lettres, Dép. de géographie, 1980. 291 p. : ill. ; 21 cm. Bibliography: p. 286-287. LC Card 87-148380
1. Togo - Population. 2. Togo - Economic conditions. 3. Togo - Social conditions. 4. Labor supply - Togo. I. Title.
HB3665.8.A3 G8 1980

Guadalajara, la gran ciudad de la pequeña industria / Patricia Arias, coordinadora. Zamora, Mich. : El Colegio de Michoacán, c1985. 301 p. : ill. ; 21 cm. Includes bibliographies. ISBN 968-7230-12-6 LC Card 86-191608
1. Small business - Mexico - Guadalajara. 2. Guadalajara (Mexico) - Industries. 3. Trade-unions - Mexico - Guadalajara. 4. Artisans - Mexico - Guadalajara. I. Arias, Patricia. II. Colegio de Michoacán.
HD2346.M42 G824 1985

GUADALAJARA (MEXICO) - INDUSTRIES.
Guadalajara, la gran ciudad de la pequeña industria /. Zamora, Mich. , c1985. 301 p. : ISBN 968-7230-12-6 LC Card 86-191608
HD2346.M42 G824 1985

Guadamuz López, Ernesto. La política agraria actual : una derrota relativa de las posiciones neoliberales / investigador, Ernesto Guadamuz López. San José, Costa Rica : Centro de Capacitación para el Desarrollo, 1986. 33 p. ; 30 cm. Includes bibliographical references. LC Card 87-402782 DDC 338.1/87286 19
1. Agriculture and state - Costa Rica. I. Centro de Capacitación para el Desarrollo (San José, Costa Rica). II. Title.
HD1803 .G83 1986

GUADELOUPE - COMMERCE.
Le Lolo . Pointe-à-Pitre [1984?] 63 p. : LC Card 86-155167
HF5473.G83 L65 1984

Guadeloupe. Conseil régional. Rapport aux assemblées régionales : troisième session ordinaire de 1982 / présenté par Marcel Gargar. [Basse-Terre] : République française, Région de Guadeloupe, [1982] 62 p. ; 30 cm. LC Card 85-136896 DDC 338.97297/6 19
1. Guadeloupe - Economic policy. 2. Guadeloupe - Social policy. I. Gargar, Marcel. II. Title.
HC158.5 .G83 1982a

GUADELOUPE - ECONOMIC CONDITIONS.
A.B.C. de l'économie guadeloupéene /. [Basse-Terre, Guadeloupe , 1986] 200 p., [27] leaves of plates : LC Card 87-125723
HC158.5 .A52 1986

Blérald, Alain Ph. Histoire économique de la Guadeloupe et de la Martinique . Paris , c1986. 336 p. : ISBN 2-86537-134-4 LC Card 86-159186
HC158.5 .B54 1986

GUADELOUPE - ECONOMIC POLICY.
A.B.C. de l'économie guadeloupéene /. [Basse-Terre, Guadeloupe , 1986] 200 p., [27] leaves of plates : LC Card 87-125723
HC158.5 .A52 1986

Guadeloupe. Conseil régional. Rapport aux assemblées régionales . [Basse-Terre] [1982] 62 p. ; LC Card 85-136896 DDC 338.97297/6 19
HC158.5 .G83 1982a

GUADELOUPE - INDUSTRIES - DIRECTORIES.
Carnet d'adresses /. [Pointe-à-Pitre, Guadeloupe] [1986?] 64 p. : LC Card 87-152834
HG3729.G862 C37 1986

GUADELOUPE - POPULATION - STATISTICS.
Démographie et emploi en Guadeloupe . Basse-Terre [1977?] 3, xix leaves, [6] leaves of plates : ISBN 2-11-062928-2 LC Card 85-230531
HA918.7 .D46 1977

GUADELOUPE - SOCIAL POLICY.
Guadeloupe. Conseil régional. Rapport aux assemblées régionales . [Basse-Terre] [1982] 62 p. ; LC Card 85-136896 DDC 338.97297/6 19
HC158.5 .G83 1982a

Guala Duca, Riccardo, 1935- I nuovi colletti bianchi : dagli impiegati ai quadri / Riccardo Guala Duca. Milano, Italy : F. Angeli, c1985. 164 p. : ill. ; 22 cm. (Sociologia del lavoro e delle organizzazioni. 25) Includes bibliographical references. LC Card 86-128292 DDC 331.7/92/0945 19
1. White collar workers - Italy. 2. Executives - Italy. I. Title.
HD8039.M4 I854 1985

GUANO INDUSTRY - NAMIBIA - HISTORY - 19TH CENTURY.
Phillips, John A. S. Deutsch-englische Komödie der Irrungen um Südwestafrika . Pfaffenhofen, West Germany , 1986. 184 p., [12] p. of plates : ISBN 3-87010-105-9 LC Card 87-146587 DDC 338.4/76686366/09688 19
HD9484.G9 N366 1986

The guarantee . Chavers-Wright, Madrue, 1916- New York , 1985. xix, 425 p. : ISBN 0-931505-02-X (pbk.) : LC Card 84-51854 DDC 338/.04/0924 B 19
HG2463.C48 C48 1985
NYPL [Sc D 86-412]

The guarantee . Chavers-Wright, Madrue, 1916- New York , 1987, c1985. xix, 427 p. : ISBN 0-931505-05-4 : LC Card 86-51447 DDC

338/.04/0924 B 19
HG2463.C48 C48 1987

GUARANTEED ANNUAL INCOME.
Büchele, Herwig, 1935- Grundeinkommen ohne Arbeit . Wien , c1985. 191 p. : ISBN 3-203-50898-2 LC Card 85-207929
HC79.I5 B83 1985

GUARANTEED ANNUAL INCOME - GREAT BRITAIN.
Lenkowsky, Leslie, 1946- Politics, economics, and welfare reform . Lanham, MD [Washington, D.C.] , c1986. vii, 207 p. ; ISBN 0-8191-5215-3 (alk. paper) : LC Card 85-29456 DDC 362.5/82 19
HC260.I5 L46 1986 ***NYPL [JLE 86-2801]***

GUARANTEED ANNUAL INCOME - UNITED STATES.
Lenkowsky, Leslie, 1946- Politics, economics, and welfare reform . Lanham, MD [Washington, D.C.] , c1986. vii, 207 p. ; ISBN 0-8191-5215-3 (alk. paper) : LC Card 85-29456 DDC 362.5/82 19
HC260.I5 L46 1986 ***NYPL [JLE 86-2801]***

Moynihan, Daniel P. (Daniel Patrick), 1927- The politics of a guaranteed income. New York [1973] xiii, 579 p. ISBN 0-394-46354-4 LC Card 77-37069 DDC 362.5
HC110.I5 M65 ***NYPL [JLE 74-384]***

GUARANTEED INCOME. see **GUARANTEED ANNUAL INCOME.**

GUARD FENCES (ROADS) see **ROADS - GUARD FENCES.**

The Guardian book of the General Strike / [edited by] R.H. Haigh, D.S. Morris, A.R. Peters. Aldershot, Hants, England : Wildwood House ; Brookfield, Vt. : Distributed in the U. S. by Gower Pub. Co., 1987. p. cm. Reports selected from the Manchester guardian. ISBN 0-7045-3081-3 : LC Card 87-25287 DDC 331.89/25/0941 19
1. General Strike, Great Britain, 1926 - History - Sources. I. Haigh, R. H. II. Morris, D. S. III. Peters, A. R. (Anthony R.). IV. Guardian (Manchester, Greater Manchester).
HD5365.A6 G8 1987

Guardian guide to the economy. Cairncross, Frances. Guide to the economy /. London , 1987. viii, 161 p. : ISBN 0-416-39600-3 (pbk.) : LC Card 87-138822 DDC 330.941/085 19
HC256.6 .C27 1987

GUARDIAN LIFE INSURANCE COMPANY - HISTORY.
Rapone, Anita. The Guardian Life Insurance Company, 1860-1920 . New York , c1987. xiv, 209 p., [10] p. of plates : ISBN 0-8147-7401-6 : LC Card 87-7913 DDC 368.3/2/0068 19
HG8963.G942 R36 1987

The Guardian Life Insurance Company, 1860-1920 . Rapone, Anita. New York , c1987. xiv, 209 p., [10] p. of plates : ISBN 0-8147-7401-6 : LC Card 87-7913 DDC 368.3/2/0068 19
HG8963.G942 R36 1987

Guardian (Manchester, Greater Manchester) The Guardian book of the General Strike /. Aldershot, Hants, England , Brookfield, Vt. , 1987. p. cm. ISBN 0-7045-3081-3 : LC Card 87-25287 DDC 331.89/25/0941 19
HD5365.A6 G8 1987

GUARDRAILS (ROADS) see **ROADS - GUARD FENCES.**

Guarracino, Scipione, 1943- Le origini dell'industria / di Scipione Guarracino. Milano, Italy : F. Angeli, c1985. 83 p. : ill. ; 22 cm. (Cultura fondamentale. Unità didattiche . 3) LC Card 86-157399
1. Industry - History. I. Title. II. Series.
HD2321 .G78 1985

Guarrasi, Vincenzo. La Questione meridionale oggi /. Caltanissetta , 1985. 186 p. ; LC Card 86-214162
HC307.S69 Q47 1985

Guatemala : las diferencias socioeconómicas de la fecundidad, 1959-1980. [Guatemala] : Dirección General de Estadística, República de Guatemala ; San José, Costa Rica : Centro Latinoamericano de Demografía, [1984] vii, 73 p. : ill. ; 27 cm. (Serie A . no. 1,045) "LC/DEM/CR/G.3, setiembre de 1984"--T.p. verso. Bibliography: p. 71-73. LC Card 86-158744
1. Fertility, Human - Guatemala - History. I. Guatemala. Dirección General de Estadística. II. CELADE (Organization). III. Series: Serie A (CELADE (Organization)) , no. 1,045.
HA755 .U5 no. 1045 HB949.A3

Guatemala . Paz Cárcamo, Guillermo. Ciudad Universitaria Rodrigo Facio [Costa Rica] , 1986. 278 p. : ISBN 997-7300-95-X LC Card 87-401521
HD1333.G9 P385 1986

Guatemala.
Informe de la obra realizada por el Gobierno Militar, período del 8 de agosto 1983/31 de diciembre 1985. Guatemala : Tip. Nacional, [1986] 192 p., [17] p. of plates : col. ill. ; 21 cm. Cover title: Gobierno Militar. LC Card 86-200374
1. Guatemala - Economic conditions - 1945-. 2. Guatemala - Politics and government - 1945-1985. I. Title. II. Title: Gobierno Militar.
HC144 .G76 1986

GUATEMALA - CENSUS, 1978.
Directorio artesanal, 1978 /. Guatemala , 1981. 6 v. ; LC Card 87-403025
HD2346.G8 D57 1981

Principales indicadores económicos . Guatemala , 1982. 487 p. ; LC Card 87-403026 DDC 331.7/94 19
HD2346.G8 P75 1982

Guatemala. Dirección General de Caminos. Sección de Estadística. Informe de caminos rurales . [Guatemala, Guatemala] [1982] 2, [6] leaves ; LC Card 85-153481
HE359.G83 R855 1982

GUATEMALA - ECONOMIC CONDITIONS - 1945-
Guatemala. Informe de la obra realizada por el Gobierno Militar, período del 8 de agosto 1983/31 de diciembre 1985. Guatemala [1986] 192 p., [17] p. of plates : LC Card 86-200374
HC144 .G76 1986

Guatemala 1986 . Ciudad de Guatemala, Guatemala , c1987. vi, 50 p. : LC Card 87-403676 DDC 330.97281/053 19
HC144 .G8135 1987

Vides de Orive, Enna. Análisis de la situación económica de Guatemala, 1965-1984 /. Guatemala, Guatemala , 1985. ii leaves, 118 p. : LC Card 86-205265 DDC 330.97281/053 19
HC144 .V53 1985

GUATEMALA - POLITICS AND GOVERNMENT - 1945-1985.
Guatemala. Informe de la obra realizada por el Gobierno Militar, período del 8 de agosto 1983/31 de diciembre 1985. Guatemala [1986] 192 p., [17] p. of plates : LC Card 86-200374
HC144 .G76 1986

GUATEMALA - POLITICS AND GOVERNMENT - 1985-
Guatemala 1986 . Ciudad de Guatemala, Guatemala , c1987. vi, 50 p. : LC Card 87-403676 DDC 330.97281/053 19
HC144 .G8135 1987

GUATEMALA - RURAL CONDITIONS.
Hintermeister, Alberto. Modernización de la agricultura y pobreza rural en Guatemala /. [Santiago, Chile] , 1982. 59 leaves : LC Card 87-403247 DDC 338.1/6/097281 19
HC144.Z9 P624 1982

Paz Cárcamo, Guillermo. Guatemala . Ciudad Universitaria Rodrigo Facio [Costa Rica] , 1986. 278 p. : ISBN 997-7300-95-X LC Card 87-401521
HD1333.G9 P385 1986

Guatemala 1986 : the year of promises. Ciudad de Guatemala, Guatemala : Inforpress Centroamericana, c1987. vi, 50 p. : ill. ; 28 cm. LC Card 87-403676 DDC 330.97281/053 19
1. Guatemala - Economic conditions - 1945-. 2. Guatemala - politics and government - 1985-. I. INFORPRESS Centroamericana.
HC144 .G8135 1987

Guatri, Luigi. Crisi e risanamento delle imprese / Luigi Guatri. Milano : A. Giuffrè, 1986. viii, 339 p. : ill. ; 25 cm. (Collana del Centro di studi sulle crisi d'impresa e sulle ristrutturazioni industriali . 2) "Appendice" (documental): p. [133]-339. ISBN 88-14-00914-7 : LC Card 86-228719
1. Corporate reorganizations - Italy. 2. Business failures - Italy. 3. Crisis management - Italy. 4. Business cycles - Italy. I. Title. II. Series.
HD58.8 .G82 1986

GUAVA - BANGLADESH.
Ali, Md. Harun, 1944- An economic study on guava cultivation in some selected areas of Bangladesh /. Mymensingh , 1986. 38 p. ; LC Card 87-902187 DDC 338.1/74421/095492 19
HD9259.G83 B353 1986

GUAVA INDUSTRY - BANGLADESH.
Ali, Md. Harun, 1944- An economic study on guava cultivation in some selected areas of Bangladesh /. Mymensingh , 1986. 38 p. ; LC Card 87-902187 DDC 338.1/74421/095492 19
HD9259.G83 B353 1986

GUAVIARE (COLOMBIA) - ECONOMIC CONDITIONS.
Molano, Alfredo. Selva adentro . Bogotá , 1987. 142 p. : ISBN 958-9012-02-7 LC Card 87-404301 DDC 986.1/65 19
HD519.G8 M65 1987

GUAVIARE (COLOMBIA) - HISTORY.
Molano, Alfredo. Selva adentro . Bogotá , 1987. 142 p. : ISBN 958-9012-02-7 LC Card 87-404301 DDC 986.1/65 19
HD519.G8 M65 1987

GUAVIARE (COLOMBIA) - SOCIAL CONDITIONS.
Molano, Alfredo. Selva adentro . Bogotá , 1987. 142 p. : ISBN 958-9012-02-7 LC Card 87-404301 DDC 986.1/65 19
HD519.G8 M65 1987

Gubaĭdullin, M. S. Industrializat͡sii͡a proizvodstva i mezhkhozi͡aĭstvennoe kooperirovanie /. Ufa , 1979. 122 p. ; LC Card 82-161458
HD9425.S653 B375 1979

Guber, A. A. (Aleksandr Andreevich)
Industry / Alexander Guber. Moscow : Novosti Press Agency Pub. House, 1985. 46 p., [16] p. of plates : ill. ; 20 cm. (The Soviet Union today and tomorrow) Title in colophon: Promyshlennost′. LC Card 86-208070 DDC 338.947 19
1. Soviet Union - Industries. 2. Soviet Union - Economic conditions - 1976-. 3. Central planning - Soviet Union. 4. Soviet Union - Economic policy. I. Title. II. Title: Promyshlennost′. III. Series.
HC336.25 .G8 1985

Nasha ėkonomika : vremi͡a peremen : voprosy, otvety, interv′i͡u / A.A. Guber. Moskva : Izd-vo polit. lit-ry, 1986. 157 p. ; 21 cm. Includes bibliographical references. LC Card 87-132459 DDC 330.947/085/3 19
1. Soviet Union - Economic policy - 1981-1985 - Miscellanea. 2. Soviet Union - Economic policy - 1986- - Miscellnea. 3. Soviet Union - Economic conditions - 1976- - Miscellanea. 4. Soviet Union - Social conditions - 1970- - Miscellanea. I. Title.
HC336.25 .G82 1986

Gucci . McKnight, Gerald. New York , c1987. xi, 362 p. : ISBN 1-556-11037-5 (alk. paper) : LC Card 86-46390 DDC 338.7/687/0945 19
HD9940.I84 G86 1987

GUCCI (FIRM)
McKnight, Gerald. Gucci . New York , c1987. xi, 362 p. : ISBN 1-556-11037-5 (alk. paper) : LC Card 86-46390 DDC 338.7/687/0945 19
HD9940.I84 G86 1987

Günter, Janne, 1937- Mündliche Geschichtsschreibung : alte Menschen im Ruhrgebiet erzählen erlebte Geschichte / Janne Günter. Mülheim/Ruhr : W.G. von Westarp-Verlag, 1982. 142, [1] p. : ill. ; 21 cm. Bibliography: p. [143] ISBN 3-923456-00-X LC Card 85-146144
1. Miners - Germany (West) - Ruhr (Region) - History. 2. Ruhr (Germany : Region) - Biography. 3. Ruhr (Germany : Region) - Economic conditions. 4. Aged - Germany (West) - Ruhr (Region) - History. 5. Oral biography. 6. Miners - Germany (West) - Ruhr (Region) - Interviews. I. Title.
HD8039.M61 G343 1982

Guerra García, R. (Roger) Problemas poblacionales peruanos II /. Lima , c1986. 402 p. : LC Card 86-228816
HB3575 .P763 1986

Guerra, Oswaldo. Empresas estatais na Bahia. Salvador, Bahia, Brasil , 1986. 134 p. : LC Card 87-137490 DDC 338.6/2/098142 19
HD4095.B33 E47 1986

Guerra, Paulo de Brito, 1914- A civilização da seca : o Nordeste é uma história mal contada /

Paulo de Brito Guerra. Fortaleza : Ministério do Interior, Departamento Nacional de Obras Contra as Secas, 1981. 324 p. : ill. (some col.) ; 22 cm. Includes bibliographies. LC Card 82-231215 DDC 361.6/0981/3 19
1. Regional planning - Brazil, Northeast. 2. Arid regions agriculture - Brazil, Northeast. 3. Droughts - Brazil, Northeast. 4. Seca. 5. Brazil, Northeast - Economic conditions. I. Title.
HT395.B72 N63 1981 ***NYPL [JLD 86-2873]***

La guerre des images /. Frèches, José. Paris , c1986. 173 p. : ISBN 2-207-23215-8 : LC Card 86-141723
HE8700.9.F7 F77 1986

Guerre du téléphone. Darmon, Jacques. Le grand dérangement . [Paris] , c1985. 269 p. : LC Card 85-242541 DDC 384/.068 19
HE8144 .D37 1985 ***NYPL [JLE 87-363]***

Guerrero Rodríguez, Milton. Casas Grieve, Luis Felipe de las. Economía y frustración social . Lima, Perú [1982?] 128 p. : LC Card 83-104684
HC227 .C27 1982

Guerrilla capitalism . Cash, Adam. Port Townsend, Wash. , c1984. 172 p. : ISBN 0-915179-16-4 (pbk.) LC Card 84-81910 DDC 343.7305/23 347.303523 19
HD2346.U5 C34 1984 ***NYPL [JLD 86-2946]***

Guerrina Soderini, Alfonso. El drama quijotesco de los oficios en la época cervantina / Alfonso Guerrina Soderini. 1a ed. Montevideo, Uruguay : [s.n.], 1980 (Montevideo : Talleres Don Bosco) 209 p., [7] : ill. ; 24 cm. "1a edición 1979." Errata slip laid in. Bibliography: p. [213]-[215] LC Card 84-132190
1. Artisans - Spain - History - 16th century. 2. Artisans - Spain - History - 17th century. I. Title.
HD2346.S7 G84 1980

Guess, George M. The politics of United States foreign aid / George M. Guess. New York : St. Martin's Press, 1987. 297 p. ; 22 cm. Bibliography: p. 273-289. Includes index. ISBN 0-312-00448-6 : LC Card 86-26301 DDC 338.91/09172/4 19
1. Economic assistance, American - Political aspects - Developing countries. 2. Military assistance, American - Political aspects - Developing countries. I. Title.
HC60 .G7383 1987

Das Güterverkehrszentrum als infrastrukturelle Schnittstelle des Güterverkehrs /. Tress, Roland. Düsseldorf , 1984. xv, 288 p. : LC Card 86-140143
HE5 .C6 Nr. 45 HE5999.Z7G2

Guevara López, Onofre. Pérez Bermúdez, Carlos. El movimiento obrero en Nicaragua . [S.l. , 1985] ([Managua, Nicaragua?] : Editorial "El Amanecer") 2 v. in 1 : LC Card 86-174663
HD6557 .P473 1985

Guggenheim, Joseph.
HUD's rental rehabilitation program, HUD's housing development grant program / [by Joseph Guggenheim]. Washington, D.C. : For additional copies write to Community Information Exchange, National Urban Coalition, [c1984] 13 p. ; 28 cm. (Technical bulletin) LC Card 87-100358 DDC 363.5/8 19
1. Rental housing - United States - Finance. 2. Rent subsidies - United States. 3. Housing rehabilitation - Government policy - United States. I. Title. II. Title: HUD's housing development grant program. III. Series: Technical bulletin (Community Information Exchange (U. S.)).
HD7288.85.U6 G84 1984

Tax credits for low income housing : new opportunities for developers, non-profit, and communities under the 1986 Tax Reform Act / Joseph Guggenheim.2nd ed. Washington, D.C. : Simon Publications, c1986. vii, 117 p. : ill. ; 28 cm. ISBN 0-941239-00-4 (pbk.) LC Card 87-112304 DDC 363.5/8 19
1. Property tax credit - United States. 2. Public housing - United States - Finance. 3. Real estate investment - United States. 4. Public housing - Finance - Law and legislation - United States. 5. Income tax - Law and legislation - United States. 6. Real property and taxation - United States. I. Title.
HJ4653.C73 G85 1986

Guglielmetti, Francis. L'indice des prix de la Martinique, base 100 en 1979 : méthodes, bilan 1979-1984 et perspectives / par Francis Guglielmetti. [Fort de France?] : INSEE, Service interrégional Antilles-Guyane, [1985] 130, xxiii p. : ill. ; 30 cm. (Les Dossiers Antilles Guyane, 0291-8706 . 10) "Juin 1985." Bibliography: p. 127. ISBN 2-11-062943-6 : LC Card 86-176702
1. Consumer price indexes - Martinique. 2. Prices - Martinique. I. Title. II. Series.
HB235.M37 G83 1985

Gührs, Eckhard. Leitfaden für Kostenermittlung und Wirtschaftlichkeitsprüfung : Hinweise für die Verwaltung der Freien und Hansestadt Hamburg / Eckhard Gührs, Gerd Hünerberg. Hamburg : Senatsamt für den Verwaltungsdienst, 1983. iii, 92 p. ; 21 cm. Includes bibliographical references and index. LC Card 85-212548
1. Finance, Public - Germany (West) - Hamburg - Accounting. 2. Finance, Public - Accounting - Law and legislation - Germany (West) - Hamburg. I. Hünerberg, Gerd. II. Hamburg (Germany). Senatsamt für den Verwaltungsdienst. III. Title.
HJ9925.G3 G84 1983

Guia ação : o guia completo do mercado de ações : nomes e endereços de onde comprar ações, as alternativas para ter ações em seu patrimônio, termos técnicos e evolução do mercado de ações. 2a. ed. ampliada e atualizada. RJ [i.e. Rio de Janeiro] : Comitê de Divulgação do Mercado de Capitais : Editoração Empresa Jornalística, [1985 or 1986] 285 p. ; 22 cm. Cover title. Spine title: O guia completo do mercado de ações. LC Card 87-405004 DDC 332.6/78/0981 19
1. Mutual funds - Brazil - Directories. 2. Investments - Brazil - Directories. 3. Stocks - Brazil - Directories. I. Comitê de Divulgação do Mercado de Capitais (Brazil). II. Title: Guia completo do mercado de ações.
HG5334.5 .G85 1985

Guia completo do mercado de ações. Guia ação . RJ [i.e. Rio de Janeiro] [1985 or 1986] 285 p. ; LC Card 87-405004 DDC 332.6/78/0981 19
HG5334.5 .G85 1985

Guía conceptual y metodológica para instructores de cursos de capacitación de INFOPLAN. Santiago de Chile : Centro Latinoamericano de Documentación Económica y Social, 1983. iv, 70 p. : ill. ; 28 cm. (Serie de manuales . no. 2) "Distr. restringida. E/CEPAL/CLADES/R. 24, 28 de septiembre de 1983. Original: español. Bibliography: p. 69-70. LC Card 87-108080
1. INFOPLAN (Information retrieval system) - Handbooks, manuals, etc. 2. Information storage and retrieval systems - Latin America - Economic conditions - Handbooks, manuals, etc. 3. Information storage and retrieval systems - Latin America - Social conditions - Handbooks, manuals, etc. I. Latin American Centre for Economic and Social Documentation. II. Series: Serie de manuales (Latin American Centre for Economic and Social Documentation) , no. 2.
HC125 .G814 1983

Guía de organizaciones gremiales, 1984 / DIL, Documentación e Información Laboral. Capital Federal, República Argentina : Ediciones DIL, [between 1984 and 1986] [12], 651 p. : ill. ; 31 cm. Spine title: Guía, 1984. "Octava edición ampliada"--Prelim. p. [3]. LC Card 87-123823 DDC 331.88/025/82 19
1. Trade-unions - Argentina - Directories. I. Documentación e Información Laboral (Buenos Aires, Argentina). II. Title: Guía, 1984.
HD6601.5 .G85 1984

Guía del Mercado Común Europeo . Tamames, Ramón, 1933- Madrid , c1986. xii, 309 p. ; ISBN 84-206-9524-6 LC Card 86-150515
HC241.25.S6 T35 1986

Guia dos produtores de insumos farmacêuticos. Brasil--guia dos produtores de insumos farmacêuticos /. Rio de Janeiro, Brasil , 1983. 71 p. ; LC Card 86-202196
HD9670.B82 B7 1983

Guía, 1984. Guía de organizaciones gremiales, 1984 /. Capital Federal, República Argentina [between 1984 and 1986] [12], 651 p. : LC Card 87-123823 DDC 331.88/025/82 19
HD6601.5 .G85 1984

Guiba (Writer)
Por qué nos confunden-- el comunismo, el capitalismo, los economistas, las elites? / Guiba. Montevideo : G. Bausero, 1981. 211 p. ; 20 cm. LC Card 82-125535 DDC 330.9/04 19
1. Economic history - 20th century. 2. World politics - 20th century. 3. Capitalism. I. Title.
HC54 .G79 1981 ***NYPL [JLC 86-320]***

Salario humano y libertad / Guillermo Bausero. 1a ed. Buenos Aires : Ediciones Marymar, 1986. viii, 155 p. ; 20 cm. Includes bibliographical references. ISBN 950-50-3130-0 LC Card 87-101595
1. Wages - Minimum wage. 2. Liberty. I. Title.
HD4917 .G85 1986

Guichard-Ayoub, Éliane. Les associations syndicales de propriétaires / Éliane Ayoub. 1ère éd. Paris : Presses universitaires de France, 1984. 127 p. ; 18 cm. (Que sais-je? 2146) Bibliography: p. 124. ISBN 2-13-038290-8
1. Agriculture, Cooperative - France. 2. Real property - France. 3. Land use - France. I. Title.
NYPL [JLC 87-57]

Guida al primo lavoro /. Ferragni, Fabrizio. Milano , 1986. 271 p. : ISBN 88-17-13617-4 : LC Card 86-193250
HD6276.I7 F47 1986

Guida alla valorizzazione agricola nei paesi in via di sviluppo / Pietro Antinori ... [et al. ; a cura di Carlo Barberis]. Milano, Italy : F. Angeli, c1983. 434 p. : ill. ; 22 cm. (Collana di studi e ricerche / Ministero degli affari esteri, Dipartimento per la cooperazione allo sviluppo . 4) At head of title: Ministero degli affari esteri, Dipartimento per la cooperazione allo sviluppo. LC Card 83-144803 DDC 338.1/09172/4 19
1. Agriculture - Economic aspects - Developing countries. 2. Agricultural development projects - Developing countries - Evaluation. I. Antinori, Pietro. II. Barberis, Carlo. III. Series: Collana di studi e ricerche (Italy. Ministero degli affari esteri. Dipartimento per la cooperazione allo sviluppo) , 4.
HD1417 .G85 1983 ***NYPL [JLD 86-3296]***

Guidance and counseling series.
Raskin, Patricia M., 1943- Vocational counseling . New York, NY , c1987. xiii, 160 p. ; ISBN 0-8077-2860-8 (pbk.) LC Card 87-1972 DDC 371.4/25 19
HF5381 .R325 1987

Guidance Associates.
Job survival skills [videorecording] . Mt. Kisco, NY , 1986, c1987. 1 videocassette (50 min.) : LC Card 86-707971 DDC 650.1 11
HF5386

Résumés that get interviews, interviews that get jobs [videorecording] /. Mt. Kisco, NY , 1986, c1987. 1 videocassette (42 min.) : LC Card 86-707973 DDC 650.1 11
HF5383

Winning the employment game [videorecording] /. Mt. Kisco, NY , 1981. 1 videocassette (52 min.) : LC Card 86-707777 DDC 650.1 11
HF5382.7

GUIDANCE, STUDENT. see **VOCATIONAL GUIDANCE.**

GUIDANCE, VOCATIONAL. see **VOCATIONAL GUIDANCE.**

Guide de la banque suisse et de ses secrets /. Chambost, Édouard. [Paris] , c1987. 317 p. : ISBN 2-7158-0626-4 : LC Card 87-132185
HG3204 .C43 1987

Guide de la consommation, des dépenses et des prix alimentaires. Hassan, Zuhair A. Handbook of food expenditures, prices, and consumption /. Ottawa , c1983. 270 p., [2] p. of plates : LC Card 86-228246 DDC 339.4/8664/00971 19
HD9014.C3 H29 1983

Guide des 150 meileures entreprises françaises. 150 meilleures entreprises françaises /. Paris , c1986. 313 p. ; ISBN 2-234-01894-3 : LC Card 87-107207
HF5382.75.F8 A13 1986

Guide d'évaluation a posteriori des opérations de développement rural. Evaluation du développement rural /. [Paris] , c1982. 201 p. : ISBN 2-11-084484-1 LC Card 84-134740
HC59.72.E44 E93 1982

Guide du spéculateur . Freymond, Joël. Paris , c1986. 175 p. : ISBN 2-226-02463-8 : LC Card 87-166254
HG6041 .F82 1986

Guide du système de gestion des politiques et des dépenses. Guide to the policy & expenditure management system. [Ottawa] , c1980. 33, 33 p. ; ISBN 0-662-51109-3 (pbk.) LC Card 81-116818
HJ7660 .G85 1980

Guide économique de la francophonie. Africascope . Paris [1985] 426 p. : LC Card

86-192167
HC945 .A65 1985

A Guide for investors. [Jakarta] : Batam Industrial Development Authority, [1984] 112 p. : col. ill., col. map, col. plan, col. ports. ; 26 cm. Includes a speech in Indonesian. Cover title. Spine title: A guide for investors, Batam island. Four apprendices in pocket. LC Card 86-942985 DDC 332.6/73225981 19
1. Batam Island (Indonesia) - Economic conditions - 1945-. 2. Investments, Foreign - Indonesia - Batam Island. I. Otorita Pengembangan Daerah Industri Pulau Batam. II. Title: Guide for investors, Batam island.
HC448.B38 G85 1984

Guide for investors, Batam island. A Guide for investors. [Jakarta] [1984] 112 p. : LC Card 86-942985 DDC 332.6/73225981 19
HC448.B38 G85 1984

Guide for occupational exploration / edited by Thomas F. Harrington, Arthur J. O'Shea. 2nd ed. [Washington, D.C.] : National Forum Foundation ; Circle Pines, Minn. : Distributed by American Guidance Service, c1984. vii, 984 p. : ill. ; 28 cm. Based on research conducted by the Division of Occupational Analysis and the Division of Testing of the United States Employment Service, Dept. of Labor. Bibliography: p. 588. LC Card 87-402857 DDC 331.7/02/0973 19
1. United States - Occupations. 2. Vocational interests - United States. 3. Vocational guidance - United States. I. Harrington, Thomas F. II. O'Shea, Arthur J. III. United States Employment Service. Division of Testing. IV. United States Employment Service. Division of Occupational Analysis.
HF5382.5.U5 G83 1984

A Guide for selecting ALM microcomputer models : a comprehensive survey / prepared by Peat, Marwick, Mitchell & Co. Washington, D.C. (1120 Connecticut Ave., N.W., Washington 20036) : American Bankers Association, c1987. iv, 147 p. : forms ; 28 cm. LC Card 87-159971 DDC 332.1/028/5416 19
1. Asset-liability management (Banking) - Computer programs - Directories. 2. Banks and banking - United States - Data processing. 3. Market surveys - United States. I. Peat, Marwick, Mitchell & Co. II. American Bankers Association.
HG1615.25 .G85 1987

Guide for the independent manager. Milling, Bryan E. Banking strategies for businesses . Radnor, PA , c1987. viii, 231 p. : ISBN 0-8019-7651-0 (pbk.) : LC Card 86-47959 DDC 658.1/592 19
HG4027.7 .M55 1987

Guide international des branches techniques par Uhland. Uhlands Internationales Technisches Branchen-Adressbuch =. Leipzig , 1926. 22, 767 p. ; LC Card 85-666352
HC282.2 .U45x 1926

Guide pratique de l'analyse financière à l'usage des banquiers /. Barbier, André. Paris , c1985. viii, 313 p. : ISBN 2-86325-038-8 : LC Card 86-165653
HF5686.C7 B32 1985

Guide pratique du financement des industries agroalimentaires / collection dirigée par François de Sars. 2me éd. Paris : AGRA Alimentation : [Diffusion, Lavoisier], [1986] 351 p. : ill. ; 30 cm. (Tec & doc) List of organizations with addresses: p. 342-351. Distributor from label on t.p. Series statement from label on t.p. LC Card 86-186921
1. Agricultural industries - France - Finance. 2. Food industry and trade - France - Finance. I. Sars, François de. II. Series: Technique & documentation.
HD9012.5 .G86 1986

Guide to ACH processor selection & evaluation : result of NACHA's private sector alternative's project. Washington, D.C. (Suite 640, 1901 L St., N.W., Washington 20036) : National Automated Clearing House Association, c1987. v, 199 p. ; 28 cm. LC Card 87-402621 DDC 332.1/028 19
1. Clearinghouse - United States - Evaluation. I. National Automated Clearing House Association.
HG2322 .G85 1987

Guide to audits of local governments /. Carmichael, D. R. Douglas R.), 1941- Fort Worth, Tex. , 1986- 2 v. (loose-leaf) : LC Card 86-206730 DDC 657/.835045 19
HJ9777.A3 C37 1986

Guide to bond and money market investments. Stigum, Marcia L. The Dow Jones-Irwin guide to bond and money market investments /. Homewood, Ill. , c1987. xiii, 298 p. : ISBN 0-87094-892-X : LC Card 86-71921
NYPL [*R-Econ. 87-1260]

Guide to China's foreign economic relations and trade. Cities newly opened to foreign investors / editors, Policy Research Department, Ministry of Foreign Economic Relations and Trade, China = Chung-kuo tui wai ching chi mao i chih nan. Hsin k'ai fang cheng shih chuan chi / Chung-kuo tui wai ching chi mao i pu cheng ts'e yen chiu shih chu pien.880-02 1st ed. Hong Kong : Economic Information and Agency, 1985. 385 p. : maps ; 27 cm. Chinese and English. ISBN 962-7063-19-3
1. Free ports and zones - China. 2. Economic zoning - China. 3. Investments, Foreign - Law and legislation - China. I. Chung-kuo tui wai ching chi mao i pu cheng ts'e yen chiu shih. II. Title: Chung-kuo tui wai ching chi mao i chih nan. Hsin k'ai fang ch'eng shih chuan chi. ***NYPL [*OVY 86-3400]***

Guide to China's foreign economic relations and trade. Investment special / editors, Policy Research Department and Foreign Investment Administration, Ministry of Foreign Economic Relations and Trade, China = Chung-kuo tui wai ching chi mao i chih nan. T'ou tzu chuan chi / Chung-kuo tui wai ching chi mao i pu cheng ts'e yen chiu shih, Wai tzu kuan li chü chu pien.880-02 1st ed. Hong Kong : Economic Information and Agency, 1983. 342 p. : ill. (some col.) ; 27 cm. Chinese and English. In Chinese. ISBN 0-9627063-8-8 : LC Card 84-177660 DDC 346.51/07 345.1067 19
1. Investments, Foreign - China. 2. Joint ventures - China. 3. Investments, Foreign - Law and legislation - China. I. Chung-kuo tui wai ching chi mao i pu cheng ts'e yen chiu shih. II. China. Wai tzu kuan li chü. III. Title: Chung-kuo tui wai ching chi mao i chih nan. T'ou tzu chuan chi.
HG5784 .G835 1983 ***NYPL [*OVY 86-3398]***

Guide to company information in Great Britain /. Norkett, P. T. C. Burnt Mill, Harlow, Essex, U.K. , c1986. xi, 208 p. : ISBN 0-582-97820-3 (pbk.) : LC Card 86-220140 DDC 338.7/4/072041 19
HD2845 .N67 1986

Guide to compilation and review engagements /. Meals, Dennis R. Fort Worth, Tex. , c1986- 3 v. (loose-leaf) : LC Card 86-224183 DDC 657/.3 19
HF5667.65 .M42 1986

Guide to computer installations in southern California . Horner, Ken. Palo Alto, Calif. , c1986. iv, 750 p. : LC Card 87-134229 DDC 004/.025/7949 19
HD9696.C63 U518343 1986

A guide to financial institutions /. Geisst, Charles R. New York , 1988. p. cm. ISBN 0-312-01132-6 : LC Card 87-13047 DDC 332.1 19
HG185.U5 G45 1988

A guide to forecasting for planners and managers /. Willis, Raymond E. (Raymond Edson), 1930- Englewood Cliffs, N.J. , c1987. xii, 404 p. : ISBN 0-13-369539-5 : LC Card 86-25532 DDC 658.4/0355 19
HD30.27 .W55 1987

Guide to forecasts and projections /. Pallais, Don. Fort Worth, Tex. , 1986. 2 v. (loose-leaf) : LC Card 87-108778 DDC 657/.3 19
HF5681.B2 P15 1986

Guide to Hong Kong's bus, light bus, rail, and ferry services / [Transport Department]. [4th ed.]. Hong Kong : Government Printer, 1986. p. D3799-D4101, 14 p. ; 21 cm. At head of p. D3799-D4101: S.s. no. 4 to gazette no. 36/1986. Includes index. LC Card 87-401055 DDC 388.4/0951/25 19
1. Local transit - Hong Kong - Handbooks, manuals, etc. I. Hong Kong. Transport Dept.
HE5080.5.H662 G85 1986

Guide to housing alternatives for older citizens /. Gold, Margaret. [Older American's guide to housing and living arrangements.] Mount Vernon, N.Y. , c1985. ix, 170 p. : ISBN 0-89043-031-4 (pbk.) : LC Card 87-401956 DDC 646/.79 19
HD7287.92.U54 G65 1985

Guide to Hugh Moore Park. Metz, Lance E. Sherman's guide to Hugh Moore Park /. Easton, PA , 1988. p. cm. ISBN 0-930973-07-0 (pbk.) : LC Card 87-25622 DDC 338.09748/22 19
HE395 .P43 1988

Guide to IFPS (Interactive Financial Planning System) /. Gray, Paul, 1930- New York , c1987. xii, 497 p. : ISBN 0-07-024394-8 (pbk.) : LC Card 86-21514 DDC 658.1/5/02855329 19
HG4012.5 .G7 1987

A guide to implementation of Statement 87 on employer's accounting for pensions . Amble, Joan Lordi. Stamford, Conn. (High Ridge Park, P.O. Box 3821, Stamford 06905-0821) , c1986. vii, 106 p. : LC Card 87-133173 DDC 657/.75
HF5686.O5 A56 1986

A Guide to industrial investment / Kingdom of Saudi Arabia, Saudi Consulting House. 7th ed. Riyadh : The House, 1986. vi, 286 p., [4] leaves of plates : ill. (some col.) ; 24 cm. LC Card 87-400301 DDC 332.6/7322538 19
1. Industrial promotion - Saudi Arabia. 2. Industry and state - Saudi Arabia. 3. Trade regulation - Saudi Arabia. 4. Investments - Saudi Arabia. 5. Saudi Arabia - Economic conditions. I. Dar al-Sa'ūdiyah lil-Khadamāt al-Istishārīyah.
HC415.33.Z9 I534 1986

A guide to information on closely held corporations /. Law, Gordon T., 1945- Buffalo, N.Y. , c1986. p. cm. ISBN 0-9615917-1-4 : LC Card 86-32812 DDC 338.7/4/072073 19
HD2785 .L38 1986

Guide to investing. The New York Institute of Finance guide to investing. New York, N.Y. , c1987. xi, 296 p. : ISBN 0-13-620436-8 (pbk.) : LC Card 87-11323 DDC 332.6/78 19
HG4921 .N53 1987

The guide to Lotus HAL . Rier, David C. Reading, Mass. [1987], c1988. xv, 266 p. : ISBN 0-201-16827-8 (pbk.) : LC Card 87-22885 DDC 005.36/9 19
HF5548.4.L68 R54 1988

Guide to market research for the computer software and services industry. ADAPSO guide to market research for the computer software and services industry. Arlington, Va. (1300 N. 17th St., Suite 300, Arlington 22209) , c1985. 71 p. ; LC Card 87-402047 DDC 005/.068/8 19
HD9696.C63 U511235 1985

Guide to personal finance . Stillman, Richard Joseph, 1917- Englewood Cliffs, N.J. , c1988. xxii, 504 p. : ISBN 0-13-370214-6 : LC Card 87-19298 DDC 332.024 19
HG179 .S84 1988

Guide to preparing financial statements /. Clay, John R. Fort Worth, Tex. , c1987- 2 v. (loose-leaf) ; LC Card 87-161098 DDC 657/.3 19
HF5681.B2 C565 1987

Guide to real estate and mortgage banking software / Ina S. Bechhoefer, editor. 4th ed. Washington, D.C. : Real Estate Solutions, 1986. 3 v. ; 24 cm. Includes indexes. ISBN 0-917935-14-4 (pbk. : set) LC Card 86-63061 DDC 333.3/028/553 19
1. Real estate business - Computer programs - Catalogs. 2. Mortgage loans - Computer programs - Catalogs. 3. Computer software industry - Directories. I. Bechhoefer, Ina S. II. Real Estate Solutions, Inc. III. Title: Real estate and mortgage banking software.
HD1380 .G85 1986a

Guide to real estate licensing examinations for salespersons and brokers /. French, William B. New York , c1986. ix, 367 p. : ISBN 0-471-87754-9 : LC Card 83-23484 DDC 333.33/0973 19
HD1375 .F74 1984
NYPL [*R-Econ. 86-3475]

Guide to retirement planning. Vicker, Ray. The Dow Jones-Irwin guide to retirement planning /. Homewood, Ill. , c1987. ix, 332 p. : ISBN 1-556-23005-2 LC Card 86-72973 DDC 332.024/01 19
HG179 .V54 1987

A Guide to small firms assistance in Europe / edited and coordinated by Gay Haskins with Allan Gibb and Tony Hubert with contributors from 17 countries. Aldershot, Hants, England ; Brookfield, Vt., U. S.A. : Gower Pub. Co., c1986. vii, 263 p. ; 35 cm. At head of title: European Association for National Productivity

Centres, European Foundation for Management Development. ISBN 0-566-05082-X : LC Card 85-27307 DDC 338.6/42/094 19
1. Small business - Government policy - Europe. 2. Industry and state - Europe. I. Haskins, Gay. II. Gibb, Allan. III. Hubert, Tony. IV. European Association for National Productivity Centres. V. European Foundation for Management Development.
HD2346.E9 G85 1986 ***NYPL [JLG 86-205]***

Guide to southern California computers. Horner, Ken. Guide to computer installations in southern California . Palo Alto, Calif. , c1986. iv, 750 p. : LC Card 87-134229 DDC 004/.025/7949 19
HD9696.C63 U518343 1986

A guide to SPSS/PC+ /. Frude, Neil. New York , 1987. p. cm. ISBN 0-387-91312-2 LC Card 87-16711 DDC 300/.285416 19
HA32 .F78 1987

Guide to state capital formation incentives and innovations / Chemical Bank ; prepared for the National Governors' Association. 2nd ed. [Washington, D.C. : National Governors' Association, 1983] vii, 154 p. ; 29 cm. "February 1983." "Judy Scherer ... prepared the guide"--"P. i. Bibliography: p. 147-152. LC Card 86-673432
1. Industrial promotion - United States - States - Directories. 2. Capital investments - Government policy - United States - States - Directories. 3. Economic development - Government policy - United States - States - Directories. I. Scherer, Judy. II. Chemical Bank (New York, N.Y.). III. National Governors' Association.
HC110.I53 G84x 1983

Guide to the economy /. Cairncross, Frances. London , 1987. viii, 161 p. : ISBN 0-416-39600-3 (pbk.) : LC Card 87-138822 DDC 330.941/085 19
HC256.6 .C27 1987

A Guide to the new consumer price index. [George Town, Grand Caymon, B.W.I.] : Statistics Unit, Dept. of Finance & Development, [1985] 26 leaves ; 28 cm. "February 1985." LC Card 86-221984 DDC 338.5/28/0972921 19
1. Consumer price indexes - Cayman Islands. 2. Prices - Cayman Islands - Statistics. I. Cayman Islands. Dept. of Finance and Development. Statistics Unit.
HB235.C29 G85 1985

Guide to the policy & expenditure management system. [Ottawa] : Government of Canada, Minister of Supply and Services Canada, c1980. 33, 33 p. ; 28 cm. English and French. Cover title. Title on added t.p.: Guide du système de gestion des politiques et des dépenses. "Cat. no. BT 32-15/1980"--T.p. verso. ISBN 0-662-51109-3 (pbk.) LC Card 81-116818
1. Canada - Appropriations and expenditures. 2. Government spending policy - Canada. I. Canada. Supply and Services Canada. II. Title: Guide du système de gestion des politiques et des dépenses.
HJ7660 .G85 1980

A Guide to the spreading and analysis of Japanese bank statements. Philadelphia, PA (1616 Philadelphia National Bank Bldg. Philadelphia 19107) : R. Morris Associates, c1986. 60 p. ; 28 cm. LC Card 86-203674 DDC 657/.833 19
1. Banks and banking - Japan - Accounting. I. Robert Morris Associates.
HG3324 .G85 1986

A guide to tracing the history of a business /. Orbell, John. Aldershot, Hants, Eng. , Brookfield, Vt., USA , c1987. p. cm. ISBN 0-566-05591-0 : LC Card 87-15505 DDC 338.7/072 19
HD2321 .O7 1987

Guide to training needs assessment / edited by Lloyd A. Stanley. Ljubljana, Yugoslavia : International Center for Public Enterprises in Developing Countries, c1984. 65 p. ; 24 cm. (ICPE training series . no. 1) At head of title: International research project on human resource development. Bibliography: p. 57-60. ISBN 92-9038-412-8 (pbk.) LC Card 85-242690 DDC 658.3/12404 19
1. Training needs. 2. Employees, Training of. I. Stanley, Lloyd A. II. International Center for Public Enterprises in Developing Countries. III. Title: International research project on human resource development. IV. Series.
HF5549.5.T7 G847 1984

Guide to world commodity markets : physical, futures & options trading / consultant editor, John Buckley.5th ed. London : K. Page ; Detroit, Mich. : Distributed exclusively in the United States, possessions, and Canada by Gale Research Co., 1986. 465 p. : ill. ; 25 cm. Includes index. ISBN 1-85091-116-9 LC Card 87-144180 DDC 332.64/4 19
1. Commodity exchanges. I. Buckley, John, 1947-.
HG6046 .G84 1986

Guided incomes policy /. Prakash, Om, 1927- New Delhi , 1983. vi, 214 p. ; LC Card 83-902415 DDC 339.5/0954 19
HC440.I5 P72 1983 ***NYPL [JLD 86-3834]***

Guideline for designing and executing small scale surveys in Botswana. Botswana. Central Statistics Office. [Gaborone] [1982] 53 p. in various pagings : LC Card 83-154943 DDC 304.6/0723 19
HB849.49 .B68 1982 ***NYPL [JLG 86-217]***

Guidelines for auditing governmental subdivisions / [Premium Audit Advisory Service]. [2nd ed.]. [New York, NY] : The Service, [c1987] ii, 50 p. ; 28 cm. Bibliography: p. 14. LC Card 87-121255 DDC 350.72/32 19
1. Finance, Public - Auditing. 2. Administrative agencies - Auditing. I. Premium Audit Advisory Service.
HJ9733 .G85 1987

Guidelines for estimating the cost effectiveness of high-occupancy vehicle lanes /. Lomax, Timothy J. College Station, Tex. , Springfield, Va. [1985] xiii, 55 p. : LC Card 86-622240 DDC 380.5 s 388.3/142 19
HE203 .T43 no. 339-5 HE356.T4

Guidelines for planning community participation activities in water supply and sanitation projects /. Whyte, Anne V. T. Geneva , Albany, NY , 1986. 53 p. : ISBN 92-4-170096-3 (pbk.) : LC Card 87-137091 DDC 333.91/009172/4 19
HD4465.D44 W49 1986

Guidelines for the planning of rural settlements and infrastructure : electrification, a methodology. Nairobi : United Nations Centre for Human Settlements (Habitat), 1985. vi, 295 p. ; 30 cm. Bibliography: p. 289-295. ISBN 92-1-131003-2 LC Card 86-981187 DDC 363/.068 19
1. Rural electrification - Planning. 2. Rural development - Planning. 3. Human settlements - Planning. 4. Infrastructure (Economics) - Planning. I. United Nations Centre for Human Settlements.
HD9688.A2 G85 1985

Guides and handbooks .
(no. 13) Spufford, Peter. Handbook of medieval exchange /. London : Woodbridge, Suffolk ; xcii, 376 p., [3] leaves of plates (1 folded) : ISBN 0-86193-105-X LC Card 86-673816
HG3942 .S68x 1986

Guides to contemporary issues .
(6) Golkin, Arline T. (Arline Tartus) Famine, a heritage of hunger . Claremont, Calif. , c1987. xvi, 168 p. : ISBN 0-941690-21-0 : LC Card 86-26138 DDC 363.8 19
HC79.F3 B63 1986 ***NYPL [JLD 87-878]***

Guidotti, Daniela. Strategia generale e azione decentrata : i precontratti dei tessili in Lombardia nel 1983 / Daniela Guidotti ; ricerca promossa dalla FILTEA CGIL Lombardia. Milano, Italy : F. Angeli, c1986. 216 p. ; 22 cm. (IRES/CGIL Lombardia. Materiali di ricerca . 3) Includes bibliographical references. LC Card 86-193797
1. Collective bargaining - Textile industry - Italy - Lombardy. 2. Collective labor agreements - Textile industry - Italy - Lombardy. I. Series: Ires/Cgil Lombardia (Series). Materiali di ricerca , 3. II. Title.
HD6976.T42 I764 1986

GUILD SOCIALISM - HISTORY.
Marucco, Dora. Fabianesimo, ghildismo, forme di democrazia industriale /. Milano, Italy , c1986. 82 p. ; LC Card 86-194327
HD6479 .M37 1986

GUILDS - EUROPE - HISTORY.
John, Peter, 1946- Handwerkskammern im Zwielicht . Köln , 1983. 304 p. ; ISBN 3-7663-0597-2 LC Card 83-127836 DDC 338.6/425/0943 19
HD2346.E9 J63 1983 ***NYPL [JLD 87-1038]***
Mackenney, Richard. Tradesmen and traders . London , c1987. xv, 289 p. : ISBN 0-7099-1763-5 LC Card 87-672566
HD6472.V4 M33x 1987b

GUILDS - EUROPE, NORTHERN - HISTORY.
Gilde und Korporation in den nordeuropäischen Städten des späten Mittelalters /. Köln , 1984. 114 p. ; ISBN 3-412-06883-3 LC Card 84-194645
HD6473.E853 G55 1984

GUILDS - GREECE - IŌANNINA - HISTORY - 19TH CENTURY.
Papageōrgiou, Giōrgos. Hoi syntechnies sta Giannena kata ton 19o kai tis arches tou 20ou aiōna (arches 19ou ai. hōs 1912) /. Iōannina : Athēna : 454 p. ; LC Card 84-137611
HD2346.G752 I566 1982

GUILDS - GREECE - IŌANNINA - HISTORY - 20TH CENTURY.
Papageōrgiou, Giōrgos. Hoi syntechnies sta Giannena kata ton 19o kai tis arches tou 20ou aiōna (arches 19ou ai. hōs 1912) /. Iōannina : Athēna : 454 p. ; LC Card 84-137611
HD2346.G752 I566 1982

GUILDS - ITALY - VENICE - HISTORY.
Mackenney, Richard. Tradesmen and traders . London , c1987. xv, 289 p. : ISBN 0-7099-1763-5 LC Card 87-672566
HD6472.V4 M33x 1987b

GUILDS - MEXICO - MEXICO CITY - HISTORY.
Castro Gutiérrez, Felipe. La extinción de la artesanía gremial /. México , 1986. 188 p. ; ISBN 968-8374-01-6 LC Card 87-104891
HD6473.M64 M483 1986

GUILDS - NEW SPAIN - HISTORY.
Castro Gutiérrez, Felipe. La extinción de la artesanía gremial /. México , 1986. 188 p. ; ISBN 968-8374-01-6 LC Card 87-104891
HD6473.M64 M483 1986

GUILDS - SPAIN - BARCELONA - HISTORY - 18TH CENTURY.
Martinell, César, 1888-1973. L'antic Gremi d'Escultors de Barcelona /. Valls , 1956. 68 p. ; LC Card 86-180958
HD6473.S73 B356 1956

Guile, Bruce R. Technology and global industry . Washington, D.C. , 1987. vi, 272 p. : ISBN 0-309-03736-0 (pbk.) LC Card 87-7765 DDC 338/.06 19
HC79.T4 T438 1987

Guiley, Rosemary. Brownstone, David M. The manager's advisor /. New York , c1987. vii, 296 p. ; ISBN 0-8144-7682-1 (pbk.) : LC Card 87-47712 DDC 658.4 19
HD38.2 .B75 1987

Guilhaume, Philippe. Une volonté d'espérance : les nouveaux démocrates / Philippe Guilhaume. Paris : Encre, c1984. 218 p. ; 22 cm. ISBN 2-86418-178-9 : LC Card 84-163185
1. France - Economic policy - 1945-. 2. France - Social policy. I. Title.
HC276.2 .G785 1984

Guilhot, Bernard-Henri. Analyse bancaire de la P.M.E. / par Bernard-Henri Guilhot. Paris : La Revue Banque, c1985. 306 p. : ill. ; 30 cm. Includes bibliographies and index. ISBN 2-86325-035-3 : LC Card 86-152256
1. Small business - Finance. 2. Small business - Accounting. 3. Financial statements. I. Title.
HG4027.7 .G85 1985

Guiliani Cury, Hugo. Glosario de terminos de renegociacíon de deuda externa = Glossary of external debt renegotiation / Hugo Guilliani [i.e. Guiliani] Cury. Santo Domingo, República Dominicana : Banco Central de la República Dominicana, 1985. 68 p. ; 21 cm. English and Spanish. LC Card 86-184550
1. Debt relief - Dictionaries - Spanish. 2. Debts, External - Dictionaries - Spanish. 3. Debt relief - Dictionaries. 4. Debts, External - Dictionaries. 5. Spanish language - Dictionaries - English. 6. English language - Dictionaries - Spanish. I. Title. II. Title: Glossary of external debt renegotiation.
HJ8046 .G85 1985

Guillemin, Christophe. Delmas, Philippe. La stabilisation des prix des matières premières . Paris , 1983. vii, 359 p. : ISBN 2-7178-0657-1 : LC Card 84-116258
HF1051 .D38 1983

Guilloteau, Jean-François. Jean, Diane. Le travail à domicile dans le vêtement pour dames . [Montréal] [1982] xi, 146, [1] p. : ISBN 2-550-02847-3 LC Card 83-242834
HD6073.C62 C25 1982

Guiltinan, Joseph P.
Marketing management : strategies and programs / Joseph P. Guiltinan, Gordon W. Paul.3rd ed. New York : McGraw-Hill, c1988. xvi, 427 p. : ill. (some col.) ; 25 cm. (McGraw-Hill series in marketing) Includes bibliographies and index. ISBN 0-07-048929-7 : LC Card 87-23186 DDC 658.8 19
1. Marketing management. I. Paul, Gordon W. II. Title.
HF5415.13 .G84 1988

Schoell, William F. Marketing . Boston , 1987. p. cm. ISBN 0-205-10569-6 LC Card 87-23178 DDC 658.8 19
HF5415 .S357 1987

Guinea-Bissau . Galli, Rosemary. London , Boulder , 1987. xvi, 217 p., [1] leaf of plates : ISBN 1-555-87025-2 (U. S. : lib. bdg.) : LC Card 86-28011 DDC 966/.5703 19
HC1080 .G35 1987

GUINEA-BISSAU - ECONOMIC CONDITIONS - TO 1974.
Galli, Rosemary. Guinea-Bissau . London , Boulder , 1987. xvi, 217 p., [1] leaf of plates : ISBN 1-555-87025-2 (U. S. : lib. bdg.) : LC Card 86-28011 DDC 966/.5703 19
HC1080 .G35 1987

GUINEA-BISSAU - ECONOMIC CONDITIONS - 1974-
Galli, Rosemary. Guinea-Bissau . London , Boulder , 1987. xvi, 217 p., [1] leaf of plates : ISBN 1-555-87025-2 (U. S. : lib. bdg.) : LC Card 86-28011 DDC 966/.5703 19
HC1080 .G35 1987

GUINEA-BISSAU - POLITICS AND GOVERNMENT - TO 1974.
Galli, Rosemary. Guinea-Bissau . London , Boulder , 1987. xvi, 217 p., [1] leaf of plates : ISBN 1-555-87025-2 (U. S. : lib. bdg.) : LC Card 86-28011 DDC 966/.5703 19
HC1080 .G35 1987

GUINEA-BISSAU - POLITICS AND GOVERNMENT - 1974-
Galli, Rosemary. Guinea-Bissau . London , Boulder , 1987. xvi, 217 p., [1] leaf of plates : ISBN 1-555-87025-2 (U. S. : lib. bdg.) : LC Card 86-28011 DDC 966/.5703 19
HC1080 .G35 1987

GUINEA-BISSAU - POPULATION.
Ribeiro, Sérgio. Situação e perspectivas dos recursos humanos na República da Guiné-Bissau /. Addis Ababa [1984 or 1985] 49, 19 p., [8] leaves : LC Card 85-981187 DDC 331.11/0966/57 19
HD5849.A6 R53 1984

GUINEA-BISSAU - SOCIAL CONDITIONS.
Galli, Rosemary. Guinea-Bissau . London , Boulder , 1987. xvi, 217 p., [1] leaf of plates : ISBN 1-555-87025-2 (U. S. : lib. bdg.) : LC Card 86-28011 DDC 966/.5703 19
HC1080 .G35 1987

Guinea. Comité militaire de redressement national. Premières mesures de mise en application du programme du CMRN. 1ère éd. [Conakry, R.G. : Comité militaire de redressement national, 1984] 84 p. ; 24 cm. "Octobre 84"--Cover. LC Card 85-143345
1. Agriculture and state - Guinea. 2. Rural development - Guinea. 3. Guinea - Social policy. I. Title.
HD2143.Z8 G85 1984

GUINEA - COMMERCE.
Guinea (Revolutionäre Volksrepublik Guinea) . Köln , 1983. viii, 89 p. : LC Card 85-104313
HC1030 .G83 1983

GUINEA - ECONOMIC CONDITIONS - 1958-
Guinea (Revolutionäre Volksrepublik Guinea) . Köln , 1983. viii, 89 p. : LC Card 85-104313
HC1030 .G83 1983

GUINEA - ECONOMIC CONDITIONS - 1984-
Où allons nous?. [Conakry] [1986?] 92 p. ; LC Card 87-115579
HC1030 .O89 1986

GUINEA - POLITICS AND GOVERNMENT - 1958-
Où allons nous?. [Conakry] [1986?] 92 p. ; LC Card 87-115579
HC1030 .O89 1986

Guinea (Revolutionäre Volksrepublik Guinea) : Wirtschaftsstruktur / Bundesstelle für Aussenhandelsinformation (BFAI) ; [... in Zusammenarbeit mit Counterpart GmbH, Consulting & Marketing Service, Erftstadt]. Köln : Die Bundesstelle, 1983. viii, 89 p. : map ; 30 cm. (Marktinformation) Cover title. Includes bibliographical references. LC Card 85-104313
1. Guinea - Economic conditions - 1958-. 2. Guinea - Commerce. I. Bundesstelle für Aussenhandelsinformation (Germany). II. Counterpart GmbH. III. Series.
HC1030 .G83 1983

GUINEA - SOCIAL POLICY.
Guinea. Comité militaire de redressement national. Premières mesures de mise en application du programme du CMRN. [Conakry, R.G. , 1984] 84 p. ; LC Card 85-143345
HD2143.Z8 G85 1984

Guinée, où allons nous? Où allons nous?. [Conakry] [1986?] 92 p. ; LC Card 87-115579
HC1030 .O89 1986

Guinet, Jean. Petro chemical industry . Paris, France [Washington, D.C.] 1985. 161 p. : ISBN 92-64-12683-X (pbk.) : LC Card 85-177511 DDC 338.4/7661804 19
HD9579.C32 P48 1985

Guiton, R. J. (Raymond J.), 1915- Der Aufbruch : Forschungsbeiträge zur Dritten Welt / R.J. Guiton. Rheinfelden : Schäuble, c1984. 2 v. : ill. ; 21 cm. (Reihe Romanistik, 0174-0946 . Nr. 46-47) Contains articles which first appeared 1952/53 and 1960/65 in Europa-Archiv. Includes indexes. Includes bibliographies. CONTENTS. - Bd. 1. Der Zerfall des französischen Kolonialreichs -- Bd. 2. Das Wagnis der Unabhängigkeit. ISBN 3-87718-746-3 (Bd. 1) LC Card 85-181833 DDC 325/.344/09 19
1. France - Colonies - History - 20th century. 2. France - Colonies - Economic conditions. 3. Developing countries - Politics and government. 4. Developing countries - Economic conditions. I. Title.
JV1818 .G85 1984 ***NYPL [JFK 86-364]***

Gujarat Energy Development Agency. Energy use in rural Gujarat /. New Delhi , c1987. iv, 186 p. : ISBN 81-204-0216-2 : LC Card 87-901949 DDC 333.79/13/095475 19
HD9502.I43 G844 1987

GUJARAT (INDIA) - APPROPRIATIONS AND EXPENDITURES - HISTORY.
Reddy, K. N. (Kaipa Narayana), 1936- Central government expenditure . New Delhi , 1984. xvi, 175 p. ; LC Card 84-901866 DDC 336.3/9/0954 19
HJ2157 .R43 1984 ***NYPL [JLD 87-66]***

GUJARAT (INDIA) - CENSUS, 1981.
Census of India, 1981. Delhi , <1983-1986. v. in : LC Card 87-915012 DDC 304.6/0954/75021 19
HA4587.G84 C46 1983

GUJARAT (INDIA) - ECONOMIC POLICY - 1980-
Gujarat (India). General Administration Dept. (Planning) Draft Seventh Five Year Plan 1985-90 and Annual Plan 1985-86. [Gandhinagar] , 1985. iii, 629 p. : LC Card 87-900571 DDC 338.954/75 19
HC437.G85 G7 1985

Gujarat (India). General Administration Dept. (Planning) Draft Seventh Five Year Plan 1985-90 and Annual Plan 1985-86. [Gandhinagar] : Planning Division, General Administration Dept., Govt. of Gujarat, 1985. iii, 629 p. : ill., folded col. maps ; 31 cm. LC Card 87-900571 DDC 338.954/75 19
1. Gujarat (India) - Economic policy - 1980-. I. Title.
HC437.G85 G7 1985

GUJARAT (INDIA) - SCHEDULED TRIBES - CASE STUDIES.
Pathy, Jaganath, 1948- Tribal peasantry dynamics of development /. New Delhi , 1984, c1983. xiii, 233 p. : LC Card 84-900095 DDC 330.954/75052 19
HD879.G8 P37 1984 ***NYPL [JLD 87-724]***

Gujarātanāṃ bandaro . Rajyagor, S. B. Amadāvāda , 1986. 6, 167 p. : LC Card 87-900295
HE559.I4 R34 1986

Gujarati, Damodar N. Basic econometrics / Damodar N. Gujarati. 2nd ed. New York : McGraw-Hill, c1988. xxv, 705 p. : ill. ; 25 cm. Includes indexes. Bibliography: p. 692-693. ISBN 0-07-025188-6 : LC Card 87-9268 DDC 330/.028 19
1. Econometrics. I. Title.
HB139 .G84 1988

Gukov, Vladimir Pavlovich. Metodologicheskie problemy formirovaniia territorial'no-proizvodstvennykh kompleksov /. Novosibirsk , 1980. 162 p. : LC Card 82-106930
HC336.25 .M46 1980

Gulati, Ashok, 1954- Agricultural price policy in India : an econometric approach, with special reference to wheat / Ashok Gulati. New Delhi : Concept Pub. Co., 1987, c1985. 196 p. : ill. ; 23 cm. Originally presented as the author's thesis (Ph. D.--University of Delhi, 1985) under the title: Some aspects of agricultural price policy-- a case study of wheat in India. Bibliography: p. [180]-192. Includes index. LC Card 86-903595 DDC 338.1/8 19
1. Agricultural prices - India. 2. Agricultural price supports - India. 3. Wheat - Prices - India. I. Title.
HD2073 .G85 1987

Gul'binskas, A. N. (Al'binas Nikodemovich) Tendentsii razvitiia passazhirskikh perevozok v Litovskoĭ SSR . Vil'nius , 1985. 179 p. : LC Card 86-199868
HE255.Z7 L577 1985

Guldimann, Werner, 1916- Mensch und Luftfahrt . Bern [1981] 177 p. : LC Card 83-116416
HE9863.A4 M45 1981

GULDIMANN, WERNER, 1916-
Mensch und Luftfahrt . Bern [1981] 177 p. : LC Card 83-116416
HE9863.A4 M45 1981

Gulf Futures, Inc. Perspective on world energy . Arlington, Va. (1911 Fort Myer Dr., Suite 403, Arlington 22209) , c1987. 3, iii, 27, [19] p. : LC Card 87-142737 DDC 333.79 19
HD9560.5 .P3847 1987

Gulf in the early twentieth century. The Gulf in the early 20th century . [Durham] , c1986. 215 p., [1] leaf of plates : LC Card 87-100795 DDC 330.953/6 19
HC415.3 .G85 1986

The Gulf in the early 20th century : foreign institutions and local responses / edited by R.I. Lawless. [Durham] : University of Durham, Centre for Middle Eastern and Islamic Studies, c1986. 215 p., [1] leaf of plates : ill. ; 21 cm. (Occasional papers series, 0307-0654 . no. 31 (1986)) Includes bibliographies. LC Card 87-100795 DDC 330.953/6 19
1. Persian Gulf region - Economic conditions. 2. Petroleum industry and trade - Persian Gulf region. 3. Persian Gulf Region - Economic policy. I. Lawless, Richard I. II. Title: Gulf in the early twentieth century. III. Series: Occasional papers series (University of Durham. Centre for Middle Eastern and Islamic Studies) , no. 31.
HC415.3 .G85 1986

GULF INTRACOASTAL WATERWAY.
The Gulf Intracoastal Waterway in Texas . [Austin] , 1982. 1 v. (various pagings) : LC Card 83-620632
HE631.T4 G44 1982

The Gulf Intracoastal Waterway in Texas : presented in response to the Texas Coastal Waterway Act of 1975 and submitted to the Sixty-eighth session of the Texas Legislature / prepared by the State Department of Highways and Public Transportation, Transportation Planning Division. [Austin] : The Division, 1982. 1 v. (various pagings) : ill. (some col.) ; 28 cm. Includes bibliography. LC Card 83-620632
1. Coastwise shipping - Texas. 2. Intracoastal waterways - Texas. 3. Gulf Intracoastal Waterway. 4. Texas - Economic conditions. I. Texas. Transportation Planning Division.
HE631.T4 G44 1982

Gulf South Research Institute. Secondary benefits associated with the Red River Waterway, Mississippi River to Shreveport, Louisiana . Baton Rouge, La. (P.O. Box 14787, Baton Rouge 70898) [1986] 2 v. : LC Card 87-620750 DDC 330.9766/6053 19
HC107.A15 S43 1986

The Gulf States =. Bazarian, Carl J. New York,

N.Y. , c1980. 577 p. : ISBN 0-916006-07-7 LC Card 80-65496
HC415.3 .B39 1980

Gullickson, Gay L. Spinners and weavers of Auffay : rural industry and the sexual division of labor in a French village, 1750-1850 / Gay L. Gullickson. Cambridge [Cambridgeshire] ; New York : Cambridge University Press, 1986. x, 256 p. : ill. ; 24 cm. Includes index. Bibliography: p. 235-250. ISBN 0-521-32280-4 LC Card 86-6808 DDC 331.4/877/02822094425 19
1. Weavers - France - Auffay - History. 2. Sexual division of labor - France - Auffay - History. 3. Auffay (France) - Occupations - History. I. Title.
HD8039.T42 F834 1986
NYPL [JLE 87-1054]

Guma, Xolile P. Small farmer credit and small farmer attitudes towards co-operatives / by Xolile P. Guma and Vakashile R. Simelane. [Kwaluseni, Swaziland] : University of Swaziland, Social Science Research Unit, [1982] 94 p. : ill. ; 30 cm. (Research paper . no. 8) "September 1982" "Under the auspices of the Social Science Research Unit, University of Swaziland for the Department of Co-operative Development, Ministry of Agriculture and co-operatives." Includes bibliographies. LC Card 86-101161 DDC 332.7/1/096813 19
1. Agriculture, Cooperative - Swaziland. 2. Agricultural credit - Swaziland. 3. Farmers - Swaziland - Attitudes. I. Simelane, Vakashile R. II. University of Swaziland. Social Science Research Unit. III. Series: Research paper (University of Swaziland. Social Science Research Unit) , no. 8. IV. Title.
HD1491.S855 G85 1982
NYPL [JLG 86-262]

Gummesson, Rolf. Finnland : frühe Ortsstempel / Rolf Gummesson. [Sweden : s.n., 1964] ([Kristianstad] : Kristianstads Länstryckeri) 96 p. : ill. ; 21 cm. Bibliography: p. 95-96. LC Card 86-209484
1. Postmarks - Finland. I. Title.
HE6185.F5 G85 1964

Gummivaruindustri : industrigummi. Stockholm : Statens industriverk, 1981. 119, [12] p. : ill. ; 30 cm. (SIND PM, 0346-573X . 1981:5) Includes bibliographical references. ISBN 91-38-06243-7 LC Card 82-241338
1. Rubber industry and trade - Sweden. 2. Rubber goods - Sweden. I. Sweden. Statens industriverk. II. Series.
HD9161.S82 G84 1981

GUMS AND RESINS INDUSTRY - INDIA.
Gurdev Singh. Resin systems in India . Bombay , 1986. xiii, 100 p. ; ISBN 0-86132-128-6 : LC Card 86-903469 DDC 338.4/766837/0954 19
HD9660.R43 I44 1986

Gunatilleke, Godfrey. Migration of Asian workers to the Arab world /. Tokyo, Japan , c1986. v, 358 p. ; ISBN 92-808-0555-X (pbk.) LC Card 87-131112 DDC 331.6/2/50174927 19
HD8656 .M53 1986

Gunda, Béla. Árucsere és migráció . Miskolc , 1986. 237 p. : ISBN 963-01-6995-9 : LC Card 87-409685
HD5856.H9 A78 1986

GUNDA, BÉLA.
Árucsere és migráció . Miskolc , 1986. 237 p. : ISBN 963-01-6995-9 : LC Card 87-409685
HD5856.H9 A78 1986

Gunderson, Ralph O. Agricultural and socioeconomic perspectives of Arkansas : counties and regions / Ralph O. Gunderson and Enrique Ospina. Morrilton, AR : Winrock International, 1987. p. cm. "May 1987." Bibliography: p. ISBN 0-933595-13-1 : LC Card 87-24146 DDC 338.1/09767 19
1. Agriculture - Economic aspects - Arkansas. I. Ospina, Enrique. II. Winrock International Institute for Agricultural Development. III. Title.
HD1775.A8 G85 1987

Gunn, Christopher Eaton. Alternatives to economic orthodoxy . Armonk, N.Y. , c1987. 348 p. : ISBN 0-87332-409-9 : LC Card 86-33899 DDC 330 19
HB171 .A47 1987

Gunn, Thomas G. Manufacturing for competitive advantage : becoming a world class manufacturer / Thomas G. Gunn. Cambridge, Mass. : Ballinger Pub. Co., c1987. xvi, 221 p. ; 24 cm. Bibliography: p. 215-216. Includes index. ISBN 0-88730-154-1 LC Card 87-1093 DDC 658 19
1. United States - Manufactures - Management. 2. Manufacturing processes - United States. 3. Competition, International. I. Title.
HD9725 .G85 1987

Gunner and Edwards on the carriage of crude oil by sea /. Gunner, T. J. London , New York , 1986. xii, 137 p. : ISBN 1-85044-073-5 (pbk.) : LC Card 86-224898 DDC 387.5/448 19
HE595.P4 G86 1986

Gunner, T. J. Gunner and Edwards on the carriage of crude oil by sea / T.J. Gunner, D.A. Edwards. London ; New York : Lloyd's of London Press, 1986. xii, 137 p. : ill. ; 21 cm. Includes bibliographies. ISBN 1-85044-073-5 (pbk.) : LC Card 86-224898 DDC 387.5/448 19
1. Petroleum - Transportation. 2. Shipping. I. Edwards, D. A. II. Title. III. Title: Carriage of crude oil by sea.
HE595.P4 G86 1986

GUNNING. see **HUNTING.**

GUNSMITHS - PENNSYLVANIA - PHILADELPHIA - REGISTERS.
Whisker, James B., 1939- Arms makers of Philadelphia /. [Morgantown, W. Va.?] [1987?] 32 p., [1] leaf of plates : LC Card 87-124428 DDC 338.7/623422/02574811 19
HD9743.U7 P48 1987

Gunston, Bill. The Grumman story / Bill Gunston. New York : Orion Books, 1988, c1987. p. cm. ISBN 0-517-56796-2 : LC Card 87-21964 DDC 338.7/6291/0973 19
1. Grumman Aerospace Corporation - History. 2. Grumman airplanes - History. 3. Aerospace industries - United States - History. 4. Aircraft industry - United States - History. I. Title.
HD9711.5.U63 G784 1988

Gunter, Erwin R. Skinner, Hubert C. The new Dietz Confederate States catalog and handbook /. Miami, Fla. (1007 Kane Concourse, Bay Harbor Islands 33154) , 1986. viii, 270 p. : LC Card 86-206685 DDC 769.56975/075/0973 19
HE6500 .S58 1986

Gunton, Tony, 1943- Business information technology : end user focus / Tony Gunton. Englewood Cliffs, N.J. : Prentice Hall International, 1988. p. cm. Bibliography: p. Includes index. ISBN 0-13-100843-9 LC Card 87-7365 DDC 658/.05 19
1. Business - Data processing. 2. Business - Communication systems. 3. Information technology. I. Title.
HF5548.2 .G86 1988

Guowaishangyeyanjiuziliao. Kuo wai shang yeh yen chiu tzu liao /. [Peking] , 1984. 3, 604 p. ;
NYPL [*OVY 86-3606]

Gup, Benton E. Principles of financial management / Benton E. Gup. 2nd ed. New York : Wiley, c1987. xii, 672, 16 p. : col. ill. ; 25 cm. Includes index. ISBN 0-471-81203-X LC Card 86-28937 DDC 658.1/5 19
1. Business enterprises - Finance. 2. Corporations - Finance. I. Title.
HG4026 .G88 1987

Gupta, Anand P. Fiscal policy and the poor / Anand P. Gupta. New Delhi : Oxford & IBH, c1984. 90 p. ; 23 cm. Includes bibliographical references. LC Card 84-900303 DDC 339.5/2/0954 19
1. Fiscal policy - India. 2. Economic assistance, Domestic - India. 3. Rural employment - Government policy - India. I. Title.
HJ1331 .G87 1984 ***NYPL [JLD 87-778]***

Gupta, B. L. (Babu Lal), 1949- Trade and commerce in Rajasthan during the 18th century / by B.L. Gupta. Jaipur : Jaipur Pub. House, 1987. iv, 274 p. : maps ; 22 cm. Originally presented as the author's thesis (Ph. D.--Rajasthan University, 1984) Bibliography: p. [250]-268. Includes index. LC Card 87-902534 DDC 380.1/0954/4 19
1. Rajasthan (India) - Commerce - History - 18th century. I. Title.
HF3789.R33 G86 1987

Gupta, B. P. Industrial relations . New Delhi , 1986. 254 p. ; LC Card 87-902682
HD8686.5.I575 1978

Gupta, D. P. (Dharm Pall), 1932- Agricultural development in Haryana / D.P. Gupta ; with a foreword by H. Laxminarayan. New Delhi, India : Agricole Pub. Academy, 1985. xiii, 120 p. : ill. ; 23 cm. (Agricultural development in India series . vol. 4) Agricole monographs ; 30 At head of title: Agricultural Economics Research Centre, University of Delhi, Delhi. Includes index. LC Card 85-901427 DDC 338.1/854558 19
1. Agriculture - Economic aspects - India - Haryana. 2. Agriculture and state - India - Haryana. I. University of Delhi. Agricultural Economics Research Centre. II. Title. III. Series.
HD2075.H3 G85 1985
NYPL [JLD 86-3862]

Gupta, Ravindra, 1942- Jilā janagaṇanā hastapustikā . [Lakhanaū] [1983] xi, 174, ii p., [5] folded leaves of plates : LC Card 86-903117
HA4587.J48 J55 1983

Gupta, S. C., 1954- Institutional financing and industrial growth : with special reference to cotton textiles industry in India / S.C. Gupta.1st ed. Jaipur : Adarsh Prakashan, 1987. xx, 316 p. (some folded) : ill. ; 22 cm. Originally presented as the author's thesis (Ph. D.--University of Rajasthan, 1985) under the title: Role of development banks in financing cotton textiles industry in India. Bibliography: p. [302]-307. Includes index. LC Card 87-900864
1. Cotton textile industry - India - Finance. 2. Development banks - India. I. Title.
HD9886.I42 G83 1987

Gupta, S. P. (Shiv Prakash), 1957- Structural dimensions of poverty in India / S.P. Gupta. Delhi, India : Mittal Publications, 1987. xii, 427 p. : ill. ; 22 cm. Bibliography: p. [372]-415. Includes index. LC Card 87-901423 DDC 362.5/0954 19
1. Poor - India. 2. Social structure - India. 3. India - Economic conditions - 1947-. I. Title.
HC440.P6 G86 1987

Gupta, Satya Prakash, 1940- The agrarian system of eastern Rajasthan, c. 1650-c. 1750 / Satya Prakash Gupta. Delhi : Manohar, 1986. xvi, 352 p. : maps (some folded) ; 23 cm. "Centre of Advanced Study in History, Aligarh Muslim University." Revision of the author's thesis (Ph. D.--Aligarh Muslim University, 1974) Bibliography: p. [317]-338. Includes index. ISBN 81-85054-11-8 : LC Card 87-900814 DDC 338.1/0954/4 19
1. Agriculture and state - India - Rajasthan - History. 2. Agricultural systems - India - Rajasthan - History. 3. Rajasthan, India - Rural conditions. I. Aligarh Muslim University. Centre of Advanced Study in History. II. Title.
HD2075.R27 G86 1986

Gupta, Shaibal. Bihar, stagnation or growth /. Patna , 1987. xxix, 404 p. ; LC Card 87-902676 DDC 330.954/12052 19
HC437.B47 B49 1987

Gupta, Uttam. Impact of credit on fertiliser consumption / [by Uttam Gupta]. New Delhi : Fertiliser Association of India, [1986] 158 p. ; 23 cm. "November 1986." Bibliography: p. 158. LC Card 87-900336 DDC 338.4/766862/0954 19
1. Fertilizer industry - India. 2. Agricultural credit - India. I. Fertiliser Association of India. II. Title.
HD9483.I42 G86 1986

Gupta, V. K. Gaikwad, V. R., 1933- Managing paddy-rice business of small farmers . Bombay , 1986. xxiii, 239 p. : ISBN 0-86132-129-4 : LC Card 86-903247 DDC 334/.68318/0954 19
HD9066.A7 G35 1986

Gurdev Singh.
Financing of kapas-cloth system / Gurdev Singh, S.P. Seetharaman. New Delhi : Oxford & IBH Pub. Co., c1987. xi, 59 p. ; 23 cm. On the role of institutional finance in cotton textile industry in India. ISBN 81-204-0217-0 : LC Card 87-902510 DDC 338.4/367721/0954 19
1. Cotton textile industry - India - Finance. I. Seetharaman, S. P. II. Title.
HD9886.I42 G87 1987

Resin systems in India : economic and management aspects / Gurdev Singh, S.R. Asokan. Bombay : Popular Prakashan, 1986. xiii, 100 p. ; 23 cm. (CMA monograph. no. 112) Bibliography: p. 99-100. ISBN 0-86132-128-6 : LC Card 86-903469 DDC 338.4/766837/0954 19
1. Gums and resins industry - India. I. Asokan, S. R. II. Title.
HD9660.R43 I44 1986

Gurevich, M. N. (Maĭia Naumovna) Shister, G. A. (Grigoriĭ Aronovich) Rukovodstvo kompartii Uzbekistana podgotovkoĭ rabochikh kadrov v usloviiakh razvitogo sotsializma /. Tashkent ,

1981. 274, [2] p. ; LC Card 82-204041
HD5797.U9 S54 1981

Gurney, Kathleen. Your money personality : how it is and how you can profit from it / Kathleen Gurney. New York : Doubleday, 1988. p. cm. Includes index. ISBN 0-385-24254-9 LC Card 87-24449 DDC 332.4/01/9 19
1. Money - Psychological aspects. I. Title.
HG222.3 .G87 1988

Gurría Gascón, José Luis.
Alvarado Corrales, Eduardo J. Extremadura . Cáceres [1984?] 101 p. : ISBN 84-600-3663-4 LC Card 86-165503
HD1333.S712 E783 1984

El paisaje de montaña en Extremadura : delimitacíon, economía y poblacíon / José L. Gurría Gascón. Cáceres : Servicio de Publicaciones de la Universidad de Extremadura, [1985?] 273 p. : ill. ; 24 cm. + 18 maps. "Un extracto de la Tesis Doctoral, presentada en la Universidad de Extremadura en setiembre de 1983"--Colophon. Includes bibliographical references. ISBN 84-600-3949-8 LC Card 87-111451
1. Estremadura, Spain - Economic conditions. 2. Estremadura (Spain) - Population. 3. Physical geography - Spain - Estremadura. 4. Land use - Spain - Estremadura. I. Title.
HC387.E7 G87 1985

Guru, D. D. Energy and economic development / D.D. Guru and Qamar Ahsan. Delhi : Amar Prakashan, c1987. xi, 257 p. : ill. ; 23 cm. Spine title: Energy & economic development. Bibliography: p. 248-251. Includes index. ISBN 81-85061-53-6 : LC Card 87-901433 DDC 333.79/0954 19
1. Power resources - India. 2. Energy policy - India. 3. India - Economic conditions - 1947-. I. Ahsan, Qamar. II. Title. III. Title: Energy & economic development.
HD9502.I4 G87 1987

Gurung, Harka B. Food systems and society in Nepal : an overview / by Harka Gurung. Kathmandu, Nepal : New ERA, 1981. 53, iii p. : 2 folded maps ; 33 cm. (New ERA occasional paper . no. 002) Bibliography: p. iii. LC Card 83-901141 DDC 338.1/9/5496 19
1. Food supply - Nepal. 2. Agriculture - Economic aspects - Nepal. 3. Agriculture and state - Nepal. I. Title. II. Series.
HD9016.N42 G87 1981 ***NYPL [JLG 86-71]***

Guseĭnova, D. S. Rabochie-moriāki Kaspiīa : 90-e gody XIX v.--1907 g. / D.S. Guseĭnova. Baku : Izd-vo "Ėlm", 1981. 113 p. ; 21 cm. Title in colophon: Khăzăr făhlă-dănizchilări. At head of title: Akademiīa nauk Azerbaĭdzhanskoĭ SSR. Institut istorii. Includes bibliographical references. LC Card 82-166385
1. Seamen - Caspian Sea - History - 19th century. 2. Seamen - Azerbaijan S.S.R. - History - 19th century. 3. Shipping - Caspian Sea - History - 19th century. 4. Shipping - Azerbaijan S.S.R. - History - 19th century. I. Title. II. Title: Khăzăr făhlă-dănizchilări.
HD8039.S42 C424 1981

Gusev, S. G. (Sergeĭ Georgievich) Razumovskiĭ, A. V. (Al'bert Vadimovich) Ėkonomika promyshlennosti stroitel'nykh materialov /. Moskva , 1986. 350 p. : LC Card 86-204591
HD9715.8.S652 R39 1986

Gushchina, V. V. Rabochie Sibiri v bor'be za sotsialisticheskuīu revoliūtsiīu i postroenie sotsializma . Novosibirsk , 1975. 119 p. ; LC Card 85-187793
HD8529.S652 R283 1975

Gutek, Barbara A. Sex role stereotyping and affirmative action policy /. Los Angeles, Calif. , c1982. 227 p. : LC Card 82-623259 DDC 331.4/133 19
HD6060 .S49 1982 ***NYPL [JLD 87-275]***

Gutenberg, Erich, 1897- Neuere Entwicklungen in der Unternehmenstheorie . Wiesbaden , c1982. xiii, 290 p. : ISBN 3-409-39810-4 LC Card 87-672661
HD35 .N4814x 1982

GUTENBERG, ERICH, 1897-
Neuere Entwicklungen in der Unternehmenstheorie . Wiesbaden , c1982. xiii, 290 p. : ISBN 3-409-39810-4 LC Card 87-672661
HD35 .N4814x 1982

Guth, Suzie. Exil sous contrat : les communautés de coopérants en Afrique francophone / Suzie Guth. Paris : Agence de coopération culturelle et technique : Silex, c1984. 479 p. : ill. ; 22 cm. Bibliography: p. 445-460. Includes index. ISBN 2-903871-53-1 : LC Card 85-141675
1. Economic assistance, French - Africa. 2. France - Foreign economic relations - Africa. I. Agence de coopération culturelle et technique. II. Title.
HC800 .G88 1984

Gutiérrez, Horácio. Costa, Iraci del Nero da. Paraná . São Paulo , 1985. 185 p. : LC Card 86-158196
HA984 .C67 1985

Gutiérrez, Miguel. Cobriza, Cobriza, 1971 /. [Lima? Peru] , 1981. 136 p. ; LC Card 83-106108
HD5361 .M612 1971

Gutiérrez, Sara. Cohen, Noemí. Trabajadores y seguridad social en América Latina /. México, D.F. [1982], c1981. 146 p. ; ISBN 968-8241-38-5 LC Card 83-140620 DDC 368.4/0098 19
HD7130.5 .C63 1982 ***NYPL [JLD 86-2768]***

Gutiérrez Urrutia, Mario. Reflexiones sobre apertura financiera : el caso chileno / Mario Gutiérrez Urrutia. Santiago : Banco Central de Chile, 1982. 36 p. : ill. ; 27 cm. (Serie de estudios económicos . no. 14) Bibliography: p. 29. LC Card 82-203323
1. Monetary policy - Chile. I. Series: Serie de estudios económicos (Banco Central de Chile) , no. 14. II. Title.
HG845 .G87 1982

Gutiérrez y Ulloa, Antonio. Libro de la razón general de hacienda nacional : de la Provincia de Guadalajara, hoy Estado Libre de Jalisco / Antonio Gutiérrez y Ulloa. Guadalajara, Jalisco, México : Gobierno de Jalisco, Secretaría General, Unidad Editorial, 1983. 222 p. ; 23 cm. (Colección Historia. Serie Estadísticas básicas . no. 2) Previously published: Guadalajara : Impr. Léon Domínguez, 1882. ISBN 968-8320-48-X LC Card 87-401751 DDC 336.72/35 19
1. Finance, Public - Mexico - Jalisco - History. I. Title. II. Series.
HJ805.J3 G87 1983

Gutiérrez Zermeño, Rodolfo, 1953- Movimiento obrero en Jalisco, período 1925-1930 / Rodolfo Gutiérrez Zermeño. Guadalajara, Jalisco, México : Gobierno de Jalisco, Secretaría General, Unidad Editorial, 1985. 64 p. ; 21 cm. (Temática jalisciense . no. 12) Bibliography: p. 63-64. ISBN 968-8322-01-6 LC Card 86-208368
1. Trade-unions - Mexico - Jalisco - History - 20th century. 2. Trade-unions - Mexico - Jalisco - Political activity - History - 20th century. I. Title. II. Series.
HD6535.J35 G88 1985

Gutkind, Peter Claus Wolfgang. International labour and the Third World . Aldershot, Hants, England , c1987. xii, 283 p. ; ISBN 0-566-00971-4 : LC Card 86-31791 DDC 331/.09172/4 19
HD8943 .I55 1987

Gutman, Herbert George, 1928- Power & culture : essays on the American working class / Herbert G. Gutman ; edited by Ira Berlin.1st ed. New York, N.Y. : Pantheon Books, c1987. xi, 452 p. ; 25 cm. Bibliography: p. [413]-444. Includes index. ISBN 0-394-56171-6 LC Card 87-43018 DDC 305.5/62/0973 19
1. Labor and laboring classes - United States - History. 2. Afro-Americans - History. 3. Slavery - United States - History. I. Berlin, Ira, 1941-. II. Title. III. Title: Power and culture.
HD8072 .G97 1987

Gutmann, Gernot. Aussenwirtschaft der DDR und innerdeutsche Wirtschaftsbeziehungen . Berlin , c1986. 98 p. ; ISBN 3-428-06121-7 LC Card 87-137949 DDC 382/.0943/0431 19
HF3570.5.Z7 G352 1986

Gutmann, Hermann. Scheidulin, Hans. Die Häfen Bremen, Bremerhaven /. Bremen , c1985. 160 p. : ISBN 3-920699-63-7 LC Card 86-124602 DDC 330.943/52 19
HC289.B72 S34 1985

Gutowski, Armin.
Indebtedness and growth in developing countries /. Hamburg , 1986. 344 p. ; ISBN 3-87895-300-3 (pbk.) LC Card 86-213057 DDC 336.3/435/091724 19
HJ8899 .I53 1986

Die Internationale Schuldenkrise . Berlin , 1986. 179 p. : ISBN 3-428-05972-7 LC Card 86-172589
HJ8899 .I58 1986

Der Neue Protektionismus /. Hamburg , 1984. 149 p. ; ISBN 3-87895-251-1 LC Card 84-222112
HF1703 .N48 1984

Guts . Lyons, John, 1940- New York, NY , c1987. viii, 317 p. : ISBN 0-8144-5537-9 LC Card 86-47816 DDC 659.1 19
HF5823 .L92 1987

Guīsaĭt, E. M. (Evgeniĭ Mikhel'evich) Vanags, I. ĪA. (Ilmar ĪAnovich) Ėffektivnoe ispol'zovanie vychislitel'noĭ tekhniki /. Moskva , 1982. 142, [2] p. : LC Card 83-165693
HF5548.2 .V345 1982

Guvenen, O. International macroeconomic modelling for policy decisions /. Dordrecht , Boston , c1986. viii, 269 p. : ISBN 90-247-3201-8 LC Card 85-13698 DDC 337/.0724 19
HF1410.5 .I577 1986 ***NYPL [JLE 86-3469]***

Guy, Dan M. Meals, Dennis R. Guide to compilation and review engagements /. Fort Worth, Tex. , c1986- 3 v. (loose-leaf) : LC Card 86-224183 DDC 657/.3 19
HF5667.65 .M42 1986

Guy, Duane F. Texas 47--Deaf Smith : a history of Deaf Smith Electric Cooperative, Inc. : 1936 to 1986, the first 50 years / by Duane F. Guy. [Hereford, Tex.] : Deaf Smith County Electric Cooperative, c1986. vii, 160 p. : ill. ; 24 cm. Illustrations on lining papers. Bibliography: p. [145]-158. Includes index. LC Card 86-210662 DDC 334/.682131/09764835 19
1. Deaf Smith Electric Cooperative - History. 2. Rural electrification - Texas - History. I. Title. II. Title: Texas forty-seven.
HD9688.U54 D434 1986

Guy F. Atkinson Company of California . Atkinson, Ray N. New York , 1985, c1986. 24 p. : LC Card 86-61271 DDC 338.7/624/0973 19
HD9715.U54 G882 1986

GUY F. ATKINSON COMPANY OF CALIFORNIA - HISTORY.
Atkinson, Ray N. Guy F. Atkinson Company of California . New York , 1985, c1986. 24 p. : LC Card 86-61271 DDC 338.7/624/0973 19
HD9715.U54 G882 1986

GUYANA - COMMERCE.
British Guiana. [British Guiana] [1962] 47 p. : LC Card 85-215673
HC207 .B75 1962

GUYANA - ECONOMIC CONDITIONS.
British Guiana. [British Guiana] [1962] 47 p. : LC Card 85-215673
HC207 .B75 1962

McLewin, Philip J., 1939- Power and economic change . New York , 1987. ii, 271 p. : ISBN 0-8240-1366-2 (alk. paper) : LC Card 87-8344 DDC 330.97292/04 19
HC154 .M36 1987

GUYANA - INDUSTRIES.
British Guiana. [British Guiana] [1962] 47 p. : LC Card 85-215673
HC207 .B75 1962

GUYANA - INDUSTRIES - DIRECTORIES.
Carnet d'adresses /. [Pointe-à-Pitre, Guadeloupe] [1986?] 64 p. : LC Card 87-152834
HG3729.G862 C37 1986

GUYANA - POLITICS AND GOVERNMENT - 1803-1966.
McLewin, Philip J., 1939- Power and economic change . New York , 1987. ii, 271 p. : ISBN 0-8240-1366-2 (alk. paper) : LC Card 87-8344 DDC 330.97292/04 19
HC154 .M36 1987

Guyenne . Desharnais, Marcel, 1924- Montréal, Québec , c1983. 182 p. : ISBN 2-89035-062-2 LC Card 84-127460
HD3450.G89 D47 1983

Guyenne-- et après-- . Desharnais, Marcel, 1924- Guyenne . Montréal, Québec , c1983. 182 p. : ISBN 2-89035-062-2 LC Card 84-127460
HD3450.G89 D47 1983

GUYENNE (QUÉBEC) - COLONIZATION - HISTORY.
Desharnais, Marcel, 1924- Guyenne . Montréal, Québec , c1983. 182 p. : ISBN 2-89035-062-2 LC Card 84-127460
HD3450.G89 D47 1983

Guyer, Jane I. Feeding African cities . Bloomington , c1987. x, 249 p. ; ISBN

0-253-32102-6 LC Card 86-46323 DDC 338.1/9/6 19
HD9017.A2 F44 1987

Guyot, F. Eléments de microéconomie / F. Guyot. Paris : Editions Technip, 1985. 310 p. : ill. ; 25 cm. (Publications de l'Institut français du pétrole) At head of title: Institut français du pétrole, Ecole nationale supérieure du pétrole et des moteurs, Centre d'études supérieures d'économie pétrolière. Bibliography: p. 291. Includes indexes. ISBN 2-7108-0479-4 LC Card 86-210675
1. Microeconomics. I. Ecole nationale supérieure du pétrole et des moteurs (France). Centre d'études supérieures d'économie pétrolière. II. Title.
HB173 .G88 1985

Guzevatyĭ, IAropolk Nikolaevich. Trudovye resursy Vostoka . Moskva , 1987. 319 p. ; LC Card 87-142995
HD5811.85.A6 T78 1987

Guzmán, Gonzalo. see **Guzmán Ortega, Gonzalo.**

Guzmán Ortega, Gonzalo.
Como justificar la pobreza en un país subdesarrollado. Guzmán Ortega, Gonzalo. Superestructuras y subdesarrollo : visión de un país tercer mundista / Gonzalo Guzmán Ortega. Quito , 1985. 178 p. : LC Card 86-132144
HC59.7 .G86 1985

Superestructuras y subdesarrollo : visión de un país tercer mundista / Gonzalo Guzmán Ortega. Quito : Casa de la Cultura Ecuatoriana, 1985. 178 p. : ill. ; 22 cm. Rev. ed. of: Como justificar la pobreza en un país subdesarrollado. 1972. Errata slip inserted. LC Card 86-132144
1. Developing countries - Economic conditions. 2. Economic development. 3. Developing countries - Social conditions. I. Guzmán Ortega, Gonzalo. Como justificar la pobreza en un país subdesarrollado. II. Casa de la Cultura Ecuatoriana. III. Title.
HC59.7 .G86 1985

Guzmán S., José I. (José Ignacio).
Hora trágica. 1983. Capelo C., J. Alejo (J. Alejo Capelo Cabello), d. 1973. El crimen del 15 de noviembre de 1922 / por J. Alejo Capelo C. Rasgos salientes de la tragedia histórica de noviembre de 1922 / por Segundo Ramos. La hora trágica : (15 de noviembre de 1922) y otros apuntes sobre el movimiento obrero / por José I. Guzmán S. [Guayaquil] , 1983. 10, 14, 19 p. : LC Card 86-114097
HD5358.A6 C36 1983

Guzzo, Richard A. Programs for productivity and quality of work life / by Richard A. Guzzo. 1st ed. New York : Pergamon Press, c1983. 38 p. ; 28 cm. (Work in America Institute studies in productivity . 32) Bibliography: p. 31-38. ISBN 0-08-030964-X (pbk.) : LC Card 83-22029 DDC 658.3/14 19
1. Labor productivity - United States - Abstracts. 2. Quality of work life - United States - Abstracts. I. Title. II. Series.
HC110.L3 G89 1983 ***NYPL [JLM 83-380 no.32]***

GWEMBE DISTRICT, ZAMBIA - ECONOMIC CONDITIONS.
Strengthening local linkages for socioeconomic development at regional level . Berlin [1986] 2 v. : LC Card 87-143388 DDC 338.96894 19
HC915.Z7 G847 1986

GWEMBE DISTRICT (ZAMBIA) - POLITICS AND GOVERNMENT.
Strengthening local linkages for socioeconomic development at regional level . Berlin [1986] 2 v. : LC Card 87-143388 DDC 338.96894 19
HC915.Z7 G847 1986

GWEMBE DISTRICT (ZAMBIA) - RURAL CONDITIONS.
Strengthening local linkages for socioeconomic development at regional level . Berlin [1986] 2 v. : LC Card 87-143388 DDC 338.96894 19
HC915.Z7 G847 1986

GWEMBE DISTRICT (ZAMBIA) - SOCIAL CONDITIONS.
Strengthening local linkages for socioeconomic development at regional level . Berlin [1986] 2 v. : LC Card 87-143388 DDC 338.96894 19
HC915.Z7 G847 1986

GWEMBE SOUTH DEVELOPMENT PROJECT (ZAMBIA)
Scudder, Thayer. An evaluation of the Gwembe South Development Project, Zambia /. Binghamton, N.Y., USA [1982] 48 p. ; LC Card 87-119502 DDC 338.96894 19
HC915.Z7 G846 1982

Gwynne, Robert N. Industrialization and urbanization in Latin America / Robert N. Gwynne. Baltimore, Md. : Johns Hopkins University Press, 1986. xiv, 259 p. : ill. ; 23 cm. Includes index. Bibliography: p. 243-253. ISBN 0-8018-3113-X LC Card 85-10079 DDC 338.098 19
1. Industry and state - Latin America. 2. Urbanization - Latin America. 3. Latin America - Industries. I. Title.
HC125 .G96 1986 ***NYPL [JLD 86-2200]***

Gwynne, S. C. (Samuel C.), 1953- Selling money / by S.C. Gwynne. New York : Penguin Books, 1987, c1986. 182 p. ; 20 cm. "A young banker's account of the great international lending boom--and bust"--Cover. Bibliography: p. 181-182. ISBN 0-14-010282-5 (pbk.) LC Card 87-6969 DDC 336.3/435 19
1. Loans, Foreign. 2. Loans, American. 3. Banks and banking, International. 4. Banks and banking, American. I. Title.
HG3891.5 .G98 1987

Gyakorlati útmutató a kötvény és a váltó használatához /. Hardy, Ilona. Budapest , 1986. 62 p. ; ISBN 963-621-315-1 LC Card 87-407776
HG5470.5.A3 H37 1986

Gyáni, Gábor. Család, háztartás és a városi cselédség / Gyáni Gábor. Budapest : Magvető, c1983. 251, [1] p. ; 18 cm. (Gyorsuló idő, 0324-7155) Bibliography: p. 245-[252] ISBN 963-271-955-7 : LC Card 84-129676
1. Women domestics - Hungary - History. I. Title.
HD6072.2.H8 G92 1983

Gyárfás, Judit. Magyar Kereskedelmi Kamara. Managers in Hungary . [Budapest?] , 1986. 368 p. ; ISBN 963-7073-09-4 (pbk.) LC Card 87-137498 DDC 658/.0025/439 19
HD38.25.H9 M34 1986

Gyarmathy, Zsigmond. Ipari üzemtörténet /. Nyíregyháza , 1979 ([Nyíregyháza] : Készült a Szabolcs-Szatmár Megyei Tanács Sokszorosító Költségvetési Üzemében) 228 p. : ISBN 963-01-2796-2 LC Card 81-173980
HC300.29.S92 I62 1979

Gydesen, Ellen. Kvinders livsgrundlag i 80-erne / Ellen Gydesen, Marianne Helms, Ulla Sønder ; vejleder, Mogens Holm. K [i.e. Copenhagen] : Sociologisk institut, [1985] 202 columns : ill. ; 21 x 30 cm. (Afhandling . nr. 3, 1985) "December 1985." Bibliography: columns 198-202. LC Card 87-168500
1. Sexual division of labor - Denmark. 2. Women - Employment - Denmark. 3. Sex role - Denmark. I. Helms, Marianne. II. Sønder, Ulla. III. Series: Afhandling (Københavns universitet. Sociologisk institut) , 1985, nr. 3. IV. Title.
HD6060.65.D4 G93 1985

Gyenes, Antal. Szövetkezetipolitikai, szövetkezetelméleti ismeretek / írta, Gyenes Antal. Vezetési ismeretek / írta, László Ferenc. Budapest : MÉM Mérnök- és Vezetőtovábbképző Intézet, 1974. 217 p. ; 29 cm. "A termelőszövetkezeti elnökök és függetlenitett elnökhelyettesek továbbképző tanfolyamának tananyaga." LC Card 87-113832
1. Cooperative societies - Hungary. 2. Cooperation - Hungary. I. László, Ferenc. Vezetési ismeretek. 1974. II. MÉM Mérnök- és Vezetőtovábbképző Intézet. III. Title.
HD3492.5.A4 G94 1974

Gylfason, Thorvaldur.
Credit policy and economic activity in developing countries with IMF stabilization programs / Thorvaldur Gylfason. Princeton, N.J. : International Finance Section, Dept. of Economics, Princeton University, c1987. 44 p. ; 23 cm. (Princeton studies in international finance, 0081-8070 . no. 60 (August 1987)) Bibliography: p. 31-32. ISBN 0-88165-232-6 (pbk.) : LC Card 87-3389 DDC 332.7/09172/4 19
1. Credit control - Developing countries. 2. Developing countries - Economic policy. 3. Economic stabilization - Developing countries. 4. International Monetary Fund. I. Series: Princeton studies in international finance, no. 60. II. Title.
HG3711.D48 G94 1987

Interest, inflation, and the aggregate consumption function / by Thorvaldur Gylfason. Stockholm, Sweden : Institute for International Economic Studies, [1979] 44 leaves : ill. ; 30 cm. (Seminar paper / Institute for International Economic Studies, 0347-8769 . no. 117) "February 1979." Bibliography: leaves 41-44. LC Card 81-114286
1. Consumption (Economics) - United States - Econometric models. 2. Interest rates - United States - Econometric models. 3. Inflation (Finance) - United States - Econometric models. I. Series: Seminar paper (Stockholms universitet. Institutet för internationell ekonomi) , no. 117. II. Title.
HC110.C6 G95 1979

Gynaikeia apascholēsē kai oikogeneia stēn Hellada kai allou /. Mousourou, Loukia M. Athēna , c1985. 220 p. : LC Card 86-205975
HD6181.83 .M68 1985

Györgypál, Katalin. A magyar szakszervezetek napjainkban : zárótanulmány / Györgypál Katalin. Budapest : Szakszervezetek Elméleti Kutató Intézete, 1984. 128 p. ; 21 cm. "A zárótanulmány az Intézet Információs- és Közvéleménykutató Részlegében készült"--T.p. verso. ISBN 963-608-062-3 LC Card 85-230460
1. Trade-unions - Hungary. I. Szakszervezetek Elméleti Kutató Intézete. Információs- és Közvéleménykutató Részleg. II. Title.
HD6680.5 .G96 1984

GYPSIES - IRELAND - ECONOMIC CONDITIONS.
Rottman, David B. The population structure and living circumstances of Irish travellers . Dublin , 1986. 134 p. : ISBN 0-7070-0084-X (pbk.) : LC Card 86-215759 DDC 330.9417 s 305.5/68 19
HC257.I6 E3 no. 131 DX217

GYPSIES - IRELAND - SOCIAL CONDITIONS.
Rottman, David B. The population structure and living circumstances of Irish travellers . Dublin , 1986. 134 p. : ISBN 0-7070-0084-X (pbk.) : LC Card 86-215759 DDC 330.9417 s 305.5/68 19
HC257.I6 E3 no. 131 DX217

Gyüge, Tamás. Lovassné Szecső, Judit. A kereskedelmi hitel és a váltó alkalmazásának 1985. évi tapasztalatai /. Budapest [1986] 62 p. ; ISBN 963-7202-84-6 LC Card 87-151536
HG3754.5.H9 L68 1986

HLDI. see **Highway Loss Data Institute.**

H. U. D. see **United States. Dept. of Housing and Urban Development.**

HWWA-Institut für Wirtschaftsforschung-Hamburg.
Neue Industriepolitik oder Stärkung der Marktkräfte? . Hamburg , 1986. xiii, 221 p. ; ISBN 3-87895-315-1 LC Card 87-408234 DDC 338.9 19
HD3616.G4 N48 1986

Der Neue Protektionismus /. Hamburg , 1984. 149 p. ; ISBN 3-87895-251-1 LC Card 84-222112
HF1703 .N48 1984

Veröffentlichungen.
Boeck, Klaus. Die DM als internationale Reservewährung . Hamburg , 1974. 75 p. ; LC Card 75-550711 ***NYPL [JLE 80-744]***

Ha nincs fék, gáz van . Cserhalmi, Imre. [Budapest] , 1984. 294 p. ; LC Card 85-183756
HE5667.5.A6 C74 1984

Ha, Seong-Kyu, 1947- Housing policy and practice in Asia /. London , New York , c1987. 197 p. : ISBN 0-7099-4711-9 LC Card 87-9091 DDC 363.5/8/095 19
HD7366.5.A3 H68 1987

Haack, W. G. C. M. Europese economische integratie . Utrecht , 1986. 304 p. : ISBN 90-274-0506-9 : LC Card 86-206597
HC241.2 .E8655 1986

Haag, F. (Franz) Interregionale Wanderungen in der Schweiz . Zürich , c1978. 2 v. : LC Card 85-215084
HB2083 .I57 1978

Haag, Ingeborg. Arbeitskommunikation, Kommunikationsarbeit : Neukozeption industriesoziologischer Arbeitsanalyse durch die systematische Einbeziehung arbeitsbezogener Kommunikation / Ingeborg Haag.1. Aufl. Berlin : Schelzky & Jeep, 1986. viii, 258 p. ; 21 cm. Bibliography: p. 248-256. ISBN 3-923024-08-8 LC Card 86-226373
1. Industrial sociology - Germany, West. 2. Industrial

productivity - Germany, West. 3. Communication in management - Germany (West). I. Title.
HD6957.G35 H33 1986

Haaland, Gunnar. Evolution of socio-economic dualism in the Maldives / Gunnar Haaland. Bergen : Chr. Michelsen Institute, DERAP (Development Research and Action Programme), [1987] 30 leaves ; 30 cm. (DERAP working papers, 0800-2045 = DERAP arbeidsnotater . A 363) Summary in Norwegian. "January 1987." Includes bibliographical references. LC Card 87-130051 DDC 330.9549/5 19
1. Maldives - Economic conditions. 2. Maldives - Social conditions. I. Series: DERAP working papers , A 363. II. Title.
HC596 .H33 1987

Haan, J. A. C. de. Omgeving, doelstellingen en organisatie . Assen , 1986. viii, 464 p. : ISBN 90-232-2208-3 : LC Card 86-182876
HG4181 .O44 1986

Haar, Elke von der. Haar, Heinrich von der. Jugendarbeitslösigkeit und soziale Sicherung . Berlin , c1982. 216 p. : ISBN 3-88114-302-5 : LC Card 83-152854 DDC 331.3/4/0943 19
HD7096.G3 H33 1982 ***NYPL [JLE 87-1214]***

Haar, Heinrich von der. Jugendarbeitslösigkeit und soziale Sicherung : eine Studie zur materiellen und sozialen Notlage arbeitsloser Jugendlicher / Heinrich von der Haar, Elke Stark-von der Haar. Berlin : Die Arbeitswelt, c1982. 216 p. : ill. ; 23 cm. Chapters 1-11 originally presented as H.v.d. Haar's thesis (doctoral)--TU Berlin, 1982. Bibliography: p. 200-216. ISBN 3-88114-302-5 : LC Card 83-152854 DDC 331.3/4/0943 19
1. Insurance, Unemployment - Germany (West). 2. Youth - Employment - Germany, West. I. Haar, Elke von der. II. Title.
HD7096.G3 H33 1982 ***NYPL [JLE 87-1214]***

Haaren, Kurt van. Befreiung der Arbeit . Bonn , c1986. 197 p. : ISBN 3-87831-429-9 LC Card 86-194157
HD6955 .B389 1986

Haarhoff, E. J. (Errol J.) Planning and financial evaluation of housing strategies /. Durban , 1983. viii, 233 p. : ISBN 0-86980-360-3 (pbk.) LC Card 86-205849 DDC 363.5/8 19
HD7287.96.S682 D876 1983

Haas, Hans-Dieter. Karibische Klein- und Mikrostaaten : wirtschatliche Aussenabhängigkeit und Integrationsbestrebungen / von H.-D. Haas, U. Bader u. J. Grumptmann. Tübingen : Attempto, 1985. xvi, 200 p. : ill. ; 21 cm. Summary in English, French, and German. Bibliography: p. 181-194. ISBN 3-921552-62-1 LC Card 86-155952
1. Caribbean area - Economic integration. 2. Caribbean Area - Dependency on foreign countries. 3. Caribbean Area - Economic conditions - 1945-. I. Bader, U. (Udo). II. Grumptmann, J. (Jörg). III. Title.
HC141 .H25 1985

Haas, Ingrid. Funktion und Wirkung von Aufklebern an Personenkraftwagen / Ingrid Haas. Köln : Bundesanstalt für Strassenwesen, Bereich Unfallforschung, [1983] 101, [13] p. : ill. ; 21 cm. (Forschungsberichte der Bundesanstalt für Strassenwesen, Bereich Unfallforschung, 0173-7066 . 85) "Bericht zum Forschungsprojekt 8262 der Bundesanstalt für Strassenwesen, Bereich Unfallforschung." "Februar 1983." Bibliography: p. 99-101. LC Card 84-147451
1. Traffic safety - Germany (West) - Cologne. 2. Advocacy advertising - Germany (West) - Cologne. I. Bundesanstalt für Strassenwesen (Germany). Bereich Unfallforschung. II. Title. III. Series.
HE5614.5.G3 H28 1983

Haás, László. A Mezőgazdasági szövetkezetek szabályozó rendszere /. [Budapest] , 1979. 119 p. ; LC Card 86-187443
HD1492.H8 M417 1979

Haas, Paul F., 1939- Browne, M. Neil, 1944- Modern economics . Englewood Cliffs, N.J. , c1987. xvi, 464 p. : ISBN 0-13-587940-X (pbk.) LC Card 86-25256 DDC 330 19
HB171.5 .B724 1987

Haber, Audrey. Runyon, Richard P. Fundamentals of behavioral statistics /. New York , c1988. p. cm. ISBN 0-394-36619-0 LC Card 87-23066 DDC 519.5 19
HA29 .R85 1988

Haberl, Othmar Nikola. Der Marshall-Plan und die europäische Linke /. [Frankfurt am Main] , c1986. 659 p. : ISBN 3-434-00475-0 LC Card 87-127508 DDC 338.91/73/04 19
HC240 .M2735 1986

HABERMAS, JÜRGEN.
Roncolini, Giuliana, 1948- La crisi della legittimità borghese . Napoli , 1978. 115 p. ; ISBN 88-20-70809-4 : LC Card 79-368996
HC54 .R64 ***NYPL [JLD 81-254]***

Habermayer, Wolfgang, 1959- Internationale Rohstoffabkommen als Beispiel des Nord-Süd Dialoges / Wolfgang Habermayer. Frankfurt am Main ; New York : P. Lang, c1985. xxxiii, 264 p. : ill. ; 21 cm. (Europäische Hochschulschriften. Reihe V, Volks- und Betriebswirtschaft, 0531-7339 . Bd. 639 = vol. 639) Originally presented as the author's thesis (doctoral)--Wirtschaftsuniversität Wien, 1984. Bibliography: p. xv-xxxii. ISBN 3-8204-8896-0 LC Card 86-111744
1. Raw materials - Developing countries. 2. Developing countries - Commerce. 3. International economic relations. I. Series: Europäische Hochschulschriften. Reihe V, Volks- und Betriebswirtschaft , Bd. 639. II. Title.
HF1054.D44 H33 1985

Habibullah, M. Management constraints of co-operatives / M. Habibullah, Mahbub Ahmed. Dhaka : Bureau of Business Research, University of Dhaka, 1986. 92 p. ; 25 cm. Study of fishing cooperatives in Bangladesh. Bibliography: p. [85]-86. LC Card 87-900945
1. Fisheries, Cooperative - Bangladesh - Management. I. Ahmed, Mahbub. II. Title.
HD1491.B3 H34 1986

Habicht, Werner. Werkssiedlung Madenfelderhof bei Landsweiler-Reden : Dokumentation im Auftrag der Saarbergwerke AG / Werner Habicht. Saarbrücken : Saarbergwerke, 1985. 54 p., [52] p. of plates : ill. ; 21 cm. Bibliography: p. 52-54. LC Card 87-408673 DDC 330.943/42 19
1. Industrial housing - Germany (West) - Schiffweiler. 2. Company towns - Germany (West) - Schiffweiler. 3. Company town architecture - Germany (West) - Schiffweiler. 4. Schiffweiler (Germany) - Economic conditions. I. Saarbergwerke. II. Title.
HD7289.5.A3 G437 1985

Habitação . Peruzzo, Dilvo, 1941- São Paulo-SP [1984] 133 p. ; LC Card 84-242125 DDC 363.5/0981 19
HD7287.6.B7 P47 1984
NYPL [JLD 86-2535]

L'habitat en Algérie . Boubekeur, Sid, 1952- Lyon , c1986. 256 p. : ISBN 2-7297-0272-5 : LC Card 86-217640
HD7372.4.A3 B68 1986

Habitat popular : experiencias y alternativas en países de América Latina / Nora Clichevsky, Beatriz Cuenya y Susana Peñalva, coordinadoras. Buenos Aires : Centro de Estudios Urbanos y Regionales, 1986. 162 p. : ill. ; 28 cm. (Cuadernos del CEUR, 0326-1417 . 16) Spanish and Portuguese. "Trabajos presentados por investigadores de la Argentina, Brasil, Chile y Uruguay en el segundo Seminario sobre el Habitat Popular realizado entre el 28 y el 30 de noviembre de 1984 en la ciudad de Buenos Aires"--Introd. Includes bibliographies. CONTENTS. - A participação dos moradores na urbinazação de uma favela / Nabil G. Bonduki -- El cooperativismo de ayuda mutua en el Uruguay / Centro Cooperativista Uruguayo (CCU) y Federación Unificadora de Cooperativas de Vivienda por Ayuda Mutua (FUCVAM) -- Diagnóstico de la situación habitacional de los sectores más carenciados de la Capital Federal / Artemio Abba, Gustavo Dardik y Ana María Facciolo, con la colaboración de Eduardo Faierman -- Asistencia técnica / Alfredo Rodríguez -- Investigación participativa en asentamientos populares / Susana Peñalava ... [et al.] -- Asociaciones populares urbanas y participación / Héctor Atilio Poggiese -- El acceso de sectores populares a la tierra urbana / Nora Clichevsky -- Población de los bajos ingresos y agua potable en Argentina / Fernando J. Brunstein. LC Card 87-404028 DDC 363.5/8 19
1. Self-help housing - Latin America - Congresses. 2. Poor - Housing - Latin America - Congresses. I. Clichevsky, Nora. II. Cuenya, Beatriz. III. Peñalava, Susana. IV. Series.
HD7305.5 .H32 1986

L'Habitat réunionnais / CAUE de l'Ile de la Réunion. Saint-Denis : Ministère de l'éducation nationale, CNDP, CDDP de la Réunion, [1983] 73 p., A-T leaves of plates : ill. ; 30 cm. Cover title. Leaves of plates (21) inserted. Bibliography: p. 73. LC Card 84-981007
1. Labor and laboring classes - Dwellings - Réunion. 2. Housing - Réunion. I. CAUE de l'Ile de la Réunion. II. Centre départemental de documentation pédagogique de la Réunion.
HD7378.9.A3 H33 1983

L'habitation sucrière au Quartier La Dumaine, Le François /. Rosélie, Roland. [Fort-deFrance? , 1986] ([Fort-de-France] : Impr. Désormeaux) 59 p. : LC Card 86-203128
HD8039.S86 M327 1986

Hablützel, Peter. Staatsverschuldung : die hintertriebene Sanierung der Bundesfinanzen / von Peter Hablützel. Basel : Helbing & Lichtenhahn, c1984. 96 p. : ill. ; 21 cm. (Standpunkte, kontrovers . Heft 3) ISBN 3-7190-0864-9 LC Card 84-159813
1. Debts, Public - Switzerland. 2. Fiscal policy - Switzerland. I. Title.
HJ8749 .H33 1984

Habtamu Wondimu. Some factors which affect peasant motivation to work in the Ethiopian agricultural producers cooperatives / Habtamu Wondimu. [Addis Ababa] : Institute of Development Research, Addis Ababa University, [1983] 60 leaves : forms ; 30 cm. (Research report . no. 21) "December 1983." Bibliography: leaves 59-60. LC Card 84-980911 DDC 334/.683/0963 19
1. Agriculture, Cooperative - Ethiopia. 2. Producer cooperatives - Ethiopia. 3. Peasantry - Ethiopia - Attitudes. 4. Motivation (Psychology). I. Addis Ababa University. Institute of Development Research. II. Series: Research report (Addis Ababa University. Institute of Development Research) , no. 21. III. Title.
HD1491.E83 H3 1983b ***NYPL [JLG 86-163]***

Hacendados y campesinos en Aguascalientes /. Gómez Serrano, Jesús. [Aguascalientes] , 1985. 221 p., [20] p. of plates : LC Card 86-217321
HD1471.M62 A384 1985

Hacia la ciudad del capital--México, 1790-1870 /. López Monjardín, Adriana. México, D.F. , 1985. 193 p. : LC Card 87-124857 DDC 330.972/53 19
HC138.M4 L66 1985

Hacia un planeamiento de la industria de la construcción en la Argentina / Centro Argentino de Ingenieros. Buenos Aires : El Centro, 1943. 289 p. : ill. ; 29 cm. Includes bibliographical references. LC Card 85-104409
1. Construction industry - Argentina. 2. Building - Argentina. I. Centro Argentino de Ingenieros.
HD9715.A72 H33 1943

Hacia un populismo petrolero? y otros temas /. Eastman, Jorge Mario. Bogotá, Colombia , 1986. viii, 145 p., [8] p. of plates : LC Card 86-227075
HD9574.C52 E18 1986

Hacia una reestructuración dirigida de la economía dominicana / Miguel Ceara Hatton ... [et al.]. Santo Domingo, República Dominicana : Fundación Friedrich Ebert : Grupo de Investigación Económica, c1986. 355 p. : ill. ; 23 cm. Bibliography: p. 327-339. LC Card 87-402158 DDC 338.97293 19
1. Dominican Republic - Economic conditions - 1961-. 2. Dominican Republic - Economic policy. I. Ceara Hatton, Miguel. II. Grupo de Investigación Económica (Dominican Republic).
HC153.5 .H33 1986

Hacia una reforma social urbana en Colombia . Toro Agudelo, Hernán. Bogotá, Colombia , 1986. 342 p. : ISBN 958-601-100-3 LC Card 87-107055
HD7325.A3 T67 1986

Hacienda colonial venezolana / contadores mayores e intendentes de ejército y real hacienda ; introducción explicativa y selección documental de Héctor García Chuecos. Caracas : Editorial Crisol, 1946. 170 p. ; 24 cm. (Publicaciones de la Comisión Preparatoria de la IV Asamblea General del Instituto Panamericano de Geografía e Historia) Includes bibliographical references. LC Card 85-105445
1. Venezuela. Real Hacienda - History - Sources. 2. Finance, Public - Venezuela - History - Sources. 3. Finance, Public - Spain - Colonies - America - History - Sources. 4. Accountants - Venezuela - Biography. 5. Intendants - Venezuela - Biography. I. García Chuecos, Héctor. II. Series.
HJ991 .H323 1946

La hacienda serrana, 1900-1930 /. Trujillo León, Jorge. Quito , 1986. 244 p. ; LC Card 87-115338 DDC 333.3/09866 19
HD1471.E2 T78 1986

Hacienda y crédito público : cifras, 1970-1985. [Bogotá, Colombia] : Ministerio de Hacienda y Crédito Público, [1986] 94 p. : ill. ; 28 cm. Chiefly tables. LC Card 87-404281 DDC 336.861 19
1. Budget - Colombia - Statistics. 2. Colombia - Appropriations and expenditures - Statistics. 3. Credit - Colombia - Statistics. I. Colombia. Ministerio de Hacienda y Crédito Público.
HJ2083 .H33 1986

HACIENDAS - ECUADOR - HISTORY.
Trujillo León, Jorge. La hacienda serrana, 1900-1930 /. Quito , 1986. 244 p. ; LC Card 87-115338 DDC 333.3/09866 19
HD1471.E2 T78 1986

Las haciendas locales de la Provincia de Granada, 1940-1983 . Martín Rodríguez, Manuel. Granada [1985?] 369 p. ; ISBN 84-338-0266-6 LC Card 86-230887
HJ9527.G7 M37 1985

HACIENDAS - MEXICO - AGUASCALIENTES (STATE) - HISTORY - CASE STUDIES.
Gómez Serrano, Jesús. Hacendados y campesinos en Aguascalientes /. [Aguascalientes] , 1985. 221 p., [20] p. of plates : LC Card 86-217321
HD1471.M62 A384 1985

HACIENDAS - MEXICO - HIDALGO (STATE) - CASE STUDIES.
Laviada, Iñigo. Vida y muerte de un latifundio /. México , 1984. xiii, 259 p., [6] leaves of plates : LC Card 86-208690
HD1471.M62 H535 1984

HACIENDAS - MEXICO - HISTORY.
Schell, William, 1950- Medieval Iberian tradition and the development of the Mexican hacienda /. Syracuse, NY , 1986. 117 p. ; ISBN 0-915984-99-7 : LC Card 85-31042 DDC 307.7/2/0972 19
HD1471.M6 S34 1986 ***NYPL [JLE 86-1697]***

HACIENDAS - MEXICO - MEXICO - CASE STUDIES.
Laviada, Iñigo. Vida y muerte de un latifundio /. México , 1984. xiii, 259 p., [6] leaves of plates : LC Card 86-208690
HD1471.M62 H535 1984

HACIENDAS - PERU - HISTORY.
Zúñiga Trelles, Washington. Las empresas azucareras y la reforma agraria /. [S.l. , 1981] ([S.l.] : EBRASA) 108 p. ; LC Card 81-204318 DDC 333.3/1/85 19
HD9114.P52 Z86 1981 ***NYPL [JLD 87-922]***

HACIENDAS - SPAIN - HISTORY.
Schell, William, 1950- Medieval Iberian tradition and the development of the Mexican hacienda /. Syracuse, NY , 1986. 117 p. ; ISBN 0-915984-99-7 : LC Card 85-31042 DDC 307.7/2/0972 19
HD1471.M6 S34 1986 ***NYPL [JLE 86-1697]***

Hackbarth, Glenn M. Ginsburg, Paul B. A private health plan option strategy for Medicare /. Santa Monica, CA [1987] xvi, 116 p. ; ISBN 0-8330-0863-3 (pbk.) LC Card 87-17593 DDC 368.4/26/00973 19
HD7102.U4 G56 1987

Hackenbroch, Inge. Zur Theorie und Politik eines supranationalen Finanzausgleichs : Gestaltungsprobleme und Gestaltungsansätze unter besonderer Berücksichtigung der EG / Inge Hackenbroch. München : Weltforum Verlag, c1983. xvi, 350 p. ; 22 cm. Bibliography: p. 319-350. ISBN 3-8039-0259-2 LC Card 83-167962
1. Finance, Public - European Economic Community Countries. 2. Transfer payments - European Economic Community countries. 3. Regional planning - European Economic Community countries. I. Title.
HJ1000.5 .H33 1983

Hackert, Klaus. Leben mit Gneisenau, hundert Jahre-- . Dortmund , Essen [1986?] 317 p. : ISBN 3-88474-323-6 LC Card 87-408388 DDC 331.7/622334/094355 19
HD8039.M62 G335 1986

Hackett, Judith C. Managing rural infrastructure : state assistance to small and rural governments for public works / authors, Judith C. Hackett, project director, Terry Busson, project co-director ; contributing researchers, Tim Barber ... [et al.]. Lexington, Ky. : Council of State Governments, State Government Research Institute, Center for Agriculture and Rural Development, c1986. iii, 36 p. : ill., maps ; 28 cm. "December 1986." Bibliography: p. 34-36. ISBN 0-87292-070-4 (pbk.) : LC Card 87-404481 DDC 363/.0973 19
1. United States - Public works - Finance. 2. Rural development - Government policy - United States - States. 3. Intergovernmental fiscal relations - United States. 4. Economic assistance, Domestic - United States - States. I. Busson, Terry. II. Center for Agriculture and Rural Development. III. Title.
HD3888 .H27 1986

Hadady, R. Earl (Robert Earl), 1920- Winning with the insiders / by R. Earl Hadady, I. Lee Finberg, Dan Rahfeldt ; edited by Martin D. Weiss. West Palm Beach, Fla. : Weiss Research, c1987. vi, 115 p. : ill ; 24 cm. ISBN 0-9613048-8-X : LC Card 87-40003 DDC 332.64/4 19
1. Investments - United States. 2. Commodity exchanges - United States. 3. Put and call transactions - United States. I. Finberg, I. Lee. II. Rahfeldt, Dan. III. Weiss, Martin D. IV. Title.
HG4910 .H18 1987

Haddad, Paulo Roberto. Dimensões do planejamento estadual no Brasil : análise de experiências / Paulo Roberto Haddad. Rio de Janeiro : IPEA/INPES, 1985. 188 p. : ill. ; 21 cm. (Série PNPE . 13) Includes bibliographical references. LC Card 86-195636
1. Minas Gerais, Brazil - Economic policy. 2. Community development - Brazil - Minas Gerais. 3. Brazil - Economic policy. I. Title. II. Series.
HC188.M6 H33 1985

Hadden, Kenneth.
Groff, William H. Income variability in Connecticut, 1980 /. Storrs, CT [1987] 32 p. : LC Card 87-621355 DDC 339.2/2/09746 19
HC107.C83 I5138 1987

Poverty in Connecticut, 1979 / by Kenneth P. Hadden. Storrs, CT : Storrs Agricultural Experiment Station, College of Agriculture and Natural Resources, University of Connecticut, [1986] 24 p. : map ; 23 cm. (Bulletin / Storrs Agricultural Experiment Station, College of Agriculture and Natural Resources, University of Connecticut . 472) Cover title. "June 1986." Bibliography: p. 20 LC Card 86-623148 DDC 362.5/09746 19
1. Connecticut - Economic conditions. 2. Connecticut - Social conditions. 3. Poor - Connecticut. I. Series: Bulletin (Storrs Agricultural Experiment Station) , 472. II. Title.
HC107.C8 H33 1986

Haddock, Patricia. Standing up for America : a biography of Lee Iacocca / Patricia Haddock. Minneapolis, Minn. : Dillon Press, c1987. 111 p. : ill. ; 24 cm. (A People in focus book) Bibliography: p. [108]. Includes index. A biography of the businessman who saved the Chrysler Corporation from bankruptcy. ISBN 0-87518-362-X : LC Card 86-32965 DDC 338.7/6292/0924 B 92 19
1. Iacocca, Lee A. - Juvenile literature. 2. Automobile industry and trade - United States - Juvenile literature. 3. Businessmen - United States - Biography - Juvenile literature. 4. Automobile industry and trade. I. Title. II. Series.
HD9710.U52 I246 1987

Hadenius, Axel, 1945- A crisis of the welfare state? : opinions about taxes and public expenditure in Sweden / by Axel Hadenius. Stockholm, Sweden : Almqvist & Wiksell International, c1986. 151 p. : ill. ; 24 cm. Bibliography: p. 146-151. ISBN 91-22-00821-7 (pbk.) : LC Card 87-127805 DDC 339.5/22/09485 19
1. Taxation - Sweden. 2. Sweden - Appropriations and expenditures. 3. Government spending policy - Sweden. I. Title.
HJ2837 .H34 1986

Hadjimatheou, George. Consumer economics after Keynes : theory and evidence of the consumption function / George Hadjimatheou. New York : St. Martin's Press, 1987. viii, 280 p. : ill. ; 23 cm. Bibliography: p. 243-270 Includes indexes. ISBN 0-312-00478-8 : LC Card 87-9427 DDC 339.4/7 19
1. Consumption (Economics) - Mathematical models. I. Title.
HB801 .H245 1987

Hadjio, Roman, 1952- Internationaler Zinsverbund / Roman Hadjio. Frankfurt am Main ; New York : P. Lang, c1985. 272 p. : ill. ; 21 cm. (Europäische Hochschulschriften. Reihe V, Volks- und Betriebswirtschaft, 0531-7339 . Bd. 630 = vol. 630 = vol. 630) Bibliography: p. 255-272. ISBN 3-8204-5691-0 LC Card 85-220128
1. Foreign exchange. 2. Monetary policy. 3. Interest rates. I. Series: Europäische Hochschulschriften. Reihe V, Volks- und Betriebswirtschaft , Bd. 630. II. Title.
HG3821 .H27 1985

Haefeli-Meylan, Traugott. Die Entstehung der Briefmarke und ihre weltweite Verbreitung / Traugott Haefeli-Meylan. Lausanne : Mondo-Verlag, c1985. 167 p. : chiefly ill. (some col.) ; 29 cm. Bibliography: p. 167. LC Card 86-202635
1. Postage-stamps - Collectors and collecting - History. I. Title.
HE6203 .H25 1985

Die Häfen Bremen, Bremerhaven /. Scheidulin, Hans. Bremen , c1985. 160 p. : ISBN 3-920699-63-7 LC Card 86-124602 DDC 330.943/52 19
HC289.B72 S34 1985

Haendel, Dan, 1950- Goldberg, Ellen S. On edge . New York , 1987. ix, 116 p. ; ISBN 0-275-92604-4 (alk. paper) : LC Card 86-25324 DDC 332.1/5 19
HG3881 .G6142 1987

Häuser, Karl, 1920-
Finanzsysteme, Ideal- und Realtypen . Berlin , c1983. 278 p. : ISBN 3-428-05419-9 LC Card 83-240120
HJ161 .F575 1983

Geyer, Herbert, 1927- Budgetpolitik im Wandel /. Berlin , c1986. 111 p. : ISBN 3-428-05922-0 LC Card 86-165210
HJ113 .G49 1986

Hafer, R. W. (Rick W.) The Monetary versus fiscal policy debate . Totowa, N.J. , 1986. 171 p. : ISBN 0-8476-7454-1 : LC Card 85-11912 DDC 339.5/2 19
HG230.3 .M64 1986 ***NYPL [JLE 86-4720]***

Haferkamp, Hans. Wohlfahrtsstaat und soziale Probleme /. Opladen , c1984. vi, 294 p. : ISBN 3-531-11701-7 ***NYPL [JLD 85-1550]***

Ḥāfiẓ, ʻUmar Zuhayr. Shaykh, Riyāḍ ʻAbd al-Ḥafiẓ. Niẓām al-iʻānah fī al-iqtiṣād al-Saʻūdī /. al-Mamlakah al-ʻArabīyah al-Suʻūdīyah , 1985. 77 p. : LC Card 86-208281
HC415.33.Z9 E447 1985

Hafskip, gjörningar og gæsluvarðhald /. Helgi Magnússon. Reykjavík , 1986. 272 p. : LC Card 87-117447
HE945.H19 H45 1986

HAFSKIP HF.
Helgi Magnússon. Hafskip, gjörningar og gæsluvarðhald /. Reykjavík , 1986. 272 p. : LC Card 87-117447
HE945.H19 H45 1986

Hagan, Jim. Australian trade unionism in documents / Jim Hagan. Melbourne, Australia : Longman Cheshire, 1986. xvi, 289 p. ; 22 cm. Bibliography: p. 282. Includes index. ISBN 0-582-71146-0 (pbk.) LC Card 86-223615 DDC 331.88/0994 19
1. Trade-unions - Australia - History - Sources. I. Title.
HD6892 .H34 1986

Hage, Jerald, 1932- Organizational change as a development strategy : models & tactics for improving third world organizations / Jerald Hage and Kurt Finsterbusch. Boulder, Colo. : L. Rienner Publishers, 1987. xvi, 293 p. ; 24 cm. (Studies in development management) Includes bibliographies and index. ISBN 1-555-87012-0 (lib. bdg. : alk. paper) : LC Card 87-12730 DDC 338.9/0068 19
1. Economic development projects - Developing countries - Management. 2. Organizational change - Developing countries. I. Finsterbusch, Kurt, 1935-. II. Title. III. Series.
HC59.72.E44 H34 1987

Hagelberg, R. Majandusteaduse ABC . Tallinn , 1985. 511 p. : LC Card 85-195109
HB61 .M225 1985

Hagelin, Björn, 1947- Kulorna rullar : ekonomi och politik kring svensk militär export / Björn Hagelin.1. uppl. Stockholm : Ordfront, 1985. 186 p. : ill. ; 22 cm. Includes bibliographical

references. ISBN 91-7324-253-5 LC Card 86-124793
1. Munitions - Sweden. 2. Munitions - Political aspects - Sweden. I. Title.
HD9743.S82 H34 1985

Hagemann, Harald.
Beschäftigung, Verteilung und Konjunktur . Bremen , 1984. 276 p. : ISBN 3-88722-088-9 : LC Card 85-176579
HB175 .B49 1984

Technischer Fortschritt und Arbeitslosigkeit /. Frankfurt/Main , New York , c1983. 372 p. : ISBN 3-593-33246-9 LC Card 84-143045
HD6331 .T39 1983 ***NYPL [JLD 87-331]***

Hagemann, Hermann. Die Formierung der rohstoffpolitischen Forderungen der Entwicklungsländer auf der Ebene der Vereinten Nationen bis zur ersten Konferenz für Handel und Entwicklung (UNCTAD 1) 1946 / Hermann Hagemann. Münster : [Institut für Politikwissenschaft der Westfälischen Wilhelms-Universität Münster], 1983. xix, 384, [14], 42 p. : ill. ; 21 cm. (Schriften des Instituts für Politikwissenschaft der Westfälischen Wilhelms-Universität Münster . Bd. 3) Bibliography: p. 374-384. ISBN 3-923676-11-5 LC Card 84-172079
1. Natural resources - Developing countries. 2. Raw materials - Developing countries. I. Title. II. Series.
HC59.7 .H27 1983

Haggai, Tom. How the best is won / Tom Haggai with Richard L. Federer. Nashville : T. Nelson, c1987. 228 p. ; 24 cm. Includes index. ISBN 0-8407-4221-5 LC Card 87-14996 DDC 658.4/09 19
1. Executive ability. 2. Leadership. I. Federer, Richard L. II. Title.
HD38.2 .H34 1987

Hagley Museum and Library.
Hagley collection guide.
Hagley Museum and Library. Trade catalogs in the Hagley Museum and Library /. Wilmington, Del. , 1987. 104 p. : ISBN 0-914650-26-2 (pbk.) LC Card 87-146349 DDC 016.3801/029/4 19
HF5861 .H234 1987

Trade catalogs in the Hagley Museum and Library / Nina de Angeli Walls. Wilmington, Del. : The Library, 1987. 104 p. : ill. ; 22 cm. (A Hagley collections guide) Includes bibliographical references and index. ISBN 0-914650-26-2 (pbk.) LC Card 87-146349 DDC 016.3801/029/4 19
1. Catalogs, Commercial. 2. Hagley Museum and Library - Catalogs. I. Walls, Nina de Angeli. II. Series: Hagley Museum and Library. Hagley collection guide. III. Title.
HF5861 .H234 1987

HAGLEY MUSEUM AND LIBRARY - CATALOGS.
Hagley Museum and Library. Trade catalogs in the Hagley Museum and Library /. Wilmington, Del. , 1987. 104 p. : ISBN 0-914650-26-2 (pbk.) LC Card 87-146349 DDC 016.3801/029/4 19
HF5861 .H234 1987

Hagskýrslur Íslands .
(II, 82) Tölfræðihandbók 1984 =. Reykjavík , 1984. 12, 268 p. ; LC Card 87-165528
HA1491 .A4 vol. II, 82

Hahn, Barbara. Der geförderte Wohnungsbau in Mannheim 1850-1985 / Barbara Hahn. Mannheim : Institut für Landeskunde und Regionalforschung der Universität Mannheim, 1986. 236 p. : ill. ; 21 cm. (Südwestdeutsche Schriften . 3) Bibliography: p. 226-236. ISBN 3-87804-185-3 LC Card 87-121543 DDC 363.5/8/0943/46 19
1. Housing - Germany (West) - Mannheim - History. 2. Housing policy - Germany (West) - Mannheim - History. 3. Public housing - Germany (West) - Mannheim - History. I. Title. II. Series.
HD7339.M35 H34 1986

Hahn, Frank.
Equilibrium and macroeconomics / Frank Hahn. Oxford : B. Blackwell, 1984. vi, 397 p. : ill. ; 24 cm. Includes bibliographies and index. ISBN 0-631-13482-4 : LC Card 87-672165
1. Economics. 2. Equilibrium (Economics). 3. Macroeconomics. I. Title.
HB171 .H23x 1984b

Money, growth, and stability / Frank Hahn. Oxford, U.K. : B. Blackwell, 1985. viii, 392 p. : ill. ; 24 cm. Includes bibliographies and index. ISBN 0-631-14354-8 LC Card 87-672166
1. Money. 2. Equilibrium (Economics). I. Title.
HG221.3 .H28x 1985b

Hahn, Gernot von, 1935- Ein Zuhause für Menschen . Frankfurt am Main , c1986. 204 p. : ISBN 3-921722-03-9 LC Card 87-133035
HD7339.A3 Z78 1986

Hahn, Hans-Werner. Geschichte des Deutschen Zollvereins / Hans-Werner Hahn. Göttingen : Vandenhoeck & Ruprecht, c1984. 214 p. ; 19 cm. (Kleine Vandenhoeck-Reihe. 1502) Bibliography: p. 200-204. Includes index. ISBN 3-525-33500-8 LC Card 85-129823
1. Deutscher Zollverein - History. 2. Tariff - Germany - History. I. Title.
HF2106 .H27 1984

Hahn, Helmut. Beiträge zur empirischen Wirtschaftsgeographie /. Bonn , c1986. 238 p. : ISBN 3-427-74191-5 LC Card 87-104279 DDC 330.9 19
HF1025 .B3495 1986

HAHN, HELMUT.
Beiträge zur empirischen Wirtschaftsgeographie /. Bonn , c1986. 238 p. : ISBN 3-427-74191-5 LC Card 87-104279 DDC 330.9 19
HF1025 .B3495 1986

Hahn, Jörg. Ökonomie, Politik und Krise : diskutiert am Beispiel der ökonomischen Konzeption Karl Schillers / Jörg Hahn. Würzburg : Königshausen + Neumann, 1984. 137 p. ; 21 cm. (Epistemata. Reihe Gesellschaftswissenschaften . Bd. 2 - 1984) Bibliography: p. 132-137. ISBN 3-88479-183-4 LC Card 85-113948
1. Economic stabilization. 2. Business cycles. 3. Economic stabilization - Germany (West). 4. Business cycles - Germany (West). 5. Schiller, Karl, 1911-. I. Series: Epistemata. Reihe Gesellschaftswissenschaften , Bd. 2. II. Title.
HB3732 .H34 1984

Hahner, June Edith, 1940- Poverty and politics : the urban poor in Brazil, 1870-1920 / June E. Hahner. Albuquerque : University of New Mexico Press, 1986. xvi, 415 p. : ill. ; 24 cm. Includes index. Bibliography: p. 373-402. ISBN 0-8263-0878-3 : LC Card 86-1258 DDC 305.5/69/0981 19
1. Urban poor - Brazil - History. 2. Urbanization - Brazil - History. 3. Laboring and laboring classes - Brazil - Political activity - History. 4. Brazil - Social conditions. 5. Brazil - Politics and government - 1822-. I. Title.
HC190.P6 H34 1986 ***NYPL [JLE 86-4407]***

Haigh, Barry. Angell, George. West of Wall Street /. [Chicago] [1987], c1988. xxiv, 215 p. ; ISBN 0-88462-623-7 LC Card 87-3003 DDC 332.63/222 19
HG6043 .A55 1988

Haigh, R. H.
The Guardian book of the General Strike /. Aldershot, Hants, England , Brookfield, Vt. , 1987. p. cm. ISBN 0-7045-3081-3 : LC Card 87-25287 DDC 331.89/25/0941 19
HD5365.A6 G8 1987

Soviet foreign policy, the League of Nations and Europe, 1917-39 / R.H. Haigh, D.S. Morris & A.R. Peters. Aldershot, Hants : Gower, 1986. x, 138 p. ; 23 cm. Includes index. Bibliography: p. 129-132.
1. League of Nations. 2. World politics - 1919-1932. 3. World politics - 1933-1945. 4. World War, 1939-1945 - Causes. 5. Russia - Foreign relations - 1917-1945. 6. Europe - Politics and government - 1918-1945. I. Morris, D. S. II. Peters, A. R. III. Title.
NYPL [JFD 86-5778]

Haigh, Robert William, 1926- Leading Virginia industries : textiles and apparel : a business update, 1986 / Robert W. Haigh, Donald W. Lindsey. Charlottesville, Va. : Business Studies Center, Tayloe Murphy Institute, Colgate Darden Graduate School of Business Administration, University of Virginia, [1986] 161 p. : ill. ; 22 x 28 cm. Includes index. LC Card 87-620837 DDC 338.4/7677/009755 19
1. Textile industry - Virginia - Statistics. 2. Textile industry - Virginia - Finance - Statistics. 3. Textile industry - Virginia - Directories. 4. Clothing trade - Virginia - Statistics. 5. Clothing trade - Virginia - Finance - Statistics. 6. Clothing trade - Virginia - Directories. I. Lindsey, Donald W. II. Title.
HD9857.V8 H35 1986

Haight, G. Timothy. REITs : new opportunities in real estate investment trust securities / G. Timothy Haight, Deborah Ann Ford. Chicago, Ill. : Probus Pub. Co., c1987. x, 227 p. : ill. ; 24 cm. Includes index. ISBN 0-917253-71-X : LC Card 87-2558 DDC 346.7304/37 347.306437 19
1. Real estate investment trusts - United States. I. Ford, Deborah Ann. II. Title.
HG5095 .H33 1987

Hain Ökonomie .
(Bd. 7) Müller, Frieder, 1944- Volkswirtschaftliche Gesamtrechnung und Preisveränderungen . Königstein/Ts. , 1984. xx, 414 p. : ISBN 3-445-02378-6 LC Card 85-142948 DDC 339.343 19
HC79.I5 M85 1984 ***NYPL [JLE 86-3225]***

Hain, Peter, 1950-
Political strikes : the state and trade unionism in Britain / Peter Hain. Harmondsworth, Middlesex, England ; New York : Viking, 1986. 357 p. ; 22 cm. Includes bibliographical references and index. ISBN 0-670-80601-3
1. Strikes and lockouts - Great Britain. 2. Trade-unions - Great Britain - Political activity. I. Title.
NYPL [JLD 87-532]

Political strikes : the state and trade unionism in Britain / Peter Hain. Harmondsworth, Middlesex, England ; New York, N.Y., U. S.A. : Viking, 1986. 357 p. ; 23 cm. Bibliography: p. [323]-344. Includes index. ISBN 0-670-80601-3 : LC Card 86-216642 DDC 331.89/2941 19
1. Political strikes - Great Britain. 2. Strikes and lockouts - Great Britain. I. Title.
HD5365.A6 H35 1986

Haine, Edgar A., 1908- Anthracite coal / by Edgar A. Haine. Chicago, Ill. : Adams Press, c1987. 214 p., ca. 250 p. of plates : ill. ; 24 cm. Bibliography: p. 197-202. Includes index. ISBN 0-9617434-0-9 LC Card 86-90990 DDC 338.2/725/09748 19
1. Anthracite coal industry - Pennsylvania - History. I. Title.
HD9547.P4 H35 1987

Haines, Lionel. How to buy a good business with little or none of your own money / Lionel Haines. 1st ed. New York : Times Books, c1987. 212 p. ; 22 cm. Includes index. ISBN 0-8129-1627-1 : LC Card 86-30017 DDC 658.1/6 19
1. Leveraged buyouts. I. Title.
HD2746.5 .H35 1987

Hainzl, Martin. Konkurrenzanalyse in der strategischen Planung / Martin Hainzl. Wien : Signum, 1985. 143 p. : ill. ; 24 cm. Bibliography: p. 131-143. ISBN 3-85436-027-4 LC Card 86-127579 DDC 658.4/012 19
1. Strategic planning. 2. Competition. I. Title.
HD30.28 .H334 1985

Haire, Mason. Modern organization theory . New York , 1987, c1959. x, 324 p. : ISBN 0-8240-8208-7 (alk. paper) : LC Card 86-27072 DDC 658 19
HD31 .M614 1987

Haiti : public expenditure review. Washington, D.C., U. S.A. : World Bank, [1987] xix, 254 p. ; 28 cm. (A World Bank country study, 0253-2123) Includes bibliographical references. ISBN 0-8213-0872-6 (pbk.) LC Card 86-32599 DDC 339.5/22/097294 19
1. Public investments - Haiti. 2. Haiti - Economic policy. 3. Haiti - Economic conditions - 1971-. I. International Bank for Reconstruction and Development. II. Series.
HC153.Z9 P834 1987

HAITI - CENSUS, 1982.
Résultats préliminaires du recensement général (septembre 1982) /. [Port-au-Prince] [1982 or 1983] vii, 60 p., [1] leaf of plates : LC Card 84-138275 DDC 304.6/097294/021 19
HD7316.A3 R47 1982 ***NYPL [JLF 86-1280]***

HAITI - DEPENDENCY ON FOREIGN COUNTRIES.
Girault, Christian A. [Commerce du café en Haïti. Spanish.] El comercio del café en Haití . Santo Domingo, República Dominicana , c1985. 426 p. : LC Card 86-200427
HD9199.H22 G5518 1985

HAITI - ECONOMIC CONDITIONS.
Mathon, Alix. [Haïti, un cas.] Haïti, un cas /. [Port-au-Prince? , 1985] (Port-au-Prince, Haïti : Impr. Le Natal) 172, 271 p. ; LC Card

86-139806 DDC 330.97294 19
HC153 .M38 1985 ***NYPL [Sc D 86-555]***

HAITI - ECONOMIC CONDITIONS - 1971-
Francisque, Édouard. La structure économique et sociale d'Haïti /. [Port-au-Prince, Haïti] [1986] 255 p. ; LC Card 87-113952
HC153 .F72 1986

Haiti . Washington, D.C., U. S.A. [1987] xix, 254 p. ; ISBN 0-8213-0872-6 (pbk.) LC Card 86-32599 DDC 339.5/22/097294 19
HC153.Z9 P834 1987

HAITI - ECONOMIC CONDITIONS - 1981-
Ronceray, Hubert de. Notre projet de société pour Haïti /. [Port-au-Prince?] [1986?] 52 p. : LC Card 86-210570
HC153 .R66 1986

HAITI - ECONOMIC POLICY.
Haiti . Washington, D.C., U. S.A. [1987] xix, 254 p. ; ISBN 0-8213-0872-6 (pbk.) LC Card 86-32599 DDC 339.5/22/097294 19
HC153.Z9 P834 1987

Ronceray, Hubert de. Notre projet de société pour Haïti /. [Port-au-Prince?] [1986?] 52 p. : LC Card 86-210570
HC153 .R66 1986

HAITI - HISTORY - 1804-
Mathon, Alix. [Haïti, un cas.] Haïti, un cas /. [Port-au-Prince? , 1985] (Port-au-Prince, Haïti : Impr. Le Natal) 172, 271 p. ; LC Card 86-139806 DDC 330.97294 19
HC153 .M38 1985 ***NYPL [Sc D 86-555]***

HAITI - POPULATION.
Francisque, Édouard. La structure économique et sociale d'Haïti /. [Port-au-Prince, Haïti] [1986] 255 p. ; LC Card 87-113952
HC153 .F72 1986

HAITI - POPULATION - STATISTICS.
Résultats préliminaires du recensement général (septembre 1982) /. [Port-au-Prince] [1982 or 1983] vii, 60 p., [1] leaf of plates : LC Card 84-138275 DDC 304.6/097294/021 19
HD7316.A3 R47 1982 ***NYPL [JLF 86-1280]***

HAITI - SOCIAL CONDITIONS.
Mathon, Alix. [Haïti, un cas.] Haïti, un cas /. [Port-au-Prince? , 1985] (Port-au-Prince, Haïti : Impr. Le Natal) 172, 271 p. ; LC Card 86-139806 DDC 330.97294 19
HC153 .M38 1985 ***NYPL [Sc D 86-555]***

HAITI - SOCIAL CONDITIONS - 1971-
Francisque, Édouard. La structure économique et sociale d'Haïti /. [Port-au-Prince, Haïti] [1986] 255 p. ; LC Card 87-113952
HC153 .F72 1986

Haïti, un cas /. Mathon, Alix. [Haïti, un cas.] [Port-au-Prince? , 1985] (Port-au-Prince, Haïti : Impr. Le Natal) 172, 271 p. ; LC Card 86-139806 DDC 330.97294 19
HC153 .M38 1985 ***NYPL [Sc D 86-555]***

HAITIANS - DOMINICAN REPUBLIC.
Lemoine, Maurice. [Sucre amer. English.] Bitter sugar /. London , 1985. 308 p., [17] p. of plates : ISBN 0-86232-445-9 LC Card 87-672356
HD4875.D44 L4513x 1985b

Lemoine, Maurice. [Sucre amer. English.] Bitter sugar /. London , c1985. 308 p., [17] p. of plates : ISBN 0-86232-445-9
NYPL [JLD 86-814]

HAITIANS - EMPLOYMENT - DOMINICAN REPUBLIC.
Plant, Roger. Sugar and modern slavery . London , Atlantic Highlands, N.J. , 1987. xiv, 177 p. : ISBN 0-86232-572-2 : LC Card 87-13315 DDC 331.7/6361/097293 19
HD8039.S86 D652 1987

Hajra, S. (Sridhar), 1936- Capital and technological progress in the Indian economy, 1950/51-1980/81 / Birla Institute of Scientific Research, Economic Research Division. New Delhi : Radiant Publishers, 1985. xvi, 198 p. : ill. ; 23 cm. Bibliography: p. [192]-198. LC Card 85-900681 DDC 338.954 19
1. Saving and investment - India. 2. Technological innovations - India. I. Birla Institute of Scientific Research. Economic Research Division. II. Title.
HC440.S3 H35 1985 ***NYPL [JLD 87-736]***

Hajrah, Hassan Hamza. Public land distribution in Saudi Arabia / Hassan Hamza Hajrah. London ; New York : Longman, 1982. xxi, 280 p. : ill. ; 24 cm. "... in association with the municipality of Jeddah and the University of Durham, Centre for Middle Eastern and Islamic Studies." Includes index. Bibliography: p. 267-273. ISBN 0-582-78301-1 LC Card 83-232929 DDC 333.1/6/09538 19
1. Land grants - Saudi Arabia. 2. Land reform - Saudi Arabia. 3. Land settlement - Saudi Arabia. 4. Saudi Arabia - Public lands. I. Jiddah (Saudi Arabia). II. University of Durham. Centre for Middle Eastern and Islamic Studies. III. Title.
HD853.Z7 H34 1982 ***NYPL [JLE 87-1566]***

Haka, Saiỳada Ājijula. Rahamāna, Matiura, 1946- Dhanikagoshṭhira luṭapāṭera kāhinī /. Ḍhākā , 1987. 136 p. : LC Card 87-902373
HG3290.6.A6 R35 1987

Hakala, Donald R. Austin, Douglas V. Modern banking . Boston , c1985. x, 406 p. : ISBN 0-87267-053-8 LC Card 84-21754 DDC 332.1/068 19
HG1615 .A98 1985 ***NYPL [JLE 85-3956]***

Hakemulder, Roel. Subcultuur en stigma van de armoede : een herziening van, en aanvulling op, Lewis' "culture of poverty" theorie / Roel Hakemulder. Leiden : Instituut voor Culturele Antropologie en Sociologie der Niet-Westerse Volken, 1985. 96 p. ; 21 cm. (ICA publikat[i]e . nr. 68) Bibliography: p. 93-96. ISBN 90-6624-058-X LC Card 86-172398
1. Poverty - Psychological aspects. 2. Lewis, Oscar, 1914-1970. 3. Poor. 4. Stigma (Social psychology). I. Series: ICA publikatie , nr. 68. II. Title.
HC79.P6 H34 1985

Hakizimana, Déo. Bahizi, Joseph. Monographie d'unités domestiques. [Bujumbura] [1985] 41 leaves ; LC Card 86-980542
HC880.Z7 M843 1985

Hakoun, Mitchell. Accountant's complete model letter book / Mitchell Hakoun, Gerald Tomlinson. Englewood Cliffs, N.J. : Prentice-Hall, c1987. xxi, 424 p. : forms ; 29 cm. Bibliography: p. 415-416. Includes index. ISBN 0-13-001199-1 : LC Card 87-11548 DDC 657 19
1. Commercial correspondence. 2. Accounting. 3. Form letters. I. Tomlinson, Gerald, 1933-. II. Title.
HF5726 .H3257 1987

HAL plain and simple . Bingham, Julie E. Reading, Mass. , c1988. vii, 296 p. : ISBN 0-201-08002-8 (pbk.) : LC Card 87-17524 DDC 005.36/9 19
HF5548.4.L68 B56 1988

HAL plain & simple. Bingham, Julie E. HAL plain and simple . Reading, Mass. , c1988. vii, 296 p. : ISBN 0-201-08002-8 (pbk.) : LC Card 87-17524 DDC 005.36/9 19
HF5548.4.L68 B56 1988

Halász, Péter. Nemzedéki vonások a mezőgazdasági kistermelésben / Halász Péter. Budapest : Agrárgazdasági Kutató Intézet, 1984. 72 p. ; 29 cm. (Agrárgazdasági Kutató Intézet, 0209-5696 . 1984/14) Bibliography: p. 71-72. ISBN 963-491-192-7 LC Card 86-198744
1. Private plot agriculture - Hungary. 2. Intergenerational relations - Hungary. I. Series: Agrárgazdasági Kutató Intézet (Series) , 1984/14. II. Title.
HD1476.H8 H252 1984

Halberstam, David. The reckoning / David Halberstam. New York : Morrow, c1986. 752 p. ; 25 cm. Includes index. Bibliography: p. [735]-740. ISBN 0-688-04838-2 LC Card 86-16427 DDC 338.4/76292/0973 19
1. Automobile industry and trade - United States. 2. Automobiles - United States - Fuel consumption. 3. Petroleum industry and trade - United States. 4. Energy consumption - United States. I. Title.
HD9710.U52 H28 1986
NYPL [JLE 86-4151]

Halbherr, Philipp. Makromodelle und Wirtschaftspolitik . Grüsch , c1985. 120 p. : ISBN 3-7253-0250-2 : LC Card 85-208009
HC397 .M26 1985

Halbzeitbilanz '85 . Barschel, Uwe. Kiel [1985] 1 v. (various pagings) : LC Card 86-211699
HC287.S35 B37 1985

Hale, William M. Turkish agriculture and Community enlargement / William M. Hale. [Ankara] : DPT, 1984. 37 p. ; 24 cm. (Yayın / Devlet Planlama Teşkilatı . no. DPT 1949. AETB ; 12) "Mart, 1984." Bibliography: p. [36]-37. LC Card 87-113782 DDC 338.9561 s 338.1/09561 19
1. Produce trade - Turkey. 2. Turkey - Commerce - European Economic Community countries. 3. European Economic Community countries - Commerce - Turkey. 4. Exports - Turkey. 5. European Economic Community - Turkey. I. Series: Yayın (Devlet Planlama Teşkilatı (Turkey)) , no. DPT 1949. II. Title.
HC401 .A356 no. 1949 HD9016.T82

Halevy, Eva Etzioni- see Etzioni-Halevy, Eva.

Haley, Charles T. To do good and do well [microform] : middle class Blacks and the depression, Philadelphia, 1929-1941 / by Charles T. Haley. 1980. x, 233 leaves ; 28 cm. Thesis (Ph. D.)--State University of New York at Binghamton, 1980. Abstract. Bibliography: leaves 223-233. Microfilm of typescript. Ann Arbor, Mich. : University Microfilms International, 1980. 1 microfilm reel ; 35 mm.
1. Afro-Americans - Pennsylvania - Philadelphia. 2. Afro-Americans - Pennsylvania - Philadelphia - Social conditions. 3. Afro-Americans - Pennsylvania - Philadelphia - Social life and customs. 4. Afro-Americans - Pennsylvania - Philadelphia - Economic conditions. 5. Depressions - 1929 - United States. 6. Middle classes - United States. I. Title.
NYPL [Sc Micro R-4654]

Haley, Charles W. Schall, Lawrence D. Introduction to financial management /. New York , c1988. xvii, 856 p. : ISBN 0-07-055112-X LC Card 87-21450 DDC 658.1/5 19
HG4011 .S33 1988

Haley, Stephen L. The value of the dollar and competitiveness of U. S. wheat exports / Stephen L. Haley, Barry Krissoff. [Washington, D.C.] : U. S. Dept. of Agriculture, Economic Research Service, International Economics Division, [1986] iv, 28 p. : ill. ; 28 cm. (ERS staff report . no. AGES 860611) Cover title. "July 1986"--p. iii. Bibliography: p. 23-24. LC Card 86-602853 DDC 382/.41311/0973 19
1. Wheat trade - United States. 2. Wheat trade. 3. Wheat - Prices. 4. Dollar, American. 5. Competition, International. I. Krissoff, Barry. II. United States. Dept. of Agriculture. Economic Research Service. International Economics Division. III. Title.
HD9049.W5 U4288 1986

Haley, Stephen W. Effective credit management in the equipment leasing and finance industry / prepared by Peat Marwick for the American Association of Equipment Lessors. Arlington, VA : The Association, c1986. ix, 121 p. : ill. ; 28 cm. "Authors: Stephen W. Haley ... Mary Ann Colihan"--T.p. verso. ISBN 0-912413-01-8 (pbk.) LC Card 87-105306 DDC 658.1/5242 19
1. Industrial equipment leases - United States - Finance. 2. Credit - United States - Management. I. Colihan, Mary Ann. II. Peat, Marwick, Mitchell & Co. III. American Association of Equipment Lessors. IV. Title.
HD39.4 .H35 1986

Half, Robert.
[Success guide for accountants]
Robert Half's success guide for accountants / Robert Half. 2nd ed. New York : McGraw-Hill, c1987. x, 167 p. ; 24 cm. (Accounting and finance practice series) Includes index. ISBN 0-07-172107-X LC Card 87-16430 DDC 657/.023/72 19
1. Accounting - Vocational guidance. I. Title. II. Title: Success guide for accountants. III. Series.
HF5657 .H34 1987

Halifax, N. S. Dalhousie University. see **Dalhousie University.**

Halim, Abdul, 1945- The effects of rice based cropping system research on women in Bangladesh / Abdul Halim, M. Hazrat Ali. Mymensingh : Graduate Training Institute, Bangladesh Agricultural University, 1986. 2, 30 leaves ; 29 cm. (GTI pub. . no. 65) Bibliography: leaf 19. LC Card 86-901954 DDC 331.4/8318/095492 19
1. Women agricultural laborers - Bangladesh. 2. Rural women - Bangladesh - Social conditions. I. Ali, M. Hazrat. II. Series: G.T.I. pub. , no. 65. III. Title.
HD1537.B3 H35 1986

Halkovics, László. A magyar vegyipar fejlődése, 1945-1980 között és eredményei a magyar népgazdaság szolgálatában / összeállította, Halkovics László. Budapest : Magyar Kémikusok Egyesülete Tervgazdasági Bizottsága, [1985] 50 p. ; 29 cm. Bibliography: p. 48-50. ISBN 963-8191-50-3 (Magy. nmz. bibl.) LC Card 86-148561

1. Chemical industry - Hungary - History. I. Title.
HD9656.H92 H35 1985

Hall, Andrew.
Baltic states revenues / by Andrew Hall. York, England : J. Barefoot, c1983. 40 p. : ill. ; 30 cm. (European philately . 9) Bibliography: p. 3. ISBN 0-906845-14-9 (pbk.) LC Card 87-100278 DDC 769.5/7 19
1. Revenue-stamps - Baltic States - Catalogs. I. Title. II. Series.
HJ5429.B34 H34 1983

Barefoot, John. Georgia /. York, England , c1983. 66 p. : ISBN 0-906845-19-X (pbk.) LC Card 87-100272 DDC 769.5694795 19
HE6185.S653 G463 1983

Hall, Bruno. Kapazitätsfestlegung in Distributionssystemen / Bruno Hall. München : Minerva Publikation, c1986. xiii, 266 p. ; 21 cm. (Wirtschaftsinformatik und quantitative Betriebswirtschaftslehre . 21) Bibliography: p. 259-266. ISBN 3-597-10558-0 LC Card 87-127684 DDC 658.7/88 19
1. Physical distribution of goods. I. Title. II. Series.
HF5415.6 .H35 1986

Hall, Gus. Working class USA : the power and the movement / by Gus Hall.1st ed. New York : International Publishers, 1987. 392 p. : ill. ; 23 cm. Bibliography: p. [373]-381. Includes index. ISBN 0-7178-0660-X : LC Card 87-3232 DDC 305.5/62/0973 19
1. Labor and laboring classes - United States - History. 2. Social conflict - United States - History. 3. Communist Party of the United States of America - History. I. Title.
HD8066 .H29 1987

Hall, Jacquelyn Dowd. Like a family . Chapel Hill , c1987. xxiii, 468 p. : ISBN 0-8078-1754-6 (alk. paper) LC Card 87-40135 DDC 305/.9677 19
HD9077.A13 L55 1987

Hall, John, 1946- Reducing industrial oil costs / John Hall and Graham Hankinson. Aldershot, Hants England ; Brookfield, Vt., U. S.A. : Gower Technical Press, c1987. xvii, 118 p. : ill. ; 31 cm. (Gower executive report) ISBN 0-291-39740-9 (U. S.) : LC Card 86-29511 DDC 338.2/3 19
1. Petroleum products - Prices. 2. Petroleum industry and trade - Costs. 3. Industry - Energy consumption - Costs. 4. Petroleum products - Great Britain - Purchasing. I. Hankinson, Graham, 1947-. II. Title. III. Series.
HD9560.4 .H35 1987

Hall, John A., 1949- Europe and the rise of capitalism /. Oxford [Oxfordshire] , New York, NY, USA , 1987. p. cm. ISBN 0-631-15006-4 : LC Card 87-12293 DDC 330.94 19
HC240.9.C3 E97 1987

Hall, John R. Pascon, Paul. [Haouz de Marrakech. English.] Capitalism and agriculture in the Haouz of Marrakesh /. London ; New York : 248 p. : ISBN 0-7103-0189-8 LC Card 87-100309 DDC 338.1/0964/6 19
HD2121.Z9 M37613 1986

Hall, Kenneth O. The Group of 77 : strengthening its negotiating capacity : a report / by Kenneth O. Hall ; with a note from Ismail-Sabri Abdalla. Nyon, Switzerland : Third World Forum, 1979. 48 p. ; 21 cm. (Occasional paper (Third World Forum) . no. 11) Bibliography: p. 39-40. LC Card 86-202645
1. Group of 77. 2. Developing countries - Commercial policy. I. 'Abd Allāh, Ismā'īl Ṣabrī. II. Series. III. Series: Occasional paper (Third World Forum) , no. 11. IV. Title.
HF1413 .H27 1979

Hall, Maximilian. The city revolution : causes and consequences / Maximilian Hall. New York : St. Martin's Press, 1987. xiii, 147 p. ; 23 cm. Bibliography: p. 141-142. Includes index. ISBN 0-312-00986-0 : LC Card 87-9684 DDC 332.6/0941 19
1. Finance - Great Britain. 2. Finance - England - London. 3. Stock Exchange (London, England). I. Title.
HG186.G7 H35 1987

Hall, Patrice A. Starr, Martin Kenneth, 1927- The performance of Japanese-owned firms in America, 1982-1985 /. [New York, NY] , c1987. ii, 41 leaves : LC Card 87-145262 DDC 338.8/8952/073 19
HD2785 .S66 1987

Hall, Peter A. Governing the economy : the politics of state intervention in Britain and France / Peter A. Hall. Cambridge, U.K. : Polity Press ; Oxford, U.K. : In association with B. Blackwell, 1986. 341 p. ; 24 cm. (Europe and the international order) Bibliography: p. [292]-321. Includes index. ISBN 0-7456-0227-4 : LC Card 87-672535
1. Great Britain - Economic policy - 1945-. 2. France - Economic policy. I. Title. II. Series.
HC256.5 .H256x 1986b

Hall, Peter Geoffrey.
The Spatial impact of technological change /. Totowa, NJ , 1987. p. cm. ISBN 0-389-20753-5 LC Card 87-11460 DDC 338/.06 19
HC79.T4 S77 1987

Western sunrise . London , Boston , 1987. xvi, 208 p. : ISBN 0-04-338142-1 LC Card 86-28755 DDC 338.6/042 19
HC260.H53 W47 1987

Hall, Peter (Peter J.), 1932- Elements of banking / Peter J. Hall, B. Julian Beecham. London ; New York : Longman, 1987. xi, 236 p. : ill. ; 22 cm. (Longman exam guides) Includes index. ISBN 0-582-29728-1 (pbk.) LC Card 86-21144 DDC 332.1 19
1. Banks and banking. 2. Finance. 3. Banks and banking - Great Britain. 4. Finance - Great Britain. I. Beecham, B. Julian, 1927-. II. Title. III. Series.
HG1601 .H25 1987

Hall, Peter, 1931- Can rail save the city? : the impacts of rail rapid transit and pedestrianisation on British and German cities / Peter Hall and Carmen Hass-Klau. Aldershot, Hants ; Brookfield, Vt., U. S.A. : Gower Pub. Co., c1985. xii, 241 p. : ill., maps ; 23 cm. Includes index. Bibliography: p. 225-239. ISBN 0-566-00947-1 : LC Card 85-17659 DDC 388.4/2/0943 19
1. Street-railroads - Germany (West) - Case studies. 2. Street-railroads - Great Britain - Case studies. 3. Subways - Germany (West) - Case studies. 4. Subways - Great Britain - Case studies. 5. Pedestrian areas - Germany (West) - Case studies. 6. Pedestrian areas - Great Britain - Case studies. 7. Central business districts - Germany (West) - Case studies. 8. Central business districts - Great Britain - Case studies. I. Hass-Klau, Carmen. II. Title.
HE4774 .H35 1985 ***NYPL [JLD 86-2622]***

Hall, Philippa. O'Donnell, Carol. Getting equal . Sidney , Boston , 1988. p. cm. ISBN 0-04-302005-4 LC Card 87-22302 DDC 331.2/1 19
HD6060.5.A8 O365 1988

Hall, R. Duane.
The corporate board : an executive guide to multinational leadership / R. Duane Hall.1st ed. New York : Random House Professional Business Publications, c1987. p. cm. Bibliography: p. Includes index. ISBN 0-394-55327-6 : LC Card 87-4937 DDC 658.4/22 19
1. Directors of corporations. 2. Comparative management. I. Title.
HD2745 .H34 1987

International purchasing : an executive guide / R. Duane Hall. New York : Random House Professional Business Publications, c1987. p. cm. Bibliography: p. Includes index. ISBN 0-394-55326-8 : LC Card 87-4926 DDC 658.7/2 19
1. Industrial procurement. 2. Purchasing. 3. Shipping. 4. Foreign trade regulation - United States. I. Title.
HD39.5 .H34 1987

Hall, Richard, 1937- The Prices Surveillance Authority / Richard Hall, John Nieuwenhuysen. Melbourne : Committee for Economic Development of Australia, [1987] 24 p. ; 29 cm. (Information paper . no. IP23) "January 1987." "CEDA study." ISBN 0-85801-167-0 (pbk.) LC Card 87-156317 DDC 338.5/26/0994 19
1. Australia. Prices Surveillance Authority. 2. Price regulation - Australia. I. Nieuwenhuysen, J. P. II. Series: Information paper (Committee for Economic Development of Australia) , no. IP 23. III. Title.
HB236.A8 H35 1987

Hall, Richard H., 1934- Organizational theory and public policy /. Beverly Hills, Calif. , c1983. 304 p. : ISBN 0-8039-2006-7 LC Card 83-9704 DDC 302.3/5 19
HD38 .O75 1983 ***NYPL [JLD 87-1123]***

Hall, Robert W. (Robert William), 1939- Media math : basic techniques of media evaluation / Robert W. Hall. Lincolnwood, Ill., U. S.A. : NTC Business Books, c1987. v, 138 p. : ill. ; 28 cm. Includes index. ISBN 0-8442-3142-8 (pbk.) : LC Card 86-62067 DDC 659.1/01/51 19
1. Advertising media planning - Mathematics. 2. Business mathematics. I. Title.
HF5826.5 .H35 1987

HALLANDS LÄN (SWEDEN) - POPULATION, RURAL.
Ydborn, Lars. Befolkningstillväxt och jordbruk . Göteborg , c1984. 214 p. : ISBN 91-7222-705-2 LC Card 84-194466
HB2498.H35 Y38 1984

HALLANDS LÄN (SWEDEN) - RURAL CONDITIONS.
Ydborn, Lars. Befolkningstillväxt och jordbruk . Göteborg , c1984. 214 p. : ISBN 91-7222-705-2 LC Card 84-194466
HB2498.H35 Y38 1984

Hallauer, Robert. Export promotion policies in Costa Rica : the works of CENPRO and development problems of the agroindustrial sector / Robert Hallauer. Austin : Office for Public Sector Studies, Institute of Latin American Studies, University of Texas at Austin, 1985. 17 p. ; 28 cm. (Technical papers series . no. 51) Bibliography: p. 15-17. LC Card 86-622254 DDC 382/.63/097286 19
1. Centro para la Promoción de las Exportaciones y las Inversiones (Costa Rica). 2. Foreign trade promotion - Costa Rica. 3. Agriculture - Economic aspects - Costa Rica. I. Title. II. Series.
HF1487 .H35 1985

HALLE BROS. CO. - HISTORY.
Wood, James M., 1939- Halle's . Cleveland, Ohio , 1987. 223 p. : ISBN 0-940601-02-8 : LC Card 87-15010 DDC 381/.45/000977132 19
HF5465.U6 H359 1987

HALLE (GERMANY : BEZIRK) - CENSUS, 1964.
Volks- und Berufszählung am 31. Dezember 1964 . [Halle] , 1966. 60 p. ; LC Card 85-123405
HA1347.H34 V64 1966

Hallensleben, Ruth. Frauenarbeit in der Industrie : Fotografien aus den Jahren 1938-1967 / Ruth Hallensleben ; herausgegeben und ausgewählt von Ursula Peters ; mit Texten von Kah Jagals ... [et al.]. Berlin-Kreuzberg : D. Nishen, c1985. 157 p. : ill. ; 20 cm. (Das Foto-Taschenbuch . 2) Includes bibliographical references. ISBN 3-88940-602-5 : LC Card 86-201457
1. Women - Employment - Germany, West. 2. Women - Employment - Germany (West) - Pictorial works. I. Peters, Ursula, 1950-. II. Jagals, Kah, 1921-. III. Title. IV. Series.
HD6149 .H27 1985

Haller, Matthias. Risiko-Management /. Wiesbaden [1986] 145 p. : ISBN 3-409-17902-X LC Card 86-161867
HD70.G2 S3 Bd. 33 HD61

Halle's . Wood, James M., 1939- Cleveland, Ohio , 1987. 223 p. : ISBN 0-940601-02-8 : LC Card 87-15010 DDC 381/.45/000977132 19
HF5465.U6 H359 1987

Hallman, G. Victor. Personal financial planning / G. Victor Hallman, Jerry S. Rosenbloom. 4th ed. New York : McGraw-Hill, c1987. xix, 475 p. : ill., forms ; 24 cm. Includes index. ISBN 0-07-025650-0 : LC Card 87-2584 DDC 332.024 19
1. Finance, Personal. I. Rosenbloom, Jerry S. II. Title.
HG179 .H24 1987

Halloran, Jack, 1931- Applied human relations : an organizational approach / Jack Halloran, Douglas Benton.3rd ed. Englewood Cliffs, N.J. : Prentice-Hall, c1987. xvi, 528 p. : ill. ; 25 cm. Includes bibliographies and index. ISBN 0-13-040742-9 LC Card 86-25336 DDC 658.3 19
1. Organizational behavior. 2. Management. 3. Personnel management. I. Benton, Douglas, 1937-. II. Title.
HD58.7 .H34 1987

Halloran, James W. The entrepreneur's guide to starting a successful business / James W. Halloran. 1st ed. Blue Ridge Summit, PA : Liberty House, c1987. ix, 243 p. : ill. ; 24 cm. Bibliography: p. 229. Includes index. ISBN 0-8306-3049-X (pbk.) : LC Card 86-27410 DDC 658.1/141 19

1. New business enterprises. 2. Entrepreneur. I. Title.
HD62.5 .H35 1987

Hallows, Karen S. Walstad, William B. An annotated catalog of microcomputer software in economics /. New York, NY (2 Park Ave., New York 10016) , c1986. viii, 160 p. ; LC Card 86-210285 DDC 330/.028/5536 19
HB74.8 .W34 1986

Halmai, Péter. Integráció és tulajdon az iparosodó mezőgazdaságban / Halmai Péter. [Budapest] : Művelődési Minisztérium Marxizmus-Leninizmus Oktatási Főosztálya, 1984. 124 p. ; 24 cm. (Politikai gazdaságtan füzetek, 0324-6396 . 43) Summary in Russian. Includes bibliographical references. ISBN 963-673-278-7 LC Card 85-126691
1. Agriculture - Economic aspects - Hungary. 2. Agricultural industries - Hungary - Consolidation. 3. Right of property - Hungary. I. Title. II. Series.
HD1940.5 .H35 1984

Halmos, Csaba. A szakszervezetek és a tervezés / [irták Halmos Csaba, Müller Lajos, Terbócs László]. Budapest : Szakszervezetek Elméleti Kutató Intézete, 1983. 178 p. ; 21 cm. Bibliography: p. 88-91. ISBN 963-608-052-6 LC Card 85-108502
1. Trade-unions - Hungary. 2. Welfare work in industry - Hungary. I. Müller, Lajos. II. Terbócs, László. III. Title.
HD6680.5 .H34 1983

Halper, Robert F. Computer data center design : a guide to planning, designing, constructing, and operating computer data centers / Robert F. Halper. New York : Wiley, c1985. xv, 189 p. : ill. ; 23 cm. "A Wiley-Interscience publication." Includes index. ISBN 0-471-82579-4 : LC Card 85-5347 DDC 658/.054 19
1. Data processing service centers - Planning. 2. Data processing service centers - Design and construction. I. Title.
HD9696.C62 H24 1985 ***NYPL [JSE 86-1294]***

Halper, Stanley D. Handbook of EDP auditing. Boston , c1986. 1 v. (various pagings) : ISBN 0-88712-597-2 (pbk.) LC Card 87-107300 DDC 657/.45/0285 19
HF5548.35 .H36 1986

Halpern, Burton M. Tell it to the world : a guide to international public relations / Burton M. Halpern. Jerusalem ; New York, N.Y. : Gefen Books, [c1982] 152 p. ; 25 cm. ISBN 965-229-004-1 LC Card 86-214902 DDC 659.2 19
1. Public relations. 2. International economic relations. 3. International relations. I. Title. II. Title: International public relations.
HD59 .H25 1982

Halpern, Diane F. Sex differences in cognitive abilities / Diane F. Halpern. Hillsdale, N.J. : Erlbaum Associates, 1986. x, 189 p. : ill. ; 24 cm. Includes indexes. Bibliography: p. 163-174. ISBN 0-89859-579-7 LC Card 86-11506 DDC 155.3/3 19
1. Cognition. 2. Sex differences (Psychology). 3. Sex role. I. Title.
BF311 .H295 1986 ***NYPL [JFE 86-4001]***

Halpern, Martin, 1945- UAW politics in the cold war era/ Martin Halpern. Albany, N.Y. : State University of New York Press, c1988. p. cm. (SUNY series in American labor history) Bibliography: p. Includes index. ISBN 0-88706-671-2 LC Card 87-13890 DDC 322/.2/0973 19
1. International Union, United Automobile, Aerospace, and Agricultural Implement Workers of America - History. 2. Trade-unions and communism - United States - History - Case studies. I. Title. II. Series.
HD6515.A82 I574 1988

Ḥalqah al-niqāshīyah .
(5) Tanmiyah al-ʻArabīyah wa-al-ʻalāqāt al-dawlīyah /. al-Kuwayt , 1983. 230, 96 p. ; LC Card 86-964623
HC498 .T349 1983

Halting the march . Mann, H. S. (Haracharan Singh), 1922- [New Delhi] [1983] 35, [1] p., [4] p. of plates : LC Card 86-204352 DDC 338.1/0954/4 19
HC437.T47 M36 1983

Halvfems plus ti. 90 plus 10 /. [Copenhagen] [1986] 39 p. : ISBN 87-7002-353-0 LC Card 86-197313
HD5799.A6 A12 1986

Hamberger, Sylvia. Bode, Peter M. Alptraum Auto . München , 1986. 237 p. : ISBN 3-922696-46-5 LC Card 87-107197 DDC 303.4/832 19
HE5613 .B63 1986

Hambleton, Ronald, 1917- The branding of America : from Levi Strauss to Chrysler, from Westinghouse to Gillette, the forgotten fathers of America's best-known brand names / by Ronald Hambleton.1st ed. Dublin, N.H. : Yankee Books, c1987. 224 p. : ill., ports. ; 29 cm. Includes index. ISBN 0-89909-101-6 : LC Card 86-80335 DDC 338/.02/0973 19
1. Brand name products - United States - History. I. Title.
HF1040.8 .H36 1987

Hambre + dignidad=ollas comunes /. Hardy, Clarisa. [Santiago, Chile] , 1986. 282 p., [16] p. of plates : ***NYPL [JLD 87-334]***

Hambre mas dignidad igual ollas comunes. Hardy, Clarisa. Hambre + dignidad=ollas comunes /. [Santiago, Chile] , 1986. 282 p., [16] p. of plates : ***NYPL [JLD 87-334]***

Hambre y dignidad igual ollas comunes. Hardy, Clarisa. Hambre + dignidad=ollas comunes /. [Santiago, Chile] , 1986. 282 p., [16] p. of plates : ***NYPL [JLD 87-334]***

Hamburg. Arbeitsgemeinschaft Deutsche Lateinamerika-Forschung. see **Arbeitsgemeinschaft Deutsche Lateinamerika-Forschung.**

Hamburg. Deutsches Orient-Institut. Mitteilungen.
(Nr. 15) Pennisi, Giuseppe. Development, manpower and migration in the Red Sea region . Hamburg , c1981. xi, 264 p. : LC Card 82-109615 DDC 331.6/2/091824 19
HD8656 .P46 1981 ***NYPL [JLF 86-1602]***

HAMBURG (GERMANY) - COMMERCE - HISTORY.
Stadt und Hafen . Hamburg , 1986. 209 p. : ISBN 3-7672-0951-9 LC Card 87-130912 DDC 387.1/0943/515 19
HE558.H3 S7 1986

HAMBURG (GERMANY) - ECONOMIC CONDITIONS.
Ahrens, Gerhard, 1939- Krisenmanagement 1857 . Hamburg , 1986. 136 p. ; ISBN 3-923356-11-0 LC Card 87-127645 DDC 338.5/4 19
HB3717 1857 .A38 1986

Arbeiter in Hamburg . Hamburg , c1983. 606 p. : ISBN 3-8103-0807-2 LC Card 86-174037
HD8460.H36 A73 1983

HAMBURG (GERMANY) - ECONOMIC POLICY.
Ahrens, Gerhard, 1939- Krisenmanagement 1857 . Hamburg , 1986. 136 p. ; ISBN 3-923356-11-0 LC Card 87-127645 DDC 338.5/4 19
HB3717 1857 .A38 1986

HAMBURG (GERMANY) - INDUSTRIES.
Die Hamburger Industrie im Anpassungsprozess. Hamburg , 1980. 31 p. : LC Card 84-216971
HC289.H2 H42 1980

Vollzug und Wirkungen regionaler Umweltpolitik . Opladen , 1984. 199 p. ; ISBN 3-8100-0392-1 LC Card 84-228636
HC290.5.E5 V65 1984

HAMBURG (GERMANY) - INDUSTRIES - LOCATION.
Pohle, Michael. Industriebrachen und extensiv genutzte Flächen in innenstadtnahen Gewerbegebieten . Paderborn , 1985. viii, 121 p. : ISBN 3-506-73577-2 : LC Card 86-183775
HC289.H2 P64 1985

Hamburg (Germany). Senatsamt für den Verwaltungsdienst. Gührs, Eckhard. Leitfaden für Kostenermittlung und Wirtschaftlichkeitsprüfung . Hamburg , 1983. iii, 92 p. ; LC Card 85-212548
HJ9925.G3 G84 1983

HAMBURG (GERMANY) - SOCIAL CONDITIONS.
Grüttner, Michael. Arbeitswelt an der Wasserkante . Göttingen , 1984. 331 p. ; ISBN 3-525-35722-2 (Deut. Bibl.) LC Card 86-139479
HD8039.L82 G4335 1984

Hamburg (Germany). Statistisches Landesamt. Das Handwerk in Hamburg . Hamburg [1979] 140 p. ; LC Card 86-133694
HA1282 .A Heft 128 HD2346.G32H3

Hamburger Arbeitskreis für Regionalgeschichte. Stadt und Hafen . Hamburg , 1986. 209 p. : ISBN 3-7672-0951-9 LC Card 87-130912 DDC 387.1/0943/515 19
HE558.H3 S7 1986

Hamburger Bankengeschichte /. Pohl, Manfred, 1944- Mainz , c1986. 264 p., [20] p. of plates : ISBN 3-7758-1136-2 LC Card 87-104548
HG3060.H22 P64 1986

Hamburger Beiträge zur Friedensforschung und Sicherheitspolitik .
(Heft 3) Wilke, Peter. Manpower conversion in defence related industry . Hamburg [1986] 62 p. : LC Card 86-212660 DDC 331.25/924 19
HC79.D4 W55 1986

Die Hamburger Industrie im Anpassungsprozess. Hamburg : Hamburgische Landesbank, 1980. 31 p. : ill. ; 21 cm. (Wirtschaftsanalysen . 3/1980) LC Card 84-216971
1. Hamburg (Germany) - Industries. 2. Germany, West - Industries. I. Hamburgische Landesbank, Girozentrale. II. Series: Wirtschaftsanalysen , 1980/3.
HC289.H2 H42 1980

Hamburger Schriften zum Genossenschaftswesen .
(Bd. 1) Bänsch, Axel. Operationalisierung des Unternehmenszieles Mitgliederförderung /. Göttingen , c1983. xv, 245 p. ; ISBN 3-525-12750-2 LC Card 83-199427
HD3498 .B35 1983

(Bd. 3) Schwenk, Andreas. Die Kreditwürdigkeit der eingetragenen Genossenschaft /. Göttingen , c1984. xiv, 287 p. ; ISBN 3-525-12752-9 LC Card 86-139501
HG3711.G3 S36 1984

(Bd. 5) Lipfert, Helmut. Mitgliederförderndes Kooperations- und Konkurrenzmanagement in genossenschaftlichen Systemen /. Göttingen , c1986. xvii, 302 p. : ISBN 3-525-12754-5 LC Card 86-235180 DDC 334/.068 19
HD3498 .L53 1986

(Bd.1) Bänsch, Axel. Operationalisierung des Unternehmenszieles, Mitgliederförderung /. Göttingen , 1983. xv, 245 p. ; ISBN 3-525-12750-2 ***NYPL [JLE 86-1770]***

Hamburger Stiftung für Sozialgeschichte des 20. Jahrhunderts. Ermittlungen gegen die Dresdner Bank, 1946 /. Nördlingen , 1986. cxxxiv, 353 p., [8] p. of plates : ISBN 3-89190-297-2 : LC Card 87-121689
HG3058.D7 E76 1986

Hamburger Universitätsreden, 0438-4822 .
(44) Die Protestantische Ethik und der Verfall des Kapitalismus . [Hamburg] , 1985. 31 p. : LC Card 86-112068
HB501 .P76 1985

Hamburgische Landesbank, Girozentrale. Dienstleistungsmetropole Hamburg . Hamburg [1980] 27 p. ; LC Card 84-216975
HD9984.8.H3 D54 1980

Die Hamburger Industrie im Anpassungsprozess. Hamburg , 1980. 31 p. : LC Card 84-216971
HC289.H2 H42 1980

Hamdan, Lawrence. Graham, Lawrence. Youthtrends . New York , c1987. xx, 282 p. ; ISBN 0-312-00704-3 : LC Card 87-4426 DDC 658.8/348 19
HC110.C6 G67 1987

Hamer, Eberhard.
Mittelstand, Träger der Marktwirtschaft : Beiträge zur Mittelstands- und Wettbewerbspolitik / Eberhard Hamer. Minden : A. Philler, c1984- v. ; 22 cm. (Schriftenreihe des Mittelstandsinstituts Niedersachsen e.V. . Bd. 10-) A collection of the author's essays previously published in various periodicals. "Festschrift für Klaus Nottbohm." ISBN 3-7907-3056-4 (Bd. 1) LC Card 85-175274 DDC 338.6/42/0943 19
1. Nottbohm, Klaus, 1927- - Addresses, essays, lectures. 2. Small business - Germany, West - Addresses, essays, lectures. 3. Industry and state - Germany, West - Addresses, essays, lectures. I. Nottbohm, Klaus, 1927-. II. Series: Schriftenreihe des Mittelstandsinstituts Niedersachsen e.V. , Bd. 10, etc. III. Title.
HD2346.G3 H215 1984 ***NYPL [JLK 86-61]***

Die Unternehmerlücke / Eberhard Hamer. Stuttgart : Poller, 1984. 238 p. ; 21 cm. Includes bibliographical references and index. ISBN 3-87959-223-3 LC Card 85-128353
1. Entrepreneurship. I. Title.
HB615 .H235 1984

Hamermesh, Daniel S. The economics of work and pay / Daniel S. Hamermesh, Albert Rees. 4th ed. New York : Harper & Row, c1988. xii, 452 p. : ill. ; 24 cm. Includes bibliographical references and indexes. ISBN 0-06-045356-7 LC Card 87-18355 DDC 331 19
1. Labor economics. I. Rees, Albert, 1921-. II. Title.
HD4901 .H18 1988

Hamermesh, Richard G. Making strategy work : how senior managers produce results / Richard G. Hamermesh. New York : Wiley, c1986. xiii, 245 p. : ill. ; 25 cm. (The Wiley management series on problem solving, decision making, and strategic thinking) Includes index. Bibliography: p. 231-240. ISBN 0-471-80319-7 : LC Card 85-12456 DDC 658.4/012 19
1. Strategic planning. 2. Industrial management - Case studies. I. Title. II. Series.
HD30.28 .H35 1986 ***NYPL [JLE 86-2018]***

Hames, M. J. Clements, R. T. The Reserve Bank econometric model of the New Zealand economy . Wellington [1986] 62 p., [2] leaves of plates : LC Card 87-142103 DDC 330.9931/00724 19
HC665 .C54 1986

Hamid, Edy Suandi, 1957- Kredit pedesaan di Indonesia /. Yogyakarta , 1986. xii, 160 p. ; LC Card 86-943011
HG2051.I65 K74 1986

Hamilton, Adrian, 1944- Oil : the price of power / edited [i.e. compiled] by Adrian Hamilton. London : M. Joseph/Rainbird in association with Channel Four Television Co., 1986. 191 p., [16] p. of plates : ill. (some col.) ; 24 cm. Bibliography: p. [180]-181. Includes index. ISBN 0-7181-2783-8 : LC Card 87-106290 DDC 338.2/7282/09 19
1. Petroleum industry and trade - History. I. Title.
HD9560.5 .H25 1986

Hamilton, Billy. Outlook for state spending and revenues in the late '80s : a speech given at the Third Annual Conference for Editors of Texas Newspapers, San Antonio, Texas, October 12, 1985 / by Billy Hamilton. College Station, Tex. : Center for Education and Research in Free Enterprise, Texas A&M University, c1985. 14 p. : ill. ; 22 cm. (Series on public issues . no. 19) ISBN 0-86599-055-7 (pbk.) LC Card 86-622256 DDC 336.764 19
1. Texas - Appropriations and expenditures. 2. Revenue - Texas. 3. Texas - Economic conditions. I. Texas A & M University. Center for Education and Research in Free Enterprise. II. Title. III. Series.
HJ2053.T5 H36 1985

Hamilton, Cheryl. Communicating for results : a guide for business and the professions / Cheryl Hamilton, Cordell Parker.2nd ed. Belmont, Calif. : Wadsworth Pub. Co., c1987. xiii, 418 p. : ill. ; 24 cm. Includes bibliographies and indexes. ISBN 0-534-07956-3 (pbk.) LC Card 86-28108 DDC 658.4/5 19
1. Communication in management. I. Parker, Cordell. II. Title.
HD30.3 .H35 1987

Hamilton, F. E. Ian.
Industrial change in advanced economies /. London , Wolfeboro, N.H. , c1987. 319 p. : ISBN 0-7099-3828-4 : LC Card 86-19661 DDC 338.09 19
HC79.T4 H35 1987 ***NYPL [JLD 87-410]***

Industrialization in developing and peripheral regions /. London , Dover, N.H. , c1986. 363 p. ; ISBN 0-7099-3827-6 : LC Card 86-4159 DDC 338.09172/4 19
HD2329 .I54 1986 ***NYPL [JLD 86-2985]***

Hamilton, Geoffrey. Red multinationals or red herrings? . London , 1986. xi, 202 p. ; ISBN 0-86187-583-4 ***NYPL [JLD 86-2751]***

Hamilton, S. W. (Stanley William), 1939- Foundations of real estate financing : the mathematical basis / by Stanley W. Hamilton, David Baxter, Daniel D. Ulinder. Vancouver : Butterworth (Western Canada), c1982. xv, 319 p. : ill. ; 25 cm. ISBN 0-409-98843-X LC Card 87-143264
1. Business mathematics - Real estate business. 2. Real estate investment - Finance - Mathematical models. I. Baxter, David, 1945-. II. Ulinder, Daniel D. III. Title.
HF5695.5.R3 H36 1982

Hamilton, Seymour, 1941- A communication audit handbook : helping organizations communicate / Seymour Hamilton. New York : Longman, c1987. x, 197 p. : ill. ; 24 cm. Bibliography: p. 193. Includes index. ISBN 0-8013-0061-4 : LC Card 87-3743 DDC 658.4/5 19
1. Communication in organizations - Auditing. 2. Management audit. I. Title.
HD30.3 .H353 1987

Hamilton, Thomas E. Forests in demand . Boston, Mass. , c1982. xv, 265 p. : ISBN 0-86569-106-1 : LC Card 81-12881 DDC 333.75/0973 19
SD565 .F58 ***NYPL [JLE 86-4465]***

Hamilton, William W. Innovations in economic development : lessons from the states / prepared for the state of Kansas by William W. Hamilton, Larry C. Ledebur, Deborah Matz. Washington, D.C. (2021 K St., Suite 711, Washington 20006) : ASLAN, [1986] 1 v. (various foliations) : ill. ; 28 cm. Cover title. "March 1986." Includes bibliographical references. LC Card 87-620522 DDC 338.973 19
1. Industrial promotion - United States - States. I. Ledebur, Larry C. II. Matz, Deborah Norelli. III. Title.
HC110.I53 H363 1986

Hämisegger, Kuno, 1956- Neue Formen des Auslandengagements : erhöhte Interdependenz in einer fragmentierten Weltwirtschaft / Kuno Hämisegger. Bern ; New York : P. Lang, c1986. 292 p. : ill. ; 21 cm. (Europäische Hochschulschriften. Reihe V, Volks- und Betriebswirtschaft . Bd. 732 = vol. 732 = vol. 732) Originally presented as the author's thesis (doctoral)--Universität Basel. Bibliography: p. 276-292. ISBN 3-261-03598-6 LC Card 86-208515
1. International economic relations. 2. Switzerland - Foreign economic relations. 3. Corporations, Swiss. I. Series: Europäische Hochschulschriften. Reihe V, Volks- und Betriebswirtschaft , Bd. 732. II. Title.
HF1411 .H253 1986

Hamlin, Alan P., 1951- Ethics, economics, and the state / Alan P. Hamlin. Brighton, Sussex : Wheatsheaf Books, 1986. x, 198 p. ; 23 cm. Includes index. Bibliography: p. 186-193.
1. Economics - Moral and ethical aspects. 2. Economics - Philosophy. 3. Political science - Philosophy. 4. Welfare economics. I. Title.
NYPL [JLD 86-3648]

Hamm, Rüdiger. Die Inzidenz sektorspezifischer Kapitalbesteuerung / Rüdiger Hamm. Krefeld : G. Marchal und H.-J. Matzenbacher, 1983. 296 p. : ill. ; 21 cm. Bibliography: p. 292-296. ISBN 3-88358-034-1 LC Card 83-218772
1. Corporations - Taxation - Econometric models. 2. Tax incidence - Econometric models. I. Title.
HD2753.A3 H36 1983

Hamm, Walter.
Aspekte zur GKV-Strukturreform /. Stuttgart , New York , 1984. x, 102 p. ; ISBN 3-437-10918-9 LC Card 84-187001
HD7102.G3 A87 1984

Eucker-Herresthal, Waltraud. Staatliche Eingriffe in den Mietwohnungsmarkt, Erfolgskontrolle und Reformvorschläge /. [Mainz] [1985?] v, 242 p. ; LC Card 87-407601 DDC 363.5/8 19
HD7288.85.G3 E92 1985

Hammer /. Hammer, Armand, 1897- New York , c1987. 544 p., [32] p. of plates : ISBN 0-399-13275-9 LC Card 86-30289 DDC 338.092/4 B 19
HC102.5.H35 A3 1987

Hammer, Armand, 1897- Hammer / Armand Hammer, with Neil Lyndon. New York : Putnam, c1987. 544 p., [32] p. of plates : ill. ; 24 cm. Includes index. ISBN 0-399-13275-9 LC Card 86-30289 DDC 338.092/4 B 19
1. Hammer, Armand, 1897-. 2. Businessmen - United States - Biography. 3. Capitalists and financiers - United States - Biography. 4. Statesmen - United States - Biography. 5. United States - Relations - Soviet Union. 6. Soviet Union - Relations - United States. I. Lyndon, Neil. II. Title.
HC102.5.H35 A3 1987

HAMMER, ARMAND, 1897-
Hammer, Armand, 1897- Hammer /. New York , c1987. 544 p., [32] p. of plates : ISBN 0-399-13275-9 LC Card 86-30289 DDC 338.092/4 B 19
HC102.5.H35 A3 1987

Laurent, Eric. La corde pour les pendre-- . Paris , c1985. 304 p. ; ISBN 2-213-01550-3 : LC Card 85-231994
HF1411 .L3645 1985

Hammer, Gottlieb, 1911- Good faith and credit / Gottlieb Hammer ; introduction by Arthur Hertzberg. New York : Cornwall Books, c1985. 258 p., [12] p. of plates : ill. ; 24 cm. Includes index. ISBN 0-8453-4798-5 (alk. paper) LC Card 85-13962 DDC 956.94/001/0973 19
1. Hammer, Gottlieb, 1911-. 2. Zionists - United States - Biography. 3. Jews - United States - Politics and government. 4. Jews - United States - Charities. 5. Israel and the Diaspora. I. Title.
DS151.H34 A34 1985
NYPL [*PWZ (Hammer, G.) 86-2026]

HAMMER, GOTTLIEB, 1911-
Hammer, Gottlieb, 1911- Good faith and credit /. New York , c1985. 258 p., [12] p. of plates : ISBN 0-8453-4798-5 (alk. paper) LC Card 85-13962 DDC 956.94/001/0973 19
DS151.H34 A34 1985
NYPL [*PWZ (Hammer, G.) 86-2026]

Hammer, Karl-Heinrich. Posttips : Geld sparen bei Post und Telefon / Karl-Heinrich Hammer, Lars Limpert.2., erw. Aufl. Bonn : Deutscher Industrie- und Handelstag, 1982. 108 p. : ill. ; 20 cm. Includes index. LC Card 83-193275
1. Postal service - Germany (West) - Rates. I. Limpert, Lars. II. Title.
HE6998 .H35 1982

Hammer, Richard, 1928- Franco, Joseph. Hoffa's man . New York , c1987. xv, 332 p., [8] p. of plates : ISBN 0-13-517764-2 : LC Card 87-42675 DDC 331.88/11388324/0924 B 19
HD6509.F69 A3 1987

Hammer, William E. Moore, James M. (James Mendon), 1925- An engineers guide to spreadsheets, word processors & data base managers /. Norcross, GA , c1986. xi, 154 p. : ISBN 0-89806-081-8 (pbk.) LC Card 87-157586 DDC 620/.0028/553 19
HF5548 .M566 1986

Hammers-Strizek, Gisela. Strizek, Helmut. Europäische Einigung . Bonn , c1984. 144 p. ; ISBN 3-87831-274-1 LC Card 84-173216
HC241 .S72 1984

Hammitt, James E.
Prague, Cary N. Programming with dBase III /. Blue Ridge Summit, Pa. , 1985. ix, 292 p. ; ISBN 0-8306-0976-8 : LC Card 84-23979 DDC 001.64/2 19
QA76.9.D3 P728 1985 ***NYPL [JSE 87-75]***

Prague, N. Cary. Programming with dBASE III PLUS /. Blue Ridge Summit, PA , c1986. vi, 375 p. : ISBN 0-8306-0326-3 : LC Card 86-5736 DDC 005.74 19
QA76.9.D3 P729 1986 ***NYPL [JSE 87-539]***

Hammond, Claire Holton, 1951- The benefits of subsidized housing programs : an intertemporal approach / Claire Holton Hammond. Cambridge [Cambridgeshire] ; New York : Cambridge University Press, 1987. ix, 140 p. ; 25 cm. Bibliography: p. 126-136. Includes index. ISBN 0-521-32752-0 LC Card 86-32638 DDC 363.5/8 19
1. Rent subsidies - United States. 2. Poor as consumers - United States. I. Title.
HD7288.83 .H36 1987

Hamouda, O. F.
Harcourt, Geoffrey Colin. Controversies in political economy . New York , 1986. 293 p. ; ISBN 0-8147-3437-5 : LC Card 85-31055 DDC 330.1 19
HB75 .H33 1986 ***NYPL [JLD 86-3571]***

Keynes and public policy after fifty years /. New York , <c1988-. v. <2 > : ISBN 0-8147-3444-8 (v. 1) : LC Card 87-20368 DDC 330.15/6 19
HB99.7 .K3815 1988

Hampe, Peter. Renten 2000 . München , c1985. 124 p. : ISBN 3-7892-7267-1 LC Card 87-118239 DDC 331.25/2/0943 19
HD7105.35.G3 R46 1985

Hampson, Fen Osler. Forming economic policy : the case of energy in Canada and Mexico / Fen Osler Hampson. London : Francis Pinter, 1986. x, 161 p. : ill. ; 24 cm. (Studies in international political economy) Includes index. Bibliography: p. [136]-156. ISBN 0-86187-628-8
1. Energy policy - Canada. 2. Energy policy - Mexico. 3. Canada - Economic policy. 4. Mexico - Economic policy 1970-. I. Title. II. Series.
NYPL [JLE 86-3813]

Hampton, David R. Organizational behavior and the practice of management / David R. Hampton, Charles E. Summer, Ross A. Webber. 5th ed. Glenview, Ill. : Scott, Foresman, c1987. 876 p. : ill. ; 24 cm. Includes bibliographies and indexes. ISBN 0-673-18303-3 LC Card 86-24798 DDC 658.4 19
1. Organizational behavior. 2. Psychology, Industrial. 3. Management. I. Summer, Charles Edgar. II. Webber, Ross A. III. Title.
HD58.7 .H35 1987

Hamrin, Carol Lee. China and the future : decision making, economic planning, and foreign policy / Carol Lee Hamrin. Boulder, Colo. : Westview Press, 1986. p. cm. Includes index. ISBN 0-8133-7364-6 : LC Card 86-28960 DDC 338.951 19
1. China - Economic policy - 1976-. 2. China - Politics and government - 1976-. I. Title.
HC427.92 .H34 1986

Hamza, M. H. IASTED Symposia on Modelling, Policy and Economics of Energy and Power Systems, and Alternative Energy Sources and Technology (1981 : San Francisco, Calif.) Proceedings of the IASTED Energy Symposia : Modelling, Policy and Economics of Energy and Power Systems [and] Alternative Energy Sources and Technology, May 20-22, 1981, San Francisco, U. S.A. /. Anaheim, Calif. [1981?] 209 p. : ISBN 0-88986-027-0
NYPL [JSF 86-1103]

Han, Fei, d. 233 B.C.
HAN FEI TZU.
Moriya, Hiroshi, 1932- Kyōsha no kanrigaku Kanpishi /. Kyōto-shi , 1984. 273 p. ; ISBN 4-569-21374-X : LC Card 85-142427
HF5387 .M67 1984 <Orien Japan>
NYPL [*OSM 87-1463]

Han Fei-tzu. Japanese & Chinese. Selections. 1984. Moriya, Hiroshi, 1932- Kyōsha no kanrigaku Kanpishi / Moriya Hiroshi. 880-03 Dai 1-han. Kyōto-shi , 1984. 273 p. ; ISBN 4-569-21374-X : LC Card 85-142427
HF5387 .M67 1984 <Orien Japan>
NYPL [*OSM 87-1463]

Hanagan, Michael P., 1947- Confrontation, class consciousness, and the labor process . Westport, Conn. , 1986. viii, 261 p. ; ISBN 0-313-25140-1 (lib. bdg. : alk. paper) LC Card 85-17734 DDC 305.5/62 19
HD4851 .C63 1986 ***NYPL [JLE 86-3558]***

Hanan, Mack. If you don't have a plan, stay in the car / Mark Hanan. New York, NY : Amacom, c1987. x, 277 p. ; 22 cm. ISBN 0-8144-5936-6 LC Card 87-47706 DDC 658.8/1 19
1. Selling. 2. Profit. I. American Management Association. II. Title.
HF5438.25 .H347 1987

Hanawalt, Barbara. Women and work in preindustrial Europe /. Bloomington , c1986. xviii, 233 p. ; ISBN 0-253-36610-0 LC Card 85-42829 DDC 331.4/094 19
HD6059.5.E85 W65 1986
NYPL [JLE 86-3381]

Hanayama, Yuzuru, 1939- Land markets and land policy in a metropolitan area : a case study of Tokyo / Yuzuru Hanayama. Boston, MA : Published by Oelgeschlager, Gunn & Hain in association with Lincoln Institute of Land Policy, 1986. xiv, 162 p. : ill. ; 24 cm. "A Lincoln Institute of Land Policy book." Includes index. Bibliography: p. [151]-153. ISBN 0-89946-197-2 LC Card 85-13867 DDC 333.77/13/0952135 19
1. Land use, Urban - Government policy - Japan - Tokyo Metropolitan Area. 2. Real property - Prices - Japan - Tokyo Metropolitan Area. 3. Real estate development - Japan - Tokyo Metropolitan Area. I. Title.
HD920.T62 H36 1986 ***NYPL [JLE 86-4398]***

HANCOCK COUNTY (ME.) - ECONOMIC CONDITIONS.
Rubertone, Patricia E. Background study of Maine coastal life . [Providence, R.I.?] , 1983. iii, 99 leaves : LC Card 86-601627 DDC 304.6/09741/45 19
HB3525.M2 R82 1983

HANCOCK COUNTY (ME.) - POPULATION - HISTORY.
Rubertone, Patricia E. Background study of Maine coastal life . [Providence, R.I.?] , 1983. iii, 99 leaves : LC Card 86-601627 DDC 304.6/09741/45 19
HB3525.M2 R82 1983

HANCOCK COUNTY (ME.) - SOCIAL CONDITIONS.
Rubertone, Patricia E. Background study of Maine coastal life . [Providence, R.I.?] , 1983. iii, 99 leaves : LC Card 86-601627 DDC 304.6/09741/45 19
HB3525.M2 R82 1983

Hancock, Keith Jackson. Japanese and Australian labour markets . Canberra [c1983] xx, 610 p. : ISBN 0-86413-004-X (pbk.) : LC Card 84-220557 DDC 331.12/0952 19
HD5850.A6 J36 1983 ***NYPL [JLE 86-630]***

Hancock, Linda. Burke, Terry, 1942- A roof over their heads . Melbourne , 1984. xiv, 178 p. : ISBN 0-642-87172-8 ***NYPL [JLD 86-2639]***

HAND WEAVING - ECONOMIC ASPECTS - PAPUA NEW GUINEA.
Philp, Norman E. The cash incentive . Canberra , 1986. xii, 135 p. : ISBN 0-86784-984-3 (pbk.) LC Card 87-150813
HD2346.P37 P46 1986

Handbook for creative and innovative managers / Robert Lawrence Kuhn, editor in chief. New York : McGraw-Hill, c1988. xx, 652 p. : ill. ; 24 cm. Includes bibliographies and index. ISBN 0-07-035607-6 : LC Card 87-3189 DDC 658.4/094 19
1. Creative ability in business. I. Kuhn, Robert Lawrence.
HD53 .H356 1988

A handbook for professional futures and options traders /. Koziol, Joseph D. New York , c1987. xvi, 325 p. : ISBN 0-471-87423-X : LC Card 87-8180 DDC 332.64/4 19
HG6024.A3 K68 1987

Handbook for raising capital : financing alternatives for emerging and growing businesses / edited by Lawrence Chimerine, Robert F. Cushman, Howard D. Ross. Homewood, Ill. : Dow Jones-Irwin, c1987. xxiv, 666 p. : ill., ports. ; 24 cm. Includes bibliographies. ISBN 0-87094-705-2 LC Card 86-71216
1. Small business - Finance - Handbooks, manuals, etc. 2. Business enterprises - Finance - Handbooks, manuals, etc. 3. Capital - Handbooks, manuals, etc. I. Chimerine, Lawrence. II. Cushman, Robert Frank, 1931-. III. Ross, Howard D. ***NYPL [*R-Econ. 87-1124]***

Handbook of accounting and auditing / editors, John C. Burton, Russell E. Palmer, Robert S. Kay. Boston : Warren, Gorham & Lamont, c1981. 1 v. (various pagings) ; 25 cm. Includes index. Kept up-to-date by cumulative "Update with cumulative index". Bibliography: p. B-1-23. ISBN 0-88712-221-3 (Update 1985) LC Card 80-53166 DDC 657/.02/02 19
1. Accounting - Handbooks, manuals, etc. 2. Auditing - Handbooks, manuals, etc. I. Burton, John C. II. Palmer, Russell E. III. Kay, Robert S. IV. Title: Handbook of accounting and auditing : update with cumulative index.
HF5635.H22 ***NYPL [*R-Econ. 85-31]***

Handbook of accounting and auditing : update with cumulative index. Handbook of accounting and auditing /. Boston , c1981. 1 v. (various pagings) ; ISBN 0-88712-221-3 (Update 1985) LC Card 80-53166 DDC 657/.02/02 19
HF5635.H22 ***NYPL [*R-Econ. 85-31]***

Handbook of alternative energy technology development and policy / by the Alternative Energy Technology Group, Science Policy Research Division. [Washington, D.C.] : Congressional Research Service, Library of Congress, 1983. xiv, 341 p. : ill. ; 28 cm. "Report no. 83-43 SPR." "March 1, 1983." Includes bibliographical references.
1. Energy development - United States. 2. Energy policy - United States. 3. Power resources - United States. I. United States. Library of Congress. Congressional Research Service. II. United States. Science Policy Researc Division. Alternative Energy Technology Group. ***NYPL [JLF 86-1486]***

Handbook of business policy /. Meidan, Arthur, 1936- [Bradford, West Yorkshire, England , Birmingham, Ala.] , c1986. 123 p. : ISBN 0-86176-273-8 (pbk.) LC Card 87-150995 DDC 658.4/012 19
HD30.28 .M42 1986

Handbook of commercial French /. Geoghegan, C., 1945- London , New York , 1988. p. cm. ISBN 0-7102-0857-X LC Card 87-16320 DDC 448/.002465 19
HF5728.F8 G46 1988

The handbook of credit and accounts receivable management /. Bukics, Rosie L. Chicago, Ill. , c1987. xi, 252 p. : ISBN 0-917253-67-1 : LC Card 87-7008 DDC 658.8/8 19
HG3751 .B85 1987

Handbook of demographics for marketing and advertising . Lazer, William. Lexington, Mass. , c1987. xxi, 211 p. : ISBN 0-669-16013-X (alk. paper) LC Card 86-46440 DDC 304.6/0973 19
HC110.C6 L39 1987

Handbook of EDP auditing. 1986 supplement / Stanley D. Halper ... [et al.]. Boston : Warren, Gorham & Lamont, c1986. 1 v. (various pagings) : ill. ; 24 cm. (Simonoff accounting series) Includes index. ISBN 0-88712-597-2 (pbk.) LC Card 87-107300 DDC 657/.45/0285 19
1. Business - Data processing - Auditing. I. Halper, Stanley D. II. Handbook of EDP auditing. III. Series.
HF5548.35 .H36 1986

Handbook of EDP auditing. Handbook of EDP auditing. Boston , c1986. 1 v. (various pagings) : ISBN 0-88712-597-2 (pbk.) LC Card 87-107300 DDC 657/.45/0285 19
HF5548.35 .H36 1986

Handbook of financial analysis, forecasting, and modeling /. Shim, Jae K. Englewood Cliffs, NJ , c1988. p. cm. ISBN 0-13-377995-5 : LC Card 87-14325 DDC 658.1/5 19
HG4011 .S46 1988

Handbook of financial markets : securities, options, and futures / edited by Frank J. Fabozzi and Frank G. Zarb.2nd ed. Homewood, Ill. : Dow Jones-Irwin, c1986. xix, 785 p. : ill. ; 24 cm. Includes bibliographical references and indexes. ISBN 0-87094-600-5 LC Card 85-71920 DDC 332.6/78 19
1. Investments - Handbooks, manuals, etc. 2. Securities - Handbooks, manuals, etc. 3. Put and call transactions - Handbooks, manuals, etc. 4. Commodity exchanges - Handbooks, manuals, etc. I. Fabozzi, Frank J. II. Zarb, Frank G.
HG4527 .H25 1986
NYPL [*R-Econ 86-3815]

Handbook of financial markets--securities, options, futures / Frank J. Fabozzi and Frank G. Zarb, editors. Homewood, Ill. : Dow Jones-Irwin, c1981. xxiii, 794 p. : ill. ; 24 cm. Includes bibliographical references and indexes. ISBN 0-87094-216-6 LC Card 80-70448 DDC 332.6/78 19
1. Investments - Handbooks, manuals, etc. 2. Securities - Handbooks, manuals, etc. 3. Financial institutions - Handbooks, manuals, etc. 4. Put and call transactions - Handbooks, manuals, etc. 5. Commodity exchanges - Handbooks, manuals, etc. I. Fabozzi, Frank J. II. Zarb, Frank G.
HG4527 .H25 ***NYPL [JLE 86-1500]***

The Handbook of fixed income securities / Frank J. Fabozzi and Irving M. Pollack, editors. 2nd ed. Homewood, Ill. : Dow Jones-Irwin, 1987. xxx, 1376 p. : ill. ; 24 cm. Includes bibliographies and indexes. ISBN 0-87094-745-1 LC Card 86-50815
1. Bonds - Handbooks, manuals, etc. 2. Preferred stocks - Handbooks, manuals, etc. 3. Money market funds - Handbooks, manuals, etc. 4. Investment trusts - Handbooks, manuals, etc. I. Pollack, Irving M., 1918-. II. Fabozzi, Frank J. III. Title: Fixed income securities.
NYPL [JLE 87-939]

Handbook of food expenditures, prices, and consumption /. Hassan, Zuhair A. Ottawa , c1983. 270 p., [2] p. of plates : LC Card 86-228246 DDC 339.4/8664/00971 19
HD9014.C3 H29 1983

The Handbook of forecasting : a manager's guide / edited by Spyros Makridakis and Steven C. Wheelwright.2nd ed. New York : Wiley, c1987. xviii, 638 p. : ill. ; 24 cm. "A Wiley-Interscience

publication." Includes bibliographies and index. ISBN 0-471-83903-5 LC Card 86-28137 DDC 658.4/0355 19
1. Business forecasting. I. Makridakis, Spyros G. II. Wheelwright, Steven C., 1943-.
HD30.27 .H36 1987

Handbook of governmental accounting and finance / edited by Nicholas G. Apostolou, D. Larry Crumbley. New York : Wiley, c1988. 1 v. (various pagings) ; 25 cm. Includes bibliographies and index. ISBN 0-471-84741-0 LC Card 87-23092 DDC 350.72/31 19
1. Finance, Public - United States - Accounting - Handbooks, manuals, etc. I. Apostolou, Nicholas G. II. Crumbley, D. Larry.
HJ9801 .H36 1988

Handbook of industrial and organizational psychology / Marvin D. Dunnette, editor. New York : Wiley, c1983. xxvii, 1740 p. : ill. ; 25 cm. "A Wiley-Interscience publication." Includes bibliographies and indexes. Reprint. Originally published: Chicago : Rand McNally College Pub. Co., c1976. ISBN 0-471-88642-4 LC Card 83-42702 DDC 158.7 19
1. Psychology, Industrial - Addresses, essays, lectures. 2. Organizational behavior - Addresses, essays, lectures. I. Dunnette, Marvin D.
HF5548.8 .H265 1983 ***NYPL [JLE 86-1120]***

Handbook of management accounting. 2nd ed. / edited by Roger Cowe. Aldershot, Hants, England ; Brookfield, Vt., U. S.A. : Gower, c1988. xxvi, 468 p. : ill. ; 24 cm. "In association with the Chartered Institute of Management Accountants." Includes bibliographies and index. ISBN 0-566-02615-5 : LC Card 86-29616 DDC 658.1/511 19
1. Managerial accounting. I. Cowe, Roger, 1951-.
HF5635 .H228 1988

Handbook of management development / edited by Alan Mumford. 2nd ed. Aldershot, Hants, England ; Brookfield, Vt., U. S.A. : Gower, c1986. xxiii, 452 p. : ill. ; 24 cm. Includes bibliographies and index. ISBN 0-566-02563-9 LC Card 86-226592 DDC 658.4/07124 19
1. Executives, Training of. I. Mumford, Alan.
HD38.2 .H36 1986

Handbook of medieval exchange /. Spufford, Peter. London : Woodbridge, Suffolk ; xcii, 376, [3] p., [1] fold. leaf : ISBN 0-86193-105-X
NYPL [JLE 86-4344]

Handbook of medieval exchange /. Spufford, Peter. London : Woodbridge, Suffolk ; xcii, 376 p., [3] leaves of plates (1 folded) : ISBN 0-86193-105-X LC Card 86-673816
HG3942 .S68x 1986

Handbook of model accounting reports and formats /. Vickman, Thomas M. Englewood Cliffs, N.J. , c1987. xvii, 350 p. : ISBN 0-13-380338-4 : LC Card 86-15068 DDC 658.1/512 19
HF5635 .V53 1987 ***NYPL [JLF 87-214]***

Handbook of motivation and cognition : foundations of social behavior / edited by Richard M. Sorrentino, E. Tory Higgins. New York : Guilford Press, c1986. x, 610 p. : ill. ; 24 cm. Includes bibliographies and indexes. ISBN 0-89862-667-6 LC Card 85-24916 DDC 153.8 19
1. Motivation (Psychology). 2. Cognition. I. Sorrentino, Richard M. II. Higgins, E. Tory (Edward Tory), 1946-.
BF503 .H36 1986 ***NYPL [JFE 86-2410]***

The handbook of multilevel marketing . Harden, Michael P. (Michael Patrick), 1952- Carrollton, TX , c1987. 138 p. : ISBN 0-938703-10-2 (pbk.) : LC Card 86-25439 DDC 658.8/4 19
HF5415.126 .H37 1987

Handbook of organizational communication : an interdisciplinary perspective / editors, Fredric M. Jablin ... [et al.]. Newbury Park, Calif. : Sage Publications, c1987. 781 p. : ill. ; 24 cm. Includes bibliographies and indexes. ISBN 0-8039-2387-2 : LC Card 87-23417 DDC 658.4/5 19
1. Communication in management. 2. Communication in organizations. I. Jablin, Fredric M.
HD30.3 .H3575 1987

Handbook of organizational communication / edited by Gerald M. Goldhaber, George A. Barnett. Norwood, N.J. : Ablex Pub. Corp., c1988. 502 p. : ill. ; 26 cm. (Communication and information science) Includes bibliographies and indexes. ISBN 0-89391-446-0 LC Card 87-19380 DDC 658.4/5 19
1. Communication in organizations. I. Goldhaber, Gerald M. II. Barnett, George A.
HD30.3 .H357 1988

Handbook of organizations / edited by James G. March. New York : Garland Pub., 1987, c1965. 2 v. (xvi, 1247 p.) : ill. ; 27 cm. (Continuity in administrative science) Reprint. Originally published: Chicago: Rand McNally, c1965. (Rand McNally sociology series) Includes bibliographies and index. ISBN 0-8240-8215-X (set : alk. paper) : LC Card 86-25797 DDC 658.4 19
1. Organizational behavior. 2. Organization. 3. Management. I. March, James G. II. Series.
HD58.7 .H365 1987

A handbook of retail promotion ideas /. Seltz, David D. Rockville Centre, N.Y. , c1985. 256 p. ; ISBN 0-87863-220-4 LC Card 84-25969 DDC 658.8/2 19
HF5438.5 .S45 1985 ***NYPL [JLF 86-1789]***

Handbook of road safety research /. Grime, G. (Geoffrey) London , Boston , 1987. ix, 149 p. : ISBN 0-408-02780-0 : LC Card 86-26427 DDC 363.1/25/0941 19
HE5614.5.G7 G77 1987

Handbook of small business valuation formulas /. Desmond, Glenn M. Los Angeles , c1987. 139 p. ; ISBN 0-930458-04-4 LC Card 87-402145 DDC 658.1/522 19
HG4028.V3 D478 1987

A handbook of software development and operating procedures for microcomputers /. Holliday, Paul, 1938- New York , c1985. xix, 181 p. : ISBN 0-02-949510-5 : LC Card 84-19384 DDC 001.64/2 19
QA76.6 .H645 1985 ***NYPL [JSE 87-332]***

Handbook of state trading organizations of developing countries = Répertoire des organismes de commerce d'etat des pays en développement = Repertorio de las organizaciones comerciales estatales de países en desarrollo = [Dalīl al-hay'āt al-tijārīyah al-ḥukūmīyah fī al-buldān al-nāmiyah] / United Nations Conference on Trade and Development (UNCTAD), International Trade Center UNCTAD/GATT (ITC).[2nd ed.]. New York : United Nations, 1985. clxxxix, 542 p. : ill. ; 30 cm. Arabic, English, French, and Spanish. Includes index. "UNCTAD/ECDC/95/Rev.1"--Verso t.p. "United Nations publication sales no. A/E/F/S.85.II.D.7"--Verso t.p. ISBN 92-1-012014-0 (pbk.) LC Card 86-233995
1. Trading companies - Developing countries - Handbooks, manuals, etc. 2. Trading companies - Developing countries - Directories. 3. Commercial products - Developing countries - Classification. I. United Nations. Conference on Trade and Development. II. International Trade Center UNCTAD/GATT. III. Title: Répertoire des organismes de commerce d'etat des pays en développement. IV. Title: Repertorio de las organizaciones comerciales estatales de países en desarrollo. V. Title: Dalīl al-hay'āt al-tijārīyah al-ḥukūmīyah fī al-buldān al-nāmiyah.
HF1009.7.D44 H35 1985

Handbook of strategic planning for nonprofit organizations /. Espy, Siri N. New York , 1986. ix, 131 p. ; ISBN 0-275-92342-8 (alk. paper) LC Card 86-21192 DDC 658.1/148 19
HD62.6 .E86 1986 ***NYPL [JLE 87-874]***

A handbook of systems analysis /. Bingham, John E. London , 1978. ix, 229 p. : ISBN 0-333-24198-3 : LC Card 79-309251
HF5548.2 .B47 1978b ***NYPL [JLE 80-2972]***

The handbook of the bond and money markets /. Darst, David M., 1947- New York , c1981. xv, 461 p. : ISBN 0-07-015401-5 LC Card 80-36816 DDC 332.63/23
HG4527 .D37 ***NYPL [JLE 87-568]***

Handbook of the money and capital markets /. Gart, Alan. New York , c1988. p. cm. ISBN 0-89930-270-X (lib. bdg. : alk. paper) LC Card 87-24938 DDC 332.63/2/0973 19
HG181 .G367 1988

Handbook of the postage stamps of Switzerland from the German of Ernst Zumstein. Zumstein, Ernst. [Germany , Southfield, MI [1986?] 61 p., 4 p. of plates : LC Card 86-202597 DDC 769.569494 19
HE6185.S92 Z78 1986

Handbook on the Houston economy. [Houston, Tex. : Center for Public Policy, 1986?] 36 p. : col. ill. ; 28 cm. Cover title. LC Card 86-622198 DDC 330.9764/1411063 19
1. Houston (Tex.) - Economic conditions - Statistics. I. University of Houston-University Park. Center for Public Policy.
HC108.H8 H36 1986

Handbuch der bayerischen Poststempel /. Winkler, Karl. Southfield, MI [198-?] 383 p., [18] p. of plates : LC Card 86-155089
HE6185.G32 B389 1980z

Handbuch der Hausfinanzierung . Grimm, Bernd Christian. Mannheim , 1985. 174, [318] p. ; LC Card 85-188627
HD7339.Z9 G75 1985

Handbuch der Landwirtschaft und Ernährung in den Entwicklungsländern / Herausgeber des Gesamtwerkes, Peter von Blanckenburg, Hans-Diedrich Cremer. 2., völlig neubearbeitete und erw. Aufl. Stuttgart : E. Ulmer, c1982- v. : ill. ; 25 cm. Includes bibliographies and indexes. CONTENTS. - Bd. 3. Grundlagen des Pflanzenbaues in den Tropen und Subtropen. ISBN 3-8001-3059-9 (Bd. 1) LC Card 84-155503 DDC 338.1/09172/4 19
1. Agriculture - Economic aspects - Developing countries - Handbooks, manuals, etc. 2. Nutrition - Developing countries - Handbooks, manuals, etc. I. Blanckenburg, Peter von. II. Cremer, Hans Diedrich, 1910-.
HD1417 .H24 1982 ***NYPL [JLL 86-257]***

Handbuch der schweizerischen Textil-, Bekleidungs- und Lederwirtschaft = Manuel suisse de l'industrie textile, de l'habillement et du cuir. 7. Aufl. Zürich : Verlag für Wirtschaftsliteratur, 1986. 214 p. : ill. ; 21 cm. Includes index. ISBN 3-909214-07-X LC Card 86-221803
1. Clothing trade - Switzerland - Directories. 2. Textile industry - Switzerland - Directories. 3. Leather industry and trade - Switzerland - Directories. I. Verlag für Wirtschaftsliteratur (Zurich, Switzerland). II. Title: Manuel suisse de l'industrie textile, de l'habillement et du cuir.
HD9940.S93 H36 1986

Handbuch des Genossenschaftsbauern. Rosenkranz, Otto. (ed) [Berlin, 1954-<1959. v. <v. 1, pt. 1-2; v. 3; in 3 > LC Card 60-21317
HD1491.G33 R6

Handbuch für Zivildienstleistende. Wer fürchtet sich vor'm schwarzen Mann? niemand! und wenn er kommt? dann lesen wir . Velbert , c1985. 95 p. : ISBN 3-922319-08-4 : LC Card 86-206116 DDC 355.2/2363/0943 19
HD4870.G3 W47 1985

Der Handel des frühen Mittelalters : Bericht über die Kolloquien der Kommission für die Altertumskunde Mittel- und Nordeuropas in den Jahren 1980 bis 1983 / herausgegeben von Klaus Düwel ... [et al.]. Göttingen : Vandenhoeck & Ruprecht, 1985. 510 p. : 67 ill. ; 25 cm. (Untersuchungen zu Handel und Verkehr der vor- und frühgeschichtlichen Zeit in Mittel- und Nordeuropa . T. 3) Abhandlungen der Akademie der Wissenschaften in Göttingen, Philologisch-Historische Klasse ; 3. Folge, Nr. 150 Includes one contribution in English. "Vorgelegt von Herrn H. Jankuhn in der Sitzung vom 30. November 1984"--T.p. verso. Bibliography: p. 502-510. ISBN 3-525-82433-5 (Deut. Bibl.) LC Card 86-209040
1. Central Europe - Commerce - History. 2. Europe, Northern - Commerce - History. I. Düwel, Klaus. II. Kommission für die Altertumskunde Mittel- und Nordeuropas. III. Series.
HF3495 .U57 1985 t. 3

Handel en wandel in de dertiende eeuw / D. Ellmers ... [et al.]. Amsterdam : Bataafsche Leeuw, c1986. 139 p. : ill. ; 25 cm. (Publicatie nr. 26 van de Stichting "Comité Out Muiderberg") Dutch and German. Includes bibliographies. CONTENTS. - Graaf Floris V en het reizen in zijn dagen / J. van Herwaarden -- Die Niederlande in Schiffahrt und Handel Nordwesteuropas im Mittelalter / D. Ellmers -- De Hollandse munt in de dertiende eeuw / H. Enno van Gelder -- Wie zal dat betalen? / M. Slingerland -- Melis Stoke en de ridderromans / A.L.H. Hage -- Edelvrouwen tussen Kerk en Heer / J.M. van Winter -- Medische kennis en praktijk in de Nederlanden in de dertiende eeuw / R. Jansen-Sieben -- Het Jeu de Robin et Marion / R.E.V. Stuip en C. Vellekoop -- Aan de vooravond van "een nieuwe tijd" / W. Prevenier. ISBN 90-6707-112-9 LC Card 86-199144
1. Netherlands - Economic conditions. 2. Netherlands - Social conditions. 3. Social history - Medieval,

500-1500. I. Ellmers, Detlev. II. Series: Publicatie ... van de Stichting Comité Oud-Muiderberg , nr. 26.
HC324 .H36 1986

Handel, Lagerung 1983 / bearbeitet im Österreichischen Statistischen Zentralamt. Wien : Das Zentralamt : Kommissionsverlag, Österreichische Staatsdruckerei, 1986- v. <1- > ; 30 cm. (Beiträge zur österreichischen Statistik . 793. Heft) LC Card 87-408429 DDC 314.36 s 380.1/09436/021 19
1. Austria - Commerce - Statistics. I. Österreichisches Statistisches Zentralamt. II. Series.
HA1173 .A27 Heft 793 HF3541.5

Handelsforschung heute : Festschrift zum 50jährigen Bestehen der Forschungsstelle für den Handel. Berlin : Duncker & Humblot, c1979. 230 p. : ill. ; 24 cm. (Schriftenreihe der Forschungsstelle für den Handel . 3. Folge, Nr. 7) Includes bibliographies. ISBN 3-428-04408-8 LC Card 87-408239 DDC 380.1 s 380.1/06/04355 19
1. Forschungsstelle für den Handel (Germany) - History. 2. Boards of trade - Berlin (Germany) - History. 3. Berlin (Germany) - Commerce - Research - History. I. Forschungsstelle für den Handel (Germany). II. Series.
HF345 .F66 Folge 3, Nr. 7 HF308

Handelshäfen im Ostseeraum / [Redaktion, Jürgen Völker, Hans-Jochen Arndt]. [Lübeck] : Industrie- und Handelskammer zu Lübeck, [1983] 232 p. : ill. ; 21 cm. (Ostsee-Jahrbuch, 0720-4868 . 1983) Includes English summaries. LC Card 84-192969
1. Harbors - Europe, Northern - Directories. 2. Harbors - North Sea Region - Directories. I. Völker, Jürgen. II. Arndt, Hans-Jochen. III. Industrie- und Handelskammer zu Lübeck. IV. Series.
HE557.A3 H36 1983

Handelshögskolan i Stockholm. Ekonomiska forskningsinstitutet. Datoriseringen i försäkringsbranschen : en branschstudie / utförd av Ekonomiska forskningsinstitutet vid Handelshögskolan i Stockholm på uppdrag av Dataeffektutredningen. [Stockholm] : Arbetsmarknadsdepartementet : LiberFörlag, [1981] 81, [36] p. : ill. ; 21 cm. Bibliography: p. 80-81. "Ds A 1981:14." ISBN 91-38-06574-6 LC Card 82-244714
1. Insurance - Sweden - Data processing. I. Sweden. Dataeffektutredningen. II. Title.
HG8673 .H35 1981

Handelskammer Braunschweig. Die Industrie-Erzeugnisse und Handelswaren des Landes Braunschweig /. Wolfenbüttel , 1921. 120 p. : LC Card 85-666348
HC289.B7 I52x 1921

Handelspolitik under skärpt konkurrens . Nilson, Bengt, 1952- Lund , c1983. 217 p. ; ISBN 91-40-04894-2 : LC Card 84-144528
HF1567 .N55 1983

Handelsserie fra Institut for øst-vest forskning, 0108-5387 .
(6) Nielsen, Margit, 1950- Udenrigsøkonomi i Østeuropa . Esbjerg , 1985. 99 p. ; ISBN 87-88521-19-2 LC Card 85-227937
HF1531 .N54 1985

HANDICAPPED - EMPLOYMENT.
Mcloughlin, Caven S. Getting employed, staying employed . Baltimore , c1987. xvi, 239 p. ; ISBN 0-933716-70-2 (pbk.) : LC Card 87-13185 DDC 650.1/4/0240816 19
HD7255 .M395 1987

Pimentel, Richard. Job placement for the industrially injured worker /. Northridge, Calif. (17624 Romar St., Northridge 91325) , c1987. v, 93, [1] leaves : LC Card 87-401986 DDC 650.1/4/0240816 19
HD7255 .P54 1987

HANDICAPPED - EMPLOYMENT - GERMANY, WEST.
Brandt, Franz. Ursachen für die Schwierigkeiten bei der Eingliederung von Schwerbehinderten auf dem allgemeinen Arbeitsmarkt /. Bonn [1984] 410 p. ; LC Card 87-408829 DDC 331.5/9/0943 19
HD7256.G3 B7 1984

Zur Problematik der Abbrecher der beruflichen Rehabilitation /. Bonn [1985?] 118, [29] p. ; LC Card 86-190824
HD7256.G3 Z87 1985

HANDICAPPED - EMPLOYMENT - GOVERNMENT POLICY - AUSTRALIA - WESTERN AUSTRALIA.
A Fair go for people with disabilities . Perth, W.A [1986] xxxv, 162 p. ; ISBN 0-7309-0332-X LC Card 87-158098 DDC 331.5/9/09941 19
HD7256.A762 W474 1986

HANDICAPPED - EMPLOYMENT - GOVERNMENT POLICY - UNITED STATES.
Barrett, John (John J.) The industrial work model . Menomonie, Wis. , c1987. v, 143 p. : ISBN 0-916671-73-9 (pbk.) LC Card 87-403218 DDC 362.0425 19
HD7256.U5 B37 1987

HANDICAPPED - EMPLOYMENT - INFORMATION SERVICES - UNITED STATES.
Rugh, Jack Leighton, 1911- Channels to employment for the disabled and ex-offenders /. San Gabriel, Calif. (5555 N. Charlotte Ave., San Gabriel 91776) , c1987. 89 p. : LC Card 87-402897 DDC 362.4/0484/02573 19
HD7256.U5 R75 1987

HANDICAPPED - EMPLOYMENT - SWEDEN.
Sweden. Samverkanskommittén. Arbetsanpassning . [Stockholm] [1984] 231 p. ; ISBN 91-38-08108-3 LC Card 84-193689
HD7256.S9 S945 1984

HANDICAPPED - EMPLOYMENT - UNITED STATES.
Barrett, John (John J.) The industrial work model . Menomonie, Wis. , c1987. v, 143 p. : ISBN 0-916671-73-9 (pbk.) LC Card 87-403218 DDC 362.0425 19
HD7256.U5 B37 1987

Greenwood, Reed. Employer concerns regarding workers with disabilities /. Hot Springs, Ark. [1985] xii, 170 p. ; LC Card 87-620863 DDC 658.3/045 19
HD7256.U5 G74 1985

Supported employment . Baltimore , c1988. x, 287 p. : ISBN 0-933716-83-4 (pbk.) : LC Card 87-14367 DDC 362/.0425 19
HD7256.U5 S86 1988

HANDICAPPED - EMPLOYMENT - UNITED STATES - ADDRESSES, ESSAYS, LECTURES.
Competitive employment issues and strategies /. Baltimore , c1986. xvii, 363 p. : ISBN 0-933716-59-1 : LC Card 85-30929 DDC 362/.0425 19
HD7256.U5 C4655 1986 ***NYPL [JLF 87-19]***

HANDICAPPED - EMPLOYMENT - UNITED STATES - CONGRESSES.
Joint Seminar on Designing Jobs for Handicapped Workers (1985 : Chicago, Ill.) Designing jobs for handicapped workers . Hot Springs, Ark. (P.O. Box 1358, Hot Spring 71902) [1986] 66 p. : LC Card 86-622317 DDC 658.3/045 19
HD7256.U5 J65 1985

HANDICAPPED - EMPLOYMENT - UNITED STATES - FORECASTING.
Hester, Edward J. Predicting which disabled employees will return to work . Topeka, Kan. (700 Jackson, 9th floor, Topeka 66603) , c1986. x, 86 p. : LC Card 86-231920 DDC 331.5/9 19
HD7256.U5 H43 1986

HANDICAPPED - EMPLOYMENT - UNITED STATES - STATES - DIRECTORIES.
National directory, training and employment programs for Americans with disabilities /. Washington, D.C. [1985] vii, 374 p. : LC Card 85-602984 DDC 362.4/0484/02573 19
HD7256.U5 N335 1985 ***NYPL [JLF 87-466]***

HANDICAPPED - INDIA - WEST BENGAL - STATISTICS.
Tables on houses and disabled population, series 23, West Bengal /. Delhi , 1986. v, 128 p. ; LC Card 87-900630
HA4587.W47 T33 1986

HANDICAPPED - REHABILITATION. see **VOCATIONAL REHABILITATION; REHABILITATION.**

HANDICAPPED - SERVICES FOR - UNITED STATES - STATES - DIRECTORIES.
National directory, training and employment programs for Americans with disabilities /. Washington, D.C. [1985] vii, 374 p. : LC Card 85-602984 DDC 362.4/0484/02573 19
HD7256.U5 N335 1985 ***NYPL [JLF 87-466]***

HANDICAPPED - TRAINING OF.
Mcloughlin, Caven S. Getting employed, staying employed . Baltimore , c1987. xvi, 239 p. ; ISBN 0-933716-70-2 (pbk.) : LC Card 87-13185 DDC 650.1/4/0240816 19
HD7255 .M395 1987

HANDICAPPED - VOCATIONAL GUIDANCE.
Mcloughlin, Caven S. Getting employed, staying employed . Baltimore , c1987. xvi, 239 p. ; ISBN 0-933716-70-2 (pbk.) : LC Card 87-13185 DDC 650.1/4/0240816 19
HD7255 .M395 1987

HANDICRAFT - ASIA - CONGRESSES.
Invisible hands . New Delhi , Newbury Park, Calif. , 1987. 273 p. ; ISBN 0-8039-9524-5 (U. S.) LC Card 87-4337 DDC 331.4/0954 19
HD6181.85 .A85 1987

HANDICRAFT - ECONOMIC ASPECTS - INDIA.
Cable, Vincent. The commerce of culture . New Delhi , 1986. 237 p. ; ISBN 81-7062-004-X : LC Card 86-902899 DDC 338.4/77455/0954 19
HF5439.H27 C33 1986

HANDICRAFT - ECONOMIC ASPECTS - NEPAL.
Upadhyay, Kiran Dutta. Handicrafts development in Nepal . Kathmandu, Nepal , 1985. ii, 126, [14] p. ; LC Card 86-902589 DDC 338.4/77455/095496 19
HD2346.N36 U63 1985

HANDICRAFT - GOVERNMENT POLICY - BRAZIL - CEARÁ (STATE)
Estudos fundamentais . Fortaleza , 1986. 120 p. : LC Card 87-120224
HD2346.B72 C44 1986

HANDICRAFT - JAPAN.
Nakae, Katsumi, 1935- Edo no shokunin . Tōkyō , 1986. 229 p. : ISBN 4-88470-522-X : LC Card 86-184888
HD2346.J3 N26 1986 <Orien Japan> ***NYPL [*OSM 87-1217]***

HANDICRAFT - LESOTHO.
Crafts and small-scale industries in Lesotho . Berlin [1982] vi, 60, 16 p., [1] leaf of plates : LC Card 84-215894 DDC 338.6/42/096816 19
HD2346.L44 C73 1982 ***NYPL [Sc F 86-141]***

HANDICRAFT - MARKETING.
Smith, Allan H. How to sell your homemade creation /. Lake Park, Fla. , 1986 printing, c1985. 146 p. : ISBN 0-931113-02-4 (pbk.) : LC Card 84-52239 DDC 745.5/068/8 19
HF5439.H27 S64 1986

HANDICRAFT - SCANDINAVIA - HISTORY - 19TH CENTURY.
Isacson, Maths, 1948- Proto-industrialisation in Scandinavia . Leamington Spa, UK ; New York : p. cm. ISBN 0-85496-514-9 : LC Card 86-32062 DDC 338.09485 19
HC375 .I8 1987

HANDICRAFT - SWEDEN - HISTORY - 19TH CENTURY.
Isacson, Maths, 1948- Proto-industrialisation in Scandinavia . Leamington Spa, UK ; New York : p. cm. ISBN 0-85496-514-9 : LC Card 86-32062 DDC 338.09485 19
HC375 .I8 1987

Isacson, Maths, 1948- Vägen till fabrikerna . [Stockholm] [Uppsala] , c1983. 195, [1] p. : ISBN 91-7021-464-6 : LC Card 84-125076
HC375 .I83 1983

HANDICRAFT - UNITED STATES - MARKETING.
Long, Steve. Marketing your arts & crafts . Sandpoint, Idaho (9395 Rapid Lightning Rd., Sandpoint 83864) [c1987] iv, 188 p. : LC Card 87-401972 DDC 745.5/068/8 19
HF5439.H27 L66 1987

Handicrafts development in Nepal . Upadhyay, Kiran Dutta. Kathmandu, Nepal , 1985. ii, 126, [14] p. ; LC Card 86-902589 DDC 338.4/77455/095496 19
HD2346.N36 U63 1985

HANDICRAFTS - HONDURAS - INTIBUCÁ (DEPT.)
Consejo Superior de Planificación Económica (Honduras). Secretaría Técnica. Proyecto de

desarrollo local de La Paz, Intibucá /. [Tegucigalpa, Honduras] [1984- v. <1 > : LC Card 86-213886
HC145.Z9 E443 1984

HANDICRAFTS - HONDURAS - LA PAZ (DEPT.)
Consejo Superior de Planificación Económica (Honduras). Secretaría Técnica. Proyecto de desarrollo local de La Paz, Intibucá /. [Tegucigalpa, Honduras] [1984- v. <1 > : LC Card 86-213886
HC145.Z9 E443 1984

Handjiiski, A. Kostov, Miroslav. ZMM metal-working machines combine, Sofia /. Sofia , 1986. [104] p. : LC Card 87-116288 DDC 338.7/621902/0949773 19
HD9703.B94 Z384 1986

Handling human performance /. Matejka, J. Kenneth. Richmond, Va. , c1982. v, 90 p. : ISBN 0-936328-20-7 (pbk.) LC Card 81-69197 DDC 658.3/14 19
HF5549.5.I5 M337 1982 ***NYPL [JLE 86-4361]***

Handloom Fabrics Survey Team (U. S.) Report on development of India's handloom fabrics for export to the United States of America, September 1957 /. [S.l. , 1957] (Delhi : Albion Press) ii, ii, 108 p., [8] p. of plates : LC Card 81-911063
HD9866.I62 R46 1957

HANDLOOM INDUSTRY - INDIA.
Report on development of India's handloom fabrics for export to the United States of America, September 1957 /. [S.l. , 1957] (Delhi : Albion Press) ii, ii, 108 p., [8] p. of plates : LC Card 81-911063
HD9866.I62 R46 1957

HANDLOOM INDUSTRY - INDIA - ASSAM.
Das, Nagen C., 1943- Development of handloom industry . New Delhi , c1986. 264 p. : LC Card 86-903222 DDC 338.4/767702822/0954162 19
HD9866.I63 A874 1986

HANDLOOM INDUSTRY - INDIA - ORISSA.
Mahapatro, P. C. (Poorna Chandra), 1944- Economics of cotton handloom industry in India /. New Delhi , 1986. xvi, 277 p. ; ISBN 81-7024-060-3 : LC Card 86-903087 DDC 338.4/774614/0954
HD9866.I63 O745 1986

The Hands that feed us : undocumented farmworkers in Florida. Washington, D.C. : American Civil Liberties Union, c1986. iii leaves, 150, 2 p., [3] leaves of plates : ill. ; 28 cm. (Public policy report / American Civil Liberties Union) "April 1986." "National Immigration and Alien Rights Project, report no. 2." Includes bibliographies. ISBN 0-86566-039-5 (pbk.) : LC Card 87-154337 DDC 331.5/44/09759 19
1. Migrant agricultural laborers - Florida. 2. Aliens, Illegal - Florida. 3. United States - Emigration and immigration - Government policy. I. American Civil Liberties Union. II. Series: Public policy report / American Civil Liberties Union.
HD1527.F6 H36 1986

Handwerk, Hauswerk, Heimarbeit . Meier, Thomas. Zürich , c1986. 435 p., [44] p. of plates : ISBN 3-905278-07-3 LC Card 86-227651
HD2346.S92 Z875 1986

Das Handwerk in Hamburg : Ergebnisse der Handwerkszählung 1977 (allgemeine Erhebung). Hamburg : Statistisches Landesamt, [1979] 140 p. ; 30 cm. (Statistik des Hamburgischen Staates, 0170-3064 . Heft 128) Chiefly tables. LC Card 86-133694
1. Small business - Germany (West) - Hamburg - Statistics. 2. Artisans - Germany (West) - Hamburg - Statistics. I. Hamburg (Germany). Statistisches Landesamt. II. Series.
HA1282 .A Heft 128 HD2346.G32H3

Handwerk in Krise und Umbruch . Simon, Manfred. Köln , 1983. xvii, 652 p. : ISBN 3-412-02983-1 : LC Card 83-221725 DDC 322/.2/0943 19
HD2346.G3 S47 1983

Handwerk in Staat und Gesellschaft . Beck, Thomas, 1950- München , c1987. xvii, 319 p. : ISBN 3-88259-415-2 LC Card 87-152203 DDC 331.7/94 19
HD2346.G32 K663 1987

Handwerk um 1700 : holländische und deutsche Kupferstiche / mit Beschreibungen von Christoph Weigel und Betrachtungen von Abraham a Sancta Clara ; ausgewählt und eingeleitet von Margarete Wagner. Hürtgenwald : Pressler, c1985. 245 p. : ill. ; 24 cm. Bibliography: p. 243-245. Includes index. ISBN 3-87646-052-2 : LC Card 85-211788
1. Artisans - Netherlands - History - 18th century. 2. Artisans - Germany - History - 18th century. 3. Abraham a Santa Clara, 1644-1709 - Views on artisans. I. Weigel, Christoph. II. Abraham a Santa Clara, 1644-1709. III. Wagner, Margarete.
HD2346.N4 H35 1985

Das Handwerk und die Berufseingliederung Jugendlicher in der Bundesrepublik Deutschland /. Maier, Hans E. Berlin [1986] 68 p. : LC Card 86-230660
HD5715.5.G4 M35 1986

Handwerker, W. Penn. Culture and reproduction . Boulder, Colo. , 1986. xix, 389 p. : ISBN 0-8133-7199-6 (pbk. : alk. paper) : LC Card 86-5671 DDC 304.6/32 19
HB887 .C85 1986 ***NYPL [JLE 86-3842]***

Handwerksgesellen und Lohnarbeiter . Schulz, Knut. Sigmaringen , 1985. vii, 477 p., [20] p. of plates : ISBN 3-7995-7026-8 LC Card 85-149930
HD4885.E8 S38 1985 ***NYPL [JLE 86-1598]***

Handwerkskammern im Zwielicht . John, Peter, 1946- Köln , 1983. 304 p. ; ISBN 3-7663-0597-2 LC Card 83-127836 DDC 338.6/425/0943 19
HD2346.E9 J63 1983 ***NYPL [JLD 87-1038]***

HANDWERSKAMMER KONSTANZ.
Beck, Thomas, 1950- Handwerk in Staat und Gesellschaft . München , c1987. xvii, 319 p. : ISBN 3-88259-415-2 LC Card 87-152203 DDC 331.7/94 19
HD2346.G32 K663 1987

Hanf, Claus-H. Intrasektorale Einkommensstreuung in der Landwirtschaft /. Münster-Hiltrup , 1983. 177 p. : ISBN 3-7843-0281-5 : LC Card 83-236007
HD1955 .I57 1983

Hanging together . Putnam, Robert D. Cambridge, Mass. , 1987. x, 293 p. ; ISBN 0-674-37226-3 (pbk.) LC Card 87-23593 DDC 337 19
HF1410.5 .P87 1987

Han'guk Kaebal Yŏn'guwŏn. Whang, In Joung. Administration of land reform in Korea /. Seoul, Korea [1982] 41 p. ; LC Card 84-148921 DDC 333.3/1/519 19
HD1333.K78 W46 1982

Han'guk Oehwan Ŭnhaeng. Chosabu. The Korean economy . Seoul, Korea , 1984. 308 p. ; LC Card 87-128969 DDC 330.9519/5043 19
HC467 .K61996 1984

Hanisch, Bärbel, 1957- Die Ergebnisrechnung nach dem Bilanzrichtlinie-Gesetzentwurf im internationalen Vergleich (BRD, Japan, USA) / Bärbel Hanisch. Frankfurt am Main ; New York : P. Lang, c1984. 286 p. : ill. ; 22 cm. (Beiträge zum Rechnungs-, Finanz- und Revisionswesen, 0721-3026 . Bd. 11) Originally presented as the author's thesis (doctoral--Universität Augsburg, 1984) Bibliography: p. 249-264. ISBN 3-8204-8559-7 : LC Card 85-164345
1. Accounting - Germany, West. 2. Accounting - Law and legislation - Germany, West. 3. Accounting - Japan. 4. Accounting - Law and legislation - Japan. 5. Accounting - United States. 6. Accounting - Law and legislation - United States. I. Title. II. Series.
HF5616.G3 H35 1984

Hanisch, Rolf, 1942- Der Staat, ländliche Armutsgruppen und legale Bauernbewegung in den Philippinen / Rolf Hanisch. 1. Aufl. Baden-Baden : Nomos Verlagsgesellschaft, 1983. xii, 432 p. ; 24 cm. (Darstellungen zur internationalen Politik und Entwicklungspolitik, 0173-1270 . Bd. 6) Originally presented as the author's Habilitationsschrift--Universität Hamburg, 1983. Bibliography: p. 407-422. Includes index. ISBN 3-7890-0980-6 LC Card 84-143058
1. Peasantry - Philippines - Political activity. 2. Agricultural laborers - Philippines - Political activity. 3. Philippines - Rural conditions. 4. Land reform - Philippines. 5. Agriculture and state - Philippines. 6. Philippines - Politics and government - 1973-. I. Title. II. Series.
HD1537.P5 H35 1983

Hanisch, Tore Jørgen, 1945- Bergh, Trond, 1946- Vitenskap og politikk . Oslo , 1984. 269 p. : ISBN 82-03-11342-7 : LC Card 84-184253
HB116.3.A2 B47 1984

Hanke, Steve H. Prospects for privatization /. New York , 1987. x, 214 p. ; LC Card 87-70470 DDC 338.973 19
HD3885 .P76 1987

Hankel, Wilhelm, 1929- Gegenkurs : von der Schuldenkrise zur Vollbeschäftigung / Wilhelm Hankel ; Mitarbeit, Helmut Kupky. Berlin : Siedler, c1984. 261 p. : ill. ; 23 cm. Includes bibliographical references and index. ISBN 3-88680-114-4 LC Card 84-174753
1. Business cycles. 2. Monetary policy. 3. Economic development. 4. Rational expectations (Economic theory). 5. Informal sector (Economics). 6. Interest rates. I. Kupky, Helmut. II. Title.
HB3723 .H26 1984

Hankinson, Graham, 1947- Hall, John, 1946- Reducing industrial oil costs /. Aldershot, Hants England , Brookfield, Vt., U. S.A. , c1987. xvii, 118 p. : ISBN 0-291-39740-9 (U. S.) : LC Card 86-29511 DDC 338.2/3 19
HD9560.4 .H35 1987

Hanlon, Joseph. SADCC : progress, projects & prospects : the trade and investment future of the Southern African Development Coordination Conference / by Joseph Hanlon. London, U.K. : Economist Intelligence Unit, c1984. 110 p. : ill. ; 30 cm. (Special report . no. 182) Bibliography: p. 103. LC Card 86-148391 DDC 332.6/732268 19
1. Africa, Southern - Economic integration. 2. Africa, Southern - Commerce. 3. Africa, Southern - Economic conditions, 1975-. 4. Investments - Africa, Southern. 5. Southern African Development Coordination Conference. I. Series: Special report (Economist Intelligence Unit (Great Britain)) , no. 182. II. Title.
HC900 .H35 1984

Hann, Danny. Government and North Sea oil / Danny Hann. Basingstoke, Hampshire : Macmillan, c1986. ix, 175 p. : ill. ; 23 cm. Includes index. Bibliography: p. 160-170. ISBN 0-333-39436-4
1. Petroleum industry and trade - Government policy - Great Britain. 2. Offshore oil industry - Government policy - Great Britain. 3. Offshore oil industry - North Sea. I. Title. ***NYPL [JLD 86-2581]***

Hanna, Michael S., 1939- Communicating in business and professional settings / by Michael S. Hanna, Gerald L. Wilson. 2nd ed. New York : Random House, c1988. p. cm. Includes bibliographies and index. ISBN 0-394-36447-3 LC Card 87-12713 DDC 658.4/5 19
1. Communication in management. 2. Communication in organizations. I. Wilson, Gerald L., 1943-. II. Title.
HD30.3 .H36 1988

Hannah, Leslie. Pension asset management . Homewood, Ill. , 1988. xiii, 178 p. : ISBN 0-256-06123-8 LC Card 87-81575 DDC 332.6/7254 19
HD7105.4 .P45 1988

Hänni, Heinz D. Raumordnungspolitik im Vollzug . Grüsch , c1985. 507 p. : ISBN 3-7253-0258-8 : LC Card 86-149201
HC397 .R36 1985

Hannington, Wal, 1895- The problem of the distressed areas / Wal Hannington. New York : Garland Pub., 1985. 286 p. : ill. ; 22 cm. (English workers and the coming of the welfare state, 1918-1945) Includes bibliographical references. Reprint. Originally published: London : V. Gollancz, 1937. ISBN 0-8240-7613-3 : LC Card 85-14663 DDC 338.941 19
1. Taxation - Great Britain. 2. Unemployment - Great Britain. 3. Great Britain - Economic policy - 1918-1945. 4. Great Britain - Economic conditions - 1918-1945. I. Title. II. Series.
HC256.3 .H265 1985 ***NYPL [JLD 86-3420]***

Hanover. Bundesanstalt für Geowissenschaften und Rohstoffe. see **Bundesanstalt für Geowissenschaften und Rohstoffe.**

HANOVER (MAN.) - ECONOMIC CONDITIONS.
Rural municipality of Hanover . [Winnipeg, Man.] [1976?] iv, 55 p. : LC Card 82-219722
HC118.H34 R87 1976

HANOVER (MAN.) - POPULATION.
Rural municipality of Hanover . [Winnipeg,

Man.] [1976?] iv, 55 p. : LC Card 82-219722
HC118.H34 R87 1976

Hanover-Niverville District Advisory Planning Commission. Rural municipality of Hanover . [Winnipeg, Man.] [1976?] iv, 55 p. : LC Card 82-219722
HC118.H34 R87 1976

Hans, Asha. The power sector in India / Asha Hans. New Delhi : Sterling Publishers, c1986. vi, 149 p. ; 23 cm. Study on electric power production and distribution. Includes bibliographies. LC Card 86-901959 DDC 333.79/32/0954 19
1. Energy policy - Social aspects - India. 2. Electric power production - Social aspects - India. 3. Electric power distribution - Social aspects - India. I. Title.
HD9502.I42 H36 1986

Hans Martin Schleyer-Stiftung. Symposium Umweltprobleme als Herausforderung der Marktwirtschaft, Neue Ideen jenseits des Dirigismus (1983 : Stuttgart, Germany) Symposium Umweltprobleme als Herausforderung der Marktwirtschaft, Neue Ideen jenseits des Dirigismus . [Köln] [Freiburg] , 1983. 300 p. ; ISBN 3-7616-0722-9 LC Card 84-152335 DDC 363.7/058 19
HC79.E5 S96 1983 ***NYPL [JLD 86-1631]***

HANSA TOWNS.
Kürtz, Hans Joachim. Zu Zeiten der Hanse . Lübeck , c1983. 128 p. : ISBN 3-87498-330-7 LC Card 87-672840
HF455 .K87x 1983

HANSA TOWNS - COMMERCE - HISTORY.
Stark, Walter. Untersuchungen zum Profit beim hansischen Handelskapital in der ersten Hälfte des 15. Jahrhunderts /. Weimar , 1985. 147 p. ; LC Card 86-148303
HF458 .S73 1985

HANSA TOWNS - ECONOMIC CONDITIONS.
Ahrens, Gerhard, 1939- Staatsverschuldung ohne Ende? /. Hamburg [1984] 37 leaves ; LC Card 85-166341
HJ8650 .A37 1984

HANSEATIC LEAGUE - COMMERCE - NORWAY - HISTORY.
Schelzel, Manfred. Hanseschiffahrt mit Norwegen /. Bergen , 1979. 33 leaves ; LC Card 85-174193
HF458 .S34 1979

Hansen, C. D. Clements, R. T. The Reserve Bank econometric model of the New Zealand economy . Wellington [1986] 62 p., [2] leaves of plates : LC Card 87-142103 DDC 330.9931/00724 19
HC665 .C54 1986

Hansen, Christian Overgård. Forbedring og rationalisering af rutebilkørsel / Christian Overgaard Hansen. Esbjerg : Sydjysk universitetsforlag, 1986. 259 p. : ill. ; 25 cm. Bibliography: p. 255-259. ISBN 87-88521-37-0 LC Card 86-205999
1. Bus lines - Denmark - Costs. 2. Transportation, Automotive - Denmark - Planning. 3. Bus lines - Denmark. I. Title.
HE5677.A6 H36 1986

Hansen, Erik Jørgen. Vor tids fattigdom /. [Copenhagen] , c1986. 130 p. : ISBN 87-412-3897-4 : LC Card 86-214667
HC79.P6 V67 1986

Hansen, Gary B. Adams, Frank T. Putting democracy to work . Eugene, OR , 1987. p. cm. ISBN 0-938493-03-5 : LC Card 87-4246 DDC 658.1/147 19
HD5650 .A3 1987

Hansen, John A. Lund, Robert T. Keeping America at work . New York , c1986. xi, 260 p. : ISBN 0-471-81563-2 LC Card 85-17900 DDC 331.12/0973 19
HD45 .L86 1985 ***NYPL [JLD 86-2101]***

Hanser, Christian. Erfolgskontrolle der Industrieansiedlungspolitik : eine empirische Überprüfung der traditionellen Regionalpolitik am Beispiel dreier Regionen im schweizerischen Berggebiet / Christian Hanser. Bern ; New York : P. Lang, c1986. 375 p. ; 21 cm. (Europäische Hochschulschriften. Reihe V, Volks- und Betriebwirtschaft . Bd. 738 = vol. 738 = vol. 738) Originally presented as the author's thesis (doctoral)--Universität Zürich, 1985/86. Bibliography: p. 284-305. ISBN 3-261-03610-9 LC Card 87-407957 DDC 338.6/042/09494 19
1. Switzerland - Industries - Location. 2. Regional planning - Switzerland. I. Series: Europäische Hochschulschriften. Reihe V, Volks- und Betriebswirtschaft , Bd. 738. II. Title.
HD58 .H36 1986

Hanseschiffahrt mit Norwegen /. Schelzel, Manfred. Bergen , 1979. 33 leaves ; LC Card 85-174193
HF458 .S34 1979

Hansmeyer, Karl-Heinrich.
Geyer, Herbert, 1927- Budgetpolitik im Wandel /. Berlin , c1986. 111 p. : ISBN 3-428-05922-0 LC Card 86-165210
HJ113 .G49 1986

Staatsfinanzierung im Wandel . Berlin , c1983. xi, 877 p. : ISBN 3-428-05420-2
NYPL [JLL 73-186 Bd. 134]

Umweltpolitisches Gespräch (1983 : Bad Godesberg, Bonn, Germany) Ökonomische Instrumente der Umweltpolitik . Berlin , c1984. 108 p. ; ISBN 3-503-02401-8 LC Card 86-152141
HC290.5.E5 U625 1983

Hansohm, Jürgen. Opitz, Otto. Zur Analyse des Personal Computer Marktes 1985 . Augsburg [1986] 35 leaves : LC Card 87-407365 DDC 380.1/4500416 19
HD9696.C62 O664 1986

Hanson, Philip. The comparative economics of research development in East and West : a survey / Philip Hanson and Keith Pavitt. Chur, Switzerland ; New York : Harwood Academic Publishers, c1987. viii, 101 ; 22 cm. (Fundamentals of pure and applied economics . v. 25.) Bibliography: p. 90-97. Includes index. ISBN 3-7186-0419-1 (pbk.) LC Card 87-23623 DDC 338/.06 19
1. Technological innovations - Economic aspects. I. Pavitt, Keith. II. Series. III. Series: Fundamentals of pure and applied economics , v. 25. IV. Title.
HC79.T4 H355 1987

Hanson, R. Employee benefits and conditions of employment in Canada : highlights of studies on prevalence, characteristics, and costs from 1967 to 1976. [Ottawa, Ont.] : Pay Research Bureau, Public Service Staff Relations Board, c1977. iv, 111 p. : ill. (some col.) ; 28 cm. ISBN 0-662-00630-5 (pbk.) LC Card 82-136152
1. Employee fringe benefits - Canada. 2. Executives - Salaries, pensions, etc. - Canada. I. Canada. Public Service Staff Relations Board. Pay Research Bureau. II. Title.
HD4928.N62 C225 1977

Hanson, Robert D. Swanson, Robert M. Century 21 accounting . Cincinnati , c1988. xi, 653 p. : ISBN 0-538-02470-4 LC Card 87-60958 DDC 657/.046 19
HF5635 .C4228 1988

Hansson, Ingemar, 1951- Skatter och samhällsekonomi / Ingemar Hansson. 1. uppl. Stockholm : SNS, c1986. 170 p. : ill. ; 21 cm. Bibliography: p. 167-170. ISBN 91-7150-280-7 : LC Card 86-215332
1. Taxation - Sweden. 2. Sweden - Economic conditions - 1945-. I. Title.
HJ2837 .H36 1986

Hansson, Lennart. Andersson, Per Magnus, 1951- Internprissättning inom offentlig förvaltning . Lund [1984] xii, 357 p. ; ISBN 91-44-43971-7 : LC Card 84-210334
HD62.45 .A53 1984

Hanthorn, Michael. Selected farm machinery statistics / Michael Hanthorn, Carlos Sisco. Washington, D.C. : U. S. Dept. of Agriculture, Economic Research Service : Supt. of Docs., U. S. G.P.O. [distributor, 1986] ii, 54 p. : ill. ; 28 cm. (Statistical bulletin . no. 743) Cover title. Distributed to depository libraries in microfiche. "July 1986"--P. i. Bibliography: p. 5. S/N 001-019-00475-4 Item 15 (microfiche) LC Card 86-602408 DDC 338.1/61/0973 19
1. Agricultural machinery industry - United States - Statistics. I. Sisco, Carlos. II. United States. Dept. of Agriculture. Economic Research Service. III. Series: Statistical bulletin (United States. Dept. of Agriculture) , no. 743. IV. Title.
HD1751 .A5 no. 743 HD9486.U4

Hanumantha Rayappa, P. (Pullikunta), 1938- Backwardness and welfare of scheduled castes and scheduled tribes in India / P. Hanumantha Rayappa, R. Mutharayappa. 1st ed. New Delhi : Ashish Pub. House, 1986. xi, 121 p. ; 22 cm. Study with reference to Karnataka. Bibliography: p. [119]-121. Includes index. ISBN 81-7024-059-X : LC Card 86-902970
1. Karnataka (India) - Scheduled tribes - Economic conditions. 2. Caste - India - Karnataka. 3. Public welfare - India - Karnataka. 4. Karnataka, India - Economic conditions. I. Mutharayappa, R. II. Title.
HC437.K27 H36 1986

Hanžel, K. 110 let městské hromadné dopravy v Praze /. [Prague] [1985] 52 p. : LC Card 86-201750
HE4759.3.Z8 P732 1985

Hapag-Lloyd . Witthöft, Hans Jürgen. Herford , 1979, c1974. 176 p. : ISBN 3-7822-0201-5 LC Card 85-178567
HE945.H424 W58 1979

HAPAG-LLOYD AG - HISTORY.
Witthöft, Hans Jürgen. Hapag-Lloyd . Herford , 1979, c1974. 176 p. : ISBN 3-7822-0201-5 LC Card 85-178567
HE945.H424 W58 1979

Haq, Mahbub ul, 1934-
Employment, distribution, and basic needs in Pakistan . Lahore , 1986. xxxiv, 408 p., [1] leaf of plates : LC Card 86-930280 DDC 330.9549/1 19
HD5820.5.A6 E47 1986

The poverty curtain : choices for the Third World / Mahbub ul Haq.[Pakistan ed.]. Lahore : Ferozsons, 1983. li, 247 p. ; 22 cm. Includes index. Bibliography: p. [239]-240. Reprint. Originally published: New York : Columbia University Press, 1976 With two additional articles. LC Card 83-931275 DDC 338.9/009172/4 19
1. Poor - Developing countries. 2. Developing countries - Economic policy. 3. Developing countries - Population policy. I. Title.
HC59.7 .H35 1983 ***NYPL [JLD 87-439]***

Haque, T. (Tajamul), 1947- Agrarian reforms and institutional changes in India / T. Haque, A.S. Sirohi. New Delhi : Concept Pub. Co., 1986, c1985. xvi, 268 p. : maps ; 23 cm. Includes index. Bibliography: p. [249]-262. LC Card 86-902575 DDC 338.1/854 19
1. Land reform - India. 2. Agriculture and state - India. 3. Agricultural cooperative credit associations - India. 4. Agricultural cridit - India. I. Sirohi, A. S. (Amar Singh), 1926-. II. Title.
HD1333.I4 H36 1986 ***NYPL [JLD 87-1547]***

Harabi, Najib. Makromodelle und Wirtschaftspolitik . Grüsch , c1985. 120 p. : ISBN 3-7253-0250-2 : LC Card 85-208009
HC397 .M26 1985

Ḥarakat al-quwá al-ʻāmilah wa-al-tanmiyah al-iqlīmīyah fī Lībiyā /. Khalaf Allāh, Ramaḍān ʻUraybī. Ṭarābulus, al-Jamāhīrīyah al-ʻArabīyah al-Lībīyah al-Shaʻbīyah al-Ishtirākīyah , 1984. 279 p. : LC Card 86-965535
HB2121.6.A3 K47 1984

Harbans Singh, 1940- Conceptual and methodological issues on agricultural marketing research in Zambia / by H.S. Aulakh and P.D. Ncube. [Lusaka, Zambia] : University of Zambia Business & Economics Association, [1979?] 19, [2] leaves ; 30 cm. (Occasional paper / The University of Zambia Business & Economics Association . no. 3) Bibliography: leaves [20]-[21] LC Card 85-980091
1. Farm produce - Zambia - Marketing - Research - Methodology. I. Ncube, Patrick Donsi. II. Series: Occasional paper (University of Zambia. Business & Economics Association) , no. 3. III. Title.
HD9017.Z32 H37 1979

Harber, Richard P. Tax policy, economic development, and regional inequality [microform] : a case study of Brazil's fiscal incentive system / Richard P. Harber, Jr. Austin : Office for Public Sector Studies, Institute of Latin American Studies, University of Texas at Austin, 1984. 33 p. ; 28 cm. (Technical papers series . no. 40 40) Summary of thesis (Ph. D.)--University of Illinois, Urbana, 1982. Bibliography: p. 33. Microfilm. New York : New York Public Library, 1986. 1 microfilm reel ; 35 mm. (MN *ZZ-25,866) LC Card 84-623077 DDC 339.5/2/09813 19
1. Tax incentives - Brazil. 2. Investments - Taxation - Brazil. 3. Regional planning - Brazil. I. Title. II. Series.
HJ2527 .H37 1984 ***NYPL [*ZT-1646 no.22]***

Harberger, Arnold C. Modern developments in public finance . Oxford, UK , New York, NY, USA , 1987. xii, 259 p. : ISBN 0-631-15595-3 : LC Card 87-6568 DDC 336 19
HJ141 .M59 1987

HARBERGER, ARNOLD C.
Modern developments in public finance . Oxford, UK , New York, NY, USA , 1987. xii, 259 p. : ISBN 0-631-15595-3 : LC Card 87-6568 DDC 336 19
HJ141 .M59 1987

HARBORS - AFRICA.
Port guide on African major ports. [Addis Ababa, Ethiopia] [1986?] ii, 256 p. ; LC Card 86-980946 DDC 387.1/096 19
HE559.5 .P68 1986

HARBORS - ALABAMA - MOBILE.
The Port of Mobile, Alabama /. Washington , Fort Belvoir, Va. , 1986. vi, 99 p. : LC Card 86-603154 DDC 387.1/09761/22 19
HE554.M7 P67 1986

HARBORS - BELGIUM - ANTWERP - MANAGEMENT.
Mester, Bernt. Marktchancen der Binnenschiffahrt im Container-Hinterlandverkehr der Häfen der Hamburg-Antwerpen-Range /. Düsseldorf , 1986. xii, 304 p. ; LC Card 87-409549
HE5 .C6 Nr. 47 HE558.H3

HARBORS - BELGIUM - ANTWERP - RATES.
Boldt, Günter. Wettbewerb und Preisbildung der Seehafenverkehrswirtschaft in nordwesteuropäischen Seehäfen . Göttingen , 1964. 120 p. ; LC Card 87-408787 DDC 380.5 s 387.1 19
HE131 .M84 Heft 30 HE558.H3

HARBORS - BRAZIL - VITÓRIA (ESPÍRITO SANTO) - HISTORY.
Siqueira, Penha. O desenvolvimento do porto de Vitória, 1870-1940 /. Vitória-ES , 1984. 162 p. : LC Card 85-144275
HE556.V5 S56 1984

HARBORS - BRITISH COLUMBIA - VANCOUVER METROPOLITAN AREA - HISTORY.
Fraser Port . Victoria, B.C. , 1986. 131 p., [16] p. of plates : ISBN 0-919203-17-5 (pbk.) LC Card 87-106756
HE554.V3 F73 1986

HARBORS - BULGARIA - VARNA - HISTORY.
Morska vrata na rodinata . Varna , 1986. 146 p., [32] p. of plates : LC Card 86-233471
HE557.B9 M67 1986

HARBORS - CALIFORNIA - JUVENILE LITERATURE.
Davis, Charlotte. Ports of California. Los Angeles [1970] 80 p. LC Card 79-114863 DDC 387.1/09794
HE554.C16 D3

HARBORS - CANADA.
Brouillette, Benoît, 1904-1979. [Perspectives de changements dans la manutention des marchandises aux ports canadiens. English.] Prospective changes for handling of commodities in Canadian ports. Montréal, Québec, Canada [1974] iv, 93, [3] p. ; LC Card 82-219246
HE553 .B7613 1974

HARBORS - DEVELOPING COUNTRIES.
Alternative Hafen- und Küstenpolitik /. Hamburg , 1985. 260 p. : ISBN 3-88876-034-8 LC Card 87-133678 DDC 387.1/094 19
HE557.G3 A55 1985

HARBORS - ECONOMIC ASPECTS.
Gorbatyĭ, M. M. (Mark Moiseevich) Teoriia i praktika optimizatsii proizvodstvennykh moshchnosteĭ morskikh portov /. Moskva , 1981. 167 p. : LC Card 82-162836
HE551 .G625 1981

HARBORS - ECONOMIC ASPECTS - CENTRAL EUROPE.
Seidenfus, Hellmuth Stefan. Die Bedeutung der Seehäfen für die Industrialisierung Mitteleuropas /. Göttingen , 1979. 20 p. ; ISBN 3-525-85769-1 LC Card 86-194319
HE131 .M84 Heft 18 HE557.A3

HARBORS - EUROPE.
Alternative Hafen- und Küstenpolitik /. Hamburg , 1985. 260 p. : ISBN 3-88876-034-8 LC Card 87-133678 DDC 387.1/094 19
HE557.G3 A55 1985

HARBORS - EUROPE - HISTORY.
See- und Flusshäfen vom Hochmittelalter bis zur Industrialisierung /. Köln , 1986. xxi, 315 p. : ISBN 3-412-07585-X LC Card 87-146564 DDC 387.1/094 19
HE557.A3 S37 1986

HARBORS - EUROPE, NORTHERN - DIRECTORIES.
Handelshäfen im Ostseeraum /. [Lübeck] [1983] 232 p. : LC Card 84-192969
HE557.A3 H36 1983

HARBORS - FRANCE - DUNKERQUE - HISTORY - 17TH CENTURY.
Pfister-Langanay, Christian. Ports, navires et négociants à Dunkerque, 1662-1792 /. Dunkerque , 1985. 677 p. : LC Card 87-115474
HD558.D85 P45 1985

HARBORS - FRANCE - DUNKERQUE - HISTORY - 18TH CENTURY.
Pfister-Langanay, Christian. Ports, navires et négociants à Dunkerque, 1662-1792 /. Dunkerque , 1985. 677 p. : LC Card 87-115474
HD558.D85 P45 1985

HARBORS - GERMANY, WEST.
Alternative Hafen- und Küstenpolitik /. Hamburg , 1985. 260 p. : ISBN 3-88876-034-8 LC Card 87-133678 DDC 387.1/094 19
HE557.G3 A55 1985

HARBORS - GERMANY (WEST) - BREMEN - RATES.
Boldt, Günter. Wettbewerb und Preisbildung der Seehafenverkehrswirtschaft in nordwesteuropäischen Seehäfen . Göttingen , 1964. 120 p. ; LC Card 87-408787 DDC 380.5 s 387.1 19
HE131 .M84 Heft 30 HE558.H3

HARBORS - GERMANY (WEST) - HAMBURG - HISTORY.
Grüttner, Michael. Arbeitswelt an der Wasserkante . Göttingen , 1984. 331 p. ; ISBN 3-525-35722-2 (Deut. Bibl.) LC Card 86-139479
HD8039.L82 G4335 1984

Stadt und Hafen . Hamburg , 1986. 209 p. : ISBN 3-7672-0951-9 LC Card 87-130912 DDC 387.1/0943/515 19
HE558.H3 S7 1986

HARBORS - GERMANY (WEST) - HAMBURG - MANAGEMENT.
Mester, Bernt. Marktchancen der Binnenschiffahrt im Container-Hinterlandverkehr der Häfen der Hamburg-Antwerpen-Range /. Düsseldorf , 1986. xii, 304 p. ; LC Card 87-409549
HE5 .C6 Nr. 47 HE558.H3

HARBORS - GERMANY (WEST) - HAMBURG - RATES.
Boldt, Günter. Wettbewerb und Preisbildung der Seehafenverkehrswirtschaft in nordwesteuropäischen Seehäfen . Göttingen , 1964. 120 p. ; LC Card 87-408787 DDC 380.5 s 387.1 19
HE131 .M84 Heft 30 HE558.H3

HARBORS - GERMANY (WEST) - WESER RIVER VALLEY.
Komp, Klaus Ulrich. Die Seehafenstädte im Weser-Jade-Raum und ihre überregionale Verflechtung /. Münster , 1982. x, 143 p. : LC Card 83-197866
HE558.W45 K66 1982

HARBORS - GOVERNMENT POLICY - CASE STUDIES - CONGRESSES.
Port development policy . Bangkok, Thailand , 1985. ix, 83 p. : LC Card 87-106926 DDC 387.1/0952 19
HE559.J3 P653 1985

HARBORS - GOVERNMENT POLICY - CONGRESSES.
Port development policy . Bangkok, Thailand , 1985. ix, 83 p. : LC Card 87-106926 DDC 387.1/0952 19
HE559.J3 P653 1985

HARBORS - GOVERNMENT POLICY - FRANCE.
France. Conseil économique et social. Les ports maritimes . Paris [1983] 1 v. (various pagings) : LC Card 83-186600
HE557.F8 F67 1983

HARBORS - GOVERNMENT POLICY - JAPAN - CASE STUDIES - CONGRESSES.
Port development policy . Bangkok, Thailand , 1985. ix, 83 p. : LC Card 87-106926 DDC 387.1/0952 19
HE559.J3 P653 1985

HARBORS - GOVERNMENT POLICY - JAPAN - CONGRESSES.
Port development policy . Bangkok, Thailand , 1985. ix, 83 p. : LC Card 87-106926 DDC 387.1/0952 19
HE559.J3 P653 1985

HARBORS - GOVERNMENT POLICY - PACIFIC COAST (U. S.)
Boschken, Herman L. Strategic design and organizational change . Tuscaloosa, Ala. , c1989. p. cm. ISBN 0-8173-0339-1 LC Card 86-14673 DDC 387.1/0979 19
HE554.A6 B67 1989

HARBORS - INDIA - GUJARAT.
Rajyagor, S. B. Gujarātanāṃ bandaro . Amadāvāda , 1986. 6, 167 p. : LC Card 87-900295
HE559.I4 R34 1986

HARBORS - ITALY - GENOA - CONGRESSES.
Convegno Genova nell'economia marittimo/portuale in Europa e nel mondo (1982 : Genoa, Italy) Atti del Convegno Genova nell'economia marittimo/portuale in Europa e nel mondo . Genova [1982?] 135 p. : LC Card 86-105783
HE558.G3 C66 1982

HARBORS - ITALY - LIGURIA.
Vallega, Adalberto. Dai porti al sistema portuale . Savona , 1985. 320 p. : LC Card 87-139096
HE558.L44 V35 1985

HARBORS - LAKE STATES - PORT CHARGES.
Impact of deep-draft user charges on the six western Great Lakes states /. [Chicago, Ill.] (310 S. Michigan Ave., Chicago 60604) [1986] 3 v. : LC Card 87-404522 DDC 387.1 19
HE952.U6 I47 1986

HARBORS - LAKE STATES - STATISTICS.
Impact of deep-draft user charges on the six western Great Lakes states /. [Chicago, Ill.] (310 S. Michigan Ave., Chicago 60604) [1986] 3 v. : LC Card 87-404522 DDC 387.1 19
HE952.U6 I47 1986

HARBORS - MASSACHUSETTS - BOSTON - HISTORY.
Weinbaum, Paul O. Hoosac docks . Boston, Mass. , 1985. vi, 95 p. : LC Card 85-603289 DDC 387.1/64/0974461 19
HE554.B6 W45 1985

HARBORS - MATHEMATICAL MODELS.
Gorbatyĭ, M. M. (Mark Moiseevich) Teoriia i praktika optimizatsii proizvodstvennykh moshchnosteĭ morskikh portov /. Moskva , 1981. 167 p. : LC Card 82-162836
HE551 .G625 1981

HARBORS - MINNESOTA.
The Ports of Duluth, MN, and Superior, WI, Taconite Harbor, Silver Bay, and Two Harbors, Mdd, and Ashland, WI /. Washington , Fort Belvoir, Va. , 1987. vi, 62 p. : LC Card 87-601753 DDC 386/.8/0977512 19
HE554.A5 P66 1987

HARBORS - NETHERLANDS - ROTTERDAM - RATES.
Boldt, Günter. Wettbewerb und Preisbildung der Seehafenverkehrswirtschaft in nordwesteuropäischen Seehäfen . Göttingen , 1964. 120 p. ; LC Card 87-408787 DDC 380.5 s 387.1 19
HE131 .M84 Heft 30 HE558.H3

HARBORS - NEW JERSEY - CAMDEN.
Levinson, Alfred Linden, 1933- Economic impact assessment of the South Jersey Port Corporation /. Newark, N.J. (323 High St., Newark 07102) [1982] 31 leaves : LC Card 86-622073 DDC 387.1/09749/88 19
HE554.C18 L48 1982

HARBORS - NORTH SEA REGION - DIRECTORIES.
Handelshäfen im Ostseeraum /. [Lübeck]

[1983] 232 p. : LC Card 84-192969
HE557.A3 H36 1983

HARBORS - NORWAY - STAVANGER - HISTORY - 19TH CENTURY.
Grude, Egil Harald, 1944- Fra brygger til storhavn . Stavanger , c1985. 167 p. : ISBN 82-00-07235-5 : LC Card 86-148407
HE558.S67 G78 1985

HARBORS - NORWAY - STAVANGER - HISTORY - 20TH CENTURY.
Grude, Egil Harald, 1944- Fra brygger til storhavn . Stavanger , c1985. 167 p. : ISBN 82-00-07235-5 : LC Card 86-148407
HE558.S67 G78 1985

HARBORS - PACIFIC COAST (U. S.)
Boschken, Herman L. Strategic design and organizational change . Tuscaloosa, Ala. , c1989. p. cm. ISBN 0-8173-0339-1 LC Card 86-14673 DDC 387.1/0979 19
HE554.A6 B67 1989

HARBORS - PACIFIC COAST (U. S.) - MANAGEMENT.
Boschken, Herman L. Strategic design and organizational change . Tuscaloosa, Ala. , c1989. p. cm. ISBN 0-8173-0339-1 LC Card 86-14673 DDC 387.1/0979 19
HE554.A6 B67 1989

HARBORS - PERU.
Flórez Nohesell, Miguel. Los puertos del Perú /. Lima, Perú , 1986. 947 p. : LC Card 86-210075
HE555.P5 F58 1986

HARBORS - PLANNING.
Frankel, Ernst G. Port planning and development /. New York , c1987. xxiv, 795 p. : ISBN 0-471-83708-3 LC Card 86-24747 DDC 387.1/068 19
HE551 .F7 1987

HARBORS - POLAND.
Kwiatkowski, Eugeniusz. Pisma o rzeczypospolitej morskiej /. Szczecin , 1985. 277 p., [24] p. of plates : ISBN 83-7007-012-4 :
NYPL [*QO 86-2539]

Organizacja i technika portów morskich /. Gdańsk , 1978. 292 p. : LC Card 81-200313
HE557.P58 O73 1978

Sójka, Zygmunt. Polska polityka morska /. Gdańsk , 1986. 237, [1] : ISBN 83-215-1646-7(pbk.) :
NYPL [*QO 87-1818]

HARBORS - QUÉBEC (PROVINCE) - QUÉBEC.
Economic impact of the Port of Québec. [Québec, Québec] [1974] [16], [18] leaves ; LC Card 85-183731 DDC 386/.8/09714471 19
HE554.Q4 E27 1974

HARBORS - SCOTLAND - ABERDEEN (GRAMPIAN) - HISTORY.
Turner, John R. (John Raymond), 1936- Scotland's North Sea gateway . Aberdeen , 1986. xvi, 228 p. : ISBN 0-08-032463-0 LC Card 87-131902 DDC 387.1/09412/35 19
HE558.A34 T87 1986

HARBORS - SPAIN - PAÍS VASCO.
Ciriquiain-Gaiztarro, M. Los puertos marítimos del País Vasco /. San Sebastián [1986?] 270 p. : ISBN 84-7148-180-4 LC Card 87-105513
HE558.P15 C57 1986

HARBORS - UNITED STATES - PORT CHARGES.
Impact of deep-draft user charges on the six western Great Lakes states /. [Chicago, Ill.] (310 S. Michigan Ave., Chicago 60604) [1986] 3 v. : LC Card 87-404522 DDC 387.1 19
HE952.U6 I47 1986

HARBORS - UNITED STATES - STATISTICS.
Impact of deep-draft user charges on the six western Great Lakes states /. [Chicago, Ill.] (310 S. Michigan Ave., Chicago 60604) [1986] 3 v. : LC Card 87-404522 DDC 387.1 19
HE952.U6 I47 1986

HARBORS - WASHINGTON (STATE)
The Ports of Tacoma, Grays Harbor, and Olympia, Washington /. Washington, D.C. , Fort Belvoir, Va. , 1983. vi, 98 p. : LC Card 83-603527 DDC 387.1/09797/7 19
HE554.T2 P67 1983 ***NYPL [JLF 85-2000]***

HARBORS - WASHINGTON (STATE) - OLYMPIA.
The Ports of Tacoma, Grays Harbor, and Olympia, Washington /. Washington, D.C. , Fort Belvoir, Va. , 1983. vi, 98 p. : LC Card 83-603527 DDC 387.1/09797/7 19
HE554.T2 P67 1983 ***NYPL [JLF 85-2000]***

HARBORS - WASHINGTON (STATE) - TACOMA.
The Ports of Tacoma, Grays Harbor, and Olympia, Washington /. Washington, D.C. , Fort Belvoir, Va. , 1983. vi, 98 p. : LC Card 83-603527 DDC 387.1/09797/7 19
HE554.T2 P67 1983 ***NYPL [JLF 85-2000]***

HARBORS - WISCONSIN.
The Ports of Duluth, MN, and Superior, WI, Taconite Harbor, Silver Bay, and Two Harbors, Mdd, and Ashland, WI /. Washington , Fort Belvoir, Va. , 1987. vi, 62 p. : LC Card 87-601753 DDC 386/.8/0977512 19
HE554.A5 P66 1987

Harbury, C. D. Workbook in introductory economics / by Colin Harbury. 4th ed. Oxford [Oxfordshire] ; New York : Pergamon Press, 1987, c1982. xvii, 176 p. : ill. ; 30 cm. ISBN 0-08-034790-8 (pbk.) : LC Card 87-19011 DDC 330/.076 19
1. Economics - Problems, exercises, etc. 2. Great Britain - Economic conditions - Problems, exercises, etc. I. Title.
HB74.6 .H37 1987

Harcourt Brace Jovanovich college outline series.
Emery, Mary Ann. Principles of accounting /. San Diego , <c1987-. v. <2- > : ISBN 0-15-600029-6 (pbk.) : LC Card 86-27103 DDC 657 19
HF5635 .E537 1987

Harcourt, Geoffrey Colin.
Controversies in political economy : selected essays of G.C. Harcourt / edited by O.F. Hamouda. New York : New York University Press, 1986. 293 p. ; ill. : 23 cm. Includes bibliographies and index. ISBN 0-8147-3437-5 : LC Card 85-31055 DDC 330.1 19
1. Economics - History - Addresses, essays, lectures. 2. Economists - Addresses, essays, lectures. 3. Capitalism - Addresses, essays, lectures. 4. Economic policy - Addresses, essays, lectures. 5. Economics - Moral and ethical aspects - Addresses, essays, lectures. I. Hamouda, O. F. II. Title.
HB75 .H33 1986 ***NYPL [JLD 86-3571]***

International monetary problems and supply-side economics . Houndmills, Basingstoke, Hampshire , 1986. viii, 162 p. : ISBN 0-333-36200-4 ***NYPL [JLD 86-4356]***

Harcsa, István.
A Háztáji és kisegitő gazdaság szerepe az életmód alakulásában . Budapest , 1983. 263 p. ; ISBN 963-02-2948-X (Magy. nemz. bibl.) LC Card 84-216989
HD1476.H8 H28 1983

Vándorlás, mobilitás, keresetalakulás : az 1983. évi társadalmi mobilitás és jövedelmi vizsgálat alapján / [készült a Központi Statisztikai Hivatal Társadalmi Statisztikai Főosztályán ; készitette, Harcsa István]. Budapest : Központi Statisztikai Hivatal, 1987. 86 p. ; 29 cm. (Társadalom statisztikai közlemények, 0133-8226) ISBN 963-340-812-1 : LC Card 87-409641
1. Migration, Internal - Hungary - Statistics. 2. Social mobility - Hungary - Statistics. 3. Income distribution - Hungary - Statistics. I. Hungary. Központi Statisztikai Hivatal. Társadalmi Statisztikai Főosztály. II. Title. III. Series.
HB2052.5.A3 H37 1987

Hard choices : a report on the increasing gap between America's infrastructure needs and our ability to pay for them : appendix : a case study / prepared for the use of the Subcommittee on Economic Goals and Intergovernmental Policy of the Joint Economic Committee, Congress of the United States. Washington : U. S. G.P.O., 1984. 23 v. : ill. ; 24 cm. (S. prt. . 98-164, App. 1-23) At head of title: 98th Congress, 2d session. Joint committee print. "February 25, 1984." Includes bibliographical references. CONTENTS. - app. 1. Alabama -- app. 2. California -- app. 3. Colorado -- app. 4. Florida -- app. 5. Indiana -- app. 6. Kentucky -- app. 7. Louisiana -- app. 8. Maine -- app. 9. Maryland -- app. 10. Massachusetts -- app. 11. Missouri -- app. 12. Montana -- app. 13. New Jersey -- app. 14. New Mexico -- app. 15. New York -- app. 16. North Carolina -- app. 17. Ohio -- app. 18. Oklahoma -- app. 19. Oregon -- app. 20. South Carolina -- app. 21. Tennessee -- app. 22. Texas -- app. 23. Washington.
1. Infrastructure (Economics) - United States. 2. Capital budget - United States - States. 3. Intergovernmental fiscal relations - United States. I. United States. Congress. Joint Economic Committee. Subcommittee on Economic Goals and Intergovernmental Policy. II. Series. III. Series: United States. Congress (98th, 2nd session : 1984). Senate. S. prt. , 98-164, App. 1-23.
NYPL [JLE 87-566 Appendix 1-23]

Hard choices . Kaplan, Marshall. Washington , 1984. xi, 230 p. : LC Card 84-602470 DDC 338.4/3363/0973 19
HC110.C3 K37 1984 ***NYPL [JLE 87-566]***

Hard coal, hard times : ethnicity and labor in the anthracite region / edited by David L. Salay ; The Scranton Anthracite Museum Associates in cooperation with the Commonwealth of Pennsylvania, Pennsylvania Historical and Museum Commission. Scranton : Anthracite Museum Press, 1984, c1983. xv, 193 p. ; 24 cm. Proceedings of a symposium held Oct. 1982 at the Scranton Anthracite Museum. Includes bibliographies. ISBN 0-917445-00-7 LC Card 85-156422 DDC 331.7/622335/0974837
1. Coal miners - Pennsylvania - Scranton Region - History - Addresses, essays, lectures. 2. Anthracite coal industry - Pennsylvania - Scranton Region - History - Addresses, essays, lectures. 3. Ethnology - Pennsylvania - Scranton Region - History - Addresses, essays, lectures. 4. Scranton Region (Pa.) - Social life and customs - Addresses, essays, lectures. I. Salay, David L., 1944-. II. Scranton Anthracite Museum. Associates. III. Pennsylvania. Historical and Museum Commission.
HD8039.M62 U633 1984
NYPL [JLE 87-1218]

Hard heads, soft hearts . Blinder, Alan S. Reading, Mass. , c1987. xi, 236 p. : ISBN 0-201-11504-2 : LC Card 87-14078 DDC 330 19
HB171 .B535 1987

Hard labour /. Sirs, Bill. London , 1985. 151 p., [8] p. of plates : ISBN 0-283-99241-7 : LC Card 86-191030 DDC 331.88/1691/0924 B 19
HD6665.S57 A3 1985

Hard times . Sutcliffe, Robert B. London , 1983. 118 p. ; ISBN 0-86104-505-X (pbk.) : LC Card 83-126438 DDC 330.9/04 19
HC59 .S8873 1983 ***NYPL [JLD 86-4088]***

Hard times cotton mill girls . Byerly, Victoria Morris. Ithaca, N.Y. , c1986. x, 223 p. : ISBN 0-87546-128-X : LC Card 86-20082 DDC 331.4/877/00922 B 19
HD6073.T42 A132 1986
NYPL [JLD 87-1241]

Harden, Michael P. (Michael Patrick), 1952-
The handbook of multilevel marketing : understanding multilevel sales programs, direct selling, and pyramids / by Michael P. Harden. Carrollton, TX : Promontory Pub., c1987. 138 p. : ill. ; 21 cm. Includes bibliographies and index. ISBN 0-938703-10-2 (pbk.) : LC Card 86-25439 DDC 658.8/4 19
1. Multilevel marketing. 2. Direct selling. I. Title. II. Title: Multilevel marketing.
HF5415.126 .H37 1987

Hardes, Heinz-Dieter. Arbeitsmarktstrukturen und Beschäftigungsprobleme im internationalen Vergleich : theoretische und empirische Analyse am Beispiel von USA, Grossbritannien und der Bundesrepublik Deutschland / von Heinz-Dieter Hardes. Tübingen : Mohr, 1981. xv, 484 p. : 17 ill. ; 24 cm. (Schriften zur angewandten Wirtschaftsforschung, 0582-0286 . 44) Includes index. Bibliography: p. 445-479. ISBN 3-16-344468-7 : LC Card 81-196609 DDC 331.13/7 19
1. Unemployment. 2. Unemployment - United States. 3. Unemployment - Great Britain. 4. Unemployment - Germany (West). I. Title. II. Series.
HD5707.5 .H37 1981 ***NYPL [JLE 86-2544]***

Hardesty, Sarah. Success and betrayal : the crisis of women in corporate America / Sarah Hardesty, Nehama Jacobs.1st Touchstone ed. New York : Simon & Schuster, 1987, c1986. 464 p. ; 22 cm. (A Touchstone book) Bibliography: p. 449-452. Includes index. ISBN 0-671-64563-3 (pbk.) : LC Card 87-17289 DDC 331.4/816584/00973 19
1. Women executives - United States. 2. Women in the professions - United States. I. Jacobs, Nehama.
HD6054.4.U6 H37 1987

Harding and Mexico . Beelen, George D. New

York , 1987. xiii, 200 p., [16] p. of plates : ISBN 0-8240-8073-4 (alk. paper) LC Card 87-23724 DDC 337.72073 19
HF1456.5.M6 B44 1987

Harding, Cynthia, 1952- Harding, Owen, 1946- How to start your own business successfully! /. Oklahoma City, OK , c1986. 102 p. ; ISBN 0-940897-01-6 (pbk.) : LC Card 86-32849 DDC 658.1/141 19
HD62.5 .H37 1986

Harding, Donald M. Penning-Rowsell, Edmund. Floods and drainage . London , Boston , 1986. xx, 199 p. : ISBN 0-04-627001-9 (alk. paper) : LC Card 85-13383 DDC 363.3/4936/0941 19
HD1676.G7 P46 1985 ***NYPL [JLE 86-3996]***

Harding, Owen, 1946- How to start your own business successfully! / by Owen & Cynthia Harding. Oklahoma City, OK : Cynoak Pub., c1986. 102 p. ; 22 cm. Includes index. ISBN 0-940897-01-6 (pbk.) : LC Card 86-32849 DDC 658.1/141 19
1. New business enterprises. I. Harding, Cynthia, 1952-. II. Title.
HD62.5 .H37 1986

Hardt, John Pearce. Tariff, legal, and credit constraints on East-West commercial relations /. Ottawa , 1975. 101 p. ; LC Card 76-379543 DDC 382.1
K3823.A55 T3 ***NYPL [JLD 86-1752]***

Hardtimes--a cartographic and graphic representation of selected aspects of the depression years, 1925-1935, in Australia /. Camm, J. C. R. (Jack Charles Robert) [Newcastle, N.S.W.] , 1985. 59, iii p. : ISBN 0-7259-0542-5 (pbk.) : LC Card 86-222404 DDC 330.994/042 19
HC603 .C36 1985

HARDWARE INDUSTRY - SWITZERLAND - DIRECTORIES.
Interferex 86 (Basel, Switzerland) Interferex 86, Intertable . Basel, Schweiz [1986] 284 p., [6] p. of plates : LC Card 87-409294 DDC 381/.18 19
HF5474.S92 B365 1986

HARDWARE INDUSTRY - UNITED STATES - HISTORY.
Kantowicz, Edward R. True Value . Chicago , 1986. 270 p., [16] p. of plates : ISBN 0-89526-580-X : LC Card 86-42795 DDC 381/.45683/0924 B 19
HD9745.U5 C655 1986 ***NYPL [JLE 87-1449]***

Hardy, C. Colburn. The blue chip investment strategy : quality, value, and timing for income and appreciation / C. Colburn Hardy. New York : F. Watts, 1987. 324 p. : ill. ; 24 cm. Includes index. ISBN 0-531-15525-0 LC Card 87-14726 DDC 332.63/22 19
1. Stocks - United States. 2. Investments - United States. I. Title.
HG4963 .H37 1987

Hardy, Clarisa. Hambre + dignidad=ollas comunes / Clarisa Hardy. 1a ed. [Santiago, Chile] : Programa de Economía del Trabajo, Academia de Humanismo Cristiano, 1986. 282 p., [16] p. of plates : ill. ; 22 cm. (Colección Experiencias populares . 3) Bibliography: p. 279-282.
1. Food relief - Chile. 2. Cooperative societies - Chile. 3. Consumers cooperatives - Chile. 4. Nutrition - Chile. I. Title. II. Title: Hambre mas dignidad igual ollas comunes. III. Title: Hambre y dignidad igual ollas comunes. IV. Series. ***NYPL [JLD 87-334]***

Hardy, Ilona. Gyakorlati útmutató a kötvény és a váltó használatához / [szerzők, Hardy Ilona, Komlós János]. Budapest : Saldo Pénzügyi Szervező és Tanácsadó Vállalat, 1986. 62 p. ; 24 cm. (Szabályozórendszer) ISBN 963-621-315-1 LC Card 87-407776
1. Bonds - Hungary. 2. Bills of exchange - Hungary. I. Komlós, János. II. Title. III. Series.
HG5470.5.A3 H37 1986

Hardy, Kenneth G., 1941- Marketing channel management : strategic planning and tactics / Kenneth G. Hardy, Allan J. Magrath. Glenview, IL : Scott, Foresman, c1988. 724 p. : ill. ; 24 cm. Includes bibliographies and indexes. ISBN 0-673-18295-9 : LC Card 87-12742 DDC 658.8/4 19
1. Marketing channels - Management. I. Magrath, Allan J. II. Title.
HF5415 .H229 1988

Hargreaves, Judith. The home-owner's guide : buying, building, improving, and running your own home / Judith Hargreaves. Cambridge [Cambridgeshire] ; Wolfeboro, N.H., USA : Woodhead-Faulkner, 1988. p. cm. (A Woodhead-Faulkner moneyguide) Includes index. ISBN 0-85941-423-X (pbk.) : LC Card 87-17388 DDC 643 19
1. Home ownership. 2. House buying. 3. House construction. I. Title. II. Series.
HD7287.8 .H37 1988

Hari Singh, Master, 1902- Agrarian scene in British Punjab / Master Hari Singh. New Delhi : People's Pub. House, 1983-c1984. 2 v. : maps ; 22 cm. Vol. 2 has title: Punjab peasant freedom struggle. Includes bibliographies. LC Card 83-905514 DDC 338.1/0954/5 19
1. Agriculture - Economic aspects - India - Punjab - History. 2. Peasantry - India - Punjab - Political activity - History. I. Title. II. Title: Punjab peasant freedom struggle.
HD2075.P8 H37 1983 ***NYPL [JLK 86-113]***

Haridasan, V., 1937- Dr. John Matthai, 1886-1959 : a biography / by V. Haridasan. Cranganore, Trichur Dist., Kerala : Sunil, 1986. xi, 192 p., [2] p. of plates : ill., port. ; 21 cm. "A commemorative volume released on the occasion of Dr. John Matthai's birth centenary celebrations on the 10th January 1986, at Dr. John Matthai Centre, Trichur." Biography of an Indian economist and administrator. Bibliography: p. [183]-186. Includes index. LC Card 86-903052 DDC 330/.092/4 B 19
1. Matthai, John, 1886-. 2. Economists - India - Biography. I. Title.
HB126.I43 M374 1986

HARIJANS. see **UNTOUCHABLES.**

Harinas compuestas. Proyecto harinas compuestas . La Paz, Bolivia , 1982. 272, [2], 3 p., [9] p. of plates : LC Card 83-195592
HD9044.B52 P76 1982

Harjinder Singh. Agricultural problems in Ethiopia / Harjinder Singh. Delhi, India : Gian Pub. House, c1987. viii, 254 p. : maps ; 22 cm. Bibliography: p. [239]-249. Includes index. ISBN 81-212-0078-4 : LC Card 87-900338 DDC 338.1/0963 19
1. Agriculture and state - Ethiopia. 2. Agriculture - Economic aspects - Ethiopia. 3. Land reform - Ethiopia. 4. Land tenure - Ethiopia. I. Title.
HD2124.5 .H37 1987

Harju, Hely. Puutteellisen asumisen parantaminen kunnissa vuosina 1985-1989 / Hely Harju. [Helsinki : Asuntohallitus, Tutkimus- ja suunnitteluosasto, 1986] 69, [16] p. : forms ; 30 cm. (Julkaisuja / Asuntohallitus, Tutkimus- ja suunnitteluosasto, 0781-6650 . 1985:2) Bibliography: p. 69. ISBN 951-46-9022-2 LC Card 86-215457
1. Housing rehabilitation - Finland. 2. Housing policy - Finland. I. Series: Julkaisuja (Finland. Asuntohallitus. Tutkimus- ja suunnitteluosasto) , 1985:2. II. Title.
HD7345.3.A3 H367 1986

Harker, Carlton. Pension plan partial terminations / Carlton Harker. Brookfield, Wis. : International Foundation of Employee Benefit Plans, c1982. 92 p. ; 27 cm. Includes index. Bibliography: p. 85. ISBN 0-89154-163-2 (pbk.) : LC Card 82-147078 DDC 344.73/01252 347.3041252 19
1. Pension trusts - Law and legislation - United States. 2. Pension trusts - United States. I. Title.
KF3512.Z9 H37 1982 ***NYPL [JLF 85-605]***

Harkess, Shirley. Women working . Mountain View, Calif. , c1988. xv, 431 p. : ISBN 0-87484-744-3 (pbk.) LC Card 87-3215 DDC 331.4/0973 19
HD6095 .W6976 1988

The Harley-Davidson Motor Company . Wright, David, 1943- Osceola, Wis., USA , c1987. 288 p. : ISBN 0-87938-245-7 : LC Card 87-5519 DDC 338.7/6292275/0973 19
HD9710.5.U54 H378 1987

HARLEY-DAVIDSON MOTOR COMPANY - HISTORY.
Wright, David, 1943- The Harley-Davidson Motor Company . Osceola, Wis., USA , c1987. 288 p. : ISBN 0-87938-245-7 : LC Card 87-5519 DDC 338.7/6292275/0973 19
HD9710.5.U54 H378 1987

Harlow, Alvin F. (Alvin Fay), 1875-1963. When horses pulled boats : a story of early canals / by Alvin F. Harlow ; introduction by William H. Shank ; illustrated by Orson Lowell and Philip J. Hoffmann. York, PA : American Canal and Transportation Center, c1983. 72 p. : ill. ; 22 cm. Reprint. Originally published: 1936. Bibliography: p. 69-70. Surveys the history of canals in America, from colonial times to the twentieth century. ISBN 0-933788-43-6 (pbk.) LC Card 87-400271 DDC 386/.48/0973 19
1. Canals - United States - History - Juvenile literature. I. Lowell, Orson, ill. II. Hoffmann, Philip J., ill. III. Title.
HE395.A3 H37 1983

Harlow, P. A. (Peter Alan)
Construction management and organisation in perspective /. London , New York , 1987. p. cm. ISBN 0-419-14020-4 LC Card 87-20548 DDC 624/.068 s 624/.068 19
HD9715.A2 M296 vol. 3

Managing construction worldwide /. London , New York , 1987. p. cm. ISBN 0-419-14030-1 (set) LC Card 87-20545 DDC 624/.068 19
HD9715.A2 M296

Productivity and human factors in construction /. London , New York , 1987. p. cm. ISBN 0-419-14010-7 LC Card 87-20547 DDC 624/.068 s 624/.068/3 19
HD9715.A2 M296 vol. 2

Systems for managing construction /. London , New York , 1987. p. cm. ISBN 0-419-14000-X LC Card 87-20546 DDC 624/.068 s 624/.068 19
HD9715.A2 M296 vol. 1

Harmer, C. H. C. (Cyril Henry Carrington) Newfoundland air mails : air stamps and flight covers from 1919 through March 31, 1949 : an update of 1953 edition / by C.H.C. Harmer ; edited by Joseph L. Eisendrath.Rev. and updated. Cinnaminson, N.J., U. S.A. : American Air Mail Society, 1984. x, 181 p. : ill. ; 24 cm. Cover title: Newfoundland air mails, 1919-1939. Rev. ed. of: Newfoundland air mails, 1919-1939 / Robert Elgar Richard Dalwick. 1953. Includes index. LC Card 87-147693 DDC 383/.144/09718 19
1. Air mail stamps - Newfoundland. I. Eisendrath, Joseph L. II. Dalwick, Robert Elgar Richard. Newfoundland air mails, 1919-1939. III. Title.
HE6185.C23 N475 1984

Harmon, Charlotte. The flea market entrepreneur / by Charlotte Harmon. Babylon, N.Y. : Pilot Industries, c1987. 31 p. ; 22 cm. (Pilot books) ISBN 0-87576-134-8 (pbk.) : LC Card 87-2223 DDC 658.8/4 19
1. Flea markets - Management. 2. Small business - Management. I. Title.
HF5482 .H36 1987

Harmon, David P., 1937- Dublin, Jack. Mid-term evaluation of the Malawi Union of Savings and Credit Co-operatives Project (612-0205) /. Lilongwe, Malawi , 1983. x, 84, [29] leaves ; LC Card 85-981350 DDC 334/.22/096897 19
HG2039.M29 D83 1983

Harmon, Paul. Expert systems : tools and applications / Paul Harmon, Rex Maus, William Morrissey. New York : Wiley, c1988. xii, 289 p. : ill. ; 24 cm. Bibliography: p. 272-274. Includes index. ISBN 0-471-83950-7 (pbk.) LC Card 87-17608 DDC 650/.028/5633 19
1. Business - Data processing. 2. Expert systems (Computer science). I. Maus, Rex. II. Morrissey, William. III. Title.
HF5548.2 .H367 1988

Harmonization of accounting standards : achievements and prospects. Paris : Organisation for Economic Co-operation and Development ; Washington, D.C. : OECD Publications and Information Centre [distributor], 1986. 147 p. ; 23 cm. ISBN 92-64-12895-6 (pbk.) : LC Card 87-124490 DDC 657/.0218 19
1. Accounting - Standards. 2. Comparative accounting. 3. Organisation for Economic Co-operation and Development. I. Organisation for Economic Co-operation and Development.
HF5611 .H37 1986

Harms, John H. U. S. News investment guide /. Washington, D.C. (2400 N. St., N.W., Washington 20037-1196) , c1987. iv, 60 p. : LC Card 87-143438 DDC 332.6/78 19
HG4910 .U25 1987

HARNEY COUNTY (OR.) - HISTORY.
Simpson, Peter K., 1930- The community of

cattlemen . Moscow, Idaho , c1987. xiv, 228 p. ; ISBN 0-89301-117-7 (pbk.) LC Card 87-5855 DDC 338.1/762/00979595 19
HD9433.U5 H277 1987

Harouel, Jean Louis. Essai sur l'inégalité / Jean-Louis Harouel. 1re éd. Paris : Presses universitaires de France, c1984. 287, [1] p. ; 22 cm. (Politique d'aujourd'hui) Bibliography: p. 287-[288] ISBN 2-13-038354-8 : LC Card 84-150958
1. Income distribution - France - History. 2. Equality - France - History. 3. France - Intellectual life. 4. International economic relations. I. Title. II. Series.
HC280.I5 H35 1984

Harper, Douglas A. Working knowledge : skill and community in a small shop / Douglas Harper. Chicago : University of Chicago Press, 1987. x, 214 p. : ill. ; 26 cm. Bibliography: p. 209-211. Includes index. ISBN 0-226-31688-2 LC Card 86-30708 DDC 302.3/4 19
1. Work. 2. Community life. 3. Repairing trades - New York (State) - Case studies. I. Title.
HD4904 .H335 1987

Harper, John Lamberton. America and the reconstruction of Italy, 1945-1948 / John Lamberton Harper. Cambridge [Cambridgeshire] ; New York : Cambridge University Press, 1986. x, 213 p. ; 24 cm. Includes index. Bibliography: p. 201-208. ISBN 0-521-32518-8 LC Card 85-30915 DDC 338.91/73/045 19
1. Economic assistance, American - Italy. 2. Reconstruction (1939-1951) - Italy. 3. United States - Foreign relations - Italy. 4. Italy - Foreign relations - United States. I. Title.
HC305 .H36 1986 ***NYPL [JLE 86-3600]***

Harper, Susan D. Traylor, Harlon D. An analysis of grain elevator bankruptcies in Louisiana /. [Baton Rouge?] [1986] iii, 77 p. ; LC Card 87-620885 DDC 338.1/09763 s 338.1/6 19
HD1775.L8 L7 no. 661 HD9037.L6

Harradine, Peter W. A. Philippine postage stamp handbook, 1854-1982 / by Peter W.A. Harradine. Jefferson, N.C. : McFarland & Co., c1987. xv, 387 p., [71] p. of plates : ill. ; 24 cm. Bibliography: p. 375-377. Includes index. ISBN 0-89950-178-8 LC Card 84-43212 DDC 769.569599 19
1. Postage-stamps - Philippines - Catalogs. I. Title.
HE6185.P52 H373 1987

Harrap's new standard French and English dictionary / [edited] by J. E. Mansion. Completely rev. and enl. ed. / by R. P. L. Ledésert and Margaret Ledésert. London : Harrap, 1980-1981. 4 v. ; 29 cm. Earlier title: Harrap's standard French and English dictionary. CONTENTS. - v. 1-2. French-English -- v. 3-4. English-French. ISBN 0-245-50972-0 (v.1)
1. French language - Dictionaries - English. 2. English language - Dictionaries - French. I. Mansion, J. E. (Jean Edmond), 1870-1942. II. Ledésert, Margaret. III. Harrap's standard French and English dictionary. IV. Title.

Harrap's slang dictionary English-French/French-English /. Marks, Georgette A. London , 1984. 476 p. ; ISBN 0-245-54047-4 ***NYPL [JFC 86-640]***

Harrap's standard French and English dictionary. Harrap's new standard French and English dictionary /. London , 1980-1981. 4 v. ; ISBN 0-245-50972-0 (v.1)

Harrigan, Anthony H. Putting America first . Washington, D.C. , c1987. 87 p. ; ISBN 0-944468-00-4 (pbk.) : LC Card 87-50998 DDC 382/.3/0973 19
HF1455 .P87 1987

Harringer, Reinhold. Nydegger, Alfred. Investitionen und Innovationen in kleineren Industriebetrieben . Diessenhofen , c1983. viii, 317 p. : ISBN 3-7253-0196-4 LC Card 83-224277 DDC 658.1/592 19
HG4027.7 .N93 1983 ***NYPL [JLD 87-633]***

Harrington, Diana R., 1940-
Modern portfolio theory and the capital asset pricing model. Harrington, Diana R., 1940- Modern portfolio theory, the capital asset pricing model, and arbitrage pricing theory : a user's guide / Diana R. Harrington.2nd ed. Englewood Cliffs, N.J. , c1987. x, 229 p. : ISBN 0-13-597261-2 (pbk.) LC Card 86-22693 DDC 332.6 19
HG4637 .H37 1987

Modern portfolio theory, the capital asset pricing model, and arbitrage pricing theory : a user's guide / Diana R. Harrington.2nd ed. Englewood Cliffs, N.J. : Prentice-Hall, c1987. x, 229 p. : ill. ; 23 cm. Previous ed. published as: Modern portfolio theory and the capital asset pricing model. 1983. Includes bibliographies and index. ISBN 0-13-597261-2 (pbk.) LC Card 86-22693 DDC 332.6 19
1. Capital assets pricing model. 2. Portfolio management. 3. Arbitrage. I. Harrington, Diana R., 1940- Modern portfolio theory and the capital asset pricing model. II. Title.
HG4637 .H37 1987

Harrington, Thomas F. Guide for occupational exploration /. [Washington, D.C.] , Circle Pines, Minn. , c1984. vii, 984 p. : LC Card 87-402857 DDC 331.7/02/0973 19
HF5382.5.U5 G83 1984

Harris, C. C. (Christopher Charles) Redundancy and recession in South Wales / C.C. Harris and the Redundancy and Unemployment Research Group, School of Social Studies, University College of Swansea. Oxford, OX, UK ; New York, NY, USA : Blackwell, 1987. p. cm. Bibliography: p. Includes index. ISBN 0-631-15106-0 : LC Card 87-6301 DDC 331.13/794294 19
1. Unemployed - Wales, South. 2. Unemployment - Wales, South. 3. Wales, South - Economic conditions. I. University of College of Swansea. School of Social Studies. Redundancy and Unemployment Research Group. II. Title.
HD5766.A6 H37 1987

Harris, Chauncy Dennison, 1914- World patterns of modern urban change . Chicago , 1986. x, 479 p. : ISBN 0-89065-122-1 : LC Card 85-23231 DDC 910 s 307.7/6 19
H31 .C514 no.217-218
NYPL [JFM 72-132 no.217-218]

HARRIS, CHAUNCY DENNISON, 1914-
World patterns of modern urban change . Chicago , 1986. x, 479 p. : ISBN 0-89065-122-1 : LC Card 85-23231 DDC 910 s 307.7/6 19
H31 .C514 no.217-218
NYPL [JFM 72-132 no.217-218]

Harris, Howell John, 1951- The right to manage : industrial relations policies of American business in the 1940s / Howell John Harris. Madison, Wis. : University of Wisconsin Press, 1982. ix, 296 p. ; 24 cm. Includes bibliographical references and index. ISBN 0-299-08640-2 : LC Card 81-69820 DDC 331./0973 19
1. Industrial relations - United States - History. 2. Industry - Social aspects - United States - History. I. Title.
HD8072 .H2874 ***NYPL [JLE 86-4147]***

Harris, Jack C., 1945-
Friedman, Jack P. Adjustable rate mortgages /. New York , c1987. viii, 293 p. ; ISBN 0-8120-3764-2 (soft) : LC Card 86-28852 DDC 332.8/2 19
HG1634 .F75 1987

Friedman, Jack P. Dictionary of real estate terms /. New York , c1987. v, 329 p. : ISBN 0-8120-3898-3 (pbk.) : LC Card 87-19869 DDC 333.33/03/21 19
HD1365 .F75 1987

1985-86 real estate review and outlook / compiled by Jack Harris ; contributors, Waldo Born ... [et al.]. College Station, Tex. : Texas Real Estate Research Center, Texas A&M University, [1985?] 22 p. ; 28 cm. "TRERC-186-1M-511." LC Card 86-621364 DDC 333.33/09764 19
1. Real estate business - Texas. 2. Real estate business - Texas - Forecasting. I. Born, Waldo L. II. Texas Real Estate Research Center. III. Title.
HD266.T4 H37 1985

Harris, John Andrew de Oliveira. Evolução e definição da moeda / John Andrew de Oliveira Harris. 1a. ed. Rio de Janeiro, RJ : FGV, Instituto de Documentação, Editora da Fundação Getúlio Vargas, 1985. 90 p. : ill. ; 22 cm. (Série Teses. no. 13) Bibliography: p. 83-87. Includes index. LC Card 87-135878 DDC 332.4/981 19
1. Money - Brazil - Mathematical models. 2. Monetary policy - Brazil - Mathematical models. 3. Inflation (Finance) - Brazil - Mathematical models. 4. Money - Mathematical models. 5. Monetary policy - Mathematical models. I. Series: Série Teses (Escola de Pós-Graduação em Economia) , no. 13. II. Title.
HG835 .H37 1985

Harris, Kenneth, 1919- The wildcatter : a portrait of Robert O. Anderson / by Kenneth Harris.1st ed. New York : Weidenfeld & Nicolson, c1987. x, 180 p., [8] p. of plates : ill., ports. ; 23 cm. Includes index. ISBN 1-555-84048-5 LC Card 87-8183 DDC 338.7/622338/0924 B 19
1. Anderson, Robert O., 1917-. 2. Businessmen - United States - Biography. 3. Petroleum industry and trade - United States - History. 4. Atlantic Richfield Co. - History. I. Title.
HD9570.A53 H37 1987

Harris, Laurence. New perspectives on the financial system /. London , New York , c1988. 410 p. : ISBN 0-7099-3741-5 LC Card 87-15723 DDC 332/.0941 19
HG186.G7 N44 1988

Harris, Lement, 1904- My tale of two worlds : USA and USSR / by Lement Harris.1st ed. New York : International Publishers, 1986. 289 p. : ill. ; 22 cm. Includes index. ISBN 0-7178-0645-6 : LC Card 86-10671 DDC 338.1/092/4 B 19
1. Harris, Lement, 1904-. 2. Farmers - United States - Biography. 3. Agriculture - United States - History - 20th century. 4. Agriculture - Soviet Union - History - 20th century. 5. Agriculture and state - United States - History - 20th century. 6. Agriculture and state - Soviet Union - History - 20th century. I. Title. II. Title: My tale of 2 worlds.
S417.H35 A36 1986 ***NYPL [JLD 87-1376]***

HARRIS, LEMENT, 1904-
Harris, Lement, 1904- My tale of two worlds . New York , 1986. 289 p. : ISBN 0-7178-0645-6 : LC Card 86-10671 DDC 338.1/092/4 B 19
S417.H35 A36 1986 ***NYPL [JLD 87-1376]***

Harris, Leo J. Central America postal history and a listing of prephilatelic postmarks =. New York [Yonkers, N.Y.?] , 1986. xiv, 142 p. : ISBN 0-912574-41-0 (pbk.) LC Card 87-402819 DDC 383/.49728 19
HE6674 .C46 1986

Harris (Louis) and Associates. see **Louis Harris and Associates.**

Harris, Milton. Dynamic economic analysis / Milton Harris. New York : Oxford University Press, 1987. x, 137 p. : ill. ; 25 cm. Includes bibliographies and index. ISBN 0-19-504406-1 (alk. paper) LC Card 86-23925 DDC 339.5 19
1. Equilibrium (Economics). 2. Statics and dynamics (Social sciences). I. Title.
HB145 .H37 1987

Harris, Myles F. Breakfast in hell : a doctor's eyewitness account of the politics of hunger in Ethiopia / Myles F. Harris. New York : Poseidon Press, c1987. 271 p. ; 23 cm. ISBN 0-671-63272-8 : LC Card 86-25504 DDC 363.8/83/0963 19
1. Famines - Ethiopia. 2. Ethiopia - Politics and government - 1974-. 3. Harris, Myles F. 4. Physicians, Foreign - Ethiopia - Biography. I. Title.
HC845.Z9 F345 1987

HARRIS, MYLES F.
Harris, Myles F. Breakfast in hell . New York , c1987. 271 p. ; ISBN 0-671-63272-8 : LC Card 86-25504 DDC 363.8/83/0963 19
HC845.Z9 F345 1987

Harris, Nigel.
The end of the Third World : newly industrializing countries and the decline of an ideology / Nigel Harris. London : I.B. Tauris, 1986. 231 p. : ill. ; 24 cm. Includes index. Bibliography: p. [204]-207. ISBN 1-85043-031-4
1. Industry and state - Developing countries. 2. Industrialization - Political aspects. 3. Developing countries - Industries. I. Title.
NYPL [JLE 87-858]

The end of the Third World : newly industrializing countries and the decline of an ideology / Nigel Harris. New York : Meredith Press, 1987, c1986. 231 p. : 10 ill. ; 24 cm. Bibliography: p. [204]-207. Includes index. ISBN 0-941533-14-X : LC Card 87-12295 DDC 330.9172/4 19
1. Developing countries - Economic conditions. 2. Developing countries - Economic policy. 3. Developing countries - Industries. 4. International economic relations. I. Title.
HC59.7 .H3536 1987

Harris, Philip R. (Philip Robert), 1926- Management in transition : transforming managerial practices and organizational strategies for a new work culture / Philip R. Harris.1st ed. San Francisco, Calif. : Jossey-Bass, c1985. xxvii, 404 p. : ill. ; 24 cm. (The Jossey-Bass management series) The Jossey-Bass social and behavioral science series Includes index. Bibliography: p. 369-384. ISBN 0-87589-660-X (alk. paper) LC Card 85-45055 DDC 658.4 19
1. Corporate culture. 2. Leadership. I. Title. II. Series.
HD58.7 .H3695 1985 ***NYPL [JLE 85-3954]***

Managing cultural differences / Philip R. Harris, Robert T. Moran. 2nd ed. Houston : Gulf Pub. Co., Book Division, c1987. xiii, 609 p. : ill. ; 24 cm. (Building blocks of human potential) Bibliography: p. 580-594. Includes indexes. ISBN 0-87201-161-5 LC Card 86-25618 DDC 658.1/8 19
1. International business enterprises - Management. 2. Acculturation. 3. Cross-cultural studies. I. Moran, Robert T., 1938-. II. Title. III. Series.
HD62.4 .H37 1987

Harris, Reuben T. Beckhard, Richard, 1918- Organizational transitions . Reading, Mass. , c1987. xii, 117 p. : ISBN 0-201-10887-9 (pbk.) : LC Card 86-25863 DDC 658.4/06 19
HD58.8 .B4 1987

Harris, Robert S., 1949- Pringle, John J. Essentials of managerial finance /. Glenview, Ill. , c1987. xxxi, 811, [98] p. : ISBN 0-673-18331-9 : LC Card 86-31333 DDC 658.1/5 19
HG4026 .P73 1987

Harris, Rosemary. Power and powerlessness in industry : an analysis of the social relations of production / Rosemary Harris. London ; New York : Tavistock Publications, 1987. viii, 245 p. : ill. ; 23 cm. Includes indexes. Bibliography: p. [238]-239. ISBN 0-422-60920-X LC Card 86-14420 DDC 338.4/766134/0941 19
1. Ammonia industry - Great Britain - Employees - Case studies. 2. Industrial sociology - Great Britain - Case studies. I. Title.
HD6956.A497 H37 1986
NYPL [JLD 87-825]

Harris, Stuart. Analysis of commodity markets for policy purposes / by Stuart Harris, Mark Salmon, and Ben Smith. London : Trade Policy Research Centre, 1978. ix, 81 p. ; 22 cm. (Thames essay, 0306-6991 . no. 17) Includes bibliographical references. ISBN 0-900842-42-3 (pbk.) LC Card 85-111455 DDC 332.64/4 19
1. Commodity exchanges. I. Salmon, Mark. II. Smith, Ben. III. Title. IV. Series.
HG6046 .H367 1978

Harrison, Clifford E., 1931- Managing staff reductions in corporations / by Clifford E. Harrison. Ann Arbor, Mich. : UMI Research Press, c1986. vi, 138 p. : ill. ; 24 cm. (Research for business decisions. 91) Revision of the author's thesis (Ph. D.)--Fairleigh Dickinson University, 1984. Includes index. Bibliography: p. [129]-134. ISBN 0-8357-1758-5 (alk. paper) LC Card 86-11223 DDC 658.3/134 19
1. Employees, Dismissal of - United States - Case studies. 2. Personnel management - United States - Case studies. I. Title.
HF5549.5.D55 H37 1986
NYPL [JLE 86-3391]

Harrison, J. F. C. (John Fletcher Clews) The common people of Great Britain : a history from the Norman Conquest to the present / J.F.C. Harrison.1st Midland book ed. Bloomington : Indiana University Press, 1985. 445 p. : map ; 21 cm. Includes index. Bibliography: p. 413-426. ISBN 0-253-20357-0 (pbk.) LC Card 84-48820 DDC 305.5/62/0942 19
1. Labor and laboring classes - Great Britain - History. 2. Peasantry - Great Britain - History. 3. Great Britain - Social conditions. I. Title.
HD8388 .H36 1985 ***NYPL [JLD 86-3656]***

Harrison, Joseph, 1944- The Spanish economy in the twentieth century / Joseph Harrison. London : Croom Helm, c1985. 207 p. : map ; 23 cm. (Croom Helm series on the contemporary economic history of Europe) Bibliography: p. 191-202. Includes index. ISBN 0-85664-721-7 : LC Card 86-674012
1. Spain - Economic conditions. 2. Spain - Economic policy. 3. Spain - Politics and government - 20th century. I. Title. II. Title: Spanish economy in the 20th century. III. Series.
HC385 .H34x 1985b

Harrison, Lawrence E. Underdevelopment is a state of mind : the Latin American case / Lawrence E. Harrison. [Cambridge, Mass.] : Center for International Affairs, Harvard University ; Lanham, MD : Madison Books, 1988, c1985. p. cm. Reprint. Originally published: Lanham, MD : Center for International Affairs, Harvard University and University Press of America, c1985. Bibliography: p. Includes index. ISBN 0-8191-6490-9 (pbk. : alk. paper) : LC Card 87-24678 DDC 330.98/0038 19
1. Latin America - Economic conditions - 1945-. 2. Economic development - Social aspects. 3. Culture. 4. Economic development - Psychological aspects. I. Harvard University. Center for International Affairs. II. Title.
HC125 .H384 1988

Harrison, M. L. (Malcolm L.) Planning control . London , Wolfeboro, N.H. , c1987. 234 p. ; ISBN 0-7099-3790-3 : LC Card 86-24079 DDC 333.73/17/0941 19
HD596 .P53 1987 ***NYPL [JLD 87-803]***

Harrison, Paul. The greening of Africa : breaking through in the battle for land and food / Paul Harrison. New York, N.Y., U. S.A. : Penguin, 1987. 380 p. : ill. ; 20 cm. "International Institute for Environment and Development, Earthscan." Bibliography: p. [359]-371. Includes index. ISBN 0-14-010192-6 (pbk.) : LC Card 87-404277 DDC 338.1/9/6 19
1. Agriculture - Economic aspects - Africa. 2. Agriculture - Environmental aspects - Africa. 3. Agriculture - Africa. 4. Agriculture and state - Africa. 5. Africa - Rural conditions. 6. Food supply - Africa. I. Earthscan. II. Title.
HD2117 .H37 1987

Harrison, Royden. Divisions of labour . Sussex [Eng.] , Urbana , 1985. ix, 254 p. ; ISBN 0-252-01189-9 LC Card 84-23988 DDC 331.7/94 19
HD8390 .D58 1985 ***NYPL [JLD 87-93]***

Harrod, Jeffrey. Power, production, and the unprotected worker / Jeffrey Harrod. New York : Columbia University Press, 1987. xviii, 347 p. ; 24 cm. (Power and production . v. 2) The Political economy of international change Includes bibliographies and indexes. ISBN 0-231-05844-6 (alk. paper) LC Card 86-26374 DDC 306/.36 19
1. Industrial relations. 2. Power (Social sciences). 3. Labor and laboring classes. 4. Peasantry. 5. Home labor. 6. Self-employed. I. Series: Cox, Robert W., 1926- Power and production , v. 2. II. Title.
HD6971 .H287 1987

Harry Gunnison Brown, economist /. Ryan, Christopher K. (Christopher Keith) Boulder , 1987. xv, 179 p. ; ISBN 0-8133-7355-7 (pbk. : alk. paper) : LC Card 86-28994 DDC 330/.092/4 B 19
HB119.B65 R93 1987

Hart, Emma. Lucas, Martin. How to survive the 9 to 5 /. London , 1986. 175 p. ; ISBN 0-423-01930-9 (pbk.) : LC Card 86-188564 DDC 158.7 19
HF5548.85 .L825 1986

Hart, Gillian Patricia. Power, labor, and livelihood : processes of change in rural Java / Gillian Hart. Berkeley : University of California Press, c1986. xvi, 228 p. : ill. ; 25 cm. Includes index. Bibliography: p. 213-222. ISBN 0-520-05499-7 (alk. paper) LC Card 85-8435 DDC 330.9598/2 19
1. Agricultural laborers - Indonesia - Jawa Tengah. 2. Income distribution - Indonesia - Jawa Tengah. 3. Jawa Tengah, Indonesia - Rural conditions. I. Title.
HD1537.I56 H37 1986
NYPL [JLE 86-3039]

Hart, Norman A.
Case studies in international marketing /. London , 1982. vii, 391 p. : ISBN 0-434-90370-1 : LC Card 82-241323 DDC 658.8/48 19
HF1009.5 .C34 1982 ***NYPL [JLE 87-1196]***

Effective corporate relations . London , New York , c1987. xii, 207 p. : ISBN 0-07-084940-4 (pbk.) : LC Card 87-21520 DDC 659.2/85 19
HD59 .E33 1987

Hart, P. E. (Peter Edward) Youth unemployment in Great Britain / P.E. Hart. Cambridge [Cambridgeshire] ; New York, NY, USA : Cambridge University Press, 1988. p. cm. (The National Institute of Economic and Social Research occasional papers . 43) ISBN 0-521-35348-3 LC Card 87-25597 DDC 331.3/4137941 19
1. Youth - Employment - Great Britain. 2. Unemployment - Great Britain. I. Series: Occasional papers (National Institute of Economic and Social Research) , 43. II. Title.
HD6276.G72 H37 1988

Hart, Robert A. Working time and employment / Robert A. Hart. Boston : Allen & Unwin, 1987. xx, 293 p. : ill. ; 23 cm. Bibliography: p. 277-286. Includes index. ISBN 0-04-331109-1 (alk. paper) LC Card 86-28815 DDC 331.25/72 19
1. Hours of labor. 2. Labor supply. I. Title.
HD5106 .H298 1987

Härtel, Hans-Hagen.
Neue Industriepolitik oder Stärkung der Marktkräfte? . Hamburg , 1986. xiii, 221 p. ; ISBN 3-87895-315-1 LC Card 87-408234 DDC 338.9 19
HD3616.G4 N48 1986

Wechselwirkungen von Geldpolitik, Inflation und Strukturwandel . Hamburg , 1984. 179 p. : ISBN 3-87895-243-0 LC Card 84-221405
HB235.G3 W42 1984

Hartgraves, Al L. Morse, Wayne J. Management accounting /. Reading, Mass. , c1988. xxiii, 840 p. : ISBN 0-201-15760-8 : LC Card 87-11570 DDC 658.1/511 19
HF5635 .M864 1988

Hartig, Hans-Jürgen. Uhlig, Karl-Heinz. Internationales Konzernmarketing /. Berlin , c1986. 143 p. : ISBN 3-349-00001-0 LC Card 87-118692 DDC 658.8/48 19
HF1009.5 .U36 1986

Hartkopf, Günter. Umweltschutz und Verwaltung . Bonn , c1986. 171 p. ; ISBN 3-87999-040-9 LC Card 87-136048 DDC 363.7/056/0943 19
HC290.5.E5 U645 1986

Hartley, Elda.
What makes Japan work [motion picture] . Cos Cob, CT , 1983. 1 film reel (11 min.) : LC Card 83-700702 DDC 181 11
HD8726.5

What makes Japan work [videorecording] . Cos Cob, CT , 1983. 1 videocassette (11 min.) : LC Card 87-705342 DDC 181 11
HD8726.5

Hartley Film Foundation.
What makes Japan work [motion picture] . Cos Cob, CT , 1983. 1 film reel (11 min.) : LC Card 83-700702 DDC 181 11
HD8726.5

What makes Japan work [videorecording] . Cos Cob, CT , 1983. 1 videocassette (11 min.) : LC Card 87-705342 DDC 181 11
HD8726.5

Hartley, Jean, 1953- Australian industrial relations . London [1986] 24 p. ; ISBN 0-902499-56-4 (pbk.) : LC Card 86-233230 DDC 331/.0994 19
HD8846.5 .A96 1986

Hartley, Jill. New electronic information services : an overview of the UK database industry in an international context / Jill Hartley, Amanda Noonan, Stan Metcalfe. Aldershot, Hants, England ; Brookfield, Vt., USA : Gower, c1987. 147 p. : ill. ; 30 cm. Bibliography: p. 140-147. ISBN 0-566-05489-2 (pbk.) : LC Card 87-23600 DDC 338.4/700574/0941 19
1. Data base industry - Great Britain. 2. Data base industry. I. Noonan, Amanda. II. Metcalfe, Stan. III. Title.
HD9696.D364 G74 1987

Hartley, Robert F. Bullseyes and blunders : stories of business success & failure / Robert F. Hartley. New York : Wiley, c1987. vii, 253 p. : ill. ; 24 cm. Includes bibliographies. ISBN 0-471-84904-9 LC Card 86-23350 DDC 658 19
1. Industrial management - Case studies. 2. Marketing management - Case studies. 3. Success in business - Case studies. 4. Business failures - Case studies. I. Title.
HD38 .H3487 1987 ***NYPL [JLE 87-1047]***

Hartley, W. C. F. An introduction to business accounting for managers / by W.C.F. Hartley. 4th ed. Oxford [Oxfordshire] ; New York : Pergamon Press, 1987. xvi, 221 p. : ill. ; 22 cm.

Includes index. ISBN 0-08-034789-4 : LC Card 87-6921 DDC 657/.024658 19
1. Accounting. 2. Managerial accounting. I. Title.
HF5635 .H335 1987

Hartman, Chester W. Critical perspectives on housing /. Philadelphia , 1986. xxi, 686 p. : ISBN 0-87722-395-5 LC Card 85-17274 DDC 363.5/0973 19
HD7293 .C738 1986 ***NYPL [JLE 86-3639]***

Hartman, Tori. Specialty modeling / Tori Hartman & Carolyn Strauss. 1st ed. New York : Dutton, c1988. x, 128 p. ; 21 cm. Bibliography: p. 127-128. ISBN 0-525-48356-X LC Card 87-22470 DDC 659.1/52 19
1. Models, Fashion - United States. I. Strauss, Carolyn. II. Title.
HD6073.M772 U55 1988

Hartmann, Heidi I.
National Research Council (U. S.). Committee on Women's Employment and Related Social Issues. Panel on Technology and Women's Employment. Computer chips and paper clips . Washington, D.C. , 1986. v. : ISBN 0-309-03688-7 (v. 1) LC Card 86-18113 DDC 331.4/8165137/0973 19
HD6331.18.M39 N38 1986
NYPL [JLL 87-129]

Women's work, men's work . Washington, D.C. , 1986. xii, 173 p. : ISBN 0-309-03429-9 (pbk.) LC Card 85-11541 DDC 331.1/33/0973 19
HD6060.5.U5 W66 1986
NYPL [JLF 86-1430]

Hartmann-Wendels, Thomas. Dividendenpolitik bei asymmetrischer Informationsverteilung / Thomas Hartmann-Wendels. Wiesbaden : Gabler, c1986. 299 p. : ill. ; 25 cm. (Beiträge zur betriebswirtschaftlichen Forschung. Bd. 59) Bibliography: p. [277]-299. ISBN 3-409-13706-8 LC Card 86-165737
1. Dividends - Mathematical models. I. Title. II. Series.
HG4028.D5 H33 1986

Hartmann, Wolf-Dietrich, 1946-
Internationaler Technologieaustausch--Kooperation oder Konfrontation? : Mythos und Realität US-amerikanischer Konzeptionen des Technologietransfers in den Ost-West-Wirtschaftsbeziehungen / Wolf-D. Hartmann, Walter Stock. Frankfurt/Main : Verlag Marxistische Blätter, 1984. 153 p. ; 20 cm. (Zur Kritik der bürgerlichen Ideologie. 104) Includes bibliographical references and index. ISBN 3-88012-633-X LC Card 85-155132 DDC 338.9/26 19
1. Technology transfer - Economic aspects. 2. Technology transfer - Economic aspects - United States. 3. East-West trade (1945-). I. Title.
HC79.T4 H36 1984

Kapitale Karrieren : Mythos und Realität profitabler Geschäfte / Wolf D. Hartmann. Berlin : Verlag Neues Leben, c1986. 154 p. : ill. ; 21 cm. (NL konkret. 70) Includes bibliographies. LC Card 86-214325
1. Capitalists and financiers - History - 20th century. 2. Capitalism - History - 20th century. I. Title.
HG172.A2 H37 1986

Hartog, H. den. Investeren in Nederland /. 's-Gravenhage [1986] 122 p. : LC Card 86-231212
HG5562 .I58 1986

Hartshorn, Gary S.
Belize . Belize City, Belize , 1984. xvi, 151 p. : LC Card 86-136310 DDC 333.7/097282 19
HC142 .B447 1984 ***NYPL [JLF 87-170]***

La República Dominicana . McLean, Va. , 1981. xii, 134 p. : LC Card 86-218146
HC153.5 .R45 1981

Hartshorn, Truman A. Economic geography / Truman A. Hartshorn, John W. Alexander. 3rd ed. Englewood Cliffs, N.J. : Prentice Hall, 1988. xiii, 385 p. : ill. ; 29 cm. Rev. ed. of: Economic geography / John W. Alexander, Lay James Gibson. 2nd ed. 1979. Includes bibliographies and index. ISBN 0-13-225160-4 LC Card 87-17407 DDC 330.9 19
1. Geography, Economic. I. Alexander, John W. (John Wesley), 1918-. II. Alexander, John W. (John Wesley), 1918- Economic geography. III. Title.
HF1025 .H296 1988

Hartung, Hans. Verfahren zur Nutzung erschöpfbarer Ressourcen : das Beispiel der Versteigerung von Offshore-Förderrechten in den USA / Hans Hartung. Tübingen : J.C.B. Mohr, 1986. ix, 172 p. : ill. ; 24 cm. (Kieler Studien, 0340-6989 . 201) Bibliography: p. 162-172. ISBN 3-16-345126-8 (Deut. Bibl. : pbk.) LC Card 86-233079
1. Offshore oil industry - United States. 2. Oil and gas leases - United States. 3. Auctions - United States. I. Title. II. Series.
HD9565 .H36 1986

Hartwich, Hans Hermann. Vollzug und Wirkungen regionaler Umweltpolitik . Opladen , 1984. 199 p. ; ISBN 3-8100-0392-1 LC Card 84-228636
HC290.5.E5 V65 1984

Hartwig, Karl-Hans. Monetäre Steuerungsprobleme in sozialistischen Planwirtschaften / von Karl-Hans Hartwig. Stuttgart ; New York ; G. Fischer, 1987. vi, 146 p. ; 23 cm. (Schriften zum Vergleich von Wirtschaftsordnungen, 0582-0243 . Heft 39) Bibliography: p. 131-140. ISBN 3-437-50295-6 LC Card 87-136038 DDC 339.5/3/0947 19
1. Monetary policy - Europe, Eastern. 2. Central planning. I. Title. II. Series.
HG925 .H37 1987

Hartzell, Hal, 1946- Birth of a cooperative : Hoedads, Inc., a worker owned forest labor co-op / Hal Hartzell, Jr.1st ed. Eugene, Or. : Hulogos'i, 1987. 351 p. : ill. ; 22 cm. "A Yew book." Includes index. ISBN 0-938493-09-4 (pbk.) : LC Card 87-2656 DDC 334/.6834956/09795 19
1. Hoedads, Inc. - History. 2. Forests and forestry, Cooperative - United States - History. I. Title.
HD9759.H64 H37 1987

Harvard Business School Project on the Auto Industry and the American Economy. Dyer, Davis. Changing alliances /. Boston, Mass. , c1987. xvi, 333 p. ; ISBN 0-87584-175-9 LC Card 86-33619 DDC 338.4/76292/0973 19
HD9710.U52 D94 1987

Harvard East Asian monographs. For earlier vols. see entry in Old Catalog.
(117) Gordon, Andrew, 1952- The evolution of labor relations in Japan . Cambridge, Mass. , 1985. xvi, 524 p. : ISBN 0-674-27130-0 (Harvard Univ. Pr.) LC Card 85-3747 DDC 331/.0952 19
HD8726 .G67 1985 ***NYPL [M-11 435 v.117]***

(117) Gordon, Andrew, 1952- The evolution of labor relations in Japan . Cambridge, Mass. , 1985. xvi, 524 p. : ISBN 0-674-27130-0 (Harvard Univ. Pr.) LC Card 85-3747 DDC 331/.0952 19
HD8726 .G67 1985 ***NYPL [M-11 435 v.117]***

(130) Perdue, Peter C., 1949- Exhausting the earth . Cambridge, Mass. , 1987. xvii, 331 p. : ISBN 0-674-27504-7 LC Card 87-5067 DDC 338.1/0951/215 19
HD2100.H86 P47 1987

Harvard economic studies. For other vols. in this series, see Old Catalog.
(v. 158) Mariger, Randall P., 1954- Consumption behavior and the effects of government fiscal policies /. Cambridge, Mass. , 1986. xi, 265 p. ; ISBN 0-674-16635-3 (alk. paper) LC Card 85-17550 DDC 339.4/7/0973 19
HC110.C6 M287 1986 ***NYPL [JLE 86-3315]***

(v. 159) Jorgenson, Dale Weldeau, 1933- Productivity and U. S. economic growth /. Cambridge, Mass. , 1987. 567 p. : ISBN 0-674-71175-0 (alk. paper) LC Card 87-12098 DDC 338/.06/0973 19
HC110.I52 J67 1987

The Harvard guide to careers /. Leape, Martha P. Cambridge, Mass. , 1987. ix, 181 p. ; ISBN 0-674-37564-5 (pbk.) LC Card 87-8409 DDC 331.7/02 19
HF5382.5.U5 L36 1987

Harvard international energy studies .
(no. 1) Natural gas trade in transition /. Cambridge, MA , c1987. 91 p. ; ISBN 0-942781-00-7 (pbk.) LC Card 87-81051 DDC 338.2/7285 19
HD9581.A2 N38 1987

Harvard studies in business history. For additional listing of contents, see Old Catalog.
(39) Tolliday, Steven. Business, banking, and politics . Cambridge, Mass. , 1987. vi, 433 p. : ISBN 0-674-08725-9 (alk. paper) LC Card 86-31944 DDC 338.4/7669142/0941 19
HD9521.5 .T64 1987

(40) Dalzell, Robert F. Enterprising elite . Cambridge, Mass. , 1987. xviii, 298 p., [11] p. of plates : ISBN 0-674-25765-0 (alk. paper) LC Card 86-33649 DDC 338.4/7677/0097444 19
HD9858.L9 D35 1987

Harvard University. Business Administration, Graduate School of. see Harvard University. Graduate School of Business Administration.

Harvard University. Center for International Affairs.
Harrison, Lawrence E. Underdevelopment is a state of mind . [Cambridge, Mass.] , Lanham, MD , 1988, c1985. p. cm. ISBN 0-8191-6490-9 (pbk. : alk. paper) : LC Card 87-24678 DDC 330.98/0038 19
HC125 .H384 1988

Land rites and wrongs . Boston , 1988. p. cm. ISBN 0-89946-222-7 LC Card 87-12186 DDC 333.73/13/0971 19
HD171.A15 L28 1988

Harvard University. Graduate School of Business Administration. Division of Research.
Goodpaster, Kenneth E., 1944- Ethics in management /. Boston , c1984. 154 p. : ISBN 0-87584-165-1 (course module : pbk.) LC Card 84-12847 DDC 174/.4 19
HF5387 .G66 1984

Harvard University. International Affairs, Center for. see Harvard University. Center for International Affairs.

Harvard University. Office of Career Services.
Leape, Martha P. The Harvard guide to careers /. Cambridge, Mass. , 1987. ix, 181 p. ; ISBN 0-674-37564-5 (pbk.) LC Card 87-8409 DDC 331.7/02 19
HF5382.5.U5 L36 1987

Harvey and Jessie . O'Connor, Jessie Lloyd, 1904- Philadelphia , 1988. p. cm. ISBN 0-87722-519-2 (alk. paper) LC Card 87-21737 DDC 322/.2/0922 B 19
HD8073.A1 O25 1988

Harvey, Charles E. The Rio Tinto Company : an economic history of a leading international mining concern, 1873-1954 / by Charles E. Harvey. Penzance, Cornwall : A. Hodge, 1981. xiv, 390 p. : ill., maps ; 22 cm. Includes index. Bibliography: p. [373]-381. ISBN 0-906720-03-6 : LC Card 82-127720 DDC 338.8/87 19
1. Rio Tinto Company - History. 2. Mineral industries - History. 3. International business enterprises - History. I. Title.
HD9506.G74 R564 1981
NYPL [JLD 86-2605]

Harvey, Charles, M.A. World prices and development /. Aldershot, Hants, England , Brookfield, Vt., U. S.A. , c1985. xi, 377 p. : ISBN 0-566-00890-4 LC Card 86-134604 DDC 338.5/2/0971724 19
HC59.7 .W684 1985 ***NYPL [JLD 86-4068]***

Harvey, David. The electronic office in the smaller business / David Harvey. Aldershot, Hants, England ; Brookfield, Vt., U. S.A. : Gower, with Philips Business Systems, c1986. vii, 214 p. : ill. ; 23 cm. Bibliography: p. 189-192. Includes index. ISBN 0-566-02578-7 LC Card 86-225568 DDC 651.8/416 19
1. Office practice - Automation. 2. Small business - Data processing. 3. Microcomputers. I. Title.
HF5547.5 .H365 1986

Harvey, Donald F. An experiential approach to organization development / Donald F. Harvey, Donald R. Brown. 3rd ed. Englewood Cliffs, N.J. : Prentice Hall, c1988. p. cm. Includes index. ISBN 0-13-295122-3 LC Card 87-26207 DDC 658.4/063 19
1. Organizational change. I. Brown, Donald R., 1945-. II. Title.
HD58.8 .H37 1988

Harvey, Greg.
Lotus 1-2-3 desktop companion / Greg Harvey. San Francisco : Sybex, c1987. ix, 976 p. : ill. ; 24 cm. (Sybex ready reference series) Includes indexes. ISBN 0-89588-385-6 : LC Card 86-63454 DDC 005.36/9 19
1. Lotus 1-2-3 (Computer program). 2. Business - Data

processing. I. Title. II. Series.
HF5548.4.L67 H38 1987

Mastering SuperCalc3 / Greg Harvey. Berkeley, CA : Sybex, c1986. xvi, 276 p. : ill. ; 23 cm. Includes index. ISBN 0-89588-312-0 (pbk.) : LC Card 87-119243 DDC 005.36/9 19
1. SuperCalc 3 (Computer program). 2. Business - Data processing. I. Title. II. Title: Mastering SuperCalc 3. III. Title: Mastering SuperCalc Three.
HF5548.4.S86 H37 1986

Mastering SuperCalc4 / Greg Harvey. San Francisco : Sybex, c1987. xix, 311 p. : ill. ; 23 cm. Includes index. ISBN 0-89588-419-4 (pbk.) : LC Card 87-60636 DDC 005.36/9 19
1. SuperCalc 4. 2. Business - Data processing. I. Title. II. Title: Mastering SuperCalc 4. III. Title: Mastering SuperCalc four.
HF5548.4.S87 H37 1987

HARYANA (INDIA) - CENSUS, 1981. Census of India, 1981. Delhi , <1981-1983. v. in : LC Card 87-915014
HA4587.H37 C46 1981

Haryana State Electricity Board. HSEB statistics, 1983-84. [Chandigarh] [1984] iii, 105 p., [7] p. of plates : LC Card 87-901651 DDC 363.6/2/0954558021 19
HD9696.A3 I5535 1984

Harza, Lajos. Az EGK szőlő- és borgazdaságának szabályozórendszere / Harza Lajos, Papp Zsolt. Budapest : Agrárgazdasági Kutató Intézet, 1985. 70 p. : ill. ; 28 cm. (Agrárgazdasági Kutató Intézet, 0209-5696 . 1985/10) Bibliography: p. 69-70. ISBN 963-491-210-9 LC Card 86-196818
1. Grape industry - European Economic Community countries. 2. Wine industry - European Economic Community countries. I. Papp, Zsolt, Dr. II. Series: Agrárgazdasági Kutató Intézet (Series) , 1985/10. III. Title.
HD9259.G7 E864 1985

Has trade protection revitalized domestic industries? Kaplan, Daniel P. Washington, D.C. [1986] xvi, 111 p. : LC Card 86-603423 DDC 382.7/3/0973 19
HF1421 .K36 1986

Hasan Ersel. see **Ersel, Hasan.**

Haschek, Helmut. Wagner, Adolph, 1835-1917. Die Ordnung des österreichischen Staatshaushaltes--1863 /. Wien , c1984. 308 p. ; ISBN 3-85447-086-X LC Card 85-223615
HJ1065 .W34 1984

Hasenfratz, Eberhard. Gemeindetypen der Pfalz : empirischer Versuch auf bevölkerungs- und sozialgeographischer Basis / von Eberhard Hasenfratz. Mannheim : Im Selbstverlag des Geographischen Instituts der Universität, 1986. 197 p. : ill., maps ; 21 cm. (Mannheimer geographische Arbeiten. Heft 20) One folded map laid in. Originally presented as the author's thesis (doctoral)--Universität Mannheim, 1985. Summary in English. Bibliography: p. 162-182. ISBN 3-923750-19-6 LC Card 86-185643
1. Rhineland-Palatinate (Germany) - Population. 2. Rhineland-Palatinate (Germany) - Social conditions. 3. Rhineland-Palatinate (Germany) - Economic conditions. I. Title. II. Series.
HB3596.R46 H37 1986

Haskamp, Clemens Heinrich, 1955- Aktienkursprognose auf Grundlage der Identifikation von Trend- und Saisonkomponente : eine empirische Untersuchung / Clemens Heinrich Haskamp. Krefeld : Marchal und Matzenbacher, 1985. 204 p. : ill. ; 21 cm. Bibliography: p. 200-204. ISBN 3-88358-052-1 LC Card 86-121480
1. Stock price forecasting. 2. Stocks - Prices - Germany, West. I. Title.
HG4637 .H38 1985

HASKINS, CHARLES WALDO, 1852-1903. Selected papers from the Charles Waldo Haskins accounting history seminars /. [University, Ala.] , 1983. iv, 172 p. ; LC Card 86-224698 DDC 657/.09 19
HF5611 .S45 1983

Haskins, Gay. A Guide to small firms assistance in Europe /. Aldershot, Hants, England , Brookfield, Vt., U. S.A. , c1986. vii, 263 p. ; ISBN 0-566-05082-X : LC Card 85-27307 DDC 338.6/42/094 19
HD2346.E9 G85 1986 ***NYPL [JLG 86-205]***

Haslam, Colin. Williams, Karel. The breakdown of Austin Rover . Leamington Spa, UK ; New York : v, 150 p. : ISBN 0-85496-515-7 : LC Card 86-24449 DDC 338.7/6292222 19
HD9710.G74 A868 1987

Hasquin, Hervé, 1942- Les Réflexions sur l'état présent du commerce, fabriques et manufactures des Païs-Bas autrichiens (1765) du négociant bruxellois, Nicolas Bacon (1710-1779), conseiller députe aux affaires du commerce / par Hervé Hasquin. Bruxelles : Académie royale de Belgique, Commission royale d'histoire, 1978. vi, 190 p. ; 22 cm. "Réflexions sur l'état présent du commerce, fabriques et manufactures des Païs-Bas autrichiens": p. [57]-157. LC Card 87-672234
1. Benelux countries - Commerce - History - 18th century. 2. Bacon, Nicolas, 1710-1779. I. Bacon, Nicolas, 1710-1779. Réflexions sur l'état présent du commerce, fabriques et manufactures des Païs-Bas autrichiens. 1978. II. Title.
HF3595 .H37x 1978

Hass-Klau, Carmen. Hall, Peter, 1931- Can rail save the city? . Aldershot, Hants , Brookfield, Vt., U. S.A. , c1985. xii, 241 p. : ISBN 0-566-00947-1 : LC Card 85-17659 DDC 388.4/2/0943 19
HE4774 .H35 1985 ***NYPL [JLD 86-2622]***

Hassan, Shabir. Public enterprises in economic development : a case study of J&K Industries Ltd. / by Shabir Hassan.1st ed. Delhi : Anmol Publications : Distributed by Anupama Publishers Distributors, 1987. xiii, 230 p. ; 23 cm. Bibliography: p. [216]-226. Includes index. LC Card 86-903835
1. Jammu & Kashmir Industries Limited - Case studies. 2. Government business enterprises - India - Jammu and Kashmir - Case studies. 3. Government business enterprises - India - Case studies. I. Title.
HD2900.12.J35 H37 1987

Hassan, Zuhair A. Handbook of food expenditures, prices, and consumption / Zuhair A. Hassan, Linda G. Robbins ; edited by Communications Branch, Agriculture Canada = Guide de la consommation, des dépenses et des prix alimentaires / Zuhair A. Hassan, Linda G. Robbins ; édition revue et corrigée par la Direction générale des communications, Agriculture Canada. Ottawa : Marketing and Economics Branch, Agriculture Canada, c1983. 270 p., [2] p. of plates : ill. ; 28 cm. (Publication . no. 83/3) English and French. Includes bibliographical references. LC Card 86-228246 DDC 339.4/8664/00971 19
1. Food consumption - Canada - Statistics. 2. Food prices - Canada - Statistics. 3. Food supply - Canada - Statistics. I. Robbins, Linda. II. Title. III. Title: Guide de la consommation, des dépenses et des prix alimentaires. IV. Series: Publication (Canada. Agriculture Canada. Marketing and Economics Branch) , no. 83/3.
HD9014.C3 H29 1983

Hasse, Rolf. Ökonometrie als Instrument der Interessenpolitik : zum Aussagewert der UNCTAD-Berechnungen über die Handelswirkungen der Tokio-Runde für die Entwicklungsländer / Rolf Hasse. Köln : Institut für Wirtschaftspolitik an der Universität zu Köln, 1985. ii, 109 p. : ill. ; 24 cm. (Untersuchungen zur Wirtschaftspolitik, 0175-7458 . 64) Includes bibliographical references and index. ISBN 3-921471-52-4 : LC Card 85-216061
1. Tariff preferences - Developing countries. 2. Tokyo Round (1973-1979). 3. Developing countries - Commerce - Econometric models. I. Title. II. Series.
HF1733.D44 H37 1985

Hassler, Hermann. Die Briefmarkenausgabe vom 12. März 1984 =. Vaduz [1984?] 41 p. : LC Card 84-248309
HE6184.F57 B75 1984

Hastings, Colin. The superteam solution : successful teamworking in organisations / Colin Hastings, Peter Bixby, and Rani Chaudhry-Lawton. San Diego, Calif. : University Associates, Inc., c1987. x, 182 p. : ill. ; 23 cm. Includes index. ISBN 0-88390-206-0 (pbk.) : LC Card 87-19185 DDC 658.4/036 19
1. Work groups. 2. Industrial management. 3. Management. I. Bixby, Peter. II. Chaudhry-Lawton, Rani. III. Title.
HD66 .H38 1987

HAT TRADE - PORTUGAL - HISTORY. Mónica, Maria Filomena, 1943- Artesãos e operários . Lisboa [1986] 228 p., [24] p. of plates : LC Card 86-229921
HD8596 .M65 1986

Hatalom, technika, világgazdaság /. Simai, Mihály. Budapest , 1985. 436 p. ; ISBN 963-221-548-6 : LC Card 86-187337
HC59 .S529 1985

Hatch, James E. Canadian commercial lending : a guide to credit decision making / James E. Hatch, Larry Wynant. Toronto ; New York : Methuen, c1986. ix, 262 p. : ill. ; 24 cm. Includes bibliographies and index. ISBN 0-458-80270-0 : LC Card 87-130576 DDC 332.1/753/0685 19
1. Credit - Canada - Management. I. Wynant, Larry, 1946-. II. Title.
HG3754.5.C2 H38 1986

Hatch, Michael T., 1945- Politics and nuclear power : energy policy in Western Europe / Michael T. Hatch. Lexington, KY : University Press of Kentucky, 1986. xi, 219 p. ; 23 cm. Includes index. Bibliography: p. [203]-214. ISBN 0-8131-1583-3 : LC Card 85-29545 DDC 333.79/24/094 19
1. Nuclear industry - Government policy - Europe. 2. Nuclear power plants - Government policy - Europe. 3. Energy policy - Europe. I. Title.
HD9698.E82 H38 1986 ***NYPL [JLD 86-2137]***

Hatékony vezetői időgazdálkodás : szakirodalmi szemle / [szerkesztette, Kozma László, Radó Lszlóné]. Budapest : Országos Vezetőképző Központ, Tudományos Tájékoztató Szolgálat, 1984. 62 p. ; 29 cm. (Szakirodalmi szemle, 0236-9885) Bibliography: p. 41-59. ISBN 963-7902-09-0 (Magy. nemz. bibl.) LC Card 85-177403
1. Executies - Time management. I. Kozma, László. II. Radó, Lászlóné. III. Series: Szakirodalmi Szemle (Országos Vezetőképző Központ (Hungary). Tudományos Tájékoztató Szolgálat).
HD69.T54 H38 1984

Hatékonyság és fejlesztési lehetőségek a mai magyar mezőgazdaságban /. Németi, László. Budapest , 1986. 189 p. : ISBN 963-232-238-X : LC Card 87-407758
HD1940.5 .N46 1986

Hathaway, Dale E. Agriculture and the GATT : rewriting the rules / Dale E. Hathaway. Washington, DC : Institute for International Economics, c1987. xii, 157 p. : ill. ; 23 cm. (Policy analyses in international economics . 20) "September 1987." Bibliography: p. 156-157. ISBN 0-88132-052-8 LC Card 87-21430 DDC 382/.41/0973 19
1. Produce trade - Government policy - United States. 2. United States - Foreign economic relations. 3. Produce trade - Government policy. 4. Tariff on farm produce. 5. General Agreement on Tariffs and Trade (Organization). 6. Agriculture and state - United States. I. Title. II. Series.
HD9006 .H28 1987

Hatmadji, Sri Harijati. Ananta, Aris. Perilaku fertilitas di beberapa daerah di Jawa /. Jakarta , 1986. vi, 56, 26 p. ; LC Card 86-946460
HB1058.J38 A52 1986

Hatten, Kenneth J.

Effective strategic management : analysis and action / Kenneth J. Hatten, Mary Louise Hatten. Englewood Cliffs, N.J. : Prentice Hall, c1988. xiv, 338 p. : ill. ; 24 cm. Bibliography: p. 315-331. Includes index. ISBN 0-13-245200-6 (pbk.) LC Card 87-20589 DDC 658.4/012 19
1. Strategic planning. I. Hatten, Mary Louise. II. Title.
HD30.28 .H383 1988

Strategic management : analysis and action / Kenneth J. Hatten, Mary Louise Hatten. Englewood Cliffs, N.J. : Prentice-Hall, c1987. xiv, 1041 p. : ill. ; 25 cm. Bibliography: p. 315-331. Includes index. ISBN 0-13-850694-9 LC Card 86-30453 DDC 658.4/012 19
1. Strategic planning. 2. Strategic planning - Case studies. I. Hatten, Mary Louise. II. Title.
HD30.28 .H384 1987

Hatten, Mary Louise.

Hatten, Kenneth J. Effective strategic management . Englewood Cliffs, N.J. , c1988. xiv, 338 p. : ISBN 0-13-245200-6 (pbk.) LC Card 87-20589 DDC 658.4/012 19
HD30.28 .H383 1988

Hatten, Kenneth J. Strategic management . Englewood Cliffs, N.J. , c1987. xiv, 1041 p. :

ISBN 0-13-850694-9 LC Card 86-30453 DDC 658.4/012 19
HD30.28 .H384 1987

Hattersley, Roy. Economic priorities for a labour government / Roy Hattersley ; edited and introduced by Doug Jones. New York : St. Martin's Press, 1987. ix, 198 p. ; 23 cm. ISBN 0-312-00987-9 : LC Card 87-9576 DDC 338.941 19
1. Great Britain - Economic policy - 1945-. 2. Fiscal policy - Great Britain. 3. Industry and state - Great Britain. 4. Labour Party (Great Britain). I. Jones, Doug, 1958-. II. Title.
HC256.6 .H385 1987

Haubrich, Kathy. (ill) Brandt, Betty. Special delivery /. Minneapolis, Minn. , c1988. 40 p. : ISBN 0-87614-312-5 (lib. bdg.) LC Card 87-15647 DDC 383/.4973 19
HE6371 .B77 1988

Hauck, David.
U. S. corporate withdrawal from South Africa : the likely impact on political change / by David Hauck. Washington, D.C. (Suite 600, 1755 Massachusetts Ave., N.W., Washington 20036) : South Africa Review Service, Investor Responsibility Research Center, [1986] 22 p. ; 28 cm. Cover title. "August 1986." LC Card 86-209299 DDC 332.6/7373/068 19
1. Investments, American - South Africa. 2. Corporations, American - South Africa. 3. Political parties - South Africa. 4. Corporate divestiture - United States. I. Investor Responsibility Research Center. South Africa Review Service. II. Title. III. Title: US corporate withdrawal from South Africa.
HG5851.A3 H39 1986

What happens when U. S. companies sell their South African operations? / by David Hauck. Washington, D.C. (Suite 600, 1755 Massachusetts Ave., N.W., Washington 20036) : South Africa Review Service, c1987. 16 p. ; 29 cm. Cover title. "May 1987." LC Card 87-163729 DDC 338.8/8973/068 19
1. Investments, American - South Africa. 2. Corporations, American - South Africa. 3. Disinvestment - South Africa. I. Investor Responsibility Research Center. South Africa Review Service. II. Title.
HG5851.A3 H392 1987

Haueisen, Peter, 1955- Unmittelbare Versorgungszusage und Direktversicherung als Gestaltungsformen der betrieblichen Altersversorgung / Peter Haueisen. Frankfurt am Main ; New York : P. Lang, c1983. xx, 297 p. : ill. ; 21 cm. (Betriebswirtschaftliche Forschungsergebnisse, 0724-2549 . Bd. 2) Originally presented as the author's thesis (doctoral--Universität Bayreuth, 1982) Bibliography: p. 258-275. Includes index. ISBN 3-8204-7592-3 LC Card 86-107083 DDC 331.25/2/0943 19
1. Old age pensions - Germany, West. I. Series: Betriebswirtschaftliche Forschungsergebnisse (Frankfurt am Main, Germany) , Bd. 2. II. Title.
HD7105.35.G3 H38 1983

Hauff, Elaine M. Berdie, Douglas R. The Yellow Pages report . St. Paul, Minn. (905 Raymond Ave., St. Paul 55114) , c1986. 109 p. ; LC Card 86-209709 DDC 659.13/2 19
HF6146.T4 B45 1986

Hauff, Hanns Joachim Paul. Aufstieg zur Macht : zur Kader- und Personalpolitik im Leitungsbereich / Hanns Joachim Paul Hauff. München : Minerva Publikation, c1983. 85 p. : ill. ; 21 cm. (Minerva-Fachserie Wirtschafts- und Sozialwissenschaften) Bibliography: p. 81-83. Includes index. ISBN 3-597-10422-3 LC Card 83-136638
1. Executive ability. 2. Leadership. 3. Organization effectiveness. I. Title. II. Series.
HD38.2 .H38 1983

Haug, Wolf, 1953- Fokkink, Manfred, 1955- Denk ja nicht, Du bist selber schuld . Gelsenkirchen-Buer , 1980. 180 p. : LC Card 82-114713
HD6276.G4 F6 1980 ***NYPL [JLE 86-1457]***

Haug, Wolfgang Fritz.
Kritik der Warenästhetik / Wolfgang Fritz Haug. Mit einer Nachbemerkung zur 8. Aufl. Frankfurt am Main : Suhrkamp, [1983], c1971. 187 p. ; 18 cm. (Edition Suhrkamp. 513) Includes bibliographical references and index. ISBN 3-518-10513-2 (pbk.) LC Card 87-673362
1. Commercial products. 2. Aesthetics. 3. Fashion and art. 4. Sensuality. I. Title.
HF1041 .H33x 1983

Pluraler Marxismus : Beiträge zur politischen Kultur / Wolfgang Fritz Haug.1. Aufl. Berlin : Argument, 1985- v. ; 22 cm. Includes bibliographies and indexes. ISBN 3-88619-303-9 (Bd. 1) LC Card 86-119293 DDC 355.43/09/04 19
1. Philosophy, Marxist. 2. Marxian school of sociology. 3. Communism - History - 20th century. I. Title.
HX40 .H27 1985 ***NYPL [JLK 86-57]***

Haugen, Robert A. Introductory investment theory / Robert A. Haugen. Englewood Cliffs, N.J. : Prentice-Hall, c1987. xv, 524 p. : ill. (some col.) ; 25 cm. Includes bibliographies and index. ISBN 0-13-501933-8 LC Card 86-25373 DDC 332.6 19
1. Investment analysis. 2. Portfolio management. I. Title.
HG4529 .H378 1987

Haugstveit, Nils. The Nicaraguan development process, 1979-85 : conflicts and constraints / Nils Haugstveit. Oslo : International Peace Research Institute, [1987] 148 p. : ill. ; 30 cm. (PRIO report, 0333-483X . 2/87) Thesis--University of Oslo, 1987. Bibliography: p. 143-148. ISBN 82-7288-136-5 (pbk.) LC Card 87-164230 DDC 338.97285 19
1. Nicaragua - Economic policy. 2. Nicaragua - Economic conditions - 1979-. I. Series: PRIO report , 87/2. II. Title.
HC146 .H38 1987

Haugwitz, Karl, Graf. Prokopp, Ludwig Ferdinand. Europäische Commerzreisen um die Mitte des 18. Jahrhunderts /. Linz , c1982. xiii, 446 p., [1] folded leaf of plates : ISBN 3-85320-296-1 LC Card 83-150921
HF3548.C36 P76 1982

Haumer, Heinrich. Sequentielle stochastische Investitionsplanung / Heinrich Haumer. Wiesbaden : Gabler, c1983. 305 p. ; 24 cm. (Beiträge zur betriebswirtschaftlichen Forschung. Bd. 55) Bibliography: p. 293-304. ISBN 3-409-13420-4 LC Card 83-190299
1. Investments - Decision making - Statistical methods. 2. Stochastic programming. 3. Sequential analysis. I. Title. II. Series.
HG4515.2 .H38 1983

Haupt, Georges. Maitron, Jean. Dictionnaire biographique du mouvement ouvrier international. Paris, 1971-<c1985. <1-2, 5 > ISBN 2-7082-1955-3 (v. 2) LC Card 72-333529
HD4851 .M34

Haupt, Hans-Georg. Die Sozialistische Gemeinschaft . Berlin , 1985. 238 p. ; LC Card 86-120025 DDC 337.1/1717 19
HC243.5 .S685 1985

Haupt, Reinhard. Produktionstheorie und Ablaufmanagement : zeitvariable Faktoreinsätze und ablaufbezogene Dispositionen in Produktionstheorie- und -planungs-Modellen / Reinhard Haupt. Stuttgart : C.E. Poeschel, c1987. xiv, 217 p. : 20 ill. ; 24 cm. (Betriebswirtschaftliche Abhandlungen . n.F., Bd. 64) A revision of the author's Habilitationsschrift--Universität zu Köln, 1984, originally issued under the title: Produktionstheorie und Ablaufplanung. Bibliography: p. 201-215. Includes index. ISBN 3-7910-0398-4 LC Card 87-134161 DDC 338.6 19
1. Production (Economic theory). 2. Production planning - Mathematical models. I. Title. II. Series.
HB241 .H37 1987

Das Haus am Wall . Förster, Walter, 1914- Bremen , c1983. 159 p. : ISBN 3-920699-45-9 LC Card 84-155521
HG1010.B7 F67 1983

HAUSAS - ECONOMIC CONDITIONS.
Jackson, Cecile, 1953- The Kano River Irrigation Project /. West Hartford, Conn. , 1985. xviii, 66 p. ; ISBN 0-931816-19-X LC Card 85-5242 DDC 331.4/83/09669 19
HD6073.F32 N64 1985
NYPL [JLF 86-1634]

Hauschildt, Elke. Polnische Arbeitsmigranten in Wilhelmsburg bei Hamburg während des Kaiserreichs und der Weimarer Republik / Elke Hauschildt. Dortmund : Forschungsstelle Ostmitteleuropa, c1986. xv, 330 p. : ill. ; 21 cm. (Veröffentlichungen der Forschungsstelle Ostmitteleuropa; Reihe A. Nr. 47) Originally presented as the author's thesis (doctoral)--Universität Hamburg, 1985. Bibliography: p. 302-307. Includes index. ISBN 3-923293-17-8 LC Card 87-127027 DDC 331.6/2/438043515 19
1. Alien labor, Polish - Germany (West) - Wilhelmsburg (Hamburg) - History - 20th century. 2. Poles - Germany (West) - Wilhemsburg (Hamburg) - History - 20th century. 3. Poles - Germany (West) - Wilhelmsburg (Hamburg) - Social life and customs. 4. Wilhelmsburg (Hamburg, Germany) - Economic conditions. I. Title.
HD8458.P65 H38 1986

Hausen, Ivan Zanoni. Segurança empresarial : manual de ação e prevenção / Ivan Zanoni Hausen.1a. ed. Brasília, Distrito Federal : Horizonte Editora, 1979. 157 p. : ill. ; 21 cm. (Movimento cultural brasileiro) Includes legislation. Bibliography: p. 157. LC Card 82-100947
1. Industrial hygiene - Brazil. 2. Industrial safety - Brazil. 3. Industrial hygiene - Law and legislation - Brazil. 4. Industrial safety - Law and legislation - Brazil. I. Title.
HD7683 .H38 1979

Hauser, Heinz-Michael. Reform der Entwicklungsfinanzierung durch "Automatisierung"? : Begründung, Ausgestaltung und Umsetzung eines internationalen Reformkonzepts / Heinz-Michael Hauser.1. Aufl. Baden-Baden : Nomos, 1986. vi, 531 p. ; 23 cm. (Internationale Kooperation. Bd. 30) A revision of the author's thesis (doctoral)--Universität Tübingen, 1984. Summary in English. Bibliography: p. 505-531. ISBN 3-7890-1235-1 LC Card 87-407969 DDC 338.91/09172/4 19
1. Economic assistance - Developing countries. I. Series. II. Series: Internationale Kooperation, 30. III. Title.
HC60 .H329 1986

Hauser, Richard, 1936- Sozialpolitik in der Beschäftigungskrise /. Berlin , c1986. 2 v. : ISBN 3-428-05949-2 (Bd. I) : LC Card 87-119211 DDC 361.6/1 19
HD5710 .S67 1986

Die Haushalte der Flächenländer unter Konsolidierungszwang / [Bearbeiter, Werner Patzig, Manfred Schlick]. Bonn : Institut "Finanzen und Steuern", 1986. 159 p. ; 30 cm. (Brief / Institut "Finanzen und Steuern" . Nr. 262) Cover title. Includes bibliographical references. LC Card 87-409459 DDC 332 s 336.43 19
1. Finance, Public - Germany, West. I. Patzig, Werner. II. Schlick, Manfred. III. Series: Brief (Institut "Finanzen und Steuern" (Germany)) , Nr. 262.
HJ1120 .B65 Nr. 262

Haushalte mit ausgewählten staatlichen Transferzahlungen : Ergebnisse der Einkommens- und Verbrauchsstichprobe 1978, ergänzt durch Ergebnisse des Mikrozensus 1979 / Manfred Euler und Frank Klanberg (Herausgeber). Stuttgart : W. Kohlhammer, c1983. 352 p. : ill. ; 30 cm. (Schriften zum Bericht der Transfer-Enquête-Kommission "Das Transfersystem in der Bundesrepublik Deutschland" . Bd. 2, Teilbd. 2) "Erschienen Januar 1983." ISBN 3-17-007631-0 LC Card 83-117808
1. Transfer payments - Germany, West. 2. Income - Germany, West. I. Euler, Manfred. II. Klanberg, Frank. III. Transfer-Enquête-Kommission (Germany). IV. Series.
HC290.5.I5 H37 1983

Die Haushalte von Reich, Ländern und Gemeinden in Deutschland von 1925 bis 1933 . Heindl, Wolfgang, 1951- Frankfurt am Main , New York , c1984. 419 p. : ISBN 3-8204-5474-8 LC Card 85-198505
HJ1119 .H36 1984

Haushalts- und mehrjährige Finanzplanung im Planspiel . Engelhardt, Gunther. Baden-Baden , 1984. 331 p. : ISBN 3-7890-0975-X LC Card 85-140583
HJ2109 .E54 1984

Haushaltsfinanzierung durch Notendruck /. Runge, Harry. Berlin , c1986. 69 p. ; ISBN 3-428-05984-0 LC Card 86-165742
HG1004 .R75 1986

Haushaltsfinanzierung durch Notendruck /. Runge, Harry. Berlin , c1986. 69 p. ; ISBN 3-428-05984-0 ***NYPL [JLE 86-2839]***

Hausmann, Friedrich Bernhard. Landhandwerk und Landwirtschaft /. Göttingen , 1964. 104 p. : LC Card 87-409231 DDC 338.1/61/0943 19
HD1955 .L17 1964

HAUSSAS. see **HAUSAS.**

Häussler, Joachim. Berufs- und Weiterbildung 1984/85 . Bonn , 1985. 201 p. : LC Card 86-171726
HF5549.5.T7 B488 1985

Hauswirtschaft und Lebenshaltung . Egner, Erich, 1901- Berlin , 1974. 249 p. ; ISBN 3-428-03093-1 : LC Card 76-511945
TX7 .B4 Heft 9 HD6995.5
NYPL [JLE 86-3436]

Hautes études médiévales et modernes. For other vols. in this series, see entry in Old Catalog: École pratique des hautes études, Paris. Centre de recherches d'histoire et de philologie. [Publications. Série] V: Hautes études médiévales et modernes.
(55) Administration et contrôle de l'économie, 1800-1914 /. Genève , Paris , 1985. 167 p. : LC Card 86-128349 DDC 338.944 19
HD3616.F82 A66 1985

Haveman, Robert H.
Jobs and the environment / by Robert H. Haveman and Greg Christainsen. Scarsdale, N.Y. : Work in America Institute, c1979. 32 p. ; 28 cm. (Work in America Institute studies in productivity, 0149-8703 . 10) Bibliography: p. 31-32. LC Card 79-15418 DDC 301.31/0973
1. Environmental policy - Economic aspects - United States. 2. Labor supply - United States. I. Christainsen, Gregory, joint author. II. Title. III. Series.
HC110.E5 H38 ***NYPL [JLM 83-380 no.10]***

Poverty policy and poverty research : the Great Society and the social sciences / Robert H. Haveman. Madison, Wis. : University of Wisconsin Press, 1987. xi, 307 p. : ill. ; 24 cm. Bibliography: p. 259-298. Includes index. ISBN 0-299-11150-4 : LC Card 86-40453 DDC 362.5/8/0973 19
1. Poverty research - United States. 2. Economic assistance, Domestic - United States. 3. United States - Social policy. I. Title.
HC110.P6 H38 1987

Havemann, Hans A., 1912-
Industrialisierungspolitik für Entwicklungsländer : Grossprojekte und die Beteiligung von mittelständischen Unternehmen / Hans A. Havemann. Aachen : Forschungsinstitut für Internationale Technische und Wirtschaftliche Zusammenarbeit der Rheinisch-Westfälischen Technischen Hochschule Aachen, 1982. 68 p. ; 30 cm. (Intertechnik . 23) Includes bibliographical references. ISBN 3-922525-06-7 LC Card 83-203761
1. Developing countries - Industries. 2. Industry and state - Developing countries. 3. Economic development projects - Developing countries. 4. Germany (West) - Foreign economic relations - Developing countries. 5. Developing countries - Foreign economic relations - Germany (West). I. Title. II. Series.
HC59.7 .H386 1982

Havnevik, Kjell J. Norsk industris internasjonalisering, rettet mot utviklingslandene . Bergen [1982] vi, 57 p. ; LC Card 83-139811
HD2932 .N67 1982

Havrilesky, Thomas M. Introduction to modern macroeconomics / Thomas M. Havrilesky. 2nd ed. Arlington Heights, Ill. : H. Davidson, c1988. p. cm. Bibliography: p. Includes indexes. ISBN 0-88295-414-8 LC Card 87-24456 DDC 339 19
1. Macroeconomics. I. Title.
HB172.5 .H38 1988

Havrylyshyn, Oli. Exports of developing countries . Washington, D.C. , c1987. viii, 168 p. : ISBN 0-8213-0870-X (pbk.) : LC Card 87-15991 DDC 382/.6/091724 19
HF4055 .E96 1987

HAWAII - COMMERCE - JAPAN - STATISTICS.
Hawaii's trade with Japan, 1976-1985 /. Honolulu, Hawaii (P.O. Box 2359, Honolulu 96804) [1986] 20 p. : LC Card 86-623207 DDC 382/.09969/052 19
HF3161.H3 H38733 1986

HAWAII - COMMERCE - NEW ZEALAND - STATISTICS.
Hawaii's trade with New Zealand, 1976-1985 /. Honolulu, Hawaii (P.O. Box 2359, Honolulu 96804) [1986] 14 p. : LC Card 87-620878 DDC 382/.09931/0969021 19
HF3161.H3 H3878 1986

HAWAII - COMMERCE - TAIWAN - STATISTICS.
Hawaii's trade with Taiwan, 1976-1985 /. Honolulu, Hawaii (P.O. Box 2359, Honolulu 96804) [1986] 18 p. ; LC Card 86-622297 DDC 382/.09969/051249021 19
HF3161.H3 H378 1986

Hawaii. Dept. of Planning and Economic Development. (Old Catalog form: Hawaii (State). Planning and economic development, Dept. of)

Hawaii. Dept. of Planning and Economic Development. Kauai Inter-Division Committee. Economic development on the island of Kauai . [Honolulu] [1985] xxii, 84 p. : LC Card 86-622084 DDC 338.9969/41 19
HC107.H32 K383 1985

Hawaii. Dept. of Planning and Economic Development. Research and Economic Analysis Division.
The Honolulu consumer price index, 1940-1986. [Honolulu] [1986] 19 p. ; LC Card 86-622085 DDC 319.69 s 338.5/28/09969 19
HA329.1 .A25 no. 187 HB235.U6

Population and economic projections for the State of Hawaii, 1980-2005 [microform]. [Honolulu, Hawaii] [1984] 22 p. ; LC Card 84-622934 DDC 304.6/2/09969021 19
HB3525.H3 P67 1984
NYPL [*ZT-1745 no.28]

HAWAII - ECONOMIC CONDITIONS - 1959- - STATISTICS.
Population and economic projections for the State of Hawaii, 1980-2005 [microform]. [Honolulu, Hawaii] [1984] 22 p. ; LC Card 84-622934 DDC 304.6/2/09969021 19
HB3525.H3 P67 1984
NYPL [*ZT-1745 no.28]

Hawaii. International Services Branch.
Hawaii's trade with Japan, 1976-1985 /. Honolulu, Hawaii (P.O. Box 2359, Honolulu 96804) [1986] 20 p. : LC Card 86-623207 DDC 382/.09969/052 19
HF3161.H3 H38733 1986

Hawaii's trade with New Zealand, 1976-1985 /. Honolulu, Hawaii (P.O. Box 2359, Honolulu 96804) [1986] 14 p. : LC Card 87-620878 DDC 382/.09931/0969021 19
HF3161.H3 H3878 1986

Hawaii's trade with Taiwan, 1976-1985 /. Honolulu, Hawaii (P.O. Box 2359, Honolulu 96804) [1986] 18 p. ; LC Card 86-622297 DDC 382/.09969/051249021 19
HF3161.H3 H378 1986

Hawaii. Planning and Economic Development, Dept. of. see **Hawaii. Dept. of Planning and Economic Development.**

HAWAII - POLITICS AND GOVERNMENT - 1900-1959.
Cooper, George. Land and power in Hawaii . Honolulu, Hawaii , c1985. x, 518 p. ; ISBN 0-9615052-0-6 : LC Card 85-72037 DDC 333.73/13/09969 19
HD266.H3 C66 1985 ***NYPL [JLE 87-361]***

HAWAII - POLITICS AND GOVERNMENT - 1959-
Cooper, George. Land and power in Hawaii . Honolulu, Hawaii , c1985. x, 518 p. ; ISBN 0-9615052-0-6 : LC Card 85-72037 DDC 333.73/13/09969 19
HD266.H3 C66 1985 ***NYPL [JLE 87-361]***

HAWAII - POPULATION - STATISTICS.
The Population of Hawaii, 1980-1985. [Honolulu] [1986] 12 p. ; LC Card 86-622982 DDC 319.69 s 304.6/09969 19
HA329.1 .A25 no. 190 HA329.5

Hawaii. State Dept. of Planning and Economic Development. see **Hawaii. Dept. of Planning and Economic Development.**

Hawaiian ordeal . Ewanchuk, Michael, 1908- Winnipeg, Man. , c1986. xii, 180 p. : ISBN 0-9690768-7-8 (pbk.) : LC Card 87-156576
HD4875.U5 E93x 1986

Hawaii's trade with Japan, 1976-1985 / compiled by International Services Branch, Department of Planning and Economic Development, State of Hawaii. Honolulu, Hawaii (P.O. Box 2359, Honolulu 96804) : The Branch, [1986] 20 p. : ill. ; 28 cm. (Trade report . no. 58) Chiefly tables. "August 1986." LC Card 86-623207 DDC 382/.09969/052 19
1. Hawaii - Commerce - Japan - Statistics. 2. Japan - Commerce - Hawaii - Statistics. I. Hawaii. International Services Branch. II. Series: Trade report (Hawaii. International Services Branch) , no. 58.
HF3161.H3 H38733 1986

Hawaii's trade with New Zealand, 1976-1985 / compiled by International Services Branch, Department of Planning and Economic Development, State of Hawaii. Honolulu, Hawaii (P.O. Box 2359, Honolulu 96804) : The Branch, [1986] 14 p. : ill. ; 28 cm. (Trade report . no. 59) "October 1986." LC Card 87-620878 DDC 382/.09931/0969021 19
1. Hawaii - Commerce - New Zealand - Statistics. 2. New Zealand - Commerce - Hawaii - Statistics. I. Hawaii. International Services Branch. II. Series: Trade report (Hawaii. International Services Branch) , no. 59.
HF3161.H3 H3878 1986

Hawaii's trade with Taiwan, 1976-1985 / compiled by International Services Branch, Department of Planning and Economic Development, State of Hawaii. Honolulu, Hawaii (P.O. Box 2359, Honolulu 96804) : The Department, [1986] 18 p. ; 28 cm. (Trade report . no. 57) LC Card 86-622297 DDC 382/.09969/051249021 19
1. Hawaii - Commerce - Taiwan - Statistics. 2. Taiwan - Commerce - Hawaii - Statistics. I. Hawaii. International Services Branch. II. Series: Trade report (Hawaii. International Services Branch) , no. 57.
HF3161.H3 H378 1986

Hawawini, Gabriel A.
European equity markets . New York , 1984. 470 p. : ISBN 0-8240-6307-4 (alk. paper) : LC Card 83-49440 DDC 332.64/094
HG5430.5.A3 E84 1984
NYPL [JLE 86-4508]

Mandatory financial information and capital market equilibrium in Belgium / Gabriel Hawawini and Pierre Michel. New York : Garland Pub., 1987. 271 p. : ill. ; 24 cm. (Accounting thought and practice through the years) Bibliography: p. 211-225. ISBN 0-8240-7852-7 (alk. paper) : LC Card 87-54 DDC 332.63/222/09493 19
1. Stocks - Prices - Belgium. 2. Capital market - Belgium. 3. Corporations - Accounting - Law and legislation - Belgium. 4. Financial disclosure - Law and legislation - Belgium. I. Michel, Pierre A. II. Title. III. Series.
HG5553 .H39 1987

Hawes, Charles A. Morris, Joseph M., 1949- Joint ventures . New York , c1987. xii, 324 p. ; ISBN 0-471-01170-3 LC Card 86-28083 DDC 658/.044 19
HD62.47 .M67 1987

Hawes, Gary, 1950- The Philippine State and the Marcos regime : the politics of export / Gary Hawes. Ithaca : Cornell University Press, 1987. 196 p. ; 25 cm. (Cornell studies in political economy) Bibliography: p. 177-192. Includes index. ISBN 0-8014-2012-1 (alk. paper) LC Card 86-29237 DDC 382/.41/09599 19
1. Produce trade - Philippines. 2. Sugar trade - Philippines. 3. Coconut industry - Philippines. 4. Fruit trade - Philippines. 5. Agriculture and state - Philippines. I. Title. II. Series.
HD9016.P52 H38 1987

Hawken, Paul. Growing a business / Paul Hawken. New York : Simon and Schuster, c1987. 251 p. ; 22 cm. Includes index. ISBN 0-671-64457-2 LC Card 87-16431 DDC 658.1/141 19
1. New business enterprises - Management. I. Title.
HD62.5 .H38 1987

Hawkes, Ellen. Feminism on trial : the Ginny Foat case and the future of the women's movement / Ellen Hawkes.1st ed. New York : Morrow, c1986. 420 p. ; 25 cm. Includes index. ISBN 0-688-04850-1 : LC Card 85-31968 DDC 305.4/2/0973 19
1. Foat, Ginny. 2. National Organization for Women. 3. Feminists - United States - Biography. 4. Feminism - United States. I. Title.
HQ1413.F63 H39 1986
NYPL [JLE 86-2863]

Hawley, James P., 1944- Dollars & borders : U. S. government attempts to restrict capital flows, 1960-1980 / James P. Hawley. Armonk, N.Y. : M.E. Sharpe, c1987. xi, 204 p. ; 24 cm. Bibliography: p. 171-196. Includes index. ISBN 0-87332-386-6 : LC Card 86-31395 DDC 332/.041 19
1. Capital movements - United States - History - 20th century. 2. Capital movements - Government policy -

United States - History - 20th century. 3. Euro-dollar market - History - 20th century. 4. Balance of payments - United States - History - 20th century. I. Title. II. Title: Dollars and borders.
HG3891 .H38 1987

Hawliczek, Ingo. Die Kreisfreien Städte und Landkreise in Rheinland-Pfalz /. Bad Ems , 1977. 420 p. : LC Card 85-244499
HC287.R7 K74 1977

Hawryszkiewycz, I. T. Database analysis and design / I.T. Hawryszkiewycz. Chicago : Science Research Associates, c1984. xx, 578 p. : ill. ; 25 cm. Includes index. Bibliography: p. 561-571. ISBN 0-574-21485-2 : LC Card 84-1341 DDC 001.64/2 19
1. Data base management. 2. System design. I. Title.
QA76.9.D3 H386 1984
NYPL [JSE 86-2113]

Hawthorne, Elizabeth M. Evaluating employee training programs : a research-based guide for human resources managers / Elizabeth M. Hawthorne. New York : Quorum Books, 1987. xiv, 196 p. : ill. ; 23 cm. Bibliography: p. [183]-192. Includes index. ISBN 0-89930-242-4 (lib. bdg. : alk. paper) LC Card 87-5984 DDC 658.3/12404 19
1. Employees, Training of - Evaluation. 2. Training needs - Evaluation. I. Title.
HF5549.5.T7 H36 1987

Hax, Arnoldo C. Planning strategies that work /. New York , 1987. xii, 287 p. : ISBN 0-19-504883-0 (alk. paper) LC Card 86-31117 DDC 658.4/012 19
HD30.28 .P555 1987

Hay, Donald A. The Economics of market dominance /. Oxford, UK , New York, NY, USA , 1987. p. cm. ISBN 0-631-14784-5 : LC Card 86-26416 DDC 338.8/2 19
HD2326 .E24 1987

Hay, Leon Edwards, 1923- Essentials of accounting for governmental and not-for-profit organizations / Leon E. Hay, John H. Engstrom. Homewood, Ill. : Irwin, 1987. x, 310 p. ; 24 cm. (The Robert N. Anthony/Willard J. Graham series in accounting) Includes bibliographies and index. ISBN 0-256-03454-0 (pbk.) LC Card 86-82587 DDC 657/.98 19
1. Finance, Public - United States - Accounting. 2. Administrative agencies - United States - Accounting. 3. Corporations, Nonprofit - United States - Accounting. I. Engstrom, John H. II. Title. III. Series.
HJ9801 .H39 1987

Hay, Peter. The book of business anecdotes / Peter Hay. New York, N.Y. : Facts on File, c1988. viii, 296 p. ; 24 cm. Bibliography: p. 279-290. Includes index. ISBN 0-8160-1522-8 LC Card 87-20211 DDC 650/.0207 19
1. Business - Anecdotes, facetiae, satire, etc. I. Title.
HF5351 .H34 1988

Hayashi, Takeshi, 1930- Gijutsu kakushin to joshi rōdō /. Tōkyō , 1985. x, 219 p. : ISBN 4-13-051068-1 ***NYPL [*OSL 87-1658]***

Hayastanė filateliayum. Arakelov, S. N. (Suren Nersesovich) Armeniia v filatelii /. Erevan , 1980. 175 p., [24] p. of plates : LC Card 82-105026
HE6183.A69 A72 1980

Hayden Macintosh library books.
Loggins, Richard, 1949- The Excel advanced user's guide /. Indianapolis, Ind., USA , c1987. x, 189 p. : ISBN 0-672-46626-0 (pbk.) : LC Card 87-60109 DDC 005.36/9 19
HF5548.4.E93 L64 1987

Haydu, Jeffrey. Between craft and class : skilled workers and factory politics in the United States and Britain, 1890-1922 / Jeffrey Haydu. Berkeley : University of California Press, c1988. p. cm. Bibliography: p. Includes index. ISBN 0-520-06060-1 (alk. paper) LC Card 87-22169 DDC 322/.2/0941 19
1. Labor and laboring classes - United States - Political activity - History. 2. Labor and laboring classes - Great Britain - Political activity - History. 3. Artisans - United States - History. 4. Artisans - Great Britain - History. 5. Social classes - United States - History. 6. Social classes - Great Britain - History. I. Title.
HD8076 .H39 1988

Hayek, Friedrich A. von (Friedrich August), 1899-
Monetary nationalism and international stability / by F.A. Hayek. Fairfield, NJ : A.M. Kelley, 1988. p. cm. (Reprints of economic classics) Reprint. Originally published: 1st ed. London : Longmans, Green, 1937. ISBN 0-678-00047-6 LC Card 87-17244 DDC 332.4 19
1. Money. 2. Currency question. 3. International finance. I. Title.
HG221 .H345 1988

HAYEK, FRIEDRICH A. VON (FRIEDRICH AUGUST), 1899-
Bofinger, Peter. Währungswettbewerb . Köln , c1985. xiv, 235 p. : ISBN 3-452-20332-8 : LC Card 86-185566
HG221 .B57455 1985

Derix, Hans-Heribert. Säkulare Inflation, kompetitive Geldordnung und "unbeschränkte Demokratie" . Stuttgart , New York , 1985. xiv, 630 p. : ISBN 3-437-50284-0 LC Card 86-110730
HG229 .D46 1985

Honeck, Gerhard. Probleme einer Privatgeldordnung . Frankfurt am Main , c1985. 93 p. ; ISBN 3-88129-964-5 LC Card 86-153829
HG230.3 .H56 1985

Sovremennyĭ konservatizm i krizis burzhuaznoĭ ėkonomicheskoĭ nauki . Moskva , 1986. 175 p. ; LC Card 87-165796
HB241 .S673 1986

Walker, Graham. The ethics of F.A. Hayek /. Lanham, MD , c1986. vii, 135 p. ; ISBN 0-8191-5250-1 (alk. paper) : LC Card 86-1515 DDC 171/.7 19
HB101.H39 W35 1986
NYPL [JFD 86-9138]

HAYEK, FRIEDRICH A. VON (FRIEDRICH AUGUST), 1899- - INFLUENCE.
Israel Zipper, Ricardo. Democracia y liberalismo /. Santiago de Chile , 1984. 56 p. ; LC Card 85-197546
HB95 .I87 1984

Hayes, Charles R., 1919- Mayer, Harold Melvin, 1916- Land uses in American cities /. Champaign, Ill. [c1983] vi, 176 p. : ISBN 0-941226-02-6 (pbk.) LC Card 82-81036 DDC 333.77/13/0973 19
HD257 .M39 1983 ***NYPL [JLD 86-3126]***

Hayes, J. P. (John Philip), 1924- Economic effects of sanctions on southern Africa / by J.P. Hayes. Aldershot, Hampshire, England ; Brookfield, Vt., USA : Gower, 1987. xii, 100 p. : ill. ; 22 cm. (Thames essay . no. 53) Published for the Trade Policy Research Centre, London. Bibliography: p. [94]-95. ISBN 0-566-05539-2 (pbk.) : LC Card 87-11674 DDC 337.68 19
1. Economic sanctions - South Africa. I. Trade Policy Research Centre. II. Title. III. Series.
HF1413.5 .H39 1987

Hayes, Peter, 1946- Industry and ideology : IG Farben in the Nazi era / Peter Hayes. Cambridge [Cambridgeshire] ; New York : Cambridge University Press, 1987. xxviii, 411 p. : ill. ; 24 cm. Includes bibliographical references and index. ISBN 0-521-32948-5 LC Card 86-28388 DDC 338.7/66/00943 19
1. Interessengemeinschaft Farbenindustrie Aktiengesellschaft - Political activity - History - 20th century. 2. Nationalsozialistische Deutsche Arbeiter-Partei - History. 3. Chemical industry - Political aspects - Germany - History - 20th century. 4. Mineral industries - Political aspects - Germany - History - 20th century. 5. Germany - Politics and government - 1933-1945. 6. World War, 1939-1945. I. Title.
HD9654.9.I5 H39 1987

Hayes, Robert H. The Uneasy alliance . Boston, Mass. , c1985. x, 485 p. : ISBN 0-87584-172-4 LC Card 85-8709 DDC 658.5 19
HD56 .U53 1985 ***NYPL [JLE 86-2361]***

Hayes-Roth, Frederick. Building expert systems /. Reading, Mass. , 1983. xvi, 444 p. : ISBN 0-201-10686-8 LC Card 82-24511 DDC 001.64/2 19
QA76.9.E96 B84 1983 ***NYPL [JSE 87-204]***

Hayes, Samuel L. Auerbach, Joseph, 1916- Investment banking and diligence . Boston, Mass. , c1986. x, 274 p. : ISBN 0-87584-171-6 (alk. paper) LC Card 86-319 DDC 332.66/0973 19
HG4910 .A94 1986 ***NYPL [JLE 86-3128]***

Haynes, Marion E. Stepping up to supervisor / Marion E. Haynes. Houston, Tex. : Executive Roundtable Publications, c1987. ix, 171 p. : ill., forms ; 22 cm. ISBN 0-941021-00-9 (pbk.) LC Card 87-124242 DDC 658.3/02 19
1. Supervision of employees. I. Title.
HF5549.12 .H39 1987

Hayward, Jack Ernest Shalom. The state and the market economy : industrial patriotism and economic intervention in France / Jack Hayward. Brighton, Sussex : Wheatsheaf Books : Distributed by Harvester Press, 1986. xv, 267 p. : ill. ; 24 cm. Bibliography: p. 237-257. Includes index. ISBN 0-7450-0012-6 LC Card 87-672693
1. Industry and state - France. 2. France - Economic policy - 1945-. I. Title.
HC276.2 .H35x 1986b

HAYWOOD, BIG BILL, 1869-1928.
Dubofsky, Melvyn, 1934- "Big Bill" Haywood /. New York , 1987. viii, 184 p. ; ISBN 0-312-01272-1 : LC Card 87-17355 DDC 331.88/6 B 19
HD6509.H3 D82 1987

A Hazai áralakulásról / [összeállította, Wiesel Iván]. [Budapest] : Kossuth, 1986. 342 p. ; 20 cm. (Vélemények/viták, 0139-4010) Includes bibliographical references. ISBN 963-09-2758-6 : LC Card 87-407741
1. Inflation (Finance) - Hungary. 2. Prices - Hungary. I. Wiesel, Iván.
HG970.5 .H39 1986

A hazai energiaszerkezet-változás fontosabb regionális kérdései /. Márton, Géza. Budapest , 1974. 271 p. : ISBN 963-05-0062-0 LC Card 86-187425
HD9502.H92 M37 1974

A hazai gazdaság négy évtizedének története, 1945-1985 /. Pető, Iván. Budapest , 1985- v. <1 > ; ISBN 963-221-553-2 (set) LC Card 87-105744
HC300.28 .P47 1985

Hazai gazdaság 4 évtizedének története, 1945-1985. Pető, Iván. A hazai gazdaság négy évtizedének története, 1945-1985 /. Budapest , 1985- v. <1 > ; ISBN 963-221-553-2 (set) LC Card 87-105744
HC300.28 .P47 1985

HAZARDOUS GOODS. see **HAZARDOUS SUBSTANCES.**

HAZARDOUS MATERIALS. see **HAZARDOUS SUBSTANCES.**

HAZARDOUS SUBSTANCES - ACCIDENTS - MANAGEMENT - CONGRESSES.
Insuring and managing hazardous risks--from Seveso to Bhopal and beyond /. Berlin , New York , c1987. ix, 534 p. : ISBN 0-387-17732-9 (U. S.) LC Card 87-4963 DDC 346.03/8 342.638 19
HG9994 .I57 1987

HAZARDOUS SUBSTANCES - MANAGEMENT - CONGRESSES.
Insuring and managing hazardous risks--from Seveso to Bhopal and beyond /. Berlin , New York , c1987. ix, 534 p. : ISBN 0-387-17732-9 (U. S.) LC Card 87-4963 DDC 346.03/8 342.638 19
HG9994 .I57 1987

HAZARDOUS SUBSTANCES - UNITED STATES - TRANSPORTATION.
Petersen, Sybil. Transportation . Arlington, Va. (P.O. Box 926, Arlington 22216) [1986] [8], 40 p. : LC Card 87-401670 DDC 363.1/7 19
HE199.5.D3 P48 1986

Hazardous waste management . Goldman, Benjamin A. Washington, D.C. , c1986. xx, 316 p. : ISBN 0-933280-30-0 : LC Card 86-2748 DDC 363.7/28 19
HD9975.U52 G65 1986
NYPL [JLE 87-1159]

HAZARDOUS WASTE MANAGEMENT INDUSTRY - NORTHEASTERN STATES - CORRUPT PRACTICES.
Rebovich, Donald. Understanding hazardous waste crime . [Trenton?] [1986] viii, 70 p. : LC Card 86-622805 DDC 364.1/42 19
HD9975.U53 A1157 1986

HAZARDOUS WASTE MANAGEMENT INDUSTRY - UNITED STATES.
Goldman, Benjamin A. Hazardous waste management . Washington, D.C. , c1986. xx, 316 p. : ISBN 0-933280-30-0 : LC Card 86-2748

DDC 363.7/28 19
HD9975.U52 G65 1986
NYPL [JLE 87-1159]

Shelton, Robert D. Hazardous waste management market assessment /. Menlo Park, CA (333 Ravenswood Ave., Menlo Park 94025) , c1986. 19 p. : LC Card 86-220787 DDC 338.4/7363728 19
HD9975.U52 S54 1986

Hazardous waste management market assessment /. Shelton, Robert D. Menlo Park, CA (333 Ravenswood Ave., Menlo Park 94025) , c1986. 19 p. : LC Card 86-220787 DDC 338.4/7363728 19
HD9975.U52 S54 1986

HAZARDOUS WASTE SITES - UNITED STATES.
Dimensions of hazardous waste politics and policy /. New York , c1988. p. cm. ISBN 0-313-25989-5 (lib. bdg. : alk. paper) LC Card 87-17792 DDC 363.7/28 19
HC110.E5 D56 1988

Goldman, Benjamin A. Hazardous waste management . Washington, D.C. , c1986. xx, 316 p. : ISBN 0-933280-30-0 : LC Card 86-2748 DDC 363.7/28 19
HD9975.U52 G65 1986
NYPL [JLE 87-1159]

HAZARDOUS WASTES - GOVERNMENT POLICY - CALIFORNIA.
California. Governor's Task Force on Toxics, Waste, and Technology. Final report /. [Sacramento, CA] [1986] 2 v. : LC Card 86-622772 DDC 363.7/28 19
HC107.C23 P553 1986

HAZARDOUS WASTES - GOVERNMENT POLICY - UNITED STATES.
Dimensions of hazardous waste politics and policy /. New York , c1988. p. cm. ISBN 0-313-25989-5 (lib. bdg. : alk. paper) LC Card 87-17792 DDC 363.7/28 19
HC110.E5 D56 1988

HAZARDOUS WASTES - LAW AND LEGISLATION - CALIFORNIA.
California. Governor's Task Force on Toxics, Waste, and Technology. Final report /. [Sacramento, CA] [1986] 2 v. : LC Card 86-622772 DDC 363.7/28 19
HC107.C23 P553 1986

Hazell, P. B. R. Crop insurance for agricultural development . Baltimore , c1986. xviii, 322 p. ISBN 0-8018-2673-X (alk. paper) LC Card 85-9810 DDC 368.1/22 19
HG9968 .C76 1985 *NYPL [JLE 86-1082]*

A Háztáji és kisegitő gazdaság szerepe az életmód alakulásában : az 1976/77. évi időmérleg felvétel adatai alapján / [készült a Központi Statisztikai Hivatal Társadalmi Statisztikai Főosztályán ; a jelentést készitette Harcsa István]. Budapest : Központi Statisztikai Hivatal, 1983. 263 p. ; 29 cm. Chiefly tables. Bibliography: p. 43. ISBN 963-02-2948-X (Magy. nemz. bibl.) LC Card 84-216989
1. Private plot agriculture - Hungary - Statistics. 2. Collective farms - Hungary - Officials and employees - Time management - Statistics. 3. Quality of life - Hungary - Statistics. I. Harcsa, István. II. Hungary. Központi Statisztikai Hivatal. Társadalmi Statisztikai Főosztály.
HD1476.H8 H28 1983

HBO. Mair, George, 1929- Inside HBO . New York , c1988. xviii, 204 p. ; ISBN 0-396-08420-6 : LC Card 87-19939 DDC 384.55/47/0973 19
HE8700.72.U6 M34 1988

HCM Rajasthan State Institute of Public Administration. Centre for Management Studies. Energy alternatives for rural development /. Jaipur , 1985. vi, 303 p. : LC Card 86-902191 DDC 333.79/0954 19
HD9556.I42 E54 1985

Head, George L., 1941- Essentials of risk control /. Malvern, Pa. , 1986. 2 v. : ISBN 0-89462-033-9 (pbk.) LC Card 86-82833 DDC 368 19
HD61 .E84 1986

Head, Robert V. Planning and implementing information resource centers for end-user computing / Robert V. Head. Wellesley, MA : QED Information Sciences, c1985. viii, 186 p. : ill. ; 24 cm. Includes index. ISBN 0-89435-123-0 : LC Card 84-61536
1. Electronic data processing departments - Management. 2. Business - Data processing - Management. 3. Office practice - Automation - Management. I. Title. *NYPL [JLE 86-2117]*

Head, Sylvia. The neighborhood mint : Dahlonega in the Age of Jackson / Sylvia Head, Elizabeth W. Etheridge. Macon, Ga. : Mercer University Press, c1986. xviii, 206 p. : ill. ; 24 cm. Bibliography: p. 197-198. Includes index. ISBN 0-86554-240-6 (alk. paper) : LC Card 86-23500 DDC 737.49758/273 19
1. Mints - Georgia - Dahlonega - History - 19th century. 2. Coinage - United States - History - 19th century. 3. Dahlonega (Ga.) - History. I. Etheridge, Elizabeth W. II. Title.
HG461.D342 H4 1986

Head, Thomas C.
Griffin, Ricky W. Instructor's manual, Practicing management, second edition /. Boston , c1987. xiii, 167 p. ; ISBN 0-395-42585-9 (pbk.) LC Card 87-400618 DDC 658 19
HD31 .G7627 1987

Griffin, Ricky W. Practicing management /. Boston , c1987. xii, 368 p. : ISBN 0-395-42584-0 (pbk.) LC Card 87-163492 DDC 658 19
HD31 .G7635 1987

Headline series, 0017-8780 .
(no. 274) Walker, Brian W. Authentic development in Africa /. New York, N.Y. , c1985. 70 p. : ISBN 0-87124-102-1 (pbk.) : LC Card 85-82567 DDC 081 s 338.96 19
E744 .H43 no. 274 HC800
NYPL [JLD 86-3400]

Heagler, Arthur M. Shuker, Iain G. W. Economic analysis of the cost structure of commercial sugar cane farms in Louisiana /. Baton Rouge, La. [1986] vi, 50 p. : LC Card 86-622542 DDC 338.1/09763 s 338.1/7361/09763021 19
HD1775.L8 L7 no. 651 HD9107.L8

HEAL & SON - HISTORY.
Gooden, Susanna. A history of Heal's . [London] , Atlantic Highlands, N.J. , 1984. 137 p. : ISBN 0-85331-488-8 (pbk.) LC Card 86-221633 DDC 381/.456841/00941 19
HD9773.G74 H434 1984

Heald, Edward S. Woodman, Byron E. Personal financial planning /. Andover, Mass. , c1987. 151 p. ; ISBN 0-931790-77-8 : LC Card 87-13229 DDC 332.024 19
HG179 .W578 1987

Healey, Michael. The Industrialization of the countryside /. Norwich [Norfolk] , c1985. xiv, 315 p. : ISBN 0-86094-202-3 LC Card 87-141251 DDC 338.9/009173/4 19
HC256.6 .I524 1985

Healey, Patsy. Gilbert, Alan, 1944- The political economy of land . Aldershot, Hants , Brookfield, Vt., U. S.A. , c1985. xv, 163 p. : ISBN 0-566-05007-2 : LC Card 85-17535 DDC 333.77/13/0987 19
HD576 .G54 1985 *NYPL [JLD 86-3632]*

HEALTH CARE. see **MEDICAL CARE.**

The health care survival curve . Miller, Irwin. Homewood, Ill. , c1984. xv, 144 p. ; ISBN 0-87094-481-9 LC Card 83-73714 DDC 338.4/73621/0973 19
RA410.53 .M55 1984 *NYPL [JLE 86-4362]*

HEALTH, COMMUNITY. see **PUBLIC HEALTH.**

HEALTH ECONOMICS. see **MEDICAL ECONOMICS.**

HEALTH - ENVIRONMENTAL ASPECTS. see **ENVIRONMENTAL HEALTH.**

HEALTH FACILITIES - TEXAS - SAN ANTONIO - CONGRESSES.
A Transcription of key addresses at San Antonio's Bio-Medical Seminar /. San Antonio, TX (8961 Tesoro Dr., Suite 308, San Antonio 78217) , c1985. v, 104, [4] leaves of plates : LC Card 87-144092 DDC 338.4/7681761/09764351 19
HD9999.B443 U667 1985

Health insurance : comparing Blue Cross and Blue Shield plans with commercial insurers : report to the Chairman, Subcommittee on Health, Committee on Ways and Means, House of Representatives / United States General Accounting Office. Washington, D.C. : The Office, 1986. 53 p. ; 28 cm. Cover title. Running title: Blue Cross and commercial insurers. "GAO/HRD-86-110." LC Card 86-603180 DDC 368.3/82/00973 19
1. Blue Cross and Blue Shield Association. 2. Insurance, Health - United States. I. United States. General Accounting Office.
HG9398.B57 H4 1986

Health insurance . California. Legislature. Assembly. Committee on Finance and Insurance. Sacramento, Calif. [1984] 359 p. : LC Card 87-621024 DDC 368.3/82/009794 19
HG9397.5.C2 C35 1984

Health insurance . New York (State). Council on Health Care Financing. Subcommittee on Health Insurance. Albany, N.Y. [1985?] 1 v. (various pagings) : LC Card 86-622080 DDC 368.3/82/009747 19
HD7102.U5 N655 1985

HEALTH INSURANCE. see **INSURANCE, HEALTH.**

Health insurance and the demand for medical care : evidence from a randomized experiment / Willard G. Manning ... [et al.]. Santa Monica, CA : Rand, 1987. p. cm. Based on data from the Rand Health Insurance Study. "Prepared under a grant from the U. S. Department of Health and Human Services." "R-3476-HHS." "June 1987." Bibliography: p. ISBN 0-8330-0864-1 LC Card 87-17587 DDC 368.3/82/00973 19
1. Insurance, Health - United States. 2. Medical care, Cost of - United States. I. Manning, Willard G. II. Rand Corporation. III. Rand Health Insurance Study.
HD7102.U4 H413 1987

HEALTH, INTERNATIONAL. see **WORLD HEALTH.**

HEALTH MAINTENANCE ORGANIZATION PATIENTS - CALIFORNIA - STATISTICS.
Medi-Cal fee-for-service eligibles and prepaid health plan enrollees by age group, sex, and county--July 1983. [Sacramento] [1984] 21 p. : LC Card 86-622329 DDC 362.1/04252/09794021 19
HD7102.U5 C3 1984

HEALTH MAINTENANCE ORGANIZATIONS.
Oberg, Charles N. Medicaid, entering the third decade . Excelsior, Minn. (P.O. Box 458, Excelsior 55331-0458) , c1986. vii, 70 p. : LC Card 86-233259 DDC 362.1/0425/0973 19
HD7102.U4 O58 1986

HEALTH MAINTENANCE ORGANIZATIONS - MARYLAND - DIRECTORIES.
Directory of licensed insurers, licensed motor clubs, licensed health maintenance organizations, licensed rating organizations, registered advisory organizations . [Baltimore, Md.] (501 St. Paul Pl., Baltimore 21202) [1985] viii, 150 p. ; LC Card 86-621407 DDC 368/.0025/752 19
HG8526.M3 D59 1985

HEALTH MAINTENANCE ORGANIZATIONS - UNITED STATES.
Miller, Irwin. The health care survival curve . Homewood, Ill. , c1984. xv, 144 p. ; ISBN 0-87094-481-9 LC Card 83-73714 DDC 338.4/73621/0973 19
RA410.53 .M55 1984 *NYPL [JLE 86-4362]*

Health of an aging population : issues on data for policy analysis. Hyattsville, Md. : U. S. Dept. of Health and Human Services, Public Health Service, National Center for Health Statistics ; Washington, D.C. : For sale by the Supt. of Docs., U. S. G.P.O., 1987. p. cm. (Series 4, Documents and committee reports . no. 25) DHHS publication ; no. (PHS) 87-1488 Includes bibliographies. ISBN 0-8406-0362-2 LC Card 86-600392 DDC 362.1/0723 s 362.1/9897/00973 19
1. Aged - Health and hygiene - United States - Statistical methods. 2. Health surveys - United States - Statistical methods. 3. Aged - Health and hygiene - United States - Statistical services. I. Manton, Kenneth G. II. National Center for Health Statistics (U. S.).
HA37 .U1693 no. 25 RA408.A3

HEALTH OF CHILDREN. see **CHILDREN - CARE AND HYGIENE.**

HEALTH OF WOMEN. see **WOMEN - HEALTH AND HYGIENE.**

HEALTH OF WORKERS. see **INDUSTRIAL HYGIENE.**

Health policy studies.
Affording access to quality care . Washington, D.C. (444 N. Capitol St., N.W., Suite 250, Washington 20001) , c1986. xx, 245 p. ; LC Card 87-127057 DDC 338.4/336210452/0973 19
HD7102.U4 A66 1986

HEALTH, PUBLIC. see **PUBLIC HEALTH.**

Health Series Research Center of InterStudy. see **InterStudy (Center)**

HEALTH SERVICES. see **PUBLIC HEALTH.**

HEALTH SURVEYS - UNITED STATES - STATISTICAL METHODS.
Health of an aging population . Hyattsville, Md. , Washington, D.C. , 1987. p. cm. ISBN 0-8406-0362-2 LC Card 86-600392 DDC 362.1/0723 s 362.1/9897/00973 19
HA37 .U1693 no. 25 RA408.A3

HEALTH, WORLD. see **WORLD HEALTH.**

Healthcare electronics / Consumer & Technology Division. Boston, MA (89 Broad St., Boston 02110) : Yankee Group, c1986. iv, 79 p. : ill. ; 28 cm. (Industry research report) At head of title: Consumer healthcare. "July 1986." LC Card 86-212563 DDC 381/.45681761 19
1. Medical electronics equipment industry - United States. I. Yankee Group. Consumer & Technology Division. II. Title: Consumer healthcare. III. Series.
HD9995.E43 U55 1986

Healy, Caroline Wells. see **Dall, Caroline Wells (Healey), 1822-1912.**

Healy, Robert G. Competition for land in the American South : agriculture, human settlement, and the environment / Robert G. Healy. Washington, D.C. : Conservation Foundation, c1985. xxxii, 333 p. : ill., maps ; 23 cm. Includes bibliographies and index. ISBN 0-89164-094-0 (pbk.) LC Card 85-25459 DDC 333.76/13/0975 19
1. Land use, Rural - Southern States. 2. Agriculture - Economic aspects - Southern States. 3. Forests and forestry - Economic aspects - Southern States. 4. Real estate development - Southern States. 5. Soil conservation - Southern States. 6. Conservation of natural resources - Southern States. I. Title.
HD266.A13 H43 1985 ***NYPL [JLE 86-2724]***

Heard, James E. Conflicts of interest in the proxy voting system / by James E. Heard and Howard D. Sherman. Washington, D.C. : Investor Responsibility Research Center, c1987. 100 p. : ill. ; 28 cm. "March 1987"--P. [2] of cover. Bibliography: p. 87-90. ISBN 0-931035-18-X (pbk.) LC Card 87-404270 DDC 338.8/3/0973 19
1. Stockholders' voting - United States. 2. Proxy - United States. I. Sherman, Howard D. II. Investor Responsibility Research Center. III. Title.
HD2743 .H43 1987

Hearn, Frank. The transformation of industrial organization : management, labor, and society in the United States / Frank Hearn. Belmont, Calif. : Wadsworth Pub. Co., c1988. xii, 370 p. ; 24 cm. Includes bibliographies. ISBN 0-534-08160-6 (pbk.) LC Card 87-17755 DDC 306/.3 19
1. Industrial organization - United States. I. Title.
HD70.U5 H42 1988

Hearne, Dana, 1943- Parnell, Anna, 1852-1911. The tale of a great sham /. Dublin , Wick, Littlehampton, West Sussex , 1986. 205 p. ; ISBN 0-905223-93-4 LC Card 86-234070 DDC 333.33/5/09415 19
HD625 .P37 1986

The heart of business . Koestenbaum, Peter, 1928- San Francisco , New York, NY , c1987. xiii, 368 p. : ISBN 0-933071-15-9 : LC Card 87-13665 DDC 658.4/09 19
HF5351 .K584 1987

Heart rhythmogram recognition system. Sistema raspoznavanii͡a ritmogramm serdtsa . Vil′ni͡us , 1980. 55 p. : LC Card 81-194159
HD38 .S715 vyp. 49 QP112.5.C3

HEAT PUMPS - GERMANY (WEST)
Ziesing, Hans-Joachim. Beurteilung der Wirtschaftlichkeitsschwelle und Analyse der Produktionskapazitäten bei neuen Technologien zur Energieeinsparung in mittel- bis längerfristiger Sicht . Berlin , 1983. 458 p. : ISBN 3-428-05497-0
NYPL [JLL 73-207 Bd. 139]

Heath, Robert L. (Robert Lawrence), 1941- Issues management : corporate public policymaking in an information society / Robert L. Heath, Richard Alan Nelson. Beverly Hills : Sage Publications, c1986. 288 p. ; 23 cm. Includes index. Bibliography: p. 257-276. ISBN 0-8039-2535-2 LC Card 85-14547 DDC 659.2 19
1. Issues management. 2. Advocacy advertising. I. Nelson, Richard Alan, 1947-. II. Title.
HD59 .H33 1986 ***NYPL [JLD 87-19]***

Heathfield, David F. An introduction to cost and production functions / David F. Heathfield and Sören Wibe. Atlantic Highlands, NJ : Humanities Press International, 1987. xv, 193 p. : ill. ; 23 cm. Bibliography: p. 183-189. Includes index. ISBN 0-391-03506-1 LC Card 86-27587 DDC 338.5 19
1. Production functions (Economic theory). 2. Cost - Mathematical models. 3. Industrial organization (Economic theory). I. Wibe, Sören. II. Title.
HB241 .H39 1987

HEATING AND VENTILATING INDUSTRY - MANAGEMENT.
Bak, Richard, 1954- Smart contracting . Troy, Mich. , c1987. 213 p. : ISBN 0-912524-39-1 (pbk.) : LC Card 86-28327 DDC 338.4/7697 19
HD9683.A2 B35 1987

HEATING EQUIPMENT INDUSTRY - UNITED STATES.
Residential heating, ventilating & cooling systems market. New York, N.Y. , c1983. iv, 269 leaves : LC Card 87-138699 DDC 381/.45697/000973 19
HD9683.U52 R47 1983

HEATING FROM CENTRAL STATIONS - ECONOMIC ASPECTS - GERMANY (WEST)
Schröter, Klaus, 1953- Die wettbewerbspolitische Behandlung der leitungsgebundenen Energiewirtschaft . Frankfurt am Main , New York , c1986. viii, 300 p. ; ISBN 3-8204-9551-7 LC Card 87-407422 DDC 363.6/2/0943 19
HD9685.G3 S375 1986

HEATING FROM CENTRAL STATIONS - ECONOMIC ASPECTS - GERMANY (WEST) - HAMBURG.
Der Ausbau von Fernwärmenetzen und seine Wirkungen auf Arbeitsmarkt und Beschäftigung, dargestellt am Beispiel der Freien und Hansestadt Hamburg . Bonn [1983] xiv, 172 p. : LC Card 85-107700
HD5780.H34 A87 1983

Heaton, Cherrill P. Ford, Robert Clayton, 1945- Organization theory . New York , c1988. xxii, 482 p. : ISBN 0-06-042124-X LC Card 87-23796 DDC 302.3/5 19
HD31 .F5726 1988

Heaver, Richard, 1952- Country commitment to development projects / Richard Heaver, Arturo Israel. Washington, D.C., U. S.A. : World Bank, [1986] 32 p. ; 28 cm. (World Bank discussion papers, 0259-210X . 4) ISBN 0-8213-0860-2 (pbk.) LC Card 86-28114 DDC 338.91 19
1. Economic development projects - Developing countries. I. Israel, Arturo. II. Title. III. Series.
HC59.72.E44 H43 1986

The heavy engineering industry in New Zealand . Gapes, R. F. (Robert Francis) [Wellington, N.Z. , 1976] 105 p. : LC Card 84-255451
HD9705.N44 G36 1976

HEBREW LANGUAGE - DICTIONARIES - ENGLISH.
Yaḳir, E. (Eli), 1929- Milon munaḥim be-khalkalah ṿe-nihul ʻasaḳim /. Tel-Aviv , 1986. 414, 38 p. : LC Card 87-162041
HB61 .Y25 1986

HEBREWS. see **JEWS.**

Hechalutz (Organization) Dies ist das Land . [Sweden] 1946 (Lund : Berlingska Boktryckeriet) 102, [1] p., [1] folded leaf of plates : LC Card 86-225837
HD850 .D54 1946

Hecker, Christian. Abschreibungsgesellschaften in Berlin (West) : Untersuchung über wirtschaftliche und rechtliche Wirkungen von Personengesellschaften in der Rechtsform der GmbH & Co. KG und der AG & Co. KG / von Christian Hecker. Köln : P. Deubner, c1982. viii, 236, xix, 78 p. : ill. ; 23 cm. Bibliography: p. i-xix (3rd group) ISBN 3-921379-96-2 LC Card 83-197457
1. Tax incentives - Berlin (Germany). 2. Depreciation allowances - Berlin (Germany). 3. Corporations - Taxation - Berlin (Germany). 4. Depreciation allowances - Law and legislation - Berlin (Germany). I. Title.
HJ4720.B45 H43 1982

Hecker, Sid. Nonverbal communication in advertising /. Lexington, Mass. , c1988. viii, 296 p. : ISBN 0-669-14172-0 (alk. paper) LC Card 87-17143 DDC 659.1/01/9 19
HF5822 .N66 1988

Heckler, F. A. J., 1912- Meijer, H., 1904- De Deli Spoorweg Maatschappij . Zutphen , c1987. 152 p. : ISBN 90-6011-540-6 : LC Card 87-157915
HE3340.D45 M45 1987

Hedberg, Bo, 1944-
Bra affärer med datorer? . [Stockholm] , 1982. 176 p. : ISBN 91-38-06989-X LC Card 83-235564
HF5429.15 .B72 1982

Jobb i framtid? . Stockholm , c1983. 121 p. : ISBN 91-7410-270-2 : LC Card 84-103510
HC375 .J53 1983

HEDGING (FINANCE) - ACCOUNTING - STANDARDS - UNITED STATES.
Accounting for options /. New York, NY (1211 Ave. of the Americas, New York 10036-8775) [1986] 182 p., [4] p. of plates (some folded) : LC Card 86-221314 DDC 657/.76 19
HF5686.I6 A28 1986

Hedging foreign exchange . Jones, Eric T. (Eric Thomas) New York , c1987. xiv, 239 p. : ISBN 0-471-84986-3 LC Card 86-26639 DDC 332.4/5 19
HG3853 .J66 1987

Hedman, Lowe. TV-tittandet och reklamen : rapport / skriven på uppdrag av TV-reklameffektutredningen av Lowe Hedman. [Stockholm] : Liber, [1986] 83 p. : ill. ; 22 cm. At head of title: Utbildningsdepartementet. "Ds U 1986:4." Bibliography: p. 82-83. ISBN 91-38-09315-4 LC Card 86-199170
1. Television advertising. 2. Television advertising - Sweden. I. Sweden. TV-reklameffektutredningen. II. Title.
HF6146.T42 H43 1986

Hedström, Håkan, 1960- Die internationale Verschuldungskrise : Ursachen, Folgen, Lösungsansätze / Håkan Hedström. Heidelberg : HVA, [1985] xvi, 273 p. : ill. ; 21 cm. (Heidelberger Dritte welt Studien . Bd. 21) Based on the author's Diplomarbeit--Universität Heidelberg, Wintersemester 1983/84. Bibliography: p. 257-273. ISBN 3-920431-50-2 LC Card 86-122591
1. Debts, External - Developing countries. I. Title. II. Series.
HJ8899 .H43 1985

HEERN Consultants. Nigeria . Hyattsville, Md. , 1975. iii, 35 p. ; LC Card 85-114200
HC1055 .N533 1975

Heerwagen, Peter D. Self directed IRAs for the active investor / Peter D. Heerwagen. Rev. ed. Chicago, Ill. : Probus Pub. Co., c1987. x, 233 p. : ill. ; 23 cm. Includes index. ISBN 0-917253-61-2 (pbk.) : LC Card 86-25312 DDC 332.024/01 19
1. Individual retirement accounts. I. Title.
HG1660.A3 H44 1987

Heffernan, Shelagh A., 1956- Sovereign risk analysis / Shelagh A. Heffernan. London ; Boston : Allen & Unwin, 1986. xvii, 181 p. : ill. ; 23 cm. Includes index. Bibliography: p. [171]-176. ISBN 0-04-332119-4 (alk. paper) LC Card 85-32069 DDC 332.1/5/0685 19
1. Loans, Foreign - Evaluation. 2. Risk. I. Title.
HG3891.5 .H44 1986 ***NYPL [JLD 86-2957]***

Hefford, Ron. Farm policy in Australia / R.K. Hefford. St. Lucia [Brisbane] ; New York : University of Queensland Press, c1985. xviii, 415 p. : ill. ; 23 cm. Includes bibliographical references and index. ISBN 0-7022-1698-4 LC Card 83-23457 DDC 338.1/894 19
1. Agriculture and state - Australia. 2. Agriculture -

Economic aspects - Australia. I. Title.
HD2153 .H43 1984 ***NYPL [JLD 87-867]***

Hegedűs, József. Értékelemzés a termékfejlesztésben / Hegedűs József. Budapest : Műszaki Könyvkiadó, 1983. 215 p., [2] p. of plates : ill. ; 19 cm. (A Gazdasági mérnök, 0324-4210) Bibliography: p. 198-199. ISBN 963-10-5784-4 LC Card 85-110177
1. New products. 2. Value analysis (Cost control). I. Title. II. Series.
HD69.N4 H38 1983

Hegedűs, Miklós. Iparunk 40 éve /. [Budapest] , 1985. 58, [37] p. : ISBN 963-382-009-X LC Card 85-228898
HC300.28 .I64 1985

Hegedüs, Zsuzsa. Il presente è l'avvenire : nuove pratiche e nuova rappresentazione sociale / Zsuzsa Hegedus. Milano, Italy : F. Angeli, c1985. 126 p. : ill. ; 22 cm. (Documenti ISVET . 77) Includes bibliographical references. LC Card 85-215705
1. Industry - Social aspects - Forecasting. 2. Technology and civilization - Forecasting. 3. Industrial relations - Forecasting. I. Title. II. Series.
HD85.I7 I68 no. 77 HD6955
NYPL [JLD 87-427]

HEGEL, GEORG WILHELM FRIEDRICH, 1770-1831 - VIEWS ON ECONOMICS.
Hegel on economics and freedom /. Macon, Ga. , c1987. viii, 236 p. ; ISBN 0-86554-256-2 (alk. paper) : LC Card 87-7887 DDC 330.1 19
HB107.H38 H44 1987

HEGEL, GEORG WILHELM FRIEDRICH, 1770-1831 - VIEWS ON LIBERTY.
Hegel on economics and freedom /. Macon, Ga. , c1987. viii, 236 p. ; ISBN 0-86554-256-2 (alk. paper) : LC Card 87-7887 DDC 330.1 19
HB107.H38 H44 1987

Hegel on economics and freedom / edited by William Maker. Macon, Ga. : Mercer University Press, c1987. viii, 236 p. ; 24 cm. Includes bibliographical references and index. ISBN 0-86554-256-2 (alk. paper) : LC Card 87-7887 DDC 330.1 19
1. Hegel, Georg Wilhelm Friedrich, 1770-1831 - Views on economics. 2. Hegel, Georg Wilhelm Friedrich, 1770-1831 - Views on liberty. I. Maker, William.
HB107.H38 H44 1987

Hegelheimer, Armin. Gleichwertigkeit von allgemeiner und beruflicher Bildung / Armin Hegelheimer ; herausgegeben vom Bundesminister für Bildung und Wissenschaft. Bonn : Der Bundesminister ; Bad Honnef : Vertrieb, K.H. Bock, 1986. v, 74 p. ; 21 cm. (Schriftenreihe Studien zu Bildung und Wissenschaft, 0175-8055 . 40) Bibliography: p. 72-74. ISBN 3-87066-628-5 : LC Card 87-409371 DDC 331.4/2592/0943 19
1. Occupational training for women - Germany (West). 2. Vocational guidance for women - Germany, West. 3. Professional education of women - Germany (West). I. Germany (West). Bundesministerium für Bildung und Wissenschaft. II. Title. III. Series.
HD6059.6.G4 H42 1986

Hegelheimer, Barbara. Berufsqualifikation und Berufschancen von Frauen in der Bundesrepublik Deutschland / Barbara Hegelheimer. Berlin : Max-Planck-Institut für Bildungsforschung, 1977. viii, 303 p. ; 30 cm. (Materialien aus der Bildungsforschung . Nr. 11) Bibliography: p. 287-303. LC Card 85-142052
1. Occupational training for women - Germany (West). 2. Vocational guidance for women - Germany, West. 3. Women - Employment - Germany, West. I. Max-Planck-Institut für Bildungsforschung. II. Title. III. Series.
HD6059.6.G4 H428 1977

Heggade, Odeyar D. Cherunilam, Francis. Housing in India /. Bombay , 1987. vi, 168 p. ; LC Card 86-903722 DDC 363.5/0954 19
HD7361.A3 C46 1987

Heggestad, Arnold A., 1943- Public policy toward corporations /. Gainesville , 1987. p. cm. ISBN 0-8130-0880-8 LC Card 87-21324 DDC 338.973 19
HD3616.U47 P82 1987

Hegner, Friedhart. Burian, Klaus. Betriebliche Erfahrungen mit neuen Arbeitszeitformen . Berlin [1984] iv, 162 p. ; LC Card 84-182592
HD5110.2.G3 B87 1984

Hegrenes, Agnar. Mekaniseringsøkonomi på enkeltbruk / av Agnar Hegrenes = Mechanisation economics for individual farms. Oslo : Norges landbruksøkonomiske institutt, 1985. 175 p. : ill. ; 21 cm. Summary in English. Bibliography: p. 169-175. ISBN 82-7077-028-0 LC Card 86-180961
1. Farm mechanization - Norway. 2. Agriculture - Economic aspects - Norway. I. Title. II. Title: Mechanisation economics for individual farms.
HD2012 .H44 1985

Hegyi, András.
Agrárgazdaság, agrártársadalom, agrárpolitika /. Szeged , 1985. 338 p. : ISBN 963-481-548-0 : LC Card 86-143859
HD1940.5 .A78 1985

Két évtized . Szeged , 1987. 116 p., [67] p. of plates : LC Card 87-407665
HD1492.H82 C765 1987

Hegyi, Anna. A külkereskedő vállalat / Somogyiné Hegyi Anna. Budapest : Közgazdasági és Jogi Könyvkiadó, 1985. 213, [1] p., [1] folded leaf of plates : ill. ; 25 cm. Bibliography: p. 209-[214] ISBN 963-221-531-1 : LC Card 86-187063
1. Trading companies - Hungary. I. Title.
HF1009.7.H8 H44 1985

Heibült, Uwe. Bopp-Schmehl, Annemarie, 1946- Technische Normung und Verbraucherinteressen im gesellschaftlichen Wandel /. Frankfurt am Main , c1984. iii, 269 p. ; ISBN 3-88129-834-7 : LC Card 85-119483
HC290.5.C6 B66 1984

Heidelberg. Universität. Stand der grenzüberschreitenden Raumordnung am Oberrhein /. [Heidelberg] , 1981. 105 p. : ISBN 3-88570-071-9 LC Card 81-197772 DDC 361.6/0943/4 19
HT395.G4 S735 1981
NYPL [L-10 4979 Heft 71]

Heidelberger betriebswirtschaftliche Studien.
Laux, Helmut. Grundfragen der Erfolgskontrolle /. Berlin , New York , c1986. x, 161 p. : ISBN 0-387-17037-5 LC Card 86-232406
HD30.23 .L39 1986

Heidelberger Dritte welt Studien .
(Bd. 16) Knapp, Johannes, 1953- Argentinien und Australien . Heidelberg , c1983. 151 p. : ISBN 3-88326-129-7 LC Card 83-240132
HC175 .K58 1983

(Bd. 20) Struktur- und Entwicklungsprobleme der Industrie Perus /. Heidelberg , c1985. 338 p. : ISBN 3-88326-165-3 LC Card 86-108518 DDC 338.0985 19
HC227 .S77 1985

(Bd. 21) Hedström, Håkan, 1960- Die internationale Verschuldungskrise . Heidelberg [1985] xvi, 273 p. : ISBN 3-920431-50-2 LC Card 86-122591
HJ8899 .H43 1985

Heidelberger geographische Arbeiten. For additional listing of contents, see Old Catalog.
(Heft 68) König, Robert. Die Wohnflächenbestände der Gemeinden der Vorderpfalz . Heidelberg , 1980. [14], 226 p. : ISBN 3-88570-068-9 LC Card 81-136631 DDC 333.73/13/0724 19
HD659.P34 K66 1980
NYPL [L-10 4979 Heft 68]

(Heft 71) Stand der grenzüberschreitenden Raumordnung am Oberrhein /. [Heidelberg] , 1981. 105 p. : ISBN 3-88570-071-9 LC Card 81-197772 DDC 361.6/0943/4 19
HT395.G4 S735 1981
NYPL [L-10 4979 Heft 71]

Heidelberger Lehrtexte. Wirtschaftswissenschaften.
Gál, Tomáš. Mathematik für Wirtschaftswissenschaftler. Berlin , New York , c1986. xi, 160 p. : ISBN 0-387-16381-6 (U. S.) LC Card 86-208763
HB135 .G35 1986

Heidelberger Wegweiser.
Spinnarke, Jürgen. Soziale Sicherheit in der Bundesrepublik Deutschland . Heidelberg , c1985. 142 p. : ISBN 3-8114-1085-7 : LC Card 86-103725
HD7179 .S63 1985

Heidemann, Claus. Heinzmann, Ute. Umzugsverhalten der Bevölkerung in ausgewählten ländlichen Teilräumen am Beispiel der Region Neckar-Alb . Tübingen , 1985. 69, [4] p. : LC Card 86-195573
HB2056.N43 H45 1985

The Heights . Baxter, Ellen. New York, N.Y. [1986] 69 leaves : LC Card 87-401534 DDC 363.5/8 19
HD7287.96.U62 N683 1986

HEIGHTS, THE (NEW YORK, N. Y.)
Baxter, Ellen. The Heights . New York, N.Y. [1986] 69 leaves : LC Card 87-401534 DDC 363.5/8 19
HD7287.96.U62 N683 1986

Heijmans, Risto. The Practice of econometrics . Dordrecht , Boston , 1987. xii, 273 p. : ISBN 90-247-3502-5 LC Card 87-4054 DDC 330/.028 19
HB139 .P7 1987

Heil, Johann. Einführung in die Ökonometrie / von Johann Heil. München : R. Oldenbourg, c1984. 320 p. : ill. ; 24 cm. Bibliography: p. [315]-317. Includes index. ISBN 3-486-28801-6 (pbk.) LC Card 87-672731
1. Econometrics. I. Title.
HB139 .H44x 1984

Heilbroner, Robert L.
Behind the veil of economics : essays in the worldly philosophy / Robert L. Heilbroner. New York : W.W. Norton, 1988. p. cm. Includes index. ISBN 0-393-02542-X LC Card 87-20392 DDC 330.12/2 19
1. Capitalism. 2. Economics. I. Title.
HB501 .H396 1988

Economics explained / Robert L. Heilbroner and Lester C. Thurow. Updated ed., updated Touchstone ed. New York : Simon & Schuster, 1987. 250 p. : ill. ; 22 cm. (A Touchstone book) Includes index. ISBN 0-671-64556-0 (pbk.) LC Card 87-12807 DDC 330 19
1. Economics. 2. United States - Economic conditions - 1945-. I. Thurow, Lester C. II. Title.
HB171 .H479 1987

Smith, Adam, 1723-1790. [Selections. 1986.] The essential Adam Smith /. Oxford [Oxfordshire] , New York , 1986. p. cm. ISBN 0-19-877270-X : LC Card 86-23856 DDC 330.15/3 19
HB161 .S6522 1986b

Heilbronner Museumshefte. see **Heilbronner Museumshefte.**

HEILBRONN (GERMANY) - HISTORY.
Sinzinger, Friedrich, 1911- Heilbronner Postgeschichte bis zur Einführung der Briefmarke 1851 /. Heilbronn , c1984. 133 p. : LC Card 87-409273 DDC 383/.494346 19
HE6185.G32 H457 1984

Heilbronner Museumshefte.
(Nr. 10) Sinzinger, Friedrich, 1911- Heilbronner Postgeschichte bis zur Einführung der Briefmarke 1851 /. Heilbronn , c1984. 133 p. : LC Card 87-409273 DDC 383/.494346 19
HE6185.G32 H457 1984

Heilbronner Postgeschichte bis zur Einführung der Briefmarke 1851 /. Sinzinger, Friedrich, 1911- Heilbronn , c1984. 133 p. : LC Card 87-409273 DDC 383/.494346 19
HE6185.G32 H457 1984

Heilbrunner, Christina. Schauer, Reinbert. Die Verwaltung als betriebliches Teilsystem . Wien , 1984. v, 258 p. : ISBN 3-85436-014-2 LC Card 84-173337
HD35 .S2655 1984

Heilig, Bernd. Die gesamtwirtschaftliche Bedeutung der Agrar- und Ernährungswirtschaft : Möglichkeiten der empirischen Untersuchung mit Hilfe der Input-Output-Analyse / Bernd Heilig. Kiel : Wissenschaftsverlag Vauk, 1986. 171 p. : ill. ; 21 cm. Bibliography: p. 167-171. ISBN 3-922553-80-X LC Card 86-177526
1. Agricultural productivity - Germany (West). 2. Input-output analysis. I. Title.
HD1955 .H38 1986

Heilmann, Martin. Lorenz von Stein und die Grundprobleme der Steuerlehre : ein Beitrag zur Geschichte der Finanzwissenschaft / von Martin Heilmann. Heidelberg : R.v. Decker, 1984. xi, 577 p. ; 24 cm. (Schriftenreihe des

Lorenz-von-Stein-Instituts für Verwaltungswissenschaften Kiel . Bd. 3) The author's Habilitationsschrift--Christian-Albrechts-Universität zu Kiel. Bibliography: p. 537-558. Includes indexes. ISBN 3-7685-0184-1 LC Card 84-236751
1. Stein, Lorenz von, 1815-1890. 2. Taxation. I. Title. II. Series.
HJ2309 .H36 1984

Heilmann, Ronald L. Great Lakes transportation in the eighties / Ronald L. Heilmann, Harold M. Mayer, Eric Schenker, with the collaboration of Patricia F. Rieselbach. Madison, WI : University of Wisconsin Sea Grant Institute, c1986. 100 p. : ill. ; 26 cm. ([Sea grant] technical report. no.) Bibliography: p. [95]-98. Includes index. ISBN 0-936287-00-4 (pbk.) : LC Card 86-622259 DDC 386/.544/0977 19
1. Shipping - Great Lakes. 2. Great Lakes region - Economic conditions. I. Mayer, Harold M. (Harold Melvin), 1916-. II. Schenker, Eric, 1931-. III. Series: Sea grant technical report (University of Wisconsin Sea Grant Institute) , no. 85-242. IV. Title.
HE398 .H45 1986

Heiman, Stephen E. Miller, Robert B. (Robert Bruce), 1931- Conceptual selling . Berkeley, Calif. , New York, N.Y. , c1987. 320 p. : ISBN 0-8050-0410-6 LC Card 86-29428 DDC 658.8/5 19
HF5438.25 .M566 1987

Heimat und Fremde . Höher, Peter. Münster , 1985. viii, 414 p., [1] p. of plates : ISBN 3-88547-290-2 LC Card 85-160726 DDC 381/.0943/42 19
HF3569.S28 H64 1985

Die heimliche Wirtschaft . Weck-Hannemann, Hannelore. Bern , c1986. 112 p. : ISBN 3-258-03541-5 LC Card 86-159961
HD2346.S9 W43 1986

Hein, Peter Ulrich. Protestkultur und Jugend : Ästhetische Opposition in der Bundesrepublik Deutschland / Peter Ulrich Hein ; unter Mitarbeit von Maria Eva Jahn. Münster : Lit, 1984. iii, 151 p. ; 21 cm. (Geschichte der Jugend . Bd. 9) Includes bibliographical references. ISBN 3-88660-109-9
1. Youth - Germany (West) - Attitudes. 2. Youth - Germany, West - Political activity. I. Title. II. Series.
NYPL [JLD 86-2444]

Heindl, Wolfgang, 1951- Die Haushalte von Reich, Ländern und Gemeinden in Deutschland von 1925 bis 1933 : öffentliche Haushalte und Krisenverschärfung / Wolfgang Heindl. Frankfurt am Main ; New York : P. Lang, c1984. 419 p. : ill. ; 21 cm. (Europäische Hochschulschriften. Reihe V, Volks- und Betriebswirtschaft, 0531-7339 . Bd. 565 = vol. 565 = vol. 565) Bibliography: p. 410-419. ISBN 3-8204-5474-8 LC Card 85-198505
1. Finance, Public - Germany - History - 20th century. 2. Business cycles - Germany - History - 20th century. 3. Germany - Economic policy - 1918-1933. 4. Germany - Social policy. I. Series: Europäische Hochschulschriften. Reihe V, Volks- und Betriebswirtschaft , Bd. 565. II. Title.
HJ1119 .H36 1984

Heineberg, Heinz.
Beiträge zur empirischen Bürostandortforschung /. Kallmünz , 1983. 167 p. : ISBN 3-7847-6050-3 : LC Card 84-176770
HF5547.25 .B45 1983

Neue Einkaufszentren im Ruhrgebiet : vergleichende Analysen der Planung, Ausstattung und Inanspruchnahme der 21 grössten Shopping-Center / Heinz Heineberg und Alois Mayr. Paderborn : Schöningh, 1986. 247 p. : ill. ; 30 cm. (Münstersche geographische Arbeiten, 0176-1064 . Heft 24) Bibliography: p. 219-222. ISBN 3-506-73224-2 LC Card 87-407591 DDC 381/.1/094355 19
1. Shopping centers - Germany (West) - Ruhr (Region). I. Mayr, Alois. II. Title. III. Series.
HF5430.6.G4 H45 1986

Heinecke, P.
Development administration in Nigeria : radical essays / by P. Heinecke.4th ed. [Nigeria : s.n., 1985?] 201 p. ; 24 cm. Includes bibliographies. LC Card 86-207544 DDC 338.9669 19
1. Nigeria - Economic policy. 2. Nigeria - Economic conditions - 1970-. I. Title.
HC1055 .H446 1985

Freedom in the grave : Nigeria and the political economy of Africa / by P. Heinecke.3rd ed. [Zaria, Nigeria] : P. Heinecke, [1985] 178 p. ; 25 cm. LC Card 86-153310 DDC 337.66906 19
1. Nigeria - Economic conditions - 1970-. 2. Nigeria - Politics and government - 1979-. 3. Nigeria - Social conditions - 1960-. 4. Africa - Economic conditions - 1960-. 5. Africa - Politics and government - 1960-. 6. Africa - Social conditions - 1960-. I. Title.
HC1055 .H45 1985

Heineken, Hermann. Der Salzhandel Lüneburgs mit Lübeck bis zum Anfang des 15. Jahrhunderts / von Hermann Heineken. Vaduz : Kraus Reprint, 1965. 150 p. ; 23 cm. Includes text in Latin. Reprint. Originally published: Berlin : E. Ebering, 1908. (Historische Studien ; Heft 63) Bibliography: p. [9]-13. LC Card 86-231350
1. Salt industry and trade - Germany (West) - Lüneburg - History. 2. Salt industry and trade - Germany (West) - Lübeck - History. 3. Lüneburg (Germany) - Commerce - History. 4. Lübeck (Germany) - Commerce - History. I. Series: Historische Studien (Matthiesen Verlag) , Heft 63. II. Title.
HD9213.G43 L864 1965

Heineman report on income maintenance. United States. President's Commission on Income Maintenance Programs. Poverty amid plenty, the American paradox. [Washington] 1969. ix, 155 p. LC Card 71-605334 DDC 362.5/0973
HC110.P63 A59 ***NYPL [JLF 86-478]***

Heinemeier, Meredith M.
Tretyakova, Albina. Cost estimates for the Soviet gas industry, 1970 to 1990 /. Washington, D.C. [1986] vii, 116 p. ; LC Card 87-601292 DDC 338.2/3 19
HD9581.S652 T74 1986

1977 consumption by industrial sector / by Meredith Heinemeier. Washington, D.C. : Center for International Research, U. S. Bureau of the Census, [1986] vii, 148 p. ; 28 cm. (CIR staff paper . no. 13) "January 1986." Bibliography: p. 141-148. LC Card 87-601286 DDC 339.2/3/0947 19
1. Input-output tables - Soviet Union. 2. Consumption (Economics) - Soviet Union. I. Title. II. Series.
HC340.I57 H45 1986

Heinen, Edmund.
Betriebswirtschaftliche Entscheidungen bei Stagnation . Wiesbaden , c1984. xvi, 327 p. : ISBN 3-409-13303-8 LC Card 84-197990
HD30.23 .B486 1984

Marzen, Walter. Betriebswirtschaftliche Forschung und Wirtschaftspraxis . Spardorf , c1986. ix, 229 p. ; ISBN 3-922919-82-0 LC Card 87-133392 DDC 658.4 19
HD35 .M276 1986

HEINEN, EDMUND.
Betriebswirtschaftliche Entscheidungen bei Stagnation . Wiesbaden , c1984. xvi, 327 p. : ISBN 3-409-13303-8 LC Card 84-197990
HD30.23 .B486 1984

Heinhuis, D. Mauretanië / D. Heinhuis, M.N. Heinhuis-Leeuwin. Amsterdam : Koninklijk Instiuut voor de Tropen ; 's-Gravenhage : Staatsuitgeverij, 1985. 46 p., [1] folded leaf of plates : ill., maps ; 24 cm. (Landendocumentatie. 1985, nr. 5) Bibliography: p. 45-46. ISBN 90-12-05188-6 LC Card 86-174578
1. Mauritania - Economic conditions. I. Heinhuis-Leeuwin, M. N. II. Title.
HC1050 .H45 1985

Heinhuis-Leeuwin, M. N. Heinhuis, D. Mauretanië /. Amsterdam , 's-Gravenhage , 1985. 46 p., [1] folded leaf of plates : ISBN 90-12-05188-6 LC Card 86-174578
HC1050 .H45 1985

Heinonen, Kerstin. Systemet med särskilda dragningsrätter : dess utveckling, egenskaper och framtid / Kerstin Heinonen. Helsingfors : Finlands bank, 1985. 65 p. ; 26 cm. (Finlands banks publikationer. Serie A, 0355-6034 . A:60) Summary in English. Bibliography: p. [59]-62. ISBN 951-686-112-1 LC Card 86-175395
1. Special drawing rights. 2. International finance. I. Title.
HG3898 .H45 1985

Heinrich, Hans, 1952- Optimale valutaområder / Hans Heinrich. [Odense] : Universitas Othiniensis, Institut for nationaløkonomi og sociologi, 1984. 142 p. : ill. ; 21 cm. Bibliography: p. 134-137. Includes index. ISBN 87-981541-2-5 : LC Card 85-129406
1. Foreign exchange. 2. Foreign exchange administration - Denmark. I. Title.
HG3957 .H45 1984

Heinrich, Herbert, 1938- Arbeitsbewertung und Disziplinierung : die Praxis der Arbeitsbewertung im Angestelltenbereich und der Wirkungsmechanismus der latenten Disziplinierung / Herbert Heinrich. Spardorf : R.F. Wilfer, c1985. v, 281 p. ; 21 cm. (Schriften zu Macht, Konflikt, technischem und sozialem Wandel in Organisationen . Bd. 6) Errata slip laid in. Bibliography: p. 255-261. Includes index. ISBN 3-922919-67-7 LC Card 86-162759
1. Job evaluation - Germany (West). 2. Labor discipline - Germany, West. 3. Collective labor agreements - Television broadcasting - Germany (West). I. Title. II. Series.
HF5549.5.J62 H36 1985

Heinrich, Lutz J. (Lutz Jürgen)
Wirtschaftsinformatik-Lexikon / von Lutz J. Heinrich und Friedrich Roithmayr. München : R. Oldenbourg, c1986. xxi, 539 p. : ill. ; 25 cm. Includes indexes. ISBN 3-486-20045-3 LC Card 87-122992 DDC 330/.03/31 19
1. Economics - Dictionaries. I. Roithmayr, Friedrich. II. Title.
HB61 .H365 1986

Heinritz, Günter. Standorte und Einzugsbereiche tertiärer Einrichtungen . Damrstadt , 1985. vi, 403 p., [1] folded leaf of plates : ISBN 3-534-08402-0 LC Card 86-228150
HF5547.25 .S73 1985

Heinsohn, Gunnar. Privateigentum, Patriarchat, Geldwirtschaft : eine sozialtheoretische Rekonstruktion zur Antike / Gunnar Heinsohn.1. Aufl. Frankfurt am Main : Suhrkamp, 1984. 218 p. ; 18 cm. (Suhrkamp Taschenbuch Wissenschaft. 455) Bibliography: p. 188-[203] Includes indexes. ISBN 3-518-28055-4 : LC Card 84-150578
1. Economic history - To 500. 2. Right of property - History. 3. Money - History. I. Title.
HC31 .H45 1984

Heintzeler, Wolfgang. Der rote Faden : fünf Jahrzehnte, Staatsdienst, Wehrmacht, chemische Industrie, Nürnberg, Marktwirtschaft, Mitbestimmung, Kirche / Wolfgang Heintzeler. Stuttgart : Seewald, c1983. 292 p. ; 22 cm. Includes bibliographical references. ISBN 3-512-00664-7 LC Card 83-183709
1. Heintzeler, Wolfgang. 2. Badische Anilin- & Soda-Fabrik - History. 3. Chemical industry - Germany (West) - History. 4. Businessman - Germany (West) - Biography. I. Title.
HD9654.9.B27 H45 1983

HEINTZELER, WOLFGANG.
Heintzeler, Wolfgang. Der rote Faden . Stuttgart , c1983. 292 p. ; ISBN 3-512-00664-7 LC Card 83-183709
HD9654.9.B27 H45 1983

Heinz, Rudolf. Hermesiade . Essen , c1986. 182 p. ; ISBN 3-89206-143-2 LC Card 86-226901 DDC 658.8/2 19
HF5438.5 .H47 1986

Heinz, Werner, Dr. phil., Dipl.-Ing. Echter, Claus-Peter. Konzepte städtischer Wohnungspolitik . Berlin , 1985. 97 p. : ISBN 3-88118-123-7 LC Card 86-145702
HD7288.78.G3 E265 1985

Heinze, Rolf G., 1951- Arbeitslosigkeit in der Arbeitsgesellschaft /. Frankfurt am Main , 1984. 350 p. ; ISBN 3-518-11212-0 : LC Card 84-192978
HD5708 .A72 1984

Heinzmann, Ute. Umzugsverhalten der Bevölkerung in ausgewählten ländlichen Teilräumen am Beispiel der Region Neckar-Alb : Kurzbericht über die Ergebnisse eines Forschungsvorhabens des Instituts für Regionalwissenschaft der Universität Karlsruhe / Ute Heinzmann und Claus Heidemann. Tübingen : IRB Verlag, 1985. 69, [4] p. : ill., maps ; 30 cm. (Veröffentlichung Nr. 159 der Forschungsgemeinschaft Bauen und Wohnen, Stuttgart) Forschungsbericht / IRB At head of title: Regionalverband Neckar-Alb. Bibliography: p. [70]-[73] LC Card 86-195573
1. Migration, Internal - Germany (West) - Neckar River (Region). I. Heidemann, Claus. II. Universität Karlsruhe. Institut für Regionalwissenschaft. III. Regionalverband Neckar-Alb. IV. Series: Veröffentlichung der Forschungsgemeinschaft Bauen

und Wohnen, Stuttgart , Nr. 159. V. Title.
HB2056.N43 H45 1985

Heipel, Gerd. Nichtkapitalistische Produktionsverhältnisse und Konkurrenz : die Entwicklung des Kapitalismus im Kaffeesektor von São Paulo, 1822-1967 / Gerd Heipel. Pfaffenweiler : Centaurus-Verlagsgesellschaft, 1986. vii, 459 p. ; 21 cm. (Reihe Sozialwissenschaften, 0177-2813 . Bd. 8) Bibliography: p. 444-459. ISBN 3-89085-116-9 LC Card 86-171832
1. Coffee trade - Brazil - São Paulo (State) - History. I. Title. II. Series.
HD9199.B8 S22 1986

Heiratstafeln versus Familienstandstafeln . Schweitzer, Walter. Wiesbaden , 1985. iii, 102 p. : LC Card 87-408703 DDC 306.8/1/0943021 19
HB1215 .S39 1985

HEIRS. see **INHERITANCE AND SUCCESSION.**

Heirs, Ben J. The professional decision-thinker : America's new management and education priority / Ben Heirs with Peter Farrell.1st ed. New York : Dodd Mead, c1987. xiv, 294 ; 24 cm. Originally published: Great Britain : Sidgwick & Jackson, 1986. Bibliography: p. [293]-294. ISBN 0-396-09203-9 : LC Card 87-15575 DDC 658.4/03 19
1. Decision-making. I. Farrell, Peter. II. Title.
HD30.23 .H445 1987

Heitger, Bernhard. Strukturwandel und realer Wechselkurs : ein Zwei-Sektoren-Modell im Test / Bernhard Heitger. Tübingen : Mohr (P. Siebeck), c1983. vii, 115 p. : ill. ; 24 cm. (Kieler Studien, 0340-6989 . 183) Bibliography: p. 106-115. ISBN 3-16-344735-X : LC Card 84-125132
1. Foreign exchange - Econometric models. 2. Foreign exchange problem - Germany (West) - Econometric models. I. Title. II. Series.
HG3823 .H43 1983

Heitmann, John Alfred. The modernization of the Louisiana sugar industry, 1830-1910 / John Alfred Heitmann. Baton Rouge : Louisiana State University Press, c1987. xii, 298 p. : ill. ; 24 cm. Bibliography: p. 273-289. Includes index. ISBN 0-8071-1324-7 LC Card 86-27639 DDC 338.4/56641/09763 19
1. Sugar trade - Louisiana - Technological innovations - History. I. Title.
HD9107.L8 H45 1987

Helberger, Christof. Beitragsäquivalenz oder interpersonelle Umverteilung in der gesetzlichen Rentenversicherung? : eine Analyse auf der Grundlage von Lebenseinkommen : Beitrag zur Tagung des Sozialpolitischen Ausschusses der Gesellschaft für Wirtschafts- und Sozialwissenschaften am 25./26. Sept. 1980 in Wien / Christof Helberger, Gert Wagner. Berlin : Wirtschaftwissenschaftliche Dokumentation, Technische Universität Berlin, 1981. 96 p. ; 30 cm. (Diskussionspapier / Wirtschaftswissenschaftliche Dokumentation, Technische Universität Berlin . 63) "Erscheint in Ph. Herder-Dorneich (Hrsg.), Intertemporaler Ausgleich in der Sozialpolitik, Berlin, München". Bibliography: p. 93-96. LC Card 81-201422 DDC 331.25/2/0943 19
1. Old age pensions - Germany (West) - Mathematical models. 2. Income distribution - Germany, West - Mathematical models. I. Wagner, Gert. II. Series: Diskussionspapier (Technische Universität Berlin. Wirtschaftswissenschaftliche Dokumentation) , 63. III. Title.
HD7105.35.G3 H44 1981
NYPL [JLM 81-818 v.63]

Helbert, Jean-Pierre, 1947- L'insurrection des patrons / Jean-Pierre Helbert ; préface de René Monory. Châteaugiron : Y. Salmon, 1984. 165 p. ; 24 cm. Errata slip inserted. Bibliography: p. 165. ISBN 2-903414-33-5 LC Card 85-180275 DDC 658/.006/044 19
1. Employers' associations - France. 2. Business and politics - France. I. Title.
HD6948.F8 H45 1984 ***NYPL [JLE 86-526]***

Held, Daniel. Marché de l'emploi : entreprises et régions / Daniel Held et Denis Maillat.1re éd. Lausanne : Presses polytechniques romandes, 1984. 205 p. : ill. ; 24 cm. (Collection "Villes, régions et sociétés") Bibliography: p. [197]-200. ISBN 2-88074-028-2
1. Labor supply - Switzerland. 2. Regional planning - Switzerland. I. Maillat, Denis. II. Title.
NYPL [JLE 86-679]

Held, Karl, 1944- Krieg und Frieden : politische Ökonomie des Weltfriedens / Karl Held, Theo Ebel.Erstausg. Frankfurt am Main : Suhrkamp, c1983. 324 p. ; 18 cm. (Edition Suhrkamp. 1149, n.F., Bd. 149) ISBN 3-518-11149-3 : LC Card 83-228517
1. Armaments - Economic aspects. 2. Imperialism. 3. Developing countries - Dependency on foreign countries. 4. Germany (West) - Foreign economic relations - Developing countries. 5. Developing countries - Foreign economic relations - Germany (West). 6. North Atlantic Treaty Organization. I. Ebel, Theo, 1942-. II. Title.
HC79.D4 H45 1983

Held, Martin, Dr. Technik von gestern für die Ziele von morgen? . Opladen , c1986. 153 p. ; ISBN 3-531-11713-0 LC Card 86-230906
HD9502.A2 T43 1986

Heldman, Robert K. Telecommunications management planning : ISDN networks, products, and services / Robert K. Heldman.1st ed. Blue Ridge Summit, PA : TAB Professional and Reference Books, c1987. xviii, 734 p. : ill. ; 25 cm. Includes index. ISBN 0-8306-2864-9 : LC Card 86-30002 DDC 658.4/038 19
1. Management - Communication systems - Planning. 2. Business enterprises - Communication systems - Planning. 3. Management information systems - Planning. 4. Telecommunication systems. 5. Telemarketing. I. Title.
HD30.335 .H45 1987

Heldt, Sven. Die Wirtschaftsplanung Gabuns / von Sven Heldt. Kiel : Institut für Weltwirtschaft an der Universität Kiel, 1978. 31 leaves ; 30 cm. (Kieler Arbeitspapiere . Arbeitspapier Nr. 70 =) Includes bibliographical references. LC Card 85-238709
1. Gabon - Economic policy. 2. Gabon - Economic conditions - 1960-. I. Series: Kieler Arbeitspapiere , Arbeitspapier Nr. 70. II. Title.
HC975 .H45 1978

Helen of delen . Korteweg, Hans. Amsterdam , 1986, c1985. 222 p. ; ISBN 90-254-6652-4 : LC Card 86-182872
HD58.8 .K66 1986

Helfert, Erich A. Techniques of financial analysis / Erich A. Helfert. 6th ed. Homewood, Ill. : Irwin, 1987. xiii, 458 p. : ill. ; 23 cm. Includes bibliographies and index. ISBN 0-256-03625-X (pbk.) LC Card 86-82589 DDC 658.1/51 19
1. Corporations - Finance. 2. Cash flow. 3. Financial statements. 4. Ratio analysis. I. Title.
HG4026 .H44 1987

Helfert, Mario. Wertewandel, Arbeit, technischer Fortschritt, Wachstum / Mario Helfert. Köln : Bund-Verlag, c1986. 149 p. : ill. ; 21 cm. (WSI-Studie zur Wirtschafts- und Sozialforschung . Nr. 50) Bibliography: p. 125-149. ISBN 3-7663-3010-1 LC Card 87-134855 DDC 331.12 19
1. Labor supply - Effect of automation. 2. Industry - Social aspects. 3. Work ethic. I. Title. II. Series.
HD6331 .H37 1986

Helgerson, Linda W. Market report on scanning products & systems /. Falls Church, VA (6609 Rosecroft Pl., Falls Church 22043) [1986]- 1 v. (loose-leaf) ; LC Card 87-151419 DDC 338.7/61006424 19
HD9696.O672 M37 1986

Helgi Magnússon. Hafskip, gjörningar og gæsluvarðhald / Helgi Magnússon. Reykjavík : Frjálst framtak, 1986. 272 p. : ill. ; 24 cm. Errata slip inserted. Includes index. LC Card 87-117447
1. Hafskip hf. 2. Shipping - Iceland. I. Title.
HE945.H19 H45 1986

Heligman, Larry. Methodologies for the collection and analysis of mortality data . Liège, Belgium , 1984. vi, 510 p. : ISBN 2-87040-032-2 (pbk.) LC Card 86-205582 DDC 304.6/4/072 19
HB1321 .M48 1984

Helios Productions.
Contract for life, the S.A.D.D. story [motion picture] /. Los Angeles, CA , 1985. 1 film reel (31 min.) : LC Card 85-700743 DDC 363.1 11
HE5620.D7

Contract for life, the S.A.D.D story [videorecording] /. Los Angeles, CA , 1985. 1 videocassette (31 min.) : LC Card 85-700744 DDC 363.1 11
HE5620.D7

Hē Hellada stēn Eurōpaikē Koinotēta : hē prōtē pentaetia : taseis, provlēmata, prooptikes / eisagōgē-epimeleia P. Kazakos, K. Stephanou. Athēna : Ekdoseis A.N. Sakkoula, 1987. 14, 565 p. ; 24 cm. (Hellēnikē Hetaireia Diethnous Dikaiou kai Diethnōn Scheseōn . 2) Title on added t.p.: Greece in the European Community. Includes bibliographical references. LC Card 87-169443
1. European Economic Community - Greece. I. Kazakos, Panos V. II. Stephanou, K. (Kōnstantinos). III. Title: Greece in the European Community. IV. Series: Hellēnikē Hetaireia Diethnous Dikaiou kai Diethnōn Scheseōn (Series) , 2.
HC241.25.G8 H43 1987

Hē Hellada stēn Eurōpē . Kontogeōrgēs, Geōrgios L. [Athens] [1985] 311 p. : LC Card 86-206722
HC241.25.G8 K65 1985

Hellēnikē emporikē nautalia, 1833-1856 . Papathanasopoulos, Kōnstantinos, 1950- Athēna , 1983. 470 p., [32] p. of plates : LC Card 83-237694
HE872.5 .P36 1983

Hellēnikē Geōgraphikē Hetaireia (Athens, Greece) Moustakas, Dion. E. Hai ploutoparagōgikai dynameis tēs nēsou Androu /. En Athēnais , 1924. 25 p. : LC Card 87-100195
HC297.A53 M68 1924

Hellēnikē Hetaireia Diethnous Dikaiou kai Diethnōn Scheseōn (Series) .
(2) Hē Hellada stēn Eurōpaikē Koinotēta . Athēna , 1987. 14, 565 p. ; LC Card 87-169443
HC241.25.G8 H43 1987

Hellēnikē Hetairia Dēmographikōn Meletōn. Dēmographikē Hēmerida (1984 : Athens, Greece) Hē Dēmographikē krisē stēn Hellada . Athēna , 1985. 205 p. : LC Card 86-192606
HB3632.5.A3 D45 1984

Hellēnikē Hetairia Dēmographikōn Meletōn (Greece) Dēmographikē Hēmerida (1984 : Athens, Greece) Hē Dēmographikē krisē stēn Hellada . Athēna , 1986. 205 p. : LC Card 86-201713
HB3632.5.A3 D45 1986

Hellēnikē Hetairia Dioikēseōs Epicheirēseōn. Hellēniko Institouto Marketinnk. Hodēgos marketinnk Hellados, 1983 /. Athēnai [1983?] 357 p. ; LC Card 84-107807
HF5415.12.G8 H63 1983

Hellēnikē koinōnia .
(3) Mousourou, Loukia M. Gynaikeia apascholēsē kai oikogeneia stēn Hellada kai allou /. Athēna , c1985. 220 p. : LC Card 86-205975
HD6181.83 .M68 1985

Hellēnikē nautilia, 1776-1835 /. Kremmydas, Vasilēs. Athēna , 1985-<1986. v. <1-2 > : LC Card 86-211031
HE872.5 .K74 1985

Hellēnikē Trapeza Viomēchanikēs Anaptyxaeōs (Greece) Hē Eurōpē tōn 10. [Athenai] [1981] 37 p. : LC Card 86-184401
HC241.25.G8 H42 1981

Hellēnikē Trapeza Viomēchanikēs Anaptyxeōs (Greece)
Hē drasteriotēta tēs ETVA to etos 1985. [Athēna] : Hē Trapeza, [1985] 43 p. ; 28 cm. Includes (1 folded leaf in pocket); Isologismos 31-12-85. LC Card 86-212959
1. Hellēnikē Trapeza Viomēchanikēs Anaptyxeōs (Greece). 2. Industrial promotion - Greece. I. Title.
HG3250.5.A8 H444 1985

Hē Hellēnikē viomēchania apo ton 19o ston 20o aiōna /. Athēna , 1985. 32 p., [22] p. of plates : LC Card 86-212947
HC295 .H373 1985

HELLĒNIKĒ TRAPEZA VIOMĒCHANIKĒS ANAPTYXEŌS (GREECE)
Hellēnikē Trapeza Viomēchanikēs Anaptyxeōs (Greece) Hē drasteriotēta tēs ETVA to etos 1985. [Athēna] [1985] 43 p. ; LC Card 86-212959
HG3250.5.A8 H444 1985

Hellēnikē Trapeza Viomēchanikēs Anaptyxeōs (Greece). Tmēma Dēmosiōn Scheseōn. Vliamos, Spyros I. Ho symvoulos epicheirēseōn . Athēna , c1985. 48 p. : LC Card 86-182906
HD69.C6 V55 1985

Hē Hellēnikē viomēchania apo ton 19o ston 20o aiōna / [egrapse Odysseas Dēmētrakopoulos ; genikē kai kallitechnikē epimeleia Lousē Bratziōtē]. Athēna : Hellēnikē Trapeza Viomēchanikēs Anaptyxeōs, 1985. 32 p., [22] p. of plates : ill. ; 28 cm. LC Card 86-212947
1. Greece - Industries - History - 19th century. 2. Greece - Industries - History - 20th century. I. Dēmētrakopoulos, Odysseas. II. Bratziōtē, Lousē. III. Hellēnikē Trapeza Viomēchanikēs Anaptyxeōs (Greece).
HC295 .H373 1985

Hellēniko syndikalistiko kinēma : praktika synedriou, Athēna 3-5 Phevrouariou, 1984 / [epimeleia keimenōn Anny Podēmata]. Athēna : Eleuthero Politiko Ergastēri, 1984. 215 p. ; 24 cm. LC Card 86-193159
1. Trade-unions - Greece - Congresses. I. Podēmata, Anny. II. Eleuthero Politiko Ergastēri (Athens, Greece).
HD6795.5 .H44 1984

Heller, Ágnes. Fehér, Ferenc, 1933- Doomsday or deterrence? . Armonk, N.Y. , c1986. 154 p. ; ISBN 0-87332-368-8 : LC Card 86-10074 DDC 327.1/74 19
JX1974.7 .F38 1986 ***NYPL [JLE 86-4319]***

Heller, Robert, 1932-
The age of the common millionaire / by Robert Heller. New York : Dutton, c1987. p. cm. "Truman Talley Books." Includes index. ISBN 0-525-24588-X LC Card 87-19973 DDC 305.5/234 19
1. Millionaires. I. Title.
HC79.W4 H45 1987

The supermarketers : marketing for success, rules of the mastermarketers, the naked marketplace / Robert Heller.1st ed. New York : Dutton, c1987. xiii, 384 p. ; 24 cm. "A Truman Talley book." Bibliography: p. 363-365. Includes index. ISBN 0-525-24520-0 LC Card 86-23977 DDC 658.8 19
1. Marketing - Case studies. 2. Success in business - Case studies. I. Title. II. Title: Super marketers.
HF5415 .H374 1987

Heller, Walter P. Social choice and public decision making /. Cambridge [Cambridgeshire] , New York , 1986. xix, 215 p. : ISBN 0-521-30454-7 LC Card 86-8580 DDC 339 19
HB846.8 .S59 1986 ***NYPL [JLE 86-4189]***

Hellinger, Doug. Hellinger, Steve. Aid for just development . Washington, D.C. (1010 Vermont Ave., N.W., Suite 521, Washington 20005) , c1987. vii, 191 p. ; LC Card 87-404422 DDC 338.91/09172/4 19
HC60 .H38516 1987

Hellinger, Steve. Aid for just development : proposals for a new development assistance structure / by Steve Hellinger, Doug Hellinger, Fred O'Regan.1st ed. Washington, D.C. (1010 Vermont Ave., N.W., Suite 521, Washington 20005) : Development Group for Alternative Policies, c1987. vii, 191 p. ; 28 cm. Bibliography: p. [182]-191. LC Card 87-404422 DDC 338.91/09172/4 19
1. Economic assistance - Developing countries. 2. Economic development projects - Developing countries. 3. Non-governmental organizations - Developing countries. 4. Project management - Developing countries - Decision making. I. Hellinger, Doug. II. O'Regan, Fred. III. Development Group for Alternative Policies. IV. Title.
HC60 .H38516 1987

Helliwell, John E. Aggregate supply in interlink . Paris, France , c1985. 60 p. : LC Card 86-205160 DDC 338.5/213 19
HB201 .A25 1985

Hellman, Judith Adler. Notes on the failure of reformist capitalism in Mexico / Judith A. Hellman. Toronto, Ont., Canada : Brazilian Studies/Latin American Research Unit, [1976] 24 p ; 28 cm. (LARU working paper . 18) "December 1976." Bibliography: p. 23-24. LC Card 85-155317 DDC 338.972 19
1. Mexico - Economic policy. 2. Capitalism - Mexico. I. Title. II. Series.
HC135 .H38 1976

Hellmuth, James G. Finding money : a businessman's guide to sources of financing / James G. Hellmuth.Rev. ed. New York, N.Y. : Boardroom Books, c1983. p. cm. Includes index. ISBN 0-932648-79-7 LC Card 86-31053 DDC 658.1/5224 19
1. Small business - United States - Finance. 2. Business enterprises - United States - Finance. I. Title.
HG4027.7 .H44 1983b

Hellriegel, Don.
Management. Sashkin, Marshall, 1944- Experiencing management / Marshall Sashkin, William C. Morris. Reading, Mass. , c1987. x, 234 p. : ISBN 0-201-11545-X (pbk.) : LC Card 86-28731 DDC 658.4/0352 19
HD30.26 .S27 1987

Hellwig, Zdzisław.
Problems of decision making based on experimental data /. Wrocław , 1985. 186 p. : LC Card 86-207027
HB9 .B7522 nr. 301 QA279.4

Statystyka i ekonometria /. Wrocław , 1978. 193 p. : LC Card 81-206821
HB9 .B7522 zesz. 141 HB135

Systemy organizacyjne /. [Wrocław] , 1981. 75 p. : LC Card 83-161920
HB9 .B7522 nr. 188 HM131

Helmbold, Lois Rita. Making choices, making do [microform] : Black and white working class women's lives and work during the Great Depression / by Lois Rita Helmbold. 1982. vii, 385 leaves Typescript. Thesis (Ph. D.)--Stanford University, 1982. Bibliography: leaves 371-385. Microfilm. Ann Arbor, Mich. : University Microfilms International, 1983. 1 microfilm reel ; 35 mm.
1. Women - United States - History - 20th century. 2. Women - United States - Economic conditions. 3. Women - United States - Social conditions. 4. Labor and laboring classes - United States - 1914-. 5. Afro-American women - Employment. I. Title.
NYPL [Sc Micro R-4672]

Helmedag, Fritz, 1953- Die Technikwahl bei linearer Einzelproduktion, oder, Die dritte Krise der Profitrate / Fritz Helmedag. Frankfurt am Main ; New York : P. Lang, c1986. viii, 301 p. : ill. ; 21 cm. (Europäische Hochschulschriften. Reihe V, Volks- und Betriebswirtschaft, 0531-7339 . Bd. 731 = vol. 731 = vol. 731) Originally presented as the author's thesis (doctoral--TH Aachen) Bibliography: p. 275-301. ISBN 3-8204-9645-9 LC Card 86-219002
1. Profit - Mathematical models. 2. Capital - Mathematical models. 3. Production functions (Economic theory). I. Title. II. Title: Dritte Krise der Profitrate. III. Series: Europäische Hochschulschriften. Reihe V, Volks- und Betriebswirtschaft , Bd. 731.
HB601 .H44 1986

Helmer, Hans-Josef. Merkantilismus und Kapitalismus im modernen Rationalisierungsprozess / Hans-Josef Helmer. Frankfurt : R.G. Fischer, c1986. iii, 223 p. ; 21 cm. Bibliography: p. 217-223. ISBN 3-88323-647-0 LC Card 87-113030 DDC 330.15/13 19
1. Mercantile system. 2. Capitalism. 3. Rational expectations (Economic theory). I. Title.
HB91 .H436 1986

Helmkamp, John G. Managerial accounting / John G. Helmkamp. 1st ed. New York : Wiley, c1987. xxiii, 720 p. : ill. (some col.) ; 26 cm. Includes index. ISBN 0-471-88910-5 LC Card 86-29021 DDC 658.1/511 19
1. Managerial accounting. I. Title.
HF5635 .H45 1987

Helmreich, Jonathan E. Gathering rare ores : the diplomacy of uranium acquisition, 1943-1954 / Jonathan E. Helmreich. Princeton, N.J. : Princeton University Press, c1986. xiv, 303 p. : map ; 25 cm. Includes index. Bibliography: p. 287-291. ISBN 0-691-04738-3 (alk. paper) : LC Card 86-4862 DDC 327.1/11 19
1. Nuclear energy - Government policy - United States - History. 2. Nuclear industry - Political aspects - History. 3. Uranium industry - Political aspects - History. 4. World politics - 1945-. 5. United States - Foreign relations - Great Britain. 6. Great Britain - Foreign relations - United States. I. Title.
HD9698.U52 H45 1986
NYPL [JLE 86-4584]

Helms, Marianne. Gydesen, Ellen. Kvinders livsgrundlag i 80-erne /. K [i.e. Copenhagen] [1985] 202 columns : LC Card 87-168500
HD6060.65.D4 G93 1985

Helmstädter, Ernst.
Die Bedingungen des Wirtschaftswachstums in Vergangenheit und Zukunft . Tübingen , 1984. viii, 321 p., [1] leaf of plates : ISBN 3-16-344727-9 LC Card 85-165269
HD84 .B415 1984

Die Input-Output-Analyse als Instrument der Strukturforschung . Tübingen , 1983. xxv, 177 p. : ISBN 3-16-344661-2 LC Card 83-206282
HB142 .I52 1983

Studien zur Entwicklung der ökonomischen Theorie /. Berlin , c1981- v. ; ISBN 3-428-04862-8 (v. 1) : LC Card 81-154218 DDC 330/.09 19
HB75 .S787 1981
NYPL [JLL 73-186 Bd.115]

Help for the troubled employee. United States. Dept. of the Interior. Division of Medical and Health Services. Washington [1975?] 57 p. ;
NYPL [JLF 86-1309]

Help in distress. Hilfe in der Not . [Bremen] [1947] 74 p. : LC Card 87-408692 DDC 338.91/73/04352 19
HC286.5 .H545 1947

HELP-WANTED ADVERTISING - HANDBOOKS, MANUALS, ETC.
Wolff, Rick, 1951- The encyclopedia of pre-written employment ads . Westbury, N.Y. , c1986. vi, 196 p. ; ISBN 0-87280-142-X (loose-leaf) : LC Card 86-26526 DDC 659.1/9331128 19
HF6125 .W65 1986

Helpers and aides /. Franck, Irene M. New York, N.Y. , c1987. x, 182 p. : ISBN 0-8160-1445-0 LC Card 86-24370 DDC 331.7 19
HF5381.2 .F68 1987

Helping handbook / by Michigan League for Human Services. 4th ed. Lansing, MI (300 N. Washington Square, Suite 401, Lansing 48933) : The League, 1986. v, 101 p. ; 28 cm. Rev. ed. of: Recession survival handbook. 3rd ed., 1982-83. c1982. LC Card 87-110874 DDC 361.6/025/774 19
1. Economic assistance, Domestic - Michigan - Handbooks, manuals, etc. I. Michigan League for Human Services. II. Recession survival handbook.
HC107.M53 P633 1986

Helping others in crisis.
Perry, Richard D. Money problems /. Elgin, Ill. , c1987. 111 p. ; ISBN 1-555-13797-0 (pbk.) LC Card 86-73209 DDC 332.024 19
HG179 .P367 1987

Helping small firms grow . Hull, Christopher J. New York , c1987. 228 p. : ISBN 0-7099-4791-7 LC Card 87-15728 DDC 338.6/42 19
HD2346.G3 .H786 1987

Helping the sexually oppressed / Harvey L. Gochros, Jean S. Gochros, Joel Fischer, editors. Englewood Cliffs, N.J. : Prentice-Hall, c1986. xix, 282 p. : ill. ; 25 cm. Includes bibliographies and indexes. ISBN 0-13-386129-5 : LC Card 85-16687 DDC 305.3 19
1. Discrimination - United States. 2. Sex discrimination - United States. 3. Sexual harassment. 4. Social service - United States. I. Gochros, Harvey L. II. Gochros, Jean S. III. Fischer, Joel.
HN57 .H46 1986 ***NYPL [JLE 86-3217]***

Helpman, Elhanan. Economic effects of the government budget /. Cambridge, Mass. , c1988. p. cm. ISBN 0-262-08172-5 LC Card 87-26187 DDC 338.9 19
HJ2005 .E25 1988

HELSINKI (FINLAND) - POPULATION - STATISTICS.
Kinturi, Jorma. Väestö, asunnot ja asuntorakentaminen suur- ja peruspiireittäin Helsingissä 1970-1983 =. Helsinki , 1984. 36 p., [1] folded leaf of plates : LC Card 85-156678
HD7345.3.H5 K563 1984

Lankinen, Leila. Asuminen Helsingissä 1950-1983 =. Helsinki , 1985. 80 p. : LC Card 86-148571
HD7345.3.H5 L35 1985

Helyzetkép az élelmiszeripari müvezetőkről /. Réder, Gyula. Budapest , 1985. 81 p. ; ISBN 963-491-205-2 LC Card 86-196825
HD9015.H82 R43 1985

Hemenway, David. Prices and choices : microeconomic vignettes / David Hemenway.2nd ed. Cambridge, Mass. : Ballinger, c1988. xii, 315 p. : ill. ; 23 cm. Includes bibliographies and indexes. ISBN 0-88730-242-4 (pbk.) LC Card 87-17437 DDC 338.5 19
1. Microeconomics. I. Title.
HB172 .H47 1988

To hēmerologio tēs peinas /. Maroudēs, Giōrgos. [Athens] , 1976. 99 p., [6] leaves of plates ; LC Card 84-107778
HC300.F3 M37 1976

Hémery, Daniel. Debeir, Jean-Claude. Les servitudes de la puissance . [Paris] , c1986. 428 p. : ISBN 2-08-211163-6 : LC Card 87-121577
HD9502.A2 D43 1986

Hemmers, K. (Karlheinz) Planung des Personalbedarfs in indirekten Bereichen / K. Hemmers. Berlin ; New York : Springer-Verlag, 1986. viii, 141 p. : 73 ill. ; 21 cm. (Forschung für die Praxis . Bd. 9) Originally presented as the author's thesis (doctoral)--TH Aachen. Bibliography: p. 111-117. ISBN 0-387-16702-1 (U. S.) : LC Card 86-200805
1. Manpower planning - Germany, West. 2. Germany, West - Occupations. 3. Germany, West - Industries. I. Title. II. Series.
HF5549.5.M3 H46 1986

Hemphill, John K. (John Knox), 1919- Dimensions of executive positions : a study of the basic characteristics of the positions of ninety-three business executives / John K. Hemphill. New York : Garland Pub., 1987, c1960. xiv, 103 p. ; 23 cm. (Continuity in administrative science) Reprint. Originally published: Columbus, Ohio : Bureau of Business Research, College of Commerce and Administration, Ohio State University, 1960. Originally published in series: Bureau of Business Research monograph. Bibliography: p. 65. ISBN 0-8240-8209-5 (alk. paper) : LC Card 86-27078 DDC 658.4 19
1. Executives. I. Title. II. Series.
HD38.2 .H46 1987

Hemphill, John Mearl, 1943- Kuriloff, Arthur H. Starting and managing the small business /. New York , c1988. xxi, 663 p. : ISBN 0-07-035665-3 : LC Card 87-3832 DDC 658/.022 19
HD62.5 .K87 1988

Hen, Paul de. Om het behoud van een explosieve stad . Muiderberg , 1986. 298 p. : ISBN 90-6283-661-5 : LC Card 86-205071
HC328.A5 O4 1986

Henderson, Dennis R. Federal marketing programs in agriculture . Danville, Ill. , c1983. x, 326 p. ; ISBN 0-8134-2292-2 : LC Card 83-80130 ***NYPL [JLE 86-4572]***

Henderson, George, 1932- International business and cultures : a human relations perspective / George Henderson, Virginia Hall Milhouse. New York, NY : Cummings & Hathaway, 1987. p. cm. Includes index. ISBN 0-943025-03-6 : LC Card 87-24378 DDC 658/.049 19
1. Commerce. 2. International business enterprises. 3. Cross-cultural studies. 4. National characteristics. 5. Business travel. I. Milhouse, Virginia Hall, 1950-. II. Title.
HF1008 .H46 1987

Henderson, J. W. (Jeffrey William), 1947- Race, class, and state housing : inequality and the allocation of public housing in Britain / Jeff Henderson and Valerie Karn. Aldershot, Hants, England ;Brookfield, Vt. : Gower Pub. Co., c1987. xxiii, 331 p. : maps ; 23 cm. (Studies in urban and regional policy . 4) Includes index. Bibliography: p. 313-320. ISBN 0-566-00785-1 :
1. Minorities - Housing - England - Birmingham (West Midlands). 2. Discrimination in housing - England - Birmingham (West Midlands). 3. Minorities - Housing - Great Britain. 4. Minorities - Housing - Government policy - Great Britain. I. Karn, Valerie Ann. II. Title. III. Series. ***NYPL [JLD 87-1476]***

Henderson, James W. Obtaining venture financing : principles and practices / James W. Henderson. Lexington, Mass. : Lexington Books, c1988. xii, 366 p. : ill. ; 24 cm. Includes bibliographies and index. ISBN 0-669-10931-2 (alk. paper) LC Card 85-40234 DDC 658.1/5224 19
1. Venture capital - United States. I. Title.
HG4963 .H44 1988

Henderson, Julie A. Lillywhite, Donald P. Virginia population projections 2000 /. Richmond, VA (P.O. Box 1422, Ninth St. Office Building, Richmond 23219) [1986] 96 p. : LC Card 87-621004 DDC 304.6/2/09755021 19
HA685 .L542 1986

Henderson, Sheila, 1950- Bard, Ray. Own your own franchise . Reading, Mass. , 1987. vii, 455 p. ; ISBN 0-201-11439-9 (pbk.) : LC Card 87-14389 DDC 658.8/708 19
HF5429.235.U5 B37 1987

Henderson, Thomas P.
Ficek, Edmund F. Real estate principles and practices /. Columbus , c1983. viii, 550 p. : ISBN 0-675-20016-4 LC Card 82-73775 DDC 346.7304/37 347.306437 19
KF2042.R4 F46 1983 ***NYPL [JLE 86-2010]***

Johnson, Ross H. Real estate finance /. Columbus, Ohio , c1985. ix, 445 p. : ISBN 0-675-20195-0 LC Card 84-61298 DDC 332.7/2 19
HG2040 .J6 1985 ***NYPL [JLE 86-3033]***

Hendrick, Kingsley. Investigating accidents with STEP / Kingsley Hendrick, Ludwig Benner, Jr. New York : M. Dekker, c1987. xviii, 454 p. : ill. ; 24 cm. (Occupational safety and health. 13) Bibliography: p. 435-438. Includes index. ISBN 0-8247-7510-4 LC Card 86-24165 DDC 363.1/065 19
1. Accidents - Investigation. 2. Industrial accidents - Investigation. I. Benner, Ludwig. II. Series: Occupational safety and health (Marcel Dekker, Inc.) , v. 13. III. Title.
HD7262.25 .H46 1987

HENDRIX' FABRIEKEN - HISTORY.
Bläsing, J. F. E. (Joachim F. E.), 1940- Op het spoor van de Körver . Leiden , 1986. xvi, 396 p. : ISBN 90-247-8065-9 : LC Card 86-214829
HD9052.N44 H453 1986

HENEQUEN INDUSTRY - MEXICO - YUCATAN.
Villanueva, Eric. Crisis henequenera y movimientos campesinos en Yucatán, 1966-1983 /. México, D.F. , 1985. 220 p., [10] p. of plates : ISBN 968-603-803-5 LC Card 86-118134 DDC 304.8/0972/65 19
HD9156.H463 M67 1985
NYPL [JLD 87-342]

HENEQUIN INDUSTRY - MEXICO - YUCATÁN (STATE) - HISTORY.
Cárdenas, Lázaro, 1895-1970. Los ejidos de Yucatán y el henequén . [Mexico City, Mexico] , c1984. 79 p. : LC Card 87-403579 DDC 333.3/1/7265 19
HD1333.M62 Y823 1984

Hengsbach, Friedhelm. Aussperrung und Streik . Mainz , 1981, c1980. 173 p. ; ISBN 3-7867-0854-1 LC Card 81-101514 DDC 331.89/2943 19
HD5378 .A97 1981 ***NYPL [JLD 86-2787]***

Henke, Emerson O. Introduction to nonprofit organization accounting / Emerson O. Henke. 3rd ed. Boston : PWS-Kent Pub. Co., c1988. xvi, 670 p. : ill. ; 25 cm. (Kent series in accounting) Bibliography: p. 644-648. Includes index. ISBN 0-534-08322-6 LC Card 87-7330 DDC 657/.98 19
1. Corporations, Nonprofit - Accounting. 2. Finance, Public - Accounting. I. Title. II. Series.
HF5686.N56 H45 1988

Henke, Klaus-Dirk. Schmähl, Winfried. Änderung der Beitragsfinanzierung in der Rentenversicherung? . Baden-Baden , 1984. 388 p. : ISBN 3-7890-1018-9 LC Card 84-206647
HD7179 .S324 1984

HENKEL FAMILY.
Schöne, Manfred, 1935- Stammwerk Henkel, 80 Jahre in Düsseldorf-Holthausen /. Düsseldorf , 1981. 148 p. : LC Card 86-216690
HD9654.9.H444 S36 1981

HENKEL KGAA.
Schöne, Manfred, 1935- Ein Vierteljahrhundert Betriebskrankenkasse Henkel, Düsseldorf /. [Düsseldorf] , 1977. 60 p. : LC Card 86-216782
HG9399.G33 B477 1977

HENKEL KGAA - HISTORY.
Goosmann, Cornelia. Ein Jahrhundert Wasserglas von Henkel /. Düsseldorf , c1985. 76 p. : ISBN 3-923324-67-8 LC Card 86-171258
HD9654.9.H444 G66 1985

Schöne, Manfred, 1935- Stammwerk Henkel, 80 Jahre in Düsseldorf-Holthausen /. Düsseldorf , 1981. 148 p. : LC Card 86-216690
HD9654.9.H444 S36 1981

Schöne, Manfred, 1935- Von der Leimabteilung zum grössten Klebstoffwerk Europas /. Düsseldorf , 1979. 68 p. : LC Card 86-216773
HD9654.9.H444 S37 1979

Henkes, Barbara. Kaatje, ben je boven? : leven en werken van Nederlandse dienstbodes, 1900-1940 / Barbara Henkes & Hanneke Oosterhof. Nijmegen : SUN, c1985. 192 p. : ill. ; 21 x 22 cm. Bibliography: p. 170-173. ISBN 90-6168-242-8 : LC Card 85-237937
1. Women domestics - Netherlands - History. 2. Women - Employment - Netherlands - History. I. Oosterhof, Hanneke. II. Title.
HD6072.2.N4 H46 1985

Henley, Ernest J. Designing for reliability and safety control / Ernest J. Henley, Hiromitsu Kumamoto. Englewood Cliffs, N.J. : Prentice-Hall, c1985. xvi, 527 p. : ill. ; 24 cm. (Prentice-Hall international series in industrial and systems engineering) Includes bibliographies and index. ISBN 0-13-201229-4 LC Card 84-17892 DDC 620/.00452 19
1. Security systems. 2. System design. I. Kumamoto, Hiromitsu. II. Title.
TA169 .H46 1985 ***NYPL [JSE 86-2491]***

Henley, N. T. (Nathaniel T.) Howell, Rate A. The legal environment of business /. Chicago , c1987. xiv, 783 p. : ISBN 0-03-008369-9 LC Card 86-4503 DDC 346.73/07 347.3067 19
KF1600 .H68 1987 ***NYPL [JLE 87-911]***

Hennicke, Martin. Zum Förderungssystem für kleine und mittlere Unternehmen : Analyse des Koordinations- und Harmonisierungsbedarfs der Förderprogramme des Bundes und der Bundesländer / Martin Hennicke, Diana de Pay. Stuttgart : Poeschel, c1986. 155 p. ; 24 cm. (Schriften zur Mittelstandsforschung . n.F., Nr. 12) Summary in English. Bibliography: p. 153-155. ISBN 3-7910-5012-5 LC Card 86-181544 DDC 338.6/42/0943 19
1. Small business - Germany, West. 2. Subsidies - Germany, West. I. Pay, Diana de. II. Title. III. Series.
HD2346.G3 H44 1986

Henning, C. Randall. Macroeconomic diplomacy in the 1980s : domestic politics and international conflict among the United States, Japan, and Europe / C. Randall Henning. London ; New York : Croom Helm for the Atlantic Institute for International Affairs, c1987. x, 76 p. ; 22 cm. (Atlantic paper . no. 65) Bibliography: p. 64-74. ISBN 0-7099-3794-6 (pbk.) LC Card 87-20041 DDC 337/.09171/3 19
1. United States - Foreign economic relations. 2. Europe - Foreign economic relations. 3. Japan - Foreign economic relations. 4. United States - Economic policy - 1981-. 5. Japan - Economic policy - 1945-. 6. Europe - Economic policy. I. Atlantic Institute for International Affairs. II. Title. III. Series.
HF1455 .H46 1987

Henning, Charles N. Financial markets and the economy / Charles N. Henning, William Pigott, Robert Haney Scott. 5th ed. Englewood Cliffs, N.J. : Prentice Hall, c1988. xvi, 638 p. : ill. ; 25 cm. Includes bibliographies and index. ISBN 0-13-316894-8 LC Card 87-24413 DDC 332/.0973 19
1. Finance - United States. 2. Financial institutions - United States. 3. Money market - United States. 4. Capital market - United States. I. Pigott, William, 1927-. II. Scott, Robert Haney. III. Title.
HG181 .H37 1988

Henning, Friedrich-Wilhelm.
Vorindustrielles Gewerbe und wirtschaftlicher Wandel im Paderborner Land im 19. Jahrhundert / von Friedrich-Wilhelm Henning. Region und Industrialisierung im Vergleich, Minden-Ravensberg und die englischen Industriegebiete / Sidney Pollard. Dortmund : Gesellschaft für Westfälische Wirtschaftsgeschichte, 1983. 67 p. ; 21 cm. (Vortragsreihe der Gesellschaft für Westfälische Wirtschaftsgeschichte . Heft 25) Cover title. Lectures by F.-W. Henning and S. Pollard held at the Gesellschaft für Westfälische Wirtschaftsgeschichte and before four other bodies. Bibliography: p. 39-41. LC Card 83-198581
1. Paderborn Region (Germany) - Economic conditions. 2. Minden Region (North Rhine-Westphalia, Germany) - Economic conditions. 3. Ravensburg Region (Germany) - Economic conditions. I. Pollard, Sidney. Region und Industrialisierung im Vergleich, Minden-Ravensberg und die englischen Industriegebiete. 1983. II. Gesellschaft für Westfälische Wirtschaftsgeschichte. III. Title. IV. Title: Region und Industrialisierung im Vergleich, Minden-Ravensberg und die englischen Industriegebiete. V. Series.
HC288.P27 H46 1983

Wirtschaftsarchive und Kammern--Aspekte wirtschaftlicher selbstverwaltung gestern und heute . Köln , 1982. 250 p. ; LC Card 86-198576
HC286 .W59 1982

Henningsen, Eckart. Aschhoff, Gunther, 1934- Das deutsche Genossenschaftswesen . Frankfurt am Main , 1985. 167 p. : ISBN 3-7819-0345-1 LC Card 86-145522
HD3038 .A77 1985

Hennock, E. P., 1926- British social reform and German precedents : the case of social insurance, 1880-1914 / E.P. Hennock. Oxford [Oxfordshire] : Clarendon Press ; New York : Oxford University Press, 1987. vi, 243 p. ; 23 cm. Bibliography: p. [216]-229. Includes index. ISBN 0-19-820127-3 : LC Card 87-11082 DDC 368.4/00941 19
1. Social security - Great Britain - History. 2. Social security - Germany - History. 3. Great Britain - Social policy. 4. Germany - Social policy. I. Title.
HD7165 .H455 1987

Heno, Rudolf. Kreditwürdigkeitsprüfung mit Hilfe von Verfahren der Mustererkennung / von Rudolf Heno. Bern : Haupt, c1983. vi, 317 p. : ill. ; 23 cm. (Bankwirtschaftliche Forschungen. Bd. 81) Bibliography: p. 302-317. ISBN 3-258-03245-9 : LC Card 83-228668
1. Credit bureaus - Germany, West. 2. Credit guides - Germany (West). I. Title. II. Series.
HG1526 .B27 Bd. 81 HG3751.9.G3

HENŌSIS HELLĒNŌN EPHOPLISTŌN (GREECE) - CONGRESSES.
Henōsis Hellēnōn Ephoplistōn (Greece). Dioikētikon Symvoulion. Ekthesis tōn pepragmemōn tou Dioikētikou Symvouliou . Athēnai , 1957. 23 p. ; LC Card 86-235109
HE564.E3 G824 1957

Henōsis Hellēnōn Ephoplistōn (Greece). Dioikētikon Symvoulion. Ekthesis tōn pepragmemōn tou Dioikētikou Symvouliou : genikē syneleusis tēs 25ēs Iouniou, 1957 / Henōsis Hellēnōn Ephoplistōn. Athēnai : Hē Henōsis, 1957. 23 p. ; 25 cm. LC Card 86-235109
1. Henōsis Hellēnōn Ephoplistōn (Greece) - Congresses. 2. Shipping - Greece - Congresses. I. Title.
HE564.E3 G824 1957

Henrich, Rudolf. Analyse und Planung des Erfolgs und der Überschussverwendung einer Krankenversicherungsaktiengesellschaft / [Rudolf Henrich]. Karlsruhe : VVW, c1983. xxi, 498 p. : ill. ; 21 cm. (Veröffentlichungen des Instituts für Versicherungswissenschaften der Universität Mannheim, 0170-2254 . Bd. 24) Bibliography: p. 441-457. Includes index. ISBN 3-88487-053-X LC Card 85-131706
1. Insurance, Health - Germany, West. I. Title. II. Series.
HG9399.G32 H46 1983

Henrichsmeyer, Wilhelm. Einkommenswirkungen von Getreidepreissenkungen /. Münster-Hiltrup , 1985. viii, 158 p. : ISBN 3-7843-0315-3 LC Card 87-408928 DDC 338.1/0943 s 338.1/331/094 19
HD1920.5 .E37 1985

Henriksen, Ingrid. Holdninger til den økonomiske fordeling = Attitudes to the distribution of incomes / Ingrid Henriksen. København : Socialforskningsinstituttet, 1985. 349 p. : ill. ; 21 cm. (Sammenligningsundersøgelsen = The Danish study on attitudes to inequality . 1) Publikation / Socialforskningsinstituttet, 0583-712X ; 138 Summary in English. Bibliography: p. 341-346. ISBN 87-7487-265-6 : LC Card 85-186400
1. Income distribution - Denmark - Public opinion. 2. Public opinion - Denmark. I. Title. II. Title: Attitudes to the distribution of incomes. III. Series: Socialforskningsinstituttet, Copenhagen. Publkationer , 138.
HC360.I5 S25 1985 vol. 1
NYPL [JLD 86-2002]

Henrique, Luiz. O salário perverso : discursos / pronunciados pelo Deputado Luiz Henrique. Brasília : Câmara dos Deputados, Centro de Documentação e Informação, Coordenação de Publicações, 1983. 129 p. ; 23 cm. (Separatas de discursos, pareceres e projetos . 47a.) LC Card 86-129394
1. Wages - Government policy - Brazil. 2. Brazil - Economic policy. I. Brazil. Congresso Nacional. Câmara dos Deputados. Centro de Documentação e Informação. Coordenação de Publicações. II. Title. III. Series.
HD5004 .H45 1983

Henriques, Diana B. The machinery of greed : public authority abuse and what to do about it / by Diana B. Henriques. Lexington, Mass. : Lexington Books, c1986. x, 161 p. ; 24 cm. Includes index. ISBN 0-669-09809-4 (alk. paper) LC Card 85-23841 DDC 364.1/68 19
1. Corporations, Government - United States - Corrupt practices. 2. Special districts - United States - Corrupt practices. I. Title.
HD3885 .H45 1986 ***NYPL [JLE 86-2739]***

Henríquez, Helia.
Barrera, Manuel. Sindicatos y estado en el Chile actual . Geneva, Switzerland , Santiago, Chile , c1985. v, 196 p. : LC Card 87-118607
HD6617 .B27 1985

Barrera, Manuel. Trade unions and the state in the present day Chile . Geneva, Switzerland , Santiago, Chile , 1986. xx, 154 p. : LC Card 87-128364 DDC 331.89/0983 19
HD6617 .B273 1986

HENRY VII, KING OF ENGLAND, 1457-1509.
Ide, Arthur Frederick. The mercantile policies of Henry VII /. Irving, Tex. , 1987. v, 78 p. : ISBN 0-938659-02-2 (pbk.) : LC Card 87-4316 DDC 382/.3/0942 19
HF1533 .I34 1987

Henry A. Wallace Center for Agricultural History and Rural Studies. Agricultural distress in the Midwest, past & present /. Iowa City , 1986. ix, 111 p. : ISBN 0-87414-049-8 : LC Card 86-29932 DDC 338.1/0977 19
HD1773.A3 A37 1986

The Henry A. Wallace series on agricultural history and rural studies.
Atack, Jeremy. To their own soil . Ames , 1987. xi, 322 p. : ISBN 0-8138-0086-2 LC Card 86-21349 DDC 338.1/0974 19
HD1773.A4 A86 1987

Henry, Brian. British television advertising . London , 1986. 528 p., xxxii p. of plates : ISBN 0-09-165800-4 : LC Card 87-120167 DDC 659.14/3/0941 19
HF6146.T42 B675 1986

Henry C. Carey and American economic development /. Morrison, Rodney J., 1934- Philadelphia , 1986. ix, 91 p. : ISBN 0-87169-763-7 (pbk.) LC Card 86-71420 DDC 338.973/0092/4 19
HB119.C3 M67 1986

Henry, Donald Putnam, 1957- The financial cost of export credit guarantee programs / Donald Putnam Henry. Santa Monica, CA : Rand, 1987. ix, 37 p. ; 23 cm. "Prepared for the Office of the Under Secretary of Defense for Policy." Bibliography: p. 37. R-3491-USDP." ISBN 0-8330-0794-7 (pbk.) LC Card 87-4630 DDC 382/.63 19
1. Export credit - United States. 2. Insurance, Export credit - United States. I. United States. Office of the Under Secretary of Defense for Policy. II. Title.
HG3754.5.U6 H46 1987

Henry, Etienne. Transports urbains et services en Amérique latine . Arcueil, France , Quito [1985- v. <1 > : ISBN 2-85782-137-9 (set) LC Card 87-153020
HE311.L29 T73 1985

Henry, Lauchland. The professional's guide to working smarter / Lauchland A. Henry. Tenafly, N.J. : Burrill-Ellsworth Associates, 1988. xv, 208 p. : ill. ; 24 cm. (People and the organization series) Bibliography: p. 205. Includes index. ISBN 0-935310-03-7 LC Card 87-23868 DDC 650.1 19
1. Professions. 2. Professional socialization. 3. Business communication. 4. Career development. 5. Time management. I. Title. II. Series.
HD8038.A1 H47 1988

Henry, Louis, writer on demography. [Fécondité des marriages. English]
Fertility of marriage : a new method of measurement / by Louis Henry ; translated by Nita Léry. New York : United Nations, 1980. iv, 136 p. : ill. ; 28 cm. (Population studies translation series . no. 3) Translation of: Fécondité des marriages. Corrigenda slip laid in. "ST/ESCAP/97." Includes bibliographical references. LC Card 81-133059
1. Fertility, Human - Measurement. I. Title. II. Series.
HB901 .H4613 1980

Henry, Porter.
Callanan, Joseph A. Sales management and motivation /. New York , 1987. xi, 204 p. : ISBN 0-531-15516-1 LC Card 86-29020 DDC 658.8/1 19
HF5438.4 .C335 1987

Secrets of the master sellers / Porter Henry. New York, NY : AMACOM, c1987. x, 294 p. : ill. ; 23 cm. Includes index. ISBN 0-8144-7688-0 (pbk.) : LC Card 87-47707 DDC 658.8/5 19
1. Selling. I. Title.
HF5438.25 .H465 1987

Hensiruk, Stepan Antonovych. Kompleksnoe ispolʹzovanie prirodnykh resursov . Kiev , 1985. 174 p. ; LC Card 86-175133
HC337.U5 K6372 1985

Henson, Mary F. Cleveland, Robert W. Income nonresponses . [Washington] [1985] iv, 87 p. : LC Card 85-603179 DDC 339.2/2/0973021 19
HC110.I5 C44 1985

Henton, Douglas C. Carlson, Richard C. Managing the changing work force . Menlo Park, Calif. (333 Ravenswood Ave., Menlo Park 94025-3476) , c1984. 44 p. : LC Card 86-212936 DDC 658.3 19
HD5706 .C29 1984

Hentze, Joachim. Unternehmungsführung und Mitbestimmung / Joachim Hentze, Peter Brose. Würzburg : Physica-Verlag, 1985. 297 p. : ill. ; 21 cm. (Physica Paperback) Bibliography: p. 279-296. ISBN 3-7908-0268-9 LC Card 85-186054
1. Industrial management - Germany (West) - Employee participation. 2. Management - Germany (West) - Employee participation. I. Brose, Peter. II. Title.
HD5660.G4 H43 1985

Heper, Metin. Development administration in Turkey : conceptual theory and methodology / Metin Heper, A. Ümit Berkman. Bebek, Istanbul : Boğaziçi University Press, [1980] vi, 116 p. ; 24 cm. (Boğaziçi University Publications. no. 164) Bibliography: p. [109]-116. LC Card 87-400032 DDC 338.9561 19
1. Turkey - Economic policy. 2. Public administration - Turkey. I. Berkman, A. Ümit. II. Title.
HC492 .H47 1980

Hepp, Ibolya. Magyar Kereskedelmi Kamara. Managers in Hungary . [Budapest?] , 1986. 368 p. ; ISBN 963-7073-09-4 (pbk.) LC Card 87-137498 DDC 658/.0025/439 19
HD38.25.H9 M34 1986

Her own business . Wilkens, Joanne. New York , c1987. xv, 245 p. ; ISBN 0-07-050854-2 : LC Card 86-27780 DDC 338.6/422/088042 19
HD2346.U5 W548 1987

A herança de Stroessner . Menezes, Alfredo da Mota, 1944- Campinas, SP [1987] 186 p. ; LC Card 87-404011 DDC 337.810892 19
HF1524.5.B7 M46 1987

Herausgebergruppe der Entropologischen Jahrbücher (Zurich, Switzerland) Arbeit, Entropie, Apokalypse . Zürich , 1982. 134 p. : LC Card 83-128724
HC106.8 .A73 1982

Herberg, Horst. Stagflation as a consequence of an expansionary monetary or fiscal policy under flexible exchange rates / by Horst Herberg. Stockholm, Sweden : Institute for International Economic Studies, [1978] 34 leaves ; 30 cm. (Seminar paper / Institute for International Economic Studies, 0347-8769 . no. 115) "December 1978." Bibliography: leaf 34. LC Card 81-116937
1. Unemployment - Effect of inflation on - Mathematical models. 2. Monetary policy - Mathematical models. 3. Foreign exchange - Mathematical models. I. Series: Seminar paper (Stockholms universitet. Institutet för internationell ekonomi) , no. 115. II. Title.
HD5710 .H47 1978

Herbert, David C. Fairfield on-scene study of collisions . [Sydney?] [1977] 120 p. : LC Card 85-170609
HE5614.5.A8 F37 1977

Herbert, Ulrich, 1951- Geschichte der Ausländer, Beschäftigung in Deutschland, 1880 bis 1980 : Saisonarbeiter, Zwangsarbeiter, Gastarbeiter / Ulrich Herbert. Berlin : J.H.W. Dietz, c1986. 272 p. : ill. ; 19 cm. (Dietz Taschenbuch . 19) Includes bibliographical references. ISBN 3-8012-3019-8 LC Card 87-113703 DDC

331.6/2/0943 19
1. Alien labor - Germany - History. 2. Seasonal labor - Germany - History. 3. Forced labor - Germany - History. 4. Labor policy - Germany - History. I. Title.
HD8458.A2 H39 1986

HERBICIDES INDUSTRY - GERMANY (WEST)
Weber, Norbert. Markttransparenz bei Pflanzenschutz- und Düngemitteln . Münster-Hiltrup , 1983. xi, 247 p. : ISBN 3-7843-0277-7 : LC Card 83-234135
HD9660.P33 G328 1983

Herbst, Erika. Alle suchen nach Lösungen : wir haben sie / Erika Herbst.1. Aufl. Feucht : Mündige Bürger ; Stuttgart : Frech-Verlag, c1984. 151 p. ; 21 cm. Cover title. ISBN 3-7724-0688-2 LC Card 85-146171
1. Economic history - 1971-. 2. Economic policy. 3. Social problems. 4. Social policy. I. Title.
HC59 .H395 1984

Herder-Dorneich, Philipp, 1928- Überwindung der Sozialstaatskrise . Baden-Baden , 1984. 317 p. : ISBN 3-7890-0925-3 LC Card 84-166713
HD7179 .U35 1984

Herdt, Hans Konradin, 1935- Bosch, 1886-1986 : Porträt eines Unternehmens / Hans Konradin Herdt ; mit Farbfotos von Dieter Blum. [Stuttgart] : Deutsche Verlags-Anstalt, [1986] 174 p., [88] p. of plates : ill. ; 26 cm. Bibliography: p. 171-174. Includes indexes. ISBN 3-421-06324-9 LC Card 86-229723
1. Robert Bosch GmbH - History. 2. Bosch, Robert, 1861-1942. I. Blum, Dieter. II. Title.
HD9710.3.G44 R634 1986

HEREDITARY SUCCESSION. see **INHERITANCE AND SUCCESSION.**

Hergarten, Lothar, 1953- Der Prospekt über steuerbegünstigte Kapitalanlagen : zur anlegerschutzorientierten Bestimmmung des Informationsgehaltes unter besonderer Berücksichtigung von Immobilieninvestitionsangeboten / Lothar Hergarten. Köln : Müller Botermann, c1986. v, 209 p. ; 21 cm. (Reihe Finanzierung, Steuern, Wirtschaftsprüfung . Bd. 1) Bibliography: p. 173-209. ISBN 3-924361-18-5 : LC Card 87-103997 DDC 332.63 19
1. Capital investments. 2. Capital investments - Taxation. I. Title. II. Series.
HG4028.C4 H456 1986

Hergert, Douglas.
Mastering Framework II / Douglas Hergert and Jonathan Kamin. Berkeley : Sybex, c1987. xvii, 509 p. : ill. ; 23 cm. Includes index. ISBN 0-89588-390-2 (pbk.) : LC Card 86-62808 DDC 650/.028/55369 19
1. Framework II (Computer program). 2. Business - Data processing. I. Kamin, Jonathan. II. Title.
HF5548.4.F72 H47 1987

Microsoft Excel with macros : maximizing the power and speed of Microsoft Excel / Douglas Hergert. Redmond, Wash. : Microsoft Press ; [New York, N.Y.] : Distributed to the book trade in the U. S. by Harper and Row, c1986. xii, 265 p. : ill. (some col.) ; 24 cm. Includes index. ISBN 0-914845-76-4 (pbk.) : LC Card 86-211548 DDC 005.36/9 19
1. Excel (Computer program). 2. Macintosh (Computer) - Programming. 3. Macro instructions (Electronic computers). 4. Business - Data processing. I. Title.
HF5548.4.E93 H474 1986

Hergeth, Helmut H. A., 1956-
Investitionsstrategien für stagnierende Branchen : dargestellt am Beispiel der Textilindustrie der Bundesrepublik Deutschland / Helmut H.A. Hergeth. Münster : Lit, [1986?] xii, 261 p. : ill. ; 21 cm. (Empirische Wirtschaftsforschung . Bd. 1) Betriebswirtschaftliche Schriftenreihe ; vol. 31 Title of 2nd series added to t.p. in manuscript. Bibliography: p. 246-261. ISBN 3-88660-338-5 LC Card 87-134812 DDC 338.4/3677/00943 19
1. Textile industry - Germany (West) - Finance. 2. Textile industry - Germany (West) - Capital investments. 3. Investments - Germany, West. I. Series. II. Series: Betriebswirtschaftliche Schriftenreihe , Bd. 31. III. Title.
HD9863.5 .H39 1986

Heri, Erwin W.
Bestimmungsgründe kurzfristiger Wechselkursfluktuationen : eine empirische Analyse flexibler Wechselkurse unter besonderer Berücksichtigung der Theorie und Empirie effizienter Märkte / Erwin W. Heri. Hamburg : Weltarchiv, 1982. v, 312 p. : ill. ; 25 cm. (Veröffentlichungen des HWWA-Institut für Wirtschaftsforschung-Hamburg) Bibliography: p. 298-312. ISBN 3-87895-225-2 LC Card 83-200160 DDC 332.4/5 19
1. Foreign exchange. 2. Foreign exchange - Econometric models. 3. Efficient market theory. I. Title.
HG3852 .H47 1982

Die Geldnachfrage : Theorie und empirische Ergebnisse für die Schweiz / Erwin W. Heri. Berlin ; New York : Springer-Verlag, c1986. 226 p. : ill. ; 25 cm. (Studies in contemporary economics) Bibliography: p. [217]-226. ISBN 0-387-17157-6 (U. S.) LC Card 86-232268
1. Demand for money - Switzerland. 2. Monetary policy - Switzerland. I. Title. II. Series.
HG226.5 .H47 1986

Herington, John. The outer city / John Herington. London ; New York : Harper & Row, 1984. 205 p. : ill., maps ; 24 cm. Includes index. Bibliography: p. [187]-200. ISBN 0-06-318237-8
1. Cities and towns - Growth - Great Britain. 2. City planning - Great Britain. 3. Urban policy - Great Britain. 4. Great Britain - Economic conditions - 1945-. I. Title. ***NYPL [JLE 86-1465]***

Heritage Foundation (Washington, D.C.)
Protecting the environment . Washington, D.C. , c1986. iii, 88 p. ; ISBN 0-89195-040-0 (pbk.) : LC Card 86-82962 DDC 363.7/056/0973 19
HC110.E5 P77 1986

The Heritage lectures, 0272-1155 .
(63) Kondratas, S. Anna. Comparable worth . Washington, D.C. [c1986] 16 p. ; LC Card 86-212973 DDC 331.2/1 19
HD6061 .K66 1986

Herken Krauer, Juan Carlos, 1953- El Paraguay rural entre 1869 y 1913 : contribución a la historia económica regional del Plata / Juan Carlos Herken Krauer.1a ed. Asunción, Paraguay : Centro Paraguayo de Estudios Sociológicos, 1984. 224 p., [10] p. of plates : ill. ; 20 cm. (Serie Historia social) Bibliography: p. 217-222. Includes indexes. LC Card 84-237050
1. Paraguay - Economic conditions. 2. Agriculture - Economic aspects - Paraguay - History. 3. Paraguay - Rural conditions. I. Title. II. Series.
HC222 .H47 1984

Herken Krauer, Pablo Alfredo. Vía crucis económico, 1982-86 / Pablo Alfredo Herken Krauer. Asunción : Arte Nuevo Editores, 1986. 523 p. ; 21 cm. (Serie Ensayos. 8) LC Card 86-226871
1. Paraguay - Economic conditions - 1954-. I. Title.
HC222 .H48 1986

Hermann, Christian, 1954- Auswirkungen industrieller Exportproduktion im Rahmen der internationalen Arbeitsteilung auf die Einkommensverteilung von Entwicklungsländern / Christian Hermann. Frankfurt am Main ; New York : P. Lang, c1984. viii, 393 p. ; 21 cm. (Europäische Hochschulschriften. Reihe V, Volks- und Betriebswirtschaft, 0531-7339 . Bd. 521 = vol. 521 = vol. 521) Bibliography: p. 369-393. ISBN 3-8204-7456-0 LC Card 85-191626
1. Developing countries - Commerce. 2. Income distribution - Developing countries. 3. Developing countries - Industries. I. Series: Europäische Hochschulschriften. Reihe V, Volks- und Betriebswirtschaft , Bd. 521. II. Title.
HF4055 .H47 1984

Hermann, Hans-Peter, 1942- Leasing als Leistungsangebot im Dienstleistungs-Marketing / Hans-Peter Hermann. Frankfurt am Main ; New York : P. Lang, c1984. ix, 275 p. : ill. ; 21 cm. (Europäische Hochschulschriften. Reihe V, Volks- und Betriebswirtschaft, 0531-7339 . Bd. 523 = vol. 523 = vol. 523) Originally presented as the author's thesis (doctoral--Johannes Gutenberg-Universität Mainz, 1984) Bibliography: p. 261-275. ISBN 3-8204-8084-6 LC Card 85-198760
1. Lease and rental services - Germany (West). 2. Lease and rental services - Taxation - Germany (West). I. Series: Europäische Hochschulschriften. Reihe V, Volks- und Betriebswirtschaft , Bd. 523. II. Title.
HD9999.L4363 G34 1984

Hermann, Hayo. Sektorale Wirtschaftsstruktur und kommunale Finanzsituation : eine empirische Studie für Kreise und Arbeitsmarktregionen der Bundesrepublik Deutschland / Hayo Hermann. München : V. Florentz, c1986. xiii, 384 p. : ill. ; 21 cm. (Schriften des Instituts für Regionalforschung der Universität Kiel . Bd. 9) Originally presented as the author's thesis (doctoral--Universität Kiel) under the title: Sektorale Wirtschaftsstruktur, kommunale Steuer- und Finanzausstattung und Finanzierungsspielraum für kommunale Infrastrukturinvestitionen. Bibliography: p. 377-384. ISBN 3-88259-405-5 LC Card 86-228161
1. Local finance - Germany, West. 2. Infrastructure (Economics) - Germany (West). 3. Labor supply - Germany, West. I. Title. II. Series.
HJ9473 .H47 1986

Hermann, Ursula. Die Implementierung betrieblicher Rationalisierungshandlungen und der personelle Widerstand : eine Anwendung des funktional-strukturellen Systemansatzes auf betriebswirtschaftliche Problemstellungen / Ursula Hermann. Göttingen : Vandenhoeck & Ruprecht, c1984. xx, 356 p. : 18 ill. ; 24 cm. (Innovative Unternehmensführung. Bd. 10) Originally presented as the author's thesis (doctoral--Universität Erlangen-Nürnberg, 1980) Bibliography: p. [330]-358. ISBN 3-525-12558-5 : LC Card 84-218331
1. Organizational change. 2. Organizational behavior. 3. Luhmann, Niklas. I. Title.
HD58.8 .H48 1984

Hermanns, Arnold.
Sport und Werbung, Präsenz und Erinnerungswirkung ausgewählter Werbeträger an Rennstrecken . München [1986] 70, lii, [iii] p. : LC Card 87-409557 DDC 659.13/42 19
HF5843 .S69 1986

Zukunftsorientiertes Marketing für Theorie und Praxis . Berlin , c1984. 340 p., [1] leaf of plates : ISBN 3-428-05651-5 LC Card 85-115141
HF5415 .Z85 1984

Hermansson, C. H. Sverige i imperialismens nät / C.H. Hermansson. 1. uppl. Stockholm : Arbetarkultur, 1986. 301 p. : ill. ; 21 cm. Bibliography: p. 297-301. ISBN 91-7014-203-3 LC Card 86-225250
1. International business enterprises - Sweden. I. Title.
HD2883 .H43 1986

Hermesiade : philosophische Tagungsbeiträge zum Tauschproblem / Rudolf Heinz (Hrsg.). Essen : Verlag Die Blaue Eule, c1986. 182 p. ; 21 cm. (Genealogica . Bd. 9) Papers originally presented at a conference held in Wuppertal in September of 1985. Includes bibliographical references. ISBN 3-89206-143-2 LC Card 86-226901 DDC 658.8/2 19
1. Sales promotion - Congresses. 2. Selling - Congresses. I. Heinz, Rudolf. II. Series.
HF5438.5 .H47 1986

Hern, Brian. South African paper money trends : standard catalogue of the banknotes of South Africa / compiled by Brian Hern.1st ed. Braamfontein, Republic of South Africa : P. & G. Coin Co., 1986. 172 p. : ill. ; 19 x 25 cm. Includes index. LC Card 86-201066 DDC 769.5/5968/0750968 19
1. Bank notes - South Africa - Catalogs. I. Title. II. Title: Trends.
HG1351.Z8 H47 1986

Hernádi, András. A távol-keleti kihívás : Japán, a "négyek" és Kína a 80-as években / Hernádi András. Budapest : Közgazdasági és Jogi Könyvkiadó, 1985. 233 p. ; 19 cm. Includes bibliographical references. ISBN 963-221-545-1 : LC Card 86-186844
1. East Asia - Economic conditions. 2. East Asia - Foreign economic relations - Hungary. 3. Hungary - Foreign economic relations - East Asia. I. Title.
HC460.5 .H47 1985

Hernández, Angela. Campesinas y políticos, 1986 . Santo Domingo, República Dominicana , 1986. 83 p. : LC Card 87-102259
HD6073.A292 D653 1986

Hernández C., Alexandra. Encuesta de consumo energético en el sector transporte / elaborado por Alexandra Hernández C. ; revisado por Gloria Villa, Hermann Hess ; aprobado por Jorge Blanco Roldán. San José, Costa Rica : Dirección Sectorial de Energía, 1985. 68, [137] p. : ill. ; 28 cm. Cover title: Encuesta de consumo energético, sector transporte. "Agencia para el Desarrollo Internacional"--Cover. Includes

bibliographical references. LC Card 86-218227
1. Transportation, Automotive - Costa Rica - Energy consumption. 2. Transportation, Automotive - Costa Rica - Energy conservation. 3. Transportation and state - Costa Rica. I. Villa, Gloria. II. Hess, Hermann. III. Costa Rica. Dirección Sectorial de Energía. IV. Title. V. Title: Encuesta de consumo energético, sector transporte.
HE5638 .H37 1985

Hernández, Carlos Nicolás, 1953- Yunis, José. Barrancabermeja . Bogotá , 1986. 102 p. : ISBN 958-9096-03-4 LC Card 87-400984 DDC 331.7/6223382/0986125 19
HD8310.B372 Y86 1986

Hernández H., Alberto (Hernández Hernández) Carrillo V., Jorge (Carrillo Viveros) Mujeres fronterizas en la industria maquiladora /. [Mexico City] , Tijuana, B.C.N. , 1985. 216 p. : ISBN 968-290-389-0 LC Card 87-400964 DDC 331.4 19
HD6073.O332 M483 1985

Hernández, Rafael.
Estados Unidos y América Latina : la conexión energética / Rafael Hernández. La Habana : Centro de Estudios sobre América, 1982. 209 p. : ill. ; 28 cm. (Avances de investigación . no. 17) Summary also in English. Bibliography: p. 197-200. LC Card 87-403785 DDC 333.8/232/0973 19
1. Petroleum industry and trade - Latin America. 2. Petroleum industry and trade - United States. 3. Investments, American - Latin America. I. Series: Avances de investigación (Havana, Cuba) , no. 17. II. Title.
HD9574.L3 H47 1982

Fernández Tabío, Luis René. Apuntes sobre el capital financiero en Estados Unidos . La Habana , 1981 [i.e. 1982] ii, 74 p. : LC Card 87-401153
HG5851.A3 F47 1982

Hernández, Zoila. El coraje de las mineras : marginalidad andino-minera en Canaria / Zoila Hernández. Lima, Perú : Asociación Aurora Vivar, 1986. 184 p. : ill. ; 21 cm. Errata slip inserted. LC Card 86-232046
1. Labor disputes - Peru - Canaria. 2. Miners' wives - Peru - Canaria - Political activity. I. Asociación Aurora Vivar. II. Title.
HD5361.Z9 C35 1986

Hernanz, Germán Rueda. see **Rueda Hernanz, Germán.**

Hernes, Gudmund, 1941- Colbjørnsen, Tom. Så samles vi på valen--? . [Oslo?] [1985] 88 p. : ISBN 82-991187-5-1 LC Card 85-220350
HD6752 .C644 1985

HEROINES. see **WOMEN.**

Herr, Edwin L. Career guidance and counseling through the life span : systematic approaches / Edwin L. Herr, Stanley H. Cramer.3rd ed. Glenview, Ill. : Scott, Foresman/Little, Brown College Division, c1988. xvi, 576 p. : ill. ; 25 cm. Bibliography: p. 500-565. Includes index. ISBN 0-673-39726-2 LC Card 87-22748 DDC 331.7/02/0973 19
1. Vocational guidance - United States. I. Cramer, Stanley H. II. Title.
HF5382.5.U5 H39 1988

Herr, Hansjörg, 1951- Geld, Kredit und ökonomische Dynamik in marktvermittelten Ökonomien, die Vision einer Geldwirtschaft / Hansjörg Herr. München : V. Florentz, c1986. ix, 240 p. ; 21 cm. (Volkswirtschaftliche Forschung und Entwicklung . Bd. 25) Bibliography: p. 228-238. Includes index. ISBN 3-88259-396-2 LC Card 87-140289 DDC 332.4/6 19
1. Monetary policy. 2. Credit. 3. Economic policy. I. Title. II. Series.
HG230.3 .H47 1986

Herr, Richard. Rural change and royal finances in Spain at the end of the old regime / Richard Herr. Berkeley : University of California Press, c1987. p. cm. Bibliography: p. Includes index. ISBN 0-520-05948-4 (alk. paper) LC Card 86-25027 DDC 333.3/0946/25 19
1. Church lands - Spain - Jaén (Province) - History - 18th century. 2. Secularization - Spain - Jaén (Province) - History - 18th century. 3. Agriculture - Economic aspects - Spain - Jaén (Province) - History - 18th century. 4. Jaén (Spain : Province) - History. 5. Church lands - Spain - Salamanca (Province) - History - 18th century. 6. Secularization - Spain - Salamanca (Province) - History - 18th century. 7. Agriculture - Economic aspects - Spain - Salamanca (Province) - History - 18th century. 8. Salamanca (Spain : Province) - History. I. Title.
HD779.J34 H47 1987

Herrenmensch und Arbeitsvölker : ausländische Arbeiter und Deutsche 1939-1945 / Autoren, Jochen August ... [et al.]. Berlin : Rotbuch Verlag, c1986. 189 p. : ill. ; 23 cm. (Beiträge zur nationalsozialistischen Gesundheits- und Sozialpolitik . 3) Includes bibliographical references and index. ISBN 3-88022-952-X (cover); 3-88022-925-X : LC Card 87-119712 DDC 331.11/732/0943 19
1. Forced labor - Germany - History. 2. World War, 1939-1945 - Conscript labor - Germany. 3. Alien labor - Germany - History. 4. Prisoners of war - Germany - History. I. August, Jochen. II. Series.
HD4875.G4 H47 1986

Herrera Canales, Inés. Alvarado Gómez, Armando. Principales productos del comercio exterior mexicano del siglo XIX /. México, D.F. , 1985. v. <1 > ; LC Card 87-401206 DDC 382/.0972 19
HF3236 .A5 1985

Herrera, César. Inflación, política devaluatoria y apertura externa en el Perú, 1978-1984 / César Herrera. Lima, Perú : Instituto de Estudios Peruanos, 1985. 55 p. : ill. ; 21 cm. (Documento de trabajo . no. 7) Serie Economía ; no. 1 Bibliography: p. 53-55. LC Card 87-104441
1. Devaluation of currency - Peru. 2. Inflation (Finance) - Peru. 3. Peru - Commercial policy. 4. Prices - Peru. I. Series: Documentos de trabajo (Instituto de Estudios Peruanos) , no. 7. II. Title.
HG895 .H47 1985

Herrera, Felipe, 1922- América Latina, desarrollo e integracíon / Felipe Herrera. [Santiago, Chile] : Editorial Emisión, [1986] 302 p., [11] p. of plates : ill. ; 22 cm. LC Card 87-115159 DDC 337.1/8 19
1. Latin America - Economic integration. 2. Economic assistance, American - Latin America. 3. Finance - Latin America. 4. Latin America - Social conditions - 1945-. I. Title.
HC125 .H466 1986

Herrera García, Antonio.
El Aljarafe durante el antiguo régimen / por Antonio Herrera García. Sevilla : Excma. Diputación Provincial, 1981. 147 p., [3] leaves of plates : ill. ; 17 cm. (Colecciones paralelas. Historia . 3) Includes bibliographical references. ISBN 84-500-4850-8 LC Card 82-142028 DDC 333.3/0946/86 19
1. Land tenure - Spain - Aljarafe - History. 2. Farm produce - Spain - Aljarafe - History. 3. Aljarafe (Spain) - Population - History. 4. Aljarafe (Spain) - Social life and customs. I. Title. II. Series.
HD779.A39 H47 1981 ***NYPL [JLC 86-126]***

El Aljarafe sevillano durante el antiguo régimen : un estudio de su evolución socioeconómica en los siglos XVI, XVII y XVIII / Antonio Herrera García ; prólogo de Julio González González. [Sevilla] : Excma. Diputación Provincial de Sevilla, 1980. 517 p., [9] leaves of plates : ill. ; 24 cm. (Publicaciones de la Excma. Diputación Provincial de Sevilla. Sección Historia . ser. 1a, no. 17) "Apéndice documental": p. [441]-481. Includes index. Bibliography: p. 431-440. ISBN 84-500-4373-5 LC Card 81-173649 DDC 946/.86 19
1. Land tenure - Spain - Aljarafe - History. 2. Farm produce - Spain - Aljarafe - History. 3. Aljarafe (Spain) - Population - History. 4. Aljarafe (Spain) - Social life and customs. I. Series. II. Series: Seville)Province). Diputación Provincial. Publicaciones. Sección: Historia. Seriel , no. 17. III. Title.
HD779.A39 H475 1980 ***NYPL [JLF 86-928]***

Herrero de Miñón, Miguel, 1940- España y la Comunidad Económica Europea : un sí para-- / Miguel Herrero de Miñón.1a ed. Barcelona, España : Planeta, 1986. 225 p. ; 20 cm. (Colección Textos. 90) "Apéndices documentales": p. [215]-221. Includes bibliographical references and index. ISBN 84-320-0661-0 LC Card 87-100785
1. European Economic Community - Spain. I. Title.
HC241.25.S6 H47 1986

Herrero Suazo, Santiago. Técnicas presupuestarias en la administración pública / Santiago Herrero Suazo, Vicente Querol Bellido. Alcalá de Henares-Madrid, España : Instituto Nacional de Administración Pública, [1984?] 382 p. : ill. ; 19 cm. (Colección Biblioteca bsica de administración pública. Serie especial) Publicaciones del Instituto Nacional de Administración Pública Bibliography: p. 325-327. ISBN 84-7351-173-5 LC Card 85-185202
1. Budget - Spain. I. Querol Bellido, Vicente. II. Title. III. Series.
HJ1248 .H47 1984

Herrgeist, Fritz, 1895-1980. Die Wasser-, Boden- und Deichverbände in Ost- und Westpreussen, 1868 bis 1938 / Fritz Herrgeist. Köln : Grote, 1983. 524 p. : ill. (1 col.), maps ; 21 cm. (Studien zur Geschichte Preussens. Bd. 32) Bibliography: p. 523-524. ISBN 3-7745-6456-6 LC Card 84-211844
1. Water districts - Poland - Prussia, West - History. 2. Water districts - Prussia, East (Poland and R.S.F.S.R.) - History. 3. Levee districts - Poland - Prussia, West - History. 4. Levee districts - Prussia, East (Poland and R.S.F.S.R.) - History. 5. Soil conservation districts - Poland - Prussia, West - History. 6. Soil conservation districts - Prussia, East (Poland and R.S.F.S.R.) - History. I. Title.
HD1697.P64 P784 1983

Herrick, Helen S. Daniels, Leroy Judson, 1882- Tales of an old horsetrader . Iowa City , 1987. viii, 235 p. : ISBN 0-87745-173-7 LC Card 87-10932 DDC 338.1/761/00924 B 19
HD9434.U6 D36 1987

Herrington, Paul.
Pricing of water services / [prepared and written by P. Herrington]. Paris : Organisation for Economic Co-operation and Development ; Washington, D.C. : OECD Publications and Information Centre [distributor], 1987. 145 p. : ill. ; 23 cm. Bibliography: p. 138-145. ISBN 92-64-12921-9 (pbk.) : LC Card 87-167536 DDC 338.4/336361 19
1. Municipal water supply - Rates. 2. Municipal water supply - Finance. 3. Water quality management - Finance. 4. Sewage disposal - Finance. I. Title.
HD4456 .H47 1987

Water demand forecasting . Norwich, U.K. , c1986. 139 p. : ISBN 0-86094-214-7 : LC Card 87-127184 DDC 333.91/13 19
HD1690.5 .W383 1986

Herrmann, Ernst. Die Deutsche Bundespost : Kommunikationsunternehmen zwischen Staat und Wirtschaft / Ernst Herrmann.1. Aufl. Baden-Baden : Nomos, 1986. 261 p. ; 23 cm. (Schriften zur öffentlichen Verwaltung und öffentlichen Wirtschaft. Bd. 99) Summary in English. Bibliography: p. 241-250. Includes indexes. ISBN 3-7890-1323-4 LC Card 87-116897 DDC 383/.4943 19
1. Postal service - Germany, West. 2. Deutsche Bundespost - Communication systems. I. Title.
HE6995 .H44 1986

Herrmann, Joachim, 1932- Ökonomie und Gesellschaft an der Wende von der Antike zum Mittelalter : zum Problem der Herausbildung der ökonomischen Grundlagen der Feudalgesellschaft im mittleren und westlichen Europa / Joachim Herrmann. Berlin : Akademie-Verlag, 1979. 72 p. : ill. ; 22 cm. (Sitzungsberichte der Akademie der Wissenschaften der DDR. Gesellschaftswissenschaften . Jahrg. 1979, Nr. 13/G) Includes bibliographical references. LC Card 85-209249
1. Economic history - To 500. 2. Europe - Economic conditions - To 1492. 3. Europe - Social conditions - To 1492. I. Title. II. Series.
HC31 .H47 1979

Herrmann, Roland. The compensatory financing system of the International Monetary Fund : an analysis of its effects and comparisons with alternative systems / by Roland Herrmann. Kiel, West-Germany : Kieler Wissenschaftsverlag Vauk, 1983. iii, 85 p. ; 21 cm. (Forum, 0721-474X . no. 4) Summary in German. Bibliography: p. 81-85. ISBN 3-922553-18-4 (pbk.) LC Card 83-227524 DDC 332.1/52 19
1. International Monetary Fund. 2. Balance of payments - Developing countries. 3. Commodity control - Developing countries. I. Series: Forum (Kiel, Germany) , no. 4. II. Title.
HG3881.5.I58 H47 1983 ***NYPL [JLD 97-7]***

Herrschaft, Krise, Überleben : Gesellschaft der Bundesrepublik in den achtziger Jahren / herausgegeben von Hans-Günter Thien und Hanns Wienold.1. Aufl. Münster : Westfälisches Dampfboot, 1986. 396 p. : ill. ; 21 cm. Includes bibliographies. ISBN 3-924550-19-0 LC Card 86-229590
1. Germany, West - Economic policy - 1974-. 2. Germany, West - Social policy. 3. Germany, West - Economic conditions - 1974-. 4. Germany, West -

Social conditions. 5. Germany (West) - Politics and government - 1982-. 6. Bureaucracy - Germany, West. I. Thien, Hans-Günter, 1947-. II. Wienold, Hanns, 1944-.
HC286.7 .H48 1986

Herrschaftsformen und Industrialisierungsprozess in Peru . Basurco Valverde, Gerardo Félix. Freiburg [Breisgau] , c1985. xi, 420 p. : ISBN 3-8107-2210-3 LC Card 86-179243
HC227 .B339 1985

Herschell Gordon Lewis on the art of writing copy /. Lewis, Herschell Gordon, 1926- Englewood Cliffs, N.J. , c1987. p. cm. ISBN 0-13-387309-9 : LC Card 87-11489 DDC 659.13/22 19
HF5825 .L44 1987

Hersey, Paul. Management of organizational behavior : utilizing human resources / Paul Hersey, Kenneth H. Blanchard.5th ed. Englewood Cliffs, N.J. : Prentice-Hall, 1988. p. cm. Bibliography: p. Includes index. ISBN 0-13-551268-9 : LC Card 87-23064 DDC 658.3 19
1. Organizational behavior. 2. Management. 3. Leadership. I. Blanchard, Kenneth H. II. Title.
HD58.7 .H47 1988

HERSFELD-ROTENBURG (GERMANY : LANDKREIS) - ECONOMIC CONDITIONS.
Spilker, Ernst Moritz. Der Wirtschaftsraum zwischen den Wirtschaftsräumen . Köln , 1986. 223 p. : LC Card 87-408201 DDC 330.943/55 19
HC288.W46 S67 1986

Hertner, Peter. Multinationals--theory and history /. Aldershot, Hants, England , Brookfield, Vt., USA , c1986. vii, 200 p. : ISBN 0-566-05078-1 : LC Card 85-24955 DDC 338.8/8 19
HD2755.5 .M86 1986 ***NYPL [JLD 86-1575]***

Hertrich, Roland, 1954- Die Reihenfolge der Informationssuche von Konsumenten : eine theoretische und empirische Untersuchung / Roland Hertrich. Frankfurt am Main ; New York : P. Lang, c1985. iv, 272 p. ; 21 cm. (Europäische Hochschulschriften. Reihe V, Volks- und Betriebswirtschaft, 0531-7339 . Bd. 652 = vol. 652 = vol. 652) Bibliography: p. 261-272. ISBN 3-8204-8594-5 LC Card 85-230707
1. Consumers - Mathematical models. I. Series: Europäische Hochschulschriften. Reihe V, Volks- und Betriebswirtschaft , Bd. 652. II. Title.
HB801 .H43 1985

Hertz, David Bendel, 1919- The expert executive : using AI and expert systems for financial management, marketing, production, and strategy / David Bendel Hertz. New York : Wiley, c1988. xvi, 238 p. ; 24 cm. Bibliography: p. 231-232. Includes index. ISBN 0-471-89677-2 LC Card 87-21682 DDC 658/.05633 19
1. Business - Data processing. 2. Management - Data processing. 3. Artificial intelligence. 4. Expert systems (Computer science). I. Title.
HF5548.2 .H455 1988

Hertz, Leah. The business amazons / Leah Hertz. London : Deutsch, 1986. xviii, 264, [1] p., [1] leaf of plates : ill. ; 25 cm. Bibliography: p. 262-[265]. ISBN 0-233-97892-5 : LC Card 86-200078 DDC 338.6/422/088042 19
1. Women-owned business enterprises - Great Britain. 2. Women-owned business enterprises - United States. 3. Women in business - Great Britain. 4. Women in business - United States. I. Title.
HD2346.G7 H47 1986

Hervé, Jean-Claude. Demornex, Jacqueline. Lancôme /. Paris , c1985. 189 p. : ISBN 2-903370-23-0 LC Card 86-201508
HD9999.P3934 L363 1985
NYPL [JSG 87-24]

Herz, H. (Hermann) Angebotsentwicklung und Preisbildung natürlicher Ressourcen /. München , 1986. vii, 148, 10 p. : ISBN 3-486-26171-1 LC Card 86-182074
HC59 .A794 1986

Herz, Martin Florian, 1917- The Role of embassies in promoting business . Lanham, MD , 1987, c1981. p. cm. ISBN 0-8191-5053-3 (pbk. : alk. paper) LC Card 87-14027 DDC 382/.3/0973 19
HF1417.5 .R64 1987

Herzberg, Frederick.
Job attitudes . New York , 1987. xii, 279 p. ; ISBN 0-8240-8210-9 (alk. paper) : LC Card 86-26935 DDC 331.25 19
HF5549.5.J63 J57 1987

The managerial choice : to be efficient and to be human / Frederick Herzberg.2nd ed., rev. Salt Lake City, Utah : Olympus Pub. Co., c1982. xviii, 360 p. : ill. ; 24 cm. Includes index. Errata slip inserted. "Bibliography of the works of Frederick Herzberg": p. 329-34. ISBN 0-913420-97-2 LC Card 81-85925 DDC 658.3/14 19
1. Incentives in industry - Addresses, essays, lectures. 2. Motivation (Psychology) - Addresses, essays, lectures. 3. Psychology, Industrial - Addresses, essays, lectures. 4. Job enrichment - Addresses, essays, lectures. I. Title.
HF5549.5.I5 H47 1982
NYPL [JLE 86-2591]

Herzig, Arno. Arbeiter in Hamburg . Hamburg , c1983. 606 p. : ISBN 3-8103-0807-2 LC Card 86-174037
HD8460.H36 A73 1983

Herzog, Philippe.
Un Chemin pour sortir de la crise /. Paris , c1985. 249 p. ; ISBN 2-209-05753-1 LC Card 86-154397
HC276.2 .C517 1985

La France peut se ressaisir / Philippe Herzog. Paris : Messidor / Editions sociales, c1987. 416 p. : ill. ; 22 cm. Includes bibliographical references. ISBN 2-209-05941-0 : LC Card 87-169995
1. France - Economic policy - 1981-. 2. France - Politics and government - 1981-. 3. Political planning - France. 4. France - Foreign economic relations. I. Title.
HC276.3 .H47 1987

Herzog, Werner. Kartographie und Bürgerbeteiligung im Rahmen der vorbereitenden Bauleitplanung : empirische Untersuchungen zur kartographischen Kommunikation / Werner Herzog. Paderborn : F. Schöningh, 1986. xi, 164 p. : 40 ill. (some col.) ; 30 cm. (Bochumer geographische Arbeiten. Heft 46) Summary in English. Supplementary material (7 pieces) in pocket. Originally presented as the author's thesis (doctoral)--Ruhr-Universität Bochum, 1985. Bibliography: p. 150-164. ISBN 3-506-71256-X LC Card 87-401386 DDC 333.73/17/028 19
1. Land use - Planning - Maps. 2. Land use - Germany (West) - Planning - Citizen participation. 3. City planning - Germany, West - Citizen participation. I. Title. II. Series.
HD108.6 .H47 1986

Heseler, Heiner. Wirtschaftsdemokratie gegen Wirtschaftskrise . Hamburg , 1986. 177 p. : ISBN 3-87975-310-5 LC Card 86-193914
HD4175 .W54 1986

Hess, Alan. Googie : fifties coffee shop architecture / Alan Hess. San Francisco, CA : Chronicle Books, [1986]. 144 p. : ill. (some col.) : 26 cm. Includes index. Bibliography: p. 142-143 ISBN 0-87701-334-9 (pbk.) : LC Card 85-17089 DDC 725/.71/0973 19
1. Coffee-houses - United States. 2. Car washes - United States. 3. Architecture, Modern - 20th century - United States. I. Title.
NA7856 .H47 1986
NYPL [3-MQWO 86-2210]

Hess, Hermann. Hernández C., Alexandra. Encuesta de consumo energético en el sector transporte /. San José, Costa Rica , 1985. 68, [137] p. : LC Card 86-218227
HE5638 .H37 1985

Hess, Karen M., 1939- Buchholz, Steve. Creating the high performance team /. New York , c1987. xiii, 202 p. : ISBN 0-471-85672-X : LC Card 86-32623 DDC 658.4/02 19
HD66 .B82 1987a

Hess, Stephan M. Liquiditätswirkungen alternativer Geldvermögensanlagen / von Stephan M. Hess. Frankfurt am Main : F. Knapp, c1983. 193 p. ; 21 cm. (Probleme des Kapitalmarkts. Monographien. 10) Originally presented as the author's thesis (doctoral)--Johann Wolfgang Goethe-Universität Frankfurt am Main. Bibliography: p. 184-193. ISBN 3-7819-2533-1 LC Card 84-109572
1. Liquidity (Economics). I. Title. II. Series.
HG173.5 .H47 1983

HESSE (GERMANY) - ECONOMIC CONDITIONS.
Krietemeyer, Hartmut, 1955- Der Erklärungsgehalt der Exportbasistheorie /. Hamburg , 1983. 224 p. : ISBN 3-87895-240-6 : LC Card 84-147595
HC287.H4 K75 1983

Wie war denn das? . Frankfurt [1983?] 30 p., [1] leaf of plates : LC Card 84-158849
HC287.H4 W47 1983

HESSE (GERMANY) - ECONOMIC POLICY.
Steger, Ulrich. Zukunft statt Wende . Bonn , c1986. 171 p. ; ISBN 3-87831-442-6 LC Card 86-226220
HC287.H4 S73 1986

Hesse (Germany). Landtag. Grünen. Geiler, Nick. Wasser konkret . Wiesbaden [1985] 199 p. : LC Card 86-162674
HD1697.G33 H474 1985

Hesse, Günter, Dr. Die Entstehung industrialisierter Volkswirtschaften : ein Beitrag zur theoretischen und empirischen Analyse der langfristigen wirtschaftlichen Entwicklung / Günter Hesse. Tübingen : J.C.B. Mohr, 1982. vi, 100 p. : ill. ; 24 cm. Includes index. Bibliography: p. [93]-97. ISBN 3-16-344559-4 : LC Card 83-153439 DDC 338.9 19
1. Industrialization. 2. Industry and weather. I. Title.
HD84 .H4718 1982 ***NYPL [JLE 87-1169]***

Hesse, Gunter, 1949- Arend, Brigitte, 1953- Vom Lohnarbeiter zum Klienten . Frankfurt am Main , c1986. 206 p. ; ISBN 3-445-02490-1 LC Card 86-231993
HD5708 .A74 1986

Hesselbach, Walter. Wirtschaftspolitik und wirtschaftliche Entwicklung . Bonn , c1985. xii, 248 p. : ISBN 3-87831-405-1 LC Card 85-142846
HD75 .W57 1985

HESSELBACH, WALTER.
Wirtschaftspolitik und wirtschaftliche Entwicklung . Bonn , c1985. xii, 248 p. : ISBN 3-87831-405-1 LC Card 85-142846
HD75 .W57 1985

Hesselmann, Hans. Das Wirtschaftsbürgertum in Bayern 1890-1914 : ein Beitrag zur Analyse der Wechselbeziehungen zwischen Wirtschaft und Politik am Beispiel des Wirtschaftsbürgertums im Bayern der Prinzregentenzeit / von Hans Hesselmann. [Stuttgart] : In Kommission bei F. Steiner Verlag Wiesbaden, 1985. 419 p. : ill. ; 23 cm. (Beiträge zur Wirtschafts- und Sozialgeschichte, 0723-5453 . Bd. 32) Bibliography: p. 380-400. Includes index. ISBN 3-515-04565-1 LC Card 86-127555
1. Bavaria (Germany) - Economic conditions. 2. Bavaria (Germany) - Politics and government - 1777-1918. 3. Social structure - Germany (West) - Bavaria - History. 4. Middle classes - Germany (West) - Bavaria - History. I. Title.
HC287.B3 H46 1985

Hessick, Michael H. Achieving quality in financial service organizations : how to identify and satisfy customer expectations / Michael H. Hessick and Robert E. Grasing. New York : Quorum Books, c1988. p. cm. Includes index. ISBN 0-89930-231-9 (lib. bdg. : alk. paper) LC Card 87-24937 DDC 332.1/2/0688 19
1. Financial institutions - United States. 2. Consumer satisfaction - United States. I. Grasing, Robert E. II. Title.
HG181 .H44 1988

Hessische Erwachsenenbildungsstätte Falkenstein (Königstein im Taunus, Germany) Processi formativi e coscienza operaia . Pisa , c1983. 509 p. ; LC Card 86-136656 DDC 658.3/124/0945 19
HF5549.5.T7 P69 1983
NYPL [JLE 87-1466]

Hessischer Jugendring. Vorstand. Angsturlaub statt Bildungsurlaub . Frankfurt am Main , c1979. 179 p. : ISBN 3-88203-044-5 LC Card 85-167471
HD5257.2.G3 A54 1979

Hessisches Statistisches Landesamt.
Gehalts- und Lohnstrukturerhebung 1978 . Wiesbaden , 1983. 285, [3] p. ; LC Card 84-217477
HA1320 .H529 n.F., Nr. 152 HD5030.H47

Die Kommunalwahlen am 20. März 1977 . Wiesbaden , 1978. 116 p. ; LC Card 86-102904
HA1320 .H529 n.F., Nr. 88 JS5471.H423E44

Hester, Edward J. Predicting which disabled employees will return to work : the Menninger RTW Scale / Edward J. Hester, Paul G. Decelles, Edwin L. Gaddis. Topeka, Kan. (700 Jackson, 9th floor, Topeka 66603) : Menninger Foundation, Will Menninger Center for Applied

Behaviorial Sciences, Division of Rehabilitation Programs, Research and Training Center, c1986. x, 86 p. : ill. ; 28 cm. Bibliography: p. 85-86. LC Card 86-231920 DDC 331.5/9 19
1. Handicapped - Employment - United States - Forecasting. 2. Vocational rehabilitation - United States - Forecasting. I. Decelles, Paul G. II. Gaddis, Edwin L. III. Menninger Rehabilitation Research and Training Center. IV. Title.
HD7256.U5 H43 1986

Heston, Thomas J. (Thomas Janney) Sweet subsidy : the economic and diplomatic effects of the U. S. sugar acts, 1934-1974 / Thomas J. Heston. New York : Garland Pub., 1987. 544 p. ; 23 cm. (Foreign economic policy of the United States) Originally presented as the author's thesis (Ph. D.)--Case Western Reserve University, 1975. Includes bibliographies and index. ISBN 0-8240-8084-X (alk. paper) : LC Card 87-23776 DDC 338.1/8 19
1. Sugar trade - United States. 2. Sugar laws and legislation - United States. 3. Subsidies - United States. 4. Sugar trade - Cuba. 5. United States - Foreign economic relations. 6. United States - Foreign relations - 20th century. I. Title. II. Series.
HD9105 .H47 1987

Het psychologisch klimaat van de economie in de Verenigde Staten en West-Europa /. Katona, George, 1901- [Aspirations and affluence. Dutch.] Utrecht , 1974. 247 p. ; ISBN 90-274-5826-X ***NYPL [JLD 86-295]***

De heta åren /. Bergquist, Sven, 1926- [Stockholm] , 1985. 319 p. : ISBN 91-7566-089-X LC Card 85-233735
HD9698.S84 S923 1985

Hetaireia Oikonomikēs kai Koinōnikēs Historias tēs Helladas. Tsokopoulos, Vasias. Peiraias, 1835-1870 . Athēna , 1984. 280 p., [8] p. of plates : LC Card 86-128354
HC298.P57 T77 1984 ***NYPL [JLD 86-171]***

Heterogene Koordinationsinstrumente im Beschäftigungssystem der DDR /. Schrimpff, Wolfgang. Münster , 1983. xv, 360 p. : ISBN 3-7923-0505-4 LC Card 85-140056
HD5780.5.A6 S37 1983

Héthy, Lajos.
Patterns of worker's behavior and the enterprise / Lajos Héthy and Csaba Makó. New Brunswick, U. S.A. : Transaction Books, c1987. p. cm. Includes bibliographies. ISBN 0-88738-177-4 LC Card 87-13958 DDC 331/.0471/09439 19
1. Metal-workers - Hungary - Case studies. 2. Industrial sociology - Hungary - Case studies. 3. Industrial relations - Hungary - Case studies. I. Makó, Csaba. II. Title.
HD6956.M5 H47 1987

A vezetők részvétele a vezetésben / [irta Héthy Lajos]. Budapest : Szakszervezetek Elméleti Kutató Intézete, 1983. 87 p. : ill. ; 21 cm. ISBN 963-608-057-7 LC Card 85-110905
1. Executives - Hungary. I. Szakszervezetek Elméleti Kutató Intézete. II. Title.
HD38.25.H9 H47 1983

Hetzler, Antoinette, 1943-
Arbetsskadeförsäkringens tillämpning : en rättssociologisk studie / Antoinette Hetzler, Kjell E. Eriksson.2. uppl. Lund : EKNA : Distribution, Infografen, [1984] 176 p. : ill. ; 21 cm. ACQ MSG: E 49-140. Bibliography: p. 172-176. ISBN 91-970351-3-0 : LC Card 84-159654
1. Workers' compensation - Sweden. 2. Workers' compensation - Law and legislation - Sweden. I. Eriksson, Kjell E. II. Title.
HD7103.65.S8 H48 1984

Heuber, Ulrich. Untersuchung der Unfälle auf Bundesautobahnen . [München?] [1976] 84 p. : LC Card 85-135444
HE5614.5.G3 U58 1976

Heuer, Kurt. Innovation und internationale Monopole /. Berlin , 1983. 85 p. ; LC Card 84-104008
HD2755.5 .I534 1983

Heuer, Wolfgang. Peru, Kolonisation und Abhängigkeit . Saarbrücken , Fort Lauderdale , 1981. 192 p. : ISBN 3-88156-165-X : LC Card 82-104103
HD1905.O75 P47 1981

Heurung, Rainer-Otto, 1952- Wirken Substanzsteuern investitionshemmend? / Rainer-Otto Heurung. Frankfurt am Main ; New York : P. Lang, c1986. xvii, 251, [93] p. : ill. ; 23 cm. (Studien zum Finanz- und Steuerrecht, 0170-9224 . Bd. 10) Bibliography: p. [71]-[93] (3rd group). ISBN 3-8204-9800-1 LC Card 87-408762 DDC 332.63 19
1. Capital investments - Germany, West. 2. Corporations - Taxation - Germany, West. I. Title. II. Series.
HG4028.C4 H49 1986

Heute Grenzen-- morgen Europa / von Dieter Rogalla ... [et al.]. Bonn : Europa Union Verlag, c1984. 107 p. : ill. ; 21 cm. ISBN 3-7713-0227-7 LC Card 85-146220
1. Tolls - European Economic Community countries. I. Rogalla, Dieter.
HE197.E86 H48 1984

Hewers of wood and drawers of water . Semyonov, Moshe. Ithaca, NY , c1987. xii, 152 p. : ISBN 0-87546-133-6 (pbk. : alk. paper) LC Card 87-2682 DDC 331.6/99275695 19
HD8660 .S45 1987

Hewes, Jeremy Joan. Wordprocessing on IBM PCs / Jeremy Joan Hewes, Bill Grout. New York : Wiley, c1985. xiii, 178 p. : ill. ; 26 cm. (Wiley IBM PC series) Includes index. "Wiley Press book." ISBN 0-471-88663-7 : LC Card 84-11966 DDC 652/.5 19
1. Word processing. 2. IBM Personal Computer - Programming. I. Grout, Bill. II. Title. III. Title: Word processing on the IBM PC.
Z52.5.I27 H48 1985 ***NYPL [JSF 87-232]***

Hewett, Charles E., 1950- Forests in demand . Boston, Mass. , c1982. xv, 265 p. : ISBN 0-86569-106-1 : LC Card 81-12881 DDC 333.75/0973 19
SD565 .F58 ***NYPL [JLE 86-4465]***

Hewison, Kevin. Southeast Asia in the 1980s . Sydney , Boston , 1987. p. cm. ISBN 0-04-301289-2 LC Card 87-19550 DDC 338.959 19
HC441 .S69 1987

HEWLETT-PACKARD COMPANY.
Change master companies [videorecording] . Chicago, IL , 1987. 1 videocassette (42 min.) : LC Card 87-705608 DDC 658.3 11
HD45

Hewlett, Sylvia Ann, 1946- A lesser life : the myth of women's liberation in America / Sylvia A. Hewlett. New York, N.Y. : W. Morrow, 1986. 461 p. : ill. ; 24 cm. Includes bibliographic notes and index. ISBN 0-688-04855-2 LC Card 85-21395 DDC 305.4/2/0973 19
1. Feminism - United States. 2. Women - United States - Social conditions. 3. Women - United States - Economic conditions. I. Title.
HQ1426 .H457 1986 ***NYPL [JLE 86-1460]***

Hexē hapla mathēmata : hē sēmerinē koinōnia kai hē palē gia to sosialismo ; Ta dekaexaselida tēs Komep : to kephalaiokratiko systēma. Thessalonikē : Ekdosē "Komep", 1945. 32, 16 p. ; 21 cm. (Dokoumenta tou Hellēnikou proodeutikou kinēmatos . 11) Cover title LC Card 87-122267
1. Capitalism. I. Title: Dekaexaselida tēs Komep. II. Series.
HB501 .H475 1945

Hexter, Kathryn Wertheim. Sweet, David C. Public utilities and the poor . New York , 1987. xxiii, 174 p. : ISBN 0-275-92572-2 (alk. paper) : LC Card 87-6979 DDC 362.5/82 19
HC110.P6 S894 1987

Hey, John Denis. Surveys in the economics of uncertainty /. Oxford, UK , New York, NY, USA , 1987. 232 p. : ISBN 0-631-15335-7 LC Card 87-10366 DDC 330 19
HB615 .S97 1987

Heyel, Carl, 1908- John Diebold on management. Foreword by Richard M. Cyert. Englewood Cliffs, N.J., Prentice-Hall [1972] ix, 282 p. illus. 29 cm. "Bibliography: selected writings of John Diebold:" p. [269]-275. ISBN 0-13-510214-6 LC Card 75-170643 DDC 658
1. Technological innovations - Addresses, essays, lectures. 2. Automation - Social aspects - Addresses, essays, lectures. 3. Business - Data processing - Addresses, essays, lectures. 4. Management - Addresses, essays, lectures. I. Diebold, John, 1926-. II. Title.
HD45 .H42 ***NYPL [JLF 73-1242]***

Heymann, Eugène. Empresas multinacionales y división internacional del trabajo /. Salamanca , 1977. 158 p. : ISBN 84-301-0465-8 LC Card 86-164261
HD2755.5 .E49 1977

Heyne, Paul T. Microeconomics / Paul Heyne. Chicago : Science Research Associates, c1988. xiv, 411 p. : ill. (some col.) ; 24 cm. Includes index. ISBN 0-574-19485-1 (pbk.) : LC Card 87-22194 DDC 338.5 19
1. Microeconomics. I. Title.
HB172 .H525 1988

Hezel, Dieter. Siedlungsformen und soziale Kosten . Frankfurt am Main , New York , c1984. vi, 219 p., [1] folded leaf of plates : ISBN 3-8204-5402-0 LC Card 85-190162
HD7339.A3 S59 1984

Hi-res graphics for the Apple II/IIe/IIc /. Tice, Robert L. Blue Ridge Summit, Pa. , 1985. vii, 197 p. : ISBN 0-8306-0849-4 : LC Card 84-23954 DDC 001.64/43 19
T385 .T52 1985 ***NYPL [JSE 86-805]***

Hibbard, W. R. (Walter Rollo) The Virginia coal industry : final report / Walter R. Hibbard. Blacksburg, Va. (617 N. Main St., Blacksburg 24061) : Virginia Center for Coal and Energy Research, Virginia Polytechnic Institute and State University, [1986] ii, 46 leaves ; 28 cm. Cover title. "October 1986." LC Card 87-620671 DDC 338.2/724/09755 19
1. Coal trade - Virginia. I. Virginia Center for Coal and Energy Research. II. Title.
HD9547.V8 H523 1986

Hibbs, Douglas A., 1944- The American political economy : macroeconomics and electoral politics / Douglas A. Hibbs, Jr. Cambridge, Mass. : Harvard University Press, 1987. xiii, 404 p. : ill. ; 24 cm. Bibliography: p. [329]-395. Includes index. ISBN 0-674-02735-3 (alk. paper) LC Card 87-155 DDC 338.973 19
1. Business cycles - Political aspects - United States. 2. Elections - United States. 3. United States - Economic policy - 1981-. 4. United States - Economic conditions - 1981-. I. Title.
HB3743 .H52 1987

Hibbs, Douglas A., 1943- The political economy of industrial democracies / Douglas A. Hibbs, Jr. Cambridge, Mass. : Harvard University Press, 1987. viii, 327 p. : ill. ; 24 cm. Includes bibliographical references and index. ISBN 0-674-68580-6 LC Card 86-9799 DDC 339.5/09171/3 19
1. Business cycles - United States. 2. Business cycles - Europe. 3. Strikes and lockouts - United States. 4. Strikes and lockouts - Europe. 5. Industry and state - United States. 6. Industry and state - Europe. I. Title.
HB3743 .H53 1987 ***NYPL [JLE 87-1430]***

Hichert, Ingo, 1944- Staatliche Exportabsicherung : die Hermes-Deckung vor dem Hintergrund der internationalen Verschuldungskrise / Ingo Hichert. Köln : Deutscher Instituts-Verlag, c1986. 302 p. : ill. ; 19 cm. (DIV-Sachbuchreihe. 44) Bibliography: p. 240-246. Includes index. ISBN 3-602-34848-2 LC Card 87-145196 DDC 368.8/7 19
1. Insurance, Export credit - Germany, West. I. Title.
HG9977.4.G3 H53 1986

Hickel, Rudolf. Wirtschaftsdemokratie gegen Wirtschaftskrise . Hamburg , 1986. 177 p. : ISBN 3-87975-310-5 LC Card 86-193914
HD4175 .W54 1986

Hickling, Allen. Friend, John. Planning under pressure . Oxford [Oxfordshire] , New York , 1987. xix, 338 p. : ISBN 0-08-018766-8 : LC Card 86-25219 DDC 658.4/012 19
HD30.28 .F75 1987

Hickman, Bert G., 1924- Macroeconomics [i.e. Macroeconomic] impacts of energy shocks /. Amsterdam ; New York : xvi, 331 p. : ISBN 0-444-70247-4 (U. S.) LC Card 87-9035 DDC 338.4/36655/0724 19
HG229 .M315 1987

Hickman, Craig R. The future 500 : creating tomorrow's organizations today / by Craig R. Hickman and Michael A. Silva. New York, N.Y. : New American Library, c1987. xiv, 274 p. ; 24 cm. "NAL books." Bibliography: p. 264-267. Includes index. ISBN 0-453-00544-6 LC Card 87-15204 DDC 658 19
1. Management. 2. Organizational effectiveness. 3. Management - History. I. Silva, Michael A., 1951-. II. Title. III. Title: Future five hundred.
HD31 .H4814 1987

Hickman, James R. Management advisory services : expanding your accounting practice / James R. Hickman. Colorado Springs, Colo. :

Shephard's/McGraw-Hill, c1987. xxiv, 510 p. : ill. ; 24 cm.' 1 diskette. (Accounting and finance practice series) Includes bibliographies and index. ISBN 0-07-172102-9 LC Card 87-4482 DDC 657/.068/8 19
1. Accounting - Marketing. 2. Business consultants. I. Title. II. Series.
HF5657 .H53 1987

Hickman, Martin Berkeley, 1925- David Matthew Kennedy : banker, statesman, churchman / by Martin Berkeley Hickman. Salt Lake City, Utah : Deseret Book Co., in cooperation with the David M. Kennedy Center for International Studies, c1987. xi, 403 p. : ill. ; 24 cm. (Monograph series of the David M. Kennedy Center for International Studies at Brigham Young University . v. 1) Bibliography: p. 367-383. Includes index. ISBN 0-87579-093-3 : LC Card 87-19898 DDC 332.1/092/4 B 19
1. Kennedy, David Matthew, 1905-. 2. Bankers - United States - Biography. 3. Statesmen - United States - Biography. 4. Church of Jesus Christ of Latter-Day Saints - Biography. I. Title. II. Series.
HG2463.K46 H53 1987

Hicks, Donald A. Automation technology and industrial renewal : adjustment dynamics in the U. S. metalworking sector / Donald A. Hicks. Washington, D.C. : American Enterprise Institute for Public Policy Research, [1985], c1986. xiii, 160 p. ; 23 cm. (AEI studies . 440) Bibliography: p. 153-160. ISBN 0-8447-3598-1 LC Card 85-31568 DDC 671 19
1. Metal-work - United States - Automation. 2. Metal-work - United States - Technological innovations. I. Series. II. Series: American Enterprise Institute for Public Policy Research. AEI studies, 440. III. Title.
HD9506.U62 H53 1986 ***NYPL [JSE 86-1901]***

Hicks, John Richard, Sir, 1904- Capital and time : a neo-Austrian theory / by John Hicks. Oxford [Oxfordshire] ; New York : Oxford University Press, 1987. p. cm. Reprint. Originally published: Oxford : Clarendon Press, 1973. Includes bibliographies. ISBN 0-19-877286-6 : LC Card 87-20233 DDC 332/.041 19
1. Capital - Mathematical models. 2. Austrian school of economists. I. Title.
HB501 .H48 1987

Hicks, John Richard, Sir, 1940- A revision of demand theory / by J.R. Hicks. Oxford [Oxfordshire] : Clarendon Press ; New York : Oxford University Press, 1986, c1956. vii, 196 p. : ill. ; 23 cm. Includes bibliographical references and index. ISBN 0-19-828110-2 LC Card 86-154241 DDC 338.5/212 19
1. Demand (Economic theory). 2. Consumption (Economics). I. Title.
HB801 .H48 1986 ***NYPL [JLD 86-3663]***

Hicks, Sam A. The use of microcomputers in accounting / Sam A. Hicks and Donald V. Saftner. St. Paul : West Pub. Co., c1985. xx, 349 p. : ill. ; 25 cm. ISBN 0-314-87064-4 (pbk.) LC Card 85-8950 DDC 657/.028/54 19
1. Accounting - Data processing. 2. Microcomputers - Programming. I. Saftner, Donald V. II. Title.
HF5679 .H535 1985 ***NYPL [JLF 86-1720]***

Hicks, Tyler Gregory, 1921-
How to borrow your way to real estate riches / Tyler G. Hicks. Rev. ed., completely updated for the new federal tax law. Rocklin, CA : Prima Pub. & Communications, c1987. 324 p. ; 23 cm. Bibliography: p. 305-311. Includes index. ISBN 0-914629-57-3 (pbk.) : LC Card 87-2426 DDC 332.63/24 19
1. Real estate investment. 2. Mortgage loans. I. Title.
HD1382.5 .H53 1987

How to start your own business on a shoestring and make up to $100,000 a year. Hicks, Tyler Gregory, 1921- How to start your own business on a shoestring and make up to $500,000 a year / Tyler G. Hicks. Rocklin, CA , New York , c1987. xi, 225 p. ; ISBN 0-914629-12-3 (pbk.) : LC Card 86-25196 DDC 658/.041 19
HD62.5 .H527 1987

How to start your own business on a shoestring and make up to $500,000 a year / Tyler G. Hicks. Rocklin, CA : Prima Pub. & Communications ; New York : Distributed to the trade and libraries by St. Martin's Press, c1987. xi, 225 p. ; 23 cm. Rev. ed. of: How to start your own business on a shoestring and make up to $100,000 a year. 1968. Bibliography: p. 241-246. Includes index. ISBN 0-914629-12-3 (pbk.) : LC Card 86-25196 DDC 658/.041 19
1. Home-based businesses. 2. New business enterprises. 3. Self-employed. 4. Success in business. I. Hicks, Tyler Gregory, 1921- How to start your own business on a shoestring and make up to $100,000 a year. II. Title.
HD62.5 .H527 1987

Hidas, János. Szilvássy, Erika. A nemzetközi pénzügyek és a külkereskedelmi fizetések gyakorlata /. Budapest , 1985. 286 p. ; ISBN 963-221-529-X : LC Card 86-190902
HG3881 .S95 1985

Hidden aspects of women's work / edited by Christine Bose, Roslyn Feldberg, and Natalie Sokoloff ; with the Women and Work Research Group. New York : Praeger, 1987. x, 380 p. ; 25 cm. Bibliography: p. 323-369. Includes index. ISBN 0-275-92415-7 (alk. paper) : LC Card 87-2449 DDC 331.4/133/0973 19
1. Sex discrimination in employment - United States - History. 2. Sex role in the work environment - United States - History. 3. Sex discrimination against women - United States - History. 4. Women - Employment - United States - History. I. Bose, Christine E. II. Feldberg, Roslyn. III. Sokoloff, Natalie J. IV. Women and Work Research Group.
HD6060.5.U5 H53 1987

Hidy, Ralph Willard, 1905- The Great Northern Railway . Boston, Mass. , c1988. xv, 360 p. : ISBN 0-87584-185-6 LC Card 87-25040 DDC 385/.065/78 19
HE2791.G775 G73 1988

Higashi, Chikara. The internationalization of the Japanese economy / Chikara Higashi, G. Peter Lauter. Boston, MA : Kluwer Academic Publishers, c1987. xi, 273 p. : ill. ; 24 cm. Bibliography: p. 231-236. Includes index. ISBN 0-89838-199-1 LC Card 87-3893 DDC 337.52 19
1. Japan - Economic conditions - 1945-. 2. Japan - Economic policy - 1945-. 3. Japan - Foreign economic relations. I. Lauter, Geza P. (Geza Peter). II. Title.
HC462.9 .H45 1987

Higgins, Benjamin Howard, 1912- Regional economic development . Boston , 1987. p. cm. ISBN 0-04-338155-3 (alk. paper) LC Card 87-16749 DDC 338.9 19
HD75 .R44 1987

Higgins, E. Tory (Edward Tory), 1946- Handbook of motivation and cognition . New York , c1986. x, 610 p. : ISBN 0-89862-667-6 LC Card 85-24916 DDC 153.8 19
BF503 .H36 1986 ***NYPL [JFE 86-2410]***

Higgins, James M. Human relations : behavior at work / James M. Higgins.2nd ed. New York : Random House Business Division, c1987. xvi, 479 p. : ill. ; 25 cm. Includes bibliographies and indexes. ISBN 0-394-35112-6 : LC Card 86-31450 DDC 658.3/145 19
1. Personnel management. 2. Communication in personnel management. 3. Organizational behavior. 4. Interpersonal relations. 5. Psychology, Industrial. I. Title.
HF5549 .H474 1987

Higgins, José Consuegra. see **Consuegra Higgins, José.**

Higgins, Winton. Ewer, Peter. Unions and the future of Australian manufacturing /. Sydney , Boston , 1987. xi, 189 p. : ISBN 0-04-330382-X (pbk.) LC Card 87-164410 DDC 338.4/767/0994 19
HD9738.A82 E93 1987

Higgott, Richard A. Southeast Asia in the 1980s . Sydney , Boston , 1987. p. cm. ISBN 0-04-301289-2 LC Card 87-19550 DDC 338.959 19
HC441 .S69 1987

Higgs, Edward, 1952- Domestic servants and households in Rochdale, 1851-1871 / Edward Higgs. New York : Garland Pub. Co., 1986. 423 p. ; 24 cm. (British economic history) Revision of thesis (Ph. D.)--Oxford, 1979. Bibliography: p. 253-257. ISBN 0-8240-6682-0 : LC Card 84-46002 DDC 305.5/6 19
1. Domestics - England - Rochdale (Greater Manchester) - History - 19th century. 2. Women domestics - England - Rochdale (Greater Manchester) - History - 19th century. 3. Domestics - England - Rochdale (Greater Manchester) - Social conditions. 4. Rochdale (Greater Manchester) - Social conditions. I. Title. II. Series.
HD8039.D52 G7755 1986
NYPL [JLE 86-4591]

Higgs, Henry, 1864-1940. The physiocrats : six lectures on the French économistes of the 18th century / by Henry Higgs. New York, N.Y. : A.M. Kelley, 1988. p. cm. (Reprints of economic classics) Reprint. Originally published: London : Macmillan, 1897. Bibliography: p. Includes index. ISBN 0-678-00398-X LC Card 87-17066 DDC 330.15/2 19
1. Physiocrats. I. Title.
HB93 .H6 1988

Higgs, Peter J. (Peter John), 1959- Adaptation and survival in Australian agriculture : a computable general equilibrium analysis of the impact of economic shocks originating outside the domestic agricultural sector / Peter J. Higgs. Melbourne ; New York : Oxford University Press, 1986. xxx, 320 p. : ill. ; 23 cm. Bibliography: p. 302-310. ISBN 0-19-554749-7 LC Card 87-133685 DDC 338.1/0994 19
1. Agriculture - Economic aspects - Australia - Econometric models. 2. Agriculture - Economic aspects - Australia - Forecasting - Econometric models. 3. Agriculture and state - Australia - Econometric models. I. Title.
HD2152 .H54 1986

High finance on a low budget /. Skousen, Mark. Alexandria, VA , c1987. 197 p. : LC Card 87-153152 DDC 332.6/78 19
HG179 .S528 1987

High impact resumes and letters /. Krannich, Ronald L. Manassas, Va. , c1987. viii, 136 p. : ISBN 0-942710-12-6 (pbk.) : LC Card 86-83117 DDC 650.1/4 19
HF5383 .K7 1987

High impact resumes & letters. Krannich, Ronald L. High impact resumes and letters /. Manassas, Va. , c1987. viii, 136 p. : ISBN 0-942710-12-6 (pbk.) : LC Card 86-83117 DDC 650.1/4 19
HF5383 .K7 1987

High impact selling . Brooks, William T. Englewood Cliffs, N.J. , 1988. p. cm. ISBN 0-13-387663-2 LC Card 87-3567 DDC 658.8/5 19
HF5438.25 .B743 1988

High interest rates and tight money. Davey, Patrick J. [New York, 1969] 25 p. LC Card 70-9411 DDC 332.8/0973
HB545 .D38

High-involvement management /. Lawler, Edward E. San Francisco, Calif. , 1986. xvii, 252 p. : ISBN 0-87589-686-3 (alk. paper) LC Card 85-45909 DDC 658.3/152 19
HD5650 .L35 1986 ***NYPL [JLE 86-3096]***

High, Jack C. A Nation in debt . Frederick, Md. , c1987. p. cm. ISBN 0-89093-963-2 : LC Card 86-28254 DDC 339.5/23/0973 19
HJ2052 .N36 1987

HIGH OCCUPANCY VEHICLE LANES.
McCasland, William R. Transitway surveillance, communications, and control /. College Station, Tex. [1986] vi, 76 p. : LC Card 87-620995 DDC 380.5 s 388.3/143 19
HE203 .T43 no. 425-2F HE336.B8

HIGH OCCUPANCY VEHICLE LANES - TEXAS - EVALUATION.
Lomax, Timothy J. Guidelines for estimating the cost effectiveness of high-occupancy vehicle lanes /. College Station, Tex. , Springfield, Va. [1985] xiii, 55 p. : LC Card 86-622240 DDC 380.5 s 388.3/142 19
HE203 .T43 no. 339-5 HE356.T4

High performance purchasing . Schorr, John E. Essex Junction, Vt. , c1986. xii, 211 p. : ISBN 0-939246-05-8 LC Card 86-201739 DDC 658.7/2 19
HD39.5 .S36 1986

High performance team. Buchholz, Steve. Creating the high performance team /. New York , c1987. xiii, 202 p. : ISBN 0-471-85672-X : LC Card 86-32623 DDC 658.4/02 19
HD66 .B82 1987a

HIGH SCHOOL DROPOUTS - EMPLOYMENT - UNITED STATES.
United States. Vice President's Task Force on Youth Employment. A summary report of the

Vice President's Task Force on Youth Employment. Washington , 1980. 70 p. : *NYPL [JLF 86-214]*

HIGH SCHOOL GRADUATES - EMPLOYMENT - GERMANY (WEST)
Abiturienten und Hochschulabsolventen beim Übergang vom Studium in den Beruf . Nürnberg , 1983. 407 p. : LC Card 84-140881
HD6278.G4 A25 1983

HIGH SCHOOL GRADUATES - EMPLOYMENT - GREAT BRITAIN.
Roberts, Kenneth, 1940- School-leavers and their prospects . Milton Keynes , 1984. viii, 133 p. ; ISBN 0-335-10418-5 (pbk.) LC Card 87-672221
HD6276.G72 R62x 1984

HIGH SCHOOL GRADUATES - EMPLOYMENT - HUNGARY.
Érettségizettek a munkaerőpiacon /. Budapest , 1985. 124 p. ; ISBN 963-404-026-8 LC Card 87-409614
HD6276.H82 E73 1985

HIGH SCHOOL GRADUATES - EMPLOYMENT - KENYA.
Cheru, Fantu. Dependence, underdevelopment, and unemployment in Kenya . Lanham, MD , c1987. xvii, 198 p. : ISBN 0-8191-6539-5 (alk. paper) : LC Card 87-13710 DDC 331.13/77/096762 19
HD6276.K42 C46 1987

HIGH SPEED TRAINS - FRANCE.
TGV atlantique . Paris [1984] 410 p., [8] folded leaves of plates : ISBN 2-11-001253-6 : LC Card 85-103473 DDC 385/.22 19
HE3065 .T34 1984

HIGH SPEED TRAINS - GERMANY (WEST)
Krummheuer, Eberhard. Intercity experimental ICE, der neue Zug der neuen Bahn . München , c1986. 200 p. : ISBN 3-923967-25-X : LC Card 86-220676
HE3080.D37 K78 1986

High-tech exporter's sourcebook . Grant, Land. Brooklyn, N.Y. , 1987. viii, 263 p. ; LC Card 87-157599 DDC 382/.6/02573 19
HC79.T4 G68 1987

High tech holocaust /. Bellini, James. Newton Abbot , c1986. 255 p. ; ISBN 0-7153-8812-6 *NYPL [JLE 87-827]*

High tech investing. Powell, James B. The Dow Jones-Irwin guide to high tech investing . Homewood, Ill. , c1986. xix, 356 p. : ISBN 0-87094-596-3 : LC Card 85-72178 DDC 332.6/7253 19
HG4521 .P63 1986 NYPL [JLE 86-2261]

High Technology . Stock, Walter. Köln , 1986. 244 p. : ISBN 3-7609-1049-1 : LC Card 86-230225
HC110.H53 S76 1986

High technology employment : Maine and U. S., 1975-1984 : selected states, 1975-1983 / Maine Department of Labor, Bureau of Employment Security, Division of Economic Analysis and Research. Augusta, Me. (20 Union St., Augusta 04330) : The Division, [1985] iii, 23 p. : ill. ; 28 cm. (Technical services monograph . LMEP-14) Labor market information services Cover title. LC Card 85-623118 DDC 331.12/57/09741 19
1. High technology industries - Maine - Employees - Supply and demand. 2. High technology industries - United States - Employees - Supply and demand. I. Maine. Bureau of Employment Security. Division of Economic Analysis and Research. II. Series.
HD5718.H542 U635 1985

A High technology gap? : Europe, America, and Japan / Andrew J. Pierre, editor ; Frank Press ... [et al.] ; introduction by Robert D. Hormats. New York, N.Y. : Council on Foreign Relations, c1987. xii, 114 p. : ill. ; 23 cm. (Europe/America . 6) Includes bibliographical references. ISBN 0-87609-021-8 (pbk.) : LC Card 87-6713 DDC 338/.06 19
1. Technological innovations - Economic aspects - Europe. 2. Technology transfer - Economic aspects - Europe. 3. Technological innovations - Economic aspects - United States. 4. Technology transfer - Economic aspects - United States. 5. Technological innovations - Economic aspects - Japan. 6. Technology transfer - Economic aspects - Japan. I. Pierre, Andrew J. II. Press, Frank. III. Series.
HC240.9.T4 H54 1987

HIGH TECHNOLOGY INDUSTRIES.
The Development of high technology industries . London , New York , c1987. 363 p. : ISBN 0-7099-3942-6 LC Card 87-9086 DDC 338.4/762 19
HC79.H53 D48 1987

Emery, James J. Technology trade with the Middle East /. Boulder , 1986. xvii, 302 p. : ISBN 0-8133-7043-4 : LC Card 85-3215 DDC 338.9/26 19
HC415.15.Z9 H533 1986
NYPL [JLE 86-2460]

Foglio, Antonio, 1940- Il commercio estero delle tecnologie, dei progetti industriali e dei know how /. Milano, Italy , 1984. 269 p. ; LC Card 86-102943
HC79.H53 F64 1984

Fusfeld, Herbert I. The technical enterprise . Cambridge, Mass. , 1986. xiii, 312 p. ; ISBN 0-88730-033-2 LC Card 86-3340 DDC 338/.06 19
HC79.T4 F87 1986 NYPL [JLE 86-3344]

Powell, James B. The Dow Jones-Irwin guide to high tech investing . Homewood, Ill. , c1986. xix, 356 p. : ISBN 0-87094-596-3 : LC Card 85-72178 DDC 332.6/7253 19
HG4521 .P63 1986 NYPL [JLE 86-2261]

Technology and trade . Washington , 1986. x, 80 p. : LC Card 86-603362 DDC 338/.06 19
HC110.T4 T393 1986

The World market for high technology industrial ceramics. New York, N.Y. [1985] 1 v. (various pagings) ; ISBN 0-931634-52-0 (pbk.) LC Card 86-201912 DDC 382/.45666 19
HD9590.5 .W67 1985

HIGH TECHNOLOGY INDUSTRIES - BRAZIL - FINANCE.
Criação de empresas de alta tecnologia . São Paulo . 192, [1] p. ; LC Card 87-403991 DDC 338.4/362/000981 19
HC190.H53 C75 1987

HIGH TECHNOLOGY INDUSTRIES - CANADA.
Technology and commodity trade [microform] /. Ottawa , c1984. 40 p. : ISBN 0-660-11447-X (pbk.) : LC Card 85-132672 DDC 382/.4562/000971 19
HC120.T4 T43 1984
*NYPL [*ZT-1745 no.16]*

HIGH TECHNOLOGY INDUSTRIES - EMPLOYEES - CONGRESSES.
Human resource management in high-technology firms /. Lexington, Mass. , 1986, c1987. x, 243 p. : ISBN 0-669-13686-7 (alk. paper) LC Card 86-45556 DDC 658.3 19
HF5549 .H875 1987 NYPL [JLE 87-1100]

HIGH TECHNOLOGY INDUSTRIES - EUROPE.
Poniatowski, Michel. Les technologies nouvelles . Paris , c1986. 334 p. ; ISBN 2-259-01439-9 : LC Card 86-182131
HC240.9.T4 P65 1986

Technologie nouvelle et ruptures régionales /. Paris , c1986. 216 p. : ISBN 2-7178-1133-8 : LC Card 86-224660
HC240.9.T4 T42 1986

HIGH TECHNOLOGY INDUSTRIES - EUROPE, GERMAN-SPEAKING - MANAGEMENT.
Seibert, Siegfried, 1954- Strategische Erfolgsfaktoren in mittleren Unternehmen . Frankfurt am Main , New York , c1987. xii, 353 p. : ISBN 3-8204-9828-1 LC Card 87-122289
HD2346.G3 S38 1987

HIGH TECHNOLOGY INDUSTRIES - FINANCE - CONGRESSES.
Financing new technology . London , 1984. 124 p. : ISBN 0-85297-126-5 (pbk.) LC Card 86-117401 DDC 338.6/041 19
HG4027.6 .F55 1984 NYPL [JLD 87-1346]

HIGH TECHNOLOGY INDUSTRIES - FRANCE.
Noir, Michel, 1944- 1988 . [Paris] , c1984. 263 p. : LC Card 84-169744
HC280.H53 N65 1984 NYPL [JLE 87-2052]

HIGH TECHNOLOGY INDUSTRIES - GERMANY (WEST)
Hochtechnologien und internationale Wettbewerbsfähigkeit der deutschen Wirtschaft /. Bonn [1984] 30 p. ; LC Card 85-184765
HF3564 .H63 1984

HIGH TECHNOLOGY INDUSTRIES - GOVERNMENT OWNERSHIP - BRAZIL.
Ramamurti, Ravi. State-owned enterprises in high technology industries . New York , 1987. xii, 306 p. ; ISBN 0-03-068767-5 (alk. paper) : LC Card 85-30751 DDC 338.4/762/00954 19
HC440.H53 R36 1986 NYPL [JLE 87-1514]

HIGH TECHNOLOGY INDUSTRIES - GOVERNMENT OWNERSHIP - INDIA.
Ramamurti, Ravi. State-owned enterprises in high technology industries . New York , 1987. xii, 306 p. ; ISBN 0-03-068767-5 (alk. paper) : LC Card 85-30751 DDC 338.4/762/00954 19
HC440.H53 R36 1986 NYPL [JLE 87-1514]

HIGH TECHNOLOGY INDUSTRIES - GOVERNMENT POLICY - CASE STUDIES.
National policies for developing high technology industries . Boulder, Colo. , c1986. xiv, 247 p. : ISBN 0-8133-7280-1 (soft : alk. paper) LC Card 86-50530 DDC 338.4/762 19
HC79.H53 N38 1986 NYPL [JLE 86-4504]

HIGH TECHNOLOGY INDUSTRIES - GOVERNMENT POLICY - GREAT BRITAIN.
Western sunrise . London , Boston , 1987. xvi, 208 p. : ISBN 0-04-338142-1 LC Card 86-28755 DDC 338.6/042 19
HC260.H53 W47 1987

HIGH TECHNOLOGY INDUSTRIES - GOVERNMENT POLICY - JAPAN.
Building an industrial structure for the 21st century . Tokyo , 1982. ii, 58 p. ; LC Card 83-201472 DDC 338.4/762/000952 19
HC465.H53 B85 1982

HIGH TECHNOLOGY INDUSTRIES - GOVERNMENT POLICY - PENNSYLVANIA.
Allen, David N. Nurturing advanced technology enterprises . New York , c1986. xvi, 268 p. ; ISBN 0-275-92136-0 (alk. paper) : LC Card 86-9411 DDC 338.4/762/0009748 19
HC107.P43 H533 1986
NYPL [JLE 86-3609]

HIGH TECHNOLOGY INDUSTRIES - GOVERNMENT POLICY - UNITED STATES.
Technology, regions, and policy /. Totowa, N.J. , 1986. xiv, 322 p. : ISBN 0-8476-7409-6 LC Card 85-24970 DDC 338.4/76213817/0973 19
HC110.H53 T43 1986 NYPL [JLE 86-3327]

HIGH TECHNOLOGY INDUSTRIES - GREAT BRITAIN - LOCATION.
Western sunrise . London , Boston , 1987. xvi, 208 p. : ISBN 0-04-338142-1 LC Card 86-28755 DDC 338.6/042 19
HC260.H53 W47 1987

HIGH TECHNOLOGY INDUSTRIES - HANDBOOKS, MANUALS, ETC.
Grant, Land. High-tech exporter's sourcebook . Brooklyn, N.Y. , 1987. viii, 263 p. ; LC Card 87-157599 DDC 382/.6/02573 19
HC79.T4 G68 1987

HIGH TECHNOLOGY INDUSTRIES - INTERNATIONAL COOPERATION.
Schunk, Gerhard. Internationale Zusammenarbeit in hochtechnologischen Bereichen . Baden-Baden , 1982. 305 p. : ISBN 3-7890-0760-9 LC Card 82-198815 DDC 338.4/76217 19
HD41 .S355 1982 NYPL [TB (Internationale Kooperation. Bd.22)]

HIGH TECHNOLOGY INDUSTRIES - ISRAEL.
Electronics-1985 . [Jerusalem , 1985] 128 p. : LC Card 86-213293 DDC 338.4/7621381/095694 19
HD9696.A3 I654 1985

HIGH TECHNOLOGY INDUSTRIES - JAPAN.
Building an industrial structure for the 21st century . Tokyo , 1982. ii, 58 p. ; LC Card 83-201472 DDC 338.4/762/000952 19
HC465.H53 B85 1982

Sautter, Christian. Les dents du géant . Paris , c1987. 323 p. ; ISBN 2-85565-362-2 : LC Card 87-169635
HC462.9 .S277 1987

HIGH TECHNOLOGY INDUSTRIES - LOCATION - CONGRESSES.
The Spatial impact of technological change /. Totowa, NJ , 1987. p. cm. ISBN 0-389-20753-5 LC Card 87-11460 DDC 338/.06 19
HC79.T4 S77 1987

HIGH TECHNOLOGY INDUSTRIES - MAINE - EMPLOYEES - SUPPLY AND DEMAND.
High technology employment . Augusta, Me. (20 Union St., Augusta 04330) [1985] iii, 23 p. : LC Card 85-623118 DDC 331.12/57/09741 19
HD5718.H542 U635 1985

HIGH TECHNOLOGY INDUSTRIES - MANAGEMENT.
Shigekawa, Marlene, 1944- Succeeding in high tech . New York , c1987. xiv, 294 p. : ISBN 0-471-85636-3 LC Card 86-33953 DDC 650.1 19
HD62.37 .S52 1987

HIGH TECHNOLOGY INDUSTRIES - NEAR EAST.
Emery, James J. Technology trade with the Middle East /. Boulder , 1986. xvii, 302 p. : ISBN 0-8133-7043-4 : LC Card 85-3215 DDC 338.9/26 19
HC415.15.Z9 H533 1986 ***NYPL [JLE 86-2460]***

HIGH TECHNOLOGY INDUSTRIES - PERSONNEL MANAGEMENT - CONGRESSES.
Human resource management in high-technology firms /. Lexington, Mass. , 1986, c1987. x, 243 p. : ISBN 0-669-13686-7 (alk. paper) LC Card 86-45556 DDC 658.3 19
HF5549 .H875 1987 ***NYPL [JLE 87-1100]***

HIGH TECHNOLOGY INDUSTRIES - SOCIAL ASPECTS.
Venerable, Grant, 1942- The paradox of the silicon savior . San Francisco , c1987. xxx, 190 p. ; ISBN 0-943425-00-X (pbk.) : LC Card 87-17232 DDC 303.4/83 19
HC79.H53 V45 1987

HIGH TECHNOLOGY INDUSTRIES - SPAIN.
Nuevas tecnologías, economía y sociedad en España /. Madrid , c1986. 2 v. (xvi, 1056 p.) : ISBN 84-206-9495-9 (set) LC Card 86-205429
HC390.T4 N84 1986

HIGH TECHNOLOGY INDUSTRIES - TECHNOLOGICAL INNOVATIONS.
Schunk, Gerhard. Internationale Zusammenarbeit in hochtechnologischen Bereichen . Baden-Baden , 1982. 305 p. : ISBN 3-7890-0760-9 LC Card 82-198815 DDC 338.4/76217 19
HD41 .S355 1982 ***NYPL [TB (Internationale Kooperation. Bd.22)]***

HIGH TECHNOLOGY INDUSTRIES - UNITED STATES.
Commercializing SDI technologies /. New York , 1987. xvi, 246 p. : ISBN 0-275-92332-0 (alk. paper) : LC Card 87-18333 DDC 338.4/762 19
HC110.H53 C65 1987

Johnston, Robert F. Entrepreneurial science . New York , 1987. 157 p. ; ISBN 0-89930-260-2 (lib. bdg. : alk. paper) LC Card 87-2518 DDC 338/.06 19
HC110.H53 J65 1987

Stock, Walter. High Technology . Köln , 1986. 244 p. : ISBN 3-7609-1049-1 : LC Card 86-230225
HC110.H53 S76 1986

Technology and trade . Washington , 1986. x, 80 p. : LC Card 86-603362 DDC 338/.06 19
HC110.T4 T393 1986

HIGH TECHNOLOGY INDUSTRIES - UNITED STATES - CASE STUDIES.
Oppenheimer, Michael F. Nontariff barriers . Boulder , 1987. xiii, 203 p. ; ISBN 0-8133-7403-0 (pbk. : alk. paper) LC Card 87-50073 DDC 338.4/762/000973 19
HC110.H53 O66 1987

HIGH TECHNOLOGY INDUSTRIES - UNITED STATES - EMPLOYEES - SUPPLY AND DEMAND.
High technology employment . Augusta, Me. (20 Union St., Augusta 04330) [1985] iii, 23 p. : LC Card 85-623118 DDC 331.12/57/09741 19
HD5718.H542 U635 1985

HIGH TECHNOLOGY INDUSTRIES - UNITED STATES - FORECASTING.
Bryant, Richard W. The Strategic Defense Initiative, business opportunities, and technological potential /. Norwalk, Conn., U. S.A. , c1986. 1 v. (various foliations) : ISBN 0-89336-477-0 (pbk.) LC Card 87-168253 DDC 338.4/762/00973 19
HC110.H53 B79 1986

HIGH TECHNOLOGY INDUSTRIES - UNITED STATES - LOCATION.
Technology, regions, and policy /. Totowa, N.J. , 1986. xiv, 322 p. : ISBN 0-8476-7409-6 LC Card 85-24970 DDC 338.4/76213817/0973 19
HC110.H53 T43 1986 ***NYPL [JLE 86-3327]***

HIGH TECHNOLOGY INDUSTRIES - UNITED STATES - STATES.
Promoting high-technology industry . Boulder , 1987. 283 p. ; ISBN 0-8133-7427-8 (pbk. : alk. paper) LC Card 87-61327 DDC 338.4/762/000973 19
HC110.H53 P76 1987

HIGH TECHNOLOGY INDUSTRIES - VOCATIONAL GUIDANCE.
Winkler, Connie. Careers in high tech /. New York, N.Y. , c1987. vi, 220 p. : ISBN 0-668-06537-0 (pbk.) LC Card 86-25277 DDC 331.7/02 19
HD8039.H54 W56 1987

HIGH TECHNOLOGY - STUDY AND TEACHING - UNITED STATES.
Bushnell, David S. Training for new technology /. New York , c1983. 41 p. ; ISBN 0-08-029508-8 : LC Card 83-17341 DDC 658.3/124 19
HD5715.2 .B87 1983 ***NYPL [JLM 83-380 no.27]***

HIGH TEMPERATURE METALLURGY. see **METALS AT HIGH TEMPERATURES.**

Higher density housing : planning, design, marketing. Washington, D.C. : National Association of Home Builders, c1986. 155 p. : ill. ; 28 cm. "With Sanford R. Goodkin, the Goodkin Group"--Cover. Bibliography: p. 155. ISBN 0-86718-271-7 (pbk.) LC Card 86-63356 DDC 690/.83 19
1. Housing development. I. Goodkin, Sanford R. II. National Association of Home Builders (U. S.).
HD1390.5 .H545 1986

Higher education for business /. Gordon, Robert Aaron. New York , 1987, c1959. xi, 491 p. ; ISBN 0-8240-8207-9 (alk. paper) : LC Card 86-25813 DDC 650/.07/1173 19
HF1131 .G6 1987

HIGHLANDS (SCOTLAND) - ECONOMIC CONDITIONS.
Richards, Eric. A history of the Highland clearances /. London , c1982-1985. 2 v. : ISBN 0-85664-496-X : LC Card 81-208122 DDC 333.33/5 19
HD1511.G7 R53 1982 ***NYPL [JLL 82-171]***

Highlights of Ninth Medium-Term Economic Development Plan for Taiwan, Republic of China, 1986-1989. Hsing cheng yüan ching chi chien she wei yüan hui (China) [Taipei? Taiwan] [1986] ii, 65 p. ; LC Card 87-400742 DDC 338.951/249 19
HC430.5 .H757 1986a

Highlights of the Tax Reform Act of 1986 / prepared by Baker & Hostetler. Boston : [Warren, Gorham & Lamont, 1986] xi, 94 p. ; 24 cm. At head of title: Special Report. Issued as part of the publisher's 1983 edition of Federal estate and gift taxation.
1. United States. Tax Reform Act of 1986. 2. Taxation - Law and legislation - United States. 3. Income tax - Law and legislation - United States. I. Baker & Hostetler. ***NYPL [JLE 87-761]***

Highlights of 1986 economic development plan for Taiwan, Republic of China. Hsing cheng yüan ching chi chien she wei yüan hui (China) [Taipei] [1986] ii, 61 p. ; LC Card 87-118523 DDC 338.951/249 19
HC430.5 .H757 1986

Highman, Arthur. Highman, Edith L. The organization woman . New York, N.Y. , c1985. 204 p. ; ISBN 0-89885-237-4 LC Card 84-27775 DDC 658.4/09/024042 19
HD6054.3 .H54 1985 ***NYPL [JLD 86-1930]***

Highman, Edith L. The organization woman : building a career--an inside report / Edith L. Highman ; surveys by Arthur Highman. New York, N.Y. : Human Sciences Press, c1985. 204 p. ; 22 cm. Includes index. Bibliography: p. 199-200. ISBN 0-89885-237-4 LC Card 84-27775 DDC 658.4/09/024042 19
1. Women supervisors. 2. Women executives. I. Highman, Arthur. II. Title.
HD6054.3 .H54 1985 ***NYPL [JLD 86-1930]***

HIGHWAY ACCIDENTS. see **TRAFFIC ACCIDENTS.**

HIGHWAY CAPACITY.
Leisch, Jack E. Capacity analysis techniques for signalized intersections /. Washington, D.C., USA (525 School St., S.W., Suite 410, Washington 20024-2729) , c1986. 46 p. : LC Card 86-212242 DDC 388.3/14 19
HE336.H48 L45 1986

HIGHWAY CAPACITY - WASHINGTON METROPOLITAN AREA - FORECASTING.
Kaufmann, Elizabeth Irwin. Traffic growth resulting from future development . Washington, D.C. (1875 Eye St., N.W., Washington 20006-5454) , c1987. ix, 53, 15 p. : LC Card 87-161086 DDC 388.4/13142/09753 19
HE356.5.W3 K38 1987

HIGHWAY CONSTRUCTION. see **ROAD CONSTRUCTION.**

Highway finance : two reports on highway finance / prepared by the Office of Highway Planning. [Washington] : U. S. Dept. of Transportation, Federal Highway Administration, [1983] iii, 96 p. ; 28 cm. "April 1983." Cover title. Includes bibliographical references. CONTENTS. - The evolution of the highway-user charge principle / N. Kent Bramlett -- State highway finance trends / Thomas W. Cooper.
1. Transportation, Automotive - Taxation - United States. 2. Roads - United States - Finance. I. Bramlett, N. Kent. Evolution of the highway-user charge principle. II. Cooper, Thomas W. State highway finance trends. III. United States. Office of Highway Planning. ***NYPL [JLF 87-431]***

HIGHWAY GUARD FENCES. see **ROADS - GUARD FENCES.**

Highway Loss Data Institute.
Comparison of the insurance loss experience of unibody and frame construction cars after a collision repair, 1981-82 models. Washington, D.C. (Watergate 600, Washington 20037) , c1985. 10 p. : LC Card 87-107697 DDC 368.5/72/00973 19
HG9970.3 .C65 1985

Consistency of model year injury claim frequency results for selected 1981-1983 models. Washington, D.C (Watergate 600, Washington 20037) , c1986. 11 p. ; LC Card 87-107714 DDC 368.5/72/00973 19
HG9970.3 .C66 1986

Highway Loss Data Institute insurance collision report . Washington, DC (Watergate 600, Washington 20037) , c1986. 24 p. ; LC Card 87-107636 DDC 368.5/72/00973021 19
HG9970.3 .H5365 1986

Highway Loss Data Institute insurance collision report . Washington, D.C. (Watergate 600, Washington 20037) , c1986. 51 p. : LC Card 86-210266 DDC 368.5/72/00973021 19
HG9970.3 .H536 1986

Highway Loss Data Institute insurance injury report . Washington, D.C. (Watergate 600, Washington 20037) , c1986. 30 p. : LC Card 87-107645 DDC 368.5/72/00973021 19
HG9970.3 .H537 1986

Highway Loss Data Institute insurance special report . Washington, D.C. (Watergate 600, Washington 20037) , c1986. 11 p. ; LC Card 86-211182 DDC 368.5/72016/09747 19
HG9970.35.N7 H55 1986

Highway Loss Data Institute insurance theft report . Washington, D.C. (Watergate 600, Washington 20037) , c1986. 44 p. ; LC Card 87-107648 DDC 368.2/32/00973021 19
HG9970.3 .H538 1986

Injury and collision losses by engine option, selected 1983 models. Washington, D.C. (Watergate 600, Washington 20037) , c1985. 11

p. ; LC Card 87-115471 DDC 368.5/72/00973 19
HG9970.3 .I524 1985

Relationships between losses and vehicle density, 1982-84 models. Washington, D.C. (Watergate 600, Washington 20037) , c1985. 24 p. : LC Card 87-107842 DDC 368.5/72/00973 19
HG9970.3 .R45 1985

Highway Loss Data Institute insurance collision report : initial results for 1986 automobiles. Washington, DC (Watergate 600, Washington 20037) : HLDI, c1986. 24 p. ; 28 cm. (Research report HLDI . R86-1) Cover title: Insurance collision report. "August 1986." LC Card 87-107636 DDC 368.5/72/00973021 19
1. Insurance, Automobile - United States - Statistics. 2. Traffic accidents - United States - Costs - Statistics. I. Highway Loss Data Institute. II. Title: Insurance collision report.
HG9970.3 .H5365 1986

Highway Loss Data Institute insurance collision report : 1985 models during their first year, 1984 models during their first two years, 1983 models during their first three years. Washington, D.C. (Watergate 600, Washington 20037) : HLDI, c1986. 38 p. : ill. ; 28 cm. (Research report HLDI . R85-2) Cover title: Insurance collision report. LC Card 86-210266 DDC 368.5/72/00973021 19
1. Insurance, Automobile - United States - Statistics. 2. Traffic accidents - United States - Costs - Statistics. I. Highway Loss Data Institute. II. Title: Insurance collision report.
HG9970.3 .H536 1986

Highway Loss Data Institute insurance injury report : 1983-1985 models. Washington, D.C. (Watergate 600, Washington 20037) : HLDI, c1986. 30 p. : ill. ; 28 cm. (Research report HLDI . I85-1) Cover title: Insurance injury report. "August 1986." LC Card 87-107645 DDC 368.5/72/00973021 19
1. Insurance, Automobile - United States - Statistics. 2. Traffic accidents - United States - Costs - Statistics. I. Highway Loss Data Institute. II. Title: Insurance injury report.
HG9970.3 .H537 1986

Highway Loss Data Institute insurance special report : a preliminary evaluation of New York and New Jersey insurance injury claim results before and after enactment of mandatory seat belt legislation : 1983-85 models. Washington, D.C. (Watergate 600, Washington 20037) : The Institute, c1986. 11 p. ; 28 cm. (Research report HLDI . A-27 (May 1986)) Cover title: Insurance special report. LC Card 86-211182 DDC 368.5/72016/09747 19
1. Insurance, Automobile - New York (State). 2. Insurance, Automobile - New Jersey. 3. Automobiles - Seat belts - Government policy - New York (State). 4. Automobiles - Seat belts - Government policy - New Jersey. I. Highway Loss Data Institute. II. Title: Insurance special report. III. Series: Research report HLDI , A-27.
HG9970.35.N7 H55 1986

Highway Loss Data Institute insurance theft report : passenger cars, vans, pickups, and utility vehicles, 1985 models during their first year, 1984 models during their first two years, 1983 models during their first three years. Washington, D.C. (Watergate 600, Washington 20037) : HLDI, c1986. 44 p. ; 28 cm. (Research report HLDI . T85-1) Cover title: Insurance theft report. "April 1986." LC Card 87-107648 DDC 368.2/32/00973021 19
1. Insurance, Automobile - United States - Statistics. 2. Automobile theft - United States - Statistics. I. Highway Loss Data Institute. II. Title: Insurance theft report.
HG9970.3 .H538 1986

Highway needs vs. anticipated funds. 1984 needs vs. funds expected to be available July 1983 through September 1990. [Columbia, S.C.] [1984] [49] leaves ; LC Card 86-622435 DDC 388.1/14/09757 19
HE356 .A57 1984

HIGHWAY PLANNING - GERMANY, WEST - CONGRESSES.
Deutscher Strassenkongress (1984 : Mannheim, Germany) Deutscher Strassenkongress, Mannheim, 1984 /. Köln [1985?] 255 p. : LC Card 87-408263 DDC 388.1/0943 19
HE363.G3 D48 1984

HIGHWAY PLANNING - KENYA - CITIZEN PARTICIPATION.
Community participation for road planning in squatter settlement upgrading . Nairobi, Kenya , 1983. 56 leaves : LC Card 86-980653 DDC 388.1/09676/2 19
HE367.K43 C584 1983

HIGHWAY PLANNING - UNITED STATES - HISTORY.
Weiner, Edward. Urban transportation planning in the United States . [Washington, D.C.] [1986] vii, 149 p. : LC Card 87-601522 DDC 388.4/068 19
HE308 .W45 1986

HIGHWAY SAFETY. see **TRAFFIC SAFETY.**

Highway safety plan and alcohol plan, fiscal year 1987. New Mexico. Traffic Safety Bureau. Highway safety plan, fiscal year 1987 /. Santa Fe, N.M. (P.O. Box 1028, Santa Fe 87504-1028) [1986] 190 leaves : LC Card 86-622688 DDC 363.1/256/09789 19
HE5614.3.N47 N49 1986

Highway safety plan, fiscal year 1987 /. New Mexico. Traffic Safety Bureau. Santa Fe, N.M. (P.O. Box 1028, Santa Fe 87504-1028) [1986] 190 leaves : LC Card 86-622688 DDC 363.1/256/09789 19
HE5614.3.N47 N49 1986

HIGHWAY TRANSPORT WORKERS - TRAINING OF - GERMANY (WEST)
Rüter, Gert. Sicherheitsorientierte Ausbildung von Berufskraftfahren /. Köln [1983] vii, 91 p. : LC Card 83-235527
HD5716.M7952 G327 1983

HIGHWAY TRANSPORTATION. see **TRANSPORTATION, AUTOMOTIVE.**

HIJACKING OF AIRCRAFT - PAKISTAN.
Pī.Ā'ī.Ae. ṭayyāre kā ighvā, dahshat gardī kī intihā, 'amle aur musāfiron ke ta'aṣṣurāt, Pishāvar, 18 Mārc, 1981. Islāmābād [1981] 27 p. ; LC Card 82-930104
HE9871.5.Z7 H56 1981

HIJACKING OF AIRCRAFT - PREVENTION.
Ashwood, Thomas M. Terror in the skies /. New York , 1987. p. cm. ISBN 0-8128-3125-X : LC Card 86-42779 DDC 363.2/876 19
HE9779 .A74 1987

Hilanderías del Fonce (Bucaramanga, Colombia) Productividad y participación . [Bucaramanga, Colombia] , c1985. 165 p. : ISBN 958-9302-15-6 LC Card 86-166141
HD5660.C7 P76 1985

Hilbert, Stephen. Jaffe, Eugene D. How to prepare for the graduate management admission test GMAT /. New York , c1987. x, 541 p. : ISBN 0-8120-3882-7 (pbk.) LC Card 87-18619 DDC 650/.076 19
HD30.413 .J33 1987

Hildebrand, David K., 1940- Statistical thinking for managers / David K. Hildebrand, Lyman Ott. 2nd ed. Boston, Mass. : Duxbury Press, c1987. xvii, 894 p. : ill. ; 25 cm. Ott's name appears first on earlier edition. Bibliography: p. 791-792. Includes index. ISBN 0-87150-036-1 LC Card 86-29222 DDC 519.5/024658 19
1. Industrial management - Statistical methods. 2. Industrial management - Statistical methods - Data processing. 3. Economics - Statistical methods. 4. Statistics - Data processing. I. Ott, Lyman. II. Title.
HD30.215 .H54 1987

Hildebrand, John R. Monetary integration : key currencies contributing equitably to development / John R. Hildebrand. Bristol, Ind., U. S.A. : Wyndham Hall Press, c1987. viii, 81 p. ; 22 cm. Includes bibliographies and index. ISBN 1-556-05004-6 (pbk.) LC Card 87-50033 DDC 332.4/6 19
1. Monetary policy. 2. Monetary unions. I. Title.
HG230.3 .H535 1987

Hildebrandt, Eckart. Organisation als soziales System . Berlin , c1986. 219 p. ; ISBN 3-924859-22-1 LC Card 87-137969 DDC 302.3/5 19
HD58.7 .O6687 1986

Hildebrandt, Herbert William, 1931-
A managerial profile : the woman manager / Herbert W. Hildebrandt, Edwin L. Miller, Stephen J. LaCivita. Ann Arbor, MI : Division of Research, Graduate School of Business Administration, University of Michigan, c1985. 31 p. ; 21 cm. (Michigan management and executive development studies . #4) ISBN 0-87712-248-2 (pbk.) LC Card 86-621187 DDC 331.4/816584/00973 19
1. Women executives - United States. I. Miller, Edwin Leroy, 1929-. II. LaCivita, Stephen J. III. Title. IV. Series.
HD6054.4.U6 H55 1985

Murphy, Herta A. Effective business communications /. New York , c1988. xx, 730 p. : ISBN 0-07-044094-8 LC Card 87-17330 DDC 651.7 19
HF5721 .M85 1988

Hildebrandt, Lutz. Konfirmatorische Analysen von Modellen des Konsumentenverhaltens / von Lutz Hildebrandt. Berlin : Duncker & Humblot, c1983. xii, 307 p. : ill. ; 24 cm. (Vertriebswirtschaftliche Abhandlungen. Heft 24) Originally presented as the author's thesis (doctoral)--Technische Universität Berlin, 1981/82. Bibliography: p. 258-[284] ISBN 3-428-05381-8 LC Card 83-190106
1. Consumers' Research. 2. Latent variables. I. Title. II. Series.
HF5415.3 .H55 1983

Hildebrandt, Reiner. Geiler, Nick. Wasser konkret . Wiesbaden [1985] 199 p. : LC Card 86-162674
HD1697.G33 H474 1985

Hilden, Patricia. Working women and socialist politics in France, 1880-1914 : a regional study / Patricia Hilden. Oxford [Oxfordshire] : Clarendon ; New York : Oxford University Press, 1986. viii, 307 p. ; 23 cm. Includes index. Bibliography: p. [280]-300. ISBN 0-19-821935-0 : LC Card 85-15487 DDC 331.4/877/0094428 19
1. Women textile workers - France - Lille Region - Case studies. 2. Women in trade-unions - France - History. 3. Socialism - France - History. I. Title.
HD6073.T42 F84 1986
NYPL [JLD 86-1838]

Hildenbrand, Werner, 1936- Advances in economic theory . Cambridge [Cambridgeshire] , New York , 1982. x, 285 p. : ISBN 0-521-24443-9 LC Card 81-38500 DDC 330/.028 19
HB21 .A33 1982 ***NYPL [JLE 85-2041]***

Hildreth, Sandra S. The A to Z of Wall Street / Sandra S. Hildreth. Chicago, Ill. : Longman Financial Services Pub., c1988. 299 p. : ill. ; 23 cm. ISBN 0-88462-711-X (pbk.) : LC Card 87-22615 DDC 332.6/03/21 19
1. Investments - Dictionaries. I. Title.
HG4513 .H56 1988

Hilfe in der Not : Bildbericht über die Verteilung von amerikanischen Liebesgabenspenden in Bremen, Juni bis Dezember 1946 : mit Lichtbildern / von H. Saebens = Help in distress : a pictorial report on the distribution of American relief gifts in the city of Bremen, from June to December 1946 : with photos / by H. Saebens. [Bremen] : Evangelisches Hilfswerk in Bremen, [1947] 74 p. : ill. ; 30 cm. English and German. LC Card 87-408692 DDC 338.91/73/04352 19
1. Economic assistance, American - Germany (West) - Bremen - History - Pictorial works. 2. Bremen (Germany) - Economic conditions - Pictorial works. I. Saebens, Hans. II. Title: Help in distress.
HC286.5 .H545 1947

Hilfer, Rudolf. Stochastische Modelle für die betriebliche Planung / Rudolf Hilfer. München : GBI-Verlag, c1985. ii, 191 p. : ill. ; 21 cm. (Betriebswirtschaftliche Forschungsbeiträge . Bd. 16) Originally presented as the author's thesis (doctoral)--Universität Göttingen, 1984. Bibliography: p. 175-188. Includes index. ISBN 3-89003-015-7 LC Card 85-189343
1. Industrial management - Mathematical models. 2. Corporate planning - Mathematical models. I. Title. II. Series.
HD30.25 .H55 1985

Hilger, James G. Soldati, John M. Risk assessments . Washington, D.C. (1120 Connecticut Ave., N.W., Washington 20036) , c1987. 21 p. : LC Card 87-148315 DDC 332.64/52 19
HG6042 .S65 1987

HILL FARMING - MEXICO - NAHUATZEN REGION.
García López, Lucía. Nahuatzen, agricultura y comercio en una comunidad serrana /. Zamora, Mich. , México, D.F. , c1984. 115 p. : ISBN 968-7230-03-7 LC Card 85-154045 DDC

338.1/0972/37 19
HD1795.N34 G37 1984 ***NYPL [JLD 87-16]***

Hill, Henry P. Accounting principles for the autonomous corporate entity / Henry P. Hill. New York : Quorum Books, 1987. xii, 144 p. : ill. ; 22 cm. Bibliography: p. 140. Includes index. ISBN 0-89930-212-2 (lib. bdg. : alk. paper) LC Card 86-25587 DDC 657/.95 19
1. Corporations - United States - Accounting. I. Title.
HF5686.C7 H55 1987

Hill, Ian, 1958- Affording access to quality care . Washington, D.C. (444 N. Capitol St., N.W., Suite 250, Washington 20001) , c1986. xx, 245 p. ; LC Card 87-127057 DDC 338.4/336210452/0973 19
HD7102.U4 A66 1986

Hill, Paul Bernhard, 1953- Determinanten der Eingliederung von Arbeitsmigranten / von Paul Bernhard Hill. Königstein/Ts. : Hanstein, c1984. 228 p. : ill. ; 21 cm. (Materialien zur Arbeitsmigration und Ausländerbeschäftigung . Bd. 10) Bibliography: p. 219-228. ISBN 3-7756-6939-6 LC Card 84-219137 DDC 331.6/2/0943 19
1. Alien labor - Germany, West. 2. Emigration and immigration - Psychological aspects. I. Title. II. Series.
HD8458.A2 H55 1984
NYPL [JLD 86-2467]

Hill Samuel & Co. Report to the World Bank, Amazônia Mineração S.A. . London [1979?] v, 57, [31] leaves : LC Card 85-154695
HD9524.B8 R46 1979

Hill, Stephen. Abercrombie, Nicholas. Sovereign individuals of capitalism /. London , Boston , 1986. 211 p. ; ISBN 0-04-301230-2 (alk. paper) LC Card 86-1122 DDC 330.12/2 19
HB501 .A23 1986 ***NYPL [JLD 86-3686]***

Hillard, John. The Economic revival of modern Britain . Aldershot, Hants, England , c1987. xv, 349 p. : ISBN 1-85278-000-2 (pbk.) : LC Card 87-170031 DDC 338.941 19
HC256.6 .E227 1987

HILLBILLY MUSIC. see **COUNTRY MUSIC.**

Hillebrand, B. Korthaus, E.
Input-Output-Tabellen für die Bundesrepublik Deutschland, 1962 bis 1975 /. Essen , 1979. 279 p. ; LC Card 87-408858 DDC 339.2/3/0943 19
HC290.5.I57 K67 1979

Hillen, Peter. Die Verplante Wohnmisere . Saarbrücken , Fort Lauderdale , 1986. 334 p. : ISBN 3-88156-329-6 LC Card 87-408292 DDC 363.5/1/096 19
HD7287.96.A4 V47 1986

Hiller, Marlene P., 1948- Krisenregion Nahost : russische Orientpolitik im Zeitalter des Imperialismus, 1900-1914 / Marlene P. Hiller. Frankfurt am Main ; New York : P. Lang, c1985. 335 p. : ill. ; 21 cm. (Europäische Hochschulschriften. Reihe III, Geschichte und ihre Hilfswissenschaften, 0531-7320 . Bd. 267 = vol. 267 = vol. 267) Originally presented as the author's thesis (doctoral--Universität Tübingen, WS 1983/84) Bibliography: p. 299-335. ISBN 3-8204-8249-0 LC Card 85-191941
1. Russia - Foreign economic relations - Turkey. 2. Turkey - Foreign economic relations - Russia. 3. Railroads - Turkey - History - 20th century. 4. Turkey - Economic policy. I. Series: Europäische Hochschulschriften. Reihe III, Geschichte und ihre Hilfswissenschaften , Bd. 267. II. Title.
HF1558.15.T8 H55 1985

Hiller, Michael D. How to get the 1 hour real estate loan : the note modification agreement / Michael D. Hiller. Encino, CA (16161 Ventura Blvd., #C-719, Encino 91436) : E & J Enterprises, c1987. 170 p. : ill. ; 22 cm. LC Card 87-154252 DDC 332.7/22/0973 19
1. Mortgage loans - United States. 2. Mortgages - United States. I. Title. II. Title: Note modification agreement.
HG2040.5.U5 H53 1987

Hillerich, Robert L., 1927-
Fitz-Gerald, Christine Maloney. I can be a textile worker /. Chicago , c1987. 29 p. : ISBN 0-516-01912-0 (lib bdg.) LC Card 87-10716 DDC 677/.0023/73 19
HD8039.C6 F57 1987

Lillegard, Dee. I can be a secretary /. Chicago , c1987. 29 p. : ISBN 0-516-01907-4 (lib. bdg.) LC Card 86-29947 DDC 651.3/741/02373 19
HF55475 .L55 1987

Hilliard, Francis, 1808?-1878. A treatise on the law of bankruptcy and insolvency [microform] / by Francis Hilliard. 3rd ed. / embracing the Bankrupt Act of 1867, and an abstract of decisions under the present bankrupt law. Philadelphia : J.B. Lippincott & Co. ; London : Trübner and Co., 1872. xxxiii, 564, 84, xxiii p. ; 24 cm. Includes index. Microfilm. New York: New York Public Library, 1986. 1 microfilm reel; 35 mm. (MN *ZZ-22263)
1. Bankruptcy - United States. 2. Bankruptcy - Great Britain. I. Title. ***NYPL [*ZT-1689]***

Hilling, David. Mountjoy, Alan B. Africa, geography and development /. Totowa, NJ , 1987. p. cm. ISBN 0-389-20722-5 LC Card 87-1306 DDC 330.96/0328 19
HC800 .M68 1987

Hillkirk, John.
Jacobson, Gary. Xerox . New York , c1986. ix, 338 p. ; ISBN 0-02-551600-0 LC Card 85-30922 DDC 338.7/68644 19
HD9802.3.U64 X475 1986
NYPL [JLE 86-2982]

Jacobson, Gary. Xerox . New York , 1987, c1986. xii, 338 p. ; ISBN 0-02-033830-9 (pbk.) LC Card 86-31009 DDC 338.7/68644 19
HD9802.3.U64 X475 1986b

Hillman, Jimmye S., 1923-
Agricultural trade and protection in Japan / by Jimmye S. Hillman and Robert A. Rothenberg. Aldershot, Hants, England ; Brookfield, Vt. : Gower Pub. Co., 1988. p. cm. (Thames essay . no. 52) "For the Trade Policy Research Centre, London." Bibliography: p. ISBN 0-566-05339-X : LC Card 87-15043 DDC 382.7/3/0952 19
1. Produce trade - Government policy - Japan. 2. Food industry and trade - Government policy - Japan. 3. Agriculture and state - Japan. 4. Tariff on farm produce - Japan. 5. Free trade and protection. I. Rothenberg, Robert A. II. Trade Policy Research Centre. III. Title. IV. Series.
HD9016.J42 H55 1988

Goldschmidt, Yaaqov. The impact of inflation on financial activity in business, with applications to the U. S. farming sector /. Totowa, N.J. , 1986. xvi, 181 p. ; ISBN 0-8476-7427-4 : LC Card 85-14196 DDC 338.1/3/0973 19
HD1761 .G645 1986 ***NYPL [JLE 86-3484]***

Hills, Stephen M. The Changing labor market . Lexington, Mass. , c1986. x, 166 p. : ISBN 0-669-11943-1 (alk. paper) LC Card 85-45710 DDC 331.12/0973 19
HD6331.2.U5 C47 1986
NYPL [JLE 86-1069]

Hillstrom, Roger. 1960-1969, a decade of corporate and international finance. Edited by Roger Hillstrom and Robert King. New York, IDD [1972] 381 p. illus. 38 cm. Running title: Corporate financing, 1960-1969. "A joint project of Investment dealers' digest and Investment Bankers Association of America." 1961 ed., by The Investment dealer's digest, published under title: Corporate financing, 1950-1960. LC Card 72-175335 DDC 332
1. Corporations - United States - Finance. 2. Investment banking - United States. 3. Securities - United States. I. King, Robert, 1944- joint author. II. Investment Bankers Association of America. III. Investment dealers' digest. Corporate financing, 1950-1960. IV. Title. V. Title: Corporate financing, 1960-1969.
HG4907 .H54 ***NYPL [JLG 73-17]***

Hilpert, Edwin J. Abelow, Daniel.
Communications in the modern corporate environment /. Englewood Cliffs, NJ , c1986. xviii, 236 p. : ISBN 0-13-153842-X LC Card 85-16942 DDC 658/.0546 19
HF5548.2 .A24 1986 ***NYPL [JLE 86-1992]***

Hilton, D. Reid. Robinson, Dean L. Network marketing /. Salt Lake City, Utah , c1983. 137 p. : LC Card 86-202974 DDC 658.8/4 19
HF5415.126 .R63 1983

Hilton, John, 1880-1943. Rich man, poor man / John Hilton. New York : Garland Pub., 1985. 174 p. ; 19 cm. (English workers and the coming of the welfare state, 1918-1945. [15]) Reprint. Originally published: London : Allen & Unwin, 1944. (Sir Halley Stewart lectures ; 1938) ISBN 0-8240-7614-1 (alk. paper) : LC Card 85-13078 DDC 339.2/2/0941 19
1. Wealth - Great Britain. 2. Great Britain - Economic conditions - 1918-1945. I. Title. II. Series.
HC256.4 .H54 1985 ***NYPL [JLC 86-342]***

Hilton, R. H. (Rodney Howard), 1916- Class conflict and the crisis of feudalism : essays in medieval social history / Rodney Hilton. London ; Ronceverte, W. Va. : Hambledon Press, 1985. 349 p. ; 24 cm. (History series . 28) Includes index. Bibliography: p. [295]-338. ISBN 0-907628-36-2 : LC Card 85-21855 DDC 305.5/0942 19
1. Peasantry - England - History - Addresses, essays, lectures. 2. Feudalism - England - History - Addresses, essays, lectures. 3. England - Social conditions - Medieval period, 1066-1485 - Addresses, essays, lectures. I. Series: History series (Hambledon Press) , v. 28. II. Title.
HD604 .H48 1985 ***NYPL [JFE 87-391]***

Hilton, Robert, 1927- U. S. maritime industries--down for the third time? / by Robert Hilton, Paula J. Pettavino, Harlan K. Ullman. Washington, D.C. : Center for Strategic and International Studies, Georgetown University, c1987. vi, 60 p. : ill. ; 23 cm. (Significant issues series, 0736-7146 . v. 9, no. 1) Bibliography: p. 56-60. ISBN 0-89206-099-9 (pbk.) LC Card 86-31768 DDC 387.5/0973 19
1. Merchant marine - United States. 2. Shipping - United States. 3. Shipbuilding industry - United States. 4. Merchant marine - Government policy - United States. 5. Shipping - Government policy - United States. 6. Shipbuilding industry - Government policy - United States. I. Pettavino, Paula J. II. Ullman, Harlan. III. Title. IV. Title: US maritime industries--down for the third time?. V. Title: United States maritime industries--down for the third time?. VI. Series.
HE745 .H66 1987

HIMACHAL PRADESH (INDIA) - CENSUS, 1981.
Census of India, 1981. Delhi , <1982-1986. <v. in > : LC Card 87-915013
HA4587.H54 C45 1982

HIMACHAL PRADESH, INDIA - ECONOMIC CONDITIONS.
Sharma, L. R., 1934- The economy of Himachal Pradesh . Delhi, India , 1987. vii, 167 p. ; LC Card 86-903541 DDC 330.954/52 19
HC437.H5 S52 1987

HIMACHAL PRADESH (INDIA) - ECONOMIC CONDITIONS - CONGRESSES.
Development administration in a changing society /. New Delhi, India , 1987. xix, 214 p. ; ISBN 81-85135-18-5 : LC Card 87-900453 DDC 338.954/52 19
HC437.H5 D48 1987

HIMACHAL PRADESH (INDIA) - SOCIAL CONDITIONS - CONGRESSES.
Development administration in a changing society /. New Delhi, India , 1987. xix, 214 p. ; ISBN 81-85135-18-5 : LC Card 87-900453 DDC 338.954/52 19
HC437.H5 D48 1987

Himachal Pradesh University. Post Graduate Centre of Public Administration.
Development administration in a changing society /. New Delhi, India , 1987. xix, 214 p. ; ISBN 81-85135-18-5 : LC Card 87-900453 DDC 338.954/52 19
HC437.H5 D48 1987

Himmelstein, Hal. Television myth and the American mind / Hal Himmelstein. New York : Praeger, 1984. xii, 336 p. : ill. ; 25 cm. Includes bibliographical references and index. ISBN 0-03-062134-8 (alk. paper) : LC Card 84-11621 DDC 302.2/345 19
1. Television programs - United States - History and criticism. 2. Television advertising - United States. 3. Television broadcasting - United States. I. Title.
PN1992.3.U5 H55 1984
NYPL [MWGT 85-394]

Hince, Kevin. Industrial relations . [Wellington] , 1986. ii, 71 p. ; LC Card 86-212248 DDC 331/.09931 19
HD8930.5 .I52 1986

Hinchliffe, Keith. Forecasting skilled-manpower needs . Paris , 1985. 259 p. : ISBN 92-803-1122-3 (pbk.) LC Card 86-214025 DDC 331.12/3 19
HD5701.55 .F67 1985

Hinckley, Ted C. Business entrepreneurs in the West /. Manhattan, Kan. , c1986. 120 p. : ISBN 0-89745-088-4 (pbk.) LC Card 87-135380 DDC 338/.04/0922 B 19
HC102.5.A2 B78 1986

Hinder, Alex, 1954- Wechselkursprognosen : Ansätze, Modelle und Erfolgsbeurteilung / Alex Hinder. Bern ; New York : Lang, c1983. xvii, 424 p. : ill. ; 23 cm. (Europäische Hochschulschriften. Reihe V, Volks- und Betriebswirtschaft . Bd. 481 = vol. 481 = vol. 481) Originally presented as the author's thesis (doctoral)--Hochschule St. Gallen. Bibliography: p. 403-424. ISBN 3-261-03345-2 LC Card 86-104957
1. Foreign exchange - Forecasting - Mathematical models. I. Series: Europäische Hochschulschriften. Reihe V, Volks- und Betriebswirtschaft , Bd. 481. II. Title.
HG3823 .H5 1983

Hinderer, Michael. Die mittelständische Unternehmung : Selbstverständnis in der Marktwirtschaft, Analyse und Strategie / Michael Hinderer. München : V. Florentz, c1984. xix, 435 p. : ill. ; 21 cm. (Hochschulschriften zur Betriebswirtschaftslehre . Bd. 30) Bibliography: p. 406-435. ISBN 3-88259-328-8 LC Card 85-152951
1. Small business. 2. Small business - Germany, West. I. Title. II. Series.
HD2341 .H56 1984

HINDI LANGUAGE.
Pāṇḍeya, Āśā. Hindī vijñāpanoṃ kī bhāshā /. Bambaī , 1986. xv, 105, [3] p. ; LC Card 87-901590
HF5827 .P36 1986

Hindī vijñāpanoṃ kī bhāshā /. Pāṇḍeya, Āśā. Bambaī , 1986. xv, 105, [3] p. ; LC Card 87-901590
HF5827 .P36 1986

Hindle, Brian Paul. Medieval roads / Brian Paul Hindle. Aylesbury, Bucks, UK : Shire Publications, 1982. 62 p. : ill., maps ; 21 cm. (Shire archaeology. 26) Includes index. Bibliography: p. 29. ISBN 0-85263-600-8 (pbk.) : LC Card 83-228901 DDC 388.1/0942 19
1. Roads - England - History. 2. Roads - Wales - History. I. Title.
HE363.G72 H56 1982 ***NYPL [JLD 86-1755]***

HINDUSTAN SHIPYARD LIMITED.
Prabhakara Rao, D. (Devisetti), 1954- Human resource accounting /. New Delhi, India , 1986. xviii, 247 p. : ISBN 81-210-0169-2 : LC Card 86-902848
HF5681.H8 P73 1986

Hines, Colin. Dinham, Barbara. Agribusiness in Africa /. Trenton, N.J. , 1984. 224 p. : ISBN 0-86543-003-9 : LC Card 85-672721
HD9017.A2 D56x 1984 ***NYPL [Sc D 86-769]***

Hines, Lawrence Gregory. The market, energy, and the environment / Lawrence Gregory Hines. Boston : Allyn and Bacon, c1988. xii, 305 p. : ill. ; 24 cm. Includes bibliographies and index. ISBN 0-205-10568-8 : LC Card 87-1037 DDC 333.7/0973 19
1. Environmental policy - United States. 2. Energy policy - United States. 3. United States - Economic policy - 1981-. I. Title.
HC110.E5 H57 1988

Hines, Mary Alice.
Financing real estate with securities / M.A. Hines. New York : Wiley, c1988. p. cm. (Real estate for professional practitioners) Bibliography: p. Includes index. ISBN 0-471-62813-1 LC Card 87-26336 DDC 332.7/2 19
1. Mortgages. 2. Securities. 3. Real estate investment. 4. Mortgages - United States. I. Title.
HG4655 .H56 1988

Investing in Japanese real estate / M.A. Hines. New York : Quorum Books, 1987. xiv, 287 p. : ill. ; 24 cm. Includes bibliographies and index. ISBN 0-89930-184-3 (lib. bdg. : alk. paper) LC Card 86-30582 DDC 332.63/24/0952 19
1. Real estate investment - Japan. I. Title.
HD918 .H55 1987

Marketing real estate internationally / M.A. Hines. New York : Quorum Books, c1988. p. cm. Includes index. ISBN 0-89930-205-X (lib. bdg. : alk. paper) LC Card 87-24935 DDC 333.33/0688 19
1. Real estate investment. 2. Real property - Foreign ownership. 3. Investments, Foreign. I. Title.
HD1382.5 .H557 1988

Real estate debt financing / M.A. Hines. New York : J. Wiley and Sons, c1987. xviii, 405 p. ; 24 cm. (Real estate for professional practitioners) Includes bibliographical references and index. ISBN 0-471-85493-X LC Card 87-6200 DDC 332.7/2/0973 19
1. Mortgage loans - United States. 2. Real estate development - United States - Finance. I. Title.
HG2040.5.U5 H55 1987

Shopping center development and investment / M.A. Hines. 2nd ed. New York : Wiley, c1987. p. cm. (Real estate for professional practitioners) Bibliography: p. Includes index. ISBN 0-471-62427-6 LC Card 87-26342 DDC 332.63/24 19
1. Shopping centers. 2. Shopping centers - United States. 3. Real estate investment. 4. Real estate investment - United States. 5. Real estate development. 6. Real estate development - United States. I. Title.
HF5430 .H56 1987

Hines, Walker Downer, 1870-1934. War history of American railroads / byWalker D. Hines. [S.l.] : J.S. Ozer, 1974. xviii, 327 p. : ill. ; 25 cm. (Economic and social history of the world war. American series) Includes index. Reprint. Originally published : New Haven : Yale University Press, 1928. LC Card 74-75240
1. World War, 1914-1918 - Transportation. 2. Railroads - United States. 3. Railroads and state - United States. I. Title. ***NYPL [JLD 87-638]***

Hinman, Felicitas.
The Future directions of employee relations /. Los Angeles, Calif. , c1985. xiv, 418 p. ; ISBN 0-89215-132-3 ***NYPL [JLD 86-3596]***

The Future directions of employee relations /. Los Angeles, Calif. , c1985. xiv, 418 p. : ISBN 0-89215-132-3 (pbk.) LC Card 86-622936 DDC 331/.0973 19
HD8072.5 .F87 1985

Hinnanasetanta, toiminta-analyyttinen tutkimus pienyrityksistä /. Neilimo, Kari, 1944- Tampere , 19. 90, [8] leaves : ISBN 951-44-1729-1 LC Card 86-140431
HF5416.5 .N45 1985

Hinojosa Tapia, Juan. La problemática de los almacenes generales de depósito como instituciones financieras no bancarias en el Perú (1970-1983) / Juan Hinojosa Tapia. Lima, Perú : Universidad de Lima, Facultad de Economía, Centro de Investigaciones Económicas y Sociales, 1985. iii, 29, [43] p. : ill. ; 30 cm. (Serie Avances de investigación . no. 7) Originally presented as the author's thesis (grado de bachiller)--Universidad de Lima. Bibliography: p. [37]-[38] LC Card 86-218257
1. Commercial credit - Peru. 2. Warehouses - Peru. 3. Granaries - Peru. I. Series: Avances de investigación (Universidad de Lima. Centro de Investigaciones Económicas y Sociales) , 7. II. Title.
HG3751.9.P4 H56 1985

Hinterbuchner, Christian. Die Entwicklung der oberösterreichischen Elektrizitätswirtschaft in den Jahren 1938-1980 / Christian Hinterbuchner. Linz : R. Trauner, c1986. 344 p. : ill., map ; 24 cm. (Linzer Schriften zur Sozial- u. Wirtschaftsgeschichte . Bd. 16) One folded map laid in. Bibliography: p. 332-344. ISBN 3-85320-370-1 : LC Card 86-225017
1. Electric utilities - Austria - Upper Austria - History - 20th century. I. Title. II. Series.
HD9685.A93 U664 1986

Hinteregger, R. (Robert), 1947- Auf dem Weg in die Freiheit . Graz , 1984. 356 p. : LC Card 87-672377
HD8419.S82 A93x 1984

Hintermeister, Alberto.
El empleo agrícola en una estructra en transformación : el caso de Nicaragua / Alberto Hintermeister. [Santiago, Chile] : Organización Internacional del Trabajo, Programa Mundial del Empleo, Programa Regional del Empleo para América Latina y el Caribe, 1982. 27 p. ; 28 cm. (Trabajo ocasional . 46) "Original: español." Cover title. "Trabajo presentado en el taller de discusión sobre 'Conceptualización de empleo rural en América Latina con propósitos de medición,' octubre 1981, organizado por la Dirección del Empleo de la Secretaría del Trabajo y Previsión Social de México, el PREALC y el Proyecto de Planificación y Promoción del Empleo (PNUD/OIT)." Includes bibliographical references. LC Card 87-403249 DDC 331.7/63/097285 19
1. Agricultural laborers - Nicaragua. 2. Peasantry - Nicaragua. 3. Collective farms - Nicaragua. 4. Cotton growing - Nicaragua. I. Series: Occasional paper (Regional Employment Program for Latin America and the Caribbean) , 46. II. Title.
HD1531.N5 H56 1982

Modernización de la agricultura y pobreza rural en Guatemala / Alberto Hintermeister. [Santiago, Chile] : Organización Internacional del Trabajo, Programa Mundial del Empleo, Programa Regional del Empleo para América Latina y el Caribe, 1982. 59 leaves : ill. ; 28 cm. (Trabajo ocasional . 45) "Original: español." Cover title. Includes bibliographies. LC Card 87-403247 DDC 338.1/6/097281 19
1. Rural poor - Guatemala. 2. Peasantry - Guatemala. 3. Agricultural laborers - Guatemala. 4. Agriculture - Economic aspects - Guatemala. 5. Guatemala - Rural conditions. I. Series: Occasional paper (Regional Employment Program for Latin America and the Caribbean) , 45. II. Title.
HC144.Z9 P624 1982

Hinze, Kenneth. Dlin, Norman. Social atlas of Shreveport, Louisiana /. Shreveport , 1985. 1 atlas (vii, 43 p.) : LC Card 86-622543 DDC 304.6/09763/99 19
HA730.S615 D57 1985

Hinzen, Eckhard. Pre-feasibility study of the integrated Ras Hafun project in north east Somalia : saltworks, fisheries, harbour, road / prepared by FGU-Kronberg Unternehmensberatung Gmbh Consulting + Engineering, Eckhard Hinzen ; commissioned by German Agency for Technical Cooperation, Ltd. Kronberg [West Germany] : FGU-Kronberg, [1981] xii, 186 leaves : ill. ; 30 cm. "Technical cooperation with Somalia, consultancy for the Ministry for National Planning, PN: 78.2016.0-01.100/1300." "September 1981." Bibliography: leaves 147-149. LC Card 85-980733
1. Economic development projects - Somalia - Case studies. I. Deutsche Gesellschaft für Technische Zusammenarbeit. II. Somalia. Wasaaradda Qorshaynta Qaranka. III. Title.
HC850.Z9 E444 1981

Hippel, Eric von. The sources of innovation / Eric von Hippel. New York : Oxford University Press, c1988. xi, 218 p. : ill. ; 25 cm. Bibliography: p. 123-130. Includes index. ISBN 0-19-504085-6 (alk. paper) LC Card 86-28620 DDC 338/.06 19
1. Technological innovations - Economic aspects. I. Title.
HC79.T4 H56 1988

HIPPIES - BRAZIL - CAMPINAS (SÃO PAULO)
A Feira hippie de Campinas . Campinas, SP, Brasil , São Paulo, SP , 1986. 73 p. ; LC Card 87-404187 DDC 381/.18/098161 19
HF5473.B72 C364 1986

Hird, Martin. Gilligan, Colin. International marketing . London , Dover N.H. , c1986. 310 p. : ISBN 0-7099-3811-X : LC Card 86-9015 DDC 658.8/48 19
HF1009.5 .G55 1986 ***NYPL [JLD 86-4466]***

Hirdt, Willi. Der Bauer im Wandel der Zeit /. Bonn , 1986. x, 340 p., [1] leaf of plates : ISBN 3-416-04010-4 LC Card 86-228506
HD1521 .B37 1986

Hiring costs and strategies : the AMA report. New York, N.Y. : American Management Association, c1986. v, 82 p. : ill. ; 28 cm. (AMACOM briefings & surveys) ISBN 0-8144-3153-4 (pbk.) LC Card 86-209862 DDC 658.4/07111/0973 19
1. Executives - United States - Recruiting - Costs - Statistics. 2. Executives - Salaries ,etc. - United States - Statistics. 3. Labor turnover - United States - Statistics. I. American Management Association. II. Series.
HD38.25.U6 H57 1986

Hiring costs and strategies : the AMA report / [Project Director, Eric Rolfe Greenberg]. New York : AMA Membership Publications Division, American Management Association, c1986. v, 82 p. : ill. ; 28 cm. (AMACOM briefings & surveys) ISBN 0-8144-3153-4
1. Employee selection - United States. 2. Recruiting of employees - United States. 3. Executives - United States - Recruiting. I. Greenberg, Eric Rolfe. II. American Management Association. AMA Membership Publications Division. III. Title: AMA survey of hiring

costs and strategies. IV. Series.
NYPL [JLF 86-960]

Hirono, Ryōkichi. Factors which hinder or help productivity improvement in the Asian region, a review and the prospect : national report-Japan / by Ryokichi Hirono. Tokyo, Japan : Asian Productivity Organization, c1980. v, 111 p. ; 22 cm. "APO basic research." Includes bibliographies. ISBN 92-833-1470-0 LC Card 81-174179 DDC 338/.06/0952 19
1. Industrial productivity - Japan. 2. Corporate planning - Japan. 3. Industry and state - Japan. I. Title. II. Title: Added t.p. has title: Factors which help or hinder productivity improvement: country report--Japan.
HD56 .H57 1980 ***NYPL [JLD 86-2287]***

Hirsch, Dagmar. Zur Theorie und Praxis imperialistischer Anpassungs- und Konfrontationspolitik in der Gegenwart /. Berlin [1986] 99 p. ; LC Card 87-409046 DDC 330.12/2 19
HB501 .Z765 1986

Hirsch, Michael D. Multifund investing : how to build a high performance portfolio of mutual funds / Michael D. Hirsch. Homewood, Ill. : Dow Jones-Irwin, c1987. xx, 237 p. : ill. ; 24 cm. Includes bibliographical references and index. ISBN 0-87094-912-8 LC Card 86-71215 DDC 332.63/27 19
1. Mutual funds. 2. Portfolio management. I. Title.
HG4530 .H57 1987

Hirsch, Paul Morris. Pack your own parachute : how to survive mergers, takeovers, and other corporate disasters / by Paul Hirsch. Reading, Mass. : Addison-Wesley Pub. Co., c1987. xix, 197 p. ; 21 cm. Bibliography: p. 173-185. Includes index. ISBN 0-201-12205-7 (pbk.) : LC Card 87-14388 DDC 658.4/09 19
1. Executives - United States - Dismissal of. 2. Consolidation and merger of corporations - United States. 3. Corporate culture - United States. I. Title.
HD38.25.U6 H578 1987

Hirsch, Ralph B. Hudson Waterfront Walkway plan and design guidelines /. [Trenton, N.J.] , 1984] 136 p. : ***NYPL [JLF 87-913]***

Hirsch, Yale. Don't sell stocks on Monday / Yale Hirsch. New York, N.Y., U. S.A. : Penguin Books, 1987, c1986. viii, 232 p. : ill. ; 23 cm. Originally published: New York, N.Y. : Facts on File, c1986. Includes index. ISBN 0-14-010375-9 (pbk.) LC Card 87-8717 DDC 332.63/22 19
1. Stocks. I. Title.
HG4661 .H57 1987

Hirschheim, R. A. (Rudy A.) IFIP TC 8 Working Conference on Office Systems (1985 : Helsinki, Finland) Office systems . Amsterdam ; New York : vii, 199 p. : ISBN 0-444-70105-2 (Elsevier Science Pub. Co.) LC Card 86-16841 DDC 651.8 19
HF5547.5 .I345 1985 ***NYPL [JLD 87-1264]***

Hirschhorn, Larry. The workplace within : the psychodynamics of organizational life / Larry Hirschhorn. Cambridge, Mass. : MIT Press, c1988. x, 265 p. ; 24 cm. (MIT Press series on organization studies . 8) Bibliography: p. [251]-258. Includes index. ISBN 0-262-08169-5 LC Card 87-20144 DDC 158.7 19
1. Psychology, Industrial. 2. Industrial sociology. 3. Organizational behavior. 4. Man-machine systems. 5. Work design. I. Title. II. Series.
HF5548.8 .H493 1988

Hirschman, Albert O. The political economy of Latin American development : seven exercises in retrospection / by Albert O. Hirschman. La Jolla, Calif. : Center for U. S.-Mexican Studies, University of California, San Diego, [1986] 57 p. ; 28 cm. (Copublications series . 3) Working paper / Center for U. S.-Mexican Studies, University of California, San Diego ; no. CE-03 Working paper / Helen Kellogg Institute for International Studies ; no. 88 "December 1986." "This paper in its original form was requested by the Silvert Award committee for presentation at the 20th International Congress of the Latin American Studies Association in Boston, Massachusetts, October 24, 1986"--P. 2. Includes bibliographical references. LC Card 87-621614 DDC 338.98 19
1. Latin America - Economic conditions - 1945-. 2. Latin America - Economic policy. I. Series. II. Series: Working paper (University of California, San Diego. Center for U. S.-Mexican Studies) , no. CE-03. III. Title.
HC125 .H544 1986

Hirschmeier, Johannes. Johannes Hirschmeier, die japanische Unternehmung : Schriften aus dem Nachlass / Willy Kraus, Erhard Louven (Hrsg.) ; [Textverarbeitung, Marie Louise Frank]. Hamburg : Institut für Asienkunde, 1986. viii, 218 p. : ill. ; 21 cm. Bibliography: p. 211-214. ISBN 3-88910-024-4 : LC Card 86-225311
1. Japan - Commerce - History. 2. Businessmen - Japan - History. 3. Industrial management - Japan - History. I. Kraus, Willy. II. Louven, Erhard. III. Title.
HF5349.J3 H573 1986

Hirshleifer, Jack. Economic behaviour in adversity / Jack Hirshleifer. Chicago : University of Chicago Press, 1987. ix, 310 p. ; 26 cm. Includes bibliographies and index. ISBN 0-226-34282-4 : LC Card 87-19846 DDC 330.9 19
1. Natural disasters - Economic aspects. 2. War - Economic aspects. I. Title.
HC79.D45 H57 1987

Hirst, Mônica. As relações dos Estados Unidos com as potências médias na América Latina, México e Brasil / Monica Hirst. [Rio de Janeiro] : Pontifícia Universidade Católica, Instituto de Relações Internacionais, 1985. 48 leaves ; 30 cm. (Textos. no. 2) Bibliography: leaves 45-48. LC Card 87-143873 DDC 337.73072 19
1. United States - Foreign economic relations - Mexico. 2. Mexico - Foreign economic relations - United States. 3. United States - Foreign economic relations - Brazil. 4. Brazil - Foreign economic relations - United States. I. Series: Textos (Pontifícia Universidade Católica do Rio de Janeiro. Instituto de Relações Internacionais) , no. 2. II. Title.
HF1456.5.M6 H57 1985

Hirszowicz, Christine. Internationale Wettbewerbsfähigkeit des Finanzplatzes Schweiz /. Bern , c1987. 131 p. : ISBN 3-258-03806-6 LC Card 87-114764 DDC 332.1 s 332.1/09494 19
HG1526 .B27 Bd. 101 HG3206

Hirway, Indira.
Denial of maternity benefits to women workers : a study of the factory sector in Gujarat / Indira Hirway. New Delhi : Oxford & IBH Pub. Co., c1986. iv, 151 p. ; 23 cm. Bibliography: p. [143]-148. Includes index. ISBN 81-204-0154-9 : LC Card 86-903013 DDC 331.4/25763 19
1. Maternity leave - India - Gujarat. 2. Maternity leave - Law and legislation - India - Gujarat. 3. Women - Employment - India - Gujarat. I. Title.
HD6065.5.I4 H57 1986

Wage employment programmes in rural development : a study of NREP in Gujarat / Indira Hirway. New Delhi : Oxford & IBH Pub. Co., c1986. vi, 112 p. ; 23 cm. Study of National Rural Employment Programme, conducted under the auspices of the Sardar Patel Institute of Economic and Social Research, Ahmedabad. Bibliography: p. [106]-109. Includes index. ISBN 81-204-0072-0 : LC Card 86-903398 DDC 331.2/95475 19
1. Rural development projects - India - Gujarat. 2. Rural poor - Employment - India - Gujarat. 3. National Rural Employment Programme (India). 4. Wages - India - Gujarat. I. Sardar Patel Institute of Economic and Social Research. II. Title.
HD5070.G85 H57 1986

Hise, Richard T. Marketing : concepts, decisions, strategies / Richard T. Hise, Peter L. Gillett, John K. Ryans, Jr.Rev. ed. Houston, Tex. : Dame Publications, 1986. xiv, 891 p. : ill. ; 25 cm. Includes bibliographical references and indexes. ISBN 0-87393-038-X LC Card 83-72200 DDC 658.8 19
1. Marketing. I. Gillett, Peter L. II. Ryans, John K. III. Title.
HF5415 .H543 1986

HISPANIC AMERICANS AS CONSUMERS.
Valencia, Humberto. The U. S. Hispanic market. New York, N.Y. [1984] 1 v. (various foliations) : ISBN 0-931634-48-2 (pbk.) LC Card 86-203027 DDC 658.8/348 19
HC110.C6 V35 1984

HISPANIC AMERICANS - ECONOMIC CONDITIONS.
Borjas, George J. The economic status of male Hispanic migrants and natives in the U. S. [microform] . Santa Barbara, Calif. , 1981. vi, 95 p. ; ***NYPL [*XME-11,311]***

Valencia, Humberto. The U. S. Hispanic market. New York, N.Y. [1984] 1 v. (various foliations) : ISBN 0-931634-48-2 (pbk.) LC Card 86-203027 DDC 658.8/348 19
HC110.C6 V35 1984

HISPANIC AMERICANS - EMPLOYMENT.
Borjas, George J. The economic status of male Hispanic migrants and natives in the U. S. [microform] . Santa Barbara, Calif. , 1981. vi, 95 p. ; ***NYPL [*XME-11,311]***

HISPANIC AMERICANS - EMPLOYMENT - NEW YORK (N.Y.)
Stafford, Walter W. Closed labor markets . New York, N.Y. (105 E. 22nd St., New York 10010) , c1985. xvi, 203, 3, [2] p. ; LC Card 85-186853 DDC 331.12/09747/1 19
HD5726.N5 S73 1985 ***NYPL [Sc F 86-274]***

HISPANOS. see **MEXICAN AMERICANS.**

Hisrich, Robert D. Entrepreneurship, intrapreneurship, and venture capital . Lexington, Mass. , 1986. xiv, 144 p. : ISBN 0-669-11867-2 (alk. paper) LC Card 85-45519 DDC 338/.04 19
HB615 .E634 1986 ***NYPL [JLE 86-3000]***

Histoire de la Bourse du travail de Romans et de ceux qui l'ont faite . Armand, Marcel. [Romans-sur-Isère , 1982] 80 p. ; LC Card 83-143101
HD5926.R66 A76 1982

Histoire de la Fédération des travailleurs du papier et de la forêt /. Vanasse, Gilbert, 1948- Montréal, Québec , 1986- v. <1 > : ISBN 2-89035-122-X (t. 1) LC Card 86-231295
HD6528.P332 F438 1986

Histoire de la navigation sur l'Allier en Bourbonnais / réalisation du Service éducatif des Archives départementales de l'Allier ; introduction, M. Lelong. Clermont-Ferrand [France] : Centre régional de documentation pédagogique, 1983. 61 p. : ill. ; 30 cm. (Annales du Centre régional de documentation pédagogique de Clermont-Ferrand. Collection Documents régionaux) Bibliography: p. 58. LC Card 84-150630
1. Allier River (France) - Navigation - History. I. Archives départementales de l'Allier. Service éducatif. II. Series.
HE668.Z7 A454 1983

Histoire de la pensée économique /. Jessua, Claude. Paris , 1981. 494, viii p. : LC Card 87-672485
HB75 .J47x 1981

Histoire de la poste et des télécommunications dans la région Nord-Pas-de-Calais : actes du colloque de Chéreng, 3 et 4 juin 1983. [Lille] : Cercle amical des P.T.T. de Lille, c1983. 156 p. : ill. ; 25 cm. (Mémoires du Cercle amical des P.T.T. de Lille, Section Histoire, 0248-9902 . t. 4) LC Card 86-115052
1. Postal service - France - Nord-Pas-de-Calais - History - Congresses. 2. Telecommunication - France - Nord-Pas-de-Calais - History - Congresses. I. Cercle amical des P.T.T. de Lille (France). II. Series.
HE6986.N67 H57 1983

Histoire des grandes liaisons françaises /. Reverdy, Georges. Paris, France , c1981-c1982. 2 v. : LC Card 83-129286
HE363.F7 R48 1981

Histoire du Brionnais aux XVIIe et XVIIIe siècles. Durix, Pierre. Les structures économiques et sociales dans le Brionnais oriental aux XVIIe et XVIIIe siècles /. Dijon [1983] xxxiii, 608 p. : LC Card 86-200732
HC277.B68 D87 1983

Histoire économique de la Guadeloupe et de la Martinique . Blérald, Alain Ph. Paris , c1986. 336 p. : ISBN 2-86537-134-4 LC Card 86-159186
HC158.5 .B54 1986

Histoire sociale des faits économiques . Le Bas, Christian. Lyon , c1984. 242 p. : ISBN 2-7297-0221-0 : LC Card 85-152656
HC275 .L45 1984

Histoires, 0246-6120.
Meyer, Jean, 1924- Le poids de l'Etat /. Paris , c1983. 304 p. : ISBN 2-13-037770-X : LC Card 83-175028
HC280.D4 M49 1983

HISTORCIAL MATERIALISM.
Lima, Rômulo de Araújo, 1949- Em busca da dialética . Campina Grande-Paraíba , 1983. 102 p. ; LC Card 86-130003
HB97.5 .L464 1983

Historia contemporánea de Soria, 1860-1936 . Romero, Carmelo, 1950- [Soria] , 1982. 510 p. : ISBN 84-85792-02-5 LC Card 85-136084
HC387.S67 R66 1982

História da reforma agrária /. Dé Carli, Gileno. [Recife?] , 1985. 524 p. ; LC Card 87-102928 DDC 333.3/1/81 19
HD1333.B6 D4 1985

Historia de Cuba. Dumpierre, Erasmo. La Esso en Cuba . La Habana , 1984. xiii, 148 p., [7] p. of plates : LC Card 86-177066
HD9574.C84 E774 1984

Historia de la deuda externa latinoamericana y entretelones del endeudamiento argentino /. Vitale, Luis. Buenos Aires, Argentina , c1986. 351 p. ; ISBN 950-37-0223-2 LC Card 87-100729
HJ8514.5 .V57 1986

Historia de la Estancia "Pozo de Correa" /. Tagle Frías de Cuenca, Matilde. [Córdoba, Argentina] , 1984. 88 p. : LC Card 86-157022
HD1471.A72 C677 1984

Historia de las luchas sociales y el movimiento obrero en Bolivia /. Taboada Terán, Néstor. Cochabamba, Bolivia , 1983- v. <1-3 > : LC Card 86-203884 DDC 331.88/0984 19
HD8275 .T32 1983

Historia del Banco de la Nación. Callegari Ramírez, Carlos. Lima, Perú , 1986. 223 p. : LC Card 87-400236 DDC 332.1/1/0985 19
HG2946 .C35 1986

Historia del contingente internacionalista de Granada. [Havana, Cuba] : Sindicato Nacional de Trabajadores de la Construcción, Secretaría de Divulgación, Comisión de Historia, [1984] 157 p. : ill. ; 21 cm. LC Card 85-213062
1. Technical assistance, Cuban - Grenada. 2. Grenada - History - American invasion, 1983. I. Sindicato Nacional de Trabajadores de la Construcción (Cuba). Comisión de Historia.
HC156.5.Z7 G844 1984

Historia del desarrollo regional en Colombia /. Jiménez, Margarita. Bogotá, Colombia , 1985. 338 p. ; ISBN 958-9061-04-4 LC Card 85-242811
HC197 .J57 1985

Historia del movimiento obrero cubano, 1865-1958 / Instituto de Historia del Movimiento Comunista y de la Revolución Socialista de Cuba, anexo al Comité Central del Partido Comunista de Cuba. La Habana : Editora Política, 1985- v. <1 > ; 23 cm. "Esta obra se publica en saludo al III Congreso del Partido Comunista de Cuba"--V. 1, p. [ii]. Includes bibliographical references and indexes. CONTENTS. - t. 1. 1865-1935 LC Card 87-401462
1. Trade-unions - Cuba - History. 2. Strikes and lockouts - Cuba - History. I. Instituto de Historia del Movimiento Comunista y de la Revolución Socialista de Cuba.
HD6577 .H57 1985

Historia del movimiento obrero ecuatoriano . Ycaza, Patricio. Quito , 1984. 371 p. :
NYPL [JLB 86-21]

Historia del papel moneda argentino / Banco Roberts. Buenos Aires, Argentina : El Banco, c1984. 47, [1] p. : ill. ; 23 x 24 cm. Bibliography: p. [48] LC Card 86-180304
1. Paper money - Argentina - History. 2. Bank notes - Argentina - History. I. Banco Roberts.
HG817 .H57 1984

História do comércio do Maranhão. Viveiros, Jerônimo de, 1884- São Luís, 1954-<1964. v. <1-3 > LC Card 55-29090
HF3409.M3 V5

História do sindicalismo no Rio Grande do Norte /. Oliveira, Geraldo Sabino de. Natal [Brazil] , 1985. 68 p., [6] leaves of plates : LC Card 87-403987 DDC 331.88/0981/32 19
HD6615.R54 O45 1985

Historia económica y social de Manabí /. Dueñas de Anhalzer, Carmen. [Quito, Ecuador] , 1986. 140 p., [4] leaves of plates : LC Card 87-107503
HC203.S83 D84 1986

Historia económica y social del norte de Manabí. Dueñas de Anhalzer, Carmen. Historia económica y social de Manabí /. [Quito, Ecuador] , 1986. 140 p., [4] leaves of plates : LC Card 87-107503
HC203.S83 D84 1986

Historia (Ediciones Cátedra). Serie menor. Rueda Hernanz, Germán. La desamortización de Mendizábal y Espartero en España /. Madrid , c1986. 200 p. ; ISBN 84-376-0592-X LC Card 86-216590
HD774 .R84 1986

História empresarial vivida / [compilada por] Cleber Aquino ; [Olacyr Francisco de Moraes ... et al.]. 2a. ed. São Paulo : Gazeta Mercantil, 1986-<1987 > v. <1-3 > ; 21 cm. Vol. 1-2 contain lectures given in the Programa História Empresarial Vivida, held by the Faculdade de Economia e Administração, Universidade de São Paulo, during 1985. Vol. 2-<3 > without ed. statement. LC Card 86-226035
1. Industrial management - Brazil. 2. Industrial management - Brazil - Case studies. I. Aquino, Cléber Pinheiro de. II. Moraes, Olacyr Francisco de. III. Universidade de São Paulo. Faculdade de Economia e Administração.
HD70.B7 H57 1986

Historia gospodarcza Polski dziewiętnastego i dwudziestego wieku. Kostrowicka, Irena. Historia gospodarcza Polski XIX i XX wieku /. Warszawa , 1984. 583 p., [3] folded leaves of plates : ISBN 83-05-11411-2 : LC Card 85-218322
HC340.3 .K67 1984

Historia gospodarcza Polski XIX i XX wieku /. Kostrowicka, Irena. Warszawa , 1984. 583 p., [3] folded leaves of plates : ISBN 83-05-11411-2 : LC Card 85-218322
HC340.3 .K67 1984

Historia gospodarcza Polski 19. i 20. wieku. Kostrowicka, Irena. Historia gospodarcza Polski XIX i XX wieku /. Warszawa , 1984. 583 p., [3] folded leaves of plates : ISBN 83-05-11411-2 : LC Card 85-218322
HC340.3 .K67 1984

Historia gráfica de las luchas populares en Costa Rica, 1870-1930. 1a ed. San José, Costa Rica : E.P. : CECADE, 1986- v. <1 > : ill., facsims., ports. ; 18 x 21 cm. Bibliography: v. 1, p. 145-146. ISBN 997-7944-12-1 (v. 1) LC Card 87-158835 DDC 305.5/62/097286 19
1. Labor and laboring classes - Costa Rica - Political activity - History. I. Editorial Porvenir. II. Centro de Capacitación para el Desarrollo (San José, Costa Rica).
HD8138 .H57 1986

Historia laboral de Honduras . Argueta, Mario. [Tegucigalpa] , 1985. 204 p. ; LC Card 85-199862
HD8155 .A74 1985

La historia laboral de las mujeres y su efecto en la tasa de salario . Pardo V., Lucía. Santiago , 1986. 44, 5 p. : LC Card 86-217486
HD6126 .P37 1986

Historia marítima del Perú. Serie Monografías . (t. 1) Flórez Nohesell, Miguel. Los puertos del Perú /. Lima, Perú , 1986. 947 p. : LC Card 86-210075
HE555.P5 F58 1986

Historia social de América /. Astesano, Eduardo. [Historia socialista de América.] Buenos Aires, Argentina [1982] 177 p. : ISBN 950-0-17004-3 LC Card 83-165516
HC94 .A83 1982

Historia tōn ethnikōn daneiōn /. Andreadēs, Andreas Michaēl, 1876-1935. Athēna , 1986- v. <1 > ; LC Card 87-112859
HJ8672 .A53 1986

Historia y realidad del movimiento popular en Bolivia.
Taboada Terán, Néstor. Historia de las luchas sociales y el movimiento obrero en Bolivia /. Cochabamba, Bolivia , 1983- v. <1-3 > : LC Card 86-203884 DDC 331.88/0984 19
HD8275 .T32 1983

Historiallisia tutkimuksia, 0073-2559 . (131) Orrman, Eljas. Bebyggelsen i Pargas, S:t Mårtens och Vemo socknar i egentliga Finland under senmedeltiden och på 1500-talet /. Helsingfors , 1986. 293 p. : ISBN 951-9254-73-0 LC Card 86-199875
HD723 .O77 1986

Historias de Edmundo Flores. Flores, Edmundo, 1918- México , 1983-<c1986. v. <1-2 > : ISBN 968-471-052-6 (v. 1) LC Card 83-199689
HB123.M43 F564 1983

HISTORIC DISTRICTS.
Bortoli, Michele. Il traffico nei centri storici /. [Lucca, Italy] , 1986. 236 p. : LC Card 87-151755
HE311.I82 L843 1986

HISTORIC DISTRICTS - ITALY - LUCCA.
Bortoli, Michele. Il traffico nei centri storici /. [Lucca, Italy] , 1986. 236 p. : LC Card 87-151755
HE311.I82 L843 1986

Historical and projected oil and gas consumption : prepared for the second session, Fourteenth Alaska Legislature / State of Alaska. [Juneau] : Alaska Dept. of Natural Resources, Division of Oil & Gas, [1986] 1 v. (in various pagings) : ill. ; 28 cm. "January 1986." LC Card 86-622301 DDC 333.8/2313/09798 19
1. Energy consumption - Alaska. 2. Petroleum industry and trade - Alaska. 3. Gas industry - Alaska. I. Alaska. Division of Oil and Gas.
HD9502.U53 A4574 1986

HISTORICAL MATERIALISM.
Tetzel, Manfred. Philosophie und Ökonomie, oder, Das Exempel Bernstein /. Berlin , 1984. 187 p. : LC Card 84-166815
HB107.B52 T48 1984

The Historical meanings of work / edited by Patrick Joyce. Cambridge [Cambridgeshire] ; New York : Cambridge University Press, 1987. v, 320 p. ; 24 cm. Bibliography: p. 258-309. Includes index. ISBN 0-521-30897-6 LC Card 87-788 DDC 306/.36 19
1. Work. 2. Leisure. 3. Work ethic. 4. Work - History. I. Joyce, Patrick.
HD4904 .H54 1987

Historical perspectives on modern economics. Koot, Gerard M. English historical economics, 1870-1926 . Cambridge [Cambridgeshire] , New York , 1987. viii, 277 p. ; ISBN 0-521-32854-3 LC Card 87-11592 DDC 330/.0941 19
HB103.A2 K65 1987

HISTORICAL RECORDS - PRESERVATION. see **ARCHIVES.**

Historical Society of New Mexico. Baxter, John O., 1927- Las carneradas . Albuquerque , c1987. x, 198 p., [4] p. of plates : ISBN 0-8263-0961-5 LC Card 86-30906 DDC 381/.4163/009789 19
HD9436.U53 N63 1987

Historical trends in Australian rural production, exports, farm income, and indexes of prices received and paid by farmers, 1952-53 to 1972-73 / Bureau of Agricultural Economics. Canberra : Australian Govt. Pub. Service, 1974. vii, 17 p. : ill. ; 21 x 31 cm. ISBN 0-642-00746-2 (pbk.) LC Card 85-126806 DDC 338.1/0994/021 19
1. Agriculture - Economic aspects - Australia - History - Statistics. 2. Agricultural prices - Australia - History - Statistics. I. Australia. Bureau of Agricultural Economics.
HD2152 .H57 1974

Historical trends in job vacancies by major occupation groups : Ontario and ten Canada Manpower Centre (C.M.C.) Management Regions, 1970-1975 / by Research Branch, Ontario Ministry of Labour. Toronto, Ont. : Ontario Ministry of Labour, Research Branch, [1976] 26 p. : ill. ; 30 cm. (Employment information series . no. 16) "March 1976." LC Card 82-213963 DDC 331.2 s 331.12/4/09713021 19
1. Job vacancies - Ontario - Statistics. 2. Ontario - Occupations - Statistics. I. Ontario. Ministry of Labour. Research Branch. II. Series.
HD5729.O6 E46 no. 16

Historisch-sozialwissenschaftliche Forschungen, 0713-2153 . (Bd. 19) Beiträge zur quantitativen vergleichenden Unternehmensgeschichte /. Stuttgart , c1985. 206 p. : ISBN 3-608-91325-4 LC Card 85-233589
HD2734 .B32 1985

Historische Anthropologie : der Mensch in der Geschichte / mit Beiträgen von Michael Erbe ... [et al.] ; herausgegeben von Hans Süssmuth. Göttingen : Vandenhoeck & Ruprecht, c1984. 166 p. ; 19 cm. (Kleine Vandenhoeck-Reihe. 1499) Bibliography: p. 162-165. CONTENTS. - Geschichte und Anthropologie / Hans Süssmuth -- Historisch-anthropologische Fragestellungen der Annales-Schule / Michael Erbe -- Fragestellungen der historischen Anthropologie / August Nitschke -- Probleme historisch-sozialanthropologischer Forschung /

Jochen Martin -- Vom Interesse der Sozialhistoriker an der Ethnologie / Hans Medick -- Neuere Alltagsgeschichte und historische Anthropologie / Detlev Peukert -- Historisch-anthropologische Fragestellungen / Jürgen Kocka -- Zur Stellung des Vaters in antiken Gesellschaften / Jochen Martin -- Modelle des Alterns in der europäischen Tradition / Rolf Sprandel -- Vom Wandel des Wirkens / August Nitschke -- Anthropologische Fragestellungen in Geschichtsbüchern / Eugen Hoffmann -- Historische Anthropologie und Alltagsgeschichte in Perspektiven der Geschichtsdidaktik / Wolfgang Hug -- Historische Anthropologie und Geschichtsdidaktik / Siegfried Quandt. ISBN 3-525-33497-4 LC Card 84-203590 DDC 306/.09 19
1. Ethnology - Addresses, essays, lectures. 2. History - Addresses, essays, lectures. 3. Social history - Addresses, essays, lectures. I. Erbe, Michael. II. Süssmuth, Hans.
GN345.2 .H57 1984 ***NYPL [JFC 86-1764]***

Historische Entwicklung und heutiger Stand der Wettbewerbstheorie . Neumann, Carl Wolfgang. Königstein/Ts. , 1982. 318 p. ; ISBN 3-7610-6362-8 : LC Card 83-154547
HB238 .N48 1982

Historische Strassen in Europa . Grieser, Dietmar, 1934- München , c1983. 95 p. : ISBN 3-87405-160-9 (pbk.) LC Card 87-672444
HE361 .G74x 1983

Historische Studien (Matthiesen Verlag) .
(Heft 274) Banze, Angelika. Die deutsch-englische Wirtschaftsrivalität . Vaduz , 1965. 105 p. ; LC Card 85-243022 DDC 337.43041 19
HF1546.15.G7 B36 1965

(Heft 63) Heineken, Hermann. Der Salzhandel Lüneburgs mit Lübeck bis zum Anfang des 15. Jahrhunderts /. Vaduz , 1965. 150 p. ; LC Card 86-231350
HD9213.G43 L864 1965

Historische Wurzeln der Sozialpartnerschaft / herausgegeben von Gerald Stourzh und Margarete Grandner. München : R. Oldenbourg, 1986. 368 p. ; 24 cm. (Wiener Beiträge zur Geschichte der Neuzeit. Bd. 12/13) Includes bibliographical references. ISBN 3-486-52971-4 LC Card 87-146580 DDC 306/.36/09436 19
1. Industrial sociology - Austria - History. 2. Labor supply - Social aspects - Austria. I. Stourzh, Gerald. II. Grandner, Margarete, 1953-.
HD6957.A9 H57 1986

Historische Zeitschrift. Beiheft .
(n.F., 9) Vereinswesen und bürgerliche Gesellschaft in Deutschland /. München , 1984. 180 p. ; ISBN 3-486-52081-4 LC Card 84-205111
HD2429.G3 V46 1984

HISTORY - ADDRESSES, ESSAYS, LECTURES.
Historische Anthropologie . Göttingen , c1984. 166 p. ; ISBN 3-525-33497-4 LC Card 84-203590 DDC 306/.09 19
GN345.2 .H57 1984 ***NYPL [JFC 86-1764]***

History and the economic past . Coleman, D. C. (Donald Cuthbert), 1920- Oxford , New York , 1987. 150 p.; ISBN 0-19-828305-9 LC Card 86-28543 DDC 330/.07/1041 19
HC28.5.G7 C65 1987

HISTORY - BIOGRAPHY. see **BIOGRAPHY.**

HISTORY, ECONOMIC. see **ECONOMIC HISTORY.**

A history of Adolf Hitler and the Third Reich in postage stamps and postal stationery /. Thomas, Earl. Silver Spring, Md. , c1987. p. cm. ISBN 0-918184-06-1 LC Card 87-755 DDC 769.56/3 19
HE6183.H53 T46 1987

History of American economic policy in the Philippines during the American colonial period, 1900-1935 /. Giesecke, Leonard F. (Leonard Frederick) New York , 1987. 279 p. ; ISBN 0-8240-8082-3 (alk. paper) : LC Card 87-23786 DDC 337.730599 19
HF1456.5.P6 G53 1987

A history of American enterprise /. Dobson, John M. Englewood Cliffs, N.J. , c1988. p. cm. ISBN 0-13-389081-3 LC Card 87-18679 DDC 338.0973 19
HF3021 .D6 1988

The History of American thought and culture. Brick, Howard, 1953- Daniel Bell and the decline of intellectual radicalism . Madison, Wis. , 1986. 215-266. ISBN 0-299-10550-4 : LC Card 85-40757 DDC 300/.92/4 19
H59.B42 B75 1986 ***NYPL [JLE 86-3046]***

A history of British trade unions since 1889 /. Clegg, Hugh Armstrong. Oxford , New York , <1987- c1985-. p. cm. ISBN 0-19-828307-5 (pbk. : v. 2) : LC Card 87-15229 DDC 331.88/0941 19
HD6664 .C3864 1987

A history of capitalism, 1500-1980 /. Beaud, Michel. [Histoire du capitalisme, 1500-1980. English.] London , 1984. 256 p. ; ISBN 0-333-35957-7 LC Card 87-673370
HC51 .B3813x 1984

The history of commodity futures trading and its regulation /. Markham, Jerry W. New York , 1987. xiv, 305 p. ; ISBN 0-275-92313-4 (alk. paper) : LC Card 86-25246 DDC 332.64/4 19
HG6049 .M37 1986 ***NYPL [JLE 87-819]***

A History of Cooper Brothers & Co., 1854-1954. New York : Garland Pub., 1986, c1954. xi, 116 p., [13] leaves of plates : ill. ; 24 cm. (Accounting thought and practice through the years) Reprint. Originally published: London: Privately published for Cooper Brothers & Co. by B.T. Batsford, 1954. Includes index. ISBN 0-8240-7881-0 (alk. paper) : LC Card 86-25720 DDC 338.7/61657/0941 19
1. Cooper Brothers & Co. - History. 2. Accounting firms - Great Britain - History. 3. Accounting - Great Britain - History. I. Cooper Brothers & Co. II. Title: History of Cooper Brothers and Company, 1854-1954. III. Series.
HF5616.G73 C665 1986

History of Cooper Brothers and Company, 1854-1954. A History of Cooper Brothers & Co., 1854-1954. New York , 1986, c1954. xi, 116 p., [13] leaves of plates : ISBN 0-8240-7881-0 (alk. paper) : LC Card 86-25720 DDC 338.7/61657/0941 19
HF5616.G73 C665 1986

A history of econometrics /. Epstein, Roy J. (Roy Jacob), 1954- Amsterdam ; New York : x, 254 p. ; ISBN 0-444-70267-9 LC Card 87-15308 DDC 330/.028 19
HB139 .E67 1987

The history of famines in Rajputana, 1858-1900 A.D. /. Maloo, Kamala, 1948- Udaipur , 1987. xii, 296 p. : ISBN 81-85167-00-1 : LC Card 87-901599 DDC 363.8/0954/4 19
HC437.R3 M28 1987

A history of financial intermediaries. Krooss, Herman Edward, 1912-1975. New York [1971] xi, 254 p. ISBN 0-394-31001-2 LC Card 78-127552 DDC 332.1/0973
HG181 .K73 ***NYPL [JLE 87-572]***

A history of Heal's . Goodden, Susanna. [London] , Atlantic Highlands, N.J. , 1984. 137 p. : ISBN 0-85331-488-8 (pbk.) LC Card 86-221633 DDC 381/.456841/00941 19
HD9773.G74 H434 1984

The history of industrial training in Britain /. Sheldrake, John, 1944- Aldershot Hants, England , Brookfield, Vt., USA , c1987. v, 75 p. ; ISBN 0-566-05294-6 : LC Card 86-29601 DDC 331.25/92 19
HD5715.5.G7 S54 1987

The history of marketing thought /. Bartels, Robert, 1913- Columbus, Ohio , c1988. p. cm. ISBN 0-942280-44-X : LC Card 87-20702 DDC 658.8/009 19
HF5415 .B36 1988

History of NUPE. Dix, Bernard. Serving the public, building the union . London , 1987- v. <1 > : ISBN 0-85315-645-X (v. 1) : LC Card 87-169851 DDC 331.88/09421 19
HD8005.2.G7 D59 1987

History of Raterpillar. Zinman, Michael. The history of the decline and fall of the Raterpillar Tractor Company . Ardsley, N.Y. , c1986. 231 p. : ISBN 0-937704-03-2 (pbk.) : LC Card 86-82887 DDC 338.7/629225 19
HD9710.4.U64 R388 1986

A history of revenue administration in Assam, 1228-1826 A.D. . Goswami, Surendra Kumar, 1929-1985. Delhi , 1986. xii, 321 p. : LC Card 86-903188 DDC 354.54/16200726/09 19
HJ2939.Z9 A874 1986

History of Royal Blue Express Services /. Anderson, Roy Claude. Newton Abbot , North Pomfret, Vt. , 1985. 216 p. : ISBN 0-7153-8654-9 : LC Card 86-136155 DDC 388.3/22/09423 19
HE5664.Z7 R63 1985

A history of taxation and expenditure in the Western world /. Webber, Carolyn. New York , c1986. 734 p. ,[16] p. of plates : ISBN 0-671-54617-1 LC Card 86-3863 DDC 336.2/009 19
HJ2250 .W42 1986 ***NYPL [JLE 86-3474]***

History of the American worker, 1933-1941. Bernstein, Irving, 1916- A caring society . Boston , 1985. 338 p., [24] p. of plates : ISBN 0-395-33116-1 : LC Card 84-25129 DDC 362.8/5/0973 19
HD8072 .B365 1985 ***NYPL [JLD 86-2102]***

The history of the British Bank of the Middle East /. Jones, Geoffrey. Cambridge [Cambridgeshire] , New York , 1986- v. : ISBN 0-521-32322-3 (v. 1) LC Card 85-31359 DDC 332.1/5/0955 19
HG3270.2.A8 B755 1986 ***NYPL [JLL 87-87]***

The history of the British coal industry. Oxford [Oxfordshire] : Clarendon Press ; New York : Oxford University Press, c1983- v. : ill., maps ; 24 cm. Includes bibliographical references and index. CONTENTS. - v. 2. 1700-1830, the Industrial Revolution / by Michael W. Flinn, with the assistance of David S. Stoker -- v. 3. 1830-1913, Victorian pre-eminence / by Roy Church, with the assistance of Alan Hall and John Kanefsky -- v. 5. 1946-1982: the nationalized industry / by William Ashworth, with the assistance of Mark Pegg. ISBN 0-19-828283-4 (v. 2) : LC Card 83-4194 DDC 338.2/724/0941 19
1. Coal trade - Great Britain - History. 2. Coal mines and mining - Great Britain - History. I. Flinn, Michael W., 1917-. II. Church, Roy. III. Title.
HD9551.5 .F58 1983 ***NYPL [JLL 84-138]***

A history of the Chillicothe and other Ross County, Ohio, post offices, 1799-1987 /. Grabb, John R., 1915- Chillicothe, Ohio (206 Caldwell St., Chillicothe 45601) , c1987. iv, 76 p. : LC Card 87-80919 DDC 383/.4977182 19
HE6376.C45 G73 1987

The history of the decline and fall of the Raterpillar Tractor Company . Zinman, Michael. Ardsley, N.Y. , c1986. 231 p. : ISBN 0-937704-03-2 (pbk.) : LC Card 86-82887 DDC 338.7/629225 19
HD9710.4.U64 R388 1986

A history of the Highland clearances /. Richards, Eric. London , c1982-1985. 2 v. : ISBN 0-85664-496-X : LC Card 81-208122 DDC 333.33/5 19
HD1511.G7 R53 1982 ***NYPL [JLL 82-171]***

The history of the Hongkong and Shanghai Banking Corporation /. King, Frank H. H. Cambridge [Cambridgeshire] , New York , 1987- p. cm. ISBN 0-521-32706-7 (v. 1) LC Card 86-28339 DDC 332.1/5/095125 19
HG1571 K56

A history of the Maryland Federation of Business and Professional Women's Clubs, Inc., 1929-1980. Maryland Federation of Business and Professional Women's Clubs. [S.l.] , c1986. iii, 206 p., [1] leaf of plates : LC Card 86-206928 DDC 061/.3 19
HD6054.4.U62 M35 1986

A history of the Oklahoma State University, College of Business Administration /. Kincaid, William M. Stillwater, Okla. , c1987. x, 227 p. : ISBN 0-914956-31-0 LC Card 87-11046 DDC 650/.07/1176634 19
HF1134.O57 K55 1987

The History of UNCTAD, 1964-1984 / United Nations Conference on Trade and Development. New York : United Nations, 1985. ix, 294 p. ; 24 cm. "UNCTAD/OSG/286"--T.p. verso. "United Nations publication. Sales no. E.85.II.D6"--T.p. verso. Includes bibliographical references. ISBN 92-1-112189-2 (pbk.) LC Card 86-202097 DDC 341.7/54 19
1. United Nations Conference on Trade and Development - History. I. United Nations. Conference on Trade and Development.
HF1411 .H516 1985

History series (Hambledon Press) .
(v. 28) Hilton, R. H. (Rodney Howard), 1916- Class conflict and the crisis of feudalism .

London , Ronceverte, W. Va. , 1985. 349 p. ; ISBN 0-907628-36-2 : LC Card 85-21855 DDC 305.5/0942 19
HD604 .H48 1985 *NYPL [JFE 87-391]*

History series (London) .
(v. 13) Fryde, E. B. Studies in medieval trade and finance /. London , 1983. 1 v. (various pagings) ; ISBN 0-907628-10-9 LC Card 83-168474 DDC 382/.0942/04 19
HF3518.E85 F79 1983 *NYPL [JLE 86-2481]*

Hitotsubashi Daigaku. Toshokan. Menger, Carl, 1840-1921. Carl Mengers erster Entwurf zu seinem Hauptwerk "Grundsätze" geschrieben als Anmerkungen zu den "Grundsätzen der Volkswirthschaftslehre" von Karl Heinrich Rau. Tokio , 1963. xxviii, 236 p., [3] leaves of plates : LC Card 85-210245
HB175 .M47 1963

Hiwsisayin Amerikayi Miats'eal Tērut'iwnk'. see **United States.**

al-Ḥizb al-Shuyūʻiyal-Faransī. see **Parti communiste français.**

Hjern, Benny. Hull, Christopher J. Helping small firms grow . New York , c1987. 228 p. : ISBN 0-7099-4791-7 LC Card 87-15728 DDC 338.6/42 19
HD2346.G3 .H786 1987

Ho, James K. K. Linear and dynamic programming with Lotus 1-2-3, Release 2 / James K. Ho. Portland, Or. : Management Information Source, c1987. xiv, 330 p. : ill. ; 24 cm. Bibliography: p. 236. Includes index. ISBN 0-943518-72-5 (pbk.) : LC Card 87-1586 DDC 005.36/9 19
1. Lotus 1-2-3 (Computer program). 2. Business - Data processing. I. Title.
HF5548.4.L67 H6 1987

Hobbs, Charles R. Time power / Charles R. Hobbs. 1st ed. New York : Harper & Row, c1987. ix, 209 p. : ill. ; 25 cm. Bibliography: p. 185-199. Includes index. ISBN 0-06-015589-2 : LC Card 86-46072 DDC 650.1 19
1. Time management. I. Title.
HD69.T54 H62 1987

Hobbs, Frank. Demographic estimates, projections, and selected social characteristics of the population of India / by Frank B. Hobbs. Washington, D.C. : Center for International Research, U. S. Bureau of the Census, [1986] vii, 148 p. : ill. ; 28 cm. (CIR staff paper . no. 21) "May 1986." Bibliography: p. 145-148. LC Card 87-601294 DDC 304.6/0954/021 19
1. Population forecasting - India - Statistics. 2. India - Population - Statistics. 3. Migration, Internal - India - Statistics. I. Center for International Research (U. S.). II. Title. III. Series.
HA4585 .H63 1986

Hobbs, James B. Corporate staying power : how America's most consistently successful corporations maintain exceptional performance / James B. Hobbs. Lexington, Mass. : Lexington Books, c1987. xi, 178 p. ; 24 cm. Includes index. Bibliography: p. [165]-172. ISBN 0-669-11153-8 (alk. paper) LC Card 85-45096 DDC 338.7/4/0973 19
1. Organizational effectiveness. 2. Industrial organization - United States. 3. Organizational effectiveness - Case studies. 4. Industrial organization - United States - Case studies. I. Title.
HD58.9 .H62 1987 *NYPL [JLE 87-1125]*

Hoben, Allan. Somalia . Boston, MA [1983] vi, 164 p. : LC Card 87-108393 DDC 330.967/7305 19
HC850 .S655 1983

Hoberg, Peter. Investitionseinzelentscheidungen : Ziele, Daten, Verfahren / Peter Hoberg. Münster : Lit, [1983?] xi, 244 p. : ill. ; 21 cm. (Betriebswirtschaftliche Schriftenreihe . Bd. 9) Bibliography: p. 235-244. ISBN 3-88660-137-4 LC Card 84-132141
1. Investments - Decision making - Econometric models. I. Title. II. Series.
HG4515.2 .H63 1983

Hobfoll, Stevan E., 1951- Stress, social support, and women /. Washington , c1986. xviii, 272 p. : ISBN 0-89116-404-9 : LC Card 84-27967 DDC 155.9 19
BF575.S75 S7739 1985 *NYPL [JFE 86-3212]*

HOBOES. see **TRAMPS.**

Hobsbawm, E. J. (Eric J.), 1917- Worlds of labour : further studies in the history of labour / E.J. Hobsbawm. London : Weidenfeld and Nicolson, c1984. x, 369 p., [4] p. of plates : ill. ; 23 cm. "Follows ... the collection first published in 1964 under the title Labouring men"--P. viii. Bibliography: p. [317]-354. Includes index. ISBN 0-297-78509-5 : LC Card 86-674019
1. Labor and laboring classes - Great Britain - History. 2. Socialism - Great Britain - History. 3. Labor and laboring classes - History. I. Title.
HD8388 .H63x 1984

Hobson, J. A. (John Atkinson), 1858-1940. The economics of unemployment / J.A. Hobson. New York : Garland Pub., 1985. 157 p. ; 19 cm. (English workers and the coming of the welfare state, 1918-1945) Reprint. Originally published: London : Allen & Unwin, 1922. ISBN 0-8240-7615-X : LC Card 85-13053 DDC 331.13/7 19
1. Consumption (Economics). 2. Unemployment. I. Title. II. Series.
HB822 .H63 1985 *NYPL [JLC 86-452]*

Mummery, A. F. (Albert Frederick), 1855-1895. The physiology of industry . Fairfield, NJ , 1988. p. cm. ISBN 0-678-00673-3 LC Card 87-17943 DDC 330.1 19
HB171 .M95 1988

Hočevar, Jože. Socialismo autogestionario en marcha . Mérida, Venezuela , 1984. 377 p. ; LC Card 87-403553 DDC 335.43/09497 19
HB108.4.A2 S65 1984

Hoch, Róbert.
Életszínvonal és közhangulat /. Budapest , 1984. 69 p. ; LC Card 86-147705
HD7027.5 .E44 1984

A gazdaság nyitottságáról : akadémiai székfoglaló, 1986. április 30. / Hoch Róbert. Budapest : Akadémiai Kiadó, c1987. 33 p. ; 20 cm. (Értekezések, emlékezések, 0236-6258) Includes bibliographical references. ISBN 963-05-4444-X : LC Card 87-425574
1. Hungary - Foreign economic relations. I. Title. II. Series.
HF1542.5 .H63 1987

Hochheiser, Robert M., 1935- How to work for a jerk / by Robert M. Hochheiser. 1st ed. New York : Vintage Books, 1987. 227 p. ; 21 cm. "A Vintage original." ISBN 0-394-74777-1 (pbk.) : LC Card 86-40163 DDC 650.1/3 19
1. Managing your boss. I. Title.
HF5548.83 .H63 1987

Hochschule der Deutschen Gewerkschaften "Fritz Heckert." Kolloquium zur Gewerkschaftlichen Interessenvertretung beim Umfassenden Aufbau des Sozialismus in der Deutschen Demokratischen Republik (1964) Protokoll über das Kolloquium zur Gewerkschaftlichen Interessenvertretung beim Umfassenden Aufbau des Sozialismus in der Deutschen Demokratischen Republik am 31. Januar 1964. [Bernau] [1964] iv, 246 p. ; LC Card 85-125499
HD6700.5 .K65 1964

Hochschule für Wirtschaft und Politik Hamburg. Staatliche Wirtschaftsregulierung in der Krise . Opladen , c1986. 241 p. ; ISBN 3-531-11805-6 LC Card 86-228864
HD84 .S69 1986

Hochschulsammlung Philosophie. Politikwissenschaft, 0720-5406 .
(Bd. 6) Basurco Valverde, Gerardo Félix. Herrschaftsformen und Industrialisierungsprozess in Peru . Freiburg [Breisgau] , c1985. xi, 420 p. : ISBN 3-8107-2210-3 LC Card 86-179243
HC227 .B339 1985

HochschulSammlung Wirtschaftswissenschaft. Volkswirtschaft, 0720-5686 .
(Bd. 10) Kaufmann-Scheuer, Brigitte. Perspektiven und Modelle einer Neuorientierung der staatlichen Wohneigentumsförderung /. Freiburg [i. Br.] , 1983. 235 p. : ISBN 3-8107-2185-9 LC Card 84-108468
HD7339.A3 K34 1983

Hochschulschriften zur Betriebswirtschaftslehre .
(Bd. 16) Weissman, Arnold. Verbraucherpanel, Informationen als Grundlage für Marketingentscheidungen im Einzelhandel /. München , c1983. xxviii, 194, [4] p. : ISBN 3-88259-242-7 LC Card 83-161472
HF5415.3 .W437 1983

(Bd. 18) Graumann, Jens. Die Dienstleistungsmarke . München , c1983. l, 197 p. : ISBN 3-88259-244-3 LC Card 83-180401
HD9984.5 .G7 1983

(Bd. 22) Bürkle, Roland. Das Modell der Ausgleichslösung . München , c1983. 210 p. : ISBN 3-88259-255-9 LC Card 83-222868
HD30.23 .B865 1983

(Bd. 24) Mähling, Friedrich W. (Friedrich Wilhelm), 1952- Werbung, Wettbewerb und Verbraucherpolitik /. München , c1983. xii, 477 p. : ISBN 3-88259-258-3 LC Card 84-144205
HF5822 .M34 1983

(Bd. 25) März, Thomas. Interdependenzen in einem Kennzahlensystem . München , c1983. iv, 296 p. : ISBN 3-88259-262-1 : LC Card 83-222369
HG4028.V3 M34 1983

(Bd. 27) Storz, Peter, 1954- Steuerplanung im Unternehmen mit einem computergestützten Modell /. München , c1984. vii, 657 p. : ISBN 3-88259-282-6 LC Card 84-174173 DDC 336.24/3/0943 19
HD2753.G3 S76 1984

(Bd. 30) Hinderer, Michael. Die mittelständische Unternehmung . München , c1984. xix, 435 p. : ISBN 3-88259-328-8 LC Card 85-152951
HD2341 .H56 1984

(Bd. 32) Weber, Rolf. Vehicle Routing- und Scheduling-Probleme unter besonderer Berücksichtigung von Dial-a-Ride-Problemen /. München , c1985. iii, 158 p. : ISBN 3-88259-349-0 LC Card 86-123392
HE305 .W4 1985

(Bd. 35) Gisteren, Roland van, 1950- Branchenorientierte Bonitätsanalyse mit Früherkennungseigenschaften . München , c1986. 2, xi, 393 p. : ISBN 3-88259-370-9 LC Card 86-173025
HD9715.G32 G57 1986

(Bd. 38) Schiller, Karla, 1955- Loglineare Modellierung mit dem Abschlusstest . München , c1986. xiii, 226 p. : ISBN 3-88259-397-0 LC Card 86-230772
HF5415.135 .S35 1986

(Bd. 40) Staudinger, Hans-Joachim, 1957- Die Überwachung der Geschäftsführung, eine betriebswirtschaftliche Betrachtung . München , c1986. lxxxvi, 340 p. ; ISBN 3-88259-412-8 LC Card 87-125378 DDC 663/.3/0685 19
HD35 .S6745 1986

(Bd. 41) Kohlmann, Ulrike, 1954- Möglichkeiten und Grenzen der Aussagefähigkeit von Teilkonzernabschlüssen /. München , c1986. viii, 180 p. ; ISBN 3-88259-419-5 LC Card 87-121768 DDC 657/.95/0943 19
HF5686.C7 K644 1986

(Bd. 42) Lubos, Günter, 1958- Die Berichterstattung der internen Revision im Grossbetrieb /. München , c1986. xxvii, 207 p. ; ISBN 3-88259-421-7 LC Card 87-121827 DDC 657/.458 19
HF5668.25 .L82 1986

(Bd. 43) Medla, Karsten, 1954- Shop-in-the-shop . München , c1987. xxxi, 207, 6 p. ; ISBN 3-88259-428-4 LC Card 87-141864 DDC 658.8/7 19
HF5429 .M36 1987

(Bd. 45) Christians, Uwe, 1957- Entwicklung und empirische Überprüfung eines konjunkturgerechten Erfolgsprognosemodells zur Unterstützung der Kreditwürdigkeitsprüfung . München , c1986. xiv, 412 p. : ISBN 3-88259-430-6 (Deut. Bibl.) LC Card 87-409324 DDC 332.7/0943 19
HG3754.5.G3 C48 1986

Hochtechnologien und internationale Wettbewerbsfähigkeit der deutschen Wirtschaft / Der Bundesminister für Wirtschaft, LP. Bonn : Bundesministerium für Wirtschaft, Referat Öffentlichkeitsarbeit, [1984] 30 p. ; 29 cm. (BMWI Dokumentation, 0342-9288 . Nr. 263) Cover title. "Juli 1984." LC Card 85-184765
1. Germany, West - Commerce. 2. Competition, International. 3. High technology industries - Germany (West). I. Germany (West). Bundesministerium für

Wirtschaft. II. Series.
HF3564 .H63 1984

Hoda, Anwarul, 1938- Developing countries in the international trading system / Anwarul Hoda. Ahmedabad : Allied Publishers, 1987. xii, 302 p. ; 22 cm. Study, with reference to the General Agreement on Tariffs and Trade (GATT), drawn up at Geneva, 1947. Bibliography: p. [285]-295. Includes index. LC Card 87-902308 DDC 382/.091724 19
1. Developing countries - Commerce. I. Title.
HF4055 .H64 1987

Hodēgos exagōgikōn diadikasiōn / [epimeleia, Giōrgos P. Nezēs]. 4. ekdosē. [Athēna] : Organismos Proōthēseōs Exagōgōn, Dieuthynsē Eidikōn Meletōn, E.O.K., [1983] 184 p. : forms ; 28 cm. (Eidikes ekdoseis) Bibliography: p. 183-184. LC Card 86-170148
1. Export marketing - European Economic Community countries - Handbooks, manuals, etc. 2. Export sales - European Economic Community countries - Forms. I. Nezēs, Giōrgos P. II. Organismos Proōthēseōs Exagōgōn (Greece). Dieuthynsē Eidikōn Meletōn-E.O.K. III. Series.
HF1009.7.E86 H63 1983

Hodēgos geōrgikōn viomēchaniōn. Athēna : Agrotikē Trapeza tēs Hellados, Dieuthynsē Meletōn & Programmatismou, 1985. 510 p. : ill. ; 28 cm. LC Card 86-193419
1. Agricultural industries - Greece - Directories. 2. Produce trade - Greece - Directories. 3. Food industry and trade - Greece - Directories. I. Agrotikē Trapeza tēs Hellados. Dieuthynsē Meletōn & Programmatismou.
HD9015.G82 H58 1985

Hodēgos marketing Hellados, 1983. Hodēgos marketinnk Hellados, 1983 /. Athēnai [1983?] 357 p. ; LC Card 84-107807
HF5415.12.G8 H63 1983

Hodēgos marketinnk Hellados, 1983 / Hellēniko Institouto Marketinnk tēs Hellēnikēs Hetairias Dioikēseōs Epicheirēseōn ; [syntaktikē ergasia Athan. Papandropoulos ... et al.]. Athēnai : D. Michaēlidēs, [1983?] 357 p. ; 25 cm. Includes index. LC Card 84-107807
1. Marketing - Greece. I. Papandropoulos, Athan. II. Hellēnikē Hetairia Dioikēseōs Epicheirēseōn. Hellēniko Institouto Marketinnk. III. Title: Hodēgos marketing Hellados, 1983.
HF5415.12.G8 H63 1983

Hodēgos synetairistikōn geōrgikōn viomēchaniōn : agrotikes synetairistikes viomēchanies. Athēna : Dieuthynsē Geōrgikōn Viomēchaniōn, 1985. 102 p. : col. ill. ; 21 cm. LC Card 86-194038
1. Food industry and trade - Greece - Directories. I. Agrotikē Trapeza tēs Hellados. Dieuthynsē Geōrgikōn Viomēchaniōn.
HD9015.G82 H59 1985

Hodēgos tachydromikōn tomeōn Athēnōn / [epimeleia Kōstas Rizos]. Athēnai : Ekd. Olympiakē Aeroporia, [1962] 124 p. : ill. ; 24 cm. At head of title: Hellēnika Tachydromeia. LC Card 86-234916
1. Zip code - Greece - Athens - Directories. I. Rizos, Kōstas.
HE7180.5.Z7 A744 1962

Hodeige, Christian H., 1958- Job-Search im strukturierten Arbeitsmarkt : zur suchtheoretischen Erklärung unfreiwilliger Arbeitslosigkeit / Christian H. Hodeige.1. Aufl. Freiburg : Rombach, c1985. 166 p. ; 23 cm. Bibliography: p. 153-166. ISBN 3-7930-0113-1 LC Card 86-142859
1. Unemployed - Mathematical models. 2. Labor supply - Mathematical models. 3. Job hunting - Mathematical models. I. Title.
HD5701.6 .H62 1985

Hodges, James A., 1932- New deal labor policy and the southern cotton textile industry, 1933-1941 / by James A. Hodges. 1st ed. Knoxville : University of Tennessee Press, c1986. xii, 252 p. : ill. ; 24 cm. Includes index. Bibliography: p. [236]-244. ISBN 0-87049-496-1 (alk. paper) : LC Card 85-20368 DDC 338.4/767721/0975 19
1. Cotton textile industry - Southern States - Employees - History. 2. New Deal, 1933-1939 - Southern States - History. 3. United States - Social conditions - 1933-1945. I. Title.
HD8039.T42 U652 1986 ***NYPL [JLE 86-3477]***

Hodgetts, Richard M.
Addison-Wesley economics / Richard M. Hodgetts, Terry L. Smart ; consultant, Jane Schaerges Lopus. Annotated teachers ed., Texas ed. Menlo Park, Calif. : Addison-Wesley Pub. Co., c1988. vi, T1-T266, 31, 548 p. : ill. (some col.) ; 27 cm. On spine: Economics and free enterprise. Includes index. ISBN 0-201-22775-4 LC Card 87-147565 DDC 330 19
1. Economics. 2. Texas - Economic conditions. I. Smart, Terry L. II. Title. III. Title: Economics and free enterprise.
HB171.5 .H676 1988

Essentials of economics and free enterprise / Richard M. Hodgetts, Terry L. Smart. Rev. ed. Menlo Park, Calif. : Addison-Wesley Pub. Co., c1987. 437 p. : ill. (some col.) ; 24 cm. Bibliography: p. 420-422. Includes index. ISBN 0-201-20719-2 LC Card 86-207031 DDC 330 19
1. Economics. 2. Capitalism - United States. 3. United States - Economic conditions. 4. United States - Economic policy. I. Smart, Terry L. II. Title.
HB171.5 .H677 1987

Luthans, Fred. Real managers /. Cambridge, Mass. , c1988. xvi, 192 p. : ISBN 0-88730-103-7 LC Card 87-19080 DDC 658.4 19
HD31 .L865 1988

Hodgson, Godfrey. Lloyd's of London : a reputation at risk / Godfrey Hodgson.Rev. and updated. Harmondsworth, Middlesex, England ; New York, N.Y., U. S.A. : Penguin Books, 1986. 414 p. ; 24 cm. Includes index. ISBN 0-14-005646-7 (pbk.) : LC Card 87-106915 DDC 368/.012/094212 19
1. Lloyd's (Firm). I. Title.
HG8039 .H62 1986

Hodgson, Philip. Interviewing skills / Philip Hodgson. London ; New York : McGraw-Hill Bk. Co. (UK), c1987. p. cm. Includes index. ISBN 0-07-084941-2 : LC Card 87-3658 DDC 658.3/1124 19
1. Employment interviewing. I. Title.
HF5549.5.I6 H58 1987

Hodin, Michael W. A national policy for organized free trade : the case of U. S. foreign trade policy for steel, 1976-1978 / Michael W. Hodin. New York : Garland Pub., 1987. 481 p. ; 23 cm. (Foreign economic policy of the United States) Originally presented as the author's thesis (Ph. D.)--Columbia, 1979. Bibliography: p. 470-481. ISBN 0-8240-8085-8 (alk. paper) : LC Card 87-23719 DDC 382/.45669142/0973 19
1. Steel industry and trade - United States. 2. Steel industry and trade. 3. United States - Commercial policy. 4. Free trade and protection - Protection. I. Title. II. Series.
HD9515 .H59 1987

Hodrick, Robert J. The empirical evidence on the efficiency of forward and futures foreign exchange markets / Robert J. Hodrick. Chur, Switzerland ; New York : Harwood Academic Publishers, c1987. viii, 174 p. ; 22 cm. (Fundamentals of pure and applied economics, 0191-1708 . v. 24.) Bibliography: p. 158-169. Includes index. ISBN 3-7186-0415-9 (pbk.) LC Card 87-17790 DDC 332.4/5 19
1. Forward exchange. 2. Foreign exchange. I. Series: Fundamentals of pure and applied economics , v. 24. II. Title.
HG3853 .H43 1987

Höcherl, Hermann, 1912- Kohl, Helmut, 1930- Soziale Marktwirtschaft, Fundament für morgen . Bonn [1987] 39 p. : ISBN 3-88991-011-4 LC Card 87-409383 DDC 338.943 19
HC286.5 .K565 1987

HOECHST AG - ARCHIVES.
US-Administration . Frankfurt (M) , 1976. 153 p. : LC Card 85-224662
HD9654.9.H64 U7 1976

HOEDADS, INC. - HISTORY.
Hartzell, Hal, 1946- Birth of a cooperative . Eugene, Or. , 1987. 351 p. : ISBN 0-938493-09-4 (pbk.) : LC Card 87-2656 DDC 334/.6834956/09795 19
HD9759.H64 H37 1987

Hoek, M. P. van der. De praktijk van de inkomensverdeling / M.P. van der Hoek. Groningen : Wolters-Noordhoff, c1987. 183 p. : ill. ; 23 cm. Bibliography: p. 173-177. Includes indexes. ISBN 90-01-39430-2 : LC Card 87-157808
1. Income distribution - Netherlands. 2. Distribution (Economic theory). I. Title.
HC329.5.I5 H634 1987

Hoel, Michael. Natural gas markets and contracts /. Amsterdam ; New York : x, 320 p. : ISBN 0-444-70206-7 (U. S.) LC Card 87-5061 DDC 380.1/42285/094 19
HD9581.E82 N37 1987 ***NYPL [TB (Contributions to economic analysis. v.161)]***

Hoel, Robert F. Contemporary issues and practices in marketing /. Boston , 1987. p. cm. ISBN 0-205-10545-9 LC Card 87-1062 DDC 658.8 19
HF5415 .C5475 1987

Hoenig, Alan. Framework with applications for the IBM PC / Alan Hoenig. Dubuque, Iowa : W.C. Brown, c1985. xiii, 213 p. : ill. ; 24 cm. (Micropower series) On t.p. the registered trademark symbol "TM" is superscript following "Framework" in the title. Includes index. ISBN 0-697-00725-1 (pbk.) : LC Card 85-60013 DDC 005.3/69 19
1. Framework (Computer program). 2. IBM Personal Computer - Programming. 3. Business - Data processing. I. Title. II. Series.
HF5548.4.F7 H64 1985 ***NYPL [JSE 86-2110]***

Höpflinger, François. Bevölkerungswandel in der Schweiz : zur Entwicklung von Heiraten, Geburten, Wanderungen und Sterblichkeit / François Höpflinger. Grüsch : Rüegger, c1986. 179 p. : ill. ; 21 cm. Bibliography: p. 165-176. ISBN 3-7253-0269-3 LC Card 86-234328
1. Switzerland - Population. 2. Switzerland - Statistics, Vital. I. Title.
HB3623 .H66 1986

Hoeraene, J. d' (Jacques) Introduction à la gestion prévisionnelle /. Lyon , c1985. 337 p. : ISBN 2-7297-0268-7 : LC Card 86-132861 DDC 658.4/0355 19
HD30.28 .I56 1985

Hoerder, Dirk. Labor migration in the Atlantic economies . Westport, Conn. , 1985. xvi, 491 p. : ISBN 0-313-24637-8 (lib. bdg. : alk. paper) LC Card 85-7975 DDC 331.12/7 19
HD8375 .L33 1985 ***NYPL [JLE 86-1127]***

Hoerr, John P., 1930- And the wolf finally came : the decline of the American steel industry / John P. Hoerr. Pittsburgh, PA : University of Pittsburgh Press, 1988. p. cm. (Pittsburgh series in social and labor history) Includes index. ISBN 0-8229-3572-4 LC Card 87-24932 DDC 338.4/7669142/097488 19
1. Steel industry and trade - Monongahela River Region (W.Va. and Pa.). 2. Steel industry and trade - Pennsylvania. 3. Steel industry and trade - West Virginia. 4. Iron and steel workers - Monongahela River Region (W.Va. and Pa.). 5. Iron and steel workers - Pennsylvania. 6. Iron and steel workers - West Virginia. 7. Collective bargaining - Monongahela River Region (W.Va. and Pa.). 8. Collective bargaining - Pennsylvania. 9. Collective bargaining - West Virginia. I. Title. II. Series.
HD9517.M85 H64 1988

Hoetjes, B. J. S., 1945- International dimension of development problems . Amsterdam , New York , 1984. 103 p. ; ISBN 0-444-85621-8 (pbk.) LC Card 85-209291 DDC 338.9 19
HD75 .I59 1984 ***NYPL [JLE 86-1391]***

Hof, Bernd. Arbeitsmarktstrukturen im Wandel / Bernd Hof. Köln : Deutscher Instituts-Verlag, c1985. 56 p. : ill. ; 21 cm. (Beiträge zur Wirtschafts- und Sozialpolitik . 137) Includes bibliographical references. ISBN 3-602-24737-6 LC Card 86-119065 DDC 331.12/5/0943 19
1. Labor supply - Germany, West. 2. Germany, West - Full employment policies. 3. Unemployment - Germany (West). I. Title.
HD5779 .H638 1985

HOFFA, JAMES R. (JAMES RIDDLE), 1913-
Franco, Joseph. Hoffa's man . New York , c1987. xv, 332 p., [8] p. of plates : ISBN 0-13-517764-2 : LC Card 87-42675 DDC 331.88/11388324/0924 B 19
HD6509.F69 A3 1987

Hoffa's man . Franco, Joseph. New York , c1987. xv, 332 p., [8] p. of plates : ISBN 0-13-517764-2 : LC Card 87-42675 DDC 331.88/11388324/0924 B 19
HD6509.F69 A3 1987

Hoffman, Cheryl. Paulson, S. Lawrence. Reagan on energy . New York, NY (850 3rd Ave.,

New York 10022) , 1981. 248 p. in various pagings ; LC Card 82-111477 DDC 333.79/0973 19
HD9502.U52 P38 *NYPL [JLF 87-368]*

Hoffman, Elizabeth, 1946- Binger, Brian R. Microeconomics with calculus /. Glenview, Ill. , c1988. 609 p. : ISBN 0-673-18002-6 LC Card 87-12132 DDC 338.5/01/515 19
HB172 .B52 1988

Hoffman, Frank. Accounting fundamentals : a Gregg text-kit in continuing adult education / Frank Hoffman, Vivian Pacsy, Esther Flashner.4th ed. New York : Gregg Division, McGraw-Hill, c1987. vi, 229 p. : ill. ; 28 cm. (Continuing education series) Includes index. ISBN 0-07-029210-8 (pbk.) : LC Card 86-27352 DDC 657 19
1. Accounting. I. Pacsy, Vivian A. II. Flashner, Esther, 1925-. III. Title.
HF5635 .H678 1987

Hoffman, Gerard H. Foreign aid? yes, but-- : a constructive critique of the "North-South" conspiracy / Gerard H. Hoffman. Toronto, Ont. : Our Canada Publications, 1981. vi, 55 p. : ill. ; 21 cm. LC Card 81-182755 DDC 338.91/71/01724 19
1. Economic assistance - Developing countries. 2. Economic assistance, Canadian - Developing countries. I. Title.
HC60 .H63 1981 *NYPL [JLD 86-3406]*

Hoffman, Kurt. Micro-electronics and clothing : the impact of technical change on a global industry / Kurt Hoffman and Howard Rush. New York : Praeger, 1988. xxxii, 253 p. ; 25 cm. "A study prepared for the International Labour Office within the framework of the World Employment Programme." Bibliography: p. 233-241. Includes index. ISBN 0-275-92798-9 (alk. paper) : LC Card 87-25736 DDC 338.4/5687 19
1. Clothing trade. 2. Clothing factories - Automation. I. Rush, Howard. II. International Labour Organization. III. Title.
HD9940.A2 H63 1988

Hoffman, Naphtali. The bank book : how to get the most for your banking dollars : the Consumer Federation of America's guide to the new financial marketplace / Naphtali Hoffman and Stephen Brobeck ; edited by Jack Gillis.1st ed. San Diego : Harcourt Brace Jovanovich, 1986. xiii, 222 p. ; 23 cm. "A Harvest/HBJ book." Includes index. ISBN 0-15-610676-0 (pbk.) : LC Card 85-27271 DDC 332.1/7/0973 19
1. Banks and banking - United States - Customer services. 2. Building and loan associations - United States. 3. Financial institutions - United States. I. Brobeck, Stephen. II. Gillis, Jack. III. Consumer Federation of America. IV. Title.
HG1616.C87 H64 1986
NYPL [JLE 86-3189]

Hoffman, Ronald, 1941- The Economy of early America . Charlottesville , 1988. xvi, 334 p. : ISBN 0-8139-1139-7 LC Card 87-6169 DDC 330.973/02 19
HC104 .E26 1988

HOFFMAN, WALTHER, G., 1903-
Die Bedingungen des Wirtschaftswachstums in Vergangenheit und Zukunft . Tübingen , 1984. viii, 321 p., [1] leaf of plates : ISBN 3-16-344727-9 LC Card 85-165269
HD84 .B415 1984

Hoffman, William, 1937- Fantasy : the incredible Cabbage Patch phenomenon / William Hoffman.1st ed. Dallas, Tex. : Taylor Pub. Co., c1984. 217 p. : ill. (some col.) ; 24 cm. ISBN 0-87833-386-X LC Card 84-8817 DDC 338.4/76887221/0973 19
1. Doll industry - United States. 2. Cabbage Patch Kids dolls. I. Title.
HD9993.D653 U64 1984
NYPL [JLE 87-218]

Hoffmann, Klaus G. Raumbedeutsamkeit von Schnellfahrstrecken im Schienenverkehr / von Klaus G. Hoffmann. Berlin : Duncker & Humblot, c1985. xxviii, 547, [1] p. : ill. ; 24 cm. (Verkehrswissenschaftliche Forschungen. Bd. 45) Bibliography: p. 529-[548] ISBN 3-428-05770-8 LC Card 85-155640
1. Railroads - Germany, West. I. Title. II. Series.
HE3078 .H64 1985

Hoffmann-Nowotny, Hans-Joachim. Ansprüche an die Arbeit . Frankfurt [am Main] , New York , c1984. 298 p. : ISBN 3-593-33390-2 LC Card 85-103333
HF5548.8 .A683 1984

Hoffmann, Philip J. (ill) Harlow, Alvin F. (Alvin Fay), 1875-1963. When horses pulled boats . York, PA , c1983. 72 p. : ISBN 0-933788-43-6 (pbk.) LC Card 87-400271 DDC 386/.48/0973 19
HE395.A3 H37 1983

Hoffmann, Traute. Reform oder Revolution? . Bonn , 1987. vi, 241, A 140 p. : LC Card 87-409091 DDC 368.4/00943 19
HD7179 .R384 1987

Hoffmann, Ulrich, Prof. Dr. sc. oec.
Politökonomische Probleme des Gebrauchswerts, der Nützlichkeit und der Bewertung von Gebrauchswerten /. Karl-Marx-Stadt [1983] 92 p. ; LC Card 84-167577
HB201 .P63 1983

Hoffmann, Walther G., 1903- Die Bedingungen des Wirtschaftswachstums in Vergangenheit und Zukunft . Tübingen , 1984. viii, 321 p., [1] leaf of plates : ISBN 3-16-344727-9 LC Card 85-165269
HD84 .B415 1984

Hoffmann, William E. Kaplan, Howard J. Scouts on stamps of the world /. [Hicksville, N.Y.] , c1986. 1 v. (loose-leaf) : LC Card 86-224816 DDC 769.56/3 19
HE6183.B63 K36 1986

Hofmann, Hans, Dr. habil. Ökonomische Strategie und Vervollkommnung der staatlichen Leitung /. Potsdam-Babelsberg , 1983. 64 p. ; LC Card 84-180104
HC290.78 .O387 1983

Hofmann, Michael. Entwicklungsmanagement . Berlin , c1982. 192 p. : ISBN 3-428-05208-0 LC Card 83-150764 DDC 338.9/0068 19
HD84 .E56 1982 *NYPL [JLE 87-1179]*

Hofmeister, Ernst, 1922- Von der Bereitschaft zum technischen Wandel /. Berlin , 1981. 278 p. : ISBN 3-8009-1339-9 LC Card 83-194263
HC79.T4 V66 1981

Hofmeyr, Bärbel E. Kok, P. C. Black migration to the PWV complex . Pretoria , 1985. viii, 79 p. : ISBN 0-7969-0313-1 (pbk.) : LC Card 86-232836 DDC 304.8/0968 19
HB2123.4.P68 K65 1985

Hofsten, Erland Adolf Gerhard von, 1911- Svensk befolkningshistoria : några grunddrag i utvecklingen från 1750 / Erland Hofsten. [Stockholm] : Raben & Sjögren, c1986. 180, [1] p. : ill. ; 22 cm. Bibliography: p. 178-[181] ISBN 91-29-57693-8 LC Card 86-194606
1. Sweden - Population - History. I. Title.
HB3617 .H768 1986

Hofstra University. School of Business. The Evolution of education in collegiate schools of business . Hempstead, N.Y. , c1987. vi, 237 p. : LC Card 87-80670 DDC 650/.07/1073 19
HF1131 .E94 1987

Hofstra University yearbook of business .
(ser. 21, v. 1) The Impact of zero base budgeting on managerial behavior /. Hempstead, N.Y. , 1986. vii, 288 p. ; LC Card 86-80005 DDC 658.1/54 19
HG4028.B8 I55 1986

Hogan, Dennis P. Cultural and economic factors in the fertility of Thai women / Dennis P. Hogan, Aphichat Chamratrithirong, and Peter Xenos. Honolulu, HI : East-West Center, [1987] p. cm. (Papers of the East-West Population Institute, 0732-0531 . no. 107) "September 1987." Bibliography: p. ISBN 0-86638-103-1 : LC Card 87-21459 DDC 304.6/32/09593 19
1. Fertility, Human - Thailand. I. Aphichat Chamratrithirong, 1948-. II. Xenos, Peter, 1943-. III. Title. IV. Series.
HB1054.55.A3 H64 1987

Hogan, Michael J., 1943- The Marshall Plan : America, Britain, and the reconstruction of Western Europe, 1947-1952 / Michael J. Hogan. Cambridge [Cambridgeshire] ; New York : Cambridge University Press, 1987. xiv, 482 p. ; 24 cm. (Studies in economic history and policy) Bibliography: p. 446-463. Includes index. ISBN 0-521-25140-0 LC Card 86-31773 DDC 338.91/73/04 19
1. Marshall Plan. 2. Reconstruction (1939-1951). 3. United States - Foreign economic relations - Europe. 4. Europe - Foreign economic relations - United States. 5. Great Britain - Foreign economic relations - Europe. 6. Europe - Foreign economic relations - Great Britain. I. Title. II. Series.
HC240 .H614 1987

Hogan, William Thomas, 1919- Minimills and integrated mills : a comparison of steelmaking in the United States / William T. Hogan. Lexington, Mass. : Lexington Books, c1987. 148 p. : ill. ; 24 cm. Bibliography: p. [137]-138. Includes index. ISBN 0-669-14021-X (alk. paper) LC Card 86-45605 DDC 338.4/7669142/0973 19
1. Steel industry and trade - United States. 2. Steel minimills - United States. I. Title.
HD9515 .H599 1987

El hogar como unidad de análisis de los datos censales . Pantelides, Edith A. Santiago de Chile , 1972. ii, 48 p. : LC Card 83-169482
HA755 .U53 no. 147 HB849.49

Hogarth, Robin M. Behavioral foundations of economic theory. Rational choice . Chicago , 1987. ix, 332 p. : ISBN 0-226-34857-1 (alk. paper) LC Card 86-27241 DDC 330/.01/9 19
HB74.P8 B44 1987

Hoge, Cecil C.
The first 100 years are the toughest / by Cecil C. Hoge, Sr. Berkeley, Calif. : Ten Speed Press, 1987. p. cm. ISBN 0-89815-221-6 LC Card 87-7077 DDC 380.1/45000/6073 19
1. Sears, Roebuck and Company - History. 2. Montgomery Ward - History. I. Title. II. Title: First one hundred years are the toughest.
HF5467.S4 H64 1987

Mail order moonlighting / by Cecil C. Hoge, Sr. [Rev. ed.]. Berkeley, Calif. : Ten Speed Press, 1987. p. cm. ISBN 0-89815-222-4 LC Card 87-17953 DDC 658.8/72 19
1. Mail-order business. 2. Supplementary employment. 3. New business enterprises. I. Title.
HF5466 .H572 1987

Hogendorn, Jan S. Economic development / Jan S. Hogendorn. New York : Harper & Row, c1987. xv, 508 p. : ill. ; 25 cm. Includes bibliographies and index. ISBN 0-06-042853-8 LC Card 86-27034 DDC 338.9 19
1. Economic development. I. Title.
HD75 .H64 1987

Höglund, Bengt. Spelet om resurserna i den svenska blandekonomin / Bengt Höglund, under medverkan av Eskil Wadensjö. Lund : Dialogos, c1984. 227 p. : ill. ; 23 cm. Errata slip inserted. Bibliography: p. 220-224. Includes index. ISBN 91-7504-041-7 : LC Card 84-200450
1. Natural resources - Government policy - Sweden. 2. Sweden - Economic conditions - 1945-. I. Wadensjö, Eskil, 1944-. II. Title.
HC373.5 .H64 1984

Högskole- och forskningspolitiska studier.
Wittrock, Björn. De stora programmens tid . Stockholm , 1984. 186 p. ; ISBN 91-7410-200-1 : LC Card 84-189613
HD9502.S82 W58 1984

Hohenberg, Paul M. Failed transitions to modern industrial society . Montreal , c1975. vii, 105 p. : ISBN 0-919958-00-1 LC Card 80-510009 DDC 303.4/094 19
HM101 .F26 *NYPL [JLE 81-166]*

Hohenheimer Arbeiten. Allgemeine Reihe.
Bakonyi, Emmerich. Mitgliedererwartungen in Bankgenossenschaften . Stuttgart , c1983. 389 p. : ISBN 3-8001-8188-6 LC Card 84-106778
HG2035 .B28 1983

Röhm, Helmut. Der Förderungsauftrag im Zielsystem der Bankgenossenschaften . Stuttgart , c1983. 306 p. ; ISBN 3-8001-8187-8 LC Card 84-106807
HG2039.G4 R568 1983

Hohenheimer volkswirtachaftliche Schriften, 0721-3085 .
(Bd. 3) Schröter, Klaus, 1953- Die wettbewerbspolitische Behandlung der leitungsgebundenen Energiewirtschaft . Frankfurt am Main , New York , c1986. viii, 300 p. ; ISBN 3-8204-9551-7 LC Card 87-407422 DDC 363.6/2/0943 19
HD9685.G3 S375 1986

Hohenheimer volkswirtschaftliche Schriften, 0721-3085 .
(Bd. 4) Mann, Hugo, 1954- Theorie und Politik

der Steuerreform in der Demokratie /. Frankfurt am Main , New York , c1987. vi, 264 p. ; ISBN 3-8204-9464-2 LC Card 87-407788 DDC 336.2/00943 19
HJ2687 .M3 1987

Höher, Peter. Heimat und Fremde : Wanderhändler des oberen Sauerlandes / Peter Höher. Münster : F. Coppenrath, 1985. viii, 414 p., [1] p. of plates : ill. ; 24 cm. (Beiträge zur Volkskultur in Nordwestdeutschland, 0724-4096 . Heft 41) Bibliography: p. 363-400. "D 6." ISBN 3-88547-290-2 LC Card 85-160726 DDC 381/.0943/42 19
1. Sauerland (Germany) - Commerce - History. 2. Merchants - Germany (West) - Sauerland - History. I. Title. II. Series.
HF3569.S28 H64 1985

Hoisington, Caroline. Food policy . Baltimore , c1987. xiv, 567 p. : ISBN 0-8018-3500-3 (pbk.) : LC Card 86-27613 DDC 363.8/56/091724 19
HD9018.D44 F665 1987

Höj och sänk pensionsåldern /. Klevmarken, N. Anders. Göteborg [1985?] 9 leaves : LC Card 86-195492
HD7203 .K57 1985

Holahan, John. Medicaid : the trade-off between cost containment and access to care / John Holahan, Joel W. Cohen. Washington, D.C. : Urban Institute Press, c1986. xvii, 124 p. ; 23 cm. (The Changing domestic priorities series) Bibliography: p. 115-117. ISBN 0-87766-406-4 LC Card 86-28100 DDC 353.0084/1045 19
1. Medicaid - Cost control. 2. Medicaid - Cost effectiveness. I. Cohen, Joel W., 1952-. II. Title. III. Series.
HD7102.U4 H59 1986

Holaschke, Irmgard. Osteuropa im Blickpunkt . Linz [1985?] 168 p. ; LC Card 87-142952 DDC 382/.091713/01717 19
HF1411 .O687 1985

Holbein, Thomas J. Evaluating the effectiveness of newspaper promotion /. Reston, Va. (11600 Sunrise Valley Dr., Reston 22091) , c1987. iii, 123 p. : LC Card 87-152731 DDC 659.13/2 19
HF6161.N4 E93 1987

Holcomb, Bonnie K. Clay, Jason W. Politics and the Ethiopian famine, 1984-1985 /. Cambridge, MA (11 Divinity Ave., Cambridge 02138) , 1985. xi, 250 p. : LC Card 86-153948 DDC 363.8/56/0963 19
HC845.Z9 F33 1985 ***NYPL [JLF 87-364]***

Holcombe, Marya W., 1944- Writing for decision makers : memos and reports with a competitive edge / Marya W. Holcombe, Judith K. Stein.2nd ed. New York : Van Nostrand Reinhold Co., c1987. xi, 219 p. : ill. ; 24 cm. Includes index. ISBN 0-442-23268-3 (pbk.) : LC Card 86-24700 DDC 808/.066658 19
1. Business report writing. I. Stein, Judith K., 1935-. II. Title.
HF5719 .H64 1987

Holcombe, Randall G. Public sector economics / Randall G. Holcombe. Belmont, Calif. : Wadsworth Pub. Co., [1987], c1988. xxxii, 414 p. : ill. ; 25 cm. Includes bibliographical references and index. ISBN 0-534-08190-8 LC Card 87-13344 DDC 338.9 19
1. Finance, Public. 2. Economic policy. I. Title.
HJ141 .H58 1988

Holden, J. David. Stegman, Michael A. Nonfederal housing programs . Washington, D.C. , 1987. viii, 231 p. ; ISBN 0-87420-673-1 LC Card 87-51080 DDC 363.5/8 19
HD7293.Z9 S75 1987

Holder, William W. Carmichael, D. R. Douglas R.), 1941- Guide to audits of local governments /. Fort Worth, Tex. , 1986- 2 v. (loose-leaf) : LC Card 86-206730 DDC 657/.835045 19
HJ9777.A3 C37 1986

HOLDING COMPANIES - ACCOUNTING.
Goodman, Hortense. Illustrations of "push down" accounting /. New York, N.Y. (1211 Ave., of the Americas, New York 10036) , c1985. 52 p. ; LC Card 87-100703 DDC 657/.3 19
HF5681.B2 G663 1985

HOLDING COMPANIES - BRAZIL - CASE STUDIES.
Suplicy, Eduardo Matarazzo, 1941- Investigando o Caso Coroa-Brastel . Brasília , 1984. 215 p. ; LC Card 86-200269
HG4109 .S85 1984

A Verdade sobre o "Caso Coroa-Brastel.". Brasília, DF , 1984. 156 p. ; LC Card 85-207657
HG4109 .V47 1984

HOLDING COMPANIES - SPAIN.
Ekaizer, Ernesto, 1949- José María Ruiz Mateos, el ultimo magnate /. Esplugues de Llobregat, Barcelona , 1985. 833 p., [16] p. of plates : ISBN 84-01-33291-5 LC Card 86-122394 DDC 332.1/6 B 19
HG4216.R85 E38 1985
NYPL [JFD 86-6856]

HOLDING COMPANIES - VENEZUELA - MANAGEMENT.
Quintas reuniones técnicas de información, evaluación y perspectivas de las empresas /. [Caracas, Venezuela] [1984?] 245 p. : LC Card 87-404408 DDC 338.8/6/09877 19
HD2843.Z75 C467 1984

Holdninger til den økonomiske fordeling =. Henriksen, Ingrid. København , 1985. 349 p. : ISBN 87-7487-265-6 : LC Card 85-186400
HC360.I5 S25 1985 vol. 1
NYPL [JLD 86-2002]

Holl, Jack M. United States civilian nuclear power policy, 1954-1984 : a summary history / by Jack M. Holl, Roger M. Anders, Alice L. Buck. Washington, D.C. : U. S. Dept. of Energy, Assistant Secretary, Management and Administration, Office of the Executive Secretariat, History Division ; Springfield, Va. : Available from National Technical Information Service, U. S. Dept. of Commerce, [1986] 46 p., [1] leaf of plates : ill. ; 28 cm. "February 1986." Bibliography: p. 33. "DOE/MA-0152; dist. category UC-2." LC Card 86-601137 DDC 333.79/24 19
1. Nuclear power plants - Government policy - United States - History. 2. Nuclear policy - United States - History. I. Anders, Roger M. II. Buck, Alice L. III. Title.
HD9698.U52 H65 1986

Höll, Otmar. Österreichische Entwicklungshilfe, 1970-1983 : kritische Analyse und internationaler Vergleich / Otmar Höll. Wien : W. Braumüller ; Laxenburg, Austria : Österreichisches Institut für Internationale Politik, c1986. 187 p. : ill. ; 24 cm. (Informationen zur Weltpolitik . 7) Bibliography: p. 183-187. Summary in English. ISBN 3-7003-0659-8 LC Card 86-192362
1. Economic assistance, Austrian - Developing countries. 2. Technical assistance, Austrian - Developing countries. 3. Economic assistance - Developing countries. 4. Technical assistance - Developing countries. I. Title. II. Series.
HC60 .H6643 1986

Holla, Michael. Die Belastung der Landwirtschaft durch Beiträge zur sozialen Sicherung im Vergleich zur Situation anderer sozialer Gruppen : im Auftrag der Bundesverbände der landwirtschaftlichen Sozialversicherungsträger Kassel / erstellt im Sekretariat der Agrarsozialen Gesellschaft e.V. durch Michael Holla. Göttingen : Die Gesellschaft, [1986] viii, 174 p. ; 21 cm. (ASG-Materialsammlung, 0344-5712 . Nr. 174) "Februar 1986." Includes bibliographical references. LC Card 87-407657 DDC 368.4/00943 19
1. Social security - Germany, West. 2. Agriculture - Economic aspects - Germany, West. I. Agrarsoziale Gesellschaft. Sekretariat. II. Title. III. Series.
HD7179 .H635 1986

Holland. see **Netherlands.**

Holland, Barbara Kamanitz. Managing single-family homes / Barbara Kamanitz Holland. Chicago, Ill. : Institute of Real Estate Management of the National Association of Realtors, c1987. xiv, 155 p. ; 28 cm. (Institute of Real Management monographs. Series on specific property types) Includes index. ISBN 0-912104-92-9 (pbk.) LC Card 87-81672 DDC 333.33/8 19
1. Real estate management. 2. Housing, Single family - Management. I. Title. II. Series.
HD1394 .H63 1987

Holland in Australia : a vocational choice theory in research and practice / edited by Jan J. Lokan & Keith F. Taylor. Melbourne : Australian Council for Educational Research, 1986. xxii, 229 p. : ill. ; 25 cm. Includes bibliographies and indexes. ISBN 0-86431-032-3 LC Card 87-164636 DDC 331.7/02/0994 19
1. Holland, John L. 2. Vocational guidance. 3. Vocational guidance - Australia. I. Lokan, Jan J. II. Taylor, Kent F.
HF5381.H56693 H65 1986

HOLLAND, JOHN L.
Holland in Australia . Melbourne , 1986. xxii, 229 p. : ISBN 0-86431-032-3 LC Card 87-164636 DDC 331.7/02/0994 19
HF5381.H56693 H65 1986

Holland, John L., 1919- Gottfredson, Gary D. Dictionary of Holland occupational codes /. Palo Alto, CA , c1982. xviii, 500 p. ; ISBN 0-89106-020-X ***NYPL [JLE 86-3992]***

Holland, Stuart.
The global economy : from meso to macroeconomics / Stuart Holland. New York : St. Martin's Press, 1987. xiv, 443 p. : ill. ; 24 cm. Bibliography: p. [424]-434. Includes index. ISBN 0-312-01323-X : LC Card 87-20566 DDC 339 19
1. Macroeconomics. 2. Commerce. I. Title.
HB172.5 .H655 1987

The market economy : from micro to mesoeconomics / Stuart Holland. New York : St. Martin's Press, 1987. xiv, 363 p. : ill. ; 25 cm. Bibliography: p. [345]-353. Includes index. ISBN 0-312-01324-8 : LC Card 87-20908 DDC 330.12/2 19
1. Capitalism. I. Title.
HB501 .H56 1987

Hollanda Filho, Sergio Buarque de. Estrutura industrial no Brasil : concentração e diversificação / Sérgio Buarque de Holanda Filho. Rio de Janeiro : IPEA/INPES, 1983. 275 p. : ill. ; 21 cm. (Série PNPE . 7) Bibliography: p. 267-275. LC Card 87-119359 DDC 338.8/0981 19
1. Industrial concentration - Brazil. 2. Diversification in industry - Brazil. I. Title. II. Series.
HD2834 .H65 1983

Hollander, Richard S. Video democracy : the vote-from-home revolution / Richard S. Hollander. Mt. Airy, Md. : Lomond Publications, c1985. ix, 161 p. : ill. ; 27 cm. Includes index. Bibliography: p. 145-155. ISBN 0-912338-51-2 LC Card 85-81818 DDC 384.55/5 19
1. Television in politics - United States. 2. Cable television - United States. 3. Political participation - United States. I. Title.
HE8700.76.U6 H65 1985
NYPL [MWGT 86-1503]

Hollander, Samuel.
Classical economics / Samuel Hollander. Oxford [Oxfordshire] ; New York, NY, USA : B. Blackwell, 1987. xiv, 485 p. : ill. ; 24 cm. Bibliography: p. [457]-471. Includes index. ISBN 0-631-13435-2 : LC Card 87-8004 DDC 330.15/3 19
1. Classical school of economics. I. Title.
HB94 .H65 1987

The economics of John Stuart Mill / Samuel Hollander. Oxford, U.K. : B. Blackwell, 1985. 2 v. (xx, 1037 p.) ; 24 cm. (Studies in classical political economy. 3) Includes index. Bibliography: p. [979]-1005. CONTENTS. - v. 1. Theory and method -- v. 2. Political economy. ISBN 0-631-14045-X (set) LC Card 86-673535
1. Mill, John Stuart, 1806-1873. 2. Economics - Great Britain - History - 19th century. I. Title.
HB103.M7 H64x 1985 ***NYPL [JLE 87-951]***

Holländska Ostindiska Kompaniet. see **Nederlandsche Oost-Indische Compagnie.**

Holler, Manfred Joseph, 1946- Trading markets and entry costs / Manfred J. Holler. Aarhus, Denmark : Institute of Economics, University of Aarhus, [1986] 15 p. ; 21 cm. (Memo . 1986-3) Bibliography: p. 14-15. LC Card 86-219580 DDC 382.1 19
1. Barriers to entry (Industrial organization). I. Series: Memo (Aarhus universitet. Økonomisk institut) , 1986-3. II. Title.
HD2756.5 .H64 1986

Hollerman, Leon. Japan, disincorporated : the economic liberalization process / Leon Hollerman. Stanford, Calif. : Hoover Institution Press, c1988. xxi, 185 p. ; 24 cm. (Hoover Press publication . 363) Bibliography: p. [157]-174. Includes index. ISBN 0-8179-8631-6 : LC Card 87-25633 DDC 338.952 19

1. Industry and state - Japan. 2. Japan - Commercial policy. I. Title.
HD3616.J33 H65 1988

Holley, H. A., 1924- Developing country debt : the role of the commercial banks / H.A. Holley. London : Royal Institute of International Affairs ; London ; 85 p. ; 22 cm. (Chatham House papers . 35) Bibliography: p. 83-85. ISBN 0-7102-1211-9 (pbk.) : LC Card 86-29838 DDC 336.3/435/091724 19
1. Loans, Foreign - Developing countries. 2. Debts, External - Developing countries. 3. Banks and banking, International. I. Series. II. Series: Chatham House papers , no. 35. III. Title.
HG3891.5 .H65 1987

Holley, Noel T., 1947- Jones, William C., 1937- The kite route . Boulder, Colo. , c1986. 159 p. : ISBN 0-87108-721-9 LC Card 86-25190 DDC 385/.5 19
HE2791.D383 J66 1986

Holley, William H.
The labor relations process / William H. Holley, Jr., Kenneth M. Jennings. 3rd ed. Chicago : Dryden Press, c1988. xix, 714 p. : ill. ; 24 cm. (The Dryden Press series in management) Includes bibliographies and indexes. ISBN 0-03-012649-5 LC Card 87-9117 DDC 658.3/15/0973 19
1. Industrial relations - United States. I. Jennings, Kenneth M. II. Title.
HD8072.5 .H64 1988

Wolters, Roger S. Labor relations . Chicago , c1988. xi, 321 p. ; ISBN 0-03-069304-7 (pbk.) LC Card 87-19941 DDC 331 19
HD8072.5 .W65 1988

Hollich, Franz. Analyse organisatorischer und personeller Einflussgrössen auf Fehlzeiten / Franz Hollich. Karlsruhe : Planta-Verlag, c1985. iii, 210 p. : ill. ; 21 cm. Bibliography: p. 161-177. ISBN 3-923485-03-4 LC Card 85-233162
1. Absenteeism (Labor) - Germany (West). 2. Absenteeism (Labor). I. Title.
HD5115.2.G4 H65 1985

Holliday, John C. Land at the centre : choices in a fast changing world / John C. Holliday. London : Shepheard-Walwyn, 1986. xiii, 241 p. : ill. ; 22 cm. Bibliography: p. 226-234. Includes index. ISBN 0-85683-084-4 (pbk.) : LC Card 87-121817 DDC 333.73/13/0941 19
1. Land use - Great Britain - Planning. 2. Land use - Europe - Planning. I. Title.
HD596 .H65 1986

Holliday, Paul, 1938- A handbook of software development and operating procedures for microcomputers / Paul Holliday. New York : Macmillan, c1985. xix, 181 p. : ill. ; 25 cm. Includes index. ISBN 0-02-949510-5 : LC Card 84-19384 DDC 001.64/2 19
1. Microcomputers - Programming. 2. Computer software - Development. I. Title.
QA76.6 .H645 1985 ***NYPL [JSE 87-332]***

Holling, C. S. Alpine Areas Workshop (1974 : Schloss Laxenburg) Alpine Areas Workshop, May 13-17, 1974 /. Laxenburg [1974] 80 p. : LC Card 82-212849
HC268.O25 A46 1974

Hollingsworth, I. Lucretia. Hornwood, Sanford W. The number one real estate investment no one talks about /. Englewood Cliffs, N.J. , c1987. xv, 239 p. : ISBN 0-13-626482-4 : LC Card 86-25482 DDC 332.63/244 19
HG4655 .H67 1987

Hollingsworth, J. Rogers (Joseph Rogers), 1932- The governance of the American economy : the role of markets, clans, hierarchies, and associative behavior / J. Rogers Hollingsworth, Leon N. Lindberg. Berlin : Wissenschaftszentrum Berlin, [1985] 60 p. ; 30 cm. (Discussion papers / IIM, Labour Market Policy, 0722-673X . IIM/LMP 85-8) Abstract in German. "Oktober 1985." Bibliography: p. 57-60. LC Card 86-205784 DDC 330.973 19
1. United States - Economic conditions - 1981-. 2. Capitalism - United States. 3. Organizational behavior. I. Lindberg, Leon N. II. Series: Discussion papers (International Institute of Management. Labour Market Policy) , IIM/LMP 85-5. III. Title.
HC106.8 .H635 1985

Hollingworth, Peter John, 1935- Australians in poverty / Peter Hollingworth. 4th ed. Melbourne, Vic. : Nelson, 1985. x, 166 p. : ill. ; 22 cm. Bibliography: p. 161-163. Includes index. ISBN 0-17-006741-6 (pbk.) : LC Card 87-108662 DDC 305.5/69/0994 19
1. Poor - Australia. 2. Australia - Economic conditions - 1945-. 3. Economic assistance, Domestic - Australia. I. Title.
HC610.P6 H62 1985

Hollins, Timothy. Beyond broadcasting : into the cable age / Timothy Hollins. London : Published for the Broadcasting Research Unit by BFI Pub., 1984. ix, 385 p. ; 22 cm. Includes index. ISBN 0-85170-148-5 (pbk.) LC Card 84-125713 DDC 384.55/563 19
1. Cable television - Great Britain - History. 2. Cable television - Canada - History. 3. Cable television - United States - History. I. British Film Institute, London. Broadcasting Research Unit. II. Title.
HE8700.72.G7 H65 1984
NYPL [JLD 86-1057]

Hollist, W. Ladd, 1947-
Food, the state, and international political economy . Lincoln , c1986. xxiii, 351 p. : ISBN 0-8032-4413-4 (alk. paper) LC Card 85-30893 DDC 338.1/9/1724 19
HD9018.D44 F67 1986
NYPL [JLD 86-3440]

Pursuing food security . Boulder , 1987. xv, 357 p. : ISBN 1-555-87032-5 (lib. bdg. : alk. paper) : LC Card 87-4524 DDC 337/.05 s 338.1/9/1724 19
HF1410 .I579 vol. 3 HD9018.D44

Hollnagel, Erik, 1941- NATO Advanced Study Institute on Intelligent Decision Support in Process Environments (1985 : San Miniato, Italy) Intelligent decision support in process environments /. Berlin , New York , c1986. xv, 524 p. : ISBN 0-387-13922-2 (U. S.) LC Card 86-6742 DDC 658.4/03 19
T57.95 .N37 1985 ***NYPL [JFE 86-4847]***

Holloway, Steven Kendall, 1951- The aluminum multinationals and the bauxite cartel / Steven Kendall Holloway. New York : St. Martin's Press, 1988. vii, 93 p. : ill. ; 22 cm. Bibliography: p. 89-91. Includes index. ISBN 0-312-00939-9 : LC Card 87-12991 DDC 338.8/87 19
1. Aluminum industry and trade. 2. International business enterprises. 3. Bauxite - Economic aspects - Developing countries. 4. Cartels. I. Title.
HD9539.A62 H64 1988

Hollyer, Mark. Maritime shipping in the 1980s / prepared by Mark R. Hollyer. Menlo Park, CA (333 Ravenswood Ave., Menlo Park 94025) : SRI International, Business Intelligence Program, c1986. 18 leaves : ill. ; 28 cm. (Datalog file . no. 86-1102) "September 1986." LC Card 87-150588 DDC 387.5 19
1. Merchant marine. 2. Merchant marine - United States. I. Title. II. Series.
HE735 .H57 1986

Holm, Erik, 1919- Fred och säkerhet . [Stockholm] , c1983. 385 p. : ISBN 91-7410-249-4 : LC Card 83-229846
JX1963 .F817 1983 ***NYPL [JLD 84-2639]***

Holm, Yngvar. Engrosomsetningsindeks / av Yngvar Holm. Oslo : Statistisk sentralbyrå : I kommisjon hos H. Aschehoug og Universitetsforlaget, 1984. 18 leaves ; 30 cm. (Rapporter fra Statistisk sentralbyrå, 0332-8422 . 84/24) ISBN 82-537-2141-2 : LC Card 85-178075
1. Wholesale price indexes - Norway. 2. Prices - Norway. I. Title. II. Series.
HB235.N6 H65 1984

Holmer, Martin R. Marquis, M. Susan. Choice under uncertainty and the demand for health insurance /. Santa Monica, CA (P.O. Box 2138, Santa Monica 90406-2138) [1986] ix, 50 p. ; LC Card 87-118503 DDC 368.3/8/00973 19
HG9396 .M268 1986

Holmes, Frank Wakefield, Sir, 1924- Recent developments in monetary policy : address to the eighteenth annual general meeting / by Sir Frank Holmes. [Wellington] : N.Z. Institute of Economic Research, [1976] 5 p. ; 21 cm. Cover title. "October 1976." LC Card 82-216052
1. Monetary policy - New Zealand. I. New Zealand Institute of Economic Research. II. Title.
HG1480.5 .H65 1976

Holmlöv, Per Gunnar, 1951- Reklam i satellit-tv : konsekvenser för svensk industri / P.G. Holmlöv, Claes-Robert Julander. Stockholm : Ekonomiska forskningsinstitutet vid Handelshögskolan i Stockholm, [1984] 147 p. ; 25 cm. Bibliography: p. 139-144. ISBN 91-7258-183-2 : LC Card 84-229824
1. Television advertising. 2. Direct broadcast satellite television. 3. Sweden - Industries. I. Julander, Claes-Robert, 1944-. II. Title.
HF6146.T42 H64 1984

Holmlund, Bertil, 1947- Albrecht, James W. Job search and the transition to employment . Göteborg [1986] 38 leaves ; LC Card 87-158051 DDC 331.12/8 19
HF5382.7 .A43 1986

Holmquist, Carin, 1948- Förhandla mer räkna mindre / Carin Holmquist, Rolf A. Lundin, Elisabeth Sundin. Uppl. 1. Stockholm : LiberFörlag, [1984] 124 p. : ill. ; 21 cm. (Forskningens frontlinjer) Bibliography: p. 122-123. ISBN 91-38-90409-8 : LC Card 84-241380
1. Managerial economics. 2. Managerial economics - Sweden. I. Lundin, A. Rolf. II. Sundin, Elisabeth. III. Title. IV. Series.
HD30.22 .H65 1984

HOLOCAUST, JEWISH (1939-1945) - POLAND - WARSAW.
American Jewish Joint Distribution Committee. [Choroba głodowa. English.] Hunger disease . New York , c1979. xiv, 261 p. : ISBN 0-471-05003-2 LC Card 78-26397 DDC 616.3/9
RC627.S7 A43 1979
NYPL [*PXV (Warsaw) 86-3505]

HOLOGRAPHY - INDUSTRIAL APPLICATIONS.
Holography, new commercial opportunities /. Stamford, Conn. , c1985. vii, 149 leaves : ISBN 0-89336-480-0 (soft) LC Card 87-165251 DDC 380.1/456213675 19
HD9707.5.H342 H64 1985

HOLOGRAPHY INDUSTRY.
Holography, new commercial opportunities /. Stamford, Conn. , c1985. vii, 149 leaves : ISBN 0-89336-480-0 (soft) LC Card 87-165251 DDC 380.1/456213675 19
HD9707.5.H342 H64 1985

Holography, new commercial opportunities / Jack T. Miskell, project analyst. Stamford, Conn. : Business Communications Co., c1985. vii, 149 leaves : ill. ; 29 cm. (Business opportunity report . GB-074) ISBN 0-89336-480-0 (soft) LC Card 87-165251 DDC 380.1/456213675 19
1. Holography industry. 2. Holography - Industrial applications. 3. Market surveys. I. Miskell, Jack T. II. Business Communications Co. III. Series.
HD9707.5.H342 H64 1985

Holoviak, Stephen J. Managing human productivity : people are your best investments / Stephen J. Holoviak and Susan Stone Sipkoff. New York : Praeger, 1987. xiii, 216 p. : ill. ; 25 cm. Bibliography: p. 203-210. Includes index. ISBN 0-275-92481-5 (alk. paper) : LC Card 86-25247 DDC 658.3/14 19
1. Personnel management - United States. 2. Manpower planning - United States. 3. Human capital - United States. 4. Industrial relations - United States. I. Sipkoff, Susan Stone. II. Title.
HF5549.2.U5 H65 1987

Holt, David H.
Management, principles and practices / David H. Holt. Englewood Cliffs, N.J. : Prentice-Hall, c1987. xxiv, 808 p. : ill. (some col.) ; 25 cm. Includes bibliographies and indexes. ISBN 0-13-548207-0 LC Card 86-25161 DDC 658.4 19
1. Management. 2. Industrial management. I. Title.
HD31 .H6225 1987

Management, principles, and practices.
Readings in management / Phillip B. DuBose, editor. Englewood Cliffs, NJ , c1988. viii, 343 p. : ISBN 0-13-755166-5 (pbk.) : LC Card 87-2301 DDC 658.4 19
HD31 .R4175 1988

Holt, Julius F. J. Yeraswork Admassie. Food-for-work in Ethiopia . Addis Abeba , 1985. viii, 102, [58] leaves : LC Card 86-980537 DDC 339.5/0963 19
HD5839.7.A6 Y47 1985

Holt, Rinehart and Winston, inc. Marketing. Fountain Valley, CA , 1985. 1 videocassette (30 min.) : LC Card 87-705967 DDC 658.8 11
HF5415

Hölter, Erich, 1955- Computergestütztes Ertragsteuersimulationsmodell der deutschen internationalen Kapitalgesellschaft : ein Führungsinstrument zur Ertragsteuerplanung und -erklärung / Erich Hölter. Giessen : Verlag der Ferber'schen Universitätsbuchhandlung, c1986. xxv, 383 p. : ill. ; 21 cm. (Schriftenreihe des Instituts für Unternehmungsplanung . Bd. 3) At head of title, cover: Institut für Unternehmungsplanung. Bibliography: p. [278]-313. ISBN 3-922730-67-1 LC Card 87-116057 DDC 336.24/3/0943 19
1. Corporations - Taxation - Germany (West) - Mathematical models. 2. Corporations, West German - Taxation - Mathematical models. 3. Corporations - Taxation - Germany (West) - Data processing. 4. Corporations, West German - Taxation - Data processing. I. Justus Liebig-Universität Giessen. Institut für Unternehmungsplanung. II. Title. III. Series.
HJ4720.A7 H65 1986

Holterhus, Gerhard. Früherkennung von Bankkrisen bei der Abschlussprüfung / von Gerhard Holterhus. Frankfurt am Main : F. Knapp, c1985. xvi, 360 p. : ill. ; 25 cm. (Schriftenreihe des Instituts für Kreditwesen der Westfälischen Wilhelms-Universität Münster . Bd. 30) Bibliography: p. 335-360. ISBN 3-7819-0348-6 LC Card 86-164226
1. Banks and banking - Germany, West - State supervision. 2. Banking law - Germany, West. I. Title. II. Series.
HG1768.G3 H64 1985

Holthus, Manfred. Indebtedness and growth in developing countries /. Hamburg , 1986. 344 p. ; ISBN 3-87895-300-3 (pbk.) LC Card 86-213057 DDC 336.3/435/091724 19
HJ8899 .I53 1986

Holtomiglan? holtodiglan? /. Lakos, Éva. Budapest , c1985. 269 p., [6] leaves of plates : ISBN 963-15-3100-7 : LC Card 86-190862
HD8420.5 .L35 1985

Holton, Stephen D.
Clay, John R. Guide to preparing financial statements /. Fort Worth, Tex. , c1987- 2 v. (loose-leaf) ; LC Card 87-161098 DDC 657/.3 19
HF5681.B2 C565 1987

Pallais, Don. Guide to forecasts and projections /. Fort Worth, Tex. , 1986. 2 v. (loose-leaf) : LC Card 87-108778 DDC 657/.3 19
HF5681.B2 P15 1986

Holtz, Herman.
Advice, a high profit business : a guide for consultants and other entrepreneurs / Herman Holtz. Englewood Cliffs, N.J. : Prentice-Hall, c1986. xii, 242 p. : ill. ; 24 cm. Includes index. ISBN 0-13-011958-X LC Card 85-24405 DDC 658.4/6/0688 19
1. Consultants - Marketing. 2. Information services - Marketing. I. Title.
HD69.C6 H618 1986 ***NYPL [JLE 86-3858]***

The business writing problem solver : instant solutions for every business / Herman R. Holtz. Homewood, Ill. : Dow Jones-Irwin, c1987. xii, 235 p. : ill. ; 29 cm. Bibliography: p. 229-232. Includes index. ISBN 0-87094-901-2 LC Card 86-72270 DDC 651.7/4 19
1. Business writing. I. Title.
HF5718.3 .H65 1987

The consultant's guide to winning clients / Herman Holtz. New York : Wiley, c1988. ix, 262 p. ; 24 cm. Includes bibliographical references and index. ISBN 0-471-62759-3 : LC Card 87-24945 DDC 658.4/6 19
1. Business consultants. 2. Consultants. I. Title.
HD69.C6 H623 1988

Expanding your consulting practice with seminars / Herman Holtz. New York : Wiley, c1987. xvi, 240 p. : ill. ; 24 cm. Includes index. ISBN 0-471-85899-4 LC Card 87-14231 DDC 658.4/6 19
1. Consultants. 2. Seminars. I. Title.
HD69.C6 H625 1987

How to make money with your micro / Herman Holtz. New York : Wiley, c1984. xiv, 324 p. : ill. ; 23 cm. Includes index. Bibliography: p. 295-298. ISBN 0-471-88455-3 (pbk.) : LC Card 84-3589 DDC 001.64 19
1. Small business - Data processing. 2. Microcomputers - Programming. I. Title.
HF5548.2 .H5925 1984
NYPL [JLE 86-2074]

2001 sources of financing for small business / Herman Holtz. New York : Arco, c1983. x, 173 p. ; 26 cm. ISBN 0-668-05468-9 LC Card 82-11366 DDC 658.1/522 19
1. Small business - United States - Finance - Directories. 2. Venture capital - United States - Directories. I. Title. II. Title: Two thousand one sources of financing for small businesses. III. Title: Two thousand and one sources of financing for small businesses.
HG4057 .A286 1983 ***NYPL [JLF 84-63]***

Höltz, Joachim. Kritik der Geldentstehungstheorien : Carl Menger, Wilhelm Gerloff und eine Untersuchung über die Entstehung des Geldes im alten Ägypten und Mesopotamien / Joachim Höltz. Berlin : Reimer, c1984. ii, 401 p. ; 21 cm. (Mainzer ethnologische Arbeiten . Bd. 5) Bibliography: p. 344-401. ISBN 3-496-00796-6 LC Card 85-147094
1. MoneyxHistory. 2. Money - Egypt - History. 3. Money - Iraq - History. 4. Egypt - Commerce - History. 5. Iraq - Commerce - History. 6. Menger, Carl, 1840-1921. 7. Gerloff, Wilhelm. I. Title. II. Series.
HG237 .H64 1984

Holtz, Uwe, 1944- Entwicklung und Rüstung . Baden-Baden , 1984. 303 p. ; ISBN 3-7890-1068-5 LC Card 85-175510
HC79.D4 E58 1984

Holzapfel, Fritz. Mehrwert heute . Berlin , c1981. 285 p. ; LC Card 82-189316 DDC 338.5/21 19
HB206 .M44 1981 ***NYPL [JLD 86-2837]***

Holzberger, Peter. Recollections of an "old China hand" / by Peter Holzberger. [Hongkong : Martin & Thomas, c1984] 233 p. : ill. ; 27 cm. LC Card 86-135690 DDC 338.092/2 B 19
1. Holzberger, Peter. 2. Businessmen - Germany - Biography. 3. Businessmen - China - Biography. 4. Businessmen - Japan - Biography. I. Title.
HC282.5.H64 A3 1984

HOLZBERGER, PETER.
Holzberger, Peter. Recollections of an "old China hand" /. [Hongkong , c1984] 233 p. : LC Card 86-135690 DDC 338.092/2 B 19
HC282.5.H64 A3 1984

Holzer, Harry J. The Black youth employment crisis /. Chicago , 1986. viii, 469 p. : ISBN 0-226-26164-6 LC Card 85-20989 DDC 331.3/46396073 19
HD6273 .B57 1986 ***NYPL [JLE 86-3726]***

Holzhausen, Walter, 1929- Vision creates hope : reflections on development issues in developing countries and in Bangladesh / Walter Holzhausen. Dhaka, Bangladesh : University Press, 1986. viii, 118 p. ; 22 cm. Includes index. LC Card 87-901565 DDC 330.9172/4 19
1. Developing countries - Economic conditions. 2. Bangladesh - Economic conditions. I. Title.
HC59.7 .H624 1986

Holzhuber, Thomas. Strategische Unternehmensführung in Klein- und Mittelbetrieben : Theorie und Fallbeispiele / Thomas Holzhuber. Wien : Signum, [1984?] 198, 5 p. : ill. ; 25 cm. Bibliography: p. 190-198. ISBN 3-85436-018-5 : LC Card 84-248354
1. Small business - Austria - Management. I. Title.
HD62.7 .H65 1984

Holzman, Franklyn D. The economics of Soviet bloc trade and finance / Franklyn D. Holzman. Boulder : Westview Press, 1987. xi, 215 p. : ill. ; 24 cm. Includes bibliographies and index. ISBN 0-8133-7274-7 (alk. paper) : LC Card 86-32598 DDC 382/.0947 19
1. Europe, Eastern - Commerce. 2. Finance - Europe, Eastern. 3. Balance of payments - Europe, Eastern. I. Title.
HF3496.5 .H62 1987

Holzwarth, Fritz. Ordnung der Wirtschaft durch Wettbewerb : Entwicklung der Ideen der Freiburger Schule / Fritz Holzwarth. Freiburg im Breisgau : R. Haufe, c1985. 217 p. ; 21 cm. (Schriftenreihe des Instituts für Allgemeine Wirtschaftsforschung der Albert-Ludwigs-Universität Freiburg i. Br. . Bd. 23) Bibliography: p. 200-217. ISBN 3-448-01510-5 LC Card 86-109043
1. Laissez-faire - History - 20th century. 2. Trade regulation - Germany - History - 20th century. 3. Economics - Germany (West) - History - 20th century. 4. Economics - Germany - History - 20th century. I. Title. II. Series.
HB95 .H65 1985

Holzwirtschaft im Wandel . Jordan, Reinhard, d. 1986. Köln , c1986. viii, 163 p. : ISBN 3-7663-0977-3 LC Card 86-211012 DDC 338.4/5674/0943 19
HD9763.5 .J67 1986

El hombre de la tierra /. Ringuelet, Andrés. [S.l. , 1984] (La Plata, Rep. Argentina : Impr. Ferrograf) 111 p. ; LC Card 85-104745
HD1531.L3 R55 1984

Hombre y sociedad (Esplugas de Llobregat, Spain)
Bayo, Eliseo. Descubro y acuso /. Esplugues de Llobregat, Barcelona , 1985,c1984. 287 p. ; ISBN 84-01-33258-3 ***NYPL [JFD 86-7111]***

Hombres y empresas . Suárez Díaz, Reynaldo. México , 1983. 388 p. : ISBN 968-241-155-6 LC Card 87-404869 DDC 658.3 19
HF5549 .S8946 1983

HOME APPLIANCES. see **HOUSEHOLD APPLIANCES.**

Home away from home /. Woititz, Janet Geringer. Pompano Beach, Fla. , c1987. x, 137 p. : ISBN 0-932194-38-9 LC Card 86-33478 DDC 658.3/045 19
HF5549.5.A4 W65 1987

HOME BANKING SERVICES - FRANCE.
Moore, L. K. S. (Linda K. S.) Videotext and home banking services in France. New York, NY (654 Madison Ave., New York 10021) , c1986. 59, 3 leaves : LC Card 86-203144 DDC 332.1/028 19
HG1711 .M66 1986

HOME-BASED BUSINESSES.
Edwards, Paul. Working from home . Los Angeles , New York , c1987. xii, 436 p. : ISBN 0-87477-457-8 (pbk.) LC Card 87-10188 DDC 658/.041 19
HD62.5 .E39 1987

Glenn, Peggy. Word processing profits at home /. Huntington Beach, CA , 1987, c1986. p. cm. ISBN 0-936930-86-1 : LC Card 87-25188 DDC 652/.5 19
HF5548.115 .G56 1987

Hicks, Tyler Gregory, 1921- How to start your own business on a shoestring and make up to $500,000 a year /. Rocklin, CA , New York , c1987. xi, 225 p. ; ISBN 0-914629-12-3 (pbk.) : LC Card 86-25196 DDC 658/.041 19
HD62.5 .H527 1987

HOME-BASED BUSINESSES - GERMANY (WEST) - DATA PROCESSING.
Schwohnke, Andreas. Teleheimarbeit als neue Rationalisierungsstrategie . Köln , 1986. vii, 237, [14] p. : ISBN 3-7609-5220-8 LC Card 86-224163
HD2336.G3 S38 1986

HOME-BASED BUSINESSES - INFORMATION SERVICES - UNITED STATES.
Paradis, Adrian A. The small business information source book /. White Hall, Va. , c1987. 136 p. ; ISBN 0-932620-81-7 (pbk.) LC Card 87-15925 DDC 658/.022/07073 19
HD2346.U5 P37 1987

HOME-BASED BUSINESSES - MANAGEMENT.
Frohbieter-Mueller, Jo. Stay home and mind your own business . White Hall, Va. , c1987. 280 p. : ISBN 0-932620-83-3 (pbk.) : LC Card 87-15922 DDC 658/.041 19
HD62.5 .F76 1987

HOME-BASED BUSINESSES - UNITED STATES.
Christensen, K. (Kathleen) Women and home-based work . New York , c1988. xv, 201 p. ; ISBN 0-8050-0386-X LC Card 87-8527 DDC 305.4/3 19
HD6072.6.U5 C47 1988

Costello, Cynthia B. (Cynthia Butler) Home-based employment . Washington, D.C. (1700 18th St., N.W., Washington 20009) , 1987. iii, 20 p. ; LC Card 87-403088 DDC 331.4/0973 19
HD2336.U5 C58 1987

Waymon, Lynne. Starting and managing a business from your home /. Washington, D.C. , 1986. vi, 48 p. ; LC Card 86-602842 DDC 658/.041 19
HD62.5 .W395 1986

Home-based employment . Costello, Cynthia B.

(Cynthia Butler) Washington, D.C. (1700 18th St., N.W., Washington 20009) , 1987. iii, 20 p. ; LC Card 87-403088 DDC 331.4/0973 19
HD2336.U5 C58 1987

HOME BOX OFFICE (FIRM)
Mair, George, 1929- Inside HBO . New York , c1988. xviii, 204 p. ; ISBN 0-396-08420-6 : LC Card 87-19939 DDC 384.55/47/0973 19
HE8700.72.U6 M34 1988

HOME BUYING.
Joseph, Joel D. How to buy your home /. Bethesda, Md. , c1988. p. cm. ISBN 0-915765-36-5 : LC Card 86-23630 DDC 643/.12 19
HD1379 .J66 1988

HOME CARE SERVICES - ECONOMIC ASPECTS - UNITED STATES.
Home healthcare products and services markets in the U. S. New York, N.Y. , c1983. 2 v. (x, 368 leaves) ; LC Card 87-144925 DDC 381/.45681761 19
HD9995.H563 U5436 1983

The Home computer software market. New York, N.Y. : Frost & Sullivan, c1983. iv, 212 p. : ill. ; 29 cm. "July 1983." "(#A1096)." LC Card 87-141858 DDC 381/.45004/0973 19
1. Computer software industry - United States. 2. Market surveys - United States. I. Frost & Sullivan.
HD9696.C63 U5183245 1983

HOME CONSTRUCTION. see **HOUSE CONSTRUCTION.**

HOME DESIGN. see **ARCHITECTURE, DOMESTIC.**

HOME ECONOMICS - BRAZIL - SÃO PAULO - ACCOUNTING.
Endo, Seiti Kaneko. Pesquisa de orçamentos familiares no município de São Paulo /. São Paulo [Rio de Janeiro] , 1984. 131 p. : LC Card 85-136517
HB235.B8 E53 1984

HOME ECONOMICS - GREAT BRITAIN.
Rose, Richard, 1933- Getting by in three economies . Glasgow , 1983. 40 p. ; LC Card 83-150133 DDC 330.941/0858 19
HC256.6 .R67 1983

HOME ECONOMICS - INDIA - SIMLA - SOCIAL ASPECTS.
Sharma, Ursula, 1941- Women's work, class, and the urban household . London , New York , 1986. 213 p. ; ISBN 0-422-79320-5 : LC Card 86-11296 DDC 305.4/3 19
HQ759 .S4616 1986 ***NYPL [JLD 87-1281]***

HOME ECONOMICS - VALUATION.
Houseworker's handbook. [Cambridge, Mass.] (c/o Women's Center, 46 Pleasant St., Cambridge 02139) [1974] 81 p. : LC Card 87-110536
HD6073.H84 H68 1974

HOME EQUITY CONVERSION - UNITED STATES - CONGRESSES.
The Future is Now: A Home Equity Conversion Conference (1985 : Washington, D.C.) Proceedings from The Future is Now, A Home Equity Conversion Conference. Washington, D.C. [1985?] ix, 76 p. ; LC Card 86-601425 DDC 332.7/22 19
HG2040.45 .F87 1985

Home healthcare products and services markets in the U. S. New York, N.Y. : Frost & Sullivan, c1983. 2 v. (x, 368 leaves) ; 29 cm. "August 1983." "A1120." LC Card 87-144925 DDC 381/.45681761 19
1. Home nursing equipment industry - United States. 2. Home care services - Economic aspects - United States. 3. Market surveys - United States. I. Frost & Sullivan.
HD9995.H563 U5436 1983

HOME LABOR - BRAZIL - RIO DE JANEIRO.
Abreu, Alice R. de Paiva. O avesso da moda . São Paulo , 1986. 302 p. ; LC Card 87-129109 DDC 331.4/887/098153 19
HD6073.C62 B62 1986

HOME LABOR - GERMANY (WEST) - DATA PROCESSING.
Schwohnke, Andreas. Teleheimarbeit als neue Rationalisierungsstrategie . Köln , 1986. vii, 237, [14] p. : ISBN 3-7609-5220-8 LC Card 86-224163
HD2336.G3 S38 1986

HOME LABOR - GOVERNMENT POLICY - UNITED STATES.
Costello, Cynthia B. (Cynthia Butler) Home-based employment . Washington, D.C. (1700 18th St., N.W., Washington 20009) , 1987. iii, 20 p. ; LC Card 87-403088 DDC 331.4/0973 19
HD2336.U5 C58 1987

HOME LABOR - HISTORY.
Abreu, Alice R. de Paiva. O avesso da moda . São Paulo , 1986. 302 p. ; LC Card 87-129109 DDC 331.4/887/098153 19
HD6073.C62 B62 1986

HOME LABOR - HUNGARY.
Bennó, Pál. A bedolgozás helye és szerepe, perspektívája a szövetkezeti iparban . Budapest , 1985. 153 p. ; LC Card 85-226119
HD2336.H9 B46 1985

HOME LABOR - ITALY.
Esposito, Gennaro, 1956- Decentramento produttivo, lavoro a domicilio e sindacato /. Milano [1983] 109 p. ; LC Card 85-150186
HD2336.I8 E86 1983

HOME LABOR - QUÉBEC (PROVINCE)
Jean, Diane. Le travail à domicile dans le vêtement pour dames . [Montréal] [1982] xi, 146, [1] p. : ISBN 2-550-02847-3 LC Card 83-242834
HD6073.C62 C25 1982

HOME NURSING EQUIPMENT INDUSTRY - UNITED STATES.
Alternate site clinical testing. Tustin, CA, U. S.A. (17722 Irvine Blvd., Tustin 92680) , c1987. 167 leaves in various foliations : LC Card 87-402110 DDC 381/.45681761 19
HD9995.L33 U5412 1987

Home healthcare products and services markets in the U. S. New York, N.Y. , c1983. 2 v. (x, 368 leaves) ; LC Card 87-144925 DDC 381/.45681761 19
HD9995.H563 U5436 1983

The home-owner's guide . Hargreaves, Judith. Cambridge [Cambridgeshire] , Wolfeboro, N.H., USA , 1988. p. cm. ISBN 0-85941-423-X (pbk.) : LC Card 87-17388 DDC 643 19
HD7287.8 .H37 1988

HOME OWNERSHIP.
Galster, George C., 1948- Homeowners and neighborhood reinvestment /. Durham , 1987. xii, 354 p. ; ISBN 0-8223-0725-1 LC Card 87-13448 DDC 307.3/36 19
HD1387 .G34 1987

Hargreaves, Judith. The home-owner's guide . Cambridge [Cambridgeshire] , Wolfeboro, N.H., USA , 1988. p. cm. ISBN 0-85941-423-X (pbk.) : LC Card 87-17388 DDC 643 19
HD7287.8 .H37 1988

The Kiplinger/Changing times guide to buying and selling a home /. Washington, DC , New York, NY , c1987. iii, 311 p. : ISBN 0-938721-02-X (pbk.) : LC Card 87-167806 DDC 643/.12 19
HD1379 .K52 1987

HOME OWNERSHIP - AUSTRIA.
Lins, Josef. Wohnungsmarkt und soziale Schicht . Linz , 1983. 89 p. : ISBN 3-85320-292-6 LC Card 84-214132 DDC 363.6/09436 19
HD7337.A3 L55 1983 ***NYPL [JLD 87-102]***

HOME OWNERSHIP - CANADA.
Che-Alford, Janet. Mortgagor [sic] households in Canada . Ottawa , c1986. 100 p. : ISBN 0-660-52986-6 (pbk.) : LC Card 86-202749 DDC 332.7/22/0971 19
HD7287.82.C2 C48 1986

HOME OWNERSHIP - NEW ZEALAND - COSTS.
Brooks, R. Inflation, tax rules, and housing in New Zealand /. Wellington, N.Z. [1986] 22, [22] p. : LC Card 87-132461 DDC 363.5/8 19
HD7387.5.A3 B76 1986

HOME OWNERSHIP - PACIFIC ISLANDS (TRUST TERRITORY) - STATISTICS.
Barr, Lorna R. Land of the Trust islands . [Victoria, B.C.] [1978] 36 p. : LC Card 83-226106 DDC 333.3/0996/5 19
HD1121.Z63 B37 1978

HOME OWNERSHIP - TEXAS.
Albrecht, Don E. A profile of 1984 Texas homebuyers /. College Station, Tex. [1986] 70 p. : LC Card 86-622194 DDC 333.33/8 19
HD7287.82.U62 T434 1986

HOME OWNERSHIP - UNITED STATES.
Thomsett, Michael C. Homeowners money management . Emmaus, Pa. , c1987. xiii, 238 p. : ISBN 0-87857-673-8 (alk. paper) : LC Card 86-26096 DDC 332.024 19
HD7287.82.U6 T47 1987

HOME PURCHASE. see **HOUSE BUYING.**

HOME RULE (IRELAND) - HISTORY.
Parnell, Anna, 1852-1911. The tale of a great sham /. Dublin , Wick, Littlehampton, West Sussex , 1986. 205 p. ; ISBN 0-905223-93-4 LC Card 86-234070 DDC 333.33/5/09415 19
HD625 .P37 1986

The Home terminal II : computers in the home--survey results 1985/86 : RECOM, residential computing / Consumer & Technology Division. [Boston, Ma.] (89 Broad St., Boston 02110) : Yankee Group, [1986] 63 leaves : ill. ; 29 cm. (Industry research report) "July 1986." LC Card 86-211108 DDC 381/.45621396/0973 19
1. Computer industry - United States - Statistics. 2. Microcomputers - United States - Statistics. 3. Market surveys - United States. I. Yankee Group. Consumer & Technology Division. II. Title: Home terminal 2. III. Title: Home terminal two. IV. Title: RECOM, residential computing. V. Series.
HD9696.C63 U518327 1986

Home terminal two. The Home terminal II . [Boston, Ma.] (89 Broad St., Boston 02110) [1986] 63 leaves : LC Card 86-211108 DDC 381/.45621396/0973 19
HD9696.C63 U518327 1986

Home terminal 2. The Home terminal II . [Boston, Ma.] (89 Broad St., Boston 02110) [1986] 63 leaves : LC Card 86-211108 DDC 381/.45621396/0973 19
HD9696.C63 U518327 1986

HOMELANDS, SOUTH AFRICA - ECONOMIC CONDITIONS.
An Introduction to economic development in Southern Africa and the role of DBSA /. Sandton, Republic of South Africa [1985] 78 p. ; LC Card 87-127414 DDC 338.968 19
HG3401.A8 D485 1985

HOMELANDS (SOUTH AFRICA) - INDUSTRIES.
Wellings, Paul. Industrial decentralisation under apartheid . Durban , 1984. 48, xxxii p. : ISBN 0-86980-455-3 (pbk.) LC Card 87-127005 DDC 338.968 19
HC905.Z9 D59 1984

HOMELESS PERSONS - HOUSING - GERMANY (WEST)
Drygala, Anke, 1950- Obdachlosenhilfe im Sozialstaat . Weinheim , 1986. 154 p. ; ISBN 3-407-58292-7 LC Card 87-103682 DDC 362.5/83 19
HD7287.96.G3 D79 1986

HOMELESS PERSONS - HOUSING - NEW YORK (N. Y.) - CASE STUDIES.
Baxter, Ellen. The Heights . New York, N.Y. [1986] 69 leaves : LC Card 87-401534 DDC 363.5/8 19
HD7287.96.U62 N683 1986

HOMELESS PERSONS - HOUSING - URUGUAY - MONTEVIDEO.
Vicario, Luis B. Lineamientos básicos del Programa Habitacional de Emergencia, 1985-86 /. [Montevideo] , 1985. 25 p. : LC Card 87-122422 DDC 363.5/8 19
HD7287.96.U82 M668 1985

HOMELESSNESS - GERMANY, WEST.
Drygala, Anke, 1950- Obdachlosenhilfe im Sozialstaat . Weinheim , 1986. 154 p. ; ISBN 3-407-58292-7 LC Card 87-103682 DDC 362.5/83 19
HD7287.96.G3 D79 1986

HOMELESSNESS - GREAT BRITAIN - HISTORY - 20TH CENTURY.
Shaw, Frederick. The homes and homeless of post-war Britain /. Carnforth, Lancashire, UK , c1985. viii, 288 p. : ISBN 1-85070-104-0
NYPL [JLG 86-278]

HOMELESSNESS - INDIA.
Housing and Urban Development Corporation. HUDCO's initiatives for IYSH. New Delhi [1987?] 49 p. : LC Card 87-902550 DDC 363.5/8

19
HD7287.96.I4 H67 1987

HOMELESSNESS - INDIA - KARNATAKA.
Parvathamma, C., 1928- Housing, rural poor, and their living conditions /. Delhi, India [1987] vi, 135 p. ; ISBN 81-212-0088-1 : LC Card 87-900831 DDC 363.5/8 19
HD7361.K27 P37 1987

Homem de Melo, Fernando Bento, 1942- Prioridade agrícola : sucesso ou fracasso? / Fernando Homem de Melo. São Paulo : Fundação Instituto de Pesquisas Econômicas : Livraria Pioneira Editora, 1985. xiii, 200 p. : ill. ; 22 cm. (Biblioteca Pioneira de ciências sociais. Economia) Estudos econômicos / FIPE/Pioneira Includes bibliographical references. LC Card 86-126447 DDC 338.1/881 19
1. Agriculture - Economic aspects - Brazil. 2. Agriculture and state - Brazil. 3. Food supply - Brazil. I. Series. II. Series: Estudos econômics (Fundação Instituto de Pesquisas Econômicas (São Paulo, Brazil)). III. Title.
HD1872 .H66 1985 ***NYPL [JLD 86-3809]***

HOMEMAKERS. see **HOUSEWIVES.**

Homemaking skills go to the office . Filbert, Judith Ann. Bozeman, Mont. (P.O. Box 6244, Bozeman 59771) , c1986. 46 p. ; LC Card 86-218123 DDC 651.3/741/02373 19
HF5547.5 .F53 1986

Os homens de ferro . Minayo, Maria Cecília de Souza. Rio de Janeiro , 1986. 244 p. : LC Card 87-129149 DDC 331.7/622341/098151 19
HD8039.M72 B86 1986

Homeowners and neighborhood reinvestment /. Galster, George C., 1948- Durham , 1987. xii, 354 p. ; ISBN 0-8223-0725-1 LC Card 87-13448 DDC 307.3/36 19
HD1387 .G34 1987

HOMEOWNERS' ASSOCIATIONS - UNITED STATES.
Dowden, C. James. Creating a community association . Washington, D.C. , Alexandria, Va. , 1986. vii, 76 p. : ISBN 0-87420-659-6 (pbk.) LC Card 86-50785 DDC 643/.2 19
HD7287.67.U5 C73 1986

HOMEOWNERS INSURANCE. see **INSURANCE, HOMEOWNERS.**

Homeowners money management . Thomsett, Michael C. Emmaus, Pa. , c1987. xiii, 238 p. : ISBN 0-87857-673-8 (alk. paper) : LC Card 86-26096 DDC 332.024 19
HD7287.82.U6 T47 1987

HOMEOWNERS - UNITED STATES - FINANCE, PERSONAL.
Thomsett, Michael C. Homeowners money management . Emmaus, Pa. , c1987. xiii, 238 p. : ISBN 0-87857-673-8 (alk. paper) : LC Card 86-26096 DDC 332.024 19
HD7287.82.U6 T47 1987

HOMES . Mason, Andrew, 1947- Honolulu, Hawaii [1987] x, 114 p. : ISBN 0-86638-102-3 (pbk.) : LC Card 87-22288 DDC 304.6/028/55329 19
HB849.49 .M38 1987

The homes and homeless of post-war Britain /. Shaw, Frederick. Carnforth, Lancashire, UK , c1985. viii, 288 p. : ISBN 1-85070-104-0
NYPL [JLG 86-278]

HOMES (Computer program) Mason, Andrew, 1947- HOMES . Honolulu, Hawaii [1987] x, 114 p. : ISBN 0-86638-102-3 (pbk.) : LC Card 87-22288 DDC 304.6/028/55329 19
HB849.49 .M38 1987

HOMES (COMPUTER PROGRAM)
Mason, Andrew, 1947- HOMES . Honolulu, Hawaii [1987] x, 114 p. : ISBN 0-86638-102-3 (pbk.) : LC Card 87-22288 DDC 304.6/028/55329 19
HB849.49 .M38 1987

HOMES (INSTITUTIONS) see **CHARITIES.**

HOMES, MOBILE. see **MOBILE HOMES.**

Homesharing and other lifestyle options /. Horne, Jo. Washington, D.C. , Glenview, Ill. , c1988. xi, 259 p. : ISBN 0-673-24886-0 (pbk.) : LC Card 87-13028 DDC 363.5/9 19
HD7287.92.U54 H65 1988

The homestead exemption . Florida. Legislature. Senate. Finance, Tax & Claims Committee. [Tallahassee, Fla.] [1986] ii leaves, 104 p. ; LC Card 86-623229 DDC 336.22 19
HJ4204.A27 F57 1986

HOMESTEAD LAW - ECONOMIC ASPECTS - WEST (U. S.) - HISTORY.
Layton, Stanford J., 1941- To no privileged class . Provo, Utah , Salt Lake City, Utah , c1987. p. cm. ISBN 0-941214-59-1 : LC Card 87-14299 DDC 333.1/6/0978 19
HD1339.U5 L39 1987

HOMESTEAD LAW - SOCIAL ASPECTS - WEST (U. S.) - HISTORY.
Layton, Stanford J., 1941- To no privileged class . Provo, Utah , Salt Lake City, Utah , c1987. p. cm. ISBN 0-941214-59-1 : LC Card 87-14299 DDC 333.1/6/0978 19
HD1339.U5 L39 1987

Homfeld, Wolfgang. Verkehrsberuhigung in Berlin (West) : Dokumentation und Analyse / Wolfgang Homfeld. Berlin : D. Reimer, c1984. 306 p. : ill. ; 21 cm. Bibliography: p. 288-301. ISBN 3-496-00782-6 LC Card 84-212018
1. City traffic - Environmental aspects - Berlin (Germany). 2. City traffic - Berlin (Germany) - Environmental aspects. 3. City planning - Berlin (Germany). 4. Traffic safety - Berlin (Germany). I. Title.
HE311.G32 B4753 1984

HOMICIDE - OREGON - STATISTICS.
Suicides and homicides, Oregon residents, 1979 to 1981. Portland, OR (1400 S.W. 5th Ave., Portland 97201) [1986] 39 p. : LC Card 87-620589 DDC 614.5/985844/09795 19
HB1323.S82 U57 1986

Hommage à Robert Laurent. Mélanges Robert Laurent . Montpellier , 1980. xxi, 296 p. : LC Card 83-151672
HC273 .M43 1980

Homme d'affaires québécois. L'Homme d'affaires québécois des années 80 /. Montréal, Québec, Canada , c1983. 418 p., [14] p. of plates : ISBN 2-89045-585-8 LC Card 83-190776
HC117.Q4 H65 1983

L'Homme d'affaires québécois des années 80 / Michel G. Bédard, Léo-Paul Lauzon, Gilbert Tarrab. Montréal, Québec, Canada : Hurtubise HMH, c1983. 418 p., [14] p. of plates : ports. ; 23 cm. "Le lecteur trouvera donc réunis ici les protocoles abrégés, revus et corrigés par les hommes d'affaires ... 36 entretiens ... rédigés à la suite d'interviews télédiffusées (entre juin 1981 et la fin de février 1982)"--Introd. ISBN 2-89045-585-8 LC Card 83-190776
1. Businessmen - Québec (Province) - Interviews. I. Bédard, Michel G. II. Lauzon, Léo-Paul, 1946-. III. Tarrab, Gilbert. IV. Title: Homme d'affaires québécois.
HC117.Q4 H65 1983

Hommes et sociétés.
Blérald, Alain Ph. Histoire économique de la Guadeloupe et de la Martinique . Paris , c1986. 336 p. : ISBN 2-86537-134-4 LC Card 86-159186
HC158.5 .B54 1986

Hommes et sociétés, 0290-6600.
Enjeux fonciers en Afrique noire /. Bondy , Paris , c1982. 425 p. ; ISBN 2-86537-057-7 : LC Card 83-130847 DDC 333.3/096 19
HD966 .E54 1982 ***NYPL [JLE 87-950]***

Espaces disputés en Afrique noire . Paris , c1986. 426 p., [8] p. of plates : ISBN 2-86537-146-8 LC Card 86-210958
HD965 .E86 1986

Honadle, George. Implementation for sustainability : lessons from integrated rural development / by George Honadle and Jerry VanSant. West Hartford, Conn. : Kumarian Press, c1985. xiv, 128 p. ; 24 cm. Includes bibliographies and index. ISBN 0-931816-47-5 LC Card 85-12538 DDC 338.9/0068 19
1. Rural development projects - Developing countries - Management. 2. Rural development projects - Developing countries - Management - Case studies. I. VanSant, Jerry. II. Title.
HD1417 .H66 1985 ***NYPL [JLE 86-3888]***

Honduras : situación y políticas de empleo en el corto plazo / Organización Internacional del Trabajo, Programa Mundial del Empleo, Programa Regional del Empleo para América Latina y el Caribe, PREALC. [Santiago, Chile] : PREALC, 1983. vii, 99 p. ; 28 cm. (Documento de trabajo / PREALC . 226) "Julio 1983, original: español." LC Card 84-225233
1. Labor supply - Honduras. 2. Labor policy - Honduras. I. Regional Employment Program for Latin America and the Caribbean. II. Series: Documento de trabajo (Regional Employment Program for Latin America and the Caribbean) , 226.
HD5736.A6 H66 1983

Honduras.
International Labour Organisation. Desarrollo de la formación profesional rural . Ginebra , 1982. ii, 30 p. : ISBN 92-2-303048-X LC Card 84-113985
HD5715.5.H8 I58 1982

HONDURAS - COMMERCE.
Imagen de la estructura económica-social y explotación de los recursos naturales /. Tegucigalpa, D.C., Honduras, C.A. , 1973. viii, 334 p. : LC Card 86-177356
HC145 .I52 1973

Honduras. Consejo Nacional de Economía. (Old Catalog form: Honduras. Economía, Consejo National de)
El Desarrollo económico de Honduras . Tegucigalpa, D.C. , 1959. [56] leaves : LC Card 86-173618
HD9014.H82 D47 1959

Honduras. Economía, Consejo Nacional de. see **Honduras. Consejo Nacional de Economía.**

HONDURAS - ECONOMIC CONDITIONS.
Molina Chocano, Guillermo. Estado liberal y desarrollo capitalista en Honduras /. Tegucigalpa, Honduras , 1985. 136 p. : LC Card 86-233622
HG5202 .M65 1985

HONDURAS - ECONOMIC CONDITIONS - 1918-
Honduras, informe general de la situación socioeconómica. Tegucigalpa, D.C., Honduras, C.A. , 1971. 2, 6, 155 leaves ; LC Card 86-120957
HC145 .H665 1971

Imagen de la estructura económica-social y explotación de los recursos naturales /. Tegucigalpa, D.C., Honduras, C.A. , 1973. viii, 334 p. : LC Card 86-177356
HC145 .I52 1973

HONDURAS - ECONOMIC CONDITIONS - 1918-1980.
Consejo Superior de Planificación Económica (Honduras) Situación actual y perspectivas económicas, 1972 . Tegucigalpa, D.C., Honduras, C.A. , 1972. 38, [18] leaves ; LC Card 86-158684
HC145 .C66 1972

HONDURAS - ECONOMIC CONDITIONS - 1980-

HONDURAS - ECONOMIC POLICY.
Molina Chocano, Guillermo. Estado liberal y desarrollo capitalista en Honduras /. Tegucigalpa, Honduras , 1985. 136 p. : LC Card 86-233622
HG5202 .M65 1985

Honduras, informe general de la situación socioeconómica. Tegucigalpa, D.C., Honduras, C.A. : Secretaría Técnica del Consejo Superior de Planificación Económica, 1971. 2, 6, 155 leaves ; 28 cm. LC Card 86-120957
1. Honduras - Economic conditions - 1918-. 2. Honduras - Social conditions. 3. Education - Honduras. I. Consejo Superior de Planificación Económica (Honduras). Secretaría Técnica.
HC145 .H665 1971

HONDURAS - POPULATION - ECONOMIC ASPECTS.
Suazo, Margarita. Problación y desarrollo socioeconómico en Honduras /. Chicago, Ill., USA (1313 E. 60th St., Chicago 60637) , c1984. 90 p., [2] leaves of plates : LC Card 85-203746
HB3540.A3 S82 1984

HONDURAS - POPULATION POLICY - PUBLIC OPINION.
Análisis de la encuesta a líderes nacionales /. Tegucigalpa, D.C. , 1983. 49, [12] leaves ; LC Card 85-203745
HB3540.A3 A52 1983

HONDURAS - SOCIAL CONDITIONS.
Honduras, informe general de la situación socioeconómica. Tegucigalpa, D.C., Honduras, C.A. , 1971. 2, 6, 155 leaves ; LC Card

86-120957
HC145 .H665 1971

Imagen de la estructura económica-social y explotación de los recursos naturales /. Tegucigalpa, D.C., Honduras, C.A. , 1973. viii, 334 p. : LC Card 86-177356
HC145 .I52 1973

Honeck, Gerhard. Probleme einer Privatgeldordnung : eine Auseinandersetzung mit den Vorstellungen F.A. von Hayeks zur Entnationalisierung des Geldes / Gerhard Honeck. Frankfurt am Main ; Haag + Herchen, c1985. 93 p. ; 21 cm. Bibliography: p. 87-93. ISBN 3-88129-964-5 LC Card 86-153829
1. Monetary policy. 2. Money. 3. Inflation (Finance). 4. Hayek, Friedrich A. von (Friedrich August), 1899-. I. Title.
HG230.3 .H56 1985

Honecker, Erich.
Mit qualitativ neuen Schritten zu höchsten Leistungen . Berlin , 1986. 80 p. ; ISBN 3-320-00807-2 LC Card 87-144292 DDC 338.9431 19
HC290.78 .M567 1986

Sozialistische Einheitspartei Deutschlands. Zentralkomitee. [Bericht des Zentralkomitees der Sozialistischen Einheitspartei Deutschlands an den XI. Parteitag der SED. English.] Report of the Central Committee of the Socialist Unity Party of Germany to the 11th Congress of the SED /. Dresden [1986] 109 p. : LC Card 86-220057 DDC 338.9431 19
HC290.78 .S66 1986

Honegger, Eric, 1946- Allenspach, Heinz. Bevorzugter Beamtenstatus, Möglichkeiten und Grenzen einer Reform . Zürich [1986] 32 p. ; LC Card 87-407830 DDC 330.9494 s 331.7/61354494 19
HC395 .Z43 Nr. 130 JN8831

Honeymoon uranium mine occupation [sound recording]. Los Angeles, Calif. : Pacifica Radio Archive, p1983. 1 sound cassette (53 min.) : analog. Radio broadcast. Producers, Nancy Atkin, Geoff Barbour, and Greg Segal. Issued also on reel. Records events which took place in May 1982 when some four hundred people rallied at Broken Hill, South Australia. Protesters speak about the need for jobs in the area, mining methods used that may contaminate the water supply, the use of uranium for nuclear weapons, aboriginal rights, and the involvement of the police. LC Card 87-752867
1. Uranium industry - Social aspects - Australia - Broken Hill (N.S.W.). 2. Uranium industry - Environmental aspects - Australia - Broken Hill (N.S.W.). 3. Antinuclear movement - Australia - Broken Hill (N.S.W.). I. Pacifica Radio Archive.
HD9539.U72

Honeywell after 100 years /. Spencer, Edson W. New York , 1985, c1986. 24 p. : LC Card 85-63243 DDC 338.7/62/000973 19
HD9729.H66 S66 1986

HONEYWELL, INC. - HISTORY.
Spencer, Edson W. Honeywell after 100 years /. New York , 1985, c1986. 24 p. : LC Card 85-63243 DDC 338.7/62/000973 19
HD9729.H66 S66 1986

HONG KONG - ECONOMIC POLICY.
The Political economy of the new Asian industrialism /. Ithaca, N.Y. , 1987. 252 p. ; ISBN 0-8014-1948-4 (alk. paper) LC Card 86-29103 DDC 338.95 19
HC460.5 .P65 1987

Rabushka, Alvin. The new China . San Francisco , Boulder, Colo. , 1987. xii, 254 p. ; ISBN 0-936488-15-8 (pbk. : alk. paper) LC Card 87-10574 DDC 338.951 19
HC427.92 .R33 1987

Hong Kong. Transport Dept. Guide to Hong Kong's bus, light bus, rail, and ferry services /. Hong Kong , 1986. p. D3799-D4101, 14 p. ; LC Card 87-401055 DDC 388.4/0951/25 19
HE5080.5.H662 G85 1986

Honger op ons bord : over politiek en voedselveiligheid / [eindredactie, Jan van Bergen, Kees Kingma en Josephine Verspaget]. Amsterdam : Evert Vermeer Stichting, 1986. 164 p. : ill. ; 20 cm. "Ter gelegenheid van de conferentie van de Evert Vermeer Stichting op 19 april 1986 te Ede"--T.p. verso. Includes bibliographies. ISBN 90-70985-05-5 : LC Card 86-166714
1. Food supply - Congresses. 2. Famines - Congresses. 3. Food relief - Congresses. 4. Food supply - Developing countries - Congresses. I. Bergen, Jan van. II. Kingma, Kees. III. Verspaget, Josephine. IV. Evert Vermeer Stichting.
HD9000.5 .H655 1986

HONGKONG AND SHANGHAI BANKING CORPORATION - HISTORY.
King, Frank H. H. The history of the Hongkong and Shanghai Banking Corporation /. Cambridge [Cambridgeshire] , New York , 1987- p. cm. ISBN 0-521-32706-7 (v. 1) LC Card 86-28339 DDC 332.1/5/095125 19
HG1571 K56

King, Frank H. H. The Hongkong Bank in the period of imperialism and war, 1895-1918 . Cambridge [Cambridgeshire] , New York , 1988. p. cm. ISBN 0-521-32707-5 LC Card 87-6349 DDC 332.1/5/095125 s 332.1/5/095125 19
HG1571 .K56 vol. 2 HG3354.H65

The Hongkong Bank in late imperial China 1864-1902 . King, Frank H. H. Cambridge [Cambridgeshire] , New York , 19. p. cm. ISBN 0-521-32706-7 LC Card 86-28341 DDC 332.1/5/095125 s 332.1/0951 19
HG1571 .K56 vol. 1 HG3338.H66

The Hongkong Bank in the period of imperialism and war, 1895-1918 . King, Frank H. H. Cambridge [Cambridgeshire] , New York , 1988. p. cm. ISBN 0-521-32707-5 LC Card 87-6349 DDC 332.1/5/095125 s 332.1/5/095125 19
HG1571 .K56 vol. 2 HG3354.H65

Hongkong Banking Group history series.
Jones, Geoffrey. The history of the British Bank of the Middle East /. Cambridge [Cambridgeshire] , New York , 1986- v. : ISBN 0-521-32322-3 (v. 1) LC Card 85-31359 DDC 332.1/5/0955 19
HG3270.2.A8 B755 1986 ***NYPL [JLL 87-87]***

Honig, Emily. Sisters and strangers : women in the Shanghai cotton mills, 1919-1949 / Emily Honig. Stanford, Calif. : Stanford University Press, 1986. ix, 299 p. : ill. ; 24 cm. Includes index. Bibliography: p. [279]-289. ISBN 0-8047-1274-3 (alk. paper) : LC Card 84-51711 DDC 331.4/87721/0951132 19
1. Women textile workers - China - Shanghai - History - 20th century. 2. Trade-unions - China - Shanghai - Political activity - History - 20th century. 3. China - Economic conditions - 1912-1949. 4. Shanghai - Economic conditions. I. Title.
HD6073.T42 C64 1986
NYPL [JLD 86-3016]

Honigman, Arch H., 1960- Downtown and regional shopping centre retailing in Winnipeg /. Winnipeg, Man., Canada , 1985. x, 90, [8] p. : ISBN 0-920213-22-7 (pbk.) LC Card 86-137592 DDC 381/.1/0971274 19
HF5429.6.C3 D69 1985
NYPL [JLF 86-1331]

Honismereti kutatások Szabolcs-Szatmárban, 0139-3650 .
(7) Ipari üzemtörténet /. Nyíregyháza , 1979 ([Nyíregyháza] : Készült a Szabolcs-Szatmár Megyei Tanács Sokszorosító Költségvetési Üzemében) 228 p. : ISBN 963-01-2796-2 LC Card 81-173980
HC300.29.S92 I62 1979

The Honolulu consumer price index, 1940-1986. [Honolulu] : Dept. of Planning & Economic Development, Research & Economic Analysis Division, State of Hawaii, [1986] 19 p. ; 28 cm. (Statistical report . 187) "May 30, 1986." LC Card 86-622085 DDC 319.69 s 338.5/28/09969 19
1. Consumer price indexes - Hawaii. 2. Prices - Hawaii. I. Hawaii. Dept. of Planning and Economic Development. Research and Economic Analysis Division. II. Series: Statistical report (Hawaii. Dept. of Planning and Economic Development) .
HA329.1 .A25 no. 187 HB235.U6

Hoof, J. A. P. van. Autonomie als arbeidssociologisch vraagstuk . Zeist , 1987. 237 p. : ISBN 90-6720-032-8 : LC Card 87-169950
HD5660.N4 A94 1987

HOOF, J. A. P. VAN.
Autonomie als arbeidssociologisch vraagstuk . Zeist , 1987. 237 p. : ISBN 90-6720-032-8 : LC Card 87-169950
HD5660.N4 A94 1987

Hoofprints on the forest . Shane, Douglas R. Philadelphia , c1986. xvi, 159 p. ; ISBN 0-89727-054-1 : LC Card 83-26585 DDC 338.1/76213/098 19
HD9433.L292 S53 1984
NYPL [JLD 86-2289]

Hooja, Rakesh. Energy alternatives for rural development /. Jaipur , 1985. vi, 303 p. : LC Card 86-902191 DDC 333.79/0954 19
HD9556.I42 E54 1985

Hooley, Richard W., 1925- Productivity growth in Philippine manufacturing : retrospect and future prospects / Richard Hooley. [Manila?] : Philippine Institute for Development Studies, c1985. ix, 128 p. : ill. ; 23 cm. (PIDS monograph series, 0115-9194 . no. 9) "December 1985"--Cover. Bibliography: p. 67-68. LC Card 87-112014 DDC 338.4/769/09599 19
1. Industrial productivity - Philippines. 2. Philippines - Manufactures. I. Title. II. Series.
HC460.I52 H66 1985

Hooper, H. Paul. Page, John R., 1949- Accounting and information systems /. Englewood Cliffs, N.J. , c1987. xiii, 738 p. : ISBN 0-13-002361-2 LC Card 86-25429 DDC 657/.028/5 19
HF5679 .P25 1987

Hoós, János. Az új növekedési pálya feltételei és követelményei / Hoós János. Budapest : Közgazdasági és Jogi Könyvkiadó, 1985. 227, [2] p. : ill. ; 19 cm. (Időszerű közgazdasági kérdések, 0324-3214) Bibliography: p. [229] ISBN 963-221-508-7 : LC Card 86-128355
1. Hungary - Economic policy - 1968-. 2. Hungary - Economic conditions - 1968-. I. Title. II. Series.
HC300.28 .H664 1985

Hoosac docks . Weinbaum, Paul O. Boston, Mass. , 1985. vi, 95 p. : LC Card 85-603289 DDC 387.1/64/0974461 19
HE554.B6 W45 1985

Hooven, Eckart van. Das Süd-Nord-Gefälle . Stuttgart , 1986. 168 p. ; ISBN 3-87959-270-5 LC Card 87-103590 DDC 330.943/0878 19
HC286.7 .S9 1986

Hoover Institution on War, Revolution, and Peace.
Below-replacement fertility in industrial societies . Cambridge [Cambridgeshire] , New York , c1987. x, 360 p. : ISBN 0-521-34324-0 LC Card 87-6371 DDC 304.6/32 19
HB901 .B45 1987b

Below-replacement fertility in industrial societies . New York, N.Y., USA , c1987. x, 360 p. : LC Card 87-2458 DDC 304.6/32 19
HB901 .B45 1987

Hoover monongraph series .
(3) Saint-Etienne, Christian, 1951- The Mitterrand and Reagan economic experiments . [Stanford, Calif.] , c1986. 36 p ; ISBN 0-8179-5082-6 (pbk.) LC Card 86-27776 DDC 338.944 19
HC276.2 .S24 1986

Hope for the family farm : trust God and care for the land / edited by LaVonne Godwin Platt ; [foreword by Gregory D. Cusack]. Newton, Kan. : Faith and Life Press, c1987. viii, 231 p. : ill. ; 23 cm. Bibliography: p. 213-215. Filmography: p. 215-217. ISBN 0-87303-126-1 (pbk.) LC Card 87-81635 DDC 338.1/6 19
1. Family farms - United States. 2. Agriculture - Economic aspects - United States. 3. Family - United States - Religious life. I. Platt, LaVonne.
HD1476.U5 H67 1987

Hope in hard times . Loeb, Paul Rogat, 1952- Lexington, Mass. , c1987. ix, 322 p. : ISBN 0-669-12929-1 LC Card 85-46044 DDC 327.1/74 19
JX1974.7 .L63 1986 ***NYPL [JLE 86-4051]***

Hope, Kempe R. Development finance and the development process : a case study of selected Caribbean countries / Kempe Ronald Hope. New York : Greenwood Press, 1987. 100 p. ; 25 cm. (Contributions in economics and economic history, 0084-9235 . no. 74) Bibliography: p. [87]-96. Includes index. ISBN 0-313-25835-X (lib. bdg. : alk. paper) LC Card 86-29617 DDC 336.729 19
1. Finance, Public - Caribbean Area - Case studies. 2. Fiscal policy - Caribbean Area - Case studies. 3. Caribbean Area - Economic conditions - 1945- - Case studies. 4. Finance - Caribbean Area - Case studies. I. Title. II. Series.
HJ844.3 .H67 1987

Hopf, Michael. Informationen für Märkte und Märkte für Informationen / von Michael Hopf. Frankfurt am Main : Barudio & Hess, 1983. iv, 237 p. : ill. ; 21 cm. (Reihe Oikos . Bd. 14) Originally presented as the author's thesis (doctoral)--Johann Wolfgang Goethe-Universität Frankfurt am Main, 1983. Bibliography: p. 228-237. ISBN 3-922182-14-3 : LC Card 84-180866
1. Information theory in economics. 2. Uncertainty (Information theory). I. Title. II. Series.
HB133 .H66 1983

Hopke, William E. The Encyclopedia of careers and vocational guidance /. Chicago, Ill. , 1987. 3 v. : ISBN 0-89434-083-2 (set) : LC Card 87-19084 DDC 331.7/02 19
HF5381 .E52 1987

Hopkin and Associates. Transition in agriculture . Washington, D.C. (1120 Connecticut Ave. N.W., Washington 20036) , c1986. 2 v. : LC Card 86-233848 DDC 332.7/1/0973 19
HG2051.U5 T68 1986

Hopkins, David M. Changing career values : professional employees in the 1980s / David Hopkins. Bethlehem, PA : CPC Foundation, 1986. x, 126 p. : ill. ; 28 cm. Bibliography: p. 124-126. ISBN 0-914885-10-3 (pbk.) LC Card 87-112752 DDC 331.25 19
1. Professional employees - United States - Attitudes - Longitudinal studies. 2. College graduates - United States - Attitudes - Longitudinal studies. 3. Career development - United States - Longitudinal studies. I. CPC Foundation. II. Title.
HD8038.U5 H66 1986

Hopkins, Mike.
Alternatives to unemployment and underemployment : the case of Colombia / Michael Hopkins. Boulder : Westview Press, 1985. xiv, 129 p. : ill. ; 23 cm. (Westview special studies on Latin America and the Caribbean) "A study prepared for the International Labour Office within the framework of the World Employment Programme." Includes bibliographies and indexes. ISBN 0-8133-0200-5 (pbk.) LC Card 85-45007 DDC 331.13/79861 19
1. Unemployment - Colombia. 2. Underemployment - Colombia. 3. Colombia - Economic policy. I. International Labor Office. II. World Employment Programme. III. Title.
HD5757.A6 H67 1985 ***NYPL [JLD 86-2149]***

Employment forecasting . London , New York , c1988. p. cm. ISBN 0-86187-938-4 : LC Card 87-21882 DDC 331.12/094 19
HD5764 .E47 1988

Hopkins, William L. People skills in action, for loan officers and processors. Chicago, Ill. , 1986. 1 videocassette (20 min.) : LC Card 86-707349 DDC 658.8 11
HG1641

Hoppe, Rudolf. Püschel, Herbert. Die Rentenversorgung der Arbeiter und Angestellten in der DDR /. Berlin , c1986. 206 p. ; ISBN 3-7303-0068-7 LC Card 87-408895 DDC 331.25/2/09431 19
HD7180.5 .P87 1986

Hoppit, Julian. Risk and failure in English business, 1700-1800 / Julian Hoppit. Cambridge [Cambridgeshire] ; New York : Cambridge University Press, 1987. vii, 228 p. : ill. ; 24 cm. Bibliography: p. 197-221. Includes index. ISBN 0-521-32624-9 LC Card 87-743 DDC 332.7/5/0942 19
1. Bankruptcy - England - History - 18th century. 2. Business enterprises - England - History - 18th century. 3. Business cycles - England - History - 18th century. I. Title.
HG3769.G73 E54 1987

HOPS INDUSTRY - ENGLAND - KENT - HISTORY.
Baker, Dennis, 1928- Agricultural prices, production, and marketing, with special reference to the hop industry . New York , 1985. 779 p. : ISBN 0-8240-6675-8 : LC Card 84-45995 DDC 338.1/7382 19
HD9019.H72 G67 1985 ***NYPL [JLE 87-63]***

Hopwood, William S. Bodnar, George H. Accounting information systems /. Boston , c1987. xvii, 892 p. : ISBN 0-205-10308-1 LC Card 86-26505 DDC 657/.028/5 19
HF5679 .B59 1987

Hora trágica. Capelo C., J. Alejo (J. Alejo Capelo Cabello), d. 1973. El crimen del 15 de noviembre de 1922 /. [Guayaquil] , 1983. 10, 14, 19 p. : LC Card 86-114097
HD5358.A6 C36 1983

Horch, Hans. Der Wandel der Gesellschafts- und Herrschaftsstrukturen in der Saarregion während der Industrialisierung (1740-1914) / Hans Horch. St. Ingbert [W. Germany] : W.J. Röhrig, 1985. 720 p. : ill. ; 21 cm. (Wissenschaftliche Reihe Soziologie) Originally presented as the author's thesis (doctoral)--Universität Hannover, 1984. Bibliography: p. 672-720. ISBN 3-924555-04-4 LC Card 85-194709
1. Saarland (Germany) - Economic conditions. 2. Saarland (Germany) - Industries - History. 3. Saarland (Germany) - Social conditions. 4. Labor and laboring classes - Germany (West) - Saarland - History. 5. Saarland (Germany) - Politics and government. I. Title. II. Series.
HC287.S23 H67 1985

Horenstein, Nadine R., 1954- Trueblood, Michael A. The Ivory Coast . Washington, DC , 1986. iv, 32 p. : LC Card 86-602806 DDC 338.1 s 382/.41/096668 19
HD1411 .F59 no. 223 HD9017.I912

Horgby, Björn. Den disciplinerade arbetaren : brottslighet och social förändring i Norrköping 1850-1910 / Björn Horgby. Stockholm : Almqvist & Wiksell international, [1986] 322 p. : ill. ; 21 cm. (Acta Universitatis Stockholmiensis. Stockholm studies in history, 0491-0842 . 36) Thesis (doctoral)--Stockholms universitet, 1986. Bibliography: p. 299-319. ISBN 91-22-00804-7 LC Card 87-105821
1. Industry - Social aspects - Sweden - Norrköping - History - 19th century. 2. Labor and laboring classes - Sweden - Norrköping - History - 19th century. 3. Crime and criminals - Sweden - Norrköping - History - 19th century. I. Title. II. Series.
HC378.N67 H67 1986

Horlacher, D. Population and socioeconomic development /. Moscow , 1986. 186 p. ; LC Card 86-226273 DDC 304.6/09172/4 19
HB849.41 .P644 1986

Horlacher, Michael. Der Wiederaufbau der deutschen Volkswirtschaft : eine Denkschrift über Deutschlands finanzielle und wirtschaftliche Not / von Michael Horlacher. Diessen vor München : Jos. C. Huber, 1919. 118 p. ; 26 cm. Includes bibliographical references. LC Card 87-409517 DDC 338.943 19
1. Germany - Economic policy - 1888-1918. 2. Germany - Economic conditions - 1888-1918. I. Title.
HC286.2 .H67 1919

Horn, Christel-Margret. Feldtheorie und Konsumverhalten / Christel-Margret Horn. Freiburg im Breisgau : R. Haufe, c1983. 121 p. : 23 ill. ; 21 cm. (Bd. 19 der Schriftenreihe des Instituts für Allgemeine Wirtschaftsforschung der Albert-Ludwigs-Universität Freiburg i. Br) Bibliography: p. 107-117. Includes index. ISBN 3-448-01293-9 LC Card 84-136042
1. Consumers - Mathematical models. 2. Consumers - Germany, West - Mathematical models. 3. Motivation research (Marketing) - Mathematical models. 4. Field theory (Social psychology). I. Series: Schriftenreihe des Instituts für Allgemeine Wirtschaftsforschung der Albert-Ludwigs-Universität Freiburg i. Br. , Bd. 19. II. Title.
HF5415.3 .H65 1983

Horn, Thomas W. Business valuation manual : an understandable, step-by-step guide to finding the value of a business / Thomas W. Horn.Newly rev. Lancaster, PA : Charter Oak Press, 1987. 224 p. : ill. ; 23 cm. Page 224 order form. Includes index. ISBN 0-87521-015-5 (pbk.) : LC Card 87-17887 DDC 658.1/522 19
1. Business enterprises - Valuation. I. Title.
HD1393.25 .H66 1987

Hornbook series student edition.
Hovenkamp, Herbert, 1948- Economics and federal antitrust law /. St. Paul, Minn. , 1985. xxvii, 414 p. : ISBN 0-314-86196-3 LC Card 84-25783 DDC 343.73/072 347.30372 19
KF1649 .H67 1985 ***NYPL [JLF 86-1373]***

Horne, Jo. Homesharing and other lifestyle options / Jo Horne with Leo Baldwin. Washington, D.C. : American Association of Retired Persons ; Glenview, Ill. : Scott, Foresman, Lifelong Learning Division, c1988. xi, 259 p. : ports. ; 21 cm. Bibliography: p. 247-252. Includes index. ISBN 0-673-24886-0 (pbk.) : LC Card 87-13028 DDC 363.5/9 19
1. Aged - United States - Dwellings. 2. Shared housing - United States. I. Baldwin, Leo. II. Title.
HD7287.92.U54 H65 1988

Horne, John (John D.) Work, employment, and unemployment / John Horne. London ; New York : Longman, 1988. p. cm. (Sociology in focus series) Bibliography: p. Includes index. Identifies the theories, trends, and issues of work and unemployment and discusses the relationship between sociology and work. ISBN 0-582-35499-4 (pbk.) LC Card 87-3671 DDC 306/.36 19
1. Work. 2. Unemployment. I. Title. II. Series.
HD4901 .H66 1988

Horne, M. K. (McDonald Kelso), 1909- The economic outlook for U. S. cotton : a report before the council's twenty-fourth annual meeting at New Orleans, Louisiana, January 29, 1962 / by M.K. Horne, Jr. Memphis, Tenn. : National Cotton Council of America, 1962. 32 p. : ill. ; 28 cm. Cover title. LC Card 86-162675
1. Cotton trade - United States. 2. Cotton textile industry - United States. I. National Cotton Council of America. II. Title. III. Title: Economic outlook for US cotton.
HD9075 .H73 1962

Horner, Ken.
DP index.
Horner, Ken. Guide to computer installations in southern California . Palo Alto, Calif. , c1986. iv, 750 p. : LC Card 87-134229 DDC 004/.025/7949 19
HD9696.C63 U518343 1986

Guide to computer installations in southern California : Nov. 1986-Nov. 1988 / editor, Ken Horner ; asst. editor, Sandra Morris. Palo Alto, Calif. : DP Index Co. : Distributed by Horner Associates, c1986. iv, 750 p. : ill. ; 22 cm. (DP index) Cover title: Guide to southern California computers. LC Card 87-134229 DDC 004/.025/7949 19
1. Computer service industry - California, Southern - Directories. 2. Data processing service centers - California, Southern - Directories. 3. Business - Data processing - Directories. I. Morris, Sandra. II. Title. III. Title: Guide to southern California computers. IV. Series: Horner, Ken. DP index.
HD9696.C63 U518343 1986

HORNEY, KAREN, 1885-1952.
Westkott, Marcia, 1943- The feminist legacy of Karen Horney /. New Haven , c1986. viii, 242 p. ; ISBN 0-300-03706-6 (alk. paper) LC Card 86-9201 DDC 305.4/2 19
HQ1206 .W47 1986 ***NYPL [JFD 86-10266]***

Horngren, Charles T., 1926-
Introduction to financial accounting / Charles T. Horngren, Gary L. Sundem. 3rd ed. Englewood Cliffs, N.J. : Prentice-Hall, c1987. xx, 795 p. ; 25 cm. (Prentice-Hall series in accounting) Bibliography: p. 769. Includes index. ISBN 0-13-483264-7 LC Card 86-25310 DDC 657 19
1. Accounting. I. Sundem, Gary L. II. Title. III. Series.
HF5635 .H813 1987

Introduction to management accounting / Charles T. Horngren, Gary L. Sundem. 7th ed. Englewood Cliffs, N.J. : Prentice-Hall, c1987. xxi, 762 p. : ill. ; 25 cm. (Prentice-Hall series in accounting) Bibliography: p. 719-722. Includes index. ISBN 0-13-487885-X LC Card 86-25138 DDC 658.1/511 19
1. Managerial accounting. I. Sundem, Gary L. II. Title. III. Series.
HF5635 .H814 1987

Hörnig, Bodo. Beteiligungs- und Fusionsvorhaben : eine entscheidungs- und investitionstheoretische Untersuchung / von Bodo Hörnig. Berlin : Duncker & Humblot, c1985. xvi, 357 p. : ill. ; 24 cm. (Betriebswirtschaftliche Schriften. Heft 117) Bibliography: p. 329-349. ISBN 3-428-05786-4 LC Card 85-168610
1. Consolidation and merger of corporations - Mathematical models. I. Title.
HD2746.5 .H67 1985

Hornschild, Kurt. Präferenzregelung der Forschungs- und Entwicklungsförderung in Berlin / Kurt Hornschild. Berlin : Duncker & Humblot, 1985. v, 55 p. ; 23 cm. (Sonderheft / Deutsches Institut für Wirtschaftsforschung . 142) Bibliography: p. 55. ISBN 3-428-05800-3 LC Card 86-156799

1. Research, Industrial - Berlin (Germany). 2. Research, Industrial - Germany, West. 3. Berlin (Germany) - Industries. 4. Germany, West - Industries. I. Series: Sonderheft / Deutsches Institut für Wirtschaftsforschung , 142. II. Title.
HD30.42.G39 H67 1985

Hornung, Daniel. Methoden zur Prognose des Wohnungsmarktgeschehens auf regionaler Ebene : dargestellt am Beispiel von Basel, Bern, Genf, Lausanne und Zürich / vorgelegt von Daniel Hornung. Diessenhofen : Rüegger, 1983. xvi, 251 p. : ill. ; 21 cm. Thesis (doctoral)--Universität Bern, 1983. Bibliography: p. 235-251. ISBN 3-7253-0214-6 LC Card 86-114266
1. Housing forecasting - Switzerland - Mathematical models. I. Title.
HD7353.A3 H66 1983

Hornwood, Sanford W. The number one real estate investment no one talks about / Sanford W. Hornwood and I. Lucretia Hollingsworth. Englewood Cliffs, N.J. : Prentice-Hall, c1987. xv, 239 p. : ill. ; 25 cm. Includes index. ISBN 0-13-626482-4 : LC Card 86-25482 DDC 332.63/244 19
1. Mortgages. I. Hollingsworth, I. Lucretia. II. Title. III. Title: Number 1 real estate investment no one talks about.
HG4655 .H67 1987

Hornziel, Ijola Maria. La condizione degli immigrati stranieri in Italia : rapporto al Ministero del lavoro dell'Istituto per gli studi sui servizi sociali / Ijola Maria Hornziel ; prefazione di Franco Foschi ; introduzione di Aurelia Florea. Milano, Italy : F. Angeli, c1986. 166 p. : ill. ; 22 cm. (La Società. 113) "Fonti documentarie": p. [135]-163. Bibliography: p. [165]-166. LC Card 86-181215
1. Alien labor - Italy. 2. Aliens - Italy - Economic conditions. 3. Aliens - Italy - Social conditions. I. Title.
HD8488.A2 H67 1986

Horowitz, Michael M., 1933- Lands at risk in the Third World . Boulder , 1987. xiii, 416 p. : ISBN 0-8133-7311-5 (pbk. : alk. paper) : LC Card 86-51423 DDC 333.73/13 19
HD1131 .L37 1987

HORSE INDUSTRY - ENGLAND - HISTORY.
Edwards, Peter (Peter Roger) The horse trade of Tudor and Stuart England /. Cambridge [Cambridgeshire] , New York , 1988. p. cm. ISBN 0-521-35058-1 LC Card 87-24243 DDC 338.1/761/00942 19
HD9434.G73 E654 1988

HORSE INDUSTRY - FRANCE.
France. Conseil économique et social. Le développement de l'élevage des équidés en France . [Paris] [1986] 166 p. in various pagings : LC Card 86-133487
HD9434.F72 F73 1986

HORSE INDUSTRY - UNITED STATES - HISTORY.
Daniels, Leroy Judson, 1882- Tales of an old horsetrader . Iowa City , 1987. viii, 235 p. : ISBN 0-87745-173-7 LC Card 87-10932 DDC 338.1/761/00924 B 19
HD9434.U6 D36 1987

A horse of a different color . Broh, C. Anthony. Washington, D.C. , 1987. xiv, 93 p. : ISBN 0-941410-54-4 (pbk.) : LC Card 87-2869 DDC 324.973/0927 19
HE8700.76.U6 B76 1987

The horse trade of Tudor and Stuart England /. Edwards, Peter (Peter Roger) Cambridge [Cambridgeshire] , New York , 1988. p. cm. ISBN 0-521-35058-1 LC Card 87-24243 DDC 338.1/761/00942 19
HD9434.G73 E654 1988

Horseling, Hannsjörg. Mahler, Karl-Werner, 1933- Der Waste Factor . München-Gräfelfing , c1983. 64 p. ; ISBN 3-8040-0321-4 LC Card 84-214297
HC290.5.W3 M34 1983

Horsfield, A. K. (Anne K.) Copeland, M. C. (Michael Campbell) Transport energy in New Zealand's overseas trade . Auckland, N.Z. [1982] iv, 130 p. : LC Card 84-159485 DDC 387.5/1 19
HE597.N4 C63 1982
NYPL [JSK 82-15 no.80]

Horta, Elisabeth Vorcaro. A mulher na cultura brasileira / Elisabeth Vorcaro Horta. Belo Horizonte : [s.n.], 1975. 122 p. ; 23 cm. Thesis--Universidade Federal de Minas Gerais, 1973. Bibliography: p. [115]-122. LC Card 75-511579
1. Women - Brazil - Social conditions. 2. Women - Employment - Brazil. I. Title.
HQ1542 .H66 ***NYPL [Sc D 86-811]***

Hörte, Sven Åke. Medbestämmande : en analys av kontaktmönster mellan parter vid arbetsställen / Sven Åke Hörte. [Göteborg] : Sociologiska institutionen, Göteborgs universitet, Arbetet, facket og medbestämmandet, c1983. 160, [28] p. : ill. ; 21 cm. (Monograph from the Department of Sociology, University of Gothenburg, 0072-5102 . no. 28) Summary in English. Includes bibliography. ISBN 91-7222-576-9 LC Card 83-173622
1. Management - Sweden - Employee participation. I. Series: Monografier utgivna av Sociologiska institutionen vid Göteborgs universitet , nr. 28. II. Title.
HD5660.S9 H67 1983

HORTICULTURAL PRODUCTS INDUSTRY - AUSTRIA - STATISTICS.
Betriebswirtschaftliche Ergebnisse von Gartenbaubetrieben 1984 /. Wien , 1985. 13 p. ; LC Card 86-194865
HD9015.A8 B47 1985

HORTICULTURAL PRODUCTS INDUSTRY - GERMANY (WEST) - LOWER SAXONY - STATISTICS.
Landwirtschaftszählung 1979, Gartenbauerhebung 1981/82 . Hannover , 1983. xv, 132 p. ; LC Card 85-117833
HD9013.7.L68 L37 1983

HORTICULTURAL PRODUCTS INDUSTRY - INDIA - JAMMU AND KASHMIR.
Sahaf, Musadiq Amin, 1958- Marketing of horticulture industry in India /. Delhi, India , 1987. xiii, 151 p. ; LC Card 86-903833 DDC 381/.414/0954 19
HD9016.I43 J367 1987

HORTICULTURAL PRODUCTS INDUSTRY - UNITED STATES - DIRECTORIES.
Directory of regional gardening resources /. New York, NY (598 Madison Ave., New York 10022) , 1987. 172 p. : LC Card 87-402229 DDC 338.7/6359/02573 19
HD9003 .D66 1987

Horváth, Imre. Ács, Rudolf. A komplex meliorációs beruházások történeti áttekintése és gazdasági hatásának vizsgálata különböző agroökológiai tipusu gazdaságokban /. Budapest , 1986. 118 p. ; ISBN 963-491-237-0 LC Card 87-137972
HD1940.5 .A65 1986

Horváth, János. Pilling, András. Az önelszámoló rendszer alkalmazásának, a kistermelők integrálásának és a kihelyezett részlegeknek a hatása a mezőgazdasági vállalatok szervezeti felépitésére, s annak müködésére /. Budapest , 1985. 89 p. ; ISBN 963-491-206-0 LC Card 86-196755
HD1492.H8 P55 1985

Horváth, Jenő. A 80-as évek kapitalizmusa . [Budapest] , 1985. 406 p. ; ISBN 963-09-2696-2 : LC Card 86-186468
HB501 .A14 1985

Horváth, Mihály, 1809-1878. Az ipar és kereskedés története Magyarországban a három utolsó század alatt / írta Horváth Mihály. [Budapest : Állami Könyvterjesztő Vállalat, 1984] xiv, 390 p. ; 21 cm. (Az Állami Könyvterjesztő Vállalat reprint sorozata, 0231-1518) Reprint. Originally published: Budán : A Magyar Kir. Egyetem Betűivel, 1840. Includes bibliographical references. ISBN 963-02-2781-9 : LC Card 85-138953
1. Hungary - Economic conditions. 2. Hungary - Industries - History. 3. Hungary - Commerce - History. I. Series: Reprint (Budapest, Hungary). II. Title.
HC300.26 .H67 1984

Horvath, Ricardo. La trama secreta de la radiodifusión argentina : los dueños de la información electrónica y el largo brazo de su poder / Ricardo Horvath. Cap. Fed. [i.e. Buenos Aires, Argentina] : Ediciones Unidad, [1986] 153 p. ; 20 cm. Bibliography: p. 150-152. ISBN 950-9458-13-9 LC Card 86-226636
1. Radio broadcasting - Argentina - History. I. Title.
HE8699.A7 H67 1986

Horvátország. see **Croatia.**

Horvitz, Paul M. Monetary policy and the financial system / Paul M. Horvitz, Richard A. Ward. 6th ed. Englewood Cliffs, N.J. : Prentice-Hall, c1987. xii, 532 p. : ill. ; 25 cm. Includes bibliographies and index. ISBN 0-13-599861-1 LC Card 86-25447 DDC 332.4/973 19
1. Monetary policy - United States. 2. Finance - United States. I. Ward, Richard Alexander, 1929-. II. Title.
HG540 .H67 1987

Hosena, Nājira, 1930- Samabāya, saṃgrāma, sādhanā / Nājira Hosena. 1. saṃskaraṇa. Ḍhākā : Thri Shṭāra Ko-apāreṭibha Mālaṭipārapāsa Sosāiṭi : Paribeśaka Jātīya Grantha Kendra, Bikraya Bibhāga, 1985. 8, 109 p., [7] p. of plates : ill. ; 23 cm. In Bengali. On the activities of a multi-purpose cooperative society. LC Card 85-904909
1. Thri Shṭāra Ko-apāreṭibha Mālaṭipārapāsa Sosaiṭi. I. Thri Shṭāra Ko-apāreṭibha Mālaṭipārapāsa Sosaiṭi. II. Title.
HD3540.6.D32 H67 1985

Hosier, Richard. Energy use in rural Kenya : household demand and rural transformation / Richard Hosier. Stockholm : Beijer Institute, Royal Swedish Academy of Sciences ; Uppsala : Scandinavian Institute of African Studies, c1985. xi, 177 p. : ill., map. ; 23 cm. (Energy, environment and development in Africa 0281-8515 . 7) Includes index. Bibliography: p. 153-163. ISBN 91-7106-241-6
1. Energy consumption - Kenya. 2. Rural development - Kenya. 3. Power resources - Kenya. I. Vetenskapsakademiens internationella institut för energi och humanekologi, Beljerinstitutet. II. Title. III. Series.
NYPL [JLD 86-2653]

Hoskin, Robert E. Financial accounting cases / Robert E. Hoskin, John S. Hughes. Chicago : Dryden Press, c1988. 201 p. : ill. ; 28 cm. ISBN 0-03-011778-X (pbk.) LC Card 87-22238 DDC 657 19
1. Accounting - Case studies. I. Hughes, John S. II. Title.
HF5635 .H817 1988

Hosmer, LaRue T. The ethics of management / LaRue Tone Hosmer. Homewood, Ill. : Irwin, 1987. xiii, 185 p. : ill. ; 24 cm. (The Irwin series in management and the behavioral sciences) Includes bibliographies and index. ISBN 0-256-03480-X LC Card 86-81804 DDC 174/.4 19
1. Business ethics. 2. Industrial management - Moral and ethical aspects. I. Title.
HF5387 .H67 1987

Hosomi, Gen, 1929- New approach to vocational training /. Islamabad, Pakistan , 1985-1986. 2 v. : ISBN 92-2-105078-5 (pbk. : v. 1) LC Card 86-221389 DDC 331.25/92/0952 19
HD5715.5.J3 N48 1985

HOSPITAL COMMUNICATION EQUIPMENT INDUSTRY - UNITED STATES.
The Medical communications market. New York, N.Y. , c1972. vi, 163 leaves : LC Card 87-141851
HD9995.H63 U5454 1972

HOSPITAL PHARMACIES.
Strategic marketing of hospital pharmacy products. Tustin, CA, U. S.A. (17722 Irvine Blvd., Tustin 92680) , c1986. iii leaves, 2, 12, 134, 111 p. : LC Card 87-149442 DDC 380.1/456151 19
HD9665.5 .S77 1986

L'Hospitalet a l'inici del S. XVIII . Massana i Llorens, Ma. Pilar. L'Hospitalet de Llobregat , 1985. 116 p. : LC Card 86-230458
HD779.H67 M37 1985

Hospitality management accounting /. Coltman, Michael M., 1930- New York , c1987. xi, 449 p. : ISBN 0-442-21777-3 : LC Card 86-28201 DDC 657/.837 19
HF5686.H75 C53 1987

HOSPITALS - ARKANSAS - STAFF - STATISTICS.
Staffing patterns for manufacturing industries and hospitals /. Little Rock, Ark. [1983?] vi leaves, 249 p. ; LC Card 86-623216 DDC 331.12/57/09767 19
HD5725.A8 S79 1983

HOSPITALS - ITALY - SIENA REGION - HISTORY.
Epstein, Stephan R., 1960- Alle origini della fattoria toscana . Firenze , c1986. 315 p. : LC

Card 87-104355
HD1470.5.I82 S544 1986

Hospodářská politika USA v oblasti energetiky /. Chlumský, Jiří. Praha , 1986. 134 p. ; LC Card 86-215183
HD9502.U52 C526 1986

Hospodářský mechanismus fungování socialistické ekonomiky / mezinárodní kolektiv ; [vedecký redaktor Miloslav Fremer]. Vyd. 1. Praha : Academia, 1985. 238 p. ; 24 cm. On p. facing t.p.: Československá akademie věd. Includes bibliographical references. LC Card 86-203712
1. Communist countries - Economic policy. 2. Industrial management - Communist countries. I. Fremer, Miloslav. II. Československá akademie věd.
HC704 .H65 1985

Hossain, Md. Akhtar. The short-run demand for real money balances in the Bangladesh economy : a theoretical and empirical analysis / by Md. Akhtar Hossain. Bundoora, Vic., Australia : School of Economics, La Trobe University, [1986] 90 p. ; 22 cm. (Discussion paper . no. 6/86) Bibliography: p. 77-90. ISBN 0-85816-784-0 (pbk.) LC Card 86-228714 DDC 332.4/14 19
1. Demand for money - Bangladesh - Mathematical models. I. Series: Economics discussion papers , 86/6. II. Title.
HG1240.6 .H67 1986

HOSTILITIES. see WAR.

Hot money and the politics of debt /. Naylor, R. T., 1945- New York, N.Y. , 1987. 463 p. ; ISBN 0-671-62319-2 LC Card 86-33739 DDC 364.1/68 19
HG3891 .N39 1987

HOT PEPPER INDUSTRY - MEXICO - HISTORY.
Long-Solís, Janet. Capsicum y cultura . México , 1986. 181 p. : ISBN 968-16-2124-7 LC Card 86-221123
HD9235.P462 M65 1986

HOT PEPPERS - MEXICO - HISTORY.
Long-Solís, Janet. Capsicum y cultura . México , 1986. 181 p. : ISBN 968-16-2124-7 LC Card 86-221123
HD9235.P462 M65 1986

Hotel Association of New York City. Uniform system of accounts for hotels. New York, N.Y. (40 W. 38th St., New York 10018) , 1986. x, 139 p. : LC Card 86-220845 DDC 657/.837 19
HF5686.H75 U55 1986

Hotel sales, room rents, and transient room taxes in Utah, 1978-1985 /. Katayama, Leslee. Salt Lake City, Utah (519 Heber Wells Bldg., Salt Lake City 84134) [1985] i, 49 leaves : LC Card 86-620905 DDC 336.2/7864794 19
HJ5715.U62 U85 1985

HOTELS, TAVERNS, ETC. - ACCOUNTING.
Coltman, Michael M., 1930- Hospitality management accounting /. New York , c1987. xi, 449 p. : ISBN 0-442-21777-3 : LC Card 86-28201 DDC 657/.837 19
HF5686.H75 C53 1987

Cote, Raymond. Understanding hospitality accounting I /. East Lansing, Mich. , c1987. p. cm. ISBN 0-86612-035-1 : LC Card 87-15724 DDC 657/.837 19
HF5686.H75 C63 1987

HOTELS, TAVERNS, ETC. - GERMANY (WEST) - RHINELAND-PALATINATE - STATISTICS.
Die Unternehmen des Gastgewerbes in Rheinland-Pfalz 1979 . Bad Ems [1982] 46 p., [2] p. of plates : LC Card 83-207906 DDC 314.3/43 s 338.4/7647/944343021 19
HA1320 .R453 Bd. 294 TX910.G4

HOTELS, TAVERNS, ETC. - SWITZERLAND - EMPLOYEES.
Diedrich, Wolfgang. Arbeitsbedingungen in der Schweizer Hotellerie . Bern , c1984. 185 p. : ISBN 3-258-03437-0 : LC Card 85-113566
HD5718.H82 S953 1984

HOTELS, TAVERNS, ETC. - TAXATION - UTAH.
Katayama, Leslee. Hotel sales, room rents, and transient room taxes in Utah, 1978-1985 /. Salt Lake City, Utah (519 Heber Wells Bldg., Salt Lake City 84134) [1985] i, 49 leaves : LC Card 86-620905 DDC 336.2/7864794 19
HJ5715.U62 U85 1985

HOTELS, TAVERNS, ETC. - UNITED STATES.
McMillon, Bill, 1942- The old lodges & hotels of our national parks /. South Bend, Ind. , 1983. ix, 130 p., [32] p. of plates : ISBN 0-89651-551-6 : LC Card 83-18456 DDC 647/.947301 19
TX909 .M34 1983 ***NYPL [JFF 86-405]***

HOTELS, TAVERNS, ETC. - UNITED STATES - ACCOUNTING.
Uniform system of accounts for hotels. New York, N.Y. (40 W. 38th St., New York 10018) , 1986. x, 139 p. : LC Card 86-220845 DDC 657/.837 19
HF5686.H75 U55 1986

Hotterbeex, M. (Marcel) Les verbos de la F.E.B. en 1979 / M. Hotterbeex. Liège : Département de science politique, Université de Liège, 1982. 20 leaves ; 30 cm. (Etudes et recherches. no 24) LC Card 83-221745
1. Fédération des entreprises de Belgique - Language. 2. Employers' associations - Belgium - Language. I. Series: Etudes et recherches (Université de Liège. Département de science politique) , no 24. II. Title.
HD6948.B4 H67 1982

Hottes, Karlheinz. Becker, Fritz, 1947- Entwicklungseffekte durch Verkehrserschliessung in der Arabischen Republik Jemen . Bochum , 1984. 50 p. : LC Card 84-241945
HE268.7 .B4 1984 ***NYPL [JLH 86-2]***

Hotuba ya Ndugu S.A. ole Saibull, mbunge, waziri wa maliasili na utalii . Ole Saibull, Solomon, 1935- Dar es Salaam, Tanzania , 1979. 56 p. ; LC Card 83-244807
HC885 .O44 1979

Houben, Piet. Ouderenhuisvesting in 'n emancipatieperspectief / Piet Houben. Delft : Delftse Universitaire Pers, 1985. 178 p. : ill. ; 24 cm. (Maatschappelijke participatie van ouderen en volkshuisvesting . 3) Bibliography: 165-168. ISBN 90-6275-118-0 : LC Card 86-149527
1. Aged - Netherlands - Dwellings. 2. Housing policy - Netherlands. I. Title. II. Series.
HD7287.92.N4 H683 1985
NYPL [JLE 86-3902]

Houck, John W., 1951- The Common good and U. S. capitalism /. Lanham, MD , c1987. viii, 425 p. ; ISBN 0-8191-6364-3 (alk. paper) : LC Card 87-8334 DDC 306/.36/0973 19
HD60.5.U5 C665 1987

Hough, George H. Morris, Peter W. G. The anatomy of major projects . Chichester , New York , c1987. p. cm. ISBN 0-471-91551-3 : LC Card 87-8176 DDC 658.4/04 19
HD69.P75 M674 1987

Hough, Richard L. Economic assistance and security : rethinking US policy / by Richard L. Hough. Fort Lesley J. McNair, Washington, D.C. : National Defense University Press : For sale by the Supt. of Docs., U. S. G.P.O., 1982. xii, 139 p. : ill., 1 map ; 23 cm. Includes bibliographical references. Item 378-H-1 008-020-00895-8 LC Card 82-600548 DDC 338.91/73/01724 19
1. Economic assistance, American - Developing countries. 2. United States - National security. 3. United States - Military policy. I. Title.
HC60 .H675 1982

Hours, Henri. Lyon, l'argent, le commerce et la soie /. Lyon , c1986. 138 p. : ISBN 2-904638-63-6 : LC Card 86-184131
HC278.L9 L96 1986

HOURS OF LABOR - ARGENTINA - STATISTICS.
Evolución de la industria manufacturera, 1982-1984. Buenos Aires, República Argentina [1986] 115 p. : LC Card 86-226786
HD4999 .E95 1986

HOURS OF LABOR - AUSTRIA.
Arbeitszeitentwicklung und Arbeitszeitpolitik /. Wien , 1984. 164 p. ; LC Card 85-137865
HD5170 .A72 1984

HOURS OF LABOR - BRAZIL.
Fernandes, Fátima Sobral. Aspectos de transporte urbano na modificação dos horários de trabalho /. Brasília, DF , 1985. 105 p. : LC Card 87-404953 DDC 331.25/72 19
HD5108.2.B6 F47 1985

HOURS OF LABOR - CALIFORNIA - ALAMEDA COUNTY.
McGuire, Nan. Survey of private sector work and family policy . San Francisco , c1986. 41 leaves ; LC Card 87-113810 DDC 331.25/72/0979461 19
HD5126.S4 M38 1986

HOURS OF LABOR - CALIFORNIA - SAN FRANCISCO.
McGuire, Nan. Survey of private sector work and family policy . San Francisco , c1986. 41 leaves ; LC Card 87-113810 DDC 331.25/72/0979461 19
HD5126.S4 M38 1986

HOURS OF LABOR - ECONOMETRIC MODELS.
Schettkat, Ronald. Generelle Arbeitszeitverkürzung . Berlin , 1984. iii, 108 p. : LC Card 84-182608
HD5106 .S3 1984

HOURS OF LABOR - EUROPE.
Flexibility and jobs . Bruxelles [1985] 157, 5 p. : LC Card 87-111122 DDC 331.25 19
HD5764.A6 F44 1985

HOURS OF LABOR, FLEXIBLE - AUSTRIA.
Arbeitszeitentwicklung und Arbeitszeitpolitik /. Wien , 1984. 164 p. ; LC Card 85-137865
HD5170 .A72 1984

HOURS OF LABOR, FLEXIBLE - CALIFORNIA - ALAMEDA COUNTY.
McGuire, Nan. Survey of private sector work and family policy . San Francisco , c1986. 41 leaves ; LC Card 87-113810 DDC 331.25/72/0979461 19
HD5126.S4 M38 1986

HOURS OF LABOR, FLEXIBLE - CALIFORNIA - SAN FRANCISCO.
McGuire, Nan. Survey of private sector work and family policy . San Francisco , c1986. 41 leaves ; LC Card 87-113810 DDC 331.25/72/0979461 19
HD5126.S4 M38 1986

HOURS OF LABOR, FLEXIBLE - EUROPEAN ECONOMIC COMMUNITY COUNTRIES - CONGRESSES.
Neue Arbeits- und Tätigkeitsformen . Dublin, Ireland [Washington, D.C.] c1986. xvi, 339 p. ; ISBN 92-825-6418-5 LC Card 87-408469 DDC 306/.36/094 19
HD6957.E86 N48 1986

HOURS OF LABOR, FLEXIBLE - GERMANY (WEST)
Arbeitskampf um Arbeitszeit . Marburg , c1985. 218 p. : ISBN 3-921630-52-5 LC Card 86-160526
HD5378 .A73 1985

Fels, Gerhard. Mehr Flexibilität am Arbeitsmarkt /. Kiel , 1986. 21 p. ; ISBN 3-925357-37-8 LC Card 87-126264 DDC 331.25/72/0943 19
HD5109.2.G3 F4 1986

Flexible Arbeitszeit gegen starre Sozialsysteme /. Baden-Baden , 1986. 254 p. ; ISBN 3-7890-1213-0 LC Card 87-101055 DDC 331.25/72/0943 19
HD5109.2.G3 F43 1986

Gaugler, Eduard. Flexibilisierung der Beschäftigungsverhältnisse /. Berlin , c1986. 85 p. ; ISBN 3-428-06070-9 LC Card 87-118519 DDC 331.25/72/0943 19
HD5109.2.G3 G38 1986

Marr, Rainer, 1942- Flexibilisierung von Arbeitszeitstrukturen . [Neubiberg? , 1986] 111 leaves : LC Card 87-409556
HD5109.2.G3 M37 1986

Müller, Christoph, 1957- Organisatorische Gestaltung des Job Sharing in der Unternehmung . Köln , c1986. xiii, 404 p. ; ISBN 3-924361-12-6 LC Card 87-114139 DDC 331.25/72 19
HD5110.2.G3 M85 1986

Weissbuch Arbeitszeitverkürzung /. Stuttgart , 1983. 152 p. : ISBN 3-87959-212-8 LC Card 84-163631
HD5108.2.G47 W45 1983

HOURS OF LABOR, FLEXIBLE - GERMANY (WEST) - CASE STUDIES.
Brumlop, Eva. Arbeitsbewertung bei flexiblem Personaleinsatz . Frankfurt , New York , c1986. 229 p. : ISBN 3-593-32744-9 LC Card 86-196323
HD5109.2.G3 B76 1986

Flexible Fertigung und Industriearbeit . Frankfurt Main , New York , c1986. v, 577, iii p. : ISBN 3-593-33648-0 LC Card 86-197535
HD5109.2.G3 F45 1986

HOURS OF LABOR, FLEXIBLE - GERMANY (WEST) - MUNICH.
Möglichkeiten und Probleme der Realisierung flexibler Arbeitszeitstrukturen in Filialen der Bayerischen Vereinsbank München /. München , 1985. 67 p. : LC Card 87-401387 DDC 331.25/72 19
HD5109.2.G32 M866 1985

HOURS OF LABOR, FLEXIBLE - UNITED STATES.
The Changing workplace . Washington, D.C. [Rockville, Md.] , c1986. iv, 140 p. : ISBN 0-87179-910-3 (pbk.) LC Card 86-221689 DDC 331.25/72 19
HD5124 .C46 1986

HOURS OF LABOR - FRANCE.
Drancourt, Michel. La fin du travail /. Paris , c1984. 329 p. : ISBN 2-01-009476-X LC Card 84-222228 DDC 306/.36 19
HD6957.F8 D7 1984 ***NYPL [JLC 86-444]***

HOURS OF LABOR - GERMANY - HISTORY.
Steinisch, Irmgard. Arbeitszeitverkürzung und sozialer Wandel . Berlin , New York , 1986. xiv, 640 p. : ISBN 3-11-010483-0 LC Card 87-110005 DDC 331.25/7/0973 19
HD5119.I52 U67 1986

HOURS OF LABOR - GERMANY - HISTORY - 19TH CENTURY.
Seifert, Eberhard. Industrielle Arbeitszeiten in Deutschland . Wuppertal , 1982. 68, [8] p. : LC Card 87-672398
HD5178 .S44x 1982

HOURS OF LABOR - GERMANY - HISTORY - 20TH CENTURY.
Seifert, Eberhard. Industrielle Arbeitszeiten in Deutschland . Wuppertal , 1982. 68, [8] p. : LC Card 87-672398
HD5178 .S44x 1982

HOURS OF LABOR - GERMANY, WEST.
Weissbuch Arbeitszeitverkürzung /. Stuttgart , 1983. 152 p. : ISBN 3-87959-212-8 LC Card 84-163631
HD5108.2.G47 W45 1983

HOURS OF LABOR - SHIFTS. see **SHIFT SYSTEMS.**

HOURS OF LABOR - SOUTH AFRICA.
Schroeder, Ighsaan. Conditions of employment . Cape Town [1985]- 1 v. (loose-leaf) ; ISBN 0-7992-1002-1 (loose-leaf) LC Card 86-232933 DDC 331.2/0968 19
HD4927.S6 S37 1985

South Africa. Commission of Inquiry into the Possible Introduction of a Five-Day Working Week in the Mining Industry. Report of the Commission of Inquiry into the Possible Introduction of a Five-Day Working Week in the Mining Industry of the Republic of South Africa. [Pretoria] , 1977. iii, 194 p. : LC Card 85-148007
HD5119.M5982 S68 1977

HOURS OF LABOR - SOVIET UNION.
Maksimov, A. L. (Alekseĭ L′vovich) Rabochee i svobodnoe vremia v usloviiakh razvitogo sotsializma /. Moskva , 1981. 95 p. ; LC Card 82-104233
HD5195 .M34 1981

HOURS OF LABOR - SWEDEN - ECONOMETRIC MODELS.
Åberg, Yngve. The impact of working hours and other factors on production and employment /. Aldershot, Hants, England , Brookfield, Vt., U. S.A. , c1987. viii, 166 p. : ISBN 0-566-05480-9 : LC Card 87-8393 DDC 331.25/7/09485 19
HD5202 .A64 1987

HOURS OF LABOR - UNITED STATES.
The Changing workplace . Washington, D.C. [Rockville, Md.] , c1986. iv, 140 p. : ISBN 0-87179-910-3 (pbk.) LC Card 86-221689 DDC 331.25/72 19
HD5124 .C46 1986

United States. Wage and Hour and Public Contracts Divisions. Laundry and cleaning services. [Washington, 1969] iii, 31, A-ii, A-67p. ***NYPL [JLF 86-586]***

HOURS OF LABOR - UNITED STATES - HISTORY.
Steinisch, Irmgard. Arbeitszeitverkürzung und sozialer Wandel . Berlin , New York , 1986. xiv, 640 p. : ISBN 3-11-010483-0 LC Card 87-110005 DDC 331.25/7/0973 19
HD5119.I52 U67 1986

HOURS OF LABOR - VERMONT - STATISTICS.
Employment and earnings, 1980-1985 . Montpelier, Vt. [1986] ii, 79 leaves : LC Card 86-622186 DDC 331.12/5/09743021 19
HD5725.V5 E46 1986

HOURS ON LABOR, FLEXIBLE - GERMANY (WEST)
Tınar, Mustafa Yaşar, 1955- Humanisierung der Arbeit und Produktivität . Frankfurt am Main , New York , c1986. xiii, 296 p. : ISBN 3-8204-9542-8 LC Card 86-233418
HF5549.5.J63 T55 1986

HOUSE BUYING - UNITED STATES.
DeBat, Don. The mortgage manual . Chicago , c1986. ix, 154 p. ; ISBN 0-8092-4890-5 (pbk.) : LC Card 86-23972 DDC 332.7/22 19
HG2040.5.U5 D423 1986

The Kiplinger/Changing times guide to buying and selling a home /. Washington, DC , New York, NY , c1987. iii, 311 p. : ISBN 0-938721-02-X (pbk.) : LC Card 87-167806 DDC 643/.12 19
HD1379 .K52 1987

Knox, Albert H. What homebuyers should know about buying a home /. New York , c1987. vii, 192 p. : ISBN 0-533-06883-5 : LC Card 85-91377 DDC 643/.12 19
HD1379 .K656 1987

HOUSE CONSTRUCTION - UNITED STATES - TECHNOLOGICAL INNOVATIONS.
Technology, trade, and the U.S residential construction industry . Washington, D.C. , 1986. x, 91 p. : LC Card 86-600575 DDC 338.4/769083/0973 19
HD9715.U52 T43 1986

HOUSE DRAINAGE. see **SANITATION; SEWERAGE.**

HOUSE NAMES - ESTONIA - REGISTERS.
Eesti ala mõisate nimestik /. Tallinn , 1981. 191 p. ; LC Card 82-143283
HD1329.E75 E37 1981
NYPL [JFD 86-6806]

The house of Getty /. Miller, Russell. London , 19. 361 p., [32] p. of plates : ISBN 0-7181-2601-7 : LC Card 86-222703 DDC 332/.092/4 B 19
HD9570.G4 M55 1986b

The house of Getty /. Miller, Russell. South Yarmouth, Ma. [1987], c1985. 669 p. [16] p. of plates : ISBN 1-555-04230-9 LC Card 86-24259 DDC 332/.092/4 B 19
HD9570.G4 M55 1987

House of Representatives (U. S.) see **United States. Congress. House.**

HOUSE PURCHASING. see **HOUSE BUYING.**

House report / 99th Congress, 2d session . (99-1009) United States. Congress. House. Committee on Science and Technology. Prospects for sustainable development in Sub-Saharan Africa . Washington , 1986. vii, 88 p. ; LC Card 86-603140 DDC 338.967 19
HD2117 .U48 1986

House Research Agency report .
(86-B) Pierce, Brad. The timber industry in interior Alaska . [Juneau] [1986] 65 p. ; LC Card 86-621755 DDC 338.1/7498/09798 19
HD9757.A7 P54 1986

(86-C) Livey, Jay. The effect of state income tax policy on the development of marginal oil fields . [Juneau] [1986] vii leaves, 52 p., [17] leaves ; LC Card 86-622190 DDC 333.8/232/09798 19
HD9560.8.U53 A445 1986

HOUSE SELLING.
Anderson, Georgia. Equity sharing /. Chicago , c1986. xiv, 136 p. : ISBN 0-8092-4836-0 (pbk.) : LC Card 86-24083 DDC 332.63/24 19
HD1382.5 .A54 1986

Bloch, H. I. Sonny. Inside real estate . New York , c1987. xx, 375 p. ; ISBN 1-555-84030-2 LC Card 86-28303 DDC 333.33/8 19
HD1379 .B515 1987

Boroson, Warren. Sell your own home! . Tucson, AZ , c1987. 238 p. : ISBN 0-89586-571-8 LC Card 87-4020 DDC 333.33/8 19
HD1379 .B645 1987

Buying or selling a home . Chicago, Ill. (4025 W. Peterson Ave., Chicago 60646) , c1986. 31 p. : LC Card 86-209128 DDC 343.7305/46 347.303546 19
HJ4182.A5 B89 1986

Chaney, Dale. Selling your house without a broker . Chicago , c1986. 98 p. : ISBN 0-8092-4833-6 (pbk.) : LC Card 86-24043 DDC 333.33/8 19
HD1379 .C48 1986

Kennedy, David W. The condominium and cooperative apartment buyer's and seller's guide /. New York , c1987. viii, 312 p. : ISBN 0-471-62732-1 (pbk.) LC Card 87-21548 DDC 333.33/8 19
HD1390.5 .K46 1987

Platt, Barbara. Residential real estate . Austin, Tex. , c1987. 206 p. : ISBN 0-941089-17-7 (lib. bdg.) LC Card 87-60697 DDC 332.63/243 19
HD1379 .P57 1987

Selling your home for the best price in the shortest time . [Norwell, Mass.] , c1986. 48 leaves : LC Card 87-150628 DDC 333.33/8 19
HD1379 .S36 1986

Wickman, Floyd. Successful strategies for real estate agents . Dubuque, Iowa , c1987. xii, 226 p. ; ISBN 0-8403-4185-7 (pbk.) : LC Card 86-82782 DDC 333.33/068/8 19
HD1382 .W53 1987

HOUSE SELLING - MARYLAND - STATISTICS.
Owen, Gail T. Residential property sales in Maryland . Baltimore, Md. (2225 N. Charles St., Baltimore 21218-5767) [1985] iv, 79 leaves : LC Card 86-622370 DDC 333.33/8 19
HD266.M3 O9 1985

HOUSE SELLING - UNITED STATES.
The Kiplinger/Changing times guide to buying and selling a home /. Washington, DC , New York, NY , c1987. iii, 311 p. : ISBN 0-938721-02-X (pbk.) : LC Card 87-167806 DDC 643/.12 19
HD1379 .K52 1987

HOUSE STYLE. see **INDUSTRIAL DESIGN COORDINATION.**

House, Verne W. Trends in the Montana economy and taxation / by Verne W. House and Douglas J. Young. Bozeman : Montana Cooperative Extension Service, Montana State University, [1986] 19 p. : ill. ; 28 cm. (Bulletin / Montana Cooperative Extension Service, Montana State University . 1343) "Prepared for 'Taxation and the Montana economy,' a conference sponsored by Montana State University and the University of Montana, Helena, MT September 5-6, 1986." LC Card 87-620963 DDC 330.9786/033 19
1. Montana - Economic conditions. 2. Economic forecasting - Montana. 3. Taxation - Montana. I. Young, Douglas J. II. Series: Bulletin (Montana State University (Bozeman). Cooperative Extension Service) , 1343. III. Title.
HC107.M9 H68 1986

House, William J. Population, poverty, and basic needs in southern Sudan : a review of the evidence / by William J. House. [Juba, Sudan : UNFPA/ILO Project SUD/79/PO6: "Population and Human Resources Development and Planning in Southern Sudan", 1985] vi, 94 leaves ; 30 cm. (Working report / UNFPA/ILO Project SUD/79/PO6 "Population and Human Resources Development and Planning in Southern Sudan . no. 4) "July 1985." "September 1985"--Cover. Bibliography: leaves 89-94. LC Card 86-981127 DDC 338.9629 19
1. Southern Region, Sudan - Economic conditions. 2. Basic needs - Sudan - Southern Region. 3. Southern Region (Sudan) - Population. I. Series: Working report / UNFPA/ILO Project SUD/79/PO6 "Population and Human Resources Development and Planning in Southern Sudan , no. 4. II. Title.
HC835.Z7 S684 1985

Household and economy . Nerlove, Marc, 1933-

Boston , 1987. xiii, 155 p. : ISBN 0-12-515752-5 LC Card 86-10764 DDC 304.6/32 19
HB901 .N47 1987 ***NYPL [JLE 87-1715]***

Household and family projections. Interim household and family projections for Canada, provinces, and territories to 2006 =. [Ottawa] [1987] 67 p. ; LC Card 87-162270 DDC 304.6/2/0971021 19
HA745 .I62 1987

Household and population projections for Canadian provinces and territories, 1981-2046. Edmonton, Alta., Canada : DemoSystems, c1984. 53 p. ; 21 x 28 cm. Bibliography: p. 5. LC Card 84-670146 DDC 312/.8/0971 19
1. Population forecasting - Canada - Statistics. 2. Households - Canada - Statistics - Forecasting. 3. Canada - Population - Statistics. I. DemoSystems (Firm).
HA745 .H69 1984 ***NYPL [JLF 86-642]***

HOUSEHOLD APPLIANCES - INDIA - ENERGY CONSERVATION.
Mayer, Hans, 1951- Energie für die Armen? . Saarbrücken , Fort Lauderdale , 1984. 195 p. : ISBN 3-88156-288-5 : LC Card 85-199309
HD9502.I42 M38 1984

Household economy and urban development . Kuznesof, Elizabeth Anne. Boulder , 1986. 216 p. : ISBN 0-8133-7181-3 : LC Card 85-31491 DDC 307.7/64/098161 19
HC188.S3 K89 1986 ***NYPL [JLE 87-711]***

HOUSEHOLD ELECTRONICS INDUSTRY - SWITZERLAND - DIRECTORIES.
Interferex 86 (Basel, Switzerland) Interferex 86, Intertable . Basel, Schweiz [1986] 284 p., [6] p. of plates : LC Card 87-409294 DDC 381/.18 19
HF5474.S92 B365 1986

Household energy in South Asia /. Leach, Gerald. London ; New York : xii, 111 p. : ISBN 1-85166-125-5 (pbk.) : LC Card 87-13177 DDC 333.79 19
HD9502.S613 H68 1987

HOUSEHOLD EQUIPMENT. see **HOUSEHOLD APPLIANCES.**

The Household expenditure survey, 1983-1984. Mahé, Seychelles : Republic of Seychelles, Statistics Section, [1986] 74 p. : ill. ; 30 cm. "Carried out by Statistics Division"--P. 7. LC Card 86-981214 DDC 339.4/7/09696 19
1. Cost and standard of living - Seychelles - Statistics. I. Seychelles. Statistics Division.
HD7068.8 .H68 1986

HOUSEHOLD EXPENSES. see **COST AND STANDARD OF LIVING.**

HOUSEHOLD GOODS. see **HOUSEHOLD APPLIANCES.**

Household Goods Carriers Bureau (U. S.) Transportation fact book. Alexandria, VA (1611 Duke St., Alexandria 22314-3482) , c1987. iii, 75 p. : LC Card 87-155218 DDC 388.3/2/0973021 19
HE5623 .T67 1987

HOUSEHOLD MANAGEMENT. see **HOME ECONOMICS.**

Household population by religion of head of household, up to C.D. block and town level, series 14, Meghalaya : paper 1 of 1985 / J. Tayeng (Director of Census Operations, Meghalaya). New Delhi : Controller of Publications, 1986. iii, 70 p. ; 31 cm. At head of title: Census of India, 1981. "PRG.507 (Meghalaya)/300-1985 (DSK-II)"--P. [4] of cover. LC Card 87-901361 DDC 304.6/0954/164021 19
1. Households - India - Meghalaya - Statistics. 2. Meghalaya (India) - Population - Statistics. 3. Meghalaya (India) - Religion - Statistics. 4. Meghalaya (India) - Census, 1981. 5. India - Census, 1981. I. Tayeng, J. II. India. Office of the Director of Census Operations, Meghalaya. III. Title: Census of India, 1981.
HA4587.M43 H68 1986

Household population by religion of head of household, upto C.D. block and town level, series 31, Mizoram : paper 1 of 1985 / P. Lalnithanga (Director of Census Operations, Mizoram). Delhi : Printed by the Manager, Govt. of India Press, Shimla for the Controller of Publications, 1986. xiii, 17 p. ; 30 cm. At head of title: Census of India, 1981. Statistical tables. "PRG.3.81 (Mizoram)/300-8985 (DSK.II)"--P. [4] of cover. LC Card 87-900232 DDC 304.6/0954/166021 19
1. Households - India - Mizoram - Statistics. 2. Mizoram (India) - Population - Statisitcs. 3. Mizoram (India) - Religion - Statistics. 4. Mizoram (India) - Census, 1981. 5. India - Census, 1981. I. Lannithanga, p., 1928-. II. India. Director of Census Operations, Mizoram. III. Title: Census of India, 1981.
HA4587.M58 H68 1986

HOUSEHOLD SCIENCE. see **HOME ECONOMICS.**

HOUSEHOLD SURVEYS.
Pantelides, Edith A. El hogar como unidad de análisis de los datos censales . Santiago de Chile , 1972. ii, 48 p. : LC Card 83-169482
HA755 .U53 no. 147 HB849.49

HOUSEHOLD SURVEYS - ARGENTINA - BELÉN (CATAMARCA)
Pantelides, Edith A. El hogar como unidad de análisis de los datos censales . Santiago de Chile , 1972. ii, 48 p. : LC Card 83-169482
HA755 .U53 no. 147 HB849.49

HOUSEHOLD SURVEYS - BRAZIL - RIO GRANDE DO SUL.
O Emprego no Rio Grande do Sul . Porto Alegre , 1985. 163 p. : LC Card 85-207909
HD5755.R54 E46 1985

HOUSEHOLD SURVEYS - CHILE.
Problemas metodológicos de una encuesta rural en Chile y estructura del empleo /. [Santiago, Chile] [c1983] ii, 27 leaves ; LC Card 84-225128
HD1531.C5 P76 1983

HOUSEHOLD SURVEYS - COLOMBIA.
Metodología de la encuesta nacional de hogares. Bogotá, D.E., Colombia [1985] 64 p. : LC Card 85-240042
HB849.49 .M48 1985

HOUSEHOLD SURVEYS - COSTA RICA.
Encuesta nacional de hogares, empleo y desempleo . San José, Costa Rica , 1982. xi, xi, 86 p. ; LC Card 82-202317
HD5734.A6 E53 1982

HOUSEHOLD SURVEYS - COSTA RICA - GRECIA.
Pantelides, Edith A. El hogar como unidad de análisis de los datos censales . Santiago de Chile , 1972. ii, 48 p. : LC Card 83-169482
HA755 .U53 no. 147 HB849.49

HOUSEHOLD SURVEYS - ETHIOPIA.
The Rural integrated household survey programme . Addis Abeba [1983] 52 leaves ; LC Card 86-980701 DDC 307.7/2/0723 19
HB2542.A3 R87 1983

Rural labour force survey, April 1981-April 1982 /. Addis Ababa , 1985. xii, 170 p. ; LC Card 86-981178 DDC 331.1/0963 19
HD5839.7.A6 R87 1985

HOUSEHOLD SURVEYS - GREAT BRITAIN.
Todd, Jean Elizabeth. Changing the definition of a household . London , 1986. viii, 43 p. : ISBN 0-11-691071-2 (pbk.) : LC Card 87-132272
HB849.49 .T63 1986

HOUSEHOLD SURVEYS - GRENADA.
Burpee, C. Gaye. 1985 household survey of Grenada . Ann Arbor, Mich. , 1986. 168 p. : ISBN 0-87944-317-0 (pbk.) LC Card 86-217405 DDC 339.4/1/0723 19
HD7009.9.Z8 G843 1986

HOUSEHOLD SURVEYS - UNITED STATES - RESPONSE RATE.
Cleveland, Robert W. Income nonresponses . [Washington] [1985] iv, 87 p. : LC Card 85-603179 DDC 339.2/2/0973021 19
HC110.I5 C44 1985

HOUSEHOLD SURVEYS - URUGUAY.
Apezechea, Héctor J., 1937- Tasas de participación y relaciobes multivariadas a partir e la información de la encuesta de hogares del segundo semestre de 1978 . [Montevideo, Uruguay] , 1980. 12, [44] leaves ; LC Card 86-157658
HD5762.A6 A64 1980

HOUSEHOLDS.
Pflaumer, Peter, 1947- Bevölkerung, Haushalte, Konsum . Frankfurt , New York , c1986. iv, 218 p. : ISBN 3-593-33674-X LC Card 87-408990 DDC 339.4/7 19
HB849.53 .P49 1986

HOUSEHOLDS - AFRICA.
Feeding African cities . Bloomington , c1987. x, 249 p. ; ISBN 0-253-32102-6 LC Card 86-46323 DDC 338.1/9/6 19
HD9017.A2 F44 1987

HOUSEHOLDS - AFRICA, SUB-SAHARAN - ADDRESSES, ESSAYS, LECTURES.
Understanding Africa's rural households and farming systems /. Boulder , 1986. xiv, 234 p. : ISBN 0-8133-7175-9 : LC Card 85-32318 DDC 338.1/0967 19
HD1476.A357 U53 1986
NYPL [JLE 86-4336]

HOUSEHOLDS - ARGENTINA - CÓRDOBA (PROVINCE) - STATISTICS.
Compendio estadístico /. Córdoba, República Argentina [1984] 110 leaves : LC Card 87-400414 DDC 304.6/0982/54021 19
HA958.C6 C64 1984

HOUSEHOLDS - BRAZIL.
Calsing, Elizeu F. Extensão e características da pobreza no Brasil /. Brasília , 1983. 44, [1] p. : LC Card 86-178277
HC190.P6 C29 1983

HOUSEHOLDS - BRAZIL - SÃO PAULO (STATE) - HISTORY.
Kuznesof, Elizabeth Anne. Household economy and urban development . Boulder , 1986. 216 p. : ISBN 0-8133-7181-3 : LC Card 85-31491 DDC 307.7/64/098161 19
HC188.S3 K89 1986 ***NYPL [JLE 87-711]***

HOUSEHOLDS - BURUNDI - MUGINA (COMMUNE)
Bahizi, Joseph. Monographie d'unités domestiques. [Bujumbura] [1985] 41 leaves ; LC Card 86-980542
HC880.Z7 M843 1985

HOUSEHOLDS - CANADA.
Che-Alford, Janet. Mortgagor [sic] households in Canada . Ottawa , c1986. 100 p. : ISBN 0-660-52986-6 (pbk.) : LC Card 86-202749 DDC 332.7/22/0971 19
HD7287.82.C2 C48 1986

Fallis, George, 1947- Housing economics /. Toronto [Ont.] , Boston , c1985. 241 p. : ISBN 0-409-82940-4 LC Card 85-177894 DDC 333.33/8 19
HD7305.A3 F35 1985 ***NYPL [JLE 87-2573]***

HOUSEHOLDS - CANADA - FORECASTING - STATISTICS.
Interim household and family projections for Canada, provinces, and territories to 2006 =. [Ottawa] [1987] 67 p. ; LC Card 87-162270 DDC 304.6/2/0971021 19
HA745 .I62 1987

HOUSEHOLDS - CANADA - STATISTICS.
Family characteristics and labour force activity . Ottawa , c1986. xxii, 131 p. ; ISBN 0-660-52240-3 (pbk.) : LC Card 86-206978
HD5728 .F36 1986

HOUSEHOLDS - CANADA - STATISTICS - FORECASTING.
Household and population projections for Canadian provinces and territories, 1981-2046. Edmonton, Alta., Canada , c1984. 53 p. ; LC Card 84-670146 DDC 312/.8/0971 19
HA745 .H69 1984 ***NYPL [JLF 86-642]***

HOUSEHOLDS - DATA PROCESSING.
Mason, Andrew, 1947- HOMES . Honolulu, Hawaii [1987] x, 114 p. : ISBN 0-86638-102-3 (pbk.) : LC Card 87-22288 DDC 304.6/028/55329 19
HB849.49 .M38 1987

HOUSEHOLDS - DOMINICAN REPUBLIC - STATISTICS.
Censo nacional de población y vivienda, 1981 . Santo Domingo, Distrito Nacional, República Dominicana , 1985- v. <1 > : LC Card 86-223758
HA886.5 1981c

HOUSEHOLDS - ECONOMIC ASPECTS.
Maierbeck, Marianne. Nutzen- und Zielprobleme privater Haushalte . Berlin , 1978. 203 p. : ISBN 3-428-04220-4 : LC Card 79-356181
TX7 .B4 Heft 13 HB201
NYPL [JLE 86-3431]

HOUSEHOLDS - ECONOMIC ASPECTS - GERMANY (WEST)
Demographische Probleme der Haushaltsökonomie /. Bochum , 1986. vii, 212

p. : ISBN 3-88339-534-X LC Card 87-137970 DDC 339.4/1/0943 19
HD7029 .D37 1986

Households, employment, and gender . England, Paula. New York , c1986. ix, 237 p. : ISBN 0-202-30322-5 (lib. bdg.) LC Card 85-18628 DDC 304.6 19
HQ536 .E54 1986 *NYPL [JLE 86-2828]*

HOUSEHOLDS - GERMANY (WEST)
Krause, Detlef. Einkommensquellen und Lebenschancen . Berlin , c1986. 189 p. : ISBN 3-428-06114-4 LC Card 87-130932 DDC 339.2/2/0943 19
HC290.5.I5 K7 1986

Leben im Jahr 2000 und danach . Berlin , c1984. 213 p. : ISBN 3-7605-8571-X LC Card 85-128359
HB3595 .L43 1984

HOUSEHOLDS - GERMANY (WEST) - ENERGY CONSUMPTION.
Suding, Paul H. Ökonomische Ansätze zur Analyse des Energieverbrauchs der Haushalte für Rauwärmzwecke /. München , 1984. ix, 252, 10 p. : ISBN 3-486-28661-7 LC Card 84-209002
HD9502.G42 S8 1984

HOUSEHOLDS - GREAT BRITAIN.
Todd, Jean Elizabeth. Changing the definition of a household . London , 1986. viii, 43 p. : ISBN 0-11-691071-2 (pbk.) : LC Card 87-132272
HB849.49 .T63 1986

HOUSEHOLDS - HAITI - STATISTICS.
Résultats préliminaires du recensement général (septembre 1982) /. [Port-au-Prince] [1982 or 1983] vii, 60 p., [1] leaf of plates : LC Card 84-138275 DDC 304.6/097294/021 19
HD7316.A3 R47 1982 *NYPL [JLF 86-1280]*

HOUSEHOLDS - HUNGARY - STATISTICAL SERVICES.
A Magyar háztartásstatisztikai megfigyelés módszertana /. Budapest , 1986. 59 p. ; LC Card 87-408579
HA37.H92 M34 1986

HOUSEHOLDS - HUNGARY - STATISTICS.
Csernák, Józsefné. A családok és háztartások előreszámítása, 1981-2001 /. Budapest , 1985. 125 p. : LC Card 86-166603
HA1201 .A64 no. 59 HA1205

HOUSEHOLDS - INDIA - MEGHALAYA - STATISTICS.
Household population by religion of head of household, up to C.D. block and town level, series 14, Meghalaya . New Delhi , 1986. iii, 70 p. ; LC Card 87-901361 DDC 304.6/0954/164021 19
HA4587.M43 H68 1986

HOUSEHOLDS - INDIA - MIZORAM - STATISTICS.
Household population by religion of head of household, upto C.D. block and town level, series 31, Mizoram . Delhi , 1986. xiii, 17 p. ; LC Card 87-900232 DDC 304.6/0954/166021 19
HA4587.M58 H68 1986

HOUSEHOLDS - INDIA - WEST BENGAL - STATISTICS.
Tables on houses and disabled population, series 23, West Bengal /. Delhi , 1986. v, 128 p. ; LC Card 87-900630
HA4587.W47 T33 1986

HOUSEHOLDS - MATHEMATICALS MODELS.
Modelling household formation and dissolution /. Oxford [Oxfordshire] , New York , c1987. p. cm. ISBN 0-19-829500-6 : LC Card 87-18581 DDC 306.8/5/0724 19
HB849.49 .M63 1987

HOUSEHOLDS - PENNSYLVANIA - HISTORY - 18TH CENTURY.
Schweitzer, Mary M. Custom and contract . New York , 1987. xii, 271 p. : ISBN 0-231-06288-5 LC Card 87-8003 DDC 338.9748 19
HC107.P4 S417 1987

HOUSEHOLDS - PHILIPPINES - BAYAWAN.
Socio-economic and marketing study of municipal fishing households, Bayawan, Negros Oriental, Philippines. Manila, Philippines [1983] vii, 94, 7 p. : LC Card 86-225887
HD8039.F652 P67 1983

HOUSEHOLDS - SOUTH AFRICA - PIETERMARITZBURG - STATISTICS.
Martins, J. H. Income and expenditure patterns of urban Indian households in Pietermaritzburg, 1985 /. Pretoria , 1986. xi, 126 p. : ISBN 0-908408-60-9 (pbk.) LC Card 87-140863 DDC 658.8/3968 s 339.4/1/0968475 19
HC517.S7 S48 no. 130, pt. 5 HD7064.4.Z8P54

HOUSEHOLDS - SOUTH AFRICA - PRETORIA - STATISTICS.
Martins, J. H. Income and expenditure patterns of urban black multiple households in Pretoria, 1985 /. Pretoria , 1986. xi, 128 p. : ISBN 0-908408-57-9 (pbk.) LC Card 86-220725 DDC 658.8/3968 s 339.4/1/0968235 19
HC517.S7 S48 no. 130, pt. 2 HD7064.4.Z8P74

HOUSEHOLDS - SOUTH ASIA - ENERGY CONSUMPTION.
Leach, Gerald. Household energy in South Asia /. London ; New York : xii, 111 p. : ISBN 1-85166-125-5 (pbk.) : LC Card 87-13177 DDC 333.79 19
HD9502.S613 H68 1987

HOUSEHOLDS - TANZANIA.
Collier, Paul. Labour and poverty in rural Tanzania . Oxford [Oxfordhire] , New York , 1986. vii, 143 p. : ISBN 0-19-828531-0 : LC Card 86-5303 DDC 307.1/4/09678 19
HN797.Z9 C625 1986 *NYPL [JLD 87-511]*

HOUSEHOLDS - TRINIDAD AND TOBAGO - STATISTICS.
1980 population and housing census . Trinidad and Tobago , c1986. 15 p. : LC Card 87-402815 DDC 304.6/097298/3 19
HA867 .A4 1980b

HOUSEHOLDS - UNITED STATES.
England, Paula. Households, employment, and gender . New York , c1986. ix, 237 p. : ISBN 0-202-30322-5 (lib. bdg.) LC Card 85-18628 DDC 304.6 19
HQ536 .E54 1986 *NYPL [JLE 86-2828]*

HOUSEHOLDS - UNITED STATES - CONGRESSES.
Survey of income and program participation and related longitudinal surveys, 1984 . [Washington, D.C.] , 1985. ix, 201 p. : LC Card 85-601676 DDC 339.2/3/0973 19
HC110.I5 S89 1985 *NYPL [JLF 86-1641]*

HOUSEHOLDS - URUGUAY - STATISTICS.
Encuesta de gastos e ingresos de los hogares, 1982-1983 . [Montevideo] [1986] 76, 96, 120 p. : LC Card 87-403151 DDC 339.4/2/09895 19
HD7020 .E53 1986

HOUSEHOLDS - WASHINGTON METROPOLITAN AREA - STATISTICS.
Growth trends to the year 2010. Washington, D.C. , c1986. i, 32 p. : LC Card 87-129483 DDC 304.6/2/09753021 19
HA305 .G76 1986

HOUSEHOLDS - ZAMBIA - CHIBALE (SERENJE DISTRICT)
Farming systems and family economy in Chibale, Serenje District. Mpika, Zambia [1985?] 74 p. : LC Card 86-981248 DDC 338.1/096894 19
HD1476.Z352 C454 1985

HOUSEHOLDS - ZAMBIA - NDUNYA.
Farming system and family economy in Ndunya, Chinsali District. Mpika, Zambia [1985?] 45 leaves, [12] leaves of plates : LC Card 86-981252 DDC 338.1/096894 19
HD1476.Z352 N384 1985

HOUSEKEEPING. see **HOME ECONOMICS.**

Houseman, Gerald L. State and local government : the new battleground / Gerald L. Houseman. Englewood Cliffs, N.J. : Prentice-Hall, c1986. xvi, 272 p. : ill. ; 23 cm. Includes bibliographies and index. ISBN 0-13-843368-2 (pbk.) LC Card 85-16981 DDC 320.973 19
1. State governments. 2. Local government - United States. 3. Intergovernmental fiscal relations - United States. 4. Federal government - United States. I. Title.
JK2408 .H79 1986 *NYPL [JLE 86-2916]*

HOUSES. see **ARCHITECTURE, DOMESTIC.**

HOUSES, APARTMENT. see **APARTMENT HOUSES.**

HOUSES, DEMOUNTABLE. see **PREFABRICATED HOUSES.**

HOUSES, PREFABRICATED. see **PREFABRICATED HOUSES.**

HOUSEWIVES.
Chabaud-Rychter, Danielle. Espace et temps du travail domestique /. Paris , 1985. 156 p. ; ISBN 2-86563-127-3 LC Card 86-165713
HD6055 .C45 1985

Houseworker's handbook. [Cambridge, Mass.] (c/o Women's Center, 46 Pleasant St., Cambridge 02139) [1974] 81 p. : LC Card 87-110536
HD6073.H84 H68 1974

HOUSEWIVES - INDIA - SIMLA - SOCIAL CONDITIONS.
Sharma, Ursula, 1941- Women's work, class, and the urban household . London , New York , 1986. 213 p. ; ISBN 0-422-79320-5 : LC Card 86-11296 DDC 305.4/3 19
HQ759 .S4616 1986 *NYPL [JLD 87-1281]*

HOUSEWIVES - ITALY.
Petrillo, Giovanna, 1952- Produttività e improduttività del lavoro domestico . Bologna , 1985. 139 p. ; LC Card 86-132212
HD8039.H842 I87 1985

HOUSEWIVES - NORWAY.
Avdem, Anna Jorunn, 1952- Oppe først og sist i seng . Oslo , 1985. 190 p. : ISBN 82-00-07512-5 LC Card 86-175305
HD8039.H842 N82 1985

HOUSEWIVES - UNITED STATES.
Blau, Francine D. The economics of women, men, and work /. Englewood Cliffs, N.J. , c1986. xiv, 365 p. : ISBN 0-13-233719-3 LC Card 85-30746 DDC 305.3/0973 19
HQ1426 .B62 1986 *NYPL [JLE 86-4254]*

Follis, Anne Bowen, 1947- I'm not a women's libber, but--and other confessions of a Christian feminist /. Nashville , c1981. 128 p. ; ISBN 0-687-18687-0 LC Card 81-1241
HQ1426 .F75 *NYPL [JLD 85-1976]*

Leghorn, Lisa. What's a wife worth? /. Somerville, Mass. [198-] 8 p. : LC Card 87-111053 DDC 331.2/8164/0973 19
HD4966.H842 U64 1980z

HOUSEWIVES - UNITED STATES - ECONOMIC CONDITIONS.
Minton, Michael H. What is a wife worth? . New York , 1984, c1983. 192 p. ; ISBN 0-07-042414-4 (pbk.) : LC Card 84-11221 DDC 331.4/28164/0973 19
HD4966.H842 U65 1984
NYPL [JLD 87-12]

Houseworker's handbook. [Cambridge, Mass.] (c/o Women's Center, 46 Pleasant St., Cambridge 02139) : [s.n., 1974] 81 p. : ill. ; 22 cm. Cover title. Prepared by Betsy Warrior, Lisa Leghorn, and others. LC Card 87-110536
1. Housewives. 2. Wages - Housewives. 3. Home economics - Valuation. 4. Sexual division of labor. I. Warrior, Betsy. II. Leghorn, Lisa.
HD6073.H84 H68 1974

Housing a divided community /. Brett, Charles Edward Bainbridge, 1928- Dublin, Ireland , 1986. xi, 171 p., [32] p. of plates : ISBN 0-906980-49-6 : LC Card 86-222853 DDC 363.5/09416 19
HD7335.5.A3 B74 1986

HOUSING - ALGERIA.
Boubekeur, Sid, 1952- L'habitat en Algérie . Lyon , c1986. 256 p. : ISBN 2-7297-0272-5 : LC Card 86-217640
HD7372.4.A3 B68 1986

HOUSING - ALGERIA - ALGIERS.
Benatia, Farouk. L'appropriation de l'espace à Alger après 1962 /. Alger , c1978. 189 p. : LC Card 81-143253
HD7372.4.A4 B45 1978

Housing America in the 1980s /. Adams, John S., 1938- New York , c1987. p. cm. ISBN 0-87154-003-7 : LC Card 86-42950 DDC 363.5/0973 19
HD7293 .A625 1987

Housing America's poor / edited by Peter D. Salins. Chapel Hill : University of North Carolina Press, c1987. ix, 203 p. ; 24 cm. (Urban and regional policy and development studies) Includes bibliographies and index. ISBN 0-8078-1738-4 LC

Card 86-40449 DDC 363.5/8 19
1. Poor - Housing - United States. 2. Housing policy - United States. 3. Public housing - United States. I. Salins, Peter D. II. Series.
HD7287.96.U5 H68 1987

Housing and neighborhoods : theoretical and empirical contributions / edited by Willem Van Vliet-- ... [et al.]. New York : Greenwood Press, 1987. xii, 319 p. : ill. ; 25 cm. (Contributions in sociology, 0084-9278 . no. 66) Includes bibliographies and indexes. ISBN 0-313-25459-1 (lib. bdg. : alk. paper) LC Card 87-7527 DDC 307.3/36 19
1. Housing. 2. Neighborhood. I. Van Vliet, Willem. II. Series.
HD7287.5 .H47 1987

HOUSING AND STATE. see **HOUSING POLICY.**

Housing and the environment /. Massa, Alison K. Sacramento, CA (921 10th St., Sacramento 95814-2774) [1985?] 2 v. : LC Card 87-621018 DDC 363.7 19
HD266.C2 M37 1985

Housing and town and country planning in the United Kingdom dependencies. Great Britain. Central Office of Information. Reference Division. [London, 1960] 51 p. LC Card 72-222605
HD7333.A3 A54 1960b

Housing and Urban Development Corporation. HUDCO's initiatives for IYSH. New Delhi : Housing and Urban Development Corp., [1987?] 49 p. : ill. (chiefly col.) ; 23 x 29 cm. Implementation of the International Year of Shelter for the Homeless program by Housing and Urban Development Corporation. LC Card 87-902550 DDC 363.5/8 19
1. Housing - India. 2. Urban renewal - India. 3. Homelessness - India. I. United Nations/International Year of Shelter for the Homeless. II. Title.
HD7287.96.I4 H67 1987

HOUSING - ARGENTINA.
Funciones y servicios de competencia municipal /. Córdoba, República Argentina , 1984. 94 leaves ; LC Card 87-121632 DDC 352.082 19
HD4629 .F86 1984

HOUSING - ARGENTINA - BUENOS AIRES METROPOLITAN AREA.
Feijoó, María del Carmen. Buscando un techo . Buenos Aires, Argentina [1984] 90, [5] p. : LC Card 85-214586
HD7321.B9 F45 1984

HOUSING - AUSTRALIA.
Burke, Terry, 1942- A roof over their heads . Melbourne , 1984. xiv, 178 p. : ISBN 0-642-87172-8 ***NYPL [JLD 86-2639]***

Design for diversification /. Canberra , Portland, OR. [1985] 57 p. : ISBN 0-909724-68-7 (pbk.) LC Card 86-222390 DDC 363.5/0994 19
HD7379.A3 D47 1985

HOUSING - AUSTRALIA - MELBOURNE (VIC.)
Logan, William Stewart, 1942- The Gentrification of inner Melbourne . St. Lucia, Qld., Australia ; New York : xxxiii, 328 p. : ISBN 0-7022-1729-8 LC Card 84-17382 DDC 307/.2 19
HD7379.M45 L64 1985
NYPL [JLD 87-798]

HOUSING - AUSTRIA.
Lins, Josef. Wohnungsmarkt und soziale Schicht . Linz , 1983. 89 p. : ISBN 3-85320-292-6 LC Card 84-214132 DDC 363.6/09436 19
HD7337.A3 L55 1983 ***NYPL [JLD 87-102]***

HOUSING - AUSTRIA - LOCATION - EVALUATION.
Grasberger, Helmut, 1941- Die Untersuchung des Wohnwertes von Wohngebieten /. Wien , New York , 1983. 108 p., [15] folded leaves of plates : ISBN 0-387-81752-2 (U. S.) LC Card 84-142695
HD7337.A3 G73 1983

HOUSING - AUSTRIA - UPPER AUSTRIA - HISTORY.
Urferer, Wilhelm. Das Wohnungswesen in Oberösterreich seit Beginn dieses Jahrhunderts im Vergleich zu seiner gesamtstaatlichen Entwicklung /. Linz , c1986. viii, 235 p. : ISBN 3-85320-384-1 LC Card 87-127729 DDC 363.5/8/094362 19
HD7337.U6 U74 1986

HOUSING - AUSTRIA - VIENNA - COSTS.
Czasny, Karl. Erfassung des Wohnungsangebotes /. Wien , 1985. 284 p. ; ISBN 3-900551-04-9 LC Card 87-103427 DDC 333.33/8 19
HD7337.V3 C93 1985

HOUSING AUTHORITIES - ENGLAND - SOUTH HAMS (DEVON)
Phillips, David R. Rural housing and the public sector /. Aldershot, Hampshire, England [Brookfield, Vt.] c1982. viii, 174 p. : ISBN 0-566-00456-9 : LC Card 82-134413 DDC 352.7/5/0941 19
HD7289.G82 S687 1982
NYPL [JLD 83-2605]

HOUSING AUTHORITIES - ONTARIO.
Peter Barnard Associates. An evaluation of the Ontario Home Renewal Program . [Toronto] , 1976. x, 43, [28] p. : LC Card 85-192287
HD7305.O6 P47 1976

HOUSING - BERLIN (GERMANY)
Sonnewald, Bernd, 1947- Die "Berliner Linie" und die Hausbesetzer-Szene /. Berlin , c1983. 149 p. ; ISBN 3-87061-170-7 LC Card 83-190228
HD7287.96.G32 B477 1983

Was wird in den besetzten Häusern gemacht? . Berlin [1982]. 65 p. : ***NYPL [JLF 87-439]***

HOUSING - BERLIN (GERMANY) - STATISTICS.
Ergebnisse der Gebäude- und Wohnungszählung in Berlin (West) am 25. Oktober 1968 . Berlin [1971] 52 p. ; LC Card 85-171262
HA1330.B6 B45 Heft 169 HD7339.B4

HOUSING - BRAZIL.
Lucena, José Mário Pereira de. O mercado habitacional no Brasil /. Rio de Janeiro, RJ , 1985. v, 185 p. : LC Card 85-208372
HD7323.A3 L83 1985

Peruzzo, Dilvo, 1941- Habitação . São Paulo-SP [1984] 133 p. ; LC Card 84-242125 DDC 363.5/0981 19
HD7287.6.B7 P47 1984
NYPL [JLD 86-2535]

HOUSING - BRAZIL - ADDRESSES, ESSAYS, LECTURES.
A Produção capitalista da casa (e da cidade) no Brasil industrial /. São Paulo , 1979. 166 p. : LC Card 80-100793
HD7323.A3 P76 1979 ***NYPL [JLD 80-3858]***

HOUSING - BRAZIL - EVORA.
Inquérito às rendas e a outras características das habitações arrendadas na cidade de Evora em 1955-56 /. Lisboa [1958] 26 p. : LC Card 85-185037
HA1571 .A32 no. 33 HD7288.85.P82E93

HOUSING - BRAZIL - FINANCE.
Brazil. Grupo de Trabalho para Reformulação do Sistema Financeiro da Habitação. Reformulação . [Brasília] , 1986. 94 leaves ; LC Card 87-144710 DDC 363.5/8 19
HD7323.A3 B7 1986

A Brazilian solution to Brazilian problems. Rio de Janeiro , 1974. 32 p. ; LC Card 86-673453
HD7323.A4 B72x 1974

HOUSING - BRAZIL - PERNAMBUCO - CONGRESSES.
Seminário Permanente de Habitação Popular (1981 : Recife, Brazil) Anais--1981 /. Recife [19]82. 178 p. ; LC Card 84-256147
HD7323.P37 S46 1981

HOUSING - BRAZIL - SÃO PAULO.
Blay, Eva Alterman. Eu não tenho onde morar . São Paulo, SP [1985] 332 p. : ISBN 85-21-30298-3 : LC Card 85-211285
HD7323.S28 B56 1985

HOUSING - BULGARIA - CONGRESSES.
Nauchno-prakticheska konferentsii͡a "Prebroi͡avane na naselenieto i zhilishtnii͡a fond--teorii͡a i praktika" (1986 : Slŭnchev bri͡ag, Bulgaria) Nauchno-prakticheska konferentsii͡a "Prebroi͡avane na naselenieto i zhilishtnii͡a fond--teorii͡a i praktika," 9-11 oktomvri 1986 g., Slŭnchev bri͡ag /. Sofii͡a , 1986- v. <1 > : LC Card 87-156528
HA1621.5 1985

HOUSING - CAMEROON - YAOUNDÉ.
Yaoundé, typologie de l'habitat . [Yaoundé, Cameroon] [197-?] [26] p. : LC Card 83-106947
HD1019.Z9 Y368 1970z

HOUSING - CANADA.
Fallis, George, 1947- Housing economics /. Toronto [Ont.] , Boston , c1985. 241 p. : ISBN 0-409-82940-4 LC Card 85-177894 DDC 333.33/8 19
HD7305.A3 F35 1985 ***NYPL [JLE 87-2573]***

HOUSING - CHILE - STATISTICS.
XV censo nacional de población y IV de vivienda--Chile, Abril 1982. [Santiago] , <[1983]-[1986]. <v. 3-14; in 15 > : LC Card 87-110013
HA994 1982d

XV Censo nacional de población y IV de vivienda--Chile, abril 1982. [Santiago] [1985-<1986]. v. <1-13 > : LC Card 87-109976
HA994 1982c

HOUSING - COLOMBIA.
Jaramillo, Samuel. Análisis de las condiciones de vivienda de los hogares colombianos, a partir de los resultados de la encuesta nacional de hogares, etapa 33, 1981 /. Bogotá, Colombia , 1985. ii, 166 p. ; LC Card 87-403605 DDC 363.5/1/09861 19
HD7325.A3 J37 1985

HOUSING, COOPERATIVE - AUSTRIA - HISTORY.
Novy, Klaus. Genossenschafts-Bewegung . Berlin , c1983. 176 p. : ISBN 3-88747-017-6 LC Card 84-190729
HD7287.72.G3 N68 1983

HOUSING, COOPERATIVE - FRANCE.
Analyse socio-économique comparée des coopératives d'habitation en France et au Québec . [Chicoutimi] [1985] xvi, 391 p. : ISBN 2-920730-04-5 LC Card 86-181851
HD7287.72.F8 A53 1985

HOUSING, COOPERATIVE - GERMANY - HISTORY.
Novy, Klaus. Genossenschafts-Bewegung . Berlin , c1983. 176 p. : ISBN 3-88747-017-6 LC Card 84-190729
HD7287.72.G3 N68 1983

HOUSING, COOPERATIVE - GERMANY (WEST)
Petersen, Paul. Wohngemeinschaft oder Grossfamilie. [Wuppertal, c1972] 224 p. LC Card 72-375103 ***NYPL [JLD 77-3003]***

HOUSING, COOPERATIVE - GERMANY (WEST) - NORTH RHINE-WESTPHALIA.
Anders leben . Berlin , 1985. 231 p. : ISBN 3-8012-0107-4 LC Card 85-189669
HD7287.72.G32 N6725 1985

HOUSING, COOPERATIVE - KENYA.
Gatabaki-Kamau, Rose. Co-operative housing development in Kenya . Nairobi, Kenya [1985] vi leaves, 131 p. : LC Card 86-980648 DDC 334/.1/096762 19
HD7287.72.K4 G37 1985

HOUSING, COOPERATIVE - KENYA - CASE STUDIES.
Gatabaki-Kamau, Rose. Co-operative housing development in Kenya . Nairobi, Kenya [1985] vi leaves, 131 p. : LC Card 86-980648 DDC 334/.1/096762 19
HD7287.72.K4 G37 1985

HOUSING, COOPERATIVE - QUÉBEC (PROVINCE)
Analyse socio-économique comparée des coopératives d'habitation en France et au Québec . [Chicoutimi] [1985] xvi, 391 p. : ISBN 2-920730-04-5 LC Card 86-181851
HD7287.72.F8 A53 1985

HOUSING, COOPERATIVE - SWITZERLAND - HISTORY.
Novy, Klaus. Genossenschafts-Bewegung . Berlin , c1983. 176 p. : ISBN 3-88747-017-6 LC Card 84-190729
HD7287.72.G3 N68 1983

HOUSING, COOPERATIVE - UNITED STATES.
Producing lower income housing . Washington, D.C. , c1986. xiv, 373 p. ; ISBN 0-87179-533-7 (pbk.) LC Card 86-26424 DDC 363.5/ 19
HD7288.78.U5 P76 1986

United States. Dept. of Housing and Urban Development. Office of Policy Development and Research. Division of Policy Studies. The conversion of rental housing to condominiums and cooperatives . [Washington, D.C.] , 1982. 95 p. : *NYPL [JLF 86-442]*

HOUSING - COSTA RICA.
Carreras, Rodrigo X. Vivienda y población en Costa Rica . Heredia, Costa Rica , 1979. 203 p. : LC Card 87-404329 DDC 363.5/097286 19
HD7308.A3 C37 1979

Costa Rica--respuesta al cuestionario del Banco Interamericano de Desarrollo /. [San José] [1962] 69 leaves (some folded) ; LC Card 85-117361
HC143 .C685 1962

HOUSING - COSTA RICA - STATISTICS.
Censo de vivienda, 1984 /. San José, Costa Rica , 1987. xxxiii, 335 p. : LC Card 87-402910 DDC 363.5/097286/021 19
HD7308.A3 C46 1987

The Housing crisis / edited by Peter Malpass. London ; Dover, N.H. : Croom Helm, c1986. 243 p.: ill. ; 23 cm. Chapters 4, 5, 7, and 8 are based on talks given at a housing forum at Bristol Polytechnic. Includes bibliographical references and index. CONTENTS. - From complacency to crisis / Peter Malpass -- The decline of public expenditure / Philip Leather and Alan Murie -- The deterioration of public sector housing / Ted Cantle -- Housing renewal : privatisation and beyond / Mike Gibson -- Growing crisis and contradiction to home ownership / Valerie Karn, John Doling, and Bruce Stafford -- Housing and class in the inner city / David Byrne -- Housing policies for older people / Christine Oldman -- The worsening crisis of single homelessness / Chris Holmes -- Housing policy and young people / Peter Malpass -- Conclusion / Peter Malpass. ISBN 0-7099-4605-8 : LC Card 85-31113 DDC 363.5/0941 19
1. Housing - Great Britain - Addresses, essays, lectures. 2. Housing policy - Great Britain - Addresses, essays, lectures. 3. Public housing - Great Britain - Addresses, essays, lectures. I. Malpass, Peter.
HD7333.A3 H684 1986
NYPL [JLD 86-2181]

HOUSING - DENMARK.
Kjær Jensen, Mogens. Unges boligsituation /. København , 1983. 139 p. : ISBN 87-7487-228-1 : LC Card 83-189408
HD7347.A3 K53 1983
NYPL [JLK 73-237 v.116]

HOUSING - DENMARK - FINANCE.
Denmark. Udvalget vedrørende byfornyelse og støtte til ejerboliger. Redegørelse om støtte til ejerboliger i forbindelse med byfornyelse . København [1981] 128 p. : ISBN 87-503-3873-0 LC Card 82-194685
HD7347.A4 D455 1981

HOUSING - DEVELOPING COUNTRIES.
Shelter, settlement, and development /. Boston , 1987. xvii, 476 p. : ISBN 0-04-711023-6 (alk. paper) LC Card 87-1038 DDC 363.5/09172/4 19
HD7391 .S54 1987

Vivienda del Tercer Mundo . Bogotá , c1986. 94 p. : ISBN 958-9054-01-3 LC Card 86-224743
HD7305.5 .V58 1986

HOUSING DEVELOPMENT.
Higher density housing . Washington, D.C. , c1986. 155 p. : ISBN 0-86718-271-7 (pbk.) LC Card 86-63356 DDC 690/.83 19
HD1390.5 .H545 1986

HOUSING DEVELOPMENTS. see **REAL ESTATE DEVELOPMENT.**

HOUSING - DOMINICAN REPUBLIC - STATISTICS.
Censo nacional de población y vivienda, 1981 . Santo Domingo, Distrito Nacional, República Dominicana , 1985- v. <1 > : LC Card 86-223758
HA886.5 1981c

Gómez, Carmen. Población y vivienda en la República Dominicana . Santo Domingo, República Dominicana , 1984. 116 p. : LC Card 85-154466
HD7316.5.A3 G65 1984
NYPL [JLF 86-1146]

HOUSING - ECONOMETRIC MODELS.
Rantala, Olavi, 1949- A study of housing investment and housing market behaviour /. Helsinki , 1986. 117 p. : ISBN 951-686-116-4 (pbk.) LC Card 86-204998 DDC 338.4/369083/0724 19
HD7287.5 .R33 1986

Housing economics /. Fallis, George, 1947- Toronto [Ont.] , Boston , c1985. 241 p. : ISBN 0-409-82940-4 LC Card 85-177894 DDC 333.33/8 19
HD7305.A3 F35 1985 NYPL [JLE 87-2573]

HOUSING - ENVIRONMENTAL ASPECTS - GERMANY (WEST)
Siedlungsformen und soziale Kosten . Frankfurt am Main , New York , c1984. vi, 219 p., [1] folded leaf of plates : ISBN 3-8204-5402-0 LC Card 85-190162
HD7339.A3 S59 1984

HOUSING - EUROPEAN ECONOMIC COMMUNITY COUNTRIES.
Employment and housing renovation in Europe /. Luxembourg , Washington, DC , 1986. 89 p. : ISBN 92-825-6422-3 : LC Card 87-136222 DDC 331.2/89/083094 19
HD5718.B92 E863 1986

HOUSING - FINANCE.
Bush, Vanessa A. How to buy a house when you're cash poor . Chicago , c1986. 92 p. ; ISBN 0-8092-4834-4 (pbk.) : LC Card 86-24053 DDC 332.7/22 19
HG2040.15 .B87 1986

Chinloy, Peter, 1950- Real estate . Boston, Mass. , c1987. p. cm. ISBN 0-89838-237-8 LC Card 87-3249 DDC 332.63/24 19
HD1382.5 .C475 1987

Johnson, Ross H. Real estate finance /. Columbus, Ohio , c1985. ix, 445 p. : ISBN 0-675-20195-0 LC Card 84-61298 DDC 332.7/2 19
HG2040 .J6 1985 NYPL [JLE 86-3033]

Knox, Albert H. What homebuyers should know about buying a home /. New York , c1987. vii, 192 p. : ISBN 0-533-06883-5 : LC Card 85-91377 DDC 643/.12 19
HD1379 .K656 1987

Miller, Peter G. The common-sense mortgage . New York , c1987. xvi, 285 p. ; ISBN 0-06-055081-3 : LC Card 86-46265 DDC 332.7/22 19
HG2040 .M54 1987

Unger, Maurice Albert, 1917- Real estate finance /. Cincinnati , c1984. vi, 426 p. : ISBN 0-538-19630-0 LC Card 83-61343 DDC 332.7/2 19
HG2040 .U53 1984 NYPL [JLE 86-4718]

Housing finance and public policy . Stegman, Michael A. New York , c1986. xiv, 290 p. : ISBN 0-442-28035-1 (pbk.) : LC Card 85-13408 DDC 332.63/24/0973 19
HD7293.Z9 S74 1986 NYPL [JLE 86-3779]

HOUSING - FINANCE - LAW AND LEGISLATION - CALIFORNIA.
California affordable housing legislation . [Sacramento] [1986?] 2 v. ; LC Card 86-622916 DDC 363.5/8 19
HD7303.C2 C275 1986

HOUSING - FINLAND - HELSINKI - STATISTICS.
Kinturi, Jorma. Väestö, asunnot ja asuntorakentaminen suur- ja peruspiireittäin Helsingissä 1970-1983 =. Helsinki , 1984. 36 p., [1] folded leaf of plates : LC Card 85-156678
HD7345.3.H5 K563 1984

Lankinen, Leila. Asuminen Helsingissä 1950-1983 =. Helsinki , 1985. 80 p. : LC Card 86-148571
HD7345.3.H5 L35 1985

HOUSING - FINLAND - STATISTICS.
Lankinen, Leila. Asuminen Helsingissä 1950-1983 =. Helsinki , 1985. 80 p. : LC Card 86-148571
HD7345.3.H5 L35 1985

HOUSING FOR THE AGED. see **AGED - DWELLINGS.**

HOUSING FORECASTING - COSTA RICA.
Carreras, Rodrigo X. Vivienda y población en Costa Rica . Heredia, Costa Rica , 1979. 203 p. : LC Card 87-404329 DDC 363.5/097286 19
HD7308.A3 C37 1979

HOUSING FORECASTING - DOMINICAN REPUBLIC - STATISTICS.
Gómez, Carmen. Población y vivienda en la República Dominicana . Santo Domingo, República Dominicana , 1984. 116 p. : LC Card 85-154466
HD7316.5.A3 G65 1984
NYPL [JLF 86-1146]

HOUSING FORECASTING - SWITZERLAND - MATHEMATICAL MODELS.
Hornung, Daniel. Methoden zur Prognose des Wohnungsmarktgeschehens auf regionaler Ebene . Diessenhofen , 1983. xvi, 251 p. : ISBN 3-7253-0214-6 LC Card 86-114266
HD7353.A3 H66 1983

HOUSING - FRANCE - COSTS - STATISTICS.
Les Logements neufs en 1978 . Paris , 1982. 40 p. : LC Card 83-176727
HD7338.A4 L64 1982

HOUSING - GERMANY - HISTORY.
Teuteberg, Hans Jürgen. Wohnalltag in Deutschland, 1850-1914 . Münster , 1985. 488 p. : ISBN 3-88547-277-5 LC Card 86-165201
HD7339.A3 T46 1985

HOUSING - GERMANY, WEST.
Bürger, es geht um Deine Gemeinde . [S.l. , 1983] ([Bonn] : Bundesdruckerei) 7 p. ; LC Card 84-198296
HD7339.A3 B97 1983

Kaufmann-Scheuer, Brigitte. Perspektiven und Modelle einer Neuorientierung der staatlichen Wohneigentumsförderung /. Freiburg [i. Br.] , 1983. 235 p. : ISBN 3-8107-2185-9 LC Card 84-108468
HD7339.A3 K34 1983

Krischausky, D. Wohnungsgemeinnützigkeit . Köln , c1984. vi, 161 p. ; ISBN 3-452-19899-5 LC Card 84-182027
HD7339.A3 K79 1984

Petersen, Paul. Wohngemeinschaft oder Grossfamilie. [Wuppertal, c1972] 224 p. LC Card 72-375103 *NYPL [JLD 77-3003]*

HOUSING - GERMANY, WEST - ADDRESSES ESSAYS, LECTURES.
Wohnen . Hamburg , c1983. 230 p. : ISBN 3-7672-0808-3 LC Card 83-219819 DDC 363.5/0943 19
HD7339.A3 W616 1983
NYPL [JLE 86-3338]

HOUSING - GERMANY, WEST - CONGRESSES.
Forum wohnen /. Freiburg i. Br. , Giessen , 1986. 158 p. : ISBN 3-89125-009-6 LC Card 86-169106
HD7339.A3 F68 1986

HOUSING - GERMANY, WEST - FINANCE.
Grimm, Bernd Christian. Handbuch der Hausfinanzierung . Mannheim , 1985. 174, [318] p. ; LC Card 85-188627
HD7339.Z9 G75 1985

HOUSING - GERMANY (WEST) - FINANCE - HISTORY.
Ein Zuhause für Menschen . Frankfurt am Main , c1986. 204 p. : ISBN 3-921722-03-9 LC Card 87-133035
HD7339.A3 Z78 1986

HOUSING - GERMANY, WEST - HAMBURG.
Neue Heimat . Hamburg , 1983. 231 p. : ISBN 3-87975-238-9 LC Card 83-150360
HD7339.H3 N48 1983

HOUSING - GERMANY (WEST) - HANNOVER - HISTORY - 19TH CENTURY.
Voigt, Wolfgang. Der Eisenbahnkönig, oder, Rumänien lag in Linden . München , 1982. 142 p. : ISBN 3-923126-15-8 (pbk.) LC Card 87-672921
HD7289.5.R1 V64x 1982

HOUSING - GERMANY, WEST - MANNHEIM.
Miodek, Wolfgang. Innerstädtische Umzüge und Stadtentwicklung in Mannheim, 1977-1983 . Mannheim , 1986. 244 p. : ISBN 3-923750-18-8 : LC Card 86-181776
HD7288.92.G32 M355 1986

HOUSING - GERMANY (WEST) - MANNHEIM - HISTORY.
Hahn, Barbara. Der geförderte Wohnungsbau in Mannheim 1850-1985 /. Mannheim , 1986. 236 p. : ISBN 3-87804-185-3 LC Card 87-121543 DDC 363.5/8/0943/46 19
HD7339.M35 H34 1986

HOUSING - GERMANY (WEST) - MATHEMATICAL MODELS - ADDRESSES, ESSAYS, LECTURES.
Microeconomic models of housing markets /. Berlin , New York , c1985. iv, 197 p. : ISBN 0-387-15193-1 (pbk.) LC Card 85-4648 DDC 381/.4569083/0724 19
HD7339.A3 M53 1985
NYPL [JLM 72-289 no.239]

HOUSING - GERMANY (WEST) - RHINELAND-PALATINATE - MATHEMATICAL MODELS.
König, Robert. Die Wohnflächenbestände der Gemeinden der Vorderpfalz . Heidelberg , 1980. [14], 226 p. : ISBN 3-88570-068-9 LC Card 81-136631 DDC 333.73/13/0724 19
HD659.P34 K66 1980
NYPL [L-10 4979 Heft 68]

HOUSING - GERMANY, WEST - STATISTICS.
Marx, G. Die Entwicklung der Wohnungsbautätigkeit in Leverkusen /. Leverkusen [1984] 37 p., [1] folded leaf of plates : LC Card 84-183932
HD9715.G33 L575 1984

HOUSING - GREAT BRITAIN - ADDRESSES, ESSAYS, LECTURES.
The Housing crisis /. London , Dover, N.H. , c1986. 243 p.: ISBN 0-7099-4605-8 : LC Card 85-31113 DDC 363.5/0941 19
HD7333.A3 H684 1986
NYPL [JLD 86-2181]

HOUSING - GREAT BRITAIN - COLONIES.
Great Britain. Central Office of Information. Reference Division. Housing and town and country planning in the United Kingdom dependencies. [London, 1960] 51 p. LC Card 72-222605
HD7333.A3 A54 1960b

HOUSING - GREAT BRITAIN - FINANCE.
Boléat, Mark. The mortgage market /. London , Boston , 1987. x, 176 p. ; ISBN 0-04-334011-3 (alk. paper) LC Card 86-28875 DDC 332.7/22 19
HG2040.5.G7 B65 1987

HOUSING - GREAT BRITAIN - HISTORY.
Gaskell, S. Martin. Model housing from the great exhibition to the festival of Britain /. London , New York , 1986. x, 180 p. : ISBN 0-7201-1834-4 : LC Card 86-23775 DDC 363.5/0941 19
HD7333.A3 G37 1986

HOUSING - GREAT BRITAIN - HISTORY - 20TH CENTURY.
Shaw, Frederick. The homes and homeless of post-war Britain /. Carnforth, Lancashire, UK , c1985. viii, 288 p. : ISBN 1-85070-104-0
NYPL [JLG 86-278]

HOUSING - HAITI - STATISTICS.
Résultats préliminaires du recensement général (septembre 1982) /. [Port-au-Prince] [1982 or 1983] vii, 60 p., [1] leaf of plates : LC Card 84-138275 DDC 304.6/097294/021 19
HD7316.A3 R47 1982 ***NYPL [JLF 86-1280]***

The Housing handbook : a guide to financing for non-profit organizations / Tamara Greeley, project director. New York, N.Y. (130 E. 59 St., New York 10022) : Neighborhood Preservation Program, Federation of Jewish Philanthropies of New York, 1986. 150 p. ; 28 cm. LC Card 87-107431 DDC 363.5/8/0681 19
1. Housing - New York (N.Y.) - Finance - Handbooks, manuals, etc. 2. Housing - United States - Finance - Handbooks, manuals, etc. I. Greeley, Tamara. II. Federation of Jewish Philanthropies of New York. Neighborhood Preservation Program.
HD7304.N5 H68 1986

HOUSING - HUNGARY - STATISTICS.
Lakásváltoztatási szándékok, lakáskörülmények az 1984. évi mikrocenzus alapján /. Budapest , 1986. 199 p. ; ISBN 963-340-798-2 LC Card 87-110348
HD7337.5.A3 L355 1986

Housing in India /. Cherunilam, Francis. Bombay , 1987. vi, 168 p. ; LC Card 86-903722 DDC 363.5/0954 19
HD7361.A3 C46 1987

Housing in urban development . Chadsri Bunnag. [Bangkok] [Rotterdam] Netherlands [1985] 49, [2] leaves : LC Card 86-915989 DDC 363.5/09593 19
HD7363.55.A3 C46 1985

HOUSING - INDIA.
Cherunilam, Francis. Housing in India /. Bombay , 1987. vi, 168 p. ; LC Card 86-903722 DDC 363.5/0954 19
HD7361.A3 C46 1987

Dholakia, Bakul H. 1947- The economics of housing in India . Delhi , 1982. xviii, 274 p. ; LC Card 83-905798 DDC 363.5/0954 19
HD7361.A3 D47 1982
NYPL [JLD 85-2908]

Housing and Urban Development Corporation. HUDCO's initiatives for IYSH. New Delhi [1987?] 49 p. : LC Card 87-902550 DDC 363.5/8 19
HD7287.96.I4 H67 1987

Mulkh Raj. Employment, income, and housing /. New Delhi , 1987. viii, 130 p. : ISBN 81-7000-025-4 : LC Card 87-901029 DDC 331.12/5/0954 19
HD7361.A3 M85 1987

Om Kumar, 1944- Sites and services in urban housing in India /. New Delhi , 1987. xii, 86 p. : ISBN 81-7000-026-2 : LC Card 87-900362 DDC 363.5/0954 19
HD7361.A3 O5 1987

HOUSING - INDIA - FINANCE.
Dholakia, Bakul H. 1947- The economics of housing in India . Delhi , 1982. xviii, 274 p. ; LC Card 83-905798 DDC 363.5/0954 19
HD7361.A3 D47 1982
NYPL [JLD 85-2908]

HOUSING - INDIA - KARNATAKA.
Parvathamma, C., 1928- Housing, rural poor, and their living conditions /. Delhi, India [1987] vi, 135 p. ; ISBN 81-212-0088-1 : LC Card 87-900831 DDC 363.5/8 19
HD7361.K27 P37 1987

HOUSING - INDIA - LOCATION.
Om Kumar, 1944- Sites and services in urban housing in India /. New Delhi , 1987. xii, 86 p. : ISBN 81-7000-026-2 : LC Card 87-900362 DDC 363.5/0954 19
HD7361.A3 O5 1987

HOUSING - ISRAEL - STATISTICS.
Tekhunot demografiyot shel ha-ukhlusiyah . Yerushalayim , 1985. 31, 175, xxxiv p. : LC Card 86-204169
HA4560 .A4 1983

Housing issues .
(1) Design for diversification /. Canberra , Portland, OR. [1985] 57 p. : ISBN 0-909724-68-7 (pbk.) LC Card 86-222390 DDC 363.5/0994 19
HD7379.A3 D47 1985

HOUSING - ITALY - CONGRESSES.
La Politica comunitaria della casa. Roma, 1971. 227 p. LC Card 74-883223
NYPL [JLD 72-3595]

HOUSING - LATIN AMERICA.
Vivienda del Tercer Mundo . Bogotá , c1986. 94 p. : ISBN 958-9054-01-3 LC Card 86-224743
HD7305.5 .V58 1986

HOUSING - LAW AND LEGISLATION - CALIFORNIA.
California affordable housing legislation . [Sacramento] [1986?] 2 v. ; LC Card 86-622916 DDC 363.5/8 19
HD7303.C2 C275 1986

Massa, Alison K. Housing and the environment /. Sacramento, CA (921 10th St., Sacramento 95814-2774) [1985?] 2 v. : LC Card 87-621018 DDC 363.7 19
HD266.C2 M37 1985

HOUSING - LOCATION - EVALUATION.
Grasberger, Helmut, 1941- Die Untersuchung des Wohnwertes von Wohngebieten /. Wien , New York , 1983. 108 p., [15] folded leaves of plates : ISBN 0-387-81752-2 (U. S.) LC Card 84-142695
HD7337.A3 G73 1983

Housing markets and policies under fiscal austerity / edited by Willem van Vliet. New York : Greenwood Press, 1987. x, 263 p. : ill. ; 25 cm. (Contributions in sociology, 0084-9278 . no. 62) Includes bibliographies and indexes. ISBN 0-313-25409-5 (lib. bdg. : alk. paper) LC Card 86-29603 DDC 363.5 19
1. Housing. 2. Housing policy. I. Van Vliet, Willem. II. Series.
HD7287 .H67 1987

HOUSING - MEXICO - CHIHUAHUA.
Verbeek, Henk. Residentiële mobiliteit in Ciudad Chihuahua, Mexico /. Utrecht [1986] iii, 142 p. : LC Card 86-172646
HD7288.92.M62 C488 1986

HOUSING - MEXICO - STATES - STATISTICS.
X censo general de población y vivienda, 1980 . México, D.F. , c1985- v. <1-6 > : ISBN 968-8099-30-9 (v. 1) LC Card 86-226718
HA761.5 1980d

HOUSING - MEXICO - STATISTICS.
X censo general de población y vivienda, 1980 . México, D.F. , c1985- v. <1-6 > : ISBN 968-8099-30-9 (v. 1) LC Card 86-226718
HA761.5 1980d

HOUSING - MOROCCO - STATISTICS.
Morocco. Maṣlaḥah al-Markazīyah lil-Iḥṣā'īyāt. Résultats préliminaires du recensement de 1960 . [Rabat] [1964?] 43 leaves ; LC Card 82-960641
HD7372.3.A3 M67 1964

HOUSING - NETHERLANDS.
Fulpen, Hans van. Volkshuisvesting in demografisch en economisch perspectief /. 's-Gravenhage , 1985. 354 p. : ISBN 90-12-05159-2 LC Card 86-169936
HD7344.A3 F85 1985

Priemus, Hugo. Nederlandse woontheorieën /. Delft , 1984. vi, 92 p. : ISBN 90-6275-126-1 : LC Card 84-226472
HD7344.A3 P67 1984 ***NYPL [JLE 86-2510]***

Toekomstverkenning volkshuisvesting . Delft , 1985. 100 p. : ISBN 90-6275-193-8 : LC Card 86-157352
HD7288.78.N4 T64 1985

HOUSING - NETHERLANDS - FINANCE.
Fulpen, Hans van. Volkshuisvesting in demografisch en economisch perspectief /. 's-Gravenhage , 1985. 354 p. : ISBN 90-12-05159-2 LC Card 86-169936
HD7344.A3 F85 1985

HOUSING - NEW YORK (N.Y.) - FINANCE - HANDBOOKS, MANUALS, ETC.
The Housing handbook . New York, N.Y. (130 E. 59 St., New York 10022) , 1986. 150 p. ; LC Card 87-107431 DDC 363.5/8/0681 19
HD7304.N5 H68 1986

HOUSING - NEW YORK (STATE) - FINANCE.
New York (State). Legislature. Legislative Commission on Expenditure Review. Mitchell-Lama housing mortgage delinquencies . Albany, N.Y. (111 Washington Ave., Albany 12210-2277) [1985] 5, ii, 44 p. : LC Card 86-620632 DDC 353.97470086/5045 19
HD7303.N7 N394 1985 ***NYPL [JLF 87-104]***

HOUSING - NORTHERN IRELAND - HISTORY.
Brett, Charles Edward Bainbridge, 1928- Housing a divided community /. Dublin, Ireland , 1986. xi, 171 p., [32] p. of plates : ISBN 0-906980-49-6 : LC Card 86-222853 DDC 363.5/09416 19
HD7335.5.A3 B74 1986

HOUSING - NORWAY - STATISTICS.
Knudsen, Jon Paschen. Boligstandard . Oslo , 1984. 66 p. : ISBN 82-537-2088-2 : LC Card 85-125379
HD7349.A3 K58 1984

HOUSING - PACIFIC ISLANDS (TRUST TERRITORY) - STATISTICS.
Barr, Lorna R. Land of the Trust islands . [Victoria, B.C.] [1978] 36 p. : LC Card 83-226106 DDC 333.3/0996/5 19
HD1121.Z63 B37 1978

HOUSING - PANAMA - PANAMA (DISTRICT)
Pacheco D., Rubén. Industria de la construcción . [Panamá] , 1974. 17, [1] leaves, [4] leaves of plates : LC Card 87-400643
HD9715.P223 P367 1974

HOUSING - PENNSYLVANIA - FINANCE.
A Sunset performance audit of the Pennsylvania Housing Finance Agency pursuant to Act 1981-142 /. Harrisburg, Pa. (Rm. 400, Finance Bldg., Harrisburg 17120) [1985] ii, 75 p. ; LC

Card 85-623018 DDC 353.97480086/5045 19
HD7303.P4 P425 1985
NYPL [JLF 86-1807]

HOUSING - POLAND - FINANCE.
Kapustka, Aleksander. Gospodarka inwestycyjna i remontowa w latach 1984-1985 /. Zielona Góra , 1984. 294 p. ; LC Card 86-670001
HC340.3.Z9 C35 1984

HOUSING - POLAND - STATISTICS.
Spis ludności i mieszkań metodą reprezentacyjną z dnia 6 XII 1984 r. . Warszawa , 1985. xx, 93 p., [2] p. of plates : LC Card 86-176185
HD7345.7.A3 S65 1985

HOUSING POLICY - AFRICA.
Die Verplante Wohnmisere . Saarbrücken , Fort Lauderdale , 1986. 334 p. : ISBN 3-88156-329-6 LC Card 87-408292 DDC 363.5/1/096 19
HD7287.96.A4 V47 1986

HOUSING POLICY - ALGERIA.
Boubekeur, Sid, 1952- L'habitat en Algérie . Lyon , c1986. 256 p. : ISBN 2-7297-0272-5 : LC Card 86-217640
HD7372.4.A3 B68 1986

Housing policy and practice in Asia / edited by Seong-Kyu Ha. London ; New York : Croom Helm, c1987. 197 p. : ill. ; 23 cm. "Published in the U. S.A. by Croom Helm in association with Methuen, Inc."--T.p. verso. Includes bibliographies and index. ISBN 0-7099-4711-9 LC Card 87-9091 DDC 363.5/8/095 19
1. Housing policy - East Asia - Case studies. 2. Housing policy - Asia, Southeastern - Case studies. 3. Housing policy - India. I. Ha, Seong-Kyu, 1947-.
HD7366.5.A3 H68 1987

HOUSING POLICY - ARGENTINA - BUENOS AIRES METROPOLITAN AREA.
Feijoó, María del Carmen. Buscando un techo . Buenos Aires, Argentina [1984] 90, [5] p. : LC Card 85-214586
HD7321.B9 F45 1984

HOUSING POLICY - ASIA, SOUTHEASTERN - CASE STUDIES.
Housing policy and practice in Asia /. London , New York , c1987. 197 p. : ISBN 0-7099-4711-9 LC Card 87-9091 DDC 363.5/8/095 19
HD7366.5.A3 H68 1987

HOUSING POLICY - AUSTRIA.
Lins, Josef. Wohnungsmarkt und soziale Schicht . Linz , 1983. 89 p. : ISBN 3-85320-292-6 LC Card 84-214132 DDC 363.6/09436 19
HD7337.A3 L55 1983 *NYPL [JLD 87-102]*

HOUSING POLICY - AUSTRIA - UPPER AUSTRIA - HISTORY.
Urferer, Wilhelm. Das Wohnungswesen in Oberösterreich seit Beginn dieses Jahrhunderts im Vergleich zu seiner gesamtstaatlichen Entwicklung /. Linz , c1986. viii, 235 p. : ISBN 3-85320-384-1 LC Card 87-127729 DDC 363.5/8/094362 19
HD7337.U6 U74 1986

HOUSING POLICY - BANGLADESH - DHAKA.
Choguill, Charles L. New communities for urban squatters . New York , c1987. xiv, 213 p. : ISBN 0-306-42545-9 LC Card 86-30501 DDC 307.3/36 19
HD7361.6.D57 C46 1987

HOUSING POLICY - BRAZIL.
Brazil. Grupo de Trabalho para Reformulação do Sistema Financeiro da Habitação. Reformulação . [Brasília] , 1986. 94 leaves ; LC Card 87-144710 DDC 363.5/8 19
HD7323.A3 B7 1986

Peruzzo, Dilvo, 1941- Habitação . São Paulo-SP [1984] 133 p. ; LC Card 84-242125 DDC 363.5/0981 19
HD7287.6.B7 P47 1984
NYPL [JLD 86-2535]

HOUSING POLICY - BRAZIL - ADDRESSES, ESSAYS, LECTURES.
A Produção capitalista da casa (e da cidade) no Brasil industrial /. São Paulo , 1979. 166 p. : LC Card 80-100793
HD7323.A3 P76 1979 *NYPL [JLD 80-3858]*

HOUSING POLICY - BRAZIL - CONGRESSES.
Matta, Nelson da. Política habitacional /. [Salvador] [1984] 59 p. : LC Card 87-138899 DDC 363.5/8 19
HD7323.A3 M37 1984

HOUSING POLICY - CALIFORNIA.
California affordable housing legislation . [Sacramento] [1986?] 2 v. ; LC Card 86-622916 DDC 363.5/8 19
HD7303.C2 C275 1986

Local government mobilehome and mobilehome park policies in California . [Sacramento, Calif.] [1986] iii, 70 p. ; LC Card 86-622920 DDC 333.33/8 19
HD7289.62.U6 L63 1986

Massa, Alison K. Housing and the environment /. Sacramento, CA (921 10th St., Sacramento 95814-2774) [1985?] 2 v. : LC Card 87-621018 DDC 363.7 19
HD266.C2 M37 1985

HOUSING POLICY - CANADA.
Fallis, George, 1947- Housing economics /. Toronto [Ont.] , Boston , c1985. 241 p. : ISBN 0-409-82940-4 LC Card 85-177894 DDC 333.33/8 19
HD7305.A3 F35 1985 *NYPL [JLE 87-2573]*

HOUSING POLICY - COLOMBIA.
Toro Agudelo, Hernán. Hacia una reforma social urbana en Colombia . Bogotá, Colombia , 1986. 342 p. : ISBN 958-601-100-3 LC Card 87-107055
HD7325.A3 T67 1986

HOUSING POLICY - DENMARK.
Denmark. Udvalget vedrørende byfornyelse og støtte til ejerboliger. Redegørelse om støtte til ejerboliger i forbindelse med byfornyelse . København [1981] 128 p. : ISBN 87-503-3873-0 LC Card 82-194685
HD7347.A4 D455 1981

HOUSING POLICY - DEVELOPING COUNTRIES.
Laquian, Aprodicio A. Basic housing . Ottawa, Canada , c1983. 163 p. : ISBN 0-88936-370-6 (pbk.) LC Card 83-231129 DDC 363.5/8/091724 19
HD7391 .L36 1983 *NYPL [JLE 86-1376]*

Shelter, settlement, and development /. Boston , 1987. xvii, 476 p. : ISBN 0-04-711023-6 (alk. paper) LC Card 87-1038 DDC 363.5/09172/4 19
HD7391 .S54 1987

Spontaneous shelter . Philadelphia , 1988. p. cm. ISBN 0-87722-507-9 (alk. paper) LC Card 87-10002 DDC 363.5/8/091724 19
HD7287.96.D44 S66 1988

HOUSING POLICY - EAST ASIA - CASE STUDIES.
Housing policy and practice in Asia /. London , New York , c1987. 197 p. : ISBN 0-7099-4711-9 LC Card 87-9091 DDC 363.5/8/095 19
HD7366.5.A3 H68 1987

HOUSING POLICY - ECUADOR.
Landivar, Jorge F. The role of housing in development models . Swansea, U.K. , 1986. 60 p. ; ISBN 0-906250-12-9 (pbk.) LC Card 87-166136 DDC 363.5/8 19
HD7287.96.E2 L36 1986

HOUSING POLICY - FINLAND.
Harju, Hely. Puutteellisen asumisen parantaminen kunnissa vuosina 1985-1989 /. [Helsinki , 1986] 69, [16] p. : ISBN 951-46-9022-2 LC Card 86-215457
HD7345.3.A3 H367 1986

HOUSING POLICY - GERMANY - HISTORY.
Teuteberg, Hans Jürgen. Wohnalltag in Deutschland, 1850-1914 . Münster , 1985. 488 p. : ISBN 3-88547-277-5 LC Card 86-165201
HD7339.A3 T46 1985

HOUSING POLICY - GERMANY, WEST.
Echter, Claus-Peter. Konzepte städtischer Wohnungspolitik . Berlin , 1985. 97 p. : ISBN 3-88118-123-7 LC Card 86-145702
HD7288.78.G3 E265 1985

Eucker-Herresthal, Waltraud. Staatliche Eingriffe in den Mietwohnungsmarkt, Erfolgskontrolle und Reformvorschläge /. [Mainz] [1985?] v, 242 p. ; LC Card 87-407601 DDC 363.5/8 19
HD7288.85.G3 E92 1985

Kaufmann-Scheuer, Brigitte. Perspektiven und Modelle einer Neuorientierung der staatlichen Wohneigentumsförderung /. Freiburg [i. Br.] , 1983. 235 p. : ISBN 3-8107-2185-9 LC Card 84-108468
HD7339.A3 K34 1983

Killat, Gerhard. Kommunalisierung der Wohnungspolitik? . Köln , 1984. xiii, 291 p. : ISBN 3-921471-50-8 : LC Card 85-137757
HD7339.A3 K49 1984

Krischausky, D. Wohnungsgemeinnützigkeit . Köln , c1984. vi, 161 p. ; ISBN 3-452-19899-5 LC Card 84-182027
HD7339.A3 K79 1984

Kujath, Hans Joachim. Die Regeneration der Stadt . Hamburg , c1986. 282 p. ; ISBN 3-7672-0943-8 LC Card 87-113493 DDC 363.5/8 19
HD7339.A3 K85 1986

Schlüsselgewalt . Dortmund , c1981. 190 p. : ISBN 3-88142-261-7 : LC Card 81-206444
HD7339.A3 S25 1981

HOUSING POLICY - GERMANY (WEST) - ADDRESSES, ESSAYS, LECTURES.
Wohnen . Hamburg , c1983. 230 p. : ISBN 3-7672-0808-3 LC Card 83-219819 DDC 363.5/0943 19
HD7339.A3 W616 1983
NYPL [JLE 86-3338]

HOUSING POLICY - GERMANY (WEST) - HISTORY.
Ein Zuhause für Menschen . Frankfurt am Main , c1986. 204 p. : ISBN 3-921722-03-9 LC Card 87-133035
HD7339.A3 Z78 1986

HOUSING POLICY - GERMANY (WEST) - MANNHEIM - CASE STUDIES.
Ipsen, Detlev. Markt und Raum . Frankfurt , New York , c1986. 250 p. : ISBN 3-593-33685-5 LC Card 87-127593 DDC 363.5/8 19
HD7339.M35 I67 1986

HOUSING POLICY - GERMANY (WEST) - MANNHEIM - HISTORY.
Hahn, Barbara. Der geförderte Wohnungsbau in Mannheim 1850-1985 /. Mannheim , 1986. 236 p. : ISBN 3-87804-185-3 LC Card 87-121543 DDC 363.5/8/0943/46 19
HD7339.M35 H34 1986

HOUSING POLICY - GERMANY (WEST) - RUHR (REGION)
Wehling, Hans-Werner, 1949- Wohnstandorte und Wohnumfeldprobleme in der Kernzone des Ruhrgebietes /. Paderborn , 1984. ix, 285 p. : ISBN 3-506-72309-X LC Card 85-121205
HD7339.R79 W44 1984

HOUSING POLICY - GREAT BRITAIN - ADDRESSES, ESSAYS, LECTURES.
The Housing crisis /. London , Dover, N.H. , c1986. 243 p.: ISBN 0-7099-4605-8 : LC Card 85-31113 DDC 363.5/0941 19
HD7333.A3 H684 1986
NYPL [JLD 86-2181]

HOUSING POLICY - INDIA.
Dholakia, Bakul H. 1947- The economics of housing in India . Delhi , 1982. xviii, 274 p. ; LC Card 83-905798 DDC 363.5/0954 19
HD7361.A3 D47 1982
NYPL [JLD 85-2908]

Housing policy and practice in Asia /. London , New York , c1987. 197 p. : ISBN 0-7099-4711-9 LC Card 87-9091 DDC 363.5/8/095 19
HD7366.5.A3 H68 1987

HOUSING POLICY - INDIA - CONGRESSES.
Public housing /. Hyderabad, A.P. , c1983. xx, 345 p. ; LC Card 85-903848 DDC 363.5/8 19
HD7288.78.I4 P83 1983
NYPL [JLF 86-1782]

HOUSING POLICY - ITALY.
La Riconversione produttiva nell'edilizia /. Milano , 1984, c1981. 319 p. :
NYPL [JLD 86-3381]

HOUSING POLICY - JAPAN.
Reed, Steven R., 1947- Japanese prefectures and policy making /. Pittsburgh, Pa. , 1986. ix, 197 p. ; ISBN 0-8229-3527-9 LC Card 85-22528 DDC 352/.00047 19
JS7373.A3 R44 1986 *NYPL [JLE 86-3757]*

HOUSING POLICY - KENYA - KISUMU DISTRICT.
Sterkenburg, J. J. Rural housing conditions in

Kisumu District, Kenya /. [Utrecht] [Nairobi] , 1982. 95 p., [6] leaves of plates : LC Card 85-981197
HD7289.K42 K67 1982

HOUSING POLICY - LATIN AMERICA.
Buscando la equidad. English. In search for equity . Aldershot, Hants, England , Brookfield, USA , c1987. xvi, 249 p. ; ISBN 0-566-05537-6 : LC Card 87-21225 DDC 338.98 19
HC130.B38 B8713 1987

Die Verplante Wohnmisere . Saarbrücken , Fort Lauderdale , 1986. 334 p. : ISBN 3-88156-329-6 LC Card 87-408292 DDC 363.5/1/096 19
HD7287.96.A4 V47 1986

HOUSING POLICY - MANITOBA - WINNIPEG.
Levin, Earl A. A model for joint public sector/private sector participation in core area housing development and core area revitalization /. [Winnipeg, Man., Canada] , 1985. ix leaves, 93 p. ; LC Card 86-137674 DDC 363.5/8 19
HD7305.M3 L48 1985 ***NYPL [JLF 86-1313]***

HOUSING POLICY - NETHERLANDS.
Fulpen, Hans van. Volkshuisvesting in demografisch en economisch perspectief /. 's-Gravenhage , 1985. 354 p. : ISBN 90-12-05159-2 LC Card 86-169936
HD7344.A3 F85 1985

Houben, Piet. Ouderenhuisvesting in 'n emancipatieperspectief /. Delft , 1985. 178 p. : ISBN 90-6275-118-0 : LC Card 86-149527
HD7287.92.N4 H683 1985 ***NYPL [JLE 86-3902]***

Priemus, Hugo. Nederlandse woontheorieën /. Delft , 1984. vi, 92 p. : ISBN 90-6275-126-1 : LC Card 84-226472
HD7344.A3 P67 1984 ***NYPL [JLE 86-2510]***

Toekomstverkenning volkshuisvesting . Delft , 1985. 100 p. : ISBN 90-6275-193-8 : LC Card 86-157352
HD7288.78.N4 T64 1985

HOUSING POLICY - NEW YORK (STATE)
Seligson, Wendy. Rural housing in N.Y.S. /. [Albany, N.Y.] [1979] [61] p. : LC Card 82-621690 DDC 363.5/8/09747 19
HD7289.U7 N77 1979 ***NYPL [JLF 86-765]***

HOUSING POLICY - NORTHERN IRELAND - HISTORY.
Brett, Charles Edward Bainbridge, 1928- Housing a divided community /. Dublin, Ireland , 1986. xi, 171 p., [32] p. of plates : ISBN 0-906980-49-6 : LC Card 86-222853 DDC 363.5/09416 19
HD7335.5.A3 B74 1986

HOUSING POLICY - POLAND.
Polish People's Republic national report to the habitat . [S.l.] 1976 (Warszawa : Dom Słowa Polskiego) 48 p. : LC Card 83-226226
HC340.3 .P656 1976

HOUSING POLICY - RUSSIAN S.F.S.R. - MOSCOW - HISTORY.
Kreis, Barbara, 1947- Moskau, 1917-35 . [Germany] , c1985. 243 p., [3] p. of plates : ISBN 3-921420-26-1 : LC Card 86-170426
HD7345.M6 K73 1985

HOUSING POLICY - SOUTH AFRICA - DURBAN METROPOLITAN AREA.
Planning and financial evaluation of housing strategies /. Durban , 1983. viii, 233 p. : ISBN 0-86980-360-3 (pbk.) LC Card 86-205849 DDC 363.5/8 19
HD7287.96.S682 D876 1983

HOUSING POLICY - SWEDEN.
Bostadsbidragen . [Stockholm] [1982] 207 p. : ISBN 91-38-72586-X LC Card 83-240044
HD7350.A3 B697 1982

Wiktorin, Marianne. Kommunal bostadsförmedling . Stockholm [1983] 107 p. : ISBN 91-540-3929-0 : LC Card 84-218864
HD7350.A3 W55 1983

HOUSING POLICY - THAILAND.
Chadsri Bunnag. Housing in urban development . [Bangkok] [Rotterdam] Netherlands [1985] 49, [2] leaves : LC Card 86-915989 DDC 363.5/09593 19
HD7363.55.A3 C46 1985

HOUSING POLICY - TURKEY.
Boratav, Korkut. Housing yearbook /. Ankara, Turkey , 1985. 32, [2] p. ; LC Card 87-403323 DDC 363.5/09561 19
HD7358.25.A3 B67 1985

HOUSING POLICY - UNITED STATES.
The Fair Housing Assistance Program evaluation /. Washington, D.C. [1985] 1 v. (various pagings) : ***NYPL [JLF 87-17]***

Gilderbloom, John Ingram. Rethinking rental housing /. Philadelphia , 1987. p. cm. ISBN 0-87722-498-6 (alk. paper) LC Card 87-1958 DDC 363.5/8 19
HD7288.85.U6 G55 1987

Housing America's poor /. Chapel Hill , c1987. ix, 203 p. ; ISBN 0-8078-1738-4 LC Card 86-40449 DDC 363.5/8 19
HD7287.96.U5 H68 1987

HOUSING POLICY - UNITED STATES - CASE STUDIES.
Stegman, Michael A. Housing finance and public policy . New York , c1986. xiv, 290 p. : ISBN 0-442-28035-1 (pbk.) : LC Card 85-13408 DDC 332.63/24/0973 19
HD7293.Z9 S74 1986 ***NYPL [JLE 86-3779]***

HOUSING POLICY - UNITED STATES - CONGRESSES.
The Urban caldron /. Boston, Mass. , 1986. 152 p. ; ISBN 0-89946-207-3 LC Card 85-21641 DDC 333.73/0973 19
HD257 .U73 1986 ***NYPL [JLE 86-4372]***

HOUSING POLICY - UNITED STATES - STATES.
Stegman, Michael A. Nonfederal housing programs . Washington, D.C. , 1987. viii, 231 p. ; ISBN 0-87420-673-1 LC Card 87-51080 DDC 363.5/8 19
HD7293.Z9 S75 1987

HOUSING POLICY - ZIMBABWE.
Report on housing and urban development in Zimbabwe . [Harare, Zimbabwe , 1986] vi, 46 p., [1] folded leaf of plates : LC Card 87-980381 DDC 363.5/8 19
HD7374.5.A3 R46 1986

HOUSING - PRICES - FRANCE.
Vincent, Maurice, 1955 or 6- La formation du prix du logement /. Paris , c1986. v, 221 p. : ISBN 2-7178-1082-X : LC Card 86-190085
HD7338.A3 V55 1986

HOUSING - PRICES - TEXAS.
Wright, A. L. (Arthur L.) The Texas housing affordability index /. College Station, TX [1986] 5, [17] p. : LC Card 86-622195 DDC 338.4/369083/09764021 19
HD7303.T4 W748 1986

Housing rehabilitation : programs, techniques, and resources. Washington, D.C. : U. S. Dept. of Housing and Urban Development, Office of Policy Development and Research, [1987] 39 p. : ill. ; 28 cm. Shipping list no.: 87-339-P. "April 1987"--P. [2] of cover. Includes bibliographical references. "HUD-1086-PDR"--P. [4] of cover. Item 582 LC Card 87-601734 DDC 363.5/8 19
1. Housing rehabilitation - United States - Abstracts. I. United States. Dept. of Housing and Urban Development. Office of Policy Development and Research.
HD7293 .H7822 1987

HOUSING REHABILITATION - EUROPEAN ECONOMIC COMMUNITY COUNTRIES.
Employment and housing renovation in Europe /. Luxembourg , Washington, DC , 1986. 89 p. : ISBN 92-825-6422-3 : LC Card 87-136222 DDC 331.2/89/083094 19
HD5718.B92 E863 1986

HOUSING REHABILITATION - FINLAND.
Harju, Hely. Puutteellisen asumisen parantaminen kunnissa vuosina 1985-1989 /. [Helsinki , 1986] 69, [16] p. : ISBN 951-46-9022-2 LC Card 86-215457
HD7345.3.A3 H367 1986

HOUSING REHABILITATION - GERMANY (WEST)
Kujath, Hans Joachim. Die Regeneration der Stadt . Hamburg , c1986. 282 p. ; ISBN 3-7672-0943-8 LC Card 87-113493 DDC 363.5/8 19
HD7339.A3 K85 1986

Versicherungen in der Altbauerneuerung /. Berlin , c1985. 83 p. ; ISBN 3-433-02219-4 LC Card 86-104351
HG9986.4.G3 V47 1985

HOUSING REHABILITATION - GOVERNMENT POLICY - ONTARIO.
Peter Barnard Associates. An evaluation of the Ontario Home Renewal Program . [Toronto] , 1976. x, 43, [28] p. : LC Card 85-192287
HD7305.O6 P47 1976

HOUSING REHABILITATION - GOVERNMENT POLICY - UNITED STATES.
Guggenheim, Joseph. HUD's rental rehabilitation program, HUD's housing development grant program /. Washington, D.C. [c1984] 13 p. ; LC Card 87-100358 DDC 363.5/8 19
HD7288.85.U6 G84 1984

HOUSING REHABILITATION - HUNGARY - STATISTICS.
Lakásváltoztatási szándékok, lakáskörülmények az 1984. évi mikrocenzus alapján /. Budapest , 1986. 199 p. ; ISBN 963-340-798-2 LC Card 87-110348
HD7337.5.A3 L355 1986

HOUSING REHABILITATION - ITALY.
La Riconversione produttiva nell'edilizia /. Milano , 1984, c1981. 319 p. : ***NYPL [JLD 86-3381]***

HOUSING REHABILITATION - ITALY - ADDRESSES, ESSAYS, LECTURES.
Riuso e riqualificazione edilizia negli anni '80 /. Milano [1981] 706 p. :ill. ; ISBN 88-20-42135-6 (pbk.) : LC Card 81-210070
HD7341.A3 R58 1981 ***NYPL [JSD 86-493]***

HOUSING REHABILITATION - MANITOBA - WINNIPEG.
Levin, Earl A. A model for joint public sector/private sector participation in core area housing development and core area revitalization /. [Winnipeg, Man., Canada] , 1985. ix leaves, 93 p. ; LC Card 86-137674 DDC 363.5/8 19
HD7305.M3 L48 1985 ***NYPL [JLF 86-1313]***

HOUSING REHABILITATION - NEW YORK (STATE)
Nolon, John R. Housing rehabilitation under the Community Development Block Grant Program . [New York, N.Y.] [1984] 150 p. in various pagings ; LC Card 86-622826 DDC 363.5/8 19
HD7303.N7 N65 1984

Housing rehabilitation under the Community Development Block Grant Program . Nolon, John R. [New York, N.Y.] [1984] 150 p. in various pagings ; LC Card 86-622826 DDC 363.5/8 19
HD7303.N7 N65 1984

HOUSING REHABILITATION - UNITED STATES.
United States. Office of Urban Rehabilitation and Community Reinvestment. FHA Title I property improvement loan insurance [microform] . Washington , 1978. 19 p. ; ***NYPL [*ZT-1564 no.11]***

HOUSING REHABILITATION - UNITED STATES - ABSTRACTS.
Housing rehabilitation . Washington, D.C. [1987] 39 p. : LC Card 87-601734 DDC 363.5/8 19
HD7293 .H7822 1987

HOUSING - RESEARCH - PANAMA.
Navarro, Hugo. La vivienda de interés social en Panamá . Panamá , 1975. 288 p. : LC Card 84-100873
HD7312.A3 N38 1975

HOUSING - RÉUNION.
L'Habitat réunionnais /. Saint-Denis [1983] 73 p., A-T leaves of plates : LC Card 84-981007
HD7378.9.A3 H33 1983

HOUSING, RURAL - BRAZIL - PERNAMBUCO - CASE STUDIES.
Construção de habitações na zona rural da microrregião do São Francisco /. Recife , 1982. 23 leaves ; LC Card 86-175009
HD7289.B72 S263 1982

HOUSING, RURAL - BRAZIL - SÃO FRANCISCO RIVER REGION.
Construção de habitações na zona rural da microrregião do São Francisco /. Recife , 1982. 23 leaves ; LC Card 86-175009
HD7289.B72 S263 1982

HOUSING, RURAL - ENGLAND - SOUTH HAMS (DEVON)
Phillips, David R. Rural housing and the public sector /. Aldershot, Hampshire, England [Brookfield, Vt.] c1982. viii, 174 p. : ISBN 0-566-00456-9 : LC Card 82-134413 DDC 352.7/5/0941 19
HD7289.G82 S687 1982
NYPL [JLD 83-2605]

HOUSING, RURAL - GERMANY (WEST) - KÖRLE - HISTORY.
Wagner, Kurt. Leben auf dem Lande im Wandel des Industrialisierung . Frankfurt am Main , 1986. 558, [1] p. : ISBN 3-458-14329-7 LC Card 87-112493 DDC 330.943/41 19
HC289.K66 W34 1986

HOUSING, RURAL - GOVERNMENT POLICY - MEXICO.
Vivienda rural, México. [Mexico City] [1982?] 40 p. : LC Card 86-174056
HD7289.M6 V58 1982

HOUSING, RURAL - GREAT BRITAIN.
Phillips, David R. Rural housing and the public sector /. Aldershot, Hampshire, England [Brookfield, Vt.] c1982. viii, 174 p. : ISBN 0-566-00456-9 : LC Card 82-134413 DDC 352.7/5/0941 19
HD7289.G82 S687 1982
NYPL [JLD 83-2605]

HOUSING, RURAL - KENYA - KISUMU DISTRICT.
Sterkenburg, J. J. Rural housing conditions in Kisumu District, Kenya /. [Utrecht] [Nairobi] , 1982. 95 p., [6] leaves of plates : LC Card 85-981197
HD7289.K42 K67 1982

HOUSING, RURAL - MEXICO.
Vivienda rural, México. [Mexico City] [1982?] 40 p. : LC Card 86-174056
HD7289.M6 V58 1982

HOUSING, RURAL - NEW YORK (STATE)
Seligson, Wendy. Rural housing in N.Y.S. /. [Albany, N.Y.] [1979] [61] p. : LC Card 82-621690 DDC 363.5/8/09747 19
HD7289.U7 N77 1979 ***NYPL [JLF 86-765]***

Housing, rural poor, and their living conditions /. Parvathamma, C., 1928- Delhi, India [1987] vi, 135 p. ; ISBN 81-212-0088-1 : LC Card 87-900831 DDC 363.5/8 19
HD7361.K27 P37 1987

HOUSING, RURAL - PORTUGAL.
Costa, F. Ramos da. Inquérito à habitação rural . Lisboa , 1944. 57 p. : LC Card 86-137838
HD7289.P67 C67 1944

HOUSING, RURAL - TANZANIA - RUVUMA REGION.
Salomon, Robert. Ruvuma region . Dar es Salaam , 1981. 32 leaves : LC Card 85-981451
HD7289.T352 R897 1981

HOUSING - RUSSIAN S.F.S.R. - MOSCOW - HISTORY.
Kreis, Barbara, 1947- Moskau, 1917-35 . [Germany] , c1985. 243 p., [3] p. of plates : ISBN 3-921420-26-1 : LC Card 86-170426
HD7345.M6 K73 1985

HOUSING, SINGLE FAMILY - MANAGEMENT.
Holland, Barbara Kamanitz. Managing single-family homes /. Chicago, Ill. , c1987. xiv, 155 p. ; ISBN 0-912104-92-9 (pbk.) LC Card 87-81672 DDC 333.33/8 19
HD1394 .H63 1987

HOUSING - SOCIAL ASPECTS - COLOMBIA - VALLE DEL CAUCA.
Mosquera Torres, Gilma. Clases, segregación y barrios /. Cali, Colombia , 1984. 126 p. : LC Card 86-218143
HD7325.V35 M67 1984

HOUSING - SOUTH AFRICA - EAST LONDON REGION - STATISTICS.
Erwee, Johannes Albertus. Trends in the construction of dwelling units in the Port Elizabeth/Uitenhage and East London/King William's town regions, 1970-1984, including additions and alterations /. Port Elizabeth [South Africa] [1985] 44 leaves : ISBN 0-86988-244-9 (pbk.) LC Card 86-229280 DDC 363.5/1/096875 19
HD7374.4.P6 E735 1985

HOUSING - SOUTH AFRICA - PORT ELIZABETH - STATISTICS.
Erwee, Johannes Albertus. Trends in the construction of dwelling units in the Port Elizabeth/Uitenhage and East London/King William's town regions, 1970-1984, including additions and alterations /. Port Elizabeth [South Africa] [1985] 44 leaves : ISBN 0-86988-244-9 (pbk.) LC Card 86-229280 DDC 363.5/1/096875 19
HD7374.4.P6 E735 1985

HOUSING - SPAIN.
El Libro blanco de la promoción-construcción. [Barcelona] , 1985. 141 p. : LC Card 86-188032
HD7351.A3 L53 1985

HOUSING - SPAIN - ASTURIAS.
Argüelles, Alfonso. Los Oscos y la Cuenca del Eo . [Asturias] [1984?] ix, 317 p. : ISBN 84-505-0237-3 LC Card 86-174593
HC387.A7 A74 1984

HOUSING - SPAIN - BARCELONA - STATISTICS.
Cens d'edificis, 1970 /. [Barcelona] [1979?] 5, 9 leaves ; LC Card 84-131679
HD7351.B3 C45 1979

Cens vivendas 1970 /. [Barcelona] [1979?] 4, 9 leaves ; LC Card 84-131705
HD7351.B3 C47 1979

HOUSING - SPAIN - CATALONIA.
El Libro blanco de la promoción-construcción. [Barcelona] , 1985. 141 p. : LC Card 86-188032
HD7351.A3 L53 1985

HOUSING - SPAIN - CATALONIA - FINANCE.
Trilla i Bellart, Carme. Finançament del l'accés a l'habitatge a Catalunya en els darrers anys /. [Barcelona] [1984] 58 p. : LC Card 86-160332
HD7351.C37 T75 1984

HOUSING - SPAIN - FINANCE.
Trilla i Bellart, Carme. La financiación del acceso a la vivienda de España, 1976-1981 /. [Barcelona] [1984] 56 p. : LC Card 86-160004
HD7351.A4 T75 1984

HOUSING - SPAIN - FINANCE - CONGRESSES.
El Mercado hipotecario . Madrid , 1984. 162 p. ; ISBN 84-85669-34-7 LC Card 86-211862
HG2040.5.S7 M47 1984

HOUSING - SPAIN - MADRID METROPOLITAN AREA - MATHEMATICAL MODELS.
El Sector vivienda . Madrid , 1982. 224 p. : ISBN 84-7088-324-0 LC Card 85-219674
HD7351.A3 S43 1982

HOUSING - SPAIN - MATHEMATICAL MODELS.
El Sector vivienda . Madrid , 1982. 224 p. : ISBN 84-7088-324-0 LC Card 85-219674
HD7351.A3 S43 1982

HOUSING - SRI LANKA - STATISTICS.
Census of population and housing, 1981. [Colombo] [1986] iv, 232 p. : LC Card 87-901055
HA4570.8 .A4 1981c

Sri Lanka census of population and housing, 1981. [Colombo] , 1985. 3 v. in 1 ; LC Card 86-903509 DDC 304.6/09549/3021 19
HA4570.8 .A4 1981b

HOUSING SUBSIDIES - AUSTRIA - UPPER AUSTRIA - HISTORY.
Urferer, Wilhelm. Das Wohnungswesen in Oberösterreich seit Beginn dieses Jahrhunderts im Vergleich zu seiner gesamtstaatlichen Entwicklung /. Linz , c1986. viii, 235 p. : ISBN 3-85320-384-1 LC Card 87-127729 DDC 363.5/8/094362 19
HD7337.U6 U74 1986

HOUSING SUBSIDIES - CALIFORNIA - LOS ANGELES.
Aroni, Samuel. How successful was Section 8 in Los Angeles? . Berkeley , 1986. 18 p. ; ISBN 0-87772-311-7 (pbk.) LC Card 86-27180 DDC 363.5/8 19
HD7288.85.U62 L73 1986

HOUSING SUBSIDIES - GERMANY (WEST)
Kaufmann-Scheuer, Brigitte. Perspektiven und Modelle einer Neuorientierung der staatlichen Wohneigentumsfoïderung /. Freiburg [i. Br.] , 1983. 235 p. : ISBN 3-8107-2185-9 LC Card 84-108468
HD7339.A3 K34 1983

HOUSING SUBSIDIES - GERMANY (WEST) - MANNHEIM - CASE STUDIES.
Ipsen, Detlev. Markt und Raum . Frankfurt , New York , c1986. 250 p. : ISBN 3-593-33685-5 LC Card 87-127593 DDC 363.5/8 19
HD7339.M35 I67 1986

HOUSING SUBSIDIES - SWEDEN.
Bostadsbidragen . [Stockholm] [1982] 207 p. : ISBN 91-38-72586-X LC Card 83-240044
HD7350.A3 B697 1982

HOUSING SUBSIDIES - UNITED STATES - STATES.
Stegman, Michael A. Nonfederal housing programs . Washington, D.C. , 1987. viii, 231 p. ; ISBN 0-87420-673-1 LC Card 87-51080 DDC 363.5/8 19
HD7293.Z9 S75 1987

HOUSING SURVEYS - COLOMBIA.
Jaramillo, Samuel. Análisis de las condiciones de vivienda de los hogares colombianos, a partir de los resultados de la encuesta nacional de hogares, etapa 33, 1981 /. Bogotá, Colombia , 1985. ii, 166 p. ; LC Card 87-403605 DDC 363.5/1/09861 19
HD7325.A3 J37 1985

HOUSING SURVEYS - PORTUGAL - EVORA.
Inquérito às rendas e a outras características das habitações arrendadas na cidade de Evora em 1955-56 /. Lisboa [1958] 26 p. : LC Card 85-185037
HA1571 .A32 no. 33 HD7288.85.P82E93

HOUSING SURVEYS - TEXAS.
Albrecht, Don E. A profile of 1984 Texas homebuyers /. College Station, Tex. [1986] 70 p. : LC Card 86-622194 DDC 333.33/8 19
HD7287.82.U62 T434 1986

HOUSING - SWEDEN.
Wiktorin, Marianne. Kommunal bostadsförmedling . Stockholm [1983] 107 p. : ISBN 91-540-3929-0 : LC Card 84-218864
HD7350.A3 W55 1983

HOUSING - SWITZERLAND.
Flückiger, Hans. Siedlungsstruktur . Bern , c1985. 118 p. : ISBN 3-258-03529-6 : LC Card 86-134805
HN603.5 .F58 1985 ***NYPL [JLE 86-3789]***

HOUSING - TEXAS.
Albrecht, Don E. A profile of 1984 Texas homebuyers /. College Station, Tex. [1986] 70 p. : LC Card 86-622194 DDC 333.33/8 19
HD7287.82.U62 T434 1986

HOUSING - THAILAND.
Chadsri Bunnag. Housing in urban development . [Bangkok] [Rotterdam] Netherlands [1985] 49, [2] leaves : LC Card 86-915989 DDC 363.5/09593 19
HD7363.55.A3 C46 1985

HOUSING - THAILAND - BANGKOK METROPOLITAN AREA.
Charoon Vitiprod. Rapid population growth, living conditions, and fertility reduction implication (Bangkok metropolis) /. [Singapore] 1979. ii, 41 leaves : LC Card 82-940038
HB3644.55.B36 C48 1979

Housing the aged : design directives and policy considerations / edited by Victor Regnier and Jon Pynoos. New York : Elsevier, c1987. xvii, 500 p. : ill. ; 27 cm. Bibliography: p. 465-487. Includes index. ISBN 0-444-01012-2 LC Card 87-5253 DDC 363.5/9
1. Aged - Dwellings. I. Regnier, Victor, 1947-. II. Pynoos, Jon.
HD7287.9 .H7 1987

Housing the poor of Paris, 1850-1902 /. Shapiro, Ann-Louise, 1944- Madison, Wis. , 1985. xx, 224 p. : ISBN 0-299-09880-X : LC Card 84-40159 DDC 363.5/8 19
HD7288.78.F82 P357 1985
NYPL [JLE 85-1534]

HOUSING - TURKEY.
Boratav, Korkut. Housing yearbook /. Ankara, Turkey , 1985. 32, [2] p. ; LC Card 87-403323 DDC 363.5/09561 19
HD7358.25.A3 B67 1985

HOUSING - UNITED STATES.
Adams, John S., 1938- Housing America in the 1980s /. New York , c1987. p. cm. ISBN

0-87154-003-7 : LC Card 86-42950 DDC 363.5/0973 19
HD7293 .A625 1987

Hughes, James W. The dynamics of America's housing /. New Brunswick, N.J. , c1987. xiv, 224 p. ; ISBN 0-88285-122-5 : LC Card 87-4515 DDC 363.5/0973 19
HD7293 .H826 1987

HOUSING - UNITED STATES - ADDRESSES, ESSAYS, LECTURES.
Critical perspectives on housing /. Philadelphia , 1986. xxi, 686 p. : ISBN 0-87722-395-5 LC Card 85-17274 DDC 363.5/0973 19
HD7293 .C738 1986 ***NYPL [JLE 86-3639]***

HOUSING - UNITED STATES - COSTS.
United States. Dept. of Housing and Urban Development. Office of Policy Development and Research. Division of Policy Studies. The conversion of rental housing to condominiums and cooperatives . [Washington, D.C.] , 1982. 95 p. : ***NYPL [JLF 86-442]***

HOUSING - UNITED STATES - FINANCE.
Bass, Gary J. A practical and simple guide to a home mortgage /. Irving, Tex. , c1987. v, 66 p. : ISBN 0-944319-00-9 (pbk.) LC Card 87-82025 DDC 332.7/22/0973 19
HG2040.5.U5 B367 1987

G-Yohannes, Arefaine. The professional's desktop guide to real estate finance /. Chicago, Ill. , c1988. p. cm. ISBN 0-917253-93-0 : LC Card 87-17918 DDC 332.7/2 19
HG2040.5.U5 G125 1988

Stegman, Michael A. Nonfederal housing programs . Washington, D.C. , 1987. viii, 231 p. ; ISBN 0-87420-673-1 LC Card 87-51080 DDC 363.5/8 19
HD7293.Z9 S75 1987

Wiedemer, John P., 1918- Real estate finance /. Englewood Cliffs, N.J. , c1987. xvi, 396 p. : ISBN 0-13-762774-2 LC Card 86-30471 DDC 332.7/2/0973 19
HG2040.5.U5 W54 1987

HOUSING - UNITED STATES - FINANCE - CASE STUDIES.
Stegman, Michael A. Housing finance and public policy . New York , c1986. xiv, 290 p. : ISBN 0-442-28035-1 (pbk.) : LC Card 85-13408 DDC 332.63/24/0973 19
HD7293.Z9 S74 1986 ***NYPL [JLE 86-3779]***

HOUSING - UNITED STATES - FINANCE - HANDBOOKS, MANUALS, ETC.
The Housing handbook . New York, N.Y. (130 E. 59 St., New York 10022) , 1986. 150 p. ; LC Card 87-107431 DDC 363.5/8/0681 19
HD7304.N5 H68 1986

HOUSING - UNITED STATES - FINANCE - STATISTICS.
Gramley, Lyle E. Real estate finance and housing . Washington, D.C. (1125 15th St., N.W., Washington 20005) , c1987. vii, 132 p. : LC Card 87-124264 DDC 332.7/2/0973021 19
HG2040.5.U5 G73 1987

HOUSING - UNITED STATES - MATHEMATICAL MODELS - ADDRESSES, ESSAYS, LECTURES.
Microeconomic models of housing markets /. Berlin , New York , c1985. iv, 197 p. : ISBN 0-387-15193-1 (pbk.) LC Card 85-4648 DDC 381/.4569083/0724 19
HD7339.A3 M53 1985
NYPL [JLM 72-289 no.239]

HOUSING - UNITED STATES - STATISTICS.
Gramley, Lyle E. Real estate finance and housing . Washington, D.C. (1125 15th St., N.W., Washington 20005) , c1987. vii, 132 p. : LC Card 87-124264 DDC 332.7/2/0973021 19
HG2040.5.U5 G73 1987

HOUSING - URUGUAY - MONTEVIDEO.
Vicario, Luis B. Algunas características del inventario de vivienda . [Montevideo] , 1985. 42 p. : LC Card 86-152477
HD7330.M64 V53 1985

HOUSING - URUGUAY - STATISTICS.
Recuentos preliminares . [Montevideo] [1986] 188 p. : LC Card 87-122427 DDC 304.6/09895/021 19
HA1074 1985

HOUSING - VENEZUELA.
Gilbert, Alan, 1944- The political economy of land . Aldershot, Hants , Brookfield, Vt., U. S.A. , c1985. xv, 163 p. : ISBN 0-566-05007-2 : LC Card 85-17535 DDC 333.77/13/0987 19
HD576 .G54 1985 ***NYPL [JLD 86-3632]***

HOUSING - VENEZUELA - STATISTICS.
Situación habitacional en Venezuela . [Caracas] [1986- v. <1 > : ISBN 980-280-043-0 LC Card 87-114711 DDC 363.5/1/0987/021 19
HD7331.A3 S57 1986

HOUSING - VIRGINIA - DIRECTORIES.
Directory of Virginia housing resources. [Richmond] [1986] iii, 153 p. : LC Card 87-620669 DDC 350.86/5/025755 19
HD7303.V8 D57 1986

Housing yearbook /. Boratav, Korkut. Ankara, Turkey , 1985. 32, [2] p. ; LC Card 87-403323 DDC 363.5/09561 19
HD7358.25.A3 B67 1985

HOUSING - ZAMBIA - STATISTICS.
1980 population and housing census of Zambia. Lusaka, Zambia , <[1985?-. v. <2-5 > : LC Card 86-981236 DDC 304.6/096894 19
HA4703 .A4 1980

HOUSING - ZIMBABWE.
Report on housing and urban development in Zimbabwe . [Harare, Zimbabwe , 1986] vi, 46 p., [1] folded leaf of plates : LC Card 87-980381 DDC 363.5/8 19
HD7374.5.A3 R46 1986

Houston Area Research Center. Promoting high-technology industry . Boulder , 1987. 283 p. ; ISBN 0-8133-7427-8 (pbk. : alk. paper) LC Card 87-61327 DDC 338.4/762/000973 19
HC110.H53 P76 1987

Houston Chamber of Commerce.
Houston Chamber of Commerce membership directory & buyers guide / prepared by Research Division, Member Services Council, Houston Chamber of Commerce. Houston, Tex. : The Chamber, c1986. xxvii, 284 p. : ill. (some col.) ; 28 cm. Includes index. LC Card 87-119626 DDC 380.1/025/7641411 19
1. Houston Chamber of Commerce - Directories. 2. Houston (Tex.) - Commerce - Directories. 3. Houston (Tex.) - Industries - Directories. I. Houston Chamber of Commerce. Research Division. II. Title.
HF296 .H68 1986

HOUSTON CHAMBER OF COMMERCE - DIRECTORIES.
Houston Chamber of Commerce. Houston Chamber of Commerce membership directory & buyers guide /. Houston, Tex. , c1986. xxvii, 284 p. : LC Card 87-119626 DDC 380.1/025/7641411 19
HF296 .H68 1986

Houston Chamber of Commerce membership directory & buyers guide /. Houston Chamber of Commerce. Houston, Tex. , c1986. xxvii, 284 p. : LC Card 87-119626 DDC 380.1/025/7641411 19
HF296 .H68 1986

Houston Chamber of Commerce. Research Division. Houston Chamber of Commerce. Houston Chamber of Commerce membership directory & buyers guide /. Houston, Tex. , c1986. xxvii, 284 p. : LC Card 87-119626 DDC 380.1/025/7641411 19
HF296 .H68 1986

Houston, Douglas C. Daicoff, Darwin W. The Kansas retail liquor industry . [Lawrence, Kan.] [1985] 53 leaves ; LC Card 86-622263 DDC 381/.456631/09781 19
HD9390.U63 K23 1985

HOUSTON (TEX.) - COMMERCE - DIRECTORIES.
Houston Chamber of Commerce. Houston Chamber of Commerce membership directory & buyers guide /. Houston, Tex. , c1986. xxvii, 284 p. : LC Card 87-119626 DDC 380.1/025/7641411 19
HF296 .H68 1986

HOUSTON (TEX.) - ECONOMIC CONDITIONS - STATISTICS.
Handbook on the Houston economy. [Houston, Tex. , 1986?] 36 p. : LC Card 86-622198 DDC 330.9764/1411063 19
HC108.H8 H36 1986

HOUSTON (TEX.) - INDUSTRIES - DIRECTORIES.
Houston Chamber of Commerce. Houston Chamber of Commerce membership directory & buyers guide /. Houston, Tex. , c1986. xxvii, 284 p. : LC Card 87-119626 DDC 380.1/025/7641411 19
HF296 .H68 1986

Houweling, Marjolein. Ondernemende vrouwen / samengesteld door Marjolein Houweling en Bernadette de Wit. Amsterdam : Aramith, c1985. 128 p. : ill. ; 22 cm. Bibliography: p. 127. ISBN 90-6834-018-2 : LC Card 86-166264
1. Women-owned business enterprises - Netherlands - Case studies. 2. Women in business - Netherlands - Case studies. 3. Success in business - Netherlands - Case studies. I. Wit, Bernadette de. II. Title.
HD2346.N4 H68 1985

Houyoux, Joseph. Kinshasa 1975 /. Kinshasa , Bruxelles [1986] 287 p. : LC Card 86-229048
HA4711.Z9 K565 1986

Houze, William C. Lenfest, David. Kaypro word processing, plain & simple /. Blue Ridge Summit, Pa. , c1985. xiv, 176 p. : ISBN 0-8306-0812-5 : LC Card 84-8720 DDC 652 19
Z52.5.K39 L46 1985 ***NYPL [JSE 87-12]***

Hovda, Gudmund. Dagbok frå bondekongressen i Moskva, oktober 1923 / Gudmund Hovda ; innledning og kommentarer ved Jens Petter Nielsen. Oslo : Universitetet i Oslo, Slavisk-baltisk institutt, 1984. 46 p. ; 21 cm. (Meddelelser / Universitetet i Oslo, Slavisk-baltisk institutt . nr. 40) Includes bibliographical references. ISBN 82-902503-1-2 LC Card 85-190754
1. International Peasants' Conference (1st : 1923 : Moscow, R.S.F.S.R.). I. Nielsen, Jens Petter. II. Series: Meddelelser / Universitetet i Oslo, Slavisk-baltisk institutt , nr. 40. III. Title.
HD1405 .H68 1984

Hovenkamp, Herbert, 1948- Economics and federal antitrust law / by Herbert Hovenkamp. St. Paul, Minn. : West Pub. Co., 1985. xxvii, 414 p. : ill. ; 26 cm. (Hornbook series student edition) Includes bibliographical references and indexes. ISBN 0-314-86196-3 LC Card 84-25783 DDC 343.73/072 347.30372 19
1. Antitrust law - United States. 2. Antitrust law - Economic aspects - United States. I. Title. II. Series.
KF1649 .H67 1985 ***NYPL [JLF 86-1373]***

How and why of rural banking /. Khemani, C. L., 1934- New Delhi , 1987. 255, [41] p. : LC Card 87-901033 DDC 332.1/0954 19
HG3288 .K44 1987

How bad is Australia's economic performance and why? . Gruen, F. H. (Fred Henry), 1921- Canberra, Australia [1985] 61 p. ; ISBN 0-949293-38-5 (pbk.) LC Card 86-228640 DDC 338.994 19
HC605 .G78 1985

How consumers view credit unions : results of a comprehensive telephone survey to determine public familiarity with and attitudes toward credit unions / by Opinion Research Corporation, Financial Services Group. New York, NY (1 Penn Plaza, Suite 1631, New York 10119) : The Corporation, c1986. 37, 7 leaves, [166] p. ; 28 cm. "ORC study #33270." LC Card 87-111937 DDC 334/.22/0973 19
1. Credit unions - United States - Public opinion. 2. Public opinion - United States. I. Opinion Research Corporation (U. S.). Financial Services Group.
HG2037 .H68 1986

How Detroit changed history /. Bolan, Nelson. Lawrenceville, Va. , c1987. v, 246 p. : ISBN 1-556-18018-7 (pbk.) : LC Card 87-70325 DDC 338.4/76292/0973 19
HD9710.U52 B55 1987

How, Douglas.
[Very private person]
Canada's mystery man of high finance : the story of Izaak Walton Killiam and his glittering wife Dorothy / Douglas How. Hantsport, N.S. : Lancelot Press, 1986. 173 p. : ports. ; 21 cm. Spine title: Mystery man of high finance. ISBN 0-88999-305-X (pbk.) LC Card 86-207291 DDC 338.092/2 B 19
1. Killam, Izaak Walton, 1885-1955. 2. Killam, Dorothy Johnston. 3. Capitalists and financiers - Canada - Biography. I. Title. II. Title: Mystery man of high finance.
HG172.K55 H68 1986

How Europe underdeveloped Africa /. Rodney, Walter. Washington, D.C. , 1981, c1972. xxiv,

312 p. ; ISBN 0-88258-105-8 LC Card 87-142601
HC800 .R62 1981b

How federal policies affect the steel industry. Washington, D.C. : Congress of the U. S., Congressional Budget Office : For sale by the Supt. of Docs., U. S. G.P.O., [1987] xii, 66 p. : ill. ; 26 cm. (A special study) Shipping list no.: 87-136-P. "February 1987"--Cover. Includes bibliographical references. S/N 052-070-06254-1 Item 1005 C LC Card 87-601115 DDC 338.4/7669142/0973 19
1. Steel industry and trade - Government policy - United States. 2. Industry and state - United States. I. United States. Congressional Budget Office. II. Series: Special study (United States. Congressional Budget Office).
HD9516 .H65 1987

HOW five. Clark, James Leland, 1929- HOW 5 . Boston, Mass. , c1988. ix, 370 p. : ISBN 0-534-87144-5 (pbk.) : LC Card 87-20155 DDC 651.7/402 19
HF5726 .C55 1988

How labor markets work : reflections on theory and practice / by John Dunlop ... [et al.] ; edited by Bruce E. Kaufman. Lexington, Mass. : Lexington Books, c1988. viii, 256 p. : port. ; 24 cm. "Selected bibliographies": p. [233]-244. Includes index. ISBN 0-669-15126-2 (alk. paper) LC Card 87-22718 DDC 331.12 19
1. Labor supply - Congresses. 2. Wages - Congresses. 3. Dunlop, John Thomas, 1914- - Congresses. 4. Kerr, Clark, 1911- - Congresses. 5. Lester, Richard Allen, 1908- - Congresses. 6. Reynolds, Lloyd George, 1910- - Congresses. I. Dunlop. John Thomas, 1914-. II. Kaufman, Bruce E.
HD5701.3 .H68 1988

How men feel . Astrachan, Anthony. Garden City, N.Y. , 1986. x, 444 p. ; ISBN 0-385-23333-7 : LC Card 85-22944 DDC 305.3/1 19
HQ1090.3 .A88 1986 ***NYPL [JLE 86-3421]***

How Miami's new image was created /. Botifoll, Luis J. Coral Gables, Fla. [1985?] 16 p. ; LC Card 87-124138
HC108.M5 B68 1985

How mighty a force? : studies of workers' consciousness and organization in the United States / Maurice Zeitlin, editor. Los Angeles : Institute of Industrial Relations, University of California, c1983. ix, 369 p. ; 22 cm. (Monograph and research series . 35) Includes bibliographies.
1. Labor and laboring classes - United States - 1914-. 2. Trade-unions - United States - History. I. Zeitlin, Maurice, 1935-. II. Series: Monograph and research series (University of California, Los Angeles. Institute of Industrial Relations) , 35.
NYPL [JLD 87-277]

How much does one percent of growth change the unemployment? . Paldam, Martin. Aarhus, Denmark [1986] 35 p. : LC Card 86-221448 DDC 331.13/7 19
HD5707.5 .P34 1986

How much say do the trade unions have? : a report from the German Democratic Republic / [translated by Intertext Verlag Zeit im Bild]. Berlin : Panorama DDR, [1986] 61 p., [16] p. of plates : ill. ; 19 cm. (First-hand information) LC Card 87-117720 DDC 331.88/09431 19
1. Trade-unions - Germany, East.
HD6700.5.Z6 H69 1986

How socialist competition is run /. DDR im Überblick. English. Berlin , 1983. 64 p. : LC Card 86-201752 DDC 338.6/048/09431 19
HC290.795.S6 D3713 1983

How state spending reductions affect economic activity /. Goldsmith, Oliver Scott. Fairbanks [1986] 40, 10 p. : LC Card 86-622972 DDC 330.9798/05 19
HJ7553 .G64 1986

How successful was Section Eight in Los Angeles? Aroni, Samuel. How successful was Section 8 in Los Angeles? . Berkeley , 1986. 18 p. ; ISBN 0-87772-311-7 (pbk.) LC Card 86-27180 DDC 363.5/8 19
HD7288.85.U62 L73 1986

How successful was Section 8 in Los Angeles? . Aroni, Samuel. Berkeley , 1986. 18 p. ; ISBN 0-87772-311-7 (pbk.) LC Card 86-27180 DDC 363.5/8 19
HD7288.85.U62 L73 1986

How the best is won /. Haggai, Tom. Nashville , c1987. 228 p. ; ISBN 0-8407-4221-5 LC Card 87-14996 DDC 658.4/09 19
HD38.2 .H34 1987

How the public works . Pagano, Michael A. Washington, D.C. , c1986. ix, 68, 6 p. : ISBN 0-933729-13-8 (pbk.) : LC Card 87-129719 DDC 338.4/3363/0973 19
HJ9145 .P343 1986

How the Queensland planters get and treat their--. Gray, William, Rev. The kanaka, or, How the Queensland planters get and treat their-- /. Adelaide , 1895. 40 p. ; LC Card 87-123897 DDC 331.6/2/960943 19
HD8848.5.P75 G73 1895

How to avoid a mid-life financial crisis /. Eisenberg, Richard, 1956- Glenview, Ill. , c1987. xxi, 426 p. : ISBN 0-673-18727-6 : LC Card 86-31647 DDC 332.024 19
HG179 .E39 1987

How to be an effective trainer . Smith, Barry J., 1947- New York , c1987. 404 p. : ISBN 0-471-85239-2 (pbk.) LC Card 86-26774 DDC 658.3/1243 19
HF5549.5.T7 S642 1987

How to become a professional model /. Addams, Jon, 1941- Philadelphia, PA , c1987. p. cm. ISBN 0-943331-01-3 : LC Card 87-20656 DDC 659.1/52 19
HD6073.M77 A33 1987

How to borrow your way to real estate riches /. Hicks, Tyler Gregory, 1921- Rocklin, CA , c1987. 324 p. ; ISBN 0-914629-57-3 (pbk.) : LC Card 87-2426 DDC 332.63/24 19
HD1382.5 .H53 1987

How to break into modeling /. Orenstein, Vik, 1960- Cincinnati, Ohio , c1987. 169 p. : ISBN 0-89879-282-7 (pbk.) : LC Card 87-21703 DDC 659.1/52 19
HD6073.M772 U56 1987

How to buy a good business with little or none of your own money /. Haines, Lionel. New York , c1987. 212 p. ; ISBN 0-8129-1627-1 : LC Card 86-30017 DDC 658.1/6 19
HD2746.5 .H35 1987

How to buy a house when you're cash poor . Bush, Vanessa A. Chicago , c1986. 92 p. ; ISBN 0-8092-4834-4 (pbk.) : LC Card 86-24053 DDC 332.7/22 19
HG2040.15 .B87 1986

How to buy an automated sales, marketing, and telemarketing system. Los Gatos, CA : International MarketVision Corp., c1985. 46 p. : ill. ; 28 cm. "MarketVision's turnkey productivity system." LC Card 86-224565 DDC 658.8/0028/5 19
1. Telemarketing - Data processing. 2. System design. I. International MarketVision Corporation (Los Gatos, Calif.).
HF5415.1265 .H68 1985

How to buy or sell a car by long distance /. Hudson, Adams, 1958- Osceola, Wis. , 1987. 80 p. ; ISBN 0-87938-259-7 (soft) LC Card 87-12185 DDC 629.2/222 19
HF5439.A8 H83 1987

How to buy or sell the closely held corporation /. Silton, Lawrence C. Englewood Cliffs, N.J. , c1987. xi, 308 p. ; ISBN 0-13-403064-8 LC Card 87-14433 DDC 658.1/6 19
HG4028.V3 S54 1987

How to buy real estate with other people's money and how to assemble a real estate investment portfolio . Barr, Andrew M. [Arlington, Va.] , c1978, 1984 printing. ix, 194 p. : LC Card 86-224399 DDC 332.63/24 19
HD1382.5 .B37 1984

How to buy tax free bonds . Howell, Dean M., 1932- Denver, Colo. , 1987. 165 p. ; LC Card 86-91807 DDC 332.63/233/0973 19
HG4952 .H68 1987

How to buy your home /. Joseph, Joel D. Bethesda, Md. , c1988. p. cm. ISBN 0-915765-36-5 : LC Card 86-23630 DDC 643/.12 19
HD1379 .J66 1988

How to check out your competition . Kelly, John M., 1949- New York , c1987. xii, 349 p. : ISBN 0-471-85670-3 (pbk.) LC Card 86-32408 DDC 658.8/02 19
HD41 .K44 1987

How to compete successfully in a public accounting practice /. Miller, Robert E. Englewood Cliffs, N.J. , c1987. xx, 250 p. ; ISBN 0-13-402157-6 LC Card 87-18677 DDC 657/.068 19
HF5627 .M54 1987

How to conduct and analyze real estate market and feasibility studies /. Barrett, G. Vincent. New York , c1988. xvii, 366 p. : ISBN 0-442-21220-8 : LC Card 87-18861 DDC 332.63/24 19
HD1390 .B37 1988

How to create a winning business plan /. Taylor, James Walter, 1933- New York, NY , 1987, c1986. p. cm. ISBN 0-87280-116-0 : LC Card 87-7685 DDC 658.4/012 19
HD62.7 .T38 1987

How to cut business travel costs /. Day, Denis W. New York , c1986. ix, 207 p. : ISBN 0-471-83633-8 : LC Card 86-9277 DDC 658.1/553 19
HD38 .D39 1986 ***NYPL [JLE 86-4235]***

How to deal with difficult people /. Weiss, Donald H., 1936- New York, N.Y. , c1987. 57 p. ; ISBN 0-8144-7674-0 (pbk.) : LC Card 86-47827 DDC 158/.2 19
HD42 .W45 1987

How to define goals and objectives [videorecording] / produced by CRM Productions, Inc. Del Mar, CA : McGraw-Hill Training Systems, 1986. 1 videocassette (18 min.) : sd., col. + 1 leader's guide. Title from data sheet. College students and adults. Issued as U-matic 3/4 in. or Beta 1/2 in. or VHS 1/2 in. Illustrates three useful assumptions about setting objectives and the corresponding pitfalls of these assumptions. Also explains how goals are derived, as well as how goals interrelate on the different management levels of an organization. ISBN 0-07-109094-0 (3/4 in.) LC Card 86-700128 DDC 658.4 11
1. Goal setting in personnel management. 2. Management by objectives. I. CRM Productions. II. McGraw-Hill Training Systems (Firm).
HF5549.5.G6

How to develop a business plan in 15 days /. Luther, William M. New York, NY , c1987. xiii, 241 p. : ISBN 0-8144-5874-2 LC Card 86-47854 DDC 658.4/012 19
HD30.28 .L88 1987

How to do business with Russians . Knight, Misha G. New York , 1987. xxiv, 311 p. : ISBN 0-89930-211-4 (lib. bdg. : alk. paper) LC Card 86-30396 DDC 658.8/48/0947 19
HF1558.5.U6 K56 1987

How to do business with the Japanese . De Mente, Boye. Lincolnwood, Ill., U. S.A. , c1987. vi, 269 p. ; ISBN 0-8442-8509-9 (pbk.) LC Card 86-62724 DDC 395/.52 19
HF5387 .D3835 1987

How to evaluate real estate partnerships /. Stanger, Robert A. Shrewsbury, N.J. , c1986. xvi, 256 p. ; ISBN 0-943570-10-7 LC Card 85-90539 DDC 332.63/247 19
HD1382.55 .S73 1986

How to find company intelligence in state documents / by Washington Researchers Publishing. Ed. 8. Washington, D.C. : Washington Researchers Pub., c1986. 110 p. ; 28 cm. (Briefcase series . bk. 6) Rev. ed. of: Sources of state information on corporations. Ed. 7. c1984. ISBN 0-934940-38-X (pbk.) LC Card 86-218108 DDC 016.3387/4/0973 19
1. Corporations - United States - Information services - United States - Directories. 2. Administrative agencies - United States - States - Directories. I. Washington Researchers Publishing. II. Sources of state information on corporations. III. Series.
HD2785 .H67 1986

How to find information about acquisition candidates /. Rosenberg, Gerald I. Washington, D.C. , c1987. 79 p. ; ISBN 0-934940-45-2 LC Card 86-51570 DDC 016.3387/4/0973 19
HD2785 .R58 1987

How to find information about companies in the telecommunications, data processing, and office automation industries / by Washington Researchers Publishing ; contributor, Michael M. Kaiser Associates. Ed. I. Washington, DC : Washington Researchers, c1987. ii, 130 p. ; 28 cm. Includes index. ISBN 0-934940-48-7 (pbk.) LC

Card 86-51630 DDC 338.7/61004/072073 19
1. Electronic industries - Information services - United States - Directories. 2. Telecommunication - Information services - United States - Directories. 3. Electronic data processing - Information services - United States - Directories. 4. Office practice - Automation - Information services - United States - Directories. 5. Office equipment and supplies - Information services - United States - Directories. I. Washington Researchers Publishing. II. Michael M. Kaiser Associates.
HD9696.A3 U559 1987

How to find information about executives / by Washington Researchers Publishing ; contributors, Leila K. Kight, Lorraine Underwood. Ed. 1. Washington, DC : Washington Researchers Pub., c1986. 72 p. ; 28 cm. (The Executive reports series) Includes bibliographies and index. ISBN 0-934940-44-4 (pbk.) : LC Card 86-51569 DDC 658.4/0072 19
1. Executives - United States - Information services - United States. I. Kight, Leila K. II. Underwood, Lorraine A. III. Washington Researchers Publishing. IV. Series.
HD38.25.U6 H69 1986

How to find information about foreign firms / by Washington Researchers Publishing ; contributors, Teresa Flynn, Olivia Page. Ed. 1. Washington, D.C. : Washington Researchers, c1987. 93 p. ; 28 cm. (Executive reports series) Includes index. ISBN 0-934940-46-0 (pbk.) : LC Card 86-51568 DDC 016.3388/8873 19
1. Corporations, Foreign - Information services - United States. 2. Corporations, Foreign - United States - Directories. 3. Corporations - Directories. I. Flynn, Teresa M. II. Page, Olivia. III. Washington Researchers Publishing. IV. Series.
HD2785 .H69 1987

How to find information about private companies / by Washington Researchers Publishing. Ed. 1. Washington, DC : Washington Researchers Pub., c1987. iii, 149 p. ; 29 cm. Includes index. ISBN 0-934940-47-9 (pbk.) : LC Card 86-51566 DDC 016.3387/4/0973 19
1. Private companies - Information services - United States - Handbooks, manuals, etc. 2. Corporations - Information services - United States - Handbooks, manuals, etc. 3. Government information - United States - Handbooks, manuals, etc. I. Washington Researchers Publishing.
HG4013.5 .H69 1987

How to get a better job quicker /. Payne, Richard A. New York , 1987. x, 242 p. ; ISBN 0-8008-3965-X : LC Card 86-23101 DDC 650.1/4 19
HF5383 .P36 1987

How to get a job in Dallas, Fort Worth . Camden, Thomas M., 1938- Chicago, IL , c1987. viii, 490 p. : ISBN 0-9609516-9-5 (pbk.) : LC Card 86-30123 DDC 650.1/4/097642812 19
HF5382.75.U6 C353 1987

How to get a mortgage in 24 hours /. Lumley, James E. A. New York , c1987. xvii, 205 p. ; ISBN 0-471-85249-X LC Card 86-28930 DDC 332.7/2 19
HG2040.15.U5 .L85 1987

How to get an honest union election /. Benson, Herman W., 1910 (ca.)- Brooklyn, N.Y. [c1987] 65 p. : ISBN 0-9602244-4-0 (pbk.) LC Card 86-73217 DDC 331.87/4/0973 19
HD6490.E42 U62 1987

How to get credit and loans . James, Christopher. Austin, TX , 1987. viii, 179 p. : ISBN 0-9618114-0-4 (pbk.) : LC Card 87-71591 DDC 332.7/43 19
HG3756.U54 J36 1987

How to get organized & increase self confidence . Vitullo, Ray, 1925- North Plainfield, N.J. , c1986. p. cm. ISBN 0-9607752-3-4 : LC Card 86-72854 DDC 650.1 19
HD69.T54 V58 1986

How to get organized and increase self confidence. Vitullo, Ray, 1925- How to get organized & increase self confidence . North Plainfield, N.J. , c1986. p. cm. ISBN 0-9607752-3-4 : LC Card 86-72854 DDC 650.1 19
HD69.T54 V58 1986

How to get the 1 hour real estate loan . Hiller, Michael D. Encino, CA (16161 Ventura Blvd., #C-719, Encino 91436) , c1987. 170 p. : LC Card 87-154252 DDC 332.7/22/0973 19
HG2040.5.U5 H53 1987

How to get your first copywriting job in advertising /. Wasserman, Dick. New York , 1987. viii, 199 p. : ISBN 0-525-48281-4 (pbk.) : LC Card 86-72833 DDC 659.13/22/02373 19
HF5825 .W29 1987

How to hire a consultant. Charnov, Bruce H. Management report . Westbury, N.Y. , c1987. 63 p. : ISBN 0-87280-120-9 (pbk.) : LC Card 87-24106 DDC 658.4/6 19
HD69.C6 C36 1987

How to influence motivation [videorecording] / produced by CRM Productions, Inc. Del Mar, CA : McGraw-Hill Training Systems, 1986. 1 videocassette (31 min.) : sd., col. + 1 leader's guide. Title from data sheet. College students and adults. Issued as U-matic 3/4 in. or Beta 1/2 in. or VHS 1/2 in. Shows how managers can foster employee motivation at three crucial stages of job performance: before a new task is begun, while the task is in progress, and after a task has been completed. ISBN 0-07-109093-2 (3/4 in.) LC Card 86-700127 DDC 658.3 11
1. Employee motivation. I. CRM Productions. II. McGraw-Hill Training Systems (Firm).
HF5549.5.M63

How to invest fifty to five thousand dollars. Dunnan, Nancy. How to invest $50-$5000 /. New York , 1987. 124 p. ; ISBN 0-06-096159-7 (pbk.) : LC Card 86-45862 DDC 332.6/78 19
HG4527 .D77 1987

How to invest in real estate with as little as $1,000 /. Dunnan, Nancy. New York , c1987. p. cm. ISBN 0-06-096042-6 (pbk.) : LC Card 86-45648 DDC 332.63/24 19
HD1382.5 .D86 1987

How to invest offshore successfully /. Marsh, Michael G., 1935- Geneva, Switzerland , c1986. 207 p. : LC Card 86-212027 DDC 332.6/73 19
HG4538 .M3635 1986

How to invest $50-$5000 /. Dunnan, Nancy. New York , 1987. 124 p. ; ISBN 0-06-096159-7 (pbk.) : LC Card 86-45862 DDC 332.6/78 19
HG4527 .D77 1987

How to lead effectively [videorecording] / produced by CRM Productions, Inc. Del Mar, CA : McGraw-Hill Training Systems, 1986. 1 videocassette (19 min.) : sd., col. + 1 leader's guide. Title from data sheet. College students and adults. Issued as U-matic 3/4 in. or Beta 1/2 in. or VHS 1/2 in. Illustrates how to use power effectively by selecting an appropriate leadership style to suit the needs of the situation and individuals. Explains and demonstrates four styles of leadership: directing, consulting, delegating, and participating. ISBN 0-07-109095-9 (3/4 in.) LC Card 86-700130 DDC 658.4 11
1. Leadership. I. CRM Productions. II. McGraw-Hill Training Systems (Firm).
HD57.7

How to learn basic bookkeeping in ten easy lessons /. Barnes, John, 1913- New York , 1987, c1978. 168 p. : ISBN 0-06-463721-2 (pbk.) : LC Card 86-45638 DDC 657/.2 19
HF5635 .B258 1987

How to lose your farm in ten easy lessons and cope with it /. Neill, Robert Hitt. Leland, Miss. , c1987. xi, 138 p. ; ISBN 0-9617591-1-9 (pbk.) : LC Card 87-14176 DDC 338.1/3/097624 19
HD1476.U6 A156 1987

How to make it when you're cash poor /. Norton, Hollis. New York , 1986. 232 p. ; ISBN 0-671-62803-8 (pbk.) LC Card 86-26174 DDC 332.63/24 19
HD1382.5 .N67 1986

How to make money with your micro /. Holtz, Herman. New York , c1984. xiv, 324 p. : ISBN 0-471-88455-3 (pbk.) : LC Card 84-3589 DDC 001.64 19
HF5548.2 .H5925 1984
NYPL [JLE 86-2074]

How to make one thousand dollars a minute. Chapman, Jack, 1945- How to make $1,000 a minute . Berkeley, Calif. , c1987. xii, 90 p. : ISBN 0-89815-191-0 (pbk.) : LC Card 86-23099 DDC 650.1/4 19
HF5549.5.P7 C48 1987

How to make profits with service contracts /. Rizzo, Michael R. New York, NY , c1987. xii, 367 p. ; ISBN 0-8144-5807-6 LC Card 86-47590 DDC 658 19
HD9980.5 .R59 1987

How to make $1,000 a minute . Chapman, Jack, 1945- Berkeley, Calif. , c1987. xii, 90 p. : ISBN 0-89815-191-0 (pbk.) : LC Card 86-23099 DDC 650.1/4 19
HF5549.5.P7 C48 1987

How to manage change effectively /. Kirkpatrick, Donald L. San Francisco , 1985. xxii, 280 p. : ISBN 0-87589-659-6 LC Card 85-45060 DDC 658.4/06 19
HD58.8 .K52 1985 ***NYPL [JLE 87-1191]***

How to manage strikes through strategy . Botha, Henk. Moreletapark , c1986. vi, 101 p. : ISBN 0-620-10384-1 LC Card 87-148504 DDC 658.3/154 19
HD5442.A6 B68 1986

How to manage your boss, yourself, and your coworkers. Grove, Andrew S. One-on-one with Andy Grove . New York , c1987. 235 p. ; ISBN 0-399-13250-3 : LC Card 86-30483 DDC 650.1/3 19
HF5548.83 .G77 1987

How to organize a co-op . Cooperative League of the U. S. A. Washington , 1969. 53 p. :
NYPL [JLF 86-590]

How to organize and operate a small business /. Baumback, Clifford Mason, 1915- Englewood Cliffs, NJ , c1988. xiii, 578 p. : ISBN 0-13-424987-9 LC Card 87-20455 DDC 658/.022 19
HD62.7 .B39 1988

How to pick up foreclosures . Cook, Wade B. Tempe, AZ , New York , c1983. xviii, 130 p. : ISBN 0-910019-04-5 LC Card 86-218222 DDC 332.63/244 19
HD1382.5 .C6694 1983

How to plan and conduct productive business meetings /. Kirkpatrick, Donald L. New York, NY , c1987. p. cm. ISBN 0-8144-7664-3 LC Card 86-47589 DDC 658.4/563 19
HD30.3 .K56 1987

How to prepare a results-driven marketing plan /. Bell, Martin L. New York, NY , c1987. p. cm. ISBN 0-8144-7690-2 LC Card 87-47717 DDC 658.8/02 19
HF5415 .B4285 1987

How to prepare for the certified public accountant examination, CPA. Person, Samuel. Barron's how to prepare for the certified public accountant examination, CPA /. New York , c1987. vi, 537 p. ; ISBN 0-8120-3880-0 (pbk.) : LC Card 87-17914 DDC 657/.076 19
HF5661 .P48 1987

How to prepare for the graduate management admission test GMAT /. Jaffe, Eugene D. New York , c1987. x, 541 p. : ISBN 0-8120-3882-7 (pbk.) LC Card 87-18619 DDC 650/.076 19
HD30.413 .J33 1987

How to prepare for the U. S. Postal Service mailhandler/mail processor examination /. Barkus, Philip. New York , c1987. viii, 295 p. : ISBN 0-8120-2995-X (pbk.) : LC Card 87-14435 DDC 383/.1/076 19
HE6499 .B296 1987

How to profit from-- buying & selling a home. The Kiplinger/Changing times guide to buying and selling a home /. Washington, DC , New York, NY , c1987. iii, 311 p. : ISBN 0-938721-02-X (pbk.) : LC Card 87-167806 DDC 643/.12 19
HD1379 .K52 1987

How to read and understand the financial news /. Warfield, Gerald. New York , c1986. 214 p. ; ISBN 0-06-015647-3 : LC Card 86-45161 DDC 332.63/2042 19
PN4888.C59 W37 1986
NYPL [JLE 87-1488]

How to run a meeting /. Linkemer, Bobbi. New York, NY , c1987. 51 p. ; ISBN 0-8144-7671-6 (pbk.) : LC Card 86-47815 DDC 658.4/563 19
HD30.3 .L55 1987

How to sell a service . McDonald, Malcolm. London , 1986. 149 p. : ISBN 0-434-91231-X (pbk.) : LC Card 86-212510 DDC 658.8 19
HF5438.25 .M396 1986

How to sell apartment buildings . Earle, Gary.

[Chicago] [1987], c1988. xiv, 183 p. : ISBN 0-88462-716-0 LC Card 87-13964 DDC 333.33/8 19
HD1394 .E24 1988

How to sell your homemade creation /. Smith, Allan H. Lake Park, Fla. , 1986 printing, c1985. 146 p. : ISBN 0-931113-02-4 (pbk.) : LC Card 84-52239 DDC 745.5/068/8 19
HF5439.H27 S64 1986

How to shake the new money tree . Dunn, Thomas G. New York, N.Y., U. S.A. , 1988. xviii, 185 p. : ISBN 0-14-046811-0 (pbk.) : LC Card 87-8795 DDC 658.1/5224 19
HG177 .D86 1988

How to solve problems [videorecording] / produced by CRM Productions, Inc. Del Mar, CA : McGraw-Hill Training Systems, 1986. 1 videocassette (22 min.) : sd., col. + 1 leader's guide. Title from data sheet. College students and adults. Issued as U-matic 3/4 in. or Beta 1/2 in. or VHS 1/2 in. Presents a systematic, step-by-step method of problem solving that allows the manager to apply both logic and creativity to the problem-solving process. ISBN 0-07-109096-7 (3/4 in.) LC Card 86-700129 DDC 658.4 11
1. Problem solving. I. CRM Productions. II. McGraw-Hill Training Systems (Firm).
HD30.29

How to start and manage a business of your own in Tennessee. Yates, M. M. (Maurice M.) Greeneville, Tenn. , c1986. ii, 66 p. : LC Card 86-209197 DDC 658.1/141/09768 19
HD62.5 .Y28 1986

How to start, finance, and manage your own small business /. Mancuso, Joseph. Englewood Cliffs, N.J. , c1984. vi, 392 p. : ISBN 0-13-434879-6 LC Card 84-13411 DDC 658/.022 19
HD62.7 .M365 1984
NYPL [*R-Econ. 84-3832]

How to start your own business on a shoestring and make up to $500,000 a year /. Hicks, Tyler Gregory, 1921- Rocklin, CA , New York , c1987. xi, 225 p. ; ISBN 0-914629-12-3 (pbk.) : LC Card 86-25196 DDC 658/.041 19
HD62.5 .H527 1987

How to start your own business successfully! /. Harding, Owen, 1946- Oklahoma City, OK , c1986. 102 p. ; ISBN 0-940897-01-6 (pbk.) : LC Card 86-32849 DDC 658.1/141 19
HD62.5 .H37 1986

How to succeed as a PAO in an era of constraints. Cost-effective management for today's public affairs, or, How to succeed as a PAO in an era of constraints /. Washington, D.C. (1255 Twenty-third St., N.W., Suite 750, Washington 20037) [c1987] xiii, 109 p. : LC Card 87-135276 DDC 659.2 19
HD59 .C645 1987

How to successfully win job interviews . Bezanson, H. A. (Harold A.), 1935- Blaine, WA , c1986. 106 leaves : ISBN 0-9691828-0-5 (pbk.) : LC Card 86-31689 DDC 650.1/4 19
HF5549.5.I6 B48 1986

How to survive and profit from the coming currency recall /. Rice, Jonathan. Chicago , c1986. xiii, 258 p. : ISBN 0-8092-4998-7 : LC Card 86-6215 DDC 332.4/973 19
HG540 .R53 1986 ***NYPL [JLE 86-3508]***

How to survive the nine to five. Lucas, Martin. How to survive the 9 to 5 /. London , 1986. 175 p. ; ISBN 0-423-01930-9 (pbk.) : LC Card 86-188564 DDC 158.7 19
HF5548.85 .L825 1986

How to survive the 9 to 5 /. Lucas, Martin. London , 1986. 175 p. ; ISBN 0-423-01930-9 (pbk.) : LC Card 86-188564 DDC 158.7 19
HF5548.85 .L825 1986

How to think about statistics /. Phillips, John L., 1923- New York , c1988. xiv, 198 p. : ISBN 0-7167-1923-1 (pbk.) LC Card 87-15056 DDC 519.5 19
HA29 .P517 1988

How to turn your MBA into a CEO /. Lear, Robert W. New York , London , c1987. xvii, 222 p. ; ISBN 0-02-569610-6 LC Card 86-28332 DDC 650/.07/1173 19
HF1131 .L39 1987

How to understand and use design and layout /. Swann, Alan, 1946- Cincinnati, Ohio , c1987. 144 p. : ISBN 0-89134-212-5 : LC Card 87-13698 DDC 659.13/24 19
HF5825 .S9 1987

How to use leverage to maximize your real estate investment return . Reed, John T. Danville, Calif. , Cambridge, MA , c1986. iii, 301 p. : ISBN 0-939224-12-7 (pbk.) LC Card 85-90486 DDC 332.63/24 19
HD1382.5 .R426 1986

How to use management ratios /. Westwick, C. A. Aldershot, Hants, England , 1987. xviii, 421 p. : ISBN 0-566-02425-X LC Card 87-126440 DDC 658.4/001/512924 19
HF5681.R25 W47 1987

How to use the business library . Johnson, H. Herbert Webster, 1906- Cincinnati , c1984. iv, 267 p. : ISBN 0-538-05750-5 (pbk.) LC Card 83-60484 DDC 027.6/9 19
Z675.B8 J6 1984 ***NYPL [JLE 86-3971]***

How to use the HP-18C in real estate /. Fournier, Rick. Chicago, Ill. , c1987. xv, 173 p. : ISBN 0-88462-592-3 (pbk.) LC Card 87-2079 DDC 333.33/028/54165 19
HF5716.R4 F68 1987

How to win customers and keep them for life /. LeBoeuf, Michael. New York , c1987. 190 p. ; ISBN 0-399-13301-1 LC Card 87-13892 DDC 658.8/12 19
HF5415.5 .L4 1987

How to work for a jerk /. Hochheiser, Robert M., 1935- New York , 1987. 227 p. ; ISBN 0-394-74777-1 (pbk.) : LC Card 86-40163 DDC 650.1/3 19
HF5548.83 .H63 1987

How to work for a woman boss, even if you'd rather not /. Bern, Paula. New York , c1987. ix, 207 p. ; ISBN 0-396-08839-2 : LC Card 86-16735 DDC 650.1/3 19
HF5548.83 .B48 1987 ***NYPL [JLE 87-1439]***

How to work the competition into the ground and have fun doing it . Molloy, John T. New York, NY , 1987. xiii, 206 p. ; ISBN 0-446-38499-2 (pbk.) : LC Card 86-24761 DDC 650.1 19
HF5386 .M72 1987

How to write a successful business plan /. Brooks, Julie K. New York, NY , c1987. vii, 231 p. : ISBN 0-8144-5873-4 LC Card 86-22355 DDC 658.4/012 19
HD30.28 .B775 1987

How to write an effective resume /. Linkemer, Bobbi. New York, NY , c1987. 58 p. ; ISBN 0-8144-7669-4 (pbk.) : LC Card 86-47813 DDC 650.1/4 19
HF5383 .L56 1987

HOW 5 . Clark, James Leland, 1929- Boston, Mass. , c1988. ix, 370 p. : ISBN 0-534-87144-5 (pbk.) : LC Card 87-20155 DDC 651.7/402 19
HF5726 .C55 1988

Howard, Geoffry S. Computer anxiety and the use of microcomputers in management / by Geoffry S. Howard. Ann Arbor, Mich. : UMI Research Press, c1986. xii, 137 p. ; 24 cm. (Research for business decisions. no. 92) Revision of thesis (D.B.A.)--Kent State University, 1984. Includes index. Bibliography: p. 129-133. ISBN 0-8357-1759-3 (alk. paper) LC Card 86-6904 DDC 658.4/0028/5 19
1. Management - Data processing - Psychological aspects. 2. Computer literacy. I. Title.
HD30.2 .H69 1986 ***NYPL [JLE 86-3451]***

Howard-Healy, Marion. Aspects of the new media in Europe / prepared by Marion Howard-Healy. Menlo Park, CA (333 Ravenswood Ave., Menlo Park 94025) : SRI International, Business Intelligence Program, c1986. 22 leaves : ill. ; 28 cm. (Datalog file . no. 86-1052) "March 1986." LC Card 86-220771 DDC 384/.094 19
1. Cable television - Europe. 2. Artificial satellites in telecommunication - Europe. 3. Videotex (Data transmission system) - Europe. I. Business Intelligence Program (SRI International). II. Title. III. Series.
HE8700.72.E85 H69 1986

Howard, Richard, 1940- Fraser Port . Victoria, B.C. , 1986. 131 p., [16] p. of plates : ISBN 0-919203-17-5 (pbk.) LC Card 87-106756
HE554.V3 F73 1986

Howe, J. D. G. F. Rural roads and poverty alleviation . London , 1984. vii, 191 p. : ISBN 0-946688-05-2 : LC Card 86-673296
HE336.R85 R87x 1984

Howe, Larry E. Pritchard, Robert E., 1941- Be your own financial advisor /. Englewood Cliffs, N.J. , c1988. xiv, 187 p. ; ISBN 0-13-071242-6 LC Card 87-14366 DDC 332.024 19
HG179 .P737 1988

Howe, Mike. Accessing private industry council funding : a dream or reality / sponsored by the American Vocational Association ; Mike Howe, author ; produced by Milt Wright and Associates. [Northridge, CA] (17624 Romar St., Northridge 91325) : M. Wright and Associates, [1987?] 24, [15] leaves ; 28 cm. "Survey of the Job Training Partnership Act eight percent set-aside": leaves 24-[30]. LC Card 87-401761 DDC 362.8/5 19
1. Occupational training - United States - Finance. 2. Occupational retraining - United States - Finance. I. American Vocational Association. II. Survey of the Job Training Partnership Act eight percent set-aside. 1987. III. Title.
HD5715.2 .H69 1987

Howell, David, 1936- Blind victory : a study in income, wealth, and power / David Howell. London : H. Hamish, 1986. xiv, 191 p. ; 23 cm. Includes bibliographical references. ISBN 0-241-11743-7 : LC Card 86-223521 DDC 338.941 19
1. Great Britain - Economic policy - 1945-. I. Title.
HC256.6 .H639 1986

Howell, Dean M., 1932- How to buy tax free bonds : the inside story / by Dean M. Howell.1st ed. Denver, Colo. : DH Pub., 1987. 165 p. ; 24 cm. LC Card 86-91807 DDC 332.63/233/0973 19
1. Municipal bonds - United States. 2. Securities, Tax-exempt - United States. I. Title.
HG4952 .H68 1987

Howell, James Edwin. Gordon, Robert Aaron. Higher education for business /. New York , 1987, c1959. xi, 491 p. ; ISBN 0-8240-8207-9 (alk. paper) : LC Card 86-25813 DDC 650/.07/1173 19
HF1131 .G6 1987

Howell, Martha C. Women, production, and patriarchy in late medieval cities / Martha C. Howell. Chicago : University of Chicago Press, 1986. xv, 285 p. ; 24 cm. (Women in culture and society) Includes index. Bibliography: p. 261-277. ISBN 0-226-35503-9 : LC Card 85-31816 DDC 331.4/094 19
1. Women - Employment - Europe, Northern - History. 2. Women - History - Middle Ages, 500-1500. 3. Patriarchy - Europe, Northern - History. I. Title. II. Series.
HD6134 .H69 1986 ***NYPL [JLE 86-4284]***

Howell, Rate A. The legal environment of business / Rate A. Howell, John R. Allison, N.T. Henley. 2nd ed. Chicago : Dryden Press, c1987. xiv, 783 p. : ill. ; 24 cm. Includes indexes. ISBN 0-03-008369-9 LC Card 86-4503 DDC 346.73/07 347.3067 19
1. Industrial laws and legislation - United States. 2. Trade regulation - United States. 3. Commercial law - United States. 4. Industry - Social aspects - United States. I. Allison, John Robert, 1948-. II. Henley, N. T. (Nathaniel T.). III. Title.
KF1600 .H68 1987 ***NYPL [JLE 87-911]***

Howell, Thomas R., 1949-
The EEC and the third Multifiber Arrangement : a study prepared for the Fiber, Fabric, and Apparel Coalition for Trade (FFACT) / by Thomas R. Howell, William A. Noellert. Washington, DC : Dewey, Ballantine, Bushby, Palmer & Wood, 1986. [14], 126, [12] p. : ill. ; 28 cm. Cover title. Includes bibliographical references. LC Card 86-224652 DDC 382/.45677/0094 19
1. Textile industry - Government policy - European Economic Community countries. 2. Clothing trade - Government policy - European Economic Community countries. 3. Import quotas - European Economic Community countries. 4. Textile industry - Government policy - Developing countries. 5. Clothing trade - Government policy - Developing countries. 6. European Economic Community countries - Foreign economic relations - Developing countries. 7. Developing countries - Foreign economic relations - European Economic Community countries. I. Noellert, William A. II. Fiber, Fabric and Apparel Coalition for Trade (U. S.). III. Title.
HD9865.E852 H68 1986

The Textile and apparel trade crisis . Washington, D.C. (1775 Pennsylvania Ave., N.W., Washington 20006) , c1985. vi, 200, [23] p. : LC Card 87-122082 DDC 382/.45677 19
HD9850.6 .T475 1985

Howell, William Smiley.
Presentational speaking for business and the professions. Howell, William Smiley. The process of presentational speaking / William S. Howell, Ernest G. Bormann. 2nd ed. New York , c19. p. cm. ISBN 0-06-042929-1 LC Card 87-8673 DDC 658.4/52 19
HF5718 .H7 1988

The process of presentational speaking / William S. Howell, Ernest G. Bormann. 2nd ed. New York : Harper & Row, c1988 p. cm. Rev. ed. of: Presentational speaking for business and the professions. 1971. ISBN 0-06-042929-1 LC Card 87-8673 DDC 658.4/52 19
1. Communication in management. 2. Meetings. 3. Oral communication. 4. Public speaking. I. Bormann, Ernest G. II. Howell, William Smiley. Presentational speaking for business and the professions. III. Title.
HF5718 .H7 1988

Howitt, Peter, 1946- Monetary policy in transition : a study of Bank of Canada policy, 1982-85 / Peter Howitt. Toronto : C.D. Howe Institute ; Scarborough, Ont. : Availabe from Prentice-Hall Canada, [1986] viii, 140 p. : ill. ; 21 cm. (Policy study, 0832-7912 . no. 1) Includes bibliographical references. ISBN 0-88806-136-6 (pbk.) LC Card 86-229489 DDC 332.1/12/0971 19
1. Monetary policy - Canada. 2. Bank of Canada. 3. Banks and banking, Central - Canada. I. Series: Policy study (C.D. Howe Institute) , no. 1. II. Title.
HG655 .H69 1986

Howson, Susan, 1945- Meade, J. E. (James Edward), 1907- [Works. 1988.] The collected papers of James Meade /. London , Boston , 1988- p. cm. ISBN 0-04-445073-7 (v. 1. : alk. paper) LC Card 87-15288 DDC 330.1 19
HD5710 .M43 1988

Hoy, Anne H. Coca-Cola : the first hundred years / text by Anne Hoy. Atlanta, Ga. : Coca-Cola Co., c1986. 159 p. : ill. (some col.) ; 29 x 36 cm. LC Card 86-209155 DDC 338.7/66362/0973 19
1. Coca-Cola Company - History. 2. Soft drink industry - United States - History. 3. Coca-Cola Company - Pictorial works. 4. Photography, Advertising. I. Coca-Cola Company. II. Title.
HD9349.S634 C64 1986

Hoyer, Wayne D.
Jacoby, Jacob. The comprehension and miscomprehension of print communications . New York, N.Y. , Hillsdale, N.J. , c1987. xvii, 273 p. : ISBN 0-8058-0087-5 (L. Erlbaum Associates) LC Card 87-1366 DDC 659.13/2 19
HF6107 .J32 1987

The Role of affect in consumer behavior . Lexington, Mass. , c1986. ix, 196 p. : ISBN 0-669-12874-0 (alk. paper) LC Card 85-46042 DDC 658.8/342 19
HF5415.3 .R65 1986 ***NYPL [JLE 86-3376]***

Hoyle, Joe Ben. Advanced accounting / Joe Ben Hoyle. 2nd ed. Plano, Tex. : Business Publications, 1987. xvii, 809 p. : ill. ; 25 cm. Includes bibliographical references and index. ISBN 0-256-03696-9 LC Card 86-72556 DDC 657/.046 19
1. Accounting. I. Title.
HF5635 .H863 1987

Hoyos Lascano, Fernando. La UNCTAD y los problemas de transporte marítimo de los países en desarrollo : el caso colombiano / Fernando Hoyos Lascano. Bogotá, D.E. : [s.n.], 1975 ([Bogotá] : Gráficas Venus) 99 p. ; 25 cm. Thesis (doctoral)--Pontificia Universidad Javeriana, 1975. Bibliography: p. 97-99. LC Card 85-205214
1. Merchant marine - Colombia. 2. United Nations. Conference on Trade and Development. I. Title.
HE807 .H69 1975

Hoyt, Douglas B. Computer security handbook /. New York, N.Y. , c1987. p. cm. ISBN 0-02-915300-X LC Card 87-1735 DDC 658.4/78 19
HF5548.37 .C64 1987

HP-18C (CALCULATOR)
Fournier, Rick. How to use the HP-18C in real estate /. Chicago, Ill. , c1987. xv, 173 p. : ISBN 0-88462-592-3 (pbk.) LC Card 87-2079 DDC 333.33/028/54165 19
HF5716.R4 F68 1987

HPS Productions.
Are you reading me? [motion picture] /. Falls Church, VA , 1985. 1 film reel (9 min.) : LC Card 85-702717 DDC 388.3 11
HE5614

Are you reading me? [videorecording] /. Falls Church, VA , 1985. 1 videocassette (9 min.) : LC Card 85-702718 DDC 388.3 11
HE5614

Hraba, Joseph. Schwieder, Dorothy, 1933- Buxton . Ames , 1987. viii, 256 p. : ISBN 0-8138-0246-6 LC Card 87-2929 DDC 305/.9622 19
HD8039.M62 U66825 1987

HRAFlex books. Cross-cultural research series. McCoid, Catherine Hodge. Carrying capacities of nation-states /. New Haven, Conn. (P.O. Box 2015, Yale Station, New Haven 06520) , 1984. x, 198 leaves : LC Card 84-152784 DDC 304.6/2 19
GN33.5 .M38 1984 ***NYPL [JFE 86-2142]***

Hrbek, R. (Rudolf) Die Deutschen Länder und die Europäischen Gemeinschaften . Baden-Baden , 1986. 294 p. ; ISBN 3-7890-1350-1 LC Card 87-141896 DDC 341.24/22 19
HC241.25.G3 D48 1986

HRC Conference. IUF Mediterranean Hotel and Restaurant Workers' Conference (1978 : Palermo, Sicily) IUF Mediterranean Hotel and Restaurant Workers' Conference, Palermo, November 15-17, 1978. Petit-Lancy, Switzerland [1978?] 1 v. (various pagings) ; LC Card 83-225538
HD6475.A2 I7836 1978

Hristache, Ilie. Trebici, Vladimir. Demografia teritorială a României /. București , 1986. 160 p. : LC Card 87-151036
HB3631 .T72 1986

Hrubec, Thomas R. The managerial accounting quizmaster / Thomas R. Hrubec, David E. Keys. New York : McGraw-Hill, c1987. xx, 216 p. : ill. ; 28 cm. ISBN 0-07-034472-8 (pbk.) LC Card 86-62759 DDC 658.1/511/076 19
1. Managerial accounting - Problems, exercises, etc. I. Keys, David E. II. Title.
HF5657.4 .H78 1987

Hrvatska. see **Croatia.**

Hrvatski pomorski regesti. Regesti marittimi croati /. Padova , 1985- v. <v. 1, pt. 1 > : LC Card 86-215640
HE565.Y8 R42 1985

HSEB statistics, 1983-84. [Chandigarh] : Haryana State Electricity Board, [1984] iii, 105 p., [7] p. of plates : col. ill. ; 29 cm. Cover title. Statistical presentation of the functioning of Haryana State Electricity Board. LC Card 87-901651 DDC 363.6/2/0954558021 19
1. Electric utilities - India - Haryana - Statistics. I. Haryana State Electricity Board.
HD9696.A3 I5535 1984

HSFK-Report.
(1986/4) Rode, Reinhard, 1947- US-Technologietransferpolitik gegenüber der UdSSR und der VR China . Frankfurt am Main [1986] 39 p. : ISBN 3-926197-01-3 LC Card 87-120584 DDC 338.9/26 19
HC340.T4 R63 1986

(4/1986) Rode, Reinhard, 1947- US-Technologietransferpolitik gegenüber der UdSSR und der VR China . Frankfurt am Main [1986] 39 p. : ISBN 3-926197-01-3 LC Card 87-120584 DDC 338.9/26 19
HC340.T4 R63 1986

Hsiao, Hsin-huang. In search of an East Asian development model /. New Brunswick, N.J., USA , c1988. xi, 243 p. ; ISBN 0-88738-686-5 (pbk.) LC Card 87-19061 DDC 338.95 19
HC460.5 .I5 1988

Hsieh, Ching-Yao, 1917- A search for synthesis in economic theory / Ching-Yao Hsieh and Stephen L. Mangum. Armonk, N.Y. : M.E. Sharpe, c1985. xii, 268 p. : ill. ; 23 cm. Bibliography: p. 257-267. ISBN 0-87332-328-9 LC Card 84-29816 DDC 330.1 19
1. Classical school of economics. 2. Keynesian economics. I. Mangum, Stephen L. II. Title.
HB71 .H73 1985 ***NYPL [JLE 87-315]***

Hsing cheng yüan ching chi chien she wei yüan hui (China)
Economic development, Taiwan, Republic of China. Taipei, Taiwan, Republic of China [1986] 46 p. : LC Card 87-119341 DDC 338.951/249 19
HC430.5 .E34 1986

Highlights of Ninth Medium-Term Economic Development Plan for Taiwan, Republic of China, 1986-1989. [Taipei? Taiwan] : Council for Economic Planning and Development, Executive Yuan, [1986] ii, 65 p. ; 15 x 21 cm. "January 1986." "Pien hao (75) 509.190"--Cover. LC Card 87-400742 DDC 338.951/249 19
1. Taiwan - Economic policy - 1975-. I. Title.
HC430.5 .H757 1986a

Highlights of 1986 economic development plan for Taiwan, Republic of China. [Taipei] : Council for Economic Planning and Development, Executive Yuan, [1986] ii, 61 p. ; 15 x 21 cm. Cover title. "January 1986." LC Card 87-118523 DDC 338.951/249 19
1. Taiwan - Economic policy - 1975-. I. Title.
HC430.5 .H757 1986

Hsing cheng yüan nung yeh fa chan wei yüan hui (China) CAPD and agricultural development in the Republic of China on Taiwan . Taipei [1984] 152 p. : LC Card 87-400057 DDC 338.1/851249 19
HD2108 .C36 1984

HSING CHENG YÜAN NUNG YEH FA CHAN WEI YÜAN HUI (CHINA)
CAPD and agricultural development in the Republic of China on Taiwan . Taipei [1984] 152 p. : LC Card 87-400057 DDC 338.1/851249 19
HD2108 .C36 1984

Hu, Sheng C. A game-theoretic approach to the design of an optimal sales policy / by Sheng C. Hu, Manohar U. Kalwani, and Kin-Nam Lau. West Lafayette, Ind. : Institute for Research in the Behavioral, Economic, and Management Sciences, Krannert Graduate School of Management, Purdue University, [1986] 30, 14 p. : ill. ; 28 cm. (Paper / Institute for Research in the Behavioral, Economic, and Management Sciences, Krannert Graduate School of Management, Purdue University . no. 900 (July 1986)) Bibliography: p. 30. LC Card 86-622755 DDC 658/.001/9 s 658.8/101 19
1. Selling - Mathematical models. I. Kalwani, Manohar U. II. Lau, Kin-Nam. III. Series: Paper (Krannert Graduate School of Management. Institute for Research in the Behavioral, Economic, and Management Sciences) , no. 900. IV. Title.
HD6483 .P8 no. 900 HF5438.25

Huang, Chung-liang, 1945- Food demand analysis . Ames , 1987. xvi, 285 p. : ISBN 0-8138-1841-9 LC Card 86-30534 DDC 338.4/76413 19
HD9000.5 .F5947 1987

Huang, Stanley S. C. Investment analysis and management / Stanley S.C. Huang, Maury R. Randall. 2nd ed. Boston : Allyn and Bacon, c1987. xiv, 605 p. : ill. ; 25 cm. Includes bibliographies and index. ISBN 0-205-10501-7 LC Card 87-986 DDC 332.6 19
1. Investment analysis. 2. Portfolio management. 3. Investments. I. Randall, Maury R. II. Title.
HG4529 .H8 1987

Huang, Wen-Yuan. Webb, Shwu-Eng. Idling erodible cropland . Washington, D.C. [1986] iii, 31 p. : LC Card 86-601632 DDC 338.1 s 338.1/62 19
HD1751 .A91854 no. 550 HD256

Hubbard, E. Dee. Cherrington, J. Owen. Cost and managerial accounting /. St. Paul , c1988. p. cm. ISBN 0-314-25327-0 : LC Card 86-24753 DDC 657/.42 19
HF5686.C8 C475 1988

Hubbard, L. Ron (La Fayette Ron), 1911- The management series / by L. Ron Hubbard. Los Angeles, Calif. : Bridge Publications, c1982- v. <1 > ; 31 cm. CONTENTS. - v. 1. Data series, establishment officer series, organizing series, target series. ISBN 0-88404-090-9 (v. 1) LC Card 82-71055 DDC 658.4
1. Management. I. Title.
HD38 .H82 1982

Hubbard, Michael. Agricultural exports and economic growth : a study of the Botswana beef industry / Michael Hubbard. London ; New York : KPI, 1986. xx, 284 p. : ill., map ; 23 cm. Includes index. Bibliography: p. 259-278. ISBN 0-7103-0121-9
1. Beef industry - Botswana. 2. Cattle trade - Botswana. I. Title. ***NYPL [Sc D 86-967]***

Hubbard, Thomas D., 1933- Auditing . Houston, TX , 1986. xvii, 919 p. : ISBN 0-87393-016-9 LC Card 86-127902 DDC 657/.45 19
HF5667 .A832 1986

Huber, Gérard. Les conséquences à long terme de la politique macroéconomique / par Gérard Huber. Berne : P. Lang, 1982. 449 p. ; 23 cm. (Collection des thèses de la Faculté des sciences économiques et sociales, 0271-7146 . thèse no 278) Thesis (doctoral)--Université de Genève, 1980. Bibliography: p. [443]-449. ISBN 3-261-04985-5 LC Card 87-672303
1. Macroeconomics. 2. Macroeconomics - Mathematical models. 3. Economic policy. 4. Equilibrium (Economics). I. Title. II. Series.
HB172.5 .H82x 1982

Huber, Peter W. (Peter William), 1952- The geodesic network : 1987 report on competition in the telephone industry / prepared by Peter W. Huber. Washington, D.C. : U. S. Dept. of Justice, Antitrust Division : For sale by the Supt. of Docs., U. S. G.P.O., 1987. 1 v. (various pagings) : ill., col. maps ; 28 cm. Shipping list no.: 87-34-P. "January 1987." "Funded by the Antitrust Division, U. S. Department of Justice." Includes bibliographical references. S/N 027-000-01267-1 Item 717 LC Card 87-601031 DDC 384/.041 19
1. Telephone - United States - Consolidation. 2. Telephone systems. 3. Antitrust law - United States. 4. Telecommunication equipment industry - United States - Consolidation. 5. Telecommunication - United States. I. United States. Dept. of Justice. Antitrust Division. II. Title. III. Title: Report on competition in the telephone industry.
HE8819 .H76 1987

Huber, Vandra L. (Vandra Lee), 1949- Readings in personnel and human resource management /. St. Paul, MN , c1988. xix, 600 p. : ISBN 0-314-33750-4 (pbk.) LC Card 86-28244 DDC 658.3 19
HF5549 .R38167 1988

Hubert H. Humphrey Institute of Public Affairs. The Industrial future of the Pacific basin /. Boulder , 1984. xvi, 285 p. : ISBN 0-86531-685-6 LC Card 83-51653 DDC 338.9/009182/3 19
HC681 .I53 1984 ***NYPL [JLD 86-3100]***

Hubert, Tony. A Guide to small firms assistance in Europe /. Aldershot, Hants, England , Brookfield, Vt., U. S.A. , c1986. vii, 263 p. ; ISBN 0-566-05082-X : LC Card 85-27307 DDC 338.6/42/094 19
HD2346.E9 G85 1986 ***NYPL [JLG 86-205]***

Hubl, Peter. Interplanetare Raumsonden / Peter Hubl. 3. Aufl. Lorch/Württemberg : H.E. Sieger, [1983?] 98 p. : ill. ; 21 cm. Philatelic material. Cover title. LC Card 83-218116
1. Postage-stamps - Topics - Outer space. 2. Postage-stamps - Topics - Space flight. I. Title.
HE6183.O95 H83 1983

Hubscher, Ronald H. Cabaud, Michel. 1900, la Française au quotidien /. Paris , c1985. 204 p. : ISBN 2-200-37097-0 LC Card 86-137649
HD6059.F8 C33 1985

HUD. see **United States. Dept. of Housing and Urban Development.**

HUDCO's initiatives for IYSH. Housing and Urban Development Corporation. New Delhi [1987?] 49 p. : LC Card 87-902550 DDC 363.5/8 19
HD7287.96.I4 H67 1987

Huddle, Norie, 1944- Island of dreams : environmental crisis in Japan / Norie Huddle & Michael Reich with Nahum Stiskin ; foreword by Paul R. Ehrlich ; afterword by Ralph Nader. Cambridge, Mass. : Schenkman Books, c1987. xxiii, 355 p. : ill. ; 22 cm. Bibliography: p. 344-349. Includes index. ISBN 0-87047-027-2 : LC Card 86-33842 DDC 363.7/00952 19
1. Environmental policy - Japan. 2. Pollution - Japan. 3. Environmental health - Japan. I. Reich, Michael, 1950-. II. Stiskin, Nahum, 1945-. III. Title.
HC465.E5 H82 1987

Hudgins, Linda Lucas, 1946- Development of the Mexican tuna industry, 1976-86 / Linda Lucas Hudgins. Honolulu, Hawaii : Pacific Islands Development Program, East-West Center, 1987. p. cm. (Research report series . no. 5) Includes bibliographies. ISBN 0-86638-091-4 LC Card 87-505 DDC 338.3/72758 19
1. Tuna industry - Mexico. I. Series: Research report series (Pacific Islands Development Program (East-West Center)) , no. 5. II. Title.
HD9469.T83 M64 1987

HUD's housing development grant program. Guggenheim, Joseph. HUD's rental rehabilitation program, HUD's housing development grant program /. Washington, D.C. [c1984] 13 p. ; LC Card 87-100358 DDC 363.5/8 19
HD7288.85.U6 G84 1984

HUD's rental rehabilitation program, HUD's housing development grant program /. Guggenheim, Joseph. Washington, D.C. [c1984] 13 p. ; LC Card 87-100358 DDC 363.5/8 19
HD7288.85.U6 G84 1984

Hudson, Adams, 1958- How to buy or sell a car by long distance / Adams Hudson. Osceola, Wis. : Motorbooks International, 1987. 80 p. ; 19 cm. ISBN 0-87938-259-7 (soft) LC Card 87-12185 DDC 629.2/222 19
1. Selling - Automobiles. 2. Automobiles - Purchasing. 3. Advertising - Automobiles. I. Title.
HF5439.A8 H83 1987

Hudson, Gladys W. Strain, Lois S. (Lois Smith) The story of Paul J. Meyer . Hollywood, Fla. , c1986. xii, 193 p. : ISBN 0-8119-0720-1 : LC Card 86-29525 DDC 338/.04/0924 B 19
HF5386 .S8832 1986

Hudson, R. W. Business computer systems : a guide for students and small businesses / R.W. Hudson, R.P. Batten. London ; New York : McGraw-Hill Book Co., c1986. x, 163 p. : ill. ; 25 cm. Includes index. ISBN 0-07-084976-5 (pbk.) : LC Card 86-10481 DDC 650/.028/5 19
1. Business - Data processing. 2. Small business - Data processing. I. Batten, R. P. II. Title.
HF5548.2 .H78 1986 ***NYPL [JLE 87-1038]***

Hudson Waterfront Walkway plan and design guidelines / prepared by Wallace Roberts & Todd, Louis Berger & Associates, Inc., Ralph B. Hirsch, for the State of New Jersey Department of Environmental Protection, Division of Coastal Resources. [Trenton, N.J.] : The Department, 1984] 136 p. : ill., maps, plans ; 28 cm. "March, 1984." Title from cover. Bibliography: p. 133-135.
1. Waterfronts - Hudson River (N.Y. and N.J.) - Planning. 2. Waterfronts - New Jersey - Planning. 3. City planning - New Jersey. I. Hirsch, Ralph B. II. Wallace, McHarg, Roberts and Todd. III. Louis Berger and Associates. IV. New Jersey. Division of Coastal Resources. ***NYPL [JLF 87-913]***

Hudson, William J. Business without economists : an irreverent guide / William J. Hudson. New York, N.Y. : AMACOM, c1987. 178 p. : ill. ; 22 cm. Bibliography: p. 167-169. Includes index. ISBN 0-8144-5896-3 : LC Card 86-47812 DDC 658.4/0355 19
1. Business forecasting. 2. Economic forecasting. 3. Economists. I. Title.
HB3730 .H83 1987

Hübl, Lothar. Strukturwandel und Strukturpolitik : eine Einführung / Lothar Hübl, Walter Schepers. Hannover : Niedersächsische Landeszentrale für Politische Bildung, 1983. 104 p. : ill. ; 21 cm. Includes bibliographical references. LC Card 84-126938
1. Germany, West - Economic conditions - 1974-. 2. Germany, West - Economic policy - 1974-. I. Schepers, Walter. II. Title.
HC286.7 .H83 1983

Huebner international series on risk, insurance, and economic security.
Rushing, William A. Social functions and economic aspects of health insurance /. Boston , c1986. vii, 226 p. ; ISBN 0-89838-219-X LC Card 86-7297 DDC 368.3/82/00973 19
HD7102.U4 R86 1986 ***NYPL [JLE 87-1237]***

Huebner, S. S. (Solomon Stephen), 1882-1964. Life insurance. Black, Kenneth. Life insurance. 11th ed. / Kenneth Black, Jr., Harold D. Skipper, Jr. Englewood Cliffs, N.J. , c1987. xiii, 608 p. : ISBN 0-13-535881-7 LC Card 86-25375 DDC 368.3/2 19
HG8771 .B55 1987

Huebner school series.
Ivers, James F. Financial planning applications /. Bryn Mawr, Pa. , c1987. 2 v. : ISBN 0-943590-13-2 (pbk. : v. 1) LC Card 87-71366 DDC 332.024 19
HG179 .C326 1987

Hueckel, Glenn R. (Glenn Russell), 1945- The Napoleonic wars and their impact on factor returns and output growth in England, 1793-1815 / Glenn R. Hueckel. New York : Garland, 1985. lvi, 212 p. ; 24 cm. (British economic history) Originally presented as the author's thesis (doctoral--University of Wisconsin, 1972) Bibliography: p. 205-212. ISBN 0-8240-6683-9 : LC Card 84-46003 DDC 330.941/073 19
1. First Coalition, War of the, 1792-1797 - Economic aspects - Great Britain. 2. Second Coalition, War of the, 1798-1801 - Economic aspects - Great Britain. 3. Napoleonic Wars, 1800-1814 - Economic aspects - Great Britain. 4. Great Britain - Economic conditions - 1760-1860. 5. Great Britain - Industries - History. I. Title. II. Series.
HC254.5 .H78 1985 ***NYPL [JLE 86-4294]***

El hueco negro . Echavarría Olózaga, Hernán. [S.l. , 1986] (Bogotá, Colombia : Editorial Andes) 244 p., [7] p. of plates : LC Card 86-209093
HC197 .E34 1986

La huelga obrera en Chile, 1890-1970 /. Pizarro, Crisóstomo. Santiago, Chile [1986] 227 p. : LC Card 87-115190 DDC 331.89/2983 19
HD5356.A6 P59 1986

Huella, cuadernos de divulgación académica . (3) Orozco, Jesús. Ideología y programa de gobierno en los discursos de toma de posesión de los presidentes de México, 1928-1982 /. Guadalajara, Jal., México , c1983. 47 p. ; ISBN 968-511-003-4 LC Card 83-191579
HC135 .O66 1983

Huellen, Karl Konrad. Die Motivation von Arbeitnehmern im Innen- und Aussendienst des Vertriebs : eine empirische Untersuchung / Karl Konrad Huellen. Münster : Lit, [1986] iv, 245 p. : ill. ; 21 cm. (Betriebswirtschaftliche Schriftenreihe . Bd. 33) Bibliography: p. 232-244. ISBN 3-88660-356-3 (Deut. Bibl.) LC Card 87-114821 DDC 658.3/14 19
1. Employee motivation - Germany, West. 2. Job satisfaction - Germany, West. 3. Leisure - Germany, West. 4. Personnel management - Germany, West. I. Title. II. Series.
HF5549.5.M63 H84 1986

Huerta González, Arturo. Economía mexicana : más allá del milagro / Arturo Huerta González.1a ed. [Mexico City, Mexico] : Ediciones de Cultura Popular, 1986. 246 p. : ill. ; 21 cm. (Economía) Originally presented as the author's thesis (doctoral)--Universidad Nacional Autónoma de México. Bibliography: p. 243-246. LC Card 87-404065 DDC 330.972/0834 19
1. Mexico - Economic conditions - 1970-. 2. Mexico - Economic policy 1970-. 3. Mexico - Manufactures. I. Series: Economía (Ediciones de Cultura Popular). II. Title.
HC135 .H84 1986

Huerta, Jesús R.- (Jesús Ruíz) Gimeno Ullastres, Juan Antonio. El nuevo Estado fiscal español . Madrid , 1981. xx, 315 p. : ISBN 84-7214-219-1 LC Card 85-176738
HJ1249.A1 G56 1981

Huertas, Josep Maria. Obrers a Catalunya : manual d'història del moviment obrer 1840-1975 / Josep M. Huertas Claveria ; assessors, Joaquim Ferrer ... [et al.].1a ed. Barcelona : L'Avenç, 1982. 409 p. : ill. ; 22 cm. (Col·lecció Clio . 1) Bibliography: p. 405-408. ISBN 84-85905-06-7 LC Card 83-101512
1. Labor and laboring classes - Spain - Catalonia - History. 2. Labor and laboring classes - Spain - Catalonia - Political activity - History. I. Title. II. Series.
HD8589.C32 H83 1982
NYPL [JLD 86-3659]

Huet, Maryse. La concentration des emplois féminins : ampleur, analyse, évolution / Maryse Huet. Paris : Institut national de la statistique et des études économiques, [1983] 138 p. : ill. ; 30 cm. (Archives & documents . no 84) "Juin 1983." Includes bibliographical references. ISBN 2-11-064535-0 : LC Card 85-176290 DDC

331.4/12/0944 19
1. Women - Employment - France. I. Series: Archives & documents (Institut national de la statistique et des études économiques (France)) , no 84. II. Title.
HD6145 .H79 1983

Hueting, Ernest. Naar groter eenheid : de geschiedenis van het Nederlands Verbond van Vakverenigingen 1906-1981 / Ernest Hueting, Frits de Jong Edz., Rob Neij. Amsterdam : Van Gennep, 1983, c1982. 432 p. : ill. ; 31 cm. (De Nederlandse arbeidersbeweging . 13) Includes index. Bibliography: p. 393-397. ISBN 90-6012-531-2 : LC Card 83-184649
1. Nederlands Verbond van Vakverenigingen - History - 20th century. 2. Trade-unions - Netherlands - History - 20th century. 3. Labor and laboring classes - Netherlands - History - 20th century. I. Jong, Frits de. II. Neij, Rob. III. Title.
HD6727 .H83 1983 ***NYPL [JLG 87-188]***

Huff, Kathryn. Developing and using microcomputer business systems / Kathryn Huff. St. Paul : West Pub. Co., c1987. xvi, 224, [29] p. : ill. ; 26 cm. (The Microcomputing series) Includes bibliographies and index. ISBN 0-314-34730-5 (pbk.) LC Card 87-2184 DDC 658/.05416 19
1. Business - Data processing. 2. Microcomputers - Programming. I. Title. II. Series.
HF5548.2 .H785 1987

Huffman, Harry. General recordkeeping / Harry Huffman, Jeffrey R. Stewart, Jr., Daisy L. Stewart. 9th ed. New York : Gregg Division, McGraw-Hill, c1988. x, 564 p. : col. ill. ; 25 cm. Includes index. ISBN 0-07-031054-8 LC Card 87-2982 DDC 657/.2 19
1. Bookkeeping. I. Stewart, Jeffrey Robert, 1932-. II. Stewart, Daisy L. III. Title.
HF5635 .H8834 1988

Hufschmidt, Maynard M.
Economic valuation techniques for the environment . Baltimore , c1986. xx, 203 p. : ISBN 0-8018-3352-3 (alk. paper) LC Card 86-2730 DDC 363.7/05/0681 19
HC79.E5 E274 1986 ***NYPL [JLE 87-677]***

Watershed resource management . Boulder , 1986. xx, 236 p. : ISBN 0-8133-7300-X (pbk. : alk. paper) : LC Card 86-18987 DDC 333.91/0095 19
HD1691 .W37 1986 ***NYPL [JLD 87-767]***

Huge Sinzheimer Gedächtnisveranstaltung. see **Otto Brenner Stiftung. Schriftenreihe.**

HUGH MOORE PARK (EASTON, PA.) - GUIDE-BOOKS.
Metz, Lance E. Sherman's guide to Hugh Moore Park /. Easton, PA , 1988. p. cm. ISBN 0-930973-07-0 (pbk.) : LC Card 87-25622 DDC 338.09748/22 19
HE395 .P43 1988

Hughes, Dean W. Financing the agricultural sector . Boulder, Colo. , 1986. xi, 256 p. : ISBN 0-8133-0055-X (pbk. : alk. paper) LC Card 86-50152 DDC 338.1/3/0973 19
HD1761 .F5 1986 ***NYPL [JLE 86-2766]***

Hughes Hallett, Andrew. Ghosh, S. Stabilizing speculative commodity markets /. Oxford [Oxfordshire] , New York , 1987. xiii, 437 p. : ISBN 0-19-828472-1 : LC Card 86-32654 DDC 332.64/4 19
HG6046 .G485 1987

Hughes, James W. The dynamics of America's housing / James W. Hughes, George Sternlieb. New Brunswick, N.J. : Center for Urban Policy Research, c1987. xiv, 224 p. ; 24 cm. Bibliography: p. 215-217. Includes index. ISBN 0-88285-122-5 : LC Card 87-4515 DDC 363.5/0973 19
1. Housing - United States. I. Sternlieb, George. II. Rutgers University. Center for Urban Policy Research. III. Title.
HD7293 .H826 1987

Hughes, John S. Hoskin, Robert E. Financial accounting cases /. Chicago , c1988. 201 p. : ISBN 0-03-011778-X (pbk.) LC Card 87-22238 DDC 657 19
HF5635 .H817 1988

Hughes Ortega, William, 1953- Gómez Pérez, José Antonio, 1950- Desarrollo, crisis, deuda y política económica en Panamá . Panamá , 1985. vii, 168 p. : LC Card 86-122320 DDC 338.97287 19
HC147 .G66 1985 ***NYPL [JLD 86-2899]***

Hughes, Theodore E. The parents' financial survival guide / Theodore E. Hughes & David Klein. Tucson, Ariz. : Body Press, c1987. 227 p. ; 22 cm. Includes index. ISBN 0-89586-644-7 : LC Card 87-10233 DDC 332.024/0431 19
1. Parents - Finance, Personal. 2. Parenting. I. Klein, David, 1919-. II. Title.
HG179 .H84 1987

Hugo, Graeme.
Australia's changing population : trends and implications / Graeme Hugo. Melbourne ; New York : Oxford University Press, 1986. x, 354 p. : ill. ; 24 cm. Bibliography: p. [329]-347. Includes index. ISBN 0-19-554680-6 LC Card 87-107294 DDC 304.6/0994 19
1. Australia - Population. 2. Population forecasting - Australia. 3. Australia - Population policy. I. Title.
HB3675 .H84 1986

The Demographic dimension in Indonesian development /. Singapore , New York , 1987. xxv, 417 p. : ISBN 0-19-582699-X : LC Card 87-11021 DDC 304.6/09598 19
HB3647 .D45 1987

Hugonnier, Bernard. Investissements directs, coopération internationale et firmes multinationales / Bernard Hugonnier. Paris : Economica, 1984. 343 p. : ill. ; 24 cm. Includes bibliographies. ISBN 2-7178-0793-4 : LC Card 85-105926
1. International business enterprises. 2. Investments, Foreign. I. Title.
HD2755.5 .H83 1984

Huh, Ko Kwang. Economic survey on Western Samoa. [Manila, Philippines] : Asian Development Bank, [1984] vii, 44 p. : col. maps ; 28 cm. (Report / Asian Development Bank . no. SAM Ec-6s) Cover title. "April 1984." "Restricted." LC Card 87-403365 DDC 330.996/14 19
1. Western Samoa - Economic conditions. I. Asian Development Bank. II. Series: Report / Asian Development Bank , no. SAM Ec-6s. III. Title.
HC687.5 .H84 1984

Huijgen, F. Autonomie als arbeidssociologisch vraagstuk . Zeist , 1987. 237 p. : ISBN 90-6720-032-8 : LC Card 87-169950
HD5660.N4 A94 1987

Huizinga, W.
Dutch agricultural development, 1600-1880. 1986. Huizinga, W. Two lectures on the historical development of Dutch agriculture, 1600-1985 / W. Huizinga, D. Strijker. Den Haag [1986] 31 p. : LC Card 86-233719
HD1987 .H85 1986

Two lectures on the historical development of Dutch agriculture, 1600-1985 / W. Huizinga, D. Strijker. Den Haag : Landbouw-Economisch Instituut, Stafafd., [1986] 31 p. : ill. ; 24 cm. (Mededeling / Landbouw-Economisch Instituut . 351) "The Hage, June 1986." Bibliography: p. 29-30. CONTENTS. - Dutch agricultural development, 1600-1880 / W. Huizinga -- Structural development towards a modern agricultural sector, 1880-1985 / D. Strijker. LC Card 86-233719
1. Agriculture - Economic aspects - Netherlands - History. I. Huizinga, W. Dutch agricultural development, 1600-1880. 1986. II. Strijker, D. III. Series: Mededeling (Landbouw-Economisch Instituut (Netherlands)) , 351. IV. Title.
HD1987 .H85 1986

Hula, Richard C., 1947- Market-based public policy /. New York , 1988. xiv, 265 p. : ISBN 0-312-00747-7 : LC Card 87-19703 DDC 361.6 19
HD3612 .M36 1988

Hulbert, James M. Capon, Noel. Corporate strategic planning /. New York , 1987. p. cm. ISBN 0-231-06380-6 LC Card 87-18239 DDC 658.4/012 19
HD30.28 .C375 1987

Huldt, Bo, 1941- Fred och säkerhet . [Stockholm] , c1983. 385 p. : ISBN 91-7410-249-4 : LC Card 83-229846
JX1963 .F817 1983 ***NYPL [JLD 84-2639]***

Hull, Christopher J. Helping small firms grow : an implementation approach / Christopher J. Hull with Benny Hjern. New York : Croom Helm in association with Methuen, c1987. 228 p. : ill. ; 23 cm. (Croom Helm small business series) Bibliography: p. 213-223. Includes index. ISBN 0-7099-4791-7 LC Card 87-15728 DDC 338.6/42 19
1. Small business - Government policy - Germany (West) - Mathematical models. 2. Job vacancies - Germany (West) - Mathematical models. 3. Industrial promotion - Germany (West) - Mathematical models. I. Hjern, Benny. II. Title. III. Series.
HD2346.G3 .H786 1987

Hull, Galen. A small business agenda : trends in a global economy / Galen Spencer Hull. Lanham, MD : University Press of America, c1986. x, 128 p. ; 22 cm. Bibliography: p. 125-127. ISBN 0-8191-5163-7 (alk. paper) : LC Card 85-26513 DDC 338.6/42/0973 19
1. Small business - United States. 2. Small business - Developing countries. I. Title.
HD2346.U5 H85 1986 ***NYPL [JLD 86-2614]***

Hulme, James A. Goldman, Benjamin A. Hazardous waste management . Washington, D.C. , c1986. xx, 316 p. : ISBN 0-933280-30-0 : LC Card 86-2748 DDC 363.7/28 19
HD9975.U52 G65 1986 ***NYPL [JLE 87-1159]***

Hulten, Michel van. Djibouti, ville et pays en voie de développement . Djibouti [c1983] 2 v. : LC Card 87-131462
HC855.Z9 E443 1983

Hultman, Charles W. An examination of issues related to multibank holding companies / Charles W. Hultman, principal investigator ; L. Randolph McGee, co-investigator ; Keith Johnson, co-investigator ; prepared by the Office for Research and Extension, College of Business and Economics, University of Kentucky, for the Department of Banking and Securities, Kentucky State government. [Frankfort, Ky. : The Department, 1983] [8], 56 leaves ; 28 cm. "August 15, 1983." Bibliography: p. 49-56. LC Card 86-620545 DDC 332.1/6 19
1. Bank holding companies - United States. 2. Bank holding companies - Kentucky. I. McGee, L. Randolph. II. Johnson, Keith (Keith H.). III. University of Kentucky. College of Business and Economics. Office for Research and Extension. IV. Kentucky. Dept. of Banking and Securities. V. Title.
HG2567 .H85 1983

Humala Tasso, Ulises. Subdesarrollo o camino al colapso : desarrollo del subdesarrollo en el Perú / Ulises Humala Tasso. [S.l. : s.n., 1987?] (Lima, Perú : Graphos 100 Editores) 175 p. ; 21 cm. Bibliography: p. 174-175. LC Card 87-403093 DDC 330.985/0633 19
1. Peru - Economic conditions. 2. Capitalism - Peru - History. I. Title. II. Title: Desarrollo del subdesarrollo en el Perú.
HC227 .H86 1987

Human aspects in office automation / edited by Barbara G.F. Cohen. Amsterdam ; New York : Elsevier, 1984. xv, 322 p. : ill. ; 25 cm. (Elsevier series in office automation . 1) Includes bibliographical references and indexes. ISBN 0-444-42327-3 : LC Card 84-5917 DDC 363.1/19651 19
1. Office practice - Automation - Addresses, essays, lectures. 2. Clerks - Effect of automation on - Addresses, essays, lectures. 3. Job stress - Addresses, essays, lectures. 4. Industrial safety - Addresses, essays, lectures. I. Cohen, Barbara G. F. II. Series.
HF5547.5 .H85 1984 ***NYPL [JLF 86-892]***

HUMAN ASSETS. see **HUMAN CAPITAL.**

Human behaviour in geographical space : essays in honour of Leo H. Klaassen / edited by J.H.P. Paelinck. Aldershot, Hants, England ; Brookfield, Vt., U. S.A. : Gower Press, c1986. x, 328 p. : ill., maps ; 23 cm. (Studies in spatial economic analysis) Includes bibliographies and index. ISBN 0-566-00807-6 : LC Card 85-5528 DDC 338.9 19
1. Klaassen, Leo H. (Leo Hendrik), 1920-. 2. Regional economics - Addresses, essays, lectures. 3. Space in economics - Addresses, essays, lectures. I. Paelinck, Jean H. P. II. Series: Studies in spatial analysis.
HT391 .H785 1986 ***NYPL [JLD 86-1630]***

Human capital . Fallows, James M. New York, N.Y. , 1988. p. cm. ISBN 0-394-56498-7 : LC Card 87-42659 DDC 306/.3 19
HC106.8 .F35 1988

HUMAN CAPITAL - ACCOUNTING.
Prabhakara Rao, D. (Devisetti), 1954- Human resource accounting /. New Delhi, India , 1986. xviii, 247 p. : ISBN 81-210-0169-2 : LC Card

86-902848
HF5681.H8 P73 1986

HUMAN CAPITAL - GERMANY (EAST)
Koziolek, Helmut. Umfassende Intensivierung und Infrastruktur /. Berlin , 1986. 68 p. ; LC Card 86-169897
HC290.795.C3 K68 1986

HUMAN CAPITAL - GERMANY (WEST) - CONGRESSES.
Arbeitsmoral und Technikfeindlichkeit . Frankfurt , New York , c1986. 274 p. : ISBN 3-593-33757-6 LC Card 86-212283
HD8444 .A73 1986

HUMAN CAPITAL - LATIN AMERICA.
Elizaga, Juan C. (Juan Carlos) Investigaciones sobre recursos humanos en América Latina . Santiago de Chile , 1972. 16 p. ; LC Card 83-103424
HA755 .U5 no. 91 HD5730.5.A6

HUMAN CAPITAL - MATHEMATICAL MODELS.
Valencia Roa, Carlos Alberto, 1944- Social investments and economic growth /. 1974. xiv, 199 leaves : *NYPL [JLD 86-2961]*

HUMAN CAPITAL - PAKISTAN - CONGRESSES.
Population, human and national resources in Pakistan /. [Karachi , 198-?] 19 p. ; LC Card 85-931341
HA4590.5 .P66 1980z

HUMAN CAPITAL - SAHEL.
Sall, Alioune. Ressources humaines pour le développement . [Dakar, Sénégal , 1984] 51 p. : LC Card 85-129264 DDC 338.91/09624 19
HC1002 .S25 1984

HUMAN CAPITAL - UNITED STATES.
Holoviak, Stephen J. Managing human productivity . New York , 1987. xiii, 216 p. : ISBN 0-275-92481-5 (alk. paper) : LC Card 86-25247 DDC 658.3/14 19
HF5549.2.U5 H65 1987

Winick, Bradley H. Making the link . [Washinton, D.C.] , c1986. i, 17 p. ; ISBN 0-88713-678-8 (pbk.) LC Card 87-106145 DDC 331.11/0973 19
HD5724 .W557 1986

Human carrying capacity of the Brazilian rain-forest /. Fearnside, Philip M. (Philip Martin) New York , 1986. xii, 293 p. : ISBN 0-231-06104-8 (alk. paper) LC Card 85-6643 DDC 330.981/1063 19
HC188.A5 F42 1986 NYPL [JLE 86-4554]

HUMAN ECOLOGY - ADDRESSES, ESSAYS, LECTURES.
Diez años después de Estocolmo . Madrid [1983?] 285 p. : ISBN 84-85633-26-3 LC Card 84-122682 DDC 304.2 19
GF49 .D54 1983 NYPL [JLE 86-1307]

HUMAN ECOLOGY - AMAZON RIVER VALLEY REGION.
Meirelles Filho, João Carlos, 1960- Amazônia--o que fazer? /. São Paulo , 1986. 85 p., [1] folded leaf of plates : LC Card 86-233275
HC187.5 .M45 1986

HUMAN ECOLOGY - AUSTRIA - OBERGURGL - MATHEMATICAL MODELS.
Alpine Areas Workshop (1974 : Schloss Laxenburg) Alpine Areas Workshop, May 13-17, 1974 /. Laxenburg [1974] 80 p. : LC Card 82-212849
HC268.O25 A46 1974

HUMAN ECOLOGY - CONGRESSES.
Umweltschutz . [Mainz] , c1984. 130 p. ; ISBN 3-7758-1086-2 LC Card 85-146233
HC290.5.E5 U64 1984

HUMAN ECOLOGY - GERMANY (WEST)
Schneewind, Klaus A., 1939- Eltern und Kinder . Stuttgart , c1983. 229 p. : ISBN 3-17-007744-9 LC Card 83-150745 DDC 303.3/23/0943 19
HQ739 .S29 1983 NYPL [JLE 87-1168]

HUMAN ECOLOGY - GERMANY (WEST) - CONGRESSES.
Umweltschutz . [Mainz] , c1984. 130 p. ; ISBN 3-7758-1086-2 LC Card 85-146233
HC290.5.E5 U64 1984

HUMAN ECOLOGY - INDIA - ADDRESSES, ESSAYS, LECTURES.
Khoshoo, T. N., 1927- Environmental concerns and strategies /. New Delhi, India , 1984. xii, 296 p. ; LC Card 84-901589
HC440.E5 K48 1984 NYPL [JLE 87-1015]

HUMAN ENGINEERING - CONGRESSES.
West European Conference on the Psychology of Work and Organization (1985 : Aachen, Germany) The psychology of work and organization . Amsterdam ; New York : xi, 407 p. : ISBN 0-444-70029-3 (U. S.) LC Card 86-8947 DDC 158.7 19
HF5548.8 .W475 1985 NYPL [JLE 86-4341]

The human factor, the sugar industry, and Mauritius . Mauritius. Commission of Inquiry into the Sugar Industry. Port Louis, Mauritius [1984] 157 p. ; LC Card 85-980119 DDC 338.1/7361/096982 19
HD9118.M45 M33 1984a

HUMAN FACTORS IN ENGINEERING DESIGN. see **HUMAN ENGINEERING.**

HUMAN GEOGRAPHY. see **ANTHROPO-GEOGRAPHY.**

HUMAN INTERACTION. see **SOCIAL INTERACTION.**

Human migration . Lewis, G. J. London , c1982. 220 p. : ISBN 0-7099-0007-4 LC Card 86-673643
HB1952 .L48x 1982b

Human relations . Higgins, James M. New York , c1987. xvi, 479 p. : ISBN 0-394-35112-6 : LC Card 86-31450 DDC 658.3/145 19
HF5549 .H474 1987

HUMAN RELATIONS. see **INTERPERSONAL RELATIONS.**

Human Relations Media, inc.
You need me [filmstrip] . Pleasantville, NY , 1986. 2 filmstrips (71 fr. each) : LC Card 86-700183 DDC 650.1 11
HF382.7

You need me [videorecording] . Pleasantville, NY , 1986. 1 videocassette (30 min.) : LC Card 87-705080 DDC 650.1 11
HF5382.7

Your job [filmstrip] . Pleasantville, NY , 1986. 2 filmstrips (ca. 74 fr. each) : LC Card 86-700184 DDC 650.1 11
HF5549.5.C35

Your job [videorecording] . Pleasantville, NY , 1986. 1 videocassette (30 min.) : LC Card 87-705039 DDC 650.1 11
HF5549.5.C35

Human resource accounting /. Prabhakara Rao, D. (Devisetti), 1954- New Delhi, India , 1986. xviii, 247 p. : ISBN 81-210-0169-2 : LC Card 86-902848
HF5681.H8 P73 1986

HUMAN RESOURCE DEVELOPMENT. see **MANPOWER POLICY.**

Human resource management /. Byars, Lloyd L. Homewood, Ill. , 1987. xiii, 540 p. : ISBN 0-256-03630-6 LC Card 86-82596 DDC 658.3 19
HF5549 .B937 1987

Human resource management in high-technology firms / edited by Archie Kleingartner, Carolyn S. Anderson (Institute of Industrial Relations, UCLA). Lexington, Mass. : Lexington Books, 1986, c1987. x, 243 p. : ill., tables ; 24 cm. Includes index. Papers presented at a seminar at the University of California, Los Angeles. Bibliography: p. [219]-233. CONTENTS. - Human resource management in high technology firms and the impact of professionalism / Carolyn S. Anderson and Archie Kleingartner -- High technology labor markets / Richard S. Belous -- The educational implications of the high technology revolution / Lewis C. Solmon and Midge A. La Porte -- The dynamic relationship between research universities and the development of high technology industry / Karl S. Pister -- Human resources at Autotel, Inc. / Fred K. Foulkes -- Compensation systems in high technology companies / George T. Milkovich -- Key human resource issues for management in high tech firms / Robert C. Miljus and Rebecca L. Smith -- Conflict resolution in the nonunion high technology firm / David Lewin -- Unions' stake in high tech development / Everett M. Kassalow -- Human resource management and business life cycles / Thomas A. Kochan -- Summary and conclusions. ISBN 0-669-13686-7 (alk. paper) LC Card 86-45556 DDC 658.3 19
1. High technology industries - Personnel management - Congresses. 2. Industrial relations - Congresses. 3. High technology industries - Employees - Congresses. I. Kleingartner, Archie. II. Anderson, Carolyn S. III. University of California, Los Angeles. Institute of Industrial Relations.
HF5549 .H875 1987 NYPL [JLE 87-1100]

Human Resource Mobilization Programme publications.
The Poor in Asia . Kuala Lumpur, Malaysia , 1985- v. <1 > ; ISBN 967-99954-0-2 (v. 1) LC Card 86-944764 DDC 362.5/8/095 19
HC415.P6 P66 1985

Human resource training & development /. Andres, Tomas Quintin D., 1942- Quezon City , c1980. viii, 134 p. : LC Card 82-102431 DDC 658.3/12404/09599 19
HF5549.5.T7 A64 1980 NYPL [JLD 87-935]

Human resource training and development. Andres, Tomas Quintin D., 1942- Human resource training & development /. Quezon City , c1980. viii, 134 p. : LC Card 82-102431 DDC 658.3/12404/09599 19
HF5549.5.T7 A64 1980 NYPL [JLD 87-935]

HUMAN RESOURCES. see **HUMAN CAPITAL.**

Human resources development in Saudi Arabia . Viola, Joy Winkie. Boston , c1986. xxvi, 291 p. : ISBN 0-88746-070-4 (IHRDC) LC Card 85-19694 DDC 303.4/8273/0538 19
HD5812.35.A6 V56 1986 NYPL [JLE 86-2188]

Human resources management : cultivating quality in rehabilitation / edited by Bettye Shofner-Hoffman and Sandra Salser Long. Springfield, Ill., U. S.A. : C.C. Thomas, c1987. xiv, 170 p. : ill. ; 26 cm. Includes bibliographies and index. ISBN 0-398-05296-4 LC Card 86-23016 DDC 362/.0425 19
1. Rehabilitation centers - Personnel management. I. Shofner-Hoffman, Bettye. II. Long, Sandra Salser.
HD7255 .H86 1987

Human resources management / edited by Jill P. Kern, John J. Riley, Louis N. Jones ; sponsored by the American Society of Quality Control, Human Resources Division. New York : M. Dekker ; Milwaukee, Wis. : ASQC Quality Press, c1987. xiv, 276 p. : ill. ; 24 cm. (Quality and reliability . 12) Includes bibliographies and index. ISBN 0-8247-7716-6 LC Card 86-29321 DDC 658.3 19
1. Personnel management. 2. Organizational change. 3. Human capital. I. Kern, Jill P. II. Riley, John J. (John Joseph), 1920-. III. Jones, Louis N. IV. American Society for Quality Control. Human Resources Division. V. Series.
HF5549 .H8727 1987

Human resources management in Indian railways /. Gangadhara Rao, M. Delhi , 1986. xvi, 245 p. ; ISBN 81-7049-004-9 : LC Card 86-900747 DDC 385/.068/3 19
HD8039.R12 I437 1986 NYPL [JLE 86-4104]

Human Resources Program (Conference Board)
Freedman, Audrey. Perspectives on employment /. New York, N.Y. (845 3rd Ave., New York 10022) , c1986. 15 p. : LC Card 86-212384 DDC 331.12 19
HD5701.3 .F74 1986

Human response in organizations . Chakraborty, S. K. Calcutta, India [1985] xv, 228 p. : LC Card 87-901782 DDC 658/.00954 19
HD58.7 .C44 1985

HUMAN RIGHTS - DEVELOPING COUNTRIES.
Glinz, Ferdinand N. Entwicklungsförderung am Wendepunkt . Zürich , c1986. 320 p. ; ISBN 3-280-01676-2 LC Card 86-227950
HC59.7 .G55 1986

HUMAN RIGHTS - EUROPE, EASTERN.
Pressler, Larry, 1942- Trip report, a visit to Eastern Europe in the wake of the 27th Soviet Party Congress and the Chernobyl nuclear accident (Czechoslovakia, Hungary, Yugoslavia, and Romania) on June 28, 1986 . Washington , 1987. vi, 58 p. ; LC Card 87-601360 DDC 337.47 19
HC244 .P744 1987

HUMAN RIGHTS - GERMANY (WEST)
Löffler, Reiner. Macht, Arbeit und Humanität .

Göttingen , c1986. v, 563 p. ; ISBN 3-921969-12-3 LC Card 86-227215
HD6957.G3 L64 1986

Human Sciences Research, inc. Airport transportation . Arlington, Va. , Washington, D.C. [1961] vii, 289, 42 leaves : LC Card 84-132332
HE9797.4.A2 A38 1961

HUMAN SERVICES - RHODE ISLAND - FINANCE.
Salamon, Lester M. Rhode Island nonprofit organizations . Washington, D.C. , Providence, RI , c1987. vii, 40 p. : LC Card 87-148803 DDC 338.7/4/09745 19
HD2769.2.U6 S25 1987

HUMAN SETTLEMENTS.
Schmidt, Aurel, 1935- Der Fremde bin ich selber . Basel , c1982. 261 p. : ISBN 3-85787-103-2 : LC Card 83-109021
HC79.E5 S284 1982

HUMAN SETTLEMENTS - GREAT ALFÖLD - HISTORY.
Blazovich, László. A Körös-Tisza-Maros köz középkori településrendje /. Békéscsaba , Szeged , 1985. 207 p., [9] folded leaves of plates : ISBN 963-01-6828-6 LC Card 87-408571
HD640.5.Z8 G743 1985

HUMAN SETTLEMENTS - INDIA - CASE STUDIES.
Ansari, Saiyad Hasan, 1952- Evolution and spatial organization of clan settlements . New Delhi , 1986. 212 p., [8] p. of plates : LC Card 86-900654
HD879.G45 A57 1986 *NYPL [JLD 86-3220]*

HUMAN SETTLEMENTS - INDIA - GHAZIPUR - CASE STUDIES.
Ansari, Saiyad Hasan, 1952- Evolution and spatial organization of clan settlements . New Delhi , 1986. 212 p., [8] p. of plates : LC Card 86-900654
HD879.G45 A57 1986 *NYPL [JLD 86-3220]*

HUMAN SETTLEMENTS - INDIA - UTTAR PRADESH.
Singh, Alok Kumar, 1958- Population and settlement in U.P. . New Delhi, India , 1985. xx, 231 p., [10] p. of plates : LC Card 86-900123 DDC 304.6/0954/2 19
HB2100.U88 S55 1985 *NYPL [JLD 86-3156]*

HUMAN SETTLEMENTS - PLANNING.
Guidelines for the planning of rural settlements and infrastructure . Nairobi , 1985. vi, 295 p. ; ISBN 92-1-131003-2 LC Card 86-981187 DDC 363/.068 19
HD9688.A2 G85 1985

HUMAN SETTLEMENTS - SWITZERLAND.
Flückiger, Hans. Siedlungsstruktur . Bern , c1985. 118 p. : ISBN 3-258-03529-6 : LC Card 86-134805
HN603.5 .F58 1985 *NYPL [JLE 86-3789]*

The Human side of advanced manufacturing technology / edited by Toby D. Wall and Chris W. Clegg and Nigel J. Kemp. Chichester [West Sussex] ; New York : Wiley, c1987. xi, 205 p. : ill. ; 24 cm. (Wiley series in psychology and productivity at work) Includes bibliographies and indexes. ISBN 0-471-90867-3 : LC Card 86-32554 DDC 331.25 19
1. Manufactures - Technological innovations. 2. Manufacturing processes - Automation. I. Wall, Toby D. II. Clegg, Chris W. III. Kemp, Nigel J. IV. Series.
HD9720.5 .H85 1987

The human side of management . Odiorne, George S. Lexington, Mass. , c1987. xiv, 236 p. ; ISBN 0-669-15350-8 (alk. paper) LC Card 86-46314 DDC 658.3 19
HD30.65 .O35 1987

Human spatial abilities . McGee, Mark G. New York , 1979. xiv, 144 p. : ISBN 0-03-052391-5 LC Card 79-16070 DDC 153.7/52
BF469 .M3 *NYPL [JFE 84-185]*

HUMANE SOCIETIES. see **CHILD WELFARE.**

Humanisierung der Arbeit und Produktivität . Tınar, Mustafa Yaşar, 1955- Frankfurt am Main , New York , c1986. xiii, 296 p. : ISBN 3-8204-9542-8 LC Card 86-233418
HF5549.5.J63 T55 1986

Humanisierung der Arbeit und Reform der beruflichen Bildung . Feuerstein, Thomas. München , c1983. 221 p. ; ISBN 3-87966-184-7 LC Card 83-222687
HD5715.5.G4 F48 1983

HUMANISM - ADDRESSES, ESSAYS, LECTURES.
Rationalism, humanism, and democracy . Meerut , 1985. xcii, 514 p., [2] p. of plates : LC Card 85-901252 DDC 144 19
B833 .R29 1985 *NYPL [JFD 86-3589]*

Tarkunde, V. M. For freedom /. New Delhi , 1984. xii, 199 p. ; LC Card 84-902126 DDC 144 19
B821 .T285 1984 *NYPL [JFD 87-1740]*

HUMANITIES - STUDY AND TEACHING (GRADUATE) - UNITED STATES.
Groneman, Carol. [Corporate Ph. D.] Corporate PhD . New York, N.Y., U. S.A. , 1987, c1985. xx, 156 p. ; ISBN 0-14-010123-3 (pbk.) LC Card 86-30654 DDC 658.4/09 19
HD38.25.U6 G76 1987

Humanum.
Das Unternehmen als Grösse der Arbeitswelt . Bonn , 1984. 291 p. ; ISBN 3-923202-02-4 LC Card 85-119845
HD6957.G3 U58 1984

Humble, Ronald. Todd, Daniel. World aerospace . London , New York , c1987. 226 p. : ISBN 0-7099-4325-3 LC Card 86-29368 DDC 338.4/76291/021 19
HD9711.5.A2 T629 1987

Humboldt-Universität zu Berlin.
Innovation und internationale Monopole /. Berlin , 1983. 85 p. ; LC Card 84-104008
HD2755.5 .I534 1983

Humboldt-Universität zu Berlin. Gesellschaftswissenschaftliche Fakultät. Zur Theorie und Praxis imperialistischer Anpassungs- und Konfrontationspolitik in der Gegenwart /. Berlin [1986] 99 p. ; LC Card 87-409046 DDC 330.12/2 19
HB501 .Z765 1986

Humboldt-Universität zu Berlin. Intersektioneller Arbeitskreis "Weltwirtschaft und Ökonomie der Entwicklungsländer." Internationale Wirtschaft und revolutionärer Weltprozess /. [Berlin] , 1983. 390 p. ; LC Card 84-167604
HF1410.5 .I592 1983

Humboldt-Universität zu Berlin. Wissenschaftsbereich Politische Ökonomie.
Sozialistisches Arbeitsverhalten als Leistungsverhalten /. Berlin [1984] 77 p. ; LC Card 84-250357
HD8460.5 .S694 1984

Hummel, Gertraude. Bottesi, Valentin, 1933- Kombinatsplanung und Leistungssteigerung /. Berlin , 1984. 120 p. ; LC Card 84-217968
HC290.795.I52 B67 1984

Hummel, Marlies.
Die steuerliche Behandlung des eigengenutzten Wohneigentums in den Ländern Bundesrepublik Deutschland, Österreich, Schweiz, Frankreich, Grossbritannien und den USA / wissenschaftliche Bearbeitung, Frankreich, Grossbritannien, USA von Marlies Hummel, Bundesrepublik Deutschland, Österreich, Schweiz von Rüdiger Parsche. München : Ifo-Institut für Wirtschaftsforschung, 1986. ii, 73 p. ; 21 cm. (Ifo Studien zur Finanzpolitik, 0081-7279 . 40) Bibliography: p. 71-73. ISBN 3-88512-021-6 : LC Card 86-215255
1. Income tax - Germany, West. 2. Income tax - Law and legislation - Germany, West. 3. Income tax - Europe. 4. Income tax - Law and legislation - Europe. 5. Income tax - United States. 6. Income tax - Law and legislation - United States. I. Parsche, Rüdiger. II. Title. III. Series.
HJ4719 .H85 1986

Subsidiaritätsprinzip als Leitlinie für einen Subventionsabbau : generelle Problematik und Fallstudien : Gutachten im Auftrag des Bundesministeriums für Wirtschaft / Bearbeiter, Marlies Hummel, unter der Mitarbeit von Klaus-Dieter Knörndel. München : Ifo-Institut für Wirtschaftsforschung, 1985. xiii, 306 p. ; 21 cm. (Ifo Studien zur Finanzpolitik, 0081-7279 . 34) Bibliography: p. 299-306. ISBN 3-88512-003-8 : LC Card 86-125424
1. Subsidies - Germany, West. 2. Subsidies - Law and legislation - Germany (West). 3. Subsidies - Europe. 4. Subsidies - Law and legislation - Europe. I. Knörndel, Klaus-Dieter. II. Germany (West). Bundesministerium für Wirtschaft. III. Title. IV. Series.
HC290.5.S9 H85 1985

Hummeltenberg, Rita. Die optimale Wahl steuerbegünstigter Kapitalanlagen unter Berücksichtigung der Einkommensteuerprogression : Entscheidungshilfen für die Anlageberatung / Rita Hummeltenberg. Berlin : E. Schmidt, c1984. xi, 276 p. : ill. ; 21 cm. (Betriebswirtschaftliche Studien. 47) Originally presented as the author's thesis (doctoral)--Universität zu Köln, 1984? Bibliography: p. 242-254. Includes index. ISBN 3-503-02437-9 LC Card 85-227381
1. Income tax - Germany, West - Mathematical models. 2. Capital investments - Germany (West) - Mathematical models. I. Title.
HJ4719 .H86 1984

Humphrey, John, 1950- Gender and work in the Third World : sexual divisions in Brazilian industry / John Humphrey. London ; New York : Tavistock Publications, 1987. p. cm. Bibliography: p. Includes index. ISBN 0-422-61900-0 (cased) LC Card 87-12416 DDC 305.4/3/00981 19
1. Sexual division of labor - Brazil. I. Title.
HD6060.65.B6 H86 1987

Humphrey, Thomas M. Essays on inflation / by Thomas M. Humphrey. 5th ed. Richmond, Va. : Federal Reserve Bank of Richmond, 1986. vii, 323 p. : ill. ; 26 cm. Includes bibliographies. LC Card 86-205422 DDC 332.4/1 19
1. Inflation (Finance). I. Title.
HG229 .H884 1986

HUNAN PROVINCE (CHINA) - POPULATION - HISTORY.
Perdue, Peter C., 1949- Exhausting the earth . Cambridge, Mass. , 1987. xvii, 331 p. : ISBN 0-674-27504-7 LC Card 87-5067 DDC 338.1/0951/215 19
HD2100.H86 P47 1987

Hundert Jahre im Dienst der Gesundheit, 1886-1986. 100 Jahre im Dienst der Gesundheit, 1886-1986 /. Ludwigshafen am Rhein , c1986. 159 p. : LC Card 87-408744 DDC 338.7/616151/0943 19
HD9669.9.K56 A15 1986

Hundert Jahre Rechts- und Wirtschaftsgeschichte an der Rechts-, Wirtschafts- und Sozialwissenschaftlichen Fakultät der Universität Freiburg = Cent ans d'histoire du droit et d'histoire économique à la Faculté de droit et des sciences économiques de l'Université de Fribourg / Louis Carlen ... [et al.]. Freiburg, Schweiz : Universitätsverlag, 1982. 96 p., [6] p. of plates : ports. ; 23 cm. French and German. Includes bibliographical references. CONTENTS. - Rechtsgeschichte an der Universität Freiburg / Louis Carlen -- Hundert Jahre römisches Recht an der Universität Freiburg i.Ü. / Felix Wubbe -- Cent ans d'enseignement et de recherches en histoire économique / Gaston Gaudard -- L'histoire économique à l'Université de Fribourg / Jean Valarché. ISBN 3-7278-0277-4 : LC Card 83-108855 DDC 340 19
1. Fribourg. Université. Faculté de droit et des sciences économiques - Addresses, essays, lectures. 2. Law - History and criticism - Addresses, essays, lectures. 3. Commercial law - Addresses, essays, lectures. 4. Trade regulation - Addresses, essays, lectures. I. Carlen, Louis. II. Title: Cent ans d'histoire du droit et d'histoire économique à la Faculté de droit et des sciences économiques de l'Université de Fribourg. III. Title: 100 Jahre Rechts- und Wirtschaftsgeschichte an der Rechts-, Wirtschafts- und Sozialwissenschaftlichen Fakultät der Universität Freiburg. IV. Title: 100 ans d'histoire du droit et d'histoire économiques à la Faculté de droit et des sciences économiques de l'Université de Fribourg.
K296 .H86 1982 *NYPL [JLD 86-676]*

Hundertfünfzig Jahre Promotion an der Wirtschaftswissenschaftlichen Fakultät der Universität Tübingen. 150 Jahre Promotion an der Wirtschaftswissenschaftlichen Fakultät der Universität Tübingen . Stuttgart , c1984. xxxvi, 809 p. : ISBN 3-8062-0409-8 LC Card 85-140557
HB74.9.G3 A15 1984 *NYPL [JFE 87-1673]*

Hünerberg, Gerd. Gührs, Eckhard. Leitfaden für Kostenermittlung und Wirtschaftlichkeitsprüfung . Hamburg , 1983. iii, 92 p. ; LC Card 85-212548
HJ9925.G3 G84 1983

Hung, Chao-shun, 1942- Greenhut, Melvin L. The economics of imperfect competition . Cambridge [Cambridgeshire] , New York , 1987. xix, 408 p. : ISBN 0-521-30552-7 LC Card 86-11707 DDC 338.6/048 19
HB238 .G74 1987 *NYPL [JLE 87-1413]*

Hungarian Academy of Sciences. see **Magyar Tudományos Akadémia, Budapest.**

Hungarian Chamber of Commerce. see **Magyar Kereskedelmi Kamara.**

The Hungarian economy in the twentieth century /. Berend, T. Iván (Tibor Iván), 1930- London , c1985. 316 p. ; ISBN 0-7099-2209-4 LC Card 86-673483
HC300.24 .B44 1985b

Hungarian economy in the 20th century. Berend, T. Iván (Tibor Iván), 1930- The Hungarian economy in the twentieth century /. London , c1985. 316 p. ; ISBN 0-7099-2209-4 LC Card 86-673483
HC300.24 .B44 1985b

The Hungarian enterprise in the context of intra-CMEA relations / edited by András Inotai. Budapest : Hungarian Scientific Council for World Economy, 1986. 93 p. ; 24 cm. (Trends in world economy, 0133-7769 . no. 54) CONTENTS. - Summary analysis / Margit Rácz -- Metallurgical enterprises in a constrained room for manoeuvre / Tamás Réti -- Intra-CMEA relations of some Hungarian chemical enterprises / András Inotai -- Intra-CMEA relations of the Hungarian engineering enterprises / Adám Török -- On the intra-CMEA relations of some Hungarian manufacturers of electronics-intensive products / Margit Rácz -- The Hungarian light manufacturers' links with the CMEA region / Gyula Pártos -- The FTOs in intra-CMEA cooperation / Mária Bábosik. ISBN 963-301-138-8 (pbk.) LC Card 87-101284 DDC 337.439 19
1. Hungary - Foreign economic relations. 2. Business enterprises - Hungary. 3. Hungary - Manufactures. 4. Trading companies - Hungary. 5. Council for Mutual Economic Assistance. I. Inotai, András. II. Series: Irányzatok a világgazdaságban , sz. 54.
HF1542.5.H8 H85 1986

Hungarian Socialist Workers' Party. see **Magyar Szocialista Munkáspárt.**

Hungarian sociological studies . (3) Economy and society in Hungary /. Budapest , 1986. 331 p. : LC Card 87-147704 DDC 330.9439/053 19
HC300.28 .E36 1986

Hungarian Workers' Party. see **Magyar Dolgozók Pártja.**

Hungarian Working People's Party. see **Magyar Dolgozók Pártja.**

HUNGARIANS - FOREIGN COUNTRIES.
Tanulmányok Magyarországról, magyarokról. [Budapest] [1985] 280 p. ; ISBN 963-01-7352-2 (Magy. nemz. bibl.) LC Card 87-408505
HC300.24 .T36 1985

Hungary--a market for products from developing countries / International Trade Centre UNCTAD/GATT. Geneva : The Centre, 1985. xi, 129 p. : ill. ; 23 cm. LC Card 87-118542 DDC 382/.09439/01724 19
1. Hungary - Commerce - Developing countries. 2. Developing countries - Commerce - Hungary. I. International Trade Centre UNCTAD/GATT.
HF3550.5.Z7 D44 1985

Hungary. Central Statistical Office. see **Hungary. Központi Statisztikai Hivatal.**

HUNGARY - COMMERCE.
Török, Ádám. Komparatív előnyök . Budapest , 1986, c1985. 225, [1] p. ; ISBN 963-221-579-6 : LC Card 87-105362
HF1412 .T67 1986

HUNGARY - COMMERCE - DEVELOPING COUNTRIES.
Hungary--a market for products from developing countries /. Geneva , 1985. xi, 129 p. : LC Card 87-118542 DDC 382/.09439/01724 19
HF3550.5.Z7 D44 1985

HUNGARY - COMMERCE - HISTORY.
Horváth, Mihály, 1809-1878. Az ipar és kereskedés története Magyarországban a három utolsó század alatt /. [Budapest , 1984] xiv, 390 p. ; ISBN 963-02-2781-9 : LC Card 85-138953
HC300.26 .H67 1984

HUNGARY - COMMERCE - STATISTICS.
Külkereskedelmi árstatisztikai adatok, 1950-1985 /. Budapest , 1986. 114 p. ; LC Card 87-409625
HB235.H8 K84 1986

Külkereskedelmi árstatisztikai adatok, 1957-1977 /. Budapest [1978] 125 p. ; LC Card 86-196922
HB235.H8 K85 1978

HUNGARY - COMMERCIAL POLICY.
Munkaügy a belkereskedelemben /. [Budapest] , 1986. 272 p. ; ISBN 963-01-7513-4 : LC Card 87-148137
HF5549.2.H85 M86 1986

Somogyi, Dorottya. A fejlett tőkés országok exportpolitikája /. Budapest , 1985. 277, [1] p. : ISBN 963-221-507-9 : LC Card 85-231848
HF1417.5 .S66 1985

HUNGARY - ECONOMIC CONDITIONS.
Berend, T. Iván (Tibor Iván), 1930- The Hungarian economy in the twentieth century /. London , c1985. 316 p. ; ISBN 0-7099-2209-4 LC Card 86-673483
HC300.24 .B44 1985b

Horváth, Mihály, 1809-1878. Az ipar és kereskedés története Magyarországban a három utolsó század alatt /. [Budapest , 1984] xiv, 390 p. ; ISBN 963-02-2781-9 : LC Card 85-138953
HC300.26 .H67 1984

Tanulmányok Magyarországról, magyarokról. [Budapest] [1985] 280 p. ; ISBN 963-01-7352-2 (Magy. nemz. bibl.) LC Card 87-408505
HC300.24 .T36 1985

HUNGARY - ECONOMIC CONDITIONS - 18TH CENTURY - MAPS.
Malmok, ipari és gazdasági létesítmények az első katonai felmérés térképszelvényein, 1782-1785 /. Budapest , 1982. 220 p., [1] leaf of plates : ISBN 963-01-4433-6 (Magy. nemz. bibl.) LC Card 83-230040
HC300.26 .M35 1982

HUNGARY - ECONOMIC CONDITIONS - 1945-
Batt, Judy. Economic reform and political change in eastern Europe . New York , 1987. p. cm. ISBN 0-312-01196-2 : LC Card 87-24065 DDC 338.9437 19
HC270.28 .B37 1987

Berend, T. Iván (Tibor Iván), 1930- Szocializmus és reform /. Budapest , 1986. 194, [1] p. ; ISBN 963-05-4386-9 : LC Card 87-407684
HC300.28 .B475 1986

Economy and society in Hungary /. Budapest , 1986. 331 p. : LC Card 87-147704 DDC 330.9439/053 19
HC300.28 .E36 1986

Hungary, pushing the limits [videorecording] /. Alexandria, VA , 1987. 1 videocassette (60 min.) : LC Card 87-707589 DDC 943.9 11
HC300.28

Nyitrai, Ferencné. A magyar gazdaság negyven éve /. [Budapest] , 1985. 385 p. ; ISBN 963-09-2570-2 : LC Card 86-104105
HC300.28 .N945 1985

Pető, Iván. A hazai gazdaság négy évtizedének története, 1945-1985 /. Budapest , 1985- v. <1 > ; ISBN 963-221-553-2 (set) LC Card 87-105744
HC300.28 .P47 1985

HUNGARY - ECONOMIC CONDITIONS - 1968-
Gazdaság és társadalom a nyolcvanas években Magyarországon /. Budapest , 1986- v. <1 > ; ISBN 963-7700-19-6 (set) LC Card 87-136629
HC300.28 .G265 1986

Gazdaságunk helyzetéről és fejlődésünk problémáiról. [Budapest] , 1985. 239 p. : ISBN 963-09-2681-4 : LC Card 86-202400
HC300.28 .G36 1985

Hoós, János. Az új növekedési pálya feltételei és követelményei /. Budapest , 1985. 227, [2] p. : ISBN 963-221-508-7 : LC Card 86-128355
HC300.28 .H664 1985

Illés, Iván. Gazdaságunk helye és rangja a világban . Budapest , 1985. 222 p. : ISBN 963-221-523-0 : LC Card 86-156571
HC300.28 .I45 1985

A Magyar szakszervezetek feladatai a gazdaságirányítás továbbfejlesztésének segítésében . Budapest , 1984. 47 p. ; ISBN 963-322-215-X LC Card 85-176937
HC300.28 .M3297 1984

Pongrácz, Antal. Gazdaságpolitika, elméletben és gyakorlatban . [Budapest] , 1985. 73 p. ; ISBN 963-422-739-2 : LC Card 87-105897
HC300.28 .P66 1985

Sándorné Szennyessy, Judit. Gazdaságpolitikai kézikönyv /. [Budapest] , 1985. 170 p. : LC Card 86-186314
HC300.28 .S26 1985

Társadalmi-gazdasági fejlődés a VI. ötéves tervidőszakban. Budapest , 1986. 131 p. ; ISBN 963-340-800-8 : LC Card 87-408587
HC300.28 .T378 1986

HUNGARY - ECONOMIC CONDITIONS - 1968- - ADDRESSES, ESSAYS, LECTURES.
Kornai, János. [Ellentmondások és dilemmák. English.] Contradictions and dilemmas . Cambridge, Mass. , 1986, c1983. ix, 165 p. : ISBN 0-262-11107-1 LC Card 85-5168 DDC 330.9439/053 19
HC300.28 .K67213 1986 *NYPL [JLC 86-254]*

HUNGARY - ECONOMIC CONDITIONS - 1968- - CONGRESSES.
A Gazdaság és társadalom viszonya a szocializmus építésének jelenlegi időszakában . Szeged , 1985. 181 p. ; LC Card 86-207975
HC300.28 .G27 1985

HUNGARY - ECONOMIC CONDITIONS - 1968- - REGIONAL DISPARITIES - STATISTICS.
Nagyné Szauter, Edit. A gazdaságilag elmaradott térségek társadalmi-gazdasági jellemzői /. Budapest , 1986. 41 p. : LC Card 86-215345
HC300.28 .N26 1986

HUNGARY - ECONOMIC POLICY - 1945-
Batt, Judy. Economic reform and political change in eastern Europe . New York , 1987. p. cm. ISBN 0-312-01196-2 : LC Card 87-24065 DDC 338.9437 19
HC270.28 .B37 1987

Hungary, pushing the limits [videorecording] /. Alexandria, VA , 1987. 1 videocassette (60 min.) : LC Card 87-707589 DDC 943.9 11
HC300.28

Pető, Iván. A hazai gazdaság négy évtizedének története, 1945-1985 /. Budapest , 1985- v. <1 > ; ISBN 963-221-553-2 (set) LC Card 87-105744
HC300.28 .P47 1985

HUNGARY - ECONOMIC POLICY - 1945-1968.
Vigvári, András. A gazdaságirányítási rendszer egyes kérdései, elmélettörténeti megközelítésben /. [Budapest] , 1985. 87 p. ; ISBN 963-673-302-3 LC Card 85-231820
HC300.28 .V53 1985

HUNGARY - ECONOMIC POLICY - 1968-
Bagota, Béla. Mit kell tudni a hetedik ötéves tervről? /. [Budapest] , 1986. 238 p. ; ISBN 963-09-2815-9 : LC Card 86-210804
HC300.28 .B319 1986

Bagota, Béla. Mit kell tudni az 1987. évi népgazdasági tervről? /. [Budapest] , 1987. 239 p. ; ISBN 963-09-3110-9 : LC Card 87-151787
HC300.28 .B329 1987

Böhm, Edward. Wechselkurspolitik in der Planwirtschaft . Hamburg , 1986. 139 p. : ISBN 3-87895-301-1 LC Card 86-210978
HG3947.5 .B64 1986

Bontó, László. Iparfejlesztés a hetedik ötéves terv időszakában /. [Budapest] , 1986. 170, [4] p. : ISBN 963-09-3001-3 : LC Card 87-138631
HC300.28 .B659 1986

Friss István emlékezete /. Budapest , 1984. 128 p. ; LC Card 86-145174
HC300.28 .F75 1984

A Gazdaságirányítás és a szakszervezetek /. Budapest , 1985. 191 p. ; ISBN 963-322-253-2 : LC Card 86-104573
HC300.28 .G349 1985

Gazdaságirányítás, 1985 /. Budapest , 1984. 175 p. ; ISBN 963-221-540-0 : LC Card 85-229856
HC300.28 .G338 1984

A Gazdaságirányítási rendszer továbbfejlesztése

/. Budapest , 1984. 171 p. ; LC Card 86-145153
HC300.28 .G339 1984

Gazdaságunk helyzetéről és fejlődésünk problémáiról. [Budapest] , 1985. 239 p. : ISBN 963-09-2681-4 : LC Card 86-202400
HC300.28 .G36 1985

Hoós, János. Az új növekedési pálya feltételei és követelményei /. Budapest , 1985. 227, [2] p. : ISBN 963-221-508-7 : LC Card 86-128355
HC300.28 .H664 1985

Juhász, Ottó. A népgazdasági szintü gazdaságpolitikai döntések végrehajtását segitő szakszervezeti munka . [Budapest] [1984] 136 p. ; ISBN 963-608-064-X LC Card 86-126615
HD6680.5 .J84 1984

Közgazdasági bizottságok kézikönyve /. Budapest , 1984. 324 p. ; ISBN 963-322-017-3 : LC Card 85-126303
HC300.28 .K68 1984

Nyitrai, Ferencné. Prioritások gazdaságunk fejlesztésében /. [Budapest] , 1986. 270 p. ; ISBN 963-09-2782-9 : LC Card 87-408568
HC300.28 .N954 1986

Pongrácz, Antal. Gazdaságpolitika, elméletben és gyakorlatban . [Budapest] , 1985. 73 p. ; ISBN 963-422-739-2 : LC Card 87-105897
HC300.28 .P66 1985

Sándorné Szennyessy, Judit. Gazdaságpolitikai kézikönyv /. [Budapest] , 1985. 170 p. : LC Card 86-186314
HC300.28 .S26 1985

Soós, Károly Attila. Terv, kampány, pénz . Budapest , 1986. 532 p. : ISBN 963-221-575-3 : LC Card 87-137237
HB3787.5 .S66 1986

Vigvári, András. A gazdaságirányítási rendszer egyes kérdései, elmélettörténeti megközelítésben /. [Budapest] , 1985. 87 p. ; ISBN 963-673-302-3 LC Card 85-231820
HC300.28 .V53 1985

La Voie hongroise . [Paris] , c1986. 319 p. : ISBN 2-7021-1378-8 : LC Card 86-221784
HC300.28 .V65 1986

HUNGARY - ECONOMIC POLICY - 1968- - CONGRESSES.
A Gazdaság és társadalom viszonya a szocializmus építésének jelenlegi időszakában . Szeged , 1985. 181 p. ; LC Card 86-207975
HC300.28 .G27 1985

Gazdasági fejlődésünk és a gazdaságirányítás továbbfejlesztése . [Budapest] , 1984. 219 p. ; ISBN 963-09-2571-0 : LC Card 85-186920
HC300.28 .G332 1984

A Vállalati magatartást motiváló gazdasági és társadalmi tényezők címü konferencia előadásai . Pécs , 1985. 2 v. : LC Card 87-408547
HD70.H8 V334 1985

Hungary. Építésügyi és Városfejlesztési Minisztérium. Építészeti és Településfejlesztési Főosztály. A Magyarországi településrendszer strukturális változása /. Budapest , 1984. 155 p., [1] folded leaf of plates : ISBN 963-03-2079-7 (Magy. nemz. bibl.) LC Card 85-231254
HD640.5 .M343 1984

HUNGARY - FOREIGN ECONOMIC RELAIONS - INDOCHINA.
Árva, László. Indokina gazdasági fejlődése és hazánk lehetőségei a térség országaival való együttműködés terén /. Budapest , 1984. 69 p. : ISBN 963-491-194-3 LC Card 86-199424
HC441 .A77 1984

HUNGARY - FOREIGN ECONOMIC RELATIONS.
Hoch, Róbert. A gazdaság nyitottságáról . Budapest , c1987. 33 p. ; ISBN 963-05-4444-X : LC Card 87-425574
HF1542.5 .H63 1987

The Hungarian enterprise in the context of intra-CMEA relations /. Budapest , 1986. 93 p. ; ISBN 963-301-138-8 (pbk.) LC Card 87-101284 DDC 337.439 19
HF1542.5.H8 H85 1986

Illés, Iván. Gazdaságunk helye és rangja a világban . Budapest , 1985. 222 p. : ISBN 963-221-523-0 : LC Card 86-156571
HC300.28 .I45 1985

Kiefer, Márta. Magyarország tőkés viszonylatu gazdasági és pénzügyi kapcsolatairól /. [Budapest] [1985] 115 p. ; ISBN 963-608-080-1 LC Card 86-228329
HF1542.5 .K54 1985

HUNGARY - FOREIGN ECONOMIC RELATIONS - EAST ASIA.
Hernádi, András. A távol-keleti kihívás . Budapest , 1985. 233 p. ; ISBN 963-221-545-1 : LC Card 86-186844
HC460.5 .H47 1985

Hungary - Government. see **Hungary - Politics and government.**

HUNGARY - INDUSTRIES.
Bontó, László. Iparfejlesztés a hetedik ötéves terv időszakában /. [Budapest] , 1986. 170, [4] p. : ISBN 963-09-3001-3 : LC Card 87-138631
HC300.28 .B659 1986

Botos, Balázs. Kérdőjelek iparunk fejlesztésében /. Budapest , 1984. 391, [1] p. ; ISBN 963-221-392-0 : LC Card 85-156613
HC300.28 .B69 1984

HUNGARY - INDUSTRIES - DIRECTORIES.
Marketing . [Budapest , 1985?] 68 p. : LC Card 86-234770 DDC 338.7/4/09439 19
HC300.227 .M37 1985

HUNGARY - INDUSTRIES - HISTORY.
Horváth, Mihály, 1809-1878. Az ipar és kereskedés története Magyarországban a három utolsó század alatt /. [Budapest , 1984] xiv, 390 p. ; ISBN 963-02-2781-9 : LC Card 85-138953
HC300.26 .H67 1984

Iparunk 40 éve /. [Budapest] , 1985. 58, [37] p. : ISBN 963-382-009-X LC Card 85-228898
HC300.28 .I64 1985

HUNGARY - INDUSTRIES - STATISTICS.
Iparunk színvonala és fejlődése nemzetközi összehasonlításban, 1970-1983 /. Budapest , 1985. 147, [1] p. ; ISBN 963-340-761-3 : LC Card 86-186336
HC300.28 .I66 1985

Az 1983. évi iparstatisztikai világprogram adatai, Magyarország /. [Budapest , 1986. 289 p. ; LC Card 86-219027
HC300.28 .A14 1986

Hungary. Kereskedelmi Kamara. see **Magyar Kereskedelmi Kamara.**

Hungary. Közlekedési Minisztérium. Közuti Főosztály. Az Ország közuthálózatának müszaki minősitése és nyilvántartása /. [Budapest] , 1983. 2 v. : LC Card 84-253458
HE363.H82 O76 1983

Hungary. Központi Statisztikai Hivatal. (Old Catalog form: Hungary. Statisztikai Hivatal.)

Hungary. Központi Statisztikai Hivatal. Agrárgazdasági Osztály. Beruházások és állóeszközök a mezőgazdaságban, 1981-1985 /. Budapest , 1987. 90 p. ; ISBN 963-02-4805-0 LC Card 87-409593
HD1940.5 .B474 1987

Hungary. Központi Statisztikai Hivatal. Ár- és Modszertani Osztály. Külkereskedelmi árstatisztikai adatok, 1957-1977 /. Budapest [1978] 125 p. ; LC Card 86-196922
HB235.H8 K85 1978

Hungary. Központi Statisztikai Hivatal. Belkereskedelmi Osztály.
Alkoholtartalmú italok kiskereskedelmi eladási forgalmának alakulása 1960-1984 években /. Budapest , 1986. 32 p. : LC Card 86-199334
HD9365.H82 A45 1986

Kiskereskedelmi áralakulás, 1981-1985 /. Budapest , 1986. 81 p. ; LC Card 86-202239
HB235.H8 K56 1986

Hungary. Központi Statisztikai Hivatal. Beruházási és Építőipari Statisztikai Főosztály. Beruházási árindexek, 1968-1971 /. [Budapest] [1972] 56 p. ; LC Card 86-189972
HB235.H8 B48 1972

Hungary. Központi Statisztikai Hivatal. Gépesitési és Munkaügyi Osztály. Munkaerőhelyzet és kereseti viszonyok az állami gazdaságokban, kombinátokban és a mezőgazdasági termelőszövetkezetekben, 1980-1985 /. Budapest , 1987. 45 p. ; LC Card 87-419798
HD1536.H9 M85 1987

Hungary. Központi Statisztikai Hivatal. Háztartásstatisztikai Osztály.
A Magyar háztartásstatisztikai megfigyelés módszertana /. Budapest , 1986. 59 p. ; LC Card 87-408579
HA37.H92 M34 1986

Salamin, Pálné. Vélemények az életszínvonalról /. Budapest , 1986. 88 p. : LC Card 86-218875
HD7027.5 .S25 1986

Hungary. Központi Statisztikai Hivatal. Iparstatisztikai Főosztály.
Az Ipari nagyüzemi munkásság jövedelmi viszonyai, élet- és munkakörülményei /. [Budapest] [1985] 94 p. ; LC Card 85-210330
HD8420.5 .I63 1985

Iparunk színvonala és fejlődése nemzetközi összehasonlításban, 1970-1983 /. Budapest , 1985. 147, [1] p. ; ISBN 963-340-761-3 : LC Card 86-186336
HC300.28 .I66 1985

Az 1983. évi iparstatisztikai világprogram adatai, Magyarország /. [Budapest , 1986. 289 p. ; LC Card 86-219027
HC300.28 .A14 1986

Hungary. Központi Statisztikai Hivatal. Iparstatisztikai Főosztály. Módszertani és Elemzési Osztály.
Adatgyűjtemény az állami iparvállalatoknál foglalkoztatottak létszám-, bér- és kereseti arányairól /. Budapest , 1986. 148 p. ; LC Card 87-407679
HD5772.5.A6 A34 1986

Az Állami iparvállalatoknál foglalkoztatottak létszámösszetétele bér- és kereseti viszonyai /. Budapest , 1986. 124 p. ; ISBN 963-02-4488-8 LC Card 86-218968
HD5772.5.A6 A57 1986

Hungary. Központi Statisztikai Hivatal. Jövedelem- és Fogyasztásstatisztikai Osztály.
A Lakosság jövedelme és fogyasztása, 1960-1973 /. [Budapest] , c1975. 91 p. ; ISBN 963-340-048-1 LC Card 86-196944
HC300.295.I5 L32 1975

A Lakosság jövedelme és fogyasztása, 1960-1983 /. Budapest , 1984. 118 p. ; ISBN 963-340-740-0 : LC Card 85-155585
HC300.295.I5 L3315 1984
NYPL [JLF 86-672]

A Lakosság jövedelme és fogyasztása, 1970-1985 /. Budapest , 1986. 97 p. ; ISBN 963-340-805-9 : LC Card 87-408026
HC300.295.I5 L3317 1986

Hungary. Központi Statisztikai Hivatal. Kereskedelmi és Közlekedési Statisztikai Főosztály. Külkereskedelmi Osztály. see **Hungary. Központi Statisztikai Hivatal. Külkereskedelmi Osztály.**

Hungary Központi Statisztikai Hivatal. Kohó- és Gépipari Osztály.
Az Ipari robotok termelésének és felhasználásának trendjei /. Budapest , 1985. 63 p. : LC Card 86-199458
HD9696.R623 H852 1985

A Kohászati és a gépipari árak alakulása, 1980-1984 /. Budapest , 1986. 91 p. ; LC Card 86-202642
HD9705.H82 K64 1986

Hungary. Központi Statisztikai Hivatal. Közgazdasági Főosztály.
A Lakosság jövedelme, társadalombiztosítás, családpolitika /. Budapest [1983] 82 p. : LC Card 83-206799
HC30.295.I5 L332 1983
NYPL [JLE 87-179]

A Lakosság jövedelmi rétegződése 1982-ben . Budapest , 1984. 50 p. ; LC Card 86-195316
HC300.295.I5 L36 1984

A Nemzeti vagyon és az állóeszközállomány 1970-1978 /. [Budapest] [1979] 140 p. ; LC Card 82-193609
HC300.295.W4 N454 1979

Hungary. Központi Statisztikai Hivatal. Külkereskedelmi Osztály. Külkereskedelmi árstatisztikai adatok, 1950-1985 /. Budapest , 1986. 114 p. ; LC Card 87-409625
HB235.H8 K84 1986

Hungary. Központi Statisztikai Hivatal. Mezőgazdasági Statisztikai Főosztály.
A Mezőgazdasági és az erdőgazdálkodási

árstatisztika módszere /. Budapest , 1986. 81 p. ; LC Card 87-408580
HD9015.H82 M486 1986

Hungary. Központi Statisztikai Hivatal. Mezőgazdasági Statisztikai Főosztály. Módszertani és Elemzési Osztály. Franciaország és Magyarország mezőgazdasága /. Budapest , 1986. 43 p. : ISBN 963-340-783-4 : LC Card 86-189634
HD1945 .F74 1986

A Jugoszláv és a magyar mezőgazdaság összehasonlítása a határmenti területeken /. Budapest , 1986. 37 p. ; LC Card 87-407672
HD1940.5 .J83 1986

A Magyar mezőgazdaság európai összehasonlításban /. Budapest , 1985. 207 p. : ISBN 963-02-3856-X (Magy. nemz. bibl.) LC Card 86-157394
HD1940.5 .M34 1985

A Mezőgazdasági termelés ár- és költségviszonyai nemzetközi összehasonlításban /. Budapest , 1986. 89 p. : LC Card 87-407682
HD1447 .M49 1986

Hungary. Központi Statisztikai Hivatal. Mezőgazdasági Statisztikai Főosztály. Összeirási Osztály. Szőlőtermelés . Budapest , 1986. 519 p. ; ISBN 963-340-777-X : LC Card 86-196884
HD9385.H82 S95 1986

Hungary. Központi Statisztikai Hivatal. Munkaerő és Foglalkozásstatisztikai Osztály. Budapest és a jelentősebb városok napi munkaerővonzási körzete népességének főbb jellemzői, 1980. január 1. /. Budapest , 1986. 106 p. : ISBN 963-02-4578-7 LC Card 87-407674
HA1205 .B83 1986

Hungary. Központi Statisztikai Hivatal. Nehézipari Osztály. Az Energiatermelés és az energiafelhasználás szerkezete . Budapest , 1970. 44 p. ; LC Card 86-189699
HD9502.H92 E54 1970

Hungary. Központi Statisztikai Hivatal. Népesedésstatisztikai Főosztály. Demograficheskie protsessy v sotsialisticheskom obshchestve. Hungarian. Demográfiai folyamatok a szocialista társadalomban az európai KGST országok példáján /. Budapest , 1984. 136 p. ; LC Card 85-154859
HB3581 .D4515 1984

Lakásváltoztatási szándékok, lakáskörülmények az 1984. évi mikrocenzus alapján /. Budapest , 1986. 199 p. ; ISBN 963-340-798-2 LC Card 87-110348
HD7337.5.A3 L355 1986

Hungary. Központi Statisztikai Hivatal. Népesedésstatisztikai Osztály. Egységes szülészeti adatszolgáltatási rendszer . Budapest , 1986. 102 p. ; LC Card 86-233497
HB1002.5.A3 E39 1986

Az 1937-68 években született nők kohorsz-termékenysége /. Budapest [1986] 77 p. ; LC Card 87-407670
HB1002.5.A3 A15 1986

Hungary. Központi Statisztikai Hivatal. Population Statistics Dept. see Hungary. Központi Statisztikai Hivatal. Népesedésstatisztikai Fóosztály.

Hungary. Központi Statisztikai Hivatal. Társadalmi Statisztikai Főosztály. Harcsa, István. Vándorlás, mobilitás, keresetalakulás . Budapest , 1987. 86 p. ; ISBN 963-340-812-1 : LC Card 87-409641
HB2052.5.A3 H37 1987

A Háztáji és kisegitő gazdaság szerepe az életmód alakulásában . Budapest , 1983. 263 p. ; ISBN 963-02-2948-X (Magy. nemz. bibl.) LC Card 84-216989
HD1476.H8 H28 1983

Hungary. Központi Statisztikai Hivatal. Termelési és Mérlegosztály. A Bolgár és a magyar mezőgazdaság összehasonlítása, 1976-1984 /. Budapest , 1987. 69 p. ; ISBN 963-02-4777-1 LC Card 87-409639 DDC 338.1/09439/021 19
HD2042 .B59 1987

HUNGARY - MANUFACTURES.
The Hungarian enterprise in the context of intra-CMEA relations /. Budapest , 1986. 93 p. ; ISBN 963-301-138-8 (pbk.) LC Card 87-101284 DDC 337.439 19
HF1542.5.H8 H85 1986

Hungary. Nehézipari Minisztérium. A Bányászat műszaki, gazdasági szakembereinek II. ágazati tanácskozása . [Budapest , 1979] (Szolnok : NKFV Nyomda) 83 p. ; LC Card 82-205242
HD9506.H92 B36 1979

Hungary. Office central de statistique. see **Hungary. Központi Statisztikai Hivatal.**

Hungary. Pénzügyminisztérium. Titkárság. Management of public budgetary institutions /. Budapest , 1986. 37 p. ; ISBN 963-03-2343-5 (pbk.) : LC Card 86-230773 DDC 336.439 19
HJ2103 .M33 1986

HUNGARY - POLITICS AND GOVERNMENT - 1945-
Batt, Judy. Economic reform and political change in eastern Europe . New York , 1987. p. cm. ISBN 0-312-01196-2 : LC Card 87-24065 DDC 338.9437 19
HC270.28 .B37 1987

Economy and society in Hungary /. Budapest , 1986. 331 p. : LC Card 87-147704 DDC 330.9439/053 19
HC300.28 .E36 1986

Gáspár, Sándor. A munkásosztály szolgálatában /. [Budapest] , c1983. 326 p., [26] p. of plates : ISBN 963-322-025-4 : LC Card 84-129952
HD6680.5.Z55 G375 1983

HUNGARY - POPULATION.
Gazdaság és társadalom a nyolcvanas években Magyarországon /. Budapest , 1986- v. <1 > ; ISBN 963-7700-19-6 (set) LC Card 87-136629
HC300.28 .G265 1986

Tanulmányok Magyarországról, magyarokról. [Budapest] [1985] 280 p. ; ISBN 963-01-7352-2 (Magy. nemz. bibl.) LC Card 87-408505
HC300.24 .T36 1985

HUNGARY - POPULATION - PUBLIC OPINION.
Pataki, Judit. Közvéleménykutatás népesedési kérdésekről /. Budapest , c1985. 75 p. ; LC Card 86-166976
HA1201 .A64 no. 60 HB3592.5.A3

HUNGARY - POPULATION - STATISTICS.
Budapest és a jelentősebb városok napi munkaerővonzási körzete népességének főbb jellemzői, 1980. január 1. /. Budapest , 1986. 106 p. : ISBN 963-02-4578-7 LC Card 87-407674
HA1205 .B83 1986

Csernák, Józsefné. A családok és háztartások előreszámítása, 1981-2001 /. Budapest , 1985. 125 p. : LC Card 86-166603
HA1201 .A64 no. 59 HA1205

Hungary. Population Statistics Dept. see **Hungary. Központi Statisztikai Hivatal. Népesedésstatisztikai Fóosztály.**

Hungary, pushing the limits [videorecording] / KCET-TV ; producers, Jeffrey Kaye, Peter Stone. Alexandria, VA : PBS Video, 1987. 1 videocassette (60 min.) : sd., col. Title from data sheet. Originally shown on television. Ages 17 through adults. Issued as U-matic 3/4 in. or Beta 1/2 in. or VHS 1/2 in. Shows Los Angeles builder Dezso Biczo returning to his native Hungary for the first time since the revolution of 1956. Examines the many changes which have occurred since he left, and describes the economic reform which allows Hungary a better standard of living than other Eastern bloc nations. LC Card 87-707589 DDC 943.9 11
1. Hungary - Economic policy - 1945-. 2. Hungary - Economic conditions - 1945-. I. Biczo, Dezso. II. KCET (Television station : Los Angeles, Calif.). III. PBS Video.
HC300.28

HUNGARY - RURAL CONDITIONS.
Simó, Tibor. Metszetek az agrártársadalom struktúrájából /. Budapest , 1985. 167 p. ; ISBN 963-7700-25-0 : LC Card 86-232606
HD1536.H9 S56 1985

Szelényi, Iván. Socialist entrepreneurs . Madison, Wis. , 1988. p. cm. ISBN 0-299-11360-4 : LC Card 87-16085 DDC 338.1/09439 19
HD1940.5 .S94 1988

Vasary, Ildiko. Beyond the plan . Boulder , 1987. xvii, 308 p. : ISBN 0-8133-7412-X (soft : alk. paper) : LC Card 87-8219 DDC 307.7/2/09439 19
HD1492.H8 V35 1987

HUNGARY - SOCIAL CONDITIONS - 1945-
Economy and society in Hungary /. Budapest , 1986. 331 p. : LC Card 87-147704 DDC 330.9439/053 19
HC300.28 .E36 1986

Tanulmányok Magyarországról, magyarokról. [Budapest] [1985] 280 p. ; ISBN 963-01-7352-2 (Magy. nemz. bibl.) LC Card 87-408505
HC300.24 .T36 1985

HUNGARY - SOCIAL CONDITIONS - 1945- - CONGRESSES.
A Gazdaság és társadalom viszonya a szocializmus építésének jelenlegi időszakában . Szeged , 1985. 181 p. ; LC Card 86-207975
HC300.28 .G27 1985

HUNGARY - SOCIAL CONDITIONS - 1945- - STATISTICS.
Nagyné Szauter, Edit. A gazdaságilag elmaradott térségek társadalmi-gazdasági jellemzői /. Budapest , 1986. 41 p. : LC Card 86-215345
HC300.28 .N26 1986

HUNGARY - SOCIAL CONDITIONS - 1968-
Gazdaság és társadalom a nyolcvanas években Magyarországon /. Budapest , 1986- v. <1 > ; ISBN 963-7700-19-6 (set) LC Card 87-136629
HC300.28 .G265 1986

Társadalmi-gazdasági fejlődés a VI. ötéves tervidőszakban. Budapest , 1986. 131 p. ; ISBN 963-340-800-8 : LC Card 87-408587
HC300.28 .T378 1986

HUNGARY - SOCIAL POLICY - CONGRESSES.
A Gazdaság és társadalom viszonya a szocializmus építésének jelenlegi időszakában . Szeged , 1985. 181 p. ; LC Card 86-207975
HC300.28 .G27 1985

HUNGARY - STATISTICAL SERVICES - HISTORY.
A Népmozgalmi statisztika fejlődése Magyarorságon. Budapest , 1985- v. <1 > ; LC Card 86-190535
HA37.H92 N46 1985

HUNGARY - STATISTICS, VITAL.
Rex-Kiss, Béla. Vizsgálatok az újszülöttek nemi arányának alakulásáról /. Budapest , 1986. 124 p. : ISBN 963-241-457-8 : LC Card 87-138601
HB1741 .R49 1986

Az 1937-68 években született nők kohorsz-termékenysége /. Budapest [1986] 77 p. ; LC Card 87-407670
HB1002.5.A3 A15 1986

HUNGARY - STATISTICS, VITAL - HISTORY.
A Népmozgalmi statisztika fejlődése Magyarorságon. Budapest , 1985- v. <1 > ; LC Card 86-190535
HA37.H92 N46 1985

HUNGARY - STATISTICS, VITAL - MATHEMATICAL MODELS.
Pollard, J. H. Mortality, expectation of life, and the Hungarian experience /. [North Ryde, N.S.W.] [1986] 59 p. ; ISBN 0-85837-578-8 (pbk.) LC Card 87-110257 DDC 304.6/4/09439 19
HB1422.5.A3 P65 1986

Hungary. Statistisches Zentralamt. see **Hungary. Központi Statisztikai Hivatal.**

Hungary. Statisztika és Gazdaságelemző Központ. Mezőgazdasági és élelmiszeripari adattár a felszabadulástól napjainkig. English. Collection of data of agriculture and food industry from the liberation till now /. Budapest , 1985. 85 p. ; ISBN 963-502-393-6 LC Card 86-230345
HD1940.5 .M49713 1985

Hungary. Statisztikai és Gazdaságelemző Központ.
Mezőgazdasági és élelmiszeripari adattár a felszabadulástól napjainkig /. Budapest , 1985. 152 p. ; ISBN 963-502-393-6 LC Card 86-202515
HD1940.5 .M497 1985

Hungary. Statisztikai és Gazdaságelemző Központ. Mezőgazdasági Költség- és Árelemzési Osztály. A Szocialista nagyüzemek főbb ágazatainak költség- és jövedelemhelyzete 1984-ben /. Budapest , 1985.

35, [46] p. ; LC Card 85-177804
HD1492.H8 S93 1985

Hungary. Statisztikai Hivatal. see **Hungary. Központi Statisztikai Hivatal.**

HUNGER.
American Jewish Joint Distribution Committee. [Choroba głodowa. English.] Hunger disease . New York , c1979. xiv, 261 p. : ISBN 0-471-05003-2 LC Card 78-26397 DDC 616.3/9
RC627.S7 A43 1979
*NYPL [*PXV (Warsaw) 86-3505]*

Castro, Josué de, 1908-1973. Fome, um tema proibido . Petrópolis , 1983. 154 p. ; LC Card 83-224629
HD9000.5 .C28 1983

Griffin, Keith B. World hunger and the world economy . New York , 1987. xvi, 274 p. ; ISBN 0-8419-1128-2 LC Card 86-33626 DDC 330.9172/4 19
HC59.7 .G749 1987

Kent, George, 1939- Fish, food, and hunger . Boulder , 1987. ix, 201 p. ; ISBN 0-8133-7409-X (pbk.) : LC Card 87-6066 DDC 338.3/7194 19
HD9450.5 .K46 1987

Semana Josué de Castro e a nova geografia da fome, Rio de Janeiro, 19-24 de setembro de 1983 . [S.l. , 1983] 90 leaves : LC Card 86-201115
HD9000.5 .S3968 1983

Solving world hunger, the U. S. stake /. Cabin John, MD , 1986. ix, 102 p. : ISBN 0-932020-42-9 (pbk.) : LC Card 86-17665 DDC 363.8/526/0973 19
HV696.F6 S65 1986 *NYPL [JLF 87-531]*

Warnock, John W., 1933- The politics of hunger . Toronto , New York , c1987. xv, 334 p. ; ISBN 0-458-80630-7 (pbk.) : LC Card 87-1659 DDC 363.8/09172/4 19
HD9018.D44 W37 1987

Hunger disease . American Jewish Joint Distribution Committee. [Choroba głodowa. English.] New York , c1979. xiv, 261 p. : ISBN 0-471-05003-2 LC Card 78-26397 DDC 616.3/9
RC627.S7 A43 1979
*NYPL [*PXV (Warsaw) 86-3505]*

Hunger, J. David, 1941- Wheelen, Thomas L. Cases in strategic management and business policy /. Reading, Mass. , c1987. xii, 530 p. : ISBN 0-201-09134-8 (pbk.) : LC Card 86-26501 DDC 658.4/012 19
HD30.28 .W428 1987

The hunger machine . Bennett, Jon. Oxford , New York , 1987. 232 p. : ISBN 0-7456-0444-7 : LC Card 87-724 DDC 363.8 19
HD9000.5 .B449 1987

Hunsdiek, Detlef.
Albach, Horst. Finanzierung mit Risikokapital /. Stuttgart , c1986. 312 p. ; ISBN 3-7910-5015-X LC Card 87-127700 DDC 332/.0415/0943 19
HG5492 .A797 1986

Entwicklungslinien und Entwicklungsrisiken neugegründeter Unternehmen / Detlef Hunsdiek, Eva May-Strobl. Stuttgart : C.E. Poeschel, c1986. x, 190 p. : ill. ; 24 cm. (Schriften zur Mittelstandsforschung . n.F., Nr. 9) Summary in English. Bibliography: p. 181-190. ISBN 3-7910-5009-5 LC Card 87-211045
1. New business enterprises - Germany (West). 2. Entrepreneurship. I. May-Strobl, Eva. II. Title. III. Series.
HD62.5 .H86 1986

Hunt, Audrey. Women and paid work . New York , 1988. p. cm. ISBN 0-312-01200-4 : LC Card 87-23477 DDC 331.2/1 19
HD6061.2.G7 W66 1988

Hunt, H. Allan. Clerical employment and technological change / H. Allan Hunt, Timothy L. Hunt. Kalamazoo, Mich. : W.E. Upjohn Institute for Employment Research, 1986. x, 296 p. : ill. ; 23 cm. Bibliography: p. 287-296. ISBN 0-88099-042-2 (pbk.) LC Card 86-26556 DDC 331.12/5165137/0973 19
1. Clerks - United States - Supply and demand. 2. Clerks - United States - Effect of technological innovations on. 3. Office practice - Automation. I. Hunt, Timothy L. II. Title.
HD5718.M392 U65 1986

Hunt, James G., 1932- Emerging leadership vistas /. Lexington, Mass. , c1988. xv, 331 p. : ISBN 0-669-15331-1 (alk. paper) LC Card 86-46310 DDC 658.4/092 19
HD57.7 .E44 1987

Hunt, Lacy H. A time to be rich : winning on Wall Street in the new economy / Lacy H. Hunt ; edited by Paul Stanwick.1st ed. New York : Rawson Associates, c1987. xvi, 282 p. : ill. ; 22 cm. Includes index. ISBN 0-89256-325-7 : LC Card 87-9431 DDC 332.6/78 19
1. Investments - United States. 2. Economic forecasting - United States. 3. Business cycles - United States. I. Title.
HG4910 .H86 1987

Hunt, Timothy L. Hunt, H. Allan. Clerical employment and technological change /. Kalamazoo, Mich. , 1986. x, 296 p. : ISBN 0-88099-042-2 (pbk.) LC Card 86-26556 DDC 331.12/5165137/0973 19
HD5718.M392 U65 1986

Hunter, Carl. Bush, Fredy. Your fortune in foreclosures . Tucson, Ariz. , c1987. ix, 221 p. : ISBN 0-89586-572-6 LC Card 86-33793 DDC 332.63/24 19
HD1382.5 .B87 1987

Hunter, Jane, 1943- Undercutting sanctions : Israel, the U. S., and South Africa : a report / by Jane Hunter ; edited by Jane Power.Rev. and updated, rev. ed. Washington, DC (918 16th St. NW, Suite 501, Washington 20006) : Washington Middle East Associates, c1987. iv, 71 p. ; 22 cm. Bibliography: p. 55-71. LC Card 87-403525 DDC 337.68 19
1. Economic sanctions - South Africa. 2. Israel - Relations - South Africa. 3. South Africa - Relations - Israel. 4. United States - Relations - Israel. 5. Israel - Relations - United States. I. Power, Jane. II. Washington Middle East Associates. III. Title.
HF1613.4 .H86 1987

Hunter, Thomas G. Button, Joe W. Synthetic fibers in asphalt paving mixtures /. College Station, Tex. [1984] vi, 153 p. : LC Card 86-620835 DDC 380.5 s 625.8/5 19
HE203 .T43 no. 319-1F TA443.A7

Hunter, W. T. Canadian financial markets / W.T. Hunter. Peterborough, Canada : Broadview Press, c1986. 193 p. : ill. ; 23 cm. Includes bibliographies. ISBN 0-921149-01-8 (pbk.) LC Card 86-206029 DDC 332.6/0973 19
1. Finance - Canada. 2. Money market - Canada. 3. Investments - Canada. 4. Securities - Canada. I. Title.
HG185.C2 H86 1986

HUNTERS - ARGENTINA - CORRIENTES - CASE STUDIES.
Proyecto Paraná Medio . Buenos Aires , 1985. 44 leaves : LC Card 86-218225
HD8039.F66 A746 1985

HUNTERS - ARGENTINA - ENTRE RÍOS - CASE STUDIES.
Proyecto Paraná Medio . Buenos Aires , 1985. 44 leaves : LC Card 86-218225
HD8039.F66 A746 1985

HUNTERS - PARANÁ RIVER VALLEY (BRAZIL-ARGENTINA) - CASE STUDIES.
Proyecto Paraná Medio . Buenos Aires , 1985. 44 leaves : LC Card 86-218225
HD8039.F66 A746 1985

HUNTING - ARGENTINA - STATISTICS.
Agricultura, caza, silvicultura y pesca . [Buenos Aires] [1982] 57 p. : LC Card 87-401763 DDC 338.1/0982/021 19
HD1862 .A58 1982

HUNTING - GOVERNMENT POLICY - ALASKA.
Alaska habitat management guide. Juneau, Alaska , 1986- 2 v. (loose-leaf) : LC Card 86-623159 DDC 333.95/09798 19
HD9457.A4 A427 1986

Huntington, Hillard G. Macroeconomics [i.e. Macroeconomic] impacts of energy shocks /. Amsterdam ; New York : xvi, 331 p. : ISBN 0-444-70247-4 (U. S.) LC Card 87-9035 DDC 338.4/36655/0724 19
HG229 .M315 1987

Hunziker, Peter, 1941- Lokales Bürgerfernsehen : die Wil-Studie / Peter Hunziker, Horst Willi Schors. Aarau : Sauerländer, c1983. 192 p. ; 23 cm. (Beiträge zur Kommunikations- und Medienpolitik . Bd. 2) Bibliography: p. 181-191. ISBN 3-7941-2369-7 : LC Card 83-141437
1. Low power television - Switzerland - Wil (Saint Gall). I. Schors, Horst Willi, 1951-. II. Title. III. Series.
HE8700.72.S95 H85 1983

Huo pi li lun yen t'ao hui, Chung-hua min kuo 75 nien 1 yüeh 3 jih chih 8 jih. Symposium on Monetary Theory (1986 : Institute of Economics, Academia Sinica) Symposium on Monetary Theory, January 3-8, 1986 =. Taipei, Taiwan, Republic of China [1986?] 2 v. (iv, 630 p.) : LC Card 87-152394 DDC 332.4 19
HG203 .S96 1986

Huppes, T. The Western edge : work and management in the information age / by Tjerk Huppes. Dordrecht ; Boston : Kluwer Academic Publishers, 1987. viii, 141 p. : ill. ; 25 cm. Bibliography: p. [171]-121. ISBN 90-247-3495-9 LC Card 87-4087 DDC 338/.06 19
1. Organizational change. 2. Work design. 3. Management - Data processing. 4. Technological innovations. I. Title.
HD58.8 .H86 1987

Hur planeras Sverige? / Rolf A. Karlson ... [et al.]. 6., omarb. uppl. Stockholm : Liber, c1986. 179 p. : ill. ; 21 cm. (Publica samhälle) Includes index. ISBN 91-38-90679-1 : LC Card 87-151788
1. Sweden - Economic policy. 2. Regional planning - Sweden. I. Karlson, Rolf A.
HC375 .H85 1986

Hurler, Peter. Gestaltungsspielräume der Arbeitsmarktpolitik auf regionalen Arbeitsmärkten . Berlin , c1984. 180 p. : ISBN 3-428-05614-0 LC Card 84-218530
HD8444 .G47 1984

Hurtado Miller, Juan Carlos. Por una causa agraria : desarrollo agrario peruano / Juan Carlos Hurtado Miller.1a ed. Lima, Perú : Centro de Investigación, Universidad del Pacífico, 1986. 348 p. : ill. ; 21 cm. Includes bibliographical references. LC Card 87-400122 DDC 338.1/885 19
1. Agriculture and state - Peru. 2. Food supply - Peru. 3. Land tenure - Law and legislation - Peru. 4. Agricultural laws and legislation - Peru. I. Title.
HD1903 .H87 1986

Hurwicz, Leonid. Social goals and social organization . Cambridge [Cambridgeshire] , New York , 1985. xii, 365 p. : ISBN 0-521-26204-6 LC Card 85-6668 DDC 330.15/5 19
HB846 .S65 1985 *NYPL [JLE 86-3786]*

Hurwicz, Michael. Networking with the IBM Network & Cluster / Michael Hurwicz ; illustrations by Maxim Hurwicz. Blue Ridge Summit, Pa. : Tab Books, 1985. x, 518 p. : ill. ; 24 cm. On t.p. the registered trademark symbol "TM" is superscript following "Network" and "Cluster" in the title. Includes index. ISBN 0-8306-0929-6 : LC Card 85-4639 DDC 001.64/404 19
1. Local area networks (Computer networks). 2. IBM Personal Computer. I. Title. II. Title: Networking with the I.B.M. Network and Cluster.
TK5105.7 .H87 1985 *NYPL [JSE 86-1975]*

Hurwitz, Leon. The European Community and the management of international cooperation / Leon Hurwitz. New York : Greenwood Press, 1987. xvii, 267 p. ; 25 cm. (Contributions in political science, 0147-1066 . no. 181) Bibliography: p. [245]-259. Includes index. ISBN 0-313-25030-8 (lib. bdg. : alk. paper) LC Card 87-229 DDC 337.1/4 19
1. European Economic Community. 2. Commission of the European Communities. 3. European Parliament. 4. European federation. I. Title. II. Series.
HC241.2 .H87 1987

A hús- és a tejgazdaság jellemző vonásai Dániában /. Kóbor, Kálmán. Budapest , 1984. 111 p. : ISBN 963-491-183-8 LC Card 86-198770
HD9425.D4 K6 1984

Husack, Glen A. More profit from your retail business : a way to achieve it and to maintain it / by Glen A. Husack. [S.l.] : Maclean-Hunter Ltd., c1977. 84 p. : ill. ; 23 cm. (A Financial Post book) ISBN 0-88896-066-2 (pbk.) LC Card 85-174558
1. Stores, Retail - Management. 2. Small business - Management. I. Title. II. Series.
HF5429 .H85 1977

Husain, M. G., 1949- Psycho-ecological dimensions of poverty /. New Delhi , 1983. x,

115 p. : LC Card 83-906411 DDC 305.5/69/0954 19
HC440.P6 P78 1983 ***NYPL [JLD 87-491]***

HUSBANDRY. see **AGRICULTURE.**

Husch, Tony, 1943- That's a great idea / by Tony Husch & Linda Foust. Berkeley, Calif. : Ten Speed Press, 1987, c1986. p. cm. Reprint. Originally published: Oakland, Calif. : Gravity Pub., c1986. Bibliography: p. Includes index. ISBN 0-89815-218-6 LC Card 87-13891 DDC 658.5/75 19
1. New products. 2. Creative ability in business. 3. Inventions. 4. New business enterprises. I. Foust, Linda, 1950-. II. Title.
HD69.N4 H87 1987

Husein, Machnun, 1941- Etika pembangunan dalam pemikiran Islam di Indonesia /. Jakarta , 1986. xi, 270 p. ; ISBN 979-421-043-9 (pbk.) LC Card 86-946413
HC447 .E78 1986

Huseman, Richard C. Business communication : strategies and skills. 3rd ed. / Richard C. Huseman, James M. Lahiff, John M. Penrose, Jr. Chicago : Dryden Press, c1988. xxxi, 702 p., [8] p. of plates : ill. (some col.) ; 25 cm. Rev. ed. of: Business communication / Richard C. Huseman ... [et al.]. 2nd ed. c1985. Bibliography: p. 696-697. Includes index. ISBN 0-03-012294-5 LC Card 87-438 DDC 658.4/5 19
1. Communication in management. I. Lahiff, James M. II. Penrose, John M. III. Business communication. IV. Title.
HF5718 .H84 1988

Hussey, D. E. (David E.) Management training and corporate strategy : how to improve competitive performance / by David E. Hussey.1st ed. Oxford [Oxfordshire] ; New York : Pergamon, 1988. x, 201 p. : ill. ; 24 cm. Includes bibliographies. ISBN 0-08-034036-9 : LC Card 87-22075 DDC 658.4/07124 19
1. Management - Study and teaching - Great Britain. 2. Executives, Training of - Great Britain. I. Title.
HD30.42.G7 H87 1988

Hussey, Denis D. Australian grain marketing : achieving lower costs / Denis Hussey. Perth, W.A. : Australian Institute for Public Policy, 1986. 72 p. : ill. ; 21 cm. (Policy paper / Australian Institute for Public Policy, 0815-9394 . no. 6) Bibliography: p. 70-72. ISBN 0-949186-11-2 (pbk.) : LC Card 86-213695 DDC 338.1/731/0994 19
1. Grain trade - Australia. I. Series: Policy paper (Australian Institute for Public Policy) , no. 6. II. Title.
HD9048.A82 H87 1986

Huston, James L., 1947- The panic of 1857 and the coming of the Civil War / James L. Huston. Baton Rouge : Louisiana State University Press, c1987. xviii, 315 p. ; 24 cm. Bibliography: p. [283]-306. Includes index. ISBN 0-8071-1368-9 LC Card 87-2705 DDC 338.5/42 19
1. Depressions - 1857 - United States. 2. United States - Economic conditions - To 1865. 3. United States - Politics and government - 1857-1861. I. Title.
HB3717 1857 .H87 1987

Huston, Ray E. Senior driver facts / authors, Ray E. Huston and Mary K. Janke. 2nd ed., rev. Sacramento, CA : State of California, Dept. of Motor Vehicles, Research and Development Section ; Springfield, VA : Available to the public through the National Technical Information Service, 1986. iii, 22 p. : ill. ; 28 cm. Cover title. Bibliography: p. 21. LC Card 86-623189 DDC 363.1/252/09794021 19
1. Traffic accidents - California - Statistics. 2. Aged automobile drivers - California - Statistics. I. Janke, Mary K. II. California. Dept. of Motor Vehicles. Research and Development Section. III. Title.
HE5614.3.C3 H87 1986

Huszár, Ernőné. Munkaügyi statisztikai és módszertani ismeretek /. Budapest , 1985. 323 p. : ISBN 963-10-6513-8 : LC Card 83-228566
HD4826.5 .M86 1985

Huszár, József. A Mezőgazdasági szövetkezetek szabályozó rendszere /. [Budapest] , 1979. 119 p. ; LC Card 86-187443
HD1492.H8 M417 1979

Hutchinson, Gillian. Recent advances in labour economics /. London , New York , c1984. 258 p. : ISBN 0-312-66575-X (St. Martin's) : LC Card 83-40628 DDC 331 19
HD4813 .R28 1984 ***NYPL [JLD 86-2455]***

Hutchinson, Harry D. Money, banking, and the United States economy / Harry D. Hutchinson. 6th ed. Englewood Cliffs, NJ : Prentice Hall, 1988. p. cm. Includes bibliographical references and index. ISBN 0-13-600156-4 LC Card 87-19299 DDC 332.1/0973 19
1. Banks and banking - United States. 2. Money - United States. 3. Monetary policy - United States. 4. United States - Economic conditions - 1945-. 5. International finance. I. Title.
HG2491 .H8 1988

Hutchinson, Van. College cash : how to earn and learn as a student entrepreneur / Van Hutchinson.1st Harvest/HBJ ed. San Diego : Harcourt Brace Jovanovich, 1987. p. cm. "A Harvest/HBJ Book." Bibliography: p. Includes index. ISBN 0-15-619150-4 (pbk.) : LC Card 87-8666 DDC 658.4/2 19
1. New business enterprises - United States. 2. Entrepreneur. 3. College students - Employment - United States. I. Title.
HD62.5 .H88 1987

Hutchison, Anna Marie. IRA investing made easy / Anna Marie Hutchison. Oakhurst, Calif. : Eagle North Communications, c1987. 158 p. : ill. ; 23 cm. "For '87 tax law"--Cover. Bibliography: p. 149. Includes index. ISBN 0-940083-07-8 (pbk.) : LC Card 86-83347 DDC 343.7305/23 347.303523 19
1. Individual retirement accounts - United States. 2. Investments - United States. I. Title.
HG1660.U5 H87 1987

Huter, Otto, 1952- Die Berliner Eigenbetriebe als Instrumente kommunaler Politik / Otto Huter, Christoph Landerer. Berlin : Berlin Verlag A. Spitz, c1984. 275 p. : ill. ; 21 cm. (Berlin Forschung . Bd. 10) "Forschungsprojekt"--P. [1] Bibliography: p. 272-275. ISBN 3-87061-910-4 LC Card 84-231849
1. Privatization - Berlin (Germany) - Case studies. 2. Berlin (Germany) - Economic policy - Case studies. I. Landerer, Christoph, 1952-. II. Title. III. Series.
HD4180.B47 H87 1984

Hutin, Stanislas. Promotion de la petite industrie dans les pays en développement /. Paris , c1985. 103 p. : ISBN 2-86844-008-8 LC Card 85-242526 DDC 338.6/42/0943 19
HD2346.5 .P76 1985 ***NYPL [JLD 86-3171]***

Hutner, Frances Cornwall. Equal pay for comparable worth : the working woman's issue of the eighties / Frances C. Hutner. New York : Praeger, 1986. xiii, 227 p. ; 25 cm. Includes index. Bibliography: p. 213-218. ISBN 0-03-062873-3 (alk. paper) : LC Card 85-19427 DDC 331.4/21/0973 19
1. Equal pay for equal work - United States. 2. Equal pay for equal work - United States - Case studies. 3. Equal pay for equal work. I. Title.
HD6061.2.U6 H86 1986
NYPL [JLE 86-2946]

Hutt, Arthur E. Computer security handbook /. New York, N.Y. , c1987. p. cm. ISBN 0-02-915300-X LC Card 87-1735 DDC 658.4/78 19
HF5548.37 .C64 1987

Hutter, Monika, 1950- Die Warenstruktur des Aussenhandels : theoretische Konzepte und empirische Untersuchungen am Beispiel Österreichs / Monika Hutter. Frankfurt am Main ; New York : P. Lang, c1987. 216 p. ; 21 cm. (Europäische Hochschulschriften. Reihe V, Volks- und Betriebswirtschaft, 0531-7339 . Bd. 778 = vol. 778 = vol. 778) Revision of the author's thesis (doctoral)--Johannes Kepler Universität, Linz, 1985. Bibliography: p. 208-216. ISBN 3-8204-8810-3 LC Card 87-407938 DDC 382/.09436 19
1. Austria - Commerce. 2. Commercial products - Austria. 3. Foreign trade and employment - Austria. I. Series: Europäische Hochschulschriften. Reihe V, Volks- und Betriebswirtschaft , Bd. 778. II. Title.
HF3546.5 .H87 1987

Hüttig, Christoph. Gemeinwirtschaft im Sozialstaat : Grenzen und Möglichkeiten eines wirtschaftspolitischen Instrumentariums / Christoph Hüttig. Frankfurt am Main : Haag + Herchen, c1986. vi, 355 p. : ill. ; 21 cm. Bibliography: p. 304-355. ISBN 3-88129-990-4 : LC Card 86-223747
1. Government business enterprises - Germany, West. 2. Welfare state. 3. Corporate state - Germany (West). 4. Germany, West - Politics and government. I. Title.
HD4175 .H83 1986

Huxley, Aldous, 1894-1963.
[Brave new world]
Brave new world ; and, Brave new world revisited / by Aldous Huxley ; with an introduction by Sybille Bedford. London : Chatto & Windus : Hogarth Press, 1984. xxii, 387 p. ; 21 p. (A Chatto twin) ISBN 0-7011-2769-4 : LC Card 84-134715 DDC 823/.912 19
1. Huxley, Aldous, 1894-1963. Brave new world. 2. Culture. 3. Propaganda. 4. Brainwashing. I. Huxley, Aldous, 1894-1963. Brave new world revisited. 1984. II. Title. III. Title: Brave new world revisited.
PR6015.U9 B65 1984 ***NYPL [JFE 86-4706]***

BRAVE NEW WORLD
Huxley, Aldous, 1894-1963. [Brave new world.] Brave new world ; and, Brave new world revisited /. London , 1984. xxii, 387 p. ; ISBN 0-7011-2769-4 : LC Card 84-134715 DDC 823/.912 19
PR6015.U9 B65 1984 ***NYPL [JFE 86-4706]***

Brave new world revisited. 1984. Huxley, Aldous, 1894-1963. [Brave new world.] Brave new world ; and, Brave new world revisited / by Aldous Huxley ; with an introduction by Sybille Bedford. London , 1984. xxii, 387 p. ; ISBN 0-7011-2769-4 : LC Card 84-134715 DDC 823/.912 19
PR6015.U9 B65 1984 ***NYPL [JFE 86-4706]***

Huynh, Frank C. H. Athukoralge, Premachandra. Export instability and growth . London , Wolfeboro, N.H. , c1987. 244 p. : ISBN 0-7099-3739-3 : LC Card 86-32833 DDC 382/.6/095493 19
HF3770.8.Z5 A84 1987

Hva blev der af dem? . Johansen, Carsten Ulstrup. Esbjerg , 1983. 168 p. : ISBN 87-85198-93-5 LC Card 83-236971
HD5717.5.D42 R55 1983

Hva' nu Larsen . Due, Jesper. [Copenhagen] , c1984. 152 p. ; ISBN 87-574-4410-2 : LC Card 84-229467
HD2429.D4 D84 1984

Hvidtfeldt, Kirsten. Strategies for integrating women into the labour market /. Copenhagen, Denmark , 1982. 347 p. : ISBN 87-88209-08-3 (pbk.) LC Card 86-673782
HD6052 .S77x 1982

H.W. Johns Manufacturing Co.
Structural decoration. [New York : H.W. Johns Manufacturing Co.], c1882. 32 p. : ill. ; 17 cm. Advertisement. Cover title. Prefatory letter signed: H.W. Johns M'f'g Co. LC Card 86-224190
1. H.W. Johns Manufacturing Co. 2. Advertising. 3. Paint. 4. Endorsements in advertising. I. Title.
HD9660.P254 H174 1882

Trade price list : January 1898 : strictly confidential, to dealers only. New York : H.W. Johns M'f'g. Co., c1898. 15 p. ; 18 cm. LC Card 86-223003
1. Building materials - United States - Catalogs. I. Title.
HD9715.8.U52 H14 1898

H.W. JOHNS MANUFACTURING CO.
H.W. Johns Manufacturing Co. Structural decoration. [New York] c1882. 32 p. : LC Card 86-224190
HD9660.P254 H174 1882

Hwang, C. L. (Ching-Lai), 1929-
Hwang, Hae-Shin. Dominant firm price leadership : an empirical examination / Hae-Shin Hwang, Charles W. Smithson. Toronto, Ont. : Ontario Ministry of Northern Development and Mines, Mines and Minerals Division, [1986] 40 p. : ill. ; 30 cm. (Mineral policy background paper, 0706-1034 . no. 23) "November 1986." Bibliography: p. 39. ISBN 0-7729-2122-9 : LC Card 87-161006 DDC 338.2/3 19
1. Nickel - Prices - Econometric models. 2. Oligopolies - Mathematical models. 3. Pricing - Mathematical models. I. Smithson, C. W. (Charles W.). II. Title. III. Series.
HD9539.N5 H93 1986

Hyde, Janet Shibley. The Psychology of gender . Baltimore , c1986. vii, 293 p. : ISBN 0-8018-2974-7 (alk. paper) LC Card 85-19822 DDC 155.3/3 19
BF692.2 .P76 1986 ***NYPL [JFE 86-2969]***

HYDOELECTRIC POWER PLANTS - BRAZIL - PASSO REAL.
Rio Grande do Sul (Brazil). Assembléia Legislativa. Comissão Especial dos Agricultores Desalojados do Passo Real. Afogados, até quando? . [Porto Alegre] [1984] 99 p. : LC Card 85-150200
HD500.P39 R56 1984

HYDRAULIC MACHINERY INDUSTRY - EUROPE.
Industrial hydraulics components market in Europe. New York, N.Y. , c1983. xxxvi, 338 p. ; LC Card 87-141832 DDC 381/.456212/094 19
HD9705.5.H933 E855 1983

Hydrick, Blair. United States. Women's Bureau. Records of the Women's Bureau of the Department of Labor, 1918-1965 [microform] /. Frederick, MD , 1987- microfilm reel ISBN 0-89093-870-9 (microfilm : pt. 1) : LC Card 87-6239 DDC 331.4/0973 19
HD6095

Hydro-Québec. Hydro-Quebéc development plan, 1986-1988 : horizon 1995. [Québec : Hydro-Québec] ; Montréal, Quebec : Centre de diffusion, Hydro-Québec [distributor, 1986] x, 143 p. : ill. ; 28 cm. "February 1986." LC Card 86-201868 DDC 333.79/32/09714 19
1. Hydro-Québec. 2. Electric utilities - Québec (Province) - Planning. 3. Electric power consumption - Québec (Province) - Forecasting. I. Title.
HD9685.C4 H857 1986

HYDRO-QUÉBEC.
Hydro-Québec. Hydro-Quebéc development plan, 1986-1988 . [Québec] Montréal, Quebec [1986] x, 143 p. : LC Card 86-201868 DDC 333.79/32/09714 19
HD9685.C4 H857 1986

Poste Des Cantons, lignes Nicolet-Des Cantons et Des Cantons-Nouvelle-Angleterre /. [Sainte-Foy, Qc] [1983] 1 v. (various pagings) ; ISBN 2-550-10466-8 LC Card 85-121505
HD9685.C3 Q455 1983

Hydro-Quebéc development plan, 1986-1988 . Hydro-Québec. [Québec] Montréal, Quebec [1986] x, 143 p. : LC Card 86-201868 DDC 333.79/32/09714 19
HD9685.C4 H857 1986

HYDROCARBONS - CONGRESSES.
Mercados mundiales de hidrocarburos . México, D.F. , 1983. 377 p. : ISBN 968-12-0231-7 LC Card 84-222729
HD9560.5 .M39 1983

HYDROELECTRIC POWER PLANTS - DEVELOPING COUNTRIES.
Evaluating electrification experience . Washington, D.C. , 1982- v. <1 > : LC Card 86-176385 DDC 333.91/4 19
HD9688.D44 E9 1982

HYDROELECTRIC POWER PLANTS - ENVIRONMENTAL ASPECTS - GOVERNMENT POLICY - AUSTRALIA - TASMANIA.
Lowe, D. A. (Douglas Ackley), 1942- The price of power . South Melbourne , 1984. viii, 184 p., [12] p. of plates : ISBN 0-333-38088-6 LC Card 84-254286 DDC 333.91/62/099466 19
HD9685.A83 T385 1984 *NYPL [JLD 87-795]*

HYDROELECTRIC POWER PLANTS - PARAGUAY - CONGRESSES.
Seminario Estrategia de Desarrollo en Condiciones de Oferta Abundante de Energía Eléctrica (1980 : Asunción, Paraguay) Memoria del Seminario Estrategia de Desarrollo en Condiciones de Oferta Abundante de Energía Eléctrica . Asunción, Paraguay [s.l.] , 1980. 165 p., [18] leaves of plates : LC Card 83-169471 DDC 363.6/2 19
HD9685.P32 S45 1980 *NYPL [JLE 87-995]*

HYDROELECTRIC POWER PLANTS - QUÉBEC (PROVINCE) - PORTNEUF (COUNTY)
Le Projet Delaney . [St-Raymond, Québec] [1983] 76 leaves in various foliations : LC Card 84-224364
HD9685.C3 Q456 1983

HYDROELECTRIC POWER PLANTS - RIO DE LA PLATA REGION (ARGENTINA AND URUGUAY)
Obras hidroeléctricas binacionales en América Latina. [Buenos Aires, Argentina] , 1985. vii leaves, 385 p., 3 leaves of plates : LC Card 86-180644
HD1696.A7 O27 1985

HYGIENE - ECONOMIC ASPECTS. see **MEDICAL ECONOMICS.**

HYGIENE, INDUSTRIAL. see **INDUSTRIAL HYGIENE.**

HYGIENE, PUBLIC. see **PUBLIC HEALTH.**

HYGIENE, SOCIAL. see **PUBLIC HEALTH.**

Hyper-performance . Korn, Errol R. New York , c1987. xi, 195 p. : ISBN 0-471-85344-5 LC Card 86-33984 DDC 650.1 19
HF5386 .K775 1987

Hypodēmata. Athēna : Organismos Proōthēseōs Exagōgōn, 1985. 86 p. : ill. ; 24 cm. (Ereuna gia tis hellēnikes exagōges stēn EOK . 8) At head of title: Ekdosē: Organismos Proōthēseōs Exagōgōn. Dieuthynsē Ereunas Agoras. LC Card 86-194391
1. Shoe industry - Greece. 2. Shoe industry - European Economic Community countries. I. Organismos Proōthēseōs Exagōgōn (Greece). Dieuthynsē Ereunas Agoras. II. Series.
HD9787.G62 H96 1985

HYPOTHECATION. see **MORTGAGES.**

Das Hypothekenbankgeschäft in den Niederlanden und in der Bundesrepublik Deutschland /. Schubäus, Klaus. Berlin , c1984. 251 p. : ISBN 3-428-05569-1 LC Card 84-250906
HG2040.5.N37 S38 1984

Hyuha, Mukwanason. Financial structure and economic development in Africa : some evidence / by Mukwanason Hyuha. Dar-es-Salaam, Tanzania : Economic Research Bureau, University of Dar-es-Salaam, c1983. 43 p. : ill. ; 30 cm. (E.R.B. paper . 83.4) Bibliography: p. 26-28. LC Card 85-981441 DDC 332/.096 19
1. Financial institutions - Africa. 2. Saving and investment - Africa. I. Chuo Kikuu cha Dar es Salaam. Economic Research Bureau. II. Title. III. Series.
HG187.5.A2 H98 1983

I. A. B. C. see **International Association of Business Communicators.**

I.A.E.A. safeguards, 1980-1985. IAEA safeguards, 1980-1985 . Vienna , 1986. 15 p. ; LC Card 87-114776 DDC 363.1/79 19
HD9698.5 .I24 1986

I. A. S. P. see **Indian Association for the Study of Population.**

I. A. T. A. see **International Air Transport Association.**

I arbetets tjänst /. Meidner, Rudolf. Stockholm , 1984. 473 p. : ISBN 91-550-2932-9 : LC Card 84-229372
HD5803 .M45 1984

I. B. A. see **Investment Bankers Association of America.**

I. B. A. M. see **Instituto Brasileiro de Administração Municipal.**

I. B. F. I. see **International Business Forms Industries.**

I. B. M. see **International Business Machines Corporation.**

I.B.M. way. Rodgers, F. G. (Francis G.) The IBM way . New York , c1986. xiv, 235 p. ; ISBN 0-06-015522-1 : LC Card 85-45223 DDC 338.7/61004/0973 19
HD9696.C64 I4875 1986 *NYPL [JLE 86-1374]*

I. B. of T. see **International Brotherhood of Teamsters, Chauffeurs, Warehousemen and Helpers of America.**

I. B. R. D. see **International Bank for Reconstruction and Development.**

I bräcklig farkost . Ahlqvist, Berndt, 1931- Stockholm , c1983. 186 p. ; ISBN 91-550-2917-5 : LC Card 83-230190
HC375 .A63 1983

I. C. A. P. see **Instituto Centroamericano de Administración Pública.**

I. C. D. S. C. see **Permanent Inter-State Committee for Drought Control in the Sahel.**

I. C. E. C. O. O. P. see **Instituto Chileno de Educación Cooperativa.**

I. C. F. T. U. see **International Confederation of Free Trade Unions.**

I. C. I. see **Imperial Chemical Industries, ltd.**

I can be a secretary /. Lillegard, Dee. Chicago , c1987. 29 p. : ISBN 0-516-01907-4 (lib. bdg.) LC Card 86-29947 DDC 651.3/741/02373 19
HF55475 .L55 1987

I can be a textile worker /. Fitz-Gerald, Christine Maloney. Chicago , c1987. 29 p. : ISBN 0-516-01912-0 (lib bdg.) LC Card 87-10716 DDC 677/.0023/73 19
HD8039.C6 F57 1987

I censo artesanal, 1978. Directorio artesanal, 1978 /. Guatemala , 1981. 6 v. ; LC Card 87-403025
HD2346.G8 D57 1981

I censo artesanal 1978. Principales indicadores económicos . Guatemala , 1982. 487 p. ; LC Card 87-403026 DDC 331.7/94 19
HD2346.G8 P75 1982

The I Ching on business and decision making . Damian-Knight, Guy. Rochester, VT , 1987. p. cm. ISBN 0-89281-173-0 : LC Card 87-15440 DDC 658.4/03 19
HD37.C47 D35 1987

I Conti finanziari dell'Emilia-Romagna / a cura di Marco Onado e Diletta P. Pedani. [Bologna] : Mulino, c1984. 157 p. : ill. ; 24 cm. (Quaderni di banca, impresa, società . 2) Bibliography: p. 155-157. ISBN 88-15-00522-6 : LC Card 84-235593 DDC 332.1/0945/4 19
1. Banks and banking - Italy - Emilia-Romagna - Accounting. 2. Financial institutions - Italy - Emilia-Romagna - Accounting. 3. Credit - Italy - Emilia-Romagna - Statistics. 4. Emilia-Romagna (Italy) - Economic conditions - Statistics. I. Onado, Marco. II. Pedani, Diletta P. III. Series.
HG3089.E45 C66 1984 *NYPL [JLE 86-3198]*

I. D. A. see **International Development Association.**

IEE control engineering series.
(28) Robots and automated manufacture /. London, U.K. , c1985. xii, 233 p. : ISBN 0-86341-053-7 *NYPL [JSK 77-191 v.28]*

IEEE Computer Society. Technical Committee on Mathematical Foundations of Computing.
Symposium on Logic in Computer Science (1986 : Cambridge, Mass.) Proceedings, Symposium on Logic in Computer Science, Cambridge, Massachusetts, June 16-18, 1986 /. Washington, D.C. , Los Angeles, CA , 1986. xi, 383 p. : ISBN 0-8186-0720-3 (pbk.) LC Card 86-81090 DDC 004 19
QA75.5 .S9813 1986 *NYPL [JSF 86-1041]*

IEEE Engineering Management Society.
Lineback, L. Kent, 1943- Being the boss . New York , c1987. xi, 177 p. ; ISBN 0-87942-212-2 LC Card 86-27751 DDC 658.3 19
HF5549 .L4945 1987

I. E. F. C. see **Illinois. Economic and Fiscal Commission.**

I. E. R. E. For corporate body represented by these initials, see: **Institution of Electronic and Radio Engineers.**

I. F. C. see **International Finance Corporation.**

I. F. R. B. see **International Frequency Registration Board.**

I.G.C.C. Workshop on Linkages Between University Based Population Activities and National Population/Family Planning Programmes. IGCC Workshop on Linkages Between University Based Population Activities and National Population/Family Planning Programmes (1978 : Bangkok, Thailand) IGCC Workshop on Linkages Between University Based Population Activities and National Population/Family Planning Programmes . Kuala Lumpur, Selangor [1978?] 111 p. : LC Card 81-941403
HB3641 .I35 1978

I. I. C. A. see **Inter-American Institute of Agricultural Sciences.**

I. I. E. P. see **International Institute for Educational Planning.**

I. I. F. T. see **Indian Institute of Foreign Trade.**

Der I. Kongress der Revolutionären Gewerkschafts-Opposition (RGO) im Bezirk Mittelrhein (Raum Aachen-Köln-Koblenz) im Jahre 1930 / Günter Bers (Hrsg.). Reinbek :

Einhorn, c1982. 136 p. : ill., col. maps ; 21 cm. (Die Arbeiterbewegung in den Rheinlanden. 17) Two folded col. maps in pocket. Summary in English and French. Includes indexes. ISBN 3-88756-024-8 : LC Card 84-135308
1. Revolutionäre Gewerkschaftsopposition (Organization) - Congresses. 2. Kommunistische Partei Deutschlands - Congresses. 3. Trade-unions - Germany (West) - Rhine River Valley - History - Congresses. I. Bers, Günter, 1940-. II. Title: 1. Kongress der Revolutionären Gewerkschafts-Opposition (RGO) im Bezirk Mittelrhein (Raum Aachen-Köln-Koblenz) im Jahre 1930. III. Series. IV. Series: Arbeiterbewegung in den Rheinlanden , Nr. 17.
HD6699.R47 I18 1982

I. Krüger A/S. Teknisk-økonomisk-organisatorisk analyse /. København [1983] 131 p. : ISBN 87-503-4561-3 LC Card 84-169883
HD4465.D4 T44 1983

I. L. A. D. E. S. see **Instituto Latinoamericano de Estudios Sociales.**

I. L. A. F. A. see **Instituto Latinoamericano del Fierro y el Acero.**

ILO. see **International Labor Office.**

I. L. O. see **International Labor Organization.**

I. L. S. see **Institut für Landes- und Stadtentwicklungsforschung des Landes Nordrhein-Westfalen.**

I Mercati creditizi africani .
(18) Mauri, Arnaldo. Moneta e banca in Etiopia /. Milano [1986] xi, 316 p. : ISBN 88-14-00769-1 LC Card 86-182310
HG3389.A6 M38 1986 *NYPL [JLE 87-1721]*

I mercati regionali del lavoro e il problema degli indicatori . Magni, Carlo. Milano [1981] 133, [3] p. : ISBN 88-20-42109-7 : LC Card 81-194409
HD5784 .M3 1981 *NYPL [JLD 87-815]*

I. N. C. R. A. see **Instituto Nacional de Colonização e Reforma Agraria.**

I. N. E. see **Instituto Nacional de Estadística (Peru)**

I. N. I. F. E. S. see **Internationales Institut für Empirische Sozialökonomie.**

I. N. T. U. C. see **Indian National Trade Union Congress.**

I. P. B. see **Institut Pertanian Bogor.**

I. P. E. A. see **Instituto de Planejamento Econômico e Social.**

I. P. S. see **Institute for Policy Studies.**

I. P. W. see **Institut für Internationale Politik und Wirtschaft der DDR.**

I Quaderni di Cooperazione .
(1) Cooperazione italiana allo sviluppo . Roma [1984] 144 p. ; ISBN 88-7621-170-5 : LC Card 85-223760 DDC 338.91/45/01724 19
HC60 .C65757 1984

I Quaderni di Ikon .
(1) Comunicazione come dominio? /. Milano [1979] 147 p. ; ISBN 88-20-41548-8 : LC Card 79-395059 DDC 302.2/3
HM258 .C5896 *NYPL [JLD 86-3359]*

(6) Il Territorio immaginario /. Milano [1980] 106 p. ; ISBN 88-20-41848-7 : LC Card 81-123209 DDC 302.2/34/0945 19
HE8700.9.I8 T47 1980
NYPL [JFD 86-8337]

(7) Il Consumo dell'audiovisivo /. Milano, Italy , c1984. 173 p. : LC Card 85-178903
HE8700.66.I8 C66 1984

I. R. F. see **International Road Federation.**

I. R. R. A. see **Industrial Relations Research Association.**

I. R. R. C. see **Investor Responsibility Research Center.**

I. S. A. see **Instrument Society of America.**

I. S. B. I. see **International Savings Banks Institute.**

I. S. E. A. S. see **Institute of Southeast Asian Studies.**

I. S. S. A. For corporate body represented by these initials, see: **International Social Security Association.**

I ser'ëzno, i kur'ëzno . Levitas, I. I͡A. (Iosif I͡Akovlevich) Moskva , 1985. 232 p. : LC Card 85-184912
HE6182 .L48 1985

I sindacalisti . Pirzio Ammassari, Gloria. Bari , c1982. 155 p. ; LC Card 82-131644 DDC 331.87/33/0945 19
HD6709 .P57 1982 *NYPL [JLD 86-2840]*

I. T. T. see **International Telephone and Telegraph Corporation.**

I. T. U. see **International Telecommunication Union.**

I. W. W. For corporate body referred to by these initials, see: **Industrial Workers of the World.**

The I.W.W. and the Paterson silk strike of 1913 /. Tripp, Anne Huber, 1934- Urbana , c1987. xiv, 317 p., [6] p. of plates : ISBN 0-252-01382-4 LC Card 86-24989 DDC 331.89/287739/0974924 19
HD5325.T42 1913 .P387 1987

I want to sell you success /. Grindle, Art, 1923- Charleston [S.C.] , c1987. p. cm. ISBN 0-931807-12-3 : LC Card 87-6962 DDC 650.1 19
HF5386 .G776 1987

I Write Books (Firm) Golden tokens . Roxbury, Conn. , c1987. p. cm. ISBN 0-941067-00-9 LC Card 86-27826 DDC 388.4/28 19
HE4211 .G58 1987

Iacocca, Lee A.
Iacocca. Iacocca, Lee A. The Iacocca tapes [sound recording] : an autobiography. Chicago, Ill. , c1985. 6 sound cassettes : LC Card 87-750990
HD9710.U I

The Iacocca tapes [sound recording] : an autobiography. Chicago, Ill. : Nightingale-Conant Corp., c1985. 6 sound cassettes : analog. Title from container. Adapted from the book: Iacocca / Lee Iacocca with William Novak. Notes inserted in container (30 cm.) Automobile executive Lee Iacocca discusses his life and labors on behalf of the automobile industry and saving the Statue of Liberty. CONTENTS. - Opening words ; The man, 1 -- The man, 2 ; The making of a manager, 1 -- The making of a manager, 2 ; The skills of salesmanship -- Marketing and the Mustang ; Advertising -- The Chrysler story, 1-2 -- The Chrysler stop1, 3 ; Straight talk. LC Card 87-750990
1. Iacocca, Lee A. 2. Businessmen - United States - Biography. 3. Automobile industry and trade - United States. 4. Statue of Liberty (New York, N.Y.) - Centennial celebrations, etc. I. Iacocca, Lee A. Iacocca. II. Title.
HD9710.U I

IACOCCA, LEE A.
Iacocca, Lee A. The Iacocca tapes [sound recording] . Chicago, Ill. , c1985. 6 sound cassettes : LC Card 87-750990
HD9710.U I

Wyden, Peter. The unknown Iacocca /. New York , c1987. 416 p. : ISBN 0-688-06616-X LC Card 87-15240 DDC 338.7/6292/0924 B 19
HD9710.U52 I28 1987

IACOCCA, LEE A. - JUVENILE LITERATURE.
Haddock, Patricia. Standing up for America . Minneapolis, Minn. , c1987. 111 p. : ISBN 0-87518-362-X : LC Card 86-32965 DDC 338.7/6292/0924 B 92 19
HD9710.U52 I246 1987

The Iacocca tapes [sound recording] . Iacocca, Lee A. Chicago, Ill. , c1985. 6 sound cassettes : LC Card 87-750990
HD9710.U I

Iaconetti, Joan. First-time manager / Joan Iaconetti, Patrick O'Hara. 1st Collier Books ed. New York : Collier Books ; London : Collier Macmillan, 1987, c1985. xii, 290 p. : ill. ; 21 cm. Includes index. ISBN 0-02-085730-6 (pbk.) : LC Card 86-24454 DDC 658.4 19
1. Executives. 2. Executives, Training of. I. O'Hara, Patrick, 1946-. II. Title.
HD38.2 .I19 1987

IAEA safeguards, 1980-1985 : a progress report. Vienna : International Atomic Energy Agency, 1986. 15 p. ; 24 cm. LC Card 87-114776 DDC 363.1/79 19
1. International Atomic Energy Agency. 2. Nuclear industry - Safety measures - Government policy - International cooperation. 3. Radioactive waste disposal - Safety measures - Government policy - International cooperation. I. International Atomic Energy Agency. II. Title: I.A.E.A. safeguards, 1980-1985.
HD9698.5 .I24 1986

IAEE Conference (5th : 1984 : New Delhi, India) Global energy interactions /. Ahmedabad , 1987. xxxi, 1290 p. : LC Card 87-902497 DDC 333.79 19
HD9502.A2 G545 1987b

I͡Agol'nit͡ser, Miron Arkad'evich. Rozin, Bent͡sian Borisovich. Statisticheskai͡a ot͡senka normativov otraslevogo planirovanii͡a /. Novosibirsk , 1986. 188, [3] p. : LC Card 86-230359
HC336.25 .R69 1986

I͡Akovenko, Evgeniĭ Georgievich. Rumi͡ant͡sev, Alekseĭ Matveevich. Instrumentariĭ ėkonomicheskoĭ nauki i praktiki . Moskva , 1985. 303 p. : LC Card 87-109217
HB61 .R86 1985

I͡Akovlev, I͡U. P. (I͡Uriĭ Prokof'evich) Ėffektivnoe ispol'zovanie kapital'nykh vlozheniĭ v sel'skom stroitel'stve / I͡U.P. I͡Akovlev. Kiev : "Budivel'nyk", 1985. 104 p. : ill. ; 20 cm. Bibliography: p. [3] of cover. LC Card 86-214694
1. Construction industry - Ukraine - Capital investments. 2. Agriculture - Ukraine - Capital investments. I. Title.
HD9715.S73 U383 1985

I͡Akovleva, O. P. (Olimpiada Pavlovna) Formirovanie i izmerenie rezervov proizvodstva / O.P. I͡Akovleva ; pod redakt͡sieĭ V.L. Klimenko. Leningrad : Izd-vo Leningradskogo universiteta, 1985. 86 p. : ill. ; 22 cm. At head of title: Ministerstvo vysshego i srednego spet͡sial'nogo obrazovanii͡a RSFSR. Includes bibliographical references. LC Card 86-168063
1. Industrial capacity - Soviet Union. I. Klimenko, V. L. (Vladimir Leonidovich). II. Title.
HC336.25 .I25 1985

I͡AKUTSKAI͡A A.S.S.R. (R.S.F.S.R.) - ECONOMIC CONDITIONS.
Ėffektivnost' kapital'nykh vlozheniĭ i novoĭ tekhniki v narodnom khozi͡aĭstve I͡Akutskoĭ ASSR . I͡Akutsk , 1981. 91 p. ; LC Card 82-217455
HC337.I23 C34 1981

I͡Uzhnai͡a I͡Akutii͡a, sot͡sial'no-ėkonomicheskiĭ aspekt . I͡Akutsk , 1985. 94 p. ; LC Card 86-180767
HC337.I2 I97 1985

Razvitie ėnergetiki I͡Akutskoĭ ASSR v svi͡azi s sooruzheniem BAM . I͡Akutsk , 1985. 99, 3 p. : LC Card 86-233736
HD9502.S653 I237 1985

I͡AKUTSKAI͡A A.S.S.R. (R.S.F.S.R.) - INDUSTRIES.
Mezhotraslevye svi͡azi v I͡Akutskoĭ ASSR . I͡Akutsk , 1985. 80 p. ; LC Card 86-193902
HC337.I23 I576 1985

I͡AKUTSKAI͡A A.S.S.R. (R.S.F.S.R.) - SOCIAL CONDITIONS.
I͡Uzhnai͡a I͡Akutii͡a, sot͡sial'no-ėkonomicheskiĭ aspekt . I͡Akutsk , 1985. 94 p. ; LC Card 86-180767
HC337.I2 I97 1985

I͡AMBOLSKI OKRŬG (BULGARIA) - ECONOMIC CONDITIONS.
Godini na vŭzkhod . I͡Ambol , 1986. 87 p., [40] p. of plates : LC Card 87-103737
HC403.Z7 I64 1986

I͡Anaev, S. I. (Saberdzhan Ismailovich) Rumi͡ant͡sev, Alekseĭ Matveevich. Instrumentariĭ ėkonomicheskoĭ nauki i praktiki . Moskva , 1985. 303 p. : LC Card 87-109217
HB61 .R86 1985

Ianchilovici, Beatriz. Goldberg, Samuel. El stock de capital en la Argentina . [Buenos Aires] , 1986. 28 leaves : LC Card 87-403996 DDC 332/.0414 19
HC180.C3 G65 1986

Iancu, Aurel. Schimburile economice internaţionale : o analiză critică a teoriei înzestrării naţiunilor cu factori de producţie / Aurel Iancu. Bucureşti : Editura Ştiinţifică şi Enciclopedică, 1983. 372 p. ; 21 cm. Table of contents in English, Romanian, and Russian. Includes bibliographical references. LC Card 85-216409
I. Title.
HF1411 .I24 1983 *NYPL [JLD 87-1962]*

ÌAremenko, ÌUriĭ Vasil'evich. Modelirovanie mezhotraslevykh vzaimodeĭstviĭ /. Moskva , 1984. 277 p. : LC Card 84-175111
HC336.25 .M6314 1984

Iarezza, Juan Carlos. Fundación de Investigaciones Económicas Latinoamericanas (Buenos Aires, Argentina) Gasto público . [Buenos Aires] , 1986. 6 v. in 8 : LC Card 87-403573 DDC 354.820072/252 19
HJ2075 .F86 1986

ÌArkin, A. P. (Anatoliĭ Pavlovich) Levin, A. I. (Aleksandr Ivanovich) Tovarnoe obrashchenie . Moskva , 1980. 286 p. ; LC Card 81-141540
HF1040.9.S65 L48 1980

ÌArmolovich, M. V. (Mikhail Viktorovich) Finansovye rychagi i material'nye stimuly sovershenstvovaniia stroitel'nogo proizvodstva / M.V. ÌArmolovich. Moskva : "Finansy i statistika", 1982. 196 p. ; 20 cm. Includes bibliographical references. LC Card 83-167253
1. Construction industry - Soviet Union - Finance. 2. Construction industry - Soviet Union - Capital investments. I. Title.
HD9715.S72 I27 1982

The IAS-System data base : a portable application of the b*-tree : final report / Harald Sonnberger ... [et al.]. Wien, Austria : Institut für Höhere Studien, [1982] ii, 151, 3 p. : ill. ; 30 cm. (Forschungsbericht = Research memorandum . no. 179 (Nov. 1982)) Bibliography: p. 67.
1. Data base management. 2. Econometrics - Data processing. I. Sonnberger, Harald. II. Series: Forschungsbericht (Institut für Höhere Studien, Vienna, Austria) , no. 179. ***NYPL [JSG 86-170]***

ÌAshkin, V. A. (Vladimir Andreevich) Planirovanie ėkonomicheskogo rosta v razvivaiushchikhsia stranakh : uchebnoe posobie / V.A. ÌAshkin, E.D. Cherevik. Moskva : Izd-vo Universiteta druzhby narodov, 1986. 120 p. ; 22 cm. At head of title: Ministerstvo vysshego i srednego spetsial'nogo obrazovaniia SSSR. Includes bibliographical references. LC Card 86-220878
1. Developing countries - Economic policy. 2. Economic development. I. Cherevik, E. D. (Evgeniĭ Dmitrievich). II. Title.
HC59.7 .I13 1986

IASTED Symposia on Modelling, Policy and Economics of Energy and Power Systems, and Alternative Energy Sources and Technology (1981 : San Francisco, Calif.) Proceedings of the IASTED Energy Symposia : Modelling, Policy and Economics of Energy and Power Systems [and] Alternative Energy Sources and Technology, May 20-22, 1981, San Francisco, U. S.A. / [editor, M.H. Hamza]. Anaheim, Calif. : Acta Press, [1981?] 209 p. : ill. ; 28 cm. Cover title. At head of title: International Association of Science and Technology for Development. Includes bibliographical references. ISBN 0-88986-027-0
1. Power resources - Economic aspects - Congresses. 2. Power resources - Mathematical models - Congresses. 3. Energy policy - Congresses. 4. Renewable energy sources - Congresses. I. Hamza, M. H. II. International Association of Science and Technology for Development. III. Title. IV. Title: Modelling, policy and economics of energy and power systems. V. Title: Alternative energy sources and technology. ***NYPL [JSF 86-1103]***

Iatros, Michaēl, 1779-1868. Spēliōtakēs, K. K. Archeion Michaēl Iatrou, 1802-1893 /. Athēna , 1983. 189 p., [4] folded leaves of plates : LC Card 85-134031
HF3750.5.S64 A3 1983 ***NYPL [JFE 86-4131]***

ÌAzykova, Valentina Spiridonovna. Distsiplina truda--delo kazhdogo /. Moskva , 1982. 77 p. ; LC Card 83-126613
HF5549.5.L3 D57 1982

Ibarz del Olmo, Carlos. González Blanch, Francisco. Implantación en España de un sistema de tarificación por el uso de la infraestructura viaria /. Madrid [1984?] 204 p. ; ISBN 84-7196-470-8 : LC Card 85-201965
HJ5956.E86 G66 1984

Ibbotson, Roger G. Investment markets : gaining the performance advantage / Roger G. Ibbotson, Gary P. Brinson. New York : McGraw-Hill, c1987. ix, 294 p. : ill. ; 24 cm. Includes bibliographies and index. ISBN 0-07-031673-2 : LC Card 86-33740 DDC 332.6 19
1. Capital market. 2. Portfolio management. I. Brinson, Gary P. II. Title.
HG4523 .I23 1987

IBC dossier . (17) Manutenzione e sostituzione . Bologna [1983] xviii, 227 p. : LC Card 84-142790
HD2346.I82 E45 1983

IBEC, 10 years. International Bank for Economic Co-operation. Moscow [1973] [27] p. : LC Card 82-216202
HG3881.5.I55 I58 1973

IBI international business intelligence. Investment incentives worldwide . London ; Boston : 518 p. : ISBN 0-408-00990-X : LC Card 87-24928 DDC 332.6/7322 19
HG4516 .I58 1987

Ibler, Josef. Nominallohnentwicklung in der Bundesrepublik Deutschland : eine empirische Untersuchung zur Bedeutung von Erwartungen und Verhandlungsmacht / Josef Ibler. Regensburg : Transfer Verlag, c1986. 256 p. : ill. ; 22 cm. (Wirtschafts- und sozialwissenschaftliche Forschungsbeiträge . Bd. 1) Bibliography: p. 245-256. ISBN 3-924956-18-9 LC Card 87-118941 DDC 331.2/943 19
1. Wages - Germany (West) - Econometric models. 2. Phillips curve - Case studies. I. Title. II. Series.
HD5029 .I2 1986

IBM . Mercer, David (David Steuart) London , 1987. 306 p. ; ISBN 1-85091-287-4 : LC Card 87-138763 DDC 338.7/61004/0973 19
HD9696.C64 I4855 1987

IBM ASSISTANT SERIES (COMPUTER PROGRAMS)
Burton, Kevin R. Advanced applications for PFS and the IBM assistant series /. Blue Ridge Summit, PA , c1985. x, 213 p. : ISBN 0-8306-0989-X : LC Card 85-9885 DDC 001.64/25 19
QA76.754 .B87 1985 ***NYPL [JSE 86-2148]***

The IBM market in Europe. New York, N.Y. : Frost & Sullivan, c1983. 2 v. (xv, 573, 9 p.) ; 29 cm. "April, 1983." "(#623)." LC Card 87-146364 DDC 380.1/45004/094 19
1. International Business Machines Corporation. 2. Computer industry - Europe. 3. Market surveys - Europe. I. Frost & Sullivan.
HD9696.C64 I4846 1983

IBM PCJR (COMPUTER) - PROGRAMMING.
Simpson, Henry. Programming the IBM PC user interface /. New York , c1985. vii, 228 p. : ISBN 0-07-057297-6 (pbk.) : LC Card 85-7924 DDC 005.265 19
QA76.8.I2594 S575 1985 ***NYPL [JSE 86-1154]***

IBM PERSONAL COMPUTER.
Add-on boards & peripherals for the IBM PC & compatibles. Norwalk, Conn., U. S.A. (6 Prowitt St., Norwalk 06855) , c1986. x, 320 leaves ; LC Card 86-235156 DDC 380.1/456213984 19
HD9696.C62 A34 1986

Cohen, Eli B. Business BASIC for the IBM PC with cases /. St. Louis , 1987. xxiv, 634 p. : ISBN 0-8016-1244-6 (pbk.) LC Card 86-23100 DDC 005.2/165 19
HF5548.5.B3 C64 1987

Hurwicz, Michael. Networking with the IBM Network & Cluster /. Blue Ridge Summit, Pa. , 1985. x, 518 p. : ISBN 0-8306-0929-6 : LC Card 85-4639 DDC 001.64/404 19
TK5105.7 .H87 1985 ***NYPL [JSE 86-1975]***

Ingalsbe, Lon. Business applications software for the IBM PC /. Columbus , c1987. 1 v. (various pagings) : ISBN 0-675-20760-6 (pbk.) LC Card 86-63664 DDC 650/.028/55365 19
HF5548.4.I24 I54 1987

IBM PERSONAL COMPUTER - PROGRAMMING.
Burgess, Ross. Office automation using the IBM personal computer systems . London , 1986. 180 p. : ISBN 0-00-383104-3 (pbk.) : LC Card 86-220136 DDC 651.8/4165 19
HF5548.2 .B783 1986

Eliason, Alan L. Program analysis and design . Chicago , c1987. ix, 134 p. : ISBN 0-574-18660-3 (pbk.) LC Card 87-4521 DDC 658/.055265 19
HF5548.2 .E4275 1987

Gane, Chris, 1938- Developing business systems in SQL . New York, NY , 1986. 1 v. (various pagings) : ISBN 0-914751-02-6 (pbk.) LC Card 87-107881 DDC 650/.028/557565 19
HF5548.5.S65 G36 1986

Hewes, Jeremy Joan. Wordprocessing on IBM PCs /. New York , c1985. xiii, 178 p. : ISBN 0-471-88663-7 : LC Card 84-11966 DDC 652/.5 19
Z52.5.I27 H48 1985 ***NYPL [JSF 87-232]***

Hoenig, Alan. Framework with applications for the IBM PC /. Dubuque, Iowa , c1985. xiii, 213 p. : ISBN 0-697-00725-1 (pbk.) : LC Card 85-60013 DDC 005.3/69 19
HF5548.4.F7 H64 1985 ***NYPL [JSE 86-2110]***

Simpson, Henry. Programming the IBM PC user interface /. New York , c1985. vii, 228 p. : ISBN 0-07-057297-6 (pbk.) : LC Card 85-7924 DDC 005.265 19
QA76.8.I2594 S575 1985 ***NYPL [JSE 86-1154]***

Sparks, L. E. Investment analysis using your IBM PC and compatibles /. Blue Ridge Summit, PA , c1985. xi, 224 p. : ISBN 0-8306-0859-1 : LC Card 85-17322 DDC 332.6/028/55365 19
HG4529 .S6 1985 ***NYPL [JLE 86-4621]***

Witkin, Ruth K. Managing your business with Multiplan . Redmond, Wash. , 1987. xv, 525 p. ; ISBN 0-914845-94-2 (pbk.) : LC Card 87-7773 DDC 005.36/9 19
HF5548.4.M74 W57 1987

Wolverton, Van, 1939- Running MS DOS . Bellevue, Wash. [New York, NY] , c1985. xv, 423 p. : ISBN 0-914845-68-3 LC Card 85-18951 DDC 005.4/469 19
QA76.76.O63 W65 1985 ***NYPL [JSE 86-1760]***

Words & Figures . Monterey, CA (411 Pacific St., Monterey 93940) , c1986. 1 v. (various pagings) : LC Card 87-111370 DDC 005.36/9 19
HF5548.4.W66 W67 1986

IBM PERSONAL COMPUTER XT - PROGRAMMING.
O'Keeffe, Linda. Statistical packages for the IBM PC family /. New York , c1986. x, 162 p. : ISBN 0-07-056320-9 : LC Card 85-18213 DDC 658/.055365 19
HF1017 .O39 1986 ***NYPL [JSE 86-1876]***

The IBM way . Rodgers, F. G. (Francis G.) New York , c1986. xiv, 235 p. ; ISBN 0-06-015522-1 : LC Card 85-45223 DDC 338.7/61004/0973 19
HD9696.C64 I4875 1986 ***NYPL [JLE 86-1374]***

IBM's evolving mainframes : information systems / Communications/Information Systems. Boston, Mass. (200 Portland St., Boston 02114) : Yankee Group, c1986. iii, 45 p. : ill. ; 28 cm. "October 1986." LC Card 86-231231 DDC 381/.4500412/0973 19
1. International Business Machines Corporation. 2. Computer industry - United States. 3. Market surveys - United States. I. Communications/Information Systems (Firm : Yankee Group).
HD9696.C64 I48466 1986

Ibrahim, José. O que todo cidadão precisa saber sobre comissões de fábrica / José Ibrahim. São Paulo, SP : Global, [1986] 96 p. : ill. ; 18 cm. (Cadernos de educação política . 11.) ISBN 85-26-00095-0 LC Card 87-402908 DDC 338.6 19
1. Works councils - Brazil. 2. Management - Brazil - Employee participation. 3. Works councils - History. 4. Management - Employee participation - History. I. Title. II. Title: Que todo cidadão precisa saber sobre comissões de fábrica. III. Title: Comissões de fábrica. IV. Series: Cadernos de educação política , 11.
HD5660.B7 I27 1986

Ibrahim, Saad Eddin. Internal migration in Egypt : a critical review / by Saad Eldin Ibrahim. Cairo, Egypt : Supreme Council for Population and Family Planning, Population and Family Planning Board, Research Office, [1982] 86, viii p. : ill. ; 29 cm. (Research monographs . series no. 5) "January 1982." Bibliography: p. 74-86. LC Card 84-960007 DDC 304.8/0962 19
1. Migration, Internal - Egypt. I. Series: Research monographs (Egypt. Jihāz Tanẓim al-Usrah wa-al-Sukkān. Maktab al-Buḥūth) , series no. 5. II.

Title.
HB2121.7.A3 I27 1982

Ibrahim, Saaduddin. Aspek-aspek proteksi dalam industri dan perdagangan / Saaduddin Ibrahim, Pranoto K. Cet. 1. Jakarta : Jaya Prasada, 1987. 251 p. : forms ; 21 cm. "Dilengkapi daftar barang impor yang mangalami perubahan bea masuk sesuai SK Menteri Keuangan RI, no. 915/KMK.05/1986." Bibliography: p. 249-251. LC Card 87-941314
1. Industry and state - Indonesia. 2. Foreign trade regulation - Indonesia. I. Kartoatmodjo, Pranoto. II. Title.
HD4304 .I27 1987

IC Institute.
Frontiers in creative and innovative management /. Cambridge, Mass. , 1985, c1986. xxv, 391 p. : ISBN 0-88730-057-X LC Card 85-15125 DDC 658.4 19
HD53 .F76 1986 NYPL [JLE 86-3614]
The Role of affect in consumer behavior . Lexington, Mass. , c1986. ix, 196 p. : ISBN 0-669-12874-0 (alk. paper) LC Card 85-46042 DDC 658.8/342 19
HF5415.3 .R65 1986 NYPL [JLE 86-3376]

ICA publikatie .
(nr. 68) Hakemulder, Roel. Subcultuur en stigma van de armoede . Leiden , 1985. 96 p. ; ISBN 90-6624-058-X LC Card 86-172398
HC79.P6 H34 1985

ICAP Hellas, S.A. Mikromesaies kai megales epicheirēseis stēn Hellēnikē viomēchania. Athēna , 1982. 32 p. ; LC Card 85-152476
HD69.S5 M54 1982

ICE BREAKING OPERATIONS - SOVIET UNION.
Zuev, V. A. (Valeriĭ Andreevich) Sredstva prodleniia navigatsii na vnutrennikh vodnykh putiakh /. Leningrad , 1986. 206 p. : LC Card 86-166974
HE675 .Z84 1986

ICE CREAM INDUSTRY - NETHERLANDS.
Bovenkerk, Frank. Italiaans ijs . Meppel [1983?] 203 p. : ISBN 90-6009-551-0 LC Card 83-179690
HD9281.N42 B68 1983

ICE CREAM INDUSTRY - UNITED STATES.
Shurtleff, William, 1941- Tofutti® & other soy ice creams . Lafayette, CA , c1985. 2 v. : ISBN 0-933332-19-X (v. 1) : LC Card 85-10829 DDC 381/.4174 19
HD9330.B323 U 1985 NYPL [JLF 86-1035]

ICE INDUSTRY - ALASKA - WOOD ISLAND - HISTORY - SOURCES.
Walker, David B., 1841 or 2-ca. 1906. Captain David B. Walker, journal and papers, 1864-1869 . Juneau, Alaska (Pouch G, Juneau 99811) , 1984. 60 p. : LC Card 84-622198
HD9481.U4 W359 1984

ICE NAVIGATION - SOVIET UNION.
Zuev, V. A. (Valeriĭ Andreevich) Sredstva prodleniia navigatsii na vnutrennikh vodnykh putiakh /. Leningrad , 1986. 206 p. : LC Card 86-166974
HE675 .Z84 1986

Icecoop. see **Instituto Chileno de Educación Cooperativa.**

Iced coffee taste test : fresh brew products, soluble products : a report to the Coffee Development Group ... / submitted by Market Facts. Van Nuys, CA (14416 Victory Blvd. Van Nuys 91401) : Market Facts, [1985] 132 p., 6, 6 leaves : ill., forms ; 28 cm. "December 1985." LC Card 87-100181 DDC 381/.4566393/0973 19
1. Coffee trade - United States. 2. Consumers' preferences - United States. 3. Consumers - United States - Attitudes. 4. Market surveys - United States. I. Coffee Development Group (U. S.). II. Market Facts, Inc.
HD9199.U48 I25 1985

ICELAND - ECONOMIC CONDITIONS.
Birgir Björn Sigurjónsson, 1949- Frjálshyggjan /. [Reykjavík] , 1981. 261 p. : LC Card 84-134561
HB95 .B55 1981

ICELAND - ECONOMIC CONDITIONS - 1918-1945.
Kjartan Jónasson. Kreppuárin á Íslandi 1930-1939 /. [Reykjavik] , 1986- v. <1 > : LC Card 87-117468
HB3717 1929 .K58 1986

ICELAND - ECONOMIC CONDITIONS - 1945-
Glässer, Ewald. Island /. Darmstadt , 1986. xii, 315 p., [20] p. of plates (4 folded) : ISBN 3-534-01225-9 LC Card 87-101040
HC360.5 .G57 1986

Iceland. Hagstofa. Tölfræðihandbók 1984 =. Reykjavík , 1984. 12, 268 p. ; LC Card 87-165528
HA1491 .A4 vol. II, 82

ICELAND - POPULATION.
Glässer, Ewald. Island /. Darmstadt , 1986. xii, 315 p., [20] p. of plates (4 folded) : ISBN 3-534-01225-9 LC Card 87-101040
HC360.5 .G57 1986

Iceland. Statistical Bureau. see **Iceland. Hagstofa.**

ICELAND - STATISTICS - PERIODICALS.
Tölfræðihandbók 1984 =. Reykjavík , 1984. 12, 268 p. ; LC Card 87-165528
HA1491 .A4 vol. II, 82

ICFTU World Conference on the Trade Union Role in Balanced Development (1981 : New Delhi, India) Souvenir, ICFTU World Conference on the Trade Union Role in Balanced Development, Vigyan Bhawan, New Delhi, India, March 18-20, 1981 /. New Delhi [1981] 68 p. : LC Card 84-901715 DDC 331.88 19
HD6475.A2 I26347 1981
NYPL [JLG 86-296]

Ichtisar tahunan tentang pelaksanaan Ketetapan MPRS no. II/MPRS/1960 mengenai pola pembangunan nasional semesta berentjana tahapan pertama, 1961-1969 jang berkenaan dengan tahun pelaksanaan pembangunan 1963. Indonesia. Majelis Permusyawaratan Rakyat. [Djakarta] [1965] 141 p. ; LC Card 86-161520
HC447 .I5534 1963

ICI . Kennedy, Carol. London , 1986. xii, 209 p., [20] p. of plates : ISBN 0-09-167300-3 : LC Card 87-121862 DDC 338.7/66/00941 19
HD9652.9.I5 K46 1986

ICIDCA. Correa, Jorge Lois. Sistemas y equipos de desmedulado en la industria del bagazo de la caña de azúcar /. Ciudad de La Habana , c1982. 77 p. : LC Card 85-198777
HD9119.B4 C83 1982

Icke-permanent stöd till tre industriföretag : fallstudier / utförda för Industristödsutredningen. [Stockholm] : Industridepartementet : LiberFörlag, [1981] 245 p. : ill. ; 21 cm. "Ds I 1981:9." ISBN 91-38-06270-4 LC Card 83-245223
1. Subsidies - Sweden - Case studies. 2. Industry and state - Sweden - Case studies. I. Sweden. Industristödsutredningen.
HD3646.S8 I25 1981

Ickis, John C., 1943- Beyond bureaucracy . West Hartford, Conn. , c1986. xii, 256 p. : ISBN 0-931816-44-0 LC Card 86-34420 DDC 338.9/0068 19
HC59.72.E44 B48 1986

ICMA management accounting in inflation series.
Allen, David. Funds flow management . London , 1980. x, 84 p. :
NYPL [JLD 86-2760]

ICMA Training Institute. Management policies in local government finance /. Washington, D.C. , c1987. 449 p. : ISBN 0-87326-075-9 : LC Card 87-2658 DDC 352.1 19
HJ9105 .M3 1987

ICPE training series .
(no. 1) Guide to training needs assessment /. Ljubljana, Yugoslavia , c1984. 65 p. ; ISBN 92-9038-412-8 (pbk.) LC Card 85-242690 DDC 658.3/12404 19
HF5549.5.T7 G847 1984

I.C.U. (SOUTH AFRICA) - HISTORY.
Bradford, Helen. A taste of freedom . New Haven , 1987. xvi, 364 p., [2] p. of plates : ISBN 0-300-03873-9 LC Card 87-10451 DDC 331.88/0968 19
HD8801.A5 I1634 1987

IDA working paper series.
Scudder, Thayer. An evaluation of the Gwembe South Development Project, Zambia /. Binghamton, N.Y., USA [1982] 48 p. ; LC Card 87-119502 DDC 338.96894 19
HC915.Z7 G846 1982

IDAHO - ECONOMIC CONDITIONS.
Idaho. Governor's Economic Research Council. Report of the Governor's Economic Research Council on the Idaho economy, submitted to John V. Evans, governor. [Boise] [1984] v, 30 p. : LC Card 86-621917 DDC 330.9796/033 19
HC107.I2 I164 1984

Idaho economy. Idaho. Governor's Economic Research Council. Report of the Governor's Economic Research Council on the Idaho economy, submitted to John V. Evans, governor. [Boise] [1984] v, 30 p. : LC Card 86-621917 DDC 330.9796/033 19
HC107.I2 I164 1984

Idaho. Governor's Economic Research Council. Report of the Governor's Economic Research Council on the Idaho economy, submitted to John V. Evans, governor. [Boise] : The Council, [1984] v, 30 p. : ill. ; 28 cm. "Annotated bibliography of ERC-sponsored research reports": p. 28-30. LC Card 86-621917 DDC 330.9796/033 19
1. Idaho - Economic conditions. I. Title. II. Title: Idaho economy.
HC107.I2 I164 1984

Idaho Oregon Onion Promotion Committee. Sweet Spanish onion : market development research : complete report / Idaho Oregon Onion Promotion Committee. Temple, Me. (Santa Claus Lake, Temple 04984) : Food Business Associates, 1986. ii, 46, 27 leaves : ill. ; 28 cm. Cover title. LC Card 87-120958 DDC 381/.41525/0973 19
1. Onion industry - United States. 2. Onion industry - Idaho. 3. Onion industry - Oregon. 4. Market surveys - United States. I. Title.
HD9235.O62 U34 1986

IDCJ working paper series .
(no. 35) Kimura, Fukunari. Industrial development of Malaysia . Tokyo, Japan , 1986. 25 p. : LC Card 86-232472 DDC 338.09595 19
HD9736.M32 K56 1986

Ide, Arthur Frederick. The mercantile policies of Henry VII / by Arthur Frederick Ide. Irving, Tex. : Scholars Books, 1987. v, 78 p. : ill. ; 21 cm. (Medieval people, 0273-3307 . v. 10) Bibliography: p. 75-76. Includes index. ISBN 0-938659-02-2 (pbk.) : LC Card 87-4316 DDC 382/.3/0942 19
1. Great Britain - Commercial policy - History - 16th century. 2. Mercantile system - Great Britain - History - 16th century. 3. Great Britain - History - Henry VII, 1485-1509. 4. Henry VII, King of England, 1457-1509. I. Title. II. Title: Mercantile policies of Henry the Seventh. III. Series.
HF1533 .I34 1987

The idea of Third World development . Alcalde Cardoza, Xavier. Lanham, MD [Charlottesville, Va.] , c1987. xxii, 236 p. ; ISBN 0-8191-6303-1 (alk. paper) : LC Card 87-8154 DDC 338.91/009172/4 19
HC60 .A4595 1987

Ideas para la cultura europea : la crisis. Barcelona : Huguin, [1980?] 64 p. : ill. ; 22 cm. "La crisis, quién la provoca y aquién beneficia"--Cover. CONTENTS. - El crack de 1929 -- La crisis -- La crisis europea y las primeras materias -- La lucha por la hegemonía mundial -- Europa, de crisis en crisis -- La crisis no es sólo económica. ISBN 84-300-3210-X LC Card 85-105410
1. Economic history - 1918-. 2. Depressions - 1929. I. Title: Crisis, quién la provoca y a quién beneficia.
HC57 .I24 1980

El IDEMA, hacia una pérdida de los objetivos sociales. Isaza Tobón, Gabriela. [Colombia? , between 1984 and 1987] ([Colombia?] : Litoarte) 126 p., [1] leaf of plates : LC Card 87-404223 DDC 381/.41/09861 19
HD9014.C72 I8 1984

Identificação e caracterização de agrupamentos industriais como subsídio à política de desenvolvimento regional. São Paulo : Coordenadoria de Ação Regional, 1981. 134, 17, 60 p. : ill. ; 23 cm. Includes bibliographical references. LC Card 86-146114
1. São Paulo (Brazil : State) - Industries - Location. 2. Urbanization - Brazil - São Paulo (State). 3. Regional planning - Brazil - São Paulo (State). I. São Paulo (Brazil : State). Secretaria do Interior. Coordenadoria de Ação Regional.
HC188.S3 I34 1981

Identification & economic analysis of small farmers /. Banerjee, B. N. (Biswa Nath), 1945- Delhi, India , 1986. viii, 127 p. : LC Card

86-903139 DDC 338.1/6 19
HD1476.I42 V373 1986

Identification and economic analysis of small farmers. Banerjee, B. N. (Biswa Nath), 1945- Identification & economic analysis of small farmers /. Delhi, India , 1986. viii, 127 p. : LC Card 86-903139 DDC 338.1/6 19
HD1476.I42 V373 1986

IDENTITY (PSYCHOLOGY)
Fast, Irene. Gender identity . Hillsdale, N.J. , 1984. vii, 189 p. ; ISBN 0-88163-014-4 LC Card 84-6366 DDC 155.3/3 19
BF692.2 .F36 1984 *NYPL [JFE 86-4829]*

Lichtenstein, Heinz, 1904- The dilemma of human identity /. New York , c1983. xiv, 399 p. ; ISBN 0-87668-677-3 : LC Card 84-45086 DDC 155.2 19
BF697 .L52 1983 *NYPL [JFE 86-2218]*

Roberts, Richard. From Eden to Eros . San Anselmo, Ca. , 1985. 166 p. : ISBN 0-942380-05-3 (pbk.) LC Card 85-51722
NYPL [JLD 87-224]

Westkott, Marcia, 1943- The feminist legacy of Karen Horney /. New Haven , c1986. viii, 242 p. ; ISBN 0-300-03706-6 (alk. paper) LC Card 86-9201 DDC 305.4/2 19
HQ1206 .W47 1986 *NYPL [JFD 86-10266]*

IDENTITY (PSYCHOLOGY) - ADDRESSES, ESSAYS, LECTURES.
The Social psychology of female-male relations . Orlando , 1986. xvi, 351 p. ; ISBN 0-12-065280-3 (alk. paper) LC Card 85-9138 DDC 305.3 19
HM132 .S569 1986 *NYPL [JLE 86-1746]*

Ideología y programa de gobierno en los discursos de toma de posesión de los presidentes de México, 1928-1982 /. Orozco, Jesús. Guadalajara, Jal., México , c1983. 47 p. ; ISBN 968-511-003-4 LC Card 83-191579
HC135 .O66 1983

Ideologías de los grupos dirigentes sindicales /. Fernández, Arturo. Buenos Aires , c1986. 2 v. ; ISBN 950-25-1403-3 (v. 1) LC Card 86-205687
HD6603.5 .F47 1986

IDEOLOGY.
Abercrombie, Nicholas. Class, structure, and knowledge . London , 1980. 196 p. ; ISBN 0-8147-0571-5 : *NYPL [JLD 80-2963]*

Akopov, Mykhaĭlo Arutiunovych. Dukhovnyĭ mir sovetskogo cheloveka /. Kiev , 1985. 124, [3] p. ; LC Card 86-139846
JN6581 .A64 1985 *NYPL [*QIK 87-3448]*

Ideology and national competitiveness . Boston, Mass. , c1987. x, 350 p. ; ISBN 0-87584-147-3 LC Card 86-19569 DDC 338.6/048 19
HF1414 .I34 1987 *NYPL [JLE 87-1046]*

Sowell, Thomas, 1930- A conflict of visions /. New York , c1987. 273 p. ; ISBN 0-688-06912-6 LC Card 86-18187 DDC 303.3/72 19
HM73 .S68 1987 *NYPL [JLD 87-823]*

Thompson, Kenneth, 1937- Beliefs and ideology /. Chichester, West Sussex : London ; 135 p. ; ISBN 0-85312-858-8 : LC Card 86-2984 DDC 306/.4 19
BL60 .T49 1986 *NYPL [JLD 86-2479]*

Ideology and abortion policy politics /. Falik, Marilyn. New York, N.Y. , 1983. 228 p. ; ISBN 0-03-062813-X LC Card 83-2402 DDC 363.4/6 19
HQ767.5.U5 F34 1983 *NYPL [JLE 85-1581]*

Ideology and national competitiveness : an analysis of nine countries / edited by George C. Lodge and Ezra F. Vogel. Boston, Mass. : Harvard Business School Press, c1987. x, 350 p. ; 24 cm. Includes index. Bibliography: p. 327-342. ISBN 0-87584-147-3 LC Card 86-19569 DDC 338.6/048 19
1. Ideology. 2. Individualism. 3. Community. I. Lodge, George C. II. Vogel, Ezra F.
HF1414 .I34 1987 *NYPL [JLE 87-1046]*

IDEOLOGY - POLITICAL ASPECTS.
Falik, Marilyn. Ideology and abortion policy politics /. New York, N.Y. , 1983. 228 p. ; ISBN 0-03-062813-X LC Card 83-2402 DDC 363.4/6 19
HQ767.5.U5 F34 1983 *NYPL [JLE 85-1581]*

IDESI (ORGANIZATION : PERU)
Aumento del ingreso y mejoramiento de las condiciones de trabajo del sector informal urbano en sietes ciudades del Perú /. [Lima, Perú?] , 1986. ii, 69, [25] leaves : LC Card 87-106249
HD2346.P4 A85 1986

Idling erodible cropland . Webb, Shwu-Eng. Washington, D.C. [1986] iii, 31 p. : LC Card 86-601632 DDC 338.1 s 338.1/62 19
HD1751 .A91854 no. 550 HD256

Idősorok és keresztmetszeti adatok együttes felhasználása az ökonometriai vizsgálatokban /. Mátyás, László. Budapest , 1985. 119 p. ; ISBN 963-491-212-5 LC Card 86-196805
HB139 .M39 1985

Időszerű közgazdasági kérdések.
Bayer, B. József. A kis- és középvállalatok és a gazdasági fejlődés . Budapest , 1986. 203, [1] p. : ISBN 963-221-914-7 : LC Card 87-138623
HD2341 .B29 1986

Időszerű közgazdasági kérdések, 0324-3214.
Bagó, Eszter. Diverzifikáció az iparban /. Budapest , 1985. 251, [1] p. : ISBN 963-221-544-3 : LC Card 86-186848
HD2755.8 .B34 1985

Botos, Balázs. Kérdőjelek iparunk fejlesztésében /. Budapest , 1984. 391, [1] p. ; ISBN 963-221-392-0 : LC Card 85-156613
HC300.28 .B69 1984

Farkas, János. Az innováció társadalmi-gazdasági akadályai /. Budapest , 1984. 350 p. ; ISBN 963-221-453-6 : LC Card 85-157214
HC300.295.T4 F36 1984

Hoós, János. Az új növekedési pálya feltételei és követelményei /. Budapest , 1985. 227, [2] p. : ISBN 963-221-508-7 : LC Card 86-128355
HC300.28 .H664 1985

Illés, Iván. Gazdaságunk helye és rangja a világban . Budapest , 1985. 222 p. : ISBN 963-221-523-0 : LC Card 86-156571
HC300.28 .I45 1985

Somogyi, Dorottya. A fejlett tőkés országok exportpolitikája /. Budapest , 1985. 277, [1] p. : ISBN 963-221-507-9 : LC Card 85-231848
HF1417.5 .S66 1985

Veress, József, Dr. A veszélyhelyzetbe került vállalatok és a gazdaságirányítás /. Budapest , 1986. 207, [1] p. ; ISBN 963-221-778-0 : LC Card 87-136695
HG3769.H94 V47 1986

IDR working paper .
(no. 18) Tegegne Teke. Cooperatives and national development . Addis Ababa, Ethiopia [1984] iii, 57 leaves ; LC Card 85-980411 DDC 334/.683/0963 19
HD1491.E83 T44 1984 *NYPL [JLG 86-173]*

IDRC (Series) .
(243s) Comercialización interna de los alimentos en América Latina . Ottawa, Canada , c1985. 253 p. : ISBN 0-88936-448-6 LC Card 87-118494 DDC 338.1/9/8 19
HD9014.L32 C66 1985

(246e) With our own hands . Ottawa, Canada , c1986. 206 p. : ISBN 0-88936-460-5 (pbk.) LC Card 86-212405 DDC 338.91/71/01724 19
HC59.72.F44 W58 1986

IDS consultancy report .
(no. 12) Vandemoortele, Jan. The wage policy in Kenya . [Nairobi] [1984] 28 leaves : LC Card 86-681105 DDC 331.2/96762 19
HC865.Z9 W248 1984

Idyll of the Kings, 1889-1979 . Mallett, Alan S. Kendal [Cumbria] , 1980. 64 p. : ISBN 0-905617-10-X (pbk.) LC Card 81-105772 DDC 387.5/065/41 19
HE945.K48 M35 1980

IEA readings, 0305-814X .
(22) Tax avoision . London , 1979. x, 134 p. ; ISBN 0-255-36126-2 (pbk.) LC Card 86-673369
HJ2348.5 .T39x 1979

IEEE Computer Society Office Automation Symposium, National Bureau of Standards, Gaithersburg, MD, 27-29 April 1987. IEEE Computer Society Office Automation Symposium (1987 : National Bureau of Standards) Washington, D.C. , Los Angeles, CA , c1987. xi, 319 p. : ISBN 0-8186-0770-X (pbk.) LC Card 86-83315 DDC 651.8 19
HF5548 .I44 1987

IEEE Computer Society Office Automation Symposium (1987 : National Bureau of Standards) IEEE Computer Society Office Automation Symposium, National Bureau of Standards, Gaithersburg, MD, 27-29 April 1987. Washington, D.C. : Computer Society Press of the IEEE ; Los Angeles, CA : Order from Computer Society of the IEEE, c1987. xi, 319 p. : ill. ; 28 cm. Includes bibliographies and index. ISBN 0-8186-0770-X (pbk.) LC Card 86-83315 DDC 651.8 19
1. Office practice - Automation - Congresses. 2. Business - Data processing - Congresses. I. IEEE Computer Society. II. Title.
HF5548 .I44 1987

IEEE Professional Communication Society.
Carnes, William T. Effective meetings for busy people . New York , c1987. xvi, 348 p. ; ISBN 0-87942-211-4 LC Card 86-27719 DDC 658.4/563 19
HD2743 .C37 1987

IEEE Professional Communications Society.
Blicq, Ron, 1925- Writing reports to get results . New York , c1987. x, 203 p. : ISBN 0-87942-228-9 LC Card 87-16850 DDC 808/.066651 19
HF5719 .B55 1987

If I could work /. Blacker, Terence. New York , c1988. p. cm. ISBN 0-397-32245-3 : LC Card 87-3972 DDC 331.7/02 19
HF5381.2 .B55 1988

If you don't have a plan, stay in the car /. Hanan, Mack. New York, NY , c1987. x, 277 p. ; ISBN 0-8144-5936-6 LC Card 87-47706 DDC 658.8/1 19
HF5438.25 .H347 1987

IFAC proceedings series .
(1987, no. 12) IFAC/IFORS/IFIP/IASC/AFCET Conference on Economics and Artificial Intelligence (1986 : Aix-en-Provence, France) Economics and artificial intelligence . Oxford [Oxfordshire] , New York , 1987. xiii, 194 p. : ISBN 0-08-034350-3 (U. S.) : LC Card 87-6943 DDC 330/.028/563 19
HB143.5 .I44 1986

IFAC/IFORS/IFIP/IASC/AFCET Conference on Economics and Artificial Intelligence (1986 : Aix-en-Provence, France) Economics and artificial intelligence : proceedings of the IFAC/IFORS/IFIP/IASC/AFCET Conference, Aix-en-Provence, France, 2-4 September, 1986 / edited by Jean-Louis Roos.1st ed. Oxford [Oxfordshire] ; New York : Published for the International Federation of Automatic Control by Pergamon Press, 1987. xiii, 194 p. : ill. ; 31 cm. (IFAC proceedings series . 1987, no. 12) Organized by Association française pour la cybernétique économique et technique (AFCET). Includes bibliographies and indexes. ISBN 0-08-034350-3 (U. S.) : LC Card 87-6943 DDC 330/.028/563 19
1. Economics - Data processing - Congresses. 2. Artificial intelligence - Data processing - Congresses. I. Roos, Jean-Louis. II. International Federation of Automatic Control. III. Association française pour la cybernétique économique et technique. IV. Title. V. Series.
HB143.5 .I44 1986

Ifeagwu, Sam. OPEC aid and the challenge of development /. London , New York , c1987. x, 130 p. ; ISBN 0-7099-1969-7 LC Card 87-9160 DDC 338.91/09172/4 19
HC60 .O5754 1987

IFIP Conference on System Modeling and Optimization (12th : 1985 : Budapest, Hungary) System modelling and optimization . Berlin , New York , c1986. xii, 1046 p. : ISBN 0-387-16854-0 (U. S.) LC Card 86-15637 DDC 003 19
QA402 .S95822 1986 *NYPL [JSE 86-1775]*

IFIP TC-7 (Organization) System modelling and optimization . Berlin , New York , c1986. xii, 1046 p. : ISBN 0-387-16854-0 (U. S.) LC Card 86-15637 DDC 003 19
QA402 .S95822 1986 *NYPL [JSE 86-1775]*

IFIP TC 8 Working Conference on Office Systems (1985 : Helsinki, Finland) Office systems : proceedings of the IFIP TC 8 Working Conference on Office Systems, Helsinki, Finland, 29 September-2 October 1985 / edited by A.A. Verrijn-Stuart, R.A. Hirschheim. Amsterdam ; New York :

North-Holland ; vii, 199 p. : ill. ; 23 cm. Includes bibliographies. ISBN 0-444-70105-2 (Elsevier Science Pub. Co.) LC Card 86-16841 DDC 651.8 19
1. Office practice - Automation - Congresses. 2. Information storage and retrieval systems - Business - Congresses. I. Verrijn Stuart, A. A. II. Hirschheim, R. A. (Rudy A.). III. Title.
HF5547.5 .I345 1985 ***NYPL [JLD 87-1264]***

IFIP TC 8/WG 8.4 Working Conference on Methods and Tools for Office Systems (1986 : Pisa, Italy) Office systems : methods and tools : proceedings of the IFIP TC 8/WG 8.4 Working Conference on Methods and Tools for Office Systems, Pisa, Italy, 22-24 October 1986 / edited by G. Bracchi and D. Tsichritzis. Amsterdam ; New York : North-Holland ; xi, 347 p. : ill. ; 23 cm. Papers presented at the conference organized by IFIP Technical Committee 8, Information Systems, International Federation for Information Processing, and co-sponsored by Consiglio nazionale delle ricerche and Associazione italiana per l'informatica e il calcolo automatico. Includes index. ISBN 0-444-70241-5 (U. S.) LC Card 87-8916 DDC 651.8 19
1. Information storage and retrieval systems - Business - Congresses. 2. Office practice - Automation - Congresses. I. Bracchi, G. (Giampio), 1944-. II. Tsichritzis, Dionysios C. III. International Federation for Information Processing. Technical Committee for Information Systems. IV. Consiglio nazionale delle ricerche (Italy). V. Associazione italiana per l'informatica e il calcolo automatico. VI. Title.
HF5548.2 .I285 1986

IFIP Working Conference on System Modelling and Optimization (1984 : Santiago, Chile) Recent advances in system modelling and optimization : proceedings of the IFIP-WG 7/1 Working Conference, Santiago, Chile, August 27-31, 1984 / edited by L. Contesse, R. Correa, and A. Weintraub. Berlin ; New York : Springer-Verlag, c1986. 199 p. : ill. ; 25 cm. (Lecture notes in control and information sciences. 87) Includes bibliographies. ISBN 0-387-17083-9 (U. S.) LC Card 86-29770 DDC 003 19
1. System analysis - Congresses. 2. Mathematical models - Congresses. 3. Mathematical optimization - Congresses. I. Contesse, L. (Luis), 1948-. II. Correa, R. (Rafael), 1947-. III. Weintraub, Andres. IV. Title.
QA402 .I43 1984 ***NYPL [JSE 87-639]***

The IFM guide to the preparation of a company policy manual. 2nd ed. Greenvale, N.Y. : Institute for Management, c1987. xv, 412 p. ; 23 cm. Includes index. ISBN 0-916592-71-5 (loose-leaf) LC Card 87-22258 DDC 658.3/01 19
1. Personnel management - Handbooks, manuals, etc. I. Institute for Management. II. Title: Company policy manual.
HF5549 .I5643 1987

Ifo Forschungsberichte der Abteilung Entwicklungsländer .
(67) Mounbaga, Emmanuel Seidou, 1957- Finanzpolitik und Wirtschaftsentwicklung in der Dritten Welt . München , c1986. 265 p. ; ISBN 3-8039-0341-6 LC Card 86-233152
HJ1620 .M68 1986

Afrika-Studien. see Afrika-Studien.

Ifo-Institut für Wirtschaftsforschung.
Wachstumsmarkt Südostasien . München , c1984. x, 807 p. : ISBN 3-8039-0292-4 : LC Card 84-249861
HF3790.8.Z5 W33 1984

Ifo-Studien zur Entwicklungsforschung. Sonderreihe "Information und Dokumentation" .
(3) Wachstumsmarkt Südostasien . München , c1984. x, 807 p. : ISBN 3-8039-0292-4 : LC Card 84-249861
HF3790.8.Z5 W33 1984

Ifo-Studien zur Finanzpolitik .
(27) Parsche, Rüdiger. Die Belastung der Einkünfte aus nichtselbständiger Arbeit mit Einkommensteuern und Sozialabgaben in den EG-Ländern und in Schweden /. München , 1981. 2 v. ; LC Card 83-115269
HJ4719 .P37 1981

Ifo Studien zur Finanzpolitik, 0081-7279 .
(32) Analyse der Wirksamkeit der Beschäftigungszulage . München , 1984. vii, 172 p. : LC Card 85-230164
HJ4720.A45 A53 1984

(34) Hummel, Marlies. Subsidiaritätsprinzip als Leitlinie für einen Subventionsabbau . München , 1985. xiii, 306 p. ; ISBN 3-88512-003-8 : LC Card 86-125424
HC290.5.S9 H85 1985

(37) Sicherung der Altersvorsorge durch Aufgabenteilung zwischen Individualversicherung und gesetzlicher Rentenversicherung . München , 1986. xi, 242 p. : ISBN 3-88512-017-8 : LC Card 86-163171
HD7105.35.G3 S53 1986

(38) Leibfritz, Willi. Berücksichtigung der zentralen Orte im kommunalen Finanzausgleich Bayern . München , 1986. vi, 151 p. : ISBN 3-88512-018-6 LC Card 86-172605
HJ9493.5.B38 L45 1986

(39) Sherman, Heidemarie C. Der Einfluss staatlicher Budgetdefizite auf die Zinsentwicklung in der Bundesrepublik Deutschland und den Vereinigten Staaten . München , c1986. xxiii, 190 p. : ISBN 3-88512-019-4 LC Card 86-192070
HJ2110 .S53 1986

(40) Hummel, Marlies. Die steuerliche Behandlung des eigengenutzten Wohneigentums in den Ländern Bundesrepublik Deutschland, Österreich, Schweiz, Frankreich, Grossbritannien und den USA /. München , 1986. ii, 73 p. ; ISBN 3-88512-021-6 : LC Card 86-215255
HJ4719 .H85 1986

(41) Uhlmann, Luitpold. Instrumentelle Aspekte der Investitionsförderung . München , 1986. vii, 270 p. : ISBN 3-88512-024-0 LC Card 86-215244 DDC 332.63 19
HG4028.C4 U367 1986

Ifo-Studien zur Industriewirtschaft .
(16) Baumann, Hans, 1931- Der deutsche Maschinenbau im Wandel der industriellen Output-Struktur . München , 1978. vi, 196 p. : LC Card 84-126586
HD9705.G4 B26 1978

IFPS (COMPUTER SYSTEM)
Gray, Paul, 1930- Guide to IFPS (Interactive Financial Planning System) /. New York , c1987. xii, 497 p. : ISBN 0-07-024394-8 (pbk.) : LC Card 86-21514 DDC 658.1/5/02855329 19
HG4012.5 .G7 1987

IFSTAD studies series .
(no. 1) Quazi, Mohammed Hanif. Food insecurity in the Muslim world /. Jeddah, Saudi Arabia (P.O. Box 9833, Jeddah) , 1985. 21, [26] p. : LC Card 87-133798 DDC 338.1/9/17671 19
HD9018.I84 Q39 1985

Iftitāḥi taqrib. Journalist Workshop on Population and Development Reporting (1981 : Islāmābād, Pakistan) Journalist Workshop on Population and Development Reporting, Oct. 31-Nov. 5, 1981, Islamabad /. [Pakistan , 1982? (Lahore : Directorate of Production and Publication) 63, 12 p. ; LC Card 83-930293 DDC 304.6 19
HB849 .J67 1981

Igazságügyi Minisztérium Tudományos és Tájékoztatási Főosztály kiadványai. Tanulmánykötet, 0236-5057 .
(12) A Föld és a népgazdaság /. [Budapest] , 1985. 514 p. ; ISBN 963-03-2232-3 LC Card 86-228739
HD640.5.Z63 F65 1985

IGCC Secretariat.
IGCC Workshop on Linkages Between University Based Population Activities and National Population/Family Planning Programmes (1978 : Bangkok, Thailand) IGCC Workshop on Linkages Between University Based Population Activities and National Population/Family Planning Programmes . Kuala Lumpur, Selangor [1978?] 111 p. : LC Card 81-941403
HB3641 .I35 1978

Seminar on the Effect of Internal Migration, Urbanization, and Resettlement in the IGCC Region on its Population/Family Planning Programmes (1980 : Jakarta, Indonesia) Seminar on the Effect of Internal Migration, Urbanization, and Resettlement in the IGCC Region on its Population/Family Planning Programmes . Kuala Lumpur, Malaysia [1980?] 131 p. : LC Card 81-941408
HB2101 .S45 1980

IGCC Workshop on Linkages Between University Based Population Activities and National Population/Family Planning Programmes . IGCC Workshop on Linkages Between University Based Population Activities and National Population/Family Planning Programmes (1978 : Bangkok, Thailand) Kuala Lumpur, Selangor [1978?] 111 p. : LC Card 81-941403
HB3641 .I35 1978

IGCC Workshop on Linkages Between University Based Population Activities and National Population/Family Planning Programmes (1978 : Bangkok, Thailand) IGCC Workshop on Linkages Between University Based Population Activities and National Population/Family Planning Programmes : a report on the IGCC Workshop on Linkages Between University Based Population Activities and National Population/Planning Programmes, held in Bangkok, 22-25 March 1978 / prepared by the IGCC Secretariat. Kuala Lumpur, Selangor : The Secretariat, [1978?] 111 p. : ill., map ; 26 cm. Cover title. At head of title: Regional Organization for Inter-governmental Cooperation and Coordination in Population and Family Planning in South East Asia. Includes bibliographies. LC Card 81-941403
1. Asia, Southeastern - Population policy - Congresses. 2. Birth control - Asia, Southeastern - Congresses. 3. Universities and colleges - Asia, Southeastern - Congresses. I. IGCC Secretariat. II. Title. III. Title: I.G.C.C. Workshop on Linkages Between University Based Population Activities and National Population/Family Planning Programmes.
HB3641 .I35 1978

Iger, Svante. Den svenska ekonomins intertnationalisering : drivkrafter och utvecklingsmönster / Svante Iger. Lund : Projektgruppen "Sveriges internationella villkor" ; Stockholm : Sekretariatet för framtidsstudier, [1976] iv, 144 p. : ill. ; 30 cm. (Framtidsstudien Sveriges internationella villkor . rapport nr 206) Bibliography: p. 138-144. ISBN 91-38-03072-1 LC Card 84-226057
1. Sweden - Commerce. 2. Sweden - Foreign economic relations. 3. Sweden - Economic conditions - 1945-. 4. Economic forecasting - Sweden. I. Title. II. Series.
HF3674 .I36 1976

Iglesias, Severo. Sindicalismo y socialismo en México / Severo Iglesias. México, D.F. : Grijalbo, 1985,c1970 194 p. ; 19 cm. (Enlace) Includes bibliographic references. ISBN 968-419-418-8
1. Trade-unions and communism - Mexico. 2. Trade-unions - Mexico - History. I. Title.
NYPL [JLC 86-406]

Iglésies, Josep, 1902- El moviment de població de les comarques de la Catalunya de sobirania francesa en el curs dels segles XIX i XX / per Josep Iglésies. Barcelona : Reial Acadèmia de Ciències i Arts de Barcelona, 1979. 63 p. ; 31 cm. (Memòries de la Reial Acadèmia de Ciències i Arts de Barcelona, 0368-8283 . 3a època, núm. 801 = vol. 44, núm. 16) Summary in French. Pages also numbered 435-495. Includes bibliographical references. LC Card 81-120813
1. Catalonia (Spain) - Population - History. 2. Roussillon (France : Province) - Population - History. 3. Migration, Internal - Spain - Catalonia - History. 4. Migration, Internal - France - Roussillon (Province) - History. I. Series: Memorias de la Real Academia de Ciencias y Artes de Barcelona , 31 época, núm. 801. II. Title.
HB3620.C3 I325 1979

Ignatenko, I. M., 1919-
Bich, M. O. Rabochee dvizhenie v Belorussii v 1861-1904 gg. /. Minsk , 1983. 278 p. ; LC Card 83-182369
HD8529.B952 B52 1983
NYPL [*QM 87-2378]

Kostiuk, Mikhail Pavlovich. Trudovoĭ vklad krest'ianstva v pobedu i uprochnenie sotsializma . Minsk , 1986. 236 p. ; LC Card 86-136452
HD1492.S652 B9252 1986

A igualdade de oportunidades de formação profissional para as mulheres /. Silva, Manuela. Lisboa , 1983. 51, [1] p. : LC Card 84-238349
HD6179 .S56 1983

Iguíñiz, Javier.
Crisis y fluctuaciones en la economía peruana, 1950-1983 : avances de investigación / Javier Iguíñiz E. Jesús María [Peru] : Tarea, [1985]

245 p. : ill. ; 17 cm. (Colección Peruanicemos el Perú) Includes bibliographies. CONTENTS. - Ciclos en la economía peruana y crisis actual -- Razones y falacias de la exportación tradicional -- Fluctuaciones económicas de los EE.UU. y terminos de intercambio en el Perú -- Comerio exterior, conceptos, experiencias y opciones -- Ciclos productivos y región en el Perú, 1971-1981 -- Perú, dinamismo económico y tensiones sociales, 1950-1983. LC Card 86-116792 DDC 338.5/42/0985 19
1. Business cycles - Peru. 2. Peru - Commerce. 3. Peru - Economic conditions - 1918-1968. 4. Peru - Economic conditions - 1968-. I. Title. II. Series.
HB3779 .I35 1985 ***NYPL [JLC 86-268]***

Política económica 1985-1986 : deslindes mirando al futuro / Javier Iguíñiz. Lima : Centro de Estudios y Promoción del Desarrollo, 1986. 153 p. : ill. ; 21 cm. (Cuadernos Desco. 5) Includes bibliographical references. LC Card 87-120200
1. Peru - Economic policy. I. Title.
HC227 .I368 1986

Igumnov, ÎU. S. (ÎUriĭ Stepanovich) Sebestoimost′ i puti ee snizheniîa v promyshlennosti / ÎU. S. Igumnov, K.F. Luchenko. Kiev : Nauk. dumka, 1986. 223 p. ; 21 cm. (Ėkonomika razvitogo sotsializma) On page facing t.p.: Akademiîa nauk Ukrainskoĭ SSR. Institut ėkonomiki promyshlennosti. Bibliography: p. 210-[220]. Includes index. LC Card 87-126676
1. Costs, Industrial - Soviet Union. I. Luchenko, Klavdiîa Fedorovna. II. Title. III. Series.
HC340.C7 I38 1986

IHK-Atlas Industrie-Ansiedlung : Daten und Fakten aus den 12 Kammerbezirken Baden-Würtembergs. Stuttgart : Arbeitsgemeinschaft der Industrie- und Handelskammern in Baden-Würtemberg, [1982?] 145 p. : maps ; 30 cm. Issued by the Arbeitsgemeinschaft der Industrie- und Handelskammern in Baden-Württemberg. Two folded col. maps laid in. LC Card 86-213370
1. Baden-Württemberg (Germany) - Economic conditions. 2. Baden-Württemberg (Germany) - Industries. I. Arbeitsgemeinschaft der Industrie- und Handelskammern in Baden-Württemberg (Germany).
HC287.B23 I38 1982

Ihonvbere, Julius Omozuanvbo. Nigeria and the international capitalist system /. Boulder, Colo. , 1988. v, 154 p. ; ISBN 1-555-87087-2 (alk. paper) : LC Card 87-23183 DDC 337.669 19
HF1616.7 .N54 1988

II censo nacional agropecuario. Resultados provisionales. [La Paz], República de Bolivia : Ministerio de Planeamiento y Coordinación, Instituto Nacional de Estadística, [1986- v. <1-3 > : ill. (some col.) ; 22 cm. Includes bibliographies. CONTENTS. - [1] Pando -- [2] Santa Cruz -- [3] Chuquisaca. LC Card 87-109107
1. Agriculture - Economic aspects - Bolivia - Statistics. 2. Bolivia - Census, 1984. I. Instituto Nacional de Estadística (Bolivia). II. Title: 2o censo nacional agropecuario. III. Title: Segundo censo nacional agropecuario.
HD1867 .A14 1986

IIASA (International Institute for Applied Systems Analysis) International Meeting on Long-Term Fluctuations in Economic Growth (1985 : Weimar, Germany) The long-wave debate : selected papers from an IIASA (International Institute for Applied Systems Analysis) International Meeting on Long-Term Fluctuations in Economic Growth, their causes and consequences, held in Weimar, GDR, June 10-14, 1985 / Tibor Vasko, editor. Berlin ; New York : Springer-Verlag, c1987. xvii, 430 p. : ill. ; 25 cm. Includes bibliographies. Includes index. ISBN 0-387-18164-4 (U. S.) LC Card 87-23256 DDC 338.5/42 19
1. Long waves (Economics) - Congresses. I. Vasko, Tibor, 1931-. II. Title.
HB3729 .I52 1985

IIC monograph series .
(no. 10) Monetary policy . New Delhi , c1986. 70 p. ; LC Card 87-900210 DDC 332.4/954 19
HG1235 .M66 1986

(no. 5) Balakrishnan, C. B. Review of a mid-year review of the economy, 1984 /. New Delhi , 1984. 132 p. ; LC Card 86-903796 DDC 330.954/052 19
HC435.2 .B323 1984

(no. 8) Kabra, Kamal Nayan. Black money . New Delhi , 1985. 47 p. ; LC Card 87-900898 DDC 381 19
HJ2348.5 .K32 1985

Iida, Tsuneo, 1932- What is really unique about the Japanese economy? / by Tsuneo Iida. Nagoya, Japan : Economic Research Center, Faculty of Economics, Nagoya University, 1985. 13 leaves ; 28 cm. (International economic conflict discussion paper . no. 23) LC Card 87-109242 DDC 331.25 19
1. Seniority, Employee - Japan. 2. Job security - Japan. 3. Company unions - Japan. 4. Personnel management - Japan. I. Title. II. Series.
HF5549.5.S4 I35 1985

III. Serie, Estudios (Centro de Investigaciones Económicas (Uruguay)) .
(no. 11) Teja, Ana María. Análisis de la encuesta sobre cambio técnico en la industria del cuero en Uruguay /. Montevideo, Uruguay [1980] 56 p., [60] leaves ; LC Card 86-157655
HD9780.U82 T45 1980

(no. 27) Forteza, Alvaro. Efectos de la política económica en el mercado de leche fluida /. Montevideo, Uruguay [1986] 126 p. : LC Card 87-121158
HD9282.U72 F67 1986

IIVG papers .
(82-207) Dohse, Knuth, 1948- [Ausländerpolitik und betriebeliche Ausländerdiskriminierung. English.] Foreign workers in the Federal Republic of Germany . Berlin [1982] 80 p. : LC Card 86-214190 DDC 331.6/2/0943 19
HD8458.A2 D6213 1982

Ikani, Azizollah. The dynamics of inflation in Iran, 1960-1977 / Azizollah Ikani. Tilburg, Netherlands : Tilburg University Press, 1987. xii, 395 p. ; 24 cm. Bibliography: p. 373-395. ISBN 90-361-9761-9 (pbk.) : LC Card 87-132510 DDC 332.4/1/0955 19
1. Inflation (Finance) - Iran - History. 2. Iran - Economic conditions - 1945-. 3. Iran - Economic policy. I. Title.
HG1220.2 .I36 1987

Ikeda, Hiroaki, 1942- Erekutoronikusu pawā shōjiten /. Tōkyō , 1985. v, 618 p. : ISBN 4-320-08454-3 : LC Card 85-229520
TK7804 .E73 1985 <Orien Japan> ***NYPL [*OSG 86-3267]***

Ikonomicheski institut (Bŭlgarska akademiîa na naukite)
Dŭrzhavno-monopolistichesko regulirane na mezhdunarodnite ikonomicheski otnosheniîa /. Sofiîa , 1986. 273 p. ; LC Card 86-195948
HF1411 .D86 1986

Krŭstīu Dobrev . Sofiîa , 1987. 80 p., [16] p. of plates : LC Card 87-170598
HB108.3.D63 K78 1987

Parichno-kreditni i finansovi otnosheniîa v sistemata na sŭvremenniîa dŭrzhavno-monopolisticheski kapitalizŭm /. Sofiîa , 1985. 245 p. : LC Card 86-153156
HG3881 .P2936 1985

Problemi na stopanskata smetka /. Sofiîa , 1981. 207 p. ; LC Card 82-133037
HC403.Z9 A865 1981

Problemy valîutnogo soîuza stran-chlenov Evropeĭskogo ėkonomicheskogo soobshchestva i razvitie mezhdunarodnoĭ valîutnoĭ sistemy kapitalizma . Sofiîa , 1984. 151 p. ; LC Card 85-224144
HG3942.8 .P76 1984

Upravlenie na narodnoto potreblenie /. Sofiîa , 1984. 235 p. : LC Card 85-212359
HC403.Z9 C628 1984

Ikonomicheski otnosheniîa ikonomicheska politika . Georgiev, Slavcho. Sofiîa , 1986. 114 p. ; LC Card 86-209756
HC403 .G47 1986

Ikonomicheskiiat podkhod i ikonomicheskoto vŭzpitanie na trudeshtite se. Sliven : Bŭlgarska komunisticheska partiîa, Okrŭzhen kom-t--Sliven : Dom za politicheska prosveta, 1984. 195 p. ; 20 cm. Includes bibliographical references. LC Card 86-102634
1. Economics - Study and teaching - Bulgaria. 2. Labor and laboring classes - Education - Bulgaria. I. Bŭlgarska komunisticheska partiîa. Okrŭzhen komitet (Sliven). II. Dom za politicheska prosveta (Sliven, Bulgaria).
HB74.9.B9 I37 1984

Ikonomika i upravlenie na kachestvoto. Svishtov : Vissh finansovo-stopanski in-t "D.A. TSenov"--Svishtov, Otd-nie za povishavane kvalifikatsiîata na kadrite, 1985. 201 p. : ill. ; 21 cm. Includes bibliographical references. LC Card 86-155955
1. Industrial productivity - Bulgaria. 2. Quality of products - Bulgaria. 3. Bulgaria - Economic policy - 1944-. I. Vissh finansovo-stopanski institut "D.A. TSenov"--Svishtov. Otdelenie za povishavane kvalifikatsiîata na kadrite.
HC403.Z9 I5239 1985

Ikonomikata na kapitalizma dnes.
Chonov, Nikola. Inflatsiîata v sŭvremennoto kapitalistichesko obshtestvo /. Sofiîa , 1985. 168 p. ; LC Card 85-243423
HG229 .C534 1985

Ikuta, Yasutoshi. American car graffiti. English. The American automobile . San Francisco , 1988. p. cm. ISBN 0-87701-451-5 (cloth) LC Card 87-25017 DDC 659.1/9629222/0973 19
HF6161.A9 A4413 1988

Il bilancio nell'economia pubblica /. Forte, Francesco, 1929- Milano [1985] 2 v. ; ISBN 88-14-00636-9 : LC Card 86-151358 DDC 350.72/2 19
HJ2005 .F67 1985 ***NYPL [JLE 86-2653]***

Il Consolidamento regionale della finanza locale / Di P. Bondonio ... [et al.]. Milano : F. Angeli, [1980] 332 p. : ill. ; 22 cm. (Programmazione regionale. Sezione 2 . [2]) Includes bibliographical references. ISBN 88-20-41859-2 : LC Card 80-143023
1. Local finance - Italy. 2. Fiscal policy - Italy. 3. Italy - Economic policy. I. Bondonio, Pier Vincenzo, 1942-. II. Series.
HJ9497 .C63 ***NYPL [JLD 87-1397]***

Il Gigante nano : il sistema radiotelevisivo in Italia, dal monopolio al satellite / a cura di Carlo Macchitella ; presentazione di Enzo Cheli. Torino : ERI, c1985. 382 p. : ill. ; 21 cm. On t.p.: 5. Includes index. LC Card 86-128171 DDC 384.54/0945 19
1. Television broadcasting - Italy. 2. Radio broadcasting - Italy. 3. Telecommunication - Italy. I. Macchitella, Carlo.
HE8689.9.I8 G54 1985
NYPL [MWGK (Italy) 86-2853]

Il Leasing e il mercato del credito in Italia / A. Bertoni ... [et al.]. [Milano] : Giuffrè, [1984] iv, 82 p. : ill. ; 25 cm. (Collana di diritto ed economia . 8) ISBN 88-14-00263-0 (pbk.) : LC Card 84-250907
1. Industrial equipment leases - Italy - Finance - Addresses, essays, lectures. 2. Credit - Italy - Addresses, essays, lectures. I. Bertoni, Alberto. II. Series.
HD39.4 .L37 1984 ***NYPL [JLE 87-509]***

Il Mezzogiorno nelle politiche nazionali e comunitarie : contributi della Svimez alla "Giornata del Mezzogiorno" (Bari, 1969-1979) / a cura di Salvatore Cafiero. Milano : Giuffrè, 1982. 379 p. ; 24 cm. (Collana di "Monografie". 47) Includes bibliographical references. LC Card 82-230171 DDC 338.945/7 19
1. European Economic Community - Italy - Addresses, essays, lectures. 2. Industrial promotion - Italy, Southern - Addresses, essays, lectures. 3. Agriculture - Economic aspects - Italy, Southern - Addresses, essays, lectures. 4. Italy, Southern - Economic policy - Addresses, essays, lectures. 5. Italy - Foreign economic relations - European Economic Community countries - Addresses, essays, lectures. 6. European Economic Community countries - Foreign economic relations - Italy - Addresses, essays, lectures. I. Cafiero, Salvatore. II. Associazione per lo sviluppo dell'industria nel Mezzogiorno. III. Series: Collana di "monografie" (Associazione per lo sviluppo dell'industria nel Mezzogiorno) , 47.
HC305 .M42156 1982 ***NYPL [JLE 86-1611]***

Il nuovo amore di coppia /. Tarizzo, Domenico. Milano , 1982. 192 p. ; LC Card 82-141135 DDC 306.7 19
HQ21 .T338 1982 ***NYPL [JLD 87-1019]***

Il Pensiero politico contemporaneo .
(11) Pesante, Maria Luisa. Economia e politica /. Milano, Italy , c1986. 94 p. ; LC Card 86-196256
HB75 .P465 1986

(14) Marucco, Dora. Fabianesimo, ghildismo, forme di democrazia industriale /. Milano, Italy , c1986. 82 p. ; LC Card 86-194327
HD6479 .M37 1986

Il Presente come storia.
Maione, Giuseppe, 1942- Tecnocrati e mercanti . Milano, Italia , c1986. 354 p. ; LC Card 86-194293
HC305 .M274 1986

Il presente è l'avvenire . Hegedüs, Zsuzsa. Milano, Italy , c1985. 126 p. : LC Card 85-215705
HD85.I7 I68 no. 77 HD6955 ***NYPL [JLD 87-427]***

Il Robot italiano : produzione e mercato della robotica industriale / a cura di Roberto Camagni ; contributi di Roberto Camagni ... [et al.].1a ed. Milano : Edizioni del sole 24 ore, 1984. 194 p. : ill. ; 21 cm. (Tecnologia e impresa) Bibliography: p. 181-187. LC Card 86-129858
1. Robot industry - Italy. I. Camagni, Roberto. II. Series.
HD9696.R623 I837 1984 ***NYPL [JLD 87-1277]***

Il sindacato /. Balducci, Cataldo. Torino , c1984. 2 v. ; ISBN 88-02-03818-X (set) : LC Card 85-158972 DDC 344.45/0188 344.504188 19
LAW ***NYPL [JLE 86-3250]***

Il Sindacato in Lombardia. Storia .
(1.2) Granata, Ivano, 1949- Sindacato e crisi della democrazia . Milano, Italy , c1986. 224 p. ; LC Card 87-103965
HD6714.M54 G724 1986

Il sistema distributivo italiano . Fruscio, Dario. [Milano] , 1983. vii, 184 p. ; LC Card 83-233439 DDC 380.1/0945 19
HF5415.6 .F78 1983 ***NYPL [JLE 86-3650]***

Il Territorio immaginario / a cura di Franco Iseppi ; scritti di C. Bodo ... [et al.]. Milano : F. Angeli, [1980] 106 p. ; 22 cm. (I Quaderni di Ikon . 6) Includes bibliographical references. ISBN 88-20-41848-7 : LC Card 81-123209 DDC 302.2/34/0945 19
1. Television - Italy - Addresses, essays, lectures. 2. Mass media - Italy - Addresses, essays, lectures. 3. Culture diffusion - Italy - Addresses, essays, lectures. I. Iseppi, Franco. II. Bodo, C. (Carla). III. Series.
HE8700.9.I8 T47 1980 ***NYPL [JFD 86-8337]***

Ilades. see **Instituto Latinoamericano de Estudios Sociales.**

ILAFA. see **Instituto Latinoamericano del Fierro y el Acero.**

Ilbery, Brian W. The Industrialization of the countryside /. Norwich [Norfolk] , c1985. xiv, 315 p. : ISBN 0-86094-202-3 LC Card 87-141251 DDC 338.9/009173/4 19
HC256.6 .I524 1985

Ilchman, Warren Frederick. New York State in the year 2000 /. Albany, N.Y. , 1988. 572 p. : ISBN 0-88706-602-X LC Card 87-6486 DDC 338.5/443/09747 19
HC107.N7 N447 1988

Ile de la Dominique. Dominique, juin 1985 . [Paris] , c1985. 102 p. : LC Card 86-209026
HC156.5.Z7 D6626 1985

Ile de Saint Vincent. St.-Vincent et les Grenadines, juin 1985 . Paris , 1985] 85 p. : LC Card 86-209310
HC156.5 .S72 1985

Ile de Sainte-Lucie. Sainte-Lucie, juin 1985 . [Paris] , 1985] 120 p. : LC Card 86-209048
HC155.5.Z7 S257 1985

ILE (Series)
Women and recession /. London , New York , 1988. xii, 294 p. ; ISBN 0-7102-0701-8 LC Card 87-20626 DDC 331.4/12 19
HD6053 .W6375 1988

Ilersic, A. R. (Alfred Roman), 1920- Tax avoision . London , 1979. x, 134 p. ; ISBN 0-255-36126-2 (pbk.) LC Card 86-673369
HJ2348.5 .T39x 1979

Ilgen, Thomas L. Trading technology : Europe and Japan in the Middle East / Thomas L. Ilgen and T.J. Pempel. New York : Praeger, 1987. x, 203 p. ; 25 cm. Includes index. Bibliography: p. 191-195. ISBN 0-275-92483-1 (alk. paper) : LC Card 86-21197 DDC 338.94/06 19
1. Technology transfer - Near East. 2. Technology transfer - Europe. 3. Technology transfer - Japan. 4. Near East - Commerce. I. Pempel, T. J., 1942-. II. Title.
HC415.15 .I45 1986 ***NYPL [JLE 87-832]***

Iliffe, John. The African poor : a history / John Iliffe. Cambridge [Cambridgeshire] ; New York : Cambridge University Press, 1987. ix, 387 p. ; 24 cm. (African studies series. 58) Bibliography: p. 356-375. Includes index. ISBN 0-521-34415-8 LC Card 87-14622 DDC 305.5/62/096 19
1. Poor - Africa - History. I. Title. II. Series.
HC800.Z9 P625 1987

Il'in, Vladimir. see **Lenin, Vladimir Il'ich, 1870-1924.**

Ilíùtovich, A. E. Chislennye metody v zadachakh optimal'nogo ėkonomicheskogo planirovaniía /. Moskva , 1983. 158 p. : LC Card 84-128729
HC336.25 .C515 1983

I'll buy that! : 50 small wonders and big deals that revolutionized the lives of consumers : a 50-year retrospective / by the editors of Consumer reports. New York : Consumer Reports Books, c1986. 240 p. : ill. ; 23 x 30 cm. ISBN 0-89043-046-2 LC Card 86-1281 DDC 303.4/83 19
1. New products - History - 20th century. 2. Inventions - History - 20th century. I. Consumer reports.
HF5415.153 .I45 1986 ***NYPL [JLG 87-125]***

Ill fares the land . George, Susan. Washington, D.C. , c1984. xviii, 102 p. ; ISBN 0-89758-039-7 (pbk.) : LC Card 84-25124 DDC 363.8 19
HD9000.5 .G385 1984 ***NYPL [JLD 86-3899]***

Illarionov, Sergeĭ Ivanovich.
Osvobodivshiesía strany : rol' vneshneėkonomicheskikh svíàzeĭ v razvitii / S.I. Illarionov. Moskva : "Mezhdunar. otnosheniía", 1987. 260, [4] p. ; 20 cm. Bibliography: p. 252-[261]. LC Card 87-118170
1. Developing countries - Foreign economic relations. 2. Developing countries - Commerce. 3. Developing countries - Economic conditions. I. Title.
HF1413 .I54 1987

Problema tovarnogo proizvodstva : perekhodnyĭ period / S.I. Illarionov. Moskva : "Ėkonomika", 1984. 109 p. ; 22 cm. Includes bibliographical references. LC Card 85-111933
1. Soviet Union - Commerce - History. 2. Finance - Soviet Union - History. 3. Soviet Union - Economic policy - 1917-1928. I. Title.
HF3626 .I64 1984

Rol' gosudarstva v razvitii ėkonomiki Pakistana : 70-e gody XX v. / S.I. Illarionov. Moskva : Izd-vo "Nauka," Glav. red. vostochnoĭ lit-ry, 1981. 196, [3] p. ; 20 cm. At head of title: Akademiía nauk SSSR. Ordena Trudovogo Krasnogo Znameni Institut vostokovedeniía. Bibliography: p. 190-[197] LC Card 82-112505
1. Pakistan - Economic policy. 2. Pakistan - Economic conditions. 3. Industry and state - Pakistan. I. Title.
HC440.5 .I39 1981

Illés, Iván. Gazdaságunk helye és rangja a világban : a magyar népgazdaság a nemzetközi összehasonlítás tükrében / Illés Iván. Budapest : Közgazdasági és Jogi Könyvkiadó, 1985. 222 p. : ill. ; 19 cm. (Időszerű közgazdasági kérdések, 0324-3214) Bibliography: p. 208-209. ISBN 963-221-523-0 : LC Card 86-156571
1. Hungary - Economic conditions - 1968-. 2. Hungary - Foreign economic relations. I. Title. II. Series.
HC300.28 .I45 1985

Illescas Ortiz, Rafael. Europa hacia el sur (al hilo de la adhesión española a la Comunidad europea) / Rafael Illescas. [Jerez] : Fundación Universitaria de Jerez, [1985], 1986 printing. 152 p. ; 20 cm. (Fundación Universitaria de Jerez . 4) Includes bibliographical references. ISBN 84-600-4184-0 LC Card 86-150722
1. European Economic Community - Spain. I. Series: Fundación Universitaria de Jerez (Series) , 4. II. Title.
HC241.25.S6 I47 1986

Illescas, Rafael. see **Illescas Ortiz, Rafael.**

ILLICIT COINING. see **COUNTERFEITS AND COUNTERFEITING.**

Illing, Gerhard. Geld und asymmetrische Information / Gerhard Illing. Berlin ; New York : Springer-Verlag, 1985. vi, 148 p. : ill. ; 25 cm. (Studies in contemporary economics . 13) Bibliography: p. [143]-148. ISBN 0-387-13999-0 (U.S.) LC Card 85-142939
1. Money - Mathematical models. 2. Money supply - Mathematical models. I. Series. II. Series: Studies in contemporary economics , v. 13. III. Title.
HG220.A2 I55 1985

Illinois : jobs for the future : five-year economic development strategy. [Springfield, Ill. : Illinois Dept. of Commerce and Community Affairs, 1985] 155 p. : ill. ; 27 cm. Cover title. Spine title: Illinois, five-year economic development strategy. LC Card 85-622626 DDC 338.9773 19
1. Employment forecasting - Illinois. 2. Labor supply - Illinois. 3. Illinois - Industries. I. Illinois. Dept. of Commerce and Community Affairs. II. Title: Jobs for the future. III. Title: Illinois, five-year economic development strategy.
HD5725.I3 I517 1985 ***NYPL [JLF 87-787]***

ILLINOIS AND MICHIGAN CANAL (ILL.) - HISTORY.
Clemensen, A. Berle. Illinois and Michigan Canal National Heritage Corridor, Illinois . [Denver, Colo.] [1985] ix, 109 p. : LC Card 85-603278 DDC 386/.48/097732 19
HE396.I4 C56 1985

ILLINOIS AND MICHIGAN CANAL NATIONAL HERITAGE CORRIDOR (ILL.) - ECONOMIC CONDITIONS.
Clemensen, A. Berle. Illinois and Michigan Canal National Heritage Corridor, Illinois . [Denver, Colo.] [1985] ix, 109 p. : LC Card 85-603278 DDC 386/.48/097732 19
HE396.I4 C56 1985

Illinois and Michigan Canal National Heritage Corridor, Illinois . Clemensen, A. Berle. [Denver, Colo.] [1985] ix, 109 p. : LC Card 85-603278 DDC 386/.48/097732 19
HE396.I4 C56 1985

Illinois. Commerce Commission. Independent power production in Illinois / Illinois Commerce Commission. Springfield, Ill. (P.O. Box 4905, Springfield 62708) : The Commission, [1986- v. <1 > : ill. ; 28 cm. "March 1986." "Printed by the authority of the State of Illinois, 200 copies, March 1986, no. 374." Includes bibliographies. CONTENTS. - phase 1. Issues overview. LC Card 86-622355 DDC 338.4/762131/09773 19
1. Electric utilities - Government policy - Illinois. 2. Electric utilities - Government policy - United States. 3. Cogeneration of electric power and heat - Illinois. 4. Cogeneration of electric power and heat - United States. 5. Electric utilities - Law and legislation - Illinois. 6. Electric utilities - Law and legislation - United States. I. Title.
HD9685.U6 I263 1986

Illinois. Dept. of Commerce and Community Affairs.
Assessing Illinois' strengths and weaknesses in a changing national economy /. Chicago, IL [1986] 117 p. : LC Card 87-620507 DDC 330.9773/043 19
HC107.I3 A75 1986

Illinois . [Springfield, Ill. , 1985] 155 p. : LC Card 85-622626 DDC 338.9773 19
HD5725.I3 I517 1985 ***NYPL [JLF 87-787]***

Illinois. Dept. of Transportation. Office of Planning and Programming. Illinois travel statistics, 1985. [Springfield, Ill.] [1986] 19 leaves : LC Card 86-622775 DDC 388.3/142/09773 19
HE371.I3 I47 1986

Illinois. Division of Water Resources. Ports Management Section. Impact of deep-draft user charges on the six western Great Lakes states /. [Chicago, Ill.] (310 S. Michigan Ave., Chicago 60604) [1986] 3 v. : LC Card 87-404522 DDC 387.1 19
HE952.U6 I47 1986

Illinois. Economic and Fiscal Commission. Tax report . Springfield, Ill. (703 Stratton Office Bldg., Springfield 62706) [1986] iv, 30, 3 leaves ; LC Card 86-622596 DDC 336.2/009773 19
HJ2403 .T39 1986

ILLINOIS - ECONOMIC CONDITIONS.
Assessing Illinois' strengths and weaknesses in a changing national economy /. Chicago, IL [1986] 117 p. : LC Card 87-620507 DDC 330.9773/043 19
HC107.I3 A75 1986

ILLINOIS - ECONOMIC CONDITIONS - SOURCES.
Illinois Writers' Project. The annals of labor and industry in Illinois 1890 for January,

February and March; <July, August, September > 1890. Chicago, Ill., 1939-<1941 > v. <1, 3 > LC Card 42-43915 DDC 331/.09773 19
HD8083.I3 I44 1939

Illinois, five-year economic development strategy. Illinois . [Springfield, Ill. , 1985] 155 p. : LC Card 85-622626 DDC 338.9773 19
HD5725.I3 I517 1985 ***NYPL [JLF 87-787]***

Illinois. General Assembly. Economic and Fiscal Commission. see Illinois. Economic and Fiscal Commission.

ILLINOIS - INDUSTRIES.
Assessing Illinois' strengths and weaknesses in a changing national economy /. Chicago, IL [1986] 117 p. : LC Card 87-620507 DDC 330.9773/043 19
HC107.I3 A75 1986

Illinois . [Springfield, Ill. , 1985] 155 p. : LC Card 85-622626 DDC 338.9773 19
HD5725.I3 I517 1985 ***NYPL [JLF 87-787]***

ILLINOIS - INDUSTRIES - HISTORY - SOURCES.
Illinois Writers' Project. The annals of labor and industry in Illinois 1890 for January, February and March; <July, August, September > 1890. Chicago, Ill., 1939-<1941 > v. <1, 3 > LC Card 42-43915 DDC 331/.09773 19
HD8083.I3 I44 1939

Illinois Postal History Society. Redlich, Paul R. The postal history of Coles County, Illinois . Des Plaines, Ill. (P.O. Box 1513, Des Plaines 60018) , c1986. v, 175 p. : LC Card 87-400110 DDC 383/.4977372 19
HE6376.A1 I58 1986

ILLINOIS - SOCIAL CONDITIONS - SOURCES.
Illinois Writers' Project. The annals of labor and industry in Illinois 1890 for January, February and March; <July, August, September > 1890. Chicago, Ill., 1939-<1941 > v. <1, 3 > LC Card 42-43915 DDC 331/.09773 19
HD8083.I3 I44 1939

Illinois. Transportation, Dept. of. see Illinois. Dept. of Transportation.

Illinois travel statistics, 1985. [Springfield, Ill.] : State of Illinois, Dept. of Transportation, Office of Planning and Programming, [1986] 19 leaves : ill. ; 28 cm. "Prepared in cooperation with the U. S. Department of Transportation, Federal Highway Administration." Tables. LC Card 86-622775 DDC 388.3/142/09773 19
1. Traffic surveys - Illinois. I. Illinois. Dept. of Transportation. Office of Planning and Programming. II. United States. Federal Highway Administration.
HE371.I3 I47 1986

Illinois Unemployment and Job Training Research Project. Job training under the new federalism . [Chicago?] , 1986. ii, 299 p. : LC Card 86-203209 DDC 331.25/92/0973 19
HD5715.2 .J63 1986

Illinois Writers' Project. The annals of labor and industry in Illinois 1890 for January, February and March; <July, August, September > 1890 Compiled by the Illinois writers' project of the Work projects administration (Illinois) Chicago, Ill., 1939-<1941 > v. <1, 3 > 28 cm. Reproduced from type-written copy. Items collected from the files of 30 periodicals. LC Card 42-43915 DDC 331/.09773 19
1. Labor and laboring classes - Illinois - History - Sources. 2. Illinois - Industries - History - Sources. 3. Illinois - Economic conditions - Sources. 4. Illinois - Social conditions - Sources. I. Title.
HD8083.I3 I44 1939

Illisz, László. Személyzeti munka, társadalmi környezet / Illisz László, Polgár Tibor, Bernát János. [Budapest] : Kossuth, 1986. 159 p. : ill. ; 20 cm. Bibliography: p. 153-[156]. ISBN 963-09-2778-0 : LC Card 87-408532
1. Personnel management - Hungary. 2. Personnel management. I. Polgár, Tibor, Dr. II. Bernát, János. III. Title.
HF5549.2.H85 I44 1986

Illustrated dictionary of geology . Watt, Alec. Beirut [Harlow, Essex] , 1982. 329 p. :
NYPL [*OG 85-2903]

An illustrated history of Canadian labour, 1800-1974 /. Seymour, Edward E. Ottawa , 1980. xiv, 95 p. :

Illustrated Lotus one-two-three. Mylius, Ralph, 1945- The illustrated Lotus 1-2-3 . Dallas , c1987. vi, 381 p. ; ISBN 0-915381-67-2 (pbk.) LC Card 86-28217 DDC 005.36/9 19
HF5548.4.L67 M95 1987

The illustrated Lotus 1-2-3 . Mylius, Ralph, 1945- Dallas , c1987. vi, 381 p. ; ISBN 0-915381-67-2 (pbk.) LC Card 86-28217 DDC 005.36/9 19
HF5548.4.L67 M95 1987

The illustrated Symphony (release 1.2) book /. Barton, Taylor J. Dallas , c1987. vii, 310 p. : ISBN 0-915381-88-5 (pbk.) LC Card 87-6135 DDC 005.36/9 19
HF5548.4.S95 B385 1987

Illustrations of accounting for pensions and for settlements and curtailments of defined benefit pension plans . Clark, Hal G. New York, N.Y. (1211 Ave. of the Americas, New York 10036-8775) , c1987. 34 p. ; LC Card 87-401762 DDC 657/.75 19
HF5686.O5 C56 1987

Illustrations of "push down" accounting /. Goodman, Hortense. New York, N.Y. (1211 Ave., of the Americas, New York 10036) , c1985. 52 p. ; LC Card 87-100703 DDC 657/.3 19
HF5681.B2 G663 1985

Illustrierte Geschichte der Gemeinwirtschaft . Novy, Klaus. Berlin , c1985. 239 p. : ISBN 3-8012-0111-2 LC Card 86-122604
HD3498 .N68 1985

ILLYRIAN LANGUAGE (SLAVIC) see SERBO-CROATIAN LANGUAGE.

Il'menskiĭ, M. D. Realizat͡sii͡a na ĖVM uchetno-planovykh rabot material'no-tekhnicheskogo snabzhenii͡a /. Moskva , 1983. 63 p. : LC Card 84-210458
HD39.5 .R43 1983

ILO Identification and Programming Mission to the Republic of the Sudan. After the famine : a programme of action to strengthen the survival strategies of affected populations : report of the ILO Identification and Programming Mission to the Republic of the Sudan, September 1985. Geneva : International Labour Office [for] Republic of the Sudan, 1986. xi, 309 p. : ill. ; 24 cm. Includes bibliographical references. ISBN 92-2-105401-2 (pbk.) LC Card 86-226792 DDC 363.8/83/09624 19
1. Famines - Sudan. 2. Rural development - Sudan. 3. Food supply - Sudan. 4. Rural development projects - Sudan. I. Title.
HC835.Z9 F35 1985

The Ilocos and Cordillera provinces . Cleto, Romeo B. Baguio City [Philippines] , Manila [1986] xvii, 265 p. : LC Card 87-111697 DDC 330.9599/1 19
HC457.L8 C56 1986

ILOCOS NORTE (PHILIPPINES) - RURAL CONDITIONS - CASE STUDIES.
Findley, Sally E. Rural development and migration . Boulder , 1987. xxiii, 308 p. : ISBN 0-8133-7326-3 (pbk. : alk. paper) : LC Card 86-33987 DDC 304.8/09599 19
HB2110.I43 F56 1987

The Ilora farm settlement in Nigeria /. Spiro, Heather M. West Hartford, Conn. , 1985. xvii, 50 p. : ISBN 0-931816-20-3 LC Card 85-5230 DDC 331.4/83/089963 19
HD6073.F3 N667 1985
NYPL [JLF 86-1629]

Im Anpassungsprozess zurückgeworfen . Schmidt, Klaus-Dieter. Tübingen , c1984. xx, 243 p. : ISBN 3-16-344755-4 LC Card 84-170512
HC286.7 .S352 1984

Im Blickpunkt der Leistungsvergleich / [Autoren, Gerhard Schilling ... et al. ; Herausgeber], Parteihochschule "Karl Marx" beim ZK der SED. Berlin : Dietz, 1985. 126 p. ; 20 cm. Includes bibliographical references. LC Card 85-155570
1. Germany, East - Economic policy. 2. Socialism - Germany (East). I. Schilling, Gerhard. II. Parteihochschule "Karl Marx" (Berlin, Germany).
HC270.28 .I56 1985

Im Kampf gegen den Hunger . Loewenfeld-Russ, Hans, 1873-1945. München , 1986. xxiv, 381 p., [1] leaf of plates : ISBN 3-486-52451-8 LC Card 86-224948
HC270.F3 L64 1986

I'm not a women's libber, but--and other confessions of a Christian feminist /. Follis, Anne Bowen, 1947- Nashville , c1981. 128 p. ; ISBN 0-687-18687-0 LC Card 81-1241
HQ1426 .F75 ***NYPL [JLD 85-1976]***

Im Prinzip, Hoffnung : Arbeiterbewegung in Vorarlberg, 1870-1946 / Kurt Greussing (Hrsg.). Bregenz : Fink's Verlag, c1984. 368 p. : ill. ; 22 cm. (Beiträge zu Geschichte und Gesellschaft Vorarlbergs . 4) Includes bibliographical references and index. CONTENTS. - Anfänge / Gerhard Oberkofler -- Wachstum und Krise / Reinhard Mittersteiner -- Italiener in Vorarlberg 1870-1914, materielle Not und sozialer Widerstand / Robert Sutterlütti -- Konjunktur der Hoffnung / Werner Dreier -- "Jeatzt würds heall, jeatzt würds liacht" / Reinhard Johler -- Integration und Widerstand / Gernot Egger -- "Deutsches Leben heisst Arbeit" / Meinrad Pichler -- Rohstoff Mensch, Fremdarbeiter und Kriegsgefangene in Vorarlberg / Hermann Brändle, Gernot Egger -- Anspruch und Wirklichkeit, der Nationalsozialismus und die Vorarlberger Arbeiterschaft / Harald Walser -- Schichtwechsel / Kurt Greussing. ISBN 3-900438-07-9 LC Card 86-120542 DDC 331.88/09436/45 19
1. Trade-unions - Austria - Vorarlberg - History. 2. Labor and laboring classes - Austria - Vorarlberg - History. I. Greussing, Kurt. II. Series.
HD6679.V67 I4 1984 ***NYPL [JLD 87-1568]***

Im Spannungsfeld von Wirtschaft, Technik und Politik : Festschrift für Bruno Fritsch / herausgegeben von Rolf Kappel. München : Olzog, c1986. 570 p., [1] leaf of plates : ill. ; 23 cm. German and English. "Schriftenverzeichnis von Bruno Fritsch, 1953-1985": p. [561]-570. Includes bibliographies. ISBN 3-7892-7282-5 LC Card 87-112967
1. International economic relations. 2. Fritsch, Bruno. I. Fritsch, Bruno. II. Kappel, Rolf.
HF1411 .I353 1986

Im Teufelskreis der Verschuldung : der Internationale Währungsfonds und die Dritte Welt / Peter Körner ... [et al.].1. Aufl. Hamburg : Junius, 1984. 261 p. : ill. ; 21 cm. Bibliography: p. 252-261. ISBN 3-88506-126-0 LC Card 85-131681
1. International Monetary Fund. 2. Debts, External - Developing countries. 3. Economic stabilization - Developing countries. I. Körner, Peter.
HG3881.5.I58 I37 1984

Im Wendekreis des Krebsens . Fels, Gerhard. Köln , c1985. 91 p. ; ISBN 3-921349-44-3 LC Card 85-200560
HC286.7 .F46 1985

Imafuku, Aishi, 1941- A Comparative study on accounting policy between Japanese and the U. S. companies /. Tokyo, Japan , c1986. iv, 56 p. : LC Card 87-169003 DDC 657/.0952 19
HF5686.C7 C635 1986

IMAGE PROCESSING EQUIPMENT INDUSTRY.
Image processing in office automation. Norwalk, Conn., U. S.A. (6 Prowitt St., Norwalk 06855) , c1986. vii, 220 leaves ; LC Card 86-228429 DDC 381/.4500642 19
HD9696.I422 I44 1986

IMAGE PROCESSING EQUIPMENT INDUSTRY - UNITED STATES.
Virtual facsimile & PC image capture/transmission/processing. Norwalk, Conn., U. S.A. (6 Prowitt St., Norwalk 06855) , c1986. vii, 208 leaves : LC Card 86-224356 DDC 381/.4500642/0973 19
HD9696.I423 U548 1986

IMAGE PROCESSING EQUIPMENT - UNITED STATES.
The Industrial vision systems market in the U. S. New York, N.Y. , c1983. v, 246 p. : LC Card 87-143523
HD9696.I423 U5445 1983

Image processing in office automation. Norwalk, Conn., U. S.A. (6 Prowitt St., Norwalk 06855) : International Resource Development, c1986. vii, 220 leaves ; 28 cm. (Report / International Resource Development Inc. . #698) "June 1986." LC Card 86-228429 DDC 381/.4500642 19
1. Image processing equipment industry. 2. Office practice - Automation. 3. Market surveys. I. International Resource Development, inc. II. Series:

Report / International Resource Development Inc. , #698.
HD9696.I422 I44 1986

Imagen de la estructura económica-social y explotación de los recursos naturales / Secretaría Técnica del Consejo Superior de Planificación Económica. Tegucigalpa, D.C., Honduras, C.A. : La Secretaría, 1973. viii, 334 p. : ill. ; 28 cm. Cover title. LC Card 86-177356
1. Honduras - Economic conditions - 1918-. 2. Honduras - Commerce. 3. Investments, Foreign - Honduras. 4. Finance, Public - Honduras. 5. Natural resources - Honduras. 6. Honduras - Social conditions. I. Consejo Superior de Planificación Económica (Honduras). Secretaría Técnica.
HC145 .I52 1973

Imagery in scientific thought . Miller, Arthur I. Boston , c1984. xiv, 355 p. : ISBN 0-8176-3196-8 LC Card 83-26649 DDC 502.8 19
Q175 .M628 1984 ***NYPL [JSE 86-1114]***

Imagery in scientific thought . Miller, Arthur I. Cambridge, Mass. , 1986, c1984. xiv, 355 p. : ISBN 0-262-63104-0 (pbk.) : LC Card 85-23212 DDC 502.8 19
Q175 .M628 1986 ***NYPL [JSE 87-67]***

Images économiques des entreprises . Cauwet, Martine. Paris [1986] 41 p. ; ISBN 2-11-064902-X : LC Card 86-229455
HD9502.F72 C38 1986

Images incorporated . Sinclair, John, 1944- London , New York , c1987. 215 p. : ISBN 0-7099-3388-6 LC Card 87-20040 DDC 659.1 19
HF5821 .S58 1987

Images of Culture.
The BBC and public service broadcasting /. Manchester , c1986. viii, 116 p. ; ISBN 0-7190-1964-8 : LC Card 86-209725 DDC 384.54/4/0941 19
HE8689.9.G7 B34 1986

Imber, Jane. Dictionary of advertising and direct mail terms / by Jane Imber and Betsy-Ann Toffler. New York : Barron's, c1987. xi, 514 p. : ill. ; 18 cm. (Barron's business guides) ISBN 0-8120-3765-0 (pbk.) : LC Card 87-1197 DDC 659.1/03/21 19
1. Advertising - Dictionaries. 2. Advertising, Direct-mail - Dictionaries. I. Toffler, Betsy-Ann. II. Title. III. Series.
HF5803 .I46 1987

Imdieke, Leroy F. Financial accounting / Leroy F. Imdieke, Ralph E. Smith. New York : Wiley, c1987. xxii, 770, [44] p. : ill. (some col.) ; 27 cm. Includes index. ISBN 0-471-80829-6 LC Card 86-28158 DDC 657 19
1. Accounting. I. Smith, Ralph Eugene, 1941-. II. Title.
HF5635 .I43 1987

The IMF and stabilisation in sub-Saharan Africa . Green, Reginald Herbold. Brighton, England [1986] ii, 70 p. ; LC Card 86-208478 DDC 332.1/52 19
HC800 .G72 1986

The IMF and third-world political instability . Sidell, Scott R. New York , 1988. p. cm. ISBN 0-312-00755-8 : LC Card 87-9880 DDC 332.1/52 19
HG3881.5.I58 S53 1988

IMF conditionality . Spraos, John. Princeton, N.J. , c1986. 34 p. ; ISBN 0-88165-073-0 (pbk.) : LC Card 86-33805 DDC 332/.042 s 332.1/52 19
HG136 .P7 no. 166 HG3881.5.I58

IMF loan to India . Saxena, R. B. Delhi, India , 1986. ix, 284 p. ; LC Card 86-903311 DDC 332.1/52 19
HG3971 .S29 1986

IMG publication series .
(2) Issues in teaching of economics in Indian universities /. New Delhi , c1987. vii, 145 p. ; ISBN 81-204-0203-0 : LC Card 87-901784 DDC 330/.07/1154 19
HB74.9.I4 I88 1987

Imia tvoe--kollektsioner /. Vigilev, A. N. (Aleksandr Nikolaevich) Moskva , 1981. 93 p. : LC Card 82-103288
HE6213 .V54 1981

Imitation and innovation . Westney, D. Eleanor. Cambridge, Mass. , 1987. viii, 252 p. : ISBN 0-674-44437-X (alk. paper) LC Card 87-273 DDC 338.6/0952 19
HD70.J3 W47 1987

Imitatsionnoe modelirovanie proizvodstvennykh protsessov : sbornik trudov teoreticheskogo seminara / pod redaktsieĭ N.B. Mironosetskogo. Novosibirsk : Akademiia nauk SSSR, Sibirskoe otd-nie, In-t ėkonomiki i organizatsii promyshlennogo proizvodstva, 1979. 152 p. : ill. ; 20 cm. Papers given at the Vsesoiuznyĭ seminar "Imitatsionnye modeli v ASU," held in Novosibirsk from Jan. 30 to Feb. 1, 1979. Includes bibliographies. LC Card 81-132238
1. Industrial management - Soviet Union - Data processing - Congresses. 2. Industrial management - Soviet Union - Mathematical models - Congresses. I. Mironosetskiĭ, Nikolaĭ Borisovich. II. Institut ėkonomiki i organizatsii promyshlennogo proizvodstva (Akademiia nauk SSSR). III. Vsesoiuznyĭ seminar "Imitatsionnye modeli v ASU" (1979 : Novosibirsk, R.S.F.S.R.).
HD70.S63 I44 1979

Imke, Frank J. Neeley, L. Paden. Accounting principles and practices /. Cincinnati , c1987. xx, 1052 p. : ISBN 0-538-01631-0 LC Card 86-63073 DDC 657 19
HF5635 .N38 1987b

Immagini di industria in Italia : il periodo giovanile, 1860-1918 : mostra presentata in occasione del convegno della Confindustria "Risorse per lo sviluppo," Torino, Lingotto, 29-30 novembre, 1985 / testi di Valerio Castronovo e Bruno Bottiglieri ; rivisitazioni fotografiche di Franco Fontana ; [a cura di Luigi Felici e Luigi Paparoni]. Roma : SIPI, c1985. [128] p. : ill., (some col.), facsims. ; 30 cm. LC Card 86-145396
1. Italy - Industries - History - Exhibitions. 2. Italy - Industries - History - Pictorial works. I. Castronovo, Valerio. II. Bottiglieri, Bruno. III. Felici, Luigi. IV. Paparoni, Luigi.
HC305 .I46 1985

Immigrant and native workers . Bailey, Thomas Raymond. Boulder , 1987. xvi, 168 p. : ISBN 0-8133-7349-2 : LC Card 86-28205 DDC 331.6/2/0973 19
HD8081.A5 B35 1987

IMMIGRANT LABOR. see **ALIEN LABOR.**

Immigrant labour and government policy . Edye, Dave, 1953- Aldershot, Hants, England , Brookfield, Vt., U. S.A. , c1987. vi, 157 p. ; ISBN 0-566-05361-6 : LC Card 86-25704 DDC 331.6/2/0943 19
HD8458.A2 E26 1987

Immigrant mortality in England and Wales, 1970-78 . Marmot, M. G. London , 1984. xii, 144 p. : ISBN 0-11-691094-1 (pbk.) : LC Card 84-222968 DDC 614.4/242 19
HB1415 .M37 1984 ***NYPL [JLG 87-55]***

Immigrant workers; their impact on American labor radicalism. Rosenblum, Gerald. New York [1973] vi, 189 p. ISBN 0-465-03207-9 LC Card 72-89280
HD8081.A5 R67 ***NYPL [JLE 73-3033]***

IMMIGRANTS - TOGO.
Dovi-Sodemekou, Folly B. (Folly Bebey) Emploi et éducation dans le 2e plan de développement économique et social du Togo /. Lomé, Togo [1985] 89, 52, 9, 2 p. : LC Card 87-131183
HD5846.5.A6 D68 1985

IMMIGRATION. see **EMIGRATION AND IMMIGRATION.**

Immobilien-Handbuch . Falk, Bernd R. Stuttgart , c1985. xlii, 972 p. : ISBN 3-17-008062-8 LC Card 86-129985
HD656 .F35 1985

Imo State Nigeria.
Anambra State, Nigeria. Government white paper on the Report of the Administrative Board of Inquiry into the Enugu Market Authority /. Enugu , 1976. 25 p. ; LC Card 86-204970
HF5475.N52 E373 1976

Anambra State, Nigeria. Government white paper on the report of the Administrative Board of Inquiry on Ministry of Works /. [Enugu, Nigeria] [1976?] 100 p. ; LC Card 86-205027 DDC 354.669/4 19
HD4365.5.Z8 E373 1976

IMPACT ANALYSIS, ENVIRONMENTAL. see **ENVIRONMENTAL IMPACT ANALYSIS.**

L'Impact de la Septième directive : la consolidation des comptes en Europe / Ernst & Whinney. Paris : Editions techniques professionnelles, c1985. 119 p. : ill. ; 28 cm. Includes appendices. ISBN 2-86658-027-3 : LC Card 86-122475
1. Financial statements, Consolidated - Europe. I. Ernst & Whinney.
HF5681.B2 I5516 1985

Impact économique du Port de Québec. Economic impact of the Port of Québec. [Québec, Québec] [1974] [16], [18] leaves ; LC Card 85-183731 DDC 386/.8/09714471 19
HE554.Q4 E27 1974

L'impact économique et financier de la Caisse de dépôt et placement du Québec /. Raynauld, André. Montréal [1983?] 23 p. ; LC Card 85-164461
HG5160.Q4 C357 1983

IMPACT FEES - UNITED STATES.
Snyder, Thomas (Thomas P.) Paying for growth . Washington, D.C. , 1986. x, 133 p. : ISBN 0-87420-663-4 (pbk.) LC Card 86-51156 DDC 338.4/3363/0973 19
HJ9156 .S69 1986

The impact of agrarian reform on women /. Palmer, Ingrid. West Hartford, Conn. , c1985. xiv, 55 p. ; ISBN 0-931816-21-1 (pbk.) LC Card 85-5250 DDC 331.4/83/091724 19
HD6073.A292 D447 1985
NYPL [JLF 86-1633]

Impact of agricultural exports for Texas /. Paggi, Mechel S. College Station, Tex. [1986] 20 leaves, [1] leaf of plates : LC Card 87-620821 DDC 382/.41/09764 19
HD1775.T4 P34 1986

Impact of agro-based industries on rural economy . Venkaiah, V., 1952- Bombay , 1987. xxi, 348 p. ; LC Card 86-903766 DDC 338.1/0954/84 19
HD9016.I43 A67 1987

Impact of credit on fertiliser consumption /. Gupta, Uttam. New Delhi [1986] 158 p. ; LC Card 87-900336 DDC 338.4/766862/0954 19
HD9483.I42 G86 1986

Impact of deep-draft user charges on the six western Great Lakes states / prepared by Ports Management Section, Division of Water Resources, Illinois Department of Transportation. [Chicago, Ill.] (310 S. Michigan Ave., Chicago 60604) : The Department, [1986] 3 v. : ill. ; 28 cm. Cover title. "January 1986." CONTENTS. - v. 1. Main report -- v. 2. Methodology -- v. 3. Analysis. LC Card 87-404522 DDC 387.1 19
1. Harbors - Lake States - Port charges. 2. Harbors - United States - Port charges. 3. Shipping - Lake States - Rates. 4. Tonnage fees - Lake States. 5. Harbors - Lake States - Statistics. 6. Harbors - United States - Statistics. I. Illinois. Division of Water Resources. Ports Management Section.
HE952.U6 I47 1986

Impact of energy costs on manufacturing employment /. Smith, Edward Joseph, 1911- Washington, D.C. [1985] iv, 16 p. : LC Card 86-603150 DDC 331.12/57/0973 19
HD5724 .S614 1985

The impact of inflation on financial activity in business, with applications to the U. S. farming sector /. Goldschmidt, Yaaqov. Totowa, N.J. , 1986. xvi, 181 p. ; ISBN 0-8476-7427-4 : LC Card 85-14196 DDC 338.1/3/0973 19
HD1761 .G645 1986 ***NYPL [JLE 86-3484]***

Impact of land reforms on rural development . Lamba, S. K. New Delhi, India , 1986 [i.e. 1985] xiv, 148 p. ; ISBN 81-85005-20-6 : LC Card 85-905086 DDC 333.3/1/54 19
HD1333.I4 L35 1986

The impact of male out-migration on women in farming /. Palmer, Ingrid. West Hartford, Conn. , c1985. xviii, 78 p. ; ISBN 0-931816-22-X (pbk.) LC Card 85-5240 DDC 331.4/83/091724 19
HD6073.A292 D4472 1985
NYPL [JLF 86-1626]

The impact of microprocessors on the small accounting practice /. Bhaskar, Krish N. Englewood Cliffs, N.J. , c1986. xvi, 167 p. ; ISBN 0-13-453291-0 (pbk.) LC Card 85-25764

DDC 657/.028/5416 19
HF5679 .B45 1986 ***NYPL [JLE 86-4067]***

The impact of Proposition 13 (the Jarvis-Gann property tax initiative) on local government programs and services /. California. Legislature. Assembly. Committee on Local Government. [Sacramento, CA.] 1978. iv, 367, 108 p. : LC Card 79-621409 DDC 352/.0794
HJ4191 .C34 1978 ***NYPL [JLF 86-1607]***

The impact of science and technology on regional economic development. Committee on Science, Technology, and Regional Economic Development. Washington, 1969. xi, 111 p. LC Card 72-604009 DDC 338.973
HC110.R4 C65 1969b ***NYPL [JLE 87-898]***

The impact of service industries on underemployment in metropolitan economies /. Sheets, Robert G. Lexington, Mass. , c1987. xii, 185 p. ; ISBN 0-669-14575-0 (alk. paper) LC Card 86-45884 DDC 331.13 19
HD5709.2.U6 S54 1987

The impact of the current exchange rate system on trade and inflation of selected developing member countries /. Rana, Pradumna Bickram, 1947- Manila, Philippines , c1983. iv, 78 p. : LC Card 87-105105 DDC 332.4/56 19
HG3877 .R36 1983

The impact of working hours and other factors on production and employment /. Åberg, Yngve. Aldershot, Hants, England , Brookfield, Vt., U. S.A. , c1987. viii, 166 p. : ISBN 0-566-05480-9 : LC Card 87-8393 DDC 331.25/7/09485 19
HD5202 .A64 1987

The Impact of world recession on children / edited by Richard Jolly and Giovanni Andrea Cornia. 1st ed. Oxford [Oxfordshire] ; New York : Pergamon Press, 1984. xiv, 221 p. : ill.; 25 cm. Includes bibliographices. ISBN 0-08-031329-9 : LC Card 84-14694 DDC 362.7/042 19
1. Child welfare - Addresses, essays, lectures. 2. Children - Economic conditions - Addresses, essays, lectures. 3. Economic policy - Addresses, essays, lectures. 4. Depressions - Addresses, essays, lectures. I. Jolly, Richard. II. Cornia, Giovanni Andrea.
HV715 .I475 1984 ***NYPL [JLE 86-2315]***

The Impact of zero base budgeting on managerial behavior / edited by Gerald D. Ramsey. Hempstead, N.Y. : Hofstra University, 1986. vii, 288 p. ; 28 cm. (Hofstra University yearbook of business . ser. 21, v. 1) Includes bibliographies. LC Card 86-80005 DDC 658.1/54 19
1. Zero-base budgeting - Case studies. 2. Budget in business - Case studies. I. Ramsey, Gerald D. II. Series.
HG4028.B8 I55 1986

El impacto de la crisis en los esquemas de integración /. Gerardi, Ricardo E. [Buenos Aires, Argentina] , 1985 [i.e. 1986] iii, 52, [26] leaves : LC Card 87-125394 DDC 337.1/8 19
HC125 .G465 1986

El impacto de la política agrícola común en la integración española /. Fernández Alvarez, Antonio. Madrid [1986?] 48 p. ; ISBN 84-7075-333-9 LC Card 87-111468
HC241.25.S6 F47 1986

Impacto do desarmamento aduaneiro português. Sousa, Fernando Freire de. A adesão de Portugal à CEE . [Porto] [1985] 96 p. ; LC Card 86-174408
HF2236 .S68 1985

O impacto político das migrações internas . Muszynski, Maria Judith de Brito. São Paulo , 1986. 169 p. : LC Card 86-234794
HB2023 .M87 1986

Impacto social del cambio tecnológico actual en los países menos desarrollados. Fuenzalida Faivovich, Edmundo. [América Latina y la concentración del poder en la arena política.] América Latina y la concentración del poder en la arena política ; El impacto social del cambio tecnológico actual en los países menos desarrollados /. [Santiago de Chile] [between 1974 and 1979] 24, 25 leaves ; LC Card 82-180082
HD2810.5 .F84 1974

Impacts of hazardous technology : the psycho-social effects of restarting TMI-1 / John Sorensen ... [et al.]. Albany : State University of New York Press, c1987. x, 233 p. : ill. ; 24 cm. (SUNY series in environmental public policy) Includes index. Bibliography: p. 205-230. ISBN 0-88706-332-2 LC Card 86-1943 DDC 363.1/79 19
1. Metropolitan Edison Company. 2. Three Mile Island Nuclear Power Plant, Pa. 3. Nuclear power plants - Accidents - Economic aspects - Pennsylvania. 4. Nuclear power plants - Accidents - Social aspects - Pennsylvania. I. Sorensen, John H. II. Series.
HD9698.U54 M475 1987
NYPL [JLE 87-1233]

L'Impasse Nord-Sud : quelles issues? : rapport du Groupe de travail Nord-Sud / présidé par Ignacy Sachs et animé par Christian Comeliau dans le cadre des travaux du Groupe long terme "Stratégie internationale de la France" présidé par André Fontaine. Paris : La Documentation française, c1984. 103 p. : ill. ; 24 cm. (Préparation du IXe plan, 1984-1988) At head of title: Commissariat général du plan. "Novembre 1983." Includes bibliographies. ISBN 2-11-001207-2 : LC Card 84-163951
1. Developing countries - Economic conditions. 2. Economic assistance, French - Developing countries. I. Sachs, Ignacy. II. Comeliau, Christian. III. Fontaine, André, 1921-. IV. France. Groupe long terme "Stratégie internationale de la France". Groupe de travail Nord-Sud. V. Series.
HC59 .I44 1984

Imperatorskaia akademiia nauk, Leningrad. see **Akademiia nauk SSSR.**

Imperfect competition and international trade : the policy aspects of intra-industry trade / edited by David Greenaway and P.K.M. Tharakan. Brighton, Sussex : Wheatsheaf Books ; Atlantic Highlands, N.J. : Humanities Press, c1986. xiv, 242 p. : ill. 23 cm. Includes index. Papers originally presented at a conference at the European Institute for Advanced Studies in Management in Brussels in June, 1984. Bibliography: p. 226-236. ISBN 0-391-03403-0 (Humanities Press) LC Card 86-660 DDC 382 19
1. International economic relations - Congresses. 2. Competition, International - Congresses. 3. Competition, Imperfect - Congresses. I. Tharakan, P. K. Mathew.
HF1411 .I354 1986 ***NYPL [JLD 86-2120]***

Imperfectly competitive markets for exhaustible resources . Thimrén, Claes. Stockholm, Sweden [1986] 94 p. : ISBN 91-7258-212-X (pbk.) LC Card 87-151530 DDC 333.7/0724 19
HB238 .T54 1986

IMPERIAL AIRWAYS - HISTORY.
Frater, Alexander, 1937- Beyond the blue horizon . New York , 1987, c1986. xviii, 430 p. : ISBN 0-684-18837-6 LC Card 87-9426 DDC 387.7/065/73 19
HE9787 .F7 1987

IMPERIAL CHEMICAL INDUSTRIES, LTD. - HISTORY.
Kennedy, Carol. ICI . London , 1986. xii, 209 p., [20] p. of plates : ISBN 0-09-167300-3 : LC Card 87-121862 DDC 338.7/66/00941 19
HD9652.9.I5 K46 1986

IMPERIALISM - ADDRESSES, ESSAYS, LECTURES.
Imperialism and transnational corporations /. Quezon City , 1980. vi, 114 p. ;
NYPL [JLD 86-2721]

Imperialism and transnational corporations / edited by Merlin M. Magallona. Quezon City : Published under the auspices of the Philippine Peace Council, 1980. vi, 114 p. ; 22 cm. "Articles ... published ... between 1975 and ... 1980 in New Perspectives, journal of the World Peace Council"--Pref.
1. International business enterprises - Addresses, essays, lectures. 2. Imperialism - Addresses, essays, lectures. I. Magallona, Merlin M. ***NYPL [JLD 86-2721]***

IMPERIALISM - CONGRESSES.
Unterdrückung, Hunger, Krieg . Göttingen [1985?] 73 p. : LC Card 86-152237
HC59.7 .U55 1985

IMPERIALISM - HISTORY - 20TH CENTURY - COLLECTED WORKS.
Lotta, Raymond. America in decline . Chicago , c1984- v. : ISBN 0-916650-12-X (v. 1) : LC Card 83-22294 DDC 330.973/0927 19
HC54 .L63 1984 ***NYPL [JLL 87-106]***

Imperializm kak noveĭshiĭ ėtap kapitalizma. Lenin, Vladimir Il'ich, 1870-1924. [Imperializm kak Vysshaia stadiia kapitalizma. Azerbaijani.] Imperijalizm kapitalizmin ăn jeni devri gibi [microform] /. Baqï , 1927. 99 p. ;
NYPL [*ZO-247 no. 1]

Imperialistische Strategie gegen die neue Internationale Wirtschaftsordnung /. Kannapin, Klaus. Berlin , 1984. 180 p. : LC Card 85-147404
HD84 .K28 1984

Imperializm--sobytiia, fakty, dokumenty ("Iskusstvo" (Firm))
Ostrogorskiĭ, V. M. (Vladimir Mikhaĭlovich) Ostorozhno--"Nemetskaia volna" . Moskva , 1985. 254 p. ; LC Card 85-197423
HE8699.G3 O86 1985

Imperijalizm kapitalizmin ăn jeni devri gibi [microform] /. Lenin, Vladimir Il'ich, 1870-1924. [Imperializm kak Vysshaia stadiia kapitalizma. Azerbaijani.] Baqï , 1927. 99 p. ;
NYPL [*ZO-247 no. 1]

El Imperio Británico en la economía de Venezuela, 1830-1870 /. Vetencourt Guerra, Lola. Caracas , 1981. 233 p. : LC Card 83-201772
HF1530.5.G7 V47 1981

IMPLANT DENTURES.
Growth areas in dentistry . Tustin, CA (17722 Irvine Blvd., Tustin 92680) , c1986. 1 v. (various foliations) : LC Card 86-212546 DDC 381/.45681761 19
HD9995.D42 G76 1986

Implantación en España de un sistema de tarificación por el uso de la infraestructura viaria /. González Blanch, Francisco. Madrid [1984?] 204 p. ; ISBN 84-7196-470-8 : LC Card 85-201965
HJ5956.E86 G66 1984

Implementation for sustainability . Honadle, George. West Hartford, Conn. , c1985. xiv, 128 p. ; ISBN 0-931816-47-5 LC Card 85-12538 DDC 338.9/0068 19
HD1417 .H66 1985 ***NYPL [JLE 86-3888]***

Implementation guidelines for online debit card systems at the point of sale /. American Bankers Association. Retail Payments Task Force. Ad Hoc Committee. [Washington, D.C.] , c1986. 1 v. (various pagings) : LC Card 86-224882 DDC 332.1/028 19
HG1710.5 .A47 1986

Implementation of capital budgeting techniques . Bierman, Harold. Tampa, FL , c1986. i, 69 p. : ISBN 0-936795-01-8 (pbk.) LC Card 86-231118 DDC 658.1/54 19
HG4028.C4 B544 1986

Implementation of the Helsinki accords . United States. Congress. Commission on Security and Cooperation in Europe. Washington , 1986. iii, 85 p. ; LC Card 86-601286 DDC 331.11/732/0947 19
HD4875.S59 U55 1986

Implementation plan for the Growth Centre Programme. Sierra Leone. Industrial Development Dept. Free Town [1985] 2, 57 leaves : LC Card 87-119663 DDC 338.6/42/09664 19
HD2346.S5 S54 1985

Die Implementierung betrieblicher Rationalisierungshandlungen und der personelle Widerstand . Hermann, Ursula. Göttingen , c1984. xx, 356 p. : ISBN 3-525-12558-5 : LC Card 84-218331
HD58.8 .H48 1984

Implementing rural development in Botswana . Fones-Sundell, Melinda. Uppsala , 1983. 75 p. : LC Card 86-215071 DDC 338.1/86811 19
HD2133 .F66 1983

Implicaciones para el sector comercio de la integración de España en el Mercado Común : novena mesa redonda / Ministerio de Comercio y Turismo, Instituto de Reforma de las Estructuras Comerciales (IRESCO). [Madrid] : IRESCO, [1979?] 106 p. ; 21 cm. CONTENTS. - Marco estructural del sector comercio en la Comunidad y en sus países miembros / por Jacques Besnard -- El problema de la armonización legislativa en relación con la competencia en el proceso de integración comunitaria / por Paul Schmitt -- Algunos aspectos de la armonización del derecho mercantil / por John Devine -- La comercialización de productos agrarios en el Mercado Común / por Rosa Ma. Marenco -- Las estructuras de distribución en Alemania y la

organización institucional del comercio / por Heinrich Gewadt -- Los principales desequilibrios en el sector distribución italiano, ante el proceso de integración / por Silvano Ferrareto -- Las políticas gubernamentales de distribución en el Mercado Común, con especial referencia a la experiencia francesa / por Serge Lacrampe -- La problemática comercial de las empresas exportadoras españolas en la distribución intracomunitaria de sus productos / por Antonio Pont Amenós, Rafael Cerezo Enríquez y Joaquín Sáez Merino. LC Card 81-116650
1. European Economic Community - Spain. 2. Spain - Commerce. I. Instituto de Reforma de las Estructuras Comerciales (Spain).
HC241.25.S6 I48 1979

Implications of population trends for U. S. foreign policy in Central America : briefing before the Committee on Foreign Affairs, U. S. House of Representatives. Washington : U. S. G.P.O., 1984. iii, 16 p. : ill. ; 24 cm. At head of title: 98th Congress, 2d session. Committee print. Distributed to some depository libraries in microfiche. "September 19, 1984." Includes bibliographical references. Item 1017-A, 1017-B (microfiche) LC Card 86-602534 DDC 304.6/09728 19
1. Central America - Population. 2. United States - Foreign relations - Central America. 3. Central America - Foreign relations - United States. I. United States. Congress. House. Committee on Foreign Affairs.
HB3533 .I55 1984

IMPORT AND EXPORT CONTROLS. see **FOREIGN TRADE REGULATION.**

IMPORT CONTROLS. see **IMPORT QUOTAS.**

Import controls and export-oriented development . Luedde-Neurath, Richard. Boulder , 1986. xiv, 249 p. ; ISBN 0-8133-7080-9 : LC Card 85-10459 DDC 382/.3/095195 19
HF1602.5 .L84 1985 ***NYPL [JLE 86-1557]***

Import/export business. Weiss, Kenneth D. (Kenneth Duane), 1940- Building an import/export business /. New York , c1987. vii, 264 p. : ISBN 0-471-84259-1 : LC Card 86-26560 DDC 658.8 19
HF1008 .W43 1987

Import insights : a comprehensive review of the imported beer market in the United States / associate editor, Benj Steinman ; associate editor, Eric Shepard. West Nyack, NY (51 Virginia Ave., West Nyack 10994) : Beer Marketer's Insights, c1986 48 p. : ill. ; 28 cm. LC Card 86-210235 DDC 382/.4566342/0973 19
1. Brewing industry - United States - Statistics. 2. Brewing industry - Statistics. I. Steinman, Benj. II. Shepard, Eric.
HD9397.U52 I47 1986

IMPORT LICENSES. see **IMPORT QUOTAS.**

IMPORT QUOTAS.
Diumulen, I. I. (Ippolit Ippolitovich) Sovremennyĭ tarifnyĭ i netarifnyĭ protektsionizm . Moskva , 1975. 277 p. ; LC Card 82-191746
HF1713 .D62 1975

Foreign regulations affecting U. S. textile/apparel exports. [Washington, D.C.] [1986] 283 p. ; LC Card 86-601588
HF2651.T42 F67 1986

Ohlinger, Hans A., 1954- Die Relevanz nicht-tarifärer Handelshemmnisse im internationalen Handel und ihre Wirkungen auf die Integration der Entwicklungsländer in die Weltwirtschaft /. Frankfurt am Main , New York , c1986. iii, 400 p. : ISBN 3-8204-8344-6 LC Card 87-407585 DDC 382/.5/091724 19
HF1430 .O38 1986

IMPORT QUOTAS - EUROPEAN ECONOMIC COMMUNITY COUNTRIES.
Howell, Thomas R., 1949- The EEC and the third Multifiber Arrangement . Washington, DC , 1986. [14], 126, [12] p. : LC Card 86-224652 DDC 382/.45677/0094 19
HD9865.E852 H68 1986

IMPORT QUOTAS - JAPAN.
Japanese import barriers to U. S. agricultural exports and the Common agricultural policy of the European Community and implications for U. S. agricultural trade . Washington , 1986. vii, 65 p. : LC Card 87-601384 DDC 382/.5/0952 19
HF1601 .J363 1986

IMPORT QUOTAS - KOREA (REPUBLIC)
Luedde-Neurath, Richard. Import controls and export-oriented development . Boulder , 1986. xiv, 249 p. ; ISBN 0-8133-7080-9 : LC Card 85-10459 DDC 382/.3/095195 19
HF1602.5 .L84 1985 ***NYPL [JLE 86-1557]***

IMPORT QUOTAS - MATHEMATICAL MODELS.
Stockhausen, Gerard Lawrence. Threats of quotas in international trade, their effect on the exporting country /. New York , 1988. 170 p. : ISBN 0-313-25785-X (lib. bdg. : alk. paper) LC Card 87-23682 DDC 382/.64 19
HF1430 .S86 1988

IMPORT QUOTAS - UNITED STATES.
Auction quotas and United States trade policy /. Washington, DC , c1987. xiii, 241 p. : ISBN 0-88132-050-1 (pbk.) LC Card 87-12948 DDC 382/.52/0973 19
HF1455 .A83 1987

IMPORT RESTRICTIONS. see **IMPORT QUOTAS.**

Import substitution and economic efficiency . Leela, Pillalamarri. Bombay , 1984. xvi, 129 p. ; LC Card 84-900166 DDC 382/.45668624/0954 19
HD94484.N6 I544 1984
NYPL [JLD 86-3888]

IMPORT SUBSTITUTION - BRAZIL - ECONOMETRIC MODELS.
Werneck, Rogério L. Furquim. Desequilíbrio externo e reorientação do crescimento e dos investimentos . Rio de Janeiro-RJ [1983?] 130 p. ; LC Card 87-403024 DDC 338.981 19
HC187 .W47 1983

IMPORT SUBSTITUTION - CHILE - HISTORY - 20TH CENTURY.
Pitts, Mary Anne, 1927- Economic development in Chile under two growth strategies, 1925-1968 /. New York , 1987. vii, 246 p. ; ISBN 0-8240-1368-9 (alk. paper) : LC Card 87-7618 DDC 338.983 19
HC192 .P627 1987

IMPORT SUBSTITUTION - INDIA.
Leela, Pillalamarri. Import substitution and economic efficiency . Bombay , 1984. xvi, 129 p. ; LC Card 84-900166 DDC 382/.45668624/0954 19
HD94484.N6 I544 1984
NYPL [JLD 86-3888]

IMPORT SUBSTITUTION - PHILIPPINES.
Snow, Robert T. The bourgeois opposition to export-oriented industrialization in the Philippines /. Diliman, Quezon City, Philippines [1983] 45 p. ; LC Card 85-196519 DDC 382/.3/09599 19
HC453 .S66 1983

L'importance des marchés de l'Europe de l'Est . Kállay, Georges Christophe de. Genève , 1986. 247 p. ; LC Card 86-179357
HF3408.Z7 E8525 1986

Importancia y significado de la encíclica sobre el trabajo humano del papa Juan Pablo II para el movimiento obrero latinoamericano /. Máspero, Emilio. [Caracas, Venezuela] [1984] 159 p. : LC Card 87-404543 DDC 261.8/5 19
HD6338 .M425 1984

Importing into the United States : formerly Exporting to the United States. Washington, D.C. : Dept. of the Treasury, U. S. Customs Service : For sale by Supt. of Docs., U. S. G.P.O., [1985] 84 p. : ill. ; 28 cm. "August 1985"--Cover. LC Card 85-603032 DDC 343.73/087 347.30387 19
1. United States - Commerce - Handbooks, manuals, etc. 2. United States - Commercial policy - Handbooks, manuals, etc. I. United States. Customs Service. II. Exporting to the United States.
HF3035 .I46 1985

Importing into the United States. Rocklin, Calif. : Prima Pub. and Communications, c1987. 83 p. : maps ; 28 cm. Cover title: The official U. S. Customs Service Guide to importing into the United States. Reprint. Originally published: Washington, D.C. : Dept. of the Treasury, U. S. Customs Service, 1985. ISBN 0-914629-35-2 (pbk.) : LC Card 87-16931 DDC 343.73/087 347.30387 19
1. United States - Commerce - Handbooks, manuals, etc. 2. United States - Commercial policy - Handbooks, manuals, etc. I. United States. Customs Service. II. Title: Official U. S. Customs Service Guide to importing into the United States.
HF3055 .I46 1987

IMPORTS.
Blades, Derek W. Discrepancies between imports and exports in OECD foreign trade statistics /. Paris, France , c1984. i, 42 p. ; LC Card 86-205155 DDC 382/.021 19
HF1016 .B569 1984

IMPORTS CONTROLS. see **TARIFF.**

IMPORTS - GOVERNMENT POLICY - MALI.
Massow, Valentin von, 1925- Dairy imports and import policy in Mali and their implications for the dairy sector in the Bamako area /. Addis Ababa, Ethiopia [1985] v leaves, 57 p., [12] leaves ; LC Card 86-981009 DDC 382/.417/096623 19
HD9275.M423 B366 1985

L'imposta diretta a Firenze nel Quattrocento (1427-1494) /. Conti, Elio. Roma , 1984. 406 p. ; LC Card 86-171245
HJ9500.F562 C65 1984

Impôt minimum au Canada. Wilson, Michael H. (Michael Holcombe), 1937- A minimum tax for Canada . [Ottawa] [1985] iii, 15, 15, iii p. ; LC Card 86-202601 DDC 336.24/2 19
HJ4661 .W55 1985

Impôt minimum au Canada. Wilson, Michael H. (Michael Holcombe), 1937- A minimum tax for Canada /. [Ottawa] [1985] vi, 52, 56, vi p. ; LC Card 86-202606 DDC 336.24/2 19
HJ4661 .W54 1985

L'Imprenditore coltivatore nella società che cambia : [atti del convegno e della tavola rotonda promossi dalla Confederazione italiana coltivatori, svolti in Roma il 20-21 dicembre 1982 / relazione al convegno è di Giuseppe Avolio ; gli interventi alla tavola rotonda sono di A. Balzani ... et al.]. [Italy] : Monteverde, [1983] (Roma : Arti grafiche Jasillo) 364 p. : ill. ; 19 cm. At head of title: Confederazione italiana coltivatori. LC Card 86-185731
1. Agriculture and state - Italy - Congresses. 2. Produce trade - Government policy - Italy - Congresses. 3. Farms, Small - Government policy - Italy - Congresses. 4. Farmers - Italy - Political activity - Congresses. 5. Confcoltivatori - Congresses. I. Avolio, Giuseppe. II. Balzani, A. (Alberto). III. Confcoltivatori.
HD1972 .I44 1983

L'impresa artigiana tra economia e territorio . Favaretto, Ilario, 1945- Milano, Italy , c1986. 212 p. : LC Card 86-193238
HD2346.I82 P464 1986

Improved program delivery. Environmental quality strategic review . [Ottawa, Canada , c1986. 170 p. ; ISBN 0-660-12148-4 (pbk.) : LC Card 86-217056 DDC 363.7/00971 19
HC120.E5 E59 1986

Improving apparel shop profits . Cash, R. Patrick. [New York, N.Y.] [c1986] 285 p. : ISBN 0-87102-131-5 LC Card 86-61313 DDC 687/.068/8 19
HD9940.A2 C37 1986

Improving domestic resource mobilization through financial development : [a study / by the Economics Office, Asian Development Bank]. Manila, Philippines : The Bank, c1985. vii, 51 p. : ill. ; 25 cm. Includes bibliographies. LC Card 87-101640 DDC 332.6/72/091724 19
1. Saving and investment - Asia. 2. Finance - Asia. I. Asian Development Bank. Economics Office.
HC415.S3 I45 1985

Improving marketing performance /. Parsons, W. J. (Will J.) Aldershot, Hants, England , Brookfield, Vt., USA , c1987. xiii, 164 p. : ISBN 0-566-02595-7 : LC Card 86-25681 DDC 658.8 19
HF5415 .P2496 1987

Improving productivity in U. S. marine container terminals / Committee on Productivity of Marine Terminals, Marine Board, Commission on Engineering and Technical Systems, National Research Council. Washington, D.C. : National Academy Press, 1986. xiv, 205 p. : ill. ; 23 cm. Includes summary report of the committee and reports and papers from the National Meeting on Productivity of U. S. Marine Terminals held Jan. 8-10, 1986, in Long Beach, Calif. ISBN 0-309-03694-1 (pbk.) LC Card 86-62194 DDC 388.5/44/068 19

1. Marine terminals - United States - Capital productivity. 2. Marine terminals - United States - Labor productivity. I. National Research Council (U. S.). Committee on Productivity of Marine Terminals. II. National Meeting on Productivity of U. S. Marine Terminals (1986 : Long Beach, Calif.).
HE553 .I45 1986

Improving public enterprise performance . Powell, Victor. Geneva , 1987. x, 226 p. : ISBN 92-2-105563-9 (pbk.) : LC Card 87-166309 DDC 350/.0092/091724 19
HD4420.8 .P68 1987

Improving urban employment and labor productivity /. Kahnert, Friedrich, 1929- Washington, D.C. [1987] 75 p. ; ISBN 0-8213-0908-0 (pbk.) LC Card 87-10538 DDC 331.11/09172/4 19
HD5852 .K34 1987

Impuesto personal a la renta . Schwarz Kalijman, Luis M. Montevideo, Uruguay , 1985. 63 p. ; LC Card 85-243408
HJ4629 .S39 1985

Impuesto sobre la renta . Esparza Cervera, José Ramón. Valencia [1982?] 1 v. (various pagings) ; ISBN 84-85672-11-9 LC Card 83-134521
HJ4744 .E86 1982

In-house computer trends for community banks /. Gillis, M. Arthur. New Orleans, LA (833 Howard Ave., Suite 501, New Orleans 70113) , 1987. 40, 18, [16] leaves : LC Card 87-147932 DDC 332.1/028/5 19
HG1709 .G525 1987

In-house t-e-l-e marketing . McCafferty, Thomas. Chicago, Ill. , c1987. x, 337 p. : ISBN 0-917253-51-5 (pbk.) LC Card 86-63991 DDC 658.8/5 19
HF5415.1265 .M34 1987

In-house telemarketing. McCafferty, Thomas. In-house t-e-l-e marketing . Chicago, Ill. , c1987. x, 337 p. : ISBN 0-917253-51-5 (pbk.) LC Card 86-63991 DDC 658.8/5 19
HF5415.1265 .M34 1987

In our time . Burgmann, Verity. Sydney , Boston , 1985. xii, 236 p., [24] p. of plates : ISBN 0-86861-529-3 LC Card 84-71572 DDC 335/.00994 19
HD8846 .B87 1985 ***NYPL [JLD 86-2788]***

In pursuit of Lakshmi . Rudolph, Lloyd I. Chicago , 1987. xvii, 529 p. ; ISBN 0-226-73138-3 : LC Card 86-24903 DDC 338.954 19
HC435 .R77 1987

In quest of El Dorado . Finney, Kenneth V. New York , 1987. xii, 454 p. ; ISBN 0-8240-1359-X (alk. paper) : LC Card 87-8342 DDC 338.2/742/097283 19
HD9536.H82 F56 1987

In quest of human dynamism : a report of APO basic research on management systems and practices and their influence on productivity at the firm level / organized under the guidance of the chief expert, Shin-ichi Takezawa. Tokyo, Japan : Asian Productivity Organization, 1986. viii, 552 p. : ill. ; 22 cm. (APO basic research) ISBN 92-833-1088-2 LC Card 86-210648 DDC 658.3/0095 19
1. Personnel management - Asia - Case studies. I. Takezawa, Shin'ichi, 1925-.
HF5549.2.A75 Q84 1986

In retrospect : 25 years of the People's Bank / edited by Susantha Goonatilake. Colombo : The Bank, 1986. 149 p. ; 27 cm. Includes bibliographies. LC Card 86-903248 DDC 334/.2/095493
1. People's Bank (Sri Lanka). 2. Banks and banking, Cooperative - Sri Lanka. I. Goonatilake, Susantha. II. People's Bank (Sri Lanka). III. Title: 25 years of the People's Bank.
HG2039.S65 I5 1986

In search for equity . Buscando la equidad. English. Aldershot, Hants, England , Brookfield, USA , c1987. xvi, 249 p. ; ISBN 0-566-05537-6 : LC Card 87-21225 DDC 338.98 19
HC130.B38 B8713 1987

In search of an East Asian development model / edited by Peter L. Berger and Hsin-Huang Michael Hsiao. New Brunswick, N.J., USA : Transaction Books, c1988. xi, 243 p. ; 23 cm. Papers originally presented at a conference sponsored by the Carnegie Council on Ethics and International Affairs held in New York in June 1985. Includes bibliographies and index. CONTENTS. -- An East Asian development model? / Peter L. Berger -- An East Asian development model / Hsin-Huang Michael Hsiao -- The new Asian capitalism / Gustav Pananek -- The new Asian capitalism / Lucian W. Pye -- The role of the entrepreneur in the new Asian capitalism / S.G. Redding -- The role of Christianity / Jan Swyngedouw -- The applicability of Asian family values to other sociocultural settings / Siu-lun Wong -- The distinctive features of Japanese development / Iwao Munakata -- The distinctive features of Taiwan's development / Rong-I Wu -- The distinctive features of South Korea's development / Kyong-Dong Kim -- The distinctive features of two city-states' development / Pan Eng Fong. ISBN 0-88738-686-5 (pbk.) LC Card 87-19061 DDC 338.95 19
1. East Asia - Economic policy - Congresses. 2. East Asia - Social life and customs - Congresses. I. Berger, Peter L. II. Hsiao, Hsin-huang. III. Carnegie Council on Ethics & International Affairs.
HC460.5 .I5 1988

In search of profitability -- agent's business plan / prepared by the Bottom Line Task Force of the Million Dollar Round Table. Des Plaines, Ill.] : Million Dollar Round Table, c1986. 124 p. : ill. ; 28 cm. "June, 1986." Bibliography: p. 114-116. LC Card 87-167903 DDC 368/.0068 19
1. Insurance, Life - Agents. 2. Insurance companies - Management. 3. Business enterprises. I. Million Dollar Round Table (Des Plaines, Ill.). Bottom Line Task Force.
HG8877 .I49 1986

In service to America /. Schwartz, Marvin, 1948- Fayetteville, AR , 1988. p. cm. ISBN 1-557-28005-3 LC Card 87-19440 DDC 361.6/09767 19
HC110.P63 S34 1988

In the shadows of Wall Street . Strebel, Paul. Englewood Cliffs, N.J. , c1988. xii, 228 p. : ISBN 0-13-455999-1 LC Card 87-42680 DDC 332.63/22 19
HG4921 .S84 1988

INAN (Institute : Brazil) Avaliação global do programa de nutrição Brasil-BIRD . [São Paulo, SP] [Brasília] , 1981- v. <1 > : LC Card 87-123819 DDC 363.8/56/0981 19
HD9014.B82 A82 1981

Incao, Maria da Conceição d'. A questão do bóia-fria / Maria Conceição d'Incao. São Paulo-Brasil : Brasiliense, 1984. 93 p. : ill. ; 16 cm. (Qualé . 7) Spine title: Bóia-fria. Bibliography: p. 93. LC Card 85-187274
1. Migrant labor - Brazil. I. Title. II. Title: Bóia-fria.
HD5856.B6 I53 1984

Incentive and development programs for Canadian industry. Ottawa, Canada : Dept. of Industry, Trade and Commerce : Information Canada, 1973, c1975. 14, 14 p. ; 28 cm. Title on added t.p.: Programmes d'encouragement et d'expansion à l'intention de l'industrie canadienne. English and French. "Cat. no.: C2-4273"--T.p. verso. LC Card 85-158119
1. Industrial promotion - Canada. I. Canada. Dept. of Industry, Trade and Commerce. II. Title: Programmes d'encouragement et d'expansion à l'intention de l'industrie canadienne.
HC120.I53 I48 1975

Incentive-based incomes policies : advances in TIP and MAP / edited by David C. Colander. Cambridge, Mass. : Ballinger Pub. Co., c1986. xxi, 263 p. : ill. ; 24 cm. Based on the proceedings of a Middlebury Conference on Economic Affairs held in 1984. Includes index. Bibliography: p. 245-255. ISBN 0-88730-082-0 LC Card 85-20090 DDC 331.2/9 19
1. Wage-price policy - Addresses, essays, lectures. 2. Economic policy - Addresses, essays, lectures. 3. Wage-price policy - United States - Addresses, essays, lectures. 4. Inflation (Finance) - Addresses, essays, lectures. I. Colander, David C. II. Middlebury Conference on Economic Affairs (1984).
HC79.W24 I465 1986 ***NYPL [JLE 86-3724]***

An incentives approach to improving the unemployment compensation system /. Burgess, Paul L. Kalamazoo, Mich. , 1987. xv, 273 p. : ISBN 0-88099-048-1 (pbk.) LC Card 87-23128 DDC 368.4/4/00973 19
HD7096.U5 B87 1987

Incentives, cooperation, and risk sharing : economic and psychological perspectives on employment contracts / edited with an introductory essay by Haig R. Nalbantian. Totowa, N.J. : Rowman & Littlefield, 1987. xvi, 239 p. : ill. ; 24 cm. Distillation of the proceedings of a conference held at New York University, March 1984, and sponsored by the C.V. Starr Center for Applied Economics. Includes bibliographies and index. ISBN 0-8476-7464-9 LC Card 87-4558 DDC 658.3/22 19
1. Compensation management - Congresses. 2. Wage payment systems - Congresses. I. Nalbantian, Haig R. II. C.V. Starr Center for Applied Economics (New York University).
HF5549.5.C67 I56 1987

INCENTIVES IN INDUSTRY - ADDRESSES, ESSAYS, LECTURES.
Herzberg, Frederick. The managerial choice . Salt Lake City, Utah , c1982. xviii, 360 p. : ISBN 0-913420-97-2 LC Card 81-85925 DDC 658.3/14 19
HF5549.5.I5 H47 1982 ***NYPL [JLE 86-2591]***

INCENTIVES IN INDUSTRY - CONGRESSES.
Economic incentives . London , 1986. xiii, 497 p. ; ISBN 0-333-40473-4 ***NYPL [JLD 87-367]***

INCENTIVES IN INDUSTRY - GERMANY, EAST.
Rogge, Werner. Die Arbeit mit dem Prämienfonds /. Berlin , c1984. 70 p. ; LC Card 86-100311 DDC 331.2/164 19
HD4928.B62 G357 1984

INCENTIVES IN INDUSTRY - HUNGARY.
Tanulmányok az anyagi érdekeltség, jövedelemszabályozás témaköréből /. [Budapest] , 1985. 126 p. : ISBN 963-673-308-2 LC Card 86-147619
HD5022.5 .T37 1985

INCENTIVES IN INDUSTRY - SOVIET UNION.
Artemov, IU. M. (IUriĭ Mikhaĭlovich) Finansovye metody material'nogo stimulirovaniia proizvodstva /. Moskva , 1983. 126 p. ; LC Card 84-118738
HF5549.5.I5 A69 1983

Ėkonomicheskoe stimulirovanie truda v usloviiakh sotsializma . Moskva , 1986. 179 p. ; LC Card 87-166364
HD5046 .E47 1986

Material'noe stimulirovanie v khoziaistvennom mekhanizme sotsialisticheskogo obshchestva . Leningrad , 1986. 152 p. ; LC Card 86-175029
HF5549.5.I5 M3385 1986

Obobshchestvlenie i ėkonomicheskie interesy v sotsialisticheskom obshchestve /. Moskva , 1983. 127 p. ; LC Card 84-204638
HD3856.R9 O26 1983

Zhelezovskaia, N. M. Stimuly k trudu na sovremennom ėtape razvitiia sotsialisticheskogo obshchestva /. Moskva , 1985. 160 p. ; LC Card 86-174895
HF5549.5.I5 Z48 1985

INCENTIVES IN INDUSTRY - SOVIET UNION, NORTHERN.
Khlystova, E. A. (Evgeniia Andreevna) Sever i Sibir' zovut molodykh /. Moskva , 1985. 109 p. : LC Card 86-153085
HF5549.5.I5 K452 1985

INCENTIVES IN INDUSTRY - UNITED STATES.
Butler, Stephen A. Management incentive compensation plans /. Montvale, N.J. , c1986. v, 55 p. ; ISBN 0-86641-140-2 (pbk.) LC Card 86-230062 DDC 658.4/07225 19
HD4965.5.U6 B86 1986

The Productivity sourcebook /. Amherst, Mass. [1987] x, 467 p. : ISBN 0-87425-075-7 (pbk.) LC Card 87-404037 DDC 658.3/14 19
HD57 .P7114 1987

Incentivos fiscais e financeiros para investimentos no Nordeste do Brasil / Ministério do Interior, Superintendência do Desenvolvimento do Nordeste [e] Banco do Nordeste do Brasil. 4a. ed., rev. e atualizada. Recife : SUDENE : BNB, 1985. 92 p. ; 21 x 22 cm. LC Card 87-404837 DDC 332.6/7322813 19
1. Tax incentives - Brazil, Northeast. 2. Industrial promotion - Brazil Northeast. 3. Investments - Brazil, Northeast. I. Brazil. Superintendência do Desenvolvimento do Nordeste. II. Banco do Nordeste

do Brasil.
HJ2529.N6 I53 1985

Inchiesta Jacini . Italy. Parlamento. Giunta per la inchiesta agraria e sulle condizioni della classe agricola. Sala Bolognese , 1978-<1987. v. <1-7, 9-10; v. 13, t. 1, fasc. 1-3; v. 11, t. 1-3; v. 13, t. 2, fasc. 4-5; in 18 > : LC Card 86-143133
HD1970 .I84 1978

INCI publication .
(nr. 28) Rey Salgado, Rafael del. La crisis de la deuda en América Latina /. [Spain] [1985] ii, 88 p. ; LC Card 86-131407
HJ8514.5 .R49 1985

INCIDENCE OF TAXATION. see **TAX INCIDENCE.**

Incidents and cases in Canadian personnel administration /. Crocker, Olga L. Toronto , New York , c1986. 216 p. : ISBN 0-458-98690-9 (pbk.) : LC Card 86-218837 DDC 658.3/00971 19
HF5549.2.C3 C76 1986

INCLOSURES - GREAT BRITAIN - HISTORY.
Turner, Michael Edward. Enclosures in Britain, 1750-1830 /. London , 1984. 96 p. : ISBN 0-333-31682-7 (pbk.) LC Card 86-673799
HD594.6 .T84x 1984

INCLOSURES - SUDAN.
Behnke, Roy H., 1947- Open-range management and property rights in pastoral Africa . London [1985] 29 p. : LC Card 86-209817 DDC 333.2 19
HD977.Z63 B44 1985

INCOME ACCOUNTING.
Baillie, John. Systems of profit measurement /. New York , 1985. viii, 112 p. ; ISBN 0-85258-234-X (pbk.) LC Card 84-21578 DDC 657/.48 19
HF5681.I48 B34 1985

Income and cost for origination and servicing of 1 to 4 unit residential loans, 1985. Washington, D.C. (1125 15th St., N.W., Washington 20005-2766) : Mortgage Bankers Association of America, c1986. 32 p. ; 28 cm. (Operations report . no. 8) Cover title. Chiefly tables. LC Card 87-106156 DDC 332.3/2/0973021 19
1. Mortgage loans - United States - Statistics. 2. Mortgage banks - United States - Statistics. I. Mortgage Bankers Association of America. II. Series: Operations report (Mortgage Bankers Association of America) , no. 8.
HG2040.5.U5 I535 1986

Income and expenditure patterns of urban Black multiple households in Durban, 1985 /. Van Wyk, H. de J. Pretoria , 1986. xi, 130 p. : ISBN 0-908408-59-5 (pbk.) LC Card 87-151639 DDC 658.8/3968 s 339.4/1/0968455021 19
HC517.S7 S48 no. 130, pt. 4 HD7064.4.Z8D8

Income and expenditure patterns of urban black multiple households in Pretoria, 1985 /. Martins, J. H. Pretoria , 1986. xi, 128 p. : ISBN 0-908408-57-9 (pbk.) LC Card 86-220725 DDC 658.8/3968 s 339.4/1/0968235 19
HC517.S7 S48 no. 130, pt. 2 HD7064.4.Z8P74

Income and expenditure patterns of urban Indian households in Pietermaritzburg, 1985 /. Martins, J. H. Pretoria , 1986. xi, 126 p. : ISBN 0-908408-60-9 (pbk.) LC Card 87-140863 DDC 658.8/3968 s 339.4/1/0968475 19
HC517.S7 S48 no. 130, pt. 5 HD7064.4.Z8P54

Income and expenditure patterns of urban Indian multiple households in Durban, 1985 /. Martins, J. H. Pretoria , 1986. xi, 126 p. : ISBN 0-908408-54-4 (pbk.) LC Card 86-208481 DDC 658.8/3968 s 339.4/1/09684 19
HC517.S7 S48 no. 130, pt. 1 HD7064.4.Z8D8

Income and poverty in New Jersey [microform] . Crowley, Charles. Trenton, N.J. [1982] 32 p. ; LC Card 83-620831 DDC 339.2/2/09749 19
HC107.N53 I5113 1982
NYPL [*ZT-1712 no.31]

Income and poverty status report for regional planning districts. Census '80 . Baltimore, Md. (2225 N. Charles St., Baltimore 21218) [1983] xv, 106 leaves : LC Card 83-622347 DDC 339.2/2/097526 19
HC108.B2 C46 1983 ***NYPL [JLF 86-1594]***

INCOME - AUSTRALIA - STATISTICS.
Moore, Jim. Trends in the disposable incomes of Australian families, 1964-65 to 1985-86 /. Woden, ACT [1986] vii, 103 p. ; ISBN 0-642-51700-2 (pbk.) LC Card 87-154435 DDC 339.394 19
HC610.I5 M66 1986

INCOME - BRAZIL - ARAPIRACA REGION.
Estudo especial . Maceió, AL. , 1983. 174 leaves : LC Card 86-167829
HC189.A69 E88 1983

INCOME - CANADA - STATISTICS.
Rashid, A. Characteristics of high income families, 1980 /. Ottawa [1986] 97 p. : ISBN 0-660-52875-4 (pbk.) : LC Card 86-210700
HC120.I5 R36 1986

INCOME - DEVELOPING COUNTRIES.
Low income countries . New Delhi , 1987. x, 106 p. ; ISBN 81-7027-101-0 : LC Card 87-900104 DDC 330.9172/4 19
HF1413 .L68 1987

INCOME DISTRIBUTION - ADDRESSES, ESSAYS, LECTURES.
Macroeconomic conflict and social institutions /. Cambridge, Mass. , c1985. xi, 249 p. : ISBN 0-88730-034-0 LC Card 84-24376 DDC 339.2 19
HC79.I5 M225 1985 ***NYPL [JLE 86-2562]***

INCOME DISTRIBUTION - AFRICA.
Nafziger, E. Wayne. Inequality in Africa . Cambridge [Cambridgeshire] , New York , c1988. p. cm. ISBN 0-521-26881-8 LC Card 87-24263 DDC 339.2/096 19
HC800.Z9 I5136 1988

INCOME DISTRIBUTION - AMERICA.
Mauro, Frédéric. [Des origines de l'inégalité entre les peuples d'Amérique. Portuguese.] Origens da desigualdade entre os povos da América /. São Paulo, SP , 1986. 113 p. : LC Card 87-120229 DDC 339.2/097 19
HC94.Z9 I56317 1986

Income distribution and economic security in Canada / François Vaillancourt, research coordinator. Toronto ; Buffalo : University of Toronto Press, c1985. xv, 321 p. : ill. ; 23 cm. (The Collected research studies, 0829-2396 . vol. 1) Includes bibliographies. CONTENTS. - Income distribution and economic security in Canada / François Vaillancourt -- The underground economy / Mireille Éthier -- The incidence of government expenditures and taxes in Canada / B.G. Dahlby -- Income security in Canada / Bernard Fortin -- Unemployment insurance and labour market adjustments / Jean-Michel Cousineau -- Survey of pension issue / Mireille Éthier -- Health care costs in Canada / Gilles Grenier -- Comprehensive income security for Canadian workers / Jonathan R. Kesselman. ISBN 0-8020-7241-0 (pbk.) LC Card 85-227851 DDC 330.971/064 19
1. Income distribution - Canada - Addresses, essays, lectures. 2. Economic security - Canada - Addresses, essays, lectures. I. Vaillancourt, François. II. Series: Collected research studies , v. 1.
HC120.I5 I53 1985 ***NYPL [JLE 86-1881]***

Income distribution and the macroeconomy /. Nolan, Brian. Cambridge [Cambridgeshire] , New York , 1987. xii, 208 p. : ISBN 0-521-32612-5 LC Card 87-6606 DDC 339.2/0941 19
HC260.I5 N65 1987

Income distribution and the structure of production /. Ghosh, A., 1921- New Delhi , c1984. ix, 186 p. ; LC Card 83-907762 DDC 339.2/0724 19
HB523 .G46 1984 ***NYPL [JLD 86-4234]***

INCOME DISTRIBUTION - ARGENTINA - CASE STUDIES.
Diéguez, Héctor L. Mercados de trabajo y distribución de ingresos en cuatro centros urbanos de Argentina, 1974-1981 /. Buenos Aires, Argentina , 1984. 49 p. ; ISBN 950-621-013-6 LC Card 87-401771 DDC 331.12/982 19
HD5749 .D54 1984

Toledo, Nora Elena. El tamaño de las ciudades y la distribución de los ingresos (Argentina y Colombia) /. San Juan, Argentina , 1985. 63 p. : LC Card 87-400258 DDC 339.2/2/09861 19
HC200.I5 T65 1985

INCOME DISTRIBUTION - AUSTRIA.
Clement, Werner. Einkommensverteilung und Qualifikation . Wien , 1984. vi, 201 p. : ISBN 3-85436-020-7 LC Card 84-191161
HC270.I5 C56 1984

Norden, Gilbert. Einkommensgerechtigkeit, was darunter verstanden wird . Wien , 1985. 304 p. : ISBN 3-205-06324-4 LC Card 86-196913
HB523 .N67 1985

INCOME DISTRIBUTION - BRAZIL.
Singer, Paul Israel, 1932- Dominação e desigualdade . Rio de Janeiro, RJ , 1981. 185 p. ; LC Card 82-148154
HC190.I5 S55 1981 ***NYPL [JLD 86-3364]***

Singer, Paul Israel, 1932- Repartição da renda . Rio de Janeiro , 1986. 95 p. ; ISBN 85-85061-40-5 : LC Card 86-157852
HC190.I5 S56 1986

INCOME DISTRIBUTION - BRAZIL - HISTORY - 20TH CENTURY - SOURCES.
Antecedentes estadísticos de la distribución del ingreso. Santiago de Chile , 1986. 50 p. ; LC Card 87-115965 DDC 339.2/0981 19
HC190.I5 A57 1986

INCOME DISTRIBUTION - CANADA - ADDRESSES, ESSAYS, LECTURES.
Income distribution and economic security in Canada /. Toronto , Buffalo , c1985. xv, 321 p. : ISBN 0-8020-7241-0 (pbk.) LC Card 85-227851 DDC 330.971/064 19
HC120.I5 I53 1985 ***NYPL [JLE 86-1881]***

INCOME DISTRIBUTION - CANADA - CONGRESSES.
International comparisons of the distribution of household wealth /. Oxford , New York , 1987. xii, 283 p. : ISBN 0-19-828511-6 : LC Card 86-31241 DDC 339.2/2/094 19
HC240.9.I5 I56 1987

INCOME DISTRIBUTION - CANADA - STATISTICS.
Rashid, A. Characteristics of high income families, 1980 /. Ottawa [1986] 97 p. : ISBN 0-660-52875-4 (pbk.) : LC Card 86-210700
HC120.I5 R36 1986

INCOME DISTRIBUTION - CARIBBEAN AREA.
Calderón González, Arnoldo. América Latina y el Caribe . México, D.F. , 1985. 51, [25] leaves ; LC Card 87-121714 DDC 332.4/98 19
HG660.5 .C35 1985

INCOME DISTRIBUTION - CENTRAL AMERICA.
Mayorga Quirós, Román. El crecimiento desigual en Centroamérica (1950-2000) /. México, D.F. , 1983. 125 p. : ISBN 968-12-0238-4 LC Card 85-242511
HC141 .M39 1983

INCOME DISTRIBUTION - CHILE - SANTIAGO METROPOLITAN AREA.
Aldunate B., Adolfo. Análisis tipológico del trabajador del Gran Santiago e impacto sobre el ingreso de las políticas redistributivas, 1970-1971 /. [Santiago, Chile?] [1972] iv, 9, [35] p. ; LC Card 83-169296
HC193.S23 A43 1972

INCOME DISTRIBUTION - COLOMBIA.
Leibovich, José. Comercio exterior y distribución de ingresos . Bogotá, Colombia , 1984. vii, 221 p. : LC Card 87-402975 DDC 382/.41373/09861 19
HD9199.C62 L45 1984

INCOME DISTRIBUTION - COLOMBIA - CASE STUDIES.
Toledo, Nora Elena. El tamaño de las ciudades y la distribución de los ingresos (Argentina y Colombia) /. San Juan, Argentina , 1985. 63 p. : LC Card 87-400258 DDC 339.2/2/09861 19
HC200.I5 T65 1985

INCOME DISTRIBUTION - COLOMBIA - HISTORY - STATISTICS.
Antecedentes estadísticos de la distribución del ingreso. Santiago de Chile , 1986. 49 p. ; LC Card 87-115916 DDC 339.2/09861 19
HC200.I5 A58 1986

INCOME DISTRIBUTION - COMMUNIST COUNTRIES.
Glas, Miroslav, 1950- Delitev po delu v socialistični družbi /. Ljubljana , 1986. 631 p. : LC Card 87-147216
HC407.Z9 I51473 1986

INCOME DISTRIBUTION - CONNECTICUT.
Groff, William H. Income variability in Connecticut, 1980 /. Storrs, CT [1987] 32 p. :

LC Card 87-621355 DDC 339.2/2/09746 19
HC107.C83 I5138 1987

INCOME DISTRIBUTION - COSTA RICA.
Trejos S., Juan Diego. Las políticas de distribución y redistribución del ingreso en Costa Rica en la década de los años setenta /. Ciudad Universitaria Rodrigo Facio , 1983. 117 p. ; LC Card 85-242016
HC143.Z9 I527 1983

INCOME DISTRIBUTION - DENMARK - PUBLIC OPINION.
Henriksen, Ingrid. Holdninger til den økonomiske fordeling =. København , 1985. 349 p. : ISBN 87-7487-265-6 : LC Card 85-186400
HC360.I5 S25 1985 vol. 1 ***NYPL [JLD 86-2002]***

INCOME DISTRIBUTION - DEVELOPING COUNTRIES.
Capitalism and equality in the Third World /. Lanham [New York] , c1987. 375 p. ; ISBN 0-8191-5574-8 (v. 2 : alk. paper) : LC Card 86-24749 DDC 330.12/2 19
HB501 .C24234 1987

Hermann, Christian, 1954- Auswirkungen industrieller Exportproduktion im Rahmen der internationalen Arbeitsteilung auf die Einkommensverteilung von Entwicklungsländern /. Frankfurt am Main , New York , c1984. viii, 393 p. ; ISBN 3-8204-7456-0 LC Card 85-191626
HF4055 .H47 1984

Midgley, James. Social security, inequality, and the Third world /. Chichester, [Sussex] , New York , c1984. x, 225 p. ; ISBN 0-471-90061-3 LC Card 84-5188 DDC 368.4/009172/4 19
HD7252 .M52 1984 ***NYPL [JLE 86-2165]***

INCOME DISTRIBUTION - DOMINICAN REPUBLIC.
Mercados financieros y distribución del ingreso /. Santo Domingo, República Dominicana , 1986. 117 p. : LC Card 87-405027 DDC 332.1/097293 19
HG185.D65 M47 1986

INCOME DISTRIBUTION - ECONOMETRIC MODELS.
Coloma C., Fernando. Los efectos de una desgravación arancelaria en el contexto de una economía con movilidad imperfecta de trabajo /. Santiago , 1985. 46 leaves : LC Card 85-203579
HF1713 .C618 1985

Funke, Michael, 1956- Wachstumszyklen und funktionale Einkommensverteilung /. München , c1985. iii, 244 p. : ISBN 3-88259-319-9 LC Card 85-175617
HB3711 .F896 1985

INCOME DISTRIBUTION - EUROPE - CONGRESSES.
International comparisons of the distribution of household wealth /. Oxford , New York , 1987. xii, 283 p. : ISBN 0-19-828511-6 : LC Card 86-31241 DDC 339.2/2/094 19
HC240.9.I5 I56 1987

INCOME DISTRIBUTION - FRANCE - EFFECT OF INFLATION ON.
Susini, Jean-Jacques. A qui profite l'inflation? /. Paris , c1985. 122 p. : ISBN 2-13-039288-1 LC Card 86-153761
HG979.5 .S87 1985

INCOME DISTRIBUTION - FRANCE - HISTORY.
Harouel, Jean Louis. Essai sur l'inégalité /. Paris , c1984. 287, [1] p. ; ISBN 2-13-038354-8 : LC Card 84-150958
HC280.I5 H35 1984

INCOME DISTRIBUTION - GERMANY, WEST.
Aussagefähigkeit von Einkommensverteilungsrechnungen für die Bundesrepublik Deutschland . Tübingen , 1986. xxiv, 436 p. : ISBN 3-88573-027-8 LC Card 87-407588 DDC 339.2/0943 19
HC290.5.I5 A93 1986

Flaig, Jürgen. Verteilungsschwankungen im Konjunkturverlauf . Freiburg im Breisgau , c1983. vi, 221 p. : ISBN 3-448-01325-0 LC Card 83-155341
HC290.5.I5 F55 1983

Intrasektorale Einkommensstreuung in der Landwirtschaft /. Münster-Hiltrup , 1983. 177 p. : ISBN 3-7843-0281-5 : LC Card 83-236007
HD1955 .I57 1983

Krause, Detlef. Einkommensquellen und Lebenschancen . Berlin , c1986. 189 p. : ISBN 3-428-06114-4 LC Card 87-130932 DDC 339.2/2/0943 19
HC290.5.I5 K7 1986

Scheer, Christian. Verteilungswirkungen der Einkommensteuer /. Göttingen , c1982. xii, 457 p. : ISBN 3-509-01260-7 : LC Card 83-150522
HJ4719 .S34 1982

Witzke, Harald von. Personelle Einkommensverteilung in der Landwirtschaft und Agrarpreise /. Berlin , 1979. 180 p. : ISBN 3-428-04303-0 LC Card 79-389988
HC290.5.I5 W57 ***NYPL [JLE 80-439]***

Zeppernick, Ralf. Transfer-Einkommen und Einkommensverteilung /. Berlin , c1986. viii, 233, [1] p. : ISBN 3-428-05990-5 LC Card 86-178831
HC290.5.I5 Z47 1986

INCOME DISTRIBUTION - GERMANY (WEST) - ECONOMETRIC MODELS.
Aussagefähigkeit von Einkommensverteilungsrechnungen für die Bundesrepublik Deutschland . Tübingen , 1986. xxiv, 436 p. : ISBN 3-88573-027-8 LC Card 87-407588 DDC 339.2/0943 19
HC290.5.I5 A93 1986

INCOME DISTRIBUTION - GERMANY (WEST) - LONGITUDINAL STUDIES.
Göbel, Dieter, 1949- Lebenseinkommen und Erwerbsbiographie . Frankfurt/Main , New York , c1983. xix, 364 p. : ISBN 3-593-33244-2 LC Card 84-132204
HC290.5.I5 G63 1983

INCOME DISTRIBUTION - GERMANY, WEST - MATHEMATICAL MODELS.
Helberger, Christof. Beitragsäquivalenz oder interpersonelle Umverteilung in der gesetzlichen Rentenversicherung? . Berlin , 1981. 96 p. ; LC Card 81-201422 DDC 331.25/2/0943 19
HD7105.35.G3 H44 1981 ***NYPL [JLM 81-818 v.63]***

Steden, Werner. Finanzpolitik und Einkommensverteilung . Frankfurt am Main ; Bern ; 378 p. ; ISBN 3-261-01763-5 LC Card 80-459125
HJ1120 .S74 ***NYPL [JLD 80-3205]***

INCOME DISTRIBUTION - GOVERNMENT POLICY.
Ringen, Stein. The possibility of politics . Oxford [Oxfordshire] : Oxford [Oxfordshire] ; x, 303 p. ; ISBN 0-19-828574-4 :$42.00 (U. S.) LC Card 86-28472 DDC 361.6/5 19
HB846.8 .R56 1987

INCOME DISTRIBUTION - GOVERNMENT POLICY - AUSTRALIA.
Kakwani, Nanak. Analyzing redistribution policies . Cambridge [Cambridgeshire] , New York , 1986. ix, 293 p. : ISBN 0-521-30838-0 LC Card 85-31342 DDC 339.5/2 19
HC610.I5 K35 1986 ***NYPL [JLE 86-3491]***

INCOME DISTRIBUTION - GOVERNMENT POLICY - PERU.
Empleo, salarios y distribución del ingreso . [Miraflores, Lima] , 1986. 186 p. : LC Card 87-403082 DDC 331.11/0985 19
HD5761.A6 E47 1986

INCOME DISTRIBUTION - GOVERNMENT POLICY - STATES - CASE STUDIES.
Kohli, Atul. The state and poverty in India . Cambridge [Cambridgeshire] , New York , 1987. x, 262 p. : ISBN 0-521-32008-9 LC Card 85-25554 DDC 333.3/1/54 19
HD1333.I4 K65 1986 ***NYPL [JLD 87-1517]***

INCOME DISTRIBUTION - GREAT BRITAIN.
Nolan, Brian. Income distribution and the macroeconomy /. Cambridge [Cambridgeshire] , New York , 1987. xii, 208 p. : ISBN 0-521-32612-5 LC Card 87-6606 DDC 339.2/0941 19
HC260.I5 N65 1987

INCOME DISTRIBUTION - GREAT BRITAIN - HISTORY.
Williamson, Jeffrey G., 1935- Did British capitalism breed inequality? /. Boston , 1985. ix, 270 p. : ISBN 0-04-942186-7 : LC Card 84-20413 DDC 339.2/2/0941 19
HC260.I5 W45 1985 ***NYPL [JLE 86-1361]***

INCOME DISTRIBUTION - HUNGARY.
Falusné Szikra, Katalin. Az első és a második gazdaság közötti bér-, illetve jövedelem-diszparitás /. Budapest , c1986. 31 p. ; ISBN 963-05-4343-5 : LC Card 87-407713
HC300.295.I5 F35 1986

INCOME DISTRIBUTION - HUNGARY - STATISTICS.
Harcsa, István. Vándorlás, mobilitás, keresetalakulás . Budapest , 1987. 86 p. ; ISBN 963-340-812-1 : LC Card 87-409641
HB2052.5.A3 H37 1987

A Lakosság jövedelmi rétegződése 1982-ben . Budapest , 1984. 50 p. ; LC Card 86-195316
HC300.295.I5 L36 1984

INCOME DISTRIBUTION - INDIA.
De Janvry, Alain. Agricultural price policy and income distribution in India /. Delhi , New York , 1986. xi, 113 p. ; ISBN 0-19-561952-8 : LC Card 86-900015 DDC 338.1/3/0954 19
HD9016.I42 D38 1986

Mehta, Vadilal Lallubhai, 1903- Unemployment, inequality, parallel economy . Ahmedabad , 1982. viii, 141 p., [1] leaf of plates : LC Card 82-900764 DDC 331.13/7954 19
HD5819 .M43 1982 ***NYPL [JLD 85-2751]***

Sundrum, R. M. Growth and income distribution in India . New Delhi , Beverly Hills , 1986. p. cm. ISBN 0-8039-9522-9 (U. S.) LC Card 86-26323 DDC 330.954/04 19
HC435.2 .S883 1986

INCOME DISTRIBUTION - INDIA - HARYANA.
Westley, John Richard, 1942- Agriculture and equitable growth . Boulder , 1986. xv, 369 p. : ISBN 0-8133-7155-4 (alk. paper) : LC Card 85-31586 DDC 338.1/85455 19
HD2075.P8 W47 1986 ***NYPL [JLE 86-1877]***

INCOME DISTRIBUTION - INDIA - KARNATAKA.
Thimmaiah, G. Inequality and poverty . Bombay , 1983. xiv, 106 p. ; LC Card 83-903408 DDC 339.4/6/095487 19
HC437.K27 T47 1983 ***NYPL [JLD 86-3792]***

INCOME DISTRIBUTION - INDIA - PUNJAB.
Inder Pal Singh, 1959- Rural income distribution . Delhi , New Delhi, India , 1986. xvi, 123 p. : ISBN 81-7018-299-9 : LC Card 86-900514 DDC 339.2/3/0954552 19
HC440.I5 I46 1986 ***NYPL [JLD 86-3077]***

Westley, John Richard, 1942- Agriculture and equitable growth . Boulder , 1986. xv, 369 p. : ISBN 0-8133-7155-4 (alk. paper) : LC Card 85-31586 DDC 338.1/85455 19
HD2075.P8 W47 1986 ***NYPL [JLE 86-1877]***

INCOME DISTRIBUTION - INDIA - TIRUCHCHIRĀPPALLI (DISTRICT) - MATHEMATICAL MODELS.
Stanislaus, M. Sebastian. New farm technology and income distribution /. New Delhi , c1984. viii, 76 p. : LC Card 84-902272 DDC 338.1/3/095482 19
HD2075.T57 S73 1984 ***NYPL [JLD 87-669]***

INCOME DISTRIBUTION - INDONESIA - JAWA TENGAH.
Hart, Gillian Patricia. Power, labor, and livelihood . Berkeley , c1986. xvi, 228 p. : ISBN 0-520-05499-7 (alk. paper) LC Card 85-8435 DDC 330.9598/2 19
HD1537.I56 H37 1986 ***NYPL [JLE 86-3039]***

INCOME DISTRIBUTION - ITALY.
Antonelli, Gilberto. Risorse umane e redditi da lavoro . Milano , c1985. 256 p. : LC Card 85-191554
HC310.I5 A66 1985

Targetti Lenti, Renata. Struttura produttiva e distribuzione personale del reddito . Milano [1984] 263 p. : ISBN 88-14-00277-0 : LC Card 84-251227 DDC 339.2/2/0945 19
HC310.I5 T346 1984 ***NYPL [JLF 86-1305]***

INCOME DISTRIBUTION - ITALY, SOUTHERN.
Boccella, Nicola Maria, 1952- Il Mezzogiorno sussidiato . Milano, Italy , c1982. 264 p. : LC Card 85-163271
HD7185.S68 B62 1982

INCOME DISTRIBUTION - KENYA.
Collier, Paul. Labour and poverty in Kenya, 1900-1980 /. Oxford , New York , 1986. xi, 296 p. : ISBN 0-19-828505-1 : LC Card 86-1352 DDC 331.12/09676/2 19
HD5840.5.A6 C65 1986
NYPL [JLE 86-3282]

INCOME DISTRIBUTION - LATIN AMERICA.
Calderón González, Arnoldo. América Latina y el Caribe . México, D.F. , 1985. 51, [25] leaves ; LC Card 87-121714 DDC 332.4/98 19
HG660.5 .C35 1985

Foxley, Alejandro. Las desigualdades económicas y la acción del estado . México , 1980. 271 p. ; ISBN 968-16-0365-6 LC Card 82-215955 DDC 339.2/098 19
HC130.I5 F69 1980 ***NYPL [JLD 86-2631]***

Poverty in Latin America . Washington, D.C., U. S.A. [1986] 25 p. ; ISBN 0-8213-0836-X (pbk.) LC Card 86-225244 DDC 330.98/0038 19
HC130.I5 P68 1986

INCOME DISTRIBUTION - LONGITUDINAL STUDIES.
Meier, Christoph. Lebenszyklus und ökonomische Ungleichheit . Freiburg, Schweiz , 1983. 235 p. : ISBN 3-7278-0298-7 : LC Card 83-244050
HB601 .M389 1983

INCOME DISTRIBUTION - MALAYSIA.
Mehmet, Ozay. Development in Malaysia . London , Dover, N.H. , c1986. 183 p. ; ISBN 0-7099-3525-0 : LC Card 85-29079 DDC 338.9595 19
HC445.5.Z9 I51834 1986
NYPL [JLD 86-2389]

INCOME DISTRIBUTION - MATHEMATICAL MODELS.
Ghosh, A., 1921- Income distribution and the structure of production /. New Delhi , c1984. ix, 186 p. ; LC Card 83-907762 DDC 339.2/0724 19
HB523 .G46 1984 ***NYPL [JLD 86-4234]***

Pohmer, Karlheinz. Mikroökonomische Theorie der personellen Einkommens- und Vermögensverteilung . Berlin , New York , c1985. ix, 214 p. : ISBN 0-387-15174-5 (U. S.) LC Card 85-164096
HB523 .P64 1985

INCOME DISTRIBUTION - NEPAL.
Employment, income distribution, and consumption patterns in Nepal . Kathmandu, Nepal , 1983. xiv, 122 p. ; LC Card 84-901199 DDC 330.9549/6 19
HD5812.9.A6 E47 1983
NYPL [JLF 86-1993]

INCOME DISTRIBUTION - NETHERLANDS.
Hoek, M. P. van der. De praktijk van de inkomensverdeling /. Groningen , c1987. 183 p. : ISBN 90-01-39430-2 : LC Card 87-157808
HC329.5.I5 H634 1987

Odink, J. G. Inkomensherverdeling . Groningen , c1985. 254 p. : ISBN 90-01-66101-7 : LC Card 86-149572
HC329.5.I5 O35 1985

INCOME DISTRIBUTION - NETHERLANDS - PUBLIC OPINION.
Szirmai, Adam, 1946- Inequality observed . Aldershot, Hants, England , Brookfield, Vt., USA , c1988. p. cm. ISBN 0-566-05549-X : LC Card 87-23071 DDC 339.2/09492 19
HC329.5.I5 S96 1988

INCOME DISTRIBUTION - NORWAY.
Skånland, Hermod, 1925- Inntektspolitikkens dilemma . [Oslo] , 1981 ([Oslo] : Joh. Nordahls trykkeri) 114 p., [1] leaf : ISBN 82-02-04872-9 (pbk.) : LC Card 81-199141
HC370.I5 S49 1981 ***NYPL [JLD 86-2672]***

INCOME DISTRIBUTION - PAKISTAN.
Employment, distribution, and basic needs in Pakistan . Lahore , 1986. xxxiv, 408 p., [1] leaf of plates : LC Card 86-930280 DDC 330.9549/1 19
HD5820.5.A6 E47 1986

INCOME DISTRIBUTION - PORTUGAL.
Ribeiro, Maria Eduarda. Aspectos analíticos da distribuição da massa salarial no período de 1972 a 1983 /. Lisboa , 1985. 58 p. : LC Card 86-132683
HC394.5.I5 R52 1985

INCOME DISTRIBUTION - STATISTICAL METHODS.
Clement, Werner. Einkommensverteilung und Qualifikation . Wien , 1984. vi, 201 p. : ISBN 3-85436-020-7 LC Card 84-191161
HC270.I5 C56 1984

Dworschak, Franz. Struktur von Arbeitseinkommen . Idstein , 1986. ix, 408 p. : ISBN 3-925196-16-1 LC Card 86-225347
HB523 .D86 1986

INCOME DISTRIBUTION - SWEDEN.
Söderström, Lars, 1940- Perspektiv på fördelningspolitiken /. [Stockholm] [1984] 83 p. : ISBN 91-7566-068-7 LC Card 85-108552
HC380.I5 S62 1984

INCOME DISTRIBUTION - SWITZERLAND.
Schmassmann, Norbert. Verteilungswirkungen von Erdölpreissteigerungen . Diessenhofen , c1983. viii, 326 p. : ISBN 3-7253-0203-0 LC Card 83-219477
HD9575.S92 S27 1983

INCOME DISTRIBUTION - SWITZERLAND - STATISTICS.
Lüthi, Ambros, 1938- Die wirtschaftliche Ungleichheit im Rentenalter in der Schweiz /. Freiburg/Schweiz , 1983. 229 p. : ISBN 3-7278-0282-0 : LC Card 83-163287
HD7105.35.S9 L87 1983

INCOME DISTRIBUTION - UNITED STATES.
Cannon, William B., 1920- New class politics . Washington, D.C. , c1986. 137 p. ; ISBN 0-89758-042-7 (pbk.) : LC Card 86-27511 DDC 336.73 19
HJ2051 .C35 1986

Capitalism and equality in America /. Lanham [New York] , c1987. ix, 306 p. : ISBN 0-8191-5572-1 (v. 1 : alk. paper) : LC Card 86-24739 DDC 330.12/2 19
HB501 .C2423 1987

The Distributional impacts of public policies /. New York , 1988. xvii, 257 p. ; ISBN 0-312-00749-3 : LC Card 87-11877 DDC 339.2/0973 19
HC110.I5 D535 1988

Kelso, Louis O. Democracy and economic power . Cambridge, Mass. , 1986. xii, 175 p. : ISBN 0-88730-115-0 : LC Card 86-14027 DDC 338.6 19
HD5660.U5 K45 1986 ***NYPL [JLE 86-4658]***

Levy, Frank, 1941- Dollars and dreams . New York , 1987. p. cm. ISBN 0-87154-523-3 : LC Card 86-42952 DDC 339.2/0973 19
HC110.I5 L47 1987

Poverty, income distribution, the family, and public policy . Washington , 1986. viii, 125 p. : LC Card 87-601355 DDC 339.2/2/0973 19
HC110.I5 P68 1986

Rose, Adam Zachery. Natural resource policy and income distribution /. Baltimore , c1988. xvi, 139 p. : ISBN 0-8018-3523-2 (alk. paper) LC Card 87-2788 DDC 333.7/0973 19
HC103.7 .R67 1988

Wolff, Nancy, 1955- Income redistribution and the Social Security program /. Ann Arbor , c1987. vi, 181 p. : ISBN 0-8357-1807-7 LC Card 87-10791 DDC 368.4/3/00973 19
HD7105.35.U6 W65 1987

INCOME DISTRIBUTION - UNITED STATES - CONGRESSES.
International comparisons of the distribution of household wealth /. Oxford , New York , 1987. xii, 283 p. : ISBN 0-19-828511-6 : LC Card 86-31241 DDC 339.2/2/094 19
HC240.9.I5 I56 1987

INCOME DISTRIBUTION - UNITED STATES - STATISTICS.
Consumer expenditure survey . Washington, D.C. [1986] vi, 193 p. : LC Card 86-602456 DDC 339.4/1/0973 19
HC110.C6 C5647 1986

INCOME DISTRIBUTION - URUGUAY.
González, José I. (José Iván), 1944- La segmentación del mercado del crédito y sus impactos sobre la distribución del ingreso /. Montevideo, Uruguay , 1984. ii, 5, 123 p. : LC Card 85-236586
HG3754.5.U8 G66 1984

Melgar, Alicia. Distribución del ingreso en el Uruguay /. Montevideo , 1981. 87 p. ; LC Card 86-160100
HC235.I5 M448 1981

INCOME DISTRIBUTION - YUGOSLAVIA.
Glas, Miroslav, 1950- Delitev po delu v socialističnі družbi /. Ljubljana , 1986. 631 p. : LC Card 87-147216
HC407.Z9 I51473 1986

INCOME DISTRIBUTION - ZAIRE - KINSHASA.
Gozo, K. M. Le secteur non structuré de Kinshasa . Addis Abéba , c1985. iii, 64, [8] p. : ISBN 92-2-100538-0 LC Card 85-981182
HD2346.Z27 K54 1985

INCOME - EFFECT OF INFLATION ON - NORWAY.
Skånland, Hermod, 1925- Inntektspolitikkens dilemma . [Oslo] , 1981 ([Oslo] : Joh. Nordahls trykkeri) 114 p., [1] leaf : ISBN 82-02-04872-9 (pbk.) : LC Card 81-199141
HC370.I5 S49 1981 ***NYPL [JLD 86-2672]***

Income, employment, and economic growth /.
Peterson, Wallace C. New York [c1988] xxiii, 750 p. : ISBN 0-393-95628-8 LC Card 87-17933 DDC 339 19
HB172.5 .P453 1988

INCOME - FRANCE.
Constat de l'évolution récente des revenus en France . Paris [1984] 220 p. : LC Card 85-127672
HC280.I5 C67 1984

INCOME - GERMANY, EAST.
Vortmann, Heinz. Geldeinkommen in der DDR von 1955 bis zu Beginn der achtziger Jahre . Berlin , 1985. 239 p. : ISBN 3-428-95952-2 LC Card 86-166538
HC281 .B33 Heft 85 HC290.795.I5

INCOME - GERMANY, WEST.
Flaig, Jürgen. Verteilungsschwankungen im Konjunkturverlauf . Freiburg im Breisgau , c1983. vi, 221 p. : ISBN 3-448-01325-0 LC Card 83-155341
HC290.5.I5 F55 1983

Francke, Hans-Hermann. Sparverhalten bei Unterbeschäftigung, stagnierendem oder sinkendem Realeinkommen /. Stuttgart [1985] 142 p. : LC Card 86-153649
HC290.5.S3 F69 1985

Freitäger, Jürgen, 1959- Erwerb und Verwendung des Einkommens von Arbeitnehmerhaushalten mit erwerbstätiger Ehefrau /. Frankfurt am Main , New York , c1986. xix, 327 p. : ISBN 3-8204-9148-1 : LC Card 86-195223
HD9850.1 .M58 Bd. 37 HD6055.2.G3

Haushalte mit ausgewählten staatlichen Transferzahlungen . Stuttgart , c1983. 352 p. : ISBN 3-17-007631-0 LC Card 83-117808
HC290.5.I5 H37 1983

Miegel, Meinhard. Die verkannte Revolution /. Stuttgart , 1983- v. : ISBN 3-87959-196-2 (Bd. 1) LC Card 83-206487 DDC 330.943/087 19
HC286.7 .M53 1983 ***NYPL [JLK 86-154]***

INCOME - GOVERNMENT POLICY - CASE STUDIES.
Cuadrado Roura, Juan R. Política de rentas . [Madrid] [1980?] 471 p. : ISBN 84-7196-297-7 LC Card 85-131138
HC390.I5 C8 1980

INCOME - GOVERNMENT POLICY - INDIA.
Prakash, Om, 1927- Guided incomes policy /. New Delhi , 1983. vi, 214 p. ; LC Card 83-902415 DDC 339.5/0954 19
HC440.I5 P72 1983 ***NYPL [JLD 86-3834]***

INCOME - GOVERNMENT POLICY - SPAIN.
Cuadrado Roura, Juan R. Política de rentas . [Madrid] [1980?] 471 p. : ISBN 84-7196-297-7 LC Card 85-131138
HC390.I5 C8 1980

INCOME - HUNGARY.
A Lakosság jövedelme, társadalombiztosítás, családpolitika /. Budapest [1983] 82 p. : LC Card 83-206799
HC30.295.I5 L332 1983
NYPL [JLE 87-179]

INCOME - HUNGARY - STATISTICS.
A Lakosság jövedelme és fogyasztása, 1960-1973 /. [Budapest] , c1975. 91 p. ; ISBN 963-340-048-1 LC Card 86-196944
HC300.295.I5 L32 1975

A Lakosság jövedelme és fogyasztása, 1960-1983 /. Budapest , 1984. 118 p. ; ISBN 963-340-740-0 : LC Card 85-155585
HC300.295.I5 L3315 1984 ***NYPL [JLF 86-672]***

A Lakosság jövedelme és fogyasztása, 1970-1984 . Budapest , 1985. 83 p. ; LC Card 86-217829
HC300.295.I5 L3316 1985

A Lakosság jövedelme és fogyasztása, 1970-1985 /. Budapest , 1986. 97 p. ; ISBN 963-340-805-9 : LC Card 87-408026
HC300.295.I5 L3317 1986

INCOME - INDIA.
Giriappa, S. Income, saving and investment patterns in rural India /. New Delhi , 1984. 82 p. ; ***NYPL [JLD 86-4357]***

Mulkh Raj. Employment, income, and housing /. New Delhi , 1987. viii, 130 p. : ISBN 81-7000-025-4 : LC Card 87-901029 DDC 331.12/5/0954 19
HD7361.A3 M85 1987

INCOME - INDIA - CASE STUDIES.
Ghadoliya, M. K. (Mahendra Kumar) Structure of employment, earnings, and assets in India . Delhi , 1986. xi, 248 p. : LC Card 86-903221 DDC 331.12/5/09544 19
HD5820.U33 G47 1986

INCOME - INDIA - KARNATAKA.
Dadibhavi, R. V. Income, productivity, and industrial structure /. Allahabad, India , 1986. xx, 295 p. ; ISBN 81-85076-02-2 : LC Card 86-902847 DDC 339.2/0954/87 19
HC437.K27 D33 1986

INCOME - INDIA - UDAIPUR (DISTRICT) - CASE STUDIES.
Ghadoliya, M. K. (Mahendra Kumar) Structure of employment, earnings, and assets in India . Delhi , 1986. xi, 248 p. : LC Card 86-903221 DDC 331.12/5/09544 19
HD5820.U33 G47 1986

INCOME - INDIANA.
Wynne, John, 1961- The Indiana economy . Indianapolis, IN [1986] 22, [2] p. : LC Card 86-622749 DDC 330.9772/043 19
HD5725.I6 W96 1986

INCOME - ITALY.
Antonelli, Gilberto. Risorse umane e redditi da lavoro . Milano , c1985. 256 p. : LC Card 85-191554
HC310.I5 A66 1985

Targetti Lenti, Renata. Struttura produttiva e distribuzione personale del reddito . Milano [1984] 263 p. : ISBN 88-14-00277-0 : LC Card 84-251227 DDC 339.2/2/0945 19
HC310.I5 T346 1984 ***NYPL [JLF 86-1305]***

INCOME - LONGITUDINAL STUDIES.
Meier, Christoph. Lebenszyklus und ökonomische Ungleichheit . Freiburg, Schweiz , 1983. 235 p. : ISBN 3-7278-0298-7 : LC Card 83-244050
HB601 .M389 1983

Income maintenance programs . Australia. Parliament. Joint Committee of Public Accounts. Canberra , 1986. viii, 49 p. ; ISBN 0-644-04993-6 (pbk.) LC Card 86-234535 DDC 362.5/82 19
HC610.I5 A95 1986

INCOME MAINTENANCE PROGRAMS.
Büchele, Herwig, 1935- Grundeinkommen ohne Arbeit . Wien , c1985. 191 p. : ISBN 3-203-50898-2 LC Card 85-207929
HC79.I5 B83 1985

INCOME MAINTENANCE PROGRAMS - AUSTRALIA.
Australia. Parliament. Joint Committee of Public Accounts. Income maintenance programs . Canberra , 1986. viii, 49 p. ; ISBN 0-644-04993-6 (pbk.) LC Card 86-234535 DDC 362.5/82 19
HC610.I5 A95 1986

Cass, Bettina. Income support for families with children /. Canberra [1986] xiii, 126 p. : ISBN 0-644-05378-X (pbk.) LC Card 87-103419 DDC 362.5/82 19
HD4925.5.A8 C37 1986

Crompton, Cathy. Too old for a job, too young for a pension? . Canberra , 1986. x, 69 p. ; ISBN 0-644-05599-5 LC Card 87-150775 DDC 368.4/4/00880564 19
HD6283.A8 C76 1986

Whiteford, Peter. Issues in assistance for families . Woden, ACT [1986] iii, 56 p. ; ISBN 0-642-51604-9 (pbk.) LC Card 86-231139 DDC 362/.0425 19
HD4925.5.A8 W47 1986

INCOME MAINTENANCE PROGRAMS - EUROPE - CONGRESSES.
Social security and employment /. Assen, The Netherlands , 1983. 116 p. : ISBN 90-232-2011-0 (pbk.) : LC Card 83-216203 DDC 331.12/094 19
HD7164 .S594 1983 ***NYPL [JLE 86-1107]***

INCOME MAINTENANCE PROGRAMS - ITALY.
Seravalli, Gilberto, 1946- Gli effetti delle integrazioni salariali sulla mobilità del lavoro /. Milano, Italy , c1986. 119 p. : LC Card 86-222523
HD5717.5.I8 S47 1986

INCOME MAINTENANCE PROGRAMS - ITALY, SOUTHERN.
Boccella, Nicola Maria, 1952- Il Mezzogiorno sussidiato . Milano, Italy , c1982. 264 p. : LC Card 85-163271
HD7185.S68 B62 1982

INCOME MAINTENANCE PROGRAMS - UNITED STATES.
Levitan, Sar A. Working but poor . Baltimore , c1987. ix, 142 p. : ISBN 0-8018-3583-6 (alk. paper) LC Card 87-16973 DDC 362.5/0973 19
HC110.I5 L468 1987

INCOME MAINTENANCE PROGRAMS - UNITED STATES - DATA PROCESSING.
Lewis, Gordon H. Income transfer analysis /. New York , c1987. p. cm. ISBN 0-915163-01-2 LC Card 86-33744 DDC 362.5/82 19
HC110.I5 L48 1987

INCOME - MARYLAND - BALTIMORE METROPOLITAN AREA - STATISTICS.
Census '80 . Baltimore, Md. (2225 N. Charles St., Baltimore 21218) [1983] xv, 106 leaves : LC Card 83-622347 DDC 339.2/2/097526 19
HC108.B2 C46 1983 ***NYPL [JLF 86-1594]***

INCOME - MATHEMATICAL MODELS.
Sell, Friedrich L. Der Konsumcharakter der Einkommensentstehung . Freiburg im Breisgau , c1982. 221 p. : ISBN 3-448-01269-6 LC Card 82-233541 DDC 339.4/7/0724 19
HB820 .S44 1982 ***NYPL [JLD 87-1580]***

INCOME - MEXICO.
Madrigal Pana, Johnny. Metodología y construcción de un indicador del ingreso familiar . San José, Costa Rica , 1986. 43 p. ; LC Card 87-404395 DDC 339.4/2/0972 19
HD6996 .M33 1986

INCOME - NEW JERSEY - STATISTICS.
Crowley, Charles. Income and poverty in New Jersey [microform] . Trenton, N.J. [1982] 32 p. ; LC Card 83-620831 DDC 339.2/2/09749 19
HC107.N53 I5113 1982
NYPL [*ZT-1712 no.31]

Income nonresponses . Cleveland, Robert W. [Washington] [1985] iv, 87 p. : LC Card 85-603179 DDC 339.2/2/0973021 19
HC110.I5 C44 1985

INCOME - POLAND.
Klank, Leszek. Czynniki kształtujące poziom dochodów w gospodarstwach indywidualnych /. Warszawa , 1985. 176 p. ; ISBN 83-01-05449-2 : ***NYPL [*QO 86-2601]***

Income, productivity, and industrial structure /. Dadibhavi, R. V. Allahabad, India , 1986. xx, 295 p. ; ISBN 81-85076-02-2 : LC Card 86-902847 DDC 339.2/0954/87 19
HC437.K27 D33 1986

Income redistribution and the Social Security program /. Wolff, Nancy, 1955- Ann Arbor , c1987. vi, 181 p. : ISBN 0-8357-1807-7 LC Card 87-10791 DDC 368.4/3/00973 19
HD7105.35.U6 W65 1987

Income replacement for long term disability . DeVol, Karen R., 1949- Cambridge, Mass. , 1986. p. cm. ISBN 0-935149-04-X : LC Card 86-28264 DDC 368.4/1/00973 19
HD7103.65.U6 D484 1986

Income, saving and investment patterns in rural India /. Giriappa, S. New Delhi , 1984. 82 p. ; ***NYPL [JLD 86-4357]***

INCOME - SOUTH AFRICA - DURBAN.
Padayachee, Vishnu. An analysis of some aspects of employment and unemployment in the African townships of Umlazi and Lamontville . Durban [South Africa] [1985] iii, 49 p. ; ISBN 0-949947-75-X (pbk.) LC Card 87-404149 DDC 331.12/5/0968455 19
HD5842.D87 P33 1985

INCOME - SOUTH AFRICA - DURBAN - STATISTICS.
Van Wyk, H. de J. Income and expenditure patterns of urban Black multiple households in Durban, 1985 /. Pretoria , 1986. xi, 130 p. : ISBN 0-908408-59-5 (pbk.) LC Card 87-151639 DDC 658.8/3968 s 339.4/1/0968455021 19
HC517.S7 S48 no. 130, pt. 4 HD7064.4.Z8D8

INCOME STATEMENTS. see FINANCIAL STATEMENTS.

Income support for families with children /. Cass, Bettina. Canberra [1986] xiii, 126 p. : ISBN 0-644-05378-X (pbk.) LC Card 87-103419 DDC 362.5/82 19
HD4925.5.A8 C37 1986

INCOME TAX - AUSTRALIA.
Norman, Neville R. The economics of personal tax escalation in Australia /. [Sydney] : Sydney ; xii, 173 p. : ISBN 0-86861-652-4 (pbk.) LC Card 84-72057 DDC 336.24/2/0994 19
HJ4802 .N67 1985 ***NYPL [JLD 86-1906]***

INCOME TAX - AUSTRIA - STATISTICS.
Lohn- und Einkommensteuerstatistik 1979 . Wien , 1985. xxxv, 59 p. : LC Card 86-233093
HJ4713.A7 L64 1985

INCOME TAX - CANADA.
Davies, James B., 1951- Reforming capital income taxation in Canada . [Ottawa] , c1987. ix, 153 p. : ISBN 0-660-12454-8 (pbk.) : LC Card 87-168079 DDC 336.24/24/0971 19
HJ4133.C2 .D38 1987

Wilson, Michael H. (Michael Holcombe), 1937- A minimum tax for Canada /. [Ottawa] [1985] vi, 52, 56, vi p. ; LC Card 86-202606 DDC 336.24/2 19
HJ4661 .W54 1985

Wilson, Michael H. (Michael Holcombe), 1937- A minimum tax for Canada . [Ottawa] [1985] iii, 15, 15, iii p. ; LC Card 86-202601 DDC 336.24/2 19
HJ4661 .W55 1985

INCOME TAX - CANADA - DEDUCTIONS.
Jobin, Jacques. Mesure et incidence des dépenses fiscales au Québec /. Montréal [1984] 27 p. ; LC Card 85-169988
HB3 .C3 vol. 8511 HJ4662.A45

Wilson, Michael H. (Michael Holcombe), 1937- A minimum tax for Canada /. [Ottawa] [1985] vi, 52, 56, vi p. ; LC Card 86-202606 DDC 336.24/2 19
HJ4661 .W54 1985

Wilson, Michael H. (Michael Holcombe), 1937- A minimum tax for Canada . [Ottawa] [1985] iii, 15, 15, iii p. ; LC Card 86-202601 DDC 336.24/2 19
HJ4661 .W55 1985

INCOME TAX - CONGRESSES.
Taxation in developed countries . Paris , Washington, D.C. , 1987. 99 p. ; ISBN 92-64-12929-4 (pbk.) : LC Card 87-163512 DDC 336.24 19
HJ4621 .T28 1987

Income tax considerations in corporate financing. Corporate Management Tax Conference (1986) Toronto, Canada , c1986. xv, 475 p. : ISBN 0-88808-027-1 : LC Card 87-153466 DDC 658.1/53 19
HG4090 .C67 1986

INCOME TAX - EUROPE.
Hummel, Marlies. Die steuerliche Behandlung des eigengenutzten Wohneigentums in den Ländern Bundesrepublik Deutschland, Österreich, Schweiz, Frankreich, Grossbritannien und den USA /. München , 1986. ii, 73 p. ; ISBN 3-88512-021-6 : LC Card

86-215255
HJ4719 .H85 1986

INCOME TAX - EUROPEAN ECONOMIC COMMUNITY COUNTRIES.
Parsche, Rüdiger. Die Belastung der Einkünfte aus nichtselbständiger Arbeit mit Einkommensteuern und Sozialabgaben in den EG-Ländern und in Schweden /. München , 1981. 2 v. ; LC Card 83-115269
HJ4719 .P37 1981

INCOME TAX - FINLAND.
Asplund, Rita. Short-run tax-push inflation in Finland /. Helsinki , 1986. 65 p. : ISBN 951-46-9876-2 (pbk.) LC Card 87-163994 DDC 332.4/1/094897 19
HJ4738.3 .A86 1986

INCOME TAX - GERMANY, WEST.
Hummel, Marlies. Die steuerliche Behandlung des eigengenutzten Wohneigentums in den Ländern Bundesrepublik Deutschland, Österreich, Schweiz, Frankreich, Grossbritannien und den USA /. München , 1986. ii, 73 p. ; ISBN 3-88512-021-6 : LC Card 86-215255
HJ4719 .H85 1986

Parsche, Rüdiger. Die Belastung der Einkünfte aus nichtselbständiger Arbeit mit Einkommensteuern und Sozialabgaben in den EG-Ländern und in Schweden /. München , 1981. 2 v. ; LC Card 83-115269
HJ4719 .P37 1981

Scheer, Christian. Verteilungswirkungen der Einkommensteuer /. Göttingen , c1982. xii, 457 p. : ISBN 3-509-01260-7 : LC Card 83-150522
HJ4719 .S34 1982

Urbas, Helmut, 1951- Die wirtschaftliche Betrachtungsweise im Steuerrecht /. Frankfurt am Main , New York , c1987. viii, 392 p. : ISBN 3-8204-0915-7 LC Card 87-409061 DDC 336.24/0943 19
HJ4719 .U7 1987

INCOME TAX - GERMANY (WEST) - DEDUCTIONS - CHARITABLE CONTRIBUTIONS.
Paqué, Karl-Heinz. Philanthropie und Steuerpolitik . Tübingen , c1986. xv, 417 p. : ISBN 3-16-345154-3 (pbk. : Deut. Bibl.) : LC Card 87-408202 DDC 343.4305/232 344.3035232 19
HJ4720.A45 P36 1986

INCOME TAX - GERMANY, WEST - DEDUCTIONS - EXPENSES.
Piltz, Detlev Jürgen. Vorschlag zur Verbesserung der Behandlung nichtabziehbarer Ausgaben im KStG 1977 /. Bonn , 1987. 42 leaves ; LC Card 87-401366 DDC 332 s 343.4305/267 332 s 344.3035267 19
HJ1120 .B65 Nr. 263 KK7226

INCOME TAX - GERMANY, WEST - MATHEMATICAL MODELS.
Bamberg, Günter, 1940- Decision-theoretic analysis of envisaged income tax reforms for FRG and U. S. /. [Augsburg] [1986] 11 leaves : LC Card 87-101962 DDC 336.24/0724 19
HJ4719 .B35 1986

Hummeltenberg, Rita. Die optimale Wahl steuerbegünstiger Kapitalanlagen unter Berücksichtigung der Einkommensteuerprogression . Berlin , c1984. xi, 276 p. : ISBN 3-503-02437-9 LC Card 85-227381
HJ4719 .H86 1984

Steden, Werner. Finanzpolitik und Einkommensverteilung . Frankfurt am Main ; Bern ; 378 p. ; ISBN 3-261-01763-5 LC Card 80-459125
HJ1120 .S74 ***NYPL [JLD 80-3205]***

INCOME TAX - GREAT BRITAIN - FOREIGN INCOME.
Blackstone, L. R. (Lance R.) UK tax savings for the higher paid (1979) /. London , c1979. 10 p. ; LC Card 81-112830
HJ4708.A7 B533 1979

INCOME TAX - HUNGARY.
László, Gyula, Dr. Utmutató és példatár az 1985. január 1-től érvényes jövedelem- és keresetszabályozási rendszer alkalmazásához /. Budapest , 1985. 153 p. ; ISBN 963-621-216-3 LC Card 85-138648
HJ4715 .L37 1985

INCOME TAX - INDIA.
Inflation and personal taxation. New Delhi [1981] 21 p. ; LC Card 82-907052 DDC 336.24/2/0954 19
HJ4766.Z7 A85 1981 ***NYPL [JLF 86-236]***

Krishna Rao, Ch. A. (Chitrothu Atchuta), 1940- Personal income taxation in India /. Allahabad, India , 1987. xii, 284 p. ; ISBN 81-85076-19-7 : LC Card 86-903664 DDC 336.24/2/0954 19
HJ4766 .K75 1987

Mittal, Satya Narayan, 1947- Central taxation of income in India since 1951 . Delhi , New Delhi , 1986. 321 p. ; ISBN 81-7018-327-8 : LC Card 86-902918 DDC 336.24/0954 19
HJ4766 .M58 1986

INCOME TAX - LAW AND LEGISLATION - EUROPE.
Hummel, Marlies. Die steuerliche Behandlung des eigengenutzten Wohneigentums in den Ländern Bundesrepublik Deutschland, Österreich, Schweiz, Frankreich, Grossbritannien und den USA /. München , 1986. ii, 73 p. ; ISBN 3-88512-021-6 : LC Card 86-215255
HJ4719 .H85 1986

INCOME TAX - LAW AND LEGISLATION - GERMANY, WEST.
Hummel, Marlies. Die steuerliche Behandlung des eigengenutzten Wohneigentums in den Ländern Bundesrepublik Deutschland, Österreich, Schweiz, Frankreich, Grossbritannien und den USA /. München , 1986. ii, 73 p. ; ISBN 3-88512-021-6 : LC Card 86-215255
HJ4719 .H85 1986

Paqué, Karl-Heinz. Philanthropie und Steuerpolitik . Tübingen , c1986. xv, 417 p. : ISBN 3-16-345154-3 (pbk. : Deut. Bibl.) : LC Card 87-408202 DDC 343.4305/232 344.3035232 19
HJ4720.A45 P36 1986

Urbas, Helmut, 1951- Die wirtschaftliche Betrachtungsweise im Steuerrecht /. Frankfurt am Main , New York , c1987. viii, 392 p. : ISBN 3-8204-0915-7 LC Card 87-409061 DDC 336.24/0943 19
HJ4719 .U7 1987

INCOME TAX - LAW AND LEGISLATION - SOUTH AFRICA.
Divaris, Costa. Old Mutual income tax guide, 1986/87 /. [S.l.] c1987 (Cape Town : Old Mutual Print. Works) xvi, 261 p. : LC Card 87-152138 DDC 343.6805/2 346.80352 19
HJ4790.4 .D58 1987

INCOME TAX - LAW AND LEGISLATION - SPAIN.
Poveda Blanco, Francisco. La valoración de bases imponibles en los impuestos sobre la renta y el patrimonio /. [Alicante] [1984?] 395 p. ; LC Card 84-216651 DDC 333.33/2/0946 19
HJ4125.S8 P68 1984 ***NYPL [JLE 86-1461]***

INCOME TAX - LAW AND LEGISLATION - UNITED STATES.
Guggenheim, Joseph. Tax credits for low income housing . Washington, D.C. , c1986. vii, 117 p. : ISBN 0-941239-00-4 (pbk.) LC Card 87-112304 DDC 363.5/8 19
HJ4653.C73 G85 1986

Hummel, Marlies. Die steuerliche Behandlung des eigengenutzten Wohneigentums in den Ländern Bundesrepublik Deutschland, Österreich, Schweiz, Frankreich, Grossbritannien und den USA /. München , 1986. ii, 73 p. ; ISBN 3-88512-021-6 : LC Card 86-215255
HJ4719 .H85 1986

Robinson, Gerald J. Federal income taxation of real estate . Boston, Mass. , c1984. ca. 750 p. in various pagings ; ISBN 0-88712-081-4 LC Card 83-50925 DDC 343.7305/2 347.30352 19
KF6535 .R6 1984 ***NYPL [JLL 87-136]***

Robinson, Gerald J. Federal income taxation of real estate . Boston, Mass. , c1987. ca. 480 p. in various pagings ; ISBN 0-88712-743-6 LC Card 83-50925
NYPL [JLL 87-136 Suppl. 1987/1]

Robinson, Gerald J. Federal income taxation of real estate : text, forms, and tax planning ideas : 4th ed. Cumulative supplement /. Boston, Mass. , c1985- v. ISBN 0-88712-305-8 (pbk.) LC Card 83-50925
NYPL [*R-Econ. 85-1660 Suppl.]

INCOME TAX - MALAWI.
Kandoole, B. F. Revenue and equity effects of the 1983 income tax reform in Malawi /. [Zomba, Malaŵi?] [1986] 20 p. ; LC Card 86-981440 DDC 336.2/0096897 19
HJ4791 .K36 1986

INCOME TAX - NEW YORK (STATE)
The President's tax reform proposal . [Albany, N.Y.] [1985] 48 leaves : LC Card 86-622434 DDC 336.2/009747 19
HJ2424 .P84 1985

The United States Senate's tax reform proposal . [Albany, N.Y.?] [1986] 18, 6, 2 leaves ; LC Card 87-620727 DDC 336.2/009747 19
HJ2424 .U55 1986

INCOME TAX - PHILIPPINES.
Diokno, Benjamin E. Revenue mobilization and responsiveness of Philippine income taxes . [Quezon City, Philippines] [1986] 26 p. : LC Card 87-120920 DDC 339.5/25/09599 19
HJ4743 .D56 1986

INCOME TAX - PRUSSIA (GERMANY) - HISTORY.
Linzbach, Peter, 1956- Der Werdegang der preussischen Einkommensteuer unter besonderer Berücksichtigung ihrer kausalen Entwicklungsfaktoren . Frankfurt am Main , New York , c1984. 259 p. ; ISBN 3-8204-5184-6 LC Card 84-169039
HJ4720.P78 L56 1984

INCOME TAX - QUÉBEC (PROVINCE)
White paper on the personal tax and transfer systems /. Québec , 1984. 380 p. : ISBN 2-551-08967-0 (pbk.) : LC Card 85-150790 DDC 336.24/215/09714 19
HJ4663.Q8 W47 1984 ***NYPL [JLF 87-360]***

INCOME TAX - SOUTH AFRICA - HANDBOOKS, MANUALS, ETC.
Divaris, Costa. Old Mutual income tax guide, 1986/87 /. [S.l.] c1987 (Cape Town : Old Mutual Print. Works) xvi, 261 p. : LC Card 87-152138 DDC 343.6805/2 346.80352 19
HJ4790.4 .D58 1987

INCOME TAX - SPAIN.
Poveda Blanco, Francisco. La valoración de bases imponibles en los impuestos sobre la renta y el patrimonio /. [Alicante] [1984?] 395 p. ; LC Card 84-216651 DDC 333.33/2/0946 19
HJ4125.S8 P68 1984 ***NYPL [JLE 86-1461]***

INCOME TAX - SPAIN - PROBLEMS, EXERCISES, ETC.
Esparza Cervera, José Ramón. Impuesto sobre la renta . Valencia [1982?] 1 v. (various pagings) ; ISBN 84-85672-11-9 LC Card 83-134521
HJ4744 .E86 1982

INCOME TAX - SWEDEN.
Parsche, Rüdiger. Die Belastung der Einkünfte aus nichtselbständiger Arbeit mit Einkommensteuern und Sozialabgaben in den EG-Ländern und in Schweden /. München , 1981. 2 v. ; LC Card 83-115269
HJ4719 .P37 1981

INCOME TAX - SWITZERLAND.
Die Kalte Progression . Bern , 1982. 107 p. : LC Card 83-128720
HJ4747 .K35 1982

INCOME TAX - SWITZERLAND - EFFECT OF INFLATION ON.
Die Kalte Progression . Bern , 1982. 107 p. : LC Card 83-128720
HJ4747 .K35 1982

INCOME TAX - TEXAS.
Greenhut, Melvin L. Report on an income tax in Texas /. College Station, Tex. , c1986. 40 p. : ISBN 0-86599-057-3 (pbk.) LC Card 86-622258 DDC 336.24/09764 19
HJ4655.T4 G74 1986

INCOME TAX - UNITED STATES - DEDUCTIONS.
Bradford, W. Murray. The Prentice Hall business tax deduction master guide /. New York , c1987. 368 p. : ISBN 0-13-108234-5 (pbk.) : LC Card 87-2252 DDC 343.7305/23 347.303523 19
HJ4653.D4 B68 1987

INCOME TAX - UNITED STATES - DEDUCTIONS - EXPENSES.
Knepp, Jay. Tax[s]aver. Menlo Park, Calif. , c1987. 143 p. : ISBN 0-376-07015-3 (pbk.) : LC Card 86-80874 DDC 343.7305/23 347.303523 19
HJ4653.D4 K56 1987

INCOME TAX - UNITED STATES - DEDUCTIONS - RETIREMENT CONTRIBUTIONS.
Curatola, Anthony P. State income tax consequences of retirement plan distributions /. Brookfield, Wis. , c1986. 20 p. ; ISBN 0-89154-324-4 (pbk.) LC Card 87-158902 DDC 336.24/16 19
HJ4653.P5 C87 1986

INCOME TAX - UNITED STATES - DEDUCTIONS - TAXES.
Dilger, Robert Jay, 1954- The deductibility of state and local taxes . Washington, D.C. [1985] 1 v. (various pagings) ; ISBN 0-933729-02-2 (pbk.) : LC Card 85-155605 DDC 336.24/216 19
HJ4653.D4 D55 1985 ***NYPL [JLF 86-412]***

INCOME TAX - UNITED STATES - FOREIGN INCOME - STATISTICS.
Statistics of income . Washington, D.C. , 1985. iii, 516 p. : ***NYPL [JLF 86-833]***

INCOME TAX - UNITED STATES - MATHEMATICAL MODELS.
Bamberg, Günter, 1940- Decision-theoretic analysis of envisaged income tax reforms for FRG and U. S. /. [Augsburg] [1986] 11 leaves : LC Card 87-101962 DDC 336.24/0724 19
HJ4719 .B35 1986

Income transfer analysis /. Lewis, Gordon H. New York , c1987. p. cm. ISBN 0-915163-01-2 LC Card 86-33744 DDC 362.5/82 19
HC110.I5 L48 1987

INCOME - UNITED STATES.
Levy, Frank, 1941- Dollars and dreams . New York , 1987. p. cm. ISBN 0-87154-523-3 : LC Card 86-42952 DDC 339.2/0973 19
HC110.I5 L47 1987

United States. President's Commission on Income Maintenance Programs. Poverty amid plenty, the American paradox. [Washington] 1969. ix, 155 p. LC Card 71-605334 DDC 362.5/0973
HC110.P63 A59 ***NYPL [JLF 86-478]***

INCOME - UNITED STATES - CONGRESSES.
Survey of income and program participation and related longitudinal surveys, 1984 . [Washington, D.C.] , 1985. ix, 201 p. : LC Card 85-601676 DDC 339.2/3/0973 19
HC110.I5 S89 1985 ***NYPL [JLF 86-1641]***

INCOME - UNITED STATES - STATISTICS.
Cleveland, Robert W. Income nonresponses . [Washington] [1985] iv, 87 p. : LC Card 85-603179 DDC 339.2/2/0973021 19
HC110.I5 C44 1985

Linking employment problems to economic status . Washington, D.C. [1986] vi, 56 p. ; LC Card 86-603148 DDC 331.13/7973 19
HD5724 .L425 1986

Taeuber, Cynthia Murray. Women in the American economy /. Washington, D.C. [1986] vi, 45 p. : LC Card 87-601515 DDC 304.6/0973/021 s 331.4/0973 19
HA203 .A218 no. 146 HD6092

INCOME - UTAH - STATISTICS.
Jensen, Kenneth E. Utah personal income, 1929-1985 /. [Salt Lake City] [1986] 114 p. : LC Card 87-621301 DDC 339.2/2/09792 19
HC107.U83 I515 1986

Income variability in Connecticut, 1980 /. Groff, William H. Storrs, CT [1987] 32 p. : LC Card 87-621355 DDC 339.2/2/09746 19
HC107.C83 I5138 1987

INCOME - WYOMING - STATISTICS.
Wyoming income and employment report /. Cheyenne, Wyo. [1986] 54, [33], iii p. : LC Card 86-623087 DDC 331.12/5/09787021 19
HD5725.W9 W97 1986

Incorporated Society of British Advertisers.
ISBA area information, 1978 /. London , 1978. 147 p. : ISBN 0-906241-00-6 (pbk.) LC Card 83-225656 DDC 381/.1/0941021 19
HA1134 .I83 1978

Incra. see **Instituto Nacional de Colonização e Reforma Agraria.**

Increasing interdependence between states but failure of international cooperation /. Myrdal, Gunnar, 1898- Göteborg , 1978. 53 p. ; ISBN 91-7360-052-0 LC Card 80-511073 DDC 327.1/7 19
JX1954 .M94 ***NYPL [JLD 81-302]***

An increasing role for the ECU . Masera, R. S. Princeton, N.J. , 1987. vi, 50 p. ; ISBN 0-88165-074-9 (pbk.) : LC Card 87-3747 DDC 332/.042 s 332.4/56094 19
HG136 .P7 no. 167 HG930.5

Increasing sales effectiveness . Sanchez, Joseph S., 1949- Lodi, N.J. [c1987] 203 p. ; ISBN 0-941315-14-2 : LC Card 87-8794 DDC 658.8/1 19
HF5438.25 .S26 1987

Incroyables gazettes et fabuleux métaux . Morineau, Michel. London ; New York : 687 p. : ISBN 0-521-25384-5 : LC Card 83-7177 DDC 330.94/022 19
HC240 .M73 1985 ***NYPL [JLE 85-1587]***

Indagine socio-demografica sugli immigrati stranieri in Sicilia . Vizzini, Sergio. Palermo [1983] 108 p. ; LC Card 86-131931
HB3600.M39 V58 1983

Indagine sulla lettura e su altri aspetti dell'impiego del tempo libero : anno 1984. [Roma] : ISTAT, 1986. 140 p., [5] p. of plates : forms ; 26 cm. (Note e relazioni, 0535-9856 . anno 1986, n. 3) Bibliography: p. 27. LC Card 87-165864
1. Reading interests - Italy - Statistics. 2. Leisure - Italy - Statistics. I. Istituto centrale di statistica (Italy). II. Series.
HA1363 .A27 no. 3 Z1003.5.I8

Indebtedness and growth in developing countries / edited by Armin Gutowski, Manfred Holthus, Dietrich Kebschull. Hamburg : Verlag Weltarchiv, 1986. 344 p. ; 24 cm. (Publication of HWWA-Institut für Wirtschaftsforschung-Hamburg) Includes bibliographies. ISBN 3-87895-300-3 (pbk.) LC Card 86-213057 DDC 336.3/435/091724 19
1. Debts, External - Developing countries - Case studies. 2. Developing countries - Economic conditions - Case studies. I. Gutowski, Armin. II. Holthus, Manfred. III. Kebschull, Dietrich. IV. Series.
HJ8899 .I53 1986

Indeksy t͡sen i produkt͡sii v kapitalisticheskikh stranakh /. Nikitin, Sergeĭ Mikhaĭlovich. Moskva , 1981. 255 p. ; LC Card 86-460234
HB225 .N52 1981

INDEMNITY INSURANCE. see **INSURANCE, LIABILITY.**

INDENTURED SERVANTS - AMERICA - HISTORY - CONGRESSES.
Colonialism and migration . Dordrecht , Higham, MA, USA , 1986. vi, 303 p. : ISBN 90-247-3253-0 LC Card 85-21809 DDC 331.11/73 19
HD4875.A837 C65 1986
NYPL [JLE 86-3920]

INDENTURED SERVANTS - PENNSYLVANIA - HISTORY.
Salinger, Sharon V. (Sharon Vineberg) "To serve well and faithfully" . Cambridge [Cambridgeshire] , New York , 1987. xiii, 192 p., [1] leaf of plates : ISBN 0-521-33442-X LC Card 87-852 DDC 306/.363/09748 19
HD4875.U5 S25 1987

Independent Broadcasting Authority. Review of the ITV and ILR levy structures, 1984-85 . London , c1986. 44 p. ; ISBN 0-86252-236-6 (pbk.) LC Card 86-202703 DDC 384.54/3 19
HE8689.9.G7 R48 1986

Independent Commission on International Development Issues. Der Nord-Süd-Dialog zu Beginn der 80er Jahre =. Baden-Baden , 1982. 99 p. ; ISBN 3-7890-0774-9
NYPL [JLE 87-1282]

Independent Commission on International Humanitarian Issues. Tokyo Forum: Ethics of Human Survival (1985) Proceedings of the Tokyo Forum: Ethics of Human Survival . Tokyo, Japan , c1986. v, 88 p. : ISBN 4-7955-1024-5 LC Card 87-142747
HD73 .T65 1985

INDEPENDENT LABOUR PARTY (GREAT BRITAIN)
Brown, J. Gordon. Maxton /. Edinburgh , 1986. 336 p., [8] p. of plates : ISBN 1-85158-042-5 ***NYPL [JFE 87-30]***

Independent power production in Illinois /. Illinois. Commerce Commission. Springfield, Ill. (P.O. Box 4905, Springfield 62708) [1986- v. <1 > : LC Card 86-622355 DDC 338.4/762131/09773 19
HD9685.U6 I263 1986

Independent Sector (Firm). Effective Sector Leadership/Management Program. Nonprofit organizational effectiveness study . Washington, D.C. (1828 L St., N.W., Washington 20036) , c1986. v, 125 p. ; LC Card 87-141542 DDC 658/.048 19
HD31 .N57 1986

Inder Pal Singh, 1959- Rural income distribution : an analytical study of Punjab / Inder Pal Singh. Delhi : B.R. Pub. Corp. ; New Delhi, India : Distributed by D.K. Publishers' Distributors, 1986. xvi, 123 p. : ill. ; 23 cm. Includes index. Bibliography: p. [104]-111. ISBN 81-7018-299-9 : LC Card 86-900514 DDC 339.2/3/0954552 19
1. Income distribution - India - Punjab. 2. Farm income - India - Punjab. 3. Rural development - India - Punjab. I. Title.
HC440.I5 I46 1986 ***NYPL [JLD 86-3077]***

Inderjit Singh. see **Singh, Inderjit, 1941-**

Index för prisregleringar. Isacsson, Göthe. Stockholm [1985?] 80 p. : ISBN 91-618-0082-1 LC Card 85-206079
HB235.S8 I83 1985

INDEX LINKING (ECONOMICS) see **INDEXATION (ECONOMICS)**

INDEX NUMBERS (ECONOMICS)
Making the grade . Washington, D.C. , c1987. ii, 142 p. : ISBN 0-9605804-4-1 (pbk.) LC Card 87-70671 DDC 330.973/0927 19
HC106.8 .M318 1987

März, Thomas. Interdependenzen in einem Kennzahlensystem . München , c1983. iv, 296 p. : ISBN 3-88259-262-1 : LC Card 83-222369
HG4028.V3 M34 1983

Meinlschmidt, Gerhard. Statistische Methoden zur Berechnung von Preisniveauindizes integrierter Wirtschaftsräume /. Göttingen , c1985. 142 p. : ISBN 3-525-11262-9 LC Card 85-213565
HB225 .M45 1985

Index numbers of parity between prices received and prices paid by the farmers in the state of Orissa. A Report on index numbers of parity between prices received and prices paid by the farmers in the state of Orissa /. Bhubaneswar, Orissa [1985] 11 p. : LC Card 87-401032 DDC 338.1/3/095413 19
HD2075.O7 R46 1985

Index options & futures . Luskin, Donald L. New York , c1987. xi, 355 p. : ISBN 0-471-85464-6 LC Card 86-28189 DDC 332.63/222 19
HG6043 .L87 1987

Index options and futures. Luskin, Donald L. Index options & futures . New York , c1987. xi, 355 p. : ISBN 0-471-85464-6 LC Card 86-28189 DDC 332.63/222 19
HG6043 .L87 1987

Index to decisions of the World Bank Administrative Tribunal /. Amerasinghe, Chittharanjan Felix, 1933- [Washington, D.C.] [c1985] vii, 32 leaves ; LC Card 86-172153 DDC 354.1/8252 19
HG3881.5.W57 A44 1985

Index, 1978-1985 and survey methodology. Menlo Park, CA (333 Ravenswood Ave., Menlo Park 94025) : Values and Lifestyles Program, [1986] vi, 45 leaves ; 28 cm. (Vals report / SRI International, Values and Lifestyles Program . no. 63) "January 1986." LC Card 86-220307 DDC 305/.0973 19
1. Values and Lifestyles Program (SRI International) - Indexes. 2. Market surveys. I. Series: VALS report , no. 63.
HF5415.3 .I47 1986

INDEXATION (ECONOMICS) - ARGENTINA.
Badillo, Juan A. El registro contable en moneda constante . Capital Federal, Argentina , 1985. 249 p. ; LC Card 85-203677
HF5658.5 .B34 1985

Oría, Gerardo J. (Gerardo Juan) Teoría y práctica de la indexación . Buenos Aires , 1985. 216 p. ; ISBN 950-9209-28-7 LC Card 86-151154
HG815 .O75 1985

INDEXATION (ECONOMICS) - BRAZIL.
Cysne, Rubens Penha. Breve retrospecto da economia brasileira entre 1979 e 1984 /. [Rio de Janeiro] [1985] 30 leaves ; LC Card 86-176751
HC187 .C98 1985

Cysne, Rubens Penha. Política macroeconômica no Brasil, 1964/66 e 1980/84 /. Rio de Janeiro, RJ [1986?] 125 p. : LC Card 86-229936
HC187 .C983 1986

Garcia, Manuel Enriquez. Salários indexados, preços e emprego . São Paulo , 1986. 149 p. : LC Card 86-234254
HD5004 .G37 1986

Marion, José Carlos. A contabilidade após a reforma monetária /. São Paulo , 1986. 196 p. : ISBN 85-22-40175-6 : LC Card 86-222982
HG835 .M37 1986

Ness, Walter L. A influência da correção monetária no sistema financeiro /. Rio de Janeiro , 1977. 205 p. : LC Card 85-206096
HG229 .N385 1977

Política salarial. [Rio de Janeiro] [19]85. 31 leaves ; LC Card 86-152437
HD5004 .P65 1985

Vianna, Pedro Jorge Ramos. Inflação vs. indexação, uma contribuição ao tema /. Fortaleza-Ceará [19]84. 121 p. : LC Card 86-130092
HG835 .V53 1984

INDEXATION (ECONOMICS) - BRAZIL - ECONOMETRIC MODELS.
Modiano, Eduardo Marco. Salários, preços e câmbio . Rio de Janeiro, RJ , 1984. 55, [5] leaves ; LC Card 84-234066
HD5004 .M56 1984

INDEXATION (ECONOMICS) - LAW AND LEGISLATION - ARGENTINA.
Troiano, Alberto C. (Alberto Carlos) Los revalúos técnicos de bienes . Buenos Aires [1982] 63, [2] p. : ISBN 950-0-37018-2 LC Card 84-237340
HF5658.5 .T76 1982

INDEXATION (ECONOMICS) - LAW AND LEGISLATION - BRAZIL.
Marion, José Carlos. A contabilidade após a reforma monetária /. São Paulo , 1986. 196 p. : ISBN 85-22-40175-6 : LC Card 86-222982
HG835 .M37 1986

INDEXATION (ECONOMICS) - UNITED STATES.
DeMilner, Lawrence E. Indexing with the consumer price index . [Washington, D.C.] , 1981. xx, 123 p. : LC Card 81-602368 DDC 338.5/28/0973 19
HG229.5 .D45 ***NYPL [JLF 85-3118]***

INDEXING (ECONOMICS) see INDEXATION (ECONOMICS)

Indexing with the consumer price index . DeMilner, Lawrence E. [Washington, D.C.] , 1981. xx, 123 p. : LC Card 81-602368 DDC 338.5/28/0973 19
HG229.5 .D45 ***NYPL [JLF 85-3118]***

India . Sukhwal, B. L., 1929- New York , 1987. viii, 200 p. : ISBN 0-938719-13-0 LC Card 86-81410 DDC 333.7/0954 19
HC433.5 .S85 1987

India.
Atomic Energy Act, 1962. 1986. The Indian atom : power & proliferation : a documentary history of nuclear policies, development, and the critics, 1958-1986 / editor, Dhirendra Sharma. New Delhi , c1986. v, 166 p. ; LC Card 87-900288 DDC 333.79/24/0954 19
HD9698.I52 I52 1986

India and East Africa . Saeed, M. (Muhammad), 1950- Delhi , 1986. vi, 264 p. ; LC Card 87-902493 DDC 382/.0954/0676 19
HF3788.A45 S23 1986

INDIA - APPROPRIATIONS AND EXPENDITURES - HISTORY.
Reddy, K. N. (Kaipa Narayana), 1936- Central government expenditure . New Delhi , 1984. xvi, 175 p. ; LC Card 84-901866 DDC 336.3/9/0954 19
HJ2157 .R43 1984 ***NYPL [JLD 87-66]***

India. Bureau of Industrial Costs & Prices.
Studies on the structure of the industrial economy. New Delhi , 1985- v. <1- > ; LC Card 86-902242 DDC 338.0954 19
HC435.2 .S84 1985

India. Census Commissioner.
Census of India, 1981. Delhi , <1981-1983. v. in : LC Card 87-915014
HA4587.H37 C46 1981

Census of India, 1981. Delhi , <1983-1985. v. in : LC Card 87-915010 DDC 304.6/0954/021 19
HA4581.5 1981g

Census of India, 1981. Delhi , <1983-1987. v. in : LC Card 87-915011 DDC 304.6/0954/12021 19
HA4587.B53 C46 1983

Census of India, 1981. Delhi , <[1983]-[1986]. v. in : LC Card 87-915017 DDC 304.6/0954/3021 19
HA4587.M32 C46 1983

Census of India, 1981. Delhi , <1984-1986. v. in : LC Card 87-915009 DDC 304.6/0954/84021 19
HA4587.A52 C46 1984

INDIA - CENSUS, 1981.
Census of India, 1981. Delhi , <1981-1983. v. in : LC Card 87-915014
HA4587.H37 C46 1981

Census of India, 1981. Delhi , <[1982]-1986. v. in : LC Card 87-915022 DDC 315.4/13 19
HA4587.O74 C46 1982

Census of India, 1981. Delhi , <[1982]-[1983?]. v. in : LC Card 87-915023 DDC 304.6/0954/552021 19
HA4587.P86 C46 1982

Census of India, 1981. Delhi , <1982-1986. <v. in > : LC Card 87-915013
HA4587.H54 C45 1982

Census of India, 1981. Delhi , <[1982]-1985. v. in : LC Card 87-915025 DDC 304.6/0954/167021 19
HA4587.S55 C46 1982

Census of India, 1981. New Delhi , <1982-[1985]. v. in : LC Card 87-915039 DDC 304.6/0954/86021 19
HA4587.P647 C46 1982

Census of India, 1981. Delhi , <1983-1985. v. in : LC Card 87-915021 DDC 304.6/0954/165021 19
HA4587.N33 C46 1983

Census of India, 1981. Delhi , <1983-[1985]. v. in : LC Card 87-915036 DDC 304.6/0954/799021 19
HA4587.W47 C46 1983

Census of India, 1981. Delhi , <1983-1985. v. in : LC Card 87-915010 DDC 304.6/0954/021 19
HA4581.5 1981g

Census of India, 1981. Delhi , <1983-[1985]. v. in : LC Card 87-915033 DDC 304.6/0954/552 19
HA4587.C52 C46 1983

Census of India, 1981. Delhi , <1983-1987. v. in : LC Card 87-915011 DDC 304.6/0954/12021 19
HA4587.B53 C46 1983

Census of India, 1981. Delhi , <[1983]-[1986]. v. in : LC Card 87-915017 DDC 304.6/0954/3021 19
HA4587.M32 C46 1983

Census of India, 1981. Delhi , <1983-1986. v. in : LC Card 87-915012 DDC 304.6/0954/75021 19
HA4587.G84 C46 1983

Census of India, 1981. Gangtok, Sikkim , <1983-1986. v. in : LC Card 87-915028 DDC 315.4/15 19
HA4587.T74 C46 1983

Census of India, 1981. Delhi , <1984-1986. v. in : LC Card 87-915009 DDC 304.6/0954/84021 19
HA4587.A52 C46 1984

Census of India, 1981. Delhi , <1984-1987. v. in : LC Card 87-915015 DDC 304.6/0954/83021 19
HA4587.K47 C46 1984

Census of India, 1981. Delhi , <1984-1986. v. in : LC Card 87-915037 DDC 304.6/0954/81021 19
HA4587.L34 C46 1984

Census of India, 1981. Delhi , <1984-1986. v. in : LC Card 87-915032 DDC 304.6/0954/163021 19
HA4587.A78 C47 1984

Census of India, 1981. Delhi , <1985-[1987]. v. in : maps (some folded) ; LC Card 87-915030 DDC 304.6/0954/14021 19
HA4587.W47 C46 1985

Census of India, 1981. Delhi , <1985-1987. v. in : LC Card 87-915019 DDC 304.6/0954/17021 19
HA4587.M36 C46 1985

Household population by religion of head of household, up to C.D. block and town level, series 14, Meghalaya . New Delhi , 1986. iii, 70 p. ; LC Card 87-901361 DDC 304.6/0954/164021 19
HA4587.M43 H68 1986

Household population by religion of head of household, upto C.D. block and town level, series 31, Mizoram . Delhi , 1986. xiii, 17 p. ; LC Card 87-900232 DDC 304.6/0954/166021 19
HA4587.M58 H68 1986

Jilā janagaṇanā hastapustikā . [Lakhanaū] [1983] xi, 174, ii p., [5] folded leaves of plates : LC Card 86-903117
HA4587.J48 J55 1983

Sinha, Sunil Kumar. Urban growth in India, 1951-81 . New Delhi , 1986. vi, 72 p. : LC Card 86-902819
HA4581.5 1981e

SRS based abridged life tables, 1976-80. New Delhi , 1986. v, 37 p. : LC Card 87-901200
HB1470 .S77 1986

Tables on houses and disabled population, series 23, West Bengal /. Delhi , 1986. v, 128 p. ; LC Card 87-900630
HA4587.W47 T33 1986

INDIA - CIVILIZATION - TO 1200.
Rāya, Śaśikānta, 1957- Prācīna Bhārata meṃ vyāvasāyika samudāya, 600 Ī. Pū. se 200 Ī. taka =. Naī Dillī , 1986. 176 p. ; LC Card 87-902475
HB3639 .R39 1986

INDIA - CIVILIZATION - 1947- - ADDRESSES, ESSAYS, LECTURES.
Rationalism, humanism, and democracy . Meerut , 1985. xcii, 514 p., [2] p. of plates : LC Card 85-901252 DDC 144 19
B833 .R29 1985 ***NYPL [JFD 86-3589]***

INDIA - COMMERCE.
Cable, Vincent. The commerce of culture . New Delhi , 1986. 237 p. ; ISBN 81-7062-004-X : LC Card 86-902899 DDC 338.4/77455/0954 19
HF5439.H27 C33 1986

Kathuria, Sanjay. India's exports, the challenge from China /. New Delhi , 1986. 106 p. ; LC Card 86-902526 DDC 382/.6/0954 19
HF3836.5 .K37 1986

Kumar, Maneet, 1952- Export marketing of non-traditional items . Delhi , 1987. xv, 274 p. ; ISBN 81-202-0185-X : LC Card 87-900875 DDC 382/.6/0954 19
HF1009.7.I4 K86 1987

Role of foreign trade in Indian economy /. New Delhi , 1986. 216 p. ; ISBN 81-7062-001-5 : LC Card 86-902110 DDC 382/.0954 19
HF3782 .R65 1986

Saxena, Usha, 1957- Role of multinationals in India's foreign trade /. New Delhi , 1987. xx, 237 p. ; ISBN 81-7024-081-6 : LC Card 87-900766 DDC 382/.0954 19
HD2899 .S29 1987

INDIA - COMMERCE - AFRICA, EAST.
Saeed, M. (Muhammad), 1950- India and East Africa . Delhi , 1986. vi, 264 p. ; LC Card 87-902493 DDC 382/.0954/0676 19
HF3788.A45 S23 1986

INDIA - COMMERCE - GERMANY, WEST.
Wiemann, Jürgen. India in transition . New Delhi , Berlin , 1986. xxi, 151 p. ; LC Card 87-900287 DDC 338.954 19
HD3616.I83 W54 1986

INDIA - COMMERCE - GREAT. BRITAIN.
Assocham Trade Mission to UK, 1984. Opportunities for Indo-British economic cooperation . New Delhi [1985] 43, xiii p., [4] p. of plates : LC Card 87-902558 DDC 337.54041 19
HF3788.G7 A87 1985

INDIA - COMMERCE - NEPAL.
Dahal, Kishor. Indo-Nepal trade . Kathmandu, Nepal , c1987. x, 66, [9] p. ; LC Card 87-902005 DDC 382/.0954/05496 19
HF3788.N45 D34 1987

INDIA - COMMERCE - PORTUGAL - HISTORY - 16TH CENTURY.
Solis, Duarte Gomes. Armadas da carreira da India de 1560 a 1590 . Lisboa , 1938. xvi, 20 p. : LC Card 86-140347
HF3698.I4 S65 1938

INDIA - COMMERCE - UNITED STATES.
Report on development of India's handloom fabrics for export to the United States of America, September 1957 /. [S.l. , 1957] (Delhi : Albion Press) ii, ii, 108 p., [8] p. of plates : LC Card 81-911063
HD9866.I62 R46 1957

INDIA - COMMERCIAL POLICY.
Kathuria, Sanjay. India's exports, the challenge from China /. New Delhi , 1986. 106 p. ; LC Card 86-902526 DDC 382/.6/0954 19
HF3836.5 .K37 1986

Modwel, Suman Kumar, 1936- Export effort of India /. New Delhi , 1986. ix, 83, [1] p. ; LC Card 86-903364 DDC 382/.6/0954 19
HF1589 .M63 1986

India. Committee to Review the Working of the Monetary System. Monetary policy . New Delhi , c1986. 70 p. ; LC Card 87-900210 DDC 332.4/954 19
HG1235 .M66 1986

India. Dept. of Personnel & Administrative Reforms. Training Division. Command area development, successes and learnings . Hyderabad , c1980. iii, 138 p. ; LC Card 83-906246 DDC 338.1/854 19
HD1741.I29 C65 1980 ***NYPL [JLD 87-597]***

India. Dept. of Surface Transport (Roads Wing) International Seminar on "Road Safety" (1986 : Srinagar, India) International Seminar on "Road Safety", Srinagar, September 17-18, 1986 /. New Delhi [1986] 1 v. (various pagings) : LC Card 87-901986 DDC 363.1/25 19
HE5614 .I5717 1986

India. Diector of Census Operations, Dadra and Nagar Haveli. Census of India, 1981. Delhi , <1984-1985. v. in : LC Card 87-915034 DDC 304.6/0954/796021 19
HA4587.D33 C46 1984

India. Director, Census Operations, Union Territory, Chandigarh. Census of India, 1981. Delhi , <1983-[1985]. v. in : LC Card 87-915033 DDC 304.6/0954/552 19
HA4587.C52 C46 1983

India. Director of Census Operations, Andhra Pradesh. Census of India, 1981. Delhi , <1984-1986. v. in : LC Card 87-915009 DDC 304.6/0954/84021 19
HA4587.A52 C46 1984

India. Director of Census Operations, Arunachal Pradesh. Census of India, 1981. Delhi , <1984-1986. v. in : LC Card 87-915032 DDC 304.6/0954/163021 19
HA4587.A78 C47 1984

India. Director of Census Operations, Bihar. Census of India, 1981. Delhi , <1983-1987. v. in : LC Card 87-915011 DDC 304.6/0954/12021 19
HA4587.B53 C46 1983

India. Director of Census Operations, Goa, Daman & Diu. Census of India, 1981. Delhi , <1983-[1985]. v. in : LC Card 87-915036 DDC 304.6/0954/799021 19
HA4587.W47 C46 1983

India. Director of Census Operations, Gujarat. Census of India, 1981. Delhi , <1983-1986. v. in : LC Card 87-915012 DDC 304.6/0954/75021 19
HA4587.G84 C46 1983

India. Director of Census Operations, Haryana. Census of India, 1981. Delhi , <1981-1983. v. in : LC Card 87-915014
HA4587.H37 C46 1981

India. Director of Census Operations, Himachal Pradesh. Census of India, 1981. Delhi , <1982-1986. <v. in > : LC Card 87-915013
HA4587.H54 C45 1982

India. Director of Census Operations, Kerala. Census of India, 1981. Delhi , <1984-1987. v. in : LC Card 87-915015 DDC 304.6/0954/83021 19
HA4587.K47 C46 1984

India. Director of Census Operations, Lakshadweep. Census of India, 1981. Delhi , <1984-1986. v. in : LC Card 87-915037 DDC 304.6/0954/81021 19
HA4587.L34 C46 1984

India. Director of Census Operations, Madhya Pradesh. Census of India, 1981. Delhi , <[1983]-[1986]. v. in : LC Card 87-915017 DDC 304.6/0954/3021 19
HA4587.M32 C46 1983

India. Director of Census Operations, Manipur. Census of India, 1981. Delhi , <1985-1987. v. in : LC Card 87-915019 DDC 304.6/0954/17021 19
HA4587.M36 C46 1985

India. Director of Census Operations, Mizoram. Household population by religion of head of household, upto C.D. block and town level, series 31, Mizoram . Delhi , 1986. xiii, 17 p. ; LC Card 87-900232 DDC 304.6/0954/166021 19
HA4587.M58 H68 1986

India. Director of Census Operations, Nagaland. Census of India, 1981. Delhi , <1983-1985. v. in : LC Card 87-915021 DDC 304.6/0954/165021 19
HA4587.N33 C46 1983

India. Director of Census Operations, Orissa. Census of India, 1981. Delhi , <[1982]-1986. v. in : LC Card 87-915022 DDC 315.4/13 19
HA4587.O74 C46 1982

India. Director of Census Operations, Punjab. Census of India, 1981. Delhi , <[1982]-[1983?]. v. in : LC Card 87-915023 DDC 304.6/0954/552021 19
HA4587.P86 C46 1982

India. Director of Census Operations, Sikkim. Census of India, 1981. Delhi , <[1982]-1985. v. in : LC Card 87-915025 DDC 304.6/0954/167021 19
HA4587.S55 C46 1982

India. Director of Census Operations, Tripura. Census of India, 1981. Gangtok, Sikkim , <1983-1986. v. in : LC Card 87-915028 DDC 315.4/15 19
HA4587.T74 C46 1983

India. Director of Census Operations, Uttar Pradesh. Jilā janagaṇanā hastapustikā . [Lakhanaū] [1983] xi, 174, ii p., [5] folded leaves of plates : LC Card 86-903117
HA4587.J48 J55 1983

India. Director of Census Operations, West Bengal.
Census of India, 1981. Delhi , <1985-[1987]. v. in : maps (some folded) ; LC Card 87-915030 DDC 304.6/0954/14021 19
HA4587.W47 C46 1985

Tables on houses and disabled population, series 23, West Bengal /. Delhi , 1986. v, 128 p. ; LC Card 87-900630
HA4587.W47 T33 1986

India. Directorate of Census Operations, Pondicherry. Census of India, 1981. New Delhi , <1982-[1985]. v. in : LC Card 87-915039 DDC 304.6/0954/86021 19
HA4587.P647 C46 1982

India. Directorate of Marketing and Inspection. Marketing of walnuts in India. Faridabad : Market Research and Planning Cell, Directorate of Marketing and Inspection, Ministry of Rural Development, Govt. of India ; Delhi : Controller of Publications, 1986. ix, 180 p. : ill. ; 22 cm. (MRPC . no. 11) "AMA.190/1000-1986 (D.S.K.II)"--P. [4] of cover. LC Card 86-903362
1. Walnut industry - India. I. India. Directorate of Marketing and Inspection. Market Research and Planning Cell. II. Series: MRPC (Series) , no. 11. III. Title.
HD9259.N7 I45 1986

Report on the marketing of sandalwood in India. Faridabad , 1986. viii, 196 p. : LC Card 86-903266 DDC 381/.41497394/0954 19
HD9769.S33 I47 1986

India. Directorate of Marketing and Inspection. Market Research and Planning Cell. India. Directorate of Marketing and Inspection. Marketing of walnuts in India. Faridabad , Delhi , 1986. ix, 180 p. : LC Card 86-903362
HD9259.N7 I45 1986

INDIA - ECONOMIC CONDITIONS.
Dhar, D. P., 1918-1975. Enterpreneurship and development /. New Delhi [pref. 1974] 23 p., [2] p. of plates : LC Card 80-908353 DDC 338.954 19
HB615 .D49 1974

Dutt, Romesh Chunder, 1848-1909. The economic history of India in the Victorian Age . London [19--] xxii, 628 p. ; LC Card 87-131511
HC435 .D975 1900z

Lakshmana Rao, V., 1940- Progress of development banking in India /. Allahabad, India , 1986. xvi, 139 p. ; ISBN 81-85076-07-3 : LC Card 86-902782 DDC 332.2 19
HG3284 .L35 1986

INDIA - ECONOMIC CONDITIONS - TO 1000.
Om Prakash, 1916- Economy and food in ancient India /. Delhi , 1987- v. <1- > ; ISBN 81-217-0027-2 : LC Card 87-902484 DDC 338.1/9/34 19
HC434 .O45 1987

INDIA - ECONOMIC CONDITIONS - 1918-1947.
Ul'i͡anovskiĭ, R. A. (Rostislav Aleksandrovich) Agrarnai͡a Indii͡a mezhdu mirovymi voĭnami . Moskva , 1981. 342, [2] p. ; LC Card 82-102795 DDC 338.1/0954 19
HD2072 .U44 1981

INDIA - ECONOMIC CONDITIONS - 1947-
Adiseshiah, Malcolm S. Mid year review of the economy, 1986-87 /. New Delhi , 1987. 193 p. : ISBN 81-7062-016-3 : LC Card 87-900477 DDC 330.954/052 19
HC435.2 .A648 1987

Ashraf, Shahid, 1959- Indian industry . Delhi, India , 1986. 100 p. ; LC Card 86-903305 DDC 338.0954 19
HC435.2 .A889 1986

Balakrishnan, C. B. Review of a mid-year review of the economy, 1984 /. New Delhi , 1984. 132 p. ; LC Card 86-903796 DDC 330.954/052 19
HC435.2 .B323 1984

Chakrabarti, Rajendra M. Underdevelopment and choices in agriculture . New Delhi , 1986. xv, 322 p. : LC Card 86-903184 DDC 338.1/0954 19
HC435.2 .C466 1986

Datta, Anindya. Growth and equity . Calcutta , New York , 1986. xii, 119 p. : ISBN 0-19-561882-3 : LC Card 87-900001 DDC 338.954 19
HD82 .D334 1986

Gupta, S. P. (Shiv Prakash), 1957- Structural dimensions of poverty in India /. Delhi, India , 1987. xii, 427 p. : LC Card 87-901423 DDC 362.5/0954 19
HC440.P6 G86 1987

Guru, D. D. Energy and economic development /. Delhi , c1987. xi, 257 p. : ISBN 81-85061-53-6 : LC Card 87-901433 DDC 333.79/0954 19
HD9502.I4 G87 1987

Kabra, Kamal Nayan. Black money . New Delhi , 1985. 47 p. ; LC Card 87-900898 DDC 381 19
HJ2348.5 .K32 1985

Narayan Prasad, P. S. C.D. Deshmukh, his contribution to monetary and economic policy /. New Delhi , c1985. xiv, 54 p., [1] leaf of plates : LC Card 85-905075 DDC 338.954 19
HC432.5.D47 N37 1985 ***NYPL [JLD 86-3239]***

Raza, Moonis. Transport geography of India . New Delhi , 1986. xii, 299 p. : LC Card

86-903251 DDC 380.5/0954 19
HE3298 .R39 1986

Role of foreign trade in Indian economy /. New Delhi , 1986. 216 p. ; ISBN 81-7062-001-5 : LC Card 86-902110 DDC 382/.0954 19
HF3782 .R65 1986

Rudolph, Lloyd I. In pursuit of Lakshmi . Chicago , 1987. xvii, 529 p. ; ISBN 0-226-73138-3 : LC Card 86-24903 DDC 338.954 19
HC435 .R77 1987

Sarma, N. A. International environment and India's economic development /. New Delhi , 1986. viii, 100 p. ; ISBN 81-7017-214-4 : LC Card 86-902210 DDC 338.954 19
HC435.2 .S273 1986

Saxena, R. B. IMF loan to India . Delhi, India , 1986. ix, 284 p. ; LC Card 86-903311 DDC 332.1/52 19
HG3971 .S29 1986

Seth, Vijay K. Industrialisation in India . Delhi, India , 1987. xii, 242 p. : ISBN 81-900026-7-8 : LC Card 87-902803 DDC 338.0954 19
HC435.2 .S418 1987

Studies on the structure of the industrial economy. New Delhi , 1985- v. <1- > ; LC Card 86-902242 DDC 338.0954 19
HC435.2 .S84 1985

Sundrum, R. M. Growth and income distribution in India . New Delhi , Beverly Hills , 1986. p. cm. ISBN 0-8039-9522-9 (U. S.) LC Card 86-26323 DDC 330.954/04 19
HC435.2 .S883 1986

Tata, J. R. D. (Jehangir Ratanji Dadabhoy), 1904- Keynote . Bombay , 1986. xviii, 155 p., [1] leaf of plates : ISBN 81-85110-00-X : LC Card 86-902369 DDC 338.0954
HC435.2 .T37 1986

Vyasulu, Vinod. Development of backward areas . New Delhi, India , 1987. xi, 188 p. : ISBN 81-85030-05-7 : LC Card 87-902689 DDC 332.6/42/0954 19
HD2346.I5 V93 1987

INDIA - ECONOMIC CONDITIONS - 1947- - CONGRESSES.

The Development process of the Indian economy /. Bombay , 1987. xxxxxxviii, 1219, 78 p. : LC Card 87-901099 DDC 338.954 19
HC435.2 .D476 1987

Development, socio-cultural dimensions /. Jaipur , 1986. xxi, 264 p. ; ISBN 81-7033-020-3 : LC Card 86-902849 DDC 306/.0954 19
HC435.2 .D478 1986

The Indian economy . Boulder, Colo. , 1988. ix, 374 p. : ISBN 0-8133-7505-3 (pbk. : alk. paper) LC Card 87-22472 DDC 330.954/05 19
HC435.2 .I555 1988

Indien, Probleme eines Schwellenlandes . Tübingen , c1984. 75 p. ; ISBN 3-922362-02-8 LC Card 85-157722
HC435.2 .I6235 1984

INDIA - ECONOMIC CONDITIONS - 1980-

Arya, Dwarika Prasas, 1922- Swastika removes India's poverty and problems within 100 days . Calcutta, West Bengal , 1982. vi, 153 p. ; LC Card 82-904556 DDC 338.954 19
HC435.2 .A887 1982

INDIA - ECONOMIC CONDITIONS - CONGRESSES.

International Congress on Economic History (8th : 1982 : Budapest, Hungary) Münzprägung, Geldumlauf und Wechselkurse . Trier , 1984. 421 p. : ISBN 3-923087-06-3 (pbk.)
HG205 1982 .I53 ***NYPL [JLE 86-3176]***

Trusteeship, the Gandhian alternative /. New Delhi , c1986. xiii, 238 p. ; LC Card 86-903783 DDC 330.1 19
HB199 .T76 1986

INDIA - ECONOMIC CONDITIONS - REGIONAL DISPARITIES.

Mandal, S. K. (Sushil Kumar), 1954- Regional disparities and imbalances in India's planned economic development /. New Delhi [1986], c1987. 380 p. ; LC Card 87-900589 DDC 338.954 19
HC435.2 .M335 1987

INDIA - ECONOMIC POLICY.

Ambirajan, S. Political economy and monetary management . Madras , c1984. viii, 203 p. ; LC Card 87-900241 DDC 332.4/954 19
HC433 .A42 1984

Chanana, Charanjit. Industrial economics in developing countries, India . New Delhi , 1983. 113 p. : LC Card 83-903832 DDC 338.0954 19
HC435.2 .C4717 1983 ***NYPL [JLD 87-674]***

Narayan Prasad, P. S. C.D. Deshmukh, his contribution to monetary and economic policy /. New Delhi , c1985. xiv, 54 p., [1] leaf of plates : LC Card 85-905075 DDC 338.954 19
HC432.5.D47 N37 1985
NYPL [JLD 86-3239]

Prakash, Om, 1927- Guided incomes policy /. New Delhi , 1983. vi, 214 p. ; LC Card 83-902415 DDC 339.5/0954 19
HC440.I5 P72 1983 ***NYPL [JLD 86-3834]***

Venkateswaran, R. J. Decision-making in Indian economy . Bombay , 1986. vii, 199 p. ; LC Card 86-902861 DDC 338.954 19
HC435.2 .V457 1986

INDIA - ECONOMIC POLICY - 1947-

Bhattacharya, Sib Nath, 1938- India's five-year plans in theory and practice /. New Delhi, India , 1987. xvi, 352 p. ; ISBN 81-200-0076-5 : LC Card 87-900413 DDC 338.954 19
HC435.2 .B45476 1987

Chakravarty, Sukhamoy. Development planning . Oxford [Oxfordshire] , New York , 1987. viii, 137 p. ; ISBN 0-19-828555-8 : LC Card 87-1554 DDC 338.954 19
HC435.2 .C467 1987

Contribution to national and regional planning problems /. Calcutta , 1983. vii, 174 p., [2] leaves of plates (some folded) : LC Card 83-907550 DDC 338.954 19
HC435.2 .C63 1983 ***NYPL [JLD 86-3868]***

Datta, Bhabatosh, 1911- Social justice in a mixed economy /. Calcutta , 1982. ii, 64 p. ; LC Card 82-905698 DDC 338.954 19
HC435.2 .D353 1982 ***NYPL [JLD 86-3172]***

Ghosh, B. N. Political economy of neocolonialism in Third World countries /. New Delhi , c1985. vii, 174 p. ; LC Card 85-903172 DDC 338.9/009172/4 19
HC59.7 .G485 1985 ***NYPL [JLD 87-1141]***

Goel, Brij Bhushan. Project management . New Delhi , c1987. 352 p. : LC Card 87-900676 DDC 338.954/0068 19
HD69.P75 G635 1987

Rudolph, Lloyd I. In pursuit of Lakshmi . Chicago , 1987. xvii, 529 p. ; ISBN 0-226-73138-3 : LC Card 86-24903 DDC 338.954 19
HC435 .R77 1987

Shanker Shetty, K. Welfare state and bank nationalisation in India /. Delhi , 1982. xvii, 345 p. ; ISBN 0-333-90729-9 : LC Card 83-903489 DDC 332.1/0954 19
HG3284 .S4823 1982 ***NYPL [JLD 86-4354]***

Sinha, R. K. (Raj Kishore), 1946- Planning in India . New Delhi , c1987. ix, 247 p. ; ISBN 81-7003-079-X : LC Card 87-901786 DDC 338.954 19
HC435.2 .S565 1987

Sudarsana Rao, R. (Rokkam) Grants-in-aid and economic development in India /. Allahabad, India , 1986. ix, 271 p. ; ISBN 81-85076-14-6 : LC Card 86-903200 DDC 338.954
HJ1338 .S83 1986

Sundrum, R. M. Growth and income distribution in India . New Delhi , Beverly Hills , 1986. p. cm. ISBN 0-8039-9522-9 (U. S.) LC Card 86-26323 DDC 330.954/04 19
HC435.2 .S883 1986

Wiemann, Jürgen. India in transition . New Delhi , Berlin , 1986. xxi, 151 p. ; LC Card 87-900287 DDC 338.954 19
HD3616.I83 W54 1986

INDIA - ECONOMIC POLICY - 1947- - ADDRESSES, ESSAYS, LECTURES.

Patel, I. G. (Indraprasad Gordhanbhai), 1924- Essays in economic policy and economic growth /. Basingstoke, Hampshire , 1986. xii, 261 p. ; ISBN 0-333-39213-2
NYPL [JLD 86-4061]

INDIA - ECONOMIC POLICY - 1947- - CONGRESSES.

Indien, Probleme eines Schwellenlandes . Tübingen , c1984. 75 p. ; ISBN 3-922362-02-8 LC Card 85-157722
HC435.2 .I6235 1984

INDIA - ECONOMIC POLICY - 1980-

Adiseshiah, Malcolm S. Mid year review of the economy, 1986-87 /. New Delhi , 1987. 193 p. : ISBN 81-7062-016-3 : LC Card 87-900477 DDC 330.954/052 19
HC435.2 .A648 1987

Arya, Dwarika Prasas, 1922- Swastika removes India's poverty and problems within 100 days . Calcutta, West Bengal , 1982. vi, 153 p. ; LC Card 82-904556 DDC 338.954 19
HC435.2 .A887 1982

Chitale, V. P. Capital output ratio in the Indian economy /. New Delhi , 1986. viii, 106 p. ; ISBN 81-7027-099-5 : LC Card 86-901894 DDC 338/.06/0954 19
HC435.2 .C4872 1986

Dubhashi, P. R. Essays in development administration /. New Delhi, India , 1987. x, 391 p. ; LC Card 87-901132 DDC 338.954 19
HC435.2 .D833 1987

Kabra, Kamal Nayan. India's black economy and maldevelopment /. New Delhi , 1986. 192 p. ; ISBN 81-7050-025-7 : LC Card 86-902668 DDC 338.954 19
HC435.2 .K26 1986

Reflections on the Indian economy /. Delhi, India , 1987. xxxi, 439 p. : ISBN 81-900026-0-0 : LC Card 87-901043 DDC 338.9 19
HC435.2 .R425 1987

Seth, Satish C. India, the next 7000 days /. New Delhi , c1985. xxiv, 312 p. [1] spolded Leaf of plates ; ISBN 0-85226-864-5 : LC Card 85-904799 DDC 338.5/443/0954 19
HC435.2 .S416 1985 ***NYPL [JLD 86-3377]***

INDIA - ECONOMIC POLICY - 1980- - CONGRESSES.

The Development process of the Indian economy /. Bombay , 1987. xxxxxxviii, 1219, 78 p. : LC Card 87-901099 DDC 338.954 19
HC435.2 .D476 1987

Public enterprise policy in India and U.K. in 1980s /. Bombay , 1987. xx, 286 p. ; LC Card 86-903771 DDC 338.6/2/0941 19
HD4293 .P775 1987

Resource mobilisation, medium and long-term issues . New Delhi [1986] viii, 98 p. ; LC Card 87-902180 DDC 338.954 19
HC435.2 .R46 1986

INDIA - ECONOMIC POLICY - 1980- - ECONOMETRIC MODELS.

Manohar Rao, M. J. Filtering and control of macroeconomic systems . Amsterdam ; New York : xii, 279 p. : ISBN 0-444-70188-5 (Elsevier Science Pub. Co.) LC Card 86-32928 DDC 339.5/0954 19
HC435.2 .M34 1987

INDIA - ECONOMIC POOLICY - 1947- - CONGRESSES.

The Indian economy . Boulder, Colo. , 1988. ix, 374 p. : ISBN 0-8133-7505-3 (pbk. : alk. paper) LC Card 87-22472 DDC 330.954/05 19
HC435.2 .I555 1988

INDIA - EMIGRATION AND IMMIGRATION.

Ly-Tio-Fane Pineo, Huguette. Lured away . Moka, Mauritius , 1984. 261 p. :
NYPL [JLD 87-587]

Studies in migration . Delhi , 1986. x, 400 p. : ISBN 81-85054-08-8 : LC Card 86-902753 DDC 304.8/0954 19
HB2099 .S78 1986

INDIA - FOREIGN ECONOMIC RELATIONS.

Ghosh, B. N. Political economy of neocolonialism in Third World countries /. New Delhi , c1985. vii, 174 p. ; LC Card 85-903172 DDC 338.9/009172/4 19
HC59.7 .G485 1985 ***NYPL [JLD 87-1141]***

Role of foreign trade in Indian economy /. New Delhi , 1986. 216 p. ; ISBN 81-7062-001-5 : LC Card 86-902110 DDC 382/.0954 19
HF3782 .R65 1986

INDIA - FOREIGN ECONOMIC RELATIONS - DEVELOPING COUNTRIES.

South-South economic cooperation . New Delhi , 1987. xii, 262 p. ; ISBN 81-7027-102-9 : LC Card 86-903797 DDC 337/.09172/4 19
HF1413 .S617 1987

INDIA - FOREIGN ECONOMIC RELATIONS - EUROPE, EASTERN.
Indo-CMEA economic relations /. New Delhi , 1987. xviii, 263 p. ; ISBN 81-7024-078-6 : LC Card 87-901620 DDC 337.54047 19
HC433 .I535 1987

INDIA - FOREIGN ECONOMIC RELATIONS - GREAT BRITAIN.
Assocham Trade Mission to UK, 1984. Opportunities for Indo-British economic cooperation . New Delhi [1985] 43, xiii p., [4] p. of plates : LC Card 87-902558 DDC 337.54041 19
HF3788.G7 A87 1985

INDIA - FOREIGN ECONOMIC RELATIONS - NEPAL.
Maass, Citha Doris. Indien, Nepal, Sri Lanka . Wiesbaden , 1982. xxi, 380 p. ; ISBN 3-515-03802-7 LC Card 86-214318
HF1590.15.N4 M33 1982

INDIA - FOREIGN ECONOMIC RELATIONS - SOVIET UNION.
Indo-CMEA economic relations /. New Delhi , 1987. xviii, 263 p. ; ISBN 81-7024-078-6 : LC Card 87-901620 DDC 337.54047 19
HC433 .I535 1987

Menon, M. S. N., 1924- Indo-Soviet trade and economic ties /. New Delhi , 1986. 229 p. ; LC Card 86-903273 DDC 337.54047 19
HF1590.5.S65 M46 1986

INDIA - FOREIGN ECONOMIC RELATIONS - SRI LANKA.
Maass, Citha Doris. Indien, Nepal, Sri Lanka . Wiesbaden , 1982. xxi, 380 p. ; ISBN 3-515-03802-7 LC Card 86-214318
HF1590.15.N4 M33 1982

INDIA - FOREIGN ECONOMIC RELATIONS - UNITED STATES.
Roy, P. C. (Prabhash Chandra), 1955- Indo-U. S. economic relations . New Delhi , c1986. 206 p. : LC Card 86-902903 DDC 337.54073 19
HF1590.15.U5 R69 1986

INDIA - FOREIGN RELATIONS - BANGLADESH.
Ābbāsa, Bi. Ema., 1911- The Ganges waters dispute /. New Delhi , c1982. xv, 157 p., 8 p. of plates : ISBN 0-7069-2080-5 : LC Card 83-900165 DDC 341.4/42 19
HD1698.G36 A23 1982

India - Government. see **India - Politics and government.**

INDIA - HISTORY - 18TH CENTURY.
Mukhopadhyay, Subhas Chandra, 1938- The agrarian policy of the British in Bengal . Allahabad, India , 1987. xi, 195 p. ; ISBN 81-85076-11-1 : LC Card 87-900481 DDC 338.1/85414 19
HJ4392.I4 M85 1987

India in transition . Wiemann, Jürgen. New Delhi , Berlin , 1986. xxi, 151 p. ; LC Card 87-900287 DDC 338.954 19
HD3616.I83 W54 1986

INDIA - INDUSTRIES.
Ashraf, Shahid, 1959- Indian industry . Delhi, India , 1986. 100 p. ; LC Card 86-903305 DDC 338.0954 19
HC435.2 .A889 1986

Chanana, Charanjit. Industrial economics in developing countries, India . New Delhi , 1983. 113 p. : LC Card 83-903832 DDC 338.0954 19
HC435.2 .C4717 1983 ***NYPL [JLD 87-674]***

Desai, Vasant, 1933- Indian industry . Bombay , 1987. xiii, 816 p. : LC Card 87-901051 DDC 338.0954 19
HC435.2 .D45 1987

Goldar, B. N. Productivity growth in Indian industry /. New Delhi , 1986, c1985. xvi, 206 p. ; ISBN 81-7023-062-4 : LC Card 86-902812 DDC 338/.06/0954 19
HC440.I52 G65 1986

Mahajan, V. S., 1923- Growth of agriculture and industry in India /. New Delhi , c1983. 176 p. ; LC Card 83-906175 DDC 338.0954 19
HD2072 .M23 1983 ***NYPL [JLD 87-671]***

Studies on the structure of the industrial economy. New Delhi , 1985- v. <1- > ; LC Card 86-902242 DDC 338.0954 19
HC435.2 .S84 1985

Tata, J. R. D. (Jehangir Ratanji Dadabhoy), 1904- Keynote . Bombay , 1986. xviii, 155 p., [1] leaf of plates : ISBN 81-85110-00-X : LC Card 86-902369 DDC 338.0954
HC435.2 .T37 1986

INDIA - INDUSTRIES - ENVIRONMENTAL ASPECTS.
Seth, Vijay K. Industrialisation in India . Delhi, India , 1987. xii, 242 p. : ISBN 81-900026-7-8 : LC Card 87-902803 DDC 338.0954 19
HC435.2 .S418 1987

India International Centre.
Role of foreign trade in Indian economy /. New Delhi , 1986. 216 p. ; ISBN 81-7062-001-5 : LC Card 86-902110 DDC 382/.0954 19
HF3782 .R65 1986

India International Centre. Economic Affairs Group. Adiseshiah, Malcolm S. Mid year review of the economy, 1986-87 /. New Delhi , 1987. 193 p. : ISBN 81-7062-016-3 : LC Card 87-900477 DDC 330.954/052 19
HC435.2 .A648 1987

India. Labour Bureau. Statistical profile on women labour. Simla [1983] v, 224 p. ; LC Card 84-900395 DDC 331.4/0954/021 19
HD5819 .S83 1983 ***NYPL [JLF 86-1946]***

INDIA - MANUFACTURES.
Little, Ian Malcolm David. Small manufacturing enterprises . New York , 1987. x, 362 p. : ISBN 0-19-520619-3 LC Card 87-12365 DDC 338.6/42/0954 19
HD9736.I52 L57 1987

India. Ministry of External Affairs. ECDC handbook . [New Delhi] , 1983. vi, 679 p. ; LC Card 83-903543 DDC 337.1/1724 19
HC59.7 .E23 1983 ***NYPL [JLF 86-1755]***

India. National Council of Applied Economic Research. see **National Council of Applied Economic Research.**

INDIA, NORTHEASTERN - ECONOMIC CONDITIONS - CONGRESSES.
Industrial development in north east India /. Guwahati , 1987. xx, 179 p. : LC Card 87-902151 DDC 338.0954/1 19
HC437.N57 I55 1987

INDIA, NORTHEASTERN - INDUSTRIES - CONGRESSES.
Industrial development in north east India /. Guwahati , 1987. xx, 179 p. : LC Card 87-902151 DDC 338.0954/1 19
HC437.N57 I55 1987

INDIA, NORTHEASTERN - POPULATION - CONGRESSES.
The Pattern & problems of population in north-east India /. New Delhi , 1986. xv, 433 p. ; ISBN 81-85024-03-0 : LC Card 86-902123 DDC 304.6/0954/1 19
HA4587.I44 P37 1986

INDIA - OCCUPATIONS - HISTORY.
Rāya, Śaśikānta, 1957- Prācīna Bhārata meṃ vyāvasāyika samudāya, 600 Ī. Pū. se 200 Ī. taka =. Naī Dillī , 1986. 176 p. ; LC Card 87-902475
HB3639 .R39 1986

India. Office of the Director of Census Operations, Meghalaya. Household population by religion of head of household, up to C.D. block and town level, series 14, Meghalaya . New Delhi , 1986. iii, 70 p. ; LC Card 87-901361 DDC 304.6/0954/164021 19
HA4587.M43 H68 1986

India. Office of the Registrar General.
Census of India, 1981. Delhi , <1981-1983. v. in : LC Card 87-915014
HA4587.H37 C46 1981

Census of India, 1981. Delhi , <[1983]-[1986]. v. in : LC Card 87-915017 DDC 304.6/0954/3021 19
HA4587.M32 C46 1983

Census of India, 1981. Delhi , <1983-1987. v. in : LC Card 87-915011 DDC 304.6/0954/12021 19
HA4587.B53 C46 1983

Census of India, 1981. Delhi , <1983-1985. v. in : LC Card 87-915010 DDC 304.6/0954/021 19
HA4581.5 1981g

Census of India, 1981. Delhi , <1984-1986. v. in : LC Card 87-915009 DDC 304.6/0954/84021 19
HA4587.A52 C46 1984

Sinha, Sunil Kumar. Urban growth in India, 1951-81 . New Delhi , 1986. vi, 72 p. : LC Card 86-902819
HA4581.5 1981e

India. Parliament. Committee on Public Undertakings.
Action taken by Government on the recommendations contained in the sixteenth report of the Committee on Public Undertakings (Sixth Lok Sabha) on Jute Corporation of India Ltd. : economic offences committed by jute trade and jute industry, Ministry of Industry, Department of Industrial Development ; sixth Lok Sabha. New Delhi : Lok Sabha Secretariat, 1979. vii, 82 p. ; 25 cm. Cover title. Errata slip inserted. LC Card 79-906770
1. Jute Corporation of India. 2. Jute industry - India. 3. Criminal investigation - India. I. Title.
HD9156.J8 I355 1979

Tenth report on public undertakings, delays in commencement of production business, under utilisation of capacity and related matters, Ministry of Finance (Bureau of Public Enterprises) : action taken by Government on the recommendations contained in the twenty-eighth report of the Committee on Public Undertakings (Sixth Lok Sabha) / Committee on Public Undertakings, 1980-81 (Seventh Lok Sabha). New Delhi : Lok Sabha Secretariat, c1981. vii, 50 p. ; 26 cm. Cover title. Spine title: Action taken by Government on the ... under utilisation of capacity and related matters, Ministry of Finance. "Presented to Lok Sabha, 16 Mar. 1981 and laid in Rajya Sabha on 16 Mar. 1981." "C.P.U. no. 417." LC Card 81-902947 DDC 354.5409/2 19
1. Government business enterprises - India. I. Title.
HD4293 .I515 1981

India. Parliament. Lok Sabha. Secretariat.
National energy policy. New Delhi , 1986. v, 67 p. ; LC Card 87-900181
HD9502.I42 N36 1986

Transport in India. New Delhi , 1986. v, 64 p. ; LC Card 87-900171 DDC 380.5/0954 19
HE271.A2 T73 1986

India. Planning Commission. Programme Evaluation Organisation. Evaluation report on essential supplies programme. New Delhi : Programme Evaluation Organisation, Planning Commission, Govt. of India, 1985. vii, 121 p. ; 31 cm. Includes statistical tables. "PPC 258/3,000-1985 (D.S.K.II)"--P. [4] of cover. LC Card 87-902422 DDC 381/.41/0954 19
1. Commercial products - India. 2. Farm produce - India. I. Title.
HF1040.9.I4 I46 1985

INDIA - POLITICS AND GOVERNMENT - 19TH CENTURY.
Dutt, Romesh Chunder, 1848-1909. The economic history of India in the Victorian Age . London [19--] xxii, 628 p. ; LC Card 87-131511
HC435 .D975 1900z

INDIA - POLITICS AND GOVERNMENT - 1857-1919.
Chatterji, Rakhahari, 1943- Working class and the nationalist movement in India . New Delhi , c1984. ix, 215 p. ; LC Card 84-902674 DDC 322.4/4/0954 19
HD8686 .C47 1984 ***NYPL [JLD 87-709]***

INDIA - POLITICS AND GOVERNMENT - 20TH CENTURY.
Ray, Renuka Mukerji, 1903- My reminiscences . New Delhi , 1982. ix, 294 p., [5] p. of plates : LC Card 82-905707 DDC 954.03/5 19
DS481.R33 A38 1982 ***NYPL [JFD 85-9372]***

INDIA - POLITICS AND GOVERNMENT - 1919-1947.
Chatterji, Rakhahari, 1943- Working class and the nationalist movement in India . New Delhi , c1984. ix, 215 p. ; LC Card 84-902674 DDC 322.4/4/0954 19
HD8686 .C47 1984 ***NYPL [JLD 87-709]***

INDIA - POLITICS AND GOVERNMENT - 1947-
Public administration in India . Allahabad ,

1983. xii, 308 p. ; LC Card 83-907416 DDC 354.54 19
JQ224 .P75 1983 NYPL [JLE 86-4197]

Rudolph, Lloyd I. In pursuit of Lakshmi . Chicago , 1987. xvii, 529 p. ; ISBN 0-226-73138-3 : LC Card 86-24903 DDC 338.954 19
HC435 .R77 1987

Singh, V. B., 1941- Profiles of political elites in India /. Delhi , 1984. xii, 178 p. : LC Card 84-900272 DDC 305.5/24/0954 19
JQ281 .S565 1984 NYPL [JLD 86-4319]

INDIA - POLITICS AND GOVERNMENT - 1977-
Dubhashi, P. R. Essays in development administration /. New Delhi, India , 1987. x, 391 p. ; LC Card 87-901132 DDC 338.954 19
HC435.2 .D833 1987

INDIA - POLITICS AND GOVERNMENT - 1977- - ADDRESSES, ESSAYS, LECTURES.
Rationalism, humanism, and democracy . Meerut , 1985. xcii, 514 p., [2] p. of plates : LC Card 85-901252 DDC 144 19
B833 .R29 1985 NYPL [JFD 86-3589]

INDIA - POPULATION.
Sukhwal, B. L., 1929- India . New York , 1987. viii, 200 p. : ISBN 0-938719-13-0 LC Card 86-81410 DDC 333.7/0954 19
HC433.5 .S85 1987

INDIA - POPULATION - CONGRESSES.
Recent advances in the techniques for demographic analysis /. Bombay , 1987. xiv, 456 p. ; LC Card 87-900498
HB849 .R42 1987

INDIA - POPULATION - STATISTICS.
Hobbs, Frank. Demographic estimates, projections, and selected social characteristics of the population of India /. Washington, D.C. [1986] vii, 148 p. : LC Card 87-601294 DDC 304.6/0954/021 19
HA4585 .H63 1986

India (Republic). Anthropological Survey. Memoir ; no. 67.
Chakrabarti, S. B., 1943- Around the plough . Calcutta , 1986. xviii, 203 p., 8 p. of plates : LC Card 86-902283
HD2075.P36 C48 1986
NYPL [L-10 8468 no.67]

India (Republic). Ministry of Irrigation. Command Area Development programme in India . New Delhi , 1981. ii, 62 p. ; LC Card 83-907584 NYPL [JLF 86-818]

India (Republic). Ministry of Works, Housing and Supply. National Buildings Organisation. see **India (Republic). National Buildings Organisation.**

India (Republic). National Buildings Organisation. (Old Catalog form: India. National Buildings Organization)
Dholakia, Bakul H. 1947- The economics of housing in India . Delhi , 1982. xviii, 274 p. ; LC Card 83-905798 DDC 363.5/0954 19
HD7361.A3 D47 1982
NYPL [JLD 85-2908]

INDIA-RUBBER INDUSTRY. see **RUBBER INDUSTRY AND TRADE.**

INDIA - RURAL CONDITIONS.
Alaev, L. B. Sel'skaia obshchina v Severnoĭ Indii . Moskva , 1981. 240 p. ; LC Card 82-101919
HD873 .A63 1981

Étienne, Gilbert. Food and poverty . New Delhi , Newbury Park, Calif. , 1987. p. cm. ISBN 0-8039-9540-7 LC Card 87-16992 DDC 338.1/0954 19
HC440.P6 E86 1987

Rural poverty in South Asia /. New York , 1988. p. cm. ISBN 0-231-06224-9 LC Card 87-9413 DDC 330.954/052/091734 19
HC440.P6 R87 1988

Ul'ianovskiĭ, R. A. (Rostislav Aleksandrovich) Agrarnaia Indiia mezhdu mirovymi voĭnami . Moskva , 1981. 342, [2] p. ; LC Card 82-102795 DDC 338.1/0954 19
HD2072 .U44 1981

INDIA - RURAL CONDITIONS - CASE STUDIES.
Kohli, Atul. The state and poverty in India . Cambridge [Cambridgeshire] , New York , 1987. x, 262 p. : ISBN 0-521-32008-9 LC Card 85-25554 DDC 333.3/1/54 19
HD1333.14 K65 1986 NYPL [JLD 87-1517]

INDIA - SCHEDULED TRIBES - ECONOMIC CONDITIONS.
Parvathamma, C., 1928- Scheduled castes and tribes . New Delhi , 1984. xiii, 310 p. ;
NYPL [JLD 87-707]

INDIA - SCHEDULED TRIBES - SOCIAL CONDITIONS.
Parvathamma, C., 1928- Scheduled castes and tribes . New Delhi , 1984. xiii, 310 p. ;
NYPL [JLD 87-707]

INDIA - SOCIAL CONDITIONS.
Mishra, G. P. Village industries and agriculture in changing agrarian situation /. New Delhi , c1985. 120 p. ; ISBN 81-7024-010-7 LC Card 85-904926 DDC 338.6/34/0954 19
HD2346.I5 M49 1985 NYPL [JLD 86-3746]

Ray, Renuka Mukerji, 1903- My reminiscences . New Delhi , 1982. ix, 294 p., [5] p. of plates : LC Card 82-905707 DDC 954.03/5 19
DS481.R33 A38 1982 NYPL [JFD 85-9372]

INDIA - SOCIAL CONDITIONS - 1947-
Tata, J. R. D. (Jehangir Ratanji Dadabhoy), 1904- Keynote . Bombay , 1986. xviii, 155 p., [1] leaf of plates : ISBN 81-85110-00-X : LC Card 86-902369 DDC 338.0954
HC435.2 .T37 1986

INDIA - SOCIAL CONDITIONS - 1947- - CONGRESSES.
Development, socio-cultural dimensions /. Jaipur , 1986. xxi, 264 p. ; ISBN 81-7033-020-3 : LC Card 86-902849 DDC 306/.0954 19
HC435.2 .D478 1986

INDIA - SOCIAL POLICY.
Chakravarty, Sukhamoy. Development planning . Oxford [Oxfordshire] , New York , 1987. viii, 137 p. ; ISBN 0-19-828555-8 : LC Card 87-1554 DDC 338.954 19
HC435.2 .C467 1987

Shanker Shetty, K. Welfare state and bank nationalisation in India /. Delhi , 1982. xvii, 345 p. ; ISBN 0-333-90729-9 : LC Card 83-903489 DDC 332.1/0954 19
HG3284 .S4823 1982 NYPL [JLD 86-4354]

Sinha, R. K. (Raj Kishore), 1946- Planning in India . New Delhi , c1987. ix, 247 p. ; ISBN 81-7003-079-X : LC Card 87-901786 DDC 338.954 19
HC435.2 .S565 1987

INDIA, SOUTH - COMMERCE - ASIA, SOUTHEASTERN - HISTORY.
Sarkar, Himansu Bhusan. Trade and commercial activities of southern India in the Malayo-Indonesian world, up to A.D. 1511 /. Calcutta , 1986- v. <1- > : LC Card 87-900744 DDC 382/.09548/059 19
HF3788.A78 S25 1986

India, the next 7000 days /. Seth, Satish C. New Delhi , c1985. xxiv, 312 p. [1] spolded Leaf of plates ; ISBN 0-85226-864-5 : LC Card 85-904799 DDC 338.5/443/0954 19
HC435.2 .S416 1985 NYPL [JLD 86-3377]

India. University Grants Commission. Mishra, M. N. (Maha Narain), 1945- Appraisal of credit facilities provided by banking institutions in rural development /. Meerut, U.P., India [1987?] x, 251, ii p. ; LC Card 87-900918 DDC 332.2 19
HG3284 .M49 1987

India. Vital Statistics Division. SRS based abridged life tables, 1976-80. New Delhi , 1986. v, 37 p. : LC Card 87-901200
HB1470 .S77 1986

Indian agricultural development since independence : a collection of essays / [editors], M.L. Dantwala and others. New Delhi : Oxford & IBH Pub. Co., c1986. viii, 519 p. ; 25 cm. Includes bibliographies and index. ISBN 81-204-0118-2 : LC Card 86-902551 DDC 338.1/0954 19
1. Agriculture - Economic aspects - India. I. Dantwala, M. L. (Mohanlal Lalloobhai), 1909-.
HD2072 .I526 1986

Indian Association for the Study of Population. Recent advances in the techniques for demographic analysis /. Bombay , 1987. xiv, 456 p. ; LC Card 87-900498
HB849 .R42 1987

Indian Association for Women's Studies. Invisible hands . New Delhi , Newbury Park, Calif. , 1987. 273 p. ; ISBN 0-8039-9524-5 (U. S.) LC Card 87-4337 DDC 331.4/0954 19
HD6181.85 .A85 1987

The Indian atom : power & proliferation : a documentary history of nuclear policies, development, and the critics, 1958-1986 / editor, Dhirendra Sharma. New Delhi : Philosophy & Social Action : Distributor, Central News Agency, c1986. v, 166 p. ; 22 cm. "The Atomic Energy Act, 1962"--P. 3-26. Bibliography: p. 166. LC Card 87-900288 DDC 333.79/24/0954 19
1. Nuclear energy - Government policy - India. I. Sharma, Dhirendra. II. India. Atomic Energy Act, 1962. 1986.
HD9698.I52 I52 1986

Indian Council for Research on International Economic Relations.
Indo-CMEA economic relations /. New Delhi , 1987. xviii, 263 p. ; ISBN 81-7024-078-6 : LC Card 87-901620 DDC 337.54047 19
HC433 .I535 1987

Kathuria, Sanjay. India's exports, the challenge from China /. New Delhi , 1986. 106 p. ; LC Card 86-902526 DDC 382/.6/0954 19
HF3836.5 .K37 1986

Indian Council of World Affairs. Issues before non-alignment . New Delhi , 1983. 190 p. ; LC Card 83-903478 DDC 327/.09171/6 19
JX1393.N54 I87 1983 NYPL [JLE 86-4176]

Indian currency and exchange, 1835-1940 /. Goswami, Prodyot Kumar, 1940- New Delhi , 1983. viii, 134 p. ; LC Card 83-903565 DDC 332.4/560954 19
HG1234 .G67 1983 NYPL [JLD 87-673]

Indian currency and finance /. Keynes, John Maynard, 1883-1946. London , 1913 (Edinburgh : R. & R. Clark) viii, 263 p., [1] folded leaf of plates ; LC Card A13-2169 DDC 332.4/954
HG1234 .K4 NYPL [*KF 1913 87-34]

The Indian economy : recent development and future prospects / edited by Robert E.B. Lucas and Gustav F. Papanek. Boulder, Colo. : Westview Press, 1988. ix, 374 p. : ill. ; 23 cm. (Westview special studies on South and Southeast Asia) Includes bibliographies. ISBN 0-8133-7505-3 (pbk. : alk. paper) LC Card 87-22472 DDC 330.954/05 19
1. India - Economic conditions - 1947- - Congresses. 2. India - Economic poolicy - 1947- - Congresses. I. Lucas, Robert E. B. II. Papanek, Gustav Fritz.
HC435.2 .I555 1988

The Indian financial system . Seshadri, R. K. Madras , 1985. ii, 287, v, iii p. ; LC Card 85-904230 DDC 336.54 19
HD4293 .S45 1985 NYPL [JLD 86-2433]

Indian industry . Ashraf, Shahid, 1959- Delhi, India , 1986. 100 p. ; LC Card 86-903305 DDC 338.0954 19
HC435.2 .A889 1986

Indian industry . Desai, Vasant, 1933- Bombay , 1987. xiii, 816 p. : LC Card 87-901051 DDC 338.0954 19
HC435.2 .D45 1987

Indian Institute of Foreign Trade. Modwel, Suman Kumar, 1936- Export effort of India /. New Delhi , 1986. ix, 83, [1] p. ; LC Card 86-903364 DDC 382/.6/0954 19
HF1589 .M63 1986

Indian Institute of Industrial Economics. Chanana, Charanjit. Industrial economics in developing countries, India . New Delhi , 1983. 113 p. : LC Card 83-903832 DDC 338.0954 19
HC435.2 .C4717 1983 NYPL [JLD 87-674]

Indian Institute of Management, Ahmedabad. Energy use in rural Gujarat /. New Delhi , c1987. iv, 186 p. : ISBN 81-204-0216-2 : LC Card 87-901949 DDC 333.79/13/095475 19
HD9502.I43 G844 1987

Gaikwad, V. R., 1933- Managing paddy-rice business of small farmers . Bombay , 1986. xxiii, 239 p. : ISBN 0-86132-129-4 : LC Card 86-903247 DDC 334/.68318/0954 19
HD9066.A7 G35 1986

Indian land-system . Mookerji, Radhakumud, 1884-1964. Alipore, Bengal , 1940. 112, v p. ; LC Card 87-123602
HD879.B4 M63 1940

INDIAN NATIONAL SATELLITE SYSTEM - CONGRESSES.
SITE to INSAT . New Delhi , 1986. viii, 165 p. : LC Card 86-902956 DDC 384.55/44/0954 19
HE8700.9.I5 S57 1986

Indian National Trade Union Congress. Souvenir, ICFTU World Conference on the Trade Union Role in Balanced Development, Vigyan Bhawan, New Delhi, India, March 18-20, 1981 /. New Delhi [1981] 68 p. : LC Card 84-901715 DDC 331.88 19
HD6475.A2 I26347 1981
NYPL [JLG 86-296]

Indian Ocean newsletter. Somalia, productive sectors of the economy /. Paris , 1985. 115 leaves : ISBN 2-905760-00-1 (pbk.) LC Card 87-124493 DDC 338.967/73 19
HC850 .S658 1985

Indian Ocean newsletter publication. Somalia, productive sectors of the economy /. Paris , 1985. 115 leaves : ISBN 2-905760-00-1 (pbk.) LC Card 87-124493 DDC 338.967/73 19
HC850 .S658 1985

Indian Roads Congress. International Seminar on "Road Safety" (1986 : Srinagar, India) International Seminar on "Road Safety", Srinagar, September 17-18, 1986 /. New Delhi [1986] 1 v. (various pagings) : LC Card 87-901986 DDC 363.1/25 19
HE5614 .I5717 1986

Indian Space Research Organisation. Development and Educational Communication Unit. SITE to INSAT . New Delhi , 1986. viii, 165 p. : LC Card 86-902956 DDC 384.55/44/0954 19
HE8700.9.I5 S57 1986

Indian Statistical Institute. Women, work, and society /. Calcutta , 1985. xvi, 430 p. : LC Card 86-900827 DDC 331.4 19
HD6052 .W565 1982 ***NYPL [JLE 87-1019]***

Indian Statistical Institute Golden Jubilee International Symposium on Women, Work and Society (1982 : New Delhi, India) Women, work, and society /. Calcutta , 1985. xvi, 430 p. : LC Card 86-900827 DDC 331.4 19
HD6052 .W565 1982 ***NYPL [JLE 87-1019]***

Indian women in subsistence and agricultural labour /. Mies, Maria. Geneva , 1986. x, 158 p. ; ISBN 92-2-105397-0 (pbk.) : LC Card 87-114124 DDC 331.4/83/0954 19
HD6073.A292 I46 1986

Indiana. Dept. of Commerce. Division of Economic Analysis. Wynne, John, 1961- The Indiana economy . Indianapolis, IN [1986] 22, [2] p. : LC Card 86-622749 DDC 330.9772/043 19
HD5725.I6 W96 1986

INDIANA - ECONOMIC CONDITIONS.
Wynne, John, 1961- The Indiana economy . Indianapolis, IN [1986] 22, [2] p. : LC Card 86-622749 DDC 330.9772/043 19
HD5725.I6 W96 1986

The Indiana economy . Wynne, John, 1961- Indianapolis, IN [1986] 22, [2] p. : LC Card 86-622749 DDC 330.9772/043 19
HD5725.I6 W96 1986

INDIANA - POPULATION.
Wynne, John, 1961- The Indiana economy . Indianapolis, IN [1986] 22, [2] p. : LC Card 86-622749 DDC 330.9772/043 19
HD5725.I6 W96 1986

Indiana University Turkish studies .
(v. 5) Turkish workers in Europe . [Bloomington, Ind. (143 Goodbody Hall, Indiana University, Bloomington 47405) , c1985. 191 p. : LC Card 85-71750 DDC 331.6/2/56104 19
HD8378.5.T8 T87 1985
NYPL [JLE 86-2980]

INDIANS - ETHNOLOGY. see **INDIANS OF NORTH AMERICA; INDIANS OF SOUTH AMERICA.**

INDIANS, MEXICAN. see **INDIANS OF MEXICO.**

INDIANS, NORTH AMERICAN. see **INDIANS OF NORTH AMERICA.**

INDIANS OF MEXICO - POPULATION.
Mora, Teresa. La Mixteca baja, su migración . México, D.F. , 1982. 129, [84] leaves ; LC Card 87-122391 DDC 304.6/0972/74 19
HB3532.O18 M67 1982

INDIANS OF MEXICO - TRIBES. See individual tribes, e. g. Mixtec Indians. For list of tribes, see under: **INDIANS OF MEXICO.**

INDIANS OF NORTH AMERICA - CANADA - MIXED BLOODS.
McCully, Al. East Prairie Metis Settlement . [Edmonton, Alta.] [1982] iii, 99 p. :Bill. ; LC Card 82-202474 DDC 333.76/17/097123 19
HD319.A4 M52 1982

INDIANS OF NORTH AMERICA - CANADA - TRADING POSTS - HISTORY.
Caron, Diane. Les postes de traite de fourrure sur la Côte-Nord et dans l'Outaouais /. [Québec] [1984] xvi, 150 p. : ISBN 2-551-06277-2 LC Card 84-220957
HD9944.C22 C34 1984

INDIANS OF NORTH AMERICA - ETHNOLOGY. see **INDIANS OF NORTH AMERICA.**

INDIANS OF NORTH AMERICA - NEW MEXICO - LAND TENURE - HISTORY.
Land, water, and culture . Albuquerque , c1987. ix, 422 p. : ISBN 0-8263-0989-5 (pbk.) LC Card 87-10957 DDC 333.1/6/09788 19
HD243.N5 L36 1987

INDIANS OF NORTH AMERICA - TRIBES. See individual tribes, e.g. Apache Indians. For list of tribes, see under: **INDIANS OF NORTH AMERICA.**

INDIANS OF SOUTH AMERICA - AMAZON RIVER REGION - ECONOMIC CONDITIONS - CONGRESSES.
Land, people, and planning in contemporary Amazonia /. [Cambridge, Cambridgeshire] , 1980. xvi, 313 p. : LC Card 87-672189
HC167.A42 L36x 1980

INDIANS OF SOUTH AMERICA - AMAZON RIVER REGION - LAND TENURE.

INDIANS OF SOUTH AMERICA - BOLIVIA - LAND TENURE.
Ovando, Jorge. El tributo indígena en las finanzas bolivianas del siglo XIX /. La Paz, Bolivia [1985] 565 p. : ***NYPL [JLC 86-407]***

INDIANS OF SOUTH AMERICA - BRAZIL - LAND TENURE.
Terra de Deus, terra de irmãos . Brasília-DF [1986] 190 p. : LC Card 86-233600
HD1333.B6 T47 1986

INDIANS OF SOUTH AMERICA - ECONOMIC CONDITIONS.
Egner, Erich, 1901- Hauswirtschaft und Lebenshaltung . Berlin , 1974. 249 p. ; ISBN 3-428-03093-1 : LC Card 76-511945
TX7 .B4 Heft 9 HD6995.5
NYPL [JLE 86-3436]

INDIANS OF SOUTH AMERICA - ECUADOR - ECONOMIC CONDITIONS.
Santana, Roberto. Campesinado indígena y el desafío de la modernidad /. [Quito, Ecuador] , 1983. 209 p. : LC Card 84-156117 DDC 330.9866/074/08998 19
F3721.3.E25 S26 1983
NYPL [HBC 86-2225]

INDIANS OF SOUTH AMERICA - ECUADOR - LOJA (PROVINCE) - ECONOMIC CONDITIONS.
Santana, Roberto. Campesinado indígena y el desafío de la modernidad /. [Quito, Ecuador] , 1983. 209 p. : LC Card 84-156117 DDC 330.9866/074/08998 19
F3721.3.E25 S26 1983
NYPL [HBC 86-2225]

INDIANS OF SOUTH AMERICA - ETHNOLOGY. see **INDIANS OF SOUTH AMERICA.**

INDIANS OF SOUTH AMERICA - PERU - LAND TENURE - HISTORY.
Burga, Manuel. La historia agraria /. Chiclayo, Perú , 1986. 196 p. ; ***NYPL [JLD 87-1524]***

INDIANS OF SOUTH AMERICA - PERU - PIURA (DEPT.) - AGRICULTURE.
Espinoza Claudio, César. Terratenientes y campesinos en Piura, ss. XVI-XIX . Lima, Perú , 1981. xxviii, 123 p., [6] leaves of plates : LC Card 82-146131
HD559.P5 E87 1981

INDIANS OF SOUTH AMERICA - PERU - PIURA (DEPT.) - LAND TENURE.
Espinoza Claudio, César. Terratenientes y campesinos en Piura, ss. XVI-XIX . Lima, Perú , 1981. xxviii, 123 p., [6] leaves of plates : LC Card 82-146131
HD559.P5 E87 1981

INDIANS OF SOUTH AMERICA - TRIBES. See individual tribes, e.g. Carib Indians. For list of tribes, see under: **INDIANS OF SOUTH AMERICA.**

INDIANS OF THE UNITED STATES. see **INDIANS OF NORTH AMERICA.**

INDIANS, SOUTH AMERICAN. see **INDIANS OF SOUTH AMERICA.**

India's black economy and maldevelopment /. Kabra, Kamal Nayan. New Delhi , 1986. 192 p. ; ISBN 81-7050-025-7 : LC Card 86-902668 DDC 338.954 19
HC435.2 .K26 1986

India's exports, the challenge from China /. Kathuria, Sanjay. New Delhi , 1986. 106 p. ; LC Card 86-902526 DDC 382/.6/0954 19
HF3836.5 .K37 1986

India's five-year plans in theory and practice /. Bhattacharya, Sib Nath, 1938- New Delhi, India , 1987. xvi, 352 p. ; ISBN 81-200-0076-5 : LC Card 87-900413 DDC 338.954 19
HC435.2 .B45476 1987

Indicadores de la migración en México. México, D.F. : Instituto Nacional de Estadística, Geografía e Informática, 1985. ix, 161 p. ; 28 cm. Chiefly tables. ISBN 968-89200-3-7 LC Card 86-217222
1. Migration, Internal - Mexico - Statistics. 2. Mexico - Emigration and immigration - Statistics. I. Instituto Nacional de Estadística, Geografía e Informática (Mexico).
HB1991 .I55 1985

Indicadores de los países del Grupo Andino. [Lima] : Junta del Acuerdo de Cartagena, Unidad de Informática, [1985] 172 p. in various pagings : ill. ; 20 x 30 cm. Chiefly tables and ill. "JUN/di 905, 15 de mayo de 1985." LC Card 86-137319 DDC 330.98/0038 19
1. Economic indicators - Andes Region. 2. Economic indicators - South America. I. Board of the Cartagena Agreement. Unidad de Informática.
HC167.A5 I52 1985

Indicadores económicos e financeiros da Central de Balanços (1978-1980). [Porto] : Banco Português do Atlântico, Direcção de Estudos Económicos, Central de Balanços, [1982] 204 p. : col. ill. ; 29 cm. (BPA cadernos) Errata slip inserted. LC Card 85-166692
1. Costs, Industrial - Portugal - Statistics. 2. Economic indicators - Portugal. I. Banco Português do Atlântico. Central de Balanços. II. Series.
HC394.5.C7 I53 1982

Indicadores económicos, I censo artesanal 1978. Principales indicadores económicos . Guatemala , 1982. 487 p. ; LC Card 87-403026 DDC 331.7/94 19
HD2346.G8 P75 1982

Indicadores económicos y sociales . Teitelboim G., Berta. Santiago, Chile , 1985. 57 p. :
NYPL [JLD 86-2146]

Indicadores económicos y sociales [microform] . Teitelboim G., Berta. Santiago, Chile [1984] 41 p. : ***NYPL [*ZT-1711 no.26]***

Indicadores económicos y sociales, 1960-1985 / Dirección de Estudios, Banco Central de Chile. Santiago, Chile : La Dirección, c1986. xvi, 415 p. : col. ill. ; 22 x 32 cm. English and Spanish. Chiefly tables. Rev. ed. of: Indicatores económicos y sociales, 1960-1982. LC Card 87-120338
1. Economic indicators - Chile. 2. Social indicators - Chile. 3. Chile - Economic conditions - Statistics. 4. Chile - Social conditions - Statistics. I. Banco Central de Chile. Dirección de Estudios. II. Indicatores económicos y sociales, 1960-1982.
HC192 .I52 1986

Indicadores para el estudio de la población económicamente activa basados en la información censal de 1970 /. Pedrero,

Mercedes. México, D.F. [1977] 495 p. ; LC Card 85-202779
HA765 .P43 1977

Indicateurs démographiques cantonaux, 1960 et 1970. Kantonale demographische Indiktoren, 1960 und 1970 =. Bern , 1977. 187 p. : LC Card 85-217076
HA1593 .B45 Heft 44 HA1604

Les indicateurs globaux de la productivité . Nadeau, Jean. Québec [1982] 41 p. : ISBN 2-551-05072-3 LC Card 83-221751
HC120.I52 N33 1982

Indicatores económicos y sociales, 1960-1982. Indicadores económicos y sociales, 1960-1985 /. Santiago, Chile , c1986. xvi, 415 p. : LC Card 87-120338
HC192 .I52 1986

L'indice des prix de la Martinique, base 100 en 1979 . Guglielmetti, Francis. [Fort de France?] [1985] 130, xxiii p. : ISBN 2-11-062943-6 : LC Card 86-176702
HB235.M37 G83 1985

Indices and data on investments in listed Italian securities (1985) Mediobanca. Indici e dati relativi ad investimenti in titoli quotati nelle borse italiane (1985) =. [Milano] [1985] v, 427 p. : LC Card 86-210524
HG5522 .M43 1985

Indices da produção industrial : séries revistas, 1975-85 / Secretaria de Planejamento da Presidência da República, Fundação Instituto Brasileiro de Geografia e Estatística, Diretoria de Economia, Superintendência de Contas Nacionais e Agregados Macroeconômicos. Rio de Janeiro : IBGE, 1986. 178 p. : ill. ; 27 cm. ISBN 85-24-00246-8 LC Card 87-403858 DDC 338.0981/021 19
1. Brazil - Industries - Statistics. I. Fundação Instituto Brasileiro de Geografia e Estatística. Superintendência de Contas Nacionais e Agregados Macroeconômicos.
HC187 .I534 1986

Indices de eficiencia económica para la industria beneficiadora de café . Rojas Rojas, Edgar. San José, Costa Rica , 1986. 14 leaves : LC Card 87-403520 DDC 338.1/6 19
HD9199.C82 R65 1986

Indices des prix des produits industriels, 1981=100. Industrial product price indexes, 1981=100 . Ottawa , c1986. 216 p. : ISBN 0-660-52876-2 (pbk.) : LC Card 87-168891
HB235.C2 I53 1986

Indici e dati relativi ad investimenti in titoli quotati nelle borse italiane (1985) =. Mediobanca. [Milano] [1985] v, 427 p. : LC Card 86-210524
HG5522 .M43 1985

Indien, Nepal, Sri Lanka . Maass, Citha Doris. Wiesbaden , 1982. xxi, 380 p. ; ISBN 3-515-03802-7 LC Card 86-214318
HF1590.15.N4 M33 1982

Indien, Probleme eines Schwellenlandes : Länderseminar / veranstaltet vom Institut für Wissenschaftliche Zusammenarbeit ; [Redaktion, Karl-Heinz W. Bechtold]. Tübingen : Institut für Wissenschaftliche Zusammenarbeit mit Entwicklungsländern, c1984. 75 p. ; 23 cm. Includes bibliographical references. CONTENTS. - Nord-Süd Dialog und Entwicklungshilfe / Dietmar Rothermund -- Die Rolle der Religion in Modernisierungsprozessen / Heinrich von Stietencron -- Agrarproduktion und Ernährungslage in Indien / Winfried von Urff -- Zerstörung bedeutet Wachstum / Detlef Kantowsky. ISBN 3-922362-02-8 LC Card 85-157722
1. India - Economic conditions - 1947- - Congresses. 2. India - Economic policy - 1947- - Congresses. 3. Religion - Economic aspects - India - Congresses. 4. Agriculture - India - Congresses. I. Bechtold, Karl-Heinz. II. Institut für Wissenschaftliche Zusammenarbeit mit Entwicklungsländern (Tübingen, Germany).
HC435.2 .I6235 1984

Indignant heart . Denby, Charles. Montréal , 1979. 295 p. : ISBN 0-919618-93-6 LC Card 87-672793
HD8039.A82 U633x 1979

Indirect remuneration . Zoeteweij, H. Geneva , 1986. viii, 82 p. ; ISBN 92-2-105360-1 (pbk.) : LC Card 86-213666 DDC 331.25/5 19
HD4928.N6 Z64 1986

INDIRECT TAXATION. see TARIFF; TAXATION.

Individual and family markets. 3rd ed. [Chicago] : Research & Review Service of America, c1986. ii, 243 p. ; 28 cm. Cover title. ISBN 0-88462-594-X (loose-leaf) LC Card 86-29692 DDC 368.3/2/0688 19
1. Insurance, Life - United States - Marketing. I. Research & Review Service of America.
HG8951 .I44 1986

The individual investor's microcomputer resource guide /. Nicholson, Norm. Chicago , c1986. viii, 216 p. ; ISBN 0-930369-17-3 (pbk.) LC Card 86-204335 DDC 332.6/028/553 19
HG4515.5 .N53 1986

INDIVIDUAL RETIREMENT ACCOUNTS.
Heerwagen, Peter D. Self directed IRAs for the active investor /. Chicago, Ill. , c1987. x, 233 p. : ISBN 0-917253-61-2 (pbk.) : LC Card 86-25312 DDC 332.024/01 19
HG1660.A3 H44 1987

Zweig, Martin E. [Winning with new IRAs.] Martin Zweig's winning with new IRAs /. New York, NY , c1987. xvi, 207 p. : ISBN 0-446-51276-1 LC Card 86-28203 DDC 332.024/01 19
HG1660.A3 Z94 1987

INDIVIDUAL RETIREMENT ACCOUNTS - UNITED STATES.
Brownstone, David M. The IRA survival guide . New York, NY , c1987. 168 p. ; ISBN 0-8144-5861-0 (pbk.) : LC Card 86-47806 DDC 332.024/01 19
HG1660.U5 B76 1987

Dunn, Pat. Script for an employee flipchart presentation titled The 401(k) plan . Chicago, Ill. , c1986. [40] p. : ISBN 0-88462-610-5 (pbk.) LC Card 86-201609 DDC 331.25/5 19
HG1660.U5 D86 1986

Hutchison, Anna Marie. IRA investing made easy /. Oakhurst, Calif. , c1987. 158 p. : ISBN 0-940083-07-8 (pbk.) : LC Card 86-83347 DDC 343.7305/23 347.303523 19
HG1660.U5 H87 1987

IRAs, the people's choice /. Washington, D.C. (1600 M St., N.W., Washington 20036) [1986?] 60 p. : LC Card 87-402800 DDC 332.024/01 19
HG1660.U5 I73 1986

Sacks, Frank. The new IRA handbook . Chicago [1987], c1986. 126 p. : ISBN 0-911445-05-6 (pbk.) : LC Card 87-130659 DDC 332.024/01 19
HG1660.U5 S23 1987

INDIVIDUAL RETIREMENT ACCOUNTS - UNITED STATES - CONGRESSES.
Pensions in the U. S. economy /. Chicago , 1988. ix, 200 p. : ISBN 0-226-06285-6 LC Card 87-19987 DDC 331.25/2/0973 19
HD7105.45.U6 P46 1988

Individualisierung der Organisation von Banken . Lippold, Dirk, 1953- Spardorf , c1982. xxiii, 170 p. : ISBN 3-922919-04-9 LC Card 83-221727
HG1615.5 .L56 1982

INDIVIDUALISM.
Abercrombie, Nicholas. Sovereign individuals of capitalism /. London , Boston , 1986. 211 p. ; ISBN 0-04-301230-2 (alk. paper) LC Card 86-1122 DDC 330.12/2 19
HB501 .A23 1986 ***NYPL [JLD 86-3686]***

Campbell, Colin, 1940- The romantic ethic and the spirit of modern consumerism /. Oxford, UK , New York, NY, USA , 1987. 301 p. ; ISBN 0-631-15539-2 : LC Card 86-30979 DDC 339.4/7 19
HC79.C6 C36 1987

Fallows, James M. Human capital . New York, N.Y. , 1988. p. cm. ISBN 0-394-56498-7 : LC Card 87-42659 DDC 306/.3 19
HC106.8 .F35 1988

Glotz, Peter, 1939- Manifest für eine Neue Europäische Linke /. Berlin , c1985. 112, [1] p. ; ISBN 3-88680-162-4 LC Card 86-100474 DDC 320.5/31/094 19
HX238.5 .G56 1985 ***NYPL [JLD 87-1162]***

Ideology and national competitiveness . Boston, Mass. , c1987. x, 350 p. ; ISBN 0-87584-147-3 LC Card 86-19569 DDC 338.6/048 19
HF1414 .I34 1987 ***NYPL [JLE 87-1046]***

INDIVIDUALISM - CONGRESSES.
Friedman, Milton, 1912- Politics and tyranny . San Francisco, Calif. , c1984. 68 p. ; ISBN 0-936488-00-X (pbk.) : LC Card 84-61364 DDC 330 19
HB98.3 .F75 1984 ***NYPL [JLE 87-857]***

Individualistische Grundlagen der evolutorischen Ökonomik /. Witt, Ulrich. Tübingen , c1987. xi, 209 p. ; ISBN 3-16-945063-8 LC Card 87-115946 DDC 330.15/5 19
HB98.2 .W57 1987

Individuella sysselsättningskonsekvenser av nedläggningar /. Edin, Per-Anders. Helsingfors [1984] 20 leaves ; ISBN 951-555-208-7 LC Card 85-151846
HD5803 .E33 1984

Individuelle und gesellschaftliche Kosten der Massenarbeitslosigkeit : psychologische Theorie und Praxis / herausgegeben von Thomas Kieselbach und Ali Wacker. Weinheim : Beltz, 1985. xxvi, 506 p. : ill. ; 21 cm. (Beltz Monographie) Includes bibliographies. ISBN 3-407-54689-0 LC Card 86-118545 DDC 331.13/7/019 19
1. Unemployment - Psychological aspects - Congresses. 2. Unemployment - Social aspects - Congresses. 3. Quality of life - Congresses. I. Kieselbach, Thomas, 1944-. II. Wacker, Ali, 1942-.
HD5708 .I53 1985 ***NYPL [JLD 87-387]***

Indo-CMEA economic relations / edited by Suresh Kumar. New Delhi : Ashish Pub. House : Indian Council for Research on International Economic Relations, 1987. xviii, 263 p. ; 22 cm. India's foreign economic relations with countries of the Council for Mutual Economic Assistance. Includes bibliographies and index. ISBN 81-7024-078-6 : LC Card 87-901620 DDC 337.54047 19
1. India - Foreign economic relations - Europe, Eastern. 2. Europe, Eastern - Foreign economic relations - India. 3. India - Foreign economic relations - Soviet Union. 4. Soviet Union - Foreign economic relations - India. 5. Council for Mutual Economic Assistance. I. Suresh Kumar, 1935-. II. Indian Council for Research on International Economic Relations.
HC433 .I535 1987

Indo-Nepal trade . Dahal, Kishor. Kathmandu, Nepal , c1987. x, 66, [9] p. ; LC Card 87-902005 DDC 382/.0954/05496 19
HF3788.N45 D34 1987

Indo-Soviet trade and economic ties /. Menon, M. S. N., 1924- New Delhi , 1986. 229 p. ; LC Card 86-903273 DDC 337.54047 19
HF1590.5.S65 M46 1986

Indo-U. S. cooperation in business and industry, 1986. [New Delhi] : U. S. Agency for International Development Mission to India, [1986] 166 p. ; 23 x 28 cm. Directory. Includes index. LC Card 86-903197
1. Corporations, American - India - Directories. 2. Corporations - India - Directories. 3. International business enterprises - India - Directories. I. United States. AID Mission to India.
HG4242 .I44 1986

Indo-U. S. economic relations . Roy, P. C. (Prabhash Chandra), 1955- New Delhi , c1986. 206 p. : LC Card 86-902903 DDC 337.54073 19
HF1590.15.U5 R69 1986

INDOCHINA - ECONOMIC CONDITIONS.
Árva, László. Indokina gazdasági fejlődése és hazánk lehetőségei a térség országaival való együttműködés terén /. Budapest , 1984. 69 p. : ISBN 963-491-194-3 LC Card 86-199424
HC441 .A77 1984

INDOCHINA - FOREIGN ECONOMIC RELATIONS - HUNGARY.
Árva, László. Indokina gazdasági fejlődése és hazánk lehetőségei a térség országaival való együttműködés terén /. Budapest , 1984. 69 p. : ISBN 963-491-194-3 LC Card 86-199424
HC441 .A77 1984

INDOCHINA WAR, 1946-1954 - FRANCE.
Rice-Maximin, Edward Francis, 1941- Accomodation and resistance . New York , 1986. xi, 175 p. ; ISBN 0-313-25355-2 (lib. bdg. : alk. paper) LC Card 86-4624 DDC 959.704/1 19
DS553.1 .R53 1986 ***NYPL [JFE 87-1024]***

Indochinese refugees in America . Strand, Paul J., 1949- Durham, N.C. , 1985. x, 182 p. ; ISBN 0-8223-0629-8 LC Card 84-25888 DDC

362.8/49592 19
HV640.5.I5 S77 1985 *NYPL [JLE 86-4772]*

Indokina gazdasági fejlődése és hazánk lehetőségei a térség országaival való együttműködés terén /. Árva, László. Budapest , 1984. 69 p. : ISBN 963-491-194-3 LC Card 86-199424
HC441 .A77 1984

Indonesia. Otten, Mariël. Transmigrasi . Copenhagen , c1986. 254 p. : LC Card 87-144670 DDC 333.3/1/598 19
HD896 .O88 1986

Indonesia. Badan Koordinasi Keluarga Berencana Nasional.
Bahan instruksional pendidikan kependudukan untuk peserta diklat Departemen P.U. Jakarta , 1982. v, 90 p. ; LC Card 83-941464
HB850.5.I5 B34 1982

Pendidikan kependudukan untuk perwira. [Jakarta] [1981] vi, 120 p. : LC Card 85-940192
HB850.5 .P46 1981

Indonesia. Badan Urusan Logistik. Inflasi dan masalah kita : aneka coretan tentang inflasi. Jakarta : Badan Urusan Logistik, Biro Analisa Harga dan Pasar, 1979. ii, 48 leaves ; 28 cm. Bibliography: leaf 22. LC Card 80-940062
1. Inflation (Finance) - Indonesia. I. Title.
HG1255 .I5 1979

INDONESIA - COMMERCE.
Analisa perkembangan perdagangan luar negeri. Jakarta, Indonesia [1985] iv, 80, 44 leaves : LC Card 85-942679
HF3806.5 .A6 1985

INDONESIA - CULTURAL POLICY.
Indonesia dan masalah-masalah pembangunan /. [Jakarta] , 1986. viii, 277 p. : LC Card 87-940526
HC447 .I555936 1986

Indonesia dan masalah-masalah pembangunan / diredaksi oleh Budhy Munawar Rachman, F.X. Baskara Tulus Wardaya. Cet. 1. [Jakarta] : Kelompok Studi Proklamasi, 1986. viii, 277 p. : ill. ; 17 cm. (Seri esensia . 04) Includes bibliographies. LC Card 87-940526
1. Indonesia - Economic policy. 2. Indonesia - Social policy. 3. Indonesia - Cultural policy. I. Rachman, Budhy Munawar. II. Wardaya, F. X. Baskara Tulus. III. Series.
HC447 .I555936 1986

Indonesia. Departemen Perindustrian.
Pelaksanaan program keterkaitan antar sektor industri dan antara sektor industri dengan sektor ekonomi lainnya : ringkasan. [Jakarta] : Biro Humas, Departemen Perindustrian, [1985] i, 59 p. ; 25 cm. "Maret 1985." "No. IU/02/85." LC Card 85-941789
1. Industry and state - Indonesia. 2. Indonesia - Industries. I. Title.
HD3616.I53 I49 1985

Soehoed, A. R. (Abdoel Raoef), 1920- Industrial development during Pelita III. [Jakarta] [1982] 23 p. ; LC Card 83-940924 DDC 338.9598 19
HD3616.I53 S629 1982

Wilayah pusat pertumbuhan industri : pengembangan wilayah dengan orientasi pertumbuhan ekomoni pada zona-zona industri yang bertolak dari pembangunan industri dasar/kunci. Ed. 1985. [Jakarta] : Departemen Perindustrian, [1985] 20, vi p. : col. folded maps ; 24 cm. "1 Maret 1985." "IU/11/85." LC Card 85-941790
1. Industrial districts - Indonesia. 2. Industry and state - Indonesia. I. Title.
HC450.D5 I53 1985

Indonesia. Direktorat Pembinaan Kesiswaan.
Pedoman pembinaan kewiraswastaan bagi siswa. Jakarta , 1985. 1 v. (various pagings) : LC Card 86-942929
HF1171.I5 P43 1985

INDONESIA - ECONOMIC CONDITIONS.
The Oriental challenge . Delft, the Netherlands , 1987. 281 p. : ISBN 90-70879-62-X (pbk.) LC Card 87-170212 DDC 332.6/732259 19
HC445 .O75 1987

INDONESIA - ECONOMIC CONDITIONS - 1945-
Abdrabboh, Bob A. Investment in Indonesia . Dearborn, Mich., U. S.A. , c1987. ix, 124 p. : ISBN 0-915597-19-7 LC Card 86-82681 DDC 332.6/7322598 19
HG5752 .A534 1987

INDONESIA - ECONOMIC CONDITIONS - 1947-
Rudianto, Doddy. Pembangunan ekonomi dan perkembangan bisnis di Indonesia /. Jakarta , 1985. 53 p. ; LC Card 86-944718
HC447 .R73 1985

INDONESIA - ECONOMIC POLICY.
Etika pembangunan dalam pemikiran Islam di Indonesia /. Jakarta , 1986. xi, 270 p. ; ISBN 979-421-043-9 (pbk.) LC Card 86-946413
HC447 .E78 1986

Indonesia dan masalah-masalah pembangunan /. [Jakarta] , 1986. viii, 277 p. : LC Card 87-940526
HC447 .I555936 1986

Indonesia. Majelis Permusyawaratan Rakyat. Ichtisar tahunan tentang pelaksanaan Ketetapan MPRS no. II/MPRS/1960 mengenai pola pembangunan nasional semesta berentjana tahapan pertama, 1961-1969 jang berkenaan dengan tahun pelaksanaan pembangunan 1963. [Djakarta] [1965] 141 p. ; LC Card 86-161520
HC447 .I5534 1963

Indonesia. President, 1967- (Soeharto) Lampiran Pidato kenegaraan Presiden Republik Indonesia di depan sidang Dewan Perwakilan Rakyat, 16 Agustus 1979 . [Jakarta] [1981?] 1203 p. in various pagings ; LC Card 86-949503
HC447 .I5559 1981

Juoro, Umar, 1959- Masalah terdepan dalam pembangunan ekonomi Indonesia /. Bandung , 1985. xii, 224 pp. ; LC Card 86-942991
HC447 .J86 1985

Rudianto, Doddy. Pembangunan ekonomi dan perkembangan bisnis di Indonesia /. Jakarta , 1985. 53 p. ; LC Card 86-944718
HC447 .R73 1985

Sastraatmaja, Entang. Ekonomi & pembangunan . Bandung , c1986. viii, 284 p. : LC Card 86-944011
HC447 .S363 1986

INDONESIA - INDUSTRIES.
Indonesia. Departemen Perindustrian. Pelaksanaan program keterkaitan antar sektor industri dan antara sektor industri dengan sektor ekonomi lainnya . [Jakarta] [1985] i, 59 p. ; LC Card 85-941789
HD3616.I53 I49 1985

Indonesia. Kantor Menteri Negara Kependudukan dan Lingkungan Hidup.
Ananta, Aris. Perilaku fertilitas di beberapa daerah di Jawa /. Jakarta , 1986. vi, 56, 26 p. ; LC Card 86-946460
HB1058.J38 A52 1986

Indonesia. Kantor Menteri Negara Urusan Peranan Wanita. Pokok-pokok petunjuk pelaksanaan Program Peningkatan Produktivitas Kerja Tenaga Kerja Wanita Melalui Pendekatan Kesejahteraan Terpadu, tahun 1984/1986 (Juklak Nakerwan). Jakarta : Kantor Menteri Negara Urusan Peranan Wanita, [1984] iii, xii, 47 p. ; 28 cm. LC Card 86-940168
1. Women - Employment - Government policy - Indonesia. 2. Labor productivity - Government policy - Indonesia. I. Title. II. Title: Petunjuk pelaksanaan Program Peningkatan Produktivitas Kerja Tenaga Kerja Wanita Melalui Pendekatan Kesejahteraan Terpadu Tahun 1984/1986. III. Title: Juklak Nakerwan.
HD6194 .I5 1984

Indonesia. Majelis Permusyawaratan Rakyat.
Ichtisar tahunan tentang pelaksanaan Ketetapan MPRS no. II/MPRS/1960 mengenai pola pembangunan nasional semesta berentjana tahapan pertama, 1961-1969 jang berkenaan dengan tahun pelaksanaan pembangunan 1963. [Djakarta] : Pertjetakan Negara, [1965] 141 p. ; 24 cm. LC Card 86-161520
1. Indonesia - Economic policy. 2. Indonesia - Social policy. I. Title.
HC447 .I5534 1963

Indonesia. People's Consultative Assembly. see **Indonesia. Majelis Permusyawaratan Rakyat.**

Indonesia. Perindustrian, Departemen. see **Indonesia. Departemen Perindustrian.**

INDONESIA - POPULATION.
The Demographic dimension in Indonesian development /. Singapore , New York , 1987. xxv, 417 p. : ISBN 0-19-582699-X : LC Card 87-11021 DDC 304.6/09598 19
HB3647 .D45 1987

Pidato kenegaraan Presiden Republik Indonesia di depan sidang Dewan Perwakilan Rakyat, 16 Agustus 1979.
Indonesia. President, 1967- (Soeharto) Lampiran Pidato kenegaraan Presiden Republik Indonesia di depan sidang Dewan Perwakilan Rakyat, 16 Agustus 1979 : pelaksanaan Repelita II (1974/75-1978/79). [Jakarta] [1981?] 1203 p. in various pagings ; LC Card 86-949503
HC447 .I5559 1981

Indonesia. President, 1967- (Soeharto)
Lampiran Pidato kenegaraan Presiden Republik Indonesia di depan sidang Dewan Perwakilan Rakyat, 16 Agustus 1979 : pelaksanaan Repelita II (1974/75-1978/79). [Jakarta] : Departemen Penerangan RI, [1981?] 1203 p. in various pagings ; 21 cm. Cover title. LC Card 86-949503
1. Indonesia - Economic policy. 2. Indonesia - Social policy. I. Indonesia. President (1967- : Soeharto). Pidato kenegaraan Presiden Republik Indonesia di depan sidang Dewan Perwakilan Rakyat, 16 Agustus 1979. II. Title.
HC447 .I5559 1981

INDONESIA - SOCIAL POLICY.
Indonesia dan masalah-masalah pembangunan /. [Jakarta] , 1986. viii, 277 p. : LC Card 87-940526
HC447 .I555936 1986

Indonesia. Majelis Permusyawaratan Rakyat. Ichtisar tahunan tentang pelaksanaan Ketetapan MPRS no. II/MPRS/1960 mengenai pola pembangunan nasional semesta berentjana tahapan pertama, 1961-1969 jang berkenaan dengan tahun pelaksanaan pembangunan 1963. [Djakarta] [1965] 141 p. ; LC Card 86-161520
HC447 .I5534 1963

Indonesia. President, 1967- (Soeharto) Lampiran Pidato kenegaraan Presiden Republik Indonesia di depan sidang Dewan Perwakilan Rakyat, 16 Agustus 1979 . [Jakarta] [1981?] 1203 p. in various pagings ; LC Card 86-949503
HC447 .I5559 1981

INDONESIA - STATISTICS, VITAL.
Recent trends in fertility and mortality in Indonesia /. Honolulu, Hawaii , 1987. xvi, 96 p. : ISBN 0-86638-092-2 (pbk.) : LC Card 87-11178 DDC 304.6/32/09598 19
HB1057 .R43 1987

INDONESIAN LANGUAGE - DICTIONARIES - ENGLISH.
Kamus istilah demografi /. Jakarta , 1985. vi, 119 p. ; LC Card 86-941191
HB849.2 .K35 1985

Kamus istilah ekonomi /. Jakarta , 1984. v, 216 p. ; LC Card 85-941380
HB61 .K26 1984

Indonesian population monograph series .
(no. 4) Streatfield, K. Fertility decline in a traditional society . [Canberra, ACT] , 1986. xvii, 177 p. : ISBN 0-86784-711-5 (pbk.) LC Card 86-213262 DDC 304.6/32/095986 19
HB1058.B34 S87 1986

Indriði G. Þorsteinsson, 1926- Fimmtán gírar áfram : saga af Pétri á Hallgilsstöðum og öðrum brautryðjendum á langferðaleiðum / Indriði G. Þorsteinsson. Reykjavík : Almenna bókafélagið, 1981. 178 p., [16] p. of plates : ill. ; 22 cm. LC Card 83-185502
1. Pétur Jónsson á Hallgilsstöðum, 1911-. 2. Truck drivers - Iceland - Biography. 3. Trucking - Iceland. I. Title.
HD8039.M7952 I25 1981

INDUSTRAT . Larréché, Jean-Claude. Englewood Cliffs, N.J. , 1987. p. cm. ISBN 0-13-651373-5 LC Card 87-7144 DDC 658.8 19
HF5415.1263 .L37 1987

Industri, fagbevægelse og lønarbejde i Kenya . Kongstad, Per. Roskilde [1983] 76 p. ; LC Card 85-238103
HC865 .K66 1983

Indústria bélica brasileira . Tavares, José, 1949- Brasília , 1983. 44 p. ; LC Card 84-235004
HC187 .T2943 1983

La Industria colombiana y la "ALALC.". [Medellín] : INCOLDA, Instituto Colombiano

de Administración, [1964] 112 p. ; 24 cm. Papers presented at a seminar held in Medellín, Oct., 1964; organized by INCOLDA. LC Card 85-111774
1. Colombia - Industries - Congresses. 2. Asociación Latinoamericana de Libre Comercio - Congresses. 3. Customs unions - Latin America - Congresses. I. Instituto Colombiano de Administración.
HC197 .I36 1964

La industria curtidora en Argentina . Remmes Lenicov, Jorge. [Buenos Aires] , 1976. 46 leaves ; LC Card 86-157645
HD9780.A52 R45 1976

A Indústria de confecções na Bahia. [Salvador] : Banco de Desenvolvimento do Estado da Bahia, [1981] 40 p. ; 26 cm. Bibliography: p. 40. LC Card 87-400671
1. Clothing trade - Brazil - Bahia (State). I. Banco de Desenvolvimento do Estado da Bahia.
HD9940.B83 B345 1981

Industria de la construcción . Pacheco D., Rubén. [Panamá] , 1974. 17, [1] leaves, [4] leaves of plates : LC Card 87-400643
HD9715.P223 P367 1974

Industria dei pezzi per autoveicoli / Missione impresariale del Governo dello Stato di São Paulo in Italia. [São Paulo] : Governo do Estado de São Paulo, Secretaria de Economia e Planejamento, Coordenadoria de Ação Regional, 1973. 1 v. (various pagings), [12] leaves of plates : col. ill. ; 28 cm. (Balcão de projetos) Cover title. LC Card 86-146007
1. Automobile supplies industry - Brazil. I. Missione impresariale del Governo dello Stato di São Paulo in Italia. II. Series.
HD9710.3.B72 I53 1973

Industria e commercio : nuovi rapporti e nuove problematiche / ISDI, Istituto di studi e ricerche sulla distribuzione commerciale, in collaborazione con la Camera di commercio, industria, artigianato e agricoltura di Milano. Milano, Italy : F. Angeli, c1985. 194 p. : ill. ; 22 cm. (Distribuzione commerciale . 6) Includes bibliographical references. LC Card 86-112174 DDC 658.7/88/0945 19
1. Physical distribution of goods - Italy. 2. Communication in marketing - Italy. 3. Delivery of goods - Italy. I. Istituto di studi e ricerche sulla distribuzione commerciale (Milan, Italy). II. Camera di commercio, industria, artigianato e agricoltura di Milano. III. Series.
HF5415.12.I8 I53 1985 ***NYPL [JLD 87-432]***

Industria e movimento operaio a Vicenza . Spagnolo, Mario. Vicenza , 1983. 107 p., [1] leaf of plate : LC Card 85-175207
HD6714.V53 S63 1983

Industria e politica nella storia d'Italia . Colombo, Giuseppe, 1836-1921. [Milano] , Roma , c1985. 497 p. : ISBN 88-420-2555-0 : LC Card 85-180231 DDC 338.945 19
HC310.I53 C65 1985 ***NYPL [JLE 86-2517]***

Indústria e reversão da polarização no Brasil /. Azzoni, Carlos Roberto. São Paulo , 1986. 176 p. : LC Card 87-138915 DDC 338.6/042/0981 19
HC190.D5 A99 1986

Industria eléctrica, 1960-1985 . Errázuriz, Enrique. [Santiago, Chile] [1986] 243 p. : LC Card 87-403870 DDC 338.4/762131/0983 19
HD9685.C52 E77 1986

La industria en una estrategia de desarrollo para Chile /. Weinstein L., Jacqueline. Santiago, Chile , 1984. 50 leaves ; LC Card 86-139143
HD3616.C52 W45 1984

A indústria extrativa do sal e a sua importância na economia do Brasil /. Duarte, Dioclécio D. Rio de Janeiro, Brasil , 1941 i.e. 1942. 218 p., [24] leaves of plates : LC Card 85-222223
HD9213.B72 D83 1942

La industria frente a la inflación . Belardi C., Arturo. Valencia [Venezuela] , 1981. 92 leaves : LC Card 85-187972
HG915 .B44 1981

A indústria gaúcha de bens de capital na dinâmica da economia brasileira . Almeida, Pedro Fernando de. Porto Alegre, RS , 1986. 257 p. ; LC Card 87-403616 DDC 338.4/76218/0981 19
HD9705.B73 R562 1986

Industria manufacturera y empleo . García, Norberto E. [Santiago, Chile] , 1982. 51 p. ; LC Card 87-403251 DDC 338.4/767/098 19
HD9734.L32 G36 1982

La Industria mexicana de la construcción. México, D.F. : Cámara Nacional de la Industria de la Construcción, Dirección Técnica, 1979. 89 p. : ill. ; 28 cm. Prepared for presentation at the 12th Congreso Mexicano de la Industria de la Construcción, Mexico City, Apr. 1979. LC Card 87-400496 DDC 338.4/7624/0972 19
1. Construction industry - Mexico. I. Cámara Nacional de la Industria de la Construcción (Mexico). Dirección Técnica.
HD9715.M4 I53 1979

Industria petrolchimica / Missione impresariale del Governo dello Stato di São Paulo in Italia. [São Paulo] : Governo do Estado de São Paulo, Secretaria de Economia e Planejamento, Coordenadoria de Ação Regional, 1973. 1 v. (various pagings), [22] leaves of plates : col. ill. ; 28 cm. (Balcão de projetos) Cover title. LC Card 86-146014
1. Petroleum chemicals industry - Brazil. I. Missione impresariale del Governo dello Stato di São Paulo in Italia. II. Series.
HD9579.C33 B7417 1973

L'Industria siderurgica : analisi di un settore in fase di ristrutturazione / A. Signora ... [et al.] ; a cura di L. Selleri e D. Velo. Milano : Giuffrè editore, [1986] 193 p. : ill. ; 25 cm. (Collana di diritto ed economia . 13) Includes bibliographical references. ISBN 88-14-00787-X : LC Card 86-222572
1. Steel industry and trade - Congresses. 2. Iron industry and trade - Congresses. 3. Steel industry and trade - Italy - Congresses. 4. Iron industry and trade - Italy - Congresses. I. Signora, A. (Andre). II. Selleri, Luigi. III. Velo, Dario. IV. Series.
HD9510.5 .I473 1986

INDUSTRIAL ACCIDENTS - BRAZIL.
Costa, Marcia Regina da. As vítimas do capital . Rio de Janeiro , 1981. 117 p. ; LC Card 82-149102
HD7262.5.B7 C67 1981
NYPL [JLD 86-2852]

INDUSTRIAL ACCIDENTS - BRAZIL - SÃO PAULO (STATE)
Costa, Marcia Regina da. As vítimas do capital . Rio de Janeiro , 1981. 117 p. ; LC Card 82-149102
HD7262.5.B7 C67 1981
NYPL [JLD 86-2852]

INDUSTRIAL ACCIDENTS - CANADA - STATISTICS.
Employment injuries and occupational illnesses . Ottawa, Ont. , c1986. 92 p. ; ISBN 0-662-54738-1 (pbk.) LC Card 87-147113 DDC 363.1/12/0971 19
HD7262.5.C3 E463 1986

INDUSTRIAL ACCIDENTS - CONGRESSES.
Brancoli, Mario. The financial aspects of insurance against employment accidents /. Geneva , 1974. 42 p. ; LC Card 84-247775
HD7260.5 .B73 1974

INDUSTRIAL ACCIDENTS - COSTS.
Andreoni, Diego. The cost of occupational accidents and diseases /. Geneva , c1986. viii, 142 p. : ISBN 92-2-103758-4 (pbk.) : LC Card 87-119442 DDC 338.4/336311 19
HD7262 .A73 1986

INDUSTRIAL ACCIDENTS - DENMARK.
Rønne, Henning. Dødelighed og førtidspensionering blandt ansatte på danske kraftværker /. København , 1985. 73 p. : ISBN 87-7359-155-6 LC Card 85-228083
HD7262.5.D4 R66 1985

INDUSTRIAL ACCIDENTS - EUROPEAN ECONOMIC COMMUNITY COUNTRIES.
Occupational accidents and diseases . Dublin, Ireland , Washington, DC , 1986. 116 p. ; ISBN 92-825-6426-6 LC Card 87-135635 DDC 363.1/1/094 19
HD7694.5 .O33 1986

INDUSTRIAL ACCIDENTS - FINLAND.
Riikonen, Eila. Työnteon turvallisuus . Tampere , 19. x, 131, [66] p. : ISBN 951-860-009-0 LC Card 86-222051
HD7262.5.F5 R55 1986

INDUSTRIAL ACCIDENTS - GERMANY, WEST.
Arnold, Alix, 1956- Kaputt und auch noch selber schuld . Reinbek bei Hamburg , c1986. 179, [1] p. : ISBN 3-499-15908-2 : LC Card 86-226114
HD7708 .A75 1986

INDUSTRIAL ACCIDENTS - INVESTIGATION.
Accident investigation and reporting . [Ottawa] , c1986. 15, 16 p. : ISBN 0-662-54332-7 (pbk.) LC Card 86-201756
HD7262.25 .A28 1986

Hendrick, Kingsley. Investigating accidents with STEP /. New York , c1987. xviii, 454 p. : ISBN 0-8247-7510-4 LC Card 86-24165 DDC 363.1/065 19
HD7262.25 .H46 1987

INDUSTRIAL ACCIDENTS - NEW MEXICO - STATISTICS.
Characteristics of occupational injuries and illnesses in New Mexico, 1982 /. Santa Fe, N.M. [1983?] 43 p. : LC Card 86-621034 DDC 363.1/12/09789021 19
HD7262.5.U62 N625 1983

Characteristics of occupational injuries and illnesses in New Mexico, 1983 /. Santa Fe, N.M. [1983] 47 p. : LC Card 86-620786 DDC 363.1/12/09789021 19
HD7262.5.U62 N626 1983

INDUSTRIAL ACCIDENTS - PAKISTAN.
Industrial democracy in India . Saddar, Karachi, Pakistan [1985] 21 p. ; LC Card 86-222345 DDC 331/.01/12095491 19
HD7262.5.P18 I53 1985

INDUSTRIAL ACCIDENTS - PREVENTION. see **INDUSTRIAL SAFETY.**

INDUSTRIAL ACCIDENTS - REPORTING - CANADA.
Accident investigation and reporting . [Ottawa] , c1986. 15, 16 p. : ISBN 0-662-54332-7 (pbk.) LC Card 86-201756
HD7262.25 .A28 1986

INDUSTRIAL ACCIDENTS - UNITED STATES.
Modern job safety and health /. Paramus, N.J. , c1987- 1 v. (loose-leaf) : LC Card 87-403957 DDC 363.1/1/068 19
HD6067.2.U6 M63 1987

INDUSTRIAL ACCIDENTS - UNITED STATES - CONGRESSES.
Proposed national strategies for the prevention of leading work-related diseases and injuries. [Washington, D.C.] , 1986- v. <1 > ; LC Card 87-111984 DDC 363.1/17/0973 19
HD7262.5.U6 P75 1986

INDUSTRIAL ACCIDENTS - UNITED STATES - STATISTICS.
Injuries to warehouse workers. Washington, D.C. , 1986. v, 24 p. : LC Card 87-601109 DDC 363.1/19381 19
HD7269.F82 I56 1986

INDUSTRIAL ADMINISTRATION. see **INDUSTRIAL MANAGEMENT.**

Industrial and agricultural potentials in Benue State. Rev. ed. Makurdi : Ministry of Information, Social Development, Youth, Sports, and Culture, 1986. 36 p. : ill. ; 24 cm. LC Card 87-102274 DDC 338.09669/5 19
1. Benue State (Nigeria) - Industries. 2. Benue State (Nigeria) - Manufactures. 3. Agriculture - Economic aspects - Nigeria - Benue State. I. Benue State (Nigeria). Ministry of Information, Social Development, Youth, Sports, and Culture.
HC1055.Z7 B455 1986

Industrial and municipal discharges. Seattle, Wash. (217 Pine St., Ste 1100, Seattle 98101) : Puget Sound Water Quality Authority, [1986] viii, 136, 14 p. : ill. ; 28 cm. (Issue paper / Puget Sound Water Quality Authority) "May 1986." Bibliography: p. 133-136. LC Card 86-622616 DDC 363.7/31 19
1. Water quality management - Government policy - Washington (State) - Puget Sound Region. 2. Water - Pollution - Washington (State) - Puget Sound Region. 3. Factory and trade waste - Law and legislation - Washington (State) - Puget Sound Region. I. Washington (State). Puget Sound Water Quality Authority. II. Series: Issue paper (Washington (State). Puget Sound Water Quality Authority).
HC107.W22 P85 1986

Industrial and social history. Collar, George. An industrial and social history of England /. London , New York [1912] 283 p. : LC Card

85-666355
HC253 .C65x 1912

An industrial and social history of England /. Collar, George. London , New York [1912] 283 p. : LC Card 85-666355
HC253 .C65x 1912

INDUSTRIAL ARBITRATION. see **ARBITRATION, INDUSTRIAL.**

INDUSTRIAL ARTS - EXHIBITIONS. see **EXHIBITIONS.**

INDUSTRIAL BETTERMENT. see **WELFARE WORK IN INDUSTRY.**

INDUSTRIAL BUILDINGS - UNITED STATES - FINANCE.
The Trade deficit in manufactured goods . [Washington] , Washington, D.C. [1986] vi, 79 p. : LC Card 86-601142 DDC 382/.4567/0973 19
HD9725 .T73 1986

INDUSTRIAL BUYING. see **INDUSTRIAL PROCUREMENT.**

INDUSTRIAL CAPACITY - BANGLADESH.
Rahman, Alimur. Capacity utilisation in the large-scale manufacturing industry in Bangladesh /. [Dhaka] [1983] 123 p. ; LC Card 83-903801 DDC 338.6/44/095492 19
HD69.C3 R34 1983 ***NYPL [JLE 86-4622]***

INDUSTRIAL CAPACITY - PLANNING - MATHEMATICAL MODELS.
Kleindorfer, Paul R. Optimal capacity planning under stagnating demand /. Berlin [1985] 18, 4 leaves : LC Card 86-205882
HD69.C3 K49 1985

INDUSTRIAL CAPACITY - SOVIET UNION.
IÂkovleva, O. P. (Olimpiada Pavlovna) Formirovanie i izmerenie rezervov proizvodstva /. Leningrad , 1985. 86 p. : LC Card 86-168063
HC336.25 .I25 1985

Industrial change and women's employment . Garnsey, Elizabeth. Geneva , 1987. ix, 100, x p. : ISBN 92-9014-411-4 (pbk.) : LC Card 87-163195 DDC 331.4/09172/4 19
HD6223 .G37 1987

Industrial change in advanced economies / edited by F.E. Ian Hamilton. London ; Wolfeboro, N.H. : Croom Helm, c1987. 319 p. : ill., maps ; 23 cm. Includes bibliographies and index. ISBN 0-7099-3828-4 : LC Card 86-19661 DDC 338.09 19
1. Technological innovations - Economic aspects. 2. Industry - Location. 3. Industrialization. I. Hamilton, F. E. Ian.
HC79.T4 H35 1987 ***NYPL [JLD 87-410]***

Industrial cogeneration in Canada . Reinsch, Anthony Ernest. Calgary, Alta. [1987] xviii, 137 p. : ISBN 0-920522-41-6 (pbk.) : LC Card 87-163062 DDC 333.79/3 19
HD9685.C2 R45 1987

Industrial collaboration with Japan /. Turner, Louis, 1942- London , New York , 1987. 117 p. ; ISBN 0-7102-1109-0 (pbk.) : LC Card 86-26048 DDC 338.8/8 19
HD62.47 .T87 1987

INDUSTRIAL COMMUNICATION. see **COMMUNICATION IN MANAGEMENT.**

INDUSTRIAL CONCENTRATION.
Böbel, Ingo. Wettbewerb und Industriestruktur . Berlin , New York , 1984. xiv, 336 p. : ISBN 0-387-13143-4 (U. S.) LC Card 85-111698
HD2757 .B63 1984

Geroski, Paul A. Do dominant firms decline? /. Berlin [1985] 23, [8] p. ; LC Card 86-213583 DDC 338.6/44 19
HD2757 .G47 1985

Müller, Hans-Erich, 1945- Konzentration . Hamburg , 1985. 239 p. : ISBN 3-87975-303-2 LC Card 87-110533 DDC 338.8 19
HD2757 .M85 1985

Weiss, Leonard W. The extent and permanence of market dominance /. Berlin [1984] 30, 7 p. ; LC Card 85-183107 DDC 338.8/2 19
HD2757.3 .W45 1984

INDUSTRIAL CONCENTRATION - AUSTRALIA - STATISTICS.
Industry concentration statistics . Canberra [1974] 194 p. ; LC Card 82-132323
HD2930 .I53 1974

INDUSTRIAL CONCENTRATION - BRAZIL.
Hollanda Filho, Sergio Buarque de. Estrutura industrial no Brasil . Rio de Janeiro , 1983. 275 p. : LC Card 87-119359 DDC 338.8/0981 19
HD2834 .H65 1983

INDUSTRIAL CONCENTRATION - CANADA.
Francis, Diane. Controlling interest . Toronto, Ont., Canada , c1986. 352 p. ; ISBN 0-7715-9744-4 LC Card 86-218086 DDC 338.8/0971 19
HD2809 .F73 1986

INDUSTRIAL CONCENTRATION - GERMANY - HISTORY.
Bechtold, Hartmut. Die Kartellierung der deutschen Volkswirtschaft und die sozialdemokratische Theorie-Diskussion vor 1933 /. Frankfurt am Main , c1986. 291 p. ; ISBN 3-89228-000-2 LC Card 86-193858
HD2757.5 .B43 1986

Proizvoditel'nye sily i monopolisticheskiĭ kapital v Rossii i Germanii v kontse XIX-nachale XX vv. /. Moskva , 1986. 223 p. ; LC Card 87-159751
HD2859 .P76 1986

INDUSTRIAL CONCENTRATION - GERMANY, WEST.
Schenk, Hans-Otto. Die Konzentration im Handel . Berlin , c1984. 341 p. : ISBN 3-428-05618-3 LC Card 84-225438
HF345 .F66 Folge 3, Nr. 9 HF3566

INDUSTRIAL CONCENTRATION - GERMANY (WEST) - ECONOMETRIC MODELS.
Stahlecker, Peter. Konzentration und gesamtwirtschaftliche Stabilität . Frankfurt am Main , New York , c1984. v, 592 p. : ISBN 3-8204-5318-0 LC Card 85-192714
HD2757 .S78 1984

INDUSTRIAL CONCENTRATION - HUNGARY.
Dévai, Katalin. A nagyvállalatok helyzetéről /. [Budapest] , 1984. 68 p. ; ISBN 963-673-293-0 LC Card 85-175237
HD2852.5 .D48 1984

INDUSTRIAL CONCENTRATION - JAPAN.
Futatsugi, Yūsaku, 1935- [Gendai Nihon no kigyō shūdan. English.] Japanese enterprise groups /. [Kobe] , 1986. 179 p. : LC Card 86-220427 DDC 338.8/0952 19
HD2756.2.J3 F8813 1986

INDUSTRIAL CONCENTRATION - MATHEMATICAL MODELS.
Stahlecker, Peter. Konzentration und gesamtwirtschaftliche Stabilität . Frankfurt am Main , New York , c1984. v, 592 p. : ISBN 3-8204-5318-0 LC Card 85-192714
HD2757 .S78 1984

INDUSTRIAL CONCENTRATION - SOVIET UNION - HISTORY.
Proizvoditel'nye sily i monopolisticheskiĭ kapital v Rossii i Germanii v kontse XIX-nachale XX vv. /. Moskva , 1986. 223 p. ; LC Card 87-159751
HD2859 .P76 1986

INDUSTRIAL CONCENTRATION - UNITED STATES.
Adams, Walter, 1922 (Aug. 27)- The bigness complex . New York , 1986. xiii, 426 p. ; ISBN 0-394-54721-7 : LC Card 86-42624 DDC 338.6/44/0973 19
HD2785 .A68 1986 ***NYPL [JLE 87-1432]***

Bain, Joe Staten, 1912- Industrial organization . Greenwich, Conn. , c1987. 2 v. ; ISBN 0-89232-702-2 (set) LC Card 87-2618 DDC 338.6 19
HD2326 .B34 1987

Caves, Richard E. American industry . Englewood Cliffs, N.J. , c1987. x, 124 p. : ISBN 0-13-027665-0 (pbk.) : LC Card 86-22706 DDC 338.0973 19
HC106.5 .C34 1987

Gort, Michael, 1923- Diversification and integration in American industry /. Westport, Conn. , 1984, c1962. xxi, 238 p. ; ISBN 0-313-24423-5 (lib. bdg.) LC Card 84-10730 DDC 338.8/0973 19
HD2756.2.U5 G67 1984
NYPL [JLE 86-4435]

Meek, Christopher. Managing by the numbers . Reading, Mass. , c1988. ix, 293 p. : ISBN 0-201-16129-X : LC Card 87-16088 DDC 338.7/4/0973 19
HD70.U5 M413 1988

INDUSTRIAL CONCENTRATION - UNITED STATES - HISTORY.
Chandler, Alfred Dupont. The coming of managerial capitalism . Homewood, Ill. , 1985. xiv, 877 p. : ISBN 0-256-03285-8 LC Card 84-82470 DDC 338.6/44/0973 19
HD2785 .C47 1985 ***NYPL [JLE 86-4418]***

Industrial co-operation and investment in Yugoslavia /. Bauwens, Jan G., 1924- Luxembourg , Washington, D.C. , 1986. viii, 161 p. : ISBN 92-825-6410-X (pbk.) : LC Card 86-216364 DDC 332.6/73/09497 19
HG5682 .B38 1986

INDUSTRIAL COSTS. see **COSTS, INDUSTRIAL.**

INDUSTRIAL COUNCILS. see **WORKS COUNCILS.**

INDUSTRIAL COUNSELING. see **EMPLOYEE COUNSELING.**

INDUSTRIAL COURTS. see **LABOR COURTS.**

Industrial decentralisation under apartheid . Wellings, Paul. Durban , 1984. 48, xxxii p. : ISBN 0-86980-455-3 (pbk.) LC Card 87-127005 DDC 338.968 19
HC905.Z9 D59 1984

Industrial demand for freight transport in Kaduna State /. Ogwude, Innocent C. (Innocent Chuka) Zaria [Nigeria] [1984] 101 p. : LC Card 86-152627 DDC 380.5/24/096695 19
HE287.7.Z7 K336 1984

Industrial democracy : strategies for community revitalization / edited by Warner Woodworth, Christopher Meek, William Foote Whyte. Beverly Hills : Sage Publications, c1985. 308 p. : ill. ; 23 cm. (Sage focus editions. v. 73) Includes bibliographies and index. ISBN 0-8039-2476-3 LC Card 85-11741 DDC 338.973/009173/2 19
1. Community development, Urban - United States. 2. Industry - Social aspects - United States. 3. Employee ownership - United States. 4. Urban renewal - United States. I. Woodworth, Warner. II. Meek, Christopher. III. Whyte, William Foote, 1914-.
HT321 .I53 1985 ***NYPL [JLD 86-3621]***

Industrial democracy in India : experiences and lessons, accidents and safety measures, termination of services. Saddar, Karachi, Pakistan : Shaikhconsults International, [1985] 21 p. ; 29 cm. (Industrial laws and labor relations) Cover title. "Pt. 2." "Series no. 7-9 (1984-85)"--Prelim. p. 1. LC Card 86-222345 DDC 331/.01/12095491 19
1. Industrial accidents - Pakistan. 2. Management - India - Employee participation. 3. Employees, Dismissal of - Law and legislation - Pakistan. I. Shaikhconsultants International. II. Series.
HD7262.5.P18 I53 1985

INDUSTRIAL DESIGN. see **DESIGN, INDUSTRIAL.**

INDUSTRIAL DESIGN COORDINATION.
Napoles, Veronica, 1951- Corporate identity design /. New York , c1988. 144 p. : ISBN 0-442-26844-0 (pbk.) : LC Card 87-6190 DDC 659.2/85 19
HD59.2 .N36 1988

Industrial Development Bank of India. Industrial sickness . Ahmedabad , c1984. xv, 459 p. ; LC Card 87-902007 DDC 363.1/19677/00954 19
HD9866.I63 A385 1984

INDUSTRIAL DEVELOPMENT CENTERS. see **INDUSTRIAL PRODUCTIVITY CENTERS.**

Industrial development during Pelita III. Soehoed, A. R. (Abdoel Raoef), 1920- [Jakarta] [1982] 23 p. ; LC Card 83-940924 DDC 338.9598 19
HD3616.I53 S629 1982

Industrial development during Pelita three. Soehoed, A. R. (Abdoel Raoef), 1920- Industrial development during Pelita III. [Jakarta] [1982] 23 p. ; LC Card 83-940924 DDC 338.9598 19
HD3616.I53 S629 1982

Industrial development during Pelita 3. Soehoed, A. R. (Abdoel Raoef), 1920- Industrial development during Pelita III. [Jakarta] [1982]

23 p. ; LC Card 83-940924 DDC 338.9598 19
HD3616.I53 S629 1982

Industrial development in north east India / [editors], D.D. Mali, P. Deka. 1st ed. Guwahati : Omsons Publications : Distributed by Western Book Depot, 1987. xx, 179 p. : ill. ; 22 cm. On small scale industries in north east India; papers of a seminar held at Guwahati, 1985. Includes bibliographies. LC Card 87-902151 DDC 338.0954/1 19
1. India, Northeastern - Industries - Congresses. 2. Small business - India, Northeastern - Congresses. 3. India, Northeastern - Economic conditions - Congresses. I. Mali, Dharani Dhar. II. Deka, P. (Phani), 1945-.
HC437.N57 I55 1987

Industrial development in Tanzania . Skarstein, Rune. Uppsala , Stockholm, Sweden , 1986. xi, 291 p. : ISBN 91-7106-254-8 (pbk.) LC Card 87-134925 DDC 338.9678 19
HC885 .S58 1986

Industrial development of Malaysia . Kimura, Fukunari. Tokyo, Japan , 1986. 25 p. : LC Card 86-232472 DDC 338.09595 19
HD9736.M32 K56 1986

INDUSTRIAL DEVELOPMENT PROJECTS - BRAZIL, NORTHEAST.

INDUSTRIAL DEVELOPMENT PROJECTS - PARAGUAY - CONGRESSES.
Seminario Estrategia de Desarrollo en Condiciones de Oferta Abundante de Energía Eléctrica (1980 : Asunción, Paraguay) Memoria del Seminario Estrategia de Desarrollo en Condiciones de Oferta Abundante de Energía Eléctrica . Asunción, Paraguay [s.l.] , 1980. 165 p., [18] leaves of plates : LC Card 83-169471 DDC 363.6/2 19
HD9685.P32 S45 1980 ***NYPL [JLE 87-995]***

Industrial development survey. Industry in the 1980s . New York , 1985. xii, 228 p. : ISBN 92-1-106207-1 (pbk.) LC Card 86-227928 DDC 338.09 19
HD9720.5 .I53 1985

INDUSTRIAL DISCIPLINE. see **LABOR DISCIPLINE.**

INDUSTRIAL DISEASES. see **OCCUPATIONAL DISEASES.**

The Industrial display market in the U. S. New York, N.Y. : Frost & Sullivan, c1983. vi, 226 leaves ; 29 cm. "January 1983." "A1203." Includes bibliographical references. LC Card 87-142373 DDC 381/.456213985/0973 19
1. Information display systems industry - United States. 2. Market surveys - United States. I. Frost & Sullivan.
HD9696.I533 U54 1983

INDUSTRIAL DISPUTES. see **LABOR DISPUTES.**

INDUSTRIAL DISTRICTS - BRAZIL - MOSSORÓ - PLANNING.
Estudos de viabilidade técnica da implantação e plano diretor do distrito industrial de Mossoró . [Natal] , 1979. ca. 250 leaves, 8 folded leaves of plates : LC Card 84-256137
HC189.M6 E86 1979

INDUSTRIAL DISTRICTS - CHINA.
Oborne, Michael West. China's special economic zones /. Paris [Washington, D.C.] 1986. 185 p. : ISBN 92-64-12801-8 (pbk.) : LC Card 86-217671 DDC 338.6/042/0951 19
HC427.92 .O27 1986

INDUSTRIAL DISTRICTS - INDIA - UTTAR PRADESH.
Agrawal, Deepak, 1955- Prospects of industrial estates in under-developed countries /. Allahabad, India , 1987. 279 p. ; ISBN 81-85076-13-8 : LC Card 86-903605 DDC 338.6/042/09542 19
HC440.D5 A37 1987

INDUSTRIAL DISTRICTS - INDONESIA.
Indonesia. Departemen Perindustrian. Wilayah pusat pertumbuhan industri . [Jakarta] [1985] 20, vi p. : LC Card 85-941790
HC450.D5 I53 1985

INDUSTRIAL DISTRICTS - UNITED STATES - LOCATION.
National emerging industries site selection guide /. Minneapolis, MN , c1986. 124 p. ; LC Card 86-231272 DDC 338.6/042/02573 19
HC110.D5 N38 1986

Industrial economics . Martin, Stephen. New York , London , c1988. xiii, 540 p. : ISBN 0-02-376780-4 LC Card 87-24031 DDC 338.9 19
HD2326 .M35 1988

INDUSTRIAL ECONOMICS. see **INDUSTRIAL ORGANIZATION (ECONOMIC THEORY)**

Industrial economics in developing countries, India . Chanana, Charanjit. New Delhi , 1983. 113 p. : LC Card 83-903832 DDC 338.0954 19
HC435.2 .C4717 1983 ***NYPL [JLD 87-674]***

Industrial economy of Orissa /. Sahu, Promod K. (Promod Kumar), 1942- Delhi , New Delhi , 1986. viii, 152 p. ; ISBN 81-7018-401-0 : LC Card 86-903551 DDC 338.0954/13 19
HC437.O7 S24 1986

INDUSTRIAL EDUCATION. see **TECHNICAL EDUCATION.**

INDUSTRIAL EFFICIENCY. see **EFFICIENCY, INDUSTRIAL.**

INDUSTRIAL EQUIPMENT - ARGENTINA.
Goldberg, Samuel. El stock de capital en la Argentina . [Buenos Aires] , 1986. 28 leaves : LC Card 87-403996 DDC 332/.0414 19
HC180.C3 G65 1986

INDUSTRIAL EQUIPMENT - BRAZIL.
Tadini, Venilton. O setor de bens de capital sob encomenda . São Paulo , 1986. 142 p. : LC Card 87-154239 DDC 332/.0414/0981 19
HC190.C3 T33 1986

INDUSTRIAL EQUIPMENT INDUSTRY.
Brondoni, Silvio M. Politiche di mercato dei beni industriali /. [Milano] [1983] ix, 279 p. : LC Card 83-234353
HD9680.A2 B76 1983

INDUSTRIAL EQUIPMENT INDUSTRY - AGENTS.
Chaponnière, R. Les fonctions des agents économiques exportant des biens d'équipement, dans le cadre des relations est-ouest et nord-sud, depuis 1970 /. [Paris] [1981] 159 leaves : LC Card 82-180468 DDC 382/.456817 19
HD9705.A2 C55 1981 ***NYPL [JLG 86-212]***

INDUSTRIAL EQUIPMENT INDUSTRY - BRAZIL - RIO GRANDE DO SUL.
Almeida, Pedro Fernando de. A indústria gaúcha de bens de capital na dinâmica da economia brasileira . Porto Alegre, RS , 1986. 257 p. ; LC Card 87-403616 DDC 338.4/76218/0981 19
HD9705.B73 R562 1986

INDUSTRIAL EQUIPMENT INDUSTRY - COMMUNIST COUNTRIES.
Chaponnière, R. Les fonctions des agents économiques exportant des biens d'équipement, dans le cadre des relations est-ouest et nord-sud, depuis 1970 /. [Paris] [1981] 159 leaves : LC Card 82-180468 DDC 382/.456817 19
HD9705.A2 C55 1981 ***NYPL [JLG 86-212]***

INDUSTRIAL EQUIPMENT INDUSTRY - DEVELOPING COUNTRIES.
Chaponnière, R. Les fonctions des agents économiques exportant des biens d'équipement, dans le cadre des relations est-ouest et nord-sud, depuis 1970 /. [Paris] [1981] 159 leaves : LC Card 82-180468 DDC 382/.456817 19
HD9705.A2 C55 1981 ***NYPL [JLG 86-212]***

Machinery and economic development /. Houndmills, Basingstoke, Hampshire , 1986. xvii, 274 p. : ISBN 0-333-36391-4
NYPL [JLD 86-4380]

Osterkamp, Rigmar. Die Investitionsgüterindustrie . München , c1986. v, 199 p. ; ISBN 3-8039-0334-3 LC Card 87-401371 DDC 338.4/76218/091724 19
HD9705.D462 O88 1986

Pack, Howard. Fostering the capital-goods sector in LDCS . Washington, D.C. (1818 H St., N.W., Washington 20433) [1980] v, 59. 2 leaves ; LC Card 80-121299
HD9680.D44 P33 1980

INDUSTRIAL EQUIPMENT INDUSTRY - DIRECTORIES.
The Standard handbook of industrial distributors. Fairfield, CT, USA , c1987- v. <1-2 > ; ISBN 0-917408-02-0 (pbk. : v. 1) LC Card 86-73258 DDC 380.1/456218/025 19
HD9680.A2 S72 1987

INDUSTRIAL EQUIPMENT INDUSTRY - FRANCE.
Chaponnière, R. Les fonctions des agents économiques exportant des biens d'équipement, dans le cadre des relations est-ouest et nord-sud, depuis 1970 /. [Paris] [1981] 159 leaves : LC Card 82-180468 DDC 382/.456817 19
HD9705.A2 C55 1981 ***NYPL [JLG 86-212]***

INDUSTRIAL EQUIPMENT INDUSTRY - GERMANY (WEST)
Weis, Hans Christian. Marketingkommunikation in der Investitionsgüterindustrie . Thun , c1983. v, 319, xxxix p. : ISBN 3-87144-741-2 : LC Card 83-159201
HF5415.123 .W45 1983

INDUSTRIAL EQUIPMENT INDUSTRY - UNITED STATES.
Industrial power systems market in the U. S. New York, N.Y. , c1983. v, 312 p. ; LC Card 87-143811 DDC 381/.4562143/0973
HD9695.U52 I53 1983

INDUSTRIAL EQUIPMENT LEASES - FINANCE.
Johnson, James M., 1947- Fundamentals of finance for equipment lessors . Arlington, Va. , c1986. xviii, 531 p. ; ISBN 0-912413-00-X LC Card 86-214227 DDC 658.1/5242 19
HD39.4 .J64 1986

INDUSTRIAL EQUIPMENT LEASES - FRANCE.
France. Conseil économique et social. Le crédit-bail . [Paris] [1985] 90 p. in various pagings : LC Card 86-184049
HD39.4 .F73 1985

INDUSTRIAL EQUIPMENT LEASES - FRANCE - MATHEMATICAL MODELS.
Kieffer, Walther. Steuerliche Wirkungen des grenzüberschreitenden Mobilien-Leasing . Berlin , c1983. xxiv, 338 p. : ISBN 3-503-02369-0 LC Card 83-233705
HD39.4 .K54 1983

INDUSTRIAL EQUIPMENT LEASES - GERMANY (WEST) - ECONOMETRIC MODELS.
Slotta, Gerd. Die Entscheidung über die Betriebspacht bzw. Betriebsverpachtung /. Hamburg , c1986. xi, 374 p. : ISBN 3-925630-00-7 LC Card 86-152904
HD39.4 .S56 1986

INDUSTRIAL EQUIPMENT LEASES - GERMANY (WEST) - MATHEMATICAL MODELS.
Kieffer, Walther. Steuerliche Wirkungen des grenzüberschreitenden Mobilien-Leasing . Berlin , c1983. xxiv, 338 p. : ISBN 3-503-02369-0 LC Card 83-233705
HD39.4 .K54 1983

INDUSTRIAL EQUIPMENT LEASES - GREAT BRITAIN - MATHEMATICAL MODELS.
Kieffer, Walther. Steuerliche Wirkungen des grenzüberschreitenden Mobilien-Leasing . Berlin , c1983. xxiv, 338 p. : ISBN 3-503-02369-0 LC Card 83-233705
HD39.4 .K54 1983

INDUSTRIAL EQUIPMENT LEASES - ITALY - FINANCE - ADDRESSES, ESSAYS, LECTURES.
Il Leasing e il mercato del credito in Italia /. [Milano] [1984] iv, 82 p. : ISBN 88-14-00263-0 (pbk.) : LC Card 84-250907
HD39.4 .L37 1984 ***NYPL [JLE 87-509]***

INDUSTRIAL EQUIPMENT LEASES - UNITED STATES.
A Competitive assessment of the United States equipment leasing industry. Washington, D.C. [1985] xvi, 116 p. : LC Card 85-601661 DDC 382/.45 19
HD9999.L4363 U63 1985
NYPL [JLF 86-1710]

Nevitt, Peter K. Equipment leasing for commercial bankers /. Philadelphia, Pa. , c1987. x, 123 p. ; ISBN 0-936742-37-2 (pbk.) : LC Card 87-5532 DDC 332.1/068/5 19
HD39.4 .N485 1987

Winders, Terry J., 1942- Profitable equipment leasing . Boston , c1987. xii, 252 p. ; ISBN 0-87267-101-1 : LC Card 86-26601 DDC 332.1/068/7 19
HD39.4 .W56 1987 ***NYPL [JLE 87-1512]***

INDUSTRIAL EQUIPMENT LEASES - UNITED STATES - FINANCE.
Haley, Stephen W. Effective credit management in the equipment leasing and finance industry /. Arlington, VA , c1986. ix, 121 p. : ISBN 0-912413-01-8 (pbk.) LC Card 87-105306 DDC 658.1/5242 19
HD39.4 .H35 1986

Johnson, James M., 1947- Fundamentals of finance for equipment lessors . Arlington, Va. , c1986. xviii, 531 p. ; ISBN 0-912413-00-X LC Card 86-214227 DDC 658.1/5242 19
HD39.4 .J64 1986

INDUSTRIAL EQUIPMENT LEASES - UNITED STATES - MATHEMATICAL MODELS.
Kieffer, Walther. Steuerliche Wirkungen des grenzüberschreitenden Mobilien-Leasing . Berlin , c1983. xxiv, 338 p. : ISBN 3-503-02369-0 LC Card 83-233705
HD39.4 .K54 1983

INDUSTRIAL EQUIPMENT - MAINTENANCE AND REPAIR - ACCOUNTING - ADDRESSES, ESSAYS, LECTURES.
Depreciation and capital maintenance /. New York , 1984. xi, 137 p. : ISBN 0-8240-6304-X (alk. paper) : LC Card 83-49437 DDC 657/.73 19
HF5681.D5 D45 1984 ***NYPL [JLE 86-1715]***

INDUSTRIAL EQUIPMENT - MARKETING.
Brondoni, Silvio M. Politiche di mercato dei beni industriali /. [Milano] [1983] ix, 279 p. : LC Card 83-234353
HD9680.A2 B76 1983

Landi, Antonio. Il marketing d'acquisto . Milano, Italy , 1986. 247 p. : ISBN 88-20-41020-6 : LC Card 86-207836
HD9680.A2 L36 1986

INDUSTRIAL EQUIPMENT - PRICES - HUNGARY - STATISTICS.
Beruházási árindexek, 1968-1971 /. [Budapest] [1972] 56 p. ; LC Card 86-189972
HB235.H8 B48 1972

INDUSTRIAL EQUIPMENT - PURCHASING.
Landi, Antonio. Il marketing d'acquisto . Milano, Italy , 1986. 247 p. : ISBN 88-20-41020-6 : LC Card 86-207836
HD9680.A2 L36 1986

INDUSTRIAL EQUIPMENT, REPLACEMENT. see **REPLACEMENT OF INDUSTRIAL EQUIPMENT.**

INDUSTRIAL EQUIPMENT - RUSSIAN S.F. S.R. - URAL MOUNTAINS REGION.
Ėkonomicheskaia ėffektivnost′ rekonstruktsii deĭstvuiushchikh predpriiatiĭ /. Sverdlovsk , 1981. 171 p. ; LC Card 83-192125
HD39.3 .E37 1981

INDUSTRIAL EQUIPMENT - SOVIET UNION.
Palamarchuk, Aleksandr Semenovich. Rekonstruktsiia predpriiatiĭ i ėffektivnost′ proizvodstva /. Moskva , 1981. 62, [2] p. ; LC Card 81-179552
HD39.3 .P34 1981

INDUSTRIAL EQUIPMENT - UKRAINE.
Liakh, L. V. (Lidiia Vasil′evna) Planovoe regulirovanie vozmeshcheniia orudiĭ truda v promyshlennosti /. Kiev , 1983. 122, [1] p. : LC Card 84-105177
HD39.3 .L53 1983

INDUSTRIAL EXHIBITIONS. see **EXHIBITIONS.**

INDUSTRIAL FABRICS INDUSTRY - UNITED STATES.
Geotextiles, geomembranes, geomatrices . Stamford, Conn., U. S.A. , c1986. xii, 133 leaves : ISBN 0-89336-496-7 (pbk.) LC Card 87-403913 DDC 668.9 19
HD9869.I533 U64 1986

Industrial families in India . Verma, H. S. (Harnam Singh), 1942- New Delhi , 1987, c1985. xvi, 248 p. ; LC Card 87-900925 DDC 338/.04/0954 19
HC432.5.A2 V47 1987

Industrial fasteners market in the U. S. New York, N.Y. : Frost & Sullivan, c1983. iv, 375 p. : ill. ; 29 cm. "April 1983." "A1176." LC Card 87-143818
1. Fasteners industry - United States. 2. Market surveys - United States. I. Frost & Sullivan.
HD9999.F33 U476 1983

INDUSTRIAL FINANCE CORPORATION OF INDIA.
Poonia, M. S. (Mohan Singh), 1955- Development banking in India /. Jaipur , 1987. 140, iii, [i] p. ; LC Card 87-901804 DDC 332.2 19
HG3284 .P66 1987

The Industrial future of the Pacific basin / edited by Roger Benjamin and Robert T. Kudrle, ; foreward by Harlan Cleveland. Boulder : Westview Press, 1984. xvi, 285 p. : ill. ; 24 cm. (Pacific basin project . no. 2) "Published in cooperation with the Hubert H. Humphrey Institute of Public Affairs, University of Minnesota, Minneapolis, Minnesota." Papers presented at a workshop held in Seoul, August 1981, cosponsored by the East-West Center in Honolulu, the Aspen Institute for Humanistic Studies, and the University of Minnesota's Hubert H. Humphrey Institute of Public Affairs. Includes index. Bibliography: p. 255-270. ISBN 0-86531-685-6 LC Card 83-51653 DDC 338.9/009182/3 19
1. Industry and state - Pacific Area - Congresses. 2. Investments, Foreign - Pacific area - Congresses. 3. Pacific Area - Industries - Congresses. I. Benjamin, Roger W. II. Kudrle, Robert T. III. Hubert H. Humphrey Institute of Public Affairs. IV. Series.
HC681 .I53 1984 ***NYPL [JLD 86-3100]***

INDUSTRIAL GAMING. see **MANAGEMENT GAMES.**

The industrial geography of Australia /. Rich, D. C. London , Wolfeboro, N.H. , c1987. xvi, 384 p. : ISBN 0-7099-2214-0 : LC Card 86-29383 DDC 338.0994 19
HC610.D5 R53 1987

INDUSTRIAL HEALTH ENGINEERING. see **INDUSTRIAL HYGIENE.**

INDUSTRIAL HOUSING - GERMANY - HISTORY - 19TH CENTURY - CONGRESSES.
Arbeitersiedlungen im 19. Jahrhundert . Bochum , c1985. 189 p. : ISBN 3-88339-427-0 LC Card 85-164690
HD7289.5.A3 G42 1985

INDUSTRIAL HOUSING - GERMANY (WEST) - HANNOVER - HISTORY - 19TH CENTURY.
Voigt, Wolfgang. Der Eisenbahnkönig, oder, Rumänien lag in Linden . München , 1982. 142 p. : ISBN 3-923126-15-8 (pbk.) LC Card 87-672921
HD7289.5.R1 V64x 1982

INDUSTRIAL HOUSING - GERMANY (WEST) - SCHIFFWEILER.
Habicht, Werner. Werkssiedlung Madenfelderhof bei Landsweiler-Reden . Saarbrücken , 1985. 54 p., [52] p. of plates : LC Card 87-408673 DDC 330.943/42 19
HD7289.5.A3 G437 1985

INDUSTRIAL HOUSING - SWITZERLAND.
Fabrikbesichtigungen /. Zürich , c1986. 206 p. : ISBN 3-85791-109-3 LC Card 87-129952 DDC 305.5/62/09494 19
HD8606.5 .F33 1986

Industrial hydraulics components market in Europe. New York, N.Y. : Frost & Sullivan, c1983. xxxvi, 338 p. ; 29 cm. Spine title: Industrial hydraulics market in Europe. "June 1983." "E610." LC Card 87-141832 DDC 381/.456212/094 19
1. Hydraulic machinery industry - Europe. 2. Market surveys - Europe. I. Frost & Sullivan. II. Title: Industrial hydraulics market in Europe.
HD9705.5.H933 E855 1983

Industrial hydraulics market in Europe. Industrial hydraulics components market in Europe. New York, N.Y. , c1983. xxxvi, 338 p. ; LC Card 87-141832 DDC 381/.456212/094 19
HD9705.5.H933 E855 1983

INDUSTRIAL HYGIENE - BRAZIL.
De que adoecem e morrem os trabalhadores /. São Paulo , 1985. 236 p. ; LC Card 85-231487
HD7683 .D4 1985

Hausen, Ivan Zanoni. Segurança empresarial . Brasília, Distrito Federal , 1979. 157 p. : LC Card 82-100947
HD7683 .H38 1979

Possas, Cristina de Albuquerque. Saúde e trabalho . Rio de Janeiro, RJ , 1981. xxxix, 324 p. : LC Card 82-132979 DDC 362.1/0981 19
RA418.3.B6 P68 1981 ***NYPL [JLD 86-1896]***

INDUSTRIAL HYGIENE - BULGARIA - CONGRESSES.
Nauchno-prakticheska konferentsiia po podobriavane na kachestvoto na razrabotvaneto na chast "Bezopasnost, khigiena na truda i pozharna bezopasnost" (BKhTPB) kŭm proektite za obektite po kapitalnoto stroitelstvo s proizvodstveno prednaznachenie (1984) Nauchno-prakticheska konferentsiia po podobriavane na kachestvoto na razrabotvaneto na chast "Bezopasnost, khigiena na truda i pozharna bezopasnost" (BKhTPB) kŭm proektite za obektite po kapitalnoto stroitelstvo s proizvodstveno prednaznachenie . [Bulgaria] [1984?] 56 p. ; LC Card 86-102624
HD7741.5 .N39 1984

INDUSTRIAL HYGIENE - CALIFORNIA.
Schaefer, Andrew. CAL-OSHA routine compliance inspections . [Sacramento, CA , 1986] 25 p. ; LC Card 86-622709 DDC 363.1/164/09796 19
HD7262.5.U62 C573 1986

INDUSTRIAL HYGIENE - CONGRESSES.
Les Effets des conditions de travail sur la santé des travailleuses . [Montréal] [1984] 230 p., [5] p. of plates : ISBN 2-920658-00-X : LC Card 86-158040
HD6067 .E34 1984

INDUSTRIAL HYGIENE - EUROPEAN ECONOMIC COMMUNITY COUNTRIES.
Occupational accidents and diseases . Dublin, Ireland , Washington, DC , 1986. 116 p. ; ISBN 92-825-6426-6 LC Card 87-135635 DDC 363.1/1/094 19
HD7694.5 .O33 1986

INDUSTRIAL HYGIENE - GERMANY, WEST.
Belastungsabbau unter Tage . Essen , 1982. 315 p. : ISBN 3-7739-0380-4 : LC Card 83-186893 DDC 363.1/1/0943 19
HD7708 .B45 1982

Köchling, Annegret, 1944- Bildschirmarbeit . Köln , c1985. 212 p. : ISBN 3-7663-0853-X ***NYPL [JLD 87-392]***

Die Zweite Stadt . Opladen , c1986. 407 p. : ISBN 3-531-11764-5 LC Card 87-497505 DDC 331.11/0943 19
HD8451 .Z94 1986

INDUSTRIAL HYGIENE - GERMANY (WEST) - DIRECTORIES.
Dienststellenverzeichnis Arbeitsschutz . Dortmund , Bremerhaven , 1983. 217 p. ; ISBN 3-88314-274-3 LC Card 83-196051
HD7708 .D55 1983

INDUSTRIAL HYGIENE - GOVERNMENT - INDIA.
Sufrin, Sidney C., 1910- Bhopal, its setting, responsibility, and challenge /. Delhi , 1985. 98 p. ; ISBN 81-202-0135-3 : LC Card 85-903246 DDC 363.1/79 19
HD7269.C452 I527 1985 ***NYPL [JLD 86-1321]***

INDUSTRIAL HYGIENE - GREAT BRITAIN.
Inspecting industry . London , 1986. 110 p. ; ISBN 0-11-751910-3 (pbk.) : LC Card 87-164869 DDC 363.1/1/0941 19
HD7695 .I63 1986

INDUSTRIAL HYGIENE - HUNGARY.
A Munkavédelem agitációs és propaganda rendszere /. Budapest , 1983. 51 p. : ISBN 963-7006-04-4 LC Card 85-110318
HD7702.5 .M85 1983

INDUSTRIAL HYGIENE - ITALY.
La Tutela del lavoro in Italia. [Roma] [1976] 144 p. ; LC Card 86-233354
HD8481 .T85 1976

INDUSTRIAL HYGIENE - KOREA (SOUTH)
International Labour Organisation. National Institute of Labour Science (NILS) (preparatory assistance), Republic of Korea . Geneva , 1976. 43 p. ; ISBN 92-2-101617-X (pbk.) LC Card 84-145790
HD7758 .I58 1976

INDUSTRIAL HYGIENE - LAW AND LEGISLATION - BRAZIL.
Hausen, Ivan Zanoni. Segurança empresarial . Brasília, Distrito Federal , 1979. 157 p. : LC Card 82-100947
HD7683 .H38 1979

INDUSTRIAL HYGIENE - LAW AND LEGISLATION - NETHERLANDS.
Advies samenloop Wet OR en ARBO-wet . Den Haag [1986] 37 p. ; ISBN 90-6587-243-4 LC Card 87-104667
HC321 .S63 1986, nr. 6 KKM1430

INDUSTRIAL HYGIENE - LAW AND LEGISLATION - UZBEK S.S.R.
Tormysheva, T. A. (Tamara Andreevna) Okhrana truda i sotsial′noe strakhovanie trudi͡ashchikhsi͡a v Uzbekskoĭ SSR /. Tashkent , 1987. 131 p. ; LC Card 87-107413
HD7345.U93 T67 1987

INDUSTRIAL HYGIENE - MEXICO.
Enfermedades de trabajo. México, D.F. , c1983. 403 p. : ISBN 968-8242-08-X LC Card 85-216152
HD7262.5.M6 E54 1983

INDUSTRIAL HYGIENE - MORAL AND ETHICAL ASPECTS - CONGRESSES.
The Environment of the workplace and human values /. New York , c1986. vii, 118 p. ; ISBN 0-8451-4205-4 LC Card 85-23908 DDC 174/.4 19
HD7260.5 .E58 1986 ***NYPL [JLF 87-151]***

INDUSTRIAL HYGIENE - NORWAY - MANAGEMENT - EMPLOYEE PARTICIPATION.
Lewis, Gary A., 1927- News from somewhere . Westport, Conn. , 1986. xii, 213 p. : ISBN 0-313-24869-9 (lib. bdg. : alk. paper) LC Card 85-27269 DDC 658.3/152 19
HD5650 .L439 1986 ***NYPL [JLD 86-3587]***

INDUSTRIAL HYGIENE - SOCIETIES, ETC. - DIRECTORIES.
Conditions of work and quality of working life . Geneva , 1986. xxi, 306 p. ; ISBN 92-2-105328-8 (pbk.) : LC Card 86-215659 DDC 306/.36/025 19
HD7260 .C64 1986

INDUSTRIAL HYGIENE - SOVIET UNION.
Prigarin, V. S. (Valentin Stepanovich) Uslovii͡a truda pri sotsializme . Leningrad , 1985. 125 p. ; LC Card 86-124818
HD7725 .P83 1985

INDUSTRIAL HYGIENE - SWITZERLAND.
Sécurité et santé au travail . Berne [1984] 47 p. ; LC Card 85-176432 DDC 363.1/1/09494 19
HD7740 .S43 1984

INDUSTRIAL HYGIENE - UKRAINE - DONETSKAI͡A OBLAST′.
Uslovii͡a truda v regione /. Kiev , 1985. 252 p. : LC Card 86-105167
HD7726.U39 U85 1985
NYPL [*QGA 87-3379]

INDUSTRIAL HYGIENE - UNITED STATES.
Irwin, Michael H. K. Risks to health and safety on the job /. New York, NY , c1986. 28 p. : ISBN 0-88291-096-5 (pbk.) : LC Card 87-402515 DDC 363.1/1/0973 19
HD7654 .I79 1986

Noble, Charles, 1948- Liberalism at work . Philadelphia , 1986. x, 292 p. : ISBN 0-87722-421-8 (alk. paper) : LC Card 86-1766 DDC 353.0083/0289 19
HD7654 .N63 1986 ***NYPL [JLE 86-4426]***

Occupational characteristics of disabled workers, 1975-1976 . Cincinnati, Ohio (4676 Columbia Pkwy., Cincinnati 45226) [1986] xix, 187 p. ; LC Card 86-602391 DDC 363.1/12/0973 19
HD7105.25.U6 O23 1986

INDUSTRIAL HYGIENE - UNITED STATES - CONGRESSES.
Proposed national strategies for the prevention of leading work-related diseases and injuries. [Washington, D.C.] , 1986- v. <1 > ; LC Card 87-111984 DDC 363.1/17/0973 19
HD7262.5.U6 P75 1986

INDUSTRIAL HYGIENE - UNITED STATES - MANAGEMENT.
Modern job safety and health /. Paramus, N.J. , c1987- 1 v. (loose-leaf) : LC Card 87-403957 DDC 363.1/1/068 19
HD6067.2.U6 M63 1987

INDUSTRIAL HYGIENE - UZBEK S.S.R.
Tormysheva, T. A. (Tamara Andreevna) Okhrana truda i sotsial′noe strakhovanie trudi͡ashchikhsi͡a v Uzbekskoĭ SSR /. Tashkent , 1987. 131 p. ; LC Card 87-107413
HD7345.U93 T67 1987

INDUSTRIAL INJURIES. see **INDUSTRIAL ACCIDENTS.**

Industrial investment schedule for small industry, 1982-85. Dhaka : Bangladesh Small & Cottage Industries Corp., Counselling & Industrial Studies Dept. : Ministry of Industries and Commerce, Industries Division, 1982. v, 283 p. ; 29 cm. Cover title: Small industry investment schedule, 1982-85. LC Card 84-900851 DDC 338.6/42/095492 19
1. Small business - Bangladesh - Finance. 2. Industry and state - Bangladesh. 3. Investments - Bangladesh. I. Bangladesh Small & Cottage Industries Corporation. Counselling & Industrial Studies Dept. II. Bangladesh. Śilpa Bibhāga. III. Title: Small industry investment schedule, 1982-85.
HD2346.B27 I53 1982 ***NYPL [JLF 87-269]***

Industrial laws and labor relations.
Industrial democracy in India . Saddar, Karachi, Pakistan [1985] 21 p. ; LC Card 86-222345 DDC 331/.01/12095491 19
HD7262.5.P18 I53 1985

Why the office staff scared of time and motion study? . Saddar, Karachi, Pakistan [1985] 1 v. (various pagings) leaves ; LC Card 86-146552
HD5070.5 .W49 1985

INDUSTRIAL LAWS AND LEGISLATION - CANADA.
Schultz, Richard, 1945- Economic regulation and the federal system /. Toronto , Buffalo , c1985. xv, 187 p. : ISBN 0-8020-7287-9 (pbk.) LC Card 86-672574
HD3616.C23 S38x 1985
NYPL [JLD 86-2821]

INDUSTRIAL LAWS AND LEGISLATION - FRANCE.
Germon, Claude. La normalisation, clé d'un nouvel essor . Paris , c1983. 156 p. ; ISBN 2-11-001026-6 : LC Card 83-217768
HD3616.F83 G47 1983

INDUSTRIAL LAWS AND LEGISLATION - GERMANY, WEST.
Gaul, Dieter. Rechtsprobleme der Innovation . München , 1984. xiv, 126 p. ; ISBN 3-88709-084-5 ***NYPL [JLD 85-2917]***

INDUSTRIAL LAWS AND LEGISLATION - GERMANY (WEST) - COMPLIANCE COSTS.
Nold, Wolfgang. Die Kosten der Gesetze und Verordnungen in Staat, Wirtschaft und Gesellschaft /. Konstanz , 1983. xii, 237 p. : ISBN 3-923200-07-2 LC Card 83-195590
HD3616.G4 N65 1983

INDUSTRIAL LAWS AND LEGISLATION - INDIA.
Baig, Nafees, 1941- Government controls and industrial expansion in India /. Aligarh , 1983. viii, 223 p. ; LC Card 83-907504 DDC 338.954 19
HD3616.I43 B35 1983
NYPL [JLD 86-4330]

INDUSTRIAL LAWS AND LEGISLATION - MOROCCO.
Les Industries mécaniques et électriques au Maroc . Casablanca [1984] 1 v. (various pagings) ; LC Card 85-206543
HD9705.M72 I53 1984

INDUSTRIAL LAWS AND LEGISLATION - UNITED ARAB EMIRATES - ABŪ ẒABY (EMIRATE)
Dalīl rajul al-aʻmāl fī al-ṣināʻah wa-al-tijārah . [Abu Ẓaby] , 1984. 305 p. : LC Card 86-965166
HF5233.A56 D35 1984

INDUSTRIAL LAWS AND LEGISLATION - UNITED STATES.
Dunfee, Thomas W. Legal aspects of government regulation of business /. New York , c1984. viii, 335 p. ; ISBN 0-471-87029-3 (pbk.) : LC Card 83-21879 DDC 346.73/07 347.3067 19
KF1600 .D86 1984 ***NYPL [JLE 86-3511]***

Howell, Rate A. The legal environment of business /. Chicago , c1987. xiv, 783 p. : ISBN 0-03-008369-9 LC Card 86-4503 DDC 346.73/07 347.3067 19
KF1600 .H68 1987 ***NYPL [JLE 87-911]***

INDUSTRIAL LOAN ASSOCIATIONS - GOVERNMENT POLICY - VENEZUELA - CONGRESSES.
Situaciones y políticas para el financiamiento industrial . [Caracas, Venezuela] [1985?] 48 p. ; LC Card 86-205909
HG185.V4 S58 1985

INDUSTRIAL LOAN ASSOCIATIONS - VENEZUELA - CONGRESSES.
Situaciones y políticas para el financiamiento industrial . [Caracas, Venezuela] [1985?] 48 p. ; LC Card 86-205909
HG185.V4 S58 1985

INDUSTRIAL MAINTENANCE. see **PLANT MAINTENANCE.**

INDUSTRIAL MANAGEMENT - ADDRESSES, ESSAYS, LECTURES.
Führung . Zürich , cop. 1979. 189 p. : ISBN 3-85743-841-X : LC Card 81-461814 DDC 658 19
HD35 .F8115 ***NYPL [JLE 82-593]***

Managing take-off in fast growth companies . New York , c1986. x, 191 p. : ISBN 0-03-005709-4 (alk. paper) : LC Card 85-16745 DDC 658.4/2 19
HD31 .T24 1986 ***NYPL [JLE 86-1303]***

Industrial management and economic reform in China, 1949-1984 /. Lee, Peter N. S., 1940- Hong Kong , New York , 1987. x, 335 p. ; ISBN 0-19-584118-2 : LC Card 87-13748 DDC 338.951 19
HD70.C5 L44 1987

INDUSTRIAL MANAGEMENT - AUSTRALIA - EMPLOYEE PARTICIPATION.
Democracy and control in the workplace /. Melbourne, Australia , 1986. 388 p. ; ISBN 0-582-71159-2 (pbk.) LC Card 87-102095 DDC 331.01/12 19
HD5660.A8 D46 1986

INDUSTRIAL MANAGEMENT - AUSTRIA.
Schauer, Reinbert. Die Verwaltung als betriebliches Teilsystem . Wien , 1984. v, 258 p. : ISBN 3-85436-014-2 LC Card 84-173337
HD35 .S2655 1984

INDUSTRIAL MANAGEMENT - BIBLIOGRAPHY.
McKell, Lynn J. A study of MAS practice and knowledge and bibliographic references for management advisory services . New York, N.Y. , c1987. 100, [iv], 72 p. ; ISBN 0-87051-002-9 (pbk.) : LC Card 87-19491 DDC 016.6584/6 19
HF5616.U5 M34 1987

INDUSTRIAL MANAGEMENT - BRAZIL.
História empresarial vivida /. São Paulo , 1986- <1987. v. <1-3 > ; LC Card 86-226035
HD70.B7 H57 1986

INDUSTRIAL MANAGEMENT - BRAZIL - CASE STUDIES.
História empresarial vivida /. São Paulo , 1986- <1987. v. <1-3 > ; LC Card 86-226035
HD70.B7 H57 1986

INDUSTRIAL MANAGEMENT - BRAZIL - EFFECT OF INFLATION ON.
Issel, Catarina Irene. Die Geldwertberichtigung in Brasilien im Rechnungswesen der Unternehmung /. Hamburg , 1983. iii, 181 p. : LC Card 84-112596 DDC 332.6/73/098 s 657/.48 19
HG5160.5.A3 P7 Nr. 10 HF5658.5
NYPL [JLK 73-84 Nr.10]

INDUSTRIAL MANAGEMENT - BULGARIA.
Opyt khozi͡aĭstvovanii͡a v ob″edinenii͡akh promyshlennosti sotsialisticheskikh stran /. Moskva , 1985. 157 p. : LC Card 87-152292
HD70.E7 O69 1985

Problemi na sot͡sialisticheskata organizat͡sii͡a na truda /. Sofii͡a , 1986. 146 p. : LC Card 87-128832
HD5811.5.A6 P76 1986

INDUSTRIAL MANAGEMENT - BULGARIA - DECISION MAKING.
Nikolaev, Ivan. Izrabotvane na kolektivnite reshenii͡a /. Sofii͡a , 1985. 69 p. ; LC Card 86-174800
HD30.23 .N55 1985

INDUSTRIAL MANAGEMENT - BURUNDI - CONGRESSES.
Comment acheter, produire et vendre dans les entreprises africaines . [Bujumbura?] [1984 or 1985] 122 p. : LC Card 85-981488
HD29 .C624 1984

INDUSTRIAL MANAGEMENT - CANADA - CONGRESSES.
Twentieth joint conference . [Charlottetown, P.E.I. , 1986] 94 p. ; LC Card 87-147512 DDC 338/.06 19
HC120.T4 T84 1986

INDUSTRIAL MANAGEMENT - CASE STUDIES.
Bartlett, Hale C. Cases in strategic management for business /. Chicago , c1988. xiii, 784 p. : ISBN 0-03-007183-6 (pbk.) LC Card 87-20208 DDC 658.4/012 19
HD30.28 .B369 1988

Buchholz, Rogene A. Management response to public issues . Englewood Cliffs, N.J. , c1985. x, 389 p. : ISBN 0-13-549940-2 (pbk.) : LC Card 84-18355 DDC 658.4/08 19
HD60 .B83 1985 NYPL [JLE 85-1984]

Hamermesh, Richard G. Making strategy work . New York , c1986. xiii, 245 p. : ISBN 0-471-80319-7 : LC Card 85-12456 DDC 658.4/012 19
HD30.28 .H35 1986 NYPL [JLE 86-2018]

Hartley, Robert F. Bullseyes and blunders . New York , c1987. vii, 253 p. : ISBN 0-471-84904-9 LC Card 86-23350 DDC 658 19
HD38 .H3487 1987 NYPL [JLE 87-1047]

Mejías, Tulio. La coordinación como consecuencia de razones y pasiones . Caracas, Venezuela , c1983. 37, [2] p. : ISBN 980-217-002-X LC Card 86-193647
HD37.S66 M37 1983

Schonberger, Richard. World class manufacturing casebook . New York , London , c1987. xxvi, 253 p. : ISBN 0-02-929340-5 LC Card 86-25822 DDC 658 19
HD31 .S3386 1987

Strategies-- successes-- senior executives speak out /. New York , c1988. xiii, 397 p. : ISBN 0-06-044354-5 (pbk.) LC Card 87-21765 DDC 658 19
HD31 .S696394 1988

INDUSTRIAL MANAGEMENT - CHINA.
Chen hsing Chung-hua chih lu--kai ko ti sung ko /. Pei-ching , 1985. 4, 3, 385 p. ; LC Card 86-106324 *NYPL [*OVY 86-3099]*

China's industrial reform /. New York , c1987. xii, 378 p. ; ISBN 0-19-520592-8 : LC Card 87-5616 DDC 338.951 19
HD3616.C63 C495 1987

Lee, Peter N. S., 1940- Industrial management and economic reform in China, 1949-1984 /. Hong Kong , New York , 1987. x, 335 p. ; ISBN 0-19-584118-2 : LC Card 87-13748 DDC 338.951 19
HD70.C5 L44 1987

Liu, Yung-ch'eng. She hui chu i ching chi tse jen chih /. [Ch'ang-ch'un shih] , 1985. 5, 264 p. ; LC Card 86-179707 DDC 658/.00951 19
*HD70.C5 L58 1985 <Orien China> NYPL [*OVY 86-4140]*

Management reforms in China /. New York , 1987. p. cm. ISBN 0-312-00849-X : LC Card 87-4772 DDC 658/.00951 19
HD70.C5 M34 1987

Pegels, C. Carl. Management and industry in China /. New York , 1987. xii, 282 p. ; ISBN 0-275-92553-6 (alk. paper) : LC Card 86-25260 DDC 658/.00951 19
HD70.C5 P44 1987 NYPL [JLE 87-1042]

INDUSTRIAL MANAGEMENT - CHINA - HISTORY.
Remyga, V. N. (Vladimir Nikolaevich) Sistema upravleniia promyshlennost'iu KNR, 1949-1980 /. Moskva , 1982. 189, [3] p. ; LC Card 82-180587
HD70.C5 R45 1982

INDUSTRIAL MANAGEMENT - COLOMBIA - EMPLOYEE PARTICIPATION - CONGRESSES.
Productividad y participación . [Bucaramanga, Colombia] , c1985. 165 p. : ISBN 958-9302-15-6 LC Card 86-166141
HD5660.C7 P76 1985

INDUSTRIAL MANAGEMENT - COMMUNICATION SYSTEMS.
Dordick, Herbert S., 1925- Innovative management using telecommunications . New York , c1986. x, 226 p. : ISBN 0-471-81296-X : LC Card 86-7797 DDC 658.4/5 19
HF5541.T4 D67 1986 NYPL [JLE 86-4425]

INDUSTRIAL MANAGEMENT - COMMUNIST COUNTRIES.
Gárciga Marrero, Rogelio, 1941- Socialismo y la dirección de la producción /. La Habana , 1986. 426 p. : LC Card 87-402070 DDC 658 19
HD37.S66 G385 1986

Hospodářský mechanismus fungování socialistické ekonomiky /. Praha , 1985. 238 p. ; LC Card 86-203712
HC704 .H65 1985

Utkin, Ė. A. (Ėduard Andreevich) Chemu uchit opyt druzeĭ /. Moskva , 1987. 141 p. ; LC Card 87-120824 DDC 658/.009171/7 19
HD70.C725 U85 1987

INDUSTRIAL MANAGEMENT - CONGRESSES.
Comment acheter, produire et vendre dans les entreprises africaines . [Bujumbura?] [1984 or 1985] 122 p. : LC Card 85-981488
HD29 .C624 1984

Kybernetik und Management . Berlin , c1983. viii, 131 p. : ISBN 3-428-05448-2 LC Card 84-109870
HD29 .K92 1983

La Maîtrise de la croissance dans l'entreprise. Paris, 1973. xx, 333 p. LC Card 73-172856 DDC 658.4
HD29 .M26 NYPL [JLE 74-55]

Technology management '85 . London , c1985. 160 p. : ISBN 0-903748-61-4
NYPL [JLG 87-124]

A Vállalati tervezés uj módszere . [Pécs] [1985?] 167 p. : LC Card 86-187131
HD29 .V35 1985

INDUSTRIAL MANAGEMENT - DATA PROCESSING.
Barakonyi, Károly. Számítógépes vállalati tervezés /. Budapest , 1984. 320, [1] p. : ISBN 963-221-456-0 (Magy. nemz. bibl.) : LC Card 85-174882
HD30.2 .B36 1984

Bersutskiĭ, IA. G. (IAkov Grigor'evich) Informatsionnaia sistema upravleniia predpriiatiem /. Kiev , 1986. 166 p. : LC Card 86-214727
HD30.35 .B47 1986

Curwin, Jon. Business studies in context . London , New York , 1987. p. cm. ISBN 0-07-707034-8 : LC Card 87-22560 DDC 658.4/0352 19
HD30.25 .C87 1987

Geis, George T. Micromanaging . Englewood Cliffs, NJ , c1987. xiv, 233 p. ; ISBN 0-13-581901-6 (pbk.) LC Card 86-30470 DDC 658/.05416 19
HD30.2 .G44 1987

Panteleev, Vladimir Dmitrievich. Kompleksnyĭ ėkonomicheskiĭ analiz v. ASUP /. Leningrad , 1981. 176 p. ; LC Card 87-462046
HD30.2 .P365 1981

Povyshenie ėffektivnosti ASUP . Kiev , 1985. 303 p. : LC Card 85-210269
*HD30.2 .P68 1985 NYPL [*QIP 87-2760]*

INDUSTRIAL MANAGEMENT - DATA PROCESSING - CONGRESSES.
Wissenschaftliche Tagung "Nutzung Ökonomisch-Mathematischer Methoden und der Elektronischen Rechentechnik zur Erhöhung der Reaktionsfähigkeit der Industriekombinate gegenüber der Bedarfsdynamik" (1983 : Technische Hochschule Karl-Marx Stadt) Wissenschaftliche Tagung "Nutzung Ökonomisch-Mathematischer Methoden und der Elektronischen Rechentechnik zur Erhöhung der Reaktionsfähigkeit der Industriekombinate gegenüber der Bedarfsdynamik," 8. Juni 1983 . Karl-Marx-Stadt [1983] iii, 56 p. ; LC Card 84-117572
HD30.25 .W56 1983

INDUSTRIAL MANAGEMENT - DECISION MAKING.
Betriebswirtschaftliche Entscheidungen bei Stagnation . Wiesbaden , c1984. xvi, 327 p. : ISBN 3-409-13303-8 LC Card 84-197990
HD30.23 .B486 1984

Betriebswirtschaftslehre und ökonomische Krise . Wiesbaden , c1984. xxix, 412 p. : ISBN 3-409-13037-3 LC Card 85-143204
HD30.23 .B49 1984

Damian-Knight, Guy. The I Ching on business and decision making . Rochester, VT , 1987. p. cm. ISBN 0-89281-173-0 : LC Card 87-15440 DDC 658.4/03 19
HD37.C47 D35 1987

Grünig, Rudolf. Verfahren zur Erarbeitung eines Grundsatzsystems für den Investitionsbereich /. Bern , c1984. 144 p. : ISBN 3-258-03442-7 : LC Card 85-139475
HG4028.C4 G75 1984

INDUSTRIAL MANAGEMENT - DECISION MAKING - MATHEMATICAL MODELS.
Bürkle, Roland. Das Modell der Ausgleichslösung . München , c1983. 210 p. : ISBN 3-88259-255-9 LC Card 83-222868
HD30.23 .B865 1983

Früh, Bernhard, 1953- Entscheidungsträgermodelle bei Planungstechniken /. Frankfurt am Main , New York , c1984. 268 p. : ISBN 3-8204-5499-3 LC Card 85-197372
HD30.23 .F78 1984

INDUSTRIAL MANAGEMENT - DENMARK.
Langebæk, Steen. Bestyrelsens idégrundlag og funktion /. København , 1985. 175 p. ; ISBN 87-12-01597-0 : LC Card 86-156403
HD70.D4 L36 1985

INDUSTRIAL MANAGEMENT - DEVELOPING COUNTRIES - ADDRESSES, ESSAYS, LECTURES.
Entwicklungsmanagement . Berlin , c1982. 192 p. : ISBN 3-428-05208-0 LC Card 83-150764 DDC 338.9/0068 19
HD84 .E56 1982 NYPL [JLE 87-1179]

INDUSTRIAL MANAGEMENT - ECUADOR.
Foro políticas de fomento industrial en el Ecuador /. [Quito, Ecuador] [c1985] 58 p. : LC Card 86-134947 DDC 658/.009866 19
HD70.E25 F67 1985

Industrial management education in the Commonwealth : a report on advisory visits paid by staff members of the British Institution of Works Managers to Singapore, Malaysia, Malta, Jamaica, Trinidad and Tobago, and Nigeria, 1972-1975. London, England : Commonwealth Foundation, [1976] 38 p. ; 25 cm. (Occasional paper / Commonwealth Foundation, 0069-7087 . no. 39) Cover title. "November 1976"--T.p. verso. LC Card 85-100411 DDC 658/.007/11171241 19
1. Industrial management - Study and teaching (Higher) - Developing countries - Case studies. 2. Commonwealth of Nations. I. Institution of Works Managers. II. Series: Occasional paper (Commonwealth Foundation (British Commonwealth)) , no. 39.
HD70.D44 I5 1976

INDUSTRIAL MANAGEMENT - EFFECT OF INFLATION ON.
Blanco Martínez, Adolfo. Dirigir con inflación . Bilbao [1983?] 239 p. : ISBN 84-234-0537-0 LC Card 85-124395
HD49.5 .B48 1983

INDUSTRIAL MANAGEMENT - EMPLOYEE PARTICIPATION.
Carrion, Rosinha Machado. Participação ou manipulação . Porto Alegre, RS , 1984. 111 p. : LC Card 84-209842 DDC 658 19
HD37.P63 C29 1984 NYPL [JLE 86-2263]

Democracy and control in the workplace /. Melbourne, Australia , 1986. 388 p. ; ISBN 0-582-71159-2 (pbk.) LC Card 87-102095 DDC 331.01/12 19
HD5660.A8 D46 1986

Körner, Ulrich. Wettbewerb und Akkumulation in der selbstverwalteten Wirtschaft /. Frankfurt , New York , c1984. 193 p. : ISBN 3-593-33257-4 LC Card 84-191794
HD5660.Y8 K623 1984

Meran, Georg. Die arbeiterselbstverwaltete Firma bei Unsicherheit und asymmetrischer Information . München , c1986. ii, 134 p. : ISBN 3-88259-403-9 LC Card 87-121443 DDC 658.3/152 19
HD5650 .M397 1986

Volkov, Aleksandr Ivanovich. Konfrontatsiia ili kompromiss? . Moskva , 1986. 234 p. [4] ; LC

Card 86-200508 DDC 658.3/152 19
HD5650 .V65 1986

Weisbord, Marvin Ross. Productive workplaces . San Francisco , 1987. xxv, 405 p. : ISBN 1-555-42054-0 (alk. paper) LC Card 87-45425 DDC 658.3/14 19
HD31 .W424 1987

INDUSTRIAL MANAGEMENT - EMPLOYEE PARTICIPATION - CONGRESSES.
Uchastie trudi͡ashchikhsi͡a v upravlenii proizvodstvom . Moskva , 1983. 192, [2] p. : LC Card 84-210286
HD5660.S65 U26 1983

INDUSTRIAL MANAGEMENT - EMPLOYEE PARTICIPATION - HISTORY.
Marucco, Dora. Fabianesimo, ghildismo, forme di democrazia industriale /. Milano, Italy , c1986. 82 p. ; LC Card 86-194327
HD6479 .M37 1986

INDUSTRIAL MANAGEMENT - EMPLOYEE PARTICIPATION - LAW AND LEGISLATION - GERMANY (WEST)
Richter, Bernd, 1954- Der mitbestimmte Aktiengesellschaftskonzern . Köln , c1983. ix, 394 p. : ISBN 3-7663-0820-3 LC Card 83-215341
HD5660.G4 R53 1983

Spie, Ulrich. Der Personalmanager im Vorstand . Stuttgart , 1985. ix, 354 p. : ISBN 3-8202-0313-3 LC Card 86-131051
HF5549.2.G3 S67 1985

INDUSTRIAL MANAGEMENT - EMPLOYEE PARTICIPATION - LAW AND LEGISLATION - NETHERLANDS.
Sociaal-Economische Raad. Commissie Ondernemingsraden. Advies vereenvoudiging Wet OR . Den Haag [1986] 61 p. ; ISBN 90-6587-254-X LC Card 87-165080
HC321 .S63 1986, nr. 14 KKM1350

INDUSTRIAL MANAGEMENT - ENVIRONMENTAL ASPECTS.
Employers and the environmental challenge /. Geneva , 1986. vii, 101 p. ; ISBN 92-2-105647-3 (pbk.) : LC Card 87-123427 DDC 363.7/056 19
HD69.P6 E46 1986

INDUSTRIAL MANAGEMENT - ESTONIA.
Kull, Eduard. Tehnilis-majandusliku ja sotsiaalse arengu planeerimine tootmiskoondistes (tööstusettevõtetes) /. Tallinn , 1985. 277 p. : LC Card 86-221274
HD70.E68 K85 1985

INDUSTRIAL MANAGEMENT - EUROPE.
Benterud, Per. Japan som veiviser . [Oslo] , c1983. 262 p. ; ISBN 82-02-09050-4 LC Card 83-195163
HD70.J3 B45 1983

INDUSTRIAL MANAGEMENT - EUROPE, EASTERN.
Kuligin, Pavel Ivanovich. Kriterii ėffektivnosti raboty predprii͡atiĭ . Moskva , 1986. 172 p. ; LC Card 86-211780
HD70.E7 K85 1986

Opyt khozi͡aĭstvovanii͡a v ob″edinenii͡akh promyshlennosti sotsialisticheskikh stran /. Moskva , 1985. 157 p. : LC Card 87-152292
HD70.E7 O69 1985

Red multinationals or red herrings? . London , 1986. xi, 202 p. ; ISBN 0-86187-583-4
NYPL [JLD 86-2751]

INDUSTRIAL MANAGEMENT - EUROPE - EMPLOYEE PARTICIPATION.
Forgács, Pál. A szakszervezetek változó szerepe a gazdaság szabályozásában az európai fejlett tőkésországokban /. Budapest , 1985. 118 p. ; ISBN 963-608-079-8 LC Card 86-228056
HD5660.E9 F67 1985

INDUSTRIAL MANAGEMENT - FINLAND.
Yritysjohdon valmennusohjelma /. [Helsinki] [1985] 2 v. : ISBN 951-859-860-6 (v. 1) LC Card 87-101417
HD37.F55 Y73 1985

INDUSTRIAL MANAGEMENT - FRANCE.
Roux, Dominique. Analyse économique et gestion de l'entreprise /. Paris , c1986- v. <1 > : ISBN 2-04-016455-3 LC Card 87-114498
HD33 .R647 1986

Le Travail . Paris , c1986. iv, 370 p. ; ISBN 2-7178-1138-9 : LC Card 87-123294
HD8428 .T72 1986

INDUSTRIAL MANAGEMENT - FRANCE - CONGRESSES.
La Maîtrise de la croissance dans l'entreprise. Paris, 1973. xx, 333 p. LC Card 73-172856 DDC 658.4
HD29 .M26 ***NYPL [JLE 74-55]***

INDUSTRIAL MANAGEMENT GAMES. see **MANAGEMENT GAMES.**

INDUSTRIAL MANAGEMENT - GERMANY.
Schalldach, Elisabeth, 1904- Rationalisierungsmassnahmen der Nachinflationszeit im Urteil der deutschen freien Gewerkschaften. Jena, 1930. ix, [1], 186 p. LC Card AC34-383
HD70.G2 S26 1930

INDUSTRIAL MANAGEMENT - GERMANY, EAST.
Rationalisierung, Intensivierung, und "Arbeitsmarkt" in der DDR /. Bonn , c1985. 43 p. ; LC Card 86-170689
HD70.G2 R32 1985

Reinhold, Otto. Mehr, besser, billiger, aber wie? /. Berlin , 1985. 80 p. : LC Card 86-179312
HD70.G22 R45 1985

INDUSTRIAL MANAGEMENT - GERMANY (EAST) - CONGRESSES.
"Ökonomische Probleme der bedarfsorientierten Produktionsdurchführung" . Karl-Marx-Stadt , 1984. 139 p. : LC Card 84-245348
HD70.G22 O35 1984

Die Sozialistische Gemeinschaftsarbeit im Territorium . Potsdam-Babelsberg , 1986. 175 p. ; LC Card 86-212526
HD3616.G48 S68 1986

Wissenschaftliche Tagung "Nutzung Ökonomisch-Mathematischer Methoden und der Elektronischen Rechentechnik zur Erhöhung der Reaktionsfähigkeit der Industriekombinate gegenüber der Bedarfsdynamik" (1983 : Technische Hochschule Karl-Marx Stadt) Wissenschaftliche Tagung "Nutzung Ökonomisch-Mathematischer Methoden und der Elektronischen Rechentechnik zur Erhöhung der Reaktionsfähigkeit der Industriekombinate gegenüber der Bedarfsdynamik," 8. Juni 1983 . Karl-Marx-Stadt [1983] iii, 56 p. ; LC Card 84-117572
HD30.25 .W56 1983

INDUSTRIAL MANAGEMENT - GERMANY - HISTORY - 20TH CENTURY.
Stollberg, Gunnar. Die Rationalisierungsdebatte 1908-1933 . Frankfurt/Main , New York , c1981. 214 p. ; ISBN 3-593-32938-7 : LC Card 81-177695 DDC 331.88/0943 19
HD70.G2 S666 1981 ***NYPL [JLD 86-1662]***

INDUSTRIAL MANAGEMENT - GERMANY, WEST.
Internationale und nationale Problemfelder der Betriebswirtschaftslehre /. Berlin , c1984. 336 p., [1] leaf of plates : ISBN 3-428-05696-5 LC Card 85-141327
HD35 .I598 1984

Krause, Hans-Ulrich. Gewinnung, Verarbeitung und Aufbereitung von Informationen für die Geschäftsfeldplanung . Giessen , c1984. xii,324 p. ; ISBN 3-922730-52-3 LC Card 85-150146
HD35 .K71215 1984

Massenberg, Jost A., 1956- Strategie und Entwicklung deutscher Grossunternehmen . Frankfurt am Main , New York , c1986. xi, 398 p. : ISBN 3-8204-9666-1 LC Card 86-220603
HD70.G2 M37 1986

INDUSTRIAL MANAGEMENT - GERMANY (WEST) - DATA PROCESSING.
Molitor, Monika. Auswirkungen von Computeranwendungen auf die Leistungsstruktur von Unternehmensorganisationen /. Frankfurt am Main , c1984. 278 p. : ISBN 3-88129-808-8 : LC Card 85-140214
HD70.G23 M64 1984

INDUSTRIAL MANAGEMENT - GERMANY (WEST) - EMPLOYEE PARTICIPATION.
Fricke, Werner. Beteiligung im Industriebetrieb . Frankfurt/Main , New York , c1985. 291 p. ; ISBN 3-593-32735-X LC Card 85-202742
HD5660.G4 F73 1985

Hentze, Joachim. Unternehmungsführung und Mitbestimmung /. Würzburg , 1985. 297 p. : ISBN 3-7908-0268-9 LC Card 85-186054
HD5660.G4 H43 1985

Memorandum '84 . Köln , c1984. 475 p. : ISBN 3-7609-0883-7 : LC Card 85-128558
HC286.7 .M465 1984

Mitarbeiterbeteiligung und Mitbestimmung im Unternehmen /. Berlin , New York , 1987, c1986. ix, 351 p. : ISBN 3-11-010668-X LC Card 87-137953 DDC 658.3/152/0943 19
HD5660.G4 M53 1987

Osswald, Richard, 1917- Lebendige Arbeitswelt . Stuttgart , c1986. 394 p. : ISBN 3-421-06309-5 LC Card 86-148169
HD9710.G44 D385 1986

Richter, Bernd, 1954- Der mitbestimmte Aktiengesellschaftskonzern . Köln , c1983. ix, 394 p. : ISBN 3-7663-0820-3 LC Card 83-215341
HD5660.G4 R53 1983

Uvarov, V. P. (Vladimir Pavlovich) Ėkonomicheskoe soupravlenie . Minsk , 1985. 159 p. ; LC Card 85-217045
HD5660.G4 U93 1985

INDUSTRIAL MANAGEMENT - GERMANY (WEST) - EMPLOYEE PARTICIPATION - CASE STUDIES.
Mitbestimmung, Norm und Wirklichkeit . Frankfurt , New York , c1984. 369 p. ; ISBN 3-593-33325-2 LC Card 85-128882
HD5658.A82 G35 1984

INDUSTRIAL MANAGEMENT - GERMANY (WEST) - EMPLOYEE PARTICIPATION - CONGRESSES.
Das Unternehmen als Grösse der Arbeitswelt . Bonn , 1984. 291 p. ; ISBN 3-923202-02-4 LC Card 85-119845
HD6957.G3 U58 1984

INDUSTRIAL MANAGEMENT - GERMANY (WEST) - EMPLOYEE PARTICIPATION - HISTORY.
40 Jahre Mitbestimmung . Köln , c1986. 293 p., [16] p. of plates : ISBN 3-7663-3012-8 LC Card 87-125207 DDC 658.3/152/0943 19
HD5660.G4 A5 1986

INDUSTRIAL MANAGEMENT - GERMANY (WEST) - EMPLOYEE PARTICIPATION - LAW AND LEGISLATION.
Mitarbeiterbeteiligung und Mitbestimmung im Unternehmen /. Berlin , New York , 1987, c1986. ix, 351 p. : ISBN 3-11-010668-X LC Card 87-137953 DDC 658.3/152/0943 19
HD5660.G4 M53 1987

INDUSTRIAL MANAGEMENT - GERMANY (WEST) - LOWER SAXONY - EMPLOYEE PARTICIPATION.
Schanz, Günther, 1943- Mitarbeiter-Kapitalbeteiligung in der Wirtschaft Niedersachsens . Spardorf , c1984. 228 p. : ISBN 3-922919-26-X : LC Card 84-162288
HD5660.G412 L687 1984

INDUSTRIAL MANAGEMENT - GERMANY, WEST - MATHEMATICAL MODELS.
Prätsch, Joachim, 1951- Langfristige Finanzplanung und Simulationsmodelle . Frankfurt am Main , New York , c1986. xii, 481 p. : ISBN 3-8204-9403-0 LC Card 86-219850
HG4157 .P73 1986

INDUSTRIAL MANAGEMENT - GREAT BRITAIN.
Minkes, A. L. Business behaviour & management structure /. London , c1985. 224 p. ; ISBN 0-7099-1795-3
NYPL [JLD 87-1113]

Thomas, R. E. (Raymond Elliott) The government of business /. Oxford, UK , Atlantic Highlands, NJ, USA , 1987. viii, 277 p. : ISBN 0-86003-548-4 LC Card 87-12647 DDC 338.0941 19
HD70.G7 T48 1987

Tomita, Teruhiko, 1937- Transferability of Japanese-style management to Britain /. Hikone, Japan [1986] 63 leaves : LC Card 87-168468 DDC 331.25 19
HD70.J3 T585 1986

INDUSTRIAL MANAGEMENT - GREAT BRITAIN - CASE STUDIES.
Lessem, Ronnie. [Enterprise development.] Intrapreneurship . Aldershot, Hants, England , Brookfield, Vt. , c1987. p. cm. ISBN 0-7045-0577-0 (pbk.) : LC Card 87-21608

DDC 658/.00941 19
HD70.G7 L45 1987

Minkes, A. L. Business behaviour & management structure /. London , c1985. 224 p. ; ISBN 0-7099-1795-3
NYPL [JLD 87-1113]

INDUSTRIAL MANAGEMENT - GREAT BRITAIN - HANDBOOKS, MANUALS, ETC.

Company administration handbook. Aldershot, Hants, England , 1982. xxiv, 770 p. : ISBN 0-566-02352-0 LC Card 83-111544 DDC 658/.00941 19
HD70.G7 C57 1982 *NYPL [JLE 86-2558]*

Company administration handbook /. Aldershot, Hants, England , Brookfield, Vt., U. S.A. , 1988. xxiv, 737 p. : ISBN 0-566-02667-8 : LC Card 86-31876 DDC 658/.00941 19
HD70.G7 C57 1988

INDUSTRIAL MANAGEMENT - HANDBOOKS, MANUALS, ETC.

The Book of business knowledge /. New York, N.Y. , c1987. p. cm. ISBN 0-932648-83-5 : LC Card 86-30962 DDC 658 19
HF5356 .B72 1987

The Boss's encyclopedia /. New York, N.Y. , c1987. xxvi, 594 p. ; ISBN 0-932648-75-4 LC Card 86-30961 DDC 658 19
HF5356 .B735 1987

Business confidential. New York, N.Y. , c1987. xi, 504 p. ; ISBN 0-932648-82-7 LC Card 86-30963 DDC 650 19
HF5356 .B9259 1987

Wells, Richard C. The right choice . New York, N.Y., U. S.A. , c1985. viii, 178 p. : ISBN 0-86604-198-2 (pbk.) LC Card 86-201105 DDC 658.4/033 19
HD31 .W457 1985

INDUSTRIAL MANAGEMENT - HUNGARY.

Antal, Iván. Vállalatok környezete, céljai, szervezete /. Budapest , 1986. 270 p. : ISBN 963-221-567-2 : LC Card 87-149512
HD70.H8 A536 1986

Botos, Balázs. Kérdőjelek iparunk fejlesztésében /. Budapest , 1984. 391, [1] p. ; ISBN 963-221-392-0 : LC Card 85-156613
HC300.28 .B69 1984

A Gazdaságirányítás és a szakszervezetek /. Budapest , 1985. 191 p. ; ISBN 963-322-253-2 : LC Card 86-104573
HC300.28 .G349 1985

Palicz, András. Az önálló vállalattá szervezés elméleti és módszertani megalapozása /. Budapest , 1984. 81 p. : ISBN 963-02-3351-7 : LC Card 86-126838
HD70.H8 P35 1984

Veress, József, Dr. A veszélyhelyzetbe került vállalatok és a gazdaságirányítás /. Budapest , 1986. 207, [1] p. ; ISBN 963-221-778-0 : LC Card 87-136695
HG3769.H94 V47 1986

INDUSTRIAL MANAGEMENT - HUNGARY - CASE STUDIES.

Szalai, Erzsébet. Kiemelt vállalat, beruházás, érdek /. Budapest , 1981. 140 p. ; ISBN 963-05-2527-5 LC Card 81-170685
HG4028.C4 S96 1981

INDUSTRIAL MANAGEMENT - HUNGARY - CONGRESSES.

Gazdaságpolitikánk az élenjáró vállalatok gyakorlatában . [Budapest] , 1985. 276 p. : ISBN 963-09-2769-1 : LC Card 87-407761
HD70.H8 G39 1985

A Vállalati magatartást motiváló gazdasági és társadalmi tényezők című konferencia előadásai . Pécs , 1985. 2 v. : LC Card 87-408547
HD70.H8 V334 1985

A Vállalati tervezés uj módszere . [Pécs] [1985?] 167 p. : LC Card 86-187131
HD29 .V35 1985

INDUSTRIAL MANAGEMENT - HUNGARY - EMPLOYEE PARTICIPATION.

Várkonyi, Margit. A vezetők véleményezése /. Budapest , 1984. 66 p. : ISBN 963-322-189-7 : LC Card 85-176949
HD70.H8 V38 1984

INDUSTRIAL MANAGEMENT - HUNGARY - EVALUATION.

Várkonyi, Margit. A vezetők véleményezése /. Budapest , 1984. 66 p. : ISBN 963-322-189-7 : LC Card 85-176949
HD70.H8 V38 1984

INDUSTRIAL MANAGEMENT - INDIA - GUJARAT.

Dave, Nalini V. Industrial sickness and key areas of management . New Delhi , c1987. 523 p. : LC Card 87-901105 DDC 658/.00954/75 19
HD2747 .D32 1987

INDUSTRIAL MANAGEMENT - INFORMATION SERVICES.

Bersutskiĭ, IA. G. (IAkov Grigor'evich) Informatsionnaia sistema upravleniia predpriiatiem /. Kiev , 1986. 166 p. : LC Card 86-214727
HD30.35 .B47 1986

INDUSTRIAL MANAGEMENT - JAPAN.

Benterud, Per. Japan som veiviser . [Oslo] , c1983. 262 p. ; ISBN 82-02-09050-4 LC Card 83-195163
HD70.J3 B45 1983

De Mente, Boye. Japanese etiquette & ethics in business /. Lincolnwood, Ill. , c1987. ix, 182 p. : ISBN 0-8442-8507-2 (pbk.) : LC Card 86-60830 DDC 395/.52 19
HF5387 .D384 1987

Grayson, C. Jackson (Charles Jackson), 1923- American business, a two-minute warning . New York , London , c1988. xvii, 368 p. : ISBN 0-02-912680-0 LC Card 87-19391 DDC 658/.00973 19
HD70.U5 G69 1988

Industrimakten Japan . Oslo , 1982. 151 p. : ISBN 82-518-1630-0 : LC Card 84-126986
HD70.J3 I549 1982

Leibenstein, Harvey. Inside the firm . Cambridge, Mass. , 1987. xiv, 276 p. : ISBN 0-674-45515-0 (alk. paper) LC Card 87-8426 DDC 302.3/5 19
HD2326 .L45 1987

Lu, David John, 1928- Inside corporate Japan . Stamford, CT , c1987. xxi, 249 p. : ISBN 0-915299-16-X (alk. paper) : LC Card 87-60546 DDC 658/.00952 19
HD70.J3 L8 1987

Marshall, F. Ray. Unheard voices . New York , c1987. xi, 339 p. : ISBN 0-465-08869-4 : LC Card 83-46084 DDC 338.6 19
HD5660.U5 M36 1987

Robotization, its implications for management /. Tokyo, Japan , c1983. vi, 316 p. :
NYPL [JLF 86-1055]

Shapiro, H. Jack (Harris Jack) Reviving industry in America . Cambridge, Mass. , c1987. xii, 204 p. : ISBN 0-88730-118-5 LC Card 87-17585 DDC 338.4/767/0973 19
HD9725 .S46 1987

Tomita, Teruhiko, 1937- Transferability of Japanese-style management to Britain /. Hikone, Japan [1986] 63 leaves : LC Card 87-168468 DDC 331.25 19
HD70.J3 T585 1986

INDUSTRIAL MANAGEMENT - JAPAN - CONGRESSES.

Productivity and role of top management. Tokyo , 1986. x, 94 p. : ISBN 92-833-2041-1 (pbk.) LC Card 87-146526 DDC 658.3/14/0952 19
HC465.I52 P76 1986

INDUSTRIAL MANAGEMENT - JAPAN - EMPLOYEE PARTICIPATION.

Quality control circles at work . Tokyo , 1984. v, 232 p. : ISBN 92-833-1074-9 LC Card 85-133901 DDC 658.5/62/0952 19
HD66 .Q36 1984 *NYPL [JLD 87-806]*

INDUSTRIAL MANAGEMENT - JAPAN - HISTORY.

Hirschmeier, Johannes. Johannes Hirschmeier, die japanische Unternehmung . Hamburg , 1986. viii, 218 p. : ISBN 3-88910-024-4 : LC Card 86-225311
HF5349.J3 H573 1986

INDUSTRIAL MANAGEMENT - KENYA.

Gershenberg, Irving. Slack in Kenya's modern manufacturing sector /. Boston, MA (270 Bay State Rd., Boston 02215) , 1985. 15 leaves ; LC Card 87-404089 DDC 338.4/767/096762 19
HD70.K4 G47 1985

INDUSTRIAL MANAGEMENT - LATIN AMERICA - EMPLOYEE PARTICIPATION - CASE STUDIES.

Grassroots development in Latin America & the Caribbean . New York , 1985. vii, 197 p. : ISBN 0-03-001689-4 (alk. paper) : LC Card 84-18180 DDC 334/.098 19
HD3450.5.A4 G72 1985

INDUSTRIAL MANAGEMENT - LAW AND LEGISLATION - ECUADOR.

Foro políticas de fomento industrial en el Ecuador /. [Quito, Ecuador] [c1985] 58 p. : LC Card 86-134947 DDC 658/.009866 19
HD70.E25 F67 1985

INDUSTRIAL MANAGEMENT - LINEAR PROGRAMMING.

Moro, Beniamino, 1945- Programmazione lineare e teoria dell'impresa /. Milano [1980] 182 p. : ISBN 88-20-41708-1 : LC Card 80-489699
T57.74 .M67 *NYPL [JLD 87-792]*

Programmnoe obespechenie ėkonomiko-matematicheskikh issledovaniĭ /. Moskva , 1982. 142 p. : LC Card 84-209065
HD30.25 .P76 1982

INDUSTRIAL MANAGEMENT - MATHEMATICAL MODELS.

Curwin, Jon. Business studies in context . London , New York , 1987. p. cm. ISBN 0-07-707034-8 : LC Card 87-22560 DDC 658.4/0352 19
HD30.25 .C87 1987

Hilfer, Rudolf. Stochastische Modelle für die betriebliche Planung /. München , c1985. ii, 191 p. : ISBN 3-89003-015-7 LC Card 85-189343
HD30.25 .H55 1985

Lagosha, Boris Aleksandrovich. Analiz i sintez v sistemakh otraslevogo upravleniia /. Moskva , 1978. 262 p., [1] folded leaf of plates : LC Card 81-167577
HD30.25 .L335 1978

Modelirovanie ėkonomicheskogo povedeniia sotsialisticheskogo predpriiatiia /. Moskva , 1984. 131 p. : LC Card 86-144437
HD30.25 .M623 1984

Mole, R. H. (Richard H.) BASIC business analysis and operations research /. London , Boston , 1987. 136 p. : ISBN 0-408-01590-X (pbk.) : LC Card 86-26398 DDC 658.4/034/0285526 19
HD30.25 .M66 1987

Püschel, Manfred, 1953- Die Wahl der optimalen Wärmeversorgungskonfiguration als betriebswirtschaftliches Produktions- und Investitionsproblem /. Frankfurt am Main , New York , c1984. iv, 298 p. : ISBN 3-8204-7432-3 LC Card 86-108875
HD30.25 .P87 1984

Vörös, József. A kockázat, haszon és a termelési szerkezet összefüggése /. Pécs , 1983. 77 leaves : LC Card 85-111246
HD61 .V67 1983

INDUSTRIAL MANAGEMENT - MATHEMATICAL MODELS - CONGRESSES.

Wissenschaftliche Tagung "Nutzung Ökonomisch-Mathematischer Methoden und der Elektronischen Rechentechnik zur Erhöhung der Reaktionsfähigkeit der Industriekombinate gegenüber der Bedarfsdynamik" (1983 : Technische Hochschule Karl-Marx Stadt) Wissenschaftliche Tagung "Nutzung Ökonomisch-Mathematischer Methoden und der Elektronischen Rechentechnik zur Erhöhung der Reaktionsfähigkeit der Industriekombinate gegenüber der Bedarfsdynamik," 8. Juni 1983 . Karl-Marx-Stadt [1983] iii, 56 p. ; LC Card 84-117572
HD30.25 .W56 1983

INDUSTRIAL MANAGEMENT - MAURITIUS - EMPLOYEE PARTICIPATION - CONGRESSES.

National Programme on Worker's Participation and Development (1983 : Mauritius) Report on the National Programme on Worker's Participation and Development, 3-14 October, 1983, Mauritius. [Mauritius? , between 1983 and 1985] 33 p. ; LC Card 86-980341 DDC

658.3/152/096982 19
HD6890.5 .N37 1983

INDUSTRIAL MANAGEMENT - MOLDAVIAN S.S.R.
Organizatsionnye formy i metody upravleniia proizvodstvom . Kishinev , 1980. 130 p. ; LC Card 81-140768
HD9015.S653 M6453 1980

Planirovanie ėkonomiki Moldavskoĭ SSR /. Kishinev , 1986. 161 p. ; LC Card 86-203680
HD9015.S653 M6457 1986

INDUSTRIAL MANAGEMENT - MORAL AND ETHICAL ASPECTS.
Hosmer, LaRue T. The ethics of management /. Homewood, Ill. , 1987. xiii, 185 p. : ISBN 0-256-03480-X LC Card 86-81804 DDC 174/.4 19
HF5387 .H67 1987

INDUSTRIAL MANAGEMENT - NIGERIA.
Anyansi-Archibong, Chi. B., 1949- Strategy and structure of enterprise in a developing country /. Aldershots, Hants, England , Brookfield, Vt., USA , c1988. xvii, 274 p. : ISBN 0-566-05471-X : LC Card 87-12020 DDC 658/.009669 19
HD70.N43 A59 1988

INDUSTRIAL MANAGEMENT - NIGERIA - CASE STUDIES.
Osaze, Bob. Es. Readings and cases in Nigerian corporate policy and strategy /. [Benin City, Nigeria] [between 1982 and 1984] vi, 185, 17, 23 p. : LC Card 84-237026 DDC 658.4/012/09669 19
HD70.N43 O83 1982

INDUSTRIAL MANAGEMENT - NORTHWEST, PACIFIC - EMPLOYEE PARTICIPATION - CASE STUDIES.
Greenberg, Edward S., 1942- Workplace democracy . Ithaca , 1986. 257 p. ; ISBN 0-8014-1921-2 (alk. paper) LC Card 86-47641 DDC 674/.834/068 19
HD5658.P622 U554 1986
NYPL [JLE 86-4586]

INDUSTRIAL MANAGEMENT - PERU - EMPLOYEE PARTICIPATION - HISTORY - 20TH CENTURY.
Neffa, Julio César. La participación de los trabajadores en la gestión empresarial en la República del Perú, 1968-1980 /. Ginebra, Suiza , 1986. vi, 112, x p. : ISBN 92-9014-410-6 LC Card 87-400930 DDC 658.3/152/0985 19
HD5660.P4 N44 1986

INDUSTRIAL MANAGEMENT - PHILIPPINES.
Franco, Ernesto A. Pinoy management /. Metro Manila, Philippines , 1986. 230 p. : ISBN 971-08-2961-0 (pbk.) LC Card 86-217631 DDC 658/.009599 19
HD70.P5 F73 1986

INDUSTRIAL MANAGEMENT - POLAND.
Prace z zakresu ekonomiki produkcji /. Poznań , 1984. 219 p. : LC Card 86-127229
HB54 .P6 nr. 122 HD70.P6

Studencki ruch naukowy /. Wrocław , 1978. 98 p. : LC Card 81-206830
HB9 .B7522 nr. 122 HD36

Wybrane problemy ekonomiki przemysłu /. Wrocław , 1985. 110 p. ; LC Card 86-155957
HB9 .B7522 nr. 304 HD70.P6

INDUSTRIAL MANAGEMENT - POLAND - EMPLOYEE PARTICIPATION.
Dąbrowski, Marek. Ekonomiczne konsekwencje samorządności pracowniczej /. Wrocław , 1986. 140 p. ; ISBN 83-04-02213-3 : LC Card 86-199502
HD5660.P6 D33 1986

INDUSTRIAL MANAGEMENT - RESEARCH - ADDRESSES, ESSAYS, LECTURES.
Der Praktische Nutzen empirischer Forschung /. Tübingen , 1981. viii, 324 p. ; ISBN 3-16-344392-3 : LC Card 81-197515 DDC 658.4/03 19
HD30.4 .P7 1981 ***NYPL [JLE 86-1360]***

INDUSTRIAL MANAGEMENT - RESEARCH - METHODOLOGY.
Manuale di ricerca sul lavoro e sulle organizzazioni /. Roma , 1985. 384 p. : LC Card 86-118313 DDC 306/.36/072 19
HD4824 .M32 1985 ***NYPL [JLD 87-1160]***

INDUSTRIAL MANAGEMENT - ROMANIA - EMPLOYEE PARTICIPATION.
Cazacu, Honorina. Democraţia socialistă în acţiune . Bucureşti , 1985. 192 p. : LC Card 86-216024
HD5660.R6 C39 1985

INDUSTRIAL MANAGEMENT - RUSSIAN S.F.S.R. - CHUVASHSKAIA A.S.S.R.
XXVI s″ezd KPSS i voprosy ėkonomiki narodnogo khoziaĭstva Chuvashskoĭ ASSR. Cheboksary , 1982. 157 p. ; LC Card 83-128420
HC337.C46 A17 1982

INDUSTRIAL MANAGEMENT - RUSSIAN S.F.S.R. - HISTORY.
Krasnykh, L. M. (Leonid Mikhaĭlovich) Partiĭnoe rukovodstvo sovershenstvovaniem upravleniia promyshlennost′iu v period stroitel′stva sotsializma, 1926-1937 . Krasnoiarsk , 1986. 150, [2] p. ; LC Card 86-226013
HD70.S63 K73 1986

INDUSTRIAL MANAGEMENT - RUSSIAN S.F.S.R. - SIBERIA, WESTERN.
Optimizatsiia perspektivnykh planov razvitiia otraslevykh sistem . Novosibirsk , 1979. 163 p. : LC Card 81-130740
HC337.R852 S546 1979

INDUSTRIAL MANAGEMENT - SAUDI ARABIA.
ʻAlāqī, Madanī ʻAbd al-Qādir. al-Idārah wa-al-bī'ah . [Jiddah] , 1985. 136 p. : LC Card 86-200390
HD70.S28 A422 1985

INDUSTRIAL MANAGEMENT - SOCIAL ASPECTS - NIGERIA.
Anyansi-Archibong, Chi. B., 1949- Strategy and structure of enterprise in a developing country /. Aldershots, Hants, England , Brookfield, Vt., USA , c1988. xvii, 274 p. : ISBN 0-566-05471-X : LC Card 87-12020 DDC 658/.009669 19
HD70.N43 A59 1988

INDUSTRIAL MANAGEMENT - SOVIET UNION.
Chebanenko, Vladimir Mikhaĭlovich. Sistema planirovaniia tekhnicheskogo urovnia otrasli /. Moskva , 1985. 118, [7] p. : LC Card 85-241451
HD70.S63 C45 1985

Deĭneko, O. A. (Oleg Aleksandrovich) Sovremennyĭ organizator proizvodstva /. Moskva , 1984. 172, [2] p. : LC Card 85-112451
HD38.25.S65 D45 1984

Intensifikatsiia sotsialisticheskogo proizvodstva i khoziaĭstvennyĭ mekhanizm /. Moskva , 1984. 228 p. ; LC Card 84-247548
HC340.I52 I58 1984

Karpunin, M. G. (Mikhail Grigor′evich) Funktsional′no-stoimostnoĭ analiz v otraslevom upravlenii ėffektivnost′iu /. Moskva , 1983. 199 p. : LC Card 84-120682
HF5686.C8 K275 1983

Mil′ner, Bentsion Zakharovich. Sistemnyĭ podkhod k organizatsii upravleniia /. Moskva , 1983. 223 p. : LC Card 83-229946
HD70.S63 M54 1983

Modelirovanie ėkonomicheskogo povedeniia sotsialisticheskogo predpriiatiia /. Moskva , 1984. 131 p. : LC Card 86-144437
HD30.25 .M623 1984

Nagdiev, S. A. (Seĭfulakh Ataevich) Ispol′zovanie ėkonomicheskikh zakonov v upravlenii sotsialisticheskim proizvodstvom /. Leningrad , 1983. 87 p. ; LC Card 84-197365
HD56 .N34 1983

Nauchnaia organizatsiia truda v promyshlennosti /. Moskva , 1986. 414 p. : LC Card 86-218434
HD36 .N323 1986

Odintsova, G. S. (Galina Sergeevna) Organizatsionnoe proektirovanie i planirovanie razvitiia sistem upravleniia /. Kiev , 1986. 158, [2] p. : LC Card 87-162923
HD2876 .O35 1986

Organizatsiia sorevnovaniia i sovershenstvovanie khoziaĭstvennogo mekhanizma /. Moskva , 1982. 206 p. ; LC Card 82-202826
HC340.S6 O684 1982

Perestroĭka i rukovoditel′ /. Moskva , 1987. 143 p. ; LC Card 87-164793
HD38.25.S65 P47 1987

Shusharin, A. L. (Aleksandr Leonidovich) Sootnoshenie khozraschetnoĭ ėkonomicheskoĭ ėffektivnosti sredstv proizvodstva s ikh narodno-khoziaĭstvennoĭ ėffektivnost′iu /. Tomsk , 1979. 159 p. ; LC Card 87-462036
HD70.S63 S55 1979

Sinavina, V. S. (Valentina Semenovna) Rezervy ėffektivnosti upravleniia proizvodstvom /. Moskva , 1984. 167 p. : LC Card 84-244689
HD70.S63 S575 1984

TSena i khozraschet /. Moskva , 1986. 144 p. ; LC Card 87-163568
HB235.S73 T72 1986

Upravlenie v sisteme proizvodstvennykh otnosheniĭ /. Novosibirsk , 1974. 82 p. ; LC Card 83-120398
HD70.S63 U68 1974

Voprosy politicheskoĭ ėkonomii . Novosibirsk , 1973. 125 p. ; LC Card 81-131624
HD8526.5 .V674 1973

INDUSTRIAL MANAGEMENT - SOVIET UNION - DATA PROCESSING.
Sinavina, V. S. (Valentina Semenovna) Rezervy ėffektivnosti upravleniia proizvodstvom /. Moskva , 1984. 167 p. : LC Card 84-244689
HD70.S63 S575 1984

INDUSTRIAL MANAGEMENT - SOVIET UNION - DATA PROCESSING - CONGRESSES.
Imitatsionnoe modelirovanie proizvodstvennykh protsessov . Novosibirsk , 1979. 152 p. : LC Card 81-132238
HD70.S63 I44 1979

INDUSTRIAL MANAGEMENT - SOVIET UNION - DECISION MAKING.
Decision-making in the Soviet energy industry . Falls Church, VA (7700 Leesburg Pike, #250, Falls Church 22043) , c1986. ix, 166 leaves ; LC Card 87-401592 DDC 333.79/0947 19
HD9502.S652 D43 1986

INDUSTRIAL MANAGEMENT - SOVIET UNION - DECISION MAKING - MATHEMATICAL MODELS.
Priniatie reshenii v upravlenii khoziaĭstvennymi sviaziami /. Moskva , 1982. 80 p. : LC Card 85-180526
HD30.23 .P745 1982

INDUSTRIAL MANAGEMENT - SOVIET UNION - EMPLOYEE PARTICIPATION.
My--khoziaeva proizvodstva . Moskva , 1984. 261 p. : LC Card 85-107808
HD5660.S65 M9 1984

Uchastie trudiashchikhsia v upravlenii proizvodstvom . Moskva , 1985. 69, [2] p. ; LC Card 85-224379
HD5660.S65 U27 1985

INDUSTRIAL MANAGEMENT - SOVIET UNION - EMPLOYEE PARTICIPATION - CONGRESSES.
Uchastie trudiashchikhsia v upravlenii proizvodstvom . Moskva , 1983. 192, [2] p. : LC Card 84-210286
HD5660.S65 U26 1983

INDUSTRIAL MANAGEMENT - SOVIET UNION - MATHEMATICAL MODELS.
Ėkonomiko-matematicheskie metody v analize khoziaĭstvennoĭ deiatel′nosti predpriiatiĭ i ob″edineniĭ /. Moskva , 1982. 194, [5] p. : LC Card 83-161166
HD30.25 .E394 1982

Ėkonomiko-matematicheskie modeli v upravlenii proizvodstvennymi ob″edineniiami /. Moskva , 1983. 190 p. : LC Card 85-199430
HD30.25 .E397 1983

Lebedev, I. P. (Igor′ Pavlovich) Proizvodstvennye resursy predpriiatiia . Moskva , 1984. 198 p. : LC Card 85-138003
HC340.I52 L42 1984

Tekhniko-ėkonomicheskie raschety na predpriiatii /. Kiev , 1984. 126 p. : LC Card 84-234261
HD70.S63 T45 1984

INDUSTRIAL MANAGEMENT - SOVIET UNION - MATHEMATICAL MODELS - CONGRESSES.
Imitatsionnoe modelirovanie proizvodstvennykh protsessov . Novosibirsk , 1979. 152 p. : LC Card 81-132238
HD70.S63 I44 1979

INDUSTRIAL MANAGEMENT - SOVIET UNION - PROBLEMS, EXERCISES, ETC.
Praktikum po organizatsii i planirovaniiu proizvodstva na promyshlennykh predpriiatiiakh /. Voronezh , 1985. 209, [3] p. ; LC Card 84-172797
HD70.S63 P69 1985

INDUSTRIAL MANAGEMENT - STATISTICAL METHODS.
Hildebrand, David K., 1940- Statistical thinking for managers /. Boston, Mass. , c1987. xvii, 894 p. : ISBN 0-87150-036-1 LC Card 86-29222 DDC 519.5/024658 19
HD30.215 .H54 1987

INDUSTRIAL MANAGEMENT - STATISTICAL METHODS - DATA PROCESSING.
Hildebrand, David K., 1940- Statistical thinking for managers /. Boston, Mass. , c1987. xvii, 894 p. : ISBN 0-87150-036-1 LC Card 86-29222 DDC 519.5/024658 19
HD30.215 .H54 1987

INDUSTRIAL MANAGEMENT - STUDY AND TEACHING (HIGHER) - DEVELOPING COUNTRIES - CASE STUDIES.
Industrial management education in the Commonwealth . London, England [1976] 38 p. ; LC Card 85-100411 DDC 658/.007/11171241 19
HD70.D44 I5 1976

INDUSTRIAL MANAGEMENT - SWEDEN.
Bergman, Åke. Den nya given . Stockholm [1986] 157 p. ; ISBN 91-550-3244-3 : LC Card 86-235012
HD70.S8 B48 1986

INDUSTRIAL MANAGEMENT - SWEDEN - DATA PROCESSING.
Sweden. Data- och elektronikkommittén. Datateknik i industriproduktionen . [Stockholm] [1981] 182 p. : ISBN 91-38-06456-1 LC Card 84-113236
HD30.2 .S92 1981

INDUSTRIAL MANAGEMENT - SWEDEN - DATA PROCESSING - FORECASTING.
Jobb i framtid? . Stockholm , c1983. 121 p. : ISBN 91-7410-270-2 : LC Card 84-103510
HC375 .J53 1983

INDUSTRIAL MANAGEMENT - SWEDEN - EMPLOYEE PARTICIPATION.
Dellenbrant, Jan Åke, 1946- Föreningsdemokrati och företagsdemokrati . [Stockholm] [1981] 85 p. ; ISBN 91-38-06488-X LC Card 83-245188
HD5660.S9 D44 1981

Ekonomisk demokrati . Stockholm [1984] ii, 169 p. : LC Card 85-108590
HD5660.S9 E38 1984

Towards a democratic rationality . Aldershot, Hants, England , Brookfield, Vt., USA , c1986. xi, 281 p. : ISBN 0-566-00761-4 : LC Card 86-14241 DDC 331/.09485 19
HD8576.5 .T69 1986 ***NYPL [JLD 86-3873]***

Trautwein, Hans-Michael, 1957- Arbeitnehmerfonds in Schweden, der dritte Weg? . Frankfurt am Main , New York , c1986. 353, 39, [116] p. : ISBN 3-8204-9336-0 LC Card 86-203867
HD4928.G342 S88 1986

INDUSTRIAL MANAGEMENT - SWITZERLAND - HISTORY.
Jaun, Rudolf, 1948- Management und Arbeiterschaft . Zürich , c1986. 505, 10 p. ; ISBN 3-905278-08-1 LC Card 87-132013 DDC 658/.009494 19
HD70.S85 J38 1986

INDUSTRIAL MANAGEMENT - TERMINOLOGY.
Williams, Chris, 1952- Words that manage . Westbury, N.Y. , c1987. xi, 157 p. ; ISBN 0-87280-131-4 : LC Card 87-17434 DDC 658.3/0014 19
HD30.17 .W55 1987

INDUSTRIAL MANAGEMENT - UKRAINE.
Ėkonomicheskiĭ mekhanizm ėksperimenta /. Kiev , 1985. 166 p. : LC Card 86-220234
HC337.U53 I524 1985

Kondratiuk, K. K. (Konstantin Konstantinovich) Profsoiuzy Ukrainy na zavershaiushchem ėtape stroitel'stva sotsializma /. L'vov , 1985. 173 p. ; LC Card 87-165263
HD6735.U5 K65 1985

Povyshenie ėffektivnosti ASUP . Kiev , 1985. 303 p. : LC Card 85-210269
HD30.2 .P68 1985 ***NYPL [*QIP 87-2760]***

Suïmenko, IE. I. Kerivnyk-orhanizator i vykhovatel' /. Kyïv , 1985. 189 p. ; LC Card 87-109649
HD38.2 .S85 1985

INDUSTRIAL MANAGEMENT - UKRAINE - DECISION MAKING.
Upravlenie ėffektivnost'iu proizvodstva /. Kiev , 1985. 125 p. : LC Card 85-181580
HD30.23 .U67 1985

INDUSTRIAL MANAGEMENT - UNITED STATES.
Behrenfeld, William H. Accountant's business manual /. New York, N.Y. , c1987- 1 v. (loose-leaf) ; ISBN 0-87051-000-2 (loose-leaf) : LC Card 87-992 DDC 657 19
HF5616.U5 B38 1987

Bittel, Lester R. Business in action . New York , c1988. vii, 597 p. : ISBN 0-07-005565-3 LC Card 87-3134 DDC 658 19
HF5343 .B57 1988

The Competitive challenge . Cambridge, Mass. , c1987. xii, 256 p. : ISBN 0-88730-178-9 LC Card 87-1190 DDC 658.4/06 19
HD70.U5 C58 1987

Ėpshteĭn, S. I. (Samuil Isaakovich) Burzhuaznaia nauka upravleniia i neupravliaemaia ėkonomika /. Moskva , 1986. 76 p. ; LC Card 86-201018 DDC 658/.00973 19
HD70.U5 E6 1986

Funkhouser, G. Ray. The pursuit of growth . Redmond, Wash. , c1987. 261 p. ; ISBN 1-556-15043-1 : LC Card 87-20230 DDC 658/.00973 19
HD70.U5 F86 1987

Grayson, C. Jackson (Charles Jackson), 1923- American business, a two-minute warning . New York , London , c1988. xvii, 368 p. : ISBN 0-02-912680-0 LC Card 87-19391 DDC 658/.00973 19
HD70.U5 G69 1988

Groneman, Carol. [Corporate Ph. D.] Corporate PhD . New York, N.Y., U. S.A. , 1987, c1985. xx, 156 p. ; ISBN 0-14-010123-3 (pbk.) LC Card 86-30654 DDC 658.4/09 19
HD38.25.U6 G76 1987

Lareau, William. Millennium management . Piscataway, NJ [1986]. ix, 214 p. : ISBN 0-8329-0431-7 : LC Card 86-18247 DDC 658.4/06 19
HD58.8 .L37 1986 ***NYPL [JLE 87-1139]***

Lee, John Y. Managerial accounting changes for the 1990s /. Artesia, Calif., U. S.A. , c1987. iv, 87 p. : ISBN 0-9617977-0-3 (pbk.) : LC Card 87-60120 DDC 658.1/511 19
HF5657.4 .L43 1987

Lieberman, Ernest D. Unfit to manage! . New York , c1988. xvii, 301 p. ; ISBN 0-07-037815-0 : LC Card 87-20891 DDC 658/.00973 19
HD70.U5 L54 1988

Martin, Doris. Corporate productivity in action . Wailuku, Hawaii , c1987. 89 p. ; ISBN 0-9615541-0-X (pbk.) LC Card 85-90446 DDC 658.3/14 19
HC110.I52 M37 1987

Meek, Christopher. Managing by the numbers . Reading, Mass. , c1988. ix, 293 p. : ISBN 0-201-16129-X : LC Card 87-16088 DDC 338.7/4/0973 19
HD70.U5 M413 1988

Melman, Seymour. Profits without production /. Philadelphia , 1987, c1983. p. cm. ISBN 0-8122-1258-4 (pbk.) LC Card 87-13796 DDC 338.0973 19
HD70.U5 M425 1987

Mitroff, Ian I. Business not as usual . San Francisco , 1987. xxi, 194 p. : ISBN 1-555-42030-3 (alk. paper) LC Card 86-46333 DDC 338.9 19
HD70.U5 M52 1987

Peters, Thomas J. Thriving on chaos . New York , 1987. xii, 561 p. : ISBN 0-394-56784-6 LC Card 87-45575 DDC 658 19
HD70.U5 P426 1987

The Productivity sourcebook /. Amherst, Mass. [1987] x, 467 p. : ISBN 0-87425-075-7 (pbk.) LC Card 87-404037 DDC 658.3/14 19
HD57 .P7114 1987

Shapiro, H. Jack (Harris Jack) Reviving industry in America . Cambridge, Mass. , c1987. xii, 204 p. : ISBN 0-88730-118-5 LC Card 87-17585 DDC 338.4/767/0973 19
HD9725 .S46 1987

Thompson, Richard E. Theory I . San Antonio, Tex. , c1986. 105 p. : ISBN 0-940555-00-X (pbk.) LC Card 86-90531 DDC 658.4/00207 19
HD70.U5 T48 1986

Vancil, Richard F. Passing the baton . Boston, Mass. , c1987. xxii, 318 p. : ISBN 0-87584-182-1 LC Card 87-11962 DDC 658.4 19
HD38.25.U6 V36 1987

INDUSTRIAL MANAGEMENT - UNITED STATES - CASE STUDIES.
Business policy . Homewood, Ill. , 1987. xx, 940 p. : ISBN 0-256-03358-7 LC Card 86-82216 DDC 658.4/012 19
HD2785 .B78 1987

Weaver, Paul, 1942 Oct. 18- The suicidal corporation /. New York , c1988. p. cm. ISBN 0-671-52378-3 LC Card 87-23468 DDC 338.7/4/0973 19
HD2785 .W38 1988

INDUSTRIAL MANAGEMENT - UNITED STATES - EMPLOYEE PARTICIPATION.
Kelso, Louis O. Democracy and economic power . Cambridge, Mass. , 1986. xii, 175 p. : ISBN 0-88730-115-0 : LC Card 86-14027 DDC 338.6 19
HD5660.U5 K45 1986 ***NYPL [JLE 86-4658]***

Marshall, F. Ray. Unheard voices . New York , c1987. xi, 339 p. : ISBN 0-465-08869-4 : LC Card 83-46084 DDC 338.6 19
HD5660.U5 M36 1987

Teamwork, joint labor-management programs in America /. New York , 1986. xvi, 199 p. : ISBN 0-08-032799-0 : LC Card 85-28397 DDC 331.01/12/0973 19
HD8072.5 .T43 1986 ***NYPL [JLE 86-3139]***

INDUSTRIAL MANAGEMENT - UNITED STATES - EMPLOYEE PARTICIPATION - CASE STUDIES.
Grenier, Guillermo J. Inhuman relations . Philadelphia , 1988. xx, 232 p. ; ISBN 0-87722-502-8 (alk. paper) : LC Card 87-10116 DDC 331.25 19
HD6490.O72 U645 1988

INDUSTRIAL MANAGEMENT - UNITED STATES - HANDBOOKS, MANUALS, ETC.
The Book of business knowledge /. New York, N.Y. , c1987. p. cm. ISBN 0-932648-83-5 : LC Card 86-30962 DDC 658 19
HF5356 .B72 1987

The Boss's encyclopedia /. New York, N.Y. , c1987. xxvi, 594 p. ; ISBN 0-932648-75-4 LC Card 86-30961 DDC 658 19
HF5356 .B735 1987

Business confidential. New York, N.Y. , c1987. xi, 504 p. ; ISBN 0-932648-82-7 LC Card 86-30963 DDC 650 19
HF5356 .B9259 1987

INDUSTRIAL MANAGEMENT - UNITED STATES - HISTORY.
ASME Management Division history, 1886-1980 /. New York, N.Y. (345 E. 47th St., New York 10017) , c1984. x, 169 p. : LC Card 84-206982 DDC 658/.006/073 19
HD28.A6233 A86 1984 ***NYPL [JLF 86-1646]***

Jaun, Rudolf, 1948- Management und Arbeiterschaft . Zürich , c1986. 505, 10 p. ; ISBN 3-905278-08-1 LC Card 87-132013 DDC 658/.009494 19
HD70.S85 J38 1986

INDUSTRIAL MANAGEMENT - UNITED STATES - HISTORY - 20TH CENTURY.
Stine, G. Harry (George Harry), 1928- The corporate survivors /. New York, N.Y. , c1986. 230 p. : ISBN 0-8144-5831-9 LC Card 86-47597 DDC 338.7/4/0973 19
HD2785 .S73 1986 ***NYPL [JLE 86-4469]***

INDUSTRIAL MANAGEMENT - YUGOSLAVIA.
Turk, Ivan. Iskazivanje i ocjenjivanje rezultata poslovanja organizacija udruženog rada /. Zagreb , 1982. x, 171 p. ; LC Card 83-110726
HD70.Y8 T87 1982

INDUSTRIAL MANAGEMENT - YUGOSLAVIA - DECISION MAKING.
Zver, Boris. Proces odlučivanja u organizacijama udruženog rada /. Zagreb , 1983. ix, 169 p. ; LC Card 85-171946
HD30.23 .Z87 1983

INDUSTRIAL MANAGEMENT - YUGOSLAVIA - EMPLOYEE PARTICIPATION.
Körner, Ulrich. Wettbewerb und Akkumulation in der selbstverwalteten Wirtschaft /. Frankfurt , New York , c1984. 193 p. : ISBN 3-593-33257-4 LC Card 84-191794
HD5660.Y8 K623 1984

Industrial marketing . Reeder, Robert R., 1935- Englewood Cliffs, N.J. , c1987. xviii, 654 p. : ISBN 0-13-461526-3 LC Card 86-25195 DDC 658.8 19
HF5415 .R355 1987

INDUSTRIAL MARKETING.
Larréché, Jean-Claude. INDUSTRAT . Englewood Cliffs, N.J. , 1987. p. cm. ISBN 0-13-651373-5 LC Card 87-7144 DDC 658.8 19
HF5415.1263 .L37 1987

Reeder, Robert R., 1935- Industrial marketing . Englewood Cliffs, N.J. , c1987. xviii, 654 p. : ISBN 0-13-461526-3 LC Card 86-25195 DDC 658.8 19
HF5415 .R355 1987

INDUSTRIAL MARKETING - CONGRESSES.
Seminar on Problem Solving in Industrial Marketing (1986 : Lucerne, Switzerland) Seminar on Problem Solving in Idustrial Marketing, Lucerne (Switzerland) 26th-28th February 1986. Amsterdam, Netherlands [1986] iv, 179 p. : ISBN 92-831-1111-7 (pbk.) : LC Card 86-213119 DDC 658.8 19
HF5415 .S3687 1986

INDUSTRIAL MARKETING - EUROPE - CASE STUDIES.
Strategies for international industrial marketing . London , Dover, N.H. , c1986. 310 p. : ISBN 0-7099-2494-1 : LC Card 85-29047 DDC 658.8/48 19
HF1009.7.E85 S77 1986
NYPL [JLD 86-1596]

INDUSTRIAL MARKETING - MANAGEMENT.
Woodside, Arch G. Industrial purchasing strategies . Lexington, Mass. , c1987. xiv, 223 p. : ISBN 0-669-06953-1 (alk. paper) LC Card 83-48132 DDC 658.7/2 19
HD39.5 .W66 1987

INDUSTRIAL MARKETING - RESEARCH - CONGRESSES.
Seminar on Problem Solving in Industrial Marketing (1986 : Lucerne, Switzerland) Seminar on Problem Solving in Idustrial Marketing, Lucerne (Switzerland) 26th-28th February 1986. Amsterdam, Netherlands [1986] iv, 179 p. : ISBN 92-831-1111-7 (pbk.) : LC Card 86-213119 DDC 658.8 19
HF5415 .S3687 1986

INDUSTRIAL MARKETING - SOUTH AFRICA.
Nel, P. A. The BM industrial register and its application in industrial marketing /. Pretoria , 1977. iii, 29, [34] p. ; ISBN 0-949951-74-9 (pbk.) LC Card 85-127469
HC905 .N45 1977

INDUSTRIAL METEOROLOGY. see **INDUSTRY AND WEATHER.**

INDUSTRIAL MINERALS - NORWAY.
Norway. Utvalg for delutredning om industrielle mineraler. Industrimineraler . Oslo [1982] 134 p. : ISBN 82-00-70754-7 LC Card 83-123304
HD9506.N72 N67 1982

INDUSTRIAL MOBILIZATION - GERMANY - HISTORY - 20TH CENTURY.
Siegfried, Klaus-Jörg, 1940- Rüstungsproduktion und Zwangsarbeit im Volkswagenwerk, 1939-1945 . Frankfurt , New York , c1986. 239 p. : ISBN 3-593-33765-7 LC Card 87-133375 DDC 338.4/76234/0943 19
HD9743.G48 S56 1986

INDUSTRIAL MOBILIZATION - RUSSIAN S.F.S.R. - URAL MOUNTAIN REGION - HISTORY.
Vasil'ev, A. F. (Aleksandr Filippovich) Promyshlennost' Urala v gody Velikoĭ Otechestvennoĭ voĭny 1941-1945 /. Moskva , 1982. 279 p., [1] folded leaf of plates : LC Card 83-165021
HC337.R852 U7387 1982

INDUSTRIAL MORALE. see **EMPLOYEE MORALE.**

Industrial organization . Bain, Joe Staten, 1912- Greenwich, Conn. , c1987. 2 v. ; ISBN 0-89232-702-2 (set) LC Card 87-2618 DDC 338.6 19
HD2326 .B34 1987

Industrial organization and antitrust . Singleton, Ross C. Columbus, Ohio , c1986. ix, 102 p. ; ISBN 0-942280-15-6 : LC Card 85-19318 DDC 338.8/0973 19
HD70.U5 S54 1986 ***NYPL [JLD 86-3251]***

INDUSTRIAL ORGANIZATION - BRAZIL.
Araujo Júnior, José Tavares de. Tecnologia, concorrência e mudança estrutural . Rio de Janeiro , 1985. 64 p. ; LC Card 87-120280 DDC 338/.06 19
HD70.B7 A7 1985

INDUSTRIAL ORGANIZATION - CONGRESSES.
Mainstreams in industrial organization /. Dordrecht , Boston , 1986. 2 v. (x, 465 p.) ; ISBN 90-247-3363-4 LC Card 86-12345 DDC 338.6 19
HD29 .M25 1986 ***NYPL [JLE 87-457]***

INDUSTRIAL ORGANIZATION - DEVELOPING COUNTRIES - CASE STUDY.
Chanana, Charanjit. Industrial economics in developing countries, India . New Delhi , 1983. 113 p. : LC Card 83-903832 DDC 338.0954 19
HC435.2 .C4717 1983 ***NYPL [JLD 87-674]***

INDUSTRIAL ORGANIZATION (ECONOMIC AND THEORY) - ADDRESSES, ESSAYS, LECTURES.
Firms and markets . London , c1986. xiii, 271 p. : ISBN 0-7099-2446-1
NYPL [JLD 86-2134]

INDUSTRIAL ORGANIZATION (ECONOMIC THEORY) - CONGRESSES.
The Economics of firm size, market structure, and social performance . [Washington, D.C.?] , 1980. viii, 388 p. ; LC Card 81-600757 DDC 338.6/4/0973 19
HD60.5.U5 E26 ***NYPL [JLF 86-704]***

The Economics of market dominance /. Oxford, UK , New York, NY, USA , 1987. p. cm. ISBN 0-631-14784-5 : LC Card 86-26416 DDC 338.8/2 19
HD2326 .E24 1987

Economische wetenschappen . Maastricht , Assen , 1985. 224 p. ; ISBN 90-232-2148-6 LC Card 86-111599
HB21 .E248 1985

The Industrial organization of futures markets /. Lexington, Mass. , c1984. vii, 312 p. : ISBN 0-669-06836-5 LC Card 83-48029 DDC 332.64/4 19
HG6024.A3 I52 1984 ***NYPL [JLE 86-4471]***

New developments in the analysis of market structure . Cambridge, Mass. , 1986. xxiv, 559 p. : ISBN 0-262-19241-1 LC Card 85-4246 DDC 338.8 19
HD2326 .N43 1986 ***NYPL [JLD 86-3570]***

INDUSTRIAL ORGANIZATION (ECONOMIC THEORY) - MATHEMATICAL MODELS.
Bowring, Joseph. Competition in a dual economy /. Princeton, N.J. , c1986. vi, 208 p. ; ISBN 0-691-04234-9 (alk. paper) : LC Card 85-43271 DDC 338.6/048/0724 19
HD41 .B687 1986 ***NYPL [JLD 86-3314]***

INDUSTRIAL ORGANIZATION (ECONOMIC THEORY) - STATISTICAL METHODS - PROBLEMS, EXERCISES, ETC.
Praktikum po statistike promyshlennosti /. Moskva , 1985. 239 p. ; LC Card 85-153243
HD30.413 .P72 1985

INDUSTRIAL ORGANIZATION - EUROPE.
Benterud, Per. Japan som veiviser . [Oslo] , c1983. 262 p. ; ISBN 82-02-09050-4 LC Card 83-195163
HD70.J3 B45 1983

Jacquemin, Alex. Economie industrielle européenne . [Paris] , c1979. xxii, 376 p. : ISBN 2-04-010465-8 LC Card 86-673881
HD70.E8 J3x 1979

INDUSTRIAL ORGANIZATION - EUROPE, EASTERN.
Opyt khoziaĭstvovaniia v ob"edineniiakh promyshlennosti sotsialisticheskikh stran /. Moskva , 1985. 157 p. : LC Card 87-152292
HD70.E7 O69 1985

INDUSTRIAL ORGANIZATION - EUROPE, GERMAN-SPEAKING.
Meyer, Petra. Die Entwicklung der Organisationswissenschaft im deutschsprachigen Raum . München , c1985. 309 p. : ISBN 3-924361-10-X LC Card 87-114143
HD70.E8 M48 1985

INDUSTRIAL ORGANIZATION - FRANCE.
Callies, Albane. France-Japon . Paris , 1986. 208 p. ; ISBN 2-86563-129-X LC Card 86-165719
HD8431 .C35 1986

INDUSTRIAL ORGANIZATION - GERMANY.
Schalldach, Elisabeth, 1904- Rationalisierungsmassnahmen der Nachinflationszeit im Urteil der deutschen freien Gewerkschaften. Jena, 1930. ix, [1], 186 p. LC Card AC34-383
HD70.G2 S26 1930

INDUSTRIAL ORGANIZATION - GERMANY - HISTORY - 20TH CENTURY.
Stollberg, Gunnar. Die Rationalisierungsdebatte 1908-1933 . Frankfurt/Main , New York , c1981. 214 p. ; ISBN 3-593-32938-7 : LC Card 81-177695 DDC 331.88/0943 19
HD70.G2 S666 1981 ***NYPL [JLD 86-1662]***

INDUSTRIAL ORGANIZATION - GREAT BRITAIN.
Global restructuring local response . London , Merstham, Redhill, Surrey , c1986. 308 p. : ISBN 0-86226-174-0 (pbk.) LC Card 86-197207 DDC 331.12/0941 19
HD6331.2.G7 G57 1986

The Organisation in its environment /. London , 1984. xiii, 624 p. : ISBN 0-421-32290-X (pbk.) : LC Card 84-242095 DDC 302.3/5 19
HD31 .O7217 1984 ***NYPL [JLD 86-2539]***

Sudarsanam, P. S. Market and industry structure and corporate cost of capital . London [1986] 33 p. ; LC Card 86-208314 DDC 338.7/4/0941 19
HG4135 .S83 1986

INDUSTRIAL ORGANIZATION - HUNGARY.
Antal, Iván. Vállalatok környezete, céljai, szervezete /. Budapest , 1986. 270 p. : ISBN 963-221-567-2 : LC Card 87-149512
HD70.H8 A536 1986

Dévai, Katalin. A nagyvállalatok helyzetéről /. [Budapest] , 1984. 68 p. ; ISBN 963-673-293-0 LC Card 85-175237
HD2852.5 .D48 1984

INDUSTRIAL ORGANIZATION - ITALY.
Organizzazione del lavoro, mobilità e aspetti formativi nella contrattazione . Milano, Italy , c1982. 172 p. ; LC Card 83-106874
HD6709 .O73 1982

INDUSTRIAL ORGANIZATION - JAPAN.
Benterud, Per. Japan som veiviser . [Oslo] , c1983. 262 p. ; ISBN 82-02-09050-4 LC Card 83-195163
HD70.J3 B45 1983

Callies, Albane. France-Japon . Paris , 1986. 208 p. ; ISBN 2-86563-129-X LC Card 86-165719
HD8431 .C35 1986

Industrimakten Japan . Oslo , 1982. 151 p. : ISBN 82-518-1630-0 : LC Card 84-126986
HD70.J3 I549 1982

Kobayashi, Kaoru, 1931- Japan, the most misunderstood country /. Tokyo , 1984. ix, 165

p. ; ISBN 4-7890-0247-0
NYPL [JLD 86-1398]

INDUSTRIAL ORGANIZATION - MATHEMATICAL MODELS.
Ovsievich, Boris L'vovich. Modeli formirovaniia organizatsionnykh struktur /. Leningrad , 1979. 157, [3] p. : LC Card 81-162540
HD30.25 .O97 1979

The Industrial organization of futures markets / edited by Ronald W. Anderson. Lexington, Mass. : Lexington Books, c1984. vii, 312 p. : ill. ; 24 cm. "This book grew out of a conference entitled 'The industrial organization of futures markets: structure and conduct' held on November 4 and 5, 1982, sponsored by the Center for Futures Market Studies at Columbia University Graduate School of Business"--P. vii. Includes bibliographies. ISBN 0-669-06836-5 LC Card 83-48029 DDC 332.64/4 19
1. Commodity exchanges - Congresses. 2. Industrial organization (Economic theory) - Congresses. I. Anderson, Ronald W., 1946-. II. Columbia University. Center for Futures Market Studies.
HG6024.A3 I52 1984 NYPL [JLE 86-4471]

INDUSTRIAL ORGANIZATION - POLAND.
Ekonomika i programowanie rozwoju przemysłu /. Kraków , 1978. 378 p. : LC Card 81-172485
HD70.P6 E38 1978

Wybrane problemy ekonomiki przemysłu /. Wrocław , 1985. 110 p. ; LC Card 86-155957
HB9 .B7522 nr. 304 HD70.P6

INDUSTRIAL ORGANIZATION - POLAND - MATHEMATICAL MODELS.
Organizacja produkcji w przemyśle /. Wrocław , 1970. 64 p. : LC Card 87-137344
HD70.P6 O745 1970

INDUSTRIAL ORGANIZATION - RESEARCH - ADDRESSES, ESSAYS, LECTURES.
Der Praktische Nutzen empirischer Forschung /. Tübingen , 1981. viii, 324 p. ; ISBN 3-16-344392-3 : LC Card 81-197515 DDC 658.4/03 19
HD30.4 .P7 1981 NYPL [JLE 86-1360]

INDUSTRIAL ORGANIZATION - SOVIET UNION.
Akhrameev, V. N. (Vasiliĭ Nikiforovich) "IUzhdizel'mash"--podgotovka k ėkonomicheskomu ėksperimentu /. Moskva , 1984. 96 p. : LC Card 85-144706
HD9705.S595 A36 1984

Problemy sovershenstvovaniia material'no-tekhnicheskoĭ bazy otrasleĭ obshchestvennogo proizvodstva . Moskva , 1983. 167 p. : LC Card 84-211670
HD70.S63 P753 1983

Proizvodstvennye ob"edineniia . Moskva , 1982. 173 p. ; LC Card 83-123241
HD70.S63 P764 1982

INDUSTRIAL ORGANIZATION - SOVIET UNION - MATHEMATICAL MODELS.
Ėkonomiko-matematicheskie metody v analize khoziaĭstvennoĭ deiatel'nosti predpriiatiĭ i ob"edineniĭ /. Moskva , 1982. 194, [5] p. : LC Card 83-161166
HD30.25 .E394 1982

INDUSTRIAL ORGANIZATION - SWEDEN - CASE STUDIES.
Auer, Peter. Industrial relations, work organisation and new technology . Berlin [1985] 17, [6] p. ; LC Card 86-205891 DDC 331/.04292/09481 19
HD9710.S84 V6413 1985

INDUSTRIAL ORGANIZATION - TAJIK S.S.R. - MATHEMATICAL MODELS.
Baĭriev, B. S. Optimizatsiia struktur upravleniia /. Ashkhabad , 1985. 169, [23] p. : LC Card 86-196466
HC337.T23 B35 1985

INDUSTRIAL ORGANIZATION - UNITED STATES.
Bain, Joe Staten, 1912- Industrial organization . Greenwich, Conn. , c1987. 2 v. ; ISBN 0-89232-702-2 (set) LC Card 87-2618 DDC 338.6 19
HD2326 .B34 1987

Hearn, Frank. The transformation of industrial organization . Belmont, Calif. , c1988. xii, 370 p. ; ISBN 0-534-08160-6 (pbk.) LC Card 87-17755 DDC 306/.3 19
HD70.U5 H42 1988

Hobbs, James B. Corporate staying power . Lexington, Mass. , c1987. xi, 178 p. ; ISBN 0-669-11153-8 (alk. paper) LC Card 85-45096 DDC 338.7/4/0973 19
HD58.9 .H62 1987 NYPL [JLE 87-1125]

Mitroff, Ian I. Business not as usual . San Francisco , 1987. xxi, 194 p. : ISBN 1-555-42030-3 (alk. paper) LC Card 86-46333 DDC 338.9 19
HD70.U5 M52 1987

Singleton, Ross C. Industrial organization and antitrust . Columbus, Ohio , c1986. ix, 102 p. ; ISBN 0-942280-15-6 : LC Card 85-19318 DDC 338.8/0973 19
HD70.U5 S54 1986 NYPL [JLD 86-3251]

Tigges, Leann M. Changing fortunes . New York , 1987. xvi, 174 p. : ISBN 0-275-92580-3 (alk. paper) : LC Card 87-2357 DDC 331.2/973 19
HD4975 .T5 1987

Tomasko, Robert M. Downsizing . New York , c1987. p. cm. ISBN 0-8144-5907-2 LC Card 87-47709 DDC 338.6/4 19
HD69.S5 T59 1987

INDUSTRIAL ORGANIZATION - UNITED STATES - CASE STUDIES.
Hobbs, James B. Corporate staying power . Lexington, Mass. , c1987. xi, 178 p. ; ISBN 0-669-11153-8 (alk. paper) LC Card 85-45096 DDC 338.7/4/0973 19
HD58.9 .H62 1987 NYPL [JLE 87-1125]

INDUSTRIAL ORGANIZATION - YUGOSLAVIA - DECISION MAKING.
Zver, Boris. Proces odlučivanja u organizacijama udruženog rada /. Zagreb , 1983. ix, 169 p. ; LC Card 85-171946
HD30.23 .Z87 1983

INDUSTRIAL ORGANIZATION - YUGOSLAVIA - RESEARCH - METHODOLOGY.
Čubra, Nikola. Naučnoistraživački i razvojni rad u organizacijama udruženog rada /. Beograd , 1982. 165 p. : LC Card 82-166181
HD30 .C83 1982

Industrial/organizational psychology . Saal, Frank E., 1947- Pacific Grove, Calif. , c1988. xxx, 578 p. : ISBN 0-534-08214-9 : LC Card 87-21824 DDC 158.7 19
HF5548.8 .S225 1988

INDUSTRIAL POISONS. see **INDUSTRIAL TOXICOLOGY.**

Industrial policies and industrialization in the Sudan /. Affan, Bodour O. Abu. Khartoum, Sudan , 1985. 180 p. ; ISBN 0-08-637205-44 (pbk.) LC Card 86-981076 DDC 338.9624 19
HC835 .A58 1985

Industrial policies and structural change / edited by Christopher T. Saunders. New York : St. Martin's Press, 1987. xii, 369 p. : ill. ; 24 cm. Includes bibliographies and index. ISBN 0-312-00935-6 LC Card 87-9833 DDC 338.9 19
1. Industry and state. 2. Agriculture and state. I. Saunders, Christopher T.
HD3611 .I377 1987

Industrial policy. Structural dynamics of industrial policy / edited by Bodo B. Gemper. New Brunswick, N.J. (U. S.A.) : Transaction Books, c1987. x, 208 p. : ill. ; 23 cm. Reprint. Originally published: Industrial policy. Hamburg : Verlag Weltarchiv, 1985. Includes bibliographies and indexes. ISBN 0-88738-679-2 (pbk.) LC Card 87-5023 DDC 338.9 19
1. Industry and state. 2. Laissez-faire. I. Gemper, Bodo B. II. Title.
HD3611 .I385 1987

Industrial policy, R&D, and U. S.-Japanese trade /. Audretsch, David B. Berlin [1986] 39 p. ; LC Card 87-156721 DDC 382/.0952/073 19
HF3127 .A93 1986

The Industrial policy debate / edited by Chalmers Johnson ; [contributors, Eugene Bardach ... et al.]. San Francisco, Calif. : ICS Press, c1984. x, 275 p. ; 24 cm. Includes index. Bibliography: p. 247-259. CONTENTS. - Introduction / Chalmers Johnson -- Squaring the political circle / Aaron Wildavsky -- How Japanese industrial policy works / Robert S. Ozaki -- "Europeanizing" the U. S. economy / Melvyn Krauss -- Implementing industrial policy / Eugene Bardach -- What is the rust belt's problem? / Murray L. Weidenbaum, Michael J. Athey -- Sustaining the innovation process in America / Regis McKenna -- Trade policy and the dangers of protectionism / Bruce Bartlett -- Banking and finance / Walter E. Hoadley -- Industrial policy and national defense / Paul Seabury -- Tax reform / Yolanda Kodrzycki Henderson -- Conclusion / Chalmers Johnson. ISBN 0-917616-65-0 : LC Card 84-6741 DDC 338.973 19
1. Industry and state - United States - Addresses, essays, lectures. 2. Industry and state - Japan - Addresses, essays, lectures. 3. Industry and state - Europe - Addresses, essays, lectures. I. Johnson, Chalmers A.
HD3616.U47 I45 1984
NYPL [JLE 86-4707]

Industrial policy of Japan / edited by Ryūtarō Komiya ... [et al.]. Tokyo ; Orlando, FL : Academic Press, 1988. p. cm. Includes index. ISBN 0-12-418650-5 (U. S. : alk. paper) LC Card 87-1409 DDC 338.952 19
1. Industry and state - Japan. I. Komiya, Ryūtarō, 1928-.
HD3616.J33 I816 1988

Industrial power systems market. Industrial power systems market in the U. S. New York, N.Y. , c1983. v, 312 p. ; LC Card 87-143811 DDC 381/.4562143/0973
HD9695.U52 I53 1983

Industrial power systems market in the U. S. New York, N.Y. : Frost & Sullivan, c1983. v, 312 p. ; 29 cm. Spine title: Industrial power systems market. "October 1983." "#1228." LC Card 87-143811 DDC 381/.4562143/0973
1. Electric machinery industry - United States. 2. Electric power plant equipment industry - United States. 3. Industrial equipment industry - United States. 4. Electric power systems - United States. 5. Market surveys - United States. I. Frost & Sullivan. II. Title: Industrial power systems market.
HD9695.U52 I53 1983

INDUSTRIAL PROCESSING. see **MANUFACTURING PROCESSES.**

INDUSTRIAL PROCUREMENT - GERMANY (WEST) - STATISTICS.
Zur Neuberechnung der Indizes des Auftragseingangs und des Auftragsbestands für das Verarbeitende Gewerbe und das Bauhauptgewerbe auf Basis 1976. English. Indices of orders received and unfilled orders /. Wiesbaden , Stuttgart , 1986. 16 p. ; LC Card 86-215307
HF5437 .Z8713 1976

INDUSTRIAL PROCUREMENT - ITALY.
Landi, Antonio. Il marketing d'acquisto . Milano, Italy , 1986. 247 p. : ISBN 88-20-41020-6 : LC Card 86-207836
HD9680.A2 L36 1986

Le Strategie di acquisto della grande impresa nell'evoluzione dei sistemi produttivi . Milano, Italy , c1985. 223 p. : LC Card 85-233748
HD85.I7 I68 no. 76 HD39.5
NYPL [JLD 87-426]

INDUSTRIAL PROCUREMENT - MANAGEMENT.
Baily, Peter J. H. Purchasing and supply management /. London , New York , 1987. viii, 296 p. : ISBN 0-412-28940-7 (pbk.) LC Card 87-11760 DDC 658.7 19
HD39.5 .B335 1987

Baily, Peter J. H. Purchasing principles and management /. London , Marshfield, Mass. , 1985. 324 p. : ISBN 0-273-02242-3 LC Card 85-16704 DDC 658.7/2 19
HF5437 .B3415 1985 NYPL [JLE 86-3321]

Zenz, Gary Joseph. Purchasing and the management of materials /. New York , c1981. xiii, 514 p. : ISBN 0-471-06091-7 LC Card 80-21649 DDC 658.7/2 19
HD39.5 .W47 1981 NYPL [JLE 86-3384]

Zenz, Gary Joseph. Purchasing and the management of materials /. New York , c1987. xvi, 542 p. : ISBN 0-471-81802-X LC Card 86-32589 DDC 658.7/2 19
HD39.5 .W47 1987

INDUSTRIAL PROCUREMENT - SOVIET UNION.
Iniutina, K. V. (Klara Vasil'evna) Povyshenie nadezhnosti i kachestva snabzheniia /.

Leningrad , 1983. 239 p. ; LC Card 84-196942
HD39.5 .I55 1983

Makhnova, V. I. (Vera Ivanovna) Teoriia khoziaistvennykh sviazeĭ /. Moskva , 1985. 197 p. : LC Card 86-107892
HC336.25 .M347 1985

Tret'iak, V. P. (Vladimir Petrovich) Priamye khoziaistvennye sviazi v sotsialisticheskoĭ ėkonomike /. Leningrad , 1986. 141 p. : LC Card 87-146709
HF5415.6 .T74 1986

INDUSTRIAL PROCUREMENT - SOVIET UNION - DATA PROCESSING.
Realizatsiia na ĖVM uchetno-planovykh rabot material'no-tekhnicheskogo snabzheniia /. Moskva , 1983. 63 p. : LC Card 84-210458
HD39.5 .R43 1983

INDUSTRIAL PROCUREMENT - SOVIET UNION - MATHEMATICAL MODELS.
Sovershenstvovanie khoziaistvennogo mekhanizma v snabzhenii /. Moskva , 1983. 127 p. : LC Card 85-180655
HD39.5 .S68 1983

INDUSTRIAL PROCUREMENT - SOVIET UNION - STATISTICAL METHODS.
Kulinich, Emel'ian Ivanovich. Statisticheskaia otsenka faktorov khoziaistvennoĭ deiatel'nosti zagotovitel'nykh organizatsiĭ /. Moskva , 1983. 191 p. : LC Card 84-165083
HD39.5 .K84 1983

INDUSTRIAL PROCUREMENT - UKRAINE.
Baskin, A. I. (Arkadiĭ Isaakovich) Planirovanie potrebnosti v material'nykh resursakh na predpriiatii /. Kiev , 1983. 48 p. ; LC Card 83-243488
HD39.5 .B37 1983

Kryzhanovskiĭ, B. N. (Boris Nikolaevich) Spetsializatsiia zagotovitel'nogo proizvodstva /. Kiev , 1985. 125, [3] p. ; LC Card 87-112143
HD9703.S653 U474 1985

INDUSTRIAL PROCUREMENT - UNITED STATES.
An evaluation of industrial purchasing and distribution trends . Cleveland, Ohio (1230 Keith Bldg., Cleveland 44115) , c1985. 173 p. : LC Card 86-219582 DDC 658.7 19
HD39.5 .E93 1985

INDUSTRIAL PROCUREMENT - UNITED STATES - MANAGEMENT.
Bhote, Keki R., 1925- Supply management . New York, N.Y. , c1987. 150 p. : ISBN 0-8144-2330-2 (pbk.) : LC Card 86-28795 DDC 658.7/2/0973 19
HD39.5 .B49 1987

Industrial product price indexes, 1981=100 : concepts and methods / Statistics Canada, Prices Division, Industrial Prices = Indices des prix des produits industriels, 1981=100 : concepts et méthodes / Statistique Canada, Division des prix, Prix industriels. Ottawa : Statistics Canada, c1986. 216 p. : ill. ; 28 cm.
English and French. "Catalogue 62-556 occasional"--Cover. "March 1986." ISBN 0-660-52876-2 (pbk.) : LC Card 87-168891
1. Price indexes. 2. Prices - Canada. 3. Canada - Manufactures - Prices. I. Statistics Canada. Industrial Prices Section. II. Title: Indices des prix des produits industriels, 1981=100.
HB235.C2 I53 1986

INDUSTRIAL PRODUCTIVITY - ADDRESSES, ESSAYS, LECTURES.
Okonomische und soziale Wirksamkeit des wissenschaftlich-technischen Fortschritts /. Berlin , 1986. 314 p. : ISBN 3-320-00713-0
NYPL [JLD 86-4381]

The Uneasy alliance . Boston, Mass. , c1985. x, 485 p. : ISBN 0-87584-172-4 LC Card 85-8709 DDC 658.5 19
HD56 .U53 1985 ***NYPL [JLE 86-2361]***

INDUSTRIAL PRODUCTIVITY - ARGENTINA.
Resultados de la encuesta sobre expectativas de producción e inversión de las empresas industriales /. Buenos Aires , 1965. 81 leaves : LC Card 85-114982
HC180.I52 R47 1965

INDUSTRIAL PRODUCTIVITY - AUSTRALIA.
Structured chaos . Melbourne , New York , 1985. viii, 111 p. : ISBN 0-19-554687-3 LC Card 86-222312 DDC 338/.06/0994 19
HC610.I52 S77 1985

INDUSTRIAL PRODUCTIVITY - AUSTRIA.
Boguszewski, Jan. Wachstum und Produktivität in der Industrie und ihren Hauptbereichen in der BRD, Österreich, Polen und Ungarn im Zeitraum, 1960-1972 /. Wien [1979] 71 p. : LC Card 84-119739
HC290.5.I52 B64 1979

INDUSTRIAL PRODUCTIVITY - BULGARIA.
Ikonomika i upravlenie na kachestvoto. Svishtov , 1985. 201 p. : LC Card 86-155955
HC403.Z9 I5239 1985

Khadzhiev, Stoian. Pechalbata pri razshirenoto sotsialistichesko vŭzproizvodstvoto . Sofiia , 1985. 147 p. ; LC Card 85-209903
HC403.Z9 P737 1985

Narŭchnik na profsŭiuzniia aktivist . [[Sofia?] , 1985. 264 p. ; LC Card 85-216969
HC403.Z9 L366 1985

Problemi na stopanskata smetka /. Sofiia , 1981. 207 p. ; LC Card 82-133037
HC403.Z9 A865 1981

Tomov, Mitko. Pŭtishta za podobriavane na kachestvoto /. Pleven , 1984. 68, [4] p. ; LC Card 85-179053
HC403.Z9 L38 1984

INDUSTRIAL PRODUCTIVITY - BYELORUSSIAN S.S.R.
Babosov, Evgeniĭ Mikhaĭlovich. XXVII s"ezd KPSS o strategii uskoreniia sotsial'no-ėkonomicheskogo razvitiia strany /. Minsk , 1987. 124 p. ; LC Card 87-166221
HC337.B93 B33 1987

INDUSTRIAL PRODUCTIVITY - CANADA.
Nadeau, Jean. Les indicateurs globaux de la productivité . Québec [1982] 41 p. : ISBN 2-551-05072-3 LC Card 83-221751
HC120.I52 N33 1982

Stuber, Gerald. The slowdown in productivity growth in the 1975-83 period . [Ottawa] [1986] 164 p. : LC Card 87-100880 DDC 338/.06/0971 19
HC120.I52 S78 1986

INDUSTRIAL PRODUCTIVITY - CASE STUDIES.
Inside productivity . New York, N.Y. , c1987. iv, 156 p. : ISBN 0-88057-671-5 (pbk.) LC Card 86-82865 DDC 338/.06 19
HD56 .I528 1987

INDUSTRIAL PRODUCTIVITY CENTERS.
Limp, Wolfgang. Productivity centers . Frankfurt am Main , 1975. 64 p. ; LC Card 82-219310
HD30.4 .L55 1975

INDUSTRIAL PRODUCTIVITY - CUBA - ADDRESSES, ESSAYS, LECTURES.
Quantitative Latin American studies . Los Angeles , 1977. xiv, 91 p. : ISBN 0-87903-227-8 LC Card 77-620011 DDC 330.9/8/003
HD5731.A6 Q36 ***NYPL [JLF 80-242]***

INDUSTRIAL PRODUCTIVITY - CZECHOSLOVAKIA.
Semotam, Josef. Sovietske skúsenosti v rozvoji tvorivej iniciatívy pracujúcich /. Bratislava , 1981. 153 p. ; LC Card 81-182787
HC340.I52 S45 1981 ***NYPL [*QT 86-5786]***

INDUSTRIAL PRODUCTIVITY - ECUADOR.
Villalobos, Fabio. La industrialización ecuatoriana y la utilización de los recursos productivos, 1976-1983 /. Quito, Ecuador , 1987. 148 p. : LC Card 87-404654 DDC 338.09866 19
HC204.5.I52 V55 1987

INDUSTRIAL PRODUCTIVITY - EUROPE, EASTERN.
Zhamin, V. A. (Vitaliĭ Alekseevich) Sotsialisticheskaia ėkonomicheskaia integratsiia--faktor povysheniia ėffektivnosti proizvodstva stran SĖV /. Moskva , Varna , 1978. 93 p. ; LC Card 81-149558
HC244 .Z46 1978

INDUSTRIAL PRODUCTIVITY - FINLAND - ECONOMETRIC MODELS.
Menzler-Hokkanen, Ingeborg. Measuring changes in intra-industry competitiveness /. Helsingfors [1986] 39 p. ; ISBN 951-555-247-8 (pbk.) LC Card 87-170429 DDC 338.6/048 19
HC79.I52 M46 1986

INDUSTRIAL PRODUCTIVITY - GERMANY, EAST.
Bottesi, Valentin, 1933- Kombinatsplanung und Leistungssteigerung /. Berlin , 1984. 120 p. ; LC Card 84-217968
HC290.795.I52 B67 1984

Intensivierung des wissenschaftlich-technischen Arbeitsprozesses /. Jena , 1985. 200 p. : LC Card 86-132567 DDC 338/.06/09431 19
HC290.795.I52 I57 1985

Produktion, Intensivierung, Effektivität /. Jena , 1978. 180 p. : LC Card 85-183724
HC290.795.I52 P75 1978

INDUSTRIAL PRODUCTIVITY - GERMANY (EAST) - HISTORY.
Roesler, Jörg. Wirtschaftswachstum in der Industrie der DDR, 1945-1970 /. Berlin , 1986. 280 p. ; ISBN 3-05-000074-0 LC Card 86-196020
HC290.78 .R64 1986

INDUSTRIAL PRODUCTIVITY - GERMANY (EAST) - MEASUREMENT - CONGRESSES.
Die Leistungsbewertung in der Industrie . Jena , 1983. 241 p. ; LC Card 84-176546
HD56.25 .L45 1983

INDUSTRIAL PRODUCTIVITY - GERMANY, WEST.
Boguszewski, Jan. Wachstum und Produktivität in der Industrie und ihren Hauptbereichen in der BRD, Österreich, Polen und Ungarn im Zeitraum, 1960-1972 /. Wien [1979] 71 p. : LC Card 84-119739
HC290.5.I52 B64 1979

Gerstenberger, Wolfgang. Strukturwandel unter verschlechterten Rahmenbedingungen . Berlin , c1984. 255 p. : ISBN 3-428-05567-5 LC Card 84-180150
HC286.7 .G46 1984

Haag, Ingeborg. Arbeitskommunikation, Kommunikationsarbeit . Berlin , 1986. viii, 258 p. ; ISBN 3-923024-08-8 LC Card 86-226373
HD6957.G35 H33 1986

INDUSTRIAL PRODUCTIVITY - GERMANY (WEST) - ECONOMETRIC MODELS.
Conrad, Klaus, 1940- Produktivitätslücken nach Wirtschaftszweigen im internationalen Vergleich . Berlin , New York , c1985. 165 p. ; ISBN 0-387-15571-6 (U. S.) LC Card 85-233665
HC110.I52 C67 1985

INDUSTRIAL PRODUCTIVITY - HUNGARY.
Boguszewski, Jan. Wachstum und Produktivität in der Industrie und ihren Hauptbereichen in der BRD, Österreich, Polen und Ungarn im Zeitraum, 1960-1972 /. Wien [1979] 71 p. : LC Card 84-119739
HC290.5.I52 B64 1979

INDUSTRIAL PRODUCTIVITY - INDIA.
Dāśagupta, Pānnālāla, 1909- Production by the masses . Calcutta , 1983. vi, 54 p. ; LC Card 83-906787 DDC 331.11/8/0954 19
HC440.I52 D37 1983 ***NYPL [JLD 87-708]***

Goldar, B. N. Productivity growth in Indian industry /. New Delhi , 1986, c1985. xvi, 206 p. ; ISBN 81-7023-062-4 : LC Card 86-902812 DDC 338/.06/0954 19
HC440.I52 G65 1986

Singh, Nar, 1952- Sharing of productivity gains in Indian industry /. Delhi , 1984. x, 180 p. ;
NYPL [JLD 86-4253]

INDUSTRIAL PRODUCTIVITY - INDIA - CONGRESSES.
National Workshop on Productivity Enhancement in Indian Cement Industry-- a Pragmatic Approach to Modernisation (1986 : New Delhi, India) National Workshop on Productivity Enhancement in Indian Cement Industry-- a Pragmatic Approach to Modernisation, 19-20 March 1986 . New Delhi [1986] 42 p. : LC Card 87-901966 DDC 338.4/766694/0954 19
HD9622.I52 N34 1986

INDUSTRIAL PRODUCTIVITY - INDIA - ECONOMETRIC MODELS.
Shrivastava, S. C., 1939- Wages, profits, and productivity in selected industries of India since 1950 . Bombay , 1984. xii, 254 p. : LC Card 84-900745 DDC 338/.06/0954 19
HD5069 .S46 1984 ***NYPL [JLD 86-4260]***

INDUSTRIAL PRODUCTIVITY - INDIA - KARNATAKA.

Dadibhavi, R. V. Income, productivity, and industrial structure /. Allahabad, India , 1986. xx, 295 p. ; ISBN 81-85076-02-2 : LC Card 86-902847 DDC 339.2/0954/87 19
HC437.K27 D33 1986

INDUSTRIAL PRODUCTIVITY - INDIA - TECHNOLOGICAL INNOVATIONS.
Behari, Bepin. Unemployment, technology & rural poverty /. New Delhi , c1983. ix, 453 p. ; ISBN 0-7069-2337-5 : LC Card 83-906129 DDC 338/.06 19
HC440.I52 B43 1983 NYPL [JLD 87-1132]

INDUSTRIAL PRODUCTIVITY - ITALY.
Esposito, Gennaro, 1956- Decentramento produttivo, lavoro a domicilio e sindacato /. Milano [1983] 109 p. ; LC Card 85-150186
HD2336.I8 E86 1983

Palazzi, Paolo. Domanda di lavoro e produttività nell'industria italiana /. Bologna , c1980. 177 p. ; LC Card 82-156294 DDC 331.13/7945 19
HD5784 .P28 1980 NYPL [JLD 86-2811]

INDUSTRIAL PRODUCTIVITY - JAPAN.
Grayson, C. Jackson (Charles Jackson), 1923- American business, a two-minute warning . New York , London , c1988. xvii, 368 p. : ISBN 0-02-912680-0 LC Card 87-19391 DDC 658/.00973 19
HD70.U5 G69 1988

Hirono, Ryōkichi. Factors which hinder or help productivity improvement in the Asian region, a review and the prospect . Tokyo, Japan , c1980. v, 111 p. ; ISBN 92-833-1470-0 LC Card 81-174179 DDC 338/.0952 19
HD56 .H57 1980 NYPL [JLD 86-2287]

Uno, Kimio. Japanese industrial performance /. Amsterdam ; New York : xix, 439 p. : ISBN 0-444-70274-1 LC Card 87-15452 DDC 338.0952 19
HC462.9 .U56 1987

INDUSTRIAL PRODUCTIVITY - JAPAN - CONGRESSES.
Productivity and role of top management. Tokyo , 1986. x, 94 p. : ISBN 92-833-2041-1 (pbk.) LC Card 87-146526 DDC 658.3/14/0952 19
HC465.I52 P76 1986

INDUSTRIAL PRODUCTIVITY - JAPAN - ECONOMETRIC MODELS.
Conrad, Klaus, 1940- Produktivitätslücken nach Wirtschaftszweigen im internationalen Vergleich . Berlin , New York , c1985. 165 p. ; ISBN 0-387-15571-6 (U. S.) LC Card 85-233665
HC110.I52 C67 1985

INDUSTRIAL PRODUCTIVITY - LATVIA.
Khozi͡aĭstvennyĭ mekhanizm proizvodstva i obrashchenii͡a tovarov narodnogo potreblenii͡a /. Riga , 1985. 115 p. ; LC Card 86-177827
HF1040.9.L38 K47 1985

INDUSTRIAL PRODUCTIVITY - LITHUANIA.
Antanaĭtis, I͡U. A. (I͡Ustinas Antanovich) Sotsialisticheskoe sorevnovanie i intensifikatsii͡a proizvodstva /. Moskva , 1987. 157 p. : LC Card 87-103350
HC337.L53 S63 1987

INDUSTRIAL PRODUCTIVITY - MANAGEMENT.
Bialek, Jacques, 1919- Productivity improvement management . San Francisco [c1986] 339 p. ; ISBN 0-941883-01-9 (pbk.) : LC Card 87-6557 DDC 658.5 19
HD56 .B49 1986

Edosomwan, Johnson Aimie, 1953- Integrating productivity and quality management /. New York , c1987. xvii, 360 p. : ISBN 0-8247-7657-7 LC Card 86-32780 DDC 658.5 19
HD56 .E28 1987

INDUSTRIAL PRODUCTIVITY - MATHEMATICAL MODELS.
Menzler-Hokkanen, Ingeborg. Measuring changes in intra-industry competitiveness /. Helsingfors [1986] 39 p. ; ISBN 951-555-247-8 (pbk.) LC Card 87-170429 DDC 338.6/048 19
HC79.I52 M46 1986

INDUSTRIAL PRODUCTIVITY - MATHEMATICAL MODELS - ADDRESSES, ESSAYS, LECTURES.
Measurement issues and behavior of productivity variables /. Boston , Hingham, MA, USA , c1986. ix, 262 p. : ISBN 0-89838-171-1 LC Card 85-8017 DDC 338/.06/0287 19
HD56.25 .M43 1986 NYPL [JLE 86-3414]

INDUSTRIAL PRODUCTIVITY - MEASUREMENT - COMPUTER PROGRAMS.
Mundel, Marvin Everett, 1916- Measuring total productivity in manufacturing organizations . Tokyo, Japan , c1986. iv [i.e. vi], 155 p. ; ISBN 92-833-1090-4 LC Card 86-211930 DDC 658.3/14 19
HD56.25 .M87 1986

INDUSTRIAL PRODUCTIVITY - MEASUREMENT - DATA PROCESSING.
Mundel, Marvin Everett, 1916- Measuring total productivity in manufacturing organizations . Tokyo, Japan , c1986. iv [i.e. vi], 155 p. ; ISBN 92-833-1090-4 LC Card 86-211930 DDC 658.3/14 19
HD56.25 .M87 1986

Mundel, Marvin Everett, 1916- Measuring total productivity in manufacturing organizations . White Plains, N.Y. , 1987. vi, 155 p. ; ISBN 0-527-91625-0 (pbk.) LC Card 87-5029 DDC 658.5/036 19
HD56.25 .M87 1987

INDUSTRIAL PRODUCTIVITY - ONTARIO.
Nadeau, Jean. Les indicateurs globaux de la productivité . Québec [1982] 41 p. : ISBN 2-551-05072-3 LC Card 83-221751
HC120.I52 N33 1982

INDUSTRIAL PRODUCTIVITY - PHILIPPINES.
Hooley, Richard W., 1925- Productivity growth in Philippine manufacturing . [Manila?] , c1985. ix, 128 p. : LC Card 87-112014 DDC 338.4/769/09599 19
HC460.I52 H66 1985

INDUSTRIAL PRODUCTIVITY - POLAND.
Boguszewski, Jan. Wachstum und Produktivität in der Industrie und ihren Hauptbereichen in der BRD, Österreich, Polen und Ungarn im Zeitraum, 1960-1972 /. Wien [1979] 71 p. : LC Card 84-119739
HC290.5.I52 B64 1979

INDUSTRIAL PRODUCTIVITY - QUÉBEC (PROVINCE)
Nadeau, Jean. Les indicateurs globaux de la productivité . Québec [1982] 41 p. : ISBN 2-551-05072-3 LC Card 83-221751
HC120.I52 N33 1982

INDUSTRIAL PRODUCTIVITY - ROMANIA.
Eficienţa economico-socială /. Craiova , 1983. 392 p. ; LC Card 84-152996
HC405.Z9 I523 1983

INDUSTRIAL PRODUCTIVITY - RUSSIA.
Semotam, Josef. Sovietske skúsenosti v rozvoji tvorivej iniciatívy pracujúcich /. Bratislava , 1981. 153 p. ; LC Card 81-182787
*HC340.I52 S45 1981 NYPL [*QT 86-5786]*

INDUSTRIAL PRODUCTIVITY - RUSSIAN S.F.S.R. - CHELI͡ABINSKAI͡A OBLAST'.
Osobennosti razvitii͡a i puti povysheniia ėffektivnosti proizvoditel'nykh sil regiona /. Sverdlovsk , 1984. 141 p. ; LC Card 86-135171
HC337.R852 C456 1984

INDUSTRIAL PRODUCTIVITY - RUSSIAN S.F.S.R. - I͡AKUTSKAI͡A A.S.S.R.
Intensifikatsii͡a i povyshenie ėffektivnosti promyshlennogo proizvodstva v uslovii͡akh Severa . I͡Akutsk , 1986. 109 p. ; LC Card 87-159706
HC337.I23 I5214 1986

INDUSTRIAL PRODUCTIVITY - RUSSIAN S.F.S.R. - IVANOVSKAI͡A OBLAST' - POSTERS.
Korchagina, A. (Aleksandra) Nagli͡adnai͡a agitatsii͡a i vstrechnye plany /. Moskva , 1978. 44 p., [16] p. of plates : LC Card 81-161419
HC340.L3 K56 1978

INDUSTRIAL PRODUCTIVITY - RUSSIAN S.F.S.R. - NON-CHERNOZEM REGION.
Partiĭnye organizatsii Nechernozem'i͡a v bor'be za povyshenie proizvodstvennoĭ i politicheskoĭ aktivnosti rabochego klassa v period postroenii͡a i razvitii͡a sotsializma /. Kalinin , 1985. 152 p. ; LC Card 86-196840
HC337.R85 P36 1985

INDUSTRIAL PRODUCTIVITY - RUSSIAN S.F.S.R. - SIBERIA, NORTHEASTERN.
Intensifikatsii͡a i povyshenie ėffektivnosti promyshlennogo proizvodstva v uslovii͡akh Severa . I͡Akutsk , 1986. 109 p. ; LC Card 87-159706
HC337.I23 I5214 1986

INDUSTRIAL PRODUCTIVITY - SOUTH AFRICA.
Mansfield, W. R. (Willard Ridgway) A management crisis in Natal . [Durban, South Africa] [1985 or 1986] 26 p. ; LC Card 87-400770 DDC 338.0968 19
HC905.Z9 I526 1985

INDUSTRIAL PRODUCTIVITY - SOVIET UNION.
Aktual'nye problemy planomernogo razvitii͡a narodnogo khozi͡aĭstva /. Moskva , 1980. 247 p. ; LC Card 81-131558
HC336.25 .A455 1980

Babosov, Evgeniĭ Mikhaĭlovich. XXVII s"ezd KPSS o strategii uskorenii͡a sotsial'no-ėkonomicheskogo razvitii͡a strany /. Minsk , 1987. 124 p. ; LC Card 87-166221
HC337.B93 B33 1987

Chernoivanov, G. E. (Gennadiĭ Efimovich) Fondoëmkost' produktsii i ėffektivnost' sotsialisticheskogo proizvodstva /. Moskva , 1980. 156 p. ; LC Card 81-134415
HC340.C3 C54 1980

Ėffektivnost' i intensifikatsii͡a . Moskva , 1986. 161 p. ; LC Card 87-163443
HC340.I52 E33 1986

Intensifikatsii͡a sotsialisticheskogo proizvodstva i khozi͡aĭstvennyĭ mekhanizm /. Moskva , 1984. 228 p. ; LC Card 84-247548
HC340.I52 I58 1984

Khozi͡aĭstvennyĭ mekhanizm i povyshenie ėffektivnosti /. Moskva , 1982. 191 p. ; LC Card 84-193531
HC340.I52 K48 1982

Khozi͡aĭstvennyĭ mekhanizm i povyshenie ėffektivnosti proizvodstva /. Moskva , 1986. 252 p. ; LC Card 86-232347
HC340.I52 K49 1986

Makhnova, V. I. (Vera Ivanovna) Teorii͡a khozi͡aĭstvennykh svi͡azeĭ /. Moskva , 1985. 197 p. : LC Card 86-107892
HC336.25 .M347 1985

Marshruty peredovogo opyta /. Moskva , 1985. 286 p., [8] p. of plates : LC Card 85-213253
HC340.L3 M235 1985

Nagdiev, S. A. (Seĭfulakh Ataevich) Ispol'zovanie ėkonomicheskikh zakonov v upravlenii sotsialisticheskim proizvodstvom /. Leningrad , 1983. 87 p. ; LC Card 84-197365
HD56 .N34 1983

Narodnokhozi͡aĭstvennai͡a ėffektivnost'--pokazateli, metody otsenki /. Moskva , 1984. 247 p. : LC Card 84-188306
HC336.25 .N3515 1984

Obshchestvennyĭ kharakter proizvodstva i sotsialisticheskai͡a sobstvennost' /. Moskva , 1985. 286 p. ; LC Card 85-173513
HC340.I52 O27 1985

Proizvoditel'nost' truda--vazhneĭshiĭ faktor povyshenii͡a ėffektivnosti proizvodstva /. Moskva , 1982. 358 p. ; LC Card 83-140430
HC340.L3 P693 1982

Siegelbaum, Lewis H. Stakhanovism and the politics of productivity in the USSR, 1935-1941 /. Cambridge , New York , 1988. xv, 326 p. : ISBN 0-521-34548-0 LC Card 87-25605 DDC 331.11/8/0947 19
HC340.S6 S515 1988

Sistemnyĭ podkhod v reshenii nekotorykh problem sotsial'no-ėkonomicheskogo optimuma /. Moskva , 1984. 88 p. ; LC Card 86-144288
HC340.I52 S57 1984

Sotsial'no-ėkonomicheskai͡a ėffektivnost' obshchestvennogo proizvodstva--sushchnost', komponenty i voprosy ikh otsenki /. Minsk , 1983. 158 p. ; LC Card 83-206045
HC340.I52 S67 1983

Sotsial'no-ėkonomicheskie problemy intensifikatsii obshchestvennogo proizvodstva /. Moskva , 1983. 91 p. : LC Card 84-114234
HD56 .S688 1983

Sovershenstvovanie planirovaniia i upravleniia intensifikatsiei obshchestvennogo proizvodstva /. Moskva , 1984. 182 p. ; LC Card 85-240311
HC336.25 .S6735 1984

Sovershenstvovanie proizvodstvennykh otnoshenii sotsializma /. Moskva , 1986. 203 p. ; *NYPL [*QIP 87-2800]*

Vozdeistvie khoziaistvennogo mekhanizma na povyshenie ėffektivnosti obshchestvennogo proizvodstva . Dnepropetrovsk , 1984. 119 p. ; LC Card 86-181397
HC340.I52 V68 1984

INDUSTRIAL PRODUCTIVITY - SOVIET UNION - CONGRESSES.
Simpozium "Nauchno-tekhnicheskii progress i intensifikatsiia obshchestvennogo proizvodstva" (1984 : Podol'sk, Moscow, R.S.F.S.R.) Formy i metody vzaimodeistviia nauki i proizvodstva /. Moskva , 1984. 237 p. ; LC Card 85-240380
HC340.T4 S48 1984

INDUSTRIAL PRODUCTIVITY - SOVIET UNION - FORECASTING - MATHEMATICAL MODELS.
Metodologiia prognozirovaniia vosproizvodstva i ispol'zovaniia resursov v ėkonomike SSSR /. Moskva , 1984. 201 p. : LC Card 85-199435
HC340.I52 M485 1984

INDUSTRIAL PRODUCTIVITY - SOVIET UNION - MATHEMATICAL MODELS.
Lebedev, I. P. (Igor' Pavlovich) Proizvodstvennye resursy predpriiatiia . Moskva , 1984. 198 p. : LC Card 85-138003
HC340.I52 L42 1984

INDUSTRIAL PRODUCTIVITY - SOVIET UNION - POSTERS - CASE STUDIES.
Korchagina, A. (Aleksandra) Nagliadnaia agitatsiia i vstrechnye plany /. Moskva , 1978. 44 p., [16] p. of plates : LC Card 81-161419
HC340.L3 K56 1978

INDUSTRIAL PRODUCTIVITY - SOVIET UNION - STATISTICS.
Ozerov, V. K. (Viktor Konstantinovich) Analiz dinamiki sotsialisticheskogo rasshirennogo vosproizvodstva /. Novosibirsk , 1984. 263 p. ; LC Card 85-151291
HC340.I52 O97 1984

INDUSTRIAL PRODUCTIVITY - SPAIN.
Maravall, Fernando. Economía y política industrial en España /. Madrid , 1987. 231 p. : ISBN 84-368-0340-X LC Card 87-121800
HC385 .M2574 1987

INDUSTRIAL PRODUCTIVITY - STATISTICS.
Brodin, Anders. The OECD Compatible Trade and Production data base, 1970-1983 /. [Paris, France] , c1986. ii, 81 p. ; LC Card 86-213116 DDC 382/.021 19
HF1016 .B68 1986

INDUSTRIAL PRODUCTIVITY - SWEDEN - ECONOMETRIC MODELS.
Åberg, Yngve. Utvecklingen av produktion och produktivitet i svensk ekonomi, 1963-1981 /. [Stockholm] [1983] 83 p. : ISBN 91-38-08070-2 LC Card 84-218343
HC380.I52 A34 1983

INDUSTRIAL PRODUCTIVITY - UKRAINE.
Ėkonomicheskii mekhanizm ėksperimenta /. Kiev , 1985. 166 p. : LC Card 86-220234
HC337.U53 I524 1985

Gorbachev, Mikhail Sergeevich, 1931- Aktivno deistvovat', ne teriat' vremeni . Moskva , 1985. 45 p. ; LC Card 86-181428
HC337.U53 I525 1985

Pliushch, M. R. Vklad robitnychoho klasu Ukraïns'koï RSR u pryskorenniia naukovo-tekhnichnoho prohresu v promyslovosti, 50-70-i roky /. Kyïv , 1981. 244 p. ; LC Card 82-200854
HC337.U53 T465 1981

Resursy narodnogo khoziaistva . Kiev , 1985. 308 p. : LC Card 86-226867
HC337.U5 P5 1985 t. 2 HC337.U53I52

Struktura obshchestvennogo proizvodstva i tendentsii ee izmeneniia . Kiev , 1979. 113 p. ; LC Card 81-130407
HC337.U53 I527 1979

INDUSTRIAL PRODUCTIVITY - UNITED STATES.
Gray, Wayne B. (Wayne Burger), 1955- Productivity versus OSHA and EPA regulations /. Ann Arbor, Mich. , c1986. xii, p. : ISBN 0-8357-1721-6 (alk. paper) LC Card 85-28873 DDC 338/.06/0973 19
HC110.I52 G73 1986 NYPL [JLE 86-2375]

Grayson, C. Jackson (Charles Jackson), 1923- American business, a two-minute warning . New York , London , c1988. xvii, 368 p. : ISBN 0-02-912680-0 LC Card 87-19391 DDC 658/.00973 19
HD70.U5 G69 1988

Jorgenson, Dale Weldeau, 1933- Productivity and U. S. economic growth /. Cambridge, Mass. , 1987. 567 p. : ISBN 0-674-71175-0 (alk. paper) LC Card 87-12098 DDC 338/.06/0973 19
HC110.I52 J67 1987

Martin, Doris. Corporate productivity in action . Wailuku, Hawaii , c1987. 89 p. ; ISBN 0-9615541-0-X (pbk.) LC Card 85-90446 DDC 658.3/14 19
HC110.I52 M37 1987

Melman, Seymour. Profits without production /. Philadelphia , 1987, c1983. p. cm. ISBN 0-8122-1258-4 (pbk.) LC Card 87-13796 DDC 338.0973 19
HD70.U5 M425 1987

Nadeau, Jean. Les indicateurs globaux de la productivité . Québec [1982] 41 p. : ISBN 2-551-05072-3 LC Card 83-221751
HC120.I52 N33 1982

National Center for Productivity and Quality of Working Life. Starting a labor-management committee in your organization . Washington , 1978. 55 p. ; LC Card 78-603560 DDC 658.31/5
HD6490.L33 N37 1978 NYPL [JLF 81-235]

Reynolds, Morgan O., 1942- Making America poorer . Washington, D.C. , c1987. ix, 218 p. ; ISBN 0-932790-63-1 LC Card 87-6569 DDC 338.5/1/0973 19
HD6508 .R435 1987

INDUSTRIAL PRODUCTIVITY - UNITED STATES - ABSTRACTS.
Weinberg, Edgar. Labor-management cooperation for productivity /. New York , c1983. 61 p. ; ISBN 0-08-029511-8 (pbk.) LC Card 83-2361 DDC 016.33111/8/0973 19
HD56 .W44 1983
NYPL [JLM 83-380 no.30]

INDUSTRIAL PRODUCTIVITY - UNITED STATES - ECONOMETRIC MODELS.
Conrad, Klaus, 1940- Produktivitätslücken nach Wirtschaftszweigen im internationalen Vergleich . Berlin , New York , c1985. 165 p. ; ISBN 0-387-15571-6 (U. S.) LC Card 85-233665
HC110.I52 C67 1985

INDUSTRIAL PRODUCTIVITY - UNITED STATES - MEASUREMENT - ADDRESSES, ESSAYS, LECTURES.
Measurement issues and behavior of productivity variables /. Boston , Hingham, MA, USA , c1986. ix, 262 p. : ISBN 0-89838-171-1 LC Card 85-8017 DDC 338/.06/0287 19
HD56.25 .M43 1986 NYPL [JLE 86-3414]

INDUSTRIAL PRODUCTIVITY - YUGOSLAVIA.
Pavlović, Dragiša, 1943- Ko radnike povezuje lažnim koncima . Beograd , 1984. 414 p. ; LC Card 84-178578
HC407.Z9 L36 1984

INDUSTRIAL PRODUCTIVITY - ZAMBIA - KITWE.
Kamya, Andrew, 1941- Factors affecting efficiency in the informal sector in Lusaka and Kitwe /. Lusaka , 1981. iii, 40 p. ; LC Card 87-980491
HD2346.Z292 L875 1981

INDUSTRIAL PRODUCTIVITY - ZAMBIA - LUSAKA.
Kamya, Andrew, 1941- Factors affecting efficiency in the informal sector in Lusaka and Kitwe /. Lusaka , 1981. iii, 40 p. ; LC Card 87-980491
HD2346.Z292 L875 1981

INDUSTRIAL PROJECT MANAGEMENT - CANADA.
Ahmed, Mumtaz. Project management . Hamilton, Ont. [1986] xv, 254 p. : ISBN 0-920212-56-5 (pbk.) LC Card 87-158681 DDC 658.4/04 19
HF5635 .A26 1986

INDUSTRIAL PROJECT MANAGEMENT - CASE STUDIES.
Kharbanda, Om Prakesh. Successful projects, with a moral for management /. Hants, England , c1986. xvii, 267 p. : ISBN 0-566-02651-1 LC Card 86-235562 DDC 658.4/04 19
HD69.P75 K55 1986

INDUSTRIAL PROMOTION.
The role of large firms in local job creation . Paris [Washington, D.C.] c1986. 31 p. ; LC Card 87-130519 DDC 331.12/4 19
HD5710.5 .R65 1986

Small business incubators . Washington, D.C. , c1984. 32 p. : LC Card 86-233015 DDC 333.33/8 19
HD1393.25 .S63 1984

Zelfstandig werken en ondernemen in middelgrote en kleine ondernemingen /. Delft , 1985. 245 p. : ISBN 90-6275-226-8 : LC Card 86-152999
HD2346.N4 Z44 1985

INDUSTRIAL PROMOTION - ARGENTINA.
Boneo, Horacio. Desarrollo regional, incentivos fiscales y localización industrial /. Buenos Aires, Argentina [1985] 160 p. : ISBN 950-95720-8-X *NYPL [JLD 86-4218]*

Ferrucci, Ricardo Jorge. La promoción industrial en Argentina /. [Buenos Aires] , c1986. 274 p. : ISBN 950-23-0307-5 LC Card 87-124151 DDC 338.982 19
HD3616.A73 F47 1986

Frediani, Ramón O. El rol del empresario mediano en el desarrollo argentino . Buenos Aires, República Argentina , c1985. 123 p. : LC Card 87-101993
HD2346.A73 F73 1985

INDUSTRIAL PROMOTION - ARIZONA.
Arizona 1986 economic profile. Phoenix, AZ (1700 W. Washington, Phoenix 85007) [1986] 28 p. : LC Card 86-622323 DDC 330.9791/053 19
HC107.A6 A763 1986

INDUSTRIAL PROMOTION - ASIA, SOUTHEASTERN.
Bhattacharya, Sib Nath, 1938- Entrepreneurship development in India and the South-East Asian countries in agricultural and industrial sectors /. New Delhi , 1983. xix, 156 p. : LC Card 83-903206 DDC 338/.04/0954 19
HC440.I53 B48 1983 NYPL [JLD 86-3764]

INDUSTRIAL PROMOTION - AUSTRALIA - WESTERN AUSTRALIA.
Goldfields-Esperance regional profile. Kalgoorlie, W.A. , Perth, W.A. [1986] 58 p. : LC Card 87-169717 DDC 330.9941/7 19
HC607.W47 G65 1986

Western Australia's North . [Perth, W.A.] [1985?] [32] p. : LC Card 86-232759 DDC 338.9941 19
HC607.W47 W485 1985

INDUSTRIAL PROMOTION - BRAZIL, CENTRAL WEST - HANDBOOKS, MANUALS, ETC.
Centro-Oeste . [Brasília] [1983] 196 p., [3] leaves of plates : LC Card 85-208305
HC188.C46 C47 1983

INDUSTRIAL PROMOTION - BRAZIL - ESPÍRITO SANTO (STATE)
Setor de informações técnicas /. [Vitória] , 1983. 54 p. ; LC Card 85-202308
HC188.E7 S47 1983

INDUSTRIAL PROMOTION - BRAZIL NORTHEAST.
Incentivos fiscais e financeiros para investimentos no Nordeste do Brasil /. Recife , 1985. 92 p. ; LC Card 87-404837 DDC 332.6/7322813 19
HJ2529.N6 I53 1985

Magalhães, Antonio Rocha. Industrialização e desenvolvimento regional . Brasília , 1983. 315 p. : LC Card 84-160221 DDC 338.981/3 19
HD3616.B84 N676 1983
NYPL [JLD 86-3120]

INDUSTRIAL PROMOTION - BURKINA FASO.
Structure et perspectives de l'artisanat et de la petite industrie du sud-ouest de la Haute-Volta .

Berlin (West) [1978] xxvi, 253 p. : LC Card 85-118488
HD2346.B82 S77 1978

INDUSTRIAL PROMOTION - CAMEROON - NORTH-WEST PROVINCE.
Discover the North West of Cameroon . [Bamenda? , 1984] 197 p., [2] p. of plates : LC Card 87-101117 DDC 330.967/11204 19
HC995.Z7 N673 1984

INDUSTRIAL PROMOTION - CANADA.
Incentive and development programs for Canadian industry. Ottawa, Canada , 1973, c1975. 14, 14 p. ; LC Card 85-158119
HC120.I53 I48 1975

INDUSTRIAL PROMOTION - CANADA, NORTHERN.
The Northern mineral sector . Ottawa [1985] 37, 37 p. : ISBN 0-662-53700-9 (pbk.) LC Card 85-162718 DDC 338.2/0971 19
HD9506.C23 N6758 1985
NYPL [JLF 86-175]

INDUSTRIAL PROMOTION - CASE STUDIES.
State, finance, and industry . Brighton, Sussex , 1986. ix, 292 p. ; ISBN 0-7108-0219-6
NYPL [JLD 86-2997]

INDUSTRIAL PROMOTION - COSTA RICA.
Inversión industrial en Costa Rica . [San José] , 1986. 171 p., [1] folded leaf of plates : LC Card 87-400481 DDC 338.97286 19
HC143.Z9 I535 1986

INDUSTRIAL PROMOTION - DEVELOPING COUNTRIES.
Development strategies reconsidered /. New Brunswick, N.J., U. S.A. , c1986. viii, 190 p. ; ISBN 0-87855-991-4 (pbk.) : LC Card 85-24582 DDC 338.9/009172/4 19
HC59.7 .D482 1986 ***NYPL [JLE 86-2976]***

INDUSTRIAL PROMOTION - DEVELOPING COUNTRIES - CONGRESSES.
Promotion de la petite industrie dans les pays en développement /. Paris , c1985. 103 p. : ISBN 2-86844-008-8 LC Card 85-242526 DDC 338.6/42/0943 19
HD2346.5 .P76 1985 ***NYPL [JLD 86-3171]***

INDUSTRIAL PROMOTION - DOMINICAN REPUBLIC.
Najri, José Antonio, 1948- Crisis, producción y desarrollo . Santo Domingo, República Dominicana , 1986 (Santo Domingo, República Dominicana : Editora Corripio) ix, 248 p. ; LC Card 87-102092
HF1502 .N34 1986

INDUSTRIAL PROMOTION - ECUADOR.
Abril-Ojeda, Galo. Política monetaria y desarrollo industrial en el Ecuador, 1970-1983 /. Quito , 1985. 118 p. : ISBN 91-85894-10-9 LC Card 86-103812
HG865 .A27 1985

INDUSTRIAL PROMOTION - EUROPE.
D'Angelillo, Massimo, 1956- Job creation . Milano, Italy , c1985. 231 p. ; LC Card 86-156936
HD5764.A6 D418 1985
NYPL [JLD 86-3248]

INDUSTRIAL PROMOTION - EUROPEAN ECONOMIC COMMUNITY COUNTRIES.
La Politica industriale della CEE . Roma , 1983. 371 p. ; LC Card 86-104849 DDC 338.94 19
HD3616.E83 P65 1983
NYPL [JLD 87-1225]

INDUSTRIAL PROMOTION - FRANCE.
France. Groupe de stratégie industrielle no 8. Sous-groupe Travaux publics. La branche des travaux publics en France et sur les marchés extérieurs /. Paris , c1985. 202 p. : ISBN 2-11-001524-1 : LC Card 86-183130
HD4168 .F69 1985

Le Renouvellement du tissu industriel . Paris [1986] 130 p. ; ISBN 2-11-001568-3 : LC Card 86-191910
HD3616.F83 R46 1986

INDUSTRIAL PROMOTION - GERMANY, WEST.
Gewerbeentwicklung und Gewerbepolitik in der Grossstadtregion /. Gerlingen , c1987. 390 p., [3] leaves of plates : ISBN 3-88350-596-X LC Card 87-146643 DDC 332.6/732243 19
HC290.5.I53 G4797 1987

INDUSTRIAL PROMOTION - GERMANY (WEST) - MATHEMATICAL MODELS.
Hull, Christopher J. Helping small firms grow . New York , c1987. 228 p. : ISBN 0-7099-4791-7 LC Card 87-15728 DDC 338.6/42 19
HD2346.G3 .H786 1987

INDUSTRIAL PROMOTION - GERMANY (WEST) - MÜNSTER IN WESTFALEN.
Burberg, Paul-Helmuth. Zielgruppenorientierte kommunale Wirtschaftsförderung . Münster , c1983. xi, 207, 16 p. : ISBN 3-88497-042-9 LC Card 84-173863
HC289.M9 B87 1983

INDUSTRIAL PROMOTION - GERMANY (WEST) - REGENSBURG - HISTORY - 20TH CENTURY.
Finke, B. (Barbara) Studien zur kommunalen Industrieförderung im 20. Jahrhundert . Regensburg , c1986. 125, [45], xxv p. : ISBN 3-924956-19-7 : LC Card 87-129091 DDC 338.943/34 19
HC289.R36 F56 1986

INDUSTRIAL PROMOTION - GREECE.
Hellēnikē Trapeza Viomēchanikēs Anaptyxeōs (Greece) Hē drastēriotēta tēs ETVA to etos 1985. [Athēna] [1985] 43 p. ; LC Card 86-212959
HG3250.5.A8 H444 1985

INDUSTRIAL PROMOTION - INDIA.
Baig, Nafees, 1941- Government controls and industrial expansion in India /. Aligarh , 1983. viii, 223 p. ; LC Card 83-907504 DDC 338.954 19
HD3616.I43 B35 1983
NYPL [JLD 86-4330]

Bhattacharya, Sib Nath, 1938- Entrepreneurship development in India and the South-East Asian countries in agricultural and industrial sectors /. New Delhi , 1983. xix, 156 p. : LC Card 83-903206 DDC 338/.04/0954 19
HC440.I53 B48 1983 ***NYPL [JLD 86-3764]***

INDUSTRIAL PROMOTION - ITALY.
Intervento straordinario e amministrazione locale nel mezzogiorno /. Milano, Italy , c1985. 348 p. ; LC Card 86-144245
HC310.I53 I58 1985

Quale strategia per l'industria? . Bologna , c1986. 221 p. : ISBN 88-15-00975-2 : LC Card 86-182300
HC310.I53 Q35 1986

Rapporto sulle partecipazioni statali /. Milano [1981] 1 v. (in various pagings) ; ISBN 88-20-42161-5 : LC Card 81-199972 DDC 338.945 19
HC310.I53 R35 ***NYPL [JLD 83-2970]***

Relazione programmatica delle partecipazioni statali per il 1984 . Roma , 1985. 563 p. ; LC Card 86-176014
HC310.I53 R45 1985

Struttura industriale e politiche macroeconomiche in Italia /. Bologna , c1986. 152 p. : ISBN 88-15-01193-5 : LC Card 87-100465
HC305 .S845 1986

Tre incognite per lo sviluppo . Milano, Italy , c1986. 383 p. : LC Card 86-198933
HC310.I53 T74 1986

INDUSTRIAL PROMOTION - ITALY - CONGRESSES.
Convegno C.I.D.I.S. (1980 : Iesolo, Italy) Credito e finanziarie regionali . Padova , c1983. vi, 148 p. ; LC Card 85-215231
HG3729.I72 C66 1980

La Crisi delle partecipazioni statali, motivi e prospettive /. Milano , c1981. 240 p. ; ISBN 88-20-42148-8 : LC Card 81-200055
HC310.I53 C74 1981 ***NYPL [JLD 86-3503]***

INDUSTRIAL PROMOTION - ITALY - CORRUPT PRACTICES.
Risanamento e riordino delle partecipazioni statali . Milano, Italy , c1986. 429 p. : LC Card 86-169331
HC310.I53 R57 1986

INDUSTRIAL PROMOTION - ITALY - FRIULI-VENEZIA GIULIA.
Grandinetti, Roberto, 1953- Sistema industriale e politiche regionali . Milano, Italy , 1984. 234 p. : LC Card 85-176111 DDC 338.945/39 19
HC307.F68 G73 1984

INDUSTRIAL PROMOTION - ITALY - HISTORY - SOURCES.
Colombo, Giuseppe, 1836-1921. Industria e politica nella storia d'Italia . [Milano] , Roma , c1985. 497 p. : ISBN 88-420-2555-0 : LC Card 85-180231 DDC 338.945 19
HC310.I53 C65 1985 ***NYPL [JLE 86-2517]***

INDUSTRIAL PROMOTION - ITALY, SOUTHERN - ADDRESSES, ESSAYS, LECTURES.
Il Mezzogiorno nelle politiche nazionali e comunitarie . Milano , 1982. 379 p. ; LC Card 82-230171 DDC 338.945/7 19
HC305 .M42156 1982 ***NYPL [JLE 86-1611]***

INDUSTRIAL PROMOTION - LESOTHO.
Crafts and small-scale industries in Lesotho . Berlin [1982] vi, 60, 16 p., [1] leaf of plates : LC Card 84-215894 DDC 338.6/42/096816 19
HD2346.L44 C73 1982 ***NYPL [Sc F 86-141]***

INDUSTRIAL PROMOTION - MASSACHUSETTS.
The Massachusetts Industrial Finance Agency . Boston, MA (Rm. 314, State House, Boston 02133) [1986] 53 p. ; LC Card 86-622280 DDC 353.97440082 19
HG3729.U6 M366 1986

INDUSTRIAL PROMOTION - MASSACHUSETTS - WORCESTOR COUNTY.
Doeringer, Peter B. Invisible factors in local economic development /. New York , 1987. vii, 144 p. : ISBN 0-19-504965-9 (alk. paper) LC Card 87-13550 DDC 338.9744/3 19
HC107.M42 W674 1987

INDUSTRIAL PROMOTION - NEW YORK (N.Y.)
New York City Partnership. The Partnership. New York, N.Y. , c1986. 44 p. : LC Card 86-223138 DDC 380.1/06/07471 19
HF296.N4 N48 1986

INDUSTRIAL PROMOTION - NEW YORK (STATE)
New York (State). Legislature. Legislative Commission on Public-Private Cooperation. Legislative Commission on Public-Private Cooperation second report . [Albany] [1984] 57 p. ; LC Card 86-622576 DDC 338.9747 19
HC107.N7 N3743 1984

New York (State). Legislature. Legislative Commission on Public-Private Cooperation. Working together for New York's economy . [Albany] [1983] 57 p. ; LC Card 86-622577 DDC 338.9747 19
HC107.N7 N3743 1983

INDUSTRIAL PROMOTION - PENNSYLVANIA.
Allen, David N. Nurturing advanced technology enterprises . New York , c1986. xvi, 268 p. ; ISBN 0-275-92136-0 (alk. paper) : LC Card 86-9411 DDC 338.4/762/0009748 19
HC107.P43 H533 1986
NYPL [JLE 86-3609]

INDUSTRIAL PROMOTION - QUÉBEC (PROVINCE)
Conseil de planification et de développement du Québec. Le réseau décisionnel en agro-alimentation au Québec . [Québec] [1979] 29 p. ; LC Card 85-102587
HD9014.C4 Q425 1979

INDUSTRIAL PROMOTION - SAUDI ARABIA.
A Guide to industrial investment /. Riyadh , 1986. vi, 286 p., [4] leaves of plates : LC Card 87-400301 DDC 332.6/7322538 19
HC415.33.Z9 I534 1986

INDUSTRIAL PROMOTION - SOUTH DAKOTA.
South Dakota in comparison. [Aberdeen, SD] (607 North 4th St., Aberdeen 57401) , 1985. 32 p. : LC Card 87-620926 DDC 330.9783/033 19
HC107.S83 I537 1985

INDUSTRIAL PROMOTION - SWEDEN.
Andersson, Göran, 1944- Industrihotell och industribyar . Stockholm [1984] 150 p. : ISBN 91-38-08268-3 LC Card 85-106828
HC375 .A72 1984

Olofsson, Christer. De regionala utvecklingsbolagen . Stockholm [1983] 118 p. ; ISBN 91-38-07479-6 LC Card 83-234309
HC380.I53 O46 1983

Omfattning och erfarenheter . Stockholm [1984] 127 p. : ISBN 91-38-08319-1 LC Card 85-106802
HC375 .O39 1984

De Regionala utvecklingsfonderna . Stockholm , 1981. 260 p. ; ISBN 91-38-06693-9 LC Card 82-234113
HC380.I53 R44 1981

INDUSTRIAL PROMOTION - UNITED STATES.
Winick, Bradley H. Making the link . [Washinton, D.C.] , c1986. i, 17 p. ; ISBN 0-88713-678-8 (pbk.) LC Card 87-106145 DDC 331.11/0973 19
HD5724 .W557 1986

INDUSTRIAL PROMOTION - UNITED STATES - DIRECTORIES.
Directory of federal & state business assistance . Springfield, VA , c1986. xii, 159 p. : ISBN 0-934213-03-8 (pbk.) : LC Card 86-601675 DDC 353.0082/025 19
HC110.I53 D57 1986

INDUSTRIAL PROMOTION - UNITED STATES - STATES.
Corporation for Enterprise Development. Building the new economy . Washington, D.C. , 1986. iv, 178 p. ; ISBN 0-9605804-2-5 (pbk.) LC Card 86-61273 DDC 338.973 19
HC110.I53 C67 1986

Hamilton, William W. Innovations in economic development . Washington, D.C. (2021 K St., Suite 711, Washington 20006) [1986] 1 v. (various foliations) : LC Card 87-620522 DDC 338.973 19
HC110.I53 H363 1986

Promoting high-technology industry . Boulder , 1987. 283 p. ; ISBN 0-8133-7427-8 (pbk. : alk. paper) LC Card 87-61327 DDC 338.4/762/000973 19
HC110.H53 P76 1987

INDUSTRIAL PROMOTION - UNITED STATES - STATES - DIRECTORIES.
Directory of federal & state business assistance . Springfield, VA , c1986. xii, 159 p. : ISBN 0-934213-03-8 (pbk.) : LC Card 86-601675 DDC 353.0082/025 19
HC110.I53 D57 1986

Guide to state capital formation incentives and innovations /. [Washington, D.C. , 1983] vii, 154 p. ; LC Card 86-673432
HC110.I53 G84x 1983

INDUSTRIAL PROMOTION - VENEZUELA.
Preliminary study report on promotion of small-medium scale industries in the Republic of Venezuela. [Tokyo] [1978] ii, 27 p. : LC Card 84-249328
HD9506.V42 P74 1978

Industrial psychology /. Tiffin, Joseph, 1905- New York , 1987, [c1942] xvi, 386 p. : ISBN 0-8240-8221-4 (alk. paper) : LC Card 86-25803 DDC 158.7 19
HF5548.8 .T5 1987

Industrial psychology /. Viteles, Morris S. (Morris Simon), 1898- New York , 1987, c1932. xviii, 652 p., 8 p. of plates : ISBN 0-8240-8224-9 (alk. paper) : LC Card 86-25817 DDC 158.7 19
HF5548.8 .V55 1987

INDUSTRIAL PSYCHOLOGY. see **PSYCHOLOGY, INDUSTRIAL.**

Industrial psychology and organizational behaviour.
Organization analysis and development . Chichester [West Sussex] , New York , c1987. xiii, 269 p. ; ISBN 0-471-91227-1 : LC Card 86-26713 DDC 658.4/06 19
HD58.7 .O669 1987

INDUSTRIAL PUBLICITY.
Cost-effective management for today's public affairs, or, How to succeed as a PAO in an era of constraints /. Washington, D.C. (1255 Twenty-third St., N.W., Suite 750, Washington 20037) [c1987] xiii, 109 p. : LC Card 87-135276 DDC 659.2 19
HD59 .C645 1987

INDUSTRIAL PURCHASING. see **INDUSTRIAL PROCUREMENT.**

Industrial purchasing strategies . Woodside, Arch G. Lexington, Mass. , c1987. xiv, 223 p. : ISBN 0-669-06953-1 (alk. paper) LC Card 83-48132 DDC 658.7/2 19
HD39.5 .W66 1987

INDUSTRIAL RECREATION.
Chelovek, svobodnoe vremi͡a i profsoi͡uzy /. Moskva , 1980. 256 p., [32] p. of plates : LC Card 81-137052
HD7395.R4 C42 1980

INDUSTRIAL RECREATION - BULGARIA.
Chelovek, svobodnoe vremi͡a i profsoi͡uzy /. Moskva , 1980. 256 p., [32] p. of plates : LC Card 81-137052
HD7395.R4 C42 1980

INDUSTRIAL RECREATION - SOVIET UNION.
Chelovek, svobodnoe vremi͡a i profsoi͡uzy /. Moskva , 1980. 256 p., [32] p. of plates : LC Card 81-137052
HD7395.R4 C42 1980

Industrial relations : a social psychological approach / edited by Geoffrey M. Stephenson and Christopher J. Brotherton. Chichester ; New York : Wiley, c1979. xii, 412 p. ; 24 cm. Includes bibliographies and indexes. ISBN 0-471-99701-3 LC Card 78-18452 DDC 301.5/5
1. Industrial relations - Addresses, essays, lectures. 2. Industrial relations - Great Britain - Addresses, essays, lectures. 3. Psychology, Industrial - Addresses, essays, lectures. 4. Social psychology - Addresses, essays, lectures. I. Stephenson, G. M. (Geoffrey Michael). II. Brotherton, Christopher J.
HD6971 .I547 ***NYPL [JLE 80-1770]***

Industrial relations : the green paper : proceedings of a seminar held at James Cook Hotel, Wellington, 11 April 1986, [and] Carter-Holt Pavilion, Auckland Showgrounds, Auckland, 18 April 1986 / edited by Kevin Hince. [Wellington] : Industrial Relations Centre, Victoria University of Wellington, 1986. ii, 71 p. ; 21 cm. Includes bibliographies. LC Card 86-212248 DDC 331/.09931 19
1. Industrial relations - New Zealand - Congresses. I. Hince, Kevin. II. Victoria University of Wellington. Industrial Relations Centre.
HD8930.5 .I52 1986

Industrial relations : some aspects / compiled and edited by B.P. Gupta. New Delhi : PHD Chamber of Commerce and Industry, 1986. 254 p. ; 22 cm. Revision of: 2nd ed., rev. and enl., 1978. LC Card 87-902682
1. Industrial relations - India. 2. Labor laws and legislation - India. I. Gupta, B. P.
HD8686.5.I575 1978

INDUSTRIAL RELATIONS - ADDRESSES, ESSAYS, LECTURES.
Comparative labour law and industrial relations /. Deventer [Netherlands] , Boston , c1985. xiii, 527 p. ; ISBN 90-6544-236-7 (pbk.) LC Card 85-10000 DDC 344/.01 342.41 19
K1705.6 .C65 1985 ***NYPL [JLE 86-2420]***

Industrial relations . Chichester , New York , c1979. xii, 412 p. ; ISBN 0-471-99701-3 LC Card 78-18452 DDC 301.5/5
HD6971 .I547 ***NYPL [JLE 80-1770]***

Job equity and other studies in industrial relations . Los Angeles , c1982. 274 p. : LC Card 82-621216 DDC 331/.0973 19
HD5708.45.U6 J6 1982 ***NYPL [JLD 87-273]***

The Jobs challenge . Cambridge, Mass. , 1986. xvi, 304 p. : ISBN 0-88410-990-9 LC Card 85-7547 DDC 331.12 19
HD5707 .J63 1985 ***NYPL [JLE 86-2190]***

Microprocessors, manpower, and society . Aldershot, Hants., England , c1984. xi, 367 p. : ISBN 0-566-00631-6 ***NYPL [JLD 86-1098]***

INDUSTRIAL RELATIONS - AFRICA.
Mesfin Gabre Michael. Labour-management relations in public enterprises in Africa. Geneva, Switzerland , 1983. 84 p. ; ISBN 92-2-103009-1 (pbk.) LC Card 86-213649 DDC 658.3 s 331/.04135/000096 19
HD6961.A1 I73 no. 60 HD8776.5

INDUSTRIAL RELATIONS - AFRICA - ADDRESSES, ESSAYS, LECTURES.
Management problems in Africa /. London , 1986. xviii, 395 p. ; ISBN 0-333-28992-7
NYPL [Sc D 86-519]

INDUSTRIAL RELATIONS - AFRICA - CONGRESSES.
Labour-relations in Africa, English-speaking countries . Geneva , c19. 159 p. ; ISBN 92-2-103467-4 (pbk.) : LC Card 86-212930 DDC 658.3 s 331/.096 19
HD6961.A1 I73 no. 64 HD8772

Industrial relations and technical change in the British, Italian, and German automobile industry : three case studies / Wolfgang Streeck (ed.). Berlin : IIM Labour Market Policy, Wissenschaftszentrum Berlin, [1985] 1 v. (various pagings) : ill. ; 30 cm. (Discussion papers, 0722-673X . IIM/LMP 85-5) "August 1985." Bibliography: p. 44-45. LC Card 86-206613 DDC 338/.04292/094 19
1. Industrial relations - Great Britain - Case studies. 2. Industrial relations - Italy - Case studies. 3. Industrial relations - Germany (West) - Case studies. 4. Automobile industry workers - Great Britain - Effect of technological innovations on - Case studies. 5. Automobile industry workers - Italy - Effect of technological innovations on - Case studies. 6. Automobile industry workers - Germany (West) - Effect of technological innovations on - Case studies. 7. Collective bargaining - Automobile industry - Great Britain - Case studies. 8. Collective bargaining - Automobile industry - Italy - Case studies. 9. Collective bargaining - Automobile industry - Germany (West) - Case studies. I. Streeck, Wolfgang, 1946-. II. Series: Discussion papers (International Institute of Management. Labour Market Policy) , IIM/LMP 85-5.
HD6976.A82 G75 1985

INDUSTRIAL RELATIONS - AUSTRALIA.
Alternatives to arbitration /. Sydney , Boston , 1986. x, 468 p. ; ISBN 0-86861-857-8 (pbk.) LC Card 85-81482 DDC 331/.0994 19
HD5630.A6 A47 1986

Australian industrial relations . London [1986] 24 p. ; ISBN 0-902499-56-4 (pbk.) : LC Card 86-233230 DDC 331/.0994 19
HD8846.5 .A96 1986

Niland, John R. Control, consensus, or chaos? . Sydney , Boston , 1985. xiv, 330 p. : ISBN 0-86861-447-5 (pbk.) LC Card 85-70461 DDC 331.89/0994 19
HD8846.5 .N55 1985 ***NYPL [JLD 87-354]***

INDUSTRIAL RELATIONS - AUSTRALIA - CONGRESSES.
Japanese and Australian labour markets . Canberra [c1983] xx, 610 p. : ISBN 0-86413-004-X (pbk.) : LC Card 84-220557 DDC 331.12/0952 19
HD5850.A6 J36 1983 ***NYPL [JLE 86-630]***

INDUSTRIAL RELATIONS - AUSTRALIA - QUEENSLAND - HISTORY - 19TH CENTURY.
Walker, Jan, 1954- Jondaryan station . St. Lucia , New York , 1988. p. cm. ISBN 0-7022-2093-0 (pbk.) LC Card 87-13816 DDC 333.3/09943 19
HD1039.Q43 W34 1988

INDUSTRIAL RELATIONS - AUSTRIA.
The Trade union situation and industrial relations in Austria . Geneva , 1986. xiii, 107 p. ; ISBN 92-2-105659-7 (pbk.) : LC Card 87-123441 DDC 331/.09436 19
HD6674 .T72 1986

INDUSTRIAL RELATIONS - BRAZIL.
Lobos, Julio A. Manual de guerrilha trabalhista . São Paulo , c1986. 142 p. : LC Card 87-130241 DDC 658.3/15/0981 19
HD6971 .L57 1986

INDUSTRIAL RELATIONS - CANADA - ADDRESSES, ESSAYS, LECTURES.
Working Canadians . Toronto , New York , c1984. x, 380 p. ; ISBN 0-458-97370-X (pbk.) : LC Card 84-222036 DDC 331/.0971 19
HD6957.C2 W67 1984 ***NYPL [JLD 87-681]***

Industrial Relations Centre, Queen's University, Kingston, Ont. see **Queen's University, Kingston, Ont. Industrial Relations Centre.**

INDUSTRIAL RELATIONS - CHINA.
Walder, Andrew George. Communist neo-traditionalism . Berkeley , c1986. xxi, 302 p. ; ISBN 0-520-05439-3 (alk. paper) LC Card 85-27093 DDC 306/.36/0951 19
HD8736.5 .W34 1986 ***NYPL [JLD 86-3749]***

INDUSTRIAL RELATIONS - CONGRESSES.
The Future directions of employee relations /. Los Angeles, Calif. , c1985. xiv, 418 p. ; ISBN 0-89215-132-3 ***NYPL [JLD 86-3596]***

Human resource management in high-technology firms /. Lexington, Mass. , 1986, c1987. x, 243 p. : ISBN 0-669-13686-7 (alk. paper) LC Card 86-45556 DDC 658.3 19
HF5549 .H875 1987 *NYPL [JLE 87-1100]*

INDUSTRIAL RELATIONS COUNCILS. see **WORKS COUNCILS.**

INDUSTRIAL RELATIONS - DICTIONARIES.

Shafritz, Jay M. The Facts on File dictionary of personnel management and labor relations /. New York, N.Y. , c1985. 534 p. : ISBN 0-8160-1234-2 LC Card 85-20823 DDC 658.3/003/21 19
HF5549.A23 S52 1985 *NYPL [JLE 86-4748]*

INDUSTRIAL RELATIONS - DICTIONARIES - POLYGLOT.

Kunhardt, Ulla von. Elsevier's dictionary of the labour market in five languages, English, German, Swedish, Spanish, and French /. Amsterdam , New York , 1988. p. cm. ISBN 0-444-42884-4 : LC Card 87-24529 DDC 331/.03 19
HD4839 .K86 1988

INDUSTRIAL RELATIONS - EFFECT OF TECHNOLOGICAL INNOVATIONS ON.

The process of technological change . Cambridge [Cambridgeshire] , New York , 1988. p. cm. ISBN 0-521-32303-7 LC Card 87-6641 DDC 658.5/14 19
HD45 .P757 1988

Technological change . Geneva , 1985. 355 p. : ISBN 92-2-105162-5 (pbk.) : LC Card 86-203534 DDC 331.12 19
HD6331 .T416 1985

INDUSTRIAL RELATIONS - EFFECT OF TECHNOLOGICAL INNOVATIONS ON - CONGRESSES.

Computers and democracy . Aldershot [Hants, England] , Brookfield [Vt.], USA , c1987. x, 434 p. : ISBN 0-566-05476-0 : LC Card 87-8398 DDC 338/.06 19
HD5650 .C65 1987

INDUSTRIAL RELATIONS - EUROPE.

La Flexibilité du travail en Europe . Paris , 1986. 330 p. : ISBN 2-7071-1598-3 : LC Card 86-173845
HD8376.5 .F57 1986

INDUSTRIAL RELATIONS - EUROPE - ADDRESSES, ESSAYS, LECTURES.

Industrial relations in Europe . London , Dover, N.H. , c1985. ix, 277 p. ; ISBN 0-7099-4212-5 : LC Card 85-21321 DDC 331/.094 19
HD8376.5 .I54 1985 *NYPL [JLD 86-1065]*

INDUSTRIAL RELATIONS - EUROPE - CONGRESSES.

West European Conference on the Psychology of Work and Organization (1985 : Aachen, Germany) The psychology of work and organization . Amsterdam ; New York : xi, 407 p. : ISBN 0-444-70029-3 (U. S.) LC Card 86-8947 DDC 158.7 19
HF5548.8 .W475 1985 *NYPL [JLE 86-4341]*

INDUSTRIAL RELATIONS - EUROPEAN ECONOMIC COMMUNITY COUNTRIES.

Dötsch, Jochen. EG und Arbeiterrechte . Berlin , 1981. 143 p. ; LC Card 81-145834 DDC 331.11/094 19
HD8380.5 .D67 1981 *NYPL [JLD 86-2739]*

Emerson, Michael. What model for Europe? /. Cambridge, Mass. , c1988. xi, 151 p. : ISBN 0-262-05036-6 LC Card 87-15151 DDC 331.11/094 19
HD8380.5 .E47 1988

INDUSTRIAL RELATIONS - FILM CATALOGS.

National industrial relations film catalogue. [Ottawa, Ont.] , c1986. 31, 21 p. ; ISBN 0-662-54352-1 (pbk.) LC Card 86-203066 DDC 016.331 19
HD6971 .N24 1986

INDUSTRIAL RELATIONS - FINLAND - HISTORY.

Mansner, Markku. Suomalaista yhteiskuntaa rakentamassa . Helsinki [1984] 552 p., [4] p. of plates : ISBN 951-9240-75-6 LC Card 85-130291
HD8533 .M345 1984

INDUSTRIAL RELATIONS - FORECASTING.

Hegedüs, Zsuzsa. Il presente è l'avvenire . Milano, Italy , c1985. 126 p. : LC Card 85-215705
HD85.I7 I68 no. 77 HD6955 *NYPL [JLD 87-427]*

INDUSTRIAL RELATIONS - FRANCE.

Aglietta, Michel. Les métamorphoses de la société salariale . Paris , c1984. 274 p. ; ISBN 2-7021-1230-7 : LC Card 84-176554 DDC 331/.0944 19
HD8431 .A36 1984 *NYPL [JLD 87-478]*

Callies, Albane. France-Japon . Paris , 1986. 208 p. ; ISBN 2-86563-129-X LC Card 86-165719
HD8431 .C35 1986

Chotard, Yvon, 1921- Les patrons et le patronat /. [Paris] , c1986. 231 p. ; ISBN 2-7021-1538-1 : LC Card 87-167099
HD6948.F8 C46 1986

Erbès-Seguin, Sabine. Syndicats et relations de travail dans la vie économique française /. [Villeneuve d'Ascq] [1985] 137 p. ; ISBN 2-85939-262-9 : LC Card 85-226210 DDC 331/.0944 19
HD6684 .E75 1985 *NYPL [JLE 86-2222]*

Le Gal, André, 1920- Entre le marteau et l'enclume /. Paris , c1984. 448 p. ; ISBN 2-214-05783-8 : LC Card 85-118954 DDC 658.3/02/0924 B 19
HD8433.L4 A34 1984 *NYPL [JLD 87-438]*

Mothé-Gautrat, Daniel, 1924- Pour une nouvelle culture d'entreprise /. Paris , 1986. 173 p. ; ISBN 2-7071-1596-7 : LC Card 86-185142
HD8431 .M63 1986

Tableaux de l'état physique et moral des salariés en France /. Paris , 1986. 237 p. ; ISBN 2-7071-1626-2 : LC Card 87-122301
HD8431 .T32 1986

Le Travail . Paris , c1986. iv, 370 p. ; ISBN 2-7178-1138-9 : LC Card 87-123294
HD8428 .T72 1986

INDUSTRIAL RELATIONS - GERMANY, WEST.

Berghahn, Volker Rolf. Industrial relations in West Germany /. Leamington Spa, UK ; New York : p. cm. ISBN 0-907582-64-8 : LC Card 87-9359 DDC 331/.0943 19
HD8451 .B45 1988

Spie, Ulrich. Der Personalmanager im Vorstand . Stuttgart , 1985. ix, 354 p. : ISBN 3-8202-0313-3 LC Card 86-131051
HF5549.2.G3 S67 1985

INDUSTRIAL RELATIONS - GERMANY, WEST - ADDRESSES, ESSAYS, LECTURES.

Ausstieg? . Hamburg , 1985. 159 p. : ISBN 3-87975-289-3 LC Card 85-219857 DDC 331/.0943 19
HD6694 .A97 1985 *NYPL [JLD 87-710]*

Economic crisis, trade unions, and the state /. London , Dover, N.H. , c1986. 295 p. ; ISBN 0-7099-1447-4 : LC Card 85-28055 DDC 331/.094 19
HD8391 .E26 1986 *NYPL [JLD 86-1301]*

INDUSTRIAL RELATIONS - GERMANY (WEST) - CASE STUDIES.

Industrial relations and technical change in the British, Italian, and German automobile industry . Berlin [1985] 1 v. (various pagings) : LC Card 86-206613 DDC 338/.04292/094 19
HD6976.A82 G75 1985

Streeck, Wolfgang, 1946- Industrial relations in West Germany . London , 1984. 178 p. ; ISBN 0-435-83839-3 LC Card 87-673421
HD6698.A8 S77x 1984b

INDUSTRIAL RELATIONS - GOVERNMENT POLICY - BRAZIL.

Os Sindicatos e a transição democrática . São Paulo , 1986. 294 p. ; LC Card 87-153581 DDC 331.88/0981 19
HD6612 .S55 1986

INDUSTRIAL RELATIONS - GOVERNMENT POLICY - JAPAN - HISTORY.

Garon, Sheldon. The state and labor in modern Japan /. Berkeley , c1987. xvi, 326 p. ; ISBN 0-520-05983-2 (alk. paper) LC Card 86-30890 DDC 331/.0952 19
HD8726 .G37 1987

INDUSTRIAL RELATIONS - GREAT BRITAIN.

The Car industry . London , New York , 1985. viii, 210 p. : ISBN 0-422-79550-X LC Card 85-14742 DDC 331/.04292/0941 19
HD6976.A82 G72 1985 *NYPL [JLD 87-403]*

Freedom and fairness . Nottingham, England , Atlantic Highlands, N.J. , 1986. 157 p. ; ISBN 0-85124-440-8 LC Card 86-28038 DDC 331.88/0942 19
HD6664 .F763 1986

MacInnes, John. Thatcherism at work . Milton Keynes, England , Philadelphia , 1987. p. cm. ISBN 0-335-15517-0 LC Card 87-24722 DDC 338.941 19
HD8391 .M26 1987

Millward, Neil. British workplace industrial relations, 1980-1984 . Aldershot, England , Brookfield, Vt. , c1986. xxi, 341 p. ; ISBN 0-566-05391-8 : LC Card 86-25625 DDC 331/.0941 19
HD8391 .M55 1986 *NYPL [JLD 87-1287]*

Minford, Patrick. Unemployment . Oxford, UK , New York, NY, USA , 1985. x, 214 p. : ISBN 0-631-14506-0 : LC Card 85-13511 DDC 331.13/7941 19
HD5765.A6 M55 1985 *NYPL [JLE 86-2297]*

Morris, Timothy, 1953- Innovations in banking . London , Wolfeboro, N.H. , c1986. 137 p. : ISBN 0-7099-4607-4 : LC Card 86-13400 DDC 332.1/068/3 19
HG2988 .M675 1986 *NYPL [JLD 87-81]*

INDUSTRIAL RELATIONS - GREAT BRITAIN - ADDRESSES, ESSAYS, LECTURES.

Economic crisis, trade unions, and the state /. London , Dover, N.H. , c1986. 295 p. ; ISBN 0-7099-1447-4 : LC Card 85-28055 DDC 331/.094 19
HD8391 .E26 1986 *NYPL [JLD 86-1301]*

Fawcett, Henry, 1833-1884. The economic position of the British labourer /. New York , 1984. vii, 256 p. ; ISBN 0-8240-5706-6 (alk. paper) : LC Card 83-48478 DDC 331/.0941 19
HD8390 .F28 1984 *NYPL [JLC 86-366]*

Industrial relations . Chichester , New York , c1979. xii, 412 p. ; ISBN 0-471-99701-3 LC Card 78-18452 DDC 301.5/5
HD6971 .I547 *NYPL [JLE 80-1770]*

INDUSTRIAL RELATIONS - GREAT BRITAIN - CASE STUDIES.

Industrial relations and technical change in the British, Italian, and German automobile industry . Berlin [1985] 1 v. (various pagings) : LC Card 86-206613 DDC 338/.04292/094 19
HD6976.A82 G75 1985

Willman, Paul. Innovation and management control . Cambridge [Cambridgeshire] , New York , 1985. viii, 215 p. ; ISBN 0-521-26802-8 LC Card 84-17481 DDC 331/.04292/0941 19
HD8039.A82 G79 1985 *NYPL [JLD 85-3102]*

INDUSTRIAL RELATIONS - GREAT BRITAIN - EFFECT OF TECHNOLOGICAL INNOVATIONS ON.

Daniel, W. W. (William Wentworth), 1938- Workplace industrial relations and technical change /. London , c1987. 312 p. : ISBN 0-86187-917-1 LC Card 87-154801 DDC 331/.0941 19
HD8391 .D3535 1987

INDUSTRIAL RELATIONS - GREAT BRITAIN - EFFECT OF TECHNOLOGICAL INNOVATIONS ON - CASE STUDIES.

New technology and the process of labour regulation /. Oxford [Oxfordshire] , New York , 1987. p. cm. ISBN 0-19-827274-X : LC Card 87-11146 DDC 331/.0941 19
HD6331.2.G7 N48 1987

INDUSTRIAL RELATIONS - HISTORY.

Cox, Robert W., 1926- Production, power, and world order . New York , 1987. xii, 500 p. ; ISBN 0-231-05808-X LC Card 86-26387
HD6971 .C78 1987

INDUSTRIAL RELATIONS - HUNGARY.

The Trade union situation and industrial relations in Hungary . Geneva , 1984. 100 p. ; ISBN 92-2-103894-7 *NYPL [JLE 85-1780]*

INDUSTRIAL RELATIONS - HUNGARY - CASE STUDIES.

Héthy, Lajos. Patterns of worker's behavior and the enterprise /. New Brunswick, U. S.A. , c1987. p. cm. ISBN 0-88738-177-4 LC Card 87-13958 DDC 331/.0471/09439 19
HD6956.M5 H47 1987

Industrial relations in Europe : the imperatives of change / edited by B.C. Roberts. London ; Dover, N.H. : C. Helm, c1985. ix, 277 p. ; 22 cm. Includes index. ISBN 0-7099-4212-5 : LC Card 85-21321 DDC 331/.094 19
1. Industrial relations - Europe - Addresses, essays, lectures. 2. Trade-unions - Europe - Political activity - Addresses, essays, lectures. I. Roberts, B. C. (Benjamin Charles), 1917-.
HD8376.5 .I54 1985 ***NYPL [JLD 86-1065]***

Industrial relations in India . Asdhir, Vijay, 1947- New Delhi , c1987. 376 p. ; LC Card 86-903540 DDC 331.89/2877/00954552 19
HD8686.5 .A85 1987

Industrial relations in public enterprises /. Mathur, Reeta. Jaipur , 1986. vii, 226 p. ; LC Card 86-902265 DDC 331/.04135454 19
HD6976.I52 M37 1986

Industrial relations in West Germany /. Berghahn, Volker Rolf. Leamington Spa, UK ; New York : p. cm. ISBN 0-907582-64-8 : LC Card 87-9359 DDC 331/.0943 19
HD8451 .B45 1988

Industrial relations in West Germany . Streeck, Wolfgang, 1946- London , 1984. 178 p. ; ISBN 0-435-83839-3 LC Card 87-673421
HD6698.A8 S77x 1984b

INDUSTRIAL RELATIONS - INDIA.
Asdhir, Vijay, 1947- Industrial relations in India . New Delhi , c1987. 376 p. ; LC Card 86-903540 DDC 331.89/2877/00954552 19
HD8686.5 .A85 1987

Industrial relations . New Delhi , 1986. 254 p. ; LC Card 87-902682
HD8686.5.I575 1978

Madhusudhana Rao, M. Labour management relations and trade union leadership . New Delhi , c1986. 392 p. ; LC Card 86-903198 DDC 331/.0954 19
HD6812 .M23 1986

Mathur, Reeta. Industrial relations in public enterprises /. Jaipur , 1986. vii, 226 p. ; LC Card 86-902265 DDC 331/.04135454 19
HD6976.I52 M37 1986

INDUSTRIAL RELATIONS - INDIA - ANDHRA PRADESH.
Saibaba, G. Labour conditions in the mining industry of Andhra Pradesh . Tirupati [1985?] v, 314 p. ; LC Card 86-901021 DDC 331/.0422/095484 19
HD8039.M61 I47 1985
NYPL [JLD 87-1057]

INDUSTRIAL RELATIONS - INDIA - PUNJAB.
Asdhir, Vijay, 1947- Industrial relations in India . New Delhi , c1987. 376 p. ; LC Card 86-903540 DDC 331.89/2877/00954552 19
HD8686.5 .A85 1987

INDUSTRIAL RELATIONS - ITALY.
Nacamulli, Raoul C. D. La razionalità contrattata . Bologna , c1986. 166 p. : ISBN 88-15-01189-7 : LC Card 87-122104
HD6709 .N296 1986

Pirzio Ammassari, Gloria. I sindacalisti . Bari , c1982. 155 p. ; LC Card 82-131644 DDC 331.87/33/0945 19
HD6709 .P57 1982 ***NYPL [JLD 86-2840]***

Relazioni industriali nell'impresa degli anni '80 . Roma , 1985. 308 p. ; LC Card 86-192682
HD8481 .R45 1985

INDUSTRIAL RELATIONS - ITALY - ADDRESSES, ESSAYS, LECTURES.
Economic crisis, trade unions, and the state /. London , Dover, N.H. , c1986. 295 p. ; ISBN 0-7099-1447-4 : LC Card 85-28055 DDC 331/.094 19
HD8391 .E26 1986 ***NYPL [JLD 86-1301]***

La Vertenza sul costo del lavoro e le relazioni industriali /. Milano, Italy , c1984. 243 p. : LC Card 84-144150 DDC 338.5/1/0945 19
HD5034 .V47 1984 ***NYPL [JLD 86-2858]***

Ricerca sociale e movimento operaio . Milano , c1982. 294 p. ; LC Card 82-246648 DDC 331/.0945 19
HD8481 .R53 1982 ***NYPL [JLD 86-3380]***

INDUSTRIAL RELATIONS - ITALY - CASE STUDIES.
Industrial relations and technical change in the British, Italian, and German automobile industry . Berlin [1985] 1 v. (various pagings) : LC Card 86-206613 DDC 338/.04292/094 19
HD6976.A82 G75 1985

INDUSTRIAL RELATIONS - JAMAICA.
Phillip, George J. A-Z of industrial relations practices at the workplace /. Kingston, Jamaica , 1987. xiii, 122 p. : ISBN 976-625-009-X (pbk.) LC Card 87-403438 DDC 331/.097292 19
HD6971 .P46 1987

INDUSTRIAL RELATIONS - JAPAN.
Callies, Albane. France-Japon . Paris , 1986. 208 p. ; ISBN 2-86563-129-X LC Card 86-165719
HD8431 .C35 1986

Koike, Kazuo, 1932- Understanding industrial relations in modern Japan /. New York , 1987. p. cm. ISBN 0-312-01301-9 : LC Card 87-24068 DDC 331/.0952 19
HD8726.5 .K548 1987

Labor unions and labor-management relations. Tokyo, Japan , 1986. 48 p. : ISBN 4-538-74002-0 : LC Card 86-220438 DDC 331/.0952 19
HD8726.5 .L33 1986

INDUSTRIAL RELATIONS - JAPAN - CONGRESSES.
Japanese and Australian labour markets . Canberra [c1983] xx, 610 p. : ISBN 0-86413-004-X (pbk.) : LC Card 84-220557 DDC 331.12/0952 19
HD5850.A6 J36 1983 ***NYPL [JLE 86-630]***

INDUSTRIAL RELATIONS - JAPAN - HISTORY.
Garon, Sheldon. The state and labor in modern Japan /. Berkeley , c1987. xvi, 326 p. ; ISBN 0-520-05983-2 (alk. paper) LC Card 86-30890 DDC 331/.0952 19
HD8726 .G37 1987

INDUSTRIAL RELATIONS - JAPAN - HISTORY - 19TH CENTURY.
Gordon, Andrew, 1952- The evolution of labor relations in Japan . Cambridge, Mass. , 1985. xvi, 524 p. : ISBN 0-674-27130-0 (Harvard Univ. Pr.) LC Card 85-3747 DDC 331/.0952 19
HD8726 .G67 1985 ***NYPL [M-11 435 v.117]***

INDUSTRIAL RELATIONS - JAPAN - HISTORY - 20TH CENTURY.
Gordon, Andrew, 1952- The evolution of labor relations in Japan . Cambridge, Mass. , 1985. xvi, 524 p. : ISBN 0-674-27130-0 (Harvard Univ. Pr.) LC Card 85-3747 DDC 331/.0952 19
HD8726 .G67 1985 ***NYPL [M-11 435 v.117]***

INDUSTRIAL RELATIONS - LATIN AMERICA.
Relaciones colectivas del trabajo en América Latina. Portuguese. As relações coletivas de trabalho na América Latina . São Paulo . 327 p. ; LC Card 87-151930 DDC 331/.098 19
HD8110.5 .R3817 1985

INDUSTRIAL RELATIONS - NEW ZEALAND - CANTERBURY - HISTORY.
Christie, Alan R. An account of major activities in the Canterbury Labour and Trades Council District, 1929-1936 /. [Wellington] , 1980. 38, [3] p. ; LC Card 81-120047
HD8930.5.Z8 C3623 1980

INDUSTRIAL RELATIONS - NEW ZEALAND - CONGRESSES.
Industrial relations . [Wellington] , 1986. ii, 71 p. ; LC Card 86-212248 DDC 331/.09931 19
HD8930.5 .I52 1986

INDUSTRIAL RELATIONS - NIGERIA.
Contemporary problems in Nigerian industrial relations /. Lagos, Nigeria , 1986. xii, 150 p. ; ISBN 978-252-200-7 LC Card 87-139560 DDC 331/.09669 19
HD8831 .C65 1986

Mesfin Gabre Michael. Labour-management relations in public enterprises in Africa. Geneva, Switzerland , 1983. 84 p. ; ISBN 92-2-103009-1 (pbk.) LC Card 86-213649 DDC 658.3 s 331/.04135/000096 19
HD6961.A1 I73 no. 60 HD8776.5

INDUSTRIAL RELATIONS - NOVA SCOTIA.
Currie, Lawrence A., 1949- A time for change . Halifax, N.S. , c1986. 64 p. : ISBN 0-88926-031-1 (pbk.) LC Card 86-230034 DDC 331.89/281388322 19
HD5329.M82 1979 .D543 1986

Industrial Relations Research Association.
Working women . Washington, D.C. , c1987. xxii, 419 p. ; ISBN 0-87179-547-7 LC Card 87-9410 DDC 331.4/0973 19
HD6095 .W742 1987

Industrial Relations Research Centre monograph, 0729-2627.
Markey, Ray. The trade union response to technological change in Australia /. Kensington, N.S.W. , 1983. iii, 56 p. ;
NYPL [JLE 87-904]

INDUSTRIAL RELATIONS - SIERRA LEONE.
Sierra Leone. Taju-Deen Commission of Inquiry. Report of the Taju-Deen Commission of Inquiry into the status, administration, and activities of the Sierra Leone Labour Congress from 1976 following the amalgamation of the then Sierra Leone Labour Congress and the Sierra Leone Council of Labour, and to inquire into all aspects of industrial relations in Sierra Leone and to make recommendations for any improvements which it may consider necessary. [Freetown] [198-] vi, 149 leaves ; LC Card 87-118833
HD8833.A5 S57 1980

INDUSTRIAL RELATIONS - SOUTH AFRICA.
Behaviour in organisations . Johannesburg , New York , 1986, c1983. 924 p. : ISBN 0-07-450690-0 (pbk.) : LC Card 87-113321 DDC 158.7/0968 19
HD58.7 .B426 1986

Gouws, P. A. (Pieter Andries), 1949- Arbeidsverhoudinge in Suid-Afrika /. Pretoria , 1986. 127 p. ; ISBN 0-627-01492-5 : LC Card 87-127172
HD8801 .G66 1986

INDUSTRIAL RELATIONS - SOUTH AFRICA - KIMBERLEY - HISTORY.
Turrell, Robert Vicat. Capital and labour on the Kimberley diamond fields, 1871-1890 /. Cambridge [Cambridgeshire] , New York , 1987. xviii, 297 p. : ISBN 0-521-33354-7 LC Card 86-32740 DDC 331.7/622382/0968711 19
HD9677.S63 K567 1987

INDUSTRIAL RELATIONS - SOVIET UNION.
Grancelli, Bruno, 1943- Le relazioni industriali di tipo sovietico . Milano, Italy , c1986. 337 p. ; LC Card 86-222589
HD8526.5 .G73 1986

Grancelli, Bruno, 1943- Soviet management and labor relations /. Boston , c1988. xvi, 248 p. ; ISBN 0-04-497040-4 : LC Card 87-11516 DDC 331/.0947 19
HD8526.5 .G74 1988

INDUSTRIAL RELATIONS - SOVIET UNION - HISTORY.
Siegelbaum, Lewis H. Stakhanovism and the politics of productivity in the USSR, 1935-1941 /. Cambridge , New York , 1988. xv, 326 p. : ISBN 0-521-34548-0 LC Card 87-25605 DDC 331.11/8/0947 19
HC340.S6 S515 1988

INDUSTRIAL RELATIONS - SPAIN.
The Trade union situation and industrial relations in Spain . Geneva , 1985. xiii, 138 p. : ISBN 92-2-105202-8 (pbk.) : LC Card 86-207841 DDC 331.88/0946 19
HD6762 .T68 1985

INDUSTRIAL RELATIONS - SRI LANKA.
Labour standards in Sri Lanka . [Colombo] , 1981. x, 164 p. ; LC Card 83-902877 DDC 331/.09549/3 19
HD8670.8 .L32 1981 ***NYPL [JLC 87-22]***

INDUSTRIAL RELATIONS - SWEDEN.
Towards a democratic rationality . Aldershot, Hants, England , Brookfield, Vt., USA , c1986. xi, 281 p. : ISBN 0-566-00761-4 : LC Card 86-14241 DDC 331/.09485 19
HD8576.5 .T69 1986 ***NYPL [JLD 86-3873]***

INDUSTRIAL RELATIONS - SWEDEN - CASE STUDIES.

Auer, Peter. Industrial relations, work organisation and new technology . Berlin [1985] 17, [6] p. ; LC Card 86-205891 DDC 331/.04292/09481 19
HD9710.S84 V6413 1985

INDUSTRIAL RELATIONS - TUNISIA.
Mesfin Gabre Michael. Labour-management relations in public enterprises in Africa. Geneva, Switzerland , 1983. 84 p. ; ISBN 92-2-103009-1 (pbk.) LC Card 86-213649 DDC 658.3 s 331/.04135/000096 19
HD6961.A1 I73 no. 60 HD8776.5

INDUSTRIAL RELATIONS - UNITED STATES.
Allen, Robert E. (Robert Edward), 1946- Contemporary labor relations /. Reading, Mass. , c1988. xi, 724 p. : ISBN 0-201-10083-5 : LC Card 87-24128 DDC 331/.0973 19
HD8072.5 .A43 1988

Balliet, Lee. Survey of labor relations /. Washington, D.C. , c1981. ix, 198 p. : ISBN 0-87179-347-4 LC Card 80-26863 DDC 331/.0973
HD8072.5 .B34 ***NYPL [JLE 86-4719]***

Balliet, Lee. Survey of labor relations /. Washington, D.C. , c1987. xi, 212 p. : ISBN 0-87179-544-2 (pbk.) LC Card 87-864 DDC 331/.0973 19
HD8072.5 .B34 1987

Cohen-Rosenthal, Edward. Mutual gains . New York , 1987. xv, 287 p. : ISBN 0-275-92204-9 (alk. paper) : LC Card 86-25249 DDC 331/.01/12 19
HD6490.L33 C64 1987

Forging new relationships among business, labor, and government /. Greenwich, Conn. , c1986. xiii, 210 p. ; ISBN 0-89232-656-5 : LC Card 86-2839 DDC 338.973 19
HD3616.U47 F583 1986 ***NYPL [JLE 86-3452]***

The Future directions of employee relations /. Los Angeles, Calif. , c1985. xiv, 418 p. : ISBN 0-89215-132-3 (pbk.) LC Card 86-622936 DDC 331/.0973 19
HD8072.5 .F87 1985

Holley, William H. The labor relations process /. Chicago , c1988. xix, 714 p. : ISBN 0-03-012649-5 LC Card 87-9117 DDC 658.3/15/0973 19
HD8072.5 .H64 1988

Holoviak, Stephen J. Managing human productivity . New York , 1987. xiii, 216 p. : ISBN 0-275-92481-5 (alk. paper) : LC Card 86-25247 DDC 658.3/14 19
HF5549.2.U5 H65 1987

Lehr, Richard I. The new unionism . New York, N.Y. , c1987. 114 p. ; ISBN 0-88057-672-3 (pbk.) LC Card 86-82864 DDC 331.88/0973 19
HD6508 .L427 1987

Moral rights in the workplace /. Albany , c1987. xii, 312 p. ; ISBN 0-88706-362-4 LC Card 86-6949 DDC 331.25 19
HD6957.U6 M67 1987 ***NYPL [JLE 87-1197]***

Perry, Charles R. Union corporate campaigns /. Philadelphia, Pa. , c1987. viii, 211 p. : ISBN 0-89546-065-3 : LC Card 86-82727 DDC 331.89/12 19
HD6490.O72 U665 1987

Sandver, Marcus H. Labor relations . Boston , c1987. xxii, 529 p. : ISBN 0-316-77024-8 LC Card 86-27314 DDC 331/.0973 19
HD8072.5 .S32 1987

Sauer, Robert L. Labor relations . Columbus, Ohio , c1987. x, 518 p. : ISBN 0-675-20207-8 LC Card 87-134391 DDC 331/.0973 19
HD8066 .S28 1987

Sloane, Arthur A. Labor relations /. Englewood Cliffs, N.J. , c1988. xiv, 543 p. : ISBN 0-13-519604-3 LC Card 87-14535 DDC 331.89/0973 19
HD8072 .S6185 1988

Teamwork, joint labor-management programs in America /. New York , 1986. xvi, 199 p. : ISBN 0-08-032799-0 : LC Card 85-28397 DDC 331.01/12/0973 19
HD8072.5 .T43 1986 ***NYPL [JLE 86-3139]***

Wolters, Roger S. Labor relations . Chicago , c1988. xi, 321 p. ; ISBN 0-03-069304-7 (pbk.) LC Card 87-19941 DDC 331 19
HD8072.5 .W65 1988

Workers, managers, and technological change . New York , c1987. xxii, 362 p. : ISBN 0-306-42450-9 LC Card 87-2327 DDC 331/.0973 19
HD6331.2.U5 W67 1987

Wren, Daniel A. White collar hobo . Ames , 1987. xii, 165 p. : ISBN 0-8138-1922-9 LC Card 87-4048 DDC 331/.092/4 B 19
HD8073.W47 W74 1987

INDUSTRIAL RELATIONS - UNITED STATES - ADDRESSES, ESSAYS, LECTURES.
Labor-management cooperation . [Washington, D.C.?] , 1984. v, 77 p. ; LC Card 85-602044 DDC 331.01/12/0973 19
HD6490.L332 U55 1984
NYPL [JLF 86-559]

INDUSTRIAL RELATIONS - UNITED STATES - CASE STUDIES.
Grenier, Guillermo J. Inhuman relations . Philadelphia , 1988. xx, 232 p. ; ISBN 0-87722-502-8 (alk. paper) : LC Card 87-10116 DDC 331.25 19
HD6490.O72 U645 1988

Wolters, Roger S. Labor relations . Chicago , c1988. xi, 321 p. ; ISBN 0-03-069304-7 (pbk.) LC Card 87-19941 DDC 331 19
HD8072.5 .W65 1988

INDUSTRIAL RELATIONS - UNITED STATES - CONGRESSES.
The Future directions of employee relations /. Los Angeles, Calif. , c1985. xiv, 418 p. ; ISBN 0-89215-132-3 ***NYPL [JLD 86-3596]***

INDUSTRIAL RELATIONS - UNITED STATES - HISTORY.
Balfour, Alan. Union-management relations in a changing economy /. Englewood Cliffs, N.J. , c1987. xiv, 482 p. : ISBN 0-13-938804-4 LC Card 86-30495 DDC 331/.0973 19
HD8066 .B34 1987

Filippelli, Ronald L. Labor in the USA . New York , c1984. xii, 315 p. ; ISBN 0-394-34149-X LC Card 83-23458 DDC 331/.0973 19
HD8066 .F54 1984 ***NYPL [JFE 86-5130]***

Harris, Howell John, 1951- The right to manage . Madison, Wis. , 1982. ix, 296 p. ; ISBN 0-299-08640-2 : LC Card 81-69820 DDC 331./0973 19
HD8072 .H2874 ***NYPL [JLE 86-4147]***

Rogulev, I͡U. N. (I͡Uriĭ Nikolaevich) Krakh rabocheĭ politiki administrat͡sii Trumėna . Moskva , 1981. 135 p. ; LC Card 82-155486
HD8072.5 .R64 1981

INDUSTRIAL RELATIONS - UNITED STATES - HISTORY - 20TH CENTURY.
Kochan, Thomas A. The transformation of American industrial relations /. New York , c1986. viii, 287 p. ; ISBN 0-465-08696-9 : LC Card 85-47502 DDC 331/.0973 19
HD8072 .K67 1986

Industrial relations, work organisation and new technology . Auer, Peter. Berlin [1985] 17, [6] p. ; LC Card 86-205891 DDC 331/.04292/09481 19
HD9710.S84 V6413 1985

INDUSTRIAL RESEARCH. see **RESEARCH, INDUSTRIAL.**

An Industrial research and development and marketing package for Australia : report of the 36th Meeting of the Science and Industry Forum, held in Sydney, October 6 and 7, 1984 / rapporteur and editor, C.D. Kimpton. [Canberra?] : Australian Academy of Science, [1984] 48, 4 leaves : ill. ; 30 cm. (Report / Science and Industry Forum . no. 20) LC Card 87-153477 DDC 338/.06 19
1. Technological innovations - Economic aspects - Australia - Congresses. 2. Research, Industrial - Australia - Congresses. 3. Technology - Australia - Marketing - Congresses. I. Kimpton, C. D. II. Australian Academy of Science. Science and Industry Forum. III. Series: Report (Australian Academy of Science. Science and Industry Forum) , no. 20.
HC610.T4 I53 1984

Industrial restructuring. International capitalism and industrial restructuring . Boston , 1987. p. cm. ISBN 0-04-338132-4 (alk. paper) LC Card 86-28870 DDC 338.7 19
HD2321 .I58 1987

INDUSTRIAL REVOLUTION. see **INDUSTRY - HISTORY.**

Industrial robots market. New York, N.Y. : Frost & Sullivan, <c1983- > v. <2 > ; 29 cm. "March 1983." "A1128." LC Card 87-166012 DDC 381/.45629892 19
1. Robot industry - United States. 2. Robots, Industrial. 3. Market surveys - United States. I. Frost & Sullivan.
HD9696.R623 U634 1983

Industrial robots market in Europe. New York, N.Y. : Frost & Sullivan, c1983. vi, 320 p. : ill. ; 29 cm. "March 1983." "E597." LC Card 87-141842 DDC 380.1/45629892 19
1. Robot industry - Europe. 2. Market surveys - Europe. I. Frost & Sullivan.
HD9696.R623 E854 1983

INDUSTRIAL SAFETY - ADDRESSES, ESSAYS, LECTURES.
Human aspects in office automation /. Amsterdam , New York , 1984. xv, 322 p. : ISBN 0-444-42327-3 : LC Card 84-5917 DDC 363.1/19651 19
HF5547.5 .H85 1984 ***NYPL [JLF 86-892]***

INDUSTRIAL SAFETY - BRAZIL.
Hausen, Ivan Zanoni. Segurança empresarial . Brasília, Distrito Federal , 1979. 157 p. : LC Card 82-100947
HD7683 .H38 1979

INDUSTRIAL SAFETY - CALIFORNIA.
Schaefer, Andrew. CAL-OSHA routine compliance inspections . [Sacramento, CA , 1986] 25 p. ; LC Card 86-622709 DDC 363.1/164/09796 19
HD7262.5.U62 C573 1986

INDUSTRIAL SAFETY - FINLAND.
Riikonen, Eila. Työnteon turvallisuus . Tampere , 19. x, 131, [66] p. : ISBN 951-860-009-0 LC Card 86-222051
HD7262.5.F5 R55 1986

Työsuojelu kunnissa ja kuntainliitoissa. Swedish. Arbetarskyddet inom kommuner och kommunalförbund /. [Helsinki] [1983] 137 p. : LC Card 83-229126
HD7727.3 .T94618 1983

INDUSTRIAL SAFETY - GERMANY, WEST.
Arnold, Alix, 1956- Kaputt und auch noch selber schuld . Reinbek bei Hamburg , c1986. 179, [1] p. : ISBN 3-499-15908-2 : LC Card 86-226114
HD7708 .A75 1986

Ochs, Peter. Analyse und Bewertung ausgewählter sozialwissenschaftlichen Forschungen /. Dortmund , Bremerhaven , 1983. 102 p. ; ISBN 3-88314-245-X LC Card 83-207278
HD7708 .O28 1983

INDUSTRIAL SAFETY - GERMANY (WEST) - DIRECTORIES.
Dienststellenverzeichnis Arbeitsschutz . Dortmund , Bremerhaven , 1983. 217 p. ; ISBN 3-88314-274-3 LC Card 83-196051
HD7708 .D55 1983

INDUSTRIAL SAFETY - GERMANY (WEST) - STATISTICS.
Arbeitssicherheit '86 . Bonn [1986] 47, 46, 22 p. : LC Card 87-409083 DDC 363.1/12/0943 19
HD7708 .A7 1986

INDUSTRIAL SAFETY - GREAT BRITAIN.
Inspecting industry . London , 1986. 110 p. ; ISBN 0-11-751910-3 (pbk.) : LC Card 87-164869 DDC 363.1/1/0941 19
HD7695 .I63 1986

INDUSTRIAL SAFETY - HUNGARY.
A Munkavédelem agitációs és propaganda rendszere /. Budapest , 1983. 51 p. : ISBN 963-7006-04-4 LC Card 85-110318
HD7702.5 .M85 1983

INDUSTRIAL SAFETY - KOREA (SOUTH)
International Labour Organisation. National Institute of Labour Science (NILS) (preparatory assistance), Republic of Korea . Geneva , 1976. 43 p. ; ISBN 92-2-101617-X (pbk.) LC Card 84-145790
HD7758 .I58 1976

INDUSTRIAL SAFETY - LAW AND LEGISLATION - BRAZIL.
Costa, Marcia Regina da. As vítimas do

capital . Rio de Janeiro , 1981. 117 p. ; LC Card 82-149102
HD7262.5.B7 C67 1981
NYPL [JLD 86-2852]

Hausen, Ivan Zanoni. Segurança empresarial . Brasília, Distrito Federal , 1979. 157 p. : LC Card 82-100947
HD7683 .H38 1979

INDUSTRIAL SAFETY - LAW AND LEGISLATION - NETHERLANDS.
Advies samenloop Wet OR en ARBO-wet . Den Haag [1986] 37 p. ; ISBN 90-6587-243-4 LC Card 87-104667
HC321 .S63 1986, nr. 6 KKM1430

INDUSTRIAL SAFETY - LAW AND LEGISLATION - SWEDEN.
Nordfors, Lennart. Makten hälsan och vinsten . Lund, Sweden , c1985. 195 p. : ISBN 91-44-23331-0 : LC Card 85-204849
HD7732 .N66 1985

INDUSTRIAL SAFETY - LAW AND LEGISLATION - UNITED STATES - COMPLIANCE COSTS.
Gray, Wayne B. (Wayne Burger), 1955- Productivity versus OSHA and EPA regulations /. Ann Arbor, Mich. , c1986. xii, p. : ISBN 0-8357-1721-6 (alk. paper) LC Card 85-28873 DDC 338/.06/0973 19
HC110.I52 G73 1986 *NYPL [JLE 86-2375]*

INDUSTRIAL SAFETY - MANAGEMENT.
The BBP safety management handbook. Waterford, CT , c1986. 1 v. (various pagings) : ISBN 0-87622-050-2 LC Card 87-119198 DDC 658.3/82 19
HD7262 .B38 1986

INDUSTRIAL SAFETY - SOCIETIES, ETC. - DIRECTORIES.
Conditions of work and quality of working life . Geneva , 1986. xxi, 306 p. ; ISBN 92-2-105328-8 (pbk.) : LC Card 86-215659 DDC 306/.36/025 19
HD7260 .C64 1986

INDUSTRIAL SAFETY - SWEDEN.
Nordfors, Lennart. Makten hälsan och vinsten . Lund, Sweden , c1985. 195 p. : ISBN 91-44-23331-0 : LC Card 85-204849
HD7732 .N66 1985

INDUSTRIAL SAFETY - SWITZERLAND.
Sécurité et santé au travail . Berne [1984] 47 p. ; LC Card 85-176432 DDC 363.1/1/09494 19
HD7740 .S43 1984

INDUSTRIAL SAFETY - UNITED STATES.
Irwin, Michael H. K. Risks to health and safety on the job /. New York, NY , c1986. 28 p. : ISBN 0-88291-096-5 (pbk.) : LC Card 87-402515 DDC 363.1/1/0973 19
HD7654 .I79 1986

Noble, Charles, 1948- Liberalism at work . Philadelphia , 1986. x, 292 p. : ISBN 0-87722-421-8 (alk. paper) : LC Card 86-1766 DDC 353.0083/0289 19
HD7654 .N63 1986 *NYPL [JLE 86-4426]*

INDUSTRIAL SAFETY - UNITED STATES - MANAGEMENT.
Modern job safety and health /. Paramus, N.J. , c1987- 1 v. (loose-leaf) : LC Card 87-403957 DDC 363.1/1/068 19
HD6067.2.U6 M63 1987

Industrial sickness : the challenge in Indian textiles / edited by V. Padaki, V. Shanbhag. Ahmedabad : Chimanlal Lalbhai Centre for Management, Ahmedabad Textile Industry's Research Association, c1984. xv, 459 p. ; 23 cm. "Including the proceedings of the Seminar, The Challenge of Sickness in the Textile Industry sponsored by Industrial Development Bank of India." Bibliography: p. 389-451. LC Card 87-902007 DDC 363.1/19677/00954 19
1. Textile industry - India - Ahmadābād - Congresses. 2. Business mortality - India - Ahmadābād - Congresses. I. Padaki, V. (Vijay). II. Shanbhag, V. (Vinod). III. Chimanlal Lalbhai Centre for Management. IV. Seminar: the Challenge of Sickness in the Textile Industry (1983 : Ahmadābād, India). V. Industrial Development Bank of India.
HD9866.I63 A385 1984

Industrial sickness and key areas of management . Dave, Nalini V. New Delhi , c1987. 523 p. : LC Card 87-901105 DDC 658/.00954/75 19
HD2747 .D32 1987

INDUSTRIAL SITES - GREAT BRITAIN.
Fothergill, Steve. Property and industrial development /. London , Wolfeboro, N.H. , 1987. 187 p. : ISBN 0-09-170741-2 (pbk.) : LC Card 87-2627 DDC 333.3/8/0941 19
HD598 .F68 1987

INDUSTRIAL SITES - UNITED STATES - LOCATION.
National emerging industries site selection guide /. Minneapolis, MN , c1986. 124 p. ; LC Card 86-231272 DDC 338.6/042/02573 19
HC110.D5 N38 1986

Industrial sociology . Travail et sa sociologie. English. London , Newbury Park, Calif. , 1987. xvi, 184 p. ; ISBN 0-8039-8053-1 LC Card 87-50308 DDC 306/.36/0944 19
HD6957.F8 T7313 1987

INDUSTRIAL SOCIOLOGY - ADDRESSES, ESSAYS, LECTURES.
Confrontation, class consciousness, and the labor process . Westport, Conn. , 1986. viii, 261 p. ; ISBN 0-313-25140-1 (lib. bdg. : alk. paper) LC Card 85-17734 DDC 305.5/62 19
HD4851 .C63 1986 *NYPL [JLE 86-3558]*

INDUSTRIAL SOCIOLOGY - AUSTRIA - HISTORY.
Historische Wurzeln der Sozialpartnerschaft /. München , 1986. 368 p. ; ISBN 3-486-52971-4 LC Card 87-146580 DDC 306/.36/09436 19
HD6957.A9 H57 1986

INDUSTRIAL SOCIOLOGY - BULGARIA.
Kupriīanov, L. A. (Leonid Aleksandrovich) Sotsial′noe planirovanie na predpriīatiīakh NRB, GDR i ChSSR /. Leningrad , 1984. 111 p. ; LC Card 85-116781
HD7741.5 .K86 1984

Petkov, Krŭst′o. Sotsiologiīa na trudoviīa kolektiv . Sofiīa , 1982. 184 p. ; LC Card 83-124278
HD6957.B85 P47 1982
*NYPL [*QK 86-4733]*

INDUSTRIAL SOCIOLOGY - CANADA - ADDRESSES, ESSAYS, LECTURES.
Working Canadians . Toronto , New York , c1984. x, 380 p. ; ISBN 0-458-97370-X (pbk.) : LC Card 84-222036 DDC 331/.0971 19
HD6957.C2 W67 1984 *NYPL [JLD 87-681]*

INDUSTRIAL SOCIOLOGY - CASE STUDIES.
Automation and industrial workers . Oxford [Oxfordshire] , New York , 1979- v. : ISBN 0-08-023339-2 (v. 1, pt. 1) : LC Card 79-40811 DDC 331
HD6331 .A93 1979 *NYPL [JLM 82-242]*

Work in market and industrial societies /. Albany , c1984. viii, 316 p. ; ISBN 0-87395-810-1 LC Card 83-9267 DDC 306/.36 19
HD4901 .A659 1984 *NYPL [JLE 86-4483]*

INDUSTRIAL SOCIOLOGY - CZECHOSLOVAKIA.
Kupriīanov, L. A. (Leonid Aleksandrovich) Sotsial′noe planirovanie na predpriīatiīakh NRB, GDR i ChSSR /. Leningrad , 1984. 111 p. ; LC Card 85-116781
HD7741.5 .K86 1984

INDUSTRIAL SOCIOLOGY - EUROPE, EASTERN.
Matejko, Aleksander. Comparative work systems . New York , 1986. xx, 237 p. ; ISBN 0-03-004492-8 (alk. paper) : LC Card 85-6354 DDC 306/.36/0947 19
HD6957.E82 M37 1985
NYPL [JLE 86-1083]

INDUSTRIAL SOCIOLOGY - FRANCE.
La Rosa, Michele, 1937- La sociologia del lavoro in Italia e in Francia /. Milano [1979] 149 p. ; ISBN 88-20-41594-1 : LC Card 79-374935
HD6957.I83 L37 *NYPL [JLD 80-4048]*

Naville, Pierre. La maîtrise du salariat /. Paris , c1984. 153 p. ; ISBN 2-7157-1099-2 : LC Card 85-100916
HD6957.F8 N38 1984 *NYPL [JLD 87-333]*

Travail et sa sociologie. English. Industrial sociology . London , Newbury Park, Calif. , 1987. xvi, 184 p. ; ISBN 0-8039-8053-1 LC Card 87-50308 DDC 306/.36/0944 19
HD6957.F8 T7313 1987

INDUSTRIAL SOCIOLOGY - FRANCE - HISTORY.
Spurk, Jan. Soziologie der französischen Arbeiterbewegung /. Berlin , c1986. 317 p. ; ISBN 3-88619-606-2 LC Card 87-235004 DDC 331.88/0944 19
HD6684 .S68 1986

INDUSTRIAL SOCIOLOGY - GERMANY (EAST)
Kupriīanov, L. A. (Leonid Aleksandrovich) Sotsial′noe planirovanie na predpriīatiīakh NRB, GDR i ChSSR /. Leningrad , 1984. 111 p. ; LC Card 85-116781
HD7741.5 .K86 1984

INDUSTRIAL SOCIOLOGY - GERMANY, WEST.
Ahrens, Gerhard, 1939- Staatsverschuldung ohne Ende? /. Hamburg [1984] 37 leaves ; LC Card 85-166341
HJ8650 .A37 1984

Burian, Klaus. Betriebliche Erfahrungen mit neuen Arbeitszeitformen . Berlin [1984] iv, 162 p. ; LC Card 84-182592
HD5110.2.G3 B87 1984

Elsenau, Detlef von. Arbeitnehmerorientierte Sozialforschung . Münster [1986] ii, 233 p. ; ISBN 3-88660-246-X LC Card 86-200305
HD6957.G3 E59 1986

Haag, Ingeborg. Arbeitskommunikation, Kommunikationsarbeit . Berlin , 1986. viii, 258 p. ; ISBN 3-923024-08-8 LC Card 86-226373
HD6957.G35 H33 1986

Klipstein, Michael von. Der Überdruss am Überfluss . München , c1984. 212 p. : ISBN 3-7892-7194-2 LC Card 84-174408
HD6957.G35 K56 1984

Löffler, Reiner. Macht, Arbeit und Humanität . Göttingen , c1986. v, 563 p. ; ISBN 3-921969-12-3 LC Card 86-227215
HD6957.G3 L64 1986

Uvarov, V. P. (Vladimir Pavlovich) Ėkonomicheskoe soupravlenie . Minsk , 1985. 159 p. ; LC Card 85-217045
HD5660.G4 U93 1985

Voss, G. Günter. Bewusstsein ohne Subjekt? . Grosshesselohe , 1984. vi, 512 p. : ISBN 3-924346-07-0 : LC Card 85-131494
HD6957.G35 V67 1984

INDUSTRIAL SOCIOLOGY - GERMANY (WEST) - CONGRESSES.
Das Unternehmen als Grösse der Arbeitswelt . Bonn , 1984. 291 p. ; ISBN 3-923202-02-4 LC Card 85-119845
HD6957.G3 U58 1984

INDUSTRIAL SOCIOLOGY - GREAT BRITAIN.
Ashton, D. N. Unemployment under capitalism . Brighton, Sussex , 1986. xiv, 225 p. : ISBN 0-7108-0163-7
NYPL [JLD 86-1049]

INDUSTRIAL SOCIOLOGY - GREAT BRITAIN - CASE STUDIES.
Harris, Rosemary. Power and powerlessness in industry . London , New York , 1987. viii, 245 p. : ISBN 0-422-60920-X LC Card 86-14420 DDC 338.4/766134/0941 19
HD6956.A497 H37 1986
NYPL [JLD 87-825]

INDUSTRIAL SOCIOLOGY - HUNGARY.
Makó, Csaba. A társadalmi viszonyok erőtere, a munkafolyamat /. Budapest , 1985. 192 p. ; ISBN 963-221-528-1 : LC Card 86-187344
HF5549 .M2953 1985

INDUSTRIAL SOCIOLOGY - HUNGARY - CASE STUDIES.
Héthy, Lajos. Patterns of worker's behavior and the enterprise /. New Brunswick, U. S.A. , c1987. p. cm. ISBN 0-88738-177-4 LC Card 87-13958 DDC 331/.0471/09439 19
HD6956.M5 H47 1987

INDUSTRIAL SOCIOLOGY - ITALY.
La Rosa, Michele, 1937- La sociologia del lavoro in Italia e in Francia /. Milano [1979] 149 p. ; ISBN 88-20-41594-1 : LC Card 79-374935
HD6957.I83 L37 *NYPL [JLD 80-4048]*

INDUSTRIAL SOCIOLOGY - ITALY - ADDRESSES, ESSAYS, LECTURES.
Ricerca sociale e movimento operaio . Milano , c1982. 294 p. ; LC Card 82-246648 DDC

331/.0945 19
HD8481 .R53 1982 ***NYPL [JLD 86-3380]***

INDUSTRIAL SOCIOLOGY - NETHERLANDS.
Autonomie als arbeidssociologisch vraagstuk . Zeist , 1987. 237 p. : ISBN 90-6720-032-8 : LC Card 87-169950
HD5660.N4 A94 1987

INDUSTRIAL SOCIOLOGY - RESEARCH - METHODOLOGY.
Manuale di ricerca sul lavoro e sulle organizzazioni /. Roma , 1985. 384 p. : LC Card 86-118313 DDC 306/.36/072 19
HD4824 .M32 1985 ***NYPL [JLD 87-1160]***

INDUSTRIAL SOCIOLOGY - RUSSIAN S.F.S.R. - URAL MOUNTAINS REGION - CONGRESSES.
Kardinal′nyĭ rost ėffektivnosti zhivogo truda--glavnyĭ faktor uskoreniia sotsial′no-ėkonomicheskogo razvitiia . Sverdlovsk , 1986. 2 v. ; LC Card 87-136690
HC337.R853 L35 1986

INDUSTRIAL SOCIOLOGY - SOVIET UNION.
Aitov, Nariman Abdrakhmanovich. Rabotniki khoroshie i plokhie /. Moskva , 1983. 134 p. ; LC Card 84-178331
HD6957.S65 A37 1983

Upravlenie sotsial′nymi protsessami v trudovykh kollektivakh /. Kishinev , 1983. 141 p. : LC Card 84-133794
HD6957.S65 U67 1983

INDUSTRIAL SOCIOLOGY - SPAIN - CANET DE BERENGUER.
Pellicer Valero, Jesús-Agustín. Sociología del trabajo en Canet de Berenguer /. Valencia , 1984. 80 p. : ISBN 84-600-3540-9 LC Card 86-216439
HD5808.C33 P45 1984

INDUSTRIAL SOCIOLOGY - SWEDEN.
Ekonomisk demokrati . Stockholm [1984] ii, 169 p. : LC Card 85-108590
HD5660.S9 E38 1984

Om lönearbete . [Stockholm] [1983] 260 p. : ISBN 91-1-833281-1 : LC Card 84-165851
HD6957.S8 O42 1983

INDUSTRIAL SOCIOLOGY - UNITED STATES.
Ashton, D. N. Unemployment under capitalism . Brighton, Sussex , 1986. xiv, 225 p. : ISBN 0-7108-0163-7
NYPL [JLD 86-1049]

Fernandez, John P., 1941- Survival in the corporate fishbowl . Lexington, Mass. , c1987. xiii, 314 p. : ISBN 0-669-10336-5 (alk. paper) LC Card 85-40021 DDC 302.3/5 19
HD6957.U6 F47 1987

Ritzer, George. Working, conflict and change /. Englewood Cliffs, N.J. , c1986. xii, 451 p. ; ISBN 0-13-967589-2 : LC Card 85-28135 DDC 306/.36/0973 19
HD6957.U6 R5 1986 ***NYPL [JLE 86-3160]***

Silver, Marc L., 1950- Under construction . Albany , c1986. xi, 251 p. ; ISBN 0-88706-308-X LC Card 85-30447 DDC 331.7/624/0973 19
HD6956.B92 U67 1986
NYPL [JLE 86-4616]

Sullivan, Patrick J., 1929- Blue collar, Roman collar, white collar . Lanham, MD , c1987. xii, 346 p. ; ISBN 0-8191-5704-X (alk. paper) : LC Card 86-24593 DDC 261.85 19
HD6338.2.U5 S85 1987

INDUSTRIAL SOCIOLOGY - UNITED STATES - HISTORY.
Life and labor . Albany , c1986. x, 343 p. ; ISBN 0-88706-173-7 LC Card 86-14362 DDC 305.5/62/0973 19
HD8066 .L54 1986 ***NYPL [JLE 86-4350]***

INDUSTRIAL STATISTICS.
Ştefan, C. Statistică industrială . Bucureşti , 1985. 223 p. ; LC Card 86-155097
HB137 .S76 1985

Industrial structure, capital markets, and the origins of British economic decline /. Kennedy, William P. (William Paca), 1944- Cambridge [Cambridgeshire] , New York , 1987. xii, 230 p. ; ISBN 0-521-23018-7 LC Card 86-24411 DDC 330.941 19
HC255 .K45 1987

INDUSTRIAL SUPERVISORS. see **SUPERVISORS, INDUSTRIAL.**

INDUSTRIAL SURVEYS - SPAIN.
El Ciclo industrial en España . Madrid [1984?] 436 p. : ISBN 84-7474-282-X LC Card 87-113099
HC385 .C49 1984

INDUSTRIAL TOXICOLOGY - GOVERNMENT POLICY - NEW YORK (STATE)
Jaffe, Susan. Toxic chemical accidents in New York State . New York, N.Y. (2 World Trade Center, New York 10047) [1986] 27, 13, 33 p. ; LC Card 86-622820 DDC 363.1/79 19
HD7269.C452 U54 1986

INDUSTRIAL TOXICOLOGY - INDIA - BHOPAL.
Chishti, Anees, 1941- Dateline Bhopal . New Delhi , 1986. 160 p. ; LC Card 86-901993 DDC 363.1/79
HD7269.C452 I5225 1986
NYPL [JLD 87-1050]

Everest, Larry. Behind the poison cloud . Chicago , 1986. 192 p. : ISBN 0-916650-26-X : LC Card 85-26863 DDC 363.1/79 19
HD7269.C452 I524 1986
NYPL [JSD 86-425]

Sufrin, Sidney C., 1910- Bhopal, its setting, responsibility, and challenge /. Delhi , 1985. 98 p. ; ISBN 81-202-0135-3 : LC Card 85-903246 DDC 363.1/79 19
HD7269.C452 I527 1985
NYPL [JLD 86-1321]

Industrial traffic management. Morse, Leon William. Practical handbook of industrial traffic management /. Washington , 1987. xiii, 642 p. : ISBN 0-87408-039-8 LC Card 86-51249 DDC 658.7/882 19
HF5761 .M74 1987

INDUSTRIAL TRAFFIC MANAGEMENT. see **SHIPMENT OF GOODS.**

Industrial training products & services markets. Norwalk, Conn., U. S.A. (6 Prowitt St., Norwalk 06855) : International Resource Development, c1987. vi, 174 leaves ; 28 cm. (Report / International Resource Development Inc. . #735) "May 1987." LC Card 87-153554 DDC 381/.45658312404 19
1. Educational technology industries. 2. Instructional materials industry. 3. Occupational training - Equipment and supplies. 4. Employees, Training of - Equipment and supplies. 5. Market surveys. I. International Resource Development, inc. II. Title. III. Title: Industrial training products and services markets. IV. Series: Report / International Resource Development Inc. , #735.
HD9811.A2 I53 1987

Industrial training products and services markets. Industrial training products & services markets. Norwalk, Conn., U. S.A. (6 Prowitt St., Norwalk 06855) , c1987. vi, 174 leaves ; LC Card 87-153554 DDC 381/.45658312404 19
HD9811.A2 I53 1987

INDUSTRIAL UNIONS. see **TRADE-UNIONS.**

The Industrial vision systems market in the U. S. New York, N.Y. : Frost & Sullivan, c1983. v, 246 p. : ill. ; 29 cm. "June 1983." "#A1217." LC Card 87-143523
1. Image processing equipment - United States. 2. Market surveys - United States. I. Frost & Sullivan.
HD9696.I423 U5445 1983

Industrial wages in Mexico City, 1939-1975 /. Bortz, Jeff. New York , 1987. ix, 529 p. ; ISBN 0-8240-1355-7 (alk. paper) : LC Card 87-8341 DDC 331.2/97253 19
HD4981.Z9 M483 1987

INDUSTRIAL WASTES. see **FACTORY AND TRADE WASTE.**

INDUSTRIAL WELFARE WORK. see **WELFARE WORK IN INDUSTRY.**

The industrial work model . Barrett, John (John J.) Menomonie, Wis. , c1987. v, 143 p. : ISBN 0-916671-73-9 (pbk.) LC Card 87-403218 DDC 362.0425 19
HD7256.U5 B37 1987

INDUSTRIAL WORKERS OF THE WORLD - HISTORY.
Dubofsky, Melvyn, 1934- "Big Bill" Haywood /. New York , 1987. viii, 184 p. ; ISBN 0-312-01272-1 : LC Card 87-17355 DDC 331.88/6 B 19
HD6509.H3 D82 1987

Dubofsky, Melvyn, 1934- We shall be all . Urbana , c1988. xviii, 561 p. ; ISBN 0-252-01408-1 (alk. paper) LC Card 87-16725 DDC 331.88/6/0973 19
HD8055.I4 D83 1988

Tripp, Anne Huber, 1934- The I.W.W. and the Paterson silk strike of 1913 /. Urbana , c1987. xiv, 317 p., [6] p. of plates : ISBN 0-252-01382-4 LC Card 86-24989 DDC 331.89/287739/0974924 19
HD5325.T42 1913 .P387 1987

Winters, Donald E. The soul of the wobblies . Westport, Conn. , 1985. 159 p. ; ISBN 0-313-24472-3 (lib. bdg.) LC Card 84-27973 DDC 331.88/6 19
HD8055.I5 W56 1985 ***NYPL [JLD 87-775]***

Wortman, Roy T., 1940- From syndicalism to trade unionism . New York , 1985. 217 p. : ISBN 0-8240-5675-2 (alk. paper) : LC Card 85-16249 DDC 331.88/6/09771 19
HD8055.I5 O38 1985 ***NYPL [JLE 86-4097]***

INDUSTRIAL WORKERS OF THE WORLD - HISTORY - 20TH CENTURY.
Golin, Steve. The fragile bridge . Philadelphia , 1988. p. cm. ISBN 0-87722-534-6 (alk. paper) : LC Card 87-24356 DDC 331.89/287739/0974924 19
HD5325.T42 1913 .P383 1988

Industrialisation in India . Seth, Vijay K. Delhi, India , 1987. xii, 242 p. : ISBN 81-900026-7-8 : LC Card 87-902803 DDC 338.0954 19
HC435.2 .S418 1987

Industrialisierung und Stadtentwicklung im ländlichen Südost-Australien /. Grotz, Reinhold. Stuttgart , 1982. 299 p. : ISBN 3-88028-098-3 : LC Card 83-215667
HC607.S68 G76 1982

Industrialisierungspolitik für Entwicklungsländer . Havemann, Hans A., 1912- Aachen , 1982. 68 p. ; ISBN 3-922525-06-7 LC Card 83-203761
HC59.7 .H386 1982

INDUSTRIALISTS - AUSTRALIA - BIOGRAPHY.
Joris, Albert, 1915- A destiny in diamonds /. Spring, Hill, Brisbane, Qld. , Portland, OR , 1986. vi, 113 p. : ISBN 0-86439-011-4 LC Card 87-161024 DDC 338.2/782/0924 B 19
HD9677.A82 J675 1986

INDUSTRIALISTS - BRAZIL - BIOGRAPHY.
Campos Netto, José Candido de, 1880-1963. O cavvaliere Aristides Germani /. [Caxias do Sul, Brazil] [Porto Alegre] , 1978. 111 p. : LC Card 79-121861
HD9056.B62 C35 1978 ***NYPL [JLD 81-342]***

INDUSTRIALISTS - CUBA - BIOGRAPHY.
Westfall, L. Glenn, 1943- Don Vicente Martinez Ybor, the man and his empire . New York , 1987. vii, 214 p. : ISBN 0-8240-1374-3 (alk. paper) : LC Card 87-8690 DDC 338.7/67972/0924 19
HD9149.C5 U777 1987

INDUSTRIALISTS - FLORIDA - BIOGRAPHY.
Westfall, L. Glenn, 1943- Don Vicente Martinez Ybor, the man and his empire . New York , 1987. vii, 214 p. : ISBN 0-8240-1374-3 (alk. paper) : LC Card 87-8690 DDC 338.7/67972/0924 19
HD9149.C5 U777 1987

INDUSTRIALISTS - GERMANY - BIOGRAPHY.
Goetzeler, Herbert. Wilhelm und Carl Friedrich von Siemens . Stuttgart , 1986. 131 p. : ISBN 3-515-04558-9 LC Card 86-141456
HD9695.G43 S514 1986

Köhler, Otto, 1935- --und heute die ganze Welt . Hamburg , c1986. 350 p. : ISBN 3-89136-081-9 LC Card 87-116787
HD9654.9.I5 K64 1986

Müller, Fr. (Friedrich), Dr. Ferdinand von Steinbeis . Tübingen , 1907. vi, 215 p. : LC Card 85-666358
HC282.5.S67 M85x 1907

INDUSTRIALISTS - GERMANY (WEST) - BIOGRAPHY.

Feyerabend, Joachim. Die leisen Milliarden . Düsseldorf , 1984. 187 p. : ISBN 3-430-12729-7 LC Card 84-176048
HC282.5.F54 F49 1984

INDUSTRIALISTS - GREAT BRITAIN - BIOGRAPHY.
Streat, Raymond, Sir. Lancashire and Whitehall . Manchester [Greater Manchester] , c1987. 2 v. : ISBN 0-7190-2390-4 (v. 1) LC Card 87-11026 DDC 338.7/67721/0924 B 19
HD9881.5.S77 A3 1987

INDUSTRIALISTS - GREAT BRITAIN - BIOGRAPHY - DICTIONARIES.
Dictionary of business biography . London , 1984. 5 v. : ISBN 0-406-27340-5 (set) LC Card 86-188034 DDC 338/.0092/2 B 19
HC252.5.A2 D53 1984 NYPL [JLM 86-569]

INDUSTRIALISTS - INDIA.
Verma, H. S. (Harnam Singh), 1942- Industrial families in India . New Delhi , 1987, c1985. xvi, 248 p. ; LC Card 87-900925 DDC 338/.04/0954 19
HC432.5.A2 V47 1987

INDUSTRIALISTS - INDIA - MAHARASHTRA - BIOGRAPHY.
Sāvanta, Śivājī, 1940- Laḍhata /. Pravarānagara , 1985-1986. 2 v. : LC Card 87-900715
HD9116.I415 M37 1985

INDUSTRIALISTS - ITALY - BIOGRAPHY.
Camerana, Oddone. L'enigma del cavalier Agnelli e altri itinerari /. Milano , c1985. 117 p. ; LC Card 85-191746
HD9710.I82 A6615 1985
NYPL [JLC 87-25]

INDUSTRIALISTS - ITALY - BIOGRAPHY - CONGRESSES.
Convegno nazionale di studi storici (1979 : Schio, Italy) Schio e Alessandro Rossi . Roma , 1985-1986. 2 v. (1487 p., [1] folded leaf of plates) : LC Card 87-110167
HC302.5.R6 C66 1979

INDUSTRIALISTS - JAPAN - BIOGRAPHY.
Morita, Akio, 1921- Made in Japan . New York , c1986. viii, 309 p., [8] p. of plates : ISBN 0-525-24465-4 : LC Card 86-11479 DDC 338.7/6213/0924 B 19
HD9696.A3 J3658 1986
NYPL [JFE 86-5112]

INDUSTRIALISTS - MEXICO.
Story, Dale, 1950- Industry, the state, and public policy in Mexico /. Austin , 1986. xii, 275 p. ; ISBN 0-292-73837-4 LC Card 85-13363 DDC 338.972 19
HD3616.M43 S76 1986 NYPL [JLE 87-656]

INDUSTRIALISTS - MEXICO - MONTERREY - HISTORY.
Cerutti, Mario. Burguesía y capitalismo en Monterrey, 1850-1910 /. México, D.F. , 1983. 214 p. ; ISBN 968-8430-10-2 LC Card 86-221932
HC138.M6 C47 1983

INDUSTRIALISTS - SINGAPORE - BIOGRAPHY.
Yong, C. F. (Ching Fatt) Tan Kah-kee, the making of an overseas Chinese legend /. Singapore , 1987 [i.e. 1986] xix, 391 p., [16] p. of plates : ISBN 0-19-582678-7 LC Card 86-946451 DDC 338/.04/0924 B 19
HC445.8.C47 Y66 1986

INDUSTRIALISTS - SOUTH AFRICA - BIOGRAPHY.
Esterhuyse, W. P. Anton Rupert . Cape Town , c1986. 150 p. ; ISBN 0-624-02429-6 LC Card 87-122279 DDC 361.7/4/0924 B 19
HC905.R87 E88 1986

INDUSTRIALISTS - SPAIN - BILBOA - BIOGRAPHY.
Gondra y Oraá, María Victoria de, 1929- El Bilbao de Julio Lazúrtegui . Bilbao , 1984. 472 p. : ISBN 84-505-0689-1 LC Card 87-125134
HC382.5.L39 G66 1984

INDUSTRIALISTS - TEXAS - BIOGRAPHY.
Pickens, T. Boone (Thomas Boone) Boone /. Boston , 1987. xii, 304 p., [8] p. of plates : ISBN 0-395-41433-4 : LC Card 86-27648 DDC 338.7/6223382/0924 B 19
HD9570.P53 A3 1987

INDUSTRIALISTS - UNITED STATES - BIOGRAPHY.
Bilby, Kenneth. The general . New York , c1986. 326 p. ; ISBN 0-06-015568-X : LC Card 85-45621 DDC 384.54/092/4 B 19
HE8689.8 B55 1985
NYPL [MWES (Sarnoff, D.) 86-4682]

Davis, Burke, 1913- War bird . Chapel Hill , c1987. viii, 267 p., [26] p. of plates : ISBN 0-8078-1752-X (alk. paper) LC Card 87-5934 DDC 338.7/67721/0924 B 19
HD9880.S67 D38 1987

Fahy, Thomas P. Richard Scott Perkin and the Perkin-Elmer Corporation /. [United States] c1987. xv, 271 p. : ISBN 0-9618075-0-4 LC Card 86-63869 DDC 338.7/666156/0973 19
HD9707.U62 P474 1987

Walker, David B., 1841 or 2-ca. 1906. Captain David B. Walker, journal and papers, 1864-1869 . Juneau, Alaska (Pouch G, Juneau 99811) , 1984. 60 p. : LC Card 84-622198
HD9481.U4 W359 1984

Wang, An, 1920- Lessons . Reading, Mass. , 1986. 248 p., [28] p. of plates : ISBN 0-201-09400-2 LC Card 86-10768 DDC 338.7/61004/0924 B 19
HD9696.C62 A3 1986 NYPL [JFE 86-5201]

Yates, W. Ross (Willard Ross) Joseph Wharton . Bethlehem , London , c1987. 413 p. : ISBN 0-934223-00-9 (alk. paper) LC Card 86-81983 DDC 338.7/6691/0924 B 19
HC102.5.W47 Y38 1987

INDUSTRIALISTS - UNITED STATES - BIOGRAPHY - JUVENILE LITERATURE.
Wade, Mary Dodson. Milk, meat biscuits, and the terraqueous machine . Austin, Tex. , c1987. 49 p. : ISBN 0-89015-605-0 : LC Card 87-6813 DDC 338.7/664/00924 B 92 19
HD9010.B65 W33 1987

Industrialização e desenvolvimento regional . Magalhães, Antonio Rocha. Brasília , 1983. 315 p. : LC Card 84-160221 DDC 338.981/3 19
HD3616.B84 N676 1983
NYPL [JLD 86-3120]

Industrialização rural no Nordeste / Luiz Fernando Correia de Araújo, coordenador ... [et al.]. Recife : Superintendência do Desenvolvimento do Nordeste, Coordenação do Planejamento Regional, c1986. 488 p. : ill. ; 23 cm. (Série Projeto Nordeste . v. 8) At head of title: Secretaria de Planejamento da Presidência da República, Instituto de Planejamento Econômico e Social, Ministério do Interior, Superintendência do Desenvolvimento do Nordeste do Brasil. Bibliography: p. 189-205. Includes index. LC Card 87-403045 DDC 338.981/3 19
1. Agricultural industries - Government policy - Brazil, Northeast. 2. Small business - Government policy - Brazil, Northeast. 3. Rural development - Brazil, Northeast. I. Araújo, Luiz Fernando Correia de. II. Brazil. Superintendência do Desenvolvimento do Nordeste.
HD9014.B83 N755 1985

La industrialización ecuatoriana y la utilización de los recursos productivos, 1976-1983 /. Villalobos, Fabio. Quito, Ecuador , 1987. 148 p. : LC Card 87-404654 DDC 338.09866 19
HC204.5.I52 V55 1987

Industrialización ecuatoriana, 1976-1983.
Villalobos, Fabio. La industrialización ecuatoriana y la utilización de los recursos productivos, 1976-1983 /. Quito, Ecuador , 1987. 148 p. : LC Card 87-404654 DDC 338.09866 19
HC204.5.I52 V55 1987

INDUSTRIALIZATION.
Garnsey, Elizabeth. Industrial change and women's employment . Geneva , 1987. ix, 100, x p. : ISBN 92-9014-411-4 (pbk.) : LC Card 87-163195 DDC 331.4/09172/4 19
HD6223 .G37 1987

Hesse, Günter, Dr. Die Entstehung industrialisierter Volkswirtschaften . Tübingen , 1982. vi, 100 p. : ISBN 3-16-344559-4 : LC Card 83-153439 DDC 338.9 19
HD84 .H4718 1982 NYPL [JLE 87-1169]

Industrial change in advanced economies /. London , Wolfeboro, N.H. , c1987. 319 p. : ISBN 0-7099-3828-4 : LC Card 86-19661 DDC 338.09 19
HC79.T4 H35 1987 NYPL [JLD 87-410]

Industrialization in developing and peripheral regions /. London , Dover, N.H. , c1986. 363 p. ; ISBN 0-7099-3827-6 : LC Card 86-4159 DDC 338.09172/4 19
HD2329 .I54 1986 NYPL [JLD 86-2985]

Luttrell, William L. Post-capitalist industrialization . New York , 1986. xv, 189 p. : ISBN 0-275-92310-X : LC Card 86-9452 DDC 338.9678 19
HD3616.T343 L88 1986
NYPL [JLE 87-351]

Partsch, Manfred. Prinzipien und Formen sozialer Sicherung in nicht-industriellen Gesellschaften /. Berlin , c1983. 168 p. ; ISBN 3-428-05484-9 LC Card 84-148527 DDC 368.4/009172/4 19
HD7252 .P37 1983 NYPL [JLE 85-1238]

Industrialization and regional development in Colombia /. Vellinga, Menno. Amsterdam, The Netherlands , 1983. 183 p. : ISBN 90-70280-80-9 LC Card 83-209247 DDC 338.09861/26 19
HC198.C296 V45 1983

Industrialization and urbanization in Latin America /. Gwynne, Robert N. Baltimore, Md. , 1986. xiv, 259 p. : ISBN 0-8018-3113-X LC Card 85-10079 DDC 338.098 19
HC125 .G96 1986 NYPL [JLD 86-2200]

INDUSTRIALIZATION - CONGRESSES.
Failed transitions to modern industrial society . Montreal , c1975. vii, 105 p. : ISBN 0-919958-00-1 LC Card 80-510009 DDC 303.4/094 19
HM101 .F26 NYPL [JLE 81-166]

INDUSTRIALIZATION - ENVIRONMENTAL ASPECTS.
Leonard, H. Jeffrey. Pollution and the struggle for the world product . Cambridge [Cambridgeshire] , New York , 1988. p. cm. ISBN 0-521-34042-X LC Card 87-17766 DDC 338.6/042 19
HD75.6 .L46 1988

Industrialization in developing and peripheral regions / edited by F.E. Ian Hamilton. London ; Dover, N.H. : Croom Helm, c1986. 363 p. ; 23 cm. Includes bibliographies and index. ISBN 0-7099-3827-6 : LC Card 86-4159 DDC 338.09172/4 19
1. Industrialization. 2. Developing countries - Industries. I. Hamilton, F. E. Ian.
HD2329 .I54 1986 NYPL [JLD 86-2985]

The Industrialization of the countryside / edited by Michael J. Healey and Brian W. Ilbery. Norwich [Norfolk] : Geo Books, c1985. xiv, 315 p. : ill., maps ; 22 cm. "Published on behalf of the Industrial Activity and Area Development and Rural Geography Study Groups of the Institute of British Geographers." Includes bibliographies and index. ISBN 0-86094-202-3 LC Card 87-141251 DDC 338.9/009173/4 19
1. Rural industry - Great Britain - Congresses. 2. Agricultural industries - Great Britain - Congresses. 3. Great Britain - Rural conditions - Congresses. I. Healey, Michael. II. Ilbery, Brian W. III. Institute of British Geographers. Study Group on Industrial Activity and Area Development. IV. Institute of British Geographers. Rural Geography Study Group.
HC256.6 .I524 1985

Industrialization policies and regional economic development in Malaysia /. Spinanger, Dean. Singapore , New York , 1986. xii, 197 p. : ISBN 0-19-582659-0 LC Card 86-207250 DDC 338.9595 19
HC445.5 .S68 1986

INDUSTRIALIZATION - POLITICAL ASPECTS.
Harris, Nigel. The end of the Third World . London , 1986. 231 p. : ISBN 1-85043-031-4
NYPL [JLE 87-858]

Industrializatsiia i kadry sel'skogo khoziaistva /. Syrovatko, V. G. (Vitaliĭ Grigor'evich) Moskva , 1986. 191 p. ; LC Card 86-229171
HD1536.S65 S97 1986

Industrializatsiia proizvodstva i mezhkhoziaistvennoe kooperirovanie / [redaktsionnaia kollegiia, A.P. Lokotchenko (otv. redaktor), M.S. Gubaĭdullin, M.V. Khalimov]. Ufa : Akademiia nauk SSSR, Bashkirskiĭ filial, 1979. 122 p. ; 22 cm. At head of title: Akademiia nauk SSSR. Bashkirskiĭ filial. Otdel ėkonomicheskikh issledovaniĭ. Includes bibliographical references. LC Card 82-161458
1. Animal industry - Russian S.F.S.R. - Bashkirskaia A.S.S.R. I. Lokotchenko, A. P. II. Gubaĭdullin, M. S.

III. Khalimov, M. V. IV. Akademiia nauk SSSR. Bashkirskiĭ filial. Otdel ėkonomicheskikh issledovaniĭ.
HD9425.S653 B375 1979

INDUSTRIALIZED BUILDING - UNITED STATES - TECHNOLOGICAL INNOVATIONS.
Technology, trade, and the U.S residential construction industry . Washington, D.C. , 1986. x, 91 p. : LC Card 86-600575 DDC 338.4/769083/0973 19
HD9715.U52 T43 1986

INDUSTRIALIZED CONSTRUCTION. see **INDUSTRIALIZED BUILDING.**

INDUSTRIAS AERONÁUTICAS Y MECÁNICAS DEL ESTADO (ARGENTINA) - HISTORY.
Angueira, María del Carmen. Capitalismo de estado, 1927-1956 /. Buenos Aires , c1986. 116 p. : ISBN 950-25-1416-5 LC Card 87-100705
HD9711.A72 A54 1986

Las industrias forestales en la Provincia de Huesca /. Cuevas, Enrique de las. Huesca , 1919. 58 p. ; LC Card 84-100478
HD9765.S7 H833 1919

Industrie- und Handelskammer zu Lübeck. Handelshäfen im Ostseeraum /. [Lübeck] [1983] 232 p. : LC Card 84-192969
HE557.A3 H36 1983

L'industrie aux champs . Dewerpe, Alain. Roma , 1985. xxxv, 543 p. : ISBN 2-7283-0081-X LC Card 86-221375
HC307.N58 D48 1985

Industrie du vêtement. Table de concertation sur l'industrie du vêtement (1985 : Montréal, Québec) Rapport de la Table de concertation sur l'industrie du vêtement . [Québec] [1985] v, 174, 12 p. ; LC Card 87-103889
HD9940.C22 Q847 1985

Die Industrie-Erzeugnisse und Handelswaren des Landes Braunschweig / zusammengestellt im Bureau der Handelskammer Braunschweig. 2., ergänzte Aufl. Wolfenbüttel : Heckners Verlag, 1921. 120 p. : ill. ; 23 cm. Includes index. LC Card 85-666348
1. Braunschweig (Germany) - Industries. I. Handelskammer Braunschweig.
HC289.B7 I52x 1921

Industrie et politique à la frontière Mexique-U. S.A. . Trabis, Roland. Paris , c1985. 241 p., [1] p. of plates : ISBN 2-222-03772-7 : LC Card 86-175728
HC138.N84 T73 1985

L'industrie française de l'armement . Dussauge, Pierre. Paris , c1985. xi, 179 p. : ISBN 2-7178-0999-6 : LC Card 86-216731
HD9743.F82 D87 1985

L'industrie horlogère suisse et ses relations avec la Chine de 1949 à 1982 /. Yang, Yuming. Geneve , 1984. 186 leaves : LC Card 85-104853
HD9999.C583 S99 1984

L'Industrie pharmaceutique, ses réalités. Ed. 1982. Paris : Syndicat national de l'industrie pharmaceutique, 1982. 54 p. : ill. (some col.) ; 29 cm. "Mise à jour 1983" (12 p.) and errata slip inserted. LC Card 85-124408
1. Pharmaceutical industry - France - Statistics. 2. Pharmaceutical industry - Statistics. I. Syndicat national de l'industrie pharmaceutique (France).
HD9668.4 .I53 1982

L'Industrie québécoise du matériel médical jetable : description et analyse. Québec : Direction des études industrielles, Direction générale de la recherche et de la planification, Ministère de l'industrie, du commerce et du tourisme, [1983] xv, 235 p. : ill. ; 28 cm. "Réalisation ... confiée à Mme Hélène Vincent"--P. [i] "Juillet 1983." Bibliography: p. [233]-235. LC Card 84-235956
1. Disposable medical supplies industry - Québec (Province). I. Vincent, Hélène. II. Québec (Province). Direction des études industrielles.
HD9995.D563 C35 1983

Industrie und Grundbedürfnisbefriedigung in Afrika . Schneider-Barthold, Wolfgang. Frankfurt/Main , New York , c1984. 264 p. ; ISBN 3-593-33350-3 LC Card 86-125217
HC1040 .S35 1984

Industrie und Region . Bochum, Ulrich, 1953- Frankfurt am Main , New York , c1984. 340, [38] p. : ISBN 3-8204-5550-7 LC Card 85-194544
HC288.R8 B57 1984

Industriebrachen und extensiv genutzte Flächen in innenstadtnahen Gewerbegebieten . Pohle, Michael. Paderborn , 1985. viii, 121 p. : ISBN 3-506-73577-2 : LC Card 86-183775
HC289.H2 P64 1985

INDUSTRIEGEWERKSCHAFT BERGBAU UND ENERGIE - HISTORY.
Lauschke, Karl. Schwarze Fahnen an der Ruhr . Marburg [/Lahn] , c1984. 400 p. : ISBN 3-921630-42-8 LC Card 84-215799
HD6698.M616 I535 1984

Industriële innovatie in Nederland . Kleinknecht, A. Assen , 1987. viii, 140 p. ; ISBN 90-232-2261-X : LC Card 87-157579
HC329.5.T4 K58 1987

Die industrielle Anwendung der Mikroelektronik in der Bundesrepublik Deutschland, Frankreich, Grossbritannien . Knetsch, Werner. Haar bei München , c1985. 142 p. : ISBN 3-89090-121-2 : LC Card 86-106735
HC290.5.A9 K5 1985

Industrielle Arbeitszeiten in Deutschland . Seifert, Eberhard. Wuppertal , 1982. 68, [8] p. : LC Card 87-672398
HD5178 .S44x 1982

Die industrielle Mikroelektronik-Anwendung im verarbeitenden Gewerbe der Bundesrepublik Deutschland . Knetsch, Werner. Haar bei München , c1986. 223 p. : ISBN 3-89090-131-X LC Card 87-132995 DDC 338/.06 19
HC290.5.A9 K524 1986

Industrielle Strukturprobleme Österreichs . Kramer, Helmut, 1939- Wien , 1980. 112 p. ; LC Card 81-103725 DDC 338.4/76691/09436 19
HD9525.A82 K73 1980 ***NYPL [JLD 86-1237]***

Industrielles Beschaffungsverhalten . Specht, Günter. Frankfurt am Main , New York , c1985. iii, 167 p. : ISBN 3-8204-8938-X LC Card 86-120719
HD9654.5 .S64 1985

Industrielles Management : Festgabe zum 60. Geburtstag von Wolfgang Lücke / herausgegeben von Jürgen Bloech. Göttingen : Vandenhoeck & Ruprecht, c1986. vi, 276 p., [1] leaf of plates : ill., port. ; 24 cm. Includes bibliographies. CONTENTS. - Wirtschaftlicher Strukturwandel und industrielle Betriebsgrössen / Gösta B. Ihde -- Unternehmenserhaltung, Kapitalstruktur und Preisuntergrenzen bei geltendem Ertragssteuerrecht / Wolfgang von Zwehl -- Zur Handhabung von Zielkonflikten / Egbert Kahle -- New Venture Analysis in japanischen Unternehmen / Yukio Gotoh -- Wachstum durch Marktdurchdringung als strategisches Projekt / Burkhard Huch -- Entstehung des Management Accounting / Kazuo Mizoguchi -- Causal Ordering und Kostenabweichungsanalyse / Tetsuo Kobayashi -- Informationssystem für ein industrielles Controlling / Hans Wegener -- Zum Einsatz von Arbeitsplatzcomputern für Managementaufgaben / Volkmar Botta -- Materialkosten-Management durch Personaleinsatzsteuerung / Jürgen Bloech. ISBN 3-525-13182-8 LC Card 87-118224 DDC 658 19
1. Industrial management. 2. Lücke, Wolfgang, 1926-. I. Lücke, Wolfgang, 1926-. II. Bloech, Jürgen, 1936-.
HD35 .I555 1986

Industriepolitik im westlichen Ausland : Rahmenbedingungen, Strategien, Aussenhandelsaspekte / Fritz Franzmeyer ... [et al.]. Berlin : Duncker & Humblot, 1987. 2 v. ; 30 cm. (Beiträge zur Strukturforschung . Heft 92) Includes bibliographies and indexes. ISBN 3-428-06143-8 (set) LC Card 87-133587 DDC 330 s 338.9 19
1. Industry and state. 2. Industry and state - Case studies. I. Franzmeyer, Fritz.
HC281 .B33 Heft 92 HD3611

INDUSTRIES. see **INDUSTRIAL MOBILIZATION; INDUSTRY.**

Les Industries agro-alimentaires : des actions pour l'avenir : rapport du Groupe de stratégie industrielle no 6 / président du groupe, Michel Bon ; l'équipe des rapporteurs était composé de Robin Edme ... [et al.]. Paris : Documentation française, [1986], c1987. 164 p. : ill. ; 30 cm. (Plan / Commissariat général du plan) At head of title: Commission nationale de l'industrie; Commissariat général du plan; Direction des industries agricoles et alimentaires. Bibliography: p. 131. ISBN 2-11-001722-8 : LC Card 87-167615
1. Food industry and trade - Government policy - France. I. Bon, Michel, 1943-. II. Edme, Robin. III. France. Groupe de stratégie industrielle no 6. IV. France. Commissariat général du plan. V. Series: Plan (France. Commissariat général du plan).
HD9012.5 .I53 1987

INDUSTRIES, CHEMICAL. see **CHEMICAL INDUSTRIES.**

INDUSTRIES - DIVERSIFICATION. see **DIVERSIFICATION IN INDUSTRY.**

INDUSTRIES - HISTORY. see **INDUSTRY - HISTORY.**

INDUSTRIES, HOME. see **HOME LABOR.**

INDUSTRIES, LOCATION OF.
Rizzieri, Juarez Alexandre Baldini. Desenvolvimento econômico e urbanização . São Paulo , 1982. 219 p. : LC Card 83-150574 DDC 330.9173/2 19
HT321 .R59 1982 ***NYPL [JLD 86-3817]***

Les Industries mécaniques et électriques au Maroc : présentation / SEREC, Société d'études de réalisations de consultant. Casablanca : La Société, [1984] 1 v. (various pagings) ; 30 cm. Cover title. Includes bibliography. LC Card 85-206543
1. Machinery industry - Morocco. 2. Mineral industries - Morocco. 3. Electric industries - Morocco. 4. Industrial laws and legislation - Morocco. 5. Morocco - Industries. I. Sharikat al-Dirāsāt wa-al-Injāzāt wa-al-Irshādāt (Morocco).
HD9705.M72 I53 1984

INDUSTRIES, SERVICE. see **SERVICE INDUSTRIES.**

INDUSTRIES, SIZE OF - CONGRESSES.
The Economics of firm size, market structure, and social performance . [Washington, D.C.?] , 1980. viii, 388 p. ; LC Card 81-600757 DDC 338.6/4/0973 19
HD60.5.U5 E26 ***NYPL [JLF 86-704]***

Ginzberg, Eli, 1911- Resizing for organizational effectiveness . New York, N.Y. (316 Uris Hall, New York 10027) , c1985. vii, 43 p. ; LC Card 86-162474 DDC 658.1/6 19
HD58.9 .G56 1985

INDUSTRIES, SIZE OF - GERMANY (WEST)
Geiser, Josef. Wachstumshemmnisse mittelständischer Industriebetriebe /. Göttingen , 1983. xi, 385 p. : ISBN 3-509-01353-0 LC Card 84-221327
HD2346.G3 G372 1983

INDUSTRIES, SIZE OF - GREECE.
Mikromesaies kai megales epicheirēseis stēn Hellēnikē viomēchania. Athēna , 1982. 32 p. ; LC Card 85-152476
HD69.S5 M54 1982

INDUSTRIES, SIZE OF - HUNGARY.
Dévai, Katalin. A nagyvállalatok helyzetéről /. [Budapest] , 1984. 68 p. ; ISBN 963-673-293-0 LC Card 85-175237
HD2852.5 .D48 1984

INDUSTRIES, SIZE OF - INDIA.
Vyasulu, Vinod. Development of backward areas . New Delhi, India , 1987. xi, 188 p. : ISBN 81-85030-05-7 : LC Card 87-902689 DDC 332.6/42/0954 19
HD2346.I5 V93 1987

INDUSTRIES, SIZE OF - INDIA - CASE STUDIES.
Thanulingom Nadar, N. Small scale industry . Coimbatore, Tamil Nadu , 1985. 194 p. ; LC Card 85-903280 DDC 338.6/42/095482 19
HD2346.I52 C648 1985 ***NYPL [JLD 86-1411]***

INDUSTRIES, SIZE OF - INDIA - COIMBATORE.
Thanulingom Nadar, N. Small scale industry . Coimbatore, Tamil Nadu , 1985. 194 p. ; LC Card 85-903280 DDC 338.6/42/095482 19
HD2346.I52 C648 1985 ***NYPL [JLD 86-1411]***

INDUSTRIES, SIZE OF - UNITED STATES.
Adams, Walter, 1922 (Aug. 27)- The bigness complex . New York , 1986. xiii, 426 p. ; ISBN 0-394-54721-7 : LC Card 86-42624 DDC 338.6/44/0973 19
HD2785 .A68 1986 ***NYPL [JLE 87-1432]***

Tomasko, Robert M. Downsizing . New York , c1987. p. cm. ISBN 0-8144-5907-2 LC Card 87-47709 DDC 338.6/4 19
HD69.S5 T59 1987

INDUSTRIES, SIZE OF - UNITED STATES - ECONOMETRIC MODELS.
Ács, Zoltán J. The determinants of innovation in large and small firms /. Berlin [1986] 39 p. ; LC Card 87-156684 DDC 338.6/4 19
HC110.T4 A59 1986

Industriesoziologie .
(Bd. 4) Elsenau, Detlef von. Arbeitnehmerorientierte Sozialforschung . Münster [1986] ii, 233 p. ; ISBN 3-88660-246-X LC Card 86-200305
HD6957.G3 E59 1986

Industrihotell och industribyar . Andersson, Göran, 1944- Stockholm [1984] 150 p. : ISBN 91-38-08268-3 LC Card 85-106828
HC375 .A72 1984

Industrija SR Srbije, 1981-1982. godina / Socijalistička Republika Srbija, Republički zavod za statistiku. Beograd : Republički zavod za statistiku SR Srbije, 1984. 76 p. ; 29 cm. (Bilten . 239) In Serbo-Croatian (roman) Tables. LC Card 86-212264
1. Serbia - Industries - Statistics. I. Republički zavod za statistiku SR Srbije. II. Series: Bilten (Republički zavod za statistiku SR Srbije) , 239.
HA1651 .A334 no. 239 HA1634.S47

Industrimakten Japan : en inspirasjon til nytenkning? : en artikkelsamling / fra Norsk produktivitetsinstitutt ; redigert av Kjell Vesterås. Oslo : Tanum-Norli, 1982. 151 p. : ill. ; 22 cm. "NPI 1242"--Cover. Bibliography: p. 151. CONTENTS. - Japan, en sårbar maskin i en trett verden / Kåre Valebrokk -- Japan, landet der teknikk, politikk og kultur møtes / Rolf Bodh -- Det japanske under--markedsførings- og globaliseringsevnen / Martin T. Tveit -- Japans sentrale planleggingssystem / Kari Blegen -- Japansk bedriftskultur / Rudolf Lindboe -- Arbeidsorganisasjon og kulturbetingelser / Einer Thorsrud -- Fagbevegelsens utvikling i Japan / Tor Andersen -- Et samfunn som lærer / G. William Ford og Bjørn Gustavsen -- Er Japan en superstat eller et avansert industriland med problemer? / Turid Grønning og Kjell Vesterås. ISBN 82-518-1630-0 : LC Card 84-126986
1. Industrial organization - Japan. 2. Industrial management - Japan. I. Vesterås, Kjell. II. Norsk produktivitetsinstitutt.
HD70.J3 I549 1982

Industrimineraler . Norway. Utvalg for delutredning om industrielle mineraler. Oslo [1982] 134 p. : ISBN 82-00-70754-7 LC Card 83-123304
HD9506.N72 N67 1982

Industrin i Södertälje 1920-1970 . Bjessmo, Lars-Erik. Stockholm , 1987. 236 p. ; ISBN 91-7146-468-9 LC Card 87-151742
HC378.S7 B54 1987

Industrins datorinvesteringar 1980-1982 / Data- och elektronikkommittén (DEK). [Stockholm] : Liber, [1983] 61, 2 p. : ill. ; 22 cm. "Ds I 1983:28." Includes bibliographical references. ISBN 91-38-08001-X LC Card 84-218410
1. Business - Sweden - Data processing. 2. Business - Sweden - Data processing - Statistics. I. Sweden. Data- och elektronikkommittén.
HF5548.2 .I4213 1983

Industrins lönsamhet, finansiering och investeringar under 1970-talet . Olsson, Hans. [Stockholm] [1981] 58 p. : ISBN 91-38-06530-4 LC Card 84-120594
HG4211 .O45 1981

Industrirådet (Denmark). Erhvervsøkonomiske afdeling. Beskatningen af aktieafkast i Danmark og i det øvrige Vesteuropa /. København [1986] 23 p. ; ISBN 87-7353-047-6 LC Card 87-144435
HJ5913.D4 B47 1986

Industry /. Guber, A. A. (Aleksandr Andreevich) Moscow , 1985. 46 p., [16] p. of plates : LC Card 86-208070 DDC 338.947 19
HC336.25 .G8 1985

INDUSTRY.
Industry in the 1980s . New York , 1985. xii, 228 p. : ISBN 92-1-106207-1 (pbk.) LC Card 86-227928 DDC 338.09 19
HD9720.5 .I53 1985

Kalleberg, Arne L. Work and industry . New York , c1987. xviii, 244 p. ; ISBN 0-306-42344-8 LC Card 87-2333 DDC 306/.36 19
HD4904 .K294 1987

Mummery, A. F. (Albert Frederick), 1855-1895. The physiology of industry . Fairfield, NJ , 1988. p. cm. ISBN 0-678-00673-3 LC Card 87-17943 DDC 330.1 19
HB171 .M95 1988

Pereira, Nilda. Economía, organización y planificación de la producción industrial /. La Habana , 1984. 2 v. : LC Card 87-401248
HD2328 .P47 1984

INDUSTRY - LOCATION.
(1978) Territorial'nye struktury promyshlennosti /. Moskva , 1978. 128 p. : LC Card 81-147566
HC340.D5 T464 1978

(1984) Molina Ibáñez, Mercedes. Capitalismo y socialismo . Madrid , c1984. 128 p. : ISBN 84-7046-358-6 LC Card 85-135836
HB501 .M694 1984

(1987) Berry, Brian Joe Lobley, 1934- Economic geography . Englewood Cliffs, N.J. , c1987. xi, 447 p. : ISBN 0-13-231440-1 : LC Card 87-2250 DDC 330.9 19
HC59 .B52 1987

(1987) Industrial change in advanced economies /. London , Wolfeboro, N.H. , c1987. 319 p. : ISBN 0-7099-3828-4 : LC Card 86-19661 DDC 338.09 19
HC79.T4 H35 1987 ***NYPL [JLD 87-410]***

Industry analysts in the federal government. Who knows about industries and markets /. Washington, D.C. , c1986. 54 p. ; ISBN 0-934940-33-9 (pbk.) LC Card 86-217691 DDC 338/.06/072073 19
HC102.2 .W48 1986

INDUSTRY AND ART. see **ART AND INDUSTRY.**

INDUSTRY AND CLIMATE. see **INDUSTRY AND WEATHER.**

INDUSTRY AND EDUCATION - GERMANY, WEST.
Angsturlaub statt Bildungsurlaub . Frankfurt am Main , c1979. 179 p. : ISBN 3-88203-044-5 LC Card 85-167471
HD5257.2.G3 A54 1979

INDUSTRY AND EDUCATION - INDIA - WEST BENGAL.
Bose, P. K. Graduate employment and higher education in West Bengal /. Paris , New Delhi , 1983. vi, 288, [1] p. : ISBN 0-85226-078-4 (pbk.) LC Card 83-163900 DDC 331.11/423 19
HD6278.I52 W473 1983 ***NYPL [JLD 86-2269]***

INDUSTRY AND EDUCATION - UNITED STATES.
Johnston, Robert F. Entrepreneurial science . New York , 1987. 157 p. ; ISBN 0-89930-260-2 (lib. bdg. : alk. paper) LC Card 87-2518 DDC 338/.06 19
HC110.H53 J65 1987

Private means--public ends . New York , 1987. xiii, 187 p. ; ISBN 0-275-92429-7 (alk. paper) : LC Card 86-25251 DDC 361.6/1/0973 19
HN65 .P69 1987 ***NYPL [JLE 87-1390]***

Industry and finance series .
(v. 20) Sheldrick, William F. World nitrogen survey /. Washington, D.C. , 1987. xxv, 227 p. : ISBN 0-8213-0895-5 LC Card 87-6203 DDC 338.4/7668624 19
HD9660.N7 S55 1987

Industry and finance series, 0256-2235 .
(v. 19) Levitsky, Jacob, 1924- Credit guarantee schemes for small and medium enterprises /. Washington, D.C. , 1987. vi, 91 p. ; ISBN 0-8213-0866-1 (pbk.) LC Card 86-32571 DDC 658.8/7 19
HG9977 .L48 1987

(v. 21) Mould, Maurice C., 1925- Financial information for management of a development finance institution . Washington, D.C. [1987] 1 v. (various pagings) : ISBN 0-8213-0913-7 (pbk.) LC Card 87-15989 DDC 332.2 19
HG3726 .M68 1987

Industry and ideology . Hayes, Peter, 1946- Cambridge [Cambridgeshire] , New York , 1987. xxviii, 411 p. : ISBN 0-521-32948-5 LC Card 86-28388 DDC 338.7/66/00943 19
HD9654.9.I5 H39 1987

INDUSTRY AND STATE - ADDRESSES, ESSAYS, LECTURES.
The Future of private enterprise /. Atlanta, Ga. , 1984-1986. 3 v. ; ISBN 0-88406-164-7 (pbk. : v. 1) LC Card 83-25386 DDC 338.6/1 19
HB501 .F83 1984 ***NYPL [JLK 87-49]***

INDUSTRY AND STATE - AFRICA.
Growth, equity, and self reliance . Boulder , 1987. xi, 162 p. ; ISBN 0-8133-0486-5 (pbk.) : LC Card 87-14290 DDC 338.96 19
HD3616.A36 G76 1987

Policies and measures to promote industrial co-operatives in Africa /. [New York] [1985] 23 p. ; LC Card 87-104469 DDC 334/.6/096 19
HD3247 .P65 1985

INDUSTRY AND STATE - AFRICA, WEST.
Transnationals and development. Manchester, England , 1984. i, 64 p. ;
NYPL [JLD 86-3224]

INDUSTRY AND STATE - ALABAMA - HISTORY.
Flynt, J. Wayne, 1940- Mine, mill & microchip . Northridge, Calif. , 1987. 376 p. : ISBN 0-89781-215-8 LC Card 87-9192 DDC 338.09761 19
HC107.A4 F57 1987

INDUSTRY AND STATE - ARABIAN PENINSULA.
Arabian gulf studies /. Nürnberg , 1985- v. <1 > : LC Card 86-205380 DDC 330.953/053 19
HC415.3 .A7 1985

INDUSTRY AND STATE - ARGENTINA.
Ferrucci, Ricardo Jorge. La promoción industrial en Argentina /. [Buenos Aires] , c1986. 274 p. : ISBN 950-23-0307-5 LC Card 87-124151 DDC 338.982 19
HD3616.A73 F47 1986

INDUSTRY AND STATE - ASIA.
Re-orientation of industrial policies . [Bangkok] [1979. iii, 196 p. ; LC Card 83-187259
HD3616.A772 R46 1979

INDUSTRY AND STATE - AUSTRALIA.
Ewer, Peter. Unions and the future of Australian manufacturing /. Sydney , Boston , 1987. xi, 189 p. : ISBN 0-04-330382-X (pbk.) LC Card 87-164410 DDC 338.4/767/0994 19
HD9738.A82 E93 1987

Rattigan, G. A. (Godfrey Alfred), 1911- Industry assistance . Carlton, Vic. , Beaverton, Or. , 1986. viii, 289 p., [4] p. of plates : ISBN 0-522-84313-1 LC Card 86-202866 DDC 338.994 19
HF2483 .R38 1986

Structured chaos . Melbourne , New York , 1985. viii, 111 p. : ISBN 0-19-554687-3 LC Card 86-222312 DDC 338/.06/0994 19
HC610.I52 S77 1985

Tsung, Stephen. Threats to private enterprise in Australia /. [Melbourne] , 1976. 80 p. ; LC Card 82-127568
HD3616.A83 T78 1976

INDUSTRY AND STATE - AUSTRIA.
Neue Industriepolitik oder Stärkung der Marktkräfte? . Hamburg , 1986. xiii, 221 p. ; ISBN 3-87895-315-1 LC Card 87-408234 DDC 338.9 19
HD3616.G4 N48 1986

Stahl und Eisen bricht . Wien [1986] xi, 202 p. : ISBN 3-900351-62-7 LC Card 87-140293 DDC 330.9436/053 19
HC265 .S736 1986

Tieber, Herbert. Verstaatliche Industrie . Wien , c1983. 91 p. : LC Card 84-169053
HD4155 .T54 1983

INDUSTRY AND STATE - BANGLADESH.
Industrial investment schedule for small industry, 1982-85. Dhaka , 1982. v, 283 p. ; LC Card 84-900851 DDC 338.6/42/095492 19
HD2346.B27 I53 1982 ***NYPL [JLF 87-269]***

Re-orientation of industrial policies . [Bangkok] [1979. iii, 196 p. ; LC Card 83-187259
HD3616.A772 R46 1979

INDUSTRY AND STATE - BELGIUM.
Escarmelle, Jean-François. L'Etat industriel dans les politiques de sortie de crise .

Louvain-la-Neuve , 1986. 237 p. : ISBN 2-87077-301-3 : LC Card 86-229137
HD3616.B43 E84 1986

INDUSTRY AND STATE - BRAZIL.
Brazil. Ministério da Indústria e do Comércio. A política industrial da nova república. [Brasília, Brazil] [1985] 44 p. ; LC Card 87-404994 DDC 338.981 19
HD3616.B83 B66 1985

Cavalcanti, Bianor Scelza. Administração da política industrial no Brasil . Rio de Janeiro , 1986. ii, 87, 10 p. : LC Card 87-102756 DDC 338.981 19
HD3616.B83 C28 1986

Magalhães, João Paulo de Almeida. Uma política industrial para o Brasil /. [Rio de Janeiro] [between 1985 and 1987] 161 p. ; LC Card 87-403992 DDC 338.981 19
HD3616.B83 M34 1985

Martins, Luciano, 1934- Estado capitalista e burocracia no Brasil pós-64 /. Rio de Janeiro, RJ , 1985. 265 p. ; LC Card 85-232969 DDC 338.981 19
HC187 .M2947 1985 ***NYPL [JLD 86-1691]***

Souza, Francisco Araújo Salles de. O estado e o cartel do leite no Brasil /. Brasília, Distrito Federal , 1981. 130 p. : LC Card 81-217015
HD9282.B72 S65 1981
NYPL [JLD 86-3366]

Tadini, Venilton. O setor de bens de capital sob encomenda . São Paulo , 1986. 142 p. : LC Card 87-154239 DDC 332/.0414/0981 19
HC190.C3 T33 1986

INDUSTRY AND STATE - BRAZIL - BAHIA (STATE) - CONGRESSES.
Seminário sobre Política Industrial da Bahia (1986 : Salvador, Brazil) Síntese das exposições e dos debates /. [Salvador] [1986] 89 p. ; LC Card 87-403843 DDC 338.981/42 19
HD3616.B84 B37 1986

INDUSTRY AND STATE - BRAZIL - CEARÁ (STATE)
Casimiro, Liana Maria Carleial de. Avaliação da política industrial do Ceará . Fortaleza , 1983. 58 p. ; LC Card 86-129541
HD3616.B84 C422 1983

INDUSTRY AND STATE - BRAZIL, NORTHEAST.
Magalhães, Antonio Rocha. Industrialização e desenvolvimento regional . Brasília , 1983. 315 p. : LC Card 84-160221 DDC 338.981/3 19
HD3616.B84 N676 1983
NYPL [JLD 86-3120]

INDUSTRY AND STATE - BRAZIL, NORTHEAST - HISTORY - 20TH CENTURY.
Tavares, José Reinaldo Carneiro. Aspectos industriais da política de desenvolvimento do Nordeste . Recife , 1985. 24 leaves ; LC Card 87-102054 DDC 338.981/3 19
HD3616.B84 N678 1985

INDUSTRY AND STATE - CANADA.
Canadian industrial policy in action /. Toronto , Buffalo , c1985. xvii, 231 p. : ISBN 0-8020-7244-5 (pbk.) LC Card 86-672572
HD3616.C23 C36x 1985
NYPL [JLD 86-2871]

Schultz, Richard, 1945- Economic regulation and the federal system /. Toronto , Buffalo , c1985. xv, 187 p. : ISBN 0-8020-7287-9 (pbk.) LC Card 86-672574
HD3616.C23 S38x 1985
NYPL [JLD 86-2821]

INDUSTRY AND STATE - CANADA - CASE STUDIES.
Borins, Sandford F., 1949- Investments in failure . Toronto , New York , c1986. x, 175 p. ; ISBN 0-458-80340-5 (pbk.) : LC Card 87-142330 DDC 354.7109/2 19
HD4005 .B67 1986

INDUSTRY AND STATE - CANADA - HISTORY - 19TH CENTURY.
Forster, Jakob Johann Benjamin. A conjunction of interests . Toronto , Buffalo , c1986. vi, 288 p. ; ISBN 0-8020-5680-6 (alk. paper) LC Card 87-108915 DDC 382.7/0971 19
HF1765 .F67 1986

INDUSTRY AND STATE - CASE STUDIES.
Buchholz, Rogene A. Management response to public issues . Englewood Cliffs, N.J. , c1985. x, 389 p. : ISBN 0-13-549940-2 (pbk.) : LC Card 84-18355 DDC 658.4/08 19
HD60 .B83 1985 ***NYPL [JLE 85-1984]***

Industriepolitik im westlichen Ausland . Berlin , 1987. 2 v. ; ISBN 3-428-06143-8 (set) LC Card 87-133587 DDC 330 s 338.9 19
HC281 .B33 Heft 92 HD3611

National policies for developing high technology industries . Boulder, Colo. , c1986. xiv, 247 p. : ISBN 0-8133-7280-1 (soft : alk. paper) LC Card 86-50530 DDC 338.4/762 19
HC79.H53 N38 1986 ***NYPL [JLE 86-4504]***

State, finance, and industry . Brighton, Sussex , 1986. ix, 292 p. ; ISBN 0-7108-0219-6
NYPL [JLD 86-2997]

States versus markets in the world-system /. Beverly Hills, Calif. , c1985. 295 p. ; ISBN 0-8039-2510-7 LC Card 85-11716 DDC 338.9 19
HD3611 .S76 1985 ***NYPL [JLD 86-3227]***

INDUSTRY AND STATE - CHILE.
Gatica, Jaime. Deindustrialization in Chile /. Boulder , 1988. p. cm. ISBN 0-8133-7392-1 : LC Card 86-32513 DDC 338.983 19
HD9734.C52 G37 1988

Weinstein L., Jacqueline. La industria en una estrategia de desarrollo para Chile /. Santiago, Chile , 1984. 50 leaves ; LC Card 86-139143
HD3616.C52 W45 1984

INDUSTRY AND STATE - CHILE - HISTORY - 20TH CENTURY.
Pitts, Mary Anne, 1927- Economic development in Chile under two growth strategies, 1925-1968 /. New York , 1987. vii, 246 p. ; ISBN 0-8240-1368-9 (alk. paper) : LC Card 87-7618 DDC 338.983 19
HC192 .P627 1987

INDUSTRY AND STATE - CHINA.
China's industrial reform /. New York , c1987. xii, 378 p. ; ISBN 0-19-520592-8 : LC Card 87-5616 DDC 338.951 19
HD3616.C63 C495 1987

INDUSTRY AND STATE - COLOMBIA - ANTIOQUIA (DEPT.)
Vellinga, Menno. Industrialization and regional development in Colombia /. Amsterdam, The Netherlands , 1983. 183 p. : ISBN 90-70280-80-9 LC Card 83-209247 DDC 338.09861/26 19
HC198.C296 V45 1983

INDUSTRY AND STATE - COLOMBIA - CAUCA RIVER REGION.
Vellinga, Menno. Industrialization and regional development in Colombia /. Amsterdam, The Netherlands , 1983. 183 p. : ISBN 90-70280-80-9 LC Card 83-209247 DDC 338.09861/26 19
HC198.C296 V45 1983

INDUSTRY AND STATE - CONGRESSES.
Economic incentives . London , 1986. xiii, 497 p. ; ISBN 0-333-40473-4 ***NYPL [JLD 87-367]***

Growth-oriented adjustment programs /. Washington, D.C. , 1987. xiii, 537 p. : ISBN 0-939934-92-2 (pbk.) LC Card 87-21361 DDC 338.9 19
HD73 .G76 1987

Mainstreams in industrial organization /. Dordrecht , Boston , 1986. 2 v. (x, 465 p.) ; ISBN 90-247-3363-4 LC Card 86-12345 DDC 338.6 19
HD29 .M25 1986 ***NYPL [JLE 87-457]***

New dimensions in foreign economic policy . Washington, DC , 1986. xiii, 118 p. ; LC Card 86-600514 DDC 337.73 19
HF1410.5 .N488 1986

Probleme der staatsmonopolistischen Wirtschaftsregulierung . Rostock , 1981. 35 p. ; LC Card 86-211250
HB501 .P694 1981

INDUSTRY AND STATE - CUBA.
Cuba's socialist economy toward the 1990s /. Boulder, Colo. , 1987. ix, 188 p. : ISBN 1-555-87080-5 (lib. bdg. : alk. paper) : LC Card 87-12867 DDC 338.97291 19
HC152.5 .C824 1987

INDUSTRY AND STATE - DENMARK.
Dansk industripolitik . [Århus] , 1983. 143 p. : LC Card 84-164502
HD3616.D43 D35 1983

INDUSTRY AND STATE - DEVELOPING COUNTRIES.
D'Angelo, Massimo. Criteri per una cooperazione industriale con i paesi in via di sviluppo /. Milano , c1981. 294 p. ; ISBN 88-20-42145-3 : LC Card 82-113466
HF1549 .D36 1981 ***NYPL [JLD 86-3318]***

Harris, Nigel. The end of the Third World . London , 1986. 231 p. : ISBN 1-85043-031-4
NYPL [JLE 87-858]

Havemann, Hans A., 1912- Industrialisierungspolitik für Entwicklungsländer . Aachen , 1982. 68 p. ; ISBN 3-922525-06-7 LC Card 83-203761
HC59.7 .H386 1982

Postimperialism . Boulder , 1987. x, 252 p. : ISBN 1-555-87046-5 (lib. bdg. : alk. paper) : LC Card 87-4455 DDC 338.8/881724 19
HD2932 .P67 1987

INDUSTRY AND STATE - DEVELOPING COUNTRIES - CASE STUDIES.
Newly industrializing countries and the political economy of south-south relations /. New York , 1988. p. cm. ISBN 0-312-01180-6 : LC Card 87-23476 DDC 337/.09172/4 19
HF1413 .N497 1988

INDUSTRY AND STATE - DEVELOPING COUNTRIES - CONGRESSES.
Stratégies d'industrialisation et maîtrise du développement. Paris , c1984. 115, [3] p. : ISBN 2-86844-002-9 LC Card 84-248894
HC59.7 .S854 1984

INDUSTRY AND STATE - DOMINICAN REPUBLIC.
Najri, José Antonio, 1948- Crisis, producción y desarrollo . Santo Domingo, Repúblic Dominicana , 1986 (Santo Domingo, República Dominicana : Editora Corripio) ix, 248 p. ; LC Card 87-102092
HF1502 .N34 1986

INDUSTRY AND STATE - ECUADOR.
Los Grupos monopólicos en el Ecuador . Quito, Ecuador , 1986. 208 p. : LC Card 87-404236 DDC 338.8/2/09866 19
HD2838 .G78 1986

Villalobos, Fabio. La industrialización ecuatoriana y la utilización de los recursos productivos, 1976-1983 /. Quito, Ecuador , 1987. 148 p. : LC Card 87-404654 DDC 338.09866 19
HC204.5.I52 V55 1987

INDUSTRY AND STATE - EUROPE.
Comparative government-industry relations . Oxford , New York , 1987. xiii, 321 p. ; ISBN 0-19-827493-9 : LC Card 86-28631 DDC 338.9 19
HD3611 .C63 1987

La Flexibilité du travail en Europe . Paris , 1986. 330 p. : ISBN 2-7071-1598-3 : LC Card 86-173845
HD8376.5 .F57 1986

A Guide to small firms assistance in Europe /. Aldershot, Hants, England , Brookfield, Vt., U. S.A. , c1986. vii, 263 p. ; ISBN 0-566-05082-X : LC Card 85-27307 DDC 338.6/42/094 19
HD2346.E9 G85 1986 ***NYPL [JLG 86-205]***

Hibbs, Douglas A., 1943- The political economy of industrial democracies /. Cambridge, Mass. , 1987. viii, 327 p. : ISBN 0-674-68580-6 LC Card 86-9799 DDC 339.5/09171/3 19
HB3743 .H53 1987 ***NYPL [JLE 87-1430]***

Jacquemin, Alex. Economie industrielle européenne . [Paris] , c1979. xxii, 376 p. : ISBN 2-04-010465-8 LC Card 86-673881
HD70.E8 J3x 1979

Managing industrial change in Western Europe /. London , New York , 1987. xii, 247 p. ; ISBN 0-86187-281-9 : LC Card 87-21875 DDC 338.94 19
HD3616.E8 M36 1987

Wilensky, Harold L. Democratic corporatism and policy linkages . Berkeley , c1987. ix, 97 p. ; ISBN 0-87725-169-X (pbk.) : LC Card 87-3525 DDC 338.9 19
HD3616.E8 W54 1987

INDUSTRY AND STATE - EUROPE - ADDRESSES, ESSAYS, LECTURES.
The Industrial policy debate /. San Francisco, Calif. , c1984. x, 275 p. ; ISBN 0-917616-65-0 :

LC Card 84-6741 DDC 338.973 19
HD3616.U47 I45 1984
NYPL [JLE 86-4707]

INDUSTRY AND STATE - EUROPE - CONGRESSES.
Economics and politics of industrial policy . Boulder , 1986. xi, 120 p. ; ISBN 0-8133-7140-6 (pbk. : alk. paper) : LC Card 85-26478 DDC 338.94 19
HD3616.U47 E34 1986
NYPL [JLE 86-4353]

INDUSTRY AND STATE - EUROPEAN ECONOMIC COMMUNITY COUNTRIES.
A Competitive future for Europe? . London , New York , c1987. 324 p. : ISBN 0-7099-5032-2 LC Card 87-9096 DDC 338.94 19
HD3616.E833 C66 1987

La Politica industriale della CEE . Roma , 1983. 371 p. ; LC Card 86-104849 DDC 338.94 19
HD3616.E83 P65 1983
NYPL [JLD 87-1225]

INDUSTRY AND STATE - FRANCE.
Dacier, Pierre. Les dossiers noirs de l'industrie française /. [Paris] , c1985. 414 p. ; ISBN 2-213-01659-3 : LC Card 86-178468
HC276.2 .D2 1985

Escarmelle, Jean-François. L'Etat industriel dans les politiques de sortie de crise . Louvain-la-Neuve , 1986. 237 p. : ISBN 2-87077-301-3 : LC Card 86-229137
HD3616.B43 E84 1986

France. Groupe de stratégie industrielle no 8. Sous-groupe Travaux publics. La branche des travaux publics en France et sur les marchés extérieurs /. Paris , c1985. 202 p. : ISBN 2-11-001524-1 : LC Card 86-183130
HD4168 .F69 1985

French industrial policy /. Washington, D.C. , c1986. xii, 228 p. : ISBN 0-8157-0098-9 : LC Card 85-48203 DDC 338.944 19
HD3616.F82 F74 1986 ***NYPL [JLE 87-211]***

Germon, Claude. La normalisation, clé d'un nouvel essor . Paris , c1983. 156 p. ; ISBN 2-11-001026-6 : LC Card 83-217768
HD3616.F83 G47 1983

Hayward, Jack Ernest Shalom. The state and the market economy . Brighton, Sussex , 1986. xv, 267 p. : ISBN 0-7450-0012-6 LC Card 87-672693
HC276.2 .H35x 1986b

Lanier, Lucien. Les entreprises dans la décentralisation /. Paris [1985] xvi, 217 p. ; ISBN 2-86658-028-1 : LC Card 85-217648 DDC 338.944 19
HD3616.F83 L28 1985 ***NYPL [JLD 87-546]***

Rapport d'exécution du plan intérimaire, 1982-1983 /. Paris , c1984. 146 p. : ISBN 2-11-001229-3 : LC Card 85-121410
HC276.2 .R32 1984

Le Renouvellement du tissu industriel . Paris [1986] 130 p. ; ISBN 2-11-001568-3 : LC Card 86-191910
HD3616.F83 R46 1986

Le Temps des initiatives /. Paris , c1983. 187 p. ; ISBN 2-226-01647-3 : LC Card 83-212781
HD3616.F83 T46 1983

Vedie, Henri-Louis, 1943- L'Etat-pieuvre /. Paris , c1986. 172 p. : LC Card 86-219134
HD4165 .V38 1986

INDUSTRY AND STATE - FRANCE - HISTORY.
Administration et contrôle de l'économie, 1800-1914 /. Genève , Paris , 1985. 167 p. : LC Card 86-128349 DDC 338.944 19
HD3616.F82 A66 1985

Godfrey, John F. Capitalism at war . Leamington Spa, UK ; New York : xiv, 313 p. ; ISBN 0-85496-519-X : LC Card 86-32708 DDC 338.944 19
HD3616.F82 G63 1987

INDUSTRY AND STATE - GERMANY, EAST.
Gothe, Richard, 1928- Zusammenwirken von örtlichen Staatsorganen und Kombinaten /. Berlin , 1983. 89 p. ; LC Card 84-166789
HD3616.G48 G67 1983

INDUSTRY AND STATE - GERMANY (EAST) - CONGRESSES.
Die Sozialistische Gemeinschaftsarbeit im Territorium . Potsdam-Babelsberg , 1986. 175 p. ; LC Card 86-212526
HD3616.G48 S68 1986

INDUSTRY AND STATE - GERMANY - HISTORY.
Abraham, David, 1946- The collapse of the Weimar Republic . New York , 1986. liii, 352 p. ; ISBN 0-8419-1083-9 LC Card 86-27033 DDC 338.0943 19
HD3616.G35 A27 1986

Proizvoditel'nye sily i monopolisticheskiĭ kapital v Rossii i Germanii v kontse XIX-nachale XX vv. /. Moskva , 1986. 223 p. ; LC Card 87-159751
HD2859 .P76 1986

INDUSTRY AND STATE - GERMANY, WEST.
Der Einfluss des Staates auf den Wettbewerb /. Berlin , c1986. 101 p. ; ISBN 3-428-06084-9 LC Card 87-132303 DDC 338.943 19
HD3616.G35 E38 1986

Jens, Uwe, 1935- Die weltwirtschaftliche Herausforderung . Baden-Baden , 1986. 182 p. : ISBN 3-7890-1335-8 (Deut. Bibl.) LC Card 87-146574
HD3616.G4 J46 1986

Memorandum '84 . Köln , c1984. 475 p. : ISBN 3-7609-0883-7 : LC Card 85-128558
HC286.7 .M465 1984

Neue Industriepolitik oder Stärkung der Marktkräfte? . Hamburg , 1986. xiii, 221 p. ; ISBN 3-87895-315-1 LC Card 87-408234 DDC 338.9 19
HD3616.G4 N48 1986

Nold, Wolfgang. Die Kosten der Gesetze und Verordnungen in Staat, Wirtschaft und Gesellschaft /. Konstanz , 1983. xii, 237 p. : ISBN 3-923200-07-2 LC Card 83-195590
HD3616.G4 N65 1983

INDUSTRY AND STATE - GERMANY, WEST - ADDRESSES, ESSAYS, LECTURES.
Hamer, Eberhard. Mittelstand, Träger der Marktwirtschaft . Minden , c1984- v. ; ISBN 3-7907-3056-4 (Bd. 1) LC Card 85-175274 DDC 338.6/42/0943 19
HD2346.G3 H215 1984 ***NYPL [JLK 86-61]***

INDUSTRY AND STATE - GERMANY (WEST) - REGENSBURG - HISTORY - 20TH CENTURY.
Finke, B. (Barbara) Studien zur kommunalen Industrieförderung im 20. Jahrhundert . Regensburg , c1986. 125, [45], xxv p. : ISBN 3-924956-19-7 : LC Card 87-129091 DDC 338.943/34 19
HC289.R36 F56 1986

INDUSTRY AND STATE - GREAT BRITAIN.
Britain's industrial future . New York , 1985. xxiv, 503 p. ; ISBN 0-8240-7605-2 (alk. paper) : LC Card 85-13042 DDC 338.941 19
HC256.3 .B728 1985 ***NYPL [JLD 86-3461]***

Hattersley, Roy. Economic priorities for a labour government /. New York , 1987. ix, 198 p. ; ISBN 0-312-00987-9 : LC Card 87-9576 DDC 338.941 19
HC256.6 .H385 1987

Neue Industriepolitik oder Stärkung der Marktkräfte? . Hamburg , 1986. xiii, 221 p. ; ISBN 3-87895-315-1 LC Card 87-408234 DDC 338.9 19
HD3616.G4 N48 1986

Perry, Martin, 1956- Small factories and economic development /. Aldershot, Hants., England , Brookfield, VT, USA , c1986. xvi, 229 p. ; ISBN 0-566-05208-3 : LC Card 86-9904 DDC 338.6/42/0941 19
HC260.D5 P47 1986 ***NYPL [JLD 86-3993]***

Quinn, Dennis Patrick, 1955- Restructuring the automobile industry . New York , 1988. p. cm. ISBN 0-231-06524-8 LC Card 87-15919 DDC 338.4/76292/0941 19
HD9710.U52 Q56 1988

Thomas, R. E. (Raymond Elliott) The government of business /. Oxford, UK , Atlantic Highlands, NJ, USA , 1987. viii, 277 p. : ISBN 0-86003-548-4 LC Card 87-12647 DDC 338.0941 19
HD70.G7 T48 1987

Vogel, David, 1947- National styles of regulation . Ithaca, N.Y. , 1986. 325 p. ; ISBN 0-8014-1658-2 LC Card 85-21332 DDC 363.7/056/0941 19
HC260.E5 V64 1986 ***NYPL [JLE 86-2434]***

INDUSTRY AND STATE - HUNGARY.
Bontó, László. Iparfejlesztés a hetedik ötéves terv időszakában /. [Budapest] , 1986. 170, [4] p. : ISBN 963-09-3001-3 : LC Card 87-138631
HC300.28 .B659 1986

Botos, Balázs. Kérdőjelek iparunk fejlesztésében /. Budapest , 1984. 391, [1] p. ; ISBN 963-221-392-0 : LC Card 85-156613
HC300.28 .B69 1984

Veress, József, Dr. A veszélyhelyzetbe került vállalatok és a gazdaságirányítás /. Budapest , 1986. 207, [1] p. ; ISBN 963-221-778-0 : LC Card 87-136695
HG3769.H94 V47 1986

INDUSTRY AND STATE - INDIA.
Baig, Nafees, 1941- Government controls and industrial expansion in India /. Aligarh , 1983. viii, 223 p. ; LC Card 83-907504 DDC 338.954 19
HD3616.I43 B35 1983
NYPL [JLD 86-4330]

Mahajan, V. S., 1923- Growth of agriculture and industry in India /. New Delhi , c1983. 176 p. ; LC Card 83-906175 DDC 338.0954 19
HD2072 .M23 1983 ***NYPL [JLD 87-671]***

Wiemann, Jürgen. India in transition . New Delhi , Berlin , 1986. xxi, 151 p. ; LC Card 87-900287 DDC 338.954 19
HD3616.I83 W54 1986

INDUSTRY AND STATE - INDIA - ADDRESSES, ESSAYS, LECTURES.
Ranadive, K. R. Accumulation, employment, and labour aristocracy . Bombay [1982] 55 p. ; LC Card 83-903051 DDC 305.5/62/0954 19
HD8686.5 .R325 1982 ***NYPL [JLF 87-500]***

INDUSTRY AND STATE - INDIA - CONGRESSES.
Workshop on Impact of Regulatory Mechanism on Corporate Sector (1984 : Bangalore, India) Workshop on Impact of Regulatory Mechanism on Corporate Sector . New Delhi [1985] 104 p. : LC Card 87-902536 DDC 338.954 19
HC435.2 .W67 1984

INDUSTRY AND STATE - INDONESIA.
Ibrahim, Saaduddin. Aspek-aspek proteksi dalam industri dan perdagangan /. Jakarta , 1987. 251 p. : LC Card 87-941314
HD4304 .I27 1987

Indonesia. Departemen Perindustrian. Pelaksanaan program keterkaitan antar sektor industri dan antara sektor industri dengan sektor ekonomi lainnya . [Jakarta] [1985] i, 59 p. ; LC Card 85-941789
HD3616.I53 I49 1985

Indonesia. Departemen Perindustrian. Wilayah pusat pertumbuhan industri . [Jakarta] [1985] 20, vi p. : LC Card 85-941790
HC450.D5 I53 1985

Soehoed, A. R. (Abdoel Raoef), 1920- Industrial development during Pelita III. [Jakarta] [1982] 23 p. ; LC Card 83-940924 DDC 338.9598 19
HD3616.I53 S629 1982

INDUSTRY AND STATE - IRELAND.
Innovation policy . Paris , Washington, D.C. , 1987. 75 p. ; ISBN 92-64-12918-9 (pbk.) : LC Card 87-164488 DDC 338/.06 19
HC260.5.Z9 T45 1987

INDUSTRY AND STATE - ITALY.
D'Angelo, Massimo. Criteri per una cooperazione industriale con i paesi in via di sviluppo /. Milano , c1981. 294 p. ; ISBN 88-20-42145-3 : LC Card 82-113466
HF1549 .D36 1981 ***NYPL [JLD 86-3318]***

Neue Industriepolitik oder Stärkung der Marktkräfte? . Hamburg , 1986. xiii, 221 p. ; ISBN 3-87895-315-1 LC Card 87-408234 DDC 338.9 19
HD3616.G4 N48 1986

Politiche tributarie e struttura industriale in Italia /. Bologna , c1986. 118 p. ; ISBN 88-15-01224-9 : LC Card 86-224989
HD2753.I7 P65 1986

Quale strategia per l'industria? . Bologna , c1986. 221 p. : ISBN 88-15-00975-2 : LC Card

86-182300
HC310.I53 Q35 1986

Rapporto sulle partecipazioni statali /. Milano [1981] 1 v. (in various pagings) ; ISBN 88-20-42161-5 : LC Card 81-199972 DDC 338.945 19
HC310.I53 R35 ***NYPL [JLD 83-2970]***

Relazione programmatica delle partecipazioni statali per il 1984 . Roma , 1985. 563 p. ; LC Card 86-176014
HC310.I53 R45 1985

Struttura industriale e politiche macroeconomiche in Italia /. Bologna , c1986. 152 p. : ISBN 88-15-01193-5 : LC Card 87-100465
HC305 .S845 1986

Tre incognite per lo sviluppo . Milano, Italy , c1986. 383 p. : LC Card 86-198933
HC310.I53 T74 1986

INDUSTRY AND STATE - ITALY - ADDRESSES, ESSAYS, LECTURES.
Per una ristrutturazione e riconversione dell'industria italiana /. Bologna , 1980. 244 p. ; LC Card 82-102594 DDC 338.945 19
HD3616.I83 P43 ***NYPL [JLD 86-599]***

INDUSTRY AND STATE - ITALY - CONGRESSES.
La Crisi delle partecipazioni statali, motivi e prospettive /. Milano , c1981. 240 p. ; ISBN 88-20-42148-8 : LC Card 81-200055
HC310.I53 C74 1981 ***NYPL [JLD 86-3503]***

INDUSTRY AND STATE - ITALY - FRIULI-VENEZIA GIULIA.
Grandinetti, Roberto, 1953- Sistema industriale e politiche regionali . Milano, Italy , 1984. 234 p. : LC Card 85-176111 DDC 338.945/39 19
HC307.F68 G73 1984

INDUSTRY AND STATE - ITALY - HISTORY - SOURCES.
Colombo, Giuseppe, 1836-1921. Industria e politica nella storia d'Italia . [Milano] , Roma , c1985. 497 p. : ISBN 88-420-2555-0 : LC Card 85-180231 DDC 338.945 19
HC310.I53 C65 1985 ***NYPL [JLE 86-2517]***

INDUSTRY AND STATE - JAPAN.
Bandō, Satoshi, 1931- Sengo rōdō kumiai undōshi . Tokyo , 1975. 278 p. ; LC Card 75-804891
HD6832 B36 ***NYPL [*OSM 86-2348]***

Comparative government-industry relations . Oxford , New York , 1987. xiii, 321 p. ; ISBN 0-19-827493-9 : LC Card 86-28631 DDC 338.9 19
HD3611 .C63 1987

Dore, Ronald Philip. Flexible rigidities . London , 1986. 278 p. ; ISBN 0-485-11269-8 LC Card 87-672689
HC462.9 .D65 1986

Hirono, Ryōkichi. Factors which hinder or help productivity improvement in the Asian region, a review and the prospect . Tokyo, Japan , c1980. v, 111 p. ; ISBN 92-833-1470-0 LC Card 81-174179 DDC 338/.06/0952 19
HD56 .H57 1980 ***NYPL [JLD 86-2287]***

Hollerman, Leon. Japan, disincorporated . Stanford, Calif. , c1988. xxi, 185 p. ; ISBN 0-8179-8631-6 : LC Card 87-25633 DDC 338.952 19
HD3616.J33 H65 1988

Industrial policy of Japan /. Tokyo , Orlando, FL , 1988. p. cm. ISBN 0-12-418650-5 (U. S. : alk. paper) LC Card 87-1409 DDC 338.952 19
HD3616.J33 I816 1988

The Japanese challenge . Stamford, Conn., U. S.A. , c1986. xii, 108 leaves : ISBN 0-89336-489-4 (pbk.) LC Card 87-404570 DDC 338/.06 19
HC465.T4 J365 1986

Laumer, Helmut. Strukturpolitik für traditionelle Industriezweige in Japan /. Berlin , c1985. 173 p. : ISBN 3-428-05920-4 LC Card 86-151482
HD3616.J32 L38 1985

Neue Industriepolitik oder Stärkung der Marktkräfte? . Hamburg , 1986. xiii, 221 p. ; ISBN 3-87895-315-1 LC Card 87-408234 DDC 338.9 19
HD3616.G4 N48 1986

Samuels, Richard J. The business of the Japanese state . Ithaca , 1987. xii, 359 p. : ISBN 0-8014-2022-9 (alk. paper) LC Card 87-5230 DDC 338.4/7621042/0952 19
HD9502.J32 S27 1987

Vogel, Ezra F. Comeback, case by case . New York , c1985. 320 p. ; ISBN 0-671-46079-X LC Card 84-22232 DDC 338.952 19
HD3616.U47 V64 1985 ***NYPL [JLE 85-2275]***

Wilensky, Harold L. Democratic corporatism and policy linkages . Berkeley , c1987. ix, 97 p. ; ISBN 0-87725-169-X (pbk.) : LC Card 87-3525 DDC 338.9 19
HD3616.E8 W54 1987

INDUSTRY AND STATE - JAPAN - ADDRESSES, ESSAYS, LECTURES.
The Industrial policy debate /. San Francisco, Calif. , c1984. x, 275 p. ; ISBN 0-917616-65-0 : LC Card 84-6741 DDC 338.973 19
HD3616.U47 I45 1984 ***NYPL [JLE 86-4707]***

INDUSTRY AND STATE - JAPAN - ECONOMETRIC MODELS.
Audretsch, David B. Industrial policy, R&D, and U. S.-Japanese trade /. Berlin [1986] 39 p. ; LC Card 87-156721 DDC 382/.0952/073 19
HF3127 .A93 1986

INDUSTRY AND STATE - KOREA (SOUTH)
Korea . Washington, D.C., U. S.A. [1987] 2 v. : ISBN 0-8213-0887-4 (pbk. : v. 1) LC Card 87-2213 DDC 338.9519/5 19
HD3616.K853 K67 1987

INDUSTRY AND STATE - LATIN AMERICA.
Gwynne, Robert N. Industrialization and urbanization in Latin America /. Baltimore, Md. , 1986. xiv, 259 p. : ISBN 0-8018-3113-X LC Card 85-10079 DDC 338.098 19
HC125 .G96 1986 ***NYPL [JLD 86-2200]***

INDUSTRY AND STATE - LIBYA.
Naur, Maja. Political mobilization and industry in Libya /. [Uppsala] , c1986. 268 p. : ISBN 87-500-2648-8 (pbk.) : LC Card 87-141231 DDC 338.961/2 19
HD3616.L752 N38 1986

INDUSTRY AND STATE - MEXICO.
Government and private sector in contemporary Mexico /. [La Jolla, Calif.] , 1987. iv, 146 p. ; LC Card 87-622060 DDC 338.972 19
HD3616.M43 G68 1987

México, una economía en transición /. México, D.F. , 1984-1985. 3 v. ; ISBN 968-18-1900-4 (v. 1) LC Card 86-235462
HC135 .M549 1985

Rey Romay, Benito. La ofensiva empresarial contra la intervención del estado /. México , 1984. 160 p. ; ISBN 968-231-283-3 LC Card 86-151140
HD4013 .R49 1984

Story, Dale, 1950- Industry, the state, and public policy in Mexico /. Austin , 1986. xii, 275 p. ; ISBN 0-292-73837-4 LC Card 85-13363 DDC 338.972 19
HD3616.M43 S76 1986 ***NYPL [JLE 87-656]***

INDUSTRY AND STATE - MEXICO - CONGRESSES.
Reunión Nacional para el Desarrollo de la Industria, el Comercio, la Distribución y Otros Servicios (1981 : Mexico City, Mexico) Memoria /. [Mexico City] , 1981. 428 p., [4] folded leaves of plates : LC Card 84-228700
HD3616.M42 R46 1981

INDUSTRY AND STATE - MEXICO - HISTORY - 19TH CENTURY.
Keremitsis, Dawn, 1921- The cotton textile industry in Porfiriato, Mexico, 1870-1910 /. New York , 1987. 232 p. : ISBN 0-8240-1364-6 (alk. paper) : LC Card 87-7619 DDC 338.4/767721/0972 19
HD9884.M42 K47 1987

INDUSTRY AND STATE - MEXICO - HISTORY - 20TH CENTURY.
Martínez Nava, Juan Manuel. Conflicto estado-empresarios en los gobiernos de Cárdenas, López Mateos y Echeverría /. México , 1984. 240 p. ; ISBN 968-429-411-5 LC Card 85-240016
HD3616.M43 M37 1984

INDUSTRY AND STATE - MEXICO - MONTERREY - HISTORY.
Cerutti, Mario. Burguesía y capitalismo en Monterrey, 1850-1910 /. México, D.F. , 1983. 214 p. ; ISBN 968-8430-10-2 LC Card 86-221932
HC138.M6 C47 1983

INDUSTRY AND STATE - MEXICO - NUEVO LEON (STATE)
Nuevo León (Mexico : State). Archivo General del Estado. Permisos y concesiones, 1890-1912 /. [Monterrey, Mexico] [1981] 43 leaves ; LC Card 81-216459
HD3616.M44 N866 1981

INDUSTRY AND STATE - NEW YORK (STATE)
New York (State). Legislature. Legislative Commission on Public-Private Cooperation. Legislative Commission on Public-Private Cooperation second report . [Albany] [1984] 57 p. ; LC Card 86-622576 DDC 338.9747 19
HC107.N7 N3743 1984

New York (State). Legislature. Legislative Commission on Public-Private Cooperation. Working together for New York's economy . [Albany] [1983] 57 p. ; LC Card 86-622577 DDC 338.9747 19
HC107.N7 N3743 1983

INDUSTRY AND STATE - NIGERIA.
Anyansi-Archibong, Chi. B., 1949- Strategy and structure of enterprise in a developing country /. Aldershots, Hants, England , Brookfield, Vt., USA , c1988. xvii, 274 p. : ISBN 0-566-05471-X : LC Card 87-12020 DDC 658/.009669 19
HD70.N43 A59 1988

INDUSTRY AND STATE - OCEANIA.
Re-orientation of industrial policies . [Bangkok] [1979. iii, 196 p. ; LC Card 83-187259
HD3616.A772 R46 1979

INDUSTRY AND STATE - PACIFIC AREA - CONGRESSES.
The Industrial future of the Pacific basin /. Boulder , 1984. xvi, 285 p. : ISBN 0-86531-685-6 LC Card 83-51653 DDC 338.9/009182/3 19
HC681 .I53 1984 ***NYPL [JLD 86-3100]***

INDUSTRY AND STATE - PAKISTAN.
Illarionov, Sergeĭ Ivanovich. Rol′ gosudarstva v razvitii ėkonomiki Pakistana . Moskva , 1981. 196, [3] p. ; LC Card 82-112505
HC440.5 .I39 1981

INDUSTRY AND STATE - PANAMA.
Correa V., Virgilio (Correa Vásquez) Centelleo de la industria en Panamá /. [Panama?] 1986 ([Panama, Panama] : Tall. Gráf. del Centro de Impresión Educativa) 279 p., [6] p. of plates : LC Card 87-404562 DDC 338.097287 19
HC147 .C67 1986

Panama . Washington, D.C., U. S.A. , c1985. xxv, 307 p., [8] p., [1] leaf of plates : ISBN 0-8213-0580-8 LC Card 85-12420 DDC 338.97287 19
HC147 .P43 1985 ***NYPL [JLF 86-1919]***

INDUSTRY AND STATE - PAPUA NEW GUINEA.
Re-orientation of industrial policies . [Bangkok] [1979. iii, 196 p. ; LC Card 83-187259
HD3616.A772 R46 1979

INDUSTRY AND STATE - PENNSYLVANIA.
Allen, David N. Nurturing advanced technology enterprises . New York , c1986. xvi, 268 p. ; ISBN 0-275-92136-0 (alk. paper) : LC Card 86-9411 DDC 338.4/762/0009748 19
HC107.P43 H533 1986 ***NYPL [JLE 86-3609]***

INDUSTRY AND STATE - PHILIPPINES.
Re-orientation of industrial policies . [Bangkok] [1979. iii, 196 p. ; LC Card 83-187259
HD3616.A772 R46 1979

INDUSTRY AND STATE - PORTUGAL - HISTORY.
Ferreira, António Fonseca. A acumulação capitalista em Portugal . Porto , 1977. 156 p. ; LC Card 85-194898
HF3696 .F47 1977

INDUSTRY AND STATE - QUÉBEC (PROVINCE)
Québec (Province). Groupe de travail sur la déréglementation. Réglementer moins et mieux . [Quebec] [1986] 2 v. ; ISBN 2-551-08729-5 (v. 1) LC Card 86-206349
HD3616.C24 Q47 1986

INDUSTRY AND STATE - SAUDI ARABIA.
A Guide to industrial investment /. Riyadh , 1986. vi, 286 p., [4] leaves of plates : LC Card

87-400301 DDC 332.6/7322538 19
HC415.33.Z9 I534 1986

INDUSTRY AND STATE - SOVIET UNION.
Falaleev, A. N. Formirovanie predpriiatiia kommunisticheskogo tipa /. Moskva , 1980. 126 p. ; LC Card 81-144517
HD3616.S472 F35 1980

INDUSTRY AND STATE - SOVIET UNION - HISTORY.
Proizvoditel'nye sily i monopolisticheskiĭ kapital v Rossii i Germanii v kontse XIX-nachale XX vv. /. Moskva , 1986. 223 p. ; LC Card 87-159751
HD2859 .P76 1986

INDUSTRY AND STATE - SPAIN.
Maravall, Fernando. Economía y política industrial en España /. Madrid , 1987. 231 p. : ISBN 84-368-0340-X LC Card 87-121800
HC385 .M2574 1987

Pascual, Julio, 1944- En defensa de la empresa . Madrid , c1984. 242 p. ; ISBN 84-7209-175-9 LC Card 85-215607
HD3616.S49 P34 1984 ***NYPL [JLD 87-1507]***

La Reconversión industrial, la crisis y reforma agraria. [Madrid] [1984] 148 p. : ISBN 84-398-1197-7 LC Card 86-216324
HC385 .R375 1984

INDUSTRY AND STATE - SPAIN - ANDALUSIA.
Plan económico para Andalucía, 1984-1986 /. Andalucía [1985?] 164 p. ; ISBN 84-505-0611-5 LC Card 86-205786
HD3616.S495 A536 1985

INDUSTRY AND STATE - SUDAN.
Affan, Bodour O. Abu. Industrial policies and industrialization in the Sudan /. Khartoum, Sudan , 1985. 180 p. ; ISBN 0-08-637205-44 (pbk.) LC Card 86-981076 DDC 338.9624 19
HC835 .A58 1985

INDUSTRY AND STATE - SWEDEN.
Lindmark, Leif. Företagsstöd och kommunalt risktagande /. Stockholm [1984] iv, 49 p. : ISBN 91-38-08297-7 LC Card 85-106839
HD3646.S8 L55 1984

Olofsson, Christer. Kommunala bolag med industriutvecklings uppgifter . Stockholm [1984] 82 p. ; ISBN 91-38-08114-8 LC Card 85-106731
HD3616.S53 O46 1984

INDUSTRY AND STATE - SWEDEN - CASE STUDIES.
Icke-permanent stöd till tre industriföretag . [Stockholm] [1981] 245 p. : ISBN 91-38-06270-4 LC Card 83-245223
HD3646.S8 I25 1981

Två samhällsekonomiska utvärderingar av icke-permanent industristöd . [Stockholm] [1981] 221 p. : ISBN 91-38-06269-0 LC Card 83-245219
HD3646.S8 T85 1981

INDUSTRY AND STATE - TANZANIA.
Luttrell, William L. Post-capitalist industrialization . New York , 1986. xv, 189 p. : ISBN 0-275-92310-X : LC Card 86-9452 DDC 338.9678 19
HD3616.T343 L88 1986 ***NYPL [JLE 87-351]***

Skarstein, Rune. Industrial development in Tanzania . Uppsala , Stockholm, Sweden , 1986. xi, 291 p. : ISBN 91-7106-254-8 (pbk.) LC Card 87-134925 DDC 338.9678 19
HC885 .S58 1986

INDUSTRY AND STATE - THAILAND.
Re-orientation of industrial policies . [Bangkok] [1979. iii, 196 p. ; LC Card 83-187259
HD3616.A772 R46 1979

INDUSTRY AND STATE - UNITED STATES.
Chamber of Commerce of the United States of America. Council on Trends and Perspective. Government regulation of business . Washington, D.C. , c1979. x, 108 p. ; ISBN 0-89834-018-7(pbk.) : LC Card 79-91604 DDC 338.973
HD3616.U46 C44 1979 ***NYPL [JLE 80-2446]***

Comparative government-industry relations . Oxford , New York , 1987. xiii, 321 p. ; ISBN 0-19-827493-9 : LC Card 86-28631 DDC 338.9 19
HD3611 .C63 1987

Forging new relationships among business, labor, and government /. Greenwich, Conn. , c1986. xiii, 210 p. ; ISBN 0-89232-656-5 : LC Card 86-2839 DDC 338.973 19
HD3616.U47 F583 1986 ***NYPL [JLE 86-3452]***

French industrial policy /. Washington, D.C. , c1986. xii, 228 p. : ISBN 0-8157-0098-9 : LC Card 85-48203 DDC 338.944 19
HD3616.F82 F74 1986 ***NYPL [JLE 87-211]***

Hibbs, Douglas A., 1943- The political economy of industrial democracies /. Cambridge, Mass. , 1987. viii, 327 p. : ISBN 0-674-68580-6 LC Card 86-9799 DDC 339.5/09171/3 19
HB3743 .H53 1987 ***NYPL [JLE 87-1430]***

How federal policies affect the steel industry. Washington, D.C. [1987] xii, 66 p. : LC Card 87-601115 DDC 338.4/7669142/0973 19
HD9516 .H65 1987

Kozlova, K. B. Institutsionalizm v amerikanskoĭ politėkonomii . Moskva , 1987. 214, [2] p. ; LC Card 87-159642
HB99.5 .K69 1987

Neue Industriepolitik oder Stärkung der Marktkräfte? . Hamburg , 1986. xiii, 221 p. ; ISBN 3-87895-315-1 LC Card 87-408234 DDC 338.9 19
HD3616.G4 N48 1986

Noble, Charles, 1948- Liberalism at work . Philadelphia , 1986. x, 292 p. : ISBN 0-87722-421-8 (alk. paper) : LC Card 86-1766 DDC 353.0083/0289 19
HD7654 .N63 1986 ***NYPL [JLE 86-4426]***

The Politics of American economic policy making /. Armonk, N.Y. , c1987. 455 p. : ISBN 0-87332-406-4 : LC Card 87-12827 DDC 338.973 19
HJ257 .P59 1987

Public policy toward corporations /. Gainesville , 1987. p. cm. ISBN 0-8130-0880-8 LC Card 87-21324 DDC 338.973 19
HD3616.U47 P82 1987

Quinn, Dennis Patrick, 1955- Restructuring the automobile industry . New York , 1988. p. cm. ISBN 0-231-06524-8 LC Card 87-15919 DDC 338.4/76292/0941 19
HD9710.U52 Q56 1988

Research funding as an investment--can we measure the returns? Washington, D.C. [1986] vi, 72 p. : LC Card 86-600525 DDC 338/.06 19
HC110.R4 R47 1986

Vogel, David, 1947- National styles of regulation . Ithaca, N.Y. , 1986. 325 p. ; ISBN 0-8014-1658-2 LC Card 85-21332 DDC 363.7/056/0941 19
HC260.E5 V64 1986 ***NYPL [JLE 86-2434]***

Vogel, Ezra F. Comeback, case by case . New York , c1985. 320 p. ; ISBN 0-671-46079-X LC Card 84-22232 DDC 338.952 19
HD3616.U47 V64 1985 ***NYPL [JLE 85-2275]***

Wilensky, Harold L. Democratic corporatism and policy linkages . Berkeley , c1987. ix, 97 p. ; ISBN 0-87725-169-X (pbk.) : LC Card 87-3525 DDC 338.9 19
HD3616.E8 W54 1987

INDUSTRY AND STATE - UNITED STATES - ADDRESSES, ESSAYS, LECTURES.
The Industrial policy debate /. San Francisco, Calif. , c1984. x, 275 p. ; ISBN 0-917616-65-0 : LC Card 84-6741 DDC 338.973 19
HD3616.U47 I45 1984 ***NYPL [JLE 86-4707]***

INDUSTRY AND STATE - UNITED STATES - CASE STUDIES.
Aram, John D., 1942- Managing business and public policy . Marshfield, Mass. , c1986. xv, 736 p. : ISBN 0-582-98830-6 LC Card 85-16955 DDC 338.973 19
HD3616.U47 A73 1985 ***NYPL [JLE 86-2593]***

DiFilippo, Anthony, 1950- Military spending and industrial decline . Westport, Conn. , c1986. x, 199 p. ; ISBN 0-313-25179-7 (lib bdg. : alk. paper) LC Card 85-27144 DDC 338.4/7621902/0973 19
HD9703.U5 D54 1986 ***NYPL [JLD 86-2930]***

Kaplan, Daniel P. Has trade protection revitalized domestic industries? Washington, D.C. [1986] xvi, 111 p. : LC Card 86-603423 DDC 382.7/3/0973 19
HF1421 .K36 1986

INDUSTRY AND STATE - UNITED STATES - CONGRESSES.
Economics and politics of industrial policy . Boulder , 1986. xi, 120 p. ; ISBN 0-8133-7140-6 (pbk. : alk. paper) : LC Card 85-26478 DDC 338.94 19
HD3616.U47 E34 1986 ***NYPL [JLE 86-4353]***

INDUSTRY AND STATE - UNITED STATES - HISTORY.
Chandler, Alfred Dupont. The coming of managerial capitalism . Homewood, Ill. , 1985. xiv, 877 p. : ISBN 0-256-03285-8 LC Card 84-82470 DDC 338.6/44/0973 19
HD2785 .C47 1985 ***NYPL [JLE 86-4418]***

Filippelli, Ronald L. Labor in the USA . New York , c1984. xii, 315 p. ; ISBN 0-394-34149-X LC Card 83-23458 DDC 331/.0973 19
HD8066 .F54 1984 ***NYPL [JFE 86-5130]***

Weaver, Paul, 1942 Oct. 18- The suicidal corporation /. New York , c1988. p. cm. ISBN 0-671-52378-3 LC Card 87-23468 DDC 338.7/4/0973 19
HD2785 .W38 1988

INDUSTRY AND STATE - UNITED STATES - HISTORY - 20TH CENTURY.
Shook, Dale N. William G. McAdoo and the development of national economic policy, 1913-1918 /. New York , 1987. 427 p. ; ISBN 0-8240-8092-0 (alk. paper) : LC Card 87-23766 DDC 338.973 19
HC106.2 .S55 1987

INDUSTRY AND STATE - UNITED STATES - STATES.
Committee for Economic Development. Research and Policy Committee. Leadership for dynamic state economies . New York, N.Y. , 1986. xii, 104 p. ; ISBN 0-87186-782-6 LC Card 86-20760 DDC 338.973 19
HC103 .C734 1986 ***NYPL [JLF 86-1832]***

The New economic role of American states . New York , 1988. x, 370 p. ; ISBN 0-19-505003-7 LC Card 87-12499 DDC 338.973 19
HC106.8 .N495 1988

The State and local industrial policy /. Chicago, Ill. , c1987. x, 195 p. : ISBN 0-918286-46-8 (pbk.) LC Card 86-72373 DDC 338.973 19
HD3616.U47 S68 1987

INDUSTRY AND STATE - VENEZUELA.
Rangel Belis, Gonzalo. Sector económico externo, industrialización y conflictos laborales en Venezuela /. Valencia , 1985. 141 p. : ISBN 980-212-007-3 LC Card 86-226708
HF1529 .R36 1985

INDUSTRY AND STATE - YUGOSLAVIA.
Stojanović, Radmila. Na putu ka visoko industrijalizovanom socijalizmu /. Beograd , 1984. 208 p. ; LC Card 85-194079
HD3611 .S77 1984

INDUSTRY AND WEATHER.
Hesse, Günter, Dr. Die Entstehung industrialisierter Volkswirtschaften . Tübingen , 1982. vi, 100 p. : ISBN 3-16-344559-4 : LC Card 83-153439 DDC 338.9 19
HD84 .H4718 1982 ***NYPL [JLE 87-1169]***

Industry assistance . Rattigan, G. A. (Godfrey Alfred), 1911- Carlton, Vic. , Beaverton, Or. , 1986. viii, 289 p., [4] p. of plates : ISBN 0-522-84313-1 LC Card 86-202866 DDC 338.994 19
HF2483 .R38 1986

INDUSTRY - AUSTRIA.
Serres, Marcel de, 1783-1862. Essai sur les arts at les manufactures de l'empire d'Autriche /. Paris , 1814-1815. 3 v. : LC Card 85-666370
HC263 .S47x 1814

Industry basics : an introduction to the history, structure, and technology of the telecommunications industry. 2nd ed. Washington, D.C. (2000 M St., N.W., Suite 550, Washington 20036) : North American

Telecommunications Association, c1986. 53 p. : ill. ; 28 cm. Bibliography: p. 53. LC Card 86-208618 DDC 384.6/0973 19
1. Telephone. 2. Telecommunication. 3. Telephone - United States. 4. Telecommunication - United States. I. North American Telecommunications Association.
HE8731 .I53 1986

INDUSTRY - CLASSIFICATION.
Nel, P. A. The BM industrial register and its application in industrial marketing /. Pretoria , 1977. iii, 29, [34] p. ; ISBN 0-949951-74-9 (pbk.) LC Card 85-127469
HC905 .N45 1977

Industry competition and the formation of the European common market /. Yamawaki, Hideki. Berlin [1986] 34, 3 p. ; LC Card 87-156700 DDC 341.24/22 19
HD41 .Y35 1986

Industry concentration statistics : details by industry class, Australia : integrated economic censuses, 1968-69. Canberra : Australian Bureau of Statistics, [1974] 194 p. ; 30 cm. Cover title. LC Card 82-132323
1. Industrial concentration - Australia - Statistics. I. Australian Bureau of Statistics. II. Title: Integrated econmic censuses, 1968-69.
HD2930 .I53 1974

INDUSTRY - COSTS. see **COSTS, INDUSTRIAL.**

INDUSTRY - ENERGY CONSERVATION.
Nosko, Herbert. Rationelle Energieverwendung im Industriebetrieb . Berlin , c1986. xiii, 289 p. : ISBN 3-503-02547-2 LC Card 86-192206
HD9502.A2 N67 1986

INDUSTRY - ENERGY CONSERVATION - ENVIRONMENTAL ASPECTS.
Nosko, Herbert. Rationelle Energieverwendung im Industriebetrieb . Berlin , c1986. xiii, 289 p. : ISBN 3-503-02547-2 LC Card 86-192206
HD9502.A2 N67 1986

INDUSTRY - ENERGY CONSUMPTION - COSTS.
Hall, John, 1946- Reducing industrial oil costs /. Aldershot, Hants England , Brookfield, Vt., U. S.A. , c1987. xvii, 118 p. : ISBN 0-291-39740-9 (U. S.) : LC Card 86-29511 DDC 338.2/3 19
HD9560.4 .H35 1987

INDUSTRY - ENVIRONMENTAL ASPECTS.
Bellini, James. High tech holocaust /. Newton Abbot , c1986. 255 p. ; ISBN 0-7153-8812-6
NYPL [JLE 87-827]

Thomé, Gotthardt, 1949- Produktgestaltung und Ökologie /. München , c1981. xii, 212 p. : ISBN 3-88259-086-6 : LC Card 81-146058
HD69.N4 T54 1981 ***NYPL [JLD 86-2800]***

INDUSTRY - GOVERNMENT CONTROL AND OWNERSHIP. see **INDUSTRY AND STATE.**

INDUSTRY - HISTORY - 18TH CENTURY.
Verley, Patrick. La révolution industrielle /. Paris , c1985. 270 p. : ISBN 2-86676-194-4 LC Card 86-116016 DDC 338.09 19
HD2321 .V47 1985

INDUSTRY - HISTORY - 19TH CENTURY.
Verley, Patrick. La révolution industrielle /. Paris , c1985. 270 p. : ISBN 2-86676-194-4 LC Card 86-116016 DDC 338.09 19
HD2321 .V47 1985

INDUSTRY - HISTORY - CONGRESSES.
Lowell Conference on Industrial History (1984) The world of the Industrial Revolution . [Andover, MA] , 1986. 177 p. : ISBN 0-937474-08-8 (pbk.) LC Card 86-31242 DDC 338.09 19
HD2321 .L69 1984

Industry in the 1980s : structural change and interdependence : regular issue of the biennial industrial development survey / United Nations Industrial Development Organization, Vienna. New York : United Nations, 1985. xii, 228 p. : ill. ; 24 cm. Spine title: Industrial development survey. "This survey was prepared by the Division for Industrial Studies (Statistics and Survey Unit) of UNIDO"--T.p. verso. Abstract in English, French, and Spanish inserted. Includes bibliographical references. "ID/331"--T.p. verso. "United Nations publication sales no. E.85.II.B.8"--T.p. verso. ISBN 92-1-106207-1 (pbk.) LC Card 86-227928 DDC 338.09 19
1. Manufactures. 2. Industry. 3. Economic history - 1971-. 4. International economic relations. I. United Nations. Industrial Development Organization. II. United Nations Industrial Development Organization. Division for Industrial Studies. Statistics and Survey Unit. III. Title: Structural change and interdependence. IV. Title: Industrial development survey.
HD9720.5 .I53 1985

INDUSTRY - INFORMATION SERVICES.
Intelligence for economic development . Leamington Spa, [Warwickshire] ; New York : xiii, 264 p. : ISBN 0-85496-520-3 : LC Card 86-32250 DDC 025/.063389 19
HD76.2 .I58 1987

INDUSTRY - LOCATION - DECISION MAKING.
Facility planning technology /. Norcross, Ga. , c1987. viii, 935 p. : ISBN 0-910436-26-6 LC Card 86-72097 DDC 658.2/1 19
HD30.28 .F33 1987

INDUSTRY - LOCATION - MATHEMATICAL MODELS.
Wäscher, Gerhard. Innerbetriebliche Standortplanung bei einfacher und mehrfacher Zielsetzung /. Wiesbaden , c1982. 389 p. : ISBN 3-409-34487-X LC Card 86-105991
HD58 .W29 1982

INDUSTRY - MORAL AND ETHICAL ASPECTS.
Wohlfarth, Karl Anton. Leistung und Ethos . Paderborn , 1984. 266 p. ; ISBN 3-506-70223-8 LC Card 84-238158
HD60 .W64 1984

INDUSTRY - ORGANIZATION. see **INDUSTRIAL ORGANIZATION.**

INDUSTRY - POWER SUPPLY.
Debeir, Jean-Claude. Les servitudes de la puissance . [Paris] , c1986. 428 p. : ISBN 2-08-211163-6 : LC Card 87-121577
HD9502.A2 D43 1986

Industry projections, occupational projections, 1985-1988, State of Iowa. [Iowa City] : Labor Market Information Unit, Iowa Dept. of Job Service, [1986] [42] leaves ; 28 cm. "In cooperation with the Iowa State Occupational Information Coordinating Committee and the Office of Planning and Programming." "April 1986." Tables. LC Card 86-622540 DDC 331.12/09777/021 19
1. Employment forecasting - Iowa - Statistics. 2. Iowa - Industries - Forecasting - Statistics. 3. Iowa - Occupations - Forecasting - Statistics. 4. Job vacancies - Iowa - Forecasting - Statistics. 5. Iowa - Forecasting - Statistics. I. Iowa. Labor Market Information Unit. II. Iowa State Occupational Information Coordinating Committee. III. Iowa. Office for Planning and Programming.
HD5725.I8 I53 1986

INDUSTRY (PSYCHOLOGY) see **WORK.**

Industry research report.
Consumer financial services . Boston, MA (200 Portland St., Boston 02114) , 1986. xvi, 83 p. : LC Card 86-230330 DDC 332.1/028 19
HD9696.B363 U543 1986

Healthcare electronics /. Boston, MA (89 Broad St., Boston 02110) , c1986. iv, 79 p. : LC Card 86-212563 DDC 381/.45681761 19
HD9995.E43 U55 1986

The Home terminal II . [Boston, Ma.] (89 Broad St., Boston 02110) [1986] 63 leaves : LC Card 86-211108 DDC 381/.45621396/0973 19
HD9696.C63 U518327 1986

Living with SNA /. Boston, MA (89 Broad St., Boston 02110) [1986] 60 p. : LC Card 86-201765 DDC 381/.4500468/0973 19
HD9696.C63 U5223 1986

Manufacturing database management systems /. Boston, MA (89 Broad St., Boston 02110) , c1986. vii, 216 p. : LC Card 86-210661 DDC 381/.4500574/0973 19
HD9696.C63 U5226 1986

INDUSTRY, SIZE OF - MATHEMATICAL MODELS.
Schoch, Hans. Size and price in oligopoly /. Königstein, Ts. , Cambridge, Mass. , 1981. viii, 151 p. : ISBN 3-445-12157-5 LC Card 80-84489 DDC 338.8/2/0724 19
HD2757.3 .S36 1981

INDUSTRY - SOCIAL ASPECTS.
Business environment and business ethics . Cambridge, Mass. , c1987. xi, 151 p. ; ISBN 0-88730-204-1 LC Card 87-3573 DDC 174/.4 19
HF5387 .B867 1987

Corporate social responsibility . Santa Barbara, Calif. , c1986. xv, 229 p. ; ISBN 0-87436-469-8 (alk. paper) : LC Card 86-3416 DDC 658.4/08 19
HD60 .C693 1986 ***NYPL [JLE 86-3089]***

Flynn, Patricia M. Facilitating technological change . Cambridge, Mass. , c1988. x, 233 p. : ISBN 0-88730-104-5 LC Card 87-17839 DDC 331.2 19
HD6331 .F56 1988

Frederick, William Crittenden, 1925- Business and society . New York , c1988. xxvii, 626 p. : ISBN 0-07-015561-5 : LC Card 87-21436 DDC 658.4/08 19
HD60 .F72 1988

Gorz, André. [Chemins du paradis. English.] Paths to paradise . London , 1985. vii, 120 p. ; ISBN 0-86104-762-1 (pbk.) :
NYPL [JLD 86-3006]

Helfert, Mario. Wertewandel, Arbeit, technischer Fortschritt, Wachstum /. Köln , c1986. 149 p. : ISBN 3-7663-3010-1 LC Card 87-134855 DDC 331.12 19
HD6331 .H37 1986

Jéquier, François. Charles Veillon . Zürich , 1985. 142 p. : LC Card 85-139330 DDC 338.092/4 B 19
HC395.5.V45 J45 1985

Organisation als soziales System . Berlin , c1986. 219 p. ; ISBN 3-924859-22-1 LC Card 87-137969 DDC 302.3/5 19
HD58.7 .O6687 1986

Pfriem, Reinhard. Betriebswirtschaftslehre in sozialer und ökologischer Dimension /. Frankfurt [am Main] , New York , c1983. 210 p. ; ISBN 3-593-33223-X LC Card 83-190294
HD35 .P45 1983

Thomé, Gotthardt, 1949- Produktgestaltung und Ökologie /. München , c1981. xii, 212 p. : ISBN 3-88259-086-6 : LC Card 81-146058
HD69.N4 T54 1981 ***NYPL [JLD 86-2800]***

Wohlfarth, Karl Anton. Leistung und Ethos . Paderborn , 1984. 266 p. ; ISBN 3-506-70223-8 LC Card 84-238158
HD60 .W64 1984

INDUSTRY - SOCIAL ASPECTS - CANADA.
Brooks, Leonard J. Canadian corporate social performance . Hamilton, Ont. , 1986. xii, 267 p. : ISBN 0-920212-54-9 (pbk.) LC Card 87-100492 DDC 658.4/08/0971 19
HD60.5.C2 B76 1986

INDUSTRY - SOCIAL ASPECTS - CASE STUDIES.
Buchholz, Rogene A. Management response to public issues . Englewood Cliffs, N.J. , c1985. x, 389 p. : ISBN 0-13-549940-2 (pbk.) : LC Card 84-18355 DDC 658.4/08 19
HD60 .B83 1985 ***NYPL [JLE 85-1984]***

Work in market and industrial societies /. Albany , c1984. viii, 316 p. ; ISBN 0-87395-810-1 LC Card 83-9267 DDC 306/.36 19
HD4901 .A659 1984 ***NYPL [JLE 86-4483]***

INDUSTRY - SOCIAL ASPECTS - DECISION MAKING.
Burke, Richard C. Decision making in complex times . Hamilton, Ont. , 1984. xii, 185 p. : ISBN 0-920212-27-1 (pbk.) LC Card 85-154342 DDC 658.4/08 19
HD60 .B86 1984 ***NYPL [JLD 86-2720]***

INDUSTRY - SOCIAL ASPECTS - DENMARK.
Rasmussen, Jørgen, 1948- Virksomheden, lønarbejderen og samfundet . [Aalborg] , 1978. 264 p. ; LC Card 86-460208
HD60.5.D4 R37 1978

INDUSTRY - SOCIAL ASPECTS - DOMINICAN REPUBLIC - CONGRESSES.
Influencia del sector privado sobre la realidad nacional. [Santo Domingo] [1986] 180 p., [1] leaf of plates : LC Card 86-190331
HC153.5 .I53 1986

INDUSTRY - SOCIAL ASPECTS - FORECASTING.
Hegedüs, Zsuzsa. Il presente è l'avvenire .

Milano, Italy , c1985. 126 p. : LC Card 85-215705
HD85.I7 I68 no. 77 HD6955
NYPL [JLD 87-427]

INDUSTRY - SOCIAL ASPECTS - GERMANY, WEST.
Ausländerintegration in deutschen Industriebetrieben /. Königstein/Ts. , c1985. viii, 273 p. : ISBN 3-7756-6935-3 LC Card 85-194662 DDC 305.8/00943 19
HD8458.A2 A9265 1985
NYPL [JLD 86-2193]

Klipstein, Michael von. Der Überdruss am Überfluss . München , c1984. 212 p. : ISBN 3-7892-7194-2 LC Card 84-174408
HD6957.G35 K56 1984

INDUSTRY - SOCIAL ASPECTS - INFORMATION SERVICES.
Burke, Richard C. Decision making in complex times . Hamilton, Ont. , 1984. xii, 185 p. : ISBN 0-920212-27-1 (pbk.) LC Card 85-154342 DDC 658.4/08 19
HD60 .B86 1984 *NYPL [JLD 86-2720]*

INDUSTRY - SOCIAL ASPECTS - ITALY - HISTORY.
La Cassetta degli strumenti . Milano, Italy , c1986. 305 p. : LC Card 86-160695
HC304 .C37 1986

INDUSTRY - SOCIAL ASPECTS - SOUTH AFRICA.
Au, Norman. Selected implications for businessmen of social responsibility in South Africa . [Cape Town] [1977] ix, 141 leaves ; LC Card 81-155073
HD60.5.S7 A92 1977

INDUSTRY - SOCIAL ASPECTS - SOVIET UNION.
Aktivnai͡a sot͡sial′nai͡a politika . Moskva , 1986. 156 p., [16] p. of plates : LC Card 86-216405 DDC 354.47001/6 19
HD60.5.S77 A38 1986

INDUSTRY - SOCIAL ASPECTS - SWEDEN - NORRKÖPING - HISTORY - 19TH CENTURY.
Horgby, Björn. Den disciplinerade arbetaren . Stockholm [1986] 322 p. : ISBN 91-22-00804-7 LC Card 87-105821
HC378.N67 H67 1986

INDUSTRY - SOCIAL ASPECTS - UNITED STATES.
Bruyn, Severyn Ten Haut, 1927- The field of social investment /. Cambridge , New York , 1987. xi, 304 p. : ISBN 0-521-33292-3 LC Card 86-26393 DDC 332.6 19
HG4910 .B77 1987

Business and society . Lexington, Mass. , c1987. xv, 654 p. : ISBN 0-669-13207-1 (pbk : alk. paper) LC Card 86-45548 DDC 658.4/08/0973 19
HD60.5.U5 B853 1987

Chamber of Commerce of the United States of America. Contact . Washington, D.C. , c1980. v, 129 p. : ISBN 0-89834-024-1 (pbk.) LC Card 80-80440 DDC 650/.07/073 19
HF5351 .C46 1980 *NYPL [JLF 86-1414]*

The Common good and U. S. capitalism /. Lanham, MD , c1987. viii, 425 p. ; ISBN 0-8191-6364-3 (alk. paper) : LC Card 87-8334 DDC 306/.36/0973 19
HD60.5.U5 C665 1987

Corporate support for community development. Washington, D.C. , c1984. 15 p. ; LC Card 87-100348 DDC 361.7/65/0973 19
HD60.5.U5 C689 1984

Howell, Rate A. The legal environment of business /. Chicago , c1987. xiv, 783 p. : ISBN 0-03-008369-9 LC Card 86-4503 DDC 346.73/07 347.3067 19
KF1600 .H68 1987 *NYPL [JLE 87-911]*

Industrial democracy . Beverly Hills , c1985. 308 p. : ISBN 0-8039-2476-3 LC Card 85-11741 DDC 338.973/009173/2 19
HT321 .I53 1985 *NYPL [JLD 86-3621]*

Kamerman, Sheila B. A workplace for people . New York , 1987. p. cm. ISBN 0-231-06480-2 LC Card 87-18223 DDC 331.2/0973 19
HD60.5.U5 K36 1987

Lydenberg, Steven D. Rating America's corporate conscience . Reading, Mass. , c1986. x, 499 p. : ISBN 0-201-15886-8 : LC Card 86-8064 DDC 338.7/4/0973 19
HD60.5.U5 L93 1986
*NYPL [*R-Econ. 87-1830]*

McAdams, Tony. Law, business, and society /. Plano, Tex. , 1986. xvi, 662, 52 p. : ISBN 0-256-03070-7 LC Card 85-73323 DDC 346.73/065 347.30665 19
KF1355 .M28 1986 *NYPL [JLE 87-891]*

Naisbitt, John. The year ahead, 1986 . New York, NY , c1985. 168 p. ; ISBN 0-446-38330-9 LC Card 85-17909 DDC 338.5/443/0973 19
HC106.8 .N35 1985 *NYPL [JLD 86-2987]*

Sealy, Albert H. Macro blueprint . New York , 1986. viii, 407, 232 p. ; ISBN 0-89192-390-X LC Card 86-218989 DDC 338.973 19
HD2785 .S412 1986

Social forces and the manager . Malabar, Fla. , 1987, c1982. xiv, 502 p. : ISBN 0-89464-225-1 (pbk.) LC Card 87-3259 DDC 658.4/08/0973 19
HD60.5.U5 S635 1987

Troy, Kathryn. Meeting human needs . New York, NY , c1986. vii, 55 p. ; ISBN 0-8237-0323-1 (pbk.) LC Card 86-207649 DDC 658.3/8 19
HD7654 .T73 1986

Zhurikhin, Ė. A. (Ėduard Alekseevich) "Filantropicheskie" fondy SShA v sisteme vlasti monopoliĭ /. Moskva , 1978. 182, [2] p. ; LC Card 81-160810
HG4028.C6 Z48 1978

INDUSTRY - SOCIAL ASPECTS - UNITED STATES - BIBLIOGRAPHY.
Corporate support for community development. Washington, D.C. , c1984. 15 p. ; LC Card 87-100348 DDC 361.7/65/0973 19
HD60.5.U5 C689 1984

INDUSTRY - SOCIAL ASPECTS - UNITED STATES - CONGRESSES.
The Economics of firm size, market structure, and social performance . [Washington, D.C.?] , 1980. viii, 388 p. ; LC Card 81-600757 DDC 338.6/4/0973 19
HD60.5.U5 E26 *NYPL [JLF 86-704]*

INDUSTRY - SOCIAL ASPECTS - UNITED STATES - HISTORY.
Harris, Howell John, 1951- The right to manage . Madison, Wis. , 1982. ix, 296 p. ; ISBN 0-299-08640-2 : LC Card 81-69820 DDC 331./0973 19
HD8072 .H2874 *NYPL [JLE 86-4147]*

INDUSTRY - STATISTICAL METHODS. see **INDUSTRIAL STATISTICS.**

INDUSTRY - STATISTICS. see **INDUSTRIAL STATISTICS.**

Industry, the state, and public policy in Mexico /. Story, Dale, 1950- Austin , 1986. xii, 275 p. ; ISBN 0-292-73837-4 LC Card 85-13363 DDC 338.972 19
HD3616.M43 S76 1986 *NYPL [JLE 87-656]*

INDUSTRY - VOCATIONAL GUIDANCE. see **VOCATIONAL GUIDANCE.**

Industry wage survey . Williams, Harry B. Washington, D.C. [1986] iv, 34 p. ; LC Card 86-602194 DDC 331.2/86553/0973021 19
HD4966.P52 U5556 1986

Der induzierte Kapitalexport /. Jacobi, Klaus, 1929- Zürich , c1959. viii, 106 p. ; LC Card 87-408198 DDC 332.4/5609494 19
HG3891 .J33 1959

INE. see **Instituto Nacional de Estadística (Peru)**

INEBRIETY. see **ALCOHOLISM.**

INEQUALITY. see **EQUALITY.**

Inequality and poverty . Thimmaiah, G. Bombay , 1983. xiv, 106 p. ; LC Card 83-903408 DDC 339.4/6/095487 19
HC437.K27 T47 1983 *NYPL [JLD 86-3792]*

Inequality in Africa . Nafziger, E. Wayne. Cambridge [Cambridgeshire] , New York , c1988. p. cm. ISBN 0-521-26881-8 LC Card 87-24263 DDC 339.2/096 19
HC800.Z9 I5136 1988

Inequality observed . Szirmai, Adam, 1946- Aldershot, Hants, England , Brookfield, Vt., USA , c1988. p. cm. ISBN 0-566-05549-X : LC Card 87-23071 DDC 339.2/09492 19
HC329.5.I5 S96 1988

INEQUALITY OF INCOME. see **INCOME DISTRIBUTION.**

Inertial inflation. Pereira, Luiz Carlos Bresser. [Inflação e recessão. English.] The theory of inertial inflation . Boulder, Colo. , 1987. xiii, 206 p. : ISBN 1-555-87007-4 (alk. paper) : LC Card 86-29832 DDC 332.4/1/0981 19
HG835 .P4413 1987

Infant and childhood mortality in India : (bio-social determinants) / K. Mahadevan ... [et al.]. Delhi, India : Mittal Publications, c1985. xiv, 120 p. : ill., map ; 22 cm. Includes index. Bibliography: p. [115]-118. LC Card 85-905202
1. Infants - India - Mortality. 2. Children - India - Mortality. I. Mahadevan, K.
NYPL [JLD 87-517]

Infant mortality in Tennessee, 1979-1982 : a birth cohort study. Nashville, Tenn. : Center for Health Statistics, Tennessee Dept. of Health and Environment, [1986] vii, 23 p. : ill. ; 28 cm. LC Card 86-622027 DDC 304.6/4/0880542 19
1. Infants - Tennessee - Mortality - Statistics. 2. Infants (Newborn) - Tennessee - Mortality - Statistics. I. Tennessee. State Center for Health Statistics.
HB1323.I42 U6385 1986

Infante Díaz, Jorge. Aproximación a la estructura económica de la provincia de Teruel / Jorge Infante Díaz. 1a ed. [Teruel] : Instituto de Estudios Turolenses, Excma. Diputación Provincial de Teruel, adscrito al Consejo Superior de Investigaciones Científicas, 1986. 59 p. : ill. (some col.) ; 20 cm. (Cartillas turolenses . no. 3) Bibliography: p. 55-56. ISBN 84-505-3546-8 LC Card 87-105066
1. Teruel (Spain : Province) - Economic conditions. I. Title. II. Series.
HC387.T4 I53 1986

INFANTS - COLOMBIA - MEDELLÍN - MORTALITY.
García Molina, Carlos. Mortalidad infantil y clases sociales . [Medellín, Colombia] [1986] 103 p. : ISBN 958-9127-05-3 LC Card 87-400685 DDC 304.6/4/0880542 19
HB1323.I42 C74 1986

INFANTS - DEVELOPING COUNTRIES - NUTRITION.
Chetley, Andrew. The politics of baby foods . London , 1986. xv, 189 p. ; ISBN 0-86187-293-2
NYPL [JLE 86-2969]

INFANTS - ENGLAND - MORTALITY - STATISTICS.
Mortality statistics . London , 1986. viii, 49 p. ; ISBN 0-11-691069-0 (pbk.) : LC Card 87-147154 DDC 614.5/992 19
HB1323.I42 G764 1984

INFANTS - FRANCE - TERRITORIES AND POSSESSIONS - MORTALITY - STATISTICS.
Statistique du mouvement de la population dans les D.O.M. . Paris [1985] 104 p. : ISBN 2-11-064898-8 : LC Card 86-216599
HB1003 .S73 1985

INFANTS - INDIA - MORTALITY.
Infant and childhood mortality in India . Delhi, India , c1985. xiv, 120 p. : LC Card 85-905202
NYPL [JLD 87-517]

INFANTS - KIRIBATI - MORTALITY.
Feeney, Griffith. [Estimating infant mortality rates from child survivorship data by age of mother. Spanish.] Estimación de tasas de mortalidad infantil a partir de información de sobrevivencia de hijos clasificados por edad de la madre /. Santiago de Chile , 1977. 19 p. : LC Card 83-176243
HB1323.I42 T87418 1977

INFANTS - MALAYSIA - MORTALITY.
Why were infant and child mortality rates highest in the poorest states of Peninsular Malaysia, 1941-75? /. Santa Monica, CA (P.O. Box 2138, Santa Monica 90406-2138) [1986] xi, 45 p. ; LC Card 86-210106 DDC 304.6/4/088054 19
HB1323.I42 M49 1986

INFANTS - MICHIGAN - MORTALITY - STATISTICS.
Southeastern Michigan minor civil divisions . Detroit, Mich. (1200 Book Bldg., Detroit 48226) , c1986. i, 285 p. : LC Card 87-105776

DDC 304.6/3/09774021 19
HB935.M5 S68 1986

INFANTS (NEWBORN) - FRANCE - TERRITORIES AND POSSESSIONS - MORTALITY - STATISTICS.
Statistique du mouvement de la population dans les D.O.M. . Paris [1985] 104 p. : ISBN 2-11-064898-8 : LC Card 86-216599
HB1003 .S73 1985

INFANTS (NEWBORN) - TENNESSEE - MORTALITY - STATISTICS.
Infant mortality in Tennessee, 1979-1982 . Nashville, Tenn. [1986] vii, 23 p. : LC Card 86-622027 DDC 304.6/4/0880542 19
HB1323.I42 U6385 1986

INFANTS - TENNESSEE - MORTALITY - STATISTICS.
Infant mortality in Tennessee, 1979-1982 . Nashville, Tenn. [1986] vii, 23 p. : LC Card 86-622027 DDC 304.6/4/0880542 19
HB1323.I42 U6385 1986

INFANTS - TUVALU - MORTALITY.
Feeney, Griffith. [Estimating infant mortality rates from child survivorship data by age of mother. Spanish.] Estimación de tasas de mortalidad infantil a partir de información de sobrevivencia de hijos clasificados por edad de la madre /. Santiago de Chile , 1977. 19 p. : LC Card 83-176243
HB1323.I42 T87418 1977

INFANTS - WALES - MORTALITY - STATISTICS.
Mortality statistics . London , 1986. viii, 49 p. ; ISBN 0-11-691069-0 (pbk.) : LC Card 87-147154 DDC 614.5/992 19
HB1323.I42 G764 1984

INFANTS - ZAMBIA - KEEMBE (CENTRAL PROVINCE) - MORTALITY.
Interrelationships among infant and childhood mortality, socio-economic factors and fertility in Zambia . Lusaka , Addis Ababa [1984?] 300 p. : LC Card 87-105950 DDC 304.6/32/096894 19
HB1323.I42 Z335 1984

INFANTS - ZAMBIA - LUSAKA - MORTALITY.
Interrelationships among infant and childhood mortality, socio-economic factors and fertility in Zambia . Lusaka , Addis Ababa [1984?] 300 p. : LC Card 87-105950 DDC 304.6/32/096894 19
HB1323.I42 Z335 1984

Inflação versus indexação, uma contribuição ao tema. Vianna, Pedro Jorge Ramos. Inflação vs. indexação, uma contribuição ao tema /. Fortaleza-Ceará [19]84. 121 p. : LC Card 86-130092
HG835 .V53 1984

Inflação x indexação, uma contribuição ao tema. Vianna, Pedro Jorge Ramos. Inflação vs. indexação, uma contribuição ao tema /. Fortaleza-Ceará [19]84. 121 p. : LC Card 86-130092
HG835 .V53 1984

Inflációelméletek és az amerikai monetáris politika /. Foltyn, Ferenc. Budapest , 1985. 126 p. ; ISBN 963-05-3905-5 : LC Card 85-191099
HG229 .F642 1985

Inflación. Los Problemas de la inflación en la República Dominicana /. Santo Domingo, República Dominicana , 1986. 111 p. : LC Card 86-208576
HG767 .P76 1986

La inflación en dos marcos cambiarios . Cervantes Islas, Joel. México, D.F. , 1985. iv, 67 leaves ; LC Card 87-108752 DDC 332.4/1/098 19
HG660.5 .C43 1985

Inflación, política devaluatoria y apertura externa en el Perú, 1978-1984 /. Herrera, César. Lima, Perú , 1985. 55 p. : LC Card 87-104441
HG895 .H47 1985

La inflación y la política económica, el caso de Costa Rica . Picado Hidalgo, Roberto. [San José] , 1985. 16, 20 p. ; LC Card 86-219388
HC143 .P52 1985

Inflasi dan masalah kita . Indonesia. Badan Urusan Logistik. Jakarta , 1979. ii, 48 leaves ; LC Card 80-940062
HG1255 .I5 1979

L'inflation /. Clerc, Denis. Paris , c1984. 126 p. : ISBN 2-86738-041-3 : LC Card 84-241799 DDC 332.4/1 19
HG229 .C548 1984

Inflation! /. Wagner, Helmut. Würzburg , c1983. 152 p. : ISBN 3-7908-0508-4 (pbk.) LC Card 86-673944
HG229 .W238x 1983

INFLATION AND DEFLATION. see **INFLATION (FINANCE)**

Inflation and personal taxation. New Delhi : Associated Chambers of Commerce & Industry of India, [1981] 21 p. ; 28 cm. LC Card 82-907052 DDC 336.24/2/0954 19
1. Inflation (Finance) and taxation - India. 2. Income tax - India. I. Associated Chambers of Commerce & Industry of India.
HJ4766.Z7 A85 1981 ***NYPL [JLF 86-236]***

INFLATION (ECONOMICS) - SOVIET UNION.
Adirim, I. G. (Itskhok Girshevich) Stagflation in the USSR /. Falls Church, VA (7700 Leesburg Pike, #212, Falls Church 22043) [1983] xi, 122 leaves ; LC Card 84-162596 DDC 332.4/1/0947 19
HC340.I5 A44 1983 ***NYPL [JLF 86-1839]***

INFLATION (FINANCE) - ADDRESSES, ESSAYS, LECTURES.
Incentive-based incomes policies . Cambridge, Mass. , c1986. xxi, 263 p. : ISBN 0-88730-082-0 LC Card 85-20090 DDC 331.2/9 19
HC79.W24 I465 1986 ***NYPL [JLE 86-3724]***

Lezioni di economia . Milano , 1979. 195 p. ; LC Card 80-451708
HG1029.5 .L49 ***NYPL [JLC 86-357]***

INFLATION (FINANCE) AND TAXATION - INDIA.
Inflation and personal taxation. New Delhi [1981] 21 p. ; LC Card 82-907052 DDC 336.24/2/0954 19
HJ4766.Z7 A85 1981 ***NYPL [JLF 86-236]***

INFLATION (FINANCE) AND UNEMPLOYMENT - CANADA.
The Determinants of negotiated wage settlements in Canada (1966-1975) . [Ottawa] , Hull, Quebec , c1979. x, 256 p. : ISBN 0-660-10162-9 : LC Card 79-313202 DDC 331.2/971
HD4979 .D44 ***NYPL [JLE 80-447]***

INFLATION (FINANCE) - ARGENTINA.
Nassif, Luís. O cruzado . São Paulo/SP , 1986. 255 p. : LC Card 86-224110
HG835 .N37 1986

Salarios e inflación, Argentina, 1970-1983 /. [Santiago, Chile] [c1984] iv, 116 p. : LC Card 85-156959
HC180.W24 S25 1984

INFLATION (FINANCE) - ARGENTINA - HISTORY - 20TH CENTURY.
Vitelli, Guillermo. Cuarenta años de inflación en la argentina, 1945-1985 /. Buenos Aires [1986] 239 p. : ISBN 950-600-086-7 LC Card 87-124167 DDC 332.4/1/0982 19
HG815 .V57 1986

INFLATION (FINANCE) - ASIA, SOUTHEASTERN.
Skully, Michael T. Financing East Asia's success . New York , 1987. xiii, 242 p. ; ISBN 0-312-00536-9 : LC Card 86-31527 DDC 332/.0959 19
HG187.E37 S68 1987

INFLATION (FINANCE) - BOLIVIA.
Cole, Julio Harold, 1955- Latin American inflation . New York , 1987. xv, 89 p. : ISBN 0-275-92809-8 (alk. paper) : LC Card 87-15156 DDC 332.4/1/098 19
HC125 .C62 1987

INFLATION (FINANCE) - BRAZIL.
Bulhões, Octávio Gouveia de. Desdobramentos inflacionários. [Salvador] [1984] 43 p. : LC Card 86-861354 DDC 332.4/1/0981 19
HG835 .B85 1984

Fischer, Bernhard, fl. 1979- Brasilien ohne Inflation? . Kiel [1986] 28 p. ; LC Card 87-120443 DDC 330 s 332.4/1/0981 19
HB44 .K45 no. 124 HG835

Franco, Luiz L. O Brasil que temos, o país que queremos /. Guarulhos, S.P. [Brazil] , c1985. 87 p. ; LC Card 86-223053
HC187 .F7315 1985

Galvêas, Ernane. Sistema financeiro e mercado de capitais /. Rio de Janeiro , 1985. 171 p. : LC Card 85-208367
HG185.B7 G35 1985

Garcia, Manuel Enriquez. Salários indexados, preços e emprego . São Paulo , 1986. 149 p. : LC Card 86-234254
HD5004 .G37 1986

Os Mistérios da inflação . São Paulo , 1986. 121 p. ; LC Card 86-189815
HG835 .M57 1986

Modiano, Eduardo Marco. Da inflação ao cruzado . Rio de Janeiro , c1986. 126 p. : ISBN 85-7001-362-0 : LC Card 87-102624
HC187 .M593 1986

Nassif, Luís. O cruzado . São Paulo/SP , 1986. 255 p. : LC Card 86-224110
HG835 .N37 1986

Ness, Walter L. A influência da correção monetária no sistema financeiro /. Rio de Janeiro , 1977. 205 p. : LC Card 85-206096
HG229 .N385 1977

Pereira, José Maria Dias. A participação da alimentação na inflação brasileira nos anos 70 . Porto Alegre, RS , 1984. 139 p. : LC Card 85-128694 DDC 338.4/36413/00981 19
HD9014.B82 P47 1984
NYPL [JLE 86-2264]

Pereira, Luiz Carlos Bresser. [Inflação e recessão. English.] The theory of inertial inflation . Boulder, Colo. , 1987. xiii, 206 p. : ISBN 1-555-87007-4 (alk. paper) : LC Card 86-29832 DDC 332.4/1/0981 19
HG835 .P4413 1987

Vianna, Pedro Jorge Ramos. Inflação vs. indexação, uma contribuição ao tema /. Fortaleza-Ceará [19]84. 121 p. : LC Card 86-130092
HG835 .V53 1984

INFLATION (FINANCE) - BRAZIL - HISTORY.
Cardoso, Eliana A. Inflation, growth and the real exchange rate . New York , 1987. 98 p. : ISBN 0-8240-1356-5 (alk. paper) : LC Card 87-8570 DDC 330.981 19
HC187 .C218 1987

INFLATION (FINANCE) - BRAZIL - MATHEMATICAL MODELS.
Harris, John Andrew de Oliveira. Evolução e definição da moeda /. Rio de Janeiro, RJ , 1985. 90 p. : LC Card 87-135878 DDC 332.4/981 19
HG835 .H37 1985

INFLATION (FINANCE) - CHILE - HISTORY - 20TH CENTURY.
Pisciotta, John L. (John Lee) Development policy, inflation, and politics in Chile, 1938-1958 . New York , 1987. v, 188 p. ; ISBN 0-8240-1367-0 (alk. paper) : LC Card 87-7617 DDC 338.983 19
HC192 .P625 1987

INFLATION (FINANCE) - COLOMBIA.
Castillo, Julián. La amortización de deudas en Colombia . Bogotá, Colombia , 1985. 162 leaves ; LC Card 86-204058 DDC 332.7/09861 19
HG4028.A5 C37 1985

INFLATION (FINANCE) - CONGRESSES.
Inflation in the world economy /. Manchester [Eng.] , 1976. xvii, 334 p. : ISBN 0-7190-0630-9 LC Card 76-356701
HG229 .I453 1976 ***NYPL [JLD 78-401]***

Mercados de capitales bajo inflación /. New York, N.Y. , c1982. xxi, 471 p. : ISBN 0-910365-00-8 : LC Card 82-50965 DDC 332.64 19
HG4523 .M47 1982 ***NYPL [JLE 86-3568]***

Wage rigidity and unemployment /. Baltimore , 1986. viii, 221 p. : ISBN 0-8018-3400-7 LC Card 86-45446 DDC 331.2/1 19
HD4909 .W26 1986 ***NYPL [JLD 86-4077]***

INFLATION (FINANCE) - COSTA RICA.
Picado Hidalgo, Roberto. La inflación y la política económica, el caso de Costa Rica . [San José] , 1985. 16, 20 p. ; LC Card 86-219388
HC143 .P52 1985

INFLATION (FINANCE) - DEVELOPING COUNTRIES.
Kapur, Basant. Studies in inflationary dynamics . Kent Ridge, Singapore , c1986. xviii,

146 p., [1] folded leaf of plates : ISBN 997-16-9099-3 (pbk.) LC Card 87-116919 DDC 332.4/1 19
HC59.7 .K276 1986

Rana, Pradumna Bickram, 1947- The impact of the current exchange rate system on trade and inflation of selected developing member countries /. Manila, Philippines , c1983. iv, 78 p. : LC Card 87-105105 DDC 332.4/56 19
HG3877 .R36 1983

INFLATION (FINANCE) - DOMINICAN REPUBLIC - CONGRESSES.
Los Problemas de la inflación en la República Dominicana /. Santo Domingo, República Dominicana , 1986. 111 p. : LC Card 86-208576
HG767 .P76 1986

INFLATION (FINANCE) - EAST ASIA.
Skully, Michael T. Financing East Asia's success . New York , 1987. xiii, 242 p. ; ISBN 0-312-00536-9 : LC Card 86-31527 DDC 332/.0959 19
HG187.E37 S68 1987

INFLATION (FINANCE) - ECONOMETRIC MODELS.
Loranger, Jean Guy, 1938- Lien entre capital fictif, markup flexible et inflation /. Montréal [1985] 30 p. ; LC Card 85-177724 DDC 332.4/1 19
HB3 .C3 vol. 8517 HG229

INFLATION (FINANCE) - EFFECT OF ENERGY COSTS ON - MATHEMATICAL MODELS.
Macroeconomics [i.e. Macroeconomic] impacts of energy shocks /. Amsterdam ; New York : xvi, 331 p. : ISBN 0-444-70247-4 (U. S.) LC Card 87-9035 DDC 338.4/36655/0724 19
HG229 .M315 1987

INFLATION (FINANCE) - EUROPE - CONGRESSES.
Nationale Wege der Inflationsbekämpfung /. Berlin , c1986. 223 p. : ISBN 3-428-06077-6 LC Card 87-132310 DDC 332.4/1/094 19
HC240 .N315 1986

INFLATION (FINANCE) - EUROPE, EASTERN.
Bokros, Lajos. Piac és pénz a modern gazdaságban /. Budapest , 1985. 340, [1] p. ; ISBN 963-221-551-6 : LC Card 86-185991
HB95 .B65 1985

INFLATION (FINANCE) - FINLAND.
Asplund, Rita. Short-run tax-push inflation in Finland /. Helsinki , 1986. 65 p. : ISBN 951-46-9876-2 (pbk.) LC Card 87-163994 DDC 332.4/1/094897 19
HJ4738.3 .A86 1986

INFLATION (FINANCE) - FRANCE.
Susini, Jean-Jacques. A qui profite l'inflation? /. Paris , c1985. 122 p. : ISBN 2-13-039288-1 LC Card 86-153761
HG979.5 .S87 1985

INFLATION (FINANCE) - GERMANY - HISTORY.
Lindenlaub, Dieter. Maschinenbauunternehmen in der Deutschen Inflation 1919-1923 . Berlin , New York , 1985. xiii, 262 p. ; ISBN 3-11-009934-9 LC Card 85-214738
HG999 .L75 1985

INFLATION (FINANCE) - GERMANY - HISTORY - 20TH CENTURY.
The Adaptation to inflation /. Berlin , New York , 1986. xvi, 512 p. : ISBN 0-89925-287-7 (U. S.) LC Card 86-29134 DDC 338.943 19
HC286.2 .A62 1986

INFLATION (FINANCE) - GERMANY, WEST.
Dieckhöner, Bruno. Rentabilitätsrisiken aus dem Hypothekargeschäft von Kreditinstituten in Zeiten der Geldentwertung /. Wiesbaden , c1984. xi, 395 p. : ISBN 3-409-14002-6 : LC Card 85-119494
HG2040.5.G4 D53 1984

Menkhoff, Lukas. Zur Theorie der nicht-monetär verursachten Inflation /. Berlin , c1986. 222 p. : ISBN 3-428-06051-2 LC Card 86-215073
HG229 .M524 1986

Runge, Harry. Haushaltsfinanzierung durch Notendruck /. Berlin , c1986. 69 p. ; ISBN 3-428-05984-0 LC Card 86-165742
HG1004 .R75 1986

Wechselwirkungen von Geldpolitik, Inflation und Strukturwandel . Hamburg , 1984. 179 p. : ISBN 3-87895-243-0 LC Card 84-221405
HB235.G3 W42 1984

INFLATION (FINANCE) - HUNGARY.
A Folyamatos árszinvonal-emelkedés társadalmi hatásai . Budapest [1985] 176 p. ; ISBN 963-608-087-9 LC Card 87-407751
HG970.5 .F65 1985

A Hazai áralakulásról /. [Budapest] , 1986. 342 p. ; ISBN 963-09-2758-6 : LC Card 87-407741
HG970.5 .H39 1986

INFLATION (FINANCE) - INDONESIA.
Indonesia. Badan Urusan Logistik. Inflasi dan masalah kita . Jakarta , 1979. ii, 48 leaves ; LC Card 80-940062
HG1255 .I5 1979

INFLATION (FINANCE) - IRAN - HISTORY.
Ikani, Azizollah. The dynamics of inflation in Iran, 1960-1977 /. Tilburg, Netherlands , 1987. xii, 395 p. ; ISBN 90-361-9761-9 (pbk.) : LC Card 87-132510 DDC 332.4/1/0955 19
HG1220.2 .I36 1987

INFLATION (FINANCE) - ITALY.
Cardillo, Giovanni. La programmabilità delle gestioni aziendali in tempi di inflazione /. Milano , 1983. 118 p. ; LC Card 84-177279 DDC 658.4/012/0945 19
HD70.I8 C27 1983 ***NYPL [JLD 86-1047]***

INFLATION (FINANCE) - ITALY - ADDRESSES, ESSAYS, LECTURES.
Lezioni di economia . Milano , 1979. 195 p. ; LC Card 80-451708
HG1029.5 .L49 ***NYPL [JLC 86-357]***

INFLATION (FINANCE) - LATIN AMERICA.
Cole, Julio Harold, 1955- Latin American inflation . New York , 1987. xv, 89 p. : ISBN 0-275-92809-8 (alk. paper) : LC Card 87-15156 DDC 332.4/1/098 19
HC125 .C62 1987

INFLATION (FINANCE) - LATIN AMERICA - CASE STUDIES.
Cervantes Islas, Joel. La inflación en dos marcos cambiarios . México, D.F. , 1985. iv, 67 leaves ; LC Card 87-108752 DDC 332.4/1/098 19
HG660.5 .C43 1985

INFLATION (FINANCE) - LATIN AMERICA - MATHEMATICAL MODELS.
Canto, Victor A. Currency substitution . Boston , c1987. viii, 196 p. ; ISBN 0-89838-195-9 LC Card 86-27747 DDC 332.4/56/098 19
HG3823 .C36 1987

INFLATION (FINANCE) - MATHEMATICAL MODELS.
Blang, Hans-Georg, 1953- Die Variabilität relativer Preisänderungen und die Varianz monetärer Aggregate /. Frankfurt am Main , New York , c1986. xxvii, 338 p. : ISBN 3-8204-9074-4 LC Card 86-156110
HG229 .B555 1986

Frenkel, Roberto. Decisiones de precio en alta inflación /. Buenos Aires, Argentina , 1979. 58 p. ; LC Card 80-125798 DDC 332.4/15 19
HF5416.5 .F73 ***NYPL [JLD 86-2701]***

Serra, Daniel. Monnaie, inflation et croissance /. Paris , 1982. xi, 306 p. : ISBN 2-7178-0478-1 : LC Card 82-153767 DDC 332.4/0724 19
HG221 .S485 1982 ***NYPL [JLE 86-1903]***

Wagner, Helmut. Inflation und Wirtschaftswachstum . Berlin , c1983. 234 p. : ISBN 3-428-05319-2 LC Card 83-219188
HG229 .W237 1983

INFLATION (FINANCE) - MEXICO.
García Alba Iduñate, Pascual, 1948- [Financial aspects of macroeconomic management in Mexico. Spanish.] Causas y efectos de la crisis económica en México /. México, D.F. , 1984. 124 p. : ISBN 968-12-0285-6 LC Card 86-138030
HC135 .G29818 1984

INFLATION (FINANCE) - PERU.
Herrera, César. Inflación, política devaluatoria y apertura externa en el Perú, 1978-1984 /. Lima, Perú , 1985. 55 p. : LC Card 87-104441
HG895 .H47 1985

Uriarte, J. Manuel. Transnational banks and the dynamics of the Peruvian foreign debt and inflation /. New York , c1986. x, 195 p. : ISBN 0-03-002599-0 (alk. paper) : LC Card 84-26307 DDC 336.3/4/0985 19
HJ8604 .U75 1985 ***NYPL [JLE 86-1384]***

INFLATION (FINANCE) - PORTUGAL.
Girão, José António. Salários, inflação e moeda . Lisboa , 1984. 50 p. : LC Card 85-157764
HG1145 .G57 1984

INFLATION (FINANCE) - QUEBEC (PROVINCE)
Fortin, Pierre. [Unemployment, inflation, and economic stabilization in Quebec. French.] Chômage, inflation et régulation de la conjoncture au Québec /. Montréal, Québec [1980] viii, 144 p. : ISBN 0-88806-063-7 (pbk.) LC Card 87-673448
HC117.Q4 F63x 1980

INFLATION (FINANCE) - SWITZERLAND.
Baltensperger, Ernst. Geldmengenpolitik und Inflationskontrolle . Diessenhofen , c1984. 132 p. : ISBN 3-7253-0224-3 : LC Card 84-178054 DDC 332.4/9494 19
HG1155 .B345 1984 ***NYPL [JLD 87-168]***

Merk, Gerhard, 1931- Ausgewählte Aufsätze zur Wirtschaftstheorie /. Zürich , 1986. 138 p. ; ISBN 3-9999462-1-1 LC Card 87-409558 DDC 330.9494/073 19
HB118.A2 M47 1986

INFLATION (FINANCE) - SWITZERLAND - EFFECT OF ENERGY COSTS ON.
Schmassmann, Norbert. Verteilungswirkungen von Erdölpreissteigerungen . Diessenhofen , c1983. viii, 326 p. : ISBN 3-7253-0203-0 LC Card 83-219477
HD9575.S92 S27 1983

INFLATION (FINANCE) - TURKEY.
Aşıkoğlu, Rıza. Sermaye piyasası aracı olarak enflasyon ortamında tahvilleri değerleme /. [Eskişehir, Turkey] , 1983. xii, 155 p. : LC Card 85-221546
HG5706.5.A3 A85 1983

INFLATION (FINANCE) - UNITED STATES.
Foltyn, Ferenc. Inflációelméletek és az amerikai monetáris politika /. Budapest , 1985. 126 p. ; ISBN 963-05-3905-5 : LC Card 85-191099
HG229 .F642 1985

Goldschmidt, Yaaqov. The impact of inflation on financial activity in business, with applications to the U. S. farming sector /. Totowa, N.J. , 1986. xvi, 181 p. ; ISBN 0-8476-7427-4 : LC Card 85-14196 DDC 338.1/3/0973 19
HD1761 .G645 1986 ***NYPL [JLE 86-3484]***

INFLATION (FINANCE) - UNITED STATES - ECONOMETRIC MODELS.
Gylfason, Thorvaldur. Interest, inflation, and the aggregate consumption function /. Stockholm, Sweden [1979] 44 leaves : LC Card 81-114286
HC110.C6 G95 1979

INFLATION (FINANCE) - UNITED STATES - HISTORY.
Olnek, Jay I. The invisible hand . Riverdale, N.Y. , c1984. 176 p. : ISBN 0-938538-01-2 LC Card 82-24634 DDC 382.7/1/0973 19
HF1455 .O49 1984 ***NYPL [JLE 87-21]***

Pick, Franz. The U. S. dollar . Bethel, CT , c1986. xvi, 103 p., [1] folded leaf of plates : ISBN 0-916373-04-5 (pbk.): LC Card 86-210094 DDC 332.4/973 19
HG539 .P5 1986

INFLATION (FINANCE) - VENEZUELA.
Belardi C., Arturo. La industria frente a la inflación . Valencia [Venezuela] , 1981. 92 leaves : LC Card 85-187972
HG915 .B44 1981

Martín-Guédez, Rafael, 1942- Vigencia de la multibanca . [Caracas? , 1982 or 1983] 122 p. ; LC Card 83-201555
HG2964 .M37 1982

Inflation, growth and the real exchange rate . Cardoso, Eliana A. New York , 1987. 98 p. : ISBN 0-8240-1356-5 (alk. paper) : LC Card 87-8570 DDC 330.981 19
HC187 .C218 1987

Inflation in the world economy / edited by Michael Parkin and George Zis. Manchester [Eng.] : Manchester University Press, 1976. xvii, 334 p. : ill. ; 23 cm. (Studies in inflation) Papers presented at a conference held at the University of Manchester from 17-19 July, 1974. Includes

bibliographical references and indexes. ISBN 0-7190-0630-9 LC Card 76-356701
1. Inflation (Finance) - Congresses. 2. Monetary policy - Congresses. I. Parkin, Michael. II. Zis, George.
HG229 .I453 1976 ***NYPL [JLD 78-401]***

Inflation, tax rules, and housing in New Zealand /. Brooks, R. Wellington, N.Z. [1986] 22, [22] p. : LC Card 87-132461 DDC 363.5/8 19
HD7387.5.A3 B76 1986

Inflation und Beschäftigung in Volkswirtschaften mit Güter- und Arbeitsmarktkontrakten /. Gröschel, Ulrich. Berlin , c1986. 252 p. ; ISBN 3-428-06149-7 LC Card 87-120985 DDC 331.13/72 19
HD5710.2 .G76 1986

Inflation und Wirtschaftswachstum . Wagner, Helmut. Berlin , c1983. 234 p. : ISBN 3-428-05319-2 LC Card 83-219188
HG229 .W237 1983

Inflat͡siia v süvremennoto kapitalistichesko obshtestvo /. Chonov, Nikola. Sofii͡a , 1985. 168 p. ; LC Card 85-243423
HG229 .C534 1985

The influence of Frank A. Vanderlip and the National City Bank on American commerce and foreign policy, 1910-1920 /. Mayer, Robert Stanley. New York , 1987. viii, 221 p. ; ISBN 0-8240-8087-4 : LC Card 87-23793 DDC 332.1/5/097471 19
HG2613.N54 N3555 1987

INFLUENCE (PSYCHOLOGY)
Winn, Denise, 1950- The manipulated mind . London , c1983. 217 p. ; ISBN 0-86304-025-X LC Card 83-184383 DDC 302.3/3 19
BF632.5 .W56 1983 ***NYPL [JFD 87-1158]***

Influences.
Courlet, Claude. L'Europe du sud au milieu du gué /. Grenoble , 1984. 122 p. ; ISBN 2-7061-0243-8 : LC Card 85-116696
HC244.5 .C68 1984

Influences externes sur l'économie suisse en changes fixes et flottants /. Genberg, Hans. Genève , c1985. ii, 202 p. : ISBN 2-8257-0127-0 : LC Card 85-235579 DDC 332.4/5609494 19
HG3963 .G46 1985 ***NYPL [JLD 86-2381]***

A influência da correção monetária no sistema financeiro /. Ness, Walter L. Rio de Janeiro , 1977. 205 p. : LC Card 85-206096
HG229 .N385 1977

Influencia del sector privado sobre la realidad nacional. [1a ed.]. [Santo Domingo] : Asociación Nacional de Jóvenes Empresarios, [1986] 180 p., [1] leaf of plates : ports. ; 21 cm. Papers presented at the Seminario ANJE '85 held in Santo Domingo July 19, 1985. LC Card 86-190331
1. Capitalism - Dominican Republic - Congresses. 2. Dominican Republic - Economic conditions - 1961- - Congresses. 3. Business enterprises - Dominican Republic - Congresses. 4. Industry - Social aspects - Dominican Republic - Congresses. 5. Church and industry - Dominican Republic - Congresses. I. Asociación Nacional de Jovenes Empresarios (Dominican Republic). II. Seminario ANJE '85 (7th : 1985 : Santo Domingo, Dominican Republic).
HC153.5 .I53 1986

INFOPLAN (INFORMATION RETRIEVAL SYSTEM) - HANDBOOKS, MANUALS, ETC.
Guía conceptual y metodológica para instructores de cursos de capacitación de INFOPLAN. Santiago de Chile , 1983. iv, 70 p. : LC Card 87-108080
HC125 .G814 1983

Información básica sobre el GATT y el desarrollo industrial y comercial de México. México : Dirección de Publicaciones del Senado de la República, c1985. 79, 62 p. ; 22 cm. (Cuadernos del Senado . 55) "Documento de trabajo de carácter informativo, cuyas opiniones y orientaciones son de las fuentes consultadas y no del Senado de la República." "LIII Legislatura, Senado de la República." "Al cuidado de Carlos Sevilla y María Eugenia Castañeda"--T.p. verso. "Acuerdo general sobre aranceles aduaneros y comercio": p. 1-62 (2nd group) LC Card 87-400559 DDC 338.0972 19
1. Mexico - Industries. 2. Mexico - Commerce. 3. Foreign trade regulation - Mexico. 4. Tariff - Law and legislation - Mexico. 5. General Agreement on Tariffs and Trade (Organization). I. Sevilla, Carlos. II. Castañeda, María Eugenia. III. Mexico. Congreso. Cámara de Senadores. IV. General Agreement on Tariffs and Trade (1947). Spanish. 1985. V. Series.
HC135 .I53 1985

Información económica.
Producto interno bruto y gasto, cuaderno 1970-1979. [Mexico City] [1980] 123 p. ; LC Card 82-197714
HC140.I5 P76 1980

Informações infra-estruturais. Setor de informações técnicas /. [Vitória] , 1983. 54 p. ; LC Card 85-202308
HC188.E7 S47 1983

Informal Black business in Durban . Nattrass, Jill. Pietermaritzburg, Natal, South Africa , 1986. xviii, 138 p. : ISBN 0-909232-58-X (pbk.) : LC Card 87-112836 DDC 381 19
HD2346.S632 D86 1986

INFORMAL SECTOR (ECONOMICS)
Les Economies non officielles /. Paris , 1984. 247 p. : ISBN 2-7071-1441-3 : LC Card 86-460169
HD2341 .E26 1984

Hankel, Wilhelm, 1929- Gegenkurs . Berlin , c1984. 261 p. : ISBN 3-88680-114-4 LC Card 84-174753
HB3723 .H26 1984

The Unofficial economy . Aldershot, Hants, England , Brookfield, Vt., USA , c1987. 345 p. : ISBN 0-566-05131-1 : LC Card 86-25634 DDC 381 19
HD2341 .U56 1987

Weck-Hannemann, Hannelore. Schattenwirtschaft . Frankfurt am Main , New York , c1983. 152 p. : ISBN 3-8204-7590-7 (pbk.) LC Card 87-672943
HD2341 .W37x 1983

INFORMAL SECTOR (ECONOMICS) - AFRICA.
The Informal sector in Africa /. Addis Ababa , 1984. 2, iii, 149 p. ; ISBN 92-2-103785-1 LC Card 87-106188 DDC 381 19
HD2346.A55 I19 1984

The Informal sector in Africa. Addis Ababa [Ethiopia] , 1985. 147 p. ; ISBN 92-2-103785-1 :
NYPL [JLE 86-1454]

INFORMAL SECTOR (ECONOMICS) - AFRICA - CONGRESSES.
JASPA Steering Group Meeting on Priority Employment Policies and Projects for Africa (1985 : Addis Ababa, Ethiopia) Report of JASPA Steering Group Meeting on Priority Employment Policies and Projects for Africa. Addis Ababa , 1986. 43 leaves ; LC Card 87-980227 DDC 331.12/042/096 19
HD5837.A6 J37 1985

INFORMAL SECTOR (ECONOMICS) - ARGENTINA.
Lindenboim, Javier. La terciarización del empleo en la Argentina. Buenos Aires , 1985. vi, 59, 50, 3 p. ; LC Card 87-122527 DDC 381 19
HD2346.A73 L56 1985

INFORMAL SECTOR (ECONOMICS) - ARGENTINA - BUENOS AIRES METROPOLITAN AREA.
Lindenboim, Javier. La terciarización del empleo en la Argentina. Buenos Aires , 1985. vi, 59, 50, 3 p. ; LC Card 87-122527 DDC 381 19
HD2346.A73 L56 1985

INFORMAL SECTOR (ECONOMICS) - BOLIVIA.
El Sector informal en Bolivia /. [La Paz, Bolivia?] [1986] 323 p. : LC Card 87-100849
HD2346.B6 S43 1986

INFORMAL SECTOR (ECONOMICS) - BRAZIL.
Economia informal, tecnologia apropriada e associativismo /. São Paulo , 1986. 176 p. : LC Card 86-233370
HC190.P6 E34 1986

INFORMAL SECTOR (ECONOMICS) - BRAZIL - PERNAMBUCO - CASE STUDIES.
Apoio ao setor informal da economia de Pernambuco . Recife , 1985. 135 p. : LC Card 87-403615 DDC 381 19
HD2346.B72 P473 1985

INFORMAL SECTOR (ECONOMICS) - BRAZIL - RIO DE JANEIRO.
Abreu, Alice R. de Paiva. O avesso da moda . São Paulo , 1986. 302 p. ; LC Card 87-129109 DDC 331.4/887/098153 19
HD6073.C62 B62 1986

INFORMAL SECTOR (ECONOMICS) - BRAZIL - SALVADOR METROPOLITAN AREA.
O gigante invisível . [Salvador] [1983] 105 p. : LC Card 84-181184
HD2346.B72 S25 1983

INFORMAL SECTOR (ECONOMICS) - BURKINA-FASO.
Dijk, Meine Pieter van. Burkina-Faso . Paris , c1986. 203 p. ; ISBN 2-85802-638-6 LC Card 86-221033
HD2346.B822 O933 1986

INFORMAL SECTOR (ECONOMICS) - BURKINA-FASO - OUAGADOUGOU.
Dijk, Meine Pieter van. Burkina-Faso . Paris , c1986. 203 p. ; ISBN 2-85802-638-6 LC Card 86-221033
HD2346.B822 O933 1986

INFORMAL SECTOR (ECONOMICS) - CASE STUDIES.
L'Altra metà dell'economia . Napoli , 1986. 345 p. : ISBN 88-20-71420-5 : LC Card 86-214178
HD2341 .A68 1986

INFORMAL SECTOR (ECONOMICS) - CENTRAL AMERICA.
Cambio y polarización ocupacional en Centroamérica. [San José, Costa Rica?] , 1986. 202 p. : ISBN 92-2-305432-X LC Card 86-231773
HD5733.A6 C36 1986

INFORMAL SECTOR (ECONOMICS) - CHILE - SANTIAGO.
Corvalán Vásquez, Oscar E., 1947- Empleo y capacitación en los talleres informales de Santiago /. Montevideo , 1984. 150 p. ; LC Card 86-127324
HD2346.C54 S263 1984

INFORMAL SECTOR (ECONOMICS) - COLOMBIA - MEDELLÍN.
López Castaño, Hugo. El comercio callejero en la ciudad de Medellín . Medellín , 1983. xv, 194 leaves : LC Card 85-131765
HF5459.C7 L67 1983

INFORMAL SECTOR (ECONOMICS) - CONGRESSES.
Schattenwirtschaft und alternative Ökonomie . Regensburg , c1984. 268 p. : ISBN 3-924956-00-6 LC Card 86-224071
HD2341 .S337 1984

INFORMAL SECTOR (ECONOMICS) - DEVELOPING COUNTRIES.
Andersson, Tommy D., 1947- Profit in small firms . Aldershot, Hants, England , Brookfield, Vt., USA , c1987. 407 p. : ISBN 0-566-05468-X : LC Card 87-21321 DDC 338.6/42/091724 19
HD2346.5 .A53 1987

Les Economies non officielles /. Paris , 1984. 247 p. : ISBN 2-7071-1441-3 : LC Card 86-460169
HD2341 .E26 1984

INFORMAL SECTOR (ECONOMICS) - EUROPE, EASTERN.
Les Economies non officielles /. Paris , 1984. 247 p. : ISBN 2-7071-1441-3 : LC Card 86-460169
HD2341 .E26 1984

INFORMAL SECTOR (ECONOMICS) - EUROPEAN ECONOMIC COMMUNITY COUNTRIES.
Buiren, S. van. The quantitative and qualitative significance of the emergence of local initiatives for employment creation . Luxembourg , Washington, D.C. , 1986. iii, 141, 14, [12] p. : ISBN 92-825-6048-1 (pbk.) : LC Card 86-222030 DDC 331.12/042/094 19
HD5764.5.A6 B85 1986

INFORMAL SECTOR (ECONOMICS) - GERMANY (WEST)
Niessen, Hans-Joachim. Schattenwirtschaft in der Bundesrepublik . Opladen , 1987. 246 p. : ISBN 3-8100-0592-4 LC Card 87-131108
HD2346.G3 N545 1987

INFORMAL SECTOR (ECONOMICS) - GERMANY (WEST) - ADDRESSES, ESSAYS, LECTURES.
Wirtschaft im Untergrund /. Reinbek bei Hamburg , 1983. 188 p. : ISBN 3-499-33035-0 :

LC Card 83-206566
HF5482.65.G3 W57 1983
NYPL *[JLC 86-265]*

INFORMAL SECTOR (ECONOMICS) - GHANA - ACCRA.
Burchards, Eckehard. Strukturen und Funktionen des informellen Sektors in Ghana . Hamburg , 1983. vii, 138 p. : ISBN 3-923519-54-0 LC Card 83-214699 DDC 381 19
HD2346.G42 A243 1983

INFORMAL SECTOR (ECONOMICS) - GOVERNMENT POLICY - BOLIVIA.
El Sector informal en Bolivia /. [La Paz, Bolivia?] [1986] 323 p. : LC Card 87-100849
HD2346.B6 S43 1986

INFORMAL SECTOR (ECONOMICS) - GREAT BRITAIN.
Rose, Richard, 1933- Getting by in three economies . Glasgow , 1983. 40 p. ; LC Card 83-150133 DDC 330.941/0858 19
HC256.6 .R67 1983

INFORMAL SECTOR (ECONOMICS) - GREAT BRITAIN - HISTORY - 20TH CENTURY.
Smithies, Edward. The black economy in England since 1914 /. London , Atlantic Highlands, N.J. , 1984. 165 p. ; ISBN 0-391-03114-7 LC Card 84-6516 DDC 364.1/33 19
HF5482.65.G7 S64 1984
NYPL *[JLD 86-2509]*

INFORMAL SECTOR (ECONOMICS) - HUNGARY.
Falusné Szikra, Katalin. Az első és a második gazdaság közötti bér-, illetve jövedelem-diszparitás /. Budapest , c1986. 31 p. ; ISBN 963-05-4343-5 : LC Card 87-407713
HC300.295.I5 F35 1986

Körösényi, András. A takarékszövetkezetek banki reformjának alternativai /. Budapest [1985] 43 p. ; LC Card 87-408585
HG1939.H82 K67 1985

INFORMAL SECTOR (ECONOMICS) - INDIA.
Kabra, Kamal Nayan. Black money . New Delhi , 1985. 47 p. ; LC Card 87-900898 DDC 381 19
HJ2348.5 .K32 1985

Mehta, Vadilal Lallubhai, 1903- Unemployment, inequality, parallel economy . Ahmedabad , 1982. viii, 141 p., [1] leaf of plates : LC Card 82-900764 DDC 331.13/7954 19
HD5819 .M43 1982 **NYPL *[JLD 85-2751]***

INFORMAL SECTOR (ECONOMICS) - KENYA - KISUMU.
Aboagye, A. A. Informal sector employment in Kenya . Addis Ababa , Geneva, Switzerland , 1986. vii, 117, [64] p. ; ISBN 92-2-105557-4 LC Card 87-980151 DDC 331.12/51381 19
HD2346.K42 N353 1986

INFORMAL SECTOR (ECONOMICS) - KENYA - MOMBASA.
Aboagye, A. A. Informal sector employment in Kenya . Addis Ababa , Geneva, Switzerland , 1986. vii, 117, [64] p. ; ISBN 92-2-105557-4 LC Card 87-980151 DDC 331.12/51381 19
HD2346.K42 N353 1986

INFORMAL SECTOR (ECONOMICS) - KENYA - NAIROBI.
Aboagye, A. A. Informal sector employment in Kenya . Addis Ababa , Geneva, Switzerland , 1986. vii, 117, [64] p. ; ISBN 92-2-105557-4 LC Card 87-980151 DDC 331.12/51381 19
HD2346.K42 N353 1986

Mitullah, W. V. Management of urban services in Nairobi . Nairobi, Kenya , 1985. 109, 106, vi p., [6] leaves of plates : LC Card 87-116360 DDC 388.4/09676/25 19
HD4720.5.N35 M57 1985

INFORMAL SECTOR (ECONOMICS) - MADAGASCAR - ANTANANARIVO.
Gozo, K. M. Le secteur non structuré d'Antananarivo . Addis-Abéba , c1985. vi, 175 p. : LC Card 85-981181
HD2346.M282 A574 1985

INFORMAL SECTOR (ECONOMICS) - MADAGASCAR - ANTSIRABE.
Le Secteur non structuré d'Antsirabe . Addis-Abéba , 1985. iii, ii, 111, 24, 71 p. : ISBN 92-2-205256-0 LC Card 87-980400
HD2346.M282 A588 1985

INFORMAL SECTOR (ECONOMICS) - MADAGASCAR - MAHAJANGA.
Le Secteur non structuré de Mahajanga . Addis Abéba , 1985. vii, 114 p. ; ISBN 92-2-205254-4 LC Card 86-981199
HD2346.M282 M347 1985

INFORMAL SECTOR (ECONOMICS) - PERU.
Soto, Hernando de, 1941- El otro sendero . [Lima] , 1986. xxxvi, 317 p. : LC Card 87-400476 DDC 381 19
HD2346.P4 S67 1986

INFORMAL SECTOR (ECONOMICS) - PERU - CASE STUDIES.
Aumento del ingreso y mejoramiento de las condiciones de trabajo del sector informal urbano en sietes ciudades del Perú /. [Lima, Perú?] , 1986. ii, 69, [25] leaves : LC Card 87-106249
HD2346.P4 A85 1986

INFORMAL SECTOR (ECONOMICS) - PERU - LIMA.
Grompone, Romeo. Talleristas y vendedores ambulantes en Lima /. Lima , 1985. 319 p. : LC Card 85-243089
HD2346.P42 L564 1985

INFORMAL SECTOR (ECONOMICS) - PORTUGAL.
Santos, J. Albano. A economia subterrânea /. Lisboa , 1983. 86 p. : LC Card 86-171907
HD2346.P8 S36 1983

INFORMAL SECTOR (ECONOMICS) - SCANDINAVIA - ECONOMETRIC MODELS.
Schneider, Friedrich. The development of the shadow economies for Denmark, Norway, and Sweden . Aarhus, Denmark [1986] 46 p. : LC Card 86-215193 DDC 381 19
HD2346.S29 S35 1986

INFORMAL SECTOR (ECONOMICS) - SENEGAL.
Dijk, Meine Pieter van. Developing the informal sector in Senegal . Dakar [1976] 47 leaves ; LC Card 84-232063
HD2346.S4 D55 1976

Dijk, Meine Pieter van. Sénégal . Paris [1986] 164 p. ; ISBN 2-85802-637-8 LC Card 86-221017
HD2346.S42 D343 1986

INFORMAL SECTOR (ECONOMICS) - SENEGAL - DAKAR.
Dijk, Meine Pieter van. Sénégal . Paris [1986] 164 p. ; ISBN 2-85802-637-8 LC Card 86-221017
HD2346.S42 D343 1986

INFORMAL SECTOR (ECONOMICS) - SOUTH AFRICA.
South Africa. National Manpower Commission. Verslag van die Nasionale Mannekragkommissie oor 'n ondersoek na die kleinsakesektor in die Republiek van Suid-Afrika, in die besonder die faktore wat die groei en ontwikkeling daarvan kan belemmer =. [Pretoria] [1983] 58 p. ; ISBN 0-620-07511-2 LC Card 85-116407 DDC 338.6/42/0968 19
HD2346.S63 S64 1983

INFORMAL SECTOR (ECONOMICS) - SOUTH AFRICA - DURBAN.
Nattrass, Jill. Informal Black business in Durban . Pietermaritzburg, Natal, South Africa , 1986. xviii, 138 p. : ISBN 0-909232-58-X (pbk.) : LC Card 87-112836 DDC 381 19
HD2346.S632 D86 1986

INFORMAL SECTOR (ECONOMICS) - SOVIET UNION.
Ėvel'son, Evgeniia. Sudebnye protsessy po ėkonomicheskim delam v SSSR . London , 1986. 370 p. ; **NYPL *[*QIX 87-4024]***

INFORMAL SECTOR (ECONOMICS) - SPAIN.
Ruesga Benito, Santos, 1953- Métodos de estimación de la economía oculta . Madrid [1985?] 55 p. : ISBN 88-470-7531-18 LC Card 87-111661
HD2346.S7 R84 1985

INFORMAL SECTOR (ECONOMICS) - SUDAN - JUBA.
Jenkins, S. J. (Susan J.) Aspects of the informal economic sector of Juba, southern Sudan /. [Jūbā, Sudan] [1981?] xiii, 217 p., [4] leaves of plates : LC Card 86-980565
HD2346.S82 J85 1981

INFORMAL SECTOR (ECONOMICS) - SURINAM - PARAMARIBO.
Onderzoek naar werkgelegenheid, inkomen en de structuur van de stedelijke economie van Paramaribo . Paramaribo, Suriname [1978] 69 leaves : LC Card 87-115836
HD5759.5.P37 O53 1978

INFORMAL SECTOR (ECONOMICS) - SWITZERLAND.
Weck-Hannemann, Hannelore. Die heimliche Wirtschaft . Bern , c1986. 112 p. : ISBN 3-258-03541-5 LC Card 86-159961
HD2346.S9 W43 1986

INFORMAL SECTOR (ECONOMICS) - TANZANIA.
Employment promotion in Tanzania . Addis Ababa , 1986. ii leaves, 107 p. ; LC Card 87-980150 DDC 331.11/09678 19
HD5841.3.A6 E46 1986

INFORMAL SECTOR (ECONOMICS) - UNITED STATES.
Cash, Adam. Guerrilla capitalism . Port Townsend, Wash. , c1984. 172 p. : ISBN 0-915179-16-4 (pbk.) LC Card 84-81910 DDC 343.7305/23 347.303523 19
HD2346.U5 C34 1984 **NYPL *[JLD 86-2946]***

INFORMAL SECTOR (ECONOMICS) - ZAIRE - KINSHASA.
Gozo, K. M. Le secteur non structuré de Kinshasa . Addis Abéba , c1985. iii, 64, [8] p. : ISBN 92-2-100538-0 LC Card 85-981182
HD2346.Z27 K54 1985

INFORMAL SECTOR (ECONOMICS) - ZAMBIA - KITWE.
Kamya, Andrew, 1941- Factors affecting efficiency in the informal sector in Lusaka and Kitwe /. Lusaka , 1981. iii, 40 p. ; LC Card 87-980491
HD2346.Z292 L875 1981

INFORMAL SECTOR (ECONOMICS) - ZAMBIA - LUSAKA.
Kamya, Andrew, 1941- Factors affecting efficiency in the informal sector in Lusaka and Kitwe /. Lusaka , 1981. iii, 40 p. ; LC Card 87-980491
HD2346.Z292 L875 1981

INFORMAL SECTOR (ECONOMICS) - ZAMBIA - MONGU DISTRICT.
The Structure of the informal sector in Mongu (Western Province) and its potential for employment creation . Lusaka, Zambia [1982] iii, 44, 10 p. ; LC Card 87-980490 DDC 331.12/51381 19
HD2346.Z292 M657 1982

Informal sector employment in Kenya . Aboagye, A. A. Addis Ababa , Geneva, Switzerland , 1986. vii, 117, [64] p. ; ISBN 92-2-105557-4 LC Card 87-980151 DDC 331.12/51381 19
HD2346.K42 N353 1986

The Informal sector in Africa / International Labour Organisation. Addis Ababa : Jobs and Skills Programme for Africa, 1984. 2, iii, 149 p. ; 30 cm. Includes bibliographies. ISBN 92-2-103785-1 LC Card 87-106188 DDC 381 19
1. Informal sector (Economics) - Africa. I. International Labor Organisation. II. Jobs and Skills Programme for Africa.
HD2346.A55 I19 1984

The Informal sector in Africa. Addis Ababa [Ethiopia] : Jobs and Skills Programme for Africa, 1985. 147 p. ; 24 cm. At head of title: International Labour Organisation. Includes bibliographical references. ISBN 92-2-103785-1 : *1. Informal sector (Economics) - Africa. 2. Small business - Africa. 3. Africa - Economic conditions - 1960-. I. International Labor Organization. II. International Labor Office. Jobs and Skills Programme for Africa.* **NYPL *[JLE 86-1454]***

Informática . Araújo, Sergio. [Brazil? , 1986?] (Guarulhos [Brazil] : Artes Gráficas Guaru) 184 p. : LC Card 87-154279 DDC 338.4/7004 19
HC79.I55 A7 1986

Informática e sociedade /. Rattner, Henrique. São Paulo-SP , 1985. 219 p. : LC Card 85-221850
HC79.T4 R387 1985

La informática nacional . Quibrera Matienzo,

Enrique. [Xochimilco, Mexico] , 1984. 133 p. ; LC Card 86-124964 DDC 338.4/7004/0972 19
HD9696.C63 M617 1984

Informatics and development . Cline, William R. Washington, D.C. (9416 Friendship Station, Washington 20016) [1987] vi, 161 p. ; LC Card 87-6819 DDC 338.4/7004/0981 19
HD9696.C63 B728 1987

Informatieverzorging.
Völlmar, H. De organisatie-aspecten van de automatisering /. Leiden , 1985. xiv, 316 p. : ISBN 90-207-1347-7 : LC Card 85-220224
HD45.2 .V65 1985

Information analysis /. Burn, Janice. London , 1987. x, 260 p. : ISBN 0-948825-50-2 (pbk.) : LC Card 87-166130 DDC 658.4/038 19
HD30.35 .B87 1987

Information and capital markets /. Strong, Norman, 1954- Oxford, UK , New York, NY, USA , 1987. x, 222 p. : ISBN 0-631-13834-X : LC Card 86-31721 DDC 332/.041 19
HG4523 .S77 1987

Information and records management /. Robek, Mary F. Encino, Calif. , c1987. vi, 580 p. : ISBN 0-02-820590-1 LC Card 87-135683 DDC 651.5 19
HF5736 .R53 1987

Information and records management . Smith, Milburn D. New York , c1986. xiv, 285 p. : ISBN 0-89930-111-8 (lib. bdg. : alk. paper) LC Card 86-638 DDC 651.5 19
HF5736 .S58 1986 ***NYPL [JLE 87-1454]***

Information and the crisis economy /. Schiller, Herbert I., 1919- New York , 1986. xv, 133 p. ; ISBN 0-19-520514-6 (pbk. : alk. paper) LC Card 86-2374 DDC 302.2/34 19
HE7651 .S34 1986 ***NYPL [JLD 86-3695]***

The information center /. Perry, William E. Englewood Cliffs, N.J. , c1987. xi, 284 p. : ISBN 0-13-464371-2 LC Card 86-25212 DDC 658.4/038 19
HF5548.2 .P47284 1987

Information center magazine. The 1986 AMA report on information centers . New York, N.Y. , c1986. viii, 92, [28] p. : ISBN 0-8144-3154-2 ***NYPL [JLF 86-1835]***

INFORMATION CENTERS. see **INFORMATION SERVICES.**

INFORMATION CONSULTANTS.
Warner, Alice Sizer. Mind your own business . New York , c1987. xii, 165 p. ; ISBN 1-555-70014-4 : LC Card 86-23641 DDC 658.1/1 19
HD62.5 .W37 1987

INFORMATION CONSULTANTS - DIRECTORIES.
The International directory of business information sources and services. London , 1986. ix, 378 p. ; ISBN 0-946653-18-6 ***NYPL [*R-Econ. 86-2525]***

INFORMATION DISPLAY SYSTEMS INDUSTRY.
Flat panel displays. Norwalk, Conn., U. S.A. (6 Prowitt St., Norwalk 06855) , c1986. vii, 204 leaves ; LC Card 86-224985 DDC 380.1/4562138195832 19
HD9696.C62 F57 1986

INFORMATION DISPLAY SYSTEMS INDUSTRY - UNITED STATES.
The Industrial display market in the U. S. New York, N.Y. , c1983. vi, 226 leaves ; LC Card 87-142373 DDC 381/.456213985/0973 19
HD9696.I533 U54 1983

The information edge /. Meyer, N. Dean. New York , c1987. xvii, 333 p. ; ISBN 0-07-041782-2 LC Card 86-222546 DDC 651.8 19
HF5547.5 .M495 1987

Information evaluation in capital markets /. Firchau, Volker. Berlin , New York , c1986. iv, 103 p. : ISBN 0-387-16462-6 (U. S.) : LC Card 86-6655 DDC 332.6/0724 19
HG4523 .F57 1986
NYPL [JLM 72-289 v.268]

L'Information financière : facteur d'interdépendance économique : colloque des 26, 27 et 28 novembre 1981 / organisé avec la collaboration de la province de Brabant. Bruxelles : E. Bruylant, 1983. 220 p. ; 24 cm. (Recueil du Centre d'études européennes de Waterloo . no 3) English and French. Organized by Centre d'études européennes de Waterloo. Includes bibliographical references. ISBN 2-8027-0298-X LC Card 84-104169
1. Communication in financial institutions - Europe - Congresses. 2. Finance - Information services - Europe - Congresses. 3. Money market - Europe - Congresses. I. Brabant (Belgium). II. Centre d'études européennes de Waterloo. III. Series.
HG151.5 .I56 1983

INFORMATION, FREEDOM OF. see **FREEDOM OF INFORMATION.**

INFORMATION, GOVERNMENT. see **GOVERNMENT INFORMATION.**

Information hotline U. S.A. /. Bly, Amy Sprecher. New York , c1987. xviii, 286 p. ; ISBN 0-452-25921-5 (pbk.) : LC Card 87-5687 DDC 384.6/025/73 19
HE8811 .B49 1987

Information hotline USA. Bly, Amy Sprecher. Information hotline U. S.A. /. New York , c1987. xviii, 286 p. ; ISBN 0-452-25921-5 (pbk.) : LC Card 87-5687 DDC 384.6/025/73 19
HE8811 .B49 1987

Information i prognosfrågor, 0082-0180 .
(1985:2) Trender och prognoser inför 90-talet. Stockholm , Örebro , 1985. 147 p. : ISBN 91-618-0001-5 LC Card 86-115921
LB2833 .S9 1985:2 HC375
NYPL [JLG 86-230]

The information imperative . Gibson, Cyrus F. Lexington, Mass. , c1987. xxii, 160 p. : ISBN 0-669-12338-2 (alk. paper) LC Card 85-45797 DDC 658/.05 19
HF5548.2 .G496 1987

INFORMATION MEASUREMENT - MATHEMATICAL MODELS.
Firchau, Volker. Information evaluation in capital markets /. Berlin , New York , c1986. iv, 103 p. : ISBN 0-387-16462-6 (U. S.) : LC Card 86-6655 DDC 332.6/0724 19
HG4523 .F57 1986
NYPL [JLM 72-289 v.268]

INFORMATION NETWORKS - CONGRESSES.
International Conference on Networks and Electronic Office Systems (1983 : University of Reading) Networks and electronic office systems . London , c1983. 240 p. : ISBN 0-903748-52-5 ***NYPL [JSG 86-298]***

International Conference on Networks and Electronic Office Systems (1985 : London, England) Networks and electronic office systems . London , c1985. 166 p. : ISBN 0-903748-60-6 ***NYPL [JSG 86-264]***

Information note on the technical cooperation programme / [prepared by the Informaton Division of FAO ; written by Steve Dembner]. Rome : Food and Agriculture Organization of the United Nations, [1985?] 29 p. : ill. ; 30 cm. LC Card 87-122600 DDC 338.9/26/091724 19
1. Technical assistance - Developing countries. 2. Agricultural assistance - Developing countries. 3. Technical assistance - Developing countries - Case studies. 4. Agricultural assistance - Developing countries - Case studies. I. Dembner, Steve. II. Food and Agriculture Organization of the United Nations. Information Division.
HC60 .I477 1985

Information og kontrol . Denmark. Direktoratet for toldvæsenet. [Copenhagen] [1985] 125, [49] p. : LC Card 86-209910
HJ6971 .D46 1985

Information om arbetsmarknaden, 0283-3719 .
(1986:7) Sveriges arbetskraft . Stockholm , Örebro [1986] 62 p. : ISBN 91-618-0162-3 : LC Card 87-151800
HD5803 .S943 1986

Information on the administration of workers' compensation programs in each state and the District of Columbia / prepared by Division of State Workers' Compensation Programs, Office of State Liaison and Legislative Analysis, Employment Standards Administration, U. S. Department of Labor. [Washington, D.C.?] : The Division, [1985] iii, 426 p. ; 28 cm. Cover title: State workers' compensation: administration profiles. "October 1985."
1. Workers' compensation - United States. 2. Workers' compensation - United States - States. I. United States. Employment Standards Administration. Division of State Workers' Compensation Programs. II. Title: State workers' compensation, administration profiles.
NYPL [JLF 86-774]

Information on the administration of workers' compensation programs in each state and the District of Columbia / prepared by Division of State Workers' Compensation Programs, Office of State Liaison and Legislative Analysis, Employment Standards Administration, U. S. Department of Labor. [Washington, D.C.?] : The Division, [1985] iii, 426 p. ; 29 cm. Cover title: State workers' compensation. "October 1985." LC Card 86-601358 DDC 368.4/1/00973 19
1. Workers' compensation - United States. I. United States. Employment Standards Administration. Division of State Workers' Compensation Programs. II. Title: State workers' compensation.
HD7103.65.U6 I55 1985

Information paper (Committee for Economic Development of Australia) .
(no. IP 23) Hall, Richard, 1937- The Prices Surveillance Authority /. Melbourne [1987] 24 p. ; ISBN 0-85801-167-0 (pbk.) LC Card 87-156317 DDC 338.5/26/0994 19
HB236.A8 H35 1987

Information paper (Victoria. Dept. of Management and Budget) .
(no. 2) Victorian public sector debt. [Melbourne, Vic.] [1986] vii, 57, [1] p. ; LC Card 87-165135 DDC 336.3/4/09945 19
HJ8857.V53 V53 1986

Information papers (Singapore. Economic Development Division. Economics Section) .
(inf. 59/G) Koh, Cher Siang. The co-operative movement in Singapore /. Singapore [1970] 26 p. ; LC Card 87-121945 DDC 334/.09595/7 19
HD3543.A4 K64 1970

INFORMATION PROCESSING SYSTEMS. see **INFORMATION STORAGE AND RETRIEVAL SYSTEMS.**

Information, promotion et coopération internationales, A.S.B.L. L'Economie des pays de l'Afrique de l'Ouest. Bruxelles [1978] 1 v. (various pagings) : LC Card 86-673818
HC1000 .E36x 1978

Information research and resource reports .
(v. 7) Microanalytic simulation models to support social and financial policy /. Amsterdam ; New York : xvii, 553 p. : ISBN 0-444-87876-9 (U. S.) LC Card 85-25231 DDC 361.6/0724 19
HD87 .M52 1986 ***NYPL [JLD 86-3485]***

INFORMATION RESOURCES MANAGEMENT.
Burn, Janice. Information analysis /. London , 1987. x, 260 p. : ISBN 0-948825-50-2 (pbk.) : LC Card 87-166130 DDC 658.4/038 19
HD30.35 .B87 1987

Smith, Milburn D. Information and records management . New York , c1986. xiv, 285 p. : ISBN 0-89930-111-8 (lib. bdg. : alk. paper) LC Card 86-638 DDC 651.5 19
HF5736 .S58 1986 ***NYPL [JLE 87-1454]***

Synnott, William R. The information weapon . New York , 1987. xi, 334 p. ; ISBN 0-471-84557-4 LC Card 86-32393 DDC 658.4/038 19
HD30.335 .S96 1987

INFORMATION RETRIEVAL SYSTEMS. see **INFORMATION STORAGE AND RETRIEVAL SYSTEMS.**

Information series (National Center for Research in Vocational Education (U. S.) .
(no. 290) Bhaerman, Robert D. Planning for adult career counseling /. Columbus, Ohio (1960 Kenny Rd., Columbus 43210-1090) , 1985. ix, 64 p. ; LC Card 87-108253 DDC 331.12/8 19
HF5381 .B4225 1985

INFORMATION SERVICES - DIRECTORIES.
The International directory of business information sources and services. London , 1986. ix, 378 p. ; ISBN 0-946653-18-6 ***NYPL [*R-Econ. 86-2525]***

Information services in rural areas . Clark, David, Ph. D. Norwich [Norfolk] , c1980. x, 122 p. : ISBN 0-86094-058-6 (pbk.) LC Card 81-149488
HE8109.L55 C55 1980

INFORMATION SERVICES - MARKETING.
Holtz, Herman. Advice, a high profit business . Englewood Cliffs, N.J. , c1986. xii, 242 p. : ISBN 0-13-011958-X LC Card 85-24405 DDC 658.4/6/0688 19
HD69.C6 H618 1986 ***NYPL [JLE 86-3858]***

INFORMATION STORAGE AND RETRIEVAL SYSTEMS - ACCOUNTING.
Accounting information systems . Reading, Mass. , c1987. p. cm. ISBN 0-201-10376-1 : LC Card 87-1155 DDC 657/.028/5 19
HF5679 .A34 1987

Bodnar, George H. Accounting information systems /. Boston , c1987. xvii, 892 p. : ISBN 0-205-10308-1 LC Card 86-26505 DDC 657/.028/5 19
HF5679 .B59 1987

Moscove, Stephen A. Accounting information systems . New York , c1987. xxi, 824 p. : ISBN 0-471-84033-5 LC Card 86-32387 DDC 657/.028/5 19
HF5679 .M62 1987

Page, John R., 1949- Accounting and information systems /. Englewood Cliffs, N.J. , c1987. xiii, 738 p. : ISBN 0-13-002361-2 LC Card 86-25429 DDC 657/.028/5 19
HF5679 .P25 1987

Sharifi, Mohsen. Integrated case studies in accounting and information systems /. Englewood Cliffs, N.J. , c1987. ix, 229 p. : ISBN 0-13-469016-8 (pbk.) LC Card 86-30297 DDC 657/.028/5 19
HF5679 .S4754 1987

INFORMATION STORAGE AND RETRIEVAL SYSTEMS - BUSINESS.
Arn, Joseph V., 1943- Office automation . Boston, MA , c1988. xxvii, 402 p., [8] p. of plates : ISBN 0-87835-232-5 LC Card 86-28359 DDC 651.8 19
HF5547.5 .A79 1988

Ellis, Clarence Arthur, 1943- Design of office information systems /. Berlin , New York , c1987. vi, 248 p. : ISBN 0-387-17810-4 (U. S.) : LC Card 87-9582 DDC 651.8 19
HF5548.2 .E445 1987

Gremillion, Lee L. (Lee Louis) Computers and information systems in business . New York , c1988. xxi, 359 p., [16] p. of plates : ISBN 0-07-051007-5 (pbk.) LC Card 87-20300 DDC 650/.028/5 19
HF5548.2 .G7196 1988

Johnson, Bonnie McDaniel, 1944- Managing organizational innovation . New York , 1987. xiv, 242 p. ; ISBN 0-231-06398-9 LC Card 87-307 DDC 652/.5 19
HF5548.115 .J64 1987

Long, Larry E. Computers in business /. Englewood Cliffs, N.J. , c1987. xxv, 609 p. : ISBN 0-13-164294-4 LC Card 86-30412 DDC 650/.028/5 19
HF5548.2 .L586 1987

Perry, William E. The information center /. Englewood Cliffs, N.J. , c1987. xi, 284 p. : ISBN 0-13-464371-2 LC Card 86-25212 DDC 658.4/038 19
HF5548.2 .P47284 1987

Robek, Mary F. Information and records management /. Encino, Calif. , c1987. vi, 580 p. : ISBN 0-02-820590-1 LC Card 87-135683 DDC 651.5 19
HF5736 .R53 1987

Simkin, Mark G. Introduction to computer information systems for business /. Dubuque, Iowa , c1987. xxvi, 678 p. : ISBN 0-697-00125-3 LC Card 86-72218 DDC 658/.05 19
HF5548.2 .S4498 1987

Vella, Carolyn M. Competitive intelligence in the computer age /. New York , 1987. xv, 189 p. ; ISBN 0-89930-169-X (lib. bdg. : alk. paper) LC Card 86-25565 DDC 651.8 19
HF5548.2 .V38 1987

INFORMATION STORAGE AND RETRIEVAL SYSTEMS - BUSINESS - CONGRESSES.
IFIP TC 8 Working Conference on Office Systems (1985 : Helsinki, Finland) Office systems . Amsterdam ; New York : vii, 199 p. : ISBN 0-444-70105-2 (Elsevier Science Pub. Co.) LC Card 86-16841 DDC 651.8 19
HF5547.5 .I345 1985 ***NYPL [JLD 87-1264]***

IFIP TC 8/WG 8.4 Working Conference on Methods and Tools for Office Systems (1986 : Pisa, Italy) Office systems . Amsterdam ; New York : xi, 347 p. : ISBN 0-444-70241-5 (U. S.) LC Card 87-8916 DDC 651.8 19
HF5548.2 .I285 1986

INFORMATION STORAGE AND RETRIEVAL SYSTEMS - BUSINESS - DIRECTORIES.
Lavin, Michael R. Business information . Phoenix, Ariz. , 1987. x, 299 p. : ISBN 0-89774-157-9 (alk. paper) : LC Card 86-42787 DDC 650/.072 19
HF5356 .L36 1987

INFORMATION STORAGE AND RETRIEVAL SYSTEMS - INDUSTRY.
Völlmar, H. De organisatie-aspecten van de automatisering /. Leiden , 1985. xiv, 316 p. : ISBN 90-207-1347-7 : LC Card 85-220224
HD45.2 .V65 1985

INFORMATION STORAGE AND RETRIEVAL SYSTEMS - LATIN AMERICA - ECONOMIC CONDITIONS - HANDBOOKS, MANUALS, ETC.
Guía conceptual y metodológica para instructores de cursos de capacitación de INFOPLAN. Santiago de Chile , 1983. iv, 70 p. : LC Card 87-108080
HC125 .G814 1983

INFORMATION STORAGE AND RETRIEVAL SYSTEMS - LATIN AMERICA - SOCIAL CONDITIONS - HANDBOOKS, MANUALS, ETC.
Guía conceptual y metodológica para instructores de cursos de capacitación de INFOPLAN. Santiago de Chile , 1983. iv, 70 p. : LC Card 87-108080
HC125 .G814 1983

INFORMATION STORAGE AND RETRIEVAL SYSTEMS - ROADS.
Az Ország közúthálózatának müszaki minősitése és nyilvántartása /. [Budapest] , 1983. 2 v. : LC Card 84-253458
HE363.H82 O76 1983

Information sur le marché du travail et renforcement des structures de la direction de l'emploi. International Labour Organisation. Côte-d'Ivoire . Genève , 1984. 94 p. : ISBN 92-2-203860-6 LC Card 86-219971
HD5846.9.A6 I57 1984

Information symposium, 23 October 1981. Inligtingsimposium, 23 Oktober 1981 /. [Pretoria] [1981] 115 p. : LC Card 86-213181 DDC 380.5/0968 19
HE284.4.A2 I55 1981

Information systems in Italian savings banks : proceedings of the MIS Working Group seminar, Rome, Italy, October 21-22, 1974. Geneva : International Savings Banks Institute, 1975. 93 p. : ill. ; 30 cm. LC Card 84-247915
1. Savings banks - Italy - Management - Congresses. 2. Management information systems - Congresses. I. International Savings Banks Institute. MIS Working Group.
HG1939.I7 I54 1975

Information systems study, 1986. Washington, D.C. (1750 K St. N.W., Washington 20006) : Research Division, Food Marketing Institute, c1986. v, 39 p. : ill. ; 28 cm. Copyright date from label on t.p. LC Card 86-220211 DDC 381/.456413/00285 19
1. Supermarkets - United States - Data processing - Costs - Statistics. 2. Grocery trade - United States - Data processing - Costs - Statistics. I. Food Marketing Institute. Research Division.
HF5469.23.U62 I543 1986

Information technology . Poppel, Harvey L. New York , c1987. xx, 207 p. : ISBN 0-07-050511-X : LC Card 86-27782 DDC 338.4/7004/0973 19
HD9696.C62 P623 1987

INFORMATION TECHNOLOGY.
Gerstein, Marc Saul. The technology connection . Reading, Mass. , c1987. xiv, 194 p. : ISBN 0-201-12188-3 (pbk.) : LC Card 86-22343 DDC 658.4/012 19
HD30.28 .G47 1987

Gibson, Cyrus F. The information imperative . Lexington, Mass. , c1987. xxii, 160 p. : ISBN 0-669-12338-2 (alk. paper) LC Card 85-45797 DDC 658/.05 19
HF5548.2 .G496 1987

Gunton, Tony, 1943- Business information technology . Englewood Cliffs, N.J. , 1988. p. cm. ISBN 0-13-100843-9 LC Card 87-7365 DDC 658/.05 19
HF5548.2 .G86 1988

Izzo, Joseph E., 1931- The embattled fortress . San Francisco , 1987. xxii, 155 p. : ISBN 1-555-42059-1 (alk. paper) LC Card 87-45429 DDC 658.4/038 19
HF5548.2 .I97 1987

Jones, Graham. Information technology and the new accounting /. London , New York , c1988. p. cm. ISBN 0-07-084179-9 : LC Card 87-22579 DDC 657/.028/5 19
HF5679 .J634 1988

Long, Richard J. New office information technology . London , New York , c1987. xix, 333 p. : ISBN 0-7099-4103-X (jacket); 0-7099-4130-X LC Card 87-3601 DDC 651.8 19
HF5547.5 .L65 1987

Martin, James, 1933- The wired world . Carnforth, Lancashire, England , 1986. xiii, 140 p. : ISBN 0-906774-49-7 (pbk.) LC Card 87-157689 DDC 384 19
HE7631 .M373 1986

Women and information technology /. Chichester , New York , c1987. viii, 283 p. : ISBN 0-471-91603-X : LC Card 87-10554 DDC 331.4 19
HD6053 .W636 1987

Information technology and the new accounting /. Jones, Graham. London , New York , c1988. p. cm. ISBN 0-07-084179-9 : LC Card 87-22579 DDC 657/.028/5 19
HF5679 .J634 1988

INFORMATION TECHNOLOGY - CONGRESSES.
Informationstechnologie im Dienstleistungsbereich . Berlin , c1985. 258 p. : ISBN 3-924859-15-9 : LC Card 86-220033 DDC 338.4/561 19
HD9980.5 .I54 1985

INFORMATION TECHNOLOGY - ECONOMIC ASPECTS.
Araújo, Sergio. Informática . [Brazil? , 1986?] (Guarulhos [Brazil] : Artes Gráficas Guaru) 184 p. : LC Card 87-154279 DDC 338.4/7004 19
HC79.I55 A7 1986

Information technology and economic prospects. Paris , Washington, D.C. , 1987. 221 p. : ISBN 92-64-12927-8 (pbk.) : LC Card 87-163173 DDC 331.1 19
HD9696.A2 I54 1987

INFORMATION TECHNOLOGY - ECONOMIC ASPECTS - PACIFIC AREA.
The Cost of thinking . Norwood, N.J. , c1988. xii, 249 p. : ISBN 0-89391-419-3 LC Card 87-22937 DDC 338.4/7004/099 19
HC681.3.I55 C67 1988

INFORMATION TECHNOLOGY - SOCIAL ASPECTS.
Araújo, Sergio. Informática . [Brazil? , 1986?] (Guarulhos [Brazil] : Artes Gráficas Guaru) 184 p. : LC Card 87-154279 DDC 338.4/7004 19
HC79.I55 A7 1986

INFORMATION THEORY IN ECONOMICS.
Economic analysis of information and contracts . Boston , c1988. p. cm. ISBN 0-89838-252-1 : LC Card 87-22508 DDC 657 19
HF5625 .E28 1988

Hopf, Michael. Informationen für Märkte und Märkte für Informationen /. Frankfurt am Main , 1983. iv, 237 p. : ISBN 3-922182-14-3 : LC Card 84-180866
HB133 .H66 1983

Knorr, Peter. Messwerte der Informationsnachfrage in komplexen Beurteilungsprozessen /. Kiel , 1986. xvi, 241 p. : ISBN 3-922553-77-X LC Card 86-149044
HB133 .K59 1986

Mälich, Wolfgang. Informationstheoretische Lösung ausgewählter Entscheidungsprobleme /. Göttingen , c1984. vi, 269 p. : ISBN 3-525-12314-0 LC Card 84-162246
HD30.23 .M345 1984

Vanags, I. I͡A. (Ilmar I͡Anovich) Ėffektivnoe ispolʹzovanie vychislitelʹnoĭ tekhniki /.

Moskva , 1982. 142, [2] p. : LC Card 83-165693
HF5548.2 .V345 1982

The information weapon . Synnott, William R. New York , 1987. xi, 334 p. ; ISBN 0-471-84557-4 LC Card 86-32393 DDC 658.4/038 19
HD30.335 .S96 1987

Informationen für Märkte und Märkte für Informationen /. Hopf, Michael. Frankfurt am Main , 1983. iv, 237 p. : ISBN 3-922182-14-3 : LC Card 84-180866
HB133 .H66 1983

Informationen zur Weltpolitik .
(7) Höll, Otmar. Österreichische Entwicklungshilfe, 1970-1983 . Wien , Laxenburg, Austria , c1986. 187 p. : ISBN 3-7003-0659-8 LC Card 86-192362
HC60 .H6643 1986

Informations- und Veränderungskosten in makroökonomischen Transmissionsmodellen /. Vollmer, Friedrich Uwe, 1958- Frankfurt am Main , New York , c1986. 169 p. : ISBN 3-8204-9142-2 LC Card 86-194476
HB221 .V64 1986

Informationsbericht (Institut für Marxistische Studien und Forschungen (Frankfurt am Main, Germany)) .
(Nr. 44) SPD wohin? . Frankfurt/Main , c1987. 114 p. ; ISBN 3-88807-047-3 LC Card 87-401340 DDC 330 s 324.243/072 19
HB97.5 .I53 Nr. 44 JN3971.A98S571712

Informationsbewertung und -effizienz auf dem Kapitalmarkt /. Wahl, Jack. Würzburg , 1983. 211 p. : ISBN 3-7908-0308-1 LC Card 84-154688
HG4515 .W34 1983

Informationsinstrumente zur Umweltplanung . Schmidt, Helmut, Dr. rer. oec. Frankfurt/Main , c1985. ix, 441 p. : ISBN 3-88129-947-5 LC Card 86-141873
HC79.E5 S285 1985

Der Informationsmarkt . Volkmann, Helmut, 1936- München , c1985. 366 p. : ISBN 3-89003-016-5 LC Card 85-195750
HD35 .V596 1985

Informationsprozesse auf spekulativen Märkten . Quick, Rolf H. Thun , c1984. vii, 291 p. : ISBN 3-87144-790-0 : LC Card 84-159793
HG3853 .Q53 1984

Informationsquellen der Konsumenten . Katz, Reinhard. Wiesbaden , c1983. xxix, 297 p. : ISBN 3-409-13602-9 LC Card 84-118615
HF5415.3 .K35 1983

Informationsseminar Alkohol am Arbeitsplatz (1985 : Obereifenberg, Schmitten, Germany) Informationsseminar Alkohol am Arbeitzplatz / veranstaltet von Gesellschaft für Strahlen- und Umweltforschung in Oberreifenberg/Taunus vom 2.-3. Mai 1985. München : Die Gesellschaft, [1985?] ii, 49 p. : ill. ; 21 cm. Bibliography: p. 47-48. LC Card 86-162315
1. Alcoholism and employment - Germany (West) - Congresses. I. Gesellschaft für Strahlen- und Umweltforschung. II. Title.
HF5549.5.A4 I54 1985

Informationsseminar Alkohol am Arbeitzplatz /. Informationsseminar Alkohol am Arbeitsplatz (1985 : Obereifenberg, Schmitten, Germany) München [1985?] ii, 49 p. : LC Card 86-162315
HF5549.5.A4 I54 1985

Informationstechnologie im Dienstleistungsbereich : Arbeitsbedingungen und Leistungsqualität / Thore Karlsen, Hagen Kühn, Maria Oppen (Hg.) ; [Internationales Institut für Vergleichende Gesellschaftsforschung/Arbeitspolitik]. Berlin : Edition Sigma, c1985. 258 p. : ill. ; 21 cm. (Wissenschaftszentrum Berlin, Internationales Institut für Vergleichende Gesellschaftsforschung/Arbeitspolitik) "Die im diesem Band vorgelegten Beiträge basieren auf Referaten, die im Rahmen des Internationalen Workshops 'Informationstechnologie im Dienstleistungsbereich--Arbeitsbedingungen und Leistungsqualität' präsentiert wurden"--Pref. Includes bibliographies. ISBN 3-924859-15-9 : LC Card 86-220033 DDC 338.4/561 19
1. Service industries - Data processing - Congresses. 2. Information technology - Congresses. I. Karlsen, Thore. II. Kühn, Hagen, 1943-. III. Oppen, Maria. IV. Internationales Institut für Vergleichende Gesellschaftsforschung/Arbeitspolitik. V. Internationaler Workshop "Informationstechnologie im Dienstleistungsbereich--Arbeitsbedingungen und Leistungsqualität" (1985?). VI. Series: Wissenschaftszentrum Berlin, Internationales Institut für Vergleichende Gesellschaftsforschung/Arbeitspolitik (Series).
HD9980.5 .I54 1985

Informationsteknologi og arbejdsproces . Matthiasen, Leo. Roskilde [1983?] 339 p. : ISBN 87-87893-19-3 LC Card 85-114664
HF5547.5 .M384 1983

Informationstheoretische Lösung ausgewählter Entscheidungsprobleme /. Mälich, Wolfgang. Göttingen , c1984. vi, 269 p. : ISBN 3-525-12314-0 LC Card 84-162246
HD30.23 .M345 1984

Informationsverhalten kleiner und mittlerer Unternehmen der elektrotechnischen Investitionsgüterindustrie bei strategischen Entscheidungen /. Klaes, Friedhelm, 1956- Frankfurt am Main , New York , c1986. xxii, 305 p. ; ISBN 3-8204-9713-7 LC Card 87-407575 DDC 658.4/03 19
HD62.7 .K586 1986

Informatique et emploi . France. Conseil économique et social. [Paris] [1984] 24, 4 p., 8 leaves, 187, 13 p. : LC Card 84-218059
HD6331.2.F8 F73 1984

L'informatisation et l'emploi /. Pastré, Olivier. Paris , 1983. 127 p. : ISBN 2-7071-1387-5 LC Card 83-161919 DDC 331.12/0944 19
HD6331.2.F8 P37 1983

Informatorovi rječnici.
Andrlić, Vlasta. Rječnik terminologije jugoslavenskog političko-ekonomskog sistema . Zagreb , 1985. viii, 135 p. ; LC Card 86-182784
HB61 .A55 1985 ***NYPL [*QKK 87-1803]***

Informat͡sionnai͡a sistema upravlenii͡a predprii͡atiem /. Bersutskiĭ, I͡A. G. (I͡Akov Grigor′evich) Kiev , 1986. 166 p. : LC Card 86-214727
HD30.35 .B47 1986

Informat͡sionno osiguri͡avane na profsi͡uznite organi . Zhecheva, Marii͡a. Sofii͡a , 1985. 138 p. : LC Card 86-192068
HD6782 .Z44 1985

Informat͡sionnyĭ bi͡ulleten′ (Problemnai͡a komissii͡a mnogostoronnego sotrudnichestva akademiĭ nauk sot͡sialisticheskikh stran "Ėkonomika i politika razvivai͡ushchikhsi͡a stran") .
(8) Razvivai͡ushchiesi͡a strany . Moskva , 1982. 307 p. ; LC Card 85-115259
HC59.7 .R33858 1982

Informe (Barcelona (Spain). Ayuntamiento. Departament d'Estudis i Programació) .
(2) Barcelona (Spain). Ayuntamiento. Departament d'Estudis i Programació. Estat d'execució dels programes d'actuació i pressupostos d'inversió de l'Ajuntament de Barcelona durant 1982. [Barcelona] [1983] 126 leaves ; LC Card 84-249883
HC388.B3 B36 1983

Informe cuatrianual, 1980-1983 / PREDESUR. Cuenca, Ecuador : PREDESUR, [1983] 222 p. : ill. (some col.) ; 30 cm. Cover title: Desarrollo regional del sur del Ecuador, El Oro, Loja, Zamora, 1980-1983 : Informe. Spine title: Informe de labores, 1980-1983. LC Card 86-206868
1. El Oro (Ecuador : Province) - Economic policy. 2. Rural development - Ecuador - El Oro (Province). 3. Loja (Ecuador : Province) - Economic policy. 4. Rural development - Ecuador - Loja (Province). 5. Zamora-Chinchipe (Ecuador) - Economic policy. 6. Rural development - Ecuador - Zamora-Chinchipe. I. Programa Regional para el Desarrollo del Sur (Ecuador). II. Title: Desarrollo regional del Sur del Ecuador, El Oro, Loja, Zamora, 1980-1983. III. Title: Informe de labores, 1980-1983.
HC203.O76 I53 1983

Informe de caminos rurales : 1ro. de enero a 31 de diciembre/82. [Guatemala, Guatemala] : Unidad de Planeamiento, Sección de Estadística, Dirección General de Caminos, [1982] 2, [6] leaves ; 22 cm. Cover title: Informe de los trabajos ejecutados por el programa de "caminos rurales" de la Dirección General de Caminos durante el año 1982. LC Card 85-153481
1. Rural roads - Guatemala - Finance. I. Guatemala. Dirección General de Caminos. Sección de Estadística. II. Title: Informe de los trabajos ejecutados por el programa de "caminos rurales" de la Dirección General de Caminos durante el año 1982.
HE359.G83 R855 1982

Informe de investigación (Madrid, Spain)
Bragulat, Jorge. La enseñanza del cooperativismo en la Universidad /. Madrid [1982] 119 p. : LC Card 85-203554
HD2955 .B72 1982

Informe de la Comisión Nombrada para Estudiar el Conflicto Surgido entre la United Fruit Company y la Cooperativa Bananera Colombiana. Colombia. Congreso. Cámara de Representantes. Comisión Nombrada para Estudiar el Conflicto Surgido entre la United Fruit Company y la Cooperativa Bananera Colombiana. Bogotá , 1930. 32 p. ; LC Card 83-189629
HD9259.B3 C728 1930

Informe de la obra realizada por el Gobierno Militar, período del 8 de agosto 1983/31 de diciembre 1985. Guatemala. Guatemala [1986] 192 p., [17] p. of plates : LC Card 86-200374
HC144 .G76 1986

Informe de labores, 1980-1983. Informe cuatrianual, 1980-1983 /. Cuenca, Ecuador [1983] 222 p. : LC Card 86-206868
HC203.O76 I53 1983

Informe de los trabajos ejecutados por el programa de "caminos rurales" de la Dirección General de Caminos durante el año 1982. Informe de caminos rurales . [Guatemala, Guatemala] [1982] 2, [6] leaves ; LC Card 85-153481
HE359.G83 R855 1982

Informe de trabajo (Universidad Nacional (Costa Rica). Instituto de Estudios Sociales en Población) .
(no. 39) Denton L., Carlos F. Población, fecundidad y desarrollo en Costa Rica, 1950-1970 /. [Heredia, Costa Rica] , 1984. iv, 150 p. : LC Card 86-117583 DDC 304.6/097286 19
HB3531 .D44 1984 ***NYPL [JLF 87-144]***

Informe del gobierno argentino sobre asuntos laborales / Comisión Especial del CIES-OEA. Buenos Aires, República Argentina : Ministerio de Trabajo y Seguridad Social, 1965. 115 leaves ; 29 cm. LC Card 85-115096
1. Labor policy - Argentina. 2. Social security - Argentina. 3. Trade-unions - Government policy - Argentina. I. Inter-American Economic and Social Council. Comisión Especial. II. Argentina. Ministerio de Trabajo y Seguridad Social.
HD8266.5 .I53 1965

Informe del Seminario Interamericano Conmemorativo de los 25 Años del BID /. Seminario Interamericano Conmemorativo de los 25 Años del BID (1985 : Rio de Janeiro, Brazil) Rio de Janeiro, RJ , 1986. 65 p. : LC Card 87-403948 DDC 332.1/538 19
HG3881.5.I44 S46 1985

Informe económico (Economic & Financial Survey (Firm)) .
(no. 8) La Deuda externa . [Santiago, Chile] , 1985. 105 leaves : LC Card 86-171251
HJ8514.5 .D47 1985

Informe especial (Centro de Documentación e Información--Bolivia)
Granado Cosio, Hugo del. Transnacionales y nación . [La Paz, Bolivia] , 1986. 24 p. ; LC Card 87-115866 DDC 338.8/87 19
HD9574.B82 G73 1986

Lazarte, Jorge. Crisis de identidad y centralidad minera . [La Paz, Bolivia] [1986] 37 p. : LC Card 87-401455 DDC 331.88/122/0984 19
HD8039.M61 B586 1986

Informe especial (Uruguay. Dirección Nacional de Recursos Humanos) .
(no. 73) Empleo y estructura ocupacional en grandes establecimientos industriales /. Montevideo , 1984. 51 leaves ; LC Card 86-174021
HB2667 .E46 1984

(no. 75) Informe sobre el mercado de empleo, 1983 /. Montevideo , 1984. 8, [19] leaves ; LC Card 86-174013
HD5762.A6 I54 1984

Informe final /. Seminario-Taller La Autogestión Empresarial Urbana (1985 : Lima, Peru) [Lima, Perú] [1986 or 1987] 112 p. ; LC Card

87-404369 DDC 338.6 19
HD5660.P4 S46 1985

Informe final del octavo período de sesiones del Comité de Desarrollo y Cooperación del Caribe (Puerto Príncipe, Haití, 6 al 12 de junio de 1984). United Nations. Caribbean Development and Co-operation Committee. [Port-au-Prince?] , 1984. iv, 36 p. ; LC Card 85-187058
HC151 .U54 1984

Informe final "estudio de oferta exportable" / Departamento de Estudios Económicos, División de Producción. Santo Domingo, República Dominicana : Centro Dominicano de Promoción de Exportaciones, [1985] 101, [57] p. ; 27 cm. Cover title: Estudio oferta exportable (1984) LC Card 85-203743
1. Dominican Republic - Industries. 2. Foreign trade promotion - Dominican Republic. I. Centro Dominicano de Promoción de Exportaciones. División de Producción. II. Title: Estudio de oferta exportable. III. Title: Estudio oferta exportable, 1984.
HC153.5 .I54 1985

Informe general y proyecto de parcelación, Antioquia # 2 (Barbosa y Santo Domingo) / por Ernesto Daza Vaca ... [et al.]. Bogotá, D.E. : Instituto Colombiano de la Reforma Agraria, Departamento de Estudios Técnicos, 1964. 2, 73, 16 leaves, [1] leaf of plates : 1 map ; 27 cm. Cover title: Proyecto de parcelación, Antioquia no. 2. LC Card 85-107102
1. Farms, Small - Colombia - Barbosa (Antioquia). 2. Farms, Small - Colombia - Santo Domingo (Antioquia). 3. Peasantry - Colombia - Barbosa (Antioquia). 4. Peasantry - Colombia - Santo Domingo (Antioquia). 5. Land tenure - Colombia - Barbosa (Antioquia). 6. Land tenure - Colombia - Santo Domingo (Antioquia). 7. Barbosa (Antioquia, Colombia) - Economic conditions. 8. Santo Domingo (Antioquia, Colombia) - Economic conditions. I. Daza Vaca, Ernesto. II. Instituto Colombiano de la Reforma Agraria. Departamento de Estudios Técnicos. III. Title: Proyecto de parcelación, Antioquia no. 2.
HD1476.C72 B375 1964

Informe juventud en España . (6) Montoro Romero, Ricardo. La inserción en la actividad económica, empleo y paro juvenil /. Barcelona , Madrid , c1985. 191 p. ; ISBN 84-86434-11-4 LC Card 86-186530
HD6276.S672 M65 1985

Informe político y de orientación ante el VIIIo Congreso de la CLAT . Máspero, Emilio. [Caracas] , 1983. 122 p. : LC Card 87-403072 DDC 305.5/62/098 19
HD8110.5.A5 C466 1983

El "informe secreto" de Mateo Alemán sobre el trabajo forzoso en las minas de Almadén /. Bleiberg, Germán, 1915- London , c1985. 150 p. ; ISBN 0-7293-0200-8 LC Card 86-178917
HD4875.S6 B58 1985

Informe sobre el mercado de empleo, 1983 / República Oriental del Uruguay, Ministerio de Trabajo y Seguridad Social, Dirección Nacional de Recursos Humanos. Montevideo : La Dirección, 1984. 8, [19] leaves ; 27 cm. (Informe especial. no. 75) LC Card 86-174013
1. Labor supply - Uruguay. I. Uruguay. Dirección Nacional de Recursos Humanos. II. Series: Informe especial (Uruguay. Dirección Nacional de Recursos Humanos) , no. 75.
HD5762.A6 I54 1984

Informe sobre la administración fiscal correspondiente a 1971 /. Panama. Contraloría General de la República. [Panama, Panama] , 1972. iii, 31 p. ; LC Card 83-183287
HJ9923.P28 P35 1972

Informe sobre la provincia de Coquimbo /. Chouteau, Eujenio. Santiago de Chile , 1887. 262 p. ; LC Card 85-165581
HC193.C64 C46 1887

Informe (Universidad Nacional (Costa Rica). Instituto de Estudios Sociales en Población) . (#19) Carreras, Rodrigo X. Vivienda y población en Costa Rica . Heredia, Costa Rica , 1979. 203 p. : LC Card 87-404329 DDC 363.5/097286 19
HD7308.A3 C37 1979

Informed (CINTERFOR (Organization)) . (no. 103) La Formación profesional ante las exigencias del desarrollo. Montevideo , 1980. 98 p. ; LC Card 86-139077
HD5715.5.L3 F664 1980

Informes (CINTERFOR (Organization)) . (no. 100) Concepto y aplicación del enfoque de sistemas en los procesos y técnicas de instrucción. Montevideo , 1980. 283 p. : LC Card 86-143811
HD5715.5.L29 C66 1980

(no. 106) Certificación ocupacional . Ciudad de México , 1981. 76 p. ; ISBN 968-8290-30-0 LC Card 86-142976
HD5715.5.L3 C47 1981

Informes de investigación del Ceur, 0326-6850 . (2) Lindenboim, Javier. Monetarismo y mercado de trabajo . Buenos Aires, Argentina , c1985. x, 471 p. : ISBN 950-9370-05-3 LC Card 87-122243 DDC 331.12/0982/73 19
HD5750.R56 L56 1985

Informes de los gerentes generales, 1969-84. Banco Nacional de Panamá. Panamá, República de Panamá , 1984. 126 p. : LC Card 85-124892
HG2773 .B35 1984

INFORPRESS Centroamericana. Guatemala 1986 . Ciudad de Guatemala, Guatemala , c1987. vi, 50 p. : LC Card 87-403676 DDC 330.97281/053 19
HC144 .G8135 1987

Infrastructural survey report for the development of the alumina resources in Rennell Island, Solomon Islands. [S.l.] : Japan International Cooperation Agency, [1976] xv, 321 p. : ill. ; 30 cm. "March 1976." Bibliography: p. 320-321. LC Card 84-230135
1. Infrastructure (Economics) - Solomon Islands - Rennell Islands. 2. Economic development projects - Solomon Islands - Rennell Island. 3. Rennell Island (Solomon Islands) - Economic conditions. 4. Aluminum hydroxide. I. Kokusai Kyōryoku Jigyōdan.
HC684.Z7 R455 1976

Infrastructure assets . Van Daniker, Relmond P., 1942- Stamford, Conn. (High Ridge Park, P.O. Box 3821, Stamford 06905-0821) , c1986. xii, 155 p. ; LC Card 86-90661 DDC 657/.835 19
HJ9816 .V35 1986

INFRASTRUCTURE - BRAZIL - ESPÍRITO SANTO (STATE)
Setor de informações técnicas /. [Vitória] , 1983. 54 p. ; LC Card 85-202308
HC188.E7 S47 1983

INFRASTRUCTURE (ECONOMICS)
Diewert, W. E. (W. Erwin) The measurement of the economic benefits of infrastructure services /. Berlin , New York , c1986. 202 p. : ISBN 3-540-16810-9 : LC Card 86-22055 DDC 363 19
HC79.C3 D48 1986

INFRASTRUCTURE (ECONOMICS) - ARGENTINA - HISTORY.
Quadri Castillo, Mario. La Argentina descentralizada /. [Buenos Aires] , c1986. 236 p. : ISBN 950-23-0322-9 LC Card 87-402244 DDC 330.982/064 19
HC175 .Q33 1986

INFRASTRUCTURE (ECONOMICS) - BRAZIL, NORTHEAST.
INFRASTRUCTURE (ECONOMICS) - BYELORUSSIAN S.S.R.
Regional'nye problemy razvitiia infrastruktury i mezhotraslevykh proizvodstv /. Minsk , 1985. 243, [4] p. ; LC Card 86-161744
HC337.B933 C37 1985
*NYPL [*QM 87-2108]*

INFRASTRUCTURE (ECONOMICS) - CONNECTICUT.
Infrastructure revitalization status report, October, 1985 /. [Hartford, Conn.] [1986?] 23 leaves ; LC Card 86-622547 DDC 363/.09746 19
HC107.C83 C35 1986

INFRASTRUCTURE (ECONOMICS) - DEVELOPING COUNTRIES.
A Review of technologies for the provision of basic infrastructure in low-income settlements. Nairobi , 1984. viii, 82 p. ; LC Card 86-980643 DDC 363/.09172/4 19
HC59.72.C3 R47 1984

INFRASTRUCTURE (ECONOMICS) - FLORIDA - PLANNING.
Florida. Public Facilities Financing Commission. Florida 2000, meeting the challenge . [Tallahassee] [1984] v, 44 p. ; LC Card 86-623234 DDC 363/.09759 19
HC107.F63 C345 1984

INFRASTRUCTURE (ECONOMICS) - FRANCE - FINANCE.
Le Financement des équipements publics de demain /. Paris , c1986. 432 p. : ISBN 2-7178-1186-9 : LC Card 87-117264
HC280.C3 F56 1986

INFRASTRUCTURE (ECONOMICS) - GERMANY (EAST)
Koziolek, Helmut. Reproduktion und Infrastruktur /. Berlin , c1986. 224 p. : ISBN 3-349-00017-7 LC Card 87-130782 DDC 363/.09431 19
HC290.795.C3 K675 1986

Koziolek, Helmut. Umfassende Intensivierung und Infrastruktur /. Berlin , 1986. 68 p. ; LC Card 86-169897
HC290.795.C3 K68 1986

Die Verantwortung der örtlichen Staatsorgane für die planmässige Entwicklung und die effektive Inanspruchnahme von Leistungen der technischen Infrastruktur /. Potsdam-Babelsberg , 1986. 57 p. ; LC Card 87-407347 DDC 363/.09431 19
HC290.795.C3 V47 1986

INFRASTRUCTURE (ECONOMICS) - GERMANY (WEST)
Entscheidungshilfen für die Infrastrukturplanung . Baden-Baden , 1984. 512 p. : ISBN 3-7890-0808-7 LC Card 84-188792
HC290.5.C3 E58 1984

Hermann, Hayo. Sektorale Wirtschaftsstruktur und kommunale Finanzsituation . München , c1986. xiii, 384 p. : ISBN 3-88259-405-5 LC Card 86-228161
HJ9473 .H47 1986

Reidenbach, Michael. Verfällt die öffentliche Infrastruktur? . Berlin , 1986. 212 p. : ISBN 3-88118-125-3 LC Card 86-233141
HC290.5.C3 R45 1986

INFRASTRUCTURE (ECONOMICS) - GERMANY (WEST) - MIESBACH.
Gräf, Peter. Zur Raumrelevanz infrastruktureller Massnahmen . Kallmünz/Regensburg , 1978. xxxvii, 259 p., [9] leaves of plates (7 folded) : ISBN 3-7847-6518-1 LC Card 85-205909
HC281 .M8 Bd. 18 HC288.M53

INFRASTRUCTURE (ECONOMICS) - GHANA - VOLTA REGION - CONGRESSES.
Seminar on Economic Development of the Volta Region (1983 : Ho, Ghana) The Volta Region . Accra , c1986. iii, 140 p., [13] leaves of plates : ISBN 996-497-032-3 LC Card 87-402835 DDC 338.9667 19
HC1060.Z7 V647 1983

INFRASTRUCTURE (ECONOMICS) - IOWA.
Iowa's infrastructure. Des Moines, Iowa (523 E. 12th St., Des Moines 50319) [1986] 89 p., [5] leaves of plates : LC Card 86-622778 DDC 363/.09777 19
HC107.I73 C35 1986

INFRASTRUCTURE (ECONOMICS) - IRELAND - HISTORY - 19TH CENTURY.
Griffiths, A. R. G., 1940- The Irish Board of Works, 1831-1878 /. New York , 1987. iii, 214 p. ; ISBN 0-8240-7810-1 (alk. paper) : LC Card 87-24495 DDC 363/.09415 19
HD4150.3 .G75 1987

INFRASTRUCTURE (ECONOMICS) - ITALY - ABRUZZI.
Piazzo, Pietrenzo, 1935- Una valutazione intersettoriale costi benefici estesa al territorio . Roma , c1984. viii, 224 p., 6 folded leaves of plates : LC Card 84-250428
HC307.A2 P53 1984

INFRASTRUCTURE (ECONOMICS) - KENYA.
Ulbrich, Wolfgang. Kenya . Hamburg , 1971. 308 p., [1] folded leaf of plates : LC Card 85-163190
HC865 .U43 1971

INFRASTRUCTURE (ECONOMICS) - MICHIGAN.
Michigan Infrastructure Coalition. Michigan's infrastructure . [Lansing, Mich.] (P.O. Box 13023, Lansing 48901) [1986] iii, 31, [5] p. : LC Card 86-622635 DDC 363/.09774 19
HC107.M53 C36 1986

INFRASTRUCTURE (ECONOMICS) - NEBRASKA.
Stauss, Connie. Nebraska can work /. [Lincoln , 1986- v. <1 > : LC Card 86-622362 DDC 363/.09782 19
HC107.N23 C37 1986

Stauss, Connie. Policy prescriptions for solving the infrastructure problem in Nebraska /. [Lincoln , 1986] xi, 101 leaves : LC Card 87-102492 DDC 363/.09782 s 363/.09782 19
HC107.N23 C37 1986 pt. 1

INFRASTRUCTURE (ECONOMICS) - NEW JERSEY.
New Jersey. Legislature. General Assembly. Transportation, Communications & High Technology Committee. Public hearing before the Assembly Transportation, Communications & High Technology Committee on transportation infrastructure . [Trenton, N.J.] [1986]. 95 p. ;
NYPL [JLF 86-1583]

INFRASTRUCTURE (ECONOMICS) - NEW YORK (STATE)
New York's highway system . Albany, N.Y. , 1986. S-2, iv, 130 p. : *NYPL [JLD 86-2346]*

INFRASTRUCTURE (ECONOMICS) - PLANNING.
Guidelines for the planning of rural settlements and infrastructure . Nairobi , 1985. vi, 295 p. ; ISBN 92-1-131003-2 LC Card 86-981187 DDC 363/.068 19
HD9688.A2 G85 1985

INFRASTRUCTURE (ECONOMICS) - POLAND.
Kapustka, Aleksander. Gospodarka inwestycyjna i remontowa w latach 1984-1985 /. Zielona Góra , 1984. 294 p. ; LC Card 86-670001
HC340.3.Z9 C35 1984

INFRASTRUCTURE (ECONOMICS) - SOLOMON ISLANDS - RENNELL ISLANDS.
Infrastructural survey report for the development of the alumina resources in Rennell Island, Solomon Islands. [S.l.] [1976] xv, 321 p. : LC Card 84-230135
HC684.Z7 R455 1976

INFRASTRUCTURE (ECONOMICS) - SOVIET UNION.
Infrastruktura i intensifikat͡sii͡a ėkonomiki /. Moskva , 1980. 192 p. ; LC Card 81-141492
HC340.C3 I54 1980

INFRASTRUCTURE (ECONOMICS) - SOVIET UNION - METHODOLOGY.
Metodicheskie rekomendat͡sii po issledovanii͡u proizvodstvennoĭ infrastruktury territorial′no-proizvodstvennykh kompleksov i promyshlennykh uzlov /. Sverdlovsk , 1983. 79 p. (some folded) ; LC Card 86-113572
HC340.C3 M416 1983

INFRASTRUCTURE (ECONOMICS) - SOVIET UNION, NORTHERN.
Krasnopol′skiĭ, B. Kh. (Boris Khananovich) Infrastruktura v sisteme regional′nogo khozi͡aĭstvennogo kompleksa Severa . Moskva , 1980. 143, [2] p. ; LC Card 81-131391
HC336.9.N65 K73 1980

INFRASTRUCTURE (ECONOMICS) - SPAIN - CATALONIA.
Conte, Jesús. La Catalunya a mig fer /. Barcelona , c1985. 259 p. ; ISBN 84-86006-64-5X LC Card 86-164880
HC387.C25 C57 1985

INFRASTRUCTURE (ECONOMICS) - SRI LANKA.
Public investment, 1983-1987. Colombo , 1983. 232 p. ; LC Card 83-905444 DDC 332.6/7252/095493 19
HC424 .P82 1983 *NYPL [JLF 87-290]*

INFRASTRUCTURE (ECONOMICS) - UNITED STATES.
Hard choices . Washington , 1984. 23 v. :
NYPL [JLE 87-566 Appendix 1-23]

Infrastructure financing [microform] . [New York] , c1983. 22, 7, 17 p. :
*NYPL [*ZT-1565 no.20]*

Kaplan, Marshall. Hard choices . Washington , 1984. xi, 230 p. : LC Card 84-602470 DDC 338.4/3363/0973 19
HC110.C3 K37 1984 *NYPL [JLE 87-566]*

Local infrastructure investment in rural America /. Boulder , 1988. xxi, 291 p. ; ISBN 0-8133-7460-X (soft : alk. paper) LC Card 87-21606 DDC 332.6/7252 19
HC110.P83 L63 1988

INFRASTRUCTURE (ECONOMICS) - UNITED STATES - ACCOUNTING.
Van Daniker, Relmond P., 1942- Infrastructure assets . Stamford, Conn. (High Ridge Park, P.O. Box 3821, Stamford 06905-0821) , c1986. xii, 155 p. ; LC Card 86-90661 DDC 657/.835 19
HJ9816 .V35 1986

INFRASTRUCTURE (ECONOMICS) - UNITED STATES - FINANCE.
Le Financement des équipements publics de demain /. Paris , c1986. 432 p. : ISBN 2-7178-1186-9 : LC Card 87-117264
HC280.C3 F56 1986

Pagano, Michael A. How the public works . Washington, D.C. , c1986. ix, 68, 6 p. : ISBN 0-933729-13-8 (pbk.) : LC Card 87-129719 DDC 338.4/3363/0973 19
HJ9145 .P343 1986

Snyder, Thomas (Thomas P.) Paying for growth . Washington, D.C. , 1986. x, 133 p. : ISBN 0-87420-663-4 (pbk.) LC Card 86-51156 DDC 338.4/3363/0973 19
HJ9156 .S69 1986

Infrastructure financing [microform] : an overview / by Dillon, Read & Co. inc. ; with assistance from Squire, Sanders & Dempsey ; [James W. Ziglar, Robert H. Olson, authors]. [New York] : Dillon, Read & Co. Inc., c1983. 22, 7, 17 p. : ill. ; 28 cm. Cover title. Microfilm. New York : New York Public Library, 1985. 1 microfilm reel ; 35 mm. (MN *ZZ-24,152)
1. Debts, Public - United States. 2. Infrastructure (Economics) - United States. I. Dillon, Read & Company. II. Squire, Sanders & Dempsey.
*NYPL [*ZT-1565 no.20]*

Infrastructure revitalization status report, October, 1985 / William A. O'Neill, governor. [Hartford, Conn.] : State of Connecticut, [1986?] 23 leaves ; 28 cm. Cover title. LC Card 86-622547 DDC 363/.09746 19
1. Infrastructure (Economics) - Connecticut. I. Connecticut. Governor (1980- : O'Neill).
HC107.C83 C35 1986

INFRASTRUCTURE - SPAIN - GERONA (PROVINCE)
Medir i Huerta, Rosa M. Les comarques gironines . Girona , 1986. 211 p. : ISBN 84-505-3103-9 LC Card 87-101047
HC387.G4 M43 1986

Infrastruktura i intensifikat͡sii͡a ėkonomiki / [nastoi͡ashchai͡a rabota napisana sledui͡ushchim kollektivom avtorov V.P. Krasovskiĭ ... et al. ; otvetstvennyĭ redaktor V.P. Krasovskiĭ]. Moskva : Izd-vo "Nauka", 1980. 192 p. ; 20 cm. (Problemy sovetskoĭ ėkonomiki) At head of title: Akademii͡a nauk SSSR. Institut ėkonomiki. Includes bibliographical references. LC Card 81-141492
1. Infrastructure (Economics) - Soviet Union. I. Krasovskiĭ, V. P. (Viktor Petrovich). II. Institut ėkonomiki (Akademii͡a nauk SSSR).
HC340.C3 I54 1980

Infrastruktura v sisteme regional′nogo khozi͡aĭstvennogo kompleksa Severa . Krasnopol′skiĭ, B. Kh. (Boris Khananovich) Moskva , 1980. 143, [2] p. ; LC Card 81-131391
HC336.9.N65 K73 1980

Infratest Sozialforschung. Datenlage zur Alterssicherung : Gutachten über Datenlage, Datennutzung und Datenlücken / erstellt im Auftrag des Bundesministers für Arbeit und Sozialordnung von Infratest Sozialforschung GmbH, München, in Zusammenarbeit mit F. Klanberg. Bonn : Der Bundesminister, 1984. 330 p. : ill. ; 30 cm. (Forschungsbericht / Der Bundesminister für Arbeit und Sozialordnung, 0174-4992 . 103.) Includes bibliographical references. LC Card 86-132439 DDC 331.25/2/0943 19
1. Old age pensions - Germany, West. 2. Pension trusts - Germany, West. 3. Civil service pensions - Germany, West. I. Klanberg, Frank. II. Germany (West). Bundesministerium für Arbeit und Sozialordnung. III. Series: Forschungsbericht (Germany (West). Bundesministerium für Arbeit und Sozialordnung) , 103. IV. Title.
HD7105.35.G3 I54 1984

Ingalls, Roger W. A scrapbook history of the Auburn Aviation Co., Inc., and the Auburn Airport at Throopsville, N.Y., 1941-1952. Auburn, N.Y. : R.W. Ingalls, c1986. 169 p. : ill. ; 18 x 27 cm. LC Card 87-125962
1. Auburn Aviation Co. - History. 2. Aeronautics, Commercial - New York - Throopsville - History. 3. Auburn Airport - History. 4. Airports - New York - Throopsville - History. I. Title.
HE9803.A97 I54 1986

Ingalsbe, Lon. Business applications software for the IBM PC / Lon Ingalsbe. 2nd ed. Columbus : Merrill Pub. Co., c1987. 1 v. (various pagings) : ill. (some col.) ; 28 cm. ISBN 0-675-20760-6 (pbk.) LC Card 86-63664 DDC 650/.028/55365 19
1. IBM Personal Computer. 2. Business - Data processing. I. Title.
HF5548.4.I24 I54 1987

Ingham, A. Demand, equilibrium, and trade . London , 1984. xx, 256 p. : ISBN 0-333-33184-2 LC Card 87-673439
HB34 .D45x 1984b

Ingham, Barbara. Development studies and colonial policy /. London , Totowa, N.J. , 1987. 292 p. : ISBN 0-7146-3231-7 : LC Card 87-6562 DDC 338.9171/241 19
HD82 .D395 1987

Ingham, Geoffrey K. Capitalism divided? : the City and industry in British social development / Geoffrey Ingham. Basingstoke, Hampshire : Macmillan, 1984. viii, 304 p. : ill. ; 23 cm. (Contemporary social theory) Theoretical traditions in the social sciences Bibliography: p. [246]-291. Includes index. ISBN 0-333-30116-1 LC Card 86-673507
1. Great Britain - Economic conditions - 19th century. 2. Great Britain - Economic conditions - 20th century. 3. Marxian economics. I. Series: Contemporary social theory (London, England). II. Title.
HC255 .I495x 1984b

Inglot, Stefan. Z dziejów wsi polskiej i rolnictwa / Stefan Inglot. Wyd. 1. Warszawa : Ludowa Spółdzielnia Wydawnicza, 1986. 448 p. : ill. ; 22 cm. Includes bibliographies and indexes. ISBN 83-205-3734-7 : LC Card 85-126716
1. Agriculture - Economic aspects - Poland - History. 2. Poland - Rural conditions. I. Title.
HD1995.7 .I54 1986

Ingram, Helen M., 1937- Brown, F. Lee (Franklin Lee) Water and poverty in the Southwest /. Tucson , c1987. xi, 226 p. : ISBN 0-8165-1038-5 (alk. paper) : LC Card 87-19217 DDC 333.91/00979 19
HD1695.A165 B76 1987

Ingram, Robert W. Financial reporting practices of local governments / Robert W. Ingram and Walter A. Robbins. Stamford, Conn. (P.O. Box 3821, Stamford 06905-0821) : Governmental Accounting Standards Board of the Financial Accounting Foundation, c1987. viii, 93 p. : ill. ; 23 cm. (Research report) LC Card 87-80564 DDC 657/.835 19
1. Local finance - Accounting - Standards - United States. I. Robbins, Walter A. II. Series: Research report (Financial Accounting Foundation. Governmental Accounting Standards Board). III. Title.
HJ9777.A3 I55 1987

INHERITANCE AND SUCCESSION - CONNECTICUT - HISTORY.
Ditz, Toby L., 1951- Property and kinship . Princeton, N.J. , c1986. xvi, 213 p. : ISBN 0-691-04735-9 (alk. paper) : LC Card 86-5051 DDC 333.33 19
HB715 .D58 1986 *NYPL [JLE 86-4624]*

INHERITANCE AND SUCCESSION - ITALY - NAPLES (KINGDOM) - HISTORY - 18TH CENTURY.
Rao, Anna Maria, 1949- L'"Amaro della feudalità" . Napoli , c1984. 382 p. ; ISBN 88-7042-265-8 : LC Card 85-200705
HD1333.I82 N367 1984

INHERITANCE AND SUCCESSION - NORWAY.
Knapskog, Kåre. Økonomiske forhold ved generasjonsskifte i landbruket =. Oslo , 1986. 95 p. : ISBN 82-7077-032-9 LC Card 86-231818
HD2012 .K6 1986

INHERITANCE AND TRANSFER TAX - INDIA.
Saraf, B. P., 1939- Capital taxation in India /. New Delhi , c1983. viii, 268 p. ; LC Card 83-902683 DDC 343.5405/3 345.40353 19
HJ4126.I45 S27 1983 *NYPL [JLD 86-3821]*

Inhuman relations . Grenier, Guillermo J. Philadelphia , 1988. xx, 232 p. ; ISBN 0-87722-502-8 (alk. paper) : LC Card 87-10116 DDC 331.25 19
HD6490.O72 U645 1988

Iniciación a la economía andaluza / Jose Vallés Ferrer (coordinador) ; Pedro Cantero Desmartines ... [et al.]. [Seville, Spain] : Servicio de Publicaciones de la Universidad de Sevilla, [1986] 196, [4] p. : ill. ; 25 cm. (Serie: Ciencias económicas y empresariales. núm. 24) Bibliography: p. [197]. ISBN 84-7405-343-9 LC Card 87-152155
1. Andalusia (Spain) - Economic conditions. 2. Andalusia (Spain) - Economic policy. I. Vallés Ferrer, José. II. Cantero Desmartines, Pedro. III. Series.
HC387.A64 I54 1986

Inifes. see **Internationales Institut für Empirische Sozialökonomie.**

Init͡siativi, dela, chelen opit. Problemi na dŭrzhavnoto i obshtestvenoto osiguri͡avane na rabotnitsite i sluzhitelite. Stara Zagora , 1984. 17 p. ; LC Card 86-204115
HD7211.5 .P75 1984

Ini͡utina, K. V. (Klara Vasil'evna) Povyshenie nadezhnosti i kachestva snabzhenii͡a / K.V. Ini͡utina. Leningrad : Izd-vo Leningradskogo universiteta, 1983. 239 p. ; 20 cm. At head of title: Ministerstvo vysshego i srednego spet͡sial'nogo obrazovanii͡a RSFSR. Bibliography: p. 232-238. LC Card 84-196942
1. Industrial procurement - Soviet Union. I. Title.
HD39.5 .I55 1983

INJURIES. see **ACCIDENTS.**

Injuries to warehouse workers. Washington, D.C. : U. S. Dept. of Labor, Bureau of Labor Statistics : For sale by the Supt. of Docs., U. S. G.P.O., 1986. v, 24 p. : ill., 1 form, 1 map : 28 cm. (Bulletin . 2257) "April 1986." S/N 029-001-02898-9 Item 768-A-1 LC Card 87-601109 DDC 363.1/19381 19
1. Warehouses - United States - Accidents - Statistics. 2. Industrial accidents - United States - Statistics. I. United States. Bureau of Labor Statistics. II. Series: Bulletin (United States. Bureau of Labor Statistics) , 2257.
HD7269.F82 I56 1986

Injury and collision losses by engine option, selected 1983 models. Washington, D.C. (Watergate 600, Washington 20037) : Highway Loss Data Institute, c1985. 11 p. ; 28 cm. (Research report HLDI . A-23 (Oct. 1985)) Insurance special report / Highway Loss Data Institute LC Card 87-115471 DDC 368.5/72/00973 19
1. Insurance, Automobile - United States - Statistics. 2. Traffic accidents - United States - Statistics. I. Highway Loss Data Institute. II. Series: Research report HLDI , A-23.
HG9970.3 .I524 1985

Injury deaths in Washington State, 1968-1983 : analysis by age, county of residence, and type of injury / prepared by Floyd Frost ... [et al.]. Seattle, Wash. (1610 NE 150th, Seattle 98155) : Epidemiology Section, Health Services Division, Dept. of Social and Health Services, [1985] 49, [78] p. : ill. ; 28 cm. "December 1985." LC Card 86-623057 DDC 363.1/02/09797021 19
1. Death - Washington (State) - Statistics. 2. Accidents - Washington (State) - Statistics. I. Frost, Floyd. II. Washington (State). Epidemiology Section.
HB1323.A22 U65 1985

Inkasso Unternehmungen /. Dietrich, Bernhard R. Neuried , c1986. xxxv, 200 p. ; ISBN 3-88893-050-2 LC Card 87-133343 DDC 658.8/8 19
HG3752.5 .D54 1986

Inkassounternehmungen. Dietrich, Bernhard R. Inkasso Unternehmungen /. Neuried , c1986. xxxv, 200 p. ; ISBN 3-88893-050-2 LC Card 87-133343 DDC 658.8/8 19
HG3752.5 .D54 1986

Inkomensherverdeling . Odink, J. G. Groningen , c1985. 254 p. : ISBN 90-01-66101-7 : LC Card 86-149572
HC329.5.I5 O35 1985

INLAND NAVIGATION - ENGLAND.
Atterbury, Paul. English rivers and canals /. London , 1984. 152 p. : ISBN 0-297-78318-1
NYPL [JFF 87-598]

INLAND NAVIGATION - FRANCE - HISTORY.
Le Sueur, Bernard. Batelleries et batelliers de France . Le Côteau [1985] 208 p. : ISBN 2-7171-0339-2 LC Card 87-106621
HE443 .L39 1985

INLAND NAVIGATION - GOVERNMENT POLICY - FRANCE.
Le Transport fluvial . Paris , c1983. 108 p. : ISBN 2-11-001087-8 : LC Card 83-170808
HE668 .T73 1983

INLAND NAVIGATION - SOVIET UNION.
Zuev, V. A. (Valerīĭ Andreevich) Sredstva prodlenii͡a navigatsii na vnutrennikh vodnykh puti͡akh /. Leningrad , 1986. 206 p. : LC Card 86-166974
HE675 .Z84 1986

INLAND STEEL COMPANY.
Whyte, William Foote, 1914- Pattern for industrial peace /. New York , 1987, c1951. ix, 245 p. : ISBN 0-8240-8227-3 (alk. paper) : LC Card 86-25790 DDC 331.89/0469142/0977/311 19
HD6515.I52 C48 1987

INLAND WATER TRANSPORTATION - BRAZIL.
Avaliação do programa de ação, 1984/85 /. [Brasília] , 1985. 90 leaves : LC Card 87-403938 DDC 354.810087/6/06 19
HE653 .A93 1985

Estudo preliminar para o establecimento de prioridades no financiamento para construção de embarcações para a navegação interior /. [Rio de Janeiro] , 1985. [84] leaves : LC Card 87-403936 DDC 386/.0981 19
HE653 .E88 1985

INLAND WATER TRANSPORTATION - FRANCE - HISTORY.
Le Sueur, Bernard. Batelleries et batelliers de France . Le Côteau [1985] 208 p. : ISBN 2-7171-0339-2 LC Card 87-106621
HE443 .L39 1985

INLAND WATER TRANSPORTATION - GERMANY (WEST) - HISTORY.
Schroiff, Franz J. Das Binnenschiffahrt-Verkehrssystem . Hannover , 1984. ix, 267 p. : ISBN 3-87870-951-X LC Card 84-221599
HE669 .S34 1984

INLAND WATER TRANSPORTATION - GERMANY (WEST) - RUHR RIVER.
Tress, Roland. Das Güterverkehrszentrum als infrastrukturelle Schnittstelle des Güterverkehrs /. Düsseldorf , 1984. xv, 288 p. : LC Card 86-140143
HE5 .C6 Nr. 45 HE5999.Z7G2

INLAND WATER TRANSPORTATION - GOVERNMENT POLICY - BANGLADESH - CONGRESSES.
Jerve, Alf Morten. From research to implementation . Fantoft-Bergen, Norway [1984] 23 leaves ; LC Card 86-228812 DDC 386/.068 19
HE691.6 .J47 1984

INLAND WATER TRANSPORTATION - MALAYSIA.
Environment, agriculture, and society in the Malay world /. Kyoto, Japan , 1986. ix, 177 p. : LC Card 86-201590 DDC 338.1/09595 19
HD2080.6 .E58 1986

INLAND WATER TRANSPORTATION - RHINE RIVER.
Tress, Roland. Das Güterverkehrszentrum als infrastrukturelle Schnittstelle des Güterverkehrs /. Düsseldorf , 1984. xv, 288 p. : LC Card 86-140143
HE5 .C6 Nr. 45 HE5999.Z7G2

INLAND WATER TRANSPORTATION - SOUTH AMERICA - PLANNING.
Interconexión de cuencas sudamericanas. [Buenos Aires] , 1986. 159 leaves, [5] leaves of plates : LC Card 86-225024
HE650 .I58 1986

INLAND WATER TRANSPORTATION - UNITED STATES - HISTORY.
Bauer, K. Jack (Karl Jack), 1926- A maritime history of the United States . Columbia, S.C. , c1988. p. cm. ISBN 0-87249-519-1 LC Card 87-19190 DDC 387.5/0973 19
HE745 .B38 1988

Inleiding tot de antieke economie /. Reekmans, T. Leuven , 1984. 129 leaves in various foliations ; ISBN 90-334-0834-1 : LC Card 86-203767
HB77 .R44 1984

Inligtingsimposium, 23 Oktober 1981 / Departement van Vervoer = Information symposium, 23 October 1981 / Department of Transport. [Pretoria] : Die Departement, [1981] 115 p. : ill. ; 30 cm. Compiled by Departement Vervoerekenomie, Randse Afrikaanse Universiteit. Afrikaans and English. LC Card 86-213181 DDC 380.5/0968 19
1. Transportation - South Africa - Congresses. 2. South Africa. Dept. of Transport - Congresses. I. South Africa. Dept. of Transport. II. Randse Afrikaanse Universiteit. Departement Vervoerekenomie. III. Title: Information symposium, 23 October 1981.
HE284.4.A2 I55 1981

Innenpolitik in Theorie und Praxis .
(15) Schultz, Reinhard. Gewinn- und Kapitalbeteiligung der Arbeitnehmer (Vermögensbildung) /. München , c1987. 256 p. ; ISBN 3-597-10525-4 LC Card 87-127356 DDC 331.2/164 19
HD3038 .S365 1987

(16) Posse, Achim Ulrich, 1960- Föderative Politikverflechtung in der Umweltpolitik /. München , c1986. xiv, 181 p. : ISBN 3-597-10526-2 LC Card 86-222201
HC290.5.E5 P67 1986

Innenpolitische Leistungsbilanz 1982-1986 / [Herausgeber, Bundesministerium des Innern ; Redaktion, Günther Wollmer]. 1. Aufl. Bonn : Der Bundesminister des Innern, 1986. 124 p. : ill. ; 21 cm. LC Card 86-215949
1. Germany, West - Economic policy - 1974-. 2. Germany, West - Social policy. 3. Germany (West) - Politics and government - 1982-. 4. Environmental policy - Germany, West. 5. Energy policy - Germany, West. I. Wollmer, Günther. II. Germany (West). Bundesministerium des Innern.
HC286.7 .I55 1986

The inner game of management . Flamholtz, Eric. New York, NY , c1987. xiv, 225 p. ; ISBN 0-8144-5867-X LC Card 87-47705 DDC 658.4/09 19
HD31 .F538 1987

Innerbetriebliche Standortplanung bei einfacher und mehrfacher Zielsetzung /. Wäscher, Gerhard. Wiesbaden , c1982. 389 p. : ISBN 3-409-34487-X LC Card 86-105991
HD58 .W29 1982

Innerstädtische Umzüge und Stadtentwicklung in Mannheim, 1977-1983 . Miodek, Wolfgang. Mannheim , 1986. 244 p. : ISBN 3-923750-18-8 : LC Card 86-181776
HD7288.92.G32 M355 1986

Az innováció társadalmi-gazdasági akadályai /. Farkas, János. Budapest , 1984. 350 p. ; ISBN 963-221-453-6 : LC Card 85-157214
HC300.295.T4 F36 1984

Innovatieproblematiek in kleine industriële bedrijven /. During, W. E. Assen , 1986. 242 p. : ISBN 90-232-2196-6 : LC Card 86-186964
HD2346.N4 D87 1986

Innovating to compete . Walton, Richard E. San Francisco , 1987. p. cm. ISBN 1-555-42056-7 LC Card 87-45426 DDC 658.4/06 19
HE736 .W35 1987

Innovation . Foster, Richard N. New York , c1986. 316 p. : ISBN 0-671-62250-1 : LC Card 86-1945 DDC 658.4/062 19
HD45 .F67 1986 ***NYPL [JLE 86-1899]***

Innovation and entrepreneurship in organizations : strategies for competitiveness, deregulation, and privatization / edited by Richard M. Burton and Børge Obel. Amsterdam ; New York : Elsevier ; vii, 207 p. : ill. ; 27 cm. Chiefly papers presented at a seminar held at the European Institute for Advanced Studies in Management, Brussels, in May 1985. "Has been published in a special issue of Technovation, vol 5 (1986), issues 1-3." Includes bibliographies and index. ISBN 0-444-42716-3 (U. S.) : LC Card 86-24207 DDC 658.4/012 19
1. Competition - Congresses. 2. Trade regulation - Congresses. 3. Privatization - Congresses. 4. Technological innovations - Management - Congresses. I. Burton, Richard M. II. Obel, Børge.
HD41 .I56 1986

Innovation and management control . Willman, Paul. Cambridge [Cambridgeshire] , New York , 1985. viii, 215 p. ; ISBN 0-521-26802-8 LC Card 84-17481 DDC 331/.04292/0941 19
HD8039.A82 G79 1985
NYPL [JLD 85-3102]

Innovation diffusion models of new product acceptance / edited by Vijay Mahajan, Yoram Wind. Cambridge, Mass. : Ballinger, 1986. xvi, 318 p. : ill. ; 24 cm. (Series on econometrics and management sciences . v. 5) Based on a conference held in Oct. 1983 at Harvard University. Includes bibliographical references and index. ISBN 0-88730-076-6 LC Card 85-23300 DDC 658.8/343 19
1. New Products - Marketing - Mathematical models - Congresses. 2. Consumers' preferences - Mathematical models - Congresses. I. Mahajan, Vijay. II. Wind, Yoram. III. Series.
HF5415.153 .I55 1986 NYPL [JLE 86-3235]

Innovation, entrepreneurs, and regional development /. Sweeney, G. P. (Gerald Patrick), 1928- London , 1987. xvi, 271 p. : ISBN 0-86187-647-4 *NYPL [JLD 87-1403]*

Innovation, entrepreneurs, and regional development /. Sweeney, G. P. (Gerald Patrick), 1928- New York , c1987. xvi, 271 p. : ISBN 0-312-00489-3 : LC Card 86-27999 DDC 338/.06/094 19
HC240.9.T4 S94 1987

Innovation for energy efficiency : proceedings of the European conference, Newcastle-upon-Tyne, UK, 15-17 September 1987 / edited by D.A. Reay.1st ed. Oxford [Oxfordshire] : Pergamon Press, 1988. p. cm. Includes index. ISBN 0-08-034798-3 : LC Card 87-19016 DDC 333.79/094 19
1. Energy policy - Europe - Congresses. 2. Energy conservation - Europe - Congresses. 3. Energy policy - Congresses. 4. Energy conservation - Congresses. I. Reay, D. A. (David Anthony).
HD9502.E8 I55 1988

Innovation im Büro . Weltz, Friedrich. Frankfurt , New York , c1983. 343 p. ; ISBN 3-593-32724-4 LC Card 83-243001
HF5548.115 .W44 1983

Innovation in electronic mail . Vervest, Peter. Amsterdam ; New York : xv, 212 p. : ISBN 0-444-70153-2 LC Card 87-11145 DDC 384.3/4 19
HE6239.E54 V47 1987

Innovation performance, learning, and government policy . Teubal, Morris. Madison, Wis. , 1987. xvi, 308 p. : ISBN 0-299-10950-X : LC Card 86-40448 DDC 338/.06 19
HC79.T4 T485 1987

Innovation policy : Ireland. Paris : Organisation for Economic Co-operation and Development ; Washington, D.C. : OECD Publications and Information Centre, [distributor], 1987. 75 p. ; 23 cm. Bibliography: p. 55. ISBN 92-64-12918-9 (pbk.) : LC Card 87-164488 DDC 338/.06 19
1. Technological innovations - Economic aspects - Ireland. 2. Technological innovations - Government policy - Ireland. 3. Industry and state - Ireland. I. Organisation for Economic Co-operation and Development.
HC260.5.Z9 T45 1987

Innovation und internationale Monopole / von einem Autorenkollektiv des Wissenschaftsbereiches Politische Ökonomie der Sektion Marxismus-Leninismus und des Wissenschaftsbereiches Wissenschaftstheorie der Sektion Wissenschaftstheorie und -Organisation der Humboldt-Universität zu Berlin sowie des Instituts für Theorie, Geschichte und Organisation der Wissenschaft der Akademie der Wissenschaften der DDR ; Leitung des Autorenkollektivs, Kurt Heuer. Berlin : Die Universität, 1983. 85 p. ; 21 cm. (Berichte, 0232-9123 . 6, 1983) Includes bibliographical references. CONTENTS. - Zur Technologie- und Marktstrategie des transnationalen Computerunternehmens IBM / Heuer, Kurt -- Innovationsstrategien der internationalen Mikroelektronikkonzerne IBM Corp. und Intel Corp. / Strasen, Sylvia -- Die Verwertungsstrategie der internationalen Erdölmonopole in den OPEC-Ländern unter den Bedingungen der 70er Jahre und die Aufgaben der OPEC in den 80er Jahren / Arnold, Karin -- Zur Innovationsstrategie des transnationalen Chemie-Konzerns HOECHST AG auf dem Gebiet der Gentechnik / Puls, Klaus -- Zur Unternehmensstrategie des transnationalen Druckkonzerns Bertelsmann AG in den 70er/Anfang der 80er Jahre / Schulzendorf, Gerhild -- Zu den Profitaktivitäten des multinationalen ARBED-Konzerns im Saarland / Damaschun, Heide -- Zur Rolle des Bundesministeriums für Forschung und Technologie (BMFT) als dem wesentlichen Leitinstrument der staatsmonopolistischen Regulierung von Forschung und Entwicklung in der BRD / Dietrich, Peter [und] Melis, Charles. LC Card 84-104008
1. International business enterprises. 2. Technological innovations. 3. Monopolies. I. Heuer, Kurt. II. Humboldt-Universität zu Berlin. III. Series: Berichte (Humboldt-Universität zu Berlin) , 1983, 6.
HD2755.5 .I534 1983

INNOVATIONS, AGRICULTURAL. see **AGRICULTURAL INNOVATIONS.**

INNOVATIONS, DIFFUSION OF. see **DIFFUSION OF INNOVATIONS.**

Innovations in banking . Morris, Timothy, 1953- London , Wolfeboro, N.H. , c1986. 137 p. : ISBN 0-7099-4607-4 : LC Card 86-13400 DDC 332.1/068/3 19
HG2988 .M675 1986 NYPL [JLD 87-81]

Innovations in economic development . Hamilton, William W. Washington, D.C. (2021 K St., Suite 711, Washington 20006) [1986] 1 v. (various foliations) : LC Card 87-620522 DDC 338.973 19
HC110.I53 H363 1986

INNOVATIONS, MEDICAL. see **MEDICAL INNOVATIONS.**

INNOVATIONS, TECHNOLOGICAL. see **TECHNOLOGICAL INNOVATIONS.**

Innovationsförderung durch Kooperation . Boehme, Joachim. Berlin , c1986. 227 p. ; ISBN 3-503-02618-5 LC Card 87-133032 DDC 338.4/762 19
HD9696.A2 B64 1986

Innovationsförderungs- und Technologietransfer-Zentrum der Hochschulen des Ruhrgebiets.
Arbeitersiedlungen im 19. Jahrhundert . Bochum , c1985. 189 p. : ISBN 3-88339-427-0 LC Card 85-164690
HD7289.5.A3 G42 1985

Strukturanalyse Ruhrgebiet . [Essen] [1983?] 185 p. : LC Card 86-218075
HD5760.R84 S77 1983

The innovative banker, T.A. Pai, his life and times /. Kamath, M. V., 1921- Manipal , Bombay , 1983. x, 247 p., [9] p. of plates : LC Card 83-904531 DDC 332.1/2/0924 B 19
HG1552.P4 K36 1983 NYPL [JFE 87-879]

Innovative capital financing /. Petersen, John E. Chicago, IL (1313 E. 60th St., Chicago 60637) , 1985. ii, 38 p. : LC Card 86-175368 DDC 336.73 19
HG4936 .P424 1985

The innovative choice . Amendola, Mario. Oxford [Oxfordshire] , New York, NY, USA , 1988. p. cm. ISBN 0-631-15791-3 : LC Card 87-25004 DDC 338/.06 19
HC79.T4 A46 1988

Innovative Housing Grants Program (Alta.)
Weideman, Donald James. A model to predict urban influenced land prices /. [Edmonton, Alta.] [1986] xi, 294 p. : ISBN 0-88654-148-4 (pbk.) LC Card 86-231786 DDC 333.33/7 19
HD319.A4 W45 1986

Innovative management using telecommunications . Dordick, Herbert S., 1925- New York , c1986. x, 226 p. : ISBN 0-471-81296-X : LC Card 86-7797 DDC 658.4/5 19
HF5541.T4 D67 1986 NYPL [JLE 86-4425]

Innovative Technologien im Vertrieb . Sandler, Christian Heinrich. Thun , c1986. xvii, 313 p. : ISBN 3-87144-926-1 LC Card 86-171131
HD9850.5 .S25 1986

INNS. see **HOTELS, TAVERNS, ETC.**

Innsbrucker Symposion (19th : 1985)
Neuorientierung des Wettbewerbsschutzes . Köln , 1986. viii, 231 p. ; ISBN 3-452-20666-1 : LC Card 87-138003
HB41 .F22 Heft 120 KK6456

Inntektspolitikkens dilemma . Skånland, Hermod, 1925- [Oslo] , 1981 ([Oslo] : Joh. Nordahls trykkeri) 114 p., [1] leaf : ISBN 82-02-04872-9 (pbk.) : LC Card 81-199141
HC370.I5 S49 1981 NYPL [JLD 86-2672]

Inongo, Sakombi. see **Sakombi Inongo.**

Inotai, András.
The Hungarian enterprise in the context of intra-CMEA relations /. Budapest , 1986. 93 p. ; ISBN 963-301-138-8 (pbk.) LC Card 87-101284 DDC 337.439 19
HF1542.5.H8 H85 1986

Az NSZK a változó világgazdaságban / Inotai András. Budapest : Közgazdasági és Jogi Könyvkiadó, 1986, c1985. 259 p. ; 21 cm. Includes bibliographical references. ISBN 963-221-584-2 : LC Card 87-136644
1. Germany, West - Economic conditions - 1974-. 2. Germany, West - Economic policy - 1974-. 3. Germany, West - Foreign economic relations. I. Title.
HC286.7 .I56 1986

[Regionális integrációk az új világgazdasági helyzetben. English]
Regional integrations in the new world economic environment / by András Inotai ; [translated by, Károly Kerepesi]. Budapest : Akadémiai Kiadó, 1986. vii, 286 p. ; 25 cm. Translation of: Regionális integrációk az új világgazdasági helyzetben. Includes bibliographical references. ISBN 963-05-4353-2 LC Card 87-111425 DDC 337.1 19
1. International economic integration. 2. International division of labor. I. Title.
HF1418.5 .I5513 1986

Válaszúton az Európai Gazdasági Közösség / Inotai András. [Budapest] : Kossuth, 1985. 369 p. ; 20 cm. Includes bibliographical references. ISBN 963-09-2587-7 : LC Card 86-228244
1. European Economic Community. 2. European Economic Community - Europe, Eastern. I. Title.
HC241.2 .I583 1985

Inovação tecnológica . Silva, Marcos Eugênio da. São Paulo , 1984. 103 p. : LC Card 85-136373
HD9703.B72 S55 1984

INPET (Organization) Seminario-Taller La Autogestión Empresarial Urbana (1985 : Lima, Peru) Informe final /. [Lima, Perú] [1986 or 1987] 112 p. ; LC Card 87-404369 DDC 338.6 19
HD5660.P4 S46 1985

The input of labour on farms in Northern Ireland /. O'Fee, J. H. Belfast , 1986. i, 41 leaves ; LC Card 86-218985 DDC 331.11/8 19
HD1535.N675 O47 1986

Die Input-Output-Analyse als Instrument der Strukturforschung : Leitungsfähigkeit und Grenzen der empirischen Anwendung der für die Bundesrepublik Deutschland vorliegenden Input-Output-Tabellen / von Ernst Helmstädter ... [et al.]. Tübingen : J.C.B. Mohr, 1983. xxv, 177 p. : ill. ; 24 cm. (Schriften zur angewandten Wirtschaftsforschung, 0582-0286 . 46) Bibliography: p. 172-177. ISBN 3-16-344661-2 LC Card 83-206282
1. Input-output analysis. 2. Input-output tables - Germany (West). I. Helmstädter, Ernst. II. Series.
HB142 .I52 1983

INPUT-OUTPUT ANALYSIS.
Heilig, Bernd. Die gesamtwirtschaftliche Bedeutung der Agrar- und Ernährungswirtschaft . Kiel , 1986. 171 p. : ISBN 3-922553-80-X LC Card 86-177526
HD1955 .H38 1986

Die Input-Output-Analyse als Instrument der Strukturforschung . Tübingen , 1983. xxv, 177 p. : ISBN 3-16-344661-2 LC Card 83-206282
HB142 .I52 1983

Lorenzen, Gunter. Adaptive Verfahren der Input-Output Analyse /. Göttingen , c1985. vii, 156 p. ; ISBN 3-525-11288-2 LC Card 85-221821
HB142 .L67 1985
NYPL [JLL 76-449 Heft 17]

Meyer, Peter. Die Bedeutung wichtiger Typen von Produktionsfunktionen für die Input-Output-Analyse /. Frankfurt , c1983. 109 p. : ISBN 3-88323-438-9 LC Card 83-206578
HB241 .M49 1983

Reich, Utz-Peter. Darstellungskonzepte der Input-Output-Rechnung /. Stuttgart , 1984. 185 p. : ISBN 3-17-003301-8
NYPL [JLE 86-1264]

Standish, Barry, 1954- The economic factors

affecting state output and employment /. Rondebosch [South Africa] [1986] 86 p. : ISBN 0-7992-1016-1 (pbk.) : LC Card 87-112894 DDC 339.2/3 19
HB846 .S73 1986

INPUT-OUTPUT ANALYSIS - DEVELOPING COUNTRIES - CASE STUDIES.
De Castro, Steve. "Turnpikes for small open economies . [Brasília] [1982] 22 leaves ; LC Card 83-156613 DDC 339.2/3/091724 19
HD82 .D376 1982

INPUT-OUTPUT ANALYSIS - EUROPE.
Klimenko, B. I. Mezhotraslevye balansy kapitalisticheskikh stran . Moskva , 1986. 150 p. ; LC Card 86-231527
HC110.I57 K65 1986

INPUT-OUTPUT ANALYSIS - EUROPEAN ECONOMIC COMMUNITY COUNTRIES.
Methodologie der EG-Agrarpreisindizes (Output und Input) =. Luxembourg , Washington, DC , 1985. 228 p. ; ISBN 92-825-5463-5 : LC Card 87-107275 DDC 338.1/3/094021 19
HD1920.5 .M47 1985

INPUT-OUTPUT ANALYSIS - GERMANY (WEST)
Lorenzen, Gunter. Adaptive Verfahren der Input-Output Analyse /. Göttingen , c1985. vii, 156 p. ; ISBN 3-525-11288-2 LC Card 85-221821
HB142 .L67 1985
NYPL [JLL 76-449 Heft 17]

INPUT-OUTPUT ANALYSIS - MATHEMATICAL MODELS.
Ghosh, A., 1921- Income distribution and the structure of production /. New Delhi , c1984. ix, 186 p. ; LC Card 83-907762 DDC 339.2/0724 19
HB523 .G46 1984 ***NYPL [JLD 86-4234]***

INPUT-OUTPUT ANALYSIS - NORWAY.
Bjerkholt, Olav, 1942- MODIS IV . Oslo , 1980. 189 p. : ISBN 82-537-1014-3 (pbk.) LC Card 81-120697 DDC 330.9481/00724 19
HC365 .B46 1980

INPUT-OUTPUT ANALYSIS - RUSSIAN S.F.S.R. - ĪAKUTSKAĪA A.S.S.R.
Mezhotraslevye svi͡azi v ĪAkutskoĭ ASSR . ĪAkutsk , 1985. 80 p. ; LC Card 86-193902
HC337.I23 I576 1985

INPUT-OUTPUT ANALYSIS - SOVIET UNION.
Atarov, N. Z. Regional′nyĭ aspekt mezhotraslevykh proizvodstv . Moskva , 1980. 173 p. : LC Card 81-132091
HD9705.S595 A73 1980

Ėkonomicheskie svi͡azi i sovershenstvovanie khozi͡aĭstvennogo mekhanizma . Kursk , 1985. 107 p. ; LC Card 86-235039
HC340.I57 E37 1985

INPUT-OUTPUT ANALYSIS - UKRAINE.
Alymov, Aleksandr Nikolaevich. Sbalansirovannost′ narodnokhozi͡aĭstvennogo razviti͡a . Kiev , 1986. 221, [3] p. ; LC Card 86-214583
HC337.U5 A793 1986

Ekonomiko-statystychne vyvchenni͡a mizhhaluzevykh narodnohospodars′kykh kompleksiv . Kyïv , 1985. 95 p. ; LC Card 86-194555
HC337.U53 I573 1985

INPUT-OUTPUT ANALYSIS - UNITED STATES.
Klimenko, B. I. Mezhotraslevye balansy kapitalisticheskikh stran . Moskva , 1986. 150 p. ; LC Card 86-231527
HC110.I57 K65 1986

Input-Output-Tabellen für die Bundesrepublik Deutschland, 1962 bis 1975 /. Korthaus, E. Essen , 1979. 279 p. ; LC Card 87-408858 DDC 339.2/3/0943 19
HC290.5.I57 K67 1979

INPUT-OUTPUT TABLES.
Reich, Utz-Peter. Darstellungskonzepte der Input-Output-Rechnung /. Stuttgart , 1984. 185 p. : ISBN 3-17-003301-8
NYPL [JLE 86-1264]

Zoidov, K. Kh. Ob approksimat͡sii makroėkonomicheskikh zavisimosteĭ posredstvom tablichnykh i splaĭnovykh proizvodstvennykh funkt͡siĭ /. Moskva , 1985. 25, [3] p. : LC Card 86-162091
HB142 .Z65 1985

INPUT-OUTPUT TABLES - AUSTRIA.
Rainer, Norbert. Anwendung der Arbeitsmarktorientierten Input-Output-Analyse am beispiel der Gastarbeiterbeschäftigung /. Wien , 1977. 47 leaves ; LC Card 86-194737
HC270.I57 R35 1977

INPUT-OUTPUT TABLES - CHILE.
Matriz de insumo-producto de la economía chilena, 1977. [Santiago] [1980 or 1981] 85 p. ; LC Card 82-199199
HC195.I57 M37 1980

INPUT-OUTPUT TABLES - CHINA.
Ch'üan kuo t'ou ju ch'an ch'u piao, 1981. English. Input-output tables of China, 1981 /. Beijing , Honolulu , 1987. p. cm. ISBN 0-86638-104-X (East-West Population Institute) LC Card 87-24457 DDC 339.2/3/0951 19
HC430.I57 C5813 1981

INPUT-OUTPUT TABLES - GERMANY (WEST)
Die Input-Output-Analyse als Instrument der Strukturforschung . Tübingen , 1983. xxv, 177 p. : ISBN 3-16-344661-2 LC Card 83-206282
HB142 .I52 1983

Korthaus, E. Input-Output-Tabellen für die Bundesrepublik Deutschland, 1962 bis 1975 /. Essen , 1979. 279 p. ; LC Card 87-408858 DDC 339.2/3/0943 19
HC290.5.I57 K67 1979

Krüger-Hemmer, Christiane. Der Staatssektor in der Input-Output-Rechnung . Essen , 1982. 175 p. ; LC Card 87-408033 DDC 339.2/3/0943 19
HC290.5.I57 K78 1982

INPUT-OUTPUT TABLES - MEXICO.
Producto interno bruto y gasto, cuaderno 1970-1979. [Mexico City] [1980] 123 p. ; LC Card 82-197714
HC140.I5 P76 1980

Input-output tables of China, 1981 /. Ch'üan kuo t'ou ju ch'an ch'u piao, 1981. English. Beijing , Honolulu , 1987. p. cm. ISBN 0-86638-104-X (East-West Population Institute) LC Card 87-24457 DDC 339.2/3/0951 19
HC430.I57 C5813 1981

INPUT-OUTPUT TABLES - SOVIET UNION.
Heinemeier, Meredith M. 1977 consumption by industrial sector /. Washington, D.C. [1986] vii, 148 p. ; LC Card 87-601286 DDC 339.2/3/0947 19
HC340.I57 H45 1986

Inquérito à habitação rural . Costa, F. Ramos da. Lisboa , 1944. 57 p. : LC Card 86-137838
HD7289.P67 C67 1944

Inquérito às rendas e a outras características das habitações arrendadas na cidade de Evora em 1955-56 / Portugal, Instituto Nacional de Estatística. Lisboa : Bertrand, [1958] 26 p. : ill. ; 27 cm. (Estudos / Portugal, Instituto Nacional de Estatística . no. 33) Cover title. Summary also in French. Includes bibliographical references. LC Card 85-185037
1. Rental housing - Portugal - Evora. 2. Housing surveys - Portugal - Evora. 3. Housing - Brazil - Evora. I. Instituto Nacional de Estatística (Portugal). II. Series: Estudos (Instituto Nacional de Estatística (Portugal)) , 33.
HA1571 .A32 no. 33 HD7288.85.P82E93

Inquéritos especiais / Secretaria de Planejamento da Presidencia da Republica, Fundação Instituto Brasileiro de Geografia e Estatística, IBGE. Rio de Janeiro, Brasil : IBGE, 1984. 4 v. in 5. ; 27 cm. (IX recenseamento geral do Brasil - 1980 . v. 6) Chiefly tables. CONTENTS. - no. 1. Produção e distribuçao de energia elétrica. Unidades autoprodutoras de energia elétrica. Abastecimento de água e esgotamento sanitário. Limpeza pública e remo
1. Public utilities - Brazil - Statistics. 2. Transportations - Brazil - Statistics. 3. Financial institutions - Brazil - Statistics. 4. Brazil - Census, 1980. 5. Brazil - Statistics. I. Fundação IBGE. II. Title: Nono recenseamento geral do Brasil--1980. III. Series.
NYPL [JLF 86-202]

Inquiry and accounting . Belkaoui, Ahmed, 1943- New York , 1987. xiv, 437 p. ; ISBN 0-89930-222-X (lib. bdg. : alk. paper) LC Card 87-2496 DDC 657 19
HF5625 .B382 1987

An Inquiry into the future of public and private pension plans : proceedings of a seminar / sponsored by the Manitoba Economic Development Advisory Board ; compiled and edited by John McGuire. Winnipeg : The Board, [1976] xiii, 54 p. ; 23 cm. "May 1976." LC Card 85-103269
1. Social security - Manitoba - Congresses. 2. Pensions - Manitoba - Congresses. I. McGuire, John. II. Manitoba. Economic Development Advisory Board.
HD7130.M36 I56 1976

An inquiry into the perception of casual relations in problems of management /. Khol, Josef, Dr. Prague , 1976. 26 p. ; LC Card 82-210887 DDC 658.4/03 19
HD30.23 .K375 1976

INRETS (Institute : France) Transports urbains et services en Amérique latine . Arcueil, France , Quito [1985- v. <1 > : ISBN 2-85782-137-9 (set) LC Card 87-153020
HE311.L29 T73 1985

L'Insegnamento dell'economia politica nella scuola secondaria superiore : problemi e proposte / scritti di Carluccio Bianchi ... [et al.] ; a cura di Francesco Campanella. Milano, Italy : F. Angeli, c1982. 261 p. ; 22 cm. (Cisem/Quaderni . 2) Bibliography: p. [260]-261. LC Card 87-673404
1. Economics - Study and teaching (Secondary) - Italy. I. Bianchi, Carluccio. II. Campanella, Francesco. III. Series: Quaderni (Cisem) , 2.
HB74.9.I8 I57x 1982

La inserción en la actividad económica, empleo y paro juvenil /. Montoro Romero, Ricardo. Barcelona , Madrid , c1985. 191 p. ; ISBN 84-86434-11-4 LC Card 86-186530
HD6276.S672 M65 1985

IN-SERVICE TRAINING. see **EMPLOYEES, TRAINING OF.**

Inside corporate Japan . Lu, David John, 1928- Stamford, CT , c1987. xxi, 249 p. : ISBN 0-915299-16-X (alk. paper) : LC Card 87-60546 DDC 658/.00952 19
HD70.J3 L8 1987

Inside country music /. Wacholtz, Larry E. New York , 1986. 254 p. ; ISBN 0-8230-7532-X (pbk. : alk. paper) LC Card 86-4234 DDC 784.5/2/002373 19
ML3790 .W24 1986 ***NYPL [JNE 86-18]***

Inside HBO . Mair, George, 1929- New York , c1988. xviii, 204 p. ; ISBN 0-396-08420-6 : LC Card 87-19939 DDC 384.55/47/0973 19
HE8700.72.U6 M34 1988

Inside Home Box Office. Mair, George, 1929- Inside HBO . New York , c1988. xviii, 204 p. ; ISBN 0-396-08420-6 : LC Card 87-19939 DDC 384.55/47/0973 19
HE8700.72.U6 M34 1988

Inside Japanese financial markets /. Viner, Aron. Homewood, Ill. , c1988. xvi, 364 p. : ISBN 1-556-23020-6 LC Card 87-71357 DDC 332/.0952 19
HG187.J3 V57 1988

Inside productivity : thirteen case studies / Michael L. Levine, editor. New York, N.Y. : Executive Enterprises Publications Co., c1987. iv, 156 p. : ill. ; 28 cm. (A National productivity review reprint series) Includes bibliographies. ISBN 0-88057-671-5 (pbk.) LC Card 86-82865 DDC 338/.06 19
1. Industrial productivity - Case studies. I. Levine, Michael L. II. Series.
HD56 .I528 1987

Inside real estate . Bloch, H. I. Sonny. New York , c1987. xx, 375 p. ; ISBN 1-555-84030-2 LC Card 86-28303 DDC 333.33/8 19
HD1379 .B515 1987

Inside the Bank of Canada's Weekly financial statistics . Martin, Peter, 1942- Vancouver, B. C. , 1985. xix, 201 p. : ISBN 0-88975-082-3
NYPL [JLF 87-456]

Inside the firm . Leibenstein, Harvey. Cambridge, Mass. , 1987. xiv, 276 p. : ISBN 0-674-45515-0 (alk. paper) LC Card 87-8426 DDC 302.3/5 19
HD2326 .L45 1987

Inside the Japanese system : readings on contemporary society and political economy / edited by Daniel I. Okimoto and Thomas P. Rohlen. Stanford, Calif. : Stanford University Press, c1988. xiii, 286 p. : ill. ; 24 cm. Includes bibliographical references and index. ISBN 0-8047-1425-8 (alk. paper) LC Card 87-18820

DDC 330.952/04 19
1. Japan - Economic conditions - 1945-. 2. Japan - Social conditions - 1945-. 3. Japan - Politics and government - 1945-. I. Okimoto, Daniel I., 1942-. II. Rohlen, Thomas P.
HC462.9 .I587 1988

Inside the new gilt-edged market /. Phillips, Patrick. Cambridge, England , Wolfeboro, N.H. , 1987. p. cm. ISBN 0-85941-346-2 : LC Card 86-24692 DDC 332.63/232/0941 19
HG5432 .P48 1987

Inside the over-the-counter market in the UK /. Wilmot, Tom (Tom G.) Westport, Conn. , 1985. xiii, 119 p. ; ISBN 0-89930-166-5 LC Card 85-24431 DDC 332.64/3/0941 19
HG5432 .W55 1985 *NYPL [JLD 86-3625]*

Inside track . Petras, Ross. New York , c1986. xv, 508 p. ; ISBN 0-394-74339-3 : LC Card 85-40868 DDC 650.1/4/0973 19
HF5382.U5 P44 1986
*NYPL [*R-Econ. 86-3454]*

Inside U. S. business . Mattera, Philip. Homewood, Ill. , c1987. xiv, 424 p. ; ISBN 0-87094-950-0 LC Card 87-70392 DDC 338.0973 19
HC106.8 .M337 1987

Inside US business. Mattera, Philip. Inside U. S. business . Homewood, Ill. , c1987. xiv, 424 p. ; ISBN 0-87094-950-0 LC Card 87-70392 DDC 338.0973 19
HC106.8 .M337 1987

INSIDER TRADING IN SECURITIES - UNITED STATES.
Frantz, Douglas. Levine & Co. . New York , c1987. x, 370 p. : ISBN 0-8050-0457-2 LC Card 87-8521 DDC 364.1/68 19
HG2463.L48 F72 1987

Madrick, Jeffrey G. Taking America . Toronto , New York , 1987. 310 p. ; ISBN 0-553-05229-2 LC Card 87-928 DDC 338.8/3/0973 19
HG4028.T4 M33 1987

Stevens, Mark, 1947- The insiders . New York , c1987. 256 p. ; LC Card 87-2537 DDC 364.1/68 19
HG4910 .S67 1987

The insiders . Stevens, Mark, 1947- New York , c1987. 256 p. ; LC Card 87-2537 DDC 364.1/68 19
HG4910 .S67 1987

The Insider's guide series.
Camden, Thomas M., 1938- How to get a job in Dallas, Fort Worth . Chicago, IL , c1987. viii, 490 p. : ISBN 0-9609516-9-5 (pbk.) : LC Card 86-30123 DDC 650.1/4/097642812 19
HF5382.75.U6 C353 1987

Insider's guide to antique bazaars in Japan /. Nedlog, D'Lanor. Tokyo, Japan , c1986. 124 p. : ISBN 4-906231-00-4 LC Card 87-123282 DDC 381/.18 19
HF5475.J3 N43 1986

The insider's guide to antique securities /. Garrison, G. H. Haley (George H. Haley) Williamsburg, Va. (P.O. Drawer JH, Williamsburg 23187) , c1987. 1 v. (various pagings) : LC Card 87-149140 DDC 332.63/2/0750973 19
HG4633 .G38 1987

The insider's guide to finding the right job /. Lewis, Diane, 1936- Nashville , c1987. 190 p. ; ISBN 0-8407-3107-8 (pbk.) : LC Card 86-33305 DDC 650.1/4 19
HF5382.75.U6 L49 1987

The insider's guide to Lotus 1-2-3 . Badgett, Tom. Glenview, Ill. , c1987. xix, 266 p. : ISBN 0-673-18718-7 (pbk.) : LC Card 87-4864 DDC 005.36/9 19
HF5548.4.L67 B33 1987

INSOLVENCY. see **BANKRUPTCY.**

Insolvenzfrüherkennung mittels praktischer Anwendung der Diskriminanzanalyse /. Bleier, Ernst. Wien , c1985. 216 p. : ISBN 3-85428-043-2 : LC Card 85-201068
HG3761 .B54 1985

Les inspecteurs des finances au XIXe siècle (1850-1914) . Chadeau, Emmanuel, 1956- Paris , c1986. iii, 184 p. : ISBN 2-7178-1175-3 : LC Card 87-131650
HJ9925.F8 C42 1986

Inspecting industry : pollution and safety : efficiency scrutiny report : report and annexes / commissioned jointly by the Secretary of State for the Environment and for Employment. London : H.M.S.O. : Available from HMSO Publications Centre, 1986. 110 p. ; 30 cm. ISBN 0-11-751910-3 (pbk.) : LC Card 87-164869 DDC 363.1/1/0941 19
1. Industrial hygiene - Great Britain. 2. Industrial safety - Great Britain. I. Great Britain. Dept. of the Environment. II. Great Britain. Dept. of Employment.
HD7695 .I63 1986

INSPECTION OF FACTORIES. see **FACTORY INSPECTION.**

INSPECTION OF FOOD. see **FOOD ADULTERATION AND INSPECTION.**

Inspectors-general . Moore, Mark Harrison. New York , c1986. 120 p. ; ISBN 0-87154-605-1 : LC Card 86-6728 DDC 353.0072/32 19
HJ9801 .M66 1987 *NYPL [JLE 87-1762]*

Instabile Exportmärkte und wirtschaftliche Entwicklung . Mayer, Thomas, 1927- Tübingen , c1983. vii, 181 p. : ISBN 3-16-344673-6 LC Card 83-218666
HF3426.5 .M39 1983

Instant millionaires . Wagman, Robert J. [Kensington, Md.] , 1986. 298 p. ; ISBN 0-933149-05-0 (pbk.) : LC Card 86-50285 DDC 795.3/092/2 19
HG6126 .W27 1986

Institución Nacional de Estadística (Bolivia)
Bolivia . [La Paz, Bolivia] [Santiago, Chile] [1985] 107 p. : LC Card 86-160849
HA954 .B64 1985

Instituciones costarricenses del siglo veinte. Las Instituciones costarricenses del siglo XX /. [San José] , 1986. 376 p. ; ISBN 997-7232-96-5 LC Card 86-231789
HC143 .I54 1986

Las Instituciones costarricenses del siglo XX / Carmen Lila Gómez ... [et al.]. 1a ed. [San José] : Editorial Costa Rica, 1986. 376 p. ; 21 cm. "Cátedra de Historia de las Instituciones de Costa Rica, Escuela de Historia y Geografía, Universidad de Costa Rica." Includes bibliographies. ISBN 997-7232-96-5 LC Card 86-231789
1. Costa Rica - Industries - History - 20th century. 2. Costa Rica - Economic conditions. 3. Costa Rica - Social conditions. 4. Costa Rica - Civilization. 5. Education - Costa Rica - History - 20th century. 6. Costa Rica - Politics and government. 7. Social institutions - Costa Rica - History - 20th century. I. Gómez U., Carmen Lila. II. Universidad de Costa Rica. Cátedra de Historia de las Instituciones de Costa Rica. III. Title: Instituciones costarricenses del siglo 20. IV. Title: Instituciones costarricenses del siglo veinte.
HC143 .I54 1986

Instituciones costarricenses del siglo 20. Las Instituciones costarricenses del siglo XX /. [San José] , 1986. 376 p. ; ISBN 997-7232-96-5 LC Card 86-231789
HC143 .I54 1986

As instituições para-estatais no estado novo /. Castro, J. Rio de Janeiro, Brasil , 1939 (Rio [de Janeiro] : Companhia Carioca) 225 p., [2] leaves of plates : LC Card 85-222446
HD4094 .C35 1939

Institut Afriki (Akademiia nauk SSSR)
Afrika v tsifrakh . Moskva , 1986. 421 p. ; LC Card 87-143124
HA4675 .A37 1986

Agrarnye preobrazovaniia v stranakh Afriki na sovremennom ėtape /. Moskva , 1982. 227 p. ; LC Card 83-143645
HD2117 .A347 1982

Nezavisimye strany Afriki . Moskva , 1986. 276 p. ; LC Card 87-110032
HG187.5.A2 N49 1986

Institut Agama Islam Negeri Sunan Kalijaga.
Etika pembangunan dalam pemikiran Islam di Indonesia /. Jakarta , 1986. xi, 270 p. ; ISBN 979-421-043-9 (pbk.) LC Card 86-946413
HC447 .E78 1986

Institut agronomique méditerranéen de Montpellier. Les Modèles de consommation et les politiques alimentaires dans les pays du Maghreb . Alger [1985?] 401 p. : LC Card 87-132818
HD9017.A24 M63 1985

Institut avtomatiki i protsessov upravleniia s vychislitel'nym tsentrom (Akademiia nauk SSSR) Avtomatizatsiia upravleniia transportnymi sistemami /. Moskva , 1984. 271 p. : LC Card 84-195421
HE255 .A93 1984

Institut de documentation, de recherches et d'études maritimes (Ivory Coast)
Gohibi, Bernard. Les incidences financières de l'assurance maritime sur l'économie ivoirienne /. Abidjan , 1984. 24 leaves ; LC Card 86-111379 DDC 368.2/2/0096668 19
HE964.5.I94 G64 1984
NYPL [JLF 86-1484]

Kouassi, Jean-Claude. Transports maritimes et balance des paiements en Côte d'Ivoire /. [Abidjan] [1982?] 23, xii leaves ; LC Card 86-111436 DDC 387.5/1 19
HE597.I9 K68 1982 *NYPL [JLF 86-1485]*

Institut de promotion commerciale (Guadeloupe)
Le Lolo . Pointe-à-Pitre [1984?] 63 p. : LC Card 86-155167
HF5473.G83 L65 1984

Institut de recherche rural. see **Agrárgazdasági Kutató Intézet.**

Institut de sociologie, Brussels. see **Brussels. Université libre. Institut de sociologie.**

Institut de sociologie Solvay, Brussels. see **Brussels. Université libre. Institut de sociologie.**

Institut der Deutschen Wirtschaft. Engels, Wolfram. Den Staat erneuern, den Markt retten /. Köln , c1983. 228 p. ; ISBN 3-602-34836-9 LC Card 84-182378
HC286 .E54 1983

Institut ėkonomiki (Akademiia fanhoi RSS Tojikiston) Narodnoe khoziaistvo Tadzhikistana v gody Velikoĭ Otechestvennoĭ voĭny . Dushanbe , 1980. 169, [3] p. ; LC Card 81-130944
HC337.T233 D45 1980

Institut ėkonomiki (Akademiia nauk SSSR)
Agrarnye problemy v svete resheniĭ XXVII s"ezda KPSS /. Moskva , 1986. 185 p. ; LC Card 87-163428
HD1992 .A645 1986

Agropromyshlennyĭ kompleks v usloviiakh razvitogo sotsializma . Moskva , 1986. 167 p. ; LC Card 87-166350
HD9015.S652 A38 1986

Ėffektivnost' i intensifikatsiia . Moskva , 1986. 161 p. ; LC Card 87-163443
HC340.I52 E33 1986

Formy i metody upravleniia NTP /. Moskva , 1987. 151 p. ; LC Card 87-143073
HC340.T4 F67 1987

Infrastruktura i intensifikatsiia ėkonomiki /. Moskva , 1980. 192 p. ; LC Card 81-141492
HC340.C3 I54 1980

Intensifikatsiia ėkonomiki i narodnoe potreblenie /. Moskva , 1983. 166 p. ; LC Card 84-227789
HC340.C6 I58 1983

Khoziaistvennyĭ mekhanizm i povyshenie ėffektivnosti /. Moskva , 1982. 191 p. ; LC Card 84-193531
HC340.I52 K48 1982

Kontseptsiia i napravleniia ratsionalizatsii narodnogo potrebleniia /. Moskva , 1985. 172 p. : LC Card 86-193920
HC340.C6 K573 1985

Obobshchestvlenie sel'skokhoziaistvennogo proizvodstva /. Moskva , 1986. 159 p. ; LC Card 86-177899
HD9015.S652 O26 1986

Osnovnye faktory rosta proizvoditel'nosti truda v sel'skom khoziaistve /. Moskva , 1986. 158 p. ; LC Card 87-163422
HD9015.S652 O85 1986

Problemy ėkonomicheskogo rosta na sovremennom ėtape. Moskva , 1984. 137 p. : LC Card 85-240336
HC336.25 .P624 1984

Problemy povysheniia ėkonomicheskoĭ ėffektivnosti kapital'nykh vlozheniĭ v territorial'nye promyshlennye kompleksy.

Moskva , 1983. 170 p. : LC Card 84-202808
HC340.C3 P747 1983

Problemy sovershenstvovaniia material'no-tekhnicheskoĭ bazy otrasleĭ obshchestvennogo proizvodstva . Moskva , 1983. 167 p. : LC Card 84-211670
HD70.S63 P753 1983

Proizvoditel'nost' truda--vazhneĭshiĭ faktor povysheniia ėffektivnosti proizvodstva /. Moskva , 1982. 358 p. ; LC Card 83-140430
HC340.L3 P693 1982

Rasshirenie samostoiatel'nosti predpriiatiĭ i nauchno-tekhnicheskoe razvitie proizvodstva /. Moskva , 1986. 205 p. ; LC Card 87-162795
HG4186 .R37 1986

Razvitie obshchestvennykh fondov potrebleniia na sovremennom ėtape /. Moskva , 1984. 140 p. ; LC Card 85-240059
HD7196 .R39 1984

Rezervy intensifikatsii vosproizvodstva osnovnykh fondov i ikh ispol'zovaniia /. Moskva , 1984. 204 p. ; LC Card 85-240369
HC340.C3 R48 1984

Rol' nauchno-tekhnicheskogo progressa v intensifikatsii obshchestvennogo proizvodstva /. Moskva , 1986. 177 p. : LC Card 87-163537
HC340.T4 R65 1986

Simpozium "Nauchno-tekhnicheskiĭ progress i intensifikatsiia obshchestvennogo proizvodstva" (1984 : Podol'sk, Moscow, R.S.F.S.R.) Formy i metody vzaimodeĭstviia nauki i proizvodstva /. Moskva , 1984. 237 p. ; LC Card 85-240380
HC340.T4 S48 1984

Sotsialisticheskoe obobshchestvlenie truda /. Moskva , 1981. 166 p. ; LC Card 82-161177
HD5796 .S633 1981

Sovershenstvovanie planirovaniia i upravleniia intensifikatsieĭ obshchestvennogo proizvodstva /. Moskva , 1984. 182 p. ; LC Card 85-240311
HC336.25 .S6735 1984

Sovershenstvovanie sistemy narodnokhoziaĭstvennogo upravleniia v sotsialisticheskikh stranakh . Moskva , 1986. 196 p. ; LC Card 87-163453
HC244 .S595115 1986

Struktura narodnogo khoziaĭstva v usloviiakh intensifikatsii ėkonomiki /. Moskva , 1986. 267 p. ; LC Card 86-212596
HC336.25 .S795 1986

TSena i khozraschet /. Moskva , 1986. 144 p. ; LC Card 87-163568
HB235.S73 T72 1986

Ukreplenie material'nykh osnov sotsialisticheskogo obraza zhizni /. Moskva , 1984. 156 p. ; LC Card 85-240384
HD8526.5 .U38 1984

Institut ėkonomiki (Akademiia nauk SSSR). Sektor finansovykh i kreditnykh otnosheniĭ. Sbalansirovannost' sotsialisticheskoĭ ėkonomiki i finansovo-kreditnyĭ mekhanizm /. Moskva , 1984. 108 p. ; LC Card 85-240300
HG186.S55 S27 1984

Institut ėkonomiki (Akademiia nauk SSSR). Sektor "Kharaktera i soderzhaniia truda pri sotsializme." Izmenenie soderzhaniia i kharaktera truda na sovremennom ėtape razvitogo sotsializma /. Moskva , 1984. 227 p. ; LC Card 85-240356
HD8526.5 .I97 1984

Institut ėkonomiki (Akademiia nauk SSSR). Sektor sotsialisticheskoĭ sobstvennosti. Napravleniia i formy realizatsii obshchenarodnoĭ sobstvennosti /. Moskva , 1986. 171 p. ; LC Card 87-163156
HD4213 .N36 1986

Institut ėkonomiki (Akademiia nauk SSSR. Ural'skiĭ nauchnyĭ tsentr) Formirovanie i razvitie rabochego klassa i promyshlennosti Urala v period stroitel'stva sotsializma, 1917-1937 . Sverdlovsk , 1982. 138 p. ; LC Card 84-211723
HD8529.U7 F67 1982

Kardinal'nyĭ rost ėffektivnosti zhivogo truda--glavnyĭ faktor uskoreniia sotsial'no-ėkonomicheskogo razvitiia . Sverdlovsk , 1986. 2 v. ; LC Card 87-136690
HC337.R853 L35 1986

Metodicheskie rekomendatsii po issledovaniiu proizvodstvennoĭ infrastruktury territorial'no-proizvodstvennykh kompleksov i promyshlennykh uzlov /. Sverdlovsk , 1983. 79 p. (some folded) ; LC Card 86-113572
HC340.C3 M416 1983

Ural i problemy regional'noĭ istoriografii. Sverdlovsk , 1986. 83 p. ; LC Card 87-159699
HC337.R852 U73853 1986

Institut ėkonomiki i organizatsii promyshlennogo proizvodstva (Akademiia nauk SSSR) Imitatsionnoe modelirovanie proizvodstvennykh protsessov . Novosibirsk , 1979. 152 p. : LC Card 81-132238
HD70.S63 I44 1979

KATĖK i razvitie otrasleĭ khoziaĭstva Sibiri /. Novosibirsk , 1984. 164 p. ; LC Card 84-167870
HC337.R852 S5246 1984

Khoziaĭstvennoe osvoenie novykh raĭonov i ėkonomicheskiĭ rost Sibiri . Novosibirsk , 1980. 173 p. : LC Card 83-182452
HC337.R852 S5247 1980

Metodologicheskie polozheniia razrabotki krupnykh territorial'nykh programm /. Novosibirsk , 1986. 303 p. : LC Card 86-211369
HC337.R853 D56 1986

Metody i modeli razvitiia regional'nykh ėkonomicheskikh sistem . Novosibirsk , 1985. 165 p. : LC Card 86-219402
HC337.R852 S52545 1985

Mezhregional'nye mezhotraslevye balansy /. Novosibirsk , 1983. 220 p. : LC Card 84-172934
HF3626.5 .M49 1983

Modeli i metody resheniia zadach vzaimodeĭstviia ėkonomicheskikh sistem /. Novosibirsk , 1982. 160 p. : LC Card 83-164468
HB137 .M6 1982

Optimizatsiia perspektivnykh planov razvitiia otraslevykh sistem . Novosibirsk , 1979. 163 p. : LC Card 81-130740
HC337.R852 S546 1979

Sovershenstvovanie planirovaniia i upravleniia neftegazovym kompleksom /. Novosibirsk , 1986. 208 p. : LC Card 87-124383
HD9575.S653 S577 1986

Territorial'no-proizvodstvennye kompleksy . Novosibirsk , 1986. 263 p. : LC Card 86-231926
HC336.25 .T467 1986

Territorial'no-proizvodstvennye kompleksy--voprosy struktury i razvitiia . Novosibirsk , 1981. 152 p. ; LC Card 82-160051
HC337.R852 S5276 1981

Upravlenie nauchno-tekhnicheskim progressom na predpriiatii /. Novosibirsk , 1986. 222 p. ; LC Card 87-124400
HD45 .U52 1986

Institut ėkonomiki i organizatsii promyshlennosti proizvodstva (Akademiia nauk SSSR) Problemy formirovaniia i upravleniia agrarno-promyshlennym kompleksom . Novosibirsk , 1979. 157 p. : LC Card 81-143766
HD9015.S652 P73 1979

Institut ėkonomiki kompleksnogo osvoeniia prirodnykh resursov Severa (Akademiia nauk SSSR) Intensifikatsiia i povyshenie ėffektivnosti promyshlennogo proizvodstva v usloviiakh Severa . IAkutsk , 1986. 109 p. ; LC Card 87-159706
HC337.I23 I5214 1986

Institut ėkonomiki (Kyrgyz SSR ilimder akademiiasy) Ėkonomicheskiĭ rost Kirgizskoĭ SSR v usloviiakh intensifikatsii obshchestvennogo proizvodstva . Frunze , 1984. 210 p. ; LC Card 85-131511
HC337.K545 E37 1984 *NYPL [*QIP 87-105]*

Sovershenstvovanie ėkonomicheskikh metodov upravleniia sel'skokhoziaĭstvennym proizvodstvom /. Frunze , 1982. 158 p. ; LC Card 83-196563
HD9015.S653 K577 1982

Institut ėkonomiki mirovoĭ sotsialisticheskoĭ sistemy (Akademiia nauk SSSR) Kuba v mezhdunarodnom sotsialisticheskom razdelenii truda /. Moskva , 1986. 146 p. : LC Card 86-232928
HF1500.5.E852 K83 1986

Soglasovanie ėkonomicheskoĭ politiki stran SĖV /. Moskva , 1986. 287 p. ; LC Card 87-120408
HC244 .S5925 1986

Vneshniaia torgovlia SSSR so stranami SĖV /. Moskva , 1986. 108, [3] p. ; LC Card 86-213259
HF3628.E9 V54 1986

Institut ėkonomiki okeana (Akademiia nauk SSSR) Ėkonomicheskie aspekty ratsional'nogo ispol'zovaniia resursov okeana i okhrany morskoĭ sredy . Vladivostok , 1984. 124 p. : LC Card 85-234774
HC92 .E37 1984

Institut ėkonomiki (Qazaq SSR ghylym akademiiasy) Ėffektivnost' territorial'noĭ organizatsii promyshlennogo proizvodstva v Kazakhstane /. Alma-Ata , 1980. 190 p. ; LC Card 82-164638
HC337.K33 D53 1980

Ėkonomicheskaia otsenka i prognozirovanie ispol'zovaniia prirodnykh resursov Kazakhstana /. Alma-Ata , 1980. 161 p. ; LC Card 82-106708
HC337.K3 E34 1980

Institut ekonomiky promyslovosti (Akademiia nauk Ukraïns'koï RSR) Povyshenie ėffektivnosti ASUP . Kiev , 1985. 303 p. : LC Card 85-210269
HD30.2 .P68 1985 *NYPL [*QIP 87-2760]*

Institut ekonomskih nauka (Belgrade, Serbia) Jugoslovenska privreda između stagnacije i razvoja /. Beograd , 1986. viii, 298 p. : LC Card 87-151260
HC407 .J83 1986

Institut "Finanzen und Steuern" (Germany) Dornbusch, Hans-Ludwig. Entwicklung wesentlicher Daten der öffentlichen Finanzwirtschaft in der Bundesrepublik Deutschland von 1973-1983 /. Bonn , 1984. 32 leaves ; LC Card 86-186300
HJ1120 .B65 Nr. 236

Gemeindehaushalte zur Haushaltswirtschaft der Städte Hannover, Düsseldorf, Köln, Frankfurt, Stuttgart, München. Bonn am Rhein , 1964. 148 p. ; LC Card 87-408349 DDC 336/.014/43 19
HJ9473 .G46 1964

Jasper, Lothar Th. Entwicklung der Realsteuerhebesätze der Gemeinden mit mehr als 50.000 Einwohnern 1984 gegenüber 1983 /. Bonn , 1984. 29 leaves ; LC Card 86-186306
HJ1120 .B65 nr. 238 HJ4125.G35

Länderhaushalte. Bonn [1964] 112 p. ; LC Card 85-185971
HJ1101 .B6 Heft 73 HJ1120

Ziele und Möglichkeiten der Privatisierung in volkswirtschaftlicher Sicht . Bonn , 1985. 83 leaves ; LC Card 86-185728
HJ1120 .B65 Nr. 244 HD4178

Institut fiziki i matematiki (Kyrgyz SSR Ilimder Akademiiasy) Primenenie ėkonomiko-matematicheskikh metodov v sovershenstvovanii upravleniia narodnym khoziaĭstvom /. Frunze , 1982. 225 p. : LC Card 83-193778
HD9115.S652 P75 1982

Institut fiziko-tekhnicheskikh problem Severa (Akademiia nauk SSSR) Razvitie ėnergetiki IAkutskoĭ ASSR v sviazi s sooruzheniem BAM . IAkutsk , 1985. 99, 3 p. : LC Card 86-233736
HD9502.S653 I237 1985

Institut für Angewandte Sozial- und Wirtschaftsforschung, Vienna. see **Vienna. Institut für Angewandte Sozial- und Wirtschaftsforschung.**

Institut für Arbeitsmarkt- und Berufsforschung. Abiturienten und Hochschulabsolventen beim Übergang vom Studium in den Beruf . Nürnberg , 1983. 407 p. : LC Card 84-140881
HD6278.G4 A25 1983

Evaluation der Berufsberatung der Bundesanstalt für Arbeit . Nürnberg , 1983. vii, 282 p. : LC Card 85-107586
HF5382.5.G3 E9 1983

Kabbert, Rainer. Jugendliche zwischen Schule und Beruf . Nürnberg , 1982. 84, [1] p. : LC Card 83-169834
HF5382.5.G3 K33 1982

Institut für Iberoamerika-Kunde. Arbeitsunterlagen und Diskussionsbeiträge. (Nr. 21) Glembotzki, Jürgen.

Landwirtschaftliche Entwicklung und Agrarreform in Nicaragua zwischen 1960 und 1982 . Hamburg , 1984. 80, xliv p. : LC Card 84-208160 DDC 333.3/1/7285 19
HD1333.N5 G57 1984
NYPL [JLM 75-816 Nr.21]

Institut für Internationale Politik und Wirtschaft der DDR. 30 Jahre DDR und das Fiasko imperialistischer Prognosen, Pläne und Propheten . [Berlin] , 1979. 40 p. ; LC Card 83-198579
HC290.78 .A14 1979

Institut für Landes- und Stadtentwicklungsforschung des Landes Nordrhein-Westfalen.
Puls, Heinz. Finanzkraft der Gemeinden und kommunaler Ausgleichsstock in NW /. Dortmund [1977] [15] p. : LC Card 86-211554
HJ9493.5.N6 P85 1977

Ruhender Verkehr in Wohngebieten /. Dortmund , c1983, [1982] 121 p. : LC Card 83-236251
HE363.G32 P377 1983

Institut für Wirtschafts-und Gesellschaftspolitik. IWG Impulse.
(Bd. 5) Miegel, Meinhard. Die verkannte Revolution /. Stuttgart , 1983- v. : ISBN 3-87959-196-2 (Bd. 1) LC Card 83-206487 DDC 330.943/087 19
HC286.7 .M53 1983 ***NYPL [JLK 86-154]***

Institut für Angewandte Sozial- und Wirtschaftsforschung (Vienna, Austria)
Schauer, Reinbert. Die Verwaltung als betriebliches Teilsystem . Wien , 1984. v, 258 p. : ISBN 3-85436-014-2 LC Card 84-173337
HD35 .S2655 1984

Institut für Asienkunde (Hamburg, Germany)
Louven, Erhard. Shanghai, Chinas Tor zur Welt /. Hamburg , 1986. 118 p. : LC Card 86-230755
HC428.S47 L68 1986

Institut für Marxismus-Leninismus beim ZK der SED.
Geschichte der internationalen Arbeiterbewegung in Daten /. Berlin , 1986. 868 p. ; ISBN 3-320-00635-5 LC Card 86-210352
HD6475.A1 G47 1986

Der Zweite Entwurf des "Kapitals" . Berlin , 1983. 360 p. ; LC Card 83-236586
HB175.M2585 Z86 1983

Institut für Ökologische Wirtschaftsforschung.
Ökologische Unternehmenspolitik /. Frankfurt , New York , c1986. 280 p. ; ISBN 3-593-33580-8 LC Card 87-407999 DDC 363.7 19
HD75.6 .O347 1986

Institut für Sozialforschung (Frankfurt am Main, Germany)
Grenzen der Frauenlohnarbeit . Frankfurt/Main , New York , c1986. 250 p. : ISBN 3-593-33628-6 LC Card 86-228323
HD6072.2.G4 G74 1986

Processi formativi e coscienza operaia . Pisa , c1983. 509 p. ; LC Card 86-136656 DDC 658.3/124/0945 19
HF5549.5.T7 P69 1983
NYPL [JLE 87-1466]

Institut für Stadt-, Regional- und Wohnforschung (Hamburg, Germany) Der Ausbau von Fernwärmenetzen und seine Wirkungen auf Arbeitsmarkt und Beschäftigung, dargestellt am Beispiel der Freien und Hansestadt Hamburg . Bonn [1983] xiv, 172 p. : LC Card 85-107700
HD5780.H34 A87 1983

Institut für Stadtforschung (Series) .
(74) Czasny, Karl. Erfassung des Wohnungsangebotes /. Wien , 1985. 284 p. ; ISBN 3-900551-04-9 LC Card 87-103427 DDC 333.33/8 19
HD7337.V3 C93 1985

Institut für Wissenschaftliche Zusammenarbeit mit Entwicklungsländern (Tübingen, Germany) Indien, Probleme eines Schwellenlandes . Tübingen , c1984. 75 p. ; ISBN 3-922362-02-8 LC Card 85-157722
HC435.2 .I6235 1984

Institut geografii Sibiri i Dal'nego Vostoka (Akademiia nauk SSSR)
Geograficheskie osobennosti formirovaniia agrarno-promyshlennykh kompleksov v Predbaĭkal'e /. Irkutsk , 1978. 145 p. : LC Card 81-162870
HD9015.S653 174 1978

Regional'nye osobennosti ratsionalizatsii prirodopol'zovaniia i okhrany sredy /. Irkutsk , 1980. 177 p. ; LC Card 82-111826
HC337.R852 S5266 1980

Institut haïtien de statistique et d'informantique. Résultats préliminaires du recensement général (septembre 1982) /. [Port-au-Prince] [1982 or 1983] vii, 60 p., [1] leaf of plates : LC Card 84-138275 DDC 304.6/097294/021 19
HD7316.A3 R47 1982 ***NYPL [JLF 86-1280]***

Institut interaméricain des sciences agricoles. see **Inter-American Institute of Agricultural Sciences.**

Institut international de finances publiques.
International Institute of Public Finance . Detroit , 1987. vi, 106 p. : ISBN 0-8143-1984-X LC Card 87-10724 DDC 336/.006/01 19
HJ203 .I57 1987

Institut international de finances publiques. see **International Institute of Public Finance.**

Institut international de planification de l'éducation. see **International Institute for Educational Planning.**

Institut international des caisses d'épargne. see **International Savings Banks Institute.**

Institut istorii, arkheologii i ėtnografii narodov Dal'nego Vostoka (Akademiia nauk SSSR)
Istoriografiia istorii rabochego klassa Dal'nego Vostoka SSSR /. Vladivostok , 1984. 78 p. ; LC Card 85-229962
HD8529.S652 I87 1984

Institut istorii, filologii i filosofii (Akademiia nauk SSR) Sotsial'nye problemy truda u narodnosteĭ Severa /. Novosibirsk , 1986. 213 p. ; LC Card 87-164784
HD5797.N75 S67 1986

Institut istorii, filologii i filosofii (Akademiia nauk SSSR)
Rabochiĭ klass Sibiri . Novosibirsk , 1986. 355 p., [16] p. of plates : LC Card 86-211294
HD5797.S5 R33 1986

Sotsial'no-ėkonomicheskoe i kul'turnoe razvitie Zabaĭkal'ia . Novosibirsk , 1980. 283 p. ; LC Card 81-132139
HC337.R852 T737 1980

Trudovye kollektivy Sibiri . Novosibirsk , 1985. 154 p. ; LC Card 86-162191
HD5797.S5 T78 1985

Institut istorii imeni akademika AN MSSR IA.S. Grosula. Rabochee dvizhenie v Moldavii, 1895-fevral' 1917 g. . Kishinev , 1985. 322 p. ; LC Card 86-100092
HD8529.M57 R32 1985

Institut istorii SSSR (Akademiia nauk SSSR)
Istoriia sovetskogo krest'ianstva . Moskva , 1986- v. : ***NYPL [*QG 87-3228]***

Iz istorii razvitiia metallurgicheskoĭ promyshlennosti Moskvy, 1883-1932 gg. . Moskva , 1981. 219 p. ; LC Card 84-163581
HD9525.S653 M64 1981
NYPL [*QIP 87-3316]

Proizvoditel'nye sily i monopolisticheskiĭ kapital v Rossii i Germanii v kontse XIX-nachale XX vv. /. Moskva , 1986. 223 p. ; LC Card 87-159751
HD2859 .P76 1986

Rabochee dvizhenie v Rossii v period imperializma . Moskva , 1982. 144 p. ; LC Card 83-174879
HD8526 .R3112 1982

Vozrozhdenie prifrontovykh i osvobozhdennykh raĭonov SSSR v gody Velikoĭ Otechestvennoĭ voĭny 1941-1945 /. Moskva , 1986. 214 p., [24] p. of plates : LC Card 86-232256
HC336.9.W47 V69 1986

Institut Jean-Baptiste Dumay. Faire l'histoire du monde du travail . [Seyssel] : [Le Creusot] : 52 p. : ISBN 2-903528-49-7 : LC Card 85-180268 DDC 305.5/62/072044 19
HD8428 .F35 1985 ***NYPL [JLD 87-1157]***

Institut kibernetiki im. V.M. Glushkova.
Problemy modelirovaniia makroėkonomicheskikh sistem . Kiev , 1982. 100 p. ; LC Card 83-144893
HB139 .P755 1982

Institut Latinskoĭ Ameriki (Akademiia nauk SSSR)
Latinskaia Amerika . Moskva , 1978. 271 p. ; LC Card 81-159488
HG185.L3 L37 1978

Latinskaia Amerika--problemy razvitiia neftianoĭ promyshlennosti /. Moskva , 1984. 192 p. : LC Card 86-181028
HD9574.L3 L4 1984

Prodovol'stvennaia problema i sel'skoe khoziaĭstvo stran Latinskoĭ Ameriki /. Moskva , 1981. 311 p. ; LC Card 82-108167
HD9014.L32 P76 1981

Institut "Lo Pla d'Urgell." Materials per a l'estudi geogràfic dels pobles de l'àrea econòmica de Bellpuig /. [Lleida , 1985. 253 p. : LC Card 87-131722
HA1559.B45 M38 1985

Institut mezhdunarodnogo rabochego dvizheniia (Akademiia nauk SSSR)
Mezhdunarodnoe rabochee dvizhenie . Moskva , 1980. 412 p. ; LC Card 81-143888
HD4854 .M474 1980

Rabochee dvizhenie v razvitykh kapitalisticheskikh stranakh . Moskva , 1987. 268 p. ; LC Card 87-164460
HD8378 .R29 1987

Rabochiĭ klass v proshlom i nastoiashchem . Moskva , 1984, c1983. 255 p. ; LC Card 84-169518
HD4854 .R273 1984

Institut mirovoĭ ėkonomiki i mezhdunarodnykh otnosheniĭ (Akademiia nauk SSSR)
Burzhuaznoe gosudarstvo i vneshneėkonomicheskie sviazi /. Moskva , 1986. 350 p. : LC Card 86-211675
HF1411 .B79 1986

Evropeĭskoe soobshchestvo . Moskva , 1986. 270 p. : LC Card 86-202812
HC241.2 .E867 1986

Problemy khoziaĭstvennogo razvitiia osvobodivshikhsia stran . Moskva , 1987. 2 v. (306 p.) ; LC Card 87-157281
HC59.7 .P7354 1987

SSSR--razvivaiushchiesia strany . Moskva , 1985. 237 p. ; LC Card 86-158191
HF1558.5.D44 S77 1985

SSSR, SShA i Kanada . Moskva , 1987. 325 p. ; LC Card 86-205359
HF3628.U5 S77 1987

Upravlenie protsessom novovvedeniĭ v kapitalisticheskoĭ firme /. Moskva , 1985. 228 p. : LC Card 86-151912
HD58.8 .U67 1985

INSTITUT NATIONAL DE FORMATION ET DE PERFECTIONNEMENT PROFESSIONNELS (CENTRAL AFRICAN REPUBLIC)
International Labour Organisation. Organisation de l'Institut national de formation et de perfectionnement professionnels de Bangui (INFPP) . Genève , 1980. 14 p. ; ISBN 92-2-202448-6 LC Card 82-214934
HD5716.M342 C335 1980

Institut national de formation professionnelle (Haiti) International Labour Organisation. Institut national de formation professionnelle (INFP) . Genève , 1982. ii, 69 p. : ISBN 92-2-203229-2 LC Card 83-234817
HD5715.5.H2 I57 1982

Institut national de formation professionnelle (INFP) . International Labour Organisation. Genève , 1982. ii, 69 p. : ISBN 92-2-203229-2 LC Card 83-234817
HD5715.5.H2 I57 1982

Institut national de la recherche agronomique (France)
Jégouzo, Guenhaël. Petite paysannerie en France /. Paris , c1984. 227 p. : ISBN 2-85340-610-5 LC Card 85-181759 DDC 338.1/6 19
HD1339.F8 J44 1984

Nicourt, Christian. Conditions de travail en agriculture . Paris , <1985-. v. <2 > : ISBN 2-85340-585-0 (v. 2) LC Card 86-218948
HD1536.F8 N53 1985

Système agraire et pratiques paysannes dans les monts Dômes /. Paris , 1983. xi, 318 p., [8] p.

of plates : ISBN 2-85340-478-1 LC Card 84-216594
HD1950.D65 S97 1983

Institut national de la recherche agronomique (France). Département d'économie et de sociologie rurales. Systèmes de production et transformations de l'agriculture /. Paris , 1985. 2 v. : ISBN 2-85340-715-2 (v. 1) LC Card 86-214407
HD1945 .S97 1985

Institut national de la recherche scientifique (Togo) Akakpo-Ahianyo, Anani. Contribution à l'étude des migrations au Togo /. Lomé , 1976. 108 p., [5] p. of plates : LC Card 87-150756
HB2125.8.A3 A38 1976

Institut national de la statistique et des études économiques (France)
France. Direction générale des collectivités locales. Instruction aux maires relative aux bulletins statistiques de l'état civil . [Paris] [1983] 50 p. : LC Card 84-112361
HA37.F8 F73 1983

Statistique du mouvement de la population dans les D.O.M. . Paris [1985] 104 p. : ISBN 2-11-064898-8 : LC Card 86-216599
HB1003 .S73 1985

Le Travail . Paris , c1986. iv, 370 p. ; ISBN 2-7178-1138-9 : LC Card 87-123294
HD8428 .T72 1986

Institut national de la statistique et des études économiques (France). Service départemental de la Guadeloupe. Démographie et emploi en Guadeloupe . Basse-Terre [1977?] 3, xix leaves, [6] leaves of plates : ISBN 2-11-062928-2 LC Card 85-230531
HA918.7 .D46 1977

Institut nauchnoĭ informat͡sii po obshchestvennym naukam (Akademii͡a nauk SSSR)
Bukhval'd, E. M. Povyshenie proizvoditel'nosti truda--kli͡uchevai͡a zadacha sovetskoĭ ėkonomiki . Moskva , 1984. 63 p. ; LC Card 85-188977
HC340.L3 B85 1984

Davidovich, I͡A. A. Rabochai͡a molodezh' SSSR v period razvitogo sotsializma . Moskva , 1985. 37 p. ; LC Card 86-187709
HD6276.S59 D38 1985

Metodiki opredelenii͡a ėkonomicheskoĭ ėffektivnosti kapital'nykh vlozheniĭ v sotsialisticheskikh stranakh . Moskva , 1981. 101 p. ; LC Card 82-204402
HC244.Z9 C35 1981

Podgotovka upravlencheskikh kadrov--opyt, problemy, perspektivy (po zarubezhnym materialam) . Moskva , 1984. 188 p. ; LC Card 85-188986
HD30.4 .P6 1984

"Problema neftedollarov" . Moskva , 1984. 231 p. ; LC Card 85-189000
HC498 .P75 1984

SĖV -- osnovnye napravlenii͡a sotrudnichestva . Moskva , 1984. 203 p. ; LC Card 85-177814
HC243.5 .S48 1984

Transnat͡sional'nye korporat͡sii v sisteme gosudarstvenno-monopolisticheskogo regulirovanii͡a ėkonomiki . Moskva , 1985. 167 p. ; LC Card 86-187630
HD2755.5 .T714 1985

Vyvoz kapitala v 80-e gody . Moskva , 1986. 247 p. ; LC Card 87-166362
HG4538 .V93 1986

Institut nauchnoĭ informat͡sii po obshchestvennym naukam (Akademii͡a nauk SSSR). Otdel kapitalisticheskikh stran Evropy i Severnoĭ Ameriki. Babashkina, M. L. Aktual'nye ėkonomicheskie i sotsial'nye problemy malykh stran Severnoĭ Evropy . Moskva , 1986. 71 p. ; LC Card 87-166353
HC343 .B34 1986

Institut nauchnoĭ informat͡sii po obshchestvennynm naukam (Akademii͡a nauk SSSR) Agropromyshlennyĭ kompleks v uslovii͡akh razvitogo sotsializma . Moskva , 1986. 167 p. ; LC Card 87-166350
HD9015.S652 A38 1986

Institut Perhubungan Raya Malaysia. Public relations . Kuala Lumpur , 1986. 259 p. : LC Card 86-944684 DDC 659.2/09595 19
HD59.6.M4 P83 1986

Institut Pertanian Bogor. Fakultas Kehutanan. Monografi sumber daya ekonomi di bidang kehutanan Kalimantan Timur . Bogor , 1975. ix, 67 leaves : LC Card 80-941771
HD9766.I73 K356 1975

Institut po istorii͡a na Bŭlgarskata komunisticheska partii͡a. Vŭznikvane, razvitie i zalez na oportiūnizma v bŭlgarskoto rabotnichesko dvizhenie, 1891/1948 /. Sofii͡a , 1986. 696 p. ; LC Card 86-200229
HD8628 .V89 1986

Institut scientifique du travail du front allemand du travail. see Deutsche Arbeitsfront. Arbeitswissenschaftliches Institut.

Institut slavi͡anovedenii͡a i balkanistiki (Akademii͡a nauk SSSR) Rabochiĭ klass i stroitel'stvo sotsializma v stranakh T͡Sentral'noĭ i I͡Ugo-Vostochnoĭ Evropy /. Moskva , 1977. 382 p. ; LC Card 81-174150
HD8376.5 .R33 1977

Institut Soedinennykh Shtatov Ameriki i Kanady (Akademii͡a nauk SSSR) Upravlencheskie novovvedenii͡a v SShA . Moskva , 1986. 244, [3] p. : LC Card 86-231514
HD70.U5 U67 1986

Institut sot͡sial'no-ėkonomicheskikh problem (Akademii͡a nauk SSSR)
Effektivnost' NTP . Leningrad , 1985. 215 p., [1] folded leaf of plates : LC Card 86-129301
HC244.Z9 T435 1985

Matematicheskie metody v upravlenii gorodskimi transportnymi sistemami /. Leningrad , 1979. 150 p. : LC Card 81-163008
HE311.S652 M675 1979

Institut sot͡siologicheskikh issledovaniĭ (Akademii͡a nauk SSSR) Nekotorye problemy internat͡sional'nogo vospitanii͡a v mnogonatsional'nom trudovom kollektive /. Moskva , 1985. 135 p. ; LC Card 86-233779
HD8526.5 .N45 1985

Institut universitaire de hautes études internationales, Geneva. see Geneva. Graduate Institute of International Studies.

Institut Valencià d'Investigació Social. Estructura social de la comarca "El Camp de Morvedre" /. Sagunt, Valencià [Madrid] , 1982. 2 v. (1133 p.) : ISBN 84-7231-763-3 (set) LC Card 85-188040
HB3620.S24 E87 1982

Institut vostokovedenii͡a (Akademii͡a nauk SSSR)
Gosudarstvo i agrarnai͡a ėvoli͡utsii͡a v razvivai͡ushchikhsi͡a stranakh Azii i Afriki /. Moskva , 1980. 227 p. ; LC Card 81-143353
HD2056 .G67 1980

Opyt stroitel'stva sot͡sialisticheskoĭ ėkonomiki v stranakh Azii /. Moskva , 1986. 290 p. ; LC Card 87-126301
HC412 .O675 1986

Sverkhmonopolii v I͡Ugo-Vostochnoĭ Azii /. Moskva , 1983. 219 p. ; LC Card 83-223670
HD2901 .S84 1983

Trudovye resursy Vostoka . Moskva , 1987. 319 p. ; LC Card 87-142995
HD5811.85.A6 T78 1987

Zarubezhnyĭ Vostok . Moskva , 1986. 126 p. ; LC Card 87-126378
HC412 .Z38 1986

Institut za historiju radničkog pokreta Hrvatske. Kongres privrednih stručnjaka Hrvatske (1943-1944 : Otočac and Čazma, Croatia) Kongres privrednih stručnjaka Hrvatske . Zagreb , 1985. 252 p., [16] p. of plates : ISBN 86-80359-01-7 LC Card 86-176200
HC407.Z7 C7637 1943

Institut za propaganda na marksizma-leninizma. Trendafilov, Toncho. Nauchno-tekhnicheskata revoli͡utsii͡a--zakonomernost na uskorenoto razvitie na sotsialisticheskoto obshtestvo /. Sofii͡a , 1985. 93 p. : LC Card 86-163246
HC403.Z9 T477 1985

Institute for Black Research (Durban, South Africa) Orkin, Mark. Disinvestment, the struggle, and the future . Johannesburg , 1986. xii, 78 p. : ISBN 0-86975-305-3 (pbk.) LC Card 87-100474 DDC 332.6/73/0968 19
HG5851.A3 O47 1986

Institute for Contemporary Studies. The Third world, premises of U. S. policy /. San Francisco , c1978. xv, 332 p. : ISBN 0-917616-30-8 : LC Card 78-67593 DDC 309.1/172/4
HC59.7 .T456 ***NYPL [JLD 81-653]***

Institute for Continuing Legal Education, New Jersey. see New Jersey Institute for Continuing Legal Education.

Institute for Defence Studies and Analyses. Nuclear proliferation and international security /. New Delhi , 1985-86 [i.e. 1985] 310 p. ; ISBN 1-85127-058-4 : LC Card 85-904278 DDC 327.1/74 19
JX1974.73 .N814 1985 ***NYPL [JLD 86-1334]***

Institute for Development Anthropology (Binghamton, N.Y.)
Leonard, David K. The political realities of African management /. Binghamton, NY, USA (P.O. Box 818, Binghamton 13902) [1984] 39 p. ; LC Card 87-153761 DDC 338.1/86 19
HD2118 .L46 1984

Scudder, Thayer. An evaluation of the Gwembe South Development Project, Zambia /. Binghamton, N.Y., USA [1982] 48 p. ; LC Card 87-119502 DDC 338.96894 19
HC915.Z7 G846 1982

Institute for Educational Affairs (New York, N. Y.)
The Best of This world /. Lanham, MD , c1986. x, 405 p. ; ISBN 0-8191-5605-1 (alk. paper) : LC Card 86-22411 DDC 261.8 19
HB72 .B5 1987 ***NYPL [JFE 86-5571]***

Capitalism and equality in America /. Lanham [New York] , c1987. ix, 306 p. : ISBN 0-8191-5572-1 (v. 1 : alk. paper) : LC Card 86-24739 DDC 330.12/2 19
HB501 .C2423 1987

Capitalism and equality in the Third World /. Lanham [New York] , c1987. 375 p. ; ISBN 0-8191-5574-8 (v. 2 : alk. paper) : LC Card 86-24749 DDC 330.12/2 19
HB501 .C24234 1987

Institute for Enterprise Advancement (U. S.) Risk to riche$. Washington, DC (600 Maryland Ave., S.W., Suite 700, Washington 20024) , c1986. vii, 204 p. : LC Card 87-158511 DDC 338/.04/088042 19
HD2346.U5 R57 1986

Institute for Financial Management and Research, Madras.
IFMR publication.
(32) Seshadri, R. K. The Indian financial system . Madras , 1985. ii, 287, v, iii p. ; LC Card 85-904230 DDC 336.54 19
HD4293 .S45 1985 ***NYPL [JLD 86-2433]***

Publication. see Institute for Financial Management and Research, Madras. IFMR publication.

Institute for Fiscal Studies (Great Britain) Taxation and incentives /. [London, England] , c1976. ii, 45 p. : LC Card 85-111944
HJ2619 .T289 1976

Institute for Food and Development Policy (San Francisco, Calif.) Rubin, Laurie, 1956- Food first curriculum /. San Francisco, CA , c1984. viii, 146 p. : ISBN 0-935028-17-X : LC Card 84-8986 DDC 372.8/3 19
HD9000.5 .R73 1984 ***NYPL [JLF 86-1436]***

Institute for Housing Studies (Netherlands) Chadsri Bunnag. Housing in urban development . [Bangkok] [Rotterdam] Netherlands [1985] 49, [2] leaves : LC Card 86-915989 DDC 363.5/09593 19
HD7363.55.A3 C46 1985

Institute for International Economics (U. S.)
Auction quotas and United States trade policy /. Washington, DC , c1987. xiii, 241 p. : ISBN 0-88132-050-1 (pbk.) LC Card 87-12948 DDC 382/.52/0973 19
HF1455 .A83 1987

Bergsten, C. Fred, 1941- The United States-Japan economic problem /. Washington, D.C. , c1985. x, 164 p. : ISBN 0-262-52108-3 LC Card 85-18106 DDC 382/.0973/052 19
HF3127 .B47 1985 ***NYPL [JLE 87-19]***

Capital flight and Third World debt /. Washington, D.C. , 1987. p. cm. ISBN

0-88132-064-1 LC Card 87-17080 DDC 332/.042 19
HG3891 .C36 1987

Destler, I. M. American trade politics . Washington, DC , New York, NY , 1986. xiii, 366 p. : ISBN 0-88132-058-7 : LC Card 86-27168 DDC 380.1/3/0973 19
HF1455 .D48 1986

Global economic imbalances /. Washington, DC , 1985. x, 116 p. ; ISBN 0-88132-038-2 (pbk.) LC Card 85-8279 DDC 330.9/048 19
HD73 .G56 1985 ***NYPL [JLE 87-1314]***

Lessard, Donald R. Capital flight . Washington, DC , 1987. x, 64 p. ; ISBN 0-88132-059-5 LC Card 87-17279 DDC 332/.042 19
HG3891 .C367 1987

Institute for International Politics and Economics (East Germany) see Institut für Internationale Politik und Wirtschaft der DDR.

Institute for Latin American Integration. El Acuerdo de Cartagena y el trato preferencial en favor de Bolivia y Ecuador. [Buenos Aires, Argentina] [1982] 148 leaves ; LC Card 86-202605 DDC 337.1/8 19
HC167.A5 A285 1982

Basco, Carlos A. El comercio intrarregional de alimentos básicos. [S.l.] , 1986. xi, 558 p. : LC Card 87-404784 DDC 382/.41/098 19
HD9014.L32 B37 1986

Comercio de granos entre la Argentina y los países del Grupo Andino. [Buenos Aires, Argentina] , 1983. ii, 154 p. : LC Card 86-201891
HD9044.A8 C65 1983

La Cooperación empresarial argentino-brasileña . [Buenos Aires] , 1983. viii, 160 p. ; LC Card 87-125370 DDC 338.8/8/0981 19
HD2829 .C66 1983

El Crecimiento desigual en Centroamérica, 1950-2000. [Buenos Aires, Argentina] [between 1982 and 1986] 133 leaves ; LC Card 86-200824
HC141 .C73 1982

Estrategias de desarrollo e integración en el Grupo Andino . Lima, Perú , 1985. 414 p. : LC Card 87-125026 DDC 337.1/8 19
HC167.A5 E87 1985

Estudio de transportes en la Región Amazónica y en el Alto Paraguay. Buenos Aires [1983- v. <1 > : LC Card 87-400601 DDC 380.5/0981/1 19
HE230 .E85 1983

Exenciones arancelarias e integración /. [Buenos Aires] , 1986. 273 p. ; LC Card 87-400577 DDC 382.7/1/098 19
HF1733.L29 E96 1986

Interconexión de cuencas sudamericanas. [Buenos Aires] , 1986. 159 leaves, [5] leaves of plates : LC Card 86-225024
HE650 .I58 1986

Obras hidroeléctricas binacionales en América Latina. [Buenos Aires, Argentina] , 1985. vii leaves, 385 p., 3 leaves of plates : LC Card 86-180644
HD1696.A7 O27 1985

El Proceso de integración en América Latina en 1985 /. Buenos Aires, República Argentina , 1986. 271 p. : LC Card 87-169476 DDC 337.1/8 19
HC125 .P768 1986

Reunión Técnica sobre el Financiamiento de la Integración Subregional en América Latina (1985 : Buenos Aires, Argentina) Reunión Técnica sobre el Financiamiento de la Integración Subregional en América Latina . [Buenos Aires, Argentina] . 335 p. : LC Card 86-217551
HC125 .R479 1985

Seminar on Economic Integration (1982 : Inter-American Development Bank) The economic integration process of Latin America in the 1980's . Washington, D.C. [1984] 318 p. : ISBN 0-940602-17-2 (pbk.) LC Card 87-159367
HC125 .S3973 1982

Servicios de transporte internacional por carretera en el GRAN . [Buenos Aires, Argentina] [1983] 3 v. : LC Card 87-404195 DDC 388.3/21/098 19
HE5650 .S47 1983

Zorn, Stephen. Minería y elaboración de minerales . Buenos Aires , 1986. ii, 84 p. ; LC Card 87-402781 DDC 338.2/098 19
HD9506.L252 Z67 1986

Institute for Latin American Integration. Sector Esquemas de Integración. Aragão, José María. La Asociación Latinoamericana de Libre Comercio (ALALC) y la Asociación Latinoamericana de Integración (ALADI) . Buenos Aires, Argentina [1984] xiii, 172 p. ; LC Card 86-201881
HC125 .A69 1984

Institute for Local Self-Reliance. Morris, David J. Garbage disposal economics . Washington, DC [1987] v, 101 p. : ISBN 0-917582-44-6 (pbk.) : LC Card 87-4182 DDC 338.4/3363728/0973 19
HD4483 .G37 1987

Morris, David J. Substituting agricultural materials for petroleum based industrial products /. Washington, D.C. , c1986. i, 33 p. ; ISBN 0-917582-46-2 (pbk.) : LC Card 86-21350 DDC 338.4/76628 19
HD9502.5.B543 U654 1986

Institute for Management. The IFM guide to the preparation of a company policy manual. Greenvale, N.Y. , c1987. xv, 412 p. ; ISBN 0-916592-71-5 (loose-leaf) LC Card 87-22258 DDC 658.3/01 19
HF5549 .I5643 1987

Institute for National Economic and Social Dialogue (U. S.) Sealy, Albert H. Macro blueprint . New York , 1986. viii, 407, 232 p. ; ISBN 0-89192-390-X LC Card 86-218989 DDC 338.973 19
HD2785 .S412 1986

Institute for Policy Studies. Dirt rich, dirt poor . New York , 1986. xii, 188 p. ; ISBN 0-7102-0378-0 LC Card 85-8274 DDC 338.1/9/73 19
HD1761 .D55 1986 ***NYPL [JLD 87-821]***

Institute for Research in History (New York, N. Y.) Groneman, Carol. [Corporate Ph. D.] Corporate PhD . New York, N.Y., U. S.A. , 1987, c1985. xx, 156 p. ; ISBN 0-14-010123-3 (pbk.) LC Card 86-30654 DDC 658.4/09 19
HD38.25.U6 G76 1987

Institute for Study of Regulation. Regulatory reform . Washington, D.C. , c1984. ii, 267 p. : ISBN 0-913097-02-0 (pbk.) LC Card 84-80846 DDC 363.6/0973 19
HD2766 .R357 1984

Institute for Transport Studies (Series) .
(1) Savage, Ian, 1960- The deregulation of bus services /. Aldershot, Hampshire, England , Brookfield, Vt., U. S.A. , c1985. xx, 267 p. : ISBN 0-566-05051-X : LC Card 85-17650 DDC 388.3/22 19
HE5663.A6 S33 1985 ***NYPL [JLD 87-123]***

(2) Douglas, Neil J., 1959- A welfare assessment of transport deregulation . Aldershot, Hampshire, England , Brookfield, Vt., USA , c1987. xxiv, 349 p. : ISBN 0-566-05350-0 : LC Card 86-25703 DDC 388.3/22/0941 19
HE5663.A6 D68 1987

(3) Mackie, Peter J., 1947- The British transport industry and the European Community . Aldershot, Hampshire, England , Brookfield, Vt., U. S.A. , c1987. xvi, 184 p. : ISBN 0-566-05368-3 : LC Card 86-24186 DDC 380.5/24/0941 19
HE199.G5 M33 1987

Institute for World Economics of the Hungarian Academy of Science. see Magyar Tudományos Akadémia, Budapest. Világgazdasági Kutató Intézet.

Institute newsletter. Stirrings of culture /. Dallas, Tex. , 1986. xix, 250 p. ; ISBN 0-911005-07-2 : LC Card 86-24028 DDC 306 19
HM101 .S786 1986 ***NYPL [JFF 87-151]***

Institute of Actuaries (Great Britain) McCutcheon, J. J. (John J.) An introduction to the mathematics of finance /. London , 1986. x, 463 p. : ISBN 0-434-91224-7 (pbk.) : LC Card 86-219539 DDC 332/.01/51 19
HF5691 .M385 1986

Institute of Agriculture, Bogor, Indonesia. see Institut Pertanian Bogor.

Institute of Bankers (Great Britain) Financing new technology . London , 1984. 124 p. : ISBN 0-85297-126-5 (pbk.) LC Card 86-117401 DDC 338.6/041 19
HG4027.6 .F55 1984 ***NYPL [JLD 87-1346]***

Institute of British Geographers. Rural Geography Study Group. The Industrialization of the countryside /. Norwich [Norfolk] , c1985. xiv, 315 p. : ISBN 0-86094-202-3 LC Card 87-141251 DDC 338.9/009173/4 19
HC256.6 .I524 1985

Institute of British Geographers. Study Group on Industrial Activity and Area Development. The Industrialization of the countryside /. Norwich [Norfolk] , c1985. xiv, 315 p. : ISBN 0-86094-202-3 LC Card 87-141251 DDC 338.9/009173/4 19
HC256.6 .I524 1985

Institute of Chartered Accountants in England and Wales. Chandler, John. Practical business planning /. London , New York , c1987. 210 p. ; ISBN 0-07-084172-1 (pbk.) : LC Card 87-3240 DDC 658.4/012 19
HD30.28 .C45 1987

Walsh, Brendan P., 1955- On-line information . Oxford, [Oxfordshire] , New York, NY, USA , 1987. xli, 327 p. : ISBN 0-631-15543-0 : LC Card 87-13154 DDC 025/.04/02465 19
HF5548.2 .W294 1987

Institute of Chartered Financial Analysts. CFA readings in fixed income securities analysis /. Charlottesville, VA (P.O. Box 3668, Charlottesville, VA 22903) , c1985. v, 255 p. :
NYPL [JLF 86-1994]

Financial Analysts Federation. Standards of practice handbook . Charlottesville, Va. , New York, N.Y. , 1986. xii, 150 p. ; ISBN 0-938367-03-X (pbk.) : LC Card 87-138043 DDC 174/.9332 19
HG4921 .F38 1986

Management Skills for Investment Managers Seminar (1982 : Washington, D.C.) Management Skills for Investment Managers Seminar . Charlottesville, Va. (P.O. Box 3668, Charlottesville 22903) , c1983. vi, 62 p. : LC Card 83-244808 DDC 658.1/52 19
HG4621 .M36 1982 ***NYPL [JLF 87-425]***

Quantitative methods for financial analysis /. Homewood, Ill. , c1987. xv, 229 p. : ISBN 0-87094-978-0 LC Card 86-72275 DDC 332.6/01/51 19
HG4515.3 .Q36 1987

Institute of Company Secretaries of India. Directorate of Research. Foreign collaborations . New Delhi , 1986. xii, 362 p. ; LC Card 86-903089 DDC 332.6/73/0954 19
HG5732 .F67 1986

Institute of Comparative Culture business series bulletin .
(no. 100) Ballon, Robert J. Salary administration in Japan . Tokyo , 1985. 44 p. ; ISBN 4-88168-100-1 LC Card 86-115944 DDC 331.2/952 19
HD5077 .B3454 1985

Institute of Cost and Management Accountants. Allen, David. Funds flow management . London , 1980. x, 84 p. :
NYPL [JLD 86-2760]

Institute of Cost & Management Accountants of Pakistan. National Conference of Management Accountants (1981 : Karachi, Pakistan) National Conference of Management Accountants . [Karachi] [1981?] 141 p. in various pagings ; LC Card 82-930763 DDC 658.1/511 19
HF5603 .N34 1981 ***NYPL [JLF 87-296]***

Institute of Electrical and Electronics Engineers. Computer Society. see IEEE Computer Society.

Institute of Electrical and Electronics Engineers. Engineering Management Society. see IEEE Engineering Management Society.

Institute of Family Studies monograph .
(no. 4) Burke, Terry, 1942- A roof over their

heads . Melbourne , 1984. xiv, 178 p. : ISBN 0-642-87172-8 ***NYPL [JLD 86-2639]***

Institute of Governmental Studies research report .
(86-2) Aroni, Samuel. How successful was Section 8 in Los Angeles? . Berkeley , 1986. 18 p. ; ISBN 0-87772-311-7 (pbk.) LC Card 86-27180 DDC 363.5/8 19
HD7288.85.U62 L73 1986

Institute of Industrial Engineers (1981-) Joint Seminar on Designing Jobs for Handicapped Workers (1985 : Chicago, Ill.) Designing jobs for handicapped workers . Hot Springs, Ark. (P.O. Box 1358, Hot Spring 71902) [1986] 66 p. : LC Card 86-622317 DDC 658.3/045 19
HD7256.U5 J65 1985

Institute of Interdisciplinary Studies. see **InterStudy (Center)**

Institute of Internal Auditors. Sawyer, Lawrence B. The practice of modern internal auditing /. Altamonte Springs, Fla. , 1981. xiv, 882 p. : ISBN 0-89413-092-7 LC Card 87-462054 DDC 657/.458 19
HF5668.25 .S28 1981

The Institute of Internal Auditors reports on fraud : two reports / prepared by the Institute of Internal Auditors for the National Commission on Fraudulent Financial Reporting. Altamonte Springs, Fla. : The Institute, c1987. xv, 74 p. : ill. ; 28 cm. "September 1986." ISBN 0-89413-164-8 (pbk.) LC Card 87-401942 DDC 657/.3 19
1. Corporations - Accounting. 2. Corporations - Accounting - Corrupt practices. 3. Fraud. 4. Auditing, Internal. I. National Commission on Fraudulent Financial Reporting (U. S.). II. Title: Reports on fraud.
HF5686.C7 I53 1987

Institute of Internal Auditors Research Foundation. Wilson, James A., 1928- Managing the behavioral dynamics of internal auditing /. Altamonte Springs, Fla. [1985] xii, 112 p. : ISBN 0-89413-130-3 (pbk.) LC Card 85-169744 DDC 657/.458/019 19
HF5668.25 .W53 1985 ***NYPL [JLE 86-4318]***

Institute of Latin American Studies, Stockholm. see **Latinamerika-institutet i Stockholm.**

Institute of Management in Government (Kerala, India) Issues in teaching of economics in Indian universities /. New Delhi , c1987. vii, 145 p. ; ISBN 81-204-0203-0 : LC Card 87-901784 DDC 330/.07/1154 19
HB74.9.I4 I88 1987

Institute of Manpower Studies (Great Britain) Rajan, Amin, 1942- Services--the second industrial revolution? . London , Boston , 1987. xviii, 257 p. : ISBN 0-408-02003-2 LC Card 86-32739 DDC 331.12/9042 19
HD9982.5 .R34 1987

UK occupation and employment trends to 1990 . London , Boston , 1986. xxiv, 249 p. : ISBN 0-408-02980-3 : LC Card 86-13617 DDC 331.12/0941 19
HD5765.A6 U38 1986 ***NYPL [JLE 86-4156]***

Institute of Mathematics and Its Applications. Analysing conflict and its resolution . Oxford [Oxfordshire] , New York , 1987. xvi, 349 p. : ISBN 0-19-853611-9 : LC Card 86-31108 DDC 658.4 19
HD42 .A52 1987

The Institute of Mathematics and Its Applications conference series .
(new ser., 8) Analysing conflict and its resolution . Oxford [Oxfordshire] , New York , 1987. xvi, 349 p. : ISBN 0-19-853611-9 : LC Card 86-31108 DDC 658.4 19
HD42 .A52 1987

Institute of Petroleum (Great Britain). Energy Economics Group. Economics of the retail petroleum market . London , c1986. i, 79 p. : LC Card 87-134547 DDC 381/.4566553827/0941 19
HD9579.G5 G63 1986

Institute of Property Taxation (Washington, D. C.) Property taxation /. Washington, D.C. , c1987. 1 v. (various pagings) ; LC Card 87-3326 DDC 336.22/0973 19
HJ4120 .P6717 1987

Institute of Public Administration (Dublin, Dublin) Public expenditure . Dublin, Ireland , 1986. 138 p. ; ISBN 0-906980-56-9 (pbk.) : LC Card 86-143826 DDC 336.3/9 19
HJ7461 .P83 1986 ***NYPL [JLD 87-553]***

Institute of Real Management monographs. Series on specific property types.
Holland, Barbara Kamanitz. Managing single-family homes /. Chicago, Ill. , c1987. xiv, 155 p. ; ISBN 0-912104-92-9 (pbk.) LC Card 87-81672 DDC 333.33/8 19
HD1394 .H63 1987

Institute of Social Change and Social Welfare (Calcutta, India) Movement for a no poverty society . Calcutta , 1980. 78 p. ; LC Card 81-902107
HC415.P6 M68 1980

Institute of Social Studies (Netherlands) Pobreza, participación y desarrollo regional /. [Bogotá, D.E., Colombia] , 1986. 536 p. : LC Card 87-103266
HC125 .P6 1986

The Re-emergence of the Chinese peasantry . London , New York , c1987. ix, 277 p. : LC Card 87-5373 DDC 305.5/63 19
HD1537.C5 R4 1987

Institute of Southeast Asian Studies. ASEAN Economic Research Unit. ASEAN-U. S. economic relations . Singapore , c1986. x, 54 p. : ISBN 997-19-8842-9 (pbk.) LC Card 87-940002 DDC 337.59073 19
HF1456.5.A7 A84 1986

Institute of Strategic and International Studies (Malaysia)
Mukerjee, Dilip. Primary commodities . Kuala Lumpur, Malaysia , c1985. 39 p. ; ISBN 967-99974-7-2 (pbk.) : LC Card 87-105669 DDC 338/.02 19
HF1040.7 .M85 1985

U. S. ASEAN relations . Washington, D.C. , 1987. xxii, 222 p. ; ISBN 0-943057-00-0 (pbk.) LC Card 87-50526 DDC 337.59073 19
HF1456.5.A7 U72 1987

Institute of Transportation Engineers. Stover, Vergil G., 1933- Transportation and land development /. Englewood Cliffs, N.J. , c1988. xiii, 239 p. : ISBN 0-13-930413-4 : LC Card 87-11419 DDC 625.7/25 19
HE335 .S76 1988

Institution of Civil Engineers, London. Computer technology in construction . London , 1985. 308 p. : ISBN 0-7277-0234-3 LC Card 85-670263 DDC 338.4/5624 19
HD9715.G72 C64 1985
NYPL [JLE 86-2586]

Institution of Electronic and Radio Engineers. International Conference on Networks and Electronic Office Systems (1983 : University of Reading) Networks and electronic office systems . London , c1983. 240 p. : ISBN 0-903748-52-5 ***NYPL [JSG 86-298]***

Technology management '85 . London , c1985. 160 p. : ISBN 0-903748-61-4
NYPL [JLG 87-124]

Institution of Electronics and Radio Engineers. International Conference on Networks and Electronic Office Systems (1985 : London, England) Networks and electronic office systems . London , c1985. 166 p. : ISBN 0-903748-60-6 ***NYPL [JSG 86-264]***

Institution of Surveyors Malaysia. The Management and development of natural resources . London [1985] 192 p. : ISBN 0-903577-33-X (pbk.) LC Card 86-206154 DDC 333.7 19
HC13 .M35 1985

Institution of Works Managers. (Old Catalog form: Institution of Works Managers, ltd., London)
Industrial management education in the Commonwealth . London, England [1976] 38 p. ; LC Card 85-100411 DDC 658/.007/11171241 19
HD70.D44 I5 1976

Institutional credit for agriculture in India /. Pany, Raj Kishor. New Delhi , 1985. xxi, 483 p. : ISBN 81-7024-009-3 : LC Card 85-904046 DDC 332.7/1/095413 19
HD2075.O7 P36 1985

Institutional development . Israel, Arturo. Baltimore , 1987. x, 214 p. : ISBN 0-8018-3554-2 : LC Card 87-45494 DDC 338.9/009172/4 19
HC59.72.E44 I77 1987

Institutional development and technical assistance in macro-economic policy formulation . Kjellstrom, Sven B., 1945- Washington, D.C., U. S.A. [1987] 69 p. ; ISBN 0-8213-0919-6 (pbk.) LC Card 87-14021 DDC 339.5/0966/81 19
HC1015 .K58 1987

INSTITUTIONAL ECONOMICS.
Elsner, Wolfram. Ökonomische Institutionenanalyse . Berlin , c1986. xv, 469 p. : ISBN 3-428-06035-0 LC Card 86-206447
HB99.5 .E47 1986

Gruchy, Allan Garfield, 1906- The reconstruction of economics . New York , 1987. xx, 173 p. ; ISBN 0-313-25679-9 (lib. bdg. : alk. paper) LC Card 86-25721 DDC 330 19
HB99.5 .G79 1987

Kozlova, K. B. Institut͡sionalizm v amerikanskoĭ politėkonomii . Moskva , 1987. 214, [2] p. ; LC Card 87-159642
HB99.5 .K69 1987

Tool, Marc R. Essays in social value theory . Armonk, N.Y. , c1986. xviii, 203 p. ; ISBN 0-87332-382-3 : LC Card 86-10163 DDC 306 19
HB99.5 .T66 1986 ***NYPL [JLE 86-3931]***

Williamson, Oliver E. The economic institutions of capitalism . New York , London , 1987, c1985. xiv, 450 p. : ISBN 0-02-934821-8 (pbk.) LC Card 87-11901 DDC 338.7 19
HB99.5 .W55 1987

INSTITUTIONAL ECONOMICS - ADDRESSES, ESSAYS, LECTURES.
Eichner, Alfred S. Toward a new economics . Armonk, N.Y. , c1985. ix, 240 p. : ISBN 0-87332-326-2 LC Card 84-27724 DDC 330 19
HB171 .E35 1985 ***NYPL [JLE 86-1977]***

Macroeconomic conflict and social institutions /. Cambridge, Mass. , c1985. xi, 249 p. : ISBN 0-88730-034-0 LC Card 84-24376 DDC 339.2 19
HC79.I5 M225 1985 ***NYPL [JLE 86-2562]***

Institutional financing and industrial growth . Gupta, S. C., 1954- Jaipur , 1987. xx, 316 p. (some folded) : LC Card 87-900864
HD9886.I42 G83 1987

Institutional financing of Indian agriculture . Kumar, Kewal. New Delhi , c1987. 232 p. : LC Card 87-900911 DDC 332.7/1/09542 19
HG2051.I5 N354 1987

Institutional investment in renewable energy technologies /. Fenn, Scott. Washington, D.C. , c1987. iii, 50 p. : ISBN 0-930135-17-1 (pbk.) LC Card 87-401940 DDC 332.6/722 19
HD9502.U52 F46 1987

INSTITUTIONAL INVESTMENTS - BRAZIL.
Pinto, Antônio Carlos Figueiredo. Investidores institucionais . Rio de Janeiro , 1985. 74 p. : LC Card 86-140523
HG5332 .P56 1985

INSTITUTIONAL INVESTMENTS - UNITED STATES.
Equity performance 1977-1986 . Washington, D.C. , c1987. 28, [A-Q] p. : LC Card 87-159010 DDC 332.1/754/0973 19
HG1616.I5 E68 1987

Fenn, Scott. Institutional investment in renewable energy technologies /. Washington, D.C. , c1987. iii, 50 p. : ISBN 0-930135-17-1 (pbk.) LC Card 87-401940 DDC 332.6/722 19
HD9502.U52 F46 1987

Mathiasen, Karen. Corporate governance and shareholder rights . Washington, DC (1755 Massachusetts Ave., N.W., Suite 600, Washington 20036) , c1986. 96 p. ; LC Card 86-230362 DDC 346.73/0666 347.306666 19
HD2743 .M34 1986

INSTITUTIONS, ASSOCIATIONS, ETC. see **ASSOCIATIONS, INSTITUTIONS, ETC.**

INSTITUTIONS, CHARITABLE AND PHILANTHROPIC. see **CHARITIES.**

Institutions de réadaptation sociale et professionnelle. Social and vocational rehabilitation resources . Geneve , 1984- v. ; ISBN 92-2-003776-9 (pbk. : v. 1) LC Card

86-126143 DDC 362/.0425 19
HD7255 .S62 1984 ***NYPL [JLL 85-184]***

INSTITUTIONS, INTERNATIONAL. see **INTERNATIONAL COOPERATION.**

Instituto Boliviano de Estudios Empresariales. Bolivia frente a la crisis del estaño . La Paz, Bolivia [1986] 62 p. ; LC Card 86-189109
HD9539.T6 B646 1986 ***NYPL [JLC 87-146]***

Instituto Brasileiro de Administração Municipal. Encontro de Trabalho sobre Descentralização dos Serviços Municipais (1983 : Rio de Janeiro, Brazil) Relatório final /. [Rio de Janeiro] [1983] 60 leaves ; LC Card 84-160735
HD4634 .E53 1983

Instituto Brasileiro de Economia. Centro de Estudos Agrícolas. Balanço e disponibilidade interna de gêneros alimentícios de origem vegetal 1975 a 1980 /. Rio de Janeiro, RJ, Brasil , 1983. 72 p. ; ***NYPL [JLG 85-94]***

Instituto Brasileiro de Relações do Trabalho. Relaciones colectivas del trabajo en América Latina. Portuguese. As relações coletivas de trabalho na América Latina . São Paulo . 327 p. ; LC Card 87-151930 DDC 331/.098 19
HD8110.5 .R3817 1985

Instituto Centroamericano de Administración Pública. (Old Catalog form: Instituto Centroamericano de Administration Publica, San José, Costa Rica)
La Política tributaria en Latinoamérica . Washington, D.C. , 1986. ix, 180 p. ; ISBN 0-8270-2496-7 (pbk.) LC Card 87-403563 DDC 336.2/0098 19
HJ3374.5 .P65 1986

Instituto Chileno de Educación Cooperativa. Manual de interpretación de estados financieros /. [Santiago, Chile] [1984] 49 p. : LC Card 85-150204
HD2965 .M35 1984

Instituto Colombiano de Administración. La Industria colombiana y la "ALALC.". [Medellín] [1964] 112 p. ; LC Card 85-111774
HC197 .I36 1964

Instituto Colombiano de la Reforma Agraria. Departamento de Estudios Técnicos. (Old Catalog form: Colombia. Instituto Colombiano de la Reforma Agraria. Estudio Técnicos, Departamento de)
Informe general y proyecto de parcelación, Antioquia # 2 (Barbosa y Santo Domingo) /. Bogotá, D.E. , 1964. 2, 73, 16 leaves, [1] leaf of plates : LC Card 85-107102
HD1476.C72 B375 1964

Instituto Colombiano de la Reforma Agraria. Estudios Técnicos, Departamento de. see **Instituto Colombiano de la Reforma Agraria. Departamento de Estudios Técnicos.**

Instituto de Análise da Conjuntura e Estudos de Planeamento (Portugal) La Conjoncture économique en Europe . Lisboa, Portugal [1982] 78 p. : LC Card 83-181663
HC240 .C588 1982

INSTITUTO DE APRENDIZAJE INDUSTRIAL (ORURO, BOLIVIA)
Alaix, Ramón. Experiencias de educación y producción de fe y alegría en Oruro y Santa Cruz . La Paz, Bolivia , 1986. 191 p. ; LC Card 86-208411 DDC 331.25/92/098413 19
HD5715.5.B52 S262 1986

Instituto de Capacitación Agraria (Mexico) Unidad Agrícola Industrial para la Mujer /. [Mexico City] , 1981. 45 p. : LC Card 84-228117
HD6073.A29 M68 1981

Instituto de Ciencias Sociales (Barcelona, Spain) Televisió, federalisme. Barcelona [1986] 209 p. ; LC Card 86-210066
HE8700.9.S63 T44 1986

Instituto de Cooperación Iberoamericana (Madrid, Spain) Promoción de las exportaciones no tradicionales . [Lima, Peru] . 145 p. ; LC Card 86-146920
HF1569 .P76 1985 ***NYPL [JLD 87-1165]***

Instituto de Crédito Oficial (Spain) Seminario sobre Consequencias para las Entidades Oficiales de Crédito de la Entrada de España en las Comunidades Europeas (1984 : Madrid, Spain) Seminario sobre Consequencias para las Entidades Oficiales de Crédito de la Entrada de España en las Comunidades Europeas /. [Madrid] [1984?] 270 p. ; ISBN 84-505-0963-7 LC Card 85-186710
HG1642.E86 S46 1984

Instituto de Desenvolvimento de Pernambuco. Apoio ao setor informal da economia de Pernambuco . Recife , 1985. 135 p. : LC Card 87-403615 DDC 381 19
HD2346.B72 P473 1985

Construção de habitações na zona rural da microrregião do São Francisco /. Recife , 1982. 23 leaves ; LC Card 86-175009
HD7289.B72 S263 1982

Instituto de Desenvolvimento Industrial de Minas Gerais. Seminários sobre Perspectivas dos Setores Produtivos de Minas Gerais (1986 : Belo Horizonte, Brazil) Seminários sobre Perspectivas dos Setores Produtivos de Minas Gerais . Belo Horizonte , 1986. 124 leaves ; LC Card 87-108000 DDC 338.0981/51 19
HC188.M6 S46 1986

Instituto de Economia da UNICAMP. Centro Acadêmico. Getúlio Vargas e a economia contemporânea /. Campinas , 1986. 179 p. ; ISBN 85-26-80033-7 LC Card 87-403048 DDC 330.981/063 19
HC187 .G45 1986

Instituto de Empresa. El Mercado hipotecario . Madrid , 1984. 162 p. ; ISBN 84-85669-34-7 LC Card 86-211862
HG2040.5.S7 M47 1984

Instituto de Estudios de Población y Desarrollo (ADPBF) Gómez, Carmen. Población y energía en la República Dominicana, 1990-2000. Santo Domingo, República Dominicana [1985] vi, 86 p. : LC Card 86-176044
HD9502.D652 G65 1985

Instituto de Estudios Ibero-Americanos, Stockholm. see **Latinamerika-institutet i Stockholm.**

Instituto de Estudios Latinoamericanos (Buenos Aires, Argentina) Argentina 1984 . [Buenos Aires?] [1984] 95 p. ; LC Card 85-132860
HJ8569 .A75 1984

Instituto de Estudios Políticos, Madrid. see **Instituto de Estudios Políticos (Spain)**

Instituto de Estudios Políticos para América Latina y Africa. Manifiesto contra el hambre en el mundo. Madrid , c1985. 95 p. ; ISBN 84-85436-23-7 (IEPALA) LC Card 86-165078
HD9018.D44 M35 1985
NYPL [JLD 87-1535]

Instituto de Estudios Políticos (Spain) (Old Catalog form: Instituto de Estudios Políticos, Madrid)
La Empresa. Madrid , 1962. 348 p. : LC Card 85-108024
HD2326 .E47 1962

Instituto de Formación y Capacitación (Bolivia) Taboada Terán, Néstor. Historia de las luchas sociales y el movimiento obrero en Bolivia /. Cochabamba, Bolivia , 1983- v. <1-3 > : LC Card 86-203884 DDC 331.88/0984 19
HD8275 .T32 1983

Instituto de Gestão Financeira das Empresas Públicas (Portugal). Comissão Instaladora. Relatório da Comissão Instaladora do Instituto de Gestão Financeira das Empresas Públicas : (elaborado nos termos do no. 2 da Resolução do Conselho de Ministros no. 17/83, Díario da República, 1a. série, de 23 de Janeiro). Lisboa : Imprensa Nacional-Casa de Moeda, 1984. 81 p. ; 21 cm. At head of title: Ministério das Finanças e do Plano. LC Card 84-240299
1. Government business enterprises - Portugal - Finance. I. Title.
HD4248 .I57 1984

Instituto de Historia del Movimiento Comunista y de la Revolución Socialista de Cuba. Historia del movimiento obrero cubano, 1865-1958 /. La Habana , 1985- v. <1 > ; LC Card 87-401462
HD6577 .H57 1985

Torras de la Luz, Jacinto, 1909-1963. [Selections. 1984.] Obras escogidas /. La Habana , 1984- v. <1 > : LC Card 87-125434 DDC 338.97291 19
HC152.5 .T662 1984

Instituto de Investigação Cientifica de Moçambique, Lourenço Marquez. see **Lourenço Marquez (City). Instituto de Investigação Cientifica de Moçambique.**

Instituto de Investigación UNSAAC-NUFFIC. Cori Castro, Wilfredo. Mercados y precios en la economía campesina . [Cuzco, Peru] , 1986. 29 p. : LC Card 86-200941
HC228.C8 C59 1986

Díaz Gómez, Jorge. Deterioro de los términos de intercambio, migración eventual y pobreza campesina en el departamento del Cusco /. [Cuzco, Peru] , 1986. 17, 3 leaves, 2 leaves of plates : LC Card 86-200938
HD1531.P4 D52 1986

Sotomayor, Octavio. Racionalidad campesina y cambio técnico /. Cusco , 1985. 23 p. ; LC Card 86-200944
HD1531.P4 S67 1985

Instituto de Investigaciones Cambio y Desarrollo (Peru) Promoción de las exportaciones no tradicionales . [Lima, Peru] . 145 p. ; LC Card 86-146920
HF1569 .P76 1985 ***NYPL [JLD 87-1165]***

Instituto de Investigaciones Económicas y Sociales (Managua, Nicaragua) Gariazzo, Alicia. El café en Nicaragua . Managua, Nicaragua , 1984. 175 p. : LC Card 85-192390
HD9199.N52 G37 1984
NYPL [JLF 86-1521]

Instituto de Investigaciones Estadísticas (Cuba) Evolución de la fecundidad de la mujer cubana en el período 1959-1984. [Havana?] , 1985. 110 p. : LC Card 87-404207 DDC 304.6/32/097291 19
HB959 .E96 1985

Instituto de Investigaciones sobre la Cuestión Judía (Series) .

INSTITUTO DE MERCADEO AGROPECUARIO (COLOMBIA)
Isaza Tobón, Gabriela. El IDEMA, hacia una pérdida de los objetivos sociales. [Colombia? , between 1984 and 1987] ([Colombia?] : Litoarte) 126 p., [1] leaf of plates : LC Card 87-404223 DDC 381/.41/09861 19
HD9014.C72 I8 1984

Instituto de Planejamento Econômico e Social. Instituto de Pesquisas. Perspectivas de longo prazo da economia brasileira /. [Rio de Janeiro, RJ] , 1985. 363 p. : LC Card 86-164342
HC187 .P415 1985

Serie Estudos para o planejamento. see **Serie Estudos para o planejamento.**

Instituto de Promoción Económico-Social del Uruguay. Producción y comercialización porcina en Uruguay . Montevideo , 1986. 91 p. : LC Card 87-401290 DDC 338.1/764/009895 19
HD9435.U82 P76 1986

Instituto de Reforma de las Estructuras Comerciales (Spain) Implicaciones para el sector comercio de la integración de España en el Mercado Común . [Madrid] [1979?] 106 p. ; LC Card 81-116650
HC241.25.S6 I48 1979

Instituto del Café de Costa Rica. Departamento de Estudios Agrícolas y Económicos. Rojas Rojas, Edgar. Indices de eficiencia económica para la industria beneficiadora de café . San José, Costa Rica , 1986. 14 leaves : LC Card 87-403520 DDC 338.1/6 19
HD9199.C82 R65 1986

Instituto Euvaldo Lodi.
Política salarial. [Rio de Janeiro] [19]85. 31 leaves ; LC Card 86-152437
HD5004 .P65 1985

Instituto Euvaldo Lodi. Núcleo Regional do Ceará.
Casimiro, Liana Maria Carleial de. Avaliação da política industrial do Ceará . Fortaleza , 1983. 58 p. ; LC Card 86-129541
HD3616.B84 C422 1983

Vianna, Pedro Jorge Ramos. Inflação vs. indexação, uma contribuição ao tema /. Fortaleza-Ceará [19]84. 121 p. : LC Card 86-130092
HG835 .V53 1984

Instituto Gulbendian de Ciência. Centro de Estudos de Economia Agrária. Prospective evolution of EEC common agricultural policy .

Lisboa , Oeiras , 1985. 122 p. : LC Card 86-221785
HD1920.5.Z8 P77 1985

Instituto Interamericano de Ciencias Agricolas. see **Inter-American Institute of Agricultural Sciences.**

Instituto Interamericano de Mercados de Capital. Bolsas de valores en América Latina y el Caribe. Caracas, Venezuela , 1985. 401 p. : LC Card 86-154738
HG5160.5 .B65 1985 ***NYPL [JLE 87-523]***

Mercados de capital en América Latina y el Caribe . Caracas, Venezuela [1986] 114 p. ; LC Card 87-103358
HG5160.5.A3 M47 1986

Instituto Internacional de Hacienda Pública. see **International Institute of Public Finance.**

Instituto Internacional de las Cajas de Ahorro. see **International Savings Banks Institute.**

Instituto Italo-Latino Americano. see **Istituto italo-latino americano.**

Instituto Latinoamericano de Estudios Sociales. Catholic Church. Pope (1978- : John Paul II) [Laborem exercens. Spanish.] Juan Pablo II y el trabajo . [Santiago, Chile] , 1984. 135 p. ; LC Card 85-197537
HD6338 .C277 1984

Instituto Latinoamericano de Planificación Económica y Social. see **Latin American Institute for Economic and Social Planning.**

Instituto Latinoamericano de Planificación Económica y Social (ILPES) . Latin American Institute for Economic and Social Planning. [Santiago, Chile] [1984] iii, 52 p. ; LC Card 84-202400
HD77.5.L29 L38 1984

Instituto Latinoamericano del Fierro y el Acero. The urgent need of Latin America to export steel [microform]. Santiago, Chile : Instituto Latinoamericano del Fierro y el Acero, Secretaría General, [1983?] 20 p. : ill. ; 30 cm. Microfilm. New York : New York Public Library, 1986. 1 microfilm reel ; 35 mm. (MN *ZZ-26,374) LC Card 84-244660 DDC 382/.45669142/098 19
1. Steel industry and trade - Latin America. 2. Export marketing - Latin America. 3. Latin America - Commerce - United States. 4. United States - Commerce - Latin America. I. Title.
HD9524.L32 I57 1983
NYPL [*ZT-1708 no.49]

Instituto Libertad y Democracia (Lima, Peru) Las Leyes de estabilidad laboral y sus efectos económicos /. Lima, Perú [1986?] 67 p. : LC Card 87-403254 DDC 331.11/0985 19
HD8344 .L49 1986

Soto, Hernando de, 1941- El otro sendero . [Lima] , 1986. xxxvi, 317 p. : LC Card 87-400476 DDC 381 19
HD2346.P4 S67 1986

Instituto Mexicano del Seguro Social. (Old Catalog form: Mexico. Seguro Social, Instituto del)

Instituto Mexicano del Seguro Social. Centro de Documentación.
Enfermedades de trabajo. México, D.F. , c1983. 403 p. : ISBN 968-8242-08-X LC Card 85-216152
HD7262.5.M6 E54 1983

Planeación familiar y cambio demográfico. México, D.F. [1983], c1982. 554 p. : ISBN 968-8241-63-6 LC Card 84-227488 DDC 304.6/0972 19
HB3531 .P57 1983 ***NYPL [JLE 86-3248]***

Instituto Mexicano del Seguro Social. Departamento de Asuntos Internacionales. Cohen, Noemí. Trabajadores y seguridad social en América Latina /. México, D.F. [1982], c1981. 146 p. ; ISBN 968-8241-38-5 LC Card 83-140620 DDC 368.4/0098 19
HD7130.5 .C63 1982 ***NYPL [JLD 86-2768]***

Instituto Mexicano del Seguro Social. Jefatura de Servicios de Planificación Familiar. Planeación familiar y cambio demográfico. México, D.F. [1983], c1982. 554 p. : ISBN 968-8241-63-6 LC Card 84-227488 DDC 304.6/0972 19
HB3531 .P57 1983 ***NYPL [JLE 86-3248]***

Instituto Mexicano Matías Romero de Estudios Diplomáticos. The U. S.-Mexico border region . [El Paso] , 1984, c1982. viii, 446 p. : ISBN 0-87404-091-4 (pbk.) LC Card 87-401861 DDC 333.7/0972/1 19
HC137.M46 U17 1984

Instituto Nacional de Antropología (Argentina). Asociación Amigos. Proyecto Paraná Medio . Buenos Aires , 1985. 44 leaves : LC Card 86-218225
HD8039.F66 A746 1985

Instituto Nacional de Assistência Médica da Previdência Social (Brazil) Fonseca, Aloysio de Salles. Reorientação da assistência à saúde no âmbito da previdência social . [Brasília] , 1983. 67 p. ; LC Card 86-171863
HD7102.B7 F66 1983

Instituto Nacional de Carnes (Uruguay). Dirección de Comercialización. Uruguay, producción y comercialización de ganado y carnes. [Montevideo, Uruguay] , 1985. 90 p. : LC Card 87-403154 DDC 338.1/760883/09895 19
HD9424.U8 U783 1985

Instituto Nacional de Carnes (Uruguay). Dirección de Estudios Económicos. Uruguay, producción y comercialización de ganado y carnes. [Montevideo, Uruguay] , 1985. 90 p. : LC Card 87-403154 DDC 338.1/760883/09895 19
HD9424.U8 U783 1985

Instituto Nacional de Colonização e Reforma Agraria.
1o. plano nacional de reforma agrária da Nova República : 1o. PNRA-NR (1985-1989) / Ministério da Reforma e do Desenvolvimento Agrário, MIRAD, Instituto Nacional de Colonização e Reforma Agrária, INCRA. Brasília, DF : O Instituto, 1985. 73 leaves : ill. ; 30 cm. LC Card 86-225850
1. Land reform - Brazil. I. Title. II. Title: Primeiro plano nacional de reforma agrária da Nova República.
HD1333.B6 I54 1985

Instituto Nacional de Colonização e Reforma Agrária. Diretoria de Cadastro e Tributação. Estatísticas cadastrais . Brasília , 1985- <v. 1-2; in 2 > : LC Card 87-117732
HD498 .E77 1985

Instituto Nacional de Estadística (Bolivia). División de Estadísticas Productivas. Código de productos y materias primas /. La Paz, Bolivia , 1981. 129 leaves ; LC Card 85-129059
HF1044.B5 C63 1981

Instituto Nacional de Estadística (Bolivia). División de Población y Vivienda. Estimación de la población potencialmente votante al 1o de julio de 1985 según departamentos, provincias, ciudades capital y cantones /. La Paz, Bolivia , 1985. 58 p. : LC Card 87-400543 DDC 304.6/0984/021 19
HA965 .E85 1985

Instituto Nacional de Estadística, Geografía e Informática (Mexico)
Estructura económica del Estado de [name of state] . México, D.F. [s.l.] , c1985-<c1987. v. <[1-7] > : ISBN 968-89202-6-6 (v. [1]) LC Card 86-229829
HC140.I5 E88 1985

Indicadores de la migración en México. México, D.F. , 1985. ix, 161 p. ; ISBN 968-89200-3-7 LC Card 86-217222
HB1991 .I55 1985

La Industria textil y del vestido en México, 1970-1982. México, D.F. , 1984. 77 p. : ISBN 968-8097-69-1 LC Card 85-203070 DDC 338.4/7677/00972021 19
HD9864.M62 I53 1984 ***NYPL [JLF 87-363]***

Mexico, a synoptic view. México, D.F. , 1986. 46 p. : LC Card 87-105428 DDC 330.972/0834 19
HC135 .M54527 1986

Proyecciones de la población de México y de las entidades federativas, 1980-2010. México, D.F. , c1985. xiii, 134 p. ; ISBN 968-8097-66-7 LC Card 86-223751
HB3531 .P78 1985

El Sector alimentario en México. México, D.F. [1984] vii, 673 p. : ISBN 968-8099-93-7 LC Card 85-205385
HD9014.M62 S26 1984

El Sistema bancario y financiero en México, 1970-1984. México, D.F. , c1985. 260 p. ; ISBN 968-89204-0-1 LC Card 86-223773
HG2714 .S57 1985

Sistema de cuentas nacionales de México . México, D.F. , 1985. xiii, 577 p. : ISBN 968-89200-8-8 LC Card 87-401458 DDC 339.372 19
HC140.I5 S5725 1985

X censo general de población y vivienda, 1980 . México, D.F. , c1985- v. <1-6 > : ISBN 968-8099-30-9 (v. 1) LC Card 86-226718
HA761.5 1980d

Instituto Nacional de Estadística (Peru). Dirección General de Demografía. Perú . Lima, Perú , 1984. 54 p. ; LC Card 86-111841 DDC 304.6/2/0985021 19
HA1055 .P46 1984 ***NYPL [JLG 86-190]***

Perú, proyecciones de población por años calendarios, según departamentos, provincias y distritos . Lima , 1985. 84 p. ; LC Card 86-173351
HA1064 .P49 1985

Instituto Nacional de Estadística (Spain) Censo agrario 1982 . Madrid , 1983. 104, 8 p. : ISBN 84-260-0803-8 LC Card 84-134551
HD2022 .C45 1983

Instituto Nacional de Estadística y Censos (Argentina)
Edificación, 1972-1984. Buenos Aires , 1986. 36 p. : LC Card 87-404780 DDC 338.4/7624/0982021 19
HD9715.A72 E35 1986

Evolución de la industria manufacturera, 1982-1984. Buenos Aires, República Argentina [1986] 115 p. : LC Card 86-226786
HD4999 .E95 1986

Exportaciones industriales . Buenos Aires, República Argentina [1987] 231 p. ; LC Card 87-405033 DDC 338.4/767/0982 19
HD9734.A7 E96 1987

Instituto Nacional de Estadísticas (Chile) XV censo nacional de población y IV de vivienda--Chile, Abril 1982. [Santiago] , <[1983]-[1986]. <v. 3-14; in 15 > : LC Card 87-110013
HA994 1982d

XV Censo nacional de población y IV de vivienda--Chile, abril 1982. [Santiago] [1985-<1986]. v. <1-13 > : LC Card 87-109976
HA994 1982c

Instituto Nacional de Estatística (Portugal) Inquérito às rendas e a outras características das habitações arrendadas na cidade de Evora em 1955-56 /. Lisboa [1958] 26 p. : LC Card 85-185037
HA1571 .A32 no. 33 HD7288.85.P82E93

Instituto Nacional de Industria (Spain). Departamento de Industrias de la Alimentación. Plan de red de transportes frigoríficos en España / Presidencia de la República, Instituto Nacional de Industria, Departamento de Industrias de la Alimentación. Madrid : El Departamento, 1965. 188 p., [1] folded leaf of plates : ill. ; 30 cm. LC Card 85-107661
1. Refrigerated transport - Government policy - Spain. I. Title.
HE199.5.R43 I57 1965

Instituto Nacional de los Recursos Naturales Renovables y del Ambiente (Colombia) Política ambiental y desarrollo . [Bogotá, Colombia] , 1986. 221 p. : LC Card 86-207035
HC130.E5 P65 1986

Instituto Nacional de Planificación Económica. Departamento Industria. Remmes Lenicov, Jorge. La industria curtidora en Argentina . [Buenos Aires] , 1976. 46 leaves ; LC Card 86-157645
HD9780.A52 R45 1976

Instituto Nacional de Planificación (Peru) Aumento del ingreso y mejoramiento de las condiciones de trabajo del sector informal urbano en sietes ciudades del Perú /. [Lima, Perú?] , 1986. ii, 69, [25] leaves : LC Card 87-106249
HD2346.P4 A85 1986

Perú siglo XXI. [Lima] [1986 or 1987] 63 p. :

LC Card 87-403080 DDC 338.985 19
HC227 .P416 1986

Planificación por la revolución y la justicia. [Lima, Peru] [1986] 43 p. : LC Card 87-402212 DDC 338.985 19
HC227 .P536 1986

Sistema de planes de desarrollo de corto plazo, 1986. [Lima] : República Peruana, Presidencia de la República, Instituto Nacional de Planificación, [1986- v. <1-35 > : ill., maps ; 30 cm. Some v. cover title. Includes bibliographical references. CONTENTS. - [1] Plan departamental de desarrollo de Amazonas -- [2] Plan departamental de desarrollo de Ancash -- [3] Plan departamental de desarrollo de Apurimac -- [4] Plan departamental de desarrollo de Arequipa -- [5] Plan departamental de desarrollo del Callao (2 pts.) -- [6] Plan departamental de desarrollo del Cuzco -- [7] Plan departamental de desarrollo de Huancavelica -- [8] Plan departamental de desarrollo de Ica -- [9] Plan departamental de desarrollo de Lambayeque (2 pts.) -- [10] Plan departamental de desarrollo de La Libertad -- [11] Plan departamental de desarrollo de Lima -- [12] Plan departamental de desarrollo de Loreto -- [13] Plan departamental de desarrollo de Moquegua -- [14] Plan departamental de desarrollo de Pasco -- [15] Plan departamental de desarrollo de Piura -- [16] Plan departamental de desarrollo de Puno -- [17] Plan departamental de desarrollo de San Martín -- [18] Plan departamental de desarrollo de Tacna -- [19] Plan departamental de desarrollo de Tumbes -- [20] Plan nacional de desarrollo -- [21] Plan nacional de desarrollo, detalle del Programa Nacional de Cooperación Técnica Internacional -- [22] Plan nacional de desarrollo, Programa de Inversiones Públicas 1986 por provectos -- [23] Plan nacional de desarrollo, síntesis de los planes y programas prioritarios -- [24] Plan operativo del sector agrario -- [25] Plan operativo del sector comercio -- [26] Plan operativo del sector educación -- [27] Plan operativo del sector energía y minas -- [28] Plan operativo del sector industrias -- [29] Plan operativo del sector integración -- [30] Plan operativo del sector interior -- [31] Plan operativo del sector pesquería -- [32] Plan operativo del sector trabajo y promoción social -- [33] Plan operativo del sector transportes y comunicaciones -- [34] Plan operativo del sector turismo -- [35] Plan operativo del sector vivienda y construcción. LC Card 86-216851
1. Peru - Economic policy. 2. Regional planning - Peru. I. Title.
HC227 .I529 1986

Sistema de planes de desarrollo de mediano plazo. [Lima] [1987- v. <1-2 > : LC Card 87-404041 DDC 338.985 19
HC227 .S496 1987

Instituto Paraguayo de Estudios Geopolíticos e Internacionales. Política internacional, economía e integración /. Asunción del Paraguay [1985] 178 p. ; LC Card 86-122468
HF1523 .P65 1985

Instituto Português de Ensino a Distância. Centro de Estudos de História e Cultura Portuguesa. Reflexões sobre história e cultura portuguesa . Lisboa , 1985. 286 p. ; LC Card 86-135021 DDC 946.9 19
HC392 .R34 1985

Instituto Progresso Social e Democracia Francisco Sá Carneiro.
A Reforma do mercado de capitais. [Lisbon] [1985] 143 p. : LC Card 87-127037 DDC 332.63 19
HG4523 .R44 1985

A Televisão em Portugal. [Lisbon] [1985] 95 p. : LC Card 87-102704 DDC 384.55/4/09469 19
HE8700.9.P8 T45 1985

Instituto Regional de Ecología Andina. Sánchez Enríquez, Rodrigo. Organización andina, drama y posibilidad /. Huancayo, Perú [1987] xxii, 219 p. : LC Card 87-404025 DDC 330.98/0038 19
HC167.A5 S26 1987

Instituto Torcuato di Tella. External debt, savings, and growth in Latin America . Washington, D.C. , Buenos Aires , 1987. xv, 207 p. ; ISBN 0-939934-95-7 (pbk.) : LC Card 87-21422 DDC 336.3/435/098 19
HJ8514.5 .E984 1987

Instituts Solvay, Brussels. Institut de sociologie. see **Brussels. Université libre. Institut de sociologie.**

Instituts͡ionalizm v amerikanskoĭ politėkonomii . Kozlova, K. B. Moskva , 1987. 214, [2] p. ; LC Card 87-159642
HB99.5 .K69 1987

Institutul de Ekonomie (Akademii͡a de Shtiints͡e a RSSM) Organizats͡ionnye formy i metody upravlenii͡a proizvodstvom . Kishinev , 1980. 130 p. ; LC Card 81-140768
HD9015.S653 M6453 1980

Institutul de Istorie a Partiduluĭ (Moldavian S. S. R.) Agrarnai͡a politika KPSS v deĭstvii /. Kishinev , 1983. 202 p. ; LC Card 84-235869
HD1993 .A38 1983

Institutul de Studii Istorice și Social-Politice de pe lîngă C.C. al P.C.R.
Condițiile istorice ale apariției și dezvoltării clasei muncitoare din România . București , 1984. 652 p. ; LC Card 84-234192
HD8648 .C65 1984

Pătrășcanu, Lucrețiu, 1900-1954. Scrieri, articole, cuvîntări . București , 1983. 415 p. ; LC Card 84-144088
HC405 .P345 1983

Instituut voor sociologie, Brussels. see **Brussels. Université libre. Institut de sociologie.**

INSTRUCTION. see **EDUCATION.**

Instruction aux maires relative aux bulletins statistiques de l'état civil . France. Direction générale des collectivités locales. [Paris] [1983] 50 p. : LC Card 84-112361
HA37.F8 F73 1983

INSTRUCTIONAL MATERIALS INDUSTRY.
Industrial training products & services markets. Norwalk, Conn., U. S.A. (6 Prowitt St., Norwalk 06855) , c1987. vi, 174 leaves ; LC Card 87-153554 DDC 381/.45658312404 19
HD9811.A2 I53 1987

INSTRUCTIONAL SYSTEMS - DESIGN.
Rogoff, Rosalind Louise. The training wheel . New York , c1987. 151 p. : ISBN 0-471-83467-X LC Card 86-32409 DDC 658.3/12404 19
HF5549.5.T7 R565 1987

Instructor's manual, Practicing management, second edition /. Griffin, Ricky W. Boston , c1987. xiii, 167 p. ; ISBN 0-395-42585-9 (pbk.) LC Card 87-400618 DDC 658 19
HD31 .G7627 1987

INSTRUMENT INDUSTRY - SOVIET UNION - MANAGEMENT.
Kiselev, A. A. (Anatoliĭ Alekseevich) Ėkonomika, organizats͡ii͡a i planirovanie priborostroitel'nogo proizvodstva . Leningrad , 1985. 271 p. : LC Card 86-127609
HD9706.S652 K57 1985

Instrument Society of America. Project management. Chicago, Ill. , 1987, c1985. 1 videocassette (30 min.) : LC Card 87-705140 DDC 658.4 11
HD69.P75

Instrumental'nye sistemy modelirovanii͡a / [redaktor N.I. Viskina]. Moskva : Akademii͡a nauk SSSR, T͡Sentr. ėkonomiko-matematicheskiĭ in-t, 1983. 97 p. : ill. ; 21 cm. Includes bibliographies. LC Card 84-210491
1. Economics - Mathematical models - Data processing. I. Viskina, N. I. II. T͡Sentral'nyĭ ėkonomiko-matematicheskiĭ institut (Akademii͡a nauk SSSR).
HB143.5 .I57 1983

Instrumentariĭ ėkonomicheskoĭ nauki i praktiki . Rumi͡ant͡sev, Alekseĭ Matveevich. Moskva , 1985. 303 p. : LC Card 87-109217
HB61 .R86 1985

Instrumentelle Aspekte der Investitionsförderung . Uhlmann, Luitpold. München , 1986. vii, 270 p. : ISBN 3-88512-024-0 LC Card 86-215244 DDC 332.63 19
HG4028.C4 U367 1986

Instrumenten van het geld- en valutamarktbeleid in Nederland /. Dunnen, Emile den. Amsterdam , Deventer , 1985. 109 p. : ISBN 90-267-0955-2 : LC Card 85-115663
HG295.N4 D86 1985 ***NYPL [JLD 86-91]***

Instrumentos tributarios de financiamientos coadyuvantes a la producción agraria de alimentos /. Ross, Jaime. Santo Domingo, R.D. [1983] i, 229 p. ; LC Card 84-159753
HJ4308 .R67 1983

INSTRUMENTS, NEGOTIABLE. see **NEGOTIABLE INSTRUMENTS.**

INSTRUMENTS OF WAR. see **MUNITIONS.**

Instytut derz͡havy i prava (Akademii͡a nauk Ukraïns'koï RSR) Pravovye problemy RASU /. Kiev , 1985. 303 p. : LC Card 86-139849
HC337.U5 P65 1985

Instytut ėkanomiki (Akadėmii͡a navuk Belaruskaĭ SSR)
Ėkonomicheskie aspekty integrat͡sii nauki i proizvodstva /. Minsk , 1986. 204, [4] p. ; LC Card 87-106384
HC337.B933 R43 1986

Regional'nye problemy razvitii͡a infrastruktury i mezhotraslevykh proizvodstv /. Minsk , 1985. 243, [4] p. ; LC Card 86-161744
HC337.B933 C37 1985 ***NYPL [*QM 87-2108]***

Sot͡sial'no-ėkonomicheskai͡a ėffektivnost' obshchestvennogo proizvodstva--sushchnost', komponenty i voprosy ikh ot͡senki /. Minsk , 1983. 158 p. ; LC Card 83-206045
HC340.I52 S67 1983

Instytut ekonomiky (Akademii͡a nauk Ukraïns'koï RSR)
Ekonomiko-statystychne vyvchenni͡a mizhhaluzevykh narodnohospodars'kykh kompleksiv . Kyïv , 1985. 95 p. ; LC Card 86-194555
HC337.U53 I573 1985

Modelirovanie i optimizat͡sionnye raschety . Kiev , 1986. 222, [2] p. : LC Card 86-233713
HD9015.S652 M62 1986

Povyshenie ėffektivnosti proizvodstva v uslovii͡akh sovershenstvovanii͡a khozi͡aĭstvennogo mekhanizma . Kiev , 1982. 106 p. ; LC Card 83-145049
HC337.U5 T46 1982

Prin͡tsipy ėkonomicheskogo upravlenii͡a nauchno-tekhnicheskim progressom . Kiev , 1982. 122 p. ; LC Card 83-143870
HC340.T4 P67 1982

Problemy optimizat͡sii mezhotraslevykh svi͡azeĭ . Kiev , 1976. 135 p. : LC Card 87-100694
HD9015.S653 U4547 1976

Rekomendat͡sii po ukreplenii͡u trudovoĭ i proizvodstvennoĭ distsipliny /. Kiev , 1984. 41 p. ; LC Card 86-181301
HF5549.5.L3 R45 1984

Sovershenstvovanie metodologii ėkonomicheskogo analiza v nauchnykh uchrezhdenii͡akh i nauchno-tekhnicheskikh kompleksakh . Kiev , 1986. 116 p. ; LC Card 87-126466
HC340.R4 S68 1986

Stanovlenie i razvitie sovetskoĭ ėkonomicheskoĭ nauki na Ukraine . Kiev , 1983. 285, [2] p. ; LC Card 84-120015 DDC 330/.072/04771 19
HB74.9.S65 S72 1983 ***NYPL [*QGA 87-275]***

Struktura obshchestvennogo proizvodstva i tendent͡sii ee izmenenii͡a . Kiev , 1979. 113 p. ; LC Card 81-130407
HC337.U53 I527 1979

Teorii͡a i praktika ėkonomiki demoprot͡sessa . Kiev , 1982. 181 p., [2] folded leaves of plates : LC Card 83-145373
HB883.5 .T46 1982

Instytut ekonomiky (Akademii͡a nauk Ukraïns'koï RSR). Kharkivs'ke viddilenni͡a.
Upravlenie trudovymi resursami . Kiev , 1986. 238 p. ; LC Card 86-233715
HD5797.U37 U67 1986

Instytut ekonomiky (Akademii͡a nauk Ukraïns'koï RSR). L'vivs'ke viddilenni͡a.
Kachestvo trudovogo potent͡siala . Kiev , 1986. 228 p. ; LC Card 87-161614
HD5797.U37 K34 1986

Instytut ekonomiky promyslovosti (Akademii͡a nauk Ukraïns'koï RSR).
Uslovii͡a truda v regione /. Kiev , 1985. 252 p. : LC Card 86-105167
HD7726.U39 U85 1985 ***NYPL [*QGA 87-3379]***

Instytut ekonomiky promyslovosti (Akademii͡a nauk Ukraïns'koï RSR). Dnipropetrovs'kyĭ viddil. Upravlenie ėffektivnost'i͡u proizvodstva /. Kiev , 1985. 125 p. : LC Card 85-181580
HD30.23 .U67 1985

Instytut filosofiï (Akademiia nauk Ukraïns'koï RSR) Sem'ia i vosproizvodstvo struktury trudovoï zaniatosti . Kiev , 1984. 238 p. : LC Card 86-142706
HB2698.U38 S46 1984

Instytut istoriï (Akademiia nauk Ukraïns'koï RSR)
Istoriia kolhospu "Zdobutok ZHovtnia" /. Kyïv , 1986. 188 p., [8] p. of plates : LC Card 87-161618
HD1492.S652 U3835 1986

Rabochiĭ klass Ukrainskoĭ SSR . Kiev , 1986. 238 p. ; LC Card 86-155918
HD8529.U42 R33 1986

Instytut Kształtowania Środowiska (Poland) Polish People's Republic national report to the habitat . [S.l.] 1976 (Warszawa : Dom Słowa Polskiego) 48 p. : LC Card 83-226226
HC340.3 .P656 1976

Instytut Nauk Ekonomicznych (Polska Akademia Nauk) Gospodarka w procesie reformowania /. Warszawa , 1986. 423 p. : ISBN 83-208-0514-7 : LC Card 87-102275
HC340.3 .G68 1986

Instytut Polityki Społecznej (Akademia Ekonomiczna w Poznaniu) Determinanty polityki kadrowej w przedsiębiorstwie . Poznań , 1984. 142 p. : LC Card 86-194984
HB54 .P6 nr. 129 HF5549.2.P6

Instytut sotsial'nykh i ekonomichnykh problem zarubizhnykh kraïn (Akademiia nauk Ukraïns'koï RSR)
Strukturnye sdvigi v mirovom kapitalisticheskom khoziaĭstve /. Kiev , 1985. 295 p. ; LC Card 86-105339
HC59 .S8345 1985 ***NYPL [*QIP 87-3473]***

Vneshneėkonomicheskie sviazi stran-chlenov SĖV v usloviiakh sotsialisticheskoĭ integratsii /. Kiev , 1983. 245 p. ; LC Card 83-189711
HC243.5 .V54 1983

Insumos estatísticos para o diagnóstico da pecuária no Estado de Goiás / Secretaria da Indústria e Comércio, Divisão de Informações Técnicas e Estatísticas. [Goiânia-Goiás] : A Divisão, [19]84. 156 leaves : maps ; 34 cm. Chiefly tables. LC Card 86-178269
1. Animal industry - Brazil - Goiás (State) - Statistics. 2. Meat industry and trade - Brazil - Goiás (State) - Statistics. 3. Milk trade - Brazil - Goiás (State) - Statistics. I. Goiás (Brazil : State). Secretaria da Indústria e Comércio. Divisão de Informações Técnicas e Estatísticas.
HD9424.B73 G655 1984

Insurance . Kennedy, David W. Tucson, Ariz. , c1987. ix, 276 p. ; ISBN 0-89586-436-3 (pbk.) : LC Card 86-33789 DDC 368 19
HG8051 .K42 1987

INSURANCE.
Bundy, Darcie. Total coverage . New York , c1987. xiv, 224 p. ; ISBN 0-06-055077-5 : LC Card 86-46050 DDC 368/.0029 19
HG8051 .B846 1987

Crockford, Neil. The administration of insurance /. Cambridge [Cambridgeshire] , Wolfeboro, N.H., USA , 1987. x, 134 p. : ISBN 0-902197-42-8 : LC Card 86-27596 DDC 368/.0068 19
HG8051 .C84 1987

Dorfman, Mark S., 1945- Introduction to insurance /. Englewood Cliffs, NJ , c1987. xix, 501 p. : ISBN 0-13-484809-8 LC Card 86-30319 DDC 368 19
HG8051 .D65 1987

Kennedy, David W. Insurance . Tucson, Ariz. , c1987. ix, 276 p. ; ISBN 0-89586-436-3 (pbk.) : LC Card 86-33789 DDC 368 19
HG8051 .K42 1987

INSURANCE, ACCIDENT - CONGRESSES.
Brancoli, Mario. The financial aspects of insurance against employment accidents /. Geneva , 1974. 42 p. ; LC Card 84-247775
HD7260.5 .B73 1974

INSURANCE, ACCIDENT - FRANCE - HISTORY.
Ewald, François. L'Etat providence /. Paris , c1986. 608 p. ; ISBN 2-246-30731-7 : LC Card 86-160935
HD7175 .E93 1986

INSURANCE - ACCOUNTING.
Macve, Richard, 1940- A survey of Lloyds syndicate accounts . Englewood Cliffs, NJ , 1986. xxv, 263 p. : ISBN 0-13-878273-3 : LC Card 85-12147 DDC 368/.012/094212 19
HG8039 .M33 1986 ***NYPL [JLE 87-864]***

Property-liability insurance accounting /. Durham, N.C. , Wingdale, N.Y. , c1986. 1 v. (loose-leaf) : LC Card 86-207635 DDC 657/.836 19
HG8077 .P7 1986

Insurance Accounting and Systems Association. Property-liability insurance accounting /. Durham, N.C. , Wingdale, N.Y. , c1986. 1 v. (loose-leaf) : LC Card 86-207635 DDC 657/.836 19
HG8077 .P7 1986

INSURANCE - ADJUSTMENT OF CLAIMS - CONGRESSES.
Benefits Processing Institute (1983 : Hollywood, Fla.) Claims processing for benefit plans, 1983 . Brookfield, Wis. , 1984. x, 82 p. : ISBN 0-89154-220-5 (pbk.) : LC Card 84-80454 DDC 331.25/5 19
HG9396 .B47 1984 ***NYPL [JLD 86-3940]***

INSURANCE - AGENTS.
Survey of advanced sales. Chicago , c1987. v, 214 p. : ISBN 0-88462-703-9 (pbk.) LC Card 87-13112 DDC 368/.0068/8 19
HG8091 .S87 1987

INSURANCE, AGRICULTURAL.
Santa María de Cárdenas, Cecilia. El seguro agrícola como factor de desarrollo económico /. Bogotá , 1978. 168, 2, [43] p. : LC Card 85-203482
HG9966 .S25 1978

INSURANCE, AGRICULTURAL - COLOMBIA.
Santa María de Cárdenas, Cecilia. El seguro agrícola como factor de desarrollo económico /. Bogotá , 1978. 168, 2, [43] p. : LC Card 85-203482
HG9966 .S25 1978

INSURANCE, AGRICULTURAL - CROPS - ADDRESSES, ESSAYS, LECTURES.
Crop insurance for agricultural development . Baltimore , c1986. xviii, 322 p. ISBN 0-8018-2673-X (alk. paper) LC Card 85-9810 DDC 368.1/22 19
HG9968 .C76 1985 ***NYPL [JLE 86-1082]***

INSURANCE, AGRICULTURAL - DOMINICAN REPUBLIC.
Tejada C., Frank A. Crédito y seguro agrícola . Santo Domingo, República Dominicana , 1986. 104 p. : LC Card 87-400183 DDC 332.7/1/097293 19
HG2051.D6 T45 1986

INSURANCE - AUSTRIA - HANDOOKS, MANUALS, ETC.
Versicherungs-Leitfaden . Wien , 1984. 79 p. : LC Card 85-198493 DDC 368/.9436 19
HG8061 .V47 1984

INSURANCE, AUTOMOBILE.
Kennedy, David W. Insurance . Tucson, Ariz. , c1987. ix, 276 p. ; ISBN 0-89586-436-3 (pbk.) : LC Card 86-33789 DDC 368 19
HG8051 .K42 1987

INSURANCE, AUTOMOBILE - AUSTRIA.
Rettenbacher, Karl. Die Kraftfahrzeughaftpflichtversicherung in Österreich . Linz , c1984. 183 p. : ISBN 3-85320-328-0 LC Card 85-162917
HG9970.4.A9 R48 1984

INSURANCE, AUTOMOBILE - LAW AND LEGISLATION - AUSTRIA.
Rettenbacher, Karl. Die Kraftfahrzeughaftpflichtversicherung in Österreich . Linz , c1984. 183 p. : ISBN 3-85320-328-0 LC Card 85-162917
HG9970.4.A9 R48 1984

INSURANCE, AUTOMOBILE - NEW JERSEY.
Highway Loss Data Institute insurance special report . Washington, D.C. (Watergate 600, Washington 20037) , c1986. 11 p. ; LC Card 86-211182 DDC 368.5/72016/09747 19
HG9970.35.N7 H55 1986

INSURANCE, AUTOMOBILE - NEW YORK (STATE)
Highway Loss Data Institute insurance special report . Washington, D.C. (Watergate 600, Washington 20037) , c1986. 11 p. ; LC Card 86-211182 DDC 368.5/72016/09747 19
HG9970.35.N7 H55 1986

INSURANCE, AUTOMOBILE - POLAND.
Zelwiański, Ryszard. Ubezpieczenia komunikacyjne . Warszawa , 1979. 177, [3] p. : ISBN 83-219-0031-3 LC Card 81-181561
HG9905.P7 Z45 1979

INSURANCE, AUTOMOBILE - RISKS - ECONOMETRIC MODELS.
Umani, Mario. Un procedimento per la ripartizione ottimale di una collettività in classi . [Trieste] , 1978. 19 p. ; LC Card 81-111875 DDC 368/.092 19
HG9970 .U46 1978 ***NYPL [TB (Triesta. Università Istituto do statistica. Pubblicazioni. n.17)]***

INSURANCE, AUTOMOBILE - UNITED STATES.
Comparison of the insurance loss experience of unibody and frame construction cars after a collision repair, 1981-82 models. Washington, D.C. (Watergate 600, Washington 20037) , c1985. 10 p. : LC Card 87-107697 DDC 368.5/72/00973 19
HG9970.3 .C65 1985

Consistency of model year injury claim frequency results for selected 1981-1983 models. Washington, D.C (Watergate 600, Washington 20037) , c1986. 11 p. ; LC Card 87-107714 DDC 368.5/72/00973 19
HG9970.3 .C66 1986

Relationships between losses and vehicle density, 1982-84 models. Washington, D.C. (Watergate 600, Washington 20037) , c1985. 24 p. : LC Card 87-107842 DDC 368.5/72/00973 19
HG9970.3 .R45 1985

INSURANCE, AUTOMOBILE - UNITED STATES - STATISTICS.
Highway Loss Data Institute insurance collision report . Washington, DC (Watergate 600, Washington 20037) , c1986. 24 p. ; LC Card 87-107636 DDC 368.5/72/00973021 19
HG9970.3 .H5365 1986

Highway Loss Data Institute insurance collision report . Washington, D.C. (Watergate 600, Washington 20037) , c1986. 51 p. : LC Card 86-210266 DDC 368.5/72/00973021 19
HG9970.3 .H536 1986

Highway Loss Data Institute insurance injury report . Washington, D.C. (Watergate 600, Washington 20037) , c1986. 30 p. : LC Card 87-107645 DDC 368.5/72/00973021 19
HG9970.3 .H537 1986

Highway Loss Data Institute insurance theft report . Washington, D.C. (Watergate 600, Washington 20037) , c1986. 44 p. ; LC Card 87-107648 DDC 368.2/32/00973021 19
HG9970.3 .H538 1986

Injury and collision losses by engine option, selected 1983 models. Washington, D.C. (Watergate 600, Washington 20037) , c1985. 11 p. ; LC Card 87-115471 DDC 368.5/72/00973 19
HG9970.3 .I524 1985

INSURANCE, AVIATION - UNITED STATES.
Rollo, Vera A. Foster. Aviation insurance /. Lanham, Md. , 1987. x, 438 p. : ISBN 0-917882-22-9 LC Card 86-62107 DDC 368/.093/0973 19
HG9972.3 .R65 1987

INSURANCE, BUSINESS - CONGRESSES.
L'Attività commerciale e industriale nello spazio . [Trieste] [1986] 192 p. : LC Card 86-215438
HD9711.75.A2 A77 1986

INSURANCE, BUSINESS - HANDBOOKS, MANUALS, ETC.
The Business insurance handbook /. Homewood, Ill. , c1981. xvii, 753 p. : ISBN 0-87094-237-9 LC Card 80-70437 DDC 368.8/1/00202 19
HG8059 .B87 ***NYPL [*R-Econ. 86-2502]***

INSURANCE, BUSINESS - ITALY.
Padoa, Fabio. L'assicurazione internazionale . Milano , c1983. 140 p. : ISBN 88-20-31384-7 LC Card 85-189997
HG8059 .P33 1983

INSURANCE, BUSINESS - UNITED STATES.
McIntyre, William Stokes. 101 ways to cut

your business insurance costs without sacrificing protection /. New York , c1988. viii, 190 p. : ISBN 0-07-045112-5 : LC Card 87-17255 DDC 368 19
HG8059 .M38 1988

INSURANCE - CALIFORNIA - STATE SUPERVISION.
California. Dept. of Finance. Program Evaluation Unit. The Conservation and Liquidation Division, Department of Insurance /. [Sacramento, Calif.] [1985] xii, 62 p. ; LC Card 85-622857 DDC 353.97940082/55 19
HG8538.C2 C35 1985

INSURANCE, CASUALTY - ACCOUNTING.
Basic concepts of accounting and taxation of property/casualty insurance companies /. New York, N.Y. , c1984. 66 p. : ISBN 0-932387-01-2 : ***NYPL [JLE 86-2615]***

INSURANCE, CASUALTY - JAPAN.
Miscellaneous casualty insurance in Japan. Tokyo, Japan [1986] xi, 315 p. ; LC Card 87-103937 DDC 368.5/00952 19
HG8705.A6 M57 1986

INSURANCE, CASUALTY - TAXATION - UNITED STATES.
Basic concepts of accounting and taxation of property/casualty insurance companies /. New York, N.Y. , c1984. 66 p. : ISBN 0-932387-01-2 : ***NYPL [JLE 86-2615]***

The insurance character of unemployment insurance /. Malisoff, Harry. Kalamazoo, Mich. [1961] 44 p. ; LC Card 87-401793 DDC 368.4/4/0973 19
HD7096.U5 M266 1961

INSURANCE - CHILE - DIRECTORIES.
Producción corredores de seguros 1985. [Chile] , 1986. 390 p. ; LC Card 87-403786 DDC 368/.0025/83 19
HG8576 .P76 1986

INSURANCE - CHILE - STATISTICS.
Producción corredores de seguros 1985. [Chile] , 1986. 390 p. ; LC Card 87-403786 DDC 368/.0025/83 19
HG8576 .P76 1986

Insurance collision report. Highway Loss Data Institute insurance collision report . Washington, DC (Watergate 600, Washington 20037) , c1986. 24 p. ; LC Card 87-107636 DDC 368.5/72/00973021 19
HG9970.3 .H5365 1986

Insurance collision report. Highway Loss Data Institute insurance collision report . Washington, D.C. (Watergate 600, Washington 20037) , c1986. 51 p. : LC Card 86-210266 DDC 368.5/72/00973021 19
HG9970.3 .H536 1986

INSURANCE COMPANIES - CAPTIVE COMPANIES.
Bawcutt, P. A. (Paul A.) Captive insurance companies . Cambridge [Cambridgeshire] , Wolfeboro, N.H. , 1987. xii, 410 p. : ISBN 0-85941-382-9 : LC Card 86-32621 DDC 368/.0068 19
HG8104 .B38 1987

INSURANCE COMPANIES - FRANCE - EMPLOYEES - EFFECT OF TECHNOLOGICAL INNOVATIONS ON - CONGRESSES.
Symposium sur les conséquences des techniques nouvelles de l'informatique sur les conditions de vie, et de travail, sur l'emploi des travailleurs des banques et des assurances (1980 : Paris, France) Symposium sur les conséquences des techniques nouvelles de l'informatique sur les conditions de vie, et de travail, sur l'emploi des travailleurs des banques et des assurances /. Berlin [1983?] 96 p. : LC Card 84-185736
HD8039.B27 F77 1980

INSURANCE COMPANIES - GERMANY - LOCATION.
Gilles, Martina, 1956- Die Standortfrage in der Versicherungswirtschaft . Köln , c1987. xv, 309 p., [4] folded leaves of plates : ISBN 3-924361-26-6 LC Card 87-144415 DDC 368/.006 19
HG8618 .G55 1987

INSURANCE COMPANIES - GERMANY (WEST) - ECONOMETRIC MODELS.
Lehnhardt-Ritter, Gerda. Das Kapitalanlageverhalten der deutschen Lebensversicherungsunternehmen im Wandel der Konjunktur . Karlsruhe , c1984. xxiii, 444 p. : ISBN 3-88487-067-X LC Card 85-171182
HG9078 .L44 1984

INSURANCE COMPANIES - GERMANY (WEST) - LOCATION.
Gilles, Martina, 1956- Die Standortfrage in der Versicherungswirtschaft . Köln , c1987. xv, 309 p., [4] folded leaves of plates : ISBN 3-924361-26-6 LC Card 87-144415 DDC 368/.006 19
HG8618 .G55 1987

INSURANCE COMPANIES - KENTUCKY - EMPLOYEES - SUPPLY AND DEMAND - STATISTICS.
Kentucky occupational profiles, finance, insurance, and real estate /. [Frankfort, Ky.] [1985] v, 33 p. : LC Card 85-622996 DDC 331.12/51/0009769 19
HD5718.B262 U66 1985

INSURANCE COMPANIES - MANAGEMENT.
Crockford, Neil. The administration of insurance /. Cambridge [Cambridgeshire] , Wolfeboro, N.H., USA , 1987. x, 134 p. : ISBN 0-902197-42-8 : LC Card 86-27596 DDC 368/.0068 19
HG8051 .C84 1987

In search of profitability -- agent's business plan /. Des Plaines, Ill.] , c1986. 124 p. : LC Card 87-167903 DDC 368/.0068 19
HG8877 .I49 1986

INSURANCE COMPANIES - MARKETING.
Benn, Alec. Advertising financial products and services . Westport, Conn. , c1986. xii, 231 p. : ISBN 0-89930-103-7 (lib bdg. : alk. paper) LC Card 85-24406 DDC 659.1/93321 19
HG1616.M3 B43 1986 ***NYPL [JLE 86-4110]***

INSURANCE COMPANIES - NORTH DAKOTA - EMPLOYEES - STATISTICS.
Finance, insurance, and real estate . Bismarck, N.D. (1000 E. Divide, Bismarck 58502) [1986] 55 p. : LC Card 86-623003 DDC 332.12/51/0009784 19
HD5718.B262 U64 1986

INSURANCE COMPANIES - SOUTH AFRICA - HISTORY.
Uberrima fides . [Johannesburg , 1985?] 69 p. : ISBN 0-620-08481-2 LC Card 87-146303 DDC 368/.006 19
HG8724.3.Z9 P758 1985

INSURANCE COMPANIES - UNITED STATES - EMPLOYEES - SUPPLY AND DEMAND - FORECASTING.
Roessner, J. David. The Impact of office automation on clerical employment, 1985-2000 . Westport, Conn. , 1985. xii, 297 p. : ISBN 0-89930-119-3 (lib. bdg. : alk. paper) LC Card 85-6523 DDC 331.12/9165137 19
HD8039.B27 U548 1986
NYPL [JLE 86-1424]

INSURANCE COMPANIES - UNITED STATES - STATISTICS.
Life solvency monitor. Hartford, Conn. (41 Lewis St., Hartford 06103) , 1985. 201 p. : LC Card 86-215848 DDC 368.3/2/006 19
HG8955 .L55 1985

Life solvency monitor. Hartford, Conn. (101 Pearl St., Hartford 06103) , 1986. 227 p. : LC Card 86-209963 DDC 368.3/2/006 19
HG8955 .L55 1986

INSURANCE COMPANIES - VIRGINIA - STATISTICS.
Insurance company statistical report, 1985 /. [Richmond, Va.] [1985] 1 v. (various pagings) ; LC Card 87-621272 DDC 368/.006 19
HG8538.V8 I574 1985

1984 insurance company statistical report /. [Richmond] [1984?] 1 v. (various pagings) ; LC Card 86-621902 DDC 368/.006 19
HG8538.V8 A53 1984

Insurance company statistical report. 1984 insurance company statistical report /. [Richmond] [1984?] 1 v. (various pagings) ; LC Card 86-621902 DDC 368/.006 19
HG8538.V8 A53 1984

Insurance company statistical report, 1985 / State Corporation Commission, Bureau of Insurance. [Richmond, Va.] : The Bureau, [1985] 1 v. (various pagings) ; 28 cm. Chiefly tables. LC Card 87-621272 DDC 368/.006 19
I. Insurance companies - Virginia - Statistics. I. Virginia. Bureau of Insurance.
HG8538.V8 I574 1985

INSURANCE, CORPORATE. see **INSURANCE, BUSINESS.**

Insurance Corporation of British Columbia. Traffic Safety Planning and Research Department.
Rethinking young drivers /. [North Vancouver, B.C.] , c1987. ii, 291 p. : ISBN 0-7726-0588-2 (pbk.) LC Card 87-167603 DDC 363.1/251 19
HE5620.J8 R47 1987

Rothe, John Peter, 1948- Young drivers involved in injury producing crashes . North Vancouver, B.C. , c1986. ii, 77 p. : ISBN 0-7726-0530-0 (pbk.) LC Card 87-167610 DDC 363.1/251 19
HE5620.J8 R67 1986

INSURANCE CRIMES - UNITED STATES - CASE STUDIES.
Kizorek, Bill. Disability or deception /. [Naperville, Ill., USA] (Suite 12, 6 S 235 Steeple Run Dr., Naperville 60540) [c1986] 140 p. : LC Card 86-206432 DDC 363.2/5 19
HD7105.25.U6 K59 1986

INSURANCE - DICTIONARIES.
Rubin, Harvey W. Dictionary of insurance terms /. New York , c1987. ix, 371 p. ; ISBN 0-8120-3772-3 (pbk.) : LC Card 87-12549 DDC 368/.003/21 19
HG8025 .R83 1987

INSURANCE, DISABILITY - CALIFORNIA.
The California Disability Insurance Program . [Sacramento] [1986] 17, 4 leaves ; LC Card 86-622336 DDC 368.3/82/009794 19
HD7105.25.U6 C35 1986

INSURANCE, DISABILITY - CONGRESSES.
Disability benefits . Greenwich, Conn. , c1987. xxii, 282 p. ; ISBN 0-89232-824-X : LC Card 87-17056 DDC 368.3/86/009492 19
HD7105.25.N4 D57 1987

INSURANCE, DISABILITY - GREAT BRITAIN - CONGRESSES.
Disability benefits . Greenwich, Conn. , c1987. xxii, 282 p. ; ISBN 0-89232-824-X : LC Card 87-17056 DDC 368.3/86/009492 19
HD7105.25.N4 D57 1987

INSURANCE, DISABILITY - NETHERLANDS - CONGRESSES.
Disability benefits . Greenwich, Conn. , c1987. xxii, 282 p. ; ISBN 0-89232-824-X : LC Card 87-17056 DDC 368.3/86/009492 19
HD7105.25.N4 D57 1987

INSURANCE, DISABILITY - UNITED STATES.
Berkowitz, Monroe, 1919- Permanent disability benefits in workers' compensation /. Kalamazoo, Mich. , 1987. xviii, 459 p. ; ISBN 0-88099-051-1 LC Card 87-22874 DDC 368.4/1/00973 19
HD7105.25.U6 B47 1987

DeVol, Karen R., 1949- Income replacement for long term disability . Cambridge, Mass. , 1986. p. cm. ISBN 0-935149-04-X : LC Card 86-28264 DDC 368.4/1/00973 19
HD7103.65.U6 D484 1986

Morris, William H., Jr. Disability insurance . Lexington, Ky. (98 Dennis Dr., Lexington 40503) , c1986. x, 93 p. : LC Card 87-402218 DDC 368.3/86/00973 19
HD7105.25.U6 M67 1986

Occupational characteristics of disabled workers, 1975-1976 . Cincinnati, Ohio (4676 Columbia Pkwy., Cincinnati 45226) [1986] xix, 187 p. ; LC Card 86-602391 DDC 363.1/12/0973 19
HD7105.25.U6 O23 1986

Principles of health & disability insurance selling. Chicago , c1987. 179 p. ; ISBN 0-88462-700-4 (pbk.) LC Card 87-16281 DDC 368.3/8/00688 19
HG9396 .P75 1987

INSURANCE, DISABILITY - UNITED STATES - FORECASTING.
Andrews, George H., 1932- Actuarial projections for the old-age, survivors, and disability insurance program of social security in the United States of America /. Itasca, Ill., U. S.A. , c1987. viii, 188 p. : LC Card 87-1101

DDC 368.4/301/0973 19
HC106.8 .A56 1987

INSURANCE, DISASTER - ADJUSTMENT OF CLAIMS.
Catastrophic losses . Oak Brook, Ill. (1200 Harger Rd., Suite 222, Oak Brook 60521) , c1986. vi, 73 p. : LC Card 87-106114 DDC 368.1/22014/0973 19
HG9979.3 .C38 1986

INSURANCE, DISASTER - UNITED STATES - ADJUSTMENT OF CLAIMS.
Catastrophic losses . Oak Brook, Ill. (1200 Harger Rd., Suite 222, Oak Brook 60521) , c1986. vi, 73 p. : LC Card 87-106114 DDC 368.1/22014/0973 19
HG9979.3 .C38 1986

INSURANCE, EARTHQUAKE - CALIFORNIA.
California earthquake zoning and probable maximum loss evaluation program . Los Angeles, Calif. (600 S. Commonwealth Ave., Los Angeles 90005) [1986] 44, 15 p. : LC Card 86-623193 DDC 368.1/22/09794 19
HG9981.35.C2 C35 1986

INSURANCE, EARTHQUAKE - UNITED STATES.
Earthquake insurance . Washington , 1987. ix, 61 p. : LC Card 87-601349 DDC 368.1/22 19
HG9981 .E17 1987

INSURANCE - EUROPEAN ECONOMIC COMMUNITY COUNTRIES - STATE SUPERVISION.
Eggerstedt, Harald. Produktwettbewerb und Dienstleistungsfreiheit auf Versicherungsmärkten /. Berlin , c1987. 320 p. : ISBN 3-428-06167-5 LC Card 87-143175 DDC 368/.94 19
HG8593.5.Z75 E34 1987

INSURANCE, EXECUTIVES' LIABILITY - UNITED STATES.
Directors and officers liability . Hartford, Conn. (101 Pearl St., Hartford 06103) , c1986. 53 p. ; LC Card 86-211342
HG8053.8 .D57 1986

INSURANCE, EXPORT CREDIT.
Pálfi, Sándor. Nemzetközi biztosítás a külkereskedelem szolgálatában /. [Budapest] [1986] 63 p. ; ISBN 963-02-4369-5 LC Card 87-425585
HG8059 .P35 1986

INSURANCE, EXPORT CREDIT - DEVELOPING COUNTRIES.
Mugglin, Markus. Exportrisikogarantie, internationale Verschuldung und schweizerische Entwicklungspolitik /. Adliswil , 1985. 56 p. : ISBN 3-7229-4036-X LC Card 85-148130
HF1574.5.D44 M84 1985

INSURANCE, EXPORT CREDIT - EUROPE.
Loubergé, Henri. Financement et assurance des crédits à l'exportation . Genève , 1985. 502 p. : ***NYPL [JLD 86-2109]***

INSURANCE, EXPORT CREDIT - GERMANY, WEST.
Hichert, Ingo, 1944- Staatliche Exportabsicherung . Köln , c1986. 302 p. : ISBN 3-602-34848-2 LC Card 87-145196 DDC 368.8/7 19
HG9977.4.G3 H53 1986

INSURANCE, EXPORT CREDIT - UNITED STATES.
Henry, Donald Putnam, 1957- The financial cost of export credit guarantee programs /. Santa Monica, CA , 1987. ix, 37 p. ; ISBN 0-8330-0794-7 (pbk.) LC Card 87-4630 DDC 382/.63 19
HG3754.5.U6 H46 1987

Insurance for unemployment /. Beenstock, Michael, 1946- London , Boston , 1986. 106 p. ; ISBN 0-04-331113-X (alk. paper) (Great Britain) LC Card 85-30704 DDC 368.4/4/00941 19
HD7096.G7 B36 1986 ***NYPL [JLD 86-3693]***

Insurance forum. Belth, Joseph M. The A.L. Williams replacement empire . Ellettsville, IN , c1987. 64 p. : ISBN 0-941173-00-3 (pbk.) : LC Card 86-27715 DDC 368.3/2/00973 19
HG8963.A44 B44 1987

INSURANCE - GERMANY, WEST.
Farny, Dieter. Die deutsche Versicherungswirtschaft . Karlsruhe [c1983] xiv, 189 p. ; ISBN 3-88487-054-8 LC Card 84-205736
HG8618 .F37 1983

Versicherungswirtschaftliches Studienwerk /. Wiesbaden , c1981. v. <8-10 > ; LC Card 86-171689
HG8618 .V47 1981

Zietsch, Dietmar. Grundlagen der Gestaltung aussenorganisationsbezogener Vertriebssteuerungssysteme in Versicherungsunternehmen /. Karlsruhe , c1985. xx, 308 p. : ISBN 3-88487-084-X LC Card 86-169097
HG8618 .Z53 1985

INSURANCE, GOVERNMENT - AUSTRALIA - QUEENSLAND - HISTORY.
Thomis, Malcolm I. From SGIO to Suncorp /. [Brisbane?] , 1986. xii, 272 p., [32] p. of plates : ISBN 0-7242-1698-7 LC Card 87-158138 DDC 368.4/009943 19
HG8220.A9 T56 1986

INSURANCE, GOVERNMENT RISKS - UNITED STATES.
Best's municipal underwriting guide . Oldwick, N.J. (Ambest Rd., Oldwick 08858) , c1986. 1 v. (various pagings) : LC Card 86-230785 DDC 368 19
HG8210 .B47 1986

Surveys on liability insurance for government entities. Oak Brook, Ill. (1200 Harger Rd., Suite 222, Oak Brook 60521) , c1986. vi, 66 p. ; LC Card 87-110891 DDC 368.5 19
HG8207 .S87 1986

INSURANCE - GREAT BRITAIN.
A Textbook of insurance broking /. Wolfeboro, N.H., USA , 1988. p. cm. ISBN 0-85941-386-1 : LC Card 87-21036 DDC 368/.941 19
HG8597 .T49 1988

INSURANCE - GREAT BRITAIN - ACCOUNTING.
Carmichael, K. S. (Keith Stanley) Taxation of Lloyd's underwriters /. London , 1980. xvi, 107 p. : ISBN 0-372-30027-8 (pbk.) : LC Card 81-107459
HG8123.G7 C37 1980

Insurance handbook for reporters / presented by the Allstate Corporate Communications Division, Allstate Insurance Group. 2nd ed., expanded and rev. Northbrook, Ill. : The Group, 1985. 304 p. ; 19 cm. Bibliography: p. 298-304. LC Card 87-110782 DDC 368/.002/02 19
1. Insurance - Handbooks, manuals, etc. I. Allstate Insurance Group. Corporate Communications Division.
HG8061 .I57 1985

INSURANCE - HANDBOOKS, MANUALS, ETC.
Insurance handbook for reporters /. Northbrook, Ill. , 1985. 304 p. ; LC Card 87-110782 DDC 368/.002/02 19
HG8061 .I57 1985

INSURANCE - HANDOOKS, MANUALS, ETC.
Versicherungs-Leitfaden . Wien , 1984. 79 p. : LC Card 85-198493 DDC 368/.9436 19
HG8061 .V47 1984

INSURANCE, HEALTH - AGENTS.
Principles of health & disability insurance selling. Chicago , c1987. 179 p. ; ISBN 0-88462-700-4 (pbk.) LC Card 87-16281 DDC 368.3/8/00688 19
HG9396 .P75 1987

INSURANCE, HEALTH - AUSTRALIA.
Brown, Malcolm C. (Malcolm Clarence), 1941- National health insurance in Canada and Australia . Canberra , 1983. vii, 108 p. ; ISBN 0-86784-281-4 (pbk.) LC Card 86-214526 DDC 368.4/2/00971 19
HD7102.A8 B75 1983

INSURANCE, HEALTH - BRAZIL.
Fonseca, Aloysio de Salles. Reorientação da assistência à saúde no âmbito da previdência social . [Brasília] , 1983. 67 p. ; LC Card 86-171863
HD7102.B7 F66 1983

INSURANCE, HEALTH - CALIFORNIA.
California. Legislature. Assembly. Committee on Finance and Insurance. Health insurance . Sacramento, Calif. [1984] 359 p. : LC Card 87-621024 DDC 368.3/82/009794 19
HG9397.5.C2 C35 1984

INSURANCE, HEALTH - CALIFORNIA - STATISTICS.
Medi-Cal fee-for-service eligibles and prepaid health plan enrollees by age group, sex, and county, July 1984. [Sacramento] [1985] 19 p. : LC Card 86-622330 DDC 362.1/04252/09794021 19
HD7102.U6 C345 1985

INSURANCE, HEALTH - CANADA.
Brown, Malcolm C. (Malcolm Clarence), 1941- National health insurance in Canada and Australia . Canberra , 1983. vii, 108 p. ; ISBN 0-86784-281-4 (pbk.) LC Card 86-214526 DDC 368.4/2/00971 19
HD7102.A8 B75 1983

INSURANCE, HEALTH - CANADA - ACCOUNTING.
Zucconi, Paul J. Accounting in life and health insurance companies /. Atlanta, Ga. , c1987. xiv, 365 p. : ISBN 0-915322-85-4 LC Card 86-82715 DDC 657/.836 19
HG8848 .Z84 1987

INSURANCE, HEALTH - CANADA - PUBLIC OPINION.
Taylor, Malcolm G. (Malcolm Gordon) Medical perspectives on Canadian Medicare . Downsview, Ont. , 1984. vii, 201 p. : ISBN 0-919762-57-3 (pbk.) LC Card 87-673411
HD7102.C2 T34x 1984

INSURANCE, HEALTH - FINANCE - PUBLIC OPINION - MATHEMATICAL MODELS.
Breyer, Friedrich. Family structure and intergenerational transfers in social health insurance . Berlin [1986] 24 p. : LC Card 87-156738 DDC 368.4/2016/0724 19
HD7101 .B73 1986

INSURANCE, HEALTH - FLORIDA - EXAMINATIONS, QUESTIONS, ETC.
Florida life and health study manual . [Chicago] , c1987. x, 358 p. : ISBN 0-88462-727-6 (pbk.) LC Card 87-17254 DDC 368.3/009759 19
HG8961.F6 F56 1987

INSURANCE, HEALTH - GERMANY, WEST.
Aspekte zur GKV-Strukturreform /. Stuttgart , New York , 1984. x, 102 p. ; ISBN 3-437-10918-9 LC Card 84-187001
HD7102.G3 A87 1984

Böckel, Thomas R., 1959- Selbstregelung und Entpolitisierung der gesetzlichen Rentenversicherung . Frankfurt am Main , New York , c1986. xvi, 305 p. ; ISBN 3-8204-8847-2 LC Card 87-407917 DDC 368.4/00943 19
HD7179 .B59 1986

Henrich, Rudolf. Analyse und Planung des Erfolgs und der Überschussverwendung einer Krankenversicherungsaktiengesellschaft /. Karlsruhe , c1983. xxi, 498 p. : ISBN 3-88487-053-X LC Card 85-131706
HG9399.G32 H46 1983

INSURANCE, HEALTH - GERMANY (WEST) - COST CONTROL.
Molinaro, Remo. Gesundheitswesen und Kostendämpfung in der Bundesrepublik . Berlin , New York , c1986. xvi, 108 p. ; ISBN 0-387-16648-3 (U. S.) LC Card 86-200720
HD7102.G3 M58 1986

INSURANCE, HEALTH - GOVERNMENT POLICY - NEW YORK (STATE)
New York (State). Council on Health Care Financing. Subcommittee on Health Insurance. Health insurance . Albany, N.Y. [1985?] 1 v. (various pagings) : LC Card 86-622080 DDC 368.3/82/009747 19
HD7102.U5 N655 1985

INSURANCE, HEALTH - LAW AND LEGISLATION - GERMANY (WEST)
Aspekte zur GKV-Strukturreform /. Stuttgart , New York , 1984. x, 102 p. ; ISBN 3-437-10918-9 LC Card 84-187001
HD7102.G3 A87 1984

INSURANCE, HEALTH - LAW AND LEGISLATION - UNITED STATES - OUTLINES, SYLLABI, ETC.
Lyons, Paula. Life & health insurance . Chicago , c1988. xvi, 351 p. : ISBN 0-88462-707-1 (pbk.) LC Card 87-18506 DDC 368.3/00973 19
HG8951 .L98 1988

INSURANCE, HEALTH - LAW AND LEGISLATIONS - FLORIDA - EXAMINATIONS, QUESTIONS, ETC.
Florida life and health study manual . [Chicago] , c1987. x, 358 p. : ISBN 0-88462-727-6 (pbk.) LC Card 87-17254 DDC 368.3/009759 19
HG8961.F6 F56 1987

INSURANCE, HEALTH - NEW YORK (STATE)
New York (State). Council on Health Care Financing. Subcommittee on Health Insurance. Health insurance . Albany, N.Y. [1985?] 1 v. (various pagings) : LC Card 86-622080 DDC 368.3/82/009747 19
HD7102.U5 N655 1985

INSURANCE, HEALTH - SOCIAL ASPECTS - UNITED STATES.
Rushing, William A. Social functions and economic aspects of health insurance /. Boston , c1986. vii, 226 p. ; ISBN 0-89838-219-X LC Card 86-7297 DDC 368.3/82/00973 19
HD7102.U4 R86 1986 ***NYPL [JLE 87-1237]***

INSURANCE, HEALTH - UNITED STATES.
America's uninsured and underinsured . Washington , 1986. vi, 13 p. ; LC Card 86-603377 DDC 368.3/8/00973 19
HD7102.U4 A755 1986

Davis, Karen, 1942- Medicare policy . Baltimore , c1986. xiii, 137 p. ; ISBN 0-8018-2874-0 (alk. paper) LC Card 85-45048 DDC 368.4/26/00973 19
HD7102.U4 D279 1986
NYPL [JLE 86-3782]

Farley, Pamela J. Private health insurance in the United States . Rockville, MD , Springfield, VA [1986] 106 p. : LC Card 86-23618 DDC 368.3/82/00973 19
HG9396 .F3 1986

Fein, Rashi. Medical care, medical costs . Cambridge, Mass. , 1986. viii, 240 p. ; ISBN 0-674-56052-3 (alk. paper) LC Card 86-7623 DDC 368.3/82/00973 19
HG9396 .F45 1986 ***NYPL [JLE 86-3975]***

Ginsburg, Paul B. A private health plan option strategy for Medicare /. Santa Monica, CA [1987] xvi, 116 p. ; ISBN 0-8330-0863-3 (pbk.) LC Card 87-17593 DDC 368.4/26/00973 19
HD7102.U4 G56 1987

Health insurance . Washington, D.C. , 1986. 53 p. ; LC Card 86-603180 DDC 368.3/82/00973 19
HG9398.B57 H4 1986

Health insurance and the demand for medical care . Santa Monica, CA , 1987. p. cm. ISBN 0-8330-0864-1 LC Card 87-17587 DDC 368.3/82/00973 19
HD7102.U4 H413 1987

Principles of health & disability insurance selling. Chicago , c1987. 179 p. ; ISBN 0-88462-700-4 (pbk.) LC Card 87-16281 DDC 368.3/8/00688 19
HG9396 .P75 1987

Rushing, William A. Social functions and economic aspects of health insurance /. Boston , c1986. vii, 226 p. ; ISBN 0-89838-219-X LC Card 86-7297 DDC 368.3/82/00973 19
HD7102.U4 R86 1986 ***NYPL [JLE 87-1237]***

Waller, Kal. Medicare . Cleveland , 1987. xvii, 146 p. : ISBN 0-939738-92-9 (pbk.) LC Card 87-156155 DDC 368.4/26/00973 19
HD7102.U4 W245 1987

INSURANCE, HEALTH - UNITED STATES - ACCOUNTING.
Measuring and funding corporate liabilities for retiree health benefits. Washington, D.C. , c1987. xxxviii, 226 p. : ISBN 0-86643-054-7 (pbk.) LC Card 87-24534 DDC 657/.75 19
HG9396 .M4 1987

Zucconi, Paul J. Accounting in life and health insurance companies /. Atlanta, Ga. , c1987. xiv, 365 p. : ISBN 0-915322-85-4 LC Card 86-82715 DDC 657/.836 19
HG8848 .Z84 1987

INSURANCE, HEALTH - UNITED STATES - CONGRESSES.
Benefits Processing Institute (1983 : Hollywood, Fla.) Claims processing for benefit plans, 1983 . Brookfield, Wis. , 1984. x, 82 p. : ISBN 0-89154-220-5 (pbk.) : LC Card 84-80454 DDC 331.25/5 19
HG9396 .B47 1984 ***NYPL [JLD 86-3940]***

Market reforms in health care . Washington , c1983. xv, 331 p. ; ISBN 0-8447-2242-1 LC Card 82-22678 DDC 362.1/0973 19
RA410.53 .M37 1983 ***NYPL [JLC 86-373]***

INSURANCE, HEALTH - UNITED STATES - ECONOMETRIC MODELS.
Marquis, M. Susan. Choice under uncertainty and the demand for health insurance /. Santa Monica, CA (P.O. Box 2138, Santa Monica 90406-2138) [1986] ix, 50 p. ; LC Card 87-118503 DDC 368.3/8/00973 19
HG9396 .M268 1986

INSURANCE, HEALTH - UNITED STATES - OUTLINES, SYLLABI, ETC.
Lyons, Paula. Life & health insurance . Chicago , c1988. xvi, 351 p. : ISBN 0-88462-707-1 (pbk.) LC Card 87-18506 DDC 368.3/00973 19
HG8951 .L98 1988

INSURANCE, HOMEOWNERS.
Kennedy, David W. Insurance . Tucson, Ariz. , c1987. ix, 276 p. ; ISBN 0-89586-436-3 (pbk.) : LC Card 86-33789 DDC 368 19
HG8051 .K42 1987

INSURANCE, HOMEOWNERS - GERMANY (WEST)
Versicherungen in der Altbauerneuerung /. Berlin , c1985. 83 p. ; ISBN 3-433-02219-4 LC Card 86-104351
HG9986.4.G3 V47 1985

INSURANCE, HOSPITALIZATION - GERMANY (WEST) - CONGRESSES.
Wirtschaftsentwicklung und soziale Sicherheit . Köln , 1983. viii, 146 p. : ISBN 3-452-19567-8 LC Card 84-106615
HG9399.G32 W57 1983

INSURANCE, INDEMNITY. see **INSURANCE, LIABILITY.**

INSURANCE, INDUSTRIAL - GERMANY (WEST)
Schöne, Manfred, 1935- Ein Vierteljahrhundert Betriebskrankenkasse Henkel, Düsseldorf /. [Düsseldorf] , 1977. 60 p. : LC Card 86-216782
HG9399.G33 B477 1977

Insurance Information Institute. Basic concepts of accounting and taxation of property/casualty insurance companies /. New York, N.Y. , c1984. 66 p. : ISBN 0-932387-01-2 :
NYPL [JLE 86-2615]

Insurance injury report. Highway Loss Data Institute insurance injury report . Washington, D.C. (Watergate 600, Washington 20037) , c1986. 30 p. : LC Card 87-107645 DDC 368.5/72/00973021 19
HG9970.3 .H537 1986

Insurance Institute of America. Essentials of risk control /. Malvern, Pa. , 1986. 2 v. : ISBN 0-89462-033-9 (pbk.) LC Card 86-82833 DDC 368 19
HD61 .E84 1986

INSURANCE, INVALIDITY. see **INSURANCE, DISABILITY.**

INSURANCE LAW - ECONOMIC ASPECTS - ADDRESSES, ESSAYS, LECTURES.
The Economics of insurance regulation . Houndmills, Basingstoke, Hampshire , 1986. xi, 300 p. : ISBN 0-333-39684-7
NYPL [JLD 87-1100]

INSURANCE LAW - MICHIGAN - EXAMINATIONS, QUESTIONS, ETC.
Michigan study manual for life and accident and health insurance. Chicago , c1987. v, 56 p. ; ISBN 0-88462-729-2 (unb.) LC Card 87-18552 DDC 368.3/009774 19
HG8101.M5 M53 1987

INSURANCE LAW - NEW JERSEY - EXAMINATIONS, QUESTIONS, ETC.
New Jersey study manual for life and accident and health insurance. Chicago , c1987. p. cm. ISBN 0-88462-726-8 LC Card 87-13103 DDC 368.3/009749 19
HG8101.N48 N47 1987

INSURANCE LAW - NEW YORK (STATE) - EXAMINATIONS, QUESTIONS, ETC.
New York study manual for life and accident and health insurance. Chicago , c1987. p. cm. ISBN 0-88462-725-X LC Card 87-13102 DDC 368.3/009747 19
HG8101.N49 N47 1987

INSURANCE LAW - NORWAY.
Forsikring i Norge /. Oslo [1983] 226 p. ; ISBN 82-00-70870-5 LC Card 84-158459
HG8668.5 .F67 1983

INSURANCE LAW - UNITED STATES.
Abraham, Kenneth S., 1946- Distributing risk . New Haven , c1986. x, 254 p. ; ISBN 0-300-03460-1 (alk. paper) LC Card 85-22459 DDC 346.73/086 347.30686 19
KF1164 .A72 1986 ***NYPL [JLE 86-4347]***

Alliance of American Insurers. Regulation of insurance . Chicago, Ill. , 1977. 68 p. ;
NYPL [JLE 86-1584]

INSURANCE, LIABILITY.
Commercial liability risk management and insurance /. Malvern, Pa. , 1986. 2 v. : ISBN 0-89463-049-0 (set) LC Card 86-72708 DDC 368.8/1 19
HG8059 .C64 1986

Willms, Herbert, 1952- Zur Grossschadenproblematik in der Kraftfahrt-Haftpflichtversicherung /. Bergisch Gladbach , c1986. 114 p. ; ISBN 3-89012-061-X LC Card 87-104056 DDC 368.5/00943 19
HG9990 .W55 1986

INSURANCE, LIABILITY - GERMANY, WEST.
Willms, Herbert, 1952- Zur Grossschadenproblematik in der Kraftfahrt-Haftpflichtversicherung /. Bergisch Gladbach , c1986. 114 p. ; ISBN 3-89012-061-X LC Card 87-104056 DDC 368.5/00943 19
HG9990 .W55 1986

INSURANCE, LIABILITY - UNITED STATES.
Mooney, James E. (James Edward) Liability risk retention . Springfield, N.J. (262 Mountain Ave., P.O. Box 50, Springfield 07081) , c1987. i, 53 p. ; LC Card 87-90408 DDC 368.5/00973 19
HG9990.3 .M66 1987

INSURANCE, LIABILITY - UNITED STATES - FORMS.
Liability insurance account handling guide /. Dallas, Tex. , New York, N.Y. , c1986. v, 71 p. : LC Card 87-401617 DDC 368.5/0068 19
HG9990.3 .L5 1986

INSURANCE, LIABILITY - UNITED STATES - HANDBOOKS, MANUALS, ETC.
Liability insurance account handling guide /. Dallas, Tex. , New York, N.Y. , c1986. v, 71 p. : LC Card 87-401617 DDC 368.5/0068 19
HG9990.3 .L5 1986

INSURANCE, LIFE - AGENTS.
In search of profitability -- agent's business plan /. Des Plaines, Ill.] , c1986. 124 p. : LC Card 87-167903 DDC 368/.0068 19
HG8877 .I49 1986

Total needs selling. Chicago , c1986. viii, 174 p. : ISBN 0-88462-564-8 (pbk.) LC Card 86-23542 DDC 368.3/2/00688 19
HG8877 .T68 1986

INSURANCE, LIFE - CANADA.
Rogers, James E., 1945- Life insurance for Canadians . Vancouver, B.C. [1980] 84 p. : ISBN 0-88908-073-9 (pbk.) LC Card 81-131363
HG8773 .R63 1980

INSURANCE, LIFE - CANADA - ACCOUNTING.
Zucconi, Paul J. Accounting in life and health insurance companies /. Atlanta, Ga. , c1987. xiv, 365 p. : ISBN 0-915322-85-4 LC Card 86-82715 DDC 657/.836 19
HG8848 .Z84 1987

INSURANCE, LIFE - FLORIDA - EXAMINATIONS, QUESTIONS, ETC.
Florida life and health study manual . [Chicago] , c1987. x, 358 p. : ISBN 0-88462-727-6 (pbk.) LC Card 87-17254 DDC 368.3/009759 19
HG8961.F6 F56 1987

INSURANCE, LIFE - GERMANY (WEST) - FINANCE - ECONOMETRIC MODELS.
Lehnhardt-Ritter, Gerda. Das Kapitalanlageverhalten der deutschen Lebensversicherungsunternehmen im Wandel der Konjunktur . Karlsruhe , c1984. xxiii, 444

p. : ISBN 3-88487-067-X LC Card 85-171182
HG9078 .L44 1984

INSURANCE, LIFE - GERMANY (WEST) - STATE SUPERVISION.
Stöffler, Michael. Markttransparenz in der Lebensversicherung . [Mainz] [1982?] vi, 248 p. : LC Card 83-202502
HG9078.Z9 S76 1982

INSURANCE, LIFE - GOVERNMENT POLICY.
Organisation for Economic Co-operation and Development. Committee on Consumer Policy. Consumers and life insurance /. Paris , Washington, D.C. , 1987. 79 p. ; ISBN 92-64-12920-0 (pbk.) : LC Card 87-163859 DDC 368.3/2 19
HG8771 .O73 1987

INSURANCE, LIFE - LAW AND LEGISLATION - FLORIDA - EXAMINATIONS, QUESTIONS, ETC.
Florida life and health study manual . [Chicago] , c1987. x, 358 p. : ISBN 0-88462-727-6 (pbk.) LC Card 87-17254 DDC 368.3/009759 19
HG8961.F6 F56 1987

INSURANCE, LIFE - LAW AND LEGISLATION - GERMANY (WEST)
Stöffler, Michael. Markttransparenz in der Lebensversicherung . [Mainz] [1982?] vi, 248 p. : LC Card 83-202502
HG9078.Z9 S76 1982

INSURANCE, LIFE - LAW AND LEGISLATION - SWITZERLAND.
Die Versicherungsbedingungen und wichtigsten Prämiensätze der in der Schweiz konzessionierten Lebensversicherungsgesellschaften /. Bern , 1986. 101 p. ; LC Card 87-124065 DDC 368.3/2/009494 19
HG9148 .V47 1986

INSURANCE, LIFE - LAW AND LEGISLATION - UNITED STATES - OUTLINES, SYLLABI, ETC.
Lyons, Paula. Life & health insurance . Chicago , c1988. xvi, 351 p. : ISBN 0-88462-707-1 (pbk.) LC Card 87-18506 DDC 368.3/00973 19
HG8951 .L98 1988

INSURANCE, LIFE - MATHEMATICS.
London, Dick, 1943- Graduation, the revision of estimates /. Winsted, Conn. , c1985. viii, 183 p. : ISBN 0-936031-00-X (pbk.) : LC Card 85-23001 DDC 519.5 19
HG8782 .L56 1985 ***NYPL [JLE 86-3272]***

INSURANCE, LIFE - PREMIUMS. see **INSURANCE, LIFE - RATES AND TABLES.**

INSURANCE, LIFE - RATES AND TABLES.
Brownlie, William D. Life insurance . Cincinnati, Ohio , 1983. xii, 201 p. : ISBN 0-87218-033-6 (pbk.) LC Card 83-61584 DDC 368.3/2015 19
HG8853 .B87 1983
NYPL [*R-Econ. 86-3488]

INSURANCE, LIFE - SWITZERLAND.
Die Versicherungsbedingungen und wichtigsten Prämiensätze der in der Schweiz konzessionierten Lebensversicherungsgesellschaften /. Bern , 1986. 101 p. ; LC Card 87-124065 DDC 368.3/2/009494 19
HG9148 .V47 1986

INSURANCE, LIFE - UNITED STATES.
Belth, Joseph M. The A.L. Williams replacement empire . Ellettsville, IN , c1987. 64 p. : ISBN 0-941173-00-3 (pbk.) : LC Card 86-27715 DDC 368.3/2/00973 19
HG8963.A44 B44 1987

Marketing life insurance in a bank or thrift /. Boulder, Colo. , 1986. xii, 233 p. ; ISBN 0-8133-7205-4 : LC Card 86-1644 DDC 332.1/7 19
HG1616.I47 M37 1986
NYPL [JLD 86-3992]

Phillips, David T. Profiting from the insurance revolution /. Alexandria, VA (1101 King St., Suite 400, Alexandria 22314) , c1987. vii, 120, 18 p. : LC Card 87-401086 DDC 368.3/2/00973 19
HG8951 .P47 1987

INSURANCE, LIFE - UNITED STATES - ACCOUNTING.
Zucconi, Paul J. Accounting in life and health insurance companies /. Atlanta, Ga. , c1987. xiv, 365 p. : ISBN 0-915322-85-4 LC Card 86-82715 DDC 657/.836 19
HG8848 .Z84 1987

INSURANCE, LIFE - UNITED STATES - MARKETING.
Individual and family markets. [Chicago] , c1986. ii, 243 p. ; ISBN 0-88462-594-X (loose-leaf) LC Card 86-29692 DDC 368.3/2/0688 19
HG8951 .I44 1986

INSURANCE, LIFE - UNITED STATES - OUTLINES, SYLLABI, ETC.
Lyons, Paula. Life & health insurance . Chicago , c1988. xvi, 351 p. : ISBN 0-88462-707-1 (pbk.) LC Card 87-18506 DDC 368.3/00973 19
HG8951 .L98 1988

INSURANCE, LIFE - UNITED STATES - STATISTICS.
Life solvency monitor. Hartford, Conn. (41 Lewis St., Hartford 06103) , 1985. 201 p. : LC Card 86-215848 DDC 368.3/2/006 19
HG8955 .L55 1985

Life solvency monitor. Hartford, Conn. (101 Pearl St., Hartford 06103) , 1986. 227 p. : LC Card 86-209963 DDC 368.3/2/006 19
HG8955 .L55 1986

1986 ordinary life insurance reference manual . Hartford, Conn. (101 Pearl St., Hartford 06103) [1986] 88 p. ; LC Card 87-163896 DDC 368/.006/073 19
HG8955 .A56 1986

INSURANCE - MANAGEMENT. see **INSURANCE COMPANIES - MANAGEMENT.**

INSURANCE, MARINE.
Kamiński, Zenon. Ubezpieczenia morskie /. Gdańsk , 1980. 191 p. ; LC Card 80-129098
HE965 .K26 1980

INSURANCE, MARINE - GERMANY (WEST)
Sasse, Jürgen. Deutsche Seeversicherung, 1958-1980 . Karlsruhe , 1982. 331 p. ; ISBN 3-88487-030-0 LC Card 83-190184
HE964.5.G7 S27 1982

INSURANCE, MARINE - GREAT BRITAIN - ACCOUNTING.
Carmichael, K. S. (Keith Stanley) Taxation of Lloyd's underwriters /. London , 1980. xvi, 107 p. : ISBN 0-372-30027-8 (pbk.) : LC Card 81-107459
HG8123.G7 C37 1980

INSURANCE, MARINE - IVORY COAST.
Gohibi, Bernard. Les incidences financières de l'assurance maritime sur l'économie ivoirienne /. Abidjan , 1984. 24 leaves ; LC Card 86-111379 DDC 368.2/2/0096668 19
HE964.5.I94 G64 1984
NYPL [JLF 86-1484]

INSURANCE, MARINE - NORWAY.
Norske vilkår for kaskoforsikring av borefartøyer og forsikring av utstyr og forsyninger til borefartøyer, med motiver. English. Norwegian conditions for hull insurance of drilling vessels and insurance of equipment and supplies for drilling vessels, with comments /. [Bergen] , 1977. 107 p. ; LC Card 84-199054
HE964.5.N6 N6713 1977

INSURANCE, MARINE - NORWAY - POLICIES.
Norske vilkår for kaskoforsikring av borefartøyer og forsikring av utstyr og forsyninger til borefartøyer, med motiver. English. Norwegian conditions for hull insurance of drilling vessels and insurance of equipment and supplies for drilling vessels, with comments /. [Bergen] , 1977. 107 p. ; LC Card 84-199054
HE964.5.N6 N6713 1977

INSURANCE, MARINE - TAXATION - GREAT BRITAIN.
Carmichael, K. S. (Keith Stanley) Taxation of Lloyd's underwriters /. London , 1980. xvi, 107 p. : ISBN 0-372-30027-8 (pbk.) : LC Card 81-107459
HG8123.G7 C37 1980

INSURANCE - MARYLAND - DIRECTORIES.
Directory of licensed insurers, licensed motor clubs, licensed health maintenance organizations, licensed rating organizations, registered advisory organizations . [Baltimore, Md.] (501 St. Paul Pl., Baltimore 21202) [1985] viii, 150 p. ; LC Card 86-621407 DDC 368/.0025/752 19
HG8526.M3 D59 1985

INSURANCE - MATHEMATICAL MODELS.
Cresta, Jean-Paul. Théorie des marchés d'assurance /. Paris , 1984. vii, 231 p. : ISBN 2-7178-0696-2 : LC Card 84-235141
HG8054.5 .C74 1984

Dimmer, Klaus. Die optimale Versicherungsentscheidung als risikopolitisches Problem . Karlsruhe , c1986. xiv, 320 p. : LC Card 87-114755 DDC 368/.0072 19
HG8054.5 .D555 1986

INSURANCE - MATHEMATICS.
Actuarial mathematics /. Itasca, Ill. , 1986. xxiii, 624 p. ; ISBN 0-938959-10-7 LC Card 86-61747 DDC 368/.01 19
HG8781 .A26 1986

INSURANCE - MICHIGAN - EXAMINATIONS, QUESTIONS, ETC.
Michigan study manual for life and accident and health insurance. Chicago , c1987. v, 56 p. ; ISBN 0-88462-729-2 (unb.) LC Card 87-18552 DDC 368.3/009774 19
HG8101.M5 M53 1987

INSURANCE, MUTUAL. see **INSURANCE.**

INSURANCE - NEW JERSEY - EXAMINATIONS, QUESTIONS, ETC.
New Jersey study manual for life and accident and health insurance. Chicago , c1987. p. cm. ISBN 0-88462-726-8 LC Card 87-13103 DDC 368.3/009749 19
HG8101.N48 N47 1987

INSURANCE - NEW YORK (STATE) - EXAMINATIONS, QUESTIONS, ETC.
New York study manual for life and accident and health insurance. Chicago , c1987. p. cm. ISBN 0-88462-725-X LC Card 87-13102 DDC 368.3/009747 19
HG8101.N49 N47 1987

INSURANCE - NORWAY.
Forsikring i Norge /. Oslo [1983] 226 p. ; ISBN 82-00-70870-5 LC Card 84-158459
HG8668.5 .F67 1983

INSURANCE, PHYSICIANS' LIABILITY - UNITED STATES.
Tobias, Andrew P. Treating malpractice . New York , 1986. ix, 70 p. ; ISBN 0-87078-173-1 (pbk.) : LC Card 86-217256 DDC 368.5 19
HG8054 .T63 1986

INSURANCE POLICIES - UNITED STATES.
Keenan, Gerald M. Insurance redlining . Chicago, Ill. , c1979. 135 p. :
NYPL [JLF 86-1590]

INSURANCE, POLLUTION LIABILITY - CONGRESSES.
Insuring and managing hazardous risks--from Seveso to Bhopal and beyond /. Berlin , New York , c1987. ix, 534 p. : ISBN 0-387-17732-9 (U. S.) LC Card 87-4963 DDC 346.03/8 342.638 19
HG9994 .I57 1987

INSURANCE, POSTAL LIFE. see **INSURANCE, LIFE.**

INSURANCE, PRODUCTS LIABILITY - UNITED STATES.
Mooney, James E. (James Edward) Liability risk retention . Springfield, N.J. (262 Mountain Ave., P.O. Box 50, Springfield 07081) , c1987. i, 53 p. ; LC Card 87-90408 DDC 368.5/00973 19
HG9990.3 .M66 1987

INSURANCE, PROPERTY - ACCOUNTING.
Basic concepts of accounting and taxation of property/casualty insurance companies /. New York, N.Y. , c1984. 66 p. : ISBN 0-932387-01-2 : ***NYPL [JLE 86-2615]***

INSURANCE, PROPERTY - TAXATION - UNITED STATES.
Basic concepts of accounting and taxation of property/casualty insurance companies /. New York, N.Y. , c1984. 66 p. : ISBN 0-932387-01-2 : ***NYPL [JLE 86-2615]***

Insurance redlining . Keenan, Gerald M. Chicago, Ill. , c1979. 135 p. : *NYPL [JLF 86-1590]*

Insurance ripoffs and dirty tricks . Willard, Harold F. San Diego, Calif. , c1987. 214 p. : ISBN 0-943061-04-0 (pbk.) : LC Card 87-166189 DDC 364.1/68 19
HG8531 .W55 1987

INSURANCE - RISK. see **RISK (INSURANCE)**

INSURANCE - SALESMANSHIP. see **INSURANCE - AGENTS.**

INSURANCE, SICKNESS. see **INSURANCE, HEALTH.**

INSURANCE, SOCIAL. see **SOCIAL SECURITY.**

Insurance special report. Highway Loss Data Institute insurance special report . Washington, D.C. (Watergate 600, Washington 20037) , c1986. 11 p. ; LC Card 86-211182 DDC 368.5/72016/09747 19
HG9970.35.N7 H55 1986

Insurance special report.
Comparison of the insurance loss experience of unibody and frame construction cars after a collision repair, 1981-82 models. Washington, D.C. (Watergate 600, Washington 20037) , c1985. 10 p. : LC Card 87-107697 DDC 368.5/72/00973 19
HG9970.3 .C65 1985

Consistency of model year injury claim frequency results for selected 1981-1983 models. Washington, D.C (Watergate 600, Washington 20037) , c1986. 11 p. ; LC Card 87-107714 DDC 368.5/72/00973 19
HG9970.3 .C66 1986

Injury and collision losses by engine option, selected 1983 models. Washington, D.C. (Watergate 600, Washington 20037) , c1985. 11 p. ; LC Card 87-115471 DDC 368.5/72/00973 19
HG9970.3 .I524 1985

Relationships between losses and vehicle density, 1982-84 models. Washington, D.C. (Watergate 600, Washington 20037) , c1985. 24 p. : LC Card 87-107842 DDC 368.5/72/00973 19
HG9970.3 .R45 1985

INSURANCE, STATE AND COMPULSORY. see **SOCIAL SECURITY.**

INSURANCE - STATE SUPERVISION - ADDRESSES, ESSAYS, LECTURES.
The Economics of insurance regulation . Houndmills, Basingstoke, Hampshire , 1986. xi, 300 p. : ISBN 0-333-39684-7
NYPL [JLD 87-1100]

INSURANCE - STATISTICAL METHODS.
London, Dick, 1943- Survival models and their estimation /. Winsted, Conn. , c1986 (1987 printing) xii, 282 p. : ISBN 0-936031-01-8 (pbk.) LC Card 87-402847 DDC 304.6/4/015195 19
HG8782 .L57 1987

INSURANCE - STUDY AND TEACHING - UNITED STATES.
Schrayer, Robert M. Opportunities in insurance careers /. Lincolnwood, Ill., U. S.A. , c1987. xi, 145 p. : ISBN 0-8442-6008-8 LC Card 87-60102 DDC 368/.0023/73 19
HG8531 .S37 1987

INSURANCE - SWEDEN - DATA PROCESSING.
Handelshögskolan i Stockholm. Ekonomiska forskningsinstitutet. Datoriseringen i försäkringsbranschen . [Stockholm] [1981] 81, [36] p. : ISBN 91-38-06574-6 LC Card 82-244714
HG8673 .H35 1981

INSURANCE - SWITZERLAND.
Steinlin-Fritzsche, Peter. Das Versicherungswesen der Schweiz . Zürich , 1961-1962. 2 v. ; LC Card 87-407799 DDC 368/.9494 19
HG8688 .S76 1961

INSURANCE - TAXATION - GREAT BRITAIN.
Carmichael, K. S. (Keith Stanley) Taxation of Lloyd's underwriters /. London , 1980. xvi, 107 p. : ISBN 0-372-30027-8 (pbk.) : LC Card 81-107459
HG8123.G7 C37 1980

Insurance theft report. Highway Loss Data Institute insurance theft report . Washington, D.C. (Watergate 600, Washington 20037) , c1986. 44 p. ; LC Card 87-107648 DDC 368.2/32/00973021 19
HG9970.3 .H538 1986

INSURANCE, TRANSPORTATION. see **INSURANCE, MARINE.**

INSURANCE, TRAVELERS' - POLAND.
Zelwiański, Ryszard. Ubezpieczenia komunikacyjne . Warszawa , 1979. 177, [3] p. : ISBN 83-219-0031-3 LC Card 81-181561
HG9905.P7 Z45 1979

INSURANCE, UNEMPLOYMENT.
Best, Fred. Reducing workweeks to prevent layoffs . Philadelphia , 1988. p. cm. ISBN 0-87722-506-0 LC Card 87-10097 DDC 331.25/72 19
HD5110.5 .B467 1988

Jonshagen, I. Employment maintenance and unemployment protection for young workers. [Geneva , 1980] 102, 69 p. : LC Card 86-219323 DDC 368.4/4 19
HD7095 .J66 1980

INSURANCE, UNEMPLOYMENT - AUSTRALIA.
Crompton, Cathy. Too old for a job, too young for a pension? . Canberra , 1986. x, 69 p. ; ISBN 0-644-05599-5 LC Card 87-150775 DDC 368.4/4/00880564 19
HD6283.A8 C76 1986

INSURANCE, UNEMPLOYMENT - BRAZIL.
Macedo, Roberto Brás Matos. FGTS e a rotatividade /. São Paulo-SP , Brasília-DF , 1985. 231 p. : ISBN 85-21-30271-1 LC Card 85-187484
HD7096.B6 M33 1985

INSURANCE, UNEMPLOYMENT - CANADA.
Newfoundland. Submission to the Federal Commission of Inquiry on Unemployment Insurance /. [St. John's] [1985] 63, vi p. : LC Card 86-215851 DDC 368.4/4/009718 19
HD7096.C2 N48 1985

Saunders, Ronald. Aid to workers in declining industries /. [Toronto, Ont.] , c1984. 72 p. : ISBN 0-7743-9007-7 (pbk.) LC Card 84-174952 DDC 331.13/77/0971 19
HD6331.2.C2 S28 1984
NYPL [JLD 86-1287]

INSURANCE, UNEMPLOYMENT - CONGRESSES.
Employment promotion and social security . Geneva , 1986. iv, 156 p. ; ISBN 92-2-105574-4 (pbk.) : LC Card 86-234498 DDC 368.4/4 19
HD7095 .E46 1986

INSURANCE, UNEMPLOYMENT - EUROPE - CONGRESSES.
Social security and employment /. Assen, The Netherlands , 1983. 116 p. : ISBN 90-232-2011-0 (pbk.) : LC Card 83-216203 DDC 331.12/094 19
HD7164 .S594 1983 *NYPL [JLE 86-1107]*

INSURANCE, UNEMPLOYMENT - EUROPEAN ECONOMIC COMMUNITY COUNTRIES.
Pérez Menayo, Vicente. La protección del desempleo en España y en los países de las Comunidades Europeas /. [Madrid] [1980?] 303 p. : ISBN 84-500-3715-8 LC Card 83-240633 DDC 368.4/4/00946 19
HD7096.S7 P47 1980 *NYPL [JLE 87-705]*

INSURANCE, UNEMPLOYMENT - GERMANY (WEST)
Haar, Heinrich von der. Jugendarbeitslösigkeit und soziale Sicherung . Berlin , c1982. 216 p. : ISBN 3-88114-302-5 : LC Card 83-152854 DDC 331.3/4/0943 19
HD7096.G3 H33 1982 *NYPL [JLE 87-1214]*

INSURANCE, UNEMPLOYMENT - GERMANY (WEST) - SAARLAND.
Kratz, Hans-Jürgen. Arbeitslosengeld /. Saarbrücken [1983] 176 p. ; ISBN 3-88968-006-2 LC Card 83-215450
HD7096.G32 S335 1983

INSURANCE, UNEMPLOYMENT - GREAT BRITAIN.
Minford, Patrick. Unemployment . Oxford, UK , New York, NY, USA , 1985. x, 214 p. : ISBN 0-631-14506-0 : LC Card 85-13511 DDC 331.13/7941 19
HD5765.A6 M55 1985
NYPL [JLE 86-2297]

INSURANCE, UNEMPLOYMENT - GREAT BRITAIN - HISTORY - 19TH CENTURY.
Beenstock, Michael, 1946- Insurance for unemployment /. London , Boston , 1986. 106 p. ; ISBN 0-04-331113-X (alk. paper) (Great Britain) LC Card 85-30704 DDC 368.4/4/00941 19
HD7096.G7 B36 1986 *NYPL [JLD 86-3693]*

INSURANCE, UNEMPLOYMENT - GREAT BRITAIN - HISTORY - 20TH CENTURY.
Beenstock, Michael, 1946- Insurance for unemployment /. London , Boston , 1986. 106 p. ; ISBN 0-04-331113-X (alk. paper) (Great Britain) LC Card 85-30704 DDC 368.4/4/00941 19
HD7096.G7 B36 1986 *NYPL [JLD 86-3693]*

INSURANCE, UNEMPLOYMENT - ITALY, SOUTHERN.
Boccella, Nicola Maria, 1952- Il Mezzogiorno sussidiato . Milano, Italy , c1982. 264 p. : LC Card 85-163271
HD7185.S68 B62 1982

INSURANCE, UNEMPLOYMENT - LAW AND LEGISLATION - GERMANY (WEST) - SAARLAND.
Kratz, Hans-Jürgen. Arbeitslosengeld /. Saarbrücken [1983] 176 p. ; ISBN 3-88968-006-2 LC Card 83-215450
HD7096.G32 S335 1983

INSURANCE, UNEMPLOYMENT - LAW AND LEGISLATION - UNITED STATES - HISTORY.
Rosbrow, James M. Fifty years of unemployment insurance--a legislative history, 1935-1985. Washington, D.C. , 1986. vii, 97 p. ; LC Card 87-601117 DDC 368.4/4/00973 s 344.73/024/0262 368.4/4/00973 s 347.304240262 19
HD7096.U5 U637 no. 86-5 KF3675

INSURANCE, UNEMPLOYMENT - NEW YORK (STATE) - FINANCE - STATISTICS.
Statistics relative to the New York State Unemployment Insurance Fund, 1936-1984. Albany, N.Y. [1985] vii, 66 p. ; LC Card 86-622164 DDC 368.4/4/009747021 19
HD7096.U6 N793 1985

INSURANCE, UNEMPLOYMENT - NEW YORK (STATE) - STATISTICS.
Statistics relative to the New York State Unemployment Insurance Fund, 1936-1984. Albany, N.Y. [1985] vii, 66 p. ; LC Card 86-622164 DDC 368.4/4/009747021 19
HD7096.U6 N793 1985

INSURANCE, UNEMPLOYMENT - NEWFOUNDLAND.
Newfoundland. Submission to the Federal Commission of Inquiry on Unemployment Insurance /. [St. John's] [1985] 63, vi p. : LC Card 86-215851 DDC 368.4/4/009718 19
HD7096.C2 N48 1985

INSURANCE, UNEMPLOYMENT - SOUTH DAKOTA - STATISTICS.
South Dakota employment & earnings covered by unemployment insurance, 1984. Aberdeen, S.D. [198-] 47 p. : LC Card 87-620925
HD5725.S8 S67 1980z

INSURANCE, UNEMPLOYMENT - SPAIN.
García Murcia, Joaquín. El fondo de garantía salarial /. Madrid , 1983. 454 p. ; ISBN 84-7434-201-5 LC Card 85-194099
HD7096.S7 G37 1983

Pérez Menayo, Vicente. La protección del desempleo en España y en los países de las Comunidades Europeas /. [Madrid] [1980?] 303 p. : ISBN 84-500-3715-8 LC Card 83-240633 DDC 368.4/4/00946 19
HD7096.S7 P47 1980 *NYPL [JLE 87-705]*

INSURANCE, UNEMPLOYMENT - UNITED STATES.
Burgess, Paul L. An incentives approach to improving the unemployment compensation system /. Kalamazoo, Mich. , 1987. xv, 273 p. : ISBN 0-88099-048-1 (pbk.) LC Card 87-23128 DDC 368.4/4/00973 19
HD7096.U5 B87 1987

The Changing labor market . Lexington, Mass. , c1986. x, 166 p. : ISBN 0-669-11943-1 (alk. paper) LC Card 85-45710 DDC 331.12/0973 19
HD6331.2.U5 C47 1986
NYPL [JLE 86-1069]

Malisoff, Harry. The insurance character of

unemployment insurance /. Kalamazoo, Mich. [1961] 44 p. ; LC Card 87-401793 DDC 368.4/4/0973 19
HD7096.U5 M266 1961

INSURANCE - UNITED STATES.
Keenan, Gerald M. Insurance redlining . Chicago, Ill. , c1979. 135 p. :
NYPL [JLF 86-1590]

INSURANCE - UNITED STATES - CORRUPT PRACTICES.
Willard, Harold F. Insurance ripoffs and dirty tricks . San Diego, Calif. , c1987. 214 p. : ISBN 0-943061-04-0 (pbk.) : LC Card 87-166189 DDC 364.1/68 19
HG8531 .W55 1987

INSURANCE - UNITED STATES - SOCIETIES, ETC. - DIRECTORIES.
Schrayer, Robert M. Opportunities in insurance careers /. Lincolnwood, Ill., U. S.A. , c1987. xi, 145 p. : ISBN 0-8442-6008-8 LC Card 87-60102 DDC 368/.0023/73 19
HG8531 .S37 1987

INSURANCE - UNITED STATES - STATE SUPERVISION.
Alliance of American Insurers. Regulation of insurance . Chicago, Ill. , 1977. 68 p. ;
NYPL [JLE 86-1584]

INSURANCE - UNITED STATES - VOCATIONAL GUIDANCE.
Schrayer, Robert M. Opportunities in insurance careers /. Lincolnwood, Ill., U. S.A. , c1987. xi, 145 p. : ISBN 0-8442-6008-8 LC Card 87-60102 DDC 368/.0023/73 19
HG8531 .S37 1987

INSURANCE, WORKING-MEN'S. see **SOCIAL SECURITY.**

INSURANCE, WORKMEN'S. see **SOCIAL SECURITY.**

Insuring and managing hazardous risks--from Seveso to Bhopal and beyond / editors, Paul R. Kleindorfer, Howard C. Kunreuther. Berlin ; New York : Springer-Verlag, c1987. ix, 534 p. : ill. ; 25 cm. Proceedings of the International Conference on Transportation, Storage, and Disposal of Hazardous Materials, held at the International Institute for Applied Systems Analysis, July 1-5, 1985, and sponsored by the Institute, the Geneva Association, and the Center for Risk and Decision Processes of the University of Pennsylvania. Includes bibliographies and index. ISBN 0-387-17732-9 (U. S.) LC Card 87-4963 DDC 346.03/8 342.638 19
1. Insurance, Pollution liability - Congresses. 2. Hazardous substances - Management - Congresses. 3. Hazardous substances - Accidents - Management - Congresses. 4. Risk management - Congresses. I. Kleindorfer, Paul R. II. Kunreuther, Howard. III. International Conference on Transportation, Storage, and Disposal of Hazardous Materials (1985 : International Institute for Applied Systems Analysis). IV. International Institute for Applied Systems Analysis. V. International Association for the Study of Insurance Economics. VI. University of Pennsylvania. Center for Risk and Decision Processes.
HG9994 .I57 1987

INSURRECTIONS. see **REVOLUTIONS.**

Inte bara ord-- : arbetarrörelsen och den internationella solidariteten. Stockholm : Tiden : AIC, c1984. 120 p., [8] p. of plates : ill. ; 21 cm. ISBN 91-550-3086-6 : LC Card 85-120867
1. Trade-unions - Sweden. 2. International labor activities.
HD6758 .I58 1984

Integráció és tulajdon az iparosodó mezőgazdaságban /. Halmai, Péter. [Budapest] , 1984. 124 p. ; ISBN 963-673-278-7 LC Card 85-126691
HD1940.5 .H35 1984

Integral HP electric motors and asociated [sic] controls. New York, N.Y. : Frost & Sullivan, c1983. xii, 280 leaves ; 29 cm. "August 1983." "(#996)." LC Card 87-143831
1. Electric motor industry - United States. 2. Market surveys - United States. I. Frost & Sullivan. II. Title: Integral HP electric motors and associated controls.
HD9697.M693 U55 1983

Integral HP electric motors and associated controls. Integral HP electric motors and asociated [sic] controls. New York, N.Y. , c1983. xii, 280 leaves ; LC Card 87-143831
HD9697.M693 U55 1983

Integrated approach to land use management in the Luangwa Valley. Lupande Development Workshop (1983 : Nyamaluma Wildlife Conservation Camp) Proceedings of the Lupande Development Workshop . Chipata, Zambia , 1984. x, 121 p. : LC Card 84-980605 DDC 333.73/17/096894 19
HD993.Z8 L835 1983 ***NYPL [JLG 87-67]***

An Integrated approach to population, food, and nutrition policies and programmes for national development : report of a regional seminar. Bangkok, Thailand : Economic and Social Commission for Asia and the Pacific, [1979 or 1980] 39 p. ; 28 cm. (Asian population studies series . no. 45) Report of the Regional Seminar on an Integrated Approach to Population, Food, and Nutrition Policies and Programmes for National Development held in Bangkok in 1979. LC Card 82-169080
1. Asia - Population - Congresses. 2. Food supply - Asia - Congresses. 3. Nutrition policy - Asia - Congresses. I. United Nations. Economic and Social Commission for Asia and the Pacific. II. Regional Seminar on an Integrated Approach to Population, Food, and Nutrition Policies and Programmes for National Development (1979 : Bangkok, Thailand). III. Series.
HA4553 .I58 1979

Integrated case studies in accounting and information systems /. Sharifi, Mohsen. Englewood Cliffs, N.J. , c1987. ix, 229 p. : ISBN 0-13-469016-8 (pbk.) LC Card 86-30297 DDC 657/.028/5 19
HF5679 .S4754 1987

INTEGRATED CIRCUITS INDUSTRY.
VHSIC . Norwalk, Conn., U. S.A. (6 Prowitt St., Norwalk 06855) , c1986. v, 219 leaves : LC Card 86-224890 DDC 381/.4562138173/0973 19
HD9696.I582 V47 1986

INTEGRATED CIRCUITS INDUSTRY - UNITED STATES.
New materials for new semiconductors /. Stamford, Conn., U. S.A. , c1986. xii, 198 leaves : ISBN 0-89336-475-4 (soft) LC Card 87-404262 DDC 381/.4562138152/0973 19
HD9696.S43 U492 1986

VHSIC . Norwalk, Conn., U. S.A. (6 Prowitt St., Norwalk 06855) , c1986. v, 219 leaves : LC Card 86-224890 DDC 381/.4562138173/0973 19
HD9696.I582 V47 1986

INTEGRATED CIRCUITS - VERY LARGE SCALE INTEGRATION.
Annaratone, Marco. Digital CMOS circuit design /. Boston , c1986. xv, 344 p. : ISBN 0-89838-224-6 LC Card 86-10646 DDC 621.395 19
TK7871.99.M44 A56 1986
NYPL [JSE 87-634]

Kowalski, Thaddeus J. An artificial intelligence approach to VLSI design /. Boston , c1985. x, 226 p. : ISBN 0-89838-169-X LC Card 85-7581 DDC 621.3819/5835 19
TK7874 .K675 1985 ***NYPL [JSE 86-1182]***

INTEGRATED DATA PROCESSING. see **ELECTRONIC DATA PROCESSING.**

Integrated desk-top environments . Seybold, Patricia B. New York , c1985. ix, 181 p. : ISBN 0-07-056324-1 (pbk.) : LC Card 84-27841 DDC 650/.028/5425 19
HF5548.4.S95 S49 1985
NYPL [JSE 86-2011]

Integrated econmic censuses, 1968-69. Industry concentration statistics . Canberra [1974] 194 p. ; LC Card 82-132323
HD2930 .I53 1974

Integrated fiscal policy : proceedings of Assocham workshop. New Delhi : Associated Chambers of Commerce and Industry of India, [1985] viii, 101 p. : ill. ; 26 cm. On the long-term fiscal policy of the Govt. of India. LC Card 87-902182 DDC 339.5/2/0954 19
1. Fiscal policy - India - Congresses. I. Associated Chambers of Commerce & Industry of India.
HJ1331 .I58 1985

Integrated office systems . Wagoner, Kathleen P. New York , c1987. xxi, 734 p., [4] p. of plates : ISBN 0-471-01195-9 LC Card 86-26793 DDC 651.8 19
HF5547 .W26 1987

Integrated renewable resource management for U. S. insular areas. Washington, DC : Congress of the U. S., Office of Technology Assessment : For sale by the Supt. of Docs., U. S. G.P.O., [1987] vi, 443 p. : ill., maps ; 26 cm. Shipping list no.: 87-357-P. "June 1987"--P. [4] of cover. Includes bibliographies and index. "OTA-F-325"--P. [4] of cover. S/N 052-003-01055-1 Item 1070-M LC Card 86-600595 DDC 333.7 19
1. Renewable natural resources - Puerto Rico - Management. 2. Renewable natural resources - Virgin Islands of the United States - Management. 3. Renewable natural resources - Pacific Islands (Trust Territory) - Management. 4. United States - Insular possessions - Management. I. United States. Congress. Office of Technology Assessment.
HC154.5 .I58 1987

Integrated rural development . Büscher, Ludger. Hamburg , 1984. xx, 238 p. : ISBN 3-87895-261-9 (pbk.) LC Card 86-672442
HD2146.5 .B87x 1984 ***NYPL [JLD 86-2789]***

Integrated Rural Development Project, Serenja-Mpika-Chinsali (Zambia) Farming system and family economy in Ndunya, Chinsali District. Mpika, Zambia [1985?] 45 leaves, [12] leaves of plates : LC Card 86-981252 DDC 338.1/096894 19
HD1476.Z352 N384 1985

Integrated Rural Development Project, Serenje-Mpika-Chinsali (Zambia)
Agricultural commercialisation and the allocation of labour time in Mpika District, northern Zambia. Mpika, Zambia [1986?] iii, 42 leaves : LC Card 86-981249 DDC 338.1/096894 19
HD2131.5.Z9 M653 1986

Farming systems and family economy in Chibale, Serenje District. Mpika, Zambia [1985?] 74 p. : LC Card 86-981248 DDC 338.1/096894 19
HD1476.Z352 C454 1985

Integrated Rural Development Project, Serenje-Mpika-Chinsali (Zambia). Monitoring and Evaluation Unit. A Survey of constraints facing small-scale farmers in Mpika and Chinsali Districts, Northern Province . [Mpika, Zambia?] [1985 or 1986] 8 p., [1] leaf of plates : LC Card 86-981416 DDC 338.1/6 19
HD1476.Z352 M657 1985

Integrated rural energy planning / editors Yehia ElMahgary, Asit K. Biswas. Guildford : Published by Butterworths for the United Nations Environment Programme and the International Society for Ecological Modelling, c1985. xii, 200 p. : ill., forms, maps ; 26 cm. Includes bibliographical references and indexes. ISBN 0-408-22166-6
1. Environmental policy - Developing countries. 2. Energy development - Environmental aspects - Developing countries. 3. Rural development - Developing countries. I. ElMahgary, Yehia. II. Biswas, Asit K. III. International Society for Ecological Modelling. ***NYPL [JLF 87-3]***

Integrated rural energy planning / editors, Yehia ElMahgary, Asit K. Biswas ; [with a forward by Mostafa Kamal Tolba]. Guildford, Surrey, England : Published by Butterworths for the United Nations Environment Programme and the International Society for Ecological Modelling, 1985. xii, 200 p. : ill. ; 26 cm. Includes bibliographies and indexes. CONTENTS. - An integrated rural energy system in Sri Lanka / B.P. Sepalage -- Rural energy systems in Indonesia / M. Pandjaitan and I.G.N. Gde Pemayun -- Integrated rural food-energy systems, technology and technology diffusion in India / C.V. Seshadri -- Bringing energy to the rural sector - the Philippines / Reynoldo D. Asprer -- Development of a new energy village - Xinbu, China / Chen Yancun, Huang Cong and Liang Pusen -- The Niaga Wolof experimental rural energy centre / Mohamed-Ali Toure -- Designing a model rural energy system for Nigeria / J. Oladipo Adejuwon -- Basaisa village integrated field project / Salah Arafa -- Dodoma rural energy project, Tanzania / H.H. Schneiders, E.C. Mjema and S.E. Mmakasa -- Process for rural energy development - Colombia / F. Navas -- Guidelines for planning, development and operation of integrated rural energy projects. ISBN 0-408-22166-6 LC Card 87-160993 DDC 333.79/09172/4 19
1. Energy development - Developing countries - Congresses. 2. Rural development - Developing countries - Congresses. I. ElMahgary, Yehia. II. Biswas, Asit K. III. United Nations. Environment Programme.

IV. International Society for Ecological Modelling.
HD9502.D442 I57 1985

INTEGRATED SERVICES DIGITAL NETWORKS.
ISDN . Boston, MA (200 Portland St., Boston 02114) , c1987. iv, 118 p. : LC Card 87-159823 DDC 380.1/450046 19
HD9696.D382 I82 1987

Integrated voice/data PBXs / Communications/Information Systems. Boston, MA (200 Portland St., Boston 02114) : Yankee Group, c1987. iv, 102 p. : ill. ; 28 cm. (Communications Systems & Services) "April 1987." LC Card 87-402843 DDC 381/.45621385 19
1. Telephone - United States. 2. Telephone - United States - Private branch exchanges. 3. Markets survey - United States. I. Communications/Information Systems (Firm : Yankee Group). II. Series: Communications Systems & Services (Series).
HE8817 .I57 1987

Integrating ethics into the MBA core curriculum /. Dunfee, Thomas W. [Philadelphia] , c1986. 169 leaves : LC Card 87-123702 DDC 174/.4/071173 19
HF5387 .D86 1986

Integrating nutrition into agricultural and rural development projects : six case studies / Nutrition Planning, Assessment, and Evaluation Service, Food Policy and Nutrition Division. Rome : Food and Agriculture Organization of the United Nations, 1984. ix, 132 p. : ill., maps ; 30 cm. (Nutrition in agriculture . no. 2) ISBN 92-5-102150-3
1. Nutrition policy - Developing countries. 2. Agriculture - Developing countries. 3. Rural development - Developing countries. I. Food and Agriculture Organization of the United Nations. Nutrition Planning, Assessment, and Evaluation Service. II. Series. ***NYPL [JLG 86-181]***

Integrating productivity and quality management /. Edosomwan, Johnson Aimie, 1953- New York , c1987. xvii, 360 p. : ISBN 0-8247-7657-7 LC Card 86-32780 DDC 658.5 19
HD56 .E28 1987

Integrating the computer with your business . Porter, James. London , 1980. 308 p. ; ISBN 0-372-30032-4 ***NYPL [JLD 86-2442]***

Integration der Informationsverarbeitung im Büro . Meyer, Rolf, 1957- Bergisch Gladbach , c1986. xiv, 327 p. : ISBN 3-89012-062-8 LC Card 87-104032 DDC 651.8 19
HF5547.5 .M497 1986

Intégration et démocratie /. Toledano Laredo, Armando. Bruxelles, Belgique , 1982. 192 p. ; ISBN 2-8004-0777-8 :c275F LC Card 83-163343
HF1418.5 .T65 1982

The integration of the Black manager into South African organizations /. Charoux, J. A. E. (J. A. Eric) Cape Town , 1986. xi, 178 p. : ISBN 0-7021-1706-4 (pbk.) LC Card 87-113544 DDC 331.6/3/968 19
HD38.25.S6 C53 1986

INTEGRATION, RACIAL. see **RACE RELATIONS.**

INTEGRATION, SOCIAL. see **SOCIAL INTEGRATION.**

Intelektualizatsiia na truda i proizvodstvoto /. Pamukchiev, Minko Stoĭchev. Sofiia , 1982. 48 p. ; LC Card 82-183037
HF5548.8 .P255 1982

INTELLECT AND PERSONALITY. see **PERSONALITY AND INTELLIGENCE.**

INTELLECTRONICS. see **ARTIFICIAL INTELLIGENCE.**

INTELLECTUALS - NEW YORK (N.Y.) - HISTORY - 20TH CENTURY.
Golin, Steve. The fragile bridge . Philadelphia , 1988. p. cm. ISBN 0-87722-534-6 (alk. paper) : LC Card 87-24356 DDC 331.89/287739/0974924 19
HD5325.T42 1913 .P383 1988

INTELLIGENCE, ARTIFICIAL. see **ARTIFICIAL INTELLIGENCE.**

Intelligence for economic development : an inquiry into the role of the knowledge industry / edited by Stevăn Dedijer & Nicolas Jéquier. Leamington Spa, [Warwickshire] ; New York : Berg ; xiii, 264 p. : ill. ; 23 cm. Includes index. ISBN 0-85496-520-3 : LC Card 86-32250 DDC 025/.063389 19
1. Economic development - Information services. 2. Industry - Information services. I. Dedijer, Stevan. II. Jéquier, Nicolas, 1941-.
HD76.2 .I58 1987

Intelligent buildings . Stotter, James. Stamford, Conn., U. S.A. , c1986. ix, 127 leaves : ISBN 0-89336-414-2 (pbk.) LC Card 87-165953 DDC 338.4/769/0973 19
HD9715.U52 S76 1986

Intelligent decision support in process environments /. NATO Advanced Study Institute on Intelligent Decision Support in Process Environments (1985 : San Miniato, Italy) Berlin , New York , c1986. xv, 524 p. : ISBN 0-387-13922-2 (U. S.) LC Card 86-6742 DDC 658.4/03 19
T57.95 .N37 1985 ***NYPL [JFE 86-4847]***

The intelligent investor's guide to profiting from stock market inefficiencies /. Coulson, Robert D. Chicago, Ill. , c1987. xii, 261 p. : ISBN 0-917253-46-9 : LC Card 86-25341 DDC 332.6 19
HG4529.5 .C68 1987

INTELLIGENT MACHINES. see **ARTIFICIAL INTELLIGENCE.**

INTEMPERANCE. see **ALCOHOLISM.**

INTENDANTS - VENEZUELA - BIOGRAPHY.
Hacienda colonial venezolana /. Caracas , 1946. 170 p. ; LC Card 85-105445
HJ991 .H323 1946

Intensifikatsiia ėkonomiki i narodnoe potreblenie / otvetstvennyĭ redaktor Agabab'ian Ė.M. Moskva : In-t ėkonomiki AN SSSR, 1983. 166 p. ; 20 cm. Includes bibliographical references. LC Card 84-227789
1. Consumption (Economics) - Soviet Union. 2. Soviet Union - Economic policy - 1981-. I. Agabab'ian, Ė. M. (Ėdgar Mikhaĭlovich). II. Institut ėkonomiki (Akademiia nauk SSSR).
HC340.C6 I58 1983

Intensifikatsiia i ėffektivnost' v usloviiakh razvitogo sotsializma /. Khachaturov, T. S. (Tigran Sergeevich), 1906- Moskva , 1978. 350 p. ; LC Card 81-167321
HC336.25 .K445 1978

Intensifikatsiia i povyshenie ėffektivnosti promyshlennogo proizvodstva v usloviiakh Severa : sbornik nauchnykh trudov / [otvetstvennye redaktory E.G. Egorov, S.N. Lishcheniuk]. IAkutsk : IAkutskiĭ filial SO AN SSSR, 1986. 109 p. ; 20 cm. At head of title: Akademiia nauk SSSR. Ordena Lenina Sibirskoe otdelenie. IAkutskiĭ filial. Institut ėkonomiki kompleksnogo osvoeniia prirodnykh resursov Severa. Includes bibliographical references. LC Card 87-159706
1. Industrial productivity - Russian S.F.S.R. - IAkutskaia A.S.S.R. 2. Industrial productivity - Russian S.F.S.R. - Siberia, Northeastern. I. Egorov, Egor Grigor'evich. II. Lishcheniuk, S. N. III. Institut ėkonomiki kompleksnogo osvoeniia prirodnykh resursov Severa (Akademiia nauk SSSR).
HC337.I23 I5214 1986

Intensifikatsiia i trudoemkost' stroitel'nogo proizvodstva /. Zarubin, Vadim Nikolaevich. Moskva , 1986. 183, [1] p. ; LC Card 85-178984
HD9715.S72 Z37 1986

Intensifikatsiia--opredeliaiushchee napravlenie sovremennogo ėkonomicheskogo razvitiia /. Drits, V. I. (Valentin Ivanovich) Minsk , 1986. 76, [4] p. ; LC Card 87-144484
HC336.25 .D75 1985

Intensifikatsiia sotsialisticheskogo proizvodstva i khoziaĭstvennyĭ mekhanizm / pod redaktsieĭ V.V. Radaeva. Moskva : Izd-vo Moskovskogo universiteta, 1984. 228 p. ; 21 cm. Includes bibliographical references. LC Card 84-247548
1. Industrial productivity - Soviet Union. 2. Industrial management - Soviet Union. I. Radaev, Valeriĭ Viktorovich.
HC340.I52 I58 1984

Intensive resettlement policies and procedures / Ministry of Lands Resettlement and Rural Development. Rev. [Harare, Zimbabwe] : The Ministry, 1985. 81 p. : ill. ; 31 cm. At head of cover title: Department of Rural Development. LC Card 87-980233 DDC 333.3/1/6891 19
1. Land settlement - Government policy - Zimbabwe. I. Zimbabwe. Ministry of Lands Resettlement and Rural Development. II. Zimbabwe. Dept. of Rural Development.
HD992 .I58 1985

Intensivierung des wissenschaftlich-technischen Arbeitsprozesses / [wissenschaftliche Redaktion, Heinz Fritsch und Ursula Küchler]. Jena : Friedrich-Schiller-Universität, 1985. 200 p. : ill. ; 21 cm. (Wissenschaftliche Beiträge der Friedrich-Schiller-Universität Jena, 0232-3753) Papers presented at a meeting held May 1984 sponsored by the Sektion Marxismus-Leninismus of the Friedrich-Schiller-Universität Jena. "Veröffentlichung der Friedrich-Schiller-Universität Jena"--T.p. verso. Includes bibliographical references. LC Card 86-132567 DDC 338/.06/09431 19
1. Industrial productivity - Germany, East. 2. Technological innovations - Germany, East. I. Fritsch, Heinz. II. Küchler, Ursula. III. Friedrich-Schiller-Universität Jena. Sektion Marxismus-Leninismus. IV. Friedrich-Schiller-Universität Jena. V. Series.
HC290.795.I52 I57 1985

Intenzifikatsiia i efektivno izpolzuvane na osnovnite fondove /. Nakev, Ĭordan V. (Ĭordan Vladimirov) Sofiia , 1985. 203 p. ; LC Card 85-243258
HC403.Z9 C356 1985

InterAction (Organization : U. S.)
Diversity in development . New York, NY , c1985. 49 p. : ISBN 0-932140-06-8 (pbk.) LC Card 86-231753 DDC 361.7/096 19
HC800.Z9 E444 1985

Diversity in development . New York, NY , c1986. xvii, 620 p. : ISBN 0-932140-07-6 (pbk.) LC Card 86-231757 DDC 361.7/025/73 19
HC800.Z9 E444 1986

INTERACTION, SOCIAL. see **SOCIAL INTERACTION.**

INTERACTIVE VIDEO.
Rogers, Everett M. Communication technology . New York , London , c1986. xii, 273 p. : ISBN 0-02-927110-X LC Card 85-27555 DDC 621.38 19
TK5102.5 .R55 1986 ***NYPL [JSE 86-1913]***

Interactive videodisk software market. New York, N.Y. : Frost & Sullivan, c1983. iv, 228 leaves ; 29 cm. "March 1983." "#A1171." LC Card 87-143767
1. Computer software industry - United States. 2. Video disk industry - United States. 3. Market surveys - United States. I. Frost & Sullivan.
HD9696.C63 U518378 1983

Inter-American Committee for Agricultural Development. Tenencia de la tierra y desarrollo socio-económico del sector agrícola. [Guayaquil] [1981] xxv, 539 p., [16] leaves of plates : LC Card 87-673171
HD526 .T46x 1981

INTER-AMERICAN DEVELOPMENT BANK - CONGRESSES.
Seminario Interamericano Conmemorativo de los 25 Años del BID (1985 : Rio de Janeiro, Brazil) Informe del Seminario Interamericano Conmemorativo de los 25 Años del BID /. Rio de Janeiro, RJ , 1986. 65 p. : LC Card 87-403948 DDC 332.1/538 19
HG3881.5.I44 S46 1985

Inter-American Economic and Social Council. Comisión Especial. Informe del gobierno argentino sobre asuntos laborales /. Buenos Aires, República Argentina , 1965. 115 leaves ; LC Card 85-115096
HD8266.5 .I53 1965

INTER-AMERICAN FOUNDATION - HISTORY.
Breslin, Patrick, 1940- Development and dignity . Rosslyn, Va. [1987] xiii, 128 p. : ISBN 0-8133-0632-9 (alk. paper) LC Card 87-3920 DDC 338.91/7308/0601 19
HC125 .B725 1987

Inter-American Institute for Cooperation on Agriculture.
Crop insurance for agricultural development . Baltimore , c1986. xviii, 322 p. ISBN 0-8018-2673-X (alk. paper) LC Card 85-9810 DDC 368.1/22 19
HG9968 .C76 1985 ***NYPL [JLE 86-1082]***

A Mulher rural e mudanças no processo de produção agrícola . [Brasília] [1984] i, 161 p. ;

LC Card 86-150197
HD6073.A292 L295 1984

Inter-American Institute of Agricultural Sciences. Agricultural marketing handbook for Caribbean Basin products. Spanish. Manual--mercadeo de productos agrícolas de la Cuenca del Caribe /. San José, Costa Rica . x, 434 p. : ISBN 92-9039-101-4 LC Card 86-204686
HD9014.C442 A4718 1986

Inter-American Social Development Institute. see **Inter-American Foundation.**

Inter-Arab Investment Guarantee Corporation. Silsilat dalīl al-mustathmir fī al-aqṭār al-'Arabiyah /. al-Kuwayt , <[1985]-. v. <2, 4-5, 7 > : LC Card 86-205217
HG5816.A3 S55 1985

InterBev (Firm) International Beverage Industry Exhibition & Congress (1986 : Dallas, Tex.) Registration list /. Washington, D.C. (1101-16th St., N.W., Washington 20036) , c1986. ca. 400 p. ; LC Card 87-107458 DDC 338.4/7663/025 19
HD9348.A2 I57 1986

INTERCHANGES (HIGHWAY ENGINEERING) see **ROADS - INTERCHANGES AND INTERSECTIONS.**

Intercity experimental ICE, der neue Zug der neuen Bahn . Krummheuer, Eberhard. München , c1986. 200 p. : ISBN 3-923967-25-X : LC Card 86-220676
HE3080.D37 K78 1986

Intercollegiate Studies Institute. Order, freedom, and the polity . Lanham, MD [Bryn Mawr, Pa.] , c1986. x, 184 p. ; ISBN 0-8191-5155-6 (alk. paper) : LC Card 85-26438 DDC 323.44 19
JC571 .O77 1986 ***NYPL [JLE 86-3182]***

Interconexión de cuencas sudamericanas. [Buenos Aires] : Banco Interamericano de Desarrollo, Instituto para la Integración de América Latina, 1986. 159 leaves, [5] leaves of plates : ill. ; 29 cm. (Publ. . no. 247) "BID.INTAL/DP.321/86." LC Card 86-225024
1. Inland water transportation - South America - Planning. 2. Canals - South America - Planning. I. Institute for Latin American Integration. II. Series: Publ. (Institute for Latin American Integration) , no. 247.
HE650 .I58 1986

Intercorporate relations : the structural analysis of business / edited by Mark S. Mizruchi, Michael Schwartz. Cambridge [Cambridgeshire] ; New York : Cambridge University Press, 1987. x, 330 p. : ill. ; 24 cm. (Structural analysis in the social sciences . 1) Includes bibliographies and indexes. ISBN 0-521-33503-5 LC Card 87-6388 DDC 338.7 19
1. Corporations. 2. Directors of corporations. 3. Capitalists and financiers. 4. Functionalism (Social sciences). I. Mizruchi, Mark S. II. Schwartz, Michael, 1942-. III. Series.
HD2741 .I585 1987

Interdependenzen in einem Kennzahlensystem . März, Thomas. München , c1983. iv, 296 p. : ISBN 3-88259-262-1 : LC Card 83-222369
HG4028.V3 M34 1983

Interdisziplinäre Fachtagung "Sibirien als Russisches und Sowjetisches Entwicklungsproblem" (2nd : 1984 : Vlotho, Germany) Sibirien, ein russisches und sowjetisches Entwicklungsproblem /. Berlin , c1986. 274 p. : ISBN 3-87061-260-6 LC Card 86-229174
HC336.9.S53 S53 1986

Interdisziplinärer Arbeitskreis für Entwicklungsländerforschung (Germany) Partnerschaftliche Entwicklungspolitik im Widerstreit der Interessen . Bochum-Querenburg , 1985. i, 184 leaves ; LC Card 87-409475 DDC 332.6/7343/01724 19
HG5993 .P37 1985

INTERDIVISIONAL TRANSFER PRICING. see **TRANSFER PRICING.**

Los intereses económicos en la producción militar de los Estados Unidos /. Fernández Tabío, Luis René. La Habana , 1982. ii, 87 p. : LC Card 87-400639 DDC 338.4/76234/0973 19
HD9743.U6 F46 1982

Interesse e profitto . Ciocca, Pierluigi, 1941- Bologna , c1982. 245 p. : LC Card 84-139966 DDC 332/.0945 19
HG186.I8 C56 1982

INTERESSENGEMEINSCHAFT FARBENINDUSTRIE AKTIENGESELLSCHAFT - BIOGRAPHY.
Köhler, Otto, 1935- --und heute die ganze Welt . Hamburg , c1986. 350 p. : ISBN 3-89136-081-9 LC Card 87-116787
HD9654.9.I5 K64 1986

INTERESSENGEMEINSCHAFT FARBENINDUSTRIE AKTIENGESELLSCHAFT - HISTORY.
Köhler, Otto, 1935- --und heute die ganze Welt . Hamburg , c1986. 350 p. : ISBN 3-89136-081-9 LC Card 87-116787
HD9654.9.I5 K64 1986

INTERESSENGEMEINSCHAFT FARBENINDUSTRIE AKTIENGESELLSCHAFT - POLITICAL ACTIVITY - HISTORY - 20TH CENTURY.
Hayes, Peter, 1946- Industry and ideology . Cambridge [Cambridgeshire] , New York , 1987. xxviii, 411 p. : ISBN 0-521-32948-5 LC Card 86-28388 DDC 338.7/66/00943 19
HD9654.9.I5 H39 1987

Interessenverbände der Unternehmer . Traxler, Franz. Frankfurt am Main , New York , c1986. xv, 410 p. ; ISBN 3-593-33584-0 LC Card 86-156435
HD2429.A9 T73 1986

INTEREST.
Crowe, Robert M. Time and money . Homewood, Ill. , c1987. 1 v. (various pagings) : ISBN 1-556-23051-6 (pbk.) LC Card 87-70621 DDC 332.024 19
HG1621 .C76 1987

Formation et rôle des taux d'intérêt /. Paris , c1982. 204 p. : ISBN 2-7178-0562-1 : LC Card 83-103493
HB539 .F63 1982

Möglichkeiten einer binnenwirtschaftlich orientierten Geldpolitik bei weltweit hohen Zinsen /. Berlin , c1985. 240 p. : ISBN 3-428-05806-2 LC Card 85-199321
HG230.3 .M63 1985

INTEREST AND USURY - MATHEMATICAL MODELS.
Reiss, Winfried, 1941- Umwegproduktion und Positivität des Zinses . Berlin , c1981. 152 p. : ISBN 3-428-05009-6 LC Card 82-146836 DDC 332.8/2/0724 19
HB539 .R423 1981 ***NYPL [JLE 86-2623]***

INTEREST AND USURY - UNITED STATES.
Davey, Patrick J. High interest rates and tight money. [New York, 1969] 25 p. LC Card 70-9411 DDC 332.8/0973
HB545 .D38

The Prospects for economic recovery. Washington, D.C. , 1982. xx, 120 p. :
NYPL [JLF 86-1215]

INTEREST - CANADA - TABLES.
Solomon, Stephen S. Canadian mortgage payments /. New York , c1987. 302 p. ; ISBN 0-8120-3939-4 (pbk.) LC Card 87-13073 DDC 332.8/0212 19
HG1634 .S654 1987

INTEREST - GREAT BRITAIN.
Locke, John, 1632-1704. Several papers relating to money, interest and trade, &c. /. Fairfield, NJ , 1988. p. cm. ISBN 0-678-00334-3 LC Card 87-17243 DDC 332.4/941 19
HG937 .L74 1988

INTEREST GROUPS. see **PRESSURE GROUPS.**

Interest, inflation, and the aggregate consumption function /. Gylfason, Thorvaldur. Stockholm, Sweden [1979] 44 leaves : LC Card 81-114286
HC110.C6 G95 1979

INTEREST - ISLAMIC COUNTRIES.
Khan, Waqar Masood. Towards an interest-free Islamic economic system . Leicester , Islamabad , c1985. 126 p. ; ISBN 0-86037-155-7
NYPL [JLD 87-381]

INTEREST (ISLAMIC LAW)
Saleh, Nabil A. Unlawful gain and legitimate profit in Islamic law . Cambridge [Cambridgeshire] , New York , 1986. xii, 130 p. ; ISBN 0-521-32298-7 LC Card 85-25547 DDC 297/.14 19
LAW ***NYPL [JLE 86-2377]***

Ṣiddīqī, Muḥammad Nejātullah, 1931- Banking without interest /. Leicester, UK , c1983. 192 p. ; ISBN 0-86037-119-0 LC Card 86-673953
HG1588 .S52x 1983

Theoretical studies in Islamic banking and finance /. Houston, Tex. , 1987. xvi, 245 p. : ISBN 0-932625-07-X : LC Card 86-83221 DDC 332.1/0917/4927 19
HG3368.A6 T47 1987

INTEREST - PROBLEMS, EXERCISES, ETC.
De Lisle, Christian. Business interest calculations /. London , c1985. ix, 274 p. ; ISBN 0-08-039231-8 ***NYPL [JLE 87-1030]***

INTEREST RATE FUTURES.
Andersen, Torben Juul. Currency and interest rate hedging . New York, N.Y. , c1987. viii, 272 p. : ISBN 0-13-195645-0 LC Card 87-7758 DDC 332.64/5 19
HG3853 .A53 1987

INTEREST RATE FUTURES - MATHEMATICAL MODELS.
Wondrak, Bernhard. Management von Zinsänderungschancen und -risiken /. Heidelberg , c1986. xv, 254 p. : ISBN 3-7908-0341-3 LC Card 86-213976
HG6024.5 .W66 1986

Interest rate linkages between North Atlantic and Caribbean economies, January 1968 to December 1976. Joefield-Napier, Wallace. Financial integration and interest rate linkages between North Atlantic and Caribbean economies, January 1968 to December 1976 /. St. Augustine, Trinidad [1980] vii, 82 p. : LC Card 81-132125 DDC 332.8/2/0724 19
HG1623.C27 J64 1980 ***NYPL [Sc E 86-329]***

Interest rate, risk, and income distribution /. Shin, Kilman. [Taegu, Korea] , c1986. v, 378 p. : LC Card 87-105107 DDC 330/.01/51 19
HG229 .S436 1986

INTEREST RATES.
Bethmann, Johann Philipp, Freiherr von, 1924- Die Zinskatastrophe . Konigstein/Ts. , c1985. 142 p. ; ISBN 3-7610-8390-4 : LC Card 86-139624
HG1621 .B48 1985

Bierwag, Gerald O. Duration analysis . Cambridge, Mass. , c1987. xvi, 341 p. : ISBN 0-88730-116-9 LC Card 86-28745 DDC 332.8/2 19
HG4515.3 .B54 1987

Brimmer, Andrew F. Monetary policy and the international diffusion of interest rates /. Miami, Fla. [1982] iii, 47 p. : LC Card 86-204514 DDC 332.4/973 19
HG540 .B75 1982

Formation et rôle des taux d'intérêt /. Paris , c1982. 204 p. : ISBN 2-7178-0562-1 : LC Card 83-103493
HB539 .F63 1982

Hadjio, Roman, 1952- Internationaler Zinsverbund /. Frankfurt am Main , New York , c1985. 272 p. : ISBN 3-8204-5691-0 LC Card 85-220128
HG3821 .H27 1985

Hankel, Wilhelm, 1929- Gegenkurs . Berlin , c1984. 261 p. : ISBN 3-88680-114-4 LC Card 84-174753
HB3723 .H26 1984

Ippisch, Wolfgang. Bankbetriebliches Zinsspannen-Management . Wien , c1984. xxiii, 365 p. : ISBN 3-85428-022-X : LC Card 84-174308
HG1621 .I66 1984

Kaufman, Henry. Interest rates, the markets, and the new financial world /. New York, N.Y. , 1986, c1985. xiii, 258 p. : ISBN 0-8129-1333-7 LC Card 86-5865 DDC 332 19
HG173 .K364 1986 ***NYPL [JLD 86-2681]***

Shin, Kilman. Interest rate, risk, and income distribution /. [Taegu, Korea] , c1986. v, 378 p. : LC Card 87-105107 DDC 330/.01/51 19
HG229 .S436 1986

INTEREST RATES - ADDRESSES, ESSAYS, LECTURES.
Controlling interest rate risk . New York , c1986. xv, 414 p. : ISBN 0-471-82354-6 : LC Card 85-22504 DDC 332.8/2 19
HG1621 .C6 1986 ***NYPL [JLE 86-2850]***

INTEREST RATES - BRAZIL.
Ness, Walter L. A influência da correção monetária no sistema financeiro /. Rio de Janeiro , 1977. 205 p. : LC Card 85-206096
HG229 .N385 1977

INTEREST RATES - CANADA - MATHEMATICAL MODELS.
Joefield-Napier, Wallace. Financial integration and interest rate linkages between North Atlantic and Caribbean economies, January 1968 to December 1976 /. St. Augustine, Trinidad [1980] vii, 82 p. : LC Card 81-132125 DDC 332.8/2/0724 19
HG1623.C27 J64 1980 ***NYPL [Sc E 86-329]***

INTEREST RATES - CARIBBEAN AREA - MATHEMATICAL MODELS.
Joefield-Napier, Wallace. Financial integration and interest rate linkages between North Atlantic and Caribbean economies, January 1968 to December 1976 /. St. Augustine, Trinidad [1980] vii, 82 p. : LC Card 81-132125 DDC 332.8/2/0724 19
HG1623.C27 J64 1980 ***NYPL [Sc E 86-329]***

Interest rates determinants and consequences for macroeconomic performance in Spain /. Mauleón, Ignacio. [Madrid] [1984?] 65 p. : ISBN 84-505-0648-7 (pbk.) LC Card 86-215058 DDC 332.8/2/0724 19
HG1623.S7 M38 1984

INTEREST RATES - EFFECT OF INFLATION ON.
Mistri, Maurizio. Tasso di inflazione, saggio di interesse e "nuova" macroeconomia /. Padova , 1985. x, 143 p. : LC Card 86-214490
HB539 .M54 1985

INTEREST RATES - MATHEMATICAL MODELS.
Kostiainen, Seppo. Capital controls under alternative exchange rate and monetary policy regimes /. Joensuu , 1986. 27 p. ; ISBN 951-696-619-5 (pbk.) LC Card 87-100851 DDC 332.4/5 19
HG3823 .K673 1986

Nowak, Felicitas. The allocation of bank credit and the efficiency of investment /. Göttingen, Rep. Fed. de Alemania [1986] 23 p. : LC Card 87-121215 DDC 332.7/0724 19
HG1641 .N68 1986

INTEREST RATES - NEW ZEALAND.
LLoyd, K. A. The term structure of interest rates in New Zealand, 1977-1985 /. Wellington, N.Z. [1986] 41, 3 p. : LC Card 86-212755 DDC 332.8/2/09931 19
HG1623.N48 L56 1986

INTEREST RATES - SPAIN - ECONOMETRIC MODELS.
Mauleón, Ignacio. Interest rates determinants and consequences for macroeconomic performance in Spain /. [Madrid] [1984?] 65 p. : ISBN 84-505-0648-7 (pbk.) LC Card 86-215058 DDC 332.8/2/0724 19
HG1623.S7 M38 1984

INTEREST RATES - SWITZERLAND.
Capitelli, René. Die Zinsstruktur der Schweiz . Frankfurt am Main , c1983. ix, 221 p. : ISBN 3-88129-700-6 LC Card 84-129042
HG1623.S9 C36 1983

INTEREST RATES - TABLES.
Thorndike, David, 1925- Thorndike encyclopedia of banking and financial tables /. Boston , c1987. 1737 p. in various pagings ; ISBN 0-88712-883-1 LC Card 87-50721 DDC 332.8/0212 19
HG1626 .T49 1987

Interest rates, the markets, and the new financial world /. Kaufman, Henry. New York, N.Y. , 1986, c1985. xiii, 258 p. : ISBN 0-8129-1333-7 LC Card 86-5865 DDC 332 19
HG173 .K364 1986 ***NYPL [JLD 86-2681]***

INTEREST RATES - UNITED STATES.
Brimmer, Andrew F. Monetary policy and the international diffusion of interest rates /. Miami, Fla. [1982] iii, 47 p. : LC Card 86-204514 DDC 332.4/973 19
HG540 .B75 1982

Economic choices 1987 /. Washington, D.C. , 1986. xii, 126 p. ; ISBN 0-8157-1040-2 LC Card 85-48278 ***NYPL [JLE 86-2737]***

INTEREST RATES - UNITED STATES - CHARTS, DIAGRAMS, ETC.
Fisher, Kenneth L. The Wall Street waltz . Chicago , c1987. xii, 210 p. : ISBN 0-8092-4797-6 : LC Card 87-5310 DDC 332.63/222/0973 19
HG4916 .F47 1987.

INTEREST RATES - UNITED STATES - ECONOMETRIC MODELS.
Gylfason, Thorvaldur. Interest, inflation, and the aggregate consumption function /. Stockholm, Sweden [1979] 44 leaves : LC Card 81-114286
HC110.C6 G95 1979

INTEREST RATES - UNITED STATES - MATHEMATICAL MODELS.
Joefield-Napier, Wallace. Financial integration and interest rate linkages between North Atlantic and Caribbean economies, January 1968 to December 1976 /. St. Augustine, Trinidad [1980] vii, 82 p. : LC Card 81-132125 DDC 332.8/2/0724 19
HG1623.C27 J64 1980 ***NYPL [Sc E 86-329]***

INTEREST - TABLES.
Financial comprehensive ARM payment tables /. Boston, Mass. , Philadelphia, PA , c1985. 255 p. ; ISBN 0-89471-379-5 (pbk.) : LC Card 85-206951 DDC 332.8/2/021 19
HG1634 .F44 1985

Friedman, Jack P. Adjustable rate mortgages /. New York , c1987. viii, 293 p. ; ISBN 0-8120-3764-2 (soft) : LC Card 86-28852 DDC 332.8/2 19
HG1634 .F75 1987

Sherman, Michael. Comprehensive compound interest tables /. Chicago , c1986. 280 p. ; ISBN 0-8092-4875-1 (pbk.) : LC Card 86-208382 DDC 332.8/2/021 19
HG1632 .S54 1986

Thorndike, David, 1925- Thorndike encyclopedia of banking and financial tables /. Boston , c1987. 1737 p. in various pagings ; ISBN 0-88712-883-1 LC Card 87-50721 DDC 332.8/0212 19
HG1626 .T49 1987

Interferex AG. Interferex 86 (Basel, Switzerland) Interferex 86, Intertable . Basel, Schweiz [1986] 284 p., [6] p. of plates : LC Card 87-409294 DDC 381/.18 19
HF5474.S92 B365 1986

Interferex Sechsundachtzig, Intertable. Interferex 86 (Basel, Switzerland) Interferex 86, Intertable . Basel, Schweiz [1986] 284 p., [6] p. of plates : LC Card 87-409294 DDC 381/.18 19
HF5474.S92 B365 1986

Interferex 86 (Basel, Switzerland) Interferex 86, Intertable : 14. Internationale Fachmesse für Eisenwaren, Werkzeuge und Haushaltartikel : mit Intertable, Fachmesse für den schön gedeckten Tisch : 7.-9. September 1986 in den Hallen der Schweizer Mustermesse Basel/Schweiz / Veranstalter, Interferex AG, Basel = 14e Salon professionnel international de la quincaillerie, de l´outillage et des arts ménagers : avec Intertable, salon professionnel des arts de la table : du 7 au 9 septembre 1986 dans les bâtiments de la Foire Suisse d´Echantillons Bâle/Suisse / organisateur, Interferex SA, Bâle = 14th International Specialized Trade Fair for Hardware, Tools and Household Goods : with Intertable, trade fair for elegant tableware : 7-9 September 1986 in the halls of the Swiss Industries Fair, Basle/Switzerland / organizer, Interferex Ltd., Basle. Basel, Schweiz : Interferex, [1986] 284 p., [6] p. of plates : ill. (some col.) ; 21 cm. Catalog. German, English, and French. LC Card 87-409294 DDC 381/.18 19
1. Interferex 86 (Basel, Switzerland). 2. Fairs - Switzerland - Basel. 3. Hardware industry - Switzerland - Directories. 4. Machine-tool industry - Switzerland - Directories. 5. Household electronics industry - Switzerland - Directories. I. Interferex AG. II. Intertable (1986 : Basel, Switzerland). III. Title. IV. Title: Interferex Sechsundachtzig, Intertable.
HF5474.S92 B365 1986

INTERFEREX 86 (BASEL, SWITZERLAND)
Interferex 86 (Basel, Switzerland) Interferex 86, Intertable . Basel, Schweiz [1986] 284 p., [6] p. of plates : LC Card 87-409294 DDC 381/.18 19
HF5474.S92 B365 1986

Interferex 86, Intertable . Interferex 86 (Basel, Switzerland) Basel, Schweiz [1986] 284 p., [6] p. of plates : LC Card 87-409294 DDC 381/.18 19
HF5474.S92 B365 1986

InterFinance Corporation. National emerging industries site selection guide /. Minneapolis, MN , c1986. 124 p. ; LC Card 86-231272 DDC 338.6/042/02573 19
HC110.D5 N38 1986

INTERGENERATIONAL RELATIONS - HUNGARY.
Halász, Péter. Nemzedéki vonások a mezőgazdasági kistermelésben /. Budapest , 1984. 72 p. ; ISBN 963-491-192-7 LC Card 86-198744
HD1476.H8 H252 1984

INTERGENERATIONAL RELATIONS - MATHEMATICAL MODELS.
Breyer, Friedrich. Family structure and intergenerational transfers in social health insurance . Berlin [1986] 24 p. : LC Card 87-156738 DDC 368.4/2016/0724 19
HD7101 .B73 1986

INTERGOVERNMENTAL COUNCIL OF COPPER EXPORTING COUNTRIES - CONGRESSES.
Chile y CIPEC ante la crisis del cobre /. Santiago de Chile , 1985. 74 p. ; LC Card 86-144485
HD9539.C7 C526 1985 ***NYPL [JLD 87-363]***

INTERGOVERNMENTAL FISCAL RELATIONS - AUSTRALIA.
Warhurst, John. Central agencies, intergovernmental managers, and Australian federal-state relations /. Canberra , 1983. vi, 27 p. : ISBN 0-86784-318-7 (pbk.) LC Card 85-217351
JQ4020.S8 W28 1983
NYPL [JLL 82-87 no.29]

INTERGOVERNMENTAL FISCAL RELATIONS - AUSTRIA.
Los Problemas financieros en el Estado regionalizado /. Madrid , 1983. 207 leaves ; LC Card 85-177739
HJ1120 .P75 1983

INTERGOVERNMENTAL FISCAL RELATIONS - BELGIUM.
Los Problemas financieros en el Estado regionalizado /. Madrid , 1983. 207 leaves ; LC Card 85-177739
HJ1120 .P75 1983

INTERGOVERNMENTAL FISCAL RELATIONS - BRAZIL.
Baptista, Lourival. Reforma tributária, federalismo e desenvolvimento nacional /. Brasília , 1983. 255 p. : LC Card 86-210783
HJ2525 .B36 1983

INTERGOVERNMENTAL FISCAL RELATIONS - CANADA.
Bricall, Josep Maria, 1936- Estat autonòmic i finances públiques . [Barcelona] , 1984. 358 p. : ISBN 84-500-9868-8 LC Card 85-106586
HJ1000 .B75 1984 ***NYPL [JLE 86-3989]***

Fiscal federalism /. Toronto , Buffalo , c1986. xvi, 211 p. ; ISBN 0-8020-7312-3 (pbk.)
HJ793 .F59 1986 ***NYPL [JLE 86-3253]***

INTERGOVERNMENTAL FISCAL RELATIONS - EUROPE.
Bricall, Josep Maria, 1936- Estat autonòmic i finances públiques . [Barcelona] , 1984. 358 p. : ISBN 84-500-9868-8 LC Card 85-106586
HJ1000 .B75 1984 ***NYPL [JLE 86-3989]***

Meadows, W. J. The response of local authorities to central government incitement to reduce expenditure . Strasbourg , 1986. 33 p. ; LC Card 87-135687 DDC 336.3/9/094 19
HJ9415 .M43 1986

INTERGOVERNMENTAL FISCAL RELATIONS - EUROPEAN ECONOMIC COMMUNITY COUNTRIES.
Kelly, G. Financial resources for local and regional authorities /. Strasbourg , 1985. 79 p. ; LC Card 86-206535 DDC 336/.014/4 19
HJ9420 .K45 1985

INTERGOVERNMENTAL FISCAL RELATIONS - GERMANY, WEST.
Massat, Dieter. Die ökonomische Problematik von Zuweisungen an Kommunen /. Thun , c1984. vii, 321 p. : ISBN 3-87144-792-7 LC Card 84-183709
HJ1121 .M37 1984

Los Problemas financieros en el Estado

regionalizado /. Madrid , 1983. 207 leaves ; LC Card 85-177739
HJ1120 .P75 1983

INTERGOVERNMENTAL FISCAL RELATIONS - GERMANY (WEST) - NORTH RHINE-WESTPHALIA.
Kops, Manfred. Die regionalen Verteilungswirkungen des kommunalen Finanzausgleichs . Thun , c1983. xvii, 537, 259 p. : ISBN 3-87144-728-5 : LC Card 83-159176
HJ9493.5.N6 K66 1983

INTERGOVERNMENTAL FISCAL RELATIONS - GERMANY (WEST) - RUHR (REGION)
Meyer, Willm Rolf. Ressourcenumverteilung zugunsten von Problemregionen . Frankfurt/Main , New York , c1982. 262 p. : ISBN 3-593-33036-9 LC Card 82-161064 DDC 336.1/85 19
HJ1121 .M49 1982 ***NYPL [JLD 86-3292]***

INTERGOVERNMENTAL FISCAL RELATIONS - GREAT BRITAIN.
Rhodes, R. A. W. The national world of local government /. London , 1986. xviii, 441 p. ; ISBN 0-04-320170-9 (alk. paper) LC Card 85-15103 DDC 352.041 19
JS3137 .R49 1986 ***NYPL [JLD 86-1931]***

INTERGOVERNMENTAL FISCAL RELATIONS - GREAT BRITAIN - HISTORY - 17TH CENTURY.
Cust, Richard. The forced loan and English politics, 1626-1628 /. Oxford [Oxfordshire] , New York , 1987. x, 358 p. ; ISBN 0-19-822951-8 : LC Card 87-7977 DDC 336.42 19
HJ1012 .C87 1987

INTERGOVERNMENTAL FISCAL RELATIONS - INDIA.
Gaur, Achal Kumar, 1959- Centre-state financial relations and finance commissions /. Allahabad, India , 1985. x, 364 p. ; LC Card 85-904373 DDC 336.54 19
HJ1334 .G38 1985

Sharda, N. K. State finances and regional development in India /. New Delhi , c1986. 248 p. ; LC Card 86-900599 DDC 336.54/52 19
HJ1339.H55 S54 1986 ***NYPL [JLD 86-3211]***

INTERGOVERNMENTAL FISCAL RELATIONS - INDIA - CASE STUDIES.
Govinda Rao, M. Political economy of tax and expenditure determination . New Delhi , 1981. vii, 212 p. ; LC Card 81-905062 DDC 336.54 19
HJ1337 .G68 1981 ***NYPL [JLD 86-2603]***

INTERGOVERNMENTAL FISCAL RELATIONS - ITALY.
Romagnoli, Gian Cesare, 1948- Nuove politiche di finanziamento degli enti locali in Italia . Milano, Italy , c1985. 260 p. : LC Card 86-169439
HJ9497 .R65 1985

INTERGOVERNMENTAL FISCAL RELATIONS - ITALY - CONGRESSES.
La Politica di bilancio in condizioni di stress fiscale . Milano, Italy , c1986. 377 p. ; LC Card 87-134343
HJ2119 .P65 1986

INTERGOVERNMENTAL FISCAL RELATIONS - MARYLAND.
Major fiscal issues at the 1983-1986 sessions of the General Assembly. Annapolis, Md. (90 State Cir., Annapolis 21401-1991) [1986] vi, 100 p. ; LC Card 86-622757 DDC 336.752 19
HJ485 .M15 1986

INTERGOVERNMENTAL FISCAL RELATIONS - MINNESOTA - ACCOUNTING.
Minnesota. Financial and compliance report on federally assisted programs for the year ended June 30, 1985 /. [Saint Paul, Minn.] [1986] x, 92 p. ; LC Card 87-620971 DDC 353.97760072/52 19
HJ515 .M55 1986

INTERGOVERNMENTAL FISCAL RELATIONS - NEW JERSEY.
New Jersey. Bureau of Urban Strategies. Proposed solutions to local fiscal resource disparities in the state of New Jersey . Trenton, N.J. [1980] vi, 353 p. ; LC Card 81-622089 DDC 336.02/749 19
HJ585 .N38 1980 ***NYPL [JLF 86-1372]***

INTERGOVERNMENTAL FISCAL RELATIONS - NEW YORK (STATE)
New York's highway system . Albany, N.Y. , 1986. S-2, iv, 130 p. : ***NYPL [JLD 86-2346]***

INTERGOVERNMENTAL FISCAL RELATIONS - PORTUGAL.
Lei das finanças locais . [Lisbon] [1980] 56 leaves ; LC Card 83-223473
HJ9529 .L45 1980

INTERGOVERNMENTAL FISCAL RELATIONS - SOVIET UNION.
Avak'ian, Suren Adibekovich. Sovety i rukovodstvo ėkonomikoĭ . Moskva , 1985. 110 p. ; LC Card 87-118114
HC336.25 .A87 1985

Bahry, Donna. Outside Moscow . New York , 1987. 236 p. : ISBN 0-231-06290-7 LC Card 87-8020 DDC 336.47 19
HJ2130 .B35 1987

INTERGOVERNMENTAL FISCAL RELATIONS - SPAIN.
Gimeno Ullastres, Juan Antonio. El nuevo Estado fiscal español . Madrid , 1981. xx, 315 p. : ISBN 84-7214-219-1 LC Card 85-176738
HJ1249.A1 G56 1981

INTERGOVERNMENTAL FISCAL RELATIONS - SPAIN - ANDALUSIA.
Junta de Andalucía. Grupo de Trabajo 14, Planificación Económica de las Corporaciones Locales y Comarcalización. Plan económico de Andalucía, 1984-1986 /. [Andalucía] , 1983. 133 p. ; ISBN 84-505-1243-3 LC Card 86-223752
HJ1249.A4 J86 1983

INTERGOVERNMENTAL FISCAL RELATIONS - SWITZERLAND.
Dürsteler, Urs. Kantonale Verteilung der Bundesausgaben 1983 . Bern , c1986. 55 p. ; ISBN 3-258-03577-6 : LC Card 86-149603
HJ1264.A2 D87 1986

Los Problemas financieros en el Estado regionalizado /. Madrid , 1983. 207 leaves ; LC Card 85-177739
HJ1120 .P75 1983

INTERGOVERNMENTAL FISCAL RELATIONS - UNITED STATES.
An Alphabetical guide to Office of Revenue Sharing account numbers /. Washington, D.C. , 1981. iii, 187 p. ; ***NYPL [JLF 87-470]***

Bricall, Josep Maria, 1936- Estat autonòmic i finances públiques . [Barcelona] , 1984. 358 p. : ISBN 84-500-9868-8 LC Card 85-106586
HJ1000 .B75 1984 ***NYPL [JLE 86-3989]***

Committee for Economic Development. Research and Policy Committee. Leadership for dynamic state economies . New York, N.Y. , 1986. xii, 104 p. ; ISBN 0-87186-782-6 LC Card 86-20760 DDC 338.973 19
HC103 .C734 1986 ***NYPL [JLF 86-1832]***

Federal-state-local fiscal relations . Washington, D.C. [1986] 2 v. (viii, 1118 p.) : LC Card 86-603179 DDC 336.73 19
HJ275 .F427 1986

Hackett, Judith C. Managing rural infrastructure . Lexington, Ky. , c1986. iii, 36 p. : ISBN 0-87292-070-4 (pbk.) : LC Card 87-404481 DDC 363/.0973 19
HD3888 .H27 1986

Hard choices . Washington , 1984. 23 v. : ***NYPL [JLE 87-566 Appendix 1-23]***

Houseman, Gerald L. State and local government . Englewood Cliffs, N.J. , c1986. xvi, 272 p. : ISBN 0-13-843368-2 (pbk.) LC Card 85-16981 DDC 320.973 19
JK2408 .H79 1986 ***NYPL [JLE 86-2916]***

Kaplan, Marshall. Hard choices . Washington , 1984. xi, 230 p. : LC Card 84-602470 DDC 338.4/3363/0973 19
HC110.C3 K37 1984 ***NYPL [JLE 87-566]***

Nathan, Richard P. Reagan and the States /. Princeton, N.J. , c1987. xv, 375 p. : ISBN 0-691-07748-7 (alk. paper) : LC Card 87-45529 DDC 353.0072/5 19
HJ2051 .N167 1987

Los Problemas financieros en el Estado regionalizado /. Madrid , 1983. 207 leaves ; LC Card 85-177739
HJ1120 .P75 1983

Project on the Federal Social Role (U. S.). Committee on Federalism and National Purpose. To form a more perfect union /. Washington, D.C. (1730 M St., Suite 911, Washington 20036) , c1985. xi, 52 p. ; ***NYPL [JLE 86-1879]***

Romagnoli, Gian Cesare, 1948- Nuove politiche di finanziamento degli enti locali in Italia . Milano, Italy , c1985. 260 p. : LC Card 86-169439
HJ9497 .R65 1985

Van Horn, Carl E. Policy implementation in the Federal system . Lexington, Mass. , c1979. xiv, 177 p. ; ISBN 0-669-02435-X LC Card 78-19929 DDC 353.007/25
HJ275 .V35 ***NYPL [JLE 80-794]***

INTERGOVERNMENTAL FISCAL RELATIONS - UNITED STATES - ADDRESSES, ESSAYS, LECTURES.
State politics and the new federalism . White Plains, N.Y. , c1986. xv, 544 p. : ISBN 0-582-28474-0 (pbk.) LC Card 85-15956 DDC 321.02/0973 19
JK325 .S77 1986 ***NYPL [JLD 86-2766]***

Intergovernmental relations and public policy / edited by J. Edwin Benton and David R. Morgan ; prepared under the auspices of the Policy Studies Organization. New York : Greenwood Press, 1986. viii, 224 p. : ill. ; 25 cm. (Contributions in political science, 147-1066 . no. 156) Includes index. Bibliography: p. [213]-216. ISBN 0-313-25443-5 (lib. bdg. : alk. paper) LC Card 86-3155 DDC 353.9/29 19
1. Federal government - United States. 2. Federal-city relations - United States. 3. State-local relations - United States. I. Benton, J. Edwin, 1950-. II. Morgan, David R. III. Policy Studies Organization.
JK325 .I575 1986 ***NYPL [JLE 87-749]***

INTERGOVERNMENTAL TAX RELATIONS - BRAZIL.
Longo, Carlos Alberto. Ajustamentos de impostos na fronteira e a alocação de receitas tributárias . São Paulo , 1979. 208 p. ; LC Card 80-152384
HJ5715.B8 L6617 ***NYPL [JLD 86-3846]***

INTERGOVERNMENTAL TAX RELATIONS - ILLINOIS.
Tax report . Springfield, Ill. (703 Stratton Office Bldg., Springfield 62706) [1986] iv, 30, 3 leaves ; LC Card 86-622596 DDC 336.2/009773 19
HJ2403 .T39 1986

INTERGOVERNMENTAL TAX RELATIONS - NEW YORK (STATE)
Lost revenue . [Albany, N.Y.?] [1986] 13, 22 leaves ; LC Card 87-620567 DDC 336.2/009747 19
HJ3324 .L67 1986

The President's tax reform proposal . [Albany, N.Y.] [1985] 48 leaves : LC Card 86-622434 DDC 336.2/009747 19
HJ2424 .P84 1985

The United States Senate's tax reform proposal . [Albany, N.Y.?] [1986] 18, 6, 2 leaves ; LC Card 87-620727 DDC 336.2/009747 19
HJ2424 .U55 1986

INTERGOVERNMENTAL TAX RELATIONS - SPAIN.
Gimeno Ullastres, Juan Antonio. El nuevo Estado fiscal español . Madrid , 1981. xx, 315 p. : ISBN 84-7214-219-1 LC Card 85-176738
HJ1249.A1 G56 1981

INTERGOVERNMENTAL TAX RELATIONS - UNITED STATES.
Dilger, Robert Jay, 1954- The deductibility of state and local taxes . Washington, D.C. [1985] 1 v. (various pagings) ; ISBN 0-933729-02-2 (pbk.) : LC Card 85-155605 DDC 336.24/216 19
HJ4653.D4 D55 1985 ***NYPL [JLF 86-412]***

Interim household and family projections for Canada, provinces, and territories to 2006 = Projections provisoires des ménages et des familles pour le Canada, les provinces et territoires jusqu'à 2006. [Ottawa] : Statistics Canada, Demography Division, Population Projections Section, [1987] 67 p. ; 28 cm. English and French. Prepared by M.V. George and others. Rev. ed. of: Household and family projections. 1981. "January 1987." Bibliography: p. 21. LC Card 87-162270 DDC 304.6/2/0971021 19

1. Households - Canada - Forecasting - Statistics. 2. Family - Canada - Forecasting - Statistics. 3. Population forecasting - Canada - Statistics. I. George, M. V. II. Statistics Canada. Population Projections Section. III. Household and family projections. IV. Title: Projections provisoires des ménages et des familles pour le Canada, les provinces et territoires jusqu'à 2006.
HA745 .I62 1987

Interim report . Australia. Industries Assistance Commission. Canberra , 1976. 36 p. ; ISBN 0-642-02317-4 (pbk.) LC Card 85-132707
HD9969.B433 A83 1976

Interim reports of the project "Transformation of the agricultural landscape in tropical archipelagos" .
(v. 4) Environment, agriculture, and society in the Malay world /. Kyoto, Japan , 1986. ix, 177 p. : LC Card 86-201590 DDC 338.1/09595 19
HD2080.6 .E58 1986

Les intérimeurs /. Tartakowsky, Pierre, 1952- Paris , c1985. 260 p., [8] p. of plates : ISBN 2-209-05678-0 : LC Card 85-152003 DDC 331.12/5 19
HD5854.2.F7 T37 1985

Interior mina . Poppe, René. La Paz, Bolivia , 1986. 236 p. ; LC Card 87-400962 DDC 331.7/622/0984 19
HD8039.M61 B634 1986

INTERIOR NAVIGATION. see **INLAND NAVIGATION.**

Interlinkages, concept, characteristics, and determining factors /. Boneo, Horacio. Austin , 1986. 17 p. : LC Card 86-622253 DDC 338.7/4/091724 19
HD4420.8 .B67 1986

Intermediate accounting /. Chasteen, Lanny G., 1942- New York , c1987. xxviii, 1328 p. : ISBN 0-394-35802-3 : LC Card 86-29865 DDC 657/.044 19
HF5635 .C474 1987

Intermediate accounting . Smith, Jay M. Cincinnati , c1987. xix, 1234 p. : ISBN 0-538-01921-2 LC Card 87-60815 DDC 657/.044 19
HF5635 .S5946 1987

INTERMEDIATION (FINANCE)
Bryant, Ralph C., 1938- International financial intermediation /. Washington, D.C. , c1987. xi, 181 p. : ISBN 0-8157-1138-7 : LC Card 87-10358 DDC 332/.042 19
HG3891.5 .B79 1987

Solberg, Ronald L., 1953- Sovereign rescheduling . London , Boston , 1988. p. cm. ISBN 0-04-332122-4 (alk. paper) LC Card 87-18805 DDC 336.3/435 19
HG3891.5 .S65 1988

INTERMEDIATION (FINANCE) - DEVELOPING COUNTRIES.
Wellons, Philip A. Banks and specialised financial intermediaries in development /. Paris , Washington, D.C. , 1986. 150 p. : ISBN 92-64-12867-0 (pbk.) : LC Card 87-114506 DDC 332.1/09172/4 19
HG3550 .W45 1986

Intern marknadsföring . Rosenlew, Andreas. [Helsinki] [1985] 51 p. : ISBN 951-555-227-3 LC Card 85-214635
HF5415 .R5795 1985

A internacional capitalista . Dreifuss, René Armand. Rio de Janeiro , 1986. 502, [40] p. : LC Card 87-126893 DDC 322/.3 19
HD2755.5 .D74 1986

A internacionalização financeira no Brasil /. Baer, Mônica. Petrópolis , 1986. 159 p. ; LC Card 86-200812
HG185.B7 B28 1986

Internal Improvement Convention (1834 : Baltimore, Md.) Journal of the Internal improvement convention, which assembled in Baltimore, on the 8th day of December, 1834. Baltimore, Printed by Sands & Neilson, 1835. 93 p., 1 l. fold. map. 23 cm. The convention was composed of delegates from Pennsylvania, Ohio, Virginia, Maryland, and the District of Columbia, and had for its principal work the raising of funds, etc., for the completion of the Chesapeake and Ohio canal. LC Card 06-22129
1. Chesapeake and Ohio Canal (Md. and Washington, D.C.). I. Title.
HE396.C5 I6

INTERNAL IMPROVEMENT MOVEMENT. see **PUBLIC WORKS.**

INTERNAL MIGRATION. see **MIGRATION, INTERNAL.**

Internal migration and fertility in Lesotho /. Makatjane, Tiisetso. [Roma, Lesotho] [1985] iii, 36 leaves ; LC Card 87-132347 DDC 304.6/32/096816 19
HB2123.7.A3 M35 1985

Internal migration and population redistribution in India . Prabhakara, N. R. New Delhi , 1986, c1985. xi, 117 p. ; LC Card 86-902406 DDC 304.8/0954/87 19
HB2100.K37 P73 1985

Internal migration in Egypt . Ibrahim, Saad Eddin. Cairo, Egypt [1982] 86, viii p. : LC Card 84-960007 DDC 304.8/0962 19
HB2121.7.A3 I27 1982

INTERNAL SECURITY - LATIN AMERICA.
Wiarda, Howard J., 1939- Population, internal unrest, and U. S. security in Latin America /. [Amherst] , 1986. 50 p. ; LC Card 87-621399 DDC 304.6/098 19
HB3530.5.A3 W5 1986

INTERNAL TRANSFER PRICING. see **TRANSFER PRICING.**

INTERNATIONAL. Projektmanagement, INTERNATIONAL /. Stuttgart , c1982. x, 244 p. : ISBN 3-7910-0339-9 LC Card 83-183718
HD69.P75 P764 1982

International African library.
Feeding African cities . Bloomington , c1987. x, 249 p. ; ISBN 0-253-32102-6 LC Card 86-46323 DDC 338.1/9/6 19
HD9017.A2 F44 1987

International Air Transport Association. Reason in the air . [S.l.] [1977] 31 p. : LC Card 85-149832 DDC 387.7/068 19
HE9777.7 .R43 1977

The international airline industry . Taneja, Nawal K. Lexington, Mass. , c1988. xvi, 167 p. : ISBN 0-669-16167-5 (alk. paper) LC Card 87-45227 DDC 387.7 19
HE9776 .T363 1988

International Association for Islamic Economics. Khan, Waqar Masood. Towards an interest-free Islamic economic system . Leicester , Islamabad , c1985. 126 p. ; ISBN 0-86037-155-7 ***NYPL [JLD 87-381]***

International Association for the Study of Insurance Economics. Insuring and managing hazardous risks--from Seveso to Bhopal and beyond /. Berlin , New York , c1987. ix, 534 p. : ISBN 0-387-17732-9 (U. S.) LC Card 87-4963 DDC 346.03/8 342.638 19
HG9994 .I57 1987

International Association of Business Communicators. Communicators' guide to marketing /. New York , c1987. xii, 226 p. : ISBN 0-582-28645-X LC Card 86-27787 DDC 658.8 19
HF5415.123 .C66 1987

International Association of Hospitality Accountants. Uniform system of accounts for hotels. New York, N.Y. (40 W. 38th St., New York 10018) , 1986. x, 139 p. : LC Card 86-220845 DDC 657/.837 19
HF5686.H75 U55 1986

International Association of Rotary Clubs. see **Rotary International.**

International Association of Science and Technology for Development. IASTED Symposia on Modelling, Policy and Economics of Energy and Power Systems, and Alternative Energy Sources and Technology (1981 : San Francisco, Calif.) Proceedings of the IASTED Energy Symposia : Modelling, Policy and Economics of Energy and Power Systems [and] Alternative Energy Sources and Technology, May 20-22, 1981, San Francisco, U. S.A. /. Anaheim, Calif. [1981?] 209 p. : ISBN 0-88986-027-0 ***NYPL [JSF 86-1103]***

International Association of Sociology. see **International Sociological Association.**

International aviation and the politics of regime change /. Jönsson, Christer, 1944- New York , 1987. vi, 185 p. : ISBN 0-312-00463-X : LC Card 86-31328 DDC 341.7/567 19
HE9762 .J65 1987

International Bank for Economic Co-operation. IBEC, 10 years. Moscow : The Bank, [1973] [27] p. : ill. (some col.) ; 26 cm. Cover title. LC Card 82-216202
1. International Bank for Economic Co-operation. 2. Communist countries - Economic conditions. I. Title.
HG3881.5.I55 I58 1973

INTERNATIONAL BANK FOR ECONOMIC CO-OPERATION.
International Bank for Economic Co-operation. IBEC, 10 years. Moscow [1973] [27] p. : LC Card 82-216202
HG3881.5.I55 I58 1973

INTERNATIONAL BANK FOR RECONSTRUCTION AND DEVELOPMENT - ADDRESSES, ESSAYS, LECTURES.
Adjustment crisis in the Third World /. New Brunswick, USA , c1984. x, 186 p. ; ISBN 0-88738-040-9 LC Card 84-8690 DDC 337/.09172/4 19
HC59.7 .A733 1984 ***NYPL [JLE 86-2491]***

INTERNATIONAL BANK FOR RECONSTRUCTION AND DEVELOPMENT. ADMINISTRATIVE TRIBUNAL - INDEXES.
Amerasinghe, Chittharanjan Felix, 1933- Index to decisions of the World Bank Administrative Tribunal /. [Washington, D.C.] [c1985] vii, 32 leaves ; LC Card 86-172153 DDC 354.1/8252 19
HG3881.5.W57 A44 1985

International Bank for Reconstruction and Development. Administrative Tribunal. Office of the Executive Secretary. Amerasinghe, Chittharanjan Felix, 1933- Index to decisions of the World Bank Administrative Tribunal /. [Washington, D.C.] [c1985] vii, 32 leaves ; LC Card 86-172153 DDC 354.1/8252 19
HG3881.5.W57 A44 1985

International Bank for Reconstruction and Development. Board of Governors. For publications, see: **International Bank for Reconstruction and Development.**

International Bank for Reconstruction and Development. Commodity Studies and Projections Division. Thigpen, M. Elton, 1932- World demand prospects for jute /. Washington, D.C. , Rome , 1987. vi, 178 p. ; ISBN 0-8213-0867-X (pbk.) LC Card 86-32522 DDC 338.4/767713 19
HD9156.J7 T46 1987

International Bank for Reconstruction and Development. Economics Dept. For publications, see: **International Bank for Reconstruction and Development.**

International Bank for Reconstruction and Development. Information and Public Affairs Dept. For publications, see: **International Bank for Reconstruction and Development.**

International Bank for Reconstruction and Development. Latin America and the Caribbean Regional Office. Panama . Washington, D.C., U. S.A. , c1985. xxv, 307 p., [8] p., [1] leaf of plates : ISBN 0-8213-0580-8 LC Card 85-12420 DDC 338.97287 19
HC147 .P43 1985 ***NYPL [JLF 86-1919]***

International Bank for Reconstruction and Development. Operations Evaluation Dept. The Jengka Triangle projects in Malaysia . Washington, D.C. , c1987. ix, 105 p., [1] leaf of plates : ISBN 0-8213-0946-3 (pbk.); 0-8213-0946-6 (cover) LC Card 87-21021 DDC 338.1/85951 19
HD2080.6.Z9 P345 1987

International banking / edited by Zuhayr Mikdashi ; introduction by Charles Iffland. New York : St. Martin's Press, 1988. p. cm. Proceedings of a colloquium sponsored by the Ecole des hautes études commerciales de l'Université de Lausanne. Bibliography: p. Includes index. ISBN 0-312-00862-7 : LC Card 87-21276 DDC 332.1/5 19
1. Banks and banking, International - Congresses. I. Université de Lausanne. Ecole des hautes études commerciales.
HG3881 .I57513 1988

International banking /. Oppenheim, Peter K. Washington, D.C. (1120 Connecticut Ave.,

N.W., Washington 20036) , 1987. xii, 398 p. : LC Card 87-403739 DDC 332.1/5 19
HG3881 .O6 1987

INTERNATIONAL BANKING. see **BANKS AND BANKING, INTERNATIONAL.**

International banking and financial systems . Mullineux, A. W. London , Boston , c1987. 243 p. ; ISBN 0-86010-916-X : LC Card 87-23605 DDC 332.1 19
HG1573 .M84 1987

International banking and global financing : proceedings of a conference held at Pace University, New York City, in May 1983 / Institute of International Banking, Lubin Schools of Business ; [contributions by Jacob Frenkel ... et al. edited by S.K. Kaushik]. New York, NY : Pace University, c1983. xiv, 257 p. : ill. ; 23 cm. The International Banking and Global Financing Conference held at Pace University, May 11, 1983. Includes bibliographies. ISBN 0-88239-015-5 (pbk.) : LC Card 84-60076 DDC 332.1/5 19
1. International finance - Congresses. 2. Banks and banking, International - Congresses. I. Frenkel, Jacob A. II. Kaushik, S. K., 1944-. III. International Banking and Global Financing Conference (1983 : Pace University). IV. Pace University. Institute of International Banking. V. Lubin School of Business Administration. VI. Lubin Graduate School of Business.
HG205 .I54 1983

International Banking and Global Financing Conference (1983 : Pace University) International banking and global financing . New York, NY , c1983. xiv, 257 p. : ISBN 0-88239-015-5 (pbk.) : LC Card 84-60076 DDC 332.1/5 19
HG205 .I54 1983

International banking and world economic growth : the outlook for the late 1980s / edited by S.K. Kaushik. New York : Praeger, 1987. xviii, 183 p. : ill. ; 25 cm. Proceedings of the Conference on International Banking held at Pace University, Mar. 27, 1986, sponsored by the Institute of International Banking. Bibliography: p. 131-168. Includes index. ISBN 0-275-92669-9 (alk. paper) : LC Card 87-7353 DDC 332.1/5 19
1. Banks and banking, International. 2. International finance. 3. Foreign exchange. 4. Economic development. I. Kaushik, S. K., 1944-. II. Conference on International Banking (1986 : Pace University). III. Pace University. Institute of International Banking.
HG3881 .I575133 1987

International Bar Association. Business Law, Section on. see **International Bar Association. Section on Business Law.**

International Bar Association. Section on Business Law. The Developing global securities market /. London ; Boston : viii, 192 p. ; ISBN 0-86010-979-8 LC Card 87-19086 DDC 332.6/5 19
HG4508 .D48 1987

International Benefits Seminar (1985 : Saint Thomas, V.I.) International benefits, 1985-1986 / edited by June M. Lehman. Brookfield, Wis. : International Foundation of Employee Benefit Plans, 1986. xi, 130 p. : ill. ; 23 cm. "International Benefits Seminar, September 22-25, 1985, St. Thomas, Virgin Islands; International Benefits Conference, March 9-12, 1986, New Orleans, Louisiana." ISBN 0-89154-306-6 (pbk.) LC Card 86-224351 DDC 331.25/5 19
1. Employee fringe benefits - Congresses. I. Lehman, June M. II. Title.
HD4928.N6 I57 1986

International benefits, 1985-1986 /. International Benefits Seminar (1985 : Saint Thomas, V.I.) Brookfield, Wis. , 1986. xi, 130 p. : ISBN 0-89154-306-6 (pbk.) LC Card 86-224351 DDC 331.25/5 19
HD4928.N6 I57 1986

International Beverage Industry Exhibition & Congress (1986 : Dallas, Tex.) Registration list / InterBev 86, the International Beverage Industry Exhibition & Congress, October 6-9, 1986, Dallas, Texas, U. S.A. Washington, D.C. (1101-16th St., N.W., Washington 20036) : InterBev, c1986. ca. 400 p. ; 28 cm. Cover title. LC Card 87-107458 DDC 338.4/7663/025 19
1. Beverage industry - Directories. 2. Beverage industry - United States - Directories. I. InterBev (Firm). II. Title.
HD9348.A2 I57 1986

International borrowing : negotiating and structuring international debt transactions / Daniel D. Bradlow, editor.2nd ed. Washington, D.C. : International Law Institute, c1986. 499 p. : ill. ; 28 cm. (International negotiation and development) Includes bibliographical references. ISBN 0-935328-40-8 LC Card 86-82157 DDC 341.7/51 19
1. Debts, External - Developing countries. 2. Debt relief - Developing countries. 3. Loans, Foreign - Law and legislation - Developing countries. I. Bradlow, Daniel D. II. International Law Institute (Washington, D.C.). III. Series.
K4450 .I576 1986 ***NYPL [JLF 86-1814]***

INTERNATIONAL BROADCASTING - CUBA.
Radio Broadcasting to Cuba (Organization). Advisory Board. Report /. Washington, D.C. (400 6th St., S.W., Washington 20547) , 1986. [16] p. ; LC Card 87-110428 DDC 384.54/46 19
HE8697.45.C9 R33 1986

Radio Broadcasting to Cuba (Organization). Advisory Board. Report by the Advisory Board for Radio Broadcasting to Cuba. Washington, D.C. (400 6th St., S.W., Rm. 3850, Washington 20547) , 1986. [20] p. : LC Card 87-402533 DDC 384.54/4 19
HE8698 .R27 1986

INTERNATIONAL BROADCASTING - EUROPE.
Picaper, Jean-Paul, 1938- Le pont invisible . Paris , c1986. 345 p. ; ISBN 2-259-01619-7; 0-225-91619-7 : LC Card 87-147835
HE8697.45.E87 P52 1986

Western broadcasting over the iron curtain /. London , 1986. 274 p. : ISBN 0-7099-4438-1
NYPL [MWGH 87-760]

INTERNATIONAL BROADCASTING - EUROPE, EASTERN.
Picaper, Jean-Paul, 1938- Le pont invisible . Paris , c1986. 345 p. ; ISBN 2-259-01619-7; 0-225-91619-7 : LC Card 87-147835
HE8697.45.E87 P52 1986

Western broadcasting over the iron curtain /. London , 1986. 274 p. : ISBN 0-7099-4438-1
NYPL [MWGH 87-760]

INTERNATIONAL BROADCASTING - NORTH AMERICA.
Western broadcasting over the iron curtain /. London , 1986. 274 p. : ISBN 0-7099-4438-1
NYPL [MWGH 87-760]

INTERNATIONAL BROADCASTING - UNITED STATES.
Radio Broadcasting to Cuba (Organization). Advisory Board. Report /. Washington, D.C. (400 6th St., S.W., Washington 20547) , 1986. [16] p. ; LC Card 87-110428 DDC 384.54/46 19
HE8697.45.C9 R33 1986

Radio Broadcasting to Cuba (Organization). Advisory Board. Report by the Advisory Board for Radio Broadcasting to Cuba. Washington, D.C. (400 6th St., S.W., Rm. 3850, Washington 20547) , 1986. [20] p. : LC Card 87-402533 DDC 384.54/4 19
HE8698 .R27 1986

INTERNATIONAL BROADCASTING - UNITED STATES - JUVENILE LITERATURE.
Fitzgerald, Merni Ingrassia. The Voice of America /. New York , c1987. ix, 118 p. : ISBN 0-396-08937-2 : LC Card 87-5346 DDC 384.54/53 19
HE8698 .F5 1987

INTERNATIONAL BROTHERHOOD OF TEAMSTERS, CHAUFFEURS, WAREHOUSEMEN AND HELPERS OF AMERICA.
Franco, Joseph. Hoffa's man . New York , c1987. xv, 332 p., [8] p. of plates : ISBN 0-13-517764-2 : LC Card 87-42675 DDC 331.88/11388324/0924 B 19
HD6509.F69 A3 1987

International business and Central Europe, 1918-1939 / edited by Alice Teichova and P.L. Cottrell. [Leicester, Leicestershire] : Leicester University Press ; New York : St. Martin's Press, 1983. xxvii, 459 p. : ill. ; 24 cm. Includes bibliographical references and indexes. ISBN 0-312-41982-1 : LC Card 83-13956 DDC 338.8/8843 19
1. Corporations, Foreign - Europe, Eastern - History - Addresses, essays, lectures. 2. International business enterprises - Europe, Eastern - History - Addresses, essays, lectures. 3. Investments, Foreign - Europe, Eastern - History - Addresses, essays, lectures. I. Teichova, Alice. II. Cottrell, P. L.
HD2844 .I57 1983 ***NYPL [JLE 86-3697]***

International business and cultures . Henderson, George, 1932- New York, NY , 1987. p. cm. ISBN 0-943025-03-6 : LC Card 87-24378 DDC 658/.049 19
HF1008 .H46 1987

INTERNATIONAL BUSINESS ENTERPRISES - ACCOUNTING.
Belkaoui, Ahmed, 1943- The new environment in international accounting . New York , c1988. p. cm. ISBN 0-89930-267-X (lib. bdg. : alk. paper) LC Card 87-7252 DDC 657/.95 19
HF5686.I56 B45 1988

Müller, Herbert, 1948- Die Umrechnung der Jahresabschlüsse ausländischer Konzernunternehmen und die Verrechnung der daraus resultierenden Umrechnungsdifferenzen . Bochum , 1986. x, 348 p. ; ISBN 3-88339-547-1 LC Card 87-143252 DDC 657/.48 19
HG3853.7 .M84 1986

Prodhan, B. Multinational accounting . London , Dover, N.H. , c1986. xi, 399 p. : ISBN 0-7099-4010-6 : LC Card 86-4521 DDC 657/.95 19
HF5686.I56 P76 1986 ***NYPL [JLD 86-2595]***

INTERNATIONAL BUSINESS ENTERPRISES - ACCOUNTING - STANDARDS.
Westwick, C. A. Accounting for overseas operations /. Aldershot, Hants, England , Brookfield, Vt. , c1986. ix, 184 p. ; ISBN 0-566-02586-8 : LC Card 85-30582 DDC 657/.95 19
HF5686.I56 W47 1986 ***NYPL [JLG 86-202]***

INTERNATIONAL BUSINESS ENTERPRISES - ADDRESSES, ESSAYS, LECTURES.
Imperialism and transnational corporations /. Quezon City , 1980. vi, 114 p. ;
NYPL [JLD 86-2721]

Multinationals and the restructuring of the world economy /. London , Dover, N.H. , c1986- viii, 389 p. : ISBN 0-7099-2457-7 (v. 2) : LC Card 85-29081 DDC 338.8/81 19
HD2755.5 .M8442 1986
NYPL [JLD 86-2089]

INTERNATIONAL BUSINESS ENTERPRISES - AFRICA.
Dinham, Barbara. Agribusiness in Africa /. Trenton, N.J. , 1984. 224 p. : ISBN 0-86543-003-9 : LC Card 85-672721
HD9017.A2 D56x 1984
NYPL [Sc D 86-769]

INTERNATIONAL BUSINESS ENTERPRISES - AFRICA, SUB-SAHARAN.
Ozadovskiĭ, A. A. (Andreĭ Andreevich) Uoll-strit protiv Afriki /. Kiev , 1985. 228, [4] p. ; LC Card 86-219442
HF1611.Z4 U556 1985

INTERNATIONAL BUSINESS ENTERPRISES - ASIA.
Rogach, A. I. (Aleksandr Igorevich) Ėkspansii͡a mezhdunarodnykh monopoliĭ v razvivai͡ushchiesi͡a strany Azii /. Kiev , 1987. 236, [4] p. ; LC Card 86-234922
HD2932 .R65 1987

INTERNATIONAL BUSINESS ENTERPRISES - ASIA, SOUTHEASTERN.
Sverkhmonopolii v I͡Ugo-Vostochnoĭ Azii /. Moskva , 1983. 219 p. ; LC Card 83-223670
HD2901 .S84 1983

INTERNATIONAL BUSINESS ENTERPRISES - BOLIVIA.
Granado Cosio, Hugo del. Transnacionales y nación . [La Paz, Bolivia] , 1986. 24 p. ; LC Card 87-115866 DDC 338.8/87 19
HD9574.B82 G73 1986

INTERNATIONAL BUSINESS ENTERPRISES - BRAZIL.
Banas, Geraldo. Os donos do Brasil . São Paulo , 1984. 330 p. ; LC Card 87-673258
HD2834 .B34 1984

INTERNATIONAL BUSINESS ENTERPRISES - CASE STUDIES.

Alschuler, Lawrence R., 1941- Multinationals and maldevelopment . New York , 1988. xii, 218 p. : ISBN 0-312-00531-8 : LC Card 87-4307 DDC 338.9 19
HD82 .A5493 1988

Casson, Mark, 1945- Multinationals and world trade . London , Boston , 1986. xi, 401 p. : ISBN 0-04-338125-1 (alk. paper) LC Card 85-15734 DDC 338.8/8 19
HD2748 .C37 1986 ***NYPL [JLD 86-1224]***

Clegg, Jeremy, 1955- Multinational enterprise and world competition . New York , 1987. xiv, 206 p. : ISBN 0-312-00852-X : LC Card 87-4735 DDC 338.8/8 19
HD2755.5 .C54 1987

Moskowitz, Milton. The global marketplace . New York , c1987. xi, 708 p. : ISBN 0-02-587590-6 LC Card 87-15897 DDC 338.8/8 19
HD2755.5 .M675 1987

Tung, Rosalie L. (Rosalie Lam), 1948- The new expatriates . Cambridge, Mass. , c1988. xiii, 200 p. : ISBN 0-88730-133-9 LC Card 87-17835 DDC 658.3/1 19
HF5549 .T82 1988

Vernon, Raymond, 1913- Manager in the international economy /. Englewood Cliffs, NJ , c1986. viii, 469 p. : ISBN 0-13-550807-X : LC Card 85-25653 DDC 658.1/8 19
HD62.4 .V48 1986 ***NYPL [JLE 86-3200]***

INTERNATIONAL BUSINESS ENTERPRISES - COLOMBIA - HISTORY - 20TH CENTURY.

Las Empresas transnacionales en el desarrollo colombiano. Santiago de Chile , Nueva York, NY , 1986. 218 p. : ISBN 92-1-321213-5 LC Card 87-402186 DDC 338.8/88861 19
HD2837 .E47 1986

INTERNATIONAL BUSINESS ENTERPRISES - CONGRESSES.

Cooperative strategies in international business /. Lexington, Mass. , c1988. xxix, 513 p. : ISBN 0-669-14927-6 (alk. paper) LC Card 86-46160 DDC 338.8/8 19
HD2755.5 .C645 1988

Multinationals as mutual invaders . London , c1985. 217 p. : ISBN 0-7099-0935-7 : LC Card 86-673843
HG4538 .M85x 1985b

Multinationals--theory and history /. Aldershot, Hants, England , Brookfield, Vt., USA , c1986. vii, 200 p. : ISBN 0-566-05078-1 : LC Card 85-24955 DDC 338.8/8 19
HD2755.5 .M86 1986 ***NYPL [JLD 86-1575]***

New theories of the multinational enterprise /. London , c1982. 303 p. : ISBN 0-7099-2224-8 LC Card 86-673671
HD2755.5 .N485x 1982

INTERNATIONAL BUSINESS ENTERPRISES - DECISION MAKING.

Ghertman, Michel. Decision-making in multinational enterprises . Geneva , 1984. v, 62 p. : ISBN 92-2-103831-9 (pbk.) : LC Card 86-213603 DDC 658.4/03 19
HD62.4 .G48 1984

INTERNATIONAL BUSINESS ENTERPRISES - DEVELOPING COUNTRIES.

Empresas multinacionales y división internacional del trabajo /. Salamanca , 1977. 158 p. : ISBN 84-301-0465-8 LC Card 86-164261
HD2755.5 .E49 1977

Jenkins, Rhys Owen, 1948- Transnational corporations and uneven development . London , New York , 1987. p. cm. ISBN 0-416-73340-9 LC Card 87-12351 DDC 338.8/83 19
HD2932 .J45 1987

Karagodin, N. A. Mezhdunarodnye korporatsii i sotsial'no-ėkonomicheskie problemy razvivaiushchikhsia stran /. Moskva , 1981. 196, [3] p. ; LC Card 82-162679
HC59.7 .K28 1981

Marsh, Lawrence. Employment and technological choice of multinational enterprises in developing countries . Geneva , 1983. iii, 37 p. ; ISBN 92-2-103353-8 (pbk.) : LC Card 86-213692 DDC 338.8/8854 19
HD2932 .M35 1983

Marton, Katherin. Multinationals, technology, and industrialization . Lexington, Mass. , c1986. xiii, 304 p. ; ISBN 0-669-13209-8 (alk. paper) LC Card 86-7218 DDC 338.8/881724 19
HD2932 .M37 1986 ***NYPL [JLE 86-3372]***

Mattsson, Jan. Nationella övertaganden av utländska dotterbolag . Stockholm [1982] 213 p. : ISBN 91-1-827592-3 LC Card 83-122459
HD2932 .M38 1982

Portilla, Belfor. Alimentos . México , 1983. 149, [53] p. : ISBN 968-429-384-4 LC Card 84-172348 DDC 338.1/9/1724 19
HD9018.D44 P67 1983
NYPL [JLD 86-1520]

Postimperialism . Boulder , 1987. x, 252 p. : ISBN 1-555-87046-5 (lib. bdg. : alk. paper) : LC Card 87-4455 DDC 338.8/881724 19
HD2932 .P67 1987

Rogach, A. I. (Aleksandr Igorevich) Ėkspansiia mezhdunarodnykh monopolii v razvivaiushchiesia strany Azii /. Kiev , 1987. 236, [4] p. ; LC Card 86-234922
HD2932 .R65 1987

Wenzel, Gilbert, 1956- Marktstrategien multinationaler Pharmaunternehmen und die Arzneimittelmärkte der Dritten Welt . Frankfurt am Main , New York , c1986. 398 p. : ISBN 3-8204-9721-8 LC Card 87-407426 DDC 381/.456151/091724 19
HD9674.D44 W46 1986

INTERNATIONAL BUSINESS ENTERPRISES - DEVELOPING COUNTRIES - MANAGEMENT.

Pearson, Charles S. Down to business . Washington, DC (1735 New York Ave., NW, Washington, DC 20006) , c1985. vii, 107 p. ; ISBN 0-915825-04-X (pbk.) : LC Card 84-52795
HD69.P6 P42 1985 ***NYPL [JLE 86-3186]***

INTERNATIONAL BUSINESS ENTERPRISES - DEVELOPING COUTRIES - CONGRESSES.

Las Transnacionales en el Paraguay /. Asunción, Paraguay [1985] 317 p. : LC Card 86-112866 DDC 338.8/88892 19
HD2840 .T7 1985 ***NYPL [JLD 86-2210]***

INTERNATIONAL BUSINESS ENTERPRISES - EMPLOYEES.

Social and labour practices of multinational enterprises in the textiles, clothing, and footwear industries. Geneva , 1984. xii, 184 p. ; ISBN 92-2-103882-3 (pbk.) : LC Card 85-183200 DDC 331.7/677 19
HF5549 .S83473 1984 ***NYPL [JLE 85-2322]***

INTERNATIONAL BUSINESS ENTERPRISES - EMPLOYEES - LEGAL STATUS, LAWS, ETC. - EUROPE - ADDRESSES, ESSAYS, LECTURES.

Employee consultation and information in multinational corporations /. London , Dover, N.H. , c1986. 265 p. ; ISBN 0-7099-2624-3 : LC Card 85-21264 DDC 331.25 19
NYPL [JLD 86-1612]

INTERNATIONAL BUSINESS ENTERPRISES - EUROPE - CONGRESSES.

Multinationals--theory and history /. Aldershot, Hants, England , Brookfield, Vt., USA , c1986. vii, 200 p. : ISBN 0-566-05078-1 : LC Card 85-24955 DDC 338.8/8 19
HD2755.5 .M86 1986 ***NYPL [JLD 86-1575]***

INTERNATIONAL BUSINESS ENTERPRISES - EUROPE, EASTERN.

Red multinationals or red herrings? . London , 1986. xi, 202 p. ; ISBN 0-86187-583-4
NYPL [JLD 86-2751]

INTERNATIONAL BUSINESS ENTERPRISES - EUROPE, EASTERN - CASE STUDIES.

Red multinationals or red herrings? . London , 1986. xi, 202 p. ; ISBN 0-86187-583-4
NYPL [JLD 86-2751]

INTERNATIONAL BUSINESS ENTERPRISES - EUROPE, EASTERN - HISTORY - ADDRESSES, ESSAYS, LECTURES.

International business and Central Europe, 1918-1939 /. [Leicester, Leicestershire] , New York , 1983. xxvii, 459 p. : ISBN 0-312-41982-1 : LC Card 83-13956 DDC 338.8/8843 19
HD2844 .I57 1983 ***NYPL [JLE 86-3697]***

INTERNATIONAL BUSINESS ENTERPRISES - EUROPE - EMPLOYEES - ADDRESSES, ESSAYS, LECTURES.

Employee consultation and information in multinational corporations /. London , Dover, N.H. , c1986. 265 p. ; ISBN 0-7099-2624-3 : LC Card 85-21264 DDC 331.25 19
NYPL [JLD 86-1612]

INTERNATIONAL BUSINESS ENTERPRISES - EUROPE - MANAGEMENT.

L'Information et la consultation des travailleurs dans les enterprises multinationales /. [Paris] [Genève?] , 1984. 290 p. ; ISBN 2-13-038651-2 (pbk.)
HD62.4 .I53 1984 ***NYPL [JLD 87-60]***

INTERNATIONAL BUSINESS ENTERPRISES - FINANCE.

Abdullah, Fuad A. (Fuad Abdul-Kader), 1930- Financial management for the multinational firm /. Englewood Cliffs, N.J. , c1987. xiii, 594 p. : ISBN 0-13-316340-7 LC Card 86-25226 DDC 658.1/599 19
HG4027.5 .A23 1987

Buckley, Adrian. Multinational finance /. Deddington, Oxford , Atlantic Highlands, N.J. , 1986. x, 398 p. : ISBN 0-86003-542-5 LC Card 86-226038 DDC 658.1/599 19
HG4027.5 .B83 1986

Klein, Jean, docteur ès sciences économiques. Gestion et stratégie financières internationales /. Paris , c1985. v, 266 p. : ISBN 2-04-015504-X : LC Card 86-192918
HG4027.5 .K58 1985

Pastuszek, Rainer. Leading und Lagging kurzfristig variierbarer gruppeninterner Geldflüsse im Währungsrisikomanagement einer internationalen Unternehmung /. Pfaffenweiler , 1986. xvi, 275 p. : ISBN 3-89085-122-3 LC Card 87-128258 DDC 658.1/55 19
HG3851 .P295 1986

Ross, Derek. International treasury management /. New York, N.Y. , c1988. p. cm. ISBN 0-13-473968-X : LC Card 87-16118 DDC 658.1/599 19
HG4027.5 .R67 1988

Shapiro, Alan C. International corporate finance . Tampa, FL , c1986. 79 p. : ISBN 0-936795-00-X (pbk.) LC Card 86-231054 DDC 658.1/599 19
HG4027.5 .S46 1986

Swinne, Axel Hilmar. Die finanzielle Führung und Kontrolle von Auslandsgesellschaften /. Frankfurt am Main , c1983. 422 p. : ISBN 3-7875-4200-0 LC Card 84-148375
HG4027.5 .S95 1983

INTERNATIONAL BUSINESS ENTERPRISES - FINANCE - CASE STUDIES.

Abdullah, Fuad A. (Fuad Abdul-Kader), 1930- Financial management for the multinational firm /. Englewood Cliffs, N.J. , c1987. xiii, 594 p. : ISBN 0-13-316340-7 LC Card 86-25226 DDC 658.1/599 19
HG4027.5 .A23 1987

INTERNATIONAL BUSINESS ENTERPRISES - FINANCE - CONGRESSES.

Finanz- und bankwirtschaftliche Probleme bei internationaler Unternehmenstätigkeit /. Stuttgart , c1985. x, 267 p. : ISBN 3-7910-0394-1 LC Card 86-121195 DDC 658.1/5 19
HG4027.5 .F56 1985

INTERNATIONAL BUSINESS ENTERPRISES - FINANCE - HANDBOOKS, MANUALS, ETC.

International finance handbook /. New York , c1983. 2 v. : ISBN 0-471-09861-2 (set) : LC Card 82-23824 DDC 332/.042 19
HG3881 .I57633 1983 ***NYPL [JLE 86-1719]***

INTERNATIONAL BUSINESS ENTERPRISES - FINANCE - PLANNING.

Schauenberg, Harald. Die taktische Finanzplanung der internationalen Unternehmung /. Königstein/Ts. , c1982. vi,

134 p. ; ISBN 3-445-02259-3 : LC Card 82-224376
HG4027.5 .S32 1982

INTERNATIONAL BUSINESS ENTERPRISES - GHANA.
Botchie, George. Employment and multinational enterprises in export processing zones . Geneva , 1984. iv, 74 p. ; ISBN 92-2-103770-3 (pbk.) : LC Card 86-213592
HF1417 .B68 1984

INTERNATIONAL BUSINESS ENTERPRISES - GOVERNMENT POLICY.
Basche, James R., 1926- Eliminating barriers to international trade and investment in services /. New York, N.Y. (845 Third Ave., New York 10022) , c1986. 15 p. ; LC Card 87-147770 DDC 382/.45 19
HD9980.6 .B37 1986

INTERNATIONAL BUSINESS ENTERPRISES - GOVERNMENT POLICY - CHINA.
Joint ventures in the People's Republic of China . Hong Kong , New York, N.Y., U. S.A. , c1985. 347 p. ; LC Card 87-404122 DDC 658.1/8 19
HD2910 .J65 1985

INTERNATIONAL BUSINESS ENTERPRISES - GOVERNMENT POLICY - COLOMBIA.
Wallace, Brian F. Ownership and development . Athens, Ohio , 1987. ix, 176 p. ; ISBN 0-89680-145-4 (pbk.) LC Card 86-33255 DDC 332.6/7322861 19
HD9734.C62 W35 1987

INTERNATIONAL BUSINESS ENTERPRISES - GOVERNMENT POLICY - INDIA.
Martinussen, John. Regulations in vain? . Roskilde, Denmark , 1986. 239 p. : LC Card 87-100775 DDC 338.8/8854 19
HD2900 .M37 1986

INTERNATIONAL BUSINESS ENTERPRISES - GOVERNMENT POLICY - INDONESIA.
Khong, Cho Oon. The politics of oil in Indonesia . Cambridge [Cambridgeshire] , New York , 1986. x, 253 p. : ISBN 0-521-30901-8 LC Card 85-22416 DDC 338.2/7282/09598 19
HD9567.I52 K48 1986 ***NYPL [JLD 86-3386]***

INTERNATIONAL BUSINESS ENTERPRISES - GREAT BRITAIN.
Stopford, John M. Britain and the multinationals /. Chichester , New York , c1985. xiv, 282 p. : ISBN 0-471-90839-8 : LC Card 85-12352 DDC 338.8/8841 19
HD2845 .S76 1985 ***NYPL [JLE 86-924]***

INTERNATIONAL BUSINESS ENTERPRISES - GUYANA.
Shahabuddeen, M., 1931- Nationalisation of Guyana's bauxite . Georgetown, Guyana , 1981. xvii, 306 p. ; LC Card 82-145233 DDC 338.2/74926 19
HD9539.A63 G888 1981 ***NYPL [Sc E 86-189]***

INTERNATIONAL BUSINESS ENTERPRISES - HISTORY.
Baumier, Jean. Ces patrons qui gagnent /. Paris , c1986. 262 p. ; ISBN 2-259-01532-8 : LC Card 87-106535
HD2855 .B38 1986

British multinationals . Aldershot, Hants , Brookfield, Vt., USA , c1986. xi, 212 p. : ISBN 0-566-00997-8 LC Card 86-222817 DDC 338.8/8941 19
HD2755.5 .B75 1986

Harvey, Charles E. The Rio Tinto Company . Penzance, Cornwall , 1981. xiv, 390 p. : ISBN 0-906720-03-6 : LC Card 82-127720 DDC 338.8/87 19
HD9506.G74 R564 1981 ***NYPL [JLD 86-2605]***

INTERNATIONAL BUSINESS ENTERPRISES - HISTORY - 19TH CENTURY.
Jones, Charles A., 1949- International business in the nineteenth century . New York , c1987. xi, 260 p. ; ISBN 0-8147-4172-X : LC Card 87-11321 DDC 338.8/8/09034 19
HF497 .J66 1987

INTERNATIONAL BUSINESS ENTERPRISES - INDIA.
Lall, Rajiv B. Multinationals from the Third World . Delhi , New York , 1986. 100 p. ; ISBN 0-19-561895-5 : LC Card 86-900021 DDC 338.8/8954 19
HG4538 .L274 1986

Patwardhan, M. S., 1927- Oil and other multinationals in India /. Bombay , 1986. xvi, 171 p. : LC Card 87-900107 DDC 338.8/87 19
HD9576.I42 P37 1986

Saxena, Usha, 1957- Role of multinationals in India's foreign trade /. New Delhi , 1987. xx, 237 p. ; ISBN 81-7024-081-6 : LC Card 87-900766 DDC 382/.0954 19
HD2899 .S29 1987

INTERNATIONAL BUSINESS ENTERPRISES - INDIA - DIRECTORIES.
Indo-U. S. cooperation in business and industry, 1986. [New Delhi] [1986] 166 p. ; LC Card 86-903197
HG4242 .I44 1986

INTERNATIONAL BUSINESS ENTERPRISES - ITALY.
Italia multinazionale . Milano , 1986. 2 v. : LC Card 87-158571
HD2864 .I82 1986

INTERNATIONAL BUSINESS ENTERPRISES - KENYA.
Gershenberg, Irving. Multinational enterprises, transfer of managerial know-how, technology choice and employment effects . Geneva , 1983. iii, 33 p. ; ISBN 92-2-103508-5 (pbk.) LC Card 86-213574 DDC 338.8/886762 19
HD2920.5 .G47 1983

INTERNATIONAL BUSINESS ENTERPRISES - LATIN AMERICA.
Arroyo, Gonzalo. Agricultura y alimentos en América Latina . México, D.F. , 1985. 267 p. ; ISBN 968-8373-33-8 LC Card 86-208283
HD9014.L32 A77 1985

Fuenzalida Faivovich, Edmundo. [América Latina y la concentración del poder en la arena política.] América Latina y la concentración del poder en la arena política ; El impacto social del cambio tecnológico actual en los países menos desarrollados /. [Santiago de Chile] [between 1974 and 1979] 24, 25 leaves ; LC Card 82-180082
HD2810.5 .F84 1974

Goodman, Louis Wolf. Small nations, giant firms /. New York , c1987. xiii, 181 p. : ISBN 0-8419-0996-2 LC Card 87-42 DDC 338.8/888 19
HD2755.5 .G66 1987

INTERNATIONAL BUSINESS ENTERPRISES - LATIN AMERICA - CASE STUDIES.
Sourrouille, Juan V. Inversiones extranjeras en América Latina . Buenos Aires [1984] viii, 142 p. : LC Card 86-183036
HG5160.5.A3 S64 1984

INTERNATIONAL BUSINESS ENTERPRISES - LATIN AMERICA - HISTORY.
Clayton, Lawrence A. Grace . Ottawa, Ill. , c1985. xiii, 403 p., [32] p. of plates : ISBN 0-915463-25-3 LC Card 85-14856 DDC 338.8/8885 19
HD9505.P4 C43 1986 ***NYPL [JLE 86-3892]***

INTERNATIONAL BUSINESS ENTERPRISES - LAW AND LEGISLATION - CONGRESSES.
International Law Symposium (1984 : Cambridge, Cambridgeshire) The United States, transnational business, and the law . New York , c1985. x, 132 p. ; ISBN 0-379-20783-4 LC Card 85-61594 DDC 346/.07 342.67 19
K1004.6 1984 ***NYPL [JLF 86-1046]***

INTERNATIONAL BUSINESS ENTERPRISES - LIBERIA.
Botchie, George. Employment and multinational enterprises in export processing zones . Geneva , 1984. iv, 74 p. ; ISBN 92-2-103770-3 (pbk.) : LC Card 86-213592
HF1417 .B68 1984

Iyanda, Olukunle. Multinationals and employment in a West African sub-region . Geneva , 1984. iv, 49 p. ; ISBN 92-2-103623-5 (pbk.) : LC Card 86-213585 DDC 388.8/88664 19
HD2928.8 .I92 1984

INTERNATIONAL BUSINESS ENTERPRISES - MANAGEMENT.
Achleitner, Paul M. Sozio-politische Strategien multinationaler Unternehmungen . Bern , c1985. ii, 334 p. : ISBN 3-258-03490-7 : LC Card 85-208760
HD62.4 .A24 1985

Connolly, Seamus G. Finding, entering, and succeeding in a foreign market /. Englewood Cliffs, N.J. , c1987. xiii, 274 p. : ISBN 0-13-316951-0 LC Card 86-25395 DDC 658.8/48 19
HF1009.5 .C59 1986 ***NYPL [JLE 87-1310]***

Diskontinuitätenmanagement . Berlin , c1984. x, 320 p. : ISBN 3-503-02446-8 LC Card 85-128271
HD62.4 .D57 1984

Doz, Yves L. Strategic management in multinational companies /. Oxford [Oxfordshire] , New York , 1986. xii, 243 p. : ISBN 0-08-031808-8 : LC Card 85-9282 DDC 658.4/012 19
HD62.4 .D69 1986 ***NYPL [JLE 86-1955]***

Duhnkrack, Thomas. Zielbildung und strategisches Zielsystem der internationalen Unternehmung /. Göttingen , c1984. xii, 287 p. : ISBN 3-525-12664-6 (Deut. Bibl.) LC Card 85-127165
HD62.4 .D86 1984

Ferguson, Henry. Tomorrow's global executive /. Homewood, Ill. , c1988. xiii, 265 p. : ISBN 1-15-562305-75 LC Card 87-71259 DDC 658/.049 19
HD62.4 .F47 1988

Gestion internationale de l'entreprise /. Paris , 1984. 393 p. : ISBN 2-247-00496-2 : LC Card 85-114907
HD62.4 .G47 1984

Harris, Philip R. (Philip Robert), 1926- Managing cultural differences /. Houston , c1987. xiii, 609 p. : ISBN 0-87201-161-5 LC Card 86-25618 DDC 658.1/8 19
HD62.4 .H37 1987

Johri, Lalit M. Business strategies of multinational corporations in India . New Delhi , 1983. v, 172 p. ; LC Card 83-906128 DDC 338.8/87 19
HD9672.I52 J63 1983 ***NYPL [JLD 86-4081]***

L'Information et la consultation des travailleurs dans les enterprises multinationales /. [Paris] [Genève?] , 1984. 290 p. ; ISBN 2-13-038651-2 (pbk.)
HD62.4 .I53 1984 ***NYPL [JLD 87-60]***

Mason, R. Hal (Robert Hal), 1929- Management . Homewood, Ill. , 1987. xii, 235 p. : ISBN 0-256-05631-5 (pbk.) LC Card 86-82592 DDC 658/.049 19
HD62.4 .M373 1987

Miller, Janice James. Issues for managers . Homewood, Ill. , 1987. xii, 139 p. : ISBN 0-256-05630-7 (pbk.) LC Card 87-80633 DDC 658/.049 19
HD62.4 .M54 1987

Miller, Robert R., 1929- Introduction to business . Homewood, Ill. , 1987. x, 138 p. : ISBN 0-256-05628-5 (pbk.) LC Card 86-82593 DDC 658/.049 19
HD62.4 .M55 1987

Prahalad, C. K. The multinational mission . New York , London , c1987. ix, 290 p. : ISBN 0-02-925050-1 LC Card 87-11970 DDC 658/.049 19
HD62.4 .P69 1987

Ting, Wenlee. Multinational risk assessment and management . New York , c1987. p. cm. ISBN 0-89930-175-4 (lib. bdg. : alk. paper) LC Card 87-5970 DDC 658 19
HD61 .T56 1987

Vernon, Raymond, 1913- Manager in the international economy /. Englewood Cliffs, NJ , c1986. viii, 469 p. : ISBN 0-13-550807-X : LC Card 85-25653 DDC 658.1/8 19
HD62.4 .V48 1986 ***NYPL [JLE 86-3200]***

INTERNATIONAL BUSINESS ENTERPRISES - MANAGEMENT - ADDRESSES, ESSAYS, LECTURES.
International marketing . Boston, Mass. , c1986.

xii, 466 p. : ISBN 0-534-06270-9 (pbk.) : LC Card 85-19820 DDC 658.8/48 19
HF1009.5 .I545 1986 ***NYPL [JLE 86-3023]***

INTERNATIONAL BUSINESS ENTERPRISES - MANAGEMENT - CASE STUDIES.
Grosse, Christine Uber. Case studies in international business /. Englewood Cliffs, N.J. , c1988. xv, 155 p. : ISBN 0-13-119314-7 (pbk.) LC Card 87-22307 DDC 658/.049 19
HD62.4 .G76 1988

Sawyer-Lauçanno, Christopher, 1951- Case studies in international management /. Englewood Cliffs, N.J. , c1987. xvii, 138 p. : ISBN 0-13-119298-1 (pbk.) LC Card 86-22724 DDC 658/.049 19
HD62.4 .S29 1987

INTERNATIONAL BUSINESS ENTERPRISES - MIDDLE EAST.
Uhlig, Christian. Internationale Produktionskooperation im Vorderen Orient . Stuttgart , c1983. xvi, 338 p. : ISBN 3-522-68000-6 LC Card 83-217029
HD2891.9 .U44 1983

INTERNATIONAL BUSINESS ENTERPRISES - NAMIBIA.
Transnational corporations in South Africa and Namibia . New York , 1986-<1987. v. <1-2, 4 > ; ISBN 92-1-104190-2 (pbk. : set) LC Card 87-403059 DDC 338.8/8868 19
HD2922 .T72 1986

INTERNATIONAL BUSINESS ENTERPRISES - NIGERIA.
Biersteker, Thomas J. Multinationals, the state, and control of the Nigerian economy /. Princeton, N.J. , c1987. xvii, 344 p. : ISBN 0-691-07728-2 (alk. paper) : LC Card 86-25214 DDC 338.8/88669 19
HG5881.A3 B54 1987

Nambudiri, C. N. S. Third World multinationals . Geneva , 1983. iv, 41 p. ; ISBN 92-2-103386-4 (pbk.) LC Card 86-213622 DDC 338.8/88669 19
HD2928 .N35 1983

Onimode, Bade. MNC's in Nigeria . Ibadan , 1983. ix, 144 p. ; ISBN 978-231-800-0 (pbk.) LC Card 86-195403 DDC 338.8/88669 19
HD2928 .O55 1983

INTERNATIONAL BUSINESS ENTERPRISES - PARAGUAY.
Parquet, Reinerio. Las empresas transnacionales en la economía del Paraguay. Santiago de Chile , 1987. 115 p. ; ISBN 92-1-321223-2 LC Card 87-404657 DDC 338.8/88892 19
HG5382 .P37 1987

INTERNATIONAL BUSINESS ENTERPRISES - PARAGUAY - CONGRESSES.
Las Transnacionales en el Paraguay /. Asunción, Paraguay [1985] 317 p. : LC Card 86-112866 DDC 338.8/88892 19
HD2840 .T7 1985 ***NYPL [JLD 86-2210]***

INTERNATIONAL BUSINESS ENTERPRISES - PERSONNEL MANAGEMENT.
Social and labour practices of multinational enterprises in the textiles, clothing, and footwear industries. Geneva , 1984. xii, 184 p. ; ISBN 92-2-103882-3 (pbk.) : LC Card 85-183200 DDC 331.7/677 19
HF5549 .S83473 1984 ***NYPL [JLE 85-2322]***

Tung, Rosalie L. (Rosalie Lam), 1948- The new expatriates . Cambridge, Mass. , c1988. xiii, 200 p. : ISBN 0-88730-133-9 LC Card 87-17835 DDC 658.3/1 19
HF5549 .T82 1988

INTERNATIONAL BUSINESS ENTERPRISES - PERU - CASE STUDIES.
Alarcón Aliaga, Carlos. Privilegios y capital transnacional . [Peru?] [1985 or 1986] 168 p. : LC Card 87-127159 DDC 338.8/87 19
HD2841.Z75 S683 1985

INTERNATIONAL BUSINESS ENTERPRISES - PERU - HISTORY.
Clayton, Lawrence A. Grace . Ottawa, Ill. , c1985. xiii, 403 p., [32] p. of plates : ISBN 0-915463-25-3 LC Card 85-14856 DDC 338.8/8885 19
HD9505.P4 C43 1986 ***NYPL [JLE 86-3892]***

INTERNATIONAL BUSINESS ENTERPRISES - PLANNING.
Doz, Yves L. Strategic management in multinational companies /. Oxford [Oxfordshire] , New York , 1986. xii, 243 p. : ISBN 0-08-031808-8 : LC Card 85-9282 DDC 658.4/012 19
HD62.4 .D69 1986 ***NYPL [JLE 86-1955]***

INTERNATIONAL BUSINESS ENTERPRISES - POLITICAL ACTIVITY.
Dreifuss, René Armand. A internacional capitalista . Rio de Janeiro , 1986. 502, [40] p. : LC Card 87-126893 DDC 322/.3 19
HD2755.5 .D74 1986

INTERNATIONAL BUSINESS ENTERPRISES - POLITICAL ASPECTS - LATIN AMERICA.
Wolffsohn, Michael. Politik als Investitionsmotor? . Frankfurt am Main , New York , c1985. 141 p. : ISBN 3-8204-7487-0 (pbk.) LC Card 87-672289
HD2810.5 W64x 1985

INTERNATIONAL BUSINESS ENTERPRISES - SAUDI ARABIA - PERSONNEL MANAGEMENT.
Viola, Joy Winkie. Human resources development in Saudi Arabia . Boston , c1986. xxvi, 291 p. : ISBN 0-88746-070-4 (IHRDC) LC Card 85-19694 DDC 303.4/8273/0538 19
HD5812.35.A6 V56 1986
NYPL [JLE 86-2188]

INTERNATIONAL BUSINESS ENTERPRISES - SECURITY MEASURES.
Scotti, Anthony J. Executive safety and international terrorism . Englewood Cliffs, N.J. , c1986. xv, 220 p. ; ISBN 0-13-294380-8 : LC Card 86-15079 DDC 658.4/73 19
HF5549.5.E45 S36 1986
NYPL [JLE 87-393]

INTERNATIONAL BUSINESS ENTERPRISES - SIERRA LEONE.
Iyanda, Olukunle. Multinationals and employment in a West African sub-region . Geneva , 1984. iv, 49 p. ; ISBN 92-2-103623-5 (pbk.) : LC Card 86-213585 DDC 388.8/88664 19
HD2928.8 .I92 1984

INTERNATIONAL BUSINESS ENTERPRISES - SOCIAL ASPECTS.
Social and labour practices of multinational enterprises in the textiles, clothing, and footwear industries. Geneva , 1984. xii, 184 p. ; ISBN 92-2-103882-3 (pbk.) : LC Card 85-183200 DDC 331.7/677 19
HF5549 .S83473 1984 ***NYPL [JLE 85-2322]***

INTERNATIONAL BUSINESS ENTERPRISES - SOCIAL ASPECTS - DEVELOPING COUNTRIES.
Multinational managers and host government interactions /. Notre Dame, Ind. , c1987. p. cm. ISBN 0-268-01364-0 : LC Card 86-40590 DDC 658.4/08/091724 19
HD2932 .M847 1987

INTERNATIONAL BUSINESS ENTERPRISES - SOUTH AFRICA.
Seidman, Ann Willcox, 1926- The roots of crisis in southern Africa /. Trenton, N.J. [1985] xvii, 209 p. : ISBN 0-86543-026-8 (pbk.) : LC Card 85-72995 DDC 968.06/3 19
E183.8.S6 S45 1985 ***NYPL [Sc E 86-368]***

Transnational corporations in South Africa and Namibia . New York , 1986-<1987. v. <1-2, 4 > ; ISBN 92-1-104190-2 (pbk. : set) LC Card 87-403059 DDC 338.8/8868 19
HD2922 .T72 1986

INTERNATIONAL BUSINESS ENTERPRISES - SOVIET UNION.
Bubnov, Boris. Foreign trade with the USSR . Oxford , New York , c1987. p. cm. ISBN 0-08-035844-6 : LC Card 87-7167 DDC 382/.0947 19
HF1557 .B83 1987

INTERNATIONAL BUSINESS ENTERPRISES - SPAIN - CATALONIA CASE STUDIES.
Cabana, Francesc, 1934- Les multinacionals a Catalunya /. Barcelona , 1986. 154 p. ; ISBN 84-7410-162-X LC Card 86-222016
HD2888.5.C38 C33 1986

INTERNATIONAL BUSINESS ENTERPRISES - SPAIN - CATALONIA - HISTORY.
Cabana, Francesc, 1934- Les multinacionals a Catalunya /. Barcelona , 1986. 154 p. ; ISBN 84-7410-162-X LC Card 86-222016
HD2888.5.C38 C33 1986

INTERNATIONAL BUSINESS ENTERPRISES - SPAIN - ZARAGOZA.
Todo para la G.M. . Madrid [1981?] 174 p. : ISBN 84-85639-19-7 LC Card 82-134601 DDC 338.8/87 19
HD9710.S754 G467 1981
NYPL [JLC 86-300]

INTERNATIONAL BUSINESS ENTERPRISES - SWEDEN.
Hermansson, C. H. Sverige i imperialismens nät /. Stockholm , 1986. 301 p. : ISBN 91-7014-203-3 LC Card 86-225250
HD2883 .H43 1986

Multinationella förtag . Lund , 1985. 196 p. : ISBN 91-578-0210-6 : LC Card 86-216456
HD2755.5 .M864 1985

De Transnationella företagens roll i världshandeln ; Gränsskydd i andra länder /. [Stockholm] [1984] 62, [36] p. ; ISBN 91-38-08406-6 LC Card 86-115056
HD9015.S86 T73 1984

INTERNATIONAL BUSINESS ENTERPRISES - TAXATION - GERMANY (WEST)
Kratz, Peter. Steuerplanung internationaler Unternehmungen . Bern , c1986. xii, 344 p. : ISBN 3-258-03586-5 : LC Card 86-171030
HJ4720.A3 K73 1986

INTERNATIONAL BUSINESS ENTERPRISES - TAXATION - SWITZERLAND.
Tinner, Hanspeter. Konzernstruktur und Steuerplanung . Bern , c1984. ix, 276 p. : ISBN 3-258-03367-6 : LC Card 84-198592
HJ4748.A3 T55 1984

INTERNATIONAL BUSINESS ENTERPRISES - UNITED STATES.
Medvedkov, S. I͡U. (Sergeĭ I͡Ur´evich) Mezhdunarodnyĭ marketing amerikanskoĭ tekhnologii /. Moskva , 1985. 189 p. : LC Card 85-187077
HF1009.6 .M43 1985

Ozadovskiĭ, A. A. (Andreĭ Andreevich) Uoll-strit protiv Afriki /. Kiev , 1985. 228, [4] p. ; LC Card 86-219442
HF1611.Z4 U556 1985

Poniachek, Harvey A. Direct foreign investment in the United States /. Lexington, Mass. , c1986. xiii, 256 p. : ISBN 0-669-11076-0 (alk. paper) LC Card 85-40457 DDC 332.6/73/0973 19
HG4910 .P66 1986 ***NYPL [JLE 86-4295]***

International Business Forms Industries.
Formsmark II, the short-run forms market /. Arlington, VA (1730 N. Lynn St., Arlington 22209) , c1986. 107 leaves : LC Card 87-146216 DDC 381/.4565129 19
HD9800.7.A2 F67 1986

FormsMark III . Arlington, VA (1730 N. Lynn St., Arlington 22209) , c1986. 154 p. : LC Card 87-401995 DDC 381/.4565129 19
HD9802.3.A2 F67 1986

International business in the nineteenth century . Jones, Charles A., 1949- New York , c1987. xi, 260 p. ; ISBN 0-8147-4172-X : LC Card 87-11321 DDC 338.8/8/09034 19
HF497 .J66 1987

INTERNATIONAL BUSINESS MACHINES CORPORATION - MANAGEMENT - HISTORY.
Mercer, David (David Steuart) IBM . London , 1987. 306 p. ; ISBN 1-85091-287-4 : LC Card 87-138763 DDC 338.7/61004/0973 19
HD9696.C64 I4855 1987

International capital flows and the United States . Thomsen, Stephen E. Washington, D.C. (1400 Eye St., N.W., Suite 510, Washington 20005) [1985] vi, 62 p. : LC Card 87-108428 DDC 332/.042/0973 19
HG4910 .T47 1985

International capital movements . Kindleberger, Charles Poor, 1910- Cambridge [Cambridgeshire] , New York , 1987. vi, 99 p. ;

ISBN 0-521-34132-9 LC Card 86-32733 DDC 332/.041 19
HG3891 .K55 1987

International capitalism and industrial restructuring : a critical analysis / edited by Richard Peet. Boston : Allen & Unwin, 1987. p. cm. Bibliography: p. Includes index. ISBN 0-04-338132-4 (alk. paper) LC Card 86-28870 DDC 338.7 19
1. Industry - History. 2. Industrial organization. 3. Economic history - 1945-. 4. Industry and state. 5. Marxian economics. 6. Capitalism. I. Peet, Richard. II. Title: Industrial restructuring.
HD2321 .I58 1987

International careers . Win, David. Charlotte, Vt. , c1987. 222 p. ; ISBN 0-913589-28-4 (pbk.) : LC Card 86-32547 DDC 650.1/4 19
HF5549.5.E45 W525 1987

International Center for Monetary and Banking Studies. Threats to international financial stability /. Cambridge , New York , 1987. xviii, 307 p. : ISBN 0-521-34556-1 LC Card 87-10310 DDC 332/.042 19
HG3881 .T495 1987

International Center for Public Enterprises in Developing Countries.
Guide to training needs assessment /. Ljubljana, Yugoslavia , c1984. 65 p. ; ISBN 92-9038-412-8 (pbk.) LC Card 85-242690 DDC 658.3/12404 19
HF5549.5.T7 G847 1984

Pricing policy and investment criteria in public enterprises . Ljubljana, Yugoslavia , 1982. 297 p. : ISBN 92-9038-024-1 (pbk.) LC Card 85-242542 DDC 338.7/4 19
HD3842 .P75 1985 ***NYPL [JLE 87-547]***

INTERNATIONAL CLEARING.
Szilvássy, Erika. A nemzetközi pénzügyek és a külkereskedelmi fizetések gyakorlata /. Budapest , 1985. 286 p. ; ISBN 963-221-529-X : LC Card 86-190902
HG3881 .S95 1985

Vrsaljko, Krešimir. Teorija i praksa domaćih i medunarodnih plaćanja /. Zagreb , 1982. xiv, 460 p. ; LC Card 84-160248
HG2341.Y82 V77 1982

INTERNATIONAL CLEARING - YUGOSLAVIA.
Vrsaljko, Krešimir. Teorija i praksa domaćih i medunarodnih plaćanja /. Zagreb , 1982. xiv, 460 p. ; LC Card 84-160248
HG2341.Y82 V77 1982

INTERNATIONAL COINAGE. see **COINAGE, INTERNATIONAL.**

International Communications Industries Association. Directory of software producers. Fairfax, Va. (3150 Spring St., Fairfax 22031-2399) , c1986. [28] p. ; LC Card 87-109219 DDC 338.7/6137139445 19
HD9696.C63 U515957 1986

International comparative advantage in manufacturing : changing profiles of resources and trade. Vienna : United Nations Industrial Development Organization, 1986. xii, 226 p. : ill. ; 24 cm. Summary in French and Spanish. Includes bibliographical references. ISBN 92-1-106210-1 (pbk.) LC Card 86-214978 DDC 382.1/042 19
1. Comparative advantage (Commerce). 2. Comparative advantage (Commerce) - Statistics. 3. Manufactures - Statistics. 4. Commercial statistics. I. United Nations. Industrial Development Organization.
HF1412 .I57 1986

International comparisons of the distribution of household wealth / edited by Edward N. Wolff. Oxford : Clarendon Press ; New York : Oxford University Press, 1987. xii, 283 p. : ill. ; 23 cm. Papers originally published at the C.V. Starr Center Conference on International Comparisons of the Distribution of Household Wealth, November 11-12, 1983 in New York City. Spine title: Distribution of household wealth. Includes bibliographies and index. ISBN 0-19-828511-6 : LC Card 86-31241 DDC 339.2/2/094 19
1. Income distribution - Europe - Congresses. 2. Income distribution - United States - Congresses. 3. Income distribution - Canada - Congresses. 4. Wealth - Europe - Congresses. 5. Wealth - United States - Congresses. 6. Wealth - Canada - Congresses. I. Wolff, Edward N. II. C. V. Starr Center Conference on International Comparisons of the Distribution of Household Wealth (1983 : New York, N.Y.). III. Title: Distribution of household wealth.
HC240.9.I5 I56 1987

INTERNATIONAL COMPETITION. see **COMPETITION, INTERNATIONAL.**

International competition in services : banking building software know-how--. Washington, DC : Congress of the U. S., Office of Technology Assessment : For sale by the Supt. of Docs., U. S. G.P.O., [1987] vii, 403 p. : ill. ; 26 cm. Shipping list no.: 87-398-P. "July 1987"--P. [4] of cover. Includes bibliographical references and index. "OTA-ITE-328"--P. [4] of cover. S/N 052-003-01067-4 Item 1070-M LC Card 87-619820 DDC 382/.45/00973 19
1. Service industries - United States. 2. Competition, International. 3. International trade. I. United States. Congress. Office of Technology Assessment.
HD9981.5 .I58 1987

INTERNATIONAL CONFEDERATION OF FREE TRADE UNIONS - CONGRESSES.
Souvenir, ICFTU World Conference on the Trade Union Role in Balanced Development, Vigyan Bhawan, New Delhi, India, March 18-20, 1981 /. New Delhi [1981] 68 p. : LC Card 84-901715 DDC 331.88 19
HD6475.A2 I26347 1981
NYPL [JLG 86-296]

International Conference on Creative and Innovative Management (2nd : 1984 : Miami, Fla.) Frontiers in creative and innovative management /. Cambridge, Mass. , 1985, c1986. xxv, 391 p. : ISBN 0-88730-057-X LC Card 85-15125 DDC 658.4 19
HD53 .F76 1986 ***NYPL [JLE 86-3614]***

International Conference on Employment and Training (1985 : Perth, W.A.) Full employment, uncertain futures / International Conference on Employment and Training, September 23-26, 1985 : Merlin Hotel, Perth, Western Australia. [Perth, W.A.] : Dept. of Employment and Training, State Govt. of Western Australia, [1985] ix, 263 p. : ill. ; 30 cm. "A collection of papers by keynote speakers"--Cover. Includes bibliographies. LC Card 86-185208 DDC 339.5 19
1. Labor supply - Congresses. 2. Manpower policy - Congresses. 3. Occupational training - Congresses. I. Western Australia. Dept. of Employment and Training. II. Title.
HD5701.3 .I55 1985

International Conference on Ethiopian Studies (7th : 1982 : Lund, Sweden) Fassil G. Kiros. Mobilizing the peasantry for rural development [microform] . [Addis Ababa , 1982] 20 leaves ; LC Card 82-980723 DDC 334/.683/0963 19
HD1538.E7 F37 1982
NYPL [*Z-3952 no.39]

International Conference on Networks and Electronic Office Systems (1983 : University of Reading) Networks and electronic office systems : University of Reading, 26th-30th September, 1983. London : The Institution of Electronic and Radio Engineers, c1983. 240 p. : ill. ; 30 cm. (IERE publication . no. 57) On cover: NEOS '83. Includes bibliographical references and index. ISBN 0-903748-52-5
1. Computer networks - Congresses. 2. Data transmission systems - Congresses. 3. Information networks - Congresses. 4. Office practice - Automation - Congresses. I. Institution of Electronic and Radio Engineers. II. Series: Publication / Institution of Electronic and Radio Engineers , no. 57. III. Title. ***NYPL [JSG 86-298]***

International Conference on Networks and Electronic Office Systems (1985 : London, England) Networks and electronic office systems : the Empire Suite, Tottenham Court Road, London Wi 17th-19th September, 1985. London : Institution of Electronic and Radio Engineers, c1985. 166 p. : ill. ; 30 cm. (Publication / Institution of Electronic and Radio Engineers . no. 63) Includes bibliographies and index. ISBN 0-903748-60-6
1. Computer networks - Congresses. 2. Data transmission systems - Congresses. 3. Information networks - Congresses. 4. Office practice - Automation - Congresses. I. Institution of Electronics and Radio Engineers. II. Series: Publication / Institution of Electronic and Radio Engineers , no. 63. III. Title. ***NYPL [JSG 86-264]***

International Conference on Quantity and Quality in Economic Research (1st : 1984 : Princeton, N.J.) Quantity and quality in economic research /. Lanham, MD , c1985- v. : ISBN 0-8191-5112-2 (v. 1 : alk. paper) : LC Card 85-26360 DDC 330/.072 19
HB135 .Q38 1985 ***NYPL [JLL 86-232]***

International Conference on Stochastic Optimization (1984 : Kiev, Ukraine) Stochastic optimization . Berlin , New York , c1985. x, 754 p. : ISBN 0-387-16659-9 (U. S.) LC Card 86-11865 DDC 629.8/312 19
QA402.3 .S778 1985 ***NYPL [JSE 86-1596]***

International Conference on Transportation, Storage, and Disposal of Hazardous Materials (1985 : International Institute for Applied Systems Analysis) Insuring and managing hazardous risks--from Seveso to Bhopal and beyond /. Berlin , New York , c1987. ix, 534 p. : ISBN 0-387-17732-9 (U. S.) LC Card 87-4963 DDC 346.03/8 342.638 19
HG9994 .I57 1987

International Conference on Women and Offshore Oil (1985 : St. John's, Nfld.) Women, work, and family in the British, Canadian, and Norwegian oilfields /. New York , 1987. p. cm. ISBN 0-312-00528-8 : LC Card 86-31393 DDC 305.4/3665 19
HD9560.5 .W66 1987

International conference report series .
(1) Tokyo Forum: Ethics of Human Survival (1985) Proceedings of the Tokyo Forum: Ethics of Human Survival . Tokyo, Japan , c1986. v, 88 p. : ISBN 4-7955-1024-5 LC Card 87-142747
HD73 .T65 1985

INTERNATIONAL CONFERENCES, CONGRESSES AND CONVENTIONS. see **CONGRESSES AND CONVENTIONS.**

International congress and symposium series .
(no. 116) Young drivers impaired by alcohol and other drugs /. London , New York, NY , c1987. p. cm. ISBN 0-905958-48-9 (pbk) : LC Card 87-20657 DDC 363.1/251 19
HE5620.D7 Y68 1987

International Congress of Logic, Methodology, and Philosophy of Science (8th : 1987 : Moscow, R.S.F.S.R.) Buračas, A. (Antanas) Metaeconomic conceptualization and social criteria of development /. Vilnius , 1987 [i.e. 1986] 60, [4] p. ; LC Card 87-672211
HB131 .B87x 1986

International Congress on Economic History (8th : 1982 : Budapest, Hungary) Münzprägung, Geldumlauf und Wechselkurse : Akten des 8th International Economic History Congress, Section C7, Budapest 1982 = Minting, monetary circulation and exchange rates / im Auftrag der Economic History Association herausgegeben von Eddy van Cauwenberghe und Franz Irsigler. Trier : Verlag Trierer Historische Forschung, 1984. 421 p. : ill. ; 24 cm. (Trierer historische Forschungen, 0720-9096 . Bd. 7) Includes bibliographies. ISBN 3-923087-06-3 (pbk.)
1. Money - Congresses. 2. Money - Europe - History - Congresses. 3. Europe - Economic conditions - Congresses. 4. India - Economic conditions - Congresses. I. Cauwenberghe, Eddy van. II. Irsigler, Franz. III. Economic History Association. IV. Title. V. Title: Minting, monetary circulation and exchange rates. VI. Series.
HG205 1982 .I53 ***NYPL [JLE 86-3176]***

The International Congress on New Dimensions in Population Planning and Development, Bandaranaike Memorial International Conference Hall, Colombo, 26-28 March 1978 /. International Congress on New Dimensions in Population Planning and Development (1978 : Colombo, Sri Lanka) Colombo, Sri Lanka , 1978. 114 p., [5] leaves of plates : LC Card 84-902651 DDC 304.6/6/095493 19
HB883.5 .I57 1978 ***NYPL [JLF 86-1970]***

International Congress on New Dimensions in Population Planning and Development (1978 : Colombo, Sri Lanka) The International Congress on New Dimensions in Population Planning and Development, Bandaranaike Memorial International Conference Hall, Colombo, 26-28 March 1978 / sponsored by the Family Planning Association of Sri Lanka as a part of their silver jubilee celebrations. Colombo, Sri Lanka : The

Association, 1978. 114 p., [5] leaves of plates : ill. ; 27 cm. Includes bibliographical references. LC Card 84-902651 DDC 304.6/6/095493 19
1. Population policy - Congresses. 2. Birth control - Congresses. 3. Rural development - Sri Lanka - Congresses. I. Family Planning Association of Sri Lanka. II. Title.
HB883.5 .I57 1978 **NYPL [JLF 86-1970]**

INTERNATIONAL COOPERATION - ADDRESSES, ESSAYS, LECTURES.
Cooperation under anarchy /. Princeton, N.J. , 1986. 260 p. ; ISBN 0-691-07695-2 : LC Card 85-42936 DDC 327.1/1 19
D445 .C736 1986 **NYPL [JLE 86-1938]**

Myrdal, Gunnar, 1898- Increasing interdependence between states but failure of international cooperation /. Göteborg , 1978. 53 p. ; ISBN 91-7360-052-0 LC Card 80-511073 DDC 327.1/7 19
JX1954 .M94 **NYPL [JLD 81-302]**

INTERNATIONAL COOPERATION - CONGRESSES.
Varna Forum (2nd : 1985 : Varna, Bulgaria) Varna Forum II . [Varna?] [s.n.] [1985] 166 p. ; LC Card 86-220415 DDC 382/.091713/01717 19
HF1410.5 .V37 1985

International cooperation for social justice . Mower, A. Glenn (Alfred Glenn) Westport, Conn. , c1985. x, 271 p. ; ISBN 0-313-24702-1 (lib. bdg.) LC Card 84-27954 DDC 341.4/81 19
K3240.4 .M676 1985 **NYPL [JLD 85-3575]**

International corporate finance . Shapiro, Alan C. Tampa, FL , c1986. 79 p. : ISBN 0-936795-00-X (pbk.) LC Card 86-231054 DDC 658.1/599 19
HG4027.5 .S46 1986

International cost differences in developing countries . Iyare, S. Durham, England [1983] 14, [9] leaves : LC Card 86-207078 DDC 338.4/367/09667 19
HD9737.G52 I97 1983

International Council for Building Research, Studies and Documentation. Working Commission 72. The Spatial impact of technological change /. Totowa, NJ , 1987. p. cm. ISBN 0-389-20753-5 LC Card 87-11460 DDC 338/.06 19
HC79.T4 S77 1987

International Council of Shopping Centers. Food courts . New York , c1987. 70 p. : ISBN 0-913598-66-6 (pbk.) LC Card 87-604 DDC 647/.9573 19
HF5430 .F66 1987

Shopping center managers and retailers . New York , c1988. p. cm. ISBN 0-913598-73-9 (pbk.) : LC Card 87-22546 DDC 658.8/7 19
HF5430 .S557 1988

International countertrade / edited by Christopher M. Korth. New York : Quorum Books, 1987. xii, 191 p. : ill. ; 24 cm. Results of a conference held at the College of Business, University of South Carolina, Spring, 1985 ; co-sponsored by the U. S. Dept. of Education. Bibliography: p. [179]-180. Includes index. ISBN 0-89930-213-0 (lib. bdg. : alk. paper) LC Card 86-25319 DDC 382 19
1. Countertrade - Congresses. I. Korth, Christopher M. II. University of South Carolina. College of Business Administration. III. United States. Dept. of Education.
HF1410.5 .I5716 1987

INTERNATIONAL COVENANT ON ECONOMIC, SOCIAL, AND CULTURAL RIGHTS.
Mower, A. Glenn (Alfred Glenn) International cooperation for social justice . Westport, Conn. , c1985. x, 271 p. ; ISBN 0-313-24702-1 (lib. bdg.) LC Card 84-27954 DDC 341.4/81 19
K3240.4 .M676 1985 **NYPL [JLD 85-3575]**

International debt . Barth, James R. Fairfax, Va. , 1984. 36 p. ; **NYPL [*ZT-1554 no.21]**

International debt and central banking in the 1980s / edited by Zannis Res and Sima Motamen. New York : St. Martin's Press, 1987. viii, 234 p. ; 23 cm. "Proceedings of two conferences held at The City University, in October 1983 and May 1984"--Introd. Includes bibliographies and index. ISBN 0-312-00530-X : LC Card 87-4300 DDC 336.3/435/091724 19
1. Debts, External - Developing countries - Congresses. 2. Banks and banking, Central - Developing countries - Congresses. I. Res, Zannis, 1941-. II. Motamen, Sima.
HJ8899 .I574 1987

The international debt crisis of the Third World . Nunnenkamp, Peter. New York , 1986. xvi, 205 p. ; ISBN 0-312-42003-X : LC Card 85-2008 DDC 336.3/435/091724 19
HJ8899 .N86 1985 **NYPL [JLD 86-2529]**

The International debt problem : lessons for the future : symposium 1985 / Institut für Weltwirtschaft an der Universität Kiel ; edited by Herbert Giersch. Tübingen : J.C.B. Mohr (P. Siebeck), 1986. vi, 193 p. : ill. ; 24 cm. Papers presented at a conference held at the Institut für Weltwirtschaft at the Universität Kiel on June 26-28, 1985. Includes bibliographies. ISBN 3-16-345084-9 (pbk.) LC Card 86-201893 DDC 336.3/435 19
1. Debts, External - Congresses. 2. Loans, Foreign - Congresses. 3. International finance - Congresses. I. Giersch, Herbert. II. Universität Kiel. Institut für Weltwirtschaft.
HG3891.5 .I557 1986

The International debt problem : lessons for the future / edited by Herbert Giersch. Boulder : Westview Press, 1987. p. cm. (Publications of the Institute of World Economics, University of Kiel) Papers presented at an international symposium, sponsored by the Kiel Institute of World Economics, on June 26-28, 1985. ISBN 0-8133-0595-0 LC Card 87-20149 DDC 336.3/435 19
1. Debts, External - Congresses. 2. Loans, Foreign - Congresses. 3. International finance - Congresses. I. Giersch, Herbert. II. Universität Kiel. Institut für Weltwirtschaft. III. Series.
HG3891.5 .I557 1987

International debt threat . Aggarwal, Vinod K. Berkeley , c1987. vii, 71 p. ; ISBN 0-87725-529-6 (pbk.) LC Card 87-80549 DDC 336.3/435 19
HG3891.5 .A38 1987

INTERNATIONAL DEBTS. see **DEBTS, EXTERNAL.**

INTERNATIONAL DEVELOPMENT ASSOCIATION.
Procurement under IBRD loans and IDA credits . Washington, D.C. , c1985. 38 p. ; ISBN 0-8213-0562-X (pbk.) LC Card 86-211637 DDC 332.1/532 19
HG3881.5.W57 P76 1985

International Development Research Centre. Laquian, Aprodicio A. Basic housing . Ottawa, Canada , c1983. 163 p. : ISBN 0-88936-370-6 (pbk.) LC Card 83-231129 DDC 363.5/8/091724 19
HD7391 .L36 1983 **NYPL [JLE 86-1376]**

International Development Research Centre (Canada)
Comercialización interna de los alimentos en América Latina . Ottawa, Canada , c1985. 253 p. : ISBN 0-88936-448-6 LC Card 87-118494 DDC 338.1/9/8 19
HD9014.L32 C66 1985

Regional Workshop on Wood Energy in East Africa (1982 : Nairobi, Kenya) Proceedings of the Regional Workshop on Wood Energy in East Africa . Ottawa, Canada [1983] 241 p. : LC Card 86-185703 DDC 333.75 19
HD9769.F843 A367 1982

With our own hands . Ottawa, Canada , c1986. 206 p. : ISBN 0-88936-460-5 (pbk.) LC Card 86-212405 DDC 338.91/71/01724 19
HC59.72.F44 W58 1986

INTERNATIONAL DEVELOPMENT RESEARCH CENTRE (CANADA)
With our own hands . Ottawa, Canada , c1986. 206 p. : ISBN 0-88936-460-5 (pbk.) LC Card 86-212405 DDC 338.91/71/01724 19
HC59.72.F44 W58 1986

International dictionary of management /. Johannsen, Hano. London , c1986. 370 p. : ISBN 0-85038-970-4 **NYPL [JLD 86-1777]**

International dimension of development problems : evaluative survey of Dutch social science research / [introduction by] B.F. Galjart ; B.J.S. Hoetjes ... [et al.]. Amsterdam ; New York : Noord-Hollandsche Uitgevers Mij., 1984. 103 p. ; 24 cm. (Handelingen / Koninklijke Nederlandse Akademie van Wetenschappen. Sociaal-Wetenschappelijke Raad . nr. 7) "Netherlands Social Science Council (Sociaal-Wetenschappelijke Raad), Advisory Council for Scientific Research in Development Problems (Raad van Advies voor het Wetenschappelijk Onderzoek in het kader van Ontwikkelingssamenwerking)." Includes bibliographies. ISBN 0-444-85621-8 (pbk.) LC Card 85-209291 DDC 338.9 19
1. Economic development - Addresses, essays, lectures. 2. Dependency - Addresses, essays, lectures. 3. Social science research - Netherlands - Addresses, essays, lectures. I. Hoetjes, B. J. S., 1945-. II. Akademie van Wetenschappen, Amsterdam. Sociaal-Wetenschappelijke Raad. III. Raad van Advies voor het Wetenschappelijk Onderzoek in het kader van Ontwikkelingssamenwerking (Netherlands). IV. Series: Akademie van Wetenschappen, Amsterdam. Sociaal-Wetenschappelijke Raad. Handelingen.
HD75 .I59 1984 **NYPL [JLE 86-1391]**

The International directory of business information sources and services. London : Europa Publications Limited, 1986. ix, 378 p. ; 25 cm. Includes bibliographical references and index. ISBN 0-946653-18-6
1. Business - Information services. - Directories. 2. Information services - Directories. 3. Information consultants - Directories.
NYPL [*R-Econ. 86-2525]

International directory of suppliers and agents for information handling equipment and logistical support services / prepared by the International Referral Centre for Information Handling Equipment, IRCIHE, with the assistance of the United Nations Educational, Scientific and Cultural Organization, UNESCO. Zagreb : IRCIHE : Referral Centre of the University of Zagreb, 1985. iii, 418 p. ; 29 cm. Bibliography: p. 411-415. Includes index. LC Card 86-220527 DDC 338.7/61004/025 19
1. Computer industry - Directories. 2. Computer service industry - Directories. I. International Referral Centre for Information Handling Equipment. II. Unesco. III. Sveuviliste u Zagrebu. Referalni centar.
HD9696.A2 I595 1985

International display and visual merchandising / from the National Retail Merchants Association's Visual Merchandising Board of Directors. Glen Cove, N.Y. : PBC Intern'l, 1987. p. cm. ISBN 0-86636-052-2 : LC Card 87-61166 DDC 659.1/5 19
1. Display of merchandise. I. National Retail Merchants Association. Visual Merchandising Board of Directors.
HF5845 .I73 1987

International diversification through the government bond market . Gheysens, Lieven. [Leuven] , 1977. 188 leaves ; LC Card 85-186317 DDC 332.63/232 19
HG4715 .G44 1977
NYPL [JLM 86-1310 nr.24]

INTERNATIONAL DIVISION OF LABOR.
Albuquerque, Marcos Cintra Cavalcanti de. Riscos e perspectivas da divisão internacional do trabalho =. Brasília, DF [1986] 19, 17, [2] p. ; LC Card 87-403241 DDC 331/.01 19
HF1411 .A3984 1986

Casson, Mark, 1945- Multinationals and world trade . London , Boston , 1986. xi, 401 p. : ISBN 0-04-338125-1 (alk. paper) LC Card 85-15734 DDC 338.8/8 19
HD2748 .C37 1986 **NYPL [JLD 86-1224]**

Cowling, Keith. Transnational monopoly capitalism /. Sussex [England] , New York , 1987. vii, 178 p. : ISBN 0-312-00954-2 (St. Martin's) : LC Card 87-4965 DDC 338.8/8 19
HD2755.5 .C68 1987

Empresas multinacionales y división internacional del trabajo /. Salamanca , 1977. 158 p. : ISBN 84-301-0465-8 LC Card 86-164261
HD2755.5 .E49 1977

Inotai, András. [Regionális integrációk az új világgazdasági helyzetben. English.] Regional integrations in the new world economic environment /. Budapest , 1986. vii, 286 p. ; ISBN 963-05-4353-2 LC Card 87-111425 DDC 337.1 19
HF1418.5 .I5513 1986

International economic restructuring and the regional community /. Aldershot, Hants, England , Brookfield, Vt., USA , c1987. x, 404 p. : ISBN 0-566-05478-7 : LC Card 87-11841 DDC 330.9 19
HF1412 .I574 1987

Kuba v mezhdunarodnom sot͡sialisticheskom

razdelenii truda /. Moskva , 1986. 146 p. : LC Card 86-232928
HF1500.5.E852 K83 1986

Planning & implementing an apparel sourcing strategy . Arlington, Va. (2500 Wilson Blvd., Suite 301, Arlington 22209) , c1986. 41 p. : LC Card 87-107327 DDC 687/.068/7 19
HD9940.U4 P52 1986

Roth, Bernhard. Weltökonomie oder Nationalökonomie? . Marburg , c1984. xiv, 377 p. : ISBN 3-921630-48-7 : LC Card 84-252964
HF1411 .R69 1984

Structure industrielle et sous-traitance /. Paris , c1983. 243 p. : ISBN 2-13-038182-0 : LC Card 84-128203 DDC 331/.01 19
HD2381 .S77 1983 ***NYPL [JLE 86-1624]***

Sulmicki, Jan. Transfer postępu naukowo-technicznego przez przedsiębiorstwa międzynarodowe a długookresowe zmiany w przedsiębiorstwa międzynarodowe a długookresowe zmiany w międzynarodowym podziale pracy /. Warszawa , 1978. 288 p. ; LC Card 81-205742
HF1411 .S876 1978

International Drivers' Behaviour Research Association. Young drivers impaired by alcohol and other drugs /. London , New York, NY , c1987. p. cm. ISBN 0-905958-48-9 (pbk) : LC Card 87-20657 DDC 363.1/251 19
HE5620.D7 Y68 1987

International economic conflict discussion paper . (no. 23) Iida, Tsuneo, 1932- What is really unique about the Japanese economy? /. Nagoya, Japan , 1985. 13 leaves ; LC Card 87-109242 DDC 331.25 19
HF5549.5.S4 I35 1985

International economic institutions /. Meerhaege, Marcel Alfons Gilbert van, 1921- [Internationale economische betrekkingen en instellingen. English.] Dordrecht , Boston , 1987. xxviii, 368 p. ; ISBN 90-247-3513-0 LC Card 87-2959 DDC 337 19
HF1411 .M433 1987

INTERNATIONAL ECONOMIC INTEGRATION - CONGRESSES.
Welthandel morgen . Stuttgart , 1984. 275 p. : ISBN 3-87959-225-X LC Card 85-132786
HF4055 .W45 1984

INTERNATIONAL ECONOMIC POLICY. see **INTERNATIONAL ECONOMIC RELATIONS.**

International Economic Policy Association. Danielian, Ronald L. The forgotten deficit . Boulder , 1987. xii, 84 p. ; ISBN 0-8133-7450-2 (pbk. : alk. paper) LC Card 87-50654 DDC 332.6/7373 19
HG3883.U7 D36 1987

Thomsen, Stephen E. International capital flows and the United States . Washington, D.C. (1400 Eye St., N.W., Suite 510, Washington 20005) [1985] vi, 62 p. : LC Card 87-108428 DDC 332/.042/0973 19
HG4910 .T47 1985

The U. S. international payments crisis . Washington, D.C. (1400 Eye St., N.W., Suite 510, Washington 20005) [1986] 31 p. : LC Card 87-108567 DDC 382.1/7/0973 19
HG3883.U7 U18 1986

INTERNATIONAL ECONOMIC RELATIONS - ADDRESSES, ESSAYS, LECTURES.
Cooperation under anarchy /. Princeton, N.J. , 1986. 260 p. ; ISBN 0-691-07695-2 : LC Card 85-42936 DDC 327.1/1 19
D445 .C736 1986 ***NYPL [JLE 86-1938]***

Croissance, échange et monnaie en économie internationale . Paris , c1985. 604 p. : ISBN 2-7178-0912-0 (pbk.) :
NYPL [JLE 86-1157]

Dependency theory and the return of high politics /. Westport, Conn. , 1986. xii, 270 p. : ISBN 0-313-24860-5 (lib. bdg. : alk. paper) LC Card 85-17745 DDC 337 19
HF1411 .D35 1986 ***NYPL [JLE 86-2911]***

Economía internacional /. México , 1979- v. in : ***NYPL [JLK 86-184]***

Floating exchange rates and the state of world trade payments /. Cambridge, Mass. , 1984. xxvi, 309 p. ; ISBN 0-88410-998-4 (pbk.) LC Card 84-2905 DDC 332.4/562 19
HG3852 .F56 1984 ***NYPL [JLD 86-2709]***

Lleras Restrepo, Carlos, Pres, 1908- Economía internacional y régimen cambiario /. [S.l. , 1981] (Bogotá, D.E. : Osprey Impresores) 298, [3] p. ; LC Card 81-204089 DDC 337/.09/048 19
HF1411 .L542 1981 ***NYPL [JLE 86-3889]***

Multinationals and the restructuring of the world economy /. London , Dover, N.H. , c1986- viii, 389 p. : ISBN 0-7099-2457-7 (v. 2) : LC Card 85-29081 DDC 338.8/81 19
HD2755.5 .M8442 1986
NYPL [JLD 86-2089]

New international economic order /. Moscow , 1984. 196 p. ; LC Card 85-151148 DDC 337/.09/047 19
HF1411 .N398 1984 ***NYPL [JLD 86-2664]***

Problemas económicos del Tercer Mundo /. Buenos Aires, República Argentina , c1983. 210 p. : ISBN 950-577-070-7 LC Card 84-120737 DDC 337/.09172/4 19
HF1413 .P75 1983 ***NYPL [JLC 86-394]***

Salvador Ortíz, S., 1917-1983. Comentarios económicos /. Santo Domingo, República Dominicana , 1984- v. ; LC Card 85-118318 DDC 330.9 19
HC125 .S2615 1984 ***NYPL [JLK 85-83]***

Strategic trade policy and the new international economics /. Cambridge, Mass. , c1986. 313 p. ; ISBN 0-262-11112-8 LC Card 86-2758 DDC 382/.3 19
HF1411 .S82 1986 ***NYPL [JLE 86-3896]***

The Third world, premises of U. S. policy /. San Francisco , c1978. xv, 332 p. : ISBN 0-917616-30-8 : LC Card 78-67593 DDC 309.1/172/4
HC59.7 .T456 ***NYPL [JLD 81-653]***

INTERNATIONAL ECONOMIC RELATIONS - CASE STUDIES.
Newly industrializing countries and the political economy of south-south relations /. New York , 1988. p. cm. ISBN 0-312-01180-6 : LC Card 87-23476 DDC 337/.09172/4 19
HF1413 .N497 1988

INTERNATIONAL ECONOMIC RELATIONS - CONGRESSES.
Castro, Fidel, 1927- [Crisis económica y social del mundo. English.] The world economic and social crisis . New Delhi , 1983. 224 p. : LC Card 83-908475 DDC 337/.097172/4 19
HC59.7 .C31472 1983 ***NYPL [JLD 87-486]***

Der Nord-Süd-Dialog zu Beginn der 80er Jahre =. Baden-Baden , 1982. 99 p. ; ISBN 3-7890-0774-9 ***NYPL [JLE 87-1282]***

Education and the new international order /. New Delhi , 1983, c1982. xx, 147 p. ; LC Card 83-902560 DDC 370/.11/5 19
HF1411 .E28 1983 ***NYPL [JLD 86-3707]***

Global energy interactions /. Ahmedabad , 1987. xxxi, 1290 p. : LC Card 87-902497 DDC 333.79 19
HD9502.A2 G545 1987b

Imperfect competition and international trade . Brighton, Sussex , Atlantic Highlands, N.J. , c1986. xiv, 242 p. : ISBN 0-391-03403-0 (Humanities Press) LC Card 86-660 DDC 382 19
HF1411 .I354 1986 ***NYPL [JLD 86-2120]***

International trade and exchange rates in the late eighties /. Amsterdam ; New York : xii, 418 p. : ISBN 2-8004-0892-8
NYPL [JLE 87-120]

International trade and the consumer . Paris [Washington, D.C. , 1986. 296 p. ; ISBN 92-64-12813-1 (pbk.) : LC Card 86-216097 DDC 382/.3 19
HF1410.5 .I585 1986 ***NYPL [JLE 87-1541]***

Internationale Wirtschaft und revolutionärer Weltprozess /. [Berlin] , 1983. 390 p. ; LC Card 84-167604
HF1410.5 .I592 1983

Issues before non-alignment . New Delhi , 1983. 190 p. ; LC Card 83-903478 DDC 327/.09171/6 19
JX1393.N54 I87 1983 ***NYPL [JLE 86-4176]***

Les Libéraux et le dialogue Nord-Sud . Bonn , c1982. 220 p. ; ISBN 3-920590-36-8 LC Card 84-204748
HC59.7 .L4177 1982

New dimensions in foreign economic policy . Washington, DC , 1986. xiii, 118 p. ; LC Card 86-600514 DDC 337.73 19
HF1410.5 .N488 1986

Putnam, Robert D. Hanging together . Cambridge, Mass. , 1987. x, 293 p. ; ISBN 0-674-37226-3 (pbk.) LC Card 87-23593 DDC 337 19
HF1410.5 .P87 1987

Souvenir, ICFTU World Conference on the Trade Union Role in Balanced Development, Vigyan Bhawan, New Delhi, India, March 18-20, 1981 /. New Delhi [1981] 68 p. : LC Card 84-901715 DDC 331.88 19
HD6475.A2 I26347 1981
NYPL [JLG 86-296]

Sviluppo della finanza internazionale e interdipendenza dei sistemi finanziari . [Italy] [1984] iv, 204 p. : ISBN 88-14-00203-7 : LC Card 84-238589 DDC 332/.042 19
HG205.S85 S85 1984 ***NYPL [JLE 86-482]***

Tariff, legal, and credit constraints on East-West commercial relations /. Ottawa , 1975. 101 p. ; LC Card 76-379543 DDC 382.1
K3823.A55 T3 ***NYPL [JLD 86-1752]***

Technik und internationale Politik /. Baden-Baden , 1986. 520 p. ; ISBN 3-7890-1239-4 (Deut. Bibl.) LC Card 87-103890 DDC 338/.06 19
HC79.T4 T422 1986

Varna Forum (2nd : 1985 : Varna, Bulgaria) Varna Forum II . [Varna?] [s.n.] [1985] 166 p. ; LC Card 86-220415 DDC 382/.091713/01717 19
HF1410.5 .V37 1985

Welthandel morgen . Stuttgart , 1984. 275 p. : ISBN 3-87959-225-X LC Card 85-132786
HF4055 .W45 1984

World petrochemicals . [Staten Island, N.Y. (139 Chestnut Ave., Staten Island 10305)] , c1985. 279 p. : LC Card 85-71088 DDC 338.4/7661804 19
HD9579.C32 W68 1985
NYPL [JLD 86-2185]

INTERNATIONAL ECONOMIC RELATIONS - DICTIONARIES - GERMAN.
Aussenwirtschafts-Alphabet . Frankfurt am Main , c1986. 396 p. ; LC Card 87-401369 DDC 382/.03/31 19
HF1001 .A86 1986

INTERNATIONAL ECONOMIC RELATIONS - DICTIONARIES - POLISH.
Białecki, Klemens. Słownik handlu zagranicznego /. Warszawa , 1986. 359 p. ; ISBN 83-208-0112-5 : LC Card 86-221378
HF1001 .B47 1986

INTERNATIONAL ECONOMIC RELATIONS - DICTIONARIES - RUSSIAN.
Kratkiĭ vneshneėkonomicheskiĭ slovar′ /. Moskva , 1984. 244 p. ; LC Card 85-156834
HF1001 .K7 1984 ***NYPL [*QCK 86-3635]***

INTERNATIONAL ECONOMIC RELATIONS - HISTORY - 20TH CENTURY.
Lieberman, Sima, 1927- The economic and political roots of the new protectionism /. Totowa, N.J. , 1987. p. cm. ISBN 0-8476-7595-5 LC Card 87-23329 DDC 382.7/3/09048 19
HF1411 .L533 1987

Von der Konkurrenz zur Rivalität . Stuttgart , 1986. 186 p. ; ISBN 3-515-04760-3 LC Card 87-134320 DDC 337/.09/04 19
HF1411 .V665 1986

INTERNATIONAL ECONOMIC RELATIONS - MATHEMATICAL MODELS.
Kattermann, Dieter. Neoricardianische Modelle zur Theorie des internationalen Handels und ihre Kritik der neoklassischen Aussenhandelstheorie . Bremen , 1981. 135, A-G p. : ISBN 3-88722-039-0 LC Card 82-177622 DDC 337/.0724 19
HF1412 .K37 1981 ***NYPL [JLD 86-2740]***

Santacoloma, Juan Francisco. Modelos

macroeconómicos en economías abiertas /. Bilbao , 1983. 3 v. : ISBN 84-7485-037-1 (set) LC Card 84-168556 DDC 339/.0724 19
HB141 .S28 1983 ***NYPL [JLL 86-351]***

INTERNATIONAL ECONOMIC RELATIONS - MATHEMATICAL MODELS - CONGRESSES.
International macroeconomic modelling for policy decisions /. Dordrecht , Boston , c1986. viii, 269 p. : ISBN 90-247-3201-8 LC Card 85-13698 DDC 337/.0724 19
HF1410.5 .I577 1986 ***NYPL [JLE 86-3469]***

INTERNATIONAL ECONOMIC RELATIONS - OUTLINES, SYLLABI, ETC.
Salvatore, Dominick. Schaum's outline of theory and problems of international economics /. New York , c1984. 231 p. : ISBN 0-07-054503-0 (pbk.) LC Card 82-21666 DDC 337 19
HF1411 .S24 1984 ***NYPL [JLF 86-1845]***

INTERNATIONAL ECONOMIC RELATIONS - PROBLEMS, EXERCISES, ETC.
Salvatore, Dominick. Schaum's outline of theory and problems of international economics /. New York , c1984. 231 p. : ISBN 0-07-054503-0 (pbk.) LC Card 82-21666 DDC 337 19
HF1411 .S24 1984 ***NYPL [JLF 86-1845]***

International economic restructuring and the regional community / edited by Herman Muegge and Walter Stöhr, with Paul Hesp and Barbara Stuckey. Aldershot, Hants, England ; Brookfield, Vt., USA : Avebury, c1987. x, 404 p. : ill. ; 23 cm. "Revised essays presented at the Symposium on Regional Development Processes and Policies and the Changing International Division of Labour, which was held at the Vienna International Centre in August 1984"--Foreword. Sponsored by the Vienna University of Economics, Interdisciplinary Institute for Urban and Regional Studies and the United Nations Industrial Development Organization, Regional and Country Studies Branch. Includes bibliographies. ISBN 0-566-05478-7 : LC Card 87-11841 DDC 330.9 19
1. International division of labor. 2. Regional planning. 3. Economic development. I. Stöhr, Walter B. II. Muegge, Herman, 1935-. III. Symposium on Regional Development Processes and Policies and the Changing International Division of Labour (1984 : Vienna International Centre). IV. Wirtschaftsuniversität Wien. Interdisciplinary Institute for Urban and Regional Studies. V. United Nations Industrial Development Organization. Regional and Country Studies Branch.
HF1412 .I574 1987

International economics / edited by Lawrence H. Officer. Boston : Kluwer Academic Publishers, c1987. x, 274 p. : ill. ; 24 cm. (Recent economic thought series) Includes bibliographies. CONTENTS. - The theory of international trade / Wilfred J. Ethier -- The issue of protection / H. Peter Gray and Ingo Walter -- International linkages, exchange-rate regimes, and the international transmission process / Kent P. Kimbrough -- National policies and the international monetary system / J. Carter Murphy. ISBN 0-89838-196-7 LC Card 86-33776 DDC 337 19
1. International economic relations. 2. International finance. 3. Commerce. I. Officer, Lawrence H. II. Series. III. Series: Recent economic thought.
HF1411 .I51725 1987

International economics . Enders, Walter, 1948- Englewood Cliffs, N.J. , c1987. xii, 542 p. : ISBN 0-13-472853-X : LC Card 86-30623 DDC 337 19
HF1411 .E49 1987

International economics . Kreinin, Mordechai Elihau, 1930- San Diego , c1987. xiii, 465 p. : ISBN 0-15-541538-7 LC Card 86-80750 DDC 337 19
HF1411 .K697 1987

International economics . Krugman, Paul R. Glenview, Ill. , 1987. xxvii, 656, [35] p. : ISBN 0-316-50475-0 LC Card 87-17229 DDC 337 19
HF1411 .K74 1987

International economics. Salvatore, Dominick. Schaum's outline of theory and problems of international economics /. New York , c1984. 231 p. : ISBN 0-07-054503-0 (pbk.) LC Card 82-21666 DDC 337 19
HF1411 .S24 1984 ***NYPL [JLF 86-1845]***

INTERNATIONAL ECONOMICS. see **INTERNATIONAL ECONOMIC RELATIONS.**

International economics I . Gandolfo, Giancarlo. Berlin , New York , c1987- p. cm. ISBN 0-387-17971-2 (U. S.) LC Card 87-23367 DDC 337 19
HF1411 .G3362 1987

International economics II . Gandolfo, Giancarlo. Berlin , New York , c1987. p. cm. ISBN 0-387-17978-X (U. S.) LC Card 87-16295 DDC 332.4/5 19
HF1411 .G3363 1987

The International economies series.
Rimmer, Douglas. The economies of West Africa /. London , c1984. xii, 308 p. : ISBN 0-297-78095-6 LC Card 87-673367
HC1000 .R56x 1984b

International environment and India's economic development /. Sarma, N. A. New Delhi , 1986. viii, 100 p. ; ISBN 81-7017-214-4 : LC Card 86-902210 DDC 338.954 19
HC435.2 .S273 1986

INTERNATIONAL EXCHANGE. see **FOREIGN EXCHANGE.**

INTERNATIONAL EXHIBITIONS. see **EXHIBITIONS.**

International experience relating to compulsory seat belt use. Marburger, Ernst-Albrecht. Internationale Erfahrungen mit der Gurtanlegepflicht =. Köln , 1982. 29, 29 p. : LC Card 83-200842
HE5614 .M288 1982

International Federation of Pedestrians. Die Sicherung des Fussgängerverkehrs. Köln , 1976. ii, 169 p. : LC Card 86-185084
HE5614.5.G3 A7 Bd. 29

International Film Bureau. Marketing and distributive education [videorecording] /. Chicago, Ill. , 1986. 2 videocassettes (24 min. each) : LC Card 86-708241 DDC 658.8 11
HF5415

INTERNATIONAL FINANCE - ADDRESSES, ESSAYS, LECTURES.
Croissance, échange et monnaie en économie internationale . Paris , c1985. 604 p. : ISBN 2-7178-0912-0 (pbk.) :
NYPL [JLE 86-1157]

Economía internacional /. México , 1979- v. in : ***NYPL [JLK 86-184]***

Floating exchange rates and the state of world trade payments /. Cambridge, Mass. , 1984. xxvi, 309 p. ; ISBN 0-88410-998-4 (pbk.) LC Card 84-2905 DDC 332.4/562 19
HG3852 .F56 1984 ***NYPL [JLD 86-2709]***

International finance and trade /. Cambridge, Mass. , c1979. 2 v. : ISBN 0-88410-680-2 LC Card 79-11158 DDC 332.4/5 19
HG3881 .I57617 ***NYPL [JLL 80-187]***

International monetary problems and supply-side economics . Houndmills, Basingstoke, Hampshire , 1986. viii, 162 p. : ISBN 0-333-36200-4 ***NYPL [JLD 86-4356]***

International finance and trade / edited by Marshall Sarnat and Giorgio P. Szegö. Cambridge, Mass. : Ballinger Pub. Co., c1979. 2 v. : ill. ; 24 cm. Includes bibliographies and indexes. ISBN 0-88410-680-2 LC Card 79-11158 DDC 332.4/5 19
1. International finance - Addresses, essays, lectures. 2. Foreign exchange problem - Addresses, essays, lectures. I. Sarnat, Marshall. II. Szegö, G. P.
HG3881 .I57617 ***NYPL [JLL 80-187]***

INTERNATIONAL FINANCE - CONGRESSES.
La Crise de l'endettement international . Paris , c1986. 410 p. : ISBN 2-7178-1127-3 : LC Card 86-222862
HJ8017 .C74 1986

The Debt crisis and financial stability . New York, NY (Attn: Comptroller, Pace Plaza, 10038) , 1985. xi, 157 p. : ISBN 0-88239-017-1 : LC Card 85-19243 DDC 336.3/435/091724 19
HG3891.5 .D4 1985 ***NYPL [JLE 86-3911]***

Deuda externa y reforma del sistema monetario internacional . Bogotá, D.E., Colombia , 1986. 235 p. ; ISBN 958-608-037-4 LC Card 87-400468 DDC 336.3/435/098 19
HJ8514.5 .D487 1986

Directions for reform . New Delhi [1984] x, 78 p. ; ISBN 0-7069-2692-7 : LC Card 84-903168 DDC 332/.042 19
HG3881 .D57 1984 ***NYPL [JLD 86-4409]***

Employment and growth . Dordrecht , Boston , 1987. xii, 310 p. : ISBN 90-247-3514-9 LC Card 87-3184 DDC 331.11 19
HD73 .E46 1987

Exchange rates and international macroeconomics /. Chicago , 1983. x, 382 p. : ISBN 0-226-26249-9 LC Card 83-14524 DDC 332.4/56 19
HG205 1981c ***NYPL [JLE 86-3231]***

Finanz- und bankwirtschaftliche Probleme bei internationaler Unternehmenstätigkeit /. Stuttgart , c1985. x, 267 p. : ISBN 3-7910-0394-1 LC Card 86-121195 DDC 658.1/5 19
HG4027.5 .F56 1985

Geldwertstabilität und Wirtschaftswachstum . Göttingen , c1984. xii, 230 p. : ISBN 3-525-13169-0 LC Card 84-232466
HG203 .G46 1984

International banking and global financing . New York, NY , c1983. xiv, 257 p. : ISBN 0-88239-015-5 (pbk.) : LC Card 84-60076 DDC 332.1/5 19
HG205 .I54 1983

The International debt problem . Tübingen , 1986. vi, 193 p. : ISBN 3-16-345084-9 (pbk.) LC Card 86-201893 DDC 336.3/435 19
HG3891.5 .I557 1986

The International debt problem . Boulder , 1987. p. cm. ISBN 0-8133-0595-0 LC Card 87-20149 DDC 336.3/435 19
HG3891.5 .I557 1987

International trade and exchange rates in the late eighties /. Amsterdam ; New York : xii, 418 p. : ISBN 2-8004-0892-8
NYPL [JLE 87-120]

Die Internationale Finanzierungskrise /. Frankfurt am Main , c1985. 153 p. ; ISBN 3-7819-2536-6 LC Card 87-146671 DDC 336.3/435 19
HG3891.5 .I587 1985

Internationaler Kapitalverkehr und Devisenhandel /. Frankfurt am Main , c1986. 133 p. ; ISBN 3-7819-0347-8 LC Card 87-164156 DDC 332/.042 19
HG3891 .I58 1986

Internationalization of banking . Seoul, Korea , c1986. 300 p. : LC Card 87-114642 DDC 332.1/5 19
HG3881 .I496 1986

KIET International Finance Conference (1985 : Seoul, Korea) International financial markets and the NICs. Seoul, Korea [1985?] viii, 144 p. : LC Card 87-129000 DDC 332/.042 19
HG205 .K54 1985

New dimensions in foreign economic policy . Washington, DC , 1986. xiii, 118 p. ; LC Card 86-600514 DDC 337.73 19
HF1410.5 .N488 1986

Sviluppo della finanza internazionale e interdipendenza dei sistemi finanziari . [Italy] [1984] iv, 204 p. : ISBN 88-14-00203-7 : LC Card 84-238589 DDC 332/.042 19
HG205.S85 S85 1984 ***NYPL [JLE 86-482]***

Welthandel morgen . Stuttgart , 1984. 275 p. : ISBN 3-87959-225-X LC Card 85-132786
HF4055 .W45 1984

World monetary system in a time of change . Budapest [1987] 283 p. ; ISBN 963-01-7937-7 (pbk.) LC Card 87-169001 DDC 332.4/5 19
HG230.3 .W68 1987

International Finance Corporation. Marine shrimp farming . Charleston, S.C., USA (P.O. Box 16190, Charleston 29412) , c1987. vi, 90 leaves : LC Card 87-404668 DDC 338.3/71543 19
HD9472.S62 M375 1987

INTERNATIONAL FINANCE - DICTIONARIES.
Walmsley, Julian. A dictionary of international finance /. Westport, Conn. , 1979. 270 p. ; ISBN 0-313-20974-X LC Card 79-17753 DDC

332/.042/0321 19
HG151 .W34 NYPL [JLD 87-1082]

INTERNATIONAL FINANCE - DICTIONARIES - GERMAN.
Aussenwirtschafts-Alphabet . Frankfurt am Main , c1986. 396 p. ; LC Card 87-401369 DDC 382/.03/31 19
HF1001 .A86 1986

International finance handbook / edited by Abraham M. George, Ian H. Giddy. New York : Wiley, c1983. 2 v. : ill. ; 24 cm. "A Wiley-Interscience publication." Includes bibliographies and index. ISBN 0-471-09861-2 (set) : LC Card 82-23824 DDC 332/.042 19
1. International finance - Handbooks, manuals, etc. 2. International business enterprises - Finance - Handbooks, manuals, etc. I. George, Abraham M. II. Giddy, Ian H.
HG3881 .I57633 1983 NYPL [JLE 86-1719]

INTERNATIONAL FINANCE - HANDBOOKS, MANUALS, ETC.
International finance handbook /. New York , c1983. 2 v. : ISBN 0-471-09861-2 (set) : LC Card 82-23824 DDC 332/.042 19
HG3881 .I57633 1983 NYPL [JLE 86-1719]

INTERNATIONAL FINANCE - HISTORY.
Brett, E. A. International money and capitalist crisis . London , Boulder, Colo. , 1983. viii, 271 p. ; ISBN 0-86531-575-2 (Westview) LC Card 82-51289 DDC 332/.042 19
HG3881 .B6738 1983 NYPL [JLD 87-1020]

Denizet, Jean. Le dollar . Paris , c1985. 259 p. ; ISBN 2-213-01626-7 : LC Card 86-148501 DDC 332.4/560973 19
HG3881 .D344 1985 NYPL [JLD 87-337]

International finance management . (Bd. 1) Swinne, Axel Hilmar. Die finanzielle Führung und Kontrolle von Auslandsgesellschaften /. Frankfurt am Main , c1983. 422 p. : ISBN 3-7875-4200-0 LC Card 84-148375
HG4027.5 .S95 1983

International financial flows to Brazil since the late 1960s . Batista Júnior, Paulo Nogueira. Washington, D.C. , 1987. 66 p. ; ISBN 0-8213-0891-2 (pbk.) LC Card 87-6065 DDC 336.3/4/0981 19
HJ8579 .B369 1987

International financial intermediation /. Bryant, Ralph C., 1938- Washington, D.C. , c1987. xi, 181 p. : ISBN 0-8157-1138-7 : LC Card 87-10358 DDC 332/.042 19
HG3891.5 .B79 1987

International financial markets /. Grabbe, J. Orlin. New York , c1986. xi, 347 p. : ISBN 0-444-01032-7 LC Card 85-32545 DDC 332.4/5 19
HG3851 .G64 1986 NYPL [JLF 87-82]

International financial markets and the NICs. KIET International Finance Conference (1985 : Seoul, Korea) Seoul, Korea [1985?] viii, 144 p. : LC Card 87-129000 DDC 332/.042 19
HG205 .K54 1985

International Föderation der Fussgängerverbände. see **International Federation of Pedestrians.**

International Food Policy Research Institute. Accelerating food production in Sub-Saharan Africa /. Baltimore , c1987. xix, 417 p. ; ISBN 0-8018-3390-6 (alk. paper) LC Card 86-10684 DDC 338.1/9/67 19
HD2117 .A33 1987 NYPL [JLE 87-1366]

Crop insurance for agricultural development . Baltimore , c1986. xviii, 322 p. ISBN 0-8018-2673-X (alk. paper) LC Card 85-9810 DDC 368.1/22 19
HG9968 .C76 1985 NYPL [JLE 86-1082]

Tshibaka, Tshikala B., 1949- The effects of trade and exchange rate policies on agriculture in Zaire /. Washington, D.C., USA , 1986. 65 p. : ISBN 0-89629-057-3 LC Card 86-27449 DDC 338.1/09675/1 19
HD2135.5 .T75 1986

International Foundation for Development Alternatives. Rist, Gilbert, 1938- Towards a new United Nations development strategy . Nyon , 1977. 74 p. ; LC Card 81-118524
HC60 .R539 1977

International Foundation Humanum. Das Unternehmen als Grösse der Arbeitswelt . Bonn , 1984. 291 p. ; ISBN 3-923202-02-4 LC Card 85-119845
HD6957.G3 U58 1984

International Foundation of Employee Benefit Plans.
Benefits Processing Institute (1983 : Hollywood, Fla.) Claims processing for benefit plans, 1983 . Brookfield, Wis. , 1984. x, 82 p. : ISBN 0-89154-220-5 (pbk.) : LC Card 84-80454 DDC 331.25/5 19
HG9396 .B47 1984 NYPL [JLD 86-3940]

Corporate Benefits Management Conferences (1986 : Phoenix, Ariz., etc.) Managing corporate benefit plans, 1986 /. Brookfield, Wis. , 1986. x, 129 p. : ISBN 0-89154-318-X (pbk.) : LC Card 87-403111 DDC 332.6/7254 19
HD7105.45.U6 C67 1986

Employee benefit plans . Brookfield, Wis. , 1987. ix, 157 p. ; ISBN 0-89154-317-1 (pbk.) LC Card 87-150660 DDC 658.3/25/0321 19
HD4928.N6 E46 1987

International Foundation of Employee Benefits Plans. Wendling, Wayne. The regulatory impact on pensions /. Brookfield, Wis. , 1986. xiii, 91 p. : ISBN 0-89154-314-7 (pbk.) : LC Card 87-129712 DDC 331.25/2/0973 19
HD7105.35.U6 W46 1986

International Frequency Registration Board. Preface to the international frequency list and the weekly IFRB circular / IFRB, International Frequency Registration Board. 11th ed. Geneva : International Telecommunication Union, 1985. 1 v. (loose-leaf) : ill. ; 32 cm. ISBN 92-71-04001-5 LC Card 86-207597 DDC 384.54/52 19
1. Radio frequency allocation. I. Title.
HE8675 .I5525 1985

International Fund for Agricultural Development. Casley, D. J. Project monitoring and evaluation in agriculture /. Baltimore , c1987. xiii, 159 p. : ISBN 0-8018-3616-6 (pbk.) LC Card 87-22632 DDC 351.82/33 19
HD1415 .C335 1987

International Geographical Union. Commission of Population Geography. Policies of population redistribution /. Oulu , 1981. 199 p. : ISBN 951-675-071-0 (pbk.) LC Card 83-148782 DDC 304.8 19
HB1952 .P65 1981

International Geographical Union. Commission on Population Geography. Population and development projects in Africa /. Cambridge [Cambridgeshire] , New York , 1985. xvi, 329 p. : ISBN 0-521-30527-6 LC Card 84-29323 DDC 304.6/096 19
HB2121.A3 P67 1985 NYPL [JLF 86-186]

International Geographical Union. Population Geography, Commission on. see **International Geographical Union. Commission on Population Geography.**

INTERNATIONAL GRANTS-IN-AID. see **ECONOMIC ASSISTANCE.**

INTERNATIONAL HEALTH. see **WORLD HEALTH.**

International Humanum Foundation. see **International Foundation Humanum.**

International Industrial Conference, 1st, San Francisco, 1957. Private investment / edited by James Daniel. New York : Arno Press, 1980, c1958. xi, 282 p. ; 23 cm. (Multinational corporations : Operations and finance) Arno Press/New York Times collection Reprint of the ed. published by McGraw-Hill, New York. ISBN 0-405-13355-3 LC Card 80-606 DDC 332.6/7314
1. Investments, Foreign - Congresses. 2. Investments, Foreign - Developing countries - Congresses. 3. Economic development - Congresses. I. Daniel, James, 1916-. II. Title. III. Series.
HG4538 .I537 1957d NYPL [JLD 81-249]

International industry and business . Ballance, Robert H. London , Boston , 1987. xxi, 357 p. ; ISBN 0-04-339037-4 (alk. paper) LC Card 86-28793 DDC 338/.09/04048 19
HC59 .B3537 1987

International inequality /. Kubálková, V. London , c1981. 293 p. : ISBN 0-7099-0221-2 LC Card 86-673398
HF1411 .K819x 1981b

International Institute for Educational Planning. (Old Catalog form: United Nations Educational, Scientific and Cultural Organization. International Institute for Educational Planning.)
Education and the new international order /. New Delhi , 1983, c1982. xx, 147 p. ; LC Card 83-902560 DDC 370/.11/5 19
HF1411 .E28 1983 NYPL [JLD 86-3707]

International Institute for Environment and Development.
Leach, Gerald. Household energy in South Asia /. London ; New York : xii, 111 p. : ISBN 1-85166-125-5 (pbk.) : LC Card 87-13177 DDC 333.79 19
HD9502.S613 H68 1987

Leonard, H. Jeffrey. Natural resources and economic development in Central America . New Brunswick, N.J., U. S.A. , c1987. xxii, 279 p. : ISBN 0-88738-722-5 (pbk.) LC Card 87-10871 DDC 333.7/09728 19
HC141 .L44 1987

International Institute for Labour Studies. Management, work, leisure . Geneva , c1986. viii, 154 p. : ISBN 92-9014-416-5 (pbk.) : LC Card 87-163300 DDC 306/.36/094 19
HD4904.6 .M35 1986

International Institute of Management. Labour Market Policy. Schettkat, Ronald. Bevölkerungs- und Erwerbsverhaltensentwicklung in Österreich, Schweden und der Bundesrepublik Deutschland /. Berlin [1984] 48 p. ; LC Card 85-198691
HD5771 .S34 1984

International Institute of Public Finance : semicentennial, 1937 to 1987 = Institut international de finances publiques / Karl W. Roskamp, editor. Detroit : Wayne State University Press, 1987. vi, 106 p. : port. ; 24 cm. Pref. in English, French, and German; text in English. ISBN 0-8143-1984-X LC Card 87-10724 DDC 336/.006/01 19
1. International Institute of Public Finance - History. 2. Finance, Public - Research - History. I. Roskamp, Karl W. II. Title: Institut international de finances publiques.
HJ203 .I57 1987

INTERNATIONAL INSTITUTE OF PUBLIC FINANCE - HISTORY.
International Institute of Public Finance . Detroit , 1987. vi, 106 p. : ISBN 0-8143-1984-X LC Card 87-10724 DDC 336/.006/01 19
HJ203 .I57 1987

INTERNATIONAL INSTITUTIONS. see **INTERNATIONAL COOPERATION.**

International investments /. Solnik, Bruno H., 1944- Reading, Mass. , c1988. xi, 387 p. : ISBN 0-201-07538-5 : LC Card 87-1345 DDC 332.6/73 19
HG4538 .S52 1988

INTERNATIONAL LABOR ACTIVITIES.
African-American Labor Center. African-American Labor Center, 1965-1970 [microform]. New York, N.Y. [1970] 16 p. : NYPL [*ZT-1646 no.23]

Barnouin, Barbara. The European labour movement and European integration /. London , Wolfeboro, N.H. , 1986. viii, 172 p. ; ISBN 0-86187-650-4 : LC Card 86-5901 DDC 331.88/091 19
HD8372.E86 B37 1986 NYPL [JLE 86-4058]

Bendiner, Burton. International labour affairs . Oxford , New York , 1987. p. cm. ISBN 0-19-827498-8 : LC Card 87-17829 DDC 331.88/091 19
HD6475.A1 B4 1987

Inte bara ord-- . Stockholm , c1984. 120 p., [8] p. of plates : ISBN 91-550-3086-6 : LC Card 85-120867
HD6758 .I58 1984

A Magyar szakszervezetek feladatai a gazdaságirányítás továbbfejlesztésének segítésében . Budapest , 1984. 47 p. ; ISBN 963-322-215-X LC Card 85-176937
HC300.28 .M3297 1984

INTERNATIONAL LABOR ACTIVITIES - HISTORY - 20TH CENTURY.
Nicholson, Marjorie. The TUC overseas . London , Boston , c1986. xvi, 329 p. ; ISBN 0-04-331103-2 (alk. paper) LC Card 85-28607

DDC 331.88/0941 19
HD8383 .N52 1986 **NYPL [JLD 86-2932]**

INTERNATIONAL LABOR ACTIVITIES - HISTORY - CHRONOLOGY.
Geschichte der internationalen Arbeiterbewegung in Daten /. Berlin , 1986. 868 p. ; ISBN 3-320-00635-5 LC Card 86-210352
HD6475.A1 G47 1986

International Labor Office.
Hopkins, Mike. Alternatives to unemployment and underemployment . Boulder , 1985. xiv, 129 p. : ISBN 0-8133-0200-5 (pbk.) LC Card 85-45007 DDC 331.13/79861 19
HD5757.A6 H67 1985
NYPL [JLD 86-2149]

Labour circulation and the labour process /. London [England] , Dover, N.H. , c1985. xvi, 416 p. : ISBN 0-7099-3342-8 : LC Card 84-14306 DDC 331.12/791 19
HD5856.D44 L33 1984
NYPL [JLD 86-2532]

The Trade union situation and industrial relations in Hungary . Geneva , 1984. 100 p. ; ISBN 92-2-103894-7 **NYPL [JLE 85-1780]**

International Labor Office. Jobs and Skills Programme for Africa. The Informal sector in Africa. Addis Ababa [Ethiopia] , 1985. 147 p. ; ISBN 92-2-103785-1 :
NYPL [JLE 86-1454]

International Labor Organisation.
The Informal sector in Africa /. Addis Ababa , 1984. 2, iii, 149 p. ; ISBN 92-2-103785-1 LC Card 87-106188 DDC 381 19
HD2346.A55 I19 1984

International Labor Organisation. World Employment Programme. Foxley, Alejandro. Las desigualdades económicas y la acción del estado . México , 1980. 271 p. ; ISBN 968-16-0365-6 LC Card 82-215955 DDC 339.2/098 19
HC130.I5 F69 1980 **NYPL [JLD 86-2631]**

International Labor Organization.
The Informal sector in Africa. Addis Ababa [Ethiopia] , 1985. 147 p. ; ISBN 92-2-103785-1 :
NYPL [JLE 86-1454]

International Labor Organization. International Labor Office. see **International Labor Office.**

International Labor Organization. Secretariat. see **International Labor Office.**

International Labor Organization. World Employment Programme. Raḍwān, Samīr Muḥammad. Agrarian change in Egypt . London , Dover, N.H. , c1986. xii, 167 p. : ISBN 0-7099-4214-1 : LC Card 85-11356 DDC 305.5/69/0962 19
HN786.A8 R33 1985 **NYPL [JLD 86-1045]**

International labour affairs . Bendiner, Burton. Oxford , New York , 1987. p. cm. ISBN 0-19-827498-8 : LC Card 87-17829 DDC 331.88/091 19
HD6475.A1 B4 1987

International labour and the Third World : the making of a new working class / edited by Rosalind E. Boyd, Robin Cohen, and Peter C.W. Gutkind. Aldershot, Hants, England ; Brookfield, Vt., USA : Avebury, c1987. xii, 283 p. ; 23 cm. Includes bibliographies and index. ISBN 0-566-00971-4 : LC Card 86-31791 DDC 331/.09172/4 19
1. Labor and laboring classes - Developing countries. 2. Trade-unions - Developing countries. I. Boyd, Rosalind E. II. Cohen, Robin. III. Gutkind, Peter Claus Wolfgang.
HD8943 .I55 1987

International Labour Conference (72nd : 1986 : Geneva, Switzerland) Report on programme implementation, 1984-85. Geneva [1986] 116 p. ; ISBN 92-2-105179-X (pbk.) : LC Card 87-101092 DDC 354.1/83 19
HD7801 .R462 1986

International Labour Conference (73rd : 1986 : Geneva, Switzerland) Employment promotion and social security . Geneva , 1986. iv, 156 p. ; ISBN 92-2-105574-4 (pbk.) : LC Card 86-234498 DDC 368.4/4 19
HD7095 .E46 1986

International Labour Office.
The Changing world of work, major issues ahead . Geneva , 1986- v. <1 > : ISBN 92-2-105165-X (pbk. : pt. 1) : LC Card 86-214807 DDC 331 19
HD4854 .C42 1986

Collective bargaining : a workers' education manual. 2nd rev. ed. Geneva : The Office, 1986. ix, 112 p. ; 24 cm. Bibliography: p. 111-112. ISBN 92-2-105284-2 (pbk.) : LC Card 86-208328 DDC 331.89 19
1. Collective bargaining - Handbooks, manuals, etc. I. Title.
HD6971.5 .I57 1986

Dynamique de l'emploi dans un système sahélien, le Niger . Addis Abéba , 1980. lxxii, 301 p. ; ISBN 92-2-202351-X : LC Card 82-980599
HD5846.7.A6 D95 1980

Economically active population . Geneva , 1986- v. ; ISBN 92-2-005345-4 (v. 1)
NYPL [JLM 87-113]

Economically active population estimates and projections, 1950-2025 =. Geneva [1986]- v. <1-5 > ; ISBN 92-2-005345-4 (pbk. : v. 1) : LC Card 86-223275 DDC 331.12/021 19
HD5712 .E26 1986

Les Effets des conditions de travail sur la santé des travailleuses . [Montréal] [1984] 230 p., [5] p. of plates : ISBN 2-920658-00-X : LC Card 86-158040
HD6067 .E34 1984

Employment forecasting . London , New York , c1988. p. cm. ISBN 0-86187-938-4 : LC Card 87-21882 DDC 331.12/094 19
HD5764 .E47 1988

Employment policy and job creation in and through the construction industry . Geneva , 1986. vi, 110 p. : ISBN 92-2-105709-7 (pbk.) : LC Card 87-167960 DDC 331.12/924 19
HD9715.A2 E42 1986

Employment promotion and social security . Geneva , 1986. iv, 156 p. ; ISBN 92-2-105574-4 (pbk.) : LC Card 86-234498 DDC 368.4/4 19
HD7095 .E46 1986

Gozo, K. M. Crise et pauvreté en Côte d'Ivoire . Addis Abéba , c1983. iv, 84 p. ; ISBN 92-2-203648-4 LC Card 85-981192
HC1025 .G69 1983

Labour inspection . Geneva , 1986. ix, 100 p. ; ISBN 92-2-105359-8 (pbk.) : LC Card 87-123437 DDC 331.25 19
HD3656 .L33 1986

Labour-relations in Africa, English-speaking countries . Geneva , c19. 159 p. ; ISBN 92-2-103467-4 (pbk.) : LC Card 86-212930 DDC 658.3 s 331/.096 19
HD6961.A1 I73 no. 64 HD8772

Land settlement policies and population redistribution in developing countries . New York , 1988. xiv, 395 p. ; ISBN 0-275-92799-7 (alk. paper) LC Card 87-15837 DDC 333.3/1/1724 19
HD1131 .L364 1988

Major stages and steps in energy manpower analysis . Geneva , 1986. viii, 80 p. : ISBN 92-2-105246-X (pbk.) : LC Card 86-222080 DDC 331.12/921042 19
HD5718.E47 M35 1986

Measures to overcome obstacles to the observance in the construction industry of ILO standards . Geneva , 1986. v, 89 p. : ISBN 92-2-105710-0 (pbk.) : LC Card 87-167948 DDC 331.25 19
HD9715.A2 M36 1986

Microelectronics, automation, and employment in the automobile industry /. Chichester [West Sussex] , New York , c1987. xix, 203 p. : ISBN 0-471-91484-3 : LC Card 86-32532 DDC 331.7/6292 19
HD8039.A8 M52 1987

Multinational enterprises . Geneva , 1985. xii, 195 p. ; ISBN 92-2-105094-7 (pbk.) : LC Card 86-210138 DDC 331.25 19
HF5549.5.M3 M85 1985

Pereira, A. (Armand) Socio-economic and policy implications of energy price increases /. Aldershot, Hants, England , Brookfield, Vt., USA , c1987. xxiv, 317 p. ; ISBN 0-566-05520-1 : LC Card 87-11955 DDC 338.2/3 19
HD9560.4 .P37 1987

Relaciones colectivas del trabajo en América Latina. Portuguese. As relações coletivas de trabalho na América Latina . São Paulo . 327 p. ; LC Card 87-151930 DDC 331/.098 19
HD8110.5 .R3817 1985

Report on programme implementation, 1984-85. Geneva [1986] 116 p. ; ISBN 92-2-105179-X (pbk.) : LC Card 87-101092 DDC 354.1/83 19
HD7801 .R462 1986

Richter, Lothar. Training needs . Geneva , 1986. viii, 83 p. : ISBN 92-2-105458-6 (pbk.) : LC Card 86-222104 DDC 331.25/92 19
HD5715 .R53 1986

Rural roads and poverty alleviation . London , 1984. vii, 191 p. : ISBN 0-946688-05-2 : LC Card 86-673296
HE336.R85 R87x 1984

Selected basic agreements and joint declarations on labour-management relations. Geneva , 1983. iv, 299 p. ; ISBN 92-2-103460-7 (pbk.) LC Card 86-213669 DDC 331.89 s 341.7/63 19
HD6961.A1 I73 no. 63 K1715

Social and labour practices of multinational enterprises in the textiles, clothing, and footwear industries. Geneva , 1984. xii, 184 p. ; ISBN 92-2-103882-3 (pbk.) : LC Card 85-183200 DDC 331.7/677 19
HF5549 .S83473 1984 **NYPL [JLE 85-2322]**

Technological change . Geneva , 1985. 355 p. : ISBN 92-2-105162-5 (pbk.) : LC Card 86-203534 DDC 331.12 19
HD6331 .T416 1985

The Trade union situation and industrial relations in Austria . Geneva , 1986. xiii, 107 p. ; ISBN 92-2-105659-7 (pbk.) : LC Card 87-123441 DDC 331/.09436 19
HD6674 .T72 1986

The Trade union situation and industrial relations in Spain . Geneva , 1985. xiii, 138 p. : ISBN 92-2-105202-8 (pbk.) : LC Card 86-207841 DDC 331.88/0946 19
HD6762 .T68 1985

Transición demográfica y oferta de fuerza de trabajo en Colombia /. [Bogotá], República de Colombia , 1986. 2 v. : ISBN 958-95096-0-6 (set) LC Card 87-113652 DDC 331.11/09861 19
HD5757.A6 T7 1986

Vocational training . Geneva , 1986. vii, 132 p. ; ISBN 92-2-105457-8 (pbk.) : LC Card 87-123102 DDC 331.25/92/0321 19
HD5715 .V63 1986

Wilke, Peter. Manpower conversion in defence related industry . Hamburg [1986] 62 p. : LC Card 86-212660 DDC 331.25/924 19
HC79.D4 W55 1986

Women, work, and demographic issues . Geneva , 1984. 159 p. ; ISBN 92-2-103886-6 : LC Card 86-673726
HD6052 .W568x 1984

Work and family life . Geneva , 1980. vi, 77 p. ; ISBN 92-2-102167-X (pbk.) LC Card 81-194978 DDC 306.8/5/0947 19
HD4904.25 .W68 1980

World labour report /. Oxford [Oxfordshire] , New York , 1987. p. cm. ISBN 0-19-828561-2 : LC Card 87-22087 DDC 331 19
HD5706 .W68 1987

INTERNATIONAL LABOUR OFFICE.
Report on programme implementation, 1984-85. Geneva [1986] 116 p. ; ISBN 92-2-105179-X (pbk.) : LC Card 87-101092 DDC 354.1/83 19
HD7801 .R462 1986

International Labour Organisation.
Aboagye, A. A. Informal sector employment in Kenya . Addis Ababa , Geneva, Switzerland , 1986. vii, 117, [64] p. ; ISBN 92-2-105557-4 LC Card 87-980151 DDC 331.12/51381 19
HD2346.K42 N353 1986

Cimillo, Elsa. La terciarización del empleo en la Argentina. [Buenos Aires] [1985] 23, [41], 3 p. ; LC Card 87-123708 DDC 381/.1/0982 19
HF5429.6.A7 C56 1985

Côte-d'Ivoire : résultats du projet et recommandations en découlant : rapport / établi pour le gouvernement de Côte-d'Ivoire par l'Organisation internationale du travail en tant qu'organisation chargée de l'exécution du projet. Genève : Organisation internationale du

travail, 1984. 94 p. : ill., map ; 30 cm. At head of title: Information sur le marché du travail et renforcement des structures de la direction de l'emploi. "IVC/80/02A." ISBN 92-2-203860-6 LC Card 86-219971
1. Labor supply - Ivory Coast. 2. Ivory Coast - Full employment policies. I. Ivory Coast. II. Title. III. Title: Résultats du projet et recommandations en découlant. IV. Title: Information sur le marché du travail et renforcement des structures de la direction de l'emploi.
HD5846.9.A6 I57 1984

Desarrollo de la formación profesional rural : Honduras : conclusiones y recomendaciones del proyecto : informe / preparado para el Gobierno de Honduras por la Organización Internacional del Trabajo en su carácter de organismo de ejecución de la Cooperación Técnica Suiza. Ginebra : DDA : La Organización, 1982. ii, 30 p. : ill. ; 30 cm. "OIT/CTS/75 HON/1, HON/80/02A/DDA." ISBN 92-2-303048-X LC Card 84-113985
1. Occupational training - Honduras. 2. Agricultural education - Honduras. I. Honduras. II. Cooperación Técnica Suiza. III. Title.
HD5715.5.H8 I58 1982

L'Emploi des femmes ... /. Addis-Abéba , 1985. 7 v. : ISBN 92-2-205192-0 (v. 1) LC Card 86-981198
HD6216 .E46 1985

Emploi et formation en Haute-Volta . Addis-Abéba , 1983. x, 142 p. : LC Card 85-981183
HD5847.5.A6 E48 1983

Employers and the environmental challenge /. Geneva , 1986. vii, 101 p. ; ISBN 92-2-105647-3 (pbk.) : LC Card 87-123427 DDC 363.7/056 19
HD69.P6 E46 1986

Formation professionnelle rurale, SEN/71/526 : Sénégal : résultats du projet et recommendations en découlant : rapport / établi pour le gouvernement du Sénégal par l'Organisation internationale du travail en tant qu'organisation chargée de l'exécution du projet pour le compte du Programme des Nations Unies pour le développement. Genève : Le Programme : L'Organisation, 1976. ii, 69 p. : ill., forms ; 30 cm. ISBN 92-2-201512-6 LC Card 84-125056
1. Agricultural laborers - Training of - Senegal. 2. Fishers - Training of - Senegal. 3. Education, Rural - Senegal. I. Senegal. II. United Nations. Development Programme. III. Title.
HD5716.A292 S385 1976

Fortalecimiento del sistema de formación profesional : Panama : conclusiones y recomendaciones del proyecto. Ginebra : Programa de las Naciones Unidas para el Desarrollo ; Organización Internacional del Trabajo, 1982. 47 p. ; 30 cm. "Preparada para el Gobierno de Panamá"--Cover p. [1] "PAN/78/002." Bibliography: p. 46-47. ISBN 92-2-303194-X LC Card 84-113933
1. Occupational training - Panama. I. United Nations. Development Programme. II. Panama. III. Title.
HD5715.5.P3 I57 1982

Institut national de formation professionnelle (INFP) : HAI/78/021 : Haïti : résultats du projet et recommandations en découlant / rapport établi pour le gouvernement d'Haïti par l'Organisation internationale du travail en tant qu'organisation chargée de l'exécution du projet pour le compte du Programme des Nations Unies pour le développement. Genève : Le Programme : L'Organisation, 1982. ii, 69 p. : ill. ; 30 cm. "Confidentiel." Includes bibliographical references. ISBN 92-2-203229-2 LC Card 83-234817
1. Occupational training - Haiti. 2. Vocational education - Haiti. 3. Employees, Training of - Haiti. I. Institut national de formation professionnelle (Haiti). II. United Nations. Development Programme. III. Title.
HD5715.5.H2 I57 1982

National Institute of Labour Science (NILS) (preparatory assistance), Republic of Korea : project findings and recommendations : report / prepared for the government of the Republic of Korea by the International Labour Organisation acting as executing agency for the United Nations Development Programme. Geneva : The Programme : ILO, 1976. 43 p. ; 30 cm. "ROK/74/003." ISBN 92-2-101617-X (pbk.) LC Card 84-145790
1. National Institute of Labour Science (Korea). 2. Industrial hygiene - Korea (South). 3. Industrial safety - Korea (South). I. United Nations. Development Programme. II. National Institute of Labour Science (Korea). III. Title.
HD7758 .I58 1976

National programme for development and training of manpower for employment, Philippines : organisation, administration, follow-up, and evaluation of the manpower training schemes : report / prepared for the government of the Philippines by the International Labour Organisation acting as executing agency for the United Nations Development Programme. Geneva : The Programme : The Organisation, 1979. ii, 54 p. ; 30 cm. "PHI/74/010 technical report no. 4." Includes bibliographical references. LC Card 81-140367 DDC 331.25/92/09599 19
1. Manpower policy - Philippines. 2. Occupational training - Philippines. I. Philippines. II. United Nations. Development Programme. III. Title.
HD5825.A6 I57 1979

National Seminar on Population, Employment, and Development Planning in Sierra Leone (1980 : Freetown, Sierra Leone) Contributed papers to the National Seminar on Population, Employment, and Development Planning in Sierra Leone . Freetown, Sierra Leone , <[1980-. v. <2 > : LC Card 87-163849 DDC 304.6/0966/4 19
HB3666.9.A3 N38 1980

Organisation de l'Institut national de formation et de perfectionnement professionnels de Bangui (INFPP) : CAF/75/010 : résultats du projet et recommandations en découlant : rapport / établi pour le gouvernement de la République centrafricaine par l'Organisation internationale du travail en tant qu'organisation chargée de l'exécution du projet pour le compte du Programme des Nations Unies pour le développement. Genève : Programme des Nations Unies pour le développement : Organisation internationale du travail, 1980. 14 p. ; 30 cm. ISBN 92-2-202448-6 LC Card 82-214934
1. Automobile mechanics - Training of - Central African Republic - Bangui. 2. Automobile driving - Study and teaching - Central African Republic - Bangui. 3. Institut national de formation et de perfectionnement professionnels (Central African Republic). I. Central African Republic. II. United Nations. Development Programme. III. Title. IV. Title: Résultats du projet et recommandations en découlant.
HD5716.M342 C335 1980

Socioeconomic aspects of renewable energy technologies . New York , 1988. p. cm. ISBN 0-275-92851-9 (alk. paper) : LC Card 87-22890 DDC 333.7/09172/4 19
HD9502.D442 S63 1988

International Labour Organisation. Advisory Committee on Rural Development.
Promotion of employment and incomes for the rural poor, including rural women, through non-farm activities . Geneva , 1983. 131 p. ; ISBN 92-2-103506-9 (pbk.) : LC Card 86-221308 DDC 331.12/042/091734 19
HD5710.8 .P76 1983

Review of ILO rural development activities since 1979 . Geneva , 1983. ii, 61 p. ; ISBN 92-2-103505-0 (pbk.) : LC Card 86-221297 DDC 331.11/09173/4 19
HD5707 .R44 1983

International Labour Organisation. Building, Civil Engineering, and Public Works Committee.
Employment policy and job creation in and through the construction industry . Geneva , 1986. vi, 110 p. : ISBN 92-2-105709-7 (pbk.) : LC Card 87-167960 DDC 331.12/924 19
HD9715.A2 E42 1986

Measures to overcome obstacles to the observance in the construction industry of ILO standards . Geneva , 1986. v, 89 p. : ISBN 92-2-105710-0 (pbk.) : LC Card 87-167948 DDC 331.25 19
HD9715.A2 M36 1986

International Labour Organisation. Iron and Steel Committee.
Policies for maintaining social development through collective bargaining, legislation, and adequate social security protection to cope with structural change in the iron and steel industry / Iron and Steel Committee, eleventh session, Geneva, 1986. Geneva : International Labour Office, 1986. 45 p. ; 30 cm. At head of title: International Labour Organisation, Sectoral Activities Programme. "Report II." Includes bibliographies. ISBN 92-2-105497-7 (pbk.) : LC Card 86-222047 DDC 331.89/0469142 19
1. Iron and steel workers - Effect of technological innovations on. 2. Iron and steel workers - Government policy. 3. Collective bargaining - Iron industry. 4. Collective bargaining - Steel industry. 5. Social security. I. International Labour Organisation. Sectoral Activities Programme. II. Title.
HD8039.I5 I6 1986

Productivity improvement and its effects on the level of employment and working conditions in the iron and steel industry / Iron and Steel Committee, eleventh session, Geneva, 1986. Geneva : International Labour Office, 1986. ii, 66 p. : ill. ; 30 cm. At head of title: International Labour Organisation, Sectoral Activities Programme. "Report III." Includes bibliographies. ISBN 92-2-105498-5 (pbk.) : LC Card 86-222063 DDC 338.4/56691 19
1. Iron industry and trade - Capital productivity. 2. Iron industry and trade - Labor productivity. 3. Steel industry and trade - Capital productivity. 4. Steel industry and trade - Labor productivity. 5. Iron and steel workers. I. International Labour Organisation. Sectoral Activities Programme. II. Title.
HD9510.5 .I525 1986

International Labour Organisation. Sectoral Activities Programme.
Employment policy and job creation in and through the construction industry . Geneva , 1986. vi, 110 p. : ISBN 92-2-105709-7 (pbk.) : LC Card 87-167960 DDC 331.12/924 19
HD9715.A2 E42 1986

International Labour Organisation. Iron and Steel Committee. Policies for maintaining social development through collective bargaining, legislation, and adequate social security protection to cope with structural change in the iron and steel industry /. Geneva , 1986. 45 p. ; ISBN 92-2-105497-7 (pbk.) : LC Card 86-222047 DDC 331.89/0469142 19
HD8039.I5 I6 1986

International Labour Organisation. Iron and Steel Committee. Productivity improvement and its effects on the level of employment and working conditions in the iron and steel industry /. Geneva , 1986. ii, 66 p. : ISBN 92-2-105498-5 (pbk.) : LC Card 86-222063 DDC 338.4/56691 19
HD9510.5 .I525 1986

Measures to overcome obstacles to the observance in the construction industry of ILO standards . Geneva , 1986. v, 89 p. : ISBN 92-2-105710-0 (pbk.) : LC Card 87-167948 DDC 331.25 19
HD9715.A2 M36 1986

International Labour Organization. Hoffman, Kurt. Micro-electronics and clothing . New York , 1988. xxxii, 253 p. ; ISBN 0-275-92798-9 (alk. paper) : LC Card 87-25736 DDC 338.4/5687 19
HD9940.A2 H63 1988

International Law Institute (Washington, D.C.) International borrowing . Washington, D.C. , c1986. 499 p. : ISBN 0-935328-40-8 LC Card 86-82157 DDC 341.7/51 19
K4450 .I576 1986 ***NYPL [JLF 86-1814]***

International Law Symposium (1984 : Cambridge, Cambridgeshire) The United States, transnational business, and the law : proceedings of the International Law Symposium of the Columbia Law School Alumni Association and the Columbia Law School Association of the United Kingdom, Cambridge, England, June, 1984 / edited by Beverly A. Allen, Christian S. Ward. New York : Oceana Publications, c1985. x, 132 p. ; 25 cm. Includes bibliographical references. ISBN 0-379-20783-4 LC Card 85-61594 DDC 346/.07 342.67 19
1. Commercial law - Congresses. 2. International business enterprises - Law and legislation - Congresses. 3. Foreign trade regulation - Congresses. 4. Commercial law - United States - Congresses. 5. Foreign trade regulation - United States - Congresses. I. Allen, Beverly A. II. Ward, Christian S. III. Columbia Law School Alumni Association. IV. Columbia Law School

Association of the United Kingdom. V. Title.
K1004.6 1984 *NYPL [JLF 86-1046]*

International leadership symposia series . (v. 8) Emerging leadership vistas /. Lexington, Mass. , c1988. xv, 331 p. : ISBN 0-669-15331-1 (alk. paper) LC Card 86-46310 DDC 658.4/092 19
HD57.7 .E44 1987

International lending, long-term credit relationships, and dynamic contract theory /. Crawford, Vincent P., 1950- Princeton, N.J. [1987] c1986. 34 p. ; ISBN 0-88165-231-8 (pbk.) : LC Card 86-33743 DDC 336.3/435 19
HG3891.5 .C7 1987

INTERNATIONAL LIQUIDITY.
Boeck, Klaus. Die DM als internationale Reservewährung . Hamburg , 1974. 75 p. ; LC Card 75-550711 *NYPL [JLE 80-744]*

International Livestock Centre for Africa.
Massow, Valentin von, 1925- Dairy imports and import policy in Mali and their implications for the dairy sector in the Bamako area /. Addis Ababa, Ethiopia [1985] v leaves, 57 p., [12] leaves ; LC Card 86-981009 DDC 382/.417/096623 19
HD9275.M423 B366 1985

INTERNATIONAL LOANS. see **LOANS, FOREIGN.**

INTERNATIONAL LONGSHOREMEN'S AND WAREHOUSEMEN'S UNION - HISTORY.
Finlay, William. Work on the waterfront . Philadelphia , 1988. p. cm. ISBN 0-87722-523-0 (alk. paper) : LC Card 87-17976 DDC 331.88/11387164/0973 19
HD6515.L82 W474 1988

International macroeconomic modelling for policy decisions / edited by P. Artus and O. Guvenen in collaboration with F. Gagey. Dordrecht ; Boston : M. Nijhoff, c1986. viii, 269 p. : ill. ; 25 cm. (Advanced studies in theoretical and applied econometrics . v. 5) "Based on an international conference organised by the Applied Econometric Association (AEA) ... which was held in Brussels at the Commission of the European Communities in December 1983"--Pref. Includes bibliographies and index. ISBN 90-247-3201-8 LC Card 85-13698 DDC 337/.0724 19
1. International economic relations - Mathematical models - Congresses. 2. Economic policy - Decision making - Congresses. I. Artus, Patrick. II. Guvenen, O. III. Gagey, F. IV. Applied Econometric Association. V. Series.
HF1410.5 .I577 1986 *NYPL [JLE 86-3469]*

The international mail-order shopping guide /. Wathey, Patricia Wogen. Englewood Cliffs, N.J. , 1984. 338 p. : ISBN 0-13-473083-6 LC Card 84-8390 DDC 381/.14/025 19
HF5466 .W38 1984
*NYPL [*R-Econ. 84-3915]*

International Maize and Wheat Improvement Center. 1985 CIMMYT World Wheat facts and trends . México, D.F. [1985] 44 p. : LC Card 87-108823 DDC 338.1/7311 19
HD9049.W4 A16 1985

International marketing : managerial perspectives / [edited by] Subhash C. Jain and Lewis R. Tucker, Jr.2nd ed. Boston, Mass. : Kent Pub. Co., c1986. xii, 466 p. : ill. ; 24 cm. Bibliography: p. 459-466. ISBN 0-534-06270-9 (pbk.) : LC Card 85-19820 DDC 658.8/48 19
1. Export marketing - Management - Addresses, essays, lectures. 2. International business enterprises - Management - Addresses, essays, lectures. I. Jain, Subhash C., 1942-. II. Tucker, Lewis R., 1943-.
HF1009.5 .I545 1986 *NYPL [JLE 86-3023]*

International marketing /. Czinkota, Michael R. Chicago , c1988. xxi, 649 p. : ISBN 0-03-070297-6 LC Card 86-32959 DDC 658.8/48 19
HF1009.5 .C95 1988

International marketing . Gilligan, Colin. London , Dover N.H. , c1986. 310 p. : ISBN 0-7099-3811-X : LC Card 86-9015 DDC 658.8/48 19
HF1009.5 .G55 1986 *NYPL [JLD 86-4466]*

International marketing management /. Jain, Subhash C., 1942- Boston, Mass. , c1987. xiv, 737 p. : ISBN 0-534-07824-9 : LC Card 86-27761 DDC 658.8/48 19
HF1009.5 .J336 1987

International marketing strategies . Wiklund, Erik. New York , c1987. xi, 195 p. ; ISBN 0-07-070176-8 : LC Card 86-21437 DDC 658.8/48 19
HF1009.5 .W555 1987

International MarketVision Corporation (Los Gatos, Calif.) How to buy an automated sales, marketing, and telemarketing system. Los Gatos, CA , c1985. 46 p. : LC Card 86-224565 DDC 658.8/0028/5 19
HF5415.1265 .H68 1985

International monetary and financial integration : the European dimension / edited by D.E. Fair and C. de Boissieu ; with contributions from Michel Aglietta ... [et al.]. Dordrecht ; Boston : Kluwer Academic Publishers, c1988. xii, 403 p. : ill. ; 25 cm. (Financial and monetary policy studies. v. 14) Papers presented at the 13th colloquium arranged by the Société universitaire européenne de recherches financières held in Luxembourg in Oct. 1986. Includes bibliographies. ISBN 90-247-3563-7 LC Card 87-3622 DDC 332.4/94 19
1. Monetary policy - European Economic Community countries - Congresses. 2. Finance - European Economic Community countries - Congresses. 3. European Monetary System (Organization) - Congresses. I. Fair, Donald E. II. Boissieu, Christian de. III. Aglietta, Michel. IV. Société universitaire européenne de recherches financières. V. Series: Financial and monetary policy studies, 14.
HG930.5 .I586 1988

International Monetary Fund.
Adjustment policies and development strategies in the Arab world /. Washington, D.C. , 1987. ix, 200 p. ; ISBN 0-939934-96-5 (pbk.) LC Card 87-21377 DDC 338.9/00917/4927 19
HC498 .A6395 1987

Crockett, Andrew. Strengthening the international monetary system . Washington, D.C. , c1987. vii, 84 p. ; LC Card 86-33750 DDC 332.4/5 19
HG3881 .C694 1987

De Vries, Margaret Garritsen, 1922- Balance of payments adjustment, 1945 to 1986 . Washington, D.C. , 1987. xi, 336 p. ; ISBN 0-939934-93-0 (pbk.) : LC Card 87-17242 DDC 332.1/52 19
HG3890 .D4 1987

The European monetary system . Washington, D.C. , c1986. vii, 75 p. : ISBN 0-939934-79-5 (pbk.) : LC Card 86-21432 DDC 332.4/5/094 19
HG930.5 .E86863 1986

External debt, savings, and growth in Latin America . Washington, D.C. , Buenos Aires , 1987. xv, 207 p. ; ISBN 0-939934-95-7 (pbk.) : LC Card 87-21422 DDC 336.3/435/098 19
HJ8514.5 .E984 1987

Geldwertstabilität und Wirtschaftswachstum . Göttingen , c1984. xii, 230 p. : ISBN 3-525-13169-0 LC Card 84-232466
HG203 .G46 1984

Growth-oriented adjustment programs /. Washington, D.C. , 1987. xiii, 537 p. : ISBN 0-939934-92-2 (pbk.) LC Card 87-21361 DDC 338.9 19
HD73 .G76 1987

Technical assistance and training services of the International Monetary Fund. Washington, D.C. : The Fund, 1985. iii, 31 p. : ill. ; 23 cm. (Pamphlet series, 0538-8759 . no. 43) LC Card 86-202820 DDC 332.1/52 19
1. International Monetary Fund. 2. Technical assistance - Developing countries. 3. Finance - Study and teaching - Developing countries. I. Series: Pamphlet series (International Monetary Fund) , no. 43. II. Title.
HG3881.5.I58 I568 1985

INTERNATIONAL MONETARY FUND.
Alcalde Cardoza, Xavier. Fondo Monetario como actor político en la escena internacional /. Lima, Perú [1986] 54 p. ; LC Card 87-400166 DDC 332.1/52 19
HG3881.5.I58 A44 1986

Barth, James R. International debt . Fairfax, Va. , 1984. 36 p. ; *NYPL [*ZT-1554 no.21]*

De Vries, Margaret Garritsen, 1922- Balance of payments adjustment, 1945 to 1986 . Washington, D.C. , 1987. xi, 336 p. ; ISBN 0-939934-93-0 (pbk.) : LC Card 87-17242 DDC 332.1/52 19
HG3890 .D4 1987

Engshuber, Wolfgang. Die Auflagenpolitik des Internationalen Währungsfonds . [München] [1985?] 32 leaves ; LC Card 85-166626
HG3881.5.I58 E54 1985

Gylfason, Thorvaldur. Credit policy and economic activity in developing countries with IMF stabilization programs /. Princeton, N.J. , c1987. 44 p. ; ISBN 0-88165-232-6 (pbk.) : LC Card 87-3389 DDC 332.7/09172/4 19
HG3711.D48 G94 1987

Herrmann, Roland. The compensatory financing system of the International Monetary Fund . Kiel, West-Germany , 1983. iii, 85 p. ; ISBN 3-922553-18-4 (pbk.) LC Card 83-227524 DDC 332.1/52 19
HG3881.5.I58 H47 1983 *NYPL [JLD 97-7]*

Im Teufelskreis der Verschuldung . Hamburg , 1984. 261 p. : ISBN 3-88506-126-0 LC Card 85-131681
HG3881.5.I58 I37 1984

International Monetary Fund. Technical assistance and training services of the International Monetary Fund. Washington, D.C. , 1985. iii, 31 p. : LC Card 86-202820 DDC 332.1/52 19
HG3881.5.I58 I568 1985

Lichtensztejn, Samuel, 1934- Fondo Monetario Internacional y Banco Mundial . San José, Costa Rica , Buenos Aires, Argentina , 1986. 215 p. : LC Card 86-233561
HG3881.5.I58 L527 1986

Schmitt, Bernard. Les pays au régime du FMI . Albeuve, Suisse , c1984. 91 p. : ISBN 2-88087-013-5 : LC Card 84-240522 DDC 382.1/7 19
HG3882 .S36 1984

Sidell, Scott R. The IMF and third-world political instability . New York , 1988. p. cm. ISBN 0-312-00755-8 : LC Card 87-9880 DDC 332.1/52 19
HG3881.5.I58 S53 1988

Spraos, John. IMF conditionality . Princeton, N.J. , c1986. 34 p. ; ISBN 0-88165-073-0 (pbk.) : LC Card 86-33805 DDC 332/.042 s 332.1/52 19
HG136 .P7 no. 166 HG3881.5.I58

Tan´kov, A. V. Mezhdunarodnyĭ valiūtnyĭ fond v usloviiākh sovremennogo kapitalizma /. Moskva , 1984. 85 p. ; LC Card 87-100183
HG3881.5.I58 T35 1984

INTERNATIONAL MONETARY FUND - ADDRESSES, ESSAYS, LECTURES.
Adjustment crisis in the Third World /. New Brunswick, USA , c1984. x, 186 p. ; ISBN 0-88738-040-9 LC Card 84-8690 DDC 337/.09172/4 19
HC59.7 .A733 1984 *NYPL [JLE 86-2491]*

INTERNATIONAL MONETARY FUND - AFRICA - CONGRESSES.
World recession and the food crisis in Africa /. London , 1986. 314 p. ; ISBN 0-85255-309-9 : LC Card 86-235333 DDC 363.8/526/096 19
HD9017.A2 W67 1986b

World recession and the food crisis in Africa /. Boulder , 1986. p. cm. ISBN 0-8133-0511-X : LC Card 86-28250 DDC 363.8/526/096 19
HD9017.A2 W67 1986

INTERNATIONAL MONETARY FUND - AFRICA, SUB-SAHARAN.
Green, Reginald Herbold. The IMF and stabilisation in sub-Saharan Africa . Brighton, England [1986] ii, 70 p. ; LC Card 86-208478 DDC 332.1/52 19
HC800 .G72 1986

The International Monetary Fund and Latin America . Pastor, Manuel. Boulder, Colo. , 1987. xvi, 228 p. : ISBN 0-8133-7373-5 (pbk. : alk. paper) : LC Card 86-32575 DDC 332.4/98 19
HG660.5 .P33 1987

INTERNATIONAL MONETARY FUND - ARAB COUNTRIES - CONGRESSES.
Adjustment policies and development strategies in the Arab world /. Washington, D.C. , 1987. ix, 200 p. ; ISBN 0-939934-96-5 (pbk.) LC Card 87-21377 DDC 338.9/00917/4927 19
HC498 .A6395 1987

INTERNATIONAL MONETARY FUND - ARGENTINA.
Argentina 1984 . [Buenos Aires?] [1984] 95 p. ; LC Card 85-132860
HJ8569 .A75 1984

Perdía, Roberto Cirilo. Existe otra Argentina posible /. Buenos Aires , 1986. 276 p. : ISBN 950-97640-0-0 LC Card 87-139879 DDC 336.3/4/0982 19
HG3881.5.I58 P47 1986

INTERNATIONAL MONETARY FUND - BRAZIL.
Alcalde Cardoza, Xavier. El poder norteamericano y la renegociación de la deuda externa brasileña, 1982-1983 /. Lima, Perú , 1985. 62 p. ; LC Card 86-223475
HJ8579 .A44 1985

Braga, Roberto Saturnino. Saturnino, o momento histórico do Congresso Nacional. Brasília , 1983. 58 p. ; LC Card 83-202638
HC187 .B76 1983

Langoni, Carlos Geraldo. A crise do desenvolvimento, uma estratégia para o futuro /. Rio de Janeiro , 1985. xix, 176 p. : ISBN 85-03-00001-6 : LC Card 85-151246 DDC 338.981 19
HG835 .L36 1985 ***NYPL [JLD 86-288]***

INTERNATIONAL MONETARY FUND - BRAZIL - CONGRESSES.
Brazil and the Ivory Coast . Greenwich, Conn. , c1987. p. cm. ISBN 0-89232-819-3 : LC Card 87-3667 DDC 332/.042/0981 19
HG3891.5 .B72 1987

International Monetary Fund. Commodities Division. Primary commodities . Washington, D.C. , 1987. p. cm. ISBN 0-939934-87-6 LC Card 87-17225 DDC 382/.4 19
HF1040.7 .P718 1987

INTERNATIONAL MONETARY FUND - DEVELOPING COUNTRIES.
L'Hériteau, Marie France. Le Fonds monétaire international et les pays du Tiers-monde /. Paris , c1986. 277 p. : ISBN 2-13-039203-2 : LC Card 86-165389
HG3881.5.I58 L52 1986

Lizano Fait, Eduardo. La condicionalidad cruzada y la deuda externa /. [San José] , 1986. 16, [1] leaves : LC Card 87-127835 DDC 336.3/435/091724 19
HJ8899 .L59 1986

INTERNATIONAL MONETARY FUND - DOMINICAN REPUBLIC - CONGRESSES.
La Situación cambiaria en la República Dominicana /. Santo Domingo, República Dominicana , 1984. 252 p. : LC Card 87-401265 DDC 338.97293 19
HC153.5 .S575 1984

INTERNATIONAL MONETARY FUND - ECUADOR.
Ecuador, política económica--teoría y realidad. [Guayaquil] [1986- v. <1-3 > ; LC Card 87-105005
HF1519 .E3 1986

INTERNATIONAL MONETARY FUND - HUNGARY.
Kiefer, Márta. Magyarország tőkés viszonylatu gazdasági és pénzügyi kapcsolatairól /. [Budapest] [1985] 115 p. ; ISBN 963-608-080-1 LC Card 86-228329
HF1542.5 .K54 1985

INTERNATIONAL MONETARY FUND - INDIA.
Saxena, R. B. IMF loan to India . Delhi, India , 1986. ix, 284 p. ; LC Card 86-903311 DDC 332.1/52 19
HG3971 .S29 1986

INTERNATIONAL MONETARY FUND - IVORY COAST - CONGRESSES.
Brazil and the Ivory Coast . Greenwich, Conn. , c1987. p. cm. ISBN 0-89232-819-3 : LC Card 87-3667 DDC 332/.042/0981 19
HG3891.5 .B72 1987

INTERNATIONAL MONETARY FUND - LATIN AMERICA.
El FMI, el Banco Mundial y la crisis latinoamericana /. México , 1986. 474 p. : ISBN 968-231-373-2 LC Card 87-127860 DDC 332.1/52 19
HG3881.5.I58 F56 1986

Pastor, Manuel. The International Monetary Fund and Latin America . Boulder, Colo. , 1987. xvi, 228 p. : ISBN 0-8133-7373-5 (pbk. : alk. paper) : LC Card 86-32575 DDC 332.4/98 19
HG660.5 .P33 1987

INTERNATIONAL MONETARY FUND - LATIN AMERICA - ADDRESSES, ESSAYS, LECTURES.
Debt, adjustment, and renegotiation in Latin America . Boulder, Colo. , 1986. x, 171 p. : ISBN 0-931477-72-7 : LC Card 85-30098 DDC 336.3/435/098 19
HJ8514.5 .D44 1986 ***NYPL [JLE 87-781]***

INTERNATIONAL MONETARY FUND - NIGERIA.
Ogunba, C. K. An ailing African economy and the IMF medicine /. Ile-Ife [Nigeria] [1985] 40, [1] p. ; LC Card 86-207586 DDC 332.1/52 19
HG3881.5.I58 O37 1985

INTERNATIONAL MONETARY FUND - PERU.
Jiménez, Félix. Perú, economía no-neoclásica, modelo de acumulación, crisis y alternativa de desarrollo no-monetarista /. Lima, Perú , 1986. 107 p. : LC Card 87-404229 DDC 338.985 19
HC227 .J53 1986

Scheetz, Thomas Edward. Peru and the International Monetary Fund /. Pittsburgh, PA , c1986. xi, 257 p. : ISBN 0-8229-3816-2 LC Card 85-40855 DDC 332.1/52 19
HG3881.5.I58 S34 1986 ***NYPL [JLD 86-2893]***

INTERNATIONAL MONETARY FUND - PHILIPPINES.
Broad, Robin. Unequal alliance . Berkeley , c1988. p. cm. ISBN 0-520-05905-0 LC Card 87-10745 DDC 332.1/52 19
HG3881.5.W57 B76 1988

International Monetary Fund. Research Dept. The Role of the SDR in the international monetary system . Washington, D.C. , 1987. vii, 62 p. : ISBN 0-939934-81-7 (pbk.) : LC Card 87-4184 DDC 332.4/5 19
HG3898 .R65 1987

Staff studies for the world economic outlook /. Washington, D.C. , c1986. xi, 195 p. : LC Card 86-202629 DDC 338.5/443 19
HC59 .S682 1986

INTERNATIONAL MONETARY FUND - TANZANIA.
Green, Reginald Herbold. The IMF and stabilisation in sub-Saharan Africa . Brighton, England [1986] ii, 70 p. ; LC Card 86-208478 DDC 332.1/52 19
HC800 .G72 1986

International Monetary Fund. Treasurer's Dept. The Role of the SDR in the international monetary system . Washington, D.C. , 1987. vii, 62 p. : ISBN 0-939934-81-7 (pbk.) : LC Card 87-4184 DDC 332.4/5 19
HG3898 .R65 1987

INTERNATIONAL MONETARY FUND - UNITED STATES.
Alcalde Cardoza, Xavier. El poder norteamericano y la renegociación de la deuda externa brasileña, 1982-1983 /. Lima, Perú , 1985. 62 p. ; LC Card 86-223475
HJ8579 .A44 1985

International monetary problems and supply-side economics : essays in honour of Lorie Tarshis / edited by Jon S. Cohen and G.C. Harcourt. Houndmills, Basingstoke, Hampshire : Macmillan, 1986. viii, 162 p. : ill., port. ; 23 cm. Includes bibliographies and index. ISBN 0-333-36200-4
1. Tarshis, Lorie. 2. International finance - Addresses, essays, lectures. 3. Keynesian economics - Addresses, essays, lectures. 4. Supply side economics - Addresses, essays, lectures. I. Tarshis, Lorie. II. Cohen, Jon S. III. Harcourt, Geoffrey Colin. ***NYPL [JLD 86-4356]***

The International monetary system and its reform : papers / prepared for the Group of Twenty-four by a United Nations project directed by Sidney Dell, 1979-1986. Amsterdam ; New York : North-Holland ; 3 v. : ill. ; 24 cm. (Contributions to economic analysis. 162) "Published in cooperation with the United Nations." Includes bibliographies. ISBN 0-444-70227-X LC Card 87-6737 DDC 332.4/5 19
1. International finance. I. Dell, Sidney Samuel. II. Group of Twenty-four. III. United Nations. IV. Series.
HG3881 .I57672 1987

INTERNATIONAL MONEY. see **COINAGE, INTERNATIONAL.**

International money and banking . Mullineux, A. W. New York , 1987. xii, 207 p. ; ISBN 0-8147-5436-8 : LC Card 87-12393 DDC 332.1/5 19
HG3881 .M815 1987

International money and capitalist crisis . Brett, E. A. London , Boulder, Colo. , 1983. viii, 271 p. ; ISBN 0-86531-575-2 (Westview) LC Card 82-51289 DDC 332/.042 19
HG3881 .B6738 1983 ***NYPL [JLD 87-1020]***

International negotiation and development. International borrowing . Washington, D.C. , c1986. 499 p. : ISBN 0-935328-40-8 LC Card 86-82157 DDC 341.7/51 19
K4450 .I576 1986 ***NYPL [JLF 86-1814]***

International Newspaper Marketing Association. Evaluating the effectiveness of newspaper promotion /. Reston, Va. (11600 Sunrise Valley Dr., Reston 22091) , c1987. iii, 123 p. : LC Card 87-152731 DDC 659.13/2 19
HF6161.N4 E93 1987

International Oil Working Group. Turner, Terisa. Trade union action to stop oil to South Africa /. Port Harcourt , c1985. v, 35 p. ; LC Card 87-673464
HF1613.4 .T87x 1985

International Olive Oil Council. Políticas oleícolas nacionales /. [S.l.] [1985] 130 p. in various pagings ; LC Card 86-131977 DDC 338.4/7664362 19
HD9490.5.O462 P65 1985

INTERNATIONAL PAYMENTS, BALANCE OF. see **BALANCE OF PAYMENTS.**

INTERNATIONAL PEASANTS' CONFERENCE (1ST : 1923 : MOSCOW, R.S.F.S.R.)
Hovda, Gudmund. Dagbok frå bondekongressen i Moskva, oktober 1923 /. Oslo , 1984. 46 p. ; ISBN 82-902503-1-2 LC Card 85-190754
HD1405 .H68 1984

International planning glossaries.
(5) Logie, Gordon. Glossary of planning and development . Amsterdam , New York , 1986. xxv, 254 p. ; ISBN 0-444-42608-6 (U. S.) : LC Card 86-521 DDC 338.9/003 19
HT391 .L64 1987 ***NYPL [JLE 86-4010]***

International political economy yearbook, 8755-8335 .
(v. 3) Pursuing food security . Boulder , 1987. xv, 357 p. : ISBN 1-555-87032-5 (lib. bdg. : alk. paper) : LC Card 87-4524 DDC 337/.05 s 338.1/9/1724 19
HF1410 .I579 vol. 3 HD9018.D44

The international politics of telecommunications /. Blatherwick, David E. S. [Berkeley, Calif.] , c1987. ix, 107 p. ; ISBN 0-87725-168-1 (pbk.) : LC Card 87-3509 DDC 384/.068 19
HE7645 .B57 1987

International Population Conference. [Proceedings]
International Population Conference (1985 : Florence, Italy) International Population Conference, Florence 1985, 5-12 June =. Liège, Belgium , c1985- v. : ISBN 2-87108-004-6 (set) LC Card 86-113476 DDC 304.6 19
HB849 .I616 1985 ***NYPL [JLL 86-265]***

International Population Conference, Florence 1985, 5-12 June =. International Population Conference (1985 : Florence, Italy) Liège, Belgium , c1985- v. : ISBN 2-87108-004-6 (set) LC Card 86-113476 DDC 304.6 19
HB849 .I616 1985 ***NYPL [JLL 86-265]***

International Population Conference (1985 : Florence, Italy) International Population Conference, Florence 1985, 5-12 June = Congrès international de la population, Florence 1985, 5-12 juin. Liège, Belgium : International Union for the Scientific Study of Population, c1985- v. : ill. ; 24 cm. (International Population Conference, 0254-5217) English and French. Addenda slip inserted in vol. 3. Includes bibliographies. ISBN 2-87108-004-6 (set) LC Card 86-113476 DDC 304.6 19
1. Demography - Congresses. 2. Population - Congresses. I. Title. II. Title: Congrès international de

la population, Florence 1985, 5-12 juin. III. Series: International Population Conference. [Proceedings].
HB849 .I616 1985 ***NYPL [JLL 86-265]***

International public relations. Halpern, Burton M. Tell it to the world . Jerusalem , New York, N.Y. [c1982] 152 p. ; ISBN 965-229-004-1 LC Card 86-214902 DDC 659.2 19
HD59 .H25 1982

International purchasing . Hall, R. Duane. New York , c1987. p. cm. ISBN 0-394-55326-8 : LC Card 87-4926 DDC 658.7/2 19
HD39.5 .H34 1987

INTERNATIONAL RAILWAY CONGRESS (4TH : 1892 : SAINT PETERSBURG, RUSSIA) - ABSTRACTS.
Leber, Maximilien, Edler von. Die Beschlüsse des internationalen Eisenbahn-Congresses zu St. Petersburg nach dem am 20.-31. August 1892 angenommenen französischen Texte in getreuer deutscher Uebersetzung /. Wien , 1893. 25 p. ; LC Card 85-666030
HE1005.I553 L4x 1893

International Referral Centre for Information Handling Equipment. International directory of suppliers and agents for information handling equipment and logistical support services /. Zagreb , 1985. iii, 418 p. ; LC Card 86-220527 DDC 338.7/61004/025 19
HD9696.A2 I595 1985

International reinsurance : a review of regulation, accounting, and taxation. [New York, N.Y.?] : Peat, Marwick, Mitchell, c1985. vii, 164 p. ; 21 cm. LC Card 85-214554 DDC 368/.012 19
1. Reinsurance. 2. Reinsurance - Law and legislation. I. Peat, Marwick, Mitchell and Company.
HG8083 .I57 1985 ***NYPL [JLD 86-2530]***

INTERNATIONAL RELATIONS - ADDRESSES, ESSAYS, LECTURES.
Cooperation under anarchy /. Princeton, N.J. , 1986. 260 p. ; ISBN 0-691-07695-2 : LC Card 85-42936 DDC 327.1/1 19
D445 .C736 1986 ***NYPL [JLE 86-1938]***

Dependency theory and the return of high politics /. Westport, Conn. , 1986. xii, 270 p. : ISBN 0-313-24860-5 (lib. bdg. : alk. paper) LC Card 85-17745 DDC 337 19
HF1411 .D35 1986 ***NYPL [JLE 86-2911]***

Fred och säkerhet . [Stockholm] , c1983. 385 p. : ISBN 91-7410-249-4 : LC Card 83-229846
JX1963 .F817 1983 ***NYPL [JLD 84-2639]***

Myrdal, Gunnar, 1898- Increasing interdependence between states but failure of international cooperation /. Göteborg , 1978. 53 p. ; ISBN 91-7360-052-0 LC Card 80-511073 DDC 327.1/7 19
JX1954 .M94 ***NYPL [JLD 81-302]***

International Research and Information Services (Cape Town, South Africa) Mobil in South Africa . [Cape Town] [1986] 64 p. : ISBN 0-620-09921-6 (pbk.) LC Card 87-126457 DDC 338.7/6223382/0968 19
HD9577.S64 M636 1986

International Research and Training Institute for the Advancement of Women. Regional Meeting on Socio-economic and Policy Aspects of Water Resources Management in Africa (1986 : Addis Ababa, Ethiopia) Regional Meeting on Socio-economic and Policy Aspects of Water Resources Management in Africa, 2-7 June 1986, Addis Ababa, Ethiopia /. [Addis Ababa?] [1986] 19 v. : LC Card 86-981006 DDC 333.91/0096 19
HD1699.A1 R44 1986

International research project on human resource development. Guide to training needs assessment /. Ljubljana, Yugoslavia , c1984. 65 p. ; ISBN 92-9038-412-8 (pbk.) LC Card 85-242690 DDC 658.3/12404 19
HF5549.5.T7 G847 1984

International Resource Development, inc.
Ada military & commercial markets. Norwalk, Conn., U. S.A. (6 Prowitt St., Norwalk 06855) , c1986. vii, 196 leaves ; LC Card 87-400056 DDC 381/.45005133/0973 19
HD9696.C63 U51123 1986

Add-on boards & peripherals for the IBM PC & compatibles. Norwalk, Conn., U. S.A. (6 Prowitt St., Norwalk 06855) , c1986. x, 320 leaves ; LC Card 86-235156 DDC 380.1/456213984 19
HD9696.C62 A34 1986

Advanced ceramics market opportunities. Norwalk, Conn., U. S.A. (6 Prowitt St., Norwalk 06855) , c1986. iv, 223 leaves ; LC Card 87-162866 DDC 380.1/45666 19
HD9590.5 .A38 1986

Artificial intelligence markets. Norwalk, Conn., U. S.A. (6 Prowitt St., Norwalk 06855) , c1986. vii, 215 leaves ; LC Card 86-227054 DDC 380.1/450063 19
HD9696.C63 U5118 1986

Bar code markets . Norwalk, Conn., U. S.A. (6 Prowitt St., Norwalk 06855) , c1987. iv, 221 leaves : LC Card 87-401927 DDC 381/.45621399 19
HD9801.6.P763 U624 1987

Biotechnology equipment & supplies. Norwalk, Conn., U. S.A. (6 Prowitt St., Norwalk 06855) , c1986. viii, 347 p. : LC Card 87-400044 DDC 380.1/4566063 19
HD9706.65.B552 B55 1986

C.A.S.E. & programmers' workstation markets. Norwalk, Conn., U. S.A. (6 Prowitt St., Norwalk 06855) , c1987. v, 221 leaves : LC Card 87-129461 DDC 380.1/450051 19
HD9696.C62 C2 1987

CD ROM markets. Norwalk, Conn., U. S.A. (6 Prowitt St., Norwalk 06855) , c1986. v, 201 leaves : LC Card 86-227050 DDC 381/.4500456 19
HD9696.O673 U627 1986

Color printer markets. Norwalk, Conn., U. S.A. (6 Prowitt St., Norwalk 06855) , c1987. vi, 188 leaves ; LC Card 87-401926 DDC 381/.456213987/0973 19
HD9696.C63 U514916 1987

Computer security markets. Norwalk, Conn., U. S.A. (6 Prowitt St., Norwalk 06855) , c1987. vii, 163 leaves ; LC Card 87-151110 DDC 380.1/450058 19
HD9696.C62 C6436 1987

Customer premises telecom equipment & the regional Bell companies. Norwalk, Conn., U. S.A. (6 Prowitt St., Norwalk 06855) , c1987. ix, 193 leaves ; LC Card 87-403216 DDC 381/.45621385 19
HD9697.T453 U5245 1987

Database management systems. Norwalk, Conn., U. S.A. (6 Prowitt St., Norwalk 06855) , c1986. iv, 149 leaves ; LC Card 86-226965 DDC 381/.4500574/0973
HD9696.C63 U515925 1986

Diamond thin film . Norwalk, Conn. , c1987. iv, 136 leaves : LC Card 87-157102 DDC 380.1/4566029453 19
HD9999.T492 D52 1987

Electronic copy boards--local & remote. Norwalk, Conn., U. S.A. (6 Prowitt St., Norwalk 06855) , c1986. iii, 101 leaves : LC Card 86-224860 DDC 381/.45621380414 19
HD9802.3.A2 E45 1986

Electronic document interchange markets . Norwalk, Conn., U. S.A. (6 Prowitt St., Norwalk 06855) , c1987. v, 192 leaves : LC Card 87-403217 DDC 384.3/1 19
HD9696.D382 E44 1987

Electronic mail . Norwalk, Conn., U. S.A. (6 Prowitt St., Norwalk 06855) , c1986. viii, 230 leaves ; LC Card 86-226979 DDC 384.3/4 19
HE6239.E54 E59 1986

Fiber optic sensors. Norwalk, Conn., U. S.A. (6 Prowitt St., Norwald 06855) , c1987. iv, 179 leaves ; LC Card 87-134996 DDC 380.1/456213692 19
HD9696.F522 F496 1987

Flat panel displays. Norwalk, Conn., U. S.A. (6 Prowitt St., Norwalk 06855) , c1986. vii, 204 leaves ; LC Card 86-224985 DDC 380.1/4562138195832 19
HD9696.C62 F57 1986

Image processing in office automation. Norwalk, Conn., U. S.A. (6 Prowitt St., Norwalk 06855) , c1986. vii, 220 leaves ; LC Card 86-228429 DDC 381/.4500642 19
HD9696.I422 I44 1986

Industrial training products & services markets. Norwalk, Conn., U. S.A. (6 Prowitt St., Norwalk 06855) , c1987. vi, 174 leaves ; LC Card 87-153554 DDC 381/.45658312404 19
HD9811.A2 I53 1987

Military electro-optics markets. Norwalk, Conn., U. S.A. (6 Prowitt St., Norwalk 06855) , c1986. vi, 238 leaves : LC Card 86-226982 DDC 380.1/456234 19
HD9744.P732 M55 1986

Non-keyboard data entry. Norwalk, Conn., U. S.A. (6 Prowitt St., Norwalk 06855) , c1986. vii, 306 leaves : LC Card 86-224995 DDC 380.1/4500476 19
HD9696.C62 N665 1986

On-line database services markets. Norwalk, Conn., U. S.A. (6 Prowitt St., Norwalk 06855) , c1984. v, 207 leaves ; LC Card 86-233709 DDC 381/.4502504/0973 19
HD9696.C62 O66 1984

Optical & "smart" cards. Norwalk, Conn., U. S.A. (6 Prowitt St., Norwalk 06855) , c1986. vi, 271 leaves : LC Card 86-226974 DDC 381/.45621399 19
HD9696.O672 O65 1986

Optical disk document storage and retrieval systems. Norwalk, Conn., U. S.A. (6 Prowitt St., Norwalk 06855) , c1987. vii, 188 leaves ; LC Card 87-146516 DDC 380.1/4562139767 19
HD9696.O672 O673 1987

Optical fiber in the local loop. Norwalk, Conn. (6 Prowitt St., Norwalk 06855) , c1986. iv, 208 leaves : LC Card 87-127281 DDC 381/.456213692/0973 19
HD9696.F522 O67 1986

Peripherals for the ISDN D-channel. Norwalk, Conn., U. S.A. (6 Prowitt St., Norwalk 06855) , c1986. iv, 153 leaves : LC Card 87-129535 DDC 380.1/45621385 19
HD9696.D382 P46 1986

Printed circuit board market opportunities. Norwalk, Conn., U. S.A. (6 Prowitt St., Norwalk 06855) [1986] v, 153 leaves : LC Card 86-224533 DDC 381/.4562/38174/0973 19
HD9696.P743 U66 1986

Seafood processing & distribution market opportunities. Norwalk, Conn., U. S.A. (6 Prowitt St., Norwalk 06855) , c1986. vii, 244 leaves : LC Card 87-129495 DDC 381/.4566494/0973 19
HD9450.5 .S4 1986

T-1 products & services. Norwalk, Conn., U. S.A. (6 Prowitt St., Norwalk 06855) , c1987. iv, 181 leaves : LC Card 87-129537 DDC 384.6/5 19
HD9697.T452 T17 1987

Talkwriters, voice mail & speech processing in office automation. Norwalk, Conn., U. S.A. (6 Prowitt St., Norwalk 06855) , c1986. iv, 145 leaves : LC Card 86-224988 DDC 381/.45621389 19
HD9696.S643 U667 1986

Third-party maintenance of computer and datacom equipment. Norwalk, Conn., U. S.A. (6 Prowitt St., Norwalk 06855) , c1987. vi, 180 leaves ; LC Card 87-129551 DDC 381/.45004/0973 19
HD9696.C62 T45 1987

U.K. consumer electronics. Norwalk, Conn., U. S.A. (6 Prowitt St., Norwalk 06855) , c1986. vi, 198 leaves ; LC Card 86-228422 DDC 381/.45621381/0941 19
HD9696.A3 G785 1986

VHSIC . Norwalk, Conn., U. S.A. (6 Prowitt St., Norwalk 06855) , c1986. v, 219 leaves : LC Card 86-224890 DDC 381/.4562138173/0973 19
HD9696.I582 V47 1986

Video telephony markets. Norwalk, Conn., U. S.A. (6 Prowitt St., Norwalk 06855) , c1986. ii, 96 leaves : LC Card 86-224725 DDC 381/.45621386 19
HD9697.T453 U58 1986

Virtual facsimile & PC image capture/transmission/processing. Norwalk, Conn., U. S.A. (6 Prowitt St., Norwalk 06855) , c1986. vii, 208 leaves : LC Card 86-224356 DDC 381/.4500642/0973 19
HD9696.I423 U548 1986

Wideband communications services & equipment markets. Norwalk, Conn., U. S.A. (6

Prowitt St., Norwalk 06855) , c1986. iii, 198 leaves : LC Card 87-129548 DDC 384/.0973 19
HD9696.T442 W53 1986

International Risk Management Institute. Liability insurance account handling guide /. Dallas, Tex. , New York, N.Y. , c1986. v, 71 p. : LC Card 87-401617 DDC 368.5/0068 19
HG9990.3 .L5 1986

International Road Federation. Shimeles Asfaw. The economic evaluation of low traffic roads . [Nairobi? , 1980?] ii, 28, 13 leaves, [2] leaves of plates : LC Card 85-981138
HE367.K43 E374 1980

International Road Transport Union. Dictionary of road transport terminology in four languages, English, French, German, and Spanish /. Amsterdam , New York , 1988. xxviii, 351 p. ; ISBN 0-444-42819-4 : LC Card 87-13397 DDC 388/.03 19
HE5613 .D53 1988

International Rural Housing Association. Vivienda rural, México. [Mexico City] [1982?] 40 p. : LC Card 86-174056
HD7289.M6 V58 1982

INTERNATIONAL SALES. see **EXPORT SALES.**

International Savings Banks Institute. (Old Catalog form: International Thrift Institute)

International Savings Banks Institute. MIS Working Group. Information systems in Italian savings banks . Geneva , 1975. 93 p. : LC Card 84-247915
HG1939.I7 I54 1975

International Scientific Forum on Changes in Energy (1981 : Mexico City, Mexico) Global energy assessment and outlook : proceedings of the International Scientific Forum on Changes in Energy, held in Mexico City, Mexico, November 9-13, 1981 / edited by Behram N. Kurşunoğlu, Arnold Perlmutter, Linda Scott. Chur, Switzerland ; New York, N.Y. : Harwood Academic Publishers, c1984. xxix, 580 p. : ill. ; 24 cm. Includes bibliographies. ISBN 3-7186-0224-5 LC Card 84-12959 DDC 333.79 19
1. Power resources - Congresses. 2. Energy policy - Congresses. I. Kurşunoğlu, Behram, 1922-. II. Perlmutter, Arnold, 1928-. III. Scott, Linda F. IV. Title.
TJ163.15 .I5678 1981 ***NYPL [JSE 86-509]***

INTERNATIONAL SECURITY. see **SECURITY, INTERNATIONAL.**

International Seminar on China's 1982 Population Census (1982 : Peking, China) A census of one billion people : papers for International Seminar on China's 1982 Population Census / chief editor, Li Chengrui ; assistant chief editors, Tie Dazhang, Wu Hui, Sun Jingxin.1st ed. [Wanchai, Hongkong : Economic Information & Agency ; Boulder, Colo. : Distribution outside China, Hongkong, Singapore, and Japan is handled by Westview Press, 1986, c1987] 704 p., [4] leaves of plates : ill. (some col.) ; 21 cm. "Population Census Office, State Statistical Bureau & Department of Population Statistics, State Statistical Bureau, People's Republic of China. Includes bibliographical references. LC Card 87-2131 DDC 304.6/0723 19
1. China - Census, 1982 - Congresses. I. Li, Ch'eng-jui. II. China. Kuo wu yüan. Jen k'ou p'u ch'a pan kung shih. III. China. Kuo chia t'ung chi chü. Jen k'ou t'ung chi ssu. IV. Title. V. Title: Census of 1,000,000,000 people.
HA4631.5 .I57 1982

International Seminar on Public Enterprise Policy in the Eighties (1985 : Hyderabad, India) Public enterprise policy in India and U.K. in 1980s /. Bombay , 1987. xx, 286 p. ; LC Card 86-903771 DDC 338.6/2/0941 19
HD4293 .P775 1987

International Seminar on Recent Improvements in Goat Production in Asia (1984 : Los Baños, Laguna, Philippines) Goat production in Asia : proceedings of the International Seminar on Recent Improvements in Goat Production in Asia, May 8-11, 1984, PCARRD, Los Baños, Laguna, Philippines. Los Baños, Laguna, Philippines : Philippine Council for Agriculture and Resources Research and Development, National Science and Technology Authority ; Taipei, Taiwan, Republic of China : Food and Fertilizer Technology Center for the Asian and Pacific Region, 1985. viii, 186 p. : ill. ; 23 cm. (Book series. no. 20/1985) Includes bibliographies. LC Card 86-200478
1. Goat industry - Asia - Congresses. 2. Goat industry - Asia - Technological innovations - Congresses. I. Philippine Council for Agriculture and Resources Research and Development. II. Asian and Pacific Council. Food & Fertilizer Technology Center. III. Series: Book series (Philippine Council for Agriculture and Resources Research and Development) , no. 1985/20. IV. Title.
HD9438.G632 A785 1984

International Seminar on "Road Safety", Srinagar, September 17-18, 1986 /. International Seminar on "Road Safety" (1986 : Srinagar, India) New Delhi [1986] 1 v. (various pagings) : LC Card 87-901986 DDC 363.1/25 19
HE5614 .I5717 1986

International Seminar on "Road Safety" (1986 : Srinagar, India) International Seminar on "Road Safety", Srinagar, September 17-18, 1986 / Indian Roads Congress & Permanent International Association of Road Congresses, Paris, in co-operation with Union Ministry of Transport, Dept. of Surface Transport (Roads Wing) ... [et al.]. New Delhi : The Congress, [1986] 1 v. (various pagings) : ill., maps ; 25 cm. "Preliminary publication." Papers. Includes bibliographies. LC Card 87-901986 DDC 363.1/25 19
1. Roads - Safety measures - Congresses. 2. Traffic safety - Congresses. I. Permanent International Association of Road Congresses. II. Indian Roads Congress. III. India. Dept. of Surface Transport (Roads Wing). IV. Title.
HE5614 .I5717 1986

International Services Guild. Ross, H. Edward. Free airline tickets-- worldwide!! . St. Paul, Minn., U. S.A. , c1986. 154 p. ; ISBN 0-9616129-0-8 (pbk.) LC Card 87-117304 DDC 387.7/1 19
HE9783.5 .R67 1986

International Social Security Association. Disability benefits . Greenwich, Conn. , c1987. xxii, 282 p. ; ISBN 0-89232-824-X : LC Card 87-17056 DDC 368.3/86/009492 19
HD7105.25.N4 D57 1987

International Society for Ecological Modelling. Integrated rural energy planning /. Guildford , c1985. xii, 200 p. : ISBN 0-408-22166-6
NYPL [JLF 87-3]

Integrated rural energy planning /. Guildford, Surrey, England , 1985. xii, 200 p. : ISBN 0-408-22166-6 LC Card 87-160993 DDC 333.79/09172/4 19
HD9502.D442 I57 1985

International Society of Statistical Science in Economics. Quantity and quality in economic research /. Lanham, MD , c1985- v. : ISBN 0-8191-5112-2 (v. 1 : alk. paper) : LC Card 85-26360 DDC 330/.072 19
HB135 .Q38 1985 ***NYPL [JLL 86-232]***

International Sociological Association. Research Committee 32 "Women in Society". Invisible hands . New Delhi , Newbury Park, Calif. , 1987. 273 p. ; ISBN 0-8039-9524-5 (U. S.) LC Card 87-4337 DDC 331.4/0954 19
HD6181.85 .A85 1987

International studies in economic modelling. Modelling the labour market /. London , New York , 1988. p. cm. ISBN 0-412-28830-3 LC Card 87-23084 DDC 331.12/0724 19
HD5765.A6 M63 1988

International studies in migration. Costello, Michael A. Mobility and employment in urban Southeast Asia . Boulder , 1987. xvi, 190 p. : ISBN 0-8133-7352-2 (pbk. : alk. paper) : LC Card 87-10649 DDC 307.2 19
HB2107 .C67 1987

The international sugar industry . Brown, James G., 1945- Washington, D.C., U. S.A. , 1987. xii, 69 p. ; ISBN 0-8213-0884-1 (pbk.) LC Card 87-6285 DDC 338.1/736 19
HD9100.5 .B76 1987

International Symposium "North-South Dialogue at the beginning of the 1980s" (1981 : Berlin, Germany) Der Nord-Süd-Dialog zu Beginn der 80er Jahre =. Baden-Baden , 1982. 99 p. ; ISBN 3-7890-0774-9 ***NYPL [JLE 87-1282]***

International Symposium on Religion, Economics, and Social Thought (1982 : Vancouver, B.C.) Morality of the market . Vancouver, B.C., Canada , c1985. xxv, 601 p. ; ISBN 0-88975-074-2 (pbk.) : LC Card 86-158049 DDC 174/.4 19
HB72 .M56 1985

International Symposium on the Role of the Asia-Pacific Region in World Economic Development (1984 : Tokyo, Japan) Proceedings of the International Symposium on the Role of the Asia-Pacific Region in World Economic Development : December 17-20, 1984. Tokyo : College of Economics, Nihon University, c1985. iv, 325 p. : ill. ; 26 cm. "In commemoration of the 80th anniversary." Includes bibliographies. LC Card 87-108109 DDC 337.9 19
1. Pacific Area - Economic policy - Congresses. 2. Pacific Area - Foreign economic relations - Congresses. 3. Economic forecasting - Pacific Area - Congresses. 4. Pacific Area cooperation - Congresses. I. Nihon Daigaku. Keizai Gakubu. II. Title. III. Title: Role of the Asia-Pacific Region in World Economic Development.
HC681 .I58 1984

International Symposium on World Trade in Forest Products (2nd : 1985 : University of Washington) World trade in forest products, 2 /. Seattle , c1986. xi, 362 p. : ISBN 0-295-96337-9 LC Card 86-234388 DDC 382/.41498 19
HD9750.5 .W67 1986

International Teamsters Union. see **International Brotherhood of Teamsters, Chauffeurs, Warehousemen and Helpers of America.**

International Telecommunication Union. Plan général de développement du réseau régional en Afrique =. Genève , 1983. 134 p. : ISBN 92-71-02066-9 LC Card 85-146412
HE8465 .P54 1983

International Telecommunication Union. International Frequency Registration Board. see **International Frequency Registration Board.**

International telecommunications markets, production & trade / Clementson Electronic Services Ltd, Nu-Markets Associates. New York, N.Y. : Stockton Press, 1986. 317 p. : ill. ; 30 cm. ISBN 0-935859-11-X (pbk.) LC Card 86-23052 DDC 338.7/62138 19
1. Telecommunication equipment industry. 2. Telephone supplies industry. I. Clementson Electronic Services. II. Nu-Markets Associates.
HD9696.T442 I578 1986

International Telephone and Telegraph Corporation. (Old Catalog form: International Telephone and Telegraph Corporation, New York)
Spain and the telephone . New York , 1925. 16 p., [1] folded leaf of plates : LC Card 85-666351
HE9324 .S63x 1925

International Tin Council. United States of America, tin in tinplate. London [1983] 89 p. : LC Card 84-216067 DDC 338.4/76736/0973 19
HD9529.T63 U67 1983

International trade : selected readings / edited by Jagdish N. Bhagwati.2nd ed. Cambridge, Mass. : MIT Press, 1987. xii, 504 p. : ill. ; 24 cm. Includes bibliographies and index. ISBN 0-262-02264-8 LC Card 87-2623 DDC 382 19
1. Commercial policy. 2. Commerce. I. Bhagwati, Jagdish N., 1934-.
HF1411 .I5185 1987

INTERNATIONAL TRADE.
Economic development and international trade /. New York , 1988. xi, 211 p. ; ISBN 0-312-01588-7 : LC Card 87-25629 DDC 382 19
HF1379 .E27 1988

International competition in services . Washington, DC [1987] vii, 403 p. : LC Card 87-619820 DDC 382/.45/00973 19
HD9981.5 .I58 1987

Pálfi, Sándor. Nemzetközi biztosítás a külkereskedelem szolgálatában /. [Budapest] [1986] 63 p. ; ISBN 963-02-4369-5 LC Card 87-425585
HG8059 .P35 1986

International trade and exchange rates in the late eighties / edited by Theo Peeters, Peter Praet, and Paul Reding. Amsterdam ; New

York : North-Holland ; xii, 418 p. : ill. ; 24 cm. Papers from a conference held June 6-8, 1985, organized by the Institut d'etudes européennes, Université libre de Bruxelles, Centrum voor Economische Studiën, Katholieke Universiteit Leuven, Facultés universitaires Notre-Dame de la Paix de Namur. Includes bibliographies. ISBN 0-444-87941-2 LC Card 86-223111 DDC 382.4/5 19
1. Foreign exchange - Congresses. 2. Commerce - Congresses. I. Peeters, Theo. II. Praet, Peter. III. Reding, Paul. IV. Université libre de Bruxelles. Institut d'études européennes. V. Katholieke Universiteit te Leuven (1970-). Centrum voor Economische Studiën. VI. Facultés universitaires Notre-Dame de la Paix, Namur.
HG203 .I58 1985

International trade and exchange rates in the late eighties / edited by Theo Peeters, Peter Praet and Paul Reding. Amsterdam ; New York : North-Holland ; xii, 418 p. : ill. ; 24 cm. A conference held June 6-8, 1985), "jointly organized by ... Institut d'études européennes, Université libre de Bruxelles; the Centrum voor Economische Studiën, Katholieke Universiteit te Leuven; Faculté des sciences économiques et sociales, Facultés universitaires Notre-Dame de la Paix, Namur."--Pref. Includes bibliographies. ISBN 2-8004-0892-8
1. International economic relations - Congresses. 2. International finance - Congresses. 3. Foreign exchange - Congresses. I. Peeters, Theo. II. Praet, Peter. III. Reding, Paul. IV. Katholieke Universiteit te Leuven (1970-). Centrum voor Economische Studiën. V. Université libre de Bruxelles. Institut d'études européenes. VI. Facultés universitaires Notre-Dame de la Paix, Namur. Faculté des sciences économiques et sociales. ***NYPL [JLE 87-120]***

International trade and the consumer : report on the 1984 OECD symposium. Paris : Organisation for Economic Co-operation and Development ; [Washington, D.C. : OECD Publications and Information Centre [distributor], 1986. 296 p. ; 23 cm. Held November 27-29, 1984 in Paris. Includes bibliographies. ISBN 92-64-12813-1 (pbk.) : LC Card 86-216097 DDC 382/.3 19
1. Commercial policy - Congresses. 2. International economic relations - Congresses. 3. Consumer protection - Congresses. I. Organization for Economic Co-operation and Development.
HF1410.5 .I585 1986 ***NYPL [JLE 87-1541]***

International Trade Center UNCTAD/GATT. Handbook of state trading organizations of developing countries =. New York , 1985. clxxxix, 542 p. : ISBN 92-1-012014-0 (pbk.) LC Card 86-233995
HF1009.7.D44 H35 1985

International Trade Centre UNCTAD/GATT. Bicycles and components . Geneva , 1985. x, 160 p. ; LC Card 86-219298 DDC 380./456292272/091724 19
HD9993.B543 D442 1985

Hungary--a market for products from developing countries /. Geneva , 1985. xi, 129 p. : LC Card 87-118542 DDC 382/.09439/01724 19
HF3550.5.Z7 D44 1985

Major import markets for builders' woodwork /. Geneva , 1985. xiii, 180 p. : LC Card 87-118537 DDC 381/.45674/094 19
HD9765.A2 M29 1985

Nicanovich, Marta Beatriz. The role fulfilled by the International Trade Centre UNCTAD/GATT within the framework of the United Nations development policy /. Genève , 1986. xii, 248, 103, xix p. : LC Card 86-225702 DDC 382/.06/01 19
HF1417.5 .N52 1986

INTERNATIONAL TRADE CONTROL. see **FOREIGN TRADE REGULATION.**

INTERNATIONAL TRADE - DICTIONARIES - HUNGARIAN.
Mádai, Edit. Külkereskedelmi tevékenységhez kapcsolódó általános fogalommeghatározások /. [Budapest , 1984] (Budapest : Datorg Nyomda) 177 p. ; ISBN 963-02-2359-7 LC Card 87-409581
HF1001 .M27 1984

International trade, employment, and structural adjustment . Gray, H. Peter. Geneva , 1986. x, 108 p. ; ISBN 92-2-105325-3 (pbk.) : LC Card 87-119470 DDC 331.12/0973 19
HD5710.75.U6 G73 1986

International trade in services. Audiovisual works. Paris : Organisation for Economic Co-operation and Development ; Washington, D.C. : OECD Publications and Information Center [distributor], 1986. 46 p. ; 27 cm. Includes bibliographical references. ISBN 92-64-12860-3 (pbk.) : LC Card 87-122911 DDC 382/.45621380282 19
1. Audio-visual equipment industry. 2. Audio-visual materials. 3. Foreign trade regulation. I. Organisation for Economic Co-operation and Development.
HD9697.A842 I58 1986

International trade in services . Kakabadse, Mario A. London , New York , c1987. 90 p. ; ISBN 0-7099-3130-1 (pbk.) LC Card 87-8951 DDC 382/.45/0009049 19
HD9980.5 .K35 1987

International trade in textiles & apparel : how is the U. S. textile import program working? : program materials, June 19, 1987, Washington, D.C. [Washington, D.C.] : Georgetown University Law Center, Continuing Legal Education Division, c1987. 1 v. (various foliations) : ill. ; 29 cm. "Co-sponsored by the International Trade Committee, Section of International Law & Practice, American Bar Association"--Cover. Includes a bibliography. LC Card 87-404516 DDC 382/.45677/00973 19
1. Textile industry - United States. 2. Clothing trade - United States. 3. Export controls - United States. 4. Textile industry - Law and legislation - United States. I. Georgetown University. Continuing Legal Education Division. II. American Bar Association. Section of International Law and Practice. International Trade Committee. III. Title: International trade in textiles and apparel.
HD9850.5 .I43 1987

International trade in textiles and apparel. International trade in textiles & apparel . [Washington, D.C.] , c1987. 1 v. (various foliations) : LC Card 87-404516 DDC 382/.45677/00973 19
HD9850.5 .I43 1987

International trade [microform] : special studies, 1982-1985 / edited by Michael C. Davis. Frederick, MD : University Publications of America, 1987. microfilm reel (The Special studies series) Accompanied by a printed reel guide, compiled by Mike Acquaviva. ISBN 0-89093-551-3 (microfilm) : LC Card 87-6240 DDC 382 19
1. Commerce. I. Davis, Michael C., 1953-. II. Acquaviva, Mike. III. University Publications of America, Inc.
HF1008

International trade regulation . McGovern, Edmond. Exeter [Devon] , 1986. xliv, 629 p. ; ISBN 0-9508463-4-1 DDC 341.7/54 19
K3943 .M4 1982 ***NYPL [JLE 86-3637]***

INTERNATIONAL TRADE REGULATION. see **FOREIGN TRADE REGULATION.**

International traffic and infrastructural needs. Paris, France : European Conference of Ministers of Transport ; [Washington, D.C. : OECD Publications and Information Centre, distributor], c1986. 92 p. : ill. ; 27 cm. ISBN 92-821-1111-3 (pbk.) : LC Card 87-167959 DDC 380.5/24/094 19
1. Freight and freightage - Europe - Congresses. 2. Freight and freightage - Government policy - Europe - Congresses. I. European Conference of Ministers of Transport.
HE199.E85 I58 1986

INTERNATIONAL TRANSIT. see **TRANSIT, INTERNATIONAL.**

International treasury management /. Ross, Derek. New York, N.Y. , c1988. p. cm. ISBN 0-13-473968-X : LC Card 87-16118 DDC 658.1/599 19
HG4027.5 .R67 1988

International Union for the Scientific Investigation of Population Problems. see **International Union for the Scientific Study of Population.**

International Union for the Scientific Study of Population.
IUSSP papers.
(no. 16) Projecting migration for integrated rural and urban development planning. Liege, Belgium , c1980. 46 p. ; LC Card 84-221919 DDC 304.8 19
HB1952 .P76 1980
NYPL [JLL 77-289 no. 16]

International Union for the Scientific Study of Population. Committee on Demographic Aspects of Family Planning Programs. Projecting migration for integrated rural and urban development planning. Liege, Belgium , c1980. 46 p. ; LC Card 84-221919 DDC 304.8 19
HB1952 .P76 1980
NYPL [JLL 77-289 no. 16]

International Union for the Scientific Study of Population. Committee on Factors Affecting Mortality and Length of Life. Methodologies for the collection and analysis of mortality data . Liège, Belgium , 1984. vi, 510 p. : ISBN 2-87040-032-2 (pbk.) LC Card 86-205582 DDC 304.6/4/072 19
HB1321 .M48 1984

International Union for the Scientific Study of Population. Committee on Urbanization and Population Redistribution. Projecting migration for integrated rural and urban development planning. Liege, Belgium , c1980. 46 p. ; LC Card 84-221919 DDC 304.8 19
HB1952 .P76 1980
NYPL [JLL 77-289 no. 16]

International Union for the Scientific Study of Population. Documents de l'Union. see **International Union for the Scientific Study of Population. IUSSP papers.**

International Union of Anthropological and Ethnological Sciences. Commission on Women. Invisible hands . New Delhi , Newbury Park, Calif. , 1987. 273 p. ; ISBN 0-8039-9524-5 (U. S.) LC Card 87-4337 DDC 331.4/0954 19
HD6181.85 .A85 1987

INTERNATIONAL UNION OF FOOD AND ALLIED WORKERS' ASSOCIATIONS.
IUF Mediterranean Hotel and Restaurant Workers' Conference (1978 : Palermo, Sicily) IUF Mediterranean Hotel and Restaurant Workers' Conference, Palermo, November 15-17, 1978. Petit-Lancy, Switzerland [1978?] 1 v. (various pagings) ; LC Card 83-225538
HD6475.A2 I7836 1978

International Union of Food and Allied Workers' Associations. Secretariat. IUF Mediterranean Hotel and Restaurant Workers' Conference (1978 : Palermo, Sicily) IUF Mediterranean Hotel and Restaurant Workers' Conference, Palermo, November 15-17, 1978. Petit-Lancy, Switzerland [1978?] 1 v. (various pagings) ; LC Card 83-225538
HD6475.A2 I7836 1978

INTERNATIONAL UNION, UNITED AUTOMOBILE, AEROSPACE, AND AGRICULTURAL IMPLEMENT WORKERS OF AMERICA - HISTORY.
Denby, Charles. Indignant heart . Montréal , 1979. 295 p. : ISBN 0-919618-93-6 LC Card 87-672793
HD8039.A82 U633x 1979

Halpern, Martin, 1945- UAW politics in the cold war era/. Albany, N.Y. , c1988. p. cm. ISBN 0-88706-671-2 LC Card 87-13890 DDC 322/.2/0973 19
HD6515.A82 I574 1988

International Union, United Steelworkers of America. see **United Steelworkers of America.**

International Workshop on Artificial Intelligence in Economics and Management (1985 : Zurich, Switzerland) Artificial intelligence in economics and management /. Amsterdam ; New York : xv, 292 p. : ISBN 0-444-87961-7 LC Card 85-31139 DDC 330/.028/563 19
HB143.5 .A78 1986 ***NYPL [JLE 86-3612]***

International Workshop on National Energy Data Systems (1982 : New Delhi, India) National energy data systems . New Delhi , 1984, c1983. xxvi, 511 p. ; LC Card 84-901310 DDC 333.79/09172/4 19
HD9502.D442 N37 1984
NYPL [JLD 86-4320]

Internationale Bauausstellung Berlin GmbH. Versicherungen in der Altbauerneuerung /. Berlin , c1985. 83 p. ; ISBN 3-433-02219-4 LC

Card 86-104351
HG9986.4.G3 V47 1985

Internationale Erfahrungen mit der Gurtanlegepflicht =. Marburger, Ernst-Albrecht. Köln , 1982. 29, 29 p. : LC Card 83-200842
HE5614 .M288 1982

Die Internationale Finanzierungskrise / Beiträge von Arno Graf von Bothmer-Plates ... [et al.]. Frankfurt am Main : F. Knapp, c1985. 153 p. ; 21 cm. (Probleme des Kapitalmarkts. Kolloquien-Beiträge. 27) Summaries in English. ISBN 3-7819-2536-6 LC Card 87-146671 DDC 336.3/435 19
1. Debts, External - Congresses. 2. Loans, Foreign - Congresses. 3. Economic history - 1971- - Congresses. 4. International finance - Congresses. I. Bothmer-Plates, Arno, Graf von. II. Series.
HG3891.5 .I587 1985

Internationale Interdependenz nationaler Geld- und Gütermärkte bei flexiblen Wechselkursen /. Ohr, Renate. Hamburg , 1980. 217 p. : ISBN 3-87895-194-9 LC Card 84-120800
HG3823 .O47 1980

Internationale Kooperation. For additional listing of contents, see Old Catalog.
(Bd. 26) Strittmatter, Gabriele. Kooperationsstrategien westeuropäischer und japanischer Banken in den ASEAN-Staaten /. Baden-Baden , 1984. 411 p. : ISBN 3-7890-1051-0 LC Card 86-134027
HG3324 .S77 1984
(Bd. 30) Hauser, Heinz-Michael. Reform der Entwicklungsfinanzierung durch "Automatisierung"? . Baden-Baden , 1986. vi, 531 p. ; ISBN 3-7890-1235-1 LC Card 87-407969 DDC 338.91/09172/4 19
HC60 .H329 1986
(22) Schunk, Gerhard. Internationale Zusammenarbeit in hochtechnologischen Bereichen . Baden-Baden , 1982. 305 p. : ISBN 3-7890-0760-9 LC Card 82-198815 DDC 338.4/76217 19
HD41 .S355 1982 ***NYPL [TB (Internationale Kooperation. Bd.22)]***
(30) Hauser, Heinz-Michael. Reform der Entwicklungsfinanzierung durch "Automatisierung"? . Baden-Baden , 1986. vi, 531 p. ; ISBN 3-7890-1235-1 LC Card 87-407969 DDC 338.91/09172/4 19
HC60 .H329 1986

Internationale Politik (Bonn, Germany) .
(27) Domitra, Michael. Mexiko . Bonn [1984] 24 p. ; LC Card 85-134274 DDC 330.972/0834 19
HC135 .D65 1984
(29) Dauderstädt, Michael. Entwicklungspolitik, Politik ohne Entwicklung . Bonn [1984] 38 p. ; LC Card 85-136902
HC59.7 .D327 1984

Internationale Produktionskooperation im Vorderen Orient . Uhlig, Christian. Stuttgart , c1983. xvi, 338 p. : ISBN 3-522-68000-6 LC Card 83-217029
HD2891.9 .U44 1983

Internationale Rohstoffabkommen als Beispiel des Nord-Süd Dialoges /. Habermayer, Wolfgang, 1959- Frankfurt am Main , New York , c1985. xxxiii, 264 p. : ISBN 3-8204-8896-0 LC Card 86-111744
HF1054.D44 H33 1985

Die Internationale Schuldenkrise : Ursachen, Konsequenzen, historische Erfahrungen / von Peter Bernholz ... [et al.] ; herausgegeben von Armin Gutowski. Berlin : Duncker & Humblot, 1986. 179 p. : ill. ; 24 cm. (Schriften des Vereins für Socialpolitik, Gesellschaft für Wirtschafts- und Sozialwissenschaften . n.F., Bd. 155) One contribution in English. Includes bibliographical references. CONTENTS. - Erfahrungen aus internationalen Finanzkrisen der Vergangenheit / Karl Erich Born -- Kriterien zur Analyse internationaler Verschuldung und Keynes' Prognose der deutschen Schuldenkrise / Karl Häuser -- Zur argentinischen Schuldenkrise 1890-1900 / Peter Bernholz -- Ansätze zur Lösung der Schuldenkrise / Wolfgang Rieke -- The international debt situation in an American view / Henry C. Wallich -- Die internationale Schuldenkrise und die Banken / Otmar Emminger -- Die Funktion des Kreditgebers der letzten Instanz bei nationalen und internationalen Finanzkrisen / Emil-Maria Claassen -- Internationale Finanzintermediation und Auslandsverschuldung / Vincenz Timmermann -- Kapitalflucht aus Entwicklungsländern / Dieter Duwendag -- Internationale Kredite mit undurchsetzbaren Forderungen / Jürg Niehans. ISBN 3-428-05972-7 LC Card 86-172589
1. Debts, External - Developing countries. 2. Loans, Foreign - Developing countries. I. Bernholz, Peter. II. Gutowski, Armin. III. Series.
HJ8899 .I58 1986

Internationale Steuervorteile /. Stern, Richard Walter. Zürich , 1977. 56 leaves : LC Card 85-173548
HJ2336 .S74 1977

Internationale Strassen-Liga. see **International Road Federation.**

Internationale und nationale Problemfelder der Betriebswirtschaftslehre / herausgegeben von Gert v. Kortzfleisch und Bernd Kaluza. Berlin : Duncker & Humblot, c1984. 336 p., [1] leaf of plates : port. ; 24 cm. (Abhandlungen aus dem Industrieseminar der Universität Mannheim . Heft 32) "Festgabe für Heinz Bergner zum 60. Geburtstag"--P. [1] Bibliography of H. Bergner's works: p. [335]-336. Includes bibliographies. ISBN 3-428-05696-5 LC Card 85-141327
1. Industrial management. 2. Economic policy. 3. Industrial management - Germany, West. 4. Germany, West - Economic policy. 5. Bergner, Heinz, 1924-. I. Bergner, Heinz, 1924-. II. Kortzfleisch, Gerd von. III. Kaluza, Bernd. IV. Series.
HD35 .I598 1984

Internationale Union für Bevölkerungswissenschaft. see **International Union for the Scientific Study of Population.**

Internationale Vereinigung für Soziale Sicherheit. see **International Social Security Association.**

Internationale vergelijking loonstructuur /. Stoffel, R. A. 's-Gravenhage [1986] 20 p. : LC Card 86-231311
HD5014 .S76 1986

Die internationale Verschuldungskrise . Hedström, Håkan, 1960- Heidelberg [1985] xvi, 273 p. : ISBN 3-920431-50-2 LC Card 86-122591
HJ8899 .H43 1985

Internationale Wettbewerbsfähigkeit des Finanzplatzes Schweiz / herausgegeben von Christine Hirszowicz. Bern : P. Haupt, c1987. 131 p. : ill. ; 23 cm. (Bankwirtschaftliche Forschungen. Bd. 101) Papers presented at a meeting of the Institut für Schweizerisches Bankwesen der Universität Zürich held Sept. 29-30, 1986. Includes bibliographical references. CONTENTS. - Die Schweizer Banken vor internationalen Herausforderungen / Rainer E. Gut -- Sind die Rahmenbedingungen des Finanzplatzes Schweiz noch attraktiv genug? / Markus Lusser -- Wettbewerbsfähigkeit der Schweizer Banken im Kreditgeschäft / Fritz Köhli -- Wettbewerbsfähigkeit der Schweizer Banken im Portfolio-Management / Hans J. Bär -- Die schweizerischen Finanzmärkte im Globalisierungsprozess / Bruno Gehrig -- Internationale Wettbewerbsfähigkeit der Schweizer Banken aus der Sicht der Eidgenössischen Bankenkommission / Kurt Hauri -- Personalengpässe des Finanzplatzes Schweiz? / Hans J. Mast -- Internationale Wettbewerbsfähigkeit der Schweizer Banken dank "Weltspitze" in der Ausbildung? / Ernst Kilgus. ISBN 3-258-03806-6 LC Card 87-114764 DDC 332.1 s 332.1/09494 19
1. Banks and banking - Switzerland - Congresses. 2. Finance - Switzerland - Congresses. 3. Competition, International - Congresses. I. Hirszowicz, Christine. II. Universität Zurich. Institut für Schweizerisches Bankwesen. III. Series.
HG1526 .B27 Bd. 101 HG3206

Internationale Wirtschaft (Bonn, Germany)
Dauderstädt, Michael. Wettbewerbsfähig durch soziale Disziplin? . Bonn [1981] 38 p. ; LC Card 85-137321
HD41 .D38 1981

Internationale Wirtschaft und revolutionärer Weltprozess / [Herausgeber, Intersektioneller Arbeitskreis "Weltwirtschaft und Ökonomie der Entwicklungsländer" an der Humboldt-Universität zu Berlin ; Redakteure, E. Karlsch, T. Nöbel]. [Berlin] : Die Humboldt-Universität, 1983. 390 p. ; 21 cm. LC Card 84-167604
1. International economic relations - Congresses. 2. Developing countries - Foreign economic relations - Congresses. I. Karlsch, E. II. Nöbel, T. III. Humboldt-Universität zu Berlin. Intersektioneller Arbeitskreis "Weltwirtschaft und Ökonomie der Entwicklungsländer.".
HF1410.5 .I592 1983

Internationale Zusammenarbeit in hochtechnologischen Bereichen . Schunk, Gerhard. Baden-Baden , 1982. 305 p. : ISBN 3-7890-0760-9 LC Card 82-198815 DDC 338.4/76217 19
HD41 .S355 1982 ***NYPL [TB (Internationale Kooperation. Bd.22)]***

Internationaler Bund Freier Gewerkschaften. see **International Confederation of Free Trade Unions.**

Internationaler Fernmeldeverein. see **International Telecommunication Union.**

Internationaler Kapitalverkehr und Devisenhandel / herausgegeben von Wolfram Engels ; mit Beiträgen von Kurt F. Viermetz ... [et al.]. Frankfurt am Main : F. Knapp, c1986. 133 p. ; 24 cm. Papers presented at the Bankwirtschaftliches Kolloquium held during the winter semester 1984/85 at the Johann Wolfgang Goethe-Universität Frankfurt am Main. One article in English. CONTENTS. - Devisenhandel einer internationalen Grossbank / von Kurt F. Viermetz -- Devisenmarktinterventionen der Deutschen Bundesbank / von Leonhard Gleske -- Kompensationsgeschäfte / von Hans Hohmann -- Fragen des Zahlungsverkehrs mit sozialistischen Ländern / von Michael N. Bauer -- The LIFFE and its perspectives for the future / von Bernard Reed -- Das europäische Währungssystem und die Rolle des ECU / von Jean Pierre Lefoulon -- Die Rolle der deutschen Banken auf den internationalen Finanzmärken / von Walter Seipp. ISBN 3-7819-0347-8 LC Card 87-164156 DDC 332/.042 19
1. Capital movements - Congresses. 2. Foreign exchange - Congresses. 3. International finance - Congresses. I. Engels, Wolfram. II. Viermetz, Kurt F. III. Bankwirtschaftliches Kolloquium (1984-1985 : Johann Wolfgang Goethe-Universität Frankfurt am Main). IV. Universität Frankfurt am Main.
HG3891 .I58 1986

Internationaler Rat für Bauforschung, -studien und -dokumentation. see **International Council for Building Research, Studies and Documentation.**

Internationaler Technologieaustausch--Kooperation oder Konfrontation? . Hartmann, Wolf-Dietrich, 1946- Frankfurt/Main , 1984. 153 p. ; ISBN 3-88012-633-X LC Card 85-155132 DDC 338.9/26 19
HC79.T4 H36 1984

Internationaler Workshop "Informationstechnologie im Dienstleistungsbereich--Arbeitsbedingungen und Leistungsqualität" (1985?)
Informationstechnologie im Dienstleistungsbereich . Berlin , c1985. 258 p. : ISBN 3-924859-15-9 : LC Card 86-220033 DDC 338.4/561 19
HD9980.5 .I54 1985

Internationaler Zinsverbund /. Hadjio, Roman, 1952- Frankfurt am Main , New York , c1985. 272 p. : ISBN 3-8204-5691-0 LC Card 85-220128
HG3821 .H27 1985

Internationales Bankgeschäft / herausgegeben und eingeleitet von Hans-Jacob Krümmel ; [Redaktion, Horst Reinhardt]. Berlin : Duncker & Humblot, c1985. 249 p. : ill. ; 24 cm. (Beihefte zu Kredit und Kapital . Heft 8) Summary in English and German. Some articles in English. Includes bibliographical references. ISBN 3-428-05790-2 LC Card 86-178830
1. Banks and banking, International. 2. International finance. I. Krümmel, Hans-Jacob. II. Series.
HG3881 .I72 1985

Internationales Bankgeschäft als Problem der Bankenaufsicht /. Zeitler, Isabella, 1956- München , c1984. viii, 353 p. : LC Card 85-103322
HG3881 .Z4 1984

Internationales Institut der Sparkassen. see **International Savings Banks Institute.**

Internationales Institut für Empirische Sozialökonomie.
Gestaltungsspielräume der Arbeitsmarktpolitik auf regionalen Arbeitsmärkten . Berlin , c1984. 180 p. : ISBN 3-428-05614-0 LC Card 84-218530
HD8444 .G47 1984

Methoden und Kriterien zur Überprüfung des Erfolgs von Aufklärungskampagnen . Köln , 1982. 99, [93] p. : LC Card 83-178796
HE5614.5.G3 M37 1982

Internationales Institut für Finanz- und Steuerwesen. see **International Institute of Public Finance.**

Internationales Institut für Umwelt und Gesellschaft. Leipert, Christian. Folgekosten des Wachstums als Wachstumsstimulans . Berlin [1985?] 35 p. : LC Card 86-116361
HD75.6 .L45 1985

Internationales Institut für Vergleichende Gesellschaftsforschung/Arbeitspolitik. Informationstechnologie im Dienstleistungsbereich . Berlin , c1985. 258 p. : ISBN 3-924859-15-9 : LC Card 86-220033 DDC 338.4/561 19
HD9980.5 .I54 1985

Internationales Konzernmarketing /. Uhlig, Karl-Heinz. Berlin , c1986. 143 p. : ISBN 3-349-00001-0 LC Card 87-118692 DDC 658.8/48 19
HF1009.5 .U36 1986

Internationalization of banking : analysis and prospects. Seoul, Korea : Korea Federation of Banks, c1986. 300 p. : ill. ; 23 cm. Proceedings of an international symposium held in 1985 and sponsored by the Korea Federation of Banks. Includes bibliographical references. LC Card 87-114642 DDC 332.1/5 19
1. Banks and banking, International - Congresses. 2. International finance - Congresses. I. Chŏn'guk Ŭnhaeng Yŏnhaphoe (Korea).
HG3881 .I496 1986

The internationalization of capital . Berberoglu, Berch. New York , 1987. xxi, 223 p. : ISBN 0-275-92169-7 (alk. paper) : LC Card 86-25259 DDC 337 19
HF1411 .B367 1987

The Internationalization of Japanese business : European and Japanese perspectives / edited by Malcolm Trevor. Boulder : Westview Press, 1986. p. cm. ISBN 0-8133-0531-4 : LC Card 87-8186 DDC 338.8/8952/04 19
1. Corporations, Japanese - European Economic Community countries. 2. Investments, Japanese - European Economic Community countries. I. Trevor, Malcolm, 1932-.
HD2844.5 .I567 1986

The internationalization of the Japanese economy /. Higashi, Chikara. Boston, MA , c1987. xi, 273 p. : ISBN 0-89838-199-1 LC Card 87-3893 DDC 337.52 19
HC462.9 .H45 1987

Internationella förutsättningar för den svenska oljeförsörjningen under 1980-talet. Stockholm : Statens industriverk, 1981. 172 p. in various pagings : ill. ; 30 cm. (SIND PM, 0346-573X . 1981:4) English and Swedish. Includes bibliographical references. ISBN 91-38-06244-5 LC Card 82-241303
1. Petroleum industry and trade - Sweden. 2. Petroleum conservation - Sweden. 3. Energy policy - Sweden. I. Sweden. Statens industriverk. II. Series.
HD9575.S82 I57 1981

Interne nota .
(330) Normen voor nieuwwaarde en afschrijving van slijtende duurzame produktiemiddelen in de fruitteelt alsmede voor de grondwaarde . Den Haag [1986] 67 p. ; LC Card 86-234475
HF5686.F7 N67 1986

Internprissättning inom offentlig förvaltning . Andersson, Per Magnus, 1951- Lund [1984] xii, 357 p. ; ISBN 91-44-43971-7 : LC Card 84-210334
HD62.45 .A53 1984

INTERNTIONAL ECONOMIC RELATIONS.
Gandolfo, Giancarlo. International economics II . Berlin , New York , c1987. p. cm. ISBN 0-387-17978-X (U. S.) LC Card 87-16295 DDC 332.4/5 19
HF1411 .G3363 1987

INTEROCEANIC CANALS. see **CANALS, INTEROCEANIC.**

INTERORGANIZATIONAL RELATIONS.
Argyris, Chris, 1923- Personality and organization . New York , 1987, c1957. xiii, 291 p. ; ISBN 0-8240-8200-1 (alk. paper) : LC Card 86-27054 DDC 658.4 19
HD58.7 .A75 1987

INTERORGANIZATIONAL RELATIONS - NETHERLANDS - CASE STUDIES.
Caris, J. Fuseren in non-profit organisaties . Nijmegen , 1986. 107 p. : ISBN 90-255-0018-8 : LC Card 86-205531
HD2746.5 .C35 1986

Interparlamentarische Konferenz über die Rheinverschmutzung (1977 : Den Haag, Netherlands) Interparlamentarische Konferenz über die Rheinverschmutzung : Binnenhof, Den Haag, 24. und 25. Februar 1977 / [herausgegeben von beiden Kammern der Generalstaaten]. 's Gravenhage : Staatsverlag, 1977. 62 p. ; 28 cm. Chiefly papers presented by the various national delegations to the conference. ISBN 90-12-01782-3 LC Card 86-149213
1. Interparlamentarische Konferenz über die Rheinverschmutzung (1977 : Den Haag, Netherlands). 2. Environmental policy - Rhine River Valley - Congresses. I. Netherlands. Staten-Generaal. Eerste Kamer. II. Netherlands. Staten-Generaal. Tweede Kamer. III. Title.
HC240.9.E5 I77 1977

INTERPARLAMENTARISCHE KONFERENZ ÜBER DIE RHEINVERSCHMUTZUNG (1977 : DEN HAAG, NETHERLANDS)
Interparlamentarische Konferenz über die Rheinverschmutzung (1977 : Den Haag, Netherlands) Interparlamentarische Konferenz über die Rheinverschmutzung . 's Gravenhage , 1977. 62 p. ; ISBN 90-12-01782-3 LC Card 86-149213
HC240.9.E5 I77 1977

Interparlamentarische Konferenz über die Rheinverschmutzung . Interparlamentarische Konferenz über die Rheinverschmutzung (1977 : Den Haag, Netherlands) 's Gravenhage , 1977. 62 p. ; ISBN 90-12-01782-3 LC Card 86-149213
HC240.9.E5 I77 1977

INTERPERSONAL COMMUNICATION.
Alves, Denise. O desencontro marcado . Petrópolis , 1985. 169 p. ; LC Card 85-226159
HQ1075 .A44 1985 ***NYPL [JFD 86-7232]***

An Introduction to communication on the telephone [videorecording] /. Del Mar, CA , 1987. 1 videocassette (7 min.) : LC Card 87-700082 DDC 658.8 11
HF5415.1265

Job survival skills [videorecording] . Mt. Kisco, NY , 1986, c1987. 1 videocassette (50 min.) : LC Card 86-707971 DDC 650.1 11
HF5386

Koestenbaum, Peter, 1928- The heart of business . San Francisco , New York, NY , c1987. xiii, 368 p. : ISBN 0-933071-15-9 : LC Card 87-13665 DDC 658.4/09 19
HF5351 .K584 1987

Mathew, Mohan, 1931- Dimensions of dialogue /. St. Louis, Mo. , c1984. 136 p. ; ISBN 0-918833-00-0 (pbk.) : LC Card 84-17009 DDC 302.5/44 19
HM291 .M392 1984 ***NYPL [JLD 86-4125]***

People skills in action, for loan officers and processors. Chicago, Ill. , 1986. 1 videocassette (20 min.) : LC Card 86-707349 DDC 658.8 11
HG1641

Person to person . Chicago, Ill. , c1986. 310 p. : ISBN 0-912857-33-1 (pbk.) LC Card 85-81996 DDC 332.1/068/8 19
HG179 .P368 1986 ***NYPL [JLE 86-3903]***

Pulvino, Charles J. Communicating with clients . Paramus, NJ , c1987. ix, 194 p. : ISBN 0-13-153578-1 (pbk.) LC Card 87-153498 DDC 332.1/068/8 19
HG179.5 .P86 1987

Sperber, Dan. Relevance . Oxford [Oxfordshire] , 1986. viii, 279 p. : ISBN 0-631-13756-4 ***NYPL [JFE 86-1728]***

Wilson, Gerald L., 1943- Organizational communication /. New York , c1986. xiv, 322 p. : ISBN 0-06-042387-0 LC Card 85-8723 DDC 658.4/5 19
HD58.7 .W55 1986 ***NYPL [JLE 86-2600]***

Wright, H. Norman. The family that listens /. Wheaton, Ill. , c1978. 142 p. ; ISBN 0-88207-633-7 : LC Card 78-57370 DDC 301.42/7
HQ734 .W9487 ***NYPL [JLD 81-655]***

INTERPERSONAL CONFLICT.
Gerstein, Arnold, 1940- Win-win approaches to conflict avoidance /. Salt Lake City, Utah , 1986. xvii, 110 p. : ISBN 0-87905-215-5 LC Card 85-26261 DDC 303.6 19
HM136 .G46 1986 ***NYPL [JLD 86-2104]***

Weiss, Donald H., 1936- How to deal with difficult people /. New York, N.Y. , c1987. 57 p. ; ISBN 0-8144-7674-0 (pbk.) : LC Card 86-47827 DDC 158/.2 19
HD42 .W45 1987

INTERPERSONAL CONFLICT - CONGRESSES.
Experimental social dilemmas /. Frankfurt am Main , New York , c1986. vi, 234 p. : ISBN 3-8204-8574-0 (pbk.) : LC Card 86-10307 DDC 302 19
HM132 .E96 1986 ***NYPL [JLD 87-1177]***

INTERPERSONAL CONFLICTS.
Madden, Tara Roth. Women vs. women . New York, NY , c1987. xxii, 266 p. ; ISBN 0-8144-5900-5 LC Card 87-47701 DDC 658.4/095/088042 19
HD6060 .M33 1987

INTERPERSONAL PERCEPTION. see **SOCIAL PERCEPTION.**

INTERPERSONAL RELATIONS - ADDRESSES, ESSAYS, LECTURES.
The Social psychology of female-male relations . Orlando , 1986. xvi, 351 p. ; ISBN 0-12-065280-3 (alk. paper) LC Card 85-9138 DDC 305.3 19
HM132 .S569 1986 ***NYPL [JLE 86-1746]***

Interplanetare Raumsonden /. Hubl, Peter. Lorch/Württemberg [1983?] 98 p. : LC Card 83-218116
HE6183.O95 H83 1983

INTERPLEADER. see **ACTIONS AND DEFENSES.**

Interpreting Mr. Keynes . Young, Warren, 1949- Boulder , 1986. p. cm. ISBN 0-8133-0533-0 : LC Card 87-10535 DDC 330.15/6 19
HB99.7 .Y68 1986

Interpreting the money supply . Graziano, Loretta. New York , 1987. xiii, 245 p. ; ISBN 0-89930-151-7 (lib. bdg. : alk. paper) LC Card 87-2539 DDC 332.4/14 19
HG226.3 .G72 1987

Interprofile conditions and impossibility /. Fishburn, Peter C. Chur, Switzerland , New York , c1987. viii, 93 p. ; ISBN 3-7186-0377-2 (pbk.) LC Card 86-31892 DDC 302/.13 19
HB846.8 .F67 1987

Interregionale Wanderungen in der Schweiz : Analyse der Volkszählung 1970 / F. Haag ... [et al.]. Zürich : Institut für Orts-, Regional- und Landesplanung, ETH, c1978. 2 v. : ill., col. maps ; 30 cm. (Berichte zur Orts-, Regional- und Landesplanung . Nr. 37a-37b) Bibliography: leaf x-xiv. CONTENTS. - Bd. 1. Ergebnisse und Beurteilung -- Bd. 2. Migrationstabellen. LC Card 85-215084
1. Migration, Internal - Switzerland. I. Haag, F. (Franz). II. Series.
HB2083 .I57 1978

Interrelationships among infant and childhood mortality, socio-economic factors and fertility in Zambia : a case study of Lusaka and Keembe. Lusaka : Central Statistical Office, Govt. of Republic of Zambia ; Addis Ababa : Population Division, United Nations Economic Commission for Africa, [1984?] 300 p. : ill. ; 29 cm. "E/ECA/POP/11." "UNFPA project No. ZAM/80/PO1." Bibliography: p. 298. LC Card 87-105950 DDC 304.6/32/096894 19
1. Infants - Zambia - Lusaka - Mortality. 2. Infants - Zambia - Keembe (Central Province) - Mortality. 3. Children - Zambia - Lusaka - Mortality. 4. Children - Zambia - Keembe (Central Province) - Mortality. 5. Fertility, Human - Zambia - Lusaka. 6. Fertility, Human - Zambia - Keembe (Central Province). 7. Lusaka (Zambia) - Statistics, Vital. 8. Keembe (Central Province, Zambia) - Statistics, Vital. I. Zambia. Central Statistical Office. II. United Nations. Economic Commission for Africa. Population Division.
HB1323.I42 Z335 1984

INTERROGATION. see **QUESTIONING.**

Interruptions de travail chez les femmes. Robinson, Patricia A. (Patricia Ann) Women's work interruptions . Ottawa [1987], c1986. 36, 40 p. ; ISBN 0-660-52895-9 (pbk.) : LC Card

87-146334 DDC 331.4/12/0971 19
HD6099 .R63 1987

INTERSECTIONS (HIGHWAY ENGINEERING) see **ROADS - INTERCHANGES AND INTERSECTIONS.**

Interstate business locational decisions and the effect of the state's tax structure on after-tax rates-of-return of manufacturing firms . New York (State). Legislature. Legislative Commission on the Modernization and Simplification of Tax Administration and the Tax Law. [Albany] [1984] 121 p. : LC Card 86-621116 DDC 336.2/07 19
HJ4655.N54 N55 1984

Interstate commerce . Burleson, Clyde W., 1934- New York , 1987. viii, 230 p. ; ISBN 0-531-15519-6 LC Card 86-29019 DDC 381/.5/0973 19
HF5387 .B856 1987

INTERSTATE COMMERCE.
Burleson, Clyde W., 1934- Interstate commerce . New York , 1987. viii, 230 p. ; ISBN 0-531-15519-6 LC Card 86-29019 DDC 381/.5/0973 19
HF5387 .B856 1987

INTERSTATE COMMERCE - TAXATION - BRAZIL - PERNAMBUCO - HISTORY.
Bezerra, Agostinho Fernandes. As tarifas internas na 1a. República /. Brasília, DF , 1986. xv, 140 p. : LC Card 87-404990 DDC 381/.5/098134 19
HJ5101.P47 B49 1986

INTERSTATE HIGHWAY SYSTEM.
St. Clair, David James, 1950- The motorization of American cities /. New York , 1986. xi, 192 p. ; ISBN 0-275-92126-3 (alk. paper) : LC Card 86-523 DDC 388.4/1321/0973 19
HE5623 .S617 1986 ***NYPL [JLE 86-3608]***

INTERSTATE HIGHWAY SYSTEM - ESTIMATES.
1987 estimate of the cost of completing the national system of interstate and defense highways in the State of Illinois, August 15, 1986 (data as of December 31, 1985) /. [Springfield] [1986?] v, 151 leaves : LC Card 87-620504 DDC 388.1/12/0973 19
HE355 .A514 1986

INTERSTATE HIGHWAY SYSTEM - ESTIMATES - VIRGINIA.
1987 estimate of the cost of completing the national system of interstate and defense highways in the Commonwealth of Virginia . [Richmond, Va.] [1986] 169 p. : LC Card 86-622650 DDC 388.1/12/09755 19
HE356.V8 A14 1986

INTERSTATE HIGHWAY SYSTEM - NEVADA - STATISTICS.
Log of the federal-aid interstate system comprising the Nevada primary state highway system, 1985 /. Carson City, Nev. [Washington] [1985] 41 leaves ; LC Card 86-622234 DDC 388.1/09793 19
HE356.N37 L632 1985

Interstate tax comparisons : individual taxpayers : a working paper / prepared by the Staff of the Legislative Commission on the Modernization and Simplification of Tax Administration and the Tax Law. [Albany, N.Y.] : The Commission, [1985] 106 p. ; 28 cm. At head of title: State of New York. "August 7, 1985." LC Card 86-621354 DDC 336.2/009747 19
1. Taxation - New York (State). 2. Taxation - United States. 3. Local taxation - New York (State). 4. Local taxation - United States. 5. Tax incidence - New York (State). 6. Tax incidence - United States. I. New York (State). Legislature. Legislative Commission on the Modernization and Simplification of Tax Administration and the Tax Law.
HJ2424 .I57 1985

InterStudy (Center) Oberg, Charles N. Medicaid, entering the third decade . Excelsior, Minn. (P.O. Box 458, Excelsior 55331-0458) , c1986. vii, 70 p. : LC Card 86-233259 DDC 362.1/0425/0973 19
HD7102.U4 O58 1986

Intertable (1986 : Basel, Switzerland) Interferex 86 (Basel, Switzerland) Interferex 86, Intertable . Basel, Schweiz [1986] 284 p., [6] p. of plates : LC Card 87-409294 DDC 381/.18 19
HF5474.S92 B365 1986

Intertechnik .
(23) Havemann, Hans A., 1912- Industrialisierungspolitik für Entwicklungsländer . Aachen , 1982. 68 p. ; ISBN 3-922525-06-7 LC Card 83-203761
HC59.7 .H386 1982

Intertemporale Produktionsentscheidungen . Wodopia, Franz-Josef. Frankfurt am Main , c1986. xx, 262 p. : ISBN 3-445-02403-0 LC Card 86-222211
HB241 .W63 1986

INTERURBAN RAILROADS. see **STREET-RAILROADS.**

A Intervenção do estado na economia : o caso café / Manoel Gonçalves Ferreira Filho ... [et al.]. Brasília, D.F. : Editora Universidade de Brasília, c1985. 83 p. ; 23 cm. (Cadernos da UnB) Includes bibliographies. CONTENTS. - Alguns aspectos da atividade de exportação de café em face de sua regulamentação interna e internacional / Manoel Gonçalves Ferreira Filho -- Notas sobre um modelo de intervencionismo estatal na economia / José Francisco Paes Landim -- A intervenção do estado no domínio econômico / Alberto Venâncio Filho -- A intervenção do estado na criação de um mercado de trabalho para a economía cafeeira no século XIX / Tereza Cristina Kirschner -- O regime jurídico da organização internacional do café / Oswaldo Trigueiro -- Fundamentos e limites constitucionais da intervenção do estado no domínio econômico / Tércio Sampaio Ferraz Júnior. ISBN 85-23-00198-0 : LC Card 87-102646 DDC 338.1/7373/0981 19
1. Coffee trade - Government policy - Brazil. I. Ferreira Filho, Manoel Gonçalves, 1934-. II. Series.
HD9199.B7 I628 1985

Intervenção no transporte : a ação da CMTC. [São Paulo, SP, Brasil : Companhia Municipal de Transportes Coletivos, 1985?] 31 leaves ; 22 cm. Cover title. LC Card 86-171230
1. CMTC (Firm : São Paulo, Brazil). 2. Bus lines - Brazil - São Paulo. I. CMTC (Firm : São Paulo, Brazil).
HE5653.S23 I58 1985

Las intervenciones financieras comunitarias /. Cuenca García, Eduardo. Madrid [1985?] 53 p. ; ISBN 84-7196-523-2 LC Card 85-200493
HJ2094.5 .C84 1985

Interventi (Guida editori) .
(27) Pasinetti, Luigi L. La ricchezza della nazioni /. Napoli , c1985. 35 p. ; ISBN 88-7042-841-9 : LC Card 86-196264
HB75 .P27 1985

L'intervento esterno nello sviluppo industriale del Mezzogiorno . Cercola, Raffaele. Napoli , c1984. 252 p. ; ISBN 88-7042-861-3 : LC Card 86-192219
HG5533.S68 C47 1984

Intervento straordinario e amministrazione locale nel mezzogiorno / di M. De Marco ... [et al.] ; a cura di Ugo De Siervo. Milano, Italy : F. Angeli, c1985. 348 p. ; 22 cm. (Istituzioni-ricerche dell'Irsi . 1) Includes bibliographical references. LC Card 86-144245
1. Industrial promotion - Italy. 2. Economic assistance, Domestic - Italy. 3. Local government - Italy. 4. Bureaucracy - Italy. I. De Marco, Maria. II. De Siervo, Ugo. III. Series.
HC310.I53 I58 1985

Interview with Professor Arthur Maass /. Reuss, Martin. Fort Belvoir, Va. , 1987. p. cm. LC Card 86-32033 DDC 333.91/15/0973 19
HD1694.A5 R46 1987

Interviewing skills /. Hodgson, Philip. London , New York , c1987. p. cm. ISBN 0-07-084941-2 : LC Card 87-3658 DDC 658.3/1124 19
HF5549.5.I6 H58 1987

INTERVIEWS - UNITED STATES.
Wacholtz, Larry E. Inside country music /. New York , 1986. 254 p. ; ISBN 0-8230-7532-X (pbk. : alk. paper) LC Card 86-4234 DDC 784.5/2/002373 19
ML3790 .W24 1986 ***NYPL [JNE 86-18]***

INTESTACY. see **INHERITANCE AND SUCCESSION.**

INTESTATE SUCCESSION. see **INHERITANCE AND SUCCESSION.**

INTOXICATION. see **ALCOHOLISM.**

Intra-industry trade and national competitiveness. MacCharles, Donald C. (Donald Clare), 1935- Trade among multinationals . London , New York , c1987. xiv, 207 p. ; ISBN 0-7099-4618-X LC Card 87-9077 DDC 382/.3 19
HF1411 .M2325 1987

INTRACOASTAL WATERWAYS - TEXAS.
The Gulf Intracoastal Waterway in Texas . [Austin] , 1982. 1 v. (various pagings) : LC Card 83-620632
HE631.T4 G44 1982

Intrapreneurship . Lessem, Ronnie. [Enterprise development.] Aldershot, Hants, England , Brookfield, Vt. , c1987. p. cm. ISBN 0-7045-0577-0 (pbk.) : LC Card 87-21608 DDC 658/.00941 19
HD70.G7 L45 1987

INTRAUTERINE CONTRACEPTIVES - COMPLICATIONS AND SEQUELAE.
Perry, Susan. Nightmare . New York , c1985. xvii, 261 p. ; ISBN 0-02-595930-1 : LC Card 85-13710 DDC 338.7/616139435 19
HD9995.C64 A236 1985
NYPL [JLE 85-3950]

INTRAUTERINE CONTRACEPTIVES INDUSTRY - UNITED STATES.
Perry, Susan. Nightmare . New York , c1985. xvii, 261 p. ; ISBN 0-02-595930-1 : LC Card 85-13710 DDC 338.7/616139435 19
HD9995.C64 A236 1985
NYPL [JLE 85-3950]

Intravenous theraphy [sic] supplies and equipment market in Europe. New York, N.Y. : Frost & Sullivan, c1983. xix, 317 p. ; 29 cm. Spine title: Intravenous therapy market in Europe. "August 1983." "#E569." LC Card 87-141784 DDC 380.1/45681761 19
1. Intravenous therapy equipment industry - Europe. 2. Market surveys - Europe. I. Frost & Sullivan. II. Title: Intravenous therapy supplies and equipment market in Europe. III. Title: Intravenous therapy market in Europe.
HD9995.I583 E854 1983

INTRAVENOUS THERAPY EQUIPMENT INDUSTRY - EUROPE.
Intravenous theraphy [sic] supplies and equipment market in Europe. New York, N.Y. , c1983. xix, 317 p. ; LC Card 87-141784 DDC 380.1/45681761 19
HD9995.I583 E854 1983

Intravenous therapy market in Europe.
Intravenous theraphy [sic] supplies and equipment market in Europe. New York, N.Y. , c1983. xix, 317 p. ; LC Card 87-141784 DDC 380.1/45681761 19
HD9995.I583 E854 1983

Intravenous therapy supplies and equipment market in Europe. Intravenous theraphy [sic] supplies and equipment market in Europe. New York, N.Y. , c1983. xix, 317 p. ; LC Card 87-141784 DDC 380.1/45681761 19
HD9995.I583 E854 1983

Introdução ao planeamento . Reigado, Felisberto Marques. Lisboa , 1983. 370 p. : LC Card 84-164510 DDC 361.2 19
HD85.P65 R45 1983 ***NYPL [JLD 86-3065]***

Introducción a la balanza de pagos de España /. Requeijo, Jaime. Madrid , 1985. 174 p. : ISBN 84-309-1221-5 LC Card 86-150983
HG3883.S69 R46 1985

Introducción a la cultura contemporánea .
(v. 3) La Presencia del tercer mundo /. San José, Costa Rica , 1982. 239 p., [1] leaf of plates : LC Card 83-161829
HC59.7 .P718 1982

Introducción a la economía para historiadores /. Tortella Casares, Gabriel. Madrid , 1986. xv, 192 p. : ISBN 84-309-1262-2 LC Card 86-219657
HB178.5 .T693 1986

Introducción a la financiación empresarial y al análisis bursátil /. Romero, Carlos, 1946- Madrid , c1984. 238 p. : ISBN 84-206-8080-X LC Card 85-135755
HG4011 .R57 1984

Introducción a la historia del movimiento obrero en Montijo : [estudio / realizado por la agrupación local del Partido Comunista de Extremadura ; y coordinado por Juan Carlos Molano Gragera]. [Montijo?] : Agrupación del Partido Comunista de España, [1982?] 103 p., 48 p. of plates : ill., ports. ; 22 cm. Bibliography: p. 103. ISBN 84-300-6966-6 LC Card 85-177027
1. Labor and laboring classes - Spain - Montijo -

History - 19th century. 2. Trade-unions - Spain - Montijo - History - 19th century. 3. Communism - Spain - Montijo - History - 19th century. I. Molano Gragera, Juan Carlos. II. Partido Comunista de España. *HD8590.M65 I57 1982*

Introducción a la teoría del crecimiento económico /. Outes Ruso, Xosé Luis, 1943- Sada, A Coruña , 1984. 359 p. : ISBN 84-7492-320-4 LC Card 87-105223 *HD75.5 .O97 1984*

Introducción a los problemas del subdesarrollo en América Latina /. Mora Forero, Jorge Rafael. Bogotá, D.E., Colombia , 1984. 96 p. ; ISBN 958-95030-9-8 LC Card 86-137776 DDC 338.98 19 *HC125 .M615 1984*

Introducción en la teoría de la planificación de la economía nacional /. Bereciuk, Román M. [Managua] , 1986. 93 leaves ; LC Card 87-403888 DDC 338.97285 19 *HC146 .B47 1986*

Introduction à la gestion prévisionnelle / sous la direction de J. D'Hoeraene, G. Chevalier, S. Lacrampe ; préface de Jules Lepidi. Lyon : Presses universitaires de Lyon, c1985. 337 p. : ill. ; 21 cm. Bibliography: p. [333]-334. ISBN 2-7297-0268-7 : LC Card 86-132861 DDC 658.4/0355 19
1. Corporate planning. 2. Management. 3. Budget in business. 4. Business forecasting. I. Hoeraene, J. d' (Jacques). II. Chevalier, Gérard. III. Lacrampe, Serge. *HD30.28 .I56 1985*

Introduction to ACH corporate payments / contributions by Patricia A. Murphy. Washington, D.C. (1901 L St., N.W., Suite 640, Washington 20036) : National Automated Clearing House Association, [c1986] 90 p. : ill. ; 23 cm. LC Card 86-222675 DDC 332.1/028 19
1. Electronic funds transfers - United States. 2. Clearinghouse - United States. 3. Corporations - United States - Finance. I. Murphy, Patricia A. II. National Automated Clearing House Association. *HG1710 .I58 1986*

An introduction to Bayesian inference in econometrics /. Zellner, Arnold. Malabar, Fla. , 1987, c1971. xv, 431 p. : ISBN 0-89874-995-6 LC Card 86-27796 DDC 330/.028 19 *HB139 .Z45 1987*

Introduction to business . Miller, Robert R., 1929- Homewood, Ill. , 1987. x, 138 p. : ISBN 0-256-05628-5 (pbk.) LC Card 86-82593 DDC 658/.049 19 *HD62.4 .M55 1987*

Introduction to business /. Straub, Joseph T. Boston, Mass. , 1988. xxi, 639, [66] p., [12] p. of plates : ISBN 0-534-87156-9 : LC Card 87-23276 DDC 658 19 *HD31 .S6965 1988*

An introduction to business accounting for managers /. Hartley, W. C. F. Oxford [Oxfordshire] , New York , 1987. xvi, 221 p. : ISBN 0-08-034789-4 : LC Card 87-6921 DDC 657/.024658 19 *HF5635 .H335 1987*

An Introduction to communication on the telephone [videorecording] / McGraw-Hill Training Systems ; [produced by] CRM Productions, Inc. ; script, Murray Krow. Del Mar, CA : McGraw-Hill Training Systems, 1987. 1 videocassette (7 min.) : sd., col. + 1 leader's guide. Title from data sheet. Telemarketing communication skills classes and senior high school through college students. Issued as U-matic 3/4 in. or VHS 1/2 in. Issued also as motion picture. Looks at communication skills used in successful telemaketing, focusing on techniques that use to full advantage the technology of today's telephone communication systems. LC Card 87-700082 DDC 658.8 11
1. Telemarketing. 2. Telephone etiquette. 3. Interpersonal communication. I. McGraw-Hill Training Systems (Firm). II. CRM Productions. *HF5415.1265*

Introduction to compiler construction with U.N.I.X. Schreiner, Axel T. Introduction to compiler construction with UNIX /. Englewood Cliffs , c1985. viii, 194 p. : ISBN 0-13-474396-2 LC Card 84-63039 ***NYPL [JSF 86-616]***

Introduction to compiler construction with UNIX /. Schreiner, Axel T. Englewood Cliffs , c1985. viii, 194 p. : ISBN 0-13-474396-2 LC Card 84-63039 ***NYPL [JSF 86-616]***

Introduction to computer information systems for business /. Simkin, Mark G. Dubuque, Iowa , c1987. xxvi, 678 p. : ISBN 0-697-00125-3 LC Card 86-72218 DDC 658/.05 19 *HF5548.2 .S4498 1987*

Introduction to corporate finance /. Maness, Terry S. New York , c1988. xxiii, 551 p. : ISBN 0-07-039934-4 : LC Card 87-21449 DDC 658.1/5 19 *HG4026 .M355 1988*

An introduction to cost and production functions /. Heathfield, David F. Atlantic Highlands, NJ , 1987. xv, 193 p. : ISBN 0-391-03506-1 LC Card 86-27587 DDC 338.5 19 *HB241 .H39 1987*

Introduction to data base management in business /. Bradley, James, 1942- New York , c1987. xii, 669 p. : ISBN 0-03-011924-3 LC Card 86-22914 DDC 658/.054 19 *HF5548.2 .B678 1987*

Introduction to database management in business. Bradley, James, 1942- Introduction to data base management in business /. New York , c1987. xii, 669 p. : ISBN 0-03-011924-3 LC Card 86-22914 DDC 658/.054 19 *HF5548.2 .B678 1987*

An introduction to econometrics /. Pokorny, Michael. Oxford, [Oxfordshire], UK , New York, NY, USA , 1987. p. cm. ISBN 0-631-15002-1 : LC Card 86-32707 DDC 330/.028 19 *HB139 .P635 1987*

An Introduction to economic development in Southern Africa and the role of DBSA / edited by R.J.W. van der Kooy. Sandton, Republic of South Africa : Development Bank of Southern Africa, [1985] 78 p. ; 30 cm. (Position paper . no. 4) "August 1985." LC Card 87-127414 DDC 338.968 19
1. Development Bank of Southern Africa. 2. Economic development. 3. Regional planning - South Africa. 4. Homelands, South Africa - Economic conditions. I. Van der Kooy, R. J. W. II. Series: Position paper (Development Bank of Southern Africa) , no. 4. *HG3401.A8 D485 1985*

Introduction to economic issues / Mahmoud H. Fouad ... [et al.]. Dubuque, Iowa : Kendall/Hunt Pub. Co., c1987. i, 220 p. : ill. ; 24 cm. Includes bibliographical references. ISBN 0-8403-4366-3 (pbk.) LC Card 87-80994 DDC 330 19
1. Economics. I. Fouad, Mahmoud H. *HB171 .I58 1987*

Introduction to economics . Robinson, Derek, 1932 (Feb. 9)- Cambridge, Cambridgeshire, England , Wolfeboro, N.H., USA , 1987. p. cm. ISBN 0-902197-53-3 (pbk.) : LC Card 87-3746 DDC 330 19 *HB171.5 .R65 1987*

Introduction to financial accounting /. Horngren, Charles T., 1926- Englewood Cliffs, N.J. , c1987. xx, 795 p. ; ISBN 0-13-483264-7 LC Card 86-25310 DDC 657 19 *HF5635 .H813 1987*

Introduction to financial management /. Schall, Lawrence D. New York , c1988. xvii, 856 p. : ISBN 0-07-055112-X LC Card 87-21450 DDC 658.1/5 19 *HG4011 .S33 1988*

Introduction to insurance /. Dorfman, Mark S., 1945- Englewood Cliffs, NJ , c1987. xix, 501 p. : ISBN 0-13-484809-8 LC Card 86-30319 DDC 368 19 *HG8051 .D65 1987*

Introduction to Japan's economic and political relations with the Middle East in the inter-war period . Shimizu, Hiroshi. Kent Ridge, Singapore [1985] v, 47 leaves ; LC Card 87-110444 DDC 337.52056 19 *HF1602.15.M626 S56 1985*

Introduction to knowledge base systems /. Frost, R. A. (Richard A.) London , 1986. xxi, 677 p. : ISBN 0-00-383114-0 ***NYPL [JFE 86-3366]***

Introduction to management accounting /. Horngren, Charles T., 1926- Englewood Cliffs, N.J. , c1987. xxi, 762 p. : ISBN 0-13-487885-X LC Card 86-25138 DDC 658.1/511 19 *HF5635 .H814 1987*

Introduction to modern macroeconomics /. Havrilesky, Thomas M. Arlington Heights, Ill. , c1988. p. cm. ISBN 0-88295-414-8 LC Card 87-24456 DDC 339 19 *HB172.5 .H38 1988*

Introduction to nonprofit organization accounting /. Henke, Emerson O. Boston , c1988. xvi, 670 p. : ISBN 0-534-08322-6 LC Card 87-7330 DDC 657/.98 19 *HF5686.N56 H45 1988*

Introduction to occupational health and safety / Joseph LaDou, editor-in-chief. Chicago, Ill. : National Safety Council, c1986. xvii, 519 p. : ill. ; 23 cm. Includes bibliographies and index. ISBN 0-87912-133-5 LC Card 84-61216 DDC 658.3/82 19
1. Industrial hygiene. 2. Industrial safety. I. LaDou, Joseph, 1938-. II. National Safety Council. *HD7261 .I68 1986*

Introduction to office systems . Bergerud, Marly, 1942- New York , c1987. xvi, 440 p., [12] p. of plates : ISBN 0-471-85532-4 (pbk.) LC Card 86-28188 DDC 652/.5 19 *HF5548.115 .B462 1987*

Introduction to social science /. Bagby, Wesley Marvin, 1922- Chicago , c1987. xv, 427 p. : ISBN 0-8304-1146-1 LC Card 86-23487 DDC 306/.0973 19 *HC106.8 .B34 1987*

An introduction to the mathematics of finance /. McCutcheon, J. J. (John J.) London , 1986. x, 463 p. : ISBN 0-434-91224-7 (pbk.) : LC Card 86-219539 DDC 332/.01/51 19 *HF5691 .M385 1986*

Introduction to the theory of traffic flow /. Leutzbach, Wilhelm. [Einführung in die Theorie des Verkehrsflusses. English.] Berlin , New York , c1988. xi, 204 p. : ISBN 0-387-17113-4 (U. S.) : LC Card 87-9839 DDC 388.3/143 19 *HE336.T7 L4813 1988*

Introductory economics /. Gordon, Sanford D. Lexington, Mass. , c1987. xviii, 490 p. : ISBN 0-669-09119-7 LC Card 86-80503 DDC 330.973/092 19 *HB171.5 .G648 1987*

Introductory economics /. McCarty, Marilu Hurt. Glenview, Ill. , c1988. xxxvii, 929 p. : ISBN 0-673-18320-3 : LC Card 87-23469 DDC 330 19 *HB171.5 .M465 1988*

Introductory investment theory /. Haugen, Robert A. Englewood Cliffs, N.J. , c1987. xv, 524 p. : ISBN 0-13-501933-8 LC Card 86-25373 DDC 332.6 19 *HG4529 .H378 1987*

Introductory macroeconomics /. McCarty, Marilu Hurt. Glenview, Ill. , c1988. xxiii, 533 p. : ISBN 0-673-18432-3 (pbk.) : LC Card 87-23434 DDC 339 19 *HB172.5 .M37 1988*

Introductory microeconomics /. McCarty, Marilu Hurt. Glenview, Ill. , c1988. xxiv, 550 p. : ISBN 0-673-18433-1 (pbk.) : LC Card 87-18046 DDC 338.5 19 *HB172 .M385 1988*

Introductory optimization dynamics . Tu, Pierre N. V. (Pierre Ninh Van) Berlin , New York , 1984. xiii, 387 p. : ISBN 0-387-13305-4 (U. S.) ***NYPL [JSE 86-1520]***

Introduktion av naturgas i Sverige : en översikt av industri- och sysselsättningspolitiska effekter. Stockholm : Statens industriverk, 1978. ii, 16, 13, 11 p. ; 30 cm. (SIND PM, 0346-573X . 1978:4) ISBN 91-38-04192-8 LC Card 83-238196
1. Gas industry - Sweden. 2. Sweden - Economic conditions - 1945-. 3. Gas, Natural - Sweden. I. Sweden. Statens industriverk. II. Series. *HD9581.S82 I58 1978*

Introduktion til ledelseslære /. Johnsen, Erik, 1928- [Copenhagen] , 1984, c1983. 109 p. : ISBN 87-17-03424-8 LC Card 85-127809 *HD57.7 .J64 1983*

Introduktion til ledelseslære /. Johnsen, Erik, 1928- [Copenhagen] , 1986, c1983. 134 p. : ISBN 87-17-03470-1 LC Card 87-108605 *HD57.7 .J64 1986*

INV .
(4) Birbuet D., Gustavo. Tierra y ganado en Pacajes . La Paz, Bolivia , 1986. 86 p. : LC

Card 87-403087 DDC 333.3/0984/12 19
HD490.C34 B57 1986

INVALIDITY INSURANCE. see **INSURANCE, DISABILITY.**

Inventaire : instituts de recherche et de formation en matière de développement en Afrique / Centre de développement de l'OCDE [et] Conseil pour le développement de la recherche économique et sociale en Afrique = Directory : development research and training institutes in Africa / OECD Development Centre [and] Council for the Development of Economic and Social Research in Africa (CODESRIA). Paris : Organisation de coopération et de développement économiques, Service des publications ; [Washington, D.C. : OECD Publications and Information Centre, distributor], 1986. xxvii, 262 p. ; 27 cm. English and French. Includes indexes. ISBN 92-64-02871-4 : LC Card 87-129509
1. Economic development - Research - Africa - Directories. 2. Economic development - Study and teaching - Africa - Directories. 3. Social sciences - Research - Africa - Directories. 4. Social sciences - Study and teaching - Africa - Directories. I. Organisation for Economic Co-operation and Development. Development Centre. II. Codesria. III. Title: Directory.
HD77.5.A34 I58 1986

Inventaire du secteur parapublic au Burundi, 1960-1984 /. Ndabahagamye, Illuminata. Bujumbura, Burundi , c1986. 211 p. : LC Card 86-981403
HD4348 .N3 1986

Inventario, evaluación e integración de los recursos naturales de la zona Esperanza-Chandles-Yaco / República del Perú, Oficina Nacional de Evaluación de Recursos Naturales (ONERN). Lima, Perú : ONERN, 1980. v, xi, 229, 24, [12] p. of plates : ill., maps (some col.) ; 29 cm. (Estudios. 50) Seven folded maps in pocket. LC Card 84-155289
1. Natural resources - Peru - Esperanza Region (Loreto). 2. Natural resources - Peru - Chandles River Valley. 3. Natural resources - Peru - Yaco River Valley. I. Peru. Oficina Nacional de Evaluación de Recursos Naturales. II. Series: Estudios (Peru. Oficina Nacional de Evaluación de Recursos Naturales) , 50.
HC228.E86 I58 1980

Inventaris van het archief van Regeringscommissariaat voor de Buitenlandse Agrarische Aangelegenheden (RECOBAA), 1946-1950 /. Plas, W. [Hague] [1985] 111 p. ; LC Card 87-101964
HD9015.N42 P55 1985

Inventing American broadcasting, 1899-1922 /. Douglas, Susan J. (Susan Jeanne), 1950- Baltimore , c1987. xxix, 363 p. : ISBN 0-8018-3387-6 (alk. paper) LC Card 87-3717 DDC 384.54/0973 19
HE8698 .D685 1987

INVENTIONS - GERMANY (WEST)
Zörgiebel, Wilhelm W. Technologie in der Wettbewerbsstrategie . Berlin , c1983. xv, 322 p. : ISBN 3-503-02361-5 LC Card 84-158275
HD9703.G42 Z67 1983

INVENTIONS - HISTORY - 20TH CENTURY.
I'll buy that! . New York , c1986. 240 p. : ISBN 0-89043-046-2 LC Card 86-1281 DDC 303.4/83 19
HF5415.153 .I45 1986 ***NYPL [JLG 87-125]***

Inventions, innovations, and economic growth in Sweden . Papachristodoulou, Christos. Uppsala , c1986. iv, 187 p. : LC Card 87-672434
HC380.T4 P36x 1986

INVENTIONS - SWEDEN.
Papachristodoulou, Christos. Inventions, innovations, and economic growth in Sweden . Uppsala , c1986. iv, 187 p. : LC Card 87-672434
HC380.T4 P36x 1986

INVENTORIES AS COLLATERAL. see **INVENTORY LOANS.**

INVENTORY CONTROL - DATA PROCESSING.
Computer models for production and inventory control /. La Jolla, Calif. , c1984. ix, 148 p. : LC Card 84-189641 DDC 658.5/0028/54 19
TS157 .C63 1984 ***NYPL [JSF 86-930]***

INVENTORY CONTROL - MATHEMATICAL MODELS.
Computer models for production and inventory control /. La Jolla, Calif. , c1984. ix, 148 p. : LC Card 84-189641 DDC 658.5/0028/54 19
TS157 .C63 1984 ***NYPL [JSF 86-930]***
Fischer, Thomas. Kontrolltheoretische Entscheidungsmodelle . Berlin , c1982. x, 343 p. : ISBN 3-428-05111-4 :
NYPL [JLE 86-3084]
Pervozvanskaia, T. N. (Tat'iana Nikolaevna) Elementy teorii upravleniia zapasami . Leningrad , 1983. 108 p. : LC Card 84-217972
HD40 .P47 1983

INVENTORY FINANCING. see **INVENTORY LOANS.**

INVENTORY LENDING. see **INVENTORY LOANS.**

INVENTORY LOANS.
Robinson, David Alexander, 1909- Accounts receivable and inventory lending . Boston , 1987. xii, 299 p. : ISBN 0-87267-104-6 LC Card 86-32252 DDC 332.1/753/068 19
HG3752.3 .R63 1987

INVENTORY MANAGEMENT. see **INVENTORY CONTROL.**

Inventory management reprints. Falls Church, Va. : American Production and Inventory Control Society, c1986. ix, 548 p. : ill. ; 23 cm. "Includes articles from publications through May, 1985"--P. iii. Includes bibliographies. ISBN 0-935406-74-3 (pbk.) LC Card 86-70610 DDC 658.7/87 19
1. Inventory control. I. American Production and Inventory Control Society.
HD40 .I575 1986

Inventory of designated roads in Malaŵi, 1983. [Lilongwe, Malawi] : Transport Planning Unit, Economic Planning Division, Office of the President and Cabinet, 1984. i, 57 leaves : maps ; 30 cm. At head of cover title: Malaŵi Government, Office of the President and Cabinet. Chiefly tables. LC Card 86-980326 DDC 388.1/096897 19
1. Roads - Malawi - Statistics. I. Malawi. Transport Planning Unit.
HE367.M32 I58 1984

Inversión industrial en Costa Rica : aspectos importantes relacionados con su ejecución / Ministerio de Industria, Energía y Minas, Secretaría Ejecutiva de Planificación del Subsector Industrial (SEPSI).2a ed. [San José] : SEPSI, 1986. 171 p., [1] folded leaf of plates : ill. (some col.) ; 21 cm. Bibliography: p. 171. LC Card 87-400481 DDC 338.97286 19
1. Industrial promotion - Costa Rica. 2. Investments, Foreign - Costa Rica. 3. Investments, Foreign - Law and legislation - Costa Rica. I. Costa Rica. Secretaría Ejecutiva de Planificación del Subsector Industrial.
HC143.Z9 I535 1986

Inversiones extranjeras en América Latina . Sourrouille, Juan V. Buenos Aires [1984] viii, 142 p. : LC Card 86-183036
HG5160.5.A3 S64 1984

Las inversiones extranjeras en la Argentina, 1860-1914 /. Regalsky, Andrés Martín. Buenos Aires , c1986. 129 p. ; ISBN 950-25-1412-2 : LC Card 87-100719
HG5312 .R44 1986

Invertir en Asturias /. Martín Alonso, Arturo. [Spain] [1984?] 72 p. : ISBN 84-398-1662-6 LC Card 85-217277
HC387.A7 M37 1984

Investeren in Nederland / H. den Hartog ... [et al.]. 's-Gravenhage : Centraal Planbureau, [1986] 122 p. : ill. ; 24 cm. (Onderzoeksmemorandum . no. 17) "April 1986." Bibliography: p. 122. LC Card 86-231212
1. Investments - Netherlands. I. Hartog, H. den. II. Series.
HG5562 .I58 1986

Investering i industrirobotar : en studie av motiv, beslutsunderlag och lönsamhet / Data- och elektronikkommittén (DEK). [Stockholm] : LiberFörlag, [1983] 263 p. : ill. ; 21 cm. "Ds I 1983:9." Bibliography: p. 261. ISBN 91-38-07833-3 LC Card 84-218538
1. Robot industry - Sweden. 2. Robots, Industrial - Sweden. 3. Market surveys - Sweden. I. Sweden. Data- och elektronikkommittén.
HD9696.R623 S845 1983

Investidores institucionais . Pinto, Antônio Carlos Figueiredo. Rio de Janeiro , 1985. 74 p. : LC Card 86-140523
HG5332 .P56 1985

Investieren und Finanzieren . Schweizer, Max. Zürich , c1984. 176 p. : ISBN 3-85565-209-0 : LC Card 84-244976
HD9715.S92 S38 1984

Investigación agraria y crisis : Venezuela, Colombia, Ecuador, Perú, Bolivia : métodos y alcances de los trabajos sobre las formaciones agrarias y las crisis del agro / editor, Lê Châu. Quito : Corporación Editora Nacional, 1986. 498 p. : ill. ; 21 cm. (Biblioteca de ciencias sociales. v. 10) "Este libro resume el Encuentro-Debate sobre las Investigaciones Agrarias en el Area Andina que tuvo lugar del 9 al 14 de septiembre de 1985 en Quito"--P. [4] of cover. "Junta del Acuerdo de Cartagena [y] Institut français de recherche scientifique pour le développement en coopération." Includes bibliographical references. LC Card 87-400125 DDC 338.1/098 19
1. Agriculture - Economic aspects - Andes Region - Congresses. 2. Peasantry - Andes Region - Congresses. 3. Agricultural innovations - Andes Region - Congresses. 4. Andes Region - Rural conditions - Congresses. I. Lê-Châu. II. Encuentro-Debate sobre las Investigaciones Agrarias en el Area Andina (1985 : Quito, Ecuador). III. Board of the Cartagena Agreement. IV. O.R.S.T.O.M. (Agency : France). V. Series: Biblioteca de ciencias sociales (Quito, Ecuador) , v. 10.
HD1860.A53 I58 1986

Investigacion en la A.N.C.A.P. Uruguay. Asemblea General. Cámara de Representantes. Investigación en la Administración, Nacional de Combustibles, Alcohol y Portland /. [Montevideo] , 1935. 352 p. ; LC Card 85-105071
HD9574.U72 U78 1935

Investigación en la Administración, Nacional de Combustibles, Alcohol y Portland /. Uruguay. Asemblea General. Cámara de Representantes. [Montevideo] , 1935. 352 p. ; LC Card 85-105071
HD9574.U72 U78 1935

Investigacion en la ANCAP. Uruguay. Asemblea General. Cámara de Representantes. Investigación en la Administración, Nacional de Combustibles, Alcohol y Portland /. [Montevideo] , 1935. 352 p. ; LC Card 85-105071
HD9574.U72 U78 1935

Investigación universitaria contra subdesarrollo /. Losada Aldana, Ramón. Caracas , 1984. 288 p. ; LC Card 87-115963 DDC 338.987/0072 19
HD77.5.V4 L67 1984

Investigaciones sobre recursos humanos en América Latina . Elizaga, Juan C. (Juan Carlos) Santiago de Chile , 1972. 16 p. ; LC Card 83-103424
HA755 .U5 no. 91 HD5730.5.A6

Investigando o Caso Coroa-Brastel . Suplicy, Eduardo Matarazzo, 1941- Brasília , 1984. 215 p. ; LC Card 86-200269
HG4109 .S85 1984

Investigating accidents with STEP /. Hendrick, Kingsley. New York , c1987. xviii, 454 p. : ISBN 0-8247-7510-4 LC Card 86-24165 DDC 363.1/065 19
HD7262.25 .H46 1987

An investigation into the utilization of white women labour in the South African industry /. Van der Walt, Sunette. Bloemfontein [1976] 45 p. ; ISBN 0-08-688017-4 LC Card 85-153291
HD6212 .V36 1976

INVESTIGATIONS, GOVERNMENTAL. see **GOVERNMENTAL INVESTIGATIONS.**

Investing and trading /. Little, Jeffrey B. New York , c1988. 47 p. : ISBN 1-555-46627-3 LC Card 87-23852 DDC 332.6/78 19
HG4553 .L58 1988

Investing in broadcast stations : course manual. [Washington, D.C.] (1120 20th St., NW, Washington 20036) : Federal Publications Inc., c1987. 318 p. in various pagings : forms, maps ; 28 cm. CONTENTS. - The economics of broadcasting / Anthony M. Hoffman -- Evaluating and financing the deal / Richard L. Geismar -- Federal controls ; The acquisition contract / Victor E. Ferrall, Jr., John T. Scott -- Tax considerations / Raymond J. Wiacek. LC Card 87-115340 DDC 384.54/3/0681 19

1. Broadcasting - United States - Finance. 2. Investments - United States. I. Federal Publications Inc.
HE8689.8 .I58 1987

Investing in Japanese real estate /. Hines, Mary Alice. New York , 1987. xiv, 287 p. : ISBN 0-89930-184-3 (lib. bdg. : alk. paper) LC Card 86-30582 DDC 332.63/24/0952 19
HD918 .H55 1987

Investing in municipal bonds . Cooner, James J. New York , c1987. xvi, 233 p. : ISBN 0-471-84941-3 LC Card 86-28911 DDC 332.63/233/0973 19
HG4952 .C66 1987

Investing in real estate /. Case, Frederick E. New York , 1988. p. cm. ISBN 0-13-503260-1 : LC Card 87-19269 DDC 332.63/24 19
HD1382.5 .C365 1988

Investir au Maroc. Pourquoi, où et comment investir /. Casablanca, Maroc [1985] 126 p. ; LC Card 86-198948
HG5832.A3 P68 1985

Investissement et emploi /. Artus, Patrick. Paris , c1986. 260 p. : ISBN 2-7178-1196-6 : LC Card 87-125878
HG4028.C4 A74 1986

L'investissement-humain dans le développement socialiste /. Senegal. Présidence du Conseil du gouvernement. Direction de l'animation. Bureau d'études. [Dakar?] [1962] 51 leaves ; LC Card 82-206645
HC1045 .S465 1962

Investissements directs, coopération internationale et firmes multinationales /. Hugonnier, Bernard. Paris , 1984. 343 p. : ISBN 2-7178-0793-4 : LC Card 85-105926
HD2755.5 .H83 1984

Investitionen und Innovationen in kleineren Industriebetrieben . Nydegger, Alfred. Diessenhofen , c1983. viii, 317 p. : ISBN 3-7253-0196-4 LC Card 83-224277 DDC 658.1/592 19
HG4027.7 .N93 1983 ***NYPL [JLD 87-633]***

Investitionsbedingungen in der ASEAN-Region /. Jungnickel, Rolf. Hamburg , 1986. 346 p. : ISBN 3-87895-296-1 LC Card 86-192978
HG5740.8.A3 J85 1986

Investitionseinzelentscheidungen . Hoberg, Peter. Münster [1983?] xi, 244 p. : ISBN 3-88660-137-4 LC Card 84-132141
HG4515.2 .H63 1983

Die Investitionsentwicklung in Nordrhein-Westfalen 1970-1980. Düsseldorf : Landesamt für Datenverarbeitung und Statistik Nordrhein-Westfalen, [1984] 94 p. : ill. ; 30 cm. (Beiträge zur Statistik des Landes Nordrhein-Westfalen . Heft 508) Chiefly tables. LC Card 87-407315 DDC 943/.55 s 332.6/0943/55021 19
1. Investments - Germany (West) - North Rhine-Westphalia - Statistics. I. Landesamt für Datenverarbeitung und Statistik Nordrhein-Westfalen. II. Series.
HA1320.N6 A32 Heft 508 HG5503.N67

Die Investitionsgüterindustrie . Osterkamp, Rigmar. München , c1986. v, 199 p. ; ISBN 3-8039-0334-3 LC Card 87-401371 DDC 338.4/76218/091724 19
HD9705.D462 O88 1986

Investitionsplanung auf der Grundlage vager Daten . Hanuscheck, Randolf. Idstein , 1986. xiii, 196 p. : ISBN 3-925196-19-6 LC Card 86-230117
HG4521 .H2385 1986

Investitionsprozess : Vorbereitung und Durchführung von Anlageninvestitionen / herausgegeben von Dieter Berger, Rolf Schulze ; [Autorenkollektiv, D. Berger ... et al.].1. Aufl. Leipzig : Deutscher Verlag für Grundstoffindustrie, c1986. 432 p. : 53 ill. ; 24 cm. Includes bibliographical references and index. LC Card 86-193837
1. Capital investments - Germany, East. I. Berger, Dieter, Dr. sc. oec. II. Schulze, Rolf, Prof. Dr.-Ing.
HG4028.C4 I534 1986

Investitionsrechnung . Liebich, Burkhardt, 1957- Frankfurt am Main , New York , c1986. viii, 170 p. ; ISBN 3-8204-9826-5 LC Card 87-109973
HG4529 .L54 1986

Investitionsstrategien für stagnierende Branchen . Hergeth, Helmut H. A., 1956- Münster [1986?] xii, 261 p. : ISBN 3-88660-338-5 LC Card 87-134812 DDC 338.4/3677/00943 19
HD9863.5 .H39 1986

Investitionsverhalten und Unternehmensgrösse /. Uhlmann, Luitpold. Berlin , c1986. 307 p. ; ISBN 3-428-06010-5 LC Card 86-216522
HG4028.C4 U37 1986

INVESTMENT ADVISERS - CONGRESSES.
Management Skills for Investment Managers Seminar (1982 : Washington, D.C.) Management Skills for Investment Managers Seminar . Charlottesville, Va. (P.O. Box 3668, Charlottesville 22903) , c1983. vi, 62 p. : LC Card 83-244808 DDC 658.1/52 19
HG4621 .M36 1982 ***NYPL [JLF 87-425]***

INVESTMENT ADVISERS - LEGAL STATUS, LAWS, ETC. - UNITED STATES.
Seglin, Jeffrey L., 1956- Personal financial planning in banks . Boston , c1986. xvii, 205 p. ; ISBN 0-87267-059-7 LC Card 85-28738 DDC 332.1/7 19
HG1616.C87 S44 1986 ***NYPL [JLE 87-820]***

INVESTMENT ADVISERS - PROFESSIONAL ETHICS - UNITED STATES - HANDBOOKS, MANUALS, ETC.
Financial Analysts Federation. Standards of practice handbook . Charlottesville, Va. , New York, N.Y. , 1986. xii, 150 p. ; ISBN 0-938367-03-X (pbk.) : LC Card 87-138043 DDC 174/.9332 19
HG4921 .F38 1986

INVESTMENT ADVISERS - UNITED STATES.
Dunton, Loren. The financial planner . Chicago , c1986. xi, 306 p. : ISBN 0-88462-544-3 LC Card 85-23821 DDC 332.024/01 19
HG179.5 .D85 1986 ***NYPL [JLE 86-4019]***

INVESTMENT ADVISERS - UNITED STATES - DIRECTORIES.
Consultant compendium. Wellesley, MA , c1986. 1 v. (various pagings) : LC Card 87-115215 DDC 332.6/2 19
HG4907 .C66 1986

INVESTMENT ANALYSIS - ADDRESSES, ESSAYS, LECTURES.
CFA readings in fixed income securities analysis /. Charlottesville, VA (P.O. Box 3668, Charlottesville, VA 22903) , c1985. v, 255 p. : ***NYPL [JLF 86-1994]***

Investment analysis and management /. Huang, Stanley S. C. Boston , c1987. xiv, 605 p. : ISBN 0-205-10501-7 LC Card 87-986 DDC 332.6 19
HG4529 .H8 1987

Investment analysis and portfolio management. Cohen, Jerome Bernard, 1915- Homewood, Ill., 1973. xiv, 946 p. ISBN 0-256-01429-9 LC Card 72-98120
HG4521 .C5296 1973 ***NYPL [JLE 74-744]***

Investment analysis and portfolio management /. Cohen, Jerome Bernard, 1915- Homewood, Ill. , 1977. xvi, 819 p. : ISBN 0-256-01883-9 LC Card 76-15739
HG4521 .C5296 1977
NYPL [*R-Econ. 78-1366]

INVESTMENT ANALYSIS - CASE STUDIES.
López Navarrete, Gregorio. Análisis y diagnóstico de la empresa . Barcelona [1983?] 377 p. : ISBN 84-300-9587-X LC Card 87-113212
HG5634.5 .L67 1983

INVESTMENT ANALYSIS - DATA PROCESSING.
Nicholson, Norm. The individual investor's microcomputer resource guide /. Chicago , c1986. viii, 216 p. ; ISBN 0-930369-17-3 (pbk.) LC Card 86-204335 DDC 332.6/028/553 19
HG4515.5 .N53 1986

Sparks, L. E. Investment analysis using your IBM PC and compatibles /. Blue Ridge Summit, PA , c1985. xi, 224 p. : ISBN 0-8306-0859-1 : LC Card 85-17322 DDC 332.6/028/55365 19
HG4529 .S6 1985 ***NYPL [JLE 86-4621]***

INVESTMENT ANALYSIS - DATA PROCESSING - INFORMATION SERVICES - UNITED STATES - DIRECTORIES.
Nicholson, Norm. The individual investor's microcomputer resource guide /. Chicago , c1986. viii, 216 p. ; ISBN 0-930369-17-3 (pbk.) LC Card 86-204335 DDC 332.6/028/553 19
HG4515.5 .N53 1986

INVESTMENT ANALYSIS - ECONOMETRIC MODELS.
Alexander, Gordon J., 1947- Portfolio analysis /. Englewood Cliffs, N.J. , c1986. xiv, 306 p. : ISBN 0-13-686825-8 : LC Card 85-28317 DDC 332.6 19
HG4521 .A42 1986 ***NYPL [JLE 86-4286]***

INVESTMENT ANALYSIS - STANDARDS - UNITED STATES - HANDBOOKS, MANUALS, ETC.
Financial Analysts Federation. Standards of practice handbook . Charlottesville, Va. , New York, N.Y. , 1986. xii, 150 p. ; ISBN 0-938367-03-X (pbk.) : LC Card 87-138043 DDC 174/.9332 19
HG4921 .F38 1986

INVESTMENT ANALYSIS - UNITED STATES.
Dunton, Loren. The financial planner . Chicago , c1986. xi, 306 p. : ISBN 0-88462-544-3 LC Card 85-23821 DDC 332.024/01 19
HG179.5 .D85 1986 ***NYPL [JLE 86-4019]***

INVESTMENT ANALYSIS - UNITED STATES - CASE STUDIES.
Weber, Nathan. Communicating with security analysts /. New York, N.Y. (845 3rd Ave., New York 10022) , c1985. 22 p. : LC Card 86-212395 DDC 658.4/5 19
HD59 .W36 1985

Investment analysis using your IBM PC and compatibles /. Sparks, L. E. Blue Ridge Summit, PA , c1985. xi, 224 p. : ISBN 0-8306-0859-1 : LC Card 85-17322 DDC 332.6/028/55365 19
HG4529 .S6 1985 ***NYPL [JLE 86-4621]***

INVESTMENT AND SAVING. see SAVING AND INVESTMENT.

Investment and securities dictionary /. Thomsett, Michael C. Jefferson, N.C. , 1986. vii, 328 p. : ISBN 0-89950-225-3 : LC Card 85-43594 DDC 332.6/03/21 19
HG4513 .T48 1986 ***NYPL [JLE 87-450]***

Investment Bankers Association of America. Hillstrom, Roger. 1960-1969, a decade of corporate and international finance. New York [1972] 381 p. LC Card 72-175335 DDC 332
HG4907 .H54 ***NYPL [JLG 73-17]***

Investment banking /. Epstein, Rachel S. New York , c1988. 48 p. : ISBN 1-555-46630-3 LC Card 87-18194 DDC 332.66 19
HG4534 .E67 1988

Investment banking and diligence . Auerbach, Joseph, 1916- Boston, Mass. , c1986. x, 274 p. : ISBN 0-87584-171-6 (alk. paper) LC Card 86-319 DDC 332.66/0973 19
HG4910 .A94 1986 ***NYPL [JLE 86-3128]***

INVESTMENT BANKING - GERMANY (WEST) - CONGRESSES.
Langfristiges Anlagengeschäft, Risiko-Management und Controlling /. Düsseldorf , c1986. 148 p. : ISBN 3-7754-0016-8 LC Card 86-227044
HG4534 .L36 1986

INVESTMENT BANKING - JUVENILE LITERATURE.
Epstein, Rachel S. Investment banking /. New York , c1988. 48 p. : ISBN 1-555-46630-3 LC Card 87-18194 DDC 332.66 19
HG4534 .E67 1988

INVESTMENT BANKING - SPAIN - CASE STUDIES.
López Navarrete, Gregorio. Análisis y diagnóstico de la empresa . Barcelona [1983?] 377 p. : ISBN 84-300-9587-X LC Card 87-113212
HG5634.5 .L67 1983

INVESTMENT BANKING - UNITED STATES.
Auerbach, Joseph, 1916- Investment banking and diligence . Boston, Mass. , c1986. x, 274 p. : ISBN 0-87584-171-6 (alk. paper) LC Card 86-319 DDC 332.66/0973 19
HG4910 .A94 1986 ***NYPL [JLE 86-3128]***

Hillstrom, Roger. 1960-1969, a decade of corporate and international finance. New York

[1972] 381 p. LC Card 72-175335 DDC 332
HG4907 .H54 ***NYPL [JLG 73-17]***

Stevens, Mark, 1947- The insiders . New York , c1987. 256 p. ; LC Card 87-2537 DDC 364.1/68 19
HG4910 .S67 1987

INVESTMENT BANKING - UNITED STATES - CORRUPT PRACTICES.
Frantz, Douglas. Levine & Co. . New York , c1987. x, 370 p. : ISBN 0-8050-0457-2 LC Card 87-8521 DDC 364.1/68 19
HG2463.L48 F72 1987

INVESTMENT BANKING - UNITED STATES - TECHNOLOGICAL INNOVATIONS.
Trading in banking . [New York?] , c1986. iv ; LC Card 87-128754 DDC 332.1/0973 19
HG2491 .T7 1986

Trading in banking . New York , c1987. x, 137 p. ; ISBN 0-939853-00-0 (pbk.) LC Card 87-404278 DDC 332.1/0973 19
HG2491 .T697 1987

INVESTMENT BANKING - URUGUAY.
Compra de carteras . Montevideo [1986] 188 p. : LC Card 87-403157 DDC 332.1/09895 19
HG2954 .C66 1986

INVESTMENT COMPANIES. see **INVESTMENT TRUSTS.**

Investment Company Institute (U. S.). Research Dept. IRAs, the people's choice /. Washington, D.C. (1600 M St., N.W., Washington 20036) [1986?] 60 p. : LC Card 87-402800 DDC 332.024/01 19
HG1660.U5 I73 1986

Investment dealers' digest.

Investment dealers' digest. Corporate financing, 1950-1960. Hillstrom, Roger. 1960-1969, a decade of corporate and international finance. New York [1972] 381 p. LC Card 72-175335 DDC 332
HG4907 .H54 ***NYPL [JLG 73-17]***

Investment in Indonesia . Abdrabboh, Bob A. Dearborn, Mich., U. S.A. , c1987. ix, 124 p. : ISBN 0-915597-19-7 LC Card 86-82681 DDC 332.6/7322598 19
HG5752 .A534 1987

INVESTMENT IN REAL ESTATE. see **REAL ESTATE INVESTMENT.**

Investment incentives worldwide : a practical guide to national funding of capital investment projects / researched and compiled by Eurofi (UK) Limited. London ; Boston : Butterworths ; 518 p. : maps ; 24 cm. (IBI international business intelligence) ISBN 0-408-00990-X : LC Card 87-24928 DDC 332.6/7322 19
1. Investments. 2. Investments - Government policy. 3. Investments, Foreign. 4. Investments, Foreign - Government policy. I. Eurofi (UK) Limited. II. Series.
HG4516 .I58 1987

Investment markets . Ibbotson, Roger G. New York , c1987. ix, 294 p. : ISBN 0-07-031673-2 : LC Card 86-33740 DDC 332.6 19
HG4523 .I23 1987

INVESTMENT OF PUBLIC FUNDS - BARBADOS.
Barbados. Duffus Commission of Enquiry. Report /. [Bridgetown, Barbados] [1978] vi, 118, 270 p. : LC Card 82-243628 DDC 354.7298/10072 19
HJ2073.B37 B37 1978 ***NYPL [JLG 86-221]***

INVESTMENT OF PUBLIC FUNDS - NEW YORK (STATE)
Lost revenue . [Albany, N.Y.?] [1986] 13, 22 leaves ; LC Card 87-620567 DDC 336.2/009747 19
HJ3324 .L67 1986

INVESTMENT OF PUBLIC FUNDS - SPAIN - CASTILLA Y LEÓN.
García Villarejo, Avelino. Estructura financiera y actividad inversora de las administraciones públicas en Castilla y León /. Valladolid , 1984. 431 p. : ISBN 84-505-0331-0 LC Card 87-108720
HJ1249.C29 G37 1984

Investment opportunities : choose wisely to make every dollar count. 3rd ed. Chicago, Ill. : Institute of Financial Education, c1987. xi, 112 p. ; 28 cm. ISBN 0-912857-38-2 (pbk.) : LC Card 86-82750 DDC 332.6/78 19
1. Investments - United States. I. Institute of Financial Education.
HG4921 .I585 1987

Investment opportunities for the mid 1980's . Sterne, George F. San Diego, Calif. , c1985. 304 p. ; ISBN 0-940398-11-7 : LC Card 78-64396
NYPL [JLE 86-1720]

Investment opportunities in the field of small scale industries in Oyo State of Nigeria. Ibadan, Oyo State of Nigeria : Ministry of Trade, Industries, and Cooperatives, [1977?] v, 94 p., [15] p. of plates : ill., forms ; 24 cm. LC Card 86-173553 DDC 658.1/592/096692 19
1. Small business - Nigeria - Oyo State - Finance. 2. Investments - Nigeria - Oyo State. I. Oyo State (Nigeria). Ministry of Trade, Industries & Co-operatives.
HD2346.N52 O965 1977

Investment opportunity in textiles & clothing, Zimbabwe. [Harare, Zimbabwe] : Standard Chartered Bank Zimbabwe, [1985?] 72 p., [12] leaves of plates : col. ill. ; 30 cm. Cover title. LC Card 87-400412 DDC 338.4/7677/0096891 19
1. Textile industry - Zimbabwe. 2. Clothing trade - Zimbabwe. 3. Investments, Foreign - Zimbabwe. I. Standard Chartered Bank Zimbabwe. II. Title: Investment opportunity in textiles and clothing, Zimbabwe.
HD9867.Z552 I58 1985

Investment opportunity in textiles and clothing, Zimbabwe. Investment opportunity in textiles & clothing, Zimbabwe. [Harare, Zimbabwe] [1985?] 72 p., [12] leaves of plates : LC Card 87-400412 DDC 338.4/7677/0096891 19
HD9867.Z552 I58 1985

The investment performance of corporate pension plans . Berkowitz, Stephen A. New York , 1988. xi, 132 p. ; ISBN 0-89930-224-6 (lib. bdg. : alk. paper) LC Card 87-19030 DDC 332.6/7154 19
HD7105.45.U6 B475 1988

Investment planning. 2nd ed. Chicago, IL : R & R Newkirk, c1987. p. cm. ISBN 0-88462-694-6 LC Card 87-15222 DDC 332.6/78 19
1. Finance, Personal. 2. Investments. I. R & R Newkirk.
HG179 .I488 1987

Investment Seminars Incorporated. San Francisco '85 . Bethesda, Md. [1986] vi, 502 p. ; LC Card 87-132666 DDC 332.6 19
HG4508 .S215 1986

INVESTMENT TAX CREDIT.
Leibfritz, Willi. Steuerliche Investitionsförderung im internationalen Vergleich /. Berlin , c1985. 255 p. : ISBN 3-428-05776-7 LC Card 85-161706
HJ4631 .L38 1985

INVESTMENT TAX CREDIT - GERMANY (WEST)
Analyse der Wirksamkeit der Beschäftigungszulage . München , 1984. vii, 172 p. : LC Card 85-230164
HJ4720.A45 A53 1984

Behrens-Ramberg, Wolfgang. Steuerliche Anreize bei innovativen Investitionen kleiner und mittlerer Industrieunternehmen unter vergleichender Berücksichtigung nichtsteuerlicher Hilfen /. Stuttgart , c1985. 299 p. ; ISBN 3-7910-5007-9 : LC Card 86-124563 DDC 336.24/316 19
HJ2337.G3 B44 1985
NYPL [JLL 73-505 Nr.6]

INVESTMENT TAX CREDIT - LAW AND LEGISLATION - GERMANY (WEST)
Analyse der Wirksamkeit der Beschäftigungszulage . München , 1984. vii, 172 p. : LC Card 85-230164
HJ4720.A45 A53 1984

The investment theme in Australia's approach to international trade /. Callaghan, Bede, Sir, 1912- [Newcastle, N.S.W.] , 1979. 16 leaves ; ISBN 0-7259-0361-9 (pbk.) LC Card 82-133660
HG5892 .C35 1979

INVESTMENT TRUSTS - HANDBOOKS, MANUALS, ETC.
The Handbook of fixed income securities /. Homewood, Ill. , 1987. xxx, 1376 p. : ISBN 0-87094-745-1 LC Card 86-50815
NYPL [JLE 87-939]

INVESTMENT TRUSTS - MEXICO - HISTORY.
Medina Cervantes, José Ramón. El estado mexicano entre la inversión extranjera directa y los grupos privados de empresarios /. México, D.F. , 1984. 268 p. : ISBN 968-434-358-2 LC Card 86-222537
HG5162 .M43 1984

Investments . Jones, Charles Parker, 1943- New York , c1988. xiv, 697 p. : ISBN 0-471-85284-8 LC Card 87-23153 DDC 332.6 19
HG4521 .J663 1988

Investments . Mayo, Herbert B. Chicago , c1988. xx, 680 p. : ISBN 0-03-009769-X LC Card 86-29129 DDC 332.6/78 19
HG4521 .M37 1988

INVESTMENTS.
El ABC de la Bolsa. Barcelona [1983?] 93 p. : ISBN 84-383-0028-6 LC Card 86-139799
HG4521 .A213 1983

Anderson, Dennis, 1937- Economic growth and the returns to investment /. Washington, D.C. [1987] 93 p. : ISBN 0-8213-0918-8 (pbk.) LC Card 87-14178 DDC 338.9 19
HD75 .A53 1987

Beckman, Robert C. The downwave . Portsmouth, Hants , 1983. 216 p. : ISBN 0-903852-38-1 ***NYPL [JLE 86-3347]***

Bernstein, Jacob, 1946- Beyond the investor's quotient . New York , c1986. x, 214 p. : ISBN 0-471-82062-8 LC Card 85-12325 DDC 332.6 19
HG4521 .B443 1986 ***NYPL [JLE 86-2936]***

Breitbard, Stanley H. The Price Waterhouse book of personal financial planning /. New York , 1988. xi, 447 p. ; ISBN 0-8050-0387-8 LC Card 87-8493 DDC 332.024 19
HG179 .B727 1988

Brosset, Michel. Multinationale Bankenverflechtungen . Bern , c1983. vii, 245 p. : ISBN 3-258-03275-0 : LC Card 83-178197
HG1526 .B27 Bd. 79 HG3881

Brown, Carolann D. (Carolann Doherty), 1946- The money manager /. Norfolk, Va. , c1987. p. cm. ISBN 0-89865-531-5 : LC Card 87-5456 DDC 332.024 19
HG4527 .B675 1987

Browne, Harry, 1933- Why the best-laid investment plans usually go wrong . New York , c1987. 557 p. : ISBN 0-688-05995-3 LC Card 87-16593 DDC 332.024 19
HG179 .B748 1987

Cistelecan, Lazăr M. Procesul investițional /. București , 1983. 264 p. : LC Card 84-135967
HG5692 .C57 1983

Craig, Malcolm. Successful investment strategy /. Cambridge, England , Wolfeboro, N.H., USA. , 1988. p. cm. ISBN 0-85941-383-7 : LC Card 87-8325 DDC 332.6/78 19
HG4521 .C858 1988

Davidson, James Dale. Blood in the streets . New York , c1987. 386 p. ; ISBN 0-671-62735-X : LC Card 87-9935 DDC 332.6 19
HG4516 .D38 1987

Enke, Harald. Der Konsumeffekt der Investitionen . Tübingen , 1986. xii, 114 p. ; ISBN 3-88573-026-X LC Card 87-407594 DDC 339.4/3 19
HG4521 .E63 1986

Goobey, Alastair Ross. The money moguls . Cambridge [Cambridgeshire] , Wolfeboro, N.H. , 1987. viii, 19 p. : ISBN 0-85941-391-8 (U. S.) : LC Card 86-26669 DDC 332.6 19
HG4521 .G5558 1986 ***NYPL [JLE 87-826]***

Griffin, Paul A. Usefulness to investors and creditors of information provided by financial reporting /. Stamford, Conn. , c1987. xii, 294 p. ; ISBN 0-910065-24-1 (pbk.) LC Card 87-81637 DDC 657/.3 19
HF5681.B2 G79 1987

Hanuscheck, Randolf. Investitionsplanung auf der Grundlage vager Daten . Idstein , 1986. xiii, 196 p. : ISBN 3-925196-19-6 LC Card 86-230117
HG4521 .H2385 1986

Huang, Stanley S. C. Investment analysis and management /. Boston , c1987. xiv, 605 p. :

ISBN 0-205-10501-7 LC Card 87-986 DDC 332.6 19
HG4529 .H8 1987

Investment incentives worldwide . London ; Boston : 518 p. : ISBN 0-408-00990-X : LC Card 87-24928 DDC 332.6/7322 19
HG4516 .I58 1987

Investment planning. Chicago, IL , c1987. p. cm. ISBN 0-88462-694-6 LC Card 87-15222 DDC 332.6/78 19
HG179 .I488 1987

Jansen, Ansgar, 1954- Desinvesititionen . Frankfurt am Main , New York , c1986. 514 p. : ISBN 3-8204-9630-0 LC Card 86-205563
HG4515 .J36 1986

Jones, Charles Parker, 1943- Investments . New York , c1988. xiv, 697 p. : ISBN 0-471-85284-8 LC Card 87-23153 DDC 332.6 19
HG4521 .J663 1988

Krause, Lawrence A., 1940- Sleep-tight money . New York , c1987. 300 p. : ISBN 0-671-64023-2 LC Card 87-14806 DDC 332.024 19
HG179 .K664 1987

Lieberman, Anne M. Mastering money . Chicago, Ill. , Naperville, IL , c1987. xi, 267 p. : ISBN 0-88462-589-3 (pbk.) : LC Card 87-3655 DDC 332.024 19
HG179 .L486 1987

Madigan, Bob, 1949- The first-time investor /. New York , c1987. xxii, 276 p. : ISBN 0-13-942376-1 (pbk.) : LC Card 87-14399 DDC 332.6/78 19
HG4521 .M217 1987

Mamis, Justin, 1929- When to sell . New York , 1986, c1977. p. cm. ISBN 0-671-63605-7 LC Card 86-26971 DDC 332.6/45 19
HG6041 .M34 1986

Marsh, Michael G., 1935- How to invest offshore successfully /. Geneva, Switzerland , c1986. 207 p. : LC Card 86-212027 DDC 332.6/73 19
HG4538 .M3635 1986

Mayo, Herbert B. Investments . Chicago , c1988. xx, 680 p. : ISBN 0-03-009769-X LC Card 86-29129 DDC 332.6/78 19
HG4521 .M37 1988

Milling, Bryan E. Banking strategies for businesses . Radnor, PA , c1987. viii, 231 p. : ISBN 0-8019-7651-0 (pbk.) : LC Card 86-47959 DDC 658.1/592 19
HG4027.7 .M55 1987

Orban, John. Money in the ground . Oklahoma City , 1985. xv, 216 p. : ISBN 0-9615776-0-6 (pbk.) : LC Card 86-120440 DDC 332.63 19
HG6047.P47 O73 1985

Oweiss, Ibrahim M. What gold investors need to know about the collapse of the oil cartel /. Bethel, CT , c1986. 37 leaves : LC Card 86-209518 DDC 332.63 19
HG293 .O84 1986

Powell, James B. The Dow Jones-Irwin guide to high tech investing . Homewood, Ill. , c1986. xix, 356 p. : ISBN 0-87094-596-3 : LC Card 85-72178 DDC 332.6/7253 19
HG4521 .P63 1986 ***NYPL [JLE 86-2261]***

Rosenthal, Daniel M. The new case for silver /. Lafayette, CA , c1986. ix, 157 p. : ISBN 0-9615814-1-7 (pbk.): LC Card 86-208965 DDC 332.63/28 19
HG305 .R67 1986

Shilling, Dana. Real life, real answers . New York , c1988. xiv, 309 p. ; ISBN 1-557-10004-7 LC Card 87-19538 DDC 332.024 19
HG179 .S465 1988

Skousen, Mark. High finance on a low budget /. Alexandria, VA , c1987. 197 p. : LC Card 87-153152 DDC 332.6/78 19
HG179 .S528 1987

Soros, George. The alchemy of finance . New York , c1987. 351 p. : ISBN 0-671-63455-0 LC Card 87-4745 DDC 332.6/78 19
HG4515 .S67 1987

Sterne, George F. Investment opportunities for the mid 1980's . San Diego, Calif. , c1985. 304 p. ; ISBN 0-940398-11-7 : LC Card 78-64396
NYPL [JLE 86-1720]

Stigum, Marcia L. The Dow Jones-Irwin guide to bond and money market investments /. Homewood, Ill. , c1987. xiii, 298 p. : ISBN 0-87094-892-X : LC Card 86-71921
NYPL [*R-Econ. 87-1260]

Successful investing . New York , 1987. 529 p. : ISBN 0-671-64762-8 (pbk.) : LC Card 87-19736 DDC 332.6/78 19
HG4521 .S823 1987

Survey of advanced sales. Chicago , c1987. v, 214 p. : ISBN 0-88462-703-9 (pbk.) LC Card 87-13112 DDC 368/.0068/8 19
HG8091 .S87 1987

Talley, Madelon DeVoe. The passionate investors . New York , c1987. 260 p. : ISBN 0-517-56563-3 : LC Card 86-24281 DDC 332.63/22 19
HG4521 .T29 1987

Tobias, Andrew P. The only other investment guide you'll ever need /. New York , c1987. 271 p. ; ISBN 0-671-64166-2 LC Card 87-20494 DDC 332.6/78 19
HG4521 .T6 1987

Verhaegen, P. H. A. M., 1950- Strategisch investeringsbeleid /. Deventer , 1986. 223 p. : ISBN 90-267-1049-6 : LC Card 86-186994
HG4521 .V475 1986

Zweig, Martin E. [Winning with new IRAs.] Martin Zweig's winning with new IRAs /. New York, NY , c1987. xvi, 207 p. : ISBN 0-446-51276-1 LC Card 86-28203 DDC 332.024/01 19
HG1660.A3 Z94 1987

INVESTMENTS - ACCOUNTING.

Fricke, Gabriele. Rechnungslegung für Beteiligungen nach der Anschaffungskostenmethode und nach der Equity-Methode /. Bochum , 1983. xv, 374 p. : ISBN 3-88339-310-X : LC Card 83-218419
HF5686.I6 F75 1983

Liebich, Burkhardt, 1957- Investitionsrechnung . Frankfurt am Main , New York , c1986. viii, 170 p. ; ISBN 3-8204-9826-5 LC Card 87-109973
HG4529 .L54 1986

INVESTMENTS - ACCOUNTING - STANDARDS - UNITED STATES.

Accounting for options /. New York, NY (1211 Ave. of the Americas, New York 10036-8775) [1986] 182 p., [4] p. of plates (some folded) : LC Card 86-221314 DDC 657/.76 19
HF5686.I6 A28 1986

INVESTMENTS - ADDRESSES, ESSAYS, LECTURES.

Controlling interest rate risk . New York , c1986. xv, 414 p. : ISBN 0-471-82354-6 : LC Card 85-22504 DDC 332.8/2 19
HG1621 .C6 1986 ***NYPL [JLE 86-2850]***

INVESTMENTS - AFRICA, SOUTHERN.

Hanlon, Joseph. SADCC . London, U.K. , c1984. 110 p. : LC Card 86-148391 DDC 332.6/732268 19
HC900 .H35 1984

INVESTMENTS, AMERICAN.

Copeland, Vincent. Expanding empire . New York, N.Y. , 1972. 62 p. ; LC Card 87-404126 DDC 338.8/8973 19
HG4538 .C668 1972

Danielian, Ronald L. The forgotten deficit . Boulder , 1987. xii, 84 p. ; ISBN 0-8133-7450-2 (pbk. : alk. paper) LC Card 87-50654 DDC 332.6/7373 19
HG3883.U7 D36 1987

Kennedy, Charles R. Political risk management . New York , 1987. xiv, 163 p. : ISBN 0-89930-157-6 (lib. bdg. : alk. paper) LC Card 86-25588 DDC 332.6/7373 19
HG4538 .K44 1987

Thomsen, Stephen E. International capital flows and the United States . Washington, D.C. (1400 Eye St., N.W., Suite 510, Washington 20005) [1985] vi, 62 p. : LC Card 87-108428 DDC 332/.042/0973 19
HG4910 .T47 1985

Trepelkov, V. P. (Vasiliĭ Petrovich) Zarubezhnyĭ biznes amerikanskikh monopoliĭ /. Moskva , 1982. 239 p ; LC Card 83-114503
HG4538 .T7 1982

INVESTMENTS, AMERICAN - AUSTRALIA.

Skully, Michael T. American depositary receipts . [Melbourne] [1986] 44 leaves : LC Card 86-229206 DDC 332.6/7373/094 19
HG5892 .S58 1986

INVESTMENTS, AMERICAN - DEVELOPING COUNTRIES.

Rodman, Kenneth Aaron. Sanctity versus sovereignty . New York , 1988. p. cm. ISBN 0-231-06448-9 LC Card 87-24970 DDC 332.6/7373/01724 19
HG5993 .R63 1988

INVESTMENTS, AMERICAN - ISLANDS OF THE PACIFIC.

Doulman, David J., 1950- Options for U. S. fisheries investment in the Pacific Islands region /. Honolulu, Hawaii, U. S.A. , 1987. vi, 30 p. ; ISBN 0-86638-097-3 (pbk.) LC Card 87-9198 DDC 338.3/72758 19
HD9469.T83 I743 1987

INVESTMENTS, AMERICAN - LATIN AMERICA.

Hernández, Rafael. Estados Unidos y América Latina . La Habana , 1982. 209 p. : LC Card 87-403785 DDC 333.8/232/0973 19
HD9574.L3 H47 1982

INVESTMENTS, AMERICAN - LATIN AMERICA - HISTORY.

Stallings, Barbara. Banker to the Third World . Berkeley , c1987. xvii, 434 p. : ISBN 0-520-05726-0 (alk. paper) LC Card 86-24988 DDC 332.6/7373/08 19
HG5160.5.A3 S73 1987

INVESTMENTS, AMERICAN - PERU - HISTORY.

Barrón Coral, Marcial. Perú . [Lima?] 1983 ([Lima] : General S.R.L.) 191 p. ; LC Card 84-253120
HC227 .B3365 1983

INVESTMENTS, AMERICAN - SOCIAL ASPECTS.

Bruyn, Severyn Ten Haut, 1927- The field of social investment /. Cambridge , New York , 1987. xi, 304 p. : ISBN 0-521-33292-3 LC Card 86-26393 DDC 332.6 19
HG4910 .B77 1987

INVESTMENTS, AMERICAN - SOUTH AFRICA.

Fernández Tabío, Luis René. Apuntes sobre el capital financiero en Estados Unidos . La Habana , 1981 [i.e. 1982] ii, 74 p. : LC Card 87-401153
HG5851.A3 F47 1982

Hauck, David. U. S. corporate withdrawal from South Africa . Washington, D.C. (Suite 600, 1755 Massachusetts Ave., N.W., Washington 20036) [1986] 22 p. ; LC Card 86-209299 DDC 332.6/7373/068 19
HG5851.A3 H39 1986

Hauck, David. What happens when U. S. companies sell their South African operations? /. Washington, D.C. (Suite 600, 1755 Massachusetts Ave., N.W., Washington 20036) , c1987. 16 p. ; LC Card 87-163729 DDC 338.8/8973/068 19
HG5851.A3 H392 1987

Seidman, Ann Willcox, 1926- The roots of crisis in southern Africa /. Trenton, N.J. [1985] xvii, 209 p. : ISBN 0-86543-026-8 (pbk.) : LC Card 85-72995 DDC 968.06/3 19
E183.8.S6 S45 1985 ***NYPL [Sc E 86-368]***

South Africa, the UC connection /. Berkeley, Calif. , 1985. 39 p. : LC Card 86-201134 DDC 332.6/73794/068 19
HG5851.A3 S63 1985

The South African quagmire . Cambridge, Mass. , c1987. xvi, 444 p. ; ISBN 0-88730-191-6 LC Card 86-28754 DDC 320.5/6 19
HF1613.4.Z4 U67 1987

U. S. investments and bank loans in South Africa (supplemental material to the hearings and markups of January 31 and February 7, 1984, serial no. 98-14, on District of Columbia South Africa divestment) . Washington , 1985. vi, 24 p.: LC Card 85-602615 DDC 332.6/7373/068 19
HG5851.A3 U17 1985

United States Catholic Conference. Administrative Board. Divestment, disinvestment, and South Africa . Washington, D.C. , c1986. 36 p. ; ISBN 1-555-86137-7 (pbk.) LC Card 87-136857 DDC 332.6/7373/068 19
HG5851.A3 U55 1986

Voorhes, Meg. Black South African views on disinvestment /. Washington, D.C. (Suite 600, 1755 Massachusetts Ave., N.W., Washington 20036) [1986] 36 p. ; LC Card 86-209279 DDC 332.6/73/0968 19
HG5851.A3 V66 1986

Williams, Oliver F. The apartheid crisis . San Francisco , 1986. xiv, 124 p. : ISBN 0-06-250951-9 (pbk.) : LC Card 85-45726 DDC 332.6/7373/068 19
HG5851.A3 W55 1986 **NYPL [JLD 86-4023]**

INVESTMENTS, AMERICAN - SOUTH AFRICA - DIRECTORIES.
Newman, Anne, 1951- Foreign investment in South Africa and Namibia . Washington, D.C. [1984] ii, 279 p. ; ISBN 0-931035-00-7 (pbk.) LC Card 85-130985 DDC 332.6/73/0968 19
HG5851.A3 N49 1984 **NYPL [Sc F 85-173]**

INVESTMENTS, AMERICAN - STATISTICS.
U. S. direct investment abroad . Washington, D.C. , 1986. x, 41 p. ; LC Card 87-600815
HG4538 .U22 1986

INVESTMENTS, AMERICAN - VENEZUELA - HISTORY.
Carreras, Charles. United States economic penetration of Venezuela and its effects on diplomacy, 1895-1906 /. New York , 1987. 252 p. : ISBN 0-8240-8077-7 (alk. paper) : LC Card 87-23723 DDC 332.6/7373/087 19
HG5412 .C45 1987

INVESTMENTS - ANECDOTES, FACETIAE, SATIRE, ETC. - DICTIONARIES.
Joy, Maurice. Not heard on the street . Chicago, Ill. , c1986. viii, 133 p. ; ISBN 0-917253-40-X : LC Card 86-3213 DDC 332.6/0207 19
HG4513 .J69 1986 **NYPL [JLD 86-2885]**

INVESTMENTS, ARAB.
Mattione, Richard P. OPEC's investments and the international financial system /. Washington, D.C. , c1985. xi, 201 p. ; ISBN 0-8157-5510-4 : LC Card 84-23242 DDC 332.6/7314 19
HG4538 .M38 1985 **NYPL [JLE 86-3698]**

"Problema neftedollarov" . Moskva , 1984. 231 p. ; LC Card 85-189000
HC498 .P75 1984

INVESTMENTS, ARAB - CONGRESSES.
Seminar on Investment Policies of Arab Oil Producing Countries (1974 : Kuwait, Kuwait) Seminar on Investment Policies of Arab Oil Producing Countries, 18-20 February 1974, Kuwait /. [Kuwait] [1974?] 216 p. ; LC Card 87-400750 DDC 332.6/7353 19
HG5816.A3 S46 1974

INVESTMENTS - ARAB COUNTRIES - CONGRESSES.
Seminar on Investment Policies of Arab Oil Producing Countries (1974 : Kuwait, Kuwait) Seminar on Investment Policies of Arab Oil Producing Countries, 18-20 February 1974, Kuwait /. [Kuwait] [1974?] 216 p. ; LC Card 87-400750 DDC 332.6/7353 19
HG5816.A3 S46 1974

INVESTMENTS - ARGENTINA.
Resultados de la encuesta sobre expectativas de producción e inversión de las empresas industriales /. Buenos Aires , 1965. 81 leaves : LC Card 85-114982
HC180.I52 R47 1965

INVESTMENTS - AUSTRALIA.
Callaghan, Bede, Sir, 1912- The investment theme in Australia's approach to international trade /. [Newcastle, N.S.W.] , 1979. 16 leaves ; ISBN 0-7259-0361-9 (pbk.) LC Card 82-133660
HG5892 .C35 1979

INVESTMENTS - BANGLADESH.
Industrial investment schedule for small industry, 1982-85. Dhaka , 1982. v, 283 p. ; LC Card 84-900851 DDC 338.6/42/095492 19
HD2346.B27 I53 1982 **NYPL [JLF 87-269]**

INVESTMENTS - BRAZIL.
Loureiro, Orozimbo Roxo. Garimpando reminiscências /. São Paulo , 1976 (São Paulo : Grafikor) 317 p. ; LC Card 85-225740
HG5332 .L68 1976

INVESTMENTS - BRAZIL, CENTRAL WEST - HANDBOOKS, MANUALS, ETC.
Centro-Oeste . [Brasília] [1983] 196 p., [3] leaves of plates : LC Card 85-208305
HC188.C46 C47 1983

INVESTMENTS - BRAZIL - DIRECTORIES.
Guia ação . RJ [i.e. Rio de Janeiro] [1985 or 1986] 285 p. ; LC Card 87-405004 DDC 332.6/78/0981 19
HG5334.5 .G85 1985

INVESTMENTS - BRAZIL - ECONOMETRIC MODELS.
Werneck, Rogério L. Furquim. Desequilíbrio externo e reorientação do crescimento e dos investimentos . Rio de Janeiro-RJ [1983?] 130 p. ; LC Card 87-403024 DDC 338.981 19
HC187 .W47 1983

INVESTMENTS - BRAZIL, NORTHEAST.
Incentivos fiscais e financeiros para investimentos no Nordeste do Brasil /. Recife , 1985. 92 p. ; LC Card 87-404837 DDC 332.6/7322813 19
HJ2529.N6 I53 1985

Magalhães, Antonio Rocha. Industrialização e desenvolvimento regional . Brasília , 1983. 315 p. : LC Card 84-160221 DDC 338.981/3 19
HD3616.B84 N676 1983
NYPL [JLD 86-3120]

INVESTMENTS, BRITISH - AFRICA - HISTORY - 19TH CENTURY.
Parfёnov, I. D. (Igor´ Danilovich) Monopoliīa i imperiīa . Saratov , 1980. 191, [1] p. ; LC Card 81-142784
HD2845 .P36 1980

INVESTMENTS, BRITISH - CHILE - HISTORY - 20TH CENTURY.
Couyoumdjian, Juan Ricardo. Chile y Gran Bretaña . [Santiago] [1986] xvi, 340 p., [4] p. of plates : LC Card 86-222403
HF1516.5.G72 C68 1986

INVESTMENTS, BRITISH - CHINA - HISTORY.
Edwards, E. W. British diplomacy and finance in China, 1895-1914 /. Oxford [Oxfordshire] , New York , 1987. 212 p. : ISBN 0-19-822916-X : LC Card 86-28567 DDC 337.41051 19
HF1534.5.C5 E39 1987

INVESTMENTS, BRITISH - DEVELOPING COUNTRIES.
Mitsotaki, Alexandra Gourdain. Public development finance corporations . Paris , 1986. 40 p. ; LC Card 86-221546 DDC 332.6/734/01724 19
HG5993 .M57 1986

Nuscheler, Franz. Die Entwicklungspolitik der Regierung Thatcher . [Bonn] [1986] 93 p. : LC Card 86-186261
HC60 .N87 1986

INVESTMENTS, BRITISH - LATIN AMERICA - HISTORY - 19TH CENTURY.
Stone, Irving, 1923- The composition and distribution of British investment in Latin America, 1865 to 1913 /. New York , 1987. xi, 502 p. : ISBN 0-8240-1372-7 : LC Card 87-8540 DDC 332.6/7341/08 19
HG5160.5.A3 S76 1987

INVESTMENTS, BRITISH - LATIN AMERICA - HISTORY - 20TH CENTURY.
Stone, Irving, 1923- The composition and distribution of British investment in Latin America, 1865 to 1913 /. New York , 1987. xi, 502 p. : ISBN 0-8240-1372-7 : LC Card 87-8540 DDC 332.6/7341/08 19
HG5160.5.A3 S76 1987

INVESTMENTS, BRITISH - NAMIBIA.
UK companies and their subsidiary or related companies in South Africa and Namibia. London [1986] [18] p. ; LC Card 87-138700 DDC 338./8941/068 19
HG5851.A3 U39 1986

INVESTMENTS, BRITISH - SOUTH AFRICA.
UK companies and their subsidiary or related companies in South Africa and Namibia. London [1986] [18] p. ; LC Card 87-138700 DDC 338./8941/068 19
HG5851.A3 U39 1986

INVESTMENTS - CANADA.
Douglas, Gordon W. Energy and regional investment in Canada /. Calgary, Alta. [1983] x, 114 p. : ISBN 0-920522-28-9 (pbk.) : LC Card 83-160268 DDC 332.6/722 19
HD9502.C32 D68 1983 **NYPL [JLD 87-996]**

Hunter, W. T. Canadian financial markets /. Peterborough, Canada , c1986. 193 p. : ISBN 0-921149-01-8 (pbk.) LC Card 86-206029 DDC 332.6/0973 19
HG185.C2 H86 1986

INVESTMENTS - COLOMBIA.
Foro de Proyectos de Inversión Colombo-Venezolanos (1986 : Cúcuta, Colombia) La frontera colombo-venezolana, una región donde invertir /. Bogotá, D.E. [1986] 96 p. ; LC Card 87-403851 DDC 332.6/09861 19
HG5352 .F67 1986

INVESTMENTS - CONGRESSES.
San Francisco '85 . Bethesda, Md. [1986] vi, 502 p. ; LC Card 87-132666 DDC 332.6 19
HG4508 .S215 1986

INVESTMENTS - DATA PROCESSING.
Nicholson, Norm. The individual investor's microcomputer resource guide /. Chicago , c1986. viii, 216 p. ; ISBN 0-930369-17-3 (pbk.) LC Card 86-204335 DDC 332.6/028/553 19
HG4515.5 .N53 1986

INVESTMENTS - DECISION MAKING - ECONOMETRIC MODELS.
Hoberg, Peter. Investitionseinzelentscheidungen . Münster [1983?] xi, 244 p. : ISBN 3-88660-137-4 LC Card 84-132141
HG4515.2 .H63 1983

INVESTMENTS - DECISION MAKING - MATHEMATICS.
Quantitative methods for financial analysis /. Homewood, Ill. , c1987. xv, 229 p. : ISBN 0-87094-978-0 LC Card 86-72275 DDC 332.6/01/51 19
HG4515.3 .Q36 1987

INVESTMENTS - DECISION MAKING - STATISTICAL METHODS.
Haumer, Heinrich. Sequentielle stochastische Investitionsplanung /. Wiesbaden , c1983. 305 p. ; ISBN 3-409-13420-4 LC Card 83-190299
HG4515.2 .H38 1983

Quantitative methods for financial analysis /. Homewood, Ill. , c1987. xv, 229 p. : ISBN 0-87094-978-0 LC Card 86-72275 DDC 332.6/01/51 19
HG4515.3 .Q36 1987

INVESTMENTS - DICTIONARIES.
Downes, John. Barron's finance and investment handbook /. Woodbury, N.Y. , c1986. xiv, 994 p. : ISBN 0-8120-5729-5 : LC Card 86-10906 DDC 332.6/78 19
HG173 .D65 1986
NYPL [*R-Econ. 86-5261]

Hildreth, Sandra S. The A to Z of Wall Street /. Chicago, Ill. , c1988. 299 p. : ISBN 0-88462-711-X (pbk.) : LC Card 87-22615 DDC 332.6/03/21 19
HG4513 .H56 1988

Pessin, Allan H. More words of Wall Street . Homewood, Ill. , 1986. v, 269 p. ; ISBN 0-87094-701-X LC Card 86-70777
NYPL [JLE 86-4060]

Scott, David Logan, 1942- Wall Street words /. Boston , c1988. xi, 404 p. : ISBN 0-395-43747-4 LC Card 87-21444 DDC 332.6/03/21 19
HG4513 .S37 1988

Thomsett, Michael C. Investment and securities dictionary /. Jefferson, N.C. , 1986. vii, 328 p. : ISBN 0-89950-225-3 : LC Card 85-43594 DDC 332.6/03/21 19
HG4513 .T48 1986 **NYPL [JLE 87-450]**

INVESTMENTS - DICTIONARIES - ANECDOTES, FACETIAE, SATIRE, ETC.
Lansky, Bruce. Wall Street bull /. Deephaven, MN , New York , c1987. iii, 111 p. : ISBN 0-88166-100-7 (pbk.) : LC Card 87-16467 DDC 332.6/0207 19
HG4513 .L29 1987

INVESTMENTS - DJIBOUTI - CONGRESSES.
Djibouti, ville et pays en voie de développement . Djibouti [c1983] 2 v. : LC Card 87-131462
HC855.Z9 E443 1983

INVESTMENTS, DUTCH.
Kox, Henk. Kapitaal-export vanuit Nederland . Amsterdam , 1985. 136 p. : ISBN 90-71284-01-8 LC Card 85-237950
HG5562 .K69 1985

INVESTMENTS, EAST INDIAN.
Lall, Rajiv B. Multinationals from the Third World . Delhi , New York , 1986. 100 p. ; ISBN 0-19-561895-5 : LC Card 86-900021 DDC 338.8/8954 19
HG4538 .L274 1986

INVESTMENTS - ECONOMETRIC MODELS.
Hanuscheck, Randolf. Investitionsplanung auf der Grundlage vager Daten . Idstein , 1986. xiii, 196 p. : ISBN 3-925196-19-6 LC Card 86-230117
HG4521 .H2385 1986

INVESTMENTS - EUROPE - CASE STUDIES.
Vlitos, Irene. The European potential for a venture capital industry /. Menlo Park, CA (333 Ravenswood Ave., Menlo Park 94025) , c1986. 13 leaves : LC Card 86-220533 DDC 332.6/6 19
HG5428 .V56 1986

INVESTMENTS - EUROPE, EASTERN.
Brabant, Jozef M. van. Adjustment, structural change, and economic efficiency . Cambridge [Cambridgeshire] , New York , 1987. xviii, 480 p. ; ISBN 0-521-33455-1 LC Card 87-785 DDC 332.4/947 19
HG186.E82 B7 1987

INVESTMENTS, EUROPEAN - ARGENTINA - SANTIAGO DEL ESTERO (PROVINCE) - HISTORY.
Dargoltz, Raúl E. (Raúl Eduardo) La alianza anglo argentina . Buenos Aires [1983] 168 p. : LC Card 84-117468
HD9764.A73 S353 1983

INVESTMENTS, EUROPEAN - CANADA.
Bruns, Claudia. Westeuropean direct investment in Canada . Hamburg [1986] 18 p. : LC Card 86-191095
HG5152 .B78 1986

INVESTMENTS - EUROPEAN ECONOMIC COMMUNITY COUNTRIES - CONGRESSES.
Industrial investment in Europe . Dordrecht ; Boston : 389 p. ; ISBN 90-247-3270-0 LC Card 85-26036 DDC 332.6/7253 19
HG5430.5.A3 I54 1985
NYPL [JLE 86-2366]

INVESTMENTS, EUROPEAN - TURKEY - HISTORY - 19TH CENTURY.
Pamuk, Şevket. The Ottoman empire and European capitalism, 1820-1913 . Cambridge [Cambridgeshire] , New York , 1987. xii, 278 p. : ISBN 0-521-33194-3 LC Card 86-28386 DDC 330.956/01 19
HF1583.4 .P36 1987

INVESTMENTS - EVALUATION.
Wahl, Jack. Informationsbewertung und -effizienz auf dem Kapitalmarkt /. Würzburg , 1983. 211 p. : ISBN 3-7908-0308-1 LC Card 84-154688
HG4515 .W34 1983

INVESTMENTS, FOREIGN - AFRICA, WEST.
Transnationals and development. Manchester, England , 1984. i, 64 p. ;
NYPL [JLD 86-3224]

INVESTMENTS, FOREIGN, AND EMPLOYMENT - GERMANY (WEST)
Jungnickel, Rolf. Eigenimporte der deutschen Industrie /. Hamburg , 1984. 392 p. : ISBN 3-87895-256-2 LC Card 84-247605
HF3566.5 .J86 1984

INVESTMENTS, FOREIGN, AND EMPLOYMENT - GERMANY (WEST) - ADDRESSES, ESSAYS, LECTURES.
Multinationale Konzerne . Köln , c1982. 478 p. : ISBN 3-7663-0506-9 LC Card 82-196963 DDC 332.6/73/0943 19
HD5710.75.G3 M84 1982
NYPL [JLD 86-2753]

INVESTMENTS, FOREIGN - ARAB COUNTRIES.
Silsilat dalīl al-mustathmir fī al-aqṭār al-ʻArabīyah /. al-Kuwayt , <[1985]-. v. <2, 4-5, 7 > : LC Card 86-205217
HG5816.A3 S55 1985

INVESTMENTS, FOREIGN - ARGENTINA - HISTORY.
Regalsky, Andrés Martín. Las inversiones extranjeras en la Argentina, 1860-1914 /. Buenos Aires , c1986. 129 p. ; ISBN 950-25-1412-2 : LC Card 87-100719
HG5312 .R44 1986

INVESTMENTS, FOREIGN - ASIA, SOUTHEASTERN.
Jungnickel, Rolf. Investitionsbedingungen in der ASEAN-Region /. Hamburg , 1986. 346 p. : ISBN 3-87895-296-1 LC Card 86-192978
HG5740.8.A3 J85 1986

Sverkhmonopolii v I͡Ugo-Vostochnoĭ Azii /. Moskva , 1983. 219 p. ; LC Card 83-223670
HD2901 .S84 1983

INVESTMENTS, FOREIGN - ASIA, SOUTHEASTERN - CONGRESSES.
Wachstumsmarkt Südostasien . München , c1984. x, 807 p. : ISBN 3-8039-0292-4 : LC Card 84-249861
HF3790.8.Z5 W33 1984

INVESTMENTS, FOREIGN - BRAZIL.
Baer, Mônica. A internacionalização financeira no Brasil /. Petrópolis , 1986. 159 p. ; LC Card 86-200812
HG185.B7 B28 1986

INVESTMENTS, FOREIGN - BRAZIL - CONGRESSES.
Brazil and the Ivory Coast . Greenwich, Conn. , c1987. p. cm. ISBN 0-89232-819-3 : LC Card 87-3667 DDC 332/.042/0981 19
HG3891.5 .B72 1987

INVESTMENTS, FOREIGN - CHINA.
Business opportunities in China . Menlo Park, Calif. (333 Ravenswood Ave., Menlo Park 94025-3476) , c1984. 32 p. : LC Card 86-210279 DDC 338.8/8851 19
HC427.92 .B85 1984

Campbell, Nigel. China strategies . [Manchester, Greater Manchester] [Hong Kong] , c1986. xxiv, 161 p. : ISBN 0-903808-51-X (pbk.) LC Card 86-235360 DDC 332.6/7314/0951 19
HD2910 .C36 1986

China economic overview . [Victoria] [1985?] 111, [2] p. : ISBN 0-7726-0465-7 (pbk.) LC Card 86-202984 DDC 330.951/058 19
HC427.92 .C68 1985

Guide to China's foreign economic relations and trade. Investment special /. Hong Kong , 1983. 342 p. : ISBN 0-9627063-8-8 : LC Card 84-177660 DDC 346.51/07 345.1067 19
HG5784 .G835 1983 ***NYPL [*OVY 86-3398]***

Mathur, Iqbal. Strategies for joint ventures in the People's Republic of China /. New York , 1987. viii, 196 p. ; ISBN 0-275-92354-1 (alk. paper) : LC Card 87-7033 DDC 338.8/8851 19
HD62.47 .M38 1987

Oborne, Michael West. China's special economic zones /. Paris [Washington, D.C.] 1986. 185 p. : ISBN 92-64-12801-8 (pbk.) : LC Card 86-217671 DDC 338.6/042/0951 19
HC427.92 .O27 1986

The Open policy at work /. Beijing, China [1985] 281 p. ; LC Card 86-219666 DDC 337.51 19
HF1604 .O63 1985

INVESTMENTS, FOREIGN - CHINA - CONGRESSES.
Foreign capital and technology in China /. New York , 1987. xvii, 191 p. : ISBN 0-275-92716-4 (alk. paper) : LC Card 87-2450 DDC 332.6/7314/0951 19
HG5782 .F67 1987

INVESTMENTS, FOREIGN - COLOMBIA.
Perfiles económicos del Valle del Cauca, Colombia. Cali, Colombia [1981?] 40 p. : LC Card 86-120381 DDC 330.9861/520632 19
HC198.V3 P47 1981

INVESTMENTS, FOREIGN - CONGRESSES.
International Industrial Conference, 1st, San Francisco, 1957. Private investment /. New York , 1980, c1958. xi, 282 p. ; ISBN 0-405-13355-3 LC Card 80-606 DDC 332.6/7314
HG4538 .I537 1957d ***NYPL [JLD 81-249]***

Multinationals as mutual invaders . London , c1985. 217 p. : ISBN 0-7099-0935-7 : LC Card 86-673843
HG4538 .M85x 1985b

INVESTMENTS, FOREIGN - COSTA RICA.
Inversión industrial en Costa Rica . [San José] , 1986. 171 p., [1] folded leaf of plates : LC Card 87-400481 DDC 338.97286 19
HC143.Z9 I535 1986

INVESTMENTS, FOREIGN - DEVELOPING COUNTRIES.
Developing with foreign investment /. London , New York , c1987. viii, 327 p. ; ISBN 0-7099-4825-5 LC Card 87-3603 DDC 332.6/73/091724 19
HG5993 .D47 1987

Dworak, Brigitte M. Das Länderrisiko als bankbetriebliches Problem /. Berlin , c1985. 168 p. : ISBN 3-428-05761-9 LC Card 85-213576
HG5993 .D86 1985

Karagodin, N. A. Mezhdunarodnye korporat͡sii i sot͡sialʹno-ėkonomicheskie problemy razvivai͡ushchikhsi͡a stran /. Moskva , 1981. 196, [3] p. ; LC Card 82-162679
HC59.7 .K28 1981

Pankova, E. A. (Evgenii͡a Afanasʹevna) Vneshneėkonomicheskie svi͡azi razvivai͡ushchikhsi͡a stran . Moskva , 1985. 158 p. ; LC Card 86-130427
HF1413 .P36 1985

Riedel, James. Myths and reality of external constraints on development /. Aldershot, Hampshire, U.K. , Brookfield, Vt., USA , 1987. xvi, 111 p. : ISBN 0-566-05336-5 (pbk.) : LC Card 86-31801 DDC 330.9172/4 19
HC59.7 .R494 1987

Status report on concessional flows, April 1986. Washington, D.C., U. S.A. , 1986. 25 p. ; ISBN 0-8213-0789-4 (pbk.) LC Card 86-214496 DDC 336.3/435/091724
HG3891 .S7 1986

Strukturelemente der Weltgesellschaft . Frankfurt am Main , 1981. v, 356 p. : ISBN 3-7875-1727-8 LC Card 83-190809
HF1411 .S845 1981

INVESTMENTS, FOREIGN - DEVELOPING COUNTRIES - CONGRESSES.
International Industrial Conference, 1st, San Francisco, 1957. Private investment /. New York , 1980, c1958. xi, 282 p. ; ISBN 0-405-13355-3 LC Card 80-606 DDC 332.6/7314
HG4538 .I537 1957d ***NYPL [JLD 81-249]***

Las Transnacionales en el Paraguay /. Asunción, Paraguay [1985] 317 p. : LC Card 86-112866 DDC 338.8/88892 19
HD2840 .T7 1985 ***NYPL [JLD 86-2210]***

INVESTMENTS, FOREIGN - DIRECTORIES.
Kehrer, Daniel M. Directory for international investors /. New York, NY, U. S.A. , c1984. 130 p. in various pagings : ISBN 0-86604-175-3 (pbk.) LC Card 86-231996 DDC 332.6/73/025 19
HG4538 .K39 1984

INVESTMENTS, FOREIGN - DOMINICAN REPUBLIC.
Najri, José Antonio, 1948- Crisis, producción y desarrollo . Santo Domingo, Repúblic Dominicana , 1986 (Santo Domingo, República Dominicana : Editora Corripio) ix, 248 p. ; LC Card 87-102092
HF1502 .N34 1986

INVESTMENTS, FOREIGN - ECUADOR.
Ecuador, política económica--teoría y realidad. [Guayaquil] [1986- v. <1-3 > ; LC Card 87-105005
HF1519 .E3 1986

INVESTMENTS, FOREIGN - EGYPT.
Caselli, Clara. L'internationalisation bancaire en Egypte /. Milano [1982] 223 p. ; LC Card 83-132087 DDC 332.1/5/0962 19
HG3386.A6 C37 1982 ***NYPL [JLE 86-1969]***

INVESTMENTS, FOREIGN - EUROPE, EASTERN - HISTORY - ADDRESSES, ESSAYS, LECTURES.
International business and Central Europe, 1918-1939 /. [Leicester, Leicestershire] , New York , 1983. xxvii, 459 p. : ISBN 0-312-41982-1 : LC Card 83-13956 DDC 338.8/8843 19
HD2844 .I57 1983 ***NYPL [JLE 86-3697]***

INVESTMENTS, FOREIGN - EUROPEAN ECONOMIC COMMUNITY COUNTRIES - CONGRESSES.
Industrial investment in Europe . Dordrecht ; Boston : 389 p. ; ISBN 90-247-3270-0 LC Card

85-26036 DDC 332.6/7253 19
HG5430.5.A3 I54 1985
NYPL [JLE 86-2366]

INVESTMENTS, FOREIGN - FRANCE.
Savary, Julien, 1944- Les conséquences économiques de l'investissement étranger en France . Toulouse [1984] 24 p. ; LC Card 85-143217
HG5472 .S28 1984

INVESTMENTS, FOREIGN - GERMANY, WEST.
Esser, Carsten, 1960- Das Fremdkapital im Unternehmen als Insolvenzursache und die Möglichkeiten rechtlicher Steuerung der Finanzierungsgrundlagen /. Frankfurt am Main , New York , c1986. xvi, 131 p. (1 folded) ; ISBN 3-8204-9398-0 LC Card 86-229108
HG5501 .E85 1986

INVESTMENTS, FOREIGN - GOVERNMENT POLICY.
Investment incentives worldwide . London ; Boston : 518 p. : ISBN 0-408-00990-X : LC Card 87-24928 DDC 332.6/7322 19
HG4516 .I58 1987

INVESTMENTS, FOREIGN - GOVERNMENT POLICY - AFRICA - CONGRESSES.
National financial policies and capital formation in Africa . Dakar, Senegal [1986] iii, 205 p. ; LC Card 87-404123 DDC 332/.096 19
HG5822 .N38 1986

INVESTMENTS, FOREIGN - GOVERNMENT POLICY - ASIA, SOUTHEASTERN.
Ahn, Doo-Soon. Government policy towards FDI and the reaction of foreign investors in DCs /. Bochum [1985] 23, 33 leaves ; LC Card 86-219920 DDC 332.6/73225195 19
HG5780.5.A3 A34 1985

INVESTMENTS, FOREIGN - GOVERNMENT POLICY - COLOMBIA.
Wallace, Brian F. Ownership and development . Athens, Ohio , 1987. ix, 176 p. ; ISBN 0-89680-145-4 (pbk.) LC Card 86-33255 DDC 332.6/7322861 19
HD9734.C62 W35 1987

INVESTMENTS, FOREIGN - GOVERNMENT POLICY - CONGRESSES.
Direct foreign investment . New York , 1987. xvii, 227 p. ; ISBN 0-275-92717-2 (alk. paper) : LC Card 87-17750 DDC 332.6732 19
HG4538 .D557 1987

INVESTMENTS, FOREIGN - GOVERNMENT POLICY - DEVELOPING COUNTRIES.
Developing with foreign investment /. London , New York , c1987. viii, 327 p. ; ISBN 0-7099-4825-5 LC Card 87-3603 DDC 332.6/73/091724 19
HG5993 .D47 1987

INVESTMENTS, FOREIGN - GOVERNMENT POLICY - HISTORY.
Sekiguchi, Sueo. Technology transfer through direct foreign investment /. Ibaraki, Osaka, Japan , 1985. 61 leaves : LC Card 86-209818 DDC 332.6/7352 19
HC60 .S416 1985

INVESTMENTS, FOREIGN - GOVERNMENT POLICY - INDONESIA.
Dickie, Robert B. Foreign investment and government policy in the Third World /. New York , 1988. p. cm. ISBN 0-312-00520-2 : LC Card 87-25076 DDC 332.6/7322598 19
HG5752 .D53 1988

INVESTMENTS, FOREIGN - GOVERNMENT POLICY - KOREA (SOUTH)
Ahn, Doo-Soon. Government policy towards FDI and the reaction of foreign investors in DCs /. Bochum [1985] 23, 33 leaves ; LC Card 86-219920 DDC 332.6/73225195 19
HG5780.5.A3 A34 1985

INVESTMENTS, FOREIGN - GOVERNMENT POLICY - PAPUA NEW GUINEA.
Daniel, Philip. Foreign investment in Papua New Guinea . Canberra , 1986. x, 144 p. : ISBN 0-86784-761-1 (pbk.) LC Card 87-151193 DDC 332.6/7322953 19
HG5982.A3 D36 1986

INVESTMENTS, FOREIGN - GREAT BRITAIN.
Stopford, John M. Britain and the multinationals /. Chichester , New York , c1985. xiv, 282 p. : ISBN 0-471-90839-8 : LC Card 85-12352 DDC 338.8/8841 19
HD2845 .S76 1985 ***NYPL [JLE 86-924]***

INVESTMENTS, FOREIGN - HANDBOOKS, MANUALS, ETC.
Kemp, L. J. (Lynette J.) The Wardley guide to world money and securities markets /. London , 1984. xvii, 472 p. ; ISBN 0-903121-66-2 ***NYPL [JLG 86-203]***

INVESTMENTS, FOREIGN - HONDURAS.
Imagen de la estructura económica-social y explotación de los recursos naturales /. Tegucigalpa, D.C., Honduras, C.A. , 1973. viii, 334 p. : LC Card 86-177356
HC145 .I52 1973

INVESTMENTS, FOREIGN - HONDURAS - HISTORY - 19TH CENTURY.
Molina Chocano, Guillermo. Estado liberal y desarrollo capitalista en Honduras /. Tegucigalpa, Honduras , 1985. 136 p. : LC Card 86-233622
HG5202 .M65 1985

INVESTMENTS, FOREIGN - INDIA.
Dhawan, O. P. Non resident Indians . New Delhi , 1984. xvi, 428 p. ; LC Card 85-900577 DDC 346.54/07 345.4067 19
HG5732 .D43 1984 ***NYPL [JLE 86-1363]***

Foreign collaborations . New Delhi , 1986. xii, 362 p. ; LC Card 86-903089 DDC 332.6/73/0954 19
HG5732 .F67 1986

Puri, Vijay Kumar. Nabhi's manual for Indian residents abroad, 1985 /. New Delhi , 1985. xv, 352 p., [1] leaf of plate : LC Card 86-901951 DDC 346.54/07 345.4067 19
HG5732 .P83 1985

INVESTMENTS, FOREIGN - INDONESIA.
Abdrabboh, Bob A. Investment in Indonesia . Dearborn, Mich., U. S.A. , c1987. ix, 124 p. : ISBN 0-915597-19-7 LC Card 86-82681 DDC 332.6/7322598 19
HG5752 .A534 1987

The Oriental challenge . Delft, the Netherlands , 1987. 281 p. : ISBN 90-70879-62-X (pbk.) LC Card 87-170212 DDC 332.6/732259 19
HC445 .O75 1987

INVESTMENTS, FOREIGN - INDONESIA - BATAM ISLAND.
A Guide for investors. [Jakarta] [1984] 112 p. : LC Card 86-942985 DDC 332.6/73225981 19
HC448.B38 G85 1984

INVESTMENTS, FOREIGN - ITALY, SOUTHERN.
Cercola, Raffaele. L'intervento esterno nello sviluppo industriale del Mezzogiorno . Napoli , c1984. 252 p. ; ISBN 88-7042-861-3 : LC Card 86-192219
HG5533.S68 C47 1984

INVESTMENTS, FOREIGN - IVORY COAST - CONGRESSES.
Brazil and the Ivory Coast . Greenwich, Conn. , c1987. p. cm. ISBN 0-89232-819-3 : LC Card 87-3667 DDC 332/.042/0981 19
HG3891.5 .B72 1987

INVESTMENTS, FOREIGN - JURISPRUDENCE. see INVESTMENTS, FOREIGN - LAW AND LEGISLATION.

INVESTMENTS, FOREIGN - KOREA (SOUTH)
Doing business in Korea /. London , New York , 1987. xvi, 121 p. : ISBN 0-89397-276-2 (Nichols) : LC Card 87-5665 DDC 330.9519/5043 19
HC467 .D58 1987

INVESTMENTS, FOREIGN - LATIN AMERICA.
Díaz Alejandro, Carlos Federico. Trade, development and the world economy . Oxford, OX, UK , New York, NY, USA , 1988. p. cm. ISBN 0-631-15687-9 : LC Card 87-20836 DDC 337.8 19
HF1480.5 .D52 1988

Foreign direct investment in Latin America . New York , c1986. iv, 28 p ; ISBN 92-1-104189-9 (pbk.) LC Card 87-104207 DDC 332.6/73/098 19
HG5160.5.A3 F67 1986

Labarca, Guillermo. Los bancos multinacionales en América Latina y la crisis del sistema capitalista /. México, D.F. , 1979. 201 p. ; ISBN 968-429-155-8 LC Card 80-123755
HG2710.5.A6 L3 ***NYPL [JLC 81-147]***

Sauvant, Karl P. Trade and foreign direct investment in data services /. Boulder Colo. , 1986. xv, 223 p. : ISBN 0-8133-7085-X : LC Card 85-22701 DDC 332.6/712 19
HD9696.C63 L387 1986
NYPL [JLD 86-3043]

Zorn, Stephen. Minería y elaboración de minerales . Buenos Aires , 1986. ii, 84 p. ; LC Card 87-402781 DDC 338.2/098 19
HD9506.L252 Z67 1986

INVESTMENTS, FOREIGN - LATIN AMERICA - CASE STUDIES.
Sourrouille, Juan V. Inversiones extranjeras en América Latina . Buenos Aires [1984] viii, 142 p. : LC Card 86-183036
HG5160.5.A3 S64 1984

INVESTMENTS, FOREIGN - LATIN AMERICA - CONGRESSES.
El Perú frente al capital extranjero . Lima, Perú [1985] xl, 399 p. : LC Card 86-109611 DDC 332.6/73/0985 19
HG5392 .P47 1985 ***NYPL [JLD 87-384]***

Foreign investment, debt, and economic growth in Latin America /. New York , 1988. xix, 250 p. : ISBN 0-312-00936-4 : LC Card 87-18808 DDC 332.6/73/098 19
HG5160.5.A3 F675 1988

INVESTMENTS, FOREIGN - LAW AND LEGISLATION - CHINA.
Guide to China's foreign economic relations and trade. Cities newly opened to foreign investors /. Hong Kong , 1985. 385 p. : ISBN 962-7063-19-3 ***NYPL [*OVY 86-3400]***

Guide to China's foreign economic relations and trade. Investment special /. Hong Kong , 1983. 342 p. : ISBN 0-9627063-8-8 : LC Card 84-177660 DDC 346.51/07 345.1067 19
HG5784 .G835 1983 ***NYPL [*OVY 86-3398]***

INVESTMENTS, FOREIGN - LAW AND LEGISLATION - COSTA RICA.
Inversión industrial en Costa Rica . [San José] , 1986. 171 p., [1] folded leaf of plates : LC Card 87-400481 DDC 338.97286 19
HC143.Z9 I535 1986

INVESTMENTS, FOREIGN - LAW AND LEGISLATION - UNITED STATES.
Ausländische Investitionen in U. S.-Grundvermögen /. Herne , 1984, c1983. 86 p. ; ISBN 3-482-69041-3 LC Card 84-203818 DDC 346.43/07 344.3067 19
K3830.4 .A97 1984 ***NYPL [JLD 86-2326]***

INVESTMENTS, FOREIGN - LIBERIA.
Iyanda, Olukunle. Multinationals and employment in a West African sub-region . Geneva , 1984. iv, 49 p. ; ISBN 92-2-103623-5 (pbk.) : LC Card 86-213585 DDC 388.8/88664 19
HD2928.8 .I92 1984

INVESTMENTS, FOREIGN - MALAYSIA - HANDBOOKS, MANUALS, ETC.
Sales & distribution guide to Malaysia /. Oxford , New York , 1988. p. cm. ISBN 0-08-034987-0 (U. S.) : LC Card 87-21043 DDC 382/.61/09595 19
HG5750.6.A3 S25 1988

INVESTMENTS, FOREIGN - MEXICO.
Gies, Christoph. Die Spielregeln für Kapitalanlagen in Mexiko . Frankfurt , c1986. ix, 314 p. : ISBN 3-88323-603-9 LC Card 86-231145
HG5162 .G48 1986

México, una economía en transición /. México, D.F. , 1984-1985. 3 v. ; ISBN 968-18-1900-4 (v. 1) LC Card 86-235462
HC135 .M549 1985

INVESTMENTS, FOREIGN - MEXICO - HISTORY.
Medina Cervantes, José Ramón. El estado mexicano entre la inversión extranjera directa y los grupos privados de empresarios /. México, D.F. , 1984. 268 p. : ISBN 968-434-358-2 LC Card 86-222537
HG5162 .M43 1984

INVESTMENTS, FOREIGN - MOROCCO.
Pourquoi, où et comment investir /. Casablanca, Maroc [1985] 126 p. ; LC Card 86-198948
HG5832.A3 P68 1985

INVESTMENTS, FOREIGN - NAMIBIA - DIRECTORIES.
Bowers, Cathy. U. S. and Canadian investment in South Africa and Namibia . Washington, D.C. , c1986. xiii, 238 p. ; ISBN 0-931035-10-4 (pbk.) LC Card 86-209149 DDC 338.8/8973/068025 19
HG5851.A3 B69 1986

INVESTMENTS, FOREIGN - NIGERIA.
Biersteker, Thomas J. Multinationals, the state, and control of the Nigerian economy /. Princeton, N.J. , c1987. xvii, 344 p. : ISBN 0-691-07728-2 (alk. paper) : LC Card 86-25214 DDC 338.8/88669 19
HG5881.A3 B54 1987

Onimode, Bade. MNC's in Nigeria . Ibadan , 1983. ix, 144 p. ; ISBN 978-231-800-0 (pbk.) LC Card 86-195403 DDC 338.8/88669 19
HD2928 .O55 1983

INVESTMENTS, FOREIGN - PACIFIC AREA.
The Pacific rim . Vancouver , 1987, c1986. ix, 319 p. : ISBN 0-7748-0266-9 (pbk.) LC Card 87-140238 DDC 330.99 19
HF4030.7 .P33 1987

INVESTMENTS, FOREIGN - PACIFIC AREA - CONGRESSES.
The Industrial future of the Pacific basin /. Boulder , 1984. xvi, 285 p. : ISBN 0-86531-685-6 LC Card 83-51653 DDC 338.9/009182/3 19
HC681 .I53 1984 ***NYPL [JLD 86-3100]***

INVESTMENTS, FOREIGN - PAKISTAN.
Ahrens, Heinz-Dietmar. Towards reducing the dependence on capital imports . Wiesbaden , 1982. xvi, 337 p. : ISBN 3-515-03853-1 (pbk.) LC Card 86-214363 DDC 338.9549/1 19
HC440.5 .A726 1982

INVESTMENTS, FOREIGN - PAPUA NEW GUINEA.
Daniel, Philip. Foreign investment in Papua New Guinea . Canberra , 1986. x, 144 p. : ISBN 0-86784-761-1 (pbk.) LC Card 87-151193 DDC 332.6/7322953 19
HG5982.A3 D36 1986

INVESTMENTS, FOREIGN - PARAGUAY.
Parquet, Reinerio. Las empresas transnacionales en la economía del Paraguay. Santiago de Chile , 1987. 115 p. ; ISBN 92-1-321223-2 LC Card 87-404657 DDC 338.8/88892 19
HG5382 .P37 1987

INVESTMENTS, FOREIGN - PARAGUAY - CONGRESSES.
Las Transnacionales en el Paraguay /. Asunción, Paraguay [1985] 317 p. : LC Card 86-112866 DDC 338.8/88892 19
HD2840 .T7 1985 ***NYPL [JLD 86-2210]***

INVESTMENTS, FOREIGN - PERU - CONGRESSES.
El Perú frente al capital extranjero . Lima, Perú [1985] xl, 399 p. : LC Card 86-109611 DDC 332.6/73/0985 19
HG5392 .P47 1985 ***NYPL [JLD 87-384]***

INVESTMENTS, FOREIGN - POLITICAL ASPECTS - EVALUATION.
Ting, Wenlee. Multinational risk assessment and management . New York , c1987. p. cm. ISBN 0-89930-175-4 (lib. bdg. : alk. paper) LC Card 87-5970 DDC 658 19
HD61 .T56 1987

INVESTMENTS, FOREIGN - SIERRA LEONE.
Iyanda, Olukunle. Multinationals and employment in a West African sub-region . Geneva , 1984. iv, 49 p. ; ISBN 92-2-103623-5 (pbk.) : LC Card 86-213585 DDC 388.8/88664 19
HD2928.8 .I92 1984

INVESTMENTS, FOREIGN - SINGAPORE.
The Oriental challenge . Delft, the Netherlands , 1987. 281 p. : ISBN 90-70879-62-X (pbk.) LC Card 87-170212 DDC 332.6/732259 19
HC445 .O75 1987

INVESTMENTS, FOREIGN - SOUTH AFRICA.
African worker under apartheid. Brussels [1984]. 109 p. : ***NYPL [Sc D 86-730]***

Jenkins, Carolyn M. (Carolyn Marion) The economic implications of disinvestment for South Africa /. [Braamfontain?] , 1986. v, 100 p. ; ISBN 0-908371-51-9 (pbk.) : LC Card 87-164832 DDC 332.6/73/0968 19
HG5851.A3 J46 1986

The South African quagmire . Cambridge, Mass. , c1987. xvi, 444 p. ; ISBN 0-88730-191-6 LC Card 86-28754 DDC 320.5/6 19
HF1613.4.Z4 U67 1987

INVESTMENTS, FOREIGN - SOUTH AFRICA - DIRECTORIES.
Bowers, Cathy. U. S. and Canadian investment in South Africa and Namibia . Washington, D.C. , c1986. xiii, 238 p. ; ISBN 0-931035-10-4 (pbk.) LC Card 86-209149 DDC 338.8/8973/068025 19
HG5851.A3 B69 1986

Newman, Anne, 1951- Foreign investment in South Africa and Namibia . Washington, D.C. [1984] ii, 279 p. ; ISBN 0-931035-00-7 (pbk.) LC Card 85-130985 DDC 332.6/73/0968 19
HG5851.A3 N49 1984 ***NYPL [Sc F 85-173]***

INVESTMENTS, FOREIGN - SOUTH AFRICA - MORAL AND ETHICAL ASPECTS.
Sincere, Richard E. The politics of sentiment . Washington, D.C. : Lanham, MD ; xiv, 164 p. : ISBN 0-89633-116-4 (alk. paper) : LC Card 87-13441 DDC 332.6/73/0968 19
HG5851.A3 S56 1987

INVESTMENTS, FOREIGN - SPAIN.
Cordón Munilla, Publio, 1935- España y las inversiones extranjeras /. Zaragoza [1968?] 79 p. ; LC Card 86-144082 DDC 332.6/73/0946 19
HG5632 .C66 1968

INVESTMENTS, FOREIGN - SRI LANKA.
Karunaratne, S. W. Potential for foreign investment in rubber products manufacture with information on special projects and a selection of local collaborators /. [Colombo] , 1985. vii, 100 p. ; LC Card 86-902791 DDC 332.6/73/095493 19
HD9161.S752 K37 1985

INVESTMENTS, FOREIGN - THAILAND.
The Oriental challenge . Delft, the Netherlands , 1987. 281 p. : ISBN 90-70879-62-X (pbk.) LC Card 87-170212 DDC 332.6/732259 19
HC445 .O75 1987

INVESTMENTS, FOREIGN - UNITED STATES.
Danielian, Ronald L. The forgotten deficit . Boulder , 1987. xii, 84 p. ; ISBN 0-8133-7450-2 (pbk. : alk. paper) LC Card 87-50654 DDC 332.6/7373 19
HG3883.U7 D36 1987

Multinational corporations, OPEC, cartels, foreign investment, and technology transfer [microform] . Frederick, MD , 1987. microfilm reel ISBN 0-89093-552-1 (microfilm) : LC Card 87-6249 DDC 338.8 19
HD2755.5

Poniachek, Harvey A. Direct foreign investment in the United States /. Lexington, Mass. , c1986. xiii, 256 p. : ISBN 0-669-11076-0 (alk. paper) LC Card 85-40457 DDC 332.6/73/0973 19
HG4910 .P66 1986 ***NYPL [JLE 86-4295]***

Thomsen, Stephen E. International capital flows and the United States . Washington, D.C. (1400 Eye St., N.W., Suite 510, Washington 20005) [1985] vi, 62 p. : LC Card 87-108428 DDC 332/.042/0973 19
HG4910 .T47 1985

Tolchin, Martin. Buying into America . New York , 1988. p. cm. ISBN 0-8129-1667-0 : LC Card 87-40198 DDC 332.6/73/0973 19
HG4910 .T65 1988

INVESTMENTS, FOREIGN - VENEZUELA - HISTORY - 20TH CENTURY.
González G., Godofredo (González González) La revolución de Los Barrosos /. Caracas, Venezuela [19]87. xii, 276 p. ; ISBN 980-263-047-0 LC Card 87-400058 DDC 338.2/7282/0987 19
HD9574.V42 G59 1987

INVESTMENTS, FOREIGN - YUGOSLAVIA.
Bauwens, Jan G., 1924- Industrial co-operation and investment in Yugoslavia /. Luxembourg , Washington, D.C. , 1986. viii, 161 p. : ISBN 92-825-6410-X (pbk.) : LC Card 86-216364 DDC 332.6/73/09497 19
HG5682 .B38 1986

INVESTMENTS, FOREIGN - ZIMBABWE.
Investment opportunity in textiles & clothing, Zimbabwe. [Harare, Zimbabwe] [1985?] 72 p., [12] leaves of plates : LC Card 87-400412 DDC 338.4/7677/0096891 19
HD9867.Z552 I58 1985

Whitsun Foundation. Project 1.07 . Harare, Zimbabwe [1983?] 2 v. ; ISBN 0-7974-0597-6 LC Card 84-981092 DDC 380.1/096891 19
HF3902 .W48 1983 ***NYPL [JLM 87-272]***

INVESTMENTS - FRANCE.
Sassier, Philippe. Les Français à la corbeille /. Paris , c1985. 268 p. ; ISBN 2-221-04729-X : LC Card 86-126750 DDC 332.64/244 19
HG4583 .S27 1985

INVESTMENTS, FRENCH - CZECHOSLOVAKIA.
Segal, Paul Harold, 1946- The French state and French private investment in Czechoslovakia, 1918-1938 . New York , 1987. vi, 379 p. ; ISBN 0-8240-8041-6 (alk. paper) : LC Card 87-252 DDC 332.6/7344/0437 19
HG5470.3.A3 S44 1987

INVESTMENTS, FRENCH - DEVELOPING COUNTRIES.
Mitsotaki, Alexandra Gourdain. Public development finance corporations . Paris , 1986. 40 p. ; LC Card 86-221546 DDC 332.6/734/01724 19
HG5993 .M57 1986

INVESTMENTS, GERMAN - CANADA - HISTORY.
Meleghy, Gyula, 1955- Die Vermittlerrolle der Banken bei deutschen Investitionen in Nord- und Mittelamerika bis zum Ersten Weltkrieg /. [Köln?] 1983 (Köln : W. Kleikamp) 330 p. : LC Card 85-229675
HG3052 .M45 1983

INVESTMENTS, GERMAN - MEXICO - HISTORY.
Meleghy, Gyula, 1955- Die Vermittlerrolle der Banken bei deutschen Investitionen in Nord- und Mittelamerika bis zum Ersten Weltkrieg /. [Köln?] 1983 (Köln : W. Kleikamp) 330 p. : LC Card 85-229675
HG3052 .M45 1983

INVESTMENTS, GERMAN - UNITED STATES - HISTORY.
Meleghy, Gyula, 1955- Die Vermittlerrolle der Banken bei deutschen Investitionen in Nord- und Mittelamerika bis zum Ersten Weltkrieg /. [Köln?] 1983 (Köln : W. Kleikamp) 330 p. : LC Card 85-229675
HG3052 .M45 1983

INVESTMENTS - GERMANY, WEST.
Götz, Gerd, 1956- Bildschirmtext . Berlin , c1985. xi, 285 p. : ISBN 3-8007-1348-9 LC Card 87-125311 DDC 384.3/5/0943 19
HD9696.T463 G346 1985

Hergeth, Helmut H. A., 1956- Investitionsstrategien für stagnierende Branchen . Münster [1986?] xii, 261 p. : ISBN 3-88660-338-5 LC Card 87-134812 DDC 338.4/3677/00943 19
HD9863.5 .H39 1986

Krist, Herbert. Bestimmungsgründe industrieller Direktinvestitionen /. Berlin , c1985. 310 p. : ISBN 3-924859-01-9 LC Card 86-225379
HG4538 .K72 1985

INVESTMENTS - GERMANY (WEST) - ACCOUNTING.
Schäfer, Harald. Bilanzierung von Beteiligungen an assoziierten Unternehmen nach der Equity-Methode . Thun , c1982. xxiii, 428 p. ; ISBN 3-87144-714-5 LC Card 83-129280
HF5686.I6 S33 1982

INVESTMENTS - GERMANY (WEST) - ECONOMETRIC MODELS.
Lehnhardt-Ritter, Gerda. Das Kapitalanlageverhalten der deutschen Lebensversicherungsunternehmen im Wandel der Konjunktur . Karlsruhe , c1984. xxiii, 444 p. : ISBN 3-88487-067-X LC Card 85-171182
HG9078 .L44 1984

INVESTMENTS - GERMANY (WEST) - NORTH RHINE-WESTPHALIA - STATISTICS.
Die Investitionsentwicklung in Nordrhein-Westfalen 1970-1980. Düsseldorf [1984] 94 p. : LC Card 87-407315 DDC 943/.55

s 332.6/0943/55021 19
HA1320.N6 A32 Heft 508 HG5503.N67

INVESTMENTS - GOVERNMENT POLICY.
Investment incentives worldwide . London ; Boston : 518 p. : ISBN 0-408-00990-X : LC Card 87-24928 DDC 332.6/7322 19
HG4516 .I58 1987

INVESTMENTS - GREAT BRITAIN.
Craig, Malcolm. Successful investment strategy /. Cambridge, England , Wolfeboro, N.H., USA. , 1988. p. cm. ISBN 0-85941-383-7 : LC Card 87-8325 DDC 332.6/78 19
HG4521 .C858 1988

INVESTMENTS - GREECE.
Baltas, Nik. K. Chrēmatodotēsē ependyseōn tou agrotikou tomea . Athēna , 1984. 142 p. ; LC Card 86-201892
HD2055.5 .B35 1984

INVESTMENTS - GREECE - CONGRESSES.
Epistēmoniko Diēmero (1984 : Athens, Greece) Ependyseis kai trapezikes chorēgēseis se periodo krisēs . Athēna , 1984. 225 p. ; LC Card 86-193395
HG5700.5.A3 E85 1984

INVESTMENTS - HANDBOOKS, MANUALS, ETC.
Band, Richard E. Contrary investing . New York , c1985. viii, 197 p. : ISBN 0-07-003604-7 : LC Card 85-99 DDC 332.6/78 19
HG4527 .B233 1985 ***NYPL [JLE 86-1234]***

Burgauer, James. The do-it-yourself investor /. Chicago, Ill. , c1987. xi, 335 p. : ISBN 0-917253-68-X : LC Card 87-7006 DDC 332.6/78 19
HG4527 .B689 1987

Darst, David M., 1947- The handbook of the bond and money markets /. New York , c1981. xv, 461 p. : ISBN 0-07-015401-5 LC Card 80-36816 DDC 332.63/23
HG4527 .D37 ***NYPL [JLE 87-568]***

Downes, John. Barron's finance and investment handbook /. Woodbury, N.Y. , c1986. xiv, 994 p. : ISBN 0-8120-5729-5 : LC Card 86-10906 DDC 332.6/78 19
HG173 .D65 1986
NYPL [*R-Econ. 86-5261]

Dunnan, Nancy. How to invest $50-$5000 /. New York , 1987. 124 p. ; ISBN 0-06-096159-7 (pbk.) : LC Card 86-45862 DDC 332.6/78 19
HG4527 .D77 1987

Gardiner, Robert M. The Dean Witter guide for today's investor /. New York, NY , c1988. p. cm. ISBN 0-453-00582-9 LC Card 87-24168 DDC 332.6/78 19
HG4527 .G37 1988

Handbook of financial markets . Homewood, Ill. , c1986. xix, 785 p. : ISBN 0-87094-600-5 LC Card 85-71920 DDC 332.6/78 19
HG4527 .H25 1986
NYPL [*R-Econ 86-3815]

Handbook of financial markets--securities, options, futures /. Homewood, Ill. , c1981. xxiii, 794 p. : ISBN 0-87094-216-6 LC Card 80-70448 DDC 332.6/78 19
HG4527 .H25 ***NYPL [JLE 86-1500]***

Kemp, L. J. (Lynette J.) The Wardley guide to world money and securities markets /. London , 1984. xvii, 472 p. ; ISBN 0-903121-66-2 ***NYPL [JLG 86-203]***

Perritt, Gerald W. Expand your investment horizons and increase your stock market profits /. Chicago, IL , c1987. viii, 288 p. : ISBN 0-930369-03-3 (pbk.) LC Card 87-401495 DDC 332.63/2 19
HG4527 .P39 1987

Stein, Lawrence M. Value investing . New York , c1988. xiv, 331 p. : ISBN 0-471-62875-1 LC Card 87-23152 DDC 332.63/22 19
HG4527 .S816 1988

INVESTMENTS - HISTORY.
Armstrong, Martin A. The greatest bull market in history . [Princeton?] , <c1986-. v. <2 > : LC Card 87-138809 DDC 332.64 19
HG4516 .A75 1986

Investments in failure . Borins, Sandford F., 1949- Toronto , New York , c1986. x, 175 p. ; ISBN 0-458-80340-5 (pbk.) : LC Card 87-142330 DDC 354.7109/2 19
HD4005 .B67 1986

INVESTMENTS - INDIA.
Dixit, R. K. (Ramesh Kumar), 1946- Behaviour of share prices and investment in India /. New Delhi , c1986. 328 p. ; LC Card 86-902907 DDC 332.63/222/0954 19
HG5733 .D59 1986

INVESTMENTS - ITALY.
Rossi, Guido. La scalata del mercato . Bologna , c1986. 152 p. ; ISBN 88-15-01123-4 : LC Card 86-180921
HG5522 .R66 1986

INVESTMENTS - ITALY - ADDRESSES, ESSAYS, LECTURES.
Per una ristrutturazione e riconversione dell'industria italiana /. Bologna , 1980. 244 p. ; LC Card 82-102594 DDC 338.945 19
HD3616.I83 P43 ***NYPL [JLD 86-599]***

INVESTMENTS, JAPANESE.
Woronoff, Jon. Japan's commercial empire /. Armonk, N.Y. , c1984. 415 p. : ISBN 0-87332-312-2 LC Card 84-22146 DDC 337.52 19
HF1601 .W66 1984 ***NYPL [JLD 87-761]***

INVESTMENTS, JAPANESE - EUROPEAN ECONOMIC COMMUNITY COUNTRIES.
The Internationalization of Japanese business . Boulder , 1986. p. cm. ISBN 0-8133-0531-4 : LC Card 87-8186 DDC 338.8/8952/04 19
HD2844.5 .I567 1986

INVESTMENTS, JAPANESE - UNITED STATES.
Starr, Martin Kenneth, 1927- The performance of Japanese-owned firms in America, 1982-1985 /. [New York, NY] , c1987. ii, 41 leaves : LC Card 87-145262 DDC 338.8/8952/073 19
HD2785 .S66 1987

Yoshida, Mamoru. Japanese direct manufacturing investment in the United States /. New York , 1987. xiv, 220 p. : ISBN 0-275-92347-9 (alk. paper) : LC Card 86-22689 DDC 332.6/7352/073 19
HG4910 .Y58 1986 ***NYPL [JLE 87-1122]***

INVESTMENTS - JUVENILE LITERATURE.
Epstein, Rachel S. Alternative investments /. New York , c1988. 47 p. : ISBN 1-555-46633-8 LC Card 87-21766 DDC 332.6/78 19
HG4521 .E685 1988

Little, Jeffrey B. Investing and trading /. New York , c1988. 47 p. : ISBN 1-555-46627-3 LC Card 87-23852 DDC 332.6/78 19
HG4553 .L58 1988

INVESTMENTS - LATIN AMERICA - CONGRESSES.
Conferenza internazionale sul tema Le zone franche industriali, nuove forme di investimento, l'America latina (1985 : Milan, Italy) Le zone franche industriali nei paesi emergenti . Milano, Italy , c1986. 207 p. ; LC Card 86-223193
HF1418 .C525 1985

INVESTMENTS, LIBYAN.
Mattes, Hanspeter. Aspekte der libyischen Ausseninvestitionspolitik, 1972-1985 /. Hamburg , c1985. iv, 169 p. : ISBN 3-89173-001-2 LC Card 86-173976
HG4538 .M376 1985

INVESTMENTS, LIBYAN - MALTA.
Mattes, Hanspeter. Aspekte der libyischen Ausseninvestitionspolitik, 1972-1985 /. Hamburg , c1985. iv, 169 p. : ISBN 3-89173-001-2 LC Card 86-173976
HG4538 .M376 1985

INVESTMENTS - MATHEMATICAL MODELS.
Büttler, Hans-Jürgen. Estimation of disequilibrium models /. Berlin , New York , c1986. vi, 114 p. : ISBN 0-387-16817-6 (U. S.) : LC Card 86-22073 DDC 339.5 19
HB145 .B88 1986
NYPL [JLM 72-289 v.279]

Müller, Sigrid, 1953- Arbitrage pricing of contingent claims /. Berlin , New York , 1985. viii, 151 p. ; ISBN 0-387-15973-8 (U. S.) LC Card 85-22170 DDC 332.6/0724 19
HG4515.2 .M85 1985
NYPL [JLM 72-289 no.254]

Nowak, Felicitas. The allocation of bank credit and the efficiency of investment /. Göttingen, Rep. Fed. de Alemania [1986] 23 p. : LC Card 87-121215 DDC 332.7/0724 19
HG1641 .N68 1986

Wallenwein, Erich, 1951- Die Bedeutung der Kapitalintensitätshypothese im neoklassischen Zwei-Sektoren-Modell und ihre empirische Überprüfung /. Frankfurt am Main , New York , c1986. x, 354 p. : ISBN 3-8204-9618-1 LC Card 86-194355
HD75.5 .W33 1986

INVESTMENTS - NETHERLANDS.
Investeren in Nederland /. 's-Gravenhage [1986] 122 p. : LC Card 86-231212
HG5562 .I58 1986

INVESTMENTS - NIGERIA - OYO STATE.
Investment opportunities in the field of small scale industries in Oyo State of Nigeria. Ibadan, Oyo State of Nigeria [1977?] v, 94 p., [15] p. of plates : LC Card 86-173553 DDC 658.1/592/096692 19
HD2346.N52 O965 1977

INVESTMENTS - PERU.
El Mercado de capitales como instrumento de la política económica /. [Miraflores, Lima] [1987] 111 p. ; LC Card 87-169408 DDC 332.6/0985 19
HG5392 .M43 1987

INVESTMENTS - PORTUGAL - EFFECT OF INFLATION ON.
Pina, Amílcar. Análise de empresas em inflação . [Porto] , 1985. 142 p. : LC Card 86-174401
HF5658.5 .P56 1985

INVESTMENTS - PSYCHOLOGICAL ASPECTS.
Bernstein, Jacob, 1946- Beyond the investor's quotient . New York , c1986. x, 214 p. : ISBN 0-471-82062-8 LC Card 85-12325 DDC 332.6 19
HG4521 .B443 1986 ***NYPL [JLE 86-2936]***

INVESTMENTS - PUERTO RICO - HISTORY.
Dietz, James L., 1947- Economic history of Puerto Rico . Princeton , c1986. xxiii, 337 p., [11] p. of plates : ISBN 0-691-07716-9 (alk. paper) : LC Card 86-12313 DDC 330.97295 19
HC154.5 .D54 1986 ***NYPL [JLE 87-1592]***

INVESTMENTS - ROMANIA.
Cistelecan, Lazăr M. Procesul investițional /. București , 1983. 264 p. : LC Card 84-135967
HG5692 .C57 1983

INVESTMENTS - SAUDI ARABIA.
A Guide to industrial investment /. Riyadh , 1986. vi, 286 p., [4] leaves of plates : LC Card 87-400301 DDC 332.6/7322538 19
HC415.33.Z9 I534 1986

INVESTMENTS - SOCIAL ASPECTS - UNITED STATES.
Bruyn, Severyn Ten Haut, 1927- The field of social investment /. Cambridge , New York , 1987. xi, 304 p. : ISBN 0-521-33292-3 LC Card 86-26393 DDC 332.6 19
HG4910 .B77 1987

INVESTMENTS - SPAIN - ASTURIAS.
Martín Alonso, Arturo. Invertir en Asturias /. [Spain] [1984?] 72 p. : ISBN 84-398-1662-6 LC Card 85-217277
HC387.A7 M37 1984

INVESTMENTS - SWEDEN - MATHEMATICAL MODELS.
Agell, Jonas. The effects of capital taxation . Uppsala , Stockholm, Sweden , 1986. 123 p. : ISBN 91-554-1938-0 (pbk.) LC Card 87-100538 DDC 330 s 336.2/009481 19
HB51 .S7 no. 9 HJ2838

INVESTMENTS - SWITZERLAND.
Schweizer, Max. Investieren und Finanzieren . Zürich , c1984. 176 p. : ISBN 3-85565-209-0 : LC Card 84-244976
HD9715.S92 S38 1984

The Swiss equity market . Westport, Conn. , 1985. xiv, 210 p. : ISBN 0-89930-147-9 (lib. bdg. : alk. paper) LC Card 85-12195 DDC 332.64/2494 19
HG5652 .M45 1985 ***NYPL [JLE 86-1965]***

INVESTMENTS - TABLES.
Thorndike, David, 1925- Thorndike encyclopedia of banking and financial tables /. Boston , c1987. 1737 p. in various pagings ; ISBN 0-88712-883-1 LC Card 87-50721 DDC

332.8/0212 19
HG1626 .T49 1987

INVESTMENTS - TAXATION.
Bradford, David F. Issues in the measurement and interpretation of effective tax rates /. Cambridge, MA (1050 Massachusetts Ave., Cambridge 02138) [1986] 21 p. : LC Card 87-108421 DDC 336.24/26 19
HJ4631 .B73 1986

Leibfritz, Willi. Steuerliche Investitionsförderung im internationalen Vergleich /. Berlin , c1985. 255 p. : ISBN 3-428-05776-7 LC Card 85-161706
HJ4631 .L38 1985

INVESTMENTS - TAXATION - BRAZIL.
Harber, Richard P. Tax policy, economic development, and regional inequality [microform] . Austin , 1984. 33 p. ; LC Card 84-623077 DDC 339.5/2/09813 19
HJ2527 .H37 1984 ***NYPL [*ZT-1646 no.22]***

INVESTMENTS - TAXATION - GREAT BRITAIN - CASE STUDIES.
Morgan, Eleanor. Corporate taxation and investment . Haldershot, Hants Gull, England , Brookfield, Vt., USA , c1986. x, 220 p. : ISBN 0-566-05265-2 : LC Card 86-25642 DDC 336.24/3/0941 19
HJ4708.A7 M63 1986

INVESTMENTS - TAXATION - ITALY.
Politiche tributarie e struttura industriale in Italia /. Bologna , c1986. 118 p. ; ISBN 88-15-01224-9 : LC Card 86-224989
HD2753.I7 P65 1986

INVESTMENTS - TAXATION - MATHEMATICAL MODELS.
Sinn, Hans-Werner. [Kapitaleinkommensbesteuerung. English.] Capital income taxation and resource allocation /. Amsterdam ; New York : xiv, 411 p. ; ISBN 0-444-70208-3 LC Card 87-9126 DDC 336.24/3 19
HD2753.A3 S47413 1987

INVESTMENTS - TAXATION - UNITED STATES.
Windish, David F. Tax-advantaged investments /. New York, N.Y. , c1985. xii, 404 p. : ISBN 0-13-884677-4 LC Card 84-25539 DDC 332.6/042 19
HJ4653.A3 W56 1985 ***NYPL [JLE 85-3677]***

Windish, David F. Tax-advantaged investments /. New York, N.Y. , c1987. xix, 407 p. : ISBN 0-13-884693-6 : LC Card 87-11156 DDC 332.6/042 19
HJ4653.A3 W56 1987

INVESTMENTS - TERMINOLOGY.
Definicje z zakresu inwestycji . Warszawa , 1977. 42 p. ; LC Card 81-172624
HG4528 .D44 1977

INVESTMENTS - UNITED STATES.
Bertot, Cathey H. The new financial planner . Homewood, Ill. , c1986. xvi, 266 p. : ISBN 0-87094-587-4 LC Card 85-52442 DDC 332.024/01 19
HG179 .B458 1986 ***NYPL [JLE 87-537]***

Chase, C. David. Mugged on Wall Street . New York , c1987. 349 p. : ISBN 0-671-62706-6 LC Card 87-4707 DDC 332.6/78 19
HG4910 .C52 1987

Cohen, Jerome Bernard, 1915- Investment analysis and portfolio management /. Homewood, Ill. , 1977. xvi, 819 p. : ISBN 0-256-01883-9 LC Card 76-15739
HG4521 .C5296 1977
NYPL [*R-Econ. 78-1366]

Currier, Chet. No cost/low cost investing /. New York , 1987. 240 p. ; ISBN 0-531-15527-7 LC Card 87-13690 DDC 332.6/78 19
HG4910 .C86 1987

Hadady, R. Earl (Robert Earl), 1920- Winning with the insiders /. West Palm Beach, Fla. , c1987. vi, 115 p. : ISBN 0-9613048-8-X : LC Card 87-40003 DDC 332.64/4 19
HG4910 .H18 1987

Hardy, C. Colburn. The blue chip investment strategy . New York , 1987. 324 p. : ISBN 0-531-15525-0 LC Card 87-14726 DDC 332.63/22 19
HG4963 .H37 1987

Hunt, Lacy H. A time to be rich . New York , c1987. xvi, 282 p. : ISBN 0-89256-325-7 : LC Card 87-9431 DDC 332.6/78 19
HG4910 .H86 1987

Hutchison, Anna Marie. IRA investing made easy /. Oakhurst, Calif. , c1987. 158 p. : ISBN 0-940083-07-8 (pbk.) : LC Card 86-83347 DDC 343.7305/23 347.303523 19
HG1660.U5 H87 1987

Investing in broadcast stations . [Washington, D.C.] (1120 20th St., NW, Washington 20036) , c1987. 318 p. in various pagings : LC Card 87-115340 DDC 384.54/3/0681 19
HE8689.8 .I58 1987

Investment opportunities . Chicago, Ill. , c1987. xi, 112 p. ; ISBN 0-912857-38-2 (pbk.) : LC Card 86-82750 DDC 332.6/78 19
HG4921 .I585 1987

Lerner, Joel J. Financial planning for the utterly confused /. New York , c1986. xi, 210 p. ; ISBN 0-07-037224-1 (pbk.) : LC Card 85-19823 DDC 332.024 19
HG179 .L45 1986 ***NYPL [JLD 86-2290]***

Little, Jeffrey B. Understanding Wall Street /. Blue Ridge Summit, PA , c1987. 219 p. : ISBN 0-8306-3120-8 : LC Card 87-3628 DDC 332.6/78 19
HG4910 .L54 1987

Little, Jeffrey B. [Wall Street library.] Understanding Wall Street /. Blue Ridge Summit, PA , 1986. p. cm. ISBN 0-8306-3010-4 (pbk.) : LC Card 86-27791 DDC 332.6/78 19
HG4921 .L63 1986

Money guide . Kansas City, Mo. , c1987. vii, 128 p. : ISBN 0-8362-2210-5 (pbk.) : LC Card 87-1200 DDC 332.63/22 19
HG4921 .M68 1987

Nelson, Charles R. The investor's guide to economic indicators /. New York , c1987. viii, 193 p. : ISBN 0-471-85902-8 LC Card 87-2134 DDC 330.973/0927 19
HC106.8 .N38 1987

The New York Institute of Finance guide to investing. New York, N.Y. , c1987. xi, 296 p. : ISBN 0-13-620436-8 (pbk.) : LC Card 87-11323 DDC 332.6/78 19
HG4921 .N53 1987

Passell, Peter. Where to put your money, 1987 /. New York, NY , c1987. 82 p. ; ISBN 0-446-38497-6 (pbk.) : LC Card 86-28917 DDC 332.6/78 19
HG179 .P27 1987

Persons, Robert H., 1922- The investor's encyclopedia of gold, silver, and other precious metals. [New York, 1974] x, 316 p. ISBN 0-394-49597-7 LC Card 74-14860 DDC 332.6/328
HG5073 .P38 ***NYPL [JLF 86-388]***

Pritchard, Robert E., 1941- Be your own financial advisor /. Englewood Cliffs, N.J. , c1988. xiv, 187 p. ; ISBN 0-13-071242-6 LC Card 87-14366 DDC 332.024 19
HG179 .P737 1988

Putnam, Bluford H. The Blackwell guide to Wall Street /. Oxford, UK , New York, NY, USA , 1987. viii, 222 p. : ISBN 0-631-14183-9 : LC Card 87-10299 DDC 332.63/2 19
HG4910 .P87 1987

Rosenthal, Daniel M. A short course in gold investing . Bethel, CT , c1986. 90 leaves : ISBN 0-938689-00-2 (pbk.) : LC Card 86-207234 DDC 332.63 19
HG295.U6 R67 1986

Rosenthal, Daniel M. The silver & gold investor's profit guide . Bethel, CT , c1986. viii, 90 leaves : ISBN 0-938689-02-9 (pbk.) : LC Card 86-232188 DDC 332.63 19
HG307.U5 R67 1986

Sobel, Robert, 1931 (Feb. 19)- The new game on Wall Street /. New York , c1987. xii, 244 p. : ISBN 0-471-84527-2 LC Card 86-33986 DDC 332.6/78 19
HG4921 .S6156 1987

Stocks, bonds, options, futures . New York, N.Y. [Englewood Cliffs, N.J.] , c1987. 332 p. : ISBN 0-13-846718-8 : LC Card 87-11324 DDC 332.6/78 19
HG4921 .S7945 1987

Strebel, Paul. In the shadows of Wall Street . Englewood Cliffs, N.J. , c1988. xii, 228 p. : ISBN 0-13-455999-1 LC Card 87-42680 DDC 332.63/22 19
HG4921 .S84 1988

Stribling, Catherine. Growing up financially . New York , 1987, c1986. 311 p. ; ISBN 0-345-33098-6 (pbk.) : LC Card 86-90719 DDC 332.6/78 19
HG179 .S846 1987

Supply-side portfolio strategies /. Westport, Conn. , 1988. xii, 180 p. : ISBN 0-89930-286-6 (lib. bdg. : alk. paper) LC Card 87-13091 DDC 332.6/0973 19
HG4910 .S775 1988

Thomsett, Michael C. Homeowners money management . Emmaus, Pa. , c1987. xiii, 238 p. : ISBN 0-87857-673-8 (alk. paper) : LC Card 86-26096 DDC 332.024 19
HD7287.82.U6 T47 1987

Train, John. The midas touch . New York , c1987. xi, 207 p. ; ISBN 0-06-015643-0 : LC Card 86-45157 DDC 332.6/092/4 B 19
HG172.B84 T72 1987

U. S. News investment guide /. Washington, D.C. (2400 N. St., N.W., Washington 20037-1196) , c1987. iv, 60 p. : LC Card 87-143438 DDC 332.6/78 19
HG4910 .U25 1987

Winning with mutual funds /. Birmingham, Ala. , c1987. 224 p. : ISBN 0-8487-0722-2 LC Card 87-61719 DDC 332.63/27 19
HG4930 .W56 1987

Zweig, Martin E. [Winning on Wall Street.] Martin Zweig's Winning on Wall Street /. New York , c1986. x, 293 p. : ISBN 0-446-51234-6 : LC Card 85-43167 DDC 332.63/22 19
HG6049 .Z87 1986 ***NYPL [JLE 86-2796]***

INVESTMENTS - UNITED STATES - CONGRESSES.
San Francisco '85 . Bethesda, Md. [1986] vi, 502 p. ; LC Card 87-132666 DDC 332.6 19
HG4508 .S215 1986

INVESTMENTS - UNITED STATES - HANDBOOKS, MANUALS, ETC.
Casey, Douglas R. Two new investment reports from Doug Casey. Arlington, VA (1300 N. 17th St., Suite 1660, Arlington 22209) , c1985. 64, 65 p. : LC Card 86-230393 DDC 332.6/78 19
HG4921 .C35 1985

Fowler, Elizabeth M. Every woman's guide to profitable investing /. New York, NY , c1986. 260 p. : ISBN 0-8144-5823-8 LC Card 85-48222 DDC 332.6/78/024042 19
HG4921 .F636 1986 ***NYPL [JLE 86-3339]***

Kennedy, David W. Money making money . New York , 1987. 215 p. ; ISBN 0-88687-296-0 : LC Card 86-62737 DDC 332.6/78 19
HG4921 .K44 1987

Rosenberg, Claude N. Stock market primer . New York, NY , c1987. xii, 372 p. ; ISBN 0-446-51257-5 LC Card 87-40163 DDC 332.63/22 19
HG4921 .R58 1987

Senchack, A. J. (Andrew J.) Personal investing . [Texas?] , c1986. 1 v. (various pagings) : LC Card 87-104863 DDC 332.6/78 19
HG4921 .S44 1986

Senchack, A. J. (Andrew J.) Smart investing . Dallas, Tex. , c1987. 1 v. (various pagings) : ISBN 0-87833-575-7 (pbk.) : LC Card 87-1923 DDC 332.6/78 19
HG4921 .S45 1987

Stoken, Dick A. Strategic investment timing . New York , London , c1984. x, 225 p. : ISBN 0-02-614810-2 LC Card 84-12576 DDC 332.6/78 19
HG4921 .S795 1984 ***NYPL [JLD 86-2041]***

INVESTMENTS - UNITED STATES - JUVENILE LITERATURE.
Little, Jeffrey B. Wall Street--how it works /. New York , c1988. 47 p. : ISBN 1-555-46621-4 LC Card 87-15139 DDC 332.64/273 19
HG4921 .L625 1988

INVESTMENTS - UNITED STATES - STATES.
Corporation for Enterprise Development. Building the new economy . Washington, D.C. , 1986. iv, 178 p. ; ISBN 0-9605804-2-5 (pbk.) LC

Card 86-61273 DDC 338.973 19
HC110.I53 C67 1986

INVESTMENTS - VENEZUELA.
Foro de Proyectos de Inversión Colombo-Venezolanos (1986 : Cúcuta, Colombia) La frontera colombo-venezolana, una región donde invertir /. Bogotá, D.E. [1986] 96 p. ; LC Card 87-403851 DDC 332.6/09861 19
HG5352 .F67 1986

INVESTMENTS - VOCATIONAL GUIDANCE.
Epstein, Rachel S. Careers in the world of investments /. New York , c1988. 47 p. : ISBN 1-555-46631-1 LC Card 87-13182 DDC 332.6/023 19
HG4528 .E67 1988

INVESTMENTS, WEST GERMAN.
Berger, Manfred, Dipl. econ. Auslandsinvestitionen kleiner und mittlerer Unternehmen . Berlin , c1985. 164 p. : ISBN 3-428-05775-9 LC Card 85-161656
HG4538 .B4538 1985

Krist, Herbert. Bestimmungsgründe industrieller Direktinvestitionen /. Berlin , c1985. 310 p. : ISBN 3-924859-01-9 LC Card 86-225379
HG4538 .K72 1985

INVESTMENTS, WEST GERMAN - ASIA, SOUTHEASTERN.
Jungnickel, Rolf. Investitionsbedingungen in der ASEAN-Region /. Hamburg , 1986. 346 p. : ISBN 3-87895-296-1 LC Card 86-192978
HG5740.8.A3 J85 1986

INVESTMENTS, WEST GERMAN - COMMUNIST COUNTRIES.
Berger, Manfred, Dipl. econ. Auslandsinvestitionen kleiner und mittlerer Unternehmen . Berlin , c1985. 164 p. : ISBN 3-428-05775-9 LC Card 85-161656
HG4538 .B4538 1985

INVESTMENTS, WEST GERMAN - DEVELOPING COUNTRIES.
Berger, Manfred, Dipl. econ. Auslandsinvestitionen kleiner und mittlerer Unternehmen . Berlin , c1985. 164 p. : ISBN 3-428-05775-9 LC Card 85-161656
HG4538 .B4538 1985

Mitsotaki, Alexandra Gourdain. Public development finance corporations . Paris , 1986. 40 p. ; LC Card 86-221546 DDC 332.6/734/01724 19
HG5993 .M57 1986

Partnerschaftliche Entwicklungspolitik im Widerstreit der Interessen . Bochum-Querenburg , 1985. i, 184 leaves ; LC Card 87-409475 DDC 332.6/7343/01724 19
HG5993 .P37 1985

INVESTMENTS, WEST GERMAN - MEXICO.
Gies, Christoph. Die Spielregeln für Kapitalanlagen in Mexiko . Frankfurt , c1986. ix, 314 p. : ISBN 3-88323-603-9 LC Card 86-231145
HG5162 .G48 1986

INVESTMENTS, WEST GERMAN - UNITED STATES.
Klose, Roland, 1954- Die Erschliessung des US-Marktes durch Direktinvestitionen mittelständischer deutscher Unternehmungen des Investitionsgüterbereichs /. [Würzburg? , 1983] (Würzburg : Dissertationsdruck, Schmitt & Meyer) v, 307 p. ; LC Card 84-195414
HG4910 .K56 1983

INVESTMENTS - YUGOSLAVIA - MATHEMATICAL MODELS.
Smiljanić, Slobodan. Sistem upravljanja investicijama /. Kragujevac , 1984. 185 p. : LC Card 86-115123
HG4234.6 .S65 1984

INVESTMENTS - ZIMBABWE.
Whitsun Foundation. Project 1.07 . Harare, Zimbabwe [1983?] 2 v. ; ISBN 0-7974-0597-6 LC Card 84-981092 DDC 380.1/096891 19
HF3902 .W48 1983 ***NYPL [JLM 87-272]***

Investor Analysis Publications (Highland Park, Ill.) Investor relations directory . Highland Park, Ill., U. S.A. (P.O. Box 1037, Highland Park 60035) , c1986. 166 p. ; LC Card 86-228008 DDC 338.7/61659285/02573 19
HD59 .I568 1986

Investor relations directory : corporate investor relations professionals and contacts, agencies providing investor relations services and their clients, extensive index for easy access to investor information. 1st ed. Highland Park, Ill., U. S.A. (P.O. Box 1037, Highland Park 60035) : Investor Analysis Publications, c1986. 166 p. ; 28 cm. Includes indexes. LC Card 86-228008 DDC 338.7/61659285/02573 19
1. Corporations - United States - Investor relations - Directories. I. Investor Analysis Publications (Highland Park, Ill.).
HD59 .I568 1986

Investor Responsibility Research Center. South Africa Review Service.
Hauck, David. U. S. corporate withdrawal from South Africa . Washington, D.C. (Suite 600, 1755 Massachusetts Ave., N.W., Washington 20036) [1986] 22 p. ; LC Card 86-209299 DDC 332.6/7373/068 19
HG5851.A3 H39 1986

Hauck, David. What happens when U. S. companies sell their South African operations? /. Washington, D.C. (Suite 600, 1755 Massachusetts Ave., N.W., Washington 20036) , c1987. 16 p. ; LC Card 87-163729 DDC 338.8/8973/068 19
HG5851.A3 H392 1987

Voorhes, Meg. Black South African views on disinvestment /. Washington, D.C. (Suite 600, 1755 Massachusetts Ave., N.W., Washington 20036) [1986] 36 p. ; LC Card 86-209279 DDC 332.6/73/0968 19
HG5851.A3 V66 1986

Investors. Talley, Madelon DeVoe. The passionate investors . New York , c1987. 260 p. : ISBN 0-517-56563-3 : LC Card 86-24281 DDC 332.63/22 19
HG4521 .T29 1987

INVESTORS. see CAPITALISTS AND FINANCIERS.

The investor's encyclopedia of gold, silver, and other precious metals. Persons, Robert H., 1922- [New York, 1974] x, 316 p. ISBN 0-394-49597-7 LC Card 74-14860 DDC 332.6/328
HG5073 .P38 ***NYPL [JLF 86-388]***

The investor's guide to economic indicators /. Nelson, Charles R. New York , c1987. viii, 193 p. : ISBN 0-471-85902-8 LC Card 87-2134 DDC 330.973/0927 19
HC106.8 .N38 1987

Invisible assets. Itami, Hiroyuki, 1945- Mobilizing invisible assets /. Cambridge, Mass. , 1987. xi, 186 p. : ISBN 0-674-57770-1 (alk. paper) LC Card 86-26972 DDC 658.4/012 19
HD30.28 .I85 1987

The invisible billionaire, Daniel Ludwig /. Shields, Jerry. Boston , 1986. xii, 401 p. : ISBN 0-395-35402-1 : LC Card 86-7519 DDC 387.5/092/4 B 19
HE569.L84 S55 1986 ***NYPL [JFE 86-3861]***

Invisible factors in local economic development /. Doeringer, Peter B. New York , 1987. vii, 144 p. : ISBN 0-19-504965-9 (alk. paper) LC Card 87-13550 DDC 338.9744/3 19
HC107.M42 W674 1987

The invisible hand . Olnek, Jay I. Riverdale, N.Y. , c1984. 176 p. : ISBN 0-938538-01-2 LC Card 82-24634 DDC 382.7/1/0973 19
HF1455 .O49 1984 ***NYPL [JLE 87-21]***

Invisible hands : women in home-based production / editors, Andrea Menefee Singh, Anita Kelles-Viitanen. New Delhi ; Newbury Park, Calif. : Sage Publications, 1987. 273 p. ; 23 cm. (Women and the household in Asia . vol. 1) Selected papers from the Regional Conference for Asia on Women and the Household held in New Delhi, Jan. 27-31, 1985 and sponsored by the Commission on Women of the International Union of Anthropological and Ethnological Sciences, Research Committee 32 "Women in Society" of the International Sociological Association, and the Indian Association for Women's Studies. Includes bibliographies and index. ISBN 0-8039-9524-5 (U. S.) LC Card 87-4337 DDC 331.4/0954 19
1. Women - Employment - Asia - Congresses. 2. Handicraft - Asia - Congresses. 3. Cottage industries - Asia - Congresses. 4. Small business - Asia - Congresses. 5. Women in development - Asia - Congresses. I. Singh, Andréa Menefee, 1943-. II. Kelles-Viitanen, Anita, 1947-. III. Regional Conference for Asia on Women and the Household (1985 : New Delhi, India). IV. International Union of Anthropological and Ethnological Sciences. Commission on Women. V. International Sociological Association. Research Committee 32 "Women in Society". VI. Indian Association for Women's Studies. VII. Series.
HD6181.85 .A85 1987

Invisible labour force . Islam, Shamima. Bangladesh , 1985. 60, [1] p. ; LC Card 85-904350 DDC 331.4/09549/2 19
HD6190.6 .I84 1985

The invisible partners . Sanford, John A. New York , c1980. 139 p. ; ISBN 0-8091-2277-4 : LC Card 79-56604 DDC 150.19/54
BF175 .S24 ***NYPL [JFE 86-5093]***

Involving managers in competitive analysis /. Morse, Diane McGinty. Menlo Park, CA (333 Ravenswood Ave., Menlo Park 94025) , c1986. 11 leaves : LC Card 86-220559 DDC 658.4/012 19
HD38.7 .M67 1986

Inwestycje w reformie . Kapustka, Aleksander. Zielona Góra , 1985. 282 p. ; LC Card 86-125896
HJ2132 .K37 1985

Die Inzidenz sektorspezifischer Kapitalbesteuerung /. Hamm, Rüdiger. Krefeld , 1983. 296 p. : ISBN 3-88358-034-1 LC Card 83-218772
HD2753.A3 H36 1983

Iorio de Souza, Ubiratan Jorge, 1946- Uma análise econômica do problema do cheque sem fundos no Brasil / Ubiratan Jorge Iorio de Souza. Rio de Janeiro : IBMEC ; [Brasília] : Banco Central do Brasil, 1985. 204 p. : ill. ; 21 cm. Bibliography: p. 201-204. LC Card 87-141390 DDC 332.7/6 19
1. Checks - Criminal provisions - Economic aspects - Brazil. I. Title. II. Title: Cheque sem fundos.
HG1691 .I58 1985

Iowa Advisory Commission on Intergovernmental Relations. Iowa's infrastructure. Des Moines, Iowa (523 E. 12th St., Des Moines 50319) [1986] 89 p., [5] leaves of plates : LC Card 86-622778 DDC 363/.09777 19
HC107.I73 C35 1986

IOWA - FORECASTING - STATISTICS.
Industry projections, occupational projections, 1985-1988, State of Iowa. [Iowa City] [1986] [42] leaves ; LC Card 86-622540 DDC 331.12/09777/021 19
HD5725.I8 I53 1986

Iowa. General Assembly. Legislative Extended Assistance Group. Otto, Daniel. Economic contribution and impacts of changes in Iowa's livestock and meat processing industries /. Oakdale, Iowa [1984] xi, 95 p. : LC Card 85-621899 DDC 338.1/76/009777021 19
HD9417.I8 O88 1984 ***NYPL [JLF 86-592]***

Iowa. Governor's Highway Safety Office. Davis, Dan J. The disposition and sentencing of operating while intoxicated (OWI) offenders in Iowa . [Des Moines, Iowa] (523 E. 12th St., Des Moines 50319) [1986] 29 leaves : LC Card 86-621927 DDC 364.1/47 19
HE5620.D7 D37 1986

IOWA - INDUSTRIES - FORECASTING - STATISTICS.
Industry projections, occupational projections, 1985-1988, State of Iowa. [Iowa City] [1986] [42] leaves ; LC Card 86-622540 DDC 331.12/09777/021 19
HD5725.I8 I53 1986

Iowa. Labor Market Information Unit.
Industry projections, occupational projections, 1985-1988, State of Iowa. [Iowa City] [1986] [42] leaves ; LC Card 86-622540 DDC 331.12/09777/021 19
HD5725.I8 I53 1986

Labor market information for Iowa (Job Training Partnership Act), State of Iowa. Des Moines, Iowa (1000 E. Grand Ave., Des Moines 50319) [1986] 125 p. : LC Card 86-622289 DDC 331.1/09777 19
HD5725.I8 L34 1986

Occupational projections, 1984-1995 . [Des Moines?] [1985] 16 v. in 1 ; LC Card 86-621925 DDC 331.12/09777/021 19
HD5725.I8 O26 1985

Unemployment by occupation, 1985 . Des Moines, Iowa (1000 E. Grand Ave., Des

Moines 50319) [1986] [12] leaves ; LC Card 86-622759 DDC 331.13/79777 19
HD5725.I8 U54 1986

IOWA - OCCUPATIONS - FORECASTING - STATISTICS.
Industry projections, occupational projections, 1985-1988, State of Iowa. [Iowa City] [1986] [42] leaves ; LC Card 86-622540 DDC 331.12/09777/021 19
HD5725.I8 I53 1986

IOWA - OCCUPATIONS - STATISTICS.
Labor market information for Iowa (Job Training Partnership Act), State of Iowa. Des Moines, Iowa (1000 E. Grand Ave., Des Moines 50319) [1986] 125 p. : LC Card 86-622289 DDC 331.1/09777 19
HD5725.I8 L34 1986

Unemployment by occupation, 1985 . Des Moines, Iowa (1000 E. Grand Ave., Des Moines 50319) [1986] [12] leaves ; LC Card 86-622759 DDC 331.13/79777 19
HD5725.I8 U54 1986

Iowa. Office for Planning and Programming. Industry projections, occupational projections, 1985-1988, State of Iowa. [Iowa City] [1986] [42] leaves ; LC Card 86-622540 DDC 331.12/09777/021 19
HD5725.I8 I53 1986

Occupational projections, 1984-1995 . [Des Moines?] [1985] 16 v. in 1 ; LC Card 86-621925 DDC 331.12/09777/021 19
HD5725.I8 O26 1985

Iowa. Office for Planning and Programming. Statistical Analysis Center. Davis, Dan J. The disposition and sentencing of operating while intoxicated (OWI) offenders in Iowa . [Des Moines, Iowa] (523 E. 12th St., Des Moines 50319) [1986] 29 leaves : LC Card 86-621927 DDC 364.1/47 19
HE5620.D7 D37 1986

Iowa. Planning and Programming Office for. see **Iowa. Office for Planning and Programming.**

Iowa State Occupational Information Coordinating Committee.
Industry projections, occupational projections, 1985-1988, State of Iowa. [Iowa City] [1986] [42] leaves ; LC Card 86-622540 DDC 331.12/09777/021 19
HD5725.I8 I53 1986

Occupational projections, 1984-1995 . [Des Moines?] [1985] 16 v. in 1 ; LC Card 86-621925 DDC 331.12/09777/021 19
HD5725.I8 O26 1985

Iowa. University. Institute of Urban and Regional Research.
Beaumont, Paul (Paul M.) Regional wage rates [microform] . Iowa City , 1982. 22 p. : ***NYPL [*ZT-1564 no.29]***

Forecasting interstate migration with limited data . Iowa City , 1982. 37 p. : ***NYPL [*ZT-1564 no.33]***

Rogerson, Peter. Job turnover and interregional migration [microform] /. Iowa City , 1981. 25 p. : ***NYPL [*ZT-1564 no.31]***

Iowa's infrastructure. Des Moines, Iowa (523 E. 12th St., Des Moines 50319) : Advisory Commission on Intergovernmental Relations, State of Iowa, [1986] 89 p., [5] leaves of plates : ill. ; 28 cm. Bibliography: p. 86-89. LC Card 86-622778 DDC 363/.09777 19
1. Infrastructure (Economics) - Iowa. I. Iowa Advisory Commission on Intergovernmental Relations.
HC107.I73 C35 1986

Az ipar és kereskedés története Magyarországban a három utolsó század alatt /. Horváth, Mihály, 1809-1878. [Budapest , 1984] xiv, 390 p. ; ISBN 963-02-2781-9 : LC Card 85-138953
HC300.26 .H67 1984

Iparfejlesztés a hetedik ötéves terv időszakában /. Bontó, László. [Budapest] , 1986. 170, [4] p. : ISBN 963-09-3001-3 : LC Card 87-138631
HC300.28 .B659 1986

Iparfejlesztés a 7-dik ötéves terv időszakában. Bontó, László. Iparfejlesztés a hetedik ötéves terv időszakában /. [Budapest] , 1986. 170, [4] p. : ISBN 963-09-3001-3 : LC Card 87-138631
HC300.28 .B659 1986

Ipargazdasági Intézet (Budapest, Hungary)
Iparunk 40 éve /. [Budapest] , 1985. 58, [37] p. : ISBN 963-382-009-X LC Card 85-228898
HC300.28 .I64 1985

Az Ipari nagyüzemi munkásság jövedelmi viszonyai, élet- és munkakörülményei / [összeállitotta a Központi Statisztikai Hivatal Iparstatisztikai Főosztálya]. [Budapest] : Központi Statisztikai Hivatal, [1985] 94 p. ; 29 cm. "1985. április." LC Card 85-210330
1. Labor and laboring classes - Hungary - Statistics. 2. Wages - Hungary - Statistics. 3. Cost and standard of living - Hungary - Statistics. I. Hungary. Központi Statisztikai Hivatal. Iparstatisztikai Főosztály.
HD8420.5 .I63 1985

Az Ipari robotok termelésének és felhasználásának trendjei / [a magyar változatot összeállitotta a KSH Iparstatisztikai Főosztály Kohó- és Gépipari Osztálya]. Budapest : Központi Statisztikai Hivatal, 1985. 63 p. : ill. ; 29 cm. (Nemzetközi szervezetek statisztikai tevékenységéből . 69. sz.) Bibliography: p. 39-40. LC Card 86-199458
1. Robot industry - Statistics. 2. Robots, Industrial - Statistics. 3. Robot industry - Hungary - Statistics. I. Hungary Központi Statisztikai Hivatal. Kohó- és Gépipari Osztály. II. Series.
HD9696.R623 H852 1985

Ipari Szövetkezetek Országos Tanácsa Oktatási Központ kiadványa.
Lukács, Lajos. Szövetkezeti gazdálkodás elemzése /. Budapest , 1983. 155 p. : ISBN 963-03-2028-2 (Magy. nemz. bibl.) LC Card 85-184472
HF5686.C67 L84 1983

Ipari szövetkezetek összevonásai a hetvenes években. Kőhegyi, Kálmán. Az ipari szövetkezetek összevonásai a 70-es években /. [Budapest] [1983] 119 p. ; LC Card 86-145163
HD3182.5.A4 K64 1983

Az ipari szövetkezetek összevonásai a 70-es években /. Kőhegyi, Kálmán. [Budapest] [1983] 119 p. ; LC Card 86-145163
HD3182.5.A4 K64 1983

Ipari üzemtörténet / [válogatta Gyarmathy Zsigmond]. Nyíregyháza : [s.n.], 1979 ([Nyíregyháza] : Készült a Szabolcs-Szatmár Megyei Tanács Sokszorosító Költségvetési Üzemében) 228 p. : ill. ; 20 cm. (Honismereti kutatások Szabolcs-Szatmárban, 0139-3650 . 7) Jósa András Múzeum kiadványai, 0133-8110 ; 14 Includes bibliographical references. ISBN 963-01-2796-2 LC Card 81-173980
1. Szabolcs-Szatmár Megye (Hungary) - Industries - History. 2. Business enterprises - Hungary - Szabolcs-Szatmár - History. I. Gyarmathy, Zsigmond. II. Series.
HC300.29.S92 I62 1979

Iparosodó mezőgazdaság, 0139-1836.
Benet, Iván. Az agráripari egyesülések útkeresése /. Budapest , 1985. 197 p. : ISBN 963-221-616-4 : LC Card 86-203013
HD9015.H82 B447 1985

Iparunk negyven éve. Iparunk 40 éve /. [Budapest] , 1985. 58, [37] p. : ISBN 963-382-009-X LC Card 85-228898
HC300.28 .I64 1985

Iparunk színvonala és fejlődése nemzetközi összehasonlításban, 1970-1983 / [összeállitotta a Központi Statisztikai Hivatal Iparstatisztikai Főosztálya]. Budapest : Központi Statisztikai Hivatel, 1985. 147, [1] p. ; 29 cm. Chiefly tables. "Források": p. 147-[148] ISBN 963-340-761-3 : LC Card 86-186336
1. Hungary - Industries - Statistics. I. Hungary. Központi Statisztikai Hivatal. Iparstatisztikai Főosztály.
HC300.28 .I66 1985

Iparunk 40 éve / [szerkesztette, Hegedűs Miklós ; írták, Balázsy Sándor ... et al ; készült ... az Ipargazdasági Intézetben]. [Budapest] : Ipari Minisztérium, 1985. 58, [37] p. : col. ill. ; 30 cm. ISBN 963-382-009-X LC Card 85-228898
1. Hungary - Industries - History. I. Hegedűs, Miklós. II. Balázsy, Sándor. III. Ipargazdasági Intézet (Budapest, Hungary). IV. Title: Iparunk negyven éve.
HC300.28 .I64 1985

Az iparvállalatok könyvvitele, 1986 /. Gábor, István. Budapest , 1986. 265 p. : ISBN 963-221-902-3 : LC Card 87-408573
HF5616.H9 G33 1986

Ipea. see **Instituto de Planejamento Econômico e Social.**

IPN (Series) .
(109) Ziefuss, Horst. Jugendliche in der gewerblich-technischen Ausbildung in Industrie und Handwerk . Kiel , c1986. 352 p. : ISBN 3-89088-011-8 LC Card 87-407898 DDC 331.3/42592/0943 19
HD5715.5.G4 Z54 1986

Ippisch, Wolfgang. Bankbetriebliches Zinsspannen-Management : instrumentelle Aspekte einer Fristen- und Rentabilitätssteuerung bei sich wandelnden Bilanzstrukturen / Wolfgang Ippisch. Wien : Service, Fachverlag an der Wirtschaftsuniversität Wien, c1984. xxiii, 365 p. : 62 ill. ; 21 cm. (Schriftenreihe des Instituts für Kredit- u. Versicherungswirtschaft, Abteilung Bankbetriebslehre . Bd. 6) Originally presented as the author's thesis (doctoral)--Wirtschaftsuniversität, Vienna. Bibliography: p. 349-365. ISBN 3-85428-022-X : LC Card 84-174308
1. Interest rates. I. Title. II. Title: Bankbetriebliches Zinsspannenmanagement. III. Series.
HG1621 .I66 1984

Ippolito, Pauline M.
Empirical approaches to consumer protection economics . Washington, D.C. [1986] ii, 484 p. : LC Card 86-602207 DDC 381/.34/0973 19
HC110.C63 E46 1986

Empirical approaches to consumer protection economics . Washington, D.C. [1986] ii, 484 p. : ***NYPL [JLE 86-3552]***

Ipsen, Detlev.
Forum wohnen /. Freiburg i. Br. , Giessen , 1986. 158 p. : ISBN 3-89125-009-6 LC Card 86-169106
HD7339.A3 F68 1986

Markt und Raum : die Verteilungswirkungen wohnungspolitischer Subventionsformen im städtischen Raum / Detlev Ipsen, Herbert Glasauer, Vera Lasch. Frankfurt ; New York : Campus, c1986. 250 p. : ill. ; 21 cm. (Campus Forschung. Bd. 509) Bibliography: p. 243-250. ISBN 3-593-33685-5 LC Card 87-127593 DDC 363.5/8 19
1. Housing subsidies - Germany (West) - Mannheim - Case studies. 2. Housing policy - Germany (West) - Mannheim - Case studies. 3. Rental housing - Germany (West) - Mannheim - Finance - Case studies. 4. Public housing - Germany (West) - Mannheim - Finance - Case studies. I. Glasauer, Herbert. II. Lasch, Vera. III. Title.
HD7339.M35 I67 1986

Ipsen, Dirk, 1939- Die Gegenwärtige Wachstumskrise . Regensburg , c1985. viii, 262 p. : ISBN 3-924956-08-1 LC Card 86-122363 DDC 338.9 19
HD73 .G43 1985

IPW-Forschungshefte .
(1984ns4) Die Rolle der Rüstung in der Wirtschaft des heutigen Kapitalismus /. Berlin [1984] 127 p. ; LC Card 85-135711
HC281 .B39 1984 Heft 4 HC79.D4

(1986/4) Staatsmonopolistische Intensivierung und Widersprüche der Reproduktion /. Berlin [1986] 127 p. ; LC Card 87-408424 DDC 330 s 338/.06 19
HC281 .B39 1986, Heft 4 HC79.I52

Iqbal, Zubair. Islamic banking / by Zubair Iqbal and Abbas Mirakhor. Washington, D.C. : International Monetary Fund, 1987. v, 62 p. ; 28 cm. (Occasional paper / International Monetary Fund, 0251-6365 . no. 49) "March 1987." Bibliography: p. 60-62. ISBN 0-939934-82-5 (pbk.) : LC Card 87-4166 DDC 332.1/0917/671 19
1. Banks and banking - Iran. 2. Banks and banking - Pakistan. 3. Banks and banking - Islamic countries. 4. Banking law (Islamic law). I. Mirakhor, Abbas. II. Series: Occasional paper (International Monetary Fund) , no. 49. III. Title.
HG3270.2.A6 I67 1987

IRA investing made easy /. Hutchison, Anna Marie. Oakhurst, Calif. , c1987. 158 p. : ISBN 0-940083-07-8 (pbk.) : LC Card 86-83347 DDC 343.7305/23 347.303523 19
HG1660.U5 H87 1987

The IRA survival guide . Brownstone, David M. New York, NY , c1987. 168 p. ; ISBN 0-8144-5861-0 (pbk.) : LC Card 86-47806

DDC 332.024/01 19
HG1660.U5 B76 1987

Irak. see **Iraq.**

IRAN - ECONOMIC CONDITIONS - 1945-
Ikani, Azizollah. The dynamics of inflation in Iran, 1960-1977 /. Tilburg, Netherlands , 1987. xii, 395 p. ; ISBN 90-361-9761-9 (pbk.) : LC Card 87-132510 DDC 332.4/1/0955 19
HG1220.2 .I36 1987

IRAN - ECONOMIC POLICY.
Ikani, Azizollah. The dynamics of inflation in Iran, 1960-1977 /. Tilburg, Netherlands , 1987. xii, 395 p. ; ISBN 90-361-9761-9 (pbk.) : LC Card 87-132510 DDC 332.4/1/0955 19
HG1220.2 .I36 1987

Iran - Government. see **Iran - Politics and government.**

IRAN - POLITICS AND GOVERNMENT - 1941-1979.
Bayat, Assef. Workers and revolution in Iran . London , Atlantic Highlands, New Jersey, USA , 1987. 227 p. : ISBN 0-86232-389-4 LC Card 87-160253 DDC 322/.2/0955 19
HD5660.I6 B39 1987

IRAN - POPULATION, RURAL.
Nattagh, Nima. Agriculture & regional development in Iran /. Wisbech, Cambridgeshire, England , 1986. 105 p. : ISBN 0-906559-26-X (pbk.) : LC Card 86-230845 DDC 338.1/0955 19
HD1565.2 .N37 1986

Irányzatok a világgazdaságban .
(sz. 54) The Hungarian enterprise in the context of intra-CMEA relations /. Budapest , 1986. 93 p. ; ISBN 963-301-138-8 (pbk.) LC Card 87-101284 DDC 337.439 19
HF1542.5.H8 H85 1986

IRAQ - COMMERCE - HISTORY.
Höltz, Joachim. Kritik der Geldentstehungstheorien . Berlin , c1984. ii, 401 p. ; ISBN 3-496-00796-6 LC Card 85-147094
HG237 .H64 1984

IRAQ - ECONOMIC POLICY.
Sassoon, Joseph. Economic policy in Iraq, 1932-1950 /. London, England , Totowa, N.J. , 1987. p. cm. ISBN 0-7146-3305-4 : LC Card 87-6577 DDC 338.9567 19
HC415.4 .S27 1987

IRAQ - FOREIGN RELATIONS - GREAT BRITAIN.
Sassoon, Joseph. Economic policy in Iraq, 1932-1950 /. London, England , Totowa, N.J. , 1987. p. cm. ISBN 0-7146-3305-4 : LC Card 87-6577 DDC 338.9567 19
HC415.4 .S27 1987

IRAQ - HISTORY - 1921-
Sassoon, Joseph. Economic policy in Iraq, 1932-1950 /. London, England , Totowa, N.J. , 1987. p. cm. ISBN 0-7146-3305-4 : LC Card 87-6577 DDC 338.9567 19
HC415.4 .S27 1987

IRAs, the people's choice / Investment Company Institute, Research Department. Washington, D.C. (1600 M St., N.W., Washington 20036) : The Institute, [1986?] 60 p. : ill. ; 22 x 28 cm. Cover title. LC Card 87-402800 DDC 332.024/01 19
1. Individual retirement accounts - United States. I. Investment Company Institute (U. S.). Research Dept.
HG1660.U5 I73 1986

IRDP occasional paper .
(no. 10) Farming system and family economy in Ndunya, Chinsali District. Mpika, Zambia [1985?] 45 leaves, [12] leaves of plates : LC Card 86-981252 DDC 338.1/096894 19
HD1476.Z352 N384 1985

(no. 5) Farming systems and family economy in Chibale, Serenje District. Mpika, Zambia [1985?] 74 p. : LC Card 86-981248 DDC 338.1/096894 19
HD1476.Z352 C454 1985

(no. 6) Agricultural commercialisation and the allocation of labour time in Mpika District, northern Zambia. Mpika, Zambia [1986?] iii, 42 leaves : LC Card 86-981249 DDC 338.1/096894 19
HD2131.5.Z9 M653 1986

IRELAND - APPROPRIATIONS AND EXPENDITURES - CONGRESSES.
Public expenditure . Dublin, Ireland , 1986. 138 p. ; ISBN 0-906980-56-9 (pbk.) : LC Card 86-143826 DDC 336.3/9 19
HJ7461 .P83 1986 ***NYPL [JLD 87-553]***

IRELAND. BOARD OF PUBLIC WORKS - HISTORY - 19TH CENTURY.
Griffiths, A. R. G., 1940- The Irish Board of Works, 1831-1878 /. New York , 1987. iii, 214 p. ; ISBN 0-8240-7810-1 (alk. paper) : LC Card 87-24495 DDC 363/.09415 19
HD4150.3 .G75 1987

IRELAND, CENSUS, 1981.
Rottman, David B. The population structure and living circumstances of Irish travellers . Dublin , 1986. 134 p. : ISBN 0-7070-0084-X (pbk.) : LC Card 86-215759 DDC 330.9417 s 305.5/68 19
HC257.I6 E3 no. 131 DX217

Ireland. Courseware Committee. Report of the Courseware Committee : a report to the Minister for Industry and Commerce on the job creation and export potential of developing computer-based instructional software. Dublin : Stationery Office, [1986] vii, 79 p. ; 30 cm. "February 1986." LC Card 86-226148 DDC 338.4/70053 19
1. Educational technology industries - Ireland. 2. Computer software industry - Ireland. 3. Computer-assisted instruction - Programming. I. Title.
HD9811.I732 I74 1986

Ireland. Dept. of Social Welfare. A National income-related pension scheme. Dublin [1976] viii, 195 p. ; LC Card 82-127069
HD7168 .N39 1976

IRELAND - ECONOMIC CONDITIONS.
Ollerenshaw, Philip, 1953- Banking in nineteenth-century Ireland . Manchester, UK , Wolfeboro, NH, USA , c1987. 263 p. : ISBN 0-7190-2276-2 : LC Card 87-11113 DDC 332.1/09416/7 19
HG950.B45 O55 1987

IRELAND - ECONOMIC CONDITIONS - 1949-
Ireland in transition /. Cork , 1986. 178 p. ; ISBN 0-85342-786-0 (pbk.) : LC Card 87-111629 DDC 306/.09417 19
HC260.5 .I735 1986

IRELAND - ECONOMIC POLICY.
FitzGerald, John D. The national debt and economic policy in the medium term /. Dublin , c1986. 62 p. : ISBN 0-7070-0089-0 (pbk.) : LC Card 87-110464 DDC 336.3/4/09417 19
HJ8630.A2 F58 1986

Ireland in transition / edited by Kieran A. Kennedy. Cork : Published in collaboration with Radio Telefís Éireann by the Mercier Press, 1986. 178 p. ; 21 cm. (The Thomas Davis lecture series) Bibliography: p. 167-178. ISBN 0-85342-786-0 (pbk.) : LC Card 87-111629 DDC 306/.09417 19
1. Ireland - Economic conditions - 1949-. 2. Ireland - Social conditions. I. Kennedy, Kieran Anthony. II. Radio Telefís Éireann. III. Series.
HC260.5 .I735 1986

IRELAND - INDUSTRIES.
Daly, J. Bowles (John Bowles) Glimpses of Irish industries /. London , 1889. xvi, 219, 16 p. ; LC Card 85-666357
HC260.5 .D35x 1889

Monsell, William, 1812-1894. On some of the impediments to Irish manufacturing industry /. Dublin , 1865. 48 p. ; LC Card 85-666368
HC260.5 .M66x 1865

Ireland, Norman J. Product differentiation and non-price competition / Norman J. Ireland. Oxford, UK ; New York, NY, USA : B. Blackwell, 1987. 192 p. : ill. ; 24 cm. Spine title: Product differentiation & non-price competition. Bibliography: p. [179]-188. Includes index. ISBN 0-631-13846-3 : LC Card 86-24504 DDC 658.8/16 19
1. Product management. 2. Competition. 3. Prices. 4. Marketing. I. Title. II. Title: Product differentiation & non-price competition.
HF5415.15 .I74 1987

Ireland. Oireachtas. Dáil. Committee on Public Expenditure. Review of Shannon Free Airport Development Company Limited : report / of the Committee on Public Expenditure = Athbhreithniú ar Chuideachta Forbartha Aerfort Neamhchustam na Sionna Teoranta : Dáil Éireann Tuarascáil ón Gcoiste um Chaiteachas Poiblí. Dublin : Stationery Office : To be purchased from the Govt. Publications Sale Office, [1983?] 79 p. : ill. ; 30 cm. "Pl. 4034." LC Card 87-146082 DDC 387.7/36/094193 19
1. Shannon Free Airport Development Company. I. Title. II. Title: Athbhreithniú ar Chuideachta Forbartha Aerfort Neamhchustam na Sionna Teoranta.
HE9797.5.I72 S54 1983

IRELAND - POPULATION POLICY.
Eastern Regional Development Organisation (Ireland) Eastern Region settlement strategy, 2011. Dublin [1985] viii, 21 p. : LC Card 87-672678
HB3589 .E27x 1985a

Eastern Regional Development Organisation (Ireland) Eastern Region settlement strategy, 2011. Dublin [1985] xviii, 269 p. : LC Card 87-672656
HB3589 .E27x 1985

IRELAND - RURAL CONDITIONS.
Russell, George William, 1867-1935. Co-operation and nationality . Dublin , c1982. 103 p. ; ISBN 0-7165-0335-2 (pbk.) LC Card 82-192895 DDC 334/.683/09417 19
HD1491.I6 R87 1982 ***NYPL [JLD 86-2358]***

IRELAND - SOCIAL CONDITIONS.
Chartism in Wales and Ireland. New York , 1986. 15, 32, 16, 18, 20 p. : ISBN 0-8240-5594-2 (alk. paper) : LC Card 86-25706 DDC 322/.2/0941 19
HD8396 .C494 1986

Ireland in transition /. Cork , 1986. 178 p. ; ISBN 0-85342-786-0 (pbk.) : LC Card 87-111629 DDC 306/.09417 19
HC260.5 .I735 1986

I.Re.R.
Conto consolidato della spesa pubblica in Lombardia /. Milano, Italy , c1982. 234 p. ; LC Card 85-147746
HJ9925.I8 C63 1982

Lavoro femminile, sviluppo tecnologico e segregazione occupazionale /. Milano, Italy , c1984. 458 p. : LC Card 84-190076 DDC 331.4/0945 19
HD6154 .L385 1984 ***NYPL [*QO 87-1143]***

Ires/Cgil Lombardia (Series). Materiali di ricerca .
(3) Guidotti, Daniela. Strategia generale e azione decentrata . Milano, Italy , c1986. 216 p. ; LC Card 86-193797
HD6976.T42 I764 1986

IRF African Highway Conference (4th : 1980 : Nairobi, Kenya) Shimeles Asfaw. The economic evaluation of low traffic roads . [Nairobi? , 1980?] ii, 28, 13 leaves, [2] leaves of plates : LC Card 85-981138
HE367.K43 E374 1980

Iriarte, Gregorio. Esquemas para la interpretación de la realidad / Gregorio Iriarte. La Paz, Bolivia : SENPAS, 1985. 10 v. : ill. ; 22 cm. CONTENTS. - 1. El mundo actual y sus problemas más graves -- 2. "El orden" (o "el desorden") económico internacional -- 3. América Latina, esperanzas, frustraciones y desafíos -- 4. Análisis de la realidad boliviano: aspectos sociales -- 5. Análisis de la realidad boliviano: aspectos económicos -- 6. Análisis de la realidad boliviana: la crisis económica actual -- 7. La política como ciencia y como praxis -- 8. El sindicalismo a nivel nacional e internacional -- 9. Teorías para analizar el subdesarrollo -- 10. Respuestas cristianas ante la problemática actual. LC Card 87-112879
1. Bolivia - Economic conditions - 1952-1982. 2. Bolivia - Social conditions. 3. Economic history - 1971-. 4. Developing countries - Economic conditions. 5. Bolivia - Economic conditions - 1982-. I. Title.
HC182 .I727 1985

Irikov, V. A. (Valeriĭ Alekseevich) Pospelov, Germogen Sergeevich. Protsedury i algoritmy formirovaniia kompleksnykh programm /. Moskva , 1985. 422, [2] p. : LC Card 86-203758
HC336.25 .P567 1985

The Irish Board of Works, 1831-1878 /.
Griffiths, A. R. G., 1940- New York , 1987. iii, 214 p. ; ISBN 0-8240-7810-1 (alk. paper) : LC Card 87-24495 DDC 363/.09415 19
HD4150.3 .G75 1987

IRISH QUESTION.
Chesterton, Gilbert Keith, 1874-1936. [Crimes of England. French.] Les crimes de l'Angleterre [microform]. Paris, 1916. 273 p. LC Card 19-16286
DA47.2 .C55 *NYPL [*Z-4049 no.7]*

Irish railways : proceedings of the deputation. London : Fores & Co., 1839. 8 p. ; 23 cm. Proceedings of a meeting held by a group of members of Parliament and others to formulate a plan for constructing railways in Ireland. LC Card 85-665175
1. Railroads - Ireland.
HE3047 .I74x 1839

Irish, Richard K. Go hire yourself an employer / Richard K. Irish. A rev. and expanded 3rd ed. New York : Anchor Press, 1987. xxviii, 280 ; 21 cm. Includes index. ISBN 0-385-23378-7 (pbk.) : LC Card 87-6896 DDC 650.1/4 19
1. Job hunting. 2. Career changes. I. Title.
HF5382.7 .I74 1987

Irkutskiĭ gosudarstvennyĭ universitet im. A.A. Zhdanova. Sotsial'noe razvitie molodezhi v trudovykh kollektivakh novykh gorodov Sibiri . Irkutsk , 1980. 158 p. ; LC Card 82-110658
HD6276.S593 S527 1980

Irland, Lloyd C. Colgan, Charles S. The natural resource industries of Maine . [Augusta, Me.] [1986] 135 p. : LC Card 87-620550 DDC 338.09741 19
HD9007.M2 C64 1986

IRON AND STEEL TRADES CONFEDERATION (GREAT BRITAIN)
Sirs, Bill. Hard labour /. London , 1985. 151 p., [8] p. of plates : ISBN 0-283-99241-7 : LC Card 86-191030 DDC 331.88/1691/0924 B 19
HD6665.S57 A3 1985

IRON AND STEEL WORKERS.
International Labour Organisation. Iron and Steel Committee. Productivity improvement and its effects on the level of employment and working conditions in the iron and steel industry /. Geneva , 1986. ii, 66 p. : ISBN 92-2-105498-5 (pbk.) : LC Card 86-222063 DDC 338.4/56691 19
HD9510.5 .I525 1986

IRON AND STEEL WORKERS - EFFECT OF TECHNOLOGICAL INNOVATIONS ON.
International Labour Organisation. Iron and Steel Committee. Policies for maintaining social development through collective bargaining, legislation, and adequate social security protection to cope with structural change in the iron and steel industry /. Geneva , 1986. 45 p. ; ISBN 92-2-105497-7 (pbk.) : LC Card 86-222047 DDC 331.89/0469142 19
HD8039.I5 I6 1986

IRON AND STEEL WORKERS - ENGLAND - CORBY (NORTHAMPTONSHIRE)
Maunders, A. R. A process of struggle . Aldershot, Hampshire, England , Brookfield, Vt., USA , c1987. xi, 283 p. : ISBN 0-566-05227-X : LC Card 86-25640 DDC 338.6/042 19
HD9521.8.C85 M38 1987
NYPL [JLD 87-1533]

IRON AND STEEL WORKERS - GOVERNMENT POLICY.
International Labour Organisation. Iron and Steel Committee. Policies for maintaining social development through collective bargaining, legislation, and adequate social security protection to cope with structural change in the iron and steel industry /. Geneva , 1986. 45 p. ; ISBN 92-2-105497-7 (pbk.) : LC Card 86-222047 DDC 331.89/0469142 19
HD8039.I5 I6 1986

IRON AND STEEL WORKERS - GOVERNMENT POLICY - UNITED STATES.
Causes and remedies for displacement of steel workers . [Washington, D.C.? , 1985] iv, 83, 2, 2 p. ; LC Card 86-601602 DDC 331.13/704 19
HD8039.I52 U524 1985

IRON AND STEEL WORKERS - INDIA.
Mathur, Reeta. Industrial relations in public enterprises /. Jaipur , 1986. vii, 226 p. ; LC Card 86-902265 DDC 331/.04135454 19
HD6976.I52 M37 1986

IRON AND STEEL WORKERS - MONONGAHELA RIVER REGION (W. VA. AND PA.)
Hoerr, John P., 1930- And the wolf finally came . Pittsburgh, PA , 1988. p. cm. ISBN 0-8229-3572-4 LC Card 87-24932 DDC 338.4/7669142/097488 19
HD9517.M85 H64 1988

IRON AND STEEL WORKERS - PENNSYLVANIA.
Hoerr, John P., 1930- And the wolf finally came . Pittsburgh, PA , 1988. p. cm. ISBN 0-8229-3572-4 LC Card 87-24932 DDC 338.4/7669142/097488 19
HD9517.M85 H64 1988

IRON AND STEEL WORKERS - PENNSYLVANIA - BETHLEHEM - HISTORY.
Strohmeyer, John, 1924- Crisis in Bethlehem . New York, N.Y., U. S.A. , 1987, c1986. xii, 244 p. ; ISBN 0-14-010370-8 (pbk.) LC Card 87-11835 DDC 338.7/669142/0974822 19
HD9519.B4 S87 1987

IRON AND STEEL WORKERS - UNITED STATES.
Causes and remedies for displacement of steel workers . [Washington, D.C.? , 1985] iv, 83, 2, 2 p. ; LC Card 86-601602 DDC 331.13/704 19
HD8039.I52 U524 1985

IRON AND STEEL WORKERS - UNITED STATES - CASE STUDIES.
Copeland, Vincent. The blast furnace brothers /. New York, N.Y. , 1973. iv, 33 p. : LC Card 87-125932 DDC 331.13/3 19
HD4903.3.B582 U63 1973

IRON AND STEEL WORKERS - WEST VIRGINIA.
Hoerr, John P., 1930- And the wolf finally came . Pittsburgh, PA , 1988. p. cm. ISBN 0-8229-3572-4 LC Card 87-24932 DDC 338.4/7669142/097488 19
HD9517.M85 H64 1988

Iron curtain lands. see **Communist countries.**

IRON FOUNDRIES - ITALY - LOMBARDY - HISTORY.
Frumento, Armando. Le repubbliche cisalpina e italiana . Milano , 1985. xii, 608 p. ; LC Card 86-215881
HD9525.I82 F72 1985

IRON INDUSTRY AND TRADE - AUSTRIA.
Kramer, Helmut, 1939- Industrielle Strukturprobleme Österreichs . Wien , 1980. 112 p. ; LC Card 81-103725 DDC 338.4/76691/09436 19
HD9525.A82 K73 1980
NYPL [JLD 86-1237]

IRON INDUSTRY AND TRADE - AUSTRIA - SYTRIA - CASE STUDIES.
Stahl und Eisen bricht . Wien [1986] xi, 202 p. : ISBN 3-900351-62-7 LC Card 87-140293 DDC 330.9436/053 19
HC265 .S736 1986

IRON INDUSTRY AND TRADE - AUSTRIA - UPPER AUSTRIA - HISTORY.
Beiträge zur Geschichte des Eisenwesens in Oberösterreich. Linz , 1949- v. <1 > : LC Card 87-117640
HD9525.A83 U663 1949

IRON INDUSTRY AND TRADE - BRAZIL - CARAJÁS MOUNTAINS REGION.
Report to the World Bank, Amazônia Mineração S.A. . London [1979?] v, 57, [31] leaves : LC Card 85-154695
HD9524.B8 R46 1979

IRON INDUSTRY AND TRADE - CAPITAL PRODUCTIVITY.
International Labour Organisation. Iron and Steel Committee. Productivity improvement and its effects on the level of employment and working conditions in the iron and steel industry /. Geneva , 1986. ii, 66 p. : ISBN 92-2-105498-5 (pbk.) : LC Card 86-222063 DDC 338.4/56691 19
HD9510.5 .I525 1986

IRON INDUSTRY AND TRADE - CONGRESSES.
L'Industria siderurgica . Milano [1986] 193 p. : ISBN 88-14-00787-X : LC Card 86-222572
HD9510.5 .I473 1986

IRON INDUSTRY AND TRADE - EUROPE - HISTORY.
Fremdling, Rainer. Technologischer Wandel und internationaler Handel im 18. und 19. Jahrhundert . Berlin , c1986. 493 p. ; ISBN 3-428-06042-3 LC Card 87-127793 DDC 382/.456691/094 19
HD9525.A2 F74 1986

IRON INDUSTRY AND TRADE - FRANCE.
Masson, Jean Louis. Demain l'acier français /. Paris , c1986. 404 p. : ISBN 2-254-86071-1 : LC Card 86-190326
HD9522.5 .M37 1986

IRON INDUSTRY AND TRADE - FRANCE - HISTORY - 18TH CENTURY.
Woronoff, Denis, 1939- L'industrie sidérurgique en France pendant la Révolution et l'Empire /. Paris , c1984. 592 p. : ISBN 2-7132-0843-2 LC Card 85-138825 DDC 338.4/76691/0944 19
HD9522.5 .W64 1984 *NYPL [JLE 86-3532]*

IRON INDUSTRY AND TRADE - FRANCE - HISTORY - 19TH CENTURY.
Woronoff, Denis, 1939- L'industrie sidérurgique en France pendant la Révolution et l'Empire /. Paris , c1984. 592 p. : ISBN 2-7132-0843-2 LC Card 85-138825 DDC 338.4/76691/0944 19
HD9522.5 .W64 1984 *NYPL [JLE 86-3532]*

IRON INDUSTRY AND TRADE - GERMANY - HISTORY.
Meyer, August. Das Syndikat . Braunschweig , c1986. 348 p. ; ISBN 3-925151-18-4 LC Card 87-129940 DDC 338.2/73/0943 19
HD9523.9.R45 M49 1986

Steinisch, Irmgard. Arbeitszeitverkürzung und sozialer Wandel . Berlin , New York , 1986. xiv, 640 p. : ISBN 3-11-010483-0 LC Card 87-110005 DDC 331.25/7/0973 19
HD5119.I52 U67 1986

IRON INDUSTRY AND TRADE - GERMANY (WEST) - HISTORY.
Gienanth, Ulrich, Freiherr von, 1907- 250 Jahre Eisenwerk Eisenberg . Eisenberg/Pfalz [1986] 68 p. : LC Card 87-409570 DDC 338.7/6691/0943 19
HD9523.9.G4 G54 1986

IRON INDUSTRY AND TRADE - GREAT BRITAIN - HISTORY.
Roberts, C. W. (Colin William), 1916- A legacy from Victorian enterprise . [Farnborough, Berkshire?] , 1983. x, 277 p. : ISBN 0-9509107-1-6 (pbk.) : LC Card 85-109000 DDC 338.7/6691/0942984 19
HD9521.9.B74 R62 1983
NYPL [JLD 86-2141]

IRON INDUSTRY AND TRADE - ITALY.
Moro, Domenico. Crisi e ristrutturazione dell'industria siderurgica italiana /. [Milano] [1984] 256 p. : LC Card 84-181172 DDC 338.4/76691/0945 19
HD9525.I82 M67 1984
NYPL [JLE 86-3649]

IRON INDUSTRY AND TRADE - ITALY - CONGRESSES.
L'Industria siderurgica . Milano [1986] 193 p. : ISBN 88-14-00787-X : LC Card 86-222572
HD9510.5 .I473 1986

IRON INDUSTRY AND TRADE - ITALY - HISTORY.
Frumento, Armando. Le repubbliche cisalpina e italiana . Milano , 1985. xii, 608 p. ; LC Card 86-215881
HD9525.I82 F72 1985

IRON INDUSTRY AND TRADE - LABOR PRODUCTIVITY.
International Labour Organisation. Iron and Steel Committee. Productivity improvement and its effects on the level of employment and working conditions in the iron and steel industry /. Geneva , 1986. ii, 66 p. : ISBN 92-2-105498-5 (pbk.) : LC Card 86-222063 DDC 338.4/56691 19
HD9510.5 .I525 1986

IRON INDUSTRY AND TRADE - PENNSYLVANIA - EASTON REGION - HISTORY - 19 CENTURY.
Metz, Lance E. Sherman's guide to Hugh Moore Park /. Easton, PA , 1988. p. cm. ISBN 0-930973-07-0 (pbk.) : LC Card 87-25622 DDC 338.09748/22 19
HE395 .P43 1988

IRON INDUSTRY AND TRADE - RUSSIAN S.F.S.R. - MOSCOW - HISTORY - SOURCES.
Iz istorii razvitiia metallurgicheskoĭ

promyshlennosti Moskvy, 1883-1932 gg. . Moskva , 1981. 219 p. ; LC Card 84-163581
HD9525.S653 M64 1981
*NYPL [*QIP 87-3316]*

IRON INDUSTRY AND TRADE - SENEGAL.
ECA/UNIDO Basic Metals and Engineering Industries Development Programme Mission. Rapport de la Mission sur le programme de développement des industries métallurgiques de base et mécaniques en République du Sénégal. [S.l.] [1979] 41, 3 p. (2 fold.) ; LC Card 80-981173
HD9506.S42 E33 1979

IRON INDUSTRY AND TRADE - SOVIET UNION - PERSONNEL MANAGEMENT.
Bakanov, K. P. (Konstantin Pavlovich) Sovershenstvovanie organizatsii truda na predpriiatiiakh chernoĭ metallurgii /. Moskva , 1981. 47 p. ; LC Card 82-104389
HD9525.S652 B355 1981

IRON INDUSTRY AND TRADE - SPAIN - ALMERÍA (PROVINCE)
Sánchez Picón, Andrés. La minería del Levante almeriense, 1838-1930 . Almería [1983] 308 p., [14] leaves of plates : ISBN 84-85219-49-X LC Card 85-126928
HD9506.S762 A457 1983

IRON INDUSTRY AND TRADE - SWEDEN.
Sweden. Malmfältsutredningen. Framtid i malmfälten . [Stockholm] [1984] 155, 5 p. : ISBN 91-38-08283-7 LC Card 86-111519
HD9506.S82 S94 1984

IRON INDUSTRY AND TRADE - TECHNOLOGICAL INNOVATIONS - EUROPE - HISTORY.
Fremdling, Rainer. Technologischer Wandel und internationaler Handel im 18. und 19. Jahrhundert . Berlin , c1986. 493 p. ; ISBN 3-428-06042-3 LC Card 87-127793 DDC 382/.456691/094 19
HD9525.A2 F74 1986

IRON INDUSTRY AND TRADE - UNITED STATES.
The Effects of semifinished steel imports on the U. S. iron and steel scrap industry . Washington, D.C. [1985] xv, 137 p. : LC Card 86-603428
HD9515 .E33 1985

The U. S. primary iron and steel industry since 1958. Washington, D.C. , 1985. xvi, 138 p. :
NYPL [JLF 86-689]

IRON INDUSTRY AND TRADE - UNITED STATES - HISTORY.
Steinisch, Irmgard. Arbeitszeitverkürzung und sozialer Wandel . Berlin , New York , 1986. xiv, 640 p. : ISBN 3-11-010483-0 LC Card 87-110005 DDC 331.25/7/0973 19
HD5119.I52 U67 1986

IRON INDUSTRY AND TRADE - WALES - BRITON FERRY (WEST GLAMORGAN) - HISTORY.
Roberts, C. W. (Colin William), 1916- A legacy from Victorian enterprise . [Farnborough, Berkshire?] , 1983. x, 277 p. : ISBN 0-9509107-1-6 (pbk.) : LC Card 85-109000 DDC 338.7/6691/0942984 19
HD9521.9.B74 R62 1983
NYPL [JLD 86-2141]

IRON MINERS - BRAZIL - DOCE RIVER VALLEY (MINAS GERAIS AND ESPÍRITO SANTO)
Minayo, Maria Cecília de Souza. Os homens de ferro . Rio de Janeiro , 1986. 244 p. : LC Card 87-129149 DDC 331.7/622341/098151 19
HD8039.M72 B86 1986

IRON MINERS - BRAZIL - ITABIRA.
Minayo, Maria Cecília de Souza. Os homens de ferro . Rio de Janeiro , 1986. 244 p. : LC Card 87-129149 DDC 331.7/622341/098151 19
HD8039.M72 B86 1986

IRON MINES AND MINING - BRAZIL - CARAJÁS MOUNTAINS REGION.
Report to the World Bank, Amazônia Mineração S.A. . London [1979?] v, 57, [31] leaves : LC Card 85-154695
HD9524.B8 R46 1979

IRON MINES AND MINING - SWEDEN.
Sweden. Malmfältsutredningen. Framtid i malmfälten . [Stockholm] [1984] 155, 5 p. : ISBN 91-38-08283-7 LC Card 86-111519
HD9506.S82 S94 1984

IRON ORES - PRICES - LATIN AMERICA - ECONOMETRIC MODELS.
Lord, Montague J. Market price models for Latin America's major commodity exports /. Washington, D.C. [1986] vii, 219 p. : LC Card 87-115208 DDC 338.5/2/098 19
HD9014.A2 L67 1986

IRON - TRADE AND STATISTICS. see **IRON INDUSTRY AND TRADE.**

IRON WORKERS. see **IRON AND STEEL WORKERS.**

IRON-WORKS - AUSTRIA - UPPER AUSTRIA - HISTORY.
Beiträge zur Geschichte des Eisenwesens in Oberösterreich. Linz , 1949- v. <1 > : LC Card 87-117640
HD9525.A83 U663 1949

Ironmonger, D. S. National income and economic progress . New York , 1988. p. cm. ISBN 0-312-01566-6 : LC Card 87-24063 DDC 339.3 19
HB141.5 .N375 1988

IRRIGATION AGRICULTURE. see **IRRIGATION FARMING.**

IRRIGATION - BANGLADESH - STATISTICS.
Thana statistics. [Dacca] , 1981- v. ; LC Card 82-903357 DDC 333.73/13/095492021 19
HD880.6.Z63 T46 1981
NYPL [JLM 87-178]

IRRIGATION - BRAZIL, NORTHEAST.
Brazil. Ministerio do Interior. Programa de Irrigação do Nordeste--PROINE . Brasília , 1986. 30 p. ; LC Card 87-400672 DDC 333.91/3/09813 19
HD1741.B82 N623 1986

A Problemática e a política da terra e água do Nordeste. Recife , 1985. 296 p. : LC Card 87-124121 DDC 333.91/00981/3 19
HD1696.B84 N675 1985

IRRIGATION - BRAZIL, NORTHEAST - CONGRESSES.
Convivência do homem com a seca e irrigação no Nordeste /. [Salvador, Brazil] [1984] 76 p. : LC Card 87-130774 DDC 333.91/3/09813 19
HD1741.B82 N624 1984

IRRIGATION CANALS AND FLUMES - PAKISTAN.
Water users associations in Pakistan. Islamabad , 1984. 108 p. ; LC Card 85-930345 DDC 333.91/3/095491 19
HD1741.P13 W37 1984

IRRIGATION - DEVELOPING COUNTRIES - FINANCE.
Irrigation investment, technology, and management strategies for development /. Boulder , 1986. xxvii, 270 p. : ISBN 0-8133-7177-5 (pbk. : alk. paper) : LC Card 85-31523 DDC 338.4/762752/091724 19
HD1741.D44 I77 1986 *NYPL [JLD 87-766]*

IRRIGATION - DEVELOPING COUNTRIES - MANAGEMENT.
Irrigation investment, technology, and management strategies for development /. Boulder , 1986. xxvii, 270 p. : ISBN 0-8133-7177-5 (pbk. : alk. paper) : LC Card 85-31523 DDC 338.4/762752/091724 19
HD1741.D44 I77 1986 *NYPL [JLD 87-766]*

Irrigation development planning : an introduction for engineers / edited by J.R. Rydzewski. Chichester ; New York : Wiley, c1987. xiv, 265 p. : ill. ; 26 cm. Includes bibliographies and index. ISBN 0-471-91506-8 : LC Card 87-2016 DDC 333.91/3 19
1. Irrigation - Planning. 2. Irrigation engineering. I. Rydzewski, J. R.
HD1714 .I77 1987

IRRIGATION DISTRICTS - INDIA - PLANNING - CONGRESSES.
Command area development, successes and learnings . Hyderabad , c1980. iii, 138 p. ; LC Card 83-906246 DDC 338.1/854 19
HD1741.I29 C65 1980 *NYPL [JLD 87-597]*

IRRIGATION - ECONOMIC ASPECTS - ATBARA RIVER REGION (ETHIOPIA AND SUDAN)
Abdel Ati, Hassan A. Lower River Atbara area (Nile Province) . [Khartoum] Sudan [1985] vii, 166 p., [19] leaves of plates : LC Card 86-981108 DDC 333.91/3/09625 19
HD1741.S852 A832 1985

IRRIGATION - ECONOMIC ASPECTS - BRAZIL, NORTHEAST.

IRRIGATION - ECONOMIC ASPECTS - INDIA.
Dhawan, B. D. Irrigation in India's agricultural development . New Delhi , Newbury Park [Calif.] , 1987. p. cm. ISBN 0-8039-9544-X LC Card 87-22521 DDC 338.1/62 19
HD1741.I29 D47 1987

IRRIGATION - ECONOMIC ASPECTS - INDIA - BIHAR.
Poddar, B. N. Development of irrigation and Indian agriculture /. New Delhi , c1987. 331 p. ; LC Card 87-901300 DDC 338.1/62 19
HD2075.B5 P63 1967

IRRIGATION ENGINEERING.
Irrigation development planning . Chichester , New York , c1987. xiv, 265 p. : ISBN 0-471-91506-8 : LC Card 87-2016 DDC 333.91/3 19
HD1714 .I77 1987

IRRIGATION ENGINEERING - ITALY - HISTORY - ADDRESSES, ESSAYS, LECTURES.
Le Bonifiche in Italia dal '700 a oggi /. Roma , 1984. viii, 437 p. : ISBN 88-420-2429-5 : LC Card 85-173148
HD1683.I8 B66 1984 *NYPL [JSD 87-50]*

IRRIGATION ENGINEERING - JAPAN - AKA RIVER WATERSHED - HISTORY.
Kelly, William W. (William Wright), 1946- Water control in Tokugawa Japan . Ithaca, N.Y. , c1982. ix, 260 p. : LC Card 83-126822
HD1741.J32 A325 1982

IRRIGATION FARMING.
A Agricultura irrigada como estratégia de desenvolvimento regional /. Brasília [198-] 56 leaves ; LC Card 87-403682 DDC 338.1/62 19
HD1741.B82 N614 1980z

IRRIGATION FARMING - BRAZIL, NORTHEAST.
A Agricultura irrigada como estratégia de desenvolvimento regional /. Brasília [198-] 56 leaves ; LC Card 87-403682 DDC 338.1/62 19
HD1741.B82 N614 1980z

IRRIGATION FARMING - ECONOMIC ASPECTS - SUDAN.
D'Silva, Brian. Sudan's irrigated subsector . Washington, D.C. , 1986. iv, 31 p. : LC Card 86-602812 DDC 333.91/3/09624 19
HD1741.S85 D75 1986

IRRIGATION FARMING - GOVERNMENT POLICY - SUDAN.
Abdel Ati, Hassan A. Lower River Atbara area (Nile Province) . [Khartoum] Sudan [1985] vii, 166 p., [19] leaves of plates : LC Card 86-981108 DDC 333.91/3/09625 19
HD1741.S852 A832 1985

IRRIGATION FARMING - LATIN AMERICA.
A Agricultura irrigada como estratégia de desenvolvimento regional /. Brasília [198-] 56 leaves ; LC Card 87-403682 DDC 338.1/62 19
HD1741.B82 N614 1980z

IRRIGATION FARMING. - UNITED STATES.
Sloggett, Gordon. Ground-water mining in the United States /. Washington, D.C , 1986. iv, 19 p. : LC Card 86-602788 DDC 338.1 s 338.1/4 19
HD1751 .A91854 no. 555 S616.U6

IRRIGATION - GOVERNMENT POLICY - CONGRESSES.
Water and water policy in world food supplies . College Station , c1987. x, 434 p. : ISBN 0-89096-278-2 : LC Card 86-23065 DDC 333.91/3 19
HD1690.5 .W38 1987

IRRIGATION - GOVERNMENT POLICY - DEVELOPING COUNTRIES.
Irrigation investment, technology, and management strategies for development /. Boulder , 1986. xxvii, 270 p. : ISBN 0-8133-7177-5 (pbk. : alk. paper) : LC Card 85-31523 DDC 338.4/762752/091724 19
HD1741.D44 I77 1986 *NYPL [JLD 87-766]*

IRRIGATION - GOVERNMENT POLICY - WEST (U. S.) - HISTORY.
Reisner, Marc. Cadillac desert . New York,

N.Y., U. S.A. , 1987, c1986. 582 p., [18] p. of plates : ISBN 0-14-010432-1 (pbk.) : LC Card 87-7602 DDC 333.91/00978 19
HD1739.A17 R45 1987

Irrigation in India's agricultural development . Dhawan, B. D. New Delhi , Newbury Park [Calif.] , 1987. p. cm. ISBN 0-8039-9544-X LC Card 87-22521 DDC 338.1/62 19
HD1741.I29 D47 1987

IRRIGATION - INDIA.
Command Area Development programme in India . New Delhi , 1981. ii, 62 p. ; LC Card 83-907584 *NYPL [JLF 86-818]*

IRRIGATION - INDIA - MANAGEMENT.
Chambers, Robert, 1932- Managing canal irrigation . Cambridge [Cambridgeshire] , New York , 1988. p. cm. ISBN 0-521-34554-5 LC Card 87-16738 DDC 333.91/3/0954 19
HD1741.I29 C45 1988

Irrigation investment, technology, and management strategies for development / edited by K. William Easter. Boulder : Westview Press, 1986. xxvii, 270 p. : ill. ; 23 cm. (Studies in water policy and management . no. 9) Includes bibliographies and indexes. ISBN 0-8133-7177-5 (pbk. : alk. paper) : LC Card 85-31523 DDC 338.4/762752/091724 19
1. Irrigation - Government policy - Developing countries. 2. Irrigation - Developing countries - Finance. 3. Irrigation - Developing countries - Management. I. Easter, K. William. II. Series.
HD1741.D44 I77 1986 *NYPL [JLD 87-766]*

IRRIGATION - ITALY - CREMONA REGION - HISTORY.
Bellabarba, Marco. Seriolanti e arzenisti . Cremona , 1986- v. <1 > : LC Card 86-167180
HD1676.I82 C743 1986

IRRIGATION - ITALY - PO RIVER PLAIN - HISTORY.
Bellabarba, Marco. Seriolanti e arzenisti . Cremona , 1986- v. <1 > : LC Card 86-167180
HD1676.I82 C743 1986

IRRIGATION - ITALY, SOUTHERN.
Barone, Giuseppe, 1947- Mezzogiorno e modernizzazione . Torino , c1986. xii, 408 p. ; ISBN 88-06-59238-6 : LC Card 86-219130
HC307.S69 B37 1986

IRRIGATION - JAPAN - AKA RIVER WATERSHED - HISTORY.
Kelly, William W. (William Wright), 1946- Water control in Tokugawa Japan . Ithaca, N.Y. , c1982. ix, 260 p. : LC Card 83-126822
HD1741.J32 A325 1982

IRRIGATION LAWS - PAKISTAN.
Water users associations in Pakistan. Islamabad , 1984. 108 p. ; LC Card 85-930345 DDC 333.91/3/095491 19
HD1741.P13 W37 1984

IRRIGATION - MANAGEMENT.
Chambers, Robert, 1932- Managing canal irrigation . Cambridge [Cambridgeshire] , New York , 1988. p. cm. ISBN 0-521-34554-5 LC Card 87-16738 DDC 333.91/3/0954 19
HD1741.I29 C45 1988

IRRIGATION - PAKISTAN.
Water users associations in Pakistan. Islamabad , 1984. 108 p. ; LC Card 85-930345 DDC 333.91/3/095491 19
HD1741.P13 W37 1984

IRRIGATION - PHILIPPINES - MANAGEMENT.
Chambers, Robert, 1932- Managing canal irrigation . Cambridge [Cambridgeshire] , New York , 1988. p. cm. ISBN 0-521-34554-5 LC Card 87-16738 DDC 333.91/3/0954 19
HD1741.I29 C45 1988

IRRIGATION - PLANNING.
Irrigation development planning . Chichester , New York , c1987. xiv, 265 p. : ISBN 0-471-91506-8 : LC Card 87-2016 DDC 333.91/3 19
HD1714 .I77 1987

IRRIGATION PUMPS - DEVELOPING COUNTRIES - CASE STUDIES.
Socioeconomic aspects of renewable energy technologies . New York , 1988. p. cm. ISBN 0-275-92851-9 (alk. paper) : LC Card 87-22890 DDC 333.7/09172/4 19
HD9502.D442 S63 1988

IRRIGATION - SOCIAL ASPECTS - PAKISTAN.
Water users associations in Pakistan. Islamabad , 1984. 108 p. ; LC Card 85-930345 DDC 333.91/3/095491 19
HD1741.P13 W37 1984

IRRIGATION - SRI LANKA - MANAGEMENT.
Chambers, Robert, 1932- Managing canal irrigation . Cambridge [Cambridgeshire] , New York , 1988. p. cm. ISBN 0-521-34554-5 LC Card 87-16738 DDC 333.91/3/0954 19
HD1741.I29 C45 1988

IRRIGATION - UNITED STATES - ENERGY CONSUMPTION - HISTORY - STATISTICS.
Sloggett, Gordon. Energy and U. S. agriculture . Washington, D.C. , 1985] iii, 43 p. : LC Card 86-600880 DDC 338.1 s 338.1/3 19
HD1751 .A91854 no. 545 S619.E53

IRRIGATION - UNITED STATES - MANAGEMENT.
Sloggett, Gordon. Ground-water mining in the United States /. Washington, D.C , 1986. iv, 19 p. : LC Card 86-602788 DDC 338.1 s 338.1/4 19
HD1751 .A91854 no. 555 S616.U6

IRRIGATION - UZBEK S.S.R.
Ėrgashev, N. (Nazirzhon) Rukovodstvo Kompartii Uzbekistana osvoeniem tselinnykh zemel′ /. Tashkent , 1985. 159 p. ; LC Card 86-231568
HD1741.S782 U84 1985

IRRIGATION WATER - AUSTRALIA - WESTERN AUSTRALIA - FINANCE.
Water Authority of Western Australia. Water Authority of Western Australia Corporate plan, 1986-1991. Appendix C, asset investment program /. Leederville, W.A. [1986] 42 p. ; LC Card 87-158833 DDC 354.9410082/325 19
HD1700.W4 W38 1986

IRRIGATION WATER - UNITED STATES.
Sloggett, Gordon. Ground-water mining in the United States /. Washington, D.C , 1986. iv, 19 p. : LC Card 86-602788 DDC 338.1 s 338.1/4 19
HD1751 .A91854 no. 555 S616.U6

IRRIGATION - WEST (U. S.) - ENERGY CONSERVATION.
Energy and water management in western irrigated agriculture /. Boulder, Colo. , 1986. xxiv, 415 p. : ISBN 0-8133-7086-8 (pbk. : alk. paper) LC Card 85-52184 DDC 333.91/3/0978 19
HD1735 .E54 1986 *NYPL [JLD 87-829]*

Irrtümer in der aktuellen Steuerdiskussion /. Fuest, Winfried, 1946- Köln , c1987. 54 p. : ISBN 3-602-24749-X LC Card 87-409547 DDC 336.2/00943 19
HJ2687 .F834 1987

Irrwege der Freiheit . Wannenmacher, Walter. München , c1986. 322 p. ; ISBN 3-7766-1429-3 LC Card 87-130925 DDC 330.9/048 19
HC59 .W279 1986

Irsigler, Franz. International Congress on Economic History (8th : 1982 : Budapest, Hungary) Münzprägung, Geldumlauf und Wechselkurse . Trier , 1984. 421 p. : ISBN 3-923087-06-3 (pbk.)
HG205 1982 .I53 *NYPL [JLE 86-3176]*

Irwin, Alan. Risk and the control of technology : public policies for road traffic safety in Britain and the United States / Alan Irwin. Manchester [Greater Manchester] ; Dover, N.H., USA : Manchester University Press, c1985. vii, 265 p. : ill. ; 23 cm. Includes index. ISBN 0-7190-1723-8 : LC Card 84-17153 DDC 363.1/25561/0941 19
1. Traffic safety - Government policy - United States. 2. Traffic safety - Government policy - Great Britain. I. Title.
HE5614.2 .I79 1985 *NYPL [JLD 87-929]*

Irwin-Dorsey series in behavioral science in business.
Social science approaches to business behavior /. New York , 1987. vii, 183 p. : ISBN 0-8240-8201-X (alk. paper) : LC Card 86-25802 DDC 658.4 19
HD58.7 .S66 1987

Irwin, Michael H. K. Risks to health and safety on the job / by Michael H.K. Irwin. 1st ed. New York, NY : Public Affairs Committee, c1986. 28 p. : ill. ; 18 cm. (Public affairs pamphlet . no. 644) Cover title. "September 1986"--T.p. verso. ISBN 0-88291-096-5 (pbk.) : LC Card 87-402515 DDC 363.1/1/0973 19
1. Industrial hygiene - United States. 2. Industrial safety - United States. I. Series: Public affairs pamphlet (Public Affairs Committee) , no. 644. II. Title.
HD7654 .I79 1986

Irwin perspectives in international business.
Cateora, Philip R. Marketing . Homewood, Ill. , 1987. xi, 172 p. : ISBN 0-256-05626-9 (pbk.) LC Card 86-83392 DDC 658.8/48 19
HF1009.5 .C37 1987

Mason, R. Hal (Robert Hal), 1929- Management . Homewood, Ill. , 1987. xii, 235 p. : ISBN 0-256-05631-5 (pbk.) LC Card 86-82592 DDC 658/.049 19
HD62.4 .M373 1987

Miller, Janice James. Issues for managers . Homewood, Ill. , 1987. xii, 139 p. : ISBN 0-256-05630-7 (pbk.) LC Card 87-80633 DDC 658/.049 19
HD62.4 .M54 1987

Miller, Robert R., 1929- Introduction to business . Homewood, Ill. , 1987. x, 138 p. : ISBN 0-256-05628-5 (pbk.) LC Card 86-82593 DDC 658/.049 19
HD62.4 .M55 1987

Irwin publications in economics.
Beal, Edwin Fletcher. The practice of collective bargaining /. Homewood, Ill. , 1985. xvi, 560 p. : ISBN 0-256-03214-9 LC Card 84-82023 DDC 331.89 19
HD6508 .B375 1985
*NYPL [*R-Econ. 86-3458]*

Irwin, Robert, 1941-
Making mortgages work for you / Robert Irwin. New York : McGraw-Hill, c1987. viii, 185 p. : ill. ; 24 cm. Rev. ed. of: The new mortgage game. c1982. Includes index. ISBN 0-07-032129-9 : LC Card 86-31270 DDC 332.7/22/0973 19
1. Mortgage loans - United States. 2. Mortgage loans, Variable rate - United States. I. Irwin, Robert, 1941- New mortgage game. II. Title.
HG2040.5.U5 I75 1987

New mortgage game. Irwin, Robert, 1941- Making mortgages work for you / Robert Irwin. New York , c1987. viii, 185 p. : ISBN 0-07-032129-9 : LC Card 86-31270 DDC 332.7/22/0973 19
HG2040.5.U5 I75 1987

The Irwin series in marketing.
Pederson, Carlton A. Selling . Homewood, Ill. , 1988. xvii, 644 p. : ISBN 0-256-03644-6 LC Card 87-81434 DDC 658.8/5 19
HF5438.25 .P42 1988

Peter, J. Paul. Consumer behavior . Homewood, Ill. , 1987. xvii, 698 p., [16] p. of plates : ISBN 0-256-03177-0 LC Card 86-81801 DDC 658.8/342 19
HF5415.3 .P468 1987

Readings and cases in basic marketing /. Homewood, Ill. , 1987. ix, 365 p. : ISBN 0-256-05795-8 (pbk.) LC Card 86-83136 DDC 658.8 19
HF5415 .R334 1987

Readings and cases in marketing management /. Homewood, Ill. , 1987. xv, 443 p. : ISBN 0-256-03161-4 (pbk.) LC Card 86-82585 DDC 658.8 19
HF5415.13 .R362 1987

IS-LM MODEL (MACROECONOMICS)
Young, Warren, 1949- Interpreting Mr. Keynes . Boulder , 1986. p. cm. ISBN 0-8133-0533-0 : LC Card 87-10535 DDC 330.15/6 19
HB99.7 .Y68 1986

Is there a moral obligation to save the family farm? / edited by Gary Comstock. 1st ed. Ames : Iowa State University Press, 1987. xxvii, 427 p. : ill. ; 23 cm. Includes bibliographies and index. ISBN 0-8138-1000-0 (pbk.) LC Card 87-13399 DDC 338.1/0973 19
1. Family farms - Government policy - United States. 2. United States - Rural conditions. 3. Agriculture - Economic aspects - United States. 4. Agriculture and state - United States. I. Comstock, Gary, 1954-.
HD1476.U5 I8 1987

ISA. see **Instrument Society of America.**

Isacson, Maths, 1948-
Proto-industrialisation in Scandinavia : craft skills in the industrial revolution / Maths Isacson, and Lars Magnusson. Leamington Spa, UK ; New York : Berg Publishers ; p. cm. Bibliography: p. Includes index. ISBN 0-85496-514-9 : LC Card 86-32062 DDC 338.09485 19
1. Sweden - Industries - History - 19th century. 2. Scandinavia - Industries - History - 19th century. 3. Handicraft - Sweden - History - 19th century. 4. Handicraft - Scandinavia - History - 19th century. 5. Sweden - Economic conditions. 6. Scandinavia - Economic conditions. I. Magnusson, Lars. II. Title.
HC375 .I8 1987

Vägen till fabrikerna : industriell tradition och yrkeskunnande i Sverige under 1800-talet / Maths Isacson & Lars Magnusson. [Stockholm] : Gidlund ; [Uppsala] : Verdandi, c1983. 195, [1] p. : ill. ; 20 cm. Bibliography: p. 185-[196] ISBN 91-7021-464-6 : LC Card 84-125076
1. Sweden - Industries - History - 19th century. 2. Handicraft - Sweden - History - 19th century. 3. Sweden - Economic conditions. I. Magnusson, Lars, 1941-. II. Title.
HC375 .I83 1983

Isacsson, Göthe. Index för prisregleringar. Stockholm : Statistiska centralbyrån, [1985?] 80 p. : ill. ; 25 cm. By Göthe Isacsson. ISBN 91-618-0082-1 LC Card 85-206079
1. Consumer price indexes - Sweden. 2. Prices - Sweden. I. Sweden. Statistiska centralbyrån. II. Title.
HB235.S8 I83 1985

Isaeva, M. G. (Muza Gavrilovna)
Ėffektivnost′ territorial′noĭ organizat͡sii promyshlennogo proizvodstva v Kazakhstane /. Alma-Ata , 1980. 190 p. ; LC Card 82-164638
HC337.K33 D53 1980

Ėkonomicheskai͡a ot͡senka i prognozirovanie ispol′zovanii͡a prirodnykh resursov Kazakhstana /. Alma-Ata , 1980. 161 p. ; LC Card 82-106708
HC337.K3 E34 1980

ʻĪsawī, Ibrāhīm Fu'ād. ʻAlāqī, Madanī ʻAbd al-Qādir. al-Idārah wa-al-bīʼah . [Jiddah] , 1985. 136 p. : LC Card 86-200390
HD70.S28 A422 1985

Isaza Tobón, Gabriela. El IDEMA, hacia una pérdida de los objetivos sociales. [Colombia? : s.n., between 1984 and 1987] ([Colombia?] : Litoarte) 126 p., [1] leaf of plates : ill. ; 25 cm. Cover title. Prepared by Gabriela Isaza Tobón and Hernando Valencia Correa. Bibliography: p. 111-115. LC Card 87-404223 DDC 381/.41/09861 19
1. Instituto de Mercadeo Agropecuario (Colombia). 2. Farm produce - Colombia - Marketing. 3. Produce trade - Colombia. I. Valencia Correa, Hernando. II. Title.
HD9014.C72 I8 1984

ISBA area information, 1978 / compiled by Research Bureau Limited. London : Incorporated Society of British Advertisers, 1978. 147 p. : maps ; 21 x 30 cm. ISBN 0-906241-00-6 (pbk.) LC Card 83-225656 DDC 381/.1/0941021 19
1. Population - Great Britain - Statistics. 2. Mass media - Great Britain - Statistics. 3. Stores, Retail - Great Britain - Statistics. 4. Retail trade - Great Britain - Statistics. 5. Market surveys - Great Britain. 6. Advertising - Great Britain - Statistics. I. Incorporated Society of British Advertisers. II. Research Bureau Limited.
HA1134 .I83 1978

**ISDN : **the implementation begins / Communications Systems & Services. Boston, MA (200 Portland St., Boston 02114) : Yankee Group, c1987. iv, 118 p. : ill. ; 28 cm. At head of title: Communications/Information Systems. LC Card 87-159823 DDC 380.1/450046 19
1. Data transmission equipment industry. 2. Digital communications. 3. Integrated services digital networks. 4. Market surveys. I. Communications Systems & Services. II. Communications/Information Systems (Firm : Yankee Group).
HD9696.D382 I82 1987

Iseppi, Franco. Il Territorio immaginario /. Milano [1980] 106 p. ; ISBN 88-20-41848-7 : LC Card 81-123209 DDC 302.2/34/0945 19
HE8700.9.I8 T47 1980
NYPL [JFD 86-8337]

ISER working paper .
(86.2) Goldsmith, Oliver Scott. How state spending reductions affect economic activity /. Fairbanks [1986] 40, 10 p. : LC Card 86-622972 DDC 330.9798/05 19
HJ7553 .G64 1986

ISÈRE (FRANCE) - ECONOMIC CONDITIONS.
Perrin, Jacqueline. L'enquête de 1848 sur le travail en Isère /. Grenoble , 1985. 251 p., [1] leaf of plates : ISBN 2-904661-03-4 : LC Card 86-227898
HC277.I8 P47 1985

ISÈRE (FRANCE) - INDUSTRIES - HISTORY.
Perrin, Jacqueline. L'enquête de 1848 sur le travail en Isère /. Grenoble , 1985. 251 p., [1] leaf of plates : ISBN 2-904661-03-4 : LC Card 86-227898
HC277.I8 P47 1985

Isern, Werner, 1950- Die Versicherung von Krediten als Instrument kreditspezifischer Risikovorsorge im Aktivgeschäft der Banken : eine theoretische Analyse der bilanziellen Auswirkungen bei aufsichtsrechtlicher Anerkennung / Werner Isern. Frankfurt am Main ; New York : P. Lang, c1984. 303 p. : ill. ; 21 cm. (Europäische Hochschulschriften. Reihe V, Volks- und Betriebswirtschaft, 0531-7339 . Bd. 505 = vol. 505 = vol. 505) Bibliography: p. 290-303. ISBN 3-8204-5319-9 LC Card 85-195374 DDC 368.8/7 19
1. Insurance, Credit. I. Series: Europäische Hochschulschriften. Reihe V, Volks- und Betriebswirtschaft , Bd. 505. II. Title.
HG9977 .I84 1984

Ishaq, Ashfaq, 1953- Cortes, Mariluz. Success in small and medium-scale enterprises . New York , c1987. xiii, 289 p. ; ISBN 0-19-520593-6 : LC Card 86-46296 DDC 338.6/42/09861 19
HD2346.C7 C69 1987

Ishikawa, Kaoru, 1915- Quality control circles at work . Tokyo , 1984. v, 232 p. : ISBN 92-833-1074-9 LC Card 85-133901 DDC 658.5/62/0952 19
HD66 .Q36 1984 ***NYPL [JLD 87-806]***

Ishmael, Cheryl. Ratemaking : a review of municipal credit ratings with emphasis upon New York State : a report to the Chairman, New York State Senate Finance Committee / Cheryl Ishmael. [Albany, N.Y.] : The Committee, [1984] xi, 152 p. : ill. ; 28 cm. "November 1984." Bibliography: p. 147-152.
1. Municipal bonds - Ratings - United States. 2. Municipal bonds - Ratings - New York (State). I. New York (State). Legislature. Senate. Finance Committe. II. Title. ***NYPL [JLF 86-598]***

Ishmuratov, Baĭron Mustafovich.
Geograficheskie osobennosti formirovanii͡a agrarno-promyshlennykh kompleksov v Predbaĭkal′e /. Irkutsk , 1978. 145 p. : LC Card 81-162870
HD9015.S653 I74 1978

Regional′nye osobennosti rat͡sionalizat͡sii prirodopol′zovanii͡a i okhrany sredy /. Irkutsk , 1980. 177 p. ; LC Card 82-111826
HC337.R852 S5266 1980

Ishwar Prakash. see **Prakash, Ishwar.**

Iskakov, B. I. (Boris Ivanovich)
Demograficheskoe modelirovanie : uchebnoe posobie / B.I. Iskakov, N.P. Tikhomirov. Moskva : MINKh im. G.V. Plekhanova, 1982. 75 p. ; 20 cm. At head of title: Ministerstvo vysshego i srednego spet͡sial′nogo obrazovanii͡a RSFSR. Moskovskiĭ ordena Trudovogo Krasnogo Znameni institut narodnogo khozi͡aĭstva im. G.V. Plekhanova. Bibliography: p. 73-74. LC Card 83-179019
1. Population - Mathematical models. 2. Soviet Union - Population - Mathematical models. I. Tikhomirov, N. P. (Nikolaĭ Petrovich). II. Title.
HB849.51 .I85 1982

Iskazivanje i ocjenjivanje rezultata poslovanja organizacija udruženog rada /. Turk, Ivan. Zagreb , 1982. x, 171 p. ; LC Card 83-110726
HD70.Y8 T87 1982

Iske, Thorsten, 1960- Verbundgeschäfte : betriebswirtschaftliche Analyse der modernen Erscheinungsformen und Möglichkeiten des Tauschhandels / Thorsten Iske. Frankfurt am Main ; New York : P. Lang, c1986. v, 267 p. : ill. ; 21 cm. (Schriften zum Investitionsgütermarketing, 0930-0015 . Bd. 1) Originally presented as the author's thesis (doctoral) Bibliography: p. 249-267. ISBN 3-8204-9756-0 LC Card 86-218131
1. Barter. 2. Counter trade. 3. Commerce. I. Title. II. Series.
HF1019 .I85 1986

Iskolakutatási témacsoport. Érettségizettek a munkaerőpiacon /. Budapest , 1985. 124 p. ; ISBN 963-404-026-8 LC Card 87-409614
HD6276.H82 E73 1985

Iskušenja marksizma . Pirec, Dušan. Beograd , 1985. 461 p. : LC Card 86-128661
HB97.5 .P498 1985

ISLAM - 20TH CENTURY.
Muslim world . Lanham, MD , c1987. viii, 190 p. : ISBN 0-8191-6558-1 (alk. paper) : LC Card 87-14087 DDC 330.917/671 19
HC499 .M875 1987

ISLAM - ECONOMIC ASPECTS.
Choudhury, Masudul Alam, 1948- Contributions to Islamic economic theory . Houndmills, Basingstoke, Hampshire , 1986. xvii, 241 p. : ISBN 0-333-38507-1 ***NYPL [JLD 86-3601]***

Khan, Muhammad Akram. Bilā sūdī bainkārī /. Lāhaur [1983] 56 p. ; LC Card 83-931274
HG3290.5.A6 K43 1983

Saʻdī, ʻAbd Allāh Jamʻān Saʻīd, 1954- Siyāsat al-māl fī al-Islām fī ʻahd ʻUmar ibn al-Khaṭṭāb wa-muqāranatuhā bi-al-anẓimah al-ḥadīthah /. al-Dawḥah, Qaṭar , 1983. 291 p. ; LC Card 86-965028
HJ1438 .S23 1983

Ṣiddīqī, Muḥammad Iqbal. Model of an Islamic bank /. Lahore, Pakistan , 1986. 90 p. ; LC Card 87-931018 DDC 332.1/0917/671 19
HG3368.A6 S54 1986

ISLAM - ECONOMIC ASPECTS - INDONESIA.
Etika pembangunan dalam pemikiran Islam di Indonesia /. Jakarta , 1986. xi, 270 p. ; ISBN 979-421-043-9 (pbk.) LC Card 86-946413
HC447 .E78 1986

Islam, Nazrul.
Bāṃlādeśera unnaẏana samasyā : bartamāna unnaẏana dhārāra saṃkaṭa ebaṃ bikalpa pathera praśna / Najarula Isalāma. Ḍhākā : Jātīẏa Sāhitya Prakāśanī, 1987. 315 p. (some folded) ; 22 cm. In Bengali. Companion volume to the author's Bāṃlādeśera unnaẏana kauśala prasaṅga, 1984. Economic development and planning in Bangladesh. Bibliography: p. 301-315. LC Card 87-902504
1. Bangladesh - Economic policy. I. Islam, Nazrul. Bāṃlādeśera unnaẏanakauśala prasaṅga. II. Title.
HC440.8 .I727 1987

Bāṃlādeśera unnaẏanakauśala prasaṅga. Islam, Nazrul. Bāṃlādeśera unnaẏana samasyā : bartamāna unnaẏana dhārāra saṃkaṭa ebaṃ bikalpa pathera praśna / Najarula Isalāma. Ḍhākā , 1987. 315 p. (some folded) ; LC Card 87-902504
HC440.8 .I727 1987

Islam, Shamima. Invisible labour force : women in poverty in Bangladesh / by Shamima Islam. Bangladesh : Center for Women and Development, 1985. 60, [1] p. ; 23 cm. Bibliography: p. [61] LC Card 85-904350 DDC 331.4/09549/2 19
1. Women - Employment - Bangladesh. 2. Women - Bangladesh - Social conditions. I. Title.
HD6190.6 .I84 1985

Islamic banking /. Iqbal, Zubair. Washington, D.C. , 1987. v, 62 p. ; ISBN 0-939934-82-5 (pbk.) : LC Card 87-4166 DDC 332.1/0917/671 19
HG3270.2.A6 I67 1987

Islamic banking and finance . Amin, S. H. (Sayed Hessan) Tehran , 1986. 72 p. : ISBN 0-946706-30-1 (pbk.) LC Card 86-209623 DDC 332.1/0955 19
HG3270.2.A6 A45 1986

The Islamic business enterprise /. El-Ashker, Ahmed Abdel-Fattah, 1943- London , Wolfboro, N.H. , c1987. xi, 242 p. : ISBN 0-7099-0985-3 : LC Card 86-24271 DDC 332.1/0917/671 19
HG3368.A6 E4 1987

ISLAMIC COUNTRIES - ECONOMIC CONDITIONS.
Muslim world . Lanham, MD , c1987. viii, 190 p. : ISBN 0-8191-6558-1 (alk. paper) : LC Card

87-14087 DDC 330.917/671 19
HC499 .M875 1987

Islamic economic series .
(5) Ṣiddīqī, Muḥammad Nejātullah, 1931- Banking without interest /. Leicester, UK , c1983. 192 p. ; ISBN 0-86037-119-0 LC Card 86-673953
HG1588 .S52x 1983

ISLAMIC EMPIRE - HISTORY - 622-661.
Sa'dī, 'Abd Allāh Jam'ān Sa'īd, 1954- Siyāsat al-māl fī al-Islām fī 'ahd 'Umar ibn al-Khaṭṭāb wa-muqāranatuhā bi-al-anẓimah al-ḥadīthah /. al-Dawḥah, Qaṭar , 1983. 291 p. ; LC Card 86-965028
HJ1438 .S23 1983

Islamic Foundation. Khan, Waqar Masood. Towards an interest-free Islamic economic system . Leicester , Islamabad , c1985. 126 p. ; ISBN 0-86037-155-7 ***NYPL [JLD 87-381]***

Islamic revivalism in a changing peasant economy . Dobbin, Christine E., 1941- London , 1983. xii, 300 p. : ISBN 0-7007-0155-9 (pbk.) : LC Card 83-127619 DDC 303.4/84 19
HD1537.I56 D63 1983
NYPL [JLD 87-1053]

ISLAMIC WOMEN. see **WOMEN, MUSLIM.**

ISLAMISM. see **ISLAM.**

İslamoğlu-İnan, Huri, 1947- Ottoman agriculture in 16th century Anatolia : stagnation or regional development / Huri İslamoğlu-İnan. Berlin : B.I.V.S., [1982] 45, [21] p. : maps ; 30 cm. (Arbeitsheft / Berliner Institut für Vergleichende Sozialforschung) Includes bibliographical references. LC Card 86-674028
1. Agriculture - Economic aspects - Turkey - History. 2. Turkey - History - Ottoman Empire, 1288-1918. I. Series: Arbeitsheft / Berliner Institut für Vergleichende Sozialforschung. II. Title.
HD2056.7 .I84x 1982

Island /. Glässer, Ewald. Darmstadt , 1986. xii, 315 p., [20] p. of plates (4 folded) : ISBN 3-534-01225-9 LC Card 87-101040
HC360.5 .G57 1986

Island of dreams . Huddle, Norie, 1944- Cambridge, Mass. , c1987. xxiii, 355 p. : ISBN 0-87047-027-2 : LC Card 86-33842 DDC 363.7/00952 19
HC465.E5 H82 1987

Island Resources Foundation (Virgin Islands of the United States) Towle, Edward L. Final report . St. Thomas, U. S.V.I. [1982] 17, 15, 4 leaves : LC Card 86-185489 DDC 333.7/097297/22 19
HC155.Z9 E56 1982

Ismailov, Makhmud. Sot͡sial'no-ėkonomicheskai͡a struktura Azerbaĭdzhana v ėpokhu imperializma / Makhmud Ismailov. Baku : Izd-vo "Ėlm", 1982. 163 p. ; 21 cm. At head of title: Akademii͡a nauk Azerbaĭdzhanskoĭ SSR. Institut istorii. Includes bibliographical references. LC Card 83-189608
1. Azerbaijan S.S.R. - Economic conditions. 2. Azerbaijan S.S.R. - Industries - History. I. Title.
HC337.A9 I85 1982

Isnenghi, Peter. Franz, Lothar. Verkehrsberuhigung in Städten und Gemeinden /. Grafenau , c1982. 134 p. : ISBN 3-88508-780-4 : LC Card 82-204794
HE311.G3 F73 1982

ISP Sozialistische Gewerkschaftspolitik .
(8) Aktive Kolleginnen und Kollegen ziehen Bilanz . Frankfurt/M. , 1984. 100 p. : ISBN 3-88332-092-7 : LC Card 85-233569 DDC 331.89/2 19
HD5378 .A64 1984

Ispol'zovanie ėkonomicheskikh zakonov v upravlenii sotsialisticheskim proizvodstvom /. Nagdiev, S. A. (Seĭfulakh Ataevich) Leningrad , 1983. 87 p. ; LC Card 84-197365
HD56 .N34 1983

Ispra courses on energy systems and technology. Management Training Seminar (1982 : Joint Research Centre, Ispra, Italy) National energy planning and management in developing countries . Dordrecht, Holland , Hingham, MA , c1983. xiii, 442 p. ; ISBN 90-277-1589-0 LC Card 83-4407 DDC 333.79/09172/4 19
HD9502.A2 M343 1982
NYPL [JLE 87-302]

ISRA .
(4) Rapetti, Vittorio, 1955- Uomini, collina e vigneto in Piemonte, da metà Ottocento agli anni trenta /. Alessandria , 1984. 342 p., [16] p. of plates : LC Card 86-151345
HD9385.I82 P547 1984

ISRAEL AND THE DIASPORA.
Hammer, Gottlieb, 1911- Good faith and credit /. New York , c1985. 258 p., [12] p. of plates : ISBN 0-8453-4798-5 (alk. paper) LC Card 85-13962 DDC 956.94/001/0973 19
DS151.H34 A34 1985
NYPL [*PWZ (Hammer, G.) 86-2026]

Israel, Arturo.
Heaver, Richard, 1952- Country commitment to development projects /. Washington, D.C., U. S.A. [1986] 32 p. ; ISBN 0-8213-0860-2 (pbk.) LC Card 86-28114 DDC 338.91 19
HC59.72.E44 H43 1986

Institutional development : incentives to performance / Arturo Israel. Baltimore : Johns Hopkins University Press, 1987. x, 214 p. : ill. ; 24 cm. "Published for the World Bank." Includes bibliographies and index. ISBN 0-8018-3554-2 : LC Card 87-45494 DDC 338.9/009172/4 19
1. Economic development projects - Developing countries. I. International Bank for Reconstruction and Development. II. Title.
HC59.72.E44 I77 1987

ISRAEL - CENSUS, 1983.
Tekhunot demografiyot shel ha-ukhlusiyah . Yerushalayim , 1985. 31, 175, xxxiv p. : LC Card 86-204169
HA4560 .A4 1983

ISRAEL - ECONOMIC POLICY.
Sharkansky, Ira. The political economy of Israel /. New Brunswick, N.J., U. S.A. , c1987. xi, 157 p. ; ISBN 0-88738-117-0 : LC Card 86-25090 DDC 338.95694/054 19
HC415.25 .S49 1987

Israel Economist Publishing Service.
Electronics-1985 . [Jerusalem , 1985] 128 p. : LC Card 86-213293 DDC 338.4/7621381/095694 19
HD9696.A3 I654 1985

ISRAEL - FOREIGN ECONOMIC RELATIONS - ARAB COUNTRIES.
Sarna, A. J. Boycott and blacklist . Totowa, N.J. , 1986. xiv, 270 p. : ISBN 0-8476-7489-4 : LC Card 86-1891 DDC 337.5694/0174927 19
HF1610.Z4 I87 1986
NYPL [*PXLB 86-6444]

ISRAEL - INDUSTRIES, RURAL.
Rural industrialization in Israel /. Boulder , 1987. xi, 193 p. ; ISBN 0-8133-7393-X (pbk. : alk. paper) : LC Card 87-2073 DDC 338.095694 19
HC415.25 .R87 1987

ISRAEL - INDUSTRIES - STATISTICS.
Aspler, I. Seḳer melai ha-hon ha-ḳavu'a be-ta'aśiyah, 1.1.1982 /. Yerushalayim , 1986. 80, xvii p. ; LC Card 87-128243
HA1931 .A354 no. 785 HC415.25.Z9C3

Israel. Lishkah ha-merkazit li-sṭaṭisṭiḳah.
Tekhunot demografiyot shel ha-ukhlusiyah . Yerushalayim , 1985. 31, 175, xxxiv p. : LC Card 86-204169
HA4560 .A4 1983

Israel. Maḥleḳet 'avodot tsiburiyot. Economic transportation survey. [Paris] [Courbevoie, Seine] , 1966. 3 v. : LC Card 87-125917
HE373.I75 E36 1966

ISRAEL - POPULATION - STATISTICS.
Tekhunot demografiyot shel ha-ukhlusiyah . Yerushalayim , 1985. 31, 175, xxxiv p. : LC Card 86-204169
HA4560 .A4 1983

ISRAEL - RELATIONS - SOUTH AFRICA.
Hunter, Jane, 1943- Undercutting sanctions . Washington, DC (918 16th St. NW, Suite 501, Washington 20006) , c1987. iv, 71 p. ; LC Card 87-403525 DDC 337.68 19
HF1613.4 .H86 1987

ISRAEL - RELATIONS - UNITED STATES.
Hunter, Jane, 1943- Undercutting sanctions . Washington, DC (918 16th St. NW, Suite 501, Washington 20006) , c1987. iv, 71 p. ; LC Card 87-403525 DDC 337.68 19
HF1613.4 .H86 1987

Israel (State) see **Israel.**

Israel Zipper, Ricardo. Democracia y liberalismo / Ricardo Israel Zipper. Santiago de Chile : Instituto de Ciencia Política, Universidad de Chile, 1984. 56 p. ; 18 cm. (Cuadernos de ciencia política, 0176-1085 . no. 7) Includes bibliographical references. LC Card 85-197546
1. Liberalism. 2. Laissez-faire. 3. Economics - Moral and ethical aspects. 4. Hayek, Friedrich A. von (Friedrich August), 1899- - Influence. 5. Political science. 6. Macpherson, C. B. (Crawford Brough), 1911- - Influence. 7. Free trade and protection. I. Series: Cuadernos de ciencia política (Santiago, Chile) , no. 7. II. Title.
HB95 .I87 1984

Israeli settlements in Gaza and the West Bank (including Jerusalem) : their nature and purpose / prepared for, and under the guidance of, the Committee on the Exercise of the Inalienable Rights of the Palestinian People. New York : United Nations, 1982. 66 p. : maps ; 22 cm. Includes bibliographical references. LC Card 82-232749 DDC 307.7/2/08992405695 19
1. Land settlement - West Bank. 2. Land settlement - Gaza Strip. 3. Israelis - West Bank. 4. Israelis - Gaza Strip. I. United Nations. Committee on the Exercise of the Inalienable Rights of the Palestinian People.
HD850.Z8 W474 1982
NYPL [*PXLB 86-5156]

ISRAELIS - GAZA STRIP.
Israeli settlements in Gaza and the West Bank (including Jerusalem) . New York , 1982. 66 p. : LC Card 82-232749 DDC 307.7/2/08992405695 19
HD850.Z8 W474 1982
NYPL [*PXLB 86-5156]

ISRAELIS - WEST BANK.
Israeli settlements in Gaza and the West Bank (including Jerusalem) . New York , 1982. 66 p. : LC Card 82-232749 DDC 307.7/2/08992405695 19
HD850.Z8 W474 1982
NYPL [*PXLB 86-5156]

ISRAELITES. see **JEWS.**

Israilov, A. (Asangazy) Razmeshchenie proizvoditel'nykh sil v Narynskoĭ oblasti / A. Israilov. Frunze : Izd-vo "Kyrgyzstan", 1978. 56 p. ; 16 cm. Includes bibliographical references. LC Card 81-147534
1. Narynskai͡a oblast' (Kirghiz S.S.R.) - Industries - Location. 2. Narynskai͡a oblast' (Kirghiz S.S.R.) - Economic conditions. I. Title.
HC337.K5452 N375 1978

ISSA Expert Meeting on Disability Research (1982 : Zoetermeer, Netherlands) Disability benefits . Greenwich, Conn. , c1987. xxii, 282 p. ; ISBN 0-89232-824-X : LC Card 87-17056 DDC 368.3/86/009492 19
HD7105.25.N4 D57 1987

Issawi, Charles Philip. The Fertile Crescent, 1800-1914 . New York , 1987. p. cm. ISBN 0-19-504951-9 LC Card 86-33275 DDC 330.956 19
HC415.15 .F47 1987

Issei, Nisei, war bride . Glenn, Evelyn Nakano. Philadelphia , 1986. xviii, 290 p. ; ISBN 0-87722-412-9 LC Card 85-25107 DDC 331.4/8164046/0899560794 19
HD6072.2.U52 C24 1986
NYPL [IEA 86-1929]

Issel, Catarina Irene. Die Geldwertberichtigung in Brasilien im Rechnungswesen der Unternehmung / Catarina Irene Issel. Hamburg : Institut für Iberoamerika-Kunde, 1983. iii, 181 p. : ill. ; 24 cm. (Private Auslandsinvestitionen in Lateinamerika. 10) Bibliography: p. 152-156. LC Card 84-112596 DDC 332.6/73/098 s 657/.48 19
1. Accounting - Brazil - Effect of inflation on. 2. Industrial management - Brazil - Effect of inflation on. I. Title. II. Series.
HG5160.5.A3 P7 Nr. 10 HF5658.5
NYPL [JLK 73-84 Nr.10]

Isserman, Andrew M. Forecasting interstate migration with limited data . Iowa City , 1982. 37 p. : ***NYPL [*ZT-1564 no.33]***

Issing, Otmar. Exporte als Herausforderung für die deutsche Wirtschaft /. Köln , c1984. 469 p. : ISBN 3-602-34842-3 LC Card 85-139543
HF3564 .E96 1984

Issledovanie odnoĭ matematicheskoĭ modeli ėkonomicheskogo rosta /. Shakhdzhakhan, Ali. Moskva , 1983. 29, [2] p. : LC Card 83-176389
HD75.5 .S52 1983

Issledovanii͡a Instituta ėkonomiki Akademii nauk Ėstonskoĭ SSR v_X pi͡atiletke : tematiko-informat͡sionnyĭ referativnyĭ sbornik / [sostavitel′, L. Apananskiĭ ; otvetstvennyĭ redaktor, K. Khabikht]. Tallin : Akademii͡a nauk Ėstonskoĭ SSR, 1983. 233 p. ; 20 cm. Russian and Estonian. At head of title: Akademii͡a nauk Ėstonskoĭ SSR. T͡Sentr nauchnoĭ informat͡sii po obshchestvennym naukam. Includes index. LC Card 86-181279
1. Economics - Research - Estonia. 2. Majanduse Instituut (Eesti NSV Teaduste Akadeemia). 3. Economics - Research - Estonia - Bibliography. I. Apananskiĭ, L. II. Khabikht, K. III. Ühiskonnateaduste Informatsioonikeskus (Eesti NSV Teaduste Akadeemia).
HB74.9.S65 I86 1983

Issue paper / Research Division, Virginia Department of Taxation .
(no. 1) Virginia's income tax age credit. [Richmond, Va.] [1984] ii, 26 leaves ; LC Card 86-622458 DDC 336.24/216 19
HJ4655.V88 A828 1984
(no. 1) The Treasury's tax reform proposal. [Richmond?] [1985] 22 leaves ; LC Card 86-622457 DDC 336.2/05 19
HJ2381 .T74 1985

Issue paper (Australia. Social Security Review) .
(no. 2) Crompton, Cathy. Too old for a job, too young for a pension? . Canberra , 1986. x, 69 p. ; ISBN 0-644-05599-5 LC Card 87-150775 DDC 368.4/4/00880564 19
HD6283.A8 C76 1986

Issue paper (Virginia. Dept. of Taxation. Research Division) .
(no. 1) Virginia's income tax age credit. [Richmond, Va.] [1984] ii, 26 leaves ; LC Card 86-622458 DDC 336.24/216 19
HJ4655.V88 A828 1984
(no. 1) The Treasury's tax reform proposal. [Richmond?] [1985] 22 leaves ; LC Card 86-622457 DDC 336.2/05 19
HJ2381 .T74 1985

Issue paper (Washington (State). Puget Sound Water Quality Authority)
Industrial and municipal discharges. Seattle, Wash. (217 Pine St., Ste 1100, Seattle 98101) [1986] viii, 136, 14 p. : LC Card 86-622616 DDC 363.7/31 19
HC107.W22 P85 1986

Issue report (Conservation Foundation)
Agriculture and the environment in a changing world economy. Washington, D.C. , c1986. xi, 66 p. : ISBN 0-89164-099-1 (pbk.) LC Card 86-24088 DDC 338.1/873 19
HD1761 .A6228 1986

Issues after a century of federal competition policy / edited by Robert L. Wills, Julie A. Caswell, John D. Culbertson. Lexington, Mass. : Lexington Books, c1987. vii, 387 p. ; 27 cm. Includes bibliographies and index. ISBN 0-669-13320-5 (alk. paper) LC Card 86-45377 DDC 338.6/048/0973 19
1. Trade regulation - United States. 2. Antitrust law - Economic aspects - United States. 3. Competition - Government policy - United States. I. Wills, Robert L., 1954-. II. Caswell, Julie A. III. Culbertson, John.
HD3616.U47 I77 1987

Issues before non-alignment : past & future / edited by Uma Vasudev. New Delhi : Indian Council of World Affairs, 1983. 190 p. ; 25 cm. Includes bibliographical references. LC Card 83-903478 DDC 327/.09171/6 19
1. Nonalignment - Congresses. 2. International economic relations - Congresses. I. Vasudev, Uma. II. Indian Council of World Affairs.
JX1393.N54 I87 1983 ***NYPL [JLE 86-4176]***

Issues for managers . Miller, Janice James. Homewood, Ill. , 1987. xii, 139 p. : ISBN 0-256-05630-7 (pbk.) LC Card 87-80633 DDC 658/.049 19
HD62.4 .M54 1987

Issues in assistance for families . Whiteford, Peter. Woden, ACT [1986] iii, 56 p. ; ISBN 0-642-51604-9 (pbk.) LC Card 86-231139 DDC 362/.0425 19
HD4925.5.A8 W47 1986

Issues in contemporary macroeconomics and distribution / edited by George R. Feiwel. London : Macmillan, 1985. xxviii, 465 p. : ill. ; 23 cm. Includes bibliographies and index. ISBN 0-333-35483-4 : LC Card 86-673473
1. Macroeconomics. 2. Distribution (Economic theory). I. Feiwel, George R.
HB172.5 .I87x 1985b

Issues in housing discrimination; a consultation/hearing of the United States Commission on Civil Rights, Washington, D.C., November 12-13, 1985. Washington, D.C. : The Commission, 1986- v. <1 > : ill., maps ; 26 cm. Shipping list no.: 86-727-P. Includes bibliographies. Item 288-A CONTENTS. - v. 1 Papers presented. LC Card 86-602528 DDC 363.5/1 19
1. Discrimination in housing - United States. 2. Discrimination in housing - Law and legislation - United States. I. United States. Commission on Civil Rights.
HD7288.76.U5 I88 1986

Issues in housing discrimination : a consultation/hearing of the United States Commission on Civil Rights, Washington, D.C., November 12-13, 1985. [Washington, D.C. : U. S. G.P.O., 1986- v. : ill., maps ; 26 cm. Includes bibliographes. CONTENTS. - V. 1. Papers presented.
1. Discrimination in housing - Law and legislation - United States. 2. Discrimination in housing - United States. ***NYPL [JLM 86-1332]***

Issues in Indian agricultural development /. Zarkovic, M. Boulder , 1987. xviii, 203 p. ; ISBN 0-8133-7451-0 (soft : alk. paper) LC Card 87-50898 DDC 338.1/0954 19
HD2072 .Z37 1987

Issues in international telecommunications policy : a sourcebook / edited and annotated by Jane H. Yurow. Washington, D.C. : George Washington University, Center for Telecommunications Studies, c1983. xviii, 260 p. ; 28 cm. Includes bibliographies and index. ISBN 0-9612072-0-5 (pbk.) LC Card 83-82231 DDC 343.73/0994 347.303994 19
1. Telecommunication - Law and legislation - United States. 2. Data transmission systems - Law and legislation - United States. 3. Foreign trade regulation - United States. 4. Data transmission systems - Law and legislation. I. Yurow, Jane H.
KF2765 .I85 1983 ***NYPL [JLF 86-1125]***

Issues in international trade and development policy /. Malloch, Theodore R. New York , 1987. ix, 178 p. ; ISBN 0-275-92356-8 (alk. paper) : LC Card 87-11697 DDC 382/.3 19
HF1411 .M3325 1987

Issues in modernization of the textile industry : proceedings of a seminar / edited by V. Shanbhag, V. Padaki. Ahmedabad : Chimanlal Lalbhai Centre for Management, Ahmedabad Textile Industry's Research Association, 1985. 87 p. : charts ; 23 cm. Organized by the Chimanlal Lalbhai Centre for Management, Ahmedabad Textile Industry's Research Association, on May 4 and 5, 1984 at New Delhi. LC Card 87-902140 DDC 338.4/7677/00954 19
1. Textile industry - India - Congresses. I. Shanbhag, V. (Vinod). II. Padaki, V. (Vijay). III. Chimanlal Lalbhai Centre for Management.
HD9866.I62 I58 1985

Issues in Nigerian development series. Okongwu, Chu S. P., 1934- The Nigerian economy . Enugu, Nigeria , 1986. vi, 453 p. : ISBN 978-15-6038-X (pbk.) : LC Card 87-132237 DDC 330.9669/05 19
HC1055 .O39 1986

Issues in teaching of economics in Indian universities / editor, M.A. Oommen. New Delhi : Oxford & IBH Pub. Co., c1987. vii, 145 p. ; 22 cm. (IMG publications series . 2) Papers presented at a workshop organized by the Institute of Management in Government, Trivandrum. Includes bibliographies and index. ISBN 81-204-0203-0 : LC Card 87-901784 DDC 330/.07/1154 19
1. Economics - Study and teaching (Higher) - India. I. Oommen, M. A., 1932-. II. Institute of Management in Government (Kerala, India). III. Series: IMG publication series , 2.
HB74.9.I4 I88 1987

Issues in the measurement and interpretation of effective tax rates /. Bradford, David F. Cambridge, MA (1050 Massachusetts Ave., Cambridge 02138) [1986] 21 p. : LC Card 87-108421 DDC 336.24/26 19
HJ4631 .B73 1986

Issues management . Heath, Robert L. (Robert Lawrence), 1941- Beverly Hills , c1986. 288 p. ; ISBN 0-8039-2535-2 LC Card 85-14547 DDC 659.2 19
HD59 .H33 1986 ***NYPL [JLD 87-19]***

ISSUES MANAGEMENT.
Heath, Robert L. (Robert Lawrence), 1941- Issues management . Beverly Hills , c1986. 288 p. ; ISBN 0-8039-2535-2 LC Card 85-14547 DDC 659.2 19
HD59 .H33 1986 ***NYPL [JLD 87-19]***

Issues of the eighties : economic and social strategy options : Vorträge des von der Zentralsparkasse und Kommerzialbank, Wien, anlässlich ihres 75jährigen Bestandes am 18. und 19. März 1982 in der Wiener Hofburg abgehaltenen Symposiums. Wien : Zentralsparkasse und Kommerzialbank, 1983. 119 p. : ill., ports. ; 21 cm. (Perspektiven) Includes bibliographical references. LC Card 83-201354 DDC 338.9 19
1. Economic policy - Congresses. 2. Social policy - Congresses. I. Zentralsparkasse und Kommerzialbank Wien. II. Symposium "Issues of the Eighties" (1982 : Vienna, Austria). III. Series. IV. Series: Perspektiven (Vienna, Austria).
HD73 .I86 1983

Issues paper.
Accounting for options /. New York, NY (1211 Ave. of the Americas, New York 10036-8775) [1986] 182 p., [4] p. of plates (some folded) : LC Card 86-221314 DDC 657/.76 19
HF5686.I6 A28 1986

Issues paper (Australia. Social Security Review) .
(no. 1) Cass, Bettina. Income support for families with children /. Canberra [1986] xiii, 126 p. : ISBN 0-644-05378-X (pbk.) LC Card 87-103419 DDC 362.5/82 19
HD4925.5.A8 C37 1986

Issues papers. National Forum on Issues in Vocational Assessment (2nd : 1986 : Dallas, Tex.) Second National Forum on Issues in Vocational Assessment . Menomonie, Wis. , c1985. vii, 236 p. : ISBN 0-916671-71-2 (pbk.) LC Card 86-217148 DDC 362/.0425 19
HD7256.U5 N336 1986

Ist die fünfunddreissig-Stunden-Woche ein Mittel zur beseitigung der Arbeitslosigkeit? Marzen, Walter. Ist die 35-Stunden-Woche ein Mittel zur Beseitigung der Arbeitslosigkeit? . Innsbruck , 1980. 29 leaves ; LC Card 85-170048
HD5108.2.A9 M37 1980

Ist die 35-Stunden-Woche ein Mittel zur Beseitigung der Arbeitslosigkeit? . Marzen, Walter. Innsbruck , 1980. 29 leaves ; LC Card 85-170048
HD5108.2.A9 M37 1980

Istamov, D. I. (Damir Istamovich)
Ėkonomicheskie problemy razvitii͡a promyshlennogo proizvodstva potrebitel′skoĭ kooperat͡sii : na primere respublik Sredneĭ Azii / D.I. Istamov. Tashkent : Izd-vo "Fan" Uzbekskoĭ SSR, 1982. 126 p. ; 23 cm. At head of title: Ministerstvo vysshego i srednego spet͡sial′nogo obrazovanii͡a Uzbekskoĭ SSR. Includes bibliographical references. LC Card 82-200979
1. Cooperation - Soviet Central Asia. 2. Consumer cooperatives - Soviet Central Asia. I. Title.
HD3517.A3 C475 1982

Gli istituti di credito speciale e il mercato finanziario, 1947-1962 /. Bagella, Michele. Milano, Italy , c1986. 289 p. ; LC Card 86-232526
HG3729.I7 B34 1986

Istituto centrale di statistica (Italy) Indagine sulla lettura e su altri aspetti dell'impiego del tempo libero . [Roma] , 1986. 140 p., [5] p. of plates : LC Card 87-165864
HA1363 .A27 no. 3 Z1003.5.I8

Istituto di studi e ricerche sulla distribuzione commerciale (Milan, Italy) Industria e commercio . Milano, Italy , c1985. 194 p. : LC Card 86-112174 DDC 658.7/88/0945 19
HF5415.12.I8 I53 1985 ***NYPL [JLD 87-432]***

Istituto di studi sulle relazioni industriali e di lavoro (Rome, Italy) L'Association des travailleurs aux choix technologiques . Luxembourg , Washington, D.C. , 1986. 45 p. :

ISBN 92-825-5880-0 : LC Card 86-179382
HD6331.2.E86 A88 1986

Istituto italo-latino americano. Report on the medium term prospects for Latin American countries. Roma , 1986. 109 p. : LC Card 86-223594 DDC 336.3/435/098 19
HJ8514.5 .R46 1986

Istituto nazionale della previdenza sociale (Italy) Costi e relativi finanziamenti dei sistemi pensionistici nei paesi europei . Roma , 1985. xi, 486 p. : LC Card 86-206925
HD7164 .C67 1985

Istituto nazionale di economia agraria. (Old Catalog form: Italy. Istituto nazionale de economia agraria)
Il programma INEA per la progettazione e le analisi statistiche di un campione rappresentativo / a cura di Claudio Scala ; presentazione di Giuseppe Barbero. Roma : INEA, 1986. 122 p. : ill. ; 28 cm. Includes bibliographical references. LC Card 86-213865
1. Agriculture - Economic aspects - Italy - Computer programs. I. Scala, Claudio. II. Title.
HD1970 .I773 1986

Istituto per i beni artistici, culturali, naturali della Regione Emilia Romagna.
Manutenzione e sostituzione . Bologna [1983] xviii, 227 p. : LC Card 84-142790
HD2346.I82 E45 1983

Istituto per la cooperazione economica internazionale (Italy) Il Sistema dei trasporti nello sviluppo della cooperazione economica internazionale . Milano, Italy , c1985. 341 p. ; LC Card 85-218403
HE2449 .S57 1985

Istituto per la ricerca sociale (Milan, Italy)
Quale strategia per l'industria? . Bologna , c1986. 221 p. : ISBN 88-15-00975-2 : LC Card 86-182300
HC310.I53 Q35 1986

Istituto per la storia della resistenza in provincia di Alessandria. Rapetti, Vittorio, 1955- Uomini, collina e vigneto in Piemonte, da metà Ottocento agli anni trenta /. Alessandria , 1984. 342 p., [16] p. of plates : LC Card 86-151345
HD9385.I82 P547 1984

Istituto per la storia della resistenza in provincia di Asti. Rapetti, Vittorio, 1955- Uomini, collina e vigneto in Piemonte, da metà Ottocento agli anni trenta /. Alessandria , 1984. 342 p., [16] p. of plates : LC Card 86-151345
HD9385.I82 P547 1984

Istituto per lo sviluppo della formazione professionale dei lavoratori.
Organizzazione del lavoro, mobilità e aspetti formativi nella contrattazione . Milano, Italy , c1982. 172 p. ; LC Card 83-106874
HD6709 .O73 1982

Rapporto ISFOL 1985 . Milano, Italy , c1985. 533 p. : LC Card 86-156267
HD5715.5.I8 R393 1985

Relazioni industriali nell'impresa degli anni '80 . Roma , 1985. 308 p. ; LC Card 86-192682
HD8481 .R45 1985

Società di terziario avanzato e professionalità . Roma [1984] 159 p. : LC Card 85-232870
HD69.C6 S66 1984

Istituto regionale di studi politici Alcide De Gasperi. Cooperazione di credito e sviluppo sociale ed economico delle campagne in Emilia Romagna . Bologna , c1983. 173 p. : LC Card 85-156690
HG2051.I82 E433 1983

Istituto regionale per la storia del movimento di liberazione nel Friuli-Venezia Giulia. --Anche l'uomo doveva essere di ferro . Milano, Italy , c1986. 441 p. : LC Card 86-213675
HD8490.T742 A53 1986

Istituzioni-ricerche dell'Irsi .
(1) Intervento straordinario e amministrazione locale nel mezzogiorno /. Milano, Italy , c1985. 348 p. ; LC Card 86-144245
HC310.I53 I58 1985

Istomin, L. A. Matematicheskie metody v prilozhenii k reshenii͡u ėkonomicheskikh zadach /. Sverdlovsk , 1985. 116 p. : LC Card 86-135187
HC337.R852 U7355 1985

Istomin, V. G. Upravlenie v sisteme proizvodstvennykh otnosheniĭ /. Novosibirsk , 1974. 82 p. ; LC Card 83-120398
HD70.S63 U68 1974

Istoricheskiĭ opyt sotrudnichestva stran SĖV /. Ladygin, Boris Nikolaevich. Moskva , 1980. 284 p. ; LC Card 81-130900
HC244 .L282 1980

Istorii͡a kolhospu "Zdobutok ZHovtni͡a" / [redaktsiĭna kolehii͡a P.T. Tron'ko (vidpovidal'nyĭ redaktor) ... et al.]. Kyïv : Nauk. dumka, 1986. 188 p., [8] p. of plates : ill. (some col.) ; 22 cm. Title in colophon: Istorii͡a kolkhoza "Zdobutok ZHovtni͡a." At head of title: Akademii͡a nauk Ukraïns'koï RSR. Instytut istoriï. Bibliography: p. 184-187. LC Card 87-161618
1. Kolhosp "Zdobutok ZHovtni͡a" (Ukraine) - History. 2. Collective farms - Ukraine - History. I. Tron'ko, Petro Tymofiĭovych. II. Instytut istoriï (Akademii͡a nauk Ukraïns'koï RSR). III. Title: Istorii͡a kolkhoza "Zdobutok ZHovtni͡a.".
HD1492.S652 U3835 1986

Istorii͡a kolkhoza imeni Kirova Takhta-Bazarskogo raĭona. Berdiev, G. Tagtabazar raĭonynyn͡g Kirov adyndaky kolkhozynyn͡g tarykhy /. Ashgabat , 1986. 79 p. : LC Card 86-198891
HD1492.S652 T873 1986

Istorii͡a kolkhoza "Zdobutok ZHovtni͡a." Istorii͡a kolhospu "Zdobutok ZHovtni͡a" /. Kyïv , 1986. 188 p., [8] p. of plates : LC Card 87-161618
HD1492.S652 U3835 1986

Istorii͡a krest'i͡anstva SSSR.
Istorii͡a sovetskogo krest'i͡anstva . Moskva , 1986- v. : ***NYPL [*QG 87-3228]***

Istorii͡a sovetskogo krest'i͡anstva /. Moskva , 1986-<1987. v. <1-3 > : LC Card 86-230318
HD1492.S65 I88 1986

Istorii͡a krest'i͡anstva v Evrope, Ėpokha feodalizma : v trekh tomakh / glavnai͡a redaktsii͡a, Z.V. Udal'tsova (glavnyĭ redaktor) ... [et al.]. Moskva : Izd-vo "Nauka", 1985- v. : ill. ; 25 cm. On leaf preceding t.p.: Akademii͡a nauk SSSR. Institut vseobshcheĭ istorii. Table of contents in v. 1-2 also in English. Includes errata. Includes bibliography (t.1-2). CONTENTS. - t. 1. Formirovanie feodal'no-zavisimogo krest'i͡anstva -- t. 2. Krest'i͡anstvo Evropy v period razvitogo feodalizma
1. Peasantry - Europe - History. 2. Feudalism - Europe - History. I. Udal'tsova, Zinaida Vladimirovna. II. Akademii͡a nauk SSSR. Institut vseobshcheĭ istorii.
NYPL [*QGS 86-1566]

Istorii͡a na kooperativnoto dvizhenie v Bŭlgarii͡a / [pod redaktsii͡ata na Minko Rusenov]. 1. izd. Sofii͡a : Izd-vo na Otechestvenii͡a front, 1986- v. <1 > ; 21 cm. At head of title: T͡Sentralen kooperativen sŭi͡uz. Includes bibliographical references. Vol. 1 has index. LC Card 87-158327
1. Cooperation - Bulgaria - History. I. Rusenov, Minko V. II. Tsentralen kooperativen sŭi͡uz.
HD3531.5.A4 I87 1986

Istorii͡a na zavod "Druzhba." Khadzhiev, Stefan. Zavod "Druzhba" . Varna , 1985. 161 p., [3] leaves of plates : LC Card 86-140096
HD8039.C62 B95 1985

Istorii͡a rabochego klassa Sibiri.
Sotsial'no-ėkonomicheskoe i kul'turnoe razvitie Zabaĭkal'i͡a . Novosibirsk , 1980. 283 p. ; LC Card 81-132139
HC337.R852 T737 1980

Istorii͡a rabochego klassa Sibiri.
Rabochiĭ klass Sibiri . Novosibirsk , 1986. 355 p., [16] p. of plates : LC Card 86-211294
HD5797.S5 R33 1986

Istorii͡a sovetskogo krest'i͡anstva / redkollegii͡a I.E. Zelenin (otvetstvennyĭ redaktor) ... [et al.]. Moskva : "Nauka", 1986-<1987 > v. <1-3 > : ill. ; 27 cm. (Istorii͡a krest'i͡anstva SSSR) At head of ser. t.p., v. <1-3 >: Akademii͡a nauk SSSR. Institut istorii SSSR. Vol. 1 edited by G.V. Sharapov. Vol. 1 has 3 maps on 2 folded sheets laid in; v. has 2 maps on 1 folded sheet laid in. Includes indexes. Includes bibliographies. CONTENTS. - 1. Krest'i͡anstvo v pervoe destiatiletie Sovetskoĭ vlasti 1917-1927 -- 2. Sovetskoe krest'i͡anstvo v period sotsialisticheskoĭ rekonstruktsii narodnogo khozi͡aĭstva, konets 1927-1937 -- 3. Krest'i͡anstvo nakanune i v gody Velikoĭ Otechestvennoĭ voĭny 1938-1945. LC Card 86-230318
1. Collectivization of agriculture - Soviet Union - History. 2. Soviet Union - Economic policy - 1928-1932. 3. Soviet Union - Economic policy - 1933-1937. 4. Peasantry - Soviet Union - Social conditions. 5. Soviet Union - Rural conditions. I. Zelenin, I. E. (Il'i͡a Evgen'evich). II. Sharapov, G. V. (German Vladimirovich). III. Series.
HD1492.S65 I88 1986

Istorii͡a sovetskogo krest'i͡anstva : v pi͡ati tomakh / V.P. Sherstobitov (glavnyĭ redaktor) ... [et al.]. Moskva : "Nauka", 1986- v. : ill., maps. ; 27 cm. (Istorii͡a krest'i͡anstva SSSR) At head of title, v. 1- : Akademii͡a nauk SSSR. Institut istorii SSSR. Folded maps inserted in v. 1 and 2. Each v. has also special t.p. Vol. 1- includes bibliographical references and indexes. CONTENTS. - 1. Krest'i͡anstvo v pervoe desi͡atiletie Sovetskoĭ vlasti, 1917-1927 -- 2. Sovetskoe krest'i͡anstvo v period sotsialisticheskoĭ rekonstuktsii narodnogo khozi͡aĭstva konets 1927-1937.
1. Peasantry - Soviet Union - History - 20th century. 2. Land tenure - Soviet Union - History - 20th century. 3. Agriculture and state - Soviet Union - History - 20th century. 4. Collectivization of agriculture - Soviet Union - History. 5. Soviet Union - Rural conditions. I. Sherstobitov, Viktor Pavlovich. II. Institut istorii SSSR (Akademii͡a nauk SSSR). III. Series.
NYPL [*QG 87-3228]

Istoriografii͡a istorii rabochego klassa Dal'nego Vostoka SSSR / pod obshcheĭ redaktsieĭ A.I. Krushanova. Vladivostok : DVNTS AN SSSR, 1984. 78 p. ; 22 cm. At head of title: Akademii͡a nauk SSSR. Dal'nevostochnyĭ nauchnyĭ t͡sentr. Institut istorii, arkheologii i ėtnografii narodov Dal'nego Vostoka. Includes bibliographies. LC Card 85-229962
1. Labor and laboring classes - Russian S.F.S.R. - Soviet Far East - Historiography. 2. Soviet Far East (R.S.F.S.R.) - Industries - Historiography. I. Krushanov, Andreĭ Ivanovich. II. Institut istorii, arkheologii i ėtnografii narodov Dal'nego Vostoka (Akademii͡a nauk SSSR).
HD8529.S652 I87 1984

Isuani, Ernesto A. (Ernesto Aldo) Los orígenes conflictivos de la seguridad social argentina / Ernesto A. Isuani. Buenos Aires : Centro Editor de América Latina, c1985. 140 p. ; 18 cm. (Biblioteca Política argentina . 129) Bibliography: p. 137-140. ISBN 950-25-0128-4 : LC Card 86-174656
1. Social security - Argentina - History - 20th century. 2. Strikes and lockouts - Argentina - History - 20th century. 3. Trade-unions - Argentina - History - 20th century. 4. Labor and laboring classes - Argentina - History - 20th century. I. Title. II. Series.
HD7149 .I88 1985

ITAIPU (POWER PLANT) - HISTORY.
Menezes, Alfredo da Mota, 1944- A herança de Stroessner . Campinas, SP [1987] 186 p. ; LC Card 87-404011 DDC 337.810892 19
HF1524.5.B7 M46 1987

Italia e Europa.
Mazzucchelli, Vanna. Catasto e volto urbano . Roma , 1983. 244 p. ; LC Card 86-106099
HD680.M54 M39 1983

Italia multinazionale : l'internazionalizzazione dell'industria italiana / a cura di R&P, Ricerche e progetti con la collaborazione di OSPRI-Università Bocconi ; indagine promossa dal CNEL ... [et al.] ; [autori dell'opera, Giovanni Balcet ... et al.].1a ed. Milano : Edizioni del sole 24 ore, 1986. 2 v. : ill. ; 24 cm. (Studi e convegni) Includes bibliographies. CONTENTS. - v. 1. La ricerca i repertori -- v. 2. Analisi di settore. LC Card 87-158571
1. Corporations, Italian - Foreign countries. 2. International business enterprises - Italy. I. Balcet, G. (Giovanni). II. Ricerche e progetti (Firm). III. Osservatorio sui processi di internazionalizzazione (Università commerciale Luigi Bocconi). IV. Consiglio nazionale dell'economia e del lavoro (Italy).
HD2864 .I82 1986

Italiaans ijs . Bovenkerk, Frank. Meppel [1983?] 203 p. : ISBN 90-6009-551-0 LC Card 83-179690
HD9281.N42 B68 1983

Italian Communist Party. see **Partito comunista italiano.**

Italian General Confederation of Labor. see **Confederazione generale italiana del lavoro.**

ITALIAN LANGUAGE - DICTIONARIES - ENGLISH.
Picchi, Fernando. Economics and business . Bologna , 1986. 1333 p. ; ISBN 88-08-04550-1 LC Card 86-201141 DDC 330/.03/51 19
HB61 .P49 1986

Reynolds, Barbara, 1914- [Cambridge Italian dictionary.] Cambridge dizionario

italiano-inglese, inglese-italiano, Signorelli . Cambridge [Cambridgeshire] ; New York : 2276 p. ; ISBN 0-521-32702-4 LC Card 86-1898 DDC 453/.21 19
PC1640 .R4 1986 *NYPL [*R-REK 86-3799]*

Spinelli, Nicola, 1881- Dizionario commerciale, italiano-inglese e inglese-italiano . Torino , 1957. 464, 683, 138 p. ; *NYPL [JLD 85-226]*

ITALIAN LANGUAGE - DICTIONARIES - FRENCH.
Emolumento, Vincenzo. Dizionario commerciale . Milano , 1983. 1150 p. ; ISBN 88-7075-068-X : LC Card 84-151136 DDC 380.1/03/41 19
HF1002 .E57 1983 *NYPL [JLD 86-1323]*

Italian manpower, 225 B.C.-A.D. 14 /. Brunt, P. A. Oxford [Oxfordshire] , 1987, c1971. xxi, 762 p. ; ISBN 0-19-814283-8 : LC Card 87-1644 DDC 304.6/0945 19
HB3599 .B77 1987

ITALIANS - MEXICO - VERACRUZ (STATE) - HISTORY.
Zilli Manica, José Benigno. Braceros italianos para México . Xalapa, México , 1986. 93 p., [6] p. of plates : ISBN 968-8340-45-6 LC Card 87-400059
HD8118.5.I83 Z55 1986

Ital'ianskaia Kommunisticheskaia partiia. see **Partito comunista italiano.**

Italien /. Wagner, Hermann, Dr. Hannover , Stuttgart , 1982. xv, 190 p., 4 folded leaves of plates : LC Card 83-235644
HD9506.I82 W34 1982

Italská komunistická strana. see **Partito comunista italiano.**

ITALTEL (FIRM : MILAN, ITALY)
Le 150 ore e la formazione professionale in azienda . Milano, Italy , c1985. 178 p. : LC Card 86-141990
HD5716.T242 I82 1985
NYPL [JFD 87-3739]

Italy. Affari esteri, Ministerio degli. see **Italy. Ministero degli affari esteri.**

ITALY - COMMERCE - ECONOMETRIC MODELS.
Bertelè, Umberto. Un modello interpretativo dell'import-export italiano, 1970-1983 /. Bologna , c1985. 172 p. : ISBN 88-15-00919-1 : LC Card 86-176592
HF3586.5 .B47 1985

ITALY - COMMERCE - HISTORY.
Abulafia, David. Italy, Sicily, and the Mediterranean, 1100-1400 /. London , 1987. 346 p. in various pagings : ISBN 0-86078-198-4 : LC Card 87-157554 DDC 330.9182/2 19
HF3585 .A29 1987

ITALY - COMMERCIAL POLICY.
D'Angelo, Massimo. Criteri per una cooperazione industriale con i paesi in via di sviluppo /. Milano , c1981. 294 p. ; ISBN 88-20-42145-3 : LC Card 82-113466
HF1549 .D36 1981 *NYPL [JLD 86-3318]*

Relazione programmatica delle partecipazioni statali per il 1984 . Roma , 1985. 563 p. ; LC Card 86-176014
HC310.I53 R45 1985

Tre incognite per lo sviluppo . Milano, Italy , c1986. 383 p. : LC Card 86-198933
HC310.I53 T74 1986

ITALY - COMMERCIAL POLICY - ADDRESSES, ESSAYS, LECTURES.
Per una ristrutturazione e riconversione dell'industria italiana /. Bologna , 1980. 244 p. ; LC Card 82-102594 DDC 338.945 19
HD3616.I83 P43 *NYPL [JLD 86-599]*

ITALY - COMMERCIAL POLICY - HISTORY - 20TH CENTURY.
Cavalcanti, Maria Luisa, 1943- La politica commerciale italiana, 1945-1952 . Napoli , c1984. 288 p. ; LC Card 86-121609 DDC 380.1/3/0945 19
HF1549 .C38 1984

ITALY - ECONOMIC CONDITIONS.
Frumento, Armando. Le repubbliche cisalpina e italiana . Milano , 1985. xii, 608 p. ; LC Card 86-215881
HD9525.I82 F72 1985

ITALY - ECONOMIC CONDITIONS - 1945-
Barberis, Corrado. La società italiana . Milano, Italy [1984?] 382 p. ; LC Card 85-201583
HC305 .B365 1984

Bieling, Thomas, 1953- Das Entwicklungsmodell der italienischen Wirtschaft . Berlin , 1982 (Berlin : Copy-Center in Dahlem) 372 p. ; LC Card 87-673359
HC305 .B46x 1982

ITALY - ECONOMIC CONDITIONS - 1976-
Turani, Giuseppe. 1985-1995, il secondo miracolo economico italiano . Milano , c1986. 147 p. : ISBN 88-20-00586-7 : LC Card 86-202136
HC305 .T85 1986

ITALY - ECONOMIC CONDITIONS - 1976- - REGIONAL DISPARITIES.
Antonelli, Gilberto. Risorse umane e redditi da lavoro . Milano , c1985. 256 p. : LC Card 85-191554
HC310.I5 A66 1985

Magni, Carlo. I mercati regionali del lavoro e il problema degli indicatori . Milano [1981] 133, [3] p. : ISBN 88-20-42109-7 : LC Card 81-194409
HD5784 .M3 1981 *NYPL [JLD 87-815]*

ITALY - ECONOMIC CONDITIONS - 1976- - REGIONAL DISPARITIES - CONGRESSES.
Convegno C.I.D.I.S. (1980 : Iesolo, Italy) Credito e finanziarie regionali . Padova , c1983. vi, 148 p. ; LC Card 85-215231
HG3729.I72 C66 1980

L'Analisi degli insediamenti umani e produttivi /. Milano, Italy , c1984. 295 p. : LC Card 84-179265 DDC 330.945/0928 19
HC305 .A6618 1984 *NYPL [JLD 86-3298]*

ITALY - ECONOMIC CONDITIONS - 1976- - STATISTICS.
L'Economia in cifre, 1971-1985 /. Roma [1986] viii, 154 p. ; LC Card 86-233222
HC305 .E246 1986

ITALY - ECONOMIC CONDITIONS - ADDRESSES, ESSAYS, LECTURES.
Teoria dell'organizzazione e realtà italiana . Milano [1980] 225 p. ; ISBN 88-20-41736-7 : LC Card 80-511472 DDC 302.3/5 19
HM131 .T4 *NYPL [JLD 81-599]*

ITALY - ECONOMIC POLICY.
Il Consolidamento regionale della finanza locale /. Milano [1980] 332 p. : ISBN 88-20-41859-2 : LC Card 80-143023
HJ9497 .C63 *NYPL [JLD 87-1397]*

Oltre la crisi . Bologna , c1986. x, 745 p. : ISBN 88-15-01249-4 : LC Card 87-149887
HC305 .O45 1986

Politica monetaria e politica dell'occupazione in Italia, in un contesto di innovazione finanziaria /. Milano , c1984. 166 p. ; LC Card 84-245111 DDC 332/.0945 19
HG1029.5 .P63 1984

Rapporto sulle partecipazioni statali /. Milano [1981] 1 v. (in various pagings) ; ISBN 88-20-42161-5 : LC Card 81-199972 DDC 338.945 19
HC310.I53 R35 *NYPL [JLD 83-2970]*

Relazione programmatica delle partecipazioni statali per il 1984 . Roma , 1985. 563 p. ; LC Card 86-176014
HC310.I53 R45 1985

Struttura industriale e politiche macroeconomiche in Italia /. Bologna , c1986. 152 p. : ISBN 88-15-01193-5 : LC Card 87-100465
HC305 .S845 1986

ITALY - ECONOMIC POLICY - CONGRESSES.
Convegno "La scienza politica in Italia, bilancio e prospettive" (1984 : Milan, Italy) Politica ed economia . Milano, Italy , c1987. 159 p. ; LC Card 87-139661
HC305 .C6767 1984

ITALY - ECONOMIC POLICY - SOURCES.
Colombo, Giuseppe, 1836-1921. Industria e politica nella storia d'Italia . [Milano] , Roma , c1985. 497 p. : ISBN 88-420-2555-0 : LC Card 85-180231 DDC 338.945 19
HC310.I53 C65 1985 *NYPL [JLE 86-2517]*

ITALY. ESERCITO - POSTAL SERVICE - HISTORY.
Buzzetti, Luciano. Il distaccamento italiano di Palestina, 1917-1921 /. Milano , c1976. 55 p. : LC Card 86-179004
HE6185.P13 B89 1976

ITALY - FOREIGN ECONOMIC RELATIONS - DEVELOPING COUNTRIES.
D'Angelo, Massimo. Criteri per una cooperazione industriale con i paesi in via di sviluppo /. Milano , c1981. 294 p. ; ISBN 88-20-42145-3 : LC Card 82-113466
HF1549 .D36 1981 *NYPL [JLD 86-3318]*

ITALY - FOREIGN ECONOMIC RELATIONS - EUROPEAN ECONOMIC COMMUNITY COUNTRIES - ADDRESSES, ESSAYS, LECTURES.
Il Mezzogiorno nelle politiche nazionali e comunitarie . Milano , 1982. 379 p. ; LC Card 82-230171 DDC 338.945/7 19
HC305 .M42156 1982 *NYPL [JLE 86-1611]*

ITALY - FOREIGN RELATIONS - 1976- - ADDRESSES, ESSAYS, LECTURES.
Gonella, Guido, 1905- Contestazioni /. Roma , 1983. 3 v. ; LC Card 84-237282 DDC 945.092 19
JN5451 .G57 1983 *NYPL [JFE 86-1367]*

ITALY - FOREIGN RELATIONS - UNITED STATES.
Harper, John Lamberton. America and the reconstruction of Italy, 1945-1948 /. Cambridge [Cambridgeshire] , New York , 1986. x, 213 p. ; ISBN 0-521-32518-8 LC Card 85-30915 DDC 338.91/73/045 19
HC305 .H36 1986 *NYPL [JLE 86-3600]*

Ortona, Egidio. Anni d'America /. Bologna , c1984- v. ; ISBN 88-15-00531-5 (v. 1) : LC Card 84-240652 DDC 338.91/73/045 19
HC305 .O78 1984 *NYPL [JLL 86-503]*

ITALY - FULL EMPLOYMENT POLICIES.
Faustini, Gino, 1930- L'obiettivo occupazione nell'esperienza italiana /. Torino , c1984. 265 p. ; LC Card 86-168096
HD5784 .F38 1984

Oltre la crisi . Bologna , c1986. x, 745 p. : ISBN 88-15-01249-4 : LC Card 87-149887
HC305 .O45 1986

Palazzi, Paolo. Domanda di lavoro e produttività nell'industria italiana /. Bologna , c1980. 177 p. ; LC Card 82-156294 DDC 331.13/7945 19
HD5784 .P28 1980 *NYPL [JLD 86-2811]*

Politica monetaria e politica dell'occupazione in Italia, in un contesto di innovazione finanziaria /. Milano , c1984. 166 p. ; LC Card 84-245111 DDC 332/.0945 19
HG1029.5 .P63 1984

ITALY - FULL EMPLOYMENT POLICIES - ADDRESSES, ESSAYS, LECTURES.
Per una ristrutturazione e riconversione dell'industria italiana /. Bologna , 1980. 244 p. ; LC Card 82-102594 DDC 338.945 19
HD3616.I83 P43 *NYPL [JLD 86-599]*

Italy - Government. see **Italy - Politics and government.**

ITALY - HISTORY - GERMAN OCCUPATION, 1943-1945.
Soldini, Bruno, 1939- Uomini da soma . [Lugano] , c1985. 289 p. : LC Card 86-136358
HJ6947 .S65 1985

ITALY - HISTORY, MILITARY.
Brunt, P. A. Italian manpower, 225 B.C.-A.D. 14 /. Oxford [Oxfordshire] , 1987, c1971. xxi, 762 p. ; ISBN 0-19-814283-8 : LC Card 87-1644 DDC 304.6/0945 19
HB3599 .B77 1987

Italy. Industria, del commercio e dell'artigianato, Ministero dell'. see **Italy. Ministero dell'industria, del commercio e dell'artigianato.**

ITALY - INDUSTRIES.
Atti del Comitato dell'inchiesta industriale (1870-1874) . [Bologna?] [1984- v. <1-3 > ; LC Card 87-123944
HC304 .A87 1984

Quale strategia per l'industria? . Bologna , c1986. 221 p. : ISBN 88-15-00975-2 : LC Card 86-182300
HC310.I53 Q35 1986

Struttura industriale e politiche macroeconomiche in Italia /. Bologna , c1986. 152 p. : ISBN 88-15-01193-5 : LC Card 87-100465
HC305 .S845 1986

ITALY - INDUSTRIES - CONGRESSES.
Failed transitions to modern industrial society . Montreal , c1975. vii, 105 p. : ISBN 0-919958-00-1 LC Card 80-510009 DDC 303.4/094 19
HM101 .F26 *NYPL [JLE 81-166]*

ITALY - INDUSTRIES - HISTORY.
La Cassetta degli strumenti . Milano, Italy , c1986. 305 p. : LC Card 86-160695
HC304 .C37 1986

ITALY - INDUSTRIES - HISTORY - 20TH CENTURY.
Maione, Giuseppe, 1942- Tecnocrati e mercanti . Milano, Italia , c1986. 354 p. ; LC Card 86-194293
HC305 .M274 1986

ITALY - INDUSTRIES - HISTORY - EXHIBITIONS.
Immagini di industria in Italia . Roma , c1985. [128] p. : LC Card 86-145396
HC305 .I46 1985

ITALY - INDUSTRIES - HISTORY - PICTORIAL WORKS.
Immagini di industria in Italia . Roma , c1985. [128] p. : LC Card 86-145396
HC305 .I46 1985

Italy. Istituto nazionale di economia agraria. see **Istituto nazionale di economia agraria.**

Italy. Ministero degli affari esteri. Dipartimento per la cooperazione allo sviluppo. D'Angelo, Massimo. Criteri per una cooperazione industriale con i paesi in via di sviluppo /. Milano , c1981. 294 p. ; ISBN 88-20-42145-3 : LC Card 82-113466
HF1549 .D36 1981 *NYPL [JLD 86-3318]*

ITALY. MINISTERO DEL TESORO - BIOGRAPHY.
Bonelli, Franco. Bonaldo Stringher . [Udine] [c1985] 169 p. : LC Card 85-220896
HJ1156.S77 B66 1985

ITALY. MINISTERO DEL TESORO - HISTORY.
Bonelli, Franco. Bonaldo Stringher . [Udine] [c1985] 169 p. : LC Card 85-220896
HJ1156.S77 B66 1985

Italy. Ministero delle partecipazioni statali. Relazione programmatica delle partecipazioni statali per il 1984 . Roma , 1985. 563 p. ; LC Card 86-176014
HC310.I53 R45 1985

Italy. Ministero dell'industria, del commercio e dell'artigianato. Conferenza nazionale sull'energia (1987 : Rome, Italy) Conferenza nazionale sull'energia . Roma [1987]- v. <1-2 > : LC Card 87-167955
HD9502.I82 C63 1987

ITALY, NORTHERN - ECONOMIC CONDITIONS.
Dewerpe, Alain. L'industrie aux champs . Roma , 1985. xxxv, 543 p. : ISBN 2-7283-0081-X LC Card 86-221375
HC307.N58 D48 1985

ITALY, NORTHERN - INDUSTRIES - HISTORY - 19TH CENTURY.
Dewerpe, Alain. L'industrie aux champs . Roma , 1985. xxxv, 543 p. : ISBN 2-7283-0081-X LC Card 86-221375
HC307.N58 D48 1985

ITALY, NORTHERN - SOCIAL CONDITIONS.
Dewerpe, Alain. L'industrie aux champs . Roma , 1985. xxxv, 543 p. : ISBN 2-7283-0081-X LC Card 86-221375
HC307.N58 D48 1985

Italy. Parlamento. Comitato dell'inchiesta industriale (1870-1874) Atti del Comitato dell'inchiesta industriale (1870-1874) . [Bologna?] [1984- v. <1-3 > ; LC Card 87-123944
HC304 .A87 1984

Italy. Parlamento. Giunta per la inchiesta agraria e sulle condizioni della classe agricola. Inchiesta Jacini : atti della Giunta per la inchiesta agraria e sulle condizioni della classe agricola. Sala Bolognese : A. Forni, 1978-<1987 > v. <1-7, 9-10; v. 13, t. 1, fasc. 1-3; v. 11, t. 1-3; v. 13, t. 2, fasc. 4-5; in 18 > : ill. (some col.) ; 32 cm. Reprint. Originally published: Roma : Forzani, 1881-1886. LC Card 86-143133
1. Agriculture - Economic aspects - Italy. 2. Agricultural laborers - Italy. 3. Italy - Rural conditions. I. Jacini, Stefano, 1827-1891. II. Title.
HD1970 .I84 1978

ITALY - POLITICS AND GOVERNMENT - 1943-1947.
D'Angelo, Lucio. Ceti medi e ricostruzione . [Milano] , 1981. vi, 287 p. ; LC Card 81-213297
JN5657.D45 D36 1981
NYPL [JLE 86-3459]

ITALY - POLITICS AND GOVERNMENT - 1945- - ADDRESSES, ESSAYS, LECTURES.
Gonella, Guido, 1905- Contestazioni /. Roma , 1983. 3 v. ; LC Card 84-237282 DDC 945.092 19
JN5451 .G57 1983 *NYPL [JFE 86-1367]*

ITALY - POLITICS AND GOVERNMENT - 1945-1976.
Mattei, Enrico. Enrico Mattei, 1945-1953 . [Matelica] [1982] 199 p. : LC Card 84-190191
HD9575.I84 E585 1982

ITALY - POLITICS AND GOVERNMENT - 1976- - CONGRESSES.
Convegno "La scienza politica in Italia, bilancio e prospettive" (1984 : Milan, Italy) Politica ed economia . Milano, Italy , c1987. 159 p. ; LC Card 87-139661
HC305 .C6767 1984

ITALY - POPULATION.
Contribution of Italian scholars to the IUSSP XX General Conference =. Roma [1985?] 320 p. : LC Card 87-169376 DDC 304.6/0945 19
HB3599 .C647 1985

ITALY - POPULATION - HISTORY.
Brunt, P. A. Italian manpower, 225 B.C.-A.D. 14 /. Oxford [Oxfordshire] , 1987, c1971. xxi, 762 p. ; ISBN 0-19-814283-8 : LC Card 87-1644 DDC 304.6/0945 19
HB3599 .B77 1987

ITALY - POPULATION - HISTORY - 19TH CENTURY - CONGRESSES.
La Popolazione italiana nell'Ottocento . Bologna [1985] xxv, 534 p. : LC Card 86-157672
HB3599 .P663 1985

ITALY - POPULATION, RURAL - STATISTICS.
Barberis, Corrado. Agricoltura e strati sociali /. Milano, Italy , c1986. 269 p. ; LC Card 86-214233
HD1536.I8 B328 1986

ITALY - RURAL CONDITIONS.
Italy. Parlamento. Giunta per la inchiesta agraria e sulle condizioni della classe agricola. Inchiesta Jacini . Sala Bolognese , 1978-<1987. v. <1-7, 9-10; v. 13, t. 1, fasc. 1-3; v. 11, t. 1-3; v. 13, t. 2, fasc. 4-5; in 18 > : LC Card 86-143133
HD1970 .I84 1978

ITALY - RURAL CONDITIONS - STATISTICS.
Barberis, Corrado. Agricoltura e strati sociali /. Milano, Italy , c1986. 269 p. ; LC Card 86-214233
HD1536.I8 B328 1986

Italy. Servizi delle informazioni e della proprietà letteraria, artistica e scientifica. La Tutela del lavoro in Italia. [Roma] [1976] 144 p. ; LC Card 86-233354
HD8481 .T85 1976

Italy, Sicily, and the Mediterranean, 1100-1400 /. Abulafia, David. London , 1987. 346 p. in various pagings : ISBN 0-86078-198-4 : LC Card 87-157554 DDC 330.9182/2 19
HF3585 .A29 1987

ITALY - SOCIAL CONDITIONS - 1945-1976.
Barberis, Corrado. La società italiana . Milano, Italy [1984?] 382 p. ; LC Card 85-201583
HC305 .B365 1984

ITALY - SOCIAL CONDITIONS - 1976-
Barberis, Corrado. La società italiana . Milano, Italy [1984?] 382 p. ; LC Card 85-201583
HC305 .B365 1984

ITALY - SOCIAL CONDITIONS - 1976- - ADDRESSES, ESSAYS, LECTURES.
Gonella, Guido, 1905- Contestazioni /. Roma , 1983. 3 v. ; LC Card 84-237282 DDC 945.092 19
JN5451 .G57 1983 *NYPL [JFE 86-1367]*

ITALY - SOCIAL CONDITIONS - ADDRESSES, ESSAYS, LECTURES.
Teoria dell'organizzazione e realtà italiana . Milano [1980] 225 p. ; ISBN 88-20-41736-7 : LC Card 80-511472 DDC 302.3/5 19
HM131 .T4 *NYPL [JLD 81-599]*

ITALY - SOCIAL POLICY - CONGRESSES.
Convegno "La scienza politica in Italia, bilancio e prospettive" (1984 : Milan, Italy) Politica ed economia . Milano, Italy , c1987. 159 p. ; LC Card 87-139661
HC305 .C6767 1984

ITALY, SOUTHERN - ECONOMIC CONDITIONS.
Massafra, Angelo. Campagne e territorio nel Mezzogiorno fra Settecento e Ottocento /. Bari , c1984. 324 p. : ISBN 88-22-06039-3 : LC Card 85-179303
HC307.S69 M37 1984

ITALY, SOUTHERN - ECONOMIC CONDITIONS - 1945-
Barone, Giuseppe, 1947- Mezzogiorno e modernizzazione . Torino , c1986. xii, 408 p. ; ISBN 88-06-59238-6 : LC Card 86-219130
HC307.S69 B37 1986

Mezzogiorno . [S.l. , 1980?] (København : Kunstakademiets trykkeri) 78 p. : LC Card 85-128057
HC307.S6 M49 1980

ITALY, SOUTHERN - ECONOMIC CONDITIONS - CONGRESSES.
La Questione meridionale oggi /. Caltanissetta , 1985. 186 p. ; LC Card 86-214162
HC307.S69 Q47 1985

ITALY, SOUTHERN - ECONOMIC POLICY.
Acocella, Giovanni, 1932- Di là dalle rovine . Napoli , c1982. 172, [4] p. ; ISBN 88-7042-185-6 : LC Card 82-181323 DDC 363.3/495 19
HC307.S69 A36 1982 *NYPL [JLD 86-485]*

ITALY, SOUTHERN - ECONOMIC POLICY - ADDRESSES, ESSAYS, LECTURES.
Il Mezzogiorno nelle politiche nazionali e comunitarie . Milano , 1982. 379 p. ; LC Card 82-230171 DDC 338.945/7 19
HC305 .M42156 1982 *NYPL [JLE 86-1611]*

ITALY, SOUTHERN - INDUSTRIES - LOCATION.
Costa, Paolo. Agglomerazione urbana, localizzazione industriale e Mezzogiorno /. Milano , 1983. viii, 240 p. : LC Card 83-186216 DDC 307.2 19
HB2060.S68 C67 1983 *NYPL [JLE 86-3657]*

ITALY, SOUTHERN - POLITICS AND GOVERNMENT.
Mezzogiorno . [S.l. , 1980?] (København : Kunstakademiets trykkeri) 78 p. : LC Card 85-128057
HC307.S6 M49 1980

ITALY, SOUTHERN - SOCIAL CONDITIONS.
Massafra, Angelo. Campagne e territorio nel Mezzogiorno fra Settecento e Ottocento /. Bari , c1984. 324 p. : ISBN 88-22-06039-3 : LC Card 85-179303
HC307.S69 M37 1984

ITALY, SOUTHERN - SOCIAL CONDITIONS - CONGRESSES.
La Questione meridionale oggi /. Caltanissetta , 1985. 186 p. ; LC Card 86-214162
HC307.S69 Q47 1985

ITALY, SOUTHERN - SOCIAL POLICY.
Acocella, Giovanni, 1932- Di là dalle rovine . Napoli , c1982. 172, [4] p. ; ISBN 88-7042-185-6 : LC Card 82-181323 DDC 363.3/495 19
HC307.S69 A36 1982 *NYPL [JLD 86-485]*

ITALY - STATISTICAL SERVICES - CONGRESSES.
Statistica e pubblica amministrazione . Milano , 1983-1985. 2 v. ; ISBN 88-14-00703-9 (v. 2) : LC Card 86-215546
HA37.I9 S7 1983

ITALY - STATISTICS.
A metà decennio . Milano, Italy , c1986. 355 p. ; LC Card 86-224676
HA1374 .A19 1986

Itami, Hiroyuki, 1945- Mobilizing invisible assets / Hiroyuki Itami with Thomas W. Roehl. Cambridge, Mass. : Harvard University Press,

1987. xi, 186 p. : ill. ; 25 cm. Bibliography: p. [175]-[179]. Includes index. ISBN 0-674-57770-1 (alk. paper) LC Card 86-26972 DDC 658.4/012 19
1. Strategic planning. I. Roehl, Thomas W. II. Title. III. Title: Invisible assets.
HD30.28 .I85 1987

ITC publications.
Wells, Jeremy. The export marketing of technical consulting services from developing countries /. Geneva , 1986. vi, 127 p. : LC Card 87-168669 DDC 658.4/6/091724 19
HD9989.D44 W46 1986

Ithaca Filmworks.
Faces in a famine [motion picture] /. New York, N.Y. , 1985. 1 film reel (51 min.) : LC Card 85-702803 DDC 963 11
HC845.Z9F3

Faces in a famine [videorecording] /. New York, N.Y. , 1985. 1 videocassette (51 min.) : LC Card 85-703663 DDC 963 11
HC845.Z9F3

ITHACA, N. Y. - BIOGRAPHY.
Sisler, Carol U., 1929- Enterprising families, Ithaca, New York . Ithaca, N.Y. (5 Cornell Walk, Ithaca 14850) , 1986. 159 p. : LC Card 86-81672 DDC 338/.092/2 B 19
HC102.5.A2 S55 1986

Ithurbide, Philippe. Bourguinat, Henri. L'entreprise française face aux variations de change . Paris , c1985. vi, 123 p. : ISBN 2-7178-0899-X : LC Card 85-190582 DDC 332.4/5 19
HG3815 .B68 1985 ***NYPL [JLE 86-494]***

Itinerari culturali del comune di Chioggia . (n. 4) Un Mestiere e un paese . Venezia , 1986. 172 p. : ISBN 88-317-4893-9 LC Card 86-219883
HD8039.S252 I85 1986

Itō, Makoto, 1936- The basic theory of capitalism : the forms and substance of the capitalist economy / Makoto Itoh. Totowa, N.J. : Barnes & Noble Books, 1987. p. cm. Bibliography: p. Includes index. ISBN 0-389-20729-2 LC Card 87-905 DDC 330.12/2 19
1. Marxian economics. 2. Capitalism. 3. Value. I. Title.
HB97.5 .I823 1987

Itō, Motoshige, 1951- Disequilibrium trade theories / Motoshige Itoh and Takashi Negishi. Chur, Switzerland ; New York : Harwood Academic Publishers, c1987. viii, 100 p. : ill. ; 22 cm. (Fundamentals of pure and applied economics, 0191-1708 . v. 23.) Bibliography: p. 94-98. Includes index. ISBN 3-7186-0412-4 LC Card 87-11834 DDC 380.1 19
1. Commerce. 2. Equilibrium (Economics). I. Negishi, Takashi, 1933-. II. Series: Fundamentals of pure and applied economics , v. 23. III. Title.
HF1008 .I855 1987

It's your money! . Scott, Gini Graham. New York, N.Y. , c1987. vii, 295 p. ; ISBN 0-380-89979-5 (pbk.) : LC Card 85-91536 DDC 658.8/8 19
HG3752.5 .S36 1987

Itskovich, I. A. (Iosif Aleksandrovich)
Kazantsev, S. V. (Sergeĭ Vladimirovich) Makromodelirovanie rasshirennogo vosproizvodstva /. Novosibirsk , 1980. 206, [2] p. ; LC Card 81-138742
HB139 .K39 1980

Val'tukh, Konstantin Kurtovich. Matematicheskiĭ i statisticheskiĭ analiz funktsii potrebleniia /. Novosibirsk , 1986. 165, [3] p. : LC Card 86-230310
HB801 .V26 1986

Iturraspe, Francisco. Participación, cogestión y autogestión en América Latina /. Caracas , 1986. 2 v. : ISBN 980-265-396-9 (set) LC Card 87-111263
HD5660.L29 P37 1986

IUdanov, A. IU. (Andreĭ IUr'evich) Teorii "otkrytoĭ ėkonomiki," doktriny i deĭstvitel'nost' / A.IU. IUdanov. Moskva : "Mysl'", 1983. 190 p. ; 20 cm. (Sovremennye burzhuaznye ėkonomicheskie teorii) Includes bibliographical references. LC Card 83-209639
1. Free trade and protection - Free trade. 2. Commercial policy. I. Title. II. Series.
HF1713 .I93 1983

IUF Mediterranean Hotel and Restaurant Workers' Conference, Palermo, November 15-17, 1978. IUF Mediterranean Hotel and Restaurant Workers' Conference (1978 : Palermo, Sicily) Petit-Lancy, Switzerland [1978?] 1 v. (various pagings) ; LC Card 83-225538
HD6475.A2 I7836 1978

IUF Mediterranean Hotel and Restaurant Workers' Conference (1978 : Palermo, Sicily) IUF Mediterranean Hotel and Restaurant Workers' Conference, Palermo, November 15-17, 1978. Petit-Lancy, Switzerland : International Union of Food and Allied Workers' Associations, Secretariat, [1978?] 1 v. (various pagings) ; 30 cm. Cover title: Mediterranean Conference, HRC. Spine title: HRC Conference. LC Card 83-225538
1. International Union of Food and Allied Workers' Associations. 2. Trade-unions - Hotels, taverns, etc. I. International Union of Food and Allied Workers' Associations. Secretariat. II. Title. III. Title: Mediterranean Conference, HRC. IV. Title: HRC Conference.
HD6475.A2 I7836 1978

IUkhimenko, V. V. (Vladimir Vasil'evich)
Izuchenie i prognozirovanie sprosa na bytovye uslugi / V.V. IUkhimenko, R.G. Puzynin, S.I. Povolotskaia. Kiev : "Tekhnika", 1983. 103 p. ; 20 cm. (Biblioteka peredovogo opyta. Tekhnologiia proizvodstva) Bibliography: p. 103. LC Card 83-218585
1. Service industries - Ukraine - Forecasting. 2. Consumption (Economics) - Ukraine - Forecasting. I. Puzynin, R. G. (Roman Gavrilovich). II. Povolotskaia, S. I. (Sarra Isaakovna). III. Series. IV. Series: Biblioteka peredovogo opyta (Tekhnika (Firm)). Tekhnologiia proizvodstva. V. Title.
HD9986.S683 U385 1983

IUkhneva, N. V. Ėtnicheskiĭ sostav i ėtnosotsial'naia struktura naseleniia Peterburga : vtoraia polovina XIX-nachalo XX veka : statisticheskiĭ analiz / N.V. IUkhnëva ; pod redaktsieĭ K.V. Chistova. Leningrad : Izd-vo "Nauka," Leningradskoe otd-nie, 1984. 220 p., [1] folded leaf of plates : ill., maps ; 23 cm. At head of title: Akademiia nauk SSSR. Institut ėtnografii im. N.N. Miklukho-Maklaia. Errata slip inserted. Includes bibliographical references. LC Card 85-116858
1. Minorities - Russian S.F.S.R. - Leningrad - History - 19th century. 2. Social classes - Russian S.F.S.R. - Leningrad - History - 19th century. 3. Leningrad (R.S.F.S.R.) - Population - History - 19th century. I. Chistov, Kirill Vasil'evich. II. Title.
HB3608.L4 I94 1984 ***NYPL [*QGK 87-925]***

IUrasova, G. (Galina) IUrasova, M. Neftianik . Moskva , 1981. 254 p. : LC Card 82-111110
HD8039.P42 S654 1981

IUrasova, M. Neftianik : dokumental'naia povest' / M. IUrasova, G. IUrasova. Moskva : "Sov. Rossiia", 1981. 254 p. : port. ; 18 cm. (Liudi Sovetskoĭ Rossii) LC Card 82-111110
1. Muravlenko, V. I. (Viktor Ivanovich). 2. Petroleum workers - Russian S.F.S.R. - Biography. I. IUrasova, G. (Galina). II. Title.
HD8039.P42 S654 1981

IUrėvich, Uladzimir Mikhaĭlavich. Syn'ooka sestra Ukraïny / V.M. IUrevich. Kyïv : Vyd-vo lit-ry Ukraïny, 1985. 158 p. ; 18 cm. Title in colophon: Sineokaia sestra Ukrainy. LC Card 87-109673
1. Byelorussian S.S.R. - Economic conditions. I. Title. II. Title: Sineokaia sestra Ukrainy.
HC337.B93 I97 1985

IUrina, V. P. Puti razvitiia infrastruktury regiona /. Ufa , 1984. 117 p. : LC Card 85-199949
HE255.Z7 B377 1984

IUshkov, V. I. (Vasiliĭ Il'ich) Zakupochnaia tsena i rasshirennoe vosproizvodstvo v sel'skom khoziaĭstve / V.I. IUshkov. Moskva : Ėkonomika, 1980. 142 p. ; 20 cm. Includes bibliographical references. LC Card 81-134864
1. Agricultural prices - Russian S.F.S.R. 2. Agriculture - Economic aspects - Russian S.F.S.R. I. Title.
HD1995.R8 I95 1980

IUsufovich, B. E. (Boris Efimovich)
Sovershenstvovanie operativnogo upravleniia osnovnym proizvodstvom mashinostroitel'nogo predpriiatiia / B.E. IUsufovich, L.N. Monetkina, V.N. Piatibratova. Moskva : "Mashinostroenie", 1982. 91 p. : ill. ; 21 cm. LC Card 82-204954
1. Machinery industry - Soviet Union - Management. I. Monetkina, L. N. (Lidiia Nikolaevna). II. Piatibratova, V. N. (Vera Nikolaevna). III. Title.
HD9705.S595 I94 1982

IUsupov, Ė. IU. Akhunova, M. A. Rabochiĭ klass Uzbekistana v usloviiakh nauchno-tekhnicheskoĭ revoliutsii /. Tashkent , 1984. 181 p. ; LC Card 85-232015
HD6331.2.S652 U93 1984

"IUzhdizel'mash"--podgotovka k ėkonomicheskomu ėksperimentu /. Akhrameev, V. N. (Vasiliĭ Nikiforovich) Moskva , 1984. 96 p. : LC Card 85-144706
HD9705.S595 A36 1984

IUzhnaia IAkutiia, sotsial'no-ėkonomicheskiĭ aspekt : sbornik nauchnykh trudov / [redkollegiia, IA.T. Vasil'ev (otvetstvennyĭ redaktor), A.I. Shurgina, V.I. Vlasov]. IAkutsk : IAkutskiĭ filial SO AN SSSR, 1985. 94 p. ; 20 cm. At head of title: Akademiia nauk SSSR. Ordena Lenina Sibirskoe otdelenie. IAkutskiĭ filial. Otdel ėkonomiki. Includes bibliographical references. LC Card 86-180767
1. IAkutskaia A.S.S.R. (R.S.F.S.R.) - Economic conditions. 2. IAkutskaia A.S.S.R. (R.S.F.S.R.) - Social conditions. I. Vasil'ev, IA. T. II. Shurgina, A. I. III. Vlasov, V. I. IV. Akademiia nauk SSSR. IAkutskiĭ filial. Otdel ėkonomiki.
HC337.I2 I97 1985

IV plano mineiro de desenvolvimento econômico e social . Minas Gerais, Brazil. [Belo Horizonte] [1983] 347 p. : LC Card 86-201630
HC188.M6 M48 1983

IV pleno del Consejo Económico Sindical de Cuenca . Consejo Económico Sindical Provincial (Cuenca, Spain) [Cuenca] , 1965. 128 p. : LC Card 85-105812
HD2025.C84 C65 1965

L'IVA en els sectors agrari i pesquer catalans. 1a ed. [Barcelona] : Generalitat de Catalunya, Departament d'Agricultura, Ramaderia i Pesca, 1985. 49 p. ; 24 cm. Annex slip inserted. ISBN 84-393-0632-6 LC Card 86-165858
1. Value-added tax - Spain - Catalonia. 2. Value-added tax - Law and legislation - Spain - Catalonia. 3. Agriculture - Taxation - Spain - Catalonia. 4. Fish trade - Taxation - Spain - Catalonia. I. Catalonia (Spain). Departament d'Agricultura, Ramaderia i Pesca.
HJ5715.S7 L58 1985

Ivancevich, John M.
Donnelly, James H. Fundamentals of management /. Plano, Tex. , 1987. xxviii, 827 p. : ISBN 0-256-03682-9 LC Card 86-71879 DDC 658 19
HD31 .D594 1987

Job stress . New York , c1987. 267 p. ; ISBN 0-86656-630-9 LC Card 87-8568 DDC 658.3/82 19
HF5548.85 .J65 1987

Matteson, Michael T. Controlling work stress . San Francisco, Calif. , 1987. xx, 378 p. ; ISBN 1-555-42062-1 (alk. paper) LC Card 87-45503 DDC 658.3/82 19
HF5548.85 .M378 1987

Organizational behavior and management / John M. Ivancevich, Michael T. Matteson. Plano, Tex. : Business Publications, Inc., 1987. xv, 780 p. : col. ill. ; 25 cm. Includes bibliographies and indexes. ISBN 0-256-05608-0 LC Card 86-72712 DDC 658.4 19
1. Organizational behavior. I. Matteson, Michael T. II. Title.
HD58.7 .I89 1987

Ivanics, András. A termelőszövetkezeti termelésirányítókról : Borsod-Abauj-Zemplén megyei vizsgálat alapján / Ivanics András. Budapest : Agrárgazdasági Kutató Intézet, 1984. 83 p. ; 29 cm. (Agrárgazdasági Kutató Intézet, 0209-5696 . 1984/5) Bibliography: p. 53-54. ISBN 963-491-179-X LC Card 86-198816
1. Collective farms - Hungary - Borsod-Abaúj-Zemplén Megye - Officials and employees. I. Series: Agrárgazdasági Kutató Intézet (Series) , 1984/5. II. Title.
HD1492.H82 B675 1984

Ivanov, E. P. (Evgeniĭ Pavlovich) Kollektivizatsiia krest'ianskikh khoziaĭstv i likvidatsiia kulachestva kak klassa na Severo-Zapade RSFSR, 1927-1937 gg. : uchebnoe posobie k spetskursu / E.P. Ivanov. Leningrad : Leningradskiĭ gos. pedagog. in-t im. A.I. Gertsena, 1983. 91 p. ; 22 cm. At head of title: Ministerstvo prosveshcheniia RSFSR. Includes

bibliographical references. LC Card 84-190520
1. Collectivization of agriculture - Russian S.F.S.R. - History. 2. Collectivization of agriculture - Soviet Union, Northwestern - History. 3. Russian S.F.S.R. - Social conditions. 4. Soviet Union, Northwestern - Social conditions. I. Title.
HD1492.S652 R875 1983 ***NYPL [*QI 87-3170]***

Ivanov, I͡U. N., d.f.-m.n. Chislennye metody v zadachakh optimal'nogo ėkonomicheskogo planirovanii͡a /. Moskva , 1983. 158 p. : LC Card 84-128729
HC336.25 .C515 1983

Ivanov, I͡Uriĭ Grigor'evich. Rabochee dvizhenie v Moldavii, 1895-fevral' 1917 g. . Kishinev , 1985. 322 p. ; LC Card 86-100092
HD8529.M57 R32 1985

Ivanov, L. G. (Leonid Grigor'evich) Ocherki ėkonomicheskoĭ istorii Shri Lanki : XVI-nachalo XX v. / L.G. Ivanov. Moskva : Izd-vo "Nauka", 1978. 222 p. ; 21 cm. At head of title: Akademii͡a nauk SSSR. Institut vostokovedenii͡a. Bibiliography: p. 209-[219] Includes index. LC Card 81-153039
1. Sri Lanka - Economic conditions. I. Title.
HC424 .I95 1978

Ivanov, Marina. Blades, Derek W. Discrepancies between imports and exports in OECD foreign trade statistics /. Paris, France , c1984. i, 42 p. ; LC Card 86-205155 DDC 382/.021 19
HF1016 .B569 1984

Ivanov, N. I. (Nikolaĭ Ivanovich)
Osnovnye fondy i proizvodstvennye moshchnosti v gornoĭ promyshlennosti /. Moskva , 1984. 207 p. : LC Card 85-138074
HD9506.S7472 O86 1984

Povyshenie ėffektivnosti ASUP . Kiev , 1985. 303 p. : LC Card 85-210269
HD30.2 .P68 1985 ***NYPL [*QIP 87-2760]***

Ivanov, S. F. (Sergeĭ Feliksovich)
Razvivai͡ushchiesi͡a strany : demograficheskiĭ vzryv / S.F. Ivanov. Moskva : Izd-vo Znanie, 1984. 63 p. : ill. ; 20 cm. (Bibliotechka Problemy mirovogo khozi͡aĭstva) "V pomoshch' lektoru." Includes bibliographical references. LC Card 85-125223
1. Developing countries - Population. I. Title. II. Series.
HB884 .I93 1984

Ivanov, Semen Aleksandrovich. Trudovoe pravo i povyshenie kachestva truda /. Moskva , 1987. 270 p. ; ***NYPL [*QIX 87-3357]***

Ivanov, Sergeĭ Ivanovich, doktor ėkonomicheskikh nauk. Sovremennyĭ kapitalizm . Leningrad , 1985. 212 p. ; LC Card 86-117888
HB501 .S824 1985

Ivanov, V. A. (Valentin Aleksandrovich)
Ėkonomicheskoe stimulirovanie povyshenii͡a ėffektivnosti intensifikatsii sovkhoznogo proizvodstva / V.A. Ivanov. Moskva : Izd-vo "Nauka", 1980. 248 p. ; 20 cm. (Problemy sovetskoĭ ėkonomiki) At head of title: Akademii͡a nauk SSSR. Komi filial. Includes bibliographical references. LC Card 81-134017
1. State farms - Soviet Union, Northwestern. 2. Agricultural productivity - Soviet Union, Northwestern. I. Title.
HD1493.S652 N65 1980

Ivanov, V. R. (Vladimir Romanovich)
Proizvoditel'nost' truda i zarabotnai͡a plata v stroitel'stve sooruzheniĭ svi͡azi / V.R. Ivanov, A.A. Klimenko. Moskva : "Radio i svi͡az'", 1985. 159 p. : ill. ; 22 cm. Bibliography: p. [158] LC Card 85-224803
1. Construction industry - Soviet Union - Labor productivity - Mathematical models. 2. Wages - Construction workers - Soviet Union - Mathematical models. I. Klimenko, A. A. (Aleksandr Aleksandrovich). II. Title.
HD9715.S72 I9 1985

Ivanov, V. V., k.ė.n.
Problemy tselevoĭ orientatsii razvitii͡a resursnogo potentsiala /. Moskva , 1984. 205 p. : LC Card 86-143993
HC333.5 .P77 1984

Sovershenstvovanie metodologii ėkonomicheskogo analiza v nauchnykh uchrezhdenii͡akh i nauchno-tekhnicheskikh kompleksakh . Kiev , 1986. 116 p. ; LC Card 87-126466
HC340.R4 S68 1986

Ivanova, R. K. (Roza Konstantinovna)
Zhelezovskai͡a, N. M. Stimuly k trudu na sovremennom ėtape razvitii͡a sotsialisticheskogo obshchestva /. Moskva , 1985. 160 p. ; LC Card 86-174895
HF5549.5.I5 Z48 1985

Ivanova, V. D. (Valentina Dmitrievna) Denisova, N. F. (Nina Fedorovna) Planirovanie otdelochnogo proizvodstva s primeneniem matematicheskikh metodov i ĖVM . Moskva , 1984. 59, [5] p. : LC Card 85-131509
HD9865.S652 D46 1984

Ivanova, Vasilka. Prinosŭt na dr. Todor Zhivkov za razvitieto na sotsialno-ikonomicheskata politika na BKP v etapa na izgrazhdane na razvitoto sotsialistichesko obshtestvo . Sofii͡a , 1983. 398 p. ; LC Card 84-103348
HC403 .P72 1983

IVème plan quinquennal de développement économique et social du Burundi, 1983-1987 /. Burundi. Ministère à la présidence chargé du plan. [Bujumbura] [1983?-] <v. 1, pt. 1; v. 2, 4, 7 > : LC Card 86-980056
HC880 .B88 1983

Ivers, James F. Financial planning applications / James F. Ivers, III. 6th ed. Bryn Mawr, Pa. : American College, c1987. 2 v. : ill. ; 28 cm. . 1 fact finder. (Huebner school series) Rev. ed. of: Financial planning applications / Gwenda L. Cannon. 5th ed. c1986. Includes bibliography and index. ISBN 0-943590-13-2 (pbk. : v. 1) LC Card 87-71366 DDC 332.024 19
1. Finance, Personal. 2. Estate planning. I. Cannon, Gwenda L. Financial planning applications. II. Title. III. Series.
HG179 .C326 1987

Iversen, Gudmund R. Analysis of variance / Gudmund R. Iversen, Helmut Norpoth. 2nd ed. Newbury Park : Sage Publications, c1987. 94 p. : ill. ; 22 cm. (Sage university papers. Quantitative applications in the social sciences . no. 07-001) Bibliography: p. 93-94. ISBN 0-8039-3001-1 (pbk.) LC Card 87-61276 DDC 519.5/35 19
1. Analysis of variance. 2. Social sciences - Statistical methods. I. Norpoth, Helmut. II. Series: Sage university papers series. Quantitative applications in the social sciences , no. 07-001. III. Title.
HA31.35 .I85 1987

Iversen, John, 1954- Om EF : en kolos på lerfødder eller en supermagt på vej? / John Iversen. København : H. Reitzel, 1984. 143 p. : ill. ; 23 cm. (Æble-serien) Bibliography: p. 141. Includes index. ISBN 87-412-3775-7 : LC Card 84-186203
1. European Economic Community. 2. European Economic Community - Denmark. I. Title. II. Title: Om E.F.
HC241.2 .I84 1984

The Ivory Coast . Trueblood, Michael A. Washington, DC , 1986. iv, 32 p. : LC Card 86-602806 DDC 338.1 s 382/.41/096668 19
HD1411 .F59 no. 223 HD9017.I912

IVORY COAST - COMMERCE.
Gohibi, Bernard. Les incidences financières de l'assurance maritime sur l'économie ivoirienne /. Abidjan , 1984. 24 leaves ; LC Card 86-111379 DDC 368.2/2/0096668 19
HE964.5.I94 G64 1984 ***NYPL [JLF 86-1484]***

IVORY COAST - COMMERCE - UNITED STATES.
Trueblood, Michael A. The Ivory Coast . Washington, DC , 1986. iv, 32 p. : LC Card 86-602806 DDC 338.1 s 382/.41/096668 19
HD1411 .F59 no. 223 HD9017.I912

Ivory Coast. Direction de la statistique.
Ahonzo, Etienne. Population de la Côte d'Ivoire . Abidjan , 1984. ix, 324 p. : LC Card 86-110796 DDC 304.6/09666/8 19
HB3666.A3 A46 1984 ***NYPL [JLF 86-1466]***

Enquête démographique à passages répétés, 1978-1979 . [Abidjan] [1980?] 270 p. : LC Card 85-213692 DDC 304.6/09666/8 19
HB3666.A3 E57 1980 ***NYPL [JLF 86-1023]***

IVORY COAST - ECONOMIC CONDITIONS - 1960-
Gozo, K. M. Crise et pauvreté en Côte d'Ivoire . Addis Abéba , c1983. iv, 84 p. ; ISBN 92-2-203648-4 LC Card 85-981192
HC1025 .G69 1983

Jakobeit, Cord. Die sozio-ökonomische Entwicklung der Elfenbeinküste seit der Unabhängigkeit . Hamburg , 1984. viii, 132 p. : ISBN 3-923519-57-5 LC Card 84-222859
HC1025 .J35 1984

IVORY COAST - ECONOMIC POLICY.
Alschuler, Lawrence R., 1941- Multinationals and maldevelopment . New York , 1988. xii, 218 p. : ISBN 0-312-00531-8 : LC Card 87-4307 DDC 338.9 19
HD82 .A5493 1988

Jakobeit, Cord. Die sozio-ökonomische Entwicklung der Elfenbeinküste seit der Unabhängigkeit . Hamburg , 1984. viii, 132 p. : ISBN 3-923519-57-5 LC Card 84-222859
HC1025 .J35 1984

Willaert, Y. Ressources humaines et développement régional en Côte d'Ivoire . [Addis Ababa] [1977] 3, 108, [6] leaves (1 folded) ; LC Card 82-980560
HD5846.9.A6 W55 1977

IVORY COAST - FULL EMPLOYMENT POLICIES.
International Labour Organisation. Côte-d'Ivoire . Genève , 1984. 94 p. : ISBN 92-2-203860-6 LC Card 86-219971
HD5846.9.A6 I57 1984

Ivory Coast. Office national de formation professionnelle. Direction Etudes et recherches. Gboizo, J. Emplois et qualifications dans le secteur métaux-mécanique-électricité en Côte d'Ivoire /. [Abidjan] , 1981. 93 leaves ; LC Card 83-234024
HD5846.9.A6 G36 1981

IVORY COAST - POLITICS AND GOVERNMENT - 1960-
Jakobeit, Cord. Die sozio-ökonomische Entwicklung der Elfenbeinküste seit der Unabhängigkeit . Hamburg , 1984. viii, 132 p. : ISBN 3-923519-57-5 LC Card 84-222859
HC1025 .J35 1984

IVORY COAST - POPULATION.
Ahonzo, Etienne. Population de la Côte d'Ivoire . Abidjan , 1984. ix, 324 p. : LC Card 86-110796 DDC 304.6/09666/8 19
HB3666.A3 A46 1984 ***NYPL [JLF 86-1466]***

Enquête démographique à passages répétés, 1978-1979 . [Abidjan] [1980?] 270 p. : LC Card 85-213692 DDC 304.6/09666/8 19
HB3666.A3 E57 1980 ***NYPL [JLF 86-1023]***

IVORY COAST - SOCIAL CONDITIONS - 1960-
Jakobeit, Cord. Die sozio-ökonomische Entwicklung der Elfenbeinküste seit der Unabhängigkeit . Hamburg , 1984. viii, 132 p. : ISBN 3-923519-57-5 LC Card 84-222859
HC1025 .J35 1984

Ivory Coast. Statistique, Direction de la. see **Ivory Coast. Direction de la statistique.**

IVORY INDUSTRY - TANZANIA - ZANZIBAR - HISTORY.
Sheriff, Abdul. Slaves, spices, & ivory in Zanzibar . London , Athens , 1987. xx, 297 p. : ISBN 0-8214-0871-2 (U. S.) LC Card 87-12339 DDC 382/.096781 19
HF3897 .S54 1987

Iwanek, Marian. Rozwój sytuacji i polityki gospodarczej w Polsce w latach 1981-1984 /. Warszawa , 1985. 161 p. ; ISBN 83-03-00866-8 : LC Card 85-229473
HC340.3 .R69 1985

IWGIA document .
(57) Otten, Mariël. Transmigrasi . Copenhagen , c1986. 254 p. : LC Card 87-144670 DDC 333.3/1/598 19
HD896 .O88 1986

IX recenseamento geral do Brasil - 1980 .
(v. 6) Inquéritos especiais /. Rio de Janeiro, Brasil , 1984. 4 v. in 5. ; ***NYPL [JLF 86-202]***

Iyanda, Olukunle. Multinationals and employment in a West African sub-region : Liberia and Sierra Leone / by Olukunle Iyanda. Geneva : International Labour Office, 1984. iv, 49 p. ; 30 cm. (Working papers / Multinational Enterprises Programme . working paper no. 29) Bibliography: p. 37-39. ISBN 92-2-103623-5 (pbk.) : LC Card 86-213585 DDC 388.8/88664 19
1. International business enterprises - Liberia. 2. International business enterprises - Sierra Leone. 3.

Investments, Foreign - Liberia. 4. Investments, Foreign - Sierra Leone. 5. Labor supply - Liberia. 6. Labor supply - Sierre Leone. I. Series: Working papers / Multinational Enterprises Programme , working paper no. 29. II. Title.
HD2928.8 .I92 1984

Iyare, S. International cost differences in developing countries : a comparison of Ghanaian and Nigerian manufacturing industries : January 1983 / by S. Iyare and N. Gemmell. Durham, England : University of Durham, Dept. of Economics, [1983] 14, [9] leaves : ill. ; 30 cm. (Working paper . no. 55) Cover title. Bibliography: p. [18]-[19] LC Card 86-207078 DDC 338.4/367/09667 19
1. Ghana - Manufactures - Costs - Econometric models. 2. Nigeria - Manufactures - Costs - Econometric models. I. Gemmell, Norman. II. Series: Working paper (University of Durham. Dept. of Economics) , no. 55. III. Title.
HD9737.G52 I97 1983

Iz istorii krest'i͡anstva Evropeĭskogo Severa, Verkhnego Povolzh'i͡a i Urala v period Velikoĭ Okti͡abr'skoĭ sot͡sialisticheskoĭ revoli͡ut͡sii i pobedy sot͡sializma v SSSR, 1917-1937 gg. / [redakt͡sionnai͡a kollegii͡a E.I. Kiri͡ukhina (otvetstvennyĭ redaktor) ... et al.]. Kirov : Kirovskiĭ gos. pedagog. in-t im. V.I. Lenina, 1979. 170 p. ; 20 cm. Includes bibliographical references. LC Card 82-103738
1. Collectivization of agriculture - Russian S.F.S.R. - History. 2. Russian S.F.S.R. - Rural conditions. 3. Agriculture - Economic aspects - Russian S.F.S.R. - History. I. Kiri͡ukhina, Elena Ivanovna. II. Kirovskiĭ gosudarstvennyĭ pedagogicheskiĭ institut imeni V.I. Lenina.
HD1492.S652 R8755 1979

Iz istorii razvitii͡a metallurgicheskoĭ promyshlennosti Moskvy, 1883-1932 gg. : dokumenty i materialy / [sostavitel' I.L. Kornakovskiĭ ; otvetstvennyĭ redaktor V.E. Poletaev]. Moskva : Akademii͡a nauk SSSR, In-t istorii SSSR, 1981. 219 p. ; 20 cm. Bibliography: p. 203-[205] LC Card 84-163581
1. Iron industry and trade - Russian S.F.S.R. - Moscow - History - Sources. 2. Steel industry and trade - Russian S.F.S.R. - Moscow - History - Sources. I. Kornakovskiĭ, I. L. II. Poletaev, Vladimir Evgen'evich. III. Institut istorii SSSR (Akademii͡a nauk SSSR).
HD9525.S653 M64 1981 NYPL [*QIP 87-3316]

Izdatel'stvo Nauka. Redakt͡sii͡a "Obshchestvennye nauki i sovremennost'."
US economic expansion . Moscow , 1986. 172 p. ; LC Card 86-204071 DDC 337.7304 19
HF3092 .U8 1986

The World socialist economy. Moscow , 1986. 279 p. ; LC Card 86-231463 DDC 338.9/009171/7 19
HC704 .W67 1986

Izmenenie soderzhanii͡a i kharaktera truda na sovremennom ėtape razvitogo sot͡sializma / otvetstvennyĭ redaktor, Zhelezovskai͡a N.M. Moskva : Akademii͡a nauk SSSR, In-t ėkonomiki, Otdel ėkon. problem truda, Sektor "Kharaktera i soderzhanii͡a truda pri sot͡sializme," 1984. 227 p. ; 21 cm. Includes bibliographical references. LC Card 85-240356
1. Labor and laboring classes - Soviet Union. 2. Labor productivity - Soviet Union. I. Zhelezovskai͡a, N. M. II. Institut ėkonomiki (Akademii͡a nauk SSSR). Sektor "Kharaktera i soderzhanii͡a truda pri sot͡sializme.".
HD8526.5 .I97 1984

Izmerenie vlii͡anii͡a nauchno-tekhnicheskogo progressa na rost natsional'nogo dokhoda /. Lazurenko, S. G. (Serafima Grigor'evna) Moskva , 1981. 127 p. ; LC Card 82-115905
HC340.T4 L39 1981

Izpolzuvaneto na reka Dunav za prevoz na tovari za i ot Sredna i Zapadna Evropa /. Petrov, Vladimir. Sofii͡a , 1985. 71 p. ; LC Card 86-105301
HE387.D2 P36 1985

Izquierda Unida (Political party) Plan laboral de Izquierda Unida. 1era ed. [Lima?] : Comisión de Política y Organización Laboral, 1986. 67 p. ; 21 cm. LC Card 87-107365
1. Labor policy - Peru. 2. Izquierda Unida (Political party). I. Title.
HD8346.5 .I97 1986

IZQUIERDA UNIDA (POLITICAL PARTY)
Izquierda Unida (Political party) Plan laboral de Izquierda Unida. [Lima?] , 1986. 67 p. ; LC Card 87-107365
HD8346.5 .I97 1986

Izquierdo de Bartolomé, Rafael. Evolución, presente y futuro de la política común de transportes / Rafael Izquierdo de Bartolomé. Madrid : Fundación Juan March, [1985?] 56 p. ; 21 cm. (Série Universitária. 226) "Edición no venal de 300 ejemplares"--Cover. ISBN 84-7075-325-8 LC Card 87-111657
1. Transportation and state - European Economic Community countries. I. Series: Serie universitaria (Fundación Juan March) , 226. II. Title.
HE242.8 .I97 1985

Izrabotvane na kolektivnite reshenii͡a /. Nikolaev, Ivan. Sofii͡a , 1985. 69 p. ; LC Card 86-174800
HD30.23 .N55 1985

Izsledvane roli͡ata na proizvodstvenata sreda, trudovite kolektivi i nastavnit͡site za formirane na komunistichesko otnoshenie kŭm truda u podrastvashchtite / [avtorski kolektiv, nauchen rŭkovoditel K. Zheli͡azkov ... et al.]. Sofii͡a : Nauchnoizsl. in-t po profesionalno obrazovanie, 1984. 150 p. ; 20 cm. Bibliography: p. 149a. LC Card 85-166784
1. Youth - Employment - Bulgaria. 2. Labor and laboring classes - Education - Bulgaria. 3. Vocational guidance - Bulgaria. 4. Socialism and youth - Bulgaria. I. Zheli͡azkov, K. II. Nauchnoizsledovatelski institut po profesionalno obrazovanie (Bulgaria).
HD6276.B82 I97 1984

Izuchenie i prognozirovanie sprosa na bytovye uslugi /. I͡Ukhimenko, V. V. (Vladimir Vasil'evich) Kiev , 1983. 103 p. ; LC Card 83-218585
HD9986.S683 U385 1983

Izuchenie problem narodonaselenii͡a v Institute ėkonomiki AN Ėstonskoĭ SSR : sbornik obzorov / [sostavitel' L.I. Apananskiĭ ; otvetstvennyĭ redaktor V. Tarmisto]. Tallin : AN ĖSSR, 1979. 78 p. ; 20 cm. At head of title: Akademii͡a nauk Ėstonskoĭ SSR. T͡Sentr nauchnoĭ informat͡sii po obshchestvennym naukam. Includes bibliographies. LC Card 81-198604
1. Demography - Study and teaching - Estonia. I. Apananskiĭ, L. II. Tarmisto, Vello. III. Ühiskonnateaduste Informatsioonikeskus (Eesti NSV Teaduste Akadeemia).
HB850.5.S65 I97 1979

Izzo, Joseph E., 1931- The embattled fortress : strategies for restoring information systems productivity / Joseph E. Izzo.1st ed. San Francisco : Jossey-Bass, 1987. xxii, 155 p. : ill. ; 24 cm. (The Jossey-Bass management series) Bibliography: p. 145-149. Includes index. ISBN 1-555-42059-1 (alk. paper) LC Card 87-45429 DDC 658.4/038 19
1. Business - Data processing. 2. Management - Data processing. 3. Information technology. I. Title. II. Series.
HF5548.2 .I97 1987

J.A.K.--en dansk krisebevægelse /. Ulrichsen, Niels. København , 1978. 202 p. ; ISBN 87-87462-13-3 LC Card 87-462108
HD2002 .U45 1978

J. D. C. see American Jewish Joint Distribution Committee.

J. Lewis Associates. California. Block Grant Advisory Task Force. Block Grant Advisory Task Force final report to the Governor and the Legislature of the State of California /. [Sacramento?] [1984] 36, [7] leaves ; LC Card 86-622537 DDC 336.1/85 19
HJ325 .C32 1984

Jaap, Christiane. Möglichkeiten betriebswirtschaftlicher Beurteilung privater Kapitalanlagen : dargestellt am Beispiel des Bauherrenmodells / von Christiane Jaap. Berlin : Duncker & Humblot, c1986. xxiii, 322 p. : ill. ; 24 cm. (Betriebswirtschaftliche Schriften. Heft 120) Originally presented as the author's thesis (doctoral--Technische Universität Berlin) Bibliography: p. 309-322. ISBN 3-428-06008-3 LC Card 86-189069
1. Capital investments - Germany (West) - Econometric models. 2. Construction industry - Germany (West) - Econometric models. I. Title.
HG4028.C4 J28 1986

Jablin, Fredric M. Handbook of organizational communication . Newbury Park, Calif. , c1987. 781 p. : ISBN 0-8039-2387-2 : LC Card 87-23417 DDC 658.4/5 19
HD30.3 .H3575 1987

Jacini, Stefano, 1827-1891. Italy. Parlamento. Giunta per la inchiesta agraria e sulle condizioni della classe agricola. Inchiesta Jacini . Sala Bolognese , 1978- <1987. v. <1-7, 9-10; v. 13, t. 1, fasc. 1-3; v. 11, t. 1-3; v. 13, t. 2, fasc. 4-5; in 18 > : LC Card 86-143133
HD1970 .I84 1978

Jack in port . Fingard, Judith. Toronto , Buffalo , c1982. 292 p., [12] p. of plates : ISBN 0-8020-2458-0 LC Card 82-216821 DDC 331.7/6138754044/09715 19
HD8039.S42 C3 1982 NYPL [JLE 86-4038]

Jackson, Anthony, Ph. D. Way of life . London [1980?] 84 p. ; ISBN 0-86226-076-0 (pbk.) LC Card 82-218547 DDC 304.8 19
HD9571.7.S36 W39 1980
NYPL [JLD 85-427]

Jackson, Barbara B. Gibson, Cyrus F. The information imperative . Lexington, Mass. , c1987. xxii, 160 p. : ISBN 0-669-12338-2 (alk. paper) LC Card 85-45797 DDC 658/.05 19
HF5548.2 .G496 1987

Jackson, Cecile, 1953- The Kano River Irrigation Project / Cecile Jackson ; prepared under the auspices of the Population Council. West Hartford, Conn. : Kumarian Press, 1985. xviii, 66 p. ; 28 cm. (Women's roles and gender differences in development . 4) On cover: Cases for planners. Bibliography : p. 65-66. ISBN 0-931816-19-X LC Card 85-5242 DDC 331.4/83/09669 19
1. Women farmers - Nigeria. 2. Women agricultural laborers - Nigeria. 3. Hausas - Economic conditions. 4. Nigeria - Rural conditions. I. Population Council, New York. II. Title. III. Series.
HD6073.F32 N64 1985
NYPL [JLF 86-1634]

Jackson, Donald Dale, 1935- Flying the mail / by Donald Dale Jackson and the editors of Time-Life Books. Alexandria, Va. : Time-Life Books, c1982. 176 p. : ill. (some col.) ; 29 cm. (The Epic of flight) Includes index. Bibliography: p. 172. ISBN 0-8094-3329-X LC Card 82-2020 DDC 383/.144/09 19
1. Air mail service - United States - History. 2. Air mail service - History. I. Time-Life Books. II. Title.
HE6496 .J3 1982 NYPL [JLF 87-386]

Jackson, Ivor L. Study of the pleasure boat industry in the British Virgin Islands with emphasis on charter boats / by Ivor L. Jackson. [S.l. : S.n., 1981?] viii, 89 p. : ill., maps ; 28 cm. "June, 1981." "Prepared under contract with the World Tourism Organization (WTO)." Bibliography: p. 89.
1. Boating industry - British Virgin Islands. 2. Boats and boating - Chartering - British Virgin Islands. I. World Tourism Organization. II. Title.
NYPL [JLF 85-543]

Jackson, J. A. (John Archer), 1929- Migration / J.A. Jackson. London ; New York : Longman, 1986. 91 p. : maps ; 21 cm. (Aspects of modern sociology: social processes) Includes index. Bibliography: p. [81]-88. ISBN 0-582-48052-3 LC Card 85-13098 DDC 304.8/0941 19
1. Migration, Internal - Great Britain. 2. Labor mobility - Great Britain. I. Title.
HB2043 .M54 1986 NYPL [JLD 86-2119]

Jackson, J. Howard (James Howard), 1928-
Tilton, Rita Sloan. Secretarial procedures and administration /. Cincinnati , c1987. vi, 874 p. : ISBN 0-538-11790-7 LC Card 86-63074 DDC 651.3/74 19
HF5547.5 .S4 1987

JACKSON, JESSE, 1941-
Broh, C. Anthony. A horse of a different color . Washington, D.C. , 1987. xiv, 93 p. : ISBN 0-941410-54-4 (pbk.) : LC Card 87-2869 DDC 324.973/0927 19
HE8700.76.U6 B76 1987

Jackson, Mary, 1936- Creative modelling with Lotus 1-2-3 / Mary Jackson. Chichester ; New York : J. Wiley, c1985. ix, 169 p. : ill. ; 26 cm. + floppy disk. On t.p. the registered trademark symbol "TM" is superscript following "Lotus 1-2-3" in the title. Includes index. ISBN 0-471-90796-0 (pbk.) LC Card 86-228784 DDC 005.36/9 19
1. Lotus 1-2-3 (Computer program). 2. Electronic

spreadsheets. 3. Business - Data processing. I. Title.
HF5548.4.L67 J33 1985b

Jackson, Mason, 1926- The building / by Mason Jackson ; illustrated by Virginia Yount. Interlaken, N.Y. : Empire State Books, 1987. 128 p. : ill. ; 23 cm. ISBN 0-932334-90-3 LC Card 86-24115 DDC 974.7/89043 19
1. White collar workers - New York (State) - Rochester - Anecdotes, facetiae, satire, etc. 2. Office buildings - Social aspects - New York (State) - Rochester - Anecdotes, facetiae, satire, etc. 3. Granite Building (Rochester, N.Y.) - Anecdotes, facetiae, satire, etc. I. Yount, Virginia. II. Title.
HD8039.M4 U54 1987

Jackson, Michael Peart. Strikes / Michael P. Jackson. Sussex : Wheatsheaf Books ; New York : St. Martin's Press, c1987. xi, 232 p. ; 23 cm. Bibliography: p. 217-226. Includes index. ISBN 0-312-01194-6 (St. Martin's Press) : LC Card 87-14376 DDC 331.89/2 19
1. Strikes and lockouts. 2. Strikes and lockouts - Australia. 3. Strikes and lockouts - United States. 4. Strikes and lockouts - Great Britain. I. Title.
HD5306 .J33 1987

Jackson, P. M. (Peter McLeod) Tobin, James, 1918- Policies for prosperity . Cambridge, Mass. , 1987. xiv, 508 p. : ISBN 0-262-20066-X LC Card 87-2967 DDC 330.15/6 19
HB99.7 .T63 1987

Jackson, Robin. Rational economics / by Robin Jackson. New York : Philosophical Library, c1987. v, 145 p. ; 24 cm. ISBN 0-8022-2529-2 : LC Card 86-30260 DDC 330.1 19
1. Capitalism. 2. Economics. 3. Rand, Ayn. I. Title.
HB501 .J27 1987

Jacob, Raúl, 1946- Algunas consideraciones acerca de la formación económica del Uruguay, 1726-1930 / Raúl Jacob. Montevideo, Uruguay : Centro Interdisciplinario de Estudios sobre el Desarrollo, Uruguay, [1985 or 1986] 56 p. ; 28 cm. (Serie Documentos de trabajo . no. 3) "Ponencia presentada al V Simposio de Historia Económica de América Latina ... Lima, 1978." Bibliography: p. 52-56. LC Card 86-202376 DDC 330.9895/065 19
1. Uruguay - Economic conditions. I. Series: Serie Documentos de trabajo (Centro Interdisciplinario de Estudios sobre el Desarrollo Uruguay) , no. 3. II. Title.
HC232 .J287 1985

Jacobi, Klaus, 1929- Der induzierte Kapitalexport / Klaus Jacobi. Zürich : Polygraphischer Verlag, c1959. viii, 106 p. ; 23 cm. (Beiträge zur praktischen Nationalökonomie . Bd. 12) Originally presented as the author's thesis (doctoral)--Universität Bern. Bibliography: p. v-viii. LC Card 87-408198 DDC 332.4/5609494 19
1. Capital movements - Switzerland. 2. Foreign exchange problem - Switzerland. I. Title. II. Series.
HG3891 .J33 1959

Jacobi, Otto. Economic crisis, trade unions, and the state /. London , Dover, N.H. , c1986. 295 p. ; ISBN 0-7099-1447-4 : LC Card 85-28055 DDC 331/.094 19
HD8391 .E26 1986 ***NYPL [JLD 86-1301]***

Jacobs, Herbert. Zur Theorie und Praxis alternativer Ökonomie : eine Untersuchung über die Möglichkeiten und Grenzen von Versuchen, anders zu leben und zu arbeiten / Herbert Jacobs. Münster : Lit, [1986] iii, 390 p. ; 21 cm. (Soziologie . Bd. 7) Bibliography: p. 300-309. ISBN 3-88660-327-7 LC Card 87-133163 DDC 330 19
1. Economics. 2. Economic development. I. Series: Soziologie (Münster in Westfalen, Germany) , Bd. 7. II. Title.
HB175 .J28 1986

Jacobs, Nehama. Hardesty, Sarah. Success and betrayal . New York , 1987, c1986. 464 p. ; ISBN 0-671-64563-3 (pbk.) : LC Card 87-17289 DDC 331.4/816584/00973 19
HD6054.4.U6 H37 1987

Jacobsen, Alf R., 1950- Eventyret Anders Jahre / Alf R. Jacobsen. Oslo : Oktober, c1982. 303 p., [16] p. of plates : ill. ; 21 cm. Bibliography: p. 301-303. ISBN 82-7094-311-8 : LC Card 83-168197
1. Jahre, Anders, 1891-. 2. Merchant marine - Norway - Biography. 3. Corporations - Norway - Corrupt practices - Case studies. I. Title.
HE569.J34 J33 1982 ***NYPL [JFD 87-4754]***

Jacobsen, Hanns-Dieter, 1944- Wirtschaftskrieg oder Entspannung? . Bonn , c1984. 328 p. ; ISBN 3-87831-392-6 LC Card 84-251713
HF4050 .W57 1984

Jacobson, Beverly. Young programs for older workers : case studies in progressive personnel policies / Beverly Jacobson. New York : Van Nostrand Reinhold, 1980. xvii, 123 p. ; 24 cm. (Van Nostrand Reinhold/Work in America Institute series) Includes index. ISBN 0-442-25405-9 LC Card 80-12621 DDC 658.3/042
1. Aged - Employment - United States - Case studies. 2. Personnel management - United States - Case studies. I. Title.
HD6280 .J3 ***NYPL [JLE 81-438]***

Jacobson, Dorothy R., 1950- McNulty, Robert H., 1940- The economics of amenity . Washington, D.C. , c1985. xvi, 157 p. : ISBN 0-941182-15-0 (pbk.) LC Card 85-6545 DDC 307.7/6/0973 19
HT321 .M36 1985 ***NYPL [JLE 86-4519]***

Jacobson, Gary.
Xerox : American samurai / Gary Jacobson and John Hillkirk. New York : Macmillan, c1986. ix, 338 p. ; 25 cm. ISBN 0-02-551600-0 LC Card 85-30922 DDC 338.7/68644 19
1. Xerox Corporation. 2. Copying machine industry - United States. 3. Corporations - History. I. Hillkirk, John. II. Title.
HD9802.3.U64 X475 1986 ***NYPL [JLE 86-2982]***

Xerox : American samurai / Gary Jaconson, John Hillkirk.1st Collier Books ed. New York : Collier Books, 1987, c1986. xii, 338 p. ; 21 cm. Originally published: New York : Macmillan, c1986. Includes index. ISBN 0-02-033830-9 (pbk.) LC Card 86-31009 DDC 338.7/68644 19
1. Xerox Corporation. 2. Copying machine industry - United States. 3. Competition, International. I. Hillkirk, John. II. Title.
HD9802.3.U64 X475 1986b

Jacobson, Jay, 1946- Advanced Symphony : a power user's guide / Jay Jacobson. New York : Wiley, c1985. vi, 282 p. : ill. ; 26 cm. Includes index. ISBN 0-471-82430-5 (pbk.) : LC Card 85-12202 DDC 001.64/25 19
1. Symphony (Computer program). 2. Business - Data processing. I. Title.
HF5548.4.S95 J3 1985 ***NYPL [JLF 86-854]***

Jacobson, Jodi L. Brown, Lester Russell, 1934- Our demographically divided world /. Washington, D.C. , c1986. 54 p. : ISBN 0-916468-75-5 (pbk.) LC Card 86-51475 DDC 304.6 19
HB871 .B744 1986

Jacobson, Maria Luiza. Relaciones colectivas del trabajo en América Latina. Portuguese. As relações coletivas de trabalho na América Latina . São Paulo . 327 p. ; LC Card 87-151930 DDC 331/.098 19
HD8110.5 .R3817 1985

Jacobstein, Helen L., 1925- The process of economic development in Costa Rica, 1948-1970 : some political factors / Helen L. Jacobstein. New York : Garland, 1987. 338 p. : ill. ; 24 cm. (South American and Latin American economic history) Thesis (Ph. D.)--University of Miami, 1972. Bibliography: p. 316-332. ISBN 0-8240-1363-8 (alk. paper) : LC Card 87-8519 DDC 338.97286 19
1. Costa Rica - Economic conditions - 1948-. 2. Costa Rica - Politics and government - 1948-. 3. Costa Rica - Economic Policy. I. Title. II. Series.
HC143 .J28 1987

Jacoby, Jacob. The comprehension and miscomprehension of print communications : an investigation of mass media magazines / Jacob Jacoby, Wayne D. Hoyer ; sponsored by the Advertising Educational Foundation. New York, N.Y. : The Foundation ; Hillsdale, N.J. : Distributed by L. Erlbaum Associates, c1987. xvii, 273 p. : ill. ; 24 cm. Bibliography: p. 147-154. Includes indexes. ISBN 0-8058-0087-5 (L. Erlbaum Associates) LC Card 87-1366 DDC 659.13/2 19
1. Advertising, Magazine. 2. Advertising, Fraudulent. 3. Mass media. I. Hoyer, Wayne D. II. Advertising Educational Foundation (New York, N.Y.). III. Title.
HF6107 .J32 1987

Jacot, Jacques-Henri. Nouvelles technologies et enjeux sociaux . Lyon , c1986. 230 p. : ISBN 2-7297-0279-2 : LC Card 86-187357
HC79.T4 N68 1986

Jacquemin, Alex. Economie industrielle européenne : structures de marché et stratégies d'entreprise / par Alexis Jacquemin ; préface de Jacques Lesourne.2e éd. [Paris] : Dunod, c1979. xxii, 376 p. : ill. ; 24 cm. (Finance et économie appliquée. v. 52) Bibliography: p. [358]-376. ISBN 2-04-010465-8 LC Card 86-673881
1. Industrial organization - Europe. 2. Trusts, Industrial - Europe. 3. Industry and state - Europe. I. Series: Finance et économie appliquée, 52. II. Title.
HD70.E8 J3x 1979

Jacquemin, Alexis. The new industrial organization : market forces and strategic behaviour / Alexis Jacquemin. Oxford [Oxfordshire] ; New York : Oxford University Press ; p. cm. Includes bibliographies and index. ISBN 0-19-828568-X : LC Card 86-23816 DDC 338.6 19
1. Industrial organization (Economic theory). I. Title.
HD2326 .J29 1987

Jäggi, Max. "Ein Chaos wollen wir nicht" . Basel , c1985. 223 p. : ISBN 3-85787-141-5 : LC Card 86-128638
HE8689.9.S95 C57 1985

JAÉN (SPAIN : PROVINCE) - HISTORY.
Herr, Richard. Rural change and royal finances in Spain at the end of the old regime /. Berkeley , c1987. p. cm. ISBN 0-520-05948-4 (alk. paper) LC Card 86-25027 DDC 333.3/0946/25 19
HD779.J34 H47 1987

JAÉN, SPAIN (PROVINCE) - ECONOMIC CONDITIONS.
Ortega Campos, Pedro. Una década de la economía jiennense, 1969-1979 /. [Jaén] [1984] 122 leaves : ISBN 84-505-0662-X LC Card 86-187312
HC387.J3 O76 1984

JAÉN, SPAIN (PROVINCE) - POPULATION.
Ortega Campos, Pedro. Una década de la economía jiennense, 1969-1979 /. [Jaén] [1984] 122 leaves : ISBN 84-505-0662-X LC Card 86-187312
HC387.J3 O76 1984

Jänicke, Martin. Staatsversagen : die Ohnmacht der Politik in der Industriegesellschaft / Martin Jänicke. München : Piper, c1986. 227 p. : ill. ; 22 cm. Includes bibliographical references. ISBN 3-492-02984-1 LC Card 86-230931
1. Economic policy. 2. Industry and state. 3. State, The. 4. Budget deficits. 5. Social conflict. I. Title.
HD84 .J36 1986

Jaffe, Eugene D. How to prepare for the graduate management admission test GMAT / by Eugene D. Jaffe, Stephen Hilbert. 7th ed. New York : Barron's Educational Series, c1987. x, 541 p. : ill. ; 28 cm. Includes bibliographical references. ISBN 0-8120-3882-7 (pbk.) LC Card 87-18619 DDC 650/.076 19
1. Graduate Management Admission Test. 2. Management - Examinations, questions, etc. 3. Business - Examinations, questions, etc. I. Hilbert, Stephen. II. Title.
HD30.413 .J33 1987

Jaffe, Susan. Toxic chemical accidents in New York State : the risk of another Bhopal / written by Susan Jaffe, Douglas H. Ward. New York, N.Y. (2 World Trade Center, New York 10047) : Environmental Protection Bureau, [1986] 27, 13, 33 p. ; 28 cm. Includes bibliographies and index. LC Card 86-622820 DDC 363.1/79 19
1. Chemical industry - New York (State) - Accidents. 2. Industrial toxicology - Government policy - New York (State). I. Ward, Douglas H. II. New York (State). Dept. of Law. Environmental Protection Bureau.
HD7269.C452 U54 1986

Jagals, Kah, 1921- Hallensleben, Ruth. Frauenarbeit in der Industrie . Berlin-Kreuzberg , c1985. 157 p. : ISBN 3-88940-602-5 : LC Card 86-201457
HD6149 .H27 1985

Jagannathan, N. S. Kabra, Kamal Nayan. Black money . New Delhi , 1985. 47 p. ; LC Card 87-900898 DDC 381 19
HJ2348.5 .K32 1985

Jäger, Hubert. Die Bewertung von konzerninternen Lieferungen und Leistungen in der operativen Planung / Hubert Jäger. Heidelberg : Physica-Verlag, c1987. xii, 345 p. ;

25 cm. (Physica-Schriften zur Betriebswirtschaft . 19) Originally presented as the author's thesis (doctoral)--Universität Saarland, 1986. Bibliography: p. 332-345. ISBN 3-7908-0367-7 LC Card 87-145912 DDC 658.1/5/0943 19
1. Corporations - Germany, West - Finance. I. Title. II. Series.
HG4156 .J336 1987

Jäggi, Christian M. Die Makroökonomik von J.M. Keynes / Christian M. Jäggi. Berlin ; New York : Springer-Verlag, c1986. xiii, 278 p. : ill. ; 25 cm. (Studies in contemporary economics) Bibliography: p. [263]-278. ISBN 0-387-16477-4 (U. S.) LC Card 86-225958
1. Keynesian economics. 2. Keynes, John Maynard, 1883-1946. 3. Macroeconomics. I. Title. II. Series.
HB99.7 .J34 1986

Jäggle, Martin. Öffentlichkeitsarbeit 3. Welt in Österreich / Martin Jäggle und Bernd Sibitz. Wien : Institut für Bildungs- und Entwicklungsforschung, 1975- v. <1 > ; 21 cm. (IBE-Forschungsdokumentation . 4) Information und Bewusstseinsbildung CONTENTS. - T. 1. Analyse und Dokumentation. LC Card 86-234031
1. Economic assistance, Austrian - Developing countries - Public opinion. 2. Public opinion - Austria. I. Sibitz, Bernd. II. Title. III. Title: Öffentlichkeitsarbeit Dritte Welt in Österreich. IV. Series: IBE-Forschungsdokumentation , 4, etc.
HC60 .J344 1975

Jagoe, A. L. (Armiger L.), 1921- The winning corporation : management practices that work! / A.L. Jagoe. Washington, D.C. : Acropolis Books, c1987. xviii, 232 p. ; 24 cm. Includes index. ISBN 0-87491-858-9 : LC Card 87-1766 DDC 658.4 19
1. Organization. 2. Corporations - Management. 3. Management. I. Title.
HD31 .J245 1987

Jagoe, John R., 1936- Export sales and marketing manual / John R. Jagoe. 1st ed. Minneapolis, MN : Export USA Publications, c1987. 1 v. (loose-leaf) ; 29 cm. Includes index. ISBN 0-943677-00-9 (loose-leaf) : LC Card 87-19952 DDC 658.8/48 19
1. Exports - United States - Handbooks, manuals, etc. 2. Export marketing - United States - Handbooks, manuals, etc. I. Title.
HF3035 .J34 1987

JAGUAR AUTOMOBILE - HISTORY.
Whyte, Andrew (Andrew John Appleton) Jaguar, the history of a great British car /. Wellingborough [Northants] , New York, N.Y. , 1985. 252 p. : ISBN 0-85059-746-3 : LC Card 85-670203 DDC 338.7/6292222/0941 19
HD9710.G74 J338 1985
NYPL [JLE 87-451]

JAGUAR CARS LTD. - HISTORY.
Whyte, Andrew (Andrew John Appleton) Jaguar, the history of a great British car /. Wellingborough [Northants] , New York, N.Y. , 1985. 252 p. : ISBN 0-85059-746-3 : LC Card 85-670203 DDC 338.7/6292222/0941 19
HD9710.G74 J338 1985
NYPL [JLE 87-451]

Jaguar, the history of a great British car /.
Whyte, Andrew (Andrew John Appleton) Wellingborough [Northants] , New York, N.Y. , 1985. 252 p. : ISBN 0-85059-746-3 : LC Card 85-670203 DDC 338.7/6292222/0941 19
HD9710.G74 J338 1985
NYPL [JLE 87-451]

Jahn, Wolfgang, 1922- Der Zweite Entwurf des "Kapitals" . Berlin , 1983. 360 p. ; LC Card 83-236586
HB175.M2585 Z86 1983

Jahrbuch des Instituts für Deutsche Geschichte. Beiheft .
(7) Frieden und Friedenssicherung in Vergangenheit und Gegenwart . München , 1984. 115 p. ; ISBN 3-7705-2147-1 (pbk.) :
NYPL [JFL 76-295 Bd. 7]

Jahrbuch für Sozialökonomie und Gesellschaftstheorie.
Staatliche Wirtschaftsregulierung in der Krise . Opladen , c1986. 241 p. ; ISBN 3-531-11805-6 LC Card 86-228864
HD84 .S69 1986

JAHRE, ANDERS, 1891-
Jacobsen, Alf R., 1950- Eventyret Anders Jahre /. Oslo , c1982. 303 p., [16] p. of plates : ISBN 82-7094-311-8 : LC Card 83-168197
HE569.J34 J33 1982 ***NYPL [JFD 87-4754]***

Jahresabschlussprüfung auf Stichprobenbasis .
Pöhlmann, Helmut. Pfaffenweiler , 1987. xii, 187 p. ; ISBN 3-89085-142-8 LC Card 87-133413 DDC 657/.458 19
HF5668.25 .P64 1987

Jahresgutachten / Sachverständigenrat zur Begutachtung der Gesamtwirtschaftlichen Entwicklung .
(1984/85) Chancen für einen langen Aufschwung /. Stuttgart , 1984. xvii, 350 p. : ISBN 3-17-003288-7 : LC Card 86-178498
HC286.7 .C48 1984

Jahrestagung 1985. Partnerschaftliche Entwicklungspolitik im Widerstreit der Interessen . Bochum-Querenburg , 1985. i, 184 leaves ; LC Card 87-409475 DDC 332.6/7343/01724 19
HG5993 .P37 1985

Ein Jahrhundert Wasserglas von Henkel /.
Goosmann, Cornelia. Düsseldorf , c1985. 76 p. : ISBN 3-923324-67-8 LC Card 86-171258
HD9654.9.H444 G66 1985

Jai Bhagwan, 1948- Municipal finance in the metropolitan cities of India : a case study of Delhi Municipal Corporation / Jai Bhagwan. New Delhi : Concept, 1983. xii, 249 p. ; 23 cm. Revision of the author's thesis (Ph. D.--University of Delhi, 1981) Includes index. Bibliography: p. [238]-246. LC Card 83-906365 DDC 352.1/0954 19
1. Municipal finance - India - Delhi. 2. Municipal finance - India - Case studies. I. Title.
HJ9065.D4 A14 1983 ***NYPL [JLD 87-890]***

J'ai créé mon entreprise . Bourg, Claude, 1935- [Paris] , c1986. 223 p. ; LC Card 86-159708
HD62.5 .B68 1986

Jain, Chaman L. An Executive's guide to econometric forecasting . Flushing, N.Y. , c1983. 74 p. : ISBN 0-932126-10-3 (pbk.) LC Card 82-90726 DDC 330/.028 19
HB3730 .E978 1983 ***NYPL [JLF 86-1166]***

Jain, L. C., 1925- Cable, Vincent. The commerce of culture . New Delhi , 1986. 237 p. ; ISBN 81-7062-004-X : LC Card 86-902899 DDC 338.4/77455/0954 19
HF5439.H27 C33 1986

Jain, Manik, 1938- The silver key to the golden treasure of Indian philately / Manik Jain, S.B. Kothari. 1st ed. Calcutta : Monika Jain, 1986. xvi, 326, [1] p. : ill., facsims., maps ; 30 cm. Bibliography: p. [327] LC Card 86-903670 DDC 769.56954 19
1. Postage-stamps - India. 2. Postage-stamps - India - History. I. Kothari, S. B. II. Title.
HE6185.I5 J35 1986

Jain, Subhash C., 1942-
International marketing . Boston, Mass. , c1986. xii, 466 p. : ISBN 0-534-06270-9 (pbk.) : LC Card 85-19820 DDC 658.8/48 19
HF1009.5 .I545 1986 ***NYPL [JLE 86-3023]***

International marketing management / Subhash C. Jain. 2nd ed. Boston, Mass. : Kent Pub. Co., c1987. xiv, 737 p. : ill. ; 25 cm. Includes bibliographies and indexes. ISBN 0-534-07824-9 : LC Card 86-27761 DDC 658.8/48 19
1. Export marketing - Management. I. Title.
HF1009.5 .J336 1987

Jaipal, Rikhi, 1916- Nuclear arms and the human race : to die or not to die / Rikhi Jaipal. New Delhi : Allied Publishers, 1986. xix, 306 p. ; 22 cm. Includes index. Bibliography: p. [293]-294. ISBN 81-7023-074-8 : LC Card 86-901813 DDC 355/.0217 19
1. Nuclear warfare. 2. Arms race - History - 20th century. 3. Nuclear disarmament. I. Title.
U263 .J35 1986 ***NYPL [JLD 87-960]***

J.A.K. - HISTORY.
Ulrichsen, Niels. J.A.K.--en dansk krisebevægelse /. København , 1978. 202 p. ; ISBN 87-87462-13-3 LC Card 87-462108
HD2002 .U45 1978

Jakarta-Raya, Indonesia.
Tenaga kerja : hasil survey tenaga kerja sub-sektor industri kecil DKI Jakarta, 1979-1980 / Pemerintah Daerah Khusus Ibukota Jakarta. Jakarta : Kanwil Dit-Jen Bina Guna DKI Jakarta : Kantor Sensus dan Statistik DKI Jakarta, [1980] 52 leaves ; 28 cm. LC Card 80-942103
1. Labor supply - Indonesia - Jakarta. 2. Small business - Indonesia - Jakarta. I. Title.
HD5824.J27 J35 1980

JAKARTA RAYA (INDONESIA). KANTOR CATATAN SIPIL.
Sukarno, H., 1948- Mengenal administrasi dan prosedur catatan sipil pada Kantor Catatan Sipil Propinsi DKI Jakarta /. Jakarta , 1985. iii, 150 p. : LC Card 86-942212
HA37.I46 J357 1985

Jakob F. Ásgeirsson, 1961- Alfreð Elíasson, 1920- Alfreðs saga og Loftleiða /. Reykjavík , 1984 (1985 printing) 372 p. : LC Card 86-101929
HD9711.I22 A443 1985
NYPL [JFE 87-1455]

Jakobeit, Cord. Die sozio-ökonomische Entwicklung der Elfenbeinküste seit der Unabhängigkeit : die politischen Rahmenbedingungen und die Nutzniesser des westafrikanischen "Wirtschaftswunders" / Cord Jakobeit. Hamburg : Institut für Afrika-Kunde im Verbund der Stiftung Deutsches Übersee-Institut, 1984. viii, 132 p. : 2 maps ; 21 cm. (Arbeiten aus dem Institut für Afrika-Kunde . 46) Summary in English and French. Bibliography: p. 122-132. ISBN 3-923519-57-5 LC Card 84-222859
1. Ivory Coast - Economic conditions - 1960-. 2. Ivory Coast - Economic policy. 3. Ivory Coast - Politics and government - 1960-. 4. Ivory Coast - Social conditions - 1960-. I. Title. II. Series.
HC1025 .J35 1984

Jakšić, Miomir. Pirec, Dušan. Iskušenja marksizma . Beograd , 1985. 461 p. : LC Card 86-128661
HB97.5 .P498 1985

Jalāl al-Dīn, Muḥammad al-'Awaḍ. Some aspects of Sudanese migration to the oil-producing Arab countries, during the 1970's / by Mohd. El Awad Galaleldin. [Khartoum] : Development Studies and Research Centre, Faculty of Economic & Social Studies, University of Khartoum, [1985] 52 p. ; 22 cm. (Monograph series. no. 24) "September 1985"--Cover. Bibliography: p. 52. LC Card 86-980666 DDC 331.6/2/62409174927 19
1. Alien labor, Sudanese - Arab countries. I. Series: Monograph series (Jāmi'at al-Kharṭūm. Markaz al-Dirāsāt wa-al-Buḥūth al-Inmā'īyah) , no. 24. II. Title.
HD8766 .J35 1985

JALISCO (MEXICO) - INDUSTRIES.
Cambio regional, mercado de trabajo y vida obrera en Jalisco /. Guadalajara, Jalisco, México , 1986. 363 p. ; ISBN 968-614-201-0 LC Card 86-218238
HD5731.J35 C36 1986

JAM INDUSTRY - UNITED STATES - HISTORY.
Ellis, William Donohue. With a name like-- /. Orrville, Ohio , c1987. vii, 161 p. : LC Card 87-169333 DDC 338.7/664152/0973 19
HD9330.J34 J154 1987

Jamaica. Central Bureau of Statistics. see **Jamaica. Dept. of Statistics.**

JAMAICA - COMMERCE - UNITED STATES.
Lyn-Cook, Marlene. Marketing guidelines for Jamaica's non-traditional exports. [Miami, FL] [1986] 83 leaves : LC Card 87-156503 DDC 382/.097292/073 19
HF1009.7.J25 L96 1986

Jamaica. Commission of Enquiry into the Banana Industry of Jamaica. Report of the Commission of Enquiry into the Banana Industry of Jamaica. Kingston : The Commission, 1959- v. <1 > ; 34 cm. Cover title. LC Card 86-221011
1. Banana trade - Government policy - Jamaica. I. Title.
HD9259.B3 J346 1959

Jamaica. Dept. of Statistics. (Old Catalog form: Jamaica. Statistics, Central Bureau of) Census of agriculture, 1978-1979 . [Kingston] [1983] vi, ix, 167 p. : LC Card 83-242227 DDC 338.1/097292 19
HD1847 .C46 1983 ***NYPL [JLF 86-1028]***

JAMAICA - ECONOMIC CONDITIONS.
Alexander, Carlton. Nation building . Kingston, Jamaica , c1983. 100 p. : LC Card 84-172595 DDC 338.97293 19
HC154 .A79 1983

Lobdell, Richard A. Economic structure and demographic performance in Jamaica,

1891-1935 /. New York , 1987. xii, 259 p. ; ISBN 0-8240-1365-4 (alk. paper) : LC Card 87-8345 DDC 304.6/097292 19
HB3553 .L63 1987

McLewin, Philip J., 1939- Power and economic change . New York , 1987. ii, 271 p. : ISBN 0-8240-1366-2 (alk. paper) : LC Card 87-8344 DDC 330.97292/04 19
HC154 .M36 1987

Manley, Michael, 1924- Up the down escalator . Washington, D.C , 1987. xv, 332 p. ; ISBN 0-88258-112-0 : LC Card 87-3872 DDC 338.97292 19
HC154 .M34 1987

JAMAICA - ECONOMIC POLICY.
Manley, Michael, 1924- Up the down escalator . Washington, D.C , 1987. xv, 332 p. ; ISBN 0-88258-112-0 : LC Card 87-3872 DDC 338.97292 19
HC154 .M34 1987

JAMAICA - EMIGRATION AND IMMIGRATION - HISTORY.
Petras, Elizabeth McLean. Jamaican labor migration . Boulder , 1988. x, 297 p. : ISBN 0-8133-7456-1 (pbk. : alk. paper) LC Card 87-20139 DDC 331.6/2/7292072875 19
HD8178 .P47 1988

Jamaica - Government. see **Jamaica - Politics and government.**

Jamaica National Export Corporation. Report 1969-1984 / Jamaica National Export Corporation. [Kingston, Jamaica] : The Corporation, [1984] x, 62, 8 p. : ill. ; 28 cm. LC Card 87-110047 DDC 354.72920082/76/06 19
1. Jamaica National Export Corporation. 2. Export trading companies - Jamaica. I. Title.
HF1009.7.J25 J35 1984

JAMAICA NATIONAL EXPORT CORPORATION.
Jamaica National Export Corporation. Report 1969-1984 /. [Kingston, Jamaica] [1984] x, 62, 8 p. : LC Card 87-110047 DDC 354.72920082/76/06 19
HF1009.7.J25 J35 1984

JAMAICA - POLITICS AND GOVERNMENT - TO 1962.
McLewin, Philip J., 1939- Power and economic change . New York , 1987. ii, 271 p. : ISBN 0-8240-1366-2 (alk. paper) : LC Card 87-8344 DDC 330.97292/04 19
HC154 .M36 1987

JAMAICA - POPULATION - HISTORY - 19TH CENTURY.
Lobdell, Richard A. Economic structure and demographic performance in Jamaica, 1891-1935 /. New York , 1987. xii, 259 p. ; ISBN 0-8240-1365-4 (alk. paper) : LC Card 87-8345 DDC 304.6/097292 19
HB3553 .L63 1987

JAMAICA - POPULATION - HISTORY - 20TH CENTURY.
Lobdell, Richard A. Economic structure and demographic performance in Jamaica, 1891-1935 /. New York , 1987. xii, 259 p. ; ISBN 0-8240-1365-4 (alk. paper) : LC Card 87-8345 DDC 304.6/097292 19
HB3553 .L63 1987

Jamaica. Statistics, Central Bureau of. see **Jamaica. Dept. of Statistics.**

Jamaica. Statistics, Dept. of. see **Jamaica. Dept. of Statistics.**

Jamaican labor migration . Petras, Elizabeth McLean. Boulder , 1988. x, 297 p. : ISBN 0-8133-7456-1 (pbk. : alk. paper) LC Card 87-20139 DDC 331.6/2/7292072875 19
HD8178 .P47 1988

Jamar, Joseph. The European Community's development policy . Bruges , 19. 285 p. : LC Card 87-135534 DDC 338.94 19
HC60 .E7626 1986

James, Christopher. How to get credit and loans : a practical guide / by Christopher James ; illustrations by Bill Spence. Austin, TX : Dejon Pub., 1987. viii, 179 p. : ill. ; 23 cm. ISBN 0-9618114-0-4 (pbk.) : LC Card 87-71591 DDC 332.7/43 19
1. Consumer credit - United States. 2. Loans, Personal - United States. I. Title.
HG3756.U54 J36 1987

James de Rothschild . Muhlstein, Anka. [Paris] , c1981. 242 p., [16] p. of plates : LC Card 82-149581 DDC 332.1/092/4 B 19
HG1552.R816 M84 1981
NYPL [*PWZ (Rothschild, J.) 86-6471]

James, Kim. Arroba, Tanya. Pressure at work . London , New York , c1987. xvi, 192 p. : ISBN 0-07-084931-5 (pbk.) : LC Card 87-3925 DDC 658.4/095 19
HF5548.85 .A77 1987

James, Patricia, 1933- Malthus, T. R. (Thomas Robert, 1766-1834. An essay on the principle of population, or, a view of its past and present effects on human happiness . Cambridge [Cambridgeshire] , New York , 1988. p. cm. ISBN 0-521-24775-6 LC Card 87-9372 DDC 304.6 19
HB861 .E7 1988

James, Robert M., 1922- Quinn, James Brian, 1928- The strategy process . Englewood Cliffs, N.J. , c1988. p. cm. ISBN 0-13-850892-5 LC Card 87-1160 DDC 658.4/012 19
HD30.28 .Q53 1988

James, Simon R. The comprehensibility of taxation : a study of taxation and communications / Simon James, Alan Lewis, and Frances Allison. Aldershot, Hants, England ; Brookfield, Vt., USA : Avebury, c1987. xiii, 314 p. : ill. ; 23 cm. Includes bibliographical references and index. ISBN 0-566-05348-9 : LC Card 86-25690 DDC 336.2/00941 19
1. Taxation - Great Britain. 2. Tax administration and procedure - Great Britain. 3. Taxation. I. Lewis, Alan, 1952-. II. Allison, Frances, 1940-. III. Title.
HJ2619 .J36 1987

James, William E.
Asian agriculture and economic development / William E. James. Manila, Philippines : Asian Development Bank, c1982. xiii, 128 p. ; 28 cm. (Asian Development Bank economic staff paper . no. 5) "March 1982"--Cover. Bibliography: p. 122-128. LC Card 87-104389 DDC 338.1/095 19
1. Agriculture - Economic aspects - Asia. 2. Asia - Economic conditions - 1945-. I. Asian Development Bank. II. Title. III. Series.
HD2056 .J35 1982

Asian agriculture in transition : key policy issues / by William E. James. Manila, Philippines : Asian Development Bank, c1983. v, 93 p. ; 28 cm. (Asian Development Bank economic staff paper . no. 19) "September 1983"--Cover. Bibliography: p. 88-93. LC Card 87-105114 DDC 338.1/095 19
1. Agriculture - Economic aspects - Asia. 2. Agriculture and state - Asia. I. Title. II. Series.
HD2056 .J355 1983

Energy conservation in the Asian region . Tokyo, Japan [Honolulu, Hawaii] , 1986. vi, 173 p. : ISBN 92-833-2038-1 LC Card 87-122915 DDC 333.79/16/095 19
HD9502.A782 E53 1986

Jameson, Robert, 1938-
Professional job changing system. Gerberg, Robert J. [Job changing system.] Robert Gerberg's job changing system : world's fastest way to get a better job / Robert J. Gerberg.14th ed. Kansas City , c1986. xxii, 265 p. : ISBN 0-8362-7932-8 : LC Card 86-17298 DDC 650.1/4 19
NYPL [JD 87-125]

Jāmi'at al-Kharṭūm. Ma'had al-Dirāsāt al-Bī'īyah. Abdel Ati, Hassan A. Lower River Atbara area (Nile Province) . [Khartoum] Sudan [1985] vii, 166 p., [19] leaves of plates : LC Card 86-981108 DDC 333.91/3/09625 19
HD1741.S852 A832 1985

Mohamed, Yagoub Abdalla. The North Kordofan rural water supply baseline survey /. Khartoum , 1982. xv, 152 p. : LC Card 85-981166
HD1699.S82 K875 1982

Jāmi'at al-Malik 'Abd al-'Azīz. Kullīyat al-Iqtiṣād wa-al-Idārah. Markaz al-Buḥūth wa-al-Tanmiyah. 'Alāqī, Madanī 'Abd al-Qādir. al-Idārah wa-al-bī'ah . [Jiddah] , 1985. 136 p. : LC Card 86-200390
HD70.S28 A422 1985

Jam'īyah al-Iqtiṣādīyah al-Kuwaytīyah. Seminar on Investment Policies of Arab Oil Producing Countries (1974 : Kuwait, Kuwait) Seminar on Investment Policies of Arab Oil Producing Countries, 18-20 February 1974, Kuwait /. [Kuwait] [1974?] 216 p. ; LC Card 87-400750 DDC 332.6/7353 19
HG5816.A3 S46 1974

Jammu and Kashmir (India). Co-operative Dept. Statistical Wing. Directory of cooperative societies, 1986. Srinagar [1986] 131 p. ; LC Card 87-900324 DDC 334/.025/546 19
HD3540.A3 J353 1986

JAMMU AND KASHMIR (INDIA) - HISTORY.
Sharma, Dewan Chand, 1898- Kashmir agriculture & land revenue system under the Sikh rule, 1819-46 A.D. /. New Delhi, India , 1986. xiv, 160 p., [8] p. of plates : LC Card 86-900128
HD2075.J35 S43 1986 ***NYPL [JLD 86-3742]***

JAMMU AND KASHMIR (INDIA) - INDUSTRIES - HISTORY.
Ahad, Abdul, 1947- Kashmir to Frankfurt . New Delhi, India , 1987. xiv, 182 p., [20] p. of plates : LC Card 86-903828
HD9969.S43 I425 1987

JAMMU AND KASHMIR (INDIA) - POPULATION.
Sadhu, Kanan K. (Kanan Kusum) Bio-demographic study of Kashmiris /. Delhi, India , c1987. viii, 217 p. : ISBN 81-212-0072-5 : LC Card 87-900298 DDC 304.6/0954/6 19
HB3640.J36 S23 1987

JAMMU & KASHMIR INDUSTRIES LIMITED - CASE STUDIES.
Hassan, Shabir. Public enterprises in economic development . Delhi , 1987. xiii, 230 p. ; LC Card 86-903835
HD2900.12.J35 H37 1987

Jämställdhet i arbetsliv och samhälle. 1. uppl. Stockholm : TCO, [1985] 129 p. : ill. ; 21 cm. (TCOs förslag till forskning) Edited by Ingrid Wahlund. Includes bibliographical references. CONTENTS. - Begreppet "kvinnoperspektiv"--några olika tolkningar / Ingrid Fredriksson -- Könsrollsidentitet och jämställdhet / Marianne Carlsson -- Papparollen / Lars Jalmert -- Rättens möjlighet för jämställdhet i samhälls- och arbetsliv / Antoinette Hetzler -- Distansarbete, det nya hemarbetet? / Monica Elling -- Forskning i ett jämställdhetsperspektiv / forskare vid Arbetslivscentrum -- Kvinnor och fackligt arbete inom tjänstemannarörelsen / Mariann Sterner -- Kvinnoarbetslöshet i dagens Sverige / Karen Davies och Joke Esseveld. ISBN 91-7168-259-7 : LC Card 86-133755
1. Sex discrimination in employment - Sweden. 2. Sex role in the work environment - Sweden. 3. Sex discrimination against women - Sweden. I. Wahlund, Ingrid, 1945-. II. Tjänstemännens centralorganisation. III. Series.
HD6060.5.S8 J36 1985

Janata, Jerrold F., 1936- Property taxation /. Washington, D.C. , c1987. 1 v. (various pagings) ; LC Card 87-3326 DDC 336.22/0973 19
HJ4120 .P6717 1987

Jancar, Barbara Wolfe, 1935- Environmental management in the Soviet Union and Yugoslavia : structure and regulation in federal communist states / Barbara Jancar. Durham : Duke University Press, 1987. xi, 481 p. : ill. ; 25 cm. (Duke Press policy studies) Bibliography: p. 407-436. Includes indexes. ISBN 0-8223-0719-7 LC Card 87-5412 DDC 363.7/06/0947 19
1. Environmental policy - Soviet Union. 2. Environmental policy - Yugoslavia. 3. Environmental law - Soviet Union. 4. Environmental law - Yugoslavia. I. Title. II. Series.
HC340.E5 J35 1987

Janetzki, Annemarie. Das Verbundwinzersystem : eine Fallstudie über Motive und Wirkungen der Kooperation von Unternehmen / von Annemarie Janetzki. Münster : Institut für Genossenschaftswesen der Westfälischen Wilhelms-Universität, 1982. xxiv, 406 p., [3] folded leaves of plates : ill. ; 24 cm. (Kooperations- und genossenschaftswissenschaftliche Beiträge . Bd. 1) Originally presented as the author's thesis (doctoral)--Universität Münster, 1982. Bibliography: p. 388-397. Includes indexes. ISBN 3-7923-0486-4 LC Card 83-157892
1. Wine industry - Germany (West). 2. Weinkellerei Pieroth (Germany). 3. Producer cooperatives - Germany (West). I. Title. II. Series.
HD9383.5 .J35 1982

Janicaud, Dominique, 1937- La puissance du rationnel / Dominique Janicaud. [Paris] : Gallimard, c1985. 386 p. ; 23 cm. (Bibliothèque des idées) Includes bibliographical references and index. ISBN 2-07-070343-6 :
1. Power (Philosophy). 2. Science - Social aspects. 3. Technology - Social aspects. 4. Rationalism. I. Title.
NYPL [JFD 86-638]

Janiewski, Dolores E., 1948- Sisterhood denied : race, gender, and class in a New South community / Dolores E. Janiewski. Philadelphia : Temple University Press, 1985. xvii, 248 p. : map ; 24 cm. (Class and culture) Includes bibliographical references and index. ISBN 0-87722-361-0 : LC Card 84-2640 DDC 305.4/2/09756563 19
1. Women tobacco workers - North Carolina - Durham Region - History. 2. Women textile workers - North Carolina - Durham Region - History. 3. Durham Region (N.C.) - Social conditions. I. Title. II. Series.
HD6073.T62 U65 1985
NYPL [Sc E 86-322]

Janik, Carolyn. Money-making real estate : your personal guide to successful investing / Carolyn Janik. New York, NY : Viking, 1988. 306 p. : forms ; 24 cm. Includes index. ISBN 0-670-81137-8 : LC Card 87-23103 DDC 332.63/24 19
1. Real estate investment. I. Title.
HD1382.5 .J35 1988

Janke, Mary K. Huston, Ray E. Senior driver facts /. Sacramento, CA , Springfield, VA , 1986. iii, 22 p. : LC Card 86-623189 DDC 363.1/252/09794021 19
HE5614.3.C3 H87 1986

Jann, Gayle. (ill) Bourne, Miriam Anne. A day in the life of a cross-country trucker /. Mahwah, N.J. , c1988. 32 p. : ISBN 0-8167-1117-8 (lib. bdg.) : LC Card 87-13582 DDC 388.3/24/02373 19
HD8039.M795 B68 1988

Jansen, Ansgar, 1954- Desinvesititionen : Ursachen, Probleme und Gestaltungsmöglichkeiten / Ansgar Jansen. Frankfurt am Main ; New York : P. Lang, c1986. 514 p. : ill. ; 21 cm. (Europäische Hochschulschriften. Reihe V, Volks- und Betriebswirtschaft, 0531-7339 . Bd. 721 = vol. 721 = vol. 721) Bibliography: p. 479-514. ISBN 3-8204-9630-0 LC Card 86-205563
1. Disinvestments. 2. Investments. 3. Investments, Foreign. I. Series: Europäische Hochschulschriften. Reihe V, Volks- und Betriebswirtschaft , Bd. 721. II. Title.
HG4515 .J36 1986

Jansen, Doris J. Zimbabwe government policy and the manufacturing sector : a study prepared for the Ministry of Industry and Energy Development, Harare, Zimbabwe, April 1983 / submitted by Doris J. Jansen. Larkspur, Calif., U. S.A. : D.J. Jansen, c1983. 22 p., 10 leaves of plates : col. ill. ; 28 cm. LC Card 87-121346 DDC 338.96891 19
1. Zimbabwe - Manufactures - Government policy. I. Zimbabwe. Ministry of Industry and Energy Development. II. Title.
HD9737.Z552 J36 1983

Jansen, Eirik G.
Chowdhury, Ashraf U. Norway's commodity assistance and import support to Bangladesh . [Oslo, Norway] [1986] 83 p. : LC Card 87-150872 DDC 338.91/481/05492 19
HC440.8 .C48 1986

Jerve, Alf Morten. From research to implementation . Fantoft-Bergen, Norway [1984] 23 leaves ; LC Card 86-228812 DDC 386/.068 19
HE691.6 .J47 1984

Jansen, Paul Günter. Arbeitsmarktatlas : arbeitsmarktrelevante Informationen für Räume in Nordrhein-Westfalen, Regierungsbezirk Arnsberg : Forschungsbericht im Auftrag des Ministers für Arbeit, Gesundheit und Soziales des Landes Nordrhein-Westfalen / Dr. Jansen, Stadt- und Regionalplanung ; Bearbeiter, Paul Günter Jansen, Manfred Thebes. [Düsseldorf] : Der Minister, [1977] 206, A19 p. : maps ; 30 cm. (Arbeit und Beruf . Bd. 20) Bibliography: p. A3-A5. Includes index. LC Card 85-173256
1. Labor supply - Germany (West) - Arnsberg (Regierungsbezirk) - Statistics. I. Thebes, Manfred. II. North Rhine-Westphalia (Germany). Ministerium für Arbeit, Gesundheit und Soziales. III. Dr. Jansen, Stadt- und Regionalplanung. IV. Series: Arbeit und Beruf (North Rhine-Westphalia (Germany). Ministerium für Arbeit, Gesundheit und Soziales) , 20. V. Title.
HD5780.A76 J36 1977

Janssen, Friedrich, 1948- Bedeutung und Ausstattung von Wandel- und Optionsanleihen / von Friedrich Janssen. Göttingen : O. Schwartz, 1982. 279 p. : ill. ; 20 cm. (Göttinger Hefte zur Bankbetriebslehre und Unternehmungsfinanzierung . Heft 9) Subtitle on half title: Eine empirische und theoretische Analyse unter besonderer Berücksichtigung der Veränderungen des Verwässerungsschutzes. Originally presented as the author's thesis (doctoral)--Universität Göttingen, 1980. Bibliography: p. 259-275. Includes indexes. ISBN 3-509-01319-0 LC Card 83-240528
1. Convertible bonds - Germany (West). 2. Convertible preferred stocks - Germany (West). 3. Option (Contract) - Germany (West). I. Title. II. Series.
HG5501 .J35 1982

Janssen, J. M. L. (Johannes Marinus Lodevicus), 1918- Ondernemingsstrategie, theorie en praktijk . Leiden , c1986. xi, 346 p. : ISBN 90-207-1424-4 : LC Card 86-199689
HD37.D8 O54 1986

"JANUARY 1984."
New York (State). Legislature. Assembly. Standing Committee on Labor. A report on the plight of the collective bargaining system /. [Albany] [1984] 64 p. ; LC Card 86-622572 DDC 331.89/0973 19
HD6508 .N49 1984

Januszkiewicz, Włodzimierz. Białecki, Klemens. Słownik handlu zagranicznego /. Warszawa , 1986. 359 p. ; ISBN 83-208-0112-5 : LC Card 86-221378
HF1001 .B47 1986

Japan and the United States today : exchange rates, macroeconomic policies, and financial market innovations / Hugh T. Patrick, Ryuichiro Tachi, editors. New York : Center on Japanese Economy and Business, Columbia University, 1986, c1987. vii, 234 p. : ill. ; 24 cm. Papers presented at a conference held in New York, June 4-5, 1986, sponsored by the Center on Japanese Economy and Business at the Graduate School of Business, Columbia University, and the Institute of Fiscal and Monetary Policy of the Japanese Ministry of Finance, together with the Foundation for Advanced Information and Research, Japan. Includes bibliographies. ISBN 0-231-06575-2 LC Card 86-32640 DDC 332/.042/0952 19
1. Foreign exchange problem - United States - Congresses. 2. Foreign exchange problem - Japan - Congresses. 3. United States - Economic policy - 1981- - Congresses. 4. Japan - Economic policy - 1945- - Congresses. 5. United States - Foreign economic relations - Japan - Congresses. 6. Japan - Foreign economic relations - United States - Congresses. I. Patrick, Hugh T. II. Tachi, Ryūichirō, 1921-. III. Columbia University. Center on Japanese Economy and Business. IV. Ōkurashō Zaisei Kin'yū Kenkyūjo (Japan). V. Foundation for Advanced Information and Research (Japan).
HG3903 .J35 1987

JAPAN - BIOGRAPHY.
Goldman, Peter Louis, 1933- The end of the world that was . New York , c1986. xiv, 129 p., [8] p. of plates : ISBN 0-525-24428-X LC Card 85-31223 DDC 920/.073 19
CT220 .G6 1986 *NYPL [JFD 86-6015]*

Japan. Bureau of Statistics. see **Japan. Sōrifu. Tōkeikyoku.**

JAPAN - CIVILIZATION - OCCIDENTAL INFLUENCES.
Westney, D. Eleanor. Imitation and innovation . Cambridge, Mass. , 1987. viii, 252 p. : ISBN 0-674-44437-X (alk. paper) LC Card 87-273 DDC 338.6/0952 19
HD70.J3 W47 1987

JAPAN - COMMERCE.
Schwab, Laurent. Le Japon . [Paris] , c1984. 115 p. : ISBN 2-86262-221-4 (pbk.) : LC Card 84-164308 DDC 330.952/048 19
HC462.9 .S338 1984 *NYPL [JLD 86-3612]*

JAPAN - COMMERCE - GERMANY (EAST)
Marwege, Ulf, 1954- Neuorientierung im Westhandel der DDR? . Bonn , c1984. iv, 122 p. : ISBN 3-7713-0221-8 : LC Card 84-196602
HF3570.5.Z7 G75 1984

JAPAN - COMMERCE - GERMANY - HISTORY.
Barth, Johannes, 1891- Als deutscher Kaufmann in Fernost . Berlin , c1984. 206 p. : ISBN 3-503-02366-6 LC Card 84-143117
HC289.B7 B373 1984

JAPAN - COMMERCE - GERMANY (WEST)
Frese, Dirk. Japan, Markt für deutsche Konsumgüter /. Düsseldorf [1978?] 32 p. : LC Card 85-242493
HF3568.J3 F74 1978

JAPAN - COMMERCE - HAWAII - STATISTICS.
Hawaii's trade with Japan, 1976-1985 /. Honolulu, Hawaii (P.O. Box 2359, Honolulu 96804) [1986] 20 p. : LC Card 86-623207 DDC 382/.09969/052 19
HF3161.H3 H38733 1986

JAPAN - COMMERCE - HISTORY.
Hirschmeier, Johannes. Johannes Hirschmeier, die japanische Unternehmung . Hamburg , 1986. viii, 218 p. : ISBN 3-88910-024-4 : LC Card 86-225311
HF5349.J3 H573 1986

JAPAN - COMMERCE - UNITED STATES.
De Mente, Boye. How to do business with the Japanese . Lincolnwood, Ill., U. S.A. , c1987. vi, 269 p. ; ISBN 0-8442-8509-9 (pbk.) LC Card 86-62724 DDC 395/.52 19
HF5387 .D3835 1987

Krasner, Stephen D., 1942- Asymmetries in Japanese-American trade . Berkeley , c1987. vii, 80 p. ; ISBN 0-87725-532-6 (pbk.) : LC Card 87-81842 DDC 382/.0973/052 19
HF3127 .K73 1987

McCreary, Don R. Japanese-U. S. business negotiations . New York , 1986. viii, 121 p. ; ISBN 0-275-92006-2 (alk. paper) : LC Card 86-554 DDC 658 19
HD58.6 .M38 1986 *NYPL [JLE 86-3074]*

Trade friction and economic policy . Cambridge [Cambridgeshire] , New York , 1987. xii, 243 p. : ISBN 0-521-34446-8 LC Card 87-11694 DDC 382/.0952/073 19
HF3828.U5 T73 1987

JAPAN - COMMERCE - UNITED STATES - CONGRESSES.
Bergsten, C. Fred, 1941- The United States-Japan economic problem /. Washington, D.C. , c1985. x, 164 p. : ISBN 0-262-52108-3 LC Card 85-18106 DDC 382/.0973/052 19
HF3127 .B47 1985 *NYPL [JLE 87-19]*

JAPAN - COMMERCE - UNITED STATES - ECONOMETRIC MODELS.
Audretsch, David B. Industrial policy, R&D, and U. S.-Japanese trade /. Berlin [1986] 39 p. ; LC Card 87-156721 DDC 382/.0952/073 19
HF3127 .A93 1986

JAPAN - COMMERCE - UNITED STATES - HISTORY - 20TH CENTURY.
Bauge, Kenneth L. (Kenneth LeRoy) Voluntary export restriction as a foreign commercial policy with special reference to Japanese cotton textiles, 1930-1962 /. New York , 1987. 277 p. ; ISBN 0-8240-8072-6 LC Card 87-23717 DDC 382/.4567721/0952 19
HD9886.J3 B38 1987

JAPAN - COMMERCE - UNITED STATES - HISTORY - 20TH CENTURY - SOURCES.
Records of the U. S. Department of State relating to commercial relations between the United States and Japan, 1910-1949 [microform]. Wilmington, Del. , c1987. microfilm reel ISBN 0-8420-3061-1 (microfilm : set) : LC Card 87-23376 DDC 337.73052 19
HF3127

JAPAN - COMMERCIAL POLICY.
Hollerman, Leon. Japan, disincorporated . Stanford, Calif. , c1988. xxi, 185 p. ; ISBN 0-8179-8631-6 : LC Card 87-25633 DDC 338.952 19
HD3616.J33 H65 1988

Japan's response to crisis and change in the world economy /. Armonk, N.Y. , c1986. xiii, 309 p. : ISBN 0-87332-405-6 LC Card 86-21907 DDC 338.952 19
HC462.9 .J355 1986 *NYPL [JLE 87-1199]*

Kraus, Willy. The economic development of the Pacific Basin . New York , London , 1986. x, 180 p., [1] leaf of plates : ISBN 0-312-00452-4

(alk. paper) : LC Card 86-26292 DDC 338.95 19
HF1591 .K73 1986

JAPAN - COMMERCIAL POLICY - HISTORY - 20TH CENTURY - SOURCES.
Records of the U. S. Department of State relating to commercial relations between the United States and Japan, 1910-1949 [microform]. Wilmington, Del. , c1987. microfilm reel ISBN 0-8420-3061-1 (microfilm : set) : LC Card 87-23376 DDC 337.73052 19
HF3127

Japan Computer Usage Development Institute. Plan for information society-a national goal toward year 2000. Italian. Verso una società dell'informazione . Milano , 1974. 157 p. :
NYPL [TB (Studi e ricerche di scienze sociali. v.60)]

Japan, disincorporated . Hollerman, Leon. Stanford, Calif. , c1988. xxi, 185 p. ; ISBN 0-8179-8631-6 : LC Card 87-25633 DDC 338.952 19
HD3616.J33 H65 1988

JAPAN - ECONOMIC CONDITIONS.
Lenz, Ilse. Kapitalistische Entwicklung, Subsistenzproduktion und Frauenarbeit . Frankfurt/Main , New York , c1984. 330 p. : ISBN 3-593-33407-0(pbk.)
NYPL [JLD 87-332]

JAPAN - ECONOMIC CONDITIONS. - 1868-
Minami, Ryōshin, 1933- [Nihon no keizai hatten. English.] The economic development of Japan . Basingstoke, Hampshire , 1986. xxvi, 487 p. : ISBN 0-333-38582-9 LC Card 87-672411
HC462.7 .M47513x 1986b

JAPAN - ECONOMIC CONDITIONS - 1945-
De Mente, Boye. How to do business with the Japanese . Lincolnwood, Ill., U. S.A. , c1987. vi, 269 p. ; ISBN 0-8442-8509-9 (pbk.) LC Card 86-62724 DDC 395/.52 19
HF5387 .D3835 1987

Freeman, Christopher. Technology, policy, and economic performance . London , New York , 1987. 155 p. : ISBN 0-86187-928-7 : LC Card 87-18553 DDC 338.952 19
HC465.T4 F74 1987

Higashi, Chikara. The internationalization of the Japanese economy /. Boston, MA , c1987. xi, 273 p. : ISBN 0-89838-199-1 LC Card 87-3893 DDC 337.52 19
HC462.9 .H45 1987

Inside the Japanese system . Stanford, Calif. , c1988. xiii, 286 p. : ISBN 0-8047-1425-8 (alk. paper) LC Card 87-18820 DDC 330.952/04 19
HC462.9 .I587 1988

Kobayashi, Kaoru, 1931- Japan, the most misunderstood country /. Tokyo , 1984. ix, 165 p. ; ISBN 4-7890-0247-0
NYPL [JLD 86-1398]

Ōmae, Ken'ichi, 1943- Beyond national borders . Homewood, Ill. , c1987. xi, 128 p. : ISBN 1-556-23017-6 LC Card 86-72864 DDC 337.52 19
HF1602.15.U6 O4 1987

The Political economy of Japan. Stanford, Calif. , 1987- v. <1 > : ISBN 0-8047-1380-4 (v. 1 : alk. paper) : LC Card 86-30037 DDC 338.952 19
HC462.9 .P57 1987

Schwab, Laurent. Le Japon . [Paris] , c1984. 115 p. : ISBN 2-86262-221-4 (pbk.) : LC Card 84-164308 DDC 330.952/048 19
HC462.9 .S338 1984 ***NYPL [JLD 86-3612]***

Uno, Kimio. Japanese industrial performance /. Amsterdam ; New York : xix, 439 p. : ISBN 0-444-70274-1 LC Card 87-15452 DDC 338.0952 19
HC462.9 .U56 1987

JAPAN - ECONOMIC CONDITIONS - 1945- - REGIONAL DISPARITIES.
Gosudarstvenno-monopolisticheskiĭ kapitalizm i razmeshchenie proizvoditel′nykh sil /. Moskva , 1984. 182 p. ; LC Card 84-239188
HC240 .G565 1984

JAPAN - ECONOMIC POLICY.
Minami, Ryōshin, 1933- [Nihon no keizai hatten. English.] The economic development of Japan . Basingstoke, Hampshire , 1986. xxvi, 487 p. : ISBN 0-333-38582-9 LC Card 87-672411
HC462.7 .M47513x 1986b

JAPAN - ECONOMIC POLICY - 1945-
Dore, Ronald Philip. Flexible rigidities . London , 1986. 278 p. ; ISBN 0-485-11269-8 LC Card 87-672689
HC462.9 .D65 1986

Henning, C. Randall. Macroeconomic diplomacy in the 1980s . London , New York , c1987. x, 76 p. ; ISBN 0-7099-3794-6 (pbk.) LC Card 87-20041 DDC 337/.09171/3 19
HF1455 .H46 1987

Higashi, Chikara. The internationalization of the Japanese economy /. Boston, MA , c1987. xi, 273 p. : ISBN 0-89838-199-1 LC Card 87-3893 DDC 337.52 19
HC462.9 .H45 1987

Japan's response to crisis and change in the world economy /. Armonk, N.Y. , c1986. xiii, 309 p. : ISBN 0-87332-405-6 LC Card 86-21907 DDC 338.952 19
HC462.9 .J355 1986 ***NYPL [JLE 87-1199]***

Katō, Kan, 1926- The Japanese economy in transition /. Tokyo, Japan , c1986. viii, 160 p. : LC Card 87-163640 DDC 330.952/047 19
HC462.9 .K35367 1986

The Political economy of Japan. Stanford, Calif. , 1987- v. <1 > : ISBN 0-8047-1380-4 (v. 1 : alk. paper) : LC Card 86-30037 DDC 338.952 19
HC462.9 .P57 1987

Renshaw, Geoffrey. Adjustment and economic performance in industrialised countries . Geneva , 1986. xiv, 180 p. ; ISBN 92-2-105510-8 (pbk.) : LC Card 87-123435 DDC 338.9/009172/2 19
HC286.7 .R46 1986

Sano, Shin'ichi, 1947- Kanryō fuyu no jidai /. Tōkyō , 1985. 6, 255 p. ; ISBN 4-8334-1266-7 : LC Card 86-179753
HC462.9 .S2534 1985 <Orien Japan>
NYPL [*OSM 87-1196]

Sautter, Christian. Les dents du géant . Paris , c1987. 323 p. ; ISBN 2-85565-362-2 : LC Card 87-169635
HC462.9 .S277 1987

Striner, Herbert E. Regaining the lead . Millwood, N.Y. , c1987. xvii, 205 p. ; ISBN 0-8046-9408-7 (pbk. : alk. paper) : LC Card 86-32218 DDC 338.973 19
HC106.8 .S77 1987

Trade friction and economic policy . Cambridge [Cambridgeshire] , New York , 1987. xii, 243 p. : ISBN 0-521-34446-8 LC Card 87-11694 DDC 382/.0952/073 19
HF3828.U5 T73 1987

JAPAN - ECONOMIC POLICY - 1945- - CONGRESSES.
Japan and the United States today . New York , 1986, c1987. vii, 234 p. : ISBN 0-231-06575-2 LC Card 86-32640 DDC 332/.042/0952 19
HG3903 .J35 1987

JAPAN - FOREIGN ECONOMIC RELATIONS.
Henning, C. Randall. Macroeconomic diplomacy in the 1980s . London , New York , c1987. x, 76 p. ; ISBN 0-7099-3794-6 (pbk.) LC Card 87-20041 DDC 337/.09171/3 19
HF1455 .H46 1987

Higashi, Chikara. The internationalization of the Japanese economy /. Boston, MA , c1987. xi, 273 p. : ISBN 0-89838-199-1 LC Card 87-3893 DDC 337.52 19
HC462.9 .H45 1987

Japan's response to crisis and change in the world economy /. Armonk, N.Y. , c1986. xiii, 309 p. : ISBN 0-87332-405-6 LC Card 86-21907 DDC 338.952 19
HC462.9 .J355 1986 ***NYPL [JLE 87-1199]***

Katō, Kan, 1926- The Japanese economy in transition /. Tokyo, Japan , c1986. viii, 160 p. : LC Card 87-163640 DDC 330.952/047 19
HC462.9 .K35367 1986

Uno, Kimio. Japanese industrial performance /. Amsterdam ; New York : xix, 439 p. : ISBN 0-444-70274-1 LC Card 87-15452 DDC 338.0952 19
HC462.9 .U56 1987

The World economy and financial markets in 1995 . Kamakura-shi, Kanagawa-ken, Japan , 1986. 183 p. : LC Card 86-201317 DDC 332.1 19
HG3881 .W597 1986

Woronoff, Jon. Japan's commercial empire /. Armonk, N.Y. , c1984. 415 p. : ISBN 0-87332-312-2 LC Card 84-22146 DDC 337.52 19
HF1601 .W66 1984 ***NYPL [JLD 87-761]***

JAPAN - FOREIGN ECONOMIC RELATIONS - CANADA.
Canadian-Japanese economic relations in a triangular perspective /. Toronto , Scarborough, Ont. [1987] vi, 54 p. : ISBN 0-88806-139-0 (pbk.) LC Card 87-169818 DDC 337.52071 19
HF1480.15.J3 C35 1987

JAPAN - FOREIGN ECONOMIC RELATIONS - CONGRESSES.
Round Table Discussions on Japan in the Global Community. Japan in the global community . [Tokyo] , c1986. 129, [38] p. : ISBN 4-13-057014-5 : LC Card 87-129161 DDC 337.52 19
HF1601 .R68 1986

JAPAN - FOREIGN ECONOMIC RELATIONS - EUROPEAN ECONOMIC COMMUNITY COUNTRIES.
Korte, Karl-Rudolf. Nippons neue Vasallen? . Bonn , c1984. 103 p. : ISBN 3-7713-0216-1 LC Card 86-230930
HF1602.15.E92 K67 1984

JAPAN - FOREIGN ECONOMIC RELATIONS - MIDDLE EAST.
Shimizu, Hiroshi. Introduction to Japan's economic and political relations with the Middle East in the inter-war period . Kent Ridge, Singapore [1985] v, 47 leaves ; LC Card 87-110444 DDC 337.52056 19
HF1602.15.M626 S56 1985

JAPAN - FOREIGN ECONOMIC RELATIONS - PHILIPPINES.
RP-Japan relations and ADB . Metro Manila, Philippines , 1986. x, 137 p. : ISBN 971-08-3156-9 (pbk.) LC Card 86-211088 DDC 337.520599 19
HF1600.15.J3 R68 1986

JAPAN - FOREIGN ECONOMIC RELATIONS - UNITED STATES.
Canadian-Japanese economic relations in a triangular perspective /. Toronto , Scarborough, Ont. [1987] vi, 54 p. : ISBN 0-88806-139-0 (pbk.) LC Card 87-169818 DDC 337.52071 19
HF1480.15.J3 C35 1987

The Japanese challenge . Stamford, Conn., U. S.A. , c1986. xii, 108 leaves : ISBN 0-89336-489-4 (pbk.) LC Card 87-404570 DDC 338/.06 19
HC465.T4 J365 1986

Ōmae, Ken'ichi, 1943- Beyond national borders . Homewood, Ill. , c1987. xi, 128 p. : ISBN 1-556-23017-6 LC Card 86-72864 DDC 337.52 19
HF1602.15.U6 O4 1987

Wheeler, Jimmy W. Beyond recrimination . Indianapolis, IN (P.O. Box 26-919, Indianapolis 46226) , c1987. xix, 218 p. : LC Card 87-165405 DDC 382/.0951249/073 19
HF1456.5.T28 W46 1987

JAPAN - FOREIGN ECONOMIC RELATIONS - UNITED STATES - CONGRESSES.
Japan and the United States today . New York , 1986, c1987. vii, 234 p. : ISBN 0-231-06575-2 LC Card 86-32640 DDC 332/.042/0952 19
HG3903 .J35 1987

JAPAN - FOREIGN RELATIONS - MIDDLE EAST.
Shimizu, Hiroshi. Introduction to Japan's economic and political relations with the Middle East in the inter-war period . Kent Ridge, Singapore [1985] v, 47 leaves ; LC Card 87-110444 DDC 337.52056 19
HF1602.15.M626 S56 1985

Japan - Government. see **Japan - Politics and government.**

JAPAN - HISTORY - TOKUGAWA PERIOD, 1600-1868.
Kelly, William W. (William Wright), 1946- Water control in Tokugawa Japan . Ithaca,

N.Y. , c1982. ix, 260 p. : LC Card 83-126822
HD1741.J32 A325 1982

JAPAN - HISTORY - MEIJI PERIOD, 1868-1912.
Westney, D. Eleanor. Imitation and innovation . Cambridge, Mass. , 1987. viii, 252 p. : ISBN 0-674-44437-X (alk. paper) LC Card 87-273 DDC 338.6/0952 19
HD70.J3 W47 1987

JAPAN - HISTORY - ALLIED OCCUPATION, 1945-1952.
Park, Sung-Jo. U. S. labor policy in postwar Japan /. [Berlin] [c1985] 157 p. : ISBN 3-88548-424-2 LC Card 86-200166 DDC 331.11/0952 19
HD5827.A6 P37 1985

Japan in the global community . Round Table Discussions on Japan in the Global Community. [Tokyo] , c1986. 129, [38] p. : ISBN 4-13-057014-5 : LC Card 87-129161 DDC 337.52 19
HF1601 .R68 1986

JAPAN - INDUSTRIES - 1945-
Dore, Ronald Philip. Flexible rigidities . London , 1986. 278 p. ; ISBN 0-485-11269-8 LC Card 87-672689
HC462.9 .D65 1986

Skorov, Mikhail Sergeevich. Nauchno-tekhnicheskiĭ progress i tīazhelaīa promyshlennost′ ÎAponii /. Moskva , 1980. 213, [3] p. ; LC Card 81-130564
HC465.T4 S56 1980

Yoshida, Satoshi, 1948- Endaka to kigyō shūeki . [Higashimurayama-shi] , Tōkyō , 1986. 137 p. : ISBN 4-315-50263-4 : LC Card 86-205176
HC462.9 .Y638 1986 <Orien Japan>
NYPL [*OSM 87-2489]

JAPAN - INDUSTRIES - 1945- - ENVIRONMENTAL ASPECTS.
Environmental protection in the industrial sector in Japan . Tokyo, Japan , c1983. 168 p. : LC Card 87-672736
HC465.P55 E58x 1983

JAPAN - INDUSTRIES - CONGRESSES.
U. S.A.-Japan Conference on Manufacturing Research (1986 : Tokyo, Japan) Manufacturing research perspectives, U. S.A.-Japan . Amsterdam , New York , 1987. viii, 198 p. : ISBN 0-444-42868-2 LC Card 87-19851 DDC 338.4/767 19
HD9725 .U17 1986

JAPAN - INDUSTRIES - HISTORY.
Blackford, Mansel G., 1944- The rise of modern business in Great Britain, the United States, and Japan /. Chapel Hill , c1988. xi, 176 p. : ISBN 0-8078-1760-0 (alk. paper) LC Card 87-10022 DDC 338.09 19
HC255 .B59 1988

JAPAN - INDUSTRIES - INFORMATION SERVICES - ADDRESSES, ESSAYS, LECTURES.
Plan for information society-a national goal toward year 2000. Italian. Verso una società dell'informazione . Milano , 1974. 157 p. :
NYPL [TB (Studi e ricerche di scienze sociali. v.60)]

JAPAN - INDUSTRIES - LOCATION.
Gosudarstvenno-monopolisticheskiĭ kapitalizm i razmeshchenie proizvoditel′nykh sil /. Moskva , 1984. 182 p. ; LC Card 84-239188
HC240 .G565 1984

Japan - Industries - Statistics. see **Japan - Industries.**

Japan Institute of Labor. see **Nihon Rōdō Kyōkai.**

Japan. Kokuzeichō. An Outline of Japanese tax administration. [Tokyo], Japan , 1985. 85 p., [1] leaf of plates : LC Card 86-209172 DDC 354.520072/4 19
HJ3627 .O87 1985

Japan, management van de toekomst? /. Fassin, Yves. Antwerpen , 1985. 131 p. : ISBN 90-6716-242-6 : LC Card 86-167503
HD70.J3 F37 1985

JAPAN - MANUFACTURES - CONGRESSES.
U. S.A.-Japan Conference on Manufacturing Research (1986 : Tokyo, Japan) Manufacturing research perspectives, U. S.A.-Japan . Amsterdam , New York , 1987. viii, 198 p. : ISBN 0-444-42868-2 LC Card 87-19851 DDC 338.4/767 19
HD9725 .U17 1986

JAPAN - MANUFACTURES - MANAGEMENT.
Shapiro, H. Jack (Harris Jack) Reviving industry in America . Cambridge, Mass. , c1987. xii, 204 p. : ISBN 0-88730-118-5 LC Card 87-17585 DDC 338.4/767/0973 19
HD9725 .S46 1987

Japan, Markt für deutsche Konsumgüter /. Frese, Dirk. Düsseldorf [1978?] 32 p. : LC Card 85-242493
HF3568.J3 F74 1978

JAPAN - POLITICS AND GOVERNMENT - 1945-
Inside the Japanese system . Stanford, Calif. , c1988. xiii, 286 p. : ISBN 0-8047-1425-8 (alk. paper) LC Card 87-18820 DDC 330.952/04 19
HC462.9 .I587 1988

Wilensky, Harold L. Democratic corporatism and policy linkages . Berkeley , c1987. ix, 97 p. ; ISBN 0-87725-169-X (pbk.) : LC Card 87-3525 DDC 338.9 19
HD3616.E8 W54 1987

JAPAN - POPULATION.
McCoid, Catherine Hodge. Carrying capacities of nation-states /. New Haven, Conn. (P.O. Box 2015, Yale Station, New Haven 06520) , 1984. x, 198 leaves : LC Card 84-152784 DDC 304.6/2 19
GN33.5 .M38 1984 ***NYPL [JFE 86-2142]***

Population of Japan /. Tokyo , c1986. 124 p. : LC Card 86-230476 DDC 304.6/0952 19
HB3651 .P67 1986

JAPAN - RELATIONS - FOREIGN COUNTRIES - CONGRESSES.
Round Table Discussions on Japan in the Global Community. Japan in the global community . [Tokyo] , c1986. 129, [38] p. : ISBN 4-13-057014-5 : LC Card 87-129161 DDC 337.52 19
HF1601 .R68 1986

Japan. Shokugyō Nōryoku Kaihatsukyoku. New approach to vocational training /. Islamabad, Pakistan , 1985-1986. 2 v. : ISBN 92-2-105078-5 (pbk. : v. 1) LC Card 86-221389 DDC 331.25/92/0952 19
HD5715.5.J3 N48 1985

JAPAN - SOCIAL CONDITIONS - 1600-1868.
Bix, Herbert P. Peasant protest in Japan, 1590-1884 /. New Haven [Conn.] , c1986. xxxix, 296 p. : ISBN 0-300-03485-7 (alk. paper) LC Card 85-17889 DDC 322.4/4/0952 19
HD1339.J3 B59 1986 ***NYPL [JLE 86-2541]***

JAPAN - SOCIAL CONDITIONS - 1945-
Inside the Japanese system . Stanford, Calif. , c1988. xiii, 286 p. : ISBN 0-8047-1425-8 (alk. paper) LC Card 87-18820 DDC 330.952/04 19
HC462.9 .I587 1988

Schwab, Laurent. Le Japon . [Paris] , c1984. 115 p. : ISBN 2-86262-221-4 (pbk.) : LC Card 84-164308 DDC 330.952/048 19
HC462.9 .S338 1984 ***NYPL [JLD 86-3612]***

JAPAN - SOCIAL LIFE AND CUSTOMS.
Kobayashi, Kaoru, 1931- Japan, the most misunderstood country /. Tokyo , 1984. ix, 165 p. ; ISBN 4-7890-0247-0
NYPL [JLD 86-1398]

JAPAN - SOCIAL LIFE AND CUSTOMS - 1912-1945.
Barth, Johannes, 1891- Als deutscher Kaufmann in Fernost . Berlin , c1984. 206 p. : ISBN 3-503-02366-6 LC Card 84-143117
HC289.B7 B373 1984

JAPAN - SOCIAL LIFE AND CUSTOMS - MISCELLANEA.
Riccomini, Donald R., 1952- Unexpected Japan . New York , 1985. iv, 132 p. ; ISBN 0-8027-0858-7 : LC Card 85-7313 DDC 658/.00952 19
HD70.J3 R53 1985 ***NYPL [JLD 86-1348]***

Japan som veiviser . Benterud, Per. [Oslo] , c1983. 262 p. ; ISBN 82-02-09050-4 LC Card 83-195163
HD70.J3 B45 1983

Japan. Sōmuchō. Population of Japan /. Tokyo , c1986. 124 p. : LC Card 86-230476 DDC 304.6/0952 19
HB3651 .P67 1986

Japan. Sōrifu. Bureau of Statistics. see **Japan. Sōrifu. Tōkeikyoku.**

Japan. Sōrifu. Tōkeikyoku. (Old Catalog form: Japan. Statistical Bureau)
Population of Japan /. Tokyo , c1986. 124 p. : LC Card 86-230476 DDC 304.6/0952 19
HB3651 .P67 1986

Japan. Statistical Bureau. see **Japan. Sōrifu. Tōkeikyoku.**

Japan, the most misunderstood country /. Kobayashi, Kaoru, 1931- Tokyo , 1984. ix, 165 p. ; ISBN 4-7890-0247-0
NYPL [JLD 86-1398]

Japan. Tōkeikyoku. see **Japan. Sōrifu. Tōkeikyoku.**

Japanese agriculture . Moore, Richard H. Boulder , 1987. p. cm. ISBN 0-8133-7406-5 LC Card 87-13553 DDC 338.1/0952/115 19
HD920.N33 M65 1987

Japanese aid to the Pacific islands region /. Edo, Junko, 1947- Honolulu, Hawaii, USA , 1986. x, 94 p. ; ISBN 0-86638-090-6 (pbk.) LC Card 87-5293 DDC 338.91/52/09 19
HC681. E36 1986

JAPANESE AMERICANS - CALIFORNIA - SOCIAL CONDITIONS.
Glenn, Evelyn Nakano. Issei, Nisei, war bride . Philadelphia , 1986. xviii, 290 p. ; ISBN 0-87722-412-9 LC Card 85-25107 DDC 331.4/8164046/0899560794 19
HD6072.2.U52 C24 1986
NYPL [IEA 86-1929]

Japanese and Australian labour markets : a comparative study / edited by Keith Hancock ... [et al.]. Canberra : Australia-Japan Research Centre, [c1983] xx, 610 p. : ill. ; 25 cm. Papers presented at the Labour Market Workshop, held July 26-28, 1982 at the Australian National University and sponsored by the Australia-Japan Research Centre and the Japan Foundation. Includes bibliographies and index. ISBN 0-86413-004-X (pbk.) : LC Card 84-220557 DDC 331.12/0952 19
1. Labor supply - Australia - Congresses. 2. Labor supply - Japan - Congresses. 3. Industrial relations - Australia - Congresses. 4. Industrial relations - Japan - Congresses. I. Hancock, Keith Jackson. II. Australia-Japan Research Centre. III. Labour Market Workshop (1982 : Australian National University).
HD5850.A6 J36 1983 ***NYPL [JLE 86-630]***

The Japanese challenge : Japanese technology and industrial strategy / Kevin Gainer, project analyst. Stamford, Conn., U. S.A. : Business Communications Co., c1986. xii, 108 leaves : ill. ; 29 cm. (Business opportunity report . GB-089) ISBN 0-89336-489-4 (pbk.) LC Card 87-404570 DDC 338/.06 19
1. Technological innovations - Economic aspects - Japan. 2. Technology transfer - Economic aspects - Japan. 3. Industry and state - Japan. 4. Japan - Foreign economic relations - United States. 5. United States - Foreign economic relations - Japan. I. Gainer, Kevin. II. Business Communications Co. III. Series.
HC465.T4 J365 1986

Japanese comm/dp/w U. S. market penetration. Japanese penetration into the United States communications data processing and office equipment markets. New York, N.Y. , c1983. v, 308 p. ; LC Card 87-143908 DDC 381/.45004/0973 19
HD9696.D383 U635 1983

The Japanese competition : phase 2 / edited by Peter J. Arnesen. Ann Arbor, MI : Center for Japanese Studies, University of Michigan, 1987. xii, 124 p. ; 23 cm. (Michigan papers in Japanese studies . no. 15) Proceedings of the Sixth U. S.-Japan Automotive Industry Conference. Includes bibliographies. ISBN 0-939512-30-0 LC Card 86-31756 DDC 338.4/76292/0952 19
1. Automobile industry and trade - Japan - Congresses. 2. Automobile industry and trade - United States - Congresses. I. Arnesen, Peter Judd, 1947-. II. U. S.-Japan Automotive Industry Conference (6th : 1987? : University of Michigan). III. Series.
HD9710.J32 J374 1987
NYPL [JFL 81-188 no.15]

Japanese direct manufacturing investment in the United States /. Yoshida, Mamoru. New

York , 1987. xiv, 220 p. : ISBN 0-275-92347-9 (alk. paper) : LC Card 86-22689 DDC 332.6/7352/073 19
HG4910 .Y58 1986 ***NYPL [JLE 87-1122]***

The Japanese economy in transition /. Katō, Kan, 1926- Tokyo, Japan , c1986. viii, 160 p. : LC Card 87-163640 DDC 330.952/047 19
HC462.9 .K35367 1986

Japanese enterprise groups /. Futatsugi, Yūsaku, 1935- [Gendai Nihon no kigyō shūdan. English.] [Kobe] , 1986. 179 p. : LC Card 86-220427 DDC 338.8/0952 19
HD2756.2.J3 F8813 1986

Japanese etiquette & ethics in business /. De Mente, Boye. Lincolnwood, Ill. , c1987. ix, 182 p. : ISBN 0-8442-8507-2 (pbk.) : LC Card 86-60830 DDC 395/.52 19
HF5387 .D384 1987

Japanese etiquette and ethics in business. De Mente, Boye. Japanese etiquette & ethics in business /. Lincolnwood, Ill. , c1987. ix, 182 p. : ISBN 0-8442-8507-2 (pbk.) : LC Card 86-60830 DDC 395/.52 19
HF5387 .D384 1987

Japanese import barriers to U. S. agricultural exports and the Common agricultural policy of the European Community and implications for U. S. agricultural trade : studies / prepared for the use of the Republican members of the Joint Economic Committee, Congress of the United States by the Congressional Research Service, Library of Congress. Washington : U. S. G.P.O. : For sale by the Supt. of Docs., Congressional Sales Office, U. S. G.P.O., 1986. vii, 65 p. : ill. ; 24 cm. (S. prt. . 99-191) At head of title: 99th Congress, 2d session. Joint Committee print. Distributed to some depository libraries in microfiche. Shipping list no.: 86-951-P. Bibliography: p. 51-65. Item 1000-B, 1000-C, (microfiche) LC Card 87-601384 DDC 382/.5/0952 19
1. Import quotas - Japan. 2. Tariff on farm produce - Japan. 3. Agriculture and state - European Economic Community countries. 4. Produce trade - European Economic Community countries. 5. Produce trade - United States. I. United States. Congress. Joint Economic Committee. II. Library of Congress. Congressional Research Service. III. Title: Japanese import barriers to US agricultural exports and the Common agricultural policy of the European Community and implications for U. S. agricultural trade. IV. Title: Common agricultural policy of the European Community and implications for U. S. agricultural trade. V. Series.
HF1601 .J363 1986

Japanese import barriers to US agricultural exports and the Common agricultural policy of the European Community and implications for U. S. agricultural trade. Japanese import barriers to U. S. agricultural exports and the Common agricultural policy of the European Community and implications for U. S. agricultural trade . Washington , 1986. vii, 65 p. : LC Card 87-601384 DDC 382/.5/0952 19
HF1601 .J363 1986

Japanese industrial performance /. Uno, Kimio. Amsterdam ; New York : xix, 439 p. : ISBN 0-444-70274-1 LC Card 87-15452 DDC 338.0952 19
HC462.9 .U56 1987

Japanese industrial relations series .
(2) Labor unions and labor-management relations. Tokyo, Japan , 1986. 48 p. : ISBN 4-538-74002-0 : LC Card 86-220438 DDC 331/.0952 19
HD8726.5 .L33 1986

JAPANESE LANGUAGE - DICTIONARIES - ENGLISH.
Akiyama, Nobuo. Talking business in Japanese /. Hauppauge, N.Y. , c1987. p. cm. ISBN 0-8120-3848-7 LC Card 87-19601 DDC 650/.03/956 19
HF1002 .A34 1987

Erekutoronikusu pawā shōjiten /. Tōkyō , 1985. v, 618 p. : ISBN 4-320-08454-3 : LC Card 85-229520
TK7804 .E73 1985 <Orien Japan> ***NYPL [*OSG 86-3267]***

Takabe, Yoshinobu, 1907- Amerika shingo jiten = The Kenkyūsha dictionary of new English /. Tokyo , 1978. 717 p. ;
NYPL [*OSG 87-2157]

Takahashi, M. (Morio), 1892-1959. Romanized English-Japanese, Japanese-English dictionary /. [Tokyo] , 1958. 457, 1226 p. ;
NYPL [*O-*OSG 87-870]

Japanese multinationals in the United States . Kujawa, Duane. New York , 1986. xii, 291 p. ; ISBN 0-03-006718-9 (alk. paper) : LC Card 85-28310 DDC 338.8/8952/073 19
HF5549.2.U5 K84 1986
NYPL [JLE 86-3833]

JAPANESE NEWSPAPERS - HISTORY.
Westney, D. Eleanor. Imitation and innovation . Cambridge, Mass. , 1987. viii, 252 p. : ISBN 0-674-44437-X (alk. paper) LC Card 87-273 DDC 338.6/0952 19
HD70.J3 W47 1987

Japanese penetration into the United States communications data processing and office equipment markets. New York, N.Y. : Frost & Sullivan, c1983. v, 308 p. ; 29 cm. Spine title: Japanese comm/dp/w U. S. market penetration. "March 1983." "#A1016." LC Card 87-143908 DDC 381/.45004/0973 19
1. Data transmission equipment industry - United States. 2. Data transmission equipment industry - Japan. 3. Telecommunication equipment industry - United States. 4. Telecommunication equipment industry - Japan. 5. Electronic office machine industry - United States. 6. Electronic office machine industry - Japan. 7. Market surveys - United States. I. Frost & Sullivan. II. Title: Japanese comm/dp/w U. S. market penetration.
HD9696.D383 U635 1983

Japanese prefectures and policy making /. Reed, Steven R., 1947- Pittsburgh, Pa. , 1986. ix, 197 p. ; ISBN 0-8229-3527-9 LC Card 85-22528 DDC 352/.00047 19
JS7373.A3 R44 1986 ***NYPL [JLE 86-3757]***

Japanese-U. S. business negotiations . McCreary, Don R. New York , 1986. viii, 121 p. ; ISBN 0-275-92006-2 (alk. paper) : LC Card 86-554 DDC 658 19
HD58.6 .M38 1986 ***NYPL [JLE 86-3074]***

Japan's commercial empire /. Woronoff, Jon. Armonk, N.Y. , c1984. 415 p. : ISBN 0-87332-312-2 LC Card 84-22146 DDC 337.52 19
HF1601 .W66 1984 ***NYPL [JLD 87-761]***

Japan's response to crisis and change in the world economy / edited by Michèle Schmiegelow. Armonk, N.Y. : M.E. Sharpe, c1986. xiii, 309 p. : ill. ; 24 cm. A Publication of the Institute of Asian Affairs, Hamburg. Includes bibliographies. ISBN 0-87332-405-6 LC Card 86-21907 DDC 338.952 19
1. Monetary policy - Japan. 2. Foreign exchange problem - Japan. 3. Japan - Economic policy - 1945-. 4. Japan - Commercial policy. 5. Japan - Foreign economic relations. I. Schmiegelow, Michèle.
HC462.9 .J355 1986 ***NYPL [JLE 87-1199]***

Jaques, Elliott. The changing culture of a factory / Elliott Jaques. New York : Garland, 1987. xvii, 341 p. ; 23 cm. (Continuity in administrative science) Reprint. Originally published: London : Tavistock, 1951. Bibliography: p. 335-336. Includes index. ISBN 0-8240-8212-5 (alk. paper) : LC Card 86-25815 DDC 671/.068 19
1. Metal-workers - Great Britain. 2. Metal-work - Great Britain - Personnel management. 3. Glacier Metal Company - Employees. I. Title. II. Series.
HD8039.M5 J37 1987

Jaquette, Jane S., 1942- A Mulher rural e mudanças no processo de produção agrícola . [Brasília] [1984] i, 161 p. ; LC Card 86-150197
HD6073.A292 L295 1984

Jaramillo de Botero, Margarita. Pobreza, participación y desarrollo regional /. [Bogotá, D.E., Colombia] , 1986. 536 p. : LC Card 87-103266
HC125 .P6 1986

Jaramillo, Samuel. Análisis de las condiciones de vivienda de los hogares colombianos, a partir de los resultados de la encuesta nacional de hogares, etapa 33, 1981 / por Samuel Jaramillo, Luis Mauricio Cuervo. Bogotá, Colombia : Centro de Estudios sobre Desarrollo Económico, Facultad de Economía, Universidad de los Andes, 1985. ii, 166 p. ; 28 cm. (Documento CEDE . 082) LC Card 87-403605 DDC 363.5/1/09861 19
1. Housing - Colombia. 2. Housing surveys - Colombia. I. Cuervo, Luis Mauricio. II. Series: Documento (Universidad de los Andes (Bogotá, Colombia). Centro de Estudios sobre Desarrollo Económico) , 082. III. Title.
HD7325.A3 J37 1985

Jarett, Jeffrey, 1940- Business forecasting methods / Jeffrey Jarrett. Oxford, UK ; New York, NY, USA : Blackwell, 1987. 346 p. : ill. ; 26 cm. Includes bibliographies and index. ISBN 0-631-15289-X : LC Card 87-6408 DDC 658.4/0355 19
1. Business forecasting. I. Title.
HD30.27 .J38 1987

Jarnagin, Bill D. Financial accounting standards : explanation and analysis / Bill D. Jarnagin, Jon A. Booker.8th ed. Chicago, Ill. (4025 W. Peterson Ave., Chicago 60646) : Commerce Clearing House, 1986. xv, 1253 p. : ill. ; 23 cm. (Topical law reports) Includes index. LC Card 87-116311 DDC 657/.0218 19
1. Accounting - Standards - United States. 2. Financial statements - Standards - United States. I. Booker, Jon A. II. Series: Topical law reports (Commerce Clearing House). III. Title.
HF5616.U5 B66 1986

Jarrell, Stephen B. Basic business statistics : an interactive approach / by Stephen B. Jarrell. Newton, Mass. : Allyn and Bacon, 1987. p. cm. Includes index. ISBN 0-205-10632-3 LC Card 87-11349 DDC 519.5 19
1. Commercial statistics. 2. Statistics. I. Title.
HF1017 .J37 1987

Jarrold, T. (Thomas), 1770-1853. Dissertations on man, philosophical, physiological, and political; in answer to Mr. Malthus's "Essay on the principle of population." By T. Jarrold, M.D. London, Cadell & Davis [etc.] 1806. vi p., 1 l., [9]-367, [1] p. 22 cm. LC Card 05-22565
1. Malthusianism. I. Title.
HB863 .J38

Jarrow, Robert A. Finance theory / Robert A. Jarrow. Englewood Cliffs, N.J. : Prentice-Hall, c1988. xiv, 298 p. : ill. ; 24 cm. Includes bibliographies and index. ISBN 0-13-314865-3 LC Card 87-2359 DDC 332/.0724 19
1. Finance. I. Title.
HG173 .J34 1988

Jarva, Vuokko. Club of Rome Conference (1984 : Helsinki, Finland) Managing global issues . [Lahti] [1985] 216 p. : ISBN 951-45-3807-2 (pbk.) LC Card 87-140928 DDC 909.82/8 19
HC13 .C56 1984

Jasinski, Irv. Airline pilot interviews : how you can succeed in getting hired / Irv Jasinski. Escondido, Calif. : Career Advancement Publications, c1987. 144 p. : ill. ; 22 cm. Includes index. ISBN 0-942195-01-9 (pbk.) LC Card 87-70680 DDC 629.132/5240423/02373 19
1. Aeronautics, Commercial - Vocational guidance. 2. Air pilots. 3. Applications for positions. I. Title.
HE9777 .J36 1987

Jasmins Pereira, Fernando. see **Pereira, Fernando Jasmins.**

Jaspa Employment Advisory Mission.
Options for a dependent economy. Employment and development in Lesotho : report of a national seminar / organized by the Government of Lesotho in collaboration with ILO's Jobs and Skills Programme for Africa (JASPA) and Southern African Team for Employment Promotion (SATEP), 24-27 May 1983. Addis Ababa , 1983. ii, 229 p. ; ISBN 92-2-103780-0 LC Card 84-980769 DDC 331.12/09681/6 19
HD5842.7.A6 E46 1983

JASPA Steering Group Meeting on Priority Employment Policies and Projects for Africa (1985 : Addis Ababa, Ethiopia) Report of JASPA Steering Group Meeting on Priority Employment Policies and Projects for Africa. Addis Ababa : International Labour Organisation, Jobs and Skills Programme for Africa, 1986. 43 leaves ; 29 cm. LC Card 87-980227 DDC 331.12/042/096 19
1. Manpower policy - Africa - Congresses. 2. Labor policy - Africa - Congresses. 3. Youth - Employment - Africa - Congresses. 4. Women - Employment - Africa - Congresses. 5. Informal sector (Economics) - Africa - Congresses. 6. Manpower planning - Africa - Congresses. I. Jobs and Skills Programme for Africa. II. Title.
HD5837.A6 J37 1985

Jasper, Lothar Th.
Entwicklung der Realsteuerhebesätze der Gemeinden mit mehr als 50.000 Einwohnern 1984 gegenüber 1983 / [Bearbeiter, Lothar Th. Jasper]. Bonn : Institut "Finanzen und Steuern", 1984. 29 leaves ; 30 cm. (Brief / Institut "Finanzen und Steuern" . Nr. 238) Cover title. LC Card 86-186306
1. Real property tax - Germany, West. 2. Local taxation - Germany, West. I. Institut "Finanzen und Steuern" (Germany). II. Series: Brief (Institut "Finanzen und Steuern" (Germany)) , Nr. 238. III. Title.
HJ1120 .B65 nr. 238 HJ4125.G35

Zur Problematik von Subventionen als Instrument der Wirtschaftspolitik /. Bonn , 1986. 97 p. : LC Card 87-408486 DDC 336/.012/43 s 338.943 19
HJ1101 .B6 Heft 259 HD3646.G4

Jaszi, George. Carson, Carol S. The use of national income and product accounts for public policy . Washington, D.C. , 1986. 26 p. : LC Card 86-601338 DDC 339.5/0973 19
HC110.I5 C37 1986

Jātīẏa Mārkeṭiṃ Seminārа, 1985 (1985 : Chātra-Śikshaka Kendra, Ḍhākā Biśvabidyālaẏa)
Mākeṭiṃ, samasyā o sambhābanā : Jātīẏa Mārkeṭiṃ Seminārа-1985 te upasthāpitabya nibandha samūhera saṃkalana / Jātīẏa Mārkeṭiṃ Seminārа-1985, sthāna, Chātra-Śikshaka Kendra, Ḍhākā Biśvabidyālaẏa, tārikha 9 o 10i Jānuẏāri 1985. [Dhaka] : Mārkeṭiṃ Bibhāga, Ḍhākā Biśvabidyālaẏa, 1985. 138 p. ; 26 cm. In Bengali. On marketing in Bangladesh; papers and proceedings of the National Marketing Seminar, 1985. Includes bibliographical references. LC Card 86-903411
1. Marketing - Bangladesh - Congresses. I. Title.
HF5415.12.B36 J38 1985

Jätteiden hyötykäyttö kansantaloudessa /. Wallin, Markku. [Helsinki] [1986] 87 p. : ISBN 951-46-9505-4 LC Card 86-216953
HD9975.F52 W35 1986

Jatun Llajta . Calderón G., Fernando. La Paz, Bolivia , 1982. v, 448 p., [8] leaves of plates : LC Card 83-111937 DDC 381/.1 19
HF5473.B62 C623 1982
NYPL [JLF 86-1794]

Jauch, Lawrence R.
Business policy and strategic management / Lawrence R. Jauch, William F. Glueck. 5th ed. New York : McGraw-Hill, c1988. xix, 940 p. : ill. ; 24 cm. (McGraw-Hill series in management) Glueck's name appears first on the earlier edition. Includes bibliographies and index. ISBN 0-7032-2347-X : LC Card 87-16859 DDC 658.4/012 19
1. Corporate planning. I. Glueck, William F. II. Title.
HD30.28 .J375 1988

Strategic management and business policy / Lawrence R. Jauch, William F. Glueck. 3rd ed. New York : McGraw-Hill, c1988. xviii, 428 p. : ill. ; 24 cm. (McGraw-Hill series in management) Glueck's name appears first on the earlier edition. Includes bibliographies and index. ISBN 0-07-032339-9 (pbk.) : LC Card 87-7191 DDC 658.4/012 19
1. Corporate planning. 2. Management. I. Glueck, William F. II. Title.
HD30.28 .J38 1988

Jaun, Rudolf, 1948- Management und Arbeiterschaft : Verwissenschaftlichung, Amerikanisierung und Rationalisierung der Arbeitsverhältnisse in der Schweiz 1873-1959 / Rudolf Jaun. Zürich : Chronos, c1986. 505, 10 p. ; 23 cm. ISBN 3-905278-08-1 LC Card 87-132013 DDC 658/.009494 19
1. Industrial management - Switzerland - History. 2. Industrial management - United States - History. 3. Switzerland - Industries - History. I. Title.
HD70.S85 J38 1986

JAUNPUR (INDIA : DISTRICT) - ECONOMIC CONDITIONS.
Shankar, Kripa. Pattern of land ownership and backwardness . New Delhi , 1986. x, 119 p. ; ISBN 81-7024-021-2 : LC Card 87-900130 DDC 333.3/23/09542 19
HD879.J37 S5 1986

Jaura, Zdeno. Planomernoe razvitie sotsialisticheskoĭ ėkonomiki /. Moskva , Bratislava , 1977. 262 p. ; LC Card 87-100683
HC336.25 .P448 1977

Javaslatok az élelmiszer-gazdaság fejlesztésére : műhelytanulmányok. Budapest : Agrárgazdasági Kutató Intézet, 1984. 279 p. : ill. ; 20 cm. Published in commemoration of the 30th anniversary of the Agrárgazdasági Kutató Intézet. Bibliography: p. [148] ISBN 963-221-500-1 LC Card 85-229874
1. Food industry and trade - Hungary. 2. Food industry and trade - Government policy - Hungary. 3. Agriculture and state - Hungary. I. Agrárgazdasági Kutató Intézet.
HD9015.H82 J38 1984

Jawa Tengah (Indonesia). Badan Perencanaan Pembangunan Daerah. Jawa Tengah membangun =. [Semarang] [1985] iii, 37 leaves : LC Card 86-943679
HC437.J39 J39 1985

JAWA TENGAH (INDONESIA) - ECONOMIC CONDITIONS - CHARTS, DIAGRAMS, ETC.
Jawa Tengah membangun =. [Semarang] [1985] iii, 37 leaves : LC Card 86-943679
HC437.J39 J39 1985

JAWA TENGAH, INDONESIA - RURAL CONDITIONS.
Hart, Gillian Patricia. Power, labor, and livelihood . Berkeley , c1986. xvi, 228 p. : ISBN 0-520-05499-7 (alk. paper) LC Card 85-8435 DDC 330.9598/2 19
HD1537.I56 H37 1986
NYPL [JLE 86-3039]

Jawa Tengah membangun = Central Java develops, 1979-1983. [Semarang] : Pemerintah Propinsi Daerah Tingkat I Jawa Tengah, Badan Perencanaan Pembangunan Daerah, [1985] iii, 37 leaves : col. ill. ; 16 x 23 cm. English and Indonesian. Cover title. LC Card 86-943679
1. Jawa Tengah (Indonesia) - Economic conditions - Charts, diagrams, etc. I. Jawa Tengah (Indonesia). Badan Perencanaan Pembangunan Daerah. II. Title: Central Java develops, 1979-1980.
HC437.J39 J39 1985

JAWBONING. see **WAGE-PRICE POLICY.**

Jaworek, Rudolf. The development of small scale industry in Kaduna State : report presented to the government of Kaduna State / by Rudolf Jaworek. Zaria : Centre for Social & Economic Research, Ahmadu Bello University, [1980] vii, 162, [44] p., [2] leaves of plates : ill. ; 33 cm. (C.S.E.R. research report . no. 6) Bibliography: p. 161-162. LC Card 84-256006
1. Small business - Nigeria - Kaduna State. 2. Small business - Government policy - Nigeria - Kaduna State. I. Series: CSER research report , no. 6. II. Title.
HD2356.N62 K34 1980

Jay, Robert. The trade card in nineteenth-century America / Robert Jay. Columbia : University of Missouri Press, 1987. 112 p. : ill. (some col.) ; 20 x 26 cm. Bibliography: p. 107-110. Includes index. ISBN 0-8262-0619-0 (alk. paper) LC Card 86-30902 DDC 769.5 19
1. Advertising cards - United States - History - 19th century. I. Title. II. Title: Trade card in 19th-century America.
HF5851 .J39 1987

Jayashankar, R., 1954- Distribution of refinery products in India / R. Jayashankar. New Delhi : Concept Pub. Co., 1986, c1985. 152 p. ; 22 cm. Study, with reference to petroleum products. Bibliography: p. [143]-148. Includes index. LC Card 86-902972 DDC 381/.4566553/0954 19
1. Petroleum products - India - Marketing. I. Title.
HD9576.I42 J39 1986

Jayawardana, W. R. M. P. Wharton, Robert B. Analysis of rice export flows from southern states /. [Baton Rouge?] [1986] iii, 44 p. ; LC Card 87-620886 DDC 338.1/09763 s 382/.41318/0975021 19
HD1775.L8 L7 no. 662 HD9066.U46A13

Jayawardena, Kumari. Kūriyan, Rēval. Vatukarayē käntā śramaya surākäma . Colombo, Sri Lanka [1984] 24 p. : LC Card 86-902479
HD6182.8 .K87 1984

Jazz . Crittenden, Vicky L. Reading, Mass. , c1986. 62 p. : ISBN 0-201-11365-1 (pbk.) LC Card 86-211796 DDC 658.8/0028/55369 19
HF5439.C67 C75 1986

JAZZ (COMPUTER PROGRAM)
Crittenden, Vicky L. Jazz . Reading, Mass. , c1986. 62 p. : ISBN 0-201-11365-1 (pbk.) LC Card 86-211796 DDC 658.8/0028/55369 19
HF5439.C67 C75 1986

Jean, Diane. Le travail à domicile dans le vêtement pour dames : enquête auprès des travailleuses à domicile inscrites au comité paritaire du vêtement pour dames / Diane Jean, Jean-François Guilloteau. [Montréal] : Centre de recherche et de statistiques sur le marché du travail, [1982] xi, 146, [1] p. : ill. ; 28 cm. (Etudes et recherches) Bibliography: p. [147] ISBN 2-550-02847-3 LC Card 83-242834
1. Women clothing workers - Québec (Province). 2. Home labor - Québec (Province). 3. Home labor. I. Guilloteau, Jean-François. II. Series: Etudes et recherches (Québec (Province). Centre de recherche et de statistiques sur le marché du travail). III. Title.
HD6073.C62 C25 1982

Jean, François. Ethiopie, du bon usage de la famine / François Jean. Paris : Médecins sans frontières, [1986] 102 p. : ill. ; 25 cm. Bibliography: p. 101-102. LC Card 87-131143
1. Famines - Ethiopia. I. Title.
HC845.Z9 F347 1986

Jean-Hansen, Viggo. Sektorberegninger for samferdselssektorene og reparasjon av kjøretøyer m.v. / av Viggo Jean-Hansen. Oslo : Statistisk sentralbyrå, 1979. 56 p. ; 30 cm. (Det Norske nasjonalregnskapet. Dokumentasjonsnotat . nr. 7) Rapporter fra Statistisk sentralbyrå ; 79/2 Bibliography: p. 52. ISBN 82-537-0968-4 LC Card 86-460231
1. Transportation - Norway - Finance. I. Title. II. Series.
HE259 .J4 1979

Jean-Louis, Elyane. Rosélie, Roland. L'habitation sucrière au Quartier La Dumaine, Le François /. [Fort-deFrance? , 1986] ([Fort-de-France] : Impr. Désormeaux) 59 p. : LC Card 86-203128
HD8039.S86 M327 1986

Jeanmaire, Claude. Basler Verkehrs-Betriebe (BVB) . Villigen AG, Schweiz , c1984. 56 p., [188] p. of plates, xv p. : ISBN 3-85649-045-0 : LC Card 84-160209
HE4919.B37 B37 1984

Jebens, Albrecht. Wirtschafts- und sozialgeographische Untersuchung über das Heimgewerbe in Nordafghanistan unter besonderer Berücksichtigung der Mittelstadt Sar-e-Pul : ein geographischer Beitrag zur Stadt-Umland-Forschung und zur Wirtschaftsform des Heimgewerbes / Albrecht Jebens. Tübingen : Im Selbstverlag des Geographischen Instituts der Universität Tübingen, 1983. xii, 415 p., [2] folded leaves of plates : ill., maps ; 24 cm. (Tübinger geographische Studien, 0564-4232 . Heft 87) Originally presented as the author's thesis (doctoral)--Universität Tübingen, 1982? Summary in English, French, Persian, and Russian. Bibliography: p. 375-393. LC Card 86-128235
1. Cottage industries - Afghanistan - Sar-e Pol. 2. Anthropo-geography - Afghanistan - Sar-e Pol. 3. Cities and towns - Afghanistan - Sar-e Pol. 4. Sar-e Pol (Afghanistan) - Economic conditions. 5. Sar-e Pol (Afghanistan) - Social conditions. I. Title. II. Series.
HD2346.A52 S275 1983

Jederström, Annika. Otter, Casten von, 1941- Medbestämmandeavtal i landsting . Stockholm [1984] 92 p. : LC Card 84-241542
HD5660.S9 O77 1984

Jedidi, Mohammed. Croissance économique et espace urbain dans le Sahel tunisien depuis l'indépendance / Mohamed Jedidi. [Tunis] : Impr. officielle de la République tunisienne, 1986. 2 v. : ill. ; 24 cm. (Publications de l'Université de Tunis, Faculté des lettres et sciences humaines de Tunis. Deuxième série, Géographie . v. 20) Bibliography: v. 2, p. 381-392. LC Card 87-123401
1. Tunisia - Economic conditions - 1956-. 2. Land use, Urban - Tunisia. I. Title. II. Series.
HC820 .J43 1986

Jedlicka, Allen D. Organizational change and the Third World : designs for the twenty-first century / Allen Jedlicka. New York : Praeger, 1987. xii, 141 p. ; 25 cm. Includes bibliographies and index. ISBN 0-275-92317-7 (alk. paper) : LC Card 87-13252 DDC 658.4/06/091724 19
1. Economic development projects - Developing countries - Management. 2. Economic development projects - Developing countries - Citizen participation. 3. Organizational change - Developing countries. 4. Organizational change. I. Title.
HC59.72.E44 J43 1987

Jeeves, Alan. Migrant labour in South Africa's mining economy : the struggle for the gold mines' labour supply, 1890-1920 / Alan H. Jeeves. Kingston, Canada : McGill-Queen's University Press, 1985. xiv, 323 p. ; 24 cm. Includes index. Bibliography: p. 309-317. ISBN 0-7735-0420-6 DDC 331.7'6223422
1. Migrant labor - South Africa. 2. Gold miners - South Africa. 3. Recruiting of employees - South Africa. 4. Blacks - Employment - South Africa. I. Title.
NYPL [JLE 85-3148]

Jeffreys, Daniel. Economics and the economy / Daniel Jeffreys. Burnt Mill, Harlow, Essex, England : Longman, 1985. 317 p. : ill. ; 22 cm. Includes index. ISBN 0-582-35452-8 (pbk.) LC Card 87-152784 DDC 330 19
1. Economics. 2. Great Britain - Economic conditions - 1945-. I. Title.
HB171.5 .J45 1985

Jeffries, Ian. The East German economy /. London , New York , c1987. 328 p. : ISBN 0-7099-1469-5 LC Card 87-17163 DDC 338.9431 19
HC290.78 .E23 1987

Jégouzo, Guenhaël. Petite paysannerie en France / Guenhaël Jégouzo. Paris : Institut national de la recherche agronomique, c1984. 227 p. : ill. ; 24 cm. Includes bibliographical references and index. ISBN 2-85340-610-5 LC Card 85-181759 DDC 338.1/6 19
1. Farms, Small. 2. Peasantry - France. 3. Rural poor - France. I. Institut national de la recherche agronomique (France). II. Title.
HD1339.F8 J44 1984

Jeleček, Leoš. Zemědělství a půdní fond v Čechách ve 2. polovině 19. století / Leoš Jeleček. Vyd. 1. Praha : Academia, 1985. 283 p. : ill. (some col.) ; 24 cm. On p. facing t.p.: Československá akademie věd. Summary in English and Russian. Bibliography: p. 262-273. LC Card 86-199876
1. Land use, Rural - Czechoslovakia - Bohemia - History - 19th century. 2. Agriculture - Czechoslovakia - Bohemia - History - 19th century. I. Title.
HD640.3.Z8 B634 1985

Jemnitz, János. Május elseje születése / Jemnitz János. [Budapest] : Kossuth, 1986. 135, [1] p. : ill. ; 22 cm. Bibliography: p. 134-[136]. ISBN 963-09-2773-X : LC Card 87-408513
1. May Day (Labor holiday) - History. I. Title.
HD7791 .J46 1986

Jen kuo chi she hui. Macao. Repartição dos Serviços de Estatística. Demográficas e sociais =. Macau [1984] [28] p. ; LC Card 86-162433
HA4643 .M33 1984

The Jengka Triangle projects in Malaysia : impact evaluation report / Operations Evaluation Department. Washington, D.C. : World Bank, c1987. ix, 105 p., [1] leaf of plates : ill., col. map ; 28 cm. (A World Bank operations evaluation study, 1011-0984) ISBN 0-8213-0946-3 (pbk.); 0-8213-0946-6 (cover) LC Card 87-21021 DDC 338.1/85951 19
1. Agricultural development projects - Malaysia - Pahang - Evaluation - Case studies. I. International Bank for Reconstruction and Development. Operations Evaluation Dept. II. Series.
HD2080.6.Z9 P345 1987

Jenkins, Carolyn M. (Carolyn Marion) The economic implications of disinvestment for South Africa / Carolyn M. Jenkins. [Braamfontain?] : South African Institute of International Affairs, 1986. v, 100 p. ; 30 cm. (Special study / South African Institute of International Affairs = Spesiale studie / Suid-Afrikaanse Instituut van Internasionale Aangeleenthede) Bibliography: p. 94-100. ISBN 0-908371-51-9 (pbk.) : LC Card 87-164832 DDC 332.6/73/0968 19
1. Disinvestment - South Africa. 2. Investments, Foreign - South Africa. I. Series: Special study (South African Institute of International Affairs). II. Title.
HG5851.A3 J46 1986

Jenkins, Gilbert. Champness, Michael. Oil tanker databook, 1985 /. London ; New York : vii, 347 p. ; ISBN 0-85334-311-X LC Card 86-217414 DDC 387.5/448 19
HE566.T3 C42 1985

Jenkins, Rhys Owen, 1948- Transnational corporations and uneven development : the internationalization of capital and the Third World / Rhys Jenkins. London ; New York : Methuen, 1987. p. cm. Bibliography: p. Includes index. ISBN 0-416-73340-9 LC Card 87-12351 DDC 338.8/83 19
1. International business enterprises - Developing countries. 2. Finance - Developing countries. I. Title.
HD2932 .J45 1987

Jenkins, Richard, 1952- Racism and recruitment : managers, organisations, and equal opportunity in the labour market / Richard Jenkins. Cambridge [Cambridgeshire] ; New York : Cambridge University Press, 1986. xi, 281 p. ; 24 cm. (Comparative ethnic and race relations) Includes index. Bibliography: p. 265-275. ISBN 0-521-32028-3 LC Card 85-17483 DDC 331.13/3/0941 19
1. Discrimination in employment - Great Britain. 2. Recruiting of employees - Great Britain. 3. Race discrimination - Great Britain. 4. Blacks - Employment - Great Britain. I. Title. II. Series.
HG4903.5.G7 J46 1986
NYPL [JLE 86-3305]

Jenkins, S. J. (Susan J.) Aspects of the informal economic sector of Juba, southern Sudan / S.J. Jenkins. [Jūbā, Sudan] : University of Juba, Population and Manpower Unit, [1981?] xiii, 217 p., [4] leaves of plates : ill. ; 30 cm. (Research paper / University of Jūbā, Population and Manpower Unit . no. 1) Bibliography: p. 213-217. LC Card 86-980565
1. Informal sector (Economics) - Sudan - Jūbā. 2. Small business - Sudan - Jūbā. 3. Jūbā (Sudan) - Economic conditions. I. Series: Research paper / University of Jūbā, Population and Manpower Unit , no. 1. II. Title.
HD2346.S82 J85 1981

Jennergren, L. Peter (Lars Peter), 1944- Discrete-events simulations models in PASCAL/MT+ on a microcomputer / L. Peter Jennergren. Lund, Sweden : Studentlitteratur, c1984. 135 p. ; 22 cm. Bibliography : p. [134]-135. ISBN 91-44-22221-1 (pbk.) :
1. Computer simulation. 2. Management - Data processing. I. Title. *NYPL [JSD 86-366]*

Jennings, Diane. Self-made women : twelve of America's leading entrepreneurs talk about success, self-image, and the superwoman / Diane Jennings. Dallas : Taylor Pub. Co., c1987. 139 p. ; 23 cm. Bibliography: p. 139. ISBN 0-87833-550-1 (pbk.) : LC Card 87-16104 DDC 338/.04/088042 19
1. Women in business. 2. Success in business. I. Title.
HD6054.3 .J46 1987

Jennings, Kenneth M. Holley, William H. The labor relations process /. Chicago , c1988. xix, 714 p. : ISBN 0-03-012649-5 LC Card 87-9117 DDC 658.3/15/0973 19
HD8072.5 .H64 1988

Jennings, Patrick C. Characteristics of occupational injuries and illnesses in New Mexico, 1983 /. Santa Fe, N.M. [1983] 47 p. : LC Card 86-620786 DDC 363.1/12/09789021 19
HD7262.5.U62 N626 1983

Jennison, Peter S. Curtis, Jane, 1918- Frederick Billings, Vermonter, pioneer lawyer, business man, conservationist . Woodstock, VT , c1986. 135 p. : ISBN 0-930985-04-4 (pbk.) : LC Card 86-28103 DDC 385/.092/4 B 19
HE2754.B5 C87 1986

Jens, Uwe, 1935- Die weltwirtschaftliche Herausforderung : Strukturwandel und zukunftsorientierte Strukturpolitik im industriellen Sektor / Uwe Jens.1. Aufl. Baden-Baden : Nomos, 1986. 182 p. : 1 ill. ; 23 cm. Bibliography: p. 179-182. ISBN 3-7890-1335-8 (Deut. Bibl.) LC Card 87-146574
1. Industry and state - Germany, West. 2. Germany, West - Industries. 3. Competition, International. I. Title.
HD3616.G4 J46 1986

Jensen, An-Magritt. Flere i yrke--færre barn? : om endringer i barnetall, utdanning og yrkesaktivitet = Working mothers--fewer children? : about changes in number of children, education, and employment / av An-Magritt Jensen. Oslo : Statistisk sentralbyrå : I kommisjon hos H. Aschehoug og Universitetsforlaget, 1983. 59 p. : ill. ; 24 cm. (Artikler fra Statistisk sentralbyrå, 0085-431X . 147) English and Norwegian. Bibliography: p. 57-59. ISBN 82-537-2007-6 : LC Card 84-163552
1. Family size - Norway. 2. Fertility, Human - Norway. 3. Women - Employment - Norway. I. Title. II. Title: Working mothers--fewer children?. III. Series.
HA1503 .A45 nr. 147 HQ762.N8

Jensen, Anne Hyldegård. Dansk industripolitik . [Århus] , 1983. 143 p. : LC Card 84-164502
HD3616.D43 D35 1983

Jensen, John, 1930- Davis, William, 1933- The corporate infighter's handbook . London , 1984. 144 p. : ISBN 0-283-99133-X (pbk.) : LC Card 85-240558 DDC 650.1 19
HF5386 .D325 1984 *NYPL [JLE 87-618]*

Jensen, Kenneth E.
Utah affirmative action information, 1985. [Salt Lake City] : Utah Dept. of Security Employment Security, [1986] i, 253 p. ; 22 x 29 cm. Cover title. LC Card 86-622873 DDC 331.11/43 19
1. Labor supply - Utah - Statistics. 2. Women - Employment - Utah - Statistics. 3. Minorities - Employment - Utah - Statistics. I. McGarry, Brad M. II. Title.
HD5725.U8 J46 1986

Utah personal income, 1929-1979. Jensen, Kenneth E. Utah personal income, 1929-1985 / prepared by Kenneth E. Jensen. [Salt Lake City] [1986] 114 p. : LC Card 87-621301 DDC 339.2/2/09792 19
HC107.U83 I515 1986

Utah personal income, 1929-1985 / prepared by Kenneth E. Jensen. [Salt Lake City] : Utah Dept. of Employment Security, [1986] 114 p. : ill. ; 28 cm. Previous ed. published as: Utah personal income, 1929-1979. "October 1986." Includes bibliographical references. LC Card 87-621301 DDC 339.2/2/09792 19
1. Income - Utah - Statistics. I. Jensen, Kenneth E. Utah personal income, 1929-1979. II. Utah. Dept. of Employment Security. III. Title.
HC107.U83 I515 1986

Jensen, Knud Erik. Landbrugsarealer, landskabeligt og rekreativt / Knud Erik Jensen. [Copenhagen] : Den Kgl. Veterinær- og landbohøjskole, 1982. 248 p. : ill., maps ; 22 cm. Cover title. Summary in English. Bibliography: p. 246-248. LC Card 84-172974
1. Land use, Rural - Denmark. 2. Landscape protection - Denmark. I. Title.
HD736 .J46 1982

Jensen, Mogens Kjaer. see **Kjær Jensen, Mogens.**

Jensen, Niels-Erik, 1939- Andersen, Erling B. Statistics for economics, business administration, and the social sciences /. Berlin , New York , c1987. xi, 439 p. : ISBN 0-387-17720-5 (pbk. : U. S.) LC Card 87-9423 DDC 519.5 19
HB137 .A525 1987

Jensen, Uffe Ellemann- see **Ellemann-Jensen, Uffe, 1941-**

Jentz, John B., 1944- German workers in Chicago . Urbana , c1988. p. cm. ISBN 0-252-01458-8 (alk. paper) LC Card 87-10780 DDC 331.6/2/43077311 19
HD8081.G4 G46 1988

Jéquier, François. Charles Veillon : 1900-1971 : essai sur l'émergence d'une éthique patronale / François Jequier. Zürich : Société d'études en matière d'histoire économique, 1985. 142 p. : ill. ; 24 cm. (Pionniers suisses de l'économie et de la technique . 9) Bibliography: p. 138-141. LC Card 85-139330 DDC 338.092/4 B 19
1. Veillon, Charles, 1900-1971. 2. Businessmen - Switzerland - Biography. 3. Business ethics. 4. Industry - Social aspects. I. Title. II. Series.
HC395.5.V45 J45 1985

Jéquier, Nicolas, 1941- Intelligence for economic development . Leamington Spa, [Warwickshire] ; New York : xiii, 264 p. : ISBN 0-85496-520-3 : LC Card 86-32250 DDC 025/.063389 19
HD76.2 .I58 1987

Jeremy, David J. Dictionary of business biography . London , 1984. 5 v. : ISBN 0-406-27340-5 (set) LC Card 86-188034 DDC 338/.0092/2 B 19
HC252.5.A2 D53 1984 *NYPL [JLM 86-569]*

Jersey Standard. see **Standard Oil Company.**

Jerve, Alf Morten.
From research to implementation : the country boats of Bangladesh and strategies for development assistance to an indigenous transport sector : papers for the work group on aid performance and policies at the fourth

General Conference of EADI, Madrid, 3-7 September, 1984 / Alf Morten Jerve and Eirik G. Jansen. Fantoft-Bergen, Norway : Chr. Michelsen Institute, [1984] 23 leaves ; 30 cm. (DERAP publications, 0800-2045 = DERAP publikasjoner . A 322) "August 1984." Bibliography: leaves 22-23. LC Card 86-228812 DDC 386/.068 19
1. Inland water transportation - Government policy - Bangladesh - Congresses. 2. Boats and boating - Bangladesh - Congresses. 3. Economic assistance, Domestic - Bangladesh - Congresses. I. Jansen, Eirik G. II. Series: DERAP publications , no. A 322. III. Title.
HE691.6 .J47 1984

Pakistan . Fantoft, Norway [1985] xvii, 414 p. : ISBN 82-905840-4-0 (pbk.) LC Card 86-235254 DDC 338.91/481/05491 19
HC440.5 .P26 1985

Jespersen, Jesper, 1948- Lille Danmark hva'nu? : en debatbog om Danmarks økonomiske problemer / Jesper Jespersen. [Copenhagen] : Akademisk forlag, c1985. 128 p. : ill. ; 22 cm. Bibliography: p. 128. ISBN 87-500-2594-5 LC Card 85-243948
1. Denmark - Economic conditions. 2. Denmark - Economic policy. I. Title.
HC353 .J47 1985

Jessua, Claude. Histoire de la pensée économique / par Claude Jessua. Paris : Cours de droit, 1981. 494, viii p. : ill. ; 24 cm. (Cours de droit. Licence) Bibliography: p. 9-10. LC Card 87-672485
1. Economics - History. I. Title. II. Series.
HB75 .J47x 1981

Jessup, Deborah A. Benson, Fred C. Hot-mix pavement stability performance versus laboratory test results /. College Station, Tex. [1985] xi, 225 p. : LC Card 86-620969 DDC 380.5 s 625.8/5 19
HE203 .T43 no. 285-1 TE200

JESUITS - MISSIONS - BRAZIL - RIO DE JANEIRO - HISTORY.
Freitas, Benedicto. Santa Cruz . Rio de Janeiro , 1985-1987. 3 v. : LC Card 86-225964
HD1471.B72 R564 1985

Jesus, Society of. see **Jesuits.**

Jeunes en transit . Galland, Olivier. Paris , c1984. 236 p. ; ISBN 2-7082-2405-0 : LC Card 85-102779 DDC 367/.94486 19
HD6276.F72 G35 1984

JEUNESSE OUVRIÈRE CHRÉTIENNE (FRANCE) - HISTORY.
Debès, Joseph. L'appel de la J.O.C., 1926-1928 /. Paris , 1986. 292 p. : ISBN 2-204-02529-1 : LC Card 86-189508
HD8430 .D37 1986

Victor Michel . Bruxelles , c1985. 263 p., [8] p. of plates : ISBN 2-87003-189-0 : LC Card 86-163882
HD6722.5.M52 V52 1985

JEWELRY TRADE - GERMANY (WEST)
Breitenacher, Michael. Strukturwandlungen und Entwicklungsperspektiven im Musikinstrumentenbau, in der Spielwaren- und Sportgeräteherstellung und in der Schmuckindustrie /. Berlin , c1984. 188 p. : ISBN 3-428-05566-7 LC Card 84-186644
HD9999.M83 G32 1984

JEWELRY TRADE - SOVIET UNION - LABOR PRODUCTIVITY.
Ėkonomicheskie funktsii upravleniia proizvoditel'nym trudom /. Kiev , 1986. 167 p. ; LC Card 87-152432
HD9705.S595 E37 1986

JEWISH ANARCHISTS - ARGENTINA - BUENOS AIRES.

JEWISH-ARAB RELATIONS - 1949-
Sarna, A. J. Boycott and blacklist . Totowa, N.J. , 1986. xiv, 270 p. : ISBN 0-8476-7489-4 : LC Card 86-1891 DDC 337.5694/0174927 19
HF1610.Z4 I87 1986
NYPL [*PXLB 86-6444]

JEWISH BANKERS - BIOGRAPHY.
Attali, Jacques. [Homme d'influence. English.] A man of influence . London , 1986. 346 p. ; ISBN 0-297-78978-3 ***NYPL [JFE 87-583]***

Attali, Jacques. [Homme d'influence. English.] A man of influence . Bethesda, Md. , 1987, c1985. xvii, 380 p. ; ISBN 0-917561-36-8 : LC Card 86-28735 DDC 332.1/092/4 B 19
HG1552.W37 A8713 1987

JEWISH HOLOCAUST (1939-1945) see **HOLOCAUST, JEWISH (1939-1945)**

JEWS AND ARABS. see **JEWISH-ARAB RELATIONS.**

JEWS - ARGENTINA - BUENOS AIRES - PERSECUTIONS.

JEWS - COLONIZATION - PALESTINE.
Bericht der Exekutive der Zionistischen Organisation an den XV. Zionisten-Kongress. Jerusalem , 1927 (Jerusalem : Azriel) 110 p., [1] folded leaf of plates : LC Card 86-122608
HD1516.P18 B525 1927

JEWS - FRANCE - BIOGRAPHY.
Muhlstein, Anka. James de Rothschild . [Paris] , c1981. 242 p., [16] p. of plates : LC Card 82-149581 DDC 332.1/092/4 B 19
HG1552.R816 M84 1981
NYPL [*PWZ (Rothschild, J.) 86-6471]

JEWS - PALESTINE - ECONOMIC CONDITIONS.
Bericht der Exekutive der Zionistischen Organisation an den XV. Zionisten-Kongress. Jerusalem , 1927 (Jerusalem : Azriel) 110 p., [1] folded leaf of plates : LC Card 86-122608
HD1516.P18 B525 1927

Bernstein, Deborah. The struggle for equality . New York , 1987. x, 208 p. : ISBN 0-275-92139-5 (alk. paper) : LC Card 86-8203 DDC 305.4/3/0095694 19
HD6182.2 .B47 1986 ***NYPL [JLE 87-1462]***

JEWS - POLAND - WARSAW - PERSECUTIONS.
American Jewish Joint Distribution Committee. [Choroba głodowa. English.] Hunger disease . New York , c1979. xiv, 261 p. : ISBN 0-471-05003-2 LC Card 78-26397 DDC 616.3/9
RC627.S7 A43 1979
NYPL [*PXV (Warsaw) 86-3505]

JEWS - SPAIN - BILBAO - HISTORY.
Lafarga Lozano, Adolfo. De Bilbao y de Vizcaya sobre sus orígenes históricos y económicos /. [Bilbao? , 1976?] (Bilbao : Gráficas Loroño) 310 p. : ISBN 84-400-1414-7 LC Card 85-142805
HF3690.B5 L34 1976

JEWS - UNITED STATES - CHARITIES.
Hammer, Gottlieb, 1911- Good faith and credit /. New York , c1985. 258 p., [12] p. of plates : ISBN 0-8453-4798-5 (alk. paper) LC Card 85-13962 DDC 956.94/001/0973 19
DS151.H34 A34 1985
NYPL [*PWZ (Hammer, G.) 86-2026]

JEWS - UNITED STATES - POLITICS AND GOVERNMENT.
Hammer, Gottlieb, 1911- Good faith and credit /. New York , c1985. 258 p., [12] p. of plates : ISBN 0-8453-4798-5 (alk. paper) LC Card 85-13962 DDC 956.94/001/0973 19
DS151.H34 A34 1985
NYPL [*PWZ (Hammer, G.) 86-2026]

Jha, Ganganand. Agricultural taxation in India : a case study of Bihar / Ganganand Jha. Delhi : Capital Pub. House, 1987. vi, 199 p. ; 23 cm. Bibliography: p. [184]-186. Includes index. LC Card 87-900333 DDC 336.2/7863/095412 19
1. Agriculture - Taxation - India - Bihar - Case studies. 2. Agriculture - Taxation - India - Case studies. I. Title.
HD1443.I42 B534 1987

Jha, S. D. (Satya Dev), 1949- Arunachal Pradesh, rich land and poor people / S.D. Jha. New Delhi : Omsons Publications ; Guwahati, Assam : Distributed by Western Book Depot, 1986. viii, 228 p. ; 22 cm. Revision of the author's thesis (Ph. D.--University of Guwahati) Bibliography: p. [219]-225. Includes index. LC Card 86-902898 DDC 306/.0954/163 19
1. Arunāchal Pradesh, India - Economic conditions. 2. Arunāchal Pradesh, India - Social conditions. 3. Arunāchal Pradesh, India - Social life and customs. I. Title.
HC437.A77 J45 1986

JHĀBUA (INDIA : DISTRICT) - ECONOMIC CONDITIONS.
Pais, H. Poverty alleviation programmes . New Delhi , 1986. xii, 48, [3] p. (some folded) : LC Card 86-903597 DDC 362.5/8/09543 19
HC437.J43 P35 1986

JHANSI (INDIA : DISTRICT) - CENSUS, 1981.
Jilā janagaṇanā hastapustikā . [Lakhanaū] [1983] xi, 174, ii p., [5] folded leaves of plates : LC Card 86-903117
HA4587.J48 J55 1983

JHANSI (INDIA : DISTRICT) - SCHEDULED TRIBES - STATISTICS.
Jilā janagaṇanā hastapustikā . [Lakhanaū] [1983] xi, 174, ii p., [5] folded leaves of plates : LC Card 86-903117
HA4587.J48 J55 1983

Jharap, S. E. The production of heavy crude oil reduces fuel oil imports in Suriname / by S.E. Jharap. Paramaribo, Suriname : State Oil Co. Suriname, 1985. [25] p. : ill. ; 25 cm. "Paper to be presented at the 3rd Unitar Conference in Long Beach, California, July 22-31, 1985." Bibliography: p. [23]. LC Card 87-103716 DDC 338.4/76655/09883 19
1. Petroleum industry and trade - Surinam. I. Title.
HD9574.S752 J47 1985

Jiddah (Saudi Arabia) Hajrah, Hassan Hamza. Public land distribution in Saudi Arabia /. London , New York , 1982. xxi, 280 p. : ISBN 0-582-78301-1 LC Card 83-232929 DDC 333.1/6/09538 19
HD853.Z7 H34 1982 ***NYPL [JLE 87-1566]***

Jiggins, Janice. Gender-related impacts and the work of the international agricultural research centers / Janice Jiggins. Washington, D.C. : World Bank, c1986. x, 95 p. ; 28 cm. (CGIAR study paper, 0257-3148 . no. 17) Bibliography: p. 87-95. ISBN 0-8213-0840-8 (pbk.) LC Card 86-24709 DDC 331.4/83/091724 19
1. Women agricultural laborers - Developing countries. 2. Agricultural laborers - Developing countries. 3. Agricultural innovations - Developing countries. I. Series: Study paper (Consultative Group on International Agricultural Research) , no. 17. II. Title.
HD6073.A292 D444 1986

Jilā janagaṇanā hastapustikā : Krama 22, Uttara Pradeśa, Jilā Jhāṃsī, prāthamika janagaṇanā sāra = District census handbook : Series 22, Uttar Pradesh, District Jhansi, primary census abstract / Ravīndra Gupta (Nideśaka, Janagaṇanā Paricālana, Uttara Pradeśa). [Lakhanaū] : Nideśaka, Janagaṇanā Paricālana, Uttara Pradeśa. [1983] xi, 174, ii p., [5] folded leaves of plates : maps ; 29 cm. English and Hindi. At head of title: Census [of India], 1981. Numbered pt. XIII-B in the scheme of the national census. Chiefly statistical tables. LC Card 86-903117
1. Jhansi (India : District) - Census, 1981. 2. India - Census, 1981. 3. Jhansi (India : District) - Scheduled tribes - Statistics. I. Gupta, Ravindra, 1942-. II. India. Director of Census Operations, Uttar Pradesh. III. Title: District census handbook, series 22, Uttar Pradesh, District Jhansi, primary census abstract. IV. Title: Census of India, 1981. V. Title: Census, 1981. VI. Title: Series 22, Uttar Pradesh.
HA4587.J48 J55 1983

Jimenez, Deanna. Albano, Tracy. California employment and payrolls, April-June, 1985 /. [Sacramento] [1985] iii, 129 p. ; LC Card 86-623197 DDC 331.12/5/09794021 19
HD5725.C2 A614 1985

Jimenez, Emmanuel, 1952- Pricing policy in the social sectors : cost recovery for education and health in developing countries / Emmanuel Jimenez. Baltimore : Published for the World Bank [by] Johns Hopkins University Press, 1987. v, 170 p. ; 26 cm. Bibliography: p. 155-163. ISBN 0-8018-3501-1 : LC Card 86-27590 DDC 338.4/33621/091724 19
1. Expenditures, Public - Developing countries. 2. Developing countries - Social policy. 3. Government spending policy - Developing countries. 4. Education - Economic aspects - Developing countries. 5. Public health - Economic aspects - Developing countries. I. International Bank for Reconstruction and Development. II. Title.
HJ7469 .J56 1987

Jiménez, Félix. Perú, economía no-neoclásica, modelo de acumulación, crisis y alternativa de desarrollo no-monetarista / Félix Jiménez. Lima, Perú : Centro de Estudios para el Desarrollo y la Participación, 1986. 107 p. : ill. ; 17 cm. (Textos de contrapunto . 3) Includes bibliographical references. LC Card 87-404229 DDC 338.985 19
1. Peru - Economic policy. 2. International Monetary Fund - Peru. 3. Neoclassical school of economics. 4. Chicago school of economics. I. Title. II. Series.
HC227 .J53 1986

Jiménez, Francisco Chacón. see **Chacón Jiménez, Francisco.**

Jiménez, Jaime. (joint author) Poveda Ramos, Gabriel. Nueva alternativa para el desarrollo . Bogotá , 1974. 249 p. : LC Card 78-345029
HD1883 1974 .P68 ***NYPL [JLE 80-482]***

Jiménez, Margarita. Historia del desarrollo regional en Colombia / Margarita Jiménez, Sandro Sideri. 1a ed. Bogotá, Colombia : CIDER : Fondo Editorial CEREC, 1985. 338 p. ; 21 cm. (Serie Textos. no. 6) Bibliography: p. 325-335. ISBN 958-9061-04-4 LC Card 85-242811
1. Colombia - Economic policy. 2. Regional planning - Colombia. I. Sideri, S., 1934-. II. Title.
HC197 .J57 1985

Jiménez Ornelas, René. Los Factores del cambio demográfico en México /. México, D.F. , 1984. 422 p. : ISBN 968-231-281-7 LC Card 85-231767
HB1361 .F33 1984 ***NYPL [JLE 87-753]***

Jiménez R., Ronulfo.
Cespedes S., Víctor Hugo. Costa Rica . San José, Costa Rica , 1986. 208 p. : ISBN 997-7210-06-3 LC Card 87-404067 DDC 330.97286/053 19
HC143 .C483 1986

Cespedes S., Víctor Hugo. Costa Rica--recuperación sin reactivación . San José, Costa Rica , 1985. 238 p. : ISBN 997-7210-05-5 LC Card 86-208956
HC143 .C484 1985

Jivkov, Todor. see **Zhivkov, Todor.**

J.M. SMUCKER COMPANY - HISTORY.
Ellis, William Donohue. With a name like-- /. Orrville, Ohio , c1987. vii, 161 p. : LC Card 87-169333 DDC 338.7/664152/0973 19
HD9330.J34 J154 1987

JMA Research Institute. Robotization, its implications for management /. Tokyo, Japan , c1983. vi, 316 p. : ***NYPL [JLF 86-1055]***

Jó munkát, jó közérzetet /. Magyar, Lajosné. [Budapest] [1986?] 52 p. ; LC Card 87-148690
HD8420.5 .M33 1986

Joanette, Francois P. Funding and asset allocation decisions in corporate pension plans / Francois P. Joanette. Brookfield, Wis. : International Foundation of Employee Benefit Plans, c1986. 17 p. : ill. ; 28 cm. (Research report . rept. 86-1) "April 1986." Bibliography: p. 15-16. ISBN 0-89154-304-X (pbk.) : LC Card 87-118785 DDC 658.2/253/0973 19
1. Pension trusts - United States. I. Series: Research report (International Foundation of Employee Benefit Plans) , rept. 86-1. II. Title.
HD7105.45.U6 J6 1986

Job analysis . Ghorpade, Jai, 1936- Englewood Cliffs, N.J. , c1988. xix, 348 p. ; ISBN 0-13-510256-1 LC Card 87-14350 DDC 658.3/06 19
HF5549.5.J6 G48 1988

JOB ANALYSIS.
Elias, Hermann-Josef, 1949- Gestaltung und Bewertung von Arbeitssystemen /. Frankfurt am Main , New York , c1985. 281 p. : ISBN 3-593-33444-5 LC Card 85-143343
HF5549.5.J6 E45 1985

Ghorpade, Jai, 1936- Job analysis . Englewood Cliffs, N.J. , c1988. xix, 348 p. ; ISBN 0-13-510256-1 LC Card 87-14350 DDC 658.3/06 19
HF5549.5.J6 G48 1988

The Job analysis handbook for business, industry, and government /. New York , c1988. 2 v. : ISBN 0-471-87237-7 (set) LC Card 87-8233 DDC 658.3/06 19
HF5549.5.J6 J63 1988

Sears, Victoria Loufakis. Staffing for optimum performance /. New York, N.Y. , c1986. iv, 191 p. : ISBN 0-88057-403-8 (pbk.) LC Card 85-80707 DDC 658.3/112 19
HF5549.5.S38 S4 1986

The Job analysis handbook for business, industry, and government / edited by Sidney Gael. New York : Wiley, c1988. 2 v. : ill. ; 25 cm. Includes bibliographies and index. ISBN 0-471-87237-7 (set) LC Card 87-8233 DDC 658.3/06 19
1. Job analysis. I. Gael, Sidney.
HF5549.5.J6 J63 1988

Job attitudes : review of research and opinion / Frederick Herzberg ... [et al.]. New York : Garland, 1987. xii, 279 p. ; 23 cm. (Continuity in administrative science) Reprint. Originally published: Pittsburgh, Pa. : Psychological Service of Pittsburgh, c1957. Includes bibliographies and indexes. ISBN 0-8240-8210-9 (alk. paper) : LC Card 86-26935 DDC 331.25 19
1. Job satisfaction literature. 2. Employee attitude surveys. I. Herzberg, Frederick. II. Series.
HF5549.5.J63 J57 1987

Job changing system. Gerberg, Robert J. [Job changing system.] Robert Gerberg's job changing system . Kansas City , c1986. xxii, 265 p. : ISBN 0-8362-7932-8 : LC Card 86-17298 DDC 650.1/4 19 ***NYPL [JD 87-125]***

Job creation . D'Angelillo, Massimo, 1956- Milano, Italy , c1985. 231 p. ; LC Card 86-156936
HD5764.A6 D418 1985
NYPL [JLD 86-3248]

Job creation in America . Birch, David L. New York , London , c1987. xi, 244 p. : ISBN 0-02-903610-0 LC Card 87-8523 DDC 331.12/4/0973 19
HD2346.U5 B54 1987

JOB DESCRIPTIONS.
Catálogo de ocupações pesquisadas em Fortaleza. [Fortaleza] . 111, [1] p. ; LC Card 83-222529
HF5382.5.B7 C38 1972

Poppe, Johann Heinrich Moritz von, 1776-1854. Ausführliche Volks-Gewerbslehre, oder, Allgemeine und besondere Technologie zur Belehrung und zum Nutzen für alle Stände /. Stuttgart , Wien , 1833- v. <1 > : LC Card 87-409525 DDC 331.7/02/024042 19
HF5382.5.E84 P66 1833

JOB DESIGN. see **WORK DESIGN.**

JOB ENRICHMENT.
Britton, Paul R., 1933- Leadership is empowering people /. Lanham, MD , c1986. xxviii, 346 p. ; ISBN 0-8191-5409-1 (alk. paper) : LC Card 86-9193 DDC 658.3/14 19
HD57.7 .B75 1986 ***NYPL [JLD 86-3818]***

Odiorne, George S. The human side of management . Lexington, Mass. , c1987. xiv, 236 p. ; ISBN 0-669-15350-8 (alk. paper) LC Card 86-46314 DDC 658.3 19
HD30.65 .O35 1987

Schmied, Volker. Alternativen der Arbeitsgestaltung und ihre Bewertung . Wiesbaden , c1982. 423 p. : ISBN 3-409-38642-4 LC Card 83-187066
HD6955 .S345 1982

JOB ENRICHMENT - ADDRESSES, ESSAYS, LECTURES.
Herzberg, Frederick. The managerial choice . Salt Lake City, Utah , c1982. xviii, 360 p. : ISBN 0-913420-97-2 LC Card 81-85925 DDC 658.3/14 19
HF5549.5.I5 H47 1982
NYPL [JLE 86-2591]

JOB ENRICHMENT - UNITED STATES.
Connolly, Paul M. Promotional practices and policies . New York , c1985. 52 p. ; ISBN 0-08-029515-0 (pbk.) : LC Card 85-3421 DDC 658.3/142 19
HF5549.2.U5 C66 1985
NYPL [JLM 83-380 no.41]

Job equity and other studies in industrial relations : essays in honor of Frederic Meyers / edited by Walter Fogel. Los Angeles : Institute of Industrial Relations, University of California, c1982. 274 p. : ill. ; 22 cm. (Monograph and research series . 30) Includes bibliographical references. LC Card 82-621216 DDC 331/.0973 19
1. Meyers, Frederic - Addresses, essays, lectures. 2. Job security - United States - Addresses, essays, lectures. 3. Right to labor - United States - Addresses, essays, lectures. 4. Employees, Dismissal of - United States - Addresses, essays, lectures. 5. Industrial relations - Addresses, essays, lectures. I. Meyers, Frederic. II. Fogel, Walter A. III. Series: Monograph and research series (University of California, Los Angeles. Institute of Industrial Relations) , 30.
HD5708.45.U6 J6 1982 ***NYPL [JLD 87-273]***

JOB EVALUATION - GERMANY (WEST)
Heinrich, Herbert, 1938- Arbeitsbewertung und Disziplinierung . Spardorf , c1985. v, 281 p. ; ISBN 3-922919-67-7 LC Card 86-162759
HF5549.5.J62 H36 1985

JOB EVALUATION - HANDBOOKS, MANUALS, ETC.
Elizur, Dov. Systematic job evaluation and comparable worth /. Aldershot, Hants, England , Brookfield, Vt., USA , c1987. xxiv, 290 p. : ISBN 0-566-05113-3 : LC Card 86-25702 DDC 658.3/06 19
HF5549.5.J62 E44 1987

JOB EVALUATION - NIGERIA.
Report on survey of job evaluation practices in some Nigerian organisations /. Lagos [1981] 2, 59, [1] leaves ; LC Card 87-110199 DDC 331.25 19
HF5549.5.J62 R46 1981

Job generation : U. S. and European perspectives : conference proceedings of the National Council on Employment Policy, April 17, 1986 / Howard Rosen, editor. Salt Lake City, Utah : Olympus Pub. Co., c1986. xiv, 138 p. ; 25 cm. Conference held in Washington, D.C. Includes bibliographies. ISBN 0-913420-89-1 (pbk.) LC Card 86-31285 DDC 331.12/094 19
1. Labor supply - United States - Congresses. 2. Unemployment - United States - Congresses. 3. Labor supply - Europe - Congresses. 4. Unemployment - Europe - Congresses. I. Rosen, Howard. II. National Council on Employment Policy.
HD5724 .J63 1986

JOB HUNTING.
Bastress, Frances. The relocating spouse's guide to employment . Chevy Chase, Md. , c1987. xviii, 258 p. : ISBN 0-937623-01-6 (pbk.) : LC Card 87-16045 DDC 650.1/4 19
HF5382.7 .B375 1987

Bolles, Richard Nelson. The new quick job-hunting map /. Berkeley, Calif. , c1985. 63 p. : ISBN 0-89815-151-1 (pbk.) : LC Card 86-220490 DDC 650.1/4
HF5382.7 .B63 1985

Cantrell, Will. 101 ways to find an overseas job /. [Merrifield, VA.] [c1987] 1 v. (various pagings) ; ISBN 0-941541-00-2 (pbk.) LC Card 86-73093 DDC 650.1/4 19
HF5549.5.E45 C33 1987

Cohen, Steve, 1950- Getting to the right job /. New York , 1987. 288 p. ; ISBN 0-89480-040-X (pbk.) : LC Card 85-40899 DDC 650.1/4 19
HF5381 .C6814 1987

Cohen, William A., 1937- The student's guide to finding a superior job /. San Diego , c1987. ix, 144 p. ; ISBN 0-932238-41-6 (pbk.) : LC Card 87-4487 DDC 650.1/4 19
HF5382.7 .C64 1987

Dickhut, Harold W., 1911- The executive résumé handbook /. New York , c1987. vii, 215 p. ; ISBN 0-13-294331-X (pbk.) : LC Card 86-22692 DDC 650.1/4/024658 19
HF5383 .D469 1987

Gerberg, Robert J. [Job changing system.] Robert Gerberg's job changing system . Kansas City , c1986. xxii, 265 p. : ISBN 0-8362-7932-8 : LC Card 86-17298 DDC 650.1/4 19
NYPL [JD 87-125]

Irish, Richard K. Go hire yourself an employer /. New York , 1987. xxviii, 280 ; ISBN 0-385-23378-7 (pbk.) : LC Card 87-6896 DDC 650.1/4 19
HF5382.7 .I74 1987

Laskin, David. Getting into advertising /. New York , 1986. xiii, 272 p. : ISBN 0-345-32598-2 (pbk.) LC Card 86-90721 DDC 659.1/023/73 19
HF5828.4 .L37 1986

Lento-McGovern, Diane, 1956- Life after college . White Hall, Va. , c1987. 179 p. ; ISBN 0-932620-77-9 (pbk.) : LC Card 87-6412 DDC 331.7/02 19
HF5381 .L354 1987

Lock, Robert D., 1930- Job search . Pacific Grove, Calif. , c1988. viii, 248 p. : ISBN 0-534-08222-X (pbk.) : LC Card 87-15838 DDC 650.1/4 19
HF5382.7 .L63 1988

McAdam, Terry W. [Careers in the nonprofit sector.] Doing well by doing good . New York, N.Y., U. S.A. , 1988, c1986. xxi, 201 p. : ISBN 0-14-046820-X (pbk.) LC Card 87-23602 DDC 650.1/4 19
HF5381 .M12 1988

Moffatt, Thomas L. Land that job! /. Madison,

Wis. , 1987, c1982. vii, 152 p. : ISBN 0-910239-09-6 (pbk.) LC Card 87-4319 DDC 650.1/4 19
HF5382.7 .M63 1987

Mrkvicka, Edward F. Moving up . New York , 1985. 193 p. ; ISBN 0-688-02427-0 : LC Card 84-27272 DDC 650.1/4 19
HF5382.7 .M75 1985 ***NYPL [JLD 86-4148]***

Osher, Bill. The blue-chip graduate . Atlanta, Ga. , c1987. 238 p. : ISBN 0-934601-19-4 (pbk.) : LC Card 86-63534 DDC 650.1/4/024375 19
HF5381 .O889 1987

Payne, Richard A. How to get a better job quicker /. New York , 1987. x, 242 p. ; ISBN 0-8008-3965-X : LC Card 86-23101 DDC 650.1/4 19
HF5383 .P36 1987

Plumez, Jacqueline Hornor. Divorcing a corporation . New York, N.Y. , 1985. xxiii, 198 p. : ISBN 0-394-54457-9 : LC Card 85-40183 DDC 650.1/4 19
HF5384 .P58 1986 ***NYPL [JLE 86-2346]***

Winning the employment game [videorecording] /. Mt. Kisco, NY , 1981. 1 videocassette (52 min.) : LC Card 86-707777 DDC 650.1 11
HF5382.7

You need me [filmstrip] . Pleasantville, NY , 1986. 2 filmstrips (71 fr. each) : LC Card 86-700183 DDC 650.1 11
HF382.7

You need me [videorecording] . Pleasantville, NY , 1986. 1 videocassette (30 min.) : LC Card 87-705080 DDC 650.1 11
HF5382.7

Zey, Michael G. The right move . New York , 1987. ix, 225 p. ; ISBN 0-531-15523-4 LC Card 86-29015 DDC 650.1/4 19
HF5382.7 .Z49 1987

JOB HUNTING - DIRECTORIES.
Schultz, Gordon F. Cruise ship employment directory /. Centralia, Wash. (131 Elma Dr., Centralia 98531) , c1987. 102 p. ; LC Card 87-166826 DDC 385/.22/02373 19
HE566.E9 S38 1987

JOB HUNTING - FLORIDA.
Fencl, George. The central Florida career guide /. Altamonte Springs, FL. , c1987. 56, 48 p. : ISBN 0-942827-00-7 (pbk.) : LC Card 87-402073 DDC 650.1/4/09759 19
HF5382.75.U62 F64 1987

JOB HUNTING - FRANCE - DIRECTORIES.
150 meilleures entreprises françaises /. Paris , c1986. 313 p. ; ISBN 2-234-01894-3 : LC Card 87-107207
HF5382.75.F8 A13 1986

JOB HUNTING - ITALY.
Ferragni, Fabrizio. Guida al primo lavoro /. Milano , 1986. 271 p. : ISBN 88-17-13617-4 : LC Card 86-193250
HD6276.I7 F47 1986

JOB HUNTING - MATHEMATICAL MODELS.
Albrecht, James W. Job search and the transition to employment . Göteborg [1986] 38 leaves ; LC Card 87-158051 DDC 331.12/8 19
HF5382.7 .A43 1986

Hodeige, Christian H., 1958- Job-Search im strukturierten Arbeitsmarkt . Freiburg , c1985. 166 p. ; ISBN 3-7930-0113-1 LC Card 86-142859
HD5701.6 .H62 1985

McKenna, C. J. Uncertainty and the labor market . New York , c1985. viii, 165 p. : ISBN 0-312-82861-6 : LC Card 85-1988 DDC 331.11 19
HD5707 .M39 1985 ***NYPL [JLD 86-3666]***

Westergård-Nielsen, Niels C. Overgangen fra uddannelse til erhverv . Aarhus [Copenhagen] [1983] iii, 41 p. : LC Card 84-125491
HD5701.6 .W47 1983

JOB HUNTING - NEW YORK (N.Y.) - DIRECTORIES.
Major employers in and around New York City. Hillsdale, N.J. (P.O. Box 294, Hillsdale 07642-0294) , c1986. iv, 112 p. ; LC Card 86-211679 DDC 338.7/4/025741 19
HF5382.75.U62 N56 1986

JOB HUNTING - STUDY AND TEACHING - UNITED STATES.
Transitional career counseling from the Air Force to the private sector . Washington, D.C. , c1987. iv, 153 leaves : LC Card 87-401057 DDC 358.4/1154/0973 19
HF5382.75.U6 T7 1987

JOB HUNTING - TEXAS - DALLAS - DIRECTORIES.
Camden, Thomas M., 1938- How to get a job in Dallas, Fort Worth . Chicago, IL , c1987. viii, 490 p. : ISBN 0-9609516-9-5 (pbk.) : LC Card 86-30123 DDC 650.1/4/097642812 19
HF5382.75.U6 C353 1987

JOB HUNTING - TEXAS - FORT WORTH - DIRECTORIES.
Camden, Thomas M., 1938- How to get a job in Dallas, Fort Worth . Chicago, IL , c1987. viii, 490 p. : ISBN 0-9609516-9-5 (pbk.) : LC Card 86-30123 DDC 650.1/4/097642812 19
HF5382.75.U6 C353 1987

JOB HUNTING - UNITED STATES.
Bastress, Frances. The relocating spouse's guide to employment . Chevy Chase, Md. , c1987. xviii, 258 p. : ISBN 0-937623-01-6 (pbk.) : LC Card 87-16045 DDC 650.1/4 19
HF5382.7 .B375 1987

Birsner, E. Patricia. The 40+ job-hunting guide . New York, NY , c1987. xx, 250 p. : ISBN 0-13-329152-9 (pbk.) : LC Card 87-2438 DDC 650.1/4/024658 19
HD38.25.U6 B53 1987

Fowler, Elizabeth M. The New York times career planner /. New York , 1987. p. cm. ISBN 0-8129-1212-8 : LC Card 87-9964 DDC 650.1/4 19
HF5382.75.U6 F68 1987

Leape, Martha P. The Harvard guide to careers /. Cambridge, Mass. , 1987. ix, 181 p. ; ISBN 0-674-37564-5 (pbk.) LC Card 87-8409 DDC 331.7/02 19
HF5382.5.U5 L36 1987

Lewis, Diane, 1936- The insider's guide to finding the right job /. Nashville , c1987. 190 p. ; ISBN 0-8407-3107-8 (pbk.) : LC Card 86-33305 DDC 650.1/4 19
HF5382.75.U6 L49 1987

Lucht, John, 1933- Rites of passage at $100,000+ . New York , c1988. ix, 547 p. ; ISBN 0-942785-07-X : LC Card 87-50459 DDC 658.4/09 19
HD38.25.U6 L83 1988

Martin, Phyllis Rodgers. Martin's magic formula for getting the right job . New York , c1987. xix, 198 p. : ISBN 0-312-01065-6 (pbk.) : LC Card 87-16302 DDC 650.1/4 19
HF5382.75.U6 M37 1987

Rugh, Jack Leighton, 1911- Channels to employment for the disabled and ex-offenders /. San Gabriel, Calif. (5555 N. Charlotte Ave., San Gabriel 91776) , c1987. 89 p. : LC Card 87-402897 DDC 362.4/0484/02573 19
HD7256.U5 R75 1987

Salzman, Marian L. Wanted, liberal arts graduates . New York , 1987. xvi, 341 p. ; ISBN 0-385-24008-2 (pbk.) : LC Card 87-8846 DDC 650.1/4 19
HF5382.75.U6 S27 1987

Job mobility and private pensions /. Sahin, Izzet. Brookfield, Wis. , c1986. xv, 49 p. ; ISBN 0-89154-305-8 (pbk.) LC Card 87-129468 DDC 331.25/2/0724 19
HD7105 .S229 1986

JOB OFFERS - MATHEMATICAL MODELS.
Albrecht, James W. Job search and the transition to employment . Göteborg [1986] 38 leaves ; LC Card 87-158051 DDC 331.12/8 19
HF5382.7 .A43 1986

JOB OPENINGS. see **JOB VACANCIES.**

Job performance and chemical dependency . Voorhees, Lynda, A. Los Altos, Calif. , c1987. iii, 81 p. : ISBN 0-931961-27-0 (pbk.) LC Card 86-73172 DDC 658.3/82 19
HF5549.5.D7 V66 1987

Job placement for the industrially injured worker /. Pimentel, Richard. Northridge, Calif. (17624 Romar St., Northridge 91325) , c1987. v, 93, [1] leaves : LC Card 87-401986 DDC 650.1/4/0240816 19
HD7255 .P54 1987

JOB RATING. see **JOB EVALUATION.**

Job resources for Colorado women . Faaborg, Barbara Laue. Colorado Springs, CO , c1986. 128 p. : ISBN 0-939411-00-8 (pbk.) : LC Card 87-103489 DDC 650.1/4/024042 19
HF5382.65 .F33 1986

Job rights in the Soviet Union . Granick, David. Cambridge , New York , 1987. ix, 344 p. ; ISBN 0-521-33295-8 LC Card 86-26392 DDC 331.11/0947 19
HD5796 .G72 1987

JOB SATISFACTION.
Britton, Paul R., 1933- Leadership is empowering people /. Lanham, MD , c1986. xxviii, 346 p. ; ISBN 0-8191-5409-1 (alk. paper) : LC Card 86-9193 DDC 658.3/14 19
HD57.7 .B75 1986 ***NYPL [JLD 86-3818]***

Caple, John. The right work . New York, N.Y. , 1977. xvi, 269 p. ; ISBN 0-396-09064-8 LC Card 87-15734 DDC 650.1/4 19
HF5381 .C2634 1987

Carmignani, Fabrizo. Assenteismo e presenteismo . Milano, Italy , c1984. 211 p. ; LC Card 84-175594 DDC 658.3/14 19
HD5115 .C37 1984 ***NYPL [JLD 86-3383]***

Enke, Harald. Konsumtive Arbeit . Freiburg im Breisgau , c1983. 354 p. : ISBN 3-448-01239-4 LC Card 83-224110
HF5549.5.J63 E54 1983

Gabriel, Jürgen. Flexibilisierung der Arbeit und wirtschaftliche Instabilität . München , c1985. x, 316 p. ; ISBN 3-597-10540-8 LC Card 86-118217 DDC 331.25/72 19
HD5109 .G33 1985

Pankow, Michael. Untersuchungen zur Verbesserung der betrieblichen Arbeitssituation unter Verwendung der Akzeptanz im Rahmen von Arbeitsanalyse und Arbeitsentwicklung /. Hamburg , c1986. 1 v. (various pagings) ; ISBN 3-925630-13-9 LC Card 87-146606 DDC 658.3/14 19
HF5549.5.J63 P345 1986

Schmied, Volker. Alternativen der Arbeitsgestaltung und ihre Bewertung . Wiesbaden , c1982. 423 p. : ISBN 3-409-38642-4 LC Card 83-187066
HD6955 .S345 1982

Sinetar, Marsha. Do what you love, the money will follow . New York , c1986. p. cm. ISBN 0-8091-2874-8 : LC Card 86-30390 DDC 650.1 19
HF5381.5 .S53 1986

Strasser, Stephen. Working it out® . Englewood Cliffs, N.J. , c1988. xix, 268 p. ; ISBN 0-13-965112-8 : LC Card 87-17197 DDC 158.7 19
HD4901 .S69 1988

JOB SATISFACTION - ABSTRACTS.
Parnes, Steven. Productivity and the quality of working life /. Scarsdale, N.Y. , c1978. 43 p. ; LC Card 78-51009 DDC 658.31/4
HD57 .P33 ***NYPL [JLM 83-380 no.2]***

JOB SATISFACTION - ETHIOPIA.
Regessa Kebede. The effect of leader behavior on worker job satisfaction and job performance in Ethiopian textile factories . [Turku] , c1987. 138 p. : LC Card 87-170154 DDC 677/.0068 19
HD5658.T42 E87 1987

JOB SATISFACTION - GERMANY, WEST.
Ansprüche an die Arbeit . Frankfurt [am Main] , New York , c1984. 298 p. : ISBN 3-593-33390-2 LC Card 85-103333
HF5548.8 .A683 1984

Briam, Karl-Heinz. Arbeiten ohne Angst . Düsseldorf , 1986. 200 p. ; ISBN 3-430-11560-4 LC Card 86-159578
HF5549.2.G3 B75 1986

Huellen, Karl Konrad. Die Motivation von Arbeitnehmern im Innen- und Aussendienst des Vertriebs . Münster [1986] iv, 245 p. : ISBN 3-88660-356-3 (Deut. Bibl.) LC Card 87-114821 DDC 658.3/14 19
HF5549.5.M63 H84 1986

Tınar, Mustafa Yaşar, 1955- Humanisierung der Arbeit und Produktivität . Frankfurt am Main , New York , c1986. xiii, 296 p. : ISBN 3-8204-9542-8 LC Card 86-233418
HF5549.5.J63 T55 1986

JOB SATISFACTION LITERATURE.
Job attitudes . New York , 1987. xii, 279 p. ;

ISBN 0-8240-8210-9 (alk. paper) : LC Card 86-26935 DDC 331.25 19
HF5549.5.J63 J57 1987

JOB SATISFACTION - UNITED STATES.
Connolly, Paul M. Promotional practices and policies . New York , c1985. 52 p. ; ISBN 0-08-029515-0 (pbk.) : LC Card 85-3421 DDC 658.3/142 19
HF5549.2.U5 C66 1985
NYPL [JLM 83-380 no.41]

Quarrey, Michael. Taking stock . Cambridge, Mass. , c1986. xxii, 176 p. ; ISBN 0-88730-131-2 LC Card 86-14045 DDC 338.7/4 19
HD5660.U5 Q37 1986 NYPL [JLE 87-49]

JOB SATISFACTION - UNITED STATES - HANDBOOKS, MANUALS, ETC.
Plunkett, Jack W. The almanac of American employers . Chicago , 1985. 340 p. ; ISBN 0-8092-5407-7 LC Card 85-14908 DDC 331.2/0973 19
HF5549.5.C67 P58 1985
*NYPL [*R-Econ. 85-3166]*

Job search . Lock, Robert D., 1930- Pacific Grove, Calif. , c1988. viii, 248 p. : ISBN 0-534-08222-X (pbk.) : LC Card 87-15838 DDC 650.1/4 19
HF5382.7 .L63 1988

Job search and the transition to employment . Albrecht, James W. Göteborg [1986] 38 leaves ; LC Card 87-158051 DDC 331.12/8 19
HF5382.7 .A43 1986

Job-Search im strukturierten Arbeitsmarkt . Hodeige, Christian H., 1958- Freiburg , c1985. 166 p. ; ISBN 3-7930-0113-1 LC Card 86-142859
HD5701.6 .H62 1985

JOB SECURITY.
Mrkvicka, Edward F. Moving up . New York , 1985. 193 p. ; ISBN 0-688-02427-0 : LC Card 84-27272 DDC 650.1/4 19
HF5382.7 .M75 1985 NYPL [JLD 86-4148]

JOB SECURITY - GERMANY (WEST) - CASE STUDIES.
Steinrücke, Margareta, 1953- Generationen im Betrieb . Frankfurt , New York , c1986. 343 p. ; ISBN 3-593-33639-1 LC Card 87-137842 DDC 331.3/0943 19
HD6283.G4 S74 1986

JOB SECURITY - JAPAN.
Iida, Tsuneo, 1932- What is really unique about the Japanese economy? /. Nagoya, Japan , 1985. 13 leaves ; LC Card 87-109242 DDC 331.25 19
HF5549.5.S4 I35 1985

JOB SECURITY - QUÉBEC (PROVINCE)
Leclerc, Claudine. La sécurité d'emploi dans l'industrie de la construction au Québec . [Quebec] , c1983. xii, 275 p. : ISBN 2-7637-7028-2 LC Card 84-126505 DDC 331.25/96 19
HD5718.B92 C248 1983
NYPL [JLE 86-3170]

JOB SECURITY - UNITED STATES - ADDRESSES, ESSAYS, LECTURES.
Job equity and other studies in industrial relations . Los Angeles , c1982. 274 p. : LC Card 82-621216 DDC 331/.0973 19
HD5708.45.U6 J6 1982 NYPL [JLD 87-273]

Job Service North Dakota. Research and Statistics Section.
Finance, insurance, and real estate . Bismarck, N.D. (1000 E. Divide, Bismarck 58502) [1986] 55 p. : LC Card 86-623003 DDC 332.12/51/0009784 19
HD5718.B262 U64 1986

Mining, second quarter, 1984 /. Bismarck, N.D. (1000 E. Divide, Bismarck 58502) [1986] 43 p. : LC Card 86-623004 DDC 331.12/522/09784 19
HD8039.M5982 N675 1986

North Dakota employment and wages, 1984 /. Bismarck, N.D. (1000 E. Divide, Bismarck 58501) [1985] [3], 13, 13 leaves ; LC Card 86-623005 DDC 331.12/5/09784021 19
HD5725.N84 N73 1985

JOB SHARING.
Glaubrecht, Helmut. Arbeitszeit im Wandel . Freiburg im Breisgau , 1985. 273 p. : ISBN 3-448-01509-1 LC Card 85-216364 DDC 331.25/72 19
HD5109 .G55 1985

Meltz, Noah M. Sharing the work . Toronto , Buffalo , 1981. viii, 90 p. : ISBN 0-8020-2383-5
NYPL [JLD 82-233]

JOB SHARING - EUROPEAN ECONOMIC COMMUNITY COUNTRIES - CONGREESSES.
Neue Arbeits- und Tätigkeitsformen . Dublin, Ireland [Washington, D.C.] c1986. xvi, 339 p. ; ISBN 92-825-6418-5 LC Card 87-408469 DDC 306/.36/094 19
HD6957.E86 N48 1986

JOB SHARING - GERMANY (WEST)
Burian, Klaus. Betriebliche Erfahrungen mit neuen Arbeitszeitformen . Berlin [1984] iv, 162 p. ; LC Card 84-182592
HD5110.2.G3 B87 1984

Müller, Christoph, 1957- Organisatorische Gestaltung des Job Sharing in der Unternehmung . Köln , c1986. xiii, 404 p. ; ISBN 3-924361-12-6 LC Card 87-114139 DDC 331.25/72 19
HD5110.2.G3 M85 1986

Job stress : from theory to suggestions / John M. Ivancevich and Daniel C. Ganster, editors. New York : Haworth Press, c1987. 267 p. ; 23 cm. "Has also been published as Journal of organizational behavior management, volume 8, number 2, fall 1986/winter 1986-87/9D/--T.p. verso. Includes bibliographies. ISBN 0-86656-630-9 LC Card 87-8568 DDC 658.3/82 19
1. Job stress. I. Ivancevich, John M. II. Ganster, Daniel C.
HF5548.85 .J65 1987

JOB STRESS.
Arroba, Tanya. Pressure at work . London , New York , c1987. xvi, 192 p. : ISBN 0-07-084931-5 (pbk.) : LC Card 87-3925 DDC 658.4/095 19
HF5548.85 .A77 1987

Bamberg, Eva, 1951- Arbeit und Freizeit . Weinheim , 1986. xiv, 306 p. ; ISBN 3-407-58288-9 LC Card 87-103692 DDC 158.7 19
HF5548.85 .B36 1986

Dy, Fe Josefina F. Visual display units . Geneva , 1985. ix, 138 p. : ISBN 92-2-105083-1 (pbk.) : LC Card 86-214267 DDC 651.8 19
HF5547.5 .D9 1985

Job stress . New York , c1987. 267 p. ; ISBN 0-86656-630-9 LC Card 87-8568 DDC 658.3/82 19
HF5548.85 .J65 1987

King, Patricia, 1941- Never work for a jerk! /. New York , 1987. 356 p. ; ISBN 0-531-15522-6 LC Card 86-29014 DDC 650.1/3 19
HF5548.83 .K56 1987

Kovach, Barbara E. Survival on the fast track /. New York , c1988. xv, 240 p. ; ISBN 0-396-09027-3 LC Card 87-19940 DDC 658.4/092 19
HD57.7 .K69 1988

London, Manuel. Career management and survival in the workplace . San Francisco , 1987. xviii, 226 p. ; ISBN 1-555-42043-5 (alk. paper) LC Card 86-46334 DDC 658.3/14 19
HF5549.5.C35 L65 1987

Lucas, Martin. How to survive the 9 to 5 /. London , 1986. 175 p. ; ISBN 0-423-01930-9 (pbk.) : LC Card 86-188564 DDC 158.7 19
HF5548.85 .L825 1986

Matteson, Michael T. Controlling work stress . San Francisco, Calif. , 1987. xx, 378 p. ; ISBN 1-555-42062-1 (alk. paper) LC Card 87-45503 DDC 658.3/82 19
HF5548.85 .M378 1987

Weiss, Donald H., 1936- Managing stress /. New York, NY , c1987. 55 p. ; ISBN 0-8144-7673-2 (pbk.) : LC Card 86-47825 DDC 158.7 19
HF5548.85 .W39 1987

Wilson, James A., 1928- Managing the behavioral dynamics of internal auditing /. Altamonte Springs, Fla. [1985] xii, 112 p. : ISBN 0-89413-130-3 (pbk.) LC Card 85-169744 DDC 657/.458/019 19
HF5668.25 .W53 1985 NYPL [JLE 86-4318]

Work stress . New York , 1987. xvii, 329 p. : ISBN 0-275-92329-0 (alk. paper) : LC Card 86-30636 DDC 616.85/2 19
HF5548.85 .W67 1987

JOB STRESS - ADDRESSES, ESSAYS, LECTURES.
Human aspects in office automation /. Amsterdam , New York , 1984. xv, 322 p. : ISBN 0-444-42327-3 : LC Card 84-5917 DDC 363.1/19651 19
HF5547.5 .H85 1984 NYPL [JLF 86-892]

Job stress and blue collar work /. Chichester [West Sussex] , New York , c1985. ix, 243 p. : ISBN 0-471-90811-8 : LC Card 85-12022 DDC 158.7 19
HF5548.85 .J64 1985 NYPL [JLE 86-2412]

Job stress and blue collar work / edited by Cary L. Cooper and Michael J. Smith. Chichester [West Sussex] ; New York : Wiley, c1985. ix, 243 p. : ill. ; 24 cm. (Wiley series on studies in occupational stress) Includes bibliographies and index. ISBN 0-471-90811-8 : LC Card 85-12022 DDC 158.7 19
1. Job stress - Addresses, essays, lectures. 2. Labor and laboring classes - Addresses, essays, lectures. I. Cooper, Cary L. II. Smith, Michael J. (Michael James), 1945-. III. Series.
HF5548.85 .J64 1985 NYPL [JLE 86-2412]

JOB STRESS - CONGRESSES.
Occupational stress and organizational effectiveness /. New York , c1987. xii, 285 p. : ISBN 0-275-92281-2 (alk. paper) : LC Card 86-25250 DDC 158.7 19
HF5548.85 .O24 1987

JOB STRESS - GERMANY (WEST)
Ochs, Peter. Analyse und Bewertung ausgewählter sozialwissenschaftlichen Forschungen /. Dortmund , Bremerhaven , 1983. 102 p. ; ISBN 3-88314-245-X LC Card 83-207278
HD7708 .O28 1983

Plänitz, Günther. Das bisschen Fahren-- . Hamburg , 1983. 317 p. : ISBN 3-87975-248-6 LC Card 84-187043
HD8039.M7952 G37 1983

JOB STRESS - GREAT BRITAIN.
Davidson, Marilyn. Stress and the woman manager /. Oxford [Oxfordshire], 1983. 230 p. ; ISBN 0-85520-623-3 *NYPL [JLE 85-1426]*

JOB STRESS - PREVENTION.
Work stress . New York , 1987. xvii, 329 p. : ISBN 0-275-92329-0 (alk. paper) : LC Card 86-30636 DDC 616.85/2 19
HF5548.85 .W67 1987

Job survival skills [videorecording] : working with others / Guidance Associates, Inc. Mt. Kisco, NY : Guidance Associates, 1986, c1987. 1 videocassette (50 min.) : sd., col. + 1 program guide. Title from data sheet. In four parts. Senior high school through college students. Issued as U-matic 3/4 in. or Beta 1/2 in. or VHS 1/2 in. Shows how to create and maintain good working relationships with coworkers, supervisors, and the public. Using different work settings, illustrates why good "people skills" are vital to success on the job. LC Card 86-707971 DDC 650.1 11
1. Success in business. 2. Interpersonal relations. 3. Interpersonal communication. I. Guidance Associates.
HF5386

A job to live . Williams, Shirley, 1930- Harmondsworth, Middlesex, England , New York, N.Y., U. S.A. , 1985. 245 p. : ISBN 0-14-008426-6 (pbk.) : LC Card 87-118827 DDC 331.1 19
HD6331 .W53 1985

JOB TRAINING. see **OCCUPATIONAL TRAINING.**

Job training under the new federalism : JTPA in the industrial heartland : report to the Subcommittee on Employment Opportunities, Committee on Education and Labor, U. S. House of Representatives / Gary Orfield ... [et al.]. [Chicago?] : Illinois Unemployment and Job Training Research Project, University of Chicago, 1986. ii, 299 p. : ill. ; 23 cm. Bibliography: p. 285-299. LC Card 86-203209 DDC 331.25/92/0973 19
1. Occupational training - United States. 2. Occupational training - Government policy - United States. I. Orfield, Gary. II. United States. Congress. House. Committee on Education and Labor. Subcommittee on Employment Opportunities. III. Illinois Unemployment and Job Training Research

Project.
HD5715.2 .J63 1986

Job turnover and interregional migration [microform] /. Rogerson, Peter. Iowa City , 1981. 25 p. : *NYPL [*ZT-1564 no.31]*

JOB VACANCIES.
The role of large firms in local job creation . Paris [Washington, D.C.] c1986. 31 p. ; LC Card 87-130519 DDC 331.12/4 19
HD5710.5 .R65 1986

JOB VACANCIES - GERMANY (WEST) - MATHEMATICAL MODELS.
Hull, Christopher J. Helping small firms grow . New York , c1987. 228 p. : ISBN 0-7099-4791-7 LC Card 87-15728 DDC 338.6/42 19
HD2346.G3 .H786 1987

JOB VACANCIES - IOWA - FORECASTING - STATISTICS.
Industry projections, occupational projections, 1985-1988, State of Iowa. [Iowa City] [1986] [42] leaves ; LC Card 86-622540 DDC 331.12/09777/021 19
HD5725.I8 I53 1986

JOB VACANCIES - MAINE - FORECASTING - STATISTICS.
Maine occupational employment in 1984 and projected to 1995 /. Augusta, Me. (20 Union St., Augusta 04330) [1986] 32 leaves ; LC Card 87-620754 DDC 331.12/09741/021 19
HD5725.M3 M386 1986

JOB VACANCIES - MAINE - STATISTICS.
Maine occupational employment in 1984 and projected to 1995 /. Auqusta, Me. (20 Union St., Augusta 04330) [1986] 32 leaves ; LC Card 87-620754 DDC 331.12/09741/021 19
HD5725.M3 M386 1986

JOB VACANCIES - NEBRASKA - STATISTICS.
Greater Nebraska job prospects, 1983-1988 /. [Lincoln, Neb.] [1985] ii, 54 p. : LC Card 86-622213 DDC 331.12/09781/021 19
HD5725.N2 G74 1985

[Nebraska job prospects] 1983-1988. [Lincoln, Neb. (550 South 16th St., Lincoln 68509) , <1985- >] v. <1, 5-9 > : LC Card 86-622062 DDC 331.12/09782/021 19
HD5725.N2 N474 1985

JOB VACANCIES - NEW JERSEY - STATISTICS.
Sheppard, Thomas M. Occupational outlook for New Jersey and JTPA labor market areas, 1982-1990 [microform]. Trenton, N.J. [1984] ii leaves, 50 p. ; LC Card 84-623480 DDC 331.12/09749 19
HD5725.N5 S47 1984
*NYPL [*ZT-1745 no.24]*

JOB VACANCIES - ONTARIO - STATISTICS.
Historical trends in job vacancies by major occupation groups . Toronto, Ont. [1976] 26 p. : LC Card 82-213963 DDC 331.2 s 331.12/4/09713021 19
HD5729.O6 E46 no. 16

JOB VACANCIES - PENNSYLVANIA - STATISTICS.
Pennsylvania occupational trends and outlook for total civilian employment, 1980 and projected 1990 /. Harrisburg, Pa. , 1984. ii, 98 p. : *NYPL [JLF 87-706]*

JOB VACANCIES - SOUTH CAROLINA.
Meeting labor needs in South Carolina . Columbia, S.C. (2221 Devine St., Suite 420, Columbia 29205) [1986] 52 leaves ; LC Card 86-623031 DDC 331.12/3/09757 19
HD5725.S6 M44 1986

JOB VACANCIES - SOUTH DAKOTA - STATISTICS.
South Dakota occupational wage information . Aberdeen, S.D. (P.O. Box 4730, Aberdeen 57402-4730) [1986] 97 p. ; LC Card 86-622996 DDC 331.2/9783 19
HD4976.S65 S68 1986

JOB VACANCIES - UNITED STATES.
Birch, David L. Job creation in America . New York , London , c1987. xi, 244 p. : ISBN 0-02-903610-0 LC Card 87-8523 DDC 331.12/4/0973 19
HD2346.U5 B54 1987

Jobb i framtid? : tankar om industriarbetet i 90-talets datorsamhälle : antologi / sammanställd av Jan-Erik Ekenhill och Bo Hedberg. Stockholm : Akademilitteratur, c1983. 121 p. : ill. ; 21 cm. ISBN 91-7410-270-2 : LC Card 84-103510
1. Economic forecasting - Sweden. 2. Sweden - Economic conditions - 1945-. 3. Business - Sweden - Data processing - Forecasting. 4. Industrial management - Sweden - Data processing - Forecasting. I. Ekenhill, Jan-Erik. II. Hedberg, Bo, 1944-.
HC375 .J53 1983

Jobin, Jacques. Mesure et incidence des dépenses fiscales au Québec / par Jacques Jobin et Jean-Marie Dufour. Montréal : Département de science économique et Centre de recherche en développement économique, Université de Montréal, [1984] 27 p. ; 28 cm. (Cahier, 0709-9231 . 8511) "Décembre 1984." Bibliography: p. 25-27. LC Card 85-169988
1. Income tax - Canada - Deductions. 2. Tax expenditures - Canada. I. Dufour, Jean-Marie. II. Series: Cahier (Université de Montréal. Département de sciences économiques) , 8511. III. Title.
HB3 .C3 vol. 8511 HJ4662.A45

JOBS. see **OCCUPATIONS; PROFESSIONS.**

Jobs and gender . Bose, Christine E. New York , 1985. xiv, 206 p. ; ISBN 0-03-071692-6 (alk. paper) : LC Card 85-6305 DDC 305.4/3/00973 19
HD6058 .B67 1985 *NYPL [JLE 86-3694]*

Jobs and Skills Programme for Africa.
Bardouille, R. (Raj) Women's employment patterns, discrimination, and promotion of equality in Zambia /. [Lusaka? , 1985]. ii, 160 leaves ; LC Card 87-980054 DDC 331.4/133/096894 19
HD6212.5 .B37 1985

Dynamique de l'emploi dans un système sahélien, le Niger . Addis Abéba , 1980. lxxii, 301 p. ; ISBN 92-2-202351-X : LC Card 82-980599
HD5846.7.A6 D95 1980

Eléments pour une stratégie d'emploi dans les zones rurales au Bénin : rapport soumis au gouvernement de la République populaire du Bénin / par une mission d'assistance technique du PECTA. Addis Abeba : Organisation internationale du travail, Programme des emplois et des compétences techniques pour l'Afrique, [1980] xii, 70, 5 p. : ill. ; 29 cm. "Juillet 1980." Bibliography: p. 3-5 (3rd group) LC Card 87-100360
1. Manpower policy, Rural - Benin. 2. Rural development - Benin. 3. Benin - Rural conditions. I. Title.
HD5846.3.A6 J63 1980

Emploi d'abord . Addis Abeba , 1982. xxxviii, 499 p. ; LC Card 84-983423
hD5846.3.A6 E47 1982

L'Emploi des femmes ... /. Addis-Abéba , 1985. 7 v. : ISBN 92-2-205192-0 (v. 1) LC Card 86-981198
HD6216 .E46 1985

Emploi et formation en Haute-Volta . Addis-Abéba , 1983. x, 142 p. : LC Card 85-981183
HD5847.5.A6 E48 1983

Emploi, potentialités et priorités au Mali . Addi Abeba , c1984. xix, 266 p. : ISBN 92-2-203954-8 : LC Card 85-980540
HD5847.3.A6 E47 1984
NYPL [JLE 86-484]

Employment and development in Lesotho . Addis Ababa , 1983. ii, 229 p. ; ISBN 92-2-103780-0 LC Card 84-980769 DDC 331.12/09681/6 19
HD5842.7.A6 E46 1983

Employment promotion in Tanzania . Addis Ababa , 1986. ii leaves, 107 p. ; LC Card 87-980150 DDC 331.11/09678 19
HD5841.3.A6 E46 1986

Gozo, K. M. Le secteur non structuré d'Antananarivo . Addis-Abéba , c1985. vi, 175 p. : LC Card 85-981181
HD2346.M282 A574 1985

Gozo, K. M. Le secteur non structuré de Kinshasa . Addis Abéba , c1985. iii, 64, [8] p. : ISBN 92-2-100538-0 LC Card 85-981182
HD2346.Z27 K54 1985

The Informal sector in Africa /. Addis Ababa , 1984. 2, iii, 149 p. ; ISBN 92-2-103785-1 LC Card 87-106188 DDC 381 19
HD2346.A55 I19 1984

JASPA Steering Group Meeting on Priority Employment Policies and Projects for Africa (1985 : Addis Ababa, Ethiopia) Report of JASPA Steering Group Meeting on Priority Employment Policies and Projects for Africa. Addis Ababa , 1986. 43 leaves ; LC Card 87-980227 DDC 331.12/042/096 19
HD5837.A6 J37 1985

Livingstone, Ian. Rural development, employment and incomes in Kenya /. Aldershot, Hants , Brookfield, Vermont , 1986. xx, 389 p. : ISBN 0-566-00990-0
NYPL [Sc D 86-728]

Livingstone, Ian. Youth employment & youth employment programmes in Africa . Addis Ababa , 1986. 7 v. : ISBN 92-2-105527-2 (pbk. : v. 1) LC Card 87-980143 DDC 331.3/4/096 19
HD6276.A32 L58 1986

Mamder, Josué Sandjiman. Les effets de la crise mondiale actuelle sur l'économie et la population gabonaises /. Addis Abéba , c1984. 34 p. ; ISBN 92-2-203795-2 LC Card 86-215256
HC975 .M36 1984

Migrations rurales et urbanisation en République populaire du Congo. Addis Ababa , 1984. x, 168 p. : LC Card 84-980878
HB2125.A3 M54 1984

Les Programmes spéciaux d'emploi et de formation de la jeunesse ... Addis Abéba , 1985- v. <1-6 > : LC Card 86-981200
HD6276.A3 P76 1985

Ribeiro, Sérgio. Situação e perspectivas dos recursos humanos na República da Guiné-Bissau /. Addis Ababa [1984 or 1985] 49, 19 p., [8] leaves : LC Card 85-981187 DDC 331.11/0966/57 19
HD5849.A6 R53 1984

Le Secteur non structuré d'Antsirabe . Addis-Abéba , 1985. iii, ii, 111, 24, 71 p. : ISBN 92-2-205256-0 LC Card 87-980400
HD2346.M282 A588 1985

Le Secteur non structuré de Mahajanga . Addis Abéba , 1985. vii, 114 p. ; ISBN 92-2-205254-4 LC Card 86-981199
HD2346.M282 M347 1985

Willaert, Y. Ressources humaines et développement régional en Côte d'Ivoire . [Addis Ababa] [1977] 3, 108, [6] leaves (1 folded) ; LC Card 82-980560
HD5846.9.A6 W55 1977

Jobs and the environment /. Haveman, Robert H. Scarsdale, N.Y. , c1979. 32 p. ; LC Card 79-15418 DDC 301.31/0973
HC110.E5 H38 *NYPL [JLM 83-380 no.10]*

The Jobs challenge : pressures and possibilities / edited by Daniel F. Burton, Jr. ... [et al.]. Cambridge, Mass. : Ballinger Pub. Co., 1986. xvi, 304 p. : ill. ; 24 cm. Based on rewritten and edited versions of papers commissioned by the UNA-USA Economic Policy Council. Includes index. ISBN 0-88410-990-9 LC Card 85-7547 DDC 331.12 19
1. Labor supply - Effect of technological innovations on. 2. Industrial relations - Addresses, essays, lectures. 3. Vocational guidance - Addresses, essays, lectures. I. Burton, Daniel F. II. United Nations Association of the United States of America. Economic Policy Council.
HD5707 .J63 1985 *NYPL [JLE 86-2190]*

Jobs for the future. Illinois . [Springfield, Ill. , 1985] 155 p. : LC Card 85-622626 DDC 338.9773 19
HD5725.I3 I517 1985 *NYPL [JLF 87-787]*

Jobs for the nineties. Jobs for the '90s [videorecording] /. Pleasantville, NY , 1987. 1 videocassette (48 min.) : LC Card 87-705264 DDC 331.7 11
HF5382

Jobs for the '90s [videorecording] / Sunburst Communications, Inc. ; producer, writer, Jack Ellis. Pleasantville, NY : Sunburst Communications, 1987. 1 videocassette (48 min.) : sd., col. + 1 teacher's guide. Title from data sheet. Photographers, John Hopkins, Ken Lax ; editor, Jean Robbins ; consultant, Sonia Scheim. Senior high school students. Issued as U-matic 3/4 in. or Beta II 1/2 in. or VHS 1/2 in. Issued also as motion picture. Helps students focus their career objectives on the most

promising job fields for the 1990s. Uses the Holland hexagon to help viewers match their job skills and abilities to the career categories described. Provides on-the-job interviews and describes each job's predicted employment opportunity for the next ten years. CONTENTS. - pt. 1. Where you fit in -- pt. 2. The doers and the thinkers -- pt. 3. The creators and the helpers -- pt. 4. The persuaders and the organizers. LC Card 87-705264 DDC 331.7 11
1. Occupations - Forecasting. 2. Professions - Forecasting. 3. Employment forecasting. I. Sunburst Communications (Firm). II. Title: Jobs for the nineties.
HF5382

JOBS, STEVEN, 1955-
Butcher, Lee. Accidental millionaire . New York , c1988. xii, 224 p., [4] p. of plates : ISBN 0-913729-79-5 LC Card 87-9414 DDC 338.7/61004/0924 B 19
HD9696.C64 A863 1988

Jobsuss . O'Connor, Nuala. Cork , cl985. 96 p. ; ISBN 0-85342-748-8 (pbk.) : LC Card 86-220513 DDC 658/.022/09417 19
HD62.7 .O36 1985

Joby, R. S. The railway builders : lives and works of the Victorian railway contractors / R.S. Joby. Newton Abbot [Devon] ; North Pomfret, Vt. : David & Charles, c1983. 200 p. : ill. ; 23 cm. Includes index. Bibliography: p. [191]-192. ISBN 0-7153-7959-3 : LC Card 84-147746 DDC 338.7/6251/00941 19
1. Railroad companies - Great Britain - History - 19th century. 2. Contractors - Great Britain - History - 19th century. 3. Railroads - Great Britain - History - 19th century. I. Title.
HE3018 .J63 1983 ***NYPL [JLD 86-918]***

Joefield-Napier, Wallace. Financial integration and interest rate linkages between North Atlantic and Caribbean economies, January 1968 to December 1976 / by W. Joefield-Napier. Trinidad busway : a user survey / by J.R. Underwood and L.G. Cadan. St. Augustine, Trinidad : Institute of Social and Economic Research, University of the West Indies, [1980] vii, 82 p. : ill. ; 25 cm. (Occasional papers / Institute of Social and Economic Research, University of the West Indies. General . 3) "July 1980." Includes bibliographies. LC Card 81-132125 DDC 332.8/2/0724 19
1. Interest rates - Caribbean Area - Mathematical models. 2. Interest rates - United States - Mathematical models. 3. Interest rates - Canada - Mathematical models. 4. Bus lanes - Trinidad. I. Underwood, John. Trinidad busway. 1980. II. Title. III. Title: Trinidad busway. IV. Title: Interest rate linkages between North Atlantic and Caribbean economies, January 1968 to December 1976. V. Series: Occasional papers (University of the West Indies (St. Augustine, Trinidad and Tobago). Institute of Social and Economic Research). General , 3.
HG1623.C27 J64 1980 ***NYPL [Sc E 86-329]***

Joerges, Bernward. Public policies and private actions . Aldershot, Hants, England , Brookfield, Vt., U. S.A. , c1987. p. cm. ISBN 0-566-05436-1 : LC Card 87-14909 DDC 333.79/16 19
HD9502.A2 P82 1987

Johan & Pieter de la Court, 1622-1660 & 1618-1685 . Wildenberg, Ivo W. (Ivo Willibrord) Amsterdam , 1986. xiii, 180 p., [21] p. of plates : ISBN 90-302-1162-8 : LC Card 87-141484
HC322.5.A2 W55 1986

Johan en Pieter de la Court, 1622-1660 & 1618-1685. Wildenberg, Ivo W. (Ivo Willibrord) Johan & Pieter de la Court, 1622-1660 & 1618-1685 . Amsterdam , 1986. xiii, 180 p., [21] p. of plates : ISBN 90-302-1162-8 : LC Card 87-141484
HC322.5.A2 W55 1986

Johanet, Gilles. Contes et mécomptes de la protection sociale / par Gilles Johanet ; préface de Pierre Mauroy. Paris : Revue politique et parlementaire : Diffusion, PUF, c1986. 175 p. : ill. ; 22 cm. (Collection de la RPP) Includes bibliographical references. ISBN 2-86702-024-4 : LC Card 86-179065
1. Social security - France. 2. France - Economic policy. 3. France - Social policy. I. Title. II. Series.
HD7175 .J64 1986

Johann Georg Bodmer (1786-1864) . Lang, Norbert. Zürich , c1987. 92 p. : LC Card 87-134606 DDC 338/.09494 s 620/.0092/4 B 19
HC395.5.A2 S3 no. 45 TJ140.B53

Johann Ulrich Aebi . Tauber, Herbert. Zürich , c1983. 84, [2] p. : LC Card 83-192282
HC395.5.A2 S3 no. 38 HD9486.S94A36

Johannes Gutenberg-Universität. Forschungsinstitut für Wirtschaftspolitik. Stöffler, Michael. Markttransparenz in der Lebensversicherung . [Mainz] [1982?] vi, 248 p. : LC Card 83-202502
HG9078.Z9 S76 1982

Johannes Gutenberg-Universität. Forschungsinstitut für Wirtschatspolitik. Die Gebührenpolitik der Deutschen Bundespost im Kleingut- und Fernmeldebereich . [Mainz] [1984?] xi, 300 p. ; LC Card 87-407592 DDC 383/.23/0943 19
HE6998 .G42 1984

Johannes Hirschmeier, die japanische Unternehmung . Hirschmeier, Johannes. Hamburg , 1986. viii, 218 p. : ISBN 3-88910-024-4 : LC Card 86-225311
HF5349.J3 H573 1986

Johannes, James M. Rasche, Robert H. Controlling the growth of monetary aggregates /. Boston , c1987. xviii, 212 p. : ISBN 0-89838-226-2 : LC Card 87-3737 DDC 332.4/6 19
HG230.3 .R37 1987

Johannes Kepler Universität Linz. Sozial- und Wirtschaftswissenschaftliche Fakultät. Moser, Reinhard. Exportmarketing /. [Linz , 1979?] 120 leaves : LC Card 84-183280
HF1009.5 .M67 1979

Johannesburg . Kallaway, Peter. Braamfontein, South Africa , c1986. v, 124 p. : ISBN 0-86975-303-7 (pbk.) LC Card 87-100567 DDC 305.5/62/0968221 19
HD8801.Z8 J6424 1986

JOHANNESBURG (SOUTH AFRICA) - RACE RELATIONS - PICTORIAL WORKS.
Kallaway, Peter. Johannesburg . Braamfontein, South Africa , c1986. v, 124 p. : ISBN 0-86975-303-7 (pbk.) LC Card 87-100567 DDC 305.5/62/0968221 19
HD8801.Z8 J6424 1986

JOHANNESBURG (SOUTH AFRICA) - SOCIAL CONDITIONS - PICTORIAL WORKS.
Kallaway, Peter. Johannesburg . Braamfontein, South Africa , c1986. v, 124 p. : ISBN 0-86975-303-7 (pbk.) LC Card 87-100567 DDC 305.5/62/0968221 19
HD8801.Z8 J6424 1986

Johannessen, Viggo. (joint author) Killi, Egil. Transportproblemer, -politikk, -forskning og -undervisning i USA. Slemdal, 1968. 65, 3, 5 l. LC Card 75-408744
HE203 .K5 ***NYPL [JLF 86-617]***

Johannsen, Hano. International dictionary of management / Hano Johannsen, G. Terry Page. 3rd ed. London : Kogan Page, c1986. 370 p. : ill., maps ; 23 cm. ISBN 0-85038-970-4
1. Management - Dictionaries. 2. Business - Dictionaries. I. Page, G. Terry. II. Title.
NYPL [JLD 86-1777]

Johansen, Alan W. Lacrosse, James. Florida index of retail activity /. [Tallahassee] [1983] [22] leaves : LC Card 86-621941 DDC 381/.1/09759021 19
HF5429.4.F6 L33 1983

Johansen, Carsten Ulstrup. Hva blev der af dem? : en analyse af mobiliteten blandt tidligere uddannelsessøgende i Ribe og Vejle amter / Carsten Ulstrup Johansen. Esbjerg : Sydjysk universitetsforlag, 1983. 168 p. : ill. ; 23 cm. Bibliography: p. 135-144. ISBN 87-85198-93-5 LC Card 83-236971
1. Labor mobility - Denmark - Ribe amt. 2. Labor mobility - Denmark - Vejle amt. 3. Labor supply - Denmark - Ribe amt - Effect of education on. 4. Labor supply - Denmark - Vejle amt - Effect of education on. I. Title.
HD5717.5.D42 R55 1983

Johansen, Leif.
[Essays. Selections]
Collected works of Leif Johansen / edited by F.R. Førsund. Amsterdam ; New York : North-Holland ; 2 v. (xiii, 974 p.) ; 25 cm. Bibliography: v. 2, p. 935-949. Includes indexes. ISBN 0-444-87833-5 (set) LC Card 87-6814 DDC 330.1 19
1. Economics - Collected works. 2. Econometric models - Collected works. 3. Economic policy - Collected works. I. Førsund, Finn R. II. Title.
HB171 .J59725 1987

Johansen, Robert C. Toward an alternative security system : moving beyond the balance of power in the search for world security / Robert C. Johansen. New York, N.Y. : World Policy Institute, c1983. 57 p. ; 23 cm. (World policy paper . no. 24) Includes bibliographical references. ISBN 0-911646-12-5 (pbk.) : LC Card 83-215670 DDC 355/.03 19
1. National security. 2. World politics - 20th century. I. World Policy Institute. II. Title. III. Series.
UA10.5 .J64 1983

Johanson, P. E. (Pär Erik) Juvonen, Risto. Sahateollisuus /. [Helsinki] . 290 p. : ISBN 951-859-690-5 LC Card 86-231276
HD9765.F4 J68 1986

Johansson, Charles B. (Charles Berthil)
Career Assessment Inventory : the enhanced version / Charles B. Johansson. [Minneapolis, Minn.] : National Computer Systems, c1986. ix, 218 p. : ill. (some col.) ; 28 cm. Bibliography: p. 217-218. LC Card 87-112723
1. Career Assessment Inventory. 2. Vocational interests - United States. 3. Vocational qualifications - United States. I. Title.
HF5381.5 .J63 1986

Manual for the Career Assessment Inventory / by Charles B. Johansson. [Minneapolis] : National Computer Systems, c1976. 93 p. : ill. (some col.) ; 28 cm. Spine title: Career Assessment Inventory. Bibliography: p. [87]. LC Card 86-219030
1. Career Assessment Inventory. 2. Vocational interests - Testing. I. Title. II. Title: Career Assessment Inventory.
HF5381.5 .J64 1976

Johansson, Mats, 1951- Frihetens idéer : USA inför 90-talet / Mats Johansson, Peter Stein. [Stockholm] : Timbro, c1986. 224 p. : ill. ; 21 cm. Bibliography: p. 216-220. Includes index. ISBN 91-7566-106-3 LC Card 86-226727
1. United States - Economic conditions - 1981-. 2. United States - Economic policy - 1981-. 3. United States - Politics and government - 1981-. I. Stein, Peter, 1953-. II. Title.
HC106.8 .J64 1986

Johansson, Per-Olov, 1949- The economic theory and measurement of environmental benefits / Per-Olov Johansson. Cambridge [Cambridgeshire] ; New York : Cambridge University Press, 1987. x, 223 p. : ill. ; 24 cm. Bibliography: p. 206-219. Includes index. ISBN 0-521-32877-2 LC Card 86-33364 DDC 339.4 19
1. Consumers' surplus. 2. Consumers' surplus - Econometric models. 3. Public goods. 4. Externalities (Economics). I. Title.
HB825 .J64 1987

John Cotter 70 years of hardware. Kantowicz, Edward R. True Value . Chicago , 1986. 270 p., [16] p. of plates : ISBN 0-89526-580-X : LC Card 86-42795 DDC 381/.45683/0924 B 19
HD9745.U5 C655 1986
NYPL [JLE 87-1449]

John Diebold on management. Heyel, Carl, 1908- Englewood Cliffs, N.J. [1972] ix, 282 p. ISBN 0-13-510214-6 LC Card 75-170643 DDC 658
HD45 .H42 ***NYPL [JLF 73-1242]***

John F. Kennedy School of Government. Energy and Environmental Policy Center. Drawing the line on natural gas regulation . New York , 1987. xiii, 267 p. : ISBN 0-89930-174-6 (lib. bdg. : alk. paper) LC Card 86-25769 DDC 338.2/7285/0973 19
HD9581.U5 D73 1987

John Hancock Financial Services. Shilling, Dana. Real life, real answers . New York , c1988. xiv, 309 p. ; ISBN 1-557-10004-7 LC Card 87-19538 DDC 332.024 19
HG179 .S465 1988

John Maynard Keynes . Skidelsky, Robert Jacob Alexander, 1939- London , 1983- v. <1 > ; ISBN 0-333-11599-6 (v. 1) : LC Card 86-217586 DDC 330.15/6 B 19
HB103.K47 S57 1983

John, Peter, 1946- Handwerkskammern im Zwielicht : 700 Jahre Unternehmerinteressen im

Gewande der Zunftidylle / Peter John.2., überarbeitete und erw. Aufl. Köln : Bund-Verlag, 1983. 304 p. ; 21 cm. Bibliography: p. 297-304. ISBN 3-7663-0597-2 LC Card 83-127836 DDC 338.6/425/0943 19
1. Artisans - Europe - History. 2. Guilds - Europe - History. 3. Small business - Europe - History. I. Title.
HD2346.E9 J63 1983 ***NYPL [JLD 87-1038]***

John Raymond Wildman . Previts, Gary John. University, Ala. , 1978. viii, 84 p. ; LC Card 86-224716
HF5604.5.W55 P74 1978

John, Richard R., 1959- Managing big business . Boston, Mass. , c1986. xxvii, 425 p. ; ISBN 0-87584-142-2 LC Card 86-7683 DDC 338.6/44/0973 19
HD2785 .M353 1986 ***NYPL [JLE 87-1360]***

John, Walter. Glasspinnerei im Isergebirge / von Walter John. Die Familien und Unternehmungen der Industriepioniere J.W. Jäckel & Co. in Wiesenthal a.N., Gebrüder Redlhammer in Gablonz a.N., Johann Schowanek in Georgenthal / von Karl Zenkner. Schwäbisch-Gmünd : Leutelt-Gesellschaft, 1984, c1974. 78 p. : ill. ; 21 cm. (Beiträge zur Geschichte der Isergebirgler und ihrer Industrie . Nr. 5) Nr. 43 der Gablonzer Bücher "Jahresgabe 1985 für die Mitglieder der Leutelt-Gesellschaft"--T.p. verso. LC Card 85-135799
1. Glass trade - Izerskie Mountains (Poland and Czechoslovakia) - History. 2. Ceramic industries - Izerskie Mountains (Poland and Czechoslovakia) - History. I. Zenkner, Karl. Familien und Unternehmungen der Industriepioniere J.W. Jäckel & Co. in Wiesenthal a.N., Gebrüder Redlhammer in Gablonz a.N., Johann Schowanek in Georgenthal. 1984. II. Title. III. Title: Familien und Unternehmungen der Industriepioniere J.W. Jäckel & Co. in Wiesenthal a.N., Gebrüder Redlhammer in Gablonz a.N., Johann Schowanek in Georgenthal. IV. Series. V. Series: Gablonzer - Bücher, Nr. 43.
HD9623.I94 J64 1984

John Wiley series in California real estate. California real estate principles /. New York , c1987. ix, 364 p. : ISBN 0-471-63274-0 LC Card 87-404650 DDC 333.33/09794 19
HD266.C2 C25 1987

The John Wiley Texas real estate series. Texas real estate finance /. New York , c1987. xviii, 365 p. : ISBN 0-471-82300-7 (pbk.) LC Card 86-29004 DDC 332.7/2/09764 19
HD266.T4 T5 1987

Johns, Gary, 1946- Organizational behavior : understanding life at work / Gary Johns.2nd ed. Glenview, Ill. : Scott, Foresman, c1988. xxii, 676 p. : ill. ; 24 cm. (The Scott, Foresman series in management and organizations) Includes bibliographies and indexes. ISBN 0-673-18418-0 (p. 4 of cover); 0-673-18418-8 LC Card 87-23296 DDC 658.3 19
1. Organizational behavior. 2. Organization. 3. Management. I. Title.
HD58.7 .J6 1988

The Johns Hopkins studies in development.
Johns Hopkins studies in development.
Morris, Cynthia Taft. Comparative patterns of economic development, 1850-1914 /. Baltimore , c1988. xi, 575 p. ; ISBN 0-8018-3507-0 (alk. paper) LC Card 87-45480 DDC 338.9/009 19
HC51 .M645 1988

Prosterman, Roy L. Land reform and democratic development /. Baltimore , c1987. xii, 313 p. ; ISBN 0-8018-3482-1 (alk. paper) LC Card 87-4188 DDC 333.3/1/1724 19
HD1333.5 .P76 1987

Riddell, Roger. Foreign aid reconsidered /. Baltimore , 1987. x, 309 p. ; ISBN 0-8018-3546-1 LC Card 87-2949 DDC 338.91 19
HC60 .R49 1987

The Johns Hopkins University studies in historical and political science. For additional listing of contents, see Old Catalog.

Johns Hopkins University studies in historical and political science .
(105th ser., 2) Nelson, John R., 1952- Liberty and property . Baltimore , c1987. xv, 221 p. : ISBN 0-8018-3440-6 (alk. paper) LC Card 86-21373 DDC 338.973 19
HC105 .N45 1987

(106th ser., 1 (1988)) Marino, John A. Pastoral economics in the Kingdom of Naples /. Baltimore , c1988. xii, 381 p. : ISBN 0-8018-3437-6 (alk. paper) LC Card 87-9196 DDC 338.1/763145/09457 19
HD9905.I73 N366 1988

(106th ser., 1) Marino, John A. Pastoral economics in the Kingdom of Naples /. Baltimore , c1988. xii, 381 p. : ISBN 0-8018-3437-6 (alk. paper) LC Card 87-9196 DDC 338.1/763145/09457 19
HD9905.I73 N366 1988

Johnsen, Erik, 1928-
Introduktion til ledelseslære / Erik Johnsen. 1. udg. [Copenhagen] : Nyt nordisk forlag : Erhvervsøkonomisk forlag, 1984, c1983. 109 p. : ill. ; 23 cm. (Virksomhedens økonomi og ledelse . 2) Bibliography: p. 99-105. Includes index. ISBN 87-17-03424-8 LC Card 85-127809
1. Leadership. 2. Management. I. Title. II. Series.
HD57.7 .J64 1983

Introduktion til ledelseslære / Erik Johnsen. 2. udg. [Copenhagen] : Nyt nordisk forlag : Erhvervsøkonomisk forlag, 1986, c1983. 134 p. : ill. ; 23 cm. (Virksomhedens økonomi og ledelse . 2) Bibliography: p. 124-130. Includes index. ISBN 87-17-03470-1 LC Card 87-108605
1. Leadership. 2. Management. I. Title. II. Series.
HD57.7 .J64 1986

Johnson-Acsadi, Gwendolyn. Acsádi, György. Policy relevance of findings of the world fertility survey for developing countries /. New York , 1986. vi, 160 p. ; LC Card 85-37681 DDC 304.6/32/091724 19
HB1108 .A28 1986

Johnson, Ampah G. Growth, equity, and self reliance . Boulder , 1987. xi, 162 p. ; ISBN 0-8133-0486-5 (pbk.) : LC Card 87-14290 DDC 338.96 19
HD3616.A36 G76 1987

Johnson and Johnson, inc.
Foster, Lawrence G., 1925- A company that cares . New Brunswick, N.J. , c1986. 175 p. : ISBN 0-9617676-1-8 LC Card 86-27478 DDC 338.7/616151/0973 19
HD9666.9.J6 F67 1986

JOHNSON AND JOHNSON, INC. - HISTORY.
Foster, Lawrence G., 1925- A company that cares . New Brunswick, N.J. , c1986. 175 p. : ISBN 0-9617676-1-8 LC Card 86-27478 DDC 338.7/616151/0973 19
HD9666.9.J6 F67 1986

Johnson, Anders. Släpp tjänsterna loss : om tjänstesamhällets myter och möjligheter / Anders Johnson. [Stockholm] : Svenska arbetsgivareföreningen, c1986. 232 p. : ill. ; 25 cm. (Tjänstesverige) Bibliography: p. 222-232. ISBN 91-7152-374-X : LC Card 86-235064
1. Service industries - Sweden. 2. Sweden - Economic conditions - 1945-. I. Title. II. Series.
HD9986.S82 J63 1986

Johnson, Arthur, 1951- Breaking the banks / Arthur Johnson. 1st ed. Toronto, Canada : Lester & O. Dennys Publishers, c1986. xi, 256 p. ; 25 cm. Includes index. ISBN 0-88619-072-X LC Card 87-120151 DDC 332.1/2/0971 19
1. Canadian Commercial Bank. 2. Northland Bank. 3. Banks and banking - Canada. I. Title.
HG2708.C36 J64 1986

Johnson, Bonnie McDaniel, 1944- Managing organizational innovation : the evolution from word processing to office information systems / Bonnie McDaniel Johnson, Ronald E. Rice. New York : Columbia University Press, 1987. xiv, 242 p. ; 24 cm. (CORPS (computing, organizations, policy, and society) series) Bibliography: p. [223]-238. Includes index. ISBN 0-231-06398-9 LC Card 87-307 DDC 652/.5 19
1. Word processing. 2. Information storage and retrieval systems - Business. 3. Office practice - Automation. I. Rice, Ronald E. II. Title. III. Series.
HF5548.115 .J64 1987

Johnson, Cameron. Goldman, Benjamin A. Hazardous waste management . Washington, D.C. , c1986. xx, 316 p. : ISBN 0-933280-30-0 : LC Card 86-2748 DDC 363.7/28 19
HD9975.U52 G65 1986 ***NYPL [JLE 87-1159]***

Johnson, Chalmers A. The Industrial policy debate /. San Francisco, Calif. , c1984. x, 275 p. ; ISBN 0-917616-65-0 : LC Card 84-6741 DDC 338.973 19
HD3616.U47 I45 1984 ***NYPL [JLE 86-4707]***

Johnson, Charles, fl. 1724-1736. see **Defoe, Daniel, 1661?-1731.**

Johnson, Charles Benjamin, 1928- Marks, Georgette A. Harrap's slang dictionary English-French/French-English /. London , 1984. 476 p. ; ISBN 0-245-54047-4 ***NYPL [JFC 86-640]***

Johnson, Charles, Captain. see **Defoe, Daniel, 1661?-1731.**

Johnson, D. Gale (David Gale), 1916- Population growth and economic development . Madison, Wis. , 1987. xiii, 702 p. ; ISBN 0-299-11130-X : LC Card 86-40447 DDC 338.9/009172/4 19
HB884 .P66547 1987

Johnson, Eugene M. Profitable service marketing / Eugene M. Johnson, Eberhard E. Scheuing, Kathleen A. Gaida. Homewood, Ill. : Dow Jones-Irwin, c1986. xiv, 303 p. : ill. ; 24 cm. Includes bibliographies and index. ISBN 0-87094-613-7 LC Card 86-70516 DDC 658.8 19
1. Service industries - Marketing. 2. Service industries - United States - Marketing. I. Scheuing, Eberhard E. (Eberhard Eugen), 1939-. II. Gaida, Kathleen A. III. Title.
HF5415.122 .J64 1986 ***NYPL [JLE 87-666]***

Johnson, Gerry. Strategic change and the management process / Gerry Johnson. Oxford, OX, UK ; New York, NY, USA : B. Blackwell, 1987. xv, 319 p. : ill. ; 24 cm. (Corporate strategy, organization, and change) "Foreword by Andrew Pettigrew"--Jacket. Bibliography: p. [301]-311. Includes indexes. ISBN 0-631-14717-9 : LC Card 87-5152 DDC 658.4/012 19
1. Strategic planning. 2. Foster Brothers - Management. I. Title. II. Series.
HD30.28 .J65 1987

Johnson, Glenn Leroy, 1918- Research methodology for economists : philosophy and practice / Glenn L. Johnson. New York : Macmillan ; London : Collier Macmillan, c1986. xx, 252 p. ; 25 cm. Includes bibliographies and index. ISBN 0-02-949840-6 LC Card 85-24240 DDC 300/.72 19
1. Economics - Research. 2. Economics - Methodology. 3. Economics - Philosophy. I. Title.
HB74.5 .J65 1986 ***NYPL [JLE 86-4300]***

Johnson, H. Herbert Webster, 1906- How to use the business library : with sources of business information / H. Webster Johnson, Anthony J. Faria, Ernest L. Maier.5th ed. Cincinnati : South-Western Pub. Co., c1984. iv, 267 p. : ill. ; 24 cm. ISBN 0-538-05750-5 (pbk.) LC Card 83-60484 DDC 027.6/9 19
1. Business libraries. 2. Business - Research - Methodology. 3. Reference books - Business - Bibliography. 4. Business - Bibliography. I. Faria, A. J. II. Maier, Ernest L. III. Title.
Z675.B8 J6 1984 ***NYPL [JLE 86-3971]***

Johnson, H. Thomas, 1938- Relevance lost : the rise and fall of management accounting / H. Thomas Johnson and Robert S. Kaplan. Boston, Mass. : Harvard Business School Press, c1987. xiii, 269 p. ; 24 cm. Includes bibliographies and index. ISBN 0-87584-138-4 LC Card 86-29474 DDC 658.1/511/09 19
1. Managerial accounting - History. 2. Managerial accounting - United States - History. I. Kaplan, Robert S. II. Title.
HF5605 .J64 1987

Johnson, Ivan C. Money and banking : a market-oriented approach / Ivan C. Johnson, William W. Roberts.3rd ed. Chicago : Dryden Press, c1988. xix, 604 p. : ill. ; 25 cm. (The Dryden Press series in economics) Includes bibliographies and index. ISBN 0-03-012518-9 LC Card 87-15002 DDC 332.1 19
1. Money. 2. Banks and banking. 3. Financial institutions. I. Roberts, William W. II. Title. III. Series.
HG221 .J667 1988

Johnson, James C., 1944- Readings in contemporary transportation /. Tulsa, OK , c1983. x, 325 p. : ISBN 0-87814-215-0 (pbk.) LC Card 82-22379 DDC 380.5 19
HE151 .R37 1983 ***NYPL [JLF 86-2000]***

Johnson, James M., 1947- Fundamentals of finance for equipment lessors : a transaction

orientation / by James M. Johnson. Arlington, Va. : American Association of Equipment Lessors, c1986. xviii, 531 p. ; 24 cm. Includes bibliographies and index. ISBN 0-912413-00-X LC Card 86-214227 DDC 658.1/5242 19
1. Industrial equipment leases - Finance. 2. Industrial equipment leases - United States - Finance. I. Title.
HD39.4 .J64 1986

Johnson, James P., 1937- New Jersey : history of ingenuity and industry / James P. Johnson.1st ed. Northridge, Calif. : Windsor Publications, 1987. 624 p. : ill. (some col.) ; 32 cm. Bibliography: p. 614-615. Includes index. ISBN 0-89781-206-9 LC Card 87-8247 DDC 338.09749 19
1. New Jersey - Economic conditions. 2. New Jersey - Industries - History. I. Title.
HC107.N5 J64 1987

Johnson, Jean, 1943- Sanitation workers, A to Z / text and photographs, Jean Johnson. New York, N.Y. : Walker, 1988. p. cm. (Community helpers series) Each letter of the alphabet introduces a topic relating to sanitation workers and their jobs. ISBN 0-8027-6772-9 LC Card 87-23129 DDC 628/.4/02373 19
1. Sanitation workers - Juvenile literature. 2. Sanitation - Juvenile literature. I. Series: Community helpers series (New York, N.Y.). II. Title.
HD8039.S257 J64 1988

Johnson, Johnny R. Auditing . Houston, TX , 1986. xvii, 919 p. : ISBN 0-87393-016-9 LC Card 86-127902 DDC 657/.45 19
HF5667 .A832 1986

Johnson, Keith (Keith H.) Hultman, Charles W. An examination of issues related to multibank holding companies /. [Frankfort, Ky. , 1983] [8], 56 leaves ; LC Card 86-620545 DDC 332.1/6 19
HG2567 .H85 1983

Johnson Library. see **Lyndon Baines Johnson Library.**

Johnson, P. S. The Structure of British industry /. London , Boston , 1988. p. cm. ISBN 0-04-338146-4 (alk. paper) LC Card 87-18803 DDC 338.0941 19
HC256.6 .S76 1988

Johnson, Paul (Paul A.) Consolidated Gold Fields : a centenary portrait / Paul Johnson. New York : St. Martin's Press, 1987. p. cm. Includes index. ISBN 0-312-00549-0 : LC Card 86-31307 DDC 338.7/6223422/0968 19
1. Consolidated Gold Fields Limited - History. 2. Gold industry - South Africa - History. 3. Gold mines and mining - History. I. Title.
HD9536.S64 C665 1987

Johnson, Peter, 1949- The British travelling post office / Peter Johnson. London : I. Allan, 1985. 104 p. : ill. ; 24 cm. Bibliography: p. 104. ISBN 0-7110-1459-0 : LC Card 86-164160 DDC 383/.143 19
1. Railway mail service - Great Britain - History. 2. Railroads - Great Britain - Rolling stock - History. I. Title.
HE6939.R2 J64 1985

Johnson, Philip McBride. Futures markets . Washington, D.C. , c1985. xiii, 325 p. : ISBN 0-8447-3592-2 LC Card 85-26705 DDC 332.64/4 19
HG6049 .F86 1985 ***NYPL [JLE 86-1532]***

Johnson, Rees C., 1938- Burns, Robert, 1938- Master forms & contracts from your copier . Tucson, AZ , c1987. 160 p. : ISBN 0-89586-513-0 (pbk.) : LC Card 86-82238 DDC 651/.29 19
HF5371 .B845 1987

Johnson, Ross H.
Ficek, Edmund F. Real estate principles and practices /. Columbus , c1983. viii, 550 p. : ISBN 0-675-20016-4 LC Card 82-73775 DDC 346.7304/37 347.306437 19
KF2042.R4 F46 1983 ***NYPL [JLE 86-2010]***

Real estate finance / Ross H. Johnson, Thomas P. Henderson. Columbus, Ohio : C.E. Merrill Pub. Co., c1985. ix, 445 p. : ill. ; 24 cm. Includes index. ISBN 0-675-20195-0 LC Card 84-61298 DDC 332.7/2 19
1. Real property - Finance. 2. Housing - Finance. 3. Real estate business. I. Henderson, Thomas P. II. Title.
HG2040 .J6 1985 ***NYPL [JLE 86-3033]***

Johnson, Stanley, 1940- World population and the United Nations : challenge and response / Stanley P. Johnson. Cambridge [Cambridgeshire] ; New York : Cambridge University Press, 1987. xxxviii, 357 p. ; 24 cm. Bibliography: p. 335-343. Includes index. ISBN 0-521-32207-3 LC Card 87-5126 DDC 363.9 19
1. United Nations - Population assistance. 2. Population policy. 3. Population. I. Title.
HB884.5 .J64 1987

Johnson, Theodore R. Katzev, Richard D. Promoting energy conservation . Boulder , 1987. xvi, 218 p. : ISBN 0-8133-7337-9 (pbk.) : LC Card 86-32587 DDC 333.79/16 19
HD9502.A2 K38 1987

Johnson, Thomas G. Local infrastructure investment in rural America /. Boulder , 1988. xxi, 291 p. ; ISBN 0-8133-7460-X (soft : alk. paper) LC Card 87-21606 DDC 332.6/7252 19
HC110.P83 L63 1988

Johnson, Virginia Anne. Greenwood, Reed. Employer concerns regarding workers with disabilities /. Hot Springs, Ark. [1985] xii, 170 p. ; LC Card 87-620863 DDC 658.3/045 19
HD7256.U5 G74 1985

Johnsson, Raoul. Yritysjohdon valmennusohjelma /. [Helsinki] [1985] 2 v. : ISBN 951-859-860-6 (v. 1) LC Card 87-101417
HD37.F55 Y73 1985

Johnston, Bruce F., 1919- U. S.-Mexico relations . Stanford, Calif. , c1987. xii, 401 p. ; ISBN 0-8047-1319-7 (alk. paper) LC Card 86-23103 DDC 338.1/872 19
HD1792 .U19 1987

Johnston, Michael, 1949- Fraud, waste, and abuse in government . Philadelphia , c1986. x, 159 p. ; ISBN 0-89727-058-4 LC Card 86-2967 DDC 336.73 19
HJ257.2 .F72 1986 ***NYPL [JLE 86-4153]***

Johnston, Moira, 1934-
Takeover : the new Wall Street warriors : the men, the money, the impact / by Moira Johnston. New York : Arbor House, c1986. xv, 395 p. ; 24 cm. Includes index. "A Belvedere book." ISBN 0-87795-784-3 : LC Card 86-10818 DDC 338.8/3/0973 19
1. Consolidation and merger of corporations - United States. 2. Tender offers (Securities) - United States. I. Title.
HD2746.5 .J64 1986 ***NYPL [JLE 86-3932]***

Takeover / Moira Johnston. New York, N.Y. : Penguin Books, 1987, c1986. xiii, 418 p. ; 20 cm. Includes index. ISBN 0-14-010505-0 (pbk.) LC Card 87-8560 DDC 338.8/3/0973 19
1. Consolidation and merger of corporations - United States. 2. Tender offers (Securities) - United States. I. Title.
HD2746.5 .J64 1987

Johnston, Robert F. Entrepreneurial science : new links between corporations, universities, and government / Robert F. Johnston and Christopher G. Edwards. New York : Quorum Books, 1987. 157 p. ; 22 cm. Bibliography: p. [141]-146. Includes index. ISBN 0-89930-260-2 (lib. bdg. : alk. paper) LC Card 87-2518 DDC 338/.06 19
1. High technology industries - United States. 2. Research, Industrial - United States. 3. Industry and education - United States. 4. Universities and colleges - United States - Graduate work. 5. Research and development contracts, Government - United States. I. Edwards, Christopher G. II. Title.
HC110.H53 J65 1987

Johnston, Tom. Demands on rural lands . Boulder, Colo. , 1987. xvi, 336 p. : ISBN 0-8133-7361-1 (pbk. : alk. paper) LC Card 87-50751 DDC 333.76/13 19
HD105 .D43 1987

Johnston, William B., 1945-
Michigan beyond 2000 / by William B. Johnston, Jane Newitt, David Reed. Lanham : University Press of America ; Indianapolis, IN : Hudson Institute, c1987. xxv, 161 p. : ill. ; 24 cm. Includes bibliographical references. ISBN 0-8191-6462-3 (alk. paper) LC Card 87-10725 DDC 338.9774 19
1. Economic forecasting - Michigan. 2. Michigan - Economic policy. 3. Michigan - Economic conditions. I. Newitt, Jane. II. Reed, David A. (David Albert), 1947-. III. Title.
HC107.M5 J64 1987

Workforce 2000 : work and workers for the 21st century / William B. Johnston, Arnold E. Packer ; with contributions by Matthew P. Jaffe ... [et al.]. Indianapolis, Ind. : Hudson Institute ; [Washington, D.C.?] : U. S. Dept. of Labor, 1987. xxvii, 117 p. : ill. ; 23 cm. Shipping list no.: 87-399-P. "June 1987." "HI-3796-RR." Item 745 LC Card 87-601910 DDC 331.12/5/0973 19
1. Labor and laboring classes - United States - Forecasting. 2. Labor and laboring classes - Research - United States. 3. United States - Economic conditions - Forecasting. 4. Twenty-first century - Forecasts. I. Packer, Arnold E. II. United States. Dept. of Labor. III. Title. IV. Title: Work and workers for the 21st century.
HD8072.5 .J64 1987

Johri, Lalit M. Business strategies of multinational corporations in India : case study of drug and pharmaceutical industry / Lalit M. Johri. New Delhi : Vision Books, 1983. v, 172 p. ; 23 cm. Spine title: Multinational corporations in India. Includes index. Bibliography: p. [165]-170. LC Card 83-906128 DDC 338.8/87 19
1. Drug trade - India - Technological innovations. 2. Corporations, Foreign - India - Management. 3. International business enterprises - Management. I. Title. II. Title: Multinational corporations in India.
HD9672.I52 J63 1983 ***NYPL [JLD 86-4081]***

Joiner, Charles W. Leadership for a change / Chares W. Joiner, Jr. ; with a foreword by William G. Ouchi. Cambridge, Mass. : Ballinger Pub., 1987. xvi, 194 p. : ill, ; 24 cm. Includes index. ISBN 0-88730-107-X LC Card 86-25940 DDC 658.4/063 19
1. Leadership. I. Title.
HD57.7 .J65 1987 ***NYPL [JLE 87-981]***

JOINT ADVENTURES. see **JOINT VENTURES.**

Joint Center for Environmental and Urban Problems. The Saddlebrook papers . [Fort Lauderdale] [Tallahassee] [1985] v leaves, 177 p. : LC Card 86-621089 DDC 338.9759 19
HC107.F63 E547 1985

Joint Conference of African Planners, Statisticians, and Demographers (4th : 1986 : Addis Ababa, Ethiopia) Agricultural credit and the mobilization of resources in rural areas. [Addis Ababa?] , 1986. 45 p. ; LC Card 86-981195 DDC 332.7/1/096 19
HG2051.A3 A73 1986

Joint Council on Economic Education. Walstad, William B. An annotated catalog of microcomputer software in economics /. New York, NY (2 Park Ave., New York 10016) , c1986. viii, 160 p. ; LC Card 86-210285 DDC 330/.028/5536 19
HB74.8 .W34 1986

Joint development financing for public works : a report for the Washington Department of Community Development / submitted by Culp, Dwyer, Guterson & Grader ... [et al.]. Olympia, Wash. (9th & Columbia Bldg., MS/GH-51, Olympia 98504) : State of Washington, Dept. of Community Development, [1986] 1 v. (various pagings) : ill. ; 28 cm. "February 3, 1986." LC Card 86-622101 DDC 338.4/3363/09797 19
1. Washington (State) - Public works - Finance. 2. Privatization - Washington (State). I. Culp, Dwyer, Guterson & Grader. II. Washington (State). Dept. of Community Development.
HD3890.W2 J65 1986

Joint Distribution Committee. see **American Jewish Joint Distribution Committee.**

Joint Donors Review and Evaluation Meeting (1982 : Nairobi, Kenya) Status of evaluation of rural access roads. Nairobi , 1982. 10 leaves ; LC Card 85-981020 DDC 388.1/09676/2 19
HE367.K43 R8578 1982

JOINT PRODUCTION COMMITTEES. see **WORKS COUNCILS.**

Joint program assessment of grain marketing in Niger : a report / prepared for the Government of Niger and the United States Agency for International Development. [Niamey, Niger] : Elliot Berg Associates : Government of Niger, [1983] 2 v. : ill. ; 28 cm. English and French. "December 1983." Includes bibliographies. CONTENTS. - v. 1. Main report -- v. 2. Background papers. LC Card 87-114421 DDC

381/.4131/096626 19
1. Grain trade - Niger. 2. Grain - Niger - Marketing. I. Niger. II. United States. Agency for International Development. III. Elliot Berg Associates.
HD9049.N552 J65 1983

Joint Seminar on Designing Jobs for Handicapped Workers. Joint Seminar on Designing Jobs for Handicapped Workers (1985 : Chicago, Ill.) Designing jobs for handicapped workers . Hot Springs, Ark. (P.O. Box 1358, Hot Spring 71902) [1986] 66 p. : LC Card 86-622317 DDC 658.3/045 19
HD7256.U5 J65 1985

Joint Seminar on Designing Jobs for Handicapped Workers (1985 : Chicago, Ill.) Designing jobs for handicapped workers : joint seminar : conference proceedings, Chicago, Illinois, December 1985 / David Alexander, chair ; Reed Greenwood, editor ; sponsors, Institute of Industrial Engineers, the President's Committee on Employment of the Handicapped. Hot Springs, Ark. (P.O. Box 1358, Hot Spring 71902) : Arkansas Research & Training Center, [1986] 66 p. : ill. ; 28 cm. Cover title: Joint Seminar on Designing Jobs for Handicapped Workers. Includes bibliographies. LC Card 86-622317 DDC 658.3/045 19
1. Vocational rehabilitation - United States - Congresses. 2. Handicapped - Employment - United States - Congresses. 3. Work design - United States - Congresses. I. Alexander, David C., 1949-. II. Greenwood, Reed. III. Institute of Industrial Engineers (1981-). IV. United States. President's Committee on Employment of the Handicapped. V. Title. VI. Title: Joint Seminar on Designing Jobs for Handicapped Workers.
HD7256.U5 J65 1985

Joint studies in public policy (National Institute of Economic and Social Research) . (13) New priorities in public spending /. Brookfield, VT , 1987. 129 p. ; ISBN 0-566-05386-1 : LC Card 86-22946 DDC 336.3/9/0941 19
HJ7764 .N49 1987

Joint Symposium on the Energy Industries: Prospects of Co-operation Between Arab Gulf States and Japan (1984 : Tokyo, Japan) The Arab Gulf States and Japan : prospects for co-operation : proceedings of a Joint Symposium on the Energy Industries--Prospects of Co-operation Between Arab Gulf States and Japan / co-sponsored by Petroleum Information Committee of the Arab Gulf States and the Japan Co-operation Center for the Middle East, and held in Tokyo, 6-7 December 1984 ; edited by Walid Sharif. London ; Dover, N.H. : Croom Helm, c1986. xiv, 216 p. : ill. ; 23 cm. Includes index. ISBN 0-7099-3393-2 : LC Card 85-12819 DDC 338.2/728/0952 19
1. Petroleum industry and trade - Persian Gulf Region - Congresses. 2. Petroleum industry and trade - Japan - Congresses. I. Sharif, Walid. II. Petroleum Information Committee of the Arab Gulf States. III. Chūtō Kyōryoku Sentā. IV. Title.
HD9576.P52 J65 1984
NYPL [JLD 86-1669]

JOINT UNDERTAKINGS. see **JOINT VENTURES.**

Joint UNDP/World Bank Energy Sector Assessment Program. Rwanda : issues and options in the energy sector. [Washington, D.C.?] : World Bank, [1982] ii, 68 p., [1] folded leaf : ill., 1 col. map ; 28 cm. (Report / Joint UNDP/World Bank Energy Sector Assessment Program . no. 3779-RW) "June 1982." LC Card 87-136863 DDC 333.79/0967/571 19
1. Energy policy - Rwanda. 2. Power resources - Rwanda. I. Series: Report / Joint UNDP/World Bank Energy Sector Assessment Program , no. 3779. II. Title.
HD9502.R932 J65 1982

JOINT-VENTURE AGREEMENTS. see **FOREIGN LICENSING AGREEMENTS; LICENSE AGREEMENTS.**

Joint ventures . Morris, Joseph M., 1949- New York , c1987. xii, 324 p. ; ISBN 0-471-01170-3 LC Card 86-28083 DDC 658/.044 19
HD62.47 .M67 1987

JOINT VENTURES - ACCOUNTING.
Morris, Joseph M., 1949- Joint ventures . New York , c1987. xii, 324 p. ; ISBN 0-471-01170-3 LC Card 86-28083 DDC 658/.044 19
HD62.47 .M67 1987

JOINT VENTURES - ARGENTINA.
La Cooperación empresarial argentino-brasileña . [Buenos Aires] , 1983. viii, 160 p. ; LC Card 87-125370 DDC 338.8/8/0981 19
HD2829 .C66 1983

JOINT VENTURES - BRAZIL.
La Cooperación empresarial argentino-brasileña . [Buenos Aires] , 1983. viii, 160 p. ; LC Card 87-125370 DDC 338.8/8/0981 19
HD2829 .C66 1983

JOINT VENTURES - CHINA.
Business opportunities in China . Menlo Park, Calif. (333 Ravenswood Ave., Menlo Park 94025-3476) , c1984. 32 p. : LC Card 86-210279 DDC 338.8/8851 19
HC427.92 .B85 1984

Campbell, Nigel. China strategies . [Manchester, Greater Manchester] [Hong Kong] , c1986. xxiv, 161 p. : ISBN 0-903808-51-X (pbk.) LC Card 86-235360 DDC 332.6/7314/0951 19
HD2910 .C36 1986

Guide to China's foreign economic relations and trade. Investment special /. Hong Kong , 1983. 342 p. : ISBN 0-9627063-8-8 : LC Card 84-177660 DDC 346.51/07 345.1067 19
HG5784 .G835 1983 ***NYPL [*OVY 86-3398]***

Joint ventures in the People's Republic of China . Hong Kong , New York, N.Y., U. S.A. , c1985. 347 p. ; LC Card 87-404122 DDC 658.1/8 19
HD2910 .J65 1985

Mathur, Iqbal. Strategies for joint ventures in the People's Republic of China /. New York , 1987. viii, 196 p. ; ISBN 0-275-92354-1 (alk. paper) : LC Card 87-7033 DDC 338.8/8851 19
HD62.47 .M38 1987

The Open policy at work /. Beijing, China [1985] 281 p. ; LC Card 86-219666 DDC 337.51 19
HF1604 .O63 1985

JOINT VENTURES - CONGRESSES.
Cooperative strategies in international business /. Lexington, Mass. , c1988. xxix, 513 p. : ISBN 0-669-14927-6 (alk. paper) LC Card 86-46160 DDC 338.8/8 19
HD2755.5 .C645 1988

JOINT VENTURES - EUROPE.
Turner, Louis, 1942- Industrial collaboration with Japan /. London , New York , 1987. 117 p. ; ISBN 0-7102-1109-0 (pbk.) : LC Card 86-26048 DDC 338.8/8 19
HD62.47 .T87 1987

JOINT VENTURES - FINANCE.
Morris, Joseph M., 1949- Joint ventures . New York , c1987. xii, 324 p. ; ISBN 0-471-01170-3 LC Card 86-28083 DDC 658/.044 19
HD62.47 .M67 1987

JOINT VENTURES - HUNGARY.
Economic associations in Hungary with foreign participation. Budapest , 1986. 24 p. ; LC Card 87-106055 DDC 346.439/068 344.390668 19
HD62.47 .E25 1986

Joint ventures in the People's Republic of China : a corporate guide. Hong Kong ; New York, N.Y., U. S.A. : Business International, c1985. 347 p. ; 28 cm. (A Business International multiclient study) Prepared by Lois Dougan Tretiak ... [et al.]. Accompanied by volume "Appendices" (355 p. ; 28 cm.). LC Card 87-404122 DDC 658.1/8 19
1. Joint ventures - China. 2. International business enterprises - Government policy - China. I. Tretiak, Lois Dougan. II. Business International Corporation. III. Series.
HD2910 .J65 1985

JOINT VENTURES - JAPAN.
Turner, Louis, 1942- Industrial collaboration with Japan /. London , New York , 1987. 117 p. ; ISBN 0-7102-1109-0 (pbk.) : LC Card 86-26048 DDC 338.8/8 19
HD62.47 .T87 1987

JOINT VENTURES - MANAGEMENT.
Morris, Joseph M., 1949- Joint ventures . New York , c1987. xii, 324 p. ; ISBN 0-471-01170-3 LC Card 86-28083 DDC 658/.044 19
HD62.47 .M67 1987

JOINT VENTURES - MIDDLE EAST.
Uhlig, Christian. Internationale Produktionskooperation im Vorderen Orient . Stuttgart , c1983. xvi, 338 p. : ISBN 3-522-68000-6 LC Card 83-217029
HD2891.9 .U44 1983

JOINT VENTURES - SOVIET UNION.
Bubnov, Boris. Foreign trade with the USSR . Oxford , New York , c1987. p. cm. ISBN 0-08-035844-6 : LC Card 87-7167 DDC 382/.0947 19
HF1557 .B83 1987

JOINT VENTURES - TAXATION - UNITED STATES.
Morris, Joseph M., 1949- Joint ventures . New York , c1987. xii, 324 p. ; ISBN 0-471-01170-3 LC Card 86-28083 DDC 658/.044 19
HD62.47 .M67 1987

JOINT VENTURES - UNITED STATES.
Turner, Louis, 1942- Industrial collaboration with Japan /. London , New York , 1987. 117 p. ; ISBN 0-7102-1109-0 (pbk.) : LC Card 86-26048 DDC 338.8/8 19
HD62.47 .T87 1987

JOINT VENTURES - YUGOSLAVIA.
Bauwens, Jan G., 1924- Industrial co-operation and investment in Yugoslavia /. Luxembourg , Washington, D.C. , 1986. viii, 161 p. : ISBN 92-825-6410-X (pbk.) : LC Card 86-216364 DDC 332.6/73/09497 19
HG5682 .B38 1986

Jolles, Paul R. Von der Handelspolitik zur Aussenwirtschaftspolitik : ausgewählte Reden und Aufsätze / Paul R. Jolles ; herausgegeben von den Direktionsmitgliedern des Bundesamtes für Aussenwirtschaft aus Anlass des vierzigjährigen Dienstjubiläums von Staatssekretär Dr. Dr. h.c. Paul R. Jolles. Bern : Stämpfli, 1983. xix, 403 p. : 1 port. ; 24 cm. French and German. Bibliography: p. 399-402. ISBN 3-7272-9209-1 : LC Card 84-119428
1. Switzerland - Foreign economic relations. 2. Switzerland - Commercial policy. 3. Jolles, Paul R. I. Switzerland. Bundesamt für Aussenwirtschaft. II. Title.
HF1573 .J65 1983

JOLLES, PAUL R.
Jolles, Paul R. Von der Handelspolitik zur Aussenwirtschaftspolitik . Bern , 1983. xix, 403 p. : ISBN 3-7272-9209-1 : LC Card 84-119428
HF1573 .J65 1983

Jolly, Richard.
Disarmament and world development /. Oxford, England , New York , 1986. xiii, 306 p. ; ISBN 0-08-031309-4 : LC Card 85-19231 DDC 338.4/7355 19
JX1974 .D515 1985 ***NYPL [JLE 86-3211]***

The Impact of world recession on children /. Oxford [Oxfordshire] , New York , 1984. xiv, 221 p. : ISBN 0-08-031329-9 : LC Card 84-14694 DDC 362.7/042 19
HV715 .I475 1984 ***NYPL [JLE 86-2315]***

Jolmes, Lothar L. V. Geschichte der Unternehmungen in der deutschen Rheinschiffahrt / von Lothar Jolmes. Köln : Handelsblatt, 1960. 164 p. : ill. ; 24 cm. (Buchreihe des Instituts für Verkehrswissenschaft an der Universität zu Köln. Nr. 17) Bibliography: p. 162-164. LC Card 85-147446
1. Shipping - Rhine River - History. 2. Shipping - Germany (West) - History. I. Title.
HE5 .C6 Nr. 17 HE619.R48

Jomo K. S. (Jomo Kwame Sundaram)
Dasar-dasar ekonomi Mahathir /. Kuala Lumpur , 1986. xvi, 187 p. : LC Card 86-943311
HC445.5 .D37 1986

Jondaryan station . Walker, Jan, 1954- St. Lucia , New York , 1988. p. cm. ISBN 0-7022-2093-0 (pbk.) LC Card 87-13816 DDC 333.3/09943 19
HD1039.Q43 W34 1988

Jones, Aubrey, 1911- Britain's economy : the roots of stagnation / Aubrey Jones. Cambridge [Cambridgeshire] ; New York : Cambridge University Press, 1985. x, 158 p. : ill. ; 22 cm. Includes index. Bibliography: p. 149-150. ISBN 0-521-30816-X LC Card 85-9649 DDC 330.941/0858 19
1. Unemployment - Great Britain - Effect of inflation on. 2. Stagnation (Economics). 3. Great Britain - Economic conditions - 1945-. I. Title.
HC256.6 .J64 1985 ***NYPL [JLD 86-1581]***

Jones, Brian. Chouraqui, Jean Claude. Public debt in a medium-term context and its implications

for fiscal policy /. [Paris, France] , c1986. 67 p. : LC Card 86-218210 DDC 339.5 19
HJ8030 .C48 1986

Jones, Bronwen. The Tunnel . Chichester , New York , 1987. xxxi, 334 p. : ISBN 0-7458-0277-X : LC Card 87-17025 DDC 385/.312/0916336 19
HE380.G73 E547 1987

Jones, Bryan D. The sustaining hand : community leadership and corporate power / Bryan D. Jones and Lynn W. Bachelor with Carter Wilson. Lawrence, Kan. : University Press of Kansas, c1986. xii, 247 p. : ill ; 24 cm. (Studies in government and public policy) Includes index. Bibliography: p. 223-239. ISBN 0-7006-0278-X : LC Card 85-24631 DDC 338.4/76292/09774 19
1. General Motors Corporation. 2. Automobile industry and trade - Michigan - Case studies. 3. Business and politics - Michigan - Case studies. 4. Michigan - Industries - Location - Case studies. I. Bachelor, Lynn W., 1947-. II. Wilson, Carter. III. Title. IV. Series.
HD9710.U53 M433 1986
NYPL [JLE 86-2386]

Jones, Charles A., 1949- International business in the nineteenth century : the rise and fall of a cosmopolitan bourgeoisie / Charles A. Jones. New York : New York University Press, c1987. xi, 260 p. ; 23 cm. Revision of thesis (doctoral)--University of Cambridge, 1974. Bibliography: p. 211-247. Includes indexes. ISBN 0-8147-4172-X : LC Card 87-11321 DDC 332.8/8/09034 19
1. Commerce - History - 19th century. 2. International business enterprises - History - 19th century. 3. Middle classes - History - 19th century. I. Title.
HF497 .J66 1987

Jones, Charles Parker, 1943- Investments : analysis and management / Charles P. Jones.2nd ed. New York : Wiley, c1988. xiv, 697 p. : ill. (some col.) ; 24 cm. Includes bibliographies and index. ISBN 0-471-85284-8 LC Card 87-23153 DDC 332.6 19
1. Investments. 2. Investment analysis. I. Title.
HG4521 .J663 1988

Jones, Christopher G. Timm, Paul R. Business communication . Englewood Cliffs, N.J. , c1987. xvi, 509 p. : ISBN 0-13-091779-6 LC Card 86-30650 DDC 658.4/5 19
HF5718 .T53 1987

Jones, Constance.
Beat the MBAs to the top! : a guide to over 500 courses most valuable to business people on their way up / Constance Jones. Reading, Mass. : Addison-Wesley Pub. Co., c1987. vii, 360 p. ; 24 cm. "A Philip Lief Group book." Includes indexes. ISBN 0-201-11310-4 (pbk.) : LC Card 87-11363 DDC 650/.07/15 19
1. Business education - United States - Directories. 2. Continuing education - United States - Directories. 3. Executives, Training of - United States - Directories. I. Title.
HF1131 .J756 1987

The 220 best franchises to buy : the sourcebook for evaluating the best franchise opportunities / Constance Jones, The Philip Lief Group, Inc. Toronto ; New York : Bantam Books, 1987. xi, 459 p. ; 23 cm. Includes index. ISBN 0-553-34385-8 (pbk.) : LC Card 86-47887 DDC 658.8/708 19
1. Franchises (Retail trade) - United States. I. Philip Lief Group. II. Title. III. Title: Two hundred twenty best franchises to buy.
HF5429.235.U5 J66 1987

Jones, David, 1954- Corporation for Enterprise Development. Building the new economy . Washington, D.C. , 1986. iv, 178 p. ; ISBN 0-9605804-2-5 (pbk.) LC Card 86-61273 DDC 338.973 19
HC110.I53 C67 1986

Jones, David C., 1935- Municipal accounting for developing countries / David C. Jones. London : Chartered Institute of Public Finance and Accountancy ; Washington, D.C. : World Bank, c1984. xii, 896 p. : ill. ; 29 cm. Includes index. ISBN 0-8213-0350-3 : LC Card 84-3623 DDC 352.1/71/091724 19
1. Municipal finance - Accounting. 2. Municipal finance - Developing countries - Accounting. I. Title.
HJ9773 .J66 1984 ***NYPL [JLF 86-1628]***

Jones, Donald L. Jones, Eric T. (Eric Thomas) Hedging foreign exchange . New York , c1987. xiv, 239 p. : ISBN 0-471-84986-3 LC Card 86-26639 DDC 332.4/5 19
HG3853 .J66 1987

Jones, Doug, 1958- Hattersley, Roy. Economic priorities for a labour government /. New York , 1987. ix, 198 p. ; ISBN 0-312-00987-9 : LC Card 87-9576 DDC 338.941 19
HC256.6 .H385 1987

Jones, E. L. (Eric Lionel) The European miracle : environments, economies, and geopolitics in the history of Europe and Asia / E.L. Jones.2nd ed. Cambridge ; New York : Cambridge University Press, 1987. xxxiii, 279 p., [1] leaf of plates : map ; 22 cm. Bibliography: p. 239-274. Includes index. ISBN 0-521-33449-7 LC Card 87-8092 DDC 330.94/02 19
1. Europe - Economic conditions. 2. Asia - Economic conditions. I. Title.
HC240 .J57 1987

Jones, Eric T. (Eric Thomas) Hedging foreign exchange : converting risk to profit / Eric T. Jones, Donald L. Jones. New York : Wiley, c1987. xiv, 239 p. : ill. ; 24 cm. Includes bibliographies and index. ISBN 0-471-84986-3 LC Card 86-26639 DDC 332.4/5 19
1. Forward exchange. 2. Foreign exchange. 3. Hedging (Finance). 4. Risk. I. Jones, Donald L. II. Title.
HG3853 .J66 1987

Jones, Geoffrey.
British multinationals . Aldershot, Hants , Brookfield, Vt., USA , c1986. xi, 212 p. : ISBN 0-566-00997-8 LC Card 86-222817 DDC 338.8/8941 19
HD2755.5 .B75 1986

The history of the British Bank of the Middle East / Geoffrey Jones ; research by Frances Bostock, Grigori Gerenstein, Judith Nichol. Cambridge [Cambridgeshire] ; New York : Cambridge University Press, 1986- v. : ill. ; 24 cm. (Hongkong Banking Group history series) Includes bibliographies and index. CONTENTS. - v. 1. Banking and empire in Iran -- v. 2. Banking and oil. ISBN 0-521-32322-3 (v. 1) LC Card 85-31359 DDC 332.1/5/0955 19
1. British Bank of the Middle East - History. 2. Banks and banking, British - Iran. 3. Banks and banking, British - Middle East. I. Bostock, Frances. II. Gerenstein, Grigori. III. Nichol, Judith. IV. Title. V. Series.
HG3270.2.A8 B755 1986 ***NYPL [JLL 87-87]***

Multinationals--theory and history /. Aldershot, Hants, England , Brookfield, Vt., USA , c1986. vii, 200 p. : ISBN 0-566-05078-1 : LC Card 85-24955 DDC 338.8/8 19
HD2755.5 .M86 1986 ***NYPL [JLD 86-1575]***

Jones, Graham. Information technology and the new accounting / Graham Jones, Terry McNamara. London ; New York : McGraw-Hill, c1988. p. cm. Bibliography: p. Includes index. ISBN 0-07-084179-9 : LC Card 87-22579 DDC 657/.028/5 19
1. Accounting - Data processing. 2. Information technology. I. Title.
HF5679 .J634 1988

Jones, H. Stanley. Marketing your financial planning services : a guide for professionals / H. Stanley Jones. New York : Wiley, c1988. xvi, 304 p. ; 25 cm. Bibliography: p. 295-298. Includes index. ISBN 0-471-85649-5 LC Card 87-26373 DDC 332.6/2 19
1. Financial planners - United States - Marketing. I. Title.
HG179.5 .J66 1988

Jones, Haydn. Accounting, costing, and cost estimation : Welsh industry, 1700-1830 / Haydn Jones ; with a foreword by Basil S. Yamey. Cardiff : University of Wales Press, 1985. ix, 285 p. ; 22 cm. Bibliography: p. [281]-283. Includes index. ISBN 0-7083-0882-1 : LC Card 85-172570 DDC 657/.09429 19
1. Accounting - Wales - History - 18th century. 2. Accounting - Wales - History - 19th century. I. Title.
HF5616.G72 W35 1985
NYPL [JLD 86-2817]

Jones-Hendrickson, S. B. (Simon B.) Public finance and monetary policy in open economies : a Caribbean perspective / Simon B. Jones-Hendrickson. [Kingston, Jamaica] : Institute of Social and Economic Research, University of the West Indies, 1985 172 p. ; 23 cm. Bibliography: p.160-170.
1. Finance, Public - Caribbean Area. 2. Monetary policy - Caribbean Area. I. Title.
NYPL [Sc D 86-830]

Jones, Jocelyn. Galli, Rosemary. Guinea-Bissau . London , Boulder , 1987. xvi, 217 p., [1] leaf of plates : ISBN 1-555-87025-2 (U. S. : lib. bdg.) : LC Card 86-28011 DDC 966/.5703 19
HC1080 .G35 1987

Jones, Lloyd, 1811-1886. Ludlow, John Malcolm Forbes, 1821-1911. Progress of the working class, 1832-1867 /. New York , 1984. xv, 304 p. ; ISBN 0-8240-5717-1 (alk. paper) : LC Card 83-48490 DDC 305.5/62/0942 19
HD8390 .L93 1984 ***NYPL [JLC 86-387]***

Jones, Lonnie L. Stoll, John R. Economic impact of the recreational boating industry in Texas /. College Station, TX [1985] xiv, 86 p. : LC Card 86-622008 DDC 330.9764/063 19
HD9993.B633 U58 1985

Jones, Louis N. Human resources management /. New York , Milwaukee, Wis. , c1987. xiv, 276 p. : ISBN 0-8247-7716-6 LC Card 86-29321 DDC 658.3 19
HF5549 .H8727 1987

Jones, Martin. Bauwens, Jan G., 1924- Industrial co-operation and investment in Yugoslavia /. Luxembourg , Washington, D.C. , 1986. viii, 161 p. : ISBN 92-825-6410-X (pbk.) : LC Card 86-216364 DDC 332.6/73/09497 19
HG5682 .B38 1986

Jones, Michael, 1937- Wilsher, Peter. Strike . London [1985] xiii, 284 p., [16] p. of plates : ISBN 0-233-97825-9 : LC Card 86-221981 DDC 331.89/2822334/0941 19
HD5365.M6152 1984 .W55 1985b

Jones, Mother, 1843?-1930.
[Selections. 1988]
The speeches and writings of Mother Jones / Edward M. Steel, editor. Pittsburgh, Pa. : University of Pittsburgh Press, 1988. p. cm. (Pittsburgh series in social and labor history) Includes index. ISBN 0-8229-3575-9 LC Card 87-25192 DDC 331.88/0973 19
1. Labor and laboring classes - United States - History. 2. Miners - United States - History. 3. Trade-unions - United States - History. I. Steel, Edward M. II. Title. III. Series.
HD8072 .J7832 1988

Jones, P. Ellis. Economics of the retail petroleum market . London , c1986. i, 79 p. : LC Card 87-134547 DDC 381/.4566553827/0941 19
HD9579.G5 G63 1986

Jones, P. M. S. Nuclear power . Chichester , New York , c1987. xvii, 416 p. : ISBN 0-471-90732-4 : LC Card 86-26714 DDC 333.79/24 19
HD9698.A2 N79 1987

Jones, Philip R., 1948- Cullis, John C. Microeconomics and the public economy . Oxford, OX, UK , New York, NY, USA , 1987. xx, 251 p. : ISBN 0-631-15552-X : LC Card 87-5169 DDC 338.5 19
HB172 .C85 1987

Jones, Robert A., MSc. Collective bargaining in South Africa / Robert A. Jones. 2nd rev. ed. Johannesburg : Macmillan South Africa, 1984. 104 p. ; 22 cm. Includes index. ISBN 0-86954-173-0
1. Collective bargaining - South Africa. 2. Trade-unions - South Africa. I. Title.
NYPL [JLD 85-1003]

Jones, Robert C., 1934- Two feet to tidewater : the Wiscasset, Waterville & Farmington Railway / Robert C. Jones & David L. Register.1st ed. Boulder, Colo. : Pruett Pub. Co., c1987. xvi, 269 p., [1] leaf of plates : ill., maps ; 29 cm. Bibliography: p. 259-261. Includes index. ISBN 0-87108-729-4 LC Card 87-2428 DDC 385/.065/741 19
1. Wiscasset, Waterville, and Farmington Railway - History. I. Register, David L., 1925-1983. II. Title.
HE2791.W76647 J66 1987

Jones, Russell, 1959- Wages and employment policy, 1936-1985 / Russell Jones with a foreword by Sir Alec Cairncross. London ; Boston : Allen & Unwin, 1987. xvii, 175 p. ; 22 cm. Includes index. Bibliography: p. 160-169. ISBN 0-04-331110-5 (alk. paper) LC Card 86-14143 DDC 339.5/0941 19
1. Wages - Great Britain - History - 20th century. 2. Unemployment - Great Britain - History - 20th century.

3. Great Britain - Full employment policies - History - 20th century. I. Title.
HD5015 .J66 1987 NYPL [JLD 87-831]

Jones, Seymour, 1931- The Coopers & Lybrand guide to growing your business / Seymour Jones, M. Bruce Cohen, Victor V. Coppola. New York : Wiley, c1988. xiii, 477 p. ; 24 cm. Includes index. ISBN 0-471-85941-9 LC Card 87-21688 DDC 658 19
1. Industrial management. 2. Business enterprises - Finance. I. Cohen, M. Bruce. II. Coppola, Victor V. III. Coopers & Lybrand WD Scott. IV. Title. V. Title: Coopers and Lybrand guide to growing your business. VI. Title: Growing your business.
HD31 .J627 1988

Jones, Stephanie (Stephanie Karen) Armstrong, John, 1944- Business documents . London , New York , 1987. xiv, 251 p. : ISBN 0-7201-1846-8 : LC Card 86-28451 DDC 651.5 19
HF5349.G7 A76 1987

Jones, Stephen F. North/south countertrade : barter and reciprocal trade with developing countries / Stephen F. Jones. London : Economist Intelligence Unit, c1984. 97 p. : ill. ; 30 cm. (Special report . no. 174) Bibliography: p. 96-97. LC Card 85-239985 DDC 382/.091722/01724 19
1. Countertrade. I. Series: Special report (Economist Intelligence Unit (Great Britain)) , no. 174. II. Title.
HF1414.3 .J65 1984

Jones, Valerie. Chavangi, Noel A. Culture as the basis for implementing self-sustaining wood fuel development programmes /. Nairobi, Kenya [1985] 24 leaves ; LC Card 87-111963 DDC 333.75 19
HD9769.F843 K433 1985

Jones, William C., 1937- The kite route : story of the Denver & Interurban Railroad / William C. Jones & Noel T. Holley.1st ed. Boulder, Colo. : Pruett Pub. Co., c1986. 159 p. : ill. (some col.) ; 29 cm. One folded leaf (ill.) inserted. Bibliography: p. 158. Includes index. ISBN 0-87108-721-9 LC Card 86-25190 DDC 385/.5 19
1. Denver & Interurban Railroad - History. I. Holley, Noel T., 1947-. II. Title.
HE2791.D383 J66 1986

Jones, Woodrow. Strand, Paul J., 1949- Indochinese refugees in America . Durham, N.C. , 1985. x, 182 p. ; ISBN 0-8223-0629-8 LC Card 84-25888 DDC 362.8/49592 19
HV640.5.I5 S77 1985 NYPL [JLE 86-4772]

Jong, Frits de. Hueting, Ernest. Naar groter eenheid . Amsterdam , 1983, c1982. 432 p. : ISBN 90-6012-531-2 : LC Card 83-184649
HD6727 .H83 1983 NYPL [JLG 87-188]

Jong, H. J. de (Herman J.) Schoonebeek, olierijk in Zuidoost-Drenthe / H.J. de Jong. [Zuidwolde] : Stichting Het Drentse Boek, 1986. 232 p. : ill. ; 28 cm. (Drentse historische reeks) Bibliography: p. 202-206. ISBN 90-6509-902-6 : LC Card 86-175279
1. Nederlandse Aardolie Maatschappij - History. 2. Petroleum industry and trade - Netherlands - Schoonebeek - History. 3. Schoonebeek (Netherlands) - History. I. Title. II. Series.
HD9575.N43 N435 1986

Jong, H. W. de. Mainstreams in industrial organization /. Dordrecht , Boston , 1986. 2 v. (x, 465 p.) ; ISBN 90-247-3363-4 LC Card 86-12345 DDC 338.6 19
HD29 .M25 1986 NYPL [JLE 87-457]

Jong, K. J. de. Schijnwerper op de detailhandel / K.J. de Jong. Deventer : Kluwer, 1986. 221 p. : ill. ; 25 cm. Includes bibliographies. ISBN 90-267-1058-5 : LC Card 86-177114
1. Retail trade - Netherlands. I. Title.
HF5429.6.N4 J663 1986

Jonshagen, I. Employment maintenance and unemployment protection for young workers. Factors and principles determining the amount and duration of unemployment insurance cash benefits : International Social Security Association, XXth General Assembly, Manila, 28 October-6 November 1980. [Geneva : General Secretariat of the ISSA, 1980] 102, 69 p. : ill. ; 30 cm. Reporter for report 19, C. Major; reporter for report 20, I. Jonshagen. Cover title. "Report 19-20." Includes bibliographical references. LC Card 86-219323 DDC 368.4/4 19
1. Insurance, Unemployment. I. Major, C. Factors and principles determining the amount and duration of unemployment insurance cash benefits. 1980. II. Title.
HD7095 .J66 1980

Jönsson, Christer, 1944- International aviation and the politics of regime change / Christer Jönsson. New York : St. Martin's Press, 1987. vi, 185 p. : ill. ; 23 cm. Bibliography: p. [167]-177. Includes index. ISBN 0-312-00463-X : LC Card 86-31328 DDC 341.7/567 19
1. Aeronautics - International cooperation. 2. Aeronautics - Government policy. 3. Aeronautics - Law and legislation. 4. Aeronautics, Commercial - International cooperation. 5. Aeronautics, Commercial - Government policy. 6. Aeronautics, Commercial - Law and legislation. I. Title.
HE9762 .J65 1987

Jonsson, Sverker, 1941- Pressen, reklamen och konkurrensen, 1935-1978 / av Sverker Jonsson. Göteborg : Ekonomisk-historiska institutionen vid Göteborgs universitet, 1982. 406 p. : ill. ; 23 cm. (Meddelanden från Ekonomisk-historiska institutionen vid Göteborgs universitet, 0072-5080 . 52) Bibliography: p. 395-406. ISBN 91-85196-24-X : LC Card 84-157282
1. Advertising, Newspaper - Sweden - History - 20th century. 2. Advertising - Sweden - History - 20th century. I. Title. II. Series.
HF6105.S8 J66 1982

Jonung, Lars. Bordo, Michael D. The long-run behavior of the velocity of circulation . Cambridge [Cambridgeshire] , New York , 1987. xiv, 181 p. : ISBN 0-521-32633-8 LC Card 86-32628 DDC 332.4/14 19
HG226.6 .B67 1987

Joosten, J. Tosco, Manuel. Aprovechamiento y dominio de las tierras en 1950-51 /. Tegucigalpa, D.C., Honduras [1952] 33 p. ; LC Card 85-197157
HD366 .T66 1952

Jordá Borrell, Rosa Ma. (Rosa Maria) Dinámica y distribución recientes de la población andaluza / Rosa Ma. Jordá Borrell. [Sevilla] : Instituto de Desarrollo Regional, Universidad de Sevilla, [1985?] 80 p. : maps ; 24 cm. (Cuadernos del I.D.R. . 1) Errata slip inserted. Bibliography: p. 78-80. ISBN 84-600-3827-0 LC Card 87-124031
1. Andalusia (Spain) - Population. 2. Population geography - Spain - Andalusia. I. Title. II. Series.
HB3620.A5 J67 1985

Jordan, A. G. Learning from local authority budgeting /. Aldershot [Hampshire] , Brookfield, Vt., USA , c1987. x, 258 p. ; ISBN 0-566-05384-5 : LC Card 87-12096 DDC 352.1/2/0941 19
HJ9423 .L43 1987

JORDAN - ECONOMIC CONDITIONS.
Seccombe, Ian J. Manpower and migration . [Durham, England] , c1981. viii, 110 p. : LC Card 84-673623
HD5812.25.A6 S42x 1981
NYPL [JLD 86-2457]

JORDAN - EMIGRATION AND IMMIGRATION.
Seccombe, Ian J. Manpower and migration . [Durham, England] , c1981. viii, 110 p. : LC Card 84-673623
HD5812.25.A6 S42x 1981
NYPL [JLD 86-2457]

Jordan, Reinhard, d. 1986. Holzwirtschaft im Wandel : ökonomische und technologische Veränderungen in der Holzbearbeitung und Holzverarbeitung / Reinhard Jordan, Hartmut Küchle, Gert Volkmann. Köln : Bund-Verlag, c1986. viii, 163 p. : ill. ; 21 cm. (WSI-Studie zur Wirtschafts- und Sozialforschung . Nr. 56) Bibliography: p. 157-163. ISBN 3-7663-0977-3 LC Card 86-211012 DDC 338.4/5674/0943 19
1. Lumber trade - Germany (West) - Automation. I. Küchle, Hartmut. II. Volkmann, G. (Gert). III. Title. IV. Series.
HD9763.5 .J67 1986

Jordan, Ronald J. Fischer, Donald E. Security analysis and portfolio management /. Englewood Cliffs, N.J. , c1987. xii, 708 p. : ISBN 0-13-798901-6 LC Card 86-25484 DDC 332.6 19
HG4529 .F57 1987

Jordan, Wayne R., 1940- Water and water policy in world food supplies . College Station , c1987. x, 434 p. : ISBN 0-89096-278-2 : LC Card 86-23065 DDC 333.91/3 19
HD1690.5 .W38 1987

Jordhl, Harold C., 1926- Wise, Gregory J. The effect of tax exempt forestland on town property tax revenues . Madison [1986] 40 leaves : LC Card 86-623093 DDC 336.22/09775 19
HJ4284.A3 W59 1986

Jorge, Antonio, 1931-
An evaluation of Cuba's post-revolutionary socioeconomic models / Antonio Jorge. Coral Gables, Fla. : Institute of Interamerican Studies, Graduate School of International Studies, University of Miami, [1984?] 26 p. ; 22 cm. (Occasional paper / Institute of Interamerican Studies, Graduate School of International Studies, University of Miami . no. 1984-1) Bibliography: p. 25-26. LC Card 87-124135 DDC 330.97291/064 19
1. Cuba - Economic conditions - 1918-1959. 2. Cuba - Economic conditions - 1959-. I. Series: Occasional papers (University of Miami. Institute of Interamerican Studies) , no. 1984-1. II. Title.
HC152.5 .J66 1984

Foreign investment, debt, and economic growth in Latin America /. New York , 1988. xix, 250 p. : ISBN 0-312-00936-4 : LC Card 87-18808 DDC 332.6/73/098 19
HG5160.5.A3 F675 1988

Jørgensen, Henning, 1949- Arbejdsmarkedsnævn i arbejdsmarkedspolitikken / Henning Jørgensen. [Aalborg] : ATA-forlaget, [1985?]-<[1986] > v. <1-2 > : ill. ; 24 cm. (Rapport / ATA-projektet . nr. 4-<5 >) "ATA-projektet." Includes bibliographies. CONTENTS. - 1-2. Forvaltning mellem stat og marked. ISBN 87-88706-12-5 LC Card 87-104729
1. Manpower policy - Denmark. 2. Labor supply - Denmark. I. ATA-projektet (Aalborg universitetscenter). II. Series: Rapport (ATA-projektet (Aalborg universitetscenter)) , nr. 4, etc. III. Title.
HD5799.A6 J64 1985

Jørgensen, Kirsten. Strategies for integrating women into the labour market /. Copenhagen, Denmark , 1982. 347 p. : ISBN 87-88209-08-3 (pbk.) LC Card 86-673782
HD6052 .S77x 1982

Jørgensen, Nils-Johan. Norge mot Europa? : EF's utvikling og norsk Europa-politikk etter folkeavstemningen / Nils-Johan Jørgensen. København : Europa, 1982. 250 p. ; 25 cm. Bibliography: p. 244-250. ISBN 87-87733-30-7 : LC Card 82-172919
1. European Economic Community - Norway. 2. Europe - Foreign relations - Norway. 3. Norway - Foreign relations - Europe. I. Title.
HC241.25.N7 J67 1982

Jorgenson, Dale Weldeau, 1933- Productivity and U. S. economic growth / Dale W. Jorgenson, Frank M. Gollop, and Barbara M. Fraumeni. Cambridge, Mass. : Harvard University Press, 1987. 567 p. : ill. ; 24 cm. (Harvard economic studies. v. 159) Bibliography: p. [541]-557. Includes index. ISBN 0-674-71175-0 (alk. paper) LC Card 87-12098 DDC 338/.06/0973 19
1. Industrial productivity - United States. 2. Capital investments - United States. 3. United States - Economic conditions - 1945-. I. Gollop, Frank M. II. Fraumeni, Barbara M., 1949-. III. Title. IV. Title: Productivity and US economic growth. V. Series.
HC110.I52 J67 1987

Joris, Albert, 1915- A destiny in diamonds / by Albert Joris. Spring, Hill, Brisbane, Qld. : Boolarong Publications ; Portland, OR : Exclusive distributor ISBS, 1986. vi, 113 p. : ill. ; 25 cm. Distributor from label on t.p. ISBN 0-86439-011-4 LC Card 87-161024 DDC 338.2/782/0924 B 19
1. Joris, Albert, 1915-. 2. Industrialists - Australia - Biography. 3. Diamond industry and trade - Australia - History. 4. Diamonds, Industrial - Australia - History. I. Title.
HD9677.A82 J675 1986

JORIS, ALBERT, 1915-
Joris, Albert, 1915- A destiny in diamonds /. Spring, Hill, Brisbane, Qld. , Portland, OR , 1986. vi, 113 p. : ISBN 0-86439-011-4 LC Card 87-161024 DDC 338.2/782/0924 B 19
HD9677.A82 J675 1986

Una jornada ferroviaria . Poblete, Martiniano O. Santiago de Chile , 1930. 2 v. : LC Card

87-162075 DDC 385/.0983 19
HE2940.F47 P63 1930

Jornadas.
(104) García Alba Iduñate, Pascual, 1948- [Financial aspects of macroeconomic management in Mexico. Spanish.] Causas y efectos de la crisis económica en México /. México, D.F. , 1984. 124 p. : ISBN 968-12-0285-6 LC Card 86-138030
HC135 .G29818 1984

(105) Velázquez, María del Carmen. Notas sobre sirvientes de las Californias y proyecto de obraje en Nuevo México /. México, D.F. [1985], c1984. 246 p. ; ISBN 968-12-0298-8 LC Card 85-243085
HD2346.U52 C294 1985

(110) Clases sociales y acción obrera en Chile /. México, D.F. , 1986. 230 p. ; ISBN 968-12-0326-7 LC Card 87-404023 DDC 331/.0983 19
HD8296.5 .C57 1986

(97) Rada, Juan F. La microelectrónica, la tecnología de la información y sus efectos en los países en vía de desarrollo /. México, D.F. , c1983. 158 p. ; ISBN 968-12-0214-7 LC Card 85-243097
HD9696.A3 D447 1983

Jornadas Hispano-Francesas sobre la Nueva Economía (1980 : Cámara Oficial de Comercio e Industria de Madrid) La Nueva economía en Francia y en España /. Madrid , c1980. 197 p. : ISBN 84-85355-27-X : LC Card 83-105425 DDC 330.944/0838 19
HB105.A2 N83 1980 ***NYPL [JLD 86-3024]***

Jornadas sobre Relaciones Internacionales, Economía e Integración (5th : 1985 : Colegio de Graduados en Ciencias Económicas del Paraguay) Política internacional, economía e integración /. Asunción del Paraguay [1985] 178 p. ; LC Card 86-122468
HF1523 .P65 1985

Jörs, Bernd.
Die Bedeutung der Buntmetallhütten des mitteleuropäischen Raumes im Rahmen der Versorgung der Bundesrepublik Deutschland : am Beispiel der Zinkhüttenindustrie / von Bernd Jörs. Frankfurt/Main : Im Selbstverlag des Seminars für Wirtschaftsgeographie der Johann Wolfgang Goethe-Universität Frankfurt/Main, 1983. 579 p. in various pagings : ill. ; 22 cm. (Frankfurter wirtschafts- und sozialgeographische Schriften. Heft 44) Spine title: Die Bedeutung der Buntmetallhütten. Originally presented as the author's thesis, Johann Wolfgang Goethe-Universität Frankfurt/Main, 1982. Bibliography: p. 367-389. LC Card 83-226662
1. Zinc industry and trade - Central Europe - Case studies. 2. Zinc industry and trade - Germany (West) - Case studies. I. Title. II. Title: Bedeutung der Buntmetallhütten. III. Series.
HD9539.Z6 C365 1983

Beiträge zur Multiplizität wirtschaftsgeographischer Forschung . Frankfurt am Main , c1986. 151 p. : ISBN 3-89228-046-0 LC Card 87-131124 DDC 330.9 19
HC59 .B464 1986

Jösch, Jutta. Konsumgenossenschaften und Food-Cooperatives : ein Vergleich der Entstehungsbedingungen von Verbraucherselbstorganisationen / von Jutta Jösch. Berlin : Duncker & Humblot, c1983. 126 p. : ill. ; 24 cm. (Schriften zum Genossenschaftswesen und zur öffentlichen Wirtschaft . Bd. 9) Bibliography: p. 120-126. ISBN 3-428-05423-7 LC Card 83-231020
1. Consumer cooperatives - Germany (West). I. Title. II. Series.
HD3338 .J67 1983

JOSÉ MARÍA CARO (SANTIAGO, CHILE)
Schkolnik, Mariana. Sobrevivir en la población José M. Caro y en Lo Hermida /. [Santiago, Chile] [1986] 150 p., [20] p. of plates : LC Card 87-400080 DDC 362.5/8/098331 19
HC193.S2 S35 1986

José María Ruiz Mateos, el ultimo magnate /. Ekaizer, Ernesto, 1949- Esplugues de Llobregat, Barcelona , 1985. 833 p., [16] p. of plates : ISBN 84-01-33291-5 LC Card 86-122394 DDC 332.1/6 B 19
HG4216.R85 E38 1985
NYPL [JFD 86-6856]

Josef Simon, Schuhmacher, Gewerkschafter, Sozialist mit Ecken und Kanten /. Simon, Josef, 1865-1949. Köln , c1985. 465 p. : ISBN 3-7663-0923-4 LC Card 85-186450
HD6695.S55 A3 1985

Josefsson, Lars. Brolin, Åke, 1924- Säljledaren /. Malmö , c1984. 140 p. : ISBN 91-38-61223-2 : LC Card 84-188808
HF5438.4 .B76 1984

Joseph, G. An econometric approach to forecasting demand for electricity in Tanzania to the year 2000 A.D. / by George Joseph. [Dar es Salaam] : Bureau of Resource Assessment and Land Use Planning, University of Dar es Salaam, [between 1978 and 1984] 42, [44] p. ; 30 cm. (Research paper / Bureau of Resource Assessment and Land Use Planning, University of Dar es Salaam . no. 38) LC Card 84-980076 DDC 333.7/09678 333.79/3213/09678 19
1. Electric power consumption - Tanzania - Forecasting. 2. Electric power consumption - Tanzania - Forecasting - Econometric models. I. Series: Research paper (Chuo Kikuu cha Dar es Salaam. Bureau of Resource Assessment and Land Use Planning) , no. 38. II. Title.
HD107 .D36 no. 38a HD9685.T352

The Joseph I. Lubin memorial lectures .
(no. 1) Brimmer, Andrew F. The world banking system . New York , 1985. 59 p. ; ISBN 0-8147-1068-9 : LC Card 85-5115 DDC 332.1/5 19
HG3881 .B677 1985 ***NYPL [JLD 86-2189]***

(no. 3) Solomon, Anthony M. The dollar, debt, and the trade deficit /. New York , 1987. 55 p. ; ISBN 0-8147-7863-1 : LC Card 86-23651 DDC 382.1/7/0973 19
HF3031 .S65 1987

Joseph, James, 1954- Saperstein, Rose, 1956- Read your way to the top with the guide /. Seattle, Wash. , c1987. 83 p. : ISBN 0-930251-00-8 (pbk.) : LC Card 87-310 DDC 428.4/3 19
HF5351 .S34 1987

Joseph, Joel D. How to buy your home / Joel D. Joseph. Bethesda, Md. : National Press, c1988. p. cm. ISBN 0-915765-36-5 : LC Card 86-23630 DDC 643/.12 19
1. Home buying. I. Title.
HD1379 .J66 1988

Joseph M. Katz Graduate School of Business. Program in Corporate Culture. Corporate transformation . San Francisco , 1988. xxxi, 553 p. : ISBN 1-555-42060-5 (alk. paper) LC Card 87-45427 DDC 658.4/063 19
HD58.8 .C66 1988

Joseph Wharton . Yates, W. Ross (Willard Ross) Bethlehem , London , c1987. 413 p. : ISBN 0-934223-00-9 (alk. paper) LC Card 86-81983 DDC 338.7/6691/0924 B 19
HC102.5.W47 Y38 1987

Joshi, Navin Chandra. Third World economy : problems and prospects / Navin Chandra Joshi. New Delhi : National, 1983. x, 134 p. ; 22 cm. Includes index. Bibliography: p. [127]-131. LC Card 83-904473 DDC 330.9172/4 19
1. Developing countries - Economic policy. 2. Developing countries - Economic conditions. I. Title.
HC59.7 .J645 1983 ***NYPL [JLD 86-3794]***

Joshi, Vidyuta. Migrant labour and related issues /. New Delhi , c1987. xii, 334 p. : ISBN 81-204-0199-9 : LC Card 87-901172
HD5856.I4 M54 1985

The Jossey-Bass management series.
Jossey-Bass management series.
Below, Patrick J. The executive guide to strategic planning /. San Francisco, Calif. , c1987. xxiii, 136 p. : ISBN 1-555-42032-X (alk. paper) LC Card 86-27863 DDC 658.4/012 19
HD30.28 .B45 1987

Bozeman, Barry. All organizations are public . San Francisco , 1987. xix, 184 p. : ISBN 1-555-42036-2 (alk. paper) LC Card 86-27699 DDC 302.3/5 19
HD58.9 .B69 1987

Brinkerhoff, Robert O. Achieving results from training . San Francisco , 1987. xx, 248 p. ; ISBN 1-555-42044-3 (alk. paper) LC Card 86-46331 DDC 658.3/12404 19
HF5549.5.T7 B65 1987

Corporate transformation . San Francisco , 1988. xxxi, 553 p. : ISBN 1-555-42060-5 (alk. paper) LC Card 87-45427 DDC 658.4/063 19
HD58.8 .C66 1988

Davis, Donald D., 1950- Managing technological innovation /. San Francisco , 1986. xxi, 302 p. : ISBN 1-555-42008-7 LC Card 86-15378 DDC 658.5/14 19
HD45 .D34 1986 ***NYPL [JLE 87-862]***

Derr, C. Brooklyn (Clyde Brooklyn) Managing the new careerists /. San Francisco , 1986. xxii, 288 p. ; ISBN 0-87589-677-4 LC Card 85-45901 DDC 658.3/02 19
HF5549.2.U5 D47 1986
NYPL [JLE 86-2427]

Desatnick, Robert L. Managing to keep the customer . San Francisco , 1987. xvi, 163 p. ; ISBN 1-555-42027-3 (alk. paper) LC Card 86-21399 DDC 658.8/12 19
HF5415.5 .D47 1987

Dyer, W. Gibb, 1954- Cultural change in family firms . San Francisco , 1986. xxi, 179 p. ; ISBN 1-555-42007-9 (alk. paper) LC Card 86-10585 DDC 658/.045 19
HD62.25 .D94 1986 ***NYPL [JLE 87-1079]***

Fox, William M. Effective group problem solving . San Francisco , 1987. xvii, 204 p. : ISBN 1-555-42033-8 (alk. paper) LC Card 86-33742 DDC 658.4/036 19
HD30.29 .F69 1987

Frame, J. Davidson. Managing projects in organizations . San Francisco , 1987. xvii, 240 p. : ISBN 1-555-42031-1 (alk. paper) LC Card 86-33707 DDC 658.4/04 19
HD69.P75 F72 1987

Harris, Philip R. (Philip Robert), 1926- Management in transition . San Francisco, Calif. , c1985. xxvii, 404 p. : ISBN 0-87589-660-X (alk. paper) LC Card 85-45055 DDC 658.4 19
HD58.7 .H3695 1985 ***NYPL [JLE 85-3954]***

Izzo, Joseph E., 1931- The embattled fortress . San Francisco , 1987. xxii, 155 p. : ISBN 1-555-42059-1 (alk. paper) LC Card 87-45429 DDC 658.4/038 19
HF5548.2 .I97 1987

Kirkpatrick, Donald L. How to manage change effectively /. San Francisco , 1985. xxii, 280 p. : ISBN 0-87589-659-6 LC Card 85-45060 DDC 658.4/06 19
HD58.8 .K52 1985 ***NYPL [JLE 87-1191]***

Kouzes, James M., 1945- The leadership challenge . San Francisco , 1987. xxx, 362 p. : ISBN 1-555-42061-3 (alk. paper) LC Card 87-45428 DDC 658.4/092 19
HD57.7 .K68 1987

Lawler, Edward E. High-involvement management /. San Francisco, Calif. , 1986. xvii, 252 p. : ISBN 0-87589-686-3 (alk. paper) LC Card 85-45909 DDC 658.3/152 19
HD5650 .L35 1986 ***NYPL [JLE 86-3096]***

Matteson, Michael T. Controlling work stress . San Francisco, Calif. , 1987. xx, 378 p. ; ISBN 1-555-42062-1 (alk. paper) LC Card 87-45503 DDC 658.3/82 19
HF5548.85 .M378 1987

Mitroff, Ian I. Business not as usual . San Francisco , 1987. xxi, 194 p. : ISBN 1-555-42030-3 (alk. paper) LC Card 86-46333 DDC 338.9 19
HD70.U5 M52 1987

Morrisey, George L. The executive guide to operational planning /. San Francisco , 1988. xxvii, 130 p. : ISBN 1-555-42064-8 (alk. paper) LC Card 87-45508 DDC 658.4/012 19
HD30.28 .M65 1988

Phillips, Jack J., 1945- Recruiting, training, and retaining new employees . San Francisco , 1987. xxii, 324 p. ; ISBN 1-555-42042-7 (alk. paper) LC Card 86-46332 DDC 658.3/14 19
HF5549.5.R44 P49 1987

Rowe, Alan J. Managing with style . San Francisco , 1987. xviii, 225 p. : ISBN 1-555-42074-5 (alk. paper) LC Card 87-45570 DDC 658.4/03 19
HD30.28 .R676 1987

The Trainer's professional development handbook /. San Francisco , 1987. xix, 327 p. : ISBN 1-555-42067-2 (alk. paper) LC Card

87-45507 DDC 658.3/124 19
HF5549.5.T7 T6633 1987

Walton, Richard E. Innovating to compete . San Francisco , 1987. p. cm. ISBN 1-555-42056-7 LC Card 87-45426 DDC 658.4/06 19
HE736 .W35 1987

Weisbord, Marvin Ross. Productive workplaces . San Francisco , 1987. xxv, 405 p. : ISBN 1-555-42054-0 (alk. paper) LC Card 87-45425 DDC 658.3/14 19
HD31 .W424 1987

Jossey-Bass public administration series.
Fielding, Gordon J. Managing public transit strategically . San Francisco , 1987. xxii, 270 p. : ISBN 1-555-42068-0 (alk. paper) LC Card 87-45497 DDC 388.4/068 19
HE4301 .F54 1987

Jourdain, Didier. Dubrulle, Louis. Comptabilité analytique de gestion . [Paris] , c1985-c1987. 2 v. : ISBN 2-04-015766-2 (v. 2) : LC Card 86-149033 DDC 668/.65/0681 19
HF5642 .D74 1985

Journal de ma vie . Ménétra, Jacques-Louis, b. 1738. Paris , c1982. 431 p. : ISBN 2-85870-022-2 : LC Card 82-166496 DDC 666/.1/0924 B 19
HD8039.G52 F73 1982
NYPL [JFD 86-6795]

Journal of commercial bank lending.
Credit analysis . Philadelphia, Pa. , c1987. 146 p. : ISBN 0-936742-38-0 (pbk.) : LC Card 86-28628 DDC 332.1/753/0685 19
HG1641 .C66 1987

Small business financing . Philadelphia, Pa. , c1987. 118 p. ; ISBN 0-936742-40-2 (pbk.) : LC Card 87-5534 DDC 332.1/753/0685 19
HG3754.5.U6 S6 1987

Journal of my life /. Ménétra, Jacques-Louis, b. 1738. [Journal de ma vie. English.] New York , 1986. xviii, 368 p., [1] leaf of plate : ISBN 0-231-06128-5 LC Card 85-28068 DDC 666/.1/0924 B 19
HD8039.G52 F7313 1986
NYPL [JFE 86-2978]

Journal of the Internal improvement convention. Internal Improvement Convention (1834 : Baltimore, Md.) Baltimore, 1835. 93 p., 1 l. LC Card 06-22129
HE396.C5 I6

Journal of the United Nations Philatelists, Inc. V. 8, no. 6 (Supplement) Lamers, Duane E. United Nations definitive & airmail stamps issued & reprinted 1958-1985 /. Chicago, IL, USA (Box 1674, Chicago 60690) , c1985. 52 p. : LC Card 87-146520 DDC 769.56/1 19
HE6246 .L36 1985

Journal of the West. Business entrepreneurs in the West /. Manhattan, Kan. , c1986. 120 p. : ISBN 0-89745-088-4 (pbk.) LC Card 87-135380 DDC 338/.04/0922 B 19
HC102.5.A2 B78 1986

JOURNALISM - BRAZIL.
Lima, Gerson Moreira, 1952- Releasemania, uma contribuição para o estudo do press-release no Brasil /. São Paulo, SP , c1985. 114 p. : LC Card 85-184576 DDC 659.2 19
HM263 .L478 1985 ***NYPL [JFD 86-2728]***

JOURNALISM - COMMERCE. see **JOURNALISM, COMMERCIAL.**

JOURNALISM, COMMERCIAL.
Evans, Fred J. Managing the media . New York , 1987. xvii, 172 p. : ISBN 0-89930-156-8 (lib. bdg. : alk. paper) : LC Card 86-25736 DDC 659.2 19
HD59 .E93 1987

JOURNALISM, COMMERCIAL - HISTORY.
McCusker, John J. European bills of entry and marine lists . Cambridge, Mass. , 1985. 75 p. : LC Card 86-673685
HE565.A3 M32 1985

JOURNALISM, COMMERCIAL - UNITED STATES.
Warfield, Gerald. How to read and understand the financial news /. New York , c1986. 214 p. ; ISBN 0-06-015647-3 : LC Card 86-45161 DDC 332.63/2042 19
PN4888.C59 W37 1986
NYPL [JLE 87-1488]

JOURNALISM - REPORTING. see **REPORTERS AND REPORTING.**

Journalist Workshop on Population and Development Reporting, Oct. 31-Nov. 5, 1981, Islamabad /. Journalist Workshop on Population and Development Reporting (1981 : Islāmābād, Pakistan) [Pakistan , 1982? (Lahore : Directorate of Production and Publication) 63, 12 p. ; LC Card 83-930293 DDC 304.6 19
HB849 .J67 1981

Journalist Workshop on Population and Development Reporting (1981 : Islāmābād, Pakistan) Journalist Workshop on Population and Development Reporting, Oct. 31-Nov. 5, 1981, Islamabad / organized by Directorate of Communication Strategy, Population Welfare Division, Government of Pakistan in collaboration with Press Foundation of Asia, Manila, Philippines. [Pakistan : s.n., 1982? (Lahore : Directorate of Production and Publication) 63, 12 p. ; 23 cm. English and Urdu. Added t.p. in Urdu: Iftitāḥī taqrīb. LC Card 83-930293 DDC 304.6 19
1. Population - Congresses. I. Pakistan. Directorate of Communication Strategy. II. Press Foundation of Asia. III. Title. IV. Title: Iftitāḥī taqrīb.
HB849 .J67 1981

JOURNALISTIC ETHICS - CONGRESSES.
Famine in Ukraine, 1932-1933 /. Edmonton , Downsview, Ont., Canada , 1986. 192 p. ; ISBN 0-09-286243-8 LC Card 87-148658 DDC 363.8/0947/71 19
HC337.U53 F314 1986

JOURNALISTS - INDIA - DIARIES.
Chishti, Anees, 1941- Dateline Bhopal . New Delhi , 1986. 160 p. ; LC Card 86-901993 DDC 363.1/79
HD7269.C452 I5225 1986
NYPL [JLD 87-1050]

JOURNALISTS - UNITED STATES.
Winans, R. Foster. Trading secrets /. New York , c1986. xiv, 320 p., [8] p. of plates : ISBN 0-312-81227-2 : LC Card 86-12700 DDC 364.1/68 19
HG4572 .W547 1986 ***NYPL [JLE 86-4323]***

Journey-to-work trends . Briggs, Dwight. Washington, D.C. , Springfield, VA [1986] 1 v. (various pagings) : LC Card 86-602387 DDC 388.4/1314/0973 19
HE371.A3 B75 1986

Jovanov, Neca. Dijagnoza samoupravljanja 1974-1981 / Neca Jovanov. Zagreb : SNL, 1983. 365 p. ; 20 cm. (Posebno izdanje / Sveučilišna naklada Liber) In Serbo-Croatian (Roman) Includes bibliographical references. LC Card 84-146844
1. Management - Yugoslavia - Employee participation. 2. Yugoslavia - Politics and government - 1945-. 3. Yugoslavia - Economic policy - 1945-. I. Title.
HD5660.Y8 J68 1983

A jövedelmezőség számításának és elemzésének módszerei az ÁFÉSZEK-nél /. Marty, János. Budapest , 1984. 228 p. : ISBN 963-7006-05-2 : LC Card 85-176220
HD3492.5.A4 M37 1984

Jovković, Ljiljana. Andrlić, Vlasta. Rječnik terminologije jugoslavenskog političko-ekonomskog sistema . Zagreb , 1985. viii, 135 p. ; LC Card 86-182784
HB61 .A55 1985 ***NYPL [*QKK 87-1803]***

Joy, Maurice. Not heard on the street : an irreverent dictionary of Wall Street / Maurice Joy. Chicago, Ill. : Probus Pub. Co., c1986. viii, 133 p. ; 21 cm. ISBN 0-917253-40-X : LC Card 86-3213 DDC 332.6/0207 19
1. Investments - Anecdotes, facetiae, satire, etc. - Dictionaries. 2. Finance - Anecdotes, facetiae, satire, etc. - Dictionaries. I. Title.
HG4513 .J69 1986 ***NYPL [JLD 86-2885]***

Joyce, M. A. S. Levitt, M. S., 1938- The growth and efficiency of public spending /. Cambridge [Cambridgeshire] , New York , 1987. xiv, 201 p. : ISBN 0-521-34621-5 (U. S.) LC Card 87-11636 DDC 339.5/22/0941 19
HJ7764 .L475 1987

Joyce, Patrick. The Historical meanings of work /. Cambridge [Cambridgeshire] , New York , 1987. v, 320 p. ; ISBN 0-521-30897-6 LC Card 87-788 DDC 306/.36 19
HD4904 .H54 1987

József Attila Tudományegyetem. Marxizmus-Leninizmus Központi Tanszékcsoport. A Gazdaság és társadalom viszonya a szocializmus építésének jelenlegi időszakában . Szeged , 1985. 181 p. ; LC Card 86-207975
HC300.28 .G27 1985

JRB Associates. La República Dominicana . McLean, Va. , 1981. xii, 134 p. : LC Card 86-218146
HC153.5 .R45 1981

Juan Pablo II y el trabajo . Catholic Church. Pope (1978- : John Paul II) [Laborem exercens. Spanish.] [Santiago, Chile] , 1984. 135 p. ; LC Card 85-197537
HD6338 .C277 1984

Juan Pablo Segundo y el trabajo. Catholic Church. Pope (1978- : John Paul II) [Laborem exercens. Spanish.] Juan Pablo II y el trabajo . [Santiago, Chile] , 1984. 135 p. ; LC Card 85-197537
HD6338 .C277 1984

Juan, Po. Chen hsing Chung-hua chih lu--kai ko ti sung ko /. Pei-ching , 1985. 4, 3, 385 p. ; LC Card 86-106324
NYPL [*OVY 86-3099]

JŪBĀ (SUDAN) - ECONOMIC CONDITIONS.
Jenkins, S. J. (Susan J.) Aspects of the informal economic sector of Juba, southern Sudan /. [Jūbā, Sudan] [1981?] xiii, 217 p., [4] leaves of plates : LC Card 86-980565
HD2346.S82 J85 1981

Jucá, Alvaro Ferraz. Gênero industrial--têxtil / por Alvaro Ferraz Jucá, Antonio Carlos Veras. [Recife] : Federação das Indústrias do Estado de Pernambuco, Departamento de Economia, [1985?] 34 leaves ; 34 cm. (Série Relatórios setoriais) LC Card 86-204296
1. Textile industry - Brazil - Pernambuco. I. Veras, Antonio Carlos. II. Federação das Indústrias do Estado de Pernambuco. Departamento de Economia. III. Title. IV. Series.
HD9864.B83 P475 1985

JUDAICA. see **JEWS.**

Judd, Bruce. Design for diversification /. Canberra , Portland, OR. [1985] 57 p. : ISBN 0-909724-68-7 (pbk.) LC Card 86-222390 DDC 363.5/0994 19
HD7379.A3 D47 1985

Judges and the cities . Clark, Gordon L. Chicago , c1985. xv, 247 p. ; ISBN 0-226-10753-1 : LC Card 85-1018 DDC 306/.0973 19
HN59.2 .C57 1985 ***NYPL [JLE 86-1068]***

JUDGMENTS - ECONOMIC ASPECTS - EUROPE.
Bürge, Alfons. Rechtsdogmatik und Wirtschaft . Berlin , c1987. 280 p. ; ISBN 3-428-06124-1 LC Card 87-134998 DDC 332.8/3/094 19
HB551 .B87 1987

JUDICIAL BEHAVIOR. see **JUDICIAL PROCESS.**

JUDICIAL DECISION-MAKING. see **JUDICIAL PROCESS.**

JUDICIAL INVESTIGATIONS. see **GOVERNMENTAL INVESTIGATIONS.**

JUDICIAL PROCESS - UNITED STATES.
Clark, Gordon L. Judges and the cities . Chicago , c1985. xv, 247 p. ; ISBN 0-226-10753-1 : LC Card 85-1018 DDC 306/.0973 19
HN59.2 .C57 1985 ***NYPL [JLE 86-1068]***

Judith, Rudolf, 1925- 40 Jahre Mitbestimmung . Köln , c1986. 293 p., [16] p. of plates : ISBN 3-7663-3012-8 LC Card 87-125207 DDC 658.3/152/0943 19
HD5660.G4 A5 1986

Jugendarbeitslosigkeit, lokale Ausprägungen und kommunale Strategien . Kunert-Schroth, Heidrun. Berlin , 1987. 172 p. ; ISBN 3-88118-135-0 LC Card 87-409103 DDC 331.3/412/0943 19
HD6276.G4 K86 1987

Jugendarbeitslösigkeit und soziale Sicherung . Haar, Heinrich von der. Berlin , c1982. 216 p. : ISBN 3-88114-302-5 : LC Card 83-152854 DDC 331.3/4/0943 19
HD7096.G3 H33 1982 ***NYPL [JLE 87-1214]***

Jugendarbeitsmarktförderung in Österreich /. Amanshauser, Wilfried. Wien [1985] ii, 71, 3 p. ; LC Card 86-165982
HD6276.A9 A43 1985

Jugendbiografie und Handlungsforschung /. Behnken, Imbke, 1941- Frankfurt [am Main] , c1984. xi, 239 p. ; ISBN 3-88704-402-9 LC Card 84-174719 DDC 331.3/425922/0943 19
HD4885.G3 B425 1984 *NYPL [JLD 86-1892]*

Jugendliche in der gewerblich-technischen Ausbildung in Industrie und Handwerk . Ziefuss, Horst. Kiel , c1986. 352 p. : ISBN 3-89088-011-8 LC Card 87-407898 DDC 331.3/42592/0943 19
HD5715.5.G4 Z54 1986

Jugendliche zwischen Schule und Arbeitswelt . Sardei-Biermann, Sabine. München , c1984. v, 318 p. ; ISBN 3-87966-219-3 LC Card 84-240405
HD5715.5.G4 S27 1984

Jugendliche zwischen Schule und Beruf . Kabbert, Rainer. Nürnberg , 1982. 84, [1] p. : LC Card 83-169834
HF5382.5.G3 K33 1982

Juglar, Clément, 1819-1905.
[Des crises commerciales. English]
A brief history of panics and their periodical occurrence in the United States / by Clement Juglar. 3rd. ed. / translated and edited with an introduction, and brought down from 1889 to date by DeCourcy W. Thom. New York, NY : A.M. Kelley, 1988. p. cm. (Reprints of economic classics) Translation of: Des crises commerciales. Includes index. ISBN 0-678-00168-5 LC Card 87-17069 DDC 338.5/42 19
1. Business cycles - United States - History. 2. United States - Economic conditions. I. Thom, DeCourcy W. (DeCourcy Wright), 1858-1932. II. Title.
HB3743 .J8513 1988

Jugoslavia . Lysestøl, Peder Martin. [Oslo] , c1985. 179 p. : ISBN 82-7094-421-1 LC Card 86-204691
HC407 .L97 1985

Jugoslavija. see **Yugoslavia.**

Jugoslawisches Aluminium und Aluminium Produkte. Yugoslav aluminum and aluminium products =. Beograd , 1986. 83 p. : LC Card 87-108615
HD9539.A63 Y89 1986

Jugoslawisches Kupfer und Kupfererzeugnisse. Yugoslav copper and copper products =. Beograd , 1986. 83 p. : LC Card 87-108608
HD9539.C7 Y87 1986

Jugoslovenska agrarna teorija i politika . Tomić, Danilo. Bačka Topola , 1985. 211 p. : LC Card 85-195818
HD2045.5.Z8 T62 1985

Jugoslovenska privreda između stagnacije i razvoja / redaktor Mihael Dlesk ; predgovor Zoran Pjanić ; autori Branko Milanović ... [et al.]. 1. izd. Beograd : In-t ekonomskih nauka, 1986. viii, 298 p. : ill. ; 21 cm. In Serbo-Croatian (roman) Includes bibliographical references. LC Card 87-151260
1. Yugoslavia - Economic conditions - 1945-. 2. Yugoslavia - Economic policy - 1945-. 3. Economic stabilization - Yugoslavia. I. Dlesk, Mihael. II. Milanović, Branko. III. Institut ekonomskih nauka (Belgrade, Serbia).
HC407 .J83 1986

Jugoslovenski centar za teoriju i praksu samoupravljanja Edvard Kardelj. Technology and work . London , Dover, N.H. , c1986. 304 p. : ISBN 0-7099-3801-2 : LC Card 86-4202 DDC 303.4/83 19
HC244.Z9 T475 1986 *NYPL [JLD 86-2160]*

A Jugoszláv és a magyar mezőgazdaság összehasonlítása a határmenti területeken / [készült a Központi Statisztikai Hivatal Mezőgazdasági Statisztikai Főosztályának Módszertani és Elemzési Osztályán]. Budapest : Központi Statisztikai Hivatal, 1986. 37 p. ; 29 cm. Bibliography: p. 37. LC Card 87-407672
1. Agriculture - Economic aspects - Hungary - Statistics. 2. Agriculture - Economic aspects - Yugoslavia - Statistics. I. Hungary. Központi Statisztikai Hivatal. Mezőgazdasági Statisztikai Főosztály. Módszertani és Elemzési Osztály.
HD1940.5 .J83 1986

Juhász, Ottó. A népgazdasági szintü gazdaságpolitikai döntések végrehajtását segitő szakszervezeti munka : zárótanulmány / [késztitette, Juhász Ottó]. [Budapest] : Szakszervezetek Elméleti Kutató Intézete, [1984] 136 p. ; 21 cm. "1984. november." Bibliography: p. 131-136. ISBN 963-608-064-X LC Card 86-126615
1. Trade-unions - Hungary. 2. Hungary - Economic policy - 1968-. 3. Labor policy - Hungary. I. Title.
HD6680.5 .J84 1984

Juklak Nakerwan. Indonesia. Kantor Menteri Negara Urusan Peranan Wanita. Pokok-pokok petunjuk pelaksanaan Program Peningkatan Produktivitas Kerja Tenaga Kerja Wanita Melalui Pendekatan Kesejahteraan Terpadu, tahun 1984/1986 (Juklak Nakerwan). Jakarta [1984] iii, xii, 47 p. ; LC Card 86-940168
HD6194 .I5 1984

Julander, Claes-Robert, 1944- Holmlöv, Per Gunnar, 1951- Reklam i satellit-tv . Stockholm [1984] 147 p. ; ISBN 91-7258-183-2 : LC Card 84-229824
HF6146.T42 H64 1984

Juliá Milanés, Ramón, 1942- Fumero Marta, Julio, 1934- Comercio exterior . La Habana , 1985. vii, 210 p. : LC Card 87-107270
HF1008 .F86 1985

JÜLICH-BERG - HISTORY.
Walz, Rainer. Stände und frühmoderner Staat . Neustadt an der Aisch , 1982. 257 p., [1] leaf of plates : ISBN 3-87707-040-9 LC Card 83-215104
HJ2675 .W35 1982

Julkaisuja (Finland. Asuntohallitus. Tutkimus- ja suunnitteluosasto) .
(1985:2) Harju, Hely. Puutteellisen asumisen parantaminen kunnissa vuosina 1985-1989 /. [Helsinki , 1986] 69, [16] p. : ISBN 951-46-9022-2 LC Card 86-215457
HD7345.3.A3 H367 1986

Julkisen sektorin työllisyyskehitys pohjoismaissa 1970-luvun aikana. Den Offentliga sektorns sysselsättningsutveckling i Norden under 1970-talet =. [Oslo] [Solna] 1983. iiii, 150 p. : ISBN 91-38-07556-3 LC Card 85-184428
HD8013.S344 O35 1983

Junankar, P. N. Programme of research and actions on the development of the labour market : costs of unemployment : main report / by P.N. Junankar. Luxembourg : Office for Official Publications of the European Communities ; [Washington, DC : European Community Information Service, distributor], 1986. vi, 76, 35 p. : ill. ; 30 cm. At head of title: Commission of the European Communities. Includes bibliographies. ISBN 92-825-6084-8 (pbk.) : LC Card 86-220947
1. Unemployment - European Economic Community countries - Costs - Case studies. I. Commission of the European Communities. II. Title.
HD5764.5.A6 J85 1986

Juncker, Flemming, 1904- Men morsomt har det været / Flemming Juncker. [Copenhagen] : Gyldendal, c1983. 423 p., [8] p. of plates : ill. ; 24 cm. Includes index. ISBN 87-00-54643-7 : LC Card 84-109657
1. Juncker, Flemming, 1904-. 2. Businessmen - Denmark - Biography. 3. Forest products industry - Denmark. I. Title.
HD9765.D42 J85 1983

JUNCKER, FLEMMING, 1904-
Juncker, Flemming, 1904- Men morsomt har det været /. [Copenhagen] , c1983. 423 p., [8] p. of plates : ISBN 87-00-54643-7 : LC Card 84-109657
HD9765.D42 J85 1983

JUNG, C. G. (CARL GUSTAV), 1875-1961.
Sanford, John A. The invisible partners . New York , c1980. 139 p. ; ISBN 0-8091-2277-4 : LC Card 79-56604 DDC 150.19/54
BF175 .S24 *NYPL [JFE 86-5093]*

Jung, Ronald, 1952- Leben im Jahr 2000 und danach . Berlin , c1984. 213 p. : ISBN 3-7605-8571-X LC Card 85-128359
HB3595 .L43 1984

Jungblut, Michael. Der Wohlstand entlässt seine Kinder : Wege aus der Krise / Michael Jungblut. Stuttgart : Deutsche Verlags-Anstalt, c1983. 303 p. ; 22 cm. Bibliography: p. 301-302. Includes index. ISBN 3-421-06164-5 LC Card 83-232938
1. Economic history - 1971-. 2. Economic policy. 3. Social history - 1970-. 4. Social policy. 5. Germany, West - Economic conditions - 1974-. 6. Germany, West - Economic policy - 1974-. 7. Germany, West - Social conditions. 8. Germany, West - Social policy. I. Title.
HC59 .J78 1983

Junge Generation der SPÖ Steiermark. Armut in Österreich . Graz , c1977. 168 p. : ISBN 3-7011-7080-0 LC Card 86-176543
HC270.P6 A75 1977

Junginger-Dittel, K.-O. Marketing Boards für Agrarexportgüter in Entwicklungsländern / von Klaus-Otto Junginger-Dittel. [Kiel] : Institut für Weltwirtschaft an der Universität Kiel, 1980. iii, 48 leaves ; 30 cm. (Kieler Arbeitspapiere . Arbeitspapier Nr. 105 =) Bibliography: leaves 47-48. LC Card 85-160428
1. Produce trade - Developing countries. 2. Boards of trade - Developing countries. 3. Export marketing - Developing countries. 4. Farm produce - Developing countries - Marketing. I. Series: Kieler Arbeitspapiere , Arbeitspapier Nr. 105. II. Title.
HD9018.D44 J86 1980

Jüngling, Elisabeth. Streiks in Bayern (1889-1914) : Arbeitskampf in der Prinzregentenzeit / Elisabeth Jüngling. München : Kommissionsverlag UNI-Druck, 1986. viii, 307 p., [24] p. of plates : ill. ; 21 cm. (Miscellanea Bavarica Monacensia . Bd. 126) Neue Schriftenreihe des Stadtarchivs München A revision of the author's thesis (doctoral)--Universität Münster, 1983. Bibliography: p. 269-290. Includes index. ISBN 3-87821-214-3 LC Card 87-408637 DDC 331.89/29433 19
1. Strikes and lockouts - Germany (West) - Bavaria - History. 2. Trade-unions - Germany (West) - Bavaria - History. 3. Bavaria (Germany) - Economic conditions. I. Series: Miscellanea Bavarica Monacensia , Heft 126. II. Title.
HD5380.B38 J86 1986

Jungnickel, Rolf.
Eigenimporte der deutschen Industrie / Rolf Jungnickel, Ulrike Maenner. Hamburg : Verlag Weltarchiv, 1984. 392 p. : ill. ; 24 cm. (Veröffentlichungen des HWWA-Institut für Wirtschaftsforschung-Hamburg) Bibliography: p. 387-392. ISBN 3-87895-256-2 LC Card 84-247605
1. Germany, West - Commerce. 2. Germany, West - Industries. 3. Investments, Foreign, and employment - Germany (West). I. Maenner, Ulrike. II. Title.
HF3566.5 .J86 1984

Investitionsbedingungen in der ASEAN-Region / Rolf Jungnickel, Axel Gerberding, Ulrike Maenner. Hamburg : Weltarchiv, 1986. 346 p. : ill. ; 24 cm. (Veröffentlichungen des HWWA-Institut für Wirtschaftsforschung-Hamburg) Bibliography: p. 333-346. ISBN 3-87895-296-1 LC Card 86-192978
1. Investments, Foreign - Asia, Southeastern. 2. Investments, West German - Asia, Southeastern. I. Gerberding, Axel. II. Maenner, Ulrike. III. Title.
HG5740.8.A3 J85 1986

Junior, José Tavares de Araujo. see **Araujo Júnior, José Tavares de.**

Junk bonds and tender offer financing /. Sherman, Howard D. Washington, D.C. , c1987. 22 p. ; ISBN 0-931035-15-5 (pbk.) LC Card 87-128796 DDC 332.63/2 19
HG4963 .S535 1987

JUNK BONDS - CONGRESSES.
Mergers and acquisitions /. Chicago , 1988. xi, 108 p. : ISBN 0-226-03209-4 LC Card 87-19035 DDC 658.1/6 19
HD2746.5 .M45 1988

JUNK BONDS - UNITED STATES.
Corporate mergers and high yield (junk) bonds . Washington , 1986. vi, 57 p. ; LC Card 87-601339 DDC 332.63/22 19
HD2746.5 .C67 1986

Sherman, Howard D. Junk bonds and tender offer financing /. Washington, D.C. , c1987. 22 p. ; ISBN 0-931035-15-5 (pbk.) LC Card 87-128796 DDC 332.63/2 19
HG4963 .S535 1987

JUNK MAIL. see **ADVERTISING, DIRECT-MAIL.**

Junkernheinrich, Martin. Zimmermann, Horst, 1934- Die Gemeindefinanzen im Ruhrgebiet . Essen , 1983. xvi, 153 p. : ISBN 3-923494-28-9

LC Card 83-228289
HJ9493.5.R8 Z76 1983

Junta de Andalucía. Consejería de Economía, Planificación, Industria y Energía. Junta de Andalucía. Grupo de Trabajo 14, Planificación Económica de las Corporaciones Locales y Comarcalización. Plan económico de Andalucía, 1984-1986 /. [Andalucía] , 1983. 133 p. ; ISBN 84-505-1243-3 LC Card 86-223752
HJ1249.A4 J86 1983

Junta de Andalucía. Grupo de Trabajo 14, Planificación Económica de las Corporaciones Locales y Comarcalización. Plan económico de Andalucía, 1984-1986 / Grupo de Trabajo 14, Planificación Económica de las Corporaciones Locales y Comarcalizacion ; presidenta, Carmen Calleja ; coordinadores, Angel Melguizo, Francisca Silva. [Andalucía] : Oficina de Planificación de la Consejería de Economía, Planificación, Industria y Energía de la Junta de Andalucía, 1983. 133 p. ; 25 cm. (Documento de trabajo . 1) Cover title: Plan económico para Andalucía, 1984-1986. Cover has subtitle: Documentos del plan. Accompanied by "Composición de los grupos de trabajos de planificación" on folded leaf inserted. Includes bibliographical references. ISBN 84-505-1243-3 LC Card 86-223752
1. Intergovernmental fiscal relations - Spain - Andalusia. 2. Municipal corporations - Taxation - Spain - Andalusia. 3. Andalusia (Spain) - Economic policy. 4. Local taxation - Spain - Andalusia. 5. Finance, Public - Spain - Andalusia. I. Calleja, Carmen. II. Melguizo, Angel. III. Silva, Francisca. IV. Junta de Andalucía. Consejería de Economía, Planificación, Industria y Energía. V. Title. VI. Title: Plan económico para Andalucía, 1984-1986. VII. Series: Documento de trabajo (Junta de Andalucía. Grupo de Trabajo 14, Planificación Económica de las Corporaciones Locales y Comarcalización) , 1.
HJ1249.A4 J86 1983

Junta Internacional de Registro de Frecuencias. see **International Frequency Registration Board.**

Junta Provincial de Historia de Córdoba . Tagle Frías de Cuenca, Matilde. Historia de la Estancia "Pozo de Correa" /. [Córdoba, Argentina] , 1984. 88 p. : LC Card 86-157022
HD1471.A72 C677 1984

Junta Provincial de Historia de Córdoba (Series)
.
(10) Tagle Frías de Cuenca, Matilde. Historia de la Estancia "Pozo de Correa" /. [Córdoba, Argentina] , 1984. 88 p. : LC Card 86-157022
HD1471.A72 C677 1984

Junto a nuestro pueblo. [Lima, Perú] : Comisión para la Participación de las Iglesias en el Desarrollo : Comisión Evangélica Latino Americana de Educación Cristiana, [1979 or 1980] 71 p. : ill. ; 30 cm. Cover title. "Número doble." "CCPD 7/8." Includes bibliographical references. LC Card 82-100009
1. Catholic Church - Latin America. 2. Church and social problems - Latin America. 3. Church and the poor - Latin America. I. Comisión Evangélica Latinoamericana de Educación Cristiana.
BX1426.2 .J86 1979 ***NYPL [JLF 86-1152]***

Juoro, Umar, 1959- Masalah terdepan dalam pembangunan ekonomi Indonesia / Umar Juoro. Bandung : Alumni, 1985. xii, 224 pp. ; 21 cm. Includes bibliographies. LC Card 86-942991
1. Indonesia - Economic policy. I. Title.
HC447 .J86 1985

Jurado Carmona, María Isabel. Propiedad y explotación agrarias en Puente Genil / María Isabel Jurado Carmona ; prólogo, Antonio López Ontiveros. Córdoba : Excma. Diputación Provincial de Córdoba, 1984. 229 p. : ill. ; 23 cm. (Coleccion Estudios cordobeses . 33) Bibliography: p. [225]-229. ISBN 84-505-0063-X LC Card 85-139166 DDC 338.1/0946/84 19
1. Agriculture - Economic aspects - Spain - Puente-Genil Region. 2. Land tenure - Spain - Puente-Genil Region. I. Title.
HD2025.P84 J87 1984
NYPL [JLD 86-2522]

JURISTIC PERSONS, FOREIGN. see **CORPORATIONS, FOREIGN.**

Jussawalla, Meheroo, 1923-
The calculus of international communications : a study in the political economy of transborder data flows / Meheroo Jussawalla and Chee-Wah Cheah ; foreword by Hans Peter Gassmann. Littleton, Colo. : Libraries Unlimited, 1987. xiv, 159 p. ; 26 cm. Includes bibliographies and index. ISBN 0-87287-503-2 : LC Card 87-2640 DDC 384/.068 19
1. Telecommunication and state. 2. Electronic data processing - Government policy. 3. Data protection - Government policy. 4. Computer networks - Government policy. I. Cheah, Chee-Wah. II. Title. III. Title: Transborder data flows.
HE7645 .J87 1987

The Cost of thinking . Norwood, N.J. , c1988. xii, 249 p. : ISBN 0-89391-419-3 LC Card 87-22937 DDC 338.4/7004/099 19
HC681.3.I55 C67 1988

Just, Flemming. Brugsforeningsbevægelsen 1866-1920 : med udgangspunkt i Ribe amt / Flemming Just. Esbjerg : Sydjysk universitetsforlag, 1984. 192 p. : ill. ; 21 cm. Bibliography: p. 173-179. Includes index. ISBN 87-88521-04-4 LC Card 85-114707
1. Cooperative societies - Denmark - Ribe (Amt) - History. 2. Cooperation - Denmark - Ribe (Amt) - History. I. Title.
HD3059.A6 R524 1984

Just-in-time . Goddard, Walter E. Essex Junction, VT , c1986. x, 199 p. : ISBN 0-939246-07-4 LC Card 86-61728 DDC 658.5 19
HD56 .G62 1986

Just-in-time manufacturing . Lubben, Richard T. New York , c1988. xiv, 246 p. : ISBN 0-07-038911-X LC Card 87-4058 DDC 658.5 19
HD9720.5 .L83 1988

Just treatment for those who work for the church. Cincinnati, OH (100 E. 8th St., Cincinnati 45202) : National Association of Church Personnel Administrators, c1986. ix, 21 p. ; 22 cm. (A NACPA position paper) Bibliography: p. 15-21. LC Card 86-228672 DDC 254/.0068/3 19
1. Personnel management. 2. Church management. I. National Association of Church Personnel Administrators (U. S.). II. Series.
HF5549 .J87 1986

Justi, Johann Heinrich Gottlob von, d. 1771. Ausführliche Abhandlung von denen Steuern und Abgaben / Johann Heinrich Gottlob von Justi. Wiesbaden : Th. Gabler, 1977. 202 p., [4] p. of plates : ill. ; 23 cm. (Gablers ökonomische Klassiker) Reprint. Originally published: Königsberg : G.L. Woltersdorffs Wittwe, 1762. ISBN 3-409-50171-1 LC Card 84-235228
1. Taxation. 2. Mercantile system. I. Title. II. Series.
HJ2300 .J87 1977

A justiça do lobo . Figueira, Ricardo Rezende, 1952- Petrópolis , 1986. 115 p. ; LC Card 87-137552 DDC 305.5/63 19
HD500.C74 F54 1986

Justice : views from the social sciences / edited by Ronald L. Cohen. New York : Plenum Press, c1986. xii, 283 p. ; 24 cm. (Critical issues in social justice) Includes bibliographies and indexes. ISBN 0-306-42256-5 LC Card 86-20503 DDC 320/.01/1 19
1. Justice. 2. Social justice. 3. Distributive justice. I. Cohen, Ronald L. (Ronald Lee), 1944-. II. Series.
JC578 .J89 1986 ***NYPL [JLE 87-304]***

JUSTICE.
Justice . New York , c1986. xii, 283 p. ; ISBN 0-306-42256-5 LC Card 86-20503 DDC 320/.01/1 19
JC578 .J89 1986 ***NYPL [JLE 87-304]***

JUSTICIALISM. see **PERONISM.**

Justiz und Recht .
(Bd. 3) Wirtschaft und Umweltschutz /. Heidelberg , 1986. vii, 147 p. : ISBN 3-8114-2786-5 LC Card 87-134163 DDC 363.7/058/0943 19
HC290.5.E5 W57 1986

JUSTUM PRETIUM. see **PRICES.**

Justus Liebig-Universität Giessen. Institut für Unternehmungsplanung. Hölter, Erich, 1955- Computergestütztes Ertragsteuersimulationsmodell der deutschen internationalen Kapitalgesellschaft . Giessen , c1986. xxv, 383 p. : ISBN 3-922730-67-1 LC Card 87-116057 DDC 336.24/3/0943 19
HJ4720.A7 H65 1986

JUTE CORPORATION OF INDIA.
India. Parliament. Committee on Public Undertakings. Action taken by Government on the recommendations contained in the sixteenth report of the Committee on Public Undertakings (Sixth Lok Sabha) on Jute Corporation of India Ltd. . New Delhi , 1979. vii, 82 p. ; LC Card 79-906770
HD9156.J8 I355 1979

JUTE INDUSTRY.
Ahmad, Qazi Kholiquzzaman, 1943- World trade in a primary commodity . Nyon, Switzerland , 1979. i, 83 p. ; LC Card 86-202627
HD9156.J7 A38 1979

JUTE INDUSTRY - FORECASTING.
Thigpen, M. Elton, 1932- World demand prospects for jute /. Washington, D.C. , Rome , 1987. vi, 178 p. ; ISBN 0-8213-0867-X (pbk.) LC Card 86-32522 DDC 338.4/767713 19
HD9156.J7 T46 1987

JUTE INDUSTRY - INDIA.
India. Parliament. Committee on Public Undertakings. Action taken by Government on the recommendations contained in the sixteenth report of the Committee on Public Undertakings (Sixth Lok Sabha) on Jute Corporation of India Ltd. . New Delhi , 1979. vii, 82 p. ; LC Card 79-906770
HD9156.J8 I355 1979

JUTE INDUSTRY - INDIA - HISTORY.
Dey, P. B. (Purnendu Bhusan), 1930- The jute industry of India . Calcutta , 1984. 12, 304, iii p. ; LC Card 86-903224 DDC 382/.4567713/0954 19
HD9156.J8 I325 1984

The jute industry of India . Dey, P. B. (Purnendu Bhusan), 1930- Calcutta , 1984. 12, 304, iii p. ; LC Card 86-903224 DDC 382/.4567713/0954 19
HD9156.J8 I325 1984

JUVENILE AUTOMOBILE DRIVERS - BRITISH COLUMBIA.
Rethinking young drivers /. [North Vancouver, B.C.] , c1987. ii, 291 p. : ISBN 0-7726-0588-2 (pbk.) LC Card 87-167603 DDC 363.1/251 19
HE5620.J8 R47 1987

Rothe, John Peter, 1948- Young drivers involved in injury producing crashes . North Vancouver, B.C. , c1986. ii, 77 p. : ISBN 0-7726-0530-0 (pbk.) LC Card 87-167610 DDC 363.1/251 19
HE5620.J8 R67 1986

JUVENILE AUTOMOBILE DRIVERS - BRITISH COLUMBIA - ATTITUDES.
Rethinking young drivers /. [North Vancouver, B.C.] , c1987. ii, 291 p. : ISBN 0-7726-0588-2 (pbk.) LC Card 87-167603 DDC 363.1/251 19
HE5620.J8 R47 1987

Rothe, John Peter, 1948- Young drivers involved in injury producing crashes . North Vancouver, B.C. , c1986. ii, 77 p. : ISBN 0-7726-0530-0 (pbk.) LC Card 87-167610 DDC 363.1/251 19
HE5620.J8 R67 1986

Juvonen, Risto. Sahateollisuus / Risto Juvonen, P.E. Johanson. [Helsinki] : Ammattikasvatushallitus : Suomen Puuteollisuusinsinöörien Yhdistys : 290 p. : ill. ; 25 cm. (Mekaaninen metsäteollisuus . 2) Includes bibliographies. ISBN 951-859-690-5 LC Card 86-231276
1. Lumber trade - Finland. I. Johanson, P. E. (Pär Erik). II. Title. III. Series.
HD9765.F4 J68 1986

Juyal, B. N.
Child labour : the twice exploited / B.N. Juyal, Sudarshan Kumari, L.M. Chandola.1st ed. Varanasi : Gandhian Institute of Studies, 1985. xiii, 161 p. ; 22 cm. Study of Varanasi. LC Card 87-901161 DDC 331.3/1/0954 19
1. Children - Employment - India. I. Sudarshan Kumari, 1924-. II. Chandola, L. M. III. Title.
HD6250.I42 J89 1985

Child labour and exploitation in the carpet industry : a Mirzapur-Bhadohi case study / B.N. Juyal. New Delhi : Indian Social Institute, c1987. 49, [1] p. ; 22 cm. (Monograph series / Indian Social Institute . 29) Study conducted in Mirzapur-Bhadohi, Uttar Pradesh. Bibliography: p. [50] LC Card 87-900920 DDC 331.3/1/0954 19
1. Children - Employment - India - Case studies. 2. Rug and carpet industry - India - Employees - Case studies. I. Series: Monograph series / Indian Social

Institute , 29. II. Title.
HD6250.I42 J87 1987

Jyothi Rani, T. Sickness in small scale industrial sector / T. Jyothi Rani. 1st ed. Warangal, Andhra Pradesh : Sandeep Pub. House, 1985. xii, 258 p. ; 23 cm. Based on the author's thesis (Ph. D.--Kakatiya University, 1985) under the title: Industrial sickness with special reference to small-scale industries in Andhra Pradesh. Bibliography: p. [247]-258. LC Card 86-902876 DDC 338.6/42/0954 19
1. Business mortality - India. 2. Small business - India. I. Title.
HD2747 .J96 1985

Jyoti Consultants Limited. Energy use in rural Gujarat /. New Delhi , c1987. iv, 186 p. : ISBN 81-204-0216-2 : LC Card 87-901949 DDC 333.79/13/095475 19
HD9502.I43 G844 1987

K. A. Mohamed Ariff, 1940- Malaysia and ASEAN economic cooperation / by Mohamed Ariff. Singapore : Institute of Southeast Asian Studies, ASEAN Economic Research Unit, 1980, cover 1981. 177 p. ; 28 cm. (Current issues / ASEAN Economic Research Unit . no. 9) Bibliography: p. 175-177. ISBN 997-19-0207-9 LC Card 82-940035
1. Asia, Southeastern - Economic integration. 2. ASEAN. 3. Malaysia - Economic conditions. 4. Asia, Southeastern - Commerce. 5. Asia, Southeastern - Industries. I. Series: Current issues (Institute of Southeast Asian Studies. ASEAN Economic Research Unit) , no. 9. II. Title.
HC441 .K18 1981

K.A.T.Ė.K. i razvitie otrasleĭ khoziaĭstva Sibiri. KATĖK i razvitie otrasleĭ khoziaĭstva Sibiri /. Novosibirsk , 1984. 164 p. ; LC Card 84-167870
HC337.R852 S5246 1984

K. B. see **Kommunistischer Bund.**

K. B. (Nord) see **Kommunistischer Bund.**

K. D. I. see **Han'guk Kaebal Yŏn'guwŏn.**

K istorii sotsial'no-ėkonomicheskikh ukladov Kirgizstana / pod redaktsieĭ V.P. Sherstobitova. Frunze : Izd-vo "Ilim", 1972. 108 p. ; 20 cm. At head of title: Akademiia nauk Kirgizskoĭ SSR. Institut istorii. Includes bibliographical references. LC Card 82-171559
1. Kirghiz S.S.R. - Economic conditions. 2. Kirghiz S.S.R. - Social conditions. I. Sherstobitov, Viktor Pavlovich. II. Tarykh institutu (Kyrgyz SSR ilimder akademiiasy).
HC337.K545 K15 1972

K. O. T. R. A. see **Taehan Muyŏk Chinhŭng Kongsa.**

K organizatsii koksokhimicheskoĭ promyshlennosti v Sredneĭ Azii. Ulitskiĭ, L. I. (Lazar' Ioakhimovich) Tashkent, 1945. 63 p. LC Card 51-55383
HD9559 .C7S68

K. P. D. see **Kommunistische Partei Deutschlands.**

K. P. F. see **Parti communiste français.**

K. P. I. see **Partito comunista italiano.**

Kaasschieter, R. H. Ondernemen en vernieuwen . Delft, Netherlands , 1985. 240 p. : ISBN 90-6275-189-X LC Card 86-113900
HD2346.N4 O53 1985

Kaatje, ben je boven? . Henkes, Barbara. Nijmegen , c1985. 192 p. : ISBN 90-6168-242-8 : LC Card 85-237937
HD6072.2.N4 H46 1985

Kabbert, Rainer. Jugendliche zwischen Schule und Beruf : Pläne, Vorbereitungen und Entscheidungen für Ausbildung und berufliche Tätigkeit / Rainer Kabbert, unter Mitarbeit von Irmgard Holzbauer, Hermine Kraft, Ingrid Mollwo. Nürnberg : Institut für Arbeitsmarkt- und Berufsforschung der Bundesanstalt für Arbeit : Bezugsmöglichkeit, Landesarbeitsamt Nordbayern, Geschäftsstelle für Veröffentlichungen, 1982. 84, [1] p. : all ill. ; 30 cm. (Beiträge zur Arbeitsmarkt- und Berufsforschung, 0173-6574 . 64) Bibliography: p. [85] LC Card 83-169834
1. Vocational guidance - Germany, West. 2. Vocational education - Germany, West. I. Institut für Arbeitsmarkt- und Berufsforschung. II. Title. III. Series.
HF5382.5.G3 K33 1982

Kabel im Haus, Satellit überm Dach . Kubicek, Herbert. Reinbek bei Hamburg , 1984. 189 p. : ISBN 3-499-15528-1 (pbk.) LC Card 87-673204
HE8700.72.G3 K83x 1984

Kabra, Govind Das, 1943- Development of weaker sections : organisational alternatives / Govind Das Kabra. New Delhi : Inter-India Publications, 1984, c1983. ix, 182 p. ; 25 cm. Includes index. Bibliography: p. [176]-180. LC Card 84-900357 DDC 338.1/8544 19
1. Farms, Small - India - Rajasthan. 2. Rural development - India - Rajasthan - Management. I. Title.
HD1476.I42 R345 1984 ***NYPL [JLE 86-4597]***

Kabra, Kamal Nayan.
Black money : comment on the NIPFP report on Aspects of black economy in India / K.N. Kabra, N.S. Jagannathan. New Delhi : India International Centre, 1985. 47 p. ; 24 cm. (IIC monograph series . no. 8) Rejoinder to: Aspects of the black economy in India / Shankar N. Acharya and associates, 1985. LC Card 87-900898 DDC 381 19
1. Tax evasion - India. 2. India - Economic conditions - 1947-. 3. Informal sector (Economics) - India. I. Jagannathan, N. S. II. Acharya, Shankar N. Aspects of the black economy in India. III. National Institute of Public Finance and Policy (India). IV. Title. V. Series.
HJ2348.5 .K32 1985

India's black economy and maldevelopment / Kamal Nayan Kabra. New Delhi : Patriot Publishers, 1986. 192 p. ; 22 cm. Includes bibliographical references and index. ISBN 81-7050-025-7 : LC Card 86-902668 DDC 338.954 19
1. India - Economic policy - 1980-. I. Title.
HC435.2 .K26 1986

Kachestvo trudovogo potentsiala : sotsial'no-ėkonomicheskiĭ aspekt / [avtory M.I. Dolishniĭ ... et al. ; otvetstvennyĭ redaktor M.I. Dolishniĭ]. Kiev : Nauk. dumka, 1986. 228 p. ; 21 cm. At head of title: Akademiia nauk Ukrainskoĭ SSR. L'vovskoe otdelenie Instituta ėkonomiki. Includes bibliographical references and index. LC Card 87-161614
1. Labor supply - Ukraine. I. Dolishniĭ, Mar'ian Ivanovich. II. Instytut ekonomiky (Akademiia nauk Ukraïns'koï RSR). L'vivs'ke viddilennia.
HD5797.U37 K34 1986

Kachestvoto na truda . Shopov, Dimitŭr. Sofiia , 1984. 202 p. : LC Card 85-117683
HC403.Z9 L375 1984

Kacprzyk, Janusz. Management decision support systems using fuzzy sets and possibility theory /. Köln , c1985. xi, 350 p. : ISBN 3-88585-143-1 (pbk.) LC Card 85-217558 DDC 658.4/033 19
HD30.23 .M353 1985 ***NYPL [JLE 86-4562]***

De kadans van de getouwen . Buter, Adriaan. Amsterdam , 1985. 160 p. : ISBN 90-10-05573-6 LC Card 86-110698
HD9865.N65 B88 1985

Kadekodi, Gopal K. Econometrics of planning and efficiency /. Dordrecht , Boston , 1988. vi, 193 p., [2] p. of plates : ISBN 90-247-3602-1 LC Card 87-21305 DDC 330/.028 19
HB139 .E32 1988

Kadiev, Ivan. Khronika za "Proletariĭ" / Ivan Kadiev. [Sofia] : Profizdat, 1985. 140, [3] p., [32] p. of plates : ill. ; 21 cm. (Poznavate li svoeto predpriiatie?) Bibliography: p. 140-[141] LC Card 86-195264
1. Kombinat "Proletariĭ" (Sofia, Bulgaria) - History. 2. Knit goods industry - Bulgaria - Sofia - History. I. Title. II. Series.
HD9969.K7 B855 1985

Kadieva, D. A. Chastotnyĭ anglo-russkiĭ slovar'. Pod"iazyk ėkonomiki. Razdely "Planirovanie" i "Ėkonomicheskaia kibernetika" / Leningrad : Izd-vo Leningradskogo universiteta, 1986. 126 p. ; 20 cm. At head of title: Leningradskiĭ ordena Lenina i ordena Trudovogo Krasnogo Znameni gosudarstvennyĭ universitet imeni A.A. Zhdanova. Includes bibliographical references. LC Card 87-146427
1. Economics - Dictionaries. 2. English language - Word frequency. 3. English language - Dictionaries - Russian. I. Markova, N. L. II. Karachan, N. B. III. Stupin, L. P. (Leonid Pavlovich). IV. Leningradskiĭ gosudarstvennyĭ universitet imeni A.A. Zhdanova. V. Title.
HB61 .K23 1986

KADUNA STATE (NIGERIA) - INDUSTRIES.
Ogwude, Innocent C. (Innocent Chuka) Industrial demand for freight transport in Kaduna State /. Zaria [Nigeria] [1984] 101 p. : LC Card 86-152627 DDC 380.5/24/096695 19
HE287.7.Z7 K336 1984

Kaergel, Siegfried. Brandt, Horst. Kostensenkung und Gewinn /. Berlin , 1985. 100 p. ; LC Card 87-144350 DDC 338.5/1/09431 19
HC290.795.C7 B7 1985

Kaffir boy . Mathabane, Mark. New York , c1986. xii, 354 p., [8] p. of plates : ISBN 0-02-581800-7 : LC Card 86-53 DDC 968/.00496024 B 19
DT779.95.M38 A34 1986 ***NYPL [Sc E 86-240]***

Kaftaniuk, IU. A. (IUriĭ Anatol'evich) Vychislitel'naia tekhnika na avtomobil'nom transporte : povyshenie ėffektivnosti ispol'zovaniia / IU.A. Kaftaniuk. Moskva : "Transport", 1985. 183 p. : ill. ; 22 cm. Bibliography: p. 181-[182] LC Card 86-163666
1. Transportation, Automotive - Soviet Union - Data processing. I. Title.
HE5613 .K36 1985

Kagera Basin Organization.
Development programme of the Kagera Basin . [Kigali] [1982] viii, 73 leaves : LC Card 85-980886 DDC 338.967 19
HC860.Z9 E444 1982

Kagera Basin Organization. Secretariat.
Development programme of the Kagera Basin . [Kigali] [1982] viii, 73 leaves : LC Card 85-980886 DDC 338.967 19
HC860.Z9 E444 1982

Kahal, Matthew I. Estomin, Steven. Updated load forecast of energy and peak demand on the Delmarva Peninsula /. Bethesda, Md. (4550 Montgomery Ave., Bethesda 20814) [1986] iv, 4, 53, [18] p. : LC Card 87-620907 DDC 333.79/3212/097521 19
HD9685.U6 A123 1986

Kahaner, Larry. On the line : how MCI took on AT&T, and won! / Larry Kahaner.Warner Books ed. New York, NY : Warner Books, 1987, c1986. 344 p., [8] p. of plates : ill. ; 21 cm. Includes index. ISBN 0-446-38550-6 (pbk.) LC Card 87-10561 DDC 384.6/065/73 19
1. MCI (Firm) - History. 2. American Telephone and Telegraph Company - Reorganization - History. 3. Telephone - United States - Long distance - History. I. Title.
HE8846.M375 K34 1987

Kahk, Juhan. Uspekhi ėkonomicheskogo i kul'turnogo razvitiia Ėstonskoĭ SSR za gody sovetskoĭ vlasti . Tallin , 1980. 222 p. ; LC Card 81-198881
HC337.E7 U86 1980

Kahler, Miles, 1949- The Politics of international debt /. Ithaca , 1986. 272 p. ; ISBN 0-8014-1911-5 (alk. paper) LC Card 85-48243 DDC 327.1/11 19
HJ8083 .P65 1986 ***NYPL [JLE 86-2405]***

Kahlon, A. S., 1923- Modernization of Punjab agriculture / A.S. Kahlon. New Delhi : Allied Publishers, 1984. vi, 145 p. ; 22 cm. Includes bibliographical references and index. LC Card 84-902491 DDC 338.1/0954/5 19
1. Agriculture - India - Punjab. 2. Agricultural innovations - India - Punjab. I. Title.
S471.I32 P845 1984 ***NYPL [JLD 86-4410]***

Kahn, Alfred J., 1919-
Kamerman, Sheila B. The responsive workplace . New York , 1987. xi, 329 p. ; ISBN 0-231-06480-2 LC Card 87-6636 DDC 658.3 19
HF5549 .K253 1987

Kamerman, Sheila B. A workplace for people . New York , 1987. p. cm. ISBN 0-231-06480-2 LC Card 87-18223 DDC 331.2/0973 19
HD60.5.U5 K36 1987

KAHN, OTTO HERMANN, 1867-
Matz, Mary Jane. The many lives of Otto Kahn /. New York [1984] x, 299 p., [8] p. of plates : ISBN 0-918728-36-3 : LC Card 83-26326 DDC 361.7/4/0924 B 19
HV28.K32 M37 1984 ***NYPL [JFD 86-2699]***

KAHN, OTTO HERMANN, 1867- - ART PATRONAGE.
Matz, Mary Jane. The many lives of Otto Kahn /. New York [1984] x, 299 p., [8] p. of plates : ISBN 0-918728-36-3 : LC Card 83-26326

DDC 361.7/4/0924 B 19
HV28.K32 M37 1984 NYPL [JFD 86-2699]

Kahne, Hilda. Reconceiving part-time work : new perspectives for older workers and women / Hilda Kahne. Totowa, N.J. : Rowman & Allanheld, 1985. xv, 180 p. : ill. ; 25 cm. Includes index. Bibliography: p. [160]-174. ISBN 0-8476-7376-6 : LC Card 85-2386 DDC 331.3/94 19
1. Part-time employment - United States. 2. Aged - Employment - United States. 3. Women - Employment - United States. I. Title.
HD5110.2.U5 K33 1985
NYPL [JLE 86-1174]

Kahnert, Friedrich, 1929- Improving urban employment and labor productivity / Friedrich Kahnert. Washington, D.C. : World Bank, [1987] 75 p. ; 28 cm. (World Bank discussion papers, 0259-210X . 10) Bibliography: p. 74-75. ISBN 0-8213-0908-0 (pbk.) LC Card 87-10538 DDC 331.11/09172/4 19
1. Manpower policy - Developing countries. 2. Labor productivity - Developing countries. 3. Urban economics. I. Title. II. Series.
HD5852 .K34 1987

Kahney, Hank. Problem solving : a cognitive approach / Hank Kahney. Milton Keynes ; Philadelphia : Open University Press, 1986. 155 p. : ill. ; 23 cm. (Open guides to psychology) Includes indexes. Bibliography: p. 150-152. ISBN 0-335-15327-5 (pbk.) LC Card 85-21651 DDC 153.4/3 19
1. Problem solving. 2. Cognition. I. Title.
BF441 .K24 1986 NYPL [JFE 86-1837]

Kai ko. English. Reform in China : challenges and choices : a summary and analysis of the CESRRI survey / by the staff of the Chinese Economic System Reform Research Institute ; edited by Bruce L. Reynolds. Armonk, N.Y., USA : M.E. Sharpe, c1987. p. cm. Translation of: Kai ko. ISBN 0-87332-458-7 : LC Card 87-23537 DDC 338.951 19
1. China - Economic policy - 1976-. I. Reynolds, Bruce Lloyd, 1944-. II. Chinese Economic System Reform Research Institute. III. Title.
HC427.92 .K32 1987

Kai kurie matematinės ekonomikos klausimai. Nekotorye voprosy matematicheskoĭ ėkonomiki . Vil'nius , 1982. 90 p. ; LC Card 83-169081
HB135 .N45 1982

Kaick, Guntolf van.
Integração cooperativista no setor agropecuário. 1986. Propostas cooperativistas / [Organização das Cooperativas do Estado do Paraná-OCEPAR] ; colaboração, Fundação Friedrich Naumann e OCB. Curitiba , 1986. 56 p. : LC Card 87-403655 DDC 334 19
HD2953 .P76 1986

Kaiero Uria, Andoni. Las elecciones sindicales en Euskadi, representación de los trabajadores en la empresa e implantación de los sindicatos : estudio y resultados de las elecciones sindicales de 1980 y de 1982 en la Comunidad Autónoma / Andoni Kaiero Uria. Vitoria : Servicio Central de Publicaciones, Gobierno Vasco, 1985. 629 p. : ill. ; 30 cm. At head of title: Gobierno Vasco, Presidencia de Gobierno, Dirección de Prospección Sociológica. Includes bibliographical references. ISBN 84-7542-199-7 LC Card 87-146467
1. Trade-Unions - Spain - País Vasco - Recognition - Elections. 2. Trade-unions - Spain - País Vasco - Recognition - Elections - Statistics. I. País Vasco (Spain). Gabinete de Prospección Sociológica. II. Title.
HD6490.R42 S74 1985

Kaiser, Joan E. Barlow, Raymond E. The glass industry in Sandwich /. Windham, N.H. , c1983- v. : ISBN 0-9610166-0-4 (v. 4) LC Card 82-73582 DDC 338.4/76661/0974492 19
HD9623.U46 S263 1983
NYPL [3-MPW+ 84-1016]

Kaiser, Manfred. Abiturienten und Hochschulabsolventen beim Übergang vom Studium in den Beruf . Nürnberg , 1983. 407 p. : LC Card 84-140881
HD6278.G4 A25 1983

Kaiser, Martin.
The New Zealand software industry : the DSIR questionnaire survey of the New Zealand software industry / Martin Kaiser ; assisted by Mervyn Rodgers. Wellington, N.Z. : Science Information Pub. Centre, DSIR, c1986. 1 v. (various pagings) : ill. ; 30 cm. (DSIR resource paper . no. 11B) Includes bibliographical references. ISBN 0-477-06783-2 (pbk.) LC Card 86-212843 DDC 381/.450053/09931 19
1. Computer software industry - New Zealand. 2. Market surveys - New Zealand. I. Rodgers, Mervyn. II. Title. III. Series.
HD9696.C63 N455 1986

The New Zealand software industry : an overview of the world and New Zealand software industries / Martin Kaiser ; assisted by Philip Bradley. Wellington, N.Z. : Science Information Pub. Centre, DSIR, c1986. 110 p. : ill. ; 30 cm. (DSIR resource paper . no. 11A) Bibliography: p. 96-97. ISBN 0-477-06781-6 (pbk.) LC Card 86-212814 DDC 338.4/70053/09931 19
1. Computer software industry - New Zealand. 2. Computer software industry. I. Bradley, Philip. II. Title. III. Series.
HD9696.C63 N454 1986

Kajian semula jadual-jadual hayat mengikut jantina dan kumpulan etnik bagi Semenanjung Malaysia, 1970 dan 1980 = Revised life tables by sex and ethnic group for Peninsular Malaysia, 1970 and 1980. Kuala Lumpur : Jabatan Perangkaan, Malaysia, [1986] v, 27, v, 38 p. : ill. ; 30 cm. (Kajian mengenai subjek demografi dan penduduk . no. 3 = no. 3) In Malay, with translation in English. "Julai 1986." ISBN 967-99995-2-1 (pbk.) : LC Card 87-941374
1. Mortality - Malaysia - Statistics. 2. Malaysia - Statistics, Vital. I. Malaysia. Jabatan Perangkaan. II. Title: Revised life tables by sex and ethnic group for Peninsular Malaysia, 1970 and 1980. III. Series: Kajian mengenai subjek demografi dan penduduk , no. 3.
HB1474.6.A3 K35 1986

Kakabadse, Andrew. People and organisations . Aldershot, Hants. , c1982. ix, 143 p. : ISBN 0-566-00373-2 LC Card 82-189914 DDC 658.3/124 19
HD31 .P375 1982 NYPL [JLD 86-2775]

Kakabadse, Mario A. International trade in services : prospects for liberalisation in the 1990s / Mario A. Kakabadse. London ; New York : Croom Helm, for the Atlantic Institute for International Affairs, c1987. 90 p. ; 22 cm. (Atlantic papers . no. 64) Bibliography: p. 86-88. ISBN 0-7099-3130-1 (pbk.) LC Card 87-8951 DDC 382/.45/0009049 19
1. Service industries - International cooperation. I. Atlantic Institute for International Affairs. II. Series: Atlantic papers (Paris, France) , no. 64. III. Title.
HD9980.5 .K35 1987

Kakwani, Nanak. Analyzing redistribution policies : a study using Australian data / Nanak Kakwani. Cambridge [Cambridgeshire] ; New York : Cambridge University Press, 1986. ix, 293 p. : ill. ; 24 cm. Includes indexes. Bibliography: p. 275-287. ISBN 0-521-30838-0 LC Card 85-31342 DDC 339.5/2 19
1. Income distribution - Government policy - Australia. 2. Taxation, Progressive - Australia. 3. Transfer payments - Australia. 4. Australia - Social conditions. I. Title.
HC610.I5 K35 1986 NYPL [JLE 86-3491]

KALAMAZOO, MICH. - ECONOMIC CONDITIONS.
A Plan for an industrial survey for Kalamazoo, August 1, 1926. New York , 1926. 30 p. ; LC Card 85-666471
HC108.K34 P52x 1926

KALAMAZOO (MICH.) - INDUSTRIES.
A Plan for an industrial survey for Kalamazoo, August 1, 1926. New York , 1926. 30 p. ; LC Card 85-666471
HC108.K34 P52x 1926

Kalas, John W. The grant system / John W. Kalas. Albany : State University of New York Press, c1987. xii, 168 p. : ill. ; 24 cm. Bibliography: p. [157]-163. Includes index. ISBN 0-88706-583-X LC Card 87-6156 DDC 001.4/4 19
1. Grants-in-aid - United States. 2. Research grants - United States. I. Title.
HJ275 .K34 1987

Kaldor, Nicholas, 1908- The scourge of monetarism / Nicholas Kaldor. 2nd ed. Oxford ; New York : Oxford University Press, 1986. xxv, 112 p. : ill. ; 22 cm. Includes bibliographical references and index. CONTENTS. - Pt. 1. The Radcliffe report and monetary policy -- Pt. 2. ISBN 0-19-877248-3
1. Monetary policy - Great Britain. 2. Chicago school of economics. I. Title. NYPL [JLD 86-2212]

Kaldor, Nicholas, 1908-1986. Economics without equilibrium / Nicholas Kaldor ; with a preface by James Tobin. Cardiff, U.K. : University College Cardiff Press, 1985. 79 p. ; 21 cm. (The Arthur M. Okun memorial lectures) Includes bibliographical references. ISBN 0-906449-87-1 LC Card 86-673866
1. Economics. 2. Equilibrium (Economics). I. Title. II. Series.
HB71 .K273x 1985b

KALDOR, NICHOLAS, 1908-1986.
Thirlwall, A. P. Nicholas Kaldor /. Washington Square, NY , 1987. xvii, 360 p., [8] pages of plates : ISBN 0-8147-8177-2 : LC Card 87-22065 DDC 330/.092/4 B 19
HB103.K36 T45 1987

KALECKI, MICHAL.
Kriesler, Peter. Kalecki's microanalysis . Cambridge , New York , 1987. xii, 132 p. : ISBN 0-521-33145-5 LC Card 86-24414 DDC 338.5/21 19
HB238 .K75 1987

Pöschl, Josef. Die Preisbildung in der industrialisierten Marktwirtschaft . Hamburg , c1987. v, 149 p. : ISBN 3-925630-12-0 LC Card 87-146592 DDC 338.5/2 19
HB221 .P65 1987

Sawyer, Malcolm C. [Macroeconomics in question.] Macro-economics in question . Brighton, Sussex , 1982. xiii, 190 p. : ISBN 0-7108-0140-8 LC Card 86-673557
HB172.5 .S28x 1982b

Kalecki's microanalysis . Kriesler, Peter. Cambridge , New York , 1987. xii, 132 p. : ISBN 0-521-33145-5 LC Card 86-24414 DDC 338.5/21 19
HB238 .K75 1987

Kaleta, Józef. Studencki ruch naukowy /. Wrocław , 1978. 98 p. : LC Card 81-206830
HB9 .B7522 nr. 122 HD36

KALIMANTAN TIMUR (INDONESIA) - ECONOMIC CONDITIONS.
Kebschull, Dietrich. Transmigration in Indonesia . Hamburg , 1984. xxiv, 134 p. ; LC Card 86-223779 DDC 304.8/09598 19
HB2107 .K4 1984

KALININ REGION (R.S.F.R.) - RURAL CONDITIONS.
Altrichter, Helmut, 1945- Die Bauern von Tver . München , 1984. 373 p. : ISBN 3-486-52071-7 LC Card 84-162284
HD1536.S65 A47 1984

Kalinin, Russia. Gosudarstvennyĭ universitet. see **Kalininskiĭ gosudarstvennyĭ universitet.**

Kalinin, Russia. Universitet. see **Kalininskiĭ gosudarstvennyĭ universitet.**

Kaliningradskiĭ gosudarstvennyĭ universitet. Povyshenie trudovoĭ i obshchestvenno-politicheskoĭ aktivnosti mass kak reshaiushchiĭ faktor uskoreniia sotsial'no-ėkonomicheskogo progressa sotsialisticheskogo obshchestva . Kaliningrad , 1986. 382 p. ; LC Card 87-136621
HD8526.5 .P62 1986

Kalininskiĭ gosudarstvennyĭ universitet. Partiĭnye organizatsii Nechernozem'ia v bor'be za povyshenie proizvodstvennoĭ i politicheskoĭ aktivnosti rabochego klassa v period postroeniia i razvitiia sotsializma /. Kalinin , 1985. 152 p. ; LC Card 86-196840
HC337.R85 P36 1985

Kaliński, Janusz. Wyższa Szkoła Handlowa, Szkoła Główna Handlowa, Miejska Szkoła Handlowa, 1906-1945 /. Warszawa , 1984. 180 p. : LC Card 85-241871
HB74.9.P7 W98 1984

Kalisiak, Jerzy. Strategy of socio-economic development . Warsaw , 1980. 122 p. : LC Card 81-107307
HD75 .S8 1980

Kalistratov, P. I. (Petr Ivanovich) Kniazeva, G. A. (Galina Alekseevna) Kompleksnoe ispol'zovanie drevesiny v Komi ASSR /. Syktyvkar , 1986. 75 p. : LC Card 86-233834
HD9765.S653 K665 1986

Kalitsounakēs, Dēmētrios E. Aristopoiēsis paragōgēs Krētēs eis to plaision tēs Eurōpaikēs Oik. Koinotētos / Dēmētriou E. Kalitsounakē. Hērakleion Krētēs : A.G. Kalokairinos, 1963. p. 167-173 ; 25 cm. Cover title. "Anatypon ek tou periodikou 'Krētika Chronika'." LC Card 86-235201
1. Farm produce - Greece - Crete - Transportation. 2. Ferries - Greece - Crete. I. Title.
HE595.F3 K35 1963

KALKUS, FRANTIŠEK, 1894-1968.
Brzoň, František. Marie a František Kalkusovi /. České Budějovice , 1985. 98 p., [64] p. of plates : LC Card 86-161741
HD8420.3.A1 B78 1985

KALKUSOVÁ, MARIE, 1893-1979.
Brzoň, František. Marie a František Kalkusovi /. České Budějovice , 1985. 98 p., [64] p. of plates : LC Card 86-161741
HD8420.3.A1 B78 1985

Kallab, Valeriana.
Adjustment crisis in the Third World /. New Brunswick, USA , c1984. x, 186 p. ; ISBN 0-88738-040-9 LC Card 84-8690 DDC 337/.09172/4 19
HC59.7 .A733 1984 ***NYPL [JLE 86-2491]***

Development strategies reconsidered /. New Brunswick, N.J., U. S.A. , c1986. viii, 190 p. ; ISBN 0-87855-991-4 (pbk.) : LC Card 85-24582 DDC 338.9/009172/4 19
HC59.7 .D482 1986 ***NYPL [JLE 86-2976]***

Uncertain future . New Brunswick, N.J. , c1984. x, 129 p. ; ISBN 0-88738-041-7 : LC Card 84-16240 DDC 332.1/5 19
HG3891.5 .U53 1984 ***NYPL [JLE 86-2494]***

Kallaus, Norman Francis, 1924- Administrative office management / Norman F. Kallaus, B. Lewis Keeling. 9th ed. Cincinnati : South-Western Pub. Co., c1987. ix, 774 p. : ill. (some col.) ; 24 cm. Keeling's name appears first on the earlier edition. Includes bibliographical references and index. ISBN 0-538-07560-0 LC Card 85-61633 DDC 651.3 19
1. Office management. I. Keeling, B. Lewis (Billy Lewis). II. Title.
HF5547 .K43 1987

Kallaway, Peter. Johannesburg : images and continuities : a history of working class life through pictures, 1885-1935 / Peter Kallaway, Patrick Pearson. Braamfontein, South Africa : Ravan Press, c1986. v, 124 p. : ill. ; 30 cm. Bibliography: p. 124. ISBN 0-86975-303-7 (pbk.) LC Card 87-100567 DDC 305.5/62/0968221 19
1. Labor and laboring classes - South Africa - Johannesburg - History - Pictorial works. 2. Johannesburg (South Africa) - Social conditions - Pictorial works. 3. Johannesburg (South Africa) - Race relations - Pictorial works. I. Pearson, Patrick. II. Title.
HD8801.Z8 J6424 1986

Kállay, Georges Christophe de. L'importance des marchés de l'Europe de l'Est : les échanges commerciaux entre le Brésil et les pays européens du C.A.E.M., de 1970 à 1983 : évolution et perspectives / par Georges Christophe de Kállay. Genève : Institut universitaire de hautes études internationales, 1986. 247 p. ; 30 cm. Thesis (diplôme)--Institut universitaire de hautes études internationales, Geneva. Bibliography: p. 219-244. LC Card 86-179357
1. Brazil - Commerce - Europe, Eastern. 2. Europe, Eastern - Commerce - Brazil. 3. Council for Mutual Economic Assistance. I. Title.
HF3408.Z7 E8525 1986

Kalleberg, Arne L. Work and industry : structures, markets, and processes / Arne L. Kalleberg and Ivar Berg ; with a foreword by John T. Dunlop. New York : Plenum Press, c1987. xviii, 244 p. ; 24 cm. (Plenum studies in work and industry) Bibliography: p. 223-230. Includes indexes. ISBN 0-306-42344-8 LC Card 87-2333 DDC 306/.36 19
1. Work. 2. Labor supply. 3. Industry. I. Berg, Ivar E. II. Title. III. Series.
HD4904 .K294 1987

Kallergēs, Dēmētrios, 1803?-1867.
Spēliōtakēs, K. K. Archeion Michaēl Iatrou, 1802-1893 /. Athēna , 1983. 189 p., [4] folded leaves of plates : LC Card 85-134031
HF3750.5.S64 A3 1983
NYPL [JFE 86-4131]

KALLERGĒS, DĒMĒTRIOS, 1803?-1867 - ARCHIVES.
Spēliōtakēs, K. K. Archeion Michaēl Iatrou, 1802-1893 /. Athēna , 1983. 189 p., [4] folded leaves of plates : LC Card 85-134031
HF3750.5.S64 A3 1983
NYPL [JFE 86-4131]

Kallio, Markku. The Global forest sector . Chichester [West Sussex] , New York , c1987. xiii, 706 p. : ISBN 0-471-91735-4 : LC Card 87-19700 DDC 338.1/749 19
HD9750.5 .G56 1987

Kalmanovitz, Salomón.
El desarrollo de la ganadería en Colombia, 1950-1972 : separata / Seminario Permanente de Problemas Colombianos, SEPROCOL, DANE ; preparado por Salomón Kalmanovitz. [Bogotá, Colombia] : República de Colombia, Departamento Administrativo Nacional de Estadística, [1978] p. 195-238 : ill. (some col.) ; 21 x 22 cm. "Tomado del Boletín mensual de estadística no. 253-54, agosto-septiembre 1972, páginas 193 a 238." Includes bibliographical references. LC Card 86-157918
1. Cattle trade - Colombia. I. Seminario Permanente de Problemas Colombianos. II. Boletín mensual de estadísticas (Colombia. Departamento Administrativo de Estadísticas). III. Title.
HD9433.C62 K35 1978

El desarrollo tardío del capitalismo : un enfoque crítico de la teoría de la dependencia / por Salomón Kalmanovitz.1a ed. [Bogotá] : Universidad Nacional : Siglo Veintiuno Editores, 1983. 285 p. ; 21 cm. (Economía y demografía) Includes bibliographical references. LC Card 84-155755 DDC 338.9/009172/4 19
1. Dependency. 2. Developing countries - Economic policy. 3. Latin America - Economic policy. I. Title.
HC59.7 .K246 1983 ***NYPL [JLD 85-2613]***

Kalmbach, Peter. Technischer Fortschritt und Arbeitslosigkeit /. Frankfurt/Main , New York , c1983. 372 p. : ISBN 3-593-33246-9 LC Card 84-143045
HD6331 .T39 1983 ***NYPL [JLD 87-331]***

Kalra, G. D. Mineral development in Bihar, 1979-80 to 1988-89 / G.D. Kalra. New Delhi : National Council of Applied Economic Research, 1983. 2 v. : ill., maps ; 25 cm. Includes bibliographical references. LC Card 83-905955 DDC 338.2/0954/12 19
1. Mineral industries - India - Bihar. 2. Mines and mineral resources - India - Bihar. I. National Council of Applied Economic Research. II. Title.
HD9506.I43 B545 1983
NYPL [JLE 86-4727]

Kalt, Joseph P. Drawing the line on natural gas regulation . New York , 1987. xiii, 267 p. : ISBN 0-89930-174-6 (lib. bdg. : alk. paper) LC Card 86-25769 DDC 338.2/7285/0973 19
HD9581.U5 D73 1987

Kalte Kommunikation : der Millionen-Poker um Videotex und andere neue Medien / herausgegeben von Jürg Frischknecht ; mit Beiträgen von, Oliver Fahrni ... [et al.]. Basel : Lenos, c1985. 256 p. : ill. ; 20 cm. (Bd. 8 der Reihe Mediaprint) CONTENTS. - Ein Medium ohne Kunden / Jürg Frischknecht -- Warten auf den Profit / Oliver Fahrni -- Für alle und alles ein Ding / Urs Meier -- Die tägliche Volkszählung / Ruth Wysseier -- Jobkiller Videotex / Monika Oettli -- Lobbies unter sich / Jürg Frischknecht -- Bluff Begleituntersuchung / Peter Hunziker -- Lernziel Skepsis / Peter Christian Hall -- Der Turm zu Babel / Matthias Loretan -- Ein Kartell wankt / Oliver Fahrni -- Die neuen Monopolisten / Fredi Hänni -- Testmarkt Basel / Peter Knechtli. ISBN 3-85787-134-2 LC Card 85-232413
1. Videotex systems - Switzerland. I. Frischknecht, Jürg, 1947-. II. Fahrni, Oliver, 1955-. III. Series: Mediaprint , Bd. 8.
HD9696.T463 S95 1985

Die Kalte Progression : Protokoll der Arbeitstagung für die Schweizer Presse vom 19.10.82 in Bern / organisiert vom Pressekomitee fuer Fiskalfragen in Zusammenarbeit mit der Interkantonalen Kommission für Steueraufklärung = La Progression à froid : procès-verbal de la séance de travail à l'intention de la presse suisse, du 19.10.82, à Berne / organisée par le Comité de presse pour les questions fiscales en collaboration avec la Commission intercantonale d'information fiscale. Bern : Informationsstelle für Steuerfragen, 1982. 107 p. : ill. ; 21 cm. French and German. Bibliography: p. 31. LC Card 83-128720
1. Income tax - Switzerland. 2. Income tax - Switzerland - Effect of inflation on. I. Pressekomitee für Fiskalfragen (Switzerland). II. Switzerland. Interkantonale Kommission für Steueraufklärung. III. Switzerland. Informationsstelle für Steuerfragen. IV. Title: Progression à froid.
HJ4747 .K35 1982

Kalter Krieg und kommunale Integration . Oltmann, Joachim. Marburg , c1987. 500 p. ; ISBN 3-921630-71-1 LC Card 87-142718 DDC 331.88/0943/52 19
HD6699.B7 O48 1987

Kaluza, Bernd. Internationale und nationale Problemfelder der Betriebswirtschaftslehre /. Berlin , c1984. 336 p., [1] leaf of plates : ISBN 3-428-05696-5 LC Card 85-141327
HD35 .I598 1984

Kälvemark, Ann-Sofie, 1941- More children of better quality? : aspects on Swedish population policy in the 1930's / Ann-Sofie Kälvemark. Uppsala : Historiska institutionen vid Uppsala universitet ; Stockholm : Distributor, Almqvist & Wiksell International, 1980. 160 p. : ill. ; 23 cm. (Acta Universitatis Upsaliensis. Studia historica Upsaliensia . 115) "Falls within the framework of the research project 'The Family in the Demographic and Social Transformation of Sweden after 1800'"--P. facing t.p. ISBN 91-554-1094-4 LC Card 81-114081
1. Sweden - Population policy. 2. Sweden - Social policy. I. Title. II. Series.
HB3617 .K34 1980

Kalwani, Manohar U. Hu, Sheng C. A game-theoretic approach to the design of an optimal sales policy /. West Lafayette, Ind. [1986] 30, 14 p. : LC Card 86-622755 DDC 658/.001/9 s 658.8/101 19
HD6483 .P8 no. 900 HF5438.25

Kamaev, V. D. (Vladimir Dorofeevich)
Simpozium "Nauchno-tekhnicheskiĭ progress i intensifikatsii͡a obshchestvennogo proizvodstva" (1984 : Podol'sk, Moscow, R.S.F.S.R.) Formy i metody vzaimodeĭstvii͡a nauki i proizvodstva /. Moskva , 1984. 237 p. ; LC Card 85-240380
HC340.T4 S48 1984

Kamali, Nasser.
Focht, Rick. Employment and gross earnings of California residents in Alaska's commercial fisheries, 1977-1982 /. Juneau, AK [1984] v, 53 p. : LC Card 86-622320 DDC 331.12/5392/09798021 19
HD4966.F652 U54 1984c

Focht, Rick. Employment and gross earnings of Oregon residents in Alaska's commercial fisheries, 1977-1982 /. Juneau, AK [1984] v, 69 p. : LC Card 86-622319 DDC 331.12/5392/09798021 19
HD4966.F652 U54 1984b

Focht, Rick. Employment and gross earnings of Washington residents in Alaska's commercial fisheries, 1977-1982 /. Juneau, AK [1984] v leaves, 126 p. ; LC Card 86-622318 DDC 331.2/8392/09797021 19
HD4966.F542 U554 1984

Kamath, M. V., 1921- The innovative banker, T.A. Pai, his life and times / M.V. Kamath. Manipal : T.A. Pai Memorial Committee ; Bombay : Distributors, Allied, 1983. x, 247 p., [9] p. of plates : ill. ; 24 cm. Bibliography: p. [246]-247. LC Card 83-904531 DDC 332.1/2/0924 B 19
1. Pai, T. A. (Tonse Ananth), 1922-1981. 2. Bank directors - India - Biography. 3. Cabinet officers - India - Biography. I. Title.
HG1552.P4 K36 1983 ***NYPL [JFE 87-879]***

Kamenit͡ser, Solomon Efremovich. Opyt khozi͡aĭstvovanii͡a v ob"edinenii͡akh promyshlennosti sotsialisticheskikh stran /. Moskva , 1985. 157 p. : LC Card 87-152292
HD70.E7 O69 1985

Kamenov, Dimitŭr. Radev, Simeon. Sot͡sialnata programa na partii͡ata-delo na trudovii͡a kolektiv /. Sofii͡a , 1984. 173 p. ; LC Card 84-172433
HD8626.5 .R32 1984

KAMER VAN KOOPHANDEL EN FABRIEKEN VOOR AMSTERDAM.
Om het behoud van een explosieve stad . Muiderberg , 1986. 298 p. : ISBN 90-6283-661-5 : LC Card 86-205071
HC328.A5 O4 1986

Kamerman, Sheila B.
Meeting family needs : the corporate response / by Sheila B. Kamerman.1st ed. New York : Pergamon Press, c1983. 45 p. ; 28 cm. (Work in America Institute studies in productivity . 33) Bibliography: p. 39-45. ISBN 0-08-030965-8 (pbk.) : LC Card 83-27159 DDC 658.3/8 19
1. Employee fringe benefits - United States. 2. Family - United States. I. Title. II. Series.
HD4928.N62 U6355 1983
NYPL [JLM 83-380 no.33]

The responsive workplace : employers and a changing labor force / Sheila B. Kamerman and Alfred J. Kahn. New York : Columbia University Press, 1987. xi, 329 p. ; 24 cm. Bibliography: p. [306]-323. Includes index. ISBN 0-231-06480-2 LC Card 87-6636 DDC 658.3 19
1. Personnel management. 2. Employee fringe benefits. I. Kahn, Alfred J., 1919-. II. Title.
HF5549 .K253 1987

A workplace for people : employers and a changing labor force / Sheila B. Kamerman and Alfred J. Kahn. New York : Columbia University Press, 1987. p. cm. Bibliography: p. Includes index. ISBN 0-231-06481-0 LC Card 87-18223 DDC 331.2/0973 19
1. Industry - Social aspects - United States. 2. Labor supply - United States. 3. Family - United States. I. Kahn, Alfred J., 1919-. II. Title.
HD60.5.U5 K36 1987

Kamin, Jonathan. Hergert, Douglas. Mastering Framework II /. Berkeley , c1987. xvii, 509 p. : ISBN 0-89588-390-2 (pbk.) : LC Card 86-62808 DDC 650/.028/55369 19
HF5548.4.F72 H47 1987

Kamin, Steven, 1957- Yagci, Fahrettin, 1944- Macroeconomic policies and adjustment in Yugoslavia . Washington, D.C. [1987] 29 p. ; ISBN 0-8213-0938-2 (pbk.) LC Card 87-16064 DDC 339.5/09497 19
HC407.Y6 Y34 1987

Kamiński, Zenon.
Dmowski, Zygmunt. Organizacja i technika handlu zagranicznego . Gdańsk , 1979. 201 p. ; LC Card 81-181043
HF1558.7 .D59 1979

Ubezpieczenia morskie / Zenon Kamiński. Wyd. 1. Gdańsk : UG, 1980. 191 p. ; 24 cm. (Skrypty uczelniane / Uniwersytet Gdański) Bibliography: p. 188-189. LC Card 80-129098
1. Insurance, Marine. I. Series: Skrypty uczelniane / Uniwersytet Gdański. II. Title.
HE965 .K26 1980

Kammer für Arbeiter und Angestellte für Salzburg. Fink, Karl, Mag. Die regionale Dynamik des Salzburger Arbeitsmarktes, 1971-1980 . Salzburg [1981?] 212 p. : LC Card 82-171635
HD5772.S24 F56 1981 ***NYPL [JLG 86-301]***

Kamody, Miklós. Észak-Magyarország hírközlésének története / Kamody, Miklós. Miskolc : Herman Ottó Múzeum, 1985. 153 p., [3] leaves of plates : ill., maps ; 20 cm. (Borsodi kismonográfiák, 0324-4563 . 22) Summary in English and German. Bibliography: p. 143-144. ISBN 963-01-6902-9 : LC Card 87-408020
1. Postal service - Hungary - History. I. Title. II. Series.
HE6980.5 .K36 1985

Kamoroff, Bernard. Small time operator : how to start your own small business, keep your books, pay your taxes & stay out of trouble : a guide and workbook / by Bernard Kamoroff.Rev. ed. Jan. 1986. Laytonville, Calif. : Bell Springs Pub., c1986. 190 p. : ill., forms ; 28 cm. Includes index. ISBN 0-917510-06-2 (pbk.) : LC Card 84-73438
1. New business enterprises - Management. 2. Small business - Handbooks, manuals, etc. I. Title.
NYPL [JLF 86-947]

Kamouzēs, Kōn/nos Ch. (Kōnstantinos Ch.), 1946- Anatomia tēs Hellēnikēs oikonomias apo to 1953 mechri sēmera / Kon/nou Ch. Kamouzē. Thessalonikē : University Studio, 1981. 197 p. : ill. ; 24 cm. Spine title: Anatomia tēs Hellēnikēs oikonomias (1953-1980) Bibliography: p. 189-197. LC Card 84-140694
1. Greece - Economic conditions. 2. Greece - Economic policy. I. Title. II. Title: Anatomia tēs Hellēnikēs oikonomias (1953-1980).
HC295 .K28 1981

Kampe, Dieter, 1953- Die Macher : Wirtschaftsreportagen aus einem satten Land / von Dieter Kampe. Pfaffenweiler : Centaurus-Verlagsgesellschaft, 1986. 191 p. ; 21 cm. Essays originally published in Trans Atlantik. ISBN 3-89085-143-6 LC Card 87-133889 DDC 338.0943 19
1. Germany, West - Industries. 2. Germany, West - Economic conditions - 1974-. I. Trans Atlantik. II. Title.
HC286.7 .K36 1986

Kampf und Arbeit : Berichte aus der Arbeit und dem Ringen deutscher Jugend in Rumänien im Jahre 1935 / herausgegeben vom Landesjugendamt der Deutschen in Rumänien und vom Landesamt für Arbeitsdienst ... Kronstadt : Das Landesjugendamt : Landesamt für Arbeitsdienst, 1936. 102 p., [1] leaf of plates : ill. ; 23 cm. LC Card 84-255742
1. Labor camps - Romania - History - 20th century. 2. Germans - Romania - History - 20th century. 3. Youth - Romania - History - 20th century. I. Landesjugendamt der Deutschen in Rumänien. II. Landesamt für Arbeitsdienst der Deutschen in Rumänien.
HD7290 .K35 1936

Kamu alacaklarının tahsili teorisi ve Türkiye'de uygulaması /. Özer, İlhan. Ankara , 1979. xv, 236 p. ; LC Card 85-968002
HJ2906.5 .O93 1979

Kamus istilah demografi / oleh Kartomo Wirosuhardjo ... [et al.]. Cet. 1. Jakarta : Pusat Pembinaan dan Pengembangan Bahasa, Departemen Pendidikan dan Kebudayaan, 1985. vi, 119 p. ; 21 cm. English and Indonesian. LC Card 86-941191
1. Demography - Dictionaries - Indonesian. 2. Indonesian language - Dictionaries - English. I. Wirosuhardjo, Kartomo.
HB849.2 .K35 1985

Kamus istilah ekonomi / oleh Daidumi Darmawan ... [et al.]. Jakarta : Pusat Pembinaan dan Pengembangan Bahasa, Departemen Pendidikan dan Kebudayaan, 1984. v, 216 p. ; 21 cm. English and Indonesian. LC Card 85-941380
1. Economics - Dictionaries - Indonesian. 2. Indonesian language - Dictionaries - English. I. Darmawan, Daidumi. II. Pusat Pembinaan dan Pengembangan Bahasa.
HB61 .K26 1984

Kamya, Andrew, 1941- Factors affecting efficiency in the informal sector in Lusaka and Kitwe / by Andrew Kamya. Lusaka : International Labour Office, World Employment Programme, Southern African Team for Employment Promotion, 1981. iii, 40 p. ; 30 cm. (Working papers) "Paper presented at a Seminar on the Prospects for Growth and Employment in the Urban Informal Sector in Zambia, organised by ILO (SATEP), Lusaka, November 3-4, 1981." Bibliography: p. 39-40. LC Card 87-980491
1. Informal sector (Economics) - Zambia - Lusaka. 2. Informal sector (Economics) - Zambia - Kitwe. 3. Industrial productivity - Zambia - Lusaka. 4. Industrial productivity - Zambia - Kitwe. 5. Lusaka (Zambia) - Economic conditions. 6. Kitwe (Zambia) - Economic conditions. I. Southern African Team for Employment Promotion. II. Series: Working papers (Southern African Team for Employment Promotion). III. Title.
HD2346.Z292 L875 1981

Kanaka. Gray, William, Rev. The kanaka, or, How the Queensland planters get and treat their-- /. Adelaide , 1895. 40 p. ; LC Card 87-123897 DDC 331.6/2/960943 19
HD8848.5.P75 G73 1895

KANAKA (NEW CALEDONIAN PEOPLE)
Gray, William, Rev. The kanaka, or, How the Queensland planters get and treat their-- /. Adelaide , 1895. 40 p. ; LC Card 87-123897 DDC 331.6/2/960943 19
HD8848.5.P75 G73 1895

The kanaka, or, How the Queensland planters get and treat their-- /. Gray, William, Rev. Adelaide , 1895. 40 p. ; LC Card 87-123897 DDC 331.6/2/960943 19
HD8848.5.P75 G73 1895

Kanchier, Carole. Questers : dare to change your job and your life / Carole Kanchier. Saratoga, Calif. : R&E Publishers, c1987. xi, 225 p. ; 23 cm. Bibliography: p. 219-225. ISBN 0-88247-767-6 (pbk.) : LC Card 87-60351 DDC 658.4/09 19
1. Career changes. 2. Executives - Interviews. I. Title. II. Title: Dare to change your job and your life.
HF5384 .K36 1987

Kandoole, B. F. Revenue and equity effects of the 1983 income tax reform in Malawi / B.F. Kandoole. [Zomba, Malaŵi?] : University of Malaŵi, Chancellor College, [1986] 20 p. ; 30 cm. (Staff seminar paper . no. 51) Cover title. "Thursday 6th February, 1986." Bibliography: p. 20. LC Card 86-981440 DDC 336.2/0096897 19
1. Income tax - Malawi. 2. Revenue - Malawi. 3. Tax incidence - Malawi. I. Series: Staff seminar paper (Chancellor College) , no. 51. II. Title.
HJ4791 .K36 1986

Kanduza, Ackson M. The political economy of underdevelopment in Northern Rhodesia, 1918-1960 : a case study of customs tariff and railway freight policies / Ackson M. Kanduza. Lanham, MD : University Press of America : Centre for African Studies, Dalhousie University, c1986. x, 336 p. : maps ; 23 cm. (Dalhousie African studies series. 5) Includes index. Bibliography: p. 287-330. ISBN 0-8191-5189-0 (alk. paper) : LC Card 85-29835 DDC 338.96894 19
1. Tariff preferences - Zambia - History. 2. Railroads - Zambia - Rates - History. 3. Zambia - Economic policy. 4. Great Britain - Colonies - Africa - Economic policy. I. Title.
HC915 .K36 1986 ***NYPL [JLD 86-2962]***

Kane, Daniel R., 1949- Principles of international finance / Daniel R. Kane. London ; New York : Croom Helm, c1988. xiv, 301 p. : ill. ; 22 cm. Bibliography: p. 291-296. Includes index. ISBN 0-7099-3134-4 (pbk.) LC Card 87-24388 DDC 332.042 19
1. International finance. I. Title.
HG3881 .K263 1988

Kane, Nancy Frances, 1954- Textiles in transition : technology, wages, and industry relocation in the U. S. textile industry, 1880-1930 / Nancy Frances Kane. New York : Greenwood Press, c1988. p. cm. (Contributions in economics and economic history, 0084-9235 . no. 79) Bibliography: p. Includes index. ISBN 0-313-25529-6 (lib. bdg. : alk. paper) LC Card 87-24950 DDC 338.4/767721/0973 19
1. Cotton textile industry - United States - History. I. Title. II. Series.
HD9875 .K3 1988

Kane, Raymond W. Cahill, Lawrence B. Environmental audits /. Rockville, Md., U. S.A. , 1987. xi, 656 p. : ISBN 0-86587-720-3 (soft) LC Card 87-404450 DDC 658.4/08 19
HC110.E5 C26 1987

Kanemoto, Yoshitsugu. Miyao, Takahiro. Urban dynamics and urban externalities /. Chur, Switzerland , New York , c1987. viii, 107 p. : ISBN 3-7186-0333-0 (pbk.) LC Card 86-25629 DDC 330.9173/2 19
HB2161 .M595 1987

Kanevskiĭ, Evgeniĭ Markovich. Aktivnaia sotsial'naia politika . Moskva , 1986. 156 p., [16] p. of plates : LC Card 86-216405 DDC 354.47001/6 19
HD60.5.S77 A38 1986

Kannapin, Klaus. Imperialistische Strategie gegen die neue Internationale Wirtschaftsordnung / Klaus Kannapin. Berlin : Dietz, 1984. 180 p. : maps ; 18 cm. Includes bibliographical references. LC Card 85-147404
1. Dependency. 2. Imperialism. 3. Developing countries - Economic conditions. I. Title.
HD84 .K28 1984

The Kano River Irrigation Project /. Jackson, Cecile, 1953- West Hartford, Conn. , 1985. xviii, 66 p. ; ISBN 0-931816-19-X LC Card 85-5242 DDC 331.4/83/09669 19
HD6073.F32 N64 1985
NYPL [JLF 86-1634]

KANO STATE (NIGERIA) - INDUSTRIES.
Bashir, Ibrahim Lawan, 1948- Sources of capital formation and accumulation among Kano entrepreneurs, 1950-1980 /. Boston, MA (270 Bay State Rd., Boston 02215) , 1986. 17 leaves ; LC Card 87-156659 DDC 332/.0415/096695 19
HC1055.Z9 S33 1986

Kanogo, Tabitha M. Squatters and the roots of Mau Mau, 1905-63 / Tabitha Kanogo. London : J. Currey ; Athens : Ohio University Press, 1987. xviii, 206 p. : maps ; 23 cm.

(Eastern African studies) Bibliography: p. [188]-197. Includes index. ISBN 0-8214-0873-9 (U.S) LC Card 87-11201 DDC 307.3/36 19

1. Migrant agricultural laborers - Kenya - History - 20th century. 2. Squatters - Kenya - History - 20th century. 3. Mau Mau - History. 4. Kikuyu (African people) - History. I. Series: East African studies (London, England). II. Title.

HD1538.K4 K36 1987

Kanpishi. Moriya, Hiroshi, 1932- Kyōsha no kanrigaku Kanpishi /. Kyōto-shi , 1984. 273 p. ; ISBN 4-569-21374-X : LC Card 85-142427

HF5387 .M67 1984 <Orien Japan>

NYPL [*OSM 87-1463]

Kanryō fuyu no jidai /. Sano, Shin'ichi, 1947- Tōkyō , 1985. 6, 255 p. ; ISBN 4-8334-1266-7 : LC Card 86-179753

HC462.9 .S2534 1985 <Orien Japan>

NYPL [*OSM 87-1196]

Kansakar, Vidya Bir Singh. Migration and employment in the tea estates of Nepal / Vidya Bir Singh Kansakar. Kathmandu : Centre for Economic Development and Administration, Tribhuvan University, Kirtipur, 1985. vii, 87, iv, xvii p. ; 30 cm. Bibliography: p. [i]-iv (3rd group) LC Card 86-903522 DDC 331.12/5372/095496 19

1. Tea plantation workers - Nepal. 2. Migration, Internal - Nepal. 3. Tea plantation workers - Employment - Nepal. I. Centre for Economic Development and Administration. II. Title.

HD8039.T182 N355 1985

Kānsamrūat kānyāithin kh Survey of migration into the Bangkok Metropolis, the vicinity of the Bangkok Metropolis, and Khon Kaen Province, 1985. [Bangkok] : Samnakngān Sathiti hæng Chāt, Samnak Nāyok Ratthamontrī, [1986] 57, 165 p. ; 32 cm. Chiefly tables. Thai and English. Cover title. "'Anukrom 'ēkkasān : publication E-SuR-Mign-no. 1-86"--1st prelim. p. Errata slip inserted. LC Card 87-915769

1. Migration, Internal - Thailand - Bangkok Region. 2. Migration, Internal - Thailand - Khon Kaen (Province). 3. Migration, Internal - Thailand - Bangkok Region - Statistics. 4. Migration, Internal - Thailand - Khon Kaen (Province) - Statistics. I. Thailand. Samnakngān Sathiti hæng Chāt. II. Title: Survey of migration into the Bangkok Metropolis, the vicinity of the Bangkok Metropolis, and Khon Kaen Province, 1985.

HB2104.55.B36 K35 1986

Kansas City Southern . Lynch, Terry, 1948- Boulder, Colo. , c1987. 223 p. : ISBN 0-87108-735-9 LC Card 87-25288 DDC 385/.065/76 19

HE2791.K17 L96 1987

KANSAS CITY SOUTHERN RAILWAY - HISTORY.

Lynch, Terry, 1948- Kansas City Southern . Boulder, Colo. , c1987. 223 p. : ISBN 0-87108-735-9 LC Card 87-25288 DDC 385/.065/76 19

HE2791.K17 L96 1987

Kansas. Dept. of Revenue. Daicoff, Darwin W. The Kansas retail liquor industry . [Lawrence, Kan.] [1985] 53 leaves ; LC Card 86-622263 DDC 381/.456631/09781 19

HD9390.U63 K23 1985

KANSAS - ECONOMIC CONDITIONS.

Kansas policy choices . Lawrence, Kan. , c1986. x, 210 p. : ISBN 0-7006-0302-6 (pbk.) LC Card 86-204211 DDC 338.9781 19

HC107.K2 K387 1986

Making do and doing without . [Lawrence, Kan.] , 1985, c1983. 98 p. ; LC Card 86-622703 DDC 330.9781/032 19

HC107.K2 M35 1985

KANSAS - ECONOMIC POLICY.

Kansas policy choices . Lawrence, Kan. , c1986. x, 210 p. : ISBN 0-7006-0302-6 (pbk.) LC Card 86-204211 DDC 338.9781 19

HC107.K2 K387 1986

Kansas. Legislature. Task Force on Business Training. Report of the Task Force on Business Training of the Legislative Commission on Economic Development. [Topeka, Kansas] : The Task Force, [1986] 1 v. (various pagings) ; 23 cm. "December 1, 1986." "Publication no. DD86-269." Includes bibliographies. LC Card 87-621700 DDC 331.25/92/09781 19

1. Occupational training - Kansas. 2. Occupational retraining - Kansas. 3. Vocational education - Kansas. 4. Manpower policy - Kansas. I. Title.

HD5715.3.K2 K37 1986

Kansas policy choices : report of the Special Commission on a Public Agenda for Kansas / edited by H. Edward Flentje. Lawrence, Kan. : University Press of Kansas, c1986. x, 210 p. : ill. ; 23 cm. Bibliography: p. 193-200. Includes index. ISBN 0-7006-0302-6 (pbk.) LC Card 86-204211 DDC 338.9781 19

1. Kansas - Economic policy. 2. Kansas - Economic conditions. 3. Education and state - Kansas. 4. Medical policy - Kansas. I. Flentje, H. Edward. II. Special Commission on a Public Agenda for Kansas.

HC107.K2 K387 1986

The Kansas retail liquor industry . Daicoff, Darwin W. [Lawrence, Kan.] [1985] 53 leaves ; LC Card 86-622263 DDC 381/.456631/09781 19

HD9390.U63 K23 1985

KANT, IMMANUEL, 1724-1804 - VIEWS ON PROPERTY.

Brocker, Manfred. Kants Besitzlehre . Würzburg , 1987. 220 p. ; ISBN 3-88479-278-4 LC Card 87-136989 DDC 330/.17 19

HB701 .B78 1987

Kanter, Jerome. Computer essays for management / Jerome Kanter. Englewood Cliffs, N.J. : Prentice-Hall, 1987, c1986. xi, 109 p. ; 26 cm. ISBN 0-13-165994-4 : LC Card 86-30651 DDC 658/.05 19

1. Management - Data processing. 2. Information storage and retrieval systems. I. Title.

HD30.2 .K36 1987

Kanter, Rosabeth Moss.

Change masters.

Change master companies [videorecording] : putting the theory into action / produced for Encyclopaedia Britannica Educational Corp. by Chuck Olin Associates. Chicago, IL , 1987. 1 videocassette (42 min.) : LC Card 87-705608 DDC 658.3 11

HD45

The Change masters [motion picture] : understanding the theory / Rosabeth Moss Kanter ; [produced by] Chuck Olin Associates, Inc. Chicago, Ill. , 1987. 1 film reel (29 min.) : LC Card 87-705269 DDC 658.3 11

HD45

The Change masters [videorecording] : understanding the theory / Rosabeth Moss Kanter ; [produced by] Chuck Olin Associates, Inc. Chicago, Ill. , 1987. 1 videocassette (29 min.) : LC Card 86-707881 DDC 658.3 11

HD45

The Change masters [motion picture] . Chicago, Ill. , 1987. 1 film reel (29 min.) : LC Card 87-705269 DDC 658.3 11

HD45

The Change masters [videorecording] . Chicago, Ill. , 1987. 1 videocassette (29 min.) : LC Card 86-707881 DDC 658.3 11

HD45

Kanton Bern (n.G.), Bilanz der erwerbstätigen Pendler, nach Gemeinden (2. 12. 1980) = Canton de Berne (n.f.), balance des travailleurs navetteurs, par communes (2. 12. 1980). Bern : Amt für Statistik des Kantons Bern : Kommissionsverlag Stauffacher, 1983. 16 p. ; 30 cm. (Beiträge zur Statistik des Kantons Bern. Bevölkerungsstatistik (Reihe A) . Heft 20 = cahier 20) French and German. LC Card 83-232809 DDC 388.3/14/094945 19

1. Commuting - Switzerland - Bern (Canton) - Statistics. I. Bern (Switzerland : Canton). Amt für Statistik. II. Title: Canton de Berne (n.f.), balance des travailleurs navetteurs, par communes (2. 12. 1980). III. Series: Beiträge zur Statistik des Kantons Bern. Bevölkerungsstatistik (Reihe A) , Heft 20.

HD5717.5.S92 B46 1983

Kantonale demographische Indiktoren, 1960 und 1970 = Indicateurs démographiques cantonaux, 1960 et 1970. Bern : Eidgenössisches Statistisches Amt, 1977. 187 p. : ill. ; 30 cm. (Beiträge zur schweizerischen Statistik . Heft 44 = 44e fasc.) Text in French and German. Chiefly tables. LC Card 85-217076

1. Switzerland - Population - Statistics. 2. Switzerland - Statistics, Vital. I. Switzerland. Eidgenössisches Statistisches Amt. II. Title: Indicateurs démographiques cantonaux, 1960 et 1970. III. Series: Beiträge zur schweizerischen Statistik , Heft 44.

HA1593 .B45 Heft 44 HA1604

Kantonale Verteilung der Bundesausgaben 1983 . Dürsteler, Urs. Bern , c1986. 55 p. ; ISBN 3-258-03577-6 : LC Card 86-149603

HJ1264.A2 D87 1986

Kantorovich, L. V. (Leonid Vital'evich), 1912- Sovershenstvovanie khoziaĭstvennogo mekhanizma na transporte /. Moskva , 1983. 223 p. : LC Card 85-199829

HE255.A2 S68 1983

Kantowicz, Edward R. True Value : John Cotter 70 years of hardware / by Edward R. Kantowicz. Chicago : Regnery Books, 1986. 270 p., [16] p. of plates : ill. ; 24 cm. Includes bibliographical references and index. ISBN 0-89526-580-X : LC Card 86-42795 DDC 381/.45683/0924 B 19

1. Cotter, John, 1904-. 2. Cotter & Company - History. 3. Hardware industry - United States - History. 4. Businessmen - United States - Biography. I. Title. II. Title: John Cotter 70 years of hardware.

HD9745.U5 C655 1986

NYPL [JLE 87-1449]

Kantrow, Alan M., 1947- The constraints of corporate tradition : doing the correct thing, not just what the past dictates / Alan M. Kantrow.1st ed. New York : Harper & Row, c1987. xvii, 216 p. ; 22 cm. Bibliography: p. 203-207. Includes index. ISBN 0-06-015753-4 : LC Card 86-46075 DDC 302.3/5 19

1. Corporate culture. 2. Organizational effectiveness. 3. Industrial management. I. Title.

HD58.7 .K375 1987

Kants Besitzlehre . Brocker, Manfred. Würzburg , 1987. 220 p. ; ISBN 3-88479-278-4 LC Card 87-136989 DDC 330/.17 19

HB701 .B78 1987

Kanuk, Leslie Lazar. Schiffman, Leon G. Consumer behavior /. Englewood Cliffs, N.J. , c1987. xviii, 724 p. : ISBN 0-13-169020-5 LC Card 86-25224 DDC 658.8/342 19

HF5415.3 .S29 1987

Kānwāngphǣn phatthanā khr Sētthaph [Bangkok] , 2524 [1981] 8, 80 leaves ; LC Card 82-920041

HD9696.T442 S47 1981

Kanyangwa, Joyce. Strengthening women's participation in food and agricultural marketing . [Lusaka] [1984] 78 p. ; LC Card 86-980282 DDC 331.4/83/096894 19

HD6073.A292 Z3374 1984

Kapadia, Kamini R. Child labour and health . Bombay , c1985. xi, 287 p. ; LC Card 86-900928 DDC 331.3/1/0956 19

HD6250.I42 C46 1985

NYPL [JLD 87-1553]

Kapal dan harta karam = Ships and sunken treasure / Mohd. Yusoff Hashim ... [et al.].Cet. 1. Kuala Lumpur : Diterbitkan oleh Persatuan Muzium Malaysia, Muzium Negara untuk Jabatan Sejarah, University Malaya, 1986. xv, 181 p. : ill., map ; 23 cm. English and Malay. "Jawatankuasa Penerbitan, Jabatan Sejarah, Universiti Malaya." "Kolokium Perdagangan dan Perkapalan di Kepulauan Melayu Sebelum 1900, anjuran Jabatan Sejarah, Universiti Malaya pada 8 September 1984"--P. [xvii] Includes bibliographies. LC Card 86-942317 DDC 387.5/09595 19

1. Malaysia - Commerce - History - Congresses. 2. Shipping - Malaysia - History - Congresses. 3. Treasure-trove - Malaysia - History - Congresses. I. Yusoff Iskandar. II. Kolokium Perdagangan dan Perkapalan di Kepulauan Malayu Sebelum 1900 (1984 : Kuala Lumpur?, Malaysia). III. Universiti Malaya. Jabatan Sejarah. IV. Title: Ships and sunken treasure.

HF3800.6 .K36 1986

Kapazitätsfestlegung in Distributionssystemen /. Hall, Bruno. München , c1986. xiii, 266 p. ; ISBN 3-597-10558-0 LC Card 87-127684 DDC 658.7/88 19

HF5415.6 .H35 1986

Kapetanakē-Sēphakē, Katerina. Hē diethnopoiēsē tou kephalaiou stēn Hellada, hē periptōsē tōn diylistēriōn : mia analysē tōn scheseōn Hellēnōn ephoplistōn-polyethnikōn hetaireiōn petrelaiou / Katerina Kapetanakē-Sēphakē. Athēna : Ekdoseis Papazēsē, 1985. 234 p. : ill. ; 21 cm. Bibliography: p. 227-234. LC Card 86-206498

1. Petroleum - Transportation. 2. Merchant ships -

Greece. I. Title.
HE595.P4 K36 1985

Kapferer, Clodwig, 1901- Ein Leben für die Information : Erfahrungen und Lehren aus sechs Jahrzehnten / Clodwig Kapferer. Zürich : Kriterion, 1983. 116 p. ; 22 cm. Includes bibliographical references. ISBN 3-906639-00-X LC Card 83-185401
1. Kapferer, Clodwig, 1901-. 2. Businessmen - Germany, West - Biography. 3. World War, 1939-1945 - Biography. I. Title.
HC282.5.K36 A3 1983

KAPFERER, CLODWIG, 1901-
Kapferer, Clodwig, 1901- Ein Leben für die Information . Zürich , 1983. 116 p. ; ISBN 3-906639-00-X LC Card 83-185401
HC282.5.K36 A3 1983

Kapitaal-export vanuit Nederland . Kox, Henk. Amsterdam , 1985. 136 p. : ISBN 90-71284-01-8 LC Card 85-237950
HG5562 .K69 1985

"Kapital" K. Marksa i ėkonomicheskie problemy razvitogo sotsializma / [redaktsionnaia kollegiia, V.N. Cherkovets (otvetstvennyĭ redaktor) ... et al.]. Moskva : Izd-vo "Nauka", 1980. 260 p. ; 20 cm. (Problemy sovetskoĭ ėkonomiki) At head of title: Akademiia nauk SSSR. Nauchnyĭ sovet "Ėkonomicheskie zakonomernosti razvitiia sotsializma i ego pererastaniia v kommunizm." Institut ėkonomiki. Includes bibliographical references. LC Card 81-134413
1. Marx, Karl, 1818-1883. Kapital. 2. Soviet Union - Economic conditions - 1918-. I. Cherkovets, Viktor Nikitich. II. Nauchnyĭ sovet "Ėkonomicheskie zakonomernosti razvitiia sotsializma i ego pererastaniia v kommunizm" (Akademiia nauk SSSR).
HB501 .K248 1980

Kapital, Zins, Währung . DIHT-Kongress (1983 : Frankfurt am Main, Germany) Bonn , 1984. 68 p. : LC Card 84-212399
HC290.5.C3 D53 1983

Das Kapitalanlageverhalten der deutschen Lebensversicherungsunternehmen im Wandel der Konjunktur . Lehnhardt-Ritter, Gerda. Karlsruhe , c1984. xxiii, 444 p. : ISBN 3-88487-067-X LC Card 85-171182
HG9078 .L44 1984

Kapitalbildning i Sverige 1750-1860 . Magnusson, Lars, 1941- Uppsala , Stockholm , 1983. 95 p. ; ISBN 91-554-1443-5 LC Card 83-228044
HC374 .M34 1983

Kapitalbildung und Altersvorsorge : dem Ehrenvorsitzenden der Gesellschaft für Versicherungswissenschaft und -gestaltung, Prof. Dr. Erwin Gaber, zur Vollendung des 80. Lebensjahres gewidmet. Köln : Die Gesellschaft ; Bergisch Gladbach : I. Vollmer, [1983?] 95 p. : 1 port. ; 21 cm. (Schriftenreihe der Gesellschaft für Versicherungswissenschaft und -gestaltung e.V. Köln . Bd. 4) Includes bibliographical references. LC Card 84-180205
1. Pension trusts - Germany, West. 2. Capital - Germany, West. 3. Gaber, Erwin, 1903-. I. Gaber, Edwin, 1903-. II. Gesellschaft für Versicherungswissenschaft und -gestaltung e.V. Köln. III. Series.
HD7105.45.G3 K37 1983

Kapitalbudgetierung in divisionalisierten Unternehmen . Leichtfuss, Reinhold. Wiesbaden , c1984. 389 p. ; ISBN 3-409-13701-7 LC Card 85-231538
HG4028.C4 L387 1984

Kapitale Karrieren . Hartmann, Wolf-Dietrich, 1946- Berlin , c1986. 154 p. : LC Card 86-214325
HG172.A2 H37 1986

Kapitaleinkommensbesteuerung . Sinn, Hans-Werner. Tübingen , 1985. xv, 352 p. : ISBN 3-16-344827-5 LC Card 85-164588
HD2753.A3 S48 1985

Kapitalerhöhungen und Aktienmarkt . Zimmermann, Heinz, 1958- Köln , 1986. 446 p. : ISBN 3-921471-57-5 LC Card 87-407823 DDC 332.63/222/09494 19
HG5653 .Z56 1986

Kapitalisticheskaia ėvoliutsiia pomeshchich'ego khoziaistva v Vostochnoĭ Gruzii. Nac'vlišvili, N. Memamuluri meurneobis kapitalisturi evoluc'ia Aġmosavlet' Sak'art'veloši /. T'bilisi , 1971. 107 p. ; LC Card 86-168887
HC337.G38 N33 1971

Der Kapitalistische Charakter der jugoslawischen Arbeiterselbstverwaltung im Lichte des 8. Kongresses des Bundes der Kommunisten Jugoslawiens. Tirana : "Naim Frasheri" Verlag, 1965. 54 p. ; 17 cm. "Veröffentlicht auf der Zeitung 'Zëri i Popullit' vom 7. Februar 1965." LC Card 85-127335
1. Management - Yugoslavia - Employee participation. 2. Works councils - Yugoslavia. 3. Capitalism - Yugoslavia.
HD5660.Y8 K27 1965

Kapitalistische Entwicklung, Subsistenzproduktion und Frauenarbeit . Lenz, Ilse. Frankfurt/Main , New York , c1984. 330 p. : ISBN 3-593-33407-0(pbk.)
NYPL [JLD 87-332]

Kapitalstock und Nutzungsdauer . Adam, Martin, 1955- Frankfurt am Main , New York , c1985. v, 151 p. : ISBN 3-8204-8860-X LC Card 85-202132 DDC 332/.0414/0943 19
HG4028.C4 A24 1985

Eine kapitaltheoretische Untersuchung zum Gesetz vom tendenziellen Fall der Profitrate einschliesslich der Bestimmung seiner empirischen Relevanz /. Weingarten, Richard. München , c1982. ix, 342 p. ; ISBN 3-597-10136-4 LC Card 83-134240
HB601 .W37 1982

Kapitonov, B. V. Ėffektivnost' i intensifikatsiia . Moskva , 1986. 161 p. ; LC Card 87-163443
HC340.I52 E33 1986

Kapitula, P. A. (Petr Andreevich) Shevchuk, L. V. (Liudmila Vladimirovna) Metodicheskie osnovy analiza i prognozirovaniia fondootdachi . Minsk , 1983. 118 p. : LC Card 84-118665
HD9715.S73 B9465 1983

Kaplan, Cynthia Sue. The party and agricultural crisis management in the USSR / Cynthia S. Kaplan. Ithaca : Cornell University Press, 1987. xvi, 203 p ; 25 cm. (Studies in Soviet history and society) Bibliography: p. 185-196. Includes index. ISBN 0-8014-2021-0 (alk. paper) LC Card 86-32223 DDC 338.1/847 19
1. Agriculture and state - Soviet Union. 2. Kommunisticheskaia partiia Sovetskogo Soiuza. 3. Agriculture - Economic aspects - Soviet Union. 4. Local government - Soviet Union. I. Series: Studies in Soviet history and society (Ithaca, N.Y.). II. Title.
HD1993 .K36 1987

Kaplan, Daniel P. Has trade protection revitalized domestic industries? Washington, D.C. : Congress of the U. S., Congressional Budget Office : For sale by the Supt. of Docs., U. S. G.P.O., [1986] xvi, 111 p. : ill. ; 26 cm. (CBO study) Shipping list no.: 86-934-P. "November 1986"--Cover. Includes bibliographical references. S/N 052-070-06206-1 Item 1005-C LC Card 86-603423 DDC 382.7/3/0973 19
1. Trade adjustment assistance - United States - Case studies. 2. Industry and state - United States - Case studies. 3. Free trade and protection - Free trade - Case studies. I. United States. Congressional Budget Office. II. Title. III. Series.
HF1421 .K36 1986

Kaplan, Howard J. Scouts on stamps of the world / by Howard J. Kaplan and William E. Hoffmann ; assistant editors, William Parkin, John B. Adams, William C. Cowan. 7th ed. [Hicksville, N.Y.] : Scouts on Stamps Society International, c1986. 1 v. (loose-leaf) : ill. ; 28 cm. Rev. ed. of: Scouts on stamps of the world / Harry D. Thorsen, Jr., Arthur McKinney. LC Card 86-224816 DDC 769.56/3 19
1. Postage-stamps - Topics - Boy Scouts. 2. Postage-stamps - Topics - Girl Scouts. I. Hoffmann, William E. II. Parkin, William. III. Adams, John B. IV. Cowan, William C. V. Thorsen, Harry D., 1913- Scouts on stamps of the world. VI. Title.
HE6183.B63 K36 1986

Kaplan, L. M. (Lev Moiseevich) Ėkonomicheskie problemy upravleniia stroitel'nym proizvodstvom na Severe / L.M. Kaplan, I.IU. Murav'eva ; pod redaktsieĭ L.M. Kaplana. Leningrad : Stroĭizdat, Leningradskoe otd-nie, 1983. 167 p. : ill. ; 22 cm. Bibliography: p. 167. LC Card 84-113191
1. Construction industry - Soviet Union, Northern - Capital investments. 2. Territorial industrial complexes - Soviet Union, Northern. I. Murav'eva, I. IU. II. Title.
HD9715.S73 N675 1983

Kaplan, Marcos. El sistema de las relaciones políticas y económicas entre los países latinoamericanos : tendencias y evolución futura : Seminario sobre Evolución y Perspectivas del Sistema Económico Latinoamericano (SELA), décimo aniversario de la suscripción del Convenio de Panamá, Caracas, 9 al 11 de octubre de 1985 / Marcos Kaplan. [Buenos Aires] : Banco Interamericano de Desarrollo, Instituto para la Integración de América Latina, [1985] 62 leaves ; 29 cm. (Publ. . no. 232) At head of title: Secretaría Permanente del Sistema Economico Internacional (SELA); Instituto para la Integración de América Latina (INTAL). "Distr. especial; BID.INTAL/DP.356.4/85. Bibliography: leaves 56-62. LC Card 86-200041
1. Sistema Económico Latinoamericano. 2. Latin America - Economic integration. 3. Latin America - Politics and government - 1945-. I. Series: Publ. (Institute for Latin American Integration) , no. 232. II. Title.
HC125 .K32 1985

Kaplan, Marshall.
(joint author) Frieden, Bernard J. The politics of neglect . Cambridge, Mass. [1975] x, 281 p. ; ISBN 0-262-06061-2 LC Card 75-6792 DDC 309.2/62/0973
HT167 .F74 ***NYPL [JLE 80-1135]***

Hard choices : a report on the increasing gap between America's infrastructure needs and our ability to pay for them : a study / prepared for the use of the Subcommittee on Economic Goals and Intergovernmental Policy of the Joint Economic Committee, Congress of the United States. Washington : U. S. G.P.O. : For sale by the Supt. of Docs., U. S. G.P.O., 1984. xi, 230 p. : ill. ; 24 cm. (S. prt. . 98-164) Accompanied by appendixes covering individual states. At head of title: 98th Congress, 2d session. Joint committee print. Distributed to some depository libraries in microfiche. "February 25, 1984." S/N 052-070-05911-7 Item 1000-B, 1000-C (microfiche) Includes bibliographical references. LC Card 84-602470 DDC 338.4/3363/0973 19
1. Infrastructure (Economics) - United States. 2. Capital budget - United States - States. 3. Intergovernmental fiscal relations - United States. I. United States. Congress. Joint Economic Committee. Subcommittee on Economic Goals and Intergovernmental Policy. II. Series. III. Series: United States. Congress (98th, 2nd session : 1984). Senate. S. prt. , 98-164. IV. Title.
HC110.C3 K37 1984 ***NYPL [JLE 87-566]***

Kaplan, Robert S.
Accounting & management . Boston, Mass. , c1987. ix, 374 p. : ISBN 0-87584-186-4 (alk. paper) LC Card 87-18373 DDC 658.4/038 19
HF5657.4 .A25 1987

Johnson, H. Thomas, 1938- Relevance lost . Boston, Mass. , c1987. xiii, 269 p. ; ISBN 0-87584-138-4 LC Card 86-29474 DDC 658.1/511/09 19
HF5605 .J64 1987

Kaplan, Steven L. Work in France . Ithaca , 1986. 576 p. : ISBN 0-8014-1697-3 (alk. paper) LC Card 85-22352 DDC 331/.0944 19
HD8428 .W67 1986 ***NYPL [JLE 86-1960]***

Kaplinskaia, Elena. Puteshestvie v Riazan' / Elena Kaplinskaia. Moskva : Izd-vo "Sov. Rossiia", 1978. 84 p. ; 17 cm. (Pisatel' i vremia. Pis'ma s zavodov i stroek) LC Card 81-155441
1. Machinists - Russian S.F.S.R. - Riazan'. I. Title. II. Series.
HD8039.M22 S654 1978

Kaplinsky, Raphael. Micro-electronics and employment revisited : a review / Raphael Kaplinsky. Geneva : International Labour Office, 1987. xiv, 181 p. : ill. ; 25 cm. Bibliography: p. 171-181. ISBN 92-2-105611-2 (pbk.) : LC Card 87-163570 DDC 331.7/6213817 19
1. Microelectronics industry - Technological innovations. 2. Labor supply - Effect of technological innovations on. I. Title.
HD9696.A2 K37 1987

Kapp, Gerald B., 1956- Agroforstliche Landnutzung in der Sahel-Sudanzone : traditionelle Bewirtschaftung, Nutzungsprobleme, Lösungsansätze durch Projekte und Forschung / von Gerald B. Kapp. München : Weltforum Verlag, c1987. xii, 397 p. : ill. ; 21 cm. (Afrika-Studien. Nr. 112) Summary

in English, French and German. Bibliography: p. 310-328. ISBN 3-8039-0347-5 LC Card 87-419915 DDC 333.76/13/0966 19
1. Land use, Rural - Sahel. 2. Forests and forestry - Sahel. 3. Agricultural development projects - Sahel. 4. Land use, Rural - Sudan. 5. Forests and forestry - Sudan. 6. Agricultural development projects - Sudan. I. Title. II. Series.
HD1010.5.Z63 K37 1987

Kappel, Rolf. Im Spannungsfeld von Wirtschaft, Technik und Politik . München , c1986. 570 p., [1] leaf of plates : ISBN 3-7892-7282-5 LC Card 87-112967
HF1411 .I353 1986

Kappus, Wolfgang. Abrüstung und Wirtschaftswachstum : die Erfahrungen der USA mit der Rekonversion, 1968-1976 / Wolfgang Kappus. Frankfurt ; New York : Campus Verlag, c1985. 329 p. : ill. ; 21 cm. (Campus Forschung. Bd. 460) Schriftenreihe des Zentrums für Nordamerika-Forschung (ZENAF), Universität Frankfurt ; Bd. 5 Bibliography: p. 311-329. ISBN 3-593-33531-X LC Card 85-232235
1. Disarmament - Economic aspects - United States. 2. Armaments - Economic aspects - United States. I. Title.
HC110.D4 K37 1985

Kapronczai, István. A Szabályozórendszerre történő reagálás főbb termelőszövetkezeti tapasztalatai /. Budapest , 1985. 68 p. ; LC Card 87-408583
HD1492.H8 S92 1985

Kapronczay, Gáspár. Magyar törvényes fizetőeszközök =. [Budapest] [1986?] [38] p. : LC Card 87-407726
HG970.5 .M34 1986

Kapur, Basant. Studies in inflationary dynamics : financial repression and financial liberalization in less developed countries / Basant K. Kapur. Kent Ridge, Singapore : Singapore University Press, National University of Singapore, c1986. xviii, 146 p., [1] folded leaf of plates : ill. ; 23 cm. Bibliography: p. 142-146. ISBN 997-16-9099-3 (pbk.) LC Card 87-116919 DDC 332.4/1 19
1. Economic stabilization - Developing countries. 2. Developing countries - Economic policy. 3. Inflation (Finance) - Developing countries. I. Title.
HC59.7 .K276 1986

Kapusta, E. C., 1925- Mudahar, Mohinder S. Fertilizer marketing systems and policies in the developing world /. Muscle Shoals, Ala. , 1987. 43 p. : ISBN 0-88090-059-8 (pbk.) LC Card 87-3152 DDC 381/.4566862/091724 19
HD9483.D44 K36 1987

Kapustin, E. I. Organizat͡sii͡a sorevnovanii͡a i sovershenstvovanie khozi͡aĭstvennogo mekhanizma /. Moskva , 1982. 206 p. ; LC Card 82-202826
HC340.S6 O684 1982

Kapustka, Aleksander.
Gospodarka inwestycyjna i remontowa w latach 1984-1985 / Aleksander Kapustka. Zielona Góra : Tow. Nauk. Organizacji i Kierownictwa, Oddz. Wojewódzki w Zielonej Górze, 1984. 294 p. ; 22 cm. Includes bibliographical references. LC Card 86-670001
1. Capital investments - Poland. 2. Poland - Economic policy - 1981-. 3. Infrastructure (Economics) - Poland. 4. Housing - Poland - Finance. I. Title.
HC340.3.Z9 C35 1984

Inwestycje w reformie : przepisy i komentarze / Aleksander Kapustka. Zielona Góra : Tow. Nauk. Organizacji i Kierownictwa, Oddział Wojewodzki w Zielonej Górze, 1985. 282 p. ; 21 cm. Includes bibliographical references. LC Card 86-125896
1. Capital budget - Poland. 2. Capital investments - Poland. 3. Poland - Economic policy - 1981-. I. Title.
HJ2132 .K37 1985

Kaputt und auch noch selber schuld . Arnold, Alix, 1956- Reinbek bei Hamburg , c1986. 179, [1] p. : ISBN 3-499-15908-2 : LC Card 86-226114
HD7708 .A75 1986

Kára, Jan. Migrace a osídlení v socialistických zemích =. Praha , 1984- v. <1 > : LC Card 87-160334
HB2041 .M526 1984

Karachan, N. B. Kadieva, D. A. Chastotnyĭ anglo-russkiĭ slovar'. Leningrad , 1986. 126 p. ; LC Card 87-146427
HB61 .K23 1986

Karagandinskiĭ gosudarstvennyĭ universitet. Problemy ukreplenii͡a trudovoĭ distsipliny i predotvrashchenii͡a tekuchesti kadrov na predprii͡atii͡akh T͡Sentral'nogo Kazakhstana . Karaganda , 1982. 126 p. ; LC Card 84-226131
HF5549.5.L3 P76 1982

Karagodin, N. A. Mezhdunarodnye korporat͡sii i sotsial'no-ėkonomicheskie problemy razvivai͡ushchikhsi͡a stran / N.A. Karagodin. Moskva : Izd-vo "Nauka," Glav. red. vostochnoĭ lit-ry, 1981. 196, [3] p. ; 20 cm. At head of title: Akademii͡a nauk SSSR. Ordena Trudovogo Krasnogo Znameni Institut mirovoĭ ėkonomiki i mezhdunarodnykh otnosheniĭ. Bibliography: p. 190-[197] LC Card 82-162679
1. Developing countries - Economic conditions. 2. International business enterprises - Developing countries. 3. Investments, Foreign - Developing countries. I. Title.
HC59.7 .K28 1981

Karakozova, Ė. V. (Ėl'vira Viktorovna) Modelirovanie v obshchestvennykh naukakh : filosofsko-metodologicheskie problemy / Ė.V. Karakozova. Moskva : "Vysshai͡a shkola", 1986. 101 p. ; 21 cm. Bibliography: p. 95-[102].
1. Social sciences - Mathematical models. 2. Social sciences - Methodology. I. Title.
NYPL [*QI 87-3444]

Karamanlis, Constantine. see **Karamanlis, Konstantinos, 1907-**

KARAMANLIS, KONSTANTINOS, 1907-
Kontogeōrgēs, Geōrgios L. Hē Hellada stēn Eurōpē . [Athens] [1985] 311 p. : LC Card 86-206722
HC241.25.G8 K65 1985

Karapetian, H. S. (Hovhannes Smbati) Sovetakan Hayastani banvor dasakargi dzevavorumĕ ev zargats'umĕ (1920-1940) / H.S. Karapetian. Erevan : Haykakan SSH GA Hratarakch'ut'yun, 1980. 272 p., [1] leaf of plates : port. ; 21 cm. Title on added t.p.: Formirovanie i razvitie rabochego klassa Sovetskoĭ Armenii (1920-1940) At head of title: Haykakan SSH Gitut'yunneri Akademia, Patmut'ian Institut. Includes bibliographical references. LC Card 83-129694
1. Labor and laboring classes - Armenia S.S.R. - History. I. Title. II. Title: Formirovanie i razvitie rabochego klassa Sovetskoĭ Armenii (1920-1940).
HD8529.A692 K37 1980

Karapetian, S. A. Regional'nye osobennosti sotsial'no-demograficheskogo razvitii͡a Armi͡anskoĭ SSR / S.A. Karapeti͡an, R.L. Ovsepi͡an. Erevan : "Aĭastan", 1986. 215 p. ; 21 cm. Includes bibliographical references. LC Card 87-118556
1. Armenian S.S.R. - Population. 2. Quality of life - Armenian S.S.R. I. Ovsepi͡an, R. L. (Rudik Levonovich). II. Title.
HB3608.A75 K37 1986

Karapostolēs, Vasilēs. Oikonomikes metamorphōseis tēs agrotikēs Helladas : historikoi stathmoi 1453-1917 / Vasilēs Karapostolēs. Athēna : Agrotikē Trapeza tēs Hellados, 1981. 52 [1] p. : ill. ; 21 cm. Bibliography: p. [53] LC Card 86-194022
1. Agriculture - Economic aspects - Greece - History. I. Title.
HD2055.5 .K36 1981

Karas, Thomas H. Die Nachfrage nach Ausrüstungsinvestitionen in der Schweiz 1963-1980 : eine ökonometrische Studie / Thomas Karas. Frankfurt am Main : Haag + Herchen, c1984. v, 91 p. : ill. ; 21 cm. (Schriftenreihe des Instituts für Empirische Wirtschaftsforschung der Universität Zürich . Bd. 13) Bibliography: p. [87]-91. ISBN 3-88129-798-7 : LC Card 84-208150
1. Armaments - Economic aspects - Switzerland - Econometric models. I. Title. II. Series.
HC400.D4 K37 1984

Kardinalität in der Nutzentheorie /. Wagener, Martin. Königstein/Ts. , c1983. xii, 160 p. ; ISBN 3-445-02289-5 LC Card 83-195855
HB201 .W17 1983

Kardinal'nyĭ rost ėffektivnosti zhivogo truda--glavnyĭ faktor uskorenii͡a sotsial'no-ėkonomicheskogo razvitii͡a : tezisy vsesoi͡uznoĭ nauchno-prakticheskoĭ konferentsii / [redaktsionnai͡a kollegii͡a M.A. Sergeev, otvetstvennyĭ redaktor ... et al.]. Sverdlovsk : In-t ėkonomiki UNTS AN SSSR, 1986. 2 v. ; 20 cm. At head of title: Akademii͡a nauk SSSR. Ural'skiĭ nauchnyĭ t͡sentr. Institut ėkonomiki. Akademii͡a obshchestvennykh nauk pri TSK KPSS. Goskomitet RSFSR po trudu i sotsial'nym voprosam. Includes bibliographical references. LC Card 87-136690
1. Labor productivity - Russian S.F.S.R. - Ural Mountains Region - Congresses. 2. Labor supply - Russian S.F.S.R. - Ural Mountains Region - Congresses. 3. Industrial sociology - Russian S.F.S.R. - Ural Mountains Region - Congresses. 4. Technological innovations - Russian S.F.S.R. - Ural Mountains Region - Congresses. I. Sergeev, Mikhail Aleksandrovich. II. Institut ėkonomiki (Akademii͡a nauk SSSR. Ural'skiĭ nauchnyĭ t͡sentr). III. Akademii͡a obshchestvennykh nauk (Moscow, R.S.F.S.R.). IV. Goskomitet RSFSR po trudu i sotsial'nym voprosam.
HC337.R853 L35 1986

Kardos, Péter. Külföldi licencek a magyar gazdaságban / Kardos Péter, Szatmári Tamás. Budapest : Közgazdasági és Jogi Könyvkiadó, 1984. 204, [1] p. : ill. ; 20 cm. Bibliography: p. 201-[205] ISBN 963-221-396-3 : LC Card 85-157267
1. Foreign licensing agreements. 2. Technology transfer - Hungary. 3. License agreements - Hungary. I. Szatmári, Tamás. II. Title.
HF1429 .K37 1984

Karels, Gordon V. Prakash, Arun J. Financial, commercial, and mortgage mathematics and their applications /. New York , 1987. x, 245 p. ; ISBN 0-275-92119-0 (alk. paper) : LC Card 86-30579 DDC 513/.93 19
HF5691 .P69 1987

KAREL'SKAI͡A A.S.S.R. (R.S.F.S.R.) - ECONOMIC CONDITIONS.
Pi͡atiletka, god vtoroĭ . Petrozavodsk , 1977. 101 p. ; LC Card 81-161405
HC337.K265 P52 1977

KAREL'SKAIA A.S.S.R. (R.S.F.S.R.) - ECONOMIC CONDITIONS - STATISTICS.
Narodnoe khozi͡aĭstvo Karel'skoĭ ASSR . Petrozavodsk , 1985. 94 p. ; LC Card 86-124957
HA1448.K32 N37 1985

KAREL'SKAI͡A A.S.S.R. (R.S.F.S.R.) - STATISTICS.
Narodnoe khozi͡aĭstvo Karel'skoĭ ASSR . Petrozavodsk , 1985. 94 p. ; LC Card 86-124957
HA1448.K32 N37 1985

Karhu, Veli. Akseleraatioteoriaan perustuvia investointifunktiokokeiluja yritystason aineistolla / Veli Karhu, Pasi Ahde. Vaasa : [Vaasan Korkeakoulu], 1982. 43, [1] leaves ; 30 cm. (Vaasan korkeakoulun julkaisuja. Tutkimuksia, 0358-9080 . n:o 85. 9) Summary in English. Bibliography: leaves 43-[44] ISBN 951-683-160-5 LC Card 83-100841 DDC 332/.0415 19
1. Capital investments - Finland - Mathematical models. 2. Acceleration principle (Economics). I. Ahde, Pasi. II. Series. III. Series: Vaasan Kauppakorkeakoulu. Julkaisuja. Tutkimuksia, n:o 85. IV. Title.
HG4028.C4 K349 1982
NYPL [JLM 73-601 n:o 85]

Karibische Klein- und Mikrostaaten . Haas, Hans-Dieter. Tübingen , 1985. xvi, 200 p. : ISBN 3-921552-62-1 LC Card 86-155952
HC141 .H25 1985

Karl Rodbertus (1805-1875) und die Grundrententheorie . Rudolph, Günther. Berlin , 1984. 332 p. ; LC Card 84-158301
HB401 .R83 1984

Karliev, B. K. Stanchin, I. M. (Ivan Mikhaĭlovich) Razvitie agropromyshlennogo kompleksa Turkmenskoĭ SSR /. Ashkhabad , 1985. 181, [3] p. : LC Card 85-185696
HD9015.S653 T878 1985

Karlik, András. Gazdálkodási és jövedelmezőségi adatok, mutatószámok a szövetkezeti bolti kiskereskedelemben /. Budapest , 1984. 113 p. ; ISBN 963-7006-24-9 : LC Card 85-154737
HF5429.6.H8 G39 1984

Karlin, P. I. (Pavel Ivanovich) Statistika zarabotnoĭ platy na ugol'nykh shakhtakh : konspekt lektsiĭ / P.I. Karlin. Donetsk : DPI, 1980. 68 p. : ill. ; 21 cm. At head of title: Ministerstvo vysshego i srednego spet͡sial'nogo obrazovanii͡a USSR. Donet͡skiĭ ordena Trudovogo Krasnogo Znameni politekhnicheskiĭ institut. Bibliography: p. 54-55. LC Card 82-175895
1. Wages - Coal miners - Ukraine - Statistical methods. I. Title.
HD4966.M63 S655 1980

Karlı͡uk, I. I͡A. (Ippolit I͡Akovlevich) Agrarno-promyshlennyĭ kompleks / I.I͡A. Karlı͡uk. Moskva : Izd-vo polit. lit-ry, 1981. 93 p. : ill. ; 20 cm. (Shagi odinnadt͡satoĭ) Includes bibliographical references. LC Card 82-148305
1. Agricultural industries - Soviet Union. 2. Agricultural productivity - Soviet Union. I. Title. II. Series.
HD9015.S652 K37 1981

Karlöf, Bengt, 1939- [Strategins kärnfrågor. English] Business strategy in practice / Bengt Karlöf ; translated by Alan J. Gilderson. Chichester, England ; New York : Wiley, c1987. viii, 184 p. : ill. ; 25 cm. Translation of: Strategins kärnfrågor. Bibliography: p. 183-184. ISBN 0-471-91620-X : LC Card 87-10452 DDC 658.4/012 19
1. Strategic planning. I. Title.
HD30.28 .K3613 1987

Karlsch, E. Internationale Wirtschaft und revolutionärer Weltprozess /. [Berlin] , 1983. 390 p. ; LC Card 84-167604
HF1410.5 .I592 1983

Karlsen, Thore. Informationstechnologie im Dienstleistungsbereich . Berlin , c1985. 258 p. : ISBN 3-924859-15-9 : LC Card 86-220033 DDC 338.4/561 19
HD9980.5 .I54 1985

Karlson, Rolf A. Hur planeras Sverige? /. Stockholm , c1986. 179 p. : ISBN 91-38-90679-1 : LC Card 87-151788
HC375 .H85 1986

Karlsruhe papers in economic policy research . (vol. 3) Space-structure-economy . Karlsruhe [San Francisco, CA] c1986. vii, 311 p. : ISBN 3-88652-680-1 (pbk.) LC Card 87-129134 DDC 330.1 19
HB107.L66 S63 1986

Karlsruher Beiträge zur Wirtschaftspolitik und Wirtschaftsforschung.
([Heft 11]) Eckstein, Werner E. Kooperative Systembildung in der Transportwirtschaft . Karlsruhe , c1985. vii, 263 p. : ISBN 3-88652-028-5 LC Card 86-135639
HE199.G3 E28 1985

(Heft 13) Blum, Ulrich. Raumwirkungen des Budgets der gesetzlichen Rentenversicherung . Karlsruhe , c1986. xii, 184, 35 p. : ISBN 3-88652-029-3 LC Card 87-124826 DDC 368.4/00943 19
HD7179 .B57 1986

Karlsruher Studien, 0179-2512 .
(Bd. 1) Schulze, Konrad. Ein ökonometrischer Ansatz zur Erklärung des Bausparens /. Bonn , c1985. xii, 150 p. : ISBN 3-87169-319-7 LC Card 86-231621
HC290.5.S3 S38 1985

Karlsson, Jan, 1948- Om lönearbete . [Stockholm] [1983] 260 p. : ISBN 91-1-833281-1 : LC Card 84-165851
HD6957.S8 O42 1983

Karluk, S. Rıdvan. Türkiye'de ihracata yönelik dış ticaret politikası ve ihracatın yapısal analizi / S. Rıdvan Karluk. Eskişehir : Eskişehir İktisadi ve Ticari İlimler Akademisi, 1981. xx, 454 p. ; 24 cm. (Eskişehir İktisadi ve Ticari İlimler Akademisi yayınları . no. 237/158) Spine title: Dış ticaret politikası. Bibliography: p. [421]-454. LC Card 82-241650
1. Turkey - Commercial policy. 2. Turkey - Commerce. I. Title. II. Title: Dış ticaret politikası. III. Series.
HF1583.4 .K37 1981

Kármán, Tamásné. A Népmozgalmi statisztika fejlődése Magyarországon. Budapest , 1985- v. <1 > ; LC Card 86-190535
HA37.H92 N46 1985

Karmanov, V. A. (Vladimir Andreevich) Tisul′ : stranitsy proshlogo i nastoi͡ashchego Tisul′skogo raĭona / V.A. Karmanov. Kemerovo : Kemerovskoe knizhnoe izd-vo, 1983. 93 p., [8] p. of plates : ill. ; 17 cm. LC Card 84-103652
1. Tisul′ Region (R.S.F.S.R.) - Economic conditions. 2. Kemerovskai͡a oblast′ (R.S.F.S.R.) - Economic conditions. I. Title.
HC337.R852 T575 1983

Karn, Valerie Ann. Henderson, J. W. (Jeffrey William), 1947- Race, class, and state housing . Aldershot, Hants, England ;Brookfield, Vt. , c1987. xxiii, 331 p. : ISBN 0-566-00785-1 :
NYPL [JLD 87-1476]

Karnataka. see **Karnataka (India)**

KARNATAKA, INDIA - ECONOMIC CONDITIONS.
Dadibhavi, R. V. Income, productivity, and industrial structure /. Allahabad, India , 1986. xx, 295 p. ; ISBN 81-85076-02-2 : LC Card 86-902847 DDC 339.2/0954/87 19
HC437.K27 D33 1986

Hanumantha Rayappa, P. (Pullikunta), 1938- Backwardness and welfare of scheduled castes and scheduled tribes in India /. New Delhi , 1986. xi, 121 p. ; ISBN 81-7024-059-X : LC Card 86-902970
HC437.K27 H36 1986

Thimmaiah, G. Inequality and poverty . Bombay , 1983. xiv, 106 p. ; LC Card 83-903408 DDC 339.4/6/095487 19
HC437.K27 T47 1983 NYPL [JLD 86-3792]

Thimmaiah, G. The political economy of land reforms /. New Delhi [1983?] xiii, 94 p. ; LC Card 84-900237 DDC 333.3/1/5487 19
HD1333.I42 K3778 1983
NYPL [JLD 87-752]

KARNATAKA (INDIA) - POPULATION.
Prabhakara, N. R. Internal migration and population redistribution in India . New Delhi , 1986, c1985. xi, 117 p. ; LC Card 86-902406 DDC 304.8/0954/87 19
HB2100.K37 P73 1985

KARNATAKA (INDIA) - SCHEDULED TRIBES - ECONOMIC CONDITIONS.
Hanumantha Rayappa, P. (Pullikunta), 1938- Backwardness and welfare of scheduled castes and scheduled tribes in India /. New Delhi , 1986. xi, 121 p. ; ISBN 81-7024-059-X : LC Card 86-902970
HC437.K27 H36 1986

KARNATAKA, INDIA - SOCIAL CONDITIONS.
Thimmaiah, G. Inequality and poverty . Bombay , 1983. xiv, 106 p. ; LC Card 83-903408 DDC 339.4/6/095487 19
HC437.K27 T47 1983 NYPL [JLD 86-3792]

Karnaukhova, E. S. (Evfrazii͡a Stepanovna) Ėkonomicheskie problemy novogo ėtapa osushchestvlenii͡a Leninskogo kooperativnogo plana /. Moskva , 1979. 365 p. ; LC Card 81-165451
HD1992 .E3593 1979

Karpiński, Wojciech. Szkice o wolności / Wojciech Karpiński. Chicago, Ill. (2886 Milwaukee Ave., Chicago, Ill. 60618) : Wydawn. "Polonia" Book Store and Publishers, 1980. 95 p. ; 22 cm. (Biblioteka "Nowa droga". nr. 9) LC Card 81-201974
1. Liberty - Addresses, essays, lectures. 2. Democracy - Addresses, essays, lectures. 3. Poland - Social conditions - Addresses, essays, lectures. 4. Soviet Union - Social conditions - Addresses, essays, lectures. I. Title.
*JC585 .K32 1980 NYPL [*QR 86-4376]*

Karpov, V. V. Ėkonomicheskie interesy i uskorenie nauchno-tekhnicheskogo progressa . Leningrad , 1984. 157 p. ; LC Card 86-186728
HC340.T4 E36 1984

Karpunin, M. G. (Mikhail Grigor′evich) Funkt͡sional′no-stoimostnoĭ analiz v otraslevom upravlenii ėffektivnost′i͡u / M.G. Karpunin, B.I. Maĭdanchik. Moskva : Ėkonomika, 1983. 199 p. : charts ; 22 cm. Bibliography: p. 197-[198] LC Card 84-120682
1. Cost accounting - Soviet Union. 2. Industrial management - Soviet Union. 3. Cost accounting. 4. Industrial management. I. Maĭdanchik, B. I. (Boris Iontelevich). II. Title.
HF5686.C8 K275 1983

Karran, Terence. Rose, Richard, 1933- Taxation by political inertia . London , Boston , 1987. viii, 264 p. : ISBN 0-04-320197-0 (alk. paper) LC Card 87-11478 DDC 336.2/00941 19
HJ2619 .R68 1987

Kärre, Karl, 1885- Engelsk-svensk ordbok . Stockholm , 1970. 2 v. ;
NYPL [JFD 87-817]

KARST (YUGOSLAVIA AND ITALY) - ECONOMIC CONDITIONS.
Davis, James C. (James Cushman) Rise from want . Philadelphia , 1986. xv, 165 p. : ISBN 0-8122-8034-2 : LC Card 86-19228 DDC 305.5/63 19
HD1536.Y8 D38 1986 NYPL [JLE 87-710]

KARST (YUGOSLAVIA AND ITALY) - SOCIAL CONDITIONS.
Davis, James C. (James Cushman) Rise from want . Philadelphia , 1986. xv, 165 p. : ISBN 0-8122-8034-2 : LC Card 86-19228 DDC 305.5/63 19
HD1536.Y8 D38 1986 NYPL [JLE 87-710]

Karsten, Detlev. Berghahn, Volker Rolf. Industrial relations in West Germany /. Leamington Spa, UK ; New York : p. cm. ISBN 0-907582-64-8 : LC Card 87-9359 DDC 331/.0943 19
HD8451 .B45 1988

Kartali, János. A friss és feldolgozott zöldségek, gyümölcsök bel- és külkereskedelmi forgalmazásának aktuális problémái / Kartali János, Orbánné Nagy Mária, Mohácsi Kálmán. Budapest : Agrárgazdasági Kutató Intézet, 1985. 108 p. ; 29 cm. (Agrárgazdasági Kutató Intézet, 0209-5696 . 1985/2) Bibliography: p. 105-108. ISBN 963-491-203-6 LC Card 86-195487
1. Vegetable trade - Hungary. I. Orbánné Nagy, Mária. II. Mohácsi, Kálmán. III. Series: Agrárgazdasági Kutazó Intézet (Series) , 1985/2. IV. Title.
HD9220.H82 K37 1985

Die Kartellierung der deutschen Volkswirtschaft und die sozialdemokratische Theorie-Diskussion vor 1933 /. Bechtold, Hartmut. Frankfurt am Main , c1986. 291 p. ; ISBN 3-89228-000-2 LC Card 86-193858
HD2757.5 .B43 1986

Kartoatmodjo, Pranoto. Ibrahim, Saaduddin. Aspek-aspek proteksi dalam industri dan perdagangan /. Jakarta , 1987. 251 p. : LC Card 87-941314
HD4304 .I27 1987

Kartographie und Bürgerbeteiligung im Rahmen der vorbereitenden Bauleitplanung . Herzog, Werner. Paderborn , 1986. xi, 164 p. : ISBN 3-506-71256-X LC Card 87-401386 DDC 333.73/17/028 19
HD108.6 .H47 1986

Karunaratne, Neil Dias, 1937- The Cost of thinking . Norwood, N.J. , c1988. xii, 249 p. : ISBN 0-89391-419-3 LC Card 87-22937 DDC 338.4/7004/099 19
HC681.3.I55 C67 1988

Karunaratne, S. W. Potential for foreign investment in rubber products manufacture with information on special projects and a selection of local collaborators / S.W. Karunaratne, H. Abeysekera. [Colombo] : Foreign Investment Advisory Committee, Ministry of Finance & Planning, 1985. vii, 100 p. ; 22 cm. Bibliography: p. 100. LC Card 86-902791 DDC 332.6/73/095493 19
1. Rubber industry and trade - Sri Lanka. 2. Investments, Foreign - Sri Lanka. I. Abeysekera, H. II. Sri Lanka. Foreign Investment Advisory Committee. III. Title.
HD9161.S752 K37 1985

Karunatilake, H. N. S. The banking and financial system of Sri Lanka / H.N.S. Karunatilake. 1st ed. Colombo : Centre for Demographic and Socio-Economic Studies, 1986. 320 p. ; 23 cm. Bibliography: p. 319-320. LC Card 87-902032 DDC 332.1/09549/3 19
1. Banks and banking - Sri Lanka. 2. Financial institutions - Sri Lanka. I. Title.
HG3270.8.A6 K37 1986

Karunatilake, Neville Sepala. see **Karunatilake, H. N. S.**

Karvel, George R. Unger, Maurice Albert, 1917- Real estate, principles, and practices /. Cincinnati , c1987. ix, 650 p. : ISBN 0-538-19761-7 LC Card 86-61595 DDC 333.33 19
HD1375 .U6 1987

Kasapēs, Stergios. Oikonomikē kai koinōnikē anaptyxis Anat. Makedonias kai Thrakēs . Kavalla [1973-] v. <1 > : LC Card 87-125407
HD2055.5 .O54 1973

Kashin, Valentin Nikolaevich. Sovershenstvovanie sistemy narodnokhozi͡aĭstvennogo upravlenii͡a v sot͡sialisticheskikh stranakh . Moskva , 1986. 196 p. ; LC Card 87-163453
HC244 .S595115 1986

Kashmir agriculture & land revenue system under the Sikh rule, 1819-46 A.D. /. Sharma, Dewan

Chand, 1898- New Delhi, India , 1986. xiv, 160 p., [8] p. of plates : LC Card 86-900128
HD2075.J35 S43 1986 ***NYPL [JLD 86-3742]***

Kashmir agriculture and land revenue system under the Sikh rule, 1819-46 A.D. Sharma, Dewan Chand, 1898- Kashmir agriculture & land revenue system under the Sikh rule, 1819-46 A.D. /. New Delhi, India , 1986. xiv, 160 p., [8] p. of plates : LC Card 86-900128
HD2075.J35 S43 1986 ***NYPL [JLD 86-3742]***

Kashmir to Frankfurt . Ahad, Abdul, 1947- New Delhi, India , 1987. xiv, 182 p., [20] p. of plates : LC Card 86-903828
HD9969.S43 I425 1987

Kas'ianov, P. S. Narodnoe khoziaistvo Kirovskoĭ oblasti v desiatoĭ piatiletke, 1976-1980 gg. . Kirov , 1981. 95 p. ; LC Card 82-146329
HC337.R852 K576 1981

Kasoff, Larry, 1949- Madigan, Bob, 1949- The first-time investor /. New York , c1987. xxii, 276 p. : ISBN 0-13-942376-1 (pbk.) : LC Card 87-14399 DDC 332.6/78 19
HG4521 .M217 1987

Kasprzyk, Daniel. Survey of income and program participation and related longitudinal surveys, 1984 . [Washington, D.C.] , 1985. ix, 201 p. : LC Card 85-601676 DDC 339.2/3/0973 19
HC110.I5 S89 1985 ***NYPL [JLF 86-1641]***

Kasprzyk, Zbigniew. Sójka, Zygmunt. Polska polityka morska /. Gdańsk , 1986. 237, [1] : ISBN 83-215-1646-7(pbk.) :
NYPL [*QO 87-1818]

KASSALA (SUDAN : PROVINCE) - ECONOMIC CONDITIONS.
Abu Sin, M. E. (Mohad E.) Socio-economic aspects of integrated resource management, with special reference to the forest resources of Kassala Province, Eastern Region . Khartoum , 1986. vi leaves, 109 p. : LC Card 87-980440 DDC 333.75/09629/2 19
HD9767.S843 K3724 1986

Kassas, Mohammed. Ahmad, Yusuf J. Desertification . West Hartford, CT. , 1987. xviii, 187 p. : ISBN 0-931816-99-8 (pbk.) : LC Card 87-3650 DDC 333.73 19
HD111 .A44 1987

Kastner, Friedrich, 1951- Entscheidungsansätze zur Rechtsformwahl : Strukturelemente der Rechtsformentscheidung und ihre Berücksichtigung im theoretischen wie praktischen Modell / Friedrich Kastner. München : UNI-Druck, c1984. xviii, 631 p. : ill. ; 21 cm. Ill. and tables on 5 folded leaves in pocket. Bibliography: p. 565-631. ISBN 3-87821-200-3 LC Card 87-136549 DDC 658.4/03/0943 19
1. Corporations - Germany (West) - Decision making. 2. Corporation law - Germany, West. I. Title.
HD2859 .K37 1984

Katalog konvertov pervogo dnia i kartmaksimumov, 1980-1983 / [sostavitel' Nataliia Mikhaĭlovna Maksimenko]. Moskva : TSentr. filatelisticheskoe agenstvo "Soiuzpechat'" Ministerstva sviazi SSSR, 1985. 221 p. : ill. ; 21 cm. Spine title: Konverty pervogo dnia i kartmaksimumy. Includes bibliographical references and indexes. LC Card 86-102861
1. First day covers (Philately) - Soviet Union - Catalogs. 2. Maximum cards - Soviet Union - Catalogs. I. Maksimenko, Nataliia Mikhaĭlovna. II. TSentral'noe filatelisticheskoe agenstvo "Soiuzpechat'.". III. Title: Konverty pervogo dnia i kartmaksimumy.
HE6184.F57 K38 1985

Katalog na bŭlgarskite poshtenski marki 1979-1984 /. Georgiev, Petŭr Borisov. Sofiia , 1985. 119 p. : LC Card 86-112123
HE6185.B82 G47 1985

Katalog specjalizowany znaków pocztowych ziem polskich 1985 / [zespół autorski Fabian Bura ... et al.]. Wyd. 2. Warszawa : Krajowa Agencja Wydawnicza, 1984-1985. 4 v. : ill. ; 21 cm. Vol. 2 includes index. ISBN 83-03-00691-6 (cz. 1-2) : LC Card 87-120964
1. Postage-stamps - Poland - Catalogs. 2. Postmarks - Poland - Catalogs. I. Bura, Fabian.
HE6185.P62 K28 1984

Katash, S. S. Mezhdunarodnyĭ kredit i vneshniaia zadolzhennost' razvivaiushchikhsia stran / S.S. Katash. Moskva : Nauchno-issl. fin. in-t, 1984. 43 p. ; 21 cm. (Aktual'nye valiutno-finansovye problemy razvivaiushchikhsia stran . vyp. 2) At head of title: Ministerstvo finansov SSSR. Nauchno-issledovatel'skiĭ finansovyĭ institut. Bibliography: p. 42. LC Card 87-100185
1. Loans, Foreign - Developing countries. 2. Debts, External - Developing countries. I. Title. II. Series.
HG3877 .K37 1984

Katayama, Leslee. Hotel sales, room rents, and transient room taxes in Utah, 1978-1985 / Leslee Katayama. Salt Lake City, Utah (519 Heber Wells Bldg., Salt Lake City 84134) : Economic & Statistical Unit, Utah State Tax Commission, [1985] i, 49 leaves : ill. ; 28 cm. (Research publication / Economic & Statistical Unit, Utah State Tax Commission . 85-10) Cover title. "September, 1985." LC Card 86-620905 DDC 336.2/7864794 19
1. Sales tax - Utah. 2. Hotels, taverns, etc. - Taxation - Utah. I. Utah State Tax Commission. Economic & Statistical Unit. II. Series: Research publication (Salt Lake City, Utah) , 85-10. III. Title.
HJ5715.U62 U85 1985

Kate, Adriaan ten. La política de protección en el desarrollo económico de México / Adriaan Ten Kate, Robert Bruce Wallace [con la cooperacíon de] Antonie Waarts, Ma. Delfina Ramírez de Wallace. 1a ed. en español. México : Fondo de Cultura Económica, 1979. 376 p. ; 21 cm. (Sección de obras de economía) Bibliography: p. 362-367. ISBN 968-16-0352-4 LC Card 87-672671
1. Free trade and protection - Protection. 2. Tariff - Mexico. 3. Mexico - Commercial policy. 4. Mexico - Economic policy. I. Wallace, Robert Bruce. II. Series: Sección de obras de economía (Fondo de Cultura Económica (Mexico)). III. Title.
HF1775 .K37x 1979

KATĖK i razvitie otrasleĭ khoziaĭstva Sibiri / otvetstvennye redaktory V.Ė. Popov, P.V. Shemetov. Novosibirsk : Izd-vo "Nauka," Sibirskoe otd-nie, 1984. 164 p. ; 20 cm. At head of title: Akademiia nauk SSSR. Sibirskoe otdelenie. Institut ėkonomiki i organizatsii promyshlennogo proizvodstva. Includes bibliographical references. LC Card 84-167870
1. Territorial production complexes - Russian S.F.S.R. - Siberia. 2. Energy minerals - Russian S.F.S.R. - Kansk-Achinsk Basin. 3. Siberia (R.S.F.S.R.) - Industries. I. Popov, V. Ė. (Vitaliĭ Ėrastovich). II. Shemetov, P. V. (Petr Vasil'evich). III. Institut ėkonomiki i organizatsii promyshlennogo proizvodstva (Akademiia nauk SSSR). IV. Title: K.A.T.Ė.K. i razvitie otrasleĭ khoziaĭstva Sibiri.
HC337.R852 S5246 1984

Kath, Dietmar. Öffentliche Finanzen, Kredit und Kapital . Berlin , c1985. xvi, 618 p., [1] leaf of plates : ISBN 3-428-05737-6 LC Card 85-164173
HJ161 .O33 1985

[Publikaties] see **Katholieke Universiteit te Leuven. Faculteit der Economische en Toegepaste Economische Wetenschappen. Reeks.**

Katholieke Universiteit te Leuven. Faculteit der Economische en Toegepaste Economische Wetenschappen.
Reeks.
(nr. 23) Verheirstraeten, A. Geld, krediet en intrest in de Belgische financiële sector /. Leuven , 1977. xxii, 337 p. : LC Card 78-345984
HG1055 .V47 ***NYPL [JLM 86-1310 nr.23]***

(nr.24) Gheysens, Lieven. International diversification through the government bond market . [Leuven] , 1977. 188 leaves ; LC Card 85-186317 DDC 332.63/232 19
HG4715 .G44 1977
NYPL [JLM 86-1310 nr.24]

Katholieke Universiteit te Leuven (1970-). Centrum voor Economische Studiën.
International trade and exchange rates in the late eighties /. Amsterdam ; New York : xii, 418 p. : ISBN 2-8004-0892-8
NYPL [JLE 87-120]

International trade and exchange rates in the late eighties /. Amsterdam ; New York : xii, 418 p. : ISBN 0-444-87941-2 LC Card 86-223111 DDC 382.4/5 19
HG203 .I58 1985

Katholisch, proletarisch und in der Einheitsgewerkschaft /. Schwarz, Heino, 1936- Mainz , c1983. 141 p. : ISBN 3-7867-1046-5 LC Card 83-193395 DDC 331.88/0943 19
HD6694 .S34 1983 ***NYPL [JLD 86-2783]***

Katholische Sozialwissenschaftliche Zentralstelle, Gladbach, Ger. see **Katholische Sozialwissenschaftliche Zentralstelle, Mönchen-Gladbach, Ger.**

Katholische Sozialwissenschaftliche Zentralstelle, Mönchen-Gladbach, Ger. Alternative Ökonomie? /. Köln , 1982. 244 p. ; ISBN 3-7616-0671-0 (pbk.) LC Card 84-109717 DDC 338.9 19
HD88 .A48 1982 ***NYPL [JLC 86-230]***

Kathuria, Sanjay. India's exports, the challenge from China / Sanjay Kathuria, Nisha Taneja. New Delhi : Indian Council for Research on International Economic Relations, 1986. 106 p. ; 23 cm. Bibliography: p. 99-102. LC Card 86-902526 DDC 382/.6/0954 19
1. China - Commerce. 2. China - Commercial policy. 3. India - Commerce. 4. India - Commercial policy. I. Taneja, Nisha. II. Indian Council for Research on International Economic Relations. III. Title.
HF3836.5 .K37 1986

Katikhin, O. V. (Oleg Vladimirovich)
Napravleniia i formy realizatsii obshchenarodnoĭ sobstvennosti /. Moskva , 1986. 171 p. ; LC Card 87-163156
HD4213 .N36 1986

Katinnulong Daguiti Umili Iti Amianan, Inc.
Cleto, Romeo B. The Ilocos and Cordillera provinces . Baguio City [Philippines] , Manila [1986] xvii, 265 p. : LC Card 87-111697 DDC 330.9599/1 19
HC457.L8 C56 1986

Katins, Sabine. All you need is freedom : report about South-Rhodesia (Zimbabwe) / author and director, Sabine Katins. Berlin : Fernsehen der DDR Programmdirektion Abteilung Öffentlichkeitsarbeit, [1977] 35 p. : ill. (some col.) ; 28 cm. (Workshop booklet . 3) "First broadcast on 9th March, 1977." LC Card 86-207107 DDC 968.91/05 19
1. Zimbabwe - Economic conditions - 1980-. 2. Zimbabwe - Social conditions - 1980-. 3. Television scripts. I. Fernsehen der DDR. Abteilung Öffentlichkeitsarbeit. II. Title. III. Series.
HC910 .K37 1977

Katlan, Alexander W. American artists' materials suppliers directory : nineteenth century : New York 1810-1899, Boston 1823-1887 / by Alexander W. Katlan. Park Ridge, N.J. : Noyes Press, c1987. xvi, 460 p. : ill., facsims. ; 25 cm. Bibliography: p. 367-374. ISBN 0-8155-5064-2 : LC Card 87-12283 DDC 338.7/617028 19
1. Artists' materials industry - United States - Directories. I. Title.
HD9791.U52 K37 1987

Katō, Kan, 1926- The Japanese economy in transition / by Hiroshi Kato. Tokyo, Japan : Toyo Keizai Shinposha : Gendai Keizai Kenkyu Center [distributor], c1986. viii, 160 p. : ill. ; 22 cm. LC Card 87-163640 DDC 330.952/047 19
1. Japan - Economic policy - 1945-. 2. Japan - Foreign economic relations. 3. Administrative agencies - Japan - Reorganization. I. Title.
HC462.9 .K35367 1986

Kato, Tsuyoshi. Environment, agriculture, and society in the Malay world /. Kyoto, Japan , 1986. ix, 177 p. : LC Card 86-201590 DDC 338.1/09595 19
HD2080.6 .E58 1986

Katona, George, 1901-
Ehrenpromotion von Prof. Dr. George Katona, Ann Arbor, Michigan am 15. Juni 1981 . Berlin [1982] 51 p. : LC Card 83-200933
HB74.P8 E35 1982

KATONA, GEORGE, 1901-
Ehrenpromotion von Prof. Dr. George Katona, Ann Arbor, Michigan am 15. Juni 1981 . Berlin [1982] 51 p. : LC Card 83-200933
HB74.P8 E35 1982

[Aspirations and affluence. Dutch]
Het psychologisch klimaat van de economie in de Verenigde Staten en West-Europa / G. Katona, B. Strumpel, E. Zahn. Utrecht : Uitg. Het Spectrum, 1974. 247 p. ; 22 cm. Includes index. Translated from the English. Bibliography: p. 235-238. ISBN 90-274-5826-X
1. Consumers - United States. 2. Consumers - Europe, West. 3. Economics - Psychological aspects. I. Strumpel, Burkhard. II. Zahn, Ernestern. III. Title.
NYPL [JLD 86-295]

Katonapolitika mindenkinek, 0209-8938. Losoncz, Miklós. Erők és érdekek . Budapest , 1986. 191 p. : ISBN 963-326-966-0 : LC Card 87-148142
HF1414.5 .L67 1986

Katsman, David. Decision-making in the Soviet energy industry . Falls Church, VA (7700 Leesburg Pike, #250, Falls Church 22043) , c1986. ix, 166 leaves ; LC Card 87-401592 DDC 333.79/0947 19
HD9502.S652 D43 1986

Kattermann, Dieter. Neoricardianische Modelle zur Theorie des internationalen Handels und ihre Kritik der neoklassischen Aussenhandelstheorie : Überblick über eine aktuelle Kontroverse / Dieter Kattermann. Bremen : Universität Bremen, 1981. 135, A-G p. : ill. ; 21 cm. Slight revision of the author's Diplomarbeit, 1980. Bibliography: p. A-G. ISBN 3-88722-039-0 LC Card 82-177622 DDC 337/.0724 19
1. International economic relations - Mathematical models. 2. Commerce - Mathematical models. I. Title.
HF1412 .K37 1981 ***NYPL [JLD 86-2740]***

The Katy railroad and the last frontier /. Masterson, V. V. Columbia , 1988. xiv, 312 p., [24] p. of plates : ISBN 0-8262-0668-9 (pbk. : alk. paper) LC Card 87-19146 DDC 385/.0978 19
HE2791.M743 M37 1988

Katz, Daniel, 1903- Productivity, supervision, and morale in an office situation, part I / Daniel Katz, Nathan Maccoby, Nancy C. Morse. New York : Garland Pub., 1987, c1950. vii, 84 p. ; 23 cm. (Continuity in administrative science) Reprint. Originally published: Ann Arbor, Mich. : Institute for Social Research, University of Michigan, 1950. Includes bibliographical references. ISBN 0-8240-8211-7 (alk. paper) : LC Card 86-25804 DDC 658.3 19
1. Personnel management. 2. Labor productivity. 3. Supervision of employees. 4. Employee morale. 5. Office management. I. Maccoby, Nathan, 1912-. II. Morse, Nancy C., 1920-. III. Title. IV. Series.
HF5549 .K282 1987

Katz, Donald R. The big store : inside the crisis and revolution at Sears / Donald R. Katz. New York : Viking, 1987. xiv, 604 p., [16] pages of plates : ill. ; 24 cm. Includes index. ISBN 0-670-80512-2 LC Card 87-40060 DDC 381/.45/000973 19
1. Sears, Roebuck and Company. I. Title.
HF5467.S4 K38 1987

Katz, Harry Charles, 1951-
Kochan, Thomas A. The transformation of American industrial relations /. New York , c1986. viii, 287 p. ; ISBN 0-465-08696-9 : LC Card 85-47502 DDC 331/.0973 19
HD8072 .K67 1986

Shifting gears : changing labor relations in the U. S. automobile industry / Harry C. Katz. Cambridge, Mass. : MIT Press, c1985. xii, 230 p. : ill. ; 24 cm. Includes index. Bibliography: p.[211]-223. ISBN 0-262-11098-9 LC Card 84-26105 DDC 331/.04292/0973 19
1. Collective bargaining - Automobile industry - United States - History. 2. Wages - Automobile industry workers - United States - History. 3. Quality of work life - United States - History. I. Title.
HD6976.A82 U528 1985
NYPL [JLE 85-2260]

Katz, Reinhard. Informationsquellen der Konsumenten : eine Analyse der Divergenzen zwischen der Beurteilung und Nutzung / Reinhard Katz. Wiesbaden : Gabler, c1983. xxix, 297 p. : ill. ; 24 cm. (Schriftenreihe Unternehmensführung und Marketing. Bd. 17) Bibliography: p. [276]-297. ISBN 3-409-13602-9 LC Card 84-118615
1. Consumers. 2. Decision-making. 3. Risk. I. Title.
HF5415.3 .K35 1983

Katzan, Harry. A manager's guide to productivity, quality circles, and industrial robots / Harry Katzan, Jr. New York : Van Nostrand Reinhold Co., c1985. vii, 136 p. : ill. ; 24 cm. Includes index. Bibliography: p. 129-132. ISBN 0-442-24823-7 LC Card 84-25739 DDC 658.5 19
1. Quality circles. 2. Robots, Industrial. I. Title.
HD56 .K377 1985 ***NYPL [JLE 86-4510]***

Katzev, Richard D. Promoting energy conservation : an analysis of behavioral research / by Richard D. Katzev & Theodore R. Johnson. Boulder : Westview Press, 1987. xvi, 218 p. : ill. ; 24 cm. (Westview special studies in natural resources and energy management) Bibliography: p. 175-195. ISBN 0-8133-7337-9 (pbk.) : LC Card 86-32587 DDC 333.79/16 19
1. Energy conservation - Psychological aspects. 2. Energy consumption - Psychological aspects. 3. Consumers - Attitudes. I. Johnson, Theodore R. II. Title.
HD9502.A2 K38 1987

Katzner, Donald W., 1938- Walrasian microeconomics : an introduction to the economic theory of market behavior / Donald W. Katzner. Reading, Mass. : Addison-Wesley, c1988. xv, 512 p. : ill. ; 25 cm. Includes bibliographies and index. ISBN 0-201-10461-X : LC Card 86-26622 DDC 338.5 19
1. Microeconomics. 2. Economics, Mathematical. 3. Capitalism. I. Title.
HB172 .K38 1988

KAUAI (HAWAII) - ECONOMIC CONDITIONS.
Economic development on the island of Kauai . [Honolulu] [1985] xxii, 84 p. : LC Card 86-622084 DDC 338.9969/41 19
HC107.H32 K383 1985

Kauer, Christian, 1951- Konfliktregelung und Mitbestimmung : Aspekte der Einbeziehung verhandlungstheoretischer Ansätze zur Erklärung des Mitbestimmungsprozesses / Christian Kauer. Frankfurt am Main ; New York : P. Lang, c1985. 393 p. : ill. ; 21 cm. (Europäische Hochschulschriften. Reihe V, Volks- und Betriebswirtschaft, 0531-7339 . Bd. 588 = vol. 588 = vol. 588) Bibliography: p. 361-393. ISBN 3-8204-5626-0 (pbk.) LC Card 87-672045
1. Management - Germany (West) - Employee participation. 2. Negotiation in business - Germany (West). 3. Conflict management - Germany (West). 4. Mineral industries - Germany (West) - Management - Employee participation. I. Series: Europäische Hochschulschriften. Reihe V, Volks- und Betriebswirtschaft , Bd. 588. II. Title.
HD5660.G4 K37x 1985

Kaufhold, Karl Heinrich. Theorie und Empirie in Wirtschaftspolitik und Wirtschaftsgeschichte . Göttingen , 1984. 242 p. : ISBN 3-509-01366-2 : LC Card 85-120064
HC240 .T45 1984

Kaufhold, Klaus, 1943- Die wirtschaftlichen Wirkungen der Fluktuation in der Einzelwirtschaft : eine theoretische Untersuchung / Klaus Kaufhold. Frankfurt am Main ; New York : P. Lang, c1985. 357 p. : ill. ; 21 cm. (Europäische Hochschulschriften. Reihe V, Volks- und Betriebswirtschaft, 0531-7339 . Bd. 607 = vol. 607 = vol. 607) Bibliography: p. 336-357. ISBN 3-8204-5665-1 LC Card 85-195373
1. Retail trade - Seasonal variations - Mathematical models. 2. Retail trade - Employees - Mathematical models. I. Series: Europäische Hochschulschriften. Reihe V, Volks- und Betriebswirtschaft , Bd. 607. II. Title.
HF5429 .K4156 1985

Das Kaufkraftargument /. Vajna, Thomas. Köln , c1982. 52 p. ; ISBN 3-602-24710-4 : LC Card 83-193844
HD5029 .V35 1982

Kaufman, Bruce E.
Critical employment issues facing the Southeast /. Atlanta, Ga. , 1986. xv, 156 p. ; ISBN 0-88406-191-4 LC Card 85-31410 DDC 331.12/5/0975 19
HD5725.S85 C75 1986
NYPL [JLD 86-2441]

How labor markets work . Lexington, Mass. , c1988. viii, 256 p. : ISBN 0-669-15126-2 (alk. paper) LC Card 87-22718 DDC 331.12 19
HD5701.3 .H68 1988

Kaufman, George G. Deregulating financial services . Cambridge, Mass. , 1986. xiii, 223 p. ; ISBN 0-88730-111-8 LC Card 86-3355 DDC 332.1/0973 19
HG2491 .R42 1986 ***NYPL [JLE 86-3307]***

Kaufman, Henry. Interest rates, the markets, and the new financial world / Henry Kaufman. 1st ed. New York, N.Y. : Times Books, 1986, c1985. xiii, 258 p. : ill. ; 22 cm. Includes index. Bibliography: p. 240-244. ISBN 0-8129-1333-7 LC Card 86-5865 DDC 332 19
1. Capital market. 2. Interest rates. I. Title.
HG173 .K364 1986 ***NYPL [JLD 86-2681]***

Kaufman, Perry J. The new commodity trading systems and methods / Perry J. Kaufman. New York : Wiley, c1987. xvi, 521 p. : ill. ; 26 cm. Bibliography: p. 499-505. Includes index. ISBN 0-471-87879-0 LC Card 87-6073 DDC 332.64/4 19
1. Commodity exchanges - Statistical methods. I. Title.
HG6036 .K38 1987

Kaufman, Stuart Bruce.
Challenge & change : the history of the Tobacco Workers International Union / by Stuart Bruce Kaufman. Kensington, Md. : Bakery, Confectionery, and Tobacco Workers International Union, c1986. ix, 163 p. : ill. ; 23 cm. Includes index. LC Card 86-229223 DDC 331.88/1797/0973 19
1. Tobacco Workers International Union - History. I. Title. II. Title: Challenge and change.
HD6515.T6 K38 1986

The Samuel Gompers papers /. Urbana , c1986- v. : ISBN 0-252-01138-4 (alk. paper : set) LC Card 84-2469 DDC 331.88/32/0924 19
HD6508 .S218 1986 ***NYPL [JLL 86-230]***

A vision of unity : the history of the Bakery and Confectionery Workers International Union / by Stuart Bruce Kaufman. Kensington, Md. : Bakery, Confectionery, and Tobacco Workers International Union, c1986. ix, 182 p. : ill. ; 23 cm. Includes index. LC Card 86-225331 DDC 331.88/1 19
1. Bakery and Confectionery Workers' International Union of America - History. I. Title.
HD6515.B2 K38 1986

Kaufman, Wallace. Finding hidden values in your home / Wallace Kaufman. New York : Macmillan ; London : Collier Macmillan, c1987. xi, 302 p. : ill., forms ; 25 cm. Includes index. ISBN 0-02-560720-0 LC Card 86-26909 DDC 333.33/2 19
1. Dwellings - Valuation. I. Title.
HD1387 .K38 1987b

Kaufmann, Albert, Dr. Czasny, Karl. Erfassung des Wohnungsangebotes /. Wien , 1985. 284 p. ; ISBN 3-900551-04-9 LC Card 87-103427 DDC 333.33/8 19
HD7337.V3 C93 1985

Kaufmann, Dwight W., 1919- Crucible : the story of a steel company / by Dwight W. Kaufmann. [Pittsburgh? Pa.] : D.W. Kaufmann, c1986. x, 298 p. : ill., ports. ; 28 cm. Cover title. LC Card 86-224545 DDC 338.7/669142/0973 19
1. Crucible Steel Company of America - History. 2. Steel industry and trade - Pennsylvania - History. I. Title.
HD9519.C7 K38 1986

Kaufmann, Elizabeth Irwin. Traffic growth resulting from future development : a regional overview : a summary of Phase 1 of the Impact Assessment Project : final report / [author, Elizabeth I. Kaufmann]. Washington, D.C. (1875 Eye St., N.W., Washington 20006-5454) : National Capital Region Transportation Planning Board, Metropolitan Washington Council of Governments, c1987. ix, 53, 15 p. : ill. ; 28 cm. "June 1967." LC Card 87-161086 DDC 388.4/13142/09753 19
1. Traffic estimation - Washington Metropolitan Area. 2. Highway capacity - Washington Metropolitan Area - Forecasting. I. National Capital Region Transportation Planning Board. II. Metropolitan Washington Council of Governments. III. Title.
HE356.5.W3 K38 1987

Kaufmann, Franz Xaver. Markt, Staat und Solidarität bei Adam Smith /. Frankfurt , New York , c1984. 238 p. ; ISBN 3-593-33338-4 LC Card 84-202891
HB103.S6 M27 1984

Kaufmann, Manfred. Die persönliche materielle Interessiertheit an der Material- und Energieökonomie / Manfred Kaufmann. Jena : Friedrich-Schiller-Universität, 1984. 112 p. : ill. ; 21 cm. (Wissenschaftliche Beiträge der Friedrich-Schiller-Universität Jena, 0232-3753) Bibliography: p. 100-112. LC Card 85-224317
1. Raw materials - Germany, East. 2. Consumption (Economics) - Germany, East. 3. Energy consumption - Germany (East). I. Title. II. Series.
HF1054.G42 K38 1984

Kaufmann, Marcel. Frey, René Leo. Die regionale Ausstrahlung der Universität Basel /. Basel , c1984. 73 p. : LC Card 84-166545 DDC 378/.103

19
HC395 .A75 no. 8 LC238.4.S92B37

Kaufmann-Scheuer, Brigitte. Perspektiven und Modelle einer Neuorientierung der staatlichen Wohneigentumsförderung / Brigitte Kaufmann-Scheuer. Freiburg [i. Br.] : HochschulVerlag, 1983. 235 p. : ill. ; 22 cm. (HochschulSammlung Wirtschaftswissenschaft. Volkswirtschaft, 0720-5686 . Bd. 10) Originally presented as the author's thesis (doctoral)--Freiburg i. Br., 1983. Bibliography: p. 227-235. ISBN 3-8107-2185-9 LC Card 84-108468
1. Housing policy - Germany, West. 2. Housing subsidies - Germany (West). 3. Housing - Germany, West. I. Title. II. Series.
HD7339.A3 K34 1983

Kaushik, S. K., 1944-
The Debt crisis and financial stability . New York, NY (Attn: Comptroller, Pace Plaza, 10038) , 1985. xi, 157 p. : ISBN 0-88239-017-1 : LC Card 85-19243 DDC 336.3/435/091724 19
HG3891.5 .D4 1985 ***NYPL [JLE 86-3911]***

International banking and global financing . New York, NY , c1983. xiv, 257 p. : ISBN 0-88239-015-5 (pbk.) : LC Card 84-60076 DDC 332.1/5 19
HG205 .I54 1983

International banking and world economic growth . New York , 1987. xviii, 183 p. : ISBN 0-275-92669-9 (alk. paper) : LC Card 87-7353 DDC 332.1/5 19
HG3881 .I575133 1987

Kaushik, S. L., 1946- Public administration in India . Allahabad , 1983. xii, 308 p. ; LC Card 83-907416 DDC 354.54 19
JQ224 .P75 1983 ***NYPL [JLE 86-4197]***

Kautsky, Karl, 1854-1938.
[Agrarfrage. English]
The agrarian question / Karl Kautsky ; translated from the German by Peter Burgess. London ; Atlantic Highlands, N.J. : Zwan Publications, 1988- p. cm. Translation of: Agrarfrage. ISBN 1-85305-024-5 (v. 2) LC Card 87-20593 DDC 338.1 19
1. Agriculture - Economic aspects - Germany. 2. Socialism - Germany. 3. Communism and agriculture - Germany. 4. e-gx. I. Title.
HD1306.G3 K315 1988

Die Vorläufer des neueren Sozialismus / von Karl Kautsky. Stuttgart : J.H.W. Dietz, 1895. 2 v. ; 26 cm. (Die Geschichte des Sozialismus in Einzeldarstellungen . Bd. 1 1) CONTENTS. - T. 1. Von Plato bis zu den Wiedertäufern.--T. 2. Von Thomas More bis zum Vorabend der französischen Revolution.
1. Communism - History. 2. Socialism - History. I. Title. II. Series. ***NYPL [JLF 85-168]***

Kawase, Tarō, 1935- Erekutoronikusu pawā shōjiten /. Tōkyō , 1985. v, 618 p. : ISBN 4-320-08454-3 : LC Card 85-229520
TK7804 .E73 1985 <Orien Japan>
NYPL [*OSG 86-3267]

Kay-Åberg, K. (Karl), 1861-1927. Sveriges industri : handbok för industriidkare och affärsmän : hufvudsakligen efter officiella källor utarbetad / af K. Key-Åberg. Stockholm : P.A. Norstedt, 1898. xvi p., 1054 columns, 1055-1071 p. ; 22 cm. LC Card 85-666356
1. Sweden - Industries - Handbooks, manuals, etc. 2. Businessmen - Sweden - Handbooks, manuals, etc. I. Title.
HC372.2 .K39x 1898

Kay, Cristóbal.

Kay, David L. The Adirondack land market : the land, its value, its buyers, 1968-1983 / David L. Kay. Ithaca, N.Y. : Dept. of Agricultual Economics, Cornell University Agricultural Experiment Station, New York State College of Agriculture and Life Sciences, [1985] 53 p. : ill. ; 28 cm. (A.E. Res. . 85-18) Cover title. "December 1985." Includes bibliographical references. LC Card 86-621939 DDC 333.33/22/0974753 19
1. Real estate business - New York (State) - Adirondack Mountains Region - Statistics. I. Series: A.E. research , 85-18. II. Title.
HD266.N72 A265 1985

Kay, Ernest. Abdel Haleem, M. A. English-Arabic business dictionary /. London , 1984. xxxii, 263 p. ; ISBN 0-86010-448-6 : LC Card 83-228731 DDC 650/.03/21 19
HF1002 .A23 1984 ***NYPL [JLD 86-2048]***

Kay, J. A. (John Anderson) Edwards, J. S. S. (Jeremy S. S.) The economic analysis of accounting profitability /. Oxford , New York , 1987. 133 p. : ISBN 0-19-877241-6 : LC Card 87-5575 DDC 657/.95 19
HF5686.C7 E34 1987

Kay, Robert S. Handbook of accounting and auditing /. Boston , c1981. 1 v. (various pagings) ; ISBN 0-88712-221-3 (Update 1985) LC Card 80-53166 DDC 657/.02/02 19
HF5635.H22 ***NYPL [*R-Econ. 85-31]***

Kay, William.
A-Z guide to money / William Kay. Rev. ed. London : Constable, 1986, c1983. 281 p. : ill. ; 23 cm. "A Constable guide"--Jacket. Bibliography: p. 281. ISBN 0-09-467160-5 : LC Card 86-224824 DDC 332/.03/21 19
1. Money - Dictionaries. 2. Finance - Dictionaries. I. Title.
HG216 .K39 1986

Battle for the high street / William Kay. London : Piatkus, 1987. 194 p., [16] p. of plates : ill. ; 24 cm. Bibliography: p. 191. Includes index. ISBN 0-86188-621-6 : LC Card 87-143764 DDC 658.8/7 19
1. Retail trade - Great Britain - Case studies. I. Title.
HF5429.6.G7 K38 1987

Kayālā śramika, jībana o saṃgrāma /. Basurāya, Sunīla. Durgāpura , Kalikātā , 1986. 239 p. ; LC Card 86-903821
HD8039.M62 I394 1986

Kayani, Ashraf K. Preparing subnational population projections : a manual for selected indirect methods / Ashraf K. Kayani. Santiago de Chile : Centro Latinoamericano de Demografía, [1980] ii, 68 p. ; 28 cm. (Serie B . no. 48) "Marzo de 1980." Bibliography: p. [65]-68. LC Card 84-256007 DDC 304.6/2/072 19
1. Population forecasting - Methodology. I. Series: Serie B (CELADE (Organization)) , no. 48. II. Title.
HB849.53 .K39 1980

Kaye, Geraldine. Finance. Oxford [Oxfordshire] , New York , 1987. xiii, 495 p. ; ISBN 0-08-034780-0 : LC Card 87-7247 DDC 332/.0941 19
HG186.G7 F53 1987

Kaynak, Erdener. World food marketing systems /. London , Boston , 1986. xviii, 333 p. : ISBN 0-407-00358-4 : LC Card 85-28371 DDC 380.1/456413 19
HD9000.5 .W587 1986
NYPL [JLE 86-3213]

Kayongo-Male, Diane. Children at work in Kenya / D. Kayongo-Male and P. Walji. Nairobi ; New York : Oxford University Press, 1984. x, 187 p. : map ; 21 cm. Includes index. Bibliography: p. [176]-184. ISBN 0-19-572546-8 (pbk.) LC Card 85-980979 DDC 331.3/1/096761 19
1. Children - Employment - Kenya. 2. Youth - Employment - Kenya. I. Walji, Parveen. II. Title.
HD6250.K4 K39 1984 ***NYPL [Sc D 86-960]***

KAYPRO COMPUTERS - PROGRAMMING.
Lenfest, David. Kaypro word processing, plain & simple /. Blue Ridge Summit, Pa. , c1985. xiv, 176 p. : ISBN 0-8306-0812-5 : LC Card 84-8720 DDC 652 19
Z52.5.K39 L46 1985 ***NYPL [JSE 87-12]***

Kaypro word processing, plain & simple /. Lenfest, David. Blue Ridge Summit, Pa. , c1985. xiv, 176 p. : ISBN 0-8306-0812-5 : LC Card 84-8720 DDC 652 19
Z52.5.K39 L46 1985 ***NYPL [JSE 87-12]***

Kaypro word processing, plain and simple. Lenfest, David. Kaypro word processing, plain & simple /. Blue Ridge Summit, Pa. , c1985. xiv, 176 p. : ISBN 0-8306-0812-5 : LC Card 84-8720 DDC 652 19
Z52.5.K39 L46 1985 ***NYPL [JSE 87-12]***

Kazakevich, I. S. (Igor' Stepanovich) Opyt stroitel'stva sotsialisticheskoĭ ėkonomiki v stranakh Azii /. Moskva , 1986. 290 p. ; LC Card 87-126301
HC412 .O675 1986

Kazakevich, V. P.
Agropromyshlennyĭ kompleks v usloviiākh razvitogo sotsializma . Moskva , 1986. 167 p. ; LC Card 87-166350
HD9015.S652 A38 1986

Ėkonomicheskoe stimulirovanie truda v usloviiākh sotsializma . Moskva , 1986. 179 p. ; LC Card 87-166364
HD5046 .E47 1986

Metodiki opredeleniia ėkonomicheskoĭ ėffektivnosti kapital'nykh vlozheniĭ v sotsialisticheskikh stranakh . Moskva , 1981. 101 p. ; LC Card 82-204402
HC244.Z9 C35 1981

Sotsialisticheskaia sobstvennost' v usloviiākh razvitogo sotsializma . Moskva , 1984. 165 p. ; LC Card 85-177805
HB701 .S59 1984

KAZAKH S.S.R. - ECONOMIC CONDITIONS.
Kunaeva, Fazilia Akhmetovna. Kazakhskaia Sovetskaia Sotsialisticheskaia Respublika /. Alma-Ata , 1978. 31 p. : LC Card 81-165585
HC337.K3 K86 1978

Shedenov, U. K. (Utegali Kadyrgalievich) Sotsial'no-ėkonomicheskie problemy sfery obsluzhivaniia naseleniia v usloviiākh nauchno-tekhnicheskogo progressa /. Alma-Ata , 1978. 197, [3] p. ; LC Card 81-149568
HD9986.S683 K398 1978

KAZAKH S.S.R. - INDUSTRIES - LOCATION.
Ėffektivnost' territorial'noĭ organizatsii promyshlennogo proizvodstva v Kazakhstane /. Alma-Ata , 1980. 190 p. ; LC Card 82-164638
HC337.K33 D53 1980

Kazakhskaia Sovetskaia Sotsialisticheskaia Respublika /. Kunaeva, Fazilia Akhmetovna. Alma-Ata , 1978. 31 p. : LC Card 81-165585
HC337.K3 K86 1978

Kazakhskoe obshchestvo druzhby i kul'turnoĭ sviazi s zarubezhnymi stranami. Kunaeva, Fazilia Akhmetovna. Kazakhskaia Sovetskaia Sotsialisticheskaia Respublika /. Alma-Ata , 1978. 31 p. : LC Card 81-165585
HC337.K3 K86 1978

Kazakos, Panos V. Hē Hellada stēn Eurōpaikē Koinotēta . Athēna , 1987. 14, 565 p. ; LC Card 87-169443
HC241.25.G8 H43 1987

Kazancigil, Ali. The State in global perspective /. Aldershot, Hants, Eng. ; Brookfield, Vt., USA : xx, 300 p. : ISBN 0-566-05160-5 (U. S.) : LC Card 85-31741 DDC 320.1 19
NYPL [JLD 86-3236]

Kazantsev, S. V. (Sergeĭ Vladimirovich) Makromodelirovanie rasshirennogo vosproizvodstva / S.V. Kazantsev ; otvetstvennyĭ redaktor I.A. Itskovich. Novosibirsk : Izd-vo "Nauka," Sibirskoe otd-nie, 1980. 206, [2] p. ; 17 cm. At head of title: Akademiia nauk SSSR. Sibirskoe otdelenie. Institut ėkonomiki i organizatsii promyshlennogo proizvodstva. Bibliography: p. 199-[207] LC Card 81-138742
1. Econometrics. I. Itskovich, I. A. (Iosif Aleksandrovich). II. Title.
HB139 .K39 1980

Kazēs, D. A. (Dēmētrēs A.)
[Licensing kai viomēchanikē anaptyxē. English]
Licensing and industrial development : the case of Greece / Dimitris A. Kazis, Charalambos I. Perrakis. Athens : Centre of Planning and Economic Research, 1986. 208 p. : ill. ; 25 cm. (Studies / Centre of Planning and Economic Research . 4) Translation of: Licensing kai viomēchanikē anaptyxē. Includes bibliographical references. LC Card 87-170691 DDC 338.09495 19
1. License agreements - Economic aspects - Greece. 2. License agreements - Greece. 3. Technology transfer - Greece. 4. Greece - Industries. I. Perrakēs, Charalambos I. II. Series: Studies (Kentron Programmatismou kai Oikonomikōn Ereunōn) , 4. III. Title.
HF1429 .K3813 1986

Kazimour, Jan, engineer. Rezervy v ekonomice / J. Kazimour, J. Vrchota, J. Laitl. Praha : Práce, 1981. 227 p. ; 20 cm. (Člověk a práce) Includes bibliographical references. LC Card 81-208368
1. Czechoslovakia - Economic conditions - 1945-. I. Vrchota, J. (Jaroslav). II. Laitl, Jan. III. Title.
HC270.28 .K38 1981

Kazin, Michael, 1948- Barons of labor : the San Francisco building trades and union power in the Progressive Era / Michael Kazin. Urbana : University of Illinois Press, c1987. xiv, 319 p.,

[14] p. of plates : ill., ports. ; 24 cm. (The Working class in American history) Includes bibliographies and index. ISBN 0-252-01345-X (alk. paper) LC Card 86-6967 DDC 331.88/124/0979461 19
1. Building Trades Council (San Francisco, Calif.) - History. 2. Trade-unions - Building trades - California - San Francisco - History. 3. Building trades - California - San Francisco - History. 4. San Francisco (Calif.) - History. I. Title.
HD6515.B9 S45 1987 **NYPL [JLE 87-1053]**

KB Göttingen (Germany). Anti-Mil Kommission. Unterdrückung, Hunger, Krieg . Göttingen [1985?] 73 p. : LC Card 86-152237
HC59.7 .U55 1985

KCET (Television station : Los Angeles, Calif.) Hungary, pushing the limits [videorecording] /. Alexandria, VA , 1987. 1 videocassette (60 min.) : LC Card 87-707589 DDC 943.9 11
HC300.28

KCI Communications, Inc.
Power investing . Alexandria, VA (P.O. Box 1467, Alexandria 22313) , c1987. vi, 42 leaves : LC Card 87-403629 DDC 332.63/22 19
HG4915 .P65 1987

Stock up on options /. Alexandria, VA (P.O. Box 1467, Alexandria 22313) , c1987. 28 leaves : LC Card 87-401634 DDC 332.64/52 19
HG6042 .S84 1987

Keane, John, 1949- After full employment / John Keane and John Owens. London ; Dover, N.H., USA : Hutchinson, 1986. 198 p. ; 22 cm. (Contemporary politics) Bibliography: p. [181]-192. Includes index. ISBN 0-09-164091-1 (pbk.) : LC Card 86-213691 DDC 339.5/0941 19
1. Unemployment - Great Britain. 2. Unemployment - United States. 3. Full employment policies. I. Owens, John. II. Title.
HD5765.A6 K42 1986

Kearney, Richard C. Bowman, Ann O'M., 1948- The resurgence of the states /. Englewood Cliffs, N.J. , c1986. x, 269 p. : ISBN 0-13-774969-4 (pbk.) LC Card 85-19213 DDC 353.9 19
JK2408 .B68 1986 **NYPL [JLE 86-4496]**

Kearsley, Greg, 1951- Training and technology : a handbook for HRD professionals / Greg Kearsley. Reading, Ma. : Addison-Wesley Pub. Co., c1984. vii, 198 p. : ill. ; 24 cm. Includes bibliographical references and indexes. ISBN 0-201-10335-4 : LC Card 83-22336 DDC 658.3/12404 19
1. Employees, Training of - Computer-assisted instruction. 2. Employees, Training of - Audio-visual aids. I. Title. II. Title: Training and technology.
HF5549.5.T7 K343 1984
NYPL [JLE 86-2641]

Keating, Michael, 1943- To the last drop : Canada and the world's water crisis / Michael Keating. Toronto, Ont., Canada : Macmillan of Canada, c1986. xviii, 265 p. : ill. ; 24 cm. Bibliography: p. 256-257. Includes index. ISBN 0-7715-9704-5 LC Card 86-224945 DDC 363.7/394/0971 19
1. Water - Pollution - Canada. 2. Water - Pollution. I. Title.
HC120.W32 K43 1986

Keaveney, Susan M. Cateora, Philip R. Marketing . Homewood, Ill. , 1987. xi, 172 p. : ISBN 0-256-05626-9 (pbk.) LC Card 86-83392 DDC 658.8/48 19
HF1009.5 .C37 1987

Keaveny, Timothy J. Allen, Robert E. (Robert Edward), 1946- Contemporary labor relations /. Reading, Mass. , c1988. xi, 724 p. : ISBN 0-201-10083-5 : LC Card 87-24128 DDC 331/.0973 19
HD8072.5 .A43 1988

Kebschull, Dietrich.
Indebtedness and growth in developing countries /. Hamburg , 1986. 344 p. ; ISBN 3-87895-300-3 (pbk.) LC Card 86-213057 DDC 336.3/435/091724 19
HJ8899 .I53 1986

Transmigration in Indonesia : an empirical analysis of motivation, expectations, and experiences / Dietrich Kebschull. Hamburg : HWWA-Institut für Wirtschaftsforschung-Hamburg, 1984. xxiv, 134 p. ; 30 cm. (TAD-report . no. 26) At head of title: East Kalimantan Transmigration Area Development Project. LC Card 86-223779 DDC 304.8/09598 19
1. Migration, Internal - Indonesia. 2. Land settlement - Indonesia - Kalimantan Timur. 3. Kalimantan Timur (Indonesia) - Economic conditions. I. East Kalimantan Transmigration Area Development Project. II. Title. III. Series.
HB2107 .K4 1984

Kedar, B. Z. Ashtor, Eliyahu, 1914- East-West trade in the medieval Mediterranean /. London , 1986. [344] p. ; ISBN 0-86078-193-3 LC Card 87-134358 DDC 382/.094/056 19
HF3756.Z7 E92 1986

Keddeman, Willem. Emploi et revenus dans le secteur agricole traditionnel au Bénin / par Willem Keddeman et Marcel Fafchamps. Addis Abéba : Programme des emplois et des compétences techniques pour l'Afrique, Bureau international du travail, 1982. 64 p. ; 30 cm. (Documents de travail / Programme des emplois et des compétences techniques pour l'Afrique = Working papers / Jobs and Skills Programme for Africa) At head of title: Où vas-tu paysan? "Version provisoire." Bibliography: p. 63-64. LC Card 87-980402
1. Agriculture - Economic aspects - Benin. I. Fafchamps, Marcel. II. Title. III. Title: Où vas-tu paysan?. IV. Series: Working papers (Jobs and Skills Programme for Africa).
HD2141 .K43 1982

Keeble, David. New firms and regional development in Europe /. London , Dover, N.H. , c1986. 322 p. : ISBN 0-7099-1577-2 : LC Card 85-28372 DDC 338.7/1/094 19
HD2346.E9 N48 1986 **NYPL [JLD 86-1597]**

Keefer, Nancy. Speculating in futures. [Chicago] , c1986. v, 65 p. : LC Card 87-100478 DDC 332.64/4 19
HG6046 .S63 1986

KEELEY CURE. see **ALCOHOLISM - TREATMENT.**

Keeley, Phil. Cairncross, Frances. Guide to the economy /. London , 1987. viii, 161 p. : ISBN 0-416-39600-3 (pbk.) : LC Card 87-138822 DDC 330.941/085 19
HC256.6 .C27 1987

Keeling, B. Lewis (Billy Lewis) Kallaus, Norman Francis, 1924- Administrative office management /. Cincinnati , c1987. ix, 774 p. : ISBN 0-538-07560-0 LC Card 85-61633 DDC 651.3 19
HF5547 .K43 1987

KEEMBE (CENTRAL PROVINCE, ZAMBIA) - STATISTICS, VITAL.
Interrelationships among infant and childhood mortality, socio-economic factors and fertility in Zambia . Lusaka , Addis Ababa [1984?] 300 p. : LC Card 87-105950 DDC 304.6/32/096894 19
HB1323.I42 Z335 1984

Keenan, David R. The south-eastern lines of the Sydney tramway system / David R. Keenan. Sydney, N.S.W., Australia : Transit Press, c1982. 120 p. : ill. ; 21 x 28 cm. ISBN 0-909338-03-5 (pbk.) LC Card 87-167855 DDC 388.4/6/09441 19
1. Street-railroads - Australia - Sydney (N.S.W.). I. Title.
HE5179.S93 K44 1982

Keenan, Gerald M. Insurance redlining : profits vs policyholders / by Gerald M. Keenan.2d ed. Chicago, Ill. : National Training and Information Center, c1979. 135 p. : ill. ; 28 cm. Includes bibliographical references.
1. Insurance - United States. 2. Insurance policies - United States. 3. Risk (Insurance) - United States. 4. Discrimination in insurance - United States. I. Title.
NYPL [JLF 86-1590]

Keep out . Plotkin, Sidney. Berkeley , c1987. xiii, 360 p. ; ISBN 0-520-05806-2 LC Card 86-30807 DDC 333.3/0973 19
HD205 .P56 1987

Keeping America at work . Lund, Robert T. New York , c1986. xi, 260 p. : ISBN 0-471-81563-2 LC Card 85-17900 DDC 331.12/0973 19
HD45 .L86 1985 **NYPL [JLD 86-2101]**

A Keesing's reference publication.
Government economic agencies of the world . Detroit , c1985. x, 546 p. ; ISBN 0-8103-2104-1 (Gale) LC Card 84-26861 DDC 351.82/025 19
HD87.25 .G68 1985
NYPL [*R-Econ 86-6573]

Kehrer, Daniel M.
Directory for international investors / by Daniel M. Kehrer. New York, NY, U. S.A. : Modern Business Reports, c1984. 130 p. in various pagings : ill. ; 28 cm. ISBN 0-86604-175-3 (pbk.) LC Card 86-231996 DDC 332.6/73/025 19
1. Investments, Foreign - Directories. I. Title.
HG4538 .K39 1984

Strategies for the successful international investor / by Daniel M. Kehrer. New York, NY, U. S.A. : Modern Business Reports, c1984. ix, 183 p. : ill. ; 28 cm. ISBN 0-86604-174-5 (pbk.) LC Card 86-232170 DDC 332.6/73 19
1. Investments, Foreign. I. Title.
HG4538 .K395 1984

Kehrle, Luiz Rodrigues. Santos, Madalena Herculano dos. Condições de vida nos municípios paraibanos /. João Pessoa (PB) : Brasília, DF : 103 p. : LC Card 87-403990 DDC 330.981/33063 19
HC188.P343 S26 1986

Keidel, Albert. China's dairy and food processing industries : prospects for processors and suppliers / prepared for Dairy and Food Industries Supply Association, Inc. by Albert Keidel with the assistance of Rosemary Draper and Robert Bruce. Washington, D.C. : Rock Creek Research, c1986. ii, 65 leaves ; 29 cm. "April 1986." LC Card 86-233105 DDC 338.1/77/0951 19
1. Dairy products industry - China. 2. Food industry and trade - China. I. Draper, Rosemary. II. Bruce, Robert, 1962-. III. Dairy & Food Industries Supply Association. IV. Title.
HD9275.C62 K45 1986

Keil, Hartmut, 1942- German workers in Chicago . Urbana , c1988. p. cm. ISBN 0-252-01458-8 (alk. paper) LC Card 87-10780 DDC 331.6/2/43077311 19
HD8081.G4 G46 1988

Keilman, Nico. Modelling household formation and dissolution /. Oxford [Oxfordshire] , New York , c1987. p. cm. ISBN 0-19-829500-6 : LC Card 87-18581 DDC 306.8/5/0724 19
HB849.49 .M63 1987

Keimena kai meletai .
(1) Dokos, Kōnstantinos. Hē Sterea Hellas kata ton Henetotourkikon polemon, 1684-1699 kai ho Salōnōn Philotheos /. Athēnai , 1985. 255 p. ; LC Card 86-211599
HB2092.5.A3 D64 1985

Keith, Robert M.
Smith, Jack L. Financial accounting /. New York , c1988. xxii, 706 p. : ISBN 0-07-059002-8 : LC Card 87-17233 DDC 657 19
HF5635 .S6445 1988

Smith, Jack L. Managerial accounting /. New York , c1988. xxv, 717 p. : ISBN 0-07-058990-9 : LC Card 87-17223 DDC 658.1/511 19
HF5657.4 .S55 1988

Keizai Dōyūkai. Building an industrial structure for the 21st century . Tokyo , 1982. ii, 58 p. ; LC Card 83-201472 DDC 338.4/762/000952 19
HC465.H53 B85 1982

A kelet-nyugati kereskedelem fejlődési tendenciái a 80-as években /. Biró, Gerd. Budapest , 1986. 152 p. ; ISBN 963-221-582-6 : LC Card 87-138649
HF4050 .B57 1986

Kell, Walter Gerry, 1921- Weygandt, Jerry J. Accounting principles /. New York , c1987. xxviii, 1167, [45] p. : ISBN 0-471-03863-6 LC Card 87-2001 DDC 657 19
HF5635 .W524 1987

Keller, Edmond J. (Edmond Joseph), 1942- Education, manpower, and development : the impact of educational policy in Kenya / Edmond J. Keller, Jr. Nairobi : Kenya Literature Bureau, 1980. xi, 251 p. ; 22 cm. Bibliography: p. [235]-251. LC Card 81-980037 DDC 379.676/2 19
1. Education and state - Kenya. 2. Manpower policy - Kenya. I. Title.
LC95.K4 K45 1980 **NYPL [Sc D 86-948]**

Keller, Friedrich Jakob, 1893- Das Ende des Kapitalismus : Inflationsmentalität, Zinsverlangen, private Grundrente, dem Frieden entgegen? / Friedrich Jakob Keller. Lyss : Helfikus, [1981] 211 p. : 1 port. ; 23 cm. LC

Card 84-104878
1. Laissez-faire. 2. Capitalism. 3. Christian democracy. I. Title.
HB95 .K33 1981

Keller, Gerald. Statistics for management and economics : a systematic approach / Gerald Keller, Brian Warrack, Henry Bartel. Belmont, Calif. : Wadsworth Pub. Co., c1988. xix, 987 p. : ill. (some col.) ; 24 cm. Includes index. ISBN 0-534-08622-5 LC Card 87-19845 DDC 658.4/033 19
1. Management - Statistical methods. 2. Economics - Statistical methods. I. Warrack, Brian. II. Bartel, Henry. III. Title.
HD30.215 .K45 1988

Keller, Thomas, 1950- Bergerud, Marly, 1942- Computers for managing information /. New York , c1988. xvi, 480 p., [32] p. of plates : ISBN 0-471-84441-1 LC Card 87-20979 DDC 650/.028/5 19
HF5548.2 .B387 1988

Kelles-Viitanen, Anita, 1947- Invisible hands . New Delhi , Newbury Park, Calif. , 1987. 273 p. ; ISBN 0-8039-9524-5 (U. S.) LC Card 87-4337 DDC 331.4/0954 19
HD6181.85 .A85 1987

Kelley, Clarence M. Security for you and your home-- : a complete handbook / by Clarence M. Kelley & Carl A. Roper.1st ed. Blue Ridge Summit, Pa. : Tab Books, c1984. viii, 391 p. : ill., ports. ; 24 cm. Includes index. ISBN 0-8306-0680-7 : LC Card 83-18134 DDC 643/.16 19
1. Security systems. 2. Self-defense. I. Roper, Carl A. II. Title.
HV7431 .K44 1984 ***NYPL [JSE 86-649]***

Kelley, Nelson Lane, 1937- Personnel management in action : skill building experiences / Lane Kelley, Arthur Whatley.4th ed. St. Paul : West Pub. Co., c1987. xiv, 338 p. : ill. ; 26 cm. Includes bibliographies. ISBN 0-314-32168-3 (pbk.) LC Card 86-32445 DDC 658.3 19
1. Personnel management. 2. Personnel management - Problems, exercises, etc. I. Whatley, Arthur A., 1939-. II. Title.
HF5549 .K344 1987

Kellogg, Douglas E. A primer for buying and selling small manufacturing companies / Douglas E. Kellogg. New York : Wiley, c1987. xiv, 225 p. : ill. ; 24 cm. Includes index. ISBN 0-471-85235-X LC Card 87-19017 DDC 658.1/6 19
1. Small business - Purchasing. 2. Business enterprises - Purchasing. 3. Business enterprises, Sale of. 4. Factories - Purchasing. I. Title.
HD2341 .K44 1987

Kelly, Alfred, 1947- The German worker . Berkeley , c1987. p. cm. ISBN 0-520-05972-7 (alk. paper) LC Card 87-5076 DDC 305.5/62/0922 B 19
HD8453.A1 G47 1987

Kelly de Escobar, Janet.
Del actor racional al cesto de basura : el desarrollo organizacional y la toma de decisiones / Janet Kelly de Escobar. Caracas, Venezuela : Ediciones IESA, c1983. 31 p., 3 leaves : ill. ; 29 cm. (Papeles de trabajo IESA . PTI-83-3) Prepared for the III Simposio sobre Desarrollo Organizacional held in Guayana City, Oct. 26-28, 1983. Bibliography: leaves [1]-3. ISBN 980-217-003-8 LC Card 86-201788
1. Decision-making. 2. Management. I. Title. II. Series.
HD30.23 .K363 1983

Opciones para la evaluación de las empresas públicas / Janet Kelly de Escobar y Julián Villalba. Caracas : Ediciones IESA, c1985. 36 p. ; 29 cm. (Papeles de trabajo IESA . PTI-85-9) Includes bibliographical references. ISBN 980-217-008-9 LC Card 86-201812
1. Government business enterprises - Management - Evaluation. I. Villalba, Julián. II. Title. III. Series.
HD62.35 .K45 1985

Kelly, G. Financial resources for local and regional authorities / report prepared under the guidance of the Committee of Experts on Local and Regional Finance of the Steering Committee for Regional and Municipal Matters, by G. Kelly. Strasbourg : Council of Europe, 1985. 79 p. ; 29 cm. (Study series, Local and regional authorities in Europe . 34) LC Card 86-206535 DDC 336/.014/4 19
1. Local finance - European Economic Community countries. 2. Intergovernmental fiscal relations - European Economic Community countries. I. Council of Europe. Committee of Experts on Local and Regional Finance. II. Series: Study series, Local and regional authorities in Europe , 34. III. Title.
HJ9420 .K45 1985

Kelly, Gene.
[Catalog of the fiscal stamps of the Kantone and Gemeinden of Switzerland]
Gene Kelly's catalog of the fiscal stamps of the Kantone and Gemeinden of Switzerland. [Diessenhofen, Switzerland] : G. Kelly, [1986- v. <1 > : ill. ; 21 cm. Cover title. LC Card 87-112466 DDC 769.5/7 19
1. Revenue-stamps - Switzerland - Catalogs. I. Title.
HJ5437.Z7 K45 1986

Kelly, Graham. Lewis, Mike. 20 activities for developing managerial effectiveness . Aldershot, Hants, England , c1986. xii, 276 p. : ISBN 0-566-02515-9 LC Card 87-147860 DDC 658.4/07124 19
HD31 .L387 1986

Kelly, Jerry S. Social choice theory : an introduction / Jerry S. Kelly. Berlin ; New York : Springer-Verlag, c1988. 163 p. : ill. ; 25 cm. Includes index. ISBN 0-387-17634-9 (U. S.) LC Card 87-12858 DDC 302/.13 19
1. Social choice. I. Title.
HB846.8 .K44 1988

Kelly, John M. Managing cash flow / John M. Kelly. New York : F. Watts, 1986. xii, 210 p. : ill. ; 24 cm. Includes index. ISBN 0-531-15509-9 LC Card 86-5657 DDC 658.1/5244 19
1. Cash flow. 2. Cash management. I. Title.
HG4028.C45 K453 1986
NYPL [JLE 86-4460]

Kelly, John M., 1949- How to check out your competition : a complete plan for investigating your market / John M. Kelly. New York : Wiley, c1987. xii, 349 p. : ill. ; 26 cm. ISBN 0-471-85670-3 (pbk.) LC Card 86-32408 DDC 658.8/02 19
1. Competition. 2. Marketing research. 3. Corporate planning. 4. Competition, International. I. Title.
HD41 .K44 1987

Kelly, Margaret. Review of 1985 property tax rates / Margaret Kelly. Jefferson City : Offices of the State Auditor of Missouri, [1986] i, 6 leaves, 109, 2 p. ; 28 cm. (Report / Offices of the State Auditor of Missouri . no. 86-62) LC Card 87-620606 DDC 336.22/2 19
1. Property tax - Missouri - Rates and tables. 2. Assessment - Missouri - Rates and tables. I. Series: Report (Missouri. State Auditor) , no. 86-62. II. Title.
HJ4121.M82 K45 1986

Kelly, Rita Mae. Comparable worth, pay equity, and public policy /. New York , 1988. xi, 280 p. ; ISBN 0-313-26014-1 (lib. bdg. : alk. paper) LC Card 87-17735 DDC 331.2/1 19
HD6061.2.U6 C656 1988

Kelly, Steve S. Fielder, Lonnie L. Agricultural statistics and prices for Louisiana, 1909-1985 /. [Baton Rouge, LA] [1986] iv, [122] p. : LC Card 87-620749 DDC 338.1/09763 s 338.1/09763/021 19
HD1775.L8 L7 no. 659

Kelly, Thomas A. (Thomas Alfred) DeBat, Don. The mortgage manual . Chicago , c1986. ix, 154 p. ; ISBN 0-8092-4890-5 (pbk.) : LC Card 86-23972 DDC 332.7/22 19
HG2040.5.U5 D423 1986

Kelly, Tim. The British computer industry : crisis and development / Tim Kelly. New York, NY : Croom Helm in association with Methuen, c1987 267 p. : ill. ; 23 cm. Bibliography: p. 234-257. Includes index. ISBN 0-7099-3123-9 : LC Card 87-569 DDC 338.4/7004/0941 19
1. Computer industry - Great Britain. I. Title.
HD9696.C63 G765 1987

Kelly, William W. (William Wright), 1946- Water control in Tokugawa Japan : irrigation organization in a Japanese river basin, 1600-1870 / by William W. Kelly. Ithaca, N.Y. : China-Japan Program, Cornell University, c1982. ix, 260 p. : ill. ; 28 cm. (Cornell University East Asia papers . no. 31) Based on the author's thesis (doctoral)--1980. Bibliography: p. 246-260. LC Card 83-126822
1. Irrigation - Japan - Aka River Watershed - History. 2. Water resources development - Japan - Aka River Watershed - History. 3. Irrigation engineering - Japan - Aka River Watershed - History. 4. Japan - History - Tokugawa period, 1600-1868. I. Cornell University. China-Japan Program. II. Title. III. Series.
HD1741.J32 A325 1982

Kelm, Ellen Jakes. Tydeman, John. New media in Europe . London , New York , c1986. xii, 260 p. : ISBN 0-07-084799-1 : LC Card 85-19839 DDC 384.55/094 19
HE8700.9.E8 T93 1986
NYPL [JLE 86-3209]

Kelso, Louis O. Democracy and economic power : extending the ESOP revolution / Louis O. Kelso and Patricia Hetter Kelso. Cambridge, Mass. : Ballinger Pub. Co., 1986. xii, 175 p. : ill. ; 24 cm. Includes index. ISBN 0-88730-115-0 : LC Card 86-14027 DDC 338.6 19
1. Industrial management - United States - Employee participation. 2. Employee ownership - United States. 3. Trade-unions - Economic aspects - United States. 4. Income distribution - United States. I. Kelso, Patricia Hetter. II. Title.
HD5660.U5 K45 1986 ***NYPL [JLE 86-4658]***

Kelso, Patricia Hetter. Kelso, Louis O. Democracy and economic power . Cambridge, Mass. , 1986. xii, 175 p. : ISBN 0-88730-115-0 : LC Card 86-14027 DDC 338.6 19
HD5660.U5 K45 1986 ***NYPL [JLE 86-4658]***

Kemeny, Pietro. Runggaldier, Ulrich. Le politiche regionali del lavoro . Milano, Italy , c1986. 160 p. ; LC Card 86-169484
HD8376.5 .R93 1986

KEMEROVSKAIA OBLAST' (R.S.F.S.R.) - ECONOMIC CONDITIONS.
Karmanov, V. A. (Vladimir Andreevich) Tisul' . Kemerovo , 1983. 93 p., [8] p. of plates : LC Card 84-103652
HC337.R852 T575 1983

A kemizálás és a magyar vegyipar /. Szekér, Gyula. Budapest , 1985. 340 p. : ISBN 963-10-6508-1 : LC Card 86-127325
HD9656.H92 S86 1985

Kemp, L. J. (Lynette J.) The Wardley guide to world money and securities markets / by Lynette J. Kemp. London : Euromoney, 1984. xvii, 472 p. ; 30 cm. Includes index. ISBN 0-903121-66-2
1. Investments - Handbooks, manuals, etc. 2. Investments, Foreign - Handbooks, manuals, etc. 3. Money market - Handbooks, manuals, etc. 4. Capital market - Handbooks, manuals, etc. I. Title. II. Title: World money and securities markets.
NYPL [JLG 86-203]

Kemp, Nigel J. The Human side of advanced manufacturing technology /. Chichester [West Sussex] , New York , c1987. xi, 205 p. : ISBN 0-471-90867-3 : LC Card 86-32554 DDC 331.25 19
HD9720.5 .H85 1987

Kempf, Theo, 1955- Theorie und Empirie betrieblicher Ausbildungsplatzangebote / Theo Kempf. Frankfurt am Main ; New York : P. Lang, c1985. 305 p. : ill. ; 21 cm. (Staatliche Allokationspolitik im marktwirtschaftlichen System, 0721-2860 . Bd. 19) Originally presented as the author's thesis (doctoral--Universität Mannheim, 1985) Bibliography: p. 286-305. ISBN 3-8204-8358-6 LC Card 86-111326
1. Employees, Training of - Germany, West. I. Title. II. Series.
HF5549.5.T7 K42 1985

Kempf, Thomas. Umsetzung organisatorischer Neuerungen : Fallbeispiele aus der öffentlichen Verwaltung im Vergleich / Thomas Kempf. Berlin : Deutsches Institut für Urbanistik, 1986. 237 p. : ill. ; 30 cm. Bibliography: p. 230-237. ISBN 3-88118-133-4 LC Card 87-114986
1. Organizational change - Germany (West). 2. Germany, West - Politics and government. I. Deutsches Institut für Urbanistik. II. Title.
HD58.8 .K46 1986

Kempton, Willett, 1948- Energy efficiency . Washington, D.C. , 1987, c1986. 333 p. : ISBN 0-918249-05-8 (pbk.) LC Card 86-28817 DDC 333.79/16/0973 19
HD9502.U52 E4883 1987

Kendall, Maurice George, Sir.
Dictionary of statistical terms. Kotz, Samuel. Russian-English, English-Russian glossary of statistical terms; prepared ... by Samuel Kotz. Edinburgh, 1971. vii, 87 p. ISBN

0-05-002446-9 LC Card 72-197391 DDC 519.5/01/4
HA17 .K62 ***NYPL [JLF 73-1241]***

Kendall, Stephanie. Employee attitude surveys : communication line to higher productivity / by Stephanie Kendall. New York, NY, U. S.A. : Modern Business Reports, c1986. x, 199, [30] p. : ill. ; 28 cm. ISBN 0-86604-209-1 (pbk.) LC Card 86-233239 DDC 658.3/14 19
1. Employee attitude surveys. I. Title.
HF5549.5.A83 K46 1986

Kende, Pierre. A Lengyel földindulás /. Malakoff , New York , 1980. 150 p. ; LC Card 81-177379
HD8537.N783 L45 1980 ***NYPL [JLB 86-24]***

Kende, R. (Richard) Czasny, Karl. Lehrjahre bei Bau-Holz . Wien , c1985. ix, 148 p. ; ISBN 3-900351-34-1 LC Card 86-227367 DDC 331.88/174/09436 19
HD6678.W62 G493 1985

Kendrick, David A. Feedback : a new framework for macroeconomic policy / by David A. Kendrick. Dordrecht ; Boston : Kluwer Academic Publishers, 1988. vi, 147 p. : ill. ; 23 cm. (Advanced studies in theoretical and applied econometrics . v. 10) Bibliography: p. 135-142. Includes index. ISBN 90-247-3593-9 LC Card 87-20990 DDC 339.5 19
1. Macroeconomics - Econometric models. 2. Control theory. I. Title. II. Series.
HB172.5 .K45 1988

The Kenkyūsha dictionary of new English. Takabe, Yoshinobu, 1907- Amerika shingo jiten = The Kenkyūsha dictionary of new English /. Tokyo , 1978. 717 p. ;
NYPL [*OSG 87-2157]

Kennedy, Carol. ICI : the company that changed our lives / Carol Kennedy. London : Hutchinson, 1986. xii, 209 p., [20] p. of plates : ill. (some col.) ; 23 cm. Includes index. ISBN 0-09-167300-3 : LC Card 87-121862 DDC 338.7/66/00941 19
1. Imperial Chemical Industries, ltd. - History. 2. Chemical industry - Great Britain - History. I. Title.
HD9652.9.I5 K46 1986

Kennedy, Charles H. Ethnic preference and public policy in developing states /. Boulder, Colo. , 1986. ix, 203 p. ; ISBN 0-931477-89-1 : LC Card 86-13505 DDC 323.1/09172/4 19
JF1063.D44 E87 1986 ***NYPL [JLE 86-4694]***

Kennedy, Charles R. Political risk management : international lending and investing under environmental uncertainty / Charles R. Kennedy, Jr. New York : Quorum Books, 1987. xiv, 163 p. : ill. ; 25 cm. Bibliography: p. [157]-159. Includes index. ISBN 0-89930-157-6 (lib. bdg. : alk. paper) LC Card 86-25588 DDC 332.6/7373 19
1. Investments, American. 2. Corporations, American. 3. Loans, American. 4. Risk management - United States. 5. Country risk. I. Title.
HG4538 .K44 1987

KENNEDY, DAVID MATTHEW, 1905- Hickman, Martin Berkeley, 1925- David Matthew Kennedy . Salt Lake City, Utah , c1987. xi, 403 p. : ISBN 0-87579-093-3 : LC Card 87-19898 DDC 332.1/092/4 B 19
HG2463.K46 H53 1987

Kennedy, David S., 1938- Schick, P. Charlene, 1943- Accounting fundamentals /. Englewood Cliffs, N.J. , c1987. xviii, 509 p. : ISBN 0-13-001918-6 LC Card 86-23732 DDC 657 19
HF5635 .S3124 1987

Kennedy, David W.
The condominium and cooperative apartment buyer's and seller's guide / David W. Kennedy. 2nd ed. New York : Wiley, c1987. viii, 312 p. : ill. ; 23 cm. Includes index. ISBN 0-471-62732-1 (pbk.) LC Card 87-21548 DDC 333.33/8 19
1. Condominiums. 2. Apartment houses, Cooperative. 3. House buying. 4. House selling. I. Title.
HD1390.5 .K46 1987

Insurance : what do you need? How much is enough? / David W. Kennedy. Tucson, Ariz. : Knight-Ridder Press, c1987. ix, 276 p. ; 23 cm. Includes index. ISBN 0-89586-436-3 (pbk.) : LC Card 86-33789 DDC 368 19
1. Insurance. 2. Insurance, Life. 3. Insurance, Disability. 4. Insurance, Health. 5. Insurance, Automobile. 6. Insurance, Homeowners. I. Title.
HG8051 .K42 1987

Money making money : a beginner's guide to investing / David W. Kennedy. New York : Pharos Books : Distributed in the U. S. by Ballantine Books, 1987. 215 p. ; 23 cm. Includes index. ISBN 0-88687-296-0 : LC Card 86-62737 DDC 332.6/78 19
1. Investments - United States - Handbooks, manuals, etc. I. Title.
HG4921 .K44 1987

Kennedy, Donald. Forging a union of steel . Ithaca, N.Y. , c1987. vii, 153 p. : ISBN 0-87546-135-2 (pbk.) LC Card 87-21508 DDC 331.88/169142/0973 19
HD6515.I5 F58 1987

Kennedy, Gavin.
Doing business abroad / Gavin Kennedy. New York : Simon and Schuster, c1985. 268 p. ; 22 cm. Rev. ed. of: Negotiate anywhere. c1985. Includes index. ISBN 0-671-55484-0 : LC Card 85-14416 DDC 658.4 19
1. Negotiation in business. 2. Success in business. 3. Business enterprises - Foreign countries. I. Kennedy, Gavin. Negotiate anywhere. II. Title.
HD58.6 .K45 1985 ***NYPL [JLD 86-2339]***

Negotiate anywhere. Kennedy, Gavin. Doing business abroad / Gavin Kennedy. New York , c1985. 268 p. ; ISBN 0-671-55484-0 : LC Card 85-14416 DDC 658.4 19
HD58.6 .K45 1985 ***NYPL [JLD 86-2339]***

Pocket negotiator / Gavin Kennedy. Oxford, OX, UK ; New York, NY, USA : Blackwell ; xi, 264 p. : ill. ; 23 cm. Bibliography: p. 263-264. ISBN 0-631-15451-5 : LC Card 87-6302 DDC 658 19
1. Negotiation in business. 2. Negotiation. I. Title.
HD58.6 .K47 1987

Kennedy, Kenneth F., 1945- Personal financial planning for local government employees /. Washington, D.C. , c1987. 203 p. : ISBN 0-87326-051-1 (pbk.) LC Card 87-2948 DDC 332.024/354 19
HG179 .P386 1987

Kennedy, Kieran Anthony. Ireland in transition /. Cork , 1986. 178 p. ; ISBN 0-85342-786-0 (pbk.) : LC Card 87-111629 DDC 306/.09417 19
HC260.5 .I735 1986

Kennedy, P. J. Norton, W. E. Australian economic statistics, 1949-50 to 1984-85 /. [Sydney] [1985] 2 v. : ISBN 0-642-09904-9 (pbk. : v. 1) LC Card 86-222671 DDC 330.994/05/021 19
HC605 .N6326 1985

Kennedy, Peter, 1954- Food and agricultural policy in Peru, 1960-1977 [microform] / Peter Kennedy. Austin (Sid Richardson Hall 1.310, Austin 78712) : Office for Public Sector Studies, Institute of Latin American Studies, University of Texas at Austin, 1983. 22 p. ; 28 cm. (Technical papers series . no. 39 39) Bibliography: p. 22. Microfilm. New York : New York Public Library, 1986. 1 microfilm reel ; 35 mm. (MN *ZZ-25,866) LC Card 83-623239 DDC 338.1/885 19
1. Agriculture and state - Peru - History - 20th century. 2. Food supply - Government policy - Peru - History - 20th century. I. Title. II. Series.
HD1903 .K46 1983 ***NYPL [*ZT-1646 no.20]***

Kennedy, Robert A. Personal economics : take command of your money and develop a winning financial plan / Robert A. Kennedy & Timothy J. Watts. Tucson, AZ : Knight-Ridder Press, c1987. xi, 315 p. : ill. ; 23 cm. Bibliography: p. 306-307. Includes index. ISBN 0-89586-517-3 (pbk.) : LC Card 86-82240 DDC 332.024 19
1. Finance, Personal. I. Watts, Timothy J. II. Title. III. Title: Take command of your money and develop a winning financial plan.
HG179 .K46 1987

Kennedy, William P. (William Paca), 1944- Industrial structure, capital markets, and the origins of British economic decline / William P. Kennedy. Cambridge [Cambridgeshire] ; New York : Cambridge University Press, 1987. xii, 230 p. ; 24 cm. Bibliography: p. [192]-225. Includes index. ISBN 0-521-23018-7 LC Card 86-24411 DDC 330.941 19
1. Great Britain - Economic conditions - 19th century. 2. Great Britain - Economic conditions - 20th century. 3. Great Britain - Industries - History. 4. Capital market - Great Britain - History. I. Title.
HC255 .K45 1987

Kenney, Martin. Biotechnology : the university-industrial complex / Martin Kenney. New Haven : Yale University Press, c1986. xvi, 306 p. : ill. ; 24 cm. Includes index. Bibliography: p. 261-293. ISBN 0-300-03392-3 (alk. paper) : LC Card 86-1694 DDC 338.4/7660/6 19
1. Biotechnology. 2. Biotechnology industries. I. Title.
TP248.2 .K46 1986 ***NYPL [JSE 86-1924]***

Kenny, Brian. Cases in business policy /. Oxford, UK , New York , 1987. ix, 538 p. : ISBN 0-631-15544-9 (pbk.) : LC Card 87-6607 DDC 658.4/012 19
HD30.28 .C379 1987

Kenny, Lawrence W. Blair, Roger D. Microeconomics with business applications /. New York , c1987. xvii, 514 p. : ISBN 0-471-88304-2 LC Card 86-26770 DDC 338.5 19
HB172 .B5413 1987

Kenrick, Catherine. Autoafirmación colectiva . México , 1983. 327 p. ; ISBN 968-16-1335-X LC Card 86-159023
HC59.7 .A92 1983

Kensicki, Peter R. The Business insurance handbook /. Homewood, Ill. , c1981. xvii, 753 p. : ISBN 0-87094-237-9 LC Card 80-70437 DDC 368.8/1/00202 19
HG8059 .B87 ***NYPL [*R-Econ. 86-2502]***

Kent, Calvin A. Entrepreneurship and the privatizing of government /. New York , 1987. x, 216 p. ; ISBN 0-89930-196-7 (lib. bdg. : alk. paper) LC Card 86-25555 DDC 338.9 19
HD3850 .E57 1987

Kent, George, 1939- Fish, food, and hunger : the potential of fisheries for alleviating malnutrition / George Kent. Boulder : Westview Press, 1987. ix, 201 p. ; 23 cm. (Westview special studies in ocean science and policy) Bibliography: p. 189-201. ISBN 0-8133-7409-X (pbk.) : LC Card 87-6066 DDC 338.3/7194 19
1. Fish trade. 2. Fisheries. 3. Food supply. 4. Hunger. 5. Malnutrition. I. Title. II. Series.
HD9450.5 .K46 1987

Kent human resource management series.
Cascio, Wayne F. Costing human resources . Boston, Mass. , c1987. xiv, 274 p. : ISBN 0-534-08034-0 (pbk.) : LC Card 87-2501 DDC 658.1/553 19
HF5681.L2 C37 1987

Kent-Koop (Society) Boratav, Korkut. Housing yearbook /. Ankara, Turkey , 1985. 32, [2] p. ; LC Card 87-403323 DDC 363.5/09561 19
HD7358.25.A3 B67 1985

Kent series in accounting.
The Kent series in accounting.
Dominiak, Geraldine F. Managerial accounting /. Boston , c1988. xxiv, 808 p. : ISBN 0-534-07740-4 : LC Card 87-21472 DDC 658.1/5 19
HF5657.4 .D66 1988

Henke, Emerson O. Introduction to nonprofit organization accounting /. Boston , c1988. xvi, 670 p. : ISBN 0-534-08322-6 LC Card 87-7330 DDC 657/.98 19
HF5686.N56 H45 1988

Kentron Programmatismou kai Oikonomikōn Ereunōn. (Old Catalog form: Kentron Oikonomikōn Ereunōn)
LaLonde, Robert John. The manpower report of KEPE . Athens, Greece , c1986. 122 p. ; LC Card 86-205504 DDC 331.1/09495 19
HD5811.83.A6 L3 1986

Kentucky. Banking and Securities, Dept. of. see **Kentucky. Dept. of Banking and Securities.**

Kentucky. Cabinet for Human Resources.
Kentucky occupational profiles, finance, insurance, and real estate /. [Frankfort, Ky.] [1985] v, 33 p. : LC Card 85-622996 DDC 331.12/51/0009769 19
HD5718.B262 U66 1985

Kentucky. Commissioner of Banking and Securities. see **Kentucky. Dept. of Banking and Securities.**

Kentucky. Council of Economic Advisors. Policy paper series .
(no. 10) Ware, Ray M. Piggybacking--the federal-state collection act of 1972 /. Lexington, Ky. , 1980. ix leaves, 35 p. ;
NYPL [JLM 79-1230 no.10]

Kentucky. Dept. of Banking and Securities. Hultman, Charles W. An examination of issues related to multibank holding companies /. [Frankfort, Ky. , 1983] [8], 56 leaves ; LC Card 86-620545 DDC 332.1/6 19
HG2567 .H85 1983

Kentucky. General Assembly. Tobacco Task Force. Final report of the Kentucky Tobacco Task Force / prepared by Andrew Cammack. Frankfort, Ky. : Legislative Research Commission, [1986] vii, 91 p. : ill. ; 28 cm. (Research report / Legislative Research Commission . no. 221) "January 1986." LC Card 86-622267 DDC 338.1/7371/09769 19
1. Tobacco industry - Kentucky. 2. Tobacco industry - Government policy - Kentucky. I. Cammack, Andrew. II. Series: Research report (Kentucky. General Assembly. Legislative Research Commission) , no. 221. III. Title.
HD9137.K4 K45 1986

Kentucky occupational profiles, finance, insurance, and real estate / prepared in affiliation with the Bureau of Labor Statistics, U. S. Department of Labor. [Frankfort, Ky.] : Kentucky Cabinet for Human Resources, [1985] v, 33 p. : ill., maps ; 28 cm. (A Labor market information publication) Cover title: Kentucky occupational profiles, finance, insurance, and real estate, 1981. "February 1985." LC Card 85-622996 DDC 331.12/51/0009769 19
1. Bank employees - Kentucky - Supply and demand - Statistics. 2. Financial institutions - Kentucky - Employees - Supply and demand - Statistics. 3. Insurance companies - Kentucky - Employees - Supply and demand - Statistics. 4. Real estate business - Kentucky - Employees - Supply and demand - Statistics. I. United States. Bureau of Labor Statistics. II. Kentucky. Cabinet for Human Resources. III. Series: Labor market information publication (Frankfort Ky.).
HD5718.B262 U66 1985

Kenwood, A. G. Capital formation in north east England, 1800-1913 / A.G. Kenwood. New York : Garland, 1985. xv, 444 p. : ill. ; 24 cm. (British economic history) Originally presented as the author's thesis (doctoral--University of London, 1962) Bibliography: p. 438-444. ISBN 0-8240-6685-5 : LC Card 84-46005 DDC 332/.0415/09428 19
1. Saving and investment - England - History. 2. Capital - England - History. 3. England - Industries - History. I. Title. II. Series.
HC260.S3 K46 1985 ***NYPL [JLE 86-3900]***

Kenya . Ulbrich, Wolfgang. Hamburg , 1971. 308 p., [1] folded leaf of plates : LC Card 85-163190
HC865 .U43 1971

KENYA - CENSUS, 1977.

KENYA - COMMERCE.
Ulbrich, Wolfgang. Kenya . Hamburg , 1971. 308 p., [1] folded leaf of plates : LC Card 85-163190
HC865 .U43 1971

KENYA - COMMERCIAL POLICY.
East African lessons on economic liberalization /. Aldershot, Hampshire, U.K. ; Brookfield, Vt., U. S.A. : xxi, 72 p. : ISBN 0-566-05337-3 (pbk.) : LC Card 86-29602 DDC 338.967 19
HC865 .E27 1987

KENYA - ECONOMIC CONDITIONS - TO 1963.
Throup, David. Economic & social origins of Mau Mau 1945-53 /. London , Athens , c1988. xvi, 304 p. : ISBN 0-8214-0883-6 LC Card 87-12387 DDC 307.3/36 19
HD2126.5 .T48 1988

KENYA - ECONOMIC CONDITIONS - 1963-
Kongstad, Per. Industri, fagbevægelse og lønarbejde i Kenya . Roskilde [1983] 76 p. ; LC Card 85-238103
HC865 .K66 1983

Ulbrich, Wolfgang. Kenya . Hamburg , 1971. 308 p., [1] folded leaf of plates : LC Card 85-163190
HC865 .U43 1971

KENYA - ECONOMIC CONDITIONS - 1963- - CONGRESSES.
The Political economy of Kenya /. New York , 1987. viii, 245 p. ; ISBN 0-275-92672-9 (alk. paper) : LC Card 87-22889 DDC 330.9676/204 19
HC865 .P65 1987

KENYA - ECONOMIC POLICY.
Cheru, Fantu. Dependence, underdevelopment, and unemployment in Kenya . Lanham, MD , c1987. xvii, 198 p. : ISBN 0-8191-6539-5 (alk. paper) : LC Card 87-13710 DDC 331.13/77/096762 19
HD6276.K42 C46 1987

East African lessons on economic liberalization /. Aldershot, Hampshire, U.K. ; Brookfield, Vt., U. S.A. : xxi, 72 p. : ISBN 0-566-05337-3 (pbk.) : LC Card 86-29602 DDC 338.967 19
HC865 .E27 1987

Wegner, Gerhard, 1953- Bauern, Kapital und Staat in Kenia . Berlin , c1983. 94 p. : ISBN 3-88619-038-2 : LC Card 85-171380
HD1538.K4 W44 1983

Kenya. Exchequer and Audit Dept. Special report of the Controller and Auditor-General on the City Council of Nairobi. Kenya. Public Accounts Committee. Report of the Public Accounts Committee on the Special report of the Controller and Auditor-General on the City Council of Nairobi. Nairobi [1981] i, 23 p. ; LC Card 85-980597
HJ9620.5.Z9 N344 1981

Kenya - Government. see **Kenya - Politics and government.**

KENYA - INDUSTRIES.
Kongstad, Per. Industri, fagbevægelse og lønarbejde i Kenya . Roskilde [1983] 76 p. ; LC Card 85-238103
HC865 .K66 1983

Ulbrich, Wolfgang. Kenya . Hamburg , 1971. 308 p., [1] folded leaf of plates : LC Card 85-163190
HC865 .U43 1971

Kenya. Lake Basin Development Authority. A socio-cultural investigation into the use and functioning of the completed shallow wells in Nyanza Province / Lake Basin Development Authority. Kisumu, [Kenya] : The Authority, 1983. 2 v. ; 28 cm. "August 1983." Includes bibliography. CONTENTS. - [1]. Main report -- [2]. Summary--main findings and recommendations. LC Card 84-983298 DDC 333.91/009676/29 19
1. Water resources development - Kenya - Nyanza Province. 2. Water resources development - Social aspects - Kenya - Nyanza Province. 3. Wells - Kenya - Nyanza Province. I. Title.
HD1699.K42 N935 1983 ***NYPL [JLF 86-575]***

KENYA - MANUFACTURES - INDUSTRIAL CAPACITY.
Gershenberg, Irving. Slack in Kenya's modern manufacturing sector /. Boston, MA (270 Bay State Rd., Boston 02215) , 1985. 15 leaves ; LC Card 87-404089 DDC 338.4/767/096762 19
HD70.K4 G47 1985

KENYA - MANUFACTURES - LABOR PRODUCTIVITY.
Gershenberg, Irving. Slack in Kenya's modern manufacturing sector /. Boston, MA (270 Bay State Rd., Boston 02215) , 1985. 15 leaves ; LC Card 87-404089 DDC 338.4/767/096762 19
HD70.K4 G47 1985

Kenya. Ministry of Co-operative Development. Development Planning Division. Research & Evaluation Unit. A Base-line study of Farm Input Supply Scheme. Nairobi , 1981. 65 leaves, [1] leaf of plates : LC Card 87-980116
HD1491.K42 K583 1981

Kenya. Ministry of Co-operative Development. Training and Manpower Development Section. Training needs for co-operative movement staff . [Nairobi?] [1984] [166] p. : LC Card 86-980729 DDC 331.12/51334/096762 19
HD3560.5.A4 T73 1984

Kenya. Ministry of Finance and Planning. Rural Planning Division. Bethke, Klaus W. Small projects for rural development . [Nairobi] [1983] 33, [34] leaves ; LC Card 86-981325 DDC 354.676/20082 19
HC865 .B48 1983

Kenya NGO Organising Committee--Forum '85. Exhibition and income generation for women . [Nairobi?] [1985] 17, 11 p. ; LC Card 85-981503 DDC 331.4/09676/2 19
HD6210.5 .E94 1985

Women and credit . [Nairobi?] [1985] 17, 2 p. ; LC Card 85-981504 DDC 332.7/088042 19
HG3756.K4 W65 1985

Women and employment in Kenya . [Nairobi] [1985] iii, 46 p. ; LC Card 85-981502 DDC 331.4/09676/2 19
HD6210.5 .W65 1985

Women in co-operatives . [Nairobi?] [1985] 30 p. ; LC Card 85-981507 DDC 334/.088042 19
HA3560.5.A4 W66 1985

KENYA - OFFICIALS AND EMPLOYEES - IN-SERVICE TRAINING.
Training needs for co-operative movement staff . [Nairobi?] [1984] [166] p. : LC Card 86-980729 DDC 331.12/51334/096762 19
HD3560.5.A4 T73 1984

KENYA - POLITICS AND GOVERNMENT - TO 1963.
Throup, David. Economic & social origins of Mau Mau 1945-53 /. London , Athens , c1988. xvi, 304 p. : ISBN 0-8214-0883-6 LC Card 87-12387 DDC 307.3/36 19
HD2126.5 .T48 1988

KENYA - POPULATION.
Population, economics, and unemployment . [Nairobi] [1982] 55 leaves ; LC Card 85-980190
HD5708.47.K4 P67 1982

Kenya. Presidential Committee on Unemployment. Population, economics, and unemployment . [Nairobi] [1982] 55 leaves ; LC Card 85-980190
HD5708.47.K4 P67 1982

Kenya. Public Accounts Committee. Report of the Public Accounts Committee on the Special report of the Controller and Auditor-General on the City Council of Nairobi. Nairobi : Govt. Printer, [1981] i, 23 p. ; 29 cm. "May 1981"--Cover. LC Card 85-980597
1. Nairobi (Kenya). City Council - Auditing. 2. Finance, Public - Kenya - Nairobi - Auditing. I. Kenya. Exchequer and Audit Dept. Special report of the Controller and Auditor-General on the City Council of Nairobi. II. Title.
HJ9620.5.Z9 N344 1981

Kenya report of the pilot study on socio-economic indicators, 1981. [Nairobi?] : Central Bureau of Statistics, Ministry of Economic Planning and Development, [1982?] 107 leaves : maps ; 30 cm. Bibliography: leaves 106-107. LC Card 87-120114 DDC 330.9676/204 19
1. Economic indicators - Kenya. 2. Social indicators - Kenya. I. Kenya. Central Bureau of Statistics.
HC865 .K486 1982

Kenya. Roads and Aerodromes Dept.
The Framework of the impact study to monitor and evaluate rural access roads in Kenya. Nairobi , 1981. ii, 97, [97] leaves ; LC Card 85-981022
HE367.K43 R8538 1981

Status of evaluation of rural access roads. Nairobi , 1982. 10 leaves ; LC Card 85-981020 DDC 388.1/09676/2 19
HE367.K43 R8578 1982

KENYA. ROADS AND AERODROMES DEPT.
Trends in road use in Kenya . Nairobi , 1981. viii, 158 p. : LC Card 87-980482 DDC 388.3/142/096762 19
HE373.K4 T73 1981

Kenya. Roads Dept.
Rural access road programme . Nairobi [1977- v. : LC Card 86-981035
HE367.K43 R8575 1976

Rural access roads programme . Nairobi [1976- v. : LC Card 86-981034
HE367.K43 R8576 1976

Rural Access Roads Programme /. Nairobi [1980?] 1 v. (various foliations) : LC Card 85-981142 DDC 388.1/09676/2 19
HE367.K43 R85746 1980

KENYA RURAL ACCESS ROADS PROGRAMME.
The Framework of the impact study to monitor and evaluate rural access roads in Kenya. Nairobi , 1981. ii, 97, [97] leaves ; LC Card 85-981022
HE367.K43 R8538 1981

Rural access road programme . Nairobi [1977- v. : LC Card 86-981035
HE367.K43 R8575 1976

Rural access roads programme . Nairobi [1976- v. : LC Card 86-981034
HE367.K43 R8576 1976

Rural Access Roads Programme /. Nairobi [1980?] 1 v. (various foliations) : LC Card 85-981142 DDC 388.1/09676/2 19
HE367.K43 R85746 1980

KENYA - RURAL CONDITIONS.
Livingstone, Ian. Rural development, employment and incomes in Kenya /. Aldershot, Hants , Brookfield, Vermont , 1986. xx, 389 p. : ISBN 0-566-00990-0
NYPL [Sc D 86-728]

Status of evaluation of rural access roads. Nairobi , 1982. 10 leaves ; LC Card 85-981020 DDC 388.1/09676/2 19
HE367.K43 R8578 1982

KENYA - SOCIAL CONDITIONS.
Throup, David. Economic & social origins of Mau Mau 1945-53 /. London , Athens , c1988. xvi, 304 p. : ISBN 0-8214-0883-6 LC Card 87-12387 DDC 307.3/36 19
HD2126.5 .T48 1988

KENYA - SOCIAL CONDITIONS - 1963- - CONGRESSES.
The Political economy of Kenya /. New York , 1987. viii, 245 p. ; ISBN 0-275-92672-9 (alk. paper) : LC Card 87-22889 DDC 330.9676/204 19
HC865 .P65 1987

KENYA - SOCIAL POLICY.
Wegner, Gerhard, 1953- Bauern, Kapital und Staat in Kenia . Berlin , c1983. 94 p. : ISBN 3-88619-038-2 : LC Card 85-171380
HD1538.K4 W44 1983

Kenya Woodfuel Development Programme.
Bradley, Phil. The district resource analysis as applied to Kakamega District /. Nairobi [1984] 11 leaves : LC Card 87-112452 DDC 333.75 19
HD9769.F843 K425 1984

Chavangi, Noel A. Culture as the basis for implementing self-sustaining wood fuel development programmes /. Nairobi, Kenya [1985] 24 leaves ; LC Card 87-111963 DDC 333.75 19
HD9769.F843 K433 1985

Kenyan smallholdings and the division of labour /. Barnes, Carolyn. Nairobi , 1982. 39 leaves ; LC Card 87-156293
HD1476.K4 B37 1982

Keoghs . Cheeks, James E. New York , c1986. xviii, 248 p. ; ISBN 0-531-15505-6 LC Card 85-31753 DDC 332.024/01 19
HG1660.U5 C48 1986 ***NYPL [JLD 86-3669]***

Kepemimpinan dan masalah pertanahan di pedesaan Jawa . Purwanto, Bambang. [Yogyakarta] , 1985. ix, 58 p. : LC Card 86-943756
HD900.N36 P87 1985

Kepenek, Yakup. Boratav, Korkut. Housing yearbook /. Ankara, Turkey , 1985. 32, [2] p. ; LC Card 87-403323 DDC 363.5/09561 19
HD7358.25.A3 B67 1985

Kerachsky, Stuart. An Evaluation of short-time compensation programs. Washington, D.C. (601 D St., N.W., Room 7422, Washington 20213) , 1986. xxv, 222 p. ; LC Card 86-602784 DDC 368.4/4/00973 s 368.4/4/00973 19
HD7096.U5 U637 no. 86-4 HD7103.65.U6

KERALA (INDIA) - CENSUS, 1981.
Census of India, 1981. Delhi , <1984-1987. v. in : LC Card 87-915015 DDC 304.6/0954/83021 19
HA4587.K47 C46 1984

KERALA, INDIA - ECONOMIC CONDITIONS.
Mahadevan, K., 1940- Social development, cultural change, and fertility decline . New Delhi , Newbury Park, Calif. , 1987. p. cm. ISBN 0-8039-9536-9 LC Card 87-15001 DDC 304.6/32/095483 19
HB1050.K47 M34 1987

KERALA (INDIA) - POPULAR CULTURE.
Mahadevan, K., 1940- Social development, cultural change, and fertility decline . New Delhi , Newbury Park, Calif. , 1987. p. cm. ISBN 0-8039-9536-9 LC Card 87-15001 DDC 304.6/32/095483 19
HB1050.K47 M34 1987

KERALA (INDIA) - RURAL CONDITIONS.
Mahadevan, K., 1940- Social development, cultural change, and fertility decline . New Delhi , Newbury Park, Calif. , 1987. p. cm. ISBN 0-8039-9536-9 LC Card 87-15001 DDC 304.6/32/095483 19
HB1050.K47 M34 1987

KERALA (INDIA) - SOCIAL CONDITIONS.
Mahadevan, K., 1940- Social development, cultural change, and fertility decline . New Delhi , Newbury Park, Calif. , 1987. p. cm. ISBN 0-8039-9536-9 LC Card 87-15001 DDC 304.6/32/095483 19
HB1050.K47 M34 1987

Paul, D. Babu (Daniel Babu), 1941- A queen's story . New Delhi , c1987. xix, 132 p. : ISBN 0-7069-3376-1 : LC Card 86-903827 DDC 387.1/0954/83 19
HE560.C56 P38 1987

Kerans, Patrick. Welfare and worker participation : eight case-studies / Patrick Kerans, Glenn Drover, and David Williams. New York : St. Martin's Press, 1987. p. cm. Bibliography: p. Includes index. ISBN 0-312-00908-9 : LC Card 87-11878 DDC 362.8/5 19
1. Welfare work in industry - Case studies. 2. Social security - Case studies. I. Drover, Glenn, 1935-. II. Williams, David, 1934-. III. Title.
HD7261 .K47 1987

Kérdőjelek iparunk fejlesztésében /. Botos, Balázs. Budapest , 1984. 391, [1] p. ; ISBN 963-721-392-0 : LC Card 85-156613
HC300.28 .B69 1984

Keremitsis, Dawn, 1921- The cotton textile industry in Porfiriato, Mexico, 1870-1910 / Dawn Keremitsis. New York : Garland Pub., 1987. 232 p. : ill. ; 24 cm. (South American and Latin American economic history) Bibliography: p. 220-232. ISBN 0-8240-1364-6 (alk. paper) : LC Card 87-7619 DDC 338.4/767721/0972 19
1. Cotton textile industry - Mexico - History - 19th century. 2. Industry and state - Mexico - History - 19th century. 3. Mexico - History - 1867-1910. I. Title. II. Series.
HD9884.M42 K47 1987

Kereskedelem, piacok és pénz az ókori Görögországban /. Polanyi, Karl, 1886-1964. [Livelihood of man. Hungarian. Selections.] Budapest , 1984. 327 p. ; ISBN 963-281-335-9 : LC Card 85-189578
HC37 .P65155 1984

A kereskedelmi hitel és a váltó alkalmazásának 1985. évi tapasztalatai /. Lovassné Szecső, Judit. Budapest [1986] 62 p. ; ISBN 963-7202-84-6 LC Card 87-151536
HG3754.5.H9 L68 1986

A kereskedelmi hitel és a váltó gyakorlata /. Baross, Jenő. Budapest , 1985. 123 p. ; LC Card 86-228454
HG3754.5.H9 B37 1985

Kereskedelmi Szervezési Intézet (Budapest, Hungary) Baross, Jenő. A kereskedelmi hitel és a váltó gyakorlata /. Budapest , 1985. 123 p. ; LC Card 86-228454
HG3754.5.H9 B37 1985

A kereskedelmi tevékenység komplex finanszirozása /. Engel, Gábor. Budapest [1985] 68 p. ; ISBN 963-7202-58-7 LC Card 86-157419
HG4026 .E517 1985

Kerhervé, Jean. L'Etat breton aux 14e et 15e siècles : les ducs, l'argent et les hommes / Jean Kerhervé ; préfaces de Jean Favier et Yves Le Gallo. Paris : Maloine, c1987. 2 v. (xii, x, 1078 p.) : ill. ; 25 cm. Bibliography: p. [955]-1017. Includes index. ISBN 2-224-01703-0 (t. 1) LC Card 87-160693
1. Finance, Public - France - Brittany - History. 2. Finance - France - Brittany - History. 3. Brittany (France) - History. I. Title. II. Title: Etat breton aux quatorzième et quinzième siècles.
HJ1078.B75 K47 1987

Kéri, István. A Vállalati tervezés uj módszere . [Pécs] [1985?] 167 p. : LC Card 86-187131
HD29 .V35 1985

Kerivnyk-orhanizator i vykhovatel′ /. Suïmenko, IE. I. Kyïv , 1985. 189 p. ; LC Card 87-109649
HD38.2 .S85 1985

KERN, ALFRED, 1850-1893.
Riedl-Ehrenberg, Renate. Alfred Kern (1850-1893), Edouard Sandoz (1853-1928) . Zürich , c1986. 90 p. : LC Card 86-159933 DDC 338/.09494 s 338.7/66/0094943 19
HC395.5.A2 S3 no. 44 QD21

Kern, Dale R. Specialty Conference on Engineering and Construction Projects (1982 : New Orleans, La.) Proceedings of the Specialty Conference on Engineering and Construction Projects . New York, N.Y. , c1982. vi, 329 p. : ISBN 0-87262-299-1 (pbk.) LC Card 82-70492 DDC 658.5 19
TA190 .S67 1982 ***NYPL [JLD 86-1905]***

Kern, Hans. Fieber, Joachim. Die effektivere Gestaltung des Personennahverkehrs im Kreis Sondershausen . Potsdam-Babelsberg , Leipzig , 1983. 75 p. : LC Card 83-241076
HE249.5.Z7 S664 1983

Kern, Jill P. Human resources management /. New York , Milwaukee, Wis. , c1987. xiv, 276 p. : ISBN 0-8247-7716-6 LC Card 86-29321 DDC 658.3 19
HF5549 .H8727 1987

Kern, Jürgen, 1951- Bilanzpolitische Forschungsprogramme : Versuch einer Bestandsaufnahme und einer programmatischen Weiterentwicklung auf real- und verhaltenswissenschaftlicher Grundlage / Jürgen Kern. Frankfurt am Main ; New York : P. Lang, c1986. ix, 456 p. : ill. ; 21 cm. (Europäische Hochschulschriften. Reihe V, Volks- und Betriebswirtschaft, 0531-7339 . Bd. 737 = vol. 737 = vol. 737) Bibliography: p. 425-449. ISBN 3-8204-9363-8 LC Card 86-218816
1. Managerial accounting. 2. Financial statements. I. Series: Europäische Hochschulschriften. Reihe V, Volks- und Betriebswirtschaft , Bd. 737. II. Title.
HF5645 .K43 1986

Kernforschungsanalge Jülich. Programmgruppe Technik und Gesellschaft. Zukünftige Energiepolitik . München , 1985. 189 p. : ISBN 3-89147-002-9 LC Card 87-104306
HD9698.G42 Z85 1985

Kernforschungsanlage Jülich. Programmgruppe Systemforschung und Technologische Entwicklung. Kortzfleisch, Gert von. Energie für den Verkehr . Frankfurt am Main , c1984. 115 p. : LC Card 84-192683
HD9710.G4 V4 Nr. 42 HE5620.E53

Kerns, Allen F. Dictionary of worker traits / Allen F. Kerns, Ralph E. Neeley. Philadelphia, PA : Vocational Research Institute, 1987- p. cm. Bibliography: v. 1, p. Includes indexes. ISBN 0-9618599-9-7 LC Card 87-12478 DDC 331.7/02/0973 19
1. United States - Occupations. 2. Occupations - Dictionaries. 3. Occupations - Classification. I. Neeley, Ralph E. II. Title.
HB2595 .K43 1987

KERR, CLARK, 1911- - CONGRESSES.
How labor markets work . Lexington, Mass. , c1988. viii, 256 p. : ISBN 0-669-15126-2 (alk. paper) LC Card 87-22718 DDC 331.12 19
HD5701.3 .H68 1988

Kerr, Kathel Austin. Blackford, Mansel G., 1944- Business enterprise in American history /. Boston , c1986. xi, 456 p. : ISBN 0-395-35155-3 (pbk.) LC Card 85-60780 DDC 338.7/4/0973 19
HD2785 .B52 1986 ***NYPL [JLE 86-3008]***

Kerromes, Armelle. Tableaux normalisés simplifiés par région et département : recensement général de la population de 1982, France métropolitaine, sondage au 1/20 / Armelle Kerromes. Paris : INSEE, [1984] 273 p. ; 30 cm. (Archives & documents . no 100) "Mars 1984." Chiefly tables. ISBN 2-11-064692-6 : LC Card 86-176720
1. France - Population - Statistics. 2. France - Census, 1982. I. Title. II. Title: Recensement général de la population de 1982, France métropolitaine, sondage au 1/20. III. Series: Archives & documents (Institut national de la statistique et des études économiques (France)) , no 100.
HA1214 1982p

Kervyn de Lettenhove, A. Employment and growth . Dordrecht , Boston , 1987. xii, 310 p. : ISBN 90-247-3514-9 LC Card 87-3184 DDC 331.11 19
HD73 .E46 1987

Keskustelualoitteita (Joensuun yliopisto. Yhteiskuntapolitiikka ja sosiologia) .

(n:o 3) Kostiainen, Seppo. Capital controls under alternative exchange rate and monetary policy regimes /. Joensuu , 1986. 27 p. ; ISBN 951-696-619-5 (pbk.) LC Card 87-100851 DDC 332.4/5 19
HG3823 .K673 1986

Kessler, Denis. Epargne et développement /. Paris , 1985. 410 p. : ISBN 2-7178-0855-8 : LC Card 86-149765
HC59.72.S3 E62 1985

Keszthelyi, Csaba. Az autonómia kérdése az olasz szakszervezeti egységért folytatott küzdelemben / Keszthelyi Csaba. [Budapest] : Művelődési Minisztérium Marxizmus-Leninizmus Oktatási Főosztálya, 1985. 75 p. ; 24 cm. (Tudományos szocializmus füzetek, 0324-5683 . 84) Summary in Russian. Includes bibliographical references. ISBN 963-673-322-8 LC Card 86-185901
1. Trade-unions - Italy - Political activity. 2. Political parties - Italy. 3. Communism - Italy. I. Title. II. Series.
HD6680.5.Z65 K47 1985

Két évtized : a mezőgazdasági szövetkezeti mozgalom érdekképviselete Csongrád megyében (1967-1987) / összeállította Farkas Miklós ; szerkesztette, Hegyi András. Szeged : Csongrád Megyei Mezőgazdasági Szövetkezetek Szövetsége, 1987. 116 p., [67] p. of plates : ill. ; 19 cm. LC Card 87-407665
1. Collective farms - Hungary - Csongrád Megye - History. 2. Agriculture, Cooperative - Hungary - Csongrád Megye - History. I. Farkas, Miklós, Dr. II. Hegyi, András. III. Title: 2 évtized. IV. Title: Mezőgazdasági szövetkezeti mozgalom érdekképviselete Csongrád megyében (1967-1987).
HD1492.H82 C765 1987

Kets de Vries, Manfred F. R. Unstable at the top : inside the troubled organization / Manfred F.R. Kets de Vries and Danny Miller. New York : New American Library, 1988, c1987. xiv, 221 p. ; 23 cm. "NAL books." Bibliography: p. 201-209. Includes index. ISBN 0-453-00562-4 LC Card 87-23182 DDC 158.7 19
1. Organizational behavior. 2. Industrial organization. I. Miller, Danny. II. Title.
HD58.7 .K475 1988

Kétszáz éves a borsodi szénbányászat, 1786-1986. 200 éves a borsodi szénbányászat, 1786-1986 /. [Miskolc , 1986] 223 p. : ISBN 963-02-4565-5 (Magy. nemz. bibl.) LC Card 87-150976
HD9555.H83 B6715 1986

Kettering, Merlyn. Silverman, Jerry M. Action-planning workshops for development management . Washington, D.C., U. S.A. , 1986. ix, 74 p. : ISBN 0-8213-0864-5 (pbk.) LC Card 86-28215 DDC 338.9/0068 19
HC59.7 .S4656 1986

Kettl, Donald F. Government by proxy : (mis?)managing federal programs / Donald F. Kettl. Washington, D.C. : CQ Press, c1988. x, 170 p. ; 23 cm. Includes bibliographies and index. ISBN 0-87187-429-6 (pbk.) : LC Card 87-13645 DDC 353.009 19
1. Public contracts - United States. 2. Grants-in-aid - United States. 3. Tax expenditures - United States. 4. Government lending - United States. 5. Trade regulation - United States. I. Title.
HD3861.U6 K47 1988

Key ideas.
Thompson, Kenneth, 1937- Beliefs and ideology /. Chichester, West Sussex : London ; 135 p. ; ISBN 0-85312-858-8 : LC Card 86-2984 DDC 306/.4 19
BL60 .T49 1986 ***NYPL [JLD 86-2479]***

Key issues in economics and business.
Barnes, Ian. The European Community /. London , New York , 1988. p. cm. ISBN 0-582-29716-8 LC Card 87-16765 DDC 337.1/42 19
HC241.2 .B293 1988

Keyder, Caglar. State and class in Turkey : a study in capitalist development / Çağlar Keyder. London ; New York : Verso, 1987. 252 p. ; 22 cm. Bibliography: p. 229-247. Includes index. ISBN 0-86091-877-7 (pbk.) : LC Card 87-14992 DDC 338.9561 19
1. Turkey - Economic conditions. 2. Capitalism - Turkey - History - 19th century. 3. Capitalism - Turkey - History - 20th century. 4. Social classes - Turkey - History - 19th century. 5. Social classes - Turkey - History - 20th century. I. Title.
HC492 .K497 1987

Keynes and after /. Stewart, Michael, 1933- Harmondsworth, Middlesex, England , New York, N.Y., U. S.A. , 1986. 230 p. ; ISBN 0-14-022646-X (pbk.) : LC Card 86-218640 DDC 330.15/6 19
HB99.7 .S7 1986

Keynes and after /. Stewart, Michael, 1933- Harmondsworth, England , 1986. 230 p. ; ISBN 0-14-022646-X ***NYPL [JLD 86-2148]***

Keynes and public policy after fifty years / edited by Omar F. Hamouda, John N. Smithin. New York : New York University Press, <c1988- > v. <2 > : ill. ; 25 cm. Papers from Conference on Keynes and Public Policy after Fifty Years held in Sept. 1986, at Glendon College, York University, Toronto. Includes bibliographies and indexes. CONTENTS. - -- v. 2. Theories and method. ISBN 0-8147-3444-8 (v. 1) : LC Card 87-20368 DDC 330.15/6 19
1. Keynesian economics - Congresses. 2. Economic policy - Congresses. I. Keynes, John Maynard, 1883-1946. II. Hamouda, O. F. III. Smithin, John N. IV. Conference on Keynes and Public Policy after Fifty Years (1986 : Glendon College).
HB99.7 .K3815 1988

Keynes, John Maynard, 1883-1946.
The Foundations of Keynesian analysis . New York , 1988. xlvi, 267 p. ; ISBN 0-312-00985-2 : LC Card 87-13048 DDC 330.15/6 19
HB99.7 .F68 1988

Indian currency and finance / by John Maynard Keynes. London : Macmillan and Co., 1913 (Edinburgh : R. & R. Clark) viii, 263 p., [1] folded leaf of plates ; 23 cm. Includes bibliographical references and index. LC Card A13-2169 DDC 332.4/954
1. Currency question - India. 2. Banks and banking - India. I. Title.
HG1234 .K4 ***NYPL [*KF 1913 87-34]***

Keynes and public policy after fifty years /. New York , <c1988-. v. <2 > : ISBN 0-8147-3444-8 (v. 1) : LC Card 87-20368 DDC 330.15/6 19
HB99.7 .K3815 1988

Wirtschaftspolitik und Arbeitnehmerinteressen . Pönitz , 1986. 198 p. ; ISBN 3-923826-06-0 LC Card 86-162801
HB99.7 .W57 1986

KEYNES, JOHN MAYNARD, 1883-1946.
Arndt, Helmut, 1911- Vollbeschäftigung . Berlin , c1984. 196 p. : ISBN 3-428-05602-7 LC Card 84-209024
HD5706 .A855 1984

Duso, Anna, 1952- L'autocritica del keynesiano /. Bari , c1985. 99 p. ; ISBN 88-22-03812-6 : LC Card 86-130684
HB99.7 .D87 1985

Jäggi, Christian M. Die Makroökonomik von J.M. Keynes /. Berlin , New York , c1986. xiii, 278 p. : ISBN 0-387-16477-4 (U. S.) LC Card 86-225958
HB99.7 .J34 1986

Prices, quantities, and expectations . Oxford [Oxfordshire] , New York , 1987. xxiv, 487 p. : ISBN 0-19-828589-2 (pbk.) : LC Card 87-7770 DDC 330.15/6 19
HB99.7 .P74 1987

Scherf, Harald. Marx und Keynes /. Frankfurt am Main , 1986. 164 p. ; ISBN 3-518-28235-2 LC Card 87-104047 DDC 330.15/6 19
HB97.5 .S283 1986

Skidelsky, Robert Jacob Alexander, 1939- John Maynard Keynes . London , 1983- v. <1 > ; ISBN 0-333-11599-6 (v. 1) : LC Card 86-217586 DDC 330.15/6 B 19
HB103.K47 S57 1983

Young, Warren, 1949- Interpreting Mr. Keynes . Boulder , 1986. p. cm. ISBN 0-8133-0533-0 : LC Card 87-10535 DDC 330.15/6 19
HB99.7 .Y68 1986

Zinn, Karl Georg. Arbeit, Konsum, Akkumulation . Hamburg , 1986. 243 p. : ISBN 3-87975-347-4 LC Card 86-230933
HB103.K47 Z56 1986

KEYNES, JOHN MAYNARD, 1883-1946 - CONGRESSES.
Wirtschaftspolitik und Arbeitnehmerinteressen . Pönitz , 1986. 198 p. ; ISBN 3-923826-06-0 LC Card 86-162801
HB99.7 .W57 1986

KEYNES, JOHN MAYNARD, 1883-1946 - CONTRIBUTIONS IN COMMERCIAL POLICY.
Cammarosano, Joseph R. The contributions of John Maynard Keynes to foreign trade theory and policy, 1909-1946 /. New York , 1987. 437 p. ; ISBN 0-8240-8076-9 (alk. paper) : LC Card 87-23775 DDC 382.1/04 19
HF1411 .C323 1987

Keynes, the Great Depression. Economics U$A. Chicago, IL , 1986. 1 videocassette (28 min.) : LC Card 86-708020 DDC 330.15 11
HB99.7

KEYNESIAN ECONOMICS.
Bober, Stanley. Modern macroeconomics . London , New York , c1988. ix, 278 p. : ISBN 0-7099-5080-2 LC Card 87-15190 DDC 339 19
HB172.5 .B62 1988

Campbell, Robert Malcolm. Grand illusions . Peterborough, Canada , Lewiston, N.Y. , c1987. 270 p. ; ISBN 0-921149-03-4 LC Card 87-147385 DDC 338.971 19
HC115 .C16 1987

Duso, Anna, 1952- L'autocritica del keynesiano /. Bari , c1985. 99 p. ; ISBN 88-22-03812-6 : LC Card 86-130684
HB99.7 .D87 1985

Economics U$A. Chicago, IL , 1986. 1 videocassette (28 min.) : LC Card 86-708020 DDC 330.15 11
HB99.7

Eichberger, Jürgen, 1952- Geld und Kredit in einer Ökonomie mit festen Preisen . Frankfurt am Main , New York , c1984. 152 p. : ISBN 3-8204-5441-1 LC Card 85-191492
HG230.3 .E53 1984

Frank, Jeff. The new Keynesian economics . Brighton , 1986. xvii, 283 p. : ISBN 0-7108-0239-0 ***NYPL [JLD 86-2534]***

Hsieh, Ching-Yao, 1917- A search for synthesis in economic theory /. Armonk, N.Y. , c1985. xii, 268 p. : ISBN 0-87332-328-9 LC Card 84-29816 DDC 330.1 19
HB71 .H73 1985 ***NYPL [JLE 87-315]***

Jäggi, Christian M. Die Makroökonomik von J.M. Keynes /. Berlin , New York , c1986. xiii, 278 p. : ISBN 0-387-16477-4 (U. S.) LC Card 86-225958
HB99.7 .J34 1986

Managing the UK economy . Cambridge, UK , 1987. xxvii, 328 p. : ISBN 0-7456-0316-5 : LC Card 86-26860 DDC 338.941 19
HC256.5 .M392 1987

Menkhoff, Lukas. Zur Theorie der nicht-monetär verursachten Inflation /. Berlin , c1986. 222 p. : ISBN 3-428-06051-2 LC Card 86-215073
HG229 .M524 1986

Prices, quantities, and expectations . Oxford [Oxfordshire] , New York , 1987. xxiv, 487 p. : ISBN 0-19-828589-2 (pbk.) : LC Card 87-7770 DDC 330.15/6 19
HB99.7 .P74 1987

Rousseas, Stephen William. Post Keynesian monetary economics /. Armonk, N.Y. , c1986. x, 126 p.; ISBN 0-87332-355-6 LC Card 85-14181 DDC 332.4/6 19
HG230.3 .R68 1986 ***NYPL [JLE 86-4326]***

Sánchez Meleán, Jorge. Reflexiones para la acción /. [Venezuela?] , 1986. xv, 322 p. : ISBN 980-232-049-8 LC Card 87-134702 DDC 338.987 19
HC237 .S275 1986

Sardoni, Claudio. Marx and Keynes on economic recession . New York , 1987. xiv, 152 p. ; ISBN 0-8147-7871-2 : LC Card 87-13749 DDC 338.5/42 19
HB3714 .S27 1987

Sawyer, James E., 1943- Why Reaganomics and Keynesian economics failed /. New York , 1987. ix, 195 p. : ISBN 0-312-00532-6 : LC Card 87-9578 DDC 338.973 19
HC106.8 .S28 1987

Sawyer, Malcolm C. [Macroeconomics in question.] Macro-economics in question .

Brighton, Sussex , 1982. xiii, 190 p. : ISBN 0-7108-0140-8 LC Card 86-673557
HB172.5 .S28x 1982b

Scherf, Harald. Marx und Keynes /. Frankfurt am Main , 1986. 164 p. ; ISBN 3-518-28235-2 LC Card 87-104047 DDC 330.15/6 19
HB97.5 .S283 1986

Spahn, Heinz-Peter. Stagnation in der Geldwirtschaft . Frankfurt , New York , c1986. 304 p. : ISBN 3-593-33691-X LC Card 86-225253
HD5710 .S68 1986

Staatliche Wirtschaftsregulierung in der Krise . Opladen , c1986. 241 p. ; ISBN 3-531-11805-6 LC Card 86-228864
HD84 .S69 1986

Staatsgrenzen . Berlin , c1982. 183 p. ; ISBN 3-88619-089-7 LC Card 84-142799
HB90 .S75 1982

Stewart, Michael, 1933- Keynes and after /. Harmondsworth, Middlesex, England , New York, N.Y., U. S.A. , 1986. 230 p. ; ISBN 0-14-022646-X (pbk.) : LC Card 86-218640 DDC 330.15/6 19
HB99.7 .S7 1986

Stewart, Michael, 1933- Keynes and after /. Harmondsworth, England , 1986. 230 p. ; ISBN 0-14-022646-X ***NYPL [JLD 86-2148]***

Tobin, James, 1918- Policies for prosperity . Cambridge, Mass. , 1987. xiv, 508 p. : ISBN 0-262-20066-X LC Card 87-2967 DDC 330.15/6 19
HB99.7 .T63 1987

Vomfelde, Werner. Abschied von Keynes? . Frankfurt am Main , New York , c1985. 205 p. : ISBN 3-593-33567-0 LC Card 86-159600
HB99.7 .V65 1985

Young, Warren, 1949- Interpreting Mr. Keynes . Boulder , 1986. p. cm. ISBN 0-8133-0533-0 : LC Card 87-10535 DDC 330.15/6 19
HB99.7 .Y68 1986

KEYNESIAN ECONOMICS - ADDRESSES, ESSAYS, LECTURES.

Couri, Sergio, 1948- Ensaios sobre a evolução dos sistemas econômicos /. Brasília-Distrito Federal [1983] 133 p. : LC Card 84-116306 DDC 330.1 19
HB97.5 .C68 1983 ***NYPL [JLE 86-3363]***

Eichner, Alfred S. Toward a new economics . Armonk, N.Y. , c1985. ix, 240 p. : ISBN 0-87332-326-2 LC Card 84-27724 DDC 330 19
HB171 .E35 1985 ***NYPL [JLE 86-1977]***

International monetary problems and supply-side economics . Houndmills, Basingstoke, Hampshire , 1986. viii, 162 p. : ISBN 0-333-36200-4 ***NYPL [JLD 86-4356]***

Post Keynesian economic theory . Sussex , Armonk, N.Y. , 1985. xii, 235 p. ; ISBN 0-87332-318-1 LC Card 84-23615 DDC 330/.09/04 19
HB87 .P62 1985 ***NYPL [JLD 87-1155]***

KEYNESIAN ECONOMICS - COLLECTED WORKS.

Meade, J. E. (James Edward), 1907- [Works. 1988.] The collected papers of James Meade /. London , Boston , 1988- p. cm. ISBN 0-04-445073-7 (v. 1. : alk. paper) LC Card 87-15288 DDC 330.1 19
HD5710 .M43 1988

KEYNESIAN ECONOMICS - CONGRESSES.

The Foundations of Keynesian analysis . New York , 1988. xlvi, 267 p. ; ISBN 0-312-00985-2 : LC Card 87-13048 DDC 330.15/6 19
HB99.7 .F68 1988

Keynes and public policy after fifty years /. New York , <c1988-. v. <2 > : ISBN 0-8147-3444-8 (v. 1) : LC Card 87-20368 DDC 330.15/6 19
HB99.7 .K3815 1988

Wirtschaftspolitik und Arbeitnehmerinteressen . Pönitz , 1986. 198 p. ; ISBN 3-923826-06-0 LC Card 86-162801
HB99.7 .W57 1986

KEYNESIAN ECONOMICS - MATHEMATICAL MODELS.

Fujino, Shozaburo, 1927- Money, employment, and interest . Tokyo, Japan , New York, NY [1987] xii, 220 p. : ISBN 4-314-00464-9 : LC Card 87-165395 DDC 330.15/6 19
HB99.7 .F85 1987

Keynote . Tata, J. R. D. (Jehangir Ratanji Dadabhoy), 1904- Bombay , 1986. xviii, 155 p., [1] leaf of plates : ISBN 81-85110-00-X : LC Card 86-902369 DDC 338.0954
HC435.2 .T37 1986

Keys, Bernard. Scanlan, Burt K. Management & organizational behavior /. Malibar, Fla. , 1987, c1983. xvi, 666 p. : ISBN 0-89464-246-4 LC Card 87-17035 DDC 658.4 19
HD31 .S3256 1987

Keys, David E. Hrubec, Thomas R. The managerial accounting quizmaster /. New York , c1987. xx, 216 p. : ISBN 0-07-034472-8 (pbk.) LC Card 86-62759 DDC 658.1/511/076 19
HF5657.4 .H78 1987

Keysers kleine Kulturgeschichte.
Grieser, Dietmar, 1934- Historische Strassen in Europa . München , c1983. 95 p. : ISBN 3-87405-160-9 (pbk.) LC Card 87-672444
HE361 .G74x 1983

Khabikht, K. Issledovaniia Instituta ėkonomiki Akademii nauk Ėstonskoĭ SSR v X piatiletke . Tallin , 1983. 233 p. ; LC Card 86-181279
HB74.9.S65 I86 1983

Khachaturov, T. S. (Tigran Sergeevich), 1906- Intensifikatsiia i ėffektivnost′ v usloviiakh razvitogo sotsializma / T.S. Khachaturov. Moskva : Izd-vo "Nauka", 1978. 350 p. ; 21 cm. (Problemy sovetskoĭ ėkonomiki) At head of title: Akademiia nauk SSSR. Otdelenie ėkonomiki. Includes bibliographical references. LC Card 81-167321
1. Soviet Union - Economic policy - 1976-1980. 2. Economics - Soviet Union. I. Title.
HC336.25 .K445 1978

Metodiki opredeleniia ėkonomicheskoĭ ėffektivnosti kapital′nykh vlozheniĭ v sotsialisticheskikh stranakh . Moskva , 1981. 101 p. ; LC Card 82-204402
HC244.Z9 C35 1981

Khader, Bichara. La question agraire dans le monde arabe : le cas de la Syrie / Bichara Khader. Louvain-la-Neuve : CIACO, 1984. 631 p. : ill. ; 24 cm. Bibliography: p. 594-623. LC Card 85-169871 DDC 338.1/095691 19
1. Agriculture - Economic aspects - Syria - History. 2. Land reform - Syria - History. 3. Land tenure - Syria - History. I. Title.
HD2057.5 .K45 1984 ***NYPL [JLE 86-654]***

Khadzhiev, Stefan. Zavod "Druzhba" : 1957-1982 / Stefan Khadzhiev, Svetla Tasheva. Varna : [s.n.], 1985. 161 p., [3] leaves of plates : ill. ; 20 cm. Cover title: Istoriia na zavod "Druzhba." Includes bibliographical references. LC Card 86-140096
1. Clothing workers - Bulgaria - Varna - History. 2. Druzhba (Factory : Varna, Bulgaria) - History. I. Tasheva, Svetla. II. Title. III. Title: Istoriia na zavod "Druzhba.".
HD8039.C62 B95 1985

Khadzhiev, Stoian. Pechalbata pri razshirenoto sotsialistichesko vŭzproizvodstvoto : teoretiko-metodologicheski problemi / St. Khadzhiev. Sofiia : Izd-vo "Nauka i izkustvo", 1985. 147 p. ; 20 cm. (Poreditsa Kategorii na politicheskata ikonomiia) Includes bibliographical references. LC Card 85-209903
1. Profit - Bulgaria. 2. Industrial productivity - Bulgaria. I. Title. II. Series.
HC403.Z9 P737 1985

Khaĭdarova, Valentina Konstantinovna. Kunaeva, Faziliia Akhmetovna. Kazakhskaia Sovetskaia Sotsialisticheskaia Respublika /. Alma-Ata , 1978. 31 p. : LC Card 81-165585
HC337.K3 K86 1978

Khaĭtun, A. D. (Alekseĭ Davydovich) Ėkspeditsionno-vakhtovoe stroitel′stvo v Zapadnoĭ Sibiri / A.D. Khaĭtun. Leningrad : Stroĭizdat, Leningradskoe otd-nie, 1982. 175, [1] p. : ill. ; 22 cm. Bibliography: p. 175-[176] LC Card 83-165812
1. Construction industry - Russian S.F.S.R. - Siberia, Western. 2. Labor supply - Russian S.F.S.R. - Siberia, Western. 3. Petroleum industry and trade - Russian S.F.S.R. - Siberia, Western. I. Title.
HD9715.S73 S565 1982

Khalaf Allāh, Ramaḍān ʻUraybī. Ḥarakat al-quwá al-ʻāmilah wa-al-tanmiyah al-iqlīmiyah fī Lībiyā / Ramaḍān ʻUraybī Khalaf Allāh. al-Ṭabʻah 1. Ṭarābulus, al-Jamāhīrīyah al-ʻArabīyah al-Lībīyah al-Shaʻbīyah al-Ishtirākīyah : al-Munshaʼah al-ʻAmmah, 1984. 279 p. : ill. ; 24 cm. Bibliography: p. 273-279. LC Card 86-965535
1. Migration, Internal - Libya. 2. Labor supply - Libya. 3. Regional planning - Libya. 4. Labor and laboring classes - Libya. I. Title.
HB2121.6.A3 K47 1984

Khalbaev, M. N. (Maksim Nikolaevich) Khatylaev, M. M. (Mikhail Mikhaĭlovich) Rabochie zolotodobyvaiushcheĭ promyshlennosti Vostochnoĭ Sibiri 1921--1937 gg. /. Novosibirsk , 1986. 171, [4] p. ; LC Card 86-231511
HD8039.M74 S545 1986

Khalimov, M. V. Industrializatsiia proizvodstva i mezhkhoziaĭstvennoe kooperirovanie /. Ufa , 1979. 122 p. ; LC Card 82-161458
HD9425.S653 B375 1979

Khan, Akbar Ali, 1944- Regional Symposium on Water Resoures Policy in Agro-Socio-Economic Development (1985 : Dhaka, Bangladesh) Water resources policy for Asia . Rotterdam , Boston , 1987. xii, 627 p. : ISBN 90-6191-684-4 LC Card 87-170039 DDC 333.91/0095 19
HD1698.A1 R45 1985

Khan, Azizur Rahman. Poverty in rural Asia /. Bangkok , 1984, c1983. xii, 276 p. ; ISBN 92-2-103286-8 (pbk.) ***NYPL [JLE 86-1050]***

Khan, Jahangir. Population, human and national resources in Pakistan /. [Karachi , 198-?] 19 p. ; LC Card 85-931341
HA4590.5 .P66 1980z

Khan, Mohd. Akbar Ali. Public housing /. Hyderabad, A.P. , c1983. xx, 345 p. ; LC Card 85-903848 DDC 363.5/8 19
HD7288.78.I4 P83 1983
NYPL [JLF 86-1782]

Khan, Mohsin S.
Growth-oriented adjustment programs /. Washington, D.C. , 1987. xiii, 537 p. : ISBN 0-939934-92-2 (pbk.) LC Card 87-21361 DDC 338.9 19
HD73 .G76 1987

Theoretical studies in Islamic banking and finance /. Houston, Tex. , 1987. xvi, 245 p. : ISBN 0-932625-07-X : LC Card 86-83221 DDC 332.1/0917/4927 19
HG3368.A6 T47 1987

Khan, Muhammad Akram. Bilā sūdī bainkārī / Muḥammad Akram Khān. Lāhaur : Markaz-i Taḥqīq, Diyāl Singh Ṭrasṭ Lāʼibrerī, [1983] 56 p. ; 21 cm. (Silsilah-yi maṭbūʻāt-i Markaz-i Taḥqīq Diyāl Singh Ṭrasṭ Lāʼibrerī . 11) In Urdu. Cover title. Bibliography: p. 56. LC Card 83-931274
1. Banks and banking - Pakistan. 2. Banks and banking - Islamic countries. 3. Banks and banking - Religious aspects - Islam. 4. Islam - Economic aspects. I. Series: Silsilah-yi maṭbūʻāt-i Markaz-i Taḥqīq-i Diyāl Singh Ṭrasṭ Lāʼibrerī , 11. II. Title.
HG3290.5.A6 K43 1983

Khan, Muhammad Jameel. Elahi, Mahboob. Rural labour market, with special reference to hired labour in Pakistan's Punjab /. Lahore, Pakistan [1983] ii, ix, 186 leaves ; LC Card 86-930467
HD1537.P2 E4 1983

Khan, Najma. Studies in human migration / Najma Khan. New Delhi : Rajesh Publications, 1983. vi, 275 p. ; 23 cm. Includes chiefly bibliographies and index. LC Card 83-907120 DDC 304.8/0954 19
1. Migration, Internal - India. 2. Migration, Internal - India - Bibliography. I. Title.
HB3639 .K48 1983 ***NYPL [JLD 86-4136]***

Khan, Waqar Masood. Towards an interest-free Islamic economic system : a theoretical analysis of prohibiting debt financing / Waqar Masood Khan. Leicester : Islamic Foundation ; Islamabad : International Association for Islamic Economics, c1985. 126 p. ; 22 cm. (Islamic economics series . 11) Includes bibliographical references and index. ISBN 0-86037-155-7
1. Interest - Islamic countries. 2. Banks and banking - Islamic countries. I. Islamic Foundation. II. International Association for Islamic Economics. III. Title. ***NYPL [JLD 87-381]***

Kharabuga, V. S. (Vasiliĭ Spiridonovich) Ėkonomika, organizatsii͡a i planirovanie konservnogo proizvodstva / V.S. Kharabuga. Moskva : Pishchevai͡a promyshl., 1977. 349 p. : ill. ; 21 cm. Authorized for instructional purposes. Bibliography: p. [343] LC Card 82-122880
1. Canning and preservation - Industry and trade - Soviet Union. I. Title.
HD9326.S62 K42 1977

Kharbanda, Om Prakesh. Successful projects, with a moral for management / O.P. Kharbanda, E.A. Stallworthy. Hants, England : Gower, c1986. xvii, 267 p. : ill. ; 23 cm. Includes bibliographies and index. ISBN 0-566-02651-1 LC Card 86-235562 DDC 658.4/04 19
1. Industrial project management - Case studies. I. Stallworthy, E. A. (Ernest A.). II. Title.
HD69.P75 K55 1986

Kharchenko, L. P. (Lii͡a Petrovna) Boi͡arskiĭ, Aron I͡Akovlevich, 1906- Praktikum po demografii /. Moskva , 1985. 141, [3] p. : LC Card 86-170070
HB3607 .B64 1985

Kharitonov, S. F. (Sergeĭ Fedorovich) Rasskaz o velikom severnom puti / S.F. Kharitonov. Petrozavodsk : "Karelii͡a", 1984. 143 p. : ill. ; 21 cm. Includes bibliographical references. LC Card 84-247171
1. Murmanskai͡a zheleznai͡a doroga - History. 2. Railroads - Russian S.F.S.R. - Kola Peninsula - History. I. Title.
HE3140.M87 K46 1984

Kharnakhoev, V. Kh. (Viktor Kharitonovich) Sotsial′noe razvitie molodezhi v trudovykh kollektivakh novykh gorodov Sibiri . Irkutsk , 1980. 158 p. ; LC Card 82-110658
HD6276.S593 S527 1980

Khatib, Ahmed S. Watt, Alec. Illustrated dictionary of geology . Beirut [Harlow, Essex] , 1982. 329 p. : ***NYPL [*OG 85-2903]***

Khatylaev, M. M. (Mikhail Mikhaĭlovich) Rabochie zolotodobyvai͡ushcheĭ promyshlennosti Vostochnoĭ Sibiri 1921--1937 gg. / M.M. Khatylaev ; otvetstvennyĭ redaktor M.N. Khalbaev. Novosibirsk : Izd-vo "Nauka," Sibirskoe otd-nie, 1986. 171, [4] p. ; 20 cm. At head of title: Akademii͡a nauk SSSR. Sibirskoe otdelenie. I͡Akutskiĭ filial. Institut i͡azyka, literatury i istorii. Bibliography: p. 154-[172] LC Card 86-231511
1. Gold miners - Russian S.F.S.R. - Siberia, Eastern. 2. Gold mines and mining - Russian S.F.S.R. - Siberia, Eastern - History. I. Khalbaev, M. N. (Maksim Nikolaevich). II. Title.
HD8039.M74 S545 1986

Khăzăr făhlă-dănizchilări. Guseĭnova, D. S. Rabochie-mori͡aki Kaspii͡a . Baku , 1981. 113 p. ; LC Card 82-166385
HD8039.S42 C424 1981

Khazzoom, J. Daniel. An econometric model integrating conservation measures in the residential demand for electricity / by J. Daniel Khazzoom. Greenwich, Conn. : JAI Press, c1986. xx, 305 p. : ill. ; 24 cm. (Contemporary studies in energy analysis and policy . v. 8) Includes index. Bibliography: p. 165-170. ISBN 0-89232-606-9 : LC Card 86-7173 DDC 333.79/3216/0724 19
1. Electric power consumption - Econometric models. 2. Dwellings - Energy conservation - Econometric models. I. Title. II. Series.
HD9685.A2 K54 1986 ***NYPL [JLE 86-4174]***

Kheĭnman, S. A. (Solomon Aronovich) Problemy sovershenstvovanii͡a material′no-tekhnicheskoĭ bazy otrasleĭ obshchestvennogo proizvodstva . Moskva , 1983. 167 p. : LC Card 84-211670
HD70.S63 P753 1983

Khemani, C. L., 1934- How and why of rural banking / by C.L. Khemani and B. Yerram Raju. New Delhi : Sagar Publications, 1987. 255, [41] p. : ill. ; 23 cm. On financing of various rural development schemes operating in India. Includes bibliographical references. LC Card 87-901033 DDC 332.1/0954 19
1. Banks and banking - India. 2. Rural development - India - Finance. I. Raju, B. Yerram, 1941-. II. Title.
HG3288 .K44 1987

Kher, Manik. Conciliation and adjudication today / Manik Kher. Pune : Times Research Foundation, c1985. 99 : ill. ; 25 cm. On collective labor agreements in India; includes implications of selected decisions of the Indian Supreme Court. 80-9 Includes bibliographies and index. LC Card 85-903388 DDC 344.54/0189143 345.404189143 19
1. Arbitration, Industrial - India. 2. Mediation and conciliation, Industrial - India. 3. Labor courts - India. I. Title.
LAW ***NYPL [JLE 86-1567]***

Khizhnyĭ, Ė. K. Babashkina, M. L. Aktual′nye ėkonomicheskie i sotsial′nye problemy malykh stran Severnoĭ Evropy . Moskva , 1986. 71 p. ; LC Card 87-166353
HC343 .B34 1986

Khlystova, E. A. (Evgenii͡a Andreevna) Sever i Sibir′ zovut molodykh / E.A. Khlystova, I.N. Orlov. Moskva : "I͡Urid. lit-ra", 1985. 109 p. : col. ill. ; 17 cm. (Sovetskiĭ zakon i I͡A) Includes bibliographical references. LC Card 86-153085
1. Incentives in industry - Soviet Union, Northern. 2. Young adults - Employment - Soviet Union, Northern. 3. Family allowances - Soviet Union, Northern. I. Orlov, I. N. (Igor′ Nikolaevich). II. Title.
HF5549.5.I5 K452 1985

Khogali, M. (Mustafa) Population and development projects in Africa /. Cambridge [Cambridgeshire] , New York , 1985. xvi, 329 p. : ISBN 0-521-30527-6 LC Card 84-29323 DDC 304.6/096 19
HB2121.A3 P67 1985 ***NYPL [JLF 86-186]***

Khol, Josef, Dr. An inquiry into the perception of casual relations in problems of management / Josef Khol. Prague : Institute of Management Prague, 1976. 26 p. ; 24 cm. (Series E . 51) Bibliography: p. 27-28. LC Card 82-210887 DDC 658.4/03 19
1. Decision-making. 2. Executive ability. I. Series: Series E (Institut řízení) , 51. II. Title.
HD30.23 .K375 1976

Khomra, Aleksandr Ul′i͡anovich. Struktura obshchestvennogo proizvodstva i tendentsii ee izmenenii͡a . Kiev , 1979. 113 p. ; LC Card 81-130407
HC337.U53 I527 1979

Khong, Cho Oon. The politics of oil in Indonesia : foreign company-host government realtions / Khong Cho Oon. Cambridge [Cambridgeshire] ; New York : Cambridge University Press, 1986. x, 253 p. : ill. ; 23 cm. (LSE monographs in international studies) Includes index. Bibliography: p. 249-250. ISBN 0-521-30901-8 LC Card 85-22416 DDC 338.2/7282/09598 19
1. Petroleum industry and trade - Government policy - Indonesia. 2. International business enterprises - Government policy - Indonesia. I. Title. II. Series.
HD9567.I52 K48 1986
NYPL [JLD 86-3386]

Khonrao tāi dai kī withī /. Sanœ ʻIntharasuksī. Krung Thēp , 2526 [1983] 620 p. ; LC Card 83-916563
HB1474.55.A3 S36 1983

Khorev, Boris Sergeevich.
Nechernozem′e . Moskva , 1977. 94 p. ; LC Card 82-107146
HB3608.N57 N43 1977

Problemy rasselenii͡a v SSSR . Moskva , 1980. 254 p. : LC Card 81-135093
HB2068.S65 P76 1980

Khoshoo, T. N., 1927- Environmental concerns and strategies / by T.N. Khoshoo. New Delhi, India : Indian Environmental Society, 1984. xii, 296 p. ; 25 cm. LC Card 84-901589
1. Environmental policy - India - Addresses, essays, lectures. 2. Human ecology - India - Addresses, essays, lectures. I. Title.
HC440.E5 K48 1984 ***NYPL [JLE 87-1015]***

Khoury, Yara Aun. As greves de 1917 em São Paulo e o processo de organização proletária / Yara Aun Khoury. São Paulo : Cortez Editora : Autores Associados, 1981. 221 p. ; 21 cm. (Coleção Teoria e prática sociais) Originally presented as the author's thesis (mestrado)--Pontifícia Universidade Católica de São Paulo. Includes bibliographical references. LC Card 81-210934 DDC 331.2/98161 19
1. Strikes and lockouts - Brazil - São Paulo (State). 2. Labor and laboring classes - Brazil - São Paulo (State). I. Title. II. Title: Greves de mil e novecentos e dezessete em São Paulo. III. Series.
HD5355.S26 K48 1981
NYPL [JLD 86-3514]

Khozi͡aĭstvennoe osvoenie novykh raĭonov i ėkonomicheskiĭ rost Sibiri : sbornik nauchnykh trudov / pod redaktsieĭ A.P. Dubnova, B.P. Orlova. Novosibirsk : Akademii͡a nauk SSSR, Sibirskoe otd-nie, In-t ėkonomiki i organizatsii promyshlennogo proizvodstva, 1980. 173 p. : ill. ; 20 cm. Includes bibliographies. LC Card 83-182452
1. Siberia (R.S.F.S.R.) - Economic conditions. 2. Regional planning - Russian S.F.S.R. - Siberia. I. Dubnov, A. P. (Aleksandr Pavlovich). II. Orlov, Boris Pavlovich. III. Institut ėkonomiki i organizatsii promyshlennogo proizvodstva (Akademii͡a nauk SSSR).
HC337.R852 S5247 1980

Khozi͡aĭstvennyĭ mekhanizm funktsionirovanii͡a sotsialisticheskoĭ ėkonomiki / [redaktsionnai͡a kollegii͡a monografii N.P. Fedorenko, N.I͡A. Petrakov otvetstvennye redaktory ... et al.]. Sovmestnoe izd. Moskva : Ėkonomika, 1982. 358 p. ; 22 cm. On p. facing t.p.: Problemnai͡a komissii͡a mnogostoronnego nauchnogo sotrudnichestva akademiĭ nauk sotsialisticheskikh stran "Voprosy sovershenstvovanii͡a planirovanii͡a i upravlenii͡a narodnym khozi͡aĭstvom stran--chlenov SĖV." Includes bibliographical references. LC Card 83-134242
1. Europe, Eastern - Economic policy - 1945-. 2. Soviet Union - Economic policy - 1917-. 3. Communist countries - Economic policy. I. Fedorenko, Nikolaĭ Prokof′evich. II. Petrakov, Nikolaĭ I͡Akovlevich. III. Problemnai͡a komissii͡a mnogostoronnego nauchnogo sotrudnichestva akademiĭ nauk sotsialisticheskikh stran "Voprosy sovershenstvovanii͡a planirovanii͡a i upravlenii͡a narodnym khozi͡aĭstvom stran--chlenov SĖV.".
HC243.5 .K47 1982

Khozi͡aĭstvennyĭ mekhanizm i povyshenie ėffektivnosti / [otvetstvennyĭ redaktor Rybin V.I.]. Moskva : Akademii͡a nauk SSSR, In-t ėkonomiki, 1982. 191 p. ; 20 cm. Includes bibliographical references. LC Card 84-193531
1. Industrial productivity - Soviet Union. I. Rybin, V. I. (Valeriĭ Ivanovich). II. Institut ėkonomiki (Akademii͡a nauk SSSR).
HC340.I52 K48 1982

Khozi͡aĭstvennyĭ mekhanizm i povyshenie ėffektivnosti proizvodstva / otvetstvennyĭ redaktor P.G. Bunich. Moskva : "Nauka", 1986. 252 p. ; 20 cm. (Problemy sovetskoĭ ėkonomiki) At head of title: Akademii͡a nauk SSSR. T͡Sentral′nyĭ ėkonomiko-matematicheskiĭ institut. Nauchnyĭ sovet po kompleksnoĭ probleme "Optimal′noe planirovanie i upravlenie narodnym khozi͡aĭstvom." Includes bibliographical references. LC Card 86-232347
1. Industrial productivity - Soviet Union. I. Bunich, Pavel Grigor′evich. II. T͡Sentral′nyĭ ėkonomiko-matematicheskiĭ institut (Akademii͡a nauk SSSR). III. Nauchnyĭ sovet po kompleksnoĭ probleme "Optimal′noe planirovanie i upravlenie narodnym khozi͡aĭstvom" (Akademii͡a nauk SSSR).
HC340.I52 K49 1986

Khozi͡aĭstvennyĭ mekhanizm i t͡senoobrazovanie / [otvetstvennyĭ redaktor Borozdin, I͡U.V.]. Moskva : Akademii͡a nauk SSSR, T͡Sentr. ėkonomiko-matematicheskiĭ in-t, 1983. 77 p. ; 21 cm. Includes bibliographies. LC Card 85-180519
1. Prices - Soviet Union - Mathematical models. 2. Soviet Union - Economic policy - 1981- - Mathematical models. I. Borozdin, I͡U. V. II. T͡Sentral′nyĭ ėkonomiko-matematicheskiĭ institut (Akademii͡a nauk SSSR).
HB235.S73 K47 1983

Khozi͡aĭstvennyĭ mekhanizm proizvodstva i obrashchenii͡a tovarov narodnogo potreblenii͡a / [redaktsionnai͡a kollegii͡a, V.R. Praude (otv. red.), I͡A.M. Bel′chikov, I.P. Vasilevskai͡a]. Riga : Latviĭskiĭ gos. universitet im. P. Stuchki, 1985. 115 p. ; 20 cm. (Sbornik nauchnykh trudov) At head of title: Ministerstvo vysshego i srednego spetsialnogo obrazovanii͡a Latviĭskoĭ SSR. Latviĭskiĭ ordena Trudovogo Krasnogo Znameni gosudarstvennyĭ universitet imeni Petra Stuchki. Kafedra upravlenii͡a narodnym khozi͡aĭstvom. Includes bibliographies. LC Card 86-177827
1. Durable goods, Consumer - Latvia. 2. Latvia - Manufactures. 3. Industrial productivity - Latvia. I. Praude, V. R. (Valeriĭ Robertovich). II. Bel′chikov, I͡A. M. III. Vasilevskai͡a, I. P. IV. Pētera Stučkas Latvijas Valsts universitāte. Kafedra upravlenii͡a narodnym khozi͡aĭstvom. V. Series: Zinātnisko rakstu krājums.
HF1040.9.L38 K47 1985

Khozi͡aĭstvennyĭ mekhanizm proizvodstvennogo ob″edineni͡i͡a / [V.F. Paliĭ ... et al.]. Moskva : "Mashinostroenie", 1985. 254 p. ; 20 cm. Bibliography: p. 252-[253] LC Card 85-238796

1. Machine-tool industry - Soviet Union - Management. I. Palii, V. F. (Vitalii Fedorovich).
HD9703.S652 K46 1985

Khoziaistvennyi mekhanizm uskoreniia nauchno-tekhnicheskogo progressa . Egorov, A. D. (Aleksandr Dmitrievich) Minsk , 1986. 61, [3] p. ; LC Card 87-144749
HC340.Z9 T44 1986

Khoziaistvennyi mekhanizm v sisteme optimal'nogo funktsionirovaniia sotsialisticheskoi ekonomiki / pod redaktsiei N.P. Fedorenko, N.IA. Petrakova. Moskva : Izd-vo "Nauka", 1985. 346 p. ; 21 cm. (Voprosy optimal'nogo planirovaniia i upravleniia sotsialisticheskoi ekonomikoi) On p. preceding t.p.: Akademiia nauk SSSR. TSentral'nyi ekonomiko-matematicheskii institut. Bibliography: p. 342-[343] LC Card 86-114802
1. Soviet Union - Economic policy - 1981-. 2. Soviet Union - Economic conditions - 1976-. I. Fedorenko, Nikolai Prokof'evich. II. Petrakov, Nikolai IAkovlevich. III. TSentral'nyi ekonomiko-matematicheskii institut (Akademiia nauk SSSR). IV. Series.
HC336.25 .K474 1985

Khoziaistvovat' umelo i effektivno / pod nauchnoi redaktsiei O.V. Kozlovoi ; [sostavitel' M.N. Tubol'tsev]. Moskva : Moskovskii rabochii, 1985. 267, [5] p. ; 21 cm. Bibliography: p. 259-[268] LC Card 85-148146
1. Moscow (R.S.F.S.R.) - Economic policy. 2. Moscow (R.S.F.S.R.) - Economic conditions. I. Kozlova, O. V. (Olimpiada Vasil'evna). II. Tubol'tsev, M. N.
HC338.M6 K47 1985

Khozin, N. P. Zherebin, V. M. Proektirovanie ekonomicheskikh informatsionnykh sistem /. Moskva , 1983. 182, [2] p., [2] folded p. of plates : LC Card 83-224346
HD30.25 .Z52 1983

Khristova, Vera. Kreditni otnosheniia na Narodna republika Bŭlgariia s razvivashtite se strani /. Sofiia , 1986. 78, [1] p. ; LC Card 86-152274
HF1578.15.D44 K74 1986

Khromov, P. A. (Pavel Alekseevich) Proizvoditel'nost' truda--vazhneishii faktor povysheniia effektivnosti proizvodstva /. Moskva , 1982. 358 p. ; LC Card 83-140430
HC340.L3 P693 1982

Khrongkān 'an n [Bangkok] : Witthayālai Kānpokkhr [2526 i.e. 1983] 221 p. (some folded), [1] leaf of plates : ill. (some col.) ; 28 cm. On national development plans as suggested by King Bhumibol Adulyadet; handbook prepared by the Academy of Local Government and Administration, Local Administration Dept. LC Card 83-916454
1. Thailand - Economic policy - Handbooks, manuals, etc. I. Bhumibol Adulyadej, King of Thailand, 1927-. II. Witthayālai Kānpokkhr
HC445 .K53 1983

Khronika za "Proletarii" /. Kadiev, Ivan. [Sofia] , 1985. 140, [3] p., [32] p. of plates : LC Card 86-195264
HD9969.K7 B855 1985

Khrushchev, A. T. ((Anatolii Timofeevich)) Geografiia promyshlennosti SSSR / A.T. Khrushchev. 3-e izd., perer. i dop. Moskva : "Mysl'", 1986. 415 p. : ill., maps ; Bibliography: p.407-[414]. LC Card 87-117010
1. Soviet Union - Industries - 1957-. 2. Soviet Union - Industries - Location. I. Title.
HC336.25 .K475 1986

Khrutskii, E. A.
Priniatie reshenii v upravlenii khoziaistvennymi sviaziami /. Moskva , 1982. 80 p. : LC Card 85-180526
HD30.23 .P745 1982

Sovershenstvovanie khoziaistvennogo mekhanizma v snabzhenii /. Moskva , 1983. 127 p. : LC Card 85-180655
HD39.5 .S68 1983

Khubenova-Delisivkova, Tatiana. Problemy valiutnogo soiuza stran-chlenov Evropeiskogo ekonomicheskogo soobshchestva i razvitie mezhdunarodnoi valiutnoi sistemy kapitalizma . Sofiia , 1984. 151 p. ; LC Card 85-224144
HG3942.8 .P76 1984

Khudozhestvennye markirovannye konverty SSSR . Orlov, V. A. (Vasilii Adamovich) Moskva , 1984. 120 p. : LC Card 84-168398
HE6185.S652 O75 1984

Khumanizatsiia na truda . Stoianov, Khristo. Sofiia , 1985. 191 p. ; LC Card 85-243365
HD6955 .S85 1985

Khvoinik, Pavel Ignat'evich. Prokhorova, Galina Nikolaevna. Mezhdunarodnye organizatsii vo vneshneekonomicheskoi politike imperializma /. Moskva , 1986. 183 p. ; LC Card 86-232949
HF1411 .P692 1986

Kiam, Victor. Going for it! : how to succeed as an entrepreneur / by Victor Kiam.1st ed. New York : Morrow, c1986. 260 p. ; 25 cm. ISBN 0-688-06060-9 : LC Card 85-61762 DDC 338/.04/0924 B 19
1. Kiam, Victor. 2. Businessmen - United States - Biography. 3. Entrepreneur - Biography. 4. Success in business - United States. I. Title.
HC102.5.K53 A34 1986
NYPL [JLE 86-2954]

KIAM, VICTOR.
Kiam, Victor. Going for it! . New York , c1986. 260 p. ; ISBN 0-688-06060-9 : LC Card 85-61762 DDC 338/.04/0924 B 19
HC102.5.K53 A34 1986
NYPL [JLE 86-2954]

Kibal'chich, Oleg Aleksandrovich. Territorial'nye struktury promyshlennosti /. Moskva , 1978. 128 p. : LC Card 81-147566
HC340.D5 T464 1978

Kibal'chich, Oleg Alekseevich. Territorial'naia organizatsiia proizvoditel'nykh sil SSSR /. Moskva , 1978. 124 p. : LC Card 81-149822
HC340.D5 T44 1978

Kibal'chich, Viktor L'vovich. see Serge, Victor, **1890-1947.**

Kibria, Ghulam. Development options : muscle or money / by Ghulam Kibria.1st ed. Karachi : Pakmedia Associates, 1984. xi, 267 p. ; 22 cm. Includes index. LC Card 84-931764 DDC 338.9549/1 19
1. Pakistan - Economic conditions. I. Title.
HC440.5 .K53 1984

Kicza, John E., 1947- Colonial entrepreneurs, families and business in Bourbon Mexico City / John E. Kicza. 1st ed. Albuquerque : University of New Mexico Press, c1983. 1 v. : ill. ; 24 cm. Revision of thesis (Ph. D.) Vol. 1 only published. Includes index. Bibliography: p. 277-291. ISBN 0-8263-0655-1 (v. 1) LC Card 82-21962 DDC 305.5/54/097253 19
1. Elite (Social sciences) - Mexico - Mexico City - History. 2. Businessmen - Mexico - Mexico City - History. 3. Mexico (City) - Commerce - History. 4. Mexico (City) - Manufactures - History. I. Title.
HF3240.M5 K52 1983 ***NYPL [JLL 83-164]***

Kiczek, Paul. Decision making for bankers : the electronic spreadsheet : tutorial handbook / by Paul Kiczek.2nd ed. Washington, D.C. (1120 Connecticut Ave., NW, Washington 20036) : American Bankers Association, c1986. 89 p. : ill. ; 26 cm. LC Card 87-115307 DDC 332.1/2/02855369 19
1. Banks and banking - Decision making - Data processing. 2. Bank management - Data processing. 3. Lotus 1-2-3 (Computer program). 4. Electronic spreadsheets. I. American Bankers Association. II. Title.
HG1709 .K53 1986

Kidron, Michael. What you need to know about business, money, and power / Michael Kidron and Ronald Segal. New York : Simon and Schuster, c1987. 187 p. : ill. (some col.) ; 26 cm. "A Pluto project." Includes index. ISBN 0-671-54113-7 : LC Card 86-31571 DDC 650 19
1. Business. 2. Finance. 3. Business enterprises - Government policy. 4. Power (Social sciences). I. Segal, Ronald, 1932-. II. Title. III. Title: Business, money, and power.
HF5351 .K473 1987

Kiechle, I. (Ignaz) Landwirtschaft und Umweltschutz, Sozialpflichtigkeit oder Entschädigung? /. Göttingen , 1987. 116 p. : LC Card 87-401359 DDC 363.7/056/0943 19
HD1957 .L355 1987

Kiefer, Márta. Magyarország tőkés viszonylatu gazdasági és pénzügyi kapcsolatairól / [Kiefer Márta]. [Budapest] : Szakszervezetek Elméleti Kutató Intézete, [1985] 115 p. ; 21 cm. Bibliography: p. 106-109. ISBN 963-608-080-1 LC Card 86-228329
1. Hungary - Foreign economic relations. 2. Foreign exchange problem - Hungary. 3. International finance. 4. Finance - Hungary. 5. International Monetary Fund - Hungary. I. Title.
HF1542.5 .K54 1985

Kiefer, Rolf. Sozialdemokratische Arbeiterbewegung in der Stadt Neuss vom Sozialistengesetz bis zum Ersten Weltkrieg / Rolf Kiefer. Reinbek : Einhorn Presse Verlag, c1982. iv, 159 p. ; 21 cm. (Nr. 18 der Schriftenreihe "Die Arbeiterbewegung in den Rheinlanden") Bibliography: p. 149-155. Includes index. ISBN 3-88756-025-6 LC Card 83-186919
1. Labor and laboring classes - Germany (West) - Neuss - History. 2. Sozialdemokratische Partei Deutschlands - History. 3. Neuss (Germany) - History. I. Series: Schriftenreihe "Die Arbeiterbewegung in den Rheinlanden" , Nr. 18. II. Title.
HD8460.N48 K54 1982

Kieffer, Walther. Steuerliche Wirkungen des grenzüberschreitenden Mobilien-Leasing : unter Berücksichtigung der steuerlichen Determinanten in Deutschland, Frankreich, Gossbritannien und USA / von Walther Kieffer. Berlin : E. Schmidt, c1983. xxiv, 338 p. : ill. ; 21 cm. (Betriebswirtschaftliche Studien. 45) Bibliography: p. 293-317. Includes index. ISBN 3-503-02369-0 LC Card 83-233705
1. Industrial equipment leases - Germany (West) - Mathematical models. 2. Industrial equipment leases - Great Britain - Mathematical models. 3. Industrial equipment leases - United States - Mathematical models. 4. Industrial equipment leases - France - Mathematical models. 5. Leases - Taxation - Germany (West). 6. Leases - Taxation - Great Britain. 7. Leases - Taxation - United States. 8. Leases - Taxation - France. I. Title.
HD39.4 .K54 1983

Kiełczew, Stanisław. Wybrane problemy ekonomiki przemysłu /. Wrocław , 1985. 110 p. ; LC Card 86-155957
HB9 .B7522 nr. 304 HD70.P6

Kieler Diskussionsbeiträge .
(103) Schatz, Klaus-Werner. Die Bedeutung kleiner und mittlerer Unternehmen im Strukturwandel /. Kiel , 1984. 32 p. ; LC Card 85-136545
HB44 .K45 no. 103 HD2346.G3

(123) Für einen anhaltenden Aufschwung . Kiel [1986] 29 p. : ISBN 3-925357-33-5 (Deut. Bibl.) : LC Card 86-234971
HB44 .K45 no. 123 HC286.7

(124) Fischer, Bernhard, fl. 1979- Brasilien ohne Inflation? . Kiel [1986] 28 p. ; LC Card 87-120443 DDC 330 s 332.4/1/0981 19
HB44 .K45 no. 124 HG835

(52) Neu, Axel Dietmar, 1942- Entkoppelung von Wirtschaftswachstum und Energieverbrauch . Kiel [1978] 91 p. : LC Card 85-174721
HB44 .K45 no. 52 HD9502.G42

(55) Glismann, Hans H. Zur Natur der Wachstumsschwäche in der Bundesrepublik Deutschland . Kiel [1978] 32 p. : LC Card 85-166323
HB44 .K45 no. 55 HB3789

Kieler Konjunkturgespräch (34th : 1986?) Für einen anhaltenden Aufschwung . Kiel [1986] 29 p. : ISBN 3-925357-33-5 (Deut. Bibl.) : LC Card 86-234971
HB44 .K45 no. 123 HC286.7

Kieler Schrifttumskunden zu Wirtschaft und Gesellschaft. For additional listing of contents, see Old Catalog.
(22) Bibliographie der EG-Zeitschriften 1952-1980 . Kiel , 1981. ix, 280 p. ; LC Card 81-122713
HB41 .K55 Bd. 22 Z7165.E8 HC241.2

Kieler Studien, 0340-6989 .
(178) Mayer, Thomas, 1927- Instabile Exportmärkte und wirtschaftliche Entwicklung . Tübingen , c1983. vii, 181 p. : ISBN 3-16-344673-6 LC Card 83-218666
HF3426.5 .M39 1983

(183) Heitger, Bernhard. Strukturwandel und realer Wechselkurs . Tübingen , c1983. vii, 115 p. : ISBN 3-16-344735-X : LC Card 84-125132
HG3823 .H43 1983

(185) Schmidt, Klaus-Dieter. Im Anpassungsprozess zurückgeworfen . Tübingen , c1984. xx, 243 p. : ISBN 3-16-344755-4 LC Card 84-170512
HC286.7 .S352 1984

(190) Langhammer, Rolf J. Wirtschaftliche Zusammenarbeit zwischen den Entwicklungsländern . Tübingen , c1984. xi, 135 p. : ISBN 3-16-344889-5 : LC Card 85-143693
HF1413 .L363 1984

(198) Dee, Philippa S. Financial markets and economic development . Tübingen , c1986. ix, 131 p. ; ISBN 3-16-345086-5 LC Card 86-190926 DDC 338.9519/5 19
HC467 .D44 1986

(201) Hartung, Hans. Verfahren zur Nutzung erschöpfbarer Ressourcen . Tübingen , 1986. ix, 172 p. : ISBN 3-16-345126-8 (Deut. Bibl. : pbk.) LC Card 86-233079
HD9565 .H36 1986

(202) Soltwedel, Rüdiger. Deregulierungspotentiale in der Bundesrepublik /. Tübingen , c1986. xi, 326 p. ; ISBN 3-16-345145-4 (Deut. Bibl. : pbk.) LC Card 87-408380 DDC 338.6/048 19
HD3616.G4 S665 1986

(203) Paqué, Karl-Heinz. Philanthropie und Steuerpolitik . Tübingen , c1986. xv, 417 p. : ISBN 3-16-345154-3 (pbk. : Deut. Bibl.) : LC Card 87-408202 DDC 343.4305/232 344.3035232 19
HJ4720.A45 P36 1986

(204) Streit, Joachim. Finanzinnovationen, Deregulierung und Geldmengensteuerung in den USA /. Tübingen , c1986. xi, 188 p. : ISBN 3-16-345156-X (pbk.) LC Card 87-408200 DDC 332/.0973 19
HG181 .S825 1986

(205) Schmidt, Rainer, Dr. Offene und verdeckte Arbeitslosigkeit in der Bundesrepublik . Tübingen , c1986. viii, 124 p. : ISBN 3-16-345158-6 LC Card 87-126258 DDC 331.13/7943 19
HD5779 .S2495 1986

(207) Boss, Alfred. Ausgabenkürzungen im öffentlichen Sektor /. Tübingen , c1987. xiii, 220 p. : ISBN 3-16-345212-4 LC Card 87-408337 DDC 336.43 19
HJ2109 .B67 1987

Kieler Vorträge, 0340-6970 .
(n.F., 110) Fels, Gerhard. Mehr Flexibilität am Arbeitsmarkt /. Kiel , 1986. 21 p. ; ISBN 3-925357-37-8 LC Card 87-126264 DDC 331.25/72/0943 19
HD5109.2.G3 F4 1986

(n.F., 111) Tangermann, Stefan. Welternährung und die Verantwortlichkeit der Industrieländer /. Kiel , 1986. 27 p. ; ISBN 3-925357-38-6 LC Card 87-126268 DDC 338.1/9/1724 19
HD9018.D44 T36 1986

Kiemelt vállalat, beruházás, érdek /. Szalai, Erzsébet. Budapest , 1981. 140 p. ; ISBN 963-05-2527-5 LC Card 81-170685
HG4028.C4 S96 1981

Kiernan, Joseph J. Bogan, Elizabeth Chapin. Macroeconomics . St. Paul, MN , c1987. xviii, 569 p. : ISBN 0-314-25867-1 : LC Card 86-24643 DDC 339 19
HB172.5 .B64 1987

Kierzkowski, Henryk. Protection and competition in international trade . Oxford [Oxfordshire] , New York, NY, USA , 1987. vi, 242 p. : ISBN 0-631-15004-8 : LC Card 86-29915 DDC 382/.3 19
HF1411 .P697 1987

Kieselbach, Thomas, 1944- Individuelle und gesellschaftliche Kosten der Massenarbeitslosigkeit . Weinheim , 1985. xxvi, 506 p. : ISBN 3-407-54689-0 LC Card 86-118545 DDC 331.13/7/019 19
HD5708 .I53 1985 ***NYPL [JLD 87-387]***

Kieso, Donald E. Weygandt, Jerry J. Accounting principles /. New York , c1987. xxviii, 1167, [45] p. : ISBN 0-471-03863-6 LC Card 87-2001 DDC 657 19
HF5635 .W524 1987

KIET International Finance Conference (1985 : Seoul, Korea) International financial markets and the NICs. Seoul, Korea : Korea Institute for Economics and Technology, [1985?] viii, 144 p. : ill., ports. ; 24 cm. LC Card 87-129000 DDC 332/.042 19
1. International finance - Congresses. 2. Finance - Developing countries - Congresses. I. Sanŏp Yŏn'guwŏn (Korea). II. Title.
HG205 .K54 1985

Kiev. Naukovo-doslidnyĭ ekonomichnyĭ instytut. see **Naukovo-doslidnyĭ ekonomichnyĭ instytut.**

KIEV (UKRAINE) - OCCUPATIONS.
Sem'i͡a i vosproizvodstvo struktury trudovoĭ zani͡atosti . Kiev , 1984. 238 p. : LC Card 86-142706
HB2698.U38 S46 1984

Kiffe, Ulrich. Die Klassifizierung in der Bundesrepublik Deutschland angebotener Personenkraftwagen mit multivariaten Analysemethoden / Ulrich Kiffe. Münster : Lit, 1984. xx, 24, 340 p. : ill. ; 21 cm. (Betriebswirtschaftliche Schriftenreihe . Bd. 12) Bibliography: p. 17-24 (2nd group) ISBN 3-88660-148-8 LC Card 84-208133
1. Automobile industry and trade - Germany, West. 2. Automobiles - Germany (West) - Specifications. 3. Automobile industry and trade. 4. Automobiles - Specifications. 5. Market segmentation. 6. Consumers' preferences. 7. Cluster analysis. I. Title. II. Series.
HD9710.G42 K48 1984

Kiger, Jack E. Accounting principles / Jack E. Kiger, Stephen E. Loeb, Gordon S. May. 2nd ed. New York : Random House, Business Division, c1987. xxvii, 1092 p. : ill. ; 27 cm. Includes indexes. ISBN 0-394-35482-6 : LC Card 86-29791 DDC 657 19
1. Accounting. I. Loeb, Stephen E. II. May, Gordon S. III. Title.
HF5635 .K53 1987

Kight, Leila K. How to find information about executives /. Washington, DC , c1986. 72 p. ; ISBN 0-934940-44-4 (pbk.) : LC Card 86-51569 DDC 658.4/0072 19
HD38.25.U6 H69 1986

Kikot', V. A. (Vil' Alekseevich) Uchastie trudi͡ashchikhsi͡a v upravlenii proizvodstvom . Moskva , 1983. 192, [2] p. : LC Card 84-210286
HD5660.S65 U26 1983

KIKUYU (AFRICAN PEOPLE) - HISTORY.
Kanogo, Tabitha M. Squatters and the roots of Mau Mau, 1905-63 /. London , Athens , 1987. xviii, 206 p. : ISBN 0-8214-0873-9 (U.S) LC Card 87-11201 DDC 307.3/36 19
HD1538.K4 K36 1987

KIKUYU (AFRICAN PEOPLE) - HISTORY - 20TH CENTURY.
Throup, David. Economic & social origins of Mau Mau 1945-53 /. London , Athens , c1988. xvi, 304 p. : ISBN 0-8214-0883-6 LC Card 87-12387 DDC 307.3/36 19
HD2126.5 .T48 1988

KIKUYU (AFRICAN PEOPLE) - SOCIAL CONDITIONS.
Nakhisa, Sellah A. Parking boys in the city of Kenya "Nairobi" /. [Nairobi , 1981?] ii, 27 leaves ; LC Card 82-980697 DDC 331.3/1 19
HE367.K43 P376 1981

KILDARE (COUNTY) - POPULATION.
Eastern Regional Development Organisation (Ireland) Eastern Region settlement strategy, 2011. Dublin [1985] viii, 21 p. : LC Card 87-672678
HB3589 .E27x 1985a

Eastern Regional Development Organisation (Ireland) Eastern Region settlement strategy, 2011. Dublin [1985] xviii, 269 p. : LC Card 87-672656
HB3589 .E27x 1985

Kilhey, Ulrike. Die Beurteilung des Erfolgs von Bankprodukten als Grundlage produktpolitischer Entscheidungen / von Ulrike Kilhey. Frankfurt am Main : F. Knapp, c1987. xiv, 289 p. : ill. ; 25 cm. (Schriftenreihe des Instituts für Kreditwesen der Westfälischen Wilhelms-Universität Münster . Bd. 33) Bibliography: p. 281-289. ISBN 3-7819-0374-5 LC Card 87-136157 DDC 332.1/068/5 19
1. Product management - Decision making. 2. Banks and banking - Germany, West. I. Title. II. Series.
HF5415.15 .K55 1987

KILLAM, DOROTHY JOHNSTON.
How, Douglas. [Very private person.] Canada's mystery man of high finance . Hantsport, N.S. , 1986. 173 p. : ISBN 0-88999-305-X (pbk.) LC Card 86-207291 DDC 338.092/2 B 19
HG172.K55 H68 1986

KILLAM, IZAAK WALTON, 1885-1955.
How, Douglas. [Very private person.] Canada's mystery man of high finance . Hantsport, N.S. , 1986. 173 p. : ISBN 0-88999-305-X (pbk.) LC Card 86-207291 DDC 338.092/2 B 19
HG172.K55 H68 1986

Killat, Gerhard. Kommunalisierung der Wohnungspolitik? : zur Dezentralisierung politischer Kompetenzen / Gerhard Killat. Köln : Institut für Wirtschaftspolitik an der Universität zu Köln, 1984. xiii, 291 p. : ill. ; 24 cm. (Untersuchungen zur Wirtschaftspolitik, 0175-7458 . 62) Originally presented as the author's thesis (doctoral)--Ruhr-Universität Bochum, 1983. Bibliography: p. 261-291. ISBN 3-921471-50-8 : LC Card 85-137757
1. Housing policy - Germany, West. 2. Local government - Germany, West. I. Title. II. Series.
HD7339.A3 K49 1984

Killi, Egil.
Transportproblemer, -politikk, -forskning og -undervisning i USA. Intrykk fra en studiereise. [Ved Egil Killi, Viggo Johannessen, Olav Dolve] Slemdal, 1968. 65, 3, 5 l. illus., col. map. 30 cm. At head of title: Transportøkonomisk institutt. Norges teknisk-naturvitenskapelige forskningsråd. Includes bibliography. LC Card 75-408744
1. Transportation - United States. 2. Transportation - Research - United States. I. Johannessen, Viggo, joint author. II. Dolve, Olav, joint author. III. Transportøkonomisk institutt. IV. Norges teknisk-naturvitenskapelige forskningsråd. V. Title.
HE203 .K5 ***NYPL [JLF 86-617]***

A killing wind . Kurzman, Dan. New York , c1987. xvi, 297 p., [16] p. of plates : ISBN 0-07-035687-4 LC Card 87-3398 DDC 363.1/79 19
HD7269.C452 I525 1987

Killough, Larry N. Cost accounting : concepts and techniques for management / Larry N. Killough, Wayne E. Leininger.2nd ed. St. Paul : West Pub. Co., c1987. xxii, 870 p. : ill. ; 26 cm. Includes index. ISBN 0-314-25865-5 : LC Card 86-26677 DDC 658.1/511 19
1. Cost accounting. I. Leininger, Wayne E. II. Title.
HF5686.C8 K488 1987

Kilmann, Ralph H. Corporate transformation . San Francisco , 1988. xxxi, 553 p. : ISBN 1-555-42060-5 (alk. paper) LC Card 87-45427 DDC 658.4/063 19
HD58.8 .C66 1988

Kilmer, Richard L. Economic efficiency in agricultural and food marketing /. Ames , 1987. xii, 315 p. ; ISBN 0-8138-0533-3 LC Card 87-2821 DDC 381/.41/0973 19
HD9000.5 .E26 1987

Kilpatrick, John A., 1942- Miller, Janice James. Issues for managers . Homewood, Ill. , 1987. xii, 139 p. : ISBN 0-256-05630-7 (pbk.) LC Card 87-80633 DDC 658/.049 19
HD62.4 .M54 1987

Kilpatrick, Michael, 1952- Business statistics using Lotus 1-2-3 / Michael Kilpatrick. New York : Wiley, c1987. ix, 326 p. : ill. ; 24 cm. Includes index. ISBN 0-471-84525-6 (pbk.) : LC Card 86-24737 DDC 519.5/028/55369 19
1. Commercial statistics - Data processing. 2. Lotus 1-2-3 (Computer program). I. Title.
HF1017 .K55 1987

Kilss, Beth. Workshop on Exact Matching Methodologies (May 9-10, 1985 : Arlington, Va.) Record linkage techniques--1985 . [Washington, D.C.] , 1985. vii, 397 p. :
NYPL [JLF 86-1723]

Kim, Chungsoo. Effects of neo-protectionism on the Korean exports / Chungsoo Kim ; with assistance of Bonghun Lee, and Sungjung Oh. [Seoul] : Korea Institute for Economics and Technology, 1986. 203 p. : ill. ; 24 cm. "May 1986"--Cover. Bibliography: p. 199-203. LC Card 86-234427 DDC 382/.095195/073 19
1. Korea (South) - Commerce - United States. 2. United States - Commerce - Korea (South). 3. Free trade and protection. I. Lee, Bonghun. II. Oh, Sungjung. III. Title.
HF3830.5.Z7 U54 1986

Kim, Ki Hang. Team theory / K.H. Kim & F.W. Roush. Chichester : E. Horwood ; New York : Halsted Press, 1987. viii, 246 p. ; 25 cm. (Ellis Horwood series in mathematics and its applications. Statistics and operational research) Bibliography: p.

[234]-238. Includes indexes. ISBN 0-7458-0154-4 : LC Card 87-4137 DDC 658.4/036 19
1. Decision-making - Mathematical models. 2. Decision-making, Group - Mathematical models. 3. Statistical decision. I. Roush, Fred William. II. Title. III. Series.
HD30.23 .K396 1987

Kim, Roy U. T. New tides in the Pacific . New York , 1987. xiii, 216 p. ; ISBN 0-313-25625-X (lib. bdg. : alk. paper) LC Card 87-8406 DDC 337.1/9 19
HC681 .N48 1987

Kim, W. Chan. The Pacific challenge in international business /. Ann Arbor, Mich. , 1987. viii, 342 p. ; ISBN 0-8357-1620-1 (alk. paper) LC Card 87-5008 DDC 338.09182/3 19
HC460.5 .P32 1987

Kimberley regional profile Western Australia. Kununurra, W.A. : Dept. of Regional Development and the North West, [1986] 36 p. : ill. (some col.) ; 30 cm. "Prepared May 1986." LC Card 87-156395 DDC 330.9941/4/063 19
1. Kimberley (W.A.) - Economic conditions. I. Western Australia. Dept. of Regional Development and the North West.
HC607.K55 K55 1986

KIMBERLEY (SOUTH AFRICA) - INDUSTRIES - HISTORY - 19TH CENTURY.
Worger, William H. South Africa's city of diamonds . New Haven , c1987. xvi, 330 p. : ISBN 0-300-03716-3 (alk. paper) LC Card 86-24724 DDC 331.7/622382/0968711 19
HD9677.S63 K568 1987

KIMBERLEY (W.A.) - ECONOMIC CONDITIONS.
Kimberley regional profile Western Australia. Kununurra, W.A. [1986] 36 p. : LC Card 87-156395 DDC 330.9941/4/063 19
HC607.K55 K55 1986

Kimpton, C. D. An Industrial research and development and marketing package for Australia . [Canberra?] [1984] 48, 4 leaves : LC Card 87-153477 DDC 338/.06 19
HC610.T4 I53 1984

Kimura, Fukunari. Industrial development of Malaysia : a study on manufacturing surveys / Fukunari Kimura. Tokyo, Japan : International Development Center of Japan, 1986. 25 p. : ill. ; 30 cm. (IDCJ working paper series . no. 35) Includes bibliographical references. LC Card 86-232472 DDC 338.09595 19
1. Malaysia - Manufactures. 2. Malaysia - Industries. I. Title. II. Series.
HD9736.M32 K56 1986

Kinard, Jerry. Management / Jerry Kinard. Lexington, Mass. : D.C. Heath, c1988. xxv, 547, A58 p. : ill. ; 25 cm. Bibliography: p. A1-A25. Includes indexes. ISBN 0-669-09223-1 LC Card 87-81817 DDC 658 19
1. Management. I. Title.
HD31 .K468 1988

Kinavwidi Lewu Niwembo. Kinshasa 1975 /. Kinshasa , Bruxelles [1986] 287 p. : LC Card 86-229048
HA4711.Z9 K565 1986

Kincaid, William M. A history of the Oklahoma State University, College of Business Administration / by William M. Kincaid, Jr. Stillwater, Okla. : Oklahoma State University, c1987. x, 227 p. : ill. ; 24 cm. (Centennial histories series) Bibliography: p. 217-220. Includes index. ISBN 0-914956-31-0 LC Card 87-11046 DDC 650/.07/1176634 19
1. Oklahoma State University. College of Business Administration - History. I. Title. II. Series.
HF1134.O57 K55 1987

Kindervatter, Suzanne. Doing a feasibility study . Washington, D.C. , c1987. 173 p. : ISBN 0-912917-07-5 (pbk.) : LC Card 86-61951 DDC 658/.022/091724 19
HD62.5 .D63 1987

Kindleberger, Charles Poor, 1910-
International capital movements : based on the Marshall lectures given at the University of Cambridge, 1985 / Charles P. Kindleberger. Cambridge [Cambridgeshire] ; New York : Cambridge University Press, 1987. vi, 99 p. ; 23 cm. Bibliography: p. [88]-95. Includes index. ISBN 0-521-34132-9 LC Card 86-32733 DDC 332/.041 19
1. Capital movements. 2. Balance of payments. 3. Foreign exchange. 4. International finance. I. Title.
HG3891 .K55 1987

Marshall Plan days / Charles P. Kindleberger. Boston : Allen & Unwin, 1987. x, 273 p., [1] leaf of plates : ill. ; 23 cm. Includes bibliographies and index. ISBN 0-04-332142-9 (alk. paper) LC Card 86-32163 DDC 338.91/73/04 19
1. Marshall Plan. 2. Economic assistance, American - Europe - History. 3. Europe - Economic conditions - 1945-. I. Title.
HC240 .K454 1987

Kinek lehet igaza? . Szathmári, Gábor. Budapest , 1985. 118 p. ; ISBN 963-322-273-7 : LC Card 86-156416
HD6955 .S975 1985

King, Catherine E.
King, Frank H. H. The history of the Hongkong and Shanghai Banking Corporation /. Cambridge [Cambridgeshire] , New York , 1987- p. cm. ISBN 0-521-32706-7 (v. 1) LC Card 86-28339 DDC 332.1/5/095125 19
HG1571 K56

King, Frank H. H. The Hongkong Bank in the period of imperialism and war, 1895-1918 . Cambridge [Cambridgeshire] , New York , 1988. p. cm. ISBN 0-521-32707-5 LC Card 87-6349 DDC 332.1/5/095125 s 332.1/5/095125 19
HG1571 .K56 vol. 2 HG3354.H65

King, David J. S.
King, Frank H. H. The history of the Hongkong and Shanghai Banking Corporation /. Cambridge [Cambridgeshire] , New York , 1987- p. cm. ISBN 0-521-32706-7 (v. 1) LC Card 86-28339 DDC 332.1/5/095125 19
HG1571 K56

King, Frank H. H. The Hongkong Bank in the period of imperialism and war, 1895-1918 . Cambridge [Cambridgeshire] , New York , 1988. p. cm. ISBN 0-521-32707-5 LC Card 87-6349 DDC 332.1/5/095125 s 332.1/5/095125 19
HG1571 .K56 vol. 2 HG3354.H65

King, Frank H. H.
The history of the Hongkong and Shanghai Banking Corporation / Frank H.H. King in association with Catherine E. King and David J.S. King. Cambridge [Cambridgeshire] ; New York : Cambridge University Press, 1987- p. cm. Bibliography: v. 1, p. Includes index. ISBN 0-521-32706-7 (v. 1) LC Card 86-28339 DDC 332.1/5/095125 19
1. Hongkong and Shanghai Banking Corporation - History. 2. Banks and banking - History. I. King, Catherine E. II. King, David J. S. III. Title.
HG1571 K56

History of the Hongkong and Shanghai Banking Corporation .
(v. 1) King, Frank H. H. The Hongkong Bank in late imperial China 1864-1902 . Cambridge [Cambridgeshire] , New York , 19. p. cm. ISBN 0-521-32706-7 LC Card 86-28341 DDC 332.1/5/095125 s 332.1/0951 19
HG1571 .K56 vol. 1 HG3338.H66

(v. 2) King, Frank H. H. The Hongkong Bank in the period of imperialism and war, 1895-1918 . Cambridge [Cambridgeshire] , New York , 1988. p. cm. ISBN 0-521-32707-5 LC Card 87-6349 DDC 332.1/5/095125 s 332.1/5/095125 19
HG1571 .K56 vol. 2 HG3354.H65

The Hongkong Bank in late imperial China 1864-1902 : 'on an even keel' / Frank H.H. King in association with Catherine E. King and David J.S. King. Cambridge [Cambridgeshire] ; New York : Cambridge University Press, 1987 p. cm. (The history of the Hongkong and Shanghai Banking Corporation . v.1) Bibliography: p. Includes index. ISBN 0-521-32706-7 LC Card 86-28341 DDC 332.1/5/095125 s 332.1/0951 19
I. Series: King, Frank H. H. History of the Hongkong and Shanghai Banking Corporation , v. 1. II. Title.
HG1571 .K56 vol. 1 HG3338.H66

The Hongkong Bank in the period of imperialism and war, 1895-1918 : focus of wealth / Frank H.H. King in association with David J.S. King and Catherine E. King. Cambridge [Cambridgeshire] ; New York : Cambridge University Press, 1988. p. cm. (The history of the Hongkong and Shanghai Banking Corporation . v. 2) Bibliography: p. Includes index. ISBN 0-521-32707-5 LC Card 87-6349 DDC 332.1/5/095125 s 332.1/5/095125 19
1. Hongkong and Shanghai Banking Corporation - History. 2. East Asia - Economic conditions. I. King, David J. S. II. King, Catherine E. III. Series: King, Frank H. H. History of the Hongkong and Shanghai Banking Corporation , v. 2. IV. Title.
HG1571 .K56 vol. 2 HG3354.H65

KING LINE (FIRM) - HISTORY.
Mallett, Alan S. Idyll of the Kings, 1889-1979 . Kendal [Cumbria] , 1980. 64 p. : ISBN 0-905617-10-X (pbk.) LC Card 81-105772 DDC 387.5/065/41 19
HE945.K48 M35 1980

King, Patricia, 1941- Never work for a jerk! / Patricia King. New York : F. Watts, 1987. 356 p. ; 22 cm. Includes index. ISBN 0-531-15522-6 LC Card 86-29014 DDC 650.1/3 19
1. Managing your boss. 2. Job stress. 3. Interpersonal relations. I. Title.
HF5548.83 .K56 1987

King, Preston T., 1936- An African winter / Preston King ; with a note on ecology and famine by Richard Leakey. Harmondsworth, Middlesex, England ; New York, N.Y., U. S.A. : Penguin Books, 1986. 249 p. : map ; 20 cm. (Penguin special) Includes index. ISBN 0-14-052365-0 (pbk.) : LC Card 87-103265 DDC 363.8/096 19
1. Famines - Africa, Northeast. I. Title.
HC840.Z9 F34 1986

King, Robert, 1944- (joint author) Hillstrom, Roger. 1960-1969, a decade of corporate and international finance. New York [1972] 381 p. LC Card 72-175335 DDC 332
HG4907 .H54 ***NYPL [JLG 73-17]***

King, William Richard, 1938- Project management handbook /. New York , 1988. p. cm. ISBN 0-442-22114-2 LC Card 87-23151 DDC 658.4/04 19
HD69.P75 P75 1988

Kingma, Kees. Honger op ons bord . Amsterdam , 1986. 164 p. : ISBN 90-70985-05-5 : LC Card 86-166714
HD9000.5 .H655 1986

Kingson, Eric R. What you must know about Social Security & Medicare / Eric R. Kingson ; introduction by Edward R. Roybal. New York : Pharos Books : Distributed in the U. S. by Ballantine Books, 1987. 120 p. ; 22 cm. Includes index. ISBN 0-88687-294-4 (pbk.) : LC Card 86-62667 DDC 368.4/3/00973 19
1. Social security - United States. 2. Medicare. I. Title.
HD7125 .K538 1987

Kingston, Jerry L. Burgess, Paul L. An incentives approach to improving the unemployment compensation system /. Kalamazoo, Mich. , 1987. xv, 273 p. : ISBN 0-88099-048-1 (pbk.) LC Card 87-23128 DDC 368.4/4/00973 19
HD7096.U5 B87 1987

Kingstone, Brett. The dynamos : who are they anyway? / Brett Kingstone. New York : Wiley, c1987. xx, 256 p. : ill., ports. ; 24 cm. Bibliography: p. 251-252. Includes index. ISBN 0-471-85827-7 LC Card 87-1754 DDC 338/.04/0922 B 19
1. Businessmen - United States - Biography. 2. Entrepreneur - Biography. 3. New business enterprises - United States - Management. I. Title.
HC102.5.A2 K56 1987

Kinh t Hà N Thông tin lý lu 1983. 154 p. ; 19 cm. At head of title: Vi LC Card 87-153552
1. Vietnam - Economic conditions. 2. Agriculture - Economic aspects - Vietnam. 3. Vietnam - Industry. I. Vi
HC444 .K56 1983

Kinnear, Thomas C., 1943- Bernhardt, Kenneth L., 1944- Cases in marketing management /. Plano, Tex. , 1985. xiii, 705 p. : ISBN 0-256-03055-3 LC Card 84-70994 DDC 658.8 19
HF5415.13 .B448 1985
NYPL [JLE 86-2513]

Kinsbruner, Jay. Petty capitalism in Spanish America : the pulperos of Puebla, Mexico City, Caracas, and Buenos Aires / Jay Kinsbruner. Boulder, Colo. : Westview Press, 1987. xxii, 159 p. : ill. ; 23 cm. (Dellplain Latin American studies . no. 21) Bibliography: p. [143]-152. Includes index. ISBN 0-8133-7272-0 (pbk.) LC Card 86-51526

DDC 381/.456413/0098 19
1. Grocery trade - Latin America - History - Case studies. 2. Grocers - Latin America - History - Case studies. I. Series: Dellplain Latin American studies , 21. II. Title.
HD9325.L29 K56 1987

Kinsey, B. H. Agribusiness and rural enterprise / B.H. Kinsey. London ; New York : Croom Helm, c1987. 228 p. ; 23 cm. Authorized revision of a reference manual prepared under contract for the Agribusiness Division in the Office of Agriculture of the United States Agency for International Development. Bibliography: p. 219-223. Includes index. ISBN 0-7099-1558-6 : LC Card 87-471 DDC 338.1/09172/4 19
1. Agricultural industries - Developing countries. 2. Small business - Developing countries. 3. Rural development projects - Developing countries. I. United States. Agency for International Development. Agribusiness Division. II. Title.
HD9018.D44 K55 1987

KINSHASA, ZAIRE - ECONOMIC CONDITIONS.
Sakombi Inongo. Regards sur Kinshasa . [Zaire] [1981?] 94 p. ; LC Card 82-226585
HC955.Z7 K497 1981

Kinshasa Zaire - Government. see **Kinshasa, Zaire - Politics and government.**

KINSHASA, ZAIRE - POLITICS AND GOVERNMENT.
Sakombi Inongo. Regards sur Kinshasa . [Zaire] [1981?] 94 p. ; LC Card 82-226585
HC955.Z7 K497 1981

KINSHASA (ZAIRE) - POPULATION - STATISTICS.
Kinshasa 1975 /. Kinshasa , Bruxelles [1986] 287 p. : LC Card 86-229048
HA4711.Z9 K565 1986

KINSHASA, ZAIRE - SOCIAL CONDITIONS.
Sakombi Inongo. Regards sur Kinshasa . [Zaire] [1981?] 94 p. ; LC Card 82-226585
HC955.Z7 K497 1981

Kinshasa 1975 / [sous la direction] de Joseph Houyoux, Kinavwúidi Niwembo. Kinshasa : Bureau d'études d'aménagement et d'urbanisme ; Bruxelles : ICHEC, [1986] 287 p. : ill. ; 21 cm. Cover title. Bibliography: p. 286-287. LC Card 86-229048
1. Kinshasa (Zaire) - Population - Statistics. I. Houyoux, Joseph. II. Kinavwidi Lewu Niwembo.
HA4711.Z9 K565 1986

KINSHIP - CONNECTICUT - HISTORY.
Ditz, Toby L., 1951- Property and kinship . Princeton, N.J. , c1986. xvi, 213 p. : ISBN 0-691-04735-9 (alk. paper) : LC Card 86-5051 DDC 333.33 19
HB715 .D58 1986 *NYPL [JLE 86-4624]*

KINSHIP - DEVELOPING COUNTRIES.
Partsch, Manfred. Prinzipien und Formen sozialer Sicherung in nicht-industriellen Gesellschaften /. Berlin , c1983. 168 p. ; ISBN 3-428-05484-9 LC Card 84-148527 DDC 368.4/009172/4 19
HD7252 .P37 1983 *NYPL [JLE 85-1238]*

Kintanar, Agustin. ASEAN-U. S. economic relations . Singapore , c1986. x, 54 p. : ISBN 997-19-8842-9 (pbk.) LC Card 87-940002 DDC 337.59073 19
HF1456.5.A7 A84 1986

Kintis, Andreas A. Anaptyxē tēs Hellēnikēs viomēchanias / Andrea A. Kintē. Athēna : Gutenberg, [1982] 180 p. ; 25 cm. Bibliography: p. 179-180. LC Card 84-132514
1. Greece - Industries - History. I. Title.
HC295 .K515 1982

Kinturi, Jorma. Väestö, asunnot ja asuntorakentaminen suur- ja peruspiireittäin Helsingissä 1970-1983 = Befolkning, bostäder och bostadsbyggande efter stordistrikt och distrikt i Helsingfors 1970-1983. Helsinki : TILK, 1984. 36 p., [1] folded leaf of plates : 1 col. map ; 30 cm. (Tilastoja. A, Väestö, työvoima, asuminen, 0781-0512 = Statistik. A, Befolkning, arbetskraft, boende . 1984 A:2) "Laatineet Jorma Kinturi, Markku Lankinen ja Virva Kuparinen"--P. 3. LC Card 85-156678
1. Housing - Finland - Helsinki - Statistics. 2. Helsinki (Finland) - Population - Statistics. I. Lankinen, Markku. II. Kuparinen, Virva. III. Title. IV. Title: Befolkning, bostäder och bostadsbyggande efter stordistrikt och distrikt i Helsingfors 1970-1983. V. Series: Tilastoja. A, Väestö, työvoima, asuminen , 1984:2.
HD7345.3.H5 K563 1984

Kintz, B. L. Bruning, James L. Computational handbook of statistics /. Glenview, Ill. , c1987. 372 p. ; ISBN 0-673-18407-2 (pbk.) LC Card 86-31593 DDC 519.5 19
HA29 .B835 1987

K.I.P. studies.
Fleming, Maureen. Microcomputers and productivity . White Plains, NY , c1984. iii, 125 p. ; ISBN 0-86729-109-5 (pbk.) LC Card 84-164284 DDC 650/.028/54 19
HF5548.2 .F49 1984 *NYPL [JLf 87-8]*

The Kiplinger/Changing times guide to buying and selling a home / by the editors of Changing times magazine. Washington, DC : Kiplinger Washington Editors ; New York, NY : Distributed by Select Magazines, c1987. iii, 311 p. : ill. ; 21 cm. Spine title: Kiplinger's buying & selling a home. Cover title: How to profit from-- buying & selling a home. Rev. ed. of: Buying and selling a home in today's market / by Joan Meyers. Includes index. ISBN 0-938721-02-X (pbk.) : LC Card 87-167806 DDC 643/.12 19
1. House buying - United States. 2. House selling - United States. 3. Home ownership. 4. Real estate business - United States. I. Meyers, Joan. Buying and selling a home in today's market. II. Changing times. III. Title: Buying and selling a home. IV. Title: Buying & selling a home. V. Title: Kiplinger's buying & selling a home. VI. Title: How to profit from-- buying & selling a home.
HD1379 .K52 1987

Kiplinger forecasts : the new American boom : exciting changes in American life and business between now and the year 2000 / by the staff of the Kiplinger Washington letter. Washington, DC : Kiplinger Washington Editors ; New York, NY : Distributed by Select Magazines, c1986. vi, 330 p. ; 21 cm. Includes index. ISBN 0-938721-01-1 (pbk.) : LC Card 86-203273 DDC 338.5/443/0973 19
1. Economic forecasting - United States. 2. United States - Economic conditions - 1981-. I. Kiplinger Washington letter. II. Title: New American boom.
HC106.8 .K56 1986

Kiplinger Washington letter. Kiplinger forecasts . Washington, DC , New York, NY , c1986. vi, 330 p. ; ISBN 0-938721-01-1 (pbk.) : LC Card 86-203273 DDC 338.5/443/0973 19
HC106.8 .K56 1986

Kiplinger's buying & selling a home. The Kiplinger/Changing times guide to buying and selling a home /. Washington, DC , New York, NY , c1987. iii, 311 p. : ISBN 0-938721-02-X (pbk.) : LC Card 87-167806 DDC 643/.12 19
HD1379 .K52 1987

Kipshagen, Lothar. Die Planung von Distributionssystemen der Konsumgüterindustrie unter besonderer Berücksichtigung der Tourenauslieferung : die Konzeption einer Modellhierarchie / Lothar Kipshagen. Thun : H. Deutsch, c1983. v, 336 p. : ill. ; 21 cm. (Reihe Wirtschaftswissenschaften, 0253-1488 . Bd. 285) Bibliography: p. 318-336. ISBN 3-87144-748-X LC Card 83-185464
1. Physical distribution of goods. I. Title. II. Series.
HF5415.6 .K56 1983

Kırbaş, Sadık. Akdoğan, Abdurrahman. Açıklamalı maliye ve vergi sözlüğü /. [Ankara?] , Yenişehir, Ankara , 1986. 229 p. ; LC Card 87-968120
HJ129.T9 A43 1986

Kirchen kämpfen mit : die VFW-Fokker-Aktion zur Erhaltung der Arbeitsplätze / herausgegeben von Heinrich Ludwig und Heinz-Georg Ludwig. Mainz : Matthias-Grünewald-Verlag, 1981. 106 p. : ill. ; 20 cm. (Reihe Arbeiterbewegung und Kirche . Nr. 3) Includes bibliographical references. ISBN 3-7867-0873-8 LC Card 81-188986 DDC 261.8/34562/094343 19
1. Zentralgesellschaft VFW-Fokker m.b.H. 2. Church and labor - Germany (West) - Speyer. 3. Plant shutdowns - Germany (West) - Speyer. I. Ludwig, Heinrich, 1942-. II. Ludwig, Heinz-Georg. III. Series. IV. Series: Reihe Arbeiterbewegung und Kirche , Nr. 3.
HD6338.2.G32 S634 1981
NYPL [JLD 86-2786]

Kireta-Katewu, Patrick R., 1953- Economic analyses of the farmer cropping system under risks and uncertainties in Sierra Leone / Patrick R. Kireta-Katewu ; H.-U. Thimm, herausgeber ... [et al.]. Hamburg : Verlag Weltarchiv, 1985. xviii, 245 p. : ill. ; 21 cm. (Studien zur integrierten ländichen Entwicklung, 0177-2503 . 4) Bibliography: p. 205-214. ISBN 3-87895-266-X (pbk.) LC Card 87-103068 DDC 338.1/62 19
1. Agriculture - Economic aspects - Sierra Leone. 2. Cropping systems - Economic aspects - Sierra Leone. I. Thimm, Heinz-Ulrich. II. Title. III. Series.
HD2146.5 .K57 1985

KIRGHIZ S.S.R. - ECONOMIC CONDITIONS.
Ėkonomicheskiĭ rost Kirgizskoĭ SSR v usloviiākh intensifikatsii obshchestvennogo proizvodstva . Frunze , 1984. 210 p. ; LC Card 85-131511
HC337.K545 E37 1984
*NYPL [*QIP 87-105]*

K istorii sotsial'no-ėkonomicheskikh ukladov Kirgizstana /. Frunze , 1972. 108 p. ; LC Card 82-171559
HC337.K545 K15 1972

Tarasov, Ivan Gavrilovich. Sled v zhizni /. Frunze , 1985. 94 p. ; LC Card 87-115075
HC337.K545 T37 1985

KIRGHIZ S.S.R. - ECONOMIC CONDITIONS - CONGRESSES.
Sipozium "Geografiia v Kirgizii" (1980 : Frunze, Kirghiz S.S.R.) Sovremennye problemy geografii Kirgizii . Frunze , 1980. 167 p. : LC Card 82-121674
HC337.K545 S56 1980

KIRGHIZ S.S.R. - ECONOMIC POLICY.
Ėkonomicheskiĭ rost Kirgizskoĭ SSR v usloviiākh intensifikatsii obshchestvennogo proizvodstva . Frunze , 1984. 210 p. ; LC Card 85-131511
HC337.K545 E37 1984
*NYPL [*QIP 87-105]*

KIRGHIZ S.S.R. - INDUSTRIES.
Abdurakhmanov, I. (Ibraim) Ėffektivnost' kapital'nykh vlozheniĭ v promyshlennosti Kirgizii /. Frunze , 1981. 174 p. ; LC Card 82-160618
HC337.K5453 C32 1981

KIRGHIZ S.S.R. - RURAL CONDITIONS.
Boldzhurova, I. S. (Ishengul' Sadykovna) Kolkhoznoe krest'ianstvo Kirgizii v usloviiākh razvitogo sotsializma /. Frunze , 1985. 148 p. ; LC Card 86-106126
HD1995.K53 B65 1985

KIRGHIZ S.S.R. - SOCIAL CONDITIONS.
K istorii sotsial'no-ėkonomicheskikh ukladov Kirgizstana /. Frunze , 1972. 108 p. ; LC Card 82-171559
HC337.K545 K15 1972

Tarasov, Ivan Gavrilovich. Sled v zhizni /. Frunze , 1985. 94 p. ; LC Card 87-115075
HC337.K545 T37 1985

Kiriakov, Kiril Todorov. Problemi na stopanskata smetka /. Sofiia , 1981. 207 p. ; LC Card 82-133037
HC403.Z9 A865 1981

Kirichenko, Ė. V. (Ėlina Vsevolodovna) Korporatsii SShA v bor'be za vneshnie rynki sbyta / Ė.V. Kirichenko. Moskva : Izd-vo "Nauka", 1981. 196 p. ; 20 cm. At head of title: Akademiia nauk SSSR. Ordena Trudovogo Krasnogo Znameni Institut mirovoĭ ėkonomiki i mezhdunarodnykh otnosheniĭ. Includes bibliographies. LC Card 82-152673
1. Corporations - United States. 2. Competition, International. I. Title.
HD2766 .K53 1981

Kirichenko, Vadim Nikitich. Osnovnye idei piatiletki / V.N. Kirichenko. Moskva : Izd-vo polit. lit-ry, 1981. 92 p. : ill. ; 20 cm. (Shagi odinnadtsatoĭ) Includes bibliographical references. LC Card 82-123953
1. Soviet Union - Economic policy - 1981-. I. Title. II. Series.
HC336.25 .K569 1981

Kirillin, A. D. (Andreĭ Dmitrievich) Mezhotraslevye sviazi v IAkutskoĭ ASSR . IAkutsk , 1985. 80 p. ; LC Card 86-193902
HC337.123 I576 1985

Kirillov, S. R. (Sergeĭ Rufovich) Soizmerenie zatrat i rezul'tatov v teorii planovogo tsenoobrazovaniia / S.R. Kirillov ; otvetstvennyĭ

redaktor A.A. Deri͡abin. Moskva : "Nauka", 1987. 188 p. ; 21 cm. At head of title: Akademii͡a nauk SSSR. Ordena Trudovogo Krasnogo Znameni Institut ėkonomiki. Includes bibliographical references. LC Card 87-157208
1. Prices - Soviet Union. 2. Costs, Industrial - Soviet Union. 3. Labor theory of value - Soviet Union. I. Deri͡abin, Anatoliĭ Aleksandrovich. II. Title.
HB235.S73 K57 1987

Kirillova, A. A. Razvitie kapitalisticheskoĭ manufaktury v Anglii i Germanii XVI-XVII vv. . Moskva , 1981. 132 p. : LC Card 83-111684
HD9735.G32 R39 1981

Kiri͡ukhina, Elena Ivanovna. Iz istorii krest'i͡anstva Evropeĭskogo Severa, Verkhnego Povolzh'i͡a i Urala v period Velikoĭ Okti͡abr'skoĭ sotsialisticheskoĭ revoli͡utsii i pobedy sotsializma v SSSR, 1917-1937 gg. /. Kirov , 1979. 170 p. ; LC Card 82-103738
HD1492.S652 R8755 1979

Kirk, David, 1937- Major bus operators : Manchester and Merseyside / David Kirk.2nd ed. Harrow Weald, Middlesex : Capital Transport, 1985. 96 p. : ill. ; 21 cm. ISBN 0-904711-66-8 (pbk.) : LC Card 86-214197 DDC 388.3/22/094273 19
1. Bus lines - England - Greater Manchester. 2. Bus lines - England - Merseyside. I. Title.
HE5664.M34 K57 1985

Kirk, Gwyn. Cook, Alice. Greenham women everywhere . Boston, Mass. , 1984, c1983. 127, [1] p. : ISBN 0-89608-199-0
NYPL [JLD 87-215]

Kirk-Kuwaye, Chris. Krupa, Arlene. Couplepower . New York , c1987. 227 p. ; ISBN 0-396-09029-X (pbk.) : LC Card 87-20065 DDC 658.4/09 19
HD62.25 .K78 1987

Kirk, Michael, 1955- Ochsenanspannung in Westafrika : Probleme der entwicklungskonformen Technologiewahl für kleinbäuerliche Betriebssysteme / Michael Kirk. Göttingen : Herodot, c1984. iv, 220 p. ; 21 cm. (Sozialökonomische Schriften zur ruralen Entwicklung, 0175-2464 . Bd. 57 = vol. 57) Summary in English. Bibliography: p. 210-220. ISBN 3-88694-057-8 LC Card 86-202167 DDC 338.1/09688 19
1. Agriculture - Economic aspects - Namibia. 2. Agricultural innovations - Namibia. I. Series: Sozialökonomische Schriften zur ruralen Entwicklung , Bd. 57. II. Title.
HD2134 .K57 1984

Kirk, T. Project 3.05, rural workshop and machinery centre : report and recommendations of the director on the proposed rural workshop and machinery centre, Sanyati T.T.L. Salisbury, Zimbabwe : Whitsun Foundation, 1977. 1 v. (various pagings) : ill. ; 30 cm. LC Card 85-104610
1. Agricultural development projects - Zimbabwe - Sanyati River Region. 2. Agricultural machinery - Zimbabwe - Sanyati River Region - Maintenance and repair. I. Whitsun Foundation. II. Title.
HD2131.Z9 S265 1977

Kirkman, Patrick R. A. Electronic funds transfer systems : the revolution in cashless banking and payment methods / Patrick Kirkman. Oxford, UK ; New York, NY : Blackwell, 1987. x, 231 p. ; 24 cm. Includes index. ISBN 0-631-15317-9 : LC Card 86-26410 DDC 332.1/028 19
1. Electronic funds transfers. I. Title.
HG1710 .K57 1987

Kirkpatrick, Donald L.
How to manage change effectively / Donald L. Kirkpatrick ; foreword by Joe D. Batten. 1st ed. San Francisco : Jossey-Bass, 1985. xxii, 280 p. : ill. ; 24 cm. (The Jossey-Bass management series) "Approaches, methods, and case examples"--P. [iii]. Includes index. Bibliography: p. 273-275. ISBN 0-87589-659-6 LC Card 85-45060 DDC 658.4/06 19
1. Organizational change - Addresses, essays, lectures. 2. Organizational effectiveness - Addresses, essays, lectures. I. Title. II. Series.
HD58.8 .K52 1985 *NYPL [JLE 87-1191]*

How to plan and conduct productive business meetings / Donald L. Kirkpatrick. 2nd ed. New York, NY : AMACOM, American Management Association, c1987. p. cm. Includes index. ISBN 0-8144-7664-3 LC Card 86-47589 DDC 658.4/563 19
1. Meetings. I. Title.
HD30.3 .K56 1987

Kirkpatrick, Thomas O., 1932- Supervision : a situational approach / Thomas O. Kirkpatrick. Boston, Mass. : Kent Pub. Co., c1987. xxiii, 588 p. : ill. ; 24 cm. Includes bibliographies and index. ISBN 0-534-07314-X : LC Card 86-21121 DDC 658.3/02 19
1. Supervision of employees. I. Title.
HF5549 .K528 1987

KIRKWOOD (SOUTH AFRICA) - CENSUS, 1980.
Bevolkingsensus 1980, uitgesoekte statistiese streek Port Elizabeth/Uitenhage/Kirkwood =. [Pretoria] [1985] xix, 317 p. : ISBN 0-621-09480-3 : LC Card 85-241531
HA4701.Z9 P673 1985

KIROV ADYNDAKY KOLKHOZ (TAKHTA-BAZARSKIĬ RAĬON, TURKMEN S.S.R.) - HISTORY.
Berdiev, G. Tagtabazar raĭonynyn͡g Kirov adyndaky kolkhozynyn͡g tarykhy /. Ashgabat , 1986. 79 p. : LC Card 86-198891
HD1492.S652 T873 1986

KIROVSKAI͡A OBLAST' (R.S.F.S.R.) - ECONOMIC CONDITIONS - STATISTICS.
Narodnoe khozi͡aĭstvo Kirovskoĭ oblasti v desi͡atoĭ pi͡atiletke, 1976-1980 gg. . Kirov , 1981. 95 p. ; LC Card 82-146329
HC337.R852 K576 1981

KIROVSKAI͡A OBLAST' (R.S.F.S.R.) - STATISTICS.
Narodnoe khozi͡aĭstvo Kirovskoĭ oblasti v desi͡atoĭ pi͡atiletke, 1976-1980 gg. . Kirov , 1981. 95 p. ; LC Card 82-146329
HC337.R852 K576 1981

Kirovskiĭ gosudarstvennyĭ pedagogicheskiĭ institut imeni V.I. Lenina. Iz istorii krest'i͡anstva Evropeĭskogo Severa, Verkhnego Povolzh'i͡a i Urala v period Velikoĭ Okti͡abr'skoĭ sotsialisticheskoĭ revoli͡utsii i pobedy sotsializma v SSSR, 1917-1937 gg. /. Kirov , 1979. 170 p. ; LC Card 82-103738
HD1492.S652 R8755 1979

Kirschke, Dieter, 1952- Agrarmarktpolitik bei Unsicherheit : Grundlagen für die theoretische Analyse und Anwendung auf das EG-System der Agrarpreisfixierung / von Dieter Kirschke. Berlin : Duncker & Humblot, c1987. 225 p. : ill. ; 24 cm. (Volkswirtschaftliche Schriften. Heft 369) Bibliography: p. [211]-225. ISBN 3-428-06111-X LC Card 87-131255 DDC 338.1/8 19
1. Farm produce - Prices - Government policy - European Economic Community countries. 2. Agricultural prices - European Economic Community countries. 3. Agriculture and state - European Economic Community countries. 4. Risk - European Economic Community countries. I. Title. II. Series.
HD1920.5 .K57 1987

Kirsten, José Tiacci. Custo de vida : metodologia de cálculo, problemas e aplicações / José Tiacci Kirsten. São Paulo : Livraria Pioneira Editora : Fundação Instituto de Pesquisas Econômicas, 1985. xi, 158 p. : ill. ; 22 cm. (Biblioteca Pioneira de estudos sociais. Economia) Estudos econômicos "Obra publicada com a colaboração da Universidade de São Paulo"--P. [v] Bibliography: p. [155]-158. LC Card 86-143942
1. Consumer price indexes - Brazil. 2. Consumer price indexes. I. Series. II. Series: Estudos econômicos (Fundação Instituto de Pesquisas Econômicas (São Paulo, Brazil)). III. Title.
HB235.B8 K57 1985

Kirtovskiĭ, I. Kh. Ocherki istorii marksistsko-leninskoĭ ėkonomicheskoĭ mysli Latvii, 1920-1980 / I.Kh. Kirtovskiĭ, M.N. Panevina, I͡U.I͡U. Saulitis. Riga : "Zinatne", 1985. 199 p. ; 22 cm. At head of title: Akademii͡a nauk Latviĭskoĭ SSR. Institut ėkonomiki. Bibliography: p. 188-[196] LC Card 86-176265
1. Marxian economics - Latvia - History. 2. Economics - Latvia - History. 3. Latvia - Economic conditions. I. Panevina, M. N. (Maĭi͡a Nikolaevna). II. Saulitis, I͡U. I͡U. (I͡Uriĭ I͡Ur'evich). III. Title.
HB97.5 .K542 1985

Kiruta, A. I͡A. (Aleksandr I͡Akovlevich) Shevi͡akov, Alekseĭ I͡Ur'evich. Modelirovanie sbalansirovannosti i soglasovanii͡a planovykh resheniĭ v sfere narodnogo blagosostoi͡anii͡a /. Moskva , 1986. 211 p. : LC Card 86-177908
HC336.25 .S525 1986

Kirzner, Israel M. Subjectivism, intelligibility, and economic understanding . Basingstoke, Hampshire , 1986. xi, 319 p. : ISBN 0-333-41788-7 *NYPL [JLD 86-2215]*

A kis- és középvállalatok és a gazdasági fejlődés . Bayer, B. József. Budapest , 1986. 203, [1] p. : ISBN 963-221-914-7 : LC Card 87-138623
HD2341 .B29 1986

Kis, Pál. A mezőgazdasági nagyüzemek pénz- és hitelrendszere / Kis Pál. Budapest : Mezőgazdasági Kiadó, 1985. 261 p. ; 24 cm. Bibliography: p. 253-255. ISBN 963-232-050-6 : LC Card 85-230947
1. Agricultural credit - Hungary. 2. Agriculture - Hungary - Finance. 3. State farms - Hungary - Finance. I. Title.
HD1440.H9 K57 1985

Kiselev, A. A. (Anatoliĭ Alekseevich) Ėkonomika, organizatsii͡a i planirovanie priborostroitel'nogo proizvodstva : uchebnik dli͡a priborostroitel'nykh spetsial'nosteĭ tekhnikumov / A.A. Kiselev, V.N. Koshelev.Izd. 2-e, perer. Leningrad : "Sudostroenie", 1985. 271 p. : ill. ; 22 cm. Bibliography: p. 268. Includes index. LC Card 86-127609
1. Instrument industry - Soviet Union - Management. I. Koshelev, V. N. (Vladimir Nikolaevich). II. Title.
HD9706.S652 K57 1985

Kiselev, L. E. Kooperativnoe dvizhenie v Sibiri . Ti͡umen' , 1984. 72 p. ; LC Card 85-179545
HD3517.A3 R875 1984

Kiselev, V. G. Abdullaev, A. Kh. Zadacha razmeshchenii͡a sel'skokhozi͡aĭstvennogo proizvodstva v ob"edinenii khozi͡aĭstv meliorativnoĭ sistemy /. Moskva , 1985. 24, [2] p. ; LC Card 86-162160
HD9015.S652 A23 1985

Kisic Wagner, Drago. Reflexiones en torno al proceso de coordinación latinoamericano sobre la deuda externa / Drago Kisic. [1era. ed.]. [Lima, Perú] : Centro Peruano de Estudios Internacionales, [1985] 29 p. ; 21 cm. (Documentos de trabajo . 1) Includes bibliographical references. LC Card 87-403187 DDC 336.3/435/098 19
1. Debts, External - Latin America. 2. Pan-Americanism. I. Series: Documentos de trabajo (Centro Peruano de Estudios Internacionales) , 1. II. Title.
HJ8514.5 .K57 1985

Kisiparosok Országos Szervezete (Hungary) A Kisiparosok Országos Szervezete VIII. országos küldöttgyűlése . Budapest , 1982. 167 p. : LC Card 83-229477
HD2346.H8 K58 1982

KISIPAROSOK ORSZÁGOS SZERVEZETE (HUNGARY) - CONGRESSES.
A Kisiparosok Országos Szervezete VIII. országos küldöttgyűlése . Budapest , 1982. 167 p. : LC Card 83-229477
HD2346.H8 K58 1982

Kisiparosok Országos Szervezete nyolcadik országos küldöttgyűlése. A Kisiparosok Országos Szervezete VIII. országos küldöttgyűlése . Budapest , 1982. 167 p. : LC Card 83-229477
HD2346.H8 K58 1982

A Kisiparosok Országos Szervezete VIII. országos küldöttgyűlése : 1981. december 5-6. Budapest : Kisiparosok Országos Szervezete, 1982. 167 p. : ports. ; 24 cm. LC Card 83-229477
1. Kisiparosok Országos Szervezete (Hungary) - Congresses. 2. Small business - Hungary - Congresses. I. Kisiparosok Országos Szervezete (Hungary). II. Title: Kisiparosok Országos Szervezete 8. országos küldöttgyűlése. III. Title: Kisiparosok Országos Szervezete nyolcadik országos küldöttgyűlése.
HD2346.H8 K58 1982

Kisiparosok Országos Szervezete 8. országos küldöttgyűlése. A Kisiparosok Országos Szervezete VIII. országos küldöttgyűlése . Budapest , 1982. 167 p. : LC Card 83-229477
HD2346.H8 K58 1982

Kisker, Klaus Peter. Multinationale Konzerne . Köln , c1982. 478 p. : ISBN 3-7663-0506-9 LC Card 82-196963 DDC 332.6/73/0943 19
HD5710.75.G3 M84 1982
NYPL [JLD 86-2753]

Kiskereskedelmi áralakulás, 1981-1985 / [összeállitotta a KSH Kereskedelmi és Közlekedési Statisztikai Főosztály Belkereskedelmi Osztálya]. Budapest : Központi Statisztikai Hivatal, 1986. 81 p. ; 29 cm. Chiefly tables. LC Card 86-202239
1. Consumer price indexes - Hungary. 2. Prices - Hungary - Statistics. I. Hungary. Központi Statisztikai Hivatal. Belkereskedelmi Osztály.
HB235.H8 K56 1986

Kissler, Leo. Vilmar, Fritz, 1929- Arbeitswelt, Grundriss einer kritischen Soziologie der Arbeit /. Opladen , c1982. 256 p. : ISBN 3-8100-0400-6 (pbk.) LC Card 87-672408
HD6971 .V534x 1982

A kisvállalatok állami támogatása két fejlett tőkés országban /. Laki, Mihály. Budapest , 1983-1985. 62 p. ; LC Card 86-218531
HD2346.G3 L24 1983

Kitay, Michael G. Land acquisition in developing countries : policies and procedures of the public sector ; with surveys and case studies from Korea, India, Thailand, and Ecuador / Michael G. Kitay. Boston : Published by Oelgeschlager, Gunn & Hain in association with the Lincoln Institute of Land Policy, c1985. xx, 199 p. ; 24 cm. "A Lincoln Institute of Land Policy book." Includes index. Bibliography: p. 185-187. ISBN 0-89946-192-1 LC Card 85-7225 DDC 333.1/3/091724 19
1. Land use, Urban - Government policy - Developing countries. 2. Government purchasing of real property - Developing countries. 3. Population forecasting - Developing countries. I. Title.
HD1131 .K58 1985 ***NYPL [JLE 86-3827]***

Kitchen, Harry M. Local government finance in Canada / Harry M. Kitchen. [Toronto, Ont.] : Canadian Tax Foundation, c1984. xvii, 495 p. ; 23 cm. (Financing Canadian federation, 0225-5103 . 5) Includes bibliographical references and index. ISBN 0-88808-020-4
1. Local finance - Canada. 2. Finance, Public - Canada. I. Title. ***NYPL [JLL 80-129 no.5]***

Kitchen, Richard L. Finance for the developing countries / Richard L. Kitchen. Chichester [West Sussex] ; New York : Wiley, c1986. xvii, 365 p. ; 24 cm. Includes indexes. Bibliography: p. 333-347. ISBN 0-471-90945-9 : LC Card 85-32331 DDC 332/.09172/4 19
1. Finance - Developing countries. 2. Economic development - Finance. I. Title.
HG195 .K58 1986 ***NYPL [JLE 86-4165]***

KITCHEN UTENSILS INDUSTRY - UNITED STATES.
Portable kitchen appliance market. New York, N.Y. , c1983. 2 v. (x, 405 p.) : LC Card 87-143951 DDC 381/.4568383/0973 19
HD9971.5.K583 U656 1983

KITCHENER (ONT.) - MANUFACTURES - FORECASTING.
Manufacturing in Kitchener-Waterloo . [Waterloo] , c1987. xiii, 220 p. : ISBN 0-921083-22-X (pbk.) LC Card 87-168616 DDC 338.4/767/0971344 19
HD9734.C3 K56 1987

KITCHENER (ONT.) - MANUFACTURES - HISTORY.
Manufacturing in Kitchener-Waterloo . [Waterloo] , c1987. xiii, 220 p. : ISBN 0-921083-22-X (pbk.) LC Card 87-168616 DDC 338.4/767/0971344 19
HD9734.C3 K56 1987

The kite route . Jones, William C., 1937- Boulder, Colo. , c1986. 159 p. : ISBN 0-87108-721-9 LC Card 86-25190 DDC 385/.5 19
HE2791.D383 J66 1986

Kitterer, Wolfgang.
Aussagefähigkeit von Einkommensverteilungsrechnungen für die Bundesrepublik Deutschland . Tübingen , 1986. xxiv, 436 p. : ISBN 3-88573-027-8 LC Card 87-407588 DDC 339.2/0943 19
HC290.5.I5 A93 1986

Effizienz- und Verteilungswirkungen des Steuersystems / Wolfgang Kitterer. Frankfurt am Main ; New York : P. Lang, c1986. 397 p. ; 22 cm. (Finanzwissenschaftliche Schriften, 0170-8252 . Bd. 30) The author's Habilitationsschrift--Universität Tübingen, 1983. Bibliography: p. 386-397. ISBN 3-8204-8528-7 LC Card 86-194183
1. Tax incidence. 2. Transfer payments. 3. Income distribution. I. Title. II. Series.
HJ2321 .K52 1986

Kitui water resources development study . Nilsson, Roy. Nairobi, Kenya [1982] 13, [31] leaves : LC Card 85-980998 DDC 333.91/009676/24 19
HD1699.K42 K586 1982

KITWE (ZAMBIA) - ECONOMIC CONDITIONS.
Kamya, Andrew, 1941- Factors affecting efficiency in the informal sector in Lusaka and Kitwe /. Lusaka , 1981. iii, 40 p. ; LC Card 87-980491
HD2346.Z292 L875 1981

Kizorek, Bill. Disability or deception / Bill Kizorek. [Naperville, Ill., USA] (Suite 12, 6 S 235 Steeple Run Dr., Naperville 60540) : [PSI Pub., c1986] 140 p. : ill. ; 25 cm. Cover title. LC Card 86-206432 DDC 363.2/5 19
1. Disability evaluation - United States - Case studies. 2. Insurance crimes - United States - Case studies. 3. Fraud investigation - United States - Case studies. 4. Photography, Legal - Case studies. I. Title.
HD7105.25.U6 K59 1986

Kjær Jensen, Mogens. Unges boligsituation / Mogens Kjær Jensen. København : I kommission hos Teknisk forlag, 1983. 139 p. : ill. ; 21 cm. (Publikation / Socialforskningsinstituttet, 0583-712X . 116) Bibliography: p. 134. ISBN 87-7487-228-1 : LC Card 83-189408
1. Housing - Denmark. 2. Youth - Housing - Denmark. I. Series: Socialforskningsinstituttet, Copenhagen. Publikationer, 116. II. Title.
HD7347.A3 K53 1983
NYPL [JLK 73-237 v.116]

Kjartan Jónasson. Kreppuárin á Íslandi 1930-1939 / Kjartan Jónasson. [Reykjavik] : Örn og Örlygur, 1986- v. <1 > : ill. ; 29 cm. Bibliography: v. 1, p. 153-154. LC Card 87-117468
1. Depressions - 1929 - Iceland. 2. Iceland - Economic conditions - 1918-1945. I. Title.
HB3717 1929 .K58 1986

Kjeldsen, Jens. Nørrung, Per. The producing commune /. Aalborg Ø., Denmark , 1985. 39 p. ; ISBN 87-88353-11-7 (pbk.) LC Card 87-100060 DDC 334/.6/09489 19
HD3209.A4 N67 1985

Kjellstrom, Sven B., 1945- Institutional development and technical assistance in macro-economic policy formulation : a case study of Togo / Sven B. Kjellstrom, Ayite-Fily d'Almeida. Washington, D.C., U. S.A. : World Bank, [1987] 69 p. ; 29 cm. (World Bank discussion papers . 13) ISBN 0-8213-0919-6 (pbk.) LC Card 87-14021 DDC 339.5/0966/81 19
1. Technical assistance - Togo. 2. Togo - Economic policy. 3. Togo - Economic conditions. I. D'Almeida, Ayite-Fily, 1949-. II. Title. III. Series.
HC1015 .K58 1987

Kjervik, Diane K., 1945- Women in health & illness . Philadelphia , 1986. x, 261 p. : ISBN 0-7216-2086-8 LC Card 86-6576 DDC 155.6/33 19
RC451.4.W6 W656 1986
NYPL [JLF 86-1463]

KLAASSEN, LEO H. (LEO HENDRIK), 1920-
Human behaviour in geographical space . Aldershot, Hants, England , Brookfield, Vt., U. S.A. , c1986. x, 328 p. : ISBN 0-566-00807-6 : LC Card 85-5528 DDC 338.9 19
HT391 .H785 1986 ***NYPL [JLD 86-1630]***

Klaes, Friedhelm, 1956- Informationsverhalten kleiner und mittlerer Unternehmen der elektrotechnischen Investitionsgüterindustrie bei strategischen Entscheidungen / Friedhelm Klaes. Frankfurt am Main ; New York : P. Lang, c1986. xxii, 305 p. ; 24 cm. (Marktorientierte Unternehmensführung, 0178-8183 . Bd. 4) Bibliography: p. 272-305. ISBN 3-8204-9713-7 LC Card 87-407575 DDC 658.4/03 19
1. Small business - Management - Decision making. 2. Strategic planning. 3. Marketing. I. Title. II. Series.
HD62.7 .K586 1986

Klages, Helmut. Überwindung der Sozialstaatskrise . Baden-Baden , 1984. 317 p. : ISBN 3-7890-0925-3 LC Card 84-166713
HD7179 .U35 1984

Klagge, Jay. O'Keeffe, Linda. Statistical packages for the IBM PC family /. New York , c1986. x, 162 p. : ISBN 0-07-056320-9 : LC Card 85-18213 DDC 658/.055365 19
HF1017 .O39 1986 ***NYPL [JSE 86-1876]***

Klanberg, Frank.
Haushalte mit ausgewählten staatlichen Transferzahlungen . Stuttgart , c1983. 352 p. : ISBN 3-17-007631-0 LC Card 83-117808
HC290.5.I5 H37 1983

Infratest Sozialforschung. Datenlage zur Alterssicherung . Bonn , 1984. 330 p. : LC Card 86-132439 DDC 331.25/2/0943 19
HD7105.35.G3 I54 1984

Klank, Leszek. Czynniki kształtujące poziom dochodów w gospodarstwach indywidualnych / Leszek Klank. Warszawa : Państwowe Wydawn. Naukowe, 1985. 176 p. ; 24 cm. (Problemy rozwoju wsi i rolnictwa) Summaries in Russian and English. Bibliography: p. 165-[172]. ISBN 83-01-05449-2 :
1. Land tenure - Poland. 2. Income - Poland. 3. Farmers - Poland. I. Title. ***NYPL [*QO 86-2601]***

Klant, J. J. Filosofie van de economische wetenschappen / J.J. Klant. Leiden : Nijhoff, c1987. 87 p. ; 21 cm. (Serie Wetenschapsfilosofie) Bibliography: p. 82-84. Includes index. ISBN 90-6890-105-2 : LC Card 87-169944
1. Economics - Philosophy. I. Title. II. Series.
HB72 .K55 1987

Klartext (Basel, Switzerland) "Ein Chaos wollen wir nicht" . Basel , c1985. 223 p. : ISBN 3-85787-141-5 : LC Card 86-128638
HE8689.9.S95 C57 1985

Die Klassifizierung in der Bundesrepublik Deutschland angebotener Personenkraftwagen mit multivariaten Analysemethoden /. Kiffe, Ulrich. Münster , 1984. xx, 24, 340 p. : ISBN 3-88660-148-8 LC Card 84-208133
HD9710.G42 K48 1984

Klassiker der österreichischen Nationalökonomie .
(Bd. 2) Wagner, Adolph, 1835-1917. Die Ordnung des österreichischen Staatshaushaltes--1863 /. Wien , c1984. 308 p. ; ISBN 3-85447-086-X LC Card 85-223615
HJ1065 .W34 1984

Klatt, Edmund. Langenscheidt's standard German dictionary / by Edmund Klatt [et al.]. Enl. and updated ed. New York : Langenscheidt, 1983-1984. 1341 p. ; 9 cm. CONTENTS. - 1st part: English-German / by Edmund Klatt and Dietrich Roy.--Enl. and updated ed. 1983.--2nd part: German-English / by Edmund Klatt, Gisela Klatt, Heinz Messinger.--Enl. and updated ed. 1984.
1. English language - Dictionaries - German. 2. German language - Dictionaries - English. I. Roy, Dietrich. II. Klatt, Gisela. III. Messinger, Heinz. IV. Title. V. Title: Standard German dictionary.
NYPL [JFC 86-781]

Klatt, Gisela. Klatt, Edmund. Langenscheidt's standard German dictionary /. New York , 1983-1984. 1341 p. ; ***NYPL [JFC 86-781]***

Klatt, Sigurd. Perspektiven verkehrswissenschaftlicher Forschung . Berlin , c1985. 606 p., [1] leaf of plates : ISBN 3-428-05738-4 LC Card 85-155542
HE151 .P44 1985

Klau, Friedrich. Labour market flexibility and external price shocks / by Friedrich Klau and Axel Mittelstädt. Paris, France : OECD, c1985. 60 p. : ill. ; 30 cm. (Working papers / Economics and Statistics Department . no. 24) Bibliography: p. 47-50. LC Card 86-205164 DDC 331.12 19
1. Labor supply. 2. Labor mobility. 3. Labor costs. I. Mittelstädt, Axel. II. Series: Working papers (Organisation for Economic Co-operation and Development. Dept. of Economics and Statistics) , no. 24. III. Title.
HD5707 .K54 1985

Klaus, Barbara. (joint author) Klönne, Arno. Die deutsche Arbeiterbewegung . Düsseldorf , Köln , 1980. 382 p. ; ISBN 3-424-00652-1 : LC Card 81-453558 DDC 322/.2/0943 19
HX276 .K547 ***NYPL [JLD 81-689]***

Klaus, Joachim. Entscheidungshilfen für die Infrastrukturplanung . Baden-Baden , 1984. 512 p. : ISBN 3-7890-0808-7 LC Card 84-188792
HC290.5.C3 E58 1984

Klause, Dieter. Wegweiser zur Weiterbildung : Berufskunde zum Fachwirt, Fachkaufmann, Betriebswirt / Dieter Klause ; [Herausgeber, Deutscher Industrie- und Handelstag]. Bonn :

Der Handelstag, 1982. 101 p. ; 21 cm. LC Card 83-206662
1. Employees, Training of - Germany, West. 2. Occupational training - Germany, West. I. Deutscher Industrie- und Handelstag. II. Title.
HF5549.5.T7 K58 1982

Kleff, Fritjof, 1950- Säumt keine Minute! . Mannheim , c1986. xiii, 683 p. : ISBN 3-923003-36-6 LC Card 87-115249 DDC 331/.0943/46 19
HD8460.M35 S28 1986

Kleiber, Achim W. Fachwörterbuch, Schweissen, Schneiden und verwandte Verfahren / von Achim W. Kleiber. Düsseldorf : Deutscher Verlag für Schweisstechnik, 1986- , c1985- v. ; 23 cm. Added t.p. in English: Dictionary, welding, cutting and allied processes. CONTENTS. - Bd. 1. Englisch/Deutsch. ISBN 3-87155-707-2 (Bd. 1) LC Card 86-149500 DDC 671.5/2/0331 19
1. Welding - Dictionaries. 2. Metal-cutting - Dictionaries. 3. English language - Dictionaries - German. 4. Welding - Dictionaries - German. 5. Metal-cutting - Dictionaries - German. 6. German language - Dictionaries - English. I. Title. II. Title: Schweissen, Schneiden und verwandte Verfahren. III. Title: Dictionary, welding, cutting and allied processes. IV. Title: Welding, cutting and allied processes.
TS227.5 .K54 1986 ***NYPL [JSK 86-83]***

Klein, Alfred, 1915- Probleme der staatsmonopolistischen Wirtschaftsregulierung . Rostock , 1981. 35 p. ; LC Card 86-211250
HB501 .P694 1981

KLEIN, ALFRED, 1915-
Probleme der staatsmonopolistischen Wirtschaftsregulierung . Rostock , 1981. 35 p. ; LC Card 86-211250
HB501 .P694 1981

Klein, David, 1919- Hughes, Theodore E. The parents' financial survival guide /. Tucson, Ariz. , c1987. 227 p. ; ISBN 0-89586-644-7 : LC Card 87-10233 DDC 332.024/0431 19
HG179 .H84 1987

Klein, Herbert S. A Transição incompleta . Rio de Janeiro-RJ , 1986. 2 v. ; LC Card 86-224684
HC187 .T72 1986

Klein, Ingomar. Sozialistisches Arbeitsverhalten als Leistungsverhalten /. Berlin [1984] 77 p. ; LC Card 84-250357
HD8460.5 .S694 1984

Klein, Jean, docteur ès sciences économiques. Gestion et stratégie financières internationales / Jean Klein, Bernard Marois. Paris : Dunod, c1985. v, 266 p. : ill. ; 24 cm. (Dunod entreprise, 0242-3812) Bibliography: p. [263]-266. ISBN 2-04-015504-X : LC Card 86-192918
1. International business enterprises - Finance. 2. International finance. I. Marois, Bernard. II. Title.
HG4027.5 .K58 1985

Klein, Jean H., 1938- The phone book : the ABC's of telephone communication / by Jean H. Klein. Norfolk : Donning Co., c1987. p. cm. ISBN 0-89865-542-0 (pbk.) : LC Card 87-20897 DDC 651.7/3 19
1. Telephone in business. 2. Telephone etiquette. I. Title.
HF5541.T4 K56 1987

Klein, Jennifer. Rainery, Richard. Alaska's public energy resources . [Juneau?] [1985] 8, 124, 3, 7 p. : LC Card 86-622191 DDC 333.79/09798 19
HD9502.U53 A473 1985

Klein, John F. (John Frederick), 1950- A day in the life of a commercial fisherman / by John F. Klein and Carol Gaskin ; photography by John F. Klein. Mahwah, N.J. : Troll Associates, c1988. 32 p. : col. ill. ; 24 cm. Follows a commercial fisherman through his day as he prepares his boat for a two-week fishing trip, leaves port in the Gulf of Mexico, operates navigational equipment and a sonar "fish finder," and unloads the day's catch. ISBN 0-8167-1109-7 (lib. bdg.) : LC Card 87-10949 DDC 639/.2/02373 19
1. Fishers - Juvenile literature. I. Gaskin, Carol. II. Title. III. Title: Commercial fisherman.
HD8039.F65 K57 1988

Klein, John J., 1929- Money and the economy / John J. Klein. 6th ed. San Diego : Harcourt Brace Jovanovich, c1986. xi, 560 p. : ill. ; 24 cm. Includes bibliographies and indexes. ISBN 0-15-564007-0 LC Card 85-80078 DDC 332.4/973 19
1. Money - United States. 2. Finance - United States. 3. Monetary policy - United States. I. Title.
HG540 .K57 1986 ***NYPL [JLE 86-3392]***

Klein, Maury, 1939- The life and legend of Jay Gould / by Maury Klein. Baltimore : Johns Hopkins University Press, c1986. xvi, 595 p., [24] p. of plates : ill. ; 25 cm. Includes index. Bibliography: p. 501-584. ISBN 0-8018-2880-5 (alk. paper) LC Card 85-24107 DDC 332/.092/4 B 19
1. Gould, Jay, 1836-1892. 2. Businessmen - United States - Biography. 3. Capitalists and financiers - United States - Biography. 4. Railroads - United States - History. I. Title.
HC102.5.G68 K55 1986
NYPL [JFE 86-2364]

Klein, Robert J. The Money book of money : your personal financial planner / Robert J. Klein and the editors of Money magazine.1st ed. Boston : Little, Brown, c1987. xvii, 522 p. ; 25 cm. Includes index. ISBN 0-316-49840-8 : LC Card 86-33777 DDC 332.024 19
1. Finance, Personal - United States. I. Money (Chicago, Ill.). II. Title.
HG179 .K57 1987

Klein, Rudolf. Day, Patricia. Accountabilities . London , New York , 1987. 259 p. : ISBN 0-422-79340-X : LC Card 87-164015 DDC 354.4109/2 19
HD4147 .D39 1987

Kleinaltenkamp, Michael. Engelhardt, Werner Hans. Der Direktvertrieb im Konsumgüterbereich . Stuttgart , c1984. 158 p. : ISBN 3-17-008550-6 : LC Card 84-234886
HF5415.126 .E54 1984

Kleindorfer, Paul R.
Insuring and managing hazardous risks--from Seveso to Bhopal and beyond /. Berlin , New York , c1987. ix, 534 p. : ISBN 0-387-17732-9 (U. S.) LC Card 87-4963 DDC 346.03/8 342.638 19
HG9994 .I57 1987

Optimal capacity planning under stagnating demand / by Paul R. Kleindorfer, Joachim Schwalbach. Berlin : Wissenchaftszentrum Berlin, [1985] 18, 4 leaves : ill. ; 30 cm. (Discussion papers / IIMV Strukturpolitik, 0722-6748 = IIM industrial policy . IIM/IP 85-12) "June 1985." Bibliography: leaf 18. LC Card 86-205882
1. Industrial capacity - Planning - Mathematical models. I. Schwalbach, Joachim. II. Series: Discussion papers (International Institute of Management. Industrial Policy) , IIM/IP 85-12. III. Title.
HD69.C3 K49 1985

Kleinebeckel, Arno. Unternehmen Braunkohle : Geschichte eines Rohstoffs, eines Reviers, einer Industrie im Rheinland / Arno Kleinebeckel.2., unveränderte Aufl. Köln : Rheinische Braunkohlenwerke Aktiengesellschaft, 1986. 287 p. : ill. (some col.) ; 30 cm. Bibliography: p. 282-286. ISBN 3-7743-0225-1 LC Card 86-193426
1. Lignite industry - Germany (West) - North Rhine-Westphalia - History. 2. North Rhine-Westphalia (Germany) - Industries - History. 3. North Rhine-Westphalia (Germany) - Economic conditions. I. Rheinische Braunkohlenwerke (Cologne, Germany). II. Title.
HD9559.L6 G36 1986

Kleinewefers, Henner.
Reformen für Wirtschaft und Gesellschaft : Utopien, Konzepte, Realitäten / Henner Kleinewefers. Frankfurt ; New York : Campus, c1985. 532 p. : ill. ; 22 cm. Bibliography: p. 517-532. ISBN 3-593-33466-6 LC Card 85-143393
1. Economic policy. 2. Social problems. 3. Democracy. 4. Capitalism. 5. Socialism. I. Title.
HD84 .K543 1985

Willy Büchi, 75 Jahre /. Freiburg, Schweiz , 1982. 105 p., [1] leaf of plates : ISBN 3-7278-0263-4 LC Card 83-184580
HB118 .W55 1982

Kleingartner, Archie. Human resource management in high-technology firms /. Lexington, Mass. , 1986, c1987. x, 243 p. : ISBN 0-669-13686-7 (alk. paper) LC Card 86-45556 DDC 658.3 19
HF5549 .H875 1987 ***NYPL [JLE 87-1100]***

Kleinknecht, A. Industriële innovatie in Nederland : een enquête-onderzoek / A. Kleinknecht met medewerking van H. Bieshaar ... [et al.]. Assen : Van Gorcum, 1987. viii, 140 p. ; 22 cm. Bibliography: p. 83-85. ISBN 90-232-2261-X : LC Card 87-157579
1. Technological innovations - Netherlands. 2. Research, Industrial - Netherlands. I. Bieshaar, H. II. Title.
HC329.5.T4 K58 1987

Kleinmann, Klaus, 1956- Die langfristige Entwicklung von Kommunikation und Staatsausgaben / Klaus Kleinmann. Frankfurt am Main ; New York : P. Lang, c1985. v, 194 p. : ill. ; 22 cm. (Europäische Hochschulschriften. Reihe V, Volks- und Betriebswirtschaft, 0531-7339 . Bd. 634 = vol. 634) Bibliography: p. 171-194. ISBN 3-8204-8873-1 LC Card 85-200073
1. Finance, Public - Decision making. 2. Communication policy. 3. Social choice. 4. Public goods. 5. Voting. 6. Democracy. I. Series: Europäische Hochschulschriften. Reihe V, Volks- und Betriebswirtschaft , Bd. 634. II. Title.
HJ131 .K56 1985

Klēmēs, Arist. N. (Aristeidēs N.), 1915- Hoi synetairismoi stēn Hellada / Arist. N. Klēmē. Athēna : Ekdoseis "I. Pitsilos", 1985- v. <1 > : ill., facsims., ports. ; 25 cm. Includes bibliographies and indexes. CONTENTS. - v. 1. Synergasies, prosynetairismoi, synetairismoi, apo tēn archaiotēta mechri kai to 1922. LC Card 86-228137
1. Cooperative societies - Greece - History. I. Title.
HD3531.83.A4 K56 1985

Klemm, Günther. Ökonomische Analyse von Streik und Aussperrung im Rahmen einer marktwirtschaftlichen Ordnung / Günther Klemm. Köln : Institut für Wirtschaftspolitik an der Universität zu Köln, 1983. viii, 214 p. : ill. ; 24 cm. (Untersuchungen / Institut für Wirtschaftspolitik an der Universität zu Köln . 55) Bibliography: p. 192-214. ISBN 3-921471-43-5 : LC Card 83-216635 DDC 331.89/2 19
1. Strikes and lockouts. 2. Strikes and lockouts - Economic aspects. I. Series: Untersuchungen (Universität zu Köln. Institut für Wirtschaftspolitik) , 55. II. Title.
HD5306 .K55 1983

Klemmer, Paul.
Abgrenzung von Fördergebieten / von Paul Klemmer, unter Mitarbeit von Burkhardt Bremicker. Bochum : Brockmeyer, 1983. 206 p. : ill. ; 21 cm. (Beiträge zur Struktur- und Konjunkturforschung . Bd. 20) Includes bibliographical references. ISBN 3-88339-298-7 LC Card 83-183564
1. Germany (West) - Economic conditions - 1974- - Regional disparities. 2. Regional planning - Germany, West. I. Bremicker, Burkhardt. II. Title. III. Series.
HC286.7 .K59 1983

Bremicker, Burckhardt. Analyse der Arbeitslosigkeit in den Regionen Nordrhein-Westfalens . Bochum , 1984. xx, 381 p. : ISBN 3-88339-362-2 LC Card 84-196621 DDC 331.13/794355 19
HD5780.N6 B74 1984 ***NYPL [JLD 86-2367]***

Die Wirtschaftliche Entwicklung in den Arbeitsmarktregionen des Bergischen Landes . Bochum , 1981. 401 p. : ISBN 3-88339-217-0 LC Card 82-164818 DDC 331/.0943/55 19
HD8459.N66 W57 1981
NYPL [JLD 86-1639]

Klempin, Arno. Contribution of state-directed land settlement to agricultural development : a comprehensive case study of the land settlement and Thai-German agricultural development project Saraburi / Arno Klempin. Saarbrücken : Verlag Breitenbach ; Fort Launderdale, 1979. viii, 169 p. : ill., graphs, maps ; 23 cm. (Publications of the Research Centre for International Agrarian Development ; 9) Bibliography: p. 162-169. ISBN 3-88156-121-8 LC Card 80-464363 DDC 333.3/1/593
1. Land settlement - Thailand. 2. Agriculture and state - Thailand. I. Series: Research Center for International Agrarian Development. Publications , 9. II. Title.
HD890.55 .K57 ***NYPL [JLE 80-1270]***

Kleppner, Otto, 1899-
[Advertising procedure]
Kleppner's advertising procedure. 10th ed. / Thomas Russell, Glenn Verrill, W. Ronald Lane. Englewood Cliffs, N.J. : Prentice Hall, 1987, c1988. p. cm. (The Prentice-Hall series in marketing) Rev. ed. of: Otto Kleppner's advertising procedure. 9th ed. c1986. Bibliography: p. Includes index. ISBN 0-13-516451-6 LC Card 87-19346 DDC 659.1 19
1. Advertising. I. Russell, Thomas, 1941-. II. Verrill, Glenn. III. Lane, W. Ronald, 1940-. IV. Title. V. Title:

Advertising procedure. VI. Series.
HF5823 .K45 1988

Kleppner's advertising procedure. Kleppner, Otto, 1899- [Advertising procedure.] Englewood Cliffs, N.J. , 1987, c1988. p. cm. ISBN 0-13-516451-6 LC Card 87-19346 DDC 659.1 19
HF5823 .K45 1988

Kleutghen, Paul P. Profitable inventory management strategies / by Paul P. Kleutghen ; [Alexander Hamilton Institute]. New York, NY, U. S.A. : Modern Business Reports, c1986. viii, 208 p. : ill. ; 28 cm. ISBN 0-86604-233-4 (pbk.) LC Card 86-205426 DDC 658.7/87 19
1. Inventory control. I. Alexander Hamilton Institute (U. S.). II. Title.
HD40 .K54 1986

KLEVE REGION (NORTH RHINE-WESTPHALIA, GERMANY) - ECONOMIC CONDITIONS.
Schanz, Hermann J. Der niederrheinische Wirtschaftsraum . Stuttgart , c1986. xxii, 466 p. ; ISBN 3-7910-5014-1 LC Card 87-135757 DDC 330.943/55 19
HC289.D755 S32 1986

Klever, W. N. A. Archeologie van de economie : de economische theorie in de Griekse oudheid / W.N.A. Klever. Nijmegen : Markant, 1986. 157 p. : ill. ; 24 cm. Includes bibliographical references. ISBN 90-6772-005-4 : LC Card 86-165833
1. Economics - Greece - History. I. Title.
HB77 .K54 1986

Klevmarken, N. Anders. Höj och sänk pensionsåldern / av N. Anders Klevmarken. Göteborg : Dept. of Economics, University of Göteborg, [1985?] 9 leaves : ill. ; 30 cm. (Memorandum / Dept. of Economics, University of Göteborg . nr. 94) LC Card 86-195492
1. Retirement age - Sweden. I. Series: Memorandum (Göteborgs universitet. Nationalekonomiska institutionen) , nr. 94. II. Title.
HD7203 .K57 1985

Kliachko, Valerie A. World diesel engine markets : international competition intensifies as overall growth slows / Valerie A. Kliachko. Menlo Park, Calif. (333 Ravenswood Ave., Menlo Park 94025-3476) : SRI International, Business Intelligence Program, c1985. 36 p. : ill. (some col.) ; 28 cm. (Report / SRI International, Business Intelligence Program . no. 713 (winter 1984-85)) Cover title. LC Card 87-145492 DDC 338.4/7621436 19
1. Diesel motor industry. 2. Market surveys. I. Series: Research report (Business Intelligence Program (SRI International)) , 713. II. Title.
HD9705.5.M672 K65 1985

Kli͡ava, G. I͡A., 1906- Pravovye voprosy RASU . Riga , 1979. 109, [3] p. ; LC Card 82-100548
HC337.L3 P722 1979

Kliche, Mario. Knetsch, Werner. Die industrielle Mikroelektronik-Anwendung im verarbeitenden Gewerbe der Bundesrepublik Deutschland . Haar bei München , c1986. 223 p. : ISBN 3-89090-131-X LC Card 87-132995 DDC 338/.06 19
HC290.5.A9 K524 1986

Kligene, Nerute. Raspoznavanie sluchaĭnykh protsessov s peremennoĭ strukturoĭ veroi͡atnostnykh raspredeleniĭ : materialy k seminaru pri Institute matematiki i kibernetiki AN Litovskoĭ SSR "Statisticheskie problemy upravleni͡ia" / pod redaktsieĭ L. Tel'ksnis. Vil'ni͡us : In-t matematiki i kibernetiki Akademii nauk Litovskoĭ SSR, 1986. 136 p. : ill. ; 21 cm. (Statisticheskie problemy upravleni͡ia, 0132-5302 . vyp. 76) Titles on added t.p.: Atsitiktinių procesų su kintama tikimybinių pasiskirtymų struktūra atpažinimas; Recognition of stochastic processes with the changing structure of probabilities distributions. At head of title: Institut matematiki i kibernetiki AN Litovskoĭ SSR. Institut fiziko-tekhnicheskikh problem ėnergetiki AN LitSSR. Litovskai͡a territorial'nai͡a gruppa NKAU SSSR Mezhdunarodnoĭ federatsii po avtomaticheskomu upravleni͡iu. Summary in English and Lithuanian. Bibliography: p. 128-134. LC Card 87-146330
1. Stochastic processes. I. Tel'ksnis, L. II. Title. III. Title: Atsitiktinių procesų su kintama tikimybinių pasiskirstymų struktūra atpažinimas. IV. Title: Recognition of stochastic processes with the changing structure of probabilities distributions. V. Series.
HD38 .S715 vyp.76 QA274

Klimenko, A. A. (Aleksandr Aleksandrovich) Ivanov, V. R. (Vladimir Romanovich) Proizvoditel'nost' truda i zarabotnai͡a plata v stroitel'stve sooruzheniĭ svi͡azi /. Moskva , 1985. 159 p. : LC Card 85-224803
HD9715.S72 I9 1985

Klimenko, B. I. Mezhotraslevye balansy kapitalisticheskikh stran : osobennosti postroeni͡ia i ispol'zovanie v ėkonomicheskom analize / B.I. Klimenko ; otvetstvennyĭ redaktor E.M. Chetyrkin. Moskva : "Nauka", 1986. 150 p. ; 22 cm. At head of title: Akademii͡a nauk SSSR. Ordena Trudovogo Krasnogo Znameni Institut mirovoĭ ėkonomiki i mezhdunarodnykh otnosheniĭ. Bibliography: p. 146-[149] LC Card 86-231527
1. Input-output analysis - United States. 2. Input-output analysis - Europe. I. Chetyrkin, Evgeniĭ Mikhaĭlovich. II. Title.
HC110.I57 K65 1986

Klimenko, V. L. (Vladimir Leonidovich) I͡Akovleva, O. P. (Olimpiada Pavlovna) Formirovanie i izmerenie rezervov proizvodstva /. Leningrad , 1985. 86 p. : LC Card 86-168063
HC336.25 .I25 1985

Klimley, Laura E. Eimicke, Victor W. Managing human resources . Oxford [Oxfordshire] , New York , 1987. x, 211 p. : ISBN 0-08-034768-1 (U. S.) : LC Card 86-25273 DDC 658.3 19
HF5549 .E44 1987

Klimov, I͡U. N. (I͡Uriĭ Nikolaevich) Partiĭnye organizatsii Nechernozem'i͡a v bor'be za povyshenie proizvodstvennoĭ i politicheskoĭ aktivnosti rabochego klassa v period postroeni͡ia i razviti͡ia sotsializma /. Kalinin , 1985. 152 p. ; LC Card 86-196840
HC337.R85 P36 1985

Klimov, N. A. (Nikolaĭ Andreevich) Upravlenie protsessom novovvedeniĭ v kapitalisticheskoĭ firme /. Moskva , 1985. 228 p. : LC Card 86-151912
HD58.8 .U67 1985

Kline, Harvey F. The coal of El Cerrejón : dependent bargaining and Colombian policy-making / Harvey F. Kline. University Park : Pennsylvania State University Press, c1987. viii, 216 p. : map ; 24 cm. Bibliography: p. [202]-210. Includes index. ISBN 0-271-00491-6 : LC Card 86-43038 DDC 333.8/2215/09861 19
1. Coal trade - Government policy - Colombia - Ejón Hill Region. 2. Colombia - Politics and government - 1974-. I. Title.
HD9554.C63 E3748 1987

Kling, John L. Atchison, Michael D. New financial instruments . Charlottesville, Va. (P.O. Box 3665, Charlottesville 22903) , c1985. viii, 108 p. ; LC Card 85-195578 DDC 332.63 19
HG6024.3 .A83 1985
NYPL [JLL 81-133 no.21]

Klingberg, Tage, 1942- Swedish national and local government programs for conservation of energy in buildings /. Gävle, Sweden [1982] 187 p. : ISBN 91-540-9134-9 (pbk.) LC Card 82-208802 DDC 333.79 19
HD9502.S82 S98 1982 ***NYPL [JLG 86-107]***

Klinger, Dieter. Personal travel in the U. S. : a report on findings from the 1983-1984 nationwide personal transportation study / [sponsored by the] Office of the Secretary [of Transportation], Federal Highway Administration, National Highway Traffic Safety Administration, Urban Mass Transportation Administration. Washington, D.C. : U. S. Dept. of Transportation, Federal Highway Administration ; Springfield, Va. : Available to the public through the National Technical Information Service, [1986] 2 v. : ill. ; 28 cm. Final report by Dieter Klinger and J. Richard Kuzmyak, Comsis Corp., Wheaton, Md., under Contract DTFH61-84-C-00098. "August 1986"--V. 1. "November 1986"--V. 2. LC Card 86-603072 DDC 380.5/22/0973021 19
1. Transportation - United States - Passenger traffic. I. Kuzmyak, J. Richard. II. United States. Federal Highway Administration. III. Comsis Corporation. IV. Title. V. Title: Personal travel in the United States. VI. Title: 1983-1984 nationwide personal transportation study.
HE199.9 .K535 1986

Klinkmüller, Erich. Über interdisziplinäre, sozialwissenschaftliche Forschung in den USA und andernorts / Erich Klinkmüller. Berlin : Osteuropa-Institut, 1986. 177 p. ; 21 cm. (Berichte des Osteuropa-Instituts an der Freien Universität Berlin, 0409-1477 . Heft 138. Nr. 47) Table of contents and summary also in English and Russian. Bibliography: p. 153-154. Includes indexes. ISBN 3-921374-37-5 LC Card 86-211120
1. Social sciences - Research - United States. I. Series: Berichte des Osteuropa-Instituts an der Freien Universität Berlin , Heft 138. II. Title.
HC244.A1 B4 Nr. 47 H62.5.U5

Klipstein, Michael von.
Gewandelte Werte, erstarrte Strukturen . Bonn , c1985. ix, 329 p. : ISBN 3-87831-423-X LC Card 86-117688 DDC 330/.0943 19
HD8451 .G54 1985

Der Überdruss am Überfluss : die Deutschen nach dem Wirtschaftswunder / Michael von Klipstein, Burkhard Strümpel.Originalausg. München : Olzog, c1984. 212 p. : ill. ; 18 cm. (Analysen und Perspektiven. Bd. 18) ISBN 3-7892-7194-2 LC Card 84-174408
1. Industrial sociology - Germany, West. 2. Industry - Social aspects - Germany, West. 3. Labor supply - Germany (West) - Effect of technological innovations on. I. Strumpel, Burkhard. II. Title.
HD6957.G35 K56 1984

Kloas, Jutta. Regionale Struktur des Personenverkehrs in der Bundesrepublik Deutschland im Jahre 1980 /. Berlin , 1985. ix, 320 p. : ISBN 3-428-05961-1 LC Card 86-165242
HC281 .B33 Heft 88 HE249

Klönne, Arno. Die deutsche Arbeiterbewegung : Geschichte, Ziele, Wirkungen / Arno Klönne, unter Mitarb. von Barbara Klaus u. Karl Theodor Stiller.1. Aufl. Düsseldorf ; Köln : Diederichs, 1980. 382 p. ; 22 cm. Includes index. Bibliography: p. 377-381. ISBN 3-424-00652-1 : LC Card 81-453558 DDC 322/.2/0943 19
1. Sozialdemokratische Partei Deutschlands - History. 2. Socialism in Germany - History. 3. Trade-unions - Germany - History. 4. Labor and laboring classes - Germany - History. I. Klaus, Barbara, joint author. II. Stiller, Karl-Theodor, joint author. III. Title.
HX276 .K547 ***NYPL [JLD 81-689]***

Kloepfer, Deanne. The Watt record : James Watt and the Bureau of Land Management lands / [Deanne Kloepfer, author in collaboration with Terry Sopher and Richard Rice]. Washington, D.C. : Wilderness Society, [1983] ii, 66, 9, 3 p. : ill. ; 28 cm. "October 1983"--Verso t.p. Includes bibliographical references. LC Card 86-232533 DDC 333.1/0973 19
1. United States. Bureau of Land Management. 2. United States - Public lands. 3. Conservation of natural resources - Government policy - United States. 4. Oil and gas leases - United States. 5. Watt, James G., 1938-. I. Sopher, Terry. II. Rice, Richard E. III. Wilderness Society. IV. Title.
HD183.L3 K58 1983

Klōnarēs, N. G. (Nikos G.) Ho syndikalismos kai to politiko mas provlēma / N.G. Klōnarēs. Athēnai : [Ergatikon Kentron Athēnōn], 1973. 78 p. ; 21 cm. (Syndikalistikē vivliothēkē . 1) LC Card 86-234658
1. Syndicalism - Greece. 2. Greece - Politics and government - 1967-1974. I. Ergatikon Kentron Athēnōn (Athens, Greece). II. Title. III. Series.
HD6795.5 .K57 1973

Klooster, Dale H. Allen, Warren W. Advanced automated accounting for the microcomputer /. Cincinnati , c1988. viii, 200 p. : ISBN 0-538-02690-0 (pbk.) LC Card 87-61619 DDC 657/.028/55369 19
HF5679 .A567 1988

Kloosterman, Robert. Werkloosheid in Nederland, 1920-1939 : een onderzoek naar regionale verschillen / [Robert Kloosterman]. Utrecht : HES, 1985. xiv, 351 p. : ill. ; 23 cm. Summary in English. Include index. Bibliography: p. 326-334. ISBN 90-6194-315-9 : LC Card 86-150980
1. Unemployment - Netherlands - Regional disparities. 2. Unemployment - Netherlands. 3. Netherlands - Economic conditions - 1918-1945. I. Title.
HD5792 .K56 1985 ***NYPL [JLD 86-3407]***

Kloppenberg, James T. Uncertain victory : social democracy and progressivism in European and American thought, 1870-1920 / James T. Kloppenberg. New York : Oxford University Press, 1986. x, 546 p. ; 25 cm. Includes index.

Bibliography: p. [511]-528. ISBN 0-19-503749-9 : LC Card 85-21636 DDC 320.5/315/094 19
1. Political science - Europe - History. 2. Political science - United States - History. 3. Socialism - Europe - History. 4. Socialism - United States - History. 5. Democracy - History. I. Title.
JA84.E9 K57 1986 ***NYPL [JLE 86-2574]***

Klose, Alfred, 1928- Marktwirtschaft und Gesellschaftsordnung . Berlin , c1983. 220 p., [1] leaf of plates : ISBN 3-428-05365-6 LC Card 83-191615
HB72 .M248 1983

Klose, Hans-Ulrich. Befreiung der Arbeit . Bonn , c1986. 197 p. : ISBN 3-87831-429-9 LC Card 86-194157
HD6955 .B389 1986

Klose, Roland, 1954- Die Erschliessung des US-Marktes durch Direktinvestitionen mittelständischer deutscher Unternehmungen des Investitionsgüterbereichs / vorgelegt von Roland Klose. [Würzburg? : s.n., 1983] (Würzburg : Dissertationsdruck, Schmitt & Meyer) v, 307 p. ; 21 cm. Thesis (doctoral)--Bayrische Julius-Maximilian-Universität Würzburg. Bibliography: p. 281-303. LC Card 84-195414
1. Investments, West German - United States. 2. Small business - Germany, West - Finance. 3. Capital investments - Germany, West. I. Title. II. Title: Erschliessung des U. S.-Marktes durch Direktinvestitionen mittelständischer deutscher Unternehmungen des Investitionsgüterbereichs.
HG4910 .K56 1983

Klugman, K. Buckley, K. D. (Kenneth D.) South Pacific focus . Sydney , Boston , 1986. 126 p. : ISBN 0-04-909030-5 LC Card 86-71304 DDC 387.5/065/94 19
HE945.B87 B83 1986

Klusoň, Václav. Teoretické otázky formování plánovitého řízení národního hospodářství ČSSR / Václav Klusoň. Praha : Ekonomický ústav ČSAV, 1986- v. <1 > ; 20 cm. (Výzkum. publ. VP . č. 252-) Includes bibliographies. CONTENTS. - 1. díl. Obecné otázky. LC Card 87-167771
1. Czechoslovakia - Economic policy - 1965-. 2. Central planning - Czechoslovakia. I. Series: VP , č. 252 etc. II. Title.
HC270.28 .K58 1986

Kluwer international series in engineering and computer science .
(SECS 4) Kowalski, Thaddeus J. An artificial intelligence approach to VLSI design /. Boston , c1985. x, 226 p. : ISBN 0-89838-169-X LC Card 85-7581 DDC 621.3819/5835 19
TK7874 .K675 1985 ***NYPL [JSE 86-1182]***

The Kluwer international series in engineering and computer science. VLSI, computer architecture, and digital signal processing.
Annaratone, Marco. Digital CMOS circuit design /. Boston , c1986. xv, 344 p. : ISBN 0-89838-224-6 LC Card 86-10646 DDC 621.395 19
TK7871.99.M44 A56 1986
NYPL [JSE 87-634]

Klykov, V. V. Metodiki opredeleniia ėkonomicheskoĭ ėffektivnosti kapital´nykh vlozheniĭ v sotsialisticheskikh stranakh . Moskva , 1981. 101 p. ; LC Card 82-204402
HC244.Z9 C35 1981

Knaap, G. A. van der. New technology and regional development /. London , Wolfeboro, N.H. , c1987. 188 p. : ISBN 0-7099-3106-9 : LC Card 86-23983 DDC 338.9/26 19
HC79.T4 N48 1987

Knapp, Horst. Wagner, Adolph, 1835-1917. Die Ordnung des österreichischen Staatshaushaltes--1863 /. Wien , c1984. 308 p. ; ISBN 3-85447-086-X LC Card 85-223615
HJ1065 .W34 1984

Knapp, Johannes, 1953- Argentinien und Australien : ein Vergleich ihrer sozio-ökonomischen Entwicklung : ein Beitrag zur Kritik der Dependenztheorie / Johannes Knapp, Gerlinde Vetter. Heidelberg : Esprint, c1983. 151 p. : ill. ; 21 cm. (Heidelberger Dritte welt Studien . Bd. 16) Bibliography: p. 136-151. ISBN 3-88326-129-7 LC Card 83-240132
1. Argentina - Economic conditions - 1945-1983. 2. Australia - Economic conditions - 1945-. 3. Argentina - Dependency on foreign countries. 4. Australia - Dependency on foreign countries. 5. Comparative economics. I. Vetter, Gerlinde, 1954-. II. Title. III. Series.
HC175 .K58 1983

Knapp, Manfred. Von der Bizonengründung zur ökonomisch- politischen Westintegration . Frankfurt am Main , c1984. v, 311 p. : ISBN 3-88129-640-9 LC Card 84-154481
HC286.5 .V64 1984

Knapp, Robert H., 1944- Energy economics . Englewood Cliffs, N.J. , c1987. viii, 328 p. : ISBN 0-13-277245-0 : LC Card 86-25254 DDC 333.79/0973 19
HD9502.U52 E4874 1987

Knapskog, Kåre. Økonomiske forhold ved generasjonsskifte i landbruket = The economic relations in connection with succession of generations in agriculture / av Kåre Knapskog. Oslo : Norsk institutt for landbruksøkonomisk forskning, 1986. 95 p. : ill. ; 21 cm. Summary in English. Bibliography: p. 94. "F-202-96." ISBN 82-7077-032-9 LC Card 86-231818
1. Agriculture - Economic aspects - Norway. 2. Inheritance and succession - Norway. I. Title. II. Title: Economic relations in connection with succession of generations in agriculture.
HD2012 .K6 1986

Knebel, Heinz. Neue Entwicklungen bei Arbeit, Entgelt und Führung /. Freiburg im Breisgau , c1984. 169 p. : ISBN 3-448-01480-X : LC Card 84-249237
HF5549.2.G3 N48 1984

Kneese, Allen V.
[Economics and the environment. Russian]
Ėkonomika i okruzhaiushchaia sreda / A. Niz. Moskva : "Ėkonomika", 1981. 189 p. : ill. ; 20 cm. Abridged translation of: Economics and the environment. Includes bibliographical references. LC Card 82-187223
1. Environmental policy. 2. Pollution - Economic aspects. 3. Factory and trade waste - Environmental aspects. I. Title.
HC79.E5 K57517 1981

Knepp, Jay. Tax[s]aver. Automobile / by Jay Knepp.1st ed. Menlo Park, Calif. : Lane Pub. Co., c1987. 143 p. : forms (some col.) ; 14 x 21 cm. At head of title: Sunset. On t.p. "s" in "Taxsaver" appears as a dollar sign. "A Sunset book"--Cover. Includes index. ISBN 0-376-07015-3 (pbk.) : LC Card 86-80874 DDC 343.7305/23 347.303523 19
1. Income tax - United States - Deductions - Expenses. 2. Automobiles - Taxation - United States. 3. Records - Management. I. Title. II. Title: Automobile. III. Title: Tax saver.
HJ4653.D4 K56 1987

Knetsch, Werner.
Die industrielle Anwendung der Mikroelektronik in der Bundesrepublik Deutschland, Frankreich, Grossbritannien : ein internationaler Vergleich / Werner Knetsch, Bérengère de Lestapis, Jim Northcott. Haar bei München : Markt & Technik, c1985. 142 p. : ill. ; 24 cm. Issued by the VDI-Technologiezentrum Informationstechnik. ISBN 3-89090-121-2 : LC Card 86-106735
1. Automation - Germany (West). 2. Automation - France. 3. Automation - Great Britain. I. Lestapis, Bérengère de. II. Northcott, Jim. III. VDI-Informationszentrum Informationstechnik. IV. Title.
HC290.5.A9 K5 1985

Die industrielle Mikroelektronik-Anwendung im verarbeitenden Gewerbe der Bundesrepublik Deutschland : nationaler Teil / Bearbeiter, Werner Knetsch, Mario Kliche ; unter Mitarbeit von Hermann Breudecke ... [et al.]. Haar bei München : Markt & Technik, c1986. 223 p. : ill. ; 24 cm. Bibliography: p. 123-127. ISBN 3-89090-131-X LC Card 87-132995 DDC 338/.06 19
1. Automation - Germany (West). 2. Automation - France. 3. Automation - Great Britain. I. Kliche, Mario. II. Title.
HC290.5.A9 K524 1986

Kniazeva, G. A. (Galina Alekseevna)
Kompleksnoe ispol´zovanie drevesiny v Komi ASSR / G.A. Kniazeva, P.I. Kalistratov. Syktyvkar : Akademiia nauk SSSR, Komi filial, 1986. 75 p. : ill. ; 22 cm. Bibliography: p. 75. LC Card 86-233834
1. Forest products industry - Russian S.F.S.R. - Komi A.S.S.R. I. Kalistratov, P. I. (Petr Ivanovich). II. Title.
HD9765.S653 K665 1986

Kniazhinskiĭ, V. B. (Vsevolod Borisovich)
Zapadnoevropeĭskaia integratsiia . Moskva , 1986. 205, [3] p. ; LC Card 86-219781 DDC 327.1/7/094 19
HC241 .Z365 1986

Knieps, Günter.
Deregulierung im Luftverkehr : neuere Entwicklungen in der Wettbewerbstheorie und ihre Auswirkungen im Linienverkehr / von Günter Knieps. Tübingen : J.C.B. Mohr, c1987. 69 p. ; 23 cm. (Vorträge und Aufsätze / Walter Eucken Institut, 0509-6065 . 111) Based on the author's Habilitationsvortrag, originally delivered at the Universität Basel, February 1985. Bibliography: p. [65]-69. ISBN 3-16-345148-9 LC Card 87-121052 DDC 387.7/1 19
1. Aeronautics, Commercial - Deregulation. 2. Airlines - Deregulation. I. Series: Vorträge und Aufsätze (Walter Eucken Institut) , 111. II. Title.
HE9776 .K6 1987

Entstaatlichung im Telekommunikationsbereich : eine theoretische und empirische Analyse der technologischen, ökonomischen und institutionellen Einflussfaktoren / Günter Knieps. Tübingen : J.C.B. Mohr, 1985. xi, 205 p. : ill. ; 24 cm. (Wirtschaftswissenschaftliche und wirtschaftsrechtliche Untersuchungen, 0083-7113 . 21) "Diese Arbeit wurde im Wintersemester 1984/85 von der Rechts- und Wirtschaftswissenschaftlichen Fakultät der Universität Bern als Habilitationsschrift angenommen"--P. [v] Bibliography: p. [193]-202. Includes index. ISBN 3-16-344955-7 LC Card 86-156485
1. Telecommunication - Germany, West. 2. Privatization - Germany (West). 3. Privatization - United States. 4. Telecommunication - Law and legislation - Germany, West. I. Title. II. Series.
HE8154 .K55 1985

Kniesner, Thomas J.
Fleisher, Belton M. Principles of macroeconomics /. Dubuque, Iowa , c1987. xix, 427 p. : ISBN 0-697-01035-X (pbk.) LC Card 86-72959 DDC 339 19
HB172.5 .F545 1987

Fleisher, Belton M. Principles of microeconomics /. Dubuque, Iowa , c1987. xxi, 458 p. : ISBN 0-697-01038-4 (pbk.) LC Card 86-72958 DDC 338.5 19
HB172 .F54 1987

Knight, Misha G. How to do business with Russians : a handbook and guide for Western world business people / Misha G. Knight ; foreword by Tom Sealy. New York : Quorum Books, 1987. xxiv, 311 p. : ill. ; 25 cm. Bibliography: p. [301]-306. Includes index. ISBN 0-89930-211-4 (lib. bdg. : alk. paper) LC Card 86-30396 DDC 658.8/48/0947 19
1. Soviet Union - Foreign economic relations - United States. 2. United States - Foreign relations - Soviet Union. 3. East-West trade (1945-). 4. Soviet Union - Economic conditions - 1976-. I. Title.
HF1558.5.U6 K56 1987

Knight, Patrick A., 1954- Saal, Frank E., 1947- Industrial/organizational psychology . Pacific Grove, Calif. , c1988. xxx, 578 p. : ISBN 0-534-08214-9 : LC Card 87-21824 DDC 158.7 19
HF5548.8 .S225 1988

Knightley, Phillip. The Vestey affair / Phillip Knightley. London : Macdonald, 1981. 159 p., [8] p. of plates : ill. ; 23 cm. ISBN 0-354-04708-6 : LC Card 81-193209 DDC 343.4104/092/2 344.10340922 19
1. Corporations - Taxation - Great Britain. 2. Vestey family. I. Title.
HD2753.G7 K55 1981

Knights, David. Gender and the labour process /. Aldershot, Hampshire, Eng. , Brookfield, Vt., U. S.A. , c1986. vii, 186 p. ; ISBN 0-566-00999-4 : LC Card 85-21977 DDC 331.4 19
HD6060.6 .G45 1986 ***NYPL [JLD 86-3900]***

Knights, raiders, and targets : the impact of the hostile takeover / edited by John C. Coffee, Jr., Louis Lowenstein, Susan Rose-Ackerman. New York : Oxford University Press, 1987. p. cm. Bibliography: p. Includes index. ISBN 0-19-504405-3 (alk. paper) LC Card 86-33293 DDC 338.8/3 19
1. Consolidation and merger of corporations. 2. Corporate reorganizations. 3. Tender offers (Securities).

I. Coffee, John C., 1944-. II. Lowenstein, Louis. III. Rose-Ackerman, Susan.
HD2746.5 .K58 1987

KNIT GOODS INDUSTRY - BULGARIA - SOFIA - HISTORY.
Kadiev, Ivan. Khronika za "Proletariĭ" /. [Sofia] , 1985. 140, [3] p., [32] p. of plates : LC Card 86-195264
HD9969.K7 B855 1985

KNIT GOODS INDUSTRY - SWITZERLAND - HISTORY.
Tanner, Albert. Das Schiffchen fliegt, die Maschine rauscht . Zürich , c1985. 214 p. : ISBN 3-293-00084-3 LC Card 86-124152
HD9865.S9 T36 1985

KNIT GOODS INDUSTRY - UNITED STATES.
Vargish, George. What's made in the U. S.A.? /. New Brunswick, U. S.A. , c1988. 160 p. : ISBN 0-88738-187-1 LC Card 87-19164 DDC 382/.3/0973 19
HF1716 .V37 1988

Knitter, Udo, 1931- Rahmentarifverträge, Gehaltstarifverträge, Vermögensbildungstarifverträge, Tabelle der Kündigungsfristen, Auslösungssätze für die technischen und kaufmännischen Angestellten und für die Poliere und Schachtmeister des Baugewerbes im Gebiet der Bundesrepublik Deutschland /. Düsseldorf , 1977. 102 p. ; ISBN 3-8041-1158-0 LC Card 85-166026
HD6698.R315 R34 1977

KNITTING, MACHINE - HISTORY.
Tanner, Albert. Das Schiffchen fliegt, die Maschine rauscht . Zürich , c1985. 214 p. : ISBN 3-293-00084-3 LC Card 86-124152
HD9865.S9 T36 1985

Knodel, John E.
Demographic behavior in the past : a study of 14 German village populations in the eighteenth and nineteenth centuries / John E. Knodel. Cambridge [Cambridgeshire] ; New York : Cambridge University Press, 1988. p. cm. (Cambridge studies in population, economy, and society in past time . 6) Bibliography: p. Includes index. ISBN 0-521-32715-6 LC Card 87-20601 DDC 304.6/0943 19
1. Germany - Population - History - 18th century. 2. Germany - Population - History - 19th century. 3. Villages - Germany - History - 18th century. 4. Villages - Germany - History - 19th century. 5. Germany - Population, Rural - History - 18th century. 6. Germany - Population, Rural - History - 19th century. I. Title. II. Series.
HB3595 .K53 1988

Thailand's reproductive revolution : rapid fertility decline in a Third-World setting / John Knodel, Apichat Chamratrithirong, Nibhon Debavalya. Madison, Wis. : University of Wisconsin Press, c1987. xiii, 251 p. : map ; 24 cm. (Social demography) Bibliography: p. 231-244. Includes index. ISBN 0-299-11050-8 LC Card 87-8172 DDC 304.6/32/09593 19
1. Fertility, Human - Thailand. 2. Demographic transition - Thailand. I. Aphichat Chamratrithirong, 1948-. II. Nibhon Debavalya. III. Title. IV. Series.
HB1054.55.A3 K576 1987

Knödgen, Gabriele, 1949- Umweltschutz und industrielle Standortentscheidung / Gabriele Knödgen. Frankfurt/Main ; New York : Campus, c1982. 219 p. : ill. ; 21 cm. (Arbeitsberichte des Wissenschaftszentrums Berlin, Internationales Institut für Umwelt und Gesellschaft) Originally presented as the author's thesis (doctoral)--Gesamthochschule Kassel, 1981. Bibliography: p. 208-219. ISBN 3-593-33158-6 LC Card 83-110653
1. Pollution - Developing countries. 2. Factory and trade waste - Environmental aspects - Developing countries. 3. Environmental policy - Developing countries. I. Title. II. Series.
HC59.72.P55 K58 1982

Knoll AG (Ludwigshafen am Rhein, Germany)
100 Jahre im Dienst der Gesundheit, 1886-1986 /. Ludwigshafen am Rhein , c1986. 159 p. : LC Card 87-408744 DDC 338.7/616151/0943 19
HD9669.9.K56 A15 1986

KNOLL AG (LUDWIGSHAFEN AM RHEIN, GERMANY) - HISTORY.
100 Jahre im Dienst der Gesundheit, 1886-1986 /. Ludwigshafen am Rhein , c1986. 159 p. : LC Card 87-408744 DDC 338.7/616151/0943 19
HD9669.9.K56 A15 1986

Knoop, Jens. Online-Kostenrechnung für die CIM-Planung : prozessorientierte Kostenrechnung zur Ablaufplanung flexibler Fertigungssysteme / von Jens Knoop. Berlin : E. Schmidt, c1986. 242 p. : 53 ill. ; 25 cm. (Betriebliche Informations- und Kommunikationssysteme . Bd. 5) Bibliography: p. 223-236. Includes index. ISBN 3-503-02569-3 LC Card 86-227596
1. Cost accounting - Data processing. I. Title. II. Series.
HF5686.C8 K5835 1986

Knop, Hans, Prof. Dr. sc. Die Energiewirtschaft der DDR und die Planung ihrer künftigen Entwicklung / Hans Knop. Berlin : Verlag Die Wirtschaft, 1960. 239 p. : ill. ; 22 cm. (Volkswirtschaftsplanung . Heft 2) Bibliography: p. 224-234. LC Card 87-407618 DDC 333.79/0943 19
1. Energy policy - Germany, East. 2. Energy development - Germany (East). I. Series: Volkswirtschaftsplanung (Berlin, Germany) , Heft 2. II. Title.
HD9502.G452 K58 1960

Knopf, Jeffrey W. Ferrari, Paul L. U. S. arms exports . Washington, DC , c1987. xii, 342 p. : ISBN 0-931035-12-0 (pbk.) LC Card 87-80032 DDC 382/.456234/0971 19
HD9743.U6 F47 1987

Knöpfel, Eckehardt. Werkbuch Jugendarbeitslosigkeit : eine Chance für die Jugend? / Eckehardt Knöpfel ; mit Beiträgen von Ernst Albrecht, Theodor Schober und Josef Stingl. Wuppertal : R. Brockhaus, c1983. 168 p. : ill. ; 21 cm. (ABCteam. 855) Bibliography: p. 162-165. Includes index. ISBN 3-417-12855-2 (pbk.) LC Card 87-672977
1. Unemployment - Germany (West). 2. Youth - Employment - Germany, West. I. Albrecht, Ernst, 1930-. II. Schober, Theodor. III. Stingl, Josef, 1919-. IV. Title.
HD5779 .K59x 1983

Knörndel, Klaus-Dieter. Hummel, Marlies. Subsidiaritätsprinzip als Leitlinie für einen Subventionsabbau . München , 1985. xiii, 306 p. ; ISBN 3-88512-003-8 : LC Card 86-125424
HC290.5.S9 H85 1985

Knorr, Peter. Messwerte der Informationsnachfrage in komplexen Beurteilungsprozessen / Peter Knorr. Kiel : Wissenschaftsverlag Vauk, 1986. xvi, 241 p. : ill. ; 21 cm. Bibliography: p. 221-241. ISBN 3-922553-77-X LC Card 86-149044
1. Information theory in economics. 2. Consumers' preferences. I. Title.
HB133 .K59 1986

KNOW-HOW ASSISTANCE AGREEMENTS. see **FOREIGN LICENSING AGREEMENTS.**

Know your government (New York, N.Y.)
Cutrona, Cheryl. The Department of Labor /. [New York] , c1988. 95 p. : ISBN 0-87754-844-7 LC Card 87-24906 DDC 353.83 19
HD8066 .C85 1988

Stefany, Wallace Charles. The Department of Transportation /. New York, NY , c1988. p. cm. ISBN 0-87754-847-1 LC Card 87-24924 DDC 353.86 19
HE206.3 .S73 1988

Van Fleet, Alanson A. The Tennessee Valley Authority /. New York , c1987. 92 p. : ISBN 1-555-46123-9 : LC Card 86-31738 DDC 353.0082/3/09768 19
HD9685.U7 T385 1987

Wolman, Paul. The U. S. Mint /. New York , c1987. 92 p. : ISBN 0-87754-829-3 (lib. bdg.) : LC Card 86-31720 DDC 353.0082/2 19
HG459 .W65 1987

Knowledge and class . Resnick, Stephen A. Chicago , c1987. vii, 352 p. ; ISBN 0-226-71021-1 LC Card 86-32631 DDC 335.4 19
HB97.5 .R48 1987

Knowledge development in marketing . Bloom, Paul N. Lexington, Mass. , c1987. xvi, 238 p. ; ISBN 0-669-12581-4 (alk. paper) LC Card 85-45938 DDC 658.83 19
HF5415.2 .B57 1987

KNOWLEDGE, THEORY OF - CONGRESSES.
Cambio cultural e imagen del hombre /. Bilbao, España , c1984. 248 p. ; ISBN 84-271-1384-6 LC Card 85-234026
CB245 .C29 1984 ***NYPL [JFD 86-6394]***

Knox, Albert H. What homebuyers should know about buying a home / Albert H. Knox. 1st ed. New York : Vantage Press, c1987. vii, 192 p. : ill. ; 24 cm. Includes index. ISBN 0-533-06883-5 : LC Card 85-91377 DDC 643/.12 19
1. House buying - United States. 2. Mortgage loans - United States. 3. Housing - Finance. I. Title.
HD1379 .K656 1987

Knudsen, Jon Paschen. Boligstandard : variasjoner innen og mellom byer / av Jon Paschen Knudsen. Oslo : Statistisk sentralbyrå : I kommisjon hos H. Aschehoug og Universitetsforlaget, 1984. 66 p. : ill. ; 30 cm. (Rapporter fra Statistisk sentralbyrå, 0332-8422 . 84/13) Bibliography: p. 55. ISBN 82-537-2088-2 : LC Card 85-125379
1. Housing - Norway - Statistics. I. Title. II. Series.
HD7349.A3 K58 1984

Knutson, Ronald D.
Cooperative involvement in issues of domestic farm policy / by Ronald D. Knutson, William E. Black, Roy B. Davis. College Station, Tex. : Dept. of Agricutural Economics, Texas Agricultural Experiment Station, Texas A&M University System, 1986. 59 p. : ill. ; 28 cm. (Departmental information report . no. 86-4) "Department of Agricultural Economics, Texas Agricultural Experiment Station, Texas A&M University System ... cooperating with Agricultural Cooperative Service, U. S. Department of Agriculture." Bibliography: p. 59. LC Card 86-623063 DDC 338.1/8764 19
1. Agriculture, Cooperative - Government policy - Texas. 2. Agriculture and state - Texas. I. Black, William E. II. Davis, Roy B. III. Texas Agricultural Experiment Station. Dept. of Agricultural Economics. IV. United States. Agricultural Cooperative Service. V. Series: Departmental information report (Texas Agricultural Experiment Station. Dept. of Agricultural Economics) , DIR 86-4. VI. Title.
HD1491.U6 T45 1986

Federal marketing programs in agriculture . Danville, Ill. , c1983. x, 326 p. ; ISBN 0-8134-2292-2 : LC Card 83-80130
NYPL [JLE 86-4572]

Ko radnike povezuje lažnim koncima . Pavlović, Dragiša, 1943- Beograd , 1984. 414 p. ; LC Card 84-178578
HC407.Z9 L36 1984

Ko, Tun-hwa, 1921- Sea lane security studies . Taipei, Taiwan, Republic of China , 1986. 100 p. ; LC Card 87-133640 DDC 359/.03 19
HE327 .S435 1986

Kobayashi, Kaoru, 1931- Japan, the most misunderstood country / "Maurie" Kaoru Kobayashi. 1st ed. Tokyo : Japan Times, 1984. ix, 165 p. ; 21 cm. "July 1984." At head pf title: Articles on Japanese society, economy, management, organization and labor. ISBN 4-7890-0247-0
1. Japan - Economic conditions - 1945-. 2. Japan - Social life and customs. 3. Management - Japan. 4. Industrial organization - Japan. 5. Labor and laboring classes - Japan. I. Title. ***NYPL [JLD 86-1398]***

Koblencz, József. A vállalat rendszerképe / Koblencz József. Budapest : Építésügyi Tájékoztatási Központ, 1984. 179 p. : ill. ; 22 cm. Bibliography: p. 165-179. ISBN 963-512-143-1 : LC Card 86-186873
1. Industrial organization. 2. Business enterprises. I. Title.
HD37.H82 K63 1984

Kóbor, Kálmán. A hús- és a tejgazdaság jellemző vonásai Dániában / Kóbor Kálmán. Budapest : Agrárgazdasági Kutató Intézet, 1984. 111 p. : map ; 29 cm. (Agrárgazdasági Kutató Intézet, 0209-5696 . 1984/9) Bibliography: p. 87-93. ISBN 963-491-183-8 LC Card 86-198770
1. Meat industry and trade - Denmark. 2. Dairy products industry - Denmark. I. Series: Agrárgazdasági Kutató Intézet (Series) , 1984/9. II. Title.
HD9425.D4 K6 1984

KOCE-TV (Television station : Huntington Beach, Calif.) Marketing. Fountain Valley, CA , 1985. 1 videocassette (30 min.) : LC Card 87-705967 DDC 658.8 11
HF5415

Koch-Arzberger, Claudia. Die schwierige Integration : die bundesrepublikanische Gesellschaft und ihre 5 Millionen Ausländer / Claudia Koch-Arzberger. Opladen : Westdeutscher Verlag, c1985. 211 p. : ill. ; 23 cm. (Beiträge zur sozialwissenschaftlichen Forschung, 0175-615X . Bd. 80) Bibliography: p. 197-211. ISBN 3-531-11785-8 LC Card 86-101159 DDC 331.6/2/0943 19
1. Alien labor - Germany, West. 2. Alien labor - Housing - Germany (West). I. Title. II. Series.
HD8458.A2 K587 1985

Koch, Carlos. Cisneros C., Antonio. La mujer trabajadora . La Paz, Bolivia [1984] 131 leaves : LC Card 85-129000 DDC 331.4/0984 19
HD6121 .C58 1984 ***NYPL [JLF 86-1704]***

Koch, Harry Walter, 1909-
A California small business handbook / by Harry Walter Koch. Completely rev. 4th ed. [San Francisco] : Ken-Book, c1986. 174 p. : ill. ; 28 cm. Rev. ed. of: A handbook for California small business men. c1968. Includes index. ISBN 0-910553-06-8 (pbk.) : LC Card 87-167776 DDC 658/.022/09794 19
1. Small business - California - Handbooks, manuals, etc. I. Koch, Harry Walter, 1909- Handbook for California small business men. II. Title.
HD2346.U52 C25 1986

Handbook for California small business men. Koch, Harry Walter, 1909- A California small business handbook / by Harry Walter Koch. Completely rev. 4th ed. [San Francisco] , c1986. 174 p. : ISBN 0-910553-06-8 (pbk.) : LC Card 87-167776 DDC 658/.022/09794 19
HD2346.U52 C25 1986

Koch, Hasso B. Funktions- und Sozialstrukturen auf Containerschiffen / Hasso B. Koch. Frankfurt am Main ; New York : P. Lang, c1986. vi, 542 p. : ill. ; 22 cm. (Europäische Hochschulschriften, 0721-3379. Reihe XXII, Soziologie . Bd. 119 = vol. 119 = vol. 119) Bibliography: p. 496-542. ISBN 3-8204-9334-4 LC Card 86-194048
1. Container ships. 2. Unitized cargo systems. 3. Organizational change. 4. Freight and freightage. I. Title.
HE566.C6 K63 1986

Koch, Helmut, 1919-
Neuere Entwicklungen in der Unternehmenstheorie . Wiesbaden , c1982. xiii, 290 p. : ISBN 3-409-39810-4 LC Card 87-672661
HD35 .N4814x 1982

Unternehmenstheorie als Entscheidungshilfe / Helmut Koch. Wiesbaden : Gabler, c1987. 199 p. : ill. ; 25 cm. Bibliography: p. 189-194. Includes indexes. ISBN 3-409-13908-7 LC Card 87-143813 DDC 658.4/2 19
1. Entrepreneurship. 2. Decision-making. I. Title.
HB615 .K63 1987

Koch, Manfred. Gesellschaftliches Selbstverständnis und politische Orientierung der Freien Berufe . Nürnberg , 1978. 144 p. : LC Card 86-170378
HD8038.G32 B384 1978

Koch, Thilo. Müllverwertung und -Beseitigung in Baden-Württemberg : Probleme, Modelle und Lösungsansätze / [Verfasser, Thilo Koch und Jürgen Seeberger, Irene Reifenhäuser]. Stuttgart : Die Grünen Baden-Württemberg, 1984. ii, 177 p. : ill. ; 21 cm. Includes bibliographies. LC Card 84-158868
1. Refuse and refuse disposal - Government policy - Germany (West) - Baden-Württemberg. I. Seeberger, Jürgen. II. Reifenhäuser, Irene. III. Title.
HD4485.G32 B335 1984

Koch, Timothy W. Bank management / Timothy W. Koch. Chicago : Dryden Press, [1987], c1988. xviii, 717 p. : ill. ; 24 cm. Includes bibliographies and indexes. ISBN 0-03-004773-0 LC Card 87-6761 DDC 332.1/068 19
1. Bank management. I. Title.
HG1615 .K625 1988

Koch, Walter, 1942- Raiffeisen, F. W. (Friedrich Wilhelm), 1818-1888. [Correspondence.] Briefe . Wien , 1986. 207 p. : ISBN 0-370-40867-2 LC Card 87-139235 DDC 332.1/092/4 B 19
HG1552.R35 A4 1986

Koch, Walter A. S. Staat, Steuern und Finanzausgleich . Berlin , c1984. 452 p., [1] leaf of plates : ISBN 3-428-05513-6 LC Card 84-166906
HJ1120 .S73 1984

Kochan, Thomas A. The transformation of American industrial relations / Thomas A. Kochan, Harry C. Katz, Robert B. McKersie. New York : Basic Books, c1986. viii, 287 p. ; 26 cm. Bibliography: p. 254-273. Includes index. ISBN 0-465-08696-9 : LC Card 85-47502 DDC 331/.0973 19
1. Industrial relations - United States - History - 20th century. 2. Labor policy - United States - History - 20th century. I. Katz, Harry Charles, 1951-. II. McKersie, Robert B. III. Title.
HD8072 .K67 1986

Kochetkov, Andreĭ Vasil'evich.
Territorial'no-proizvodstvennyĭ kompleks . Moskva , 1982. 107 p. : LC Card 83-200414
HC337.R852 K3685 1982

Köchling, Annegret, 1944- Bildschirmarbeit : Gesundheitsregeln und Gesundheitsschutz / Annegret Köchling. Köln : Bund, c1985. 212 p. : ill. ; 21 cm. (Reihe der Hans-Böckler-Stiftung, Wissenschaft im Arbeitnehmerinteresse . Bd. 3) Bibliography: p. 197-212. ISBN 3-7663-0853-X
1. Industrial hygiene - Germany, West. 2. Office management - Hygienic aspects. 3. Occupational diseases - Germany (West). I. Series: Wissenschaft im Arbeitnehmerinteresse , Bd. 3. II. Title.
NYPL [JLD 87-392]

Kochubeeva, M. T. (Mariīa Tikhonovna)
Ėkonomika, organizatsiīa i planirovanie spirtovogo i likerno-vodochnogo proizvodstva / M.T. Kochubeeva. Moskva : Pishchevaīa promyshl., 1977. 342 p. : ill. ; 21 cm. Authorized for instructional purposes. Bibliography: p. 338-[339] LC Card 82-122783
1. Alcoholic beverage industry - Soviet Union. I. Title.
HD9365.S652 K63 1977

Kock, Suzan de, 1949- Milieuvervuiling en milieubeleid economisch bekeken / Suzan de Kock. Antwerpen : Nederlandsche Boekhandel, [1977] 140 p. ; 22 cm. (Leefmilieu nu ; 13) Bibliography: p. 131-134. ISBN 90-289-0313-1 : LC Card 78-384758
1. Environmental policy - Belgium. 2. Pollution - Economic aspects - Belgium. 3. Environmental policy - Netherlands. 4. Pollution - Economic aspects - Netherlands. I. Title.
HC320.E5 K6 ***NYPL [JLD 80-3195]***

Kocka, Jürgen.
Arbeiter und Bürger im 19. Jahrhundert . München , 1986. xiv, 342 p. ; ISBN 3-486-52871-8 LC Card 86-212379
HD8376 .A72 1986

Europäische Arbeiterbewegungen im 19. Jahrhundert . Göttingen , c1983. 169 p. ; ISBN 3-525-33488-5 (pbk.) LC Card 87-672976
HD8378 .E97x 1983

Lohnarbeit und Klassenbildung : Arbeiter und Arbeiterbewegung in Deutschland 1800-1875 / Jürgen Kocka. Berlin : J.H.W. Dietz, c1983. 207 p. ; 18 cm. Includes bibliographical references. ISBN 3-8012-0088-4 LC Card 83-169041
1. Labor and laboring classes - Germany - History - 19th century. 2. Germany - Economic conditions - 19th century. I. Title.
HD8449 .K63 1983

Kockázat és társadalom / a kötetet szerkesztette, Vári Anna. Budapest : Akadémiai Kiadó, 1987. 309 p. : ill. ; 20 cm. (Rendszerkutatási tanulmányok, 0139-2352 . 3) Selected papers of a conference held at the Magyar Tudományos Akadémia, Jan. 31-Feb. 1, 1984. Includes bibliographies. ISBN 963-05-4450-4 : LC Card 87-425562
1. Risk. 2. Risk management. I. Vári, Anna. II. Magyar Tudományos Akadémia. III. Series.
HD61 .K6 1987

A kockázat, haszon és a termelési szerkezet összefüggése /. Vörös, József. Pécs , 1983. 77 leaves : LC Card 85-111246
HD61 .V67 1983

Kockelke, Wilhelm. Untersuchung der Vorfahrtregelung "Rechts vor Links" unter dem Aspekt der Verkehrssicherheit / Wilhelm Kockelke, Jürgen Steinbrecher. Bergisch Gladbach : Bundesanstalt für Strassenwesen, Bereich Unfallforschung, [1983] 63, 3 p. : ill. ; 21 cm. (Forschungsberichte der Bundesanstalt für Strassenwesen, Bereich Unfallforschung, 0173-7066 . 90) "August 1983." Bibliography: p. 59-62. LC Card 84-147884
1. Roads - Germany (West) - Right of way. 2. Roads - Germany (West) - Interchanges and intersections. 3. Traffic safety - Germany (West) - Cologne. I. Steinbrecher, Jürgen. II. Title. III. Series.
HE363.G32 U744 1983

Kodinov, Stoil.
Dŭrzhavno-monopolistichesko regulirane na mezhdunarodnite ikonomicheski otnosheniīa /. Sofiīa , 1986. 273 p. ; LC Card 86-195948
HF1411 .D86 1986

Parichno-kreditni i finansovi otnosheniīa v sistemata na sŭvremenniīa dŭrzhavno-monopolisticheski kapitalizŭm /. Sofiīa , 1985. 245 p. : LC Card 86-153156
HG3881 .P2936 1985

Koeder, Kurt W. Berufsbegleitendes Studium : Studienkonzeptionen, historische Entwicklung und vergleichende Betrachtung / Kurt W. Koeder ; mit einem Vorwort von Barbara Hopf. Grafenau/Württ. : Expert Verlag, c1983. 286 p. : ill. ; 21 cm. (Beruf + Bildung . Bd. 9) Bibliography: p. 259-284. ISBN 3-88508-901-7 LC Card 84-185882
1. Occupational training - History. 2. Vocational education - History. 3. Adult education - History. I. Title. II. Series.
HD5715 .K63 1983

Köhler, Claus. Wirtschaftspolitik und wirtschaftliche Entwicklung . Bonn , c1985. xii, 248 p. : ISBN 3-87831-405-1 LC Card 85-142846
HD75 .W57 1985

Kölner bankwirtschaftliche Studien.
(Bd. 6) Reuschenbach, Ruth. Ziele, Instrumente und Bedingungen der Geschäftsstellenorganisation im filialisierten Universalbankbetrieb /. Köln , c1984. 385 p. ; ISBN 3-87951-122-5 LC Card 85-131689
HG1616.B7 R48 1984

(Bd. 7) Wiegel, Klaus Dieter. Rentabilität und Risiko im Kreditgeschäft der Banken . Köln , c1985. 342 p. : ISBN 3-87951-125-X LC Card 87-140074 DDC 332.1/753 19
HG1641 .W54 1985

(Bd. 8) Tüchter, Ulrich. Cash Management . Köln , c1985. 122 p. : ISBN 3-87951-126-8 LC Card 87-152212 DDC 332.1/2/0681 19
HG4028.C45 T83 1985

König, Heinz, 1927-
Kontrolltheoretische Ansätze in makroökonometrischen Modellen /. Frankfurt am Main , New York , c1985. 170 p. : ISBN 3-8204-8314-4 LC Card 86-156081
HB3732 .K68 1985

Mathematische Wirtschaftstheorie : mit einer Einführung in die konvexe Analysis / Heinz König, Michael Neumann. Königstein/Ts. : Hain, c1986. x, 239 p. : ill. ; 23 cm. (Mathematical systems in economics. 100) Bibliography: p. 232-239. ISBN 3-445-02393-X : LC Card 86-188816
1. Economics, Mathematical. 2. Equilibrium (Economics). 3. Convex sets. 4. Fixed point theory. I. Neumann, Michael, 1950-. II. Title.
HB135 .K66 1986

Koepke, Frank J., 1929- Stover, Vergil G., 1933- Transportation and land development /. Englewood Cliffs, N.J. , c1988. xiii, 239 p. : ISBN 0-13-930413-4 : LC Card 87-11419 DDC 625.7/25 19
HE335 .S76 1988

Koepp, Cynthia J. Work in France . Ithaca , 1986. 576 p. : ISBN 0-8014-1697-3 (alk. paper) LC Card 85-22352 DDC 331/.0944 19
HD8428 .W67 1986 ***NYPL [JLE 86-1960]***

Körner, Heiko. Die Zukunft der Globalsteuerung /. Bern , c1986. 268 p. ; ISBN 3-258-03573-3 : LC Card 86-182288
HC286.7 .Z82 1986

Körner, Peter. Im Teufelskreis der Verschuldung . Hamburg , 1984. 261 p. : ISBN 3-88506-126-0 LC Card 85-131681
HG3881.5.I58 I37 1984

Die Körperschaftsteuer in der Europäischen Gemeinschaft . Lutz, Stefan. Pfaffenweiler , 1984. xii, 346 p. : ISBN 3-89085-037-5 : LC Card 85-142851
HD2753.E8 L87 1984

Koestenbaum, Peter, 1928- The heart of business : ethics, power, and philosophy / by Peter Koestenbaum. San Francisco : Saybrook

Pub. Co. ; New York, NY : Distributed by Norton, c1987. xiii, 368 p. : ill. ; 24 cm. ISBN 0-933071-15-9 : LC Card 87-13665 DDC 658.4/09 19
1. Business. 2. Philosophy. 3. Intellect. 4. Interpersonal communication. 5. Leadership. 6. Business ethics. I. Title.
HF5351 .K584 1987

Kofler, Herbert. Die Prüfung der Geschäftsführung : Entwicklung, Möglichkeiten und Grenzen / Herbert Kofler. Wien : Industrieverlag P. Linde, 1985. 196 p. ; 24 cm. Bibliography: p. 177-193. Includes index. ISBN 3-85122-183-4 : LC Card 86-203497
1. Auditing, Internal. I. Title.
HF5668.25 .K68 1985

Kofler, Leo. Beherrscht uns die Technik? : technologische Rationalität im Spätkapitalismus / Leo Kofler ; mit einer Einleitung von Werner Seppmann. Hamburg : VSA-Verlag, 1983. 160 p. ; 21 cm. Includes bibliographical references. ISBN 3-87975-249-4 LC Card 84-181044
1. Labor supply - Effect of technological innovations on. 2. Microelectronics - Social aspects. 3. Automation. 4. Technological innovations. I. Title.
HD6331 .K685 1983

KOFO (Series) .
(Nr. 006) Lee, Mu-Choon. Entwicklungen in der Umweltpolitik Südkoreas im Widerspruch zwischen Industrialisierung und Umweltschutz /. Offenbach/Main, West Germany [1984] 21 p. : LC Card 86-172511
HC79.P55 L44 1984

Kogan, A. M. (Al'bert Moiseevich) V tvorcheskoĭ laboratorii Karla Marksa : plan ėkonomicheskikh issledovaniĭ 1857-1859 gg. i "Kapital" / A.M. Kogan. Moskva : "Mysl'", 1983. 172, [4] p. ; 20 cm. Errata slip inserted. Bibliography: p. 168-[173] LC Card 83-166605
1. Marx, Karl, 1818-1883. Kapital. I. Title.
HB501 .K57 1983

Kogan, Ninel. New standards for evaluating technological innovation in the USSR : the petro-chemical machine building industry : a case study / Ninel Kogan. Falls Church, VA (7700 Leesburg Pike, #250, Falls Church 22043) : Delphic Associates, c1986. xii, 103 leaves (some folded) : ill. ; 28 cm. (Monograph series on Soviet Union) The Delphic emigre series LC Card 87-151964 DDC 338.4/7681766/0947 19
1. Chemical plant equipment industry - Technological innovations - Evaluation - Standards - Soviet Union. I. Title. II. Series.
HD9579.C33 S654 1986

Kogō, Hiroshi, 1921- Erekutoronikusu pawā shōjiten /. Tōkyō , 1985. v, 618 p. : ISBN 4-320-08454-3 : LC Card 85-229520
TK7804 .E73 1985 <Orien Japan>
NYPL [*OSG 86-3267]

Koh, Cher Siang. The co-operative movement in Singapore / by Koh Cher Siang. Singapore : Economics Section, Economic Development Division, Ministry of Finance, [1970] 26 p. ; 28 cm. (Information papers / Economics Section . inf. 59/G) At head of title: General. "October 1970." LC Card 87-121945 DDC 334/.09595/7 19
1. Cooperative societies - Singapore. I. Singapore. Economic Development Division. Economics Section. II. Series: Information papers (Singapore. Economic Development Division. Economics Section) , inf. 59/G. III. Title.
HD3543.A4 K64 1970

A Kohászati és a gépipari árak alakulása, 1980-1984 / [összeálította, Iparstatisztikai Főosztály Kohó- és Gépipari Osztálya]. Budapest : Központi Statisztikai Hivatal, 1986. 91 p. ; 29 cm. Tables. LC Card 86-202642
1. Machinery industry - Prices - Hungary - Statistics. 2. Machinery - Prices - Hungary - Statistics. 3. Metals - Prices - Hungary - Statistics. I. Hungary Központi Statisztikai Hivatal. Kohó- és Gépipari Osztály.
HD9705.H82 K64 1986

Kőhegyi, Kálmán. Az ipari szövetkezetek összevonásai a 70-es években / Kőhegyi Kálmán. [Budapest] : Szövetkezeti Kutató Intézet, [1983] 119 p. ; 29 cm. (Közlemények / Szövetkezeti Kutató Intézet) "Belső használatra." Bibliography: p. 110. LC Card 86-145163
1. Producer cooperatives - Hungary. I. Title. II. Title: Ipari szövetkezetek összevonásai a hetvenes években. III. Series: Közlemények / Szövetkezeti Kutató Intézet.
HD3182.5.A4 K64 1983

Kohl, Benjamin G. Lane Frederic Chapin, 1900- Studies in Venetian social and economic history /. London , 1987. 346 p. in various pagings : ISBN 0-86078-202-6 LC Card 87-160893 DDC 945/.31 19
HC308.V4 L36 1987

Kohl, Helmut, 1930- Soziale Marktwirtschaft, Fundament für morgen : Festveranstaltung zum 90. Geburtstag von Professor Dr. Ludwig Erhard am Mittwoch, dem 4. Februar 1987, in der Redoute zu Bonn-Bad Godesberg. Bonn : Ludwig-Erhard-Stiftung, [1987] 39 p. : 1 ill. ; 24 cm. (Standpunkte, 0179-549X . 3) PARTIAL CONTENTS. - Das Erbe Ludwig Erhards Herausforderung für die Wirtschaftspolitik / Helmut Kohl -- Das Phänomen Erhard / Hermann Höcherl. ISBN 3-88991-011-4 LC Card 87-409383 DDC 338.943 19
1. Germany, West - Economic policy. 2. Erhard, Ludwig. I. Erhard, Ludwig. II. Höcherl, Hermann, 1912-. III. Ludwig Erhard-Stiftung. IV. Series: Standpunkte (Bonn, Germany) , 3. V. Title.
HC286.5 .K565 1987

Kohl, Heribert, 1940-
Mitbestimmung in der Krise--Krise der Mitbestimmung? . Köln , c1984. 192 p. : ISBN 3-7663-0895-5 LC Card 85-113842
HD5660.G4 M563 1984

Neue Technologien und Arbeitswelt . Köln , c1984. 197 p. : ISBN 3-7663-0893-9 LC Card 85-160745
HD6331.2.G28 N475 1984
NYPL [JLD 86-3861]

Köhler, Axel, 1938- Konturen bundesdeutscher Rohstoffpolitik / Axel Köhler. Köln : Deutscher Instituts-Verlag, c1983. 56 p. : ill. ; 21 cm. (Beiträge zur Wirtschafts- und Sozialpolitik . 113, 2/1983) Includes bibliographical references. ISBN 3-602-24713-9 LC Card 83-215016
1. Raw materials - Germany, West. 2. Energy policy - Germany, West. I. Series: Beiträge zur Wirtschafts- und Sozialpolitik , 113. II. Title.
HF1054.G4 K64 1983

Köhler, Eberhard. Neue Arbeits- und Tätigkeitsformen . Dublin, Ireland [Washington, D.C.] c1986. xvi, 339 p. ; ISBN 92-825-6418-5 LC Card 87-408469 DDC 306/.36/094 19
HD6957.E86 N48 1986

KOHLER, ERIC LOUIS, 1892-1976.
Wagner, Nancy A. Eric Louis Kohler in the accounting profession /. Atlanta, Ga. , 1987. vi, 210 p. ; ISBN 0-88406-196-5 (pbk.) : LC Card 86-25633 DDC 657/.092/4 19
HF5604.5.K64 W34 1987

Köhler, Gerd, 1944- Forum wohnen /. Freiburg i. Br. , Giessen , 1986. 158 p. : ISBN 3-89125-009-6 LC Card 86-169106
HD7339.A3 F68 1986

Köhler, H. (Heinz) Thurn und Taxis, Kurhessen 1816-1867 : Handbuch der Ortsstempel / zusammengestellt von H. Köhler und C. Vigelahn. Kassel : H. Köhler, [1970?]- v. <1 > : ill. ; 21 cm. Cover title. Vol. 1, 12 p. of supplemental material laid in. CONTENTS. - T. 1. Niederhessen. LC Card 86-235280
1. Postmarks - Germany (West) - Hesse-Kassel (Electorate) - Catalogs. I. Vigelahn, C. II. Title. III. Title: Kurhessen 1816-1867.
HE6185.G32 H474 1970

Kohler, Heinz, 1934- Statistics for business and economics / Heinz Kohler. 2nd ed. Glenview, Ill. : Scott, Foresman, c1988. 775, [153] p. : ill. ; 24 cm. Includes indexes. ISBN 0-673-18444-7 LC Card 87-11781 DDC 519.5/02433 19
1. Commercial statistics. 2. Statistics. I. Title.
HF1017 .K64 1988

Köhler, Helmut, 1944- Nachfragewettbewerb und Marktbeherrschung / von Helmut Köhler. Tübingen : J.C.B. Mohr, 1986. 121 p. ; 23 cm. (Vorträge und Aufsätze / Walter Eucken Institut, 0509-6065 . 110) Includes bibliographical references. ISBN 3-16-345124-1 (Deut. Bibl.) LC Card 86-223313
1. Monopsonies. I. Series: Vorträge und Aufsätze (Walter Eucken Institut) , 110. II. Title.
HD2757.4 .K64 1986

Köhler, Holm-Detlev, 1956- Ökonomie und Autonomie : historische und aktuelle Entwicklungen genossenschaftlicher Bewegungen / Holm-Detlev Köhler. Frankfurt : Brandes & Apsel, c1986. 213 p. ; 21 cm. (Wissen & Praxis , 4) Bibliography: p. 199-213. ISBN 3-925798-24-2 LC Card 87-108165 DDC 334/.0943 19
1. Cooperation - Germany (West) - History. I. Title. II. Series.
HD3498 .K63 1986

Kohler-Koch, Beate, 1941- Technik und internationale Politik /. Baden-Baden , 1986. 520 p. ; ISBN 3-7890-1239-4 (Deut. Bibl.) LC Card 87-103890 DDC 338/.06 19
HC79.T4 T422 1986

Köhler, Otto, 1935- --und heute die ganze Welt : die Geschichte der IG Farben und ihrer Väter / Otto Köhler. Hamburg : Rasch und Röhring, c1986. 350 p. : ill. ; 22 cm. Bibliography: p. 341-345. Includes index. ISBN 3-89136-081-9 LC Card 87-116787
1. Interessengemeinschaft Farbenindustrie Aktiengesellschaft - History. 2. Interessengemeinschaft Farbenindustrie Aktiengesellschaft - Biography. 3. Industrialists - Germany - Biography. 4. Chemical industry - Germany - History. I. Title.
HD9654.9.I5 K64 1986

Köhler, Walter. Struktur und Dynamik der Wirtschaft . Freiburg im Breisgau , c1983. 530 p. : ISBN 3-448-01348-X : LC Card 83-184564 DDC 330 19
HB44 .S77 1983

Kohli, Atul. The state and poverty in India : the politics of reform / Atul Kohli. Cambridge [Cambridgeshire] ; New York : Cambridge University Press, 1987. x, 262 p. : maps ; 23 cm. (Cambridge South Asian studies. 37) Includes index. Bibliography: p. 245-254. ISBN 0-521-32008-9 LC Card 85-25554 DDC 333.3/1/54 19
1. Land reform - India - States - Case studies. 2. Manpower policy - India - States - Case studies. 3. Rural poor - Government policy - India - States - Case studies. 4. Income distribution - Government policy - States - Case studies. 5. Political parties - India - States - Case studies. 6. India - Rural conditions - Case studies. I. Title.
HD1333.I4 K65 1986 ***NYPL [JLD 87-1517]***

Kohlmann, James D. Make them choose you : the executive selection process, replacing mystery with strategy / James D. Kohlmann. Englewood Cliffs, N.J. : Prentice Hall, c1988. xiv, 178 p. ; 24 cm. ISBN 0-13-547878-2 LC Card 87-17435 DDC 650.1/4 19
1. Employment interviewing. I. Title.
HF5549.5.I6 K58 1988

Kohlmann, Ulrike, 1954- Möglichkeiten und Grenzen der Aussagefähigkeit von Teilkonzernabschlüssen / Ulrike Kohlmann. München : V. Florentz, c1986. viii, 180 p. ; 21 cm. (Hochschulschriften zur Betriebswirtschaftslehre . Bd. 41) Bibliography: p. 151-177. Includes index. ISBN 3-88259-419-5 LC Card 87-121768 DDC 657/.95/0943 19
1. Corporations - Germany, West - Accounting. 2. Corporations - Accounting - Law and legislation - Germany (West). I. Title. II. Series.
HF5686.C7 K644 1986

Kohls, Richard L. Marketing of agricultural products / Richard L. Kohls, Joseph N. Uhl. 6th ed. New York : Macmillan ; London : Collier Macmillan, c1985. xi, 624 p. : ill. ; 25 cm. Includes bibliographies and index. ISBN 0-02-365670-0 LC Card 84-817 DDC 381/.41 19
1. Produce trade - United States. 2. Farm produce - United States - Marketing. I. Uhl, Joseph N. II. Title.
HD9000.5 .K57 1985 ***NYPL [JLE 86-4145]***

Köhn, Doris. Die Verschuldung lateinamerikanischer Länder / Doris Köhn. Hamburg : Verlag Weltarchiv, 1984. 148 p. ; 24 cm. (Veröffentlichungen des HWWA-Institut für Wirtschaftsforschung-Hamburg) A slight revision of the author's Diplomarbeit. Bibliography: p. 137-148. ISBN 3-87895-259-7 LC Card 85-134749
1. Debts, External - Latin America. 2. Latin America - Economic conditions - 1945-. I. Title.
HJ8514.5 .K64 1984

Kohn, Stephen M. (Stephen Martin) Protecting environmental & nuclear whistleblowers : a litigation manual / by Stephen Kohn. Washington, D.C. : Nuclear Information and Resource Service, Government Accountability Project, c1985. xiii, 346 p. : forms ; 23 cm. "July 1985." Includes bibliographical references and index. ISBN 0-9615323-0-0 (pbk.) LC Card 85-61844

DDC 342.73/0684 347.302684 19
1. Discrimination in employment - Law and legislation - United States. 2. Whistle blowing - Law and legislation - United States. 3. Environmental law - United States. 4. Nuclear energy - Law and legislation - United States. 5. Actions and defenses - United States. I. Title. II. Title: Protecting environmental and nuclear whistleblowers.
KF5342 .K64 1985 *NYPL [JLE 86-1787]*

Kohrs-Barrmeyer, Andrea. Die Problematik der Informationsgewinnung und -verarbeitung bei der Bewertung von Sand- und Kiesabbaugelände / Andrea Kohrs-Barrmeyer. Münster : Lit, [1986] xviii, 379 p. : ill. ; 22 cm. (Betriebswirtschaftliche Schriftenreihe . Bd. 27) Bibliography: p. 361-379. ISBN 3-88660-330-X LC Card 86-223939 DDC 622/.3622/068 19
1. Sand and gravel industry - Management. I. Title. II. Series.
HD9585.S162 K64 1986

Koĭchuev, T. K. (Turar Koĭchuevich) Ėkonomicheskiĭ rost Kirgizskoĭ SSR v usloviiakh intensifikatsii obshchestvennogo proizvodstva . Frunze , 1984. 210 p. ; LC Card 85-131511
HC337.K545 E37 1984
*NYPL [*QIP 87-105]*

Koike, Kazuo, 1932- Understanding industrial relations in modern Japan / Kazuo Koike ; translated by Mary Saso. New York : St. Martin's Press, 1987. p. cm. Bibliography: p. Includes index. ISBN 0-312-01301-9 : LC Card 87-24068 DDC 331/.0952 19
1. Industrial relations - Japan. I. Title.
HD8726.5 .K548 1987

Kok, P. C. Black migration to the PWV complex : selective, spatial, and motivational aspects / P.C. Kok, Bärbel E. Hofmeyr, D. Gelderblom. Pretoria : Human Sciences Research Council, 1985. viii, 79 p. : ill. ; 30 cm. (Report S-122) Bibliography: p. 61-62. ISBN 0-7969-0313-1 (pbk.) : LC Card 86-232836 DDC 304.8/0968 19
1. Migration, Internal - South Africa. 2. Blacks - South Africa - Pretoria - Economic conditions. 3. Blacks - South Africa - Witwatersrand - Economic conditions. 4. Blacks - South Africa - Vereeniging - Economic conditions. 5. Rural-urban migration - South Africa. I. Hofmeyr, Bärbel E. II. Gelderblom, D. III. Series: Verslag S , nr. 122. IV. Title.
HB2123.4.P68 K65 1985

Kokalj, Ljuba. Albach, Horst. Finanzierung mit Risikokapital /. Stuttgart , c1986. 312 p. ; ISBN 3-7910-5015-X LC Card 87-127700 DDC 332/.0415/0943 19
HG5492 .A797 1986

Kokorev, Mikhail Vladimirovich. Aktual'nye problemy sotsial'no-ėkonomicheskogo razvitiia SSSR v sovremennyĭ period /. Moskva , 1984. 153 p. ; LC Card 85-205938
HC336.25 .A46 1984

Kokusai Fukkō Kaihatsu Ginkō. see **International Bank for Reconstruction and Development.**

Kokusai Kyōryoku Jigyōdan.
Estudio del Plan de desarrollo carbonífero de la zona de Valle del Cauca en la República de Colombia. Tokio, Japon , 1977. v, 149 leaves : LC Card 84-244429
HD9554.C63 V34 1977

Infrastructural survey report for the development of the alumina resources in Rennell Island, Solomon Islands. [S.l.] [1976] xv, 321 p. : LC Card 84-230135
HC684.Z7 R455 1976

Preliminary study report on promotion of small-medium scale industries in the Republic of Venezuela. [Tokyo] [1978] ii, 27 p. : LC Card 84-249328
HD9506.V42 P74 1978

Kol, J. European trade policies and the developing world /. London , New York , c1988. x, 368 p. ; ISBN 0-7099-4672-4 LC Card 87-8969 DDC 382/.3/094 19
HF1492 .E87 1988

Kol, uran och gas för kristid. Sweden. 1980 års oljelagringskommitté. [Stockholm] [1981] 192 p. : ISBN 91-38-06450-2 LC Card 83-107879
HD9502.S82 S88 1981

Kołaczyk, Zdzisław. Ekonomiczne i prawne problemy przedsiębiorstwa uspołecznionego /. Poznań , 1981. 137 p. ; LC Card 83-167540
HB54 .P6 nr. 101 HD4215.7

Kolar-Dimitrijević, Mira. Kongres privrednih stručnjaka Hrvatske (1943-1944 : Otočac and Čazma, Croatia) Kongres privrednih stručnjaka Hrvatske . Zagreb , 1985. 252 p., [16] p. of plates : ISBN 86-80359-01-7 LC Card 86-176200
HC407.Z7 C7637 1943

Kolari, James W. Bank costs, structure, and performance / James Kolari, Asghar Zardkoohi. Lexington, Mass. : Lexington Books, c1987. x, 240 p. : ill. ; 24 cm. Bibliography: p. [227]-232. Includes index. ISBN 0-669-11282-8 (alk. paper) LC Card 85-45295 DDC 332.1/068/1 19
1. Banks and banking - Costs. 2. Banks and banking - United States - Costs. I. Zardkoohi, Asghar. II. Title.
HG1616.C6 K65 1987

Kolarik, William F. A model for the study of international trade politics : the United States business community and Soviet-American relations, 1975-1976 / William F. Kolarik, Jr. New York : Garland Pub., 1987. 613 p. : ill. ; 23 cm. (Foreign economic policy of the United States) Originally presented as the author's thesis (Ph. D.)--Kent State University, 1981. Bibliography: p. 545-613. ISBN 0-8240-8086-6 (alk. paper) : LC Card 87-23788 DDC 382/.0947/0730724 19
1. United States - Commerce - Soviet Union - Mathematical models. 2. Soviet Union - Commerce - United States - Mathematical models. 3. United States - Foreign relations - Soviet Union. 4. Soviet Union - Foreign relations - United States. 5. Businessmen - United States - Attitudes. I. Title. II. Series.
HF3105 .K64 1987

Kolarovski raĭonen komitet na BKP--Sofiia. Prinosŭt na dr. Todor Zhivkov za razvitieto na sotsialno-ikonomicheskata politika na BKP v etapa na izgrazhdane na razvitoto sotsialistichesko obshtestvo . Sofiia , 1983. 398 p. ; LC Card 84-103348
HC403 .P72 1983

Kolbeck, Rosemarie.
Bankinnovationen . Frankfurt am Main , c1986. 131 p. ; ISBN 3-7819-0363-X LC Card 87-120955 DDC 332.1/0943 19
HG3048 .B287 1986

Risikovorsorge . Frankfurt am Main , c1985. 130 p. : ISBN 3-7819-0323-0 LC Card 85-217569
HG1615 .R57 1985

Kolesov, Nikolai Dmitrievich.
Neposredstvenno-obshchestvennoe proizvodstvo v usloviiakh razvitogo sotsializma /. Leningrad , 1984. 212 p. ; LC Card 84-248045
HB97.5 .N434 1984

Kolev, Blagoĭ. Petkov, Krŭst'o. Sotsiologiia na trudoviia kolektiv . Sofiia , 1982. 184 p. ; LC Card 83-124278
HD6957.B85 P47 1982
*NYPL [*QK 86-4733]*

KOLHOSP "ZDOBUTOK ZHOVTNIA" (UKRAINE) - HISTORY.
Istoriia kolhospu "Zdobutok ZHovtnia" /. Kyïv , 1986. 188 p., [8] p. of plates : LC Card 87-161618
HD1492.S652 U3835 1986

Kolk, David. Rose, Adam Zachary. Forecasting natural gas demand in a changing world /. Greenwich, Conn. , c1987. xix, 152 p. : ISBN 0-89232-838-X : LC Card 87-21390 DDC 333.8/23312 19
HD9581.A2 R67 1987

Kolkhoznoe krest'ianstvo Kirgizii v usloviiakh razvitogo sotsializma /. Boldzhurova, I. S. (Ishengul' Sadykovna) Frunze , 1985. 148 p. ; LC Card 86-106126
HD1995.K53 B65 1985

Kolkhoznoe krest'ianstvo Uzbekistana na puti k razvitomu sotsializmu /. Aminova, R. Kh. Tashkent , 1983. 358 p. ; LC Card 84-192680
HD1492.S652 U922 1983

Köll, Anu-Mai. Tradition och reform i västra Södermanlands jordbruk, 1810-1890 : agrar teknik i kapitalismens inledningsskede / Anu-Mai Köll. Stockholm : A.-M. Köll : Distr., Almqvist & Wiksell International, 1983. 252 p. : ill. ; 25 cm. (Acta Universitatis Stockholmiensis. Stockholm studies in economic history . 7) Summary in English. Thesis (doctoral)--Stockholms universitet, 1983. Extra t.p. with thesis statement and abstract in English inserted. Bibliography: p. 246-252. ISBN 91-22-00633-8 LC Card 84-114628
1. Agriculture - Economic aspects - Sweden - Södermanland län - History - 19th century. 2. Agriculture - Social aspects - Sweden - Södermanland län - History - 19th century. I. Title. II. Series.
HD2020.S63 K65 1983

Koll, Hermann Josef. Mobilität und Beruf : Faktoren, Daten, Ansätze, Probleme : eine Studie zur Berufs- und Mobilitätspädagogik / Hermann Josef Koll. Opladen : Westdeutscher Verlag, 1981. xviii, 564 p. ; 23 cm. (Beiträge zur sozialwissenschaftlichen Forschung. Bd. 18) Bibliography: p. 529-554. Includes index. ISBN 3-531-11551-0 : LC Card 81-158683
1. Occupational mobility - Germany, West. 2. Labor mobility - Germany, West. I. Title.
HD5717.5.G3 K64 1981

Kollar, François, 1904- La France travaille / François Kollar ; [compilation] Anne-Claude Lelieur, Raymond Bachollet. Paris : Chêne, c1986. 238 p. : ill. ; 32 cm. Photographs by François Kollar, whose work illustrated the sections of Le Visage de la France known as La France travaille. ISBN 2-85108-435-6 LC Card 87-108516
1. Labor and laboring classes - France - Pictorial works. 2. France - Occupations - Pictorial works. I. Lelieur, Anne-Claude. II. Bachollet, Raymond. III. Visage de la France. France travaille. IV. Title.
HD8430 .K65 1986

Das kollektive Bausparen . Bock, Hartmut. Frankfurt am Main , New York , c1984. 204 p. : ISBN 3-8204-5341-5 LC Card 85-199145
HC290.5.S3 B63 1984

Kollektivizatsiia krest'ianskikh khoziaĭstv i likvidatsiia kulachestva kak klassa na Severo-Zapade RSFSR, 1927-1937 gg. . Ivanov, E. P. (Evgeniĭ Pavlovich) Leningrad , 1983. 91 p. ; LC Card 84-190520
HD1492.S652 R875 1983
*NYPL [*QI 87-3170]*

Kollektivmacht und Individualschutz im amerikanischen Arbeitsrecht /. Gassner, Peter, 1941- Frankfurt am Main , c1981. 155 p. ; ISBN 3-8204-6119-1 : LC Card 82-164604 DDC 344.73/0189 347.304189 19
KF3408.Z94 G474 1981
NYPL [JLD 86-1212]

Kollektivnyĭ podriad v sel'skom khoziaĭstve /. Zakharchenko, A. G. (Alekseĭ Gavrilovich) Kiev , 1985. 107 p. : LC Card 86-222274
HD1492.S652 U389 1985

Koller, Sándor. Forgalomtechnika és közlekedéstervezés / Koller Sándor. Budapest : Műszaki Könyvkiadó, 1986. 291 p. : ill. ; 25 cm. Bibliography: p. 254-259. ISBN 963-10-6412-3 : LC Card 87-148352
1. Traffic engineering. I. Title.
HE333 .K575 1986

Kolloquium zur Gewerkschaftlichen Interessenvertretung beim Umfassenden Aufbau des Sozialismus in der Deutschen Demokratischen Republik (1964) Protokoll über das Kolloquium zur Gewerkschaftlichen Interessenvertretung beim Umfassenden Aufbau des Sozialismus in der Deutschen Demokratischen Republik am 31. Januar 1964. [Bernau] : Hochschule der Deutschen Gewerkschaften "Fritz Heckert", [1964] iv, 246 p. ; 21 cm. Includes bibliographical references. LC Card 85-125499
1. Trade-unions - Germany (East) - Congresses. 2. Trade-unions and communism - Germany (East) - Congresses. I. Hochschule der Deutschen Gewerkschaften "Fritz Heckert.". II. Title.
HD6700.5 .K65 1964

Kolloquium zwanzig Jahre Weiterbildungs- und Forschungsarbeit. Kolloquium 20 Jahre Weiterbildungs- und Forschungsarbeit (1987 : Leipzig, Germany) Kolloquium 20 Jahre Weiterbildungs- und Forschungsarbeit . [Leipzig] , 1986. 64 p. ; LC Card 87-408852 DDC 338.9431 19
HC290.78 .K64 1987

Kolloquium 20 Jahre Weiterbildungs- und Forschungsarbeit (1987 : Leipzig, Germany) Kolloquium 20 Jahre Weiterbildungs- und Forschungsarbeit : 26. Mai 1987 in Leipzig, DDR / Institut für Sozialistische Wirtschaftsführung ; [Redakteur, Ursula Sebastian]. [Leipzig] : Der Rektor der Technischen Hochschule Leipzig, 1986. 64 p. ; 20 cm. (Wissenschaftliche Berichte der Technischen

Hochschule Leipzig, 0138-3809 . Heft 18, 1986) Papers presented at the conference. Cover title. Includes bibliographies. CONTENTS. - 20 Jahre Weiterbildungs- und Forschungsarbeit am Institut für Sozialistische Wirtschaftsführung der Technischen Hochschule Leipzig / R. Hiller -- Inhaltliche methodische Aufgaben der Weiterbildung von Führungskadern nach dem XI. Parteitag der SED am Institut für Sozialistische Wirtschaftsführung Bauwesen / K.-H. Senf -- Organisationssystem zur Überprüfung der persönlichen Befähigung zur Ausübung einer Tätigkeit im Bauwesen in der Slowakischen Sozialistischen Republik / P. Cuzy -- Ergebnisse und Erfahrungen aus der Zusammenarbeit der Bezirksakademien mit dem ISW Bauwesen der TH Leipzig bei der Weiterbildung der Leitungskader der Nomenklatur III des Bauwesens / W. Stechert -- Leitungsorganisation eines Stadtbauamtes unter Berücksichtigung der komplexen Reproduktion baulicher Grundfonds im innerstädtischen Bereich / G. Linsel -- Zur Stellung der marxistisch-leninistischen Theorie bei der Weiterbildung von Führungskadern / R. Sperl -- Inhaltliche und pädagogische Aspekte der Leiterweiterbildung für die Erhöhung der ökonomischen Wirksamkeit von Wissenschaft und Technik in den Industriebaukombinaten / W. Günther, R. Sander -- Zu Anforderungen an die Arbeit der Wohnungsbaukombinate als Grundlage abzuleitender Weiterbildungskonsequenzen für die Leiter / W. Schröter -- Der Beitrag der Bibliothek im 20jährigen Bestehen des Institutes für Sozialistische Wirtschaftsführung Bauwesen / I. Beck. LC Card 87-408852 DDC 338.9431 19
1. Germany East - Economic policy - Congresses. 2. Socialism - Germany (East) - Congresses. I. Sebastian, Ursula. II. Technische Hochschule Leipzig. Institut für Sozialistische Wirtschaftsführung. III. Title. IV. Title: Kolloquium zwanzig Jahre Weiterbildungs- und Forschungsarbeit. V. Series: Wissenschaftliche Berichte der Technischen Hochschule Leipzig , 1986, Heft 18.
HC290.78 .K64 1987

Kolloquium 20 Jahre Weiterbildungs- und Forschungsarbeit . Kolloquium 20 Jahre Weiterbildungs- und Forschungsarbeit (1987 : Leipzig, Germany) [Leipzig] , 1986. 64 p. ; LC Card 87-408852 DDC 338.9431 19
HC290.78 .K64 1987

Kolm, Serge Christophe. La bonne économie : la réciprocité générale / Serge-Christophe Kolm.1re éd. Paris : Presses universitaires de France, 1984. 472 p. : ill. ; 22 cm. (Politique d'aujourd'hui) Bibliography: p. [459]-472. ISBN 2-13-038695-4 : LC Card 84-254896 DDC 330 19
1. Economics. 2. Altruism - Economic aspects. I. Title. II. Series.
HB173 .K64 1984

Kolms, Heinz, 1914- Staat, Steuern und Finanzausgleich . Berlin , c1984. 452 p., [1] leaf of plates : ISBN 3-428-05513-6 LC Card 84-166906
HJ1120 .S73 1984

KOLMS, HEINZ, 1914-
Staat, Steuern und Finanzausgleich . Berlin , c1984. 452 p., [1] leaf of plates : ISBN 3-428-05513-6 LC Card 84-166906
HJ1120 .S73 1984

Kölner ethnologische Studien .
(Bd. 8) Busch, Angelika. Migration und psychische Belastung . Berlin , 1983. 351 p. ; ISBN 3-496-00733-8 LC Card 83-193476
HD8458.I8 B87 1983

Kölner Genossenschaftswissenschaft .
(Bd. 6) Krauss, Hans-Ulrich. Erfolgsindikatoren und Betriebsvergleich bei Kreditgenossenschaften /. Gelsenkirchen , 1983. 217 p. : ISBN 3-88485-471-2 LC Card 84-153354
HG2039.G4 K73 1983

Kölner Genossenschaftswissenschaft, 0175-9582 .
(Bd. 8) Deppenkemper, Bernhard. Mitgliederversammlungen und Willensbildung in Genossenschaften /. Gelsenkirchen , 1984. 316 p. : ISBN 3-88485-473-9 LC Card 85-114636
HG2039.G4 D45 1984

Kölner Schriften zur Betriebswirtschaft und Organisation, 0721-3123 .
(Bd. 5) Müller, Rainer, 1953- Krisenmanagement in der Unternehmung . Frankfurt am Main , New York , c1986. xxvii, 773 p. : ISBN 3-8204-7479-X LC Card 87-409055 DDC 658.4 19
HD49 .M84 1986

Kölner Vorträge und Abhandlungen zur Sozial- und Wirtschaftsgeschichte .
(Heft 38) Spilker, Ernst Moritz. Der Wirtschaftsraum zwischen den Wirtschaftsräumen . Köln , 1986. 223 p. : LC Card 87-408201 DDC 330.943/55 19
HC288.W46 S67 1986

Kolodziej, Edward A. Making and marketing arms : the French experience and its implications for the international system / Edward A. Kolodziej. Princeton, N.J. : Princeton University Press, c1987. xxv, 518 p. : ill. ; 25 cm. Includes bibliographies and index. ISBN 0-691-07734-7 (alk. paper) : LC Card 86-30567 DDC 338.4/76234/0944 19
1. Munitions - France. 2. Military assistance, French. 3. World politics - 1945-. I. Title.
HD9743.F82 K64 1987

Kolokium Perdagangan dan Perkapalan di Kepulauan Malayu Sebelum 1900 (1984 : Kuala Lumpur?, Malaysia) Kapal dan harta karam =. Kuala Lumpur , 1986. xv, 181 p. : LC Card 86-942317 DDC 387.5/09595 19
HF3800.6 .K36 1986

Kolomiĭtsev, Valentin Fedorovich. Rabochiĭ klass i profsoiuzy Frantsii v bor'ybe protiv monopoliĭ, 1968-1981 gody / V.F. Kolomiĭtsev. Moskva : Profizdat, 1981. 173 p. ; 20 cm. Includes bibliographical references. LC Card 82-134380
1. Labor and laboring classes - France - Political activity. 2. France - Economic conditions - 1945-. 3. France - Politics and government - 1969-. I. Title.
HD8435 .K65 1981

Kolos na ladoni : sbornik publitsistiki / [redaktsionnaia kollegiia V.B. Bushmanov ... et al.]. Voronezh : TSentr.-Chernozemnoe knizhnoe izd-vo, 1985. 237 p. : ill. ; 21 cm. LC Card 86-195464
1. Agricultural laborers - Russian S.F.S.R. - Social conditions. 2. Agriculture - Russian S.F.S.R. 3. Russian S.F.S.R. - Rural conditions. I. Bushmanov, V. B.
HD1536.S65 K65 1985

Kolozsvári, Ernő. Szemelvények a szakszervezetek agitációs, propaganda- és kulturális tevékenységéből, 1948-1980 / [írta és összeállította Kolozsvári Ernő]. Budapest : Népszava, 1982. 43 p. : ill. ; 20 cm. (Tények, adatok a szakszervezeti mozgalomról) ISBN 963-321-957-4 LC Card 83-229170
1. Trade-unions - Hungary. 2. Public relations - Trade-unions. I. Title. II. Series.
HD6680.5.Z6 K64 1982

Kolte, Lars. Det danske valutamarked / Lars Kolte. København : Erhvervsøkonomisk forlag : Nyt nordisk forlag, 1984, c1983. 215 p. : ill. ; 20 cm. (Småskrifter fra Institut for udenrigshandel . nr. 17) Bibliography: p. 209-213. Includes index. ISBN 87-17-03415-9 LC Card 85-127552
1. Foreign exchange administration - Denmark. 2. Foreign exchange. I. Title. II. Series.
HG3957 .K64 1984

Komáromi, Gábor. Az Állami vállalatok szervezete, vezetése, működése és irányítása /. Budapest , 1985. 262 p. ; ISBN 963-322-140-4 : LC Card 86-202934
HD4160.5 .A78 1985

Komarov, E. I. (Evgeniĭ Ivanovich) Perestroĭka i rukovoditel' /. Moskva , 1987. 143 p. ; LC Card 87-164793
HD38.25.S65 P47 1987

KOMBINAT "PROLETARIĬ" (SOFIA, BULGARIA) - HISTORY.
Kadiev, Ivan. Khronika za "Proletariĭ" /. [Sofia] , 1985. 140, [3] p., [32] p. of plates : LC Card 86-195264
HD9969.K7 B855 1985

Kombinationserbjudanden. Vällingby : Konsumentverket, [1984] 269, [45] p. : ill. ; 25 cm. (Rapport 1984:4-O3) ISBN 91-7398-243-1 LC Card 85-115578
1. Sales promotion. 2. Merchandising. I. Sweden. Konsumentverket. II. Series: Rapport (Sweden. Konsumentverket) , 1984:4-O3.
HF5438.5 .K66 1984

Kombinatsplanung und Leistungssteigerung /. Bottesi, Valentin, 1933- Berlin , 1984. 120 p. ; LC Card 84-217968
HC290.795.I52 B67 1984

Komitee zur Verteidigung Demokratischer Grundrechte (Berlin, Germany) Gesinnungs überprüft! . Berlin [1978] 263 p. : LC Card 84-198533
HD4903.5.G4 G47 1978

Komiya, Ryūtarō, 1928- Industrial policy of Japan /. Tokyo , Orlando, FL , 1988. p. cm. ISBN 0-12-418650-5 (U. S. : alk. paper) LC Card 87-1409 DDC 338.952 19
HD3616.J33 I816 1988

Komkov, N. I. (Nikolaĭ Ivanovich) Kompleksnaia organizatsiia issledovaniĭ . Moskva , 1981. 191 p. : LC Card 82-130582
HC340.R4 K66 1981

Komlós, János. Hardy, Ilona. Gyakorlati útmutató a kötvény és a váltó használatához /. Budapest , 1986. 62 p. ; ISBN 963-621-315-1 LC Card 87-407776
HG5470.5.A3 H37 1986

Kommerzielle Bankkredite. Zellweger, Bruno. Ueberwachung kommerzieller Bankkredite /. Bern , c1983. xx, 330 p. : ISBN 3-258-03246-7 : LC Card 83-214274
HG1526 .B27 Bd. 77 HG1642.S95

Kommission der Europäischen Gemeinschaften. see **Commission of the European Communities.**

Kommission für die Altertumskunde Mittel- und Nordeuropas. Der Handel des frühen Mittelalters . Göttingen , 1985. 510 p. : ISBN 3-525-82433-5 (Deut. Bibl.) LC Card 86-209040
HF3495 .U57 1985 t. 3

Kommission für Konjunkturfragen (Switzerland) Baltensperger, Ernst. Geldmengenpolitik und Inflationskontrolle . Diessenhofen , c1984. 132 p. : ISBN 3-7253-0224-3 : LC Card 84-178054 DDC 332.4/9494 19
HG1155 .B345 1984 ***NYPL [JLD 87-168]***

Kommunal bostadsförmedling . Wiktorin, Marianne. Stockholm [1983] 107 p. : ISBN 91-540-3929-0 : LC Card 84-218864
HD7350.A3 W55 1983

Kommunal energiplanering . Sweden. Statens industriverk. Stockholm , 1980. 51 p. ; ISBN 91-38-05802-2 LC Card 82-236900
HD9502.S82 S97 1980

Kommunal näringspolitik.
Andersson, Göran, 1944- Industrihotell och industribyar . Stockholm [1984] 150 p. : ISBN 91-38-08268-3 LC Card 85-106828
HC375 .A72 1984

Lindmark, Leif. Företagsstöd och kommunalt risktagande /. Stockholm [1984] iv, 49 p. : ISBN 91-38-08297-7 LC Card 85-106839
HD3646.S8 L55 1984

Olofsson, Christer. Kommunala bolag med industriutvecklings uppgifter . Stockholm [1984] 82 p. ; ISBN 91-38-08114-8 LC Card 85-106731
HD3616.S53 O46 1984

Omfattning och erfarenheter . Stockholm [1984] 127 p. : ISBN 91-38-08319-1 LC Card 85-106802
HC375 .O39 1984

Kommunal- und Europawahl am 17. Juni 1984. Saarbrücken : Statistisches Amt des Saarlandes, 1984. 115 p. : ill. ; 30 cm. (Einzelschriften zur Statistik des Saarlandes, 0558-0838 . Nr. 67) "Zugl. Statistischer Bericht B VII 3-3, B VII 5-3 und B VII 5-4." Chiefly tables. CONTENTS. - T. 1. Repräsentative Europawahlstatistik -- T. 2. Endgültige Wahlergebnisse. ISBN 3-88718-020-8 : LC Card 85-130989
1. Elections - Germany (West) - Saarland - Statistics. 2. Local elections - Germany (West) - Saarland - Statistics. 3. European Parliament - Elections - Statistics. I. Saarland (Germany). Statistisches Amt. II. Series.
HA1320 .S244 Nr. 67 JN4945.S265

Kommunala bolag med industriutvecklings uppgifter . Olofsson, Christer. Stockholm [1984] 82 p. ; ISBN 91-38-08114-8 LC Card 85-106731
HD3616.S53 O46 1984

Kommunale Arbeitsgemeinschaft Bergisch Land. Die Wirtschaftliche Entwicklung in den Arbeitsmarktregionen des Bergischen Landes . Bochum , 1981. 401 p. : ISBN 3-88339-217-0 LC Card 82-164818 DDC 331/.0943/55 19
HD8459.N66 W57 1981
NYPL [JLD 86-1639]

Kommunale Forschung in Österreich. (38) Linzer Kommunalwissenschaftliche Tagung (1978) Privatisierung kommunaler Aufgaben? . Linz , c1978. 62 p. ; ISBN 3-7141-7871-6 LC Card 85-185084
HD4651 .L56 1978

Kommunale Wirtschafts- und Finanzpolitik in Bayern zur Zeit der Weimarer Republik . Pohl, Harald. Regensburg , c1985. xiv, 312 p. : ISBN 3-924956-01-4 LC Card 86-230648
HJ9494.I53 P63 1985

Kommunale Wirtschaftsförderung, kritische Bestandsaufnahme ihrer Funktionen und Organisation /. Grätz, Christian. Bochum , 1983. xiii, 263 p. : ISBN 3-88339-340-1 : LC Card 84-138569
HC290.5.D5 G74 1983

Kommunale Wirtschaftsunternehmen /. Sander, Otfried. Köln , 1982. xiv, 144 p. : ISBN 3-555-00464-6 LC Card 81-192097
HD4659 .S26 1982

Kommunalisierung der Wohnungspolitik? . Killat, Gerhard. Köln , 1984. xiii, 291 p. : ISBN 3-921471-50-8 : LC Card 85-137757
HD7339.A3 K49 1984

Kommunalverband Ruhrgebiet.
Noll, Wulf. Lokales Informationssystem Arbeitsmarkt (LISA) /. Essen , 1986. 262 p. ; ISBN 3-923494-64-5 LC Card 87-409105 DDC 331.12/5/094355 19
HD5780.R82 N65 1986

Schlieper, Andreas. 150 Jahre Ruhrgebiet . Düsseldorf , 1986. 224 p. : ISBN 3-590-18150-8 LC Card 86-231681
HC288.R8 S34 1986

Strukturanalyse Ruhrgebiet . [Essen] [1983?] 185 p. : LC Card 86-218075
HD5760.R84 S77 1983

Wechsel auf die Zukunft /. Essen [1984] 25 p. : LC Card 85-105225
HC288.R8 W43 1984

Zimmermann, Horst, 1934- Die Gemeindefinanzen im Ruhrgebiet . Essen , 1983. xvi, 153 p. : ISBN 3-923494-28-9 LC Card 83-228289
HJ9493.5.R8 Z76 1983

Kommunalverband Ruhrgebiet. Abteilung Öffentlichkeitsarbeit. Nahwanderungen im Ruhrgebiet, 1976-1984 /. Essen , c1986. 61 p. : ISBN 3-923494-67-X LC Card 87-408772 DDC 330.943/55 19
HC288.R8 N34 1986

Kommunalverband Ruhrgebiet. Abteilung Planung. Radverkehrskonzept Sprockhövel /. Essen , c1985. 55 p., [3] folded col. leaves of plates : ISBN 3-923494-51-3 LC Card 86-113993
HE5739.G3 R33 1985

Kommunalverband Ruhrgebiet. Abteilung Wirtschaftsstruktur, EDV, Statistik. Nahwanderungen im Ruhrgebiet, 1976-1984 /. Essen , c1986. 61 p. : ISBN 3-923494-67-X LC Card 87-408772 DDC 330.943/55 19
HC288.R8 N34 1986

Zimmermann, Horst, 1934- Die Gemeindefinanzen im Ruhrgebiet . Essen , 1983. xvi, 153 p. : ISBN 3-923494-28-9 LC Card 83-228289
HJ9493.5.R8 Z76 1983

Kommunalwahlen am zwanzigsten März 1977. Die Kommunalwahlen am 20. März 1977 . Wiesbaden , 1978. 116 p. ; LC Card 86-102904
HA1320 .H529 n.F., Nr. 88 JS5471.H423E44

Die Kommunalwahlen am 20. März 1977 : Ergebnisse der Gemeindewahlen und Kreiswahlen. Wiesbaden : Hessisches Statistisches Landesamt, 1978. 116 p. ; 30 cm. (Beiträge zur Statistik Hessens . n.F., Nr. 88) Chiefly tables. LC Card 86-102904
1. Local elections - Germany (West) - Hesse - Statistics. I. Hessisches Statistisches Landesamt. II. Title: Kommunalwahlen am zwanzigsten März 1977. III. Series.
HA1320 .H529 n.F., Nr. 88 JS5471.H423E44

Kommunalwissenschaftliches Dokumentationszentrum (Vienna, Austria)
Bauer, Helfried. Fahrradfreundliche Verkehrspolitik in Stadt und Land . Wien , 1984. 87 p. : LC Card 85-150945
HE5739.A9 B38 1984

Kommunerna och framtiden : programskrift med skiss till kommunala omvärldsbilder 2000. [Stockholm] : Sekretariatet för framtidsstudier : Förlagstjänsten, FRN, [distributor, 1984] 224 p. : ill. ; 21 cm. Bibliography: p. 219-224. ISBN 91-38-08484-8 : LC Card 85-107984
1. Economic forecasting - Sweden. 2. Social prediction - Sweden. 3. Sweden - Economic conditions - 1945-. 4. Sweden - Social conditions - 1945-. 5. Cities and towns - Sweden. I. Sweden. Sekretariatet för framtidsstudier.
HC375 .K654 1984

Kommunerna och näringslivet : ett näringslivspolitiskt dilemma / Leif Melin ... [et al.].1. uppl. Stockholm : LiberFörlag, c1984. 173 p. : ill. ; 21 cm. (Publica) Bibliography: p. [170]-173. ISBN 91-38-90331-8 : LC Card 84-253511
1. Sweden - Economic conditions - 1945-. 2. Sweden - Economic policy. 3. Cities and towns - Sweden. 4. Local government - Sweden. I. Melin, Leif.
HC375 .K655 1984

Kommunerna och sysselsättningspolitiken . Öhman, Berndt, 1940- [Stockholm] [1985] 212 p. ; ISBN 91-38-08745-6 LC Card 86-114034
HD5803 .O36 1985

Kommunikationszentrum Idstein (Germany). Projektgruppe "Rüstungsexport." Rüstungsexport, ein todsicheres Geschäft . Idstein/Ts. , 1984. 1 v. (various pagings) : LC Card 86-152420
HD9743.D442 R87 1984

Kommunisticheskaia partiia Frantsii. see **Parti communiste français.**

KOMMUNISTICHESKAIA PARTIIA SOVETSKOGO SOIUZA - HISTORY.
Krasnykh, L. M. (Leonid Mikhaĭlovich) Partiĭnoe rukovodstvo sovershenstvovaniem upravleniia promyshlennost'iu v period stroitel'stva sotsializma, 1926-1937 . Krasnoiarsk , 1986. 150, [2] p. ; LC Card 86-226013
HD70.S63 K73 1986

Kommunisticheskaya Partiya Sovetskovo Soyuza. see **Kommunisticheskaia partiia Sovetskogo Soiuza.**

KOMMUNISTISCHE PARTEI DER SCHWEIZ - HISTORY.
Wandeler, Josef, 1949- Die KPS und die Wirtschaftskämpfe, 1930-1933 . Zürich , c1978. 277 p. : ISBN 3-85854-003-X LC Card 87-409249 DDC 331.89/29494 19
HD5410.A6 W36 1978

KOMMUNISTISCHE PARTEI DEUTSCHLANDS - CONGRESSES.
Der I. Kongress der Revolutionären Gewerkschafts-Opposition (RGO) im Bezirk Mittelrhein (Raum Aachen-Köln-Koblenz) im Jahre 1930 /. Reinbek , c1982. 136 p. : ISBN 3-88756-024-8 : LC Card 84-135308
HD6699.R47 I18 1982

Kommunistische Partei Frankreichs. see **Parti communiste français.**

Kommunistische Partei Indiens. see **Communist Party of India.**

Kommunistische Partei Russlands. see **Kommunisticheskaia partiia Sovetskogo Soiuza.**

Kommunistischer Bund. Wer WAA sät wird Widerstand ernten! /. Hamburg [1979] 31 p. : LC Card 85-171252
HD9698.G42 W47 1979

Kommunistischer Bund (Nord) see **Kommunistischer Bund.**

Komogortsev, I. I. (Ivan Ivanovich)
Rabochiĭ klass Sibiri . Novosibirsk , 1986. 355 p., [16] p. of plates : LC Card 86-211294
HD5797.S5 R33 1986

Sotsial'no-ėkonomicheskoe i kul'turnoe razvitie Zabaĭkal'ia . Novosibirsk , 1980. 283 p. ; LC Card 81-132139
HC337.R852 T737 1980

Komons, Nick A. The third man : a history of the airline crew complement controversy, 1947-1981 / by Nick A. Komons. Washington, D.C. : Dept. of Transportation, Federal Aviation Administration, 1987. iv, 162 p. : ill. ; 22 cm. Bibliography: p. 115-120. Includes index. LC Card 87-21267 DDC 363.1/2475 19
1. Flight crews - United States. 2. Airlines - United States - Employees. 3. Air Line Pilots Association. 4. United States. Federal Aviation Administration. I. Title. II. Title: Airline crew complement controversy.
HD8039.A42 U54 1987

Komp, Klaus Ulrich. Die Seehafenstädte im Weser-Jade-Raum und ihre überregionale Verflechtung / Klaus Ulrich Komp. Münster : Im Selbstverlag der Geographischen Kommission für Westfalen, 1982. x, 143 p. : ill., maps ; 23 cm. (Westfälische geographische Studien. 38) "Promotionsschrift," Universität Münster, 1977. Six folded maps in pocket. Summary also in English and French. Bibliography: p. 123-128. LC Card 83-197866
1. Harbors - Germany (West) - Weser River Valley. 2. Weser River Valley (Germany) - Economic conditions. I. Title. II. Series.
HE558.W45 K66 1982

Komparatív előnyök . Török, Ádám. Budapest , 1986, c1985. 225, [1] p. ; ISBN 963-221-579-6 : LC Card 87-105362
HF1412 .T67 1986

Kompendium C .
(nr. 9) Møllmann Boye, Erik. Miljøstatistik og lidt forureningsøkonomi . [Århus] , 1978. 53 leaves : LC Card 86-460199
HC79.P55 M65 1978

Kompetenzvermittlung durch Sachliteratur . Nordmann-Werner, Karin, 1945- Frankfurt am Main , New York , c1984. 391 p. ; ISBN 3-8204-5278-8 LC Card 85-193184
HB74.9.G3 N67 1984

Kompleksinis subalansuotas statybos planavimas / [redakcinė kolegija K. Antanavičius (atsak. redaktorius) ... et al.] = Kompleksnoe sbalansirovannoe planirovanie stroitel'stva / [redaktsionnaia kollegiia K. Antanavichius ... et al.]. Vilnius : "Mokslas", 1983. 115 p. : ill. ; 22 cm. (Lietuvos TSR aukštųjų mokyklų mokslo darbai. Statybos ekonomika ir organizavimas = Nauchnye trudy vysshikh uchebnykh zavedeniĭ Litovskoĭ SSR. Ėkonomika i organizatsiia stroitel'stva) Text in Lithuanian and Russian; summaries in either language and English. Includes bibliographies. LC Card 83-187666
1. Construction industry - Soviet Union - Planning. I. Antanavičius, K. (Kazimieras). II. Kompleksnoe sbalansirovannoe planirovanie stroitel'stva. III. Series: Lietuvos TSR aukštųjų mokyklų mokslo darbai. Statybos ekonomika ir organizavimas.
HD9715.S72 K66 1983

Kompleksnaia organizatsiia issledovaniĭ : [Sb. stateĭ] / Akademiia nauk SSSR, TSentral'nyĭ ėkonomiko-matematicheskiĭ institut ; [Otv. red. N.I. Komkov]. Moskva : Izd-vo "Nauka," 1981. 191 p. : ill. ; 20 cm. (Problemy sovetskoĭ ėkonomiki) Includes bibliographies. LC Card 82-130582
1. Research - Economic aspects - Soviet Union. 2. Research, Industrial - Soviet Union. I. Komkov, N. I. (Nikolaĭ Ivanovich). II. TSentral'nyĭ ėkonomiko-matematicheskiĭ institut (Akademiia nauk SSSR).
HC340.R4 K66 1981

Kompleksnoe ispol'zovanie drevesiny v Komi ASSR /. Kniazeva, G. A. (Galina Alekseevna) Syktyvkar , 1986. 75 p. : LC Card 86-233834
HD9765.S653 K665 1986

Kompleksnoe ispol'zovanie prirodnykh resursov : sbornik nauchnykh trudov / [redkol. S.A. Gensiruk (otv. red.) ... et al.]. Kiev : Akademiia nauk Ukr. SSR, Sovet po izucheniiu proizvoditel'nykh sil USSR, 1985. 174 p. ; 20 cm. Includes bibliographical references. LC Card 86-175133
1. Natural resources - Ukraine. 2. Environmental policy - Ukraine. I. Hensiruk, Stepan Antonovych. II. Rada po vyvchenniu produktyvnykh syl URSR.
HC337.U5 K6372 1985

Kompleksnoe sbalansirovannoe planirovanie stroitel'stva. Kompleksinis subalansuotas statybos planavimas /. Vilnius , 1983. 115 p. : LC Card 83-187666
HD9715.S72 K66 1983

Kompleksnye problemy obespecheniia ėkonomiki mineral'nym syr'em / [otvetstvennye redaktory A.A. Arbatov, A.IU. Reteium]. Moskva : Vses. nauchno-issl. in-t sistemnykh issledovaniĭ, 1984. 115 p. : ill. ; 26 cm. (Sbornik trudov . vyp. 7) Includes bibliographies. LC Card 85-192528
1. Raw materials. 2. Raw materials - Soviet Union. 3. Natural resources. 4. Natural resources - Soviet Union. I. Arbatov, A. A. (Aleksandr Arkad'evich). II. Reteium,

Alekseĭ I͡Ur'evich. III. Series: Sbornik trudov (Vsesoi͡uznyĭ nauchno-issledovatel'skiĭ institut sistemnykh issledovaniĭ) , 1984, vyp. 7.
HF1051 .K64 1984

Kompleksnyĭ analiz proektnogo proizvodstva na primere promyshlennogo proektirovanii͡a /. Sidorov, A. I. (Alekseĭ Ivanovich) Moskva , 1985. 197, [3] p. : LC Card 86-129875
HD9715.S72 S57 1985

Kompleksnyĭ ėkonomicheskiĭ analiz v. A.S.U.P. Panteleev, Vladimir Dmitrievich. Kompleksnyĭ ėkonomicheskiĭ analiz v. ASUP /. Leningrad , 1981. 176 p. ; LC Card 87-462046
HD30.2 .P365 1981

Kompleksnyĭ ėkonomicheskiĭ analiz v. ASUP /. Panteleev, Vladimir Dmitrievich. Leningrad , 1981. 176 p. ; LC Card 87-462046
HD30.2 .P365 1981

A komplex meliorációs beruházások történeti áttekintése és gazdasági hatásának vizsgálata különböző agroökológiai tipusu gazdaságokban /. Ács, Rudolf. Budapest , 1986. 118 p. ; ISBN 963-491-237-0 LC Card 87-137972
HD1940.5 .A65 1986

Komsomol'sko-molodezhnyĭ kollektiv /. Kuzin, V. Moskva , 1981. 157 p. ; LC Card 82-152678
HD6276.S592 K89 1981

Køn og ledelse . Carlsen, Anne Marie Sloth. København , 1986. 251 p. : ISBN 87-87749-29-7 (pbk.) :kr149.00 LC Card 87-145777
HD6054.4.D4 C37 1986

Konarzewska-Gubała, Ewa. Systemy organizacyjne /. [Wrocław] , 1981. 75 p. : LC Card 83-161920
HB9 .B7522 nr. 188 HM131

Koncepcia ďalšieho rozvoja plánovitého riadenia efektívneho využívania pracovnej sily . Fusko, Zoltán. Bratislava , 1982. 62 p. ; LC Card 83-113861
HD5772.3.A6 F87 1982

Koncepció és kritika : vita Liska Tibor "szocialista vállalkozási szektor" javaslatáról / [szerkesztette, Síklaky István]. Budapest : Magvető, c1985. 387 p. ; 18 cm. (Gyorsuló idő, 0324-7155) Includes bibliographical references. ISBN 963-14-0359-9 : LC Card 86-104222
1. Entrepreneur. 2. Small business - Hungary. 3. Small business - Communist countries. 4. Liska, Tibor. I. Síklaky, István. II. Title: Szocialista vállalkozási szektor.
HB615 .K66 1985

Kondarev, Nikolaĭ. Lekov, Kostadin. Nasoki za usŭvŭrshenstvuvane na sistemata za upravlenie na truda /. Sofii͡a , 1985. 103 p. ; LC Card 86-230344
HF5549.2.B9 L46 1985

Kondrashenkov, Alekseĭ Alekseevich. Osnovnye kategorii krest'i͡an v period pozdnego feodalizma, XVII--pervai͡a polovina XIX vv. . Smolensk , 1985. 134 p., [1] leaf of plates : LC Card 86-120158
HD1536.S65 O86 1985

Kondratas, S. Anna. Comparable worth : pay equity or social engineering? : a debate between S. Anna Kondratas and Eleanor Smeal. Washington, D.C. : Heritage Foundation, [c1986] 16 p. ; 28 cm. (The Heritage lectures, 0272-1155 . 63) LC Card 86-212973 DDC 331.2/1 19
1. Pay equity. I. Smeal, Eleanor. II. Title. III. Series.
HD6061 .K66 1986

Kondratenkov, A. E. (Aleksandr Erofeevich) Osnovnye kategorii krest'i͡an v period pozdnego feodalizma, XVII--pervai͡a polovina XIX vv. . Smolensk , 1985. 134 p., [1] leaf of plates : LC Card 86-120158
HD1536.S65 O86 1985

Kondrati͡uk, K. K. (Konstantin Konstantinovich) Profsoi͡uzy Ukraïny na zavershai͡ushchem ėtape stroitel'stva sotsializma / K.K. Kondrati͡uk. L'vov : Izd-vo pri L'vovskom gos. universitete Izdatel'skogo ob"edinenii͡a "Vyshcha shkola", 1985. 173 p. ; 21 cm. LC Card 87-165263
1. Trade-unions - Ukraine. 2. Ukraine - Social policy. 3. Industrial management - Ukraine. I. Title.
HD6735.U5 K65 1985

Kondufor, I͡Uriĭ I͡Ur'evich. Rabochiĭ klass Ukrainskoĭ SSR . Kiev , 1986. 238 p. ; LC Card 86-155918
HD8529.U42 R33 1986

Konferensie Vakbondwese in Suid-Afrika . Konferensie Vakbondwese in Suid-Afrika (1984 : Randse Afrikaanse Universiteit) Johannesburg [1984] 73 p. ; ISBN 0-86970-252-1 LC Card 87-126320
HD6870.5 .K65 1984

Konferensie Vakbondwese in Suid-Afrika (1984 : Randse Afrikaanse Universiteit) Konferensie Vakbondwese in Suid-Afrika : rewolusie of vrede? : 1 oktober 1984 / Sentrum vir die Ondersoek na Rewolusionêre Bedrywighede. Johannesburg : Randse Afrikaanse Universiteit, [1984] 73 p. ; 21 cm. (SORB . 6) Afrikaans and English. Cover title. CONTENTS. - Politisering van vakbonde / N.E. Wiehahn -- The aspirations of trade unions in South Africa / L. Mvubelo -- The advantages and disadvantages of trade unionism in South Africa / R.M. Godsell -- Vakbondwese en rewolusie / P.J. Coetzee-- Die regeringsbeleid met betrekking tot die vakbondwese / L. Wessels -- Die beleid van die amptelike opposisie met betrekking tot die vakbondwese / N.J.J. Olivier. ISBN 0-86970-252-1 LC Card 87-126320
1. Trade-unions - South Africa - Congresses. I. Title. II. Title: Vakbondwese in Suid-Afrika. III. Series: SORB (Series) , 6.
HD6870.5 .K65 1984

Konferent͡sii͡a molodykh uchenykh-ėkonomistov respublik Pribaltiki (1978 : Riga, Latvia) Ėkonomika razvitogo sotsializma : tezisy dokladov Konferentsii molodykh uchenykh-ėkonomistov respubliki Pribaltiki / [nauchnyĭ redaktor I.G. Adirim]. Riga : "Zinatne", 1978. 110 p. ; 20 cm. At head of title: Akademii͡a nauk Latviĭskoĭ SSR. Institut ėkonomiki. Includes bibliographies. LC Card 82-100692
1. Baltic States - Economic conditions - Congresses. 2. Baltic States - Economic policy - Congresses. 3. Baltic States - Economic conditions - Abstracts. 4. Baltic States - Economic policy - Abstracts. I. Adirim, I. G. (Itskhok Girshevich). II. Ekonomikas instituts (Latvijas PSR Zinātņu akadēmija). III. Title.
HC243 .K66 1978

Konferent͡sii͡a OON po torgovle i razvitii͡u. see **United Nations. Conference on Trade and Development.**

Konfirmatorische Analysen von Modellen des Konsumentenverhaltens /. Hildebrandt, Lutz. Berlin , c1983. xii, 307 p. : ISBN 3-428-05381-8 LC Card 83-190106
HF5415.3 .H55 1983

Konflikt und Kooperation der Dritten Welt mit Industrieländern /. Moser, Beat. Diessenhofen , c1985. xi, 352 p. : ISBN 3-7253-0236-7 : LC Card 85-139491
HF1413 .M66 1985

Konflikt und Kooperation in Arbeitgeberverbänden /. Mühlfeld, Claus, 1940- Augsburg , 1985. 403 p. ; ISBN 3-87512-138-4 : LC Card 86-152717
HD2429.G3 M84 1985

Konflikt und Kooperation zwischen Ost und West . Wettig, Gerhard. Bonn , c1981. 217 p. ; ISBN 3-7894-0082-3 LC Card 82-225671 DDC 327.1/7 19
D849 .W47 1981 ***NYPL [JLE 86-4503]***

Konflikte der Industrialisierung . Siegenthaler, Jürg K., 1939- Bern , New York , c1985. 249 p. : ISBN 3-261-04012-2 LC Card 85-226977
HC398.G55 S54 1985

Konflikti razvojnih ciljeva u samoupravnom društvu /. Korać, Slobodan. Beograd , 1981. 304 p. : LC Card 82-166028
HD42 .K67 1981

Konfliktregelung und Mitbestimmung . Kauer, Christian, 1951- Frankfurt am Main , New York , c1985. 393 p. : ISBN 3-8204-5626-0 (pbk.) LC Card 87-672045
HD5660.G4 K37x 1985

Konflikttraining /. Berkel, Karl. Heidelberg , c1985. 82 p. : ISBN 3-7938-7735-3 LC Card 85-188803
HD42 .B47 1985

Konformität und Nichtkonformität im Betrieb . Lenssen, Adolf K. Konstanz , 1986. 400 p. : ISBN 3-89191-064-9 (p. 4. of cover); 3-89191-064-7 LC Card 87-109576 DDC 658.3/001/9 19
HF5549 .L4619 1986

Konfrontat͡sii͡a ili kompromiss? . Volkov, Aleksandr Ivanovich. Moskva , 1986. 234 p. [4] ; LC Card 86-200508 DDC 658.3/152 19
HD5650 .V65 1986

Kongeåen, eller, Den gamle grænse /. Eliassen, Peter. [København, Amaliegade 44, 1256 K] [Esbjerg] , 1980. 357, [4] p. : ISBN 87-87796-02-3 : LC Card 81-107972
HJ6971 .E45 1980

Kongres privrednih stručnjaka Hrvatske . Kongres privrednih stručnjaka Hrvatske (1943-1944 : Otočac and Čazma, Croatia) Zagreb , 1985. 252 p., [16] p. of plates : ISBN 86-80359-01-7 LC Card 86-176200
HC407.Z7 C7637 1943

Kongres privrednih stručnjaka Hrvatske (1943-1944 : Otočac and Čazma, Croatia) Kongres privrednih stručnjaka Hrvatske : Otočac, 15-17. XII-Čazma, 20-22. I 1944 : prilog istraživanju ekonomike oslobođenih krajeva Hrvatske 1941-1945. s posebnim osvrtom na ekonomiku agrara / Nikola Rapajić, Mira Kolar-Dimitrijević. Zagreb : Savez poljoprivrednih inženjera i tehničara SRH : Institut za historiju radničkog pokreta Hrvatske, 1985. 252 p., [16] p. of plates : ill. ; 25 cm. In Serbo-Croatian (roman) Summary in English. Bibliography: p. 247. ISBN 86-80359-01-7 LC Card 86-176200
1. Croatia - Economic conditions - Congresses. 2. World War, 1939-1945 - Economic aspects - Yugoslavia - Croatia - Congresses. I. Rapajić, Nikola. II. Kolar-Dimitrijević, Mira. III. Savez poljoprivrednih inženjera i tehničara SRH. IV. Institut za historiju radničkog pokreta Hrvatske. V. Title.
HC407.Z7 C7637 1943

Kongress "Ausländerpolitik und Menschenrechte" (1983 : Frankfurt am Main, Germany) Reader zum Kongress "Ausländerpolitik und Menschenrechte" / Koordinationsbüro "Frankfurter Appell" (Hrsg.). Frankfurt : Das Koordinationsbüro, 1984. 60 p. ; 29 cm. LC Card 87-133583 DDC 331.6/2/0943 19
1. Alien labor - Government policy - Germany (West) - Congresses. 2. Alien labor - Germany (West) - Social conditions - Congresses. 3. Germany (West) - Ethnic relations - Congresses. I. Koordinationsbüro "Frankfurter Appell.". II. Title.
HD8458.A2 K594 1983

Kongstad, Per. Industri, fagbevægelse og lønarbejde i Kenya : kapitalismens fremgang og krise / Per Kongstad og Britha Mikkelsen. Roskilde : Roskilde universitetscenter, Institut for geografi, samfundsanalyse og datalogi, [1983] 76 p. ; 30 cm. (Publikationer fra Institut for geografi, samfundsanalyse og datalogi. Arbejdspapir, 0106-5920 . nr. 36, 1983) "Juni 1983." Bibliography: p. 73-76. LC Card 85-238103
1. Kenya - Industries. 2. Trade-unions - Kenya. 3. Labor and laboring classes - Kenya. 4. Kenya - Economic conditions - 1963-. 5. Capitalism - Kenya. I. Mikkelsen, Britha. II. Series: Publikationer fra Institut for geografi, samfundsanalyse og datalogi, Roskilde universitetscenter. Arbejdspapir , nr. 36. III. Title.
HC865 .K66 1983

König, Robert. Die Wohnflächenbestände der Gemeinden der Vorderpfalz : Bestandsaufnahme, Typisierung und zeitliche Begrenzung der Flächenverfügbarkeit raumfordernder Wohnfunktionsprozesse / von Robert König. Heidelberg : Im Selbstverlag des Geographischen Institutes der Universität Heidelberg, 1980. [14], 226 p. : maps ; 24 cm. (Heidelberger geographische Arbeiten. Heft 68) Summary in English. Originally presented as the author's thesis (doctoral)--Heidelberg, 1979. One folded map in pocket. Bibliography: p. 200-209. ISBN 3-88570-068-9 LC Card 81-136631 DDC 333.73/13/0724 19
1. Land use - Germany (West) - Rhineland-Palatinate - Mathematical models. 2. Housing - Germany (West) - Rhineland-Palatinate - Mathematical models. 3. Rhineland-Palatinate (Germany) - Population density - Mathematical models. I. Title. II. Series.
HD659.P34 K66 1980
NYPL [L-10 4979 Heft 68]

Konijn, Peter A. B. Kalker. Disability benefits . Greenwich, Conn. , c1987. xxii, 282 p. ; ISBN 0-89232-824-X : LC Card 87-17056 DDC 368.3/86/009492 19
HD7105.25.N4 D57 1987

Konings, Piet. The state and rural class formation in Ghana : a comparative analysis / Piet Konings ; [edited by James J. Ravell]. London ; Boston : KPI : xvi, 391 p. : maps ; 23 cm.

Includes index. Bibliography: p. 356-377. ISBN 0-7103-0117-0 LC Card 85-28109 DDC 305.5/09667 19
1. Social classes - Ghana. 2. Agriculture and state - Ghana. 3. Cocoa trade - Ghana. 4. Rice trade - Ghana. 5. Ghana - Rural conditions. I. Ravell, James J. II. Title.
HN832.Z9 S65 1986 ***NYPL [Sc D 86-574]***

Konjunktur und Wachstum . Reetz, Norbert. St. Gallen , 1983. viii, 121 p. : LC Card 83-141234
HD75.5 .R44 1983

Konjunkturinstitutet (Sweden) Sveriges varuexport 1977-1983 . [Stockholm] [1979] 168 p. : ISBN 91-38-04928-7 LC Card 83-241226
HF3676.5 .S84 1979

Konjunkturpolitik und Wahlen . Schenkluhn, Brigitte, 1951- Bergisch Gladbach , 1985. xi, 482 p. : ISBN 3-89012-017-2 LC Card 85-153982
HB3789 .S34 1985

Konjunkturzyklen . Schlager, Errol, 1950- Augsburg , 1986. ii, 99 p. : ISBN 3-925274-08-1 LC Card 87-127445 DDC 338.5/42 19
HB3716 .S35 1986

Konkurrenz und Gleichgewicht als Fundamente von Gesellschaft . Reheis, Fritz. Berlin , c1986. xi, 401 p. : ISBN 3-428-06102-0 LC Card 87-131057 DDC 339.5 19
HB238 .R44 1986

Konkurrenzanalyse in der strategischen Planung /. Hainzl, Martin. Wien , 1985. 143 p. : ISBN 3-85436-027-4 LC Card 86-127579 DDC 658.4/012 19
HD30.28 .H334 1985

Konnik, I. I. (Iosif Isaakovich) Denezhnoe obrashchenie v protsesse rasshirennogo sotsialisticheskogo vosproizvodstva / I.I. Konnik. Moskva : "Finansy i statistika", 1982. 269 p. ; 20 cm. Includes bibliographical references. LC Card 83-165373
1. Finance - Soviet Union. 2. Money - Soviet Union. 3. Credit - Soviet Union. I. Title.
HG186.S55 K65 1982

Kononov, IU. D. Vliianie energeticheskikh strategiĭ na energopotreblenie / IU.D. Kononov. Irkutsk : Akademiia nauk SSSR, Sibirskoe otd-nie, Sibirskiĭ energ. in-t, 1985. 106 p. : ill. ; 20 cm. Bibliography: p. 102-106. LC Card 86-233835
1. Energy policy - Soviet Union. 2. Energy consumption - Soviet Union. I. Sibirskiĭ energeticheskiĭ institut. II. Title.
HD9502.S652 K65 1985

Konovalov, L. A. (Leopol'd Anatol'evich) Bakanov, K. P. (Konstantin Pavlovich) Sovershenstvovanie organizatsii truda na predpriiatiiakh chernoĭ metallurgii /. Moskva , 1981. 47 p. ; LC Card 82-104389
HD9525.S652 B355 1981

Konovalov, Vladimir. Fiji, a transition to manufacturing. Washington, D.C., U. S.A. , c1987. xvi, 107 p., [1] folded leaf of plates : ISBN 0-8213-0962-5 LC Card 87-23067 DDC 338.4/767/099611 19
HD9738.F55 F55 1987

Konovalova, N. A. (Nina Alekseevna) Mezhdunarodnye transportnye tarify / N.A. Konovalova. Moskva : "Transport", 1985. 278 p. ; 22 cm. Bibliography: p. 278. LC Card 86-127719
1. Transportation - Europe, Eastern - Rates. 2. Transportation - Rates. I. Title.
HE195.5.E852 K65 1985

KONRAD-ADENAUER-STIFTUNG. Kress, Roland, 1961- Die politischen Stiftungen in der Entwicklungspolitik . Bochum , 1985. iv, 224 p. ; ISBN 3-88339-426-2 : LC Card 85-175519
HC60 .K727 1985

Konrad-Adenauer-Stiftung. Bildungswerk. Die Notwendige Hilfe . Melle [1986] 207 p. : ISBN 3-88368-111-3 : LC Card 86-197696
HC60 .N69 1986

Konrad-Adenauer-Stiftung. Sozialwissenschaftliches Forschungsinstitut. Die Wirtschaft der Vereinigten Staaten und der Bundesrepublik Deutschland . Bonn , c1977. 106 p. ; ISBN 3-87198-079-X LC Card 86-104673
HC106.7 .W57 1977

Konstantinov, IU. A. (IUriĭ Anatol'evich) Mezhdunarodnaia valiutnaia sistema stran--chlenov SEV / IU.A. Konstantinov. Moskva : "Finansy i statistika," 1982. 231 p. ; 21 cm. Includes bibliographical references. LC Card 82-210094
1. Foreign exchange problem - Europe, Eastern. 2. Currency question - Europe, Eastern. 3. Europe, Eastern - Economic integration. 4. Finance - Europe, Eastern. I. Title.
HG3942 .K67 1982

Konstanzer Dissertationen .
(Bd. 133) Lenssen, Adolf K. Konformität und Nichtkonformität im Betrieb . Konstanz , 1986. 400 p. : ISBN 3-89191-064-9 (p. 4. of cover); 3-89191-064-7 LC Card 87-109576 DDC 658.3/001/9 19
HF5549 .L4619 1986

(133) Lenssen, Adolf K. Konformität und Nichtkonformität im Betrieb . Konstanz , 1986. 400 p. : ISBN 3-89191-064-9 (p. 4. of cover); 3-89191-064-7 LC Card 87-109576 DDC 658.3/001/9 19
HF5549 .L4619 1986

(82) Schmidt, Peter M. Unweltthemen in der öffentlichen Diskussion /. Konstanz , 1985. ix, 296 p. : ISBN 3-89191-001-0 LC Card 86-155948
HC290.5.E5 S37 1985

Konstellationsadäquate Beschaffungspolitik im Handel. Mertens, Jürgen. Zur Entwicklung und zum konstellationsadäquaten Einsatz eines Beschaffungsmarketinginstrumentariums im Einzelhandel /. Köln , 1986. 379 p. : ISBN 3-922292-13-7 LC Card 87-143182 DDC 658.8/7 19
HF5429.225 .M47 1986

Konstitutionella begränsningar i Riksdagens finansmakt . Lybeck, Johan A., 1944- [Stockholm] [1984] 147 p. : ISBN 91-38-08365-5 (Sve. bok.) : LC Card 84-240503
HJ1238 .L92 1984

Konsum und Verhalten .
(Bd. 5) Bleicker, Ulrike. Produktbeurteilung der Konsumenten . Würzburg , c1983. 245 p. : ISBN 3-7908-0292-1 LC Card 83-191583
HF5415.3 .B52 1983

Der Konsumeffekt der Investitionen . Enke, Harald. Tübingen , 1986. xii, 114 p. ; ISBN 3-88573-026-X LC Card 87-407594 DDC 339.4/3 19
HG4521 .E63 1986

Konsument- och lantbrukskooperation i Sverige . Kylebäck, Hugo, 1930- Stockholm [1984] 277 p. ; ISBN 91-85196-18-5 : LC Card 86-120646
HD3524.A1 K663 1984

Konsumenteninformation und ihre Nutzer /. Bauer, Fritz. Linz , 1986. ii, 113 p. : ISBN 3-85320-388-4 LC Card 87-134585 DDC 381/.3/09436 19
HC270.C6 B38 1986

Konsumentenpsychologie und Markenartikel / herausgegeben von Fritz Unger ; mit Beiträgen von L. Berekoven ... [et al.]. Heidelberg : Physica-Verlag, c1986. xiii, 238 p. ; 25 cm. Includes bibliographies and index. ISBN 3-7908-0353-7 LC Card 87-127600 DDC 658.8/342 19
1. Marketing. I. Unger, Fritz. II. Berekoven, Ludwig.
HF5415 .K598 1986

Konsumentenreaktion auf Preise /. Feider, Josef. Göttingen , c1985. xii, 303 p. : ISBN 3-525-12667-0 LC Card 85-203330
HF5415.3 .F39 1985

Konsumentenverhalten in der Bundesrepublik Deutschland 1958-1982 . Schöll, Wolfgang. Thun , c1985. 226, 70, [9] p. : ISBN 3-87144-900-8 (Deut. Bibl.) : LC Card 85-232693
HC290.5.C6 S35 1985

Konsumentenzufriedenheit und Beschwerden . Bruhn, Manfred. Frankfurt am Main , Bern , 1982. xiv, 211 p. ; ISBN 3-8204-5712-7 LC Card 82-131889
HF5415.3 .B78 1982

Konsumenter, konsumentpolitik, rationalitet och välfärd . Wolvén, Lars-Erik. Umeå , 1981. 83 leaves ; LC Card 82-105540 DDC 658.8/342/09485 19
HC380.C63 W64 ***NYPL [JLM 74-106 no.61]***

Konsumentscheidung und Informationsüberlastung . Berndt, Hermann, 1956- München , c1983. 368 p. : ISBN 3-89003-002-5 LC Card 84-192993
HF5821 .B42 1983

Konsumgenossenschaften und Food-Cooperatives . Jösch, Jutta. Berlin , c1983. 126 p. : ISBN 3-428-05423-7 LC Card 83-231020
HD3338 .J67 1983

Konsumpcja a wykorzystanie możliwości produkcyjnej w gospodarce socjalistycznej /. Libura, Urszula. Warszawa , 1979. 242 p. ; ISBN 83-01-00103-8 LC Card 81-192720
HC710.C6 L53 1979

Konsumtion i förändring : en sammanställning. Vällingby : Konsumentverket, [1985] 87 p. : ill. ; 30 cm. At head of title: "Allmänna byrån 1985:6-04." Bibliography: p. 79-82. LC Card 86-224791
1. Consumption (Economics) - Sweden. 2. Consumers - Sweden. 3. Sweden - Economic conditions - 1945-. I. Sweden. Konsumentverket.
HC380.C6 K675 1985

Konsumtive Arbeit . Enke, Harald. Freiburg im Breisgau , c1983. 354 p. : ISBN 3-448-01239-4 LC Card 83-224110
HF5549.5.J63 E54 1983

Konsumverhalten und wirtschaftliche Entwicklung . Gerhardt, Gisela, 1955- München , c1984. 224 p. : ISBN 3-88259-278-8 LC Card 84-220049
HC79.C6 G47 1984

Kontakt & Studium.
(Bd. 80) Franz, Lothar. Verkehrsberuhigung in Städten und Gemeinden /. Grafenau , c1982. 134 p. : ISBN 3-88508-780-4 : LC Card 82-204794
HE311.G3 F73 1982

(Bd. 80) Franz, Lothar. Verkehrsberuhigung in Städten und Gemeinden /. Grafenau , c1982. 134 p. : ISBN 3-88508-780-4 : LC Card 82-204794
HE311.G3 F73 1982

Konten und Statistiken des Staates, 1970-1981. Regnskaber og statistikker for den offentlige sektor 1970-1981 =. Luxembourg , Washington, DC , 1983. clxxii, 279 p. ; ISBN 92-825-4066-9 LC Card 84-174459
HC240.9.I5 R45 1983

Kontinuität und Wandel in vier Jahrzehnten deutscher Wirtschaftspolitik / mit Beiträgen von Kurt H. Biedenkopf ... [et al.] ; Redaktion, Hartmut Pick. Stuttgart ; New York : G. Fischer, 1986. 111 p. ; 25 cm. "Ein Symposion der Ludwig-Erhard-Stiftung Bonn am 16. Januar 1986"--P. facing t.p. Bibliography: p. 105-106. Includes index. ISBN 3-437-50310-3 LC Card 87-116017 DDC 338.943 19
1. Germany, West - Economic policy - Congresses. I. Biedenkopf, Kurt H. II. Pick, Hartmut. III. Ludwig Erhard-Stiftung.
HC286.5 .K618 1986

Kontogeōrgēs, Geōrgios L. Hē Hellada stēn Eurōpē : hē poreia pros tēn henōsē kai hē politikē tou Karamanlē / Geōrgiou L. Kontogeōrgē. [Athens] : Pankosmios Ekdot. Organismos, Chrēstos Giovanēs A.E.V.E., [1985] 311 p. : col. ports. ; 21 cm. LC Card 86-206722
1. European Economic Community - Greece. 2. Karamanlis, Konstantinos, 1907-. I. Title.
HC241.25.G8 K65 1985

Kontorarbejde . Agervold, Mogens. [Copenhagen] , c1983. 126 p. ; ISBN 87-500-2489-2 : LC Card 84-126389
HF5547.5 .A43 1983

Kontos, Maria. Verbandsstrategien zur Ausländerbeschäftigung in der Bundesrepublik : eine Analyse der Integrationsstrategien der Unternehmerverbände und der Gewerkschaften gegenüber den ausländischen Arbeitern / von Maria Kontos. Königstein/Ts. : Hanstein, c1983. viii, 235 p. ; 21 cm. (Materialien zur Arbeitsmigration und Ausländerbeschäftigung . Bd. 9) Originally presented as the author's thesis (doctoral)--Universität Frankfurt, 1981. Bibliography: p. 221-235. ISBN 3-7756-6938-8 LC Card 83-190064 DDC 331.6/2/0943 19
1. Alien labor - Germany, West. 2. Employers associations - Germany, West. 3. Trade-unions - Germany, West. I. Title. II. Series.
HD8458.A2 K598 1983
NYPL [JLD 86-2465]

Kontrol´ i analiz deiatel´nosti predpriiatiĭ po zagotovkam sel´skokhoziaĭstvennoĭ produktsii /. Murashko, V. M. (Vasiliĭ Maksimovich) Moskva , 1981. 144 p. ; LC Card 82-177216
HF5686.A36 M87 1981

Kontrolltheoretische Ansätze in makroökonometrischen Modellen / Heinz König (Hrsg.). Frankfurt am Main ; New York : P. Lang, c1985. 170 p. : ill. ; 21 cm. (Staatliche Allokationspolitik im marktwirtschaftlichen System, 0721-2860 . Bd. 18) "Diese Arbeit ist im Sonderforschungsbereich 5, 'Staatliche Allokationspolitik' Mannheim entstanden"--T.p. verso. "Die in diesem Band veröffentlichten Studien wurden im Rahmen des von der Deutschen Forschungsgemeinschaft unterstützen Projektes 'Stochastische Stabilisierungspolitik' angefertigt, dessen Arbeit eng mit Projekten des Sonderforschungsbereichs 5 verbunden ist."--P. 12. Includes bibliographies. CONTENTS. - Einführung in das Thema und Übersicht über die Beiträge / Heinz König -- Adaptive Entscheidungsmodelle / Harald Frommholz -- Stabilisierungspolitik im Rahmen eines stochastischen Kontrollansatzes : eine empirische Analyse für die Bundesrepublik Deutschland / Wolfgang Franz, Theo Kempf, Horst Kräger -- Kontrolltheoretische Ansätze zur Bestimmung von Feedback-Regeln : eine Sensitivitätsanalyse / Harald Frommholz, Jürgen Wolters. ISBN 3-8204-8314-4 LC Card 86-156081
1. Economic stabilization - Econometric models. 2. Economic stabilization - Germany (West) - Econometric models. 3. Control theory - Econometric models. I. König, Heinz, 1927-. II. Series.
HB3732 .K68 1985

Kontrolltheoretische Entscheidungsmodelle . Fischer, Thomas. Berlin , c1982. x, 343 p. : ISBN 3-428-05111-4 :
NYPL [JLE 86-3084]

Kontroversen um Markt und Plan . Nienhaus, Volker. Darmstadt , 1984. vi, 171 p. ; ISBN 3-534-08700-3 LC Card 84-181049
HB95 .N47 1984

Kontseptsii obshchestvennogo razvitiia. Spanish. Concepciones del desarrollo social. Moscú : Redacción "Ciencias Sociales Contemporáneas", Academia de Ciencias de la URSS, <1984- > v. <2 > ; 22 cm. (América Latina, estudios de científicos soviéticos . <25- >) Translation of: Kontseptsii obshchestvennogo razvitiia. Includes bibliographies. LC Card 87-124757
1. Latin America - Economic conditions - 1945-. 2. Latin America - Politics and government - 1948-. I. Title. II. Series.
HC125 .K65517 1984

Kontseptsii vzaimodeĭstviia ėkonomiki i prirody /. Bartov, Vladimir Fotievich. Moskva , 1984. 157 p. ; LC Card 84-225876
HC79.E5 B369 1984

Kontseptsiia i napravleniia ratsionalizatsii narodnogo potrebleniia / otvetstvennyĭ redaktor Ė.M. Agabab´ian. Moskva : In-t ėkonomiki AN SSSR, 1985. 172 p. : ill. ; 20 cm. Includes bibliographical references. LC Card 86-193920
1. Consumption (Economics) - Soviet Union. I. Agabab´ian, Ė. M. (Ėdgar Mikhaĭlovich). II. Institut ėkonomiki (Akademiia nauk SSSR).
HC340.C6 K573 1985

Konturen bundesdeutscher Rohstoffpolitik /. Köhler, Axel, 1938- Köln , c1983. 56 p. : ISBN 3-602-24713-9 LC Card 83-215016
HF1054.G4 K64 1983

Konverty pervogo dnia i kartmaksimumy. Katalog konvertov pervogo dnia i kartmaksimumov, 1980-1983 /. Moskva , 1985. 221 p. : LC Card 86-102861
HE6184.F57 K38 1985

Könyvelésről és pénzgazdálkodásról vállalati vezetőknek . Bánhidi, Ferenc. Budapest , 1986, c1985. 215 p. ; ISBN 963-221-649-0 : LC Card 87-118825
HF5655.H9 B36 1986

Konzentration . Müller, Hans-Erich, 1945- Hamburg , 1985. 239 p. : ISBN 3-87975-303-2 LC Card 87-110533 DDC 338.8 19
HD2757 .M85 1985

Die Konzentration im Handel . Schenk, Hans-Otto. Berlin , c1984. 341 p. : ISBN 3-428-05618-3 LC Card 84-225438
HF345 .F66 Folge 3, Nr. 9 HF3566

Konzentration und gesamtwirtschaftliche Stabilität . Stahlecker, Peter. Frankfurt am Main , New York , c1984. v, 592 p. : ISBN 3-8204-5318-0 LC Card 85-192714
HD2757 .S78 1984

Das Konzept rationaler Preiserwartungen /. Wittmann, Uli. Berlin , New York , c1985. xi, 310 p. : ISBN 0-387-15221-0 LC Card 86-194342
HB221 .W56 1985

Konzepte der Organisationspsychologie . Greif, Siegfried. Bern , c1983. 320 p. : ISBN 3-456-81262-0 LC Card 83-240680
HD58.7 .G72 1983

Konzepte städtischer Wohnungspolitik . Echter, Claus-Peter. Berlin , 1985. 97 p. : ISBN 3-88118-123-7 LC Card 86-145702
HD7288.78.G3 E265 1985

Konzernrechnungslegung. Nadvornik, Wolfgang. Konzernrechnungslegung in Österreich . Linz , c1985. ii, 109 p. ; ISBN 3-85320-341-8 : LC Card 85-218757
HF5686.C7 N27 1985

Konzernrechnungslegung in Österreich . Nadvornik, Wolfgang. Linz , c1985. ii, 109 p. ; ISBN 3-85320-341-8 : LC Card 85-218757
HF5686.C7 N27 1985

Konzernstruktur und Steuerplanung . Tinner, Hanspeter. Bern , c1984. ix, 276 p. : ISBN 3-258-03367-6 : LC Card 84-198592
HJ4748.A3 T55 1984

Koontz, Harold, 1908- Management / Harold Koontz, Heinz Weihrich. 9th ed. New York : McGraw-Hill, c1988. xxix, 685 p. : ill. (some col.) ; 25 cm. (McGraw-Hill series in management) Includes bibliographies and indexes. ISBN 0-07-035552-5 : LC Card 87-21519 DDC 658.4 19
1. Management. 2. Industrial management. I. Weihrich, Heinz. II. Title.
HD31 .K6 1988

Kooperations- und genossenschaftswissenschaftliche Beiträge .
(Bd. 1) Janetzki, Annemarie. Das Verbundwinzersystem . Münster , 1982. xxiv, 406 p., [3] folded leaves of plates : ISBN 3-7923-0486-4 LC Card 83-157892
HD9383.5 .J35 1982

(Bd. 15) Berger, Axel. Mitgliederförderung in Strassenverkehrsgenossenschaften /. Münster , 1985. 455 p. ; ISBN 3-7923-0537-2 (Deut. Bibl.) LC Card 86-148185
HD6698.T72 B863 1985

(Bd. 8) Schrimpff, Wolfgang. Heterogene Koordinationsinstrumente im Beschäftigungssystem der DDR /. Münster , 1983. xv, 360 p. : ISBN 3-7923-0505-4 LC Card 85-140056
HD5780.5.A6 S37 1983

Kooperationsführer Kamerun / erstellt durch TWD, Technisch-Wirtschaftlicher Dienst der Ländervereine, in Zusammenarbeit mit Luso Consult, Gesellschaft für Agrarentwicklung und Regionalplanung. Köln : Deutsche Gesellschaft für Technische Zusammenarbeit : [zu beziehen bei, Bundesstelle für Ausenhandelsinformation], 1986. 70 p. : ill. ; 24 cm. (Betriebliche Kooperation mit Unternehmen in Entwicklungsländern . 4) Includes bibliographical references. LC Card 87-408425 DDC 330.967/1104 19
1. Cameroon - Economic conditions - 1960-. 2. Cameroon - Commerce. I. Technisch-Wirtschaftlicher Dienst der Ländervereine. II. Luso Consult, Gesellschaft für Agrarentwicklung und Regionalplanung. III. Series.
HC995 .K66 1986

Kooperationsstrategien westeuropäischer und japanischer Banken in den ASEAN-Staaten /. Strittmatter, Gabriele. Baden-Baden , 1984. 411 p. : ISBN 3-7890-1051-0 LC Card 86-134027
HG3324 .S77 1984

KOOPERATIVA FÖRBUNDET - HISTORY - 20TH CENTURY.
Kylebäck, Hugo, 1930- Konsument- och lantbrukskooperation i Sverige . Stockholm [1984] 277 p. ; ISBN 91-85196-18-5 : LC Card 86-120646
HD3524.A1 K663 1984

Kooperative Systembildung in der Transportwirtschaft . Eckstein, Werner E. Karlsruhe , c1985. vii, 263 p. : ISBN 3-88652-028-5 LC Card 86-135639
HE199.G3 E28 1985

Kooperativnoe dvizhenie v Sibiri : sbornik nauchnykh trudov / [redaktsionnaia kollegiia Kiselev L.E. (otv. redaktor) ... et al.]. Tiumen´ : Tiumenskiĭ gos. universitet, 1984. 72 p. ; 20 cm. At head of title: Ministerstvo vysshego i srednego spetsial´nogo obrazovaniia RSFSR. Tiumenskiĭ gosudarstvennyĭ universitet. Includes bibliographical references. LC Card 85-179545
1. Cooperation - Russian S.F.S.R. - Siberia - History. 2. Collectivization of agriculture - Russian S.F.S.R. - Siberia - History. I. Kiselev, L. E. II. Tiumenskiĭ gosudarstvennyĭ universitet.
HD3517.A3 R875 1984

Kooperirovannoe aratstvo M.N.R.--izmeneniia v urovne zhizni, 1960-1980. Graĭvoronskiĭ, Vladimir Viktorovich. Kooperirovannoe aratstvo MNR--izmeneniia v urovne zhizni, 1960-1980 /. Moskva , 1982. 213 p. : LC Card 82-213253
HD1491.M55 G73 1982

Kooperirovannoe aratstvo MNR--izmeneniia v urovne zhizni, 1960-1980 /. Graĭvoronskiĭ, Vladimir Viktorovich. Moskva , 1982. 213 p. : LC Card 82-213253
HD1491.M55 G73 1982

Koopman, A. F. Vrouwen zelfstandig : perspectieven op ondernemerschap. Den Haag : Emancipatieraad, [1986] 70 p. ; 30 cm. "Maart 1986." Prepared by A.F. Koopman with the cooperation of C. Walvis. Bibliography: p. 69-70. ISBN 90-346-0762-3 LC Card 86-172683
1. Women-owned business enterprises - Netherlands. 2. Entrepreneur. 3. Women in business. I. Walvis, C. II. Emancipatieraad (Netherlands). III. Title.
HD2346.N4 K66 1986

Koordinationsbüro "Frankfurter Appell." Kongress "Ausländerpolitik und Menschenrechte" (1983 : Frankfurt am Main, Germany) Reader zum Kongress "Ausländerpolitik und Menschenrechte" /. Frankfurt , 1984. 60 p. ; LC Card 87-133583 DDC 331.6/2/0943 19
HD8458.A2 K594 1983

Köörna, A. Upravlenie nauchno-tekhnicheskim progressom v soiuznykh respublikakh /. Tallin , 1986. 158 p. ; LC Card 87-123175
HC340.T4 U77 1986

Koot, Gerard M. English historical economics, 1870-1926 : the rise of economic history and neomercantilism / Gerard M. Koot. Cambridge [Cambridgeshire] ; New York : Cambridge University Press, 1987. viii, 277 p. ; 24 cm. (Historical perspectives on modern economics) Bibliography: p. 260-268. Includes index. ISBN 0-521-32854-3 LC Card 87-11592 DDC 330/.0941 19
1. Economics - Great Britain - History. 2. Economic history. I. Title. II. Title: Neomercantilism. III. Series.
HB103.A2 K65 1987

Kopach, N. L. (Nikolaĭ Leont´evich) Agrarnye problemy v svete resheniĭ XXVII s˝ezda KPSS /. Moskva , 1986. 185 p. ; LC Card 87-163428
HD1992 .A645 1986

Kopanev, A. I. (Aleksandr Il´ich) Krest´iane Russkogo Severa v XVII v. / A.I. Kopanev ; pod redaktsieĭ N.E. Nosova. Leningrad : "Nauka", Leningradskoe otd-nie, 1984. 242 p. ; 23 cm. At head of title: Akademiia nauk SSSR. Institut istorii SSSR. Leningradskoe otdelenie. Includes bibliographical references and indexes. LC Card 84-170666
1. Land tenure - Russian S.F.S.R. - History - 17th century. 2. Peasantry - Russian S.F.S.R. - History - 17th century. I. Nosov, Nikolaĭ Evgen´evich. II. Title. III. Title: Krest´iane Russkogo Severa v semnadtsatom v. IV. Title: Krest´iane Russkogo Severa v 17-om v.
HD719.R88 K67 1984 ***NYPL [*QG 86-3646]***

Kopanev, N. G. Prodovol´stvennaia programma SSSR . Moskva , 1986. 285 p. ; LC Card 87-110478 DDC 338.1/9/47 19
HD9015.S652 P743 1986

Kopcsó, István. Minőségfejlesztés az élelmiszer-termelésben : eszközök, módszerek / Kopcsó István, Sánta István. Budapest : Mezőgazdasági Kiadó, 1984. 253 p. : ill. ; 20 cm. Bibliography: p. 251-253. ISBN 963-231-707-6 : LC Card 85-183244
1. Food industry and trade - Quality control. 2. Food industry and trade - Technological innovations. 3. Food industry and trade - Hungary - Quality control. 4. Food industry and trade - Hungary - Technological innovations. I. Sánta, István. II. Title.
HD9000.5 .K644 1984

Kopec, Frank J. Barban, Arnold M. Essentials of media planning . Lincolnwood, Ill., U. S.A. , c1987. xii, 160 p. : ISBN 0-8442-3018-9 (pbk.) : LC Card 86-51055 DDC 659.1/11 19
HF5826.5 .B37 1987

Kopeck, Ronald F. Micro to mainframe links / Ronald F. Kopeck. Berkeley, Calif. : Osborne McGraw-Hill, c1986. xviii, 286 p. : ill. ; 24 cm. Includes index. ISBN 0-07-881228-3 (pbk.) LC Card 86-210460 DDC 004.6 19
1. Business - Data processing. 2. Microcomputers. 3. Local area networks (Computer networks). I. Title.
HF5548.2 .K628 1986

Kopernik, Mikołaj. see **Copernicus, Nicolaus, 1473-1543.**

Kopernikus, Nikolaus. see **Copernicus, Nicolaus, 1473-1543.**

Kopits, George. Structural reform, stabilization, and growth in Turkey / by George Kopits. Washington, D.C. : International Monetary Fund : External Relations Dept., Publication Services, IMF [distributor], c1987. v, 46 p. : col. ill. ; 28 cm. (Occasional paper. no. 52) "May 1987." Bibliography: p. 46. ISBN 0-939934-84-1 (pbk.) : LC Card 87-3583 DDC 338.9561 19
1. Turkey - Economic policy. 2. Turkey - Economic conditions - 1960-. 3. Fiscal policy - Turkey. I. Series: Occasional paper (International Monetary Fund) , no. 52. II. Title.
HC492 .K67 1987

Köpplinger, Herbert, 1954- Risiken im Auslandsgeschäft : eine theoretische und empirische Untersuchung des politischen Investitionsklimas / Herbert Köpplinger, Bernd Wolfrum. Nürnberg : Pauli-Balleis, 1986. xli, 227 p. : ill. ; 21 cm. (Schriftenreihe Internationales Management . Bd. 1) Bibliography: p. xxxi-xli. ISBN 3-89078-005-9 LC Card 87-145527 DDC 332.6/73 19
1. Investments, Foreign. 2. Venture capital. I. Wolfrum, Bernd, 1956-. II. Title. III. Series.
HG4538 .K64 1986

Kopras, Andrew. Trading with South Africa / Andrew Kopras. [Canberra] : Parliament of the Commonwealth of Australia, Legislative Research Service, Dept. of the Parliamentary Library, 1986. 14 p. ; 30 cm. (Current issues brief / Legislative Research Service, 0726-3244 . no. 3, 1986-87) Includes bibliographical references. LC Card 87-164241 DDC 382/.0968/094021 19
1. South Africa - Commerce - Statistics. 2. South Africa - Commerce - Australia - Statistics. 3. Australia - Commerce - South Africa - Statistics. I. Series: Current issues brief , 1986-87/3. II. Title.
HF3901.A45 K66 1986

Kops, Manfred. Die regionalen Verteilungswirkungen des kommunalen Finanzausgleichs : mit einer empirischen Analyse des nordrhein-westfälischen kommunalen Finanzausgleichs des Jahres 1975 / Manfred Kops. Thun : H. Deutsch, c1983. xvii, 537, 259 p. : ill. ; 21 cm. (Reihe Wirtschaftswissenschaften, 0253-1488 . Bd. 276) Bibliography: p. 219-259 (2d group) ISBN 3-87144-728-5 : LC Card 83-159176
1. Municipal finance - Germany (West) - North Rhine-Westphalia. 2. Municipal finance - Germany (West) - North Rhine-Westphalia - Accounting. 3. Intergovernmental fiscal relations - Germany (West) - North Rhine-Westphalia. I. Title. II. Series.
HJ9493.5.N6 K66 1983

Kopylov, Pierre. Ahonzo, Etienne. Population de la Côte d'Ivoire . Abidjan , 1984. ix, 324 p. : LC Card 86-110796 DDC 304.6/09666/8 19
HB3666.A3 A46 1984 ***NYPL [JLF 86-1466]***

Korać, Slobodan. Konflikti razvojnih ciljeva u samoupravnom društvu / Slobodan Korać. Beograd : Izdavačka radna organizacija "Rad," 1981. 304 p. : ill. ; 20 cm. (Teorijski spisi) In Serbo-Croatian (Roman) Bibliography: p. 295-[301] LC Card 82-166028
1. Conflict management - Yugoslavia. I. Title. II. Series.
HD42 .K67 1981

Korale, R. B. M. Foreign employment . [Colombo] [1985] x, 202 p. ; LC Card 87-900211 DDC 331.6/2/5493 19
HD8670.8 .F67 1985

KORAPUT (INDIA : DISTRICT) - ECONOMIC CONDITIONS.
Mahapatro, Prafulla Ch. Economic development of tribal India /. New Delhi , 1987. xvi, 408 p. : ISBN 81-7024-077-8 : LC Card 87-900212 DDC 338.954/13 19
HC437.K63 M34 1987

Korb, Penelope. U. S. and world food, beverages, and tobacco expenditures, 1970-83 / Penelope Korb. Washington, D.C. : U. S. Dept. of Agriculture, Economics Research Service, International Economics Division, 1986. iv, 84 p. : ill. ; 28 cm. (ERS staff report . no. AGES860920) Cover title. "October 1986." "This report was reproduced for limited distribution to the research community outside the U. S. Department of Agriculture"--P. ii. Item 42-W-1 (microfiche) LC Card 86-603160 DDC 339.4/8664/0021 19
1. Food industry and trade - Statistics. 2. Beverage industry - Statistics. 3. Alcoholic beverage industry - Statistics. 4. Tobacco industry - Statistics. 5. Food industry and trade - United States - Statistics. 6. Beverage industry - United States - Statistics. 7. Alcoholic beverage industry - United States - Statistics. 8. Tobacco industry - United States - Statistics. I. United States. Dept. of Agriculture. Economic Research Service. International Economics Division. II. Title. III. Title: US and world food, beverages, and tobacco expenditures, 1970-1983. IV. Series: ERS staff report , no. AGES 860920.
HD9000.4 .K67 1986

Körber-Weik, Margot. Wirtschaftskraft und Wirtschaftsentwicklung in den Bundesländern seit 1970 : eine vergleichende Analyse : Gutachten im Auftrag des Bundesministers für Wirtschaft / Margot Körber-Weik, Susanne Wied-Nebbeling, unter Mitarbeit von Harald Enke ... [et al.]. Tübingen : Institut für Angewandte Wirtschaftsforschung Tübingen, 1986. x, 271 p. ; 30 cm. (Forschungsberichte / Institut für Angewandte Wirtschaftsforschung Tübingen. Serie B . Nr. 6) Bibliography: p. 263-271. ISBN 3-88573-303-X LC Card 87-401375 DDC 330.943/0878 19
1. Germany (West) - Economic conditions - Regional disparities. I. Wied-Nebbeling, Susanne. II. Germany (West). Bundesministerium für Wirtschaft. III. Series: Forschungsberichte / Institut für Angewandte Wirtschaftsforschung Tübingen. Serie B , Nr. 6. IV. Title.
HC286.6 .K67 1986

Korchagina, A. (Aleksandra) Nagli͡adnai͡a agitatsii͡a i vstrechnye plany / A. Korchagina, V. Markov. Moskva : Izd-vo "Plakat", 1978. 44 p., [16] p. of plates : ill. ; 22 cm. Includes bibliographical references. LC Card 81-161419
1. Industrial productivity - Soviet Union - Posters - Case studies. 2. Industrial productivity - Russian S.F.S.R. - Ivanovskai͡a oblastʹ - Posters. 3. Employee motivation - Soviet Union - Posters - Case studies. 4. Employee motivation - Russian S.F.S.R. - Ivanovskai͡a oblastʹ - Posters. I. Markov, V. (Vladimir). II. Title.
HC340.L3 K56 1978

Korea : managing the industrial transition. Washington, D.C., U. S.A. : World Bank, [1987] 2 v. : ill. (some col.) ; 28 cm. (A World Bank country study) Report written by D.M. Leipziger and others. Includes bibliographical references. CONTENTS. - v. 1. The conduct of industrial policy -- v. 2. Selected topics and case studies. ISBN 0-8213-0887-4 (pbk. : v. 1) LC Card 87-2213 DDC 338.9519/5 19
1. Industry and state - Korea (South). 2. Korea (South) - Commercial policy. 3. Monetary policy - Korea (South). 4. Korea (South) - Economic policy. I. Leipziger, Danny M. II. International Bank for Reconstruction and Development. III. Series.
HD3616.K853 K67 1987

KOREA - COMMERCE - HISTORY.
Yu, Wŏn-dong. Le déclin des marchands privilégiés en Corée . [Paris] , 1984. 104 p. : ISBN 2-905358-03-3 : LC Card 85-131336
HF3830.5 .Y78 1984

Korea Development Institute. see **Han'guk Kaebal Yŏn'guwŏn.**

KOREA - HISTORY - 1864-1910.
Cook, Harold F., 1929- Pioneer American businessman in Korea . Seoul, Korea , 1981. ix, 104 p. : LC Card 83-140523 DDC 382/.09519/0730924 B 19
HF3023.T68 C66 1981
NYPL [JFE 86-4650]

KOREA - MANUFACTURES - HISTORY.
Yu, Wŏn-dong. Le déclin des marchands privilégiés en Corée . [Paris] , 1984. 104 p. : ISBN 2-905358-03-3 : LC Card 85-131336
HF3830.5 .Y78 1984

KOREA (NORTH) - ECONOMIC CONDITIONS.
Opyt stroitelʹstva sot͡sialisticheskoĭ ėkonomiki v stranakh Azii /. Moskva , 1986. 290 p. ; LC Card 87-126301
HC412 .O675 1986

Starrels, John M. The Korean economy in congressional perspective . Washington , 1986. v, 13 p. ; LC Card 87-601385 DDC 330.9519/043 19
HC467 .S724 1986

KOREA (SOUTH) - COMMERCE.
Doing business in Korea /. London , New York , 1987. xvi, 121 p. : ISBN 0-89397-276-2 (Nichols) : LC Card 87-5665 DDC 330.9519/5043 19
HC467 .D58 1987

KOREA (SOUTH) - COMMERCE - UNITED STATES.
Dyck, John H. South Korea . Washington, D.C. [1986] v, 74 p. : LC Card 86-602006 DDC 338.1 s 382/.41/095195 19
HD1411 .F59 no. 216 HD9005

Kim, Chungsoo. Effects of neo-protectionism on the Korean exports /. [Seoul] , 1986. 203 p. : LC Card 86-234427 DDC 382/.095195/073 19
HF3830.5.Z7 U54 1986

KOREA (SOUTH) - COMMERCIAL POLICY.
Korea . Washington, D.C., U. S.A. [1987] 2 v. : ISBN 0-8213-0887-4 (pbk. : v. 1) LC Card 87-2213 DDC 338.9519/5 19
HD3616.K853 K67 1987

KOREA (SOUTH) - ECONOMIC CONDITIONS - 1945-
Chung, Shin-Yung, d. 1962. Der Zwangssparprozess als Werkzeug der Entwicklungspolitik . Bonn , c1982. xiv, 204 p., [1] leaf of plates : LC Card 83-214728
HC470.S3 C48 1982

Starrels, John M. The Korean economy in congressional perspective . Washington , 1986. v, 13 p. ; LC Card 87-601385 DDC 330.9519/043 19
HC467 .S724 1986

KOREA (SOUTH) - ECONOMIC CONDITIONS - 1960-
Dee, Philippa S. Financial markets and economic development . Tübingen , c1986. ix, 131 p. ; ISBN 3-16-345086-5 LC Card 86-190926 DDC 338.9519/5 19
HC467 .D44 1986

Doing business in Korea /. London , New York , 1987. xvi, 121 p. : ISBN 0-89397-276-2 (Nichols) : LC Card 87-5665 DDC 330.9519/5043 19
HC467 .D58 1987

The Korean economy . Seoul, Korea , 1984. 308 p. ; LC Card 87-128969 DDC 330.9519/5043 19
HC467 .K61996 1984

Mukerjee, Dilip. Lessons from Korea's industrial experience /. Kuala Lumpur, Malaysia , c1986. vi, 81 p. ; ISBN 967-94701-3-X (pbk.) LC Card 86-944002 DDC 338.09519/5 19
HC467 .M84 1986

KOREA (SOUTH) - ECONOMIC POLICY.
Korea . Washington, D.C., U. S.A. [1987] 2 v. : ISBN 0-8213-0887-4 (pbk. : v. 1) LC Card 87-2213 DDC 338.9519/5 19
HD3616.K853 K67 1987

The Political economy of the new Asian industrialism /. Ithaca, N.Y. , 1987. 252 p. ; ISBN 0-8014-1948-4 (alk. paper) LC Card 86-29103 DDC 338.95 19
HC460.5 .P65 1987

KOREA (SOUTH) - ECONOMIC POLICY - 1960-
Alschuler, Lawrence R., 1941- Multinationals and maldevelopment . New York , 1988. xii, 218 p. : ISBN 0-312-00531-8 : LC Card 87-4307 DDC 338.9 19
HD82 .A5493 1988

Dee, Philippa S. Financial markets and economic development . Tübingen , c1986. ix, 131 p. ; ISBN 3-16-345086-5 LC Card 86-190926 DDC 338.9519/5 19
HC467 .D44 1986

KOREA (SOUTH) - FOREIGN ECONOMIC RELATIONS - UNITED STATES.
Wheeler, Jimmy W. Beyond recrimination . Indianapolis, IN (P.O. Box 26-919, Indianapolis 46226) , c1987. xix, 218 p. : LC Card 87-165405 DDC 382/.0951249/073 19
HF1456.5.T28 W46 1987

KOREA (SOUTH) - INDUSTRIES.
Mukerjee, Dilip. Lessons from Korea's industrial experience /. Kuala Lumpur, Malaysia , c1986. vi, 81 p. ; ISBN 967-94701-3-X (pbk.) LC Card 86-944002 DDC 338.09519/5 19
HC467 .M84 1986

KOREA (SOUTH) - INDUSTRIES - 1960- - CASE STUDIES.
Enos, John L. (John Lawrence), 1924- The adoption and diffusion of imported technology . New York , c1988. 272 p. : ISBN 0-7099-2030-X LC Card 87-19894 DDC 338.9519/506 19
HC470.T4 E56 1987

Korea Trade Promotion Corporation. see **Taehan Muyŏk Chinhŭng Kongsa.**

KOREAN AMERICAN BUSINESS ENTERPRISES - GEORGIA - ATLANTA.
Min, Pyong Gap, 1942- Ethnic business enterprise . Staten Island, N.Y. , 1988. p. cm. ISBN 0-934733-15-5 : LC Card 86-33366 DDC 338.6/422/0899570758231 19
HD2346.U52 A845 1988

The Korean economy : review and prospects / [prepared by Research Department, Korea Exchange Bank].6th ed. Seoul, Korea : The Department, 1984. 308 p. ; 28 cm. LC Card 87-128969 DDC 330.9519/5043 19
1. Korea (South) - Economic conditions - 1960-. I. Han'guk Oehwan Ŭnhaeng. Chosabu.
HC467 .K61996 1984

The Korean economy in congressional perspective . Starrels, John M. Washington , 1986. v, 13 p. ; LC Card 87-601385 DDC 330.9519/043 19
HC467 .S724 1986

The Korean onggi potter /. Sayers, Robert. Washington, D.C. , 1987. 288 p. : LC Card 86-600366 DDC 338.4/77382/095195 19
HD9617.K82 S29 1987

Korean parts directory. [Seoul] : Korea Trade Promotion Corp., 1986. 514 p. ; 23 cm. Includes indexes. LC Card 86-231593
1. Machine parts industry - Korea (South) - Directories. I. Taehan Muyŏk Chinhŭng Kongsa.
HD9705.5.P373 K676 1986

KOREAN POTTERY. see **POTTERY, KOREAN.**

Korennye i priezzhie /. Vasil'ev, Ivan Afanas'evich. Moskva , 1980. 86 p. ; LC Card 81-178115
HD1536.S65 V375 1980

KÖRLE (GERMANY) - ECONOMIC CONDITIONS.
Wagner, Kurt. Leben auf dem Lande im Wandel des Industrialisierung . Frankfurt am Main , 1986. 558, [1] p. : ISBN 3-458-14329-7 LC Card 87-112493 DDC 330.943/41 19
HC289.K66 W34 1986

KÖRLE (GERMANY) - SOCIAL CONDITIONS.
Wagner, Kurt. Leben auf dem Lande im Wandel des Industrialisierung . Frankfurt am Main , 1986. 558, [1] p. : ISBN 3-458-14329-7 LC Card 87-112493 DDC 330.943/41 19
HC289.K66 W34 1986

Kormendi, Roger C. Deregulating financial services . Cambridge, Mass. , 1986. xiii, 223 p. ; ISBN 0-88730-111-8 LC Card 86-3355 DDC 332.1/0973 19
HG2491 .R42 1986 ***NYPL [JLE 86-3307]***

Korn, Errol R. Hyper-performance : the A.I.M. strategy for releasing your business potential / Errol R. Korn, George J. Pratt with Peter T. Lambrou. New York : Wiley, c1987. xi, 195 p. : ill. ; 24 cm. Bibliography: p. 189-192. Includes index. ISBN 0-471-85344-5 LC Card 86-33984 DDC 650.1 19
1. Success in business. 2. Workaholics. I. Pratt, George J. II. Lambrou, Peter T. III. Title.
HF5386 .K775 1987

Korn, Lester. The winning edge : how to get the job you've always wanted / by Lester Korn. New York : Simon and Schuster, c1988. p. cm. ISBN 0-671-55263-5 LC Card 87-23249 DDC 658.4/09 19
1. Executive ability. 2. Executives - Recruiting. 3. Chief executive officers - Recruiting. 4. Success in business. 5. Corporate culture. I. Title.
HD38.2 .K67 1988

Kornai, János.
[Ellentmondások és dilemmák. English]
Contradictions and dilemmas : studies on the socialist economy and society / by János Kornai ; [translated by Ilona Lukács ... et al.].1st MIT Press ed. Cambridge, Mass. : MIT Press, 1986, c1983. ix, 165 p. : ill. ; 19 cm. Translation of: Ellentmondások és dilemmák. Bibliography: p. [161]-165. ISBN 0-262-11107-1 LC Card 85-5168 DDC 330.9439/053 19
1. Economics - Addresses, essays, lectures. 2. Marxian economics - Addresses, essays, lectures. 3. Hungary - Economic conditions - 1968- - Addresses, essays, lectures. I. Title.
HC300.28 .K67213 1986 ***NYPL [JLC 86-254]***

La Voie hongroise . [Paris] , c1986. 319 p. : ISBN 2-7021-1378-8 : LC Card 86-221784
HC300.28 .V65 1986

Kornakovskiĭ, I. L. Iz istorii razvitiia metallurgicheskoĭ promyshlennosti Moskvy, 1883-1932 gg. . Moskva , 1981. 219 p. ; LC Card 84-163581
HD9525.S653 M64 1981 ***NYPL [*QIP 87-3316]***

Kornblith, Miriam. Estado y gasto público en Venezuela, 1936-1980 / Miriam Kornblith, Thais Maingón. Caracas : Universidad Central de Venezuela, Ediciones de la Biblioteca, 1985. 287, [10] p. : ill. ; 22 cm. (Colección Ciencias económicas y sociales. 31) Bibliography: p. 279-[288] LC Card 86-172043
1. Venezuela - Appropriations and expenditures - History - 20th century. 2. Venezuela - Politics and government - 1935-1958. 3. Venezuela - Politics and government - 1958-. I. Maingón, Thais. II. Title.
HJ2093 .K67 1985

Kornbluh, Elaine H. Barron's regents exams and answers. Bookkeeping-accounting / Elaine H. Kornbluh. Woodbury, N.Y. : Barron's Educational Series, Inc., c1987. 318 p. in various pagings ; forms ; 20 cm. "18 actual regents exams with over 800 questions--marked for use in studying for the new one-year exam. Complete answer keys with model journal entries and financial statements. Glossary of important terms. Includes the latest regents exams!"--Cover. Rev. ed. of: Barron's regents exams and answers. Bookkeeping / Murray Neinstein, Elaine H. Kornbluh. c1982. ISBN 0-8120-3185-7 (pbk.) : LC Card 87-403397 DDC 657/2/076 19
1. Bookkeeping - Examinations, questions, etc. I. Neinstein, Murray. Barron's regents exams and answers. Bookkeeping. II. Barron's Educational Series, inc. III. Title. IV. Title: Bookkeeping-accounting.
HF5661 .N4 1987

Kornblum, Hans-Joachim. Therapie in der Berufsschule? : das "Krefelder Modell" erziehungstherapeutischen Unterrichts mit Jungarbeitern / Hans-Joachim Kornblum. München : Minerva Publikation, c1984. x, 458 p. : ill. ; 21 cm. (Berichte zur Erziehungstherapie und Eingliederungshilfe . 33) Bibliography: p. 389-437. ISBN 3-597-10503-3 : LC Card 85-105593
1. Occupational training - Germany, West. 2. Vocational education - Germany, West. 3. Youth - Mental health - Germany (West). I. Title. II. Series.
HD5715.5.G4 K67 1984

Kornblum, William. Williams, Terry (Terry M.) Growing up poor /. Lexington, MA , c1985. xvi, 136 p. ; ISBN 0-669-09687-3 (alk. paper) LC Card 84-48564 DDC 362.7/044 19
HV1431 .W55 1985 ***NYPL [JLE 85-2236]***

Körner, Ulrich. Wettbewerb und Akkumulation in der selbstverwalteten Wirtschaft / Ulrich Körner. Frankfurt ; New York : Campus, c1984. 193 p. : ill. ; 21 cm. (Campus Forschung. Bd. 356) Bibliography: p. 185-193. ISBN 3-593-33257-4 LC Card 84-191794
1. Industrial management - Yugoslavia - Employee participation. 2. Industrial management - Employee participation. I. Title.
HD5660.Y8 K623 1984

Kornhardt, Ullrich. Entwicklungstendenzen im Konsumgüterhandwerk / von Ullrich Kornhardt. Göttingen : O. Schwartz, 1986. 385 p. : ill. ; 23 cm. (Göttinger handwerkswirtschaftliche Studien. Bd. 37) Bibliography: p. 364-385. ISBN 3-509-01418-9 LC Card 86-197187
1. Small business - Germany, West. 2. Self-employed - Germany, West. 3. Commercial products - Germany, West. I. Title.
HD2341.A1 G6 Bd. 37 HD2346.G3

Kornienko, V. P. Sotsial'no-ėkonomicheskaia sushchnost' obshchenarodnogo khoziaĭstvennogo mekhanizma /. Kiev , 1985. 342 p. ; LC Card 86-197710
HC336.25 .S668 1985

A Környezeti erőforrások gazdasági értékelésének módszertani kérdései / [szerkesztő Fodor István]. Pécs : Magyar Tudományos Akadémia Dunántúli Tudományos Intézete ; [Budapest] : Országos Környezet- és Természetvédelmi Hivatal, 1981. 78 leaves ; 25 cm. (Környezetvédelmi tanulmányok, 0230-5437 . 2) Bibliography: leaves [73]-78. LC Card 82-202704
1. Energy development - Environmental aspects - Europe, Eastern. 2. Environmental impact analysis - Europe, Eastern. 3. Land use, Rural - Environmental aspects - Hungary. I. Fodor, István, 1938-. II. Series.
HD9502.E83 K68 1981 ***NYPL [JLE 87-219]***

Környezetvédelmi tanulmányok, 0230-5437 .
(2) A Környezeti erőforrások gazdasági értékelésének módszertani kérdései /. Pécs [Budapest] , 1981. 78 leaves ; LC Card 82-202704
HD9502.E83 K68 1981 ***NYPL [JLE 87-219]***

Korobkina, Z. V. (Zoia Vasil'evna)
Tovarovedenie vkusovykh tovarov / Z.V. Korobkina. Izd. 2-e, perer. Moskva : "Ėkonomika", 1986. 207 p. ; 20 cm. Authorized for instructional purposes. Includes bibliographical references. LC Card 86-220308
1. Food industry and trade - Soviet Union. 2. Beverages industry - Soviet Union. 3. Condiments - Soviet Union. I. Title.
HD9015.S652 K67 1986

Korolev, I. S. (Ivan Sergeevich) Valiutnye otnosheniia kapitalizma : ėkonomika i politika / I.S. Korolev ; otvetstvennyĭ redaktor M.M. Maksimova. Moskva : "Nauka", 1986. 228 p. ; 22 cm. At head of title: Akademiia nauk SSSR. Ordena Trudovogo Krasnogo Znameni Institut mirovoĭ ėkonomiki i mezhdunarodnykh otnosheniĭ. Includes bibliographical references. LC Card 86-232369
1. Monetary policy. 2. Capitalism. I. Maksimova, M. M. (Margarita Matveevna). II. Title.
HG6230.3 .K66 1986

Korolev, L. P. (Leonid Pavlovich) Trudovye resursy i ikh ispol'zovanie / L.P. Korolev. Moskva : Moskovskiĭ rabochiĭ, 1982. 139 p. ; 20 cm. (Za ėffektivnost' i kachestvo) Includes bibliographical references. LC Card 82-158161
1. Labor supply - Russian S.F.S.R. - Moscow (Oblast). 2. Labor supply - Russian S.F.S.R. - Moscow. 3. Manpower policy - Russian S.F.S.R. - Moscow (Oblast). 4. Manpower policy - Russian S.F.S.R. - Moscow. I. Title. II. Series.
HD5797.M66 K67 1982

Korol'kov, N. V. (Nikolaĭ Vasil'evich) Agrarnaia politika Kommunisticheskoĭ partii na ėtape stroitel'stva MTS, 1929-1939 . Vladimir , 1985. 132 p. ; ***NYPL [*QIK 87-3394]***

Korop, P. N. (Petr Nikolaevich) USSR--looking at an economic map / Pyotr Korop ; [translater, Igor Okov]. [Moscow] : Novosti Press Agency Pub. House, c1985. 250 p., [3] p. of plates : ill. ; 20 cm. Title on colophon: SSSR--razmyshleniia u ekonomicheskoi karty. LC Card 86-207488 DDC 330.947/0854 19
1. Soviet Union - Economic conditions - 1976-. I. Title. II. Title: U. S.S.R.--looking at an economic map.
HC336.25 .K66 1985

A Körös-Tisza-Maros köz középkori településrendje /. Blazovich, László. Békéscsaba , Szeged , 1985. 207 p., [9] folded leaves of plates : ISBN 963-01-6828-6 LC Card 87-408571
HD640.5.Z8 G743 1985

Körösényi, András. A takarékszövetkezetek banki reformjának alternativai / Körösényi András. Budapest : Szövetkezeti Kutató Intézet, [1985] 43 p. ; 29 cm. (Közlemények, 0133-4905 . 195) "1985. szeptember." Includes bibliographical references. LC Card 87-408585
1. Savings-banks - Hungary. 2. Banks and banking, Cooperative - Hungary. 3. Banking law - Hungary. 4.

Informal sector (Economics) - Hungary. I. Series: Közlemények / Szövetkezeti Kutató Intézet, 195. II. Title.
HG1939.H82 K67 1985

Korostelev, Gennadiĭ Mikhaĭlovich. Burzhuaznye kontseptsii narodonaseleniia : kriticheskiĭ analiz / G.M. Korostelev, V.S. Kraev. Moskva : "Finansy i statistika", 1981. 158 p. ; 20 cm. Includes bibliographical references. LC Card 82-140945
1. Demography - History. 2. Sociology - History. I. Kraev, V. S. (Vladimir Semenovich). II. Title.
HB851 .K65 1981

Kőrösy, Gyula. Gazdálkodási és jövedelmezőségi adatok, mutatószámok a szövetkezeti bolti kiskereskedelemben /. Budapest , 1984. 113 p. ; ISBN 963-7006-24-9 : LC Card 85-154737
HF5429.6.H8 G39 1984

Korovin, IU. V. Matematicheskie metody v ėkonomike i narodnom khoziaĭstve . Moskva , 1985. 121 p. ; LC Card 87-152514
HC336.25 M377 1985

Korporative Repräsentation der Gewerkschaften . Süllow, Bernd. Frankfurt , New York , c1982. 146 p. ; ISBN 3-593-33169-1 LC Card 83-153450
HD4177 .S85 1982

Korporatsii SShA v bor'be za vneshnie rynki sbyta /. Kirichenko, Ė. V. (Ėlina Vsevolodovna) Moskva , 1981. 196 p. ; LC Card 82-152673
HD2766 .K53 1981

Korsakova, Tat'iana Aleksandrovna. Molodost', trud, romantika . Moskva , 1985. 183 p., [8] p. of plates : LC Card 86-113851
HD4870.S65 M65 1985

Korszerű nevelés, 0324-704X.
Ritoók, Pálné. Személyiségfejlesztés és pályaválasztás /. Budapest , 1986. 192 p. ; ISBN 963-17-8713-3 : LC Card 87-408516
HF5381 .R635 1986

Kortare kredittid för skatter på energi m.m. . Sweden. Skattekreditutredningen. [Stockholm] [1983] 109 p. ; ISBN 0-913807-27-9 LC Card 84-218594
HJ5715.S84 S87 1983

Korte, Hermann, 1937- Migration und ihre sozialen Folgen : Förderung der Gastarbeiterforschung durch die Stiftung Volkswagenwerk, 1974-1981 / Hermann Korte, Alfred Schmidt. Göttingen : Vandenhoeck & Ruprecht, c1983. 170 p. ; 21 cm. (Schriftenreihe der Stiftung Volkswagenwerk, 0172-164X . Bd. 23) Bibliography: p. 163-169. ISBN 3-525-85366-1 LC Card 84-150019
1. Alien labor - Research - Germany (West) - History. 2. Social integration - Research - Germany (West) - History. 3. Stiftung Volkswagenwerk - History. I. Schmidt, Alfred, 1945-. II. Title. III. Series.
HD8458.A2 K65 1983

Korte, Karl-Rudolf. Nippons neue Vasallen? : die Japanpolitik der Europäischen Gemeinschaft / Karl-Rudolf Korte. Bonn : Europa Union, c1984. 103 p. : ill. ; 23 cm. (Mainzer Beiträge zur europäischen Einigung, 0722-5466 . Bd. 3) Bibliography: p. 93-100. Includes index. ISBN 3-7713-0216-1 LC Card 86-230930
1. Japan - Foreign economic relations - European Economic Community countries. 2. European Economic Community countries - Foreign economic relations - Japan. I. Title. II. Series.
HF1602.15.E92 K67 1984

Korten, David C. Community management . West Hartford, Conn. , c1986. xxii, 328 p. : ISBN 0-931816-40-8 (pbk.) LC Card 86-27691 DDC 338.95 19
HD75.6 .C65 1986

Korteweg, Hans. Helen of delen : over de transformatie van mens en organisatie / Hans Korteweg en Jaap Voigt. Amsterdam : Contact, 1986, c1985. 222 p. ; 21 cm. Bibliography: p. 218-222. ISBN 90-254-6652-4 : LC Card 86-182872
1. Organizational change. 2. Organizational change - Netherlands. 3. Organizational behavior. I. Voigt, Jaap. II. Title.
HD58.8 .K66 1986

Korth, Christopher M. International countertrade /. New York , 1987. xii, 191 p. : ISBN 0-89930-213-0 (lib. bdg. : alk. paper) LC Card 86-25319 DDC 382 19
HF1410.5 .I5716 1987

Korthaus, E. Input-Output-Tabellen für die Bundesrepublik Deutschland, 1962 bis 1975 / [von E. Korthaus und R. Rettig ; unter Mitarbeit von B. Hillebrand]. Essen : RWI Essen, 1979. 279 p. ; 30 cm. (RWI-Papiere . Nr. 8) Chiefly tables. Bibliography: p. 28-32. LC Card 87-408858 DDC 339.2/3/0943 19
1. Input-output tables - Germany (West). I. Rettig, Rudi. II. Hillebrand, B. III. Title. IV. Series.
HC290.5.I57 K67 1979

Kortzfleisch, Gerd von. Internationale und nationale Problemfelder der Betriebswirtschaftslehre /. Berlin , c1984. 336 p., [1] leaf of plates : ISBN 3-428-05696-5 LC Card 85-141327
HD35 .I598 1984

Kortzfleisch, Gert von.
Energie für den Verkehr : eine zusammengefasste Darstellung der Ergebnisse einer systemanalytischen Untersuchung der langfristigen Perspektiven des Verkehrssektors und seiner Versorgung mit Energie / Gert v. Kortzfleisch, Alfred Voss ; Bearbeiter, K. Bellman ... [et al.]. Frankfurt am Main : Verband der Automobilindustrie, c1984. 115 p. : ill. ; 21 cm. (Schriftenreihe des Verbandes der Automobilindustrie e.V. (VDA) . Nr. 42) "Erstellt im Auftrag und mit Unterstützung der Forschungsvereinigung Automobiltechnik e.V. vom Industrieseminar der Universität Mannheim (ISM) und der Programmgruppe Systemforschung und Technologische Entwicklung (STE) der Kernforschungsanlage Jülich." Bibliography: p. 88-90. LC Card 84-192683
1. Transportation, Automotive - Germany (West) - Energy conservation. 2. Automobiles - Germany (West) - Fuel consumption. I. Voss, Alfred. II. Bellmann, Klaus. III. Forschungsvereinigung Automobiltechnik (Germany). IV. Universität Mannheim. Industrieseminar. V. Kernforschungsanlage Jülich. Programmgruppe Systemforschung und Technologische Entwicklung. VI. Series. VII. Series: Schriftenreihe des Verbandes der Automobilindustrie e.V. (VDA) , 42. VIII. Title.
HD9710.G4 V4 Nr. 42 HE5620.E53

Erfolgskontrolle bei der Verausgabung öffentlicher Mittel /. Baden-Baden , 1986. 133 p. : ISBN 3-7890-1208-4 LC Card 86-164102
HJ7793 .E73 1986

Korzeniewicz, Richard. British economic and social history, 1700-1950 / by Richard Korzeniewicz. London : Regency, c1985. 261 p. : ill. ; 20 cm. Bibliography: p. 259. Includes index. ISBN 0-7212-0711-1 : LC Card 87-144405 DDC 330.941 19
1. Great Britain - Economic conditions - 18th century. 2. Great Britain - Economic conditions - 19th century. 3. Great Britain - Economic conditions - 20th century. 4. Great Britain - Social conditions - 18th century. 5. Great Britain - Social conditions - 19th century. 6. Great Britain - Social conditions - 20th century. I. Title.
HC254.5 .K67 1985

Kosacoff, Bernardo P. Sourrouille, Juan V. Inversiones extranjeras en América Latina . Buenos Aires [1984] viii, 142 p. : LC Card 86-183036
HG5160.5.A3 S64 1984

Kōsai, Yutaka, 1933- Round Table Discussions on Japan in the Global Community. Japan in the global community . [Tokyo] , c1986. 129, [38] p. : ISBN 4-13-057014-5 : LC Card 87-129161 DDC 337.52 19
HF1601 .R68 1986

Koschnick, Wolfgang J., 1942-
Standard-Lexikon für Marketing, Marktkommunikation, Markt- und Mediaforschung / Wolfgang J. Koschnick. München ; New York : K.G. Saur, 1987. vi, 940 p. : ill. ; 22 cm. ISBN 3-598-10583-5 LC Card 87-143648 DDC 380.1/03/31 19
1. Marketing - Dictionaries - German. 2. Commerce - Dictionaries - German. 3. Mass media - Dictionaries - German. I. Title.
HF5415 .K617 1987

Standard-Wörterbuch für Werbung, Massenmedien und Marketing, Deutsch-Englisch / Wolfgang J. Koschnick. Berlin ; New York : W. de Gruyter, 1987. 590 p. ; 22 cm. Title on added t.p.: Standard dictionary of advertising, mass media, and marketing, German-English. Spine title: Wörterbuch für Werbung--Dictionary of advertising. ISBN 0-89925-293-1 (U. S.) : LC Card 87-19928 DDC 659.1/03/21 19
1. Advertising - Dictionaries. 2. Mass media - Dictionaries. 3. Marketing - Dictionaries. 4. English language - Dictionaries - German. I. Title. II. Title: Standard dictionary of advertising, mass media, and marketing, English-German. III. Title: Wörterbuch für Werbung. IV. Title: Dictionary of advertising.
HF5803 .K67 1987

Kosev, Konstantin. Osnovnye prichiny i usloviia vozniknoveniia PTP s tiazhelymi posledstviiami, puti i metody ikh ustraneniia. Bulgarian. Osnovni prichini i usloviia za vŭznikvane na PTP s tezhki posledstviia, pŭtishta i metodi za tiakhnoto otstraniavane /. Sofiia , 1985. 95 p. : LC Card 87-101607
HF5614.5.S62 O7516 1985

Koshelev, V. N. (Vladimir Nikolaevich) Kiselev, A. A. (Anatoliĭ Alekseevich) Ėkonomika, organizatsiia i planirovanie priborostroitel'nogo proizvodstva . Leningrad , 1985. 271 p. : LC Card 86-127609
HD9706.S652 K57 1985

Kosiński, Leszek A.
Policies of population redistribution /. Oulu , 1981. 199 p. : ISBN 951-675-071-0 (pbk.) LC Card 83-148782 DDC 304.8 19
HB1952 .P65 1981

Population and development projects in Africa /. Cambridge [Cambridgeshire] , New York , 1985. xvi, 329 p. : ISBN 0-521-30527-6 LC Card 84-29323 DDC 304.6/096 19
HB2121.A3 P67 1985 **NYPL [JLF 86-186]**

Population redistribution and development in South Asia /. Dordrecht , Boston , 1985. 243 p. : ISBN 90-277-1938-1 : LC Card 84-26260 DDC 304.8/0959 19
HB2096.5 .P66 1985 **NYPL [JLE 86-3852]**

Kositsyn, N. S. (Nikolaĭ Stepanovich)
Sovershenstvovanie metodologii ėkonomicheskogo analiza v nauchnykh uchrezhdeniiakh i nauchno-tekhnicheskikh kompleksakh . Kiev , 1986. 116 p. ; LC Card 87-126466
HC340.R4 S68 1986

Koslovski, João Paulo. Propostas cooperativistas /. Curitiba , 1986. 56 p. : LC Card 87-403655 DDC 334 19
HD2953 .P76 1986

Koslowski, Peter, 1952- Economics and philosophy /. Tübingen , 1985. ix, 284 p. : ISBN 3-16-244944-8 LC Card 85-236925 DDC 330 19
HB72 .E27 1985 **NYPL [JFE 86-2159]**

Kosobchuk, S. N. (Svetlana Nikolaevna)
Latinskaia Amerika . Moskva , 1978. 271 p. ; LC Card 81-159488
HG185.L3 L37 1978

Kosta, H. G., Jiří, 1921- Crisis and reform in socialist economies /. Boulder , 1987. xi, 196 p. ; ISBN 0-8133-7332-8 (pbk. : alk. paper) : LC Card 86-32602 DDC 338.9/009171/7 19
HC704 .C75 1987

Kostakov, V. G. (Vladimir Georgievich)
Chelovecheskiĭ faktor--zaniatost', blagosostoianie / V.G. Kostakov, V.M. Rutgaĭzer. Moskva : Izd-vo polit. lit-ry, 1981. 78 p. : ill. ; 20 cm. (Shagi odinnadtsatoĭ) Includes bibliographical references. LC Card 82-164831
1. Labor supply - Soviet Union. I. Rutgaĭzer, V. M. (Valeriĭ Maksovich). II. Title. III. Series.
HD5796 .K567 1981

Problemy ėffektivnosti ispol'zovaniia trudovykh resursov /. Moskva , 1981. 147 p. ; LC Card 82-150334
HC340.L3 P64 1981

Kosten der Arbeit . Albach, Horst. Stuttgart , c1985. xi, 179 p. : ISBN 3-7910-5003-6 : LC Card 86-162885 DDC 658.3/00943 19
HD5029 .A43 1985
NYPL [JLL 73-505 Nr.2]

Die Kosten der Gesetze und Verordnungen in Staat, Wirtschaft und Gesellschaft /. Nold, Wolfgang. Konstanz , 1983. xii, 237 p. : ISBN 3-923200-07-2 LC Card 83-195590
HD3616.G4 N65 1983

Die Kosten- und Leistungsrechnung im Handelsbetrieb . Röhrenbacher, Hans. Berlin , c1985. 176 p. : ISBN 3-428-05808-9 LC Card 86-129151 DDC 657/.42 19
HF5686.C8 R583 1985

Die Kosten von Hitlers Krieg . Boelcke, Willi A. Paderborn , c1985. 220 p. : ISBN 3-506-77471-9 LC Card 86-143362
HJ1119 .B66 1985

Kostenrechnung . Dieterle, Robert. Bern , c1983. 258 p. : ISBN 3-258-03210-6 : LC Card 83-185404
HF5686.C8 D53 1983

Kostenrechnung in Klein- und Mittelbetrieben . Winkler, Wigbert M. Graz , c1986. vi, 287 p. : ISBN 3-7041-0150-8 LC Card 87-409225
HF5686.C8 W683 1986

Kostensenkung und Gewinn /. Brandt, Horst. Berlin , 1985. 100 p. ; LC Card 87-144350 DDC 338.5/1/09431 19
HC290.795.C7 B7 1985

Kostensteuern, der Einfluss von Steuern auf kurzfristige Produktions- und Absatzentscheidungen /. Döring, Ulrich. Stuttgart , c1984. x, 228 p. ; ISBN 3-7910-0369-0 LC Card 86-134925
HD2753.G3 D73 1984

Köster, Thomas. Die Entwicklung kommunaler Finanzsysteme am Beispiel Grossbritanniens, Frankreichs und Deutschlands, 1790-1980 / von Thomas Köster. Berlin : Duncker & Humblot, c1984. 422 p. : ill. ; 24 cm. (Finanzwissenschaftliche Forschungsarbeiten . n.F., Bd. 54) Bibliography: p. 398-422. ISBN 3-428-05677-9 LC Card 85-127874
1. Local finance - Great Britain - History. 2. Local finance - France - History. 3. Local finance - Germany - History. I. Series: Finanzwissenschaftliche Forschungsarbeiten , n.F., Heft 54. II. Title.
HJ9422.A4 K67 1984

Kostiainen, Seppo. Capital controls under alternative exchange rate and monetary policy regimes / Seppo Kostiainen and Heikki Taimio. Joensuu : University of Joensuu, Faculty of Social Sciences, 1986. 27 p. ; 25 cm. (Keskustelualoitteita / Joensuun yliopisto, Kansantaloustiede, 0781-0814 . n:o 3 =) Summary in Finnish. Bibliography: p. 27. ISBN 951-696-619-5 (pbk.) LC Card 87-100851 DDC 332.4/5 19
1. Foreign exchange - Mathematical models. 2. Monetary policy - Mathematical models. 3. Interest rates - Mathematical models. I. Taimio, Heikki. II. Series: Keskustelualoitteita (Joensuun yliopisto. Yhteiskuntapolitiikka ja sosiologia) , n:o 3. III. Title.
HG3823 .K673 1986

Kostin, Leonid Alekseevich. Proizvodstvo tovarov narodnogo potrebleniia : sotsial'no-ėkonomicheskiĭ aspekt / L.A. Kostin. Moskva : Ėkonomika, 1980. 212 p. ; 21 cm. Includes bibliographical references. LC Card 87-107901
1. Durable goods, Consumer - Soviet Union. 2. Commercial products - Soviet Union. 3. Food industry and trade - Soviet Union. 4. Consumption (Economics) - Soviet Union. I. Title.
HF1040.9.S65 K67 1980

Kostiuk, Mikhail Pavlovich. Trudovoĭ vklad krest'ianstva v pobedu i uprochnenie sotsializma : na materialakh BSSR / M.P. Kostiuk ; nauchnyĭ redaktor I.M. Ignatenko. Minsk : "Nauka i tekhnika", 1986. 236 p. ; 21 cm. At head of title: Akademiia nauk Belorusskoĭ SSR. Institut istorii. Includes bibliographical references. LC Card 86-136452
1. Collectivization of agriculture - Byelorussian S.S.R. - History. 2. Byelorussian S.S.R. - Industries - History. I. Ignatenko, I. M., 1919-. II. Title.
HD1492.S652 B9252 1986

Kostov, Ivan Dimitrov.
Obshtestvenata sobstvenost pri sotsializma / Ivan Kostov. 1. izd. Sofiia : Izd-vo "Nauka i izkustvo", 1985. 111 p. ; 20 cm. (Poreditsa Kategorii na politicheskata ikonomiia) Includes bibliographical references. LC Card 86-122395
1. Government ownership - Bulgaria. I. Title. II. Series.
HD4263 .K67 1985

Proizvoditel'nost' truda v razvitom sotsialisticheskom obshchestve /. Moskva , 1982. 214 p. ; LC Card 83-166417
HC340.L3 P687 1982

Kostov, Miroslav. ZMM metal-working machines combine, Sofia / [author Miroslav Kostov ; photos by Antonii Handjiiski]. Sofia : Sofia Press, 1986. [104] p. : chiefly col. ill. ; 29 cm. LC Card 87-116288 DDC 338.7/621902/0949773 19
1. Zavod za metalorezheshti mashini (Sofia, Bulgaria). 2. Machine-tool industry - Bulgaria - Sofia. I. Handjiiski, A. II. Title.
HD9703.B94 Z384 1986

Kostrowicka, Irena. Historia gospodarcza Polski XIX i XX wieku / Irena Kostrowicka, Zbigniew Landau, Jerzy Tomaszewski. Wyd. 4., uzup. Warszawa : Książka i Wiedza, 1984. 583 p., [3] folded leaves of plates : maps ; 25 cm. Bibliography: p. [547]-553. Includes index. ISBN 83-05-11411-2 : LC Card 85-218322
1. Poland - Economic conditions. I. Landau, Zbigniew. II. Tomaszewski, Jerzy, 1930-. III. Title. IV. Title: Historia gospodarcza Polski 19. i 20. wieku. V. Title: Historia gospodarcza Polski dziewiętnastego i dwudziestego wieku.
HC340.3 .K67 1984

Koszó, Károly. Munkaügy a belkereskedelemben /. [Budapest] , 1986. 272 p. ; ISBN 963-01-7513-4 : LC Card 87-148137
HF5549.2.H85 M86 1986

Kotelkin, V. I. Material'noe stimulirovanie v khoziaĭstvennom mekhanizme sotsialisticheskogo obshchestva . Leningrad , 1986. 152 p. ; LC Card 86-175029
HF5549.5.I5 M3385 1986

Kothari, S. B. Jain, Manik, 1938- The silver key to the golden treasure of Indian philately /. Calcutta , 1986. xvi, 326, [1] p. : LC Card 86-903670 DDC 769.56954 19
HE6185.I5 J35 1986

Kothari, Vinod. Lease, financing & hire-purchase : including venture capital, mutual funds, factoring, and merchant banking / by Vinod Kothari.2nd ed., thoroughly rev. and enl. Nagpur, India : Wadhwa and Co., : Authorised agents, Wadhwa Sales Corp., 1986. xxvii, 799 p. ; 25 cm. In the Indian context. Includes bibliographical references and index. LC Card 87-902268
1. Lease and rental services - India. 2. Sales, Conditional - India. I. Title. II. Title: Lease, financing and hire-purchase.
HD9999.L4363 I446 1986

Kotios, A. Arampatzēs, E. Hē mesogeiakē politikē tēs EOK . Thessalonikē , 1983. 268 p. ; LC Card 84-185339
HC241.25.M4 A73 1983

Kotios, Angelos, 1957- Die neuere Diskussion über den Zusammenhang von Wechselkursflexibilität und Inflation / Angelos Kotios. Köln : Institut für Wirtschaftspolitik an der Universität zu Köln, 1986. 384 p. ; 24 cm. (Untersuchungen zur Wirtschaftspolitik, 0175-7458 . 70) Bibliography: p. 356-384. ISBN 3-921471-58-3 LC Card 87-407838 DDC 332.4/5 19
1. Foreign exchange. 2. Inflation (Finance). I. Title. II. Series.
HG3821 .K67 1986

Kotler, Philip.
Marketing for nonprofit organizations. Kotler, Philip. Strategic marketing for nonprofit organizations / Philip Kotler, Alan R. Andreasen. 3rd ed. Englewood Cliffs, N.J. , c1987. xvi, 670 p. : LC Card 86-25538 DDC 658.8 19
HF5415 .K6312 1987

Marketing management : analysis, planning, implementation, and control / Philip Kotler.6th ed. Englewood Cliffs, NJ : Prentice Hall, 1988. p. cm. Includes bibliographical references and index. ISBN 0-13-556150-7 LC Card 87-19301 DDC 658.8 19
1. Marketing management. I. Title.
HF5415.13 .K64 1988

Marketing management and strategy . Englewood Cliffs, NJ , c1988. x, 406 p. : ISBN 0-13-558453-1 (pbk.) LC Card 87-18849 DDC 658.8 19
HF5415.13 .M3524 1988

Strategic marketing for nonprofit organizations / Philip Kotler, Alan R. Andreasen. 3rd ed. Englewood Cliffs, N.J. : Prentice-Hall, c1987. xvi, 670 p. : ill. ; 24 cm. (The Prentice-Hall series in marketing) Rev. ed. of: Marketing for nonprofit organizations / Philip Kotler. 2nd ed. 1982. Includes bibliographies and indexes. LC Card 86-25538 DDC 658.8 19
1. Corporations, Nonprofit - Marketing. 2. Corporations, Nonprofit - United States - Marketing - Case studies. I. Andreasen, Alan R., 1934-. II. Kotler, Philip. Marketing for nonprofit organizations. III. Title. IV. Series.
HF5415 .K6312 1987

Strategic marketing for nonprofit organizations . Englewood Cliffs, NJ , c1987. x, 386 p. : ISBN 0-13-851312-0 (pbk.) : LC Card 86-25262 DDC 658.8 19
HF5415 .C2854 1987

Kotliarov, Vladimir Fedorovich. Bezrabotitsa v SShA i ee gosudarstvenno-monopolisticheskoe regulirovanie v sovremennykh usloviiakh / Kotliarov Vladimir Fedorovich. Leningrad : Leningradskiĭ gos. pedagog. in-t im. A.I. Gertsena, 1977. 18 p. ; 22 cm. Thesis Master's--Leningradskiĭ gosudarstvennyĭ pedagogicheskiĭ institut imeni A.I. Gertsena, 1977. Includes bibliographical references. LC Card 81-166000
1. Unemployment - United States - Abstracts. 2. Manpower policy - United States - Abstracts. I. Title.
HD5724 .K67 1977

Kotlikoff, Laurence J. Auerbach, Alan J. Dynamic fiscal policy /. Cambridge [Cambridgeshire] , New York , 1987. xv, 196 p. : ISBN 0-521-30041-X LC Card 86-24447 DDC 339.5/2 19
HJ131 .A94 1987

Kotowski-Ziss, Joanna. Ziss, Roland. Baumaterialien und Selbsthilfe . Saarbrücken , Fort Lauderdale, Fl. , 1986. 319 p. : ISBN 3-88156-333-4 LC Card 86-197177
HD7287.96.M6 Z57 1986

Kotra. see **Taehan Muyŏk Chinhŭng Kongsa.**

Kotscho, Ricardo. Serra Pelada : uma ferida aberta na selva / Ricardo Kotscho ; fotos, Jorge Araújo. São Paulo : Brasiliense, 1984. 106 p., [16] p. of plates : ill. ; 21 cm. "Essas reportagens foram publicadas originalmente na Folha de S. Paulo"--T.p. verso. LC Card 84-206686
1. Gold miners - Brazil - Serra Pelada. 2. Gold mines and mining - Brazil - Serra Pelada. I. Title.
HD8039.M732 B75 1984

Kotsev, Tsvetan. Formirane i izpolzvane na parichnite fondove v stopanskite organizatsii / TSvetan Kotsev, Kaliu Donev, Nikola Bakalov. 1. izd. Varna : Kn-vo "Georgi Bakalov", 1985. 117 p. ; 20 cm. Bibliography: p. 116. LC Card 85-213610
1. Capital productivity - Bulgaria. 2. Business enterprises - Bulgaria - Finance. I. Donev, Kaliu. II. Bakalov, Nikola. III. Title.
HC403.Z9 C347 1985

KOTTAYAM (INDIA : DISTRICT) - ECONOMIC CONDITIONS.
Verghese, K. E. Socio-economic change in Kerala /. New Delhi , 1986. x, 211 p. ; ISBN 81-7024-061-1 : LC Card 86-903145 DDC 330.954/83 19
HC437.K645 V47 1986

KOTTAYAM (INDIA : DISTRICT) - SOCIAL CONDITIONS.
Verghese, K. E. Socio-economic change in Kerala /. New Delhi , 1986. x, 211 p. ; ISBN 81-7024-061-1 : LC Card 86-903145 DDC 330.954/83 19
HC437.K645 V47 1986

Kotter, John P., 1947- The leadership factor / John P. Kotter. New York : Free Press ; London : Collier Macmillan, c1988. ix, 161 p. ; 25 cm. Bibliography: p. 153-155. Includes index. ISBN 0-02-918331-6 LC Card 87-19805 DDC 658.4/092 19
1. Leadership. 2. Industrial management. I. Title.
HD57.7 .K67 1988

Kotz, Samuel. Russian-English, English-Russian glossary of statistical terms; prepared ... by Samuel Kotz. Edinburgh, Oliver and Boyd for the International Statistical Institute, 1971. vii, 87 p. 26 cm. Based on "A dictionary of statistical terms", by M. G. Kendall and W. R. Buckland. ISBN 0-05-002446-9 LC Card 72-197391 DDC 519.5/01/4
1. Statistics - Dictionaries - Russian. 2. Russian language - Dictionaries - English. 3. Statistics - Dictionaries. 4. English language - Dictionaries - Russian. I. Kendall, Maurice George, Sir. Dictionary of statistical terms. II. Title.
HA17 .K62 ***NYPL [JLF 73-1241]***

Kotzé, D. J. (David Jacobus) Energy projections for South Africa / D.J. Kotzé and C.J. Cooper. Johannesburg, Republic of South Africa : Institute for Energy Studies, Rand Afrikaans University, 1985. 125 p. : ill. ; 30 cm.

Bibliography: p. 124-125. ISBN 0-86970-259-9 (pbk.) : LC Card 86-219416 DDC 333.79/13/0968 19
1. Energy consumption - South Africa - Forecasting. 2. Energy industries - South Africa - Forecasting. I. Cooper, C. J. II. Title.
HD9502.S56 K68 1985

Kouassi, Jean-Claude. Transports maritimes et balance des paiements en Côte d'Ivoire / Kouassi Jean-Claude. [Abidjan] : République de Côte d'Ivoire, Ministère de la marine, Institut de documentation, de recherches et d'études maritimes, [1982?] 23, xii leaves ; 28 cm. Cover title. Includes bibliographical references. LC Card 86-111436 DDC 387.5/1 19
1. Shipping - Ivory Coast - Rates. 2. Balance of payments - Ivory Coast. I. Institut de documentation, de recherches et d'études maritimes (Ivory Coast). II. Title.
HE597.I9 K68 1982 ***NYPL [JLF 86-1485]***

Kousgaard, Nils. Andersen, Erling B. Statistics for economics, business administration, and the social sciences /. Berlin , New York , c1987. xi, 439 p. : ISBN 0-387-17720-5 (pbk. : U. S.) LC Card 87-9423 DDC 519.5 19
HB137 .A525 1987

Kouzes, James M., 1945- The leadership challenge : how to get extraordinary things done in organizations / James M. Kouzes, Barry Z. Posner ; foreword by Thomas J. Peters.1st ed. San Francisco : Jossey-Bass, 1987. xxx, 362 p. : ill. ; 24 cm. (The Jossey-Bass management series) Bibliography: p. 323-344. Includes index. ISBN 1-555-42061-3 (alk. paper) LC Card 87-45428 DDC 658.4/092 19
1. Leadership. 2. Executive ability. 3. Management. I. Posner, Barry Z. II. Title. III. Series.
HD57.7 .K68 1987

Kovač, Josef. Neuerungen in den Aussenwirtschafts- und Devisenvorschriften Jugoslawiens / Josef Kovač. Hamburg : Verlag Dr. Kovač, c1985. 100 p. : 2 ill. ; 21 cm. Fifteen articles originally published in "Jugoslavija-Wirtschaft," 1983-1985. Continues the collection: Grundlagen des Aussenwirtschafts- und Devisensystems der SFR Jugoslawien. 1983. Bibliography: p. 84. ISBN 3-9800762-9-6 LC Card 86-160924
1. Foreign exchange administration - Yugoslavia. 2. Yugoslavia - Commerce. I. Title.
HG3965.5 .K68 1985

Kovach, Barbara E. Survival on the fast track / Barbara E. Kovach. 1st ed. New York : Dodd, Mead, c1988. xv, 240 p. ; 24 cm. Bibliography: p. 225-233. Includes index. ISBN 0-396-09027-3 LC Card 87-19940 DDC 658.4/092 19
1. Leadership. 2. Executive ability. 3. Job stress. 4. Organizational behavior. I. Title.
HD57.7 .K69 1988

Kovacic, Anton. Suppe genug, aber Seele kaputt : die neue Armut in der Bundesrepublik / Anton Kovacic.Originalausg. München : W. Heyne, c1986. 185 p. ; 18 cm. (Heyne Report . Nr. 10/10) Heyne Bücher ; 780 ISBN 3-453-43075-1 : LC Card 86-230927
1. Poor - Germany, West. 2. Unemployed - Germany, West. I. Title.
HC290.5.P6 K68 1986

Kovács, György, 1925- A Vízgazdálkodás távlati fejlesztésének prognózisai /. Budapest , 1983. 176 p. : ISBN 963-602-278-X LC Card 85-109619
HD1697.H8 V59 1983

Kovács, Kálmán. Tervezési szintek érdekeltségének összehangolása gazdaságszabályozási eszközökkel : koncepció és módszer / Kovács Kálmán, Nagy József, Spitálszky Márta. Budapest : Agrárgazdasági Kutató Intézet, 1984. 50 p. : ill. ; 29 cm. (Agrárgazdasági Kutató Intézet, 0209-5696 . 1984/11) Bibliography: p. 45-47. ISBN 963-491-189-7 LC Card 86-198789
1. Agriculture and state - Hungary - Mathematical models. 2. Central planning - Hungary - Mathematical models. I. Nagy, József. II. Spitálszky, Márta. III. Series: Agrárgazdasági Kutató Intézet (Series) , 1984/11. IV. Title.
HD1940.5.Z8 K68 1984

Kovács, Mihályné. Baross, Jenő. A kereskedelmi hitel és a váltó gyakorlata /. Budapest , 1985. 123 p. ; LC Card 86-228454
HG3754.5.H9 B37 1985

Kovács, Tibor. Nagyné Szauter, Edit. A gazdaságilag elmaradott térségek társadalmi-gazdasági jellemzői /. Budapest , 1986. 41 p. : LC Card 86-215345
HC300.28 .N26 1986

Koval', Boris Iosifovich. Mezhdunarodnoe rabochee dvizhenie . Moskva , 1980. 412 p. ; LC Card 81-143888
HD4854 .M474 1980

Kovalev, A. I. (Anatoliĭ Ivanovich) Odint͡sova, G. S. (Galina Sergeevna) Organizatsionnoe proektirovanie i planirovanie razvitii͡a sistem upravlenii͡a /. Kiev , 1986. 158, [2] p. : LC Card 87-162923
HD2876 .O35 1986

Kovalev, I͡U. A. Nekotorye problemy internatsional'nogo vospitanii͡a v mnogonatsional'nom trudovom kollektive /. Moskva , 1985. 135 p. ; LC Card 86-233779
HD8526.5 .N45 1985

Kovanov, S. I. (Stanislav Ivanovich) Val'ter, S. B. (Semen Borisovich) Spravochnik po finansovo-ėkonomicheskim raschetam v sel'skokhozi͡aĭstvennykh predprii͡atii͡akh /. Moskva , 1982. 411 p. ; LC Card 83-160870
HF5686.A36 V35 1982

Kovrigin, E. B. (Evgeniĭ Borisovich) Protivorechii͡a i perspektivy formirovanii͡a "Tikhookeanskogo soobshchestva" / E.B. Kovrigin. Moskva : "Mezhdunar. otnoshenii͡a", 1986. 173, [3] p. ; 20 cm. Bibliography: p. 169-[174] LC Card 86-200677
1. Pacific Area cooperation. 2. Pacific Area - Economic integration. I. Title.
HC681 .K68 1986

Kowalczyk, David S., 1946- Cadmus' operational auditing / David S. Kowalczyk. New York : Wiley, c1987. x, 422 p. ; 24 cm. (The Wiley/Ronald-Institute of Internal Auditors professional book series) Includes index. ISBN 0-471-82660-X LC Card 87-23267 DDC 657/.458 19
1. Auditing, Internal. 2. Auditing. I. Title. II. Title: Operational auditing. III. Series.
HF5668.25 .K696 1987

Kowalski, Thaddeus J. An artificial intelligence approach to VLSI design / Thaddeus J. Kowalski. Boston : Kluwer, c1985. x, 226 p. : ill. ; 24 cm. (The Kluwer international series in engineering and computer science . SECS 4.) Includes index. Bibliography: p. [106]-114. ISBN 0-89838-169-X LC Card 85-7581 DDC 621.3819/5835 19
1. Integrated circuits - Very large scale integration. 2. Expert systems (Computer science). I. Series: Kluwer international series in engineering and computer science , SECS 4. II. Title.
TK7874 .K675 1985 ***NYPL [JSE 86-1182]***

KOWLOON (HONG KONG) - ECONOMIC CONDITIONS.
Šimko, Dušan. Strassenverkäufer und die Versorgung der Arbeiterfamilien von Kowloon (Hong Kong) im Umfeld der staatlichen Planungspolitik /. Basel , 1983. 196 p., [9] p. of plates : ISBN 3-85977-129-9 : LC Card 83-238672
HF5459.H6 S56 1983

KOWLOON (HONG KONG) - SOCIAL CONDITIONS.
Šimko, Dušan. Strassenverkäufer und die Versorgung der Arbeiterfamilien von Kowloon (Hong Kong) im Umfeld der staatlichen Planungspolitik /. Basel , 1983. 196 p., [9] p. of plates : ISBN 3-85977-129-9 : LC Card 83-238672
HF5459.H6 S56 1983

Kowtun, Józef. Rola, funkcje i zadania mistrza w systemie dokształcania i wychowania robotników / Józef Kowtun, Kiejstut R. Szymański. Wyd. 1. Warszawa : Wydawnictwa Akcydensowe, 1979. 151, [1] p. ; 21 cm. (Biblioteka pedagogiczna . P-37) At head of title: Związek Zakładów Doskonalenia Zawodowego. Bibliography: p. 149-[152] LC Card 81-180277
1. Employees, Training of - Poland. 2. Occupational retraining - Poland. I. Szymański, Kiejstut R. II. Title. III. Series.
HF5549.5.T7 K687 1979

Kox, Henk. Kapitaal-export vanuit Nederland : in relatie met binnenlandse investeringen, concernstrategieën, kontrolemogelijkheden / Henk Kox & Leo van Velzen. Amsterdam : Stichting Onderzoek Multinationale Ondernemingen, 1985. 136 p. : ill. ; 22 cm. Includes bibliographical references. ISBN 90-71284-01-8 LC Card 85-237950
1. Investments, Dutch. 2. Netherlands - Foreign economic relations. I. Velzen, Leo van. II. Title.
HG5562 .K69 1985

Koy, Kevin. Steidlmayer, J. Peter. Markets and market logic /. Chicago , c1986. 161 p. ; ISBN 0-941275-00-0 LC Card 87-401422 DDC 332.64 19
HG6046 .S673 1986

Kozak, Gregor. Versicherungs-Leitfaden . Wien , 1984. 79 p. : LC Card 85-198493 DDC 368/.9436 19
HG8061 .V47 1984

Közgazdasági bizottságok kézikönyve / [szerzők, Szűcs Ferenc ... et al. ; szerkesztette Pintér György]. Budapest : Népszava, 1984. 324 p. ; 20 cm. ISBN 963-322-017-3 : LC Card 85-126303
1. Hungary - Economic policy - 1968-. 2. Trade-unions - Hungary. I. Szűcs, Ferenc. II. Pintér, György, 1921-.
HC300.28 .K68 1984

A közgazdasági szabályozás és az élelmiszeripari szakágazatok gazdasági eredményeinek összefüggései és problémái az 1977-82 közötti években /. Szénay, Lászlóné. Budapest , 1984. 161 p. ; ISBN 963-491-196-X LC Card 86-199432
HD9015.H82 S935 1984

Koziara, Karen Shallcross. Working women . Washington, D.C. , c1987. xxii, 419 p. ; ISBN 0-87179-547-7 LC Card 87-9410 DDC 331.4/0973 19
HD6095 .W742 1987

Koziol, Joseph D. A handbook for professional futures and options traders / Joseph D. Koziol. New York : Wiley, c1987. xvi, 325 p. : ill. ; 26 cm. Bibliography: p. 307-313. Includes index. ISBN 0-471-87423-X : LC Card 87-8180 DDC 332.64/4 19
1. Commodity exchanges. 2. Financial futures. 3. Option (Contract). I. Title.
HG6024.A3 K68 1987

Koziolek, Helmut.
Marx' Aussagen über die produktive Infrastruktur vor allem in den "Grundrissen" und im "Kapital." 1986.
Koziolek, Helmut. Umfassende Intensivierung und Infrastruktur / Helmut Koziolek. Berlin , 1986. 68 p. ; LC Card 86-169897
HC290.795.C3 K68 1986

Reproduktion und Infrastruktur / Helmut Koziolek, Werner Ostwald, Hans Stürz. Berlin : Verlag Die Wirtschaft, c1986. 224 p. : ill. (some col.), col. maps ; 24 cm. Bibliography: p. 215-220. Includes index. ISBN 3-349-00017-7 LC Card 87-130782 DDC 363/.09431 19
1. Infrastructure (Economics) - Germany (East). 2. Germany, East - Population. I. Ostwald, Werner. II. Stürz, Hans. III. Title.
HC290.795.C3 K675 1986

Umfassende Intensivierung und Infrastruktur / Helmut Koziolek. Berlin : Akademie-Verlag, 1986. 68 p. ; 22 cm. (Sitzungsberichte der Akademie der Wissenschaften der DDR. Gesellschaftswissenschaften, 0138-4015 . Jahrg. 1986, Nr. 2/G) "Erweiterter Vortrag von Helmut Koziolek, ordentliches Mitglied und Vorsitzender der Klasse Gesellschaftswissenschaften I der Akademie der Wissenschaften der DDR in der Sitzung der Klasse am 16. Mai 1985."--T.p. verso. "Anlage 1: Marx' Aussagen über die produktive Infrastruktur vor allem in den 'Grundrissen' und im 'Kapital.'": p. 43-66. Includes bibliographies. LC Card 86-169897
1. Infrastructure (Economics) - Germany (East). 2. Human capital - Germany (East). 3. Germany, East - Economic policy. 4. Marxian economics. I. Koziolek, Helmut. Marx' Aussagen über die produktive Infrastruktur vor allem in den "Grundrissen" und im "Kapital." 1986. II. Title. III. Series.
HC290.795.C3 K68 1986

Közlekedés- és Postaügyi Minisztérium Postafőosztályának kiadványa.
Postai szakkifejezések ötnyelvű szótára . Budapest , 1978. 349 p. ; LC Card 84-248004
HE6035 .P67 1978

Közlemények (Szövetkezeti Kutató Intézet) ; v189.
Meszticzky, András. Termelőszövetkezeti szakemberek munkahelyváltoztatása . [Budapest] , 1985. 165 p. : LC Card 86-218526
HD1492.H8 M37 1985

Kozlov, A. F. Valentik, I. I͡A. (Ivan I͡Akovlevich) Ėkonomicheskie osnovy intensifikatsii lesnogo khozi͡aĭstva Karel'skoĭ ASSR /. Leningrad ,

1986. 135, [1] p. : LC Card 87-125199
HD9765.S653 K378 1986

Kozlov, I. D. (Igor' Dmitrievich) Ėnergeticheskoe khozīaĭstvo stran SĖV : problemy, perspektivy / I.D. Kozlov. Moskva : Izd-vo "Nauka", 1980. 158 p. ; 20 cm. At head of title: Akademiia nauk SSSR. Institut ėkonomiki mirovoĭ sotsialisticheskoĭ sistemy. Includes bibliographical references. LC Card 87-107887
1. Energy industries - Europe, Eastern - International cooperation. 2. Fuel trade - Europe, Eastern - International cooperation. 3. Council for Mutual Economic Assistance. I. Title.
HD9502.E83 K686 1980

Kozlov, IUriĭ Markovich. Ataev, M. (Murruk) Gosudarstvennoe upravlenie ispol'zovaniem i okhranoĭ vod /. Ashkhabad , 1982. 175 p. ; LC Card 82-244366
HD1697.S653 T873 1982

Kozlov, Leonard Aleksandrovich. Martynov, G. V. (Gennadiĭ Viktorovich) Mnogootraslevye kompleksy--problemy i metody optimizatsii /. Moskva , 1986. 229, [3] p. : LC Card 86-232408
HC333 .M285 1986

Kozlov, P. T. (Petr Tikhonovich) Sovershenstvovanie khozīaĭstvennogo mekhanizma v neftīanoĭ i gazovoĭ promyshlennosti / P.T. Kozlov, A.K. Kuvanyshev, T.Ė. Baīanskiĭ. Alma-Ata : Izd-vo "Nauka" Kazakhskoĭ SSR, 1983. 134 p. : ill. ; 20 cm. At head of title: Akademiia nauk Kazakhskoĭ SSR. Sovet po izucheniiu proizvoditel'nykh sil Kazakhstana. Includes bibliographical references. LC Card 83-194289
1. Petroleum industry and trade - Soviet Union. 2. Gas, Natural - Soviet Union. I. Kuvanyshev, A. K. II. Baīanskiĭ, T. Ė. (Timur Ėmirovich). III. Title.
HD9575.S652 K69 1983

Kozlova, K. B. Institutsionalizm v amerikanskoĭ politėkonomii : ideĭno-teoreticheskie osnovy liberal'nogo reformizma / K.B. Kozlova ; otvetstvennyĭ redaktor I.M. Osadchaia. Moskva : "Nauka", 1987. 214, [2] p. ; 22 cm. At head of title: Akademiia nauk SSSR. Ordena Trudovogo Krsnogo Znameni Institut mirovoĭ ėkonomiki i mezhdunarodnykh otnosheniĭ. Bibliography: p. 198-[215]. LC Card 87-159642
1. Institutional economics. 2. United States - Economic policy - 1981-. 3. Industry and state - United States. 4. Monopolies - United States. 5. Liberalism - United States. I. Osadchaia, Irina Mikhaĭlovna. II. Title.
HB99.5 .K69 1987

Kozlova, O. V. (Olimpiada Vasil'evna) Khozīaĭstvovat' umelo i ėffektivno /. Moskva , 1985. 267, [5] p. ; LC Card 85-148146
HC338.M6 K47 1985

Kozlovskaia, L. V. Regional'nye problemy razvitiia infrastruktury i mezhotraslevykh proizvodstv /. Minsk , 1985. 243, [4] p. ; LC Card 86-161744
HC337.B933 C37 1985 *NYPL [*QM 87-2108]*

Kozlowski, Joseph G. Complete guide to cost-effective employee benefit programs / Joseph G. Kozlowski and Walter Oleksy. Englewood Cliffs, N.J. : Prentice-Hall, c1987. xix, 276 p. : ill. ; 27 cm. Includes index. ISBN 0-13-160037-0 LC Card 87-11816 DDC 658.3/25 19
1. Employee fringe benefits - United States. I. Oleksy, Walter G., 1930-. II. Title.
HD4928.N62 U636 1987

Kozma, László. Hatékony vezetői időgazdálkodás . Budapest , 1984. 62 p. ; ISBN 963-7902-09-0 (Magy. nemz. bibl.) LC Card 85-177403
HD69.T54 H38 1984

A Központi Statisztikai Hivatal Népességtudományi Kutató Intézetének és a Magyar Tudományos Akadémia Demográfiai Bizottságának közleményei, 0134-0093 .

Központi Statisztikai Hivatal Népességtudományi Kutató Intézetének és a Magyar Tudományos Akadémia Demográfiai Bizottságának közleményei, 0134-0093 .
(59) Csernák, Józsefné. A családok és háztartások előreszámítása, 1981-2001 /. Budapest , 1985. 125 p. : LC Card 86-166603
HA1201 .A64 no. 59 HA1205

(60) Pataki, Judit. Közvéleménykutatás népesedési kérdésekről /. Budapest , c1985. 75 p. ; LC Card 86-166976
HA1201 .A64 no. 60 HB3592.5.A3

(62) Pongrácz, Tiborné. A terhességmegszakításon átesett 18 éven aluli hajadonok társadalmi-demográfiai jellemzői /. Budapest , c1986. 115 p. ; LC Card 87-409645
HA1201 .A64 no. 62 HQ767.5.H8

A Központi Statisztikai Hivatal Népességtudományi Kutató Intézetének kutatási jelentései, 0236-736X .
(22) Szukicsné Serfőző, Klára. Budapest és Pest megye népességfejlődése, az ezredfordulóig várható tendenciák /. Budapest , 1984. 88 p. : LC Card 86-157549
HA1208.B96 S98 1984

Központi Statisztikai Hivatal Népességtudományi Kutató Intézetének történeti demográfiai füzetei .
(1, etc) A Népmozgalmi statisztika fejlődése Magyarországon. Budapest , 1985- v. <1 > ; LC Card 86-190535
HA37.H92 N46 1985

Közvéleménykutatás népesedési kérdésekről /. Pataki, Judit. Budapest , c1985. 75 p. ; LC Card 86-166976
HA1201 .A64 no. 60 HB3592.5.A3

K.P. development monograph .
(no. 3) Bryant, Coralie. Managing rural development with small farmer participation /. West Hartford, CT. , c1984. xiii, 79 p. : ISBN 0-931816-52-1 (pbk.) LC Card 84-4445 DDC 307.7/2 19
HD1417 .B79 1984 *NYPL [JLE 87-1352]*

Die KPS und die Wirtschaftskämpfe, 1930-1933 . Wandeler, Josef, 1949- Zürich , c1978. 277 p. : ISBN 3-85854-003-X LC Card 87-409249 DDC 331.89/29494 19
HD5410.A6 W36 1978

KPSS i kolkhoznoe krest'īanstvo v 1945-1959 gg. /. Krivoded, V. V. Rostov-na-Donu , 1984. 190 p. ; LC Card 87-100194
HD1492.S652 C384 1984

Kraak, Bernhard. Berufliche Motivation und berufliches Verhalten : zur Frage geschlechtstypischer Unterschiede / von Bernhard Kraak und Dietlinde Nord-Rüdiger. Göttingen : C.J. Hogrefe, c1984. i, 145 p. ; 21 cm. (Studien zur pädagogischen Psychologie . Bd. 21) Bibliography: p. 75-78. ISBN 3-8017-0218-9 LC Card 85-100278
1. Employee motivation. 2. Sex discrimination against women. I. Nord-Rüdiger, Dietlinde. II. Title. III. Series.
HF5549.5.M63 K73 1984

KRABI (THAILAND : PROVINCE) - STATISTICS.
Sathiti thī samkhan, 2512, Čhangwat Krabī =. [Bangkok] [19]71. [8], 36 leaves, [1] leaf of plates : LC Card 83-921122
HA4600.55 .S275 1971

Krabs, Otto. Verwaltung und Planung im Wandel /. Köln , 1979. 112 p. ; ISBN 3-7745-6438-8 : LC Card 81-473982
HT395.G4 V48 *NYPL [JLE 86-2107]*

Krack, Jürgen. Lieber besser statt mehr? : qualitative Tarifpolitik in der Wirtschaftskrise / Jürgen Krack, Egon Kutscher. Köln : Bund-Verlag, c1985. 306, [2] p. : ill. ; 21 cm. Bibliography: p. [308] ISBN 3-7663-0569-7 LC Card 85-125869
1. Wages - Germany, West. 2. Trade-unions - Germany, West. 3. Germany, West - Economic conditions - 1974-. I. Kutscher, Egon, 1953-. II. Title.
HD5029 .K72 1985

Krämer, Georg. Pädagogische Aspekte entwicklungspolitischer Öffentlichkeitsarbeit / Georg Krämer. Frankfurt/Main : Haag + Herchen, 1980. 233 p. : ill. ; 21 cm. (Friedenskonzepte. Bd. 3 0170-1746) Bibliography: p. 223-233. ISBN 3-88129-332-9 LC Card 81-466304
1. Publicity. 2. Public opinion - Germany, West. 3. Developing countries - Economic conditions. 4. Developing countries - Public opinion. I. Title.
HC59.7 .K687 *NYPL [JLD 87-528]*

Krätke, Michael. Kritik der Staatsfinanzen : zur politischen Ökonomie des Steuerstaats / Michael Krätke. Hamburg : VSA-Verlag, 1984. 297 p. ; 24 cm. Bibliography: p. 284-297. ISBN 3-87975-247-8 LC Card 84-186778
1. Taxation - Germany, West. I. Title.
HJ2687 .K67 1984

Kraev, V. S. (Vladimir Semenovich) Korostelev, Gennadiĭ Mikhaĭlovich. Burzhuaznye kontseptsii narodonaseleniia . Moskva , 1981. 158 p. ; LC Card 82-140945
HB851 .K65 1981

Kraeva, M. I. Ėkonomicheskie aspekty ratsional'nogo ispol'zovaniia resursov okeana i okhrany morskoĭ sredy . Vladivostok , 1984. 124 p. : LC Card 85-234774
HC92 .E37 1984

Kraft, Alfred. Aspekte der Regionalen wirtschaftlichen Integration zwischen Entwicklungsländern : das Beispiel der Asean / von Alfred Kraft. Wiesbaden : F. Steiner, 1982. x, 298 p. : ill. ; 24 cm. (Beiträge zur Südasienforschung. Bd. 68) Summary in English. Bibliography: p. 274-289. ISBN 3-515-03801-9 LC Card 85-136228
1. ASEAN. 2. Asia, Southeastern - Economic integration. 3. Developing countries - Economic integration. I. Title. II. Series.
HC441 .K69 1982

Kraft, Joseph. The Mexican rescue / Joseph Kraft. New York : Group of Thirty, 1984. 66 p. ; 23 cm. LC Card 84-10354 DDC 336.3/4/0972 19
1. Debts, External - Mexico. 2. Loans, Foreign - Mexico. 3. Mexico - Economic policy 1970-. I. Title.
HJ8519 .K73 1984 *NYPL [JLE 86-2931]*

Kraft, Kornelius.
Mitarbeiterbeteiligung und Mitbestimmung im Unternehmen /. Berlin , New York , 1987, c1986. ix, 351 p. : ISBN 3-11-010668-X LC Card 87-137953 DDC 658.3/152/0943 19
HD5660.G4 M53 1987

Wettbewerbssituation und Marktzutrittsbarrieren bei spezifischen Qualifikationen / von Kornelius Kraft. Berlin : Wissenschaftszentrum Berlin, [1985] 35, 6 p. : ill. ; 30 cm. (Discussion papers / IIM/Industrial Policy, 0722-6748 . IIM/IP 85-39) Summary in English. Bibliography: p. 30-35. LC Card 86-211574
1. Unskilled labor. 2. Employees, Training of. I. Series: Discussion papers (International Institute of Management. Industrial Policy) , IIM/IP 85-39. II. Title.
HD5707 .K73 1985

Die Kraftfahrzeughaftpflichtversicherung in Österreich . Rettenbacher, Karl. Linz , c1984. 183 p. : ISBN 3-85320-328-0 LC Card 85-162917
HG9970.4.A9 R48 1984

Krahl, Hans-Jürgen. Vom Ende der abstrakten Arbeit : die Aufhebung der sinnlosen Arbeit ist in der Transzendentalität des Kapitals angelegt und in der Verweltlichung der Philosophie begründet / Hans Jürgen Krahl ; herausgegeben und eingeleitet von Walter Neumann.Erstausg. Frankfurt : Materialis, 1984. 209 p. ; 21 cm. (Materialis Programm . MP 23.) Includes bibliographical references. ISBN 3-88535-075-0 LC Card 84-188656
1. Work - Psychological aspects. 2. Human capital. I. Neumann, Walter. II. Series: Materialis Programm , MP 23. III. Title.
HD4904 .K6915 1984

Krahn, H. Working Canadians . Toronto , New York , c1984. x, 380 p. ; ISBN 0-458-97370-X (pbk.) : LC Card 84-222036 DDC 331/.0971 19
HD6957.C2 W67 1984 *NYPL [JLD 87-681]*

Kraiukhin, G. A. Sbornik zadach i khozīaĭstvennykh situatsiĭ po ėkonomike i planirovaniiu mashinostroitel'noĭ promyshlennosti /. Moskva , 1985. 246 p. ; LC Card 86-110747
HD9703.S652 S28 1985

Krakh rabocheĭ politiki administratsii Trumėna . Rogulev, IU. N. (IUriĭ Nikolaevich) Moskva , 1981. 135 p. ; LC Card 82-155486
HD8072.5 .R64 1981

Krakh zubatovshchiny na Ukraine. Ovsiīenko, O. F. Krakh zubatovshchyny na Ukraïni /. Kyïv , 1987. 137, [3] p. ; LC Card 87-161669
HD8529.U43 O97 1987

Krakh zubatovshchyny na Ukraïni /. Ovsiīenko, O. F. Kyïv , 1987. 137, [3] p. ; LC Card 87-161669
HD8529.U43 O97 1987

KRAKÓW (POLAND) - ECONOMIC CONDITIONS.

Prace z zakresu socjologii /. Kraków , 1979. 137 p. ; LC Card 80-129964
HB9 .K53 nr. 117 HC340.3.Z7K7

Kraljevina Jugoslavije. see **Yugoslavia.**

Kraljevina Srba, Hrvata i Slovenaca. see **Yugoslavia.**

Kramer, Arthur, 1908- Among the livewires : 100 years of Puget Power / by Arthur Kramer. [Edmonds, Wash. : Creative Communications, c1986] 141 p. : ill. ; 28 cm. Bibliography: p. 137. Includes index. ISBN 0-939116-14-6 (pbk.) LC Card 86-91152 DDC 338.7/6136362/09797 19
1. Puget Sound Power and Light Company - History. 2. Electric utilities - Washington (State) - History. I. Title.
HD9685.U7 P925 1986

Kramer, Helgard. Grenzen der Frauenlohnarbeit . Frankfurt/Main , New York , c1986. 250 p. : ISBN 3-593-33628-6 LC Card 86-228323
HD6072.2.G4 G74 1986

Kramer, Helmut.
Strukturpolitik als Dimension der Vollbeschäftigungspolitik /. Stuttgart , c1983. 103 p. : ISBN 3-437-50276-X : LC Card 83-233394
HD5706 .S82 1983

Vom Nachzügler zum Vorbild(?) . Stuttgart , c1985. 183 p. : ISBN 3-437-50303-0 LC Card 86-200243
HC265 .V65 1985

Kramer, Helmut, 1939- Industrielle Strukturprobleme Österreichs : dargestellt am Beispiel der Eisen- und Metallverarbeitung / Helmut Kramer ; herausgegeben vom Institut für Angewandte Sozial- und Wirtschaftsforschung. Wien : Signum-Verlag, 1980. 112 p. ; 21 cm. Bibliography: p. 103-108. LC Card 81-103725 DDC 338.4/76691/09436 19
1. Iron industry and trade - Austria. 2. Metal-work - Austria. I. Vienna. Institut für Angewandte Sozial- und Wirtschaftsforschung. II. Title.
HD9525.A82 K73 1980 *NYPL [JLD 86-1237]*

Krannich, Ronald L. High impact resumes and letters / Ronald L. Krannich, William J. Banis. 2nd ed. Manassas, Va. : Impact Publications, c1987. viii, 136 p. : ill., forms ; 28 cm. Cover title: High impact resumes & letters. Includes index. ISBN 0-942710-12-6 (pbk.) : LC Card 86-83117 DDC 650.1/4 19
1. Résumés (Employment). 2. Commercial correspondence. I. Banis, William J. II. Title. III. Title: High impact resumes & letters.
HF5383 .K7 1987

Krantz, Frederick. Failed transitions to modern industrial society . Montreal , c1975. vii, 105 p. : ISBN 0-919958-00-1 LC Card 80-510009 DDC 303.4/094 19
HM101 .F26 *NYPL [JLE 81-166]*

Krasavchenko, S. N.
Perestroĭka i rukovoditel´ /. Moskva , 1987. 143 p. ; LC Card 87-164793
HD38.25.S65 P47 1987

Podgotovka upravlencheskikh kadrov--opyt, problemy, perspektivy (po zarubezhnym materialam) . Moskva , 1984. 188 p. ; LC Card 85-188986
HD30.4 .P6 1984

Krasavina, L. N. Denezhnoe obrashchenie i kredit kapitalisticheskikh stran /. Moskva , 1977. 342 p. ; LC Card 82-196677
HG173.6.R8 D46 1977

Krasil´nikov, S. A. (Sergeĭ Aleksandrovich)
Shishkin, V. I. (Vladimir Ivanovich) Sotsialisticheskoe stroitel´stvo v sibirskoĭ derevne, noiabr´ 1919-mart 1921 g. /. Novosibirsk , 1985. 316 p. ; LC Card 86-164936
HD1995.S5 S45 1985

Krasnaia liniia : sbornik ocherkov i dokumental´nykh povesteĭ / [redaktor V.F. Trusova]. Moskva : Profizdat, 1986. 382 p. : ill. ; 21 cm. CONTENTS. - Glavnaia liniia zhizni / Al´bert Kubarev -- Lichnoe delo Agarkova / Nelli Zasypkina -- Tropa k ėdel´veĭsu / Genrikh Kuvitanov -- Rodom iz brigady / Al´bert Speranskiĭ -- Shtrikhi k portretu / IAkov Tavrov -- Dva kryla / Mikola Riabyĭ -- Krasnaia liniia / Vladimir Franiuk. LC Card 86-112685
1. Work groups - Soviet Union. I. Trusova, V. F.
HD8526.5 .K73 1986

Krasnenkov, Vladimir. Ne pole pereĭti-- / Vladimir Krasnenkov. Moskva : Moskovskiĭ rabochiĭ, 1986. 174 p. ; 20 cm. (Vremia i my) LC Card 86-132520
1. Agriculture - Economic aspects - Russian S.F.S.R. - Non-Chernozem Region. 2. Non-Chernozem Region (R.S.F.S.R.) - Rural conditions. I. Title. II. Series.
HD1995.N515 K73 1986

Krasner, Stephen D., 1942-
Krasnick, Mark R. Fiscal federalism /. Toronto , Buffalo , c1986. xvi, 211 p. ; ISBN 0-8020-7312-3 (pbk.)
HJ793 .F59 1986 *NYPL [JLE 86-3253]*

Krasnopol´skiĭ, B. Kh. (Boris Khananovich)
Infrastruktura v sisteme regional´nogo khoziaĭstvennogo kompleksa Severa : metodicheskie osobennosti issledovaniia / B.Kh. Krasnopol´skiĭ. Moskva : Izd-vo "Nauka", 1980. 143, [2] p. ; 20 cm. (Problemy sovetskoĭ ėkonomiki) At head of title: Akademiia nauk SSSR. Dal´nevostochnyĭ nauchnyĭ tsentr. Severo-Vostochnyĭ kompleksnyĭ nauchno-issledovatel´skiĭ institut. Bibliography: p. 140-[144] LC Card 81-131391
1. Infrastructure (Economics) - Soviet Union, Northern. 2. Natural resources - Soviet Union, Northern. 3. Territorial production complexes - Soviet Union, Northern. I. Title.
HC336.9.N65 K73 1980

Krasnykh, L. M. (Leonid Mikhaĭlovich)
Krasnykh, L. M. (Leonid Mikhaĭlovich) Partiĭnoe rukovodstvo sovershenstvovaniem upravleniia promyshlennost´iu v period stroitel´stva sotsializma, 1926-1937 . Krasnoiarsk , 1986. 150, [2] p. ; LC Card 86-226013
HD70.S63 K73 1986

Partiĭnoe rukovodstvo sovershenstvovaniem upravleniia promyshlennost´iu v period stroitel´stva sotsializma, 1926-1937 : na materialakh RSFSR / L.M. Krasnykh. Krasnoiarsk : Izd-vo Krasnoiarskogo universiteta, 1986. 150, [2] p. ; 21 cm. Bibliography: p. 137-[151] LC Card 86-226013
1. Industrial management - Russian S.F.S.R. - History. 2. Communist leadership - Russian S.F.S.R. - History. 3. Kommunisticheskaia partiia Sovetskogo Soiuza - History. I. Krasnykh, L. M. (Leonid Mikhaĭlovich). II. Title.
HD70.S63 K73 1986

Krasovskiĭ, V. P. (Viktor Petrovich)
Infrastruktura i intensifikatsiia ėkonomiki /. Moskva , 1980. 192 p. ; LC Card 81-141492
HC340.C3 I54 1980

Krasucka, Alicja. Organizacja transportu samochodowego / Alicja Krasucka, Henryk Woźniak. Wyd. 1. Gdańsk : Uniwersytet Gdański, 1984. 181 p., [8] leaves of plates (7 folded) : ill. ; 24 cm. (Skrypty uczelniane / Uniwersytet Gdański) Bibliography: p. 178-181. ISBN 83-7017-058-7 : LC Card 86-173836
1. Transportation, Automotive - Poland - Management. I. Woźniak, Henryk. II. Series: Skrypty uczelniane / Uniwersytet Gdański. III. Title.
HE5675.7.A6 K7 1984

Kratkiĭ vneshneėkonomicheskiĭ slovar´ / pod redaktsieĭ O.S. Bogdanova. Moskva : "Mezhdunarodnye otnosheniia", 1984. 244 p. ; 20 cm. Includes index. LC Card 85-156834
1. Commerce - Dictionaries - Russian. 2. International economic relations - Dictionaries - Russian. I. Bogdanov, Oleg Semenovich.
HF1001 .K7 1984 *NYPL [*QCK 86-3635]*

Kratz, Hans-Jürgen.
Arbeitslosengeld / [Bearbeitung, Hans-Jürgen Kratz, Hans-Joachim Kühner ; Redaktion, Hans Günther Schanne ; Herausgeber, Arbeitskammer des Saarlandes, Referat Presse und Information]. 2. Aufl. Saarbrücken : Die Arbeitskammer, [1983] 176 p. ; 21 cm. Updated ed. of: Arbeitslosengeld 81. 1. Aufl. 1981. ISBN 3-88968-006-2 LC Card 83-215450
1. Insurance, Unemployment - Germany (West) - Saarland. 2. Insurance, Unemployment - Law and legislation - Germany (West) - Saarland. I. Kühner, Hans-Joachim. II. Schanne, Hans Günther. III. Kratz, Hans-Jürgen. Arbeitslosengeld 81. IV. Arbeitskammer des Saarlandes. Referat Presse und Information. V. Title.
HD7096.G32 S335 1983

Arbeitslosengeld 81. Kratz, Hans-Jürgen. Arbeitslosengeld / [Bearbeitung, Hans-Jürgen Kratz, Hans-Joachim Kühner ; Redaktion, Hans Günther Schanne ; Herausgeber, Arbeitskammer des Saarlandes, Referat Presse und Information]. 2. Aufl. Saarbrücken [1983] 176 p. ; ISBN 3-88968-006-2 LC Card 83-215450
HD7096.G32 S335 1983

Kratz, Peter. Steuerplanung internationaler Unternehmungen : System und Methode / Peter Kratz. Bern : Haupt, c1986. xii, 344 p. : ill. ; 23 cm. (Schriftenreihe Finanzwirtschaft und Finanzrecht. Bd. 47) Bibliography: p. 321-344. ISBN 3-258-03586-5 : LC Card 86-171030
1. International business enterprises - Taxation - Germany (West). 2. Tax planning - Germany (West). I. Title. II. Series.
HJ4720.A3 K73 1986

Kraus, Herbert, 1937- Schrumpfende Märkte . Wien , 1986. vi, 241 p. : ISBN 3-85436-037-1 LC Card 86-227304 DDC 658.8 19
HF5351 .S4125 1986

Kraus, Rudolf, 1953- Vorkalkulation bei langfristiger Einzelfertigung / Rudolf Kraus. Frankfurt am Main ; New York : P. Lang, c1986. iii, 299 p. : ill. ; 21 cm. (Beiträge zum Rechnungs-, Finanz- und Revisionswesen, 0721-3026 . Bd. 15) Bibliography: p. 270-289. ISBN 3-8204-0000-1 LC Card 86-233181
1. Costs, Industrial. 2. Cost control. I. Title. II. Series.
HD47.3 .K73 1986

Kraus, Willy.
The economic development of the Pacific Basin : growth dynamics, trade relations, and emerging cooperation / Willy Kraus, Wilfried Lütkenhorst. New York : St. Martin's Press ; London : C. Hurst, 1986. x, 180 p., [1] leaf of plates : map ; 23 cm. Bibliography: p. 162-177. Includes index. ISBN 0-312-00452-4 (alk. paper) : LC Card 86-26292 DDC 338.95 19
1. Asia, Southeastern - Commercial policy. 2. Japan - Commercial policy. I. Lütkenhorst, Wilfried. II. Title.
HF1591 .K73 1986

Hirschmeier, Johannes. Johannes Hirschmeier, die japanische Unternehmung . Hamburg , 1986. viii, 218 p. : ISBN 3-88910-024-4 : LC Card 86-225311
HF5349.J3 H573 1986

Krause, Chester L. Standard catalog of U. S. paper money / by Chester L. Krause and Robert F. Lemke ; pricing editor, Robert E. Wilhite ; special consultants, Frederick J. Bart ... [et al.]. 4th ed. Iola, WI : Krause Publications, c1985. 192 p. : ill. ; 28 cm. Cover title: Standard catalog of United States paper money. ISBN 0-87341-078-5 (pbk.) LC Card 86-223149 DDC 769.5/5973/0750973 19
1. Paper money - United States - Catalogs. I. Lemke, Robert F. II. Title. III. Title: Standard catalog of United States paper money.
HG591 .K7 1985

Krause, Detlef. Einkommensquellen und Lebenschancen : eine Untersuchung zur Einkommenssituation der Haushalte in der Bundesrepublik Deutschland / von Detlef Krause und Gerhard Schäuble. Berlin : Duncker & Humblot, c1986. 189 p. : ill. ; 24 cm. (Sozialpolitische Schriften. Heft 55) Bibliography: p. [181]-186. ISBN 3-428-06114-4 LC Card 87-130932 DDC 339.2/2/0943 19
1. Income distribution - Germany, West. 2. Households - Germany (West). 3. Cost and standard of living - Germany, West. I. Series: Sozialpolitische Schriften (Duncker & Humblot) , Heft 55. II. Title.
HC290.5.I5 K7 1986

Krause, Hans-Ulrich. Gewinnung, Verarbeitung und Aufbereitung von Informationen für die Geschäftsfeldplanung : auf der Grundlage der morphologischen Methode der Relevanzbaum-Methode / Hans-Ulrich Krause. Giessen : Verlag der Ferber'schen Universitätsbuchhandlung, c1984. xii,324 p. ; 21 cm. Bibliography: p. 298-324. ISBN 3-922730-52-3 LC Card 85-150146
1. Industrial management - Germany, West. 2. Marketing - Germany, West. 3. Technological innovations - Economic aspects - Germany, West. I. Title.
HD35 .K71215 1984

Krause-Junk, Gerold. Geyer, Herbert, 1927- Budgetpolitik im Wandel /. Berlin , c1986. 111 p. : ISBN 3-428-05922-0 LC Card 86-165210
HJ113 .G49 1986

Krause, Lawrence A., 1940- Sleep-tight money : a guide to managing your money safely and achieving financial peace of mind / Lawrence A. Krause. New York : Simon and Schuster, c1987. 300 p. : ill. ; 25 cm. Includes index. ISBN 0-671-64023-2 LC Card 87-14806 DDC 332.024 19
1. Finance, Personal. 2. Investments. I. Title.
HG179 .K664 1987

Krauss, Hans-Ulrich. Erfolgsindikatoren und Betriebsvergleich bei Kreditgenossenschaften / Hans-Ulrich Krauss. Gelsenkirchen : Mannhold, 1983. 217 p. : ill. ; 21 cm. (Kölner Genossenschaftswissenschaft . Bd. 6) Bibliography: p. 207-217. ISBN 3-88485-471-2 LC Card 84-153354
1. Bank and banking, Cooperative - Germany (West). I. Title. II. Series.
HG2039.G4 K73 1983

Kraut, Robert E.
National Research Council (U. S.). Committee on Women's Employment and Related Social Issues. Panel on Technology and Women's Employment. Computer chips and paper clips . Washington, D.C. , 1986. v. : ISBN 0-309-03688-7 (v. 1) LC Card 86-18113 DDC 331.4/8165137/0973 19
HD6331.18.M39 N38 1986
NYPL [JLL 87-129]
Technology and the transformation of white-collar work /. Hillsdale, N.J. , 1987. x, 281 p. : ISBN 0-89859-633-5 : LC Card 86-29039 DDC 331.7/92/0973 19
HD8039.M4 U577 1987

Krauth, Wolf-Hagen. Wirtschaftsstruktur und Semantik : wissenssoziologische Studien zum wirtschaftlichen Denken in Deutschland zwischen dem 13. und 17. Jahrhundert / von Wolf-Hagen Krauth. Berlin : Duncker & Humblot, c1984. 278 p. ; 24 cm. (Soziologische Schriften. Bd. 42) Revision of the author's thesis (doctoral)--Freie Universität Berlin, 1982. Bibliography: p. [265]-278. ISBN 3-428-05728-7 LC Card 85-143046
1. Economics - Germany - History. I. Title.
HB107.A2 K69 1984

Kravchenko, L. P. (Leonid Petrovich)
Preemstvennost' stakhanovskikh traditsiĭ . Moskva , 1985. 222 p. ; LC Card 85-234107
HC340.S6 P68 1985

Krawchenko, Bohdan, 1946- Famine in Ukraine, 1932-1933 /. Edmonton , Downsview, Ont., Canada , 1986. 192 p. ; ISBN 0-09-286243-8 LC Card 87-148658 DDC 363.8/0947/71 19
HC337.U53 F314 1986

Kreativ personalplanering . Egemo, Jerry, 1931- Malmö , c1984. 99 p. ; ISBN 91-38-61248-8 : LC Card 84-188831
HF5549 .E425 1984

Kredit i intensifikatsiia sovkhoznogo proizvodstva /. Shirinskaia, Z. G. (Zinaida Grigor'evna) Moskva , 1980. 142 p. ; LC Card 81-138434
HD1493.S65 S55 1980

Kredit pedesaan di Indonesia / Dumairy ... [et al.] ; penyunting, Mubyarto dan Edy Suandi Hamid. Cet. 1. Yogyakarta : BPFE, 1986. xii, 160 p. ; 22 cm. "Diterbitkan oleh BPFE Yogyakarta untuk P3PK UGM." Bibliography: p. 151-152. LC Card 86-943011
1. Agricultural credit - Indonesia. I. Dumairy, 1956-. II. Mubyarto. III. Hamid, Edy Suandi, 1957-. IV. Universitas Gadjah Mada. Pusat Penelitian dan Studi Pedesaan & Kawasan.
HD2051.I65 K74 1986

Kreditanstalt für Wiederaufbau. Uhlmann, Luitpold. Instrumentelle Aspekte der Investitionsförderung . München , 1986. vii, 270 p. : ISBN 3-88512-024-0 LC Card 86-215244 DDC 332.63 19
HG4028.C4 U367 1986

Kreditni otnosheniia na Narodna republika Bŭlgariia s razvivashtite se strani / avtori Vera Khristova ... [et al. ; nauchen redaktor Khristina Vucheva]. Sofiia : Bŭlgarska tŭrgovsko-promishlena palata, 1986. 78, [1] p. ; 21 cm. (Biblioteka / Bŭlgarska tŭrgovsko-promishlena palata . no. 214) Bibliography: p. 76-[79] LC Card 86-152274
1. Bulgaria - Foreign economic relations - Developing countries. 2. Developing countries - Foreign economic relations - Bulgaria. I. Khristova, Vera. II. Vucheva, Khristina. III. Series: Biblioteka / Bŭlgarska tŭrgovsko-promishlena palata , kn. 214.
HF1578.15.D44 K74 1986

Kreditnye otnosheniia mezhdu stranami-chlenami SEV /. Belichenko, A. N. (Al'bert Nikolaevich) Moskva , 1983. 134 p. : LC Card 84-171632
HG3729.E932 B45 1983

Die Kreditüberwachung im Bankbetrieb . Dierkes, Friedhelm. Berlin , c1986. 139 p. : ISBN 3-428-05987-5 LC Card 86-161146
HG3705 .D54 1986

Die Kreditwirtschaft als wettbewerbspolitischer Ausnahmebereich . Kupitz, Rolf. Thun , c1983. 300 p. ; ISBN 3-87144-773-0 : LC Card 84-129435
HG3754.5.G3 K86 1983

Die Kreditwürdigkeit der eingetragenen Genossenschaft /. Schwenk, Andreas. Göttingen , c1984. xiv, 287 p. ; ISBN 3-525-12752-9 LC Card 86-139501
HG3711.G3 S36 1984

Kreditwürdigkeitsprüfung mit Hilfe von Verfahren der Mustererkennung /. Heno, Rudolf. Bern , c1983. vi, 317 p. : ISBN 3-258-03245-9 : LC Card 83-228668
HG1526 .B27 Bd. 81 HG3751.9.G3

Krefetz, Gerald. All about saving / Gerald Krefetz. New York : J. Wiley, c1987. xvi, 224 p. : ill. ; 22 cm. Includes index. ISBN 0-471-83793-8 LC Card 86-28085 DDC 332.024/01 19
1. Banks and banking - United States. 2. Saving and thrift - United States. I. Title.
HG2491 .K74 1987

Kreiken, J., 1925- Ondernemingsstrategie, theorie en praktijk . Leiden , c1986. xi, 346 p. : ISBN 90-207-1424-4 : LC Card 86-199689
HD37.D8 O54 1986

Kreinecker, Günther. Die Anfänge der Raiffeisenkassen in Oberösterreich (1889-1914) : die wirtschaftliche Entwicklung und ihre sozioökonomische Bedeutung für Gesellschaft und Wirtschaft / Günther Kreinecker. Linz : R. Trauner, c1982. xvi, 276 p. : ill. ; 25 cm. (Linzer Schriften zur Sozial- u. Wirtschaftsgeschichte . Bd. 6) Originally presented as the author's thesis (doctoral) Bibliography: p. 257-276. ISBN 3-85320-279-9 LC Card 83-224597
1. Agricultural cooperative credit associations - Austria - Upper Austria - History. I. Title. II. Series.
HG2051.A89 U64 1982
NYPL [JLE 87-2440]

Kreinin, Mordechai Elihau, 1930- International economics : a policy approach / Mordechai E. Kreinin.5th ed. San Diego : Harcourt Brace Jovanovich, c1987. xiii, 465 p. : ill. ; 25 cm. Bibliography: p. 453-455. Includes index. ISBN 0-15-541538-7 LC Card 86-80750 DDC 337 19
1. International economic relations. 2. Commerce. 3. Commercial policy. I. Title.
HF1411 .K697 1987

Kreis, Barbara, 1947- Moskau, 1917-35 : vom Wohnungsbau zum Städtebau / Barbara Kreis. [Germany] : Edition Marzona, c1985. 243 p., [3] p. of plates : ill. ; 27 cm. Originally presented as the author's thesis (doctoral)--Hochschule für Bildende Künste in Hamburg, 1984. Bibliography: p. 236-242. ISBN 3-921420-26-1 : LC Card 86-170426
1. Housing - Russian S.F.S.R. - Moscow - History. 2. Housing policy - Russian S.F.S.R. - Moscow - History. 3. City planning - Russian S.F.S.R. - Moscow - History. I. Title.
HD7345.M6 K73 1985

Die Kreisfreien Städte und Landkreise in Rheinland-Pfalz / [Autoren, Joachim Gebauer ... et al. ; Redaktion, Joachim Gebauer, Ingo Hawliczek, Fred Kuch]. Bad Ems : Statistisches Landesamt Rheinland-Pfalz, 1977. 420 p. : ill., maps ; 25 cm. One col. map in pocket. LC Card 85-244499
1. Rhineland-Palatinate (Germany) - Economic conditions. 2. Rhineland-Palatinate (Germany) - Population. 3. Rhineland-Palatinate (Germany) - Politics and government. 4. Rhineland-Palatinate (Germany) - Maps. I. Gebauer, Joachim. II. Hawliczek, Ingo. III. Kuch, Fred.
HC287.R7 K74 1977

Kreiten, Kurt. Gestalt und Wandel der nebenberuflichen Landwirtschaft in Nordrhein-Westfalen / von Kurt Kreiten. Bonn : Forschungsgesellschaft für Agrarpolitik und Agrarsoziologie, 1985. xi, 225 p. : ill., maps ; 21 cm. (Schriftenreihe der Forschungsgesellschaft für Agrarpolitik und Agrarsoziologie e.V. Bonn, 0532-2359 . 272) Two maps with transparencies laid in. Bibliography: p. 214-225. ISBN 3-88488-272-4 LC Card 86-205281
1. Part-time farming - Germany (West) - North Rhine-Westphalia. 2. Farmers, Part-time - Germany (West) - North Rhine-Westphalia. I. Series: Schriftenreihe der Forschungsgesellschaft für Agrarpolitik und Agrarsoziologie , 272. II. Title.
HD1960.N67 K74 1985

Krelle, Wilhelm. Wachstum bei Erschöpfbaren Ressourcen, gibt es das? : Ehrenbürgerwürde der Westfälischen Wilhelms-Universität für Karl Mönkemeyer / Wilhelm Krelle. Münster : Aschendorff, c1982. 59 p. : ill. ; 21 cm. (Schriften der Gesellschaft zur Förderung der Westfälischen Wilhelms-Universität zu Münster . Heft 70) "7. Mai 1981"--P. 5. Bibliography: p. 59. ISBN 3-402-04434-X LC Card 83-215135
1. Renewable natural resources. 2. Businessmen - Germany, West. 3. Mönkemeyer, Karl, 1916-. I. Mönkemeyer, Karl, 1916-. II. Title. III. Series.
HC55 .K74 1982

Kremer, Manfred. Assimilation ausländischer Arbeitnehmer in der Bundesrepublik Deutschland : Forschungsbericht / von Manfred Kremer, Helga Spangenberg, unter Mitarbeit von Lothar Jäger, Stephan Schnitzler. Königstein/Ts. : Hanstein, 1980. 203, 64 p. ; 21 cm. (Materialien zur Arbeitsmigration und Ausländerbeschäftigung . Bd. 5) Includes bibliographical references. ISBN 3-7756-6934-5 LC Card 80-151671 DDC 303.4/8243 19
1. Alien labor - Germany (West) - Social conditions. 2. Germanization. I. Spangenberg, Helga. II. Title. III. Series.
HD8458.A2 K73 1980 ***NYPL [JLD 86-2549]***

Kremeyer, Heinz. Eigenfertigung und Fremdbezug unter finanzwirtschaftlichen Aspekten / Heinz Kremeyer. Wiesbaden : Gabler, c1982. 330 p. : ill. ; 24 cm. (Neue betriebswirtschaftliche Forschung . 22) Bibliography: p. [309]-330. ISBN 3-409-37340-3 LC Card 83-148058
1. Vertical integration. 2. Industrial equipment leases. I. Series. II. Series: Neue betriebswirtschaftliche Forschung , Bd. 22. III. Title.
HD2748 .K74 1982

Kremmidas, Vasilis. see **Kremmydas, Vasilēs.**

Kremmydas, Basilēs. see **Kremmydas, Vasilēs.**

Kremmydas, Vasilēs. Hellēnikē nautilia, 1776-1835 / Vasilēs Kremmydas. Athēna : Historiko Archeio, Emporikē Trapeza tēs Hellados, 1985-<1986 > v. <1-2 > : ill. ; 24 cm. (Meletes neoellēnikēs historias . 2) Includes bibliographical references and indexes. CONTENTS. - t. 1. Opseis tēs mesogeiakēs nausiploias -- Hoi mechanismoi. LC Card 86-211031
1. Merchant marine - Greece - History. I. Title. II. Series.
HE872.5 .K74 1985

K.R.E.M.U. technical report series .
(no. 72) Agatsiva, J. L. Land use mapping of Kenya using remote sensing techniques /. [Nairobi] , 1982. iv, 39 p. : LC Card 84-980919 DDC 333.73/13/028 19
HD983.Z7 A38 1982

Krengel, Rolf. Das Deutsche Institut für Wirtschaftsforschung (Institut für Konjunkturforschung), 1925-1979 / von Rolf Krengel. Berlin : Duncker & Humblot, c1986. xi, 229 p. ; 24 cm. Bibliography: p. 209-[228]. ISBN 3-428-06074-1 LC Card 87-112851 DDC 330/.0943 19
1. Deutsches Institut für Wirtschaftsforschung - History. 2. Economics - Research - Germany - History. 3. Economics - Research - Germany (West) - History. I. Title.
HB74.9.G3 K74 1986

Krepche stali /. Zakariadze, M. Tbilisi , 1986. 51 p., [16] p. of plates : LC Card 85-172385
HD9525.S653 G469 1986

Kreppuárin á Íslandi 1930-1939 /. Kjartan Jónasson. [Reykjavik] , 1986- v. <1 > : LC Card 87-117468
HB3717 1929 .K58 1986

Kress, George. Marketing research / George Kress. 3rd ed. Englewood Cliffs, N.J. : Prentice Hall, c1988. p. cm. Includes index. ISBN 0-13-558438-8 LC Card 87-17408 DDC 658.8/3 19

1. Marketing research. I. Title.
HF5415.2 .K75 1988

Kress Library of Business and Economics. Coin and conscience . [Boston, Mass.] , 1986. [28] p. : LC Card 86-203197 DDC 332.4/94 19
HG925 .C65 1986

KRESS LIBRARY OF BUSINESS AND ECONOMICS - CATALOGS.
Coin and conscience . [Boston, Mass.] , 1986. [28] p. : LC Card 86-203197 DDC 332.4/94 19
HG925 .C65 1986

Kress, Roland, 1961- Die politischen Stiftungen in der Entwicklungspolitik : eine Analyse der Kooperation von Friedrich-Ebert-Stiftung und Konrad-Adenauer-Stiftung mit politischen Partnern in Entwicklungsländern / Roland Kress. Bochum : Studienverlag N. Brockmeyer, 1985. iv, 224 p. ; 21 cm. (Politikwissenschaftliche Paperbacks . Bd. 4) Bibliography: p. 207-224. ISBN 3-88339-426-2 : LC Card 85-175519
1. Economic assistance, West German - Developing countries. 2. Technical assistance, West German - Developing countries. 3. Economic assistance - Developing countries. 4. Technical assistance - Developing countries. 5. Friedrich-Ebert-Stiftung. 6. Konrad-Adenauer-Stiftung. 7. Non-governmental organizations - Germany (West). I. Title. II. Series.
HC60 .K727 1985

Krest'iane Russkogo Severa v semnadtsatom v. Kopanev, A. I. (Aleksandr Il'ich) Krest'iane Russkogo Severa v XVII v. /. Leningrad , 1984. 242 p. ; LC Card 84-170666
HD719.R88 K67 1984 ***NYPL [*QG 86-3646]***

Krest'iane Russkogo Severa v XVII v. /. Kopanev, A. I. (Aleksandr Il'ich) Leningrad , 1984. 242 p. ; LC Card 84-170666
HD719.R88 K67 1984 ***NYPL [*QG 86-3646]***

Krest'iane Russkogo Severa v 17-om v. Kopanev, A. I. (Aleksandr Il'ich) Krest'iane Russkogo Severa v XVII v. /. Leningrad , 1984. 242 p. ; LC Card 84-170666
HD719.R88 K67 1984 ***NYPL [*QG 86-3646]***

Kretlow, William J. Moyer, R. Charles, 1945- Contemporary financial management /. St. Paul , c1988. xxiv, 793, 24 p. : ISBN 0-314-64227-7 LC Card 87-24201 DDC 658.1/5 19
HG4026 .M68 1988

Kretschmann, Rolf. Möglichkeiten des Berufswechsels von Haupterwerbslandwirten unter besonderer Berücksichtigung von Agrarstruktur und Arbeitsmarkt / im Auftrag des Bundesministeriums für Ernährung, Landwirtschaft und Forsten erstellt im Sekretariat der Agrarsozialen Gesellschaft e.V., durch Rolf Kretschmann, Reinhard Schneemann. Göttingen : Agrarsoziale Gesellschaft, 1986. xi, 109 p. : ill. ; 21 cm. (ASG-Materialsammlung, 0344-5712 . Nr. 175) Bibliography: p. 93-95. LC Card 87-408871 DDC 331.25/924 19
1. Farmers - Training of - Germany (West). 2. Agricultural laborers - Training of - Germany (West). 3. Career changes - Germany (West). 4. Occupational retraining - Germany, West. I. Schneemann, Reinhard. II. Agrarsoziale Gesellschaft. Sekretariat. III. Title. IV. Series.
HD1536.G3 K746 1986

Krieg und Frieden . Held, Karl, 1944- Frankfurt am Main , c1983. 324 p. ; ISBN 3-518-11149-3 : LC Card 83-228517
HC79.D4 H45 1983

Krieger, Winfried. Computergestützte Auswahl interkontinentaler Distributionsverfahren / von Winfried Krieger. Berlin : Duncker & Humblot, c1984. 143 p. : ill. ; 24 cm. (Schriften zur Betriebswirtschaftslehre des Verkehrs) Bibliography: p. 133-[141] Includes index. ISBN 3-428-05617-5 LC Card 84-219069
1. Shipment of goods - Data processing - Case studies. 2. Aeronautics, Commercial - Freight - Data processing - Case studies. 3. Shipping - Data processing - Case studies. I. Title. II. Series.
HF5765 .K75 1984

Kriegsvorbereitung im Hunsrück . Stange, Sabine. Essen , 1985. 157, [35] p., [4] folded leaves of plates : ISBN 3-88474-409-7 : LC Card 86-148061
HC290.5.D4 S84 1985

KRIEKEN, J., 1925-
Ondernemingsstrategie, theorie en praktijk . Leiden , c1986. xi, 346 p. : ISBN 90-207-1424-4 : LC Card 86-199689
HD37.D8 O54 1986

Kriesi, Hanspeter. Wirtschaftsverbände in der Schweiz . Grüsch , c1986. xv, 294 p. : ISBN 3-7253-0260-X : LC Card 86-136455 DDC 322/.3/09494 19
HD2429.S92 W57 1986
NYPL [JLD 86-2919]

Kriesler, Peter. Kalecki's microanalysis : the development of Kalecki's analysis of pricing and distribution / Peter Kriesler. Cambridge ; New York : Cambridge University Press, 1987. xii, 132 p. : ill. ; 24 cm. Revision of thesis (master's)--University of Sydney, 1981. Bibliography: p. [122]-129. Includes index. ISBN 0-521-33145-5 LC Card 86-24414 DDC 338.5/21 19
1. Competition, Imperfect. 2. Prices. 3. Distribution (Economic theory). 4. Kalecki, Michał. I. Title.
HB238 .K75 1987

Krietemeyer, Hartmut, 1955- Der Erklärungsgehalt der Exportbasistheorie / Hartmut Krietemeyer. Hamburg : Weltarchiv, 1983. 224 p. : ill. ; 23 cm. (Schriften des Zentrums für Regionale Entwicklungsforschung der Justus-Liebig-Universität Giessen, 0170-1614 . Bd. 25) Originally presented as the author's thesis (doctoral)--Justus-Liebig-Universität Giessen, 1982. Bibliography: p. 215-224. ISBN 3-87895-240-6 : LC Card 84-147595
1. Hesse (Germany) - Economic conditions. 2. Regional planning - Germany (West) - Hesse - Econometric models. I. Title. II. Series.
HC287.H4 K75 1983

Kriminologische Forschungsberichte aus dem Max-Planck-Institut für Ausländisches und Internationales Strafrecht, Freiburg .
(Bd. 15) Pitsela, Angelika. Straffälligkeit und Viktimisierung ausländischer Minderheiten in der Bundesrepublik Deutschland . Freiburg [i.B.] , 1986. xxvii, 479 p. ; ISBN 3-922498-16-7 LC Card 87-131111 DDC 331.6/2/495043 19
HD8458.G7 P57 1986

Kripa, Shankar. see **Shankar, Kripa.**

Krischausky, D. Wohnungsgemeinnützigkeit : zwischen bedarfswirtschaftlicher Tradition und wohnungspolitischer Neuorientierung / von D. Krischausky und K. Mackscheidt. Köln : C. Heymann, c1984. vi, 161 p. ; 21 cm. Bibliography: p. 155-161. ISBN 3-452-19899-5 LC Card 84-182027
1. Housing policy - Germany, West. 2. Housing - Germany, West. I. Mackscheidt, K. II. Title.
HD7339.A3 K79 1984

Krischker, Gerhard C. Bamberg in alten Zeitungsanzeigen . Bamberg , c1981. 120 p. : ISBN 3-87052-442-1 LC Card 82-214699
HF6105.G4 B36 1981

Die Krise der deutschen Gewerkschaften . Müller-Vogg, Hugo. Stuttgart , c1986. 96 p. ; ISBN 3-87959-284-5 LC Card 87-104011
HD6694 .M847 1986

Krisenbevorratung von Rohstoffen unter spezieller Berücksichtigung einer Finanzierung aus Währungsreserven der Deutschen Bundesbank /. Eschenbaum, Gerhard. Bochum , 1983. xix, 464 p. : ISBN 3-88339-314-2 : LC Card 83-218426
HF1054.G4 E83 1983

Krisenmanagement in der Unternehmung . Müller, Rainer, 1953- Frankfurt am Main , New York , c1986. xxvii, 773 p. : ISBN 3-8204-7479-X LC Card 87-409055 DDC 658.4 19
HD49 .M84 1986

Krisenmanagement 1857 . Ahrens, Gerhard, 1939- Hamburg , 1986. 136 p. ; ISBN 3-923356-11-0 LC Card 87-127645 DDC 338.5/4 19
HB3717 1857 .A38 1986

Krisenregion Nahost . Hiller, Marlene P., 1948- Frankfurt am Main , New York , c1985. 335 p. : ISBN 3-8204-8249-0 LC Card 85-191941
HF1558.15.T8 H55 1985

Krisenverschärfung durch Angebotspolitik : zur Kritik der wirtschaftspolitischen Konzeption des Sachverständigenrats / Matthes Buhbe ... [et al.]. Köln : Bund-Verlag, c1984. 104 p. ; 21 cm. Bibliography: p. 100-104. ISBN 3-7663-0877-7 LC Card 84-215633
1. Germany, West - Economic conditions - 1974-. 2. Unemployment - Germany (West). I. Buhbe, Matthes, 1949-.
HC286.7 .K75 1984

Krishna Rao, Ch. A. (Chitrothu Atchuta), 1940- Personal income taxation in India / Ch. A. Krishna Rao. Allahabad, India : Chugh Publications, 1987. xii, 284 p. ; 22 cm. Revision of the author's thesis (Ph. D.--Andhra University, 1981) Study in the context of changes took place during 1951-52 to 1979-80. Bibliography: p. [264]-281. Includes index. ISBN 81-85076-19-7 : LC Card 86-903664 DDC 336.24/2/0954 19
1. Income tax - India. I. Title.
HJ4766 .K75 1987

Krishna Rao, Y. V. Growth of capitalism in agriculture : a case study of Andhra Pradesh / Y.V. Krishna Rao ; foreword by Waheeduddin Khan. Vijayawada : Visalaandhra Pub. House, 1984. x, 62 p. ; 23 cm. Bibliography: p. 61-62. LC Card 84-900585 DDC 338.1/3/095484 19
1. Agriculture - Economic aspects - India - Andhra Pradesh. 2. Agriculture - Economic aspects - India - Case studies. 3. Capitalism - India - Andhra Pradesh. 4. Capitalism - India - Case studies. I. Title.
HD2075.A5 K75 1984 ***NYPL [JLD 86-4256]***

Krishnan-Kutty, G.
Economic theory and its applications / G. Krishnan-Kutty. Delhi, India : Mittal Publications, 1987. viii, 131 p. ; 23 cm. Articles, in Indian context. Includes bibliographies and index. LC Card 87-900548 DDC 330.1 19
1. Economics. 2. Economics - India - History. I. Title.
HB71 .K68 1987

Peasantry in India / G. Krishnan-Kutty. New Delhi : Abhinav Publications, 1986. 129 p. ; 22 cm. Includes bibliographies and index. ISBN 81-7017-215-2 : LC Card 86-903053 DDC 305.5/63 19
1. Peasantry - India. 2. Peasant uprisings - India. I. Title.
HD1537.I4 K75 1986

Krishnarao Prahalad, Coimbatore. see **Prahalad, C. K.**

Krissoff, Barry. Haley, Stephen L. The value of the dollar and competitiveness of U. S. wheat exports /. [Washington, D.C.] [1986] iv, 28 p. : LC Card 86-602853 DDC 382/.41311/0973 19
HD9049.W5 U4288 1986

Krist, Herbert. Bestimmungsgründe industrieller Direktinvestitionen / Herbert Krist. Berlin : Edition Sigma, c1985. 310 p. : ill. ; 23 cm. On p. facing t.p.: Wissenschaftszentrum Berlin, Internationales Institut für Management und Verwaltung/Strukturpolitik. Bibliography: p. 279-293. ISBN 3-924859-01-9 LC Card 86-225379
1. Investments, West German. 2. Investments - Germany, West. I. Title.
HG4538 .K72 1985

KRISTIANSEN, KRISTIAN ENGELBRECHT, 1882-
Ulrichsen, Niels. J.A.K.--en dansk krisebevægelse /. København , 1978. 202 p. ; ISBN 87-87462-13-3 LC Card 87-462108
HD2002 .U45 1978

Kristiansen, Stein. U-hjelp og handel : en undersøkelse av sammenhenger mellom norsk u-hjelp og Norges handel med u-land / Stein Kristiansen. Bergen : Chr. Michelsens institutt, DERAP (Forsknings- og aksjonsprogrammet for utviklingsland), [1982] iv, 325 p. : ill. ; 30 cm. (DERAP publikasjon . nr. 141) Bibliography: p. 310-325. LC Card 83-139901
1. Economic assistance, Norwegian - Developing countries. 2. Norway - Commerce - Developing countries. I. Series: DERAP publications , no. 141. II. Title.
HC60 .K76 1982

Kristofersen, Lars. Borgan, Jens-Kristian. Dødelighet i yrker og sosioøkonomiske grupper 1970-1980 /. Oslo , 1986. 217 p. : ISBN 82-537-2339-3 : LC Card 86-231576
HB1445 .B66 1986

Kristoferson, Lars A. Renewable energy technologies : their applications in developing countries / L.A. Kristoferson & V. Bokalders.1st ed. Oxford [Oxfordshire] ; New York : Pergamon Press, 1986. xviii, 319 p. : ill. ; 31 cm. A study by the Beijer Institute, the Royal Swedish Academy of Sciences. ISBN 0-08-034061-X : LC Card 86-766 DDC 621.042 19
1. Renewable energy sources. 2. Renewable energy

sources - Developing countries. I. Bokalders, Varis, 1944-. II. Beijer Institute. III. Kungliga Svenska vetenskapsakademien. IV. Title.
TJ808 .K75 1986 **NYPL [JSG 87-45]**

Kriterii ėffektivnosti raboty predpriiatiĭ . Kuligin, Pavel Ivanovich. Moskva , 1986. 172 p. ; LC Card 86-211780
HD70.E7 K85 1986

Kritik an deutschen Wirtschaftsprüfern, ein Glaubwürdigkeitsproblem? . Binz, Hans-Bert, 1954- Bergisch Gladbach , 1984. ix, 325 p. : ISBN 3-89012-004-0 : LC Card 84-174776
HF5627 .B55 1984

Kritik der "Drei Welten Theorie" durch die TKP/ML . Türkiye Komünist Partisi/Marksist-Leninist. Wien [1978] 1 v. (various pagings) ; LC Card 85-134265
HC59.7 .T867 1978

Kritik der Geldentstehungstheorien . Höltz, Joachim. Berlin , c1984. ii, 401 p. ; ISBN 3-496-00796-6 LC Card 85-147094
HG237 .H64 1984

Kritik der Staatsfinanzen . Krätke, Michael. Hamburg , 1984. 297 p. ; ISBN 3-87975-247-8 LC Card 84-186778
HJ2687 .K67 1984

Kritik der Warenästhetik /. Haug, Wolfgang Fritz. Frankfurt am Main [1983], c1971. 187 p. ; ISBN 3-518-10513-2 (pbk.) LC Card 87-673362
HF1041 .H33x 1983

Kritika antimarksistskikh ėkonomicheskikh teoriĭ v prepodavanii politicheskoĭ ėkonomii / pod redaktsieĭ A.D. Smirnova ; [V.V. Golosov ... et al.]. Moskva : "Vysshaia shkola", 1981. 356 p. ; 22 cm. Authorized for instructional purposes. Includes bibliographical references and index. LC Card 82-107917
1. Economics. 2. Marxian economics. 3. Economics - Study and teaching. 4. Marxian economics - Study and teaching. I. Smirnov, Aleksandr Dmitrievich, economist. II. Golosov, V. V.
HB178 .K7 1981

Kritika antimarksistskikh vzgliadov po problemam NTR / otvetstvennyĭ redaktor IU.IA. Ol'sevich. Moskva : "Nauka", 1987. 157 p. ; 22 cm. (Ideologicheskaia bor'ba v sovremennom mire) At head of title: Akademiia nauk SSSR. Ordena Trudovogo Krasnogo Znameni Institut ėkonomiki. Includes bibliographical references. LC Card 87-164887
1. Technological innovations - Economic aspects - Soviet Union. 2. Technology and state - Soviet Union. 3. Capitalism. I. Ol'sevich, IU. IA. (IUriĭ IAkovlevich).
HC340.T4 K75 1987

Kritika burzhuaznykh vzgliadov na ėkonomicheskoe sotrudnichestvo stran SĖV /. Burova, S. E. (Stella Efimovna) Moskva , 1986. 154 p. ; LC Card 86-232355
HC243.5 .B87 1986

Kritika Kominternom revizionistskikh vzgliadov na ėkonomiku sotsializma /. Suvorova, M. I. (Mariia Il'inichna) Moskva , 1985. 115 p. ; LC Card 84-219550
HB97.5 .S86 1985 **NYPL [*QIP 87-2751]**

Kritische Wachstumsschwellen in der Unternehmensentwicklung /. Albach, Horst. Stuttgart , c1985. xxvii, 490 p. : ISBN 3-7910-5008-7 : LC Card 86-156636
HD35 .A64 1985

KRITSMAN, L. (LEV), 1890-1938.
Cox, Terry. Peasants, class, and capitalism . Oxford [Oxfordshire] ; New York : xii, 271 p. ; ISBN 0-19-878014-1 : LC Card 86-2362 DDC 305.5/63 19
HD1536.S65 C69 1986 **NYPL [JLD 86-3986]**

Kritzman, Mark P. Quantitative methods for financial analysis /. Homewood, Ill. , c1987. xv, 229 p. : ISBN 0-87094-978-0 LC Card 86-72275 DDC 332.6/01/51 19
HG4515.3 .Q36 1987

Krivoded, V. V. KPSS i kolkhoznoe krest'ianstvo v 1945-1959 gg. / V.V. Krivoded ; otvetstvennyĭ redaktor I.I. Alekseenko. Rostov-na-Donu : Izd-vo Rostovskogo universiteta, 1984. 190 p. ; 21 cm. At head of title: Kubanskiĭ gosudarstvennyĭ universitet. Includes bibliographical references. LC Card 87-100194
1. Collective farms - Russian S.F.S.R. - Caucasus, Northern. 2. Agricultural laborers - Russian S.F.S.R. - Caucasus, Northern. 3. Agriculture and state - Russian S.F.S.R. - Caucasus, Northern. I. Alekseenko, I. I. II. Title.
HD1492.S652 C384 1984

Krizis biudzhetno-finansovogo regulirovaniia ėkonomiki kapitalizma /. Dubinin, S. K. (Sergeĭ Konstantinovich) Moskva , 1984. 100 p. ; LC Card 84-222701
HJ236 .D82 1984

Kroatien. see **Croatia.**

Kröber, Günter.
Innovation und Wissenschaft . Berlin , 1985. 328 p. : LC Card 86-121669
HC290.795.T4 I56 1985

Intensivierung der Forschung . Berlin , 1984. 354 p. ; LC Card 84-195559
HD30.42.G4 I57 1984

Kroker, Rolf.
Fuest, Winfried, 1946- Irrtümer in der aktuellen Steuerdiskussion /. Köln , c1987. 54 p. : ISBN 3-602-24749-X LC Card 87-409547 DDC 336.2/00943 19
HJ2687 .F834 1987

Fuest, Winfried, 1946- Quantitative und qualitative Konsolidierung /. Köln , c1986. 44 p. : ISBN 3-602-24741-4 LC Card 86-214118
HJ2110 .F84 1986

Kroll on futures trading strategy /. Kroll, Stanley. Homewood, Ill. , c1988. xvi, 203 p. : ISBN 1-556-23033-8 LC Card 87-71359 DDC 332.64/4 19
HG6024.A3 K76 1988

Kroll, Stanley. Kroll on futures trading strategy / Stanley Kroll. Homewood, Ill. : Dow Jones-Irwin, c1988. xvi, 203 p. : ill. ; 24 cm. Includes bibliographical references and index. ISBN 1-556-23033-8 LC Card 87-71359 DDC 332.64/4 19
1. Futures. 2. Futures market. I. Title. II. Title: Futures trading strategy.
HG6024.A3 K76 1988

Kroneberg, Jürgen. Die mitbestimmte selbständige Aktiengesellschaft / Jürgen Kroneberg. Göttingen : WiRe Verlagsgesellschaft für Wirtschafts- und Steuerrecht, 1982. xii, 211 p. ; 21 cm. (Abhandlungen zum Handels-, Gesellschafts- und Wirtschaftsrecht . Bd. 11) Originally presented as the author's thesis (doctoral)--Universität Bayreuth, Wintersemester 1981/1982. Bibliography: p. 187-208. ISBN 3-88415-554-7 : LC Card 83-159183 DDC 346.43/0664 344.306664 19
1. Management - Employee participation - Law and legislation - Germany (West). 2. Corporation law - Germany, West. I. Series. II. Series: Abhandlungen zum Handels-, Gesellschafts-, Wirtschafts- und Arbeitsrecht , Bd. 11. III. Title.
KK3000 .K76 1982 **NYPL [JLD 86-1552]**

Kronstein, Max. Rocket mail flights of the world to 1986 / by Max Kronstein ; edited by Joseph L. Eisendrath. Cinnaminson, N.J. : American Air Mail Society, 1986. 191 p. : ill. ; 24 cm. LC Card 87-400297 DDC 383/.144 19
1. Rocket mail - History. 2. Postage-stamps - Topics - Rocket mail. I. Eisendrath, Joseph L. II. American Air Mail Society. III. Title.
HE6239.R6 K76 1986

Krooss, Herman Edward, 1912-1975. A history of financial intermediaries [by] Herman E. Krooss [and] Martin R. Blyn. [1st ed.] New York, Random House [1971] xi, 254 p. 25 cm. (Random House books in finance) Includes index. Bibliography: p. 247-250. ISBN 0-394-31001-2 LC Card 78-127552 DDC 332.1/0973
1. Financial institutions - United States - History. 2. Finance - United States - History. I. Blyn, Martin R., joint author. II. Title.
HG181 .K73 **NYPL [JLE 87-572]**

Kropatkin, Philip. Management and the audit network : internal auditors, CPAs, and the CEO / Philip Kropatkin. New York : Wiley, 1987. xii, 188 p. : ill. ; 25 cm. (The Wiley Institute of Internal Auditors professional book series) Includes index. ISBN 0-471-83286-3 LC Card 86-33983 DDC 657/.45 19
1. Auditing. I. Title. II. Series.
HF5667 .K74 1987

Krotov, M. I. (Mikhail Iosifovich) Potrebitel'naia stoimost' pri sotsializme / M.I. Krotov. Moskva : Ėkonomika, 1983. 151 p. ; 20 cm. Includes bibliographical references. LC Card 83-166303
1. Value. 2. Socialism. I. Title.
HB201 .K965 1983

Krotz, Esteban. Cooperativas agrarias y conflictos políticos en el sur de Jalisco /. México, D.F. , 1985 [i.e. 1986] 201 p. ; ISBN 968-8401-93-5 LC Card 87-405021 DDC 334/.683/097235 19
HD1491.M42 J353 1986

KṚSHAKASABHĀ (INDIA)
Ghosha, Madana. Bhūmibyabasthā, Kaṃgresa, o Kṛshakasabhā /. Bardhamāna [1986?] 100 p. ; LC Card 87-900325
HD875 .G56 1986

Krucker, Philippe. Glück auf! . Paris [1986] 117 p. : ISBN 2-86738-115-0 : LC Card 86-178958
HD8039.M6152 F84 1986

Krug, Walter, Prof. Dr. Quantifizierung des systematischen Fehlers in wirtschafts- und sozialstatistischen Daten : dargest. an d. Statistik d. Erwerbstätigkeit / von Walter Krug.1. Aufl. Berlin : Duncker und Humblot, 1976. 109 p. : graphs ; 23 cm. (Volkswirtschaftliche Schriften ; Heft 251) Includes indexes. Bibliography: p. [102]-106. ISBN 3-428-03710-3 LC Card 76-487801
1. Labor supply - statistical methods. 2. Error analysis (Mathematics). I. Title.
HD5711 .K78 **NYPL [JLE 80-187]**

Kruger, Gudrun. Development region D : a comparative study of socio-economic/demographic features based on the 1970/1980 population censusses [sic] / by Gudrun Kruger, J.F. Potgieter. Port Elizabeth : Institute for Planning Research, University of Port Elizabeth, [1985] iv, 89 p. : ill. ; 30 cm. (Series C . report no. 3) "November 1985." Bibliography: p. 87. ISBN 0-86988-274-0 (pbk.) LC Card 86-233113 DDC 304.6/09687/5 19
1. Cape of Good Hope (South Africa) - Population - Statistics. 2. Ciskei (South Africa) - Population - Statistics. 3. Transkei (South Africa) - Population - Statistics. 4. South Africa - Census, 1970. 5. South Africa - Census, 1980. 6. Cape of Good Hope (South Africa) - Economic conditions - Statistics. 7. Ciskei (South Africa) - Economic conditions - Statistics. 8. Transkei (South Africa) - Economic conditions - Statistics. I. Potgieter, J. F. II. Series: Reeks C (University of Port Elizabeth. Institute for Planning Research) , verslag nr. 3. III. Title.
HA4701.Z9 C354 1985

Krüger-Hemmer, Christiane. Der Staatssektor in der Input-Output-Rechnung : die Input-Output-Verflechtung des Staates in den Jahren 1974 bis 1978 / von Christiane Krüger-Hemmer ; [herausgegeben vom Rheinisch-Westfälischen Institut für Wirtschaftsforschung Essen]. Essen : RWI, 1982. 175 p. ; 30 cm. (RWI-Papiere . Nr. 16) Includes bibliographical references. LC Card 87-408033 DDC 339.2/3/0943 19
1. Input-output tables - Germany (West). I. Rheinisch-Westfälisches Institut für Wirtschaftsforschung Essen. II. Title. III. Series.
HC290.5.I57 K78 1982

Kruger, Joseph. Rosenbaum, Virginia K. Antitakeover charter amendments . Washington, D.C. , 1986. 100 p. : ISBN 0-931035-07-4
NYPL [JLF 86-1964]

Krugman, Paul R.
International economics : theory and policy / Paul R. Krugman, Maurice Obstfeld. Glenview, Ill. : Little, Brown, 1987. xxvii, 656, [35] p. : ill. ; 26 cm. Includes index. ISBN 0-316-50475-0 LC Card 87-17229 DDC 337 19
1. International economic relations. 2. International finance. I. Obstfeld, Maurice. II. Title.
HF1411 .K74 1987

Strategic trade policy and the new international economics /. Cambridge, Mass. , c1986. 313 p. ; ISBN 0-262-11112-8 LC Card 86-2758 DDC 382/.3 19
HF1411 .S82 1986 **NYPL [JLE 86-3896]**

Kruijer, G. J. (Gerardus Johannes), 1919- Development through liberation : Third World problems and solutions / Gerald J. Kruijer ; translated by Arnold Pomerans. Atlantic Highlands, NJ : Humanities Press International, 1987. x, 257 p. ; 23 cm. Bibliography: p. 242-252. Includes index. ISBN 0-391-03538-X LC Card 87-3710 DDC 338.9/009172/4 19
1. Poor - Developing countries. 2. Developing countries - Economic policy. 3. Developing countries -

Politics and government. 4. National liberation movements - Developing countries. I. Title.
HC59.72.P6 K78 1987

Kruijt, Dirk. Vellinga, Menno. Industrialization and regional development in Colombia /. Amsterdam, The Netherlands , 1983. 183 p. : ISBN 90-70280-80-9 LC Card 83-209247 DDC 338.09861/26 19
HC198.C296 V45 1983

Kruk, Max. Eugen Schmalenbach . Stuttgart , 1984. xvii, 478 p. : ISBN 3-8202-0295-1 LC Card 84-215889
HF5616.G3 E93 1984

Krulis-Randa, Jan S., 1926- Strategisches Marketing und Management . Bern , c1986. 205 p. : ISBN 3-258-03566-0 : LC Card 86-159360
HF5415.135 .S77 1986

Krumme, Dwane. Banking and the plastic card / Dwane Krumme. Washington, D.C. (1120 Connecticut Ave., N.W., Washington 20036) : American Bankers Association, c1987. xi, 263 p. : ill. ; 25 cm. Cover title: Banking & the plastic card. Includes index. LC Card 87-159373 DDC 332.7/6 19
1. Bank credit cards - United States. I. Title. II. Title: Banking & the plastic card.
HG1643 .K79 1987

Krümmel, Hans-Jacob.
Internationales Bankgeschäft /. Berlin , c1985. 249 p. : ISBN 3-428-05790-2 LC Card 86-178830
HG3881 .I72 1985

Tagung Strategische Bankplanung (1982 : Bonn, Germany) Strategische Bankplanung . Frankfurt am Main , c1983. 345 p. : ISBN 3-7819-0293-5 LC Card 83-233043
HG1615 .T34 1982

Krummheuer, Eberhard. Intercity experimental ICE, der neue Zug der neuen Bahn : Abfahrt ins Jahr 2000, mit 350 km/h in die Zukunft / Eberhard Krummheuer. München : ELV Verlag, c1986. 200 p. : ill., maps (some col.) ; 31 cm. One folded col. map laid in. Includes English summary. ISBN 3-923967-25-X : LC Card 86-220676
1. Deutsche Bundesbahn. 2. High speed trains - Germany (West). I. Title.
HE3080.D37 K78 1986

Krupa, Arlene. Couplepower : how to be partners in love and business / Arlene Krupa with Chris Kirk-Kuwaye.1st ed. New York : Dodd, Mead, c1987. 227 p. ; 24 cm. "A Gamut book." Includes index. ISBN 0-396-09029-X (pbk.) : LC Card 87-20065 DDC 658.4/09 19
1. Family corporations. 2. New business enterprises. 3. Partnership. 4. Married people - Employment. I. Kirk-Kuwaye, Chris. II. Title.
HD62.25 .K78 1987

KRUPP, ALFRED, 1812-1887.
Blencke, Fritz. Alfred Krupp /. Leipzig , 1898. 127 p. : LC Card 85-665721
HD9523.9.K7 B53x 1898

Krupp, Rudolf. Marburger, Ernst-Albrecht. Internationale Erfahrungen mit der Gurtanlegepflicht =. Köln , 1982. 29, 29 p. : LC Card 83-200842
HE5614 .M288 1982

Kruse, Wilfried, 1947- Arbeitsmarkterfahrungen und Berufsorientierungen Jugendlicher . München , c1983. 177 p. : ISBN 3-87966-202-9 LC Card 84-170074
HD6276.G4 A73 1983

Krusell, Per. The demand for money in Sweden, 1970-1983 / by Per Krusell. Stockholm, Sweden : Stockholm School of Economics, the Economic Research Institute, [1986] 91 p. ; 30 cm. (Research report / Ekonomiska forskningsinstitutet vid Handelshögskolan i Stockholm) "April 1986." Bibliography: p. 90-91. ISBN 0-917258-21-5 (pbk.) LC Card 87-151531 DDC 332.4/14 19
1. Demand for money - Sweden - Econometric models. I. Series. II. Series: Research report (Handelshögskolan i Stockholm. Ekonomiska forskningsinstitutet). III. Title.
HG1125 .K78 1986

Krushanov, Andreĭ Ivanovich. Istoriografiia istorii rabochego klassa Dal′nego Vostoka SSSR /. Vladivostok , 1984. 78 p. ; LC Card 85-229962
HD8529.S652 I87 1984

Krüsselberg, Hans-Günter.
Gaugler, Eduard. Flexibilisierung der Beschäftigungsverhältnisse /. Berlin , c1986. 85 p. ; ISBN 3-428-06070-9 LC Card 87-118519 DDC 331.25/72/0943 19
HD5109.2.G3 G38 1986

Markt, Staat und Solidarität bei Adam Smith /. Frankfurt , New York , c1984. 238 p. ; ISBN 3-593-33338-4 LC Card 84-202891
HB103.S6 M27 1984

Krŭstiu Dobrev : biobibliografiia / [pod redaktsiiata na Rositsa Gocheva ; sostaviteli Nikola Vŭlchev ... et al.]. Sofiia : Izd-vo na Bŭlgarskata akademiia na naukite, 1987. 80 p., [16] p. of plates : ill. ; 20 cm. (Biobibliografii na bulgarski ucheni) At head of title: Bŭlgarska akademiia na naukite. TSentralna biblioteka. Ikonomicheski institut. Includes indexes. LC Card 87-170598
1. Dobrev, Krŭstiu, 1903-1976. 2. Economists - Bulgaria - Biography. 3. Bulgaria - Economic conditions - Bibliography. 4. Economics - Bio-bibliography. I. Gocheva, Rositsa. II. Vŭlchev, Nikola. III. Ikonomicheski institut (Bŭlgarska akademiia na naukite).
HB108.3.D63 K78 1987

Krute, Stan.
Commodore 64 graphics & sound programming. Krute, Stan. Commodore 64/128 graphics and sound programming / Stan Krute. 2nd ed. Blue Ridge Summit, PA , 1986. xv, 253 p. : ISBN 0-8306-0440-5 : LC Card 85-14694 DDC 006.6/765 19
T385 .K77 1986 ***NYPL [JSE 87-266]***

Commodore 64/128 graphics and sound programming / Stan Krute. 2nd ed. Blue Ridge Summit, PA : Tab Books, 1986. xv, 253 p. : ill. ; 25 cm. Rev. ed. of: Commodore 64 graphics & sound programming. 1st ed. c1983. Includes index. "No. 2640." ISBN 0-8306-0440-5 : LC Card 85-14694 DDC 006.6/765 19
1. Speech processing systems. 2. Commodore 64 (Computer) - Programming. 3. Commodore 128 (Computer) - Programming. I. Krute, Stan. Commodore 64 graphics & sound programming. II. Title. III. Title: Commodore sixty-four/one hundred twenty-eight graphics and sound programming.
T385 .K77 1986 ***NYPL [JSE 87-266]***

Kryka, Milan, 1926- Persönlich, an den Manager : Strategien zum Entfalten der persönlichen Fähigkeiten : ein Aktionsprogramm / Milan Kryka. Zürich : ATW Verlag, c1983. 143 p. : ill. ; 23 cm. Bibliography: p. 141. Includes index. ISBN 3-85505-050-3 LC Card 83-152577
1. Personnel management. 2. Psychology, Industrial. I. Title.
HF5549 .K765 1983

Krylov, L. S. Ėkonomicheskie sviazi proizvodstva i potrebleniia pri sotsializme . Riga , 1978. 152 p. ; LC Card 81-168062
HF1040.9.S65 E36 1978

Krylov, N. V. (Nikolaĭ Vladimirovich) Steklov Seminar (1984 : Steklov Institute of Mathematics) [Statistika i upravlenie sluchaĭnykh protsessov. English.] Statistics and control of stochastic processes /. New York, N.Y. , c1985. xiii, 506 p. ; ISBN 0-911575-18-9 LC Card 85-8851 DDC 519.5 19
QA276.A1 .S7513 1984 ***NYPL [JSE 86-729]***

Krylov, V. F. (Vladimir Fedorovich) Sravnitel′nyĭ analiz deiatel′nosti predpriiatiĭ / V.F. Krylov. Moskva : "Finansy i statistika", 1981. 69 p. ; 20 cm. LC Card 82-112692
1. Labor productivity - Soviet Union - Statistical methods. 2. Efficiency, Industrial - Soviet Union - Statistical methods. I. Title.
HC340.L3 K75 1981

Krylov, V. V. Agrarnye preobrazovaniia v stranakh Afriki na sovremennom ėtape /. Moskva , 1982. 227 p. ; LC Card 83-143645
HD2117 .A347 1982

KRYMSKAIA OBLAST′ (UKRAINE) - RURAL CONDITIONS.
Shchedrost′ zemli krymskoĭ . Simferopol′ , 1985. 158 p. ; LC Card 86-128000
HD9015.S653 K797 1985

Kryteria i metody oceny efektywności przedsięwzięć organizatorskich w przedsiębiorstwie /. Lichtarski, Jan. [Wrocław] , 1982. 197 p. : LC Card 83-153426
HB9 .B7522 nr. 216 HD58.9

Kryzhanovskiĭ, B. N. (Boris Nikolaevich)
Spetsializatsiia zagotovitel′nogo proizvodstva / B.N. Kryzhanovskiĭ, P.P. Zharkov, I.V. Shetelo ; pod obshcheĭ redaktsieĭ B.N. Kryzhanovskogo. Kiev : "Tekhnika", 1985. 125, [3] p. ; 20 cm. Bibliography: p. 121-[126]. LC Card 87-112143
1. Machine-tool industry - Ukraine. 2. Industrial procurement - Ukraine. I. Zharkov, P. P. (Pavel Petrovich). II. Shetelo, I. V. (Ivan Vasil′evich). III. Title.
HD9703.S653 U474 1985

Vspomogatel′noe proizvodstvo mashinostroeniia : organizatsiia, ėffektivnost′, perspektivy / B.N. Kryzhanovskiĭ. Kiev : Nauk. dumka, 1983. 334 p. : ill. ; 21 cm. At head of title: Akademiia nauk Ukrainskoĭ SSR. Sovet po izucheniiu proizvoditel′nykh sil Ukrainskoĭ SSR. Includes bibliographical references. LC Card 83-238314
1. Machine-tool industry - Ukraine. I. Title.
HD9703.S653 U475 1983

Krzeczkowska, Eugenia. Polska 1973 . Warszawa , 1973. 199 p., [8] p. of plates : LC Card 82-102013
HA1455 .P66 1973

Krzysztofiak, Mirosław. Ekonometria . Warszawa , 1978. 371 p. : LC Card 81-212730
HB139 .E386 1978

Kuba v mezhdunarodnom sotsialisticheskom razdelenii truda / otvetstvennyĭ redaktor M.A. Manasov. Moskva : "Nauka", 1986. 146 p. : ill. ; 22 cm. At head of title: Akademiia nauk SSSR. Institut ėkonomiki mirovoĭ sotsialisticheskoĭ sistemy. Includes bibliographies. LC Card 86-232928
1. Cuba - Foreign economic relations - Europe, Eastern. 2. Europe, Eastern - Foreign economic relations - Cuba. 3. International division of labor. I. Manasov, M. A. II. Institut ėkonomiki mirovoĭ sotsialisticheskoĭ sistemy (Akademiia nauk SSSR).
HF1500.5.E852 K83 1986

Kubadinski, Pencho P. Brigadirski ogn′ove : pogled vŭrkhu razvitieto na mladezhkoto brigadirsko dvizhenie / Pencho Kubadinski.1. izd. Sofiia : Nar. mladezh, 1986. 119 p., [24] p. of plates : ill. ; 18 cm. LC Card 86-235041
1. Labor service - Bulgaria - History. 2. Youth - Employment - Bulgaria - History. I. Title.
HD4870.B9 K83 1986

Kubálková, V. International inequality / V. Kubálková and A.A. Cruickshank. London : Croom Helm, c1981. 293 p. : ill. ; 23 cm. Includes bibliographies and index. ISBN 0-7099-0221-2 LC Card 86-673398
1. International economic relations. 2. Equality. 3. International relations. I. Cruickshank, A. A. II. Title.
HF1411 .K819x 1981b

Kubicek, Herbert. Kabel im Haus, Satellit überm Dach : ein Informationsbuch zur aktuellen Mediensdiskussion / Herbert Kubicek.Originalausg. Reinbek bei Hamburg : Rowohlt, 1984. 189 p. : ill. ; 19 cm. (Rororo aktuell) Includes bibliographical references and index. ISBN 3-499-15528-1 (pbk.) LC Card 87-673204
1. Cable television - Social aspects - Germany (West). I. Title.
HE8700.72.G3 K83x 1984

Kubin, Ernst. Linzer Kommunalwissenschaftliche Tagung (1978) Privatisierung kommunaler Aufgaben? . Linz , c1978. 62 p. ; ISBN 3-7141-7871-6 LC Card 85-185084
HD4651 .L56 1978

Kublank, Peter. Balances energéticos del Ecuador : serie histórica, 1979-1982 : proyecto, actualización de los balances energéticos del Ecuador / Peter Kublank, Hernán López. Quito, Ecuador : Instituto Nacional de Energía, Planificación Energética, 1983. 1 v. (various foliations) : ill. ; 30 cm. Includes bibliography. LC Card 86-153116
1. Energy consumption - Ecuador. 2. Power resources - Ecuador. I. López, Hernán. II. Title.
HD9502.E22 K82 1983

Kubr, Milan. Management consulting . Geneva , 1986. xv, 611 p. : ISBN 92-2-105479-9 LC Card 87-131654 DDC 658.4/6/02373 19
HD69.C6 M36 1986

Kuch, Fred. Die Kreisfreien Städte und Landkreise in Rheinland-Pfalz /. Bad Ems , 1977. 420 p. : LC Card 85-244499
HC287.R7 K74 1977

Kucher, Eckhard. Scannerdaten und Preissensitivität bei Konsumgütern / Eckhard Kucher. Wiesbaden : Gabler, c1985. 282 p. : ill. ; 29 cm. (Beiträge zur betriebswirtschaftlichen

Forschung. Bd. 58) Bibliography: p. [267]-282. ISBN 3-409-13608-8 LC Card 86-128961
1. Consumers - Mathematical models. 2. Prices - Mathematical models. I. Title. II. Series.
HB801 .K789 1985

Küchle, Hartmut. Jordan, Reinhard, d. 1986. Holzwirtschaft im Wandel . Köln , c1986. viii, 163 p. : ISBN 3-7663-0977-3 LC Card 86-211012 DDC 338.4/5674/0943 19
HD9763.5 .J67 1986

Küchler, Ursula. Intensivierung des wissenschaftlich-technischen Arbeitsprozesses /. Jena , 1985. 200 p. : LC Card 86-132567 DDC 338/.06/09431 19
HC290.795.I52 I57 1985

Kuczmarski, Thomas D., 1951- Managing new products : competing through excellence / Thomas D. Kuczmarski. Englewood Cliffs, N.J. : Prentice Hall, c1988. xv, 304 p. : ill. ; 24 cm. Includes index. ISBN 0-13-550716-2 LC Card 87-26208 DDC 658.5/75 19
1. New products. 2. Product management. 3. Marketing. I. Title.
HF5415.153 .K83 1988

Kudiss, Reinhard, 1952- Die Bestimmung des Produktionspotentials in Theorie und Empirie : ein Beitrag zur Stagflationserklärung / Reinhard Kudiss. Frankfurt am Main ; New York : P. Lang, c1984. xvi, 198 p. : ill. ; 21 cm. (Europäische Hochschulschriften. Reihe V, Volks- und Betriebswirtschaft, 0531-7339 . Bd. 548 = vol. 548 = vol. 548) Revision of the author's thesis. Bibliography: p. 181-198. ISBN 3-8204-5579-5 LC Card 85-189908
1. Economic forecasting - Mathematical models. 2. Unemployment - Effect of inflation on - Mathematical models. 3. Monetary policy - Mathematical models. 4. Economic forecasting - Germany (West) - Econometric models. 5. Germany (West) - Economic policy - Econometric models. 6. Unemployment - Germany (West) - Effect of inflation on - Econometric models. 7. Monetary policy - Germany (West) - Econometric models. I. Series: Europäische Hochschulschriften. Reihe V, Volks- und Betriebswirtschaft , Bd. 548. II. Title.
HB3730 .K766 1984

Kudriashov, N. A. Sovet ėkonomicheskoĭ vzaimopomoshchi . Moskva , 1984. 29 p. : LC Card 86-203121
HC243.5 .S683 1984

Kudriavtsev, A. A. (Alekseĭ Andreevich) Analiz khoziaĭstvennoĭ deiatel'nosti kooperativnykh organizatsiĭ / A.A. Kudriavtsev. Moskva : Izd-vo "Ėkonomika," 1977. 262 p. ; 21 cm. Authorized for instructional purposes. Includes bibliographical references. LC Card 82-124930
1. Cooperative societies - Soviet Union. I. Title.
HD3515 .K78 1977

Kudrle, Robert T. The Industrial future of the Pacific basin /. Boulder , 1984. xvi, 285 p. : ISBN 0-86531-685-6 LC Card 83-51653 DDC 338.9/009182/3 19
HC681 .I53 1984 ***NYPL [JLD 86-3100]***

Kühne, Karl. Öffentliche Unternehmen in Rezession und Aufschwung . Berlin , 1977. 165 p. : LC Card 85-180964
HD3845 .G43 Heft 14 HD3842

Kümmel, Reiner, 1939- Energie und Gerechtigkeit /. München , c1984. xii, 254 p. : ISBN 3-597-10259-X LC Card 84-175053
HD9502.A2 E5192 1984

Künne, Wilfried. Die Aussenwanderung jugoslawischer Arbeitskräfte : e. Beitr. zur Analyse internat. Arbeitskräftewanderungen / von Wilfried Künne. Königstein/Ts. : Hanstein, 1979. xii, 269 p. : ill. ; 21 cm. (Materialien zur Arbeitsmigration und Ausländerbeschäftigung . Bd. 2) Summary in English and Serbo-Croatian. Bibliography: p. 251-263. ISBN 3-7756-6931-0 : LC Card 79-394439
1. Labor and laboring classes - Yugoslavia. 2. Alien labor, Yugoslav - Germany, West. 3. Labor supply - Yugoslavia. 4. Yugoslavia - Emigration and immigration. I. Title. II. Series.
HD8633.5 .K83 ***NYPL [JLD 87-1148]***

Kuenstler, Gail Baugher. The desk guide to training and work advisement / by Gail Baugher Kuenstler. Springfield, Ill., U. S.A. : C.C. Thomas, c1988. p. cm. Bibliography: p. Includes index. ISBN 0-398-05414-2 LC Card 87-25626 DDC 331.7/02/0973 19
1. Vocational guidance - United States. I. Title.
HF5382.5.U5 K84 1988

Kuenstler, P. Centre for Employment Initiatives (Great Britain) Cooperation in the field of employment . Luxembourg , Washington, DC , 1986. 55 p. ; ISBN 92-825-6086-4 (pbk.) : LC Card 87-134296 DDC 331.12/042/094 19
HD5764.A6 C45 1986

Kürbisch, Friedrich G. Entlassen ins Nichts . Berlin , c1983. 255 p. ; ISBN 3-8012-0089-2 (pbk.) LC Card 87-672743
HD5779 .E57x 1983

Küttler, Wolfgang. Lenins Formationsanalyse der bürgerlichen Gesellschaft in Russland vor 1905 : ein Beitrag zur Theorie und Methode historischer Untersuchung von Gesellschaftsformationen / Wolfgang Küttler. Berlin : Akademie-Verlag, 1978. 331 p. ; 25 cm. Originally presented as the author's thesis (doctoral--Akademie der Wissenschaft der DDR, 1976) under the title: Lenins Formationsanalyse für Russland (1893-1904) Bibliography: p. [321]-328. Includes index. LC Card 86-102733
1. Soviet Union - Economic conditions - 1861-1917. 2. Capitalism - Soviet Union - History. 3. Lenin, Vladimir Il'ich, 1870-1924. I. Title.
HC334.5 .K87 1978

Kühl, Jürgen. Staat und Beschäftigung . Nürnberg , 1985. 471 p. : LC Card 86-674027
HD5713 .S72x 1985

Kühl, Rainer. Wettbewerbstheoretische Analyse des Landwarenmarktes in der Bundesrepublik Deutschland : Arbeit aus dem Institut für Landwirtschaftliche Betriebs- und Arbeitslehre der Christian-Albrechts-Universität zu Kiel / von Rainer Kühl. Kiel : Wissenschaftsverlag Vauk, 1986. 77 p. : ill. ; 21 cm. (Agrarökonomische Studien, 0721-4731 . Bd. 11) Bibliography: p. 75-77. ISBN 3-922553-79-6 LC Card 86-172903
1. Produce trade - Germany, West. 2. Competition, International. I. Universität Kiel. Institut für Landwirtschaftliche Betriebs- und Arbeitslehre. II. Title. III. Series.
HD9013.5 .K84 1986

Kühn, Hagen, 1943- Informationstechnologie im Dienstleistungsbereich . Berlin , c1985. 258 p. : ISBN 3-924859-15-9 : LC Card 86-220033 DDC 338.4/561 19
HD9980.5 .I54 1985

Kuhn, Raymond. The Politics of broadcasting /. New York , 1985. 305 p. ; ISBN 0-312-62660-6 : LC Card 84-15996 DDC 384.54 19
HE8689.4 .P65 1985 ***NYPL [MWGT 86-5102]***

Kuhn, Robert Lawrence.
Commercializing SDI technologies /. New York , 1987. xvi, 246 p. : ISBN 0-275-92332-0 (alk. paper) : LC Card 87-18333 DDC 338.4/762 19
HC110.H53 C65 1987

Dealmaker : all the negotiating skills and secrets you need / Robert Lawrence Kuhn. New York : Wiley, c1988. xi, 316 p. : ill. ; 24 cm. Includes index. ISBN 0-471-62465-9 LC Card 87-21543 DDC 658 19
1. Negotiation in business. 2. Deals. I. Title. II. Title: Deal maker.
HD58.6 .K84 1988

Frontiers in creative and innovative management /. Cambridge, Mass. , 1985, c1986. xxv, 391 p. : ISBN 0-88730-057-X LC Card 85-15125 DDC 658.4 19
HD53 .F76 1986 ***NYPL [JLE 86-3614]***

Geis, George T. Micromanaging . Englewood Cliffs, NJ , c1987. xiv, 233 p. ; ISBN 0-13-581901-6 (pbk.) LC Card 86-30470 DDC 658/.05416 19
HD30.2 .G44 1987

Handbook for creative and innovative managers /. New York , c1988. xx, 652 p. : ISBN 0-07-035607-6 : LC Card 87-3189 DDC 658.4/094 19
HD53 .H356 1988

Managing take-off in fast growth companies . New York , c1986. x, 191 p. : ISBN 0-03-005709-4 (alk. paper) : LC Card 85-16745 DDC 658.4/2 19
HD31 .T24 1986 ***NYPL [JLE 86-1303]***

Kühner, Hans-Joachim. Kratz, Hans-Jürgen. Arbeitslosengeld /. Saarbrücken [1983] 176 p. ; ISBN 3-88968-006-2 LC Card 83-215450
HD7096.G32 S335 1983

Kühnlein, Gertrud. Arbeitsmarkterfahrungen und Berufsorientierungen Jugendlicher . München , c1983. 177 p. : ISBN 3-87966-202-9 LC Card 84-170074
HD6276.G4 A73 1983

Kuijsten, Anton. Modelling household formation and dissolution /. Oxford [Oxfordshire] , New York , c1987. p. cm. ISBN 0-19-829500-6 : LC Card 87-18581 DDC 306.8/5/0724 19
HB849.49 .M63 1987

Kuiper, J. H. Distribution of distances in pregeographical space / J.H. Kuiper. Brookfield, Vt. : Gower Pub. Co., 1986. viii, 296 p. : ill. ; 23 cm. Bibliography: p. 293-296. ISBN 0-566-05214-8 : LC Card 86-7673 DDC 910 19
1. Regional economics - Mathematical models. 2. Space in economics - Mathematical models. 3. Distance geometry. I. Title.
HT391.3 .K85 1986 ***NYPL [JSD 86-605]***

Kujath, Hans Joachim. Die Regeneration der Stadt : Ökonomie und Politik des Wandels im Wohnungsbestand / Hans Joachim Kujath. Hamburg : Christian, c1986. 282 p. ; 24 cm. (Band 7 der Reihe Stadt, Planung, Geschichte) A revision of the author's thesis (doctoral--Universität Frankfurt am Main) under the title: Die ökonomische Regeneration stagnierender Städte. Summary in English. Bibliography: p. 258-278. ISBN 3-7672-0943-8 LC Card 87-113493 DDC 363.5/8 19
1. Housing rehabilitation - Germany (West). 2. Housing policy - Germany, West. I. Series: Stadt, Planung, Geschichte , Bd. 7. II. Title.
HD7339.A3 K85 1986

Kujawa, Duane. Japanese multinationals in the United States : case studies / Duane Kujawa. New York : Praeger, 1986. xii, 291 p. ; 24 cm. Includes bibliographical references and index. ISBN 0-03-006718-9 (alk. paper) : LC Card 85-28310 DDC 338.8/8952/073 19
1. Corporations, Japanese - United States - Personnel management - Case studies. 2. Corporations, Japanese - United States - Case studies. I. Title.
HF5549.2.U5 K84 1986
NYPL [JLE 86-3833]

Kukche Puhŭng Kaebal Unhaeng. see **International Bank for Reconstruction and Development.**

Kuklinski, Antoni. Space-structure-economy . Karlsruhe [San Francisco, CA] c1986. vii, 311 p. : ISBN 3-88652-680-1 (pbk.) LC Card 87-129134 DDC 330.1 19
HB107.L66 S63 1986

Kukuck, Horst-Albert, 1939- Die Gewerkschaften von der Stabilisierung bis zur Weltwirtschaftskrise, 1924-1930 /. Köln , c1986. 2 v. (1586 p.) ; ISBN 3-7663-0902-1 (Bd. 1) LC Card 87-123987
HD6694 .Q44 1985 Bd. 3

Kukushkin, V. E. Potentsial ėffektivnosti /. IUzhno-Sakhalinsk , 1985. 67 p. ; LC Card 87-100690
HD8039.F32 S656 1985

Kukushkin, Vladimir IUr'evich. Neft' i razvitie, Liviia, Alzhir / V.IU. Kukushkin. Moskva : Izd-vo "Nauka", Glav. red. vostochnoĭ lit-ry, 1985. 227 p. ; 22 cm. At head of title: Akademiia nauk SSSR. Institut Afriki. Summary in English. Bibliography: p. 215-227. LC Card 85-180876
1. Petroleum industry and trade - Libya. 2. Petroleum industry and trade - Algeria. 3. Libya - Economic conditions. 4. Algeria - Economic conditions. I. Title.
HD9577.L52 K85 1985
NYPL [*QIP 87-3410]

Külföldi licencek a magyar gazdaságban /. Kardos, Péter. Budapest , 1984. 204, [1] p. : ISBN 963-221-396-3 : LC Card 85-157267
HF1429 .K37 1984

Kulibanov, V. S. (Vadim Sergeevich) Problemy razvitiia narodnogo khoziaĭstva Severo-Zapada SSSR : v pomoshch' lektoru / V.S. Kulibanov. Leningrad : Ob-vo "Znanie" RSFSR, Leningradskaia organizatsiia, 1980. 33, [3] p. ; 20 cm. Bibliography: p. [35] LC Card 82-115046
1. Soviet Union, Northwestern - Economic conditions. 2. Soviet Union, Northwestern - Economic policy. I.

Title.
HC336.9.N65 K85 1980

Kulidasein oder Klassenkampf : was die Kommunisten den deutschen Arbeitern heute zu sagen haben. Berlin : Vereinigung Internationaler Verlags-Anstalten, 1925. 31 p. ; 22 cm. Cover title. Issued by the KPD. Includes bibliographical references. LC Card 86-207601
1. Labor and laboring classes - Germany, West. 2. Kommunistische Partei Deutschlands. I. Kommunistische Partei Deutschlands.
HD8451 .K84 1925

Kuligin, Pavel Ivanovich. Kriterii ėffektivnosti raboty predpriiatiĭ : iz opyta stran SĖV / P.I. Kuligin ; otvetstvennyĭ redaktor R.N. Evstigneev. Moskva : "Nauka", 1986. 172 p. ; 20 cm. At head of title: Akademiia nauk SSSR. Institut ėkonomiki mirovoĭ sotsialisticheskoĭ sistemy. Includes bibliographies. LC Card 86-211780
1. Industrial management - Europe, Eastern. 2. Business enterprises - Europe, Eastern - Management. I. Evstigneev, Ruben Nikolaevich. II. Title.
HD70.E7 K85 1986

Kulikov, V. V. Soderzhanie i struktura edinogo narodno-khoziaĭstvennogo kompleksa SSSR /. Moskva , 1986. 229 p. ; LC Card 87-126348
HC336.25 .S643 1986

Kulinich, Emel'ian Ivanovich. Statisticheskaia otsenka faktorov khoziaĭstvennoĭ deiatel'nosti zagotovitel'nykh organizatsiĭ / E.I. Kulinich. Moskva : Finansy i statistika, 1983. 191 p. : ill. ; 20 cm. Bibliography: p. 191. LC Card 84-165083
1. Industrial procurement - Soviet Union - Statistical methods. I. Title.
HD39.5 .K84 1983

Kulish, N. E. (Nikolaĭ Efimovich) Upravlenie agropromyshlennymi ob"edineniiami v usloviiakh integrirovannoĭ ėkonomiki / N.E. Kulish. Kiev : Gol. izd-vo izdatel'skogo ob"edineniia "Vyshcha shkola", 1985. 174 p. : ill. ; 20 cm. (Voprosy agropromyshlennoĭ integratsii) Bibliography: p. 168-[173]. LC Card 87-104750
1. Agricultural industries - Ukraine - Management. 2. Agriculture - Economic aspects - Ukraine. I. Series: Voprosy agropromyshlennoĭ integratsii (Kiev, Ukraine). II. Title.
HD9015.S653 U4425 1985 *NYPL [*QIP 87-4125]*

Kulke, Ulrich. Betriebsnahe Tarifpolitik zur Stärkung der gewerkschaftlichen Basis / Ulrich Kulke. Berlin : Verlag Die Arbeitswelt, 1977. 108 p. ; 21 cm. (Gewerkschaftspolitische Studien ; Bd. 11) Diplomarbeit--Freie Universität, Berlin, 1975. Bibliography: p. 101-108. ISBN 3-88114-215-0 : LC Card 80-489437
1. Trade-unions - Germany, West. 2. Wages - Germany, West. I. Title.
HD6694 .K82 *NYPL [JLD 81-350]*

Külkereskedelmi árstatisztikai adatok, 1950-1985 / [összeállította a KSH Kereskedelmi és Közlekedési Statisztikai Főosztály Külkereskedelmi Osztálya]. Budapest : Központi Statisztikai Hivatal, 1986. 114 p. ; 29 cm. Tables. LC Card 87-409625
1. Prices - Hungary - Statistics. 2. Hungary - Commerce - Statistics. I. Hungary. Központi Statisztikai Hivatal. Külkereskedelmi Osztály.
HB235.H8 K84 1986

Külkereskedelmi árstatisztikai adatok, 1957-1977 / [összeállította a KSH Kereskedelmi és Közlekedési Statisztikai Főosztály Ár- és Módszertani Osztálya ; szerkesztette, Marton Ádám]. Budapest : Központi Statisztikai Hivatal, [1978] 125 p. ; 29 cm. "1978. május 8." Chiefly tables. LC Card 86-196922
1. Prices - Hungary - Statistics. 2. Hungary - Commerce - Statistics. I. Marton, Ádám. II. Hungary. Központi Statisztikai Hivatal. Ár- és Modszertani Osztály.
HB235.H8 K85 1978

Külkereskedelmi tevékenységhez kapcsolódó általános fogalommeghatározások /. Mádai, Edit. [Budapest , 1984] (Budapest : Datorg Nyomda) 177 p. ; ISBN 963-02-2359-7 LC Card 87-409581
HF1001 .M27 1984

A külkereskedő vállalat /. Hegyi, Anna. Budapest , 1985. 213, [1] p., [1] folded leaf of plates : ISBN 963-221-531-1 : LC Card 86-187063
HF1009.7.H8 H44 1985

Kull, Eduard. Tehnilis-majandusliku ja sotsiaalse arengu planeerimine tootmiskoondistes (tööstusettevõtetes) / Eduard Kull. Tallinn : "Valgus", 1985. 277 p. : ill. ; 23 cm. Title in colophon: Tekhniko-ėkonomicheskoe i sotsial'noe planirovanie v proizvodstvennykh ob"edineniiakh, na predpriiatiiakh. Bibliography: p. [274] LC Card 86-221274
1. Industrial management - Estonia. I. Title. II. Title: Tekhniko-ėkonomicheskoe i sotsial'noe planirovanie v proizvodstvennykh ob"edineniiakh, na predpriiatiiakh.
HD70.E68 K85 1985

Kulli, John E. Rugh, Jack Leighton, 1911- Channels to employment for the disabled and ex-offenders /. San Gabriel, Calif. (5555 N. Charlotte Ave., San Gabriel 91776) , c1987. 89 p. : LC Card 87-402897 DDC 362.4/0484/02573 19
HD7256.U5 R75 1987

Kulorna rullar . Hagelin, Björn, 1947- Stockholm , 1985. 186 p. : ISBN 91-7324-253-5 LC Card 86-124793
HD9743.S82 H34 1985

Kulshreshtha, V. D. (Visheshwar Dayal), 1922- Government regulation of financial management of private corporate sector in India / prepared by V.D. Kulshreshtha. Ed. 1986. Bombay : N.M. Tripathi, 1986. xxiv, 306 p. ; 25 cm. "Under the auspices of the Indian Law Institute, New Delhi." Bibliography: p. 293-300. Includes index. LC Card 87-902600
1. Corporations - India - Finance. 2. Private companies - India - Finance. 3. Corporations - Finance - Law and legislation - India. 4. Private companies - Finance - Law and legislation - India. I. Indian Law Institute. II. Title.
HG4241 .K85 1986

Kultur und Entwicklung in Brasilien . Chacon, Vamireh. Dortmund , 1970. v, 308 p. ; LC Card 86-172094
HC187 .C44 1970

Kulturen und Ideen.
Überlebenslesebuch . Reinbek bei Hamburg [1984], c1983. 316 p. : ISBN 3-499-17672-6 : LC Card 85-168871
HC79.D4 U24 1984

Kultursociologiske skrifter. For earlier file, whose numbering it continues, see: Copenhagen. Universitet. Institut for kultursociologi. Småskrifter.
(bd. 8) Christoffersen, Mads. Fysisk planlægning og samfundsmæssige reproduktionsproblemer . København , 1980, c1979. 317 p. ; ISBN 87-500-1922-8
NYPL [JLD 86-2303]

Kulturstudien. Sonderband .
(2) Proletariat . Wien , 1986. 275 p. : ISBN 3-205-00561-9 LC Card 86-673962
HD4853 .P76x 1986

Kumamoto, Hiromitsu. Henley, Ernest J. Designing for reliability and safety control /. Englewood Cliffs, N.J. , c1985. xvi, 527 p. : ISBN 0-13-201229-4 LC Card 84-17892 DDC 620/.00452 19
TA169 .H46 1985 *NYPL [JSE 86-2491]*

Kumar, Jainendra, 1935- Land use analysis : a case study of Nalanda District, Bihar / Jainendra Kumar. New Delhi, India : Inter-India Publications, 1986, c1985. xvii, 292 p., [7] p. of plates : ill., maps ; 23 cm. Includes index. Bibliography: p. [269]-287. ISBN 81-210-0063-7 : LC Card 86-901583 DDC 333.76/13/095412
1. Land use, Rural - India - Nālandā District - Case studies. 2. Land use, Rural - India - Case studies. I. Title.
HD879.N34 K86 1986 *NYPL [JLD 87-75]*

Kumar, Kewal. Institutional financing of Indian agriculture : with special reference to commercial banks / Kewal Kumar. New Delhi : Deep & Deep Publications, c1987. 232 p. : ill. ; 22 cm. Empirical study based on data collected from Nainital District, Uttar Pradesh. Bibliography: p. [223]-228. Includes index. LC Card 87-900911 DDC 332.7/1/09542 19
1. Agricultural credit corporations - India - Naini Tal (District). 2. Agriculture credit - India - Naini Tal (District). 3. Agriculture - India - Naini Tal (District) - Finance. 4. Banks and banking, Cooperative - India - Naini Tal (District). I. Title.
HG2051.I5 N354 1987

Kumar, Krishna, 1940- Casley, D. J. Project monitoring and evaluation in agriculture /. Baltimore , c1987. xiii, 159 p. : ISBN 0-8018-3616-6 (pbk.) LC Card 87-22632 DDC 351.82/33 19
HD1415 .C335 1987

Kumar, Maneet, 1952- Export marketing of non-traditional items : problems and prospects / Maneet Kumar. Delhi : Ajanta Publications (India) : Distributors, Ajanta Books International, 1987. xv, 274 p. ; 22 cm. Bibliography: p. [257]-272. Includes index. ISBN 81-202-0185-X : LC Card 87-900875 DDC 382/.6/0954 19
1. Export marketing - India. 2. India - Commerce. I. Title.
HF1009.7.I4 K86 1987

Kumar Misra, Girish. see **Misra, Girish Kumar, 1941-**

Kumar, Pradeep. Recent wage deceleration : short-run response or structural change? / Pradeep Kumar. Kingston, Ont., Canada : Industrial Relations Centre, Queen's University, 1987. 21, [12] p. ; 28 cm. (Queen's papers in industrial relations . 1987-1) "A preliminary version of this paper was presented at the annual meeting of the Canadian Industrial Relations Association held in Winnipeg in May 1986." Bibliography: p. 20-21. ISBN 0-88886-158-3 (pbk.) LC Card 87-163251 DDC 331.2/971 19
1. Wages - Canada. I. Title. II. Series.
HD4979 .K816 1987

Kumar Puri, Vijay. see **Puri, Vijay Kumar.**

Kumar, V. K. (Virendra Kumar), 1954- Singh, Anil K., 1953- Forest resource, economy, and environment /. New Delhi , 1987. xv, 124 p. : LC Card 87-901902 DDC 333.78/4 19
HD9766.I63 U887 1987

Kumari, Krishna, 1951- Mies, Maria. Indian women in subsistence and agricultural labour /. Geneva , 1986. x, 158 p. ; ISBN 92-2-105397-0 (pbk.) : LC Card 87-114124 DDC 331.4/83/0954 19
HD6073.A292 I46 1986

Kumari, Lalita K. Mies, Maria. Indian women in subsistence and agricultural labour /. Geneva , 1986. x, 158 p. ; ISBN 92-2-105397-0 (pbk.) : LC Card 87-114124 DDC 331.4/83/0954 19
HD6073.A292 I46 1986

Kumari, Sudarshan. see **Sudarshan Kumari, 1924-**

Kumarian Press library of management for development.
Beyond bureaucracy . West Hartford, Conn. , c1986. xii, 256 p. : ISBN 0-931816-44-0 LC Card 86-34420 DDC 338.9/0068 19
HC59.72.E44 B48 1986

Community management . West Hartford, Conn. , c1986. xxii, 328 p. : ISBN 0-931816-40-8 (pbk.) LC Card 86-27691 DDC 338.95 19
HD75.6 .C65 1986

Uphoff, Norman Thomas. Local institutional development . West Hartford, CT , c1986. xv, 421 p. ; ISBN 0-931816-45-9 LC Card 86-15288 DDC 302.3/5 19
HC59.7 .U64 1986 *NYPL [JLE 87-1200]*

Kumka, Donald S. Mortimer, Jeylan T., 1943- Work, family, and personality . Norwood, N.J. , c1986. viii, 267 p. : ISBN 0-89391-293-X LC Card 85-20951 DDC 306/.36/09774 19
HD4904.25 .M67 1986 *NYPL [JLE 87-869]*

Kummer, Evaldo José. Carvão mineral /. [Porto Alegre] [19]84. 56 p. ; LC Card 86-163115
HD9554.B83 S683 1984

Kunaeva, Faziliia Akhmetovna. Kazakhskaia Sovetskaia Sotsialisticheskaia Respublika / [Faziliia Akhmetovna Kunaeva, Valentina Konstantinovna Khaĭdarova]. Alma-Ata : Izd-vo "Kazakhstan", 1978. 31 p. : col. ill. ; 20 cm. At head of title: Kazakhskoe obshchestvo druzhby i kul'turnoĭ sviazi s zarubezhnymi stranami. LC Card 81-165585
1. Kazakh S.S.R. - Economic conditions. I. Khaĭdarova, Valentina Konstantinovna. II. Kazakhskoe obshchestvo druzhby i kul'turnoĭ sviazi s zarubezhnymi stranami. III. Title.
HC337.K3 K86 1978

Kundenbediente Datenstationen als marktpolitische Instrumente des Bankbetriebs /. Cordewener, Karl-Friedrich, 1951- Göttingen , 1982. 268 p. : ISBN 3-509-01312-3

LC Card 84-182492
HG3048 .C67 1982

Kundenfreundliches Verhalten . Metz, Matthias. Frankfurt am Main , c1985. xxi, 349 p. : ISBN 3-7819-0326-5 LC Card 85-202352
HG1616.P8 M47 1985

Kundu, Amitabh, 1948- Location of public enterprises and regional development / Amitabh Kundu, Girish K. Misra, Rajkishor Meher. New Delhi : Concept Pub. Co., 1986. xv, 178 p. ; 23 cm. Economic study of the impact of Bharat Heavy Electricals Limited on Bhopal City. Bibliography: p. [170]-174. Includes index. LC Card 86-903373 DDC 338.954 19
1. Bharat Heavy Electricals Limited. 2. Government business enterprises - India - Location. 3. Regional planning - India. I. Misra, Girish Kumar, 1941-. II. Meher, Rajkishor. III. Title.
HD9697.A3 I45 1986

Kunert-Schroth, Heidrun. Jugendarbeitslosigkeit, lokale Ausprägungen und kommunale Strategien : eine empirische Untersuchung in zehn Städten / Heidrun Kunert-Schroth, Nizan Rauch, H.-Jörg Siewert. Berlin : Deutsches Institut für Urbanistik, 1987. 172 p. ; 30 cm. Bibliography: p. 166-170. ISBN 3-88118-135-0 LC Card 87-409103 DDC 331.3/412/0943 19
1. Youth - Employment - Germany, West. 2. Unemployment - Germany (West). I. Rauch, Nizan. II. Siewert, Hans-Jörg. III. Title.
HD6276.G4 K86 1987

Kungl. Vitterhets historie och antikvitets akademiens handlingar. Historiska serien . (8 d) Soom, Arnold. Der baltische Getreidehandel im 17. Jahrhundert /. Stockholm , 1961. 350 p. ; LC Card 85-122593 DDC 380.1/4131/09474 19
HD9045.S63 B37 1961

Kungliga Svenska vetenskapsakademien. Kristoferson, Lars A. Renewable energy technologies . Oxford [Oxfordshire] , New York , 1986. xviii, 319 p. : ISBN 0-08-034061-X : LC Card 86-766 DDC 621.042 19
TJ808 .K75 1986 ***NYPL [JSG 87-45]***

Kunhardt, Ulla von. Elsevier's dictionary of the labour market in five languages, English, German, Swedish, Spanish, and French / compiled by Ulla von Kunhardt and Ingrid Llistosella-Matzky. Amsterdam ; New York : Elsevier, 1988. p. cm. English, French, German, Spanish, and Swedish. Bibliography: p. ISBN 0-444-42884-4 : LC Card 87-24529 DDC 331/.03 19
1. Industrial relations - Dictionaries - Polyglot. 2. Dictionaries, Polyglot. I. Llistosella-Matzky, Ingrid. II. Title.
HD4839 .K86 1988

Kunkel, Klaus. Wende wohin? . Köln , c1983. 139 p. ; ISBN 3-921349-34-6 LC Card 84-150290
HC286.7 .W4 1983 ***NYPL [JFC 87-1258]***

Kunreuther, Howard. Insuring and managing hazardous risks--from Seveso to Bhopal and beyond /. Berlin , New York , c1987. ix, 534 p. : ISBN 0-387-17732-9 (U. S.) LC Card 87-4963 DDC 346.03/8 342.638 19
HG9994 .I57 1987

Kunstakademiet (Denmark). Arkitektskolen. Mezzogiorno . [S.l. , 1980?] (København : Kunstakademiets trykkeri) 78 p. : LC Card 85-128057
HC307.S6 M49 1980

Kuntsche, Siegfried. Wie wir angefangen haben . Berlin , 1985. 326 p. : LC Card 85-217979
HD1333.G35 W54 1985

Küntzel, Matthias. Der Sofortige Ausstieg ist möglich . Bonn [1986] 35 cm : LC Card 87-409511 DDC 333.79/24/0943 19
HD9698.G42 S64 1986

Kunwar, Upendra. Banking and agricultural growth : a study of land development bank / Upendra Kunwar. New Delhi : Deep & Deep Publications, c1987. 167 p. ; 23 cm. Bibliography: p. [161]-164. Includes index. LC Card 87-901193 DDC 334/.2/0954 19
1. Agricultural cooperative credit associations - India. I. Title.
HG2051.I4 K86 1987

Kunz, Diane B., 1952- The battle for Britain's gold standard in 1931 / Diane B. Kunz. London ; New York : Croom Helm, c1987. viii, 207 p. ; 23 cm. "Published in ... association with Methuen, Inc."--Verso t.p. Bibliography: p. 194-202. Includes index. ISBN 0-7099-3120-4 LC Card 87-9065 DDC 332.4/222/0941 19
1. Monetary policy - Great Britain - History. 2. Gold standard - History. I. Title.
HG939 .K85 1987

Kunz, Norbert, 1958- Ökologie und Sozialismus . Köln , c1986. 369 p. ; ISBN 3-7663-0983-8 LC Card 87-107373 DDC 363.7/056/0943 19
HC290.E5 O39 1986

Künzel, Rainer, 1942- Die Gegenwärtige Wachstumskrise . Regensburg , c1985. viii, 262 p. : ISBN 3-924956-08-1 LC Card 86-122363 DDC 338.9 19
HD73 .G43 1985

Künzli, Ernst. Forschungs- und Entwicklungsplanung : eine situative Betrachtung / Ernst Künzli. Bern : P. Haupt, c1984. 292 p. : ill. ; 23 cm. (Schriftenreihe des Instituts für Betriebswirtschaftliche Forschung an der Universität Zürich . Bd. 45) Bibliography: p. 278-292. ISBN 3-258-03351-X : LC Card 84-178059
1. Research, Industrial. 2. Leadership. 3. Organizational effectiveness. I. Title. II. Series.
HD30.4 .K86 1984

Kuo chia chi hua wei yüan hui ching chi yü ts'e chung hsin (China) Ch'üan kuo t'ou ju ch'an ch'u piao, 1981. English. Input-output tables of China, 1981 /. Beijing , Honolulu , 1987. p. cm. ISBN 0-86638-104-X (East-West Population Institute) LC Card 87-24457 DDC 339.2/3/0951 19
HC430.I57 C5813 1981

Kuo wai shang yeh yen chiu tzu liao / Shang yeh ching chi yen chiu so tzu liao shih pien. 880-02 Ti 1 pan. [Peking] : Chung-kuo shang yeh ch'u pan she : Hsin hua shu tien Pei-ching fa hsing so fa hsing, 1984. 3, 604 p. ; 21 cm. Title also in pinyin on cover: Guowaishangyeyanjiuziliao. In Chinese. Includes bibliographical references.
1. Commerce - Addresses, essays, lectures. 2. Commercial policy - Addresses, essays, lectures. I. Shang yeh ching chi yen chiu so (China). Tzu liao shih. II. Title: Guowaishangyeyanjiuziliao.
NYPL [*OVY 86-3606]

Kuo, Wen-t'ao. Chung-kuo ch'uan t'ung nung yeh yü hsien tai nungyeh /. Pei-ching , 1986. 312 p. : ***NYPL [*OVL 87-1966]***

Kuparinen, Virva.
Kinturi, Jorma. Väestö, asunnot ja asuntorakentaminen suur- ja peruspiireittäin Helsingissä 1970-1983 =. Helsinki , 1984. 36 p., [1] folded leaf of plates : LC Card 85-156678
HD7345.3.H5 K563 1984

Lankinen, Leila. Asuminen Helsingissä 1950-1983 =. Helsinki , 1985. 80 p. : LC Card 86-148571
HD7345.3.H5 L35 1985

Kupitz, Rolf. Die Kreditwirtschaft als wettbewerbspolitischer Ausnahmebereich : ein Beitrag zur ökonomischen Begründung der Regelungen des Gesetzes über das Kreditwesen und des Gesetzes gegen Wettbewerbsbeschränkungen / Rolf Kupitz. Thun : H. Deutsch, c1983. 300 p. ; 21 cm. (Reihe Wirtschaftswissenschaften, 0253-1488 . Bd. 293) Bibliography: p. 266-300. ISBN 3-87144-773-0 : LC Card 84-129435
1. Credit - Germany, West. 2. Credit - Law and legislation - Germany (West). I. Title. II. Series.
HG3754.5.G3 K86 1983

Kupka, P. F. (Peter Friedrich), 1846- Die Eisenbahnen Österreich-Ungarns, 1822-1867 / von P.F. Kupka. Leipzig : Duncker & Humblot, 1888. x, 386 p. : ill. ; 23 cm. Includes index. LC Card 83-217358
1. Railroads - Austria - History - 19th century. 2. Railroads - Hungary - History - 19th century. I. Title.
HE3058 .K86 1888

Kupky, Helmut. Hankel, Wilhelm, 1929- Gegenkurs . Berlin , c1984. 261 p. : ISBN 3-88680-114-4 LC Card 84-174753
HB3723 .H26 1984

Kupriianov, A. B. (Alekseĭ Borisovich) Razvivaiushchiesia strany i mezhdunarodnoe sotrudnichestvo : regional'nyĭ aspekt / A.B. Kupriianov. Moskva : Izd-vo "Nauka", 1980. 262 p. ; 20 cm. At head of title: Akademiia nauk SSSR. Institut ėkonomiki mirovoĭ sotsialisticheskoĭ sistemy. Includes bibliographical references. LC Card 81-131557
1. Developing countries - Economic conditions. 2. Developing countries - Foreign economic relations - Communist countries. 3. Communist countries - Foreign economic relations - Developing countries. I. Title.
HC59.7 .K863 1980

Kupriianov, L. A. (Leonid Aleksandrovich) Sotsial'noe planirovanie na predpriiatiiakh NRB, GDR i ChSSR / L.A. Kupriianov ; pod redaktsieĭ V.R. Polozova. Leningrad : Izd-vo "Nauka," Leningradskoe otd-nie, 1984. 111 p. ; 20 cm. At head of title: Akademiia nauk SSSR. Institut sotsial'no-ėkonomicheskikh problem. Bibliography: p. 100-111. LC Card 85-116781
1. Welfare work in industry - Bulgaria. 2. Welfare work in industry - Germany (East). 3. Welfare work in industry - Czechoslovakia. 4. Industrial sociology - Bulgaria. 5. Industrial sociology - Germany (East). 6. Industrial sociology - Czechoslovakia. I. Polozov, Vladimir Romanovich. II. Title.
HD7741.5 .K86 1984

Kupsh, Joyce. The electronic office / Joyce Kupsh, Sandra Whitcomb. Mission Hills, Calif. : Glencoe Pub. Co., c1987. x, 307 p. : ill. ; 24 cm. Includes index. ISBN 0-02-803510-0 (pbk.) LC Card 87-402084 DDC 651.8 19
1. Office practice - Automation. I. Whitcomb, Sandra. II. Title.
HF5548 .K85 1987

KURA DISTRICT (NIGERIA) - ECONOMIC CONDITIONS - CASE STUDIES.
Dottridge, M. B. Aspects of social and economic development in southern Kura District before the implementation of the Kano River Project irrigation scheme /. Zaria, Nigeria , 1980. v, 47 p., [1] p. of plates : LC Card 84-256142
HC1055.Z7 K873 1980

KURA DISTRICT (NIGERIA) - POLITICS AND GOVERNMENT - CASE STUDIES.
Dottridge, M. B. Aspects of social and economic development in southern Kura District before the implementation of the Kano River Project irrigation scheme /. Zaria, Nigeria , 1980. v, 47 p., [1] p. of plates : LC Card 84-256142
HC1055.Z7 K873 1980

KURA DISTRICT (NIGERIA) - SOCIAL CONDITIONS - CASE STUDIES.
Dottridge, M. B. Aspects of social and economic development in southern Kura District before the implementation of the Kano River Project irrigation scheme /. Zaria, Nigeria , 1980. v, 47 p., [1] p. of plates : LC Card 84-256142
HC1055.Z7 K873 1980

Kuramda ve Türkiye'de istikrar politikası açısından parasal ve mali işlemler /. Ataç, Beyhan. Eskişehir [1979?] iv, 173 p. ; LC Card 82-245649
HG1206.5 .A79 1979

Kuře, Miroslav. Alternativní strategie rozvoje rozvojových zemí / Miroslav Kuře. Praha : Ekonomický ústav ČSAV, 1986. 94 p. ; 21 cm. (Inform. publ. IP . č. 166) Bibliography: p. 91-94. LC Card 86-227984
1. Developing countries - Economic policy. 2. Economic development. I. Series: IP, č. 166. II. Title.
HC59.7 .K866 1986

Kurhessen 1816-1867. Köhler, H. (Heinz) Thurn und Taxis, Kurhessen 1816-1867 . Kassel [1970?]- v. <1 > : LC Card 86-235280
HE6185.G32 H474 1970

Kuriloff, Arthur H.
Schöllhammer, Hans, 1933- Entrepreneurship and small business management /. Malabar, Fla. , 1988. xvi, 608 p. : ISBN 0-89464-235-9 LC Card 87-14818 DDC 658/.022 19
HD62.5 .S354 1988

Starting and managing the small business / Arthur H. Kuriloff, John M. Hemphill, Jr. 2nd ed. New York : McGraw-Hill, c1988. xxi, 663 p. : ill. ; 25 cm. Includes bibliographies and index. ISBN 0-07-035665-3 : LC Card 87-3832 DDC 658/.022 19
1. New business enterprises. 2. Small business - Management. 3. New business enterprises - Case studies. 4. Small business - Management - Case studies. I. Hemphill, John Mearl, 1943-. II. Title.
HD62.5 .K87 1988

Kurilov, A. E. (Alekseĭ Evgrafovich) Pospelov, Germogen Sergeevich. Protsedury i algoritmy formirovaniia kompleksnykh programm /. Moskva , 1985. 422, [2] p. : LC Card 86-203758
HC336.25 .P567 1985

Kūriyan, Rēval. Vatukarayē kāntā śramaya surākāma : tē vatuvala Demaḷa kāntā kamraruvō = The exploitation of women on the plantations : Tamil women workers on the tea plantations / Rēval Kūriyan saha Kumāri Jayawardhana. Colombo, Sri Lanka : Kāntā Adhyāpana Kavaya, [1984] 24 p. : ill. ; 22 cm. In Sinhalese. LC Card 86-902479
1. Women - Employment - Sri Lanka. 2. Tea plantation workers - Sri Lanka. 3. Tamils - Employment - Sri Lanka. I. Jayawardena, Kumari. II. Title.
HD6182.8 .K87 1984

Kurmann, Bernadette, 1950- Firmenkultur am Beispiel der Sarna / Bernadette Kurmann. Bern : P. Haupt, [1985] 119 p. ; 23 cm. Bibliography: p. 119. ISBN 3-258-03560-1 : LC Card 86-123837 DDC 338.7/6684/09494 19
1. Sarna Kunststoff AG - Management. 2. Plastics industry and trade - Switzerland - Management - Case studies. 3. Corporate culture - Switzerland - Case studies. I. Title.
HD9661.S94 S275 1985
NYPL [JLD 86-4028]

KURNOOL (INDIA : DISTRICT) - RURAL CONDITIONS - CASE STUDIES.
Wade, Robert. Village republics . Cambridge [Cambridgeshire] , New York , 1988. p. cm. ISBN 0-521-30146-7 LC Card 86-33389 DDC 334/.683/095484 19
HD1491.I392 K878 1988

Kurochkin, ÎU. P. (ÎUriĭ Petrovich) Sotsial′no-ėkonomicheskaia priroda i formy neobkhodimogo produkta pri sotsializme / ÎU.P. Kurochkin. Leningrad : Izd-vo Leningradskogo universiteta, 1984. 135 p. ; 22 cm. At head of title: Ministerstvo vysshego i srednego spetsial′nogo obrazovaniia RSFSR. Includes bibliographical references. LC Card 84-218003
1. Basic needs - Soviet Union. 2. Consumption (Economics) - Soviet Union. I. Title.
HC340.B38 K87 1984

Kuromiya, Hiroaki. Stalin's industrial revolution : politics and workers, 1928-1932 / Hiroaki Kuromiya. Cambridge [Cambridgeshire] ; New York : Cambridge University Press, 1988. p. cm. Bibliography: p. ISBN 0-521-35157-X LC Card 87-25010 DDC 338.947 19
1. Central planning - Soviet Union. 2. Soviet Union - Economic policy - 1928-1932. 3. Soviet Union - Industries - History. 4. Labor and laboring classes - Soviet Union - History. 5. Soviet Union - Politics and government - 1917-1936. 6. Stalin, Joseph, 1879-1953. I. Title.
HC335.4 .K87 1988

Kurs mata uang sebagai alat kebijakan di negara sedang berkembang (NSB) /. Damanik, Konta I. Salatiga , 1980. ii, 21 leaves ; LC Card 85-941470
HG1496 .D35 1980

Kursany, Ibrahim. The dynamics and limits of capitalist development in Sudanese agriculture / by Ibrahim Kursany. Khartoum : Development Studies and Research Centre, Faculty of Economic and Social Studies, University of Khartoum, 1982- v. ; 29 cm. (DSRC seminar series. Discussion paper . no. 16) "September 1982." Includes bibliographical references. LC Card 83-980112 DDC 338.1/09624 19
1. Agriculture - Economic aspects - Sudan. 2. Land tenure - Sudan. I. Title. II. Series.
HD2123.5 .K87 1982 ***NYPL [JLM 86-825]***

Kurskiĭ gosudarstvennyĭ pedagogicheskiĭ institut. Ėkonomicheskie sviazi i sovershenstvovanie khoziaĭstvennogo mekhanizma . Kursk , 1985. 107 p. ; LC Card 86-235039
HC340.I57 E37 1985

Kursom na sotsialisticheskuiu industrializatsiiu /. Sokolov, V. N. (Viacheslav Nikolaevich) Kiev , 1985. 158, [2] p. ; LC Card 87-113771
HD9656.S56 U377 1985

Kursom uskoreniia /. Abalkin, L. I. (Leonid Ivanovich) Moskva , 1986. 213 p. ; LC Card 87-123506 DDC 338.947/009/48 19
HC336.25 .A33 1986

Kursschwankungen des Schweizerfrankens in ihren Auswirkungen auf Produktion, Export, Import und Fremdenverkehr . Zenger, Christoph. Bern , c1982. vi, 263 p. : ISBN 3-258-03172-X : LC Card 83-242397 DDC 332.4/9494 19
HG1155 .Z46 1982

Kurst, Charlotte. The Official guide to MBA programs /. [Los Angeles, Calif.] , Princeton, N.J. , c1986. 603 p. ; ISBN 0-446-38437-2 (pbk.) : LC Card 87-102516 DDC 658/.007/1173 19
HF1131 .O359 1986

Kurşunoğlu, Behram, 1922- International Scientific Forum on Changes in Energy (1981 : Mexico City, Mexico) Global energy assessment and outlook . Chur, Switzerland , New York, N.Y. , c1984. xxix, 580 p. : ISBN 3-7186-0224-5 LC Card 84-12959 DDC 333.79 19
TJ163.15 .I5678 1981 ***NYPL [JSE 86-509]***

Kurthen, Hermann. Politische Ökonomie und Persönlichkeitstheorie : Aneignung und Individualität in der bürgerlichen Gesellschaft / Hermann Kurthen. Köln : Pahl-Rugenstein, 1985. 245 p. ; 21 cm. (Pahl-Rugenstein Hochschulschriften Gesellschafts- und Naturwissenschaften . 181) Originally presented as the author's thesis (doctoral)--Freie Universität Berlin, 1984. Bibliography: p. 237-245. ISBN 3-7609-5181-3 LC Card 85-155083
1. Economics - Psychological aspects. 2. Capitalism - Psychological aspects. 3. Personality and culture. I. Title. II. Series.
HB74.P8 K87 1985

Kurtys, Edmund. Prace z zakresu ekonomiki produkcji /. Poznań , 1984. 219 p. : LC Card 86-127229
HB54 .P6 nr. 122 HD70.P6

Kurtz, David L. Boone, Louis E. Management /. New York , c1987. xv, 677, [48] p. : ISBN 0-394-36305-1 : LC Card 86-27957 DDC 658 19
HD31 .B619 1987

Kürtz, Hans Joachim. Zu Zeiten der Hanse : Handel und Wandel in den Hansekontoren Bergen, Brügge, London und Nowgorod / Hans Joachim Kürtz. Lübeck : LN-Verlag, c1983. 128 p. : ill. (some col.) ; 19 cm. Bibliography: p. 126-127. ISBN 3-87498-330-7 LC Card 87-672840
1. Hansa towns. 2. Commerce - History - Medieval, 500-1500. 3. Europe - Commerce - History. I. Title.
HF455 .K87x 1983

Kurz, Heinz-Dieter. Beschäftigung, Verteilung und Konjunktur . Bremen , 1984. 276 p. : ISBN 3-88722-088-9 : LC Card 85-176579
HB175 .B49 1984

Kurzberichte zur Landes- und Stadtentwicklungsforschung.
Döhne, Ulrich. Analyse der Ansiedlung von Einkaufszentren und Verbrauchermärkten in Nordrhein-Westfalen /. Dortmund , Essen , 1977. 39 p. : LC Card 86-181973
HF5429.6.G42 D64 1977

Puls, Heinz. Finanzkraft der Gemeinden und kommunaler Ausgleichsstock in NW /. Dortmund [1977] [15] p. : LC Card 86-211554
HJ9493.5.N6 P85 1977

Der kurze Traum immerwährender Prosperität . Lutz, Burkart, 1925- Frankfurt/Main , New York , c1984. 272 p. ; ISBN 3-593-33418-6 LC Card 85-131822
HC240 .L88 1984

Kurzfristige Finanzplanung und Grossprojektfertigung /. Fietz, Günter. Frankfurt am Main , New York , c1986. iv, 269 p. : ISBN 3-8204-9322-0 LC Card 86-156212
HG4012 .F53 1986

Kurzfristiges Leading und Lagging gruppeninterner Geldflüsse. Pastuszek, Rainer. Leading und Lagging kurzfristig variierbarer gruppeninterner Geldflüsse im Währungsrisikomanagement einer internationalen Unternehmung /. Pfaffenweiler , 1986. xvi, 275 p. : ISBN 3-89085-122-3 LC Card 87-128258 DDC 658.1/55 19
HG3851 .P295 1986

Kurzfristprognosen für die Textilwirtschaft anhand von Bestimmungsfaktoren für Saisonschwankungen /. Siegmann, Frank, 1956- Frankfurt am Main , New York , c1986. xxxi,/ 386 p. : ISBN 3-8204-9647-5 LC Card 86-233371
HD9850.1 .M58 Bd. 39 HD9863.5

Kurzman, Dan. A killing wind : inside union carbide and the Bhopal catastrophe / Dan Kurzman. New York : McGraw-Hill, c1987. xvi, 297 p., [16] p. of plates : ports. ; 23 cm. Bibliography: p. 261-288. Includes index. ISBN 0-07-035687-4 LC Card 87-3398 DDC 363.1/79 19
1. Bhopal Union Carbide Plant Disaster, Bhopal, India, 1984. 2. Pesticides industry - India - Bhopal - Accidents. 3. Methyl isocyanate - Environmental aspects - India - Bhopal. 4. Union Carbide Ltd. (India). I. Title.
HD7269.C452 I525 1987

Kusch, Franz. Macht, Profit & Kollegen : die Affäre Neue Heimat / Franz Kusch. Stuttgart : Bonn Aktuell, [1986] 184 p. : ill. ; 21 cm. Includes index. ISBN 3-87959-272-1 LC Card 86-182407
1. Trade-unions - Germany (West) - Corrupt practices. 2. Deutscher Gewerkschaftsbund. I. Title.
HD6490.C642 G35 1986

Kuszczak, John. A VAR analysis of economic interdependence : Canada, the United States, and the rest of the world / by John Kuszczak and John D. Murray. [Ottawa] : Bank of Canada, [1987] ii, 55 p. : ill. ; 28 cm. (Technical report . 46) Abstract in French. "March 1987." Bibliography: p. 53-55. LC Card 87-167407 DDC 338.5/42/0971 19
1. Business cycles - Canada - Econometric models. 2. Business cycles - United States - Econometric models. I. Murray, John D. II. Series: Technical report (Bank of Canada) , 46. III. Title.
HB3755 .K87 1987

Kutil, Jaroslav. Czechoslovak agriculture / Jaroslav Kutil ; [translated from the Czech by Vladimír Kosina]. Prague : Orbis Press Agency, 1983. 125 p., [48] p. of plates : ill. (some col.) ; 21 cm. LC Card 84-109068 DDC 338.1/09437 19
1. Agriculture and state - Czechoslovakia. 2. Agriculture - Economic aspects - Czechoslovakia. I. Title.
HD1940.3.Z8 K87 1983
NYPL [JLD 86-2294]

Kutscher, Egon, 1953- Krack, Jürgen. Lieber besser statt mehr? . Köln , c1985. 306, [2] p. : ISBN 3-7663-0569-7 LC Card 85-125869
HD5029 .K72 1985

Kutter, Markus, 1925- Werbung in der Schweiz : Geschichte einer unbekannten Branche / Markus Kutter. [Zürich] : Ringier, 1983. 271 p., xvi p. of plates : ill. ; 19 cm. (3. Band der Ringier Reihe Kommunikation) Includes index. ISBN 3-85859-202-1 : LC Card 84-142450
1. Advertising - Switzerland - History. I. Series: Ringier Reihe Kommunikation , 3. Bd. II. Title.
HF5813.S94 K87 1983

Kutty G. Krishnan- see **Krishnan-Kutty, G.**

Kuvanyshev, A. K. Kozlov, P. T. (Petr Tikhonovich) Sovershenstvovanie khoziaĭstvennogo mekhanizma v neftianoĭ i gazovoĭ promyshlennosti /. Alma-Ata , 1983. 134 p. : LC Card 83-194289
HD9575.S652 K69 1983

Kuzin, V. Komsomol′sko-molodezhnyĭ kollektiv / V. Kuzin, I. Smirnov. Moskva : "Molodaia gvardiia", 1981. 157 p. ; 17 cm. (Biblioteka komsomol′skogo aktivista) Includes bibliographical references. LC Card 82-152678
1. Youth - Employment - Soviet Union. 2. Work groups - Soviet Union. 3. Vsesoiuznyĭ leninskiĭ kommunisticheskiĭ soiuz molodezhi. I. Smirnov, Igor′ Pavlovich. II. Title.
HD6276.S592 K89 1981

Kuziuk, V. A. Zoidov, K. Kh. Ob approksimatsii makroėkonomicheskikh zavisimosteĭ posredstvom tablichnykh i splaĭnovykh proizvodstvennykh funktsiĭ /. Moskva , 1985. 25, [3] p. : LC Card 86-162091
HB142 .Z65 1985

Kuz′minov, Ivan Ivanovich. Aktual′nye problemy planomernogo razvitiia narodnogo khoziaĭstva /. Moskva , 1980. 247 p. ; LC Card 81-131558
HC336.25 .A455 1980

Kuzmyak, J. Richard. Klinger, Dieter. Personal travel in the U. S. . Washington, D.C. , Springfield, Va. [1986] 2 v. : LC Card 86-603072 DDC 380.5/22/0973021 19
HE199.9 .K535 1986

Kuznesof, Elizabeth Anne. Household economy and urban development : São Paulo, 1765-1836 / Elizabeth Anne Kuznesof. Boulder : Westview Press, 1986. 216 p. : ill. ; 23 cm. (Dellplain Latin American studies . 18) Includes index. Bibliography: p. 199-211. ISBN 0-8133-7181-3 : LC Card 85-31491 DDC 307.7/64/098161 19
1. Households - Brazil - São Paulo (State) - History. 2. Community development - Brazil - São Paulo (State) - History. 3. São Paulo, Brazil (State) - Economic conditions. I. Title.
HC188.S3 K89 1986 ***NYPL [JLE 87-711]***

KUZNETS, SIMON SMITH, 1901-
Datta, Anindya. Growth and equity . Calcutta , New York , 1986. xii, 119 p. : ISBN 0-19-561882-3 : LC Card 87-900001 DDC 338.954 19
HD82 .D334 1986

KUZNETSK BASIN (R.S.F.S.R.) - ECONOMIC CONDITIONS.
Stroim Kuzbass /. Kemerovo , 1984. 417 p., [56] p. of plates : LC Card 84-103662
HC337.R852 K8975 1984

KUZNETSK BASIN (R.S.F.S.R.) - INDUSTRIES.
Stroim Kuzbass /. Kemerovo , 1984. 417 p., [56] p. of plates : LC Card 84-103662
HC337.R852 K8975 1984

Kuznetsov, I. I. (Il'ia Innokent'evich)
Ulymzhiev, D. B. (Dashi Batuevich) Put' mongol'skogo aratstva k sotsializmu /. Novosibirsk , 1987. 283, [5] p. ; LC Card 87-159668
HD1491.M55 U49 1987

Kuznetsov, IU. I. (IUriĭ Igorevich)
Russko-angliĭskiĭ razgovornik dlia neftekhimikov i khimikov-neorganikov / IU.I. Kuznetsov, V.M. Sloushcher. Moskva : "Russkiĭ iazyk", 1985. 359 p. ; 21 cm. Title on added t.p.: Russian-English phrase-book for the petrochemical and inorganic chemical industries. LC Card 86-138945 DDC 660/.03/9171 19
1. Petroleum chemicals industry - Dictionaries - Russian. 2. Petroleum industry and trade - Dictionaries - Russian. 3. Chemical industry - Dictionaries - Russian. 4. Russian language - Dictionaries - English. I. Sloushcher, V. M. (Vitaliĭ Mironovich). II. Title. III. Title: Russian-English phrase-book for the petrochemical and inorganic chemical industries.
HD9579.C32 K88 1985
NYPL [*QAD 86-3599]

Kuznetsov, N. K. Sotsial'noe razvitie molodezhi v trudovykh kollektivakh novykh gorodov Sibiri . Irkutsk , 1980. 158 p. ; LC Card 82-110658
HD6276.S593 S527 1980

Kuznetsova, T. E. Proizvodstvennaia sfera sovremennogo sela / T.E. Kuznetsova ; otvetstvennyĭ redaktor L.V. Nikiforov. Moskva : "Nauka", 1986. 199 p. ; 20 cm. (Problemy sovetskoĭ ėkonomiki) At head of title: Akademiia nauk SSSR. Institut ėkonomiki. Includes bibliographical references. LC Card 86-164902
1. Agricultural industries - Soviet Union. 2. Agricultural laborers - Soviet Union. I. Nikiforov, L. V. II. Title.
HD9015.S652 K89 1986

Kvartalsvis nasjonalregnskap 1978-1983 = Quarterly national accounts, 1978-1983. Oslo : Statistisk sentralbyrå : I kommisjon hos H. Aschehoug og Universitetsforlaget, 1984. 99 p. ; 30 cm. (Norges offisielle statistikk . B 510) ISBN 82-537-2143-9 : LC Card 85-223735
1. National income - Norway - Accounting. I. Norway. Statistisk sentralbyrå. II. Title: Quarterly national accounts, 1978-1983. III. Series.
HA1501 B, nr. 510 HC370.I5

Kvindeforskning.
Markussen, Randi. Det fleksible køn . [Copenhagen] , c1984. 163 p. ; ISBN 87-7445-159-6 : LC Card 84-187146
HD6169 .M37 1984

Kvindeliv--hverdagsliv : arbejderkvinders levevilkår i Danmark 1880-1930 / Agnete Birger Madsen ... [et al.].1. udg. Copenhagen : Gyldendal, 1985. 111 p. : ill. ; 23 cm. Includes bibliographies. ISBN 87-00-65962-2 : LC Card 86-156606
1. Women - Employment - Denmark - History - 19th century - Sources. 2. Women - Employment - Denmark - History - 20th century - Sources. 3. Women - Denmark - Social conditions - Sources. I. Madsen, Agnete Birger.
HD6169 .K855 1985

Kvinders livsgrundlag i 80-erne /. Gydesen, Ellen. K [i.e. Copenhagen] [1985] 202 columns : LC Card 87-168500
HD6060.65.D4 G93 1985

Kvinner i arbeid : økonomiske og sosiologiske perspektiver / Tor Rødseth og Kristin Dale Titlestad (red.). Oslo : Universitetsforlaget, c1984. 290 p. : ill. ; 21 cm. (Serien Kvinners levekår og livsløp) Bibliography: p. 269-[277] ISBN 82-00-06835-8 : LC Card 85-102185
1. Women - Employment - Norway. I. Rødseth, Tor, 1928-. II. Titlestad, Kirstin Dale, 1951-. III. Series.
HD6170 .K85 1984

Kvinnoplats . Granath, Erna. Stockholm , c1985. 141 p. ; ISBN 91-38-90602-3 : LC Card 85-236327
HD6073.M392 S84 1985
NYPL [JLE 86-3898]

Kvinnor forskar.
Arbetets döttrar /. [Stockholm] , c1986. 2 v. ; ISBN 91-7410-337-7 : LC Card 86-216247
HD6173 .A79 1986

KWANDEBELE (SOUTH AFRICA) - ECONOMIC CONDITIONS.
McCaul, Colleen. Satellite in revolt . Johannesburg, South Africa , 1987. 125 p., [11] p. of plates : ISBN 0-86982-314-0 (pbk.) LC Card 87-157406 DDC 330.9682/95063 19
HC905.Z7 K785 1987

Kwantlen College. Fraser Port . Victoria, B.C. , 1986. 131 p., [16] p. of plates : ISBN 0-919203-17-5 (pbk.) LC Card 87-106756
HE554.V3 F73 1986

KWARA STATE (NIGERIA) - ECONOMIC CONDITIONS.
Welcome, Mr. President, to Kwara State. Ilorin [1980 or 1981] 28 p. : LC Card 86-194780 DDC 966.9/5 19
HC1055.Z7 K898 1980

Kwara State (Nigeria). Information Division.
Welcome, Mr. President, to Kwara State. Ilorin [1980 or 1981] 28 p. : LC Card 86-194780 DDC 966.9/5 19
HC1055.Z7 K898 1980

KWARA STATE (NIGERIA) - POLITICS AND GOVERNMENT.
Welcome, Mr. President, to Kwara State. Ilorin [1980 or 1981] 28 p. : LC Card 86-194780 DDC 966.9/5 19
HC1055.Z7 K898 1980

KWARA STATE (NIGERIA) - SOCIAL CONDITIONS.
Welcome, Mr. President, to Kwara State. Ilorin [1980 or 1981] 28 p. : LC Card 86-194780 DDC 966.9/5 19
HC1055.Z7 K898 1980

KWAZULU (SOUTH AFRICA) - ECONOMIC POLICY.
Spies, P. H. Perspectives on the future of Natal/KwaZulu /. Pietermaritzburg , 1986. 149 p. : ISBN 0-909232-59-8 (pbk.) : LC Card 87-166530 DDC 361.2/5/09684 s 361.6/1/09684 19
HC517.N3 A44 vol. 69 JQ2224

Kwiatkowski, Eugeniusz. Pisma o rzeczypospolitej morskiej / Eugeniusz Kwiatkowski ; [wyboru dokonał i wstępem opatrzył Marian Marek Drozdowski]. Wyd. 1. Szczecin : Glob, 1985. 277 p., [24] p. of plates : ill., port. ; 25 cm. Includes bibliographical references. ISBN 83-7007-012-4 :
1. Merchant marine - Poland. 2. Shipping - Poland. 3. Harbors - Poland. 4. Pomerelia (Poland) - Economic conditions. I. Drozdowski, Marian Marek, 1932-. II. Title. ***NYPL [*QO 86-2539]***

Kwiatkowski, Vernon. Van Daniker, Relmond P., 1942- Infrastructure assets . Stamford, Conn. (High Ridge Park, P.O. Box 3821, Stamford 06905-0821) , c1986. xii, 155 p. ; LC Card 86-90661 DDC 657/.835 19
HJ9816 .V35 1986

Kwitny, Jonathan. The crimes of patriots : a true tale of dope, dirty money, and the CIA / Jonathan Kwitny. New York : W.W. Norton, c1987. 424 p., [8] p. of plates : ill. ; 24 cm. Includes index. ISBN 0-393-02387-7 : LC Card 87-22032 DDC 364.1/0994 19
1. Nugan Hand Bank - Corrupt practices. 2. Money laundering - Australia. 3. Murder - Australia. 4. United States. Central Intelligence Agency. 5. Narcotics, Control of. I. Title.
HG3448.N846 K95 1987

KYANON KAMERA KABUSHIKI KAISHA - MANAGEMENT - EMPLOYEE PARTICIPATION.
Kyanon no seisan kakushin. English. Canon production system . Stamford, Conn. , c1987. xxi, 230 p. : ISBN 0-915299-06-2 : LC Card 85-63498 DDC 681/.418/0683 19
HD9708.5.C354 K92513 1987

Kyanon no seisan kakushin. English. Canon production system : creative involvement of the total workforce / compiled by the Japan Management Association ; translated by Alan T. Campbell ; edited by Constance E. Dyer ; preface by Norman Bodek. Stamford, Conn. : Productivity Press, c1987. xxi, 230 p. : ill., ports. ; 24 cm. Translation of: Kyanon no seisan kakushin. Includes index. ISBN 0-915299-06-2 : LC Card 85-63498 DDC 681/.418/0683 19
1. Kyanon Kamera Kabushiki kaisha - Management - Employee participation. 2. Camera industry - Japan - Management - Employee participation - Case studies. 3. Production management - Japan - Case studies. I. Dyer, Constance E. II. Title. III. Title: Nihon Nōritsu Kyōkai.
HD9708.5.C354 K92513 1987

Kybernetik und Management : ein Round Table-Gespräch / herausgegeben von Jörg Baetge. Berlin : Duncker & Humblot, c1983. viii, 131 p. : ill. ; 24 cm. (Wirtschaftskybernetik und Systemanalyse. Bd. 9) Papers presented at the 3rd Round Table-Gespräch held Feb. 26-27, 1983 in Sindelfingen and sponsored by the Gesellschaft für Wirtschafts- und Sozialkybernetik. Includes bibliographical references. CONTENTS. - Der Nutzen der Kybernetik für das Unternehmensmanagement / von Karl W. Deutsch -- Kybernetische Kontrollsysteme / von Jörg Baetge -- Ein kybernetisches Modell zur Ergebnisplanung unter bilanzpolitischem Einsatz der Pensionsrückstellungen / von Wolfgang Hardes -- Kapitalbindung durch die betriebliche Altersversorgung / von Edzard Reuter. ISBN 3-428-05448-2 LC Card 84-109870
1. Industrial management - Congresses. 2. Cybernetics - Congresses. I. Baetge, Jörg. II. Gesellschaft für Wirtschafts- und Sozialkybernetik.
HD29 .K92 1983

Kyle, C. Donald. Kyle, Robert C. Property management /. Chicago, IL , c1988. x, 422 p. : ISBN 0-88462-669-5 (pbk.) LC Card 87-17906 DDC 332.63/24/068 19
HD1394 .K94 1988

Kyle, Robert C. Property management / Robert Kyle ; contributing editor, Floyd M. Baird ; consulting editor, C. Donald Kyle. 3rd ed. Chicago, IL : Real Estate Education Co., c1988. x, 422 p. : ill. ; 28 cm. Includes index. ISBN 0-88462-669-5 (pbk.) LC Card 87-17906 DDC 332.63/24/068 19
1. Real estate management. I. Baird, Floyd M. II. Kyle, C. Donald. III. Title.
HD1394 .K94 1988

Kylebäck, Hugo, 1930- Konsument- och lantbrukskooperation i Sverige : utveckling, samarbets- och konkurrensförhållanden före andra världskriget / Hugo Kylebäck.Uppl. 2. Stockholm : Kooperativa institutet, [1984] 277 p. ; 23 cm. Bibliography: p. 269-275. ISBN 91-85196-18-5 : LC Card 86-120646
1. Cooperation - Sweden - History - 20th century. 2. Kooperativa förbundet - History - 20th century. 3. Agriculture, Cooperative - Sweden - History - 20th century. 4. Sweden - Politics and government - 1905-1950. I. Title.
HD3524.A1 K663 1984

Kyng, Morten, 1950- Computers and democracy . Aldershot [Hants, England] , Brookfield [Vt.], USA , c1987. x, 434 p. : ISBN 0-566-05476-0 : LC Card 87-8398 DDC 338/.06 19
HD5650 .C65 1987

Kyōsha no kanrigaku Kanpishi /. Moriya, Hiroshi, 1932- Kyōto-shi , 1984. 273 p. ; ISBN 4-569-21374-X : LC Card 85-142427
HF5387 .M67 1984 <Orien Japan>
NYPL [*OSM 87-1463]

Kyoto. Center for Southeast Asian Studies. see **Kyōto Daigaku. Tōnan Ajia Kenkyū Sentā.**

Kyōto Daigaku. Center for Southeast Asian Studies. see **Kyōto Daigaku. Tōnan Ajia Kenkyū Sentā.**

Kyōto Daigaku. Southeast Asian Studies, Center for. see **Kyōto Daigaku. Tōnan Ajia Kenkyū Sentā.**

Kyōto Daigaku. Tōnan Ajia Kenkyū Sentā. Environment, agriculture, and society in the Malay world /. Kyoto, Japan , 1986. ix, 177 p. : LC Card 86-201590 DDC 338.1/09595 19
HD2080.6 .E58 1986

Kypke, Ulrich. Bopp-Schmehl, Annemarie, 1946- Technische Normung und Verbraucherinteressen im gesellschaftlichen Wandel /. Frankfurt am Main , c1984. iii, 269 p. ; ISBN 3-88129-834-7 : LC Card 85-119483
HC290.5.C6 B66 1984

Kypros. see **Cyprus.**

L. A. F. T. A. see **Asociación Latinoamericana de Libre Comercio.**

La Agricultura y la pesca españolas en 1981. Madrid : Ministerio de Agricultura, Pesca y Alimentación, Secretaría General Técnica, [1982?] 299 p. : ill. ; 27 cm. (Publicaciones agrarias) ISBN 84-7479-164-2 : LC Card 83-125330 DDC 338.1/0946 19
1. Agriculture - Economic aspects - Spain. 2. Fisheries - Economic aspects - Spain. 3. Fish trade - Spain. I. Spain. Ministerio de Agricultura, Pesca y Alimentación. Secretaría General Técnica.
HD2022 .A657 1982 ***NYPL [JLF 87-236]***

La Amenaza de guerra nuclear / edición preparada por Antonio Remiro Brotons ; F. de Bordejé Morencos ... [et al.]. 2a ed. Madrid : Ediciones de la Universidad Autónoma de Madrid, 1985. 129 p. ; 21 cm. (Colección de bolsillo. 1) Includes bibliographical references. ISBN 84-7477-027-0 LC Card 86-100273 DDC 355/.0217 19
1. Nuclear warfare. 2. Nuclear disarmament. I. Bordejé y Morencos, Fernando de. II. Series: Colección de bolsillo (Universidad Autónoma de Madrid) , 1.
U263 .A44 1985 ***NYPL [JLD 86-2519]***

La Banque nationale d'Haïti . Marcelin, Frédéric, 1848-1917. Port-au-Prince, Haïti , 1985. xi, 118 p. : LC Card 86-125803 DDC 332.1/1/097294 19
HG2813 .M3 1985 ***NYPL [Sc D 86-690]***

La caída del bolívar /. Cantó, Leandro. Caracas, Venezuela [1983 or 1984] 223 p. ; LC Card 84-186552 DDC 332.4/987 19
HG915 .C36 1983 ***NYPL [JLD 87-2426]***

La conflictiva y nunca acabada construcción del orden deseado /. Lechner, Norbert, 1939- [Santiago, Chile] [1984] 204 p. ; ISBN 84-89401-05-5 LC Card 84-227472 DDC 320.982 19
JL2624 .L43 1984 ***NYPL [JLE 87-2137]***

LA CONVENCIÓN (PERU) - BIOGRAPHY.
La Convención, el trabajo y sus luchas sociales /. [Peru? , 1983] (Cusco, Perú : Impr. AMAUTA) 152, vii p., [12] leaves of plates : LC Card 87-127171 DDC 330.985/3 19
HC228.C65 C66 1983

LA CONVENCIÓN (PERU) - ECONOMIC CONDITIONS.
La Convención, el trabajo y sus luchas sociales /. [Peru? , 1983] (Cusco, Perú : Impr. AMAUTA) 152, vii p., [12] leaves of plates : LC Card 87-127171 DDC 330.985/3 19
HC228.C65 C66 1983

LA CONVENCIÓN (PERU) - HISTORY.
La Convención, el trabajo y sus luchas sociales /. [Peru? , 1983] (Cusco, Perú : Impr. AMAUTA) 152, vii p., [12] leaves of plates : LC Card 87-127171 DDC 330.985/3 19
HC228.C65 C66 1983

La crise démographique en Grèce. Dēmographikē Hēmerida (1984 : Athens, Greece) Hē Dēmographikē krisē stēn Hellada . Athēna , 1985. 205 p. : LC Card 86-192606
HB3632.5.A3 D45 1984

La crise démographique en Grèce. Dēmographikē Hēmerida (1984 : Athens, Greece) Hē Dēmographikē krisē stēn Hellada . Athēna , 1986. 205 p. : LC Card 86-201713
HB3632.5.A3 D45 1986

La crise 1974-1982 . Mandel, Ernest. Paris , c1985. 352 p. : ISBN 2-08-081151-7
NYPL [JLC 86-204]

La crisi della legittimità borghese . Roncolini, Giuliana, 1948- Napoli , 1978. 115 p. ; ISBN 88-20-70809-4 : LC Card 79-368996
HC54 .R64 ***NYPL [JLD 81-254]***

La Crisi delle partecipazioni statali, motivi e prospettive / [relazioni] di Giuseppe Bognetti ... [et al.] ; a cura di Emilio Gerelli e Giuseppe Bognetti. Milano : F. Angeli, c1981. 240 p. ; 22 cm. (Collana dell'Istituto di finanza dell'Università di Pavia . 8) Includes bibliographical references. ISBN 88-20-42148-8 : LC Card 81-200055
1. Industrial promotion - Italy - Congresses. 2. Industry and state - Italy - Congresses. I. Bognetti, Giuseppe. II. Gerelli, Emilio. III. Series: Pavia. Università. Istituto di finanza. Collana, 8.
HC310.I53 C74 1981 ***NYPL [JLD 86-3503]***

La crisis de la industria automotriz (1971-1982) /. Sirumbal, Luis Miguel. Lima, Perú [1983] 54 p. : LC Card 84-123601 DDC 338.4/76292/0985 19
HD9710.P382 S57 1983
NYPL [JLD 86-365]

La cumpăna a două epoci, 1849-1877 /. Pătroiu, Ion. Craiova , 1983. 316 p. ; LC Card 84-234959
HD1333.R62 O475 1983

La derrota de Andahuaylas (1974) /. Méndez S., José Fernando. Lima , 1981. 126 p. :
NYPL [JLB 86-27]

La diplomatie . R'emy, Ernst. Port-au-Prince , 1983. 299 p. ; ***NYPL [Sc D 85-315]***

La Duron, Joannes, 17th-18th cent. Vrywillighe Liefde Broeders van S. Huybrecht Liefde, ingestelt door het Vrye Vleesvercoopers Ambacht a[nn]o 1714. [1715-1718?] [126] leaves (leaves [1], [7], [43-123], and [125-126] blank) : ill. ; 44 cm. Ms. A book honoring officers and members of the Vrywillighe Liefde Broeders van S. Huybrecht Liefde, a fraternal association established by the Brussels butchers' guild. Most of the leaves name an individual officer, usually giving his office (with a date, from 1714 to as late as 1718), a coat of arms, and a large allegorical or religious picture (often a patron saint). Leaves [43]ff. were probably intended for additions of the same nature. Seven rules of the society, numbered 3-9, are written on the recto and verso of leaf [124]. Title from leaf [11]. The dedication (leaf [4]) is dated from the writer's study, presumably in Brussels, Oct. 5, 1715, and signed: Joannes La Duron. Brown ink on paper, with gold, green, and gray coloring. The pictorial work includes calligraphic figures. Bound in contemporary gold-tooled red morocco. Signatures: [1^2 $2\text{-}17^8$ $18\text{-}19^2$]. [$3]_2$ (content unknown) has been excised. [$17]_{1\text{-}3}$ (probably blank) are also missing. Leaves [2-42] are numbered 1-41 in modern pencil. Gift of Ian Woodner, 1986. LC Card 86-222905
1. Vrywillighge Liefde Broeders van S. Huybrecht Liefde (Brussels, Belgium). 2. Vrywillighe Liefde Broeders van S. Huybrecht Liefde (Brussels, Belgium) - Officials and employees. I. Vrywillighe Liefde Broeders van S. Huybrecht Liefde (Brussels, Belgium). II. Title.
HD6473.N35 L3 1715

La empresa exportadora española frente a Iberoamérica y la CEE /. Alonso, José Antonio. Madrid , 1985. xiii, 263 p. ; ISBN 84-7232-380-3 LC Card 86-199177
HF3688.L3 A46 1985 ***NYPL [JLE 87-56]***

La fin du travail /. Drancourt, Michel. Paris , c1984. 329 p. : ISBN 2-01-009476-X LC Card 84-222228 DDC 306/.36 19
HD6957.F8 D7 1984 ***NYPL [JLC 86-444]***

La finanza pubblica in cifre, 1965-1983 /. Ghessi, Giuseppe. Milano, Italy , c1985. 186 p. : LC Card 85-180958 DDC 336.45 19
HJ1185 .G43 1985 ***NYPL [JLF 87-249]***

La France industrielle.
La Verrerie champenoise, Charbonneaux-B.S.N. Reims, de 1870 à nos jours /. Die , c1984. 279 p. : ISBN 2-904638-12-1 : LC Card 84-247744
HD9623.F8 V47 1984

La Fuente, Germán. Cisneros C., Antonio. La mujer trabajadora . La Paz, Bolivia [1984] 131 leaves : LC Card 85-129000 DDC 331.4/0984 19
HD6121 .C58 1984 ***NYPL [JLF 86-1704]***

La fuerza de trabajo en el agro . Gandásegui, Marco A. Panamá, R.P. , c1985. 404 p. : ISBN 84-8385-002-X LC Card 86-111074 DDC 331.7/63/097287 19
HD1822 .G36 1985 ***NYPL [JLF 86-1350]***

La ganadería vacuna uruguaya . Barbato de Silva, Celia. Montevideo, Uruguay [1980] 77 leaves ;
NYPL [JLF 86-1101]

La gestione marketing nella banca . Caselli, Mario, 1944- Milano [1977] 332 p. : LC Card 77-553379
HG1616.M3 C37 ***NYPL [JLD 80-3228]***

La Grange, A. B. DBSA in the southern African development framework / compiled by A.B. la Grange. Sandton, Republic of South Africa : Development Bank of Southern Africa, [1985] 36 p. : ill. ; 30 cm. (Position paper . no. 1) "June 1985." Bibliography: p. 36. LC Card 87-150256 DDC 332.2 19
1. Africa, Southern - Economic conditions. 2. Fiscal policy - Africa, Southern. 3. Economic assistance - Africa, Southern. 4. Development Bank of Southern Africa. I. Series: Position paper (Development Bank of Southern Africa) , no. 1. II. Title.
HC900 .L3 1985

LA GUAJIRA, COLOMBIA (DEPT.) - ECONOMIC CONDITIONS.
Acosta M., Amylkar (Acosta Medina), 1950- [Selections. 1986.] Escritos, 1978-1986 /. Medellín, Colombia , 1986. 201 p. ; LC Card 87-404338 DDC 330.9861/0632 19
HC197 .A5562 1986

La Guerre des ondes : histoire des radios de langue française pendant la Deuxième Guerre mondiale / Communauté des radios publiques de langue française ; ouvrage publié sous la direction d'Hélène Eck ; préf. de Jean-Noël Jeanneney. Paris : A. Colin ; Lausanne : Payot, c1985. 382 p. : ill. ; 24 cm. Bibliography: p. [369]-373. CONTENTS. - France / par Jean-Louis Crémieux-Brilhac et Hélène Eck, avec le concours de Charles Louis Foulon -- Belgique / par Jean Duhardin -- Suisse / par Geneviève Billeter -- Province de Québec / par Gérard Laurence. ISBN 2-601-00475-4 (Payot)
1. Radio broadcasting - France. 2. Radio broadcasting - Belgium. 3. Radio broadcasting - Switzerland, French-speaking. 4. Radio broadcasting - Canada - Québec. 5. Radio in propaganda. I. Eck, Hélène. II. Communauté des radios publiques de langue française.
NYPL [MWGK (France) 87-550]

La historia agraria /. Burga, Manuel. Chiclayo, Perú , 1986. 196 p. ; ***NYPL [JLD 87-1524]***

La Industria textil y del vestido en México, 1970-1982. México, D.F. : Instituto Nacional de Estadística, Geografía e Informática, 1984. 77 p. : ill. ; 28 cm. Chiefly tables. ISBN 968-8097-69-1 LC Card 85-203070 DDC 338.4/7677/00972021 19
1. Textile industry - Mexico - Statistics. 2. Clothing trade - Mexico - Statistics. 3. Textile industry - Statistics. 4. Clothing trade - Statistics. I. Instituto Nacional de Estadística, Geografía e Informática (Mexico).
HD9864.M62 I53 1984 ***NYPL [JLF 87-363]***

La Izquierda europea : análisis de las crisis de las ideologías de izquierda en la Europa occidental / [Manuel Mella Márquez (comp.) ; Francisco Alburquerque Llorens ... et al.].1a ed. Barcelona : Teide, 1985. 282 p. ; 22 cm. (Colección ciencias sociales. 7) Includes bibliographical references and index. ISBN 84-307-7438-6 LC Card 86-186087
1. Socialism - Europe. 2. Communism - Europe. I. Mella Márquez, Manuel. II. Alburquerque Llorens, Francisco.
HX238.5 .I97 1985 ***NYPL [JLD 86-4090]***

La lutte des classes aujourd'hui, 1950-1981 /. Bron, Jean. Paris , 1982. 318 p. ; ISBN 2-7082-0349-5 ***NYPL [JLD 86-1408]***

La Maîtrise de la croissance dans l'entreprise; colloque national de Cannes, 1971. Avant-propos d'Edgar Faure. Préf. de Henri Hierche. Paris, Dunod, 1973. xx, 333 p. illus. 24 cm. LC Card 73-172856 DDC 658.4
1. Industrial management - Congresses. 2. Business enterprises - Finance - Congresses. 3. Industrial management - France - Congresses.
HD29 .M26 ***NYPL [JLE 74-55]***

La maîtrise du salariat /. Naville, Pierre. Paris , c1984. 153 p. ; ISBN 2-7157-1099-2 : LC Card 85-100916
HD6957.F8 N38 1984 ***NYPL [JLD 87-333]***

La Molina, Peru. Universidad Nacional Agraria. see **Universidad Nacional Agraria.**

La mujer trabajadora . Cisneros C., Antonio. La Paz, Bolivia [1984] 131 leaves : LC Card 85-129000 DDC 331.4/0984 19
HD6121 .C58 1984 ***NYPL [JLF 86-1704]***

La Nueva economía en Francia y en España /

publicación realizada con la colaboración de la Embajada de Francia en España. Madrid : Fundación Universidad Empresa, c1980. 197 p. : ill. ; 22 cm. (Colección Forum Universidad Empresa) "Conferencias y ponencias desarrolladas con ocasión de las "Jornadas Hispano-Francesas sobre la Nueva Economía" ... 17 y 18 de enero de 1980 en la Cámara Oficial de Comercio e Industria de Madrid, organizadas por la Fundación Universidad-Empresa"--P. [7] ISBN 84-85355-27-X : LC Card 83-105425 DDC 330.944/0838 19
1. Economics - France - Congresses. 2. Economics - Spain - Congresses. I. France. Ambassade (Spain). II. Fundación Universidad-Empresa (Madrid, Spain). III. Jornadas Hispano-Francesas sobre la Nueva Economía (1980 : Cámara Oficial de Comercio e Industria de Madrid).
HB105.A2 N83 1980 NYPL [JLD 86-3024]

La paix par la vérité [microform]. Doumergue, Émile, 1844-1937. Paris, 1922-1924. 2 v. LC Card 26-3809
*D511 .D67 NYPL [*Z-4048 no. 1]*

La Paz, Bolivia. Centro de Investigación y Promoción del Campesinado. see **Centro de Investigación y Promoción del Campesinado.**

La planificación en empresas agropecuarias . Tealdo, Armando. Lima, Perú [1985], c1983. 157 p. : LC Card 85-174266 DDC 630/.68 19
HD9000.5 .T4 1985 NYPL [JLD 86-1283]

La Politica comunitaria della casa. Atti del Convegno nazionale tenuto a Roma il 26-27 aprile 1969 sul tema: Per una urbanistica operante: ravvivare gli impulsi dell'efficacia della legge 167, promosso dall'Ufficio problemi urbanistici della DC. Roma, Cinque lune, 1971. 227 p. 22 cm. LC Card 74-883223
1. City planning - Italy - Congresses. 2. Housing - Italy - Congresses. I. Partito della democrazia cristiana.
NYPL [JLD 72-3595]

La Politica industriale della CEE : documentazione generale e settoriale. Roma : Camera dei deputati, Servizio relazioni comunitarie e internazionali, 1983. 371 p. ; 21 cm. (Quaderni di documentazione . 5) Includes bibliographical references. LC Card 86-104849 DDC 338.94 19
1. Industry and state - European Economic Community countries. 2. Industrial promotion - European Economic Community countries. 3. European Economic Community countries - Commercial policy. 4. European Economic Community countries - Foreign economic relations. I. Series: Quaderni di documentazione (Italy. Parlamento. Camera dei deputati. Servizio relazioni comunitarie e internazionali) , 5.
HD3616.E83 P65 1983
NYPL [JLD 87-1225]

La politique de l'emploi-formation au Maghreb, 1970-1980 /. Bernard, Chantal. Paris , 1982. 472 p. ; *NYPL [JLE 86-568]*

La politique française d'amenagement du territoire de 1950 à 1985 /. Laborie, Jean Paul. Paris , 1985. 176 p., [8] p. of plates : ISBN 2-11-001488-1(pbk.) : *NYPL [JLG 87-38]*

La Potestà impositiva dei comuni e delle province / a cura di Antonino Tramontana. Rimini : Maggioli, c1985. 109 p. ; 24 cm. (Collana di finanza locale . 3) "Atti dell'incontro di studio svoltosi a Perugia il 12 maggio 1983"--P. [5]. Includes bibliographical references. CONTENTS. - La potestà impositiva degli enti locali / Emilio Giardina -- Le imposte comunali minori / Federico Pica -- La potestà impositiva locale : il ruolo delle province / Giancarlo Guasticchi -- Capacità impositiva e autonomia finanziaria dei comuni / Ermanno Pianesi. LC Card 85-194391 DDC 336.2/014/45 19
1. Local taxation - Italy - Congresses. 2. Local finance - Italy - Congresses. I. Tramontana, Antonino. II. Series.
HJ9498 .P68 1985 NYPL [JLE 86-4120]

La Problemática del endeudamiento externo y el financiamiento del desarrollo agropecuario latinoamericano. Lima, Perú : Asociación Latinoamericana de Instituciones Financieras de Desarrollo, [1985] 131 p. : ill. ; 21 cm. Bibliography: p. 127-131. LC Card 86-122361 DDC 336.3/435/098 19
1. Debts, External - Latin America. 2. Agricultural credit - Latin America.
HJ8514.5 .P76 1985 NYPL [JLD 86-3143]

La programmabilità delle gestioni aziendali in tempi di inflazione /. Cardillo, Giovanni. Milano , 1983. 118 p. ; LC Card 84-177279 DDC 658.4/012/0945 19
HD70.I8 C27 1983 NYPL [JLD 86-1047]

La protección del desempleo en España y en los países de las Comunidades Europeas /. Pérez Menayo, Vicente. [Madrid] [1980?] 303 p. : ISBN 84-500-3715-8 LC Card 83-240633 DDC 368.4/4/00946 19
HD7096.S7 P47 1980 NYPL [JLE 87-705]

La puissance du rationnel /. Janicaud, Dominique, 1937- [Paris] , c1985. 386 p. ; ISBN 2-07-070343-6 : *NYPL [JFD 86-638]*

La question agraire dans le monde arabe . Khader, Bichara. Louvain-la-Neuve , 1984. 631 p. : LC Card 85-169871 DDC 338.1/095691 19
HD2057.5 .K45 1984 NYPL [JLE 86-654]

La Red de Jonás. México y Latinoamérica . (14) Medina Cervantes, José Ramón. El estado mexicano entre la inversión extranjera directa y los grupos privados de empresarios /. México, D.F. , 1984. 268 p. : ISBN 968-434-358-2 LC Card 86-222537
HG5162 .M43 1984

La Riconversione produttiva nell'edilizia / di V. Bentivegna ... [e altri] ; a cura di Enrico Fattinnanzi. Milano : F. Angeli, 1984, c1981. 319 p. : ill. ; 22 cm. On cover: Cespe, Centro studi di politica economica Partito comunista italiano. Includes bibliographical references.
1. Construction industry - Italy. 2. Housing rehabilitation - Italy. 3. Housing policy - Italy. 4. Buildings - Repair and reconstruction - Economic aspects - Italy. 5. Buildings - Remodeling for other use - Economic aspects - Italy. I. Bentivegna, V. (Vincenzo). II. Fattinnanzi, Enrico. III. CESPE (Organization). NYPL [JLD 86-3381]

La Riforma del salario / G. Benvenuto ... [et al.]. Milano : F. Angeli, c1984. 150 p. ; 22 cm. (Lavoro italiano/temi d'oggi . 1.2) LC Card 84-251133 DDC 331.2/945 19
1. Wages - Italy - Congresses. 2. Collective bargaining - Italy - Congresses. I. Benvenuto, Giorgio.
HD5034 .R54 1984 NYPL [JLD 86-1082]

La Riforma della legge bancaria : temi e prospettive / a cura di Pietro Abbadessa. Milano : Giuffrè, [1984] 283 p. ; 25 cm. (Quaderni di banca, borsa e titoli di credito . 5) Includes bibliographical references. ISBN 88-14-00126-X : LC Card 84-190853 DDC 346.45/082 344.50682 19
1. Banking law - Italy. 2. Credit - Law and legislation - Italy. I. Abbadessa, Pietro. II. Series.
LAW NYPL [JLE 86-3654]

La Rioja (Argentina : Province). Gabinete de Estudios Económicos y Territoriales. Análisis de la problemática actual y perspectivas futuras de las industrias vinícola y conservera hortofrutícola en La Rioja. [La Rioja, Argentina] , 1981. 97 p., [3] p. of plates : ISBN 84-7359-144-5 LC Card 86-146432
HD9384.A8 L323 1981

La Rosa, Michele, 1937- La sociologia del lavoro in Italia e in Francia / Michele La Rosa ; presentazione di Giuseppe Bonazzi. Milano : F. Angeli, [1979] 149 p. ; 22 cm. (Collana di sociologia ; 35) Bibliography: p. [145]-149. ISBN 88-20-41594-1 : LC Card 79-374935
1. Industrial sociology - Italy. 2. Industrial sociology - France. I. Title.
HD6957.I83 L37 NYPL [JLD 80-4048]

La sécurité d'emploi dans l'industrie de la construction au Québec . Leclerc, Claudine. [Quebec] , c1983. xii, 275 p. : ISBN 2-7637-7028-2 LC Card 84-126505 DDC 331.25/96 19
HD5718.B92 C248 1983
NYPL [JLE 86-3170]

La Serre, Françoise de. La Grande-Bretagne et la Communauté européenne / Françoise de La Serre. 1re éd. Paris : Presses universitaires de France, c1987. 223, [1] p. : ill., map ; 22 cm. (Perspectives internationales, 0243-2331) Bibliography: p. 223-[224]. ISBN 2-13-040114-7 : LC Card 87-165122
1. European Economic Community - Great Britain. 2. Great Britain - Economic policy - 1945-. 3. Great Britain - Politics and government - 1945-. 4. European Economic Community. I. Title. II. Series.
HC241.25.G7 L118 1987

La sociologia del lavoro in Italia e in Francia /. La Rosa, Michele, 1937- Milano [1979] 149 p. ; ISBN 88-20-41594-1 : LC Card 79-374935
HD6957.I83 L37 NYPL [JLD 80-4048]

La Televisión en España mañana : modelos televisivos y opciones ideológicas / edición a cargo de Enrique Bustamante y Justo Villafañe.1a ed. Madrid : Ente Público Radiotelevisión Madrid : Siglo XXI de España, 1986. 331 p. ; 22 cm. ISBN 84-323-0563-X LC Card 86-199326
1. Television broadcasting - Spain. 2. Public television - Spain. I. Bustamante Ramírez, Enrique. II. Villafañe, Justo.
HE8700.9.S63 T45 1986
NYPL [MWGV (Spain) 87-2054]

La valoración de bases imponibles en los impuestos sobre la renta y el patrimonio /. Poveda Blanco, Francisco. [Alicante] [1984?] 395 p. ; LC Card 84-216651 DDC 333.33/2/0946 19
HJ4125.S8 P68 1984 NYPL [JLE 86-1461]

La valutazione economica della vita umana . Tasgian, Astrig. Torino , 1980. 117 p. : LC Card 81-124532 DDC 331/.01/1 19
HD4904.7 .T34 1980 NYPL [JLE 86-1600]

La Vendée ouvrière . Regourd, Florence. Les Sables-d'Olonne [1981] 353 p., [16] p. of plates : ISBN 2-7188-0098-4 : LC Card 82-161939 DDC 331.89/294461 19
HD5376.V46 R43 1981
NYPL [JLF 85-1433]

La Vertenza sul costo del lavoro e le relazioni industriali / di G. Altieri ... [et al.]. Milano, Italy : F. Angeli, c1984. 243 p. : ill. ; 22 cm. (IRES CGIL . 1) Includes bibliographical references. LC Card 84-144150 DDC 338.5/1/0945 19
1. Labor costs - Italy - Addresses, essays, lectures. 2. Costs, Industrial - Italy - Addresses, essays, lectures. 3. Wages - Italy - Addresses, essays, lectures. 4. Collective labor agreements - Italy - Addresses, essays, lectures. 5. Industrial relations - Italy - Addresses, essays, lectures. I. Altieri, Giovanna.
HD5034 .V47 1984 NYPL [JLD 86-2858]

Laan, G. van der. The Computation and modelling of economic equilibria /. Amsterdam ; New York : xiv, 229 p. : ISBN 0-444-70285-7 LC Card 87-15666 DDC 339/.0724 19
HB145 .C64 1987

Labarca, Guillermo. Los bancos multinacionales en América Latina y la crisis del sistema capitalista / Guillermo Labarca ; [portada, Alberto Diez]. 1. ed. México, D.F. : Editorial Nueva Imagen, 1979. 201 p. ; 20 cm. (Serie Sociedad, proceso, coyuntura) Includes bibliographical references. ISBN 968-429-155-8 LC Card 80-123755
1. Banks and banking, Foreign - Latin America. 2. Investments, Foreign - Latin America. 3. Loans, Foreign - Latin America. 4. Latin America - Economic conditions - 1945-. I. Title.
HG2710.5.A6 L3 NYPL [JLC 81-147]

Labarge, Margaret Wade. Women in medieval life : a small sound of the trumpet / by Margaret Wade Labarge. London : Hamish Hamilton, 1986. xiv, 271 p. : ill. ; 24 cm. Includes index. Bibliography: p. [253]-257. ISBN 0-241-11809-3 :
1. Women - History - Middle Ages, 500-1500. 2. Women - Social conditions. I. Title.
NYPL [JLE 86-3838]

LABELS.
Conen, Dieter, 1951- Wirkung von Werbesprache . München , c1985. iii, 162 p., [7] p. of plates : ISBN 3-89003-021-1 LC Card 86-159595
HF5822 .C58 1985

Labidi, M. (Mourad) Comptabilité nationale / M. Labidi. Alger : Office des publications universitaires : Entreprise algérienne de presse, 1982. 381 p. : ill. ; 24 cm. Bibliography: p. 380-381. LC Card 84-237940
1. National income - Algeria - Accounting. I. Title.
HC815.Z9 I515 1982

LABOR ABSENTEEISM. see **ABSENTEEISM (LABOR)**

LABOR AGREEMENTS. see **COLLECTIVE LABOR AGREEMENTS.**

LABOR AND CAPITAL. see **INDUSTRIAL RELATIONS.**

LABOR AND CHRISTIANITY. see **CHURCH AND LABOR.**

Labor and development. Special issue.
Martens, George R. Trade unionism and politics in Niger. Lome, Togo [1986] 93 p. ; LC Card 86-172446 DDC 322/.2/09669 19
HD6882.Z65 M37 1986

Trade unionism in the republic of Mali . [Lome, Togo] [1983] 78 p. : LC Card 87-107028 DDC 331.88/0966/23 19
HD8827.A5 U557 1983

LABOR AND LABORING CLASSES - 1970-
The Changing world of work, major issues ahead . Geneva , 1986- v. <1 > : ISBN 92-2-105165-X (pbk. : pt. 1) : LC Card 86-214807 DDC 331 19
HD4854 .C42 1986

LABOR AND LABORING CLASSES - ACCIDENTS. see INDUSTRIAL ACCIDENTS.

LABOR AND LABORING CLASSES - ADDRESSES, ESSAYS, LECTURES.
Confrontation, class consciousness, and the labor process . Westport, Conn. , 1986. viii, 261 p. ; ISBN 0-313-25140-1 (lib. bdg. : alk. paper) LC Card 85-17734 DDC 305.5/62 19
HD4851 .C63 1986 ***NYPL [JLE 86-3558]***

Job stress and blue collar work /. Chichester [West Sussex] , New York , c1985. ix, 243 p. : ISBN 0-471-90811-8 : LC Card 85-12022 DDC 158.7 19
HF5548.85 .J64 1985 ***NYPL [JLE 86-2412]***

Les Sauvages dans la cité . Seyssel , c1985. 229 p. ; ISBN 2-903528-53-5
NYPL [JLD 86-1133]

LABOR AND LABORING CLASSES - AFRICA - ADDRESSES, ESSAYS, LECTURES.
Struggle for the city . Beverly Hills , c1983. 319 p. : ISBN 0-8039-2067-9 LC Card 83-11196 DDC 305.5/62/096 19
HD8774 .S87 1983 ***NYPL [JLD 83-3496]***

LABOR AND LABORING CLASSES - AFRICA, SUB-SAHARAN - HISTORY.
Coquery-Vidrovitch, Catherine. [Afrique noire. English.] Africa . Berkeley , c1988. p. cm. ISBN 0-520-05679-5 (alk. paper) LC Card 87-15316 DDC 967 19
HC800 .C67513 1988

LABOR AND LABORING CLASSES - ARGENTINA - CONGRESSES.
La Clase obrera argentina . Buenos Aires , 1986. 136 p. ; LC Card 86-206788
HD8266.5 .C57 1986

LABOR AND LABORING CLASSES - ARGENTINA - HISTORY.
Falcón, Ricardo. El mundo del trabajo urbano, 1890-1914 /. Buenos Aires , c1986. 141 p. ; ISBN 950-25-1414-2 : LC Card 87-101423
HD8266 .F35 1986

LABOR AND LABORING CLASSES - ARGENTINA - HISTORY - 20TH CENTURY.
Isuani, Ernesto A. (Ernesto Aldo) Los orígenes conflictivos de la seguridad social argentina /. Buenos Aires , c1985. 140 p. ; ISBN 950-25-0128-4 : LC Card 86-174656
HD7149 .I88 1985

LABOR AND LABORING CLASSES - ARGENTINA - MENDOZA (PROVINCE) - HISTORY - 20TH CENTURY.
Vélez, Roberto. Reseña histórica del 1o de mayo en Mendoza . Buenos Aires , 1983. 125 p. : LC Card 87-400123 DDC 394.2/683 19
HD7791 .V4 1983

LABOR AND LABORING CLASSES - ARGENTINA - POLITICAL ACTIVITY - HISTORY.
Fernández, Arturo. Ideologías de los grupos dirigentes sindicales /. Buenos Aires , c1986. 2 v. ; ISBN 950-25-1403-3 (v. 1) LC Card 86-205687
HD6603.5 .F47 1986

LABOR AND LABORING CLASSES - ARMENIA S.S.R. - HISTORY.
Karapetian, H. S. (Hovhannes Smbati) Sovetakan Hayastani banvor dasakargi dzevavorumě ev zargats'umě (1920-1940) /. Erevan , 1980. 272 p., [1] leaf of plates : LC Card 83-129694
HD8529.A692 K37 1980

LABOR AND LABORING CLASSES - AUSTRALIA - HISTORY - 19TH CENTURY.
Burgmann, Verity. In our time . Sydney , Boston , 1985. xii, 236 p., [24] p. of plates : ISBN 0-86861-529-3 LC Card 84-71572 DDC 335/.00994 19
HD8846 .B87 1985 ***NYPL [JLD 86-2788]***

LABOR AND LABORING CLASSES - AUSTRIA - HISTORY.
Riesenfellner, Stefan. Der Sozialreporter . Wien , c1987. vi, 278 p. ; ISBN 3-900351-67-8 LC Card 87-137993 DDC 305.5/62/09436 19
HD8410 .R54 1987

LABOR AND LABORING CLASSES - AUSTRIA - STYRIA - HISTORY - 19TH CENTURY.
Auf dem Weg in die Freiheit . Graz , 1984. 356 p. : LC Card 87-672377
HD8419.S82 A93x 1984

LABOR AND LABORING CLASSES - AUSTRIA - STYRIA - HISTORY - 20TH CENTURY.
Auf dem Weg in die Freiheit . Graz , 1984. 356 p. : LC Card 87-672377
HD8419.S82 A93x 1984

LABOR AND LABORING CLASSES - AUSTRIA - VORARLBERG - HISTORY.
Im Prinzip, Hoffnung . Bregenz , c1984. 368 p. : ISBN 3-900438-07-9 LC Card 86-120542 DDC 331.88/09436/45 19
HD6679.V67 I4 1984 ***NYPL [JLD 87-1568]***

LABOR AND LABORING CLASSES - BIOGRAPHY - DICTIONARIES.
Maitron, Jean. Dictionnaire biographique du mouvement ouvrier international. Paris, 1971-<c1985. <1-2, 5 > ISBN 2-7082-1955-3 (v. 2) LC Card 72-333529
HD4851 .M34

LABOR AND LABORING CLASSES - BOLIVIA - HISTORY.
Bolivia, hoy /. México, D.F. , 1983. 240 p. ; LC Card 84-148626 DDC 330.984/05 19
HC182 .B565 1983 ***NYPL [JLD 86-2825]***

LABOR AND LABORING CLASSES - BOLIVIA - HISTORY - COLLECTED WORKS.
Taboada Terán, Néstor. Historia de las luchas sociales y el movimiento obrero en Bolivia /. Cochabamba, Bolivia , 1983- v. <1-3 > : LC Card 86-203884 DDC 331.88/0984 19
HD8275 .T32 1983

LABOR AND LABORING CLASSES - BOLIVIA - LA PAZ.
Sector formal de la ciudad de La Paz . La Paz, Bolivia , 1980. 77 leaves ; LC Card 81-212597 DDC 331.1/0984/12 19
HD5751.L36 S42 1980 ***NYPL [JLF 87-369]***

LABOR AND LABORING CLASSES - BOLIVIA - POLITICAL ACTIVITY.

LABOR AND LABORING CLASSES - BRAZIL.
Singer, Paul Israel, 1932- A formação da classe operária /. Campinas-SP , São Paulo-SP [1986] 80 p. : LC Card 86-224636
HD4841 .S32 1986

LABOR AND LABORING CLASSES - BRAZIL - HISTORY.
Penteado Neto, Alfredo Camargo, 1939- Organizações de trabalhadores . São Paulo , 1986. 112 p. : LC Card 87-403488 DDC 338.6 19
HD5650 .P37 1986

LABOR AND LABORING CLASSES - BRAZIL - HISTORY - PICTORIAL WORKS.
1o. de maio . [São Paulo] , 1985. 80 p. : LC Card 86-200658
HD8286 .A13 1985

LABOR AND LABORING CLASSES - BRAZIL - MARANHÃO - POLITICAL ACTIVITY - HISTORY.
Corrêa, Rossini. Mudança social no Nordeste . São Luís , 1986. 176 p., [6] p. of plates : LC Card 87-152221 DDC 322/.2/098121 19
HD8289.M37 C67 1986

LABOR AND LABORING CLASSES - BRAZIL - SÃO PAULO (STATE)
Khoury, Yara Aun. As greves de 1917 em São Paulo e o processo de organização proletária /. São Paulo , 1981. 221 p. ; LC Card 81-210934 DDC 331.2/98161 19
HD5355.S26 K48 1981
NYPL [JLD 86-3514]

LABOR AND LABORING CLASSES - BRITISH COLUMBIA - HISTORY - 20TH CENTURY.
Fighting heritage . Vancouver [1986?] 159 p., [32] p. of plates : ISBN 0-9692365-0-6 (pbk.) LC Card 86-231043 DDC 331.88/09711 19
HD8109.B72 F54 1986

LABOR AND LABORING CLASSES - BULGARIA.
Bâldescu, Emil. Din istoria legăturilor revoluționare româno-bulgare (1909-1916) [microform]. [București, 1966] 181 p. LC Card 81-475045
HD8646 .B34 ***NYPL [*ZT-1732 no.1]***

Petkov, Todor (Todor Iliev) Stopanska samostoi͡atelnost i stopanska otgovornost /. Sofii͡a , 1985. 237 p. ; LC Card 85-134177
HD8626.5 .P48 1985

LABOR AND LABORING CLASSES - BULGARIA - DEVNI͡A - BIOGRAPHY.
Biografii͡a ot mnogo imena . Sofii͡a , 1983. 232 p. : LC Card 84-163061
HD8627.A1 B56 1983

LABOR AND LABORING CLASSES - BULGARIA - POLITICAL ACTIVITY - HISTORY.
Vŭznikvane, razvitie i zalez na oportiūnizma v bŭlgarskoto rabotnichesko dvizhenie, 1891/1948 /. Sofii͡a , 1986. 696 p. ; LC Card 86-200229
HD8628 .V89 1986

LABOR AND LABORING CLASSES - BULGARIA - VARNENSKI OKRŬG - HISTORY.
Rabotnicheskoto profsŭi͡uzno dvizhenie vŭv Varnenski okrŭg /. Sofii͡a , 1985. 348 p., [16] p. of plates : LC Card 86-111781
HD8629.V372 R37 1985

LABOR AND LABORING CLASSES - BYELORUSSIAN S.S.R. - HISTORY - 19TH CENTURY.
Bich, M. O. Rabochee dvizhenie v Belorussii v 1861-1904 gg. /. Minsk , 1983. 278 p. ; LC Card 83-182369
HD8529.B952 B52 1983
NYPL [*QM 87-2378]

LABOR AND LABORING CLASSES - CANADA - ADDRESSES, ESSAYS, LECTURES.
Working Canadians . Toronto , New York , c1984. x, 380 p. ; ISBN 0-458-97370-X (pbk.) : LC Card 84-222036 DDC 331/.0971 19
HD6957.C2 W67 1984 ***NYPL [JLD 87-681]***

LABOR AND LABORING CLASSES - CANADA - HISTORY.
Seymour, Edward E. An illustrated history of Canadian labour, 1800-1974 /. Ottawa , 1980. xiv, 95 p. :

LABOR AND LABORING CLASSES - CASE STUDIES.
Automation and industrial workers . Oxford [Oxfordshire] , New York , 1979- v. : ISBN 0-08-023339-2 (v. 1, pt. 1) : LC Card 79-40811 DDC 331
HD6331 .A93 1979 ***NYPL [JLM 82-242]***

Work in market and industrial societies /. Albany , c1984. viii, 316 p. ; ISBN 0-87395-810-1 LC Card 83-9267 DDC 306/.36 19
HD4901 .A659 1984 ***NYPL [JLE 86-4483]***

LABOR AND LABORING CLASSES - CHILD LABOR. see CHILDREN - EMPLOYMENT.

LABOR AND LABORING CLASSES - CHILE.
Clases sociales y acción obrera en Chile /. México, D.F. , 1986. 230 p. ; ISBN 968-12-0326-7 LC Card 87-404023 DDC 331/.0983 19
HD8296.5 .C57 1986

Ruiz-Tagle P., Jaime. El sindicalismo chileno después del plan laboral /. Santiago, Chile [1985?] 211 p. ; ***NYPL [JLD 87-1182]***

LABOR AND LABORING CLASSES - CHINA.
Walder, Andrew George. Communist neo-traditionalism . Berkeley , c1986. xxi, 302 p. ; ISBN 0-520-05439-3 (alk. paper) LC Card

85-27093 DDC 306/.36/0951 19
HD8736.5 .W34 1986 ***NYPL [JLD 86-3749]***

LABOR AND LABORING CLASSES - CHINA - HISTORY - 20TH CENTURY.
Chung-kuo kung jen yün tung ti hsien ch'ü. Pei-ching , 1983- v. : LC Card 84-231479 DDC 322/.2/0951 19
HD8736 .C496 1983 <Orien China> ***NYPL [*OVY 87-4134]***

LABOR AND LABORING CLASSES - COLLECTED WORKS.
Gauny, Gabriel, 1806-1889. [Selections. 1983.] Le philosophe plébéien /. Paris , Saint-Denis , c1983. 205 p. ; ISBN 2-7071-1420-0 : LC Card 84-105473
HD4853 .G382 1983

LABOR AND LABORING CLASSES - COLOMBIA - BARRANCABERMEJA.
Yunis, José. Barrancabermeja . Bogotá , 1986. 102 p. : ISBN 958-9096-03-4 LC Card 87-400984 DDC 331.7/6223382/0986125 19
HD8310.B372 Y86 1986

LABOR AND LABORING CLASSES - CONDUCT OF LIFE.
Szathmári, Gábor. Kinek lehet igaza? . Budapest , 1985. 118 p. ; ISBN 963-322-273-7 : LC Card 86-156416
HD6955 .S975 1985

LABOR AND LABORING CLASSES - CONNECTICUT.
Asher, Robert. Connecticut workers and technological change . Storrs , c1983. 100 p. : LC Card 83-62409 DDC 306/.3/09746 19
HD8083.C7 A83 1983 ***NYPL [JLE 86-1507]***

LABOR AND LABORING CLASSES - CONNECTICUT - INTERVIEWS.
Palmer, Michele. Catalogue of interviews . [Storrs, Conn.] , 1983. ii, 79 p. ; LC Card 86-621476 DDC 331.12/09746 19
HD6331.2.U52 C86 1983

LABOR AND LABORING CLASSES - COSTA RICA - HISTORY.
Acuña Ortega, Víctor H. Los orígenes de la clase obrera en Costa Rica . San José [1986] 85 p. : LC Card 87-402904 DDC 331/.097286 19
HD8136 .A28 1986

LABOR AND LABORING CLASSES - COSTA RICA - POLITICAL ACTIVITY - HISTORY.
Historia gráfica de las luchas populares en Costa Rica, 1870-1930. San José, Costa Rica , 1986- v. <1 > : ISBN 997-7944-12-1 (v. 1) LC Card 87-158835 DDC 305.5/62/097286 19
HD8138 .H57 1986

LABOR AND LABORING CLASSES - CUBA.
Cantón Navarro, José, 1925- Algunas ideas de José Martí en relación con la clase obrera y el socialismo /. La Habana , 1981, c1980. 174 p. ; LC Card 82-233789 DDC 320.5/31/097291 19
HX159 .C33 1981 ***NYPL [JLD 86-1423]***

LABOR AND LABORING CLASSES - CUBA - HISTORY.
Córdova, Efrén. Castro and the Cuban labor movement . Lanham, MD , c1987. xii, 341 p. ; ISBN 0-8191-5952-2 (alk. paper) : LC Card 86-28159 DDC 322/.2/097291 19
HD6578.5 .C67 1987

LABOR AND LABORING CLASSES - CUBA - POLITICAL ACTIVITY.
Riesgo, Rodolfo. Cuba, el movimiento obrero y su entorno socio-politico, 1865-1983 /. Miami , 1985. 251 p. ; ISBN 0-917049-02-0 (pbk.) LC Card 86-673864
HD6578.5 .R53x 1985

LABOR AND LABORING CLASSES - CZECHOSLOVAKIA - BIOGRAPHY.
Brzoň, František. Marie a František Kalkusovi /. České Budějovice , 1985. 98 p., [64] p. of plates : LC Card 86-161741
HD8420.3.A1 B78 1985

LABOR AND LABORING CLASSES - CZECHOSLOVAKIA - HISTORY.
Riesenfellner, Stefan. Der Sozialreporter . Wien , c1987. vi, 278 p. ; ISBN 3-900351-67-8 LC Card 87-137993 DDC 305.5/62/09436 19
HD8410 .R54 1987

LABOR AND LABORING CLASSES - DĄBROWA BASIN (POLAND AND CZECHOSLOVAKIA) - HISTORY.
Walczak, Jan. Robotnicze drogi Śląska i Zagłębia Dąbrowskiego do roku 1939 /. Katowice , 1985. 493 p. ; ISBN 83-7008-096-0 : LC Card 86-101066
HD8539.S52 W35 1985

LABOR AND LABORING CLASSES - DENMARK - FÅBORG (FYNS AMT) - HISTORY - 19TH CENTURY.
Venge, Mikael. Arbejdere og socialdemokrater i Faaborg omkring 1900 /. [Fåborg] , 1986. 72 p. : ISBN 87-88421-01-5 LC Card 87-144687
HD6745.F33 V46 1986

LABOR AND LABORING CLASSES - DENMARK - HISTORY - 19TH CENTURY.
Christiansen, Niels Finn. Arbejderbevægelsens forhistorie . [Copenhagen] , 1986. 188 p. : ISBN 87-87739-21-6 : LC Card 87-145749
HD6742 .C495 1986

LABOR AND LABORING CLASSES - DEVELOPING COUNTRIES.
International labour and the Third World . Aldershot, Hants, England , c1987. xii, 283 p. ; ISBN 0-566-00971-4 : LC Card 86-31791 DDC 331/.09172/4 19
HD8943 .I55 1987

LABOR AND LABORING CLASSES - DICTIONARIES - GERMAN.
Siderēs, Euthymios G., 1957- Germanoellēniko lexiko horologias /. Athēna , 1984. 183 p. ; LC Card 86-180116
HD4839 .S56 1984

LABOR AND LABORING CLASSES - DISCIPLINE. see **LABOR DISCIPLINE.**

LABOR AND LABORING CLASSES - DOMINICAN REPUBLIC.
Duarte, Isis. Trabajadores urbanos . Santo Domingo, República Dominicana , c1986. 314 p. ; LC Card 87-402153 DDC 331/.097293 19
HD8218.5 .D83 1986

LABOR AND LABORING CLASSES - DOMINICAN REPUBLIC - HISTORY.
Orbe, Justino José del. Mauricio Báez y la clase obrera /. Santo Domingo, República Dominicana , 1981. 158 p. : LC Card 82-138627 DDC 331.88/092/4 B 19
HD6584.Z55 B346 1981 ***NYPL [JLE 86-3246]***

LABOR AND LABORING CLASSES - DWELLINGS - ALGERIA.
Boubekeur, Sid, 1952- L'habitat en Algérie . Lyon , c1986. 256 p. : ISBN 2-7297-0272-5 : LC Card 86-217640
HD7372.4.A3 B68 1986

LABOR AND LABORING CLASSES - DWELLINGS - BRAZIL - SÃO PAULO.
Blay, Eva Alterman. Eu não tenho onde morar . São Paulo, SP [1985] 332 p. : ISBN 85-21-30298-3 : LC Card 85-211285
HD7323.S28 B56 1985

LABOR AND LABORING CLASSES - DWELLINGS - DOMINICAN REPUBLIC - STATISTICS.
Gómez, Carmen. Población y vivienda en la República Dominicana . Santo Domingo, República Dominicana , 1984. 116 p. : LC Card 85-154466
HD7316.5.A3 G65 1984 ***NYPL [JLF 86-1146]***

LABOR AND LABORING CLASSES - DWELLINGS - GERMANY - HISTORY - 19TH CENTURY - CONGRESSES.
Arbeitersiedlungen im 19. Jahrhundert . Bochum , c1985. 189 p. : ISBN 3-88339-427-0 LC Card 85-164690
HD7289.5.A3 G42 1985

LABOR AND LABORING CLASSES - DWELLINGS - RÉUNION.
L'Habitat réunionnais /. Saint-Denis [1983] 73 p., A-T leaves of plates : LC Card 84-981007
HD7378.9.A3 H33 1983

LABOR AND LABORING CLASSES - DWELLINGS - UNITED STATES - ADDRESSES, ESSAYS, LECTURES.
Critical perspectives on housing /. Philadelphia , 1986. xxi, 686 p. : ISBN 0-87722-395-5 LC Card 85-17274 DDC 363.5/0973 19
HD7293 .C738 1986 ***NYPL [JLE 86-3639]***

LABOR AND LABORING CLASSES - ECUADOR - HISTORY.
Ycaza, Patricio. Historia del movimiento obrero ecuatoriano . Quito , 1984. 371 p. :
NYPL [JLB 86-21]

LABOR AND LABORING CLASSES - ECUADOR - HISTORY - 20TH CENTURY.
Capelo C., J. Alejo (J. Alejo Capelo Cabello), d. 1973. El crimen del 15 de noviembre de 1922 /. [Guayaquil] , 1983. 10, 14, 19 p. : LC Card 86-114097
HD5358.A6 C36 1983

Masas, luchas, solidaridad /. [S.l. , 1985] ([Guayaquil] : Litografía e Impr. de la Universidad de Guayaquil) 298 p. : LC Card 86-177888
HD8316 .M37 1985

LABOR AND LABORING CLASSES - ECUADOR - HISTORY - SOURCES.
Movimiento obrero del Ecuador, 1970-1979 . Guayaquil, Ecuador [1985] 300 p. ; LC Card 86-105256 DDC 331.88/09866 19
HD6627 .M68 1985 ***NYPL [JLD 86-3140]***

LABOR AND LABORING CLASSES - EDUCATION - BULGARIA.
Ikonomicheskiiat podkhod i ikonomicheskoto vŭzpitanie na trudeshtite se. Sliven , 1984. 195 p. ; LC Card 86-102634
HB74.9.B9 I37 1984

Izsledvane roliata na proizvodstvenata sreda, trudovite kolektivi i nastavnitsite za formirane na komunistichesko otnoshenie kŭm truda u podrastvashchtite /. Sofiia , 1984. 150 p. ; LC Card 85-166784
HD6276.B82 I97 1984

LABOR AND LABORING CLASSES - EDUCATION - EUROPE.
Verso un sistema di orientamento . Rimini , c1984. 290 p. : LC Card 85-119196 DDC 370.11/3/094 19
LC5056.I8 V47 1984 ***NYPL [JLE 86-1555]***

LABOR AND LABORING CLASSES - EDUCATION - ITALY.
Verso un sistema di orientamento . Rimini , c1984. 290 p. : LC Card 85-119196 DDC 370.11/3/094 19
LC5056.I8 V47 1984 ***NYPL [JLE 86-1555]***

LABOR AND LABORING CLASSES - EGYPT - HISTORY.
Beinin, Joel, 1948- Workers on the Nile . Princeton, N.J. , c1987. xix, 488 p. : ISBN 0-691-05506-8 (alk. paper) : LC Card 87-45510 DDC 305.5/62/0962 19
HD8786 .B45 1987

LABOR AND LABORING CLASSES - EGYPT - POLITICAL ACTIVITY.
Goldberg, Ellis. Tinker, tailor, and textile worker . Berkeley , 1986. xiii, 234 p. : ISBN 0-520-05353-2 (alk. paper) LC Card 85-16472 DDC 322.4/4/0962 19
HD8786 .G65 1986 ***NYPL [JLE 87-500]***

LABOR AND LABORING CLASSES - ENGLAND - DURHAM (COUNTY) - HISTORY - 20TH CENTURY.
But the world goes on the same . Whitley Bay, Tyne & Wear , 1979. 106 p. : LC Card 81-107503
HD8399.D872 B87 1979

LABOR AND LABORING CLASSES - ENGLAND - PRESTON (LANCASHIRE) - POLITICAL ACTIVITY - HISTORY.
Savage, Michael. The dynamics of working-class politics . Cambridge [Cambridgeshire] , New York , 1987. xii, 280 p. : LC Card 87-14636 DDC 322/.2/0941 19
HD8397.P74 S28 1987

LABOR AND LABORING CLASSES - EUROPE.
La Flexibilité du travail en Europe . Paris , 1986. 330 p. : ISBN 2-7071-1598-3 : LC Card 86-173845
HD8376.5 .F57 1986

LABOR AND LABORING CLASSES - EUROPE - CONGRESSES.
Technology and work . London , Dover, N.H. , c1986. 304 p. : ISBN 0-7099-3801-2 : LC Card 86-4202 DDC 303.4/83 19
HC244.Z9 T475 1986 ***NYPL [JLD 86-2160]***

LABOR AND LABORING CLASSES - EUROPE, EASTERN.
Matejko, Aleksander. Comparative work

systems . New York , 1986. xx, 237 p. ; ISBN 0-03-004492-8 (alk. paper) : LC Card 85-6354 DDC 306/.36/0947 19
HD6957.E82 M37 1985
NYPL [JLE 86-1083]

Rabochiĭ klass i stroitel'stvo sotsializma v stranakh TSentral'noĭ i IUgo-Vostochnoĭ Evropy /. Moskva , 1977. 382 p. ; LC Card 81-174150
HD8376.5 .R33 1977

LABOR AND LABORING CLASSES - EUROPE, EASTERN - CONGRESSES.
Technology and work . London , Dover, N.H. , c1986. 304 p. : ISBN 0-7099-3801-2 : LC Card 86-4202 DDC 303.4/83 19
HC244.Z9 T475 1986 ***NYPL [JLD 86-2160]***

LABOR AND LABORING CLASSES - EUROPE - HISTORY - 19TH CENTURY.
Labor migration in the Atlantic economies . Westport, Conn. , 1985. xvi, 491 p. : ISBN 0-313-24637-8 (lib. bdg. : alk. paper) LC Card 85-7975 DDC 331.12/7 19
HD8375 .L33 1985 ***NYPL [JLE 86-1127]***

LABOR AND LABORING CLASSES - EUROPE - HISTORY - 19TH CENTURY - CONGRESSES.
Arbeiter und Bürger im 19. Jahrhundert . München , 1986. xiv, 342 p. ; ISBN 3-486-52871-8 LC Card 86-212379
HD8376 .A72 1986

LABOR AND LABORING CLASSES - EUROPE - POLITICAL ACTIVITY.
Rabochee dvizhenie v razvitykh kapitalisticheskikh stranakh . Moskva , 1987. 268 p. ; LC Card 87-164460
HD8378 .R29 1987

LABOR AND LABORING CLASSES - EUROPE - POLITICAL ACTIVITY - HISTORY - 19TH CENTURY.
Europäische Arbeiterbewegungen im 19. Jahrhundert . Göttingen , c1983. 169 p. ; ISBN 3-525-33488-5 (pbk.) LC Card 87-672976
HD8378 .E97x 1983

LABOR AND LABORING CLASSES - FINLAND - HISTORY.
Mansner, Markku. Suomalaista yhteiskuntaa rakentamassa . Helsinki [1984] 552 p., [4] p. of plates : ISBN 951-9240-75-6 LC Card 85-130291
HD8533 .M345 1984

LABOR AND LABORING CLASSES - FORECASTING - CONGRESSES.
Arbeit 2000 . Hamburg , 1985. 236 p. : ISBN 3-87975-314-8 LC Card 86-143070
HD4813 .A68 1985

LABOR AND LABORING CLASSES - FRANCE.
Aglietta, Michel. Les métamorphoses de la société salariale . Paris , c1984. 274 p. ; ISBN 2-7021-1230-7 : LC Card 84-176554 DDC 331/.0944 19
HD8431 .A36 1984 ***NYPL [JLD 87-478]***

Naville, Pierre. La maîtrise du salariat /. Paris , c1984. 153 p. ; ISBN 2-7157-1099-2 : LC Card 85-100916
HD6957.F8 N38 1984 ***NYPL [JLD 87-333]***

Tableaux de l'état physique et moral des salariés en France /. Paris , 1986. 237 p. ; ISBN 2-7071-1626-2 : LC Card 87-122301
HD8431 .T32 1986

LABOR AND LABORING CLASSES - FRANCE - HISTORY.
Bron, Jean. La lutte des classes aujourd'hui, 1950-1981 /. Paris , 1982. 318 p. ; ISBN 2-7082-0349-5 ***NYPL [JLD 86-1408]***

Debès, Joseph. L'appel de la J.O.C., 1926-1928 /. Paris , 1986. 292 p. : ISBN 2-204-02529-1 : LC Card 86-189508
HD8430 .D37 1986

LABOR AND LABORING CLASSES - FRANCE - HISTORY - 20TH CENTURY.
Delaunay, Jean Claude. Salariat et plus-value en France depuis la fin du XIXe siècle /. Paris , c1984. xiv, 304 p. : ISBN 2-7246-0488-1 : LC Card 84-172193 DDC 331.2/944 19
HB206 .D45 1984 ***NYPL [JLD 86-426]***

Rabochiĭ klass v proshlom i nastoiashchem . Moskva , 1984, c1983. 255 p. ; LC Card 84-169518
HD4854 .R273 1984

LABOR AND LABORING CLASSES - FRANCE - HISTORY - CONGRESSES.
Work in France . Ithaca , 1986. 576 p. : ISBN 0-8014-1697-3 (alk. paper) LC Card 85-22352 DDC 331/.0944 19
HD8428 .W67 1986 ***NYPL [JLE 86-1960]***

LABOR AND LABORING CLASSES - FRANCE - INFORMATION SERVICES - FRANCE.
Faire l'histoire du monde du travail . [Seyssel] : [Le Creusot] : 52 p. : ISBN 2-903528-49-7 : LC Card 85-180268 DDC 305.5/62/072044 19
HD8428 .F35 1985 ***NYPL [JLD 87-1157]***

LABOR AND LABORING CLASSES - FRANCE - PICTORIAL WORKS.
Kollar, François, 1904- La France travaille /. Paris , c1986. 238 p. : ISBN 2-85108-435-6 LC Card 87-108516
HD8430 .K65 1986

LABOR AND LABORING CLASSES - FRANCE - POLITICAL ACTIVITY.
Kolomiĭtsev, Valentin Fedorovich. Rabochiĭ klass i profsoiuzy Frantsii v bor'ybe protiv monopoliĭ, 1968-1981 gody /. Moskva , 1981. 173 p. ; LC Card 82-134380
HD8435 .K65 1981

Lash, Scott. The militant worker . London , 1984. vii, 264 p. ; ISBN 0-435-82516-X LC Card 87-673366
HD8076 .L37x 1984b

LABOR AND LABORING CLASSES - FRANCE - RESEARCH - FRANCE.
Faire l'histoire du monde du travail . [Seyssel] : [Le Creusot] : 52 p. : ISBN 2-903528-49-7 : LC Card 85-180268 DDC 305.5/62/072044 19
HD8428 .F35 1985 ***NYPL [JLD 87-1157]***

LABOR AND LABORING CLASSES - FRANCE - VENDÉE - HISTORY.
Regourd, Florence. La Vendée ouvrière . Les Sables-d'Olonne [1981] 353 p., [16] p. of plates : ISBN 2-7188-0098-4 : LC Card 82-161939 DDC 331.89/294461 19
HD5376.V46 R43 1981
NYPL [JLF 85-1433]

LABOR AND LABORING CLASSES - FRENCH GUIANA - CONGRESSES.
Les Travailleurs antillais, guyanais, réunionnais en lutte contre le colonialisme et le racisme, pour le droit à la différence et l'unité des travailleurs. Paris , c1980. 89 p., [4] p. of plates : ISBN 2-903033-10-2 LC Card 84-164737
HD8250 .T73 1980

LABOR AND LABORING CLASSES - GERMANY.
Germanskiĭ trudovoĭ front . Berlin , 1943. 69 leaves : LC Card 85-204295
HD8443.D43 G47 1943

LABOR AND LABORING CLASSES - GERMANY - ATTITUDES - HISTORY - 19TH CENTURY.
Simon, Dan, 1937- Das Frankreichbild der deutschen Arbeiterbewegung 1859-1865 /. [Gerlingen] , 1984. 334 p. ; ISBN 3-88350-451-3 LC Card 84-173175
HD8450 .S56 1984 ***NYPL [JLD 86-2711]***

LABOR AND LABORING CLASSES - GERMANY - BIOGRAPHY.
Eberle, Eugen, 1908- Die schlaflosen Nächte des Eugen E. . Stuttgart , 1982. 281 p. : ISBN 3-922836-06-2 LC Card 83-173587 DDC 305.5/62/0924 B 19
HD8453.E2 A37 1982 ***NYPL [JFD 87-3745]***

The German worker . Berkeley , c1987. p. cm. ISBN 0-520-05972-7 (alk. paper) LC Card 87-5076 DDC 305.5/62/0922 B 19
HD8453.A1 G47 1987

LABOR AND LABORING CLASSES - GERMANY, EAST.
Berlin. Parteihochschule "Karl Marx." Lehrstuhl Wissenschaftlicher Kommunismus. Zur Entwicklung der Klassen und Schichten in der DDR /. Berlin , 1977. 147 p. ; LC Card 78-358768
HN460.5.Z9 S62 ***NYPL [JLD 79-2817]***

LABOR AND LABORING CLASSES - GERMANY - HISTORY.
Klönne, Arno. Die deutsche Arbeiterbewegung . Düsseldorf , Köln , 1980. 382 p. ; ISBN 3-424-00652-1 : LC Card 81-453558 DDC 322/.2/0943 19
HX276 .K547 ***NYPL [JLD 81-689]***

Population, labour, and migration in 19th- and 20th-century Germany /. Leamington Spa [UK] ; New York : xii, 200 p. : ISBN 0-85496-503-3 : LC Card 86-24470 DDC 331.6/2/0943 19
HD5856.G3 P66 1987

Surmann, Rolf. Die Münzenberg-Legende . Köln , c1983. 307 p. : ISBN 3-922009-53-0 LC Card 83-155325
HD8450 .S87 1983

LABOR AND LABORING CLASSES - GERMANY - HISTORY - 19TH CENTURY.
The German worker . Berkeley , c1987. p. cm. ISBN 0-520-05972-7 (alk. paper) LC Card 87-5076 DDC 305.5/62/0922 B 19
HD8453.A1 G47 1987

Kocka, Jürgen. Lohnarbeit und Klassenbildung . Berlin , c1983. 207 p. ; ISBN 3-8012-0088-4 LC Card 83-169041
HD8449 .K63 1983

LABOR AND LABORING CLASSES - GERMANY - HISTORY - 20TH CENTURY.
Eberle, Eugen, 1908- Die schlaflosen Nächte des Eugen E. . Stuttgart , 1982. 281 p. : ISBN 3-922836-06-2 LC Card 83-173587 DDC 305.5/62/0924 B 19
HD8453.E2 A37 1982 ***NYPL [JFD 87-3745]***

Smelser, Ronald, 1942- Robert Ley, Hitler's labor leader /. New York , 1988. p. cm. ISBN 0-85496-161-5 : LC Card 87-20960 DDC 331/.092/4 B 19
HD8453.L49 S64 1988

Stollberg, Gunnar. Die Rationalisierungsdebatte 1908-1933 . Frankfurt/Main , New York , c1981. 214 p. ; ISBN 3-593-32938-7 : LC Card 81-177695 DDC 331.88/0943 19
HD70.G2 S666 1981 ***NYPL [JLD 86-1662]***

LABOR AND LABORING CLASSES - GERMANY, WEST.
Arbeiterklasse, gibt's die noch? /. Wien , c1985. 246 p. : ISBN 3-900351-46-5 LC Card 86-123225
HD8451 .A836 1985

Kulidasein oder Klassenkampf . Berlin , 1925. 31 p. ; LC Card 86-207601
HD8451 .K84 1925

Voss, G. Günter. Bewusstsein ohne Subjekt? . Grosshesselohe , 1984. vi, 512 p. : ISBN 3-924346-07-0 : LC Card 85-131494
HD6957.G35 V67 1984

LABOR AND LABORING CLASSES - GERMANY, WEST - ATTITUDES.
Gewandelte Werte, erstarrte Strukturen . Bonn , c1985. ix, 329 p. : ISBN 3-87831-423-X LC Card 86-117688 DDC 330/.0943 19
HD8451 .G54 1985

LABOR AND LABORING CLASSES - GERMANY (WEST) - BERGISCHES LAND - CONGRESSES.
Die Wirtschaftliche Entwicklung in den Arbeitsmarktregionen des Bergischen Landes . Bochum , 1981. 401 p. : ISBN 3-88339-217-0 LC Card 82-164818 DDC 331/.0943/55 19
HD8459.N66 W57 1981
NYPL [JLD 86-1639]

LABOR AND LABORING CLASSES - GERMANY (WEST) - BIOGRAPHY.
Deppe, Wilfried. Drei Generationen Arbeiterleben . Frankfurt/Main , New York , c1982. 419 p. ; ISBN 3-593-33018-0 LC Card 82-167833 DDC 305.5/62/0922 19
HD6957.G3 D38 1982
NYPL [JLD 86-2569]

LABOR AND LABORING CLASSES - GERMANY (WEST) - DÜSSELDORF - HISTORY - 19TH CENTURY.
Lenger, Friedrich. Zwischen Kleinbürgertum und Proletariat . Göttingen , c1986. 332 p. ; ISBN 3-525-35731-1 LC Card 87-134322 DDC 331/.0943/55 19
HD8460.D872 L46 1986

LABOR AND LABORING CLASSES - GERMANY (WEST) - HAMBURG - HISTORY.
Arbeiter in Hamburg . Hamburg , c1983. 606 p. : ISBN 3-8103-0807-2 LC Card 86-174037
HD8460.H36 A73 1983

LABOR AND LABORING CLASSES - GERMANY (WEST) - HISTORY - 20TH CENTURY.
Reese, Hartmut. Arbeiterbewegung in der Zusammenbruchsgesellschaft . Münster [1984?] 209 p. ; ISBN 3-88660-133-1 LC Card 85-128699
HD6694 .R35 1984

LABOR AND LABORING CLASSES - GERMANY (WEST) - INTERVIEWS.
Deppe, Wilfried. Drei Generationen Arbeiterleben . Frankfurt/Main , New York , c1982. 419 p. ; ISBN 3-593-33018-0 LC Card 82-167833 DDC 305.5/62/0922 19
HD6957.G3 D38 1982 *NYPL [JLD 86-2569]*

LABOR AND LABORING CLASSES - GERMANY (WEST) - MANNHEIM - HISTORY - SOURCES.
Säumt keine Minute! . Mannheim , c1986. xiii, 683 p. : ISBN 3-923003-36-6 LC Card 87-115249 DDC 331/.0943/46 19
HD8460.M35 S28 1986

LABOR AND LABORING CLASSES - GERMANY (WEST) - NEUSS - HISTORY.
Kiefer, Rolf. Sozialdemokratische Arbeiterbewegung in der Stadt Neuss vom Sozialistengesetz bis zum Ersten Weltkrieg /. Reinbek , c1982. iv, 159 p. ; ISBN 3-88756-025-6 LC Card 83-186919
HD8460.N48 K54 1982

LABOR AND LABORING CLASSES - GERMANY (WEST) - NORTH RHINE-WESTPHALIA - HISTORY - 20TH CENTURY.
"Die Menschen machen ihre Geschichte nicht aus freien Stücken, aber sie machen sie selbst" . Berlin [1984] 267 p. : ISBN 3-8012-0101-5 LC Card 84-204204
HC287.N6 M46 1984

LABOR AND LABORING CLASSES - GERMANY (WEST) - PENZBERG - POLITICAL ACTIVITY - HISTORY - 20TH CENTURY.
Tenfelde, Klaus. Proletarische Provinz . München , 1982. xvii, 409 p. : ISBN 3-486-50701-X : LC Card 83-124119
HD8460.P452 T46 1982

LABOR AND LABORING CLASSES - GERMANY, WEST - RECREATION.
Mikolaschek, Cornelia. Freizeit als Gegenstand der Politik . Frankfurt [am Main] , New York , c1984. 202 p. : ISBN 3-593-33346-5 LC Card 84-175844
HD7395.R4 M55 1984

LABOR AND LABORING CLASSES - GERMANY (WEST) - RUHR (REGION) - HISTORY.
Arbeit und Arbeitserfahrung in der Geschichte /. Göttingen , c1986. 128 p. ; ISBN 3-525-33516-4 LC Card 86-226588
HD4904 .A6644 1986

LABOR AND LABORING CLASSES - GERMANY (WEST) - RUHR (REGION) - HISTORY - 20TH CENTURY.
Baroth, Hans Dieter, 1937- Das Gras wuchs ja umsonst /. Köln , c1983. 232 p. ; ISBN 3-462-01577-X LC Card 83-227195
HD8459.R82 B37 1983

LABOR AND LABORING CLASSES - GERMANY (WEST) - SAARLAND - HISTORY.
Horch, Hans. Der Wandel der Gesellschafts- und Herrschaftsstrukturen in der Saarregion während der Industrialisierung (1740-1914) /. St. Ingbert [W. Germany] , 1985. 720 p. : ISBN 3-924555-04-4 LC Card 85-194709
HC287.S23 H67 1985

LABOR AND LABORING CLASSES - GERMANY (WEST) - SAARLAND - HISTORY - 19TH CENTURY.
Steffens, Horst. Autorität und Revolte . Weingarten , c1987. 419 p. : ISBN 3-924027-47-1 LC Card 87-141439 DDC 331/.0422334/094342 19
HD8039.M61 G383 1987

LABOR AND LABORING CLASSES - GREAT BRITAIN.
Pollert, Anna. Girls, wives, factory lives /. London, England , 1981. 251 p. ; ISBN 0-333-29177-8 *NYPL [JLD 83-884]*

Ramdin, Ron. The making of the Black working class in Britain /. Aldershot, Hants, England , Brookfield, Vt., USA , c1987. x, 626 p. ; ISBN 0-566-00943-9 LC Card 87-127153 DDC 305.5/62 19
HD8398.B55 R36 1987

Robins, David, 1944- We hate humans /. Harmondsworth, Middlesex, England , New York, N.Y. , 1984. 155 p. ; ISBN 0-14-007062-1
NYPL [JLD 86-4404]

LABOR AND LABORING CLASSES - GREAT BRITAIN - ADDRESSES, ESSAYS, LECTURES.
Fawcett, Henry, 1833-1884. The economic position of the British labourer /. New York , 1984. vii, 256 p. ; ISBN 0-8240-5706-6 (alk. paper) : LC Card 83-48478 DDC 331/.0941 19
HD8390 .F28 1984 *NYPL [JLC 86-366]*

LABOR AND LABORING CLASSES - GREAT BRITAIN - BIOGRAPHY.
Davies, Paul, 1951- A.J. Cook /. Wolfeboro, NH , c1987. p. cm. ISBN 0-7190-2160-X LC Card 87-11114 DDC 331.88/122/0924 B 19
HD8393.C63 D38 1987

Testaments of radicalism . London , c1977. vii, 246 p., [3] leaves of plates : ISBN 0-905118-01-4 : LC Card 77-377253 DDC 322/.2/0922 B
HD8383.7.A1 T47 *NYPL [JLE 86-4274]*

LABOR AND LABORING CLASSES - GREAT BRITAIN - HISTORY.
Harrison, J. F. C. (John Fletcher Clews) The common people of Great Britain . Bloomington , 1985. 445 p. : ISBN 0-253-20357-0 (pbk.) LC Card 84-48820 DDC 305.5/62/0942 19
HD8388 .H36 1985 *NYPL [JLD 86-3656]*

Hobsbawm, E. J. (Eric J.), 1917- Worlds of labour . London , c1984. x, 369 p., [4] p. of plates : ISBN 0-297-78509-5 : LC Card 86-674019
HD8388 .H63x 1984

Littler, Craig R. The development of the labour process in capitalist societies . London , Exeter, N.H. , 1982. 226 p. : ISBN 0-435-82540-2 : LC Card 82-210245 DDC 306/.36 19
HD8390 .L48 1982 *NYPL [JLD 87-1005]*

Marrocu, Luciano. Laburismo e trade unions . Bari , 1981. 183 p. ; LC Card 81-137615 DDC 331.88/0941 19
HD6664 .M24 *NYPL [JLD 86-3453]*

LABOR AND LABORING CLASSES - GREAT BRITAIN - HISTORY - 19TH CENTURY.
Ludlow, John Malcolm Forbes, 1821-1911. Progress of the working class, 1832-1867 /. New York , 1984. xv, 304 p. ; ISBN 0-8240-5717-1 (alk. paper) : LC Card 83-48490 DDC 305.5/62/0942 19
HD8390 .L93 1984 *NYPL [JLC 86-387]*

LABOR AND LABORING CLASSES - GREAT BRITAIN - HISTORY - 20TH CENTURY.
The Worst of times . London , 1985. 201 p., [8] p. of plates : ISBN 0-7045-0513-4
NYPL [JLD 86-1799]

LABOR AND LABORING CLASSES - GREAT BRITAIN - POLITICAL ACTIVITY - HISTORY.
Haydu, Jeffrey. Between craft and class . Berkeley , c1988. p. cm. ISBN 0-520-06060-1 (alk. paper) LC Card 87-22169 DDC 322/.2/0941 19
HD8076 .H39 1988

Marrocu, Luciano. Laburismo e trade unions . Bari , 1981. 183 p. ; LC Card 81-137615 DDC 331.88/0941 19
HD6664 .M24 *NYPL [JLD 86-3453]*

Testaments of radicalism . London , c1977. vii, 246 p., [3] leaves of plates : ISBN 0-905118-01-4 : LC Card 77-377253 DDC 322/.2/0922 B
HD8383.7.A1 T47 *NYPL [JLE 86-4274]*

Wright, D. G. Popular radicalism . London , New York , 1988. p. cm. ISBN 0-582-49440-0 LC Card 87-4093 DDC 322/.2/0942 19
HD8395 .W75 1988

LABOR AND LABORING CLASSES - GREAT BRITAIN - POLITICAL ACTIVITY - HISTORY - 19TH CENTURY.
Rothstein, Theodore. From chartism to labourism /. New York , 1984. vi, 365 p. ; ISBN 0-8240-5722-8 (alk. paper) : LC Card 83-48495 DDC 335/.1 19
HX249 .R68 1984 *NYPL [JLD 86-1828]*

LABOR AND LABORING CLASSES - GUADELOUPE - CONGRESSES.
Les Travailleurs antillais, guyanais, réunionnais en lutte contre le colonialisme et le racisme, pour le droit à la différence et l'unité des travailleurs. Paris , c1980. 89 p., [4] p. of plates : ISBN 2-903033-10-2 LC Card 84-164737
HD8250 .T73 1980

LABOR AND LABORING CLASSES - HISTORY.
Arbeit und Arbeitserfahrung in der Geschichte /. Göttingen , 1986. 128 p. ; ISBN 3-525-33516-4 *NYPL [JLC 87-12]*

Capitalismo e classe operária no Brasil /. Petrópolis , 1984. 69 p. ; LC Card 86-222585
HC51 .C35 1984

Cornell, Lasse. Arbete och arbetsformernas utveckling /. Göteborg , 1986. 161 p. : ISBN 91-85196-27-4 LC Card 86-212110
HD4851 .C67 1986

Hobsbawm, E. J. (Eric J.), 1917- Worlds of labour . London , c1984. x, 369 p., [4] p. of plates : ISBN 0-297-78509-5 : LC Card 86-674019
HD8388 .H63x 1984

LABOR AND LABORING CLASSES - HISTORY - 19TH CENTURY.
Proletariat . Wien , 1986. 275 p. : ISBN 3-205-00561-9 LC Card 86-673962
HD4853 .P76x 1986

LABOR AND LABORING CLASSES - HISTORY - 20TH CENTURY.
Mezhdunarodnoe rabochee dvizhenie . Moskva , 1980. 412 p. ; LC Card 81-143888
HD4854 .M474 1980

Rabochiĭ klass v proshlom i nastoi͡ashchem . Moskva , 1984, c1983. 255 p. ; LC Card 84-169518
HD4854 .R273 1984

LABOR AND LABORING CLASSES - HONDURAS - HISTORY.
Argueta, Mario. Historia laboral de Honduras . [Tegucigalpa] , 1985. 204 p. ; LC Card 85-199862
HD8155 .A74 1985

LABOR AND LABORING CLASSES - HONG KONG - HISTORY.
Šimko, Dušan. Strassenverkäufer und die Versorgung der Arbeiterfamilien von Kowloon (Hong Kong) im Umfeld der staatlichen Planungspolitik /. Basel , 1983. 196 p., [9] p. of plates : ISBN 3-85977-129-9 : LC Card 83-238672
HF5459.H6 S56 1983

LABOR AND LABORING CLASSES - HUNGARY.
Magyar, Lajosné. Jó munkát, jó közérzetet /. [Budapest] [1986?] 52 p. ; LC Card 87-148690
HD8420.5 .M33 1986

LABOR AND LABORING CLASSES - HUNGARY - HISTORY.
Ez az a munkásság-- /. Budapest , 1984. 225 p., [40] p. of plates : ISBN 963-322-103-X LC Card 85-184724
HD6680.5 .E95 1984

Munkásosztályunk fejlődése 1945-ig . Győr , 1985. 126 p. ; LC Card 86-186895
HD8420.5 .M85 1985

Shman'ko, G. I. Rabochiĭ klass Narodnoĭ Vengrii . Kiev , 1982. 165 p. ; LC Card 83-143426
HD8420.5 .S55 1982

LABOR AND LABORING CLASSES - HUNGARY - INTERVIEWS.
Lakos, Éva. Holtomiglan? holtodiglan? /. Budapest , c1985. 269 p., [6] leaves of plates : ISBN 963-15-3100-7 : LC Card 86-190862
HD8420.5 .L35 1985

LABOR AND LABORING CLASSES - HUNGARY - STATISTICS.
Az Ipari nagyüzemi munkásság jövedelmi viszonyai, élet- és munkakörülményei /. [Budapest] [1985] 94 p. ; LC Card 85-210330
HD8420.5 .I63 1985

LABOR AND LABORING CLASSES - ILLINOIS - CHICAGO - HISTORY - SOURCES.
German workers in Chicago . Urbana , c1988. p. cm. ISBN 0-252-01458-8 (alk. paper) LC Card

87-10780 DDC 331.6/2/43077311 19
HD8081.G4 G46 1988

LABOR AND LABORING CLASSES - ILLINOIS - HISTORY - SOURCES.
Illinois Writers' Project. The annals of labor and industry in Illinois 1890 for January, February and March; <July, August, September > 1890. Chicago, Ill., 1939-<1941 > v. <1, 3 > LC Card 42-43915 DDC 331/.09773 19
HD8083.I3 I44 1939

LABOR AND LABORING CLASSES - INDIA - ADDRESSES, ESSAYS, LECTURES.
Aziz, Abdul, 1937- Labour problems of a developing economy /. New Delhi , c1984. viii, 157 p. ; LC Card 84-901201 DDC 331/.0954 19
HD8686.5 .A95 1984 ***NYPL [JLD 86-4216]***

Ranadive, K. R. Accumulation, employment, and labour aristocracy . Bombay [1982] 55 p. ; LC Card 83-903051 DDC 305.5/62/0954 19
HD8686.5 .R325 1982 ***NYPL [JLF 87-500]***

LABOR AND LABORING CLASSES - INDIA - MAHARASHTRA - BIOGRAPHY.
Tāvare, Rāmacandra. Thāpaṭanā /. Mumbaī , 1986. 179 p. ; LC Card 87-900532
HD5820.M29 T38 1986

LABOR AND LABORING CLASSES - INDIA - POLITICAL ACTIVITY.
Chatterji, Rakhahari, 1943- Working class and the nationalist movement in India . New Delhi , c1984. ix, 215 p. ; LC Card 84-902674 DDC 322.4/4/0954 19
HD8686 .C47 1984 ***NYPL [JLD 87-709]***

LABOR AND LABORING CLASSES - INDIA - PUNE.
Lambert, Richard D. The transformation of an Indian labor market . Amsterdam , Philadelphia , 1986. ix, 249 p. ; ISBN 0-915027-63-1 (alk. paper) : LC Card 86-26900 DDC 331.11/0954/792 19
HD5820.P78 L36 1986

LABOR AND LABORING CLASSES - INSURANCE. see **INSURANCE, HEALTH; INSURANCE, UNEMPLOYMENT; OLD AGE PENSIONS.**

LABOR AND LABORING CLASSES - IRAN - POLITICAL ACTIVITY.
Bayat, Assef. Workers and revolution in Iran . London , Atlantic Highlands, New Jersey, USA , 1987. 227 p. : ISBN 0-86232-389-4 LC Card 87-160253 DDC 322/.2/0955 19
HD5660.I6 B39 1987

LABOR AND LABORING CLASSES - ITALY.
De Michelis, G. (Gianni) Il piano del lavoro /. Roma , 1986. xii, 267 p. : ISBN 88-420-2753-7 : LC Card 86-219772
HD8481 .D42 1986

LABOR AND LABORING CLASSES - ITALY - ADDRESSES, ESSAYS, LECTURES.
Ricerca sociale e movimento operaio . Milano , c1982. 294 p. ; LC Card 82-246648 DDC 331/.0945 19
HD8481 .R53 1982 ***NYPL [JLD 86-3380]***

LABOR AND LABORING CLASSES - ITALY - HISTORY - 20TH CENTURY.
D'Angelo, Lucio. Ceti medi e ricostruzione . [Milano] , 1981. vi, 287 p. ; LC Card 81-213297
JN5657.D45 D36 1981
NYPL [JLE 86-3459]

LABOR AND LABORING CLASSES - ITALY - LUNIGIANA - HISTORY - 20TH CENTURY.
Bianchi, Antonio. Lotte sociali e dittatura in Lunigiana storica e Versilia (1919-1930) /. [Firenze] , 1981. xii, 309 p. ; ISBN 88-22-23028-0 LC Card 82-125955
HD8489.L86 B5 1981

LABOR AND LABORING CLASSES - ITALY - LUNIGIANA - POLITICAL ACTIVITY - HISTORY - 20TH CENTURY.
Bianchi, Antonio. Lotte sociali e dittatura in Lunigiana storica e Versilia (1919-1930) /. [Firenze] , 1981. xii, 309 p. ; ISBN 88-22-23028-0 LC Card 82-125955
HD8489.L86 B5 1981

LABOR AND LABORING CLASSES - ITALY - NOVARA (PROVINCE) - SOCIETIES, ETC. - HISTORY.
Bermani, Cesare, 1937- Dalla grande associazione degli operai di Novara al Circolo operaio agricolo della Bicocca . Novara [1983] 345 p., [31] p. of plates : LC Card 85-148843
HD6714.N68 B47 1983

LABOR AND LABORING CLASSES - ITALY - SCHIO - HISTORY - 19TH CENTURY - CONGRESSES.
Convegno nazionale di studi storici (1979 : Schio, Italy) Schio e Alessandro Rossi . Roma , 1985-1986. 2 v. (1487 p., [1] folded leaf of plates) : LC Card 87-110167
HC302.5.R6 C66 1979

LABOR AND LABORING CLASSES - ITALY - TRIESTE REGION - HISTORY - 20TH CENTURY.
--Anche l'uomo doveva essere di ferro . Milano, Italy , c1986. 441 p. : LC Card 86-213675
HD8490.T742 A53 1986

LABOR AND LABORING CLASSES - ITALY - VENETO - ATTITUDES.
Operai e scelte politiche . Milano, Italy , c1986. 267 p., 45 p. of plates : LC Card 86-169148
HD8439.V462 O64 1986

LABOR AND LABORING CLASSES - ITALY - VERSILIA PLAIN - HISTORY - 20TH CENTURY.
Bianchi, Antonio. Lotte sociali e dittatura in Lunigiana storica e Versilia (1919-1930) /. [Firenze] , 1981. xii, 309 p. ; ISBN 88-22-23028-0 LC Card 82-125955
HD8489.L86 B5 1981

LABOR AND LABORING CLASSES - ITALY - VERSILIA PLAIN - POLITICAL ACTIVITY - HISTORY - 20TH CENTURY.
Bianchi, Antonio. Lotte sociali e dittatura in Lunigiana storica e Versilia (1919-1930) /. [Firenze] , 1981. xii, 309 p. ; ISBN 88-22-23028-0 LC Card 82-125955
HD8489.L86 B5 1981

LABOR AND LABORING CLASSES - ITALY - VICENZA (PROVINCE) - HISTORY.
Spagnolo, Mario. Industria e movimento operaio a Vicenza . Vicenza , 1983. 107 p., [1] leaf of plate : LC Card 85-175207
HD6714.V53 S63 1983

LABOR AND LABORING CLASSES - JAMAICA - HISTORY.
Petras, Elizabeth McLean. Jamaican labor migration . Boulder , 1988. x, 297 p. : ISBN 0-8133-7456-1 (pbk. : alk. paper) LC Card 87-20139 DDC 331.6/2/7292072875 19
HD8178 .P47 1988

LABOR AND LABORING CLASSES - JAPAN.
Kobayashi, Kaoru, 1931- Japan, the most misunderstood country /. Tokyo , 1984. ix, 165 p. ; ISBN 4-7890-0247-0
NYPL [JLD 86-1398]

LABOR AND LABORING CLASSES - JAPAN - HISTORY.
Littler, Craig R. The development of the labour process in capitalist societies . London , Exeter, N.H. , 1982. 226 p. : ISBN 0-435-82540-2 : LC Card 82-210245 DDC 306/.36 19
HD8390 .L48 1982 ***NYPL [JLD 87-1005]***

LABOR AND LABORING CLASSES - KENYA.
Kongstad, Per. Industri, fagbevægelse og lønarbejde i Kenya . Roskilde [1983] 76 p. ; LC Card 85-238103
HC865 .K66 1983

LABOR AND LABORING CLASSES - LATIN AMERICA.
Difrieri, Jorge A. (Jorge Alberto) Progresos de la administración del trabajo en las últimas décadas . Lima, Perú , 1985. 19 p. ; LC Card 86-152814
HD8110.5 .D54 1985

Vargas, Ines. The NIEO and the situatuon of workers . Oslo [1985] xiv, 290 p. ; ISBN 82-7288-121-7 (pbk.) LC Card 86-205407 DDC 331/.098 19
HD6530.5 .V36 1985

Vargas, Ines. The situation of workers in Latin America /. Oslo , 1985. 92 p. ; ISBN 82-7288-123-3 (pbk.) LC Card 86-205392 DDC 331/.098 19
HD6530.5 .V37 1985

LABOR AND LABORING CLASSES - LATIN AMERICA - CONGRESSES.
Máspero, Emilio. Informe político y de orientación ante el VIIIo Congreso de la CLAT . [Caracas] , 1983. 122 p. : LC Card 87-403072 DDC 305.5/62/098 19
HD8110.5.A5 C466 1983

LABOR AND LABORING CLASSES - LATIN AMERICA - HISTORY.
Godio, Julio. Sindicalismo y política en América Latina /. Caracas, Venezuela [1983] 315 p. ; LC Card 83-157510 DDC 322/.2/098 19
HD8110.5 .G64 1983 ***NYPL [JLD 86-1758]***

Latin American labor organizations /. New York , 1987. xiv, 929 p. ; ISBN 0-313-22834-5 (lib. bdg. : alk. paper) LC Card 86-33613 DDC 331.88/098 19
HD6530.5 .L38 1987

LABOR AND LABORING CLASSES - LATIN AMERICA - HISTORY - 20TH CENTURY.
García, Norberto E. Industria manufacturera y empleo . [Santiago, Chile] , 1982. 51 p. ; LC Card 87-403251 DDC 338.4/767/098 19
HD9734.L32 G36 1982

LABOR AND LABORING CLASSES - LIBYA.
Khalaf Allāh, Ramaḍān 'Uraybī. Ḥarakat al-quwá al-'āmilah wa-al-tanmiyah al-iqlīmiyah fī Lībiyā /. Ṭarābulus, al-Jamāhīrīyah al-'Arabīyah al-Lībīyah al-Sha'bīyah al-Ishtirākīyah , 1984. 279 p. : LC Card 86-965535
HB2121.6.A3 K47 1984

LABOR AND LABORING CLASSES - MARTINIQUE - CONGRESSES.
Les Travailleurs antillais, guyanais, réunionnais en lutte contre le colonialisme et le racisme, pour le droit à la différence et l'unité des travailleurs. Paris , c1980. 89 p., [4] p. of plates : ISBN 2-903033-10-2 LC Card 84-164737
HD8250 .T73 1980

LABOR AND LABORING CLASSES - MEXICO.
El Proceso de trabajo en México /. [Iztapalapa, Mexico] [1983 or 1984] 227 p. : LC Card 87-401038 DDC 331/.0972 19
HD8116.5 .P76 1983

LABOR AND LABORING CLASSES - MEXICO - JALISCO.
Cambio regional, mercado de trabajo y vida obrera en Jalisco /. Guadalajara, Jalisco, México , 1986. 363 p. ; ISBN 968-614-201-0 LC Card 86-218238
HD5731.J35 C36 1986

LABOR AND LABORING CLASSES - MEXICO - MEXICO CITY METROPOLITAN AREA.
El Terremoto del 19 de septiembre y los trabajadores mexicanos. [Mexico City, Mexico?] [1985] 114 p. ; LC Card 86-144990
HC138.M4 T47 1985 ***NYPL [JLC 87-130]***

LABOR AND LABORING CLASSES - MEXICO - MEXICO - HISTORY.
García Luna O., Margarita (García Luna Ortega) El movimiento obrero en el Estado de México . Toluca, Estado de México , 1984. 302 p. : ISBN 968-514-014-6 LC Card 86-173738
HC137.M473 G37 1984

LABOR AND LABORING CLASSES - MEXICO - POLITICAL ACTIVITY - CONGRESSES.
Movimientos sociales en el noroeste de México /. México , 1985. 282 p. ; ISBN 968-590-072-8 LC Card 87-102068
HD1531.M6 M684 1985

LABOR AND LABORING CLASSES - MIDDLE EAST - HISTORY.
Labor in the ancient Near East /. New Haven, Conn. , 1987. xiv, 289 p. : ISBN 0-940490-68-4 LC Card 86-32227 DDC 305.5/62/09394 19
HD8656 .L33 1987 ***NYPL [*OAC (American Oriental series)]***

LABOR AND LABORING CLASSES - MOLDAVIAN S. S. R.
Trud i ego problemy na sovremennom ėtape razvitiia sotsialisticheskogo obshchestva . Kishinev , 1986. 133 p. ; LC Card 87-144606
HD8529.M57 T78 1986

LABOR AND LABORING CLASSES - MOLDAVIAN S.S.R. - HISTORY - SOURCES.
Rabochee dvizhenie v Moldavii, 1895-fevral' 1917 g. . Kishinev , 1985. 322 p. ; LC Card

86-100092
HD8529.M57 R32 1985

LABOR AND LABORING CLASSES - NETHERLANDS - HISTORY - 1849-
Op een beteren weg . Amsterdam , 1985. 239 p. : ISBN 90-6012-654-8 : LC Card 85-236523
HD8516 .O6 1985 ***NYPL [JLD 86-3427]***

LABOR AND LABORING CLASSES - NETHERLANDS - HISTORY - 20TH CENTURY.
Hueting, Ernest. Naar groter eenheid . Amsterdam , 1983, c1982. 432 p. : ISBN 90-6012-531-2 : LC Card 83-184649
HD6727 .H83 1983 ***NYPL [JLG 87-188]***

LABOR AND LABORING CLASSES - NEW SPAIN - HISTORY - 18TH CENTURY.
Velázquez, María del Carmen. Notas sobre sirvientes de las Californias y proyecto de obraje en Nuevo México /. México, D.F. [1985], c1984. 246 p. ; ISBN 968-12-0298-8 LC Card 85-243085
HD2346.U52 C294 1985

LABOR AND LABORING CLASSES - NICARAGUA - POLITICAL ACTIVITY.
Vilas, Carlos María. Democracia y participación obrera en la Revolución Sandinista /. Morelia, Michoacán , 1985. 44 p., [6] p. of plates : LC Card 87-128110 DDC 322/.2/097285 19
HD8168 .V55 1985

LABOR AND LABORING CLASSES - NORWAY - HISTORY - 19TH CENTURY.
Arbeiderbevegelsens historie i Norge /. Oslo , 1985-<1987. v. <1, 5 > : ISBN 82-10-02750-6 : LC Card 87-116315
HD6752 .A74 1985

LABOR AND LABORING CLASSES - NORWAY - HISTORY - 20TH CENTURY.
Arbeiderbevegelsens historie i Norge /. Oslo , 1985-<1987. v. <1, 5 > : ISBN 82-10-02750-6 : LC Card 87-116315
HD6752 .A74 1985

LABOR AND LABORING CLASSES - PENNSYLVANIA - PHILADELPHIA - SOCIAL CONDITIONS.
Scranton, Philip. Work sights . Philadelphia , 1986. 279 p. : ISBN 0-87722-341-6 : LC Card 85-26132 DDC 305.9/009748/11 19
HC108.P5 S37 1986 ***NYPL [JLF 86-1959]***

LABOR AND LABORING CLASSES - PENNSYLVANIA - PHILADELPHIA - SOCIAL CONDITIONS - PICTORIAL WORKS.
Scranton, Philip. Work sights . Philadelphia , 1986. 279 p. : ISBN 0-87722-341-6 : LC Card 85-26132 DDC 305.9/009748/11 19
HC108.P5 S37 1986 ***NYPL [JLF 86-1959]***

LABOR AND LABORING CLASSES - PERU.
Parodi Solari, Jorge. Ser obrero es algo relativo-- . Lima [1986] 184 p. ; LC Card 87-405297 DDC 331.7/671/0985 19
HD8039.M52 P46 1986

LABOR AND LABORING CLASSES - PERU - LA CONVENCIÓN - HISTORY.
La Convención, el trabajo y sus luchas sociales /. [Peru? , 1983] (Cusco, Perú : Impr. AMAUTA) 152, vii p., [12] leaves of plates : LC Card 87-127171 DDC 330.985/3 19
HC228.C65 C66 1983

LABOR AND LABORING CLASSES - PERU - LIMA.
Galin, Pedro. Asalariados y clases populares en Lima /. Lima [1986] 127 p. ; LC Card 87-400199 DDC 331/.0985/25 19
HD8350.L562 G35 1986

LABOR AND LABORING CLASSES - PHILIPPINES.
Labor day celebration, May, 1, 1960 . [Manila?, Philippines , 1960?] 98 p. : LC Card 85-191411
HD7791 .L17 1960

LABOR AND LABORING CLASSES - POLAND - BIELSKO-BIAŁA - HISTORY.
Wurbs, Gerhard. Die deutsche Arbeiterbewegung in Bielitz und Biala /. Stuttgart , 1983. 133 p. : LC Card 84-194473
HD8539.5.B542 W87 1983

LABOR AND LABORING CLASSES - POLAND - ŁÓDŹ - HISTORY.
W dymach czarnych budzi się Łódź . Łódź , 1985. 507 p. ; ISBN 83-218-0280-X : LC Card 85-218768
HD8539.5.L62 W16 1985

LABOR AND LABORING CLASSES - POLAND - RADOM (VOIVODESHIP) - POLITICAL ACTIVITY - HISTORY.
Zdrojkowski, Józef. Rola partii robotniczych w życiu społeczno-politycznym Ziemi Radomskiej w latach 1930-1939 /. Radom , 1983. 168 p. : LC Card 86-100120
HD8539.R332 Z38 1983

LABOR AND LABORING CLASSES - POMERANIA (POLAND AND GERMANY) - POLITICAL ACTIVITY - HISTORY.
Głowacki, Andrzej. Ruch robotniczy na Pomorzu Zachodnim do 1914 roku /. Warszawa , 1979. 160 p. ; ISBN 83-01-01306-0 LC Card 81-107475
HD8457.P66 G56 1979

LABOR AND LABORING CLASSES - PORTUGAL - HISTORY.
Mónica, Maria Filomena, 1943- Artesãos e operários . Lisboa [1986] 228 p., [24] p. of plates : LC Card 86-229921
HD8596 .M65 1986

LABOR AND LABORING CLASSES - RESEARCH - METHODOLOGY.
Manuale di ricerca sul lavoro e sulle organizzazioni /. Roma , 1985. 384 p. : LC Card 86-118313 DDC 306/.36/072 19
HD4824 .M32 1985 ***NYPL [JLD 87-1160]***

LABOR AND LABORING CLASSES - RESEARCH - UNITED STATES.
Johnston, William B., 1945- Workforce 2000 . Indianapolis, Ind. [Washington, D.C.?] , 1987. xxvii, 117 p. : LC Card 87-601910 DDC 331.12/5/0973 19
HD8072.5 .J64 1987

LABOR AND LABORING CLASSES - RÉUNION - CONGRESSES.
Les Travailleurs antillais, guyanais, réunionnais en lutte contre le colonialisme et le racisme, pour le droit à la différence et l'unité des travailleurs. Paris , c1980. 89 p., [4] p. of plates : ISBN 2-903033-10-2 LC Card 84-164737
HD8250 .T73 1980

LABOR AND LABORING CLASSES - ROMANIA.
Bâldescu, Emil. Din istoria legăturilor revoluționare româno-bulgare (1909-1916) [microform]. [București, 1966] 181 p. LC Card 81-475045
HD8646 .B34 ***NYPL [*ZT-1732 no.1]***

LABOR AND LABORING CLASSES - ROMANIA - CONGRESSES.
Congress of Working People of Romania (3rd : 1986 : Bucharest, Romania) Third Congress of Working People of Romania. Bucharest [1986?] ii, 56 p. ; LC Card 86-225999 DDC 331/.09498 19
HD8642 .C59 1986

LABOR AND LABORING CLASSES - ROMANIA - POLITICAL ACTIVITY - HISTORY - 19TH CENTURY.
Condițiile istorice ale apariției și dezvoltării clasei muncitoare din România . București , 1984. 652 p. ; LC Card 84-234192
HD8648 .C65 1984

LABOR AND LABORING CLASSES - RUSSIAN S.F.S.R. - KALININGRADSKAIA OBLAST′ - BIOGRAPHY.
Rasskazy o kalinintsakh. Moskva , 1978. 172 p. : LC Card 81-147895
HD8529.K3162 R37 1978

LABOR AND LABORING CLASSES - RUSSIAN S.F.S.R. - KAREL′SKAIA A.S.S.R.
Piatiletka, god vtoroĭ . Petrozavodsk , 1977. 101 p. ; LC Card 81-161405
HC337.K265 P52 1977

LABOR AND LABORING CLASSES - RUSSIAN S.F.S.R. - LENINGRAD - BIOGRAPHY.
"Chastitsa serdtsa moego--" . Leningrad , 1981. 331 p. : LC Card 82-179000
HD8530.L5 C42 1981

LABOR AND LABORING CLASSES - RUSSIAN S.F.S.R. - LENINGRAD - HISTORY.
Share, Michael. The Central Workers' Circle of St. Petersburg, 1889-1894 . New York , 1987. xi, 396 p., [6] p. of plates : ISBN 0-8240-8063-7 (alk. paper) : LC Card 87-374 DDC 305.5/62/0947453 19
HD8522.T753 S53 1987

LABOR AND LABORING CLASSES - RUSSIAN S.F.S.R. - MOSCOW.
Orlova, Zhanna. Dobroe imia /. Moskva , 1986. 124 p. ; LC Card 86-131980
HD8530.M62 O75 1986

LABOR AND LABORING CLASSES - RUSSIAN S.F.S.R. - MOSCOW REGION - BIOGRAPHY.
Synov′iam v nasledstvo /. Moskva , 1986. 204 p. : LC Card 86-132407
HD8529.M62 S97 1986

LABOR AND LABORING CLASSES - RUSSIAN S.F.S.R. - SIBERIA - HISTORY.
Rabochie Sibiri v bor′be za sotsialisticheskuiu revoliutsiiu i postroenie sotsializma . Novosibirsk , 1975. 119 p. ; LC Card 85-187793
HD8529.S652 R283 1975

Voprosy istorii dorevoliutsionnoĭ Sibiri /. Tomsk , 1983. 177 p. ; ***NYPL [*QI 87-171]***

LABOR AND LABORING CLASSES - RUSSIAN S.F.S.R. - SOVIET FAR EAST - HISTORIOGRAPHY.
Istoriografiia istorii rabochego klassa Dal′nego Vostoka SSSR /. Vladivostok , 1984. 78 p. ; LC Card 85-229962
HD8529.S652 I87 1984

LABOR AND LABORING CLASSES - RUSSIAN S.F.S.R. - URAL MOUNTAINS REGION - BIOGRAPHY.
Rabochie dinastii Urala /. Sverdlovsk , 1977. 340 p. : LC Card 81-170557
HD8527.A1 R33 1977

LABOR AND LABORING CLASSES - RUSSIAN S.F.S.R. - URAL MOUNTAINS REGION - HISTORY.
Formirovanie i razvitie rabochego klassa i promyshlennosti Urala v period stroitel′stva sotsializma, 1917-1937 . Sverdlovsk , 1982. 138 p. ; LC Card 84-211723
HD8529.U7 F67 1982

LABOR AND LABORING CLASSES - SCANDINAVIA.
Buvollen, H. P. (Hans Petter) The situation of workers in the industrialised countries with special reference to Scandinavia /. Oslo [1985] 24 p. ; LC Card 86-205580 DDC 331.13/7948 19
HD8540 .B86 1985

LABOR AND LABORING CLASSES - SCOTLAND - GLASGOW (STRATHCLYDE) - HISTORY.
The working class in Glasgow, 1750-1914 /. London , Wolfeboro, N.H. , c1987. xix, 203 p. ; ISBN 0-7099-3415-7 : LC Card 86-24059 DDC 305.5/62/0941443 19
HD8400.G57 W67 1987

LABOR AND LABORING CLASSES - SILESIA - HISTORY.
Walczak, Jan. Robotnicze drogi Śląska i Zagłębia Dąbrowskiego do roku 1939 /. Katowice , 1985. 493 p. ; ISBN 83-7008-096-0 : LC Card 86-101066
HD8539.S52 W35 1985

LABOR AND LABORING CLASSES - SOCIAL CONDITIONS.
Proletariat . Wien , 1986. 275 p. : ISBN 3-205-00561-9 LC Card 86-673962
HD4853 .P76x 1986

LABOR AND LABORING CLASSES - SOUTH AFRICA.
Gouws, P. A. (Pieter Andries), 1949- Arbeidsverhoudinge in Suid-Afrika /. Pretoria , 1986. 127 p. ; ISBN 0-627-01492-5 : LC Card 87-127172
HD8801 .G66 1986

Webster, Eddie. Cast in a racial mould . Johannesburg , 1985. xv, 299 p., [8] p. of plates : ISBN 0-86975-285-5
NYPL [JLD 87-780]

LABOR AND LABORING CLASSES - SOUTH AFRICA - CAPE OF GOOD HOPE.
Goldin, Ian. The poverty of Coloured labour preference . Cape Town [1984] ii, 97 p. :

ISBN 0-7992-0570-2 (pbk.) LC Card 84-195453
HD8801.Z8 C324 1984

LABOR AND LABORING CLASSES - SOUTH AFRICA - JOHANNESBURG - HISTORY - PICTORIAL WORKS.
Kallaway, Peter. Johannesburg . Braamfontein, South Africa , c1986. v, 124 p. : ISBN 0-86975-303-7 (pbk.) LC Card 87-100567 DDC 305.5/62/0968221 19
HD8801.Z8 J6424 1986

LABOR AND LABORING CLASSES - SOUTH AFRICA - TRANSKEI.
May, Julian. Migrant labour in Transkei . Durban , 1985. 34, vii p. ; ISBN 0-86980-467-7 (pbk.) : LC Card 86-190553 DDC 331.6/2/0968791 19
HD5856.S6 M39 1985

LABOR AND LABORING CLASSES - SOUTH AMERICA - HISTORY.
Bergquist, Charles W. Labor in Latin America . Stanford, Calif. , 1986. xiv, 397, [8] p. of plates : ISBN 0-8047-1253-0 (alk. paper) : LC Card 84-51648 DDC 331/.0968 19
HD8256 .B47 1986 ***NYPL [JLE 86-2972]***

LABOR AND LABORING CLASSES - SOVIET UNION.
Grancelli, Bruno, 1943- Soviet management and labor relations /. Boston , c1988. xvi, 248 p. ; ISBN 0-04-497040-4 : LC Card 87-11516 DDC 331/.0947 19
HD8526.5 .G74 1988

Grimali͡uk, V. A. (Viktor Andreevich) Neposredstvenno obobshchestvlennyĭ trud /. Moskva , 1985. 110, [2] p. ; LC Card 86-111859
HD5796 .G75 1985

Izmenenie soderzhanii͡a i kharaktera truda na sovremennom ėtape razvitogo sotsializma /. Moskva , 1984. 227 p. ; LC Card 85-240356
HD8526.5 .I97 1984

Mordasova, L. A. (Lidii͡a Andrianovna) Trudovye resursy v torgovle /. Moskva , 1985. 128 p. ; LC Card 86-158800
HD8526.5 .M54 1985

Nauchnai͡a organizat͡sii͡a truda v promyshlennosti /. Moskva , 1986. 414 p. : LC Card 86-218434
HD36 .N323 1986

Report of the Union Delegation to the U. S.S.R. . London [1946?] iii, 40 p. : LC Card 87-100506
HD8526.5 .R46 1946

Sot͡sialisticheskoe obobshchestvlenie truda /. Moskva , 1981. 166 p. ; LC Card 82-161177
HD5796 .S633 1981

Sot͡sial'noe upravlenie trudovym kollektivom . Moskva , 1987. 181 p. ; LC Card 87-103391
HF5549.2.S65 S675 1987

Ukreplenie material'nykh osnov sotsialisticheskogo obraza zhizni /. Moskva , 1984. 156 p. ; LC Card 85-240384
HD8526.5 .U38 1984

Voprosy metodologii issledovanii͡a obshchestvennogo truda pri sotsializme /. Voronezh , 1979. 163 p. ; LC Card 81-142810
HD5796 .V65 1979

Voprosy politicheskoĭ ėkonomii . Novosibirsk , 1973. 125 p. ; LC Card 81-131624
HD8526.5 .V674 1973

LABOR AND LABORING CLASSES - SOVIET UNION - ATTITUDES.
Sot͡sial'no-ėkonomicheskie problemy intensifikatsii obshchestvennogo proizvodstva /. Moskva , 1983. 91 p. : LC Card 84-114234
HD56 .S688 1983

LABOR AND LABORING CLASSES - SOVIET UNION - CONGRESSES.
Povyshenie trudovoĭ i obshchestvenno-politicheskoĭ aktivnosti mass kak reshai͡ushchiĭ faktor uskorenii͡a sot͡sial'no-ėkonomicheskogo progressa sotsialisticheskogo obshchestva . Kaliningrad , 1986. 382 p. ; LC Card 87-136621
HD8526.5 .P62 1986

LABOR AND LABORING CLASSES - SOVIET UNION - HISTORY.
Kuromiya, Hiroaki. Stalin's industrial revolution . Cambridge [Cambridgeshire] , New York , 1988. p. cm. ISBN 0-521-35157-X LC Card 87-25010 DDC 338.947 19
HC335.4 .K87 1988

McDaniel, Tim. Autocracy, capitalism, and the revolution in Russia /. Berkeley , c1987. p. cm. ISBN 0-520-05532-2 (alk. paper) LC Card 86-30790 DDC 322.4/2/0947 19
HD8526 .M385 1987

Rabochee dvizhenie v Rossii v period imperializma . Moskva , 1982. 144 p. ; LC Card 83-174879
HD8526 .R3112 1982

LABOR AND LABORING CLASSES - SOVIET UNION - PICTORIAL WORKS.
Glaeser, Ernst, 1902-1963. Der Staat ohne Arbeitslose . Berlin , c1931. viii, 198 p. : LC Card 87-409524 DDC 305.5/62/0947 19
HD8526 .G53 1931

LABOR AND LABORING CLASSES - SOVIET UNION - POLITICAL ACTIVITY - CONGRESSES.
Povyshenie trudovoĭ i obshchestvenno-politicheskoĭ aktivnosti mass kak reshai͡ushchiĭ faktor uskorenii͡a sot͡sial'no-ėkonomicheskogo progressa sotsialisticheskogo obshchestva . Kaliningrad , 1986. 382 p. ; LC Card 87-136621
HD8526.5 .P62 1986

LABOR AND LABORING CLASSES - SPAIN.
Baranova, T. N. (Tat'i͡ana Nikolaevna) Rabochiĭ klass Ispanii boret͡si͡a . Moskva , 1978. 151 p. ; LC Card 81-147187
HD8586.5 .B37 1978

LABOR AND LABORING CLASSES - SPAIN - ANDALUSIA - HISTORY - 19TH CENTURY.
Seis estudios sobre el proletariado andaluz (1868-1939). [Córdoba] , 1984. 247 p. ; ISBN 84-500-9584-0 LC Card 86-142680 DDC 305.5/62/09468 19
HD8589.A52 S45 1984
NYPL [JLD 87-1550]

LABOR AND LABORING CLASSES - SPAIN - ANDALUSIA - HISTORY - 20TH CENTURY.
Seis estudios sobre el proletariado andaluz (1868-1939). [Córdoba] , 1984. 247 p. ; ISBN 84-500-9584-0 LC Card 86-142680 DDC 305.5/62/09468 19
HD8589.A52 S45 1984
NYPL [JLD 87-1550]

LABOR AND LABORING CLASSES - SPAIN - CANTABRIA - HISTORY - 20TH CENTURY.
Argos Villar, José Carlos. El movimiento obrero en Cantabria (1955-1977) /. [Santander?] [1982?] 227 p. ; ISBN 84-300-6979-8 LC Card 86-203186
HD8589.C3 A74 1982

LABOR AND LABORING CLASSES - SPAIN - CATALONIA - HISTORY.
Huertas, Josep Maria. Obrers a Catalunya . Barcelona , 1982. 409 p. : ISBN 84-85905-06-7 LC Card 83-101512
HD8589.C32 H83 1982
NYPL [JLD 86-3659]

LABOR AND LABORING CLASSES - SPAIN - CATALONIA - POLITICAL ACTIVITY - HISTORY.
Huertas, Josep Maria. Obrers a Catalunya . Barcelona , 1982. 409 p. : ISBN 84-85905-06-7 LC Card 83-101512
HD8589.C32 H83 1982
NYPL [JLD 86-3659]

LABOR AND LABORING CLASSES - SPAIN - GALICIA (REGION) - HISTORY.
Dende Galicia, Marx . Sada, A Coruña [1985?] 258 p. : ISBN 84-7492-241-0 LC Card 86-215077
HB97.5 .D413 1985

LABOR AND LABORING CLASSES - SPAIN - MONTIJO - HISTORY - 19TH CENTURY.
Introducción a la historia del movimiento obrero en Montijo . [Montijo?] [1982?] 103 p., 48 p. of plates : ISBN 84-300-6966-6 LC Card 85-177027
HD8590.M65 I57 1982

LABOR AND LABORING CLASSES - SPAIN - ORENSE.
Azcárate, Blanca, 1954- Ursachen, Umfang und Auswirkungen der Abwanderung im ländlichen Bereich Galiciens am Beispiel der Provinz Orense /. Frankfurt am Main , New York , c1985. 213 p. : ISBN 3-8204-8166-4 LC Card 85-190546
HD8589.O74 A92 1985

LABOR AND LABORING CLASSES - SPAIN - VALLADOLID (PROVINCE) - POLITICAL ACTIVITY - HISTORY.
Prado Moura, Angel de. El movimiento obrero en Valladolid durante la II República, 1931-1936 /. [Castilla y León] , 1985. 234 p. : ISBN 84-505-2341-9 LC Card 86-214605
HD8119.V34 P72 1985

LABOR AND LABORING CLASSES - SRI LANKA - HISTORY.
Voronin, S. V. Rabochiĭ klass Shri Lanki . Moskva , 1979. 278, [2] p. ; LC Card 81-147848
HD8670.8 .V67 1979

LABOR AND LABORING CLASSES - STATISTICAL METHODS.
Munkaügyi statisztikai és módszertani ismeretek /. Budapest , 1985. 323 p. : ISBN 963-10-6513-8 : LC Card 83-228566
HD4826.5 .M86 1985

LABOR AND LABORING CLASSES - STUDY AND TEACHING - LATIN AMERICA.
Feuer, Björn. Consideraciones aproximativas en torno a la investigación laboral en América Latina /. Stockholm [1985] 18 p. ; LC Card 85-205735
HD4824.5.L29 F48 1985

LABOR AND LABORING CLASSES - SWEDEN.
Towards a democratic rationality . Aldershot, Hants, England , Brookfield, Vt., USA , c1986. xi, 281 p. : ISBN 0-566-00761-4 : LC Card 86-14241 DDC 331/.09485 19
HD8576.5 .T69 1986 ***NYPL [JLD 86-3873]***

LABOR AND LABORING CLASSES - SWEDEN - HISTORY.
Lundh, Christer. Den svenska debatten om industriell demokrati 1919-1924 /. Lund , 1987- v. <1 > ; ISBN 91-85611-17-4 LC Card 87-151790
HD5660.S9 L87 1987

LABOR AND LABORING CLASSES - SWEDEN - NORRKÖPING - HISTORY - 19TH CENTURY.
Horgby, Björn. Den disciplinerade arbetaren . Stockholm [1986] 322 p. : ISBN 91-22-00804-7 LC Card 87-105821
HC378.N67 H67 1986

LABOR AND LABORING CLASSES - SWITZERLAND.
Fabrikbesichtigungen /. Zürich , c1986. 206 p. : ISBN 3-85791-109-3 LC Card 87-129952 DDC 305.5/62/09494 19
HD8606.5 .F33 1986

LABOR AND LABORING CLASSES - SWITZERLAND -BASEL - HISTORY.
Degen, Bernard, 1952- Das Basel der andern . Basel , 1986. 199 p. : ISBN 3-85990-073-6 LC Card 87-137650 DDC 331.88/09494/3 19
HD6775.B29 D44 1986

LABOR AND LABORING CLASSES - TASMANIA - SOCIAL CONDITIONS.
Marwood, Jim, 1932- Ways of working /. Kenthurst , 1986. 160 p. : ISBN 0-86417-101-3 (pbk.) LC Card 87-105782 DDC 305.5/62/09946 19
HD8849.T372 M37 1986

LABOR AND LABORING CLASSES - TASMANIA - SOCIAL CONDITIONS - PICTORIAL WORKS.
Marwood, Jim, 1932- Ways of working /. Kenthurst , 1986. 160 p. : ISBN 0-86417-101-3 (pbk.) LC Card 87-105782 DDC 305.5/62/09946 19
HD8849.T372 M37 1986

LABOR AND LABORING CLASSES - UKRAINE.
Pli͡ushch, M. R. Vklad robitnychoho klasu Ukraïns'koï RSR u pryskorenni͡a naukovo-tekhnichnoho prohresu v promyslovosti, 50-70-i roky /. Kyïv , 1981. 244 p. ; LC Card 82-200854
HC337.U53 T465 1981

LABOR AND LABORING CLASSES - UKRAINE - HISTORY - 20TH CENTURY.
Rabochiĭ klass Ukrainskoĭ SSR . Kiev , 1986.

238 p. ; LC Card 86-155918
HD8529.U42 R33 1986

LABOR AND LABORING CLASSES - UKRAINE - ODESSA - POLITICAL ACTIVITY - HISTORY.
Weinberg, Robert. Social democracy and workers in Odessa . Pittsburgh, Pa. (4E23 Forbes Quad, Pittsburgh 15260) [1986] 34 p. ; LC Card 86-199472
HD8530.O32 W45 1986

LABOR AND LABORING CLASSES - UNITED STATES.
Moore, Gary A. Labor and the economy . Cincinnati , c1983. viii, 502 p. : ISBN 0-538-08750-1 LC Card 81-85863 DDC 331/.0973 19
HD4901 .M825 1983 ***NYPL [JLE 87-831]***

Ritzer, George. Working, conflict and change /. Englewood Cliffs, N.J. , c1986. xii, 451 p. ; ISBN 0-13-967589-2 : LC Card 85-28135 DDC 306/.36/0973 19
HD6957.U6 R5 1986 ***NYPL [JLE 86-3160]***

Rosen, Ellen Israel. Bitter choices . Chicago , 1987. x, 220 p. : ISBN 0-226-72644-4 LC Card 87-5867 DDC 331.4/125/0973 19
HD6095 .R74 1987

LABOR AND LABORING CLASSES - UNITED STATES - 1914-
Bernstein, Irving, 1916- A caring society . Boston , 1985. 338 p., [24] p. of plates : ISBN 0-395-33116-1 : LC Card 84-25129 DDC 362.8/5/0973 19
HD8072 .B365 1985 ***NYPL [JLD 86-2102]***

Helmbold, Lois Rita. Making choices, making do [microform] . 1982. vii, 385 leaves
NYPL [Sc Micro R-4672]

How mighty a force? . Los Angeles , c1983. ix, 369 p. ; ***NYPL [JLD 87-277]***

Pesotta, Rose, 1896- Bread upon the waters /. Ithaca, N.Y. , c1987. xxiv, 435 p., [10] p. of plates : ISBN 0-87546-127-1 (pbk. : alk. paper) LC Card 87-2953 DDC 331.88/0973 19
HD8072 .P375 1987

LABOR AND LABORING CLASSES - UNITED STATES - 1914- - ADDRESSES, ESSAYS, LECTURES.
Vorse, Mary Heaton, 1874-1966. Rebel pen . New York , c1985. 345 p. : ISBN 0-85345-669-0 : LC Card 85-7130 DDC 331.4/0973 19
HD8072 .V755 1985 ***NYPL [JLD 86-2459]***

LABOR AND LABORING CLASSES - UNITED STATES - 1914- - SOURCES.
Slaves of the Depression . Ithaca, N.Y. , 1987. x, 229 p. ; ISBN 0-8014-9464-8 (pbk. : alk. paper) LC Card 87-6671 DDC 331.25/0973 19
HD8072 .S6164 1987

LABOR AND LABORING CLASSES - UNITED STATES - 1970- - ADDRESSES, ESSAYS, LECTURES.
Editorial research reports on the American work ethic. Washington [1973] iii, 180 p. ISBN 0-87187-042-8 LC Card 72-94080 DDC 331.1/1/0973
HD8072 .E34 ***NYPL [JLD 86-1374]***

LABOR AND LABORING CLASSES - UNITED STATES - BIOGRAPHY.
Dubofsky, Melvyn, 1934- "Big Bill" Haywood /. New York , 1987. viii, 184 p. ; ISBN 0-312-01272-1 : LC Card 87-17355 DDC 331.88/6 B 19
HD6509.H3 D82 1987

O'Connor, Jessie Lloyd, 1904- Harvey and Jessie . Philadelphia , 1988. p. cm. ISBN 0-87722-519-2 (alk. paper) LC Card 87-21737 DDC 322/.2/0922 B 19
HD8073.A1 O25 1988

Wren, Daniel A. White collar hobo . Ames , 1987. xii, 165 p. : ISBN 0-8138-1922-9 LC Card 87-4048 DDC 331/.092/4 B 19
HD8073.W47 W74 1987

LABOR AND LABORING CLASSES - UNITED STATES - FORECASTING.
Johnston, William B., 1945- Workforce 2000 . Indianapolis, Ind. [Washington, D.C.?] , 1987. xxvii, 117 p. : LC Card 87-601910 DDC 331.12/5/0973 19
HD8072.5 .J64 1987

LABOR AND LABORING CLASSES - UNITED STATES - HISTORY.
Brody, David. Workers in industrial America . New York , 1981, 1980. ix, 257 p. ; ISBN 0-19-502491-5 (pbk.) LC Card 78-27157
NYPL [JLD 86-3729]

Filippelli, Ronald L. Labor in the USA . New York , c1984. xii, 315 p. ; ISBN 0-394-34149-X LC Card 83-23458 DDC 331/.0973 19
HD8066 .F54 1984 ***NYPL [JFE 86-5130]***

Form, William Humbert, 1917- Divided we stand . Urbana , c1985. xviii, 306 p. ; ISBN 0-252-01168-6 (alk. paper) LC Card 85-16537 DDC 305.5/62/0973 19
HD8072.5 .F667 1985 ***NYPL [JLE 86-1940]***

Gutman, Herbert George, 1928- Power & culture . New York, N.Y. , c1987. xi, 452 p. ; ISBN 0-394-56171-6 LC Card 87-43018 DDC 305.5/62/0973 19
HD8072 .G97 1987

Hall, Gus. Working class USA . New York , 1987. 392 p. : ISBN 0-7178-0660-X : LC Card 87-3232 DDC 305.5/62/0973 19
HD8066 .H29 1987

Jones, Mother, 1843?-1930. [Selections. 1988.] The speeches and writings of Mother Jones /. Pittsburgh, Pa. , 1988. p. cm. ISBN 0-8229-3575-9 LC Card 87-25192 DDC 331.88/0973 19
HD8072 .J7832 1988

Life and labor . Albany , c1986. x, 343 p. ; ISBN 0-88706-173-7 LC Card 86-14362 DDC 305.5/62/0973 19
HD8066 .L54 1986 ***NYPL [JLE 86-4350]***

Littler, Craig R. The development of the labour process in capitalist societies . London , Exeter, N.H. , 1982. 226 p. : ISBN 0-435-82540-2 : LC Card 82-210245 DDC 306/.36 19
HD8390 .L48 1982 ***NYPL [JLD 87-1005]***

LABOR AND LABORING CLASSES - UNITED STATES - HISTORY - 19TH CENTURY.
Labor migration in the Atlantic economies . Westport, Conn. , 1985. xvi, 491 p. : ISBN 0-313-24637-8 (lib. bdg. : alk. paper) LC Card 85-7975 DDC 331.12/7 19
HD8375 .L33 1985 ***NYPL [JLE 86-1127]***

Sorge, Friedrich A. (Friedrich Adolf), 1828-1906. Friedrich A. Sorge's labor movement in the United States . New York , c1987. xiii, 196 p. ; ISBN 0-313-25518-0 (lib. bdg. : alk. paper) LC Card 86-31792 DDC 331/.0973 19
HD8072 .S7175 1987

LABOR AND LABORING CLASSES - UNITED STATES - HISTORY - 20TH CENTURY.
Fantasia, Rick. Cultures of solidarity . Berkeley , c1988. p. cm. ISBN 0-520-06053-9 (alk. paper) LC Card 87-16748 DDC 331.8/0973 19
HD8072.5 .F36 1988

LABOR AND LABORING CLASSES - UNITED STATES - HISTORY - SOURCES.
The Samuel Gompers papers /. Urbana , c1986- v. : ISBN 0-252-01138-4 (alk. paper : set) LC Card 84-2469 DDC 331.88/32/0924 19
HD6508 .S218 1986 ***NYPL [JLL 86-230]***

LABOR AND LABORING CLASSES - UNITED STATES - POLITICAL ACTIVITY.
Lash, Scott. The militant worker . London , 1984. vii, 264 p. ; ISBN 0-435-82516-X LC Card 87-673366
HD8076 .L37x 1984b

Rabochee dvizhenie v razvitykh kapitalisticheskikh stranakh . Moskva , 1987. 268 p. ; LC Card 87-164460
HD8378 .R29 1987

Rosenblum, Gerald. Immigrant workers; their impact on American labor radicalism. New York [1973] vi, 189 p. ISBN 0-465-03207-9 LC Card 72-89280
HD8081.A5 R67 ***NYPL [JLE 73-3033]***

LABOR AND LABORING CLASSES - UNITED STATES - POLITICAL ACTIVITY - HISTORY.
Haydu, Jeffrey. Between craft and class . Berkeley , c1988. p. cm. ISBN 0-520-06060-1 (alk. paper) LC Card 87-22169 DDC 322/.2/0941 19
HD8076 .H39 1988

LABOR AND LABORING CLASSES - URUGUAY - HISTORY - 20TH CENTURY - ADDRESSES, ESSAYS, LECTURES.
El Primer batllismo . Montevideo [1985] 159 p. : LC Card 85-233561 DDC 338.9895 19
HC232 .P75 1985 ***NYPL [JLC 86-259]***

LABOR AND LABORING CLASSES - WAGES. see **WAGES.**

LABOR AND LABORING CLASSES - WEST INDIES, BRITISH.
Lewis, W. Arthur (William Arthur), 1915- Labour in the West Indies . London , 1977. 104 p., [12] p. of plates : ISBN 0-901241-25-3 (pbk.) LC Card 86-232414
HD6595.4 .L49 1977

LABOR AND LABORING CLASSES - WEST (U. S.) - HISTORY - 20TH CENTURY.
Labor in the West /. Manhattan, Kan., USA , c1986. 88 p. : ISBN 0-89745-090-6 (pbk.) LC Card 87-400877 DDC 331/.0978 19
HD8083.A17 L32 1986

LABOR AND LABORING CLASSES - YUGOSLAVIA.
Künne, Wilfried. Die Aussenwanderung jugoslawischer Arbeitskräfte . Königstein/Ts. , 1979. xii, 269 p. : ISBN 3-7756-6931-0 : LC Card 79-394439
HD8633.5 .K83 ***NYPL [JLD 87-1148]***

Labor and social change.
Best, Fred. Reducing workweeks to prevent layoffs . Philadelphia , 1988. p. cm. ISBN 0-87722-506-0 LC Card 87-10097 DDC 331.25/72 19
HD5110.5 .B467 1988

Finlay, William. Work on the waterfront . Philadelphia , 1988. p. cm. ISBN 0-87722-523-0 (alk. paper) : LC Card 87-17976 DDC 331.88/11387164/0973 19
HD6515.L82 W474 1988

Grenier, Guillermo J. Inhuman relations . Philadelphia , 1988. xx, 232 p. ; ISBN 0-87722-502-8 (alk. paper) : LC Card 87-10116 DDC 331.25 19
HD6490.O72 U645 1988

Noble, Charles, 1948- Liberalism at work . Philadelphia , 1986. x, 292 p. : ISBN 0-87722-421-8 (alk. paper) : LC Card 86-1766 DDC 353.0083/0289 19
HD7654 .N63 1986 ***NYPL [JLE 86-4426]***

Worker participation and the politics of reform /. Philadelphia , 1987. ix, 371 p. ; ISBN 0-87722-464-1 (alk. paper) : LC Card 86-23006 DDC 658.3/152 19
HD5650 .W645 1987

LABOR AND STATE. see **LABOR POLICY.**

LABOR AND THE CHURCH. see **CHURCH AND LABOR.**

Labor and the economy . Moore, Gary A. Cincinnati , c1983. viii, 502 p. : ISBN 0-538-08750-1 LC Card 81-85863 DDC 331/.0973 19
HD4901 .M825 1983 ***NYPL [JLE 87-831]***

LABOR BUREAUS - ITALY.
La Tutela del lavoro in Italia. [Roma] [1976] 144 p. ; LC Card 86-233354
HD8481 .T85 1976

LABOR CAMPS - ROMANIA - HISTORY - 20TH CENTURY.
Kampf und Arbeit . Kronstadt , 1936. 102 p., [1] leaf of plates : LC Card 84-255742
HD7290 .K35 1936

The labor climate in Brazil /. Andrade, Luis F. Philadelphia, Pa. , c1985. viii, 133 p. ; ISBN 0-89546-057-2 (pbk.) LC Card 85-81947 DDC 331/.0981 19
HD8286.5 .A67 1985 ***NYPL [JLF 86-1201]***

LABOR CONTRACT.
Cooper, Russell W., 1955- Wage and employment patterns in labor contracts . Chur, Switzerland , New York , c1987. viii, 80 p. : ISBN 3-7186-0378-0 (pbk.) LC Card 86-31947 DDC 331.12/5 19
HD4909 .C57 1987

LABOR CONTRACT - ECONOMETRIC MODELS.
Adolph, Brigitte. Rationale Erwartungen, Arbeitsverträge und Wirtschaftspolitik /. München , c1986. ii, 127 p. : ISBN 3-88259-346-6 LC Card 87-104701 DDC 330/.01/9 19
HB175 .A26 1986

LABOR CONTRACT - UNITED STATES.
Gassner, Peter, 1941- Kollektivmacht und Individualschutz im amerikanischen Arbeitsrecht /. Frankfurt am Main , c1981. 155 p. ; ISBN 3-8204-6119-1 : LC Card 82-164604 DDC 344.73/0189 347.304189 19
KF3408.Z94 G474 1981 ***NYPL [JLD 86-1212]***

LABOR CONTRACTS, COLLECTIVE. see **COLLECTIVE BARGAINING; COLLECTIVE LABOR AGREEMENTS.**

LABOR COSTS.
Flexibility in the labour market . Paris [Washington, D.C.] 1986. 146 p. ; ISBN 92-64-12892-1 (pbk.) LC Card 87-123763 DDC 331.12 19
HD5707 .F59 1986

Klau, Friedrich. Labour market flexibility and external price shocks /. Paris, France , c1985. 60 p. : LC Card 86-205164 DDC 331.12 19
HD5707 .K54 1985

LABOR COSTS - ACCOUNTING.
Cascio, Wayne F. Costing human resources . Boston, Mass. , c1987. xiv, 274 p. : ISBN 0-534-08034-0 (pbk.) : LC Card 87-2501 DDC 658.1/553 19
HF5681.L2 C37 1987

LABOR COSTS - GERMANY (WEST)
Albach, Horst. Kosten der Arbeit . Stuttgart , c1985. xi, 179 p. : ISBN 3-7910-5003-6 : LC Card 86-162885 DDC 658.3/00943 19
HD5029 .A43 1985 ***NYPL [JLL 73-505 Nr.2]***

LABOR COSTS - ITALY - ADDRESSES, ESSAYS, LECTURES.
La Vertenza sul costo del lavoro e le relazioni industriali /. Milano, Italy , c1984. 243 p. : LC Card 84-144150 DDC 338.5/1/0945 19
HD5034 .V47 1984 ***NYPL [JLD 86-2858]***

LABOR COURTS - INDIA.
Kher, Manik. Conciliation and adjudication today /. Pune , c1985. 99 : LC Card 85-903388 DDC 344.54/0189143 345.404189143 19
LAW ***NYPL [JLE 86-1567]***

Labor day celebration, May, 1, 1960 : souvenir program. [Manila?, Philippines : s.n., 1960?] 98 p. : ill. ; 31 cm. Cover title. Accompanied by the program of the May Day celebration. LC Card 85-191411
1. May Day (Labor holiday) - Philippines. 2. Labor and laboring classes - Philippines.
HD7791 .L17 1960

LABOR DISCIPLINE - GERMANY, EAST.
Möbis, Harry. Ordnung, Disziplin, Sicherheit . Berlin , 1983. 95 p. ; LC Card 83-186990
HF5549.5.L3 M63 1983

LABOR DISCIPLINE - GERMANY, WEST.
Heinrich, Herbert, 1938- Arbeitsbewertung und Disziplinierung . Spardorf , c1985. v, 281 p. ; ISBN 3-922919-67-7 LC Card 86-162759
HF5549.5.J62 H36 1985

LABOR DISCIPLINE - KAZAKH S.S.R.
Problemy ukreplenii͡a trudovoĭ distsipliny i predotvrashchenii͡a tekuchesti kadrov na predprii͡atii͡akh T͡Sentral′nogo Kazakhstana . Karaganda , 1982. 126 p. ; LC Card 84-226131
HF5549.5.L3 P76 1982

LABOR DISCIPLINE - LAW AND LEGISLATION - KAZAKH S.S.R.
Problemy ukreplenii͡a trudovoĭ distsipliny i predotvrashchenii͡a tekuchesti kadrov na predprii͡atii͡akh T͡Sentral′nogo Kazakhstana . Karaganda , 1982. 126 p. ; LC Card 84-226131
HF5549.5.L3 P76 1982

LABOR DISCIPLINE - LAW AND LEGISLATION - UNITED STATES.
Chilnick, Lawrence D. The complete guide to drug testing . New York, N.Y. , c1987. p. cm. ISBN 0-394-56058-2 : LC Card 87-9631 DDC 658.3/82 19
HF5549.5.D7 C46 1987

Denenberg, Tia Schneider. Alcohol and drugs . Washington, D.C. , c1983. xv, 201 p. : ISBN 0-87179-410-1 LC Card 83-7560 DDC 344.73/01255 347.3041255 19
KF3540 .D46 1983 ***NYPL [JLE 86-2348]***

LABOR DISCIPLINE - SOVIET UNION.
Distsiplina truda--delo kazhdogo /. Moskva , 1982. 77 p. ; LC Card 83-126613
HF5549.5.L3 D57 1982

Voprosy ukreplenii͡a trudovoĭ i proizvodstvennoĭ distsipliny v deiatel′nosti profsoi͡uznykh organizatsiĭ . Moskva , 1984. 77 p. ; LC Card 86-181312
HF5549.5.L3 V67 1984

LABOR DISCIPLINE - UKRAINE.
Danchenko, M. I. (Mykola Ivanovych) Dystsyplina pratsi /. Kyïv , 1983. 110 p. ; LC Card 83-215106
HF5549.5.L3 D34 1983

Rekomendat͡sii po ukreplenii͡u trudovoĭ i proizvodstvennoĭ distsipliny /. Kiev , 1984. 41 p. ; LC Card 86-181301
HF5549.5.L3 R45 1984

LABOR DISPUTES - BRAZIL - SÃO PAULO (STATE) - DIRECTORIES.
Data-base . [São Paulo] , 1986. 259 p. : LC Card 87-403668 DDC 331.88/025/8161 19
HD6615.S32 D37 1986

LABOR DISPUTES - ENGLAND - HISTORY - 20TH CENTURY.
Morgan, Jane. Conflict and order . Oxford [Oxfordshire] , New York , c1987. p. cm. ISBN 0-19-820128-1 : LC Card 87-11027 DDC 331.89/2942 19
HD5366.A6 M67 1987

LABOR DISPUTES - FRANCE - CLERMONT-FERRAND.
Barrière, Antoine. Michelin . Nonette , 1983. 289 p. ; ISBN 2-902894-20-1
NYPL [JLD 86-4467]

LABOR DISPUTES - GERMANY, WEST.
Arbeitskampf um Arbeitszeit . Marburg , c1985. 218 p. : ISBN 3-921630-52-5 LC Card 86-160526
HD5378 .A73 1985

Osswald, Richard, 1917- Lebendige Arbeitswelt . Stuttgart , c1986. 394 p. : ISBN 3-421-06309-5 LC Card 86-148169
HD9710.G44 D385 1986

LABOR DISPUTES - GREAT BRITAIN - HISTORY - 20TH CENTURY.
Davies, Paul, 1951- A.J. Cook /. Wolfeboro, NH , c1987. p. cm. ISBN 0-7190-2160-X LC Card 87-11114 DDC 331.88/122/0924 B 19
HD8393.C63 D38 1987

LABOR DISPUTES - INDIA.
Asdhir, Vijay, 1947- Industrial relations in India . New Delhi , c1987. 376 p. ; LC Card 86-903540 DDC 331.89/2877/00954552 19
HD8686.5 .A85 1987

Sharma, B. D. (Banarsi Das), 1921- Art of conciliation and industrial unrest /. Bombay , 1985. xvi, 366 p. ; LC Card 87-902679 DDC 331.89/14/0954 19
HD5998.A3 S48 1985

LABOR DISPUTES - INDIA - PUNJAB.
Asdhir, Vijay, 1947- Industrial relations in India . New Delhi , c1987. 376 p. ; LC Card 86-903540 DDC 331.89/2877/00954552 19
HD8686.5 .A85 1987

LABOR DISPUTES - ITALY.
Bezza, Bruno. Le lotte degli elettromeccanici /. Milano , c1981. 179 p. : ISBN 88-20-42149-6 : LC Card 81-200954 DDC 331.89/282131/0945 19
HD5384.E3 B49 1981 ***NYPL [JLD 86-2898]***

LABOR DISPUTES - ITALY - VICENZA (PROVINCE) - HISTORY.
Spagnolo, Mario. Industria e movimento operaio a Vicenza . Vicenza , 1983. 107 p., [1] leaf of plate : LC Card 85-175207
HD6714.V53 S63 1983

LABOR DISPUTES - PERU - CANARIA.
Hernández, Zoila. El coraje de las mineras . Lima, Perú , 1986. 184 p. : LC Card 86-232046
HD5361.Z9 C35 1986

LABOR DISPUTES - SCOTLAND - CASE STUDIES.
Foster, John. The politics of the UCS work-in . London , Atlantic Highlands, N.J. , 1986. 446 p. : ISBN 0-85315-663-8 (pbk.) : LC Card 86-235159 DDC 331.89/282383/094141 19
HD5365.S512 1971 .C584 1986

LABOR DISPUTES - UNITED STATES - CASE STUDIES.
Fantasia, Rick. Cultures of solidarity . Berkeley , c1988. p. cm. ISBN 0-520-06053-9 (alk. paper) LC Card 87-16748 DDC 331.8/0973 19
HD8072.5 .F36 1988

LABOR DISPUTES - UNITED STATES - HISTORY - 19TH CENTURY.
Sorge, Friedrich A. (Friedrich Adolf), 1828-1906. Friedrich A. Sorge's labor movement in the United States . New York , c1987. xiii, 196 p. ; ISBN 0-313-25518-0 (lib. bdg. : alk. paper) LC Card 86-31792 DDC 331/.0973 19
HD8072 .S7175 1987

LABOR DISPUTES - WALES - HISTORY - 20TH CENTURY.
Morgan, Jane. Conflict and order . Oxford [Oxfordshire] , New York , c1987. p. cm. ISBN 0-19-820128-1 : LC Card 87-11027 DDC 331.89/2942 19
HD5366.A6 M67 1987

LABOR ECONOMICS.
Ehrenberg, Ronald G. Modern labor economics . Glenview, Ill. [1987], c1988. 721 p. : ISBN 0-673-18964-3 LC Card 87-9789 DDC 331 19
HD4901 .E34 1988

Friedrich, Horst, 1935- Die Produktionsverhältnisse /. Berlin , 1981. 228 p. ; LC Card 81-175348
HC79.I52 F75 1981

Hamermesh, Daniel S. The economics of work and pay /. New York , c1988. xii, 452 p. : ISBN 0-06-045356-7 LC Card 87-18355 DDC 331 19
HD4901 .H18 1988

Moore, Gary A. Labor and the economy . Cincinnati , c1983. viii, 502 p. : ISBN 0-538-08750-1 LC Card 81-85863 DDC 331/.0973 19
HD4901 .M825 1983 ***NYPL [JLE 87-831]***

Reynolds, Lloyd George, 1910- Economics of labor /. Englewood Cliffs, NJ , c1987. x, 518 p. : ISBN 0-13-225772-6 LC Card 86-25149 DDC 331 19
HD4901 .R469 1987

Zinn, Karl Georg. Arbeit, Konsum, Akkumulation . Hamburg , 1986. 243 p. : ISBN 3-87975-347-4 LC Card 86-230933
HB103.K47 Z56 1986

LABOR ECONOMICS - ADDRESSES, ESSAYS, LECTURES.
Confrontation, class consciousness, and the labor process . Westport, Conn. , 1986. viii, 261 p. ; ISBN 0-313-25140-1 (lib. bdg. : alk. paper) LC Card 85-17734 DDC 305.5/62 19
HD4851 .C63 1986 ***NYPL [JLE 86-3558]***

LABOR ECONOMICS - COLOMBIA.
López, Alejandro, 1876-1940. [Selections. 1983.] Obras selectas /. Bogotá, D.E. , 1983. xiii, 458 p. ; LC Card 86-233252
HC197 .L6172 1983

LABOR ECONOMICS - CONGRESSES.
Economische wetenschappen . Maastricht , Assen , 1985. 224 p. ; ISBN 90-232-2148-6 LC Card 86-111599
HB21 .E248 1985

Recent advances in labour economics /. London , New York , c1984. 258 p. : ISBN 0-312-66575-X (St. Martin's) : LC Card 83-40628 DDC 331 19
HD4813 .R28 1984 ***NYPL [JLD 86-2455]***

LABOR ECONOMICS - SOVIET UNION.
Ėkonomika trudovykh resursov /. Minsk , 1985. 159 p. ; LC Card 87-156829
HD5796 .E35 1985

LABOR FORCE. see **LABOR SUPPLY.**

LABOR FORCE PARTICIPATION. see **LABOR SUPPLY.**

Labor force participation of black and white youth /. Williams, Donald R., 1956- Ann Arbor, Mich. , c1987. 125 p. ; ISBN 0-8357-1804-2 (alk. paper) LC Card 87-5868 DDC 331.3/412/0973 19
HD6273 .W48 1987

LABOR, FOREIGN. see **ALIEN LABOR.**

LABOR, HOURS OF. see **HOURS OF LABOR.**

Labor in crisis . Brody, David, 1930- Urbana , 1987, c1965. 218 p. ; ISBN 0-252-01373-5 (pbk. : alk. paper) LC Card 86-30880 DDC 331.89/269142/0973 19
HD5325.I5 1919 .B7 1987

Labor in Latin America . Bergquist, Charles W. Stanford, Calif. , 1986. xiv, 397, [8] p. of plates : ISBN 0-8047-1253-0 (alk. paper) : LC Card 84-51648 DDC 331/.0968 19
HD8256 .B47 1986 NYPL [JLE 86-2972]

Labor in the ancient Near East / edited by Marvin A. Powell. New Haven, Conn. : American Oriental Society, 1987. xiv, 289 p. : ill. ; 27 cm. (American Oriental series. v. 68) Includes bibliographies and indexes. ISBN 0-940490-68-4 LC Card 86-32227 DDC 305.5/62/09394 19
1. Labor and laboring classes - Middle East - History. 2. Slave labor - Middle East - History. 3. Middle East - History - To 622. I. Powell, Marvin A. II. Series.
*HD8656 .L33 1987 NYPL [*OAC (American Oriental series)]*

Labor in the U. S.A. Filippelli, Ronald L. Labor in the USA . New York , c1984. xii, 315 p. ; ISBN 0-394-34149-X LC Card 83-23458 DDC 331/.0973 19
HD8066 .F54 1984 NYPL [JFE 86-5130]

Labor in the USA . Filippelli, Ronald L. New York , c1984. xii, 315 p. ; ISBN 0-394-34149-X LC Card 83-23458 DDC 331/.0973 19
HD8066 .F54 1984 NYPL [JFE 86-5130]

Labor in the West / edited by Hugh T. Lovin. Manhattan, Kan., USA : Sunflower University Press, c1986. 88 p. : ill. ; 28 cm. "From the April 1986 Journal of the West, with two additional articles." Includes bibliographies and index. CONTENTS. - Some trends in labor history writings in this century / Hugh T. Lovin -- Labor in the Pacific Slope timber industry / William G. Robbins -- Labor in the Western oil industry / George N. Green -- Labor's fight for recognition in the Western coalfields / Allan Kent Powell -- The West Coast teamsters' and longshoremen's unions in the twentieth century / Jonathan Dembo -- Railroad labor relations in the Great War and after, 1917-1921 / W. Thomas White -- The national railroad strike of 1922 and the decline of organized labor in Nevada / Phillip I. Earl and Guy Louis Rocha -- Indians in the work force / Patricia K. Ourada -- Mexican labor in the United States : the view from Mexican cantinas / Manuel A. Machado, Jr. -- Twentieth-Century migrant farm labor / Merle Wells -- Women in the hop harvest from New York to Washington / Susan Armitage and Joan M. Jensen -- Idaho's food production army in World War II / Patricia K. Ourada. ISBN 0-89745-090-6 (pbk.) LC Card 87-400877 DDC 331/.0978 19
1. Labor and laboring classes - West (U. S.) - History - 20th century. 2. Trade-unions - West (U. S.) - History - 20th century. I. Lovin, Hugh T.
HD8083.A17 L32 1986

LABOR INCENTIVES. see **INCENTIVES IN INDUSTRY.**

LABOR INSPECTION.
Labour inspection . Geneva , 1986. ix, 100 p. ; ISBN 92-2-105359-8 (pbk.) : LC Card 87-123437 DDC 331.25 19
HD3656 .L33 1986

LABOR INSPECTION - LATIN AMERICA.
Galin, Pedro. Condiciones de trabajo y coordinación de las inspecciones /. Lima, Perú , 1986. 19 p. ; LC Card 87-401748 DDC 331.25 19
HD6957.L29 G35 1986

LABOR - JURISPRUDENCE. see **LABOR LAWS AND LEGISLATION.**

LABOR LAWS AND LEGISLATION - ADDRESSES, ESSAYS, LECTURES.
Comparative labour law and industrial relations /. Deventer [Netherlands] , Boston , c1985. xiii, 527 p. ; ISBN 90-6544-236-7 (pbk.) LC Card 85-10000 DDC 344/.01 342.41 19
K1705.6 .C65 1985 NYPL [JLE 86-2420]

LABOR LAWS AND LEGISLATION - BULGARIA.
Petkov, Todor (Todor Iliev) Stopanska samostoi͡atelnost i stopanska otgovornost /. Sofii͡a , 1985. 237 p. ; LC Card 85-134177
HD8626.5 .P48 1985

LABOR LAWS AND LEGISLATION - CANADA.
Carter, D. D. The changing face of Canadian labour relations law /. Kingston, Ont., Canada , 1985. 15 p. ; ISBN 0-88886-126-5 (pbk.) LC Card 86-145328 DDC 331 s 344.71/01 331 s 347.1041 19
HD8102 .K52 no. 54 KE3009

LABOR LAWS AND LEGISLATION - FRANCE.
Ortscheidt, Pierre. L'entreprise face au nouveau droit de travail /. Paris , c1985. 221 p. ; ISBN 2-7178-0915-5 : LC Card 85-191518
KJV3399 .O78 1985 NYPL [JLE 87-358]

LABOR LAWS AND LEGISLATION - GREAT BRITAIN - HISTORY - 19TH CENTURY.
Ludlow, John Malcolm Forbes, 1821-1911. Progress of the working class, 1832-1867 /. New York , 1984. xv, 304 p. ; ISBN 0-8240-5717-1 (alk. paper) : LC Card 83-48490 DDC 305.5/62/0942 19
HD8390 .L93 1984 NYPL [JLC 86-387]

LABOR LAWS AND LEGISLATION - INDIA.
Anonymous struggles . New Delhi , 1983. 24 p. ; LC Card 83-904576 DDC 344.54/01 345.4041 19
LAW NYPL [JLD 86-3877]

Industrial relations . New Delhi , 1986. 254 p. ; LC Card 87-902682
HD8686.5.I575 1978

LABOR LAWS AND LEGISLATION - ITALY.
Balducci, Cataldo. Il sindacato /. Torino , c1984. 2 v. ; ISBN 88-02-03818-X (set) : LC Card 85-158972 DDC 344.45/0188 344.504188 19
LAW NYPL [JLE 86-3250]

La Tutela del lavoro in Italia. [Roma] [1976] 144 p. ; LC Card 86-233354
HD8481 .T85 1976

LABOR LAWS AND LEGISLATION - JAPAN.
Labor unions and labor-management relations. Tokyo, Japan , 1986. 48 p. : ISBN 4-538-74002-0 : LC Card 86-220438 DDC 331/.0952 19
HD8726.5 .L33 1986

LABOR LAWS AND LEGISLATION - PAKISTAN - CASES.
Why the office staff scared of time and motion study? . Saddar, Karachi, Pakistan [1985] 1 v. (various pagings) leaves ; LC Card 86-146552
HD5070.5 .W49 1985

LABOR LAWS AND LEGISLATION - PERU.
Las Leyes de estabilidad laboral y sus efectos económicos /. Lima, Perú [1986?] 67 p. : LC Card 87-403254 DDC 331.11/0985 19
HD8344 .L49 1986

LABOR LAWS AND LEGISLATION - SOVIET UNION.
Trudovoe pravo i povyshenie kachestva truda /. Moskva , 1987. 270 p. ;
*NYPL [*QIX 87-3357]*

LABOR LAWS AND LEGISLATION - SRI LANKA.
Labour standards in Sri Lanka . [Colombo] , 1981. x, 164 p. ; LC Card 83-902877 DDC 331/.09549/3 19
HD8670.8 .L32 1981 NYPL [JLC 87-22]

LABOR LAWS AND LEGISLATION - UNITED STATES.
Gassner, Peter, 1941- Kollektivmacht und Individualschutz im amerikanischen Arbeitsrecht /. Frankfurt am Main , c1981. 155 p. ; ISBN 3-8204-6119-1 : LC Card 82-164604 DDC 344.73/0189 347.304189 19
KF3408.Z94 G474 1981
NYPL [JLD 86-1212]

Sandver, Marcus H. Labor relations . Boston , c1987. xxii, 529 p. : ISBN 0-316-77024-8 LC Card 86-27314 DDC 331/.0973 19
HD8072.5 .S32 1987

LABOR LAWS AND LEGISLATION - UNITED STATES - COMPLIANCE COSTS.
Reynolds, Morgan O., 1942- Making America poorer . Washington, D.C. , c1987. ix, 218 p. ; ISBN 0-932790-63-1 LC Card 87-6569 DDC 338.5/1/0973 19
HD6508 .R435 1987

LABOR LAWS AND LEGISLATION - UNITED STATES - HISTORY - 20TH CENTURY.
The Cold war against labor . Berkeley, CA , c1987. 2 v. (xxii, 915 p.) : ISBN 0-913876-19-4 (set); 0-913876-20-4 (set) : LC Card 87-18510 DDC 331.88/0973 19
HD6508 .C62 1987

LABOR-MANAGEMENT COMMITTEES - UNITED STATES.
Cohen-Rosenthal, Edward. Mutual gains . New York , 1987. xv, 287 p. : ISBN 0-275-92204-9 (alk. paper) : LC Card 86-25249 DDC 331/.01/12 19
HD6490.L33 C64 1987

National Center for Productivity and Quality of Working Life. Starting a labor-management committee in your organization . Washington , 1978. 55 p. ; LC Card 78-603560 DDC 658.31/5
HD6490.L33 N37 1978 NYPL [JLF 81-235]

LABOR-MANAGEMENT COMMITTEES - UNITED STATES - ABSTRACTS.
Weinberg, Edgar. Labor-management cooperation for productivity /. New York , c1983. 61 p. ; ISBN 0-08-029511-8 (pbk.) LC Card 83-2361 DDC 016.33111/8/0973 19
HD56 .W44 1983
NYPL [JLM 83-380 no.30]

LABOR-MANAGEMENT COMMITTEES - UNITED STATES - ADDRESSES, ESSAYS, LECTURES.
Labor-management cooperation . [Washington, D.C.?] , 1984. v, 77 p. ; LC Card 85-602044 DDC 331.01/12/0973 19
HD6490.L332 U55 1984
NYPL [JLF 86-559]

Labor-management cooperation : perspectives from the labor movement. [Washington, D.C.?] : U. S. Dept. of Labor, Bureau of Labor-Management Relations and Cooperative Programs, 1984. v, 77 p. ; 28 cm. Includes bibliographical references. LC Card 85-602044 DDC 331.01/12/0973 19
1. Labor-management committees - United States - Addresses, essays, lectures. 2. Industrial relations - United States - Addresses, essays, lectures. 3. Quality of work life - United States - Addresses, essays, lectures. I. United States. Dept. of Labor. Bureau of Labor-Management Relations and Cooperative Programs.
HD6490.L332 U55 1984
NYPL [JLF 86-559]

Labor-management cooperation for productivity /. Weinberg, Edgar. New York , c1983. 61 p. ; ISBN 0-08-029511-8 (pbk.) LC Card 83-2361 DDC 016.33111/8/0973 19
HD56 .W44 1983
NYPL [JLM 83-380 no.30]

LABOR-MANAGEMENT RELATIONS. see **INDUSTRIAL RELATIONS.**

LABOR MARKET. see **LABOR SUPPLY.**

Labor market information for Iowa (Job Training Partnership Act), State of Iowa. Des Moines, Iowa (1000 E. Grand Ave., Des Moines 50319) : Iowa Dept. of Job Service, Audit and Analysis Dept., Labor Market Information Unit, [1986] 125 p. : ill. ; 28 cm. "April 1986." LC Card 86-622289 DDC 331.1/09777 19
1. Labor supply - Iowa - Statistics. 2. Employment forecasting - Iowa - Statistics. 3. Iowa - Occupations - Statistics. I. Iowa. Labor Market Information Unit.
HD5725.I8 L34 1986

Labor market information publication (Frankfort Ky.)
Kentucky occupational profiles, finance, insurance, and real estate /. [Frankfort, Ky.] [1985] v, 33 p. : LC Card 85-622996 DDC 331.12/51/0009769 19
HD5718.B262 U66 1985

LABOR, MIGRANT. see **MIGRANT LABOR.**

Labor migration in the Atlantic economies : the European and North American working classes during the period of industrialization / edited by Dirk Hoerder. Westport, Conn. : Greenwood Press, 1985. xvi, 491 p. : ill. ; 25 cm. (Contributions in labor history 0146-3608 . no. 16) Includes index. Bibliography: p. [449]-465. ISBN 0-313-24637-8 (lib. bdg. : alk. paper) LC Card 85-7975 DDC 331.12/7 19
1. Labor and laboring classes - Europe - History - 19th century. 2. Migration, Internal - Europe - History - 19th century. 3. Alien labor - United States - History - 19th century. 4. Labor and laboring classes - United

States - History - 19th century. I. Hoerder, Dirk.
HD8375 .L33 1985 ***NYPL [JLE 86-1127]***

LABOR, MIGRATORY. see **MIGRANT LABOR.**

Labor mobility and economic opportunity : essays / by E. Wight Bakke ... [et al.] ; preface by Paul Webbink. Westport, Conn. : Greenwood Press, 1987, c1954. vii, 118 p. ; 24 cm. Reprint. Originally published: Cambridge, Mass. Technology Press of Massachusetts Institute of Technology ; New York : Wiley, c1954. Includes bibliographical references and index. ISBN 0-313-24975-X (lib. bdg. : alk. paper) LC Card 86-25763 DDC 331.12/7973 19
1. Labor mobility - United States. I. Bakke, E. Wight (Edward Wight), 1903-.
HD5717.5.U6 L33 1987

LABOR MOBILITY - BRAZIL.
Macedo, Roberto Brás Matos. FGTS e a rotatividade /. São Paulo-SP , Brasília-DF , 1985. 231 p. : ISBN 85-21-30271-1 LC Card 85-187484
HD7096.B6 M33 1985

LABOR MOBILITY - DENMARK - RIBE AMT.
Johansen, Carsten Ulstrup. Hva blev der af dem? . Esbjerg , 1983. 168 p. : ISBN 87-85198-93-5 LC Card 83-236971
HD5717.5.D42 R55 1983

LABOR MOBILITY - DENMARK - VEJLE AMT.
Johansen, Carsten Ulstrup. Hva blev der af dem? . Esbjerg , 1983. 168 p. : ISBN 87-85198-93-5 LC Card 83-236971
HD5717.5.D42 R55 1983

LABOR MOBILITY - DEVELOPING COUNTRIES - ADDRESSES, ESSAYS, LECTURES.
Labour circulation and the labour process /. London [England] , Dover, N.H. , c1985. xvi, 416 p. : ISBN 0-7099-3342-8 : LC Card 84-14306 DDC 331.12/791 19
HD5856.D44 L33 1984
NYPL [JLD 86-2532]

LABOR MOBILITY - ECONOMETRIC MODELS.
Coloma C., Fernando. Los efectos de una desgravación arancelaria en el contexto de una economía con movilidad imperfecta de trabajo /. Santiago , 1985. 46 leaves : LC Card 85-203579
HF1713 .C618 1985

LABOR MOBILITY - GERMANY (EAST)
Schaefer, Reinhard. Disponibilität--Mobilität--Fluktuation /. Berlin , 1982. 70 p. : LC Card 83-225572
HD5717.5.G35 S3 1982

LABOR MOBILITY - GERMANY, WEST.
Koll, Hermann Josef. Mobilität und Beruf . Opladen , 1981. xviii, 564 p. ; ISBN 3-531-11551-0 : LC Card 81-158683
HD5717.5.G3 K64 1981

LABOR MOBILITY - GERMANY (WEST) - BERGISCHES LAND - CONGRESSES.
Die Wirtschaftliche Entwicklung in den Arbeitsmarktregionen des Bergischen Landes . Bochum , 1981. 401 p. : ISBN 3-88339-217-0 LC Card 82-164818 DDC 331/.0943/55 19
HD8459.N66 W57 1981
NYPL [JLD 86-1639]

LABOR MOBILITY - GREAT BRITAIN.
Jackson, J. A. (John Archer), 1929- Migration /. London , New York , 1986. 91 p. : ISBN 0-582-48052-3 LC Card 85-13098 DDC 304.8/0941 19
HB2043 .M54 1986 ***NYPL [JLD 86-2119]***

Standing, Guy. Unemployment and labour market flexibility . Geneva , 1986. xi, 147 p. : ISBN 92-2-105291-5 (pbk.) : LC Card 87-114658 DDC 331.13/7941 19
HD5765.A6 S72 1986

LABOR MOBILITY - HUNGARY - STATISTICS.
Budapest és a jelentősebb városok napi munkaerővonzási körzete népességének főbb jellemzői, 1980. január 1. /. Budapest , 1986. 106 p. : ISBN 963-02-4578-7 LC Card 87-407674
HA1205 .B83 1986

LABOR MOBILITY - INDIA.
Pande, Sunanda. Trends in occupational mobility among migrants /. Jaipur , 1986. xii, 232 p. ; ISBN 81-7033-023-8 : LC Card 86-902816 DDC 331.5/44/0954 19
HD5856.I4 P36 1986

LABOR MOBILITY - ITALY.
Seravalli, Gilberto, 1946- Gli effetti delle integrazioni salariali sulla mobilità del lavoro /. Milano, Italy , c1986. 119 p. : LC Card 86-222523
HD5717.5.I8 S47 1986

LABOR MOBILITY - NETHERLANDS.
Vissers, A. M. C. Arbeidsmarktgedrag ten tijde van massale werkloosheid . 's-Gravenhage , 1986. 106 p. : ISBN 90-12-05302-1 LC Card 87-108930
HD5717.5.N45 V57 1986

LABOR MOBILITY - NIGERIA - ILORIN.
Watts, Susan J. Population mobility and multilocality in Ilorin, Kwara State, Nigeria /. [Liverpool , 1981-] v. <1 > : LC Card 86-226489 DDC 304.8/09669/5 19
HB2126.7.I46 W37 1981

LABOR MOBILITY - SOVIET UNION.
Nekotorye problemy internatsional'nogo vospitaniia v mnogonatsional'nom trudovom kollektive /. Moskva , 1985. 135 p. ; LC Card 86-233779
HD8526.5 .N45 1985

LABOR MOBILITY - SWITZERLAND.
Leibundgut, Hansjörg, 1947- Die Bedeutung der beruflichen Mobilität als arbeitsmarktlicher Ausgleichsprozess . Bern , New York , c1986. ix, 235 p. : ISBN 3-261-03630-3 LC Card 87-122350 DDC 331.12/79494 19
HD5717.5.S9 L45 1986

LABOR MOBILITY - UKRAINE - KIEV.
Sem'ia i vosproizvodstvo struktury trudovoĭ zaniatosti . Kiev , 1984. 238 p. : LC Card 86-142706
HB2698.U38 S46 1984

LABOR MOBILITY - UNITED STATES.
Labor mobility and economic opportunity . Westport, Conn. , 1987, c1954. vii, 118 p. ; ISBN 0-313-24975-X (lib. bdg. : alk. paper) LC Card 86-25763 DDC 331.12/7973 19
HD5717.5.U6 L33 1987

Labor movement in the United States. Sorge, Friedrich A. (Friedrich Adolf), 1828-1906. Friedrich A. Sorge's labor movement in the United States . New York , c1987. xiii, 196 p. ; ISBN 0-313-25518-0 (lib. bdg. : alk. paper) LC Card 86-31792 DDC 331/.0973 19
HD8072 .S7175 1987

LABOR ORGANIZATIONS. see **TRADE-UNIONS.**

LABOR, ORGANIZED. see **TRADE-UNIONS.**

LABOR OUTPUT. see **LABOR PRODUCTIVITY.**

Labor Party (Great Britain) see **Labour Party (Great Britain)**

LABOR POLICY - AFRICA - CONGRESSES.
JASPA Steering Group Meeting on Priority Employment Policies and Projects for Africa (1985 : Addis Ababa, Ethiopia) Report of JASPA Steering Group Meeting on Priority Employment Policies and Projects for Africa. Addis Ababa , 1986. 43 leaves ; LC Card 87-980227 DDC 331.12/042/096 19
HD5837.A6 J37 1985

LABOR POLICY - ARGENTINA.
Informe del gobierno argentino sobre asuntos laborales /. Buenos Aires, República Argentina , 1965. 115 leaves ; LC Card 85-115096
HD8266.5 .I53 1965

LABOR POLICY - AUSTRIA.
Schettkat, Ronald. Bevölkerungs- und Erwerbsverhaltensentwicklung in Österreich, Schweden und der Bundesrepublik Deutschland /. Berlin [1984] 48 p. ; LC Card 85-198691
HD5771 .S34 1984

LABOR POLICY - BELGIUM.
Struktur und Arbeitsweise von Arbeitsverwaltungen in EG-Ländern Frankreich, Belgien, Italien . Nürnberg , 1982. 206 p. : LC Card 83-174401
HD8431 .S77 1982

LABOR POLICY - BERLIN (GERMANY) - CONGRESSES.
DIW-Symposion (1983 : Berlin, Germany) Strategien für mehr Arbeitsplätze in Berlin . Berlin , c1984. 209 p. : ISBN 3-87061-277-0 LC Card 84-202956
HD5780.B4 D58 1983

LABOR POLICY - BOLIVIA - HISTORY.
Alvarez España, Waldo. Memorias del primer ministro obrero . La Paz, Bolivia , 1986. 300 p., [6] leaves of plates : LC Card 87-403477 DDC 331.88/0984 19
HD6608.5.A55 A3 1986

LABOR POLICY - BRAZIL.
Andrade, Luis F. The labor climate in Brazil /. Philadelphia, Pa. , c1985. viii, 133 p. ; ISBN 0-89546-057-2 (pbk.) LC Card 85-81947 DDC 331/.0981 19
HD8286.5 .A67 1985 ***NYPL [JLF 86-1201]***

LABOR POLICY - BRAZIL - SÃO PAULO (STATE) - HISTORY - 19TH CENTURY.
Salles, Iraci Galvão. Trabalho, progresso e a sociedade civilizada . São Paulo [Brasília] , 1986. 145 p. ; LC Card 86-224281
HD8289.S282 S24 1986

LABOR POLICY - BULGARIA.
Radev, Simeon. Sotsialnata programa na partiiata-delo na trudoviia kolektiv /. Sofiia , 1984. 173 p. ; LC Card 84-172433
HD8626.5 .R32 1984

LABOR POLICY - CANADA.
Adapting to change . Toronto [Ont.] , Buffalo , c1986. xv, 221 p. ; ISBN 0-8020-7260-7 (pbk.) LC Card 86-673029 DDC 331.12/0971 19
HD5728 .A596 1986 ***NYPL [JLD 87-1967]***

Canadian Railway Labour Association. CRLA submission to the government of Canada /. Ottawa [1977] 28, 31 p. ; LC Card 84-256714
HE2807 .C33 1977

LABOR POLICY - CHILE.
Barrera, Manuel. Sindicatos y estado en el Chile actual . Geneva, Switzerland , Santiago, Chile , c1985. v, 196 p. : LC Card 87-118607
HD6617 .B27 1985

Barrera, Manuel. Trade unions and the state in the present day Chile . Geneva, Switzerland , Santiago, Chile , 1986. xx, 154 p. : LC Card 87-128364 DDC 331.89/0983 19
HD6617 .B273 1986

Cruz, María Elena. Chile--opciones y desafíos del sindicalismo rural, 1973-1985 /. Santiago, Chile , 1985. 57 p. ; LC Card 87-100897
HD6619.A29 C78 1985

LABOR POLICY - EUROPE.
La Flexibilité du travail en Europe . Paris , 1986. 330 p. : ISBN 2-7071-1598-3 : LC Card 86-173845
HD8376.5 .F57 1986

LABOR POLICY - EUROPE - CASE STUDIES.
Runggaldier, Ulrich. Le politiche regionali del lavoro . Milano, Italy , c1986. 160 p. ; LC Card 86-169484
HD8376.5 .R93 1986

LABOR POLICY - EUROPEAN ECONOMIC COMMUNITY COUNTRIES.
Dötsch, Jochen. EG und Arbeiterrechte . Berlin , 1981. 143 p. ; LC Card 81-145834 DDC 331.11/094 19
HD8380.5 .D67 1981 ***NYPL [JLD 86-2739]***

Emerson, Michael. What model for Europe? /. Cambridge, Mass. , c1988. xi, 151 p. : ISBN 0-262-05036-6 LC Card 87-15151 DDC 331.11/094 19
HD8380.5 .E47 1988

LABOR POLICY - FRANCE.
Aglietta, Michel. Les métamorphoses de la société salariale . Paris , c1984. 274 p. ; ISBN 2-7021-1230-7 : LC Card 84-176554 DDC 331/.0944 19
HD8431 .A36 1984 ***NYPL [JLD 87-478]***

Struktur und Arbeitsweise von Arbeitsverwaltungen in EG-Ländern Frankreich, Belgien, Italien . Nürnberg , 1982. 206 p. : LC Card 83-174401
HD8431 .S77 1982

LABOR POLICY - GERMANY - HISTORY.
Herbert, Ulrich, 1951- Geschichte der Ausländer, Beschäftigung in Deutschland, 1880 bis 1980 . Berlin , c1986. 272 p. : ISBN 3-8012-3019-8 LC Card 87-113703 DDC

331.6/2/0943 19
HD8458.A2 H39 1986

LABOR POLICY - GERMANY, WEST.

Bernschneider, Wolfgang. Staat, Gewerkschaft und Arbeitsprozess . Opladen , c1986. viii, 291 p. : ISBN 3-531-11797-1 LC Card 86-222066
HD5710.75.G3 B47 1986

Löffler, Reiner. Macht, Arbeit und Humanität . Göttingen , c1986. v, 563 p. ; ISBN 3-921969-12-3 LC Card 86-227215
HD6957.G3 L64 1986

Schettkat, Ronald. Bevölkerungs- und Erwerbsverhaltensentwicklung in Österreich, Schweden und der Bundesrepublik Deutschland /. Berlin [1984] 48 p. ; LC Card 85-198691
HD5771 .S34 1984

Die Zweite Stadt . Opladen , c1986. 407 p. : ISBN 3-531-11764-5 LC Card 87-497505 DDC 331.11/0943 19
HD8451 .Z94 1986

LABOR POLICY - GERMANY, WEST - ADDRESSES, ESSAYS, LECTURES.

Wenig Arbeit--aber viel zu tun . Opladen , c1985. 195 p. : ISBN 3-531-11724-6
NYPL [JLE 86-1602]

LABOR POLICY - GERMANY, WEST - CONGRESSES.

Gestaltungsspielräume der Arbeitsmarktpolitik auf regionalen Arbeitsmärkten . Berlin , c1984. 180 p. : ISBN 3-428-05614-0 LC Card 84-218530
HD8444 .G47 1984

LABOR POLICY - GREAT BRITAIN.

Britain's industrial future . New York , 1985. xxiv, 503 p. ; ISBN 0-8240-7605-2 (alk. paper) : LC Card 85-13042 DDC 338.941 19
HC256.3 .B728 1985 *NYPL [JLD 86-3461]*

LABOR POLICY - GREAT BRITAIN - HISTORY.

Morris, Jenny, 1950- Women workers and the sweated trades . Aldershot, Hants, England , Brookfield, Vt., USA , c1986. 248 p. ; ISBN 0-566-05188-5 : LC Card 86-9850 DDC 331.4/23 19
HD2339.G7 M67 1986
NYPL [JLD 86-4089]

LABOR POLICY - HONDURAS.

Honduras . [Santiago, Chile] , 1983. vii, 99 p. ; LC Card 84-225233
HD5736.A6 H66 1983

LABOR POLICY - HUNGARY.

Juhász, Ottó. A népgazdasági szintü gazdaságpolitikai döntések végrehajtását segitő szakszervezeti munka . [Budapest] [1984] 136 p. ; ISBN 963-608-064-X LC Card 86-126615
HD6680.5 .J84 1984

LABOR POLICY - INDIA - ADDRESSES, ESSAYS, LECTURES.

Aziz, Abdul, 1937- Labour problems of a developing economy /. New Delhi , c1984. viii, 157 p. ; LC Card 84-901201 DDC 331/.0954 19
HD8686.5 .A95 1984 *NYPL [JLD 86-4216]*

Ranadive, K. R. Accumulation, employment, and labour aristocracy . Bombay [1982] 55 p. ; LC Card 83-903051 DDC 305.5/62/0954 19
HD8686.5 .R325 1982 *NYPL [JLF 87-500]*

Labor Policy Institute (AFL-CIO) The Environment of the workplace and human values /. New York , c1986. vii, 118 p. ; ISBN 0-8451-4205-4 LC Card 85-23908 DDC 174/.4 19
HD7260.5 .E58 1986 *NYPL [JLF 87-151]*

LABOR POLICY - INTERNATIONAL COOPERATION - CONGRESSES.

Souvenir, ICFTU World Conference on the Trade Union Role in Balanced Development, Vigyan Bhawan, New Delhi, India, March 18-20, 1981 /. New Delhi [1981] 68 p. : LC Card 84-901715 DDC 331.88 19
HD6475.A2 I26347 1981
NYPL [JLG 86-296]

LABOR POLICY - ITALY.

De Michelis, G. (Gianni) Il piano del lavoro /. Roma , 1986. xii, 267 p. : ISBN 88-420-2753-7 : LC Card 86-219772
HD8481 .D42 1986

Struktur und Arbeitsweise von Arbeitsverwaltungen in EG-Ländern Frankreich, Belgien, Italien . Nürnberg , 1982. 206 p. : LC Card 83-174401
HD8431 .S77 1982

La Tutela del lavoro in Italia. [Roma] [1976] 144 p. ; LC Card 86-233354
HD8481 .T85 1976

LABOR POLICY - JAPAN - HISTORY.

Park, Sung-Jo. U. S. labor policy in postwar Japan /. [Berlin] [c1985] 157 p. : ISBN 3-88548-424-2 LC Card 86-200166 DDC 331.11/0952 19
HD5827.A6 P37 1985

LABOR POLICY - JAPAN - HISTORY - 20TH CENTURY.

Gordon, Andrew, 1952- The evolution of labor relations in Japan . Cambridge, Mass. , 1985. xvi, 524 p. : ISBN 0-674-27130-0 (Harvard Univ. Pr.) LC Card 85-3747 DDC 331/.0952 19
HD8726 .G67 1985 *NYPL [M-11 435 v.117]*

LABOR POLICY - KENYA.

Cheru, Fantu. Dependence, underdevelopment, and unemployment in Kenya . Lanham, MD , c1987. xvii, 198 p. : ISBN 0-8191-6539-5 (alk. paper) : LC Card 87-13710 DDC 331.13/77/096762 19
HD6276.K42 C46 1987

LABOR POLICY - PERU.

Izquierda Unida (Political party) Plan laboral de Izquierda Unida. [Lima?] , 1986. 67 p. ; LC Card 87-107365
HD8346.5 .I97 1986

Las Leyes de estabilidad laboral y sus efectos económicos /. Lima, Perú [1986?] 67 p. : LC Card 87-403254 DDC 331.11/0985 19
HD8344 .L49 1986

LABOR POLICY - RED SEA REGION.

Pennisi, Giuseppe. Development, manpower and migration in the Red Sea region . Hamburg , c1981. xi, 264 p. : LC Card 82-109615 DDC 331.6/2/091824 19
HD8656 .P46 1981 *NYPL [JLF 86-1602]*

LABOR POLICY - ROMANIA - CONGRESSES.

Congress of Working People of Romania (3rd : 1986 : Bucharest, Romania) Third Congress of Working People of Romania. Bucharest [1986?] ii, 56 p. ; LC Card 86-225999 DDC 331/.09498 19
HD8642 .C59 1986

LABOR POLICY - SOUTH AFRICA - CAPE OF GOOD HOPE.

Goldin, Ian. The poverty of Coloured labour preference . Cape Town [1984] ii, 97 p. : ISBN 0-7992-0570-2 (pbk.) LC Card 84-195453
HD8801.Z8 C324 1984

LABOR POLICY - SOVIET UNION - HISTORY.

McDaniel, Tim. Autocracy, capitalism, and the revolution in Russia /. Berkeley , c1987. p. cm. ISBN 0-520-05532-2 (alk. paper) LC Card 86-30790 DDC 322.4/2/0947 19
HD8526 .M385 1987

LABOR POLICY - SRI LANKA.

Labour standards in Sri Lanka . [Colombo] , 1981. x, 164 p. ; LC Card 83-902877 DDC 331/.09549/3 19
HD8670.8 .L32 1981 *NYPL [JLC 87-22]*

LABOR POLICY - SWEDEN.

Meidner, Rudolf. I arbetets tjänst /. Stockholm , 1984. 473 p. : ISBN 91-550-2932-9 : LC Card 84-229372
HD5803 .M45 1984

Öhman, Berndt, 1940- Kommunerna och sysselsättningspolitiken . [Stockholm] [1985] 212 p. ; ISBN 91-38-08745-6 LC Card 86-114034
HD5803 .O36 1985

Schettkat, Ronald. Bevölkerungs- und Erwerbsverhaltensentwicklung in Österreich, Schweden und der Bundesrepublik Deutschland /. Berlin [1984] 48 p. ; LC Card 85-198691
HD5771 .S34 1984

Towards a democratic rationality . Aldershot, Hants, England , Brookfield, Vt., USA , c1986. xi, 281 p. : ISBN 0-566-00761-4 : LC Card 86-14241 DDC 331/.09485 19
HD8576.5 .T69 1986 *NYPL [JLD 86-3873]*

LABOR POLICY - UKRAINE - HISTORY - 20TH CENTURY.

Ovsiīenko, O. F. Krakh zubatovshchyny na Ukraïni /. Kyïv , 1987. 137, [3] p. ; LC Card 87-161669
HD8529.U43 O97 1987

LABOR POLICY - UNITED STATES.

Allen, Robert E. (Robert Edward), 1946- Contemporary labor relations /. Reading, Mass. , c1988. xi, 724 p. : ISBN 0-201-10083-5 : LC Card 87-24128 DDC 331/.0973 19
HD8072.5 .A43 1988

LABOR POLICY - UNITED STATES - HISTORY.

Bernstein, Irving, 1916- A caring society . Boston , 1985. 338 p., [24] p. of plates : ISBN 0-395-33116-1 : LC Card 84-25129 DDC 362.8/5/0973 19
HD8072 .B365 1985 *NYPL [JLD 86-2102]*

Fairchild, Byron. The Army and industrial manpower /. Westport, Conn. , 1987. xiv, 291 p. : ISBN 0-313-25480-X (lib. bdg. : alk. paper) LC Card 86-25738 DDC 331.11/0973 19
HD5724 .F25 1987

Rogulev, ĪU. N. (ĪUriĭ Nikolaevich) Krakh rabocheĭ politiki administratsii Trumėna . Moskva , 1981. 135 p. ; LC Card 82-155486
HD8072.5 .R64 1981

You may call her madam secretary [motion picture] /. West Tisbury, MA , 1987. 1 film reel (57 min., 40 sec.) : LC Card 87-706816 DDC 973.917 11
HD8073.P38

You may call her madam secretary [videorecording] /. West Tisbury, MA , 1987. 1 videocassette (57 min., 40 sec.) : LC Card 87-706817 DDC 973.917 11
HD8073.P38

LABOR POLICY - UNITED STATES - HISTORY - 20TH CENTURY.

Kochan, Thomas A. The transformation of American industrial relations /. New York , c1986. viii, 287 p. ; ISBN 0-465-08696-9 : LC Card 85-47502 DDC 331/.0973 19
HD8072 .K67 1986

Vittoz, Stanley. New Deal labor policy and the American industrial economy /. Chapel Hill , c1987. 241 p. ; ISBN 0-8078-1729-5 LC Card 86-24911 DDC 331/.0973 19
HD8072 .V715 1987

LABOR PRODUCTIVITY - ABSTRACTS.

Parnes, Steven. Productivity and the quality of working life /. Scarsdale, N.Y. , c1978. 43 p. ; LC Card 78-51009 DDC 658.31/4
HD57 .P33 *NYPL [JLM 83-380 no.2]*

LABOR PRODUCTIVITY - ACCOUNTING. see **PRODUCTIVITY ACCOUNTING.**

LABOR PRODUCTIVITY - ADDRESSES, ESSAYS, LECTURES.

Okonomische und soziale Wirksamkeit des wissenschaftlich-technischen Fortschritts /. Berlin , 1986. 314 p. : ISBN 3-320-00713-0
NYPL [JLD 86-4381]

LABOR PRODUCTIVITY AND WAGES. see **WAGES AND LABOR PRODUCTIVITY.**

LABOR PRODUCTIVITY - AUSTRALIA.

Structured chaos . Melbourne , New York , 1985. viii, 111 p. : ISBN 0-19-554687-3 LC Card 86-222312 DDC 338/.06/0994 19
HC610.I52 S77 1985

LABOR PRODUCTIVITY - BRAZIL.

Reis, Ulysses A. (Ulysses Alves) Educação & produtividade /. Salvador-BA [Rio de Janeiro] , 1984. 184 p. : ISBN 85-85023-05-8 LC Card 87-130042 DDC 331.11/8/0981 19
HC190.L3 R45 1984

LABOR PRODUCTIVITY - BULGARIA.

Aktualni ikonomicheski problemi . Sofiīa , 1985. 227 p. ; LC Card 86-205815
HC403 .A67 1985

Bliznakov, Ĭordan Petrov. Sotsialisticheskoto sŭrevnovanie v usloviīata na intenzifikatsiīata na proizvodstvoto /. Sofiīa , 1983. 101 p. : LC Card 85-140845
HC403.Z9 S613 1983

Dimitrov, Boris. Elitnite īadra na trudovite kolektivi /. Sofiīa , 1985. 80 p. ; LC Card 86-140524
HD8626.5 .D55 1985

Narŭchnik na profsŭīuzniīa aktivist . [[Sofia?] , 1985. 264 p. ; LC Card 85-216969
HC403.Z9 L366 1985

Pamukchiev, Minko Stoĭchev. Intelektualizatsiia na truda i proizvodstvoto /. Sofiia , 1982. 48 p. ; LC Card 82-183037
HF5548.8 .P255 1982

Proizvoditel'nost' truda v razvitom sotsialisticheskom obshchestve /. Moskva , 1982. 214 p. ; LC Card 83-166417
HC340.L3 P687 1982

Shopov, Dimitŭr. Kachestvoto na truda . Sofiia , 1984. 202 p. : LC Card 85-117683
HC403.Z9 L375 1984

Tomov, Mitko. Pŭtishta za podobriavane na kachestvoto /. Pleven , 1984. 68, [4] p. ; LC Card 85-179053
HC403.Z9 L38 1984

LABOR PRODUCTIVITY - CHINA.
Song, Du-Yul, 1944- Sowjetunion und China . Frankfurt/Main , New York , c1984. 255 p. : ISBN 3-593-33351-1 LC Card 84-169164
HC340.L3 S66 1984

LABOR PRODUCTIVITY - COSTA RICA.
Pucci, Carlos. Los precios sociales en la evaluación de proyectos en Costa Rica /. San José, Costa Rica , 1979. [108] leaves ; LC Card 83-238167
HC143.Z9 L36 1979

LABOR PRODUCTIVITY - DEVELOPING COUNTRIES.
Kahnert, Friedrich, 1929- Improving urban employment and labor productivity /. Washington, D.C. [1987] 75 p. ; ISBN 0-8213-0908-0 (pbk.) LC Card 87-10538 DDC 331.11/09172/4 19
HD5852 .K34 1987

LABOR PRODUCTIVITY - ECONOMETRIC MODELS.
Schettkat, Ronald. Generelle Arbeitszeitverkürzung . Berlin , 1984. iii, 108 p. : LC Card 84-182608
HD5106 .S3 1984

LABOR PRODUCTIVITY - GERMANY, EAST.
Bedürfnisse und Interessen als Triebkräfte unseres Handelns /. Berlin , 1984. 155 p. ; LC Card 84-229147
HC290.795.C3 B43 1984

LABOR PRODUCTIVITY - GERMANY, WEST.
Pusse, Leo. Arbeitsproduktivität und Beschäftigung . Freiburg im Breisgau , c1984. viii, 311 p. : ISBN 3-448-01512-1 LC Card 85-138794
HC290.5.L3 P87 1984

Tınar, Mustafa Yaşar, 1955- Humanisierung der Arbeit und Produktivität . Frankfurt am Main , New York , c1986. xiii, 296 p. : ISBN 3-8204-9542-8 LC Card 86-233418
HF5549.5.J63 T55 1986

LABOR PRODUCTIVITY - GOVERNMENT POLICY - INDONESIA.
Indonesia. Kantor Menteri Negara Urusan Peranan Wanita. Pokok-pokok petunjuk pelaksanaan Program Peningkatan Produktivitas Kerja Tenaga Kerja Wanita Melalui Pendekatan Kesejahteraan Terpadu, tahun 1984/1986 (Juklak Nakerwan). Jakarta [1984] iii, xii, 47 p. ; LC Card 86-940168
HD6194 .I5 1984

LABOR PRODUCTIVITY - INDIA.
Singh, Nar, 1952- Sharing of productivity gains in Indian industry /. Delhi , 1984. x, 180 p. ;
NYPL [JLD 86-4253]

LABOR PRODUCTIVITY - RUSSIAN S.F.S.R.
Vinogradov, I. P. (Igor' Petrovich) Proizvoditel'nost' truda--glavnoe zveno ėffektivnosti /. Moskva , 1980. 192 p. ; LC Card 81-134882
HC340.L3 V459 1980

LABOR PRODUCTIVITY - RUSSIAN S.F.S.R. - DAGESTANSKAIA A.S.S.R.
Sovershenstvovanie khoziaĭstvennogo mekhanizma i ratsional'noe ispol'zovanie resursov . Makhachkala , 1985. 190 p. : LC Card 87-136485
HC337.D3 S655 1985

LABOR PRODUCTIVITY - RUSSIAN S.F.S.R. - NON-CHERNOZEM REGION.
Partiĭnye organizatsii Nechernozem'ia v bor'be za povyshenie proizvodstvennoĭ i politicheskoĭ aktivnosti rabochego klassa v period postroeniia i razvitiia sotsializma /. Kalinin , 1985. 152 p. ; LC Card 86-196840
HC337.R85 P36 1985

LABOR PRODUCTIVITY - RUSSIAN S.F.S.R. - URAL MOUNTAINS REGION - CONGRESSES.
Kardinal'nyĭ rost ėffektivnosti zhivogo truda--glavnyĭ faktor uskoreniia sotsial'no-ėkonomicheskogo razvitiia . Sverdlovsk , 1986. 2 v. ; LC Card 87-136690
HC337.R853 L35 1986

LABOR PRODUCTIVITY - SOVIET UNION.
Artemov, IU. M. (IUriĭ Mikhaĭlovich) Finansovye metody material'nogo stimulirovaniia proizvodstva /. Moskva , 1983. 126 p. ; LC Card 84-118738
HF5549.5.I5 A69 1983

Babakov, V. M. (Viktor Mikhaĭlovich) Protsent sverkh plana /. Volgograd , 1986. 45 p. : LC Card 86-220320
HC340.S6 B23 1986

Bohynia, D. P. Ėffektivnost' obshchestvennogo truda v usloviiakh razvitogo sotsializma . Kiev , 1982. 316 p. ; LC Card 82-200989
HC340.L3 B56 1982

Bukhval'd, E. M. Povyshenie proizvoditel'nosti truda--kliuchevaia zadacha sovetskoĭ ėkonomiki . Moskva , 1984. 63 p. ; LC Card 85-188977
HC340.L3 B85 1984

Izmenenie soderzhaniia i kharaktera truda na sovremennom ėtape razvitogo sotsializma /. Moskva , 1984. 227 p. ; LC Card 85-240356
HD8526.5 .I97 1984

Marshruty peredovogo opyta /. Moskva , 1985. 286 p., [8] p. of plates : LC Card 85-213253
HC340.L3 M235 1985

Material'noe stimulirovanie v khoziaĭstvennom mekhanizme sotsialisticheskogo obshchestva . Leningrad , 1986. 152 p. ; LC Card 86-175029
HF5549.5.I5 M3385 1986

Nemtsev, F. L. (Fedor Logvinovich) Upravlenie trudom v usloviiakh nauchno-tekhnicheskogo progressa /. Minsk , 1985. 125 p. ; LC Card 85-231066
HF5549.2.S65 N45 1985

Problemy ėffektivnosti ispol'zovaniia trudovykh resursov /. Moskva , 1981. 147 p. ; LC Card 82-150334
HC340.L3 P64 1981

Proizvoditel'nost' truda v razvitom sotsialisticheskom obshchestve /. Moskva , 1982. 214 p. ; LC Card 83-166417
HC340.L3 P687 1982

Proizvoditel'nost' truda--vazhneĭshiĭ faktor povysheniia ėffektivnosti proizvodstva /. Moskva , 1982. 358 p. ; LC Card 83-140430
HC340.L3 P693 1982

Song, Du-Yul, 1944- Sowjetunion und China . Frankfurt/Main , New York , c1984. 255 p. : ISBN 3-593-33351-1 LC Card 84-169164
HC340.L3 S66 1984

Sotsial'no-ėkonomicheskie problemy intensifikatsii obshchestvennogo proizvodstva /. Moskva , 1983. 91 p. : LC Card 84-114234
HD56 .S688 1983

Trudovoe pravo i povyshenie kachestva truda /. Moskva , 1987. 270 p. ;
NYPL [*QIX 87-3357]

Vinogradov, I. P. (Igor' Petrovich) Proizvoditel'nost' truda--glavnoe zveno ėffektivnosti /. Moskva , 1980. 192 p. ; LC Card 81-134882
HC340.L3 V459 1980

Vozdeĭstvie khoziaĭstvennogo mekhanizma na povyshenie ėffektivnosti obshchestvennogo proizvodstva . Dnepropetrovsk , 1984. 119 p. ; LC Card 86-181397
HC340.I52 V68 1984

LABOR PRODUCTIVITY - SOVIET UNION - CONGRESSES.
Povyshenie trudovoĭ i obshchestvenno-politicheskoĭ aktivnosti mass kak reshaiushchiĭ faktor uskoreniia sotsial'no-ėkonomicheskogo progressa sotsialisticheskogo obshchestva . Kaliningrad , 1986. 382 p. ; LC Card 87-136621
HD8526.5 .P62 1986

LABOR PRODUCTIVITY - SOVIET UNION - MEASUREMENT - DATA PROCESSING.
Ėkonomicheskie funktsii upravleniia proizvoditel'nym trudom /. Kiev , 1986. 167 p. ; LC Card 87-152432
HD9705.S595 E37 1986

LABOR PRODUCTIVITY - SOVIET UNION - STATISTICAL METHODS.
Krylov, V. F. (Vladimir Fedorovich) Sravnitel'nyĭ analiz deiatel'nosti predpriiatiĭ /. Moskva , 1981. 69 p. ; LC Card 82-112692
HC340.L3 K75 1981

Statisticheskoe izuchenie proizvoditel'nosti truda /. Moskva , 1981. 407 p. ; LC Card 82-155063 DDC 330/.018 s 331.11/8/0947 19
HA1.A38 A15 t. 41 HC340.L3
NYPL [*QIP 87-1311]

LABOR PRODUCTIVITY - STATISTICAL METHODS.
Statisticheskoe izuchenie proizvoditel'nosti truda /. Moskva , 1981. 407 p. ; LC Card 82-155063 DDC 330/.018 s 331.11/8/0947 19
HA1.A38 A15 t. 41 HC340.L3
NYPL [*QIP 87-1311]

LABOR PRODUCTIVITY - UNITED STATES.
The Productivity sourcebook /. Amherst, Mass. [1987] x, 467 p. : ISBN 0-87425-075-7 (pbk.) LC Card 87-404037 DDC 658.3/14 19
HD57 .P7114 1987

LABOR PRODUCTIVITY - UNITED STATES - ABSTRACTS.
Guzzo, Richard A. Programs for productivity and quality of work life /. New York , c1983. 38 p. ; ISBN 0-08-030964-X (pbk.) : LC Card 83-22029 DDC 658.3/14 19
HC110.L3 G89 1983
NYPL [JLM 83-380 no.32]

LABOR PRODUCTIVITY - YUGOSLAVIA.
Pavlović, Dragiša, 1943- Ko radnike povezuje lažnim koncima . Beograd , 1984. 414 p. ; LC Card 84-178578
HC407.Z9 L36 1984

Labor relations . Sandver, Marcus H. Boston , c1987. xxii, 529 p. : ISBN 0-316-77024-8 LC Card 86-27314 DDC 331/.0973 19
HD8072.5 .S32 1987

Labor relations . Sauer, Robert L. Columbus, Ohio , c1987. x, 518 p. : ISBN 0-675-20207-8 LC Card 87-134391 DDC 331/.0973 19
HD8066 .S28 1987

Labor relations /. Sloane, Arthur A. Englewood Cliffs, N.J. , c1988. xiv, 543 p. : ISBN 0-13-519604-3 LC Card 87-14535 DDC 331.89/0973 19
HD8072 .S6185 1988

Labor relations . Wolters, Roger S. Chicago , c1988. xi, 321 p. ; ISBN 0-03-069304-7 (pbk.) LC Card 87-19941 DDC 331 19
HD8072.5 .W65 1988

LABOR RELATIONS. see **INDUSTRIAL RELATIONS.**

Labor relations and public policy series, 0075-7470 .
(no. 21) O'Reilly, James T., 1947- Unions' rights to company information /. Philadelphia, Pa. , c1987. xiii, 312 p. ; ISBN 0-89546-060-2 LC Card 85-82257
NYPL [JLL 74-174 no.21]

The labor relations process /. Holley, William H. Chicago , c1988. xix, 714 p. : ISBN 0-03-012649-5 LC Card 87-9117 DDC 658.3/15/0973 19
HD8072.5 .H64 1988

Labor research report .
(1985, no. 4) Statistics relative to the New York State Unemployment Insurance Fund, 1936-1984. Albany, N.Y. [1985] vii, 66 p. ; LC Card 86-622164 DDC 368.4/4/009747021 19
HD7096.U6 N793 1985

LABOR, RIGHT TO. see **RIGHT TO LABOR.**

Labor-saving techniques in food processing .
Nath, Kamla. Boston, MA (270 Bay State Rd., Boston 02215) , 1985. 26 leaves ; LC Card 87-155092 DDC 331.4/25 19
HD6073.A292 G256 1985

LABOR SERVICE - BULGARIA - HISTORY.
Kubadinski, Pencho P. Brigadirski ogn'ove . Sofiia , 1986. 119 p., [24] p. of plates : LC

Card 86-235041
HD4870.B9 K83 1986

40 brigadirski leta /. Sofiia, 1986. 173 p., [12] p. of plates : LC Card 87-103049
HD4870.B9 A15 1986

LABOR SERVICE - SOVIET UNION - PICTORIAL WORKS.
Molodost', trud, romantika . Moskva , 1985. 183 p., [8] p. of plates : LC Card 86-113851
HD4870.S65 M65 1985

LABOR SUPPLY - AFRICA, NORTH.
La Politique de l'emploi-formation au Maghreb, 1970-1980 /. Paris , 1982. 472 p. : ISBN 2-222-03122-2 LC Card 84-222103 DDC 331.11/0961 19
HD5838 .P65 1982

LABOR SUPPLY - ALASKA - STATISTICS.
Alaska occupational information /. Juneau, Alaska , 1986. 126 p. : LC Card 86-623154 DDC 331.12/09798/021 19
HD5725.A4 A62 1986

LABOR SUPPLY - ALGERIA.
Bernard, Chantal. La politique de l'emploi-formation au Maghreb, 1970-1980 /. Paris , 1982. 472 p. ; ***NYPL [JLE 86-568]***

Voss, Timm. Die algerisch-französische Arbeitsmigration . Königstein/Ts. , 1981. xiii, 193 p. : ISBN 3-7756-6937-X : LC Card 81-176949 DDC 331.6/2/65044 19
HD8438.A4 V67 1981 ***NYPL [JLD 86-2466]***

LABOR SUPPLY - AMERICA - HISTORY - CONGRESSES.
Colonialism and migration . Dordrecht , Higham, MA, USA , 1986. vi, 303 p. : ISBN 90-247-3253-0 LC Card 85-21809 DDC 331.11/73 19
HD4875.A837 C65 1986
NYPL [JLE 86-3920]

LABOR SUPPLY - ARGENTINA.

LABOR SUPPLY - ARGENTINA - CASE STUDIES.
Diéguez, Héctor L. Mercados de trabajo y distribución de ingresos en cuatro centros urbanos de Argentina, 1974-1981 /. Buenos Aires, Argentina , 1984. 49 p. ; ISBN 950-621-013-6 LC Card 87-401771 DDC 331.12/982 19
HD5749 .D54 1984

LABOR SUPPLY - ARGENTINA - RÍO NEGRO.
Lindenboim, Javier. Monetarismo y mercado de trabajo . Buenos Aires, Argentina , c1985. x, 471 p. : ISBN 950-9370-05-3 LC Card 87-122243 DDC 331.12/0982/73 19
HD5750.R56 L56 1985

LABOR SUPPLY - ARKANSAS.
Occupational trends, 1982-1995. Little Rock, AR (P.O. Box 2981, Little Rock, AR 72203) [1986]- v. ; ***NYPL [JLM 87-353]***

LABOR SUPPLY - ARKANSAS - STATISTICS.
Occupational employment statistics program . [Little Rock, Ark.] (P.O. Box 2981, Little Rock 72203) [1986] v leaves, 223 p. ; LC Card 87-620868 DDC 331.12/51/0009767021 19
HD5725.A8 O264 1986

Staffing patterns for manufacturing industries and hospitals /. Little Rock, Ark. [1983?] vi leaves, 249 p. ; LC Card 86-623216 DDC 331.12/57/09767 19
HD5725.A8 S79 1983

LABOR SUPPLY - ASIA.
Trudovye resursy Vostoka . Moskva , 1987. 319 p. ; LC Card 87-142995
HD5811.85.A6 T78 1987

LABOR SUPPLY - AUSTRALIA.
Bosworth, Derek L. Labour utilisation in Australia . [Bedford Park, S. Aust.] [1986] i, 205 p. : LC Card 86-229498 DDC 331.12/5/0994 19
HD5850.A6 B67 1986

LABOR SUPPLY - AUSTRALIA - CONGRESSES.
Japanese and Australian labour markets . Canberra [c1983] xx, 610 p. : ISBN 0-86413-004-X (pbk.) : LC Card 84-220557 DDC 331.12/0952 19
HD5850.A6 J36 1983 ***NYPL [JLE 86-630]***

LABOR SUPPLY - AUSTRALIA - EFFECT OF TECHNOLOGICAL INNOVATIONS ON - CONGRESSES.
The Future impact of technology on work and education /. London , New York , 1987. p. cm. ISBN 1-85000-083-2 : LC Card 87-13641 DDC 331.12/0994 19
HD6331.2.A8 F87 1987

Work, leisure, and technology /. Melbourne, Australia , 1986. vi, 273 p. : ISBN 0-582-71151-7 (pbk.) LC Card 87-105477 DDC 303.4/83/0994 19
HD6331.2.A8 W67 1986

LABOR SUPPLY - AUSTRIA.
Schettkat, Ronald. Bevölkerungs- und Erwerbsverhaltensentwicklung in Österreich, Schweden und der Bundesrepublik Deutschland /. Berlin [1984] 48 p. ; LC Card 85-198691
HD5771 .S34 1984

Wirtschaftskarten von Österreich /. Berlin , 1938. 38 p. : LC Card 86-179061
HC265 .W554 1938

LABOR SUPPLY - AUSTRIA - CARINTHIA - STATISTICS.
Die Entwicklung der Beschäftigungslage in Kärnten seit 1960 /. Klagenfurt [1979] 23 leaves : LC Card 85-143747
HD5772.C37 E57 1979

LABOR SUPPLY - AUSTRIA - ECONOMETRIC MODELS.
Böhm, Walter. Längsschnittanalyse des österreichischen Arbeitsmarktes . Wien , 1986. 138 p. : ISBN 3-85369-654-6 LC Card 87-142156 DDC 331.12/5/09436 19
HD5771 .B64 1986

LABOR SUPPLY - AUSTRIA - MAPS.
Wirtschaftskarten von Österreich /. Berlin , 1938. 38 p. : LC Card 86-179061
HC265 .W554 1938

LABOR SUPPLY - AUSTRIA - SALZBURG (LAND) - REGIONAL DISPARITIES - STATISTICS.
Fink, Karl, Mag. Die regionale Dynamik des Salzburger Arbeitsmarktes, 1971-1980 . Salzburg [1981?] 212 p. : LC Card 82-171635
HD5772.S24 F56 1981 ***NYPL [JLG 86-301]***

LABOR SUPPLY - AUSTRIA - STATISTICS.
Ergebnisse der nichtlandwirtschaftlichen Betriebszählung vom 1. September 1954 /. Wien , 1958. 84 p. ; LC Card 84-252994
HD5779 .E74 1958

LABOR SUPPLY - BENIN.
Emploi d'abord . Addis Abeba , 1982. xxxviii, 499 p. ; LC Card 84-983423
hD5846.3.A6 E47 1982

LABOR SUPPLY - BERLIN (GERMANY)
Albrecht, Christoph, 1950- Beschäftigungsentwicklung und Qualifikationsstruktur in Berlin 1977-1983 . Berlin [1985] 2 v. : LC Card 86-204299
HD5780.B4 A43 1985

LABOR SUPPLY - BERLIN (GERMANY) - CONGRESSES.
DIW-Symposion (1983 : Berlin, Germany) Strategien für mehr Arbeitsplätze in Berlin . Berlin , c1984. 209 p. : ISBN 3-87061-277-0 LC Card 84-202956
HD5780.B4 D58 1983

LABOR SUPPLY - BOLIVIA - LA PAZ.
Sector formal de la ciudad de La Paz . La Paz, Bolivia , 1980. 77 leaves ; LC Card 81-212597 DDC 331.1/0984/12 19
HD5751.L36 S42 1980 ***NYPL [JLF 87-369]***

LABOR SUPPLY - BRAZIL.
Emprego urgente /. Curitiba , 1984. vii, 75 p. ; LC Card 86-177208
HD5713 .E47 1984

Grupos homogêneos no mercado de trabalho assalariado . Brasília , 1985. 56 p. : LC Card 85-231654
HD5004 .G78 1985

O Mercado de trabalho no Brasil . São Paulo , 1986. 263 p. : LC Card 86-221361
HD5754 .M47 1986

Oliveira, Lúcia Elena Garcia de. O lugar do negro na força de trabalho /. Rio de Janeiro , 1983. 86 p. ; ISBN 85-24-00024-4 LC Card 86-129924
HD8288.5.B55 O45 1983

A Transição incompleta . Rio de Janeiro-RJ , 1986. 2 v. ; LC Card 86-224684
HC187 .T72 1986

Vieira, Cláudio Afonso. Urbanização e custo de reprodução da força de trabalho /. São Paulo , 1984. 175 p., [5] folded leaves of plates :

LABOR SUPPLY - BRAZIL - ARAPIRACA REGION.
Estudo especial . Maceió, AL. , 1983. 174 leaves : LC Card 86-167829
HC189.A69 E88 1983

LABOR SUPPLY - BRAZIL - DISTRITO FEDERAL - STATISTICS.
Caracterização da população do Distrito Federal . Brasília , 1984. 56, [1] p. : LC Card 86-130173 DDC 331.12/0981/74021 19
HA988.D5 C37 1984

LABOR SUPPLY - BRAZIL - FORTALEZA.
Casimiro, Liana Maria Carleial de. Acumulação capitalista, emprego e crise . São Paulo , 1986. 216 p. : LC Card 87-152202 DDC 331.12/0981/31 19
HD5755.F6 C37 1986

LABOR SUPPLY - BRAZIL, NORTHEAST.
Grupos homogêneos no mercado de trabalho assalariado . Brasília , 1985. 56 p. : LC Card 85-231654
HD5004 .G78 1985

LABOR SUPPLY - BRAZIL, NORTHEAST - CONGRESSES.
Dinâmica da economia e absorção de mão-de-obra . Recife , 1984. 79 p. ; ISBN 85-7019-063-8 LC Card 85-156612 DDC 338.981/3 19
HD5755.N63 D56 1984
NYPL [JLE 86-3545]

LABOR SUPPLY - BRAZIL - RIO GRANDE DO SUL.
O Emprego no Rio Grande do Sul . Porto Alegre , 1985. 163 p. : LC Card 85-207909
HD5755.R54 E46 1985

LABOR SUPPLY - BRAZIL - SALVADOR METROPOLITAN AREA.
O gigante invisível . [Salvador] [1983] 105 p. : LC Card 84-181184
HD2346.B72 S25 1983

LABOR SUPPLY - BRAZIL - SÃO PAULO.
Vieira, Cláudio Afonso. Urbanização e custo de reprodução da força de trabalho /. São Paulo , 1984. 175 p., [5] folded leaves ; LC Card 85-136502
HD5755.S3 V54 1984

LABOR SUPPLY - BRAZIL - SÃO PAULO (STATE)
Grupos homogêneos no mercado de trabalho assalariado . Brasília , 1985. 56 p. : LC Card 85-231654
HD5004 .G78 1985

LABOR SUPPLY - BRAZIL - SAÕ PAULO (STATE) - STATISTICS.
Zingg, Rosa Lúcia. O SENAI e o mercado de trabalho industrial paulista . [São Paulo] , 1986. 37 leaves ; LC Card 87-402164 DDC 331.12/5/098161021 19
HD5755.S3 Z56 1986

LABOR SUPPLY - BRAZIL - STATISTICS.
Cadastro geral de empregados e desempregados (Lei 4,923/65) . [Brasília, Brazil] , 1985. [61] leaves ; LC Card 86-178290
HD5754 .C26 1985

LABOR SUPPLY - BULGARIA.
Problemi na sotsialisticheskata organizatsiia na truda /. Sofiia , 1986. 146 p. : LC Card 87-128832
HD5811.5.A6 P76 1986

LABOR SUPPLY - BULGARIA - EFFECT OF TECHNOLOGICAL INNOVATIONS ON - CONGRESSES.
Nauchno-tekhnicheskiiat progres i problemite na truda . Sofiia , 1986. 297 p. : LC Card 86-196075
HD6331.2.B9 N38 1986

LABOR SUPPLY - BURKINA FASO.
Emploi et formation en Haute-Volta . Addis-Abéba , 1983. x, 142 p. : LC Card 85-981183
HD5847.5.A6 E48 1983

LABOR SUPPLY - CALIFORNIA - STATISTICS.

Albano, Tracy. California employment and payrolls, April-June, 1985 /. [Sacramento] [1985] iii, 129 p. ; LC Card 86-623197 DDC 331.12/5/09794021 19
HD5725.C2 A614 1985

LABOR SUPPLY - CANADA.
Adapting to change . Toronto [Ont.] , Buffalo , c1986. xv, 221 p. ; ISBN 0-8020-7260-7 (pbk.) LC Card 86-673029 DDC 331.12/0971 19
HD5728 .A596 1986 ***NYPL [JLD 87-1967]***

Foot, David K. A challenge of the 1980s . [Toronto] , c1981. 99 p. in various pagings : ***NYPL [JLF 86-1304]***

Ornstein, Michael D. The work experience of immigrants to Canada [microform] . Downsview, Ont. , 1983. 48 leaves ; ***NYPL [*ZT-1732 no.16]***

LABOR SUPPLY - CANADA - EFFECT OF TECHNOLOGICAL INNOVATIONS ON.
Adapting to change . Toronto [Ont.] , Buffalo , c1986. xv, 221 p. ; ISBN 0-8020-7260-7 (pbk.) LC Card 86-673029 DDC 331.12/0971 19
HD5728 .A596 1986 ***NYPL [JLD 87-1967]***

LABOR SUPPLY - CANADA - STATISTICS.
Family characteristics and labour force activity . Ottawa , c1986. xxii, 131 p. ; ISBN 0-660-52240-3 (pbk.) : LC Card 86-206978
HD5728 .F36 1986

LABOR SUPPLY - CENTRAL AMERICA.
Cambio y polarización ocupacional en Centroamérica. [San José, Costa Rica?] , 1986. 202 p. : ISBN 92-2-305432-X LC Card 86-231773
HD5733.A6 C36 1986

LABOR SUPPLY - CHILE.
Riveros C., Luis. Structural reforms and wage setting across sectors . Santiago , 1984. 37, [5], 13 p. ; ***NYPL [JLF 87-136]***

Rojas Ramos, Patricio. Demanda dinámica por trabajo /. Santiago , 1986. 58 p. : LC Card 87-404328 DDC 331.12/5/0983 19
HD5756.A6 R65 1986

Vega F., Humberto (Vega Fernández) Política económica y movimiento laboral . Santiago, Chile , 1986. 52 p. : LC Card 87-101128
HC192 .V355 1986

LABOR SUPPLY - CHILE - ECONOMETRIC MODELS.
Coeymans, Juan Eduardo. Determinants of sectoral annual real wages in a developing economy /. Santiago , 1986. 32, [4] leaves : LC Card 87-404007 DDC 331.12/5/0983 19
HD5006 .C64 1986

LABOR SUPPLY - CHILE - SANTIAGO.
Corvalán Vásquez, Oscar E., 1947- Empleo y capacitación en los talleres informales de Santiago /. Montevideo , 1984. 150 p. ; LC Card 86-127324
HD2346.C54 S263 1984

LABOR SUPPLY - CHINA.
Taylor, Jeffrey R., 1954- Employment outlook for China to the year 2000 /. Washington, D.C. [1986] 43 leaves, 2 p. ; LC Card 87-601289 DDC 331.12/3/0951021 19
HD5830.A6 T375 1986

LABOR SUPPLY - COLOMBIA.
Pérez P., María José. La oferta y la demanda de empleos . Bogotá, Colombia , c1984. 64 p. ; ISBN 84-8276-322-9 LC Card 84-241503
HD5757.A6 P47 1984

Reproducción de fuerza de trabajo, educación y migración en el sector rural colombiano /. Bogotá, Colombia , 1985. 98, [52] p. : LC Card 87-402979 DDC 331.1/09861 19
HD5757.A6 R46 1985

Transición demográfica y oferta de fuerza de trabajo en Colombia /. [Bogotá], República de Colombia , 1986. 2 v. : ISBN 958-95096-0-6 (set) LC Card 87-113652 DDC 331.11/09861 19
HD5757.A6 T7 1986

LABOR SUPPLY - CONGRESSES.
How labor markets work . Lexington, Mass. , c1988. viii, 256 p. : ISBN 0-669-15126-2 (alk. paper) LC Card 87-22718 DDC 331.12 19
HD5701.3 .H68 1988

International Conference on Employment and Training (1985 : Perth, W.A.) Full employment, uncertain futures /. [Perth, W.A.] [1985] ix, 263 p. : LC Card 86-185208 DDC 339.5 19
HD5701.3 .I55 1985

Tripartite Technical Meeting for the Food Products and Drink Industries, 2d, Geneva, 1978. Labour and social problems arising out of seasonal fluctuations of the food products and drink industries /. Geneva , 1978. ii, 51 p. ; ISBN 92-2-101879-2 (pbk.) : LC Card 80-477150 DDC 331.2/0464
HD9000.1 .T75 1978a ***NYPL [JLE 80-1039]***

LABOR SUPPLY - CONNECTICUT - EFFECT OF TECHNOLOGICAL INNOVATIONS ON - HISTORY - 20TH CENTURY - SOURCES.
Palmer, Michele. Catalogue of interviews . [Storrs, Conn.] , 1983. ii, 79 p. ; LC Card 86-621476 DDC 331.12/09746 19
HD6331.2.U52 C86 1983

LABOR SUPPLY - COSTA RICA - STATISTICS.
Encuesta nacional de hogares, empleo y desempleo . San José, Costa Rica , 1982. xi, xi, 86 p. ; LC Card 82-202317
HD5734.A6 E53 1982

LABOR SUPPLY - DATA PROCESSING.
Fiorito, Riccardo, 1947- Mercato del lavoro e politica economica . Venezia , 1984. 247 p. : ISBN 88-317-4733-9 : LC Card 86-163951
HD5701.6 .F56 1984

LABOR SUPPLY - DENMARK.
Jørgensen, Henning, 1949- Arbejdsmarkedsnævn i arbejdsmarkedspolitikken /. [Aalborg] [1985?]-<[1986]. v. <1-2 > : ISBN 87-88706-12-5 LC Card 87-104729
HD5799.A6 J64 1985

90 plus 10 /. [Copenhagen] [1986] 39 p. : ISBN 87-7002-353-0 LC Card 86-197313
HD5799.A6 A12 1986

LABOR SUPPLY - DENMARK - EFFECT OF AUTOMATION ON.
Vedel, Gitte. Om kvindearbejdets igangværende udvikling og perspektiver, i relation til den teknologiske udvikling /. Roskilde , 1982. 103 leaves : LC Card 83-172895
HD6060.65.D4 V42 1982

LABOR SUPPLY - DENMARK - EFFECT OF EDUCATION ON - STATISTICS.
De Nyuddannedes indplacering på arbejdsmarkedet 1981-1983 . [Copenhagen , 1986] 1 v. (various pagings) : ISBN 87-503-6320-4 LC Card 87-127126
HD6278.D4 N98 1986

LABOR SUPPLY - DENMARK - MATHEMATICAL MODELS.
Arbejdsløshed og beskæftigelse . Aarhus [Copenhagen] [1983] 34 p. ; LC Card 84-125513
HD5701.6 .A73 1983

LABOR SUPPLY - DENMARK - RIBE AMT - EFFECT OF EDUCATION ON.
Johansen, Carsten Ulstrup. Hva blev der af dem? . Esbjerg , 1983. 168 p. : ISBN 87-85198-93-5 LC Card 83-236971
HD5717.5.D42 R55 1983

LABOR SUPPLY - DENMARK - VEJLE AMT - EFFECT OF EDUCATION ON.
Johansen, Carsten Ulstrup. Hva blev der af dem? . Esbjerg , 1983. 168 p. : ISBN 87-85198-93-5 LC Card 83-236971
HD5717.5.D42 R55 1983

LABOR SUPPLY - DEVELOPING COUNTRIES.
Marsh, Lawrence. Employment and technological choice of multinational enterprises in developing countries . Geneva , 1983. iii, 37 p. ; ISBN 92-2-103353-8 (pbk.) : LC Card 86-213692 DDC 338.8/8854 19
HD2932 .M35 1983

Population growth and economic development . Madison, Wis. , 1987. xiii, 702 p. ; ISBN 0-299-11130-X : LC Card 86-40447 DDC 338.9/009172/4 19
HB884 .P66547 1987

LABOR SUPPLY - ECONOMETRIC MODELS.
Fiorito, Riccardo, 1947- Mercato del lavoro e politica economica . Venezia , 1984. 247 p. : ISBN 88-317-4733-9 : LC Card 86-163951
HD5701.6 .F56 1984

Riese, Martin. Die Messung der Arbeitslosigkeit /. Berlin , c1986. 199 p. : ISBN 3-428-06034-2 LC Card 86-215265 DDC 331.12/0724 19
HD5707.5 .R54 1986

LABOR SUPPLY - ECUADOR.
El Ecuador en la encrucijada . Quito , 1986. 307 p. : LC Card 87-400394 DDC 331.12/09866 19
HD5758.A6 E28 1986

LABOR SUPPLY - ECUADOR - MACHALA SUBURBAN REGION.
Maldonado Calderón, Arturo. Actividad económica del hombre del suburbio /. Machala, Ecuador , 1985. 168 p., [3] folded leaves of plates : LC Card 87-110202 DDC 330.9866/31 19
HC203.M33 M35 1985

LABOR SUPPLY - EFFECT OF AUTOMATION.
Helfert, Mario. Wertewandel, Arbeit, technischer Fortschritt, Wachstum /. Köln , c1986. 149 p. : ISBN 3-7663-3010-1 LC Card 87-134855 DDC 331.12 19
HD6331 .H37 1986

LABOR SUPPLY - EFFECT OF AUTOMATION ON.
Information technology and economic prospects. Paris , Washington, D.C. , 1987. 221 p. : ISBN 92-64-12927-8 (pbk.) : LC Card 87-163173 DDC 331.1 19
HD9696.A2 I54 1987

LABOR SUPPLY - EFFECT OF AUTOMATION ON - CONGRESSES.
Arbeitsplätze morgen /. Stuttgart , c1986. 431 p. : ISBN 3-519-02446-2 LC Card 86-171663
HD6331 .A695 1986

LABOR SUPPLY - EFFECT OF TECHNOLOGICAL INNOVATIONS.
Befreiung der Arbeit . Bonn , c1986. 197 p. : ISBN 3-87831-429-9 LC Card 86-194157
HD6955 .B389 1986

LABOR SUPPLY - EFFECT OF TECHNOLOGICAL INNOVATIONS ON.
Armour, Hazel. New technology in the office environment /. Aldershot, Hampshire, England , Brookfield, Vt., USA , c1986. viii, 138 p. : ISBN 0-566-05031-5 LC Card 86-215701 DDC 338.4/561651 19
HF5547.5 .A786 1986

Flynn, Patricia M. Facilitating technological change . Cambridge, Mass. , c1988. x, 233 p. : ISBN 0-88730-104-5 LC Card 87-17839 DDC 331.2 19
HD6331 .F56 1988

Francis, Arthur. New technology at work /. Oxford [Oxfordshire] , New York , 1986. vi, 216 p. ; ISBN 0-19-878016-8 : LC Card 86-12705 DDC 338/.06 19
HD6331 .F66 1987 ***NYPL [JLD 87-912]***

The Jobs challenge . Cambridge, Mass. , 1986. xvi, 304 p. : ISBN 0-88410-990-9 LC Card 85-7547 DDC 331.12 19
HD5707 .J63 1985 ***NYPL [JLE 86-2190]***

Kaplinsky, Raphael. Micro-electronics and employment revisited . Geneva , 1987. xiv, 181 p. : ISBN 92-2-105611-2 (pbk.) : LC Card 87-163570 DDC 331.7/6213817 19
HD9696.A2 K37 1987

Kofler, Leo. Beherrscht uns die Technik? . Hamburg , 1983. 160 p. ; ISBN 3-87975-249-4 LC Card 84-181044
HD6331 .K685 1983

Leach, Donald. Future employment & technological change /. London , 1986. 264 p. : ISBN 1-85091-017-0 (pbk.) : LC Card 86-180981 DDC 331.12/5 19
HD6331 .L34 1986

Nouvelles technologies et enjeux sociaux . Lyon , c1986. 230 p. : ISBN 2-7297-0279-2 : LC Card 86-187357
HC79.T4 N68 1986

Technological change . Geneva , 1985. 355 p. : ISBN 92-2-105162-5 (pbk.) : LC Card 86-203534 DDC 331.12 19
HD6331 .T416 1985

Vasil′chuk, I͡U. A. Nauchno-tekhnicheskai͡a revoli͡utsii͡a i rabochiĭ klass pri kapitalizme . Moskva , 1980. 295 p. : LC Card 81-130590
HD6331 .V22 1980

Williams, Shirley, 1930- A job to live . Harmondsworth, Middlesex, England , New York, N.Y., U. S.A. , 1985. 245 p. : ISBN 0-14-008426-6 (pbk.) : LC Card 87-118827

DDC 331.1 19
HD6331 .W53 1985

World labour report /. Oxford [Oxfordshire] , New York , 1987. p. cm. ISBN 0-19-828561-2 : LC Card 87-22087 DDC 331 19
HD5706 .W68 1987

LABOR SUPPLY - EFFECT OF TECHNOLOGICAL INNOVATIONS ON - CONGRESSES.
Arbeitsplätze morgen /. Stuttgart , c1986. 431 p. : ISBN 3-519-02446-2 LC Card 86-171663
HD6331 .A695 1986

Freedman, Audrey. Perspectives on employment /. New York, N.Y. (845 3rd Ave., New York 10022) , c1986. 15 p. : LC Card 86-212384 DDC 331.12 19
HD5701.3 .F74 1986

International Symposium on Technological Change and Employment: Urban and Regional Dimensions (1985 : Zandvoort, Netherlands) Technological change, employment, and spatial dynamics . Berlin , New York , c1986. vii, 466 p. : ISBN 0-387-16478-2 (U. S. : pbk.) LC Card 86-10081 DDC 331.12 19
HD6331 .I6 1985
NYPL [JLM 72-289 v.270]

Mehr Technik, weniger Arbeit? . Karlsruhe , c1984. 228 p. : ISBN 3-7880-9697-7 LC Card 85-108996
HD6331 .M384 1984

LABOR SUPPLY - ENGLAND - LONDON.
Weatheritt, L. Manufacturing industry in Greater London /. London , c1975. ii, 26 p. ; ISBN 0-7168-0853-6 (pbk.) LC Card 82-213745
HD5766.L66 W43 1975

LABOR SUPPLY - ESTONIA.
Tööjõu kasutamise probleeme Eesti NSV-s /. Tallinn , 1986. 179 p. ; LC Card 87-107003
HD5797.E75 T66 1986

LABOR SUPPLY - ETHIOPIA - STATISTICS.
Rural labour force survey, April 1981-April 1982 /. Addis Ababa , 1985. xii, 170 p. ; LC Card 86-981178 DDC 331.1/0963 19
HD5839.7.A6 R87 1985

LABOR SUPPLY - EUROPE.
Flexibility and jobs . Bruxelles [1985] 157, 5 p. : LC Card 87-111122 DDC 331.25 19
HD5764.A6 F44 1985

Rymarczyk, Jan. Migracja siły roboczej do krajów EWG i jej konsekwencje społeczno-gospodarcze /. [Wrocław] , 1982. 239 p., [4] folded leaves ; LC Card 83-153742
HB9 .B7522 nr. 218 HD8378.5.A2

LABOR SUPPLY - EUROPE - CONGRESSES.
Centre for Employment Initiatives (Great Britain) Cooperation in the field of employment . Luxembourg , Washington, DC , 1986. 55 p. ; ISBN 92-825-6086-4 (pbk.) : LC Card 87-134296 DDC 331.12/042/094 19
HD5764.A6 C45 1986

Convegno "Il lavoro si crea" (1985 : Ravenna, Italy) Il lavoro si crea . Milano, Italy , c1986. 305 p. : LC Card 86-232529
HD5764.A6 C68 1985

Job generation . Salt Lake City, Utah , c1986. xiv, 138 p. ; ISBN 0-913420-89-1 (pbk.) LC Card 86-31285 DDC 331.12/094 19
HD5724 .J63 1986

Social security and employment /. Assen, The Netherlands , 1983. 116 p. : ISBN 90-232-2011-0 (pbk.) : LC Card 83-216203 DDC 331.12/094 19
HD7164 .S594 1983 ***NYPL [JLE 86-1107]***

LABOR SUPPLY - EUROPEAN ECONOMIC COMMUNITY COUNTRIES.
Morgan-Gérard, Florence. Equal opportunities and vocational training . Berlin [1982] 69 p. ; ISBN 92-825-2489-2 ***NYPL [JLD 87-1318]***

LABOR SUPPLY - EUROPEAN ECONOMIC COMMUNITY COUNTRIES - EFFECT OF TECHNOLOGICAL INNOVATIONS ON.
L'Association des travailleurs aux choix technologiques . Luxembourg , Washington, D.C. , 1986. 45 p. : ISBN 92-825-5880-0 : LC Card 86-179382
HD6331.2.E86 A88 1986

La Formation des syndicalistes aux nouvelles technologies de l'information et à leur introduction dans les entreprises . Luxembourg , Washington, D.C. , 1986. 52, 13, 7 p. : ISBN 92-825-5881-9 : LC Card 86-179989
HD6331.2.E86 F67 1986

LABOR SUPPLY - FRANCE.
Comptes de l'emploi . Paris , c1984. 219 p. : ISBN 2-11-001264-1 : LC Card 85-132416
HD5775 .C5344 1984

LABOR SUPPLY - FRANCE - EFFECT OF AUTOMATION ON.
Pastré, Olivier. L'informatisation et l'emploi /. Paris , 1983. 127 p. : ISBN 2-7071-1387-5 LC Card 83-161919 DDC 331.12/0944 19
HD6331.2.F8 P37 1983

LABOR SUPPLY - FRANCE - EFFECT OF TECHNOLOGICAL INNOVATIONS ON.
France. Conseil économique et social. Informatique et emploi . [Paris] [1984] 24, 4 p., 8 leaves, 187, 13 p. : LC Card 84-218059
HD6331.2.F8 F73 1984

LABOR SUPPLY - FRANCE - GRENOBLE METROPOLITAN AREA - HISTORY.
Tiger, Henri. Restructuration industrielle et filières de main-d'œuvre . Paris , 1979. 389 p. : LC Card 85-126419
HD5776.G74 T54 1979

LABOR SUPPLY - GABON.
Mamder, Josué Sandjiman. Les effets de la crise mondiale actuelle sur l'économie et la population gabonaises /. Addis Abéba , c1984. 34 p. ; ISBN 92-2-203795-2 LC Card 86-215256
HC975 .M36 1984

LABOR SUPPLY - GEORGIA.
Oliveira, Victor J. Distribution of rural employment growth by race . Washington, D.C. [1986] vii, 17 p. : LC Card 86-601118 DDC 331.6/09758 19
HD5725.G4 O56 1986

LABOR SUPPLY - GERMAN-SPEAKING COUNTRIES - EFFECT OF TECHNOLOGICAL INNOVATIONS ON.
Gensior, Sabine. Mikroelektronik-Anwendung und ihre Bedeutung für die Qualifikationen . Berlin , 1986. 39, 118 p. ; LC Card 87-409403 DDC 338/.06 19
HD6331.2.G27 G46 1986

LABOR SUPPLY - GERMANY, EAST.
Schrimpff, Wolfgang. Heterogene Koordinationsinstrumente im Beschäftigungssystem der DDR /. Münster , 1983. xv, 360 p. : ISBN 3-7923-0505-4 LC Card 85-140056
HD5780.5.A6 S37 1983

LABOR SUPPLY - GERMANY, WEST.
Dräger, Heinrich, 1898- Zu wenig Arbeit für zu viele Menschen . Stuttgart , 1984. 125 p. : ISBN 3-87959-220-9 LC Card 84-198317
HD5779 .D68 1984

Feldmann, Berthold. Unternehmenskonzentration, Marktmacht und Lohnniveau . Göttingen , c1984. xii, 260 p. : ISBN 3-525-12269-1 LC Card 85-162393
HD2746.5 .F45 1984

Friderichs, Hans. Lohndispersionen auf strukturierten Arbeitsmärkten . Pfaffenweiler , 1986. xvi, 404 p. : ISBN 3-89085-133-9 LC Card 87-134875 DDC 331.2/943 19
HD5029 .F75 1986

Gerstenberger, Wolfgang. Strukturwandel unter verschlechterten Rahmenbedingungen . Berlin , c1984. 255 p. : ISBN 3-428-05567-5 LC Card 84-180150
HC286.7 .G46 1984

Hermann, Hayo. Sektorale Wirtschaftsstruktur und kommunale Finanzsituation . München , c1986. xiii, 384 p. : ISBN 3-88259-405-5 LC Card 86-228161
HJ9473 .H47 1986

Hof, Bernd. Arbeitsmarktstrukturen im Wandel /. Köln , c1985. 56 p. : ISBN 3-602-24737-6 LC Card 86-119065 DDC 331.12/5/0943 19
HD5779 .H638 1985

Pusse, Leo. Arbeitsproduktivität und Beschäftigung . Freiburg im Breisgau , c1984. viii, 311 p. : ISBN 3-448-01512-1 LC Card 85-138794
HC290.5.L3 P87 1984

Schettkat, Ronald. Bevölkerungs- und Erwerbsverhaltensentwicklung in Österreich, Schweden und der Bundesrepublik Deutschland /. Berlin [1984] 48 p. ; LC Card 85-198691
HD5771 .S34 1984

Strukturwandel des Ausländerproblems . Bochum , c1986. 309 p. : ISBN 3-88339-529-3 LC Card 87-121913 DDC 331.6/2/0943 19
HD8458.A2 S786 1986

LABOR SUPPLY - GERMANY (WEST) - ADDRESSES, ESSAYS, LECTURES.
Wenig Arbeit--aber viel zu tun . Opladen , c1985. 195 p. : ISBN 3-531-11724-6
NYPL [JLE 86-1602]

LABOR SUPPLY - GERMANY (WEST) - ARNSBERG (REGIERUNGSBEZIRK) - STATISTICS.
Jansen, Paul Günter. Arbeitsmarktatlas . [Düsseldorf] [1977] 206, A19 p. : LC Card 85-173256
HD5780.A76 J36 1977

LABOR SUPPLY - GERMANY (WEST) - BERGISCHES LAND - CONGRESSES.
Die Wirtschaftliche Entwicklung in den Arbeitsmarktregionen des Bergischen Landes . Bochum , 1981. 401 p. : ISBN 3-88339-217-0 LC Card 82-164818 DDC 331/.0943/55 19
HD8459.N66 W57 1981
NYPL [JLD 86-1639]

LABOR SUPPLY - GERMANY (WEST) - CONGRESSES.
Regionalisierte Arbeitsmarkt- und Beschäftigungspolitik /. Frankfurt/Main , New York , c1983. 322 p. : ISBN 3-593-33241-8 LC Card 84-106151
HC286.7 .R44 1983

LABOR SUPPLY - GERMANY (WEST) - ECONOMETRIC MODELS.
Müller, Jürgen, 1943- Sektorale Struktur und Entwicklung der industriellen Beschäftigung in den Regionen der Bundesrepublik Deutschland /. Berlin , c1983. xiii, 200 p. : ISBN 3-428-05449-0 LC Card 84-109872
HC286.7 .M8 1983

LABOR SUPPLY - GERMANY (WEST) - EFFECT OF AUTOMATION ON.
Arbeiterklasse, gibt's die noch? /. Wien , c1985. 246 p. : ISBN 3-900351-46-5 LC Card 86-123225
HD8451 .A836 1985

Widersprüche der Automationsarbeit . West-Berlin , c1987. 228 p. ; ISBN 3-88619-362-4 LC Card 87-145099 DDC 331.12/0943 19
HD6331.2.G28 W55 1987

LABOR SUPPLY - GERMANY (WEST) - EFFECT OF AUTOMATION ON - CONGRESSES.
Neue Entwicklungen bei Arbeit, Entgelt und Führung /. Freiburg im Breisgau , c1984. 169 p. : ISBN 3-448-01480-X : LC Card 84-249237
HF5549.2.G3 N48 1984

LABOR SUPPLY - GERMANY (WEST) - EFFECT OF TECHNOLOGICAL INNOVATIONS ON.
Dachrodt, Heinz-G., 1944- Arbeit und Gesellschaft im Umbruch . Köln [1987], c1986. 128 p. : ISBN 3-7663-0961-7 LC Card 87-139264 DDC 331.12/0943 19
HD6331.2.G28 D33 1987

Fels, Gerhard. Mehr Flexibilität am Arbeitsmarkt /. Kiel , 1986. 21 p. ; ISBN 3-925357-37-8 LC Card 87-126264 DDC 331.25/72/0943 19
HD5109.2.G3 F4 1986

Grumbach, Jürgen. Energieforschung und Arbeitnehmerinteressen . Frankfurt , New York , c1986. 307 p. ; ISBN 3-593-33655-3 LC Card 87-127360 DDC 331.1/0943 19
HC290.5.E5 G74 1986

Klipstein, Michael von. Der Überdruss am Überfluss . München , c1984. 212 p. : ISBN 3-7892-7194-2 LC Card 84-174408
HD6957.G35 K56 1984

Technologische Entwicklung und Beschäftigung /. Bonn [1985] 10 p. ; LC Card 86-154491
HC290.5.T4 T44 1985

LABOR SUPPLY - GERMANY (WEST) - EFFECT OF TECHNOLOGICAL INNOVATIONS ON - ADDRESSES, ESSAYS, LECTURES.
Ausstieg? . Hamburg , 1985. 159 p. : ISBN 3-87975-289-3 LC Card 85-219857 DDC

331/.0943 19
HD6694 .A97 1985 **NYPL [JLD 87-710]**

Neue Technologien und Arbeitswelt . Köln , c1984. 197 p. : ISBN 3-7663-0893-9 LC Card 85-160745
HD6331.2.G28 N475 1984
NYPL [JLD 86-3861]

LABOR SUPPLY - GERMANY (WEST) - EFFECT OF TECHNOLOGICAL INNOVATIONS ON - CASE STUDIES.
Flexible Fertigung und Industriearbeit . Frankfurt Main , New York , c1986. v, 577, iii p. : ISBN 3-593-33648-0 LC Card 86-197535
HD5109.2.G3 F45 1986

LABOR SUPPLY - GERMANY (WEST) - EFFECT OF TECHNOLOGICAL INNOVATIONS ON - CONGRESSES.
Arbeitsmoral und Technikfeindlichkeit . Frankfurt , New York , c1986. 274 p. : ISBN 3-593-33757-6 LC Card 86-212283
HD8444 .A73 1986

Rembser, Josef. Die Förderung des wirtschaftlichen und sozialen Wandels durch die Forschungs- und Entwicklungspolitik als präventive Strukturpolitik /. Dortmund , 1977. 100 p. : LC Card 84-130876
HD30 .A7 Heft 184 HD6331.2.G28

LABOR SUPPLY - GERMANY (WEST) - EFFECT OF TECHNOLOGICAL INNOVATIONS ON - HISTORY.
Der Dressierte Arbeiter . München , c1984. 211 p. : ISBN 3-406-09286-1 LC Card 84-181068 DDC 331.25 19
HD6331.2.G28 D74 1984

LABOR SUPPLY - GERMANY (WEST) - HAMBURG.
Der Ausbau von Fernwärmenetzen und seine Wirkungen auf Arbeitsmarkt und Beschäftigung, dargestellt am Beispiel der Freien und Hansestadt Hamburg . Bonn [1983] xiv, 172 p. : LC Card 85-107700
HD5780.H34 A87 1983

LABOR SUPPLY - GERMANY (WEST) - NORTH RHINE-WESTPHALIA - HISTORY - 20TH CENTURY.
Bremicker, Burckhardt. Analyse der Arbeitslosigkeit in den Regionen Nordrhein-Westfalens . Bochum , 1984. xx, 381 p. : ISBN 3-88339-362-2 LC Card 84-196621 DDC 331.13/794355 19
HD5780.N6 B74 1984 **NYPL [JLD 86-2367]**

LABOR SUPPLY - GERMANY (WEST) - RUHR (REGION) - CONGRESSES.
Strukturanalyse Ruhrgebiet . [Essen] [1983?] 185 p. : LC Card 86-218075
HD5760.R84 S77 1983

LABOR SUPPLY - GERMANY (WEST) - RUHR (REGION) - EFFECT OF TECHNOLOGICAL INNOVATIONS ON - CONGRESSES.
Strukturanalyse Ruhrgebiet . [Essen] [1983?] 185 p. : LC Card 86-218075
HD5760.R84 S77 1983

LABOR SUPPLY - GERMANY (WEST) - RUHR (REGION) - STATISTICS.
Noll, Wulf. Lokales Informationssystem Arbeitsmarkt (LISA) /. Essen , 1986. 262 p. ; ISBN 3-923494-64-5 LC Card 87-409105 DDC 331.12/5/094355 19
HD5780.R82 N65 1986

LABOR SUPPLY - GHANA.
Botchie, George. Employment and multinational enterprises in export processing zones . Geneva , 1984. iv, 74 p. ; ISBN 92-2-103770-3 (pbk.) : LC Card 86-213592
HF1417 .B68 1984

LABOR SUPPLY - GREAT BRITAIN.
Assessment of the employment effects of economic development projects funded under the Urban Programme /. London , 1986. vi, 52 p. : ISBN 0-11-751859-X (pbk.) : LC Card 86-197217 DDC 331.12/0941 19
HD5765.A6 A87 1986

Changing places . London , Baltimore, Md., USA , 1987. xv, 144 p. : ISBN 0-7131-6498-0 (pbk.) : LC Card 87-148942 DDC 331.12/5/0941 19
HD5765.A6 C49 1987

Standing, Guy. Unemployment and labour market flexibility . Geneva , 1986. xi, 147 p. : ISBN 92-2-105291-5 (pbk.) : LC Card 87-114658 DDC 331.13/7941 19
HD5765.A6 S72 1986

LABOR SUPPLY - GREAT BRITAIN - ECONOMETRIC MODELS.
Modelling the labour market /. London , New York , 1988. p. cm. ISBN 0-412-28830-3 LC Card 87-23084 DDC 331.12/0724 19
HD5765.A6 M63 1988

LABOR SUPPLY - GREAT BRITAIN - EFFECT OF TAXATION ON - CONGRESSES.
Taxation and incentives /. [London, England] , c1976. ii, 45 p. : LC Card 85-111944
HJ2619 .T289 1976

LABOR SUPPLY - GREAT BRITAIN - EFFECT OF TECHNOLOGICAL INNOVATIONS ON.
Global restructuring local response . London , Merstham, Redhill, Surrey , c1986. 308 p. : ISBN 0-86226-174-0 (pbk.) LC Card 86-197207 DDC 331.12/0941 19
HD6331.2.G7 G57 1986

Technical change and full employment /. Oxford, UK , New York, NY, USA , 1987. vii, 279 p. : ISBN 0-631-14099-9 : LC Card 87-6637 DDC 331.12/5/0941 19
HD6331.2.G7 T39 1987

LABOR SUPPLY - GREECE.
LaLonde, Robert John. The manpower report of KEPE . Athens, Greece , c1986. 122 p. ; LC Card 86-205504 DDC 331.1/09495 19
HD5811.83.A6 L3 1986

LABOR SUPPLY - GREECE - STATISTICS.
LaLonde, Robert John. The manpower report of KEPE . Athens, Greece , c1986. 122 p. ; LC Card 86-205504 DDC 331.1/09495 19
HD5811.83.A6 L3 1986

LABOR SUPPLY - GUADELOUPE - STATISTICS.
Démographie et emploi en Guadeloupe . Basse-Terre [1977?] 3, xix leaves, [6] leaves of plates : ISBN 2-11-062928-2 LC Card 85-230531
HA918.7 .D46 1977

LABOR SUPPLY - GUINEA-BISSAU.
Ribeiro, Sérgio. Situação e perspectivas dos recursos humanos na República da Guiné-Bissau /. Addis Ababa [1984 or 1985] 49, 19 p., [8] leaves : LC Card 85-981187 DDC 331.11/0966/57 19
HD5849.A6 R53 1984

LABOR SUPPLY - GUYANA - EFFECT OF EDUCATION ON.
Abdulah, Norma. The availability and utilization of skills in Guyana /. St. Augustine, Trinidad [1981] xv, 105 p. ; LC Card 84-146702 DDC 331.11/422 19
HD5759.3.A6 A24 1981
NYPL [JLE 86-4442]

LABOR SUPPLY - HONDURAS.
Honduras . [Santiago, Chile] , 1983. vii, 99 p. ; LC Card 84-225233
HD5736.A6 H66 1983

LABOR SUPPLY - HUNGARY - STATISTICS.
Adatgyűjtemény az állami iparvállalatoknál foglalkoztatottak létszám-, bér- és kereseti arányairól /. Budapest , 1986. 148 p. ; LC Card 87-407679
HD5772.5.A6 A34 1986

Az Állami iparvállalatoknál foglalkoztatottak létszámösszetétele bér- és kereseti viszonyai /. Budapest , 1986. 124 p. ; ISBN 963-02-4488-8 LC Card 86-218968
HD5772.5.A6 A57 1986

LABOR SUPPLY - ILLINOIS.
Illinois . [Springfield, Ill. , 1985] 155 p. : LC Card 85-622626 DDC 338.9773 19
HD5725.I3 I517 1985 **NYPL [JLF 87-787]**

LABOR SUPPLY - INDIA.
Chaudhary, S. K. Planning and employment trends in India /. New Delhi , c1987. 300 p. ; LC Card 86-903543 DDC 331.11/0954/12 19
HD5819 .C47 1987

Mulkh Raj. Employment, income, and housing /. New Delhi , 1987. viii, 130 p. : ISBN 81-7000-025-4 : LC Card 87-901029 DDC 331.12/5/0954 19
HD7361.A3 M85 1987

LABOR SUPPLY - INDIA - BIHAR.
Chaudhary, S. K. Planning and employment trends in India /. New Delhi , c1987. 300 p. ; LC Card 86-903543 DDC 331.11/0954/12 19
HD5819 .C47 1987

LABOR SUPPLY - INDIA - BOMBAY.
Brahm Prakash. The urban dead-end? . Bombay , 1983. xii, 138 p., [5] p. of plates : LC Card 84-900007 DDC 331.12/5/0954792 19
HD5820.B6 B72 1983 **NYPL [JLD 86-3828]**

LABOR SUPPLY - INDIA - CASE STUDIES.
Ghadoliya, M. K. (Mahendra Kumar) Structure of employment, earnings, and assets in India . Delhi , 1986. xi, 248 p. : LC Card 86-903221 DDC 331.12/5/09544 19
HD5820.U33 G47 1986

LABOR SUPPLY - INDIA - DELHI METROPOLITAN AREA.
Banerjee, Biswajit. Rural to urban migration and the urban labour market . Bombay , 1986. xviii, 285 p. ; LC Card 86-900684
HD5820.D44 B36 1986
NYPL [JLD 86-4110]

LABOR SUPPLY - INDIA - KARNATAKA.
Prabhakara, N. R. Population growth and unemployment in India /. New Delhi , 1986. ix, 102 p. ; ISBN 81-7024-041-7 : LC Card 86-902156 DDC 331.13/795487 19
HD5820.K37 P7 1986

LABOR SUPPLY - INDIA - PUNE.
Lambert, Richard D. The transformation of an Indian labor market . Amsterdam , Philadelphia , 1986. ix, 249 p. ; ISBN 0-915027-63-1 (alk. paper) : LC Card 86-26900 DDC 331.11/0954/792 19
HD5820.P78 L36 1986

LABOR SUPPLY - INDIA - STATISTICS.
Statistical profile on women labour. Simla [1983] v, 224 p. ; LC Card 84-900395 DDC 331.4/0954/021 19
HD5819 .S83 1983 **NYPL [JLF 86-1946]**

LABOR SUPPLY - INDIA - UDAIPUR (DISTRICT) - CASE STUDIES.
Ghadoliya, M. K. (Mahendra Kumar) Structure of employment, earnings, and assets in India . Delhi , 1986. xi, 248 p. : LC Card 86-903221 DDC 331.12/5/09544 19
HD5820.U33 G47 1986

LABOR SUPPLY - INDIANA.
Wynne, John, 1961- The Indiana economy . Indianapolis, IN [1986] 22, [2] p. : LC Card 86-622749 DDC 330.9772/043 19
HD5725.I6 W96 1986

LABOR SUPPLY - INDONESIA - CASE STUDIES.
Costello, Michael A. Mobility and employment in urban Southeast Asia . Boulder , 1987. xvi, 190 p. : ISBN 0-8133-7352-2 (pbk. : alk. paper) : LC Card 87-10649 DDC 307.2 19
HB2107 .C67 1987

LABOR SUPPLY - INDONESIA - JAKARTA.
Jakarta-Raya, Indonesia. Tenaga kerja . Jakarta [1980] 52 leaves ; LC Card 80-942103
HD5824.J27 J35 1980

LABOR SUPPLY - IOWA - STATISTICS.
Labor market information for Iowa (Job Training Partnership Act), State of Iowa. Des Moines, Iowa (1000 E. Grand Ave., Des Moines 50319) [1986] 125 p. : LC Card 86-622289 DDC 331.1/09777 19
HD5725.I8 L34 1986

Occupational projections, 1984-1995 . [Des Moines?] [1985] 16 v. in 1 ; LC Card 86-621925 DDC 331.12/09777/021 19
HD5725.I8 O26 1985

Unemployment by occupation, 1985 . Des Moines, Iowa (1000 E. Grand Ave., Des Moines 50319) [1986] [12] leaves ; LC Card 86-622759 DDC 331.13/79777 19
HD5725.I8 U54 1986

LABOR SUPPLY - ITALY.
Antonelli, Gilberto. Risorse umane e redditi da lavoro . Milano , c1985. 256 p. : LC Card 85-191554
HC310.I5 A66 1985

Magni, Carlo. I mercati regionali del lavoro e il problema degli indicatori . Milano [1981] 133, [3] p. : ISBN 88-20-42109-7 : LC Card 81-194409
HD5784 .M3 1981 **NYPL [JLD 87-815]**

Palazzi, Paolo. Domanda di lavoro e produttività nell'industria italiana /. Bologna , c1980. 177 p. ; LC Card 82-156294 DDC 331.13/7945 19
HD5784 .P28 1980 ***NYPL [JLD 86-2811]***

LABOR SUPPLY - ITALY - EFFECT OF TECHNOLOGICAL INNOVATIONS ON.
Rapporto ISFOL 1985 . Milano, Italy , c1985. 533 p. : LC Card 86-156267
HD5715.5.I8 R393 1985

LABOR SUPPLY - ITALY - GORIZIA (PROVINCE)
Albertini, Sergio. Il consolidamento strutturale dell'occupazione in specifiche aree con particolare riguardo alla provincia di Gorizia /. Milano , c1984. 184 p. ; LC Card 84-234951 DDC 331.12/0945/392 19
HD5785.G67 A42 1984

LABOR SUPPLY - ITALY - NUORO (SARDINIA : PROVINCE)
L'Osservatorio provinciale sul lavoro e sulle professioni . Milano, Italy , c1984. 143 p. : LC Card 84-190423
HD5785.N86 O87 1984
NYPL [JLD 86-1275]

LABOR SUPPLY - IVORY COAST.
Ahonzo, Etienne. Population de la Côte d'Ivoire . Abidjan , 1984. ix, 324 p. : LC Card 86-110796 DDC 304.6/09666/8 19
HB3666.A3 A46 1984 ***NYPL [JLF 86-1466]***

Gboizo, J. Emplois et qualifications dans le secteur métaux-mécanique-électricité en Côte d'Ivoire /. [Abidjan] , 1981. 93 leaves ; LC Card 83-234024
HD5846.9.A6 G36 1981

Gozo, K. M. Crise et pauvreté en Côte d'Ivoire . Addis Abéba , c1983. iv, 84 p. ; ISBN 92-2-203648-4 LC Card 85-981192
HC1025 .G69 1983

International Labour Organisation. Côte-d'Ivoire . Genève , 1984. 94 p. : ISBN 92-2-203860-6 LC Card 86-219971
HD5846.9.A6 I57 1984

Willaert, Y. Ressources humaines et développement régional en Côte d'Ivoire . [Addis Ababa] [1977] 3, 108, [6] leaves (1 folded) ; LC Card 82-980560
HD5846.9.A6 W55 1977

LABOR SUPPLY - JAPAN - CONGRESSES.
Japanese and Australian labour markets . Canberra [c1983] xx, 610 p. : ISBN 0-86413-004-X (pbk.) : LC Card 84-220557 DDC 331.12/0952 19
HD5850.A6 J36 1983 ***NYPL [JLE 86-630]***

LABOR SUPPLY - JORDAN.
Seccombe, Ian J. Manpower and migration . [Durham, England] , c1981. viii, 110 p. : LC Card 84-673623
HD5812.25.A6 S42x 1981
NYPL [JLD 86-2457]

LABOR SUPPLY - KENYA.
Collier, Paul. Labour and poverty in Kenya, 1900-1980 /. Oxford , New York , 1986. xi, 296 p. : ISBN 0-19-828505-1 : LC Card 86-1352 DDC 331.12/09676/2 19
HD5840.5.A6 C65 1986
NYPL [JLE 86-3282]

LABOR SUPPLY - LATIN AMERICA.
Cohen, Noemí. Trabajadores y seguridad social en América Latina /. México, D.F. [1982], c1981. 146 p. ; ISBN 968-8241-38-5 LC Card 83-140620 DDC 368.4/0098 19
HD7130.5 .C63 1982 ***NYPL [JLD 86-2768]***

Elizaga, Juan C. (Juan Carlos) Investigaciones sobre recursos humanos en América Latina . Santiago de Chile , 1972. 16 p. ; LC Card 83-103424
HA755 .U5 no. 91 HD5730.5.A6

García, Norberto E. Absorción creciente con subempleo persistente (América Latina, 1950-80) /. [Santiago, Chile] , 1982. 35 p. ; LC Card 87-403250 DDC 331.12/098 19
HD5730.5.A6 G355 1982

Poverty in Latin America . Washington, D.C., U. S.A. [1986] 25 p. ; ISBN 0-8213-0836-X (pbk.) LC Card 86-225244 DDC 330.98/0038 19
HC130.I5 P68 1986

Tokman, Víctor E. Desarrollo desigual y absorción de empleo . [Santiago, Chile] , 1982. 34 p. ; LC Card 87-403246 DDC 330.98/0038 19
HC125 .T57 1982

Vargas, Ines. The situation of workers in Latin America /. Oslo , 1985. 92 p. ; ISBN 82-7288-123-3 (pbk.) LC Card 86-205392 DDC 331/.098 19
HD6530.5 .V37 1985

LABOR SUPPLY - LESOTHO.
Senaoana, M. P. Research on rural-non farm employment in Lesotho . Roma, Lesotho [1984] 88 leaves : LC Card 86-214032 DDC 331.12/5/096816 19
HD5842.7.A6 S46 1984

LABOR SUPPLY - LESOTHO - CONGRESSES.
Employment and development in Lesotho . Addis Ababa , 1983. ii, 229 p. ; ISBN 92-2-103780-0 LC Card 84-980769 DDC 331.12/09681/6 19
HD5842.7.A6 E46 1983

LABOR SUPPLY - LESOTHO - STATISTICS.
Senaoana, M. P. Research on rural-non farm employment in Lesotho . Roma, Lesotho [1984] 88 leaves : LC Card 86-214032 DDC 331.12/5/096816 19
HD5842.7.A6 S46 1984

LABOR SUPPLY - LIBERIA.
Botchie, George. Employment and multinational enterprises in export processing zones . Geneva , 1984. iv, 74 p. ; ISBN 92-2-103770-3 (pbk.) : LC Card 86-213592
HF1417 .B68 1984

Iyanda, Olukunle. Multinationals and employment in a West African sub-region . Geneva , 1984. iv, 49 p. ; ISBN 92-2-103623-5 (pbk.) : LC Card 86-213585 DDC 388.8/88664 19
HD2928.8 .I92 1984

LABOR SUPPLY - LIBYA.
Khalaf Allāh, Ramaḍān 'Uraybī. Ḥarakat al-quwá al-'āmilah wa-al-tanmiyah al-iqlīmīyah fī Lībiyā /. Ṭarābulus, al-Jamāhīrīyah al-'Arabīyah al-Lībīyah al-Sha'bīyah al-Ishtirākīyah , 1984. 279 p. : LC Card 86-965535
HB2121.6.A3 K47 1984

LABOR SUPPLY - MADAGASCAR - MAHAJANGA.
Le Secteur non structuré de Mahajanga . Addis Abéba , 1985. vii, 114 p. ; ISBN 92-2-205254-4 LC Card 86-981199
HD2346.M282 M347 1985

LABOR SUPPLY - MAINE - STATISTICS.
Maine occupational employment in 1984 and projected to 1995 /. Auqusta, Me. (20 Union St., Augusta 04330) [1986] 32 leaves ; LC Card 87-620754 DDC 331.12/09741/021 19
HD5725.M3 M386 1986

LABOR SUPPLY - MALI.
Emploi, potentialités et priorités au Mali . Addi Abeba , c1984. xix, 266 p. : ISBN 92-2-203954-8 : LC Card 85-980540
HD5847.3.A6 E47 1984
NYPL [JLE 86-484]

LABOR SUPPLY - MARYLAND - STATISTICS.
Affirmative action data . Baltimore, Md. (1100 N. Eutaw St., Baltimore 21201) [1985] [17] leaves ; LC Card 86-622599 DDC 331.11/43 19
HD5725.M35 A68 1985

Employment and labor force in Maryland . Baltimore, Md. (301 W. Preston St., Baltimore) [1986] xliv, 164, [51] p. : LC Card 86-622107 DDC 331.12/5/09752 19
HD5725.M35 E43 1986

Zoned employment and unemployment statistics . Baltimore, Md. (1100 N. Eutaw St., Baltimore 21201) [1986] [51] p. : LC Card 86-622109 DDC 331.12/5/09752021 19
HD5725.M35 Z67 1986

LABOR SUPPLY - MASSACHUSETTS - STATISTICS.
Foley, Catherine. Massachusetts industrial employment projected changes, 1984-1995 /. [Boston] [1986] vi leaves, 37 p. : LC Card 87-620528 DDC 331.12/5/09744 19
HD5725.M4 F64 1986

Occupations in services, finance, insurance, real estate, and construction, 1984 /. [Boston, MA] [1985] 185 p. : LC Card 87-621853 DDC 331.7/009744 19
HD5725.M4 O26 1985

LABOR SUPPLY - MATHEMATICAL MODELS.
Arbejdsløshed og beskæftigelse . Aarhus [Copenhagen] [1983] 34 p. ; LC Card 84-125513
HD5701.6 .A73 1983

Bronsard, Camille. Systems of demand equations (including labour supply) for different states of the markets and for different regimes /. Montréal [198-] 28 p. ; LC Card 83-222220 DDC 338.5/212 19
HB801 .B77 1980z

Büttler, Hans-Jürgen. Estimation of disequilibrium models /. Berlin , New York , c1986. vi, 114 p. : ISBN 0-387-16817-6 (U. S.) : LC Card 86-22073 DDC 339.5 19
HB145 .B88 1986
NYPL [JLM 72-289 v.279]

Fiorito, Riccardo, 1947- Mercato del lavoro e politica economica . Venezia , 1984. 247 p. : ISBN 88-317-4733-9 : LC Card 86-163951
HD5701.6 .F56 1984

Hodeige, Christian H., 1958- Job-Search im strukturierten Arbeitsmarkt . Freiburg , c1985. 166 p. ; ISBN 3-7930-0113-1 LC Card 86-142859
HD5701.6 .H62 1985

McKenna, C. J. Uncertainty and the labor market . New York , c1985. viii, 165 p. : ISBN 0-312-82861-6 : LC Card 85-1988 DDC 331.11 19
HD5707 .M39 1985 ***NYPL [JLD 86-3666]***

Pedersen, Peder J. Dynamiska processer på arbejdsmarkedet /. Aarhus [Copenhagen] [1982] 33 p. : LC Card 84-125613
HD5701.6 .P43 1982

Westergård-Nielsen, Niels C. Overgangen fra uddannelse til erhverv . Aarhus [Copenhagen] [1983] iii, 41 p. : LC Card 84-125491
HD5701.6 .W47 1983

LABOR SUPPLY - MEXICO.
Fernández, Sonia. Análisis comparativo de la información sobre población ocupada . México, D.F. [1977] 28 p. ; LC Card 84-227473
HD5731.A6 F46 1977

Gregory, Peter. The myth of market failure . Baltimore , 1986. viii, 299 p. ; ISBN 0-8018-3343-4 : LC Card 85-45927 DDC 331.12/0972 19
HD5731.A6 G74 1986 ***NYPL [JLE 86-3065]***

LABOR SUPPLY - MEXICO - ADDRESSES, ESSAYS, LECTURES.
Quantitative Latin American studies . Los Angeles , 1977. xiv, 91 p. : ISBN 0-87903-227-8 LC Card 77-620011 DDC 330.9/8/003
HD5731.A6 Q36 ***NYPL [JLF 80-242]***

LABOR SUPPLY - MEXICO - CHIAPAS.
Thompson G., Roberto. Problemática agraria y política petrolera en Chiapas /. Tuxtla Gutiérrez, Chiapas , 1983. 37 p., [1] leaf of plates : LC Card 84-243074
HD9574.M63 C457 1983

LABOR SUPPLY - MEXICO - GUADALAJARA.
Escobar Latapí, Agustín. Con el sudor de tu frente . Guadalajara, Jalisco, México , c1986. 312 p. ; ISBN 968-614-200-2 LC Card 86-209222
HD5731.G84 E83 1986

LABOR SUPPLY - MEXICO - JALISCO.
Cambio regional, mercado de trabajo y vida obrera en Jalisco /. Guadalajara, Jalisco, México , 1986. 363 p. ; ISBN 968-614-201-0 LC Card 86-218238
HD5731.J35 C36 1986

LABOR SUPPLY - MEXICO - MONTERREY - HISTORY.
Cerutti, Mario. Burguesía y capitalismo en Monterrey, 1850-1910 /. México, D.F. , 1983. 214 p. ; ISBN 968-8430-10-2 LC Card 86-221932
HC138.M6 C47 1983

LABOR SUPPLY - MEXICO - STATISTICS.
Pedrero, Mercedes. Indicadores para el estudio de la población económicamente activa basados en la información censal de 1970 /. México, D.F. [1977] 495 p. ; LC Card 85-202779
HA765 .P43 1977

LABOR SUPPLY - MIDDLE ATLANTIC STATES - STATISTICS.

Fuller, Theodore, 1929- The Mid-Atlantic region in transition . Washington, D.C. [1986] v, 13 p. : LC Card 86-602014 DDC 331.12/0974 19
HD5725.A12 F85 1986

LABOR SUPPLY - MONTANA - STATISTICS.
Occupational employment statistics . Helena, Mont. (P.O. Box 1728, Helena 59624) [1986] ii, 93 p. : LC Card 86-622803 DDC 331.12/51/0009786021 19
HD5725.M9 O256 1986

LABOR SUPPLY - MOROCCO.
Bernard, Chantal. La politique de l'emploi-formation au Maghreb, 1970-1980 /. Paris , 1982. 472 p. ; ***NYPL [JLE 86-568]***

LABOR SUPPLY - NEBRASKA - STATISTICS.
Greater Nebraska job prospects, 1983-1988 /. [Lincoln, Neb.] [1985] ii, 54 p. : LC Card 86-622213 DDC 331.12/09781/021 19
HD5725.N2 G74 1985

Women in numbers . Lincoln, Neb. (Box 94600, Lincoln 68509-4600) , 1985. iii, 168 p. : LC Card 86-622214 DDC 331.4/125/09782 19
HD6096.N3 W66 1985

LABOR SUPPLY - NEPAL.
Employment, income distribution, and consumption patterns in Nepal . Kathmandu, Nepal , 1983. xiv, 122 p. ; LC Card 84-901199 DDC 330.9549/6 19
HD5812.9.A6 E47 1983
NYPL [JLF 86-1993]

LABOR SUPPLY - NETHERLANDS.
Arbeidsmarkt op drift . [Amsterdam] , 1986. 190 p. : ISBN 90-6287-549-1 : LC Card 86-154853
HD5792 .A72 1986 ***NYPL [JLD 86-4417]***

Bakker, G. J. Op arbeid bezuinigd? . 's-Gravenhage , 1986. 116 p. ; ISBN 90-12-05321-8 LC Card 87-108889
HJ9507 .B35 1986

Dijk, Jouke van. Migratie en arbeidsmarkt /. Assen , 1986. 239 p. : ISBN 90-232-2213-X : LC Card 86-215033
HB2065 .D54 1986

Enige aspecten van arbeid in de toekomst . 's-Gravenhage , 1986. 178 p. : ISBN 90-12-05246-7 LC Card 87-101491
HD5792 .E47 1986

LABOR SUPPLY - NEVADA - STATISTICS.
Nevada occupational information system . [Carson City, Nev.] (505 E. King St., Carson City 89710) [1986] vii, 385 p. : LC Card 86-622271 DDC 331.12/09793/021 19
HD5725.N3 N45843 1986

LABOR SUPPLY - NEW JERSEY - STATISTICS.
County business growth. Trenton, N.J. (CN 824, Trenton 08625-0824) [1987] 2 v. : LC Card 87-404521 DDC 331.12/09749/021 19
HD5725.N5 C68 1987

Sheppard, Thomas M. Occupational outlook for New Jersey and JTPA labor market areas, 1982-1990 [microform]. Trenton, N.J. [1984] ii leaves, 50 p. ; LC Card 84-623480 DDC 331.12/09749 19
HD5725.N5 S47 1984
NYPL [*ZT-1745 no.24]

LABOR SUPPLY - NEW MEXICO - STATISTICS.
New Mexico youth in the labor force. [Albuquerque, N.M.] (P.O. Box 1928, Albuquerque 87103) [1986] v leaves, 74 p. : LC Card 87-620614 DDC 331.3/4/09789 19
HD6274.N6 N49 1986

LABOR SUPPLY - NEW YORK (N.Y.)
Stafford, Walter W. Closed labor markets . New York, N.Y. (105 E. 22nd St., New York 10010) , c1985. xvi, 203, 3, [2] p. ; LC Card 85-186853 DDC 331.12/09747/1 19
HD5726.N5 S73 1985 ***NYPL [Sc F 86-274]***

LABOR SUPPLY - NIGER.
Dynamique de l'emploi dans un système sahélien, le Niger . Addis Abéba , 1980. lxxii, 301 p. ; ISBN 92-2-202351-X : LC Card 82-980599
HD5846.7.A6 D95 1980

LABOR SUPPLY - NIGERIA.
Nambudiri, C. N. S. Third World multinationals . Geneva , 1983. iv, 41 p. ; ISBN 92-2-103386-4 (pbk.) LC Card 86-213622 DDC 338.8/88669 19
HD2928 .N35 1983

LABOR SUPPLY - NORTH DAKOTA - STATISTICS.
North Dakota employment and wages, 1984 /. Bismarck, N.D. (1000 E. Divide, Bismarck 58501) [1985] [3], 13, 13 leaves ; LC Card 86-623005 DDC 331.12/5/09784021 19
HD5725.N84 N73 1985

LABOR SUPPLY - NORWAY.
Luihn, Hans. Arbeid og samfunn . [Oslo] , c1986. 372 p. : ISBN 82-508-0574-7 : LC Card 87-157793
HD5800.A6 L85 1986

LABOR SUPPLY - NORWAY - AUST-AGDER FYLKE.
Fylkesplan for Aust-Agder . [Norway] [1983] 125 p. : LC Card 84-146306
HD5800.A95 F95 1983

LABOR SUPPLY - NORWAY - HISTORY - 19TH CENTURY.
Drivenes, Einar-Arne. Fiskarbonde og gruveslusk /. Oslo , c1985. 161, [1] p. : ISBN 82-00-07480-3 LC Card 86-204801
HD9506.N72 D75 1985

LABOR SUPPLY - NORWAY - MATHEMATICAL MODELS.
Stølen, Nils Martin. Etterspørsel etter arbeidskraft i norske industrinæringer /. Oslo , 1983. 66 p. : ISBN 82-537-2001-7 : LC Card 84-191739
HD5800.A6 S76 1983

LABOR SUPPLY - NORWAY - MØRE OG ROMSDAL FYLKE.
4-årige arbeidskraftprognoser, Møre og Romsdal 1983-1986(1987). [Molde] [1983?] 59 p. ; LC Card 84-146499
HD5800.M67 A14 1983

LABOR SUPPLY - NORWAY - REGIONAL DISPARITIES.
Skoglund, Tor. Regionale strukturendringer belyst ved sysselsettingstall /. Oslo , 1983. 52 p. ; ISBN 82-537-2003-3 : LC Card 84-161751
HD5800.A6 S58 1983

LABOR SUPPLY - NORWAY - TELEMARK FYLKE.
4-årig arbeidskraftprognose for perioden 1983-1987, Telemark fylke. [Telemark] [1983] 154 leaves ; LC Card 84-145787
HD5800.T44 A14 1983

LABOR SUPPLY - PAKISTAN.
Employment, distribution, and basic needs in Pakistan . Lahore , 1986. xxxiv, 408 p., [1] leaf of plates : LC Card 86-930280 DDC 330.9549/1 19
HD5820.5.A6 E47 1986

LABOR SUPPLY - PAKISTAN - STATISTICS.
Growth of R & D manpower and expenditure in Pakistan. Islamabad , 1985. 66 p. ; LC Card 85-932022 DDC 331.12/510014/095491021 19
HC440.5.Z9 R44 1985

LABOR SUPPLY - PANAMA.
Gandásegui, Marco A. La fuerza de trabajo en el agro . Panamá, R.P. , c1985. 404 p. : ISBN 84-8385-002-X LC Card 86-111074 DDC 331.7/63/097287 19
HD1822 .G36 1985 ***NYPL [JLF 86-1350]***

Panama . Washington, D.C., U. S.A. , c1985. xxv, 307 p., [8] p., [1] leaf of plates : ISBN 0-8213-0580-8 LC Card 85-12420 DDC 338.97287 19
HC147 .P43 1985 ***NYPL [JLF 86-1919]***

LABOR SUPPLY - PENNSYLVANIA - STATISTICS.
Pennsylvania occupational trends and outlook for total civilian employment, 1980 and projected 1990 /. Harrisburg, Pa. , 1984. ii, 98 p. : ***NYPL [JLF 87-706]***

LABOR SUPPLY - PERSIAN GULF STATES.
Nadwat Tanmiyat al-Mawārid al-Basharīyah fī al-Khalīj al-ʻArabī (1975 : Bahrain) Nadwat Tanmiyat al-Mawārid al-Basharīyah fī al-Khalīj al-ʻArabī . al-Kuwayt [1975?] 361, 404 p. : LC Card 86-964662
HD5715.5.P39 N33 1975

LABOR SUPPLY - PERU.
Migraciones laborales en el Perú . [Monterrico] [c1984] 47 p. : LC Card 84-235623 DDC 331.12/7985 19
HD5761 .M53 1984 ***NYPL [JLF 86-799]***

LABOR SUPPLY - PERU - CUZCO (DEPT.)
Díaz Gómez, Jorge. Deterioro de los términos de intercambio, migración eventual y pobreza campesina en el departamento del Cusco /. [Cuzco, Peru] , 1986. 17, 3 leaves, 2 leaves of plates : LC Card 86-200938
HD1531.P4 D52 1986

LABOR SUPPLY - PERU - LIMA METROPOLITAN AREA.
Migraciones laborales en el Perú . [Monterrico] [c1984] 47 p. : LC Card 84-235623 DDC 331.12/7985 19
HD5761 .M53 1984 ***NYPL [JLF 86-799]***

LABOR SUPPLY - PHILIPPINES - CASE STUDIES.
Costello, Michael A. Mobility and employment in urban Southeast Asia . Boulder , 1987. xvi, 190 p. : ISBN 0-8133-7352-2 (pbk. : alk. paper) : LC Card 87-10649 DDC 307.2 19
HB2107 .C67 1987

LABOR SUPPLY - PORTUGAL.
Moura, João. Problemas e política de emprego no continente /. Lisboa , 1977. 56 p. ; LC Card 85-214189
HD5809.A6 M68 1977

A População de Portugal /. [Lisbon] , 1976. 116 p., [1] folded leaf of plates : LC Card 85-204353
HB3621 .P67 1976

LABOR SUPPLY - PORTUGAL - MATHEMATICAL MODELS.
Barbosa, Manuel P. (Manuel Pinto), 1944- Growth, migration, and the balance of payments in a small open economy, Portugal /. New York , 1984. xv, 212 p. : ISBN 0-8240-4169-0 : LC Card 79-53646 DDC 382.1/7/0724 19
HD5809.A6 B37 1984 ***NYPL [JLE 86-4171]***

LABOR SUPPLY - RED SEA REGION.
Pennisi, Giuseppe. Development, manpower and migration in the Red Sea region . Hamburg , c1981. xi, 264 p. : LC Card 82-109615 DDC 331.6/2/091824 19
HD8656 .P46 1981 ***NYPL [JLF 86-1602]***

LABOR SUPPLY - REGIONAL DISPARITIES.
Regional labour markets . Amsterdam ; New York : xvii, 500 p. : ISBN 0-444-70323-3 LC Card 87-22200 DDC 331.12 19
HD5707 .R37 1987

LABOR SUPPLY - RÍO DE LA PLATA REGION (ARGENTINA AND URUGUAY)
Chackiel, Juan. La fuerza de trabajo en los países de la Cuenca del Plata según los censos de 1960 /. San José, Costa Rica , 1976. iv, 81 p. : LC Card 83-169596
HD5746.A6 C42 1976

LABOR SUPPLY - RUSSIAN S.F.S.R. - CHUVASHSKAI͡A A.S.S.R.
Sotsial´no-ėkonomicheskie problemy ispol´zovanii͡a trudovykh resursov /. Cheboksary , 1986. 70 p. ; LC Card 87-137786
HD5797.C56 S68 1986

LABOR SUPPLY - RUSSIAN S.F.S.R. - MOSCOW.
Korolev, L. P. (Leonid Pavlovich) Trudovye resursy i ikh ispol´zovanie /. Moskva , 1982. 139 p. ; LC Card 82-158161
HD5797.M66 K67 1982

LABOR SUPPLY - RUSSIAN S.F.S.R. - MOSCOW (OBLAST)
Korolev, L. P. (Leonid Pavlovich) Trudovye resursy i ikh ispol´zovanie /. Moskva , 1982. 139 p. ; LC Card 82-158161
HD5797.M66 K67 1982

LABOR SUPPLY - RUSSIAN S.F.S.R. - NON-CHERNOZEM REGION.
Smekalov, Pavel Vasil´evich. Sel´skie kadry nechernozem´i͡a /. Moskva , 1981. 190 p. ; LC Card 82-177714
HD1536.S65 S64 1981

LABOR SUPPLY - RUSSIAN S.F.S.R. - SIBERIA.
Rabochiĭ klass Sibiri . Novosibirsk , 1986. 355 p., [16] p. of plates : LC Card 86-211294
HD5797.S5 R33 1986

Trudovye kollektivy Sibiri . Novosibirsk , 1985.

154 p. ; LC Card 86-162191
HD5797.S5 T78 1985

LABOR SUPPLY - RUSSIAN S.F.S.R. - SIBERIA, WESTERN.
Khaĭtun, A. D. (Alekseĭ Davydovich) Ėkspeditsionno-vakhtovoe stroitel′stvo v Zapadnoĭ Sibiri /. Leningrad , 1982. 175, [1] p. : LC Card 83-165812
HD9715.S73 S565 1982

LABOR SUPPLY - RUSSIAN S.F.S.R. - URAL MOUNTAINS REGION - CONGRESSES.
Kardinal′nyĭ rost ėffektivnosti zhivogo truda--glavnyĭ faktor uskoreniia sotsial′no-ėkonomicheskogo razvitiia . Sverdlovsk , 1986. 2 v. ; LC Card 87-136690
HC337.R853 L35 1986

LABOR SUPPLY - SCANDINAVIA.
Buvollen, H. P. (Hans Petter) The situation of workers in the industrialised countries with special reference to Scandinavia /. Oslo [1985] 24 p. ; LC Card 86-205580 DDC 331.13/7948 19
HD8540 .B86 1985

Den Offentliga sektorns sysselsättningsutveckling i Norden under 1970-talet =. [Oslo] [Solna] 1983. iiii, 150 p. : ISBN 91-38-07556-3 LC Card 85-184428
HD8013.S344 O35 1983

Vargas, Ines. The NIEO and the situatuon of workers . Oslo [1985] xiv, 290 p. ; ISBN 82-7288-121-7 (pbk.) LC Card 86-205407 DDC 331/.098 19
HD6530.5 .V36 1985

LABOR SUPPLY - SIERRE LEONE.
Iyanda, Olukunle. Multinationals and employment in a West African sub-region . Geneva , 1984. iv, 49 p. ; ISBN 92-2-103623-5 (pbk.) : LC Card 86-213585 DDC 388.8/88664 19
HD2928.8 .I92 1984

LABOR SUPPLY - SINGAPORE.
Saw, Swee-Hock, 1931- The labour force of Singapore /. Singapore [1984] xi, 78 p. : ISBN 997-19-1416-6 (pbk.) LC Card 86-946447 DDC 331.11/09595/7 19
HD5823.A6 S28 1984

LABOR SUPPLY - SINGAPORE - EFFECT OF EDUCATION ON - ADDRESSES, ESSAYS, LECTURES.
Pang, Eng Fong. Education, manpower, and development in Singapore /. Kent Ridge, Singapore , c1982. 242 p. : ISBN 997-16-9053-5 (bound) LC Card 83-941002 DDC 331.11/09595/7 19
HD5823.A6 P35 1982 ***NYPL [JLD 86-2364]***

LABOR SUPPLY - SINGAPORE - STATISTICS.
Saw, Swee-Hock, 1931- The labour force of Singapore /. Singapore [1984] xi, 78 p. : ISBN 997-19-1416-6 (pbk.) LC Card 86-946447 DDC 331.11/09595/7 19
HD5823.A6 S28 1984

LABOR SUPPLY - SOCIAL ASPECTS - AUSTRIA.
Historische Wurzeln der Sozialpartnerschaft /. München , 1986. 368 p. ; ISBN 3-486-52971-4 LC Card 87-146580 DDC 306/.36/09436 19
HD6957.A9 H57 1986

LABOR SUPPLY - SOUTH AFRICA - CAPE OF GOOD HOPE.
Goldin, Ian. The poverty of Coloured labour preference . Cape Town [1984] ii, 97 p. : ISBN 0-7992-0570-2 (pbk.) LC Card 84-195453
HD8801.Z8 C324 1984

LABOR SUPPLY - SOUTH AFRICA - DURBAN.
Padayachee, Vishnu. An analysis of some aspects of employment and unemployment in the African townships of Umlazi and Lamontville . Durban [South Africa] [1985] iii, 49 p. ; ISBN 0-949947-75-X (pbk.) LC Card 87-404149 DDC 331.12/5/0968455 19
HD5842.D87 P33 1985

LABOR SUPPLY - SOUTH AFRICA - TRANSKEI.
Muller, N. D. Unemployment and the search for work in Transkei . Umtata, Transkei [1982] 19 leaves ; LC Card 86-206957 DDC 331.13/7968791 19
HD5842.T73 M85 1982

LABOR SUPPLY - SOUTH DAKOTA - STATISTICS.
South Dakota employment & earnings covered by unemployment insurance, 1984. Aberdeen, S.D. [198-] 47 p. : LC Card 87-620925
HD5725.S8 S67 1980z

LABOR SUPPLY - SOVIET UNION.
Bohynia, D. P. Ėffektivnost′ obshchestvennogo truda v usloviiakh razvitogo sotsializma . Kiev , 1982. 316 p. ; LC Card 82-200989
HC340.L3 B56 1982

Ėkonomika trudovykh resursov /. Minsk , 1985. 159 p. ; LC Card 87-156829
HD5796 .E35 1985

Granick, David. Job rights in the Soviet Union . Cambridge , New York , 1987. ix, 344 p. ; ISBN 0-521-33295-8 LC Card 86-26392 DDC 331.11/0947 19
HD5796 .G72 1987

Grimaliuk, V. A. (Viktor Andreevich) Neposredstvenno obobshchestvlennyĭ trud /. Moskva , 1985. 110, [2] p. ; LC Card 86-111859
HD5796 .G75 1985

Kostakov, V. G. (Vladimir Georgievich) Chelovecheskiĭ faktor--zaniatost′, blagosostoianie /. Moskva , 1981. 78 p. : LC Card 82-164831
HD5796 .K567 1981

Mordasova, L. A. (Lidiia Andrianovna) Trudovye resursy v torgovle /. Moskva , 1985. 128 p. ; LC Card 86-158800
HD8526.5 .M54 1985

Problemy ėffektivnosti ispol′zovaniia trudovykh resursov /. Moskva , 1981. 147 p. ; LC Card 82-150334
HC340.L3 P64 1981

Sotsialisticheskoe obobshchestvlenie truda /. Moskva , 1981. 166 p. ; LC Card 82-161177
HD5796 .S633 1981

Voprosy metodologii issledovaniia obshchestvennogo truda pri sotsializme /. Voronezh , 1979. 163 p. ; LC Card 81-142810
HD5796 .V65 1979

LABOR SUPPLY - SOVIET UNION - HISTORY - 20TH CENTURY - CONGRESSES.
Labour and employment in the USSR /. Brighton, Sussex , 1986. xviii, 280 p. : ISBN 0-7450-0038-X LC Card 86-673709
HD5796 .L33x 1986b

LABOR SUPPLY - SOVIET UNION, NORTHERN.
Sotsial′nye problemy truda u narodnosteĭ Severa /. Novosibirsk , 1986. 213 p. ; LC Card 87-164784
HD5797.N75 S67 1986

LABOR SUPPLY - SOVIET UNION - STATISTICS.
Rapawy, Stephen. Civilian employment in the U. S.S.R., 1950 to 1983 /. Washington, D.C. [1985] 35 leaves ; LC Card 87-601284 DDC 331.12/5/0947021 19
HD5796 .R358 1985

LABOR SUPPLY - SPAIN.
Albentosa Puche, Luis. El paro en España /. Madrid , c1983. 349 p. : ISBN 84-85719-34-4 LC Card 86-121124 DDC 331.11/0946 19
HD5807 .A44 1983 ***NYPL [JLC 87-37]***

LABOR SUPPLY - SPAIN - CANET DE BERENGUER.
Pellicer Valero, Jesús-Agustín. Sociología del trabajo en Canet de Berenguer /. Valencia , 1984. 80 p. : ISBN 84-600-3540-9 LC Card 86-216439
HD5808.C33 P45 1984

LABOR SUPPLY - SPAIN - MURCIA (REGION) - STATISTICS.
Bel Adell, María del Carmen. Datos básicos para el estudio de la población en la región de Murcia /. [Murcia] , c1985. 223 p. ; ISBN 84-600-3907-2 LC Card 86-218876
HA1558.M8 B44 1985

LABOR SUPPLY - SRI LANKA.
Foreign employment . [Colombo] [1985] x, 202 p. ; LC Card 87-900211 DDC 331.6/2/5493 19
HD8670.8 .F67 1985

LABOR SUPPLY - STATISTICAL METHODS.
Krug, Walter, Prof. Dr. Quantifizierung des systematischen Fehlers in wirtschafts- und sozialstatistischen Daten . Berlin , 1976. 109 p. : ISBN 3-428-03710-3 LC Card 76-487801
HD5711 .K78 ***NYPL [JLE 80-187]***

Munkaügyi statisztikai és módszertani ismeretek /. Budapest , 1985. 323 p. : ISBN 963-10-6513-8 : LC Card 83-228566
HD4826.5 .M86 1985

LABOR SUPPLY - STATISTICS.
Economically active population . Geneva , 1986- v. ; ISBN 92-2-005345-4 (v. 1)
NYPL [JLM 87-113]

Economically active population estimates and projections, 1950-2025 =. Geneva [1986]- v. <1-5 > ; ISBN 92-2-005345-4 (pbk. : v. 1) : LC Card 86-223275 DDC 331.12/021 19
HD5712 .E26 1986

LABOR SUPPLY - SURINAM - PARAMARIBO.
Onderzoek naar werkgelegenheid, inkomen en de structuur van de stedelijke economie van Paramaribo . Paramaribo, Suriname [1978] 69 leaves : LC Card 87-115836
HD5759.5.P37 O53 1978

LABOR SUPPLY - SWEDEN.
Öhman, Berndt, 1940- Kommunerna och sysselsättningspolitiken . [Stockholm] [1985] 212 p. ; ISBN 91-38-08745-6 LC Card 86-114034
HD5803 .O36 1985

Schettkat, Ronald. Bevölkerungs- und Erwerbsverhaltensentwicklung in Österreich, Schweden und der Bundesrepublik Deutschland /. Berlin [1984] 48 p. ; LC Card 85-198691
HD5771 .S34 1984

Sveriges arbetskraft . Stockholm , Örebro [1986] 62 p. : ISBN 91-618-0162-3 : LC Card 87-151800
HD5803 .S943 1986

LABOR SUPPLY - SWEDEN - ECONOMETRIC MODELS.
Åberg, Yngve. The impact of working hours and other factors on production and employment /. Aldershot, Hants, England , Brookfield, Vt., U. S.A. , c1987. viii, 166 p. : ISBN 0-566-05480-9 : LC Card 87-8393 DDC 331.25/7/09485 19
HD5202 .A64 1987

LABOR SUPPLY - SWEDEN - EFFECT OF EDUCATION ON.
Studerandepopulation och arbetsmarknad . [Stockholm] [1986] 78 p. : ISBN 91-38-09464-9 LC Card 87-106834
HD6278.S75 S78 1986

LABOR SUPPLY - SWITZERLAND.
Held, Daniel. Marché de l'emploi . Lausanne , 1984. 205 p. : ISBN 2-88074-028-2
NYPL [JLE 86-679]

LABOR SUPPLY - THAILAND.
Ræengngān Thai. Krung Thēp , 2528 [1985] 53 p. ; LC Card 86-915944
HD5822.55.A6 R35 1985

LABOR SUPPLY - TOGO.
Dovi-Sodemekou, Folly B. (Folly Bebey) Emploi et éducation dans le 2e plan de développement économique et social du Togo /. Lomé, Togo [1985] 89, 52, 9, 2 p. : LC Card 87-131183
HD5846.5.A6 D68 1985

Gù-Konu, E. Y. Population et progrès socio-économique au Togo /. Lome , 1980. 291 p. : LC Card 87-148380
HB3665.8.A3 G8 1980

LABOR SUPPLY - TUNISIA.
Bernard, Chantal. La politique de l'emploi-formation au Maghreb, 1970-1980 /. Paris , 1982. 472 p. ; ***NYPL [JLE 86-568]***

LABOR SUPPLY - UKRAINE.
Kachestvo trudovogo potentsiala . Kiev , 1986. 228 p. ; LC Card 87-161614
HD5797.U37 K34 1986

Resursy narodnogo khoziaistva . Kiev , 1985. 308 p. : LC Card 86-226867
HC337.U5 P5 1985 t. 2 HC337.U53I52

Upravlenie trudovymi resursami . Kiev , 1986. 238 p. ; LC Card 86-233715
HD5797.U37 U67 1986

Vosproizvodstvo trudovykh resursov /. Kiev , 1984. 177, [3] p. ; LC Card 86-189052
HD5797.U37 V67 1984

LABOR SUPPLY - UKRAINE - KIEV.
Sem´i͡a i vosproizvodstvo struktury trudovoĭ zani͡atosti . Kiev , 1984. 238 p. : LC Card 86-142706
HB2698.U38 S46 1984

LABOR SUPPLY - UNITED STATES.
Employment policies . Washington, D.C. , 1986. 16, [2] p. ; ISBN 0-88713-611-7 (pbk.) LC Card 87-127759 DDC 331.12/042/0973 19
HD5724 .E449 1986

Employment projections for 1995 . Washington, D.C. , 1986. v, 131 p. : LC Card 86-602460 DDC 331.12/0723 19
HD5724 .E47 1986

Haveman, Robert H. Jobs and the environment /. Scarsdale, N.Y. , c1979. 32 p. ; LC Card 79-15418 DDC 301.31/0973
HC110.E5 H38 ***NYPL [JLM 83-380 no.10]***

Kamerman, Sheila B. A workplace for people . New York , 1987. p. cm. ISBN 0-231-06480-2 LC Card 87-18223 DDC 331.2/0973 19
HD60.5.U5 K36 1987

Moore, Sylvia F. The short-term effects of marital disruption on the labor supply behavior of young women /. Columbus, Ohio (Suite 585, 1375 Perry St., Columbus, Ohio, 43201) , 1979. v, 133 p. ; ***NYPL [JLF 86-649]***

LABOR SUPPLY - UNITED STATES - CONGRESSES.
Job generation . Salt Lake City, Utah , c1986. xiv, 138 p. ; ISBN 0-913420-89-1 (pbk.) LC Card 86-31285 DDC 331.12/094 19
HD5724 .J63 1986

LABOR SUPPLY - UNITED STATES - EFFECT OF ENERGY COSTS ON.
Smith, Edward Joseph, 1911- Impact of energy costs on manufacturing employment /. Washington, D.C. [1985] iv, 16 p. : LC Card 86-603150 DDC 331.12/57/0973 19
HD5724 .S614 1985

LABOR SUPPLY - UNITED STATES - EFFECT OF TAXATION ON - CONGRESSES.
Taxation and incentives /. [London, England] , c1976. ii, 45 p. : LC Card 85-111944
HJ2619 .T289 1976

LABOR SUPPLY - UNITED STATES - EFFECT OF TECHNOLOGICAL INNOVATIONS ON.
The Changing labor market . Lexington, Mass. , c1986. x, 166 p. : ISBN 0-669-11943-1 (alk. paper) LC Card 85-45710 DDC 331.12/0973 19
HD6331.2.U5 C47 1986
NYPL [JLE 86-1069]

Light, John J. Realistic economics /. Indianapolis, IN (P.O. Box 1606, Indianapolis 46206) , c1984. 111 p. ; ISBN 0-933021-00-3 : LC Card 84-249506 DDC 331.12/0973 19
HD5724 .L4236 1984 ***NYPL [JLE 86-4650]***

Lund, Robert T. Keeping America at work . New York , c1986. xi, 260 p. : ISBN 0-471-81563-2 LC Card 85-17900 DDC 331.12/0973 19
HD45 .L86 1985 ***NYPL [JLD 86-2101]***

Rochell, Carlton C. Dreams betrayed . Lexington, Mass. , c1987. 138 p. ; ISBN 0-669-11105-8 (alk. paper) LC Card 85-45019 DDC 331.25 19
HD6331.2.U5 R63 1987

Workers, managers, and technological change . New York , c1987. xxii, 362 p. : ISBN 0-306-42450-9 LC Card 87-2327 DDC 331/.0973 19
HD6331.2.U5 W67 1987

LABOR SUPPLY - UNITED STATES - EFFECT OF TECHNOLOGICAL INNOVATIONS ON - CONGRESSES.
The Future impact of technology on work and education /. London , New York , 1987. p. cm. ISBN 1-85000-083-2 : LC Card 87-13641 DDC 331.12/0994 19
HD6331.2.A8 F87 1987

Technology and employment . Washington, D.C. , 1987. xiii, 225 p. : ISBN 0-309-03744-1 (pbk.) : LC Card 87-42807 DDC 331.12/0973 19
HD6331.2.U5 T43 1987

LABOR SUPPLY - UNITED STATES - HISTORY.
Fairchild, Byron. The Army and industrial manpower /. Westport, Conn. , 1987. xiv, 291 p. : ISBN 0-313-25480-X (lib. bdg. : alk. paper) LC Card 86-25738 DDC 331.11/0973 19
HD5724 .F25 1987

LABOR SUPPLY - UNITED STATES - STATISTICS.
Barnes, William R. Employment problems and America's cities /. [Washington, D.C.] , 1984. xiii, 66, 33 p. ; ***NYPL [JLF 86-1]***

Linking employment problems to economic status . Washington, D.C. [1986] vi, 56 p. ; LC Card 86-603148 DDC 331.13/7973 19
HD5724 .L425 1986

LABOR SUPPLY - URUGUAY.
Argenti, Gisela. Cambio técnico, trabajo y educación . Montevideo , 1985. 91, 70 leaves : LC Card 87-124118
HC235.T4 A74 1985

Fortuna, Juan Carlos. Las bases de un desarrollo social diferente . Montevideo [1985] 117 p. ; LC Card 86-131906
HC232 .F76 1985

Informe sobre el mercado de empleo, 1983 /. Montevideo , 1984. 8, [19] leaves ; LC Card 86-174013
HD5762.A6 I54 1984

LABOR SUPPLY - URUGUAY - STATISTICS.
Apezechea, Héctor J., 1937- Tasas de participación y relaciobes multivariadas a partir e la información de la encuesta de hogares del segundo semestre de 1978 . [Montevideo, Uruguay] , 1980. 12, [44] leaves ; LC Card 86-157658
HD5762.A6 A64 1980

Empleo y estructura ocupacional en grandes establecimientos industriales /. Montevideo , 1984. 51 leaves ; LC Card 86-174021
HB2667 .E46 1984

Lombardi, Nelly Niedworok de. Algunas cifras sobre la fuerza de trabajo en el Uruguay /. [Montevideo] [1979] 18 leaves : LC Card 86-164130
HD5762.A6 L66 1979

LABOR SUPPLY - UTAH - STATISTICS.
Jensen, Kenneth E. Utah affirmative action information, 1985. [Salt Lake City] [1986] i, 253 p. ; LC Card 86-622873 DDC 331.11/43 19
HD5725.U8 J46 1986

LABOR SUPPLY - UZBEK S.S.R.
Lubin, Nancy. Labour and nationality in Soviet Central Asia . London , 1984. xix, 305 p. : ISBN 0-333-36739-1 LC Card 87-672162
HD5797.U9 L83x 1984b

LABOR SUPPLY - UZBEK S.S.R. - EFFECT OF TECHNOLOGICAL INNOVATIONS ON.
Akhunova, M. A. Rabochiĭ klass Uzbekistana v uslovii͡akh nauchno-tekhnicheskoĭ revoli͡utsii /. Tashkent , 1984. 181 p. ; LC Card 85-232015
HD6331.2.S652 U93 1984

LABOR SUPPLY - VENEZUELA - STATISTICS.
Estadísticas sociales . Caracas, Venezuela , 1983. 2 v. ; LC Card 84-183391 DDC 312/.0987 19
HA1095 .E88 1983 ***NYPL [JLM 85-550]***

LABOR SUPPLY - VERMONT - STATISTICS.
Employment and earnings, 1980-1985 . Montpelier, Vt. [1986] ii, 79 leaves : LC Card 86-622186 DDC 331.12/5/09743021 19
HD5725.V5 E46 1986

LABOR SUPPLY - WASHINGTON (STATE) - PUGET SOUND REGION - STATISTICS.
Pethick, Donald R. Population and employment forecasts and distribution for the central Puget Sound region, 1975-1990 /. Seattle, Wash. [1969] 26 p., [2] leaves of plates : LC Card 87-400702 DDC 304.6/2/097977021 19
HA697.P84 P47 1969

LABOR SUPPLY - WEST (U. S.)
Western employment trends, 1947-58. San Francisco, Calif. [1959] 18 p. ; LC Card 87-400419 DDC 331.12/5/0978 19
HD5725.A17 W47 1959

LABOR SUPPLY - WEST VIRGINIA - STATISTICS.
State of West Virginia Job Training Partnership Act . Charleston, W.Va. (112 California Ave., Charleston 25305-0112) [1986] vi, 233 p. ; LC Card 86-622901 DDC 331.1/09754/021 19
HD5725.W4 S7 1986

State of West Virginia Job Training Partnership Act planning statistics /. Charleston, W. Va. (112 California Ave., Charleston 25305-0112) [1985] v, 122 p. ; LC Card 85-623225 DDC 331.1/09754/021 19
HD5725.W4 S7 1985

LABOR SUPPLY - WISCONSIN.
Tienda, Marta. The structural transformation of employment in Wisconsin, 1960-1980 /. Madison, WI (Rm. 245, 30 N. Murray St., Madison 53715) [1986] ii, 47 p. ; LC Card 86-623091 DDC 331.12/09775 19
HD5725.W5 T54 1986

LABOR SUPPLY - WYOMING - STATISTICS.
Wyoming income and employment report /. Cheyenne, Wyo. [1986] 54, [33], iii p. : LC Card 86-623087 DDC 331.12/5/09787021 19
HD5725.W9 W97 1986

LABOR SUPPLY - YUGOSLAVIA.
Čelenković, Teodosije. Radna snaga u samoupravnom društvu . Beograd , 1980. 241 p. ; LC Card 82-166188
HD5811.6.A6 C45 1980

Künne, Wilfried. Die Aussenwanderung jugoslawischer Arbeitskräfte . Königstein/Ts. , 1979. xii, 269 p. : ISBN 3-7756-6931-0 : LC Card 79-394439
HD8633.5 .K83 ***NYPL [JLD 87-1148]***

LABOR SUPPLY - ZAIRE - KINSHASA.
Gozo, K. M. Le secteur non structuré de Kinshasa . Addis Abéba , c1985. iii, 64, [8] p. : ISBN 92-2-100538-0 LC Card 85-981182
HD2346.Z27 K54 1985

LABOR SUPPLY - ZAMBIA - MONGU DISTRICT.
The Structure of the informal sector in Mongu (Western Province) and its potential for employment creation . Lusaka, Zambia [1982] iii, 44, 10 p. ; LC Card 87-980490 DDC 331.12/51381 19
HD2346.Z292 M657 1982

LABOR THEORY OF VALUE.
La Forma-valore . Manduria , 1984. 301 p. : LC Card 86-130626 DDC 335.4/12 19
HB206 .F67 1984

Roland, Marcos M. O valor de uso em Marx /. [Brasília] [19]81. 52, [2] leaves ; LC Card 85-228336
HB206 .R65 1981

Solé, Miguel José. Las condiciones de vida y de trabajo de los tamberos de la pampa húmeda . Stockholm , 1983. 33 p. ; LC Card 84-107283
HD1865.P35 S65 1983

Takenaga, Susumu. Valeur, formes de la valeur et étapes dans la pensée de Marx /. Berne , New York , c1985. 243 p. ; ISBN 3-261-04026-2 LC Card 86-196366
HB206 .T35 1985

LABOR THEORY OF VALUE - SOVIET UNION.
Kirillov, S. R. (Sergeĭ Rufovich) Soizmerenie zatrat i rezul´tatov v teorii planovogo tsenoobrazovanii͡a /. Moskva , 1987. 188 p. ; LC Card 87-157208
HB235.S73 K57 1987

LABOR TURNOVER - GERMANY (EAST)
Schaefer, Reinhard. Disponibilität--Mobilität--Fluktuation /. Berlin , 1982. 70 p. : LC Card 83-225572
HD5717.5.G35 S3 1982

LABOR TURNOVER - HUNGARY.
Meszticzky, András. Termelőszövetkezeti szakemberek munkahelyváltoztatása . [Budapest] , 1985. 165 p. : LC Card 86-218526
HD1492.H8 M37 1985

LABOR TURNOVER - KAZAKH S.S.R.
Problemy ukreplenii͡a trudovoĭ distsipliny i predotvrashchenii͡a tekuchesti kadrov na predprii͡atii͡akh TSentral´nogo Kazakhstana . Karaganda , 1982. 126 p. ; LC Card 84-226131
HF5549.5.L3 P76 1982

LABOR TURNOVER - MATHEMATICAL MODELS.
Romanov, A. K. (Arnol´d Konstantinovich) Matematicheskoe modelirovanie dvizhenii͡a kadrov v organizatsii͡akh /. Moskva , 1986. 154

p. : LC Card 87-158073
HF5549.5.T8 R56 1986

LABOR TURNOVER - SOVIET UNION.
Granick, David. Job rights in the Soviet Union . Cambridge , New York , 1987. ix, 344 p. ; ISBN 0-521-33295-8 LC Card 86-26392 DDC 331.11/0947 19
HD5796 .G72 1987

LABOR TURNOVER - UNITED STATES.
Rogerson, Peter. Job turnover and interregional migration [microform] /. Iowa City , 1981. 25 p. : ***NYPL [*ZT-1564 no.31]***

LABOR TURNOVER - UNITED STATES - STATISTICS.
Hiring costs and strategies . New York, N.Y. , c1986. v, 82 p. : ISBN 0-8144-3153-4 (pbk.) LC Card 86-209862 DDC 658.4/07111/0973 19
HD38.25.U6 H57 1986

LABOR UNIONS. see **TRADE-UNIONS.**

Labor unions and labor-management relations. 2nd revision. Tokyo, Japan : Japan Institute of Labour, 1986. 48 p. : ill. ; 28 cm. (Japanese industrial relations series . 2) ISBN 4-538-74002-0 : LC Card 86-220438 DDC 331/.0952 19
1. Industrial relations - Japan. 2. Trade-unions - Japan. 3. Labor laws and legislation - Japan. I. Nihon Rōdō Kyōkai. II. Series.
HD8726.5 .L33 1986

LABOR, UNSKILLED. see **UNSKILLED LABOR.**

LABORAND LABORING CLASSES - MOZAMBIQUE - MAPUTO - HISTORY.
Capela, José. O movimento operário em Lourenço Marques, 1898-1927 /. [Porto?] [1981?] 281, [1] p. ; LC Card 87-401260 DDC 331.88/0967/9 19
HD6869.Z8 M363 1981

Laboratory experimentation in economics : six points of view / edited by Alvin E. Roth. Cambridge ; New York : Cambridge University Press, 1987. ix, 219 p. : ill. ; 24 cm. Based on a conference held at the University of Pittsburgh, May 16-18, 1985. Includes bibliographies. CONTENTS. - Bargaining phenomena and bargaining theory / Alvin E. Roth -- Equity and coalition bargaining in experimental three-person games / Reinhard Selten -- The psychology of choice and the assumptions of economics / Richard Thaler -- Hypothetical valuations and preference reversals in the context of asset trading / Marc Knez and Vernon L. Smith -- Economics according to the rats (and pigeons too) / John H. Kagel -- Dimensions of parallelism / Charles R. Plott. ISBN 0-521-33392-X LC Card 87-10343 DDC 330/.0724 19
1. Economics - Experiments. I. Roth, Alvin E., 1951-.
HB131 .L32 1987

LABORERS. see **LABOR AND LABORING CLASSES; UNSKILLED LABOR.**

Laborie, Jean Paul. La politique française d'amenagement du territoire de 1950 à 1985 / Jean-Paul Laborie, Jean-François Langumier, Priscilla De Roo. Paris : Documentation française, 1985. 176 p., [8] p. of plates : ill., maps (some col.) ; 30 cm. At head of title: Coopération et aménagement, Agence française pour l'aménagement et le développement à l'étranger. Includes bibliographical references. ISBN 2-11-001488-1(pbk.) :
1. France. Délégation à l'aménagement du territoire et à l'action régionale. 2. Regional planning - France. 3. Decentralization in government - France. I. Langumier, Jean-François. II. De Roo, Priscilla. III. Coopération et aménagement (France). IV. Title.
NYPL [JLG 87-38]

LABORING AND LABORING CLASSES - BRAZIL - POLITICAL ACTIVITY - HISTORY.
Hahner, June Edith, 1940- Poverty and politics . Albuquerque , 1986. xvi, 415 p. : ISBN 0-8263-0878-3 : LC Card 86-1258 DDC 305.5/69/0981 19
HC190.P6 H34 1986 ***NYPL [JLE 86-4407]***

Labour and employment in the USSR / edited by David Lane. Brighton, Sussex : Wheatsheaf Books : Distributed by Harvester Press, 1986. xviii, 280 p. : ill. ; 23 cm. Title on spine: Labour & employment in the USSR. Papers presented at a conference organized at the University of Birmingham in May 1984. Includes bibliographies and index. ISBN 0-7450-0038-X LC Card 86-673709
1. Labor supply - Soviet Union - History - 20th century - Congresses. 2. Soviet Union - Full employment policies - History - 20th century - Congresses. I. Lane, David Stuart. II. Title: Labour & employment in the USSR.
HD5796 .L33x 1986b

Labour & employment in the USSR. Labour and employment in the USSR /. Brighton, Sussex , 1986. xviii, 280 p. : ISBN 0-7450-0038-X LC Card 86-673709
HD5796 .L33x 1986b

Labour and nationality in Soviet Central Asia . Lubin, Nancy. London , 1984. xix, 305 p. : ISBN 0-333-36739-1 LC Card 87-672162
HD5797.U9 L83x 1984b

Labour and poverty in Kenya, 1900-1980 /. Collier, Paul. Oxford , New York , 1986. xi, 296 p. : ISBN 0-19-828505-1 : LC Card 86-1352 DDC 331.12/09676/2 19
HD5840.5.A6 C65 1986
NYPL [JLE 86-3282]

Labour and poverty in rural Tanzania . Collier, Paul. Oxford [Oxfordhire] , New York , 1986. vii, 143 p. : ISBN 0-19-828531-0 : LC Card 86-5303 DDC 307.1/4/09678 19
HN797.Z9 C625 1986 ***NYPL [JLD 87-511]***

Labour and social problems arising out of seasonal fluctuations of the food products and drink industries /. Tripartite Technical Meeting for the Food Products and Drink Industries, 2d, Geneva, 1978. Geneva , 1978. ii, 51 p. ; ISBN 92-2-101879-2 (pbk.) : LC Card 80-477150 DDC 331.2/0464
HD9000.1 .T75 1978a ***NYPL [JLE 80-1039]***

Labour and unions in Asia and Africa / edited by Roger Southall. New York : St. Martin's Press, 1987. p. cm. Includes index. ISBN 0-312-01362-0 : LC Card 87-21475 DDC 331.88/095 19
1. Trade-unions - Asia. 2. Trade-unions - Africa. I. Southall, Roger.
HD6796 .L3 1987

Labour circulation and the labour process / edited by Guy Standing. London [England] ; Dover, N.H. : Croom Helm, c1985. xvi, 416 p. : ill. ; 23 cm. "A study prepared for the International Labour Office within the framework of the World Employment Programme." Includes bibliographical references and index. ISBN 0-7099-3342-8 : LC Card 84-14306 DDC 331.12/791 19
1. Migrant labor - Developing countries - Addresses, essays, lectures. 2. Labor mobility - Developing countries - Addresses, essays, lectures. 3. Migration, Internal - Developing countries - Addresses, essays, lectures. I. Standing, Guy. II. International Labor Office. III. World Employment Programme.
HD5856.D44 L33 1984
NYPL [JLD 86-2532]

Labour conditions in the mining industry of Andhra Pradesh . Saibaba, G. Tirupati [1985?] v, 314 p. ; LC Card 86-901021 DDC 331/.0422/095484 19
HD8039.M61 I47 1985
NYPL [JLD 87-1057]

Labour force estimates and projections. Economically active population . Geneva , 1986- v. ; ISBN 92-2-005345-4 (v. 1)
NYPL [JLM 87-113]

Labour force estimates and projections, 1950-2000. Economically active population estimates and projections, 1950-2025 =. Geneva [1986]- v. <1-5 > ; ISBN 92-2-005345-4 (pbk. : v. 1) : LC Card 86-223275 DDC 331.12/021 19
HD5712 .E26 1986

The labour force of Singapore /. Saw, Swee-Hock, 1931- Singapore [1984] xi, 78 p. : ISBN 997-19-1416-6 (pbk.) LC Card 86-946447 DDC 331.11/09595/7 19
HD5823.A6 S28 1984

Labour force projections. Economically active population . Geneva , 1986- v. ; ISBN 92-2-005345-4 (v. 1) ***NYPL [JLM 87-113]***

Labour History Group (South Africa) The 1922 white mineworker's strike. Salt River [South Africa] [1986?] 44 p. : LC Card 86-195260 DDC 331.89/28223422/0968 19
HD5442.M73 A15 1986

Labour in the West Indies . Lewis, W. Arthur (William Arthur), 1915- London , 1977. 104 p., [12] p. of plates : ISBN 0-901241-25-3 (pbk.) LC Card 86-232414
HD6595.4 .L49 1977

Labour inspection : a workers' education manual. Geneva : International Labour Office, 1986. ix, 100 p. ; 24 cm. Bibliography: p. 99-100. ISBN 92-2-105359-8 (pbk.) : LC Card 87-123437 DDC 331.25 19
1. Labor inspection. 2. Factory inspection. I. International Labour Office.
HD3656 .L33 1986

Labour inspection in agriculture in Southeast Asia . Sub-regional Symposium on Labour Inspection in Agriculture (1982 : Denpasar, Indonesia) Bangkok , 1983. 218 p. : ISBN 92-2-103533-6 LC Card 86-915732
HD1537.A785 S8 1982

Labour management relations and trade union leadership . Madhusudhana Rao, M. New Delhi , c1986. 392 p. ; LC Card 86-903198 DDC 331/.0954 19
HD6812 .M23 1986

Labour-management relations in public enterprises in Africa. Mesfin Gabre Michael. Geneva, Switzerland , 1983. 84 p. ; ISBN 92-2-103009-1 (pbk.) LC Card 86-213649 DDC 658.3 s 331/.04135/000096 19
HD6961.A1 I73 no. 60 HD8776.5

Labour-management relations series, 0538-8325 .
(60) Mesfin Gabre Michael. Labour-management relations in public enterprises in Africa. Geneva, Switzerland , 1983. 84 p. ; ISBN 92-2-103009-1 (pbk.) LC Card 86-213649 DDC 658.3 s 331/.04135/000096 19
HD6961.A1 I73 no. 60 HD8776.5

(63) Selected basic agreements and joint declarations on labour-management relations. Geneva , 1983. iv, 299 p. ; ISBN 92-2-103460-7 (pbk.) LC Card 86-213669 DDC 331.89 s 341.7/63 19
HD6961.A1 I73 no. 63 K1715

(64) Labour-relations in Africa, English-speaking countries . Geneva , c19. 159 p. ; ISBN 92-2-103467-4 (pbk.) : LC Card 86-212930 DDC 658.3 s 331/.096 19
HD6961.A1 I73 no. 64 HD8772

Labour market flexibility : report by a high-level group of experts to the Secretary-General. Paris : Organisation for Economic Co-operation and Development ; Washington, D.C. : OECD Publications and Information Centre [distributor], 1986. 23 p. ; 24 cm. LC Card 86-215799 DDC 331.12 19
1. Labor supply. 2. Labor mobility. 3. Unemployment. 4. Quality of life. I. Organisation for Economic Co-operation and Development.
HD5707 .L28 1986

Labour market flexibility and external price shocks /. Klau, Friedrich. Paris, France , c1985. 60 p. : LC Card 86-205164 DDC 331.12 19
HD5707 .K54 1985

Labour Market Workshop (1982 : Australian National University) Japanese and Australian labour markets . Canberra [c1983] xx, 610 p. : ISBN 0-86413-004-X (pbk.) : LC Card 84-220557 DDC 331.12/0952 19
HD5850.A6 J36 1983 ***NYPL [JLE 86-630]***

Labour mobility between New Zealand and Australia /. St. Hill, R. L. Canterbury, N.Z. [1986] ix, 68 p. : LC Card 87-109510 DDC 331.12/791 19
HD8848.5.N45 S7 1986

LABOUR PARTY (GREAT BRITAIN) - HISTORY.
Marrocu, Luciano. Laburismo e trade unions . Bari , 1981. 183 p. ; LC Card 81-137615 DDC 331.88/0941 19
HD6664 .M24 ***NYPL [JLD 86-3453]***

Savage, Michael. The dynamics of working-class politics . Cambridge [Cambridgeshire] , New York , 1987. xii, 280 p. : LC Card 87-14636 DDC 322/.2/0941 19
HD8397.P74 S28 1987

LABOUR PARTY (GREAT BRITAIN) - HISTORY - 19TH CENTURY.
Rothstein, Theodore. From chartism to labourism /. New York , 1984. vi, 365 p. ; ISBN 0-8240-5722-8 (alk. paper) : LC Card 83-48495 DDC 335/.1 19
HX249 .R68 1984 ***NYPL [JLD 86-1828]***

LABOUR PARTY (GREAT BRITAIN) - HISTORY - 20TH CENTURY.
Nicholson, Marjorie. The TUC overseas . London , Boston , c1986. xvi, 329 p. ; ISBN 0-04-331103-2 (alk. paper) LC Card 85-28607 DDC 331.88/0941 19
HD8383 .N52 1986 ***NYPL [JLD 86-2932]***

Labour problems of a developing economy /. Aziz, Abdul, 1937- New Delhi , c1984. viii, 157 p. ; LC Card 84-901201 DDC 331/.0954 19
HD8686.5 .A95 1984 ***NYPL [JLD 86-4216]***

Labour-relations in Africa, English-speaking countries : proceedings of and documents submitted to a symposium (Nairobi, 22-26 November 1982). Geneva : International Labour Office, c1983 159 p. ; 25 cm. (Labour-management relations series, 0538-8325 . 64) Proceedings of the Symposium on the Development of Sound Labour Relations in English-Speaking African Countries. Bibliography: p. 48-49. ISBN 92-2-103467-4 (pbk.) : LC Card 86-212930 DDC 658.3 s 331/.096 19
1. Industrial relations - Africa - Congresses. I. International Labour Office. II. Symposium on the Development of Sound Labour Relations in English-Speaking African Countries (1982 : Nairobi, Kenya). III. Series.
HD6961.A1 I73 no. 64 HD8772

Labour Representation Committee. see **Labour Party (Great Britain)**

Labour research series .
(v. 4, etc) Schroeder, Ighsaan. Conditions of employment . Cape Town [1985]- 1 v. (loose-leaf) ; ISBN 0-7992-1002-1 (loose-leaf) LC Card 86-232933 DDC 331.2/0968 19
HD4927.S6 S37 1985

Labour sharing in agriculture /. Gasson, Ruth M. [London] [1979] 117 p. ; ISBN 0-901859-82-6 (pbk.) LC Card 83-226074 DDC 331.25/72 19
HD5119.A292 G744 1979

Labour standards in Sri Lanka : recent trends. [1st ed.] [Colombo] : Sri Lanka Foundation Institute, 1981. x, 164 p. ; 20 cm. (Sri Lanka Foundation Institute pocket book . 7) Includes bibliographical references. LC Card 83-902877 DDC 331/.09549/3 19
1. Labor policy - Sri Lanka. 2. Industrial relations - Sri Lanka. 3. Labor laws and legislation - Sri Lanka. I. Sri Lanka Foundation Institute. II. Series.
HD8670.8 .L32 1981 ***NYPL [JLC 87-22]***

Labour utilisation in Australia . Bosworth, Derek L. [Bedford Park, S. Aust.] [1986] i, 205 p. : LC Card 86-229498 DDC 331.12/5/0994 19
HD5850.A6 B67 1986

LABRADOR (NFLD.) - ECONOMIC CONDITIONS.
Royal Commission on Labrador. Ten years after . [St. John's, Nfld.] , 1986. iv, 116 p. ; LC Card 86-212404 DDC 361.6/1/097182 19
HC117.L2 R69 1986

LABRADOR (NFLD.) - ECONOMIC POLICY.
Royal Commission on Labrador. Ten years after . [St. John's, Nfld.] , 1986. iv, 116 p. ; LC Card 86-212404 DDC 361.6/1/097182 19
HC117.L2 R69 1986

LABRADOR (NFLD.) - SOCIAL CONDITIONS.
Royal Commission on Labrador. Ten years after . [St. John's, Nfld.] , 1986. iv, 116 p. ; LC Card 86-212404 DDC 361.6/1/097182 19
HC117.L2 R69 1986

LABRADOR (NFLD.) - SOCIAL POLICY.
Royal Commission on Labrador. Ten years after . [St. John's, Nfld.] , 1986. iv, 116 p. ; LC Card 86-212404 DDC 361.6/1/097182 19
HC117.L2 R69 1986

Laburismo e trade unions . Marrocu, Luciano. Bari , 1981. 183 p. ; LC Card 81-137615 DDC 331.88/0941 19
HD6664 .M24 ***NYPL [JLD 86-3453]***

Lacaita, Carlo G. Colombo, Giuseppe, 1836-1921. Industria e politica nella storia d'Italia . [Milano] , Roma , c1985. 497 p. : ISBN 88-420-2555-0 : LC Card 85-180231 DDC 338.945 19
HC310.I53 C65 1985 ***NYPL [JLE 86-2517]***

Lacaz, Francisco A. de Castro (Francisco Antonio de Castro) De que adoecem e morrem os trabalhadores /. São Paulo , 1985. 236 p. ; LC Card 85-231487
HD7683 .D4 1985

LACE INDUSTRY - ENGLAND - NOTTINGHAM - HISTORY - SOURCES - BIBLIOGRAPHY - CATALOGS.
University of Nottingham. Dept. of Manuscripts. Miscellaneous lace records /. [Nottingham] [c1985] 12 p. ; LC Card 87-116493 DDC 016.3384/7677653/0942527 19
HD9933.G73 N688 1985

Lachmann, Ludwig M.
Subjectivism, intelligibility, and economic understanding . Basingstoke, Hampshire , 1986. xi, 319 p. : ISBN 0-333-41788-7
NYPL [JLD 86-2215]

LACHMANN, LUDWIG M. - ADDRESSES, ESSAYS, LECTURES.
Subjectivism, intelligibility, and economic understanding . Basingstoke, Hampshire , 1986. xi, 319 p. : ISBN 0-333-41788-7
NYPL [JLD 86-2215]

Lachmann, Richard. From manor to market : structural change in England, 1536-1640 / Richard Lachmann. Madison, Wis. : University of Wisconsin Press, 1987. xiv, 166 p. : ill. ; 24 cm. Rev. version of the author's thesis (Ph. D.)--Harvard University. Bibliography: p. 155-162. Includes index. ISBN 0-299-11420-1 : LC Card 87-40146 DDC 330.942/05 19
1. England - Economic conditions. 2. England - Social conditions. 3. Feudalism - England - History. 4. Capitalism - England - History. I. Title.
HC254 .L33 1987

LaCivita, Stephen J. Hildebrandt, Herbert William, 1931- A managerial profile . Ann Arbor, MI , c1985. 31 p. ; ISBN 0-87712-248-2 (pbk.) LC Card 86-621187 DDC 331.4/816584/00973 19
HD6054.4.U6 H55 1985

LACKAWANNA STEEL COMPANY - HISTORY.
Leary, Thomas E., 1946- From fire to rust . Buffalo, N.Y. , c1987. 134 p. : ISBN 0-939032-00-7 (pbk.) LC Card 87-692 DDC 338.7/669142/0974796 19
HD9519.L2 L43 1987

Lackinger, Otto.
Zur Beschäftigungsproblematik in Oberösterreich. 1984. Arbeitsmarktpolitik für die Landwirtschaft und den ländlichen Raum / mit Beiträgen von Otto Lackinger, Karl Pelz, Manfred Sinz ; [Herausgeber, Hans Bach]. Graz , c1984. 138 p. : ISBN 3-900307-15-6 LC Card 85-186643
HD1536.A9 A73 1984

Lacour, Claude. Croissance urbaine : mobilité et desserte des zones périphériques par les transports collectifs / Claude Lacour, Michèle Baratra, Danièle Leymarie. Paris : Editions du Centre national de la recherche scientifique, 1981. 219 p. : ill., maps ; 30 cm. (Actions thématiques programmées . no 2954.) Bibliography: p. [209]-215. ISBN 2-222-02928-7 (pbk.) : LC Card 82-153821 DDC 388.4/068 19
1. Local transit - France. 2. Urbanization - France. 3. City planning - France. 4. Suburbs - France. I. Baratra, Michèle. II. Leymarie, Danièle. III. Université de Bordeaux I. Institut d'économie régionale du Sud-Ouest. IV. Series: Actions thématiques programmées. A. T. P.: Sciences humaines, no 2954. V. Title.
HE4764 .L3 1981 ***NYPL [JLG 86-56]***

Lacrampe, Serge. Introduction à la gestion prévisionnelle /. Lyon , c1985. 337 p. : ISBN 2-7297-0268-7 : LC Card 86-132861 DDC 658.4/0355 19
HD30.28 .I56 1985

Lacroix, Robert. Dussault, François. Les modèles scandinaves et la détermination des ententes salariales des industries manufacturières canadiennes . Montréal [1982] 21, [11] p. ; LC Card 82-196710
HD4979 .D875 1982

Lacrosse, James. Florida index of retail activity / by James Lacrosse, Alan W. Johansen. [Tallahassee] : Division of Economic and Demographic Research, Joint Legislative Management Committee, [1983] [22] leaves : ill. ; 28 cm. LC Card 86-621941 DDC 381/.1/09759021 19
1. Retail trade - Florida - Statistics. I. Johansen, Alan W. II. Florida. Legislature. Joint Legislative Management Committee. Division of Economic and Demographic Research. III. Title.
HF5429.4.F6 L33 1983

Ladbrook, Denis A. Disadvantaged youth in an isolated region : towards a youth policy for the eastern Pilbara / Denis A. Ladbrook, with Alison Moss, Mary Del Casale. [Pilbara, W.A.] : Hedland College, [1985] ix, 125 p. : ill. ; 30 cm. (Occasional papers / Hedland College . no. 3) "February 1985." Bibliography: p. 114-117. LC Card 87-121044 DDC 331.3/4/099413 19
1. Socially handicapped youth - Employment - Australia - Pilbara (W.A. : Region). I. Moss, Alison. II. Del Casale, Mary. III. Series: Occasional papers / Hedland College , no. 3. IV. Title.
HD6276.A83 P555 1985

Ladd, Doris M. The making of a strike : Mexican silver workers' struggles in Real del Monte, 1766-1775 / Doris M. Ladd. Lincoln : University of Nebraska Press, c1988. x, 205 p. ; 24 cm. Bibliography: p. [191]-200. Includes index. ISBN 0-8032-2876-7 (alk. paper) LC Card 87-5897 DDC 331.8/928223423/097246 19
1. Miners' Strike, Mineral del Monte, Mexico, 1766. 2. Compañía Real del Monte y Pachuca - History - 18th century. 3. Silver miners - Mexico - Pachuca Region - History - 18th century. I. Title.
HD5331.M72 1766 .P325 1988

Ladensack, Klaus. Bohring, Günther. Wie Leiter den wissenschaftlich-technischen Fortschritt bewältigen /. Berlin , 1986. 168 p. : ISBN 3-320-00704-1 LC Card 87-112384 DDC 338/.06 19
HD45 .B59 1986

Ladenschluss kontrovers : Beiträge zur aktuellen Diskussion / Herausgeber Hartwig Piepenbrock. Stuttgart : Seewald, [1984] 232 p. : ill. ; 21 cm. (Schriftenreihe des Vereins für Wirtschaftliche und Soziale Fragen e.V. Stuttgart . 19) Includes bibliographical references. ISBN 3-512-00712-0 LC Card 85-138606
1. Store hours - Germany, West. 2. Store hours - Law and legislation - Germany (West). I. Piepenbrock, Hartwig. II. Series.
HD5178 .L33 1984

Ladhari, Noë.
Labour-management relations in Tunisian public enterprises. 1983. Mesfin Gabre Michael. Labour-management relations in public enterprises in Africa. Geneva, Switzerland , 1983. 84 p. ; ISBN 92-2-103009-1 (pbk.) LC Card 86-213649 DDC 658.3 s 331/.04135/000096 19
HD6961.A1 I73 no. 60 HD8776.5

Laḍhata /. Sāvanta, Śivājī, 1940- Pravarānagara , 1985-1986. 2 v. : LC Card 87-900715
HD9116.I415 M37 1985

LADIES' LAND LEAGUE - HISTORY.
Parnell, Anna, 1852-1911. The tale of a great sham /. Dublin , Wick, Littlehampton, West Sussex , 1986. 205 p. ; ISBN 0-905223-93-4 LC Card 86-234070 DDC 333.33/5/09415 19
HD625 .P37 1986

LaDou, Joseph, 1938- Introduction to occupational health and safety /. Chicago, Ill. , c1986. xvii, 519 p. : ISBN 0-87912-133-5 LC Card 84-61216 DDC 658.3/82 19
HD7261 .I68 1986

LaDue, Eddy L. Carraro, Kenneth C. An economic evaluation of alternative sources of funding for agricultural lending by commercial banks /. Ithaca, N.Y. [1985] 48 p. ; LC Card 86-622432 DDC 332.7/1/09747 19
HG2051.U6 N53 1985

Ladybucks /. Bohigian, Valerie. New York, N.Y. , c1987. 246 p. ; ISBN 0-396-08852-X LC Card 86-29227 DDC 650.1/024042 19
HD6072.6.U5 B64 1987

Ladygin, Boris Nikolaevich. Istoricheskiĭ opyt sotrudnichestva stran SĖV / B.N. Ladygin, V.I. Sedov, R.R. Ultanbaev. Moskva : "Myslʹ", 1980. 284 p. ; 21 cm. Includes bibliographical references. LC Card 81-130900
1. Europe, Eastern - Economic integration - History. 2. Communist countries - Economic integration - History. I. Sedov, V. I. (Vladimir Ilʹich). II. Ultanbaev, R. R. (Rafaėlʹ Rafilʹbenovich). III. Title.
HC244 .L282 1980

Laederach, Monique, 1938- Fabrikbesichtigungen /. Zürich , c1986. 206 p. : ISBN 3-85791-109-3

LC Card 87-129952 DDC 305.5/62/09494 19
HD8606.5 .F33 1986

LAELIGER, WALTER.
Loeliger, Walter. Sind Sie frei? . Basel , 1982. 99 p. : ISBN 3-85816-043-1 : LC Card 83-100470
HD8039.T162 L64 1982

Laemmel, Christof. Lebensmittel und Getränke aus der Schweiz =. Zürich , 1984. 113 p. : ISBN 0-390-92140-3 *NYPL [JFE 86-3409]*

Länderhaushalte. Bonn : Institut "Finanzen und Steuern" : Vertrieb, W. Stollfuss, [1964] 112 p. ; 21 cm. (Institut "Finanzen und Steuern" . Heft 73) LC Card 85-185971
1. Finance, Public - Germany, West. I. Institut "Finanzen und Steuern" (Germany). II. Series: Schriftenreihe (Institut "Finanzen und Steuern" (Germany)) , Heft 73.
HJ1101 .B6 Heft 73 HJ1120

Das Länderrisiko als bankbetriebliches Problem /. Dworak, Brigitte M. Berlin , c1985. 168 p. : ISBN 3-428-05761-9 LC Card 85-213576
HG5993 .D86 1985

Längsschnittanalyse des österreichischen Arbeitsmarktes . Böhm, Walter. Wien , 1986. 138 p. : ISBN 3-85369-654-6 LC Card 87-142156 DDC 331.12/5/09436 19
HD5771 .B64 1986

Läsker, Lothar. Intensivierung der Forschung . Berlin , 1984. 354 p. ; LC Card 84-195559
HD30.42.G4 I57 1984

Lafarga, Adolfo. see **Lafarga Lozano, Adolfo.**

Lafarga Lozano, Adolfo. De Bilbao y de Vizcaya sobre sus orígenes históricos y económicos / por Adolfo Lafarga Lozano. [Bilbao? : s.n., 1976?] (Bilbao : Gráficas Loroño) 310 p. : ill., maps ; 23 cm. Bibliography: p. 303-308. ISBN 84-400-1414-7 LC Card 85-142805
1. Bilbao (Spain) - Commerce - History. 2. Vizcaya (Spain) - Commerce - History. 3. Jews - Spain - Bilbao - History. 4. Bilbao, Spain - History. 5. Vizcaya, Spain - History. I. Title.
HF3690.B5 L34 1976

Laffer, Arthur B. Supply-side portfolio strategies /. Westport, Conn. , 1988. xii, 180 p. : ISBN 0-89930-286-6 (lib. bdg. : alk. paper) LC Card 87-13091 DDC 332.6/0973 19
HG4910 .S775 1988

L'affidamento bancario . Spedale, Domenico L. Milano , 1985. 204 p. :
NYPL [JLD 86-3241]

L'Affiliazione commerciale : organizzazione di un sistema italiano di franchising distributivo / scritti di Antonio Barrese ... [et al.] ; contributi di Corrado Bertin ... [et al.] ; a cura di Giancarlo Ravazzi.2a ed. Milano : F. Angeli, 1986. 100 p. : ill. ; 22 cm. (Distribuzione commerciale . 1)
1. Franchises (Retail trade) - Italy. 2. Marketing channels - Italy. 3. Physical distribution of goods - Italy. I. Barrese, Antonio. II. Bertin, Corrado. III. Ravazzi, Giancarlo. IV. Series.
NYPL [JLD 87-531]

Laffont, Jean-Jacques, 1947-
[Fondements de l'économie publique. English] Fundamentals of public economics / Jean-Jacques Laffont ; translated by John P. Bonin and Hélène Bonin. Rev. English language ed. Cambridge, Mass. : MIT Press, c1987. p. cm. Translation of: Fondements de l'économie publique. Bibliography: p. Includes index. ISBN 0-262-12127-1 LC Card 87-21895 DDC 338.5 19
1. Microeconomics. I. Title.
HB173 .L23713 1987

Lafontaine, Oskar, 1943- Der andere Fortschritt : Verantwortung statt Verweigerung / Oskar Lafontaine. Hamburg : Hoffmann und Campe, c1985. 222 p. ; 22 cm. ISBN 3-455-08248-3 LC Card 85-146223
1. Germany, West - Economic conditions - 1974-. 2. Germany, West - Economic policy - 1974-. 3. Germany (West) - Politics and government - 1982-. 4. Sozialdemokratische Partei Deutschlands. 5. Developing countries - Economic conditions. I. Title.
HC286.7 .L33 1985

Laganier, Jean. Courlet, Claude. L'Europe du sud au milieu du gué /. Grenoble , 1984. 122 p. ; ISBN 2-7061-0243-8 : LC Card 85-116696
HC244.5 .C68 1984

Lagerqvist, Lars O. Vad kostade det? : priser och löner från medeltid till våra dagar / Lars O. Lagerqvist, Ernst Nathorst-Böös.2., rev. uppl. Stockholm : LT, c1884 115 p. : ill. ; 20 cm. Includes index. ISBN 91-36-02399-X : LC Card 86-158743
1. Cost and standard of living - Sweden - History. 2. Wages - Sweden - History. I. Nathorst-Böös, Ernst, 1918-. II. Title.
HD7040 .L34 1985

Lagerström, Tomas, 1939- Carlzon, Jan. Riv pyramiderna! . [Stockholm] , c19. 219 p. : ISBN 91-0-046844-4 LC Card 86-139896
HE9860.S28 C375 1986

Lagos (City). Nigerian Institute of International Affairs. see **Nigerian Institute of International Affairs.**

Lagos, Luis Felipe.
Aedo, Cristián. Protección efectiva en Chile, 1974-1979 /. Santiago [1984] 56 leaves ; LC Card 85-152465
HF1956 .A35 1984

Coloma C., Fernando. Algunas consideraciones sobre los efectos distributivos del proceso de liberalización comercial /. Santiago , 1982. 31 leaves ; LC Card 87-102072
HF1713 .C617 1982

Coloma C., Fernando. Los efectos de una desgravación arancelaria en el contexto de una economía con movilidad imperfecta de trabajo /. Santiago , 1985. 46 leaves : LC Card 85-203579
HF1713 .C618 1985

El efecto de los shocks externos sobre el producto : un análisis para la economía chilena / Luis Felipe Lagos Marchant. Santiago, Chile : Pontificia Universidad Católica de Chile Instituto de Economía, Oficina de Publicaciones, 1985. 15, [8] leaves : ill. ; 27 cm. (Documento de trabajo . # 104) Bibliography: leaf 15. LC Card 87-404321 DDC 339.383 19
1. Gross national product - Chile - Econometric models. 2. Chile - Economic policy - Econometric models. 3. Foreign exchange problem - Chile - Econometric models. I. Series: Documento de trabajo (Universidad Católica de Chile. Instituto de Economía) , no. 104. II. Title.
HC195.I5 L34 1985

Lagosha, Boris Aleksandrovich.
Analiz i sintez v sistemakh otraslevogo upravlenii͡a / B.A. Lagosha, V.G. Sharkovich. Moskva : Izd-vo "Nauka", 1978. 262 p., [1] folded leaf of plates : ill. ; 20 cm. (Problemy sovetskoĭ ėkonomiki) At head of title: Akademii͡a nauk SSSR. T͡Sentral'nyĭ ėkonomiko-matematicheskiĭ institut. Bibliography: p. 257-[261] LC Card 81-167577
1. Industrial management - Mathematical models. I. Sharkovich, V. G. II. Title.
HD30.25 .L335 1978

Baĭriev, B. S. Optimizat͡sii͡a struktur upravlenii͡a /. Ashkhabad , 1985. 169, [23] p. : LC Card 86-196466
HC337.T23 B35 1985

L'agriculture marocaine face au deuxième élargissement de la CEE /. Qarouach, Mostafa. [S.l.] 1983 (Casablanca : Editions maghrébines) 117 p. ; LC Card 83-192279 DDC 382/.41/0964 19
HD9017.M82 Q37 1983
NYPL [JLD 86-4326]

Lahiff, James M. Huseman, Richard C. Business communication . Chicago , c1988. xxxi, 702 p., [8] p. of plates : ISBN 0-03-012294-5 LC Card 87-438 DDC 658.4/5 19
HF5718 .H84 1988

Laidler, David E. W. Monetarist perspectives / David Laidler. Deddington, Oxford : P. Allan, 1982. xii, 218 p. ; 23 cm. Bibliography: p. [195]-209. Includes indexes. ISBN 0-86003-042-3 LC Card 86-673565
1. Monetary policy. 2. Macroeconomics. I. Title.
HG230.3 .L34x 1982b

Laĭliev, Dzh. S. Ėkonomicheskiĭ rost Kirgizskoĭ SSR v usloviiakh intensifikatsii obshchestvennogo proizvodstva . Frunze , 1984. 210 p. ; LC Card 85-131511
HC337.K545 E37 1984
*NYPL [*QIP 87-105]*

Lainé, François Bloch- see **Bloch-Lainé, François.**

LAISSEZ-FAIRE - ADDRESSES, ESSAYS, LECTURES.
The Future of private enterprise /. Atlanta, Ga. , 1984-1986. 3 v. ; ISBN 0-88406-164-7 (pbk. : v. 1) LC Card 83-25386 DDC 338.6/1 19
HB501 .F83 1984 *NYPL [JLK 87-49]*

LAISSEZ-FAIRE - CONGRESSES.
Friedman, Milton, 1912- Politics and tyranny . San Francisco, Calif. , c1984. 68 p. ; ISBN 0-936488-00-X (pbk.) : LC Card 84-61364 DDC 330 19
HB98.3 .F75 1984 *NYPL [JLE 87-857]*

LAISSEZ-FAIRE - HISTORY.
Folsom, Burton W. Entrepreneurs versus the historians /. Washington, DC , New York, NY , c1987. p. cm. ISBN 0-89526-573-7 : LC Card 87-23390 DDC 338/.04/0973 19
HG181 .F647 1987

Nelson, John R., 1952- Liberty and property . Baltimore , c1987. xv, 221 p. : ISBN 0-8018-3440-6 (alk. paper) LC Card 86-21373 DDC 338.973 19
HC105 .N45 1987

LAISSEZ-FAIRE - HISTORY - 20TH CENTURY.
Holzwarth, Fritz. Ordnung der Wirtschaft durch Wettbewerb . Freiburg im Breisgau , c1985. 217 p. ; ISBN 3-448-01510-5 LC Card 86-109043
HB95 .H65 1985

Withers, William, 1905-1987. Politics and economic policy . New York, N.Y. , c1986. 240 p. : ISBN 0-8062-2722-2 : LC Card 86-201185 DDC 338.973 19
HC106 .W82 1986

LAISSEZ-FAIRE - MORAL AND ETHICAL ASPECTS.
Wogaman, J. Philip. Economics and ethics . Philadelphia , c1986. xiii, 145 p. ; ISBN 0-8006-1904-8 (pbk.) LC Card 85-45478 DDC 261.8/5 19
HB72 .W633 1986 *NYPL [JLD 86-3984]*

Laitko, Hubert. Intensivierung der Forschung . Berlin , 1984. 354 p. ; LC Card 84-195559
HD30.42.G4 I57 1984

Laitl, Jan. Kazimour, Jan, engineer. Rezervy v ekonomice /. Praha , 1981. 227 p. ; LC Card 81-208368
HC270.28 .K38 1981

Lajo, Manuel. Agricultura y alimentación . [Lima] , 1982. 536 p. : LC Card 83-174688 DDC 338.1/9/85 19
HD9014.P52 A57 1982 *NYPL [JLD 86-268]*

Lakásváltoztatási szándékok, lakáskörülmények az 1984. évi mikrocenzus alapján / [készült a Központi Statisztikai Hivatal Népesedésstatisztikai Főosztályán]. Budapest : Központi Statisztikai Hivatal, 1986. 199 p. ; 29 cm. Chiefly tables. ISBN 963-340-798-2 LC Card 87-110348
1. Housing - Hungary - Statistics. 2. Residential mobility - Hungary - Statistics. 3. Housing rehabilitation - Hungary - Statistics. I. Hungary. Központi Statisztikai Hivatal. Népesedésstatisztikai Föosztály.
HD7337.5.A3 L355 1986

Lakatos, Ernő. Mezőgazdasági szövetkezetek Pest megyében, 1985 . Budapest , 1985. 442 p. : ISBN 963-02-4206-0 LC Card 87-137365
HD1492.H82 P475 1985

Lakatos, Miklós. Budapest és a jelentősebb városok napi munkaerővonzási körzete népességének főbb jellemzői, 1980. január 1. /. Budapest , 1986. 106 p. : ISBN 963-02-4578-7 LC Card 87-407674
HA1205 .B83 1986

Lake, Linda K. Connor, Patrick E. Managing organizational change /. New York , 1988. xii, 192 p. : ISBN 0-275-92335-5 (alk. paper) : LC Card 87-12475 DDC 658.4/06 19
HD58.8 .C653 1988

Laki, Mihály. A kisvállalatok állami támogatása két fejlett tőkés országban / Laki Mihály. Budapest : Szövetkezeti Kutató Intézet, 1983-1985. 62 p. ; 29 cm. (Közlemények, 0133-4905 . 190) Bibliography: p. 55-56. LC Card 86-218531
1. Small business - Germany, West. 2. Small business - Government policy - Germany (West). 3. Small business - United States. 4. Small business -

Government policy - United States. I. Series: Közlemények / Szövetkezeti Kutató Intézet, 190. II. Title.
HD2346.G3 L24 1983

Lakos, Éva. Holtomiglan? holtodiglan? / Lakos Éva. Budapest : Szépirodalmi Könyvkiadó, c1985. 269 p., [6] leaves of plates : ports. ; 19 cm. ISBN 963-15-3100-7 : LC Card 86-190862
1. Labor and laboring classes - Hungary - Interviews. I. Title.
HD8420.5 .L35 1985

A Lakosság jövedelme és fogyasztása, 1960-1973 / [készült a KSH Közgazdasági Főosztálya Jövedelem- és Fogyasztásstatisztikai Osztályán ; szerkesztette, Zafír Mihály]. [Budapest] : Központi Statisztikai Hivatal, c1975. 91 p. ; 29 cm. (Statisztikai időszaki közlemények . 349. köt.) "1975. július 14." Tables. ISBN 963-340-048-1 LC Card 86-196944
1. Income - Hungary - Statistics. 2. Consumption (Economics) - Hungary - Statistics. I. Zafír, Mihály. II. Hungary. Központi Statisztikai Hivatal. Jövedelem- és Fogyasztásstatisztikai Osztály. III. Series.
HC300.295.I5 L32 1975

A Lakosság jövedelme és fogyasztása, 1960-1983 / [készült a KSH Közgazdasági Főosztálya Jövedelem- és Fogyasztásstatisztikai Osztályán ; szerkesztette, Zafír Mihály]. Budapest : Központi Statisztikai Hivatal, 1984. 118 p. ; 29 cm. Chiefly tables. ISBN 963-340-740-0 : LC Card 85-155585
1. Income - Hungary - Statistics. 2. Consumption (Economics) - Hungary - Statistics. I. Zafír, Mihály. II. Hungary. Központi Statisztikai Hivatal. Jövedelem- és Fogyasztásstatisztikai Osztály.
HC300.295.I5 L3315 1984
NYPL [JLF 86-672]

A Lakosság jövedelme és fogyasztása, 1970-1984 : függelék. Budapest : Központi Statisztikai Hivatal, 1985. 83 p. ; 29 cm. Tables. LC Card 86-217829
1. Income - Hungary - Statistics. 2. Consumption (Economics) - Hungary - Statistics. I. Hungary. Központi Statisztikai Hivatal.
HC300.295.I5 L3316 1985

A Lakosság jövedelme és fogyasztása, 1970-1985 / [készült a KSH Közgazdasági Főosztálya Jövedelem- és Fogyasztásstatisztikai Osztályán ; szerkesztette, Fajth Gáspár]. Budapest : Központi Statisztikai Hivatal, 1986. 97 p. ; 29 cm. Tables. ISBN 963-340-805-9 : LC Card 87-408026
1. Income - Hungary - Statistics. 2. Consumption - Hungary - Statistics. I. Fajth, Gáspár. II. Hungary. Központi Statisztikai Hivatal. Jövedelem- és Fogyasztásstatisztikai Osztály.
HC300.295.I5 L3317 1986

A Lakosság jövedelme, társadalombiztosítás, családpolitika / [készült a Központi Statisztikai Hivatal Közgazdasági Főosztályán ; összeállította Zafír Mihály és Fekete Gyula ; munkatársak, Fajth Gáspár ... et al.]. Budapest : Statisztikai Kiadó Vállalat, [1983] 82 p. : ill. (some col.) ; 24 cm. (Életszínvonal-füzetek . 4. sz.) LC Card 83-206799
1. Income - Hungary. 2. Social security - Hungary. 3. Family policy - Hungary. I. Zafír, Mihály. II. Fekete, Gyula, Dr. III. Hungary. Központi Statisztikai Hivatal. Közgazdasági Főosztály. IV. Series.
HC30.295.I5 L332 1983
NYPL [JLE 87-179]

A Lakosság jövedelmi rétegződése 1982-ben : az 1983. évi Jövedelmi felmérés főbb adatai / [készült a Központi Statisztikai Hivatal Közgazdasági Főosztályán]. Budapest : Központi Statisztikai Hivatal, 1984. 50 p. ; 29 cm. LC Card 86-195316
1. Income distribution - Hungary - Statistics. I. Hungary. Központi Statisztikai Hivatal. Közgazdasági Főosztály.
HC300.295.I5 L36 1984

Lakossági pénzügyek, pénzintézeti tevékenység /. Szentiványi, Iván. Budapest , 1985. 563, [1] p. ; ISBN 963-221-602-4 : LC Card 86-186953
HG186.H8 S94 1985

Lakot ja yhteiskunnan muutos . Alasoini, Tuomo. Helsinki [1983] ii, 132 p. : ISBN 951-46-7101-5 LC Card 84-168540
HD5306 .A42 1983

LAKSHADWEEP (INDIA) - CENSUS, 1981. Census of India, 1981. Delhi , <1984-1986. v. in : LC Card 87-915037 DDC 304.6/0954/81021 19
HA4587.L34 C46 1984

Lakshmana Rao, V., 1940- Progress of development banking in India / V. Lakshmana Rao ; foreword by P.L. Sanjeeva Reddy. 1st ed. Allahabad, India : Chugh Publications, 1986. xvi, 139 p. ; 22 cm. Bibliography: p. 20. Includes index. ISBN 81-85076-07-3 : LC Card 86-902782 DDC 332.2 19
1. Development banks - India. 2. Banks and banking - India. 3. India - Economic conditions. I. Title.
HG3284 .L35 1986

Lal, Deepak.
Collier, Paul. Labour and poverty in Kenya, 1900-1980 /. Oxford , New York , 1986. xi, 296 p. : ISBN 0-19-828505-1 : LC Card 86-1352 DDC 331.12/09676/2 19
HD5840.5.A6 C65 1986
NYPL [JLE 86-3282]

Stagflation, savings, and the state . New York , 1986. xii, 402 p. : ISBN 0-19-520496-4 LC Card 85-31981 DDC 330.9172/4 19
HG229 .S74 1986 NYPL [JLE 86-2621]

Trade liberalization in Sri Lanka / by Deepak Lal and Sarath Rajapatirana. Aldershop, Hants, England ; Brookfield, Vt. : Gower Pub. Co., 1988. p. cm. (Thames essay . no. 51) Bibliography: p. ISBN 0-566-05340-3 : LC Card 87-15044 DDC 382/.3/095493 19
1. Sri Lanka - Commercial policy. I. Rajapatirana, Sarath. II. Title. III. Series.
HF1586.8 .L35 1988

Lal, Mohan. Financing small businesses / by Mohan Lal. Palmerston North, N.Z. : Dept. of Business Studies, Faculty of Business, Massey University, [1977] 25, [2] p. ; 26 cm. (Occasional paper / Department of Business Studies, Faculty of Business, Massey University . no. 23) Bibliography: p. [27] LC Card 85-151230
1. Small business - New Zealand - Finance. I. Series: Occasional paper (Massey University. Dept. of Business Studies) , no. 23. II. Title.
HG4027.7 .L35 1977

Lal, Shyam, 1942- Price policy and economic development in India / Shyam Lal ; foreword by H.K. Manmohan Singh. Delhi : Anmol Publications, 1987. xiii, 272 p. : ill. ; 23 cm. Originally presented as the author's thesis (Ph. D.--Punjabi University, Patiala) With special reference to Punjab, India. Bibliography: p. 265-272. LC Card 87-900801 DDC 338.5/26/0954552 19
1. Price policy - India - Punjab. 2. Punjab (India) - Economic policy. I. Title.
HB236.I4 L35 1987

Lala, R. M. Tata, J. R. D. (Jehangir Ratanji Dadabhoy), 1904- Keynote . Bombay , 1986. xviii, 155 p., [1] leaf of plates : ISBN 81-85110-00-X : LC Card 86-902369 DDC 338.0954
HC435.2 .T37 1986

Lall Nigam, Brij Mohan. see **Nigam, Brij Mohan Lall, 1935-**

Lall, Rajiv B. Multinationals from the Third World : Indian firms investing abroad / Rajiv B. Lall. Delhi ; New York : Oxford University Press, 1986. 100 p. ; 22 cm. Based on the author's thesis (Ph. D.--Columbia University, New York, 1984) Bibliography: p. [95]-98. Includes index. ISBN 0-19-561895-5 : LC Card 86-900021 DDC 338.8/8954 19
1. Investments, East Indian. 2. International business enterprises - India. I. Title.
HG4538 .L274 1986

Lall, Sanjaya. Theory and reality in development . Basingstoke, Hampshire , 1986. xii, 291 p. : ISBN 0-333-39824-6
NYPL [JLD 86-1827]

Lallubhai Mehta, Vadilal. see **Mehta, Vadilal Lallubhai, 1903-**

LaLonde, Robert John. The manpower report of KEPE : the characteristics of the Greek labor market / Robert LaLonde, Nick Papandreou. Athens, Greece : Centre of Planning and Economic Research, c1986. 122 p. ; 29 cm. (Analyses of statistical data . 4) "Athens, January 1986." Bibliography: p. 121-122. LC Card 86-205504 DDC 331.1/09495 19
1. Labor supply - Greece. 2. Labor supply - Greece - Statistics. I. Papandreou, Nicholas C. II. Kentron Programmatismou kai Oikonomikōn Ereunōn. III. Title. IV. Series.
HD5811.83.A6 L3 1986

Lam, Manuel. Louisiana crude oil and natural gas report and severance and royalty sensitivity to price, second half 1985 / prepared by Manuel Lam. Baton Rouge, La (P.O. Box 44156, Baton Rouge 70804-4156) : Dept. of Natural Resources, Energy Division, Technology Assessment Section, [1986] iii, 31 p. : ill. ; 28 cm. "April 14, 1986." LC Card 86-621907 DDC 338.2/728/09763 19
1. Petroleum - Taxation - Louisiana. 2. Gas, Natural - Taxation - Louisiana. 3. Petroleum products - Prices - Louisiana. 4. Gas, Natural - Prices - Louisiana. 5. Oil and gas leases - Louisiana. 6. Severance tax - Louisiana. 7. Revenue - Louisiana. I. Louisiana. Dept. of Natural Resources. Energy Division. Technology Assessment Section. II. Title.
HD9560.8.U53 L65 1986

Lama, Luciano.
Cari compagni : con una scelta delle lettere pervenute al Segretario generale della Cgil dal 1970 al 1986 / Luciano Lama ; prefazione di Ottaviano Del Turco ; a cura di Pasquale Cascella. Roma : Ediesse, c1986. vii, 184 p. ; 21 cm. (Primopiano) LC Card 87-155314
1. Lama, Luciano - Correspondence. 2. Trade-unions - Italy - Officials and employees - Correspondence. 3. Confederazione generale italiana del lavoro - Officials and employees - Correspondence. I. Cascella, Pasquale. II. Confederazione generale italiana del lavoro. III. Title.
HD6710.L35 A4 1986

LAMA, LUCIANO - CORRESPONDENCE. Lama, Luciano. Cari compagni . Roma , c1986. vii, 184 p. ; LC Card 87-155314
HD6710.L35 A4 1986

Lama, Mahendra P. Tea plantation workers in the eastern Himalayas . Delhi , 1986. xxxi, 255 p. : ISBN 81-7043-055-0 : LC Card 86-903466
HD8039.T182 I48 1986

LAMAISM. see **BUDDHISM.**

Lamanna, Mary Ann. (joint author) Liu, William Thomas, 1930- Transition to nowhere . Nashville , c1979. 214 p., [2] leaves of plates : ISBN 0-8202-0189-8 : LC Card 78-21129 DDC 361.5/3/09597
HV640.5.V5 L58 NYPL [JLD 87-670]

Lamb, Charles W. Strategic marketing for nonprofit organizations . Englewood Cliffs, NJ , c1987. x, 386 p. : ISBN 0-13-851312-0 (pbk.) : LC Card 86-25262 DDC 658.8 19
HF5415 .C2854 1987

Lamb, Geoffrey, 1944- Managing economic policy change : institutional dimensions / Geoffrey Lamb. Washington, D.C., U. S.A. : World Bank, [1987] x, 27 p. ; 27 cm. (World Bank discussion papers, 0259-210X . 14) Includes bibliographical references. ISBN 0-8213-0921-8 (pbk.) LC Card 87-14824 DDC 338.9 19
1. Economic policy. I. Title. II. Series.
HD87 .L36 1987

Lamb, Robert. Municipal bonds / Robert Lamb, Stephen P. Rappaport. 2nd ed. New York : McGraw-Hill, c1987. xx, 327 p. ; 24 cm. Includes index. ISBN 0-07-036084-7 : LC Card 86-27539 DDC 336.3/1 19
1. Municipal finance - United States. 2. Municipal bonds - United States. I. Rappaport, Stephen P. II. Title.
HJ9145 .L35 1987

Lamb, Robert, 1941- Running American business : top CEOs rethink their major decisions / Robert Boyden Lamb. New York : Basic Books, c1987. x, 315 p. ; 25 cm. Bibliography: p. 305-307. Includes indexes. ISBN 0-465-07150-3 : LC Card 86-47732 DDC 658.4/03 19
1. Strategic planning. 2. Decision-making. I. Title.
HD30.28 .L355 1987

Lamb, Sandra. Anderson, Georgia. Equity sharing /. Chicago , c1986. xiv, 136 p. : ISBN 0-8092-4836-0 (pbk.) : LC Card 86-24083 DDC 332.63/24 19
HD1382.5 .A54 1986

Lamba, S. K. Impact of land reforms on rural development : a critical appraisal of India, Republic of China, and some other selected countries / S.K. Lamba, J.S. Tomar.1st ed. New Delhi, India : Agricole Pub. Academy, 1986 [i.e. 1985] xiv, 148 p. ; 23 cm. (Agricole

monographs . 34) ISBN 81-85005-20-6 : LC Card 85-905086 DDC 333.3/1/54 19
1. Land reform - India. 2. Land reform - Taiwan. 3. Rural development - India. 4. Rural development - Taiwan. I. Tomar, J. S., 1943-. II. Title.
HD1333.I4 L35 1986

LAMBAYEQUE (PERU : DEPT.) - HISTORY - BIBLIOGRAPHY.
Burga, Manuel. La historia agraria /. Chiclayo, Perú , 1986. 196 p. ; ***NYPL [JLD 87-1524]***

LAMBAYEQUE, PERU (DEPT.) - RURAL CONDITIONS.
Simons Munaro, Yehude. Lambayeque, producción ganadera, comunidades campesinas [microform] /. Chiclayo, Perú , 1983. 45 p. ; LC Card 84-204537 DDC 338.1/76/0098514 19
HD9424.P43 L367 1983
NYPL [*ZT-1708 no.72]

Lambayeque, producción ganadera, comunidades campesinas [microform] /. Simons Munaro, Yehude. Chiclayo, Perú , 1983. 45 p. ; LC Card 84-204537 DDC 338.1/76/0098514 19
HD9424.P43 L367 1983
NYPL [*ZT-1708 no.72]

Lambden, William.
Bus and coach operation. Faulks, Rex William. Bus and coach operation / R.W. Faulks. 5th ed. London , Boston , 1987. xi, 259 p. : ISBN 0-408-02810-6 : LC Card 87-10966 DDC 388.3/22/068 19
HE5613 .F38 1987

Lambert, Denis Clair. Le mimétisme technologique des Tiers-Mondes : plaidoyer pour le recours á des techniques intermédiaires et différenciées / Denis-Clair Lambert.2e éd. entièrement rev. et augm. Paris : Economica, 1983. 223 p. : ill. ; 24 cm. Bibliography: p. [191]-199. Includes index. ISBN 2-7178-0597-4 : LC Card 83-233513
1. Technology transfer - Developing countries. 2. Appropriate technology - Developing countries. I. Title.
HC59.72.T4 L35 1983

Lambert, Jean-Paul, 1952- Disequilibrium macroeconomic models : theory and estimation of rationing models using business survey data / Jean-Paul Lambert. Cambridge [Cambridgeshire] ; New York : Cambridge University Press, 1988. p. cm. Bibliography: p. Includes index. ISBN 0-521-32209-X LC Card 86-24966 DDC 339.5/0724 19
1. Equilibrium (Economics) - Econometric models. 2. Macroeconomics - Econometric models. 3. Rationing, Consumer - Econometric models. 4. Belgium - Manufactures - Econometric models. I. Title.
HB145 .L36 1988

Lambert, Peter J. Surveys in the economics of uncertainty /. Oxford, UK , New York, NY, USA , 1987. 232 p. : ISBN 0-631-15335-7 LC Card 87-10366 DDC 330 19
HB615 .S97 1987

Lambert, Richard D. The transformation of an Indian labor market : the case of Pune / by Richard D. Lambert, Ralph B. Ginsberg, Sarah J. Moore. Amsterdam ; Philadelphia : J. Benjamins Pub. Co., 1986. ix, 249 p. ; 23 cm. (University of Pennsylvania studies on South Asia, 0169-0361 . v. 3) Includes bibliographical references and index. ISBN 0-915027-63-1 (alk. paper) : LC Card 86-26900 DDC 331.11/0954/792 19
1. Labor supply - India - Pune. 2. Labor and laboring classes - India - Pune. 3. Quality of work life - India - Pune. I. Ginsberg, Ralph B. II. Moore, Sarah J. III. Title. IV. Series.
HD5820.P78 L36 1986

Lamberton, D. M. see **Lamberton, Donald Mclean.**

Lamberton, D. M. (Donald McLean), 1927- The Cost of thinking . Norwood, N.J. , c1988. xii, 249 p. : ISBN 0-89391-419-3 LC Card 87-22937 DDC 338.4/7004/099 19
HC681.3.I55 C67 1988

Lamberton, Donald Mclean. The Trouble with technology . London , 1983. x, 224 p. : ISBN 0-86187-285-1 ***NYPL [JLE 86-1128]***

Lambrou, Peter T. Korn, Errol R. Hyper-performance . New York , c1987. xi, 195 p. : ISBN 0-471-85344-5 LC Card 86-33984 DDC 650.1 19
HF5386 .K775 1987

Lamers, Duane E. United Nations definitive & airmail stamps issued & reprinted 1958-1985 / by Duane E. Lamers. Chicago, IL, USA (Box 1674, Chicago 60690) : United Nations Philatelists, c1985. 52 p. : ill. ; 22 cm. (UNP monogaph [sic] . no. 5) "Supplement to the Journal of the United Nations Philatelists, Inc., August 1985, volume 8, number 6, whole number 48"--Cover. LC Card 87-146520 DDC 769.56/1 19
1. United Nations - Postal service. I. Journal of the United Nations Philatelists, Inc. V. 8, no. 6 (Supplement). II. Title. III. Title: United Nations definitive and airmail stamps issued and reprinted 1958-1985. IV. Series: UNP monograph , 5.
HE6246 .L36 1985

Lamm, Robert P. Bennett, Peter D. Marketing /. New York , c1988. xxvii, 763 p. : ISBN 0-07-004721-9 : LC Card 87-17335 DDC 658.8 19
HF5415 .B4293 1988

Lammioni Vezzadini, Anna Maria. Franchini, Augusto. Le aziende di credito . Bologna , <1986-. v. <2 > ; LC Card 87-170318
HG3751 .F73 1986

Lamorlette, Corine. 10 études de cas de fiscalité avec corrigés détaillés : préparation DECS, facultés, écoles de commerce, expertise comptable / Corine et Thierry Lamorlette. Paris : Economica, 1984. 95 p. : ill. ; 24 cm. (Collection Bibliothèque de gestion. Série Enseignement) ISBN 2-7178-0802-7 : LC Card 85-129474
1. Tax accounting - France - Problems, exercises, etc. I. Lamorlette, Thierry. II. Title. III. Title: Dix études de cas de fiscalité avec corrigés détaillés. IV. Series.
HF5681.T3 L28 1984

Lamorlette, Thierry. Lamorlette, Corine. 10 études de cas de fiscalité avec corrigés détaillés . Paris , 1984. 95 p. : ISBN 2-7178-0802-7 : LC Card 85-129474
HF5681.T3 L28 1984

LaMotte, Kelly. Contacts . San Rafael, CA (1724 Lincoln Ave., San Rafael 94901) [c1986] 252 p. ; LC Card 86-217208 DDC 332.1/028 19
HG1710 .C66 1986

Lampe, John R. The Bulgarian economy in the twentieth century / John R. Lampe. London : Croom Helm, c1986. x, 245 p. : ill. ; 23 cm. (Croom Helm series on the contemporary economic history of Europe) Bibliography: p. 231-236. Includes index. ISBN 0-7099-1644-2 LC Card 86-673485
1. Bulgaria - Economic conditions. 2. Bulgaria - Economic policy. I. Title. II. Title: Bulgarian economy in the 20th century. III. Series.
HC403 .L36x 1986b

Lamphere, Louise. From working daughters to working mothers : immigrant women in a New England industrial community / Louise Lamphere. Ithaca : Cornell University Press, 1987. xviii, 390 p. : ill. ; 23 cm. (Anthropology of contemporary issues) Bibliography: p. 371-380. Includes index. ISBN 0-8014-9441-9 (pbk. : alk. paper) LC Card 86-32952 DDC 331.4/09745/1 19
1. Women - Employment - Rhode Island - Central Falls - History. 2. Alien labor - Rhode Island - Central Falls - History. 3. Women immigrants - Rhode Island - Central Falls - History. I. Title. II. Series.
HD6096.R4 L36 1987

Lampiran Pidato kenegaraan Presiden Republik Indonesia di depan sidang Dewan Perwakilan Rakyat, 16 Agustus 1979 . Indonesia. President, 1967- (Soeharto) [Jakarta] [1981?] 1203 p. in various pagings ; LC Card 86-949503
HC447 .I5559 1981

Lampreave Pérez, José Luis. La empresa española ante el impuesto sobre el valor añadido, medidas de adaptación y ajuste / José Luis Lampreave Pérez, Juan Antonio Gimeno Ullastres y Alberto Terol Esteban ; prólogo, César Albiñana García-Quintana. Madrid, España : Instituto de Estudios Fiscales, Ministerio de Economía y Hacienda, 1985. 493 p. : ill. ; 24 cm. (Estudios de hacienda pública) Includes bibliographical references. ISBN 84-7196-571-2 : LC Card 86-208329
1. Value-added tax - Spain. 2. Business enterprises - Spain. I. Gimeno Ullastres, Juan Antonio. II. Terol Esteban, Alberto. III. Title.
HJ5715.S7 L36 1985

Lamur, Carlo. The American takeover : industrial emergence and Alcoa's expansion in Guyana and Suriname 1914-1921 / Carlo Lamur. Dordrecht, Holland ; Cinnaminson, N.J., U. S.A. : Foris Publications, 1985. vi, 209 p., [6] p. of plates : ill. ; 25 cm. (Caribbean series / Koninklijk Instituut voor Taal-, Land- en Volkenkunde . 1) English and Dutch. Appendices in Dutch. Revised ed. of author's thesis (doctoral)--Rotterdam, 1983. Bibliography: p. [153]-198. Includes indexes. ISBN 90-6765-078-1 (pbk.) : LC Card 86-181373 DDC 338.8/87 19
1. Aluminum industry and trade - Guyana - History. 2. Aluminum industry and trade - Surinam - History. 3. Aluminum Company of America - History. I. Series: Caribbean series (Koninklijk Instituut voor Taal-, Land- en Volkenkunde (Netherlands)) , 1. II. Title.
HD9539.A63 G886 1985

Lamy, José Alfredo. Lemgruber, Antonio Carlos. O controle da base monetária e as flutuações dos multiplicadores monetários e creditícios /. [Brasília] [1981?] 118 p. : LC Card 85-154853
HG835 .L35 1981

L'Analisi degli insediamenti umani e produttivi / a cura di Giorgio Leonardi e Giovanni A. Rabino ; scritti di C.S. Bertuglia ... [et al.]. Milano, Italy : F. Angeli, c1984. 295 p. : ill. ; 22 cm. (Scienze regionali . 1) Includes bibliographies. LC Card 84-179265 DDC 330.945/0928 19
1. Cities and towns - Italy - Congresses. 2. Urban economics - Congresses. 3. Space in economics - Congresses. 4. Italy - Economic conditions - 1976- - Regional disparities - Congresses. I. Leonardi, Giorgio. II. Rabino, Giovanni A. III. Bertuglia, Cristoforo Sergio. IV. Series.
HC305 .A6618 1984 ***NYPL [JLD 86-3298]***

Lancashire and Whitehall . Streat, Raymond, Sir. Manchester [Greater Manchester] , c1987. 2 v. : ISBN 0-7190-2390-4 (v. 1) LC Card 87-11026 DDC 338.7/67721/0924 B 19
HD9881.5.S77 A3 1987

LANCASHIRE, ENG. - ECONOMIC CONDITIONS.
Fleischman, Richard K. Conditions of life among the cotton workers of southeastern Lancashire, 1780-1850 /. New York , 1985. 475 p. ; ISBN 0-8240-6681-2 (alk. paper) : LC Card 84-46001 DDC 305/.9677/094276 19
HD8039.T42 G74 1985
NYPL [JLE 86-3899]

LANCASHIRE, ENG. - SOCIAL CONDITIONS.
Fleischman, Richard K. Conditions of life among the cotton workers of southeastern Lancashire, 1780-1850 /. New York , 1985. 475 p. ; ISBN 0-8240-6681-2 (alk. paper) : LC Card 84-46001 DDC 305/.9677/094276 19
HD8039.T42 G74 1985
NYPL [JLE 86-3899]

Lancaster, Kelvin. Mathematical economics / Kelvin Lancaster. New York : Dover Publications, 1987, c1968. xiii, 411 p. : ill. ; 22 cm. Reprint. Originally published: New York : Macmillan, c1968. Bibliography: p. 385-392. Includes index. ISBN 0-486-65391-9 (pbk.) LC Card 87-5459 DDC 330/.01/51 19
1. Economics, Mathematical. I. Title.
HB135 .L355 1987

LANCASTER, KELVIN.
Riepe, Claudia. Produkteigenschaften und das Nachfrageverhalten von Konsumenten . Thun , c1984. 341 p. : ISBN 3-87144-841-9 LC Card 85-113523
HB801 .R45 1984

Lancer International. Role of foreign trade in Indian economy /. New Delhi , 1986. 216 p. ; ISBN 81-7062-001-5 : LC Card 86-902110 DDC 382/.0954 19
HF3782 .R65 1986

Lancôme /. Demornex, Jacqueline. Paris , c1985. 189 p. : ISBN 2-903370-23-0 LC Card 86-201508
HD9999.P3934 L363 1985
NYPL [JSG 87-24]

LANCÔME (FIRM) - HISTORY.
Demornex, Jacqueline. Lancôme /. Paris , c1985. 189 p. : ISBN 2-903370-23-0 LC Card 86-201508
HD9999.P3934 L363 1985
NYPL [JSG 87-24]

LAND. see **LAND USE.**

Land- und Forstwirtschaftliche Landes-Buchführung-Gesellschaft.
Landeswirtschaftlicher Paritätsspiegel . Wien

[1982] 11 leaves ; LC Card 86-181563
HD1935 .L325 1982

Land- und Forstwirtschaftliche Landes-Buchführungs-Gesellschaft. Betriebswirtschaftliche Ergebnisse von Gartenbaubetrieben 1984 /. Wien , 1985. 13 p. ; LC Card 86-194865
HD9015.A8 B47 1985

Land acquisition in developing countries . Kitay, Michael G. Boston , c1985. xx, 199 p. ; ISBN 0-89946-192-1 LC Card 85-7225 DDC 333.1/3/091724 19
HD1131 .K58 1985 *NYPL [JLE 86-3827]*

Land and class in Kenya /. Leo, Christopher. Toronto , Buffalo [N.Y.] , c1984. xii, 244 p. : ISBN 0-8020-2532-3 *NYPL [JLE 86-1242]*

Land and politics in Malawi, 1875-1975 /. Pachai, Bridglal. Kingston, Ontario, Canada , c1978. xiv, 245 p., [20] p. of plates : ISBN 0-919642-82-9 LC Card 86-673708
HD997 .P32x 1978

Land and power in Hawaii . Cooper, George. Honolulu, Hawaii , c1985. x, 518 p. ; ISBN 0-9615052-0-6 : LC Card 85-72037 DDC 333.73/13/09969 19
HD266.H3 C66 1985 *NYPL [JLE 87-361]*

Land and power in late medieval Ferrara . Dean, Trevor. Cambridge , New York , 1988. xiv, 212 p. : ISBN 0-521-33127-7 LC Card 87-6583 DDC 333.3/0945/45 19
HD679.F47 D43 1988

Land at the centre . Holliday, John C. London , 1986. xiii, 241 p. : ISBN 0-85683-084-4 (pbk.) : LC Card 87-121817 DDC 333.73/13/0941 19
HD596 .H65 1986

LAND CAPABILITY FOR AGRICULTURE - AMAZON RIVER REGION.
Fearnside, Philip M. (Philip Martin) Human carrying capacity of the Brazilian rain-forest /. New York , 1986. xii, 293 p. : ISBN 0-231-06104-8 (alk. paper) LC Card 85-6643 DDC 330.981/1063 19
HC188.A5 F42 1986 *NYPL [JLE 86-4554]*

LAND CAPABILITY FOR AGRICULTURE - ITALY - LAZIO - COLLECTED WORKS.
Produttività potenziale e classificazione dei terreni. Roma , 1985- v. <1 > in <5 > : LC Card 87-105342
HD679.L39 P76 1985

LAND CAPABILITY FOR AGRICULTURE - ITALY - SACCO RIVER VALLEY.
Produttività potenziale e classificazione dei terreni. Roma , 1985- v. <1 > in <5 > : LC Card 87-105342
HD679.L39 P76 1985

LAND CAPABILITY FOR AGRICULTURE - SWITZERLAND.
Grundsätze für die Bewertung von Kulturland bei Güterzusammenlegungen . [Bern? , 1973?] 1 v. (loose leaf) : LC Card 86-184960
HD798 .G78 1973

The Land commissioners of Texas : 150 years of the General Land Office / commissioner, Garry Mauro ; preface by Ralph Yarborough. Austin (1700 N. Congress Ave., Austin 78701) : Texas General Land Office, 1986. vii, 133 p., [2] leaves of plates : ill. ; 23 cm. LC Card 87-620990 DDC 353.97640071/32/0922 B 19
1. Texas. General Land Office - History. 2. Texas. General Land Office - Officials and employees - Biography. I. Mauro, Garry.
HD243.T4 L28 1986

Land Conservation Council (Vic.) Wimmera area : final recommendations, November 1986. Melbourne, Vic. : Land Conservation Council, [1986] iii, 84 p., 3 p. of plates : maps (some col.) ; 30 cm. One col. map on folded leaf in pocket. ISBN 0-7241-9146-1 (pbk.) LC Card 87-161929 DDC 333.73/13/099458 19
1. Land use - Australia - Wimmera River Watershed (Vic.). I. Title.
HD1039.V5 L36 1986

LAND CREDIT. see **AGRICULTURAL CREDIT.**

Land degradation : problems and policies / edited by Anthony Chisholm and Robert Dumsday. Cambridge [Cambridgeshire] ; New York : Cambridge University Press, c1987. p. cm. (CRES monograph . no. 18) "Published in association with Centre for Resource and Environmental Studies, Australia National University." Bibliography: p. Includes index. ISBN 0-521-34079-9 LC Card 87-13170 DDC 333.73/16 19
1. Soil conservation - Government policy - Australia - Congresses. 2. Soil degradation - Australia - Congresses. I. Chisholm, Anthony. II. Dumsday, Robert. III. Series.
HD1036 .L36 1987

LAND DEVELOPMENT. see **REAL ESTATE DEVELOPMENT.**

LAND DRAINAGE. see **DRAINAGE.**

LAND GRANTS - COLORADO - HISTORY.
Land, water, and culture . Albuquerque , c1987. ix, 422 p. : ISBN 0-8263-0989-5 (pbk.) LC Card 87-10957 DDC 333.1/6/09788 19
HD243.N5 L36 1987

LAND GRANTS - NEW MEXICO - HISTORY.
Land, water, and culture . Albuquerque , c1987. ix, 422 p. : ISBN 0-8263-0989-5 (pbk.) LC Card 87-10957 DDC 333.1/6/09788 19
HD243.N5 L36 1987

LAND GRANTS - SAUDI ARABIA.
Hajrah, Hassan Hamza. Public land distribution in Saudi Arabia /. London , New York , 1982. xxi, 280 p. : ISBN 0-582-78301-1 LC Card 83-232929 DDC 333.1/6/09538 19
HD853.Z7 H34 1982 *NYPL [JLE 87-1566]*

LAND LAWS. see **LAND REFORM - LAW AND LEGISLATION.**

Land markets and land policy in a metropolitan area . Hanayama, Yuzuru, 1939- Boston, MA , 1986. xiv, 162 p. : ISBN 0-89946-197-2 LC Card 85-13867 DDC 333.77/13/0952135 19
HD920.T62 H36 1986 *NYPL [JLE 86-4398]*

Land of the Trust islands . Barr, Lorna R. [Victoria, B.C.] [1978] 36 p. : LC Card 83-226106 DDC 333.3/0996/5 19
HD1121.Z63 B37 1978

Land ownership and land use in the Scottish Highlands /. Armstrong, A. M. [Aberdeen, Grampian] , 1983. vii, 150 p. : LC Card 83-209521 DDC 333.3/09411/5 19
HD616 .A76 1983 *NYPL [JLF 86-457]*

Land, people, and planning in contemporary Amazonia / editor, Françoise Barbira-Scazzocchio. [Cambridge, Cambridgeshire] : Cambridge University, 1980. xvi, 313 p. : ill. ; 24 cm. (Occasional publication / Centre of Latin American Studies . no. 3) "Proceedings of the Conference on the Development of Amazonia in Seven Countries, Cambridge, 23-26 September 1979"--Cover. Errata slip laid in. Bibliography: p. 269-296. Includes index. LC Card 87-672189
1. Amazon River Region - Economic conditions - Congresses. 2. Amazon River Region - Economic policy - Congresses. 3. Land use - Amazon River Region - Congresses. 4. Indians of South America - Amazon River Region - Economic conditions - Congresses. I. Barbira-Freedman, Françoise. II. Conference on the Development of Amazonia in Seven Countries (1979 : University of Cambridge, Centre of Latin American Studies). III. Series: Occasional publication (University of Cambridge. Centre of Latin American Studies) , no. 3.
HC167.A42 L36x 1980

Land, power, and poverty . Brockett, Charles D., 1946- Boston , c1988. p. cm. ISBN 0-04-497027-7 LC Card 87-22746 DDC 338.1/09728 19
HD1797 .B76 1988

LAND QUESTION. see **LAND TENURE.**

LAND, RECLAMATION OF. see **RECLAMATION OF LAND.**

LAND REFORM - AFRICA.
Espaces disputés en Afrique noire . Paris , c1986. 426 p., [8] p. of plates : ISBN 2-86537-146-8 LC Card 86-210958
HD965 .E86 1986

LAND REFORM - ALGERIA.
Lesbet, Djaffar. Les 1000 villages socialistes en Algérie /. Alger , Paris , c1983. 335 p. : ISBN 2-86738-008-1 : LC Card 84-156989 DDC 335/.00965 19
HX441.5.A6 L47 1983 *NYPL [JLD 87-236]*

Land reform and democratic development /. Prosterman, Roy L. Baltimore , c1987. xii, 313 p. ; ISBN 0-8018-3482-1 (alk. paper) LC Card 87-4188 DDC 333.3/1/1724 19
HD1333.5 .P76 1987

LAND REFORM - ASIA - CASE STUDIES.
The Poor in Asia . Kuala Lumpur, Malaysia , 1985- v. <1 > ; ISBN 967-99954-0-2 (v. 1) LC Card 86-944764 DDC 362.5/8/095 19
HC415.P6 P66 1985

LAND REFORM - BOLIVIA.
Antezana Ergueta, Luis. Evaluación económico-política de la reforma agraria /. La Paz, Bolivia , 1986. 113 p. : LC Card 87-400948 DDC 333.3/1/84 19
HD1333.B5 A56 1986

Segunda reforma agraria . La Paz, Bolivia [1987] 287 p. : LC Card 87-403057 DDC 333.3/1/84 19
HD1333.B5 S44 1987

LAND REFORM - BOLIVIA - HISTORY.
Espinoza C., Jorge. Reforma agraria en Bolivia /. Cochabamba, Bolivia , 1984. 78 p. ; LC Card 86-166584
HD1333.B5 E87 1984

LAND REFORM - BRAZIL.
Albuquerque, Marcos Cintra Cavalcanti de. Algumas considerações sobre a reforma agrária /. Brasília, DF [19]86. 23 p. ; LC Card 87-403236 DDC 333.3/1/81 19
HD1333.B6 A4 1986

Aspectos econômicos, jurídicos e sociais da Reforma Agrária /. São Paulo-SP Brasil [1985] 75 p. ; LC Card 86-220237
HD1333.B6 A85 1985

Callado, Antônio. Entre o deus e a vasilha . Rio de Janeiro , c1985. 67 p. : LC Card 85-218767
HD496 .C23 1985

Ferreira, Benedito, 1932- A questão fundiária /. Brasília , 1986. 171 p. ; LC Card 86-229678
HD496 .F42 1986

Instituto Nacional de Colonização e Reforma Agraria. 1o. plano nacional de reforma agrária da Nova República . Brasília, DF , 1985. 73 leaves : LC Card 86-225850
HD1333.B6 I54 1985

Oliveira, Plinio Corrêa de, 1908- A propriedade privada e a livre iniciativa no tufão agro-reformista /. [São Paulo] [1985] xvi, 174 p., [16] p. of plates : LC Card 87-104428
HD1333.B6 O385 1985

Pinheiro, Saramago. Reforma agrária . Brasília , 1986. 46 p. ; LC Card 86-228887
HD1333.B6 P56 1986

Terra de Deus, terra de irmãos . Brasília-DF [1986] 190 p. : LC Card 86-233600
HD1333.B6 T47 1986

Vinhas, M. A terra, o homem, as reformas /. Rio de Janeiro (R. Hermenegildo de Barros, 31-A Glória, Rio de Janeiro) , 1980. xiii, 151 p. ; *NYPL [JLD 86-783]*

LAND REFORM - BRAZIL - GOIÁS (STATE)
Catholic Church. Comissão Pastoral da Terra (Brazil) CPT . Petrópolis , 1983. 105 p. ; LC Card 86-209008
HD499.G65 C38 1983

LAND REFORM - BRAZIL - HISTORY.
Dé Carli, Gileno. História da reforma agrária /. [Recife?] , 1985. 524 p. ; LC Card 87-102928 DDC 333.3/1/81 19
HD1333.B6 D4 1985

LAND REFORM - BRAZIL, NORTHEAST.
A Problemática e a política da terra e água do Nordeste. Recife , 1985. 296 p. : LC Card 87-124121 DDC 333.91/00981/3 19
HD1696.B84 N675 1985

LAND REFORM - BRAZIL - SÃO PAULO (STATE)
Política agrária /. Porto Alegre-RS , 1985. 79 p. : LC Card 86-198513
HD1531.B7 P65 1985

LAND REFORM - CENTRAL AMERICA.
Barry, Tom, 1950- Roots of rebellion . Boston , c1987. xii, 220 p. : ISBN 0-89608-288-1 : LC Card 87-4519 DDC 338.1/9/728 19
HD9014.C462 B37 1987

Brockett, Charles D., 1946- Land, power, and poverty . Boston , c1988. p. cm. ISBN 0-04-497027-7 LC Card 87-22746 DDC 338.1/09728 19
HD1797 .B76 1988

LAND REFORM - CHINA - HISTORY - 20TH CENTURY.
La Politique agraire en Chine . Ottignies, Louvain-la-Neuve, Belgique [1981] 84 leaves ; LC Card 86-203953
HD926 .P65 1981

LAND REFORM - CONGRESSES.
Reforma agraria como proceso social . Piura, Perú [1984] 163 p. : LC Card 84-232526 DDC 333.3/1/85 19
HD1333.P4 R44 1984 NYPL [JLD 86-2537]

LAND REFORM - CUBA.
Barro y Segura, Antonio. Rebuttal and commentaries to the third report on the progress of land reform in Cuba as rendered by the United Nations in 1962. Miami, Fla. , 1963. 17 p. ; LC Card 86-181697
HD1333.C9 B37 1963

LAND REFORM - DENMARK - ROSKILDE AMT - HISTORY - 18TH CENTURY.
Godsejerrøster . København , 1984. 320 p. : ISBN 87-7526-018-2 : LC Card 84-224395
HD1333.D42 R674 1984

LAND REFORM - DEVELOPING COUNTRIES.
Palmer, Ingrid. The impact of agrarian reform on women /. West Hartford, Conn. , c1985. xiv, 55 p. ; ISBN 0-931816-21-1 (pbk.) LC Card 85-5250 DDC 331.4/83/091724 19
HD6073.A292 D447 1985
NYPL [JLF 86-1633]

Prosterman, Roy L. Land reform and democratic development /. Baltimore , c1987. xii, 313 p. ; ISBN 0-8018-3482-1 (alk. paper) LC Card 87-4188 DDC 333.3/1/1724 19
HD1333.5 .P76 1987

LAND REFORM - DEVELOPING COUNTRIES - ADDRESSES, ESSAYS, LECTURES.
Studies on agrarian reform and rural poverty /. Rome , New York, N.Y. , 1984. vii, 104 p. : ISBN 92-5-101371-3 (pbk.) LC Card 85-183713 DDC 338.9/009172/4 19
HD1333.5 .S78 1984 NYPL [JLE 86-2720]

LAND REFORM - ECUADOR - HISTORY.
Pensamiento agrario ecuatoriano /. Quito, Ecuador , 1986. 741 p. : LC Card 87-403503 DDC 333.3/1/866 19
HD1333.E2 P46 1986

LAND REFORM - ETHIOPIA.
Harjinder Singh. Agricultural problems in Ethiopia /. Delhi, India , c1987. viii, 254 p. : ISBN 81-212-0078-4 : LC Card 87-900338 DDC 338.1/0963 19
HD2124.5 .H37 1987

LAND REFORM - GERMANY (EAST) - HISTORY - 20TH CENTURY - SOURCES.
Wie wir angefangen haben . Berlin , 1985. 326 p. : LC Card 85-217979
HD1333.G35 W54 1985

LAND REFORM - GOVERNMENT POLICY - INDIA - KARNATAKA.
Thimmaiah, G. The political economy of land reforms /. New Delhi [1983?] xiii, 94 p. ; LC Card 84-900237 DDC 333.3/1/5487 19
HD1333.I42 K3778 1983
NYPL [JLD 87-752]

LAND REFORM - GUATEMALA.
Paz Cárcamo, Guillermo. Política agraria . San José, Costa Rica , 1986. 84 p. ; LC Card 87-106764
HD1333.G9 P39 1986

LAND REFORM - GUATEMALA - HISTORY - 20TH CENTURY.
Paz Cárcamo, Guillermo. Guatemala . Ciudad Universitaria Rodrigo Facio [Costa Rica] , 1986. 278 p. : ISBN 997-7300-95-X LC Card 87-401521
HD1333.G9 P385 1986

LAND REFORM - HUNGARY - HISTORY.
Simon, Péter, 1926- A magyar parasztság sorsfordulója, 1946-1949 /. [Budapest] , 1984. 212 p. : ISBN 963-09-2475-7 :
HD1333.H9 S57 1984 NYPL [JLD 86-3163]

LAND REFORM - INDIA.
Agrarian struggles in India after independence /. Delhi , 1986. xxvi, 666 p. :
NYPL [JLD 86-3896]

Bergmann, Theodor. Agrarian reform in India . New Delhi, India , 1984. viii, 216 p. ; LC Card 84-900254 DDC 333.3/1/54 19
HD1333.I4 B46 1984 NYPL [JLD 86-3823]

Ghosh, Tushar Kanti. Operation Barga and land reforms . Delhi , New Delhi, India , 1986. vii, 200 p. ; ISBN 81-7018-315-4 : LC Card 86-900505 DDC 333.3/1/54 19
HD1478.I5 G48 1986 NYPL [JLD 86-4347]

Haque, T. (Tajamul), 1947- Agrarian reforms and institutional changes in India /. New Delhi , 1986, c1985. xvi, 268 p. : LC Card 86-902575 DDC 338.1/854 19
HD1333.I4 H36 1986 NYPL [JLD 87-1547]

Lamba, S. K. Impact of land reforms on rural development . New Delhi, India , 1986 [i.e. 1985] xiv, 148 p. ; ISBN 81-85005-20-6 : LC Card 85-905086 DDC 333.3/1/54 19
HD1333.I4 L35 1986

Singh, Sita Ram. Land reforms in India /. Allahabad , 1987. iv, 176 p. ; LC Card 87-901297 DDC 333.3/1/54 19
HD1333.I4 S56 1987

LAND REFORM - INDIA - ASSAM - CASE STUDIES.
Agnihotri, S. K. Rural development through land reforms . Delhi , 1986. viii, 3, 206 p. ; LC Card 87-900356 DDC 333.3/1/54162 19
HD1333.I42 A773 1986

LAND REFORM - INDIA - CASE STUDIES.
Agnihotri, S. K. Rural development through land reforms . Delhi , 1986. viii, 3, 206 p. ; LC Card 87-900356 DDC 333.3/1/54162 19
HD1333.I42 A773 1986

LAND REFORM - INDIA - KARNATAKA.
Rajan, M. A. S. (Mandyam Anandampullai Srirangarajan), 1921- Land reforms in Karnataka . Delhi , 1986. viii, 178 p. : LC Card 86-902976 DDC 333.3/1/5487 19
HD1333.I42 K377 1986

Thimmaiah, G. The political economy of land reforms /. New Delhi [1983?] xiii, 94 p. ; LC Card 84-900237 DDC 333.3/1/5487 19
HD1333.I42 K3778 1983
NYPL [JLD 87-752]

LAND REFORM - INDIA - KARNATAKA - HISTORY.
Pani, Narendar, 1954- Reforms to pre-empt change . New Delhi , 1983. ix, 122 p. ; LC Card 83-902691 DDC 333.3/1/5487 19
HD1333.I42 K376 1983
NYPL [JLD 86-3841]

LAND REFORM - INDIA, NORTHEASTERN.
Land reforms and peasant movement . New Delhi , Guwahati , c1986. xix, 232 p. ; LC Card 86-902255 DDC 333.3/1/541 19
HD1333.I42 N65 1986

LAND REFORM - INDIA - STATES - CASE STUDIES.
Kohli, Atul. The state and poverty in India . Cambridge [Cambridgeshire] , New York , 1987. x, 262 p. : ISBN 0-521-32008-9 LC Card 85-25554 DDC 333.3/1/54 19
HD1333.I4 K65 1986 NYPL [JLD 87-1517]

LAND REFORM - INDONESIA - CIREBON (KABUPATEN) - HISTORY.
Breman, Jan. Control of land and labour in colonial Java . Dordrecht, Netherlands , Cinnaminson, N.J., U. S.A. , 1983. xi, 158 p. : ISBN 90-6765-048-X (pbk.) LC Card 86-145678 DDC 333.3/1/5982 19
HD1333.I52 C573 1983

LAND REFORM - IRELAND - HISTORY.
Parnell, Anna, 1852-1911. The tale of a great sham /. Dublin , Wick, Littlehampton, West Sussex , 1986. 205 p. ; ISBN 0-905223-93-4 LC Card 86-234070 DDC 333.33/5/09415 19
HD625 .P37 1986

LAND REFORM - ITALY - BOLOGNA - HISTORY.
Monti, Aldino. Alle origini della borghesia urbana . Bologna , c1985. 469 p. : ISBN 88-15-00833-0 : LC Card 86-110136 DDC 333.3/0945/41 19
HD680.B65 M66 1985 NYPL [JLD 87-481]

LAND REFORM - ITALY - NAPLES (KINGDOM) - HISTORY - 18TH CENTURY.
Rao, Anna Maria, 1949- L'"Amaro della feudalità" . Napoli , c1984. 382 p. ; ISBN 88-7042-265-8 : LC Card 85-200705
HD1333.I82 N367 1984

LAND REFORM - KENYA - HISTORY - 20TH CENTURY.
Leo, Christopher. Land and class in Kenya /. Toronto , Buffalo [N.Y.] , c1984. xii, 244 p. : ISBN 0-8020-2532-3 *NYPL [JLE 86-1242]*

LAND REFORM - KOREA.
Whang, In Joung. Administration of land reform in Korea /. Seoul, Korea [1982] 41 p. ; LC Card 84-148921 DDC 333.3/1/519 19
HD1333.K78 W46 1982

LAND REFORM - KOREA (SOUTH)
Whang, In Joung. Administration of land reform in Korea /. Seoul, Korea [1982] 41 p. ; LC Card 84-148921 DDC 333.3/1/519 19
HD1333.K78 W46 1982

LAND REFORM - LATIN AMERICA - CONGRESSES.
Reforma agraria como proceso social . Piura, Perú [1984] 163 p. : LC Card 84-232526 DDC 333.3/1/85 19
HD1333.P4 R44 1984 NYPL [JLD 86-2537]

LAND REFORM - LAW AND LEGISLATION - BRAZIL.
Aspectos econômicos, jurídicos e sociais da Reforma Agrária /. São Paulo-SP Brasil [1985] 75 p. ; LC Card 86-220237
HD1333.B6 A85 1985

LAND REFORM - LAW AND LEGISLATION - ECUADOR - HISTORY.
Pensamiento agrario ecuatoriano /. Quito, Ecuador , 1986. 741 p. : LC Card 87-403503 DDC 333.3/1/866 19
HD1333.E2 P46 1986

LAND REFORM - LAW AND LEGISLATION - INDIA - ASSAM - CASES.
Agnihotri, S. K. Rural development through land reforms . Delhi , 1986. viii, 3, 206 p. ; LC Card 87-900356 DDC 333.3/1/54162 19
HD1333.I42 A773 1986

LAND REFORM - LAW AND LEGISLATION - INDIA - CASES.
Agnihotri, S. K. Rural development through land reforms . Delhi , 1986. viii, 3, 206 p. ; LC Card 87-900356 DDC 333.3/1/54162 19
HD1333.I42 A773 1986

LAND REFORM - LAW AND LEGISLATION - INDIA - KARNATAKA.
Thimmaiah, G. The political economy of land reforms /. New Delhi [1983?] xiii, 94 p. ; LC Card 84-900237 DDC 333.3/1/5487 19
HD1333.I42 K3778 1983
NYPL [JLD 87-752]

LAND REFORM - LAW AND LEGISLATION - INDIA - KARNATAKA - HISTORY.
Pani, Narendar, 1954- Reforms to pre-empt change . New Delhi , 1983. ix, 122 p. ; LC Card 83-902691 DDC 333.3/1/5487 19
HD1333.I42 K376 1983
NYPL [JLD 86-3841]

LAND REFORM - LAW AND LEGISLATION - INDIA, NORTHEASTERN.
Land reforms and peasant movement . New Delhi , Guwahati , c1986. xix, 232 p. ; LC Card 86-902255 DDC 333.3/1/541 19
HD1333.I42 N65 1986

LAND REFORM - LAW AND LEGISLATION - PERU.
Méndez S., José Fernando. La derrota de Andahuaylas (1974) /. Lima , 1981. 126 p. :
NYPL [JLB 86-27]

LAND REFORM - MEXICO.
Estructura agraria y desarrollo agrícola en México . México , 1974 (1979 printing) xvi, 1174 p. : LC Card 81-126616 DDC 338.1/0972 19
HD1792 .E85 1974 NYPL [JLE 81-372]

LAND REFORM - MEXICO - HISTORY - 20TH CENTURY.

LAND REFORM - MEXICO - SAN PEDRO AMUZGOS - HISTORY.
Egli, Walter, 1945- San Pedro Amuzgos, ein mexikanisches Dorf kämpft um sein Land . Zürich , c1982. 406 p. : ISBN 3-85791-059-3 LC Card 83-139253
HD1333.M62 S264 1982

LAND REFORM - MEXICO - YAUTEPEC (MORELOS) - HISTORY.
Rounds, Christopher R., 1945- From hacienda to ejido . New York , 1987. viii, 268 p. ; ISBN 0-8240-1369-7 (alk. paper) : LC Card 87-8526

DDC 333.3/1/7249 19
HD1333.M62 Y387 1987

LAND REFORM - MEXICO - YUCATÁN (STATE) - HISTORY.
Cárdenas, Lázaro, 1895-1970. Los ejidos de Yucatán y el henequén . [Mexico City, Mexico] , c1984. 79 p. : LC Card 87-403579 DDC 333.3/1/7265 19
HD1333.M62 Y823 1984

LAND REFORM - NICARAGUA.
Glembotzki, Jürgen. Landwirtschaftliche Entwicklung und Agrarreform in Nicaragua zwischen 1960 und 1982 . Hamburg , 1984. 80, xliv p. : LC Card 84-208160 DDC 333.3/1/7285 19
HD1333.N5 G57 1984
NYPL [JLM 75-816 Nr.21]

Revolución y mujeres del campo . Managua [1985] 46 p. : LC Card 86-231936
HD1333.N5 R48 1985

Thielen, Helmut, 1941- Agrarreformen in Lateinamerika zwischen Ökonomie und Ökologie . Frankfurt am Main , c1985. 518 p. : ISBN 3-88129-958-0 LC Card 86-153251 DDC 333.3/1/7285 19
HD1333.N5 T48 1985 ***NYPL [JLD 87-467]***

Wheelock, Jaime. Entre la crisis y la agresión . Managua, Nicaragua [1985] 148 p. : LC Card 85-241401 DDC 333.3/1/7285 19
HD1333.N5 W48 1985 ***NYPL [JLC 86-312]***

LAND REFORM - PERU.
Méndez S., José Fernando. La derrota de Andahuaylas (1974) /. Lima , 1981. 126 p. :
NYPL [JLB 86-27]

Monheim, Felix. Die Entwicklung der peruanischen Agrarreform 1969-1979 und ihre Durchführung im Departement Puno [microform] /. Wiesbaden , 1981. 37 p. ; ISBN 3-515-03629-6 : LC Card 82-113404 DDC 333.3/1/8536 19
HD1333.P42 P955 1981
NYPL [*ZT-1647 no.11]

LAND REFORM - PERU - CONGRESSES.
Reforma agraria como proceso social . Piura, Perú [1984] 163 p. : LC Card 84-232526 DDC 333.3/1/85 19
HD1333.P4 R44 1984 ***NYPL [JLD 86-2537]***

LAND REFORM - PERU - HISTORY.
Zúñiga Trelles, Washington. Las empresas azucareras y la reforma agraria /. [S.l. , 1981] ([S.l.] : EBRASA) 108 p. ; LC Card 81-204318 DDC 333.3/1/85 19
HD9114.P52 Z86 1981 ***NYPL [JLD 87-922]***

LAND REFORM - PERU - PUNO (DEPT.)
Monheim, Felix. Die Entwicklung der peruanischen Agrarreform 1969-1979 und ihre Durchführung im Departement Puno [microform] /. Wiesbaden , 1981. 37 p. ; ISBN 3-515-03629-6 : LC Card 82-113404 DDC 333.3/1/8536 19
HD1333.P42 P955 1981
NYPL [*ZT-1647 no.11]

LAND REFORM - PHILIPPINES.
Hanisch, Rolf, 1942- Der Staat, ländliche Armutsgruppen und legale Bauernbewegung in den Philippinen /. Baden-Baden , 1983. xii, 432 p. ; ISBN 3-7890-0980-6 LC Card 84-143058
HD1537.P5 H35 1983

LAND REFORM - PORTUGAL - BAIXO ALENTEJO - CASE STUDIES.
Barros, Afonso de. Do latifundismo à reforma agrária . Oeiras [Portugal] , 1986. 636 p. : LC Card 87-404938 DDC 333.3/1/46955 19
HD1333.P82 B353 1986

LAND REFORM - ROMANIA - OLTENIA - HISTORY - 19TH CENTURY.
Pătroiu, Ion. La cumpăna a două epoci, 1849-1877 /. Craiova , 1983. 316 p. ; LC Card 84-234959
HD1333.R62 O475 1983

LAND REFORM - SAUDI ARABIA.
Hajrah, Hassan Hamza. Public land distribution in Saudi Arabia /. London , New York , 1982. xxi, 280 p. : ISBN 0-582-78301-1 LC Card 83-232929 DDC 333.1/6/09538 19
HD853.Z7 H34 1982 ***NYPL [JLE 87-1566]***

LAND REFORM - SPAIN.
La Reconversión industrial, la crisis y reforma agraria. [Madrid] [1984] 148 p. : ISBN 84-398-1197-7 LC Card 86-216324
HC385 .R375 1984

LAND REFORM - SPAIN - ESTREMADURA.
Alvarado Corrales, Eduardo J. Extremadura . Cáceres [1984?] 101 p. : ISBN 84-600-3663-4 LC Card 86-165503
HD1333.S712 E783 1984

LAND REFORM - SPAIN - GRANADA (PROVINCE) - HISTORY - 19TH CENTURY.
Gómez Oliver, Miguel. La desamortización de Mendizábal en Granada /. Granada [1983] 226 p. : LC Card 85-135214
HD479.G73 G65 1983

LAND REFORM - SYRIA - HISTORY.
Khader, Bichara. La question agraire dans le monde arabe . Louvain-la-Neuve , 1984. 631 p. : LC Card 85-169871 DDC 338.1/095691 19
HD2057.5 .K45 1984 ***NYPL [JLE 86-654]***

LAND REFORM - TAIWAN.
Lamba, S. K. Impact of land reforms on rural development . New Delhi, India , 1986 [i.e. 1985] xiv, 148 p. ; ISBN 81-85005-20-6 : LC Card 85-905086 DDC 333.3/1/54 19
HD1333.I4 L35 1986

LAND REFORM - VENEZUELA.
Portocarrero de Guzmán, Blancanieve. El capitalismo dependiente y su incidencia en el problema agrario venezolano /. Valencia, Venezuela , c1985. 189 p. : LC Card 86-226697
HD1333.V4 P67 1985

Land reforms and peasant movement : a study of north-east India / ed. by Atul Goswami. New Delhi : Omsons Publications ; Guwahati : Distributed by Western Book Depot, c1986. xix, 232 p. ; 22 cm. Papers presented at a seminar organized by the North-East India Council for Social Science Research. Includes bibliographies. LC Card 86-902255 DDC 333.3/1/541 19
1. Land reform - India, Northeastern. 2. Land tenure - India, Northeastern. 3. Land reform - Law and legislation - India, Northeastern. 4. Land tenure - Law and legislation - India, Northeastern. I. Goswani, A., 1937-. II. North-East India Council for Social Science Research.
HD1333.I42 N65 1986

Land reforms in India /. Singh, Sita Ram. Allahabad , 1987. iv, 176 p. ; LC Card 87-901297 DDC 333.3/1/54 19
HD1333.I4 S56 1987

Land reforms in Karnataka . Rajan, M. A. S. (Mandyam Anandampullai Srirangarajan), 1921- Delhi , 1986. viii, 178 p. : LC Card 86-902976 DDC 333.3/1/5487 19
HD1333.I42 K377 1986

Land revenue administration in the Punjab, 1849-1901 /. Sharma, Inderjit. New Delhi , c1985. xi, 369 p. : LC Card 85-904617 DDC 354.54/552007242 19
HD879.P8 S53 1985 ***NYPL [JLD 87-552]***

Land revenue policy of the Indian government. 2nd ed. Delhi, India : Sri Satguru Publications : Distributed by Indian Books Centre, 1986. vi, 291 p. ; 23 cm. Includes index. ISBN 81-7030-004-5 : LC Card 85-905141 DDC 336.22/0954 19
1. Land value taxation - India - History.
HD878 .A3 1986

Land rights and wrongs. Land rites and wrongs . Boston , 1988. p. cm. ISBN 0-89946-222-7 LC Card 87-12186 DDC 333.73/13/0971 19
HD171.A15 L28 1988

Land rites and wrongs : the management, regulation, and use of land in Canada and the United States / Elliot J. Feldman, Michael Goldberg, editors ; sponsored by the Lincoln Institute of Land Policy and the University Consortium for Research on North America. Boston : OGH Pub., 1988. p. cm. "In 1984-85 the draft papers were the vehicle for the Seminar on Canadian-United States Relations of the University Consortium for Research on North America at the Harvard University Center for International Affairs"--P. Bibliography: p. Includes index. ISBN 0-89946-222-7 LC Card 87-12186 DDC 333.73/13/0971 19
1. Land use - United States - Congresses. 2. Land use - Canada - Congresses. 3. Land use - Government policy - United States - Congresses. 4. Land use - Government policy - Canada - Congresses. I. Feldman, Elliot J. II. Goldberg, Michael A. III. Lincoln Institute of Land Policy. IV. University Consortium for Research on North America. V. Seminar on Canadian-United States Relations (1984-1985 : Harvard University Center for International Affairs). VI. Harvard University. Center for International Affairs. VII. Title: Land rights and wrongs.
HD171.A15 L28 1988

Land, Robert D. Zucconi, Paul J. Accounting in life and health insurance companies /. Atlanta, Ga. , c1987. xiv, 365 p. : ISBN 0-915322-85-4 LC Card 86-82715 DDC 657/.836 19
HG8848 .Z84 1987

LAND SETTLEMENT - AFRICA, EASTERN - CONGRESSES.
Proceedings of the workshop on the "Interrelationship between agricultural settlement, agricultural development, and population change" in selected Eastern Africa Countries, Ethiopia, Kenya, Sudan, and Tanzania, held at the Population Studies and Research Institute, University of Nairobi, April 13-16, 1981. Nairobi [1981] 304 p. : LC Card 85-980248 DDC 338.1/09676 19
HD982.Z63 P76 1981

LAND SETTLEMENT - AMAZON RIVER VALLEY REGION.
Meirelles Filho, João Carlos, 1960- Amazônia--o que fazer? /. São Paulo , 1986. 85 p., [1] folded leaf of plates : LC Card 86-233275
HC187.5 .M45 1986

LAND SETTLEMENT - ARGENTINA - CHACO.
Borrini, Héctor R. El proceso de colonización en el impenetrable chaqueño /. Corrientes , 1981. 60 leaves : LC Card 86-204205 DDC 333.3/1/8234 19
HD479.C47 B67 1981

LAND SETTLEMENT - ARGENTINA - COMAHUE REGION.
Reboratti, Carlos E. Condicionantes físicos del asentamiento humano en el norte de la Patagonia /. Buenos Aires , 1982. 47 p. : LC Card 83-185201
HD479.C57 R43 1982

LAND SETTLEMENT - ARGENTINA - SAN JUAN (PROVINCE) - HISTORY.
Marzo, Miguel. La conquista del espacio territorial sanjuanino /. Mendoza , 1968. 89 p., [12] leaves of plates : LC Card 82-166187
HD479.S25 M37 1968

LAND SETTLEMENT - ASIA, SOUTHEASTERN - CONGRESSES.
Seminar on the Effect of Internal Migration, Urbanization, and Resettlement in the IGCC Region on its Population/Family Planning Programmes (1980 : Jakarta, Indonesia) Seminar on the Effect of Internal Migration, Urbanization, and Resettlement in the IGCC Region on its Population/Family Planning Programmes . Kuala Lumpur, Malaysia [1980?] 131 p. : LC Card 81-941408
HB2101 .S45 1980

LAND SETTLEMENT - BANGLADESH.
Shawkat Ali, A. M. M. Politics and land system in Bangladesh /. Dhaka , 1986. x, 354 p. ; LC Card 86-900954 DDC 333.3/1/5492 19
HD880.6 .S53 1986 ***NYPL [JLD 86-4018]***

LAND SETTLEMENT - BENIN - CASE STUDIES.
Ewusi, Kodwo. The development and resettlement of oncho-freed zones in the Volta River Basin of West Africa . [Legon, Ghana] [1985] 89 p. ; LC Card 87-127503 DDC 333.3/1/667 19
HD1022.Z8 V654 1985

LAND SETTLEMENT - BOLIVIA.
Wiggins, Steve. Colonización en Bolivia /. Sucre, Bolivia [1976?] iv, 112 p. : LC Card 83-203672
HD486 .W54 1976

LAND SETTLEMENT - BOLIVIA - SANTA CRUZ (DEPT.)
Gill, Lesley. Peasants, entrepreneurs, and social change . Boulder , 1987. xiv, 246 p. : ISBN 0-8133-7339-5 (pbk. : alk. paper) : LC Card 86-28207 DDC 303.4/0984/3 19
HD1870.S25 G54 1987

LAND SETTLEMENT - BRAZIL - MEL MOUNTAINS REGION (RIO GRANDE DO NORTE) - CASE STUDIES.
PDRI-Serra do Mel . Natal , 1981. 52 leaves :

LC Card 84-246626
HD499.M45 P37 1981

LAND SETTLEMENT - BRAZIL, NORTHEAST.
Simas, José Ribamar. Subsídios para uma proposta de ocupação racional de novas áreas com agricultura de sequeiro no Nordeste brasileiro /. Recife , 1985 [i.e. 1986] 28, [16] p. : LC Card 87-404827 DDC 338.1/8 19
HD499.N67 S56 1986

LAND SETTLEMENT - BRAZIL - RIO GRANDE DO SUL - HISTORY - 18TH CENTURY.
Santos, Corcino Medeiros dos. Economia e sociedade do Rio Grande do Sul . São Paulo, SP, Brasil , 1984. xxi, 216 p. : ISBN 85-04-00203-9 : LC Card 85-199838
HF3409.R56 S25 1984

LAND SETTLEMENT - BURKINA FASO - CASE STUDIES.
Ewusi, Kodwo. The development and resettlement of oncho-freed zones in the Volta River Basin of West Africa . [Legon, Ghana] [1985] 89 p. ; LC Card 87-127503 DDC 333.3/1/667 19
HD1022.Z8 V654 1985

LAND SETTLEMENT - CAMEROON - YAOUNDÉ.
Yaoundé, typologie de l'habitat . [Yaoundé, Cameroon] [197-?] [26] p. : LC Card 83-106947
HD1019.Z9 Y368 1970z

LAND SETTLEMENT - COLOMBIA - CALDAS (DEPT.) - HISTORY.
Giraldo Zuluaga, Luisa Fernanda, 1957- La colonización antioqueña y la fundación de Manizales /. Manizales, Colombia [1983] 217 p. : LC Card 84-107745
HD519.C35 G57 1983

LAND SETTLEMENT - COLOMBIA - GUAVIARE - HISTORY.
Molano, Alfredo. Selva adentro . Bogotá , 1987. 142 p. : ISBN 958-9012-02-7 LC Card 87-404301 DDC 986.1/65 19
HD519.G8 M65 1987

LAND SETTLEMENT - COLOMBIA - NARIÑO (DEPT.)
Cerón Solarte, Benhur. Contexto socioeconómico de las migraciones internas en Nariño /. Pasto [Colombia] , 1985. i, 276, 51 p. : LC Card 87-102199
HB2028.N37 C47 1985

LAND SETTLEMENT - ENVIRONMENTAL ASPECTS - AMAZON RIVER REGION.
Mueller, Charles Curt. Expansão da fronteira agrícola e meio-ambiente . [S.l. , between 1979 and 1985] 38, [4] leaves, [1] leaf of plates : LC Card 86-197353
HD499.C45 M83 1979

LAND SETTLEMENT - ENVIRONMENTAL ASPECTS - BRAZIL, CENTRAL WEST.
Mueller, Charles Curt. Expansão da fronteira agrícola e meio-ambiente . [S.l. , between 1979 and 1985] 38, [4] leaves, [1] leaf of plates : LC Card 86-197353
HD499.C45 M83 1979

LAND SETTLEMENT - ETHIOPIA.
Malhuret, Claude. Mass deportations in Ethiopia /. [Paris] [1985] 65 leaves ; LC Card 86-181587 DDC 333.3/1/63 19
HD979 .M34 1985

Niggli, Peter, 1950- [Äthiopien, Deportationen und Zwangsarbeitslager. English.] Ethiopia, deportations and forced-labour camps . [Berlin , 1986] 86 p., [1] leaf of plates : LC Card 87-131977 DDC 333.3/1/63 19
HD979 .N3413 1986

LAND SETTLEMENT - FINLAND - TURUN JA PORIN LÄÄNI - HISTORY.
Orrman, Eljas. Bebyggelsen i Pargas, S:t Mårtens och Vemo socknar i egentliga Finland under senmedeltiden och på 1500-talet /. Helsingfors , 1986. 293 p. : ISBN 951-9254-73-0 LC Card 86-199875
HD723 .O77 1986

LAND SETTLEMENT - GAZA STRIP.
Israeli settlements in Gaza and the West Bank (including Jerusalem) . New York , 1982. 66 p. : LC Card 82-232749 DDC 307.7/2/08992405695 19
HD850.Z8 W474 1982
*NYPL [*PXLB 86-5156]*

LAND SETTLEMENT - GHANA - VOLTA RIVER REGION.
Ewusi, Kodwo. The development and resettlement of oncho-freed zones in the Volta River Basin of West Africa . [Legon, Ghana] [1985] 89 p. ; LC Card 87-127503 DDC 333.3/1/667 19
HD1022.Z8 V654 1985

LAND SETTLEMENT - GOVERNMENT POLICY - BANGLADESH.
Shawkat Ali, A. M. M. Politics and land system in Bangladesh /. Dhaka , 1986. x, 354 p. ; LC Card 86-900954 DDC 333.3/1/5492 19
HD880.6 .S53 1986 *NYPL [JLD 86-4018]*

LAND SETTLEMENT - GOVERNMENT POLICY - DEVELOPING COUNTRIES - CASE STUDIES.
Land settlement policies and population redistribution in developing countries . New York , 1988. xiv, 395 p. ; ISBN 0-275-92799-7 (alk. paper) LC Card 87-15837 DDC 333.3/1/1724 19
HD1131 .L364 1988

LAND SETTLEMENT - GOVERNMENT POLICY - ETHIOPIA.
Ethiopia's bitter medicine, settling for disaster . London , 1986. 55 p. : ISBN 0-946592-01-2 (pbk.) LC Card 86-232852 DDC 333.3/1/63
HD979.Z63 E74 1986

LAND SETTLEMENT - GOVERNMENT POLICY - INDONESIA - HISTORY - 20TH CENTURY.
Otten, Mariël. Transmigrasi . Copenhagen , c1986. 254 p. : LC Card 87-144670 DDC 333.3/1/598 19
HD896 .O88 1986

LAND SETTLEMENT - GOVERNMENT POLICY - ZIMBABWE.
Intensive resettlement policies and procedures /. [Harare, Zimbabwe] , 1985. 81 p. : LC Card 87-980233 DDC 333.3/1/6891 19
HD992 .I58 1985

LAND SETTLEMENT - GREAT ALFÖLD - HISTORY.
Blazovich, László. A Körös-Tisza-Maros köz középkori településrendje /. Békéscsaba , Szeged , 1985. 207 p., [9] folded leaves of plates : ISBN 963-01-6828-6 LC Card 87-408571
HD640.5.Z8 G743 1985

LAND SETTLEMENT - HUNGARY.
Beluszky, Pál. Magyarország falutipusai /. Budapest , 1982. 167 p. : ISBN 963-7321-96-9 LC Card 84-159502
HD640.5.Z7 B44 1982

A Magyarországi településrendszer strukturális változása /. Budapest , 1984. 155 p., [1] folded leaf of plates : ISBN 963-03-2079-7 (Magy. nemz. bibl.) LC Card 85-231254
HD640.5 .M343 1984

LAND SETTLEMENT - INDIA - CASE STUDIES.
Ansari, Saiyad Hasan, 1952- Evolution and spatial organization of clan settlements . New Delhi , 1986. 212 p., [8] p. of plates : LC Card 86-900654
HD879.G45 A57 1986
NYPL [JLD 86-3220]

LAND SETTLEMENT - INDIA - GHAZIPUR - CASE STUDIES.
Ansari, Saiyad Hasan, 1952- Evolution and spatial organization of clan settlements . New Delhi , 1986. 212 p., [8] p. of plates : LC Card 86-900654
HD879.G45 A57 1986
NYPL [JLD 86-3220]

LAND SETTLEMENT - INDIA - UTTAR PREDESH.
Singh, Alok Kumar, 1958- Population and settlement in U.P. . New Delhi, India , 1985. xx, 231 p., [10] p. of plates : LC Card 86-900123 DDC 304.6/0954/2 19
HB2100.U88 S55 1985
NYPL [JLD 86-3156]

LAND SETTLEMENT - INDONESIA - KALIMANTAN TIMUR.
Kebschull, Dietrich. Transmigration in Indonesia . Hamburg , 1984. xxiv, 134 p. ; LC Card 86-223779 DDC 304.8/09598 19
HB2107 .K4 1984

LAND SETTLEMENT - ISRAEL - HISTORY.
Dies ist das Land . [Sweden] 1946 (Lund : Berlingska Boktryckeriet) 102, [1] p., [1] folded leaf of plates : LC Card 86-225837
HD850 .D54 1946

LAND SETTLEMENT - LLANOS ORIENTALES (COLOMBIA AND VENEZUELA)
Pedraja Tomán, René de la. Los Llanos . Bogotá, Colombia , 1984. 101 p. : LC Card 84-221343
HC198.L56 P4 1984

LAND SETTLEMENT - MAURITIUS.
Mauritius. Legislative Assembly. Public Accounts Committee. Special report of the Public Accounts Committee for the 1980 session . Port Louis, Mauritius , 1981. 13 p. ; LC Card 82-980151 DDC 333.1/6/09697 19
HD1030.3.Z63 M38 1981

LAND SETTLEMENT - MEXICO - PAPALOAPAN RIVER VALLEY.
Ewell, Peter T., 1947- Uxpanapa . Ithaca, N.Y. [1982] xiv, 218 p., [35] leaves of plates : LC Card 84-621492 DDC 338.1/0972/6 19
HD1795.P3 E94 1982

LAND SETTLEMENT - MEXICO - QUINTANA ROO (STATE)
Proyecto EI-5-3 . México, D.F. [1977] ca. 150 p. : LC Card 82-119251
HC137.Q5 P76 1977

LAND SETTLEMENT - NEW SPAIN - HISTORY.
Baxter, John O., 1927- Las carneradas . Albuquerque , c1987. x, 198 p., [4] p. of plates : ISBN 0-8263-0961-5 LC Card 86-30906 DDC 381/.4163/009789 19
HD9436.U53 N63 1987

LAND SETTLEMENT - PARAGUAY - CAAGUAZU (DEPT.)
Fogel, Ramón B. Movimientos campesinos en el Paraguay /. Asunción, Paraguay , 1986. 230 p., [1] leaf of plates : LC Card 86-189517
HD1531.P3 F64 1986

LAND SETTLEMENT PATTERNS - EUROPE, EASTERN.
Migrace a osídlení v socialistických zemích =. Praha , 1984- v. <1 > : LC Card 87-160334
HB2041 .M526 1984

LAND SETTLEMENT - PERU - ORIENTE.
Peru, Kolonisation und Abhängigkeit . Saarbrücken , Fort Lauderdale , 1981. 192 p. : ISBN 3-88156-165-X : LC Card 82-104103
HD1905.O75 P47 1981

Land settlement policies and population redistribution in developing countries : achievements, problems, prospects / edited by A.S. Oberai. New York : Praeger, 1988. xiv, 395 p. ; 24 cm. "Study prepared for the International Labour Office." Includes bibliographies and index.
ISBN 0-275-92799-7 (alk. paper) LC Card 87-15837 DDC 333.3/1/1724 19
1. Land settlement - Government policy - Developing countries - Case studies. I. Oberai, A. S. II. International Labour Office.
HD1131 .L364 1988

LAND SETTLEMENT - SAUDI ARABIA.
Hajrah, Hassan Hamza. Public land distribution in Saudi Arabia /. London , New York , 1982. xxi, 280 p. : ISBN 0-582-78301-1 LC Card 83-232929 DDC 333.1/6/09538 19
HD853.Z7 H34 1982 *NYPL [JLE 87-1566]*

LAND SETTLEMENT - SOUTH AFRICA - HISTORY.
Christopher, A. J. The Crown lands of British South Africa, 1853-1914 /. Kingston, Ont., Canada , 1984. vii, 247 p., [8] p. of plates : ISBN 0-919642-04-7 LC Card 85-125786 DDC 333.1/0968 19
HD991 .C49 1984 *NYPL [Sc E 85-373]*

LAND SETTLEMENT - SOUTH AFRICA - VERLOREVLEI.
Sinclair, Sharyn. The rural settlement of Verlorenvlei in historical perspective /. Rondebosch, South Africa [1980] 234 leaves : LC Card 86-210654
HD991.Z9 V477 1980

LAND SETTLEMENT - SUDAN - CASE STUDIES.

Amin, Nasr El Din Osman. Nomadism versus sedenterization . [Khartoum?] Sudan , 1986. 105 leaves : LC Card 86-981112
HD977 .A65 1986

LAND SETTLEMENT - SWEDEN - HISTORY - 17TH CENTURY.
Larsson, Lars-Olof, 1934- Bönder och gårdar i stormaktspolitikens skugga . Växjö , 1983. 260 p. : ISBN 91-7636-011-3 : LC Card 84-159659
HD763 .L37 1983

LAND SETTLEMENT - SWEDEN - HISTORY - 18TH CENTURY.
Larsson, Lars-Olof, 1934- Bönder och gårdar i stormaktspolitikens skugga . Växjö , 1983. 260 p. : ISBN 91-7636-011-3 : LC Card 84-159659
HD763 .L37 1983

LAND SETTLEMENT - THAILAND.
Klempin, Arno. Contribution of state-directed land settlement to agricultural development . Saarbrücken , Fort Launderdale, 1979. viii, 169 p. : ISBN 3-88156-121-8 LC Card 80-464363 DDC 333.3/1/593
HD890.55 .K57 ***NYPL [JLE 80-1270]***

LAND SETTLEMENT - TROPICS.
Les Phénomènes de "frontière" dans les pays tropicaux . Paris , 1981. vii, 456 p. : LC Card 83-122397
HD1131 .P47 1981

LAND SETTLEMENT - WEST BANK.
Israeli settlements in Gaza and the West Bank (including Jerusalem) . New York , 1982. 66 p. : LC Card 82-232749 DDC 307.7/2/08992405695 19
HD850.Z8 W474 1982
NYPL [*PXLB 86-5156]

LAND SUBDIVISION - PACIFIC ISLANDS (TRUST TERRITORY) - STATISTICS.
Barr, Lorna R. Land of the Trust islands . [Victoria, B.C.] [1978] 36 p. : LC Card 83-226106 DDC 333.3/0996/5 19
HD1121.Z63 B37 1978

LAND SURVEYING. see **SURVEYING.**

LAND TAX. see **REAL PROPERTY TAX.**

LAND - TAXATION. see **REAL PROPERTY TAX.**

LAND TENURE - AFRICA.
Espaces disputés en Afrique noire . Paris , c1986. 426 p., [8] p. of plates : ISBN 2-86537-146-8 LC Card 86-210958
HD965 .E86 1986

LAND TENURE - AFRICA, SUB-SAHARAN.
Enjeux fonciers en Afrique noire /. Bondy , Paris , c1982. 425 p. ; ISBN 2-86537-057-7 : LC Card 83-130847 DDC 333.3/096 19
HD966 .E54 1982 ***NYPL [JLE 87-950]***

LAND TENURE - AMAZON RIVER REGION.

LAND TENURE - ARGENTINA - CHACO.
Borrini, Héctor R. El proceso de colonización en el impenetrable chaqueño /. Corrientes , 1981. 60 leaves : LC Card 86-204205 DDC 333.3/1/8234 19
HD479.C47 B67 1981

LAND TENURE - AUSTRALIA - QUEENSLAND - HISTORY - 19TH CENTURY.
Walker, Jan, 1954- Jondaryan station . St. Lucia , New York , 1988. p. cm. ISBN 0-7022-2093-0 (pbk.) LC Card 87-13816 DDC 333.3/09943 19
HD1039.Q43 W34 1988

LAND TENURE - AUSTRALIA - WESTERN AUSTRALIA.
Western Australia. Pastoral Tenure Study Group. Final report on pastoral land tenure. Perth, W.A. [1986] [28], 63, 4 p. ; LC Card 87-120095 DDC 333.3/09941 19
HD1641.A9 W47 1986

LAND TENURE - AUSTRIA - LOWER AUSTRIA - HISTORY.
Feigl, Helmuth. Die niederösterreichische Grundherrschaft . [Wien] , 1964. 379 p. ; LC Card 85-127367
HD639.L6 F45 1964

LAND TENURE - BOLIVIA.
Ovando, Jorge. El tributo indígena en las finanzas bolivianas del siglo XIX /. La Paz, Bolivia [1985] 565 p. : ***NYPL [JLC 86-407]***

Segunda reforma agraria . La Paz, Bolivia [1987] 287 p. : LC Card 87-403057 DDC 333.3/1/84 19
HD1333.B5 S44 1987

LAND TENURE - BOLIVIA - CAQUIAVIRI.
Birbuet D., Gustavo. Tierra y ganado en Pacajes . La Paz, Bolivia , 1986. 86 p. : LC Card 87-403087 DDC 333.3/0984/12 19
HD490.C34 B57 1986

LAND TENURE - BOLIVIA - COMANCHE.
Birbuet D., Gustavo. Tierra y ganado en Pacajes . La Paz, Bolivia , 1986. 86 p. : LC Card 87-403087 DDC 333.3/0984/12 19
HD490.C34 B57 1986

LAND TENURE - BOTSWANA.
Wily, Liz. The TGLP and hunter-gatherers . Gaborone, Botswana , 1981. ii, 102 p. ; LC Card 82-207525
DT797 W55 1981 ***NYPL [JLG 87-6]***

LAND TENURE - BRAZIL.
Ferreira, Benedito, 1932- A questão fundiária /. Brasília , 1986. 171 p. ; LC Card 86-229678
HD496 .F42 1986

Terra de Deus, terra de irmãos . Brasília-DF [1986] 190 p. : LC Card 86-233600
HD1333.B6 T47 1986

LAND TENURE - BRAZIL - CONCEIÇÃO DO ARAGUAIA.
Figueira, Ricardo Rezende, 1952- A justiça do lobo . Petrópolis , 1986. 115 p. ; LC Card 87-137552 DDC 305.5/63 19
HD500.C74 F54 1986

LAND TENURE - BRAZIL - GOIÁS (STATE)
Catholic Church. Comissão Pastoral da Terra (Brazil) CPT . Petrópolis , 1983. 105 p. ; LC Card 86-209008
HD499.G65 C38 1983

LAND TENURE - BRAZIL, NORTHEAST.
A Problemática e a política da terra e água do Nordeste. Recife , 1985. 296 p. : LC Card 87-124121 DDC 333.91/00981/3 19
HD1696.B84 N675 1985

LAND TENURE - BRAZIL - PASSO REAL.
Rio Grande do Sul (Brazil). Assembléia Legislativa. Comissão Especial dos Agricultores Desalojados do Passo Real. Afogados, até quando? . [Porto Alegre] [1984] 99 p. : LC Card 85-150200
HD500.P39 R56 1984

LAND TENURE - BRAZIL - PINDARÉ RIVER VALLEY.
Luna, Regina Celi Miranda Reis. A terra era liberta . São Luís, MA , 1985. xxvii, 146 p. : LC Card 87-135907 DDC 333.3/0981/21 19
HD499.P46 L86 1985

LAND TENURE - BRAZIL - SÃO PAULO (STATE)
Fleury, Maria Tereza Leme. A organização do trabalho na lavoura algodoeira paulista /. [São Paulo, Brasil] 1984. 208 p. : LC Card 85-145302 DDC 338.1/7351/098161 19
HD9084.B62 S264 1984
NYPL [JLE 86-1740]

LAND TENURE - BRAZIL - STATISTICS.
Estatísticas cadastrais . Brasília , 1985- <v. 1-2; in 2 > : LC Card 87-117732
HD498 .E77 1985

LAND TENURE - CENTRAL AMERICA.
Barry, Tom, 1950- Roots of rebellion . Boston , c1987. xii, 220 p. : ISBN 0-89608-288-1 : LC Card 87-4519 DDC 338.1/9/728 19
HD9014.C462 B37 1987

Brockett, Charles D., 1946- Land, power, and poverty . Boston , c1988. p. cm. ISBN 0-04-497027-7 LC Card 87-22746 DDC 338.1/09728 19
HD1797 .B76 1988

LAND TENURE - CHILE.
Lira, Luis Felipe. Estructura agraria, crecimiento de la población y migraciones . Santiago, Chile , 1976. 90 p. ; LC Card 83-169710
HB2025 .L57 1976

LAND TENURE - COLOMBIA - BARBOSA (ANTIOQUIA)
Informe general y proyecto de parcelación, Antioquia # 2 (Barbosa y Santo Domingo) /. Bogotá, D.E. , 1964. 2, 73, 16 leaves, [1] leaf of plates : LC Card 85-107102
HD1476.C72 B375 1964

LAND TENURE - COLOMBIA - SANTO DOMINGO (ANTIOQUIA)
Informe general y proyecto de parcelación, Antioquia # 2 (Barbosa y Santo Domingo) /. Bogotá, D.E. , 1964. 2, 73, 16 leaves, [1] leaf of plates : LC Card 85-107102
HD1476.C72 B375 1964

LAND TENURE - COSTA RICA.
Costa Rica--respuesta al cuestionario del Banco Interamericano de Desarrollo /. [San José] [1962] 69 leaves (some folded) ; LC Card 85-117361
HC143 .C685 1962

LAND TENURE - ECUADOR.
Tenencia de la tierra y desarrollo socio-económico del sector agrícola. [Guayaquil] [1981] xxv, 539 p., [16] leaves of plates : LC Card 87-673171
HD526 .T46x 1981

LAND TENURE - ECUADOR - CHIMBORAZO - HISTORY.
Sylva Charvet, Paola. Gamonalismo y lucha campesina . [Quito] , 1986. 250 p., [3] leaves of plates : LC Card 87-101122
HD529.C47 S95 1986

LAND TENURE - ECUADOR - COTOPAXI.
Farrell, Gilda. Tenencia de la tierra y movimiento campesino en el Ecuador /. Quito, Ecuador , 1981. 158 p., [2] leaves of plates : LC Card 86-174088
HD529.C67 F37 1981

LAND TENURE - ECUADOR - PICHINCHA (PROVINCE)
Farrell, Gilda. Tenencia de la tierra y movimiento campesino en el Ecuador /. Quito, Ecuador , 1981. 158 p., [2] leaves of plates : LC Card 86-174088
HD529.C67 F37 1981

LAND TENURE - ECUADOR - TUNGURAHUA.
Farrell, Gilda. Tenencia de la tierra y movimiento campesino en el Ecuador /. Quito, Ecuador , 1981. 158 p., [2] leaves of plates : LC Card 86-174088
HD529.C67 F37 1981

LAND TENURE - EGYPT - HISTORY.
Stuchevskiĭ, I. A. (Iosif Aleksandrovich) Zemledel′tsy gosudarstvennogo khozi͡aĭstva drevnego Egipta ėpokhi Ramessidov /. Moskva , 1982. 254, [2] p. ; LC Card 82-186646
HD2123 .S78 1982

LAND TENURE - ETHIOPIA.
Harjinder Singh. Agricultural problems in Ethiopia /. Delhi, India , c1987. viii, 254 p. : ISBN 81-212-0078-4 : LC Card 87-900338 DDC 338.1/0963 19
HD2124.5 .H37 1987

LAND TENURE - FRANCE.
La Propriété foncière /. Paris , c1984. vii, 252 p. : ISBN 2-7178-0783-7 LC Card 84-249621
HD643 .N49 1984

LAND TENURE - GREECE - ATHENS - HISTORY.
Finley, M. I. (Moses I.), 1912- Studies in land and credit in ancient Athens, 500-200 B.C. . New Brunswick, U. S.A. , c1985. xli, 332 p. ; ISBN 0-88738-066-2 : LC Card 85-14091 DDC 333.3/0938/5 19
HD134 .F5 1985 ***NYPL [JLE 86-4293]***

LAND TENURE - GUATEMALA.
Paz Cárcamo, Guillermo. Guatemala . Ciudad Universitaria Rodrigo Facio [Costa Rica] , 1986. 278 p. : ISBN 997-7300-95-X LC Card 87-401521
HD1333.G9 P385 1986

LAND TENURE - HONDURAS - STATISTICS.
Tosco, Manuel. Aprovechamiento y dominio de las tierras en 1950-51 /. Tegucigalpa, D.C., Honduras [1952] 33 p. ; LC Card 85-197157
HD366 .T66 1952

LAND TENURE - HUNGARY.
A Föld és a népgazdaság /. [Budapest] , 1985. 514 p. ; ISBN 963-03-2232-3 LC Card 86-228739
HD640.5.Z63 F65 1985

LAND TENURE - INDIA.
Ghosha, Madana. Bhūmibyabasthā, Kaṃgresa, o Kṛshakasabhā /. Bardhamāna [1986?] 100 p. ; LC Card 87-900325
HD875 .G56 1986

LAND TENURE - INDIA - BARDOLI TALUKA - HISTORY.
Mehta, Shirin. The peasantry and nationalism . New Delhi , 1984. x, 215 p. : LC Card 84-901701 DDC 322.4/4/095475 19
HD1339.I4 M44 1984 NYPL [JLD 86-4424]

LAND TENURE - INDIA - BENGAL - HISTORY.
Mookerji, Radhakumud, 1884-1964. Indian land-system . Alipore, Bengal , 1940. 112, v p. ; LC Card 87-123602
HD879.B4 M63 1940

Nag Chowdhury-Zilly, Aditee. The vagrant peasant . Wiesbaden , 1982. xv, 196 p. : ISBN 3-515-03855-8 (pbk.) LC Card 86-214350
HD1537.I4 N327 1982

LAND TENURE - INDIA - HISTORY.
Alaev, L. B. Sel′skaia obshchina v Severnoĭ Indii . Moskva , 1981. 240 p. ; LC Card 82-101919
HD873 .A63 1981

LAND TENURE - INDIA - JAUNPUR (DISTRICT)
Shankar, Kripa. Pattern of land ownership and backwardness . New Delhi , 1986. x, 119 p. ; ISBN 81-7024-021-2 : LC Card 87-900130 DDC 333.3/23/09542 19
HD879.J37 S5 1986

LAND TENURE - INDIA, NORTHEASTERN.
Land reforms and peasant movement . New Delhi , Guwahati , c1986. xix, 232 p. ; LC Card 86-902255 DDC 333.3/1/541 19
HD1333.I42 N65 1986

LAND TENURE - INDIA - PUNJAB.
Sharma, Inderjit. Land revenue administration in the Punjab, 1849-1901 /. New Delhi , c1985. xi, 369 p. : LC Card 85-904617 DDC 354.54/552007242 19
HD879.P8 S53 1985 NYPL [JLD 87-552]

LAND TENURE - INDIA - WEST BENGAL.
Rudra, Ashok. Agrarian relations in West Bengal . Bombay , c1983. x, 104 p. ; LC Card 83-902673 DDC 338.1/0954/14 19
HD879.W4 R83 1983 NYPL [JLD 86-3785]

LAND TENURE - INDONESIA - BANTUL (KABUPATEN) - CASE STUDIES.
Maurer, Jean-Luc. Modernisation agricole, développement économique et changement social . Paris , c1986. 323 p. : ISBN 2-13-039622-4 : LC Card 86-175394
HD2085.B37 M38 1986

LAND TENURE - INDONESIA - NAMPU.
Purwanto, Bambang. Kepemimpinan dan masalah pertanahan di pedesaan Jawa . [Yogyakarta] , 1985. ix, 58 p. : LC Card 86-943756
HD900.N36 P87 1985

LAND TENURE - INDONESIA - NGANDAGAN.
Purwanto, Bambang. Kepemimpinan dan masalah pertanahan di pedesaan Jawa . [Yogyakarta] , 1985. ix, 58 p. : LC Card 86-943756
HD900.N36 P87 1985

LAND TENURE - IRELAND - HISTORY.
Parnell, Anna, 1852-1911. The tale of a great sham /. Dublin , Wick, Littlehampton, West Sussex , 1986. 205 p. ; ISBN 0-905223-93-4 LC Card 86-234070 DDC 333.33/5/09415 19
HD625 .P37 1986

LAND TENURE - ITALY - BOLOGNA - HISTORY.
Monti, Aldino. Alle origini della borghesia urbana . Bologna , c1985. 469 p. : ISBN 88-15-00833-0 : LC Card 86-110136 DDC 333.3/0945/41 19
HD680.B65 M66 1985 NYPL [JLD 87-481]

LAND TENURE - ITALY - EMILIA-ROMAGNA - HISTORY.
Dean, Trevor. Land and power in late medieval Ferrara . Cambridge , New York , 1988. xiv, 212 p. : ISBN 0-521-33127-7 LC Card 87-6583 DDC 333.3/0945/45 19
HD679.F47 D43 1988

LAND TENURE - ITALY - FERRARA (PROVINCE) - HISTORY.
Dean, Trevor. Land and power in late medieval Ferrara . Cambridge , New York , 1988. xiv, 212 p. : ISBN 0-521-33127-7 LC Card 87-6583 DDC 333.3/0945/45 19
HD679.F47 D43 1988

LAND TENURE - ITALY - LOMBARDY - HISTORY - 18TH CENTURY.
La Proprietà fondiaria in Lombardia dal catasto teresiano all'età napoleonica /. Milano , 1986. 2 v. ; ISBN 88-343-0341-5 (set) : LC Card 87-108100
HD679.L6 P76 1986

LAND TENURE - ITALY - MILAN - HISTORY - 18TH CENTURY.
Mazzucchelli, Vanna. Catasto e volto urbano . Roma , 1983. 244 p. ; LC Card 86-106099
HD680.M54 M39 1983

LAND TENURE - ITALY - OTRANTO REGION - HISTORY - 19TH CENTURY - SOURCES - EXHIBITIONS.
La Questione demaniale in Terra d'Otranto nel XIX secolo . [Roma] [Lecce] [1985?] 183 p., [6] leaves of plates : LC Card 86-180857
HD680.O87 Q47 1985

LAND TENURE - ITALY - PUGLIA - HISTORY - 20TH CENTURY.
Snowden, Frank M. (Frank Martin), 1946- Violence and great estates in the south of Italy . Cambridge [Cambridgeshire] , New York , 1986. x, 245 p. : ISBN 0-521-30731-7 LC Card 85-11675 DDC 322.4/4/094575 19
HD679.P83 S66 1986 NYPL [JLD 86-1627]

LAND TENURE - ITALY - VENICE REGION - HISTORY - 16TH CENTURY.
Corazzol, Gigi, 1945- Livelli stipulati a Venezia nel 1591 . Pisa , c1986. 167 p., [8] leaves of plates : LC Card 86-192693
HD680.V4 C67 1986

LAND TENURE - JAPAN - NAKADA-CHŌ (MIYAGI-KEN)
Moore, Richard H. Japanese agriculture . Boulder , 1987. p. cm. ISBN 0-8133-7406-5 LC Card 87-13553 DDC 338.1/0952/115 19
HD920.N33 M65 1987

LAND TENURE - KENYA - HISTORY.
Leo, Christopher. Land and class in Kenya /. Toronto , Buffalo [N.Y.] , c1984. xii, 244 p. : ISBN 0-8020-2532-3 NYPL [JLE 86-1242]

LAND TENURE - KOREA - HISTORY.
Vanin, ÎUriĭ Vasil′evich. Agrarnyĭ stroĭ feodal′noĭ Korei XV-XVI vv. /. Moskva , 1981. 309 p. ; LC Card 83-462393
*HD1331.K6 V36 1981 NYPL [*QI 86-3898]*

LAND TENURE - LAW AND LEGISLATION - HUNGARY.
A Föld és a népgazdaság /. [Budapest] , 1985. 514 p. ; ISBN 963-03-2232-3 LC Card 86-228739
HD640.5.Z63 F65 1985

LAND TENURE - LAW AND LEGISLATION - INDIA, NORTHEASTERN.
Land reforms and peasant movement . New Delhi , Guwahati , c1986. xix, 232 p. ; LC Card 86-902255 DDC 333.3/1/541 19
HD1333.I42 N65 1986

LAND TENURE - LAW AND LEGISLATION - ITALY - NAPLES (KINGDOM) - HISTORY - 18TH CENTURY.
Rao, Anna Maria, 1949- L'"Amaro della feudalità" . Napoli , c1984. 382 p. ; ISBN 88-7042-265-8 : LC Card 85-200705
HD1333.I82 N367 1984

LAND TENURE - LAW AND LEGISLATION - PERU.
Hurtado Miller, Juan Carlos. Por una causa agraria . Lima, Perú , 1986. 348 p. : LC Card 87-400122 DDC 338.1/885 19
HD1903 .H87 1986

LAND TENURE - LAW AND LEGISLATION - PORTUGAL.
Rau, Virginia. Sesmarias medievais portuguesas /. Lisboa [1982] 288 p. : LC Card 87-673341
HD784 .R3x 1982

LAND TENURE - MEXICO - SONORA (STATE) - HISTORY.
Radding, Cynthia. [Acumulación originaria de capital agrario en Sonora.] La acumulación originaria de capital agrario en Sonora ; Registro de los archivos del Estado de Sonora /. [Hermosillo, Sonora] , 1981. 90 p. : LC Card 82-118209
HD329.S6 R33 1981

LAND TENURE - MEXICO - YAUTEPEC (MORELOS) - HISTORY.
Rounds, Christopher R., 1945- From hacienda to ejido . New York , 1987. viii, 268 p. ; ISBN 0-8240-1369-7 (alk. paper) : LC Card 87-8526 DDC 333.3/1/7249 19
HD1333.M62 Y387 1987

LAND TENURE - PERU - CUZCO (DEPT.) - HISTORY - 19TH CENTURY.
Mörner, Magnus. Compraventas de tierras en el Cuzco, 1825-1869 /. Estocolmo , 1984. 66 p. : LC Card 87-403757 DDC 333.3/0985/37 19
HD559.C87 M67 1984

LAND TENURE - PERU - HISTORY.
Burga, Manuel. La historia agraria /. Chiclayo, Perú , 1986. 196 p. ; NYPL [JLD 87-1524]

LAND TENURE - PERU - PIURA (DEPT.) - HISTORY.
Espinoza Claudio, César. Terratenientes y campesinos en Piura, ss. XVI-XIX . Lima, Perú , 1981. xxviii, 123 p., [6] leaves of plates : LC Card 82-146131
HD559.P5 E87 1981

LAND TENURE - POLAND.
Klank, Leszek. Czynniki kształtujące poziom dochodów w gospodarstwach indywidualnych /. Warszawa , 1985. 176 p. ; ISBN 83-01-05449-2 : NYPL [*QO 86-2601]

LAND TENURE - PORTUGAL.
Rau, Virginia. Sesmarias medievais portuguesas /. Lisboa [1982] 288 p. : LC Card 87-673341
HD784 .R3x 1982

LAND TENURE - RUSSIAN S.F.S.R. - HISTORY - 17TH CENTURY.
Kopanev, A. I. (Aleksandr Il′ich) Krest′iane Russkogo Severa v XVII v. /. Leningrad , 1984. 242 p. ; LC Card 84-170666
*HD719.R88 K67 1984 NYPL [*QG 86-3646]*

LAND TENURE - RUSSIAN S.F.S.R. - SIBERIA, WESTERN - HISTORY.
Vlasova, I. V. (Irina Vladimirovna) Traditsii krest′ianskogo zemlepol′zovaniia v Pomor′e i Zapadnoĭ Sibiri v XVII-XVIII vv. /. Moskva , 1984. 230 p. : LC Card 85-174592
HD719.W45 V55 1984

LAND TENURE - RUSSIAN S.F.S.R. - WHITE SEA REGION - HISTORY.
Vlasova, I. V. (Irina Vladimirovna) Traditsii krest′ianskogo zemlepol′zovaniia v Pomor′e i Zapadnoĭ Sibiri v XVII-XVIII vv. /. Moskva , 1984. 230 p. : LC Card 85-174592
HD719.W45 V55 1984

LAND TENURE - SCOTLAND.
Armstrong, A. M. Land ownership and land use in the Scottish Highlands /. [Aberdeen, Grampian] , 1983. vii, 150 p. : LC Card 83-209521 DDC 333.3/09411/5 19
HD616 .A76 1983 NYPL [JLF 86-457]

LAND TENURE - SENEGAL - SINE-SALOUM.
Benoit-Cattin, Michel. L'exploitation agricole familiale en Afrique soudano-sahélienne /. Paris , c1982. 94 p. : ISBN 2-85319-106-0 LC Card 86-116718
HD1476.S382 S563 1982

LAND TENURE - SOVIET UNION.
Shinn, William T., 1936- The decline of the Russian peasant household /. New York , 1987. xvii, 122 p. ; ISBN 0-275-92767-9 (alk. paper) LC Card 87-2554 DDC 338.1/0947 19
HD1992 .S4735 1987

LAND TENURE - SOVIET UNION - HISTORY - 20TH CENTURY.
Istoriia sovetskogo krest′ianstva . Moskva , 1986- v. : NYPL [*QG 87-3228]

LAND TENURE - SOVIET UNION - HISTORY - MATHEMATICAL MODELS - ADDRESSES, ESSAYS, LECTURES.
Soviet quantitative history /. Beverly Hills , c1984. 216 p. : ISBN 0-8039-2082-2 LC Card 83-19196 DDC 306/.072047 19
HD715 .S5956 1984 NYPL [JLD 87-841]

LAND TENURE - SPAIN - ALCOY - HISTORY - 18TH CENTURY.
Romeo Mateo, María Cruz, 1960- Realengo y municipio . Alicante , 1986. 171 p. : ISBN 84-505-3131-4 LC Card 87-137181
HD780.A435 R66 1986

LAND TENURE - SPAIN - ALJARAFE - HISTORY.
Herrera García, Antonio. El Aljarafe durante el antiguo régimen /. Sevilla , 1981. 147 p., [3] leaves of plates : ISBN 84-500-4850-8 LC Card

82-142028 DDC 333.3/0946/86 19
HD779.A39 H47 1981 NYPL [JLC 86-126]

Herrera García, Antonio. El Aljarafe sevillano durante el antiguo régimen . [Sevilla] , 1980. 517 p., [9] leaves of plates : ISBN 84-500-4373-5 LC Card 81-173649 DDC 946/.86 19
HD779.A39 H475 1980 NYPL [JLF 86-928]

LAND TENURE - SPAIN - AMPURDÁN (REGION)
El Baix Empordà . Barcelona , c1984. xii, 303 p. : ISBN 84-505-0289-6 LC Card 85-186183
HC387.A636 B35 1984

LAND TENURE - SPAIN - ANDALUSIA - HISTORY - 19TH CENTURY.
González do Molina Navarro, Manuel. Desamortización, deuda pública y crecimiento económico, Andalucía, 1820/1823 /. Granada , Córdoba :bFundación Paco Natera [1985?] 443 p. : ISBN 84-505-1053-8 LC Card 86-210676
HD779.A4 G66 1985

LAND TENURE - SPAIN - BADAJOZ (PROVINCE) - HISTORY.
Bohoyo Velázquez, Isidoro Francisco. Situación socio-económica y condiciones de vida en la Provincia de Badajoz, 1880-1902 /. Badajoz [1984?] 149 p., [3] p. of plates : ISBN 84-309-1055-7 LC Card 86-151914
HC387.B14 B64 1984

LAND TENURE - SPAIN - CASTILLA Y LEÓN - HISTORY.
Robledo Hernández, Ricardo. La renta de la tierra en Castilla la Vieja y León (1836-1913) /. [Madrid] [1984?] 245 p. : ISBN 84-505-0885-1 LC Card 87-104999
HJ4375.C27 R63 1984

LAND TENURE - SPAIN - CATALONIA - HISTORY.
Terra, treball i propietat . Barcelona , c1986. 346 p. ; ISBN 84-7423-287-2 LC Card 86-216973
HD2025.C35 T47 1986

LAND TENURE - SPAIN - CENETE - HISTORY.
Arias Abellán, Jesús. Propiedad y usos de la tierra en el Marquesado del Cenete /. [Granada] , 1984. iv, 439 p. : ISBN 84-338-0229-1 LC Card 86-214060
HD779.C4 A75 1984

LAND TENURE - SPAIN - ESTREMADURA.
Alvarado Corrales, Eduardo J. Extremadura . Cáceres [1984?] 101 p. : ISBN 84-600-3663-4 LC Card 86-165503
HD1333.S712 E783 1984

LAND TENURE - SPAIN - HISTORY.
Rueda Hernanz, Germán. La desamortización de Mendizábal y Espartero en España /. Madrid , c1986. 200 p. ; ISBN 84-376-0592-X LC Card 86-216590
HD774 .R84 1986

LAND TENURE - SPAIN - HOSPITALET DE LLOBREGAT - HISTORY - 18TH CENTURY.
Massana i Llorens, Ma. Pilar. L'Hospitalet a l'inici del S. XVIII . L'Hospitalet de Llobregat , 1985. 116 p. : LC Card 86-230458
HD779.H67 M37 1985

LAND TENURE - SPAIN - LOGROÑO - HISTORY - 19TH CENTURY.
Bilbao Díez, Juan Carlos. La desamortización de Pascual Madoz en la ciudad de Logroño y su partido judicial (1855-1856) . Logroño , 1983. 303 p. : ISBN 84-85379-12-8 LC Card 86-215897
HD780.L64 B55 1983

LAND TENURE - SPAIN - PILAS (SEVILLE) - HISTORY.
Camacho Rueda, Eduardo. Propiedad y explotación agrarias en el aljarafe sevillano . Sevilla , 1984. 199 p. : ISBN 84-500-9772-X LC Card 85-135028
HD773 .C18 1984

LAND TENURE - SPAIN - PUENTE-GENIL REGION.
Jurado Carmona, María Isabel. Propiedad y explotación agrarias en Puente Genil /. Córdoba , 1984. 229 p. : ISBN 84-505-0063-X LC Card 85-139166 DDC 338.1/0946/84 19
HD2025.P84 J87 1984
NYPL [JLD 86-2522]

LAND TENURE - SPAIN - RANDA REGION - HISTORY.
Sastre de Sá Torreta, Antoni. Quaderns d'història d'Algaida . Algaida , 1983. 139 p., [8] p. of plates : LC Card 86-181627
HD780.R36 S27 1983

LAND TENURE - SPAIN - TIERRA DE CAMPOS REGION - HISTORY.
Martínez Sopena, Pascual. La Tierra de Campos occidental . [Valladolid] , 1985. 843 p. : ISBN 84-505-1390-1 LC Card 86-231937
HD779.T54 M37 1985

LAND TENURE - SPAIN - VERDÚ - HISTORY - SOURCES.
Bertran i Roigé, Prim. Noves aportacions sobre la repoblació de Verdú en el centenari de la seva carta de Franquesa (1184-1984) /. Lleida , 1984. 23 p., [1] leaf of plates : ISBN 84-00-05783-X LC Card 86-140657
HD780.V44 B47 1984

LAND TENURE - SUDAN.
Kursany, Ibrahim. The dynamics and limits of capitalist development in Sudanese agriculture /. Khartoum , 1982- v. ; LC Card 83-980112 DDC 338.1/09624 19
HD2123.5 .K87 1982 NYPL [JLM 86-825]

LAND TENURE - SWITZERLAND - ZURICH (CANTON) - STATISTICS.
Der Grundeigentumswechsel im Kanton Zürich 1973-1980 . [Zürich] [1982] 74 p. : LC Card 85-161363
HA1608.Z6 A3 Heft 107, Folge 3 HD799.Z8

LAND TENURE - SYRIA - HISTORY.
Khader, Bichara. La question agraire dans le monde arabe . Louvain-la-Neuve , 1984. 631 p. : LC Card 85-169871 DDC 338.1/095691 19
HD2057.5 .K45 1984 NYPL [JLE 86-654]

LAND TENURE - UGANDA - ANKOLE.
Low, G. C. Report of the commissioner appointed to inquire into the operation of the land tenure scheme in Ankole. Entebbe, Uganda [1961?] 30 p. ; LC Card 85-208468
HD994.Z8 A55 1961

LAND TENURE - VANUATU - LONGANA.
Rodman, Margaret, 1947- Masters of tradition . Vancouver , 1987. 198 p. : ISBN 0-7748-0234-0 LC Card 87-158135 DDC 333.3/0993/4 19
HD1125.Z9 L657 1987

LAND TENURE - VIETNAM - HISTORY.
Trng, H Ch Hà N 1982-1983. 2 v. ; LC Card 87-142403
HD890.5 .T78 1982

Land that job! /. Moffatt, Thomas L. Madison, Wis. , 1987, c1982. vii, 152 p. : ISBN 0-910239-09-6 (pbk.) LC Card 87-4319 DDC 650.1/4 19
HF5382.7 .M63 1987

LAND TITLES - REGISTRATION AND TRANSFER - UNITED STATES - STATES - DIRECTORIES.
Williams, 1949- The national recorder /. Denver, CO , c1983. ii, 456 p. ; LC Card 87-106311 DDC 353.9/382326/025 19
HD255 .W54 1983

LAND TRANSFER. see **LAND TITLES - REGISTRATION AND TRANSFER.**

LAND USE - AFRICA.
Espaces disputés en Afrique noire . Paris , c1986. 426 p., [8] p. of plates : ISBN 2-86537-146-8 LC Card 86-210958
HD965 .E86 1986

Timberlake, Lloyd. Africa in crisis . Philadelphia , 1986. 232 p. : ISBN 0-86571-082-1
NYPL [Sc D 87-100]

LAND USE - AFRICA, SUB-SAHARAN.
Enjeux fonciers en Afrique noire /. Bondy , Paris , c1982. 425 p. ; ISBN 2-86537-057-7 : LC Card 83-130847 DDC 333.3/096 19
HD966 .E54 1982 NYPL [JLE 87-950]

LAND USE - ALBERTA - CLYDE - PLANNING.
McCully, Al. Clyde growth report, 1985 /. [Edmonton] [1985] iii, 66 p. : LC Card 86-228996 DDC 338.97123/3 19
HD320.C5 M33 1985

LAND USE - ALBERTA - EAST PRAIRIE RIVER WATERSHED - PLANNING.
McCully, Al. East Prairie Metis Settlement . [Edmonton, Alta.] [1982] iii, 99 p. :Bill. ; LC Card 82-202474 DDC 333.76/17/097123 19
HD319.A4 M52 1982

LAND USE - AMAZON RIVER REGION - CONGRESSES.
Land, people, and planning in contemporary Amazonia /. [Cambridge, Cambridgeshire] , 1980. xvi, 313 p. : LC Card 87-672189
HC167.A42 L36x 1980

Land use analysis . Kumar, Jainendra, 1935- New Delhi, India , 1986, c1985. xvii, 292 p., [7] p. of plates : ISBN 81-210-0063-7 : LC Card 86-901583 DDC 333.76/13/095412
HD879.N34 K86 1986 NYPL [JLD 87-75]

LAND USE - AUSTRALIA - WIMMERA RIVER WATERSHED (VIC.)
Land Conservation Council (Vic.) Wimmera area . Melbourne, Vic. [1986] iii, 84 p., 3 p. of plates : ISBN 0-7241-9146-1 (pbk.) LC Card 87-161929 DDC 333.73/13/099458 19
HD1039.V5 L36 1986

LAND USE - BANGLADESH - STATISTICS.
Thana statistics. [Dacca] , 1981- v. ; LC Card 82-903357 DDC 333.73/13/095492021 19
HD880.6.Z63 T46 1981
NYPL [JLM 87-178]

LAND USE - BRAZIL - GOIÁS (STATE)
Catholic Church. Comissão Pastoral da Terra (Brazil) CPT . Petrópolis , 1983. 105 p. ; LC Card 86-209008
HD499.G65 C38 1983

LAND USE - BRAZIL - SÃO PAULO METROPOLITAN AREA.
Sócrates, Jodete Rios. A cidade invade as águas . [São Paulo] , 1985. 296 p., [2] folded leaves of plates : LC Card 87-118596 DDC 333.91/00981/61 19
HD1696.B84 S427 1985

LAND USE - CALIFORNIA - PLANNING.
Local government mobilehome and mobilehome park policies in California . [Sacramento, Calif.] [1986] iii, 70 p. ; LC Card 86-622920 DDC 333.33/8 19
HD7289.62.U6 L63 1986

LAND USE - CALIFORNIA - SAN FRANCISCO.
Dowall, David E. Back-offices and San Francisco's office development growth cap /. [Berkeley] [1986] 23 p. : LC Card 86-622513 DDC 333.77/17/0979461 19
HD268.S4 D68 1986

LAND USE - CANADA - CONGRESSES.
Land rites and wrongs . Boston , 1988. p. cm. ISBN 0-89946-222-7 LC Card 87-12186 DDC 333.73/13/0971 19
HD171.A15 L28 1988

LAND USE - CENTRAL AMERICA.
Brockett, Charles D., 1946- Land, power, and poverty . Boston , c1988. p. cm. ISBN 0-04-497027-7 LC Card 87-22746 DDC 338.1/09728 19
HD1797 .B76 1988

LAND USE - CONGRESSES.
The management and development of land and seabed resources . London [1985] 139 p. : ISBN 0-903577-29-1 (pbk.) LC Card 86-104896 DDC 333.7 19
HD105 .M36 1985

The Management and development of natural resources . London [1985] 192 p. : ISBN 0-903577-33-X (pbk.) LC Card 86-206154 DDC 333.7 19
HC13 .M35 1985

LAND USE - ENGLAND - LONDON.
Weatheritt, L. Manufacturing industry in Greater London /. London , c1975. ii, 26 p. ; ISBN 0-7168-0853-6 (pbk.) LC Card 82-213745
HD5766.L66 W43 1975

LAND USE - ENVIRONMENTAL ASPECTS.
Vink, A. P. A. [Landschapsecologie en landgebruik. English.] Landscape ecology and land use /. London , New York , 1983, c1980. vi, 264 p. : ISBN 0-582-30077-0 (pbk.) : LC Card 82-10030 DDC 333.73/13 19
HD108.6 .V5613 1983 NYPL [JLE 86-3886]

LAND USE - ENVIRONMENTAL ASPECTS - AUSTRIA - OBERGURGL - MATHEMATICAL MODELS.
Alpine Areas Workshop (1974 : Schloss Laxenburg) Alpine Areas Workshop, May 13-17, 1974 /. Laxenburg [1974] 80 p. : LC Card 82-212849
HC268.O25 A46 1974

LAND USE - ENVIRONMENTAL ASPECTS - KENYA.
Yeager, Rodger. Wildlife, wild death . Albany, NY , c1986. xvi, 173 p. : ISBN 0-88706-168-0 LC Card 86-5791 DDC 333.95/16/09676 19
QL84.6.K4 Y43 1986 ***NYPL [JLE 86-3870]***

LAND USE - ENVIRONMENTAL ASPECTS - TANZANIA.
Yeager, Rodger. Wildlife, wild death . Albany, NY , c1986. xvi, 173 p. : ISBN 0-88706-168-0 LC Card 86-5791 DDC 333.95/16/09676 19
QL84.6.K4 Y43 1986 ***NYPL [JLE 86-3870]***

LAND USE - EUROPE - PLANNING.
Holliday, John C. Land at the centre . London , 1986. xiii, 241 p. : ISBN 0-85683-084-4 (pbk.) : LC Card 87-121817 DDC 333.73/13/0941 19
HD596 .H65 1986

LAND USE - FRANCE.
Guichard-Ayoub, Éliane. Les associations syndicales de propriétaires /. Paris , 1984. 127 p. ; ISBN 2-13-038290-8 ***NYPL [JLC 87-57]***

LAND USE - GERMANY (WEST)
Fuchs, Gerhard, 1939- Die Bundesrepublik Deutschland . Stuttgart , 1983. 296 p. : ISBN 3-12-922191-3 LC Card 83-166769 DDC 330.943/087 19
HD656 .F8 1983 ***NYPL [JLE 86-578]***

LAND USE - GERMANY (WEST) - PLANNING - CITIZEN PARTICIPATION.
Herzog, Werner. Kartographie und Bürgerbeteiligung im Rahmen der vorbereitenden Bauleitplanung . Paderborn , 1986. xi, 164 p. : ISBN 3-506-71256-X LC Card 87-401386 DDC 333.73/17/028 19
HD108.6 .H47 1986

LAND USE - GERMANY (WEST) - REMOTE SENSING.
Angewandte Fernerkundung . Hannover , 1984. x, 285 p. : ISBN 3-87870-904-8 LC Card 85-147235
HD108.8 .A54 1984

LAND USE - GERMANY (WEST) - RHINELAND-PALATINATE.
Scholz, Bernhard, 1948- Bodenschutz zwischen Datenschwemme und Informationsdefizit . Speyer [1986] iii leaves, 385, 4 p. : LC Card 87-126271 DDC 333.73/13/094343 19
HD659.R54 S36 1986

LAND USE - GERMANY (WEST) - RHINELAND-PALATINATE - MATHEMATICAL MODELS.
König, Robert. Die Wohnflächenbestände der Gemeinden der Vorderpfalz . Heidelberg , 1980. [14], 226 p. : ISBN 3-88570-068-9 LC Card 81-136631 DDC 333.73/13/0724 19
HD659.P34 K66 1980
NYPL [L-10 4979 Heft 68]

LAND USE - GERMANY (WEST) - RUHR (REGION) - PLANNING.
Rau, Thomas. Bodenallokation und Bodenpolitik im Ruhrgebiet . Bochum , 1982. viii, 323 p. : ISBN 3-88339-269-3 LC Card 83-130477 DDC 333.73/13/094355 19
HD659.R8 R38 1982 ***NYPL [JLD 86-1715]***

LAND USE - GERMANY (WEST) - STUTTGART - CASE STUDIES.
Borcherdt, Christoph. Der "Landverbrauch," seine Erfassung und Bewertung . Stuttgart , 1985. 196 p. : ISBN 3-88028-104-1 LC Card 87-136211 DDC 333.77/13/094347 19
HD660.S83 B67 1985

LAND USE - GOVERNMENT POLICY - ALASKA.
Maas, Kenneth M. Availability of land for mineral exploration and development in northern Alaska, 1986 /. [Washington, D.C.] [1987] iv, 34 p. : LC Card 86-607920 DDC 333.73 19
HD243.A3 M32 1987

LAND USE - GOVERNMENT POLICY - CANADA - CONGRESSES.
Land rites and wrongs . Boston , 1988. p. cm. ISBN 0-89946-222-7 LC Card 87-12186 DDC 333.73/13/0971 19
HD171.A15 L28 1988

LAND USE - GOVERNMENT POLICY - GERMANY (WEST)
Schlüsselgewalt . Dortmund , c1981. 190 p. : ISBN 3-88142-261-7 : LC Card 81-206444
HD7339.A3 S25 1981

LAND USE - GOVERNMENT POLICY - GERMANY (WEST) - RUHR (REGION)
Rau, Thomas. Bodenallokation und Bodenpolitik im Ruhrgebiet . Bochum , 1982. viii, 323 p. : ISBN 3-88339-269-3 LC Card 83-130477 DDC 333.73/13/094355 19
HD659.R8 R38 1982 ***NYPL [JLD 86-1715]***

LAND USE - GOVERNMENT POLICY - GREAT BRITAIN.
Ambrose, Peter J. Whatever happened to planning? /. London , New York , 1986. xiv, 288 p. : ISBN 0-416-37100-0 LC Card 86-12415 DDC 333.73/17/0941 19
HD596 .A43 1986 ***NYPL [JLD 87-1402]***

Planning control . London , Wolfeboro, N.H. , c1987. 234 p. ; ISBN 0-7099-3790-3 : LC Card 86-24079 DDC 333.73/17/0941 19
HD596 .P53 1987 ***NYPL [JLD 87-803]***

LAND USE - GOVERNMENT POLICY - HAWAII.
Cooper, George. Land and power in Hawaii . Honolulu, Hawaii , c1985. x, 518 p. ; ISBN 0-9615052-0-6 : LC Card 85-72037 DDC 333.73/13/09969 19
HD266.H3 C66 1985 ***NYPL [JLE 87-361]***

LAND USE - GOVERNMENT POLICY - UNITED STATES.
Black, Peter E. Conservation of water and related land resources /. Totowa, N.J. , 1987. xvi, 336 p. : ISBN 0-8476-7567-X LC Card 87-4770 DDC 333.91/16/0973 19
HD1694 .A5105 1987

Plotkin, Sidney. Keep out . Berkeley , c1987. xiii, 360 p. ; ISBN 0-520-05806-2 LC Card 86-30807 DDC 333.3/0973 19
HD205 .P56 1987

LAND USE - GOVERNMENT POLICY - UNITED STATES - CONGRESSES.
Land rites and wrongs . Boston , 1988. p. cm. ISBN 0-89946-222-7 LC Card 87-12186 DDC 333.73/13/0971 19
HD171.A15 L28 1988

LAND USE - GREAT BRITAIN.
Fothergill, Steve. Property and industrial development /. London , Wolfeboro, N.H. , 1987. 187 p. : ISBN 0-09-170741-2 (pbk.) : LC Card 87-2627 DDC 333.3/8/0941 19
HD598 .F68 1987

LAND USE - GREAT BRITAIN - PLANNING.
Holliday, John C. Land at the centre . London , 1986. xiii, 241 p. : ISBN 0-85683-084-4 (pbk.) : LC Card 87-121817 DDC 333.73/13/0941 19
HD596 .H65 1986

LAND USE - HISTORY.
Cosgrove, Denis E. Social formation and symbolic landscape /. Totowa, N.J. , 1985, c1984. 293 p. : ISBN 0-389-20540-0 LC Card 84-21629 DDC 304.2 19
GF90 .C67 1985 ***NYPL [JLD 86-2206]***

LAND USE - HONG KONG - PLANNING.
Bristow, M. R. (M. Roger) Land-use planning in Hong Kong . Hong Kong , New York , 1987, c1984. xii, 328 p., [16] p. of plates : ISBN 0-19-581577-7 (pbk.) : LC Card 87-5524 DDC 333.73/17/095125 19
HD943.2 .B75 1987

LAND USE - HUNGARY.
A Föld és a népgazdaság /. [Budapest] , 1985. 514 p. ; ISBN 963-03-2232-3 LC Card 86-228739
HD640.5.Z63 F65 1985

A Magyarországi településrendszer strukturális változása /. Budapest , 1984. 155 p., [1] folded leaf of plates : ISBN 963-03-2079-7 (Magy. nemz. bibl.) LC Card 85-231254
HD640.5 .M343 1984

LAND USE - ILLINOIS - EAST PEORIA - PLANNING.
Urban Land Institute. R.S. Wallace Station, East Peoria, Illinois . Washington, D.C. (1090 Vermont Ave., N.W., Washington 20005) , c1986. 36 p. : LC Card 86-216045 DDC 333.77/17/0977352 19
HD268.E26 U73 1986

LAND USE - INDIA.
Bora, Ajit Kumar, 1942- Pattern of land utilization in Assam /. Delhi , 1986. x, 203 p. ; ISBN 81-7049-012-X : LC Card 86-902810 DDC 333.73/13/0954162 19
HD873 .B67 1986

LAND USE - INDIA - ASSAM.
Bora, Ajit Kumar, 1942- Pattern of land utilization in Assam /. Delhi , 1986. x, 203 p. ; ISBN 81-7049-012-X : LC Card 86-902810 DDC 333.73/13/0954162 19
HD873 .B67 1986

LAND USE - INDIA, NORTHEASTERN - CONGRESSES.
Land use pattern in north-east India /. Ludhiana , c1986. 167 p. : LC Card 86-903235 DDC 333.73/13/09541 19
HD879.I425 L36 1986

LAND USE - ISRAEL - PLANNING - HISTORY.
Dies ist das Land . [Sweden] 1946 (Lund : Berlingska Boktryckeriet) 102, [1] p., [1] folded leaf of plates : LC Card 86-225837
HD850 .D54 1946

LAND USE - ITALY - ABRUZZI.
Piazzo, Pietrenzo, 1935- Una valutazione intersettoriale costi benefici estesa al territorio . Roma , c1984. viii, 224 p., 6 folded leaves of plates : LC Card 84-250428
HC307.A2 P53 1984

LAND USE - ITALY - LAZIO - CLASSIFICATION - COLLECTED WORKS.
Produttività potenziale e classificazione dei terreni. Roma , 1985- v. <1 > in <5 > : LC Card 87-105342
HD679.L39 P76 1985

LAND USE - ITALY - LOMBARDY - HISTORY - 18TH CENTURY.
La Proprietà fondiaria in Lombardia dal catasto teresiano all'età napoleonica /. Milano , 1986. 2 v. ; ISBN 88-343-0341-5 (set) : LC Card 87-108100
HD679.L6 P76 1986

LAND USE - ITALY - SACCO RIVER VALLEY - CLASSIFICATION.
Produttività potenziale e classificazione dei terreni. Roma , 1985- v. <1 > in <5 > : LC Card 87-105342
HD679.L39 P76 1985

LAND USE - KANSAS - LENEXA.
Bedford Properties, Lenexa, Kansas . Washington, D.C. (1090 Vermont Ave., N.W., Washington 20005) [1986?] 37 p. : LC Card 87-141440 DDC 333.3/8/09781675 19
HD268.L46 B43 1986

LAND USE - KENYA - KAKAMEGA DISTRICT.
Bradley, Phil. The district resource analysis as applied to Kakamega District /. Nairobi [1984] 11 leaves : LC Card 87-112452 DDC 333.75 19
HD9769.F843 K425 1984

LAND USE - KENYA - REMOTE SENSING.
Agatsiva, J. L. Land use mapping of Kenya using remote sensing techniques /. [Nairobi] , 1982. iv, 39 p. : LC Card 84-980919 DDC 333.73/13/028 19
HD983.Z7 A38 1982

LAND USE - LAW AND LEGISLATION - BRAZIL - SÃO PAULO (STATE)
Sócrates, Jodete Rios. A cidade invade as águas . [São Paulo] , 1985. 296 p., [2] folded leaves of plates : LC Card 87-118596 DDC 333.91/00981/61 19
HD1696.B84 S427 1985

LAND USE - LAW AND LEGISLATION - GREAT BRITAIN.
Planning control . London , Wolfeboro, N.H. , c1987. 234 p. ; ISBN 0-7099-3790-3 : LC Card 86-24079 DDC 333.73/17/0941 19
HD596 .P53 1987 ***NYPL [JLD 87-803]***

LAND USE - LAW AND LEGISLATION - HUNGARY.
A Föld és a népgazdaság /. [Budapest] , 1985. 514 p. ; ISBN 963-03-2232-3 LC Card 86-228739
HD640.5.Z63 F65 1985

LAND USE - LUANGWA RIVER WATERSHED (ZAMBIA AND MOZAMBIQUE) - CONGRESSES.
Lupande Development Workshop (1983 : Nyamaluma Wildlife Conservation Camp) Proceedings of the Lupande Development Workshop . Chipata, Zambia , 1984. x, 121 p. : LC Card 84-980605 DDC 333.73/17/096894 19
HD993.Z8 L835 1983 ***NYPL [JLG 87-67]***

LAND USE - MALAWI.
Pachai, Bridglal. Land and politics in Malawi, 1875-1975 /. Kingston, Ontario, Canada , c1978. xiv, 245 p., [20] p. of plates : ISBN 0-919642-82-9 LC Card 86-673708
HD997 .P32x 1978

LAND USE - MANITOBA.
Rural municipality of Hanover . [Winnipeg, Man.] [1976?] iv, 55 p. : LC Card 82-219722
HC118.H34 R87 1976

Land use mapping of Kenya using remote sensing techniques /. Agatsiva, J. L. [Nairobi] , 1982. iv, 39 p. : LC Card 84-980919 DDC 333.73/13/028 19
HD983.Z7 A38 1982

LAND USE - MATHEMATICAL MODELS.
Foot, David H.S. A comparison of some land-use allocation/interaction models [microform] /. Reading [Berkshire] , 1974. 36 p. : ISBN 0-7049-0338-5
*NYPL [*ZT-1712 no.13]*

LAND USE - MEXICO - QUINTANA ROO (STATE)
Quintana Roo . Puerto Morelos, Q.R. , 1980. iv, 203 p., [32] leaves of plates : LC Card 84-222175
HC137.Q5 Q55 1980

LAND USE - NEPAL - CHITAWAN (DISTRICT) - PLANNING.
LAND USE - NEPAL - PARSA (DISTRICT) - PLANNING.
LAND USE - NEW ZEALAND - HECTOR MOUNTAINS REGION - PLANNING.
The Remarkables and Hector mountains, Otago, New Zealand . Dunedin, N.Z. , 1977. 215 p., [9] leaves of plates (some folded) : LC Card 85-115616
HD1120.5.Z8 R457 1977

LAND USE - NEW ZEALAND - REMARKABLES, THE, REGION - PLANNING.
The Remarkables and Hector mountains, Otago, New Zealand . Dunedin, N.Z. , 1977. 215 p., [9] leaves of plates (some folded) : LC Card 85-115616
HD1120.5.Z8 R457 1977

LAND USE - PACIFIC ISLANDS (TRUST TERRITORY) - STATISTICS.
Barr, Lorna R. Land of the Trust islands . [Victoria, B.C.] [1978] 36 p. : LC Card 83-226106 DDC 333.3/0996/5 19
HD1121.Z63 B37 1978

LAND USE - PANAMA - ALBROOK - PLANNING.
Panama. Ministerio de Vivienda. Redeterminación de usos del suelo en Ancón y redelimitación del sitio de defensa de Albrook /. [Panama, Panama] [between 1981 and 1987] [15] leaves : LC Card 87-403861 DDC 333.73/17/097287 19
HD385.A4 P36 1981

Land use pattern in north-east India / edited by B.B. Dutta. Ludhiana : Gagan Publishers, c1986. 167 p. : ill. ; 23 cm. Papers presented at a seminar. Includes bibliographies and index. LC Card 86-903235 DDC 333.73/13/09541 19
1. Land use - India, Northeastern - Congresses. I. Dutta, B. B.
HD879.I425 L36 1986

LAND USE - PENNSYLVANIA - HISTORY - 18TH CENTURY.
Schweitzer, Mary M. Custom and contract . New York , 1987. xii, 271 p. : ISBN 0-231-06288-5 LC Card 87-8003 DDC 338.9748 19
HC107.P4 S417 1987

LAND USE - PLANNING.
Vink, A. P. A. [Landschapsecologie en landgebruik. English.] Landscape ecology and land use /. London , New York , 1983, c1980. vi, 264 p. : ISBN 0-582-30077-0 (pbk.) : LC Card 82-10030 DDC 333.73/13 19
HD108.6 .V5613 1983 NYPL [JLE 86-3886]

LAND USE - PLANNING - ENVIRONMENTAL ASPECTS.
Marsh, William M. Landscape planning . New York , 1986. p. cm. ISBN 0-471-85434-4 LC Card 86-28951 DDC 712 19
HD108.6 .M37 1986

Land-use planning in Hong Kong . Bristow, M. R. (M. Roger) Hong Kong , New York , 1987, c1984. xii, 328 p., [16] p. of plates : ISBN 0-19-581577-7 (pbk.) : LC Card 87-5524 DDC 333.73/17/095125 19
HD943.2 .B75 1987

LAND USE - PLANNING - MAPS.
Herzog, Werner. Kartographie und Bürgerbeteiligung im Rahmen der vorbereitenden Bauleitplanung . Paderborn , 1986. xi, 164 p. : ISBN 3-506-71256-X LC Card 87-401386 DDC 333.73/17/028 19
HD108.6 .H47 1986

LAND USE - REMOTE SENSING.
Angewandte Fernerkundung . Hannover , 1984. x, 285 p. : ISBN 3-87870-904-8 LC Card 85-147235
HD108.8 .A54 1984

LAND USE - REMOTE SENSING - CONGRESSES.
Remote sensing and tropical land management /. [New York] , c1986. xii, 365 p., [16] p. of plates : ISBN 0-471-90889-4 : LC Card 85-17932 DDC 333.73/13/028 19
HD108.8 .R45 1986 NYPL [JLE 87-943]

LAND USE, RURAL - ALBERTA.
Swinnerton, Guy S. Recreation on agricultural land in Alberta /. Edmonton, Alta. [1982] x, 211 p. : LC Card 83-149875 DDC 333.76/17/097123 19
HD319.A4 S94 1982 NYPL [JLF 86-851]

LAND USE, RURAL - BRAZIL - CEARÁ (STATE)
O Norte cearense /. Recife , 1985. 303 p. : LC Card 86-209022
HD1875.C4 N67 1985

LAND USE, RURAL - BRAZIL - SÃO SEBASTIÃO REGION (SÃO PAULO)
Silva, Armando Corrêa da. O litoral norte do Estado de São Paulo . São Paulo , 1975. 273 p. : LC Card 85-134276
HC189.S343 S58 1975

LAND USE, RURAL - BRAZIL - STATISTICS.
Estatísticas cadastrais . Brasília , 1985- <v. 1-2; in 2 > : LC Card 87-117732
HD498 .E77 1985

LAND USE, RURAL - CANADA.
Gierman, D. M. Rural to urban land conversion =. [Ottawa] , Hull, Que. , c1977. xvii, 74 p. ; ISBN 0-662-01301-8
NYPL [JLM 80-106 no.16]

LAND USE, RURAL - CHINA - HUNAN PROVINCE - HISTORY.
Perdue, Peter C., 1949- Exhausting the earth . Cambridge, Mass. , 1987. xvii, 331 p. : ISBN 0-674-27504-7 LC Card 87-5067 DDC 338.1/0951/215 19
HD2100.H86 P47 1987

LAND USE, RURAL - CONGRESSES.
Demands on rural lands . Boulder, Colo. , 1987. xvi, 336 p. : ISBN 0-8133-7361-1 (pbk. : alk. paper) LC Card 87-50751 DDC 333.76/13 19
HD105 .D43 1987

LAND USE, RURAL - CZECHOSLOVAKIA - BOHEMIA - HISTORY - 19TH CENTURY.
Jeleček, Leoš. Zemědělství a půdní fond v Čechách ve 2. polovině 19. století /. Praha , 1985. 283 p. : LC Card 86-199876
HD640.3.Z8 B634 1985

LAND USE, RURAL - DENMARK.
Jensen, Knud Erik. Landbrugsarealer, landskabeligt og rekreativt /. [Copenhagen] , 1982. 248 p. : LC Card 84-172974
HD736 .J46 1982

LAND USE, RURAL - ENVIRONMENTAL ASPECTS - DEVELOPING COUNTRIES.
Ellenberg, Heinz, 1913- [Desarrollar sin destruir. German.] Entwicklung ohne Rückschläge . Eschborn , 1984. 139 p. : ISBN 3-88085-228-6 LC Card 86-168369
HD1131 .E4515 1984

Lands at risk in the Third World . Boulder , 1987. xiii, 416 p. : ISBN 0-8133-7311-5 (pbk. : alk. paper) : LC Card 86-51423 DDC 333.73/13 19
HD1131 .L37 1987

LAND USE, RURAL - ENVIRONMENTAL ASPECTS - HUNGARY.
A Környezeti erőforrások gazdasági értékelésének módszertani kérdései /. Pécs [Budapest] , 1981. 78 leaves ; LC Card 82-202704
HD9502.E83 K68 1981 NYPL [JLE 87-219]

LAND USE, RURAL - ENVIRONMENTAL ASPECTS - TROPICS.
Ellenberg, Heinz, 1913- [Desarrollar sin destruir. German.] Entwicklung ohne Rückschläge . Eschborn , 1984. 139 p. : ISBN 3-88085-228-6 LC Card 86-168369
HD1131 .E4515 1984

LAND USE, RURAL - GERMANY (WEST) - DATA PROCESSING.
Filter, Wolfgang, 1952- Aufbau und Ergebnisse einer Gesamtrechnung für das land- und forstwirtschaftliche Bodenvermögen in der Bundesrepublik Deutschland /. Frankfurt am Main , New York , c1984. xiii, 288 p. : ISBN 3-8204-5290-7 LC Card 85-198973
HD658 .F55 1984

LAND USE, RURAL - GERMANY (WEST) - LOWER SAXONY - STATISTICS.
Landwirtschaftszählung 1979, Gartenbauerhebung 1981/82 . Hannover , 1983. xv, 132 p. ; LC Card 85-117833
HD9013.7.L68 L37 1983

LAND USE, RURAL - GERMANY WEST - MATHEMATICAL MODELS.
Bauer, Jürgen. Quantitative Entwicklungsplanung für ländliche Regionen . Bochum , 1979. 382 p. in various pagings : ISBN 3-88339-087-9 : LC Card 80-470152
HT395.G4 B39 1979 NYPL [JLD 86-1628]

LAND USE, RURAL - GERMANY (WEST) - NORTH RHINE-WESTPHALIA - STATISTICS.
Agrarberichterstattung Nordrhein-Westfalen 1983 . Düsseldorf [1984] 263 p. ; LC Card 87-407317 DDC 943/.55 s 338.1/0943/55021 19
HA1320.N6 A32 Heft 532 HD1960.N67

Agrarberichterstattung Nordrhein-Westfalen 1983 . Düsseldorf [1985] 191 p. ; LC Card 87-407316 DDC 943/.55 s 338.1/0943/55021 19
HA1320.N6 A32 Heft 531 HD1960.N67

LAND USE, RURAL - GERMANY (WEST) - PLANNING.
Filter, Wolfgang, 1952- Aufbau und Ergebnisse einer Gesamtrechnung für das land- und forstwirtschaftliche Bodenvermögen in der Bundesrepublik Deutschland /. Frankfurt am Main , New York , c1984. xiii, 288 p. : ISBN 3-8204-5290-7 LC Card 85-198973
HD658 .F55 1984

LAND USE, RURAL - GOVERNMENT POLICY - GREAT BRITAIN.
Countryside conflicts . Aldershot, Hants, England , Brookfield, Vt., U. S. A. , c1986. vi, 378 p. [4] leaves of plates : ISBN 0-566-05088-9 : LC Card 85-24603 DDC 333.76/17/0941 19
HD596 .C675 1986 NYPL [JLD 86-2487]

LAND USE, RURAL - GOVERNMENT POLICY - ITALY - MILAN REGION.
Metropoli e agricoltura /. Milano , c1982. 319 p. : LC Card 82-246692 DDC 333.76/13/094521 19
HD680.M54 M47 1982
NYPL [JLD 86-3678]

LAND USE, RURAL - GOVERNMENT POLICY - NEW ENGLAND.
Schnidman, Frank. Retention of land for agriculture . Boston, MA , 1988. p. cm. ISBN 0-89946-219-7 LC Card 87-5580 DDC 333.76/16/0974 19
HD266.A11 S36 1988

LAND USE, RURAL - GOVERNMENT POLICY - NEW JERSEY.
New Jersey. Dept. of Agriculture. Grassroots, an agriculture retention and development program for New Jersey. [Trenton, N.J.] [1980] 65 p. : LC Card 81-621630 DDC 333.76/17/09749 19
HD211.N5 N47 1980 NYPL [JLF 86-1575]

LAND USE, RURAL - GOVERNMENT POLICY - ONTARIO.
Ontario. Foodland preservation . Toronto, Ont. [1986?] 16 p. : LC Card 86-226909 DDC 333.76/16/09713 19
HD319.O5 O5 1986

LAND USE, RURAL - GOVERNMENT POLICY - UNITED STATES.

Webb, Shwu-Eng. Idling erodible cropland . Washington, D.C. [1986] iii, 31 p. : LC Card 86-601632 DDC 338.1 s 338.1/62 19
HD1751 .A91854 no. 550 HD256

LAND USE, RURAL - GREAT BRITAIN.
Countryside conflicts . Aldershot, Hants, England , Brookfield, Vt., U. S.A. , c1986. vi, 378 p. [4] leaves of plates : ISBN 0-566-05088-9 : LC Card 85-24603 DDC 333.76/17/0941 19
HD596 .C675 1986 ***NYPL [JLD 86-2487]***

LAND USE, RURAL - HONDURAS - STATISTICS.
Tosco, Manuel. Aprovechamiento y dominio de las tierras en 1950-51 /. Tegucigalpa, D.C., Honduras [1952] 33 p. ; LC Card 85-197157
HD366 .T66 1952

LAND USE, RURAL - HUNGARY.
Beluszky, Pál. Magyarország falutipusai /. Budapest , 1982. 167 p. : ISBN 963-7321-96-9 LC Card 84-159502
HD640.5.Z7 B44 1982

LAND USE, RURAL - INDIA.
Bora, Ajit Kumar, 1942- Pattern of land utilization in Assam /. Delhi , 1986. x, 203 p. ; ISBN 81-7049-012-X : LC Card 86-902810 DDC 333.73/13/0954162 19
HD873 .B67 1986

LAND USE, RURAL - INDIA - ASSAM.
Bora, Ajit Kumar, 1942- Pattern of land utilization in Assam /. Delhi , 1986. x, 203 p. ; ISBN 81-7049-012-X : LC Card 86-902810 DDC 333.73/13/0954162 19
HD873 .B67 1986

LAND USE, RURAL - INDIA - CASE STUDIES.
Kumar, Jainendra, 1935- Land use analysis . New Delhi, India , 1986, c1985. xvii, 292 p., [7] p. of plates : ISBN 81-210-0063-7 : LC Card 86-901583 DDC 333.76/13/095412
HD879.N34 K86 1986 ***NYPL [JLD 87-75]***

LAND USE, RURAL - INDIA - NĀLANDĀ DISTRICT - CASE STUDIES.
Kumar, Jainendra, 1935- Land use analysis . New Delhi, India , 1986, c1985. xvii, 292 p., [7] p. of plates : ISBN 81-210-0063-7 : LC Card 86-901583 DDC 333.76/13/095412
HD879.N34 K86 1986 ***NYPL [JLD 87-75]***

LAND USE, RURAL - INDIA - PUNJAB - MATHEMATICAL MODELS.
Astroth, Joseph H., 1955- Understanding peasant agriculture . Chicago, Ill. , 1987. p. cm. ISBN 0-89065-127-2 (pbk.) : LC Card 87-15099 DDC 333.76/13/0724 19
HD879.P8 A77 1987

LAND USE, RURAL - KENYA - HISTORY.
Leo, Christopher. Land and class in Kenya /. Toronto , Buffalo [N.Y.] , c1984. xii, 244 p. : ISBN 0-8020-2532-3 ***NYPL [JLE 86-1242]***

LAND USE, RURAL - PLANNING - CONGRESSES.
Demands on rural lands . Boulder, Colo. , 1987. xvi, 336 p. : ISBN 0-8133-7361-1 (pbk. : alk. paper) LC Card 87-50751 DDC 333.76/13 19
HD105 .D43 1987

LAND USE, RURAL - PRAIRIE PROVINCES - HISTORY.
Breen, David. The Canadian prairie west and the ranching frontier, 1874-1924 /. Toronto , Buffalo , c1983. xiii, 302 p., [4] p. of plates : ISBN 0-8020-5548-6 LC Card 83-143575 DDC 338.1/762/009712 19
HD9433.C22 P733 1983 ***NYPL [HY 87-755]***

LAND USE, RURAL - SAHEL.
Kapp, Gerald B., 1956- Agroforstliche Landnutzung in der Sahel-Sudanzone . München , c1987. xii, 397 p. : ISBN 3-8039-0347-5 LC Card 87-419915 DDC 333.76/13/0966 19
HD1010.5.Z63 K37 1987

LAND USE, RURAL - SCOTLAND.
Armstrong, A. M. Land ownership and land use in the Scottish Highlands /. [Aberdeen, Grampian] , 1983. vii, 150 p. : LC Card 83-209521 DDC 333.3/09411/5 19
HD616 .A76 1983 ***NYPL [JLF 86-457]***

LAND USE, RURAL - SOUTH AFRICA - VERLOREVLEI.
Sinclair, Sharyn. The rural settlement of Verlorenvlei in historical perspective /. Rondebosch, South Africa [1980] 234 leaves : LC Card 86-210654
HD991.Z9 V477 1980

LAND USE, RURAL - SOUTHERN STATES.
Healy, Robert G. Competition for land in the American South . Washington, D.C. , c1985. xxxii, 333 p. : ISBN 0-89164-094-0 (pbk.) LC Card 85-25459 DDC 333.76/13/0975 19
HD266.A13 H43 1985 ***NYPL [JLE 86-2724]***

LAND USE, RURAL - SUDAN.
Behnke, Roy H., 1947- Open-range management and property rights in pastoral Africa . London [1985] 29 p. : LC Card 86-209817 DDC 333.2 19
HD977.Z63 B44 1985

Kapp, Gerald B., 1956- Agroforstliche Landnutzung in der Sahel-Sudanzone . München , c1987. xii, 397 p. : ISBN 3-8039-0347-5 LC Card 87-419915 DDC 333.76/13/0966 19
HD1010.5.Z63 K37 1987

LAND USE, RURAL - UNITED STATES.
Waterfield, Larry W. Conflict and crisis in rural America /. New York , 1986. iv, 235 p. : ISBN 0-03-006074-5 (alk. paper) : LC Card 85-19366 DDC 333.76/0973 19
HD256 .W35 1986 ***NYPL [JLE 86-2792]***

LAND USE, RURAL - UNITED STATES - PLANNING.
Planning and zoning for farmland protection . East Lansing, MI , c1987. 58 p. : LC Card 87-119320 DDC 333.76/17/0973 19
HD256 .P57 1987

LAND USE, RURAL - ZAMBIA - LUSAKA REGION.
Van den Berg, L. M. Anticipating urban growth in Africa . Lusaka, Zambia , 1984. viii, 167 p., [4] p. of plates : LC Card 86-980297 DDC 307.7/6/096894 19
HD993.Z9 L88 1984

LAND USE - SCANDINAVIA - CLASSIFICATION.
Nordisk arealklassifikation /. København [1985] 19 p. ; ISBN 87-88083-23-3 LC Card 86-162708
HD730 .N67 1985

LAND USE - SENEGAL.
Agroforstliche Landnutzung im Einzugsbereich zentraler Orte im Sahel . Köln , 1983. ix, 374 p. : ISBN 3-8039-0276-2 LC Card 87-102956 DDC 333.73/13/09663 19
HD1019.Z63 A38 1983

LAND USE - SPAIN - CENETE - HISTORY.
Arias Abellán, Jesús. Propiedad y usos de la tierra en el Marquesado del Cenete /. [Granada] , 1984. iv, 439 p. : ISBN 84-338-0229-1 LC Card 86-214060
HD779.C4 A75 1984

LAND USE - SPAIN - ESTREMADURA.
Gurría Gascón, José Luis. El paisaje de montaña en Extremadura . Cáceres [1985?] 273 p. : ISBN 84-600-3949-8 LC Card 87-111451
HC387.E7 G87 1985

LAND USE - SPAIN - RANDA REGION - HISTORY.
Sastre de Sá Torreta, Antoni. Quaderns d'història d'Algaida . Algaida , 1983. 139 p., [8] p. of plates : LC Card 86-181627
HD780.R36 S27 1983

LAND USE - SPAIN - SEGOVIA - HISTORY.
Martínez Moro, Jesús. La tierra en la comunidad de Segovia . [Valladolid] [Salamanca] , c1985. 252 p. : ISBN 84-86192-37-4 LC Card 86-211593
HD780.S44 M37 1985

LAND USE - STUDY AND TEACHING - CONGRESSES.
Land, water, and mineral resources in science education /. Oxford , New York , 1987. xii, 312 p. : ISBN 0-08-033915-8 : LC Card 86-30527 DDC 333.7/07/101724 19
HC28 .L27 1987

LAND USE - STUDY AND TEACHING - DEVELOPING COUNTRIES - CONGRESSES.
Land, water, and mineral resources in science education /. Oxford , New York , 1987. xii, 312 p. : ISBN 0-08-033915-8 : LC Card 86-30527 DDC 333.7/07/101724 19
HC28 .L27 1987

LAND USE SURVEYS - NEW ZEALAND - HECTOR MOUNTAINS REGION.
The Remarkables and Hector mountains, Otago, New Zealand . Dunedin, N.Z. , 1977. 215 p., [9] leaves of plates (some folded) : LC Card 85-115616
HD1120.5.Z8 R457 1977

LAND USE SURVEYS - NEW ZEALAND - REMARKABLES, THE, REGION.
The Remarkables and Hector mountains, Otago, New Zealand . Dunedin, N.Z. , 1977. 215 p., [9] leaves of plates (some folded) : LC Card 85-115616
HD1120.5.Z8 R457 1977

LAND USE - SWEDEN.
Markanvändningen i Sverige. Stockholm , 1983. 86 p. : ISBN 91-38-08032-X (LiberFörlag) LC Card 84-173942
HD766 .M37 1983

LAND USE - SWITZERLAND.
Flückiger, Hans. Siedlungsstruktur . Bern , c1985. 118 p. : ISBN 3-258-03529-6 : LC Card 86-134805
HN603.5 .F58 1985 ***NYPL [JLE 86-3789]***

Rumley, Pierre-Alain. Aménagement du territoire et utilisation du sol . Zürich , c1984. x, 176 p. : LC Card 85-104773
HD796 .R86 1984

LAND USE - SWITZERLAND - PLANNING.
Rumley, Pierre-Alain. Aménagement du territoire et utilisation du sol . Zürich , c1984. x, 176 p. : LC Card 85-104773
HD796 .R86 1984

LAND USE - SWITZERLAND - ZURICH (CANTON) - STATISTICS.
Der Grundeigentumswechsel im Kanton Zürich 1973-1980 . [Zürich] [1982] 74 p. : LC Card 85-161363
HA1608.Z6 A3 Heft 107, Folge 3 HD799.Z8

LAND USE - TROPICS - CONGRESSES.
Remote sensing and tropical land management /. [New York] , c1986. xii, 365 p., [16] p. of plates : ISBN 0-471-90889-4 : LC Card 85-17932 DDC 333.73/13/028 19
HD108.8 .R45 1986 ***NYPL [JLE 87-943]***

LAND USE - UNITED STATES - CONGRESSES.
Land rites and wrongs . Boston , 1988. p. cm. ISBN 0-89946-222-7 LC Card 87-12186 DDC 333.73/13/0971 19
HD171.A15 L28 1988

LAND USE - UNITED STATES - PLANNING.
Cervero, Robert. Suburban gridlock /. New Brunswick, N.J. , c1986. xxiii, 248 p. : ISBN 0-88285-115-2 : LC Card 86-2628 DDC 388.4/13142/0973 19
HE355.3.C64 C47 1986
NYPL [JLE 86-4446]

LAND USE - UNITED STATES - PLANNING - CASE STUDIES.
Growth management . Washington, D.C. , c1986. iv, 218 p. : ISBN 0-87420-655-3 (pbk.) LC Card 86-50332 DDC 307.1/4/0973 19
HD205 .G76 1986 ***NYPL [JLE 87-558]***

LAND USE - UNITED STATES - PLANNING - CONGRESSES.
Facility location and land use . New York, N.Y. , c1986. vii, 40 p. : ISBN 0-87262-574-5 (pbk.) LC Card 86-25926 DDC 338.6/042 19
HD171.A15 F33 1986

LAND USE, URBAN.
Lungo, Mario. El problema de la tierra urbana . Ciudad Universitaria Rodrigo Facio [Costa Rica] , 1986. 42 p. ; LC Card 87-127789 DDC 333.77/13 19
HD1391 .L86 1986

Stover, Vergil G., 1933- Transportation and land development /. Englewood Cliffs, N.J. , c1988. xiii, 239 p. : ISBN 0-13-930413-4 : LC Card 87-11419 DDC 625.7/25 19
HE335 .S76 1988

LAND USE, URBAN - ALBERTA - FORECASTING - MATHEMATICAL MODELS.
Weideman, Donald James. A model to predict urban influenced land prices /. [Edmonton, Alta.] [1986] xi, 294 p. : ISBN 0-88654-148-4 (pbk.) LC Card 86-231786 DDC 333.33/7 19
HD319.A4 W45 1986

LAND USE, URBAN - BRAZIL - COLLECTED WORKS.
Pesquisas sobre o problema fundiário urbano. [São Paulo] [Brasília?] , 1983. 6 v. in 8 ; LC Card 87-404400 DDC 333.77/13/0981 19
HD496 .P47 1983

LAND USE, URBAN - BRAZIL - PORTO ALEGRE.
Clichevsky, Nora. O mercado de terra na região metropolitana de Porto Alegre /. Porto Alegre , 1982. 60 p. : LC Card 84-256219
HD500.P67 C57 1982

LAND USE, URBAN - CALIFORNIA.
Massa, Alison K. Housing and the environment /. Sacramento, CA (921 10th St., Sacramento 95814-2774) [1985?] 2 v. : LC Card 87-621018 DDC 363.7 19
HD266.C2 M37 1985

LAND USE, URBAN - CAMEROON - YAOUNDÉ.
Yaoundé, typologie de l'habitat . [Yaoundé, Cameroon] [197-?] [26] p. : LC Card 83-106947
HD1019.Z9 Y368 1970z

LAND USE, URBAN - COLOMBIA - VALLE DEL CAUCA.
Mosquera Torres, Gilma. Clases, segregación y barrios /. Cali, Colombia , 1984. 126 p. : LC Card 86-218143
HD7325.V35 M67 1984

LAND USE, URBAN - DEVELOPING COUNTRIES.
Durand-Lasserve, Alain. L'exclusion des pauvres dans les villes du Tiers-Monde . Paris , c1986. 198 p. : ISBN 2-85802-613-8 LC Card 87-111461
HD7391 .D79 1986

LAND USE, URBAN - ECUADOR - QUITO REGION.
Tierras para asentamientos populares . Quito, Ecuador , 1985. 378 p. : LC Card 87-400165 DDC 333.77/13/0986613 19
HD530.Q58 T54 1985

LAND USE, URBAN - ENERGY CONSUMPTION.
Energy and cities /. New Brunswick, U. S.A. , c1985. 173 p. : ISBN 0-87855-813-6 (pbk.) LC Card 84-24074 DDC 333.79/13/091732 19
HD108.2 .E525 1985 ***NYPL [JLE 86-4441]***

LAND USE, URBAN - ENGLAND - LONDON - FORECASTING.
The London property market in AD 2000 /. London , New York , 1986. xi, 155 p. : ISBN 0-419-14100-6 : LC Card 86-217227 DDC 333.33/22/09421 19
HD610.L6 L66 1986

LAND USE, URBAN - GOVERNMENT POLICY - BRAZIL - COLLECTED WORKS.
Pesquisas sobre o problema fundiário urbano. [São Paulo] [Brasília?] , 1983. 6 v. in 8 ; LC Card 87-404400 DDC 333.77/13/0981 19
HD496 .P47 1983

LAND USE, URBAN - GOVERNMENT POLICY - DEVELOPING COUNTRIES.
Kitay, Michael G. Land acquisition in developing countries . Boston , c1985. xx, 199 p. ; ISBN 0-89946-192-1 LC Card 85-7225 DDC 333.1/3/091724 19
HD1131 .K58 1985 ***NYPL [JLE 86-3827]***

LAND USE, URBAN - GOVERNMENT POLICY - JAPAN - TOKYO METROPOLITAN AREA.
Hanayama, Yuzuru, 1939- Land markets and land policy in a metropolitan area . Boston, MA , 1986. xiv, 162 p. : ISBN 0-89946-197-2 LC Card 85-13867 DDC 333.77/13/0952135 19
HD920.T62 H36 1986 ***NYPL [JLE 86-4398]***

LAND USE, URBAN - GOVERNMENT POLICY - UNITED STATES - CONGRESSES.
The Urban caldron /. Boston, Mass. , 1986. 152 p. ; ISBN 0-89946-207-3 LC Card 85-21641 DDC 333.73/0973 19
HD257 .U73 1986 ***NYPL [JLE 86-4372]***

LAND USE, URBAN - INDIA.
Dange, Manohar N. Theory and practice of urban land values in India /. Bombay , 1983. xii, 132 p. ; LC Card 83-903969 DDC 333.33/2/0954 19
HD878 .D36 1983 ***NYPL [JLD 87-729]***

LAND USE, URBAN - INDIA - UTTAR PRADESH.
Chaurasia, B. P. (Bhanu Pratap) Urban land use and planning /. Allahabad, India , 1987. xxiii, 347 p. : ISBN 81-85076-20-0 : LC Card 87-900386 DDC 333.77/17/09542 19
HD879.U8 C53 1987

LAND USE, URBAN - ITALY - MILAN - HISTORY - 18TH CENTURY.
Mazzucchelli, Vanna. Catasto e volto urbano . Roma , 1983. 244 p. ; LC Card 86-106099
HD680.M54 M39 1983

LAND USE, URBAN - LATIN AMERICA - CONGRESSES.
Abitazione e periferie urbane nei paesi in via di sviluppo . Milano, Italy , c1985. 450 p. : LC Card 86-132019
HD7287.96.L29 A25 1985
NYPL [JLD 87-1173]

LAND USE, URBAN - MEDITERRANEAN REGION - CONGRESSES.
Abitazione e periferie urbane nei paesi in via di sviluppo . Milano, Italy , c1985. 450 p. : LC Card 86-132019
HD7287.96.L29 A25 1985
NYPL [JLD 87-1173]

LAND USE, URBAN - MEXICO.
Legorreta, Jorge. La autoconstrucción de vivienda en México . [México, D.F.] [1984] 204 p. : LC Card 86-232442
HD7306.A3 L44 1984

LAND USE, URBAN - PLANNING. see **CITY PLANNING.**

LAND USE, URBAN - TUNISIA.
Jedidi, Mohammed. Croissance économique et espace urbain dans le Sahel tunisien depuis l'indépendance /. [Tunis] , 1986. 2 v. : LC Card 87-123401
HC820 .J43 1986

LAND USE, URBAN - UNITED STATES.
Mayer, Harold Melvin, 1916- Land uses in American cities /. Champaign, Ill. [c1983] vi, 176 p. : ISBN 0-941226-02-6 (pbk.) LC Card 82-81036 DDC 333.77/13/0973 19
HD257 .M39 1983 ***NYPL [JLD 86-3126]***

Weiss, Marc A. (Marc Allan) The rise of the community builders . New York , 1987. xii, 228 p. : ISBN 0-231-06504-3 LC Card 87-5115 DDC 333.77/17/0973 19
HD257 .W46 1987

LAND USE, URBAN - UNITED STATES - CONGRESSES.
ULI/UMTA Policy Forum on Joint Development of Rail Transit Facilities (1986 : Washington, D.C.) ULI-UMTA Policy Forum on Joint Development of Rail Transit Facilities . [Washington, D.C.] [1987] iv, 107 p. : ISBN 0-87420-671-5 (pbk.) LC Card 87-82098 DDC 333.3/8 19
HD257 .U43 1986

LAND USE, URBAN - VENEZUELA.
Gilbert, Alan, 1944- The political economy of land . Aldershot, Hants , Brookfield, Vt., U. S.A. , c1985. xv, 163 p. : ISBN 0-566-05007-2 : LC Card 85-17535 DDC 333.77/13/0987 19
HD576 .G54 1985 ***NYPL [JLD 86-3632]***

LAND USE - ZAMBIA - CONGRESSES.
Lupande Development Workshop (1983 : Nyamaluma Wildlife Conservation Camp) Proceedings of the Lupande Development Workshop . Chipata, Zambia , 1984. x, 121 p. : LC Card 84-980605 DDC 333.73/17/096894 19
HD993.Z8 L835 1983 ***NYPL [JLG 87-67]***

Land uses in American cities /. Mayer, Harold Melvin, 1916- Champaign, Ill. [c1983] vi, 176 p. : ISBN 0-941226-02-6 (pbk.) LC Card 82-81036 DDC 333.77/13/0973 19
HD257 .M39 1983 ***NYPL [JLD 86-3126]***

LAND VALUATION. see **REAL PROPERTY - VALUATION.**

LAND VALUE TAXATION - INDIA - BENGAL - HISTORY.
Mukhopadhyay, Subhas Chandra, 1938- The agrarian policy of the British in Bengal . Allahabad, India , 1987. xi, 195 p. ; ISBN 81-85076-11-1 : LC Card 87-900481 DDC 338.1/85414 19
HJ4392.I4 M85 1987

LAND VALUE TAXATION - INDIA - HISTORY.
Land revenue policy of the Indian government. Delhi, India , 1986. vi, 291 p. ; ISBN 81-7030-004-5 : LC Card 85-905141 DDC 336.22/0954 19
HD878 .A3 1986

LAND VALUE TAXATION - INDIA - JAMMU AND KASHMIR - HISTORY.
Sharma, Dewan Chand, 1898- Kashmir agriculture & land revenue system under the Sikh rule, 1819-46 A.D. /. New Delhi, India , 1986. xiv, 160 p., [8] p. of plates : LC Card 86-900128
HD2075.J35 S43 1986 ***NYPL [JLD 86-3742]***

LAND VALUE TAXATION - INDIA - PUNJAB.
Sharma, Inderjit. Land revenue administration in the Punjab, 1849-1901 /. New Delhi , c1985. xi, 369 p. : LC Card 85-904617 DDC 354.54/552007242 19
HD879.P8 S53 1985 ***NYPL [JLD 87-552]***

LAND VALUE TAXATION - SPAIN - CASTILLA Y LEÓN - HISTORY.
Robledo Hernández, Ricardo. La renta de la tierra en Castilla la Vieja y León (1836-1913) /. [Madrid] [1984?] 245 p. : ISBN 84-505-0885-1 LC Card 87-104999
HJ4375.C27 R63 1984

LAND VALUES. see **REAL PROPERTY - VALUATION.**

Land, water, and culture : new perspectives on Hispanic land grants / edited by Charles L. Briggs & John R. Van Ness.1st ed. Albuquerque : University of New Mexico, c1987. ix, 422 p. : ill., maps ; 23 cm. (New Mexico land grant series) Includes bibliographies and index. ISBN 0-8263-0989-5 (pbk.) LC Card 87-10957 DDC 333.1/6/09788 19
1. Land grants - New Mexico - History. 2. Land grants - Colorado - History. 3. Pueblo Indians - Land tenure - History. 4. Indians of North America - New Mexico - Land tenure - History. 5. Mexican Americans - New Mexico - History. 6. Mexican Americans - Colorado - History. I. Briggs, Charles L., 1953-. II. Van Ness, John R. III. Series.
HD243.N5 L36 1987

Land, water, and mineral resources in science education / edited by Norman J. Graves. 1st ed. Oxford ; New York : Published for the ICSU Press by Pergamon Press, 1987. xii, 312 p. : ill. ; 24 cm. (Science and technology education and future human needs . vol. 4) "[Based on] a workshop held in Bangalore, India, in August 1985. The workshop was one of eight within a large conference"--P. vii. Includes bibliographies and index. ISBN 0-08-033915-8 : LC Card 86-30527 DDC 333.7/07/101724 19
1. Natural resources - Study and teaching - Congresses. 2. Land use - Study and teaching - Congresses. 3. Natural resources - Study and teaching - Developing countries - Congresses. 4. Land use - Study and teaching - Developing countries - Congresses. I. Graves, Norman John. II. Series.
HC28 .L27 1987

Landarbeiter und Sozialdemokratie in Ostholstein, 1872 bis 1878 . Rüdel, Holger. Neumünster , 1986. 581 p. ; ISBN 3-529-02909-2 LC Card 87-119718 DDC 331.88/13/0943512 19
HD6699.O88 R83 1986

Landau, J. J. Deutsche Industrie, deutsche Kultur /. Berlin , 1900-1902. xvi, 388 p. : LC Card 85-666344
HC283 .D48x 1900

Landau, Zbigniew.
Kostrowicka, Irena. Historia gospodarcza Polski XIX i XX wieku /. Warszawa , 1984. 583 p., [3] folded leaves of plates : ISBN 83-05-11411-2 : LC Card 85-218322
HC340.3 .K67 1984

The Polish economy in the twentieth century / Zbigniew Landau and Jerzy Tomaszewski ; translated by Wojciech Roszkowski. London : Croom Helm, c1985. vi, 346 p. ; 23 cm. (Croom Helm series on the contemporary economic history of Europe) Translated from the Polish. Bibliography: p. 323-332. Includes index. ISBN 0-7099-1607-8 LC Card 86-673496
1. Poland - Economic conditions - 1918-. 2. Poland - Economic policy. I. Tomaszewski, Jerzy, 1930-. II. Title. III. Title: Polish economy in the 20th century. IV. Series.
HC340.3 .L36x 1985b

Wirtschaftsgeschichte Polens im 19. und 20. Jahrhundert / Zbigniew Landau, Jerzy Tomaszewski ; ins Deutsche übertragen und herausgegeben von Berthold Puchert. Berlin : Akademie-Verlag, 1986. vi, 300 p. : 1 folded map ; 25 cm. (Forschungen zur Wirtschaftsgeschichte. Bd. 19) One folded map in pocket. Includes bibliographical references and indexes. LC Card 86-223591
1. Poland - Economic conditions. 2. Poland - Economic policy. I. Tomaszewski, Jerzy, 1930-. II. Puchert, Berthold. III. Title. IV. Title: Wirtschaftsgeschichte Polens im neunzehnten und zwanzigsten Jahrhundert.
HC340.3 .L367 1986

Landbohistorisk selskab. Godsejerrøster . København , 1984. 320 p. : ISBN 87-7526-018-2 : LC Card 84-224395
HD1333.D42 R674 1984

Landbouw-Economisch Instituut (Netherlands) Normen voor nieuwwaarde en afschrijving van slijtende duurzame produktiemiddelen in de fruitteelt alsmede voor de grondwaarde . Den Haag [1986] 67 p. ; LC Card 86-234475
HF5686.F7 N67 1986

Landbrugets informationskontor. Noter over dansk landbrugshistorie. Greve Strand , 1982. 53 p. : ISBN 87-7470-314-5 : LC Card 83-170741
HD2002 .N67 1982

Landbrugsarealer, landskabeligt og rekreativt /. Jensen, Knud Erik. [Copenhagen] , 1982. 248 p. : LC Card 84-172974
HD736 .J46 1982

Landerer, Christoph, 1952- Huter, Otto, 1952- Die Berliner Eigenbetriebe als Instrumente kommunaler Politik /. Berlin , c1984. 275 p. : ISBN 3-87061-910-4 LC Card 84-231849
HD4180.B47 H87 1984

Landesamt für Arbeitsdienst der Deutschen in Rumänien. Kampf und Arbeit . Kronstadt , 1936. 102 p., [1] leaf of plates : LC Card 84-255742
HD7290 .K35 1936

Landesamt für Datenverarbeitung und Statistik Nordrhein-Westfalen.
Agrarberichterstattung Nordrhein-Westfalen 1981 . Düsseldorf [1983] 189 p. ; LC Card 87-407320 DDC 943/.55 s 338.1/0943/55021 19
HA1320.N6 A32 Heft 490 HD1960.N67

Agrarberichterstattung Nordrhein-Westfalen 1981 . Düsseldorf [1983] 131, [5] p. ; LC Card 87-407319 DDC 943/.55 s 338.1/0943/55021 19
HA1320.N6 A32 Heft 489 HD9013.7.N6

Agrarberichterstattung Nordrhein-Westfalen 1983 . Düsseldorf [1984] 241, [5] p. ; LC Card 87-407318 DDC 943/.55 s 338.1/76/0094355021 19
HA1320.N6 A32 Heft 533 HD9423.7.N6

Agrarberichterstattung Nordrhein-Westfalen 1983 . Düsseldorf [1984] 263 p. ; LC Card 87-407317 DDC 943/.55 s 338.1/0943/55021 19
HA1320.N6 A32 Heft 532 HD1960.N67

Agrarberichterstattung Nordrhein-Westfalen 1983 . Düsseldorf [1985] 191 p. ; LC Card 87-407316 DDC 943/.55 s 338.1/0943/55021 19
HA1320.N6 A32 Heft 531 HD1960.N67

Die Investitionsentwicklung in Nordrhein-Westfalen 1970-1980. Düsseldorf [1984] 94 p. : LC Card 87-407315 DDC 943/.55 s 332.6/0943/55021 19
HA1320.N6 A32 Heft 508 HG5503.N67

Das Textilgewerbe in Nordrhein-Westfalen 1977 bis 1980. Düsseldorf [1982] 109 p. : LC Card 87-407312 DDC 943/.55 s 338.4/7677/0094355021 19
HA1320.N6 A32 Heft 477 HD9863.7.N67

Vorausberechnung der Bevölkerung in den kreisfreien Städten und Kreisen Nordrhein-Westfalens . Düsseldorf [1983] 103 p. : LC Card 86-202728
HA1320.N6 A32 Heft 500

Landesamt für Statistik des Landes Nordrhein-Westfalen. Zensus im Bergbau und verarbeitenden Gewerbe Nordrhein-Westfalen 1979 . Düsseldorf [1983] 109 p. ; LC Card 87-407314 DDC 943/.55 s 338.2/0943/55021 19
HA1320.N6 A32 Heft 497 HD9506.G23N6

Landesarbeitsamt Kärnten. Die Entwicklung der Beschäftigungslage in Kärnten seit 1960 /. Klagenfurt [1979] 23 leaves : LC Card 85-143747
HD5772.C37 E57 1979

Landesbank Rheinland-Pfalz Girozentrale. Banken . Frankfurt am Main , c1983. 216 p. ; ISBN 3-7819-0297-8 : LC Card 83-217788
HG3048 .B27 1983

LANDESBANK RHEINLAND-PFALZ GIROZENTRALE.
Banken . Frankfurt am Main , c1983. 216 p. ; ISBN 3-7819-0297-8 : LC Card 83-217788
HG3048 .B27 1983

Landesentwicklungsplan sechs.
Landesentwicklungsplan VI . [Düsseldorf] [1977] [4] p., [17] leaves of plates : LC Card 86-105018
HC287.N6 L28 1977

Landesentwicklungsplan VI : "Festlegung von Gebieten für flächenintensive Grossvorhaben (einschliesslich Standorte für die Energieerzeugung), die für die Wirtschaftsstruktur des Landes von besonderer Bedeutung sind" : Entwurf. [Düsseldorf] : Ministerpräsident des Landes Nordrhein-Westfalen, Landesplanungsbehörde, [1977] [4] p., [17] leaves of plates : maps ; 30 cm. Cover title. LC Card 86-105018
1. North Rhine-Westphalia (Germany) - Economic policy. 2. North Rhine-Westphalia (Germany) - Economic policy - Maps. I. North Rhine-Westphalia (Germany). Landesplanungsbehörde. II. Title: Landesentwicklungsplan 6. III. Title: Landesentwicklungsplan sechs.
HC287.N6 L28 1977

Landesentwicklungsplan 6.
Landesentwicklungsplan VI . [Düsseldorf] [1977] [4] p., [17] leaves of plates : LC Card 86-105018
HC287.N6 L28 1977

Landesjugendamt der Deutschen in Rumänien. Kampf und Arbeit . Kronstadt , 1936. 102 p., [1] leaf of plates : LC Card 84-255742
HD7290 .K35 1936

Landesprogramme von Hörfunk und Fernsehen in Hamburg . Renckstorf, Karsten. Hamburg , c1985. xlvii, vi, 388 p. : ISBN 3-87296-067-9 (pbk.) LC Card 86-109817 DDC 384.54/43/0943515 19
HE8700.9.G4 R45 1985 ***NYPL [MWGK (Germany, West) 86-4239]***

Landeswirtschaftlicher Paritätsspiegel : Indexbericht der Betriebsstatistischen Abteilung / Land- und forstwirtschaftliche Landes-Buchführungsgesellschaft m.b.H (LBG) ; [für den Inhalt verantwortlich, Wolfgang Schosserer]. Wien : Die Gesellschaft, [1982] 11 leaves ; 30 cm. Chiefly tables. LC Card 86-181563
1. Agricultural prices - Austria - Statistics. 2. Price indexes. I. Schosserer, Wolfgang. II. Land- und Forstwirtschaftliche Landes-Buchführung-Gesellschaft.
HD1935 .L325 1982

Landeszentralbank im Saarland.
Landeszentralbank im Saarland : Hauptverwaltung der Deutschen Bundesbank : 1985 / [Redaktion, Volkswirtschaftliche Abteilung]. Saarbrücken : Landeszentralbank im Saarland, 1986. 45, xii p. : ill. ; 30 cm. Title on p. 7: Die Wirtschaft des Saarlandes 1985. LC Card 86-176290
1. Saarland (Germany) - Economic conditions. 2. Saarland (Germany) - Industries. 3. Banks and banking - Germany (West) - Saarland. 4. Landeszentralbank im Saarland. I. Landeszentralbank im Saarland. Volkswirtschaftliche Abteilung. II. Title: Wirtschaft des Saarlandes 1985.
HC287.S23 L35 1986

LANDESZENTRALBANK IM SAARLAND.
Landeszentralbank im Saarland. Landeszentralbank im Saarland . Saarbrücken , 1986. 45, xii p. : LC Card 86-176290
HC287.S23 L35 1986

Landeszentralbank im Saarland. Volkswirtschaftliche Abteilung.
Landeszentralbank im Saarland. Landeszentralbank im Saarland . Saarbrücken , 1986. 45, xii p. : LC Card 86-176290
HC287.S23 L35 1986

Landhandwerk und Landwirtschaft / mit Beiträgen von Friedrich Bernhard Hausmann ... [et al.]. Göttingen : O. Schwartz, 1964. 104 p. : ill. ; 23 cm. (Göttinger handwerkswirtschaftliche Studien) Includes bibliographical references. CONTENTS. - Die Nachfrage der Landwirtschaft nach Leistungen des Handwerks / Friedrich Bernhard Hausmann -- Neuere Entwicklungslinien der Landtechnik / Reinhard Adelhelm -- Die Stellung des Handwerks auf dem Markt landwirtschaftlicher Maschinen / Christian Behrends -- Die Anpassung landhandwerklicher Betriebe an sich ändernde Marktverhältnisse / Hermann-Adolf Ihle -- Landhandwerk und Siedlungsstruktur / Gerhard Stavenhagen. LC Card 87-409231 DDC 338.1/61/0943 19
1. Farm mechanization - Germany (West). 2. Agricultural innovations - Germany (West). 3. Agricultural laborers - Germany, West. I. Hausmann, Friedrich Bernhard.
HD1955 .L17 1964

Landi, Antonio. Il marketing d'acquisto : guida pratica ad uso dei dirigenti e degli addetti all'approvvigionamento / Antonio Landi.Nuova ed. ampliata. Milano, Italy : F. Angeli, 1986. 247 p. : ill. ; 22 cm. (Azienda moderna. 147) ISBN 88-20-41020-6 : LC Card 86-207836
1. Industrial equipment - Marketing. 2. Industrial equipment - Purchasing. 3. Industrial procurement - Italy. I. Title.
HD9680.A2 L36 1986

Landivar, Jorge F. The role of housing in development models : the case of Ecuador, 1962-1982 / Jorge F. Landivar. Swansea, U.K. : Centre for Development Studies, University of College of Swansea, 1986. 60 p. ; 21 cm. (Centre for Development Studies, University College of Swansea . new ser., no. 1) Bibliography: p. 55-60. ISBN 0-906250-12-9 (pbk.) LC Card 87-166136 DDC 363.5/8 19
1. Poor - Housing - Ecuador. 2. Poor - Housing - Government policy - Ecuador. 3. Poor - Housing - Ecuador - Finance. 4. Housing policy - Ecuador. I. Series: University College of Swansea. Centre for Development Studies (Series) , new ser., no. 1. II. Title.
HD7287.96.E2 L36 1986

Landkreis Waiblingen / herausgegeben vom Innenministerium und Wirtschaftsministerium Baden-Württemberg : Bearbeitung und Druck, Statistisches Landesamt Baden-Württemberg. [Stuttgart] : Innenministerium und Wirtschaftsministerium, [1965?] 25 p. : maps (some col.) ; 30 cm. (Die Stadt- und Landkreise Baden-Württembergs in Wort und Zahl . Heft 23) Cover title. LC Card 85-230943
1. Waiblingen (Germany : Landkreis) - Economic conditions. 2. Waiblingen (Germany : Landkreis) - Economic conditions - Statistics. 3. Waiblingen (Germany : Landkreis) - Social conditions. 4. Waiblingen (Germany : Landkreis) - Social conditions - Statistics. I. Baden-Württemberg (Germany). Innenministerium. II. Baden-Württemberg (Germany). Wirtschaftsministerium. III. Statistisches Landesamt Baden-Württemberg. IV. Series.
HC288.W34 L36 1965

LANDLORD AND TENANT - INDIA - PUNJAB.
Sharma, Inderjit. Land revenue administration in the Punjab, 1849-1901 /. New Delhi , c1985. xi, 369 p. : LC Card 85-904617 DDC 354.54/552007242 19
HD879.P8 S53 1985 ***NYPL [JLD 87-552]***

LANDLORD AND TENANT - NEW YORK (N. Y.) - HISTORY - 20TH CENTURY.
The Tenant movement in New York City, 1904-1984 /. New Brunswick, N.J. , c1986. xiv, 289 p. : ISBN 0-8135-1203-4 (pbk.) : LC Card 85-27894 DDC 333.33/8 19
HD7288.85.U62 N58 1986
NYPL [JLE 86-4565]

LANDLORD AND TENANT - NEW ZEALAND - CHRISTCHURCH.
The Private residential landlord and tenant in Christchurch . Wellington, N.Z. [1986] viii, 105 p. : ISBN 0-477-03810-7 (pbk.) LC Card 87-147647 DDC 333.33/8 19
HD7288.85.N452 C576 1986

LANDOWNERS - AUSTRIA - LOWER AUSTRIA - HISTORY.
Feigl, Helmuth. Die niederösterreichische Grundherrschaft . [Wien] , 1964. 379 p. ; LC Card 85-127367
HD639.L6 F45 1964

LANDOWNERS - BRAZIL - SÃO PAULO (STATE) - HISTORY - 19TH CENTURY.
Mello, Zélia Maria Cardoso de. Metamorfoses da riqueza, São Paulo, 1845-1895 . São Paulo ,

1985. 188 p. : LC Card 85-207635
HC188.S3 M49 1985

LANDOWNERS - ECUADOR - CHIMBORAZO - POLITICAL ACTIVITY - HISTORY.
Sylva Charvet, Paola. Gamonalismo y lucha campesina . [Quito] , 1986. 250 p., [3] leaves of plates : LC Card 87-101122
HD529.C47 S95 1986

LANDOWNERS - ITALY - MILAN - HISTORY - 18TH CENTURY.
Mazzucchelli, Vanna. Catasto e volto urbano . Roma , 1983. 244 p. ; LC Card 86-106099
HD680.M54 M39 1983

LANDOWNERS - SPAIN - HISTORY - 18TH CENTURY.
Romeo Mateo, María Cruz, 1960- Realengo y municipio . Alicante , 1986. 171 p. : ISBN 84-505-3131-4 LC Card 87-137181
HD780.A435 R66 1986

LANDOWNERS - SPAIN - PILAS (SEVILLE) - HISTORY.
Camacho Rueda, Eduardo. Propiedad y explotación agrarias en el aljarafe sevillano . Sevilla , 1984. 199 p. : ISBN 84-500-9772-X LC Card 85-135028
HD773 .C18 1984

Landrum, Roger L. The role of the Peace Corps in education in developing countries : a sector study / Roger L. Landrum. Washington, D.C. : Peace Corps, Information Collection and Exchange, [1984] iv, 258 p. ; 28 cm. (Appropriate technologies for development) Reprint series ; R-49 "July 1984." Includes bibliographical references. LC Card 86-601664 DDC 371.2/07 19
1. Peace Corps (U. S.). 2. Educational assistance. 3. Educational planning - Developing countries. I. Series. II. Series: Reprint series (Peace Corps (U. S.). Information Collection and Exchange) , R-49. III. Title.
HC60.5 .L27 1984

Lands at risk in the Third World : local-level perspectives / edited by Peter D. Little and Michael M. Horowitz with A. Endre Nyerges ; foreword by Gilbert F. White. Boulder : Westview Press, 1987. xiii, 416 p. : ill. ; 24 cm. (Monographs in development anthropology) Includes bibliographies and index. ISBN 0-8133-7311-5 (pbk. : alk. paper) : LC Card 86-51423 DDC 333.73/13 19
1. Land use, Rural - Environmental aspects - Developing countries. I. Little, Peter D. II. Horowitz, Michael M., 1933-. III. Series.
HD1131 .L37 1987

LANDSCAPE ARCHITECTURE - ENVIRONMENTAL ASPECTS.
Marsh, William M. Landscape planning . New York , 1986. p. cm. ISBN 0-471-85434-4 LC Card 86-28951 DDC 712 19
HD108.6 .M37 1986

LANDSCAPE ASSESSMENT - HISTORY.
Cosgrove, Denis E. Social formation and symbolic landscape /. Totowa, N.J. , 1985, c1984. 293 p. : ISBN 0-389-20540-0 LC Card 84-21629 DDC 304.2 19
GF90 .C67 1985 ***NYPL [JLD 86-2206]***

LANDSCAPE DESIGN. see **LANDSCAPE ARCHITECTURE.**

Landscape ecology and land use /. Vink, A. P. A. [Landschapsecologie en landgebruik. English.] London , New York , 1983, c1980. vi, 264 p. : ISBN 0-582-30077-0 (pbk.) : LC Card 82-10030 DDC 333.73/13 19
HD108.6 .V5613 1983 ***NYPL [JLE 86-3886]***

Landscape planning . Marsh, William M. New York , 1986. p. cm. ISBN 0-471-85434-4 LC Card 86-28951 DDC 712 19
HD108.6 .M37 1986

LANDSCAPE PROTECTION - DENMARK.
Jensen, Knud Erik. Landbrugsarealer, landskabeligt og rekreativt /. [Copenhagen] , 1982. 248 p. : LC Card 84-172974
HD736 .J46 1982

Landscapes of poverty /. Seabrook, Jeremy, 1939- Oxford, U.K. , 1985. x, 175 p. ; ISBN 0-631-14508-7 : LC Card 86-673976
HC79.P6 S36x 1985

Landskron, Ferdinand. Von der Bauernfaust zur Bauernkammer / von Ferdinand Landskron. Totzenbach : Verein der Freunde Totzenbachs, [1983] 194 p. ; 21 cm. (Verein der Freunde Totzenbachs . Heft 12) Bibliography: p. 190-194. LC Card 84-168829
1. Peasantry - Austria - Totzenbach Region - History. 2. Totzenbach Region (Austria) - History. I. Series: Verein der Freunde Totzenbachs (Series) , Heft 12. II. Title.
HD1536.A9 L36 1983

LANDSKRONA (SWEDEN) - ECONOMIC CONDITIONS.
Schunnesson, Torgny. Framtidsstaden . [Stockholm] , c1985. 166 p. : ISBN 91-7054-498-0 LC Card 86-105915
HC378.L35 S38 1985

LANDSKRONA (SWEDEN) - SOCIAL CONDITIONS.
Schunnesson, Torgny. Framtidsstaden . [Stockholm] , c1985. 166 p. : ISBN 91-7054-498-0 LC Card 86-105915
HC378.L35 S38 1985

Landsudvalget for fjerkræ (Denmark) Den danske fjerkræsektor 1985, en beskrivelse : problemstilling, behov og opgaver 1985-1995/2000 : forslag til tilpasning : rapport / udarbejdet af en gruppe nedsat af Landsudvalget for fjerkræ. [Denmark? : s.n., 1986] 152 p. ; 30 cm. Cover title. LC Card 86-224129
1. Poultry industry - Denmark. 2. Landsudvalget for fjerkræ (Denmark). I. Title.
HD9437.D42 L35 1986

LANDSUDVALGET FOR FJERKRÆ (DENMARK)
Landsudvalget for fjerkræ (Denmark) Den danske fjerkræsektor 1985, en beskrivelse . [Denmark? , 1986] 152 p. ; LC Card 86-224129
HD9437.D42 L35 1986

Der "Landverbrauch," seine Erfassung und Bewertung . Borcherdt, Christoph. Stuttgart , 1985. 196 p. : ISBN 3-88028-104-1 LC Card 87-136211 DDC 333.77/13/094347 19
HD660.S83 B67 1985

Der Landwarenhandel in der Bundesrepublik Deutschland . Prüsse, Dieterich. Münster-Hiltrup , 1983. viii, 188, [9], 21 p. : ISBN 3-7843-0291-2 : LC Card 84-141310
HD9013.5 .P78 1983

Landwirtschaft am Niederrhein . Ebel, Friedhelm. Bonn , 1976. 223 p. : LC Card 87-408419
HD1407 .L3 Heft 33 HD1960.R48

Landwirtschaft und Umweltschutz, Sozialpflichtigkeit oder Entschädigung? / mit Beiträgen von I. Kiechle ... [et al.]. Göttingen : ASG, 1987. 116 p. : ill. ; 21 cm. (Schriftenreihe für ländliche Sozialfragen, 0080-7133 . Heft 96) Papers presented at a meeting held by the Agrarsoziale Gesellschaft, Dec. 4-5, 1985, in Göttingen. CONTENTS. - Landwirtschaft und Umweltschutz im nationalen Alleingang oder im europäischen Gleichschritt? / Ignaz Kiechle -- Ökologische Restriktionen und einzelbetriebliche Wirkungen / Hartwig de Haen und Hans-Friedrich Finck -- Berufsständische Forderungen an die Umweltpolitik / Reiner Latten -- Was die Landwirtschaft für den Umweltschutz tun kann / Hubert Weiger -- Nitratbelastung / Eckart Toussaint -- Berücksichtigung ökologischer Belange in der Beratung ... / Konrad Grass -- Zu den Konsequenzen aus der Unterschutzstellung landwirtschaftlich genutzter Flächen / Manfred Merforth -- Mehrfachbeschäftigung / Hartwig Spitzer. LC Card 87-401359 DDC 363.7/056/0943 19
1. Agricultural ecology - Government policy - Germany (West) - Congresses. I. Kiechle, I. (Ignaz). II. Agrarsoziale Gesellschaft. III. Series.
HD1957 .L355 1987

Landwirtschaft--angewandte Wissenschaft. Germany (West). Bundesministerium für Ernährung, Landwirtschaft und Forsten. Wissenschaftlicher Beirat. Gutachten des Wissenschaftlichen Beirats beim Bundesministerium für Ernährung, Landwirtschaft und Forsten /. Hiltrup bei Münster (Westf.) [1960?] 98 p. ; LC Card 86-185959
HD1957 .G47 1960

Landwirtschaftliche Entwicklung und Agrarreform in Nicaragua zwischen 1960 und 1982 . Glembotzki, Jürgen. Hamburg , 1984. 80, xliv p. : LC Card 84-208160 DDC 333.3/1/7285 19
HD1333.N5 G57 1984
NYPL [JLM 75-816 Nr.21]

Die landwirtschaftliche Modernisierung Saudi-Arabiens im 20. Jahrhundert /. Philipp, Hans-Jürgen. Hamburg , c1984. 132 p. : LC Card 85-166668
HD2060.Z8 P48 1984

Landwirtschaftliche Produktionsalternativen am Beispiel Ethanol, Ölsaaten und Eiweissfutterpflanzen / [Herausgeber], Beirat für Wirtschafts- und Sozialfragen. Wien : C. Ueberreuter, 1985. 141 p. : ill. ; 24 cm. LC Card 86-108149 DDC 338.1/09436 19
1. Agriculture - Economic aspects - Austria. 2. Alcohol fuel industry - Austria. 3. Energy crops - Austria. 4. Oil industries - Austria. 5. Oilseeds - Austria. 6. Flour and feed trade - Austria. 7. Cropping systems - Austria. I. Beirat für Wirtschafts- und Sozialfragen.
HD1935 .L33 1985

Landwirtschaftliche Übergangsbetriebe in Niedersachsen : Ursachen und Konsequenzen sozioökonomischer Probleme : Pilotstudie / gefördert vom Niedersächsischen Ministerium für Ernährung, Landwirtschaft und Forsten ; erstellt im Sekretariat der Agrarsozialen Gesellschaft e.V. durch Ernst Otto Bendixen, unter Mitarbeit von Hermann Clausen. Göttingen : Agrarsoziale Gesellschaft, 1985. xiii, 105 p. ; 21 cm. (ASG-Materialsammlung, 0344-5712 . Nr. 172) Bibliography: p. 104-105. LC Card 86-185987
1. Agricultural industries - Germany (West) - Lower Saxony. 2. Agricultural credit corporations - Germany (West) - Lower Saxony. 3. Lower Saxony (Germany) - Economic conditions. 4. Lower Saxony (Germany) - Rural conditions. 5. Peasantry - Germany (West) - Lower Saxony. I. Bendixen, Ernst Otto. II. Clausen, Hermann. III. Lower Saxony (Germany). Ministerium für Ernährung, Landwirtschaft und Forsten. IV. Agrarsoziale Gesellschaft. Sekretariat. V. Series.
HD9013.7.L68 L36 1985

Landwirtschaftszählung 1979, Gartenbauerhebung 1981/82 : Ergebnisse der Nacherhebung zur Landwirtschaftszählung 1979. Hannover : Niedersächsisches Landesverwaltungsamt, Statistik, 1983. xv, 132 p. ; 30 cm. (Statistik Niedersachsen . Bd. 387) Statistischer Bericht ; C/Landwirtschaftszählung 1979 Chiefly tables. LC Card 85-117833
1. Horticultural products industry - Germany (West) - Lower Saxony - Statistics. 2. Agriculture - Economic aspects - Germany (West) - Lower Saxony - Statistics. 3. Greenhouses - Germany (West) - Lower Saxony - Statistics. 4. Orchards - Germany (West) - Lower Saxony - Statistics. 5. Farms - Germany (West) - Lower Saxony - Statistics. 6. Land use, Rural - Germany (West) - Lower Saxony - Statistics. I. Niedersächsisches Landesverwaltungsamt. Statistik. II. Series: Statistik von Niedersachsen , Bd. 387.
HD9013.7.L68 L37 1983

Lane, A. T. Solidarity or survival? : American labor and European immigrants, 1830-1924 / A.T. Lane. New York : Greenwood Press, 1987. xii, 230 p. ; 25 cm. (Contributions in labor studies, 0886-8239 . no. 21) Bibliography: p. [215]-221. Includes index. ISBN 0-313-25544-X (lib. bdg. : alk. paper) LC Card 86-25735 DDC 331.6/2/0973 19
1. Alien labor - United States - History. 2. United States - Emigration and immigration - History. 3. Trade-unions - United States - Political activity. I. Title. II. Series.
HD8081.A5 L36 1987

Lane, David Stuart. Labour and employment in the USSR /. Brighton, Sussex , 1986. xviii, 280 p. : ISBN 0-7450-0038-X LC Card 86-673709
HD5796 .L33x 1986b

Lane Frederic Chapin, 1900-
Money and banking in medieval and Renaissance Venice / Frederic C. Lane, Reinhold C. Mueller. Baltimore : Johns Hopkins University Press, c1985- v. : ill. ; 24 cm. Includes index. Bibliography: v. 1, p. 637-670. CONTENTS. - v. 1. Coins and moneys of account. ISBN 0-8018-3157-1 (v. 1) LC Card 84-47947 DDC 332.1/0945/31 19
1. Money - Italy - Venice - History. 2. Banks and banking - Italy - Venice - History. 3. Venice - Economic conditions. I. Mueller, Reinhold C. II. Title.
HG1040.V46 L36 1985 ***NYPL [JLL 86-121]***

Studies in Venetian social and economic history / Frederic C. Lane ; edited by Benjamin G. Kohl and Reinhold C. Mueller. London : Variorum Reprints, 1987. 346 p. in various pagings : ill. ; 23 cm. (Variorum reprint. CS254)

English, French, and Italian. Includes bibliographies and index. ISBN 0-86078-202-6 LC Card 87-160893 DDC 945/.31 19
1. Venice (Italy) - Economic conditions. 2. Venice (Italy) - Commerce. 3. Venice (Italy) - Social conditions. I. Kohl, Benjamin G. II. Mueller, Reinhold C. III. Title.
HC308.V4 L36 1987

Lane, Frederick M. The Psychology of men . New York , c1986. x, 310 p. ; ISBN 0-465-06718-2 LC Card 85-48022 DDC 155.3/32 19
BF692.5 .P78 1986 ***NYPL [JFE 86-2975]***

Lane, Irving M. Siegel, Laurence. Personnel and organizational psychology /. Homewood, Ill. , 1987. xviii, 617 p. : ISBN 0-256-03369-2 LC Card 86-82591 DDC 158.7 19
HF5548.8 .S512 1987

Lane, Theodore. Developing America's northern frontier /. Lanham, MD , c1987. xx, 250 p. ; ISBN 0-8191-6081-4 (alk. paper) : LC Card 86-28233 DDC 338.9719 19
HC117.N48 D48 1987

Lane, W. Ronald, 1940- Kleppner, Otto, 1899- [Advertising procedure.] Kleppner's advertising procedure. Englewood Cliffs, N.J. , 1987, c1988. p. cm. ISBN 0-13-516451-6 LC Card 87-19346 DDC 659.1 19
HF5823 .K45 1988

Lang, Harald. Albrecht, James W. Job search and the transition to employment . Göteborg [1986] 38 leaves ; LC Card 87-158051 DDC 331.12/8 19
HF5382.7 .A43 1986

Láng, István, 1931-
A biomassza hasznosításának távlatai : akadémiai székfoglaló, 1985. december 4. / Láng István. Budapest : Akadémiai Kiadó, c1986. 28 p. ; 20 cm. (Értekezések, emlékezések, 0236-6258) ISBN 963-05-4357-5 : LC Card 87-407709
1. Biomass energy industries - Hungary. 2. Biomass energy - Hungary. I. Title. II. Series.
HD9502.5.B543 H95 1986

A Biomassza komplex hasznosításának lehetőségei /. Budapest , 1985. 249 p. : ISBN 963-232-215-0 : LC Card 87-115648
HD9502.5.B543 H93 1985

Lang, Kevin. Unemployment and the structure of labor markets /. New York, NY, USA , 1987. vi, 253 p. : ISBN 0-631-15378-0 : LC Card 86-24478 DDC 331.13/7 19
HD5707.5 .U545 1987

Lang, Norbert. Johann Georg Bodmer (1786-1864) : Maschinenbauer und Erfinder / von Norbert Lang. Zürich : Verein für wirtschaftshistorische Studien, c1987. 92 p. : ill. ; 24 cm. (Schweizer Pioniere der Wirtschaft und Technik. 45) Bibliography: p. 91-92. LC Card 87-134606 DDC 338/.09494 s 620/.0092/4 B 19
1. Bodmer, Johann Georg, (1786-1864). 2. Mechanical engineers - Switzerland - Biography. I. Bodmer, Johann Georg, (1786-1864). II. Title. III. Series.
HC395.5.A2 S3 no. 45 TJ140.B53

Lang, Sigrun. Stand der grenzüberschreitenden Raumordnung am Oberrhein /. [Heidelberg] , 1981. 105 p. : ISBN 3-88570-071-9 LC Card 81-197772 DDC 361.6/0943/4 19
HT395.G4 S735 1981
NYPL [L-10 4979 Heft 71]

Lang, Walter. Gesellschaftliches Selbstverständnis und politische Orientierung der Freien Berufe . Nürnberg , 1978. 144 p. : LC Card 86-170378
HD8038.G32 B384 1978

Lange, Diedrich. Zur sozialphilosophischen Gestalt der Marktwirtschaftstheorie bei Adam Smith / Diedrich Lange. München : V. Florentz, c1983. 230 p. : ill. ; 21 cm. (Volkswirtschaftliche Forschung und Entwicklung . Bd. 2) Bibliography: p. 204-226. Includes index. ISBN 3-88259-267-2 LC Card 84-150199
1. Smith, Adam, 1723-1790. 2. Economics. I. Title. II. Series.
HB103.S6 L36 1983

Lange, G. F. Summary report on a mission to southern Africa from 9 July to 21 August 1985 for the development of coal resources in Malawi, Swaziland, Mozambique, Zambia, and Zimbabwe. [Addis Ababa] : United Nations Economic Commission for Africa, [1985] ii, 60 p. ; 29 cm. Cover title. "September 1985." Bibliography: p. 55-58. LC Card 85-981333 DDC 338.2/724/0968 19
1. Coal trade - Africa, Southern. I. United Nations. Economic Commission for Africa. II. Title.
HD9557.A356 L36 1985

Lange, Michael. Uhlig, Christian. Internationale Produktionskooperation im Vorderen Orient . Stuttgart , c1983. xvi, 338 p. : ISBN 3-522-68000-6 LC Card 83-217029
HD2891.9 .U44 1983

Langebæk, Steen. Bestyrelsens idégrundlag og funktion / Steen Langebæk. København : Gad, 1985. 175 p. ; 24 cm. Bibliography: p. 174. ISBN 87-12-01597-0 : LC Card 86-156403
1. Industrial management - Denmark. I. Title.
HD70.D4 L36 1985

Langemeyer, Gerhard. Leben mit Gneisenau, hundert Jahre-- . Dortmund , Essen [1986?] 317 p. : ISBN 3-88474-323-6 LC Card 87-408388 DDC 331.7/622334/094355 19
HD8039.M62 G335 1986

Langemo, Mark. Barber, Donald T. Filing dynamics . Emeryville, Calif. , 1987. 92 p. : ISBN 0-941151-00-X LC Card 87-60316 DDC 651.5/3 19
HF5741 .B44 1987

Langenbach, Peter. Wettbewerb und staatliche Sachausgaben / Peter Langenbach. Bochum : Studienverlag Brockmeyer, 1981. viii, 316 p. ; 21 cm. (Bochumer wirtschaftswissenschaftliche Studien. Nr. 79) Originally presented as the author's thesis (doctoral)--Ruhr-Universität Bochum, 1981. Bibliography: p. 278-316. ISBN 3-88339-194-8 : LC Card 81-205020 DDC 336.3/9 19
1. Competition. 2. Competition - Germany, West. 3. Germany, West - Appropriations and expenditures. I. Title.
HJ7461 .L36 1981 ***NYPL [JLD 86-2579]***

Langenheim, Christian. Naumann, Thomas. Stadtbahn für Würzburg . Würzburg , 1985. 237 p., [3] leaves of plates : LC Card 86-166915
HE4779.W84 N38 1985

Langenscheidt's standard German dictionary /. Klatt, Edmund. New York , 1983-1984. 1341 p. ; ***NYPL [JFC 86-781]***

Langer, Gary F. The coming of age of political economy, 1815-1825 / Gary F. Langer. New York : Greenwood Press, 1987. x, 224 p. : ill. ; 25 cm. (Contributions in economics and economic history, 0084-9235 . no. 72) Bibliography: p. [209]-217. Includes index. ISBN 0-313-25645-4 (lib. bdg. : alk. paper) LC Card 86-31802 DDC 330/.0941 19
1. Economics - Great Britain - History - 19th century. I. Title. II. Series.
HB103.A2 L36 1987

Langer, Steven.
The Accounting/financial report /. Crete, IL (548 First St., Crete 60417) , c1983. 2 v. ; LC Card 83-152793 DDC 331.2/81657/0973 19
HF5627 .A23 1983 ***NYPL [JLM 86-1500]***

Compensation and benefits in research & development /. Crete, IL , c1987. 692 p. ; ISBN 0-916506-34-7 (pbk.) LC Card 87-403067 DDC 331.2/816584/00973021 19
HD4965.5.U6 C656 1987

Compensation in the accounting/financial field /. Crete, IL , c1987. 489 p. ; ISBN 0-916506-36-3 (pbk.) LC Card 87-153325 DDC 331.12/81657/0973021 19
HF5627 .C57 1987

Langewiesche, Dieter. Arbeiter in Hamburg . Hamburg , c1983. 606 p. : ISBN 3-8103-0807-2 LC Card 86-174037
HD8460.H36 A73 1983

Langford, Jay. Economic trends in metropolitan Washington, 1980-1985 ; [author, Jay Langford, Vetoria S. Alston]. Washington, D.C. (1875 Eye St., NW., Suite 200, Washington 20006) : Dept. of Metropolitan Development Information Resources, Metropolitan Washington Council of Governments, c1986. viii, 68 p. : ill. ; 28 cm. "September 1986." Bibliography: p. 67-68. LC Card 87-105032 DDC 330.9753/04 19
1. Washington metropolitan area - Economic conditions. 2. Washington Metropolitan Area - Economic conditions - Statistics. I. Alston, Vetoria S. II. Metropolitan Washington Council of Governments. Dept. of Metropolitan Development and Information Resources. III. Title.
HC108.W3 L36 1986

Langfristige Automobilmarktprognosen . Schülen, Heinrich, 1957- Idstein , 1985. 221 p. : ISBN 3-925196-14-5 LC Card 86-120500 DDC 338.4/76292/0943 19
HD9710.G42 S32 1985

Die langfristige Entwicklung von Kommunikation und Staatsausgaben /. Kleinmann, Klaus, 1956- Frankfurt am Main , New York , c1985. v, 194 p. : ISBN 3-8204-8873-1 LC Card 85-200073
HJ131 .K56 1985

Langfristige Finanzplanung und Simulationsmodelle . Prätsch, Joachim, 1951- Frankfurt am Main , New Yo[illegible] xii, 481 p. : ISBN 3-8204-9403-[illegible] 86-219850
HG4157 .P73 1986

Langfristiges Anlagengeschäft, Risiko-Management und Controlling / herausgegeben von Joachim Funk und Gert Lassmann. Düsseldorf : Verlagsgruppe Handelsblatt, c1986. 148 p. : ill. ; 24 cm. (Schmalenbachs Zeitschrift für betriebswirtschaftliche Forschung. Sonderheft . 20, 1986) Papers presented at the Schmalenbach-Tagung 1986 held Apt. 29 in Düsseldorf sponsored by the Schmalenbach-Gesellschaft--Deutsche Gesellschaft für Betriebswirtschaft. Bibliography: p. 142-145. Includes index. CONTENTS. - Volkswirtschaftliche Bedeutuung und betriebswirtschaftliche Besonderheiten des industriellen Anlagengeschäfts / Joachim Funk -- Risiken und Risiko-Management im Anlagenbau / Klaus von Lindeiner -Wildau -- Ansätze zur Beurteilung von Länderrisiken / Klaus Backhaus -- Beurteilung von Zinsrisiken der Absatzfinanzierung / Andreas Kley -- Planungs- und Kontrollrechnung im Anlagengeschäft / Helmut Hay -- Das Anlagengeschaft im Jahresabschluss / Ernst Höffken. ISBN 3-7754-0016-8 LC Card 86-227044
1. Investment banking - Germany (West) - Congresses. 2. Risk management - Germany (West) - Congresses. 3. Controllership - Congresses. I. Funk, Joachim. II. Lassmann, Gert. III. Schmalenbach-Tagung 1986 (1986 : Düsseldorf, Germany). IV. Schmalenbach-Gesellschaft--Deutsche Gesellschaft für Betriebswirtschaft.
HG4534 .L36 1986

Langhammer, Rolf J.
Economic impact of generalized tariff preferences / Rolf J. Langhammer and André Sapir. Aldershot, Hants, England ; Brookfield, Vt. : Gower Pub. Co., 1988. p. cm. (Thames essays. no. 49) Bibliography: p. ISBN 0-566-05338-1 : LC Card 87-15045 DDC 382.7/53 19
1. Tariff preferences. 2. Tariff preferences - United States. 3. Tariff preferences - European Economic Community countries. 4. Developing countries - Commerce. I. Sapir, André. II. Series. III. Series: Thames essay , no. 49. IV. Title.
HF1721 .L35 1988

Wirtschaftliche Zusammenarbeit zwischen den Entwicklungsländern : Chancen und Risiken / Rolf J. Langhammer, Dean Spinanger. Tübingen : J.C.B. Mohr, c1984. xi, 135 p. : ill. ; 24 cm. (Kieler Studien, 0340-6989 . 190) Bibliography: p. 126-135. ISBN 3-16-344889-5 : LC Card 85-143693
1. Developing countries - Economic integration. 2. International economic integration. I. Spinanger, Dean. II. Title. III. Series.
HF1413 .L363 1984

Langhoff, Gary M., 1952- Assessment jurisdictions and agency resources in the United States : summary report of 1986 survey / by Gary M. Langhoff. Chicago, Ill. : International Association of Assessing Officers, Professional Services Dept., 1987. p. cm. (Research and information series . no. 6) "January 1987." ISBN 0-88329-061-8 : LC Card 87-4101 DDC 336.22/2 19
1. Assessment - United States. 2. Tax administration and procedure - United States. I. Title. II. Series.
HJ3241 .L36 1987

Langholm, Odd Inge, 1928- The Aristotelian analysis of usury / Odd Langholm. Bergen [Norway] : Universitetsforlaget ; New York, NY : Columbia University Press [distributor], c1984. 153 p. ; 23 cm. Bibliography: p. [152]-153. ISBN 82-00-07290-8 LC Card 85-167906 DDC 332.8/3/09 19
1. Usury - Moral and ethical aspects - History. 2. Economics - History - To 1800. I. Title.
HB551 .L36 1984 ***NYPL [JLD 86-2545]***

Langkamp, Peter. Die Erfassung von Carryover-Effekten im Marketing : kritische Analyse ökonometrischer Modelle zur Messung periodenübergreifender Werbewirkungen / Peter Langkamp. Thun : H. Deutsch, c1984. 335 p. : ill. ; 21 cm. (Reihe Wirtschaftswissenschaften, 0253-1488 . Bd. 320) Bibliography: p. 313-335. ISBN 3-87144-844-3 : LC Card 85-113501
1. Market surveys - Econometric models. 2. Consumers' preferences - Econometric models. I. Title. II. Series.
HF5415.3 .L36 1984

Langkau, Jochem. Wirtschaftspolitik und wirtschaftliche Entwicklung . Bonn , c1985. xii, 248 p. : ISBN 3-87831-405-1 LC Card 85-142846
HD75 .W57 1985

Langmantel, Erich. Sherman, Heidemarie C. Der Einfluss staatlicher Budgetdefizite auf die Zinsentwicklung in der Bundesrepublik Deutschland und den Vereinigten Staaten . München , c1986. xxiii, 190 p. : ISBN 3-88512-019-4 LC Card 86-192070
HJ2110 .S53 1986

Langmár, Andrásné. A Német Szövetségi Köztársaság bankrendszere / készítette, Langmár Andrásné. Budapest : Magyar Nemzeti Bank, [1987] 71 p. : 2 ill. ; 29 cm. (MNB Közgazdasági Főosztály közleményei, 0231-259X . 13) "1987. március hó." Bibliography: p. 71. ISBN 963-7103-59-7 LC Card 87-409642
1. Banks and banking - Germany, West. 2. Deutsche Bundesbank. I. Title. II. Series.
HG3048 .L47 1987

Langoni, Carlos Geraldo. A crise do desenvolvimento, uma estratégia para o futuro / Carlos Geraldo Langoni. Rio de Janeiro : J. Olympio Editora, 1985. xix, 176 p. : ill. ; 21 cm. Bibliography: p. 174-176. ISBN 85-03-00001-6 : LC Card 85-151246 DDC 338.981 19
1. International Monetary Fund - Brazil. 2. Monetary policy - Brazil. 3. Monetary policy - Latin America. 4. Balance of payments - Brazil. I. Title.
HG835 .L36 1985 ***NYPL [JLD 86-288]***

Langton, Stuart. Citizen participation in public decision making /. Westport, Conn. , 1987. xii, 237 p. ; ISBN 0-313-25478-8 (lib. bdg. : alk. paper) : LC Card 86-7571 DDC 323/.042/0973 19
JK1764 .C525 1987 ***NYPL [JLD 87-932]***

LANGUAGE AND LANGUAGES - STUDY AND TEACHING - HUNGARY - CONGRESSES.
A Vállalati magatartást motiváló gazdasági és társadalmi tényezők című konferencia előadásai . Pécs , 1985. 2 v. : LC Card 87-408547
HD70.H8 V334 1985

La langue de l'économie, de la technique à la banalisation /. Richelle Giampiccoli, Emma. Torino [1983] 114 p. ; LC Card 84-141597
HB62 .R53 1983

LANGUE D'OÏL. see **FRENCH LANGUAGE.**

Langumier, Jean-François. Laborie, Jean Paul. La politique française d'amenagement du territoire de 1950 à 1985 /. Paris , 1985. 176 p., [8] p. of plates : ISBN 2-11-001488-1(pbk.) :
NYPL [JLG 87-38]

Langwell, Kathryn M. A synthesis of research on competition in the financing and delivery of health services / Kathryn M. Langwell, Sylvia F. Moore. Hyattsville, MD. : U. S. Dept. of Health and Human Services, Public Health Service, Office of Health Research, Statistics, and Technology, National Center for Health Services Research ; Springfield, VA : Available from National Technical Information Service, 1982. 85 p. ; 28 cm. (NCHSR research report series) DHHS publication ; no. (PHS) 83-3327 "Applied Management Sciences, Inc."--T.p. verso. "October 1982." "Contract 233-81-3031"--T.p. verso. Item 491-B-13 Bibliography: p. 75-85. LC Card 82-600612 DDC 338.4/73621/0973 19
1. Medical care - United States - Marketing. 2. Competition - United States. 3. Medical care, Cost of - United States. I. Moore, Sylvia F. II. National Center for Health Services Research. III. Applied Management Sciences, inc. IV. Title. V. Series.
RA410.53 .L36 1982 ***NYPL [JLF 86-422]***

LANHEZES (PORTUGAL) - POPULATION - HISTORY.
Brettell, Caroline. Men who migrate, women who wait . Princeton , c1986. xv, 329 p., [8] p. of plates : ISBN 0-691-09424-1 (alk. paper) : LC Card 86-11270 DDC 304.6/09469/12 19
HB2082.L36 B74 1986 ***NYPL [JLE 87-1417]***

Lanier, Lucien. Les entreprises dans la décentralisation / Lucien Lanier. Paris : ETP, [1985] xvi, 217 p. ; 21 cm. At head of title: CNPF. Cover title. "Novembre 1984"--P. i. ISBN 2-86658-028-1 : LC Card 85-217648 DDC 338.944 19
1. Industry and state - France. 2. Decentralization in government - France. I. Title.
HD3616.F83 L28 1985 ***NYPL [JLD 87-546]***

Lanin, V. P. (Vladimir Petrovich) Deiatel'nost' partiĭnykh organizatsiĭ po razvitiiu promyshlennosti Urala v period razvitogo sotsializma . Perm' , 1984. 96 p. ; LC Card 86-181271
HC337.R852 U734 1984

Lankinen, Leila. Asuminen Helsingissä 1950-1983 = Boende i Helsingfors 1950-1983 / [tekijä(t), Lankinen, Leila]. Helsinki : TILK, 1985. 80 p. : ill. ; 30 cm. (Helsingin kaupungin Tilastokeskuksen tilastoja, 0781-0512. A, Väestö, työvoima, asuminen = Helsingfors stads Statistikcentrals statistik. A, Befolkning, arbetskraft, boende . 1985 A:2) Prepared by Leila Lankinen and Virva Kuparinen. Bibliography: p. 79-80. LC Card 86-148571
1. Housing - Finland - Helsinki - Statistics. 2. Housing - Finland - Statistics. 3. Helsinki (Finland) - Population - Statistics. I. Kuparinen, Virva. II. Title. III. Title: Boende i Helsingfors 1950-1983. IV. Series: Tilastoja. A, Väestö, työvoima, asuminen , 1985:2.
HD7345.3.H5 L35 1985

Lankinen, Markku. Kinturi, Jorma. Väestö, asunnot ja asuntorakentaminen suur- ja peruspiireittäin Helsingissä 1970-1983 =. Helsinki , 1984. 36 p., [1] folded leaf of plates : LC Card 85-156678
HD7345.3.H5 K563 1984

Lanning, Greg. Making cars . London , Boston , c1985. ix, 131 p. : ISBN 0-7102-0272-5 : LC Card 84-13398 DDC 338.4/76292/0942574 19
HD8039.A82 G75 1984
NYPL [JLE 86-2303]

Lannithanga, p., 1928- Household population by religion of head of household, upto C.D. block and town level, series 31, Mizoram . Delhi , 1986. xiii, 17 p. ; LC Card 87-900232 DDC 304.6/0954/166021 19
HA4587.M58 H68 1986

Lannon, John M. Dumont, Raymond A. Business communications /. Boston , c1987. xxii, 602 p. : ISBN 0-316-19536-7 LC Card 86-21125 DDC 808/.066651 19
HF5718 .D845 1987

Lansbury, Russell D. Democracy and control in the workplace /. Melbourne, Australia , 1986. 388 p. ; ISBN 0-582-71159-2 (pbk.) LC Card 87-102095 DDC 331.01/12 19
HD5660.A8 D46 1986

LANSING, MICH. - HISTORY.
Whitford, Craig A. Postmarked . Lansing, Mich. (P.O. Box 14225, Lansing 48901) , c1987. 27 p., [2] p. of plates : LC Card 87-402869 DDC 769.56/7/0977427 19
HE6185.U7 M59 1987

Lansky, Bruce. Wall Street bull / Bruce Lansky. Deephaven, MN : Meadowbrook ; New York : Distributed by Simon and Schuster, c1987. iii, 111 p. : ill. ; 21 cm. ISBN 0-88166-100-7 (pbk.) : LC Card 87-16467 DDC 332.6/0207 19
1. Investments - Dictionaries - Anecdotes, facetiae, satire, etc. 2. Finance - Dictionaries - Anecdotes, facetiae, satire, etc. I. Title.
HG4513 .L29 1987

Lansley, Peter R.
Construction management and organisation in perspective /. London , New York , 1987. p. cm. ISBN 0-419-14020-4 LC Card 87-20548 DDC 624/.068 s 624/.068 19
HD9715.A2 M296 vol. 3

Managing construction worldwide /. London , New York , 1987. p. cm. ISBN 0-419-14030-1 (set) LC Card 87-20545 DDC 624/.068 19
HD9715.A2 M296

Productivity and human factors in construction /. London , New York , 1987. p. cm. ISBN 0-419-14010-7 LC Card 87-20547 DDC 624/.068 s 624/.068/3 19
HD9715.A2 M296 vol. 2

Systems for managing construction /. London , New York , 1987. p. cm. ISBN 0-419-14000-X LC Card 87-20546 DDC 624/.068 s 624/.068 19
HD9715.A2 M296 vol. 1

Lant, Jeffrey L. Money talks : the complete guide to creating a profitable workshop or seminar in any field / Jeffrey Lant. Cambridge, Mass. : JLA Publications, c1985. vii, 302 p. : ill. ; 28 cm. ISBN 0-940374-08-0 (pbk.) LC Card 87-105725 DDC 001 19
1. Consultants - Handbooks, manuals, etc. 2. Congresses and conventions - Handbooks, manuals, etc. 3. Seminars - Handbooks, manuals, etc. 4. Selling - Handbooks, manuals, etc. I. Title.
HD69.C6 L27 1985

Lanu Imchen. Roy Burman, B. K. Towards poverty alleviation programmes in Nagaland and Manipur /. Delhi , 1984. xxxi, 123 p. ; LC Card 84-902780 DDC 338.954/165 19
HC437.N25 R69 1984 ***NYPL [JLD 87-903]***

Lányfalvi, Sándor. Adalékok a tartósítóipar hosszútávu fejlesztésének megalapozásához / Lányfalvi Sándor, Vajda János. Budapest : Agrárgazdasági Kutató Intézet, 1984. 115 p. ; 29 cm. (Agrárgazdasági Kutató Intézet, 0209-5696 . 1984/21) Errata slip inserted. Bibliography: p. 91-93. ISBN 963-491-199-4 LC Card 86-199120
1. Canning and preserving - Industry and trade - Hungary. I. Vajda, János. II. Series: Agrárgazdasági Kutató Intézet (Series) , 1984/21. III. Title.
HD9326.H82 L36 1984

Lanzanova, Lucia. Il Sistema dei trasporti nello sviluppo della cooperazione economica internazionale . Milano, Italy , c1985. 341 p. ; LC Card 85-218403
HE2449 .S57 1985

Lanzaro, Jorge Luis. Sindicatos y sistema político : relaciones corporativas en el Uruguay, 1940-1985 / Jorge Luis Lanzaro.1a ed. Montevideo, Uruguay : Fundación de Cultura Universitaria, 1986. 132 p. ; 22 cm. (Temas nacionales. 14) Bibliography: p. 127-132. LC Card 87-403149 DDC 322/.2/09895 19
1. Corporate state - Uruguay - History - 20th century. 2. Trade-unions - Uruguay - History - 20th century. 3. Uruguay - Politics and government - 1904-1973. 4. Uruguay - Politics and government - 1973-. I. Series. II. Series: Colección TN , 14. III. Title.
HD3616.U72 L36 1986

Laos.
Rapport sur la situation économique et sociale, stratégie de développement et besoins d'assistance, 1986-1990 : rapport principal préparé pour la IIème Table ronde des pays les moins avancés d'Asie et du Pacifique, en exécution du Nouveau programme substantiel d'action pour les années quatre-vingt / République démocratique populaire Lao. Genève : La République démocratique, [1986- v. <1 > : maps ; 30 cm. "Avril 1986." LC Card 86-204475
1. Laos - Economic conditions. 2. Laos - Social conditions. 3. Laos - Economic policy. I. Title.
HC443 .L36 1986

LAOS - ECONOMIC CONDITIONS.
Laos. Rapport sur la situation économique et sociale, stratégie de développement et besoins d'assistance, 1986-1990 . Genève [1986- v. <1 > : LC Card 86-204475
HC443 .L36 1986

Opyt stroitel'stva sotsialisticheskoĭ ėkonomiki v stranakh Azii /. Moskva , 1986. 290 p. ; LC Card 87-126301
HC412 .O675 1986

LAOS - ECONOMIC POLICY.
Laos. Rapport sur la situation économique et sociale, stratégie de développement et besoins d'assistance, 1986-1990 . Genève [1986- v. <1 > : LC Card 86-204475
HC443 .L36 1986

LAOS - SOCIAL CONDITIONS.
Laos. Rapport sur la situation économique et sociale, stratégie de développement et besoins d'assistance, 1986-1990 . Genève [1986- v. <1 > : LC Card 86-204475
HC443 .L36 1986

Lapan, Harvey. Enders, Walter, 1948- International economics . Englewood Cliffs, N.J. , c1987. xii, 542 p. : ISBN 0-13-472853-X : LC Card 86-30623 DDC 337 19
HF1411 .E49 1987

Lapham, Lewis H. Money and class in America : notes and observations on a civil religion / Lewis H. Lapham.1st ed. New York : Weidenfeld & Nicolson, 1988, c1987. p. cm. Includes index. ISBN 1-555-84109-0 LC Card 87-22515 DDC 305.5/234/0973 19
1. Wealth - United States. 2. Money - United States. 3. Social classes - United States. 4. Millionaires - United States. I. Title.
HC110.W4 L24 1988

Lapides, Kenneth. The battle of the boycott : free speech for labor / Kenny Lapides. New York, N.Y. : Center for United Labor Action, 1974. 22 p., [3] p. of plates : ill. ; 21 cm. LC Card 87-125953 DDC 331.89/3 19
1. Farah Manufacturing Company Strike, 1972-1974. 2. Boycotts - New York - Rochester. I. Center for United Labor Action. II. Title.
HD5325.C62 1972 .L36 1974

Lapidus, Gail Warshofsky. Women in Soviet society : equality, development, and social change / Gail Warshofsky Lapidus. Berkeley : University of California Press, c1978. x, 381 p. ; 25 cm. Includes index. Bibliography: p. 347-361. ISBN 0-520-02868-6 : LC Card 74-16710 DDC 305.4/0947
1. Women - Soviet Union - Social conditions. 2. Women's rights - Soviet Union. 3. Sex role. I. Title.
HQ1663 .L33 ***NYPL [JLE 80-1771]***

Lapin, Lawrence L. Statistics for modern business decisions / Lawrence L. Lapin. 4th ed. San Diego : Harcourt Brace Jovanovich, c1987. xxxiii, 825 p. : ill. (some col.) ; 25 cm. Bibliography: p. 761-763. Includes index. ISBN 0-15-583737-0 LC Card 85-82633 DDC 519.5/024658 19
1. Social sciences - Statistical methods. 2. Commercial statistics. 3. Statistics. I. Title.
HA29 .L2664 1987

Lapitskiĭ, Mark Isaakovich. The tragedy of millions : social and psychological aspects of unemployment / Mark Lapitsky ; [translated from the Russian by Andrei Ogorodnev ; translation edited by George Wood]. Moscow : Novosti Press Agency Pub. House, 1985. 54 p., [8] p. of plates : ill. ; 17 cm. Title on verso t.p.: Tragediia millionov. Includes bibliographical references. LC Card 87-100047 DDC 331.13/7 19
1. Unemployment. 2. Unemployment - Psychological aspects. 3. Capitalism. I. Title. II. Title: Tragediia millionov.
HD5708 .L36 1985

Lapointe, Alain. Les industries québécoises de services télématiques : analyse économique / Alain Lapointe, Jean-Pierre LeGoff ; collaborateurs, René Poirier, Diane Therrien, Odette Voyer. Montréal : Institut d'économie appliquée, Ecole des hautes études commerciales, [1984] x, 305 p. : ill. ; 28 cm. Bibliography: p. 257-266. ISBN 2-551-06190-3 LC Card 84-230415 DDC 384/.09714 19
1. Telecommunication - Québec (Province). 2. Telecommunication equipment industry - Québec (Province). I. Legoff, Jean-Pierre, 1946-. II. Title.
HE7818.Q4 L36 1984 ***NYPL [JLF 86-1397]***

Laporte, Robert. Pakistan's development priorities . Karachi , 1984. 390 p. ; LC Card 85-930745 DDC 338.9549/1 19
HC440.5 .P3624 1984b

Lapp, Robert. Developing effective telephone skills / Robert Lapp. 2nd ed. Eau Claire, WI : Professional Education Systems, c1987. 56 p. : ill. ; 23 cm. ISBN 0-941161-20-X (pbk.) LC Card 87-403090 DDC 651.7/3 19
1. Telephone in business. 2. Telephone etiquette. I. Title.
HF5541.T4 L36 1987

Lappé, Frances Moore. Betraying the national interest / Francis Moore Lappé, Rachel Schurman, Kevin Danaher. 1st ed. New York : Grove Press, 1987, c1986. p. cm. "A Food first book." Bibliography: p. ISBN 0-8021-0012-0 LC Card 87-12067 DDC 338.91 19
1. Economic assistance - Developing countries. I. Schurman, Rachel. II. Danaher, Kevin. III. Title.
HC60 .L325 1987

Laquian, Aprodicio A. Basic housing : policies for urban sites, services, and shelter in developing countries / Aprodicio A. Laquian. Ottawa, Canada : International Development Research Centre, c1983. 163 p. : ill. ; 25 cm. (IDRC. 208e) Abstract in French and Spanish. Bibliography: p. [159]-163. ISBN 0-88936-370-6 (pbk.) LC Card 83-231129 DDC 363.5/8/091724 19
1. Housing policy - Developing countries. 2. Community development, Urban - Developing countries. I. International Development Research Centre. II. Title.
HD7391 .L36 1983 ***NYPL [JLE 86-1376]***

Larcombe, Graham. Markey, Ray. The trade union response to technological change in Australia /. Kensington, N.S.W. , 1983. iii, 56 p. ; ***NYPL [JLE 87-904]***

Lardy, Nicholas R. China's entry into the world economy : implications for northeast Asia and the United States / by Nicholas R. Lardy. Lanham, MD : University Press of America ; New York, N.Y. : Asia Society, c1987. xviii, 57 p. : ill. ; 24 cm. (Asian agenda report . 11) Bibliography: p. 56. ISBN 0-8191-6371-6 (alk. paper) : LC Card 87-10625 DDC 382/.0951 19
1. China - Commerce - East Asia. 2. East Asia - Commerce - China. 3. China - Commerce - United States. 4. United States - Commerce - China. 5. China - Commerce - Europe, Eastern. 6. Europe, Eastern - Commerce - United States. I. Title. II. Series.
HF3820.5 .L37 1987

Lareau, William. Millennium management : last chance for American business / William Lareau. Piscataway, NJ : New Century Publishers, [1986]. ix, 214 p. : ill. ; 24 cm. Includes index. ISBN 0-8329-0431-7 : LC Card 86-18247 DDC 658.4/06 19
1. Organization effectiveness. 2. Industrial management - United States. I. Title.
HD58.8 .L37 1986 ***NYPL [JLE 87-1139]***

Lárez, Ronald. Análisis económico social de las comunidades pesqueras del Estado Sucre / Ronald Lárez. 2a ed. [Carúpano, Venezuela] : Colegio Universitario de Carúpano, 1983. 217, 19, 8 p. : ill. ; 21 cm. "Este trabajo fue presentado como requisito para optar a la categoría de profesor asociado en el Colegio Universitario de Carúpano"--Front flap. Bibliography: p. 213-217. LC Card 87-115222 DDC 338.3/72/098753 19
1. Fishers - Venezuela - Sucre (State). 2. Fish trade - Venezuela - Sucre (State). 3. Fishing villages - Venezuela - Sucre (State). I. Title.
HD8039.F652 V45 1983

Larkin, V. A. (Vladimir Alekseevich) Sotsial'no-ėkonomicheskie problemy kompleksnoĭ mekhanizatsii sel'skokhoziaĭstvennogo proizvodstva / V.A. Larkin. Moskva : "Mysl'", 1981. 148 p. ; 20 cm. Includes bibliographical references. LC Card 82-157096
1. Agricultural productivity - Soviet Union. 2. Agricultural machinery - Soviet Union. I. Title.
HD1992 .L375 1981

Laroque, Guy. Fondements de l'analyse macroéconomique à court terme / par Guy Laroque. Paris : Editions du Centre national de la recherche scientifique : Diffusion, Presses du CNRS, 1986. 98 p. : ill. ; 25 cm. (Monographies d'économétrie) Bibliography: p. [97]-98. ISBN 2-222-03757-3 : LC Card 87-103537
1. Macroeconomics. I. Title. II. Series.
HB173 .L35 1986

Larousse Spanish dictionary. The American heritage Larousse Spanish dictionary . Boston , c1986. xxx, 532, xviii, 572 p. ; ISBN 0-395-32429-7 : LC Card 86-7202 DDC 463/.21 19
PC4640 .A54 1986
NYPL [*R-RGK 86-5942]

Larraín P., Christian. Subsidiariedad o intervencionismo? : las funciones económicas del estado, 1980-1985 / Christian Larraín P., Mario Velásquez P. [Santiago, Chile] : Programa de Economía del Trabajo, Academia de Humanismo Cristiano, [1986] 137 p. ; 22 cm. (Colección Estudios económicos . 1) Bibliography: p. 117-120. LC Card 87-401544 DDC 338.983 19
1. Chile - Economic policy. 2. Chile - Economic conditions - 1970-. I. Velásquez P., Mario. II. Title. III. Series.
HC192 .L36 1986

Larrazábal, Radamés. Los planes del capitalismo para la década de los 80 / Radamés Larrazábal. [Caracas, Venezuela? : s.n., 1982] (Caracas, Venezuela : Cooperative Mixta de Trabajadores Gráficos) 81 p. ; 23 cm. Bibliography: p. 81. LC Card 83-201901
1. Venezuela - Economic policy. 2. Capitalism - Venezuela. I. Title.
HC237 .L325 1982

Larrea Stacey, Eduardo, 1911- Pensamiento monetario y financiero /. Quito, Ecuador , 1986. 2 v. : LC Card 87-150740 DDC 332.4/9866 19
HG862 .P46 1986

Larréché, Jean-Claude. INDUSTRAT : the strategic industrial marketing simulation / Jean-Claude Larréché, David Weinstein. Englewood Cliffs, N.J. : Prentice Hall, 1987. p. cm. Includes index. ISBN 0-13-651373-5 LC Card 87-7144 DDC 658.8 19
1. Industrial marketing. 2. Management games. I. Weinstein, David, 1943-. II. Title.
HF5415.1263 .L37 1987

Larsen, E. John. Modern advanced accounting / E. John Larsen, A.N. Mosich. 4th ed. New York : McGraw-Hill, c1988. xx, 1002 p. ; 24 cm. Rev. ed. of: Modern advanced accounting / A.N. Mosich, E. John Larsen. 3rd ed. 1983. Includes bibliographical references and index. ISBN 0-07-036508-3 : LC Card 87-22621 DDC 657/.046 19
1. Accounting. I. Mosich, A. N. II. Mosich, A. N. Modern advanced accounting. III. Title.
HF5635 .M8756 1988

Larsen, Flemming. Parkeringsbehov i ældre tætte bydele : rapport. København : Miljøministeriet, Planstyrelsen, 1985. 250 p. : ill. ; 30 cm. Prepared by Flemming Larsen and Per Thost. LC Card 86-165642
1. Automobile parking - Denmark. 2. City traffic - Denmark. I. Thost, Per. II. Denmark. Planstyrelsen. III. Title.
HE336.P37 L37 1985

Larson, Elwin S. Brooklyn Union Gas : fueling growth and change in New York City / Elwin S. Larson. New York : Newcomen Society of the United States, 1987. 23 p. : ill. ; 23 cm. (Newcomen publication. no. 1286) "Address ... delivered at a '1987 national meeting' of the Newcomen Society of the United States held in New York City ... on April 22nd, 1987"--P. 1. LC Card 87-60614 DDC 338.7/6657/0974723 19
1. Brooklyn Union Gas Company - History. 2. Gas companies - New York (N.Y.) - History. 3. Gas industry - New York (N.Y.) - History. I. Newcomen Society of the United States. II. Title.
HD9581.U53 B765 1987

Larson, Kermit D.
Fundamental accounting principles /. Homewood, Ill. , 1987. xvii, 1230 p. : ISBN 0-256-03601-2 LC Card 86-83105 DDC 657 19
HF5635 .P975 1987b

Fundamental accounting principles / Kermit D. Larson, William W. Pyle. 11th ed. Homewood, Ill. : Irwin, 1987. xxxi, 1076 p. : col. ill. ; 26 cm. (The Robert N. Anthony/Willard J. Graham series in accounting) Pyle's name appears 1st on 10th ed. Includes index. ISBN 0-256-03574-1 LC Card 86-81958 DDC 657 19
1. Accounting. I. Pyle, William W. II. Title. III. Series.
HF5635 .P975 1987

Larson, Simeon, 1925- Theories of the labor movement /. Detroit, Mich. , 1987. xi, 395 p. ; ISBN 0-8143-1815-0 : LC Card 86-32414 DDC 331.88/09 19
HD6476 .T47 1987

Larsson, Folke. Varuhandeln. [Stockholm] : LiberFörlag, [1981] 137 p. : ill. ; 21 cm. By Folke Larsson and Per Nellevad. "LU 80, bilaga 3." Includes bibliographical references. "Ds E 1981:1." ISBN 91-38-06014-0 LC Card 84-120411
1. Retail trade - Sweden. 2. Wholesale trade - Sweden. I. Nellevad, Per. II. Sweden. Ekonomidepartementet. Långtidsutredningen 1980. III. Title.
HF5429.6.S9 L368 1981

Larsson, Janerik, 1944- Vändpunkten : boken om 4 oktober 1983 / av Janerik Larsson. [Stockholm] : Timbro, [1983] 125 p. : ill. (some col.) ; 25 cm. ISBN 91-7566-040-7 : LC Card 84-189468
1. Employee ownership - Political aspects - Sweden. 2. Demonstrations - Sweden - Stockholm. I. Title.
HD5660.S9 L35 1983

Larsson, Lena. Granath, Erna. Kvinnoplats . Stockholm , c1985. 141 p. ; ISBN

91-38-90602-3 : LC Card 85-236327
HD6073.M392 S84 1985
NYPL [JLE 86-3898]

Larsson, Mats, 1953- Arbete och lön vid Bredsjö bruk : en studie av löneprinciper och lönenivåer för olika yrkeskategorier vid Bredsjö bruk 1828-1905 / Mats Larsson. Uppsala : [Universitetet] ; Stockholm : Distributor, Almqvist & Wiksell International, 1986. 233 p. : ill. ; 22 cm. (Acta Universitatis Upsaliensis. Uppsala studies in economic history, 0346-6493 . 26) Thesis (doctoral)--Uppsala universitet, 1986. Summary in English. Bibliography: p. 217-219. ISBN 91-554-1822-8 LC Card 86-212849
1. Wages - Iron and steel workers - Sweden - History - 19th century - Case studies. I. Title. II. Series.
HD4966.I52 S845 1986

LARU working paper .
(18) Hellman, Judith Adler. Notes on the failure of reformist capitalism in Mexico /. Toronto, Ont., Canada [1976] 24 p ; LC Card 85-155317 DDC 338.972 19
HC135 .H38 1976

Larwood, Laurie. Strategies-- successes-- senior executives speak out /. New York , c1988. xiii, 397 p. : ISBN 0-06-044354-5 (pbk.) LC Card 87-21765 DDC 658 19
HD31 .S696394 1988

Las artesanías de cuero y tejido en el Paraguay . Morínigo, José N. Asunción , 1979. 106, [1] p. : LC Card 83-219583
HD9780.P373 A866 1979
NYPL [JLF 86-1810]

Las carneradas . Baxter, John O., 1927- Albuquerque , c1987. x, 198 p., [4] p. of plates : ISBN 0-8263-0961-5 LC Card 86-30906 DDC 381/.4163/009789 19
HD9436.U53 N63 1987

Las cooperativas en el Perú, su situación actual y legislación vigente /. Torres y Torres Lara, Carlos. Lima, Perú , 1985. 144 p. ; LC Card 86-110544 DDC 346.85/0668 348.506668 19
KHQ1370 .T67 1985 *NYPL [JLD 86-2183]*

Las Derrotas obreras, 1946-1952 / Víctor M. Durand Ponte, coordinador ; Guadalupe Cortés A. ... [et al.]. 1a ed. México : Universidad Nacional Autónoma de México, Instituto de Investigaciones Sociales, 1984. 204 p. ; 23 cm. Includes bibliographies. ISBN 968-580-647-0 LC Card 84-255708 DDC 331.88/0972 19
1. Trade-unions - Mexico - History. 2. Strikes and lockouts - Mexico - History. I. Durand Ponte, Víctor Manuel. II. Cortés A., Guadalupe. III. Universidad Nacional Autónoma de México. Instituto de Investigaciones Sociales.
HD6532 .D36 1984 *NYPL [JLE 86-4685]*

Las desigualdades económicas y la acción del estado . Foxley, Alejandro. México , 1980. 271 p. ; ISBN 968-16-0365-6 LC Card 82-215955 DDC 339.2/098 19
HC130.I5 F69 1980 *NYPL [JLD 86-2631]*

Las empresas azucareras y la reforma agraria /. Zúñiga Trelles, Washington. [S.l. , 1981] ([S.l.] : EBRASA) 108 p. ; LC Card 81-204318 DDC 333.3/1/85 19
HD9114.P52 Z86 1981 *NYPL [JLD 87-922]*

Las formas de consumo en Colombia . Salazar T., Boris. [Cali, Colombia] [1982] 118, [45] p. ; LC Card 85-192219 DDC 658.8/343/0986152 19
HC200.C6 S25 1982 *NYPL [JLD 86-1935]*

Las Transnacionales en el Paraguay / Ricardo Rodríguez Silvero ... [et al.]. Asunción, Paraguay : Editorial Histórica : Fundación Friedrich Naumann, [1985] 317 p. : ill. ; 20 cm. Includes bibliographies. LC Card 86-112866 DDC 338.8/88892 19
1. International business enterprises - Paraguay - Congresses. 2. International business enterprises - Developing coutries - Congreses. 3. Investments, Foreign - Paraguay - Congresses. 4. Investments, Foreign - Developing countries - Congresses. I. Rodríguez Silvero, Ricardo.
HD2840 .T7 1985 *NYPL [JLD 86-2210]*

Lasch, Vera. Ipsen, Detlev. Markt und Raum . Frankfurt , New York , c1986. 250 p. : ISBN 3-593-33685-5 LC Card 87-127593 DDC 363.5/8 19
HD7339.M35 I67 1986

Laser . Caldas, Maria das Graças Conde. [São Paulo] , c1986. 95 p. ; LC Card 87-143863 DDC 338.4/7621366/0981 19
HD9999.L323 B63 1986

LASER INDUSTRY - BRAZIL.
Caldas, Maria das Graças Conde. Laser . [São Paulo] , c1986. 95 p. ; LC Card 87-143863 DDC 338.4/7621366/0981 19
HD9999.L323 B63 1986

LASER PHOTOGRAPHY. see **HOLOGRAPHY.**

LaserWrite it! . Cavuoto, James. Reading, Mass. , 1986. viii, 198 p. : ISBN 0-201-11327-9 : LC Card 86-3406 DDC 070.5/028/5 19
Z286.E43 C38 1986 *NYPL [JSE 86-1226]*

LASERWRITER (PRINTER)
Cavuoto, James. LaserWrite it! . Reading, Mass. , 1986. viii, 198 p. : ISBN 0-201-11327-9 : LC Card 86-3406 DDC 070.5/028/5 19
Z286.E43 C38 1986 *NYPL [JSE 86-1226]*

Lash, Scott.
The end of organized capitalism / Scott Lash and John Urry. Madison, Wis. : University of Wisconsin Press, c1987. 383 p. : ill. ; 24 cm. Bibliography: p. [314]-377. Includes index. ISBN 0-299-11670-0 : LC Card 87-14248 DDC 330.12/2 19
1. Capitalism. 2. Organizational change. 3. Decentralization in management. I. Urry, John. II. Title.
HB501 .L278 1987

The militant worker : class and radicalism in France and America / Scott Lash. London : Heinemann Educational, 1984. vii, 264 p. ; 23 cm. Based on the author's thesis (Ph. D.)--London School of Economics. Bibliography: p. [242]-258. Includes index. ISBN 0-435-82516-X LC Card 87-673366
1. Labor and laboring classes - United States - Political activity. 2. Labor and laboring classes - France - Political activity. 3. Social conflict - United States. 4. Social conflict - France. 5. Radicalism - United States. 6. Radicalism - France. I. Title.
HD8076 .L37x 1984b

Lasker, Saidur R., 1940- Thigpen, M. Elton, 1932- World demand prospects for jute /. Washington, D.C. , Rome , 1987. vi, 178 p. ; ISBN 0-8213-0867-X (pbk.) LC Card 86-32522 DDC 338.4/767713 19
HD9156.J7 T46 1987

Laskin, David. Getting into advertising / David Laskin. 1st ed. New York : Ballantine Books, 1986. xiii, 272 p. : ill. ; 24 cm. Bibliography: p. 255-264. Includes index. ISBN 0-345-32598-2 (pbk.) LC Card 86-90721 DDC 659.1/023/73 19
1. Advertising - Vocational guidance. 2. Job hunting. 3. Advertising agencies. 4. Executives - Interviews. I. Title.
HF5828.4 .L37 1986

Lasok, Dominik. The customs law of the European Economic Community / by D. Lasok and W. Cairns. Deventer, Netherlands ; Boston : Kluwer Law and Taxation Publishers, c1983. xxiii, 292 p. : ill. ; 24 cm. Spine title: The customs law of the EEC. Includes index. Bibliography: p. 287-289. ISBN 90-6544-077-1 (pbk.) : LC Card 84-148702 DDC 343.405/6 344.0356 19
1. Customs administration - Law and legislation - European Economic Community countries. 2. Tariff - Law and legislation - European Economic Community countries. 3. Foreign trade regulation - European Economic Community countries. I. Cairns, W. II. Title. III. Title: Customs law of the EEC. IV. Title: Customs law of the E.E.C.
LAW *NYPL [JLE 86-2073]*

Lasserve, Allain Durand- see **Durand-Lasserve, Alain.**

Lassmann, Gert.
Busse von Colbe, Walther. Betriebswirtschaftstheorie /. Berlin , New York , <c1986-. v. <3 > : ISBN 0-387-16407-3 (Bd. 3 : U. S.) LC Card 87-103759
HD35 .B88 1986

Langfristiges Anlagengeschäft, Risiko-Management und Controlling /. Düsseldorf , c1986. 148 p. : ISBN 3-7754-0016-8 LC Card 86-227044
HG4534 .L36 1986

Last chance for peace . Vance, A. Boulder, Colo. , c1985. xviii, 256 p. : ISBN 0-930705-01-7 (pbk.) : LC Card 84-18831 DDC 172/.24 19
BL65.P4 V36 1985 *NYPL [JLD 86-2214]*

The Last word on management / compiled by Rolf B. White. Secaucus, N.J. : Lyle Stuart, c1987. vi, 280 p. ; 24 cm. Includes index. ISBN 0-8184-0452-3 : LC Card 87-18005 DDC 658 19
1. Management - Quotations, maxims, etc. I. White, Rolf B.
HD38 .L345 1987

Laszlo, Ervin, 1932- Europe in the contemporary world . New York , c1986. ix, 297 p. : ISBN 0-677-21520-7 (pbk.) LC Card 86-212695 DDC 330.94/0558 19
HC240 .E8176 1986

László, Ferenc.
Vezetési ismeretek. 1974. Gyenes, Antal. Szövetkezetipolitikai, szövetkezetelméleti ismeretek / írta, Gyenes Antal. Vezetési ismeretek / írta, László Ferenc. Budapest , 1974. 217 p. ; LC Card 87-113832
HD3492.5.A4 G94 1974

László, Gyula, Dr. Utmutató és példatár az 1985. január 1-től érvényes jövedelem- és kere-.szabályozási rendszer alkalmazásához / [szerző, László Gyula]. Budapest : PM Szervezési és Ügyvitelgépesítési Vállalat, 1985. 153 p. ; 24 cm. ISBN 963-621-216-3 LC Card 85-138648
1. Income tax - Hungary. 2. Business enterprises - Taxation - Hungary. 3. Business enterprises - Hungary - Finance. I. Title.
HJ4715 .L37 1985

Latah County Historical Society. Petersen, Keith. Company town . Pullman, Wash. , Moscow, Idaho , 1987. xix, 284 p., [32] p. of plates : ISBN 0-87422-036-X (alk. paper) : LC Card 87-14980 DDC 307.7/67/0979686 19
HD9759.P63 P47 1987

Latané, Henry A. The Social science of organization[s] . New York , 1987. ix, 182 p. : ISBN 0-8240-8213-3 (alk. paper) : LC Card 86-27069 DDC 658.4/03 19
HD58.7 .S67 1987

Latchinian, Sarkis. Nouvelles technologies et enjeux sociaux . Lyon , c1986. 230 p. : ISBN 2-7297-0279-2 : LC Card 86-187357
HC79.T4 N68 1986

Lateinamerikanische Gewerkschaften zwischen staatlicher Gängelung und Autonomie : Fallstudien zu Argentinien, Brasilien, Chile, Costa Rica, Ecuador und Guyana / Luiz Ramalho (Hrsg.). Saarbrücken ; Fort Lauderdale : Breitenbach, 1985. 306 p. ; 21 cm. (ASA Studien, 0176-8433 . 6) Includes bibliographies. CONTENTS. - Argentinien, die Gewerkschaften in der neuen Demokratie / Jutta Borner, Leopoldo Marmora -- Argentinien, Konzentrierung der Wirtschaftspolitik und innergewerkschaftliche Demokratie / Rodolfo Casabonne -- Die Gewerkschaften Brasiliens heute / Joachim Berndt -- Landarbeitergewerkschaften im Nordosten Brasiliens / Clêyde Nadja Barrêto Souza -- Sindiquímica-Gewerkschaft der Arbeiter in der petrochemischen Industrie der Stadtregion Salvador / Dorit Gasiorowski-Ferreira de Andrade, Luiz Ramalho -- Die chilenische Gewerkschaftsbewegung zwischen Opposition und Widerstand (1973-1984) / Renate Brunner -- Die Gewerkschaften der Bananenarbeiter in Costa Rica / Ronald Grass -- Die Bananenarbeitergewerkschaften Costa Ricas zwischen Staat, nationalen und internationalen Kapitalinteressen / Sönke Schmidt -- Gewerkschaftliche Bündnispolitik in Ecuador / Renate Brunner -- Gewerkschaften in Guyana / Elke Pieper, Monika Rulfs. ISBN 3-88156-315-6 LC Card 87-135045 DDC 331.88/098 19
1. Trade-unions - Latin America -History. I. Ramalho, Luiz. II. Series.
HD6571 .L38 1985

LATENT VARIABLES.
Hildebrandt, Lutz. Konfirmatorische Analysen von Modellen des Konsumentenverhaltens /. Berlin , c1983. xii, 307 p. : ISBN 3-428-05381-8 LC Card 83-190106
HF5415.3 .H55 1983

LATEX, SYNTHETIC.
Vinyl and acrylic latices markets in Europe. New York, N.Y. , c1983. 2 v. (xxxv, 328 leaves) : LC Card 87-143984 DDC 380.1/456684232/094 19
HD9661.E82 V55 1983

LATIFUNDIO - MEXICO - HIDALGO (STATE) - CASE STUDIES.

Laviada, Iñigo. Vida y muerte de un latifundio /. México , 1984. xiii, 259 p., [6] leaves of plates : LC Card 86-208690
HD1471.M62 H535 1984

LATIFUNDIO - MEXICO - JALISCO - CASE STUDIES.
Gómez Serrano, Jesús. El mayorazgo Rincón Gallardo . [Aguascalientes] [1984] 156 p., [24] p. of plates : LC Card 84-175622
HD329.Z3 G65 1984 ***NYPL [JLD 87-138]***

LATIFUNDIO - MEXICO - MEXICO - CASE STUDIES.
Laviada, Iñigo. Vida y muerte de un latifundio /. México , 1984. xiii, 259 p., [6] leaves of plates : LC Card 86-208690
HD1471.M62 H535 1984

LATIFUNDIO - MEXICO - ZACATECAS (STATE) - CASE STUDIES.
Gómez Serrano, Jesús. El mayorazgo Rincón Gallardo . [Aguascalientes] [1984] 156 p., [24] p. of plates : LC Card 84-175622
HD329.Z3 G65 1984 ***NYPL [JLD 87-138]***

LATIFUNDIO - PORTUGAL - BAIXO ALENTEJO - CASE STUDIES.
Barros, Afonso de. Do latifundismo à reforma agrária . Oeiras [Portugal] , 1986. 636 p. : LC Card 87-404938 DDC 333.3/1/46955 19
HD1333.P82 B353 1986

LATIN AMERCIA - COMMERCIAL POLICY - CASE STUDIES.
Lejavitzer, Moisés. Políticas de incentivos a la exportación de manufacturas en América Latina . México, D.F. , 1985. iv, 155 leaves ; LC Card 87-122013 DDC 382/.4567/098 19
HF1480.5 .L44 1985

Latin America . Chilcote, Ronald H. Boulder , 1986. xv, 175 p. ; ISBN 0-8133-0239-0 (pbk.) : LC Card 85-13899 DDC 338.98 19
HC125 .C487 1986 ***NYPL [JLE 86-4264]***

Latin America . Petras, James F., 1937- Totowa, N.J. , 1986. xi, 187 p. ; ISBN 0-8476-7505-X : LC Card 86-1885 DDC 337.8 19
HC125 .P4643 1986 ***NYPL [JLE 86-4366]***

LATIN AMERICA - APPROPRIATIONS AND EXPENDITURES.
Pfeffermann, Guy Pierre. Public expenditure in Latin America . Washington, D.C. , 1987. 38 p. ; ISBN 0-8213-0906-4 (pbk.) LC Card 87-10650 DDC 336.3/9/098 19
HJ7664.5 .P44 1987

Latin America at the crossroads . Wiarda, Howard J., 1939- Boulder, Colo. , Washington, D.C. , 1987. xiii, 114 p. ; ISBN 0-8133-0423-7 (alk. paper) : LC Card 86-18997 DDC 330.98/003 19
HC125 .W47 1987 ***NYPL [JLE 87-835]***

LATIN AMERICA - CHURCH HISTORY.
Antoncich, Ricardo. [Cristianos ante la injusticia. English.] Christians in the face of injustice . Maryknoll, N.Y. , c1987. xvi, 181 p. ; ISBN 0-88344-413-5 (pbk.) LC Card 86-23529 DDC 261.8 19
BX1753 .A5813 1987 ***NYPL [JLE 87-1051]***

LATIN AMERICA - COMMERCE.
Lejavitzer, Moisés. Los efectos del neoproteccionismo en América Latina /. México, D.F. , 1983. i, 231 p. ; LC Card 85-149154 DDC 382.7/3/098 19
HF3230.5.Z5 L45 1983 ***NYPL [JLD 86-434]***

LATIN AMERICA - COMMERCE - CASE STUDIES.
El Efecto que tendrían los aumentos de los peajes del Canal de Panamá sobre países seleccionados de América Latina y el Caribe . Washington, D.C. [1982] iii, 76 p. ; LC Card 85-176637
HE538.R3 E34 1982

LATIN AMERICA - COMMERCE - SPAIN.
Alonso, José Antonio. Efectos de la adhesión de España a la CEE sobre las exportaciones de Iberoamérica /. Madrid , 1983. 316 p. : ISBN 84-7232-299-8 LC Card 87-116624
HF3688.L3 A45 1983

Alonso, José Antonio. La empresa exportadora española frente a Iberoamérica y la CEE /. Madrid , 1985. xiii, 263 p. ; ISBN 84-7232-380-3 LC Card 86-199177
HF3688.L3 A46 1985 ***NYPL [JLE 87-56]***

LATIN AMERICA - COMMERCE - UNITED STATES.
Instituto Latinoamericano del Fierro y el Acero. The urgent need of Latin America to export steel [microform]. Santiago, Chile [1983?] 20 p. : LC Card 84-244660 DDC 382/.45669142/098 19
HD9524.L32 I57 1983
NYPL [*ZT-1708 no.49]

LATIN AMERICA - COMMERCIAL POLICY.
Economic reform and stabilization in Latin America /. New York , c1986. xxiii, 348 p. : ISBN 0-275-92307-X (alk. paper) : LC Card 86-9405 DDC 338.98 19
HC125 .E374 1986 ***NYPL [JLE 87-1073]***

Report on the medium term prospects for Latin American countries. Roma , 1986. 109 p. : LC Card 86-223594 DDC 336.3/435/098 19
HJ8514.5 .R46 1986

LATIN AMERICA - DEPENDENCY ON FOREIGN COUNTRIES.
Abreu, Antonio. Dependencia y brechas entre ricos y pobres /. Bogotá , 1987. 112 p. ; ISBN 958-625-058-X LC Card 87-403548 DDC 337.8 19
HC125 .A23 1987

Benítez, José Antonio, 1921- La dependencia, el subdesarrollo y la publicidad comercial capitalista /. La Habana, Cuba , 1986. 133 p., [2] p. of plates : LC Card 87-404231 DDC 659.1/098 19
HF5813.L29 B46 1986

Fuenzalida Faivovich, Edmundo. [América Latina y la concentración del poder en la arena política.] América Latina y la concentración del poder en la arena política ; El impacto social del cambio tecnológico actual en los países menos desarrollados /. [Santiago de Chile] [between 1974 and 1979] 24, 25 leaves ; LC Card 82-180082
HD2810.5 .F84 1974

Urien, Julio César. Un aporte para la liberación /. Buenos Aires, Argentina , c1985. 51 p. ; ISBN 950-9235-13-X LC Card 85-201095
HC125 .U75 1985

LATIN AMERICA - ECONOMIC CONDITIONS.
Abreu, Antonio. Dependencia y brechas entre ricos y pobres /. Bogotá , 1987. 112 p. ; ISBN 958-625-058-X LC Card 87-403548 DDC 337.8 19
HC125 .A23 1987

Búfalo, Enzo del. El pensamiento crítico latinoamericano /. [México?] , 1979. 236 p. ; LC Card 79-120323
HC59.7 .B84 ***NYPL [JLC 80-383]***

LATIN AMERICA - ECONOMIC CONDITIONS - 1945-
Baez, René. Ciencia y transformación social . Quito, Ecuador , 1986. 141 p. ; LC Card 86-214736 DDC 330.9/0038 19
HC125 .B195 1986

Bordering on trouble . Bethesda, Md. , 1986. xii, 448 p. : ISBN 0-917561-25-2 (pbk.) LC Card 86-7941 DDC 338.98 19
HC125 .B594 1986 ***NYPL [JLE 86-4501]***

Buen L., Néstor de (Buen Lozano) Sindicatos, democracia y crisis /. México , 1985. xii, 122 p. ; ISBN 968-452-054-9 LC Card 86-209080
HD6532 .B84 1985

Castro, Fidel, 1927- [Nada podrá detener la marcha de la historia. Selections.] Si no hay solución a la crisis, habrá explosiones sociales generalizadas de carácter revolucionario. La Habana , 1985. 97 p. ; LC Card 87-115245 DDC 338.9 19
HC125 .C37825 1985

Chilcote, Ronald H. Latin America . Boulder , 1986. xv, 175 p. ; ISBN 0-8133-0239-0 (pbk.) : LC Card 85-13899 DDC 338.98 19
HC125 .C487 1986 ***NYPL [JLE 86-4264]***

Cole, Julio Harold, 1955- Latin American inflation . New York , 1987. xv, 89 p. : ISBN 0-275-92809-8 (alk. paper) : LC Card 87-15156 DDC 332.4/1/098 19
HC125 .C62 1987

Díaz Alejandro, Carlos Federico. Trade, development and the world economy . Oxford, OX, UK , New York, NY, USA , 1988. p. cm. ISBN 0-631-15687-9 : LC Card 87-20836 DDC 337.8 19
HF1480.5 .D52 1988

Díaz Arenas, Pedro Agustín. Latinoamérica, hiel y miel /. Bogotá , 1982. 120 p. : LC Card 83-103872
HC125 .D535 1982

Eastman, Jorge Mario. Hacia un populismo petrolero? y otros temas /. Bogotá, Colombia , 1986. viii, 145 p., [8] p. of plates : LC Card 86-227075
HD9574.C52 E18 1986

The Economic crisis . Santiago, Chile , New York, NY, USA , 1986. 132 p. : ISBN 92-1-121132-8 (pbk.) LC Card 87-404540 DDC 338.98 19
HC125 .E368 1986

Economic panorama of Latin America, 1986 . Santiago, Chile [1986] 82 p. : LC Card 87-107353 DDC 330.98/0038 19
HC125 .E373 1986

Economic reform and stabilization in Latin America /. New York , c1986. xxiii, 348 p. : ISBN 0-275-92307-X (alk. paper) : LC Card 86-9405 DDC 338.98 19
HC125 .E374 1986 ***NYPL [JLE 87-1073]***

El FMI, el Banco Mundial y la crisis latinoamericana /. México , 1986. 474 p. : ISBN 968-231-373-2 LC Card 87-127860 DDC 332.1/52 19
HG3881.5.I58 F56 1986

Gavagnin Taffarel, Osvaldo. La deuda externa de América Latina . Lima, Perú , 1986. 157 p. : LC Card 86-235251
HJ8514.5 .G37 1986

Gerardi, Ricardo E. El impacto de la crisis en los esquemas de integración /. [Buenos Aires, Argentina] , 1985 [i.e. 1986] iii, 52, [26] leaves : LC Card 87-125394 DDC 337.1/8 19
HC125 .G465 1986

Gómez Pérez, José Antonio, 1950- Desarrollo, crisis, deuda y política económica en Panamá . Panamá , 1985. vii, 168 p. : LC Card 86-122320 DDC 338.97287 19
HC147 .G66 1985 ***NYPL [JLD 86-2899]***

Harrison, Lawrence E. Underdevelopment is a state of mind . [Cambridge, Mass.] , Lanham, MD , 1988, c1985. p. cm. ISBN 0-8191-6490-9 (pbk. : alk. paper) : LC Card 87-24678 DDC 330.98/0038 19
HC125 .H384 1988

Hirschman, Albert O. The political economy of Latin American development . La Jolla, Calif. [1986] 57 p. ; LC Card 87-621614 DDC 338.98 19
HC125 .H544 1986

Köhn, Doris. Die Verschuldung lateinamerikanischer Länder /. Hamburg , 1984. 148 p. ; ISBN 3-87895-259-7 LC Card 85-134749
HJ8514.5 .K64 1984

Kontseptsii obshchestvennogo razvitiia. Spanish. Concepciones del desarrollo social. Moscú , <1984-. v. <2 > ; LC Card 87-124757
HC125 .K65517 1984

Labarca, Guillermo. Los bancos multinacionales en América Latina y la crisis del sistema capitalista /. México, D.F. , 1979. 201 p. ; ISBN 968-429-155-8 LC Card 80-123755
HG2710.5.A6 L3 ***NYPL [JLC 81-147]***

Latin America's economic development . Boulder , 1987. xii, 304 p. ; ISBN 1-555-87067-8 (lib. bdg. : alk. paper) : LC Card 87-10046 DDC 338.98 19
HC125 .L3536 1987

Lay, Jean-Benoît. Vers la libération de l'Amérique latine /. Paris , c1985. 215 p. : ISBN 2-85802-433-X LC Card 85-136403
HC123 .L39 1985

Mora Forero, Jorge Rafael. Introducción a los problemas del subdesarrollo en América Latina /. Bogotá, D.E., Colombia , 1984. 96 p. ; ISBN 958-95030-9-8 LC Card 86-137776 DDC 338.98 19
HC125 .M615 1984

Rangel, Domingo Alberto. Fin de fiesta /. Valencia, Venezuela , 1982. 181 p. ; LC Card 83-200321
HC125 .R29 1982

Sheahan, John, 1923- Patterns of development in Latin America . Princeton, N.J. , c1987. x, 399 p. : ISBN 0-691-07735-5 (alk. paper) : LC

Card 87-2853 DDC 338.98 19
HC125 .S498 1987

Vela, Gil. Deuda externa latinoamericana /. Ecuador , 1984. 180 p. ; LC Card 85-180466 DDC 336.3/435/098 19
HJ8514.5 .V45 1984 ***NYPL [JLD 86-308]***

Wiarda, Howard J., 1939- Latin America at the crossroads . Boulder, Colo. , Washington, D.C. , 1987. xiii, 114 p. ; ISBN 0-8133-0423-7 (alk. paper) : LC Card 86-18997 DDC 330.98/003 19
HC125 .W47 1987 ***NYPL [JLE 87-835]***

Wionczek, Miguel S. Capital y tecnología en México y América Latina /. México , 1981. 413 p. ; ISBN 968-470-018-0
NYPL [JLE 87-377]

LATIN AMERICA - ECONOMIC CONDITIONS - 1945- - ADDRESSES, ESSAYS, LECTURES.

Petras, James F., 1937- Latin America . Totowa, N.J. , 1986. xi, 187 p. ; ISBN 0-8476-7505-X : LC Card 86-1885 DDC 337.8 19
HC125 .P4643 1986 ***NYPL [JLE 86-4366]***

Salvador Ortíz, S., 1917-1983. Comentarios económicos /. Santo Domingo, República Dominicana , 1984- v. ; LC Card 85-118318 DDC 330.9 19
HC125 .S2615 1984 ***NYPL [JLK 85-83]***

LATIN AMERICA - ECONOMIC CONDITIONS - 1945- - COLLECTED WORKS.

Estudio económico de América Latina, 1981. [Santiago, Chile?] [1982- v. <l-9 > : LC Card 86-202465
HC125 .E89 1982

LATIN AMERICA - ECONOMIC CONDITIONS - 1945- - CONGRESSES.

Foreign investment, debt, and economic growth in Latin America /. New York , 1988. xix, 250 p. : ISBN 0-312-00936-4 : LC Card 87-18808 DDC 332.6/73/098 19
HG5160.5.A3 F675 1988

Mesa Redonda sobre la Carta de Punta del Este (1961 : Universidad Nacional Autónoma de México) Memoria del ciclo de conferencias de Mesa Redonda sobre la Carta de Punta del Este /. México , 1962. 224 p. : LC Card 85-105213
HC125 .M48 1961

Políticas de ajuste y grupos más vulnerables en América Latina . [Bogotá, Colombia] , 1987. 278 p. : ISBN 958-9093-01-9 LC Card 87-404285 DDC 338.98 19
HC125 .P647 1987

LATIN AMERICA - ECONOMIC CONDITIONS - 1945- - REGIONAL DISPARATIES.

Tokman, Víctor E. Desarrollo desigual y absorción de empleo . [Santiago, Chile] , 1982. 34 p. ; LC Card 87-403246 DDC 330.98/0038 19
HC125 .T57 1982

LATIN AMERICA - ECONOMIC INTEGRATION.

Aragão, José María. La Asociación Latinoamericana de Libre Comercio (ALALC) y la Asociación Latinoamericana de Integración (ALADI) . Buenos Aires, Argentina [1984] xiii, 172 p. ; LC Card 86-201881
HC125 .A69 1984

Coers, Hermann Max. El Banco Central Latinaoamericano . México , 1972. xv, 78 p. ; LC Card 87-401518 DDC 332.1/1/098 19
HG2710.5.A7 C6 1972

Echegaray, Alfredo. Evolución y perspectivas de la cooperación financiera en América Latina /. Buenos Aires , 1982. 147 p. ; LC Card 86-198731
HG185.L3 E25 1982

Exenciones arancelarias e integración /. [Buenos Aires] , 1986. 273 p. ; LC Card 87-400577 DDC 382.7/1/098 19
HF1733.L29 E96 1986

Gerardi, Ricardo E. El impacto de la crisis en los esquemas de integración /. [Buenos Aires, Argentina] , 1985 [i.e. 1986] iii, 52, [26] leaves : LC Card 87-125394 DDC 337.1/8 19
HC125 .G465 1986

Herrera, Felipe, 1922- América Latina, desarrollo e integracíon /. [Santiago, Chile] [1986] 302 p., [11] p. of plates : LC Card 87-115159 DDC 337.1/8 19
HC125 .H466 1986

Kaplan, Marcos. El sistema de las relaciones políticas y económicas entre los países latinoamericanos . [Buenos Aires] [1985] 62 leaves ; LC Card 86-200041
HC125 .K32 1985

El Proceso de integración en América Latina en 1985 /. Buenos Aires, República Argentina , 1986. 271 p. : LC Card 87-169476 DDC 337.1/8 19
HC125 .P768 1986

Toledano Laredo, Armando. Intégration et démocratie /. Bruxelles, Belgique , 1982. 192 p. ; ISBN 2-8004-0777-8 :c275F LC Card 83-163343
HF1418.5 .T65 1982

Tussie, Diana. The less developed countries and the world trading system . London , 1987. viii, 162 p. ; ISBN 0-86187-614-8
NYPL [JLE 87-1597]

LATIN AMERICA - ECONOMIC INTEGRATION - CONGRESSES.

Política internacional, economía e integración /. Asunción del Paraguay [1985] 178 p. ; LC Card 86-122468
HF1523 .P65 1985

Por una visión del desarrollo latinoamericano con autodeterminación, democracia y paz /. San Isidro, Lima, Perú [1984] 191 p. ; LC Card 86-226515
HC167.A5 P67 1984

Reunión Técnica sobre el Financiamiento de la Integración Subregional en América Latina (1985 : Buenos Aires, Argentina) Reunión Técnica sobre el Financiamiento de la Integración Subregional en América Latina . [Buenos Aires, Argentina] . 335 p. : LC Card 86-217551
HC125 .R479 1985

Seminar on Economic Integration (1982 : Inter-American Development Bank) The economic integration process of Latin America in the 1980's . Washington, D.C. [1984] 318 p. : ISBN 0-940602-17-2 (pbk.) LC Card 87-159367
HC125 .S3973 1982

LATIN AMERICA - ECONOMIC POLICY.

Bacha, Edmar Lisboa. El milagro y la crisis . México , 1986. 468 p. : ISBN 968-16-2152-2 LC Card 87-400019 DDC 338.981 19
HC187 .B128 1986

Betancur, Belisario, 1923- Un semáforo en rojo . [Bogotá] [1984] 12, 12, 12 p. ; LC Card 87-125515 DDC 338.98 19
HC125 .B42 1984

Bordering on trouble . Bethesda, Md. , 1986. xii, 448 p. : ISBN 0-917561-25-2 (pbk.) LC Card 86-7941 DDC 338.98 19
HC125 .B594 1986 ***NYPL [JLE 86-4501]***

Conesa, Eduardo R. Fuga de capitales . Buenos Aires , 1986. 78 p. : LC Card 87-400256 DDC 332.4/5 19
HG3931 .C66 1986

Deere, Carmen Diana. The peasantry in political economy . [Amherst, MA] , 1987. 76 p. ; LC Card 87-404080 DDC 305.5/63 19
HD1531.L3 D44 1987

Deuda externa latinoamericana y proceso de ajuste . Bogotá, Colombia , 1985. 335 p. : LC Card 86-164491
HJ8514.5 .D484 1985

The Economic crisis . Santiago, Chile , New York, NY, USA , 1986. 132 p. : ISBN 92-1-121132-8 (pbk.) LC Card 87-404540 DDC 338.98 19
HC125 .E368 1986

The Economy of Latin America and the Caribbean . Washington, D.C. [1986] v, 30 p. ; ISBN 0-8270-2333-2 (pbk.) : LC Card 86-203268 DDC 336.3/435/09729 19
HJ8514.5 .E34 1986

Foxley, Alejandro. Las desigualdades económicas y la acción del estado . México , 1980. 271 p. ; ISBN 968-16-0365-6 LC Card 82-215955 DDC 339.2/098 19
HC130.15 F69 1980 ***NYPL [JLD 86-2631]***

From crisis to equitable growth ; a new development agenda for Latin America /. Aldershot , Brookfield, USA , 1987. ix, 144 p. ; ISBN 0-566-05536-8 : LC Card 87-21135 DDC 338.98 19
HC130.B38 F76 1987

Gómez Pérez, José Antonio, 1950- Desarrollo, crisis, deuda y política económica en Panamá . Panamá , 1985. vii, 168 p. : LC Card 86-122320 DDC 338.97287 19
HC147 .G66 1985 ***NYPL [JLD 86-2899]***

Hirschman, Albert O. The political economy of Latin American development . La Jolla, Calif. [1986] 57 p. ; LC Card 87-621614 DDC 338.98 19
HC125 .H544 1986

Kalmanovitz, Salomón. El desarrollo tardío del capitalismo . [Bogotá] , 1983. 285 p. ; LC Card 84-155755 DDC 338.9/009172/4 19
HC59.7 .K246 1983 ***NYPL [JLD 85-2613]***

Latin America's economic development . Boulder , 1987. xii, 304 p. ; ISBN 1-555-87067-8 (lib. bdg. : alk. paper) : LC Card 87-10046 DDC 338.98 19
HC125 .L3536 1987

Pacheco, Lucas. La política económica en el Ecuador . Quito, Ecuador , 1985. 219 p. ; LC Card 87-400294 DDC 338.9866 19
HC202 .P26 1985

Pobreza, participación y desarrollo regional /. [Bogotá, D.E., Colombia] , 1986. 536 p. : LC Card 87-103266
HC125 .P6 1986

Políticas macro-económicas . Santiago de Chile [1986] 409 p. : LC Card 87-403669 DDC 338.98 19
HC125 .P657 1986

Report on the medium term prospects for Latin American countries. Roma , 1986. 109 p. : LC Card 86-223594 DDC 336.3/435/098 19
HJ8514.5 .R46 1986

Rey Salgado, Rafael del. La crisis de la deuda en América Latina /. [Spain] [1985] ii, 88 p. ; LC Card 86-131407
HJ8514.5 .R49 1985

Schatan, Jacobo. [América Latina, deuda externa y desarrollo. English.] World debt . London , Atlantic Highlands, N.J., USA , 1987. xv, 126 p. ; ISBN 0-86232-688-5 : LC Card 87-13330 DDC 336.3/435/098 19
HJ8514.5 .S313 1987

Urien, Julio César. Un aporte para la liberación /. Buenos Aires, Argentina , c1985. 51 p. ; ISBN 950-9235-13-X LC Card 85-201095
HC125 .U75 1985

Urquidi, Víctor L. Basic issues in Latin American development prospects /. Coral Gables, Fla. [between 1983 and 1986] 27 p. ; LC Card 87-118247 DDC 338.98 19
HC125 .U765 1983

Vuscovic, Pedro. Notas para una discusión sobre política económica y la experiencia latinoamericana. Montevideo, Uruguay [1983] 29 p. ; LC Card 86-160128
HC125 .V87 1983

LATIN AMERICA - ECONOMIC POLICY - CASE STUDIES.

Cartas, José María. Precondiciones para la implementación de la economía social de mercado en América Latina . Buenos Aires, República Argentina , c1985. 80 p. ; LC Card 87-101628
HC125 .C374 1985

LATIN AMERICA - ECONOMIC POLICY - CONGRESSES.

Conferencia Económica Latinoamericana (1984 : Quito, Ecuador) Documentación relacionada con la Conferencia Económica Latino Americana, Quito, 9-13 enero, 1984. [Rome, Italy] , 1984. 62 p. ; LC Card 86-134389 DDC 338.98 19
HC125 .C6555 1984

Escenarios políticos y sociales del desarrollo latinoamericano /. [S.l.] [Buenos Aires] , c1986. 231 p. ; ISBN 950-23-0274-5 LC Card 87-400175 DDC 338.98 19
HC125 .E82 1986

External debt, savings, and growth in Latin America . Washington, D.C. , Buenos Aires , 1987. xv, 207 p. ; ISBN 0-939934-95-7 (pbk.) :

LC Card 87-21422 DDC 336.3/435/098 19
HJ8514.5 .E984 1987

Políticas de ajuste y grupos más vulnerables en América Latina . [Bogotá, Colombia] , 1987. 278 p. : ISBN 958-9093-01-9 LC Card 87-404285 DDC 338.98 19
HC125 .P647 1987

Silva Ruete, Javier. La respuesta de Latinoamérica a la crisis internacional /. [Lima, Peru?] [1984] 99 p. ; LC Card 86-154728
HF1480.5 .S55 1984

LATIN AMERICA - EMIGRATION AND IMMIGRATION.
Estructura política y políticas de población /. [Santiago, Chile] [1977] 442 p. ; LC Card 83-168971
HB3530.5 .E88 1977

LATIN AMERICA - EMIGRATION AND IMMIGRATION - CONGRESSES.
Fachtagung "Bevölkerungsentwicklung, Bevölkerungswanderung und Urbanisierung in Lateinamerika" (1984 : Eichstätt, Germany) Desarrollo demográfico, migraciones y urbanización en América Latina . Regensburg , c1986. 432 p. : LC Card 86-181152
HB3530.5.A3 F33 1984

LATIN AMERICA - FOREIGN ECONOMIC REALTIONS - UNITED STATES.
América Latina, Estados Unidos . México , 1986. 223 p. : ISBN 968-231-378-3 LC Card 87-128005 DDC 337.7308 19
HF1456.5.L3 A44 1986

LATIN AMERICA - FOREIGN ECONOMIC RELATIONS.
Díaz Alejandro, Carlos Federico. Trade, development and the world economy . Oxford, OX, UK , New York, NY, USA , 1988. p. cm. ISBN 0-631-15687-9 : LC Card 87-20836 DDC 337.8 19
HF1480.5 .D52 1988

García Bocanegra, Angela Victoria. Posición de los países en desarrollo frente a la crisis económica mundial /. Bogotá, D.E. , 1984. 146 p. ; LC Card 85-205412
HF1413 .G312 1984

Glower, Carlos J., 1952- América Latina y el sistema monetario internacional /. [Mexico City, Mexico] [1986] iv, 28 leaves : LC Card 87-400944 DDC 332.4/56098 29
HG3881 .G577 1986

Vargas, Ines. Conclusions from "The NIEO and the situation of workers" . Oslo :International Peace Research Institute, [1986] 21 p. ; LC Card 87-128390 DDC 337.8 19
HF1480.5 .V37 1986

LATIN AMERICA - FOREIGN ECONOMIC RELATIONS - ADDRESSES, ESSAYS, LECTURES.
Problemas económicos del Tercer Mundo /. Buenos Aires, República Argentina , c1983. 210 p. : ISBN 950-577-070-7 LC Card 84-120737 DDC 337/.09172/4 19
HF1413 .P75 1983 ***NYPL [JLC 86-394]***

LATIN AMERICA - FOREIGN ECONOMIC RELATIONS - CONGRESSES.
Silva Ruete, Javier. La respuesta de Latinoamérica a la crisis internacional /. [Lima, Peru?] [1984] 99 p. ; LC Card 86-154728
HF1480.5 .S55 1984

LATIN AMERICA - FOREIGN ECONOMIC RELATIONS - GERMANY, WEST.
Wolffsohn, Michael. Politik als Investitionsmotor? . Frankfurt am Main , New York , c1985. 141 p. : ISBN 3-8204-7487-0 (pbk.) LC Card 87-672289
HD2810.5 W64x 1985

LATIN AMERICA - FOREIGN ECONOMIC RELATIONS - UNITED STATES.
Clayton, Lawrence A. Grace . Ottawa, Ill. , c1985. xiii, 403 p., [32] p. of plates : ISBN 0-915463-25-3 LC Card 85-14856 DDC 338.8/8885 19
HD9505.P4 C43 1986 ***NYPL [JLE 86-3892]***

Rosenberg, Emily S., 1944- World War I and the growth of United States predominance in Latin America /. New York , 1987. p. cm. ISBN 0-8240-8089-0 : LC Card 87-23683 DDC 337.7308 19
HF1456.5.L3 R67 1987

US economic expansion . Moscow , 1986. 216 p. ; LC Card 87-112029 DDC 337.7308 19
HF1456.5.L3 U8 1986

Latin America - Government. see **Latin America - Politics and government.**

LATIN AMERICA - INDUSTRIES.
Gwynne, Robert N. Industrialization and urbanization in Latin America /. Baltimore, Md. , 1986. xiv, 259 p. : ISBN 0-8018-3113-X LC Card 85-10079 DDC 338.098 19
HC125 .G96 1986 ***NYPL [JLD 86-2200]***

LATIN AMERICA - MANUFACTURES - CASE STUDIES.
Lejavitzer, Moisés. Políticas de incentivos a la exportación de manufacturas en América Latina . México, D.F. , 1985. iv, 155 leaves ; LC Card 87-122013 DDC 382/.4567/098 19
HF1480.5 .L44 1985

LATIN AMERICA - MANUFACTURES - HISTORY - 20TH CENTURY.
García, Norberto E. Industria manufacturera y empleo . [Santiago, Chile] , 1982. 51 p. ; LC Card 87-403251 DDC 338.4/767/098 19
HD9734.L32 G36 1982

LATIN AMERICA - NEUTRALITY - HISTORY.
Rosenberg, Emily S., 1944- World War I and the growth of United States predominance in Latin America /. New York , 1987. p. cm. ISBN 0-8240-8089-0 : LC Card 87-23683 DDC 337.7308 19
HF1456.5.L3 R67 1987

LATIN AMERICA - OCCUPATIONS - LICENSES.
Agudelo Mejía, Santiago. Lineamientos para la implantación de un servicio de certificación ocupacional /. Montevideo , 1983. 67 p. : LC Card 86-142627
HD5715.5.L3 A348 1983

LATIN AMERICA - POLITICS AND GOVERNMENT - 1945-
Kaplan, Marcos. El sistema de las relaciones políticas y económicas entre los países latinoamericanos . [Buenos Aires] [1985] 62 leaves ; LC Card 86-200041
HC125 .K32 1985

LATIN AMERICA - POLITICS AND GOVERNMENT - 1948-
Bordering on trouble . Bethesda, Md. , 1986. xii, 448 p. : ISBN 0-917561-25-2 (pbk.) LC Card 86-7941 DDC 338.98 19
HC125 .B594 1986 ***NYPL [JLE 86-4501]***

Díaz Arenas, Pedro Agustín. Latinoamérica, hiel y miel /. Bogotá , 1982. 120 p. : LC Card 83-103872
HC125 .D535 1982

Kontseptsii obshchestvennogo razvitiia. Spanish. Concepciones del desarrollo social. Moscú , <1984-. v. <2 > ; LC Card 87-124757
HC125 .K65517 1984

Rangel, Domingo Alberto. Fin de fiesta /. Valencia, Venezuela , 1982. 181 p. ; LC Card 83-200321
HC125 .R29 1982

Sheahan, John, 1923- Patterns of development in Latin America . Princeton, N.J. , c1987. x, 399 p. : ISBN 0-691-07735-5 (alk. paper) : LC Card 87-2853 DDC 338.98 19
HC125 .S498 1987

Wiarda, Howard J., 1939- Latin America at the crossroads . Boulder, Colo. , Washington, D.C. , 1987. xiii, 114 p. ; ISBN 0-8133-0423-7 (alk. paper) : LC Card 86-18997 DDC 330.98/003 19
HC125 .W47 1987 ***NYPL [JLE 87-835]***

LATIN AMERICA - POLITICS AND GOVERNMENT - 1948- - CONGRESSES.
Escenarios políticos y sociales del desarrollo latinoamericano /. [S.l.] [Buenos Aires] , c1986. 231 p. ; ISBN 950-23-0274-5 LC Card 87-400175 DDC 338.98 19
HC125 .E82 1986

LATIN AMERICA - POLITICS AND GOVERNMENT - ADDRESSES, ESSAYS, LECTURES.
Quantitative Latin American studies . Los Angeles , 1977. xiv, 91 p. : ISBN 0-87903-227-8 LC Card 77-620011 DDC 330.9/8/003
HD5731.A6 Q36 ***NYPL [JLF 80-242]***

LATIN AMERICA - POPULATION.
Bordering on trouble . Bethesda, Md. , 1986. xii, 448 p. : ISBN 0-917561-25-2 (pbk.) LC Card 86-7941 DDC 338.98 19
HC125 .B594 1986 ***NYPL [JLE 86-4501]***

Wiarda, Howard J., 1939- Population, internal unrest, and U. S. security in Latin America /. [Amherst] , 1986. 50 p. ; LC Card 87-621399 DDC 304.6/098 19
HB3530.5.A3 W5 1986

LATIN AMERICA - POPULATION - CONGRESSES.
Fachtagung "Bevölkerungsentwicklung, Bevölkerungswanderung und Urbanisierung in Lateinamerika" (1984 : Eichstätt, Germany) Desarrollo demográfico, migraciones y urbanización en América Latina . Regensburg , c1986. 432 p. : LC Card 86-181152
HB3530.5.A3 F33 1984

LATIN AMERICA - POPULATION DENSITY - CONGRESSES.
Fachtagung "Bevölkerungsentwicklung, Bevölkerungswanderung und Urbanisierung in Lateinamerika" (1984 : Eichstätt, Germany) Desarrollo demográfico, migraciones y urbanización en América Latina . Regensburg , c1986. 432 p. : LC Card 86-181152
HB3530.5.A3 F33 1984

LATIN AMERICA - POPULATION - MAPS.
Wilkie, Richard W., 1938- Latin American population and urbanization analysis . Los Angeles, Calif. , c1984. xxii, 433 p. : ISBN 0-87903-242-1 (alk. paper) : LC Card 83-620019 DDC 312/.098 19
HB3530.5 .W54 1984 ***NYPL [JLF 87-298]***

LATIN AMERICA - POPULATION POLICY.
Estructura política y políticas de población /. [Santiago, Chile] [1977] 442 p. ; LC Card 83-168971
HB3530.5 .E88 1977

LATIN AMERICA - POPULATION - STATISTICS.
Wilkie, Richard W., 1938- Latin American population and urbanization analysis . Los Angeles, Calif. , c1984. xxii, 433 p. : ISBN 0-87903-242-1 (alk. paper) : LC Card 83-620019 DDC 312/.098 19
HB3530.5 .W54 1984 ***NYPL [JLF 87-298]***

LATIN AMERICA - RELATIONS - UNITED STATES - ADDRESSES, ESSAYS, LECTURES.
Petras, James F., 1937- Latin America . Totowa, N.J. , 1986. xi, 187 p. ; ISBN 0-8476-7505-X : LC Card 86-1885 DDC 337.8 19
HC125 .P4643 1986 ***NYPL [JLE 86-4366]***

LATIN AMERICA - SOCIAL CONDITIONS - 1945-
Chilcote, Ronald H. Latin America . Boulder , 1986. xv, 175 p. ; ISBN 0-8133-0239-0 (pbk.) : LC Card 85-13899 DDC 338.98 19
HC125 .C487 1986 ***NYPL [JLE 86-4264]***

Díaz Arenas, Pedro Agustín. Latinoamérica, hiel y miel /. Bogotá , 1982. 120 p. : LC Card 83-103872
HC125 .D535 1982

Egner, Erich, 1901- Hauswirtschaft und Lebenshaltung . Berlin , 1974. 249 p. ; ISBN 3-428-03093-1 : LC Card 76-511945
TX7 .B4 Heft 9 HD6995.5 ***NYPL [JLE 86-3436]***

Herrera, Felipe, 1922- América Latina, desarrollo e integracíon /. [Santiago, Chile] [1986] 302 p., [11] p. of plates : LC Card 87-115159 DDC 337.1/8 19
HC125 .H466 1986

Pérez Aguirre, Luis. Predicaciones en la plaza /. Montevideo , 1985. 228 p. ; LC Card 85-225854 DDC 282/.8 19
BX1426.2 .P46 1985 ***NYPL [JLE 87-456]***

Vela, Gil. Deuda externa latinoamericana /. Ecuador , 1984. 180 p. ; LC Card 85-180466 DDC 336.3/435/098 19
HJ8514.5 .V45 1984 ***NYPL [JLD 86-308]***

Wiarda, Howard J., 1939- Latin America at the crossroads . Boulder, Colo. , Washington, D.C. , 1987. xiii, 114 p. ; ISBN 0-8133-0423-7 (alk. paper) : LC Card 86-18997 DDC 330.98/003 19
HC125 .W47 1987 ***NYPL [JLE 87-835]***

LATIN AMERICA - SOCIAL CONDITIONS - ADDRESSES, ESSAYS, LECTURES.
Quantitative Latin American studies . Los Angeles , 1977. xiv, 91 p. : ISBN 0-87903-227-8 LC Card 77-620011 DDC 330.9/8/003
HD5731.A6 Q36 ***NYPL [JLF 80-242]***

LATIN AMERICA - SOCIAL POLICY - CONGRESSES.
Escenarios políticos y sociales del desarrollo latinoamericano /. [S.l.] [Buenos Aires] , c1986. 231 p. ; ISBN 950-23-0274-5 LC Card 87-400175 DDC 338.98 19
HC125 .E82 1986

Latin America studies .
(30) Gianotten, Vera. Organización campesina . Amsterdam , Cinnaminson, N.J. , c1985. ix, 531 p., [4] p. of plates : ISBN 90-6765-162-1 LC Card 85-200688
HD1531.P4 G5 1985

Latin American Centre for Economic and Social Documentation. Guía conceptual y metodológica para instructores de cursos de capacitación de INFOPLAN. Santiago de Chile , 1983. iv, 70 p. : LC Card 87-108080
HC125 .G814 1983

Latin American Common Market. see **Asociación Latinoamericana de Libre Comercio.**

Latin American Economic System. see **Sistema Económico Latinoamericano.**

Latin American inflation . Cole, Julio Harold, 1955- New York , 1987. xv, 89 p. : ISBN 0-275-92809-8 (alk. paper) : LC Card 87-15156 DDC 332.4/1/098 19
HC125 .C62 1987

Latin American Institute for Economic and Social Planning. Instituto Latinoamericano de Planificación Económica y Social (ILPES) : perspectivas futuras y síntesis de atividades, 1981-1984 / ILPES. [Santiago, Chile] : Naciones Unidas, Consejo Económico y Social, [1984] iii, 52 p. ; 28 cm. At head of title: Instituto Latinoamericano de Planificación Económica y Social. Includes bibliographical references. "E/CEPAL/ILPES/G.21; E/CEPAL/SES.20/G.23 17 de febrero de 1984. Original: español." LC Card 84-202400
1. Latin American Institute for Economic and Social Planning. 2. Economic policy - Study and teaching (Higher) - Latin America. 3. Social policy - Study and teaching (Higher) - Latin America. I. Title.
HD77.5.L29 L38 1984

LATIN AMERICAN INSTITUTE FOR ECONOMIC AND SOCIAL PLANNING.
Latin American Institute for Economic and Social Planning. Instituto Latinoamericano de Planificación Económica y Social (ILPES) . [Santiago, Chile] [1984] iii, 52 p. ; LC Card 84-202400
HD77.5.L29 L38 1984

Latin American Iron and Steel Institute. see **Instituto Latinoamericano del Fierro y el Acero.**

Latin American labor organizations / edited by Gerald Michael Greenfield and Sheldon L. Maram. New York : Greenwood Press, 1987. xiv, 929 p. ; 24 cm. Includes bibliographies and index. ISBN 0-313-22834-5 (lib. bdg. : alk. paper) LC Card 86-33613 DDC 331.88/098 19
1. Trade-unions - Latin America -History. 2. Labor and laboring classes - Latin America - History. I. Greenfield, Gerald Michael. II. Maram, Sheldon L.
HD6530.5 .L38 1987

Latin American monographs. For other vols. in this series, see Old Catalog.
(no. 66) Story, Dale, 1950- Industry, the state, and public policy in Mexico /. Austin , 1986. xii, 275 p. ; ISBN 0-292-73837-4 LC Card 85-13363 DDC 338.972 19
HD3616.M43 S76 1986 ***NYPL [JLE 87-656]***

Latin American monographs (University of Texas at Austin. Institute of Latin American Studies) .
(no. 71) Topik, Steven. The political economy of the Brazilian State, 1889-1930 /. Austin , 1987. xii, 241 p. : ISBN 0-292-76500-2 LC Card 87-5835 DDC 338.981 19
HC187 .T558 1987

Latin American oil companies and the politics of energy / edited by John D. Wirth. Lincoln : University of Nebraska Press, c1985. xxxix, 282 p. : ill. ; 23 cm. (Latin American studies series) Includes bibliographies and index. ISBN 0-8032-4728-1 (alk. paper) LC Card 84-29457 DDC 338.7/6223382/098 19
1. Petroleum industry and trade - Latin America - Case studies. 2. Petroleum industry and trade - Government ownership - Latin America - Case studies. I. Wirth, John D.
HD9574.L3 L38 1985 ***NYPL [JLD 86-1289]***

Latin American perspectives series .
(no. 3) Chilcote, Ronald H. Latin America . Boulder , 1986. xv, 175 p. ; ISBN 0-8133-0239-0 (pbk.) : LC Card 85-13899 DDC 338.98 19
HC125 .C487 1986 ***NYPL [JLE 86-4264]***

Latin American population and urbanization analysis . Wilkie, Richard W., 1938- Los Angeles, Calif. , c1984. xxii, 433 p. : ISBN 0-87903-242-1 (alk. paper) : LC Card 83-620019 DDC 312/.098 19
HB3530.5 .W54 1984 ***NYPL [JLF 87-298]***

LATIN AMERICANS - SWEDEN.
Latinamerikaner i Sverige . [Stockholm] [1984] 62 p. ; ISBN 91-38-08192-X LC Card 84-218936
HD8578.5.L37 L37 1984

Latin America's debt crisis : adjusting to the past or planning for the future? / edited by Robert A. Pastor. Boulder, Colo. : L. Rienner, 1987. xiii, 176 p. ; 24 cm. "This book grew our a two-day symposium at the Carter Center of Emory University in April 1986"--P. xi. Bibliography: p. 163-166. Includes index. ISBN 1-555-87053-8 (lib. bdg. : alk. paper) : LC Card 87-4956 DDC 336.3/435/098 19
1. Debts, External - Latin America - Congresses. 2. Loans, Foreign - Latin America - Congresses. I. Pastor, Robert A.
HJ8514.5 .L395 1987

Latin America's economic development : institutionalist and structuralist perspectives / edited by James L. Dietz and James H. Street. Boulder : Lynne Rienner Publishers, 1987. xii, 304 p. ; 24 cm. Includes bibliographies and index. ISBN 1-555-87067-8 (lib. bdg. : alk. paper) : LC Card 87-10046 DDC 338.98 19
1. Latin America - Economic policy. 2. Latin America - Economic conditions - 1945-. I. Dietz, James L., 1947-. II. Street, James H. (James Harry), 1915-.
HC125 .L3536 1987

Latinamerika-institutet i Stockholm. The Debt crisis in Latin America. Stockholm , 1986. 199 p. : ISBN 91-87134-01-2 LC Card 87-108739 DDC 336.3/435/098 19
HJ8514.5 .D45 1986

Latinamerikaner i Sverige : en översikt : rapport / från en Arbetsgrupp inom regeringskansliet. [Stockholm] : Liber, [1984] 62 p. ; 21 cm. At head of title: Arbetsmarknadsdepartementet. "Ds A 1984:3." ISBN 91-38-08192-X LC Card 84-218936
1. Alien labor, Latin American - Sweden. 2. Latin Americans - Sweden.
HD8578.5.L37 L37 1984

Latinoamérica, hiel y miel /. Díaz Arenas, Pedro Agustín. Bogotá , 1982. 120 p. : LC Card 83-103872
HC125 .D535 1982

Latinoamérica, su deuda externa . López Hurtado, José. Bogotá, D.E., Colombia , 1987. xxii, 156 p. : ISBN 958-9074-43-X LC Card 87-404201 DDC 336.3/435/098 19
HJ8514.5 .L66 1987

LATINOS (UNITED STATES) see **HISPANIC AMERICANS.**

Latinskaia Amerika : valiutno-finansovoe polozhenie v 70-kh godakh / [avtorskiĭ kollektiv S.N. Kosobchuk ... et al. ; otvetstvennyĭ redaktor S.N. Kosobchuk]. Moskva : Akademiia nauk SSSR, In-t Latinskoĭ Ameriki, 1978. 271 p. ; 21 cm. Includes bibliographical references. LC Card 81-159488
1. Finance - Latin America. I. Kosobchuk, S. N. (Svetlana Nikolaevna). II. Institut Latinskoĭ Ameriki (Akademiia nauk SSSR).
HG185.L3 L37 1978

Latinskaia Amerika--problemy razvitiia neftianoĭ promyshlennosti / [otvetstvennye redaktory, V.V. Vol'skiĭ, K.S. Tarasov]. Moskva : Akademiia nauk SSSR, In-t Latinskoĭ Ameriki, 1984. 192 p. : ill. ; 20 cm. Includes bibliographies. LC Card 86-181028
1. Petroleum industry and trade - Latin America. I. Vol'skiĭ, Viktor Vatslavovich. II. Tarasov, K. S. (Konstantin Sergeevich). III. Institut Latinskoĭ Ameriki (Akademiia nauk SSSR).
HD9574.L3 L4 1984

Latorre, Emilio. Transporte y crecimiento regional en Colombia / Emilio Latorre. 1a ed. Bogotá, Colombia : CIDER, UNIANDES : CEREC, 1986. 137 p. : ill., maps ; 19 cm. Includes bibliographical references. ISBN 958-9061-14-1 LC Card 87-115019 DDC 380.5/09861 19
1. Transportation - Colombia. 2. Transportation and state - Colombia. 3. Regional planning - Colombia. I. Title.
HE235 .L37 1986

Latouche, Serge, 1940- Faut-il refuser le développement? : essai sur l'anti-économique du Tiers-monde / Serge Latouche.1re éd. Paris : Presses universitaires de France, c1986. 216 p. ; 22 cm. (Economie en liberté, 0768-0988) Bibliography: p. [205]-213. Includes index. ISBN 2-13-039202-4 : LC Card 86-160202
1. Economic development. 2. Developing countries - Economic conditions. 3. Developing countries. I. Title. II. Series.
HD83 .L324 1986

Latsis, O. R. (Otto Rudol'fovich) Samorukova, A. N. (Angara Nikolaevna) Promyshlennost' Sotsialisticheskoĭ Respubliki Rumynii /. Moskva , 1986. 143 p. ; LC Card 86-202797
HC405 .S253 1986

Latter-Day Saints. see **Church of Jesus Christ of Latter-Day Saints.**

Lattmann, Charles. Die verhaltenswissenschaftlichen Grundlagen der Führung des Mitarbeiters / Charles Lattmann. Bern : P. Haupt, c1981. 565 p. : ill. ; 25 cm. (Schriftenreihe Unternehmung und Unternehmungsführung . 9) Includes index. Bibliography: p. 533-558. ISBN 3-258-03094-4 : LC Card 82-163528 DDC 658.3 19
1. Organizational behavior. 2. Leadership. I. Series. II. Series: Unternehmung und Unternehmungsführung, 9. III. Title.
HD58.7 .L36 1981 ***NYPL [JLE 86-1595]***

Latuch, Mikołaj.
Migracje wewnętrzne ludności . Warszawa , 1980. xvi, 389 p. ; LC Card 86-215694
HB2068.7.A3 M54 1980

Rozwój ludności krajów socjalistycznych . Warszawa , Moskva , 1978. 381 p. ; LC Card 81-206832
HB3608.7.A3 R69 1978

LATVIA - COMMERCE.
Ėkonomika i upravlenie torgovleĭ v razvitom sotsialisticheskom obshchestve . Riga , 1980. 123 p. : LC Card 82-102627
HF3629.L37 E38 1980

LATVIA - COMMERCIAL POLICY.
Ėkonomika i upravlenie torgovleĭ v razvitom sotsialisticheskom obshchestve . Riga , 1980. 123 p. : LC Card 82-102627
HF3629.L37 E38 1980

LATVIA - ECONOMIC CONDITIONS.
Feodālisms Baltijas reģionā . Riga , 1985. 147 p. : LC Card 86-177836
HC243 .F46 1985

Kirtovskiĭ, I. Kh. Ocherki istorii marksistsko-leninskoĭ ėkonomicheskoĭ mysli Latvii, 1920-1980 /. Riga , 1985. 199 p. ; LC Card 86-176265
HB97.5 .K542 1985

LATVIA - ECONOMIC CONDITIONS - ECONOMETRIC MODELS.
Metodicheskie polozheniia po prognozirovaniiu ėkonomicheskogo i sotsial'nogo razvitiia soiuznoĭ respubliki /. Riga , 1979. 275 p. : LC Card 81-215536
HC337.L3 M35 1979

LATVIA - ECONOMIC POLICY - DATA PROCESSING.
Pravovye voprosy RASU . Riga , 1979. 109, [3] p. ; LC Card 82-100548
HC337.L3 P722 1979

LATVIA - HISTORY - 1562-1918.
Feodālisms Baltijas reģionā . Riga , 1985. 147 p. : LC Card 86-177836
HC243 .F46 1985

LATVIA - MANUFACTURES.
Khoziaĭstvennyĭ mekhanizm proizvodstva i obrashcheniia tovarov narodnogo potrebleniia /.

Riga , 1985. 115 p. ; LC Card 86-177827
HF1040.9.L38 K47 1985

LATVIA - POPULATION.
Problemy urovnia zhizni i demografii . Riga , 1979. 175 p. ; LC Card 82-106660
HD7035.Z8 L376 1979

Lau, Kin-Nam. Hu, Sheng C. A game-theoretic approach to the design of an optimal sales policy /. West Lafayette, Ind. [1986] 30, 14 p. : LC Card 86-622755 DDC 658/.001/9 s 658.8/101 19
HD6483 .P8 no. 900 HF5438.25

Lau, Lorrie A. Y. Analysis of national and regional travel trends / by Lorrie A.Y. Lau. Washington, D.C. : Dept. of Transportation, Federal Highway Administration, 1986. iii, 78, 32 p. : ill., 1 map ; 28 cm. Shipping list no.: 87-42-P. "October 1986." "HPM-30/12-86 (500)QE"--P. [4] of cover. Item 982-G-5 LC Card 87-601033 DDC 388.3/14/0973 19
1. Travel time (Traffic engineering) - United States. 2. Traffic surveys - United States. 3. Transportation, Automotive - United States. I. United States. Federal Highway Administration. II. Title.
HE370.T74 L38 1986

Laucoin, G. Funel, Jean Marie. Politiques d'aménagement hydro-agricole /. Paris , c1980. 212 p. : ISBN 2-85319-083-8 LC Card 86-112826
HD1699.S37 F86 1980

Lauer, Deborah. Certified professional secretary examination review series. [Kansas City, Mo.?] , New York , c1986- v. <1, 6 > : ISBN 0-471-84353-9 (pbk. : v. 1) LC Card 87-100577 DDC 651.3/74/076 19
HF5547.5 .C44 1986

Laufer, Heinz, 1933- Bürokratisierte Demokratie? / Heinz Laufer. Zürich : Edition Interfrom, c1983. 123 p. ; 20 cm. (Texte + Thesen) Bibliography: p. 117-123. ISBN 3-7201-5157-3 LC Card 83-168788
1. Bureaucracy - Germany, West. 2. Bureaucracy. I. Title.
HD38.4 .L38 1983

Laufer, Leopold Yehuda.
U. S. aid to Israel : problems and perspectives : U. S.--Israel project / by Leopold Yehuda Laufer. [Jerusalem] : Hebrew University of Jerusalem, Leonard Davis Institute for International Relations, [1983] 55 p. : ill. ; 25 cm. (Policy oriented publications . *7) "U. S.--Israel Project." "May 1983." Bibliography: p. 53-55. LC Card 87-400279 DDC 338.91/73/05694 19
1. Economic assistance, American - Israel - History. I. Title. II. Title: US aid to Israel. III. Title: United States aid to Israel. IV. Series: Pirsumim mekhuvane mediniyut , 7.
HC415.25 .L38 1983

U. S. aid to the West Bank and Gaza : policy dilemmas / by Leopold Yehuda Laufer. [Jerusalem] : Hebrew University of Jerusalem, Leonard Davis Institute for International Relations, [1985] 54 p. ; 25 cm. (Policy studies . *12) "May 1985." Bibliography: p. 52-54. LC Card 87-400340 DDC 338.91/73/056951 19
1. Economic assistance, American - West Bank. 2. Economic assistance, American - Gaza Strip. 3. Palestinian Arabs - Government policy - Israel. 4. Palestinian Arabs - Governemnt policy - United States. 5. Middle East - Relations - United States. 6. United States - Relations - Middle East. I. Title. II. Title: US aid to the West Bank and Gaza. III. Title: United States aid to the West Bank and Gaza. IV. Series: Policy studies (Makhon li-yeḥasim benle'umiyim 'al-shem Le'onard Deiṿis) , 12.
HC415.25.Z7 W4735 1985

Lauksaimniecības uzņēmumu saimnieciskās darbības analīze /. Vaikulis, J. (Jānis) Riga , 1986. 185 p. ; LC Card 86-199301
HD1492.S652 L38 1986

Laulajainen, Risto. Spatial strategies in retailing / by Risto Laulajainen. Dordrecht ; Boston : D. Reidel ; xiii, 253 p. : ill., maps ; 25 cm. (The GeoJournal library) Bibliography: p. 247-251. ISBN 90-277-2595-0 LC Card 87-20803 DDC 658.8/7 19
1. Store location. 2. Retail trade. I. Title. II. Series.
HF5429.275 .L38 1987

Laumer, Helmut.
Strukturpolitik für traditionelle Industriezweige in Japan / von Helmut Laumer und Wolfgang Ochel, unter Mitarbeit von Sueo Sekiguchi und Jens-Uwe G. Jungnickel. Berlin : Duncker & Humblot, c1985. 173 p. : ill. ; 24 cm. (Schriftenreihe des IFO-Instituts für Wirtschaftsforschung . Nr. 118) Bibliography: p. [168]-173. ISBN 3-428-05920-4 LC Card 86-151482
1. Industry and state - Japan. 2. Japan - Industries. I. Ochel, Wolfgang, 1943-. II. Title. III. Series.
HD3616.J32 L38 1985

Wachstumsmarkt Südostasien . München , c1984. x, 807 p. : ISBN 3-8039-0292-4 : LC Card 84-249861
HF3790.8.Z5 W33 1984

LAUNDRESSES - ENGLAND - HISTORY.
Malcolmson, Patricia E., 1944- English laundresses . Urbana , c1986. xv, 220 p. ; ISBN 0-252-01293-3 LC Card 85-24599 DDC 305.4/3648/0942 19
HD6073.L32 G75 1986 ***NYPL [JLE 86-4640]***

LAUNDRESSES - ENGLAND - SOCIAL CONDITIONS.
Malcolmson, Patricia E., 1944- English laundresses . Urbana , c1986. xv, 220 p. ; ISBN 0-252-01293-3 LC Card 85-24599 DDC 305.4/3648/0942 19
HD6073.L32 G75 1986 ***NYPL [JLE 86-4640]***

Laundry and cleaning services. United States. Wage and Hour and Public Contracts Divisions. [Washington, 1969] iii, 31, A-ii, A-67p. ***NYPL [JLF 86-586]***

LAUNDRY INDUSTRY - SOUTH AFRICA - STATISTICS.
Sensus van wassery-, skoonmaak- en kleurdienste, 1980 =. Pretoria [1984?] xiv, 59 p., [1] folded leaf of plates : ISBN 0-621-08730-0 : LC Card 86-122444
HD9999.L383 S67 1984

LAUNDRY WORKERS - ENGLAND - HISTORY.
Malcolmson, Patricia E., 1944- English laundresses . Urbana , c1986. xv, 220 p. ; ISBN 0-252-01293-3 LC Card 85-24599 DDC 305.4/3648/0942 19
HD6073.L32 G75 1986 ***NYPL [JLE 86-4640]***

LAUNDRY WORKERS - UNITED STATES.
Siu, Paul C. P. (Paul Chan Pang), 1906- The Chinese laundryman . New York , c1987. xlii, 311 p. : ISBN 0-8147-7859-3 : LC Card 87-5609 DDC 331.6/2/51073 19
HD8039.L32 U675 1987

Laurence, Michael. Social control of the drinking driver /. Chicago , 1988. p. cm. ISBN 0-226-46953-0 : LC Card 87-19111 DDC 363.1/256 19
HE5620.D7 S66 1988

Laurent, Eric. La corde pour les pendre-- : relations entre milieux d'affaires occidentaux et régimes communistes de 1917 à nos jours / Eric Laurent. Paris : Fayard, c1985. 304 p. ; 24 cm. Bibliography: p. [299]-304. ISBN 2-213-01550-3 : LC Card 85-231994
1. International economic relations. 2. East-West trade (1945-). 3. Hammer, Armand, 1897-. I. Title.
HF1411 .L3645 1985

Laurent, Robert. Mélanges Robert Laurent . Montpellier , 1980. xxi, 296 p. : LC Card 83-151672
HC273 .M43 1980

LAURENT, ROBERT, 1908-
Mélanges Robert Laurent . Montpellier , 1980. xxi, 296 p. : LC Card 83-151672
HC273 .M43 1980

Lauritzen, Niels, 1947- Rapporter / udarbejdet af Forvaltningshøjskolen og Miljøstyrelsens økonomifunktion. København : Miljøministeriet, [1983] 59 p. : ill. ; 24 cm. "Rapportbilag II til Vandprisudvalgets betænkning." "Oktober 1983." CONTENTS. - Statistiske oplysninger om vandforbrug, takster og vandforsyningernes økonomi / [af Niels Lauritzen og Johan Nielsen] -- Overvejelser vedrørende takstpolitik og vandpriser / [af Johan Nielsen] ISBN 87-503-4574-5 LC Card 84-169893
1. Municipal water supply - Denmark - Rates. 2. Water consumption - Denmark. I. Nielsen, Johan, 1948-. II. Denmark. Udvalget til undersøgelse af vandforsyningernes økonomiske baggrund. Vandpriser. III. Title.
HD4465.D4 L38 1983

Laursen, Karsten. Udviklingslandenes økonomi / Karsten Laursen. Århus : Økonomisk institut, Aarhus universitet : Institut for nationaløkonomi og statistik, [1986] ii, 203 p. : ill. ; 20 cm. (Notat . 1986-1) Includes bibliographies. LC Card 86-215996
1. Developing countries - Economic conditions. I. Series: Notat (Aarhus universitet. Økonomisk institut) , 1986-1. II. Title.
HC59.7 .L3243 1986

Lauschke, Karl. Schwarze Fahnen an der Ruhr : die Politik der IG Bergbau und Energie während der Kohlenkrise 1958-1968 / Karl Lauschke. Marburg [/Lahn] : Verlag Arbeiterbewegung und Gesellschaftswissenschaft, c1984. 400 p. : ill. ; 21 cm. (Schriftenreihe der Studiengesellschaft für Sozialgeschichte und Arbeiterbewegung . Bd. 42) Bibliography: p. 382-400. ISBN 3-921630-42-8 LC Card 84-215799
1. Industriegewerkschaft Bergbau und Energie - History. 2. Trade-unions - Coal miners - Germany (West) - History. I. Title. II. Series.
HD6698.M616 I535 1984

Lauter, Geza P. (Geza Peter) Higashi, Chikara. The internationalization of the Japanese economy /. Boston, MA , c1987. xi, 273 p. : ISBN 0-89838-199-1 LC Card 87-3893 DDC 337.52 19
HC462.9 .H45 1987

Lauterbach, Jeffrey R.
Gourgues, Harold W. Revolution in financial services /. Washington, D.C. , c1987. xiii, 248 p. : ISBN 0-87179-561-2 LC Card 87-18390 DDC 332.1/0973 19
HG2491 .G68 1987

Seglin, Jeffrey L., 1956- Personal financial planning in banks . Boston , c1986. xvii, 205 p. ; ISBN 0-87267-059-7 LC Card 85-28738 DDC 332.1/7 19
HG1616.C87 S44 1986 ***NYPL [JLE 87-820]***

Lauth, Thomas P. Abney, Glenn. The politics of state and city administration /. Albany, N.Y. , c1986. xvi, 260 p. ; ISBN 0-88706-255-5 LC Card 85-14873 DDC 353.9 19
JK2408 .A26 1986 ***NYPL [JLE 86-3711]***

L'automazione dei processi di produzione . Vannini, Walter, 1958- Milano, Italy , c1985. 344 p. : LC Card 85-204836 DDC 338.4/54 19
HD9720.5 .V36 1985 ***NYPL [JLD 86-2523]***

Lauwerier, O. L. J. (O. L. Jeroen) The Oriental challenge . Delft, the Netherlands , 1987. 281 p. : ISBN 90-70879-62-X (pbk.) LC Card 87-170212 DDC 332.6/732259 19
HC445 .O75 1987

Laux, Helmut. Grundfragen der Erfolgskontrolle / H. Laux, F. Liermann. Berlin ; New York : Springer-Verlag, c1986. x, 161 p. : ill. ; 25 cm. (Heidelberger betriebswirtschaftliche Studien) Bibliography: p. [159]-161. ISBN 0-387-17037-5 LC Card 86-232406
1. Decision-making. 2. Uncertainty. I. Liermann, F. (Felix). II. Title. III. Series.
HD30.23 .L39 1986

Laux, Jeanne Kirk, 1942- State capitalism : public enterprise in Canada / Jeanne Kirk Laux and Maureen Appel Molot. Ithaca : Cornell University Press, 1988. ix, 250 p. ; 24 cm.. (Cornell studies in political economy) Bibliography: p. 205-241. Includes index. ISBN 0-8014-2079-2 (alk. paper) LC Card 87-47600 DDC 338.6/2/0971 19
1. Government business enterprises - Canada. I. Molot, Maureen Appel, 1941-. II. Title. III. Series.
HD4005 .L38 1988

Lauzon, Léo-Paul, 1946- L'Homme d'affaires québécois des années 80 /. Montréal, Québec, Canada , c1983. 418 p., [14] p. of plates : ISBN 2-89045-585-8 LC Card 83-190776
HC117.Q4 H65 1983

Lava Yamben. Roy Burman, B. K. Towards poverty alleviation programmes in Nagaland and Manipur /. Delhi , 1984. xxxi, 123 p. ; LC Card 84-902780 DDC 338.954/165 19
HC437.N25 R69 1984 ***NYPL [JLD 87-903]***

Lave, Lester B. Risk assessment and management /. New York , c1987. xii, 740 p. : ISBN 0-306-42683-8 LC Card 87-21288 DDC 658 19
HD61 .R5684 1987

L'avenir en face /. Minc, Alain. Paris , c1984. 255 p. ; ISBN 2-02-006828-1 : LC Card 84-218171
HC276 .M6126 1984 ***NYPL [JLE 87-2165]***

Laviada, Iñigo. Vida y muerte de un latifundio / Iñigo Laviada. 1a ed. México : Editorial Porrúa, 1984. xiii, 259 p., [6] leaves of plates : ill. ; 21 cm. Includes bibliographies. LC Card 86-208690
1. Latifundio - Mexico - Hidalgo (State) - Case studies. 2. Latifundio - Mexico - Mexico - Case studies. 3. Haciendas - Mexico - Hidalgo (State) - Case studies. 4. Haciendas - Mexico - Mexico - Case studies. I. Title.
HD1471.M62 H535 1984

Lavin, Don. Barrett, John (John J.) The industrial work model . Menomonie, Wis. , c1987. v, 143 p. : ISBN 0-916671-73-9 (pbk.) LC Card 87-403218 DDC 362.0425 19
HD7256.U5 B37 1987

Lavin, Michael R. Business information : how to find it, how to use it / by Michael R. Lavin. Phoenix, Ariz. : Oryx Press, 1987. x, 299 p. : ill. ; 29 cm. Includes bibliographies and indexes. ISBN 0-89774-157-9 (alk. paper) : LC Card 86-42787 DDC 650/.072 19
1. Business - Research - Handbooks, manuals, etc. 2. Reference books - Business - Bibliography. 3. Business - Bibliography. 4. Information storage and retrieval systems - Business - Directories. I. Title.
HF5356 .L36 1987

Lavoisier, Antoine Laurent, 1743-1794. L'art de fabriquer le salin, et la potasse ... / par les Régisseurs-généraux des poudres & salpêtres. A Paris : De l'imprimerie royale, 1779. [2], viij, 84 p., IV, [1] folded leaves of plates : ill. (engravings) ; 19 cm. (8vo) Published anonymously. By Antoine Laurent Lavoisier. Cf. BN. Signatures: pi1 a^4 A-E^8 F^2. Includes bibliographical references. LC Card 85-666435
1. Alkalai industry and trade - Early works to 1800. 2. Potash industry and trade - Early works to 1800. I. Title.
HD9660.A42 L38x 1779

Il lavoro di gruppo . Muti, Pier Luigi, 1922- Milano, Italy , c1986. 129 p. : LC Card 86-181088
HD66 .M87 1986

Lavoro femminile, sviluppo tecnologico e segregazione occupazionale / ricerca condotta da G. Barile ... [et al.] ; a cura di Giuseppe Barile. Milano, Italy : F. Angeli, c1984. 458 p. : ill. ; 22 cm. (Collana IReR . 22) At head of title: IReR. Includes bibliographies. LC Card 84-190076 DDC 331.4/0945 19
1. Women - Employment - Italy - Addresses, essays, lectures. 2. Women - Employment - Italy - Lombardy - Addresses, essays, lectures. I. Barile, Giuseppe. II. I.Re.R. III. Series.
HD6154 .L385 1984 ***NYPL [*QO 87-1143]***

Il lavoro si crea . Convegno "Il lavoro si crea" (1985 : Ravenna, Italy) Milano, Italy , c1986. 305 p. : LC Card 86-232529
HD5764.A6 C68 1985

Lavrikov, IUriĭ Aleksandrovich. Proizvodstvennye ob"edineniia . Moskva , 1982. 173 p. ; LC Card 83-123241
HD70.S63 P764 1982

Lavrushin, O. I. (Oleg Ivanovich) Rol' finansovo-kreditnogo mekhanizma v povyshenii ėffektivnosti obshchestvennykh zatrat . Moskva , 1984. 153 p. ; LC Card 86-113408
HG186.S55 R64 1984

LAW, ADVERTISING. see **ADVERTISING LAWS.**

LAW, AGRICULTURAL. see **AGRICULTURAL LAWS AND LEGISLATION.**

LAW, BANKING. see **BANKING LAW.**

Law, business, and society /. McAdams, Tony. Plano, Tex. , 1986. xvi, 662, 52 p. : ISBN 0-256-03070-7 LC Card 85-73323 DDC 346.73/065 347.30665 19
KF1355 .M28 1986 ***NYPL [JLE 87-891]***

LAW, COMMERCIAL. see **COMMERCIAL LAW.**

LAW, CORPORATION. see **CORPORATION LAW.**

LAW - DICTIONARIES.
Erdsiek, Gerhard. Wörterbuch für Recht, Wirtschaft und Politik. Bleckede bei Hamburg [1964-1968] 2 v. LC Card 65-42077
NYPL [JLE 85-408]

LAW ENFORCEMENT - UNITED STATES.
United States. President's Commission on Organized Crime. Organized crime . Washington, D.C. , 1983. vi, 159 p. :
NYPL [JLE 86-1587]

Law, Gordon T., 1945- A guide to information on closely held corporations / Gordon T. Law, Jr., Michael E. Reilly. Buffalo, N.Y. : Extension and Public Service Division, New York State School of Industrial and Labor Relations, Western District, Cornell University, c1986. p. cm. Includes bibliographies. ISBN 0-9615917-1-4 : LC Card 86-32812 DDC 338.7/4/072073 19
1. Close corporations - United States - Information services. 2. Close corporations - United States - Legal research. 3. Close corporations - New York (State) - Erie County - Legal research. I. Reilly, Michael E., 1947-. II. Title.
HD2785 .L38 1986

LAW - HISTORY AND CRITICISM - ADDRESSES, ESSAYS, LECTURES.
Hundert Jahre Rechts- und Wirtschaftsgeschichte an der Rechts-, Wirtschafts- und Sozialwissenschaftlichen Fakultät der Universität Freiburg =. Freiburg, Schweiz , 1982. 96 p., [6] p. of plates : ISBN 3-7278-0277-4 : LC Card 83-108855 DDC 340 19
K296 .H86 1982 ***NYPL [JLD 86-676]***

LAW, HOMESTEAD. see **HOMESTEAD LAW.**

LAW, INDUSTRIAL. see **INDUSTRIAL LAWS AND LEGISLATION; INDUSTRY AND STATE; LABOR LAWS AND LEGISLATION.**

LAW, LABOR. see **LABOR LAWS AND LEGISLATION.**

LAW OF SUCCESSION. see **INHERITANCE AND SUCCESSION.**

LAW OF SUPPLY AND DEMAND. see **SUPPLY AND DEMAND.**

The law of the land . Opie, John, 1934- Lincoln , c1987. xxi, 231 p. : ISBN 0-8032-3553-4 (alk. paper) LC Card 86-30860 DDC 338.1/873 19
HD1761 .O65 1987

LAW REFORM - GERMANY, WEST.
Zwei Jahre Politik der Erneuerung . Bonn [1984] 110 p. : LC Card 85-180111
HC286.7 .Z865 1984

LAW, SUNDAY. see **SUNDAY LEGISLATION.**

Lawler, Edward E. High-involvement management / Edward E. Lawler III. 1st ed. San Francisco, Calif. : Jossey-Bass, 1986. xvii, 252 p. : ill. ; 24 cm. (The Jossey-Bass management series) The Jossey-Bass social and behavioral science series Includes index. Bibliography: p. 235-241. ISBN 0-87589-686-3 (alk. paper) LC Card 85-45909 DDC 658.3/152 19
1. Management - Employee participation. 2. Quality of work life. I. Title. II. Series.
HD5650 .L35 1986 ***NYPL [JLE 86-3096]***

Lawless, Richard I.
The Gulf in the early 20th century . [Durham] , c1986. 215 p., [1] leaf of plates : LC Card 87-100795 DDC 330.953/6 19
HC415.3 .G85 1986

Symposium on the Energy Economy (1984 : Durham, Durham) Prospects for the world oil industry . London , Dover, N.H. , c1985. 131 p. : ISBN 0-7099-4104-8 : LC Card 85-4186 DDC 338.2/7282 19
HD9560.5 .S96 1985 ***NYPL [JLD 85-2430]***

Lawrence Chilnick & Associates. Gold, Mark S. Stop drugs at work ; implementation manual /. New York, N.Y. , c1986. p. cm. ISBN 0-394-55091-9 LC Card 86-26168 DDC 658.3/822 19
HF5549.5.E42 G65 1986

Lawrence, Peter R.
World recession and the food crisis in Africa /. London , 1986. 314 p. ; ISBN 0-85255-309-9 : LC Card 86-235333 DDC 363.8/526/096 19
HD9017.A2 W67 1986b

World recession and the food crisis in Africa /. Boulder , 1986. p. cm. ISBN 0-8133-0511-X : LC Card 86-28250 DDC 363.8/526/096 19
HD9017.A2 W67 1986

Lawrence, Robert Z., 1949- Saving free trade : a pragmatic approach / Robert Z. Lawrence, Robert E. Litan. Washington, D.C. : Brookings Institution, c1986. xii, 132 p. ; 24 cm. Includes bibliographical references and index. ISBN 0-8157-5178-8 LC Card 86-14705 DDC 382.7/1/0973 19
1. Trade adjustment assistance - United States. 2. Free trade and protection - Free trade. 3. United States - Commercial policy. I. Litan, Robert E., 1950-. II. Title.
HF1455 .L39 1986 ***NYPL [JLE 86-4368]***

Lawson, Adeyemi O. Growth, equity, and self reliance . Boulder , 1987. xi, 162 p. ; ISBN 0-8133-0486-5 (pbk.) : LC Card 87-14290 DDC 338.96 19
HD3616.A36 G76 1987

Lawson, Ronald, 1940- The Tenant movement in New York City, 1904-1984 /. New Brunswick, N.J. , c1986. xiv, 289 p. : ISBN 0-8135-1203-4 (pbk.) : LC Card 85-27894 DDC 333.33/8 19
HD7288.85.U62 N58 1986
NYPL [JLE 86-4565]

Laxer, James. Leap of faith : free trade and the future of Canada / James Laxer. Edmonton : Hurtig, c1986. 140 p. ; 21 cm. Bibliography: p. 138-140. ISBN 0-88830-298-3 : LC Card 87-101958 DDC 382.7/1/0971 19
1. Canada - Foreign economic relations - United States. 2. United States - Foreign economic relations - Canada. 3. Tariff - Canada. 4. Canada - Economic policy. I. Title.
HF1480.15.U5 L39 1986

Lay, Jean-Benoît. Vers la libération de l'Amérique latine / Jean-Benoît Lay ; présentation de Antonio Fragoso ; préface de Camilo Moncada. Paris : L'Harmattan, c1985. 215 p. : ill. ; 22 cm. Bibliography: p. 211-213. ISBN 2-85802-433-X LC Card 85-136403
1. Latin America - Economic conditions - 1945-. 2. Church and social problems - Latin America - Catholic Church. I. Title.
HC123 .L39 1985

Layard, P. R. G. (P. Richard G.)
The Fight against unemployment . Cambridge, Mass. , 1987. xii, 204 p. : ISBN 0-262-12122-0 LC Card 87-5356 DDC 339.5/094 19
HD5764.A6 F54 1987

The Rise in unemployment /. Oxford, UK , New York, NY, USA , 1987, c1986. 382 p. : ISBN 0-631-15419-1 (pbk.) : LC Card 87-699 DDC 331.13/7 19
HD5707.5 .R57 1987

Layman, Thomas A. Dickie, Robert B. Foreign investment and government policy in the Third World /. New York , 1988. p. cm. ISBN 0-312-00520-2 : LC Card 87-25076 DDC 332.6/7322598 19
HG5752 .D53 1988

LAYOFFS.
United States. Secretary of Labor's Task Force on Economic Adjustment and Worker Dislocation. Economic adjustment and worker dislocation in a competitive society . Washington, D.C. [1986] 189 p. in various pagings : LC Card 87-601034 DDC 331.13/7973 19
HC106.8 .U545 1986

LAYOUT, OFFICE. see **OFFICE LAYOUT.**

Layton, Stanford J., 1941- To no privileged class : the rationalization of homesteading and rural life in the early twentieth-century American West / by Stanford J. Layton. Provo, Utah : Brigham Young University, Charles Redd Center for Western Studies ; Salt Lake City, Utah : Distributed by Signature Books, c1987. p. cm. (Charles Redd monographs in western history. no. 17) Includes index. ISBN 0-941214-59-1 : LC Card 87-14299 DDC 333.1/6/0978 19
1. Homestead law - Economic aspects - West (U. S.) - History. 2. Homestead law - Social aspects - West (U. S.) - History. 3. Frontier and pioneer life - West (U. S.) - History. 4. Public lands - West (U. S.) - History. I. Title. II. Series.
HD1339.U5 L39 1987

Lazarte, Jorge. Crisis de identidad y centralidad minera : informe especial / Jorge Lazarte. [La Paz, Bolivia] : CEDOIN, [1986] 37 p. : ill. ; 29 cm. (Informe especial) Cover title. "Los mineros de ayer y de hoy"--P. 1 of cover. CONTENTS. - Preámbulo necesario -- Crisis de identidad y centralidad minera / Jorge Lazarte -- Cronología del XXI Congreso de Trabajadores Mineros de Bolivia -- Informe de la Comisión de Poderes -- Tesis de Catavi (aprobada en el XXI congreso) -- Tesis del eje de convergencia

patriótica -- Carta de renuncia de Juan Lechín Oquendo -- Acuerdo FSTMB-gobierno, 13 septiembre 1986 -- Documento del EX-CEN de la FSTMB. LC Card 87-401455 DDC 331.88/122/0984 19
1. Trade-unions - Miners - Bolivia. 2. Mineral industries - Bolivia. 3. Congreso Nacional Minero (20th : 1984 : Distrito Minero de Matilde, Bolivia). I. Title. II. Title: Mineros de ayer y de hoy. III. Series: Informe especial (Centro de Documentación e Información--Bolivia).
HD8039.M61 B586 1986

Lazer, William. Handbook of demographics for marketing and advertising : sources and trends on the U. S. consumer / William Lazer. Lexington, Mass. : Lexington Books, c1987. xxi, 211 p. : ill. ; 24 cm. Includes bibliographies and index. ISBN 0-669-16013-X (alk. paper) LC Card 86-46440 DDC 304.6/0973 19
1. Consumers - United States. I. Title.
HC110.C6 L39 1987

Lazin, Frederick A., 1943- Aroni, Samuel. How successful was Section 8 in Los Angeles? . Berkeley , 1986. 18 p. ; ISBN 0-87772-311-7 (pbk.) LC Card 86-27180 DDC 363.5/8 19
HD7288.85.U62 L73 1986

Lazio (Italy). Assessorato agricoltura, foreste, caccia e pesca. Produttività potenziale e classificazione dei terreni. Roma , 1985- v. <1 > in <5 > : LC Card 87-105342
HD679.L39 P76 1985

Lazonick, William. The Decline of the British economy /. Oxford [Oxfordshire] , New York , 1987, c1986. vii, 310 p. ; ISBN 0-19-877281-5 (pbk.) : LC Card 87-5479 DDC 330.941/08 19
HC255 .D43 1987

Lazurenko, S. G. (Serafima Grigor′evna) Izmerenie vlii͡anii͡a nauchno-tekhnicheskogo progressa na rost nat͡sional′nogo dokhoda / S.G. Lazurenko. Moskva : Izd-vo "Nauka", 1981. 127 p. ; 20 cm. (Problemy sovetskoĭ ėkonomiki) At head of title: Akademii͡a nauk SSSR. Institut ėkonomiki. Includes bibliographical references. LC Card 82-115905
1. Technological innovations - Soviet Union. 2. National income - Soviet Union. I. Title.
HC340.T4 L39 1981

LAZÚRTEGUI, JULIO.
Gondra y Oraá, María Victoria de, 1929- El Bilbao de Julio Lazúrtegui . Bilbao , 1984. 472 p. : ISBN 84-505-0689-1 LC Card 87-125134
HC382.5.L39 G66 1984

Lazzati, Santiago. Análisis de normas sobre contabilidad e inflación : Resolución 183/79, Resolución 148/81, otras resoluciones / Santiago C. Lazzati, Hugo O. de la Torre. Buenos Aires : Ediciones Macchi, [1981] 157 p. ; 23 cm. Includes bibliographical references. LC Card 82-216941
1. Accounting - Argentina - Effect of inflation on. I. Torre, Hugo O. de la. II. Title.
HF5658.5 .L39 1981

Le Bas, Christian. Histoire sociale des faits économiques : la France au XIXe siècle, introduction / C. Le Bas. Lyon : Presses universitaires de Lyon, c1984. 242 p. : ill. ; 21 cm. (Analyse, épistémologie, histoire économiques) Bibliography: p. 211-233. ISBN 2-7297-0221-0 : LC Card 85-152656
1. France - Economic conditions - 19th century. I. Title. II. Series.
HC275 .L45 1984

Le Bonifiche in Italia dal '700 a oggi / a cura di Piero Bevilacqua e Manlio Rossi-Doria. Roma : Laterza, 1984. viii, 437 p. : ill. ; 22 cm. (Storia e società) Includes bibliographical references. ISBN 88-420-2429-5 : LC Card 85-173148
1. Drainage - Italy - History - Addresses, essays, lectures. 2. Reclamation of land - Italy - History - Addresses, essays, lectures. 3. Irrigation engineering - Italy - History - Addresses, essays, lectures. 4. Agricultural engineering - Italy - History - Addresses, essays, lectures. I. Bevilacqua, Piero, 1944-. II. Rossi-Doria, Manlio, 1905-. III. Series: Storia e società (Editori Laterza).
HD1683.I8 B66 1984 ***NYPL [JSD 87-50]***

Le Bris, Émile.
Enjeux fonciers en Afrique noire /. Bondy , Paris , c1982. 425 p. ; ISBN 2-86537-057-7 : LC Card 83-130847 DDC 333.3/096 19
HD966 .E54 1982 ***NYPL [JLE 87-950]***
Espaces disputés en Afrique noire . Paris , c1986. 426 p., [8] p. of plates : ISBN 2-86537-146-8 LC Card 86-210958
HD965 .E86 1986

Le Capitalisme monopoliste d'État. Paris, Éditions sociales [1971] 2 v. 18 cm. At head of title: Traité marxiste d'économie politique. "Ce traité est l'œuvre des collaborateurs de la Section économique du Comité central du Parti communiste français et de la revue Économie et politique." LC Card 75-585406
1. Economic history - 1945-1971. 2. Capitalism. I. Title: Traité marxiste d'économie politique.
HC59 .C26 ***NYPL [JLC 71-28]***

Lê-Châu. Investigación agraria y crisis . Quito , 1986. 498 p. : LC Card 87-400125 DDC 338.1/098 19
HD1860.A53 I58 1986

Le Consommateur averti /. Neirynck, Jacques. Lausanne , 1979. 173 p. ; ISBN 2-8289-0029-X : LC Card 79-394845 DDC 381/.34
HC79.C63 N43 ***NYPL [JLD 86-2606]***

Le courrier des militaires belges internés aux Pays-Bas et en Suisse 1914-1919, et essai de classement des marques néerlandaises de censure et autres /. Silverberg, René. Bruxelles , 1978. 154 p. : LC Card 80-452392 DDC 769.56/7
HE6184.C3 S55 ***NYPL [JFD 81-1659]***

Le dollar . Denizet, Jean. Paris , c1985. 259 p. ; ISBN 2-213-01626-7 : LC Card 86-148501 DDC 332.4/560973 19
HG3881 .D344 1985 ***NYPL [JLD 87-337]***

Le facteur et ses métamorphoses /. Charbon, Paul. Barembach , c1984. 266 p., [24] p. of plates : ISBN 2-902912-40-4 LC Card 85-118656 DDC 383/.4944 19
HE6989.P4 C48 1984 ***NYPL [JLG 86-165]***

LE FRANÇOIS (MARTINIQUE) - SOCIAL CONDITIONS.
Rosélie, Roland. L'habitation sucrière au Quartier La Dumaine, Le François /. [Fort-deFrance? , 1986] ([Fort-de-France] : Impr. Désormeaux) 59 p. : LC Card 86-203128
HD8039.S86 M327 1986

Le Gal, André, 1920- Entre le marteau et l'enclume / André Le Gal. Paris : Pensée universelle, c1984. 448 p. ; 22 cm. ISBN 2-214-05783-8 : LC Card 85-118954 DDC 658.3/02/0924 B 19
1. Le Gal, André, 1920-. 2. Supervisors - France - Biography. 3. Industrial relations - France. I. Title.
HD8433.L4 A34 1984 ***NYPL [JLD 87-438]***

LE GAL, ANDRÉ, 1920-
Le Gal, André, 1920- Entre le marteau et l'enclume /. Paris , c1984. 448 p. ; ISBN 2-214-05783-8 : LC Card 85-118954 DDC 658.3/02/0924 B 19
HD8433.L4 A34 1984 ***NYPL [JLD 87-438]***

Le Goff, Jacques, 1924-
[Bourse et la vie. English]
Your money or your life : economy and religion in the Middle Ages / Jacques Le Goff ; translated by Patricia Ranum. New York : Zone Books ; Cambridge, Mass. : Distributed by MIT Press, 1988. 116 p. ; 24 cm. Translation of: La bourse et la vie. Bibliography: p. 111-116. ISBN 0-942299-14-0 (alk. paper) : LC Card 87-25248 DDC 330.94/01 19
1. Economic history - Medieval, 500-1500. 2. Church history - Middle Ages, 600-1500. I. Title.
HC41 .L43 1988

Le grand dérangement . Darmon, Jacques. [Paris] , c1985. 269 p. : LC Card 85-242541 DDC 384/.068 19
HE8144 .D37 1985 ***NYPL [JLE 87-363]***

Le grand inventaire . Paillet, Marc. Paris , c1985. 176 p. ; ISBN 2-207-23172-0 : LC Card 86-127029 DDC 338.944 19
HD4168 .P35 1985 ***NYPL [JLE 87-1232]***

Le Guen, René. Oxygène pour tous les cerveaux / René Le Guen. Paris : Messidor/Editions sociales, c1985. 204 p. : ill. ; 22 cm. (Politique) Includes bibliographical references. ISBN 2-209-05743-4 : LC Card 86-117864 DDC 331.7/12/0944 19
1. Professional employees - France. 2. Skilled labor - France. 3. Technicians in industry - France. 4. Executives - France. 5. Supervisors - France. I. Title.
HD8038.F7 L4 1985

Le Iniziative locali per l'occupazione : una risposta alla crisi nei paesi dell'area Ocse / G. Cambra ... [et al.] ; a cura di Renato Cibin e Luigi Saba. Milano, Italy : F. Angeli, c1985. 244 p. : ill. ; 22 cm. (Documenti ISVET . 75) Papers originally delivered at a seminar held at Castelgondolfo, September 7-9, 1983. Includes bibliographical references. LC Card 85-221711 DDC 331 s 331.12/042 19
1. Organisation for Economic Co-operation and Development - Congresses. 2. Public service employment - Congresses. 3. Full employment policies - Congresses. 4. Youth - Employment - Government policy - Congresses. 5. Local government - Congresses. I. Cambra, G. (Gaétan). II. Cibin, Renato. III. Saba, Luigi, 1940-. IV. Series.
HD85.I7 I68 no. 75 HD5713.5 ***NYPL [JLD 87-446]***

Le Japon . Schwab, Laurent. [Paris] , c1984. 115 p. : ISBN 2-86262-221-4 (pbk.) : LC Card 84-164308 DDC 330.952/048 19
HC462.9 .S338 1984 ***NYPL [JLD 86-3612]***

Le Lamer, Christian. Energie et décentralisation /. Paris , 1984. 297 p. : ISBN 2-7178-0782-9 : LC Card 84-249613
HD9502.F72 E5334 1984

Le lotte degli elettromeccanici /. Bezza, Bruno. Milano , c1981. 179 p. : ISBN 88-20-42149-6 : LC Card 81-200954 DDC 331.89/282131/0945 19
HD5384.E3 B49 1981 ***NYPL [JLD 86-2898]***

Le Mené, Michel. Les campagnes angevines à la fin du Moyen Age : (vers 1350-vers 1530) : étude économique / par Michel Le Mené. Nantes : Cid, c1982. 534 p., [1] folded leaf of plates : ill., maps ; 24 cm. Bibliography: p. 13-31. Includes index. LC Card 87-672705
1. Anjou (France) - Economic conditions. 2. Anjou (France) - Rural conditions. I. Title.
HC277.A55 L45x 1982

Le mouvement ouvrier /. Touraine, Alain. [Paris] , c1984. 438 p. : ISBN 2-213-01361-6 : LC Card 84-202370 DDC 322/.2/0944 19
HD6684 .T655 1984 ***NYPL [JLE 86-279]***

Le Moyne College. Institute of Industrial Relations. Collective bargaining in American industry . Lexington, Mass. , c1987. ix, 351 p. ; ISBN 0-669-12594-6 (alk. paper) LC Card 85-45936 DDC 331.89/0973 19
HD6508 .C656 1987

Le Paz, Bolivia. Instituto Nacional de Estadística. see **Instituto Nacional de Estadística (Bolivia)**

Le Roy, E. (Etienne)
Enjeux fonciers en Afrique noire /. Bondy , Paris , c1982. 425 p. ; ISBN 2-86537-057-7 : LC Card 83-130847 DDC 333.3/096 19
HD966 .E54 1982 ***NYPL [JLE 87-950]***
Espaces disputés en Afrique noire . Paris , c1986. 426 p., [8] p. of plates : ISBN 2-86537-146-8 LC Card 86-210958
HD965 .E86 1986

Le secteur rural et le développement économique . Rachidzadeh, Esfandiar. Genève , 1978. ix, 389 p. : LC Card 79-376015 DDC 338.1/0955
HD2065.2 .R3 ***NYPL [JLE 80-2370]***

Le Strategie di acquisto della grande impresa nell'evoluzione dei sistemi produttivi : contributi di una ricerca sull'indotto di fornitura / Lorenzo Caselli ... [et al.]. Milano, Italy : F. Angeli, c1985. 223 p. : ill. ; 22 cm. (Documenti ISVET . 76) Includes bibliographical references. LC Card 85-233748
1. Industrial procurement - Italy. 2. Vertical integration - Italy. 3. Consolidation and merger of corporations - Italy. I. Caselli, Lorenzo. II. Series.
HD85.I7 I68 no. 76 HD39.5 ***NYPL [JLD 87-426]***

Le Sueur, Bernard. Batelleries et bateliers de France : histoire illustrée de la navigation intérieure / Bernard Le Sueur. Le Côteau : Horvath, [1985] 208 p. : ill. (some col.), facsims., maps, ports. ; 28 cm. Bibliography: p. 207. ISBN 2-7171-0339-2 LC Card 87-106621
1. Inland water transportation - France - History. 2. Inland navigation - France - History. 3. Boatmen - France - History. I. Title.
HE443 .L39 1985

Le technocrate et le paysan . Muller, Pierre. Paris , c1984. 173 p. ; ISBN 2-7082-2347-X :

LC Card 84-171796 DDC 338.1/6 19
HD1947 .M85 1984 ***NYPL [JLD 86-3738]***

Le Tiers Monde peut se nourrir . Lenoir, René. [Paris] , c1984. 210 p. : ISBN 2-213-01385-3 : LC Card 84-188021 DDC 338.1/8/091724 19
HD1417 .L46 1984 ***NYPL [JLD 85-1065]***

Le Vaillant de Folleville, Patrice, 1954-
Nicht-sequentielle Suche, Preiswerbung und Marktgleichgewicht / Patrice Le Vaillant de Folleville. Frankfurt am Main ; New York : P. Lang, c1986. 198 p. : ill. ; 21 cm. (Europäische Hochschulschriften. Reihe V, Volks- und Betriebswirtschaft, 0531-7339 . Bd. 679 = vol. 679 = vol. 679) Originally presented as the author's thesis (doctoral)--Universität Essen, 1985. Bibliography: p. 189-198. ISBN 3-8204-9058-2 LC Card 86-153194
1. Prices - Mathematical models. 2. Advertising - Mathematical models. 3. Equilibrium (Economics) - Mathematical models. I. Series: Europäische Hochschulschriften. Reihe V, Volks- und Betriebswirtschaft , Bd. 679. II. Title.
HB221 .L42 1986

Le zone franche industriali nei paesi emergenti . Conferenza internazionale sul tema Le zone franche industriali, nuove forme di investimento, l'America latina (1985 : Milan, Italy) Milano, Italy , c1986. 207 p. ; LC Card 86-223193
HF1418 .C525 1985

Le 150 ore e la formazione professionale in azienda : il caso Italtel / P. Caciari ... [et al.] ; presentazione di M. Colasanto ; a cura di Barbara Mapelli ; coordinatori della ricerca L. Erlicher e W. Pieroni. Milano, Italy : F. Angeli, c1985. 178 p. : ill. ; 22 cm. (Cisem-Centro per l'innovazione e la sperimentazione educativa milanese/Quaderni . 10) Includes bibliographies. LC Card 86-141990
1. Italtel (Firm : Milan, Italy). 2. Telecommunication - Employees - Training of - Italy - Milan. 3. Adult education - Italy - Milan. 4. Continuing education - Italy - Milan. I. Caciari, P. (Paola). II. Mapelli, Barbara. III. Erlicher, L. (Luisella). IV. Pieroni, W. (Walter). V. Title: Centocinquante ore e la formazione professionale in azienda. VI. Series: Quaderni (Cisem) , 10.
HD5716.T242 I82 1985
NYPL [JFD 87-3739]

Leach, Donald. Future employment & technological change / Donald Leach and Howard Wagstaff with Anne-Marie Bostyn, Colin Pritchard, and Daniel Wight. London : Kogan Page, 1986. 264 p. : ill. ; 22 cm. Includes bibliographies and index. ISBN 1-85091-017-0 (pbk.) : LC Card 86-180981 DDC 331.12/5 19
1. Labor supply - Effect of technological innovations on. I. Wagstaff, Howard. II. Bostyn, Anne-Marie. III. Title. IV. Title: Future employment and technological change.
HD6331 .L34 1986

Leach, Gerald.
Energy and growth . London , Boston , 1986. xvii, 199 p. : ISBN 0-408-02560-3 : LC Card 85-31336 DDC 333.79/13 19
HD9502.A2 E542 1986
NYPL [JLE 86-2717]

Household energy in South Asia / Gerald Leach (International Institute for Environment and Development). London ; New York : Elsevier Applied Science ; xii, 111 p. : ill. ; 25 cm. Bibliography: p. 107-111. ISBN 1-85166-125-5 (pbk.) : LC Card 87-13177 DDC 333.79 19
1. Households - South Asia - Energy consumption. 2. Energy consumption - South Asia. I. International Institute for Environment and Development. II. Title.
HD9502.S613 H68 1987

Lead bank scheme . Singh, Awadh Bihari Prasad, 1946- Delhi , 1987. v, 223 p. ; LC Card 87-900328 DDC 332.1/0954/12 19
HG3289.B53 S57 1987

LEAD INDUSTRY AND TRADE - SPAIN - ALMERÍA (PROVINCE)
Sánchez Picón, Andrés. La minería del Levante almeriense, 1838-1930 . Almería [1983] 308 p., [14] leaves of plates : ISBN 84-85219-49-X LC Card 85-126928
HD9506.S762 A457 1983

The Leader-manager / John N. Williamson, editor. New York : Wiley, c1986. xi, 511 p. : ill. ; 24 cm. Bibliography: p. 507-508. ISBN 0-471-83693-1 : LC Card 86-1316 DDC 658.4/092 19
1. Executives - Addresses, essays, lectures. 2. Leadership - Addresses, essays, lectures. 3. Personnel management - Addresses, essays, lectures. I. Williamson, John N.
HD38.2 .L42 1986 ***NYPL [JLE 86-2930]***

Leadership / A. Dale Timpe, editor. New York, N.Y. : Facts on File, c1987. xi, 368 p. : ill. ; 24 cm. (The Art and science of business management . v. 3) Bibliography: p. 357-360. Includes index. ISBN 0-8160-1462-0 : LC Card 86-24167 DDC 658.4/092 19
1. Leadership. 2. Management. I. Timpe, A. Dale. II. Series.
HD57.7 .L43 1987

LEADERSHIP.
Britton, Paul R., 1933- Leadership is empowering people /. Lanham, MD , c1986. xxviii, 346 p. ; ISBN 0-8191-5409-1 (alk. paper) : LC Card 86-9193 DDC 658.3/14 19
HD57.7 .B75 1986 ***NYPL [JLD 86-3818]***

Crosby, Philip B. Running things . New York , 1987, c1986. p. cm. ISBN 0-452-25915-0 LC Card 86-28508 DDC 658.4/092 19
HD57.7 .C76 1987

Dansk ledelse '90 i et internationalt perspektiv . [Copenhagen] , 1983. 226 p. : ISBN 87-7553-128-3 : LC Card 83-185958
HD57.7 .D38 1983

Emerging leadership vistas /. Lexington, Mass. , c1988. xv, 331 p. : ISBN 0-669-15331-1 (alk. paper) LC Card 86-46310 DDC 658.4/092 19
HD57.7 .E44 1987

Follett, Mary Parker, 1868-1933. Freedom & co-ordination . New York , 1987. xvii, 89 p. ; ISBN 0-8240-8229-X (alk. paper) : LC Card 86-27079 DDC 658.4/092 19
HD57.7 .F66 1987

Friedman, Stewart D. Leadership succession systems and corporate performance /. New York, N.Y. (316 Uris Hall, New York, N.Y. 10027) , c1985. ix, 141 p. :
NYPL [JLF 87-255]

Gardner, John William, 1912- The nature of leadership . Washington, D.C. (1828 L St., N.W., Washington 20036) , c1986. 20 p. ; LC Card 87-167132 DDC 303.3/4 19
HD57.7 .G37 1986

Haggai, Tom. How the best is won /. Nashville , c1987. 228 p. ; ISBN 0-8407-4221-5 LC Card 87-14996 DDC 658.4/09 19
HD38.2 .H34 1987

Harris, Philip R. (Philip Robert), 1926- Management in transition . San Francisco, Calif. , c1985. xxvii, 404 p. : ISBN 0-87589-660-X (alk. paper) LC Card 85-45055 DDC 658.4 19
HD58.7 .H3695 1985 ***NYPL [JLE 85-3954]***

Hauff, Hanns Joachim Paul. Aufstieg zur Macht . München , c1983. 85 p. : ISBN 3-597-10422-3 LC Card 83-136638
HD38.2 .H38 1983

Hersey, Paul. Management of organizational behavior . Englewood Cliffs, N.J. , 1988. p. cm. ISBN 0-13-551268-9 : LC Card 87-23064 DDC 658.3 19
HD58.7 .H47 1988

How to lead effectively [videorecording] /. Del Mar, CA , 1986. 1 videocassette (19 min.) : ISBN 0-07-109095-9 (3/4 in.) LC Card 86-700130 DDC 658.4 11
HD57.7

Johnsen, Erik, 1928- Introduktion til ledelseslære /. [Copenhagen] , 1984, c1983. 109 p. : ISBN 87-17-03424-8 LC Card 85-127809
HD57.7 .J64 1983

Johnsen, Erik, 1928- Introduktion til ledelseslære /. [Copenhagen] , 1986, c1983. 134 p. : ISBN 87-17-03470-1 LC Card 87-108605
HD57.7 .J64 1986

Joiner, Charles W. Leadership for a change /. Cambridge, Mass. , 1987. xvi, 194 p. : ISBN 0-88730-107-X LC Card 86-25940 DDC 658.4/063 19
HD57.7 .J65 1987 ***NYPL [JLE 87-981]***

Koestenbaum, Peter, 1928- The heart of business . San Francisco , New York, NY , c1987. xiii, 368 p. : ISBN 0-933071-15-9 : LC Card 87-13665 DDC 658.4/09 19
HF5351 .K584 1987

Kotter, John P., 1947- The leadership factor /. New York , London , c1988. ix, 161 p. ; ISBN 0-02-918331-6 LC Card 87-19805 DDC 658.4/092 19
HD57.7 .K67 1988

Kouzes, James M., 1945- The leadership challenge . San Francisco , 1987. xxx, 362 p. : ISBN 1-555-42061-3 (alk. paper) LC Card 87-45428 DDC 658.4/092 19
HD57.7 .K68 1987

Kovach, Barbara E. Survival on the fast track /. New York , c1988. xv, 240 p. ; ISBN 0-396-09027-3 LC Card 87-19940 DDC 658.4/092 19
HD57.7 .K69 1988

Künzli, Ernst. Forschungs- und Entwicklungsplanung . Bern , c1984. 292 p. : ISBN 3-258-03351-X : LC Card 84-178059
HD30.4 .K86 1984

Lattmann, Charles. Die verhaltenswissenschaftlichen Grundlagen der Führung des Mitarbeiters /. Bern , c1981. 565 p. : ISBN 3-258-03094-4 : LC Card 82-163528 DDC 658.3 19
HD58.7 .L36 1981 ***NYPL [JLE 86-1595]***

Leadership /. New York, N.Y. , c1987. xi, 368 p. : ISBN 0-8160-1462-0 : LC Card 86-24167 DDC 658.4/092 19
HD57.7 .L43 1987

Manske, Fred A., 1939- Secrets of effective leadership /. Memphis, TN , 1987. ix, 206 p. : ISBN 0-943703-00-X LC Card 87-16870 DDC 658.4/09 19
HD57.7 .M37 1987

Otto, Werner, 1909- Die Otto-Gruppe . Düsseldorf , 1983, c1982. 319 p., [32] p. of plates : ISBN 3-430-17322-1 : LC Card 83-199344
HD2860.O77 O78 1982

Peters, Thomas J. The Skunk Camp promises /. New York , 1987. p. cm. ISBN 0-394-75314-3 (pbk.) : LC Card 86-46226 DDC 658.4/09 19
HD57.7 .P47 1987

Plaschka, Gerhard. Unternehmenserfolg . Wien , c1986. viii, 228 p. ; LC Card 87-103428 DDC 658.4/09 19
HD38.2 .P55 1986

Singh, V. B., 1941- Profiles of political elites in India /. Delhi , 1984. xii, 178 p. : LC Card 84-900272 DDC 305.5/24/0954 19
JQ281 .S565 1984 ***NYPL [JLD 86-4319]***

Tannenbaum, Robert. Leadership and organization . New York , 1987, c1961. xiv, 456 p. : ISBN 0-8240-8219-2 (alk. paper) : LC Card 86-27019 DDC 303.3/4 19
HD57.7 .T36 1987

Tarkenton, Francis A. Playing to win . New York , c1984. viii, 116 p. ; ISBN 0-06-015242-7 : LC Card 83-48390 DDC 650.1 19
HF5386 .T22 1984 ***NYPL [JLD 86-3515]***

Whyte, William Foote, 1914- Pattern for industrial peace /. New York , 1987, c1951. ix, 245 p. : ISBN 0-8240-8227-3 (alk. paper) : LC Card 86-25790 DDC 331.89/0469142/0977/311 19
HD6515.I52 C48 1987

LEADERSHIP - ADDRESSES, ESSAYS, LECTURES.
The Leader-manager /. New York , c1986. xi, 511 p. : ISBN 0-471-83693-1 : LC Card 86-1316 DDC 658.4/092 19
HD38.2 .L42 1986 ***NYPL [JLE 86-2930]***

Managing take-off in fast growth companies . New York , c1986. x, 191 p. : ISBN 0-03-005709-4 (alk. paper) : LC Card 85-16745 DDC 658.4/2 19
HD31 .T24 1986 ***NYPL [JLE 86-1303]***

Leadership and organization . Tannenbaum, Robert. New York , 1987, c1961. xiv, 456 p. : ISBN 0-8240-8219-2 (alk. paper) : LC Card 86-27019 DDC 303.3/4 19
HD57.7 .T36 1987

The leadership challenge . Kouzes, James M., 1945- San Francisco , 1987. xxx, 362 p. : ISBN 1-555-42061-3 (alk. paper) LC Card 87-45428 DDC 658.4/092 19
HD57.7 .K68 1987

LEADERSHIP - EVALUATION.
Ficher, Michael. Die Messung des

Führungsverhaltens . Bochum , 1981. v, 366 p. : ISBN 3-88339-193-X : LC Card 81-205568
HD57.7 .F65 1981 ***NYPL [JLD 86-2580]***

The leadership factor /. Kotter, John P., 1947- New York , London , c1988. ix, 161 p. ; ISBN 0-02-918331-6 LC Card 87-19805 DDC 658.4/092 19
HD57.7 .K67 1988

Leadership for a change /. Joiner, Charles W. Cambridge, Mass. , 1987. xvi, 194 p. : ISBN 0-88730-107-X LC Card 86-25940 DDC 658.4/063 19
HD57.7 .J65 1987 ***NYPL [JLE 87-981]***

Leadership for dynamic state economies . Committee for Economic Development. Research and Policy Committee. New York, N.Y. , 1986. xii, 104 p. ; ISBN 0-87186-782-6 LC Card 86-20760 DDC 338.973 19
HC103 .C734 1986 ***NYPL [JLF 86-1832]***

Leadership is empowering people /. Britton, Paul R., 1933- Lanham, MD , c1986. xxviii, 346 p. ; ISBN 0-8191-5409-1 (alk. paper) : LC Card 86-9193 DDC 658.3/14 19
HD57.7 .B75 1986 ***NYPL [JLD 86-3818]***

Leadership papers .
(1) Gardner, John William, 1912- The nature of leadership . Washington, D.C. (1828 L St., N.W., Washington 20036) , c1986. 20 p. ; LC Card 87-167132 DDC 303.3/4 19
HD57.7 .G37 1986

LEADERSHIP - SIMULATION METHODS.
Christopher, Elizabeth M. Leadership training through gaming . New York , 1987. 187 p. : ISBN 0-89397-284-3 : LC Card 87-12362 DDC 658.4/07353 19
HD57.7 .C53 1987

Leadership Studies Program (Independent Sector) Gardner, John William, 1912- The nature of leadership . Washington, D.C. (1828 L St., N.W., Washington 20036) , c1986. 20 p. ; LC Card 87-167132 DDC 303.3/4 19
HD57.7 .G37 1986

Leadership succession / edited by Stewart D. Friedman. New Brunswick, [N.J.], U. S.A. : Transaction Books, 1987. x, 157 p. : ill. ; 24 cm. "Published also as v. 25, no. 2 (summer 1986) of Human resource management"--T.p. verso. Includes bibliographies and index. ISBN 0-88738-162-6 : LC Card 87-10947 DDC 658.4 19
1. Chief executive officers - United States - Succession. I. Friedman, Stewart D.
HD38.25.U6 L43 1987

Leadership succession systems and corporate performance /. Friedman, Stewart D. New York, N.Y. (316 Uris Hall, New York, N.Y. 10027) , c1985. ix, 141 p. :
NYPL [JLF 87-255]

Leadership succession systems and corporate performance /. Friedman, Stewart D. New York, N.Y. (316 Uris Hall, New York 10027) , c1985. ix, 141 p. ; LC Card 86-162460 DDC 331.25/96 19
HD38.2 .F73 1985

Leadership training series (Columbus, Ohio) . (no. 66) National Center for Research in Vocational Education (U. S.) A National entrepreneurship education agenda for action /. Columbus, Ohio , 1984. xiv, 114 p. : LC Card 86-201272 DDC 658.4/2 19
HF1131 .N28 1984

Leadership training through gaming . Christopher, Elizabeth M. New York , 1987. 187 p. : ISBN 0-89397-284-3 : LC Card 87-12362 DDC 658.4/07353 19
HD57.7 .C53 1987

The leading edge . Potts, Mark. New York , c1987. iv, 220 p. ; ISBN 0-07-050599-3 LC Card 86-10567 DDC 658.4/06 19
HD58.8 .P68 1987 ***NYPL [JLE 87-33]***

Leading und Lagging kurzfristig variierbarer gruppeninterner Geldflüsse im Währungsrisikomanagement einer internationalen Unternehmung /. Pastuszek, Rainer. Pfaffenweiler , 1986. xvi, 275 p. : ISBN 3-89085-122-3 LC Card 87-128258 DDC 658.1/55 19
HG3851 .P295 1986

Leading Virginia industries . Haigh, Robert William, 1926- Charlottesville, Va. [1986] 161 p. : LC Card 87-620837 DDC 338.4/7677/009755 19
HD9857.V8 H35 1986

LEAFLETS. see PAMPHLETS.

League of Arab States. Idārah al-ʻĀmmah lil-Shuʼūn al-Iqtiṣādīyah. Zakī, Ramzī. al-Duyūn wa-al-tanmiyah . al-Qāhirah , 1985. 271 p. : LC Card 86-960543
HJ8824 .Z34 1985

LEAGUE OF NATIONS.
Haigh, R. H. Soviet foreign policy, the League of Nations and Europe, 1917-39 /. Aldershot, Hants , 1986. x, 138 p. ;
NYPL [JFD 86-5778]

League of Nations. International Labor Office. see **International Labor Office.**

League of Oregon Cities. Making the right turn . [Salem? Or.] [1986] iv, 39 p. : LC Card 87-621891 DDC 388.1/14/09795 19
HE356.O7 M35 1986

Leal, Luiz Octávio Pires. Agricultura : uma opção de investimento / Luiz Octávio Pires Leal. Rio de Janeiro : Bloch, 1985. 114 p. ; 21 cm. LC Card 87-140475 DDC 338.1/3/0981 19
1. Agriculture - Brazil - Finance. I. Title.
HD1872 .L4 1985

Leaman, Jeremy, 1947- The political economy of West Germany, 1945-85 : an introduction / Jeremy Leaman. New York : St. Martin's Press, 1988. xii, 287 p. : ill. ; 22 cm. Bibliography: p. 270-276. Includes index. ISBN 0-312-00541-5 : LC Card 87-9458 DDC 338.943 19
1. Germany, West - Economic conditions. 2. Germany, West - Economic policy. I. Title.
HC286.5 .L4 1988

Leap of faith . Laxer, James. Edmonton , c1986. 140 p. ; ISBN 0-88830-298-3 : LC Card 87-101958 DDC 382.7/1/0971 19
HF1480.15.U5 L39 1986

Leape, Martha P. The Harvard guide to careers / Martha P. Leape and Susan M. Vacca. Rev. ed. Cambridge, Mass. : Distributed for the Office of Career Services, Faculty of Arts and Sciences, Harvard University by Harvard University Press, 1987. ix, 181 p. ; 21 cm. Includes bibliographies and index. ISBN 0-674-37564-5 (pbk.) LC Card 87-8409 DDC 331.7/02 19
1. Vocational guidance - United States. 2. Job hunting - United States. 3. Vocational guidance - United States - Bibliography. 4. Vocational guidance - United States - Information services. 5. College graduates - Employment - United States. I. Vacca, Susan M., 1954-. II. Harvard University. Office of Career Services. III. Title.
HF5382.5.U5 L36 1987

Lear, Robert N. Groneman, Carol. [Corporate Ph. D.] Corporate PhD . New York, N.Y., U. S.A. , 1987, c1985. xx, 156 p. ; ISBN 0-14-010123-3 (pbk.) LC Card 86-30654 DDC 658.4/09 19
HD38.25.U6 G76 1987

Lear, Robert W. How to turn your MBA into a CEO / Robert W. Lear with Elisabetta di Cagno. New York : Macmillan ; London : Collier Macmillan Publishers, c1987. xvii, 222 p. ; 22 cm. Bibliography: p. 209-216. Includes index. ISBN 0-02-569610-6 LC Card 86-28332 DDC 650/.07/1173 19
1. Master of business administration degree - United States. 2. Executives - Vocational guidance - United States. I. Di Cagno, Elisabetta. II. Title.
HF1131 .L39 1987

Learning from local authority budgeting / edited by Howard Elcock, Grant Jordan. Aldershot [Hampshire] ; Brookfield, Vt., USA : Avebury, c1987. x, 258 p. ; 23 cm. Bibliography: p. 256-258. ISBN 0-566-05384-5 : LC Card 87-12096 DDC 352.1/2/0941 19
1. Local budgets - Great Britain - Case studies. I. Elcock, H. J. (Howard James). II. Jordan, A. G.
HJ9423 .L43 1987

Learning in the workplace / edited by Victoria J. Marsick. London ; New York : Croom Helm, c1987. 217 p. ; 23 cm. (Croom Helm series on theory and practice of adult education in North America) Includes bibliographies and index. ISBN 0-7099-4659-7 LC Card 87-20062 DDC 658.3/1243 19
1. Employees, Training of. 2. Adult education. 3. Learning. I. Marsick, Victoria J. II. Series.
HF5549.5.T7 L38 1987

Learning to use Lotus 1-2-3 /. Metzelaar, Lawrence C. Menlo Park, Calif. , c1987. xi, 286 p. : ISBN 0-8053-6736-5 (pbk.) LC Card 86-214400 DDC 005.36/9 19
HF5548.4.L67 M47 1987

Learning to use SPSSx /. Einstein, Gilles O., 1950- Englewood Cliffs, N.J. , c1987. viii, 183 p. : ISBN 0-13-528050-8 (pbk.) LC Card 86-30263 DDC 005.3/29 19
HA32 .E45 1987

Leary, Thomas E., 1946- From fire to rust : business, technology, and work at the Lackawanna Steel Plant, 1899-1983 / Thomas E. Leary, Elizabeth C. Sholes.1st ed. Buffalo, N.Y. : Buffalo and Erie County Historical Society, c1987. 134 p. : ill. ; 28 cm. Bibliography: p. 133-134. ISBN 0-939032-00-7 (pbk.) LC Card 87-692 DDC 338.7/669142/0974796 19
1. Lackawanna Steel Company - History. 2. Bethlehem Steel Corporation - History. 3. Steel industry and trade - United States - History. I. Sholes, Elizabeth C., 1946-. II. Title.
HD9519.L2 L43 1987

LEASE AND RENTAL SERVICES - GERMANY (WEST)
Hermann, Hans-Peter, 1942- Leasing als Leistungsangebot im Dienstleistungs-Marketing /. Frankfurt am Main , New York , c1984. ix, 275 p. : ISBN 3-8204-8084-6 LC Card 85-198760
HD9999.L4363 G34 1984

LEASE AND RENTAL SERVICES - GERMANY (WEST) - COST EFFECTIVENESS - ECONOMETRIC MODELS.
Slotta, Gerd. Die Entscheidung über die Betriebspacht bzw. Betriebsverpachtung /. Hamburg , c1986. xi, 374 p. : ISBN 3-925630-00-7 LC Card 86-152904
HD39.4 .S56 1986

LEASE AND RENTAL SERVICES - INDIA.
Kothari, Vinod. Lease, financing & hire-purchase . Nagpur, India , 1986. xxvii, 799 p. ; LC Card 87-902268
HD9999.L4363 I446 1986

LEASE AND RENTAL SERVICES - TAXATION - GERMANY (WEST)
Hermann, Hans-Peter, 1942- Leasing als Leistungsangebot im Dienstleistungs-Marketing /. Frankfurt am Main , New York , c1984. ix, 275 p. : ISBN 3-8204-8084-6 LC Card 85-198760
HD9999.L4363 G34 1984

LEASE AND RENTAL SERVICES - UNITED STATES.
A Competitive assessment of the United States equipment leasing industry. Washington, D.C. [1985] xvi, 116 p. : LC Card 85-601661 DDC 382/.45 19
HD9999.L4363 U63 1985
NYPL [JLF 86-1710]

Lease, financing & hire-purchase . Kothari, Vinod. Nagpur, India , 1986. xxvii, 799 p. ; LC Card 87-902268
HD9999.L4363 I446 1986

Lease, financing and hire-purchase. Kothari, Vinod. Lease, financing & hire-purchase . Nagpur, India , 1986. xxvii, 799 p. ; LC Card 87-902268
HD9999.L4363 I446 1986

LEASE SERVICES. see LEASE AND RENTAL SERVICES.

LEASES.
Unger, Maurice Albert, 1917- Real estate finance /. Cincinnati , c1984. vi, 426 p. : ISBN 0-538-19630-0 LC Card 83-61343 DDC 332.7/2 19
HG2040 .U53 1984 ***NYPL [JLE 86-4718]***

LEASES - FRANCE.
France. Conseil économique et social. Le crédit-bail . [Paris] [1985] 90 p. in various pagings : LC Card 86-184049
HD39.4 .F73 1985

LEASES, INDUSTRIAL EQUIPMENT. see INDUSTRIAL EQUIPMENT LEASES.

LEASES - TAXATION - FRANCE.
Kieffer, Walther. Steuerliche Wirkungen des grenzüberschreitenden Mobilien-Leasing . Berlin , c1983. xxiv, 338 p. : ISBN 3-503-02369-0 LC Card 83-233705
HD39.4 .K54 1983

LEASES - TAXATION - GERMANY (WEST)
Kieffer, Walther. Steuerliche Wirkungen des grenzüberschreitenden Mobilien-Leasing . Berlin , c1983. xxiv, 338 p. : ISBN 3-503-02369-0 LC Card 83-233705
HD39.4 .K54 1983

LEASES - TAXATION - GREAT BRITAIN.
Kieffer, Walther. Steuerliche Wirkungen des grenzüberschreitenden Mobilien-Leasing . Berlin , c1983. xxiv, 338 p. : ISBN 3-503-02369-0 LC Card 83-233705
HD39.4 .K54 1983

LEASES - TAXATION - UNITED STATES.
Kieffer, Walther. Steuerliche Wirkungen des grenzüberschreitenden Mobilien-Leasing . Berlin , c1983. xxiv, 338 p. : ISBN 3-503-02369-0 LC Card 83-233705
HD39.4 .K54 1983

Leasing als Leistungsangebot im Dienstleistungs-Marketing /. Hermann, Hans-Peter, 1942- Frankfurt am Main , New York , c1984. ix, 275 p. : ISBN 3-8204-8084-6 LC Card 85-198760
HD9999.L4363 G34 1984

LEATHER INDUSTRY AND TRADE - ARGENTINA.
Remmes Lenicov, Jorge. La industria curtidora en Argentina . [Buenos Aires] , 1976. 46 leaves ; LC Card 86-157645
HD9780.A52 R45 1976

LEATHER INDUSTRY AND TRADE - INDIA - UTTAR PRADESH.
Prasad, R. R., 1955- Change and continuity among the scheduled caste leather workers /. Hyderabad , 1986. 132 p., [4] leaves of plates : LC Card 87-902216
HD8039.L42 I575 1986

LEATHER INDUSTRY AND TRADE - ITALY - HISTORY.
Il Pappagallo giallo . [Pisa] , Firenze , c1986. 194 p., [1] leaf of plates : LC Card 86-212573
HD9780.I82 P37 1986

LEATHER INDUSTRY AND TRADE - PARAGUAY.
Morínigo, José N. Las artesanías de cuero y tejido en el Paraguay . Asunción , 1979. 106, [1] p. : LC Card 83-219583
HD9780.P373 A866 1979
NYPL [JLF 86-1810]

LEATHER INDUSTRY AND TRADE - PARAGUAY - ASUNCIÓN REGION.
Morínigo, José N. Las artesanías de cuero y tejido en el Paraguay . Asunción , 1979. 106, [1] p. : LC Card 83-219583
HD9780.P373 A866 1979
NYPL [JLF 86-1810]

LEATHER INDUSTRY AND TRADE - SWITZERLAND - DIRECTORIES.
Handbuch der schweizerischen Textil-, Bekleidungs- und Lederwirtschaft =. Zürich , 1986. 214 p. : ISBN 3-909214-07-X LC Card 86-221803
HD9940.S93 H36 1986

LEATHER INDUSTRY AND TRADE - URUGUAY.
Teja, Ana María. Análisis de la encuesta sobre cambio técnico en la industria del cuero en Uruguay /. Montevideo, Uruguay [1980] 56 p., [60] leaves ; LC Card 86-157655
HD9780.U82 T45 1980

LEATHER INDUSTRY AND TRADE - URUGUAY - TECHNOLOGICAL INNOVATIONS.
Teja, Ana María. Análisis de la encuesta sobre cambio técnico en la industria del cuero en Uruguay /. Montevideo, Uruguay [1980] 56 p., [60] leaves ; LC Card 86-157655
HD9780.U82 T45 1980

LEATHER - MANUFACTURE. see **LEATHER INDUSTRY AND TRADE.**

LEATHER - TRADE AND STATISTICS. see **LEATHER INDUSTRY AND TRADE.**

LEATHER WORKERS - INDIA - UTTAR PRADESH.
Prasad, R. R., 1955- Change and continuity among the scheduled caste leather workers /. Hyderabad , 1986. 132 p., [4] leaves of plates : LC Card 87-902216
HD8039.L42 I575 1986

LEAVE OF ABSENCE.
Rubin, Bonnie Miller. Time out . New York , c1987. p. cm. LC Card 87-5723 DDC 640 19
HD5255 .R82 1987

Leaver, Donald B. Dietl, Clara-Erika. Commercial dictionary . Wiesbaden , c1985-c1987. 2 v. ; ISBN 3-409-19900-4 (v. 1) LC Card 86-160868
HF1002 .D493 1985
NYPL [*R-Econ. 87-1271]

Leavitt, Harold J.
Managerial psychology : managing behavior in organizations / Harold J. Leavitt and Homa Bahrami.5th ed. Chicago : University of Chicago Press, 1988. x, 353 p. : ill. ; 24 cm. Bibliography: p. 339-344. Includes index. ISBN 0-226-46973-5 : LC Card 87-16820 DDC 158.7 19
1. Psychology, Industrial. I. Bahrami, Homa. II. Title.
HF5548.8 .L35 1988

The Social science of organization[s] . New York , 1987. ix, 182 p. : ISBN 0-8240-8213-3 (alk. paper) : LC Card 86-27069 DDC 658.4/03 19
HD58.7 .S67 1987

Lebanese economic report. Beirut : Edit-Eco Sarl, [1986] 137 p. : ill. ; 30 cm. "Edited by E.C.E. (Etudes et consultations economiques sarl)"--T.p. verso. "April 1986." Includes bibliographies. LC Card 86-231596 DDC 330.95692/044 19
1. Lebanon - Economic conditions. I. Etudes et consultations économiques sarl.
HC415.24 .L43 1986

LEBANON - COMMERCE - EUROPEAN ECONOMIC COMMUNITY COUNTRIES.
Mesropian, André. Les relations du Liban avec la Communauté économique européenne /. Beyrouth, Liban [between 1972 and 1984] 65 p. ; LC Card 84-196415
HF1583.9.Z4 E865 1972

LEBANON - ECONOMIC CONDITIONS.
Lebanese economic report. Beirut [1986] 137 p. : LC Card 86-231596 DDC 330.95692/044 19
HC415.24 .L43 1986

Yachoui, Elie. Restructuration et croissance de l'économie libanaise /. Beyrouth , 1983. 230 p. ; LC Card 86-148239
HC415.24 .Y32 1983

LEBANON - FOREIGN ECONOMIC RELATIONS - EUROPEAN ECONOMIC COMMUNITY COUNTRIES.
Mesropian, André. Les relations du Liban avec la Communauté économique européenne /. Beyrouth, Liban [between 1972 and 1984] 65 p. ; LC Card 84-196415
HF1583.9.Z4 E865 1972

Lebanon - Government. see **Lebanon - Politics and government.**

LEBANON - POLITICS AND GOVERNMENT - 1975-
Yachoui, Elie. Restructuration et croissance de l'économie libanaise /. Beyrouth , 1983. 230 p. ; LC Card 86-148239
HC415.24 .Y32 1983

Lebas, Michel. Glossary of accounting = Glossaire d'anglais comptable / Michel Lebas et Alfred Fontenilles. Paris : A. Colin : Longman, c1985. 124 p. ; 21 cm. English and French. Includes index. ISBN 2-86644-065-X (pbk.) : LC Card 86-179932
1. Accounting - Dictionaries. 2. English language - Dictionaries - French. 3. Accounting - Dictionaries - French. 4. French language - Dictionaries - English. I. Fontenilles, Alfred. II. Title. III. Title: Glossaire d'anglais comptable.
HF5621 .L42 1985

Lebedev, I. P. (Igor´ Pavlovich)
Proizvodstvennye resursy predpriiatiia : ėffektivnoe ispol´zovanie / I.P. Lebedev, A.A. Esiutin. Moskva : "Ėkonomika", 1984. 198 p. : ill. ; 20 cm. Bibliography: p. 195-[196] LC Card 85-138003
1. Industrial productivity - Soviet Union - Mathematical models. 2. Industrial management - Soviet Union - Mathematical models. I. Esiutin, A. A. (Anatoliĭ Aleksandrovich). II. Title.
HC340.I52 L42 1984

Lebedinskiĭ, IUriĭ Petrovich.
Ėkonomika ispol´zovaniia vodnykh resursov /. Kiev , 1980. 185 p. ; LC Card 87-462040
HD1697.S653 U374 1980

Territorial´nye osobennosti razmeshcheniia pishchevoĭ promyshlennosti USSR /. Kiev , 1982. 282 p. ; LC Card 83-197067
HD9015.S653 U476 1982

Lebelle, P. Besluitvorming . Deventer , 1986. 151 p. : ISBN 90-267-1065-8 LC Card 86-201119
HD30.23 .B476 1986

Leben auf dem Lande im Wandel des Industrialisierung . Wagner, Kurt. Frankfurt am Main , 1986. 558, [1] p. : ISBN 3-458-14329-7 LC Card 87-112493 DDC 330.943/41 19
HC289.K66 W34 1986

Ein Leben für die Information . Kapferer, Clodwig, 1901- Zürich , 1983. 116 p. ; ISBN 3-906639-00-X LC Card 83-185401
HC282.5.K36 A3 1983

Leben im Jahr 2000 und danach : Perspektiven für die nächsten Generationen : Ergebnisse einer Studie über die Auswirkungen der Bevölkerungs-Entwicklung auf die künftigen Lebensbedingungen in der Bundesrepublik Deutschland (ABEL-Projekt) / herausgegeben von Rainer Mackensen, Eberhard Umbach, Ronald Jung. Berlin : Arani, c1984. 213 p. : ill. ; 20 cm. "Neue Zukunft, Bd. 1"--Deut. Bibl. & advertisement. Bibliography: p. [203]-207. ISBN 3-7605-8571-X LC Card 85-128359
1. Population forecasting - Germany, West. 2. Households - Germany (West). 3. Family - Germany, West. 4. Germany, West - Population. 5. Economic forecasting - Germany, West. 6. Germany, West - Economic conditions - 1974-. I. Mackensen, Rainer, 1927-. II. Umbach, Eberhard. III. Jung, Ronald, 1952-. IV. Title: Neue Zukunft.
HB3595 .L43 1984

Leben mit Gneisenau, hundert Jahre-- : eine Zeche zwischen Dortmund und Lünen : Begleitbuch zur Ausstellung der VHS Dortmund im Museum für Kunst und Kulturgeschichte der Stadt Dortmund vom 12.9.-26.10.1986 / [herausgegeben im Auftrag der Dortmunder Museumsgesellschaft zur Pflege der Bildenden Kunst e.V. für das Museum für Kunst und Kulturgeschichte der Stadt Dortmund von Gerhard Langemeyer ; mit Beiträgen von Klaus Hackert ... et al., unter Mitarbeit von Heinz Balzereit ... et al. ; Redaktion, Gisela Framke ... et al.]. Dortmund : Museum für Kunst und Kulturgeschichte der Stadt Dortmund ; Essen : Klartext, [1986?] 317 p. : chiefly ill. ; 29 cm. Exhibition catalog. Ill. on lining papers. ISBN 3-88474-323-6 LC Card 87-408388 DDC 331.7/622334/094355 19
1. Coal-miners - Germany (West) - Dortmund - History - Exhibitions. 2. Gneisenau Mine (Germany) - History - Exhibitions. 3. Derne (Dortmund, Germany) - Social conditions - Exhibitions. 4. Dortmund (Germany) - Social conditions - Exhibitions. I. Langemeyer, Gerhard. II. Hackert, Klaus. III. Balzereit, Heinz. IV. Volkshochschule Dortmund. V. Museum für Kunst und Kulturgeschichte der Stadt Dortmund.
HD8039.M62 G335 1986

Leben mit kurzfristigem Denken . Biermann, Ingrid, 1955- Weinheim , 1985. 224 p. ; ISBN 3-407-58260-9 LC Card 86-106693
HD6053.6.G3 B54 1985
NYPL [JLD 86-3122]

Lebendige Arbeitswelt . Osswald, Richard, 1917- Stuttgart , c1986. 394 p. : ISBN 3-421-06309-5 LC Card 86-148169
HD9710.G44 D385 1986

Lebenseinkommen und Erwerbsbiographie . Göbel, Dieter, 1949- Frankfurt/Main , New York , c1983. xix, 364 p. : ISBN 3-593-33244-2 LC Card 84-132204
HC290.5.I5 G63 1983

Lebensmittel- und Agrarwissenschaften /. Gergely, Stefan M. Wien , 1983. iii, 317 p. ; ISBN 3-205-06103-9 LC Card 87-407964 DDC 338.1/9/4360285 19
HD9015.A8 G47 1983

Lebensmittel und Getränke aus der Schweiz = Produits alimentaires et des boissons de la Suisse = Food and beverages from Switzerland. 2. Aufl. Zürich : Verlag für Wirtschaftsliteratur, 1984. 113 p. : ill. (some col.) ; 24 cm. German, French and English. Compiled by: Christof Laemmel. Includes "Firm index." ISBN 0-390-92140-3
1. Food industry and trade - Switzerland. 2. Beverage industry - Switzerland. I. Laemmel, Christof. II. Title:

Produits alimentaires et des boissons de la Suisse. III. Title: Food and beverages from Switzerland.
NYPL [JFE 86-3409]

Lebensmittelüberwachung . Groebel, Wilhelm. Dortmund , 1976. 84 p. : LC Card 86-170104
HD30 .A7 Heft 167 HD9000.9

Lebensraum . Sack, Manfred, 1928- Bonn , 1982. 81 p. : ISBN 3-922153-01-1 LC Card 85-128580
HE363.G3 S23 1982

Lebenszyklus und ökonomische Ungleichheit . Meier, Christoph. Freiburg, Schweiz , 1983. 235 p. : ISBN 3-7278-0298-7 : LC Card 83-244050
HB601 .M389 1983

Leber, Maximilien, Edler von. Die Beschlüsse des internationalen Eisenbahn-Congresses zu St. Petersburg nach dem am 20.-31. August 1892 angenommenen französischen Texte in getreuer deutscher Uebersetzung / wiedergegeben und mit vielen fachlichen Bemerkungen ergänzt von Max Edlen von Leber. Wien : Otto Maass, 1893. 25 p. ; 27 cm. "Separat-Abdruck aus Nr. 67 ex 1893 des Verordnungsblattes des k.k. Handelsministeriums für Eisenbahnen und Schiffahrt." LC Card 85-666030
1. International Railway Congress (4th : 1892 : Saint Petersburg, Russia) - Abstracts. 2. Railroads - Congresses. I. Title.
HE1005.I553 L4x 1893

Lebin, Dmitriĭ Alekseevich. Bykov, A. N. (Aleksandr Naumovich) Sotsialisticheskaia integratsiia i nauchno-tekhnicheskaia revoliutsiia /. Moskva , 1981. 343 p. ; LC Card 82-101911
HC244.Z9 T43 1981

Leblanc, Raynald. La Compensation des charges familiales au Québec /. [Quebec] [1986] xxi, 197 p. ; ISBN 2-551-08707-4 LC Card 86-179318
HD4925.5.C2 C65 1986

LeBlond, Geoffrey T. Como usar Lotus 1-2-3 : la herramienta para gerenciar la productividad / por Geoffrey T. LeBlond, Douglas Ford Cobb ; revisado para la versión 2.0 por Thomas W. Carlton. Miami, Fla. : Macrobit Corp., 1986- p. cm. Includes index. LC Card 86-23629 DDC 005.36/9 19
1. Lotus 1-2-3 (Computer program). 2. Business - Data processing. I. Cobb, Douglas Ford. II. Carlton, Thomas W. III. Title.
HF5548.4.L67 L418 1986

LeBoeuf, Michael. How to win customers and keep them for life / Michael LeBoeuf. New York : Putnam's Sons, c1987. 190 p. ; 23 cm. Includes index. ISBN 0-399-13301-1 LC Card 87-13892 DDC 658.8/12 19
1. Customer relations. 2. Customer service. I. Title.
HF5415.5 .L4 1987

Lebovics, Herman. The alliance of iron and wheat in the Third French Republic, 1860-1914 : origins of the new conservatism / Herman Lebovics. Baton Rouge : Louisiana State University Press, c1988. p. cm. Bibliography: p. Includes index. ISBN 0-8071-1350-6 LC Card 87-21386 DDC 338.944 19
1. France - Economic policy. 2. France - Social policy. 3. France - Politics and government - 1870-1940. 4. France - Politics and government - 1852-1870. 5. France - History - Third Republic, 1870-1940. 6. Conservatism - France - History. I. Title.
HC276 .L354 1988

Leboyer, Claude Lévy- see Lévy-Leboyer, Claude.

Lecaillon, Jacques.
Economic policies and agricultural performance : the case of Burkina Faso / by Jacques Lecaillon and Christian Morrisson. Paris : Development Centre of the Organisation for Economic Co-operation and Development, 1985. 158 p. ; 23 cm. (Development Centre papers) Bibliography: p. 153-156. LC Card 86-216027 DDC 338.1/86625 19
1. Agriculture - Economic aspects - Burkina Faso. 2. Agriculture and state - Burkina Faso. 3. Agriculture - Burkina Faso. 4. Burkina Faso - Economic conditions. I. Morrisson, Christian. II. Title. III. Series.
HD2144 .L42 1985

Economic policies and agricultural performance : the case of Mali, 1960-1983 / by Jacques Lecaillon and Christian Morrisson. Paris : Development Centre of the Organisation for Economic Co-operation and Development, 1986. 174 p. ; 23 cm. (Development Centre papers) Bibliography: p. 155-157. LC Card 87-158595 DDC 338.1/86623 19
1. Agriculture and state - Mali. 2. Agriculture - Economic aspects - Mali. I. Morrisson, Christian. II. Title. III. Series.
HD2143.5.Z8 L43 1986

Leccisotti, Mario. Politiche dell'impresa e sistema tributario / Mario Leccisotti. 2a ed. Napoli : Liguori, 1984. 174 p. : ill. ; 21 cm. (Testi e contributi di economia . 6) Includes bibliographies. ISBN 88-20-70883-3 :
1. Corporations - Taxation - Italy. 2. Corporations - Italy - Accounting. 3. Corporations - Italy - Finance. I. Title. II. Series. ***NYPL [JLD 86-3651]***

LECHÍN OQUENDO, PERO JUAN.
Calla, Ricardo. La derrota de Lechín . La Paz, Bolivia , 1986. 79 p. : LC Card 87-105127
HD6609.M62 F433 1986

Lechner, Norbert, 1939- La conflictiva y nunca acabada construcción del orden deseado / Norbert Lechner. [Santiago, Chile] : Facultad Latinoamericana de Ciencias Sociales, [1984] 204 p. ; 23 cm. (Serie Libros FLACSO-Chile . 10) Includes bibliographical references. ISBN 84-89401-05-5 LC Card 84-227472 DDC 320.982 19
1. Authoritarianism - Chile. 2. Socialism - Chile. 3. Chile - Politics and government - 1970-. I. Title. II. Series.
JL2624 .L43 1984 ***NYPL [JLE 87-2137]***

Leclerc, Claudine. La sécurité d'emploi dans l'industrie de la construction au Québec : un rêve impossible? / Claudine Leclerc et Jean Sexton. [Quebec] : Les Presses de l'Université Laval, c1983. xii, 275 p. : forms ; 24 cm. (Collection Relations du travail) Includes legislation. Bibliography: p. [170]-193. ISBN 2-7637-7028-2 LC Card 84-126505 DDC 331.25/96 19
1. Construction workers - Québec (Province) - Supply and demand. 2. Construction industry - Québec (Province) - Employees - Supply and demand. 3. Job security - Québec (Province). 4. Construction industry - Québec (Province) - Seasonal variations. 5. Collective labor agreements - Construction industry - Québec (Province). I. Sexton, Jean. II. Title.
HD5718.B92 C248 1983
NYPL [JLE 86-3170]

LECLERC, EDOUARD, 1926-
Chavane, Laurence. Le phénomène Leclerc . Paris , c1986. 253 p., [16] p. of plates : ISBN 2-259-01481-X : LC Card 86-186372
HF5469.23.F72 L422 1986

LECLERC, MICHEL-EDOUARD.
Chavane, Laurence. Le phénomène Leclerc . Paris , c1986. 253 p., [16] p. of plates : ISBN 2-259-01481-X : LC Card 86-186372
HF5469.23.F72 L422 1986

Lecomber, Richard, 1937- Economics, growth, and sustainable environments . New York , 1988. viii, 205 p. : ISBN 0-312-01240-3 : LC Card 87-12520 DDC 363.7 19
HC79.E5 E2774 1988

LECOMBER, RICHARD, 1937-
Economics, growth, and sustainable environments . New York , 1988. viii, 205 p. : ISBN 0-312-01240-3 : LC Card 87-12520 DDC 363.7 19
HC79.E5 E2774 1988

L'economia a una svolta critica /. Di Nardi, Giuseppe. Milano , 1984- v. ; LC Card 84-216905 DDC 330 19
HB177 .D48 1984 ***NYPL [JLL 73-173 v.25]***

L'économie du populisme et le projet de passage au socialisme proposé par l'Unité populaire au Chili /. Vega Tapia, Héctor. [Brussels] , 1984. 511 p. ; LC Card 85-146534 DDC 338.983 19
HC192 .V37 1984 ***NYPL [JLE 86-3663]***

L'économie sociale, mythes et réalités /. Boursier, François, 1947- Lyon [1984] 108 p. : ISBN 2-85008-045-4 : LC Card 84-154709 DDC 334/.0944 19
HD3494 .B63 1984 ***NYPL [JLD 87-330]***

Leçons d'économie politique /. Vaté, Michel. Paris , c1985. 433 p. : ISBN 2-7178-1021-8 : LC Card 86-141680 DDC 330 19
HB173 .V367 1985

Lecturas en materia de seguridad social.
Enfermedades de trabajo. México, D.F. , c1983. 403 p. : ISBN 968-8242-08-X LC Card 85-216152
HD7262.5.M6 E54 1983

Planeación familiar y cambio demográfico. México, D.F. [1983], c1982. 554 p. : ISBN 968-8241-63-6 LC Card 84-227488 DDC 304.6/0972 19
HB3531 .P57 1983 ***NYPL [JLE 86-3248]***

Lecture notes in biomathematics.
(62) West, Bruce J. An essay on the importance of being nonlinear /. Berlin , New York , c1985. viii, 204 p. : ISBN 0-387-16038-8 (U. S.)
NYPL [JSK 75-186 v.62]

Lecture on international monetary issues /. Machlup, Fritz, 1902- Islamabad , 1982. vi, 49 p. ; LC Card 85-217227 DDC 332.4/5 19
HG3881 .M25 1982

Lecture series / Arthur Andersen & Co.
Zeff, Stephen A. Forging accounting principles in five countries . Champaign, Ill. , 1971, c1972. xvii, 332 p. ; LC Card 86-226472
HF5605 .Z44 1972

Lectures and conferences on mathematical statistics and probability. Neyman, Jerzy, 1894- Washington, 1952. vii, 274 p. LC Card Agr52-278 DDC 311.2
HA29 .N48 1952

Lectures in agricultural economics : Bicentennial year lectures / Theodore W. Schultz ... [et al.] ; sponsored by the Economic Research Service, U. S. Department of Agriculture. [Washington? : s.n., 1977] ix, 165 p. : ports. ; 24 cm. Includes bibliographical references. LC Card 77-603242
1. Agriculture - Economic aspects - United States - Addresses, essays, lectures. 2. Agriculture and state - United States - Addresses, essays, lectures. 3. Agriculture - Economic aspects - Addresses, essays, lectures. I. Schultz, Theodore William, 1902-. II. United States. Dept. of Agriculture. Economic Research Service.
HD1759 .L4 ***NYPL [JLE 79-149]***

Lectures in development economics .
(no. 2) Machlup, Fritz, 1902- Lecture on international monetary issues /. Islamabad , 1982. vi, 49 p. ; LC Card 85-217227 DDC 332.4/5 19
HG3881 .M25 1982

Ledebur, Larry C. Hamilton, William W. Innovations in economic development . Washington, D.C. (2021 K St., Suite 711, Washington 20006) [1986] 1 v. (various foliations) : LC Card 87-620522 DDC 338.973 19
HC110.I53 H363 1986

Lederman, Jess. The Secondary mortgage market . Chicago, Ill. , c1987. xvi, 648 p. : ISBN 0-917253-74-4 : LC Card 87-2303 DDC 332.63/244 19
HG2040.25 .S43 1987

Ledésert, Margaret. Harrap's new standard French and English dictionary /. London , 1980-1981. 4 v. ; ISBN 0-245-50972-0 (v.1)

Ledning, produktion & marknadsföring av tjänster : i teori & praktik / red., Johan Arndt, Alfred Friman. Malmö : Liber, c1981. 318 p. : ill. ; 25 cm. Bibliography: p. 302-313. ISBN 91-40-54058-8 : LC Card 81-174255
1. Service industries - Sweden - Marketing. 2. Marketing - Sweden. I. Arndt, Johan. II. Friman, Alfred, 1937-. III. Title: Marknadsföring av tjänster. IV. Title: Ledning, produktion och marknadsföring av tjänster.
HD9986.S82 L43 1981

Ledning, produktion och marknadsföring av tjänster. Ledning, produktion & marknadsföring av tjänster . Malmö , c1981. 318 p. : ISBN 91-40-54058-8 : LC Card 81-174255
HD9986.S82 L43 1981

Leduc, Michel. Stratégies d'industrialisation et maîtrise du développement. Paris , c1984. 115, [3] p. : ISBN 2-86844-002-9 LC Card 84-248894
HC59.7 .S854 1984

Leduc, Renato. Los diablos del petróleo / Renato Leduc. [Mexico City, Mexico] : Editorial "Nuestra América", [1986] 131 p. ; 21 cm. (Colección Testimonios) LC Card 86-219535 DDC 338.2/7282/0972 19
1. Petroleum industry and trade - Government ownership - Mexico. 2. Petróleos mexicanos. 3. Mexico - Politics and government - 1970-. I. Title.
HD9574.M62 P3745 1986

Ledvinka, James. Scarpello, Vida Gulbinas, 1940- Personnel/human resource management . Boston, Mass. , c1988. xxii, 794 p. : ISBN 0-534-08346-3 LC Card 87-13678 DDC 658.3

19
HF5549 .S186 1988

Lee, Bonghun. Kim, Chungsoo. Effects of neo-protectionism on the Korean exports /. [Seoul] , 1986. 203 p. : LC Card 86-234427 DDC 382/.095195/073 19
HF3830.5.Z7 U54 1986

Lee, Dwight R. Taxation and the deficit economy . San Francisco, Calif. , c1986. xxvii, 554 p. : ISBN 0-936488-13-1 : LC Card 85-63549 DDC 339.5/2/0973 19
HJ257.2 .T385 1986 ***NYPL [JLE 86-4136]***

Lee, Eddy.
Poverty in rural Asia /. Bangkok , 1984, c1983. xii, 276 p. ; ISBN 92-2-103286-8 (pbk.)
NYPL [JLE 86-1050]

Raḍwān, Samīr Muḥammad. Agrarian change in Egypt . London , Dover, N.H. , c1986. xii, 167 p. : ISBN 0-7099-4214-1 : LC Card 85-11356 DDC 305.5/69/0962 19
HN786.A8 R33 1985 ***NYPL [JLD 86-1045]***

Lee, James L. Pulvino, Charles J. Communicating with clients . Paramus, NJ , c1987. ix, 194 p. : ISBN 0-13-153578-1 (pbk.) LC Card 87-153498 DDC 332.1/068/8 19
HG179.5 .P86 1987

Lee, John Y. Managerial accounting changes for the 1990s / John Y. Lee. Artesia, Calif., U. S.A. : McKay Business Systems, c1987. iv, 87 p. : ill. ; 23 cm. Includes bibliographies and index. ISBN 0-9617977-0-3 (pbk.) : LC Card 87-60120 DDC 658.1/511 19
1. Managerial accounting. 2. Industrial management. 3. Industrial management - United States. I. Title.
HF5657.4 .L43 1987

Lee, Mu-Choon. Entwicklungen in der Umweltpolitik Südkoreas im Widerspruch zwischen Industrialisierung und Umweltschutz / Lee, Mu-Choon. Offenbach/Main, West Germany : Korea Forschungsgemeinschaft, [1984] 21 p. : ill. ; 29 cm. (KOFO, 0176-1773 . Nr. 006) Cover title. Bibliography: p. 20-21. LC Card 86-172511
1. Pollution - Korea (South). 2. Pollution - Economic aspects - Korea (South). I. Series: KOFO (Series) , Nr. 006. II. Title.
HC79.P55 L44 1984

Lee, Peter N. S., 1940- Industrial management and economic reform in China, 1949-1984 / Peter N.S. Lee. Hong Kong ; New York : Oxford University Press, 1987. x, 335 p. ; 23 cm. Bibliography: p. [290]-301. Includes index. ISBN 0-19-584118-2 : LC Card 87-13748 DDC 338.951 19
1. Industrial management - China. 2. China - Economic policy - 1949-. I. Title.
HD70.C5 L44 1987

Lee, Ronald Demos, 1941-
Economics of changing age distributions in developed countries /. Oxford [Oxfordshire] , Topsfield, Mass. , 1987. p. cm. ISBN 0-19-829503-0 : LC Card 86-25098 DDC 304.6/2/091722 19
HB1531 .E28 1987

Population growth and economic development . Madison, Wis. , 1987. xiii, 702 p. ; ISBN 0-299-11130-X : LC Card 86-40447 DDC 338.9/009172/4 19
HB884 .P66547 1987

Lee, S. Y. (Sheng-Yi) The monetary and banking development of Singapore and Malaysia / Lee Sheng-yi. 2nd & rev. ed. Singapore : Singapore University Press, National University of Singapore, 1986. 298 p. : ill. ; 23 cm. Bibliography: p. 281-292. Includes index. ISBN 997-16-9098-5 (pbk.) LC Card 86-943034 DDC 332.4/9595 19
1. Money - Singapore. 2. Money - Malaysia. 3. Banks and banking - Singapore. 4. Banks and banking - Malaysia. I. Title.
HG1250.67 .L43 1986

Lee, Stewart Munro.
Economics for consumers. Lee, Stewart Munro. Personal finance for consumers / Stewart M. Lee, Mel J. Zelenak. Columbus, Ohio , c1987. xiii, 518 p. : ISBN 0-942280-33-4 : LC Card 86-30503 DDC 381/.3/0973 19
HB301 .L256 1987

(joint author) Gordon, Leland James, 1897- Economics for consumers /. New York , c1977. ix, 693 p. : ISBN 0-442-22242-4 LC Card 76-50515 DDC 381/.3/0973 19
HB801 .G6 1977 ***NYPL [JLE 86-1506]***

Personal finance for consumers / Stewart M. Lee, Mel J. Zelenak. Columbus, Ohio : Publishing Horizons, c1987. xiii, 518 p. : ill. ; 24 cm. Rev. ed. of: Economics for consumers, c1982. Includes bibliographies and index. ISBN 0-942280-33-4 : LC Card 86-30503 DDC 381/.3/0973 19
1. Consumption (Economics). 2. Consumers - United States. 3. Consumer education. 4. Consumer protection - United States. I. Zelenak, Mel J. II. Lee, Stewart Munro. Economics for consumers. III. Title.
HB301 .L256 1987

Lee, Susan, 1943-
[ABZs of economics]
Susan Lee's ABZs of economics / introduction by Leonard Silk ; illustrations by Robert Mansfield. New York : Poseidon Press, c1987. 224 p. : ill. ; 22 cm. ISBN 0-671-55711-4 LC Card 86-25481 DDC 330/.03 19
1. Economics - Dictionaries. I. Title. II. Title: ABZs of economics.
HB61 .L34 1987

Lee, Thomas Alexander.
Company auditing / Tom Lee. 3rd ed. Wokingham, Berkshire, England : Van Nostrand Reinhold (UK), 1986. x, 197 p. ; 21 cm. "A Gee book." Includes bibliographies and index. ISBN 0-85258-243-9 (pbk.) LC Card 85-22537 DDC 657/.45 19
1. Corporations - Auditing. 2. Auditing. I. Title.
HF5667 .L387 1986 ***NYPL [JLD 86-3477]***

The evolution of corporate financial reporting / T.A. Lee & R.H. Parker. New York : Garland, 1984. x, 307 p. ; 23 cm. (Accounting history and the development of a profession) Includes bibliographies and index. Reprint. Originally published: Middlesex : T. Nelson, 1979. (Nelson series in accounting and finance) ISBN 0-8240-6332-5 (alk. paper) : LC Card 83-49431 DDC 657/.3 19
1. Corporations - Accounting - History - Addresses, essays, lectures. 2. Financial statements - History - Addresses, essays, lectures. I. Parker, Robert Henry. II. Title. III. Series.
HF5686.C7 L43 1984 ***NYPL [JLD 86-2835]***

Leeds, Dorothy. Smart questions : a new strategy for successful managers / Dorothy Leeds. New York : McGraw-Hill, c1987. x, 309 p. ; 25 cm. Bibliography: p. 285-295. Includes index. ISBN 0-07-036996-8 LC Card 86-27469 DDC 658.4/52 19
1. Management. 2. Personnel management. 3. Questioning. I. Title.
HD38 .L3867 1987

Leeds transport /. Soper, J. [Bramham, Wetherby, West Yorkshire] , 1985- v. <1 > : ISBN 0-9510280-0-6 (v. 1) : LC Card 87-103287 DDC 388.4/09428/19 19
HE4719.L4 S67 1985

Leedy, Jack J., 1921- Executive retirement management : a manager's guide to the planning and implementation of a successful retirement / Jack J. Leedy, James Wynbrandt. New York, N.Y. : Facts on File, c1987. xi, 260 p. ; 24 cm. Bibliography: p. 251-253. Includes index. ISBN 0-8160-1286-5 LC Card 86-24010 DDC 658.4/07132 19
1. Executives - United States - Retirement - Management. 2. Retirement - United States - Management. I. Wynbrandt, James. II. Title.
HD7125 .L43 1987

De leefsituatie van Surinamers en Antillianen in Nederland, 1985 /. Beek, P. van. 's-Gravenhage , 1986- v. <1 > : ISBN 90-357-0558-0 : LC Card 87-120083
HD8518.5.S87 B44 1986

De Leefsituatie van Turken en Marokkanen in Nederland 1984 / Centraal Bureau voor de Statistiek, Hoofdafdeling Sociaal-Culturele Statistieken. 's-Gravenhage : Staatsuitgeverij/CBS-publikaties, 1985-<1987 > v. <1-3 > : ill. ; 30 cm. Title on p. [4] of cover of v. 1: The quality of life of Turks and Moroccans in the Netherlands 1984. Summary in Arabic, English, and Turkish. CONTENTS. - d. 1. Eerste uitkomsten -- d. 2. Kerncijfers -- d. 3. Huishoudens en migratie. ISBN 90-357-0457-6 : LC Card 86-234067
1. Alien labor, Turkish - Netherlands - Statistics. 2. Alien labor, Moroccan - Netherlands - Statistics. 3. Quality of life - Netherlands - Statistics. I. Netherlands. Centraal Bureau voor de Statistiek. Hoofdafdeling Sociaal-Culturele Statistieken. II. Title: Quality of life of Turks and Moroccans in the Netherlands 1984.
HD8518.5.T87 L44 1985

Leela, Pillalamarri. Import substitution and economic efficiency : a microlevel study / Pillalamarri Leela.1st ed. Bombay : Himalaya Pub. House, 1984. xvi, 129 p. ; 23 cm. Revision of the author's thesis (Ph. D.--Andhra University) Bibliography: p. [124]-129. LC Card 84-900166 DDC 382/.45668624/0954 19
1. Fertilizer industry - India. 2. Import substitution - India. I. Title.
HD94484.N6 I544 1984
NYPL [JLD 86-3888]

Leenders, Michiel R. Reverse marketing : the new buyer-supplier relationship / Michiel R. Leenders, David L. Blenkhorn. New York : Free Press ; London : Collier Macmillan, c1988. ix, 198 p. : ill. ; 25 cm. Bibliography: p. 189-190. Includes index. ISBN 0-02-918381-2 LC Card 87-15146 DDC 658.7/2 19
1. Industrial procurement. I. Blenkhorn, David L. II. Title.
HD39.5 .L435 1988

Lees, Francis A. Financing export sales / by Francis A. Lees. New York, N.Y. (845 3rd Ave., New York 10022) : Conference Board, c1986. 12 p. : ill. ; 28 cm. (Research bulletin / The Conference Board . no. 183) Cover title. LC Card 86-212400 DDC 658.1/5 19
1. Export sales - United States. 2. Export credit - United States. 3. Domestic international sales corporations - Taxation - United States. 4. Foreign sales corporations - Taxation - United States. I. Series: Research bulletin (Conference Board) , no. 183. II. Title.
HF3031 .L36 1986

Leeworthy, Vernon R. Bell, Frederick W. An economic analysis of the importance of saltwater beaches in Florida /. Gainesville, FL [1986] xi, 166 p. : LC Card 86-622310 DDC 333.91/7/09759 19
HD266.F6 B45 1986

LEEZEN (GERMANY) - POPULATION - HISTORY.
Gehrmann, Rolf. Leezen 1720-1870 . Neumünster , 1984. 366 p. : ISBN 3-529-02907-6 : LC Card 85-217552
HB3596.L44 G44 1984

Leezen 1720-1870 . Gehrmann, Rolf. Neumünster , 1984. 366 p. : ISBN 3-529-02907-6 : LC Card 85-217552
HB3596.L44 G44 1984

Lefébure, Marcus.
Christian ethics and economics . Edinburgh , New York , c1980. xii, 114 p. ; ISBN 0-8164-2282-6 (Seabury Press : pbk.) LC Card 80-50892
HF1411 .C422 1980

Unemployment and the right to work /. Edinburgh , New York , c1982. x, 98 p. ; ISBN 0-8164-2391-1 (Seabury Press : pbk.) LC Card 87-150638
HD5707.5 .U544 1982

Lefebvre, André, docteur en droit. Planification et aménagement des communes, des départements et des régions / André Lefebvre, Jean-Claude Meyer. Paris : Berger-Levrault, c1985. 335 p. : ill. ; 21 cm. Includes index. Bibliography: p. 319-328. ISBN 2-7013-0620-5 : LC Card 86-113657 DDC 338.944 19
1. Regional planning - France. 2. Regionalism - France. 3. Decentralization in government - France. I. Meyer, Jean Claude. II. Title.
HT395.F7 L43 1985 ***NYPL [JLD 87-1577]***

Lefenfeld, Robert M. Owen, Gail T. Residential property sales in Maryland . Baltimore, Md. (2225 N. Charles St., Baltimore 21218-5767) [1985] iv, 79 leaves : LC Card 86-622370 DDC 333.33/8 19
HD266.M3 O9 1985

Leff, Enrique. Los Problemas del conocimiento y la perspectiva ambiental del desarrollo /. México, D.F. , 1986. 476 p., [1] folded leaf of plates : ISBN 968-231-372-4 LC Card 87-119336 DDC 363.7/0098 19
HD75.6 .P76 1986

Leffler, George Leland, 1899-
Stock market. Teweles, Richard Jack, 1924- The stock market / Richard J. Teweles, Edward S. Bradley. 5th ed. New York , c1987. xii, 526 p. ; ISBN 0-471-82044-X LC Card 86-33950 DDC 332.64/2 19
HG4551 .T48 1987

Lefkowitz, Rochelle, 1951- For crying out loud . New York , c1986. ix, 397 p. ; ISBN 0-8298-0581-8 (pbk.) : LC Card 86-9302 DDC 305.4/2/0973 19
HQ1426 .F757 1986 ***NYPL [JLD 86-3989]***

Leftwich, Richard H.
Eckert, Ross D. The price system and resource allocation. Chicago , c1988. xviii, 648 p. : ISBN 0-03-012533-2 LC Card 87-5068 DDC 338.5/2 19
HB172 .L45 1988

Sharp, Ansel Miree, 1924- Economics of social issues /. Plano, Tex. , 1988. xiii, 431 p. : ISBN 0-256-06173-4 (pbk.) LC Card 87-71674 DDC 330 19
HB171.5 .S5498 1988

A legacy from Victorian enterprise . Roberts, C. W. (Colin William), 1916- [Farnborough, Berkshire?] , 1983. x, 277 p. : ISBN 0-9509107-1-6 (pbk.) : LC Card 85-109000 DDC 338.7/6691/0942984 19
HD9521.9.B74 R62 1983
NYPL [JLD 86-2141]

Legal aspects of government regulation of business /. Dunfee, Thomas W. New York , c1984. viii, 335 p. ; ISBN 0-471-87029-3 (pbk.) : LC Card 83-21879 DDC 346.73/07 347.3067 19
KF1600 .D86 1984 ***NYPL [JLE 86-3511]***

The legal environment of business /. Howell, Rate A. Chicago , c1987. xiv, 783 p. : ISBN 0-03-008369-9 LC Card 86-4503 DDC 346.73/07 347.3067 19
KF1600 .H68 1987 ***NYPL [JLE 87-911]***

LEGAL PHOTOGRAPHY. see **PHOTOGRAPHY, LEGAL.**

LEGAL STATUS OF WOMEN. see **WOMEN - LEGAL STATUS, LAWS, ETC.**

LEGAL TENDER - HUNGARY.
Magyar törvényes fizetőeszközök =. [Budapest] [1986?] [38] p. : LC Card 87-407726
HG970.5 .M34 1986

Legal tenders of Hungary. Magyar törvényes fizetőeszközök =. [Budapest] [1986?] [38] p. : LC Card 87-407726
HG970.5 .M34 1986

Légár, János. Munkaügyi statisztikai és módszertani ismeretek /. Budapest , 1985. 323 p. : ISBN 963-10-6513-8 : LC Card 83-228566
HD4826.5 .M86 1985

Legay, Marie-Agnès. Réduction de la durée du travail et changement des modes de vie : le cas du travail à temps partiel féminin : rapport d'enquête / présenté par Marie-Agnès Legay, sous la responsabilité scientifique de Guy Roustang. Aix-en-Provence : Centre d'études, de recherches et de formation institutionnelles du Sud-Est, [1984] ix, 366 p. : ill. ; 30 cm. Cover title. At head of title: C.E.R.F.I.S.E. et Commissariat général du plan. "Décembre 1984." Includes appendices. Bibliography: p. 365-366. LC Card 86-185902
1. Part-time employment - France. 2. Women - Employment - France. 3. Women automobile industry workers - France - Attitudes. 4. Automobiles Peugeot (Firm) - Employees - Attitudes. I. Roustang, Guy. II. Centre d'études, de recherches et de formation institutionnelles du Sud-Est (France). III. France. Commissariat général du plan. IV. Title.
HD6066.F8 L44 1984

Die Legende von der Systemkonkurrenz . Damus, Renate. Frankfurt , New York , c1986. 245 p. ; ISBN 3-593-33590-5 LC Card 86-196924
HB90 .D36 1986

Leghorn, Lisa.
Houseworker's handbook. [Cambridge, Mass.] (c/o Women's Center, 46 Pleasant St., Cambridge 02139) [1974] 81 p. : LC Card 87-110536
HD6073.H84 H68 1974

Necessity of wages for housework. 1980. Leghorn, Lisa. What's a wife worth? / by Lisa Leghorn & Betsy Warrior. Somerville, Mass. [198-] 8 p. : LC Card 87-111053 DDC 331.2/8164/0973 19
HD4966.H842 U64 1980z

What's a wife worth? / by Lisa Leghorn & Betsy Warrior. Somerville, Mass. : New England Free Press, [198-] 8 p. : ill. ; 28 cm. Cover title. CONTENTS. - Slavery or a labor of love? / Betsy Warrior -- Women's work / The necessity of wages for housework / Lisa Leghorn. LC Card 87-111053 DDC 331.2/8164/0973 19
1. Wages - Housewives - United States. 2. Housewives - United States. I. Warrior, Betsy. II. Warrior, Betsy. Slavery or a labor of love? 1980. III. Leghorn, Lisa. Women's work. 1980. IV. Leghorn, Lisa. Necessity of wages for housework. 1980. V. Title.
HD4966.H842 U64 1980z

Women's work. 1980. Leghorn, Lisa. What's a wife worth? / by Lisa Leghorn & Betsy Warrior. Somerville, Mass. [198-] 8 p. : LC Card 87-111053 DDC 331.2/8164/0973 19
HD4966.H842 U64 1980z

Legion, pseud. see **Defoe, Daniel, 1661?-1731.**

LEGISLATION, INDUSTRIAL. see **INDUSTRIAL LAWS AND LEGISLATION.**

LEGISLATION, SOCIAL. see **SOCIAL LEGISLATION.**

Legislative Commission on Public-Private Cooperation second report . New York (State). Legislature. Legislative Commission on Public-Private Cooperation. [Albany] [1984] 57 p. ; LC Card 86-622576 DDC 338.9747 19
HC107.N7 N3743 1984

LEGISLATIVE, EXECUTIVE, AND JUDICIAL APPROPRIATIONS BILLS. see **UNITED STATES - APPROPRIATIONS AND EXPENDITURES.**

LEGISLATIVE INVESTIGATION. see **GOVERNMENTAL INVESTIGATIONS.**

LEGISLATIVE OVERSIGHT - INDIA.
Surya Prakash. Parliamentary control over public enterprises in India /. Allahabad, India , 1985. 293 p. ; LC Card 85-903454 DDC 354.5409/2 19
HD4293 .S87 1985 ***NYPL [JLD 87-325]***

LEGISLATORS - INDIA - BIOGRAPHY.
Ray, Renuka Mukerji, 1903- My reminiscences . New Delhi , 1982. ix, 294 p., [5] p. of plates : LC Card 82-905707 DDC 954.03/5 19
DS481.R33 A38 1982 ***NYPL [JFD 85-9372]***

Legoff, Jean-Pierre, 1946- Lapointe, Alain. Les industries québécoises de services télématiques . Montréal [1984] x, 305 p. : ISBN 2-551-06190-3 LC Card 84-230415 DDC 384/.09714 19
HE7818.Q4 L36 1984 ***NYPL [JLF 86-1397]***

Legorreta, Jorge. La autoconstrucción de vivienda en México : el caso de las ciudades petroleras / Jorge Legorreta.[1a ed.]. [México, D.F.] : Centro de Ecodesarrollo, [1984] 204 p. : ill. ; 23 cm. Bibliography: p. 199-204. LC Card 86-232442
1. Self-help housing - Mexico. 2. Land use, Urban - Mexico. I. Title.
HD7306.A3 L44 1984

Lehigh University. Blank, Thomas O., 1947- Older persons and their homes, today and tomorrow . [Harrisburg] [1986] 60 leaves : LC Card 86-623023 DDC 363.5/9 19
HD7287.92.U54 B55 1986

Lehman Brothers. Auletta, Ken. Greed and glory on Wall Street . Boston, Mass. , 1987, c1986. xii, 423 p. (large print) ; ISBN 0-8161-4189-4 (lg. print) : LC Card 86-26968 DDC 332.66/09747/1 19
HG5129.N5 A8 1987b

LEHMAN BROTHERS.
Auletta, Ken. Greed and glory on Wall Street . New York , c1986. xiii, 253 p., [16] p. of plates : ISBN 0-394-54410-2 : LC Card 85-10700 DDC 332.66/09747/1 19
HG5129.N5 A8 1986 ***NYPL [JLE 86-856]***

Auletta, Ken. Greed and glory on Wall Street . Boston, Mass. , 1987, c1986. xii, 423 p. (large print) ; ISBN 0-8161-4189-4 (lg. print) : LC Card 86-26968 DDC 332.66/09747/1 19
HG5129.N5 A8 1987b

Auletta, Ken. Greed and glory on Wall Street . New York, N.Y. [1987], c1986. xi, 260 p., [16] p. of plates : ISBN 0-446-38406-2 (pbk.) LC Card 86-23416 DDC 332.66/09747/1 19
HG5129.N5 A8 1987

Lehman, Carol M.
Lehman, Mark W. Using the microcomputer in cost accounting . St. Paul , c1988. x, 396 p. : ISBN 0-314-34729-1 (pbk.) LC Card 87-10632 DDC 657/.42/02855369 19
HF5686.C8 L34 1988

Lehman, Mark W. Using the microcomputer in managerial accounting . St. Paul , c1987. x, 406 p. : ISBN 0-314-98515-8 (pbk.) LC Card 87-2194 DDC 658.1/511/02855369 19
HF5657.4 .L44 1987

Lehman, June M.
Employee benefit plans . Brookfield, Wis. , 1987. ix, 157 p. ; ISBN 0-89154-317-1 (pbk.) LC Card 87-150660 DDC 658.3/25/0321 19
HD4928.N6 E46 1987

International Benefits Seminar (1985 : Saint Thomas, V.I.) International benefits, 1985-1986 /. Brookfield, Wis. , 1986. xi, 130 p. : ISBN 0-89154-306-6 (pbk.) LC Card 86-224351 DDC 331.25/5 19
HD4928.N6 I57 1986

Lehman, Mark W.
Using the microcomputer in cost accounting : Lotus 1-2-3 edition / Mark W. Lehman, Carol M. Lehman, Troy E. Daniel. St. Paul : West Pub. Co., c1988. x, 396 p. : ill. ; 28 cm. (Microcomputing in accounting series) Includes index. ISBN 0-314-34729-1 (pbk.) LC Card 87-10632 DDC 657/.42/02855369 19
1. Cost accounting - Data processing. 2. Lotus 1-2-3 (Computer program). I. Lehman, Carol M. II. Daniel, Troy E. III. Title. IV. Series.
HF5686.C8 L34 1988

Using the microcomputer in managerial accounting : Lotus 1-2-3 edition / Mark W. Lehman, Carol M. Lehman, Troy E. Daniel. St. Paul : West Pub. Co., c1987. x, 406 p. : ill. ; 29 cm. (Microcomputing in accounting series) Includes index. ISBN 0-314-98515-8 (pbk.) LC Card 87-2194 DDC 658.1/511/02855369 19
1. Managerial accounting - Data processing. 2. Lotus 1-2-3 (Computer program). 3. Microcomputers. I. Lehman, Carol M. II. Daniel, Troy E. III. Title. IV. Series.
HF5657.4 .L44 1987

Lehmann, Hans G. (Hans Georg), 1939- Maxeiner, Dirk, 1953- Testfahrer und Autospione . Stuttgart , 1985. 214 p. : ISBN 3-613-01022-4 : LC Card 85-170273
HD9710.A2 M385 1985

Lehmann, Michael B. The Dow Jones-Irwin guide to using the Wall Street journal / Michael B. Lehmann. 2nd ed. Homewood, Ill. : Dow Jones-Irwin, c1987. xii, 282 p. : ill. ; 24 cm. Includes index. ISBN 0-87094-923-3 LC Card 86-71441 DDC 332/.05 19
1. Business cycles - United States. 2. Economic indicators - United States. 3. Wall Street journal. I. Dow Jones-Irwin. II. Wall Street journal. III. Title.
HB3743 .L44 1987

Lehner, Susanna Walpurga.
Unternehmensanalyse : Vorschlag für ein umfassendes Informationssystem zur Beurteilung und laufenden Beobachtung des Bonitätsrisikos / Susanna Walpurga Lehner. Wien : Service, c1984. 243 p. : ill. ; 21 cm. (Schriftenreihe des Instituts für Kredit- u. Versicherungswirtschaft, Abteilung Bankbetriebslehre . Bd. 7) Bibliography: p. 236-242. ISBN 3-85428-023-8 : LC Card 84-173011
1. Credit guides. 2. Credit bureaus. I. Title. II. Series.
HG3751.5 .L44 1984

Lehnhardt-Ritter, Gerda. Das Kapitalanlageverhalten der deutschen Lebensversicherungsunternehmen im Wandel der Konjunktur : eine spektralanalystische und ökonometrische Untersuchung / von Gerda Lehnhardt-Ritter. Karlsruhe : Verlag Versicherungswirtschaft, c1984. xxiii, 444 p. : ill. ; 21 cm. (Veröffentlichungen des Instituts für Versicherungswissenschaft der Universität Mannheim, 0170-2254 . Bd. 25) Bibliography: p. 413-441. Includes index. ISBN 3-88487-067-X LC Card 85-171182
1. Insurance, Life - Germany (West) - Finance - Econometric models. 2. Investments - Germany (West) - Econometric models. 3. Insurance companies - Germany (West) - Econometric models. 4. Business cycles - Germany (West) - Econometric models. I. Title. II. Series.
HG9078 .L44 1984

Lehota, József. Magyar-Lengyel Agrárközgazdasági Konferencia (1984 : Gödöllő, Hungary) A nagyüzemek és a kisüzemek termelésének fejlődése, kapcsolatuk az iparosodó mezőgazdaságban =. Gödöllő , 1984. 174 p. ; LC Card 86-145249
HD1995.7 .M32 1984

Lehr, Jay H., 1936- Orbital management : beyond the hierarchy / by Jay H. Lehr and Jose E. Rodriguez. Lanham, MD : Hamilton Press ; [Cambridge, MA] : Abt Books, c1987. xvi, 104 p. : ill. ; 24 cm. Includes bibliographical references and index. ISBN 0-8191-6264-7 (alk. paper) : LC Card 87-143 DDC 658.4/02 19
1. Decentralization in management. I. Rodriguez, Jose E., 1958-. II. Title.
HD50 .L44 1987

Lehr, Richard I. The new unionism : a blueprint for the future / Richard I. Lehr and David J. Middlebrooks. New York, N.Y. : Executive Enterprises Publications Co., c1987. 114 p. ; 28 cm. ISBN 0-88057-672-3 (pbk.) LC Card 86-82864 DDC 331.88/0973 19
1. Trade-unions - United States. 2. Industrial relations - United States. I. Middlebrooks, David J. II. Title.
HD6508 .L427 1987

Lehrbuch der Altenpflege. Seddig, Gert. Hannover , c1983. 95 p. : ISBN 3-87870-204-3 LC Card 83-230557
HF5728.G3 S49 1983

Lehre und Berufsausübung . Gaulke, Klaus-Peter. Berlin , 1986. 122 p. ; ISBN 3-428-06000-8 LC Card 86-166545
HC281 .B33 Heft 89 HD5715.5.G42B47

Lehrjahre bei Bau-Holz . Czasny, Karl. Wien , c1985. ix, 148 p. ; ISBN 3-900351-34-1 LC Card 86-227367 DDC 331.88/174/09436 19
HD6678.W62 G493 1985

Lehrman, Stevanne Ruth. Local area networking with microcomputers : a guide for the business decision-maker / Stevanne Ruth Lehrman. New York, N.Y. : Prentice Hall Press, c1986. xx, 261 p. : ill. ; 24 cm. "A Brady book." Includes index. ISBN 0-89303-640-4 (pbk.) : LC Card 86-91466 DDC 650/.028/5468 19
1. Business - Data processing. 2. Local area networks (Computer networks). I. Title.
HF5548.2 .L392 1986 ***NYPL [JLE 87-121]***

Lei das finanças locais : repercussões espaciais da sua aplicação / Centro de Estudos de Planeamento. [Lisbon] : CEP, [1980] 56 leaves ; 29 cm. (Estudos urbanos e regionais . no. 19) Cover title. "Fevereiro de 1980." Includes bibliographical references. LC Card 83-223473
1. Local finance - Portugal. 2. Intergovernmental fiscal relations - Portugal. I. Centro de Estudos de Planeamento. II. Series: Estudos urbanos e regionais , estudo no. 19.
HJ9529 .L45 1980

Leibenstein, Harvey. Inside the firm : the inefficiencies of hierarchy / Harvey Leibenstein. Cambridge, Mass. : Harvard University Press, 1987. xiv, 276 p. : ill. ; 25 cm. Bibliography: p. [263]-268. Includes index. ISBN 0-674-45515-0 (alk. paper) LC Card 87-8426 DDC 302.3/5 19
1. Industrial organization (Economic theory). 2. Competition, Imperfect. 3. Industrial management - Japan. I. Title.
HD2326 .L45 1987

Leibfried, Stephan, 1944- Politik der Armut und die Spaltung des Sozialstaats /. Frankfurt am Main , 1985. 474 p. : ISBN 3-518-11233-3 : LC Card 85-183026
HC290.5.P6 P65 1985

Leibfritz, Willi.
Berücksichtigung der zentralen Orte im kommunalen Finanzausgleich Bayern : Gutachten im Auftrag des Bayerischen Städtetages, München / von Willi Leibfritz, Benedikt Thanner. München : Ifo-Institut für Wirtschaftsforschung, 1986. vi, 151 p. : ill. ; 21 cm. (Ifo Studien zur Finanzpolitik, 0081-7279 . 38) Bibliography: p. 151. ISBN 3-88512-018-6 LC Card 86-172605
1. Local finance - Germany (West) - Bavaria. 2. Local taxation - Germany (West) - Bavaria. I. Thanner, Benedikt. II. Title. III. Series.
HJ9493.5.B38 L45 1986

Sicherung der Altersvorsorge durch Aufgabenteilung zwischen Individualversicherung und gesetzlicher Rentenversicherung . München , 1986. xi, 242 p. : ISBN 3-88512-017-8 : LC Card 86-163171
HD7105.35.G3 S53 1986

Steuerliche Investitionsförderung im internationalen Vergleich / von Willi Leibfritz, Cornelia Meurer. Berlin : Duncker & Humblot, c1985. 255 p. : ill. ; 24 cm. (Schriftenreihe des IFO-Instituts für Wirtschaftsforschung . Nr. 117) Bibliography: p. [253]-255. ISBN 3-428-05776-7 LC Card 85-161706
1. Investment tax credit. 2. Tax incentives. 3. Investments - Taxation. I. Meurer, Cornelia. II. Title. III. Series.
HJ4631 .L38 1985

Leibnitz, Heinz Maier- see **Maier-Leibnitz, Heinz.**

Leibovich, José. Comercio exterior y distribución de ingresos : análisis para el caso del café colombiano / por José Leibovich. Bogotá, Colombia : Centro de Estudios sobre Desarrollo Económico, Universidad de los Andes, 1984. vii, 221 p. : ill. ; 28 cm. (Documento CEDE . 073) Bibliography: p. 219-221. LC Card 87-402975 DDC 382/.41373/09861 19
1. Coffee trade - Colombia. 2. Colombia - Commerce. 3. Income distribution - Colombia. I. Series: Documento (Universidad de los Andes (Bogotá, Colombia). Centro de Estudios sobre Desarrollo Económico) , 073. II. Title.
HD9199.C62 L45 1984

Leibowitz, Dennis. The cellular communications industry / Dennis Leibowitz, Eric Buck, James McCabe. New York, N.Y. (140 Broadway, New York 10005) : Donaldson, Lufkin & Jenrette, c1985. ii, 67 p. : ill. ; 28 cm. Cover title. LC Card 86-201572 DDC 384.5/33/0973 19
1. Cellular radio equipment industry - United States. 2. Telephone - United States. 3. Market surveys - United States. I. Buck, Eric. II. McCabe, James (James M.). III. Donaldson, Lufkin & Jenrette, inc. IV. Title.
HD9696.R363 U65 1985

Leibundgut, Hansjörg, 1947- Die Bedeutung der beruflichen Mobilität als arbeitsmarktlicher Ausgleichsprozess : eine empirische Untersuchung aufgrund der Eidgenössischen Volkszählung 1980 / Hansjörg Leibundgut. Bern ; New York : P. Lang, c1986. ix, 235 p. : ill. ; 21 cm. (Europäische Hochschulschriften. Reihe V, Volks- und Betriebswirtschaft . Bd. 749 = vol. 749 = vol. 749) Originally presented as the author's thesis (doctoral)--Universität Bern, 1985. Bibliography: p. 229-235. ISBN 3-261-03630-3 LC Card 87-122350 DDC 331.12/79494 19
1. Labor mobility - Switzerland. 2. Occupational mobility - Switzerland. 3. Switzerland - Census, 1980. I. Series: Europäische Hochschulschriften. Reihe V, Volks- und Betriebswirtschaft , Bd. 749. II. Title.
HD5717.5.S9 L45 1986

Leichtfuss, Reinhold. Kapitalbudgetierung in divisionalisierten Unternehmen : Untersuchungen zur Koordinationseffizienz von Dekompositionsprinzipien / Reinhold Leichtfuss. Wiesbaden : Gabler, c1984. 389 p. ; 24 cm. (Beiträge zur betriebswirtschaftlichen Forschung. Bd. 57) Bibliography: p. [367]-387. ISBN 3-409-13701-7 LC Card 85-231538
1. Capital budget. 2. Capital investments. I. Title. II. Series.
HG4028.C4 L387 1984

Comparative studies in overseas history. see **Comparative studies in overseas history.**

Leiden development studies .
(no. 1) Participatie, toegang tot ontwikkeling . Leiden , 1982, c1983. 313 p. ; ISBN 90-6624-043-1 LC Card 87-158868
HC59.72.E44 P37 1983

Leidig, Guido, 1953- Weimar, Robert. Die Umweltvorsorge im Rahmen der Landesplanung Nordrhein-Westfalen . Frankfurt am Main , New York , c1983. xxiii, 313 p. : ISBN 3-8204-7669-5 LC Card 83-206670
HC287.N6 W44 1983

Leienbach, Volker. Demographische Entwicklung und kapitalbildende Altersversorgungssysteme /. Bergisch Gladbach , 1984. iii, 67 p. ; LC Card 85-154174
HD7091 .D46 1984

Leimdorfer, F. (François) Enjeux fonciers en Afrique noire /. Bondy , Paris , c1982. 425 p. ; ISBN 2-86537-057-7 : LC Card 83-130847 DDC 333.3/096 19
HD966 .E54 1982 ***NYPL [JLE 87-950]***

Leinbach, Thomas R., 1941- Costello, Michael A. Mobility and employment in urban Southeast Asia . Boulder , 1987. xvi, 190 p. : ISBN 0-8133-7352-2 (pbk. : alk. paper) : LC Card 87-10649 DDC 307.2 19
HB2107 .C67 1987

Leininger, Wayne E. Killough, Larry N. Cost accounting . St. Paul , c1987. xxii, 870 p. : ISBN 0-314-25865-5 : LC Card 86-26677 DDC 658.1/511 19
HF5686.C8 K488 1987

Leipert, Christian. Folgekosten des Wachstums als Wachstumsstimulans : zur Notwendigkeit der Entwicklung eines bereinigten Nettokonsumindikators und eines Tableaus defensiver Ausgaben : eine Orientierungspapier / Christian Leipert. Berlin : Internationales Institut für Umwelt und Gesellschaft, [1985?] 35 p. : ill. ; 30 cm. (IIUG discussion papers, 0175-8918) "IIUG dp 85-7." Summary in English and German. Bibliography: p. 34-35. LC Card 86-116361
1. Economic policy - Environmental aspects. 2. Economic development - Environmental aspects. I. Internationales Institut für Umwelt und Gesellschaft. II. Series: Papers from the International Institute for Environment and Society of the Science Center Berlin. III. Title.
HD75.6 .L45 1985

Leipold, Helmut. Zur Interdependenz von Unternehmens- und Wirtschaftsordnung /. Stuttgart , New York , 1986. x, 280 p. ; ISBN 3-437-50296-4 LC Card 87-134241 DDC 338.9 19
HB95 .Z87 1986

Leipziger Beiträge zur Revolutionsforschung, 0323-6714 .
(Lehrheft 15) Die Übergangsperiode . [Leipzig] , 1986. 80 p. ; LC Card 87-407523 DDC 338.9/009171/7 19
HC704 .U24 1986

Leipziger, Danny M. Korea . Washington, D.C., U. S.A. [1987] 2 v. : ISBN 0-8213-0887-4 (pbk. : v. 1) LC Card 87-2213 DDC 338.9519/5 19
HD3616.K853 K67 1987

Leisch, Jack E. Capacity analysis techniques for signalized intersections / Jack E. Leisch. Washington, D.C., USA (525 School St., S.W., Suite 410, Washington 20024-2729) : Institute of Transportation Engineers, c1986. 46 p. : ill. ; 28 cm. Bibliography: p. 29. LC Card 86-212242 DDC 388.3/14 19
1. Highway capacity. 2. Roads - Interchanges and intersections. I. Title.
HE336.H48 L45 1986

Die leisen Milliarden . Feyerabend, Joachim. Düsseldorf , 1984. 187 p. : ISBN 3-430-12729-7 LC Card 84-176048
HC282.5.F54 F49 1984

Leisinger, Klaus M. Studien zur Entwicklungsökonomie / Klaus M. Leisinger, Thomas Straubhaar, Egon Tuchtfeldt. Bern : P. Haupt, c1986. 130 p. : ill. ; 25 cm. (Sozioökonomische Forschungen. Bd. 20) Bibliography: p. 127-130. ISBN 3-258-03665-9 LC Card 87-124013 DDC 338.9/009172/7 19
1. Economic development projects - Developing countries. 2. Economic development projects - Madagascar - Case studies. I. Straubhaar, Thomas. II. Tuchtfeldt, Egon, 1923-. III. Title.
HC59.72.E44 L45 1986

Leisner, Walter, 1929- Gaugler, Eduard. Flexibilisierung der Beschäftigungsverhältnisse /. Berlin , c1986. 85 p. ; ISBN 3-428-06070-9 LC Card 87-118519 DDC 331.25/72/0943 19
HD5109.2.G3 G38 1986

Leistritz, F. Larry.
Coon, Randal C. North Dakota lignite industry's contribution to the state economy /. Fargo, N.D. [1986] v, 40 p. : LC Card 86-623006 DDC 338.2/722/09784 19
HD9559.L6 U5525 1986

The Farm financial crisis . Boulder , 1988. xvi, 205 p. : ISBN 0-8133-7186-4 (pbk. : alk. paper) : LC Card 86-32601 DDC 338.1/3/0973 19
HD1761 .F295 1988

Leistung und Ethos . Wohlfarth, Karl Anton. Paderborn , 1984. 266 p. ; ISBN 3-506-70223-8

LC Card 84-238158
HD60 .W64 1984

Die Leistungsbewertung in der Industrie : unter besonderer Berücksichtigung nationaler und internationaler Realisierungsbedingungen / [wissenschaftliche Bearbeitung, Werner Weise, Harald Löser und Ernst Pohle]. Jena : Frierich-Schiller-Universität, 1983. 241 p. ; 21 cm. (Wissenschaftliche Beiträge der Friedrich-Schiller-Universität Jena, 0232-3753) Papers read at an international scientific conference of the Sektion Wirtschaftswissenschaften der Friedrich-Schiller-Universität Jena. "Veröffentlichung der Friedrich-Schiller-Universität Jena"--T.p. verso. Includes bibliographies. LC Card 84-176546
1. Industrial productivity - Germany (East) - Measurement - Congresses. 2. Europe, Eastern - Economic policy - Congresses. 3. Government business enterprises - Management - Evaluation - Congresses. I. Weise, Werner. II. Löser, Harald. III. Pohle, Ernst. IV. Friedrich-Schiller-Universität Jena. Sektion Wirtschaftswissenschaften. V. Series.
HD56.25 .L45 1983

Leistungswettbewerb und ruinöse Konkurrenz in ihrem Einfluss auf Wohlfahrt und Beschäftigung . Arndt, Helmut, 1911- Berlin , c1986. 147 p. ; ISBN 3-428-06078-4 LC Card 87-112253 DDC 338.9 19
HD41 .A755 1986

LEISURE.
Arbeit, Arbeit über alles? . Köln , 1985. 160 p. : ISBN 3-8025-2167-6 LC Card 86-148728
HD4854 .A725 1985

Bamberg, Eva, 1951- Arbeit und Freizeit . Weinheim , 1986. xiv, 306 p. ; ISBN 3-407-58288-9 LC Card 87-103692 DDC 158.7 19
HF5548.85 .B36 1986

Delden, P. J. van, 1949- De toekomst van de vrije tijd /. [Deventer] , c1986. 102 p. ; ISBN 90-6001-973-3 : LC Card 86-199367
HD4904.6 .D45 1986

Gasparini, Giovanni, 1940- Il tempo e il lavoro /. Milano, Italy , c1986. 178 p. ; LC Card 86-180970
HD5106 .G37 1986

The Historical meanings of work /. Cambridge [Cambridgeshire] , New York , 1987. v, 320 p. ; ISBN 0-521-30897-6 LC Card 87-788 DDC 306/.36 19
HD4904 .H54 1987

Neven, Peter, 1953- Arbeits- und Freizeitpädagogik . Düsseldorf [1982?] 424 p. ; ISBN 3-87864-087-0 LC Card 84-119072
HD4901 .N47 1982

Ravaioli, Carla. Tempo da vendere, tempo da usare . Milano, Italy , c1986. 142 p. ; LC Card 86-182560
HD5106 .R357 1986

Rubin, Bonnie Miller. Time out . New York , c1987. p. cm. LC Card 87-5723 DDC 640 19
HD5255 .R82 1987

LEISURE - ADDRESSES, ESSAYS, LECTURES.
Duncan, A. R. C. (Alastair Robert Campbell), 1915- The concept of leisure. Kingston, Ont. [1970?] 8 p. LC Card 70-534907 DDC 331/.08 s
HD8102 .K52 no. 5

LEISURE - AUSTRALIA - CONGRESSES.
Work, leisure, and technology /. Melbourne, Australia , 1986. vi, 273 p. : ISBN 0-582-71151-7 (pbk.) LC Card 87-105477 DDC 303.4/83/0994 19
HD6331.2.A8 W67 1986

LEISURE - CONGRESSES.
Travail, loisirs, culture. [Bruxelles] [Zwevegem]] 1970. ix, 163 p. LC Card 71-856101
HD4904.7 .T7 1970

LEISURE - EUROPE - BIBLIOGRAPHY.
Management, work, leisure . Geneva , c1986. viii, 154 p. : ISBN 92-9014-416-5 (pbk.) : LC Card 87-163300 DDC 306/.36/094 19
HD4904.6 .M35 1986

LEISURE - EUROPE, EASTERN - BIBLIOGRAPHY.
Management, work, leisure . Geneva , c1986. viii, 154 p. : ISBN 92-9014-416-5 (pbk.) : LC Card 87-163300 DDC 306/.36/094 19
HD4904.6 .M35 1986

LEISURE - FRANCE.
Drancourt, Michel. La fin du travail /. Paris , c1984. 329 p. : ISBN 2-01-009476-X LC Card 84-222228 DDC 306/.36 19
HD6957.F8 D7 1984 ***NYPL [JLC 86-444]***

LEISURE - GERMANY, WEST.
Huellen, Karl Konrad. Die Motivation von Arbeitnehmern im Innen- und Aussendienst des Vertriebs . Münster [1986] iv, 245 p. : ISBN 3-88660-356-3 (Deut. Bibl.) LC Card 87-114821 DDC 658.3/14 19
HF5549.5.M63 H84 1986

Mikolaschek, Cornelia. Freizeit als Gegenstand der Politik . Frankfurt [am Main] , New York , c1984. 202 p. : ISBN 3-593-33346-5 LC Card 84-175844
HD7395.R4 M55 1984

LEISURE - ITALY - STATISTICS.
Indagine sulla lettura e su altri aspetti dell'impiego del tempo libero . [Roma] , 1986. 140 p., [5] p. of plates : LC Card 87-165864
HA1363 .A27 no. 3 Z1003.5.I8

LEISURE - NETHERLANDS.
Delden, P. J. van, 1949- De toekomst van de vrije tijd /. [Deventer] , c1986. 102 p. ; ISBN 90-6001-973-3 : LC Card 86-199367
HD4904.6 .D45 1986

LEISURE - RESEARCH - EUROPE.
Management, work, leisure . Geneva , c1986. viii, 154 p. : ISBN 92-9014-416-5 (pbk.) : LC Card 87-163300 DDC 306/.36/094 19
HD4904.6 .M35 1986

LEISURE - RESEARCH - EUROPE, EASTERN.
Management, work, leisure . Geneva , c1986. viii, 154 p. : ISBN 92-9014-416-5 (pbk.) : LC Card 87-163300 DDC 306/.36/094 19
HD4904.6 .M35 1986

LEISURE - SOVIET UNION.
Maksimov, A. L. (Alekseĭ L′vovich) Rabochee i svobodnoe vremi͡a v uslovii͡akh razvitogo sotsializma /. Moskva , 1981. 95 p. ; LC Card 82-104233
HD5195 .M34 1981

Leitão, Renato de Castro. Uma visão de Rotary / Renato de Castro Leitão. Olinda [Brazil : s.n.], 1985. 55 p. ; 21 cm. LC Card 86-158781
1. Rotary International. I. Title.
HF5001 .L47 1985

Leite, José Alfredo A. A sócio-economia do semi-árido / José Alfredo A. Leite. João Pessoa : Governo do Estado da Paraíba, 1985. 47 p. : ill. ; 22 cm. (Coleção IV centenário . 10) Bibliography: p. 47. LC Card 87-141315 DDC 330.981/33/063 19
1. Agriculture - Economic aspects - Brazil - Paraíba (State). 2. Paraíba, Brazil (State) - Economic conditions. 3. Paraíba (Brazil : State) - Social conditions. 4. Seca. I. Title. II. Series.
HD1875.P34 L45 1985

Leite, Manoel Marques. Relações externas da economia do Rio Grande do Sul, 1949/79 / Manoel Marques Leite. 1a. ed. [Porto Alegre] : Universidade Federal do Rio Grande do Sul, Editora da Universidade, 1985. 114 p. : ill. ; 30 cm. ISBN 85-7025-097-5 : LC Card 87-104433 DDC 382/.098165 19
1. Rio Grande do Sul (Brazil) - Commerce - History - 20th century. 2. Balance of trade - Brazil - Rio Grande do Sul - History - 20th century. 3. Balance of payments - Brazil - Rio Grande do Sul - History - 20th century. I. Title.
HF3409.R5 L45 1985

Leitfaden für Kostenermittlung und Wirtschaftlichkeitsprüfung . Gührs, Eckhard. Hamburg , 1983. iii, 92 p. ; LC Card 85-212548
HJ9925.G3 G84 1983

Leiva, Alicia. Errázuriz, Enrique. Industria eléctrica, 1960-1985 . [Santiago, Chile] [1986] 243 p. : LC Card 87-403870 DDC 338.4/762131/0983 19
HD9685.C52 E77 1986

Lejavitzer, Moisés.
Los efectos del neoproteccionismo en América Latina / Moisés Lejavítzer. 1a ed. México, D.F. : Centro de Estudios Monetarios Latinoamericanos, 1983. i, 231 p. ; 21 cm. (Estudios) Bibliography: p. 231. LC Card 85-149154 DDC 382.7/3/098 19
1. Free trade and protection - Protection. 2. Latin America - Commerce. I. Series: Estudios (Centro de Estudios Monetarios Latinoamericanos). II. Title.
HF3230.5.Z5 L45 1983 ***NYPL [JLD 86-434]***

Políticas de incentivos a la exportación de manufacturas en América Latina : estudio comparativo de los esquemas de Argentina, Brasil, Colombia y México / Moisés Lejavitzer. México, D.F. : Centro de Estudios Monetarios Latinoamericanos, Departamento de Investigaciones, 1985. iv, 155 leaves ; 28 cm. (Serie Cuadernos de investigación . núm. 4) Summary also in English, French, and Portuguese. Bibliography: leaves 149-155. LC Card 87-122013 DDC 382/.4567/098 19
1. Foreign trade promotion - Argentina. 2. Foreign trade promotion - Brazil. 3. Foreign trade promotion - Colombia. 4. Foreign trade promotion - Mexico. 5. Latin America - Manufactures - Case studies. 6. Latin Amercia - Commercial policy - Case studies. I. Series: Serie Cuadernos de investigación (Centro de Estudios Monetarios Latinoamericanos, Departamento de Investigaciones) , núm. 4. II. Title.
HF1480.5 .L44 1985

Lekov, Kostadin. Nasoki za usŭvŭrshenstvuvane na sistemata za upravlenie na truda / Kostadin Lekov, Nikolaĭ Kondarev, Vladimir Todorovski. Sofii͡a : Nauchnoizsledovatelski in-t po truda, 1985. 103 p. ; 21 cm. Summary in English and Russian. Includes bibliographical references. LC Card 86-230344
1. Personnel management - Bulgaria. I. Kondarev, Nikolaĭ. II. Todorovski, Vladimir. III. Title.
HF5549.2.B9 L46 1985

Leksiko-semanticheskie osobennosti politiko-ėkonomicheskoĭ terminologii /. T͡Sagolova, R. S. (Rufʹ Sergeevna) Moskva , 1985. 146 p. ; LC Card 86-106188
HB62 .T76 1985

Lele, Milind M. The customer is key : gaining an unbeatable advantage through customer satisfaction / Milind M. Lele with Jagdish N. Sheth. New York : Wiley, c1987. xii, 260 p. : ill. ; 24 cm. Includes bibliographical references and index. ISBN 0-471-82859-9 LC Card 87-21549 DDC 658.8/12 19
1. Consumer satisfaction. I. Sheth, Jagdish N. II. Title.
HF5415.3 .L45 1987

Lelieur, Anne-Claude. Kollar, François, 1904- La France travaille /. Paris , c1986. 238 p. : ISBN 2-85108-435-6 LC Card 87-108516
HD8430 .K65 1986

LeMay, Michael C., 1941- The struggle for influence : the impact of minority groups on politics and public policy in the United States / Michael C. LeMay. Lanham : University Press of America, c1985. xv, 452 p. : ill. ; 24 cm. Bibliography: p. 433-452. ISBN 0-8191-4653-6 (alk. paper) : LC Card 85-6105 DDC 323.1/73 19
1. Minorities - United States - Political activity. 2. Political participation - United States. 3. United States - Politics and government - 1945-. I. Title.
E184.A1 L44 1985 ***NYPL [IE 85-3562]***

Lembaga Keluarga Berencana ABRI. Pendidikan kependudukan untuk perwira. [Jakarta] [1981] vi, 120 p. : LC Card 85-940192
HB850.5 .P46 1981

Lemby, Lars. Magnusson, Åke, 1943- Ekonomi styrning av projekt /. Stockholm [1984] 66 p., [3] folded leaves of plates : ISBN 91-524-0729-2 LC Card 85-149256
HD69.P75 M34 1984

Leme, Dulce M. Pompêo C. (Dulce Maria Pompêo de Camargo) Trabalhadores ferroviários em greve / Dulce M. Pompêo C. Leme. Campinas [Brazil] : Editora da Unicamp, 1986. 269 p. : ill. ; 23 cm. (Série Teses) Bibliography: p. 225-230. ISBN 85-26-80007-8 : LC Card 87-102922 DDC 331.89/281385/098161 19
1. Companhia Paulista de Estradas de Ferro Strike, 1906. 2. Companhia Paulista de Estradas de Ferro - History. 3. Strikes and lockouts - Brazil - São Paulo (State) - History. 4. Strikes and lockouts - Railroads - Brazil - São Paulo (State) - History. I. Series: Série Teses (Editora da UNICAMP). II. Title.
HD5354.R12 1906 .S365 1986

Lemgruber, Antonio Carlos.
O controle da base monetária e as flutuações dos multiplicadores monetários e creditícios / Antonio Carlos Lemgruber e José Alfredo Lamy. [Brasília] : Banco Central do Brasil, [1981?] 118 p. : ill. ; 21 cm. LC Card 85-154853

1. Money supply - Brazil. 2. Credit control - Brazil. 3. Monetary policy - Brazil. I. Lamy, José Alfredo. II. Banco Central do Brasil. III. Title.
HG835 .L35 1981

Daly, Herman E. Crescimento ou economia estacionária. [Salvador] [1983] 56 p. : LC Card 87-127979 DDC 338.9 19
HD85.S7 D35 1983

Lemieux-Pépin, Madeleine. P'tit train va loin : histoires de vie de trois cheminots / Madeleine Lemieux-Pépin. Ottawa : Musées nationaux du Canada, 1985. vii, 191 p. ; 28 cm. (Collection Mercure, 0316-1854 = Mercury series, 0316-1854) Dossier / Centre canadien d'études sur la culture traditionnelle, 0316-1897 ; no 55 = Paper / Canadian Centre for Folk Culture Studies, 0316-1897 ; Bibliography: p. 179. Summary in English. LC Card 86-177382
1. Canadian National - Employees - Interviews. 2. Gosselin, Jean, 1921- - Interviews. 3. Gervais, Roland, 1906- - Interviews. 4. Morneau, Michel, 1895- - Interviews. 5. Railroads - Québec (Province) - Employees - Interviews. I. Title. II. Title: Petit train va loin. III. Series: Mercury series.
HE2808.1 .L45 1985

L'émission de timbres-poste du 12 mars 1984. Die Briefmarkenausgabe vom 12. März 1984 =. Vaduz [1984?] 41 p. : LC Card 84-248309
HE6184.F57 B75 1984

Lemke, Heinz. Finanztransaktionen und Aussenpolitik : deutsche Banken und Russland im Jahrzehnt vor dem Ersten Weltkrieg / Heinz Lemke ; [herausgegeben im Auftrag des Direktors des Zentralinstituts für Geschichte der Akademie der Wissenschaften der DDR]. Berlin : Akademie der Wissenschaften der DDR, Zentralinstitut für Geschichte, 1985. 215 p. ; 21 cm. (Studien zur Geschichte, 0232-8933 . Bd. 4) Includes bibliographical references and index. LC Card 86-196601
1. Loans, German - Soviet Union - History - 20th century. 2. Banks and banking, German - Soviet Union - History - 20th century. 3. Germany - Foreign relations - Soviet Union. 4. Soviet Union - Foreign relations - Germany. I. Akademie der Wissenschaften der DDR. Zentralinstitut für Geschichte. II. Title.
HG3955 .L45 1985

Lemke, Robert F. Krause, Chester L. Standard catalog of U. S. paper money /. Iola, WI , c1985. 192 p. : ISBN 0-87341-078-5 (pbk.) LC Card 86-223149 DDC 769.5/5973/0750973 19
HG591 .K7 1985

Lemoine, Maurice.
[Sucre amer. English]
Bitter sugar / Maurice Lemoine ; translated from the French by Andrea Johnston. London : Zed Books, 1985. 308 p., [17] p. of plates : ill. ; 23 cm. Translation of: Sucre amer. ISBN 0-86232-445-9 LC Card 87-672356
1. Contract labor - Dominican Republic. 2. Sugar workers - Dominican Republic. 3. Haitians - Dominican Republic. I. Title.
HD4875.D44 L4513x 1985b

Bitter sugar / Maurice Lemoine ; translated from the French by Andrea Johnston. London : Zed Books, c1985. 308 p., [17] p. of plates : ill. ; 22 cm. (Third World books) Translation of: Sucre amer. ISBN 0-86232-445-9
1. Contract labor - Dominican Republic. 2. Sugar workers - Dominican Republic. 3. Haitians - Dominican Republic. I. Title. II. Series. ***NYPL [JLD 86-814]***

Lena . Pletnev, V. Moskva , 1925. 103 p., [4] leaves of plates : LC Card 85-217266
HD9536.S653 S536 1925

Lenat, Douglas B. Building expert systems /. Reading, Mass. , 1983. xvi, 444 p. : ISBN 0-201-10686-8 LC Card 82-24511 DDC 001.64/2 19
QA76.9.E96 B84 1983 ***NYPL [JSE 87-204]***

Lenchek, Tom. Superinsulated design and construction : a guide for building energy-efficient homes / Thomas Lenchek, Chris Mattock, John Raabe ; illustrated by Richard Fedoruk. New York : Van Nostrand Reinhold Co., c1987. ix, 172 p. : ill. ; 29 cm. Includes index. Bibliography: p. 167. ISBN 0-442-26051-2 : LC Card 86-7089 DDC 693.8/32 19
1. Dwellings - Energy conservation. 2. Dwellings - Insulation. I. Mattock, Chris. II. Raabe, John. III. Title.
TJ163.5.D86 L46 1987 ***NYPL [JSF 87-235]***

Lendi, Martin. Usteri, Martin. Bodenrecht in Bewegung . Zürich [1985] 27 p. ; LC Card 86-195037
HC395 .Z43 Nr. 126 KKW683

LENDING. see **LOANS.**

Lending in international commercial banking /. Donaldson, T. H. (Thomas Hay), 1936- New York , c1987. p. cm. ISBN 0-471-63597-9 LC Card 87-19841 DDC 332.1/5 19
HG3891.5 .D65 1987

The lending procedures of commercial banks in the United States, the United Kingdom, Japan, Germany and France /. Ohinata, Yo. [Manchester] [1983] 138 p. ; ISBN 0-903808-34-X (pbk.) LC Card 86-132282 DDC 332.1/753 19
HG1642.U5 O35 1983

Leney, Julie M. Lowell as a laboratory : an experiment in public housing / by Julie M. Leney. [Lowell, Mass.?] : Lowell Pub. Co., 1987. 92 p. : ill. ; 23 cm. "Lowell Housing Authority, 1937-1987"--Cover. Bibliography: p. 91-92. LC Card 87-158220 DDC 363.5/8 19
1. Lowell Housing Authority - History. 2. Public housing - Massachusetts - Lowell - History. I. Title.
HD7288.78.U52 M44 1987

Lenfest, David.
Kaypro word processing, plain & simple / David Lenfest & William Houze. 1st ed. Blue Ridge Summit, Pa. : Tab Books, c1985. xiv, 176 p. : ill. ; 24 cm. Includes index. ISBN 0-8306-0812-5 : LC Card 84-8720 DDC 652 19
1. Word processing. 2. Kaypro computers - Programming. I. Houze, William C. II. Title. III. Title: Kaypro word processing, plain and simple.
Z52.5.K39 L46 1985 ***NYPL [JSE 87-12]***

Mac Multiplan / David Lenfest & Linda K. Woods. 1st ed. Blue Ridge Summit, Pa. : Tab Books, c1984. ix, 259 p. : ill. ; 25 cm. On t.p. the registered trademark symbol "TM" is superscript following "Multiplan." Includes index. ISBN 0-8306-0851-6 : LC Card 84-8796 DDC 001.64/25 19
1. Multiplan (Computer program). 2. Macintosh (Computer) - Programming. I. Woods, Linda K. II. Title.
HF5548.4.M74 L46 1984 ***NYPL [JSE 86-1870]***

Lenger, Friedrich. Zwischen Kleinbürgertum und Proletariat : Studien zur Sozialgeschichte der Düsseldorfer Handwerker, 1816-1878 / von Friedrich Lenger. Göttingen : Vandenhoeck & Ruprecht, c1986. 332 p. ; 24 cm. (Kritische Studien zur Geschichtswissenschaft. Bd. 71) Bibliography: p. 310-328. Includes index. ISBN 3-525-35731-1 LC Card 87-134322 DDC 331/.0943/55 19
1. Labor and laboring classes - Germany (West) - Düsseldorf - History - 19th century. 2. Trade-unions - Germany (West) - Düsseldorf - History - 19th century. 3. Artisans - Germany (West) - Düsseldorf - History - 19th century. I. Title.
HD8460.D872 L46 1986

A Lengyel földindulás / [a szerkesztésért és kiadásért felelős, Kende Péter]. Malakoff : Dialogues européens ; New York : Püski-Corvin [distributor], 1980. 150 p. ; 17 cm. (Magyar füzetek. 7) Cover title. LC Card 81-177379
1. NSZZ "Solidarność" (Labor organization). 2. Trade-unions - Poland. 3. Strikes and lockouts - Poland. 4. Public opinion - Hungary. 5. Poland - Politics and government - 1980-. 6. Poland - Politics and government - 1980- - Public opinion. I. Kende, Pierre.
HD8537.N783 L45 1980 ***NYPL [JLB 86-24]***

Lengyel, Zsuzsa. Gazdaság és társadalom a nyolcvanas években Magyarországon /. Budapest , 1986- v. <1 > ; ISBN 963-7700-19-6 (set) LC Card 87-136629
HC300.28 .G265 1986

Lenhardt, Helmut, 1923- Teure neue Medien : Schwierigkeiten, Irrtümer, Chancen / Helmut Lenhardt ; mit einem Geleitwort von Michael Schmolke. Salzburg : Amt der Salzburger Landesregierung, Landespressebüro, 1983. 152 p. ; 21 cm. (Salzburg Dokumentationen. Nr. 77) Bibliography: p. 133-134. ISBN 3-85015-012-7 LC Card 84-107910
1. Cable television - Austria - Salzburg (Land). 2. Subscription television - Austria - Salzburg (Land). I. Series: Salzburg Dokumentationen, Bd. Nr. 77. II. Title.
HE8700.72.A9 L46 1983

L'enigma del cavalier Agnelli e altri itinerari /. Camerana, Oddone. Milano , c1985. 117 p. ; LC Card 85-191746
HD9710.I82 A6615 1985 ***NYPL [JLC 87-25]***

Lenin Academy of Agricultural Sciences, Moscow. see **Vsesoiuznaia akademiia sel'skokhoziaistvennykh nauk imeni V.I. Lenina.**

Lenin, Vladimir Il'ich, 1870-1924.
LENIN, VLADIMIR IL'ICH, 1870-1924 - VIEWS ON ELECTRIFICATION.
Steklov, Vladimir IUr'evich. V.I. Lenin i ėlektrifikatsiia /. Moskva , 1982. 511 p., [1] leaf of plates : LC Card 83-133950
HD9685.S762 S84 1982

LENIN, VLADIMIR IL'ICH, 1870-1924 - VIEWS ON MONOPOLIES.
Shishkin, M. V. (Mikhail Vladislavovich) Genezis teorii monopolii v marksistsko-leninskoi i burzhuaznoi literature (1840-1930-e gody) /. Leningrad , 1985. 151 p. ; LC Card 86-140591
HD2757.2 .S49 1985

[Imperializm kak Vysshaia stadiia kapitalizma. Azerbaijani]
Imperijalizm kapitalizmin ăn jeni devri gibi [microform] / N. Lenin (V.I. Yejanof) ; Mutărcimi G.R. Kăsimbăjli ; redaktory R. Axyndof. Baqï : Azărnăshr, 1927. 99 p. ; 23 cm. (Leninin Seçilmă ăsărläri) In Azerbaijani. Colophon title in Russian: Imperializm kak noveishii ėtap kapitalizma. Allworth no. 242. Microfilm. New York: New York Public Library, 1987. 1 microfilm reel; 35 mm. (MN *ZZ-23637)
1. Azerbaijani language - Texts. 2. Capitalism. 3. Economic history - 1750-1918 - Addresses, essays, lectures. I. Title. II. Title: Imperialism kak noveishii ėtap kapitalizma. ***NYPL [*ZO-247 no. 1]***

LENINGRAD (R.S.F.S.R.) - ECONOMIC CONDITIONS.
Share, Michael. The Central Workers' Circle of St. Petersburg, 1889-1894 . New York , 1987. xi, 396 p., [6] p. of plates : ISBN 0-8240-8063-7 (alk. paper) : LC Card 87-374 DDC 305.5/62/0947453 19
HD8522.T753 S53 1987

LENINGRAD (R.S.F.S.R.) - POPULATION.
Baranov, A. V. (Al'bert Vasil'evich) Sotsial'no-demograficheskoe razvitie krupnogo goroda /. Moskva , 1981. 189 p. : LC Card 82-114309
HB3608.L4 B37 1981

Naselenie Leningrada /. Moskva , 1981. 94 p. : LC Card 82-118662
HB2278.L46 N37 1981

LENINGRAD (R.S.F.S.R.) - POPULATION - HISTORY - 19TH CENTURY.
IUkhneva, N. V. Ėtnicheskii sostav i ėtnosotsial'naia struktura naseleniia Peterburga . Leningrad , 1984. 220 p., [1] folded leaf of plates : LC Card 85-116858
HB3608.L4 I94 1984 ***NYPL [*QGK 87-925]***

LENINGRAD (R.S.F.S.R.) - SOCIAL CONDITIONS.
Baranov, A. V. (Al'bert Vasil'evich) Sotsial'no-demograficheskoe razvitie krupnogo goroda /. Moskva , 1981. 189 p. : LC Card 82-114309
HB3608.L4 B37 1981

Share, Michael. The Central Workers' Circle of St. Petersburg, 1889-1894 . New York , 1987. xi, 396 p., [6] p. of plates : ISBN 0-8240-8063-7 (alk. paper) : LC Card 87-374 DDC 305.5/62/0947453 19
HD8522.T753 S53 1987

Leningradskie farforisty /. Agarkova, G. D. (Galina Dmitrievna) Moskva , 1984. 61 p. : LC Card 85-111565
HD9616.S653 L463 1984

Leningradskii gosudarstvennyi pedagogicheskii institut imeni A.I. Gertsena. Ėkonomicheskie interesy i uskorenie nauchno-tekhnicheskogo progressa . Leningrad , 1984. 157 p. ; LC Card 86-186728
HC340.T4 E36 1984

Leningradskii gosudarstvennyi universitet imeni A. A. Zhdanova.
Dolgosrochnoe sotsial'no-ėkonomicheskoe planirovanie /. Leningrad , 1986. 165 p. : LC

Card 87-146872
HC338.T5 D65 1986

Kadieva, D. A. Chastotnyĭ anglo-russkiĭ slovar'. Leningrad , 1986. 126 p. ; LC Card 87-146427
HB61 .K23 1986

Neposredstvenno-obshchestvennoe proizvodstvo v uslovii͡akh razvitogo sotsializma /. Leningrad , 1984. 212 p. ; LC Card 84-248045
HB97.5 .N434 1984

Sovremennyĭ kapitalizm . Leningrad , 1985. 212 p. ; LC Card 86-117888
HB501 .S824 1985

Leningradskiĭ gosudarstvennyĭ universitet imeni A. A. Zhdanova. Ėkonomicheskiĭ fakul'tet. Osobennosti khozi͡aĭstvennogo mekhanizma v zarubezhnykh stranakh--chlenakh SĖV . Leningrad , 1984. 54 p. ; LC Card 85-153742
HC244 .O723 1984

Lenins Formationsanalyse der bürgerlichen Gesellschaft in Russland vor 1905 . Küttler, Wolfgang. Berlin , 1978. 331 p. ; LC Card 86-102733
HC334.5 .K87 1978

Leninskie raboty 90-kh godov i sovremennost' /. Pokrytan, A. K. (Anatoliĭ Karpovich) Kiev , 1985. 159 p. ; LC Card 87-113578
HB97.5 .P538 1985

Leninskite printsipi i uchastieto na trudeshtite se v upravlenieto /. Vidinski, Lenin. Sofii͡a , 1982. 196 p. : LC Card 83-130010
HC403 .V495 1982

Lenkerberechtigungen im Jahre 1977 / bearbeitet im Österreichischen Statistischen Zentralamt. Wien : Kommissionsverlag, C. Ueberreuter, 1978. 69 p. ; 30 cm. (Beiträge zur österreichischen Statistik . 490. Heft) Chiefly tables. LC Card 86-196229
1. Automobile drivers' licenses - Austria - Statistics. I. Österreichisches Statistisches Zentralamt. II. Series.
HA1173 .A27 Heft 490 HE5667.A6

Lenkowsky, Leslie, 1946- Politics, economics, and welfare reform : the failure of the negative income tax in Britain and the United States / Leslie Lenkowsky. Lanham, MD : University Press of America ; [Washington, D.C.] : American Enterprise Institute for Public Policy Research, University Press of America, c1986. vii, 207 p. ; 24 cm. Bibliography: p. 195-206. ISBN 0-8191-5215-3 (alk. paper) : LC Card 85-29456 DDC 362.5/82 19
1. Negative income tax - Great Britain. 2. Guaranteed annual income - Great Britain. 3. Negative income tax - United States. 4. Guaranteed annual income - United States. I. Title.
HC260.I5 L46 1986 ***NYPL [JLE 86-2801]***

Lenoir, René. Le Tiers Monde peut se nourrir : les communautés de base, acteurs du développement : rapport au Club de Rome / René Lenoir. [Paris] : Fayard, c1984. 210 p. : ill. ; 22 cm. "Ce rapport ... a été présenté et discuté au Club de Rome lors de sa session de septembre 1983 à Budapest"--P. [9]. Bibliography: p. [160]-165. ISBN 2-213-01385-3 : LC Card 84-188021 DDC 338.1/8/091724 19
1. Agriculture and state - Developing countries. 2. Food supply - Government policy - Developing countries. 3. Agricultural innovations - Government policy - Developing countries. I. Title.
HD1417 .L46 1984 ***NYPL [JLD 85-1065]***

Lenskai͡a, L. V. (Lilii͡a Vasil'evna) Okhrana truda v trubnom proizvodstve /. Moskva , 1986. 151, [1] p. : LC Card 85-163240
HD9529.P53 S686 1986

Lenskai͡a, S. A. (Svetlana Alekseevna) Proizvodstvennye fondy kak ėkonomicheskai͡a kategorii͡a / S.A. Lenskai͡a. Moskva : "Ėkonomika", 1982. 126 p. ; 22 cm. Includes bibliographical references. LC Card 83-134249
1. Capital productivity - Soviet Union. 2. Capital investments - Soviet Union. I. Title.
HC340.C3 L396 1982

LENSLESS PHOTOGRAPHY. see **HOLOGRAPHY.**

Lenssen, Adolf K. Konformität und Nichtkonformität im Betrieb : eine theoretische Diskussion / Adolf K. Lenssen.1. Aufl. Konstanz : Hartung-Gorre, 1986. 400 p. : 21 ill. ; 21 cm. (Konstanzer Dissertationen . Bd. 133) Bibliography: p. 371-400. ISBN 3-89191-064-9 (p. 4. of cover); 3-89191-064-7 LC Card 87-109576 DDC 658.3/001/9 19
1. Personnel management - Psychological aspects. 2. Conformity. I. Series. II. Series: Konstanzer Dissertationen , 133. III. Title.
HF5549 .L4619 1986

Lento-McGovern, Diane, 1956- Life after college : so you graduated-- now what? / Diane Lento-McGovern. White Hall, Va. : Betterway Publications, c1987. 179 p. ; 23 cm. Bibliography: p. 171-172. Includes index. ISBN 0-932620-77-9 (pbk.) : LC Card 87-6412 DDC 331.7/02 19
1. Vocational guidance. 2. College graduates - Employment. 3. Universities and colleges - Graduate work. 4. Job hunting. I. Title.
HF5381 .L354 1987

L'entreprise face au nouveau droit de travail /. Ortscheidt, Pierre. Paris , c1985. 221 p. ; ISBN 2-7178-0915-5 : LC Card 85-191518
KJV3399 .O78 1985 ***NYPL [JLE 87-358]***

L'entreprise française face aux variations de change . Bourguinat, Henri. Paris , c1985. vi, 123 p. : ISBN 2-7178-0899-X : LC Card 85-190582 DDC 332.4/5 19
HG3815 .B68 1985 ***NYPL [JLE 86-494]***

Lentz, Carola. Mariano, Alfonso, José, Lorenzo, Manuel . Quito, Ecuador , 1985. 128 p., [8] leaves of plates : LC Card 86-136793
HD1531.E2 M37 1985

Lenz, Ilse. Kapitalistische Entwicklung, Subsistenzproduktion und Frauenarbeit : der Fall Japan / Ilse Lenz. Frankfurt/Main ; New York : Campus Verlag, c1984. 330 p. : map ; 21 cm. (Campus Forschung. Bd. 395) Revision of the author's dissertation -- FU Berlin, 1982. -- p. 11. Bibliography: p. 313-330. ISBN 3-593-33407-0(pbk.)
1. Agriculture - Economic aspects - Japan - History. 2. Women - Employment - Japan - History. 3. Subsistence economy. 4. Japan - Economic conditions. I. Title.
NYPL [JLD 87-332]

Lenz, Matias Martinho. Schneider, José Odelso. Realidade brasileira . Porto Alegre-RS , c1986. 438 p. : LC Card 87-119174
HC187 .S393 1986

Lenz, Matthew. Risk management manual / author, Matthew Lenz, Jr. Santa Monica, Calif. (P.O. Box 955, Santa Monica 90406) : Merritt Co., <1972- > 3 v. (loose-leaf) : ill. ; 30 cm. Includes bibliographies and index. LC Card 86-209050
1. Risk (Insurance) - United States - Handbooks, manuals, etc. 2. Risk management - United States - Handbooks, manuals, etc. I. Merritt Company. II. Title.
HG8054.5 .L46 1972

Leo, Christopher. Land and class in Kenya / Christopher Leo. Toronto ; Buffalo [N.Y.] : University of Toronto Press, c1984. xii, 244 p. : maps ; 24 cm. (Political economy of world poverty . 3) Includes index. Bibliography: p. [231]-236. ISBN 0-8020-2532-3
1. Land reform - Kenya - History - 20th century. 2. Agriculture - Social aspects - Kenya - History. 3. Social classes - Kenya - History. 4. Land tenure - Kenya - History. 5. Land use, Rural - Kenya - History. I. Title. II. Series. ***NYPL [JLE 86-1242]***

León Almeida, Pedro.
Ensayo de categorización de los municipios de Córdoba / Pedro León Almeida. Córdoba, Argentina : Instituto de Ciencias de la Administración, Universidad Católica de Córdoba, 1984. 74 leaves : ill. ; 29 cm. (Cuadernos de administración pública, 0326-0003 . no. 39) Chiefly tables. LC Card 87-403755 DDC 330.982/54062/021 19
1. Córdoba (Argentina) - Economic conditions - Statistics. 2. Córdoba (Argentina) - Administrative and political divisions - Statistics. I. Series: Cuadernos de administración pública (Universidad Católica de Córdoba. Centro de Investigación y Perfeccionamiento en Ciencias Económicas y Administración Pública) , 39. II. Title.
HC177.C7 L46 1984

Funciones y servicios de competencia municipal /. Córdoba, República Argentina , 1984. 94 leaves ; LC Card 87-121632 DDC 352.082 19
HD4629 .F86 1984

León B., Arturo. Aldunate B., Adolfo. Análisis tipológico del trabajador del Gran Santiago e impacto sobre el ingreso de las políticas redistributivas, 1970-1971 /. [Santiago, Chile?] [1972] iv, 9, [35] p. ; LC Card 83-169296
HC193.S23 A43 1972

León Ch., Carlos Amat y. see **Amat y León Ch., Carlos.**

León, I. Josefina. El quantum de exportaciones del Ecuador (1970-1983) / I. Josefina León. [Guayaquil] : Departamento de Publicaciones de la Facultad de Ciencias Económicas de la Universidad de Guayaquil, 1985. 93 p. : ill. ; 29 cm. Thesis (tesis de grado)--Universidad de Guayaquil. Bibliography: p. 91-93. LC Card 87-123381 DDC 382/.6/09866 19
1. Ecuador - Commerce. I. Title.
HF3431.5 .L46 1985

Leonard, David K. The political realities of African management / by David K. Leonard. Binghamton, NY, USA (P.O. Box 818, Binghamton 13902) : Institute for Development Anthropology, [1984] 39 p. ; 28 cm. "This paper was prepared as background material for the AID Workshop on the Evaluation of Managment [sic] in African Agricultural Development Projects." "September 1984." Bibliography: p. 37-39. LC Card 87-153761 DDC 338.1/86 19
1. Agricultural development projects - Management - Political aspects - Africa. 2. Agricultural development projects - Africa - Management. I. Institute for Development Anthropology (Binghamton, N.Y.). II. Title.
HD2118 .L46 1984

Leonard, H. Jeffrey.
Natural resources and economic development in Central America : a regional environmental profile / H. Jeffrey Leonard ; International Institute for Environment and Development. New Brunswick, N.J., U. S.A. : Transaction Books, c1987. xxii, 279 p. : ill. 23 cm. Bibliography: p. 245-267. Includes index. ISBN 0-88738-722-5 (pbk.) LC Card 87-10871 DDC 333.7/09728 19
1. Natural resources - Central America. 2. Economic assistance, American - Central America. 3. Central America - Economic policy. 4. Central America - Economic conditions - 1979-. 5. Central America - Population. I. International Institute for Environment and Development. II. Title.
HC141 .L44 1987

Pollution and the struggle for the world product : multinational corporations, environment, and international comparative advantage / H. Jeffrey Leonard. Cambridge [Cambridgeshire] ; New York : Cambridge University Press, 1988. p. cm. Includes index. ISBN 0-521-34042-X LC Card 87-17766 DDC 338.6/042 19
1. Industrialization - Environmental aspects. 2. Pollution. 3. International business enterprises. 4. Comparative advantage (Commerce). I. Title.
HD75.6 .L46 1988

Leonard, Jonathan S. (Jonathan Shawn)
Unemployment and the structure of labor markets /. New York, NY, USA , 1987. vi, 253 p. : ISBN 0-631-15378-0 : LC Card 86-24478 DDC 331.13/7 19
HD5707.5 .U545 1987

Leonardi, Giorgio. L'Analisi degli insediamenti umani e produttivi /. Milano, Italy , c1984. 295 p. : LC Card 84-179265 DDC 330.945/0928 19
HC305 .A6618 1984 ***NYPL [JLD 86-3298]***

Leone, Robert A. Who profits : winners, losers, and government regulation / Robert A. Leone. New York : Basic Books, 1986. xiii, 248 p. ; 22 cm. Includes index. Bibliography: p. [231]-237. ISBN 0-465-09183-0 : LC Card 85-47992 DDC 338.973 19
1. Trade regulation - United States. 2. Business and politics - United States. 3. Costs, Industrial - United States. I. Title.
HD3616.U47 L44 1986
NYPL [JLD 86-2410]

Leong, Jerrold K. (Jerrold Kim), 1947- Economic implications of import barriers to protect the U. S. sugar industry with particular reference to Hawaii / by Jerrold K. Leong, Frank S. Scott, Jr., PingSun Leung. Manoa : Hawaii Institute of Tropical Agriculture and Human Resources, College of Tropical Agriculture and Human Resources, University of Hawaii at Manoa, 1987. p. cm. (Research series, 0197-9310) Bibliography: p. LC Card 87-11855 DDC 382/.456641/09969 19
1. Sugar trade - Hawaii - Mathematical models. 2. Sugar trade - Government policy - United States - Mathematical models. I. Scott, F. S. (Frank Sanford), 1921-. II. Leung, PingSun, 1952-. III. Series: Research

series (Hawaii Institute of Tropical Agriculture and Human Resources). IV. Title.
HD9107.H3 L46 1987

Leonhard, Martin. Umweltverbände : zur Organisation von Umweltschutzinteressen in der Bundesrepublik Deutschland / Martin Leonhard ; mit einem Geleitwort von Thomas Ellwein. Opladen : Westdeutscher Verlag, c1986. xiii, 352 p. ; 23 cm. (Beiträge zur sozialwissenschaftlichen Forschung, 0175-615X . Bd. 89) Bibliography: p. [327]-343. ISBN 3-531-11820-X LC Card 86-192568
1. Environmental policy - Germany, West. 2. Environmental protection - Germany, West. 3. Pressure groups - Germany, West. I. Title. II. Series.
HC290.5.E5 L46 1986

Leonov, A. A. (Aleksandr Alekseevich) Andrianov, V. V. Za slovom--delo /. Moskva , 1985. 124 p. ; LC Card 85-213388
HC338.S87 A53 1985

Leont'ev, A. M. Vozdeĭstvie khoziaĭstvennogo mekhanizma na povyshenie ėffektivnosti obshchestvennogo proizvodstva . Dnepropetrovsk , 1984. 119 p. ; LC Card 86-181397
HC340.I52 V68 1984

Lepage, Francine. Rheault, Sylvie. Les femmes et l'emploi /. [Québec] [1983] 64 p. ; ISBN 2-550-10471-4 LC Card 85-108850 DDC 331.4/09714 19
HD6100.Q4 R44 1983

Lépine, Ginette. Vous autres au syndicat-- / Ginette Lépine, Pierre Cormier. Montréal, Québec : Québec/Amérique, c1984. 179 p. ; 23 cm. (Dossiers, documents) Includes bibliographical references. ISBN 2-89037-214-6 LC Card 85-101458
1. Trade-unions - Government employees - Québec (Province) - Montréal. 2. Université du Québec à Montréeal - Employees. 3. Syndicat des employé(e)s de l'UQAM. I. Cormier, P. (Pierre). II. Title.
HD8005.2.C23 M665 1984

Lepisto, Ė. (Ėndel') Druzhba i sotrudnichestvo /. Tallin , 1985. 85 p. : LC Card 86-108625
HC243.Z9 S63 1985

Leppard, John. McDonald, Malcolm. How to sell a service . London , 1986. 149 p. : ISBN 0-434-91231-X (pbk.) : LC Card 86-212510 DDC 658.8 19
HF5438.25 .M396 1986

L'Epreuve des faits.
Weber, Henri. Le parti des patrons . Paris , c1986. 437 p. ; ISBN 2-02-009352-9 : LC Card 87-106644
HD6948.F8 W43 1986

Leptin, Gert, 1929- Sibirien, ein russisches und sowjetisches Entwicklungsproblem /. Berlin , c1986. 274 p. : ISBN 3-87061-260-6 LC Card 86-229174
HC336.9.S53 S53 1986

Lerbinger, Paul, 1955- P & F charts : ein neuer Weg zum Anlageerfolg / Paul Lerbinger. Niederglatt : Fortuna Finanz-Verlag, c1984. 231 p. : ill. ; 23 cm. Bibliography: p. 231. ISBN 3-85684-031-1 : LC Card 84-119357
1. Stocks - Charts, diagrams, etc. 2. Speculation. I. Title.
HG6041 .L47 1984

Lercari Carlos, Barrenechea. see **Barrenechea Lercari, Carlos.**

Lerche, Dietrich, 1943- Grundlagen und Perspektiven des Euro-Arabischen Dialogs / Dietrich Lerche. Berlin : Deutsches Institut für Entwicklungspolitik, 1977. iii, 78 p. : ill. ; 24 cm. (Schriften des Deutschen Instituts für Entwicklungspolitik, DIE . Bd. 46) Bibliography: p. 77. LC Card 85-129693
1. European Economic Community countries - Foreign economic relations - Arab countries. 2. Arab countries - Foreign economic relations - European Economic Community countries. I. Title. II. Series.
HF1532.5.Z4 A735 1977

Lerche, Karl. Gothe, Richard, 1928- Zusammenwirken von örtlichen Staatsorganen und Kombinaten /. Berlin , 1983. 89 p. ; LC Card 84-166789
HD3616.G48 G67 1983

LÉRIDA (SPAIN) - ECONOMIC CONDITIONS.
Barrull Pelegrí, Jaume, 1947- Les comarques de Lleida durant la segona república, 1930-1936 /. Barcelona , 1986. 503 p. : ISBN 84-85905-23-7 LC Card 86-203986
HC388.L4 B37 1986

LÉRIDA (SPAIN) - POLITICS AND GOVERNMENT.
Barrull Pelegrí, Jaume, 1947- Les comarques de Lleida durant la segona república, 1930-1936 /. Barcelona , 1986. 503 p. : ISBN 84-85905-23-7 LC Card 86-203986
HC388.L4 B37 1986

LÉRIDA (SPAIN) - SOCIAL CONDITIONS.
Barrull Pelegrí, Jaume, 1947- Les comarques de Lleida durant la segona república, 1930-1936 /. Barcelona , 1986. 503 p. : ISBN 84-85905-23-7 LC Card 86-203986
HC388.L4 B37 1986

Lerner, Gerda, 1920- The majority finds its past : placing women in history / Gerda Lerner. New York : Oxford University Press, 1979. xxxii, 217 p. ; 22 cm. Includes bibliographical references and index. ISBN 0-19-502597-0 LC Card 79-14048 DDC 301.41/2/0973
1. Women - United States - History. 2. Afro-American women - History. 3. Feminism - United States - History. 4. Women's rights - United States - History. I. Title.
HQ1426 .L47 **NYPL [JLD 86-3348]**

Lerner, Joel J.
Financial planning for the utterly confused / Joel Lerner. New York : McGraw-Hill, c1986. xi, 210 p. ; 21 cm. Includes index. "McGraw Hill paperbacks." ISBN 0-07-037224-1 (pbk.) : LC Card 85-19823 DDC 332.024 19
1. Finance, Personal - United States. 2. Investments - United States. I. Title.
HG179 .L45 1986 **NYPL [JLD 86-2290]**

Schaum's outline of theory and problems of bookkeeping and accounting / Joel J. Lerner. 2nd ed. New York : McGraw-Hill, c1988. 311 p. : ill. ; 28 cm. (Schaum's outline series in accounting) Schaum's outline series Includes index. ISBN 0-07-037231-4 (pbk.) LC Card 87-3800 DDC 657/.076 19
1. Bookkeeping - Problems, exercises, etc. 2. Accounting - Problems, exercises, etc. I. Title. II. Title: Bookkeeping and accounting. III. Series.
HF5661 .L46 1988

Lernschock Tschernobyl /. Maier-Leibnitz, Heinz. Zürich , c1986. 137 p. ; ISBN 3-7201-5191-3 : LC Card 87-120438
HD9698.S653 C485 1986

Leroux, François, 1945- Que nous a appris la crise de l'endettement international? / par François Leroux. Montréal, Québec, Canada : Ecole des hautes études commerciales, [1985] 41 leaves ; 28 cm. (Cahiers de recherche / Institut d'économie appliquée, 0825-8643 . IEA-85-01) "Juin 1985." Bibliography: leaf 40-41. LC Card 86-144447 DDC 336.3/4/091724 19
1. Debts, External - Developing countries. 2. Debt relief - Developing countries. I. Series: Cahiers de recherche (Ecole des hautes études commerciales (Montréal, Québec). Institut d'économie appliquée) , IEA-85-01. II. Title.
HJ8899 .L47 1985

Les associations syndicales de propriétaires /. Guichard-Ayoub, Éliane. Paris , 1984. 127 p. ; ISBN 2-13-038290-8 **NYPL [JLC 87-57]**

Les Aventures du marxisme / collectif sous la direction de René Gallissot. Paris : Syros, c1984. 415 p. ; 22 cm. (Collection Histoire et théorie) "Organisé en 1983 par les universités de Paris VII et VIII et la Fondation nationale des sciences politiques, avec le concours du Ministère de la recherche, le Colloque Marx-marxismes a rassemblé un grand nombre de spécialistes ou de chercheurs, à l'occasion du centenaire de la mort de Karl Marx"--P. [4] of cover. Includes bibliographical references. ISBN 2-86738-025-1 (pbk.)
1. Communism - Congresses. 2. Communism - Soviet Union - Congresses. 3. Communism - Developing countries - Congresses. I. Gallissot, René. II. Series.
NYPL [JLD 87-212]

Les carriéristes . Wickham, Alexandre. Paris , c1983. 358 p. ; ISBN 2-85956-348-2 : LC Card 84-122542 DDC 650.1/4 19
HF5386 .W494 1983 **NYPL [JLE 86-4124]**

Les Collections monétaires .
(VII, 2) Thierry, François. Monnaies d'Extrême Orient /. Paris , <[1986- v. <2 > : ISBN 2-11-080873-X (v. 2) : LC Card 86-218568
HG1250.5 .T45 1986

Les Communications dans la péninsule Ibérique au Moyen-Age : actes du Colloque de Pau, 28-29 mars 1980 / Maison des pays ibériques ; [sous la direction de P. Tucoo-Chala]. Paris : Éditions du Centre national de la recherche scientifique, 1981. 208 p. : ill. ; 30 cm. (Collection de la Maison des pays ibériques . 4) French and Spanish. Includes bibliographical references. ISBN 2-222-02922-8 : LC Card 81-213698 DDC 380.5/0946 19
1. Transportation - Spain - History - Congresses. 2. Transportation - France - History - Congresses. 3. Spain - Commerce - France - History - Congresses. 4. France - Commerce - Spain - History - Congresses. I. Tucoo-Chala, Pierre. II. Maison des pays ibériques. III. Series.
HE261.A5 C65 1981 **NYPL [JLG 86-113]**

Les compagnies financières à Paris à la fin du XVIIIe siècle--tome II [microform] ... /. Bouchary, Jean. Paris , 1941. 212 p. ;
NYPL [*ZT-1711 no.28]

Les Conférences socio-économiques du Québec.
Conférence sur les communications (1983 : Montréal, Québec) La Conférence sur les communications . [Québec] [1984] ix, 489 p. ; ISBN 2-551-06176-8 LC Card 85-103400
HE7818.Q4 C46 1983

Le Meuble . [Québec] [1983] xiii, 109 p. : ISBN 2-550-10196-0 LC Card 85-124226
HD9773.C23 Q425 1983

Table de concertation sur l'industrie du vêtement (1985 : Montréal, Québec) Rapport de la Table de concertation sur l'industrie du vêtement . [Québec] [1985] v, 174, 12 p. ; LC Card 87-103889
HD9940.C22 Q847 1985

Les contrats de souscription à forfait de valeurs mobilières /. Bréard, Jean-Pierre. Montréal , 1984. xv, 158 p. : ISBN 2-89266-018-1 (pbk.) :
NYPL [JLD 87-662]

Les crimes de l'Angleterre [microform].
Chesterton, Gilbert Keith, 1874-1936. [Crimes of England. French.] Paris, 1916. 273 p. LC Card 19-16286
DA47.2 .C55 **NYPL [*Z-4049 no.7]**

Les Dossiers Antilles Guyane, 0291-8706 .
(10) Guglielmetti, Francis. L'indice des prix de la Martinique, base 100 en 1979 . [Fort de France?] [1985] 130, xxiii p. : ISBN 2-11-062943-6 : LC Card 86-176702
HB235.M37 G83 1985

Les Dossiers de l'INSEE Rhône-Alpes .
(no 24) Robert, Jacqueline. 1977 à 1982 . [Lyon] [1985] 143 p. ; LC Card 86-187676
HC277.R58 R62 1985

Les Dossiers du CETUR, 0247-1159 .
(dossier no 18) Les Rues mixtes . [Bagneux] [1982] 40 p. : ISBN 2-11-083325-4 : LC Card 84-104398
HE363.F72 P437 1982

Les entreprises dans la décentralisation /. Lanier, Lucien. Paris [1985] xvi, 217 p. ; ISBN 2-86658-028-1 : LC Card 85-217648 DDC 338.944 19
HD3616.F83 L28 1985 **NYPL [JLD 87-546]**

Les fonctions des agents économiques exportant des biens d'équipement, dans le cadre des relations est-ouest et nord-sud, depuis 1970 /. Chaponnière, R. [Paris] [1981] 159 leaves : LC Card 82-180468 DDC 382/.456817 19
HD9705.A2 C55 1981 **NYPL [JLG 86-212]**

Les greniers du monde /. Charvet, Jean-Paul. Paris , c1985. 368 p. : ISBN 2-7178-0925-2 : LC Card 85-191889 DDC 338.1/731 19
HD9030.5 .C47 1985 **NYPL [JLE 86-488]**

Les incidences financières de l'assurance maritime sur l'économie ivoirienne /. Gohibi, Bernard. Abidjan , 1984. 24 leaves ; LC Card 86-111379 DDC 368.2/2/0096668 19
HE964.5.I94 G64 1984
NYPL [JLF 86-1484]

Les industries québécoises de services télématiques . Lapointe, Alain. Montréal [1984] x, 305 p. : ISBN 2-551-06190-3 LC Card 84-230415 DDC 384/.09714 19
HE7818.Q4 L36 1984 **NYPL [JLF 86-1397]**

Les métamorphoses de la société salariale .

Aglietta, Michel. Paris , c1984. 274 p. ; ISBN 2-7021-1230-7 : LC Card 84-176554 DDC 331/.0944 19
HD8431 .A36 1984 ***NYPL [JLD 87-478]***

Les riches . Courchaure, Stéphane. [Paris] , c1985. 261 p. ; ISBN 2-7158-0537-3 : LC Card 86-111316 DDC 305.5/234 19
HC79.C6 C68 1985 ***NYPL [JLD 86-4451]***

Les Sauvages dans la cité : auto-emancipation du peuple et instruction des prolétaires au XIXe siècle / avant-propos de Jacques Derrida ; présentation de Jean Borreil ; textes de Jean-Claude Beaune ... [et al.]. Seyssel : Champ Vallon, c1985. 229 p. ; 21 cm. (Collection Milieux, 0291-7157) "Les textes ... ont fait l'objet d'une communication lors d'un colloque tenu au Creusot dans le cadre de l'Institut Jean-Baptiste Durnay les 6 et 7 1984 et placé sous la direction de Jacques Derrida." Includes bibliographical references. ISBN 2-903528-53-5
1. Proletariat - Addresses, essays, lectures. 2. Labor and laboring classes - Addresses, essays, lectures. 3. Social history - 19th century - Addresses, essays, lectures. I. Derrida, Jacques. II. Beaune, Jean-Claude.
NYPL [JLD 86-1133]

Les télévisions étrangères . Caron, André H. [Montréal] , 1983. ix, 166 p., 12 leaves : ISBN 2-920396-86-2 : LC Card 83-157210 DDC 302.2/345/09714 19
HE8700.9.C2 C37 1983
NYPL [MWGS 86-2473]

Les termes pétroliers . Arnould, Michel. Paris , c1981. xii, 267 p. ; ISBN 2-04-011414-9 LC Card 82-167169 DDC 665.5/03/21 19
TN865 .A66 1981 ***NYPL [JSE 84-171]***

Les 1000 villages socialistes en Algérie /. Lesbet, Djaffar. Alger , Paris , c1983. 335 p. : ISBN 2-86738-008-1 : LC Card 84-156989 DDC 335/.00965 19
HX441.5.A6 L47 1983 ***NYPL [JLD 87-236]***

Lesbet, Djaffar. Les 1000 villages socialistes en Algérie / Djaffar Lesbet ; préface d'Anatole Kopp. Alger : Office des publications universitaires ; Paris : Syros, c1983. 335 p. : ill. ; 22 cm. Originally presented as the author's thesis (doctoral--Université de Paris VIII, 1979) under the title: La politigue des 1000 villages socialistes en Algérie. Includes bibliographical references. ISBN 2-86738-008-1 : LC Card 84-156989 DDC 335/.00965 19
1. Socialism - Algeria. 2. Villages - Algeria. 3. Land reform - Algeria. 4. Algeria - Rural conditions. I. Title. II. Title: Mille villages socialistes en Algérie.
HX441.5.A6 L47 1983 ***NYPL [JLD 87-236]***

Lesko, Matthew. Getting yours : the complete guide to government money / by Matthew Lesko.3rd ed. New York, N.Y., U. S. A. : Penguin Books, 1987. x, 368 p. ; 20 cm. (A Penguin handbook) Includes index. ISBN 0-14-046760-2 (pbk.) : LC Card 86-22688 DDC 658.1/5224 19
1. Economic assistance, Domestic - United States - Directories. 2. Administrative agencies - United States - Directories. I. Title.
HC110.P63 L37 1987

Leslie, Joanne. Food policy . Baltimore , c1987. xiv, 567 p. : ISBN 0-8018-3500-3 (pbk.) : LC Card 86-27613 DDC 363.8/56/091724 19
HD9018.D44 F665 1987

Leslie, Winsome J. The World Bank & structural transformation in developing countries : a case of Zaire / Winsome J. Leslie. Boulder, Colo. : L. Rienner Publishers, 1987. xi, 208 p. : 1 map ; 24 cm. Bibliography: p. 187-202. Includes index. ISBN 1-555-87036-8 (lib. bdg. : alk. paper) : LC Card 87-3358 DDC 338.9675/1 19
1. World Bank - Zaire. 2. Zaire - Economic policy. I. Title. II. Title: World Bank and structural transformation in developing countries.
HG3881.5.W57 L47 1987

Lesotho.
Employment and development in Lesotho . Addis Ababa , 1983. ii, 229 p. ; ISBN 92-2-103780-0 LC Card 84-980769 DDC 331.12/09681/6 19
HD5842.7.A6 E46 1983

LESOTHO - COLONIAL INFLUENCE - CONGRESSES.
Employment and development in Lesotho . Addis Ababa , 1983. ii, 229 p. ; ISBN 92-2-103780-0 LC Card 84-980769 DDC 331.12/09681/6 19
HD5842.7.A6 E46 1983

LESOTHO - ECONOMIC CONDITIONS - 1966- - CONGRESSES.
Employment and development in Lesotho . Addis Ababa , 1983. ii, 229 p. ; ISBN 92-2-103780-0 LC Card 84-980769 DDC 331.12/09681/6 19
HD5842.7.A6 E46 1983

LESOTHO - POPULATION.
Sembajwe, I. S. L. (Israel Serwano Lubwama), 1947- Urban population growth rates in Africa with special reference to Lesotho /. [Roma, Lesotho] [1985] 31 leaves : LC Card 87-132328 DDC 307.2 19
HB3663.7.A3 S46 1985

LESOTHO - POPULATION - STATISTICS - BIBLIOGRAPHY.
Makatjane, Tiisetso. Sources of population statistics in Lesotho /. [Roma, Lesotho] [1985] iii, 29 leaves ; LC Card 87-132320 DDC 304.6/09681/6 19
HA37.L52 M35 1985

LESOTHO - RURAL CONDITIONS.
Senaoana, M. P. Research on rural-non farm employment in Lesotho . Roma, Lesotho [1984] 88 leaves : LC Card 86-214032 DDC 331.12/5/096816 19
HD5842.7.A6 S46 1984

LESOTHO - STATISTICAL SERVICES.
Makatjane, Tiisetso. Sources of population statistics in Lesotho /. [Roma, Lesotho] [1985] iii, 29 leaves ; LC Card 87-132320 DDC 304.6/09681/6 19
HA37.L52 M35 1985

L'Esprit d'entreprise.
Dacier, Pierre. Les dossiers noirs de l'industrie française /. [Paris] , c1985. 414 p. ; ISBN 2-213-01659-3 : LC Card 86-178468
HC276.2 .D2 1985

The less developed countries and the world trading system . Tussie, Diana. London , 1987. viii, 162 p. ; ISBN 0-86187-614-8
NYPL [JLE 87-1597]

Less than forever . Meyerhuber, Carl I., 1940- Selinsgrove , London , c1987. 235 p. ; ISBN 0-941664-27-9 (alk. paper) LC Card 86-62504 DDC 331.88/09748 19
HD6517.P4 M49 1987

Lessard, Donald R.
Capital flight : the problem and policy responses / Donald R. Lessard and John Williamson. Washington, DC : Institute for International Economics, 1987. x, 64 p. ; 23 cm. (Policy analyses in international economics . 23) Papers presented at a conference held October 1986. Bibliography: p. 59-60. ISBN 0-88132-059-5 LC Card 87-17279 DDC 332/.042 19
1. Capital movements - Congresses. 2. Capital movements - Developing countries - Congresses. I. Williamson, John, 1937-. II. Institute for International Economics (U. S.). III. Series.
HG3891 .C367 1987

Capital flight and Third World debt /. Washington, D.C. , 1987. p. cm. ISBN 0-88132-064-1 LC Card 87-17080 DDC 332/.042 19
HG3891 .C36 1987

Lessem, Ronnie.
[Enterprise development]
Intrapreneurship : developing the individual in business / Ronnie Lessem. Aldershot, Hants, England : Wildwood House ; Brookfield, Vt. : Gower Pub. Co., c1987. p. cm. Originally published 1986 under title: Enterprise development. ISBN 0-7045-0577-0 (pbk.) : LC Card 87-21608 DDC 658/.00941 19
1. Industrial management - Great Britain - Case studies. 2. Entrepreneurship - Case studies. I. Title.
HD70.G7 L45 1987

Lessenberry, D. D. (David Daniel), 1896- College typewriting. College keyboarding/typewriting : complete course / Charles H. Duncan ... [et al.].11th ed. Cincinnati , c1985. 396, xvi p. : ISBN 0-538-20750-7 LC Card 84-50474 DDC 652.3 19
Z49 .C65 1985 ***NYPL [JSF 86-1142]***

Lesser Antilles. see Antilles, Lesser.

A lesser life . Hewlett, Sylvia Ann, 1946- New York, N.Y. , 1986. 461 p. : ISBN 0-688-04855-2 LC Card 85-21395 DDC 305.4/2/0973 19
HQ1426 .H457 1986 ***NYPL [JLE 86-1460]***

Lessner-Abdin, Dietlinde. Bruchhaus, Eva-Maria. Frauen in Entwicklungsländern . Freiburg im Breisgau , 1979. iii, 182 p. ; LC Card 81-121677 DDC 305.4/09172/4 19
HQ1870.9 .B78 1979 ***NYPL [JLG 86-106]***

Lessons . Wang, An, 1920- Reading, Mass. , 1986. 248 p., [28] p. of plates : ISBN 0-201-09400-2 LC Card 86-10768 DDC 338.7/61004/0924 B 19
HD9696.C62 A3 1986 ***NYPL [JFE 86-5201]***

Lessons from Korea's industrial experience /. Mukerjee, Dilip. Kuala Lumpur, Malaysia , c1986. vi, 81 p. ; ISBN 967-94701-3-X (pbk.) LC Card 86-944002 DDC 338.09519/5 19
HC467 .M84 1986

Lessons from the Caribbean Basin initiative /. Mukerjee, Dilip. Kuala Lumpur, Malaysia , c1985. 36 p. ; ISBN 967-99974-6-4 (pbk.) LC Card 87-101396 DDC 338.91/73/0729 19
HF1456.5.C27 M85 1985

Lestapis, Bérengère de. Knetsch, Werner. Die industrielle Anwendung der Mikroelektronik in der Bundesrepublik Deutschland, Frankreich, Grossbritannien . Haar bei München , c1985. 142 p. : ISBN 3-89090-121-2 : LC Card 86-106735
HC290.5.A9 K5 1985

Lester, James P., 1944- Dimensions of hazardous waste politics and policy /. New York , c1988. p. cm. ISBN 0-313-25989-5 (lib. bdg. : alk. paper) LC Card 87-17792 DDC 363.7/28 19
HC110.E5 D56 1988

LESTER, RICHARD ALLEN, 1908- - CONGRESSES.
How labor markets work . Lexington, Mass. , c1988. viii, 256 p. : ISBN 0-669-15126-2 (alk. paper) LC Card 87-22718 DDC 331.12 19
HD5701.3 .H68 1988

Lester, Robert. The War on poverty, 1964-1968 [microform] . Frederick, MD , c1986- microfilm reel ISBN 0-89093-495-9 (microfilm : set) : LC Card 87-10510 DDC 338.973 19
HC110 .P63

Let's talk business /. Michulka, Jean H. Cincinnati, Ohio , c1988. x, 370 p. : ISBN 0-538-05920-6 (pbk.) LC Card 86-63174 DDC 658.4/52 19
HF5718 .M5 1988

A letter on the subject of the projected rail road between Liverpool & Manchester . Sandars, Joseph. Liverpool , 1825. 46 p. ; LC Card 85-666157
HE3018 .S36x 1825

Letter to Joseph Locke, Esq. ... in reference to his bill "to regulate Sunday travelling on railways" /. Scotchman. Glasgow , 1849. 16 p. ; LC Card 85-666156
HE3037. S36x 1849

Letters that sell /. Werz, Edward W. Chicago , c1987. 163 p. ; ISBN 0-8092-4684-8 (pbk.) LC Card 87-20064 DDC 808/.066651 19
HF5730 .W47 1987

LETTING OF CONTRACTS. see CONTRACTS, LETTING OF.

Lettre de l'océan Indien (Firm). Service des études documentaires. Madagascar . Paris , 1986, c1985. 184 p. : ISBN 2-905760-02-8 LC Card 87-123718
HC895 .M34 1986

Leube, Kurt R. Friedman, Milton, 1912- The essence of Friedman /. Stanford, Calif. , c1987. xxxiv, 566 p., [1] p. of plates : ISBN 0-8179-8661-8 LC Card 87-4003 DDC 330.1 19
HB171 .F774 1987

Leung, PingSun, 1952- Leong, Jerrold K. (Jerrold Kim), 1947- Economic implications of import barriers to protect the U. S. sugar industry with particular reference to Hawaii /. Manoa , 1987. p. cm. LC Card 87-11855 DDC 382/.456641/09969 19
HD9107.H3 L46 1987

L'Europe verte sous influence . Carfantan, Jean Yves. Paris , c1985. 282 p. ; ISBN 2-02-008982-3 : LC Card 86-140900 DDC 338.1/094 19
HD1920.5 .C37 1985 ***NYPL [JLE 87-526]***

Leutzbach, Wilhelm.
[Einführung in die Theorie des Verkehrsflusses. English]
Introduction to the theory of traffic flow / Wilhelm Leutzbach. Berlin ; New York : Springer-Verlag, c1988. xi, 204 p. : ill. ; 25 cm. Translation of: Einführung in die Theorie des Verkehrsflusses. Bibliography: p. [195]-200. Includes index. ISBN 0-387-17113-4 (U. S.) : LC Card 87-9839 DDC 388.3/143 19
1. Traffic flow - Mathematical models. 2. Traffic flow - Statistical methods. I. Title.
HE336.T7 L4813 1988

Levačić, Rosalind.
Economic policy-making / Rosalind Levačić. Sussex : Wheatsheaf Books ; Totowa, N.J. : Barnes & Noble Books, 1987. xii, 372 p. : ill. ; 24 cm. Bibliography: p. 363-365. Includes index. ISBN 0-389-20741-1 (Barnes & Noble) LC Card 87-11543 DDC 338.941 19
1. Economic policy. 2. Great Britain - Economic policy. I. Title.
HD75 .L48 1987

Managing the UK economy . Cambridge, UK , 1987. xxvii, 328 p. : ISBN 0-7456-0316-5 : LC Card 86-26860 DDC 338.941 19
HC256.5 .M392 1987

Lévai, Béla. Rádió-televízió anno-- / Lévai Béla, Szabó Miklós. Budapest : RTV-Minerva, 1985. 94 p. : chiefly ill. ; 29 cm. ISBN 963-223-331-X : LC Card 86-128497
1. Magyar Rádió - History. 2. Magyar Televízió - History. 3. Broadcasting - Hungary - History. I. Szabó, Miklós. II. Title.
HE8689.9.H8 L49 1985

LEVCIK, FRIEDRICH.
Socialist economy and economic policy /. Wien , New York , 1985. 279 p. : ISBN 0-387-81903-7 (pbk.) LC Card 86-201536
HC704 .S557 1985

LEVEE DISTRICTS - POLAND - PRUSSIA, WEST - HISTORY.
Herrgeist, Fritz, 1895-1980. Die Wasser-, Boden- und Deichverbände in Ost- und Westpreussen, 1868 bis 1938 /. Köln , 1983. 524 p. : ISBN 3-7745-6456-6 LC Card 84-211844
HD1697.P64 P784 1983

LEVEE DISTRICTS - PRUSSIA, EAST (POLAND AND R.S.F.S.R.) - HISTORY.
Herrgeist, Fritz, 1895-1980. Die Wasser-, Boden- und Deichverbände in Ost- und Westpreussen, 1868 bis 1938 /. Köln , 1983. 524 p. : ISBN 3-7745-6456-6 LC Card 84-211844
HD1697.P64 P784 1983

Levenson, Bob. Bill Bernbach's book : a history of the advertising that changed the history of advertising / by Bob Levenson.1st ed. New York : Villard Books, 1987. xvii, 219 p. : ill. (some col.) ; 32 cm. ISBN 0-394-54920-1 : LC Card 86-40103 DDC 659.1/0973 19
1. Advertising - United States - History. 2. Bernbach, Bill. I. Title.
HF5813.U6 L48 1987

LEVERAGED BUYOUTS.
Crawford, Edward K., 1933- A management guide to leveraged buyouts /. New York , c1987. x, 257 p. ; ISBN 0-471-83232-4 LC Card 86-32390 DDC 658.1/6 19
HD2746.5 .C7 1987

Haines, Lionel. How to buy a good business with little or none of your own money /. New York , c1987. 212 p. ; ISBN 0-8129-1627-1 : LC Card 86-30017 DDC 658.1/6 19
HD2746.5 .H35 1987

Logue, John, 1947- Buyout! . [Kent, Ohio] [1986] vi, 98 p. : ISBN 0-933522-15-0 (pbk.) LC Card 86-623028 DDC 658.1/6 19
HD2746.5 .L64 1986

LEVERAGED BUYOUTS - CASE STUDIES.
Crawford, Edward K., 1933- A management guide to leveraged buyouts /. New York , c1987. x, 257 p. ; ISBN 0-471-83232-4 LC Card 86-32390 DDC 658.1/6 19
HD2746.5 .C7 1987

Leverkusen (Germany)
Marx, G. Die Entwicklung der Wohnungsbautätigkeit in Leverkusen /. Leverkusen [1984] 37 p., [1] folded leaf of plates : LC Card 84-183932
HD9715.G33 L575 1984

Leverkusen (Germany). Amt für Wahlen und Meldewesen. Marx, G. Die Entwicklung der Wohnungsbautätigkeit in Leverkusen /. Leverkusen [1984] 37 p., [1] folded leaf of plates : LC Card 84-183932
HD9715.G33 L575 1984

LEVERKUSEN (GERMANY) - INDUSTRIES - STATISTICS.
Marx, G. Die Entwicklung der Wohnungsbautätigkeit in Leverkusen /. Leverkusen [1984] 37 p., [1] folded leaf of plates : LC Card 84-183932
HD9715.G33 L575 1984

LEVERKUSEN (GERMANY) - MANUFACTURES - STATISTICS.
Marx, G. Die Entwicklung der Wohnungsbautätigkeit in Leverkusen /. Leverkusen [1984] 37 p., [1] folded leaf of plates : LC Card 84-183932
HD9715.G33 L575 1984

Levet, Jean-Louis. Dacier, Pierre. Les dossiers noirs de l'industrie française /. [Paris] , c1985. 414 p. ; ISBN 2-213-01659-3 : LC Card 86-178468
HC276.2 .D2 1985

Levey, Irv. Rodgers, F. G. (Francis G.) Getting the best out of yourself and others /. New York , c1987. xi, 227 p. ; ISBN 0-06-015670-8 : LC Card 86-46125 DDC 658.3/4 19
HF5549.5.M63 R63 1987

Leviathan (Düsseldorf, Germany). Sonderheft . (7) Die Zweite Stadt . Opladen , c1986. 407 p. : ISBN 3-531-11764-5 LC Card 87-497505 DDC 331.11/0943 19
HD8451 .Z94 1986

Levich, Richard M. The ECU market . Lexington, Mass. , c1987. xiii, 246 p. : ISBN 0-669-13833-9 (alk. paper) LC Card 87-4185 DDC 332.4/56094 19
HG930.5 .E27 1987

Levidow, Les. Radical science essays /. London , Atlantic Highlands, N.J. , 1986. 230 p. : LC Card 86-7425 DDC 303.4/83 19
Q175.55 .R33 1986 ***NYPL [JLD 87-615]***

Levin, A. I. (Aleksandr Ivanovich) Tovarnoe obrashchenie : problemy prognozirovaniia i upravleniia / A.I. Levin, A.P. IArkin. Moskva : Izd-vo "Nauka", 1980. 286 p. ; 21 cm. (Problemy sovetskoĭ ėkonomiki) At head of title: Akademiia nauk SSSR. TSentral'nyĭ ėkonomiko-matematicheskiĭ institut. Nauchnyĭ sovet po problemam nauchno-tekhnicheskogo i sotsial'no-ėkonomicheskogo prognozirovaniia pri Prezidiume AN SSSR i Goskomitete po nauke i tekhnike. Includes bibliographical references. LC Card 81-141540
1. Commercial products - Soviet Union. 2. Durable goods, Consumer - Soviet United States. 3. Consumption (Economics) - Soviet Union. I. IArkin, A. P. (Anatoliĭ Pavlovich). II. Title.
HF1040.9.S65 L48 1980

Levin, A. P. Razvitie i razmeshchenie mashinostroeniia v investitsionnom komplekse /. Moskva , 1986. 128 p. : LC Card 86-232328
HD9705.S595 R39 1986

Levin, Jack S., 1936- Tax, SEC, and accounting aspects of corporate acquisitions, 1984 /. New York, N.Y. (810 Seventh Ave., New York 10019) , c1984. 584 p. : LC Card 84-231882 DDC 343.7306/7 347.30367 19
KF6499.M4 T39 1984 ***NYPL [JLD 87-57]***

Levine & Co. . Frantz, Douglas. New York , c1987. x, 370 p. : ISBN 0-8050-0457-2 LC Card 87-8521 DDC 364.1/68 19
HG2463.L48 F72 1987

Levine and Co. Frantz, Douglas. Levine & Co. . New York , c1987. x, 370 p. : ISBN 0-8050-0457-2 LC Card 87-8521 DDC 364.1/68 19
HG2463.L48 F72 1987

Levine, David, 1946- Reproducing families : the political economy of English population history / David Levine. Cambridge [Cambridgeshire] ; New York : Cambridge University Press, 1987. ix, 251 p. ; 24 cm. (Themes in the social sciences) Bibliography: p. 217-248. Includes index. ISBN 0-521-33256-7 LC Card 86-26372 DDC 304.6/0942 19
1. England - Population - History. 2. Fertility, Human - England - History. 3. Demographic transition - England. 4. England - Economic conditions. 5. England - Social conditions. 6. Family demography - England. I. Title.
HB3585 .L48 1987

Levine, David M., 1946- Using Minitab with Basic business statistics / David M. Levine, Mark L. Berenson, David Stephan. 3rd ed. Englewood Cliffs, N.J. : Prentice-Hall, c1986. viii, 160 p. : ill. ; 28 cm. Bibliography: p. 156. Includes index. ISBN 0-13-057779-0 (pbk.) LC Card 87-400304 DDC 519.5/028/55369 19
1. Minitab (Computer system). 2. Commercial statistics - Data processing. 3. Statistics - Data processing. I. Berenson, Mark L. II. Stephan, David. III. Title.
HF1017 .L425 1986

LEVINE, DENNIS, 1952-
Frantz, Douglas. Levine & Co. . New York , c1987. x, 370 p. : ISBN 0-8050-0457-2 LC Card 87-8521 DDC 364.1/68 19
HG2463.L48 F72 1987

Levine, Michael. The corporate address book : how to reach the 1000 most important companies in the U. S. / Michael Levine. New York, N.Y. : G.P. Putnam's, c1987. 268 p. ; 23 cm. "A Perigee book." Includes index. ISBN 0-399-51384-1 (pbk.) LC Card 87-11162 DDC 338.7/4/02573 19
1. Corporations - United States - Directories. I. Title.
HG4057 .A288 1987

Levine, Michael L. Inside productivity . New York, N.Y. , c1987. iv, 156 p. : ISBN 0-88057-671-5 (pbk.) LC Card 86-82865 DDC 338/.06 19
HD56 .I528 1987

Levine, Stuart M. The construction manager : course manual / [by Stuart M. Levine]. [Washington, D.C.] (1120 20th St., NW, Washington 20036) : Federal Publications, c1986. ii, 218 p. : ill. ; 28 cm. Includes bibliographical references. LC Card 87-109137 DDC 624/.068 19
1. Construction industry - Management. 2. Construction industry - United States - Management. I. Federal Publications Inc. II. Title.
HD9715.A2 L43 1986

Levine, Victor. Allen, David N. Nurturing advanced technology enterprises . New York , c1986. xvi, 268 p. ; ISBN 0-275-92136-0 (alk. paper) : LC Card 86-9411 DDC 338.4/762/0009748 19
HC107.P43 H533 1986
NYPL [JLE 86-3609]

Levinson, Alfred Linden, 1933- Economic impact assessment of the South Jersey Port Corporation / by Alfred Levinson. Newark, N.J. (323 High St., Newark 07102) : New Jersey Institute of Technology, [1982] 31 leaves : ill. ; 28 cm. Cover title. "March 1982." Bibliography: leaf 28. LC Card 86-622073 DDC 387.1/09749/88 19
1. Harbors - New Jersey - Camden. 2. South Jersey Port Corporation. I. Title.
HE554.C18 L48 1982

Levinson, Jay Conrad. Quit your job! : making the decision, making the break, making it work / Jay Conrad Levinson. New York : Dodd, Mead, c1987. 216 p. ; 22 cm. Bibliography: p. 205-211. Includes index. ISBN 0-396-08882-1 LC Card 87-15545 DDC 650.1 19
1. Career changes. 2. Self-employed. I. Title.
HF5384 .L48 1987

Levinson, Richard. Off camera : conversations with the makers of prime-time television / by Richard Levinson and William Link. New York, N.Y. : New American Library, c1986. 279 p. ; 21 cm. "A Plume book." Includes index. ISBN 0-452-25873-1 LC Card 86-18089 DDC 384.55/023/73 19
1. Television broadcasting - Vocational guidance. 2. Television industry - Vocational guidance. I. Link, William. II. Title.
HE8700.4 .L48 1986
NYPL [MWGR 87-881]

Leviste, Jose P., 1945-
Food for thought : management of Philippine agriculture : an alternative for the Third World / Jose P. Leviste, Jr. Los Baños, Laguna, Philippines : Southeast Asian Regional Center for Graduate Study and Research in Agriculture, c1985. 150 p. : ill. ; 24 cm. Bibliography: p. [145]-150. LC Card 86-193278 DDC 338.1/8599 19
1. Agriculture and state - Philippines. 2. Nutrition

policy - Philippines. I. Title.
HD2088 .L48 1985

The Pacific lake . Manila, Philippines , c1986. xvi, 248 p. : LC Card 87-111641 DDC 337.1/9 19
HF1600.15.P16 P33 1986

Levit, I. Ė. (Iziaslav Ėlikovich) Shornikov, P. M. (Petr Mikhaĭlovich) Promyshlennost′ i rabochiĭ klass Moldavskoĭ SSR v gody Velikoĭ Otechestvennoĭ voĭny /. Kishinev , 1986. 148, [4] p. ; LC Card 86-141169
HC337.M553 D47 1986

Levitan, Sar A. Working but poor : America's contradiction / Sar A. Levitan and Isaac Shapiro. Baltimore : Johns Hopkins University Press, c1987. ix, 142 p. : ill. ; 24 cm. Bibliography: p. [131]-137. Includes index. ISBN 0-8018-3583-6 (alk. paper) LC Card 87-16973 DDC 362.5/0973 19
1. Income maintenance programs - United States. 2. Poor - Employment - United States. 3. Manpower policy - United States. 4. Wages - United States. 5. United States - Economic conditions - 1981-. 6. United States - Social conditions - 1980-. I. Shapiro, Isaac, 1957-. II. Title.
HC110.I5 L468 1987

Levitas, I. IA. (Iosif IAkovlevich) I ser′ëzno, i kur′ëzno : filatelisticheskiĭ kaleĭdoskop / I.IA. Levitas. Moskva : "Radio i sviaz′", 1985. 232 p. : col. ill. ; 17 cm. Bibliography: p. 232. LC Card 85-184912
1. Postage-stamps - History - Miscellanea. 2. Postage-stamps - Collectors and collecting - Miscellanea. I. Title.
HE6182 .L48 1985

Levitsky, Jacob, 1924- Credit guarantee schemes for small and medium enterprises / Jacob Levitsky and Ranga N. Prasad. Washington, D.C. : World Bank, 1987. vi, 91 p. ; 28 cm. (Industry and finance series, 0256-2235 . v. 19) World Bank technical paper, 0253-7494 ; no. 58 Bibliography: p. 89-91. ISBN 0-8213-0866-1 (pbk.) LC Card 86-32571 DDC 658.8/7 19
1. Insurance, Credit. I. Prasad, Ranga N., 1957-. II. Series. III. Series: World Bank technical paper , no. 58. IV. Title.
HG9977 .L48 1987

Levitt, M. S., 1938-
The growth and efficiency of public spending / M.S. Levitt and M.A.S. Joyce. Cambridge [Cambridgeshire] ; New York : Cambridge University Press, 1987. xiv, 201 p. : ill. ; 24 cm. (Occasional papers / the National Institute of Economic and Social Research . 41) Bibliography: p. 189-194. Includes index. ISBN 0-521-34621-5 (U. S.) LC Card 87-11636 DDC 339.5/22/0941 19
1. Great Britain - Appropriations and expenditures. 2. Government spending policy - Great Britain. 3. Government productivity - Great Britain. I. Joyce, M. A. S. II. Series: Occasional papers (National Institute of Economic and Social Research) , 41. III. Title.
HJ7764 .L475 1987

New priorities in public spending /. Brookfield, VT , 1987. 129 p. ; ISBN 0-566-05386-1 : LC Card 86-22946 DDC 336.3/9/0941 19
HJ7764 .N49 1987

Levkovskiĭ, Alekseĭ Ivanovich. Perspektivy resheniia prodovol′stvennoĭ problemy v razvivaiushchikhsia stranakh . Moskva , 1985. 142 p. ; LC Card 85-188217
HD9018.D44 P47 1985

Levkovsky, A. I. see Levkovskiĭ, Alekseĭ Ivanovich.

Levnadsförhållanden, 0347-7193 .
(rapport nr. 36) Arbetslöshetens offer. Stockholm , 1983. 56 p. : ISBN 91-38-07637-3 LC Card 83-181664
HD5803 .A72 1983

Levy, Frank, 1941- Dollars and dreams : the changing American income distribution / Frank Levy. New York : Russell Sage Foundation for the National Committee for Research on the 1980 Census, 1987. p. cm. (The Population of the United States in the 1980s) Bibliography: p. Includes index. ISBN 0-87154-523-3 : LC Card 86-42952 DDC 339.2/0973 19
1. Income distribution - United States. 2. Income - United States. 3. United States - Economic conditions - 1945-. I. National Committee for Research on the 1980 Census. II. Title. III. Series.
HC110.I5 L47 1987

Lévy-Leboyer, Claude. La crise des motivations / par Claude Lévy-Leboyer. 1re éd. Paris : Presses universitaires de France, c1984. 135 p. ; 22 cm. Includes bibliographical references. ISBN 2-13-038772-1 : LC Card 85-115430
1. Employee motivation. I. Title.
HF5549.5.M63 L47 1984

Levy, Maurice, 1922- United Nations University Symposium on Energy and Agriculture Futures--Policy Implications of Global Models (1982 : Paris, France) Energy and agriculture . [Chur, Switzerland , New York] , c1984. xii, 370 p. : ISBN 3-7186-0187-7 LC Card 83-18363 DDC 333.79 19
HD1405 .E53 1983 ***NYPL [JLD 86-1837]***

Levy, Norman J. New York (State). Legislature. Legislative Commission on Critical Transportation Choices. Conrail . [Albany] [1986] i, 134 p. ; LC Card 87-620569 DDC 385/.065/73 19
HE2791.C899 N48 1986

Levy, Sidney J., 1921- Attitudes toward vended coffee /. [Chicago? , 1983] 1 v. (various pagings) : LC Card 86-235525 DDC 381/.4566393 19
HD9199.U48 A88 1983

Lewanski, Rodolfo. Il controllo degli inquinamenti delle acque : l'attuazione di una politica pubblica / Rodolfo Lewanski. Milano : Giuffrè, 1986. 194 p. : ill. ; 24 cm. (Quaderni I.S.A.P. . 22.) Includes bibliographical references. ISBN 88-14-00753-5 : LC Card 86-160300
1. Water quality management - Government policy - Italy. 2. Water - Pollution - Law and legislation - Italy. I. Series: Quaderni I.S.A.P. , 22. II. Title.
HC310.W32 L48 1986

Lewchuk, Wayne. American technology and the British vehicle industry / Wayne Lewchuk. Cambridge [Cambridgeshire] ; New York : Cambridge University Press, 1987. viii, 304 p. : ill. ; 24 cm. Bibliography: p. [272]-294. Includes index. ISBN 0-521-30269-2 LC Card 86-30994 DDC 338.4/56292/0941 19
1. Automobile industry and trade - Great Britain - History. 2. Automobiles - Great Britain - Technological innovations - History. 3. Mass production - Great Britain - History. 4. Automobile industry and trade - United States - History. 5. Automobiles - United States - Technological innovations - History. I. Title.
HD9710.G72 L48 1987

Lewin, David, 1943-
Public sector labor relations . Lexington, Mass. , c1988. xi, 648 p. ; ISBN 0-669-12893-7 (alk. paper) LC Card 82-64038 DDC 331.89/041353 19
HD8005.6.U5 P83 1988

Public sector labor relations. Public sector labor relations : analysis and readings / [edited by] David Lewin ... [et al.].[3rd ed.]. Lexington, Mass. , c1988. xi, 648 p. ; ISBN 0-669-12893-7 (alk. paper) LC Card 82-64038 DDC 331.89/041353 19
HD8005.6.U5 P83 1988

Lewin, Elizabeth.
Financial fitness through divorce : a guide to the financial realities of divorce / Elizabeth S. Lewin. New York, N.Y. : Facts on File, c1987. vii, 146 p. : forms ; 28 cm. Includes index. ISBN 0-8160-1323-3 (pbk.) : LC Card 86-24383 DDC 332.024 19
1. Divorced people - Finance, Personal. I. Title.
HG179 .L477 1987

Your personal financial fitness program / Elizabeth S. Lewin. 1987 ed. New York, N.Y. : Facts on File, c1987. p. cm. Includes index. ISBN 0-8160-1580-5 LC Card 86-29093 DDC 332.024 19
1. Finance, Personal. I. Title.
HG179 .L48 1987

Lewin-Epstein, Noah. Semyonov, Moshe. Hewers of wood and drawers of water . Ithaca, NY , c1987. xii, 152 p. : ISBN 0-87546-133-6 (pbk. : alk. paper) LC Card 87-2682 DDC 331.6/99275695 19
HD8660 .S45 1987

Lewin, Gordon, 1951- Car-free in Boston . Cambridge, MA (P.O. Box 192, Cambridge 02238) , c1986. 160 p. : LC Card 86-231024 DDC 388.4/09744 19
HE4491.B8 C37 1986

Lewin, Leonard, 1919- Telecommunications . Dedham, MA , c1984. xxii, 687 p. : ISBN 0-89006-140-8 LC Card 84-70225 DDC 384 19
HE7631 .T443 1984 ***NYPL [JLE 86-1167]***

Lewis, Alan, 1952- James, Simon R. The comprehensibility of taxation . Aldershot, Hants, England , Brookfield, Vt., USA , c1987. xiii, 314 p. : ISBN 0-566-05348-9 : LC Card 86-25690 DDC 336.2/00941 19
HJ2619 .J36 1987

Lewis, Colin David. Managing with micros : management uses of microputers / Colin Lewis.2nd ed. Oxford, England : Blackwell, 1984. 200 p. : ill. ; 24 cm. (The Economist books) Includes index. LC Card 85-103102 DDC 658/.054 19
1. Business - Data processing. 2. Management - Data processing. 3. Microcomputers - Programming. I. Title. II. Series.
HF5548.2 .L425 1984 ***NYPL [JLE 86-2215]***

Lewis, D. M. (Dale M.) Lupande Development Workshop (1983 : Nyamaluma Wildlife Conservation Camp) Proceedings of the Lupande Development Workshop . Chipata, Zambia , 1984. x, 121 p. : LC Card 84-980605 DDC 333.73/17/096894 19
HD993.Z8 L835 1983 ***NYPL [JLG 87-67]***

Lewis, Diane, 1936-
The insider's guide to finding the right job / Diane Lewis with Joe Carroll. Nashville : T. Nelson, c1987. 190 p. ; 21 cm. ISBN 0-8407-3107-8 (pbk.) : LC Card 86-33305 DDC 650.1/4 19
1. Job hunting - United States. 2. Employment interviewing - United States. I. Carroll, Joe. II. Title.
HF5382.75.U6 L49 1987

Why women fail in business / by Diane Lewis with J.J. Carroll. Nashville : T. Nelson, c1987. p. cm. ISBN 0-8407-4219-3 : LC Card 87-15370 DDC 658.4/09088042 19
1. Sex role in the work environment. 2. Women - Psychology. 3. Women in business. 4. Success in business. 5. Promotions. I. Carroll, Joe. II. Title.
HD6054.3 .L48 1987

Lewis, Donald E. Work, leisure, and technology /. Melbourne, Australia , 1986. vi, 273 p. : ISBN 0-582-71151-7 (pbk.) LC Card 87-105477 DDC 303.4/83/0994 19
HD6331.2.A8 W67 1986

Lewis, G. J. Human migration : a geographical perspective / G.J. Lewis. London : Croom Helm, c1982. 220 p. : ill. ; 23 cm. (Croom Helm series in geography and environment) Bibliography: p. 192-216. Includes index. ISBN 0-7099-0007-4 LC Card 86-673643
1. Migration, Internal. I. Title.
HB1952 .L48x 1982b

Lewis, Gary A., 1927- News from somewhere : connecting health and freedom at the workplace / Gary A. Lewis. Westport, Conn. : Greenwood Press, 1986. xii, 213 p. : ill. ; 22 cm. (Contributions in political science. no. 151) Includes index. Bibliography: p. [185]-195. ISBN 0-313-24869-9 (lib. bdg. : alk. paper) LC Card 85-27269 DDC 658.3/152 19
1. Management - Employee participation. 2. Management - Norway - Employee participation. 3. Industrial hygiene - Norway - Management - Employee participation. I. Title.
HD5650 .L439 1986 ***NYPL [JLD 86-3587]***

Lewis, Gordon H. Income transfer analysis / Gordon H. Lewis, Richard J. Morrison. New York : Immergut & Siolek, c1987. p. cm. Bibliography: p. Includes index. ISBN 0-915163-01-2 LC Card 86-33744 DDC 362.5/82 19
1. Income maintenance programs - United States - Data processing. 2. MAPSIT (Computer program). I. Morrison, Richard J. II. Title.
HC110.I5 L48 1987

Lewis, Herschell Gordon, 1926- Herschell Gordon Lewis on the art of writing copy / Herschell Gordon Lewis. Englewood Cliffs, N.J. : Prentice-Hall, c1987. p. cm. Includes index. ISBN 0-13-387309-9 : LC Card 87-11489 DDC 659.13/22 19
1. Advertising copy. I. Title.
HF5825 .L44 1987

Lewis, Jane (Jane E.) Women, work, and family in the British, Canadian, and Norwegian oilfields /. New York , 1987. p. cm. ISBN

0-312-00528-8 : LC Card 86-31393 DDC 305.4/3665 19
HD9560.5 .W66 1987

Lewis, John Prior.
Asian development : the role of development assistance / by John P. Lewis. Lanham, MD : University Press of America ; New York : Asia Society, c1987. 49 p. ; 23 cm. (Asian agenda report . 7) Bibliography: p. 48. ISBN 0-8191-6590-5 (pbk.) : LC Card 87-21599 DDC 338.91/095 19
1. Economic assistance - Asia - History - 20th century. 2. Asia - Economic policy. I. Title. II. Series.
HC412 .L45 1987

Development strategies reconsidered /. New Brunswick, N.J., U. S.A. , c1986. viii, 190 p. ; ISBN 0-87855-991-4 (pbk.) : LC Card 85-24582 DDC 338.9/009172/4 19
HC59.7 .D482 1986 ***NYPL [JLE 86-2976]***

Lewis, Lawrence. African environments and resources / L.A. Lewis and L. Berry. Boston : Allen & Unwin, 1987. p. cm. Bibliography: p. Includes index. ISBN 0-04-916010-9 (alk. paper) LC Card 87-16751 DDC 333.7/096 19
1. Natural resources - Africa. 2. Ecology - Africa. 3. Natural resources - Government policy - Africa. 4. Environmental policy - Africa. I. Berry, Leonard, 1930-. II. Title.
HC800 .L48 1987

Lewis, Mervyn.
Domestic and international banking / M.K. Lewis and K.T. Davis. 1st MIT Press ed. Cambridge, Mass. : MIT Press, 1987. ix, 440 p. : ill. ; 24 cm. Cover title: Domestic & international banking. Bibliography: p. 395-414. Includes indexes. ISBN 0-262-12126-3 LC Card 87-2962 DDC 332.1 19
1. Banks and banking. 2. Banks and banking, International. I. Davis, Kevin. II. Title. III. Title: Domestic & international banking.
HG1586 .L39 1987

Personal financial markets . Deddington, Oxford , Atlantic Highlands, N.J. , 1986. viii, 279 p. : ISBN 0-86003-540-9 LC Card 86-235455 DDC 332.1/7 19
HG186.G7 P38 1986

Lewis, Mike. 20 activities for developing managerial effectiveness : a management skills training manual / Mike Lewis and Graham Kelly. Aldershot, Hants, England : Gower, c1986. xii, 276 p. : ill. ; 32 cm. ISBN 0-566-02515-9 LC Card 87-147860 DDC 658.4/07124 19
1. Management - Handbooks, manuals, etc. 2. Executives - Training of - Handbooks, manuals, etc. 3. Executive ability - Handbooks, manuals, etc. I. Kelly, Graham. II. Title. III. Title: Twenty activities for developing managerial effectiveness.
HD31 .L387 1986

Lewis, Normande. Le travail à temps partiel, le partage du travail comme mesure de sécurité d'emploi et la sous-traitance : recueil de clauses-types / [préparé pour le] Centre de recherche et de statistiques sur le marché du travail par Normande Lewis et André Desjardins. [Quebec] : Gouvernement du Québec, Ministère du travail, Centre de recherche et de statistiques sur le marché du travail, c1985. 90 p. ; 28 cm. "Le contenu de cette publication a été réalisé par le Ministère du travail du Québec"--P. before t.p. Includes bibliographical references. CONTENTS. - Le travail à temps partiel / Normande Lewis -- Partage du travail comme mesure de sécurité d'emploi / André Desjardins -- La sous-traitance / Normande Lewis. ISBN 2-551-08998-0 LC Card 85-213545
1. Part-time employment - Québec (Province). 2. Work sharing - Québec (Province). 3. Subcontracting - Québec (Province). I. Desjardins, André. II. Québec (Province). Centre de recherche et de statistiques sur le marché du travail. III. Québec (Province). Ministère du travail.
HD5110.2.C22 Q45 1985

Lewis, Oscar, 1914-1970.
Rigdon, Susan M., 1943- The culture facade . Urbana , c1988. p. cm. ISBN 0-252-01495-2 (alk. paper) LC Card 87-19063 DDC 305.5/69 19
HC79.P6 R57 1988

LEWIS, OSCAR, 1914-1970.
Hakemulder, Roel. Subcultuur en stigma van de armoede . Leiden , 1985. 96 p. ; ISBN 90-6624-058-X LC Card 86-172398
HC79.P6 H34 1985

LEWIS, OSCAR, 1914-1970 - VIEWS ON POVERTY.
Rigdon, Susan M., 1943- The culture facade . Urbana , c1988. p. cm. ISBN 0-252-01495-2 (alk. paper) LC Card 87-19063 DDC 305.5/69 19
HC79.P6 R57 1988

Lewis, Ronald L., 1940- Black coal miners in America : race, class, and community conflict, 1780-1980 / Ronald L. Lewis. Lexington, Ky. : University Press of Kentucky, c1987. xv, 239 p., [8] p. of plates : ill. ; 25 cm. Bibliography: p. [227]-231. Includes index. ISBN 0-8131-1610-4 : LC Card 87-2086 DDC 331.6/396073 19
1. Afro-American coal miners - History. I. Title.
HD8039.M62 U6443 1987

Lewis, W. Arthur (William Arthur), 1915- Labour in the West Indies : the birth of a worker's movement / by W. Arthur Lewis ; with an afterwork "Germs of an Idea" by Susan Craig. London : New Beacon Books, 1977. 104 p., [12] p. of plates : ill. ; 21 cm. Bibliography: p. 82-84. ISBN 0-901241-25-3 (pbk.) LC Card 86-232414
1. Trade-unions - West Indies, British. 2. Labor and laboring classes - West Indies, British. I. Craig, Susan. Germs of an idea. 1977. II. Title.
HD6595.4 .L49 1977

LEWIS, W. ARTHUR (WILLIAM ARTHUR), 1915-
Datta, Anindya. Growth and equity . Calcutta , New York , 1986. xii, 119 p. : ISBN 0-19-561882-3 : LC Card 87-900001 DDC 338.954 19
HD82 .D334 1986

Lewis, W. David (Walter David), 1931- The airway to everywhere : a history of All American Aviation, 1937-1953 / W. David Lewis, William F. Trimble. Pittsburgh, PA : University of Pittsburgh Press, [1988] p. cm. Bibliography: p. Includes index. ISBN 0-8229-3579-1 LC Card 87-25176 DDC 387.7/065/73 19
1. All American Aviation (Firm) - History. 2. Airlines - United States - History. I. Trimble, William F., 1947-. II. Title.
HE9803.A944 L48 1988

Lewis, William, 1946-
Fast-track careers : a guide to the highest-paying jobs / William Lewis, Nancy Schuman. New York : Wiley, c1987. x, 212 p. ; 23 cm. (Career blazers) Includes bibliographies and index. ISBN 0-471-83801-2 (pbk.) : LC Card 87-10045 DDC 331.7/02/0973 19
1. Vocational guidance - United States. 2. Success in business - United States. 3. Executives - Employment - United States. 4. Baby boom generation - United States. I. Schuman, Nancy. II. Title. III. Series.
HF5382.5.U5 L45 1987

The Prentice-Hall directory of executive search firms / William Lewis & Carol Milano. New York : Prentice-Hall, c1986. v, 328 p. ; 24 cm. Includes index. Bibliography: p. 307-308. ISBN 0-671-55518-9 (pbk.) LC Card 85-30190 DDC 658.4/07111/02573 19
1. Executives - United States - Recruiting. 2. Executives - United States - Recruiting - Directories. I. Milano, Carol. II. Title. III. Title: Directory of executive search firms.
HD38.25.U6 L49 1986 ***NYPL [*R-Econ. 87-1586]***

Profitable careers in nonprofit / William Lewis, Carol Milano. New York : Wiley, c1987. vi, 202 p. ; 24 cm. Bibliography: p. 194-199. ISBN 0-471-83699-0 (pbk.) : LC Card 87-6102 DDC 331.7/02 19
1. Vocational guidance - United States. 2. Corporations, Nonprofit - United States. I. Milano, Carol. II. Title.
HF5382.5.U5 L44 1987

Lewty, Peter J., 1934- To the Columbia gateway : the Oregon Railway and the Northern Pacific, 1879-1884 / Peter J. Lewty. Pullman, Wash. : Washington State University Press, 1987. p. cm. Bibliography: p. Includes index. ISBN 0-87422-030-0 (alk. paper) : LC Card 87-21041 DDC 385/.09795 19
1. Northern Pacific Railroad Company - History - 19th century. 2. Oregon Pacific & Eastern Railway - History - 19th century. 3. Railroads - United States - History - 19th century. I. Title.
HE2791.N855 L48 1987

Lexikon Stadtverkehr. Transpress Lexikon Stadtverkehr /. Berlin , 1985. 487 p., 33 p. of plates : LC Card 86-166711
HE305 .T78 1985

Lexikon Wirtschaftspolitik : die Institutionen / herausgegeben von Wolfgang Bohling und Dieter Masberg. München : C.H. Beck, c1986. 236 p. : ill. ; 18 cm. (Beck'sche schwarze Reihe. Bd. 310) Includes bibliographies and index. ISBN 3-406-31302-7 LC Card 86-221788
1. Finance - Germany (West) - Dictionaries - German. 2. Finance, Public - Germany (West) - Dictionaries - German. 3. Germany (West) - Politics and government - Dictionaries - German. I. Bohling, Wolfgang. II. Masberg, Dieter.
HG151 .L45 1986

Lexington Books/Salomon Brothers Center series on financial institutions and markets.
The ECU market . Lexington, Mass. , c1987. xiii, 246 p. : ISBN 0-669-13833-9 (alk. paper) LC Card 87-4185 DDC 332.4/56094 19
HG930.5 .E27 1987

Lexique des termes. Glossary of terms . [Ottawa] [1981]-1984. 3 v. ; ISBN 0-662-52389-X (v. 2) LC Card 81-180363 DDC 350/.0003/41 19
JA61 .G55 ***NYPL [JLF 87-379]***

LEY, ROBERT, 1890-1945.
Smelser, Ronald, 1942- Robert Ley, Hitler's labor leader /. New York , 1988. p. cm. ISBN 0-85496-161-5 : LC Card 87-20960 DDC 331/.092/4 B 19
HD8453.L49 S64 1988

Las Leyes de estabilidad laboral y sus efectos económicos / [investigación, Róger Espinosa Reyes ; asistentes, Clara Ogata y Andrés Medina ; informes legales, Pedro Morales Corrales, Mario Pasco Cosmópolis]. Lima, Perú : Instituto Libertad y Democracia, [1986?] 67 p. : ill. ; 21 cm. (Cuaderno de trabajo . 2) LC Card 87-403254 DDC 331.11/0985 19
1. Labor policy - Peru. 2. Labor laws and legislation - Peru. I. Espinosa Reyes, Róger. II. Instituto Libertad y Democracia (Lima, Peru). III. Series: Cuaderno de trabajo (Instituto Libertad y Democracia (Lima, Peru)) , 2.
HD8344 .L49 1986

Leyland. see **British Leyland Motor Corporation.**

Leymarie, Danièle. Lacour, Claude. Croissance urbaine . Paris , 1981. 219 p. : ISBN 2-222-02928-7 (pbk.) : LC Card 82-153821 DDC 388.4/068 19
HE4764 .L3 1981 ***NYPL [JLG 86-56]***

Leyton, José I. García Elizalde, Pedro. El desarrollo frutícola y forestal en Chile y sus derivaciones sociales. Santiago de Chile , 1986. 234 p. : ISBN 92-1-321204-6 LC Card 86-175421
HD9254.C52 G37 1986

Lezioni di economia : l'inflazione / a cura di Ferdinando Targetti ; saggi di Filippo Cavazzuti ... [et al.].1a ed. Milano : Feltrinelli economica, 1979. 195 p. ; 18 cm. (I Nuovi testi. 194) Lessons previously given at the Casa della Cultura di Milano in 1976-1977. Includes bibliographies. LC Card 80-451708
1. Inflation (Finance) - Italy - Addresses, essays, lectures. 2. Inflation (Finance) - Addresses, essays, lectures. I. Targetti, Ferdinando. II. Cavazzuti, Filippo, 1942-.
HG1029.5 .L49 ***NYPL [JLC 86-357]***

Leznik, A. D. (Aleksandr Davidovich) Upravlenie mezhdunarodnoĭ spetsializatsieĭ proizvodstva stran SĖV / A.D. Leznik. Moskva : Izd-vo "Nauka", 1982. 143 p. ; 20 cm. At head of title: Akademiia nauk SSSR. Institut ėkonomiki mirovoĭ sotsialisticheskoĭ sistemy. Includes bibliographical references. LC Card 83-123508
1. Europe, Eastern - Economic integration. 2. Europe, Eastern - Industries. 3. Council for Mutual Economic Assistance. I. Title.
HC244 .L466 1982

L'Hériteau, Marie France. Le Fonds monétaire international et les pays du Tiers-monde / Marie-France L'Hériteau. 1re éd. Paris : Presses universitaires de France : I.E.D.E.S., c1986. 277 p. : ill. ; 24 cm. (Collection Tiers monde, 0223-5870) Includes bibliographical references. ISBN 2-13-039203-2 : LC Card 86-165389
1. International Monetary Fund - Developing countries. 2. Developing countries - Economic policy. 3. Finance - Developing countries. I. Title. II. Series.
HG3881.5.I58 L52 1986

Li, Ch'eng-jui. International Seminar on China's 1982 Population Census (1982 : Peking, China) A census of one billion people . [Wanchai, Hongkong , Boulder, Colo. , 1986, c1987] 704 p., [4] leaves of plates : LC Card 87-2131 DDC 304.6/0723 19
HA4631.5 .I57 1982

Li, Kuo-ting. The evolution of policy behind Taiwan's development success / by K.T. Li ; with introductory essays by Gustav Ranis and John C.H. Fei. New Haven : Yale University Press, c1988. p. cm. Includes index. ISBN 0-300-04080-6 LC Card 87-23035 DDC 338.951/249 19
1. Taiwan - Economic policy - 1945-. 2. Taiwan - Economic conditions - 1945-. I. Ranis, Gustav. II. Fei, John C. H. III. Title.
HC430.5 .L4725 1988

LIABILITIES (ACCOUNTING)
Measuring and funding corporate liabilities for retiree health benefits. Washington, D.C. , c1987. xxxviii, 226 p. : ISBN 0-86643-054-7 (pbk.) LC Card 87-24534 DDC 657/.75 19
HG9396 .M4 1987

LIABILITY INSURANCE. see **INSURANCE, LIABILITY.**

Liability insurance account handling guide / written by the staff of International Risk Management Institute, Inc. Dallas, Tex. : The Institute ; New York, N.Y. : Independent Insurance Agents of America, c1986. v, 71 p. : ill. ; 28 cm. LC Card 87-401617 DDC 368.5/0068 19
1. Insurance, Liability - United States - Handbooks, manuals, etc. 2. Insurance, Liability - United States - Forms. I. International Risk Management Institute.
HG9990.3 .L5 1986

Liability insurance for government entities. Surveys on liability insurance for government entities. Oak Brook, Ill. (1200 Harger Rd., Suite 222, Oak Brook 60521) , c1986. vi, 66 p. ; LC Card 87-110891 DDC 368.5 19
HG8207 .S87 1986

Liability risk retention . Mooney, James E. (James Edward) Springfield, N.J. (262 Mountain Ave., P.O. Box 50, Springfield 07081) , c1987. i, 53 p. ; LC Card 87-90408 DDC 368.5/00973 19
HG9990.3 .M66 1987

Liaison Committee for Food Corps Programmes International. Women farmers in Africa . Syracuse, N.Y. , 1986. xvi, 212 p. : ISBN 0-8156-2358-5 (alk. paper) LC Card 85-27771 DDC 331.4/83/096 19
HD6073.A292 A358 1986 ***NYPL [JLE 86-2556]***

Li͡akh, L. V. (Lidii͡a Vasil'evna) Planovoe regulirovanie vozmeshchenii͡a orudiĭ truda v promyshlennosti / L.V. Li͡akh. Kiev : Nauk. dumka, 1983. 122, [1] p. : ill. ; 20 cm. At head of title: Akademii͡a nauk Ukrainskoĭ SSR. Institut ėkonomiki. Bibliography: p. 121-[123] LC Card 84-105177
1. Industrial equipment - Ukraine. 2. Replacement of industrial equipment. I. Title.
HD39.3 .L53 1983

Li͡aporov, Nikolaĭ Danilovich. Marshruty peredovogo opyta /. Moskva , 1985. 286 p., [8] p. of plates : LC Card 85-213253
HC340.L3 M235 1985

Liban. see **Lebanon.**

Libbey, Mary Beth. Chaney, Dale. Selling your house without a broker . Chicago , c1986. 98 p. : ISBN 0-8092-4833-6 (pbk.) : LC Card 86-24043 DDC 333.33/8 19
HD1379 .C48 1986

Libby, Ronald T. The politics of economic power in southern Africa / Ronald T. Libby. Princeton, N.J. : Princeton University Press, c1987. xxii, 361 p. : maps ; 23 cm. Bibliography: p. [329]-354. Includes index. ISBN 0-691-07723-1 (alk. paper) : LC Card 87-2406 DDC 337.68 19
1. Africa, Southern - Foreign economic relations - South Africa. 2. South Africa - Foreign economic relations - Africa, Southern. 3. Africa, Southern - Economic conditions. 4. Africa, Southern - Economic policy. 5. Africa, Southern - Politics and government. I. Title.
HF1613.3.Z4 S65 1987

Liber focorum Regni Neapolis. 1986. Cozzetto, Fausto. Mezzogiorno e demografia nel XV secolo /. Soveria M.lli, CZ , c1986. ix, 202 p. ; LC Card 86-213782
HB3600.N37 C69 1986

Liberal Industrial Inquiry (Great Britain) Britain's industrial future . New York , 1985. xxiv, 503 p. ; ISBN 0-8240-7605-2 (alk. paper) : LC Card 85-13042 DDC 338.941 19
HC256.3 .B728 1985 ***NYPL [JLD 86-3461]***

Liberal Party of Canada. Les Libéraux et le dialogue Nord-Sud . Bonn , c1982. 220 p. ; ISBN 3-920590-36-8 LC Card 84-204748
HC59.7 .L4177 1982

Liberal utilitarianism . Riley, Jonathan, 1955- Cambridge [Cambridgeshire] , New York , 1987. p. cm. ISBN 0-521-30692-2 LC Card 87-6598 DDC 302/.13 19
HB846.8 .R55 1987

LIBERALISM.
Dahrendorf, Ralf. Die Chancen der Krise . Stuttgart , c1983. 240 p. ; ISBN 3-421-06148-3 ***NYPL [JFD 87-2528]***

Israel Zipper, Ricardo. Democracia y liberalismo /. Santiago de Chile , 1984. 56 p. ; LC Card 85-197546
HB95 .I87 1984

Nicholson, Linda J. Gender and history . New York , 1986. x, 238 p. ; ISBN 0-231-06220-6 (alk. paper) LC Card 85-21281 DDC 323.3/4/01 19
HQ1206 .N7 1986 ***NYPL [JLE 86-1987]***

Noble, Charles, 1948- Liberalism at work . Philadelphia , 1986. x, 292 p. : ISBN 0-87722-421-8 (alk. paper) : LC Card 86-1766 DDC 353.0083/0289 19
HD7654 .N63 1986 ***NYPL [JLE 86-4426]***

Riley, Jonathan, 1955- Liberal utilitarianism . Cambridge [Cambridgeshire] , New York , 1987. p. cm. ISBN 0-521-30692-2 LC Card 87-6598 DDC 302/.13 19
HB846.8 .R55 1987

Soler, Sebastián. Temas antiliberales, marxistas y autoritarios /. Buenos Aires , 1977. 179 p. ; LC Card 80-469614
JC571 .S7173 ***NYPL [JLC 80-]***

Walker, Graham. The ethics of F.A. Hayek /. Lanham, MD , c1986. vii, 135 p. ; ISBN 0-8191-5250-1 (alk. paper) : LC Card 86-1515 DDC 171/.7 19
HB101.H39 W35 1986 ***NYPL [JFD 86-9138]***

Wohlfarth, Karl Anton. Leistung und Ethos . Paderborn , 1984. 266 p. ; ISBN 3-506-70223-8 LC Card 84-238158
HD60 .W64 1984

Zwass, Adam. Zwei Weltsysteme . Wien , c1985. 264 p. ; ISBN 3-203-50891-5 LC Card 85-240587 DDC 338.9 19
HB501 .Z93 1985 ***NYPL [JLD 87-226]***

Liberalism at work . Noble, Charles, 1948- Philadelphia , 1986. x, 292 p. : ISBN 0-87722-421-8 (alk. paper) : LC Card 86-1766 DDC 353.0083/0289 19
HD7654 .N63 1986 ***NYPL [JLE 86-4426]***

LIBERALISM - COLOMBIA.
López, Alejandro, 1876-1940. [Selections. 1983.] Obras selectas /. Bogotá, D.E. , 1983. xiii, 458 p. ; LC Card 86-233252
HC197 .L6172 1983

Toro Agudelo, Hernán. Hacia una reforma social urbana en Colombia . Bogotá, Colombia , 1986. 342 p. : ISBN 958-601-100-3 LC Card 87-107055
HD7325.A3 T67 1986

LIBERALISM - FRANCE.
Séguin, Philippe, 1943- Réussir l'alternance . Paris , c1985. 220 p. ; ISBN 2-221-04633-1 : LC Card 85-187945 DDC 944.083/8 19
JN2594.2 .S37 1985 ***NYPL [JLC 87-46]***

LIBERALISM - UNITED STATES.
Brick, Howard, 1953- Daniel Bell and the decline of intellectual radicalism . Madison, Wis. , 1986. 215-266. ISBN 0-299-10550-4 : LC Card 85-40757 DDC 300/.92/4 19
H59.B42 B75 1986 ***NYPL [JLE 86-3046]***

Falik, Marilyn. Ideology and abortion policy politics /. New York, N.Y. , 1983. 228 p. ; ISBN 0-03-062813-X LC Card 83-2402 DDC 363.4/6 19
HQ767.5.U5 F34 1983 ***NYPL [JLE 85-1581]***

Kozlova, K. B. Institut͡sionalizm v amerikanskoĭ politėkonomii . Moskva , 1987. 214, [2] p. ; LC Card 87-159642
HB99.5 .K69 1987

McCann, Michael W., 1952- Taking reform seriously . Ithaca , 1986. 345 p. ; ISBN 0-8014-1952-2 LC Card 86-47647 DDC 322.4/3/0973 19
JK1118 .M37 1986 ***NYPL [JLE 87-1009]***

Osiatyński, Wiktor, 1945- Współczesny konserwatyzm i liberalizm amerykański /. Warszawa , 1984. 552 p. ; ISBN 83-01-04929-4 (pbk.) : ***NYPL [*QO 86-3450]***

LIBERALISM - UNITED STATES - HISTORY.
Nelson, John R., 1952- Liberty and property . Baltimore , c1987. xv, 221 p. : ISBN 0-8018-3440-6 (alk. paper) LC Card 86-21373 DDC 338.973 19
HC105 .N45 1987

LIBERALISM - UNITED STATES - HISTORY - 20TH CENTURY.
Withers, William, 1905-1987. Politics and economic policy . New York, N.Y. , c1986. 240 p. : ISBN 0-8062-2722-2 : LC Card 86-201185 DDC 338.973 19
HC106 .W82 1986

Liberalismo, intervencionismo e o caso português : apontamentos de história das finaças [i.e. finanças] públicas. [Lisbon] : Abdulcadre, [1982] 44 p. ; 21 cm. Cover title. "O texto ... constitui uma síntese dos conhecimentos bebidos nas aulas plenárias da cadeira de finanças públicas ... em 1979, na Faculdade de Direito de Lisboa"--P. 1. "Tiragem: 100 exemplares"--Cover p. 4. Bibliography: p. 2. LC Card 86-132673
1. Finance, Public - Portugal. 2. Finance, Public. 3. Economic policy. I. Universidade de Lisboa. Faculdade de Direito.
HJ1252 .L52 1982

Liberalización financiera [microform] . Susano Lucero, Aurelio Reynaldo. Lima , c1982. [40] p. : LC Card 84-227503 DDC 332.1/0985 19
HG2944 .S93 1982 ***NYPL [*ZT-1745 no.6]***

Les Libéraux et le dialogue Nord-Sud : perspectives sur le dialogue Nord-Sud, selon le point de vue libéral : compte-rendu du colloque internationale [sic] d'Ottawa 1979 / organisé par la Fondation Friedrich Naumann et le Parti libéral du Canada. Bonn : La Fondation, c1982. 220 p. ; 21 cm. ("Entwicklungspolitische Texte") "Octobre 1979"--P. 5. CONTENTS. - 1e ptie. Résultats du dialogue Nord-Sud selon le point de vue libéral -- 2e ptie. Développement social, économique et culturel dans le Tiers Monde -- 3e ptie. Conflit et coopération entre le Nord et le Sud -- 4e ptie. Droits de l'homme et droits civiques -- 5e ptie. Les perspectives pour les années 1980. ISBN 3-920590-36-8 LC Card 84-204748
1. Developing countries - Economic conditions - Congresses. 2. Developing countries - Social conditions - Congresses. 3. Political rights - Developing countries - Congresses. 4. Civil rights - Developing countries - Congresses. 5. International economic relations - Congresses. I. Friedrich Naumann Stiftung. II. Liberal Party of Canada. III. Series.
HC59.7 .L4177 1982

LIBEREC (CZECHOSLOVAKIA) - INDUSTRIES - HISTORY.
Album der Industrie des Reichenberger Handelskammer-Bezirks. [Praha] , 1981. 2 v. in 1 : LC Card 84-190839
HC270.292.L52 A42 1981

Liberia /. Cockrill, Philip. Newbury, Berkshire, England [198-?] 15 v. in 2 : LC Card 86-217641
HE6185.L49 C63 1980z

LIBERIA - ECONOMIC CONDITIONS - 1980-
Economic recovery program, 1986/87-1988/89. Monrovia, Liberia [1986] 76, a-n p. ; LC Card 87-104460 DDC 338.9666/2 19
HC1075 .E25 1986

LIBERIA - ECONOMIC POLICY.
Economic recovery program, 1986/87-1988/89. Monrovia, Liberia [1986] 76, a-n p. ; LC Card 87-104460 DDC 338.9666/2 19
HC1075 .E25 1986

Liberia. Ministry of Planning and Economic Affairs. Economic recovery program, 1986/87-1988/89. Monrovia, Liberia [1986] 76, a-n p. ; LC Card 87-104460 DDC 338.9666/2 19
HC1075 .E25 1986

Liberia. Planning and Economic Affairs, Ministry of. see **Liberia. Ministry of Planning and Economic Affairs.**

LIBERTINAGE. see **LIBERTINISM.**

LIBERTINISM.
Velarde Fuertes, Juan. El libertino y el nacimiento del capitalismo /. Madrid , c1981. 158 p. ; ISBN 84-368-0178-4 LC Card 82-101990
HB501 .V39 1981

El libertino y el nacimiento del capitalismo /. Velarde Fuertes, Juan. Madrid , c1981. 158 p. ; ISBN 84-368-0178-4 LC Card 82-101990
HB501 .V39 1981

LIBERTY - ADDRESSES, ESSAYS, LECTURES.
Karpiński, Wojciech. Szkice o wolności /. Chicago, Ill. (2886 Milwaukee Ave., Chicago, Ill. 60618) , 1980. 95 p. ; LC Card 81-201974
JC585 .K32 1980 *NYPL [*QR 86-4376]*

Tarkunde, V. M. For freedom /. New Delhi , 1984. xii, 199 p. ; LC Card 84-902126 DDC 144 19
B821 .T285 1984 *NYPL [JFD 87-1740]*

Liberty and property . Nelson, John R., 1952- Baltimore , c1987. xv, 221 p. : ISBN 0-8018-3440-6 (alk. paper) LC Card 86-21373 DDC 338.973 19
HC105 .N45 1987

LIBERTY - CONGRESSES.
Freedom and control in a democratic society /. New York , c1976. 107 p. ;
NYPL [JLD 80-3590]

Friedman, Milton, 1912- Politics and tyranny . San Francisco, Calif. , c1984. 68 p. ; ISBN 0-936488-00-X (pbk.) : LC Card 84-61364 DDC 330 19
HB98.3 .F75 1984 *NYPL [JLE 87-857]*

Order, freedom, and the polity . Lanham, MD [Bryn Mawr, Pa.] , c1986. x, 184 p. ; ISBN 0-8191-5155-6 (alk. paper) : LC Card 85-26438 DDC 323.44 19
JC571 .O77 1986 *NYPL [JLE 86-3182]*

LIBERTY OF EMPLOYMENT. see **FREE CHOICE OF EMPLOYMENT.**

LIBERTY OF INFORMATION. see **FREEDOM OF INFORMATION.**

LIBERTY OF OCCUPATION. see **FREE CHOICE OF EMPLOYMENT.**

Librairie du Liban. Dictionaries Dept. A Dictionary of economics & commerce . Beirut , 1983. 383 p. ; LC Card 83-961782 DDC 330/.03/21 19
HB61 .D4896 1983 *NYPL [*OEO 87-1397]*

LIBRARIES, BUSINESS. see **BUSINESS LIBRARIES.**

LIBRARIES - REFERENCE BOOKS. see **REFERENCE BOOKS.**

LIBRARY EMPLOYEES - NETHERLANDS.
Boon, Irene. Mannen in een vrouwenberoep . Den Haag , 1984. 139 p. : ISBN 90-6252-426-5 : LC Card 84-243593
Z682.4.W65 B66 1984 *NYPL [JLG 87-4]*

Library of Congress. Congressional Research Service.
Agriculture in the GATT . Washington , 1986. v, 47 p. ; LC Card 86-603393 DDC 382/.41/0973 19
HD9006 .A77 1986

The Competitiveness of American metal mining and processing . Washington , 1986. x, 186 p. ; LC Card 86-603391 DDC 338.2/74/0973 19
HD9506.U62 C63 1986

Corporate debt . Washington , 1986. v, 31 p. : LC Card 86-603382 DDC 338.7/4/0973 19
HG4028.D3 C67 1986

Corporate mergers and high yield (junk) bonds . Washington , 1986. vi, 57 p. ; LC Card 87-601339 DDC 332.63/22 19
HD2746.5 .C67 1986

Japanese import barriers to U. S. agricultural exports and the Common agricultural policy of the European Community and implications for U. S. agricultural trade . Washington , 1986. vii, 65 p. : LC Card 87-601384 DDC 382/.5/0952 19
HF1601 .J363 1986

Poland's renewal and U. S. options . Washington , 1987. xv, 41 p. : LC Card 87-601374 DDC 337.438073 19
HC340.3 .P646 1987

Library of Congress. Foreign Affairs and National Defense Division.
Feeding the world's population . Washington , 1984. xii, 779 p. : LC Card 86-602524 DDC 363.8 19
HD9000.5 .F35 1986

Foreign indebtedness and basic human needs in four African countries . Washington , 1986. ii, 54 p. : LC Card 86-603396 DDC 336.3/435/0967
HC800 .F67 1986

Trends in foreign aid, 1977-86 . Washington , 1986. vii, 21 p. : LC Card 87-601358 DDC 338.91/73 19
HC60 .T69 1986

El Libro blanco de la promoción-construcción. [Barcelona] : APCE, 1985. 141 p. : ill. ; 21 cm. LC Card 86-188032
1. Housing - Spain. 2. Housing - Spain - Catalonia. 3. Construction industry - Spain - Catalonia. 4. Construction industry - Spain. I. Asociación de Promotores Constructores de Edificios de Barcelona (Spain).
HD7351.A3 L53 1985

Libro de la razón general de hacienda nacional . Gutiérrez y Ulloa, Antonio. Guadalajara, Jalisco, México , 1983. 222 p. ; ISBN 968-8320-48-X LC Card 87-401751 DDC 336.72/35 19
HJ805.J3 G87 1983

Libros de bolsillo (Valencia, Spain) .
(5) Reig Martínez, Ernest. La política agraria de la Comunidad Económica Europea . [Valencia] [1986?] 129 p. ; ISBN 84-00-06370-8 LC Card 87-125600
HD1920.5.Z8 R45 1986

Libura, Urszula. Konsumpcja a wykorzystanie możliwości produkcyjnej w gospodarce socjalistycznej / Urszula Libura. Wyd. 1. Warszawa : Państwowe Wydawn. Nauk., 1979. 242 p. ; 20 cm. Bibliography: p. 234-[237] ISBN 83-01-00103-8 LC Card 81-192720
1. Consumption (Economics) - Communist countries. I. Title.
HC710.C6 L53 1979

LIBYA - ECONOMIC CONDITIONS.
Kukushkin, Vladimir I͡Ur′evich. Neft′ i razvitie, Livii͡a, Alzhir /. Moskva , 1985. 227 p. ; LC Card 85-180876
HD9577.L52 K85 1985
*NYPL [*QIP 87-3410]*

Shamleh, Omar. Erdölinduzierte sozioökonomische Entwicklung in den OAPEC-Staaten . Frankfurt am Main , New York , c1986. 410 p. ; ISBN 3-8204-9097-3 LC Card 86-157642
HC825 .S55 1986

LIBYA - ECONOMIC POLICY.
Mattes, Hanspeter. Aspekte der libyischen Ausseninvestitionspolitik, 1972-1985 /. Hamburg , c1985. iv, 169 p. : ISBN 3-89173-001-2 LC Card 86-173976
HG4538 .M376 1985

Shamleh, Omar. Erdölinduzierte sozioökonomische Entwicklung in den OAPEC-Staaten . Frankfurt am Main , New York , c1986. 410 p. ; ISBN 3-8204-9097-3 LC Card 86-157642
HC825 .S55 1986

LIBYA - FOREIGN ECONOMIC RELATIONS - MALTA.
Mattes, Hanspeter. Aspekte der libyischen Ausseninvestitionspolitik, 1972-1985 /. Hamburg , c1985. iv, 169 p. : ISBN 3-89173-001-2 LC Card 86-173976
HG4538 .M376 1985

LIBYA - SOCIAL CONDITIONS.
Shamleh, Omar. Erdölinduzierte sozioökonomische Entwicklung in den OAPEC-Staaten . Frankfurt am Main , New York , c1986. 410 p. ; ISBN 3-8204-9097-3 LC Card 86-157642
HC825 .S55 1986

LICENSE AGREEMENTS - ECONOMIC ASPECTS - GREECE.
Kazēs, D. A. (Dēmētrēs A.) [Licensing kai viomēchanikē anaptyxē. English.] Licensing and industrial development . Athens , 1986. 208 p. : LC Card 87-170691 DDC 338.09495 19
HF1429 .K3813 1986

LICENSE AGREEMENTS - GREECE.
Kazēs, D. A. (Dēmētrēs A.) [Licensing kai viomēchanikē anaptyxē. English.] Licensing and industrial development . Athens , 1986. 208 p. : LC Card 87-170691 DDC 338.09495 19
HF1429 .K3813 1986

LICENSE AGREEMENTS - HUNGARY.
Kardos, Péter. Külföldi licencek a magyar gazdaságban /. Budapest , 1984. 204, [1] p. : ISBN 963-221-396-3 : LC Card 85-157267
HF1429 .K37 1984

LICENSE SYSTEM - NEW ZEALAND.
New Zealand. Working Party on Liquor. The sale of liquor in New Zealand . [Wellington, N.Z. , 1986] 212, [1] p. : LC Card 87-147518 DDC 338.4/76631/09931 19
HD9390.N452 N49 1986

LICENSED BEVERAGE INDUSTRY. see **DISTILLING INDUSTRIES.**

Licensed occupations in Louisiana / Louisiana State Occupational Information Coordinating Committee. [Rev.]. [Baton Rouge, La.] (P.O. Box 94094, Baton Rouge 70804-9094) : LOICC, [1986] ix, 85 p. ; 28 cm. Cover title. LC Card 87-620751 DDC 331.7/02/09763 19
1. Louisiana - Occupations - Licenses. I. Louisiana State Occupational Information Coordinating Committee.
HD3630.U7 L529 1986

LICENSES, EXPORT. see **EXPORT CONTROLS.**

LICENSES - FRANCE.
Taxe professionelle . [Paris] [1983] v, 80, [23] p. ; LC Card 85-129298
HJ5412 .T39 1983

LICENSES - LOUISIANA - HANDBOOKS, MANUALS, ETC.
Reference guide of permits and licenses. Baton Rouge, La. (P.O. Box 94185, Baton Rouge 71808-9185) [1986?] ix, 222 p. ; LC Card 86-621904 DDC 353.97630082/4046 19
HD3630.U7 R44 1986

LICENSES - MEXICO - NUEVO LEÓN (STATE)
Nuevo León (Mexico : State). Archivo General del Estado. Permisos y concesiones, 1890-1912 /. [Monterrey, Mexico] [1981] 43 leaves ; LC Card 81-216459
HD3616.M44 N866 1981

LICENSES - TEXAS.
Mercer, Kent. Directory of licensed occupations and apprenticeship programs in Texas. [Austin, Tex.] [1985] iv, 102 p. ; LC Card 86-622006 DDC 331.7/02/09764 19
HF5382.5.U6 T45 1985

LICENSING AGREEMENTS. see **LICENSE AGREEMENTS.**

Licensing and industrial development . Kazēs, D. A. (Dēmētrēs A.) [Licensing kai viomēchanikē anaptyxē. English.] Athens , 1986. 208 p. : LC Card 87-170691 DDC 338.09495 19
HF1429 .K3813 1986

Lichev, Licho.
Bliznakov, Iordan Petrov. Sot͡sialisticheskoto sŭrevnovanie v uslovii͡ata na intenzifikat͡sii͡ata na proizvodstvoto /. Sofii͡a , 1983. 101 p. : LC Card 85-140845
HC403.Z9 S613 1983

Narŭchnik na profsŭi͡uznii͡a aktivist . [[Sofia?] , 1985. 264 p. ; LC Card 85-216969
HC403.Z9 L366 1985

Narŭchnik na profsŭi͡uznii͡a aktivist po proizvodstveno-masovata rabota /. Sofii͡a , 1986. 200 p. ; LC Card 86-197739
HC403.Z9 S658 1986

Lichnoe potreblenie v uslovii͡akh ėkonomicheskoĭ integrat͡sii stran--chlenov SĖV /. Bondarenko, E. L. (Evgenii͡a Lavrent′eva) Moskva , 1984. 110 p. ; LC Card 84-222687
HC244.Z9 C613 1984

Lichnoe potreblenie v uslovii͡akh razvitogo sot͡sializma /. Makhmutov, A. Kh. (Anas Khusainovich) Kazan′ , 1980. 249 p. ; LC Card

82-162621
HC340.C6 M29 1980

Licht, Walter, 1946- Scranton, Philip. Work sights . Philadelphia , 1986. 279 p. : ISBN 0-87722-341-6 : LC Card 85-26132 DDC 305.9/009748/11 19
HC108.P5 S37 1986 ***NYPL [JLF 86-1959]***

Lichtarski, Jan. Kryteria i metody oceny efektywności przedsięwzięć organizatorskich w przedsiębiorstwie / Jan Lichtarski. [Wrocław] : Wydawn. Uczelniane Akademii Ekonomicznej we Wrocławiu, 1982. 197 p. : ill. ; 24 cm. (Prace naukowe Akademii Ekonomicznej im. Oskara Langego we Wrocławiu . nr. 216. nr. 6) Summary in English and Russian. Bibliography: p. [184]-192. LC Card 83-153426
1. Organizational change. 2. Organizational effectiveness. I. Series: Prace naukowe Akademii Ekonomicznej imienia Oskara Langego we Wrocławiu , nr. 216. II. Title.
HB9 .B7522 nr. 216 HD58.9

Lichtenstein, Grace. Bloch, H. I. Sonny. Inside real estate . New York , c1987. xx, 375 p. ; ISBN 1-555-84030-2 LC Card 86-28303 DDC 333.33/8 19
HD1379 .B515 1987

Lichtenstein, Heinz, 1904- The dilemma of human identity / Heinz Lichtenstein. New York : J. Aronson : Distributed by Scribner Bk. Companies, c1983. xiv, 399 p. ; 24 cm. Includes index. Bibliography: p. [369]-390. ISBN 0-87668-677-3 : LC Card 84-45086 DDC 155.2 19
1. Identity (Psychology). 2. Psychoanalysis. 3. Existential psychology. I. Title.
BF697 .L52 1983 ***NYPL [JFE 86-2218]***

Lichtensztejn, Samuel, 1934- Fondo Monetario Internacional y Banco Mundial : estrategias y políticas del poder financiero / Samuel Lichtensztejn, Monica Baer.1a. ed. San José, Costa Rica : Editorial Nueva Sociedad ; Buenos Aires, Argentina : Centro de Estudios Transnacionales, 1986. 215 p. : ill. ; 20 cm. Includes bibliographical references. LC Card 86-233561
1. International Monetary Fund. 2. World Bank. I. Baer, Mônica. II. Centro de Economía Transnacional. III. Title.
HG3881.5.I58 L527 1986

Lições de economia II . Castro, Armando. Lisboa , c1986. 223 p. ; LC Card 87-106195 DDC 330 19
HB178.5 .C37 1986

Liebenau, Jonathan.
The Challenge of new technology . Aldershot, Hants, England , Brookfield, Vt., U. S.A. , c1988. x, 155 p. : ISBN 0-566-05147-8 : LC Card 87-8592 DDC 338/.06 19
HC260.T4 C46 1988

Medical science and medical industry : the formation of the American pharmaceutical industry / Jonathan Liebenau. Baltimore : Johns Hopkins University Press, 1987. ix, 207 p. ; 23 cm. Bibliography: p. 183-199. Includes indexes. ISBN 0-8018-3356-6 LC Card 86-27346 DDC 338.4/76151/0973 19
1. Pharmaceutical industry - United States - History. 2. Pharmaceutical policy - United States - History. 3. Medical innovations - United States - History. I. Title.
HD9666.5 .L54 1987

Lieber besser statt mehr? . Krack, Jürgen. Köln , c1985. 306, [2] p. : ISBN 3-7663-0569-7 LC Card 85-125869
HD5029 .K72 1985

Lieberman, Anne M. Mastering money : how to create your own financial plan / Anne M. Lieberman, J. Edson Clinton. Chicago, Ill. : Longman Financial Services Pub. ; Naperville, IL : Distributed by Longman Trade, c1987. xi, 267 p. : ill. ; 28 cm. Includes index. ISBN 0-88462-589-3 (pbk.) : LC Card 87-3655 DDC 332.024 19
1. Finance, Personal. 2. Investments. I. Clinton, James Edson. II. Title.
HG179 .L486 1987

Lieberman, Annette. Unbalanced accounts : why women are still afraid of money / by Annette Lieberman & Vicki Lindner.1st ed. New York : Atlantic Monthly Press, c1987. xx, 281 p. ; 24 cm. Bibliography: p. [277]-281. ISBN 0-87113-141-2 LC Card 86-28845 DDC 332.4/01/9 19
1. Women - Finance, Personal. 2. Money - Psychological aspects. 3. Women - Attitudes. I. Lindner, Vicki, 1944-. II. Title.
HG179 .L49 1987

Lieberman, Ernest D. Unfit to manage! : how mis-management endangers America and what working people can do about it / Ernest D. Lieberman. New York : McGraw-Hill, c1988. xvii, 301 p. ; 24 cm. Includes index. ISBN 0-07-037815-0 : LC Card 87-20891 DDC 658/.00973 19
1. Industrial management - United States. I. Title.
HD70.U5 L54 1988

Lieberman, Frank. Curtis, Jane, 1918- Frederick Billings, Vermonter, pioneer lawyer, business man, conservationist . Woodstock, VT , c1986. 135 p. : ISBN 0-930985-04-4 (pbk.) : LC Card 86-28103 DDC 385/.092/4 B 19
HE2754.B5 C87 1986

Lieberman, Sima, 1927- The economic and political roots of the new protectionism / Sima Lieberman. Totowa, N.J. : Rowman & Littlefield, 1987. p. cm. Bibliography: p. Includes index. ISBN 0-8476-7595-5 LC Card 87-23329 DDC 382.7/3/09048 19
1. International economic relations - History - 20th century. 2. Free trade and protection - Protection - History - 20th century. 3. Economic history - 20th century. 4. World politics - 20th century. I. Title.
HF1411 .L533 1987

Liebert, Robert, 1930- The Psychology of men . New York , c1986. x, 310 p. ; ISBN 0-465-06718-2 LC Card 85-48022 DDC 155.3/32 19
BF692.5 .P78 1986 ***NYPL [JFE 86-2975]***

Lieberthal, Kenneth. Bureaucratic politics and Chinese energy development / by Kenneth Lieberthal and Michel Oksenberg. [Washington, D.C.] : U. S. Department of Commerce, International Trade Administration : For sale by the Superintendent of Documents, U. S. G.P.O., [1986] xii, 405 p. ; 28 cm. "Prepared for the Department of Commerce, contract number 50-SATA-4-16230." "August 1986." Bibliography: p. 395-405. LC Card 86-602422 DDC 333.79/0951 19
1. Energy policy - China. 2. Energy development - China. 3. Energy industries - China. 4. Bureaucracy - China. 5. China - Politics and government - 1976-. I. Oksenberg, Michel, 1938-. II. United States. Dept. of Commerce. III. Title.
HD9502.C62 L54 1986

Liebich, Burkhardt, 1957- Investitionsrechnung : von exakten Methoden zu verkürzten Verfahren / Burkhardt Liebich. Frankfurt am Main ; New York : P. Lang, c1986. viii, 170 p. ; 21 cm. (Europäische Hochschulschriften. Reihe V, Volks- und Betriebswirtschaft, 0531-7339 . Bd. 759 = vol. 759 = vol. 759) Originally presented as the author's thesis (doctoral)--Johann Wolfgang Goethe-Universität Frankfurt, 1986. Bibliography: p. 164-170. ISBN 3-8204-9826-5 LC Card 87-109973
1. Investment analysis. 2. Investments - Accounting. I. Series: Europäische Hochschulschriften. Reihe V, Volks- und Betriebswirtschaft , Bd. 759. II. Title.
HG4529 .L54 1986

Liebl, Anton J. Offizieller Jubiläumsband der Deutschen Bundesbahn . München , 1985. 239 p. : ISBN 3-923967-03-9 LC Card 86-168073
HE3078 .O44 1985b

Liebst, Torben. By i forvandling . Copenhagen , 1984. 93 p. : ISBN 87-87589-42-7 LC Card 87-155193
HE4859.C68 B92 1984

Liechtenstein.
Die Briefmarkenausgabe vom 12. März 1984 =. Vaduz [1984?] 41 p. : LC Card 84-248309
HE6184.F57 B75 1984

Liechtenstein. Amt für Volkswirtschaft.
Statistische Information : Sonderausgabe der Zivilstandsstatistik von 1980-1984 : Sterbetafel, durchschnittliche Lebenserwartung. Vaduz, Fürstentum Liechtenstein : Amt für Volkswirtschaft, [1985] 18 leaves ; 30 cm. Cover title. LC Card 85-228548
1. Liechtenstein - Population - Statistics. I. Title. II. Title: Zivilstandsstatistik von 1980-1984.
HB3592.9.A3 L54 1985

Liechtenstein. Amt für Briefmarkengestaltung.
Die Briefmarkenausgabe vom 12. März 1984 =. Vaduz [1984?] 41 p. : LC Card 84-248309
HE6184.F57 B75 1984

LIECHTENSTEIN - POPULATION - STATISTICS.
Liechtenstein. Amt für Volkswirtschaft. Statistische Information . Vaduz, Fürstentum Liechtenstein [1985] 18 leaves ; LC Card 85-228548
HB3592.9.A3 L54 1985

Liechtenstein. Volkswirtschaft, Amt für. see **Liechtenstein. Amt für Volkswirtschaft.**

Liedman, Sven-Eric, 1939- Den synliga handen : Anders Berch och ekonomiämnena vid 1700-talets svenska universitet / Sven-Eric Liedman. [Stockholm] : Arbetarkultur, [1986] 268 p. ; 21 cm. Summary in English. Bibliography: p. 251-264. Includes index. ISBN 91-7014-210-6 : LC Card 86-215138
1. Berch, Anders, 1711-1774. 2. Economists - Sweden - Biography. 3. Economics - Sweden - History - 18th century. I. Title.
HB116.5.B47 L54 1986

Liegenschaftenbuchhaltung / CRB. Zürich : Kommissionsverlag, SKV Verlag des Schweizerischen Kaufmännischen Vereins, c1977. 128 p. : ill. ; 31 cm. Bibliography: p. 126-127. Includes index. ISBN 3-85567-073-1 LC Card 85-141656
1. Real estate business - Accounting. I. Schweizerische Zentralstelle für Baurationalisierung.
HF5686.R3 L54 1977

Lien entre capital fictif, markup flexible et inflation /. Loranger, Jean Guy, 1938- Montréal [1985] 30 p. ; LC Card 85-177724 DDC 332.4/1 19
HB3 .C3 vol. 8517 HG229

Lienker, Heinrich. Ziefuss, Horst. Jugendliche in der gewerblich-technischen Ausbildung in Industrie und Handwerk . Kiel , c1986. 352 p. : ISBN 3-89088-011-8 LC Card 87-407898 DDC 331.3/42592/0943 19
HD5715.5.G4 Z54 1986

Lientz, Bennet P. Data communications for business / Bennet P. Lientz, Kathryn P. Rea. 1st ed. St. Louis : Times Mirror/Mosby College Pub., 1987. xx, 326 p. : ill. (some col.), map ; 25 cm. (Times Mirror/Mosby data processing and information systems series) Bibliography: p. 300-302. Includes index. ISBN 0-8016-3013-4 LC Card 86-23012 DDC 650/.028/546 19
1. Business - Data processing. 2. Data transmission systems. 3. Computer networks. I. Rea, Kathryn P. II. Title. III. Series.
HF5548.2 .L535 1987

Liermann, F. (Felix) Laux, Helmut. Grundfragen der Erfolgskontrolle /. Berlin , New York , c1986. x, 161 p. : ISBN 0-387-17037-5 LC Card 86-232406
HD30.23 .L39 1986

Lierop, Wal F. J. van.
Economic-ecological modeling /. Amsterdam ; New York : x, 329 p. : ISBN 0-444-70298-9 LC Card 87-20048 DDC 333.7/0724 19
HC79.E5 E267 1987

Spatial interaction modelling and residential choice analysis / Wal van Lierop. Aldershot, Hants, England ; Brookfield, Vt., USA : Gower, c1986. xii, 286 p. : ill., map ; 23 cm. Includes indexes. Bibliography: p. 259-278. ISBN 0-566-05036-6
1. Residential mobility - Mathematical models. 2. Spatial analysis (Statistics). I. Title.
NYPL [JLD 87-695]

Lietuva. see **Lithuania.**

Lietuvos TSR aukštųjų mokyklų mokslo darbai. Statybos ekonomika ir organizavimas.
Kompleksinis subalansuotas statybos planavimas /. Vilnius , 1983. 115 p. : LC Card 83-187666
HD9715.S72 K66 1983

Lietuvos TSR Mokslų akademija. Matematikos ir kibernetikos institutas.
Pervichnoe opisanie signalov rechi . Vil'nius , 1980. 67 p. : LC Card 82-107723
HD38 .S715 vyp. 42 TK7882.S65

Razrabotka i issledovanie algoritmov dinamicheskoĭ klassifikatsii protsessov . Vil'nius , 1979. 93 p. : LC Card 82-150323
HD38 .S715 vyp. 37 T57.83

Sistema raspoznavaniia ritmogramm serdtsa . Vil'nius , 1980. 55 p. : LC Card 81-194159
HD38 .S715 vyp. 49 QP112.5.C3

Lietuvos TSR žemės ūkio tvarkymo sistema /

[sudarytojas V. Štuikys]. Vilnius : "Mokslas", 1985. 453 p. ; 23 cm. Title from colophon: Sistema vedeniia sel'skogo khoziaistva v Litovskoĭ SSR. "TSKP XXVII suvažiavimui." Includes summary in Russian. Includes bibliographies. LC Card 86-215158
1. Agriculture - Economic aspects - Lithuania. 2. Agricultural industries - Lithuania. I. Štuikys, V. (Vytautas). II. Title: Sistema vedeniia sel'skogo khoziaistva v Litovskoĭ SSR.
HD1995.L5 L535 1985

Life & labor. Life and labor . Albany , c1986. x, 343 p. ; ISBN 0-88706-173-7 LC Card 86-14362 DDC 305.5/62/0973 19
HD8066 .L54 1986 **NYPL [JLE 86-4350]**

Life after college . Lento-McGovern, Diane, 1956- White Hall, Va. , c1987. 179 p. ; ISBN 0-932620-77-9 (pbk.) : LC Card 87-6412 DDC 331.7/02 19
HF5381 .L354 1987

Life & health insurance . Lyons, Paula. Chicago , c1988. xvi, 351 p. : ISBN 0-88462-707-1 (pbk.) LC Card 87-18506 DDC 368.3/00973 19
HG8951 .L98 1988

Life and health insurance. Lyons, Paula. Life & health insurance . Chicago , c1988. xvi, 351 p. : ISBN 0-88462-707-1 (pbk.) LC Card 87-18506 DDC 368.3/00973 19
HG8951 .L98 1988

Life and labor : dimensions of American working-class history / edited by Charles Stephenson and Robert Asher. Albany : State University of New York Press, c1986. x, 343 p. ; 24 cm. (American labor history series) Cover title: Life & labor. Includes index. Bibliography: p. 283-333. ISBN 0-88706-173-7 LC Card 86-14362 DDC 305.5/62/0973 19
1. Labor and laboring classes - United States - History. 2. Industrial sociology - United States - History. 3. Trade-unions - United States - History. I. Stephenson, Charles. II. Asher, Robert. III. Title: Life & labor.
HD8066 .L54 1986 **NYPL [JLE 86-4350]**

The life and legend of Jay Gould /. Klein, Maury, 1939- Baltimore , c1986. xvi, 595 p., [24] p. of plates : ISBN 0-8018-2880-5 (alk. paper) LC Card 85-24107 DDC 332/.092/4 B 19
HC102.5.G68 K55 1986
NYPL [JFE 86-2364]

LIFE CHANGE EVENTS.
Women in health & illness . Philadelphia , 1986. x, 261 p. : ISBN 0-7216-2086-8 LC Card 86-6576 DDC 155.6/33 19
RC451.4.W6 W656 1986
NYPL [JLF 86-1463]

LIFE, ECONOMIC. see ECONOMIC LIFE (OF ECONOMIC GOODS)

LIFE EXPECTANCY - HUNGARY - MATHEMATICAL MODELS.
Pollard, J. H. Mortality, expectation of life, and the Hungarian experience /. [North Ryde, N.S.W.] [1986] 59 p. ; ISBN 0-85837-578-8 (pbk.) LC Card 87-110257 DDC 304.6/4/09439 19
HB1422.5.A3 P65 1986

LIFE EXPECTANCY - INDIA - STATISTICS.
SRS based abridged life tables, 1976-80. New Delhi , 1986. v, 37 p. : LC Card 87-901200
HB1470 .S77 1986

Life insurance. Black, Kenneth. Englewood Cliffs, N.J. , c1987. xiii, 608 p. : ISBN 0-13-535881-7 LC Card 86-25375 DDC 368.3/2 19
HG8771 .B55 1987

Life insurance . Brownlie, William D. Cincinnati, Ohio , 1983. xii, 201 p. : ISBN 0-87218-033-6 (pbk.) LC Card 83-61584 DDC 368.3/2015 19
HG8853 .B87 1983
NYPL [*R-Econ. 86-3488]

LIFE INSURANCE. see INSURANCE, LIFE.

Life insurance for Canadians . Rogers, James E., 1945- Vancouver, B.C. [1980] 84 p. : ISBN 0-88908-073-9 (pbk.) LC Card 81-131363
HG8773 .R63 1980

Life Office Management Association. Life Management Institute. Zucconi, Paul J. Accounting in life and health insurance companies /. Atlanta, Ga. , c1987. xiv, 365 p. : ISBN 0-915322-85-4 LC Card 86-82715 DDC 657/.836 19
HG8848 .Z84 1987

LIFE SCIENCES - STATISTICAL METHODS.
Alfred, Braxton M. Elements of statistics for the life and social sciences /. New York , c1987. xiii, 190 p. : ISBN 0-387-96500-9 : LC Card 87-4964 DDC 300/.1/5195 19
HA29 .A53 1987

Life solvency monitor. Hartford, Conn. (41 Lewis St., Hartford 06103) : Conning, 1985. 201 p. : ill. ; 28 cm. LC Card 86-215848 DDC 368.3/2/006 19
1. Insurance, Life - United States - Statistics. 2. Insurance companies - United States - Statistics. I. Conning & Company.
HG8955 .L55 1985

Life solvency monitor. Hartford, Conn. (101 Pearl St., Hartford 06103) : Conning, 1986. 227 p. : ill. ; 28 cm. "June, 1986"--Cover. LC Card 86-209963 DDC 368.3/2/006 19
1. Insurance, Life - United States - Statistics. 2. Insurance companies - United States - Statistics. I. Conning & Company.
HG8955 .L55 1986

LIFE STYLE.
Earl, Peter E. Lifestyle economics . Brighton, Sussex , 1986. xiii, 314 p. : ISBN 0-7450-0083-5
NYPL [JLD 86-3424]

Lifecareer . Miller-Tiedeman, Anna, 1934- Vista, CA , c1988. v, 65 p. ; ISBN 0-9613436-3-X (pbk.) LC Card 87-17298 DDC 331.7/02 19
HF5381 .M496 1988

LIFELONG EDUCATION. see CONTINUING EDUCATION.

Lifestyle economics . Earl, Peter E. Brighton, Sussex , 1986. xiii, 314 p. : ISBN 0-7450-0083-5
NYPL [JLD 86-3424]

The lifetime book of money management /. Weinstein, Grace W. New York , c1987. xv, 621 p. : ISBN 0-452-25893-6 (pbk.) LC Card 86-28644 DDC 332.024 19
HG179 .W439 1987

Lifetree Software Inc. Words & Figures . Monterey, CA (411 Pacific St., Monterey 93940) , c1986. 1 v. (various pagings) : LC Card 87-111370 DDC 005.36/9 19
HF5548.4.W66 W67 1986

Liga dwudziestu i arabska nafta /. Rudnicki, Bohdan. Warszawa , 1979. 469, [3] p. : LC Card 81-109444
HD9578.A55 R83 1979

Light, Donald H. Adding value to product through service / by Donald H. Light. Menlo Park, CA (333 Ravenswood Ave., Menlo Park 94025) : SRI International, Business Intelligence Program, c1986. 21 leaves : ill. ; 28 cm. (Datalog file . no. 86-1103) LC Card 87-149955 DDC 658.8/12 19
1. Customer service. I. Title. II. Series.
HF5415.5 .L54 1986

LIGHT FISHING.
Paiva, Francisco Ismar Martins. Projeto Pesca Industrial à Vela. [Natal, Brazil] [1982 or 1983] 91 p. : LC Card 85-102872
HD9464.B73 R487 1982

Light, John J. Realistic economics / by John J. Light. Indianapolis, IN (P.O. Box 1606, Indianapolis 46206) : B.I. Publishers, c1984. 111 p. ; 23 cm. Includes bibliographical references. ISBN 0-933021-00-3 : LC Card 84-249506 DDC 331.12/0973 19
1. Labor supply - United States - Effect of technological innovations on. 2. Robots, Industrial. 3. United States - Full employment policies. I. Title.
HD5724 .L4236 1984 **NYPL [JLE 86-4650]**

Lighthouse Publishing. Benjamin, Louis. The complete book of Excel macros /. Berkeley, Calif. , c1986. xviii, 123 p. : ISBN 0-07-881214-3 (pbk.) LC Card 86-106041 DDC 650/.028/55369 19
HF5548.4.E93 B46 1986
NYPL [JSE 87-239]

Les lignes Latécoère . Danel, Raymond. Toulouse , c1986. 208 p., [16] p. of plates : ISBN 2-7089-8611-2 : LC Card 87-165510
HE9848.C66 D36 1986 vol. 1

LIGNITE INDUSTRY - GERMANY (WEST) - NORTH RHINE-WESTPHALIA - HISTORY.
Kleinebeckel, Arno. Unternehmen Braunkohle . Köln , 1986. 287 p. : ISBN 3-7743-0225-1 LC Card 86-193426
HD9559.L6 G36 1986

LIGNITE INDUSTRY - NORTH DAKOTA.
Coon, Randal C. North Dakota lignite industry's contribution to the state economy /. Fargo, N.D. [1986] v, 40 p. : LC Card 86-623006 DDC 338.2/722/09784 19
HD9559.L6 U5525 1986

Like a family : the making of a Southern cotton mill world / by Jacquelyn Dowd Hall ... [et al.]. Chapel Hill : University of North Carolina Press, c1987. xxiii, 468 p. : ill., maps ; 24 cm. (The Fred W. Morrison series in Southern studies) Bibliography: p. [415]-444. Includes index. ISBN 0-8078-1754-6 (alk. paper) LC Card 87-40135 DDC 305/.9677 19
1. Cotton trade - Southern States - History. 2. Cotton trade - Southern States - Employees - History. 3. Southern States - Social conditions. 4. Textile factories - Southern States - History. I. Hall, Jacquelyn Dowd.
HD9077.A13 L55 1987

Likert, Rensis, 1903- New patterns of management / Rensis Likert. New York : Garland Pub., 1987. vii, 279 p. : ill. ; 23 cm. (Continuity in administrative science) Reprint. Originally published: New York : McGraw-Hill, 1961. Bibliography: p. 249-263. Includes index. ISBN 0-8240-8214-1 (alk. paper) : LC Card 86-25800 DDC 658.4 19
1. Industrial management. I. Title. II. Series.
HD31 .L43 1987

Lille Danmark hva'nu? . Jespersen, Jesper, 1948- [Copenhagen] , c1985. 128 p. : ISBN 87-500-2594-5 LC Card 85-243948
HC353 .J47 1985

Lillegard, Dee. I can be a secretary / by Dee Lillegard ; prepared under the direction of Robert Hillerich. Chicago : Childrens Press, c1987. 29 p. : col. ill. ; 25 cm. Includes index. Explains the many important tasks that secretaries perform and describes the special training and skills they need for the job. ISBN 0-516-01907-4 (lib. bdg.) LC Card 86-29947 DDC 651.3/741/02373 19
1. Secretaries - Juvenile literature. I. Hillerich, Robert L., 1927-. II. Title.
HF55475 .L55 1987

Lillywhite, Donald P. Virginia population projections 2000 / [authors, Donald P. Lillywhite and Larry E. Robinson, in association with Julie A. Henderson]. Richmond, VA (P.O. Box 1422, Ninth St. Office Building, Richmond 23219) : Source of copies, Dept. of Planning and Budget, Research Section, [1986] 96 p. : ill. ; 22 x 28 cm. "October 1986"--T.p. verso. LC Card 87-621004 DDC 304.6/2/09755021 19
1. Virginia - Population - Statistics. 2. Population forecasting - Virginia - Statistics. I. Robinson, Larry E. II. Henderson, Julie A. III. Virginia. Dept. of Planning and Budget. Research Section. IV. Title.
HA685 .L542 1986

Lim, David. Asean-Australia trade in manufactures /. Melbourne, Australia , c1985. xiii, 263 p. ; ISBN 0-582-71147-9 (pbk.) LC Card 86-228309 DDC 382/.4567/0994 19
HD9738.A82 A83 1985

Lim, Kit Siang. BMF, scandal of scandals / Lim Kit Siang. Petaling Jaya : Democratic Action Party, [1986] ix, 68 p. : ill., ports. ; 22 cm. Cover title: BMF, the scandal of scandals. LC Card 86-943248 DDC 364.1/68/09595 19
1. Bumiputra Malaysia Finance. 2. Banks and banking - Malaysia - Corrupt practices. 3. Misconduct of office - Malaysia. I. Title. II. Title: BMF, the scandal of scandals.
HG3300.6.A6 L553 1986

Lima, Almir Freire. Comercialização de alimentos na região norte, 1985 /. Brasília, DF , 1985. 51 p. ; LC Card 86-129086
HD9014.B83 N673 1985

Lima, Gerson Moreira, 1952- Releasemania, uma contribuição para o estudo do press-release no Brasil / Gerson Moreira Lima. São Paulo, SP : Summus Editorial, c1985. 114 p. : facsims. ; 21 cm. (Novas buscas em comunicação . v. 2) Bibliography: p. 113-114. LC Card 85-184576 DDC 659.2 19
1. Press releases. 2. Publicity. 3. Journalism - Brazil. I. Title. II. Series.
HM263 .L478 1985 **NYPL [JFD 86-2728]**

Lima, José Luiz. Estatísticas básicas do setor agrícola no Brasil / José Luiz Lima, Iraci del Nero da Costa, Francisco Vidal Luna. São Paulo : Instituto de Pesquisas Econômicas, 1983- v. : ill. ; 23 cm. (Série Estatísticas básicas da economia brasileira . no. 2, 3) Chiefly tables. LC Card 83-219032 DDC 338.1/0981 19
1. Produce trade - Brazil - Statistics - History. 2. Export sales - Brazil - Statistics - History. I. Costa, Iraci del Nero da. II. Luna, Francisco Vidal. III. Brazil (City). Universidade. São Paulo, Instituto de Pesquisas Econômicas. IV. Title. V. Series.
HD9014.B82 L55 1983 ***NYPL [JLL 86-432]***

LIMA (PERU) - CENSUS, 1700.
Numeracion general de todas las personas de ambos sexos, edades y calidades q[ue] se hà hecho en esta ciudad de Lima, año de 1700 /. Lima , 1985. xv, 358 p. : LC Card 87-400680
HA1069.L7 N86 1985

LIMA (PERU) - POPULATION - STATISTICS.
Numeracion general de todas las personas de ambos sexos, edades y calidades q[ue] se hà hecho en esta ciudad de Lima, año de 1700 /. Lima , 1985. xv, 358 p. : LC Card 87-400680
HA1069.L7 N86 1985

Lima. Pontificia Universidad Católica del Perú. (Old Catalog form: Lima (City). Universidad Católica del Perú)
Agricultura y alimentación . [Lima] , 1982. 536 p. : LC Card 83-174688 DDC 338.1/9/85 19
HD9014.P52 A57 1982 ***NYPL [JLD 86-268]***

Lima, Rômulo de Araújo, 1949- Em busca da dialética : apontamentos acerca do conceito de modo de produção / Rômulo de Araújo Lima. Campina Grande-Paraíba : Universidade Regional do Nordeste, Editora Universitária, 1983. 102 p. ; 21 cm. Bibliography: p. 99-102. LC Card 86-130003
1. Marxian economics. 2. Capitalism. 3. Work. 4. Historcial materialism. I. Title.
HB97.5 .L464 1983

Lima, Rubens Soares de. Almeida, Pedro Fernando de. A indústria gaúcha de bens de capital na dinâmica da economia brasileira . Porto Alegre, RS , 1986. 257 p. ; LC Card 87-403616 DDC 338.4/76218/0981 19
HD9705.B73 R562 1986

Lima Sobrinho, Antonio Estevam de. Fome, agricultura e política no Brasil : a chantagem alimentar / Antonio Estevam de Lima Sobrinho. Petrópolis : Vozes, 1981. 120 p. ; 21 cm. Bibliography: p. 119-120. LC Card 81-185801 DDC 338.1/0981 19
1. Food supply - Brazil. 2. Malnutrition - Brazil. 3. Agriculture and state - Brazil. I. Title.
HD9014.B82 L56 1981
NYPL [JLD 86-3297]

Lima tahun kepemimpinan Gubernur Kepala Daerah Tingkat I Sulawesi Utara, G.H. Mantik, 1980-1985. [Manado : Biro Hubungan Masyarakat, Kant. Gubernur Kepala Daerah Tingkat I Sulut, 1985] 2 v. : coll. ill., col. port. ; 33 cm. CONTENTS. - [1] Edisi data -- [2] Edisi gambar. LC Card 86-940586
1. Sulawesi Utara (Indonesia) - Economic policy. 2. Sulawesi Utara (Indonesia) - Social policy. 3. Mantik, G. H. I. Mantik, G. H. II. Sulawesi Utara (Indonesia). Gubernur. III. Sulawesi Utara (Ind nesia). Gubernur. Biro Hubungan Masyarakat.
HC448.S785 L55 1985

Lima, Tony. dBASE II for beginners / Tony Lima. Englewood Cliffs, N.J. : Prentice-Hall, c1985. xix, 234 p. : ill. ; 24 cm. (Prentice-Hall personal computing series) Includes index. ISBN 0-13-196098-9 : LC Card 84-22897 DDC 001.64/2 19
1. Data base management. 2. dBASE II (Computer program). I. Title. II. Title: d.B.A.S.E. II for beginners. III. Title: dBASE two for beginners. IV. Title: dBASE 2 for beginners.
QA76.9.D3 L56 1985 ***NYPL [JSE 87-247]***

Lima. Universidad Católica del Perú. see **Lima. Pontificia Universidad Católica del Perú.**

Lima. Universidad Nacional Agraria. see **Universidad Nacional Agraria.**

Lima.bBolsa de Valores. see **Bolsa de Valores de Lima.**

LIME INDUSTRY - BRAZIL - MINAS GERAIS.
Programa de modernização e expansão da indústria de cal em Minas Gerais. Belo Horizonte , 1977. 57 leaves, [8] leaves of plates : LC Card 79-123546
HD9585.L52 B77 1977

LIME INDUSTRY - GERMANY (WEST) - HISTORY.
Schöne, Manfred, 1935- Von der Leimabteilung zum grössten Klebstoffwerk Europas /. Düsseldorf , 1979. 68 p. : LC Card 86-216773
HD9654.9.H444 S37 1979

LIMITATION OF ARMAMENT. see **DISARMAMENT.**

LIMITATIONS, CONTRACTUAL. see **CONTRACTS.**

LIMITATIONS (LAW) see **REAL PROPERTY.**

LIMITED COMPANIES. see **CORPORATIONS.**

The limits of national liberation . Fforde, Adam. London , New York , c1987. 246 p. ; ISBN 0-7099-1036-3 LC Card 87-8977 DDC 338.9597 19
HC444 .F46 1987

The limits of power . Rosen, Christine Meisner, 1951- Cambridge [Cambridgeshire] , New York , 1986. xii, 395 p. : ISBN 0-521-30319-2 LC Card 85-7753 DDC 307.7/6/0973 19
HT371 .R67 1986 ***NYPL [JLE 86-2388]***

The Limits to growth; a report for the Club of Rome's project on the predicament of mankind [by] Donella H. Meadows [and others] New York, Universe Books [1972] 205 p. illus. 21 cm. "A Potomac Associates book." Bibliography: p. 198-200. ISBN 0-87663-165-0 LC Card 73-187907 DDC 330.9/04
1. Economic history - 1971-. 2. Social history - 1945-. I. Meadows, Donella H.
HC59 .L54 ***NYPL [JLD 75-167]***

The limits to rational expectations /. Pesaran, M. Hashem, 1946- Oxford, UK , New York, NY, USA , 1988, c1987. x, 325 p. : ISBN 0-631-14036-0 : LC Card 87-20877 DDC 339 19
HB172.5 .P445 1988

LIMÓN (COSTA RICA : PROVINCE) - ECONOMIC CONDITIONS.
Análisis de indicadores socioeconómicos, Subregión Limón . [San José] [1981] 26 p. ; LC Card 83-240958
HC143.Z7 L554 1981

LIMÓN (COSTA RICA : PROVINCE) - SOCIAL CONDITIONS.
Análisis de indicadores socioeconómicos, Subregión Limón . [San José] [1981] 26 p. ; LC Card 83-240958
HC143.Z7 L554 1981

Limp, Wolfgang. Productivity centers : purpose, program, working methods / by Wolfgang Limp. Frankfurt am Main : Rationalisierungs-Kuratorium der Deutschen Wirtschaft (RKW) e.V., 1975. 64 p. ; 29 cm. "Abbreviated translation of the RKW brochure "Produktivitätszentralen." LC Card 82-219310
1. Management - Study and teaching. 2. Industrial productivity centers. I. Rationalisierungs-Kuratorium der Deutschen Wirtschaft. II. Title.
HD30.4 .L55 1975

Limpert, Lars. Hammer, Karl-Heinrich. Posttips . Bonn , 1982. 108 p. : LC Card 83-193275
HE6998 .H35 1982

L'imposta e il deposito previo sugli acquisti di valuta e la crisi della lira del 1976 . Tasgian, Astrig. Milano , c1983. 139 p. : LC Card 83-187693 DDC 332.4/945 19
HG1029.5 .T37 1983 ***NYPL [JLD 87-813]***

Lin, Leesha. U. S. essential air services study / by Leesha Lin. Ottawa-Hull : Canadian Transport Commission, Research Branch, Economic and Social Research, c1986. viii, 118 p. : ill. ; 28 cm. (Report / Canadian Transport Commission, Research Branch, Economic and Social Research . no. 1985/06E) "August 1985." Bibliography: p. [43] ISBN 0-662-14800-2 (pbk.) LC Card 87-102545 DDC 387.7/1 19
1. Aeronautics, Commercial - United States - Deregulation. 2. Aeronautics, Commercial - Law and legislation - United States. 3. Aeronautics, Commercial - Canada. I. Title. II. Title: US essential air services study. III. Series: Report (Canadian Transport Commission. Research Branch) , no. 1985/06E.
HE9803.A4 L55 1986

Lin, Ming-Jeng, 1947- Hwang, C. L. (Ching-Lai), 1929- Group decision making under multiple criteria . Berlin , New York , c1987. xi, 400 p. : ISBN 0-387-17177-0 (U. S. : pbk.) : LC Card 86-29729 DDC 658.4/036 19
HD30.23 .H87 1987

Lincoln Institute monograph.
(#86-1) Growth management . Washington, D.C. , c1986. iv, 218 p. : ISBN 0-87420-655-3 (pbk.) LC Card 86-50332 DDC 307.1/4/0973 19
HD205 .G76 1986 ***NYPL [JLE 87-558]***
(no. 86-1) Growth management . Washington, D.C. , c1986. iv, 218 p. : ISBN 0-87420-655-3 (pbk.) LC Card 86-50332 DDC 307.1/4/0973 19
HD205 .G76 1986 ***NYPL [JLE 87-558]***

Lincoln, Yvonna S. Organizational theory and inquiry . Beverly Hills , c1985. 231 p. ; ISBN 0-8039-2494-1 LC Card 85-8137 DDC 302/.072 19
HM131 .O683 1985 ***NYPL [JLD 86-3567]***

LINCOLNSHIRE - RURAL CONDITIONS.
Clark, David, Ph. D. Information services in rural areas . Norwich [Norfolk] , c1980. x, 122 p. : ISBN 0-86094-058-6 (pbk.) LC Card 81-149488
HE8109.L55 C55 1980

Lindberg, Leon N. Hollingsworth, J. Rogers (Joseph Rogers), 1932- The governance of the American economy . Berlin [1985] 60 p. ; LC Card 86-205784 DDC 330.973 19
HC106.8 .H635 1985

Linde, Hans. Theorie der säkularen Nachwuchsbeschränkung 1800 bis 2000 / Hans Linde. Frankfurt [am Main] ; New York : Campus, c1984. 201 p. ; 21 cm. (Forschungsberichte des Instituts für Bevölkerungsforschung und Sozialpolitik (IBS), Universität Bielefeld . Bd. 8) Includes bibliographical references. ISBN 3-593-33385-6 LC Card 85-131521
1. Fertility, Human. 2. Family size. I. Title. II. Series.
HB901 .L55 1984

Linde, R. ADAC. Strassenverkehr 2000 . München [1979] 24 p. : LC Card 85-147077
HE363.G3 A33 1979

Lindegaard, Henning. 90 plus 10 /. [Copenhagen] [1986] 39 p. : ISBN 87-7002-353-0 LC Card 86-197313
HD5799.A6 A12 1986

Lindeman, J. Bruce (John Bruce) Friedman, Jack P. Dictionary of real estate terms /. New York , c1987. v, 329 p. : ISBN 0-8120-3898-3 (pbk.) : LC Card 87-19869 DDC 333.33/03/21 19
HD1365 .F75 1987

Linden, Eugene. Wang, An, 1920- Lessons . Reading, Mass. , 1986. 248 p., [28] p. of plates : ISBN 0-201-09400-2 LC Card 86-10768 DDC 338.7/61004/0924 B 19
HD9696.C62 A3 1986 ***NYPL [JFE 86-5201]***

LINDEN (HANNOVER, GERMANY) - SOCIAL CONDITIONS.
Voigt, Wolfgang. Der Eisenbahnkönig, oder, Rumänien lag in Linden . München , 1982. 142 p. : ISBN 3-923126-15-8 (pbk.) LC Card 87-672921
HD7289.5.R1 V64x 1982

Linden, Ronald Haly. Communist states and international change : Romania and Yugoslavia in comparative perspective / Ronald H. Linden. Boston : Allen & Unwin, c1987. xviii, 201 p. ; 22 cm. Includes bibliographies and index. ISBN 0-04-497050-1 : LC Card 87-11389 DDC 337.497 19
1. Romania - Foreign economic relations. 2. Romania - Politics and government - 1944-. 3. Yugoslavia - Foreign economic relations. 4. Yugoslavia - Politics and government - 1945-. 5. International economic relations. 6. Economic history - 1971-. 7. World politics - 1975-1985. I. Title.
HF1581 .L56 1987

Lindenboim, Javier.
Monetarismo y mercado de trabajo : Río Negro, 1976-1981 / Javier Lindenboim, Mabel Manzanal ; colaboradora, Nora Marqués. Buenos Aires, Argentina : Centro de Estudios Urbanos y Regionales, c1985. x, 471 p. : ill. ; 28 cm. (Informes de investigación del Ceur, 0326-6850 . 2) Errata sheet inserted. Includes bibliographical references. ISBN 950-9370-05-3 LC Card 87-122243 DDC 331.12/0982/73 19

1. Labor supply - Argentina - Río Negro. 2. Fruit trade - Argentina - Río Negro. 3. Monetary policy - Argentina. 4. Argentina - Economic policy. I. Manzanal, Mabel. II. Marqués, Nora. III. Title. IV. Series.
HD5750.R56 L56 1985

La terciarización del empleo en la Argentina. Una perspectiva regional. Buenos Aires : República Argentina, Ministerio de Trabajo y Seguridad Social : Secretaría de Planificación, 1985. vi, 59, 50, 3 p. ; 30 cm. (Estudios y documentos de trabajo sobre empleo, remuneraciones y recursos humanos) "Proyecto Gobierno Argentino, Programa de las Naciones Unidas para el Desarrollo, Organización Internacional del Trabajo, ARG/84/029." Includes bibliographical references. LC Card 87-122527 DDC 381 19
1. Informal sector (Economics) - Argentina. 2. Women - Employment - Argentina. 3. Migration, Internal - Argentina. 4. Informal sector (Economics) - Argentina - Buenos Aires Metropolitan Area. 5. Women - Employment - Argentina - Buenos Aires Metropolitan Area. 6. Buenos Aires Metropolitan Area (Argentina) - Population. I. Title. II. Series.
HD2346.A73 L56 1985

Lindenlaub, Dieter. Maschinenbauunternehmen in der Deutschen Inflation 1919-1923 : unternehmenshistorische Untersuchungen zu einigen Inflationstheorien / Dieter Lindenlaub. Berlin ; New York : de Gruyter, 1985. xiii, 262 p. ; 24 cm. (Beiträge zu Inflation und Wiederaufbau in Deutschland und Europa 1914-1924 . Bd. 4) Veröffentlichungen der Historischen Kommission zu Berlin ; Bd. 61 Revision of the author's Habilitationsschrift--Universität Tübingen, 1982. Bibliography: p. [239]-253. Includes indexes. ISBN 3-11-009934-9 LC Card 85-214738
1. Inflation (Finance) - Germany - History. 2. Germany - Economic conditions - 1918-1945. 3. Machinery industry - Germany - History. I. Series. II. Series: Veröffentlichungen der Historischen Kommission zu Berlin beim Friedrich-Meinecke-Institut der Freien Universität Berlin , Bd. 61. III. Title.
HG999 .L75 1985

Lindmark, Leif. Företagsstöd och kommunalt risktagande / Leif Lindmark. Stockholm : Liber, [1984] iv, 49 p. : ill. ; 25 cm. (Kommunal näringspolitik) SIND, 0346-5748 ; 1984:6 Bibliography: p. 48-49. ISBN 91-38-08297-7 LC Card 85-106839
1. Subsidies - Sweden. 2. Risk - Sweden. 3. Industry and state - Sweden. 4. Economic development projects - Sweden. I. Title. II. Series.
HD3646.S8 L55 1984

Lindmüller, Peter. Remscheid und Solingen im industriegeographischen Entwicklungsvergleich / Peter Lindmüller. Bochum : N. Brockmeyer, 1986. 423 p. : ill., maps ; 21-36 cm. (Beiträge zur Struktur- und Konjunkturforschung . Bd. 26) Accompanied by Bd. 2 maps ; 36 cm. Originally presented as the author's thesis (doctoral)--Ruhruniversität Bochum, 1986. Bibliography: p. 409-423. ISBN 3-88339-544-7 LC Card 87-146590 DDC 330.943/55 19
1. Remscheid (Germany) - Economic conditions. 2. Remscheid (Germany) - Industries - History. 3. Solingen (Germany) - Economic conditions. 4. Solingen (Germany) - Industries - History. I. Title. II. Series.
HC289.R38 L56 1986

Lindner, Eberhard. Ausweg aus der Weltkrise : Bestandsaufnahme und Wegweisung : Natur- und geisteswissenschaftliche Synthese / Eberhard Lindner. Karlsruhe : M. Lindner, 1984. 319 p. : ill. ; 22 cm. Includes bibliographical references and indexes. ISBN 3-921653-15-0 LC Card 85-104217 DDC 363.7 19
1. Economic development - Environmental aspects. 2. Civilization, Modern - 1950-. I. Title.
HD75.6 .L56 1984 ***NYPL [JLD 87-484]***

Lindner, Helmut. Aussagefähigkeit von Einkommensverteilungsrechnungen für die Bundesrepublik Deutschland . Tübingen , 1986. xxiv, 436 p. : ISBN 3-88573-027-8 LC Card 87-407588 DDC 339.2/0943 19
HC290.5.I5 A93 1986

Lindner, Vicki, 1944- Lieberman, Annette. Unbalanced accounts . New York , c1987. xx, 281 p. ; ISBN 0-87113-141-2 LC Card 86-28845 DDC 332.4/01/9 19
HG179 .L49 1987

Lindqvist, Lars-Johan. Marknadsföring till handeln : en studie av förhandlingar mellan dagligvaruleverantörer och distributörsblock i Finland = Marketing to the trade : a study of negotiations between convenience goods suppliers and their distributors in Finland / Lars-Johan Lindqvist. Helsingfors : Svenska handelshögskolan, 1983. 309 p. : ill. ; 25 cm. (Ekonomi och samhälle. nr. 32) Thesis (doctoral)--Svenska handelshögskolan, 1983. Extra t.p. with thesis statement inserted. Summary in English. Bibliography: p. 273-281. ISBN 951-555-183-8 LC Card 84-103976
1. Wholesale trade - Finland - Case studies. 2. Marketing - Finland - Case studies. I. Title. II. Title: Marketing to the trade. III. Series: Ekonomi och samhälle (Svenska handelshögskolan (Helsinki, Finland)) , nr. 32.
HF5421.5.F5 L56 1983

Lindsell, Sheryl L. CPS®--Certified Professional Secretary® examination / Sheryl L. Lindsell and Stanley L. Alpert. New York, N.Y. : Prentice Hall Press : Distributed by Prentice Hall Trade, c1987. xxx, 286 p. : ill. ; 28 cm. (Professional certification & licensing examination series) "An Arco book." Spine title: Arco's Certified Professional Secretary® (CPS®) examination. Bibliography: p. 281-286. ISBN 0-13-122805-6 (pbk.) : LC Card 87-11381 DDC 651.3/741/076 19
1. Secretaries - Examinations, questions, etc. 2. Office practice - Examinations, questions, etc. I. Alpert, Stanley L. II. Title. III. Title: Certified Professional Secretary® examination. IV. Title: Arco's Certified Professional Secretary® (CPS®) examination. V. Series.
HF5547.5 .L554 1987

Lindsey, Donald W.
Haigh, Robert William, 1926- Leading Virginia industries . Charlottesville, Va. [1986] 161 p. : LC Card 87-620837 DDC 338.4/7677/009755 19
HD9857.V8 H35 1986

Taxable sales in Virginia, 1985 / Donald W. Lindsey. Charlottesville, Va. (2015 Ivy Rd., Charlottesville 22903-1780) : University of Virginia, Colgate Darden Graduate School of Business Administration, Tayloe Murphy Institute, [1986] 16 p. : ill. ; 28 cm. "July 1986." LC Card 86-622891 DDC 336.2/713/09755021 19
1. Sales tax - Virginia - Statistics. I. Tayloe Murphy Institute. II. Title.
HJ5715.U62 V85 1986

Lindström, Stefan. Wittrock, Björn. De stora programmens tid . Stockholm , 1984. 186 p. ; ISBN 91-7410-200-1 : LC Card 84-189613
HD9502.S82 W58 1984

L'industrie sidérurgique en France pendant la Révolution et l'Empire /. Woronoff, Denis, 1939- Paris , c1984. 592 p. : ISBN 2-7132-0843-2 LC Card 85-138825 DDC 338.4/76691/0944 19
HD9522.5 .W64 1984 ***NYPL [JLE 86-3532]***

Lineamientos básicos del Programa Habitacional de Emergencia, 1985-86 /. Vicario, Luis B. [Montevideo] , 1985. 25 p. : LC Card 87-122422 DDC 363.5/8 19
HD7287.96.U82 M668 1985

Lineamientos generales para el Plan de Desarrollo, 1984-1988. Versión corr. Quito, Ecuador : Consejo Nacional de Desarrollo, Secretaría General de Planificación, 1985. ii, 42 leaves ; 30 cm. Errata slip inserted. LC Card 86-149211
1. Ecuador - Economic policy. 2. Ecuador - Social policy. I. Consejo Nacional de Desarrollo (Ecuador). Secretaría General de Planificación.
HC202 .L52 1985

Lineamientos para la implantación de un servicio de certificación ocupacional /. Agudelo Mejía, Santiago. Montevideo , 1983. 67 p. : LC Card 86-142627
HD5715.5.L3 A348 1983

Linear and dynamic programming with Lotus 1-2-3, Release 2 /. Ho, James K. K. Portland, Or. , c1987. xiv, 330 p. : ISBN 0-943518-72-5 (pbk.) : LC Card 87-1586 DDC 005.36/9 19
HF5548.4.L67 H6 1987

LINEAR MODELS (STATISTICS)
Gallant, A. Ronald, 1942- A unified theory of estimation and inference for nonlinear dynamic models /. Oxford [Oxfordshire] , New York, NY, USA. , 1988. p. cm. ISBN 0-631-15765-4 : LC Card 87-25602 DDC 330/.028 19
HB141 .G33 1988

LINEAR PROGRAMMING.
(1958) Dorfman, Robert. Linear programming and economic analysis /. New York , 1987, c1986. p. cm. ISBN 0-486-65491-5 (pbk.) LC Card 87-24382 DDC 330/.0724 19
HB135 .D67 1987

(1980) Moro, Beniamino, 1945- Programmazione lineare e teoria dell'impresa /. Milano [1980] 182 p. : ISBN 88-20-41708-1 : LC Card 80-489699
T57.74 .M67 ***NYPL [JLD 87-792]***

(1983) Zimmermann, Rainer. Demographische Variablen in linearen Produktionsmodellen /. Bochum , 1983. 263 p. : ISBN 3-88339-327-4 LC Card 84-107454
HB241 .Z56 1983

Linear programming and economic analysis /. Dorfman, Robert. New York , 1987, c1986. p. cm. ISBN 0-486-65491-5 (pbk.) LC Card 87-24382 DDC 330/.0724 19
HB135 .D67 1987

LINEAR SYSTEM THEORY. see **SYSTEM ANALYSIS.**

Lineback, L. Kent, 1943- Being the boss : the craft of managing people / L. Kent Lineback. New York : IEEE Press, c1987. xi, 177 p. ; 24 cm. "Published under the sponsorship of the IEEE Engineering Management Society." Bibliography: p. 167-171. Includes index. ISBN 0-87942-212-2 LC Card 86-27751 DDC 658.3 19
1. Personnel management. I. IEEE Engineering Management Society. II. Title.
HF5549 .L4945 1987

LINEN INDUSTRY - NORTHERN IRELAND - MAGHERA REGION (LONDONDERRY) - HISTORY.
Clark, Wallace, 1926- Linen on the green . Belfast , 1983, c1982. xii, 183 p., [16] p. of plates : ISBN 0-9509042-0-1 LC Card 84-242010 DDC 338.4/76771164/0941629 19
HD9930.G73 N625 1983

Linen on the green . Clark, Wallace, 1926- Belfast , 1983, c1982. xii, 183 p., [16] p. of plates : ISBN 0-9509042-0-1 LC Card 84-242010 DDC 338.4/76771164/0941629 19
HD9930.G73 N625 1983

L'Informatica nella società italiana, 1984 : primo rapporto realizzato con il patrocinio della Finsiel / CENSIS, Centro studi investimenti sociali ; [realizzato nel 1983 da un gruppo di lavoro diretto da Michele Dau e composto da Livio Barnabò ... et al.]. Milano : F. Angeli, [1984] 257 p. ; 23 cm. (Materiali di ricerca . 17) LC Card 84-249272 DDC 338.4/7004/0945 19
1. Computer industry - Italy. 2. Market surveys - Italy. I. Dau, Michele. II. Finsiel. III. Series. IV. Series: Material di ricerca (Centro studi investimenti sociali) , 17.
HD9696.C63 I85 1984
NYPL [JLD 86-3303]

L'Information et la consultation des travailleurs dans les enterprises multinationales / sous la direction de Jacques Vandamme (président du Groupe d'études politiques européennes) ; avec la collaboration de Roger Blanpain ... [et al.] ; commentaires de Ernst Piehl et Bernard Sassen. 1re éd. [Paris] : P[resses] u[niversitaires de] F[rance] ; [Genève?] : IRM, 1984. 290 p. ; 22 cm. (Collection de l'Institut de recherche et d'information sur les multinationales) Includes bibliographies. ISBN 2-13-038651-2 (pbk.)
1. International business enterprises - Management. 2. International business enterprises - Europe - Management. 3. Management information systems. 4. Management - Employee participation. I. Vandamme, J. II. Blanpain, R. (Roger), 1942-. III. Groupe d'études politiques européennes. IV. Series.
HD62.4 .I53 1984 ***NYPL [JLD 87-60]***

Linhas de ação. Federação do Comércio Varejista do Estado do Paraná. Empresa forte, mais trabalho . [Curitiba] , 1983. 67 leaves : LC Card 83-225279
HF5429.6.B7 F44 1983

Linhas de ação para o desenvolvimento de Sergipe . Sergipe (Brazil) [Aracaju] [1984] 218 p. ; LC Card 85-207558
HC188.S45 S45 1984

Link, Albert N. Strategies for technology-based competition : meeting the new global challenge / Albert N. Link, Gregory Tassey. Lexington, Mass. : Lexington Books, c1987. xii, 142 p. :

ill. ; 24 cm. Bibliography: p. [135]-139. Includes index. ISBN 0-669-14574-2 (alk. paper) LC Card 86-45885 DDC 338.6/048 19
1. Competition, International. 2. Technological innovations. 3. Research, Industrial. 4. Technology and state. 5. Industrial management. I. Tassey, Gregory. II. Title.
HF1414 .L55 1987

Link, Jörg. Organisation der strategischen Planung : Aufbau und Bedeutung strategischer Geschäftseinheiten sowie strategischer Planungsorgane / Jörg Link. Heidelberg : Physica-Verlag, c1985. xvii, 178 p. : ill. ; 25 cm. Bibliography: p. [167]-176. Includes index. ISBN 3-7908-0333-2 LC Card 86-160239 DDC 658.4/012 19
1. Strategic planning. I. Title.
HD30.28 .L545 1985

Link, William. Levinson, Richard. Off camera . New York, N.Y. , c1986. 279 p. ; ISBN 0-452-25873-1 LC Card 86-18089 DDC 384.55/023/73 19
HE8700.4 .L48 1986 *NYPL [MWGR 87-881]*

Linkage effects and small industry development . Symposium on Linkage Between Large and Small Industries (1985 : Kuala Lumpur, Malaysia) Tokyo , 1986. iv, 191 p. : ISBN 92-833-2037-3 LC Card 87-137082 DDC 338.6/42/09595 19
HD2341 .S96 1985

Linkemer, Bobbi.
How to run a meeting / Bobbi Linkemer. New York, NY : AMACOM, c1987. 51 p. ; 18 cm. (The Successful office skills series) Includes index. ISBN 0-8144-7671-6 (pbk.) : LC Card 86-47815 DDC 658.4/563 19
1. Meetings. I. Title. II. Series.
HD30.3 .L55 1987

How to write an effective resume / Bobbi Linkemer. New York, NY : AMACOM, c1987. 58 p. ; 18 cm. (The Successful office skills series) Includes index. ISBN 0-8144-7669-4 (pbk.) : LC Card 86-47813 DDC 650.1/4 19
1. Résumés (Employment). I. Title. II. Series.
HF5383 .L56 1987

Linking data /. Fielding, Nigel. Beverly Hills , c1986. 96 p. ; ISBN 0-8039-2518-2 (pbk.) LC Card 85-62290 DDC 300/.72 19
H62 .F425 1986 *NYPL [JLD 86-3863]*

Linking employment problems to economic status : 1984 survey. Washington, D.C. : U. S. Dept. of Labor, Bureau of Labor Statistics : For sale by the Supt. of Docs., U. S. G.P.O., [1986] vi, 56 p. ; 28 cm. (Bulletin . 2270) Shipping list no.: 86-856-P. "September 1986." Includes bibliographical references. S/N 029-001-02912-8 Item 768-A-1 LC Card 86-603148 DDC 331.13/7973 19
1. Unemployed - United States - Statistics. 2. Labor supply - United States - Statistics. 3. Income - United States - Statistics. I. United States. Bureau of Labor Statistics. II. Series: Bulletin (United States. Bureau of Labor Statistics) , 2270.
HD5724 .L425 1986

Linking macroeconomic and agricultural policies for adjustment with growth . Thomas, Vinod, 1949- Baltimore , c1985. xv, 252 p. ; ISBN 0-8018-3121-0 : LC Card 85-45105 DDC 338.9861 19
HC197 .T38 1985 *NYPL [JLE 86-1438]*

LINN COUNTY (OR.) - POPULATION - STATISTICS.
Population trends, Linn County, Oregon . [Eugene] [1964] 20 leaves : LC Card 85-209473
HA597.L56 P66 1964

Linn, Marcia C. The Psychology of gender . Baltimore , c1986. vii, 293 p. : ISBN 0-8018-2974-7 (alk. paper) LC Card 85-19822 DDC 155.3/3 19
BF692.2 .P76 1986 *NYPL [JFE 86-2969]*

Lins, David A. Seger, Daniel J. Financing Illinois agricultural exports /. [Urbana?] [1985] 74 p. : LC Card 86-621070 DDC 382/.63 19
HD9007.I3 S44 1985

Lins, Josef. Wohnungsmarkt und soziale Schicht : eine soziologische Studie über das Publikum geförderter Eigentumswohnungen / Josef Lins ; mit einem Vorwort von Hubert Zeitlhofer.2. Aufl. Linz : R. Trauner, 1983. 89 p. : ill. ; 21 cm. (Sozialwissenschaftliche Materialien . Bd. 3) Includes bibliographical references. ISBN 3-85320-292-6 LC Card 84-214132 DDC 363.6/09436 19
1. Housing - Austria. 2. Housing policy - Austria. 3. Home ownership - Austria. I. Title. II. Series.
HD7337.A3 L55 1983 *NYPL [JLD 87-102]*

L'insurrection des patrons /. Helbert, Jean-Pierre, 1947- Châteaugiron , 1984. 165 p. ; ISBN 2-903414-33-5 LC Card 85-180275 DDC 658/.006/044 19
HD6948.F8 H45 1984 *NYPL [JLE 86-526]*

L'internationalisation bancaire en Egypte /. Caselli, Clara. Milano [1982] 223 p. ; LC Card 83-132087 DDC 332.1/5/0962 19
HG3386.A6 C37 1982 *NYPL [JLE 86-1969]*

Linzbach, Peter, 1956- Der Werdegang der preussischen Einkommensteuer unter besonderer Berücksichtigung ihrer kausalen Entwicklungsfaktoren : ein Beitrag zur Theorie der Durchsetzbarkeit der Einkommensteuer / Peter Linzbach. Frankfurt am Main ; New York : P. Lang, c1984. 259 p. ; 21 cm. (Europäische Hochschulschriften. Reihe V, Volks- und Betriebswirtschaft, 0531-7339 . Bd. 503 = vol. 503 = vol. 503) Bibliography: p. 235-259. ISBN 3-8204-5184-6 LC Card 84-169039
1. Income tax - Prussia (Germany) - History. I. Series: Europäische Hochschulschriften. Reihe V, Volks- und Betriebswirtschaft , Bd. 503. II. Title.
HJ4720.P78 L56 1984

Linzer Kommunalwissenschaftliche Tagung (1978) Privatisierung kommunaler Aufgaben? : Beiträge aus Anlass der Linzer Kommunalwissenschaftlichen Tagung vom 13. Juni 1978 / Herausgeber, Ludwig Fröhler, Ernst Kubin. Linz : Institut für Kommunalwissenschaften und Unweltschutz, c1978. 62 p. ; 24 cm. (Kommunale Forschung in Österreich. 38) ISBN 3-7141-7871-6 LC Card 85-185084
1. Municipal services - Austria - Congresses. 2. Privatization - Austria - Congresses. I. Fröhler, Ludwig. II. Kubin, Ernst. III. Title. IV. Series.
HD4651 .L56 1978

Linzer Schriften zur Sozial- u. Wirtschaftsgeschichte .
(Bd. 11) Rettenbacher, Karl. Die Kraftfahrzeughaftpflichtversicherung in Österreich . Linz , c1984. 183 p. : ISBN 3-85320-328-0 LC Card 85-162917
HG9970.4.A9 R48 1984

(Bd. 16) Hinterbuchner, Christian. Die Entwicklung der oberösterreichischen Elektrizitätswirtschaft in den Jahren 1938-1980 /. Linz , c1986. 344 p. : ISBN 3-85320-370-1 : LC Card 86-225017
HD9685.A93 U664 1986

(Bd. 18) Urferer, Wilhelm. Das Wohnungswesen in Oberösterreich seit Beginn dieses Jahrhunderts im Vergleich zu seiner gesamtstaatlichen Entwicklung /. Linz , c1986. viii, 235 p. : ISBN 3-85320-384-1 LC Card 87-127729 DDC 363.5/8/094362 19
HD7337.U6 U74 1986

(Bd. 2) Weigl, Franz, 1948- Die Entwicklung der oberösterreichischen Elektrizitätswirtschaft von den Anfängen bis zum Jahre 1938 /. Linz [1980] 210, xi p. : ISBN 3-85320-232-2 : LC Card 81-137632
HD9685.A93 U669 1980

(Bd. 5) Prokopp, Ludwig Ferdinand. Europäische Commerzreisen um die Mitte des 18. Jahrhunderts /. Linz , c1982. xiii, 446 p., [1] folded leaf of plates : ISBN 3-85320-296-1 LC Card 83-150921
HF3548.C36 P76 1982

(Bd. 6) Kreinecker, Günther. Die Anfänge der Raiffeisenkassen in Oberösterreich (1889-1914) . Linz , c1982. xvi, 276 p. : ISBN 3-85320-279-9 LC Card 83-224597
HG2051.A89 U64 1982
NYPL [JLE 87-2440]

(Bd. 9) Otruba, Gustav. A. Hitler's "Tausend-Mark-Sperre" und die Folgen für Österreichs Fremdenverkehr (1933-1938) /. Linz , c1983. iii, 205 p. ; ISBN 3-85320-308-6 LC Card 84-213145
HG999 .O87 1983

Lipari, D. (Domenico) Strategia dei servizi per l'agricoltura . [Roma] [1983] 158 p. : LC Card 85-155420
HD9475.I82 S77 1983

Lipfert, Helmut. Mitgliederförderndes Kooperations- und Konkurrenzmanagement in genossenschaftlichen Systemen / Helmut Lipfert. Göttingen : Vandenhoeck & Ruprecht, c1986. xvii, 302 p. : 30 ill. ; 24 cm. (Hamburger Schriften zum Genossenschaftswesen . Bd. 5) Bibliography: p. [272]-290. Includes indexes. ISBN 3-525-12754-5 LC Card 86-235180 DDC 334/.068 19
1. Cooperation - Germany (West) - Management. 2. Competition - Germany, West. I. Title. II. Series.
HD3498 .L53 1986

Lipko, A. G. (Alekseĭ Gennad'evich) Proizvodstvo i potreblenie v regione / A.G. Lipko, K.M. Misko ; otvetstvennyĭ redaktor E.D. Silaev. Moskva : "Nauka", 1986. 142 p. : ill. ; 20 cm. (Problemy sovetskoĭ ėkonomiki) At head of title: Akademiia nauk SSSR. Gosplan SSSR. Sovet po izucheniiu proizvoditel'nykh sil. Includes bibliographical references. LC Card 86-211374
1. Soviet Union - Economic conditions - 1976- - Regional disparities. 2. Soviet Union - Industries - 1957-. 3. Consumption (Economics) - Soviet Union. I. Misko, K. M. (Konstantin Mikhaĭlovich). II. Silaev, E. D. III. Title.
HC336.25 .L56 1986

Lipnowski, Irwin. Macroeconomic conflict and social institutions /. Cambridge, Mass. , c1985. xi, 249 p. : ISBN 0-88730-034-0 LC Card 84-24376 DDC 339.2 19
HC79.I5 M225 1985 *NYPL [JLE 86-2562]*

Lipowatz, Thanos, 1943- Litz, Hans Peter. Amtliche Statistik in marktwirtschaftlich organisierten Industriegesellschaften . Frankfurt , New York , c1986. xii, 312 p. : ISBN 3-593-33752-5 LC Card 87-108767 DDC 350.81/9 19
HA37.G3 L58 1986

Lipp, Robert. Silkman, Richard H. Subsidizing inefficiency . New York , 1985. xviii, 101 p.: ISBN 0-03-000662-7 (alk. paper) : LC Card 84-26628 DDC 336.1/85 19
HJ275 .S53 1985 *NYPL [JLE 85-2261]*

Lippold, Dirk, 1953- Individualisierung der Organisation von Banken : aufgrund einer Untersuchung der Leistungsmotivation und Arbeitszufriedenheit von Bankmitarbeitern / Dirk Lippold. Spardorf : R.F. Wilfer, c1982. xxiii, 170 p. : ill. ; 22 cm. Originally presented as the author's thesis (doctoral)--Philipps-Universität zu Marburg. Bibliography: p. viii-xiii. ISBN 3-922919-04-9 LC Card 83-221727
1. Banks and banking - Personnel management. I. Title.
HG1615.5 .L56 1982

Lippsett, Brian. Petersen, Sybil. Transportation . Arlington, Va. (P.O. Box 926, Arlington 22216) [1986] [8], 40 p. : LC Card 87-401670 DDC 363.1/7 19
HE199.5.D3 P48 1986

Lipset, Seymour Martin.
The confidence gap : business, labor, and government in the public mind / Seymour Martin Lipset and William Schneider.Rev. ed., John Hopkins paperbacks ed. Baltimore : Johns Hopkins University Press, 1987. xxiv, 460 p. : ill. ; 23 cm. "A Johns Hopkins paperback"--Cover. Includes bibliographical references and indexes. ISBN 0-8018-3044-3 (pbk.) LC Card 86-27416 DDC 303.3/8/0973 19
1. Corporations - United States - Public opinion. 2. Trade regulation - United States - Public opinion. 3. Trade-unions - United States - Public opinion. 4. Politicians - United States - Public opinion. 5. Public opinion - United States. I. Schneider, William, 1941-. II. Title.
HD2785 .L53 1987

Unions in transition . San Francisco, Calif. , c1986. xviii, 506 p. : ISBN 0-917616-74-X : LC Card 86-10256 DDC 331.88 19
HD .U46 1986 *NYPL [JLE 86-4238]*

Lipsey, Richard G., 1928- Economics / Richard G. Lipsey, Peter O. Steiner, Douglas D. Purvis. 8th ed. New York : Harper & Row, c1987. xxvii, 942 p. : ill. ; 27 cm. Includes index. ISBN 0-06-043917-3 LC Card 86-29422 DDC 330 19
1. Economics. I. Steiner, Peter Otto, 1922-. II. Purvis, Douglas D. III. Title.
HB171.5 .L733 1987

Lipsky, David B., 1939- Collective bargaining in American industry . Lexington, Mass. , c1987. ix, 351 p. ; ISBN 0-669-12594-6 (alk. paper) LC

Card 85-45936 DDC 331.89/0973 19
HD6508 .C656 1987

Liptser, Robert Shevilevich. Steklov Seminar (1984 : Steklov Institute of Mathematics) [Statistika i upravlenie sluchaĭnykh protsessov. English.] Statistics and control of stochastic processes /. New York, N.Y. , c1985. xiii, 506 p. ; ISBN 0-911575-18-9 LC Card 85-8851 DDC 519.5 19
QA276.A1 .S7513 1984 ***NYPL [JSE 86-729]***

LIQUEFIED NATURAL GAS INDUSTRY - SOVIET UNION.
Sagers, Matthew J. Natural gas liquids and the Soviet gas processing industry /. Washington, D.C. [1986] viii, 72, 2 p. : LC Card 87-601287 DDC 338.4/766573 19
HD9581.2.L573 S657 1986

LIQUEFIED PETROLEUM GAS - BRAZIL - MATO GROSSO (STATE) - TRANSPORTATION.
Brazil. Superintendência Nacional da Marinha Mercante. Alternativa rodo-ferro-hidroviária para o abastecimento de gás liquefeito de petróleo-GLP às regiões oeste do Estado de Mato Grosso e leste do Estado de Rondônia /. [Rio de Janeiro] [1984] 41 leaves : LC Card 85-197972
HE199.5.L43 B73 1984

LIQUEFIED PETROLEUM GAS - BRAZIL - RONDÔNIA (STATE) - TRANSPORTATION.
Brazil. Superintendência Nacional da Marinha Mercante. Alternativa rodo-ferro-hidroviária para o abastecimento de gás liquefeito de petróleo-GLP às regiões oeste do Estado de Mato Grosso e leste do Estado de Rondônia /. [Rio de Janeiro] [1984] 41 leaves : LC Card 85-197972
HE199.5.L43 B73 1984

LIQUEFIED PETROLEUM GAS INDUSTRY - BRAZIL - MATO GROSSO (STATE)
Alternativa rodo-ferro-hidroviária para o abastecimento de gás liquefeito de petróleo-GLP às regiões oeste do Estado de Mato Grosso e leste do Estado de Rondônia /. [Rio de Janeiro] [19]84. 41 leaves : LC Card 87-403939 DDC 338.4/7665773 19
HE199.5.L43 A44 1984

LIQUEFIED PETROLEUM GAS INDUSTRY - BRAZIL - RONDÔNIA (STATE)
Alternativa rodo-ferro-hidroviária para o abastecimento de gás liquefeito de petróleo-GLP às regiões oeste do Estado de Mato Grosso e leste do Estado de Rondônia /. [Rio de Janeiro] [19]84. 41 leaves : LC Card 87-403939 DDC 338.4/7665773 19
HE199.5.L43 A44 1984

LIQUEFIED PETROLEUM GAS - TRANSPORTATION.
Alternativa rodo-ferro-hidroviária para o abastecimento de gás liquefeito de petróleo-GLP às regiões oeste do Estado de Mato Grosso e leste do Estado de Rondônia /. [Rio de Janeiro] [19]84. 41 leaves : LC Card 87-403939 DDC 338.4/7665773 19
HE199.5.L43 A44 1984

Liquid assets . Sokolin, William. New York , c1987. 163 p. : ISBN 0-02-612300-2 LC Card 86-31284 DDC 332.63 19
HD9370.5 .S65 1987

LIQUIDATION - DECISION MAKING.
Allerkamp, Ferdinand. Tilgungsplanung . Frankfurt am Main , c1983. xii, 288 p. : ISBN 3-7819-0296-X LC Card 85-239167
HD2747 .A53 1983

LIQUIDATION - GERMANY, WEST.
Stauf, Wolfgang. Der wichtige Grund bei der personengesellschaftlichen Auflösungs- und Ausschliessungsklage . Göttingen , 1980. xiv, 80 p. ; ISBN 3-88415-549-0 : LC Card 80-150978 DDC 346.73/07 347.3067 19
KK2435.7 .S7 1980 ***NYPL [JLD 86-1591]***

Wöbbeking, Karlheinz. Die Planung von Liquidationsstrategien . Münster [1986] vii, 273 p. : ISBN 3-88660-328-8 LC Card 86-213801
HD2747 .W6 1986

LIQUIDATION - ITALY.
Masciocchi, Giuseppe. Crisi di impresa . Milano , 1983. viii, 112 p. ; LC Card 84-141092 DDC 657/.73 19
HD2747 .M37 1983 ***NYPL [JLE 86-4053]***

Liquiditätswirkungen alternativer Geldvermögensanlagen /. Hess, Stephan M. Frankfurt am Main , c1983. 193 p. ; ISBN 3-7819-2533-1 LC Card 84-109572
HG173.5 .H47 1983

LIQUOR INDUSTRY - GOVERNMENT POLICY - NEW ZEALAND.
New Zealand. Working Party on Liquor. The sale of liquor in New Zealand . [Wellington, N.Z. , 1986] 212, [1] p. : LC Card 87-147518 DDC 338.4/76631/09931 19
HD9390.N452 N49 1986

LIQUOR INDUSTRY - KANSAS.
Daicoff, Darwin W. The Kansas retail liquor industry . [Lawrence, Kan.] [1985] 53 leaves ; LC Card 86-622263 DDC 381/.456631/09781 19
HD9390.U63 K23 1985

Lira, Enrique Astorga. see **Astorga Lira, Enrique.**

Lira, Luis Felipe. Estructura agraria, crecimiento de la población y migraciones : el caso de la zona central de Chile, 1952-1970 / Luis Felipe Lira. Santiago, Chile : Unidad Central del Programa de Investigaciones Sociales sobre Problemas de Población Relevantes para Políticas de Población en América Latina : Consejo Latinoamericano de Ciencias Sociales, Comisión de Población y Desarrollo, 1976. 90 p. ; 28 cm. (Documento de trabajo . no. 14) Includes bibliographical references. LC Card 83-169710
1. Migration, Internal - Chile. 2. Chile - Population, Rural. 3. Land tenure - Chile. I. Series: Documento de trabajo (Programa de Investigaciones Sociales sobre Problemas de Población Relevantes para Políticas de Población en América Latina. Unidad Central) , no. 14. II. Title.
HB2025 .L57 1976

Lis, Michał. Odbudowa podstaw gospodarki Śląska Opolskiego na przykładzie przemysłu, 1945-1949 / Michał Lis. Wyd. 1. [Opole] : Wydawn. Instytutu Śląskiego w Opolu, 1978. 254 p. : ill. ; 24 cm. At head of title: Instytut Śląski w Opolu. Bibliography: p. 238-[247] Includes indexes. LC Card 81-201084
1. Opole (Poland : Voivodeship) - Industries - History. 2. Reconstruction (1939-1951) - Poland - Opole (Voivodeship). I. Title.
HC340.Z7 O665 1978

Lisboa Bacha, Edmar. see **Bacha, Edmar Lisboa.**

Lischka, J. R. (Johannes Richard), 1933- Ludwig Mond and the British alkali industry / J.R. Lischka. New York : Garland, 1985. 233 p. ; 21 cm. (British economic history) Revision of thesis--Duke University, 1970. Bibliography: p. 218-233. ISBN 0-8240-6686-3 (alk. paper) : LC Card 84-46006 DDC 338.4/7673725/0924 19
1. Mond, Ludwig. 2. Alkali industry and trade - Great Britain - History - 19th century. 3. Chemists - Great Britain - Biography. I. Title. II. Series.
HD9660.A43 G75 1985 ***NYPL [JSD 86-547]***

Lishcheniuk, S. N. Intensifikatsiia i povyshenie ėffektivnosti promyshlennogo proizvodstva v usloviiakh Severa . IAkutsk , 1986. 109 p. ; LC Card 87-159706
HC337.I23 I5214 1986

LISKA, TIBOR.
Koncepció és kritika . Budapest , c1985. 387 p. ; ISBN 963-14-0359-9 : LC Card 86-104222
HB615 .K66 1985

Liskó, Ilona. Érettségizettek a munkaerőpiacon /. Budapest , 1985. 124 p. ; ISBN 963-404-026-8 LC Card 87-409614
HD6276.H82 E73 1985

List-Gesellschaft. (Old Catalog form: Friedrich List Gesellschaft)
Was trennt Europa? /. Baden-Baden , 1986. 147 p. ; ISBN 3-7890-1320-X LC Card 87-108024 DDC 337.1/42 19
HC241.2 .W394 1986

List, H. L. (Harvey L.), 1924- Petrochemical technology : an overview for decision makers in the international petrochemical industry / H.L. List. Englewood Cliffs, N.J. : Prentice-Hall, c1986. xxxi, 271 p. : ill. ;24 cm. Includes bibliographies and index. ISBN 0-13-661992-4 : LC Card 85-19225 DDC 661/.804 19
1. Petroleum chemicals industry - Technological innovations. 2. Petroleum chemicals. I. Title.
HD9579.C32 L44 1986 ***NYPL [JSE 86-1624]***

List of aid worth projects, 1984. [Dhaka] : Ministry of Planning, Planning Commission, Govt. of the People's Republic of Bangladesh, [1984] 431 p. ; 29 cm. LC Card 85-904102 DDC 338.9549/2 19
1. Economic development projects - Bangladesh. I. Bangladesh. Parikalpanā Kamiśana.
HC440.8.Z9 E445 1984

List of post offices in the United States, March 1, 1876. Post offices in the United States, 1876 /. Melber, Ky. [1986] 125 p. ; LC Card 87-400310 DDC 383/.42/0973 19
HE6366 .P67 1986

List Society. see **List-Gesellschaft.**

List, Stephan, 1959- Arbeitnehmerbeteiligung bei Personengesellschaften : eine theoretische Analyse der steuerlichen Probleme / Stephan List. Spardorf : R.F. Wilfer, c1985. v, 167 p. ; 21 cm. Bibliography: p. 147-165. ISBN 3-922919-50-2 LC Card 86-141876
1. Management - Germany (West) - Employee participation. 2. Business enterprises - Taxation - Germany, West. I. Title.
HD5660.G4 L55 1985

Listen to the people . Salmen, Lawrence F., 1942- New York , c1987. x, 149 p. : ISBN 0-19-520545-6 : LC Card 86-23672 DDC 338.984/12 19
HC185.E44 S25 1987

Lister, Timothy R. DeMarco, Tom. Peopleware . New York, NY , c1987. x, 188 p. : ISBN 0-932633-05-6 (pbk.) : LC Card 87-22293 DDC 658.3/14 19
HD31 .D42185 1987

Liston, Linda L. Facility planning technology /. Norcross, Ga. , c1987. viii, 935 p. : ISBN 0-910436-26-6 LC Card 86-72097 DDC 658.2/1 19
HD30.28 .F33 1987

Litan, Robert E., 1950-
Lawrence, Robert Z., 1949- Saving free trade . Washington, D.C. , c1986. xii, 132 p. ; ISBN 0-8157-5178-8 LC Card 86-14705 DDC 382.7/1/0973 19
HF1455 .L39 1986 ***NYPL [JLE 86-4368]***

What should banks do? / Robert E. Litan. Washington, D.C. : Brookings Institution, c1987. xi, 207 p. : ill. ; 24 cm. Includes bibliographical references and index. ISBN 0-8157-5270-9 : LC Card 87-18235 DDC 332.1/0973 19
1. Banks and banking - United States. I. Title.
HG2491 .L58 1987

LITERACY - UNITED STATES.
Workplace literacy /. New York , c1986. 74 p. : ISBN 0-8144-2325-6 LC Card 86-14013 DDC 331.25/92 19
HF5549.5.T7 W66 1986
NYPL [JLE 86-3510]

LITHUANIA - COMMERCE - CONGRESSES.
Problemy razvitiia i sovershenstvovaniia material'no-tekhnicheskoĭ bazy torgovli i obshchestvennogo pitaniia v dvenadtsatoĭ piatiletke . Vil'nius , 1985. 169 p. ; LC Card 86-102743
HF3629.L5 P76 1985

LITHUANIA - ECONOMIC CONDITIONS - 1945- - ECONOMETRIC MODELS.
Regional'noe modelirovanie obshchestvennogo vosproizvodstva . Vil'nius , 1980. 280 p. : LC Card 81-191307
HC337.L5 R44 1980

LITHUANIA - INDUSTRIES - STATISTICAL METHODS.
Matematicheskie metody v organizatsii sotsialisticheskogo sorevnovaniia . Vil'nius , 1986. 238 p. : LC Card 87-130668
HC337.L53 S65 1986

O litoral norte do Estado de São Paulo . Silva, Armando Corrêa da. São Paulo , 1975. 273 p. : LC Card 85-134276
HC189.S343 S58 1975

Litovka, Oleg Petrovich. Ėkonomicheskaia i sotsial'naia geografiia . Leningrad , 1984. 149 p. : LC Card 85-191961
HC336.25 .E3812 1984

Little, Alan. Loading the law : a study of transmitted deprivation, ethnic minorities and affirmative action / Alan Little, Diana Robbins.1st ed. London : Commission for

Racial Equality, 1982. 67 p. ; 21 cm. Bibliography: p. 63-67. ISBN 0-902355-98-8 (pbk.)
1. Race discrimination - Great Britain. 2. Minorities - Great Britain. 3. Affirmative action programs - United States. I. Robbins, Diana. II. Title.
NYPL [JLD 87-1941]

Little, Geoffrey, 1956- Mitroff, Ian I. Business not as usual . San Francisco , 1987. xxi, 194 p. : ISBN 1-555-42030-3 (alk. paper) LC Card 86-46333 DDC 338.9 19
HD70.U5 M52 1987

Little, Ian Malcolm David. Small manufacturing enterprises : a comparative study of India and other economies / Ian M.D. Little, Dipak Mazumdar, John M. Page, Jr. New York : Oxford University Press, 1987. x, 362 p. : ill. ; 24 cm. (A World Bank research publication) "Published for the World Bank." Bibliography: p. 337-345. Includes index. ISBN 0-19-520619-3 LC Card 87-12365 DDC 338.6/42/0954 19
1. India - Manufactures. 2. Small business - India. 3. Developing countries - Manufactures. 4. Small business - Developing countries. I. Mazumdar, Dipak, 1932-. II. Page, John M., 1949-. III. International Bank for Reconstruction and Development. IV. Title.
HD9736.I52 L57 1987

Little, Jeffrey B.
Growth stocks / Jeffrey B. Little ; Paul A. Samuelson, senior editorial consultant. New York : Chelsea House, c1988. p. cm. (The Basic investor's library) Bibliography: p. Includes index. Examines growth stocks as shares of companies whose sales and profits are increasing faster than their particular industry or the economy in general. ISBN 1-555-46624-9 LC Card 87-24482 DDC 332.63/22 19
1. Stocks - Juvenile literature. I. Samuelson, Paul Anthony 1915-. II. Title. III. Series.
HG4661 .L57 1988

Investing and trading / Jeffrey B. Little ; Paul A. Samuelson, senior editorial consultant. New York : Chelsea House Publishers, c1988. 47 p. : ill. ; 21 cm. (The Basic investor's library) Bibliography: p. 44. Includes index. Offers advice on selecting a stockbroker and explains various aspects of trading and investing, including margin accounts, investment clubs, and mutual funds. ISBN 1-555-46627-3 LC Card 87-23852 DDC 332.6/78 19
1. Stock-exchange - Juvenile literature. 2. Investments - Juvenile literature. I. Samuelson, Paul Anthony 1915-. II. Title. III. Series.
HG4553 .L58 1988

Understanding a company / Jeffrey B. Little ; Paul A. Samuelson, senior editorial consultant. New York : Chelsea House Publishers, c1988. 47 p. : ill. ; 21 cm. (The Basic investor's library) Bibliography: p. 45. Includes index. Explains how to identify and learn more about the best companies in which to invest, with an emphasis on the reading of financial statements and the basics of analysis. ISBN 1-555-46622-2 LC Card 87-17654 DDC 657/.33 19
1. Financial statements - Juvenile literature. 2. Corporations - Finance - Juvenile literature. I. Samuelson, Paul Anthony 1915-. II. Title. III. Series.
HG4028.B2 L57 1988

Understanding Wall Street / by Jeffrey B. Little and Lucien Rhodes. 2nd ed. Blue Ridge Summit, PA : Liberty House, c1987. 219 p. : ill. ; 22 cm. Includes index. ISBN 0-8306-3120-8 : LC Card 87-3628 DDC 332.6/78 19
1. Investments - United States. 2. Stocks - United States. 3. Stock-exchange - United States. 4. Wall Street. I. Rhodes, Lucien. II. Title.
HG4910 .L54 1987

Wall Street--how it works / Jeffrey B. Little ; Paul A. Samuelson, senior editorial consultant. New York : Chelsea House, c1988. 47 p. : ill. ; 21 cm. (The Basic investor's library) Bibliography: p. 46. Includes index. Presents a brief history of Wall Street and explains how stocks and bonds are traded in the U. S. securities market. ISBN 1-555-46621-4 LC Card 87-15139 DDC 332.64/273 19
1. Investments - United States - Juvenile literature. 2. Stocks - United States - Juvenile literature. 3. Stock-exchange - United States - Juvenile literature. 4. Wall Street - Juvenile literature. I. Samuelson, Paul Anthony 1915-. II. Title. III. Series.
HG4921 .L625 1988

[Wall Street library]
Understanding Wall Street / Jeffrey B. Little and Lucien Rhodes. Blue Ridge Summit, PA : Liberty House, 1986. p. cm. Previously published as: Wall Street library. Includes index. ISBN 0-8306-3010-4 (pbk.) : LC Card 86-27791 DDC 332.6/78 19
1. Investments - United States. 2. Stocks - United States. 3. Stock-exchange - United States. 4. Wall Street. I. Rhodes, Lucien. II. Title.
HG4921 .L63 1986

What is a share of stock? / Jeffrey B. Little ; Paul A. Samuelson, senior editorial consultant. New York : Chelsea House, c1988. 47 p. : ill. ; 21 cm. (The Basic investor's library) Bibliography: p. 46. Includes index. Explains how a stock is created, how a new company is founded and financed, why investors invest in companies, and how an established company is organized and raises money for its operations. ISBN 1-555-46620-6 LC Card 87-13788 DDC 332.63/22 19
1. Stocks - Juvenile literature. 2. Business enterprises - Finance - Juvenile literature. I. Samuelson, Paul Anthony 1915-. II. Title. III. Series.
HG4521 .L736 1988

Little, Joseph R. Nguyen, Tim K. Applied 1-2-3 . New York, N.Y. , c1987. p. cm. ISBN 0-13-729542-1 : LC Card 87-11390 DDC 005.36/9 19
HF5548.4.L67 N48 1987

Little, Peter D. Lands at risk in the Third World . Boulder , 1987. xiii, 416 p. : ISBN 0-8133-7311-5 (pbk. : alk. paper) : LC Card 86-51423 DDC 333.73/13 19
HD1131 .L37 1987

Little, Richard. McKinlay, Robert D. Global problems and world order /. Madison, Wis. , c1986. 292 p. ; ISBN 0-299-11384-1 (pbk.) : LC Card 86-40489 DDC 337 19
HF1411 .M376 1986

Little Russia. see **Ukraine.**

Littler, Craig R. The development of the labour process in capitalist societies : a comparative study of the transformation of work organization in Britain, Japan, and the USA / Craig R. Littler. London ; Exeter, N.H. : Heinemann Educational, 1982. 226 p. : ill. ; 22 cm. Includes index. Bibliography: p. [205]-215. ISBN 0-435-82540-2 : LC Card 82-210245 DDC 306/.36 19
1. Labor and laboring classes - Great Britain - History. 2. Labor and laboring classes - Japan - History. 3. Labor and laboring classes - United States - History. 4. Comparative organization. 5. Bureaucracy. I. Title.
HD8390 .L48 1982 ***NYPL [JLD 87-1005]***

Littman, Jonathan, 1958- Once upon a time in ComputerLand : the amazing, billion-dollar tale of Bill Millard / Jonathan Littman. Tucson, AZ : Knight-Ridder Press, c1987. xiii, 296 p., [8] p. of plates : ports. ; 24 cm. ISBN 0-89586-502-5 : LC Card 87-3823 DDC 381/.4500416/0973 19
1. ComputerLand (Firm) - History. 2. Millard, Bill. 3. Computer industry - United States - History. 4. Businessmen - United States - Biography. I. Title.
HD9696.C64 C655 1987

Litva. see **Lithuania.**

Litvinova, L. N. (Lı͡udmila Nikolaevna) Shevchuk, L. V. (Lı͡udmila Vladimirovna) Metodicheskie osnovy analiza i prognozirovanii͡a fondootdachi . Minsk , 1983. 118 p. : LC Card 84-118665
HD9715.S73 B9465 1983

Litwa. see **Lithuania.**

Litwin, George H. Tagiuri, Renato. Organizational climate. Boston, 1968. viii, 246 p. LC Card 68-8418 DDC 301.4
HM131 .T27 ***NYPL [JLD 86-684]***

Litz, Hans Peter. Amtliche Statistik in marktwirtschaftlich organisierten Industriegesellschaften : eine vergleichende Untersuchung der amtlichen Statistik der Bundesrepublik Deutschlands, der Niederlande und Frankreichs / Hans Peter Litz, Thanos Lipowatz ; unter Mitarbeit von Sander America und Rik Verhorst. Frankfurt ; New York : Campus, c1986. xii, 312 p. : ill. ; 21 cm. (Campus Forschung. Bd. 512) Bibliography: p. 298-312. ISBN 3-593-33752-5 LC Card 87-108767 DDC 350.81/9 19
1. Germany, West - Statistical services. 2. France - Statistical services. 3. Netherlands - Statistical services. I. Lipowatz, Thanos, 1943-. II. Title.
HA37.G3 L58 1986

Liu, Alan P. L., 1937- Phoenix and the lame lion : modernization in Taiwan and mainland China, 1950-1980 / Alan P.L. Liu. Stanford, Calif. : Hoover Institution Press, Stanford University, c1987. x, 182 p. ; 24 cm. Bibliography: p. [163]-179. Includes index. ISBN 0-8179-8581-6 LC Card 87-13555 DDC 338.951 19
1. Taiwan - Economic policy - 1945-. 2. China - Economic policy - 1949-. I. Title.
HC430.5 .L568 1987

Liu, Shih-pai. She hui chu i so yu chih yen chiu / Liu Shih-pai chu. 880-03 Ti 1 pan. Shang-hai : Shang-hai jen min ch'u pan she : Hsin hua shu tien Shang-hai fa hsing so fa hsing, 1985. 2, 6, 223 p. ; 19 cm. Title also in pinyin on cover: Shehuizhuyi suoyouzhi yanjiu. In Chinese. Includes bibliograhical references.
1. Production (Economic theory). 2. Marxian economics. I. Title. II. Title: Shehuizhuyi suoyouzhi yanjiu. ***NYPL [*OVY 86-3647]***

Liu, William Thomas, 1930- Transition to nowhere : Vietnamese refugees in America / by William T. Liu, Maryanne [i.e. Mary Ann] Lamanna, Alice Murata. Nashville : Charter House, c1979. 214 p., [2] leaves of plates : ill. ; 22 cm. (The Asian American mental health monograph series) Bibliography: p. 211-214. ISBN 0-8202-0189-8 : LC Card 78-21129 DDC 361.5/3/09597
1. Refugees - Vietnam. 2. Refugees - United States. 3. Vietnamese Conflict, 1961-1975 - Refugees. 4. Refugees, Political - Psychology. I. Lamanna, Mary Ann, joint author. II. Murata, Alice, joint author. III. Title.
HV640.5.V5 L58 ***NYPL [JLD 87-670]***

Liu, Yung-ch'eng. She hui chu i ching chi tse jen chih / Liu Yung-ch'eng chu. 880-03 Ti 1 pan. [Ch'ang-ch'un shih] : Chi-lin ta hsüeh ch'u pan she : Chi-lin sheng hsin hua shu tien fa hsing, 1985. 5, 264 p. ; 18 cm. In Chinese. Includes bibliographical references. LC Card 86-179707 DDC 658/.00951 19
1. Industrial management - China. 2. Agricultural productivity - China. 3. Farm production quotas - China. I. Title.
HD70.C5 L58 1985 <Orien China>
NYPL [*OVY 86-4140]

Lı͡ubenova, Temenuzhka. Morska vrata na rodinata . Varna , 1986. 146 p., [32] p. of plates : LC Card 86-233471
HE557.B9 M67 1986

Lı͡ubimoe pole /. Rotov, Viktor. Moskva , 1980. 149 p. ; LC Card 81-143989
HD1492.S652 K76 1980

Lı͡utov, Atanas N. Upravlenie na narodnoto potreblenie /. Sofii͡a , 1984. 235 p. : LC Card 85-212359
HC403.Z9 C628 1984

Live births by estimated marital status of mother, California, 1981. Mielke, Robert B. [Sacramento] [1984] 22 p. : LC Card 86-622328 DDC 304.6/32/09794 19
HB935.C2 M54 1984

Livelli stipulati a Venezia nel 1591 . Corazzol, Gigi, 1945- Pisa , c1986. 167 p., [8] leaves of plates : LC Card 86-192693
HD680.V4 C67 1986

Liverēs, Anastasēs I. Politikē oikonomia gia holous : to politiko alphavēto tēs laikēs henotētas : hena aitēma tou kairou mas / A.I. Liverēs. Athēna : Dōrikos, 1985. 424 p. ; 21 cm. LC Card 86-178760
1. Marxian economics. 2. Greece - Economic conditions - 1974-. I. Title.
HB97.5 .L555 1985

Liverpool papers in human geography . (no. 1) Watts, Susan J. Population mobility and multilocality in Ilorin, Kwara State, Nigeria /. [Liverpool , 1981-] v. <1 > : LC Card 86-226489 DDC 304.8/09669/5 19
HB2126.7.I46 W37 1981

Lives of the laureates : seven Nobel economists / edited by William Breit and Roger W. Spencer. Cambridge, Mass. : MIT Press, c1986. xii, 135 p. : ports. ; 22 cm. The papers were originally delivered at Trinity University, San Antonio, Tex. in a lecture series organized by W. Breit. Includes bibliographies. CONTENTS. - W. Arthur Lewis -- Lawrence R. Klein -- Kenneth J. Arrow -- Paul A. Samuelson -- Milton Friedman -- George J. Stigler --

James Tobin. ISBN 0-262-02255-9 LC Card 86-2919 DDC 330/.092/2 B 19
1. Economists - Biography. 2. Nobel prizes - Biography. I. Breit, William. II. Spencer, Roger W. III. Trinity University (San Antonio, Tex.).
HB76 .L58 1986 *NYPL [JFD 86-9827]*

Lives of the left.
Davies, Paul, 1951- A.J. Cook /. Wolfeboro, NH , c1987. p. cm. ISBN 0-7190-2160-X LC Card 87-11114 DDC 331.88/122/0924 B 19
HD8393.C63 D38 1987

Livestock and meat marketing /. McCoy, John Henry, 1912- New York , c1988. vii, 642 p. : ISBN 0-442-20488-4 LC Card 87-23136 DDC 381/.416/00973 19
HD9415 .M25 1988

LIVESTOCK - CANADA.
Canadian farming . Toronto , 1881. 432 p., [4] folded leaves of plates : LC Card 85-666092
HD1783 .C3x 1881

LIVESTOCK - CHINA.
China, the livestock sector. Washington, D.C., U. S.A. , 1987. vii, 195 p. ; ISBN 0-8213-0940-4 (pbk.) LC Card 87-16089 DDC 338.1/76/00951 19
HD9426.C62 C475 1987

LIVESTOCK - ECONOMIC ASPECTS - AFRICA - CASE STUDIES.
Addis Anteneh. Financing livestock services in some countries of east and southern Africa /. Addis Ababa, Ethiopia [1985] 26 p. ; LC Card 86-980745 DDC 338.1/36/0096 19
HD9427.A2 A33 1985

LIVESTOCK FACTORIES - UNITED STATES.
Fox, Michael W., 1937- Agricide . New York , 1986. xv, 194 p., [10] p. of plates : ISBN 0-8052-4013-6 LC Card 85-27690 DDC 338.1/6/0973 19
S441 .F69 1986 *NYPL [JLD 86-2542]*

LIVESTOCK - GERMANY (WEST) - NORTH RHINE-WESTPHALIA - STATISTICS.
Agrarberichterstattung Nordrhein-Westfalen 1983 . Düsseldorf [1984] 241, [5] p. ; LC Card 87-407318 DDC 943/.55 s 338.1/76/0094355021 19
HA1320.N6 A32 Heft 533 HD9423.7.N6

Agrarberichterstattung Nordrhein-Westfalen 1983 . Düsseldorf [1985] 191 p. ; LC Card 87-407316 DDC 943/.55 s 338.1/0943/55021 19
HA1320.N6 A32 Heft 531 HD1960.N67

Livey, Jay. The effect of state income tax policy on the development of marginal oil fields : an analysis of the impact of House Bill 353 / Jay Livey. [Juneau] : House Research Agency, Alaska State Legislature, [1986] vii leaves, 52 p., [17] leaves : ill. ; 28 cm. (House Research Agency report . 86-C) Cover title: The effects of state income tax policy on the development of marginal oil fields. "January 1986." Includes bibliographical references. LC Card 86-622190 DDC 333.8/232/09798 19
1. Petroleum - Taxation - Alaska. 2. Petroleum industry and trade - Alaska - Finance. 3. Oil fields - Alaska. 4. Petroleum - Taxation - Law and legislation - Alaska. I. Title. II. Title: Effects of state income tax policy on the development of marginal oil fields. III. Series.
HD9560.8.U53 A445 1986

LIVING, COST OF. see COST AND STANDARD OF LIVING.

LIVING EXPENSES. see COST AND STANDARD OF LIVING.

LIVING, STANDARD OF. see COST AND STANDARD OF LIVING.

Living with SNA / Communications/Information Systems Planning Service and Critical Path Planning Service. Boston, MA (89 Broad St., Boston 02110) : Yankee Group, [1986] 60 p. : ill. ; 28 cm. (Industry research report) "June 1986." LC Card 86-201765 DDC 381/.4500468/0973 19
1. Computer industry - United States. 2. Local area networks (Computer networks). 3. Market surveys - United States. I. Communications/Information Systems Planning Service and Critical Path Planning Service (Form : Yankee Group). II. Series.
HD9696.C63 U5223 1986

Livingston, James, 1949- Origins of the Federal Reserve System : money, class, and corporate capitalism, 1890-1913 / James Livingston. Ithaca : Cornell University Press, 1986. 250 p. ; 24 cm. Includes bibliographical references and index. ISBN 0-8014-1844-5 (alk. paper) LC Card 85-48199 DDC 332.1/1/0973 19
1. United States. Board of Governors of the Federal Reserve System - History. 2. Capitalism - United States - History. 3. Money - United States - History. I. Title.
HG2563 .L58 1986 *NYPL [JLE 86-2522]*

Livingstone, Ian.
Rural development, employment and incomes in Kenya / Ian Livingstone. Aldershot, Hants ; Brookfield, Vermont : Gower Pub. Co., 1986. xx, 389 p. : ill. ; 23 cm. "A study prepared for the International Labour Office within the framework of the jobs and skills program for Africa (JASPA)"--T.p. verso. Includes bibliographical references. ISBN 0-566-00990-0
1. Rural development - Kenya. 2. Agricultural laborers - Kenya. 3. Kenya - Rural conditions. I. Jobs and Skills Programme for Africa. II. Title.
NYPL [Sc D 86-728]

Youth employment & youth employment programmes in Africa : a comparative sub-regional study : the case of [name of country]. Addis Ababa : International Labour Organisation, Jobs & Skills Programme for Africa, 1986. 7 v. : ill. ; 29 cm. Cover title: Youth employment and youth employment programmes in Africa. Includes bibliographies. CONTENTS. - [1] Botswana -- [2] Ethiopia -- [3] Kenya -- [4] Malawi -- [5] Mauritius -- [6] Somalia -- [7] Zambia. ISBN 92-2-105527-2 (pbk. : v. 1) LC Card 87-980143 DDC 331.3/4/096 19
1. Youth - Employment - Africa. 2. Youth - Government policy - Africa. 3. Occupational training - Africa. I. Jobs and Skills Programme for Africa. II. Title. III. Title: Youth employment and youth employment programmes in Africa.
HD6276.A32 L58 1986

Livingstone, John Leslie. Management planning and control . Beavercreek, Ohio , c1987. xvii, 249 p. : ISBN 0-939787-00-8 (pbk.) : LC Card 86-24930 DDC 658.1/511 19
HF5635 .M236 1987

Die Livländische Gemeinnützige und Ökonomische Sozietät (1792-1939) .
Engelhardt, Hans Dieter von. Köln , 1983. ix, 215 p., [3] leaves of plates : ISBN 3-412-04282-X LC Card 84-117318
HD1486.S65 E54 1983

LIVLÄNDISCHE GEMEINNÜTZIGE UND ÖKONOMISCHE SOZIETÄT - HISTORY.
Engelhardt, Hans Dieter von. Die Livländische Gemeinnützige und Ökonomische Sozietät (1792-1939) . Köln , 1983. ix, 215 p., [3] leaves of plates : ISBN 3-412-04282-X LC Card 84-117318
HD1486.S65 E54 1983

Livre blanc de l'environnement :
Basse-Normandie : documents. [S.l. : s.n., 1982] (Caen : Impr. P.A.C.) 1 portfolio (32 p.) : ill. ; 31 cm. (Etats régionaux de l'environnement) Cover title. LC Card 83-209058
1. Environmental policy - France - Basse-Normandie. I. Series.
HC277.B28 L58 1982

Livros de contas da ilha da Madeira, 1504-1537 / prefácio, leitura e notas de Fernando Jasmins Pereira e José Pereira da Costa. Coimbra : Biblioteca Geral da Universidade, 1985- v. <1 > ; 26 cm. Errata slip inserted in v. 1. Bibliography; v. 1, p. 155-189. Includes index. CONTENTS. - 1. Almoxarifados e alfândegas. LC Card 86-232733
1. Finance, Public - Madeira Islands - Accounting - History - 16th century. 2. Tariff - Madeira Islands - Accounting - History - 16th century. 3. Customs administration - Madeira Islands - History - 16th century. I. Pereira, Fernando Jasmins. II. Costa, José Pereira da. III. Universidade de Coimbra. Biblioteca Geral.
HJ9930.3.M33 L58 1985

Livshits, V. I. (Vadim Isaevich)
Obobshchestvlenie i ėkonomicheskie interesy v sotsialisticheskom obshchestve /. Moskva , 1983. 127 p. ; LC Card 84-204638
HD3856.R9 O26 1983

Lizano, Eduardo. see Lizano Fait, Eduardo.

Lizano Fait, Eduardo. La condicionalidad cruzada y la deuda externa / Eduardo Lizano, Silvia Charpentier. [San José] : Banco Central de Costa Rica, 1986. 16, [1] leaves : ill. ; 28 cm. (Serie "Comentarios sobre asuntos económicos" . no. 59) "Ponencia presentada ... en la XXIII Reunión de Gobernadores de Bancos Centrales del Continente Americano celebrada en Buenos Aires, Argentina, entre el 10 y 11 de marzo de 1986." Bibliography: leaf [17]. LC Card 87-127835 DDC 336.3/435/091724 19
1. Debts, External - Developing countries. 2. International Monetary Fund - Developing countries. I. Charpentier, Silvia. II. Title. III. Series.
HJ8899 .L59 1986

Lizárraga Bobbio, Raúl. Estrategias para la descentralización y el desarrollo regional / Raúl Lizárraga Bobbio. Lima, Perú : Centro Peruano de Estudios para el Desarrollo Regional, c1985. 356 p. : ill. ; 22 cm. Includes bibliographical references. LC Card 86-146658
1. Regional planning - Peru. 2. Decentralization in government - Peru. 3. Peru - Economic conditions - 1968-. I. Title.
HT395.P4 L59 1985 *NYPL [JLD 87-1315]*

Ljunggren, Sten. Fredriksson, Carl, 1947- Kooperationens industrisektor i 1980-talets industri-Sverige . [Stockholm] [1981] iv, 196, 24, 11 p. : ISBN 91-38-06535-5 LC Card 83-147552
HD3522 .F74 1981

Los Llanos . Pedraja Tomán, René de la. Bogotá, Colombia , 1984. 101 p. : LC Card 84-221343
HC198.L56 P4 1984

LLANOS ORIENTALES (COLOMBIA AND VENEZUELA) - ECONOMIC CONDITIONS.
Pedraja Tomán, René de la. Los Llanos . Bogotá, Colombia , 1984. 101 p. : LC Card 84-221343
HC198.L56 P4 1984

Lleras Restrepo, Carlos, Pres, 1908- Economía internacional y régimen cambiario / Carlos Lleras Restrepo. [S.l. : s.n., 1981] (Bogotá, D.E. : Osprey Impresores) 298, [3] p. ; 24 cm. "Obras del autor": p. [299]-[301] CONTENTS. - La economía de guerra -- El Fondo Monetario Internacional -- La misión de las Naciones Unidas en el campo económico -- La Carta de comercio y empleo -- La Conferencia de Comercio y Desarrollo de las Naciones Unidas -- La política cambiaria -- El Banco Interamericano de Desarrollo -- El nueve orden económico -- Las inversiones extranjeras en países desarrollados y en países en vía de desarrollo -- Informe sobre el desarrollo económico mundial -- El drama de las monedas. LC Card 81-204089 DDC 337/.09/048 19
1. International economic relations - Addresses, essays, lectures. 2. Foreign exchange - Addresses, essays, lectures. I. Title.
HF1411 .L542 1981 *NYPL [JLE 86-3889]*

Llewellyn, Ralph A. Patterns of energy consumption in Florida, 1970-1983 : main report / Ralph A. Llewellyn. Tallahassee, Fla. : State of Florida, Governor's Energy Office, [1985] xiv, 147 p. : ill. ; 28 cm. "November 1985." Bibliography: p. 145-147. LC Card 86-622312 DDC 333.79/13/09759 19
1. Energy consumption - Florida. 2. Florida - Industries - Energy consumption. I. Florida. Governor's Energy Office. II. Title.
HD9502.U53 F5846 1985

Llistosella-Matzky, Ingrid. Kunhardt, Ulla von. Elsevier's dictionary of the labour market in five languages, English, German, Swedish, Spanish, and French /. Amsterdam , New York , 1988. p. cm. ISBN 0-444-42884-4 : LC Card 87-24529 DDC 331/.03 19
HD4839 .K86 1988

Lloyd, Christopher, 1950- Explanation in social history / Christopher Lloyd. Oxford, UK ; New York, NY, USA : B. Blackwell, 1986. xi, 375 p. : ill. ; 24 cm. Includes index. Bibliography: p. 318-365. ISBN 0-631-13113-2 : LC Card 85-13359 DDC 301/.09 19
1. Social history - Philosophy. 2. Social history - Methodology. 3. Criticism (Philosophy). I. Title.
HN28 .L58 1986 *NYPL [JLE 86-1677]*

LLoyd, K. A. The term structure of interest rates in New Zealand, 1977-1985 / K.A. Lloyd. Wellington, N.Z. : Economic Dept., Reserve Bank of New Zealand, [1986] 41, 3 p. : ill. ; 30 cm. (Discussion paper . G86/2) "July 1986." Bibliography: p. [1]-3 (2nd sequence) Includes index. LC Card 86-212755 DDC 332.8/2/09931 19
1. Interest rates - New Zealand. I. Series: Discussion paper (Reserve Bank of New Zealand. Economic

Dept.) , G86/2. II. Title.
HG1623.N48 L56 1986

LLOYD'S (FIRM)
Hodgson, Godfrey. Lloyd's of London . Harmondsworth, Middlesex, England , New York, N.Y., U. S.A. , 1986. 414 p. ; ISBN 0-14-005646-7 (pbk.) : LC Card 87-106915 DDC 368/.012/094212 19
HG8039 .H62 1986

Macve, Richard, 1940- A survey of Lloyds syndicate accounts . Englewood Cliffs, NJ , 1986. xxv, 263 p. : ISBN 0-13-878273-3 : LC Card 85-12147 DDC 368/.012/094212 19
HG8039 .M33 1986 NYPL [JLE 87-864]

Lloyd's of London . Hodgson, Godfrey. Harmondsworth, Middlesex, England , New York, N.Y., U. S.A. , 1986. 414 p. ; ISBN 0-14-005646-7 (pbk.) : LC Card 87-106915 DDC 368/.012/094212 19
HG8039 .H62 1986

LLOYD'S UNDERWRITERS' ASSOCIATION.
Carmichael, K. S. (Keith Stanley) Taxation of Lloyd's underwriters /. London , 1980. xvi, 107 p. : ISBN 0-372-30027-8 (pbk.) : LC Card 81-107459
HG8123.G7 C37 1980

Lluch, Ernest, 1937-
Acaecimientos de Manuel Belgrano, fisiócrata, y su traducción de las "Máximas generales del gobierno económico de un reyno agricultor" de François Quesnay / Ernest Lluch. Madrid : Ediciones Cultura Hispánica, 1984. 107 p. ; 17 cm. Includes bibliographical references. ISBN 84-7232-332-3 LC Card 85-179398
1. Quesnay, François, 1694-1774. Maximes générales du gouvernement économique d'un royaume agricole. 2. Economics. 3. Agriculture - Economic aspects. 4. Belgrano, Manuel, 1770-1820 - Knowledge - Economics. 5. Physiocrats - Argentina - Biography. I. Title.
HB159 .L58 1984

Agronomía y fisiocracia en España, 1750-1820 / Ernest Lluch y Lluís Argemí i d'Abadal ; prólogo y epílogo por Fabián Estapé. Valencia : Institución Alfonso el Magnánimo : Institució Valenciana d'Estudis i Investigació, [1985?] lxi, 215 p. ; 21 cm. (Estudios universitarios. 11) Includes bibliographical references and index. ISBN 84-00-05965-4 LC Card 85-240630
1. Agriculture - Economic aspects - Spain - History - 18th century. 2. Agriculture - Economic aspects - Spain - History - 19th century. 3. Physiocrats. I. Argemí i d'Abadal, Lluís, 1945-. II. Series: Estudios universitarios (Institución Alfonso el Magnánimo) , 11. III. Title.
HD2022 .L58 1985

LO HERMIDA (SANTAIGO, CHILE)
Schkolnik, Mariana. Sobrevivir en la población José M. Caro y en Lo Hermida /. [Santiago, Chile] [1986] 150 p., [20] p. of plates : LC Card 87-400080 DDC 362.5/8/098331 19
HC193.S2 S35 1986

Load management / edited by Sarosh Talukdar, Clark W. Gellings. New York : IEEE Press, c1987. vii, 207 p. : ill. ; 29 cm. (IEEE Press selected reprint series) Includes bibliographies and indexes. ISBN 0-87942-214-9 LC Card 86-33824 DDC 363.6/2 19
1. Electric utilities - United States. 2. Electric power systems - United States - Load dispatching. 3. Electric utilities - United States - Rates - Time-of-use pricing. I. Talukdar, Sarosh. II. Gellings, Clark W.
HD9685.U5 L58 1987

LOADING AND UNLOADING.
Seiffert, Bernd. Zahlungsmittelbewirtschaftung im Verkehrsbetrieb /. Berlin , c1986. 187 p. : ISBN 3-428-06094-6 : LC Card 87-143799 DDC 380.5/24/0943 19
HE5999.Z7 G374 1986

Loading the law . Little, Alan. London , 1982. 67 p. ; ISBN 0-902355-98-8 (pbk.)
NYPL [JLD 87-1941]

LOAN ASSOCIATIONS. see **BUILDING AND LOAN ASSOCIATIONS.**

LOAN CLOSING COSTS. see **SETTLEMENT COSTS.**

Loan interviewing handbook. Washington, D.C. (1120 Connecticut Ave., NW, Washington 20036) : American Bankers Association, c1986. 55 p. : ill. ; 26 cm. Cover title. LC Card 86-210702 DDC 332.1/753/0685 19
1. Loans. 2. Loan officers. 3. Interviewing. I. American Bankers Association.
HG1641 .L48 1986

LOAN OFFICERS.
Loan interviewing handbook. Washington, D.C. (1120 Connecticut Ave., NW, Washington 20036) , c1986. 55 p. : LC Card 86-210702 DDC 332.1/753/0685 19
HG1641 .L48 1986

LOAN OFFICERS - TRAINING OF.
People skills in action, for loan officers and processors. Chicago, Ill. , 1986. 1 videocassette (20 min.) : LC Card 86-707349 DDC 658.8 11
HG1641

LOAN OFFICERS - UNITED STATES.
Ruth, George E. Commercial lending /. Washington, D.C. (1120 Connecticut Ave., N.W., Washington 20036) , c1987. vi, 427 p. : LC Card 87-405117 DDC 332.1/753/0685 19
HG1642.U5 R88 1987

LOAN OFFICERS - UNITED STATES - TRAINING OF.
Pace, Edmond E. Developing a basic loan training program /. Philadelphia, Pa. , c1987. 108 p. ; ISBN 0-936742-41-0 (pbk.) : LC Card 87-7936 DDC 332.1/753/0683 19
HG1642.U5 P33 1987

LOANS.
Loan interviewing handbook. Washington, D.C. (1120 Connecticut Ave., NW, Washington 20036) , c1986. 55 p. : LC Card 86-210702 DDC 332.1/753/0685 19
HG1641 .L48 1986

Rennhoff, Harley A. Get that business loan . Gretna, La. , 1987. viii, 163 p. ; ISBN 0-88289-602-4 LC Card 87-2245 DDC 658.1/5224 19
HG4027.7 .R46 1987

LOANS, AMERICAN.
Gwynne, S. C. (Samuel C.), 1953- Selling money /. New York , 1987, c1986. 182 p. ; ISBN 0-14-010282-5 (pbk.) LC Card 87-6969 DDC 336.3/435 19
HG3891.5 .G98 1987

Kennedy, Charles R. Political risk management . New York , 1987. xiv, 163 p. : ISBN 0-89930-157-6 (lib. bdg. : alk. paper) LC Card 86-25588 DDC 332.6/7373 19
HG4538 .K44 1987

LOANS, AMERICAN - BRAZIL.
Alcalde Cardoza, Xavier. El poder norteamericano y la renegociación de la deuda externa brasileña, 1982-1983 /. Lima, Perú , 1985. 62 p. ; LC Card 86-223475
HJ8579 .A44 1985

LOANS, AMERICAN - EUROPE - HISTORY - 20TH CENTURY.
Pullen, William George. World War debts and United States foreign policy, 1919-1929 /. New York , 1987. 157 p. ; ISBN 0-8240-8088-2 : LC Card 87-23789 DDC 337.7304 19
HF1456.5.E8 P84 1987

LOANS, AMERICAN - GERMANY - HISTORY - 20TH CENTURY.
McNeil, William C. American money and the Weimar Republic . New York , 1986. x, 352 p. : ISBN 0-231-06236-2 LC Card 85-29962 DDC 336.3/4/0943 19
HG3949 .M38 1986 NYPL [JLE 86-3268]

LOANS, AMERICAN - LATIN AMERICA - HISTORY.
Stallings, Barbara. Banker to the Third World . Berkeley , c1987. xvii, 434 p. : ISBN 0-520-05726-0 (alk. paper) LC Card 86-24988 DDC 332.6/7373/08 19
HG5160.5.A3 S73 1987

LOANS - COLOMBIA.
Castillo, Julián. La amortización de deudas en Colombia . Bogotá, Colombia , 1985. 162 leaves ; LC Card 86-204058 DDC 332.7/09861 19
HG4028.A5 C37 1985

LOANS FOR CONSUMPTION. see **LOANS.**

LOANS, FOREIGN - ARAB COUNTRIES.
Zakī, Ramzī. al-Duyūn wa-al-tanmiyah . al-Qāhirah , 1985. 271 p. : LC Card 86-960543
HJ8824 .Z34 1985

LOANS, FOREIGN - BOLIVIA.
Devlin, Robert. External debt in Bolivia /. Boulder, Colo. , 1987. p. cm. ISBN 0-8133-7366-2 : LC Card 87-2088 DDC 336.3/4/0984 19
HJ8574 .D48 1987

LOANS, FOREIGN - BRAZIL.
Batista Júnior, Paulo Nogueira. International financial flows to Brazil since the late 1960s . Washington, D.C. , 1987. 66 p. ; ISBN 0-8213-0891-2 (pbk.) LC Card 87-6065 DDC 336.3/4/0981 19
HJ8579 .B369 1987

Calcagnotto, Gilberto. Brasilien 1974-1981 . Hamburg [1983] xi, 78 p. : LC Card 83-222930
HC187 .C143 1983

LOANS, FOREIGN - BRAZIL - CONGRESSES.
Brazil and the Ivory Coast . Greenwich, Conn. , c1987. p. cm. ISBN 0-89232-819-3 : LC Card 87-3667 DDC 332/.042/0981 19
HG3891.5 .B72 1987

LOANS, FOREIGN - CONGRESSES.
La Crise de l'endettement international . Paris , c1986. 410 p. : ISBN 2-7178-1127-3 : LC Card 86-222862
HJ8017 .C74 1986

The International debt problem . Tübingen , 1986. vi, 193 p. : ISBN 3-16-345084-9 (pbk.) LC Card 86-201893 DDC 336.3/435 19
HG3891.5 .I557 1986

The International debt problem . Boulder , 1987. p. cm. ISBN 0-8133-0595-0 LC Card 87-20149 DDC 336.3/435 19
HG3891.5 .I557 1987

Die Internationale Finanzierungskrise /. Frankfurt am Main , c1985. 153 p. ; ISBN 3-7819-2536-6 LC Card 87-146671 DDC 336.3/435 19
HG3891.5 .I587 1985

LOANS, FOREIGN - DEVELOPING COUNTRIES.
Aggarwal, Vinod K. International debt threat . Berkeley , c1987. vii, 71 p. ; ISBN 0-87725-529-6 (pbk.) LC Card 87-80549 DDC 336.3/435 19
HG3891.5 .A38 1987

Barth, James R. International debt . Fairfax, Va. , 1984. 36 p. ; NYPL [*ZT-1554 no.21]

Cline, William R. Mobilizing bank lending to debtor countries /. Washington, DC , 1987. viii, 92 p. : ISBN 0-88132-062-5 (pbk.) LC Card 87-16857 DDC 332.1/5 19
HG3891.5 .C58 1987

Dillon, K. Burke. Recent experience with multilateral official debt rescheduling /. Washington, D.C. , c1987. v, 22 p. : LC Card 87-2633 DDC 336.3/435 19
HG3891.5 .D55 1987

Dworak, Brigitte M. Das Länderrisiko als bankbetriebliches Problem /. Berlin , c1985. 168 p. : ISBN 3-428-05761-9 LC Card 85-213576
HG5993 .D86 1985

Financing foreign development of non-fuel mineral resources . [Washington, D.C.] [1986] 308 p. : LC Card 86-602175 DDC 332.1/5 19
HD9506.D452 F56 1986

Holley, H. A., 1924- Developing country debt . London : London ; 85 p. ; ISBN 0-7102-1211-9 (pbk.) : LC Card 86-29838 DDC 336.3/435/091724 19
HG3891.5 .H65 1987

Die Internationale Schuldenkrise . Berlin , 1986. 179 p. : ISBN 3-428-05972-7 LC Card 86-172589
HJ8899 .I58 1986

Katash, S. S. Mezhdunarodnyĭ kredit i vneshni͡a͡ia zadolzhennostʹ razvivai͡ushchikhsi͡a stran /. Moskva , 1984. 43 p. ; LC Card 87-100185
HG3877 .K37 1984

Lomax, David F. The developing country debt crisis /. Basingstoke, Hampshire , 1986. xxiv, 317 p. : ISBN 0-333-38581-0 LC Card 86-674010
HJ8899 .L64x 1986b

Lomax, David F. The developing country debt crisis /. London , 1986. xxiv, 317 p. ; ISBN 0-333-38581-0 NYPL [JLD 86-3497]

Milivojević, Marko, 1957- The debt rescheduling process /. London , 1985. xvi, 240

p. : ISBN 0-86187-575-3 LC Card 87-672863
HG3891.5 .M55x 1985b

Pankova, E. A. (Evgeniia Afanas'evna) Vneshneėkonomicheskie sviazi razvivaiushchikhsia stran . Moskva , 1985. 158 p. ; LC Card 86-130427
HF1413 .P36 1985

Status report on concessional flows, April 1986. Washington, D.C., U. S.A. , 1986. 25 p. ; ISBN 0-8213-0789-4 (pbk.) LC Card 86-214496 DDC 336.3/435/091724
HG3891 .S7 1986

Wellons, Philip A. Passing the buck . Boston, Mass. , c1987. xiv, 342 p. : ISBN 0-87584-146-5 (alk. paper) LC Card 86-19508 DDC 332.1/53 19
HG3891.5 .W46 1987 ***NYPL [JLE 87-1072]***

LOANS, FOREIGN - DEVELOPING COUNTRIES - ADDRESSES, ESSAYS, LECTURES.
Uncertain future . New Brunswick, N.J. , c1984. x, 129 p. ; ISBN 0-88738-041-7 : LC Card 84-16240 DDC 332.1/5 19
HG3891.5 .U53 1984 ***NYPL [JLE 86-2494]***

LOANS, FOREIGN - DEVELOPING COUNTRIES - CONGRESSES.
The Debt crisis and financial stability . New York, NY (Attn: Comptroller, Pace Plaza, 10038) , 1985. xi, 157 p. : ISBN 0-88239-017-1 : LC Card 85-19243 DDC 336.3/435/091724 19
HG3891.5 .D4 1985 ***NYPL [JLE 86-3911]***

LOANS, FOREIGN - DEVELOPING COUNTRIES - HANDBOOKS, MANUALS, ETC.
Disbursement handbook. Washington, D.C., U. S.A. , c1986. iv, 58 p. : ISBN 0-8213-0746-0 (pbk.) LC Card 86-210947 DDC 332.1/532/0685 19
HG3881.5.W57 D57 1986

LOANS, FOREIGN - DEVELOPING COUNTRIES - STATISTICS - FORECASTING.
Status report . Philadelphia, PA (3624 Science Center, Philadelphia 19104) , c1987. iii, 67 p. : LC Card 87-153448 DDC 336.3/435/091724 19
HJ8899 .S72 1987

LOANS, FOREIGN - DOMINICAN REPUBLIC.
Renegociación de la deuda externa, 1985 /. Santo Domingo, República Dominicana , 1985. iv, 168 p. ; LC Card 86-186407
HJ8548 .R46 1985

LOANS, FOREIGN - EUROPE, EASTERN.
Barth, James R. International debt . Fairfax, Va. , 1984. 36 p. ; ***NYPL [*ZT-1554 no.21]***

LOANS, FOREIGN - EVALUATION.
Heffernan, Shelagh A., 1956- Sovereign risk analysis /. London , Boston , 1986. xvii, 181 p. : ISBN 0-04-332119-4 (alk. paper) LC Card 85-32069 DDC 332.1/5/0685 19
HG3891.5 .H44 1986 ***NYPL [JLD 86-2957]***

LOANS, FOREIGN - INDIA.
Saxena, R. B. IMF loan to India . Delhi, India , 1986. ix, 284 p. ; LC Card 86-903311 DDC 332.1/52 19
HG3971 .S29 1986

LOANS, FOREIGN - IVORY COAST - CONGRESSES.
Brazil and the Ivory Coast . Greenwich, Conn. , c1987. p. cm. ISBN 0-89232-819-3 : LC Card 87-3667 DDC 332/.042/0981 19
HG3891.5 .B72 1987

LOANS, FOREIGN - LATIN AMERICA.
The Debt crisis in Latin America. Stockholm , 1986. 199 p. : ISBN 91-87134-01-2 LC Card 87-108739 DDC 336.3/435/098 19
HJ8514.5 .D45 1986

The Economy of Latin America and the Caribbean . Washington, D.C. [1986] v, 30 p. ; ISBN 0-8270-2333-2 (pbk.) : LC Card 86-203268 DDC 336.3/435/09729 19
HJ8514.5 .E34 1986

Labarca, Guillermo. Los bancos multinacionales en América Latina y la crisis del sistema capitalista /. México, D.F. , 1979. 201 p. ; ISBN 968-429-155-8 LC Card 80-123755
HG2710.5.A6 L3 ***NYPL [JLC 81-147]***

Rey Salgado, Rafael del. La crisis de la deuda en América Latina /. [Spain] [1985] ii, 88 p. ; LC Card 86-131407
HJ8514.5 .R49 1985

Schinke, Rolf. Ursachen der Verschuldungskrise . Göttingen [1987] 33 p. : LC Card 87-409568 DDC 336.3/435/098 19
HJ8514.5 .S34 1987

LOANS, FOREIGN - LATIN AMERICA - CONGRESSES.
Latin America's debt crisis . Boulder, Colo. , 1987. xiii, 176 p. ; ISBN 1-555-87053-8 (lib. bdg. : alk. paper) : LC Card 87-4956 DDC 336.3/435/098 19
HJ8514.5 .L395 1987

LOANS, FOREIGN - LAW AND LEGISLATION - DEVELOPING COUNTRIES.
International borrowing . Washington, D.C. , c1986. 499 p. : ISBN 0-935328-40-8 LC Card 86-82157 DDC 341.7/51 19
K4450 .I576 1986 ***NYPL [JLF 86-1814]***

LOANS, FOREIGN - MEXICO.
Bailey, Norman A. The Mexican time bomb /. New York , 1987. vi, 61 p. ; ISBN 0-87078-209-6 (pbk.) : LC Card 87-400092 DDC 336.3/4/0972 19
HJ8519 .B26 1987

Kraft, Joseph. The Mexican rescue /. New York , 1984. 66 p. ; LC Card 84-10354 DDC 336.3/4/0972 19
HJ8519 .K73 1984 ***NYPL [JLE 86-2931]***

LOANS, FOREIGN - NIGERIA.
Ogunba, C. K. An ailing African economy and the IMF medicine /. Ile-Ife [Nigeria] [1985] 40, [1] p. ; LC Card 86-207586 DDC 332.1/52 19
HG3881.5.I58 O37 1985

LOANS, FOREIGN - PERU.
Scheetz, Thomas Edward. Peru and the International Monetary Fund /. Pittsburgh, PA , c1986. xi, 257 p. : ISBN 0-8229-3816-2 LC Card 85-40855 DDC 332.1/52 19
HG3881.5.I58 S34 1986
NYPL [JLD 86-2893]

Uriarte, J. Manuel. Transnational banks and the dynamics of the Peruvian foreign debt and inflation /. New York , c1986. x, 195 p. : ISBN 0-03-002599-0 (alk. paper) : LC Card 84-26307 DDC 336.3/4/0985 19
HJ8604 .U75 1985 ***NYPL [JLE 86-1384]***

LOANS, FOREIGN - POLITICAL ASPECTS - ADDRESSES, ESSAYS, LECTURES.
The Politics of international debt /. Ithaca , 1986. 272 p. ; ISBN 0-8014-1911-5 (alk. paper) LC Card 85-48243 DDC 327.1/11 19
HJ8083 .P65 1986 ***NYPL [JLE 86-2405]***

LOANS, FOREIGN - SOVIET UNION.
Neu, C. R. (Carl Richard), 1949- Toward a profile of Soviet behavior in international financial markets /. Santa Monica, CA [1987] xv, 58 p. : ISBN 0-8330-0865-X (pbk.) LC Card 87-13084 DDC 332/.042/0947 19
HG3955 .N48 1987

LOANS, FOREIGN - URUGUAY.
Compra de carteras . Montevideo [1986] 188 p. : LC Card 87-403157 DDC 332.1/09895 19
HG2954 .C66 1986

LOANS, GERMAN - SOVIET UNION - HISTORY - 20TH CENTURY.
Lemke, Heinz. Finanztransaktionen und Aussenpolitik . Berlin , 1985. 215 p. ; LC Card 86-196601
HG3955 .L45 1985

LOANS - GOVERNMENT GUARANTY - UNITED STATES - HANDBOOKS, MANUALS, ETC.
FmHA guaranteed lending manual /. Washington, D.C. (1120 Connecticut Ave., N.W., Washington 20036) , c1986. xi, 88, [59] p. : LC Card 86-226067 DDC 332.1/753 19
HG2051.U5 F55 1986

LOANS, INTERNATIONAL. see **LOANS, FOREIGN.**

LOANS, PERSONAL - UNITED STATES.
Beares, Paul. Consumer lending /. Washington, D.C. (1120 Connecticut Ave., N.W., Washington 20036) , c1987. xi, 335 p. : LC Card 87-410019 DDC 332.1/753/0685 19
HG3755 .B39 1987

James, Christopher. How to get credit and loans . Austin, TX , 1987. viii, 179 p. : ISBN 0-9618114-0-4 (pbk.) : LC Card 87-71591 DDC 332.7/43 19
HG3756.U54 J36 1987

LOANS - UNITED STATES.
Ruth, George E. Commercial lending /. Washington, D.C. (1120 Connecticut Ave., N.W., Washington 20036) , c1987. vi, 427 p. : LC Card 87-405117 DDC 332.1/753/0685 19
HG1642.U5 R88 1987

LOANS - UNITED STATES - GOVERNMENT GUARANTY.
Bosworth, Barry, 1942- The economics of federal credit programs /. Washington, D.C. , c1987. xii, 214 p. : ISBN 0-8157-1038-0 : LC Card 85-48205 DDC 336.3/44/0973 19
HJ8119 .B67 1987

LOBBYING - UNITED STATES.
Browne, William Paul, 1945- Private interests, public policy, and American agriculture /. Lawrence, Kan. , c1988. p. cm. ISBN 0-7006-0334-4 : LC Card 87-23131 DDC 338.1/873 19
HD1761 .B73 1988

Lobdell, Richard A. Economic structure and demographic performance in Jamaica, 1891-1935 / Richard A. Lobdell. New York : Garland Pub., 1987. xii, 259 p. ; 24 cm. (South American and Latin American economic history) Originally presented as the author's thesis (Ph. D.)--McGill University. Bibliography: p. 253-259. ISBN 0-8240-1365-4 (alk. paper) : LC Card 87-8345 DDC 304.6/097292 19
1. Jamaica - Population - History - 19th century. 2. Jamaica - Population - History - 20th century. 3. Agriculture - Economic aspects - Jamaica - History - 19th century. 4. Agriculture - Economic aspects - Jamaica - History - 20th century. 5. Jamaica - Economic conditions. I. Title. II. Series.
HB3553 .L63 1987

Lobos, Julio A. Manual de guerrilha trabalhista : para gerentes e supervisores / Julio Lobos. São Paulo : Melhoramentos, c1986. 142 p. : ill. ; 23 cm. LC Card 87-130241 DDC 658.3/15/0981 19
1. Industrial relations. 2. Industrial relations - Brazil. I. Title.
HD6971 .L57 1986

Lobov, Aleksandr. Gazovyĭ most . Sverdlovsk , 1985. 206 p. : LC Card 86-186324
HD9581.S653 S54 1985

LOCAL ADMINISTRATION. see **LOCAL GOVERNMENT.**

Local area networking with microcomputers . Lehrman, Stevanne Ruth. New York, N.Y. , c1986. xx, 261 p. : ISBN 0-89303-640-4 (pbk.) : LC Card 86-91466 DDC 650/.028/5468 19
HF5548.2 .L392 1986 ***NYPL [JLE 87-121]***

Local area networks : new developments in a growth industry / Eve Oppenheim, project analyst. Stamford, Conn., U. S.A. : Business Communications Co., c1986. xvi, 186 leaves : ill. ; 29 cm. (Business opportunity report . G-074R) "June 1986"--T.p. verso. ISBN 0-89336-438-X (pbk.) LC Card 87-404428 DDC 381/.4500468/0973 19
1. Local area networks industry - United States. 2. Local area networks (Computer networks). 3. Data transmission systems. 4. Data transmission equipment industry - United States. I. Oppenheim, Eve. II. Business Communications Co. III. Series.
HD9696.C63 U52253 1986

LOCAL AREA NETWORKS (COMPUTER NETWORKS)
Hurwicz, Michael. Networking with the IBM Network & Cluster /. Blue Ridge Summit, Pa. , 1985. x, 518 p. : ISBN 0-8306-0929-6 : LC Card 85-4639 DDC 001.64/404 19
TK5105.7 .H87 1985 ***NYPL [JSE 86-1975]***

Kopeck, Ronald F. Micro to mainframe links /. Berkeley, Calif. , c1986. xviii, 286 p. : ISBN 0-07-881228-3 (pbk.) LC Card 86-210460 DDC 004.6 19
HF5548.2 .K628 1986

Lehrman, Stevanne Ruth. Local area networking with microcomputers . New York, N.Y. , c1986. xx, 261 p. : ISBN 0-89303-640-4 (pbk.) : LC Card 86-91466 DDC 650/.028/5468 19
HF5548.2 .L392 1986 ***NYPL [JLE 87-121]***

Living with SNA /. Boston, MA (89 Broad St., Boston 02110) [1986] 60 p. : LC Card

86-201765 DDC 381/.4500468/0973 19
HD9696.C63 U5223 1986

Local area networks . Stamford, Conn., U. S.A. , c1986. xvi, 186 leaves : ISBN 0-89336-438-X (pbk.) LC Card 87-404428 DDC 381/.4500468/0973 19
HD9696.C63 U52253 1986

LOCAL AREA NETWORKS INDUSTRY - UNITED STATES.
Local area networks . Stamford, Conn., U. S.A. , c1986. xvi, 186 leaves : ISBN 0-89336-438-X (pbk.) LC Card 87-404428 DDC 381/.4500468/0973 19
HD9696.C63 U52253 1986

LOCAL BUDGETS.
Forte, Francesco, 1929- Il bilancio nell'economia pubblica /. Milano [1985] 2 v. ; ISBN 88-14-00636-9 : LC Card 86-151358 DDC 350.72/2 19
HJ2005 .F67 1985 ***NYPL [JLE 86-2653]***

LOCAL BUDGETS - EUROPEAN ECONOMIC COMMUNITY COUNTRIES.
Forte, Francesco, 1929- Il bilancio nell'economia pubblica /. Milano [1985] 2 v. ; ISBN 88-14-00636-9 : LC Card 86-151358 DDC 350.72/2 19
HJ2005 .F67 1985 ***NYPL [JLE 86-2653]***

LOCAL BUDGETS - GREAT BRITAIN - CASE STUDIES.
Learning from local authority budgeting /. Aldershot [Hampshire] , Brookfield, Vt., USA , c1987. x, 258 p. ; ISBN 0-566-05384-5 : LC Card 87-12096 DDC 352.1/2/0941 19
HJ9423 .L43 1987

LOCAL BUDGETS - ITALY.
Forte, Francesco, 1929- Il bilancio nell'economia pubblica /. Milano [1985] 2 v. ; ISBN 88-14-00636-9 : LC Card 86-151358 DDC 350.72/2 19
HJ2005 .F67 1985 ***NYPL [JLE 86-2653]***

LOCAL BUDGETS - SPAIN - GRANADA (PROVINCE) - HISTORY - 20TH CENTURY - STATISTICS.
Martín Rodríguez, Manuel. Las haciendas locales de la Provincia de Granada, 1940-1983 . Granada [1985?] 369 p. ; ISBN 84-338-0266-6 LC Card 86-230887
HJ9527.G7 M37 1985

LOCAL BUDGETS - UNITED STATES - MATHEMATICAL MODELS.
Wacht, Richard F. A new approach to capital budgeting for city and county governments /. Atlanta, Ga. , 1987. ix, 149 p. : ISBN 0-88406-190-6 (pbk.) : LC Card 87-21157 DDC 352.1/2 19
HJ9147 .W33 1987

Local economic development agencies. Winick, Bradley H. Making the link . [Washinton, D.C.] , c1986. i, 17 p. ; ISBN 0-88713-678-8 (pbk.) LC Card 87-106145 DDC 331.11/0973 19
HD5724 .W557 1986

LOCAL ELECTIONS - GERMANY (WEST) - HESSE - STATISTICS.
Die Kommunalwahlen am 20. März 1977 . Wiesbaden , 1978. 116 p. ; LC Card 86-102904
HA1320 .H529 n.F., Nr. 88 JS5471.H423E44

LOCAL ELECTIONS - GERMANY (WEST) - SAARLAND - STATISTICS.
Kommunal- und Europawahl am 17. Juni 1984. Saarbrücken , 1984. 115 p. : ISBN 3-88718-020-8 : LC Card 85-130989
HA1320 .S244 Nr. 67 JN4945.S265

LOCAL FINANCE.
Management policies in local government finance /. Washington, D.C. , c1987. 449 p. : ISBN 0-87326-075-9 : LC Card 87-2658 DDC 352.1 19
HJ9105 .M3 1987

Rosenfeld, Martin. Ausgabeneffekte kommunaler Funktionalreformen . Baden-Baden , 1985. 395 p. : ISBN 3-7890-1077-4 LC Card 86-156503
HJ9493.5.L6 R67 1985

LOCAL FINANCE - ACCOUNTING - STANDARDS - UNITED STATES.
Ingram, Robert W. Financial reporting practices of local governments /. Stamford, Conn. (P.O. Box 3821, Stamford 06905-0821) , c1987. viii, 93 p. : LC Card 87-80564 DDC 657/.835 19
HJ9777.A3 I55 1987

LOCAL FINANCE - AUDITING - STANDARDS - UNITED STATES - HANDBOOKS, MANUALS, ETC.
Carmichael, D. R. Douglas R.), 1941- Guide to audits of local governments /. Fort Worth, Tex. , 1986- 2 v. (loose-leaf) : LC Card 86-206730 DDC 657/.835045 19
HJ9777.A3 C37 1986

LOCAL FINANCE - BRAZIL - ARAGUAIA RIVER REGION - STATISTICS.
Finanças públicas municipais da região do PRODIAT /. Brasília , 1985. 420 p. ; LC Card 86-195656
HJ9388.A2 A734 1985

LOCAL FINANCE - BRAZIL - TOCANTINS RIVER REGION - STATISTICS.
Finanças públicas municipais da região do PRODIAT /. Brasília , 1985. 420 p. ; LC Card 86-195656
HJ9388.A2 A734 1985

LOCAL FINANCE - CALIFORNIA.
California. Legislature. Assembly. Committee on Local Government. The impact of Proposition 13 (the Jarvis-Gann property tax initiative) on local government programs and services /. [Sacramento, CA.] 1978. iv, 367, 108 p. : LC Card 79-621409 DDC 352/.0794
HJ4191 .C34 1978 ***NYPL [JLF 86-1607]***

LOCAL FINANCE - CANADA.
Bricall, Josep Maria, 1936- Estat autonòmic i finances públiques . [Barcelona] , 1984. 358 p. : ISBN 84-500-9868-8 LC Card 85-106586
HJ1000 .B75 1984 ***NYPL [JLE 86-3989]***

Kitchen, Harry M. Local government finance in Canada /. [Toronto, Ont.] , c1984. xvii, 495 p. ; ISBN 0-88808-020-4
NYPL [JLL 80-129 no.5]

LOCAL FINANCE - CANADA - CONGRESSES.
State and local finance . Madison, Wis. , 1983. x, 243 p. : ISBN 0-299-09340-9 : LC Card 83-47757 DDC 336.73 19
HJ275 .S675 1983 ***NYPL [JLE 86-4001]***

LOCAL FINANCE - ENGLAND - ACCOUNTING.
Performance review in local government . [London , 1986] 1 v. (various pagings) : ISBN 0-11-701302-1 (loose-leaf : set) : LC Card 87-144582 DDC 352.1/72/0942 19
HJ9779.G7 P47 1986

LOCAL FINANCE - EUROPE.
Bricall, Josep Maria, 1936- Estat autonòmic i finances públiques . [Barcelona] , 1984. 358 p. : ISBN 84-500-9868-8 LC Card 85-106586
HJ1000 .B75 1984 ***NYPL [JLE 86-3989]***

Meadows, W. J. The response of local authorities to central government incitement to reduce expenditure . Strasbourg , 1986. 33 p. ; LC Card 87-135687 DDC 336.3/9/094 19
HJ9415 .M43 1986

LOCAL FINANCE - EUROPEAN ECONOMIC COMMUNITY COUNTRIES.
Kelly, G. Financial resources for local and regional authorities /. Strasbourg , 1985. 79 p. ; LC Card 86-206535 DDC 336/.014/4 19
HJ9420 .K45 1985

LOCAL FINANCE - FRANCE - ACCOUNTING.
Sources et méthodes d'élaboration des comptes nationaux. [Paris] [1983] 481 p. ; LC Card 84-161813
HC271 .A218 no. 440-441 HJ9925.F8

LOCAL FINANCE - FRANCE - HISTORY.
Köster, Thomas. Die Entwicklung kommunaler Finanzsysteme am Beispiel Grossbritanniens, Frankreichs und Deutschlands, 1790-1980 /. Berlin , c1984. 422 p. : ISBN 3-428-05677-9 LC Card 85-127874
HJ9422.A4 K67 1984

LOCAL FINANCE - GERMANY - HISTORY.
Köster, Thomas. Die Entwicklung kommunaler Finanzsysteme am Beispiel Grossbritanniens, Frankreichs und Deutschlands, 1790-1980 /. Berlin , c1984. 422 p. : ISBN 3-428-05677-9 LC Card 85-127874
HJ9422.A4 K67 1984

LOCAL FINANCE - GERMANY, WEST.
Gornas, Jürgen. Zur Berücksichtigung der finanziellen Leistungsfähigkeit in kommunalen Investitions- und Finanzplanungsmodellen /. Hamburg , 1984. 40 p. ; LC Card 85-166310
HJ9473 .G67 1984

Hermann, Hayo. Sektorale Wirtschaftsstruktur und kommunale Finanzsituation . München , c1986. xiii, 384 p. : ISBN 3-88259-405-5 LC Card 86-228161
HJ9473 .H47 1986

Rickert, Heinrich. Der Sozialvertrag für die Finanzierung kommunaler Einrichtungen und Gemeinschaftsaufgaben . Stuttgart , c1982. 268 p. : ISBN 3-17-007760-0 : LC Card 83-152669
HJ9473 .R53 1982

Zeidler, Achim, 1952- Möglichkeiten zur Fortsetzung der Gemeindefinanzreform . Frankfurt am Main , New York , c1985. xx, 301 p. : ISBN 3-8204-8534-1 LC Card 86-125215 DDC 336/.014/43 19
HJ9473 .Z4 1985

LOCAL FINANCE - GERMANY (WEST) - BAVARIA.
Leibfritz, Willi. Berücksichtigung der zentralen Orte im kommunalen Finanzausgleich Bayern . München , 1986. vi, 151 p. : ISBN 3-88512-018-6 LC Card 86-172605
HJ9493.5.B38 L45 1986

LOCAL FINANCE - GERMANY (WEST) - LOWER SAXONY.
Finanzwirtschaftliche Folgen kommunaler Gebiets- und Funktionalreformen . Baden-Baden , 1986. 209 p. : ISBN 3-7890-1163-0 (Deut. Bibl.) LC Card 86-169111
HJ1121 .F55 1986

Rosenfeld, Martin. Ausgabeneffekte kommunaler Funktionalreformen . Baden-Baden , 1985. 395 p. : ISBN 3-7890-1077-4 LC Card 86-156503
HJ9493.5.L6 R67 1985

LOCAL FINANCE - GERMANY, WEST - NORTH RHINE-WESTPHALIA.
Puls, Heinz. Finanzkraft der Gemeinden und kommunaler Ausgleichsstock in NW /. Dortmund [1977] [15] p. : LC Card 86-211554
HJ9493.5.N6 P85 1977

LOCAL FINANCE - GERMANY (WEST) - RUHR (REGION)
Zimmermann, Horst, 1934- Die Gemeindefinanzen im Ruhrgebiet . Essen , 1983. xvi, 153 p. : ISBN 3-923494-28-9 LC Card 83-228289
HJ9493.5.R8 Z76 1983

LOCAL FINANCE - GREAT BRITAIN.
Midwinter, Arthur F. Rates reform . Edinburgh , 1987. 182 p. ; ISBN 1-85158-062-X : LC Card 87-167866 DDC 336/.014/41 19
HJ9421 .M53 1987

LOCAL FINANCE - GREAT BRITAIN - HISTORY.
Köster, Thomas. Die Entwicklung kommunaler Finanzsysteme am Beispiel Grossbritanniens, Frankreichs und Deutschlands, 1790-1980 /. Berlin , c1984. 422 p. : ISBN 3-428-05677-9 LC Card 85-127874
HJ9422.A4 K67 1984

LOCAL FINANCE - ITALY.
Il Consolidamento regionale della finanza locale /. Milano [1980] 332 p. : ISBN 88-20-41859-2 : LC Card 80-143023
HJ9497 .C63 ***NYPL [JLD 87-1397]***

Romagnoli, Gian Cesare, 1948- Nuove politiche di finanziamento degli enti locali in Italia . Milano, Italy , c1985. 260 p. : LC Card 86-169439
HJ9497 .R65 1985

LOCAL FINANCE - ITALY - CONGRESSES.
La Potestà impositiva dei comuni e delle province /. Rimini , c1985. 109 p. ; LC Card 85-194391 DDC 336.2/014/45 19
HJ9498 .P68 1985 ***NYPL [JLE 86-4120]***

LOCAL FINANCE - JAPAN.
Yonehara, Junshichirō. Local public finance in Japan /. Canberra , Miami, Fla., USA , 1981. xi, 112 p. : ISBN 0-908160-89-5 : LC Card 80-68801 DDC 352.1/0952 19
HJ9585 .Y663 1981
NYPL [JLM 75-1302 no. 36]

LOCAL FINANCE - LAW AND LEGISLATION - JAPAN.
Yonehara, Junshichirō. Local public finance in

Japan /. Canberra , Miami, Fla., USA , 1981. xi, 112 p. : ISBN 0-908160-89-5 : LC Card 80-68801 DDC 352.1/0952 19
HJ9585 .Y663 1981
NYPL [JLM 75-1302 no. 36]

LOCAL FINANCE - OREGON.
Oregon county finances, fiscal 1984. Eugene, OR [1985] 17, [12] p. ; LC Card 86-622281 DDC 336/.014/795 19
HJ9302 .O725 1985

LOCAL FINANCE - PORTUGAL.
Lei das finanças locais . [Lisbon] [1980] 56 leaves ; LC Card 83-223473
HJ9529 .L45 1980

LOCAL FINANCE - SASKATCHEWAN.
Saskatchewan Local Government Finance Commission. Final report of the Local Government Finance Commission, September 1986 /. [Regina, Canada] [1986] xiii, 440 p. : LC Card 87-163885 DDC 336/.014/7124 19
HJ9352.S3 S37 1986

LOCAL FINANCE - SPAIN - CONGRESSES.
Las Finanzas municipales en el estado de las autonomías . [Barcelona] , 1985. 178 p. ; ISBN 84-505-1593-9 LC Card 85-240344
HJ9525 .F55 1985

LOCAL FINANCE - SPAIN - GRANADA (PROVINCE) - HISTORY - 20TH CENTURY - STATISTICS.
Martín Rodríguez, Manuel. Las haciendas locales de la Provincia de Granada, 1940-1983 . Granada [1985?] 369 p. ; ISBN 84-338-0266-6 LC Card 86-230887
HJ9527.G7 M37 1985

LOCAL FINANCE - UNITED STATES.
Bricall, Josep Maria, 1936- Estat autonòmic i finances públiques . [Barcelona] , 1984. 358 p. : ISBN 84-500-9868-8 LC Card 85-106586
HJ1000 .B75 1984 ***NYPL [JLE 86-3989]***

Long-term financial planning . Washington, D.C. , 1987. 188 p. ; ISBN 0-87326-076-7 (pbk.) : LC Card 87-2613 DDC 352.1/0973 19
HJ275 .L66 1987

Romagnoli, Gian Cesare, 1948- Nuove politiche di finanziamento degli enti locali in Italia . Milano, Italy , c1985. 260 p. : LC Card 86-169439
HJ9497 .R65 1985

LOCAL FINANCE - UNITED STATES - ACCOUNTING.
Van Daniker, Relmond P., 1942- Infrastructure assets . Stamford, Conn. (High Ridge Park, P.O. Box 3821, Stamford 06905-0821) , c1986. xii, 155 p. ; LC Card 86-90661 DDC 657/.835 19
HJ9816 .V35 1986

LOCAL FINANCE - UNITED STATES - CASE STUDIES.
Nathan, Richard P. Reagan and the States /. Princeton, N.J. , c1987. xv, 375 p. : ISBN 0-691-07748-7 (alk. paper) : LC Card 87-45529 DDC 353.0072/5 19
HJ2051 .N167 1987

LOCAL FINANCE - UNITED STATES - CONGRESSES.
State and local finance . Madison, Wis. , 1983. x, 243 p. : ISBN 0-299-09340-9 : LC Card 83-47757 DDC 336.73 19
HJ275 .S675 1983 ***NYPL [JLE 86-4001]***

LOCAL FINANCE - WALES - ACCOUNTING.
Performance review in local government . [London , 1986] 1 v. (various pagings) : ISBN 0-11-701302-1 (loose-leaf : set) : LC Card 87-144582 DDC 352.1/72/0942 19
HJ9779.G7 P47 1986

LOCAL FINANCE - WISCONSIN - HANDBOOKS, MANUALS, ETC.
Financial administration . Madison, WI , c1986. vi, 97 p. : LC Card 87-620662 DDC 352.1/09775 19
HJ9338 .F56 1986

Local fiscal issues in the Philadelphia metropolitan area /. Luce, Thomas F. Philadelphia , c1987. xii, 248 p., [2] p. of plates : ISBN 0-8122-1255-X (pbk.) LC Card 87-25486 DDC 336.748/11 19
HJ9307.P4 L83 1987

Local food prices . Nyanteng, V. K. [Ghana] , 1978. 37 p. : LC Card 87-403379 DDC 338.4/3664/009667 19
HD9017.G452 N92 1978

LOCAL GOVERNMENT. Here are entered works which deal with local government of districts, counties, townships, etc. Works dealing with government of municipalities only are entered under Municipal government; those dealing with government of counties only are entered under County government.

LOCAL GOVERNMENT - CALIFORNIA.
Local government mobilehome and mobilehome park policies in California . [Sacramento, Calif.] [1986] iii, 70 p. ; LC Card 86-622920 DDC 333.33/8 19
HD7289.62.U6 L63 1986

LOCAL GOVERNMENT - CONGRESSES.
Le Iniziative locali per l'occupazione . Milano, Italy , c1985. 244 p. : LC Card 85-221711 DDC 331 s 331.12/042 19
HD85.I7 I68 no. 75 HD5713.5
NYPL [JLD 87-446]

LOCAL GOVERNMENT - ECUADOR - CHIMBORAZO - HISTORY.
Sylva Charvet, Paola. Gamonalismo y lucha campesina . [Quito] , 1986. 250 p., [3] leaves of plates : LC Card 87-101122
HD529.C47 S95 1986

LOCAL GOVERNMENT - EGYPT.
Adams, Richard H. Development and social change in rural Egypt /. Syracuse, N.Y. , 1986. xii, 231 p. : ISBN 0-8156-2362-3 (alk. paper) LC Card 85-30251 DDC 307.1/4/0962 19
HN786.Z9 C63 1986 ***NYPL [JLE 86-1999]***

Local government finance in Canada /. Kitchen, Harry M. [Toronto, Ont.] , c1984. xvii, 495 p. ; ISBN 0-88808-020-4
NYPL [JLL 80-129 no.5]

LOCAL GOVERNMENT - FLORIDA.
The Saddlebrook papers . [Fort Lauderdale] [Tallahassee] [1985] v leaves, 177 p. : LC Card 86-621089 DDC 338.9759 19
HC107.F63 E547 1985

LOCAL GOVERNMENT - FRANCE.
Tuppen, John N. France under recession, 1981-1986 /. Albany , c1988. p. cm. ISBN 0-88706-580-5 LC Card 87-1980 DDC 338.944 19
HC276.3 .T86 1988

LOCAL GOVERNMENT - GERMANY, EAST.
Gothe, Richard, 1928- Zusammenwirken von örtlichen Staatsorganen und Kombinaten /. Berlin , 1983. 89 p. ; LC Card 84-166789
HD3616.G48 G67 1983

Die Verantwortung der örtlichen Staatsorgane für die planmässige Entwicklung und die effektive Inanspruchnahme von Leistungen der technischen Infrastruktur /. Potsdam-Babelsberg , 1986. 57 p. ; LC Card 87-407347 DDC 363/.09431 19
HC290.795.C3 V47 1986

LOCAL GOVERNMENT - GERMANY - HISTORY.
Roloff, Otto, 1937- Umweltschutz in öffentlichen Budgets /. Regensburg , c1986. 278 p. : ISBN 3-924956-14-6 LC Card 87-129127 DDC 363.7/00943 19
HC290.5.E5 R65 1986

LOCAL GOVERNMENT - GERMANY, WEST.
Killat, Gerhard. Kommunalisierung der Wohnungspolitik? . Köln , 1984. xiii, 291 p. : ISBN 3-921471-50-8 : LC Card 85-137757
HD7339.A3 K49 1984

LOCAL GOVERNMENT - GERMANY (WEST) - LOWER SAXONY.
Finanzwirtschaftliche Folgen kommunaler Gebiets- und Funktionalreformen . Baden-Baden , 1986. 209 p. : ISBN 3-7890-1163-0 (Deut. Bibl.) LC Card 86-169111
HJ1121 .F55 1986

LOCAL GOVERNMENT - GERMANY (WEST) - NORDRHEIN-WESTFALEN.
Roloff, Otto, 1937- Umweltschutz in öffentlichen Budgets /. Regensburg , c1986. 278 p. : ISBN 3-924956-14-6 LC Card 87-129127 DDC 363.7/00943 19
HC290.5.E5 R65 1986

LOCAL GOVERNMENT - GREAT BRITAIN.
Rhodes, R. A. W. The national world of local government /. London , Boston , 1986. xviii, 441 p. ; ISBN 0-04-320170-9 (alk. paper) LC Card 85-15103 DDC 352.041 19
JS3137 .R49 1986 ***NYPL [JLD 86-1931]***

LOCAL GOVERNMENT - GREAT BRITAIN - CONGRESSES.
Developing local economic strategies . Milton Keynes [England] , Philadelphia , 1987. p. cm. ISBN 0-335-15522-7 LC Card 87-22681 DDC 338.941 19
HC256.6 .D48 1987

LOCAL GOVERNMENT - ITALY.
Intervento straordinario e amministrazione locale nel mezzogiorno /. Milano, Italy , c1985. 348 p. ; LC Card 86-144245
HC310.I53 I58 1985

LOCAL GOVERNMENT - JAPAN.
Reed, Steven R., 1947- Japanese prefectures and policy making /. Pittsburgh, Pa. , 1986. ix, 197 p. ; ISBN 0-8229-3527-9 LC Card 85-22528 DDC 352/.00047 19
JS7373.A3 R44 1986 ***NYPL [JLE 86-3757]***

LOCAL GOVERNMENT - LAW AND LEGISLATION - UNITED STATES - INTERPRETATION AND CONSTRUCTION.
Clark, Gordon L. Judges and the cities . Chicago , c1985. xv, 247 p. ; ISBN 0-226-10753-1 : LC Card 85-1018 DDC 306/.0973 19
HN59.2 .C57 1985 ***NYPL [JLE 86-1068]***

Local government mobilehome and mobilehome park policies in California : a survey of city and county planning directors pursuant to SB 1802 (Leroy Greene, Chapter 1443, Statutes of 1984) / State of California, Department of Housing and Community Development ; contributing staff, Don Crow, Melody Hartman, Bill Murphy. [Sacramento, Calif.] : The Department, [1986] iii, 70 p. ; 28 cm. LC Card 86-622920 DDC 333.33/8 19
1. Mobile homes - Government policy - California. 2. Mobile home parks - Government policy - California. 3. Local government - California. 4. City planning - California. 5. Land use - California - Planning. 6. Housing policy - California. I. California. Dept. of Housing and Community Development.
HD7289.62.U6 L63 1986

LOCAL GOVERNMENT - RUSSIAN S.F.S.R.
Shiri͡aev, A. V. (Andreĭ Vasil'evich) RAPO . Moskva , 1985. 155 p. ; LC Card 86-142380
HD9015.S653 R8775 1985

LOCAL GOVERNMENT - SOVIET UNION.
Avak'i͡an, Suren Adibekovich. Sovety i rukovodstvo ėkonomikoĭ . Moskva , 1985. 110 p. ; LC Card 87-118114
HC336.25 .A87 1985

Kaplan, Cynthia Sue. The party and agricultural crisis management in the USSR /. Ithaca , 1987. xvi, 203 p ; ISBN 0-8014-2021-0 (alk. paper) LC Card 86-32223 DDC 338.1/847 19
HD1993 .K36 1987

LOCAL GOVERNMENT - SWEDEN.
Kommunerna och näringslivet . Stockholm , c1984. 173 p. : ISBN 91-38-90331-8 : LC Card 84-253511
HC375 .K655 1984

Lokal samverkan--fördelar för näringsliv och kommun? . Stockholm [1982] 185 p. : ISBN 91-38-07027-8 LC Card 82-236501
HC375 .L786 1982

Otter, Casten von, 1941- Medbestämmandeavtal i landsting . Stockholm [1984] 92 p. : LC Card 84-241542
HD5660.S9 O77 1984

Sweden. Statens industriverk. Kommunal energiplanering . Stockholm , 1980. 51 p. ; ISBN 91-38-05802-2 LC Card 82-236900
HD9502.S82 S97 1980

LOCAL GOVERNMENT - UNITED STATES.
Burns, James MacGregor. State and local politics . Englewood Cliffs, N.J. , c1984. xi, 266 p. : ISBN 0-13-843524-3 (pbk.) LC Card 83-21259 DDC 320.973 19
JK2408 .B87 1984 ***NYPL [JLE 87-142]***

Clark, Gordon L. Judges and the cities . Chicago , c1985. xv, 247 p. ; ISBN 0-226-10753-1 : LC Card 85-1018 DDC 306/.0973 19
HN59.2 .C57 1985 ***NYPL [JLE 86-1068]***

Houseman, Gerald L. State and local government . Englewood Cliffs, N.J. , c1986. xvi, 272 p. : ISBN 0-13-843368-2 (pbk.) LC Card

85-16981 DDC 320.973 19
JK2408 .H79 1986 ***NYPL [JLE 86-2916]***

Local infrastructure investment in rural America /. Boulder , 1988. xxi, 291 p. ; ISBN 0-8133-7460-X (soft : alk. paper) LC Card 87-21606 DDC 332.6/7252 19
HC110.P83 L63 1988

Silkman, Richard H. Subsidizing inefficiency . New York , 1985. xviii, 101 p.: ISBN 0-03-000662-7 (alk. paper) : LC Card 84-26628 DDC 336.1/85 19
HJ275 .S53 1985 ***NYPL [JLE 85-2261]***

Stegman, Michael A. Nonfederal housing programs . Washington, D.C. , 1987. viii, 231 p. ; ISBN 0-87420-673-1 LC Card 87-51080 DDC 363.5/8 19
HD7293.Z9 S75 1987

Winick, Bradley H. Making the link . [Washinton, D.C.] , c1986. i, 17 p. ; ISBN 0-88713-678-8 (pbk.) LC Card 87-106145 DDC 331.11/0973 19
HD5724 .W557 1986

LOCAL GOVERNMENT - UNITED STATES - ADDRESSES, ESSAYS, LECTURES.
Rural public administration . Westport, Conn. , 1986. ix, 208 p. ; ISBN 0-313-25246-7 (lib. bdg. : alk. paper) LC Card 85-27253 DDC 352/.00722/0973 19
JS425 .R87 1986 ***NYPL [JLE 86-4005]***

State politics and the new federalism . White Plains, N.Y. , c1986. xv, 544 p. : ISBN 0-582-28474-0 (pbk.) LC Card 85-15956 DDC 321.02/0973 19
JK325 .S77 1986 ***NYPL [JLD 86-2766]***

Local infrastructure investment in rural America / edited by Thomas G. Johnson, Brady J. Deaton, and Eduardo Segarra. Boulder : Westview Press, 1988. xxi, 291 p. ; 23 cm. Bibliography: p. 265-291. ISBN 0-8133-7460-X (soft : alk. paper) LC Card 87-21606 DDC 332.6/7252 19
1. Public investments - United States. 2. Infrastructure (Economics) - United States. 3. United States - Rural conditions. 4. Local government - United States. I. Johnson, Thomas G. II. Deaton, Brady J. III. Segarra, Eduardo.
HC110.P83 L63 1988

Local institutional development . Uphoff, Norman Thomas. West Hartford, CT , c1986. xv, 421 p. ; ISBN 0-931816-45-9 LC Card 86-15288 DDC 302.3/5 19
HC59.7 .U64 1986 ***NYPL [JLE 87-1200]***

LOCAL MASS MEDIA - QUÉBEC (PROVINCE)
Programme d'aide aux médias communautaires, 1979-80 . [Québec] [1979] 97 leaves ; LC Card 83-200428
HE8689.9.C3 P755 1979

LOCAL OFFICIALS AND EMPLOYEES - UNITED STATES - FINANCE, PERSONAL.
Personal financial planning for local government employees /. Washington, D.C. , c1987. 203 p. : ISBN 0-87326-051-1 (pbk.) LC Card 87-2948 DDC 332.024/354 19
HG179 .P386 1987

Local planning in practice /. Bruton, Michael J. London , 1987. 452 p. : ISBN 0-09-165381-9
NYPL [JLE 87-1201]

Local public finance in Japan /. Yonehara, Junshichirō. Canberra , Miami, Fla., USA , 1981. xi, 112 p. : ISBN 0-908160-89-5 : LC Card 80-68801 DDC 352.1/0952 19
HJ9585 .Y663 1981
NYPL [JLM 75-1302 no. 36]

LOCAL TAXATION - CONNECTICUT.
Tax districts. [Hartford, Conn.] [1985] 53 p. ; LC Card 86-620827 DDC 352.1/3/09746 19
HJ9210 .T39 1985

LOCAL TAXATION - GERMANY, WEST.
Jasper, Lothar Th. Entwicklung der Realsteuerhebesätze der Gemeinden mit mehr als 50.000 Einwohnern 1984 gegenüber 1983 /. Bonn , 1984. 29 leaves ; LC Card 86-186306
HJ1120 .B65 nr. 238 HJ4125.G35

Rickert, Heinrich. Der Sozialvertrag für die Finanzierung kommunaler Einrichtungen und Gemeinschaftsaufgaben . Stuttgart , c1982. 268 p. : ISBN 3-17-007760-0 : LC Card 83-152669
HJ9473 .R53 1982

Zeidler, Achim, 1952- Möglichkeiten zur Fortsetzung der Gemeindefinanzreform . Frankfurt am Main , New York , c1985. xx, 301 p. : ISBN 3-8204-8534-1 LC Card 86-125215 DDC 336/.014/43 19
HJ9473 .Z4 1985

LOCAL TAXATION - GERMANY (WEST) - BAVARIA.
Leibfritz, Willi. Berücksichtigung der zentralen Orte im kommunalen Finanzausgleich Bayern . München , 1986. vi, 151 p. : ISBN 3-88512-018-6 LC Card 86-172605
HJ9493.5.B38 L45 1986

LOCAL TAXATION - ITALY - CONGRESSES.
La Potestà impositiva dei comuni e delle province /. Rimini , c1985. 109 p. ; LC Card 85-194391 DDC 336.2/014/45 19
HJ9498 .P68 1985 ***NYPL [JLE 86-4120]***

LOCAL TAXATION - LAW AND LEGISLATION - ROME.
Pack, Edgar. Städte und Steuern in der Politik Julians . Bruxelles , 1986. 420 p. ; ISBN 2-87031-134-6 LC Card 87-105922 DDC 336.2/014/37 19
HJ9497.A3 P33 1986

LOCAL TAXATION - MINNESOTA.
Minnesota tax handbook . [St. Paul] [1985] iii, 70 p. ; LC Card 86-620842 DDC 343.77604 347.76034 19
HJ2415 .M49 1985

LOCAL TAXATION - NEW YORK (STATE)
Baynes, Peter A. Distribution of local sales tax revenue . Albany, N.Y. (119 Washington Ave., Albany 12210) [1986] 13 p. : LC Card 87-106773 DDC 336.2/713/09747 19
HJ5715.U62 N72 1986

Interstate tax comparisons . [Albany, N.Y.] [1985] 106 p. ; LC Card 86-621354 DDC 336.2/009747 19
HJ2424 .I57 1985

LOCAL TAXATION - ROME.
Pack, Edgar. Städte und Steuern in der Politik Julians . Bruxelles , 1986. 420 p. ; ISBN 2-87031-134-6 LC Card 87-105922 DDC 336.2/014/37 19
HJ9497.A3 P33 1986

LOCAL TAXATION - SPAIN - ANDALUSIA.
Junta de Andalucía. Grupo de Trabajo 14, Planificación Económica de las Corporaciones Locales y Comarcalización. Plan económico de Andalucía, 1984-1986 /. [Andalucía] , 1983. 133 p. ; ISBN 84-505-1243-3 LC Card 86-223752
HJ1249.A4 J86 1983

LOCAL TAXATION - UNITED STATES.
Interstate tax comparisons . [Albany, N.Y.] [1985] 106 p. ; LC Card 86-621354 DDC 336.2/009747 19
HJ2424 .I57 1985

LOCAL TAXATION - VIRGINIA.
Ware, Peggy M. Virginia, an outline of the state and local taxes /. Richmond, Va. (1000 Washington Bldg., Richmond 23219) [1986] iv, 26 p. ; LC Card 86-622876 DDC 343.75504/3 347.550343 19
HJ2438 .W37 1986

LOCAL TRANSIT - BRAZIL.
Fernandes, Fátima Sobral. Aspectos de transporte urbano na modificação dos horários de trabalho /. Brasília, DF , 1985. 105 p. : LC Card 87-404953 DDC 331.25/72 19
HD5108.2.B6 F47 1985

LOCAL TRANSIT - BRAZIL - EMPLOYEES.
Fernandes, Fátima Sobral. Aspectos de transporte urbano na modificação dos horários de trabalho /. Brasília, DF , 1985. 105 p. : LC Card 87-404953 DDC 331.25/72 19
HD5108.2.B6 F47 1985

LOCAL TRANSIT - BRAZIL - EVALUATION.
Daibert, José Ricardo Motta. Avaliação do desempenho de transporte coletivo por ônibus /. Brasília, DF , 1985. 73 p. : LC Card 87-113224 DDC 388.4/1322/0981 19
HE5653.A6 D35 1985

LOCAL TRANSIT - BRAZIL - SÃO PAULO.
Lopes, Miriam B. P. Oelsner (Miriam Bettina Paulina Oelsner) Pequena história dos transportes públicos de São Paulo. São Paulo [1985] 91 p. : LC Card 86-158179
HE5653.Z7 C675 1985

LOCAL TRANSIT - CALIFORNIA - SAN FRANCISCO BAY AREA - FINANCE.
California. Legislature. Joint Legislative Budget Committee. Legislative Analyst. A review of Bay Area public transportation financing. Sacramento, Calif. (925 L St., Suite 650, Sacramento 95814) [1986] 57 p. : LC Card 86-621890 DDC 388.4/042 19
HE4491.S45 C33 1986

LOCAL TRANSIT - CZECHOSLOVAKIA - PRAGUE.
110 let městské hromadné dopravy v Praze /. [Prague] [1985] 52 p. : LC Card 86-201750
HE4759.3.Z8 P732 1985

LOCAL TRANSIT - DENMARK - COPENHAGEN - HISTORY.
By i forvandling . Copenhagen , 1984. 93 p. : ISBN 87-87589-42-7 LC Card 87-155193
HE4859.C68 B92 1984

LOCAL TRANSIT - ENGLAND - COVENTRY (WEST MIDLANDS) - HISTORY.
Denton, A. S. Coventry transport . Birmingham [West Midlands, England] , c1985- v. <1 > : ISBN 0-905103-05-X (pbk.) : LC Card 86-224227 DDC 388.4/09424/98 19
HE4719.C68 D46 1985

LOCAL TRANSIT - ENGLAND - LEEDS (WEST YORKSHIRE) - HISTORY.
Soper, J. Leeds transport /. [Bramham, Wetherby, West Yorkshire] , 1985- v. <1 > : ISBN 0-9510280-0-6 (v. 1) : LC Card 87-103287 DDC 388.4/09428/19 19
HE4719.L4 S67 1985

LOCAL TRANSIT - FARES.
Co-ordinated urban transport pricing . Paris [Washington, D.C.] 1985. 151 p. : ISBN 92-64-12692-9 (pbk.) : LC Card 86-125699 DDC 388.4/042 19
HE305 .C58 1985

LOCAL TRANSIT - FRANCE.
Lacour, Claude. Croissance urbaine . Paris , 1981. 219 p. : ISBN 2-222-02928-7 (pbk.) : LC Card 82-153821 DDC 388.4/068 19
HE4764 .L3 1981 ***NYPL [JLG 86-56]***

Les Rues mixtes . [Bagneux] [1982] 40 p. : ISBN 2-11-083325-4 : LC Card 84-104398
HE363.F72 P437 1982

LOCAL TRANSIT - FRANCE - PARIS METROPOLITAN AREA.
Régie autonome des transports parisiens. RATP plan d'entreprise 1983/1987. Paris [1982] 164 p. : LC Card 83-203335
HE4769.P33 R47 1982

LOCAL TRANSIT - FRANCE - STATISTICS.
Cent un réseaux urbains de transports collectifs . [Paris] [1982] 48 p. : LC Card 83-227229
HE4764 .C45 1982

LOCAL TRANSIT - FRANCE - TECHNOLOGICAL INNOVATIONS.
France. Conseil économique et social. L'évolution des transports urbains de voyageurs face aux nouvelles technologies . [Paris] [1986] 184 p. in various pagings : LC Card 86-179126
HE4764 .F73 1986

LOCAL TRANSIT - GERMANY, WEST.
Aufbereitung von Ergebnissen der Stadtverkehrsforschung . Hof/Saale , 1986. 2 v. : LC Card 87-408335 DDC 388.4/0943 19
HE4774 .A94 1986

LOCAL TRANSIT - HONG KONG - HANDBOOKS, MANUALS, ETC.
Guide to Hong Kong's bus, light bus, rail, and ferry services /. Hong Kong , 1986. p. D3799-D4101, 14 p. ; LC Card 87-401055 DDC 388.4/0951/25 19
HE5080.5.H662 G85 1986

LOCAL TRANSIT - MANAGEMENT.
Fielding, Gordon J. Managing public transit strategically . San Francisco , 1987. xxii, 270 p. : ISBN 1-555-42068-0 (alk. paper) LC Card 87-45497 DDC 388.4/068 19
HE4301 .F54 1987

LOCAL TRANSIT - MASSACHUSETTS - BOSTON METROPOLITAN AREA - HANDBOOKS, MANUALS, ETC.
Car-free in Boston . Cambridge, MA (P.O. Box 192, Cambridge 02238) , c1986. 160 p. : LC Card 86-231024 DDC 388.4/09744 19
HE4491.B8 C37 1986

LOCAL TRANSIT - NEW ENGLAND - HANDBOOKS, MANUALS, ETC.
Car-free in Boston . Cambridge, MA (P.O. Box 192, Cambridge 02238) , c1986. 160 p. : LC Card 86-231024 DDC 388.4/09744 19
HE4491.B8 C37 1986

LOCAL TRANSIT - NEW YORK (N.Y.) - FINANCE.
Staff report on proposed modification no. 86-12 to New York City's financial plan relating to the New York City Transit Authority and Staten Island Rapid Transit Operating Authority. [Albany] [1986] 27 leaves ; LC Card 86-622415 DDC 388.4/042 19
HE4491.N65 S7 1986

LOCAL TRANSIT - NEW YORK REGION - HISTORY - 20TH CENTURY.
Baxter, Raymond J., 1928- Railroad ferries of the Hudson . Woodcliff Lake, NJ , 1987. viii, 254 p. : ISBN 0-910389-01-2 : LC Card 87-22782 DDC 386/.2234/097473 19
HE5774. B39 1987

LOCAL TRANSIT - PENNSYLVANIA - FINANCE.
Pennsylvania. General Assembly. Legislative Budget and Finance Committee. A report on mass transit funding needs in Pennsylvania /. Harrisburg, Pa. (Rm. 400, Finance Bldg., Harrisburg 17120) [1986] ii, 151 p. ; LC Card 86-622848 DDC 388.4/042 19
HE4487.P4 P44 1986

LOCAL TRANSIT - PENNSYLVANIA - PHILADELPHIA METROPOLITAN AREA - HANDBOOKS, MANUALS, ETC.
Philadelphia bus & rail directory . [Phila., Pa.] (437 Chestnut St., Suite 209, Philadelphia 19106) [c1986] 88 p. : LC Card 87-110517 DDC 388.4/09748/11 19
HE4491.P52 P48 1986

LOCAL TRANSIT - QUÉBEC (PROVINCE) - MONTRÉAL REGION.
Bussière, Yves. Vieillissement de la population et demande de transport dans la région de Montréal . Montréal, Québec [1983] 83 p. : ISBN 2-89228-036-2 LC Card 84-177163
HE4509.M68 B88 1983

LOCAL TRANSIT - RESEARCH - UNITED STATES.
Research for public transit . Washington, D.C. , 1987. vi, 146 p. : ISBN 0-309-04461-8 (pbk.) LC Card 87-22878 DDC 388.4/0973 19
HE4451 .R47 1987

LOCAL TRANSIT - SOVIET UNION.
Artynov, Aleksandr Petrovich. Prigorodnye passazhirskie perevozki /. Moskva , 1985. 160 p. : LC Card 86-208093
HE4834 .A78 1985

LOCAL TRANSIT - SPAIN - BARCELONA REGION - MANAGEMENT - PUBLIC OPINION.
Estudi motivacional i d'opinió sobre els transports públics a la conurbació barcelonina ; Estudi de comunicació per a la campanya publicitària del foment de l'ús del transport col·lectiu /. [Barcelona] [1982?] 80 p. : ISBN 84-393-0087-5 LC Card 86-209206
HE4899.B43 E87 1982

LOCAL TRANSIT - SPAIN - BARCELONA REGION - PUBLIC OPINION.
Estudi motivacional i d'opinió sobre els transports públics a la conurbació barcelonina ; Estudi de comunicació per a la campanya publicitària del foment de l'ús del transport col·lectiu /. [Barcelona] [1982?] 80 p. : ISBN 84-393-0087-5 LC Card 86-209206
HE4899.B43 E87 1982

LOCAL TRANSIT - TEXAS.
Bullard, Diane L. Texas public transit reference manual /. College Station, Tex. [1985] xv, 279 p. : LC Card 86-623065 DDC 388.4/09764 19
HE4426.T4 B84 1985

LOCAL TRANSIT - UNITED STATES - CONGRESSES.
ULI/UMTA Policy Forum on Joint Development of Rail Transit Facilities (1986 : Washington, D.C.) ULI-UMTA Policy Forum on Joint Development of Rail Transit Facilities . [Washington, D.C.] [1987] iv, 107 p. : ISBN 0-87420-671-5 (pbk.) LC Card 87-82098 DDC 333.3/8 19
HD257 .U43 1986

LOCAL TRANSIT - UNITED STATES - DIRECTORIES.
A Directory of rural and specialized transit operators /. Washington, D.C. , 1986- v. <1-3 > : LC Card 86-603414 DDC 388.3/22/0973 19
HE203 .D57 1986

LOCAL TRANSIT - UNITED STATES - EMPLOYEES.
MacDorman, Littleton C. Use of part-time operators /. Washington, D.C. [1986] 33 p. : ISBN 0-309-04403-0 (pbk.) LC Card 86-51175 DDC 331.25/72 19
HD8039.S82 U65 1986

LOCAL TRANSIT - UNITED STATES - FINANCE.
Bloch, Arnold J. Interstate highway trade-in process. Vol. 1. Assessment /. New York , 1982. [45] p. : ***NYPL [*XME-11,324]***

United States. Office of Highway Planning. Urban Planning and Transportation Management Division. Review of Federal-Aid Urban System program. [Washington, D.C.?] [1985] 55 p. : ***NYPL [JLF 86-340]***

LOCAL TRANSIT - UNITED STATES - HISTORY - 20TH CENTURY.
St. Clair, David James, 1950- The motorization of American cities /. New York , 1986. xi, 192 p. ; ISBN 0-275-92126-3 (alk. paper) : LC Card 86-523 DDC 388.4/1321/0973 19
HE5623 .S617 1986 ***NYPL [JLE 86-3608]***

LOCAL TRANSIT - UNITED STATES - MARKETING.
Marketing public transit . New York , 1987. x, 228 p. : ISBN 0-275-92499-8 (alk. paper) : LC Card 87-11583 DDC 388.4/068/8 19
HE4456 .M37 1987

LOCAL TRANSIT - WASHINGTON METROPOLITAN AREA - RIDERSHIP - STATISTICS.
1986 D.C. Core Cordon Count of vehicular and passenger volumes /. [Washington, D.C.] , c1986. iv, 34 p., [66] p. : LC Card 87-105302 DDC 388.4/13142/09753 19
HE372.W3 A15 1986

Localidades pobladas. XV censo nacional de población y IV de vivienda--Chile, Abril 1982. [Santiago] , <[1983]-[1986]. <v. 3-14; in 15 > : LC Card 87-110013
HA994 1982d

La localisation de l'industrie pharmaceutique au Canada /. Martin, Fernand. [Ottawa] , c1986. 48 p. ; ISBN 0-662-93544-6 LC Card 86-206756
HD9670.C22 M37 1986

Locarek, Hermann. Opitz, Otto. Zur Analyse des Personal Computer Marktes 1985 . Augsburg [1986] 35 leaves : LC Card 87-407365 DDC 380.1/4500416 19
HD9696.C62 O664 1986

LOCATION IN BUSINESS. see **INDUSTRIES, LOCATION OF.**

LOCATION OF INDUSTRIES. see **INDUSTRIES, LOCATION OF.**

LOCATION OF OFFICES. see **OFFICES - LOCATION.**

Location of public enterprises and regional development /. Kundu, Amitabh, 1948- New Delhi , 1986. xv, 178 p. ; LC Card 86-903373 DDC 338.954 19
HD9697.A3 I45 1986

LOCATION OF STORES. see **STORE LOCATION.**

Location strategies for retail and service firms /. Ghosh, Avijit. Lexington, Mass. , c1987. x, 212 p. : ISBN 0-669-12032-4 (alk. paper) LC Card 85-45583 DDC 658.1/1 19
HF5429.275 .G47 1987

Locational pattern of agricultural production/purchases . Ahmad, Nisar. Lilongwe [Malawi] , 1984. ii, 33 leaves ; LC Card 86-980325 DDC 380.1/41/096897 19
HE199.5.F3 A38 1984

L'occidentalisation des pays du Tiers Monde . Dahmani, Mohamed. Paris , Alger , c1983. 217 p. ; ISBN 2-7178-0623-7 : LC Card 83-162697 DDC 909/.09724082 19
HC59.7 .D273 1983 ***NYPL [JLE 86-566]***

Lock, Dennis. The Gower handbook of management /. Aldershot, Hants, England , Brookfield, Vt., U. S.A. , 1987. p. cm. ISBN 0-566-02662-7 : LC Card 87-144 DDC 658 19
HD31 .G684 1987

Lock, Robert D., 1930-
Career planning guidebook .
(bk. 1) Lock, Robert D., 1930- Taking charge of your career direction /. Pacific Grove, Calif. , c1988. xv, 377 p. : ISBN 0-534-08220-3 (pbk.) : LC Card 87-11637 DDC 650.1/4 19
HF5381 .L59 1988

Job search : career planning guidebook, book II / Robert D. Lock. Pacific Grove, Calif. : Brooks/Cole Pub. Co., c1988. viii, 248 p. : ill. ; 24 cm. Includes bibliographies and index. ISBN 0-534-08222-X (pbk.) : LC Card 87-15838 DDC 650.1/4 19
1. Job hunting. I. Title.
HF5382.7 .L63 1988

Taking charge of your career direction / Robert D. Lock. Pacific Grove, Calif. : Brooks/Cole, c1988. xv, 377 p. : ill. ; 24 cm. (Career planning guidebook . bk. 1) Includes bibliographies and index. ISBN 0-534-08220-3 (pbk.) : LC Card 87-11637 DDC 650.1/4 19
1. Vocational guidance. I. Series: Lock, Robert D., 1930- Career planning guidebook , bk. 1. II. Title.
HF5381 .L59 1988

Locke, John, 1632-1704. Several papers relating to money, interest and trade, &c. / by John Locke. Fairfield, NJ : A.M. Kelley, 1988. p. cm. (Reprints of economic classics) Reprint. Originally published: London : Printed for A. & J. Churchill, 1696. CONTENTS. - Some considerations of the consequences of the lowering of interest, and raising the value of money (1691) -- Some observations on a printed paper intituled, For encouraging the coining silver money in England, and after for keeping it here (1695) -- Further considerations concerning raising the value of money (1695). ISBN 0-678-00334-3 LC Card 87-17243 DDC 332.4/941 19
1. Money - Great Britain. 2. Interest - Great Britain. 3. Usury - Great Britain. I. Title.
HG937 .L74 1988

Locke, Joseph, 1805-1860. Scotchman. Letter to Joseph Locke, Esq. ... in reference to his bill "to regulate Sunday travelling on railways" /. Glasgow , 1849. 16 p. ; LC Card 85-666156
HE3037. S36x 1849

Lockman, Zachary. Beinin, Joel, 1948- Workers on the Nile . Princeton, N.J. , c1987. xix, 488 p. : ISBN 0-691-05506-8 (alk. paper) : LC Card 87-45510 DDC 305.5/62/0962 19
HD8786 .B45 1987

LOCKOUTS. see **STRIKES AND LOCKOUTS.**

Locoh, Thérèse.
Comprendre les problèmes de population : cours d'initiation à la démographie / par Thérèse Locoh, avec la collaboration de Kuakuvi Gbenyon et Kokou Vignikin.Version rév. Lomé, Togo : Université du Bénin, Unité de recherche démographique, 1984. 72, [3], 3 p. : ill. ; 30 cm. (Etudes togolaises de population . no 1) Bibliography: p. [74]-[75]. LC Card 87-131146
1. Population. 2. Togo - Population. 3. Africa - Population. I. Gbenyon, Kuakuvi. II. Vignikin, Kokou. III. Title. IV. Series.
HB871 .L57 1984

La fécondité en Afrique noire / Thérèse Locoh. Pour une mesure indirecte de la mortalité : la méthode de Courbage-Farques : adéquation ou inadéquation au cas du Togo en 1971? / Kuakuvi Gbenyon. Lomé : Université du Benin, Unité de recherche démographique, [1985] 36, 22 leaves : ill. ; 30 cm. (Etudes togolaises de population . no 9) Cover title. At head of title: République togolaise, Ministère de l'éducation nationale et de la recherche scientifique. Includes bibliographical references. LC Card 87-126644
1. Fertility, Human - Africa, Sub-Saharan. 2. Africa, Sub-Saharan - Population. 3. Mortality - Togo. 4. Togo - Statistics, Vital. I. Gbenyon, Kuakuvi. Pour une mesure indirecte de la mortalitè. 1985. II. Togo. Ministère de l'éducation nationale et de la recherche scientifique. III. Title. IV. Title: Pour une mesure indirecte de la mortalité. V. Series.
HB1071 .L63 1985

LOCOMOTIVE ENGINEERS - FRANCE - BIOGRAPHY.
Péroche, Marcel, 1907- Les mémoires de Marcel Péroche, "sénateur" du rail /. Paris , c1984. 256 p., [8] p. of plates : ISBN

2-7013-0556-X : LC Card 84-206923
HD8039.R322 F87 1984

LOCOMOTIVE ENGINEERS - FRANCE - HISTORY - 19TH CENTURY.
Stein, Margot B. (Margot Ballou), 1945- The social origins of a labor elite . New York , 1987. xxiv, 515 p. : ISBN 0-8240-8043-2 (alk. paper) : LC Card 87-6913 DDC 305/.9385 19
HD8039.R322 F88 1987

Loddon-Campaspe Resources Co-ordination Committee. The Bendigo and Loddon-Campaspe employment and training study /. [Australia] [1982-1984] 5 v. : ISBN 0-9592508-0-8 (pbk. : v. 1) LC Card 87-168391 DDC 330.9945/4 19
HC608.B46 B46 1982

Loderer, Eugen. Metallgewerkschaften in Südafrika /. [Köln] , c1983. 217 p. ; ISBN 3-7663-0530-1 LC Card 85-232412 DDC 331.88/171/0968 19
HD6870.5.Z7 M54 1983
NYPL [JLD 87-1964]

Lodge, George C. Ideology and national competitiveness . Boston, Mass. , c1987. x, 350 p. ; ISBN 0-87584-147-3 LC Card 86-19569 DDC 338.6/048 19
HF1414 .I34 1987 ***NYPL [JLE 87-1046]***

Lodge, Joseph H., 1942- Drug and alcohol abuse in the workplace : an assessment of economic and productivity losses / Joseph H. Lodge. New York : M. Dekker, c1987. xi, 91 p. ; 30 cm. Includes index. ISBN 0-8247-7769-7 LC Card 87-627 DDC 658.3/822 19
1. Drugs and employment - United States. 2. Alcoholism and employment - United States. I. Title.
HF5549.5.D7 L63 1987

LODGING-HOUSES - INDIA.
Chauhan, Indira, 1949- The dilemma of working women hostelers . Delhi , New Delhi , 1986. 70 p. : ISBN 81-7018-374-X : LC Card 86-902619 DDC 305.4/0954/792 19
HD6189 .C42 1986

LODGING-HOUSES - INDIA - MAHARASHTRA.
Chauhan, Indira, 1949- The dilemma of working women hostelers . Delhi , New Delhi , 1986. 70 p. : ISBN 81-7018-374-X : LC Card 86-902619 DDC 305.4/0954/792 19
HD6189 .C42 1986

Loeb, Marshall. Money minutes / Marshall Loeb. 1st ed. Boston : Little, Brown, c1987. ix, 210 p. ; 21 cm. ISBN 0-316-53058-1 (pbk.) : LC Card 87-10245 DDC 332.024 19
1. Finance, Personal. I. Title.
HG179 .L553 1987

Loeb, Paul Rogat, 1952- Hope in hard times : America's peace movement and the Reagan era / by Paul Rogat Loeb. Lexington, Mass. : Lexington Books, c1987. ix, 322 p. : ill. ; 24 cm. Includes index. Bibliography: p. [305]-306. ISBN 0-669-12929-1 LC Card 85-46044 DDC 327.1/74 19
1. Nuclear disarmament. 2. Antinuclear movement - United States. I. Title.
JX1974.7 .L63 1986 ***NYPL [JLE 86-4051]***

Loeb, Stephen E. Kiger, Jack E. Accounting principles /. New York , c1987. xxvii, 1092 p. : ISBN 0-394-35482-6 : LC Card 86-29791 DDC 657 19
HF5635 .K53 1987

Loebbecke, James K. Arens, Alvin A. Auditing, an integrated approach /. Englewood Cliffs, N.J. , c1988. p. cm. ISBN 0-13-051814-X LC Card 87-26359 DDC 657/.45 19
HF5667 .A69 1988

Loebel, Hansgeorg. Frauen und neue Technologien /. Hannover , 1986. 112 p. ; LC Card 87-407392 DDC 331.4/0943 19
HD6059.G3 F74 1986

Loebl, Herbert. Government factories and the origins of British regional policy, 1934-1948 : including a case study of North Eastern Trading Estates Ltd. / Herbert Loebl. Aldershot, Hants, England ; Brookfield, Vt., USA : Gower, c1987. p. cm. Bibliography: p. Includes index. ISBN 0-566-05343-8 LC Card 87-23075 DDC 338.6/2/0941 19
1. Government business enterprises - Great Britain. 2. Regional planning - Great Britain. 3. North Eastern Trading Estates Ltd. I. Title.
HD4145 .L64 1987

Loeliger, Walter. Sind Sie frei? : Geschichten eines Taxifahrers / Walter Loeliger.1. Aufl. Basel : Nachtmaschine, 1982. 99 p. : ill. ; 20 cm. (Reihe Unterhaltungsliteratur) ISBN 3-85816-043-1 : LC Card 83-100470
1. Laeliger, Walter. 2. Taxicab drivers - Switzerland - Basel - Biography. 3. Basel (Switzerland) - Social life and customs. 4. Basel (Switzerland) - Biography. I. Title. II. Series.
HD8039.T162 L64 1982

Löschner, Ernst. Souveräne Risken und internationale Verschuldung / von Ernst Löschner. Wien : Manzsche Verlags- und Universitätsbuchhandlung, 1983. 187 p. : ill. ; 23 cm. (Recht, Wirtschaft, Aussenhandel . Bd. 6) Includes index. Bibliography: p. [180]-184. ISBN 3-214-06553-X : LC Card 84-152762 DDC 336.3/435/091724 19
1. Debts, Public - Developing countries. 2. Debts, External - Developing countries. I. Title. II. Series.
HJ8899 .L67 1983 ***NYPL [JLE 86-1553]***

Loewenfeld-Russ, Hans, 1873-1945. Im Kampf gegen den Hunger : aus den Erinnerungen des Staatssekretärs für Volksernährung, 1918-1920 / Hans Loewenfeld-Russ ; herausgegeben und bearbeitet von Isabella Ackerl. München : Oldenbourg, 1986. xxiv, 381 p., [1] leaf of plates : ill. ; 24 cm. (Studien und Quellen zur österreichischen Zeitgeschichte . Bd. 6) Includes bibliographical references and indexes. ISBN 3-486-52451-8 LC Card 86-224948
1. Famines - Austria - History. 2. Food supply - Government policy - Austria - History. 3. Food relief - Austria - History. 4. World War, 1914-1918 - Food supply - Austria. I. Ackerl, Isabella. II. Title. III. Series.
HC270.F3 L64 1986

Löffelholz, Herbert. Marburger, Ernst-Albrecht. Internationale Erfahrungen mit der Gurtanlegepflicht =. Köln , 1982. 29, 29 p. : LC Card 83-200842
HE5614 .M288 1982

Löffler, Reiner. Macht, Arbeit und Humanität : zur Pathologie organisierter Arbeitssituationen / Reiner Löffler, Wolfgang Sofsky ; Vorwort, Hans Paul Bahrdt. Göttingen : J. Cromm, c1986. v, 563 p. ; 24 cm. "WiSoMed." Bibliography: p. 550-563. ISBN 3-921969-12-3 LC Card 86-227215
1. Industrial sociology - Germany, West. 2. Labor policy - Germany, West. 3. Human rights - Germany (West). 4. Work. I. Sofsky, Wolfgang. II. Title.
HD6957.G3 L64 1986

Löffler, Reiner, 1959- STRATEGOS : ein dynamisches und computergestütztes Planspiel des Wettbewerbs zwischen Unternehmen zur Unterstützung des strategischen Managements / vorgelegt von Reiner Löffler. Mannheim : [s.n.], 1986 (Darmstadt : Copy Shop) 246, [49] p. : ill. ; 21 cm. Thesis (doctoral)--Universität Mannheim, 1986. Bibliography: p. 237-246. LC Card 87-408452 DDC 658.4/0353/0285 19
1. Management games - Data processing. 2. Strategic planning - Data processing. 3. Game theory - Data processing. I. Title.
HD30.26 .L64 1986

LOFTLEIÐIR (AIRLINE) - HISTORY.
Alfreð Elíasson, 1920- Alfreðs saga og Loftleiða /. Reykjavík , 1984 (1985 printing) 372 p. : LC Card 86-101929
HD9711.I22 A443 1985
NYPL [JFE 87-1455]

Loftus, Simon. Anatomy of the wine trade : Abe's sardines and other stories / Simon Loftus ; edited and introduced by Jancis Robinson.1st U. S. ed. New York : Harper & Row, c1985. 179 p. ; 25 cm. Includes index. ISBN 0-06-015785-2 : LC Card 87-45066 DDC 380.1/456632 19
1. Wine industry. I. Robinson, Jancis. II. Title.
HD9370.5 .L64 1985

Log of the federal-aid interstate system comprising the Nevada primary state highway system, 1985 / State of Nevada, Department of Transportation, Planning. Carson City, Nev. : Inventory and Road Life ; [Washington] : U. S. Dept. of Transportation, Federal Highway Administration, [1985] 41 leaves ; 28 cm. Cover title: Federal aid, interstate routes, 1985. On cover: State of Nevada, Dept. of Transportation, Research Division. "December 31, 1984." LC Card 86-622234 DDC 388.1/09793 19
1. Interstate Highway System - Nevada - Statistics. 2. Roads - Nevada - Statistics. I. Nevada. Dept. of Transportation. Planning Division. II. Nevada. Dept. of Transportation. Research Division. III. Title: Federal aid interstate routes, 1985.
HE356.N37 L632 1985

Logan, William Stewart, 1942- The Gentrification of inner Melbourne : a political geography of inner city housing / William Stewart Logan. St. Lucia, Qld., Australia ; New York : University of Queensland Press ; xxxiii, 328 p. : ill. (some col.), maps, ports. ; 23 cm. (Scholars' library) Includes index. Bibliography: p. [305]-315. ISBN 0-7022-1729-8 LC Card 84-17382 DDC 307/.2 19
1. Housing - Australia - Melbourne (Vic.). 2. Urban renewal - Australia - Melbourne (Vic.). 3. Gentrification - Australia - Melbourne (Vic.). I. Series: University of Queensland Press scholars' library. II. Title.
HD7379.M45 L64 1985
NYPL [JLD 87-798]

Les Logements neufs en 1978 : prix de revient et parc énergétique / Ministère de l'urbanisme et du logement, Direction des affaires économiques et internationales, Service des statistiques, Division des enquêtes sur le marché du bâtiment. Paris : Documentation française, 1982. 40 p. : ill. ; 30 cm. (Collections statistiques du Ministère de l'urbanisme et du logement. Statistiques et études générales, 0184-6892 . no 79) LC Card 83-176727
1. Housing - France - Costs - Statistics. 2. Dwellings - France - Costs - Statistics. 3. Dwellings - France - Insulation - Costs - Statistics. 4. Dwellings - France - Heating and ventilation - Equipment and supplies - Costs - Statistics. I. France. Division des enquêtes sur le marcheé du bâtiment. II. Series. III. Series: Statistiques et études générales , no. 79.
HD7338.A4 L64 1982

LOGGERS - MICHIGAN - BIOGRAPHY.
Corrigan, George A., 1896-1981. Calked boots and cant hooks /. Ashland, WI , 1986, c1976. xxi, 265 p. : ISBN 0-9613961-5-6 (pbk.) : LC Card 87-401439 DDC 331.7/634982/0924 B 19
HD8039.L92 U535 1986

LOGGERS - WISCONSIN - BIOGRAPHY.
Corrigan, George A., 1896-1981. Calked boots and cant hooks /. Ashland, WI , 1986, c1976. xxi, 265 p. : ISBN 0-9613961-5-6 (pbk.) : LC Card 87-401439 DDC 331.7/634982/0924 B 19
HD8039.L92 U535 1986

Loggins, Richard, 1949- The Excel advanced user's guide / Richard Loggins. 1st ed. Indianapolis, Ind., USA : Hayden Books, c1987. x, 189 p. : ill. ; 24 cm. (Hayden Macintosh library books) Includes index. ISBN 0-672-46626-0 (pbk.) : LC Card 87-60109 DDC 005.36/9 19
1. Excel (Computer program). 2. Business - Data processing. I. Title. II. Series.
HF5548.4.E93 L64 1987

Logic in computer science. Symposium on Logic in Computer Science (1986 : Cambridge, Mass.) Proceedings, Symposium on Logic in Computer Science, Cambridge, Massachusetts, June 16-18, 1986 /. Washington, D.C. , Los Angeles, CA , 1986. xi, 383 p. : ISBN 0-8186-0720-3 (pbk.) LC Card 86-81090 DDC 004 19
QA75.5 .S9813 1986 ***NYPL [JSF 86-1041]***

Logic of economic-mathematical modelling. Biliarski, Dimitŭr. Logikata i ikonomiko-matematicheskoto modelirane /. Sofiia , 1985. 307 p., [1] folded leaf of plates : LC Card 85-213972
HB135 .B523 1985

LOGIC, SYMBOLIC AND MATHEMATICAL - CONGRESSES.
Symposium on Logic in Computer Science (1986 : Cambridge, Mass.) Proceedings, Symposium on Logic in Computer Science, Cambridge, Massachusetts, June 16-18, 1986 /. Washington, D.C. , Los Angeles, CA , 1986. xi, 383 p. : ISBN 0-8186-0720-3 (pbk.) LC Card 86-81090 DDC 004 19
QA75.5 .S9813 1986 ***NYPL [JSF 86-1041]***

LOGIC, UNIVERSAL. see **LOGIC, SYMBOLIC AND MATHEMATICAL.**

Logie, Gordon. Glossary of planning and development : English-French-Italian-Dutch-German-Swedish / Gordon Logie. Amsterdam ; New York :

Elsevier, 1986. xxv, 254 p. ; 24 cm. (International planning glossaries. 5) Includes indexes. Bibliography: p. 251-252. ISBN 0-444-42608-6 (U. S.) : LC Card 86-521 DDC 338.9/003 19
1. Regional planning - Dictionaries - Polyglot. 2. Economic development - Dictionaries - Polyglot. 3. Economic policy - Dictionaries - Polyglot. I. Title. II. Series.
HT391 .L64 1987 ***NYPL [JLE 86-4010]***

Logika ėkonomiko-matematicheskogo modelirovanii͡a. Biliarski, Dimitŭr. Logikata i ikonomiko-matematicheskoto modelirane /. Sofii͡a , 1985. 307 p., [1] folded leaf of plates : LC Card 85-213972
HB135 .B523 1985

Logikata i ikonomiko-matematicheskoto modelirane /. Biliarski, Dimitŭr. Sofii͡a , 1985. 307 p., [1] folded leaf of plates : LC Card 85-213972
HB135 .B523 1985

Loginov, V. P. Struktura narodnogo khozi͡aĭstva v uslovii͡akh intensifikatsii ėkonomiki /. Moskva , 1986. 267 p. ; LC Card 86-212596
HC336.25 .S795 1986

Logistik als Instrument zur Steigerung der Marktleistungsfähigkeit von Stahlhandlungen /. Reutersberg, Bernhard. Göttingen , 1985. 301 p. : ISBN 3-525-85697-0 : LC Card 86-162333
HE131 .M8 Heft 107 HE199.5.M4

Logistik einer Grossbank . Gross, Peter, Dr. Bern , c1983. 52 p. : ISBN 3-258-03274-2 : LC Card 83-181853
HG1526 .B27 Bd. 80 HG3208.U54

Loglineare Modellierung mit dem Abschlusstest . Schiller, Karla, 1955- München , c1986. xiii, 226 p. : ISBN 3-88259-397-0 LC Card 86-230772
HF5415.135 .S35 1986

LOGOTYPE.
Napoles, Veronica, 1951- Corporate identity design /. New York , c1988. 144 p. : ISBN 0-442-26844-0 (pbk.) : LC Card 87-6190 DDC 659.2/85 19
HD59.2 .N36 1988

Logsdon, Tom, 1937- Striking it rich in space / by Tom Logsdon. New York : Crown Publishers, 1988. p. cm. Bibliography: p. Includes index. LC Card 87-22294 DDC 332.6/78/0919 19
1. Space industrialization. I. Title.
HD9711.75.A2 L65 1988

Logue, Dennis E. Berkowitz, Stephen A. The investment performance of corporate pension plans . New York , 1988. xi, 132 p. ; ISBN 0-89930-224-6 (lib. bdg. : alk. paper) LC Card 87-19030 DDC 332.6/7154 19
HD7105.45.U6 B475 1988

Logue, John, 1947- Buyout! : employee ownership as an alternative to plant shutdowns : the Ohio experience / John Logue, James B. Quilligan, and Barbara J. Weissmann ; foreword by William F. Whyte. [Kent, Ohio] : Kent Popular Press, [1986] vi, 98 p. : ill. ; 28 cm. Bibliography: p. 96-97. ISBN 0-933522-15-0 (pbk.) LC Card 86-623028 DDC 658.1/6 19
1. Leveraged buyouts. 2. Plant shutdowns - Ohio. 3. Employee ownership - Ohio. I. Quilligan, James B. II. Weissmann, Barbara J. III. Title.
HD2746.5 .L64 1986

Loh, Wolfram W. Das S.W.I.F.T.-System : die moderne Datenübertragung im internationalen Zahlungsverkehr / von Wolfram W. Loh. Frankfurt am Main : F. Knapp, c1983. vii, 198 p. : ill. ; 21 cm. Bibliography: p. 190-198. ISBN 3-7819-0285-4 : LC Card 83-211180
1. Banks and banking, International - Communication systems. 2. Society for Worldwide Interbank Financial Telecommunication. I. Title. II. Title: SWIFT-System.
HG1708.5 .L64 1983

Lohmann, Jens. Den mellemamerikanske drøm : mellemamerika mellem storpolitik og revolution / Jens Lohmann. [Copenhagen] : Vindrose, c1984. 184 p. : map ; 20 cm. Bibliography: p. 170-[174] Includes index. ISBN 87-7456-194-4 LC Card 84-193120
1. Central America - Economic conditions. 2. Central America - Politics and government. 3. Central America - Social conditions. I. Title.
HC141 .L64 1984

Lohmar, Ceil. Buy more home for less money / by Ceil Lohmar. Crystal Bay, Minn. (P.O. Box 61, Crystal Bay 55323) : Lohmar Pub., c1987. 121 p. : forms ; 23 cm. Includes index. ISBN 0-940641-00-3 (pbk.) LC Card 87-401647 DDC 643/.12 19
1. House buying. I. Title.
HD1379 .L646 1987

Lohn- und Einkommensteuerstatistik 1979 : Zusammenführung / bearbeitet im Österreichischen Statistischen Zentralamt. Wien : Das Amt : Kommissionsverlag, Österreichische Staatsdruckerei, 1985. xxxv, 59 p. : ill. ; 30 cm. LC Card 86-233093
1. Wages - Taxation - Austria - Statistics. 2. Income tax - Austria - Statistics. I. Österreichisches Statistisches Zentralamt.
HJ4713.A7 L64 1985

Lohn- und Gehaltsstruktur 1978/79 : Hauptergebnisse. Lønstrukturen 1978/79 . Luxembourg , Washington, D.C. , <1983-1986. v. <2-3, 6-7, 10 > ; ISBN 92-825-3817-6 (set) : LC Card 86-211360
HD5014.5 .L66 1983

Lohnarbeit und Klassenbildung . Kocka, Jürgen. Berlin , c1983. 207 p. ; ISBN 3-8012-0088-4 LC Card 83-169041
HD8449 .K63 1983

Lohndispersionen auf strukturierten Arbeitsmärkten . Friderichs, Hans. Pfaffenweiler , 1986. xvi, 404 p. : ISBN 3-89085-133-9 LC Card 87-134875 DDC 331.2/943 19
HD5029 .F75 1986

Die Lohnentwicklung deutscher Industrieaktiengesellschaften /. Wanik, Bernhard. Bonn , 1981. vii, 268 p. : LC Card 85-165602
HD5029 .W36 1981

Lohnentwicklung und Lohnpolitik als Bestimmungsgründe konjunktureller Verläufe und struktureller Verschiebungen . Basler, Hans-Peter. Berlin , 1981. 102 p. : ISBN 3-428-04970-5 LC Card 82-100546 DDC 330 s 331.2/943 19
HB41 .B4 Nr. 134 HD5029
NYPL [JLL 73-207 Heft 134]

Lohnpolitik im Betrieb . Teschner, Eckart, 1940- Frankfurt/Main , New York , c1977. 226 p. : ISBN 3-593-32244-7 LC Card 85-134281 DDC 331.2/943 19
HD4966.M44 G48 1977

Löhr, Paul. Arbeitslose Jugendliche, eine Zielgruppe für Fernsehen und Hörfunk? /. München , New York , 1985. 157 p. : ISBN 3-598-20759-X LC Card 86-153843
HD6276.G39 A73 1985

Loiacono, Nicholas. Work of the purchase and sales department / Nicholas Loiacono. New York, NY : New York Institute of Finance, c1987. p. cm. Includes index. ISBN 0-13-965104-7 : LC Card 87-7734 DDC 332.6/068/7 19
1. Brokers. 2. Purchasing. 3. Selling. I. Title.
HG4621 .L64 1987

LOIRE (FRANCE : DEPT.) - ECONOMIC POLICY.
Comité d'expansion de la Loire. Bilan socio-économique de la Loire /. Saint Etienne [1983] 270 p., [2] leaves of plates : LC Card 85-104338
HC277.L6 C66 1983

LOIRE (FRANCE : DEPT.) - INDUSTRIES.
Comité d'expansion de la Loire. Bilan socio-économique de la Loire /. Saint Etienne [1983] 270 p., [2] leaves of plates : LC Card 85-104338
HC277.L6 C66 1983

LOIRE (FRANCE : DEPT.) - SOCIAL POLICY.
Comité d'expansion de la Loire. Bilan socio-économique de la Loire /. Saint Etienne [1983] 270 p., [2] leaves of plates : LC Card 85-104338
HC277.L6 C66 1983

LOIRE, FRANCE (DEPT.) - ECONOMIC CONDITIONS.
Comité d'expansion de la Loire. Bilan socio-économique de la Loire /. Saint Etienne [1983] 270 p., [2] leaves of plates : LC Card 85-104338
HC277.L6 C66 1983

LOIRE, FRANCE (DEPT.) - SOCIAL CONDITIONS.
Comité d'expansion de la Loire. Bilan socio-économique de la Loire /. Saint Etienne [1983] 270 p., [2] leaves of plates : LC Card 85-104338
HC277.L6 C66 1983

LOJA (ECUADOR : PROVINCE) - ECONOMIC POLICY.
Informe cuatrianual, 1980-1983 /. Cuenca, Ecuador [1983] 222 p. : LC Card 86-206868
HC203.O76 I53 1983

Lokal samverkan--fördelar för näringsliv och kommun? : erfarenheter från en decentraliserad industripolitik byggd på lokala initiativ / Statens industriverk. Stockholm : LiberFörlag, [1982] 185 p. : ill. ; 25 cm. (SIND, 0346-5748 . 1982:7) Bibliography: p. 183-185. ISBN 91-38-07027-8 LC Card 82-236501
1. Sweden - Industries. 2. Sweden - Economic conditions - 1945-. 3. Local government - Sweden. I. Sweden. Statens industriverk. II. Series.
HC375 .L786 1982

Lokales Bürgerfernsehen . Hunziker, Peter, 1941- Aarau , c1983. 192 p. ; ISBN 3-7941-2369-7 : LC Card 83-141437
HE8700.72.S95 H85 1983

Lokales Informationssystem Arbeitsmarkt (LISA) /. Noll, Wulf. Essen , 1986. 262 p. ; ISBN 3-923494-64-5 LC Card 87-409105 DDC 331.12/5/094355 19
HD5780.R82 N65 1986

Lokan, Jan J. Holland in Australia . Melbourne , 1986. xxii, 229 p. : ISBN 0-86431-032-3 LC Card 87-164636 DDC 331.7/02/0994 19
HF5381.H56693 H65 1986

Lőkös, László.
Agrárgazdaságtan /. Budapest , 1984. 465 p. : ISBN 963-231-719-X : LC Card 85-229778
HD1415 .A27 1984

Magyar-Lengyel Agrárközgazdasági Konferencia (1984 : Gödöllő, Hungary) A nagyüzemek és a kisüzemek termelésének fejlődése, kapcsolatuk az iparosodó mezőgazdaságban =. Gödöllő , 1984. 174 p. ; LC Card 86-145249
HD1995.7 .M32 1984

Lokotchenko, A. P. Industrializatsii͡a proizvodstva i mezhkhozi͡aĭstvennoe kooperirovanie /. Ufa , 1979. 122 p. ; LC Card 82-161458
HD9425.S653 B375 1979

Le Lolo : réalites et devenir. Pointe-à-Pitre : Institut de promotion commerciale : Chambre de commerce et d'industrie, [1984?] 63 p. : ill. ; 29 cm. Includes bibliographical references. LC Card 86-155167
1. Markets - Guadeloupe. 2. Guadeloupe - Commerce. I. Institut de promotion commerciale (Guadeloupe). II. Chambre de commerce et d'industrie de Pointe-à-Pitre.
HF5473.G83 L65 1984

Lomax, David F.
The developing country debt crisis / David F. Lomax. London : Macmillan, 1986. xxiv, 317 p. ; 23 cm. Includes bibliographical references and index. ISBN 0-333-38581-0
1. Debts, External - Developing countries. 2. Loans, Foreign - Developing countries. I. Title.
NYPL [JLD 86-3497]

The developing country debt crisis / David F. Lomax ; foreword by Samuel Brittan. Basingstoke, Hampshire : Macmillan, 1986. xxiv, 317 p. : ill. ; 23 cm. Bibliography: p. 303-309. Includes index. ISBN 0-333-38581-0 LC Card 86-674010
1. Debts, External - Developing countries. 2. Loans, Foreign - Developing countries. I. Title.
HJ8899 .L64x 1986b

Lomax, Timothy J.
Guidelines for estimating the cost effectiveness of high-occupancy vehicle lanes / by Timothy J. Lomax, Daniel E. Morris ; sponsored by State Department of Highways and Public Transportation in cooperation with the U. S. Department of Transportation, Federal Highway Administration. College Station, Tex. : Texas Transportation Institute, Texas A&M University System ; Springfield, Va. : Available through National Technical Information Service, [1985] xiii, 55 p. : ill. ; 28 cm. (Research report / Texas Transportation Institute, Texas A&M University System . 339-5) "November 1985." "Research study number 2-10-85-339." Bibliography: p. 55. LC Card 86-622240 DDC 380.5 s 388.3/142 19
1. High occupancy vehicle lanes - Texas - Evaluation. I.

Morris, Daniel E. II. Texas. State Dept. of Highways and Public Transportation. III. United States. Federal Highway Administration. IV. Series: Research report (Texas Transportation Institute) , 339-5. V. Title.
HE203 .T43 no. 339-5 HE356.T4

Relative mobility in Texas cities, 1975 to 1984 / by Timothy J. Lomax ; sponsored by State Department of Highways and Public Transportation in cooperation with the U. S. Department of Transportation, Federal Highway Administration. College Station, Tex. : Texas Transportation Institute, Texas A&M University System, [1986] xiii, 30, 9 p. : ill. ; 28 cm. (Research report . 339-8) "Improving urban mobility through application of high-occupancy vehicle priority treatments." "HOV priority treatment"--Cover. "December 1986." "Research study number 2-10-84-339." Bibliography: p. 29-30. LC Card 87-620994 DDC 380.5 s 388.4/1314/09764 19
1. Traffic congestion - Texas. 2. Traffic flow - Texas. 3. City traffic - Texas. I. Texas. State Dept. of Highways and Public Transportation. II. Texas Transportation Institute. III. Series: Research report (Texas Transportation Institute) , 339-8. IV. Title.
HE203 .T43 no. 339-8 HE356.T4

Lombardi, Nelly Niedworok de. Algunas cifras sobre la fuerza de trabajo en el Uruguay / Nelly Niedworok. [Montevideo] : CIESU, [1979] 18 leaves : ill. ; 29 cm. (Serie Documentos de trabajo . 10/79) Chiefly tables. LC Card 86-164130
1. Labor supply - Uruguay - Statistics. I. Centro de Informaciones y Estudios del Uruguay. II. Series: Serie Documentos de trabajo (Centro de Informaciones y Estudios del Uruguay) , 79/10. III. Title.
HD5762.A6 L66 1979

LOMBARDY (ITALY) - APPROPRIATIONS AND EXPENDITURES - ACCOUNTING.
Conto consolidato della spesa pubblica in Lombardia /. Milano, Italy , c1982. 234 p. ; LC Card 85-147746
HJ9925.I8 C63 1982

LOMBARDY (ITALY) - COMMERCE - HISTORY.
Commercio in Lombardia /. Milano , c1986- v. <1 > : LC Card 87-158732
HF3589.L65 C65 1986

LOMBARDY (ITALY) - ECONOMIC POLICY.
Gario, Giuseppe. Discontinuità e permanenza . Milano, Italy , c1986. 262 p. : LC Card 87-149940
HC307.L8 G37 1986

LOMBARDY (ITALY) - HISTORY - AUSTRIAN RULE, 1714-1796.
Grab, Alexander I., 1946- La politica del pane . Milano, Italy , c1986. 180 p. ; LC Card 86-168239
HD9015.I85 L664 1986

Migliavacca, Giorgio. The postal history of Lombardy under Austrian rule, 1707-1796 . [S.l.] , 1985. [40] p. : ISBN 0-934139-03-2 (pbk.) LC Card 87-149625 DDC 383/.49452 19
HE7016.L66 M54 1985

La Proprietà fondiaria in Lombardia dal catasto teresiano all'età napoleonica /. Milano , 1986. 2 v. ; ISBN 88-343-0341-5 (set) : LC Card 87-108100
HD679.L6 P76 1986

LOMBARDY (ITALY) - INDUSTRIES - HISTORY.
Commercio in Lombardia /. Milano , c1986- v. <1 > : LC Card 87-158732
HF3589.L65 C65 1986

LOMBARDY (ITALY) - NAPOLEONIC RULE, 1796-1813.
Bressan, E. (Edoardo) Povertà e assistenza in Lombardia nell'età napoleonica /. [Milano] , Bari , c1985. viii, 339 p. : ISBN 88-420-2653-0 : LC Card 86-162978
HC307.L8 B74 1985

LOMBARDY (ITALY) - SOCIAL POLICY.
Bressan, E. (Edoardo) Povertà e assistenza in Lombardia nell'età napoleonica /. [Milano] , Bari , c1985. viii, 339 p. : ISBN 88-420-2653-0 : LC Card 86-162978
HC307.L8 B74 1985

Lombeya Bosongo L. Organisation coopérative et développement rural / Lombeya Bosongo L. [Kinshasa] : Presses universitaires du Zaïre, 1985. 173 p. ; 19 cm. Bibliography: p. [165]-168. Includes index. LC Card 86-185252
1. Agriculture, Cooperative - Developing countries. 2. Rural development - Developing countries. I. Title.
HD1491.5 .L66 1985

Lomonosov, ÎU. (ÎUriĭ), 1876-1952.
Tekhnicheskie perspektivy zheleznodorozhnogo transporta v blizhaĭshee vremi͡a. Moskva, Transpechatʹ, 1924. 67 p. 22 cm. LC Card 60-59178
1. Railroads - Soviet Union. I. Title.
HE3135 .L6

The London and New York stock exchanges, 1850-1914 /. Michie, R. C., 1949- London , Boston , 1987. xv, 312 p. ; ISBN 0-04-332117-8 (alk. paper) LC Card 87-1394 DDC 332.64/241 19
HG4577 .M52 1987

London Business School. see **London Graduate School of Business Studies.**

London Capital Group Limited (formerly British Bangladesh Trust Limited) . Sherrard, Michael. London , 1977. vi, 376 p. : ISBN 0-11-512127-7 (pbk.) LC Card 85-164377
HG4135 .S46 1977

LONDON CAPITAL GROUP LTD.
Sherrard, Michael. London Capital Group Limited (formerly British Bangladesh Trust Limited) . London , 1977. vi, 376 p. : ISBN 0-11-512127-7 (pbk.) LC Card 85-164377
HG4135 .S46 1977

London. Central Council for Agricultural and Horticultural Co-operation. see **Central Council for Agricultural and Horticultural Co-operation.**

London Conference on Taxes and Growth . London Conference on Taxes and Growth (1986) New York, NY [1986] 61 p. ; LC Card 87-404887 DDC 339.5/25 19
HJ2279 .L655 1986

London Conference on Taxes and Growth (1986)
London Conference on Taxes and Growth : St. James Court Hotel, London, England, Tuesday, October 14, 1986 / co-directed by the Manhattan Institute for Policy Research (New York) and the Adam Smith Institute (London). New York, NY : Manhattan Institute, [1986] 61 p. ; 28 cm. Bibliography: p. 60-61. LC Card 87-404887 DDC 339.5/25 19
1. Taxation - Congresses. 2. Taxation - United States - Congresses. 3. Taxation - Great Britain - Congresses. 4. Fiscal policy - United States - Congresses. 5. Fiscal policy - Great Britain - Congresses. I. Manhattan Institute for Policy Research. II. Adam Smith Institute. III. Title.
HJ2279 .L655 1986

London, Dick, 1943-
Graduation, the revision of estimates / Dick London. Winsted, Conn. : ACTEX Publications, c1985. viii, 183 p. : ill. ; 23 cm. Includes index. Bibliography: p. 157-160. ISBN 0-936031-00-X (pbk.) : LC Card 85-23001 DDC 519.5 19
1. Insurance, Life - Mathematics. 2. Graduation (Statistics). I. Title.
HG8782 .L56 1985 ***NYPL [JLE 86-3272]***

Survival models and their estimation / Dick London. Winsted, Conn. : Actex Publications, c1986 (1987 printing) xii, 282 p. : ill. ; 28 cm. Bibliography: p. 280-282. ISBN 0-936031-01-8 (pbk.) LC Card 87-402847 DDC 304.6/4/015195 19
1. Insurance - Statistical methods. 2. Mortality - Statistical methods. 3. Population forecasting - Statistical methods. I. Title.
HG8782 .L57 1987

LONDON (ENGLAND) - ECONOMIC CONDITIONS.
Weatheritt, L. Manufacturing industry in Greater London /. London , c1975. ii, 26 p. ; ISBN 0-7168-0853-6 (pbk.) LC Card 82-213745
HD5766.L66 W43 1975

LONDON (ENGLAND) - MANUFACTURES - EMPLOYEES.
Weatheritt, L. Manufacturing industry in Greater London /. London , c1975. ii, 26 p. ; ISBN 0-7168-0853-6 (pbk.) LC Card 82-213745
HD5766.L66 W43 1975

London Graduate School of Business Studies.
(Old Catalog form: London Business School.) Public enterprise policy in India and U.K. in 1980s /. Bombay , 1987. xx, 286 p. ; LC Card 86-903771 DDC 338.6/2/0941 19
HD4293 .P775 1987

London House (Firm : Park Ridge, Ill.) Baehr, Melany E. Experience and background inventory . [Park Ridge, Ill.] (1550 Northwest Highway, Park Ridge 60068) [c1986] 48 p. ; LC Card 87-404267 DDC 658.3/112 19
HF5549.5.S38 B34 1986

London. Institute of Cost and Management Accountants. see **Institute of Cost and Management Accountants.**

London. Institution of Civil Engineers. see **Institution of Civil Engineers, London.**

London, Manuel. Career management and survival in the workplace : helping employees make tough career decisions, stay motivated, and reduce career stress / Manuel London, Edward M. Mone.1st ed. San Francisco : Jossey-Bass, 1987. xviii, 226 p. ; 24 cm. (A joint publication in the Jossey-Bass management series and the Jossey-Bass social and behavioral science series) Bibliography: p. 213-219. Includes index. ISBN 1-555-42043-5 (alk. paper) LC Card 86-46334 DDC 658.3/14 19
1. Career development. 2. Employee motivation. 3. Job stress. I. Mone, Edward M. II. Series: Jossey-Bass social and behavioral science series. III. Title.
HF5549.5.C35 L65 1987

London Postal History Group. London's postal history /. [London] , c1978. 16 p. : LC Card 84-172225
HE6946.L6 L65 1978

The London property market in AD 2000 / edited by Clive Darlow on behalf of the Continuing Professional Development Foundation. London ; New York : E. & F.N. Spon, 1986. xi, 155 p. : ill. ; 24 cm. ISBN 0-419-14100-6 : LC Card 86-217227 DDC 333.33/22/09421 19
1. Real estate business - England - London - Forecasting. 2. Real estate investments - England - London - Forecasting. 3. Land use, Urban - England - London - Forecasting. I. Darlow, Clive.
HD610.L6 L66 1986

Londoño Botero, Rocío. Gómez Buendía, Hernando. Sindicalismo y política económica /. Bogotá, Colombia , 1986. 324 p. : ISBN 958-9061-16-8 LC Card 87-401441 DDC 331.88/09861 19
HD6622 .G64 1986

Londoño Mejía, Mario. Restrepo Correa, Alejandro. Manual de crédito industrial y agropecuario . [Bogotá, D.E. , 1985] 270, 30, 4 p. : LC Card 86-110073
HG3751.9.C7 R47 1985

London's postal history / London Postal History Group. [London] : The Group, c1978. 16 p. : ill. ; 30 cm. LC Card 84-172225
1. Postal service - England - London - History. 2. Postage-stamps - England - London - History. 3. Postmarks - England - London - History. I. London Postal History Group.
HE6946.L6 L65 1978

Lönebildningsforskning i Finland /. Blomqvist, H. C. (Hans-Christer), 1947- [Helsinki] [1984] 23 leaves : ISBN 951-555-207-9 LC Card 85-137027
HD5047.3 .B57 1984

Long, Cindy. Long, Steve. Marketing your arts & crafts . Sandpoint, Idaho (9395 Rapid Lightning Rd., Sandpoint 83864) [c1987] iv, 188 p. : LC Card 87-401972 DDC 745.5/068/8 19
HF5439.H27 L66 1987

Long cycles . Goldstein, Joshua S., 1952- New Haven , c1988. p. cm. ISBN 0-300-03994-8 (alk. paper) LC Card 87-10723 DDC 338.5/42 19
HB3729 .G64 1988

Long, David. Goldman, Barbara. Final report on the San Diego job search and work experience demonstration /. New York, N.Y. (3 Park Ave., New York 10016) , c1986. xliv, 269 p. : LC Card 87-118376 DDC 331.12/042/0979498 19
HD5713.6.U542 S395 1986

LONG ISLAND (N.Y.) - HISTORY.
Matthiessen, Peter. Men's lives /. New York , 1988, c1986. xvi, 335 p. ; ISBN 0-394-75560-X (pbk.) : LC Card 87-40095 DDC 338.3/72709747/21 19
HD8039.F66 U5 1988

Long, J. Scott. vrmmon problems/proper solutions . Newbury Park, CA , 1987. p. cm. ISBN 0-8039-2806-8 : LC Card 87-20625

DDC 300/.72 19
HA29 .C7325 1987

Long, Larry E. Computers in business / Larry Long. Englewood Cliffs, N.J. : Prentice-Hall, c1987. xxv, 609 p. : ill. (some col.) ; 27 cm. Includes index. ISBN 0-13-164294-4 LC Card 86-30412 DDC 650/.028/5 19
1. Business - Data processing. 2. Basic (Computer program language). 3. Information storage and retrieval systems - Business. 4. Microcomputers. 5. Business - Computer-assisted instruction. I. Title.
HF5548.2 .L586 1987

Long, Michael. Widmann, Richard H. Ohio timber products output--1983 /. Broomall, PA [1986] 29 p. : LC Card 86-603412 DDC 338.1/7498/09771021 19
HD9757.O3 W53 1986

Long, Richard J. New office information technology : human and managerial implications / Richard J. Long. London ; New York : Croom Helm, c1987. xix, 333 p. : ill. ; 23 cm. (UWIST/Croom Helm series on management and new information technology) "Published in the USA ... in association with Methuen, Inc."--Verso t.p. Bibliography: p. 306-327. Includes index. ISBN 0-7099-4103-X (jacket); 0-7099-4130-X LC Card 87-3601 DDC 651.8 19
1. Office practice - Automation. 2. Office management. 3. Office practice - Automation - Psychological aspects. 4. Information technology. I. Title. II. Series.
HF5547.5 .L65 1987

The long-run behavior of the velocity of circulation . Bordo, Michael D. Cambridge [Cambridgeshire] , New York , 1987. xiv, 181 p. : ISBN 0-521-32633-8 LC Card 86-32628 DDC 332.4/14 19
HG226.6 .B67 1987

Long, Sandra Salser. Human resources management . Springfield, Ill., U. S.A. , c1987. xiv, 170 p. : ISBN 0-398-05296-4 LC Card 86-23016 DDC 362/.0425 19
HD7255 .H86 1987

Long-Solís, Janet. Capsicum y cultura : la historia del chilli / Janet Long-Solís.1a ed. México : Fondo de Cultura Económica, 1986. 181 p. : ill. ; 23 cm. Bibliography: p. 162-177. ISBN 968-16-2124-7 LC Card 86-221123
1. Hot pepper industry - Mexico - History. 2. Hot peppers - Mexico - History. I. Title.
HD9235.P462 M65 1986

Long, Steve. Marketing your arts & crafts : step up to financial independence and work for yourself at home. Sandpoint, Idaho (9395 Rapid Lightning Rd., Sandpoint 83864) : Idahome Publications, [c1987] iv, 188 p. : ill. ; 28 cm. Cover title. Written by Steve and Cindy Long. LC Card 87-401972 DDC 745.5/068/8 19
1. Selling - Handicraft. 2. Handicraft - United States - Marketing. I. Long, Cindy. II. Title. III. Title: Marketing your arts and crafts.
HF5439.H27 L66 1987

LONG-TERM CARE FACILITIES - UNITED STATES.
Davis, Karen, 1942- Medicare policy . Baltimore , c1986. xiii, 137 p. ; ISBN 0-8018-2874-0 (alk. paper) LC Card 85-45048 DDC 368.4/26/00973 19
HD7102.U4 D279 1986 ***NYPL [JLE 86-3782]***

Long-term financial planning : creative strategies for local government / edited by Jeffrey I. Chapman. Washington, D.C. : ICMA, 1987. 188 p. ; 23 cm. (Practical management series) Bibliography: p. [185]-188. ISBN 0-87326-076-7 (pbk.) : LC Card 87-2613 DDC 352.1/0973 19
1. Local finance - United States. I. Chapman, Jeffrey I. II. International City Management Association. III. Series.
HJ275 .L66 1987

The long-wave debate . IIASA (International Institute for Applied Systems Analysis) International Meeting on Long-Term Fluctuations in Economic Growth (1985 : Weimar, Germany) Berlin , New York , c1987. xvii, 430 p. : ISBN 0-387-18164-4 (U. S.) LC Card 87-23256 DDC 338.5/42 19
HB3729 .I52 1985

LONG WAVES (ECONOMICS)
Booth, Douglas E. Regional long waves, uneven growth, and the cooperative alternative /. New York , 1987. 121 p. ; ISBN 0-275-92567-6 (alk. paper) : LC Card 87-2348 DDC 338.973 19
HB3729 .B66 1987

Goldstein, Joshua S., 1952- Long cycles . New Haven , c1988. p. cm. ISBN 0-300-03994-8 (alk. paper) LC Card 87-10723 DDC 338.5/42 19
HB3729 .G64 1988

Petersen, Ib Damgaard. The political economy of long waves . København, Denmark [1986] 10, [1] p. : ISBN 87-7393-042-3 (pbk.) LC Card 86-214084 DDC 338.9 19
HB3729 .P47 1986

LONG WAVES (ECONOMICS) - ADDRESSES, ESSAYS, LECTURES.
Design, innovation, and long cycles in economic development /. London , 1986. 248 p. : ISBN 0-86187-616-4
NYPL [JLE 86-3312]

LONG WAVES (ECONOMICS) - CONGRESSES.
IIASA (International Institute for Applied Systems Analysis) International Meeting on Long-Term Fluctuations in Economic Growth (1985 : Weimar, Germany) The long-wave debate . Berlin , New York , c1987. xvii, 430 p. : ISBN 0-387-18164-4 (U. S.) LC Card 87-23256 DDC 338.5/42 19
HB3729 .I52 1985

LONG WAVES (ECONOMICS) - ECONOMETRIC MODELS.
Schulte, Heinrich. Statistisch-methodische Untersuchungen zum Problem langer Wellen /. Königstein/Ts. , 1981. x, 186 p. : ISBN 3-445-02189-9 LC Card 81-176113 DDC 338.9 19
HB3729 .S38 1981

Solomou, Solomos. Phases of economic growth, 1850-1973 . Cambridge [Cambridgeshire] , New York , 1987. p. cm. ISBN 0-521-33457-8 LC Card 86-34324 DDC 338.9 19
HB3729 .S65 1987

Longévité et tables de mortalité chronologiques (abrégées) Nagnur, D. N. Longevity and historical life tables . Ottawa , c1986. 215 p. : ISBN 0-660-52882-7 (pbk.) : LC Card 86-215300
HB1359.N34 1986

Longevity and historical life tables . Nagnur, D. N. Ottawa , c1986. 215 p. : ISBN 0-660-52882-7 (pbk.) : LC Card 86-215300
HB1359.N34 1986

LONGITUDITAL METHOD.
Federal longitudinal surveys /. [Washington, D.C.?] [Springfield, VA] 1986. v, 159 p. : LC Card 86-603413 DDC 001.4/33 19
HA31.2 .F43 1986

Longman economics series.
Cobham, David P. Macroeconomic analysis . London , New York , 1987. viii, 159 p. : ISBN 0-582-29708-7 (pbk.) LC Card 86-27825 DDC 339 19
HB172.5 .C63 1987

Longman exam guides.
Beecham, B. Julian, 1927- Monetary economics /. London , New York , 1988. p. cm. ISBN 0-582-02042-5 LC Card 87-17142 DDC 332.4 19
HG221 .B424 1988

Daff, Trevor. Cost and management accounting /. London , New York , 1988. p. cm. ISBN 0-582-46924-4 LC Card 87-3715 DDC 657/.42 19
HF5686.C8 D17 1988

Hall, Peter (Peter J.), 1932- Elements of banking /. London , New York , 1987. xi, 236 p. : ISBN 0-582-29728-1 (pbk.) LC Card 86-21144 DDC 332.1 19
HG1601 .H25 1987

Longman series in public communication.
Communicators' guide to marketing /. New York , c1987. xii, 226 p. : ISBN 0-582-28645-X LC Card 86-27787 DDC 658.8 19
HF5415.123 .C66 1987

Longo, Carlos Alberto. Ajustamentos de impostos na fronteira e a alocação de receitas tributárias : o caso do ICM / Carlos Alberto Longo. São Paulo : Instituto de Pesquisas Econômicas, 1979. 208 p. ; 22 cm. (Série Ensaios econômicos . v.03) Translation of the author's thesis (doctoral--Rice University), 1978, originally presented under the title: Border tax adjustments and the allocation of tax revenues. Bibliography p. 195-208. LC Card 80-152384
1. Value-added tax - Brazil. 2. Intergovernmental tax relations - Brazil. 3. Revenue sharing - Brazil. 4. Sales tax - Brazil. I. Series: Ensaios econômicos (Universidade de São Paulo. Instituto de Pesquisas Econômicas) , 03. II. Title.
HJ5715.B8 L6617 ***NYPL [JLD 86-3846]***

Longva, Svein. Bjerkholt, Olav, 1942- MODIS IV . Oslo , 1980. 189 p. : ISBN 82-537-1014-3 (pbk.) LC Card 81-120697 DDC 330.9481/00724 19
HC365 .B46 1980

Lønstrukturen 1978/79 : vigtigste resultater = Lohn- und Gehaltsstruktur 1978/79 : Hauptergebnisse = Structure of earnings, 1978/79 : principal results. Luxembourg : Europæiske fælleskabers statistiske kontor ; Washington, D.C. : European Community Information Service [distributor for the U. S.], <1983-1986 > v. <2-3, 6-7, 10 > ; 30 cm. Text in Danish, Dutch, English, French, German, Greek, and Italian. CONTENTS. - -- vol. 2. France -- vol. 3. Luxembourg -- vol. 6. Nederland -- vol. 7. BR Deutschland -- vol. 10. United Kingdom. ISBN 92-825-3817-6 (set) : LC Card 86-211360
1. Wages - European Economic Community countries - Statistics. I. Statistical Office of the European Communities. II. Title: Lohn- und Gehaltsstruktur 1978/79 : Hauptergebnisse. III. Title: Structure of earnings, 1978/79 : principal results.
HD5014.5 .L66 1983

Loo, L. Frank van, 1945- Armelui : armoede en bedeling te Alkmaar, 1850-1914 / L. Frank van Loo. Bergen (NH) : Octavo, 1986. 285 p. ; 23 cm. Bibliography: p. 278-282. Includes index. ISBN 90-70805-10-3 : LC Card 86-205672
1. Urban poor - Netherlands - Alkmaar - History. 2. Alkmaar (Netherlands) - Economic conditions. 3. Alkmaar (Netherlands) - Social conditions. I. Title.
HC328.A44 L66 1986

Looff, Carolyn S. Business and economics funding guide /. Washington, D.C. , c1987. 122 p. ; ISBN 0-88044-087-2 (alk. paper) : LC Card 87-17436 DDC 001.4/4 19
HF1131 .B78 1987

Looise, J. C., 1949- Vakbeweging in verandering . Deventer , 1986. 191 p. : ISBN 90-267-1082-8 : LC Card 86-224831
HD6727 .V29 1986

A look at the credit approval process /. Davis, John A., 1947- Philadelphia, Pa. , c1987. 55 p. : ISBN 0-936742-36-4 (pbk.) LC Card 86-23855 DDC 332.7 19
HG1642.U5 D38 1987

Look before you leap . Davidson, Jeffrey P. New York , 1988. p. cm. ISBN 0-8027-1012-3 LC Card 87-23274 DDC 658.4/2 19
HD62.5 .D38 1988

Loparto, Leonard W. Rubertone, Patricia E. Background study of Maine coastal life . [Providence, R.I.?] , 1983. iii, 99 leaves : LC Card 86-601627 DDC 304.6/09741/45 19
HB3525.M2 R82 1983

Lopata, Helena Znaniecka, 1925- Widows and dependent wives : from social problem to federal program / Helena Znaniecka Lopata, Henry P. Brehm. New York : Praeger, 1986. xxi, 242 p. ; 25 cm. Includes bibliographies and index. ISBN 0-03-046301-7 (alk. paper) : LC Card 85-16753 DDC 362.8/382 19
1. Survivors' benefits - United States. 2. Mothers' pensions - United States. 3. Social security - United States. 4. Widows - United States - Economic conditions. I. Brehm, Henry P. II. Title. III. Title: Dependent wives.
HV699 .L67 1985 ***NYPL [JLE 86-2182]***

Lopatnikov, L. I. (Leonid Isidorovich) Ėkonomiko-matematicheskiĭ slovarʹ / L.I. Lopatnikov ; otvetstvennyĭ redaktor N.P. Fedorenko. Moskva : "Nauka", 1987. 509 p. : ill. ; 23 cm. At head of title: Akademiiā nauk SSSR. T͡Sentralʹnyĭ ėkonomiko-matematicheskiĭ institut. Bibliography: p. [507]. Includes indexes. LC Card 87-164866
1. Economics, Mathematical - Dictionaries - Russian. I. Fedorenko, Nikolaĭ Prokofʹevich. II. Title.
HB135 .L64 1987

Lopes, Francisco Lafaiete. Sistemas alternativos de política salarial / Francisco Lafaiete Lopes. Rio de Janeiro, RJ : Departamento de

Economia, Pontifícia Universidade Católica do Rio de Janeiro, 1984. 51 leaves : ill. ; 30 cm. (Texto para discussão . no. 66) Bibliography: leaves 49-51. LC Card 86-178892
1. Wage-price policy - Mathematical models. I. Series: Texto para discussão (Pontifícia Universidade Católica do Rio de Janeiro. Departamento de Economia) , no. 66. II. Title.
HC79.W24 L66 1984

Lopes, Luiz Martins. Martone, Celso L. (Celso Luiz) Mercado financeiro e ajustamento macroeconômico brasileiro, 1978-1985 /. São Paulo , 1986. 82 p. : LC Card 87-120453 DDC 332.4/981 19
HG835 .M375 1986

Lopes, Marcos José. Atendimento ao mercado de energia elétrica do Nordeste / Marcos José Lopes. Recife, PE : Companhia Hidro Elétrica do São Francisco, [1984] 2 v. in 4 : ill. ; 30 cm. (Ciclo de debates . no. 6-7) Papers presented at the Seminário "A CHESF e o Sistema Elétrico Brasileiro." CONTENTS. - 1a. pt. Palestra proferida no dia 09.03.84 -- 2a. pt. Palestra proferida no dia 16.04.84 (3 v.) LC Card 86-166126
1. Electric utilities - Brazil, Northeast - Congresses. 2. Power resources - Brazil, Northeast - Congresses. 3. Water resources development - Brazil - Saõ Francisco River Watershed - Congresses. 4. Electric power production - Brazil - Congresses. 5. Energy policy - Brazil, Northeast - Congresses. I. Title. II. Series.
HD9685.B83 N675 1984

Lopes, Miriam B. P. Oelsner (Miriam Bettina Paulina Oelsner) Pequena história dos transportes públicos de São Paulo. São Paulo : Museu CMTC dos Transportes Públicos, [1985] 91 p. : ill. ; 22 cm. Bibliography: p. 89-91. LC Card 86-158179
1. CMTC (Firm : São Paulo, Brazil). 2. Local transit - Brazil - São Paulo. I. Museu CMTC dos Transportes Públicos (São Paulo, Brazil). II. Title.
HE5653.Z7 C675 1985

López, Alejandro, 1876-1940.
[Selections. 1983]
Obras selectas / Alejandro López ; Jorge Mario Eastman, presentación y compilación. Bogotá, D.E. : Camara de Representantes, 1983. xiii, 458 p. ; 24 cm. (Colección "Pensadores políticos colombianos" . t. 9) Includes bibliographical references. LC Card 86-233252
1. Colombia - Economic conditions - 1918-1970. 2. Labor economics - Colombia. 3. Liberalism - Colombia. 4. Economics. I. Eastman, Jorge Mario. II. Title. III. Series.
HC197 .L6172 1983

López Alonso, Carmen. Los rostros y la realidad de la pobreza en la sociedad castellana medieval (siglos XIII-XV) / Carmen López Alonso. Madrid : Fundación Juan March, [1983?] 54 p. ; 21 cm. (Serie universitaria (Fundación Juan March) . 209) Abstract of a study which was later enlarged and presented as the author's thesis (doctoral--Universidad Complutense de Madrid) under the title: La concepción sociopolítica de los pobres y la pobreza en la sociedad castellana medieval. "Edición ... de 300 ejemplares"--Cover. Includes bibliographical references. ISBN 84-7075-284-7 LC Card 87-110606
1. Poor - Spain - Castile - History. 2. Castile (Spain) - Social conditions. I. Series. II. Series: Serie universitaria (Fundación Juan March) , 209. III. Title.
HC387.C244 L66 1983

López, Antonio [i. e. Antonio López Nieto] see **López Nieto, Antonio.**

López Aparicio, Alfonso. Alamán, primer economista de México / Alfonso López Aparicio. México : Editorial Jus, [1986] 118 p. ; 22 cm. Half title: Alamán. Bibliography: p. 115-116. ISBN 968-423-013-3 LC Card 87-403286 DDC 330/.092/4 B 19
1. Alamán, Lucas, 1792-1853. 2. Economists - Mexico - Biography. I. Title. II. Title: Alamán.
HB123.M43 A435 1986

López Castaño, Hugo. El comercio callejero en la ciudad de Medellín : aspectos microeconómicos / Hugo López Castaño. Medellín : Universidad de Antioquia, Centro de Investigaciones Económicas, 1983. xv, 194 leaves : ill. ; 28 cm. Includes bibliographical references. LC Card 85-131765
1. Peddlers and peddling - Colombia - Medellín. 2. Informal sector (Economics) - Colombia - Medellín. I. Universidad de Antioquia. Centro de Investigaciones Económicas. II. Title.
HF5459.C7 L67 1983

López Castro, Gustavo. La casa dividida : un estudio de caso sobre la migración a Estados Unidos en un pueblo michoacano / Gustavo López Castro. Zamora, Mich. [i.e. Michoacán] : Colegio de Michoacán ; [S.l.] : Asociación Mexicana de Población, 1986. 169 p. : ill. ; 23 cm. Bibliography: p. 141-147. ISBN 968-7230-19-3 LC Card 87-400954 DDC 304.8/73/07237 19
1. Gómez Farías (Michoacán de Ocampo, Mexico) - Population. 2. Gómez Farías (Michoacán de Ocampo, Mexico) - Economic conditions. 3. Gómez Farías (Michoacán de Ocampo, Mexico) - Social conditions. 4. Mexico - Emigration amd immigration. 5. United States - Emigration and immigration. I. Title.
HB3532.G66 L66 1986

López Díaz, Pedro. Crítica de la economía y la política / Pedro López Díaz. 1a ed. de la UAS. México : Universidad Autónoma de Sinaloa, 1985. 255 p. ; 21 cm. (Colección Renovación . 11) Includes bibliographical references. ISBN 968-590-060-4 LC Card 86-156378
1. Capitalism. 2. Mexico - Economic conditions - 1970-. I. Series: Renovación , 11. II. Title.
HB501 .L856 1985

López, Francisco [i. e. Francisco López Serrano] see **López Serrano, Francisco.**

López González, Pedro. La población de Tepic bajo la organización regional, 1530-1821 / Pedro López González. 1a ed. Tepic, Nay. : Universidad Autónoma de Nayarit, 1984. 80 p. : ill. ; 27 cm. "Padrón de habitantes de la ciudad de Tepic del año de 1762": p. 55-77. Bibliography: p. 78-79. LC Card 86-119610
1. Tepic (Mexico) - Population - History. 2. Tepic (Mexico) - Economic conditions. 3. Tepic (Mexico) - Genealogy. I. Title.
HB3532.T47 L66 1984

López, Hernán. Kublank, Peter. Balances energéticos del Ecuador . Quito, Ecuador , 1983. 1 v. (various foliations) : LC Card 86-153116
HD9502.E22 K82 1983

López Hurtado, José. Latinoamérica, su deuda externa : entre el colapso económico y el desafío democrático / José López Hurtado ; prólogo del doctor Víctor Mosquera Chaux.1a ed. Bogotá, D.E., Colombia : Ecoe, 1987. xxii, 156 p. : ill. ; 20 cm. Errata slip inserted. Bibliography: p. 155-156. ISBN 958-9074-43-X LC Card 87-404201 DDC 336.3/435/098 19
1. Debts, External - Latin America. I. Title.
HJ8514.5 .L66 1987

López, Jorge Cejudo. see **Cejudo López, Jorge.**

López, José Roberto.
La economía del banano en Centroamérica / José Roberto López. San José, Costa Rica : Departamento Ecuménico de Investigaciones, c1986. 236 p. : ill. ; 22 cm. (Colección universitaria) Bibliography: p. 229-233. ISBN 997-7904-31-6 LC Card 87-404078 DDC 338.1/74772/09728 19
1. Banana trade - Central America. I. Series: Colección universitaria (San José, Costa Rica). II. Title.
HD9259.B3 C4554 1986

Gallardo, María Eugenia. Centroamérica . San José, Costa Rica , 1986. 259 p. : ISBN 92-9039-110-3 LC Card 87-401731 DDC 330.9728/053 19
HC141 .G35 1986

Rivera, Eugenio. Centroamérica, política económica y crisis /. San José, Costa Rica , c1986. 201 p. : ISBN 997-7904-37-5 LC Card 87-404079 DDC 338.9728 19
HC141 .R58 1986

López Leal, Carlos Roberto. La Presencia del tercer mundo /. San José, Costa Rica , 1982. 239 p., [1] leaf of plates : LC Card 83-161829
HC59.7 .P718 1982

López Monjardín, Adriana. Hacia la ciudad del capital--México, 1790-1870 / Adriana López Monjardín. 1a ed. México, D.F. : Dirección de Estudios Históricos, Instituto Nacional de Antropología e Historia, 1985. 193 p. : ill. ; 28 cm. (Cuaderno de trabajo . 46) Includes bibliographies. LC Card 87-124857 DDC 330.972/53 19
1. Mexico City (Mexico) - Economic conditions. 2. Markets - Mexico - Mexico City - History. 3. City planning - Mexico - Mexico City - History. 4. Urbanization - Mexico - Mexico City - History. I. Series: Cuaderno de trabajo (Instituto Nacional de Antropología e Historia (Mexico). Dirección de Estudios Históricos) , no. 46. II. Title.
HC138.M4 L66 1985

López Navarrete, Gregorio. Análisis y diagnóstico de la empresa : desde la banca y cajas de ahorros : casos prácticos / Gregorio López Navarrete. Barcelona : G. López Navarrete, [1983?] 377 p. : ill. ; 24 cm. ISBN 84-300-9587-X LC Card 87-113212
1. Investment banking - Spain - Case studies. 2. Investment analysis - Case studies. I. Title.
HG5634.5 .L67 1983

López Nieto, Antonio. Los costes de las obras a cargo del sector público : una minimización de los costes de las obras mediante el análisis de sistemas / por Antonio López Nieto ; prólogo por Agustín Cotorruelo Sendagorta. Madrid : Ministerio de Obras Públicas, Centro de Estudios Hidrográficos, 1962. xiv, 214 p. : ill. ; 21 cm. Includes bibliographical references. LC Card 85-107655
1. Public works - Costs. I. Title.
HD3856.S7 L66 1962

López-Orihuela, Alcides, 1926- El pacto y la democracia sociales / Alcides López-Orihuela. Caracas, Venezuela : [s.n., 1986] (Caracas : Editorial Greco) xvi, 129 p. ; 22 cm. Cover title. Includes bibliographical references. ISBN 90-826548-5-X LC Card 87-402941 DDC 338.987 19
1. Venezuela - Economic policy. 2. Venezuela - Social policy. 3. Venezuela - Politics and government - 1958-. 4. Acción Democrática (Venezuela). I. Title.
HC237 .L667 1986

Lopez, Robert Sabatino. The shape of medieval monetary history / Robert S. Lopez. London : Variorum Reprints, 1986. 330 p. 1 v. (various pagings) : ill. ; 24 cm. (Variorum reprint. CS247) English, French, and Italian. Includes bibliographical references and index. ISBN 0-86078-195-X LC Card 87-133292 DDC 332.4/94 19
1. Money - History. 2. Economic history - Medieval, 500-1500. I. Title.
HG243 .L67 1986

López, Roberto. Los orígenes económicos de la crisis en Centroamérica / Roberto López. San José, Costa Rica : Instituto Centroamericano de Documentación e Investigación Social, [1986] 134 p. : ill. ; 28 cm. (Proyecto crisis y alternativas en Centroamérica--documentos de trabajo) Includes bibliographical references. LC Card 87-106423
1. Central America - Economic conditions. I. Title. II. Series.
HC141 .L67 1986

López Serrano, Francisco. Del desierto a la selva / Francisco López Serrano. 1a ed. México : Editorial Diana, 1984. 215 p. : ill. ; 23 cm. Includes bibliographical references. ISBN 968-13-1608-8 LC Card 86-189936
1. Agricultural colonies - Candelaria River Valley (Guatemala and Mexico). 2. Agricultural colonies - Mexico - Case studies. I. Title.
HD1516.M5 L66 1984

L'or, la parole, l'Etat . Martine, Joël. Paris , c1983. 296 p. : ISBN 2-7157-1065-8 LC Card 83-133521
HX542 .M32 1983 ***NYPL [JLD 87-872]***

Lora, Guillermo. Control obrero colectivo y co-gestión : programa revolucionario o programa de adaptación a la burguesía / Guillermo Lora.2a ed. actualizada. La Paz, Bolivia : Ediciones Masas, 1982. 45 p. ; 19 cm. LC Card 83-204234
1. Management - Employee participation. I. Title.
HD5650 .L73 1982

Lora, Víctor Carlos.
Población y tecnología. 1985. Comunicación y tecnología en la investigación demográfica / Centro Peruano de Investigación Aplicada. Lima , 1985. vi, 38 p. ; LC Card 86-168814
HB849.6 .C65 1985

Lorandi, D. (Daniela) Metropoli e agricoltura /. Milano , c1982. 319 p. : LC Card 82-246692 DDC 333.76/13/094521 19
HD680.M54 M47 1982
NYPL [JLD 86-3678]

Lorange, Peter. Cooperative strategies in international business /. Lexington, Mass. , c1988. xxix, 513 p. : ISBN 0-669-14927-6 (alk. paper) LC Card 86-46160 DDC 338.8/8 19
HD2755.5 .C645 1988

Loranger, Jean Guy, 1938- Lien entre capital fictif, markup flexible et inflation / par Jean-Guy Loranger. Montréal : Département de science économique, Université de Montréal, [1985] 30 p. ; 28 cm. (Cahier, 0709-9231 . 8517) Summary in English and French. Bibliography: p. [29]-30. LC Card 85-177724 DDC 332.4/1 19
1. Inflation (Finance) - Econometric models. I. Series: Cahier (Université de Montréal. Département de sciences économiques) , 8517. II. Title.
HB3 .C3 vol. 8517 HG229

Lorber, Lawrence Z.
Lorber, Lawrence Z. Sex and salary . Alexandria, Va. , 1985. v, 61 p. ;
NYPL [JLF 86-417]

Sex and salary : a legal and personnel analysis of "comparable worth" / Lawrence Z. Lorber ... [et al.] Alexandria, Va. : ASPA Foundation, 1985. v, 61 p. ; 28 cm. Includes bibliographical references.
1. Equal pay for equal work - United States. 2. Equal pay for equal work - Law and legislation - United States. I. Lorber, Lawrence Z. II. ASPA Foundation.
NYPL [JLF 86-417]

Lorca, Alejandro. Viernes europeos 81 . Madrid [1984?] 494 p. : LC Card 85-178055
HC241.25.S6 V48 1984

Lord Grenville's manuscript notes on Malthus /. Pullen, J. M. [Newcastle] [1986] 94 p. ; ISBN 0-7259-0557-3 (pbk.) LC Card 87-150102 DDC 330.15/3 19
HB161.M28 P85 1986

Lord, Kenniston W. Office automation systems handbook / Kenniston W. Lord, Jr. Blue Ridge Summit, PA. : TAB Books, 1988. p. cm. Includes index. ISBN 0-8306-2899-1 : LC Card 87-7112 DDC 650/.028/5 19
1. Business - Data processing. 2. Office practice - Automation. I. Title.
HF5548.2 .L589 1988

Lord, Montague J. Market price models for Latin America's major commodity exports / by Montague J. Lord ; with research assistance by Greta R. Boye and Stephane Conte. Washington, D.C. : International Economics Section, Economic and Social Development Dept., Inter-American Development Bank, [1986] vii, 219 p. : ill. ; 28 cm. (Working paper / Economic and Social Development Department, International Economics Section . 86/1) "August 1986." Bibliography: p. 183-187. LC Card 87-115208 DDC 338.5/2/098 19
1. Food prices - Latin America - Econometric models. 2. Cotton - Prices - Latin America - Econometric models. 3. Copper - Prices - Latin America - Econometric models. 4. Iron ores - Prices - Latin America - Econometric models. 5. Exports - Prices - Latin America - Econometric models. I. Boye, Greta R. II. Conte, Stephane. III. Inter-American Development Bank. IV. Series: Working paper (Inter-American Development Bank. International Economics Section) , 86/1. V. Title.
HD9014.A2 L67 1986

The lords of creation. Allen, Frederick Lewis, 1890-1954. New York, London, 1935. xii, 483 p. LC Card 35-20649 DDC 332.0973
HG181 .A57 ***NYPL [JLD 86-1097]***

Lorence, Jon. Mortimer, Jeylan T., 1943- Work, family, and personality . Norwood, N.J. , c1986. viii, 267 p. : ISBN 0-89391-293-X LC Card 85-20951 DDC 306/.36/09774 19
HD4904.25 .M67 1986 ***NYPL [JLE 87-869]***

Lorensen, Leonard.
Clark, Hal G. Illustrations of accounting for pensions and for settlements and curtailments of defined benefit pension plans . New York, N.Y. (1211 Ave. of the Americas, New York 10036-8775) , c1987. 34 p. ; LC Card 87-401762 DDC 657/.75 19
HF5686.O5 C56 1987

Goodman, Hortense. Illustrations of "push down" accounting /. New York, N.Y. (1211 Ave., of the Americas, New York 10036) , c1985. 52 p. ; LC Card 87-100703 DDC 657/.3 19
HF5681.B2 G663 1985

Lorenz, Christopher, 1946- The Uneasy alliance . Boston, Mass. , c1985. x, 485 p. : ISBN 0-87584-172-4 LC Card 85-8709 DDC 658.5 19
HD56 .U53 1985 ***NYPL [JLE 86-2361]***

Lorenz, Hans-Walter, 1951- Gabisch, Günter, 1943- Business cycle theory . Berlin , New York , c1987. vii, 229 p. : ISBN 0-387-17188-6 (U. S. : pbk.) LC Card 86-31539 DDC 338.5/42/01 19
HB3711 .G19 1987

Lorenz von Stein und die Grundprobleme der Steuerlehre . Heilmann, Martin. Heidelberg , 1984. xi, 577 p. ; ISBN 3-7685-0184-1 LC Card 84-236751
HJ2309 .H36 1984

Lorenzen, Gunter. Adaptive Verfahren der Input-Output Analyse / Gunter Lorenzen. Göttingen : Vandenhoeck & Ruprecht, c1985. vii, 156 p. ; 25 cm. (Studien zur angewandten Wirtschaftsforschung und Statistik aus dem Institut für Statistik und Ökonometrie der Universität Hamburg . Heft 17) Bibliography: p. [153]-156. ISBN 3-525-11288-2 LC Card 85-221821
1. Input-output analysis. 2. Input-output analysis - Germany (West). I. Series. II. Series: Studien zur angewandten Wirtschaftsforschung und Statistik, 17. III. Title.
HB142 .L67 1985
NYPL [JLL 76-449 Heft 17]

Loriaux, M. Economie, population et politique démographique / Michel Loriaux. Louvain-la-Neuve : CIACO, [c1984] 169 p. : ill. ; 24 cm. (Politiques de population . no 3-4) Cover title. Bibliography: p. [164]-169. ISBN 2-87085-041-7 : LC Card 86-144677
1. Population policy. 2. Economic policy. I. Title. II. Series.
HB883.5 .L67 1984

Loring, Jaime. Los sectores agrarios de Andalucía ante la integración en la C.E.E. / Jaime Loring Miró, Luis Godoy López, José J. Romero Rodríguez. Madrid : Banco de Crédito Agrícola, 1984. 303 p. : ill. ; 22 cm. (Biblioteca de economía agraria del Banco de Crédito Agrícola) Includes bibliographical references. ISBN 84-7114-149-3 LC Card 86-152628
1. Agriculture - Economic aspects - Spain - Andalusia. 2. Agriculture - Economic aspects - Spain. 3. Agriculture - Economic aspects - European Economic Community countries. 4. European Economic Community - Spain. I. Godoy López, Luis. II. Romero Rodríguez, José J. III. Title. IV. Series.
HD2025.A5 L67 1984

LORRAINE (FRANCE) - SOCIAL LIFE AND CUSTOMS - PICTORIAL WORKS.
Glück auf! . Paris [1986] 117 p. : ISBN 2-86738-115-0 : LC Card 86-178958
HD8039.M6152 F84 1986

Lorriaux, Jean-Pierre. Economie politique contemporaine : économie générale BTS-DUT-DEUG-CPECF-BP / Jean-Pierre Lorriaux.3e éd., rev. et augm. Paris : Economica, c1985. iv, 565 p. : ill. ; 24 cm. Bibliography: p. 535-542. ISBN 2-7178-0937-6 : LC Card 86-116111 DDC 330 19
1. Economics. 2. France - Economic conditions - 1945-. I. Title.
HB173 .L784 1985

LOS ANDES (VENEZUELA) - HISTORY - 19TH CENTURY.
Muñoz, Arturo Guillermo. El Táchira fronterizo . Caracas , 1985. 315 p. ; ISBN 980-265-178-8 LC Card 87-402928 DDC 330.987/120633 19
HC238.T3 M86 1985

Los Angeles and the automobile . Bottles, Scott L. Berkeley , c1987. xiii, 301 p. : ISBN 0-520-05795-3 (alk. paper) LC Card 86-14660 DDC 388.4/1321/0979494 19
HE5634.L7 B68 1987

Los Angeles. University. see **California. University. University at Los Angeles.**

Los Angeles. University of California. see **California. University. University at Los Angeles.**

Los bancos multinacionales en América Latina y la crisis del sistema capitalista /. Labarca, Guillermo. México, D.F. , 1979. 201 p. ; ISBN 968-429-155-8 LC Card 80-123755
HG2710.5.A6 L3 ***NYPL [JLC 81-147]***

Los efectos del neoproteccionismo en América Latina /. Lejavitzer, Moisés. México, D.F. , 1983. i, 231 p. ; LC Card 85-149154 DDC 382.7/3/098 19
HF3230.5.Z5 L45 1983 ***NYPL [JLD 86-434]***

Los Factores del cambio demográfico en México / por Raúl Benítez Zenteno ... [et al.] ; coordinado por René Jiménez Ornelas y Alberto Minujin Zmud. 1a ed. México, D.F. : Siglo Veintiuno Editores, 1984. 422 p. : ill. ; 24 cm. (Economía y demografía) Includes bibliographies. ISBN 968-231-281-7 LC Card 85-231767
1. Mortality - Mexico - Addresses, essays, lectures. 2. Fertility, Human - Mexico - Addresses, essays, lectures. 3. Migration, Internal - Mexico - Addresses, essays, lectures. 4. Mexico - Emigration and immigration - Addresses, essays, lectures. 5. United States - Emigration and immigration - Addresses, essays, lectures. I. Benítez Zenteno, Raúl. II. Jiménez Ornelas, René. III. Minujin Z., Alberto. IV. Series: Economía y demografía (Mexico City, Mexico).
HB1361 .F33 1984 ***NYPL [JLE 87-753]***

Los problemas del socialismo en nuestra tiempo [microform]. México, Ediciones Ibero Americanas, 1944. 119 p. 20 cm. At head of title: Victor Serge, Julián Gorkin, Marceau Pivert, Paul Chevalier. Microfilm. New York : New York Public Library, 1986. 1 microfilm reel ; 35 mm. (MN *ZZ-26,232) DDC 335.082
1. Socialism - History. 2. World politics. I. Serge, Victor, 1890-1947. II. Gorkin, Julián, 1901-. III. Pivert, Marceau, 1895-. IV. Chevalier, Paul.
HX40 .P73 ***NYPL [*ZT-1711 no.21]***

Losada Aldana, Ramón. Investigación universitaria contra subdesarrollo / Ramón Losada Aldana. Caracas : Consejo de Profesores Universitarios Jubilados U.C.V., 1984. 288 p. ; 22 cm. Bibliography: p. 279-288. LC Card 87-115963 DDC 338.987/0072 19
1. Economic development - Research - Venezuela. 2. Venezuela - Learned institutions and societies. I. Title.
HD77.5.V4 L67 1984

Lösch, August, 1906-1945.
Space-structure-economy . Karlsruhe [San Francisco, CA] c1986. vii, 311 p. : ISBN 3-88652-680-1 (pbk.) LC Card 87-129134 DDC 330.1 19
HB107.L66 S63 1986

LÖSCH, AUGUST, 1906-1945.
Space-structure-economy . Karlsruhe [San Francisco, CA] c1986. vii, 311 p. : ISBN 3-88652-680-1 (pbk.) LC Card 87-129134 DDC 330.1 19
HB107.L66 S63 1986

Löser, Harald. Die Leistungsbewertung in der Industrie . Jena , 1983. 241 p. ; LC Card 84-176546
HD56.25 .L45 1983

Losoncz, Miklós. Erők és érdekek : nyugati stratégiai koncepciók a kelet-nyugati gazdasági kapcsolatokban / Losoncz Miklós. Budapest : Zrínyi Katonai Kiadó, 1986. 191 p. : ill. ; 19 cm. (Katonapolitika mindenkinek, 0209-8938) Bibliography: p. 189-[190]. ISBN 963-326-966-0 : LC Card 87-148142
1. Export controls. 2. East-West trade (1945-). 3. Export controls - United States. 4. United States - National security. I. Title. II. Series.
HF1414.5 .L67 1986

Losoto, Oleg Pavlovich. Adresa svershenіĭ /] Moskva , 1980. 271 p., [16] p. of plates : LC Card 81-130832
HC336.25 .A35 1980

L'Osservatorio provinciale sul lavoro e sulle professioni : il caso Nuoro / a cura di Rosario Scalia. Milano, Italy : F. Angeli, c1984. 143 p. : ill. ; 22 cm. (AFM-Europa. Sezione Italia . 1) Bibliography: p. 86. LC Card 84-190423
1. Labor supply - Italy - Nuoro (Sardinia : Province). 2. Occupational training - Italy - Nuoro (Sardinia : Province). 3. Artisans - Italy - Nuoro (Sardinia : Province). 4. Unemployment - Italy - Nuoro (Sardinia : Province). 5. Nuoro (Sardinia : Province) - Occupations. 6. Nuoro (Sardinia : Province) - Industries. I. Scalia, Rosario, 1949-. II. Series: AFM-Europa. Sezione Italia (Series) , 1.
HD5785.N86 O87 1984
NYPL [JLD 86-1275]

Lost initiatives . Gillis, R. Peter. New York , 1986. 326 p. : ISBN 0-313-25415-X (lib. bdg. : alk. paper) LC Card 86-3122 DDC 333.75/0971 19
HD9764.C3 G55 1986 ***NYPL [JLE 87-947]***

Lost revenue : a study of the collection & investment of tax money by A) towns on behalf of counties, B) counties on behalf of the state / Assembly Standing Committee on Local Governments. [Albany, N.Y.?] : The

Committee, [1986] 13, 22 leaves ; 28 cm. "March 1986." LC Card 87-620567 DDC 336.2/009747 19
1. Intergovernmental tax relations - New York (State). 2. Tax collection - New York (State). 3. Investment of public funds - New York (State). I. New York (State). Legislature. Assembly. Committee on Local Governments.
HJ3324 .L67 1986

Lotions, potions, and liniments pure . Wilder, Joseph E., 1896- Winnipeg, Man. , c1982. 100 p. : ISBN 0-919576-34-6 (pbk.) : LC Card 83-121333 DDC 381/.456151/0971274 19
HD9670.C23 W568 1982
NYPL [JLE 87-1213]

Lotta, Raymond. America in decline : an analysis of the developments toward war and revolution, in the U. S. and worldwide, in the 1980s / by Raymond Lotta with Frank Shannon. Chicago : Banner Press, c1984- v. : ill. ; 23 cm. Includes bibliographical references and index. ISBN 0-916650-12-X (v. 1) : LC Card 83-22294 DDC 330.973/0927 19
1. Economic history - 20th century - Collected works. 2. Imperialism - History - 20th century - Collected works. 3. United States - Foreign economic relations - Collected works. I. Shannon, Frank, 1947-. II. Title.
HC54 .L63 1984 *NYPL [JLL 87-106]*

Lotte sociali e dittatura in Lunigiana storica e Versilia (1919-1930) /. Bianchi, Antonio. [Firenze] , 1981. xii, 309 p. ; ISBN 88-22-23028-0 LC Card 82-125955
HD8489.L86 B5 1981

LOTTERIES - UNITED STATES.
Wagman, Robert J. Instant millionaires . [Kensington, Md.] , 1986. 298 p. ; ISBN 0-933149-05-0 (pbk.) : LC Card 86-50285 DDC 795.3/092/2 19
HG6126 .W27 1986

LOTTERY WINNERS - UNITED STATES.
Wagman, Robert J. Instant millionaires . [Kensington, Md.] , 1986. 298 p. ; ISBN 0-933149-05-0 (pbk.) : LC Card 86-50285 DDC 795.3/092/2 19
HG6126 .W27 1986

Lotus Books. The Lotus guide to learning Symphony macros . Reading, Mass. , c1986. viii, 243 p. : ISBN 0-201-16684-4 (pbk.) LC Card 86-213051 DDC 005.36/9 19
HF5549.4.S95 L67 1986

Lotus Development Corporation. Lotus Freelance Plus . Cambridge, MA (55 Cambridge Pkwy., Cambridge 02142) , c1987. 3 v. : LC Card 87-404478 DDC 650/.028/566869 19
HF5548.4.L676 L68 1987

Lotus Freelance Plus : introductory course. Cambridge, MA (55 Cambridge Pkwy., Cambridge 02142) : Lotus Development Corp., c1987. 3 v. : ill. ; 28 cm. CONTENTS. - [1] Guide to the course -- [2] Book one -- [3] Book two. LC Card 87-404478 DDC 650/.028/566869 19
1. Lotus Freelance Plus (Computer program). 2. Business - Graphic methods. I. Lotus Development Corporation.
HF5548.4.L676 L68 1987

LOTUS FREELANCE PLUS (COMPUTER PROGRAM)
Lotus Freelance Plus . Cambridge, MA (55 Cambridge Pkwy., Cambridge 02142) , c1987. 3 v. : LC Card 87-404478 DDC 650/.028/566869 19
HF5548.4.L676 L68 1987

The Lotus guide to learning Symphony macros : includes Release 1.1. Reading, Mass. : Addison-Wesley Pub. Co., c1986. viii, 243 p. : ill. (some col.) ; 24 cm. (The Lotus learning series) "Lotus Books." Includes index. ISBN 0-201-16684-4 (pbk.) LC Card 86-213051 DDC 005.36/9 19
1. Symphony (Computer program). 2. Macro instructions (Electronic computers). 3. Business - Data processing. I. Lotus Books. II. Series.
HF5549.4.S95 L67 1986

The Lotus guide to 1-2-3 advanced macro commands : programming techniques. Reading, Mass. : Addison-Wesley, [1987], c1986. x, 278 p. : ill. ; 23 cm. Includes index. ISBN 0-201-16822-7 (pbk.) : LC Card 86-32213 DDC 005.36/9 19
1. Lotus 1-2-3 (Computer program). 2. Macroprogramming. 3. Business - Data processing. I. Title: Lotus guide to 123 advanced macro commands.
HF5548.4.L67 L64 1987

Lotus guide to 123 advanced macro commands. The Lotus guide to 1-2-3 advanced macro commands . Reading, Mass. [1987], c1986. x, 278 p. : ISBN 0-201-16822-7 (pbk.) : LC Card 86-32213 DDC 005.36/9 19
HF5548.4.L67 L64 1987

LOTUS HAL (COMPUTER PROGRAM)
Bingham, Julie E. HAL plain and simple . Reading, Mass. , c1988. vii, 296 p. : ISBN 0-201-08002-8 (pbk.) : LC Card 87-17524 DDC 005.36/9 19
HF5548.4.L68 B56 1988

Campbell, Mary V. Mastering Lotus HAL /. San Francisco , c1987. xxi, 342 p. : ISBN 0-89588-422-4 (pbk.) : LC Card 87-60797 DDC 005.36/9 19
HF5548.4.L68 C35 1987

Postman, Andrew. Using HAL . Berkeley, Calif. , c1987. xvi, 557 p. : ISBN 0-07-881268-2 (pbk.) : LC Card 87-403738 DDC 005.36/9 19
HF5548.4.L68 P67 1987

Rier, David C. The guide to Lotus HAL . Reading, Mass. [1987], c1988. xv, 266 p. : ISBN 0-201-16827-8 (pbk.) : LC Card 87-22885 DDC 005.36/9 19
HF5548.4.L68 R54 1988

The Lotus learning series.
The Lotus guide to learning Symphony macros . Reading, Mass. , c1986. viii, 243 p. : ISBN 0-201-16684-4 (pbk.) LC Card 86-213051 DDC 005.36/9 19
HF5549.4.S95 L67 1986

Lotus Manuscript (Computer program) Nelson, Kay Yarborough. Using Lotus Manuscript /. Berkeley, Calif. , c1987. xvii, 410 p. : ISBN 0-07-881003-5 (pbk.) : LC Card 87-401628 DDC 652/.5 19
HF5548.115 .N45 1987

LOTUS MANUSCRIPT (COMPUTER PROGRAM)
Nelson, Kay Yarborough. Using Lotus Manuscript /. Berkeley, Calif. , c1987. xvii, 410 p. : ISBN 0-07-881003-5 (pbk.) : LC Card 87-401628 DDC 652/.5 19
HF5548.115 .N45 1987

Lotus One-Two-Three. Mazursky, Alan D., 1955- Lotus 1-2-3 . Chicago , c1988. 480 p. : ISBN 0-574-18645-X (pbk.) : LC Card 87-4675 DDC 005.36/9 19
HF5548.4.L67 M32 1988

Lotus one-two-three financial models. Tymes, Elna. Lotus 1-2-3 financial models /. Indianapolis, Ind. , c1988. vi, 307 p. ; ISBN 0-672-48410-2 (pbk.) LC Card 87-72205 DDC 005.36/9 19
HF5548.4.L67 T95 1988

Lotus one-two-three simplified. Bolocan, David. Lotus 1-2-3 simplified /. Blue Ridge Summit, PA , c1986. xii, 255 p. : ISBN 0-8306-0448-0 : LC Card 86-5820 DDC 005.36/9 19
HF5548.4.L67 B64 1986
NYPL [JSE 87-276]

Lotus 1-2-3 . Mazursky, Alan D., 1955- Chicago , c1988. 480 p. : ISBN 0-574-18645-X (pbk.) : LC Card 87-4675 DDC 005.36/9 19
HF5548.4.L67 M32 1988

Lotus 1-2-3 applications with disk /. Martin, Dale R. Englewood Cliffs, N.J. , c1986. viii, 120 p. : ISBN 0-13-540717-6 (pbk.) LC Card 86-200542 DDC 657/.044/02855369 19
HF5679 .M37 1986

LOTUS 1-2-3 (COMPUTER PROGRAM)
Badgett, Tom. The insider's guide to Lotus 1-2-3 . Glenview, Ill. , c1987. xix, 266 p. : ISBN 0-673-18718-7 (pbk.) : LC Card 87-4864 DDC 005.36/9 19
HF5548.4.L67 B33 1987

Baker, Keith, 1938- Public budgeting with Lotus 1-2-3 /. Portland, Or. , 1988. p. cm. ISBN 0-943518-46-6 : LC Card 87-24020 DDC 350.72/2/02855369 19
HJ2009 .B34 1988

Baras, Edward M. The advanced guide to Lotus 1-2-3 /. Berkeley, Calif. , c1986. xiii, 234 p. : ISBN 0-07-881237-2 (pbk.) LC Card 86-215569 DDC 005.36/9 19
HF5548.4.L67 B36 1986

Bidgoli, Hossein. Working with Lotus 1-2-3 . St. Paul , c1988. xxii, 397 p. : ISBN 0-314-65031-8 (pbk.) LC Card 87-25268 DDC 005.36/9 19
HF5548.4.L67 B53 1988

Bingham, Julie E. HAL plain and simple . Reading, Mass. , c1988. vii, 296 p. : ISBN 0-201-08002-8 (pbk.) : LC Card 87-17524 DDC 005.36/9 19
HF5548.4.L68 B56 1988

Bolocan, David. Lotus 1-2-3 simplified /. Blue Ridge Summit, PA , c1986. xii, 255 p. : ISBN 0-8306-0448-0 : LC Card 86-5820 DDC 005.36/9 19
HF5548.4.L67 B64 1986
NYPL [JSE 87-276]

Campbell, Mary V. 1-2-3, the complete reference /. Berkeley, Calif. , c1986. xii, 892 p. : ISBN 0-07-881005-1 (pbk.) : LC Card 86-230048 DDC 005.36/9 19
HF5548.4.L67 C35 1986

Gorham, Kenneth D. Personal productivity with Lotus 1-2-3 /. Dubuque, Iowa , c1987. x, 164 p. : ISBN 0-697-05227-3 (pbk.) LC Card 87-70158 DDC 005.36/9 19
HF5548.4 L67 G67 1987

Greenfield, W. M. Accounting with 1-2-3 /. Englewood Cliffs, N.J. , 1987. p. cm. ISBN 0-13-001686-1 LC Card 87-12485 DDC 657/.028/55369 19
HF5679 .G737 1987

Harvey, Greg. Lotus 1-2-3 desktop companion /. San Francisco , c1987. ix, 976 p. : ISBN 0-89588-385-6 : LC Card 86-63454 DDC 005.36/9 19
HF5548.4.L67 H38 1987

Ho, James K. K. Linear and dynamic programming with Lotus 1-2-3, Release 2 /. Portland, Or. , c1987. xiv, 330 p. : ISBN 0-943518-72-5 (pbk.) : LC Card 87-1586 DDC 005.36/9 19
HF5548.4.L67 H6 1987

Jackson, Mary, 1936- Creative modelling with Lotus 1-2-3 /. Chichester , New York , c1985. ix, 169 p. : ISBN 0-471-90796-0 (pbk.) LC Card 86-228784 DDC 005.36/9 19
HF5548.4.L67 J33 1985b

Kiczek, Paul. Decision making for bankers . Washington, D.C. (1120 Connecticut Ave., NW, Washington 20036) , c1986. 89 p. : LC Card 87-115307 DDC 332.1/2/02855369 19
HG1709 .K53 1986

Kilpatrick, Michael, 1952- Business statistics using Lotus 1-2-3 /. New York , c1987. ix, 326 p. : ISBN 0-471-84525-6 (pbk.) : LC Card 86-24737 DDC 519.5/028/55369 19
HF1017 .K55 1987

LeBlond, Geoffrey T. Como usar Lotus 1-2-3 . Miami, Fla. , 1986- p. cm. LC Card 86-23629 DDC 005.36/9 19
HF5548.4.L67 L418 1986

Lehman, Mark W. Using the microcomputer in cost accounting . St. Paul , c1988. x, 396 p. : ISBN 0-314-34729-1 (pbk.) LC Card 87-10632 DDC 657/.42/02855369 19
HF5686.C8 L34 1988

Lehman, Mark W. Using the microcomputer in managerial accounting . St. Paul , c1987. x, 406 p. : ISBN 0-314-98515-8 (pbk.) LC Card 87-2194 DDC 658.1/511/02855369 19
HF5657.4 .L44 1987

The Lotus guide to 1-2-3 advanced macro commands . Reading, Mass. [1987], c1986. x, 278 p. : ISBN 0-201-16822-7 (pbk.) : LC Card 86-32213 DDC 005.36/9 19
HF5548.4.L67 L64 1987

Lunsford, E. Michael. Macros, menus, and miracles for Lotus 1-2-3 /. New York , c1987. xix, 234 p. : ISBN 0-471-85996-6 (pbk.) : LC Card 87-14285 DDC 005.36/9 19
HF5548.4.L67 L86 1987

Lunsford, E. Michael. Power user's guide to 1-2-3 /. San Francisco , c1988. xx, 367 p. : ISBN 0-89588-421-6 (pbk.) LC Card 87-61528 DDC 005.36/9 19
HF5548.4.L67 L87 1988

Martin, Dale R. Lotus 1-2-3 applications with disk /. Englewood Cliffs, N.J. , c1986. viii, 120 p. : ISBN 0-13-540717-6 (pbk.) LC Card 86-200542 DDC 657/.044/02855369 19
HF5679 .M37 1986

Mazursky, Alan D., 1955- Lotus 1-2-3 . Chicago , c1988. 480 p. : ISBN 0-574-18645-X (pbk.) : LC Card 87-4675 DDC 005.36/9 19
HF5548.4.L67 M32 1988

Metzelaar, Lawrence C. Learning to use Lotus 1-2-3 /. Menlo Park, Calif. , c1987. xi, 286 p. : ISBN 0-8053-6736-5 (pbk.) LC Card 86-214400 DDC 005.36/9 19
HF5548.4.L67 M47 1987

Mylius, Ralph, 1945- The illustrated Lotus 1-2-3 . Dallas , c1987. vi, 381 p. ; ISBN 0-915381-67-2 (pbk.) LC Card 86-28217 DDC 005.36/9 19
HF5548.4.L67 M95 1987

Nguyen, Tim K. Applied 1-2-3 . New York, N.Y. , c1987. p. cm. ISBN 0-13-729542-1 : LC Card 87-11390 DDC 005.36/9 19
HF5548.4.L67 N48 1987

Person, Ron, 1948- [1-2-3 business formula handbook. Spanish.] 1-2-3 en el mundo de las finanzas . Miami, Fla., E.U.A. , 1988. p. cm. ISBN 0-939573-02-4 LC Card 87-20916 DDC 005.36/9 19
HF5548.4.L67 P4718 1988

Rier, David C. The guide to Lotus HAL . Reading, Mass. [1987], c1988. xv, 266 p. : ISBN 0-201-16827-8 (pbk.) : LC Card 87-22885 DDC 005.36/9 19
HF5548.4.L68 R54 1988

Ross, Steven C. Understanding and using Lotus 1-2-3 . St. Paul , c1987. xv, 232, [34] p. : ISBN 0-314-34741-0 (pbk.) LC Card 86-33964 DDC 650/.028/55369 19
HF5548.4.L67 R673 1987

Ross, Steven S. SPREADSTAT . New York , c1988. p. cm. ISBN 0-07-053909-X : LC Card 87-22811 DDC 005.36/9 19
HF1017 .R67 1988

Shaffer, Daniel N. Macro programming for 1-2-3 . Indianapolis, Ind. , c1987. xiv, 283 p. : ISBN 0-672-46573-6 (pbk.) LC Card 86-63301 DDC 005.36/9 19
HF5548.4.L67 S48 1987

Stark, Robin. Encyclopedia of Lotus 1-2-3 /. Blue Ridge Summit, PA , c1987. x, 484 p. : ISBN 0-8306-7891-3 : LC Card 87-19839 DDC 005.36/9 19
HF5548.4.L67 S675 1987

Tymes, Elna. Lotus 1-2-3 financial models /. Indianapolis, Ind. , c1988. vi, 307 p. ; ISBN 0-672-48410-2 (pbk.) LC Card 87-72205 DDC 005.36/9 19
HF5548.4.L67 T95 1988

Using 1-2-3 /. Carmel, Ind. , c1987. xxviii, 905 p. : ISBN 0-88022-332-4 (pbk.) LC Card 87-61897 DDC 005.36/9 19
HF5548.4.L67 U85 1987

Wells, Nancy E., 1946- Straight forward managerial accounting applications . Burlington, VT , 1987, c1986. p. cm. ISBN 0-9612704-1-1 LC Card 87-22393 DDC 658.1/511/02855369 19
HF5657.4 .W44 1987

Williams, Mark M., 1948- Expert advisor, 1-2-3 . Reading, Mass. , 1988. p. cm. ISBN 0-201-18238-6 (pbk.) : LC Card 87-19286 DDC 005.36/9 19
HF5548.4.L67 W536 1988

Wolf, Douglas, 1948- Compute!'s quick & easy guide to learning Lotus 1-2-3 /. Greensboro, N.C. , c1987. vi, 139 p. : ISBN 0-87455-106-4 (pbk.) : LC Card 87-163385 DDC 005.36/9 19
HF5548.4.L67 W65 1987

Lotus 1-2-3 desktop companion /. Harvey, Greg. San Francisco , c1987. ix, 976 p. : ISBN 0-89588-385-6 : LC Card 86-63454 DDC 005.36/9 19
HF5548.4.L67 H38 1987

Lotus 1-2-3 financial models /. Tymes, Elna. Indianapolis, Ind. , c1988. vi, 307 p. ; ISBN 0-672-48410-2 (pbk.) LC Card 87-72205 DDC 005.36/9 19
HF5548.4.L67 T95 1988

Lotus 1-2-3 simplified /. Bolocan, David. Blue Ridge Summit, PA , c1986. xii, 255 p. : ISBN 0-8306-0448-0 : LC Card 86-5820 DDC 005.36/9 19
HF5548.4.L67 B64 1986
NYPL [JSE 87-276]

Lotz, J. Policies with regard to grants to local authorities . Strasbourg , 1986. 35 p. : LC Card 86-218329 DDC 336.1/85 19
HJ1000 .P65 1986

Loubergé, Henri. Financement et assurance des crédits à l'exportation : aspects théoriques et pratiques en vigueur dans les pays européens / Henri Loubergé et Pierre Maurer.1ère éd. Genève : Librairie Droz, 1985. 502 p. : ill. ; 22 cm. (Travaux de droit, d'économie, de sciences politiques, de sociologie et d'anthropologie . no. 148) Bibliography: p. [477]-478.
1. Export credit - Europe. 2. Insurance, Export credit - Europe. I. Maurer, Pierre. II. Title. III. Series.
NYPL [JLD 86-2109]

Loubser, M. G.
Income and expenditure patterns of urban Black multiple households in Pretoria, 1980. Martins, J. H. Income and expenditure patterns of urban black multiple households in Pretoria, 1985 / by J.H. Martins. Pretoria , 1986. xi, 128 p. : ISBN 0-908408-57-9 (pbk.) LC Card 86-220725 DDC 658.8/3968 s 339.4/1/0968235 19
HC517.S7 S48 no. 130, pt. 2 HD7064.4.Z8P74

Louderback, Joseph G. Dominiak, Geraldine F. Managerial accounting /. Boston , c1988. xxiv, 808 p. : ISBN 0-534-07740-4 : LC Card 87-21472 DDC 658.1/5 19
HF5657.4 .D66 1988

Lougheed, A. L. Trends in international trade and Australia's performance / by Alan L. Lougheed. Canberra, Australia : Australian Institute of International Affairs, 1986. 16, [4] p. : ill. ; 30 cm. (Occasional paper / Australian Institute of International Affairs, 0816-4584 . no. 2) Includes bibliographical references. ISBN 0-909992-18-5 (pbk.) LC Card 87-107912 DDC 382/.0994 19
1. Australia - Commerce. 2. Australia - Commerce - Statistics. I. Series: Occasional paper (Australian Institute of International Affairs) , no. 2. II. Title.
HF3946.5 .L68 1986

Louis Berger and Associates. Hudson Waterfront Walkway plan and design guidelines /. [Trenton, N.J.] , 1984] 136 p. :
NYPL [JLF 87-913]

Louis Berger International, inc. Nilsson, Roy. Kitui water resources development study . Nairobi, Kenya [1982] 13, [31] leaves : LC Card 85-980998 DDC 333.91/009676/24 19
HD1699.K42 K586 1982

Louis Harris and Associates. A Study of the attitudes toward and an assessment of the Financial Accounting Standards Board /. Stamford, CT , 1985. x, 141 p. : LC Card 86-230871 DDC 657/.0218 19
HF5616.U5 S78 1985

Louis, Marie Victoire. Galland, Olivier. Jeunes en transit . Paris , c1984. 236 p. ; ISBN 2-7082-2405-0 : LC Card 85-102779 DDC 367/.94486 19
HD6276.F72 G35 1984

LOUISIANA - APPROPRIATIONS AND EXPENDITURES.
Louisiana. Legislature. Joint Legislative Committee on Economies in State Government. Final report /. [Baton Rouge] [1986] 62, 74, 105, [40] p. ; LC Card 86-621905 DDC 353.97630072 19
HJ2053.L8 L66 1986

Louisiana crude oil and natural gas report and severance and royalty sensitivity to price, second half 1985 /. Lam, Manuel. Baton Rouge, La (P.O. Box 44156, Baton Rouge 70804-4156) [1986] iii, 31 p. : LC Card 86-621907 DDC 338.2/728/09763 19
HD9560.8.U53 L65 1986

Louisiana. Dept. of Natural Resources. Energy Division. Technology Assessment Section. Lam, Manuel. Louisiana crude oil and natural gas report and severance and royalty sensitivity to price, second half 1985 /. Baton Rouge, La (P.O. Box 44156, Baton Rouge 70804-4156) [1986] iii, 31 p. : LC Card 86-621907 DDC 338.2/728/09763 19
HD9560.8.U53 L65 1986

Louisiana. General Assembly. see **Louisiana. Legislature.**

Louisiana. Legislature. Joint Legislative Committee on Economies in State Government. Final report / Joint Legislative Committee on Economies in State Government. [Baton Rouge] : The Committee, [1986] 62, 74, 105, [40] p. ; 28 cm. "April 21, 1986." LC Card 86-621905 DDC 353.97630072 19
1. Louisiana - Appropriations and expenditures. 2. Administrative agencies - Louisiana - Finance. I. Title.
HJ2053.L8 L66 1986

LOUISIANA - OCCUPATIONS - LICENSES.
Licensed occupations in Louisiana /. [Baton Rouge, La.] (P.O. Box 94094, Baton Rouge 70804-9094) [1986] ix, 85 p. ; LC Card 87-620751 DDC 331.7/02/09763 19
HD3630.U7 L529 1986

Louisiana. Office of Commerce & Industry. Reference guide of permits and licenses. Baton Rouge, La. (P.O. Box 94185, Baton Rouge 71808-9185) [1986?] ix, 222 p. ; LC Card 86-621904 DDC 353.97630082/4046 19
HD3630.U7 R44 1986

Louisiana State Occupational Information Coordinating Committee. Licensed occupations in Louisiana /. [Baton Rouge, La.] (P.O. Box 94094, Baton Rouge 70804-9094) [1986] ix, 85 p. ; LC Card 87-620751 DDC 331.7/02/09763 19
HD3630.U7 L529 1986

Louisville Area Chamber of Commerce. Economic Development Group. Louisville statistical abstract . [Louisville, KY] 1985. 86 p. : LC Card 86-219117 DDC 317.69/44 19
HC108.L6 L6515 1985

LOUISVILLE (KY.) - ECONOMIC CONDITIONS - STATISTICS.
Louisville statistical abstract . [Louisville, KY] 1985. 86 p. : LC Card 86-219117 DDC 317.69/44 19
HC108.L6 L6515 1985

LOUISVILLE (KY.) - POPULATION - STATISTICS.
Louisville statistical abstract . [Louisville, KY] 1985. 86 p. : LC Card 86-219117 DDC 317.69/44 19
HC108.L6 L6515 1985

Louisville statistical abstract : a compendium of economic and demographic data, 1955-1985. [Louisville, KY : Economic Development Group, Louisville Chamber of Commerce], 1985. 86 p. : ill. (some col.) ; 28 cm. Cover title. LC Card 86-219117 DDC 317.69/44 19
1. Louisville (Ky.) - Economic conditions - Statistics. 2. Louisville (Ky.) - Population - Statistics. I. Louisville Area Chamber of Commerce. Economic Development Group.
HC108.L6 L6515 1985

Loureiro, Antônio José Souto. A grande crise : (1908-1916) / Antônio José Souto Loureiro. Manaus, Amazonas, Brasil : T. Loureiro & Cia., 1986. 282 p. : ill., ports. ; 23 cm. LC Card 86-222988
1. Rubber industry and trade - Brazil - History. I. Title.
HD9161.B8 L68 1986

Loureiro, Orozimbo Roxo. Garimpando reminiscências / Orozimbo Roxo Loureiro ; prefácio, Benedito Ferri de Barros. São Paulo : [s.n.], 1976 (São Paulo : Grafikor) 317 p. ; 21 cm. LC Card 85-225740
1. Investments - Brazil. 2. Banks and banking - Brazil. 3. Loureiro, Orozimbo Roxo. I. Title.
HG5332 .L68 1976

LOUREIRO, OROZIMBO ROXO.
Loureiro, Orozimbo Roxo. Garimpando reminiscências /. São Paulo , 1976 (São Paulo : Grafikor) 317 p. ; LC Card 85-225740
HG5332 .L68 1976

Loureiro, Violeta Refkalefsky. Os parceiros do mar : natureza e conflito social na pesca da Amazônia / Violeta Refkalefsky Loureiro. [Brasília] : CNPq ; [Belém] : Museu Paraense Emílio Goeldi, 1985. 227 p. : ill. ; 22 cm. Bibliography: p. 205-207. LC Card 85-211634
1. Fish trade - Amazon River Estuary. 2. Fish trade - Brazil - Vigia (Pará). 3. Vigia (Pará, Brazil) - Economic conditions. I. Title.
HD9464.A4 L68 1985

Lourenço Marquez (City). Instituto de Investigação Cientifica de Moçambique. Wuyts, Marc. Camponeses e economia rural em Moçambique [microform] /. Maputo , 1978. 31, A1-A6 p. ; LC Card 80-980386 DDC

338.1/0967/9 19
HD2129 .W89 1978
NYPL [*ZT-1564 no.14]

Lourenço Marquez (City) Mozambique Institute of Scientific Research. see **Lourenço Marquez (City). Instituto de Investigação Cientifica de Moçambique.**

LOUVAIN (BELGIUM) - ECONOMIC CONDITIONS.
Stadsboek Leuven /. Leuven , c1985. 259 p. : ISBN 90-6303-137-8 : LC Card 86-204792
HC318.L6 S73 1985

LOUVAIN (BELGIUM) - POLITICS AND GOVERNMENT.
Stadsboek Leuven /. Leuven , c1985. 259 p. : ISBN 90-6303-137-8 : LC Card 86-204792
HC318.L6 S73 1985

LOUVAIN (BELGIUM) - SOCIAL CONDITIONS.
Stadsboek Leuven /. Leuven , c1985. 259 p. : ISBN 90-6303-137-8 : LC Card 86-204792
HC318.L6 S73 1985

Louvain psychology series studia psychologica. Nuttin, Jozef, 1909- [Théorie de la motivation humaine. English.] Motivation, planning, and action . Leuven, Belgium , Hillsdale, N.J. , c1984. viii, 251 p. ; ISBN 0-89859-332-8 (L. Erlbaum) LC Card 83-16416 DDC 153.8 19
BF503 .N8713 1984 ***NYPL [JFE 86-2315]***

Louven, Erhard.
Hirschmeier, Johannes. Johannes Hirschmeier, die japanische Unternehmung . Hamburg , 1986. viii, 218 p. : ISBN 3-88910-024-4 : LC Card 86-225311
HF5349.J3 H573 1986

Shanghai, Chinas Tor zur Welt / Institut für Asienkunde ; [die Autoren, Erhard Louven, Peter Schier, Brunhild Staiger]. Hamburg : Landeszentrale für Politische Bildung, 1986. 118 p. : ill., maps ; 21 cm. Bibliography: p. 116-118. LC Card 86-230755
1. Shanghai (China) - Economic conditions. I. Schier, Peter, 1950-. II. Staiger, Brunhild. III. Institut für Asienkunde (Hamburg, Germany). IV. Title.
HC428.S47 L68 1986

Lovassné Szecső, Judit.
Engel, Gábor. A kereskedelmi tevékenység komplex finanszirozása /. Budapest [1985] 68 p. ; ISBN 963-7202-58-7 LC Card 86-157419
HG4026 .E517 1985

A kereskedelmi hitel és a váltó alkalmazásának 1985. évi tapasztalatai / [szerzők, Lovassné Szecső Judit, Gyüge Tamás, Tamás Gábor]. Budapest : Belkereskedelmi Kutató Intézet, [1986] 62 p. ; 29 cm. (Tanulmány / Belkereskedelmi Kutató Intézet) "1986. március". Bibliography: p. 61-62. ISBN 963-7202-84-6 LC Card 87-151536
1. Commercial credit - Hungary. I. Gyüge, Tamás. II. Tamás, Gábor. III. Series: Tanulmány (Budapest, Hungary). IV. Title.
HG3754.5.H9 L68 1986

Love, Cohn, 1938- Conflicts over closure : the Laurence Scott affair / by Cohn Love. Aldershot, Hants, England ; Brookfield, Vt., U. S.A. : Gower Pub. Co., [1987] p. cm. Includes indexes. ISBN 0-566-05367-5 : LC Card 86-29496 DDC 338.6/042 19
1. Plant shutdowns - Great Britain - Case studies. I. Title.
HD5708.55.G7 L68 1987

Love, Douglas O. The minimum cost of living in Nebraska / Douglas O. Love. [Lincoln] : Bureau of Business Research, College of Business Administration, University of Nebraska-Lincoln, [1986] 2 v. : ill. ; 28 cm. "January 14, 1986." Bibliography: v. 2, leaves 424-430. LC Card 87-620964 DDC 339.4/2/09782 19
1. Cost and standard of living - Nebraska. I. Title.
HD6993.N4 L68 1986

Loveday, Peter. Economy and people in the north /. Darwin , 1985. v, 294 p. : ISBN 0-86784-591-0 (pbk.) : LC Card 86-159263 DDC 330.9719/03 19
HC607.N6 E27 1985

Lovell, Malcolm Read, 1921- United States. Secretary of Labor's Task Force on Economic Adjustment and Worker Dislocation. Economic adjustment and worker dislocation in a competitive society . Washington, D.C. [1986] 189 p. in various pagings : LC Card 87-601034 DDC 331.13/7973 19
HC106.8 .U545 1986

Lovelock, Christopher H. Marketing public transit . New York , 1987. x, 228 p. : ISBN 0-275-92499-8 (alk. paper) : LC Card 87-11583 DDC 388.4/068/8 19
HE4456 .M37 1987

Loven, Walter T. Bukics, Rosie L. The handbook of credit and accounts receivable management /. Chicago, Ill. , c1987. xi, 252 p. : ISBN 0-917253-67-1 : LC Card 87-7008 DDC 658.8/8 19
HG3751 .B85 1987

Lovett, A. F. Weatheritt, L. Manufacturing industry in Greater London /. London , c1975. ii, 26 p. ; ISBN 0-7168-0853-6 (pbk.) LC Card 82-213745
HD5766.L66 W43 1975

Lovett, William Anthony. World trade rivalry : trade equity and competing industrial policies / William A. Lovett. Lexington, Mass. : Lexington Books, c1987. xxxv, 260 p. : ill. ; 24 cm. Includes bibliographies and index. ISBN 0-669-11027-2 (alk. paper) LC Card 85-40388 DDC 382/.3 19
1. Commerce. 2. Industry and state. 3. Competition, International. 4. United States - Commercial policy. I. Title.
HF1008 .L68 1987

Lovin, Hugh T. Labor in the West /. Manhattan, Kan., USA , c1986. 88 p. : ISBN 0-89745-090-6 (pbk.) LC Card 87-400877 DDC 331/.0978 19
HD8083.A17 L32 1986

LOW-CALORIE DIET.
(1986) Diet foods . Stamford, Conn., U. S.A. , c1986. xv, 195 leaves : ISBN 0-89336-487-8 (pbk.) LC Card 87-160485 DDC 381/.4166463/0973 19
HD9005 .D53 1986

Low cost investing. Currier, Chet. No cost/low cost investing /. New York , 1987. 240 p. ; ISBN 0-531-15527-7 LC Card 87-13690 DDC 332.6/78 19
HG4910 .C86 1987

Low-cost marketing strategies . Deran, Elisabeth. New York , 1987. ix, 151 p. ; ISBN 0-275-92341-X (alk. paper) : LC Card 86-30640 DDC 658.8 19
HF5415 .D458 1987

Low, G. C. Report of the commissioner appointed to inquire into the operation of the land tenure scheme in Ankole. Entebbe, Uganda : Printed by the Govt. Printer, [1961?] 30 p. ; 25 cm. Cover title. At head of title: Uganda Protectorate. Includes bibliographical references. LC Card 85-208468
1. Land tenure - Uganda - Ankole. I. Title.
HD994.Z8 A55 1961

Low income countries : problems and prospects / Govind R. Agrawal ... [et al.]. New Delhi : Radiant Publishers, 1987. x, 106 p. ; 23 cm. "Issued under the auspices of the Research and Information System for the Nonaligned and Other Developing Countries." Includes index. ISBN 81-7027-101-0 : LC Card 87-900104 DDC 330.9172/4 19
1. Developing countries - Foreign economic relations. 2. Developing countries - Economic conditions. 3. Income - Developing countries. I. Agrawal, Govind Ram. II. Research and Information System for the Nonaligned and Other Developing Countries.
HF1413 .L68 1987

LOW INCOME HOUSING. see **HOUSING.**

Low-income housing in the Durban metropolitan region .
(project report no. 4) Planning and financial evaluation of housing strategies /. Durban , 1983. viii, 233 p. : ISBN 0-86980-360-3 (pbk.) LC Card 86-205849 DDC 363.5/8 19
HD7287.96.S682 D876 1983

LOW POWER TELEVISION - SWITZERLAND - WIL (SAINT GALL)
Hunziker, Peter, 1941- Lokales Bürgerfernsehen . Aarau , c1983. 192 p. ; ISBN 3-7941-2369-7 : LC Card 83-141437
HE8700.72.S95 H85 1983

Low wages and hard work. Dall, Caroline Wells (Healey), 1822-1912. "Woman's right to labor," or, Low wages and hard work . Boston , 1860. xv, 184 p. ; LC Card 87-162350
HD6053 .D27 1860

Lowe, Adolph, 1893-
Beschäftigung, Verteilung und Konjunktur . Bremen , 1984. 276 p. : ISBN 3-88722-088-9 : LC Card 85-176579
HB175 .B49 1984

Essays in political economics : public control in a democratic society / Adolph Lowe ; edited and introduced by Allen Oakley. New York : New York University Press, 1987. 257 p. ; 24 cm. "Bibliography of the works of Adolph Lowe": p. 251-256. Includes bibliographies. ISBN 0-8147-6168-2 LC Card 87-11219 DDC 338.9 19
1. Economic development. 2. Economic policy. I. Oakley, Allen. II. Title.
HD82 .L693 1987

LOWE, ADOLPH, 1893-
Beschäftigung, Verteilung und Konjunktur . Bremen , 1984. 276 p. : ISBN 3-88722-088-9 : LC Card 85-176579
HB175 .B49 1984

Lowe, D. A. (Douglas Ackley), 1942- The price of power : the politics behind the Tasmanian dams case / Doug Lowe. South Melbourne : Macmillan, 1984. viii, 184 p., [12] p. of plates : ill. ; 23 cm. Includes index. ISBN 0-333-38088-6 LC Card 84-254286 DDC 333.91/62/099466 19
1. Hydroelectric power plants - Environmental aspects - Government policy - Australia - Tasmania. 2. Dams - Environmental aspects - Government policy - Australia - Tasmania. 3. Wilderness areas - Government policy - Australia - Tasmania. I. Title.
HD9685.A83 T385 1984
NYPL [JLD 87-795]

Lowe, Graham S. Working Canadians . Toronto , New York , c1984. x, 380 p. ; ISBN 0-458-97370-X (pbk.) : LC Card 84-222036 DDC 331/.0971 19
HD6957.C2 W67 1984 ***NYPL [JLD 87-681]***

Lowe, John S., 1941- Oil and gas in a nutshell / by John S. Lowe. St. Paul, Minn. : West Pub. Co., 1983. xlvii, 443 p. ; 19 cm. (Nutshell series) Includes index. ISBN 0-314-73469-4 LC Card 83-6811 DDC 346.7304/6823 347.30646823 19
1. Petroleum law and legislation - United States. 2. Gas, Natural - Law and legislation - United States. I. Title.
KF1850 .L68 1983 ***NYPL [JLC 86-226]***

Lowe, Mifflin. The cheapskate's handbook : a guide to the subtleties, intricacies, and pleasures of being a tightwad / by Mifflin Lowe. Los Angeles : Price/Stern/Sloan, 1986. 104 p. : ill. ; 18 cm. ISBN 0-8431-1246-8 (pbk.): LC Card 86-207189 DDC 332.024 19
1. Saving and thrift - Anecdotes, facetiae, satire, etc. 2. Finance, Personal - Anecdotes, facetiae, satire, etc. I. Title.
HG7931 .L68 1986

Lowe, Philip. Countryside conflicts . Aldershot, Hants, England , Brookfield, Vt., U. S.A. , c1986. vi, 378 p. [4] leaves of plates : ISBN 0-566-05088-9 : LC Card 85-24603 DDC 333.76/17/0941 19
HD596 .C675 1986 ***NYPL [JLD 86-2487]***

Lowell as a laboratory . Leney, Julie M. [Lowell, Mass.?] , 1987. 92 p. : LC Card 87-158220 DDC 363.5/8 19
HD7288.78.U52 M44 1987

Lowell Conference on Industrial History (1984) The world of the Industrial Revolution : comparative and international aspects of industrialization : essays from the Lowell Conference on Industrial History, 1984 / edited by Robert Weible. [Andover, MA] : Museum of American Textile History, 1986. 177 p. : ill. ; 23 cm. Includes bibliographies. ISBN 0-937474-08-8 (pbk.) LC Card 86-31242 DDC 338.09 19
1. Industry - History - Congresses. I. Weible, Robert. II. Title.
HD2321 .L69 1984

LOWELL HOUSING AUTHORITY - HISTORY.
Leney, Julie M. Lowell as a laboratory . [Lowell, Mass.?] , 1987. 92 p. : LC Card 87-158220 DDC 363.5/8 19
HD7288.78.U52 M44 1987

Lowell, Orson. (ill) Harlow, Alvin F. (Alvin Fay), 1875-1963. When horses pulled boats . York, PA , c1983. 72 p. : ISBN 0-933788-43-6 (pbk.) LC Card 87-400271 DDC 386/.48/0973 19
HE395.A3 H37 1983

Lowenstein, Louis. Knights, raiders, and targets . New York , 1987. p. cm. ISBN 0-19-504405-3 (alk. paper) LC Card 86-33293 DDC 338.8/3 19
HD2746.5 .K58 1987

LOWER AUSTRIA (AUSTRIA) - GENEALOGY.
Feigl, Helmuth. Die niederösterreichische Grundherrschaft . [Wien] , 1964. 379 p. ; LC Card 85-127367
HD639.L6 F45 1964

Lower River Atbara area (Nile Province) . Abdel Ati, Hassan A. [Khartoum] Sudan [1985] vii, 166 p., [19] leaves of plates : LC Card 86-981108 DDC 333.91/3/09625 19
HD1741.S852 A832 1985

Lower Saxony (Germany)
2. Nachtragshaushalt des Landes Niedersachsen . [West Germany , 1981?] 178 p. ; LC Card 85-123229
HJ2110.5.L68 A12 1981

LOWER SAXONY (GERMANY) - APPROPRIATIONS AND EXPENDITURES - STATISTICS.
2. Nachtragshaushalt des Landes Niedersachsen . [West Germany , 1981?] 178 p. ; LC Card 85-123229
HJ2110.5.L68 A12 1981

LOWER SAXONY (GERMANY) - ECONOMIC CONDITIONS.
Landwirtschaftliche Übergangsbetriebe in Niedersachsen . Göttingen , 1985. xiii, 105 p. ; LC Card 86-185987
HD9013.7.L68 L36 1985

Schumacher, Karl-Edzard. Entwicklungsmöglichkeiten landwirtschaftlicher Übergangsbetriebe in Niedersachsen . Göttingen , 1985. 234, vi p. : LC Card 86-186858
HD9013.7.L68 S38 1985

LOWER SAXONY (GERMANY) - FOREIGN ECONOMIC RELATIONS - DEVELOPING COUNTRIES.
Menck, Karl Wolfgang. Mittelstand und Entwicklungsländer . Hamburg , 1986. 192 p. ; ISBN 3-87895-318-6 LC Card 87-407405 DDC 337.43/59/01724 19
HF1546.19.L68 M46 1986

LOWER SAXONY (GERMANY) - INDUSTRIES.
Schanz, Günther, 1943- Mitarbeiter-Kapitalbeteiligung in der Wirtschaft Niedersachsens . Spardorf , c1984. 228 p. : ISBN 3-922919-26-X : LC Card 84-162288
HD5660.G412 L687 1984

Lower Saxony (Germany). Ministerium für Ernährung, Landwirtschaft und Forsten.
Landwirtschaftliche Übergangsbetriebe in Niedersachsen . Göttingen , 1985. xiii, 105 p. ; LC Card 86-185987
HD9013.7.L68 L36 1985

LOWER SAXONY (GERMANY) - RURAL CONDITIONS.
Landwirtschaftliche Übergangsbetriebe in Niedersachsen . Göttingen , 1985. xiii, 105 p. ; LC Card 86-185987
HD9013.7.L68 L36 1985

Lowery, David. Berry, William Dale. Understanding United States government growth . New York , 1987. xiv, 212 p. : ISBN 0-275-92509-9 (alk. paper) : LC Card 87-11818 DDC 336.73 19
HJ257.2 .B47 1987

Lowry, S. Todd. The archaeology of economic ideas : the classical Greek tradition / S. Todd Lowry. Durham : Duke University Press, 1987. xviii, 366 p. ; 25 cm. Bibliography: p. [327]-349. Includes index. ISBN 0-8223-0774-X LC Card 87-15507 DDC 330/.0938 19
1. Economics - Greece - History. 2. Public administration - Greece - History. 3. Greece - Economic conditions - To 146 B.C. I. Title.
HB108.A2 L68 1987

LOYALTY.
Shea, Gordon F., 1925- Company loyalty . New York, N.Y. , c1987. 86 p. : ISBN 0-8144-2331-0 (pbk.) : LC Card 86-28883 DDC 650.1 19
HD58.9 .S48 1987

Lozano, Adolfo Lafarga. see **Lafarga Lozano, Adolfo.**

Lozano Irueste, José María, 1920- Glosario de términos de economía y hacienda / José Ma. Lozano Irueste [con la colaboración de] Ramón Carbajo, Valentín Edo e Isabel Verdeja. [Madrid] : Instituto de Estudios Fiscales, Ministerio de Economía y Hacienda, [1986] 56 p. ; 25 cm. Cover title. Includes English-Spanish list of terms. Bibliography: p. 55-56.
1. Economics - Terminology. 2. Spanish language - Glossaries, vocabularies, etc. I. Title.
NYPL [JLF 87-148]

LPU working paper .
(no. 8) Massow, Valentin von, 1925- Dairy imports and import policy in Mali and their implications for the dairy sector in the Bamako area /. Addis Ababa, Ethiopia [1985] v leaves, 57 p., [12] leaves ; LC Card 86-981009 DDC 382/.417/096623 19
HD9275.M423 B366 1985

LPU working paper ; no. 6.
Addis Anteneh. Financing livestock services in some countries of east and southern Africa /. Addis Ababa, Ethiopia [1985] 26 p. ; LC Card 86-980745 DDC 338.1/36/0096 19
HD9427.A2 A33 1985

LSE monographs in international studies.
Khong, Cho Oon. The politics of oil in Indonesia . Cambridge [Cambridgeshire] , New York , 1986. x, 253 p. : ISBN 0-521-30901-8 LC Card 85-22416 DDC 338.2/7282/09598 19
HD9567.I52 K48 1986
NYPL [JLD 86-3386]

LSMS working paper .
(no. 24) Grootaert, Christiaan, 1950- Measuring and analyzing levels of living in developing countries . Washington, D.C., U. S.A. , c1986. x, 139 p. : ISBN 0-8213-0758-4 (pbk.) LC Card 86-5611 DDC 339.4/7/091724 19
HD7067 .G76 1986b

Lu, David John, 1928-
Inside corporate Japan : the art of fumble-free management / David J. Lu ; foreword by Norman Bodek. Stamford, CT : Productivity Press, c1987. xxi, 249 p. : ill. ; 24 cm. Bibliography: p. 225-231. Includes index. ISBN 0-915299-16-X (alk. paper) : LC Card 87-60546 DDC 658/.00952 19
1. Industrial management - Japan. I. Title.
HD70.J3 L8 1987

Nemoto, Masao. [TQC to toppu bu-kachō no yakuwari. English.] Total quality control for management . Englewood Cliffs, N.J. , c1987. xix, 238 p. : ISBN 0-13-925637-7 : LC Card 87-2329 DDC 658.4/036 19
HD66 .N4613 1987

Lü se ko ming. On rolls the green revolution /. Beijing, China [1984] 142 p., [36] p. of plates : LC Card 86-115054 DDC 338.1/0951 19
HD2097 .O5 1984 ***NYPL [JLK 83-122 no.9]***

Luangwa Development Project (Zambia)
Lupande Development Workshop (1983 : Nyamaluma Wildlife Conservation Camp) Proceedings of the Lupande Development Workshop . Chipata, Zambia , 1984. x, 121 p. : LC Card 84-980605 DDC 333.73/17/096894 19
HD993.Z8 L835 1983 ***NYPL [JLG 87-67]***

Lubben, Richard T. Just-in-time manufacturing : an aggressive manufacturing strategy / Richard T. Lubben. New York : McGraw-Hill, c1988. xiv, 246 p. : ill. ; 24 cm. Bibliography: p. 237. Includes index. ISBN 0-07-038911-X LC Card 87-4058 DDC 658.5 19
1. Manufactures - Management. 2. Manufactures - Quality control. 3. Manufacturing processes. 4. Competition, International. I. Title.
HD9720.5 .L83 1988

LÜBECK (GERMANY) - COMMERCE - HISTORY.
Heineken, Hermann. Der Salzhandel Lüneburgs mit Lübeck bis zum Anfang des 15. Jahrhunderts /. Vaduz , 1965. 150 p. ; LC Card 86-231350
HD9213.G43 L864 1965

LÜBECK (GERMANY) - ECONOMIC CONDITIONS.
Lübecker Weinhandel . Lübeck , 1985. 260 p. : ISBN 3-924214-27-1 LC Card 86-145675
HD9383.8.L82 L82 1985

Lubin Graduate School of Business. International banking and global financing . New York, NY , c1983. xiv, 257 p. : ISBN 0-88239-015-5 (pbk.) : LC Card 84-60076 DDC 332.1/5 19
HG205 .I54 1983

Lubin, Nancy. Labour and nationality in Soviet Central Asia : an uneasy compromise / Nancy Lubin ; foreword by Murray Feshbach. London : Macmillan in association with St. Antony's College, Oxford, 1984. xix, 305 p. : 1 map ; 23 cm. (St Antony's/Macmillan series) Bibliography: p. 255-293. Includes index. ISBN 0-333-36739-1 LC Card 87-672162
1. Labor supply - Uzbek S.S.R. 2. Discrimination in employment - Uzbek S.S.R. 3. Ethnology - Uzbek S.S.R. I. Title.
HD5797.U9 L83x 1984b

Lubin School of Business Administration.
International banking and global financing . New York, NY , c1983. xiv, 257 p. : ISBN 0-88239-015-5 (pbk.) : LC Card 84-60076 DDC 332.1/5 19
HG205 .I54 1983

Lubitz, Karl-Joachim. Bankmarketing gegenüber mittelständischen Betrieben / von Karl-Joachim Lubitz. Frankfurt am Main : Knapp, c1984. 299 p. ; 23 cm. (Bank- und Geldmarketing) Bibliography: p. 272-298. ISBN 3-7819-3012-2 LC Card 85-153969
1. Small business - Germany, West - Finance. 2. Bank marketing - Germany (West). I. Title.
HG4027.7 .L83 1984

Lubos, Günter, 1958- Die Berichterstattung der internen Revision im Grossbetrieb / Günter Lubos. München : V. Florentz, c1986. xxvii, 207 p. ; 21 cm. (Hochschulschriften zur Betriebswirtschaftslehre . Bd. 42) Bibliography: p. xi-xxiv. Includes index. ISBN 3-88259-421-7 LC Card 87-121827 DDC 657/.458 19
1. Auditing, Internal. 2. Corporations - Auditing. I. Title. II. Series.
HF5668.25 .L82 1986

Luca, Walmor de. Moratória com diretas já : os números da dívida e a submissão ao FMI : discursos / pronunciados pelo Deputado Walmor de Luca. Brasília : Câmara dos Deputados, Centro de Documentação e Informação, Coordenação de Publicações, 1984. 69 p. ; 23 cm. (Separatas de discursos, pareceres e projetos . 47a. Legislatura--2a. Sessão Legislativa, no. 13) Speeches given 8/10/83-4/12/84 in the Câmara dos Deputados, Brazil. LC Card 86-152773
1. Santa Catarina (Brazil : State) - Economic policy. 2. Brazil - Economic policy. I. Brazil. Congresso Nacional. Câmara dos Deputados. Centro de Documentação e Informação. Coordenação de Publicações. II. Title. III. Series.
HC188.S26 L83 1984

Lucas, Martin. How to survive the 9 to 5 / Martin Lucas, Kim Wilson, and Emma Hart. London : Thames Methuen, 1986. 175 p. ; 20 cm. Bibliography: p. [170] Includes index. ISBN 0-423-01930-9 (pbk.) : LC Card 86-188564 DDC 158.7 19
1. Job stress. I. Wilson, Kim. II. Hart, Emma. III. Title. IV. Title: How to survive the nine to five.
HF5548.85 .L825 1986

Lucas, Robert E. B.
The Indian economy . Boulder, Colo. , 1988. ix, 374 p. : ISBN 0-8133-7505-3 (pbk. : alk. paper) LC Card 87-22472 DDC 330.954/05 19
HC435.2 .I555 1988

Motivations to remit : evidence from Botswanna [sic] / by Robert E.B. Lucas and Oded Stark. [Tel Aviv] : David Horowitz Institute for the Research of Developing Countries, Tel Aviv University, [1985] 27 leaves ; 27 cm. (Paper / The David Horowitz Institute for the Research of Developing Countries . no. 2/85) Bibliography: leaves 21-22. LC Card 86-177234
1. Emigrant remittances - Botswana - Psychological aspects. I. Stark, Oded. II. Series: Paper (Mekhon Horovits le-ḥeḳer aratsot mitpatḥot) , no. 85/2. III. Title.
HG3984.9 .L83 1985

Luce, Thomas F.
Local fiscal issues in the Philadelphia metropolitan area / Thomas F. Luce and Anita A. Summers. Philadelphia : University of Pennsylvania Press, c1987. xii, 248 p., [2] p. of plates : ill. ; 26 cm. Bibliography: p. [133]-142. Includes index. ISBN 0-8122-1255-X (pbk.) LC Card 87-25486 DDC 336.748/11 19
1. Finance, Public - Pennsylvania - Philadelphia

Metropolitan Area. I. Summers, Anita A. II. Title.
HJ9307.P4 L83 1987

Summers, Anita A. Economic development within the Philadelphia metropolitan area /. Philadelphia , c1987. xiv, 268 p. : ISBN 0-8122-1231-2 (pbk.) LC Card 86-25091 DDC 338.9748/11 19
HC108.P5 S85 1987

Lucena, José Mário Pereira de. O mercado habitacional no Brasil / José Mário Pereira de Lucena. 1a. ed. Rio de Janeiro, RJ : FGV-Instituto de Documentação, Editora da Fundação Getulio Vargas, 1985. v, 185 p. : ill. ; 21 cm. (Série Teses. no. 9) Originally presented as the author's thesis (doctoral--Escola de Pós-Graduação em Economia) Bibliography: p. 177-179. Includes index. LC Card 85-208372
1. Housing - Brazil. I. Series: Série Teses (Escola de Pós-Graduação em Economia) , no. 9. II. Title.
HD7323.A3 L83 1985

Lucena Salmoral, Manuel. Vísperas de la independencia americana : Caracas / Manuel Lucena Salmoral.1a ed. Madrid : Alhambra, 1986. vii, 389 p. ; 20 cm. (Estudios. 31) Includes bibliographical references. ISBN 84-205-1308-3 LC Card 86-205153
1. Caracas Region (Venezuela) - Commerce - History - 19th century. 2. Agriculture - Economic aspects - Venezuela - Caracas Region - History - 19th century. 3. Agricultural productivity - Venezuela - Caracas Region - History - 19th century. 4. Cattle trade - Venezuela - Caracas Region - History - 19th century. I. Title.
HF3490.C37 L83 1986

LUCERNE (SWITZERLAND) - POPULATION - HISTORY.
Schüpbach, Werner. Die Bevölkerung der Stadt Luzern 1850-1914 . Luzern , 1983. 323 p., [17] p. of plates : ISBN 3-7252-0432-2 LC Card 83-201416
HB3624.L8 S38 1983

LUCERNE (SWITZERLAND) - STATISTICS, MEDICAL - HSITORY.
Schüpbach, Werner. Die Bevölkerung der Stadt Luzern 1850-1914 . Luzern , 1983. 323 p., [17] p. of plates : ISBN 3-7252-0432-2 LC Card 83-201416
HB3624.L8 S38 1983

LUCERNE (SWITZERLAND) - STATISTICS, VITAL - HISTORY.
Schüpbach, Werner. Die Bevölkerung der Stadt Luzern 1850-1914 . Luzern , 1983. 323 p., [17] p. of plates : ISBN 3-7252-0432-2 LC Card 83-201416
HB3624.L8 S38 1983

La lucha contra la pobreza /. Barco, Virgilio. [Bogotá] , 1985. 193 p. ; ISBN 958-9044-11-5 LC Card 85-239429
HC197 .B2765 1985

Lucha y polémica sindical, 1968-1973. [Montevideo?] : Centro Uruguay Independiente, 1985. 4 v. ; 19 cm. (Documentos sindicales . no. 4-7) Articles previosuly published in "El Popular" and "Marcha," covering a series of debates, written by Héctor Rodríguez and others. CONTENTS. - 1. Cómo luchar por el programa? -- 2. Movimiento sindical y potencial de lucha. -- 3. CNT: Documentos y congresos/1. -- 4. CNT: Documentos y congresos/2. LC Card 86-107744 DDC 322/.2/09895 19
1. Trade-unions - Uruguay. 2. Trade-unions - Uruguay - Political activity. I. Rodríguez, Héctor, 1918-. II. Centro Uruguay Independiente. III. Series.
HD6647 .L83 1985 ***NYPL [JLC 86-368]***

Luchando por nuestros derechos : organizaciones campesinas de América Latina. Quito : Ecuarunari : FENOC, 1984. 50 p. : ill. ; 21 cm. Cover title. "Publicación realizada con la colaboración de ALAI, Oficina Regional Andina"--P. [2] of cover. Includes bibliographical references. LC Card 86-174980
1. Peasantry - Latin America - Political activity - Case studies. I. Ecuarunari (Organization). II. Federación Nacional de Organizaciones Campesinos (Ecuador). III. ALAI (Organization). Oficina Regional Andina.
HD1531.L3 L79 1984

Luchenko, Klavdiia Fedorovna. Igumnov, IU. S. (IUriĭ Stepanovich) Sebestoimost' i puti ee snizheniia v promyshlennosti /. Kiev , 1986. 223 p. ; LC Card 87-126676
HC340.C7 I38 1986

Luchinova, S. (Svetlana) TSygankov, P. A. (Pavel Afanas'evich) V bor'be protiv vsevlastiia kapitala /. Moskva , 1986. 139 p. ; LC Card 86-132423
HB501 .T78 1986

Lucht, John, 1933- Rites of passage at $100,000+ : the insider's guide to absolutely everything about executive job-changing / John Lucht. New York : Viceroy Press : Distributed to the trade in the USA by H. Holt & Co., c1988. ix, 547 p. ; 24 cm. Includes index. ISBN 0-942785-07-X : LC Card 87-50459 DDC 658.4/09 19
1. Executives - United States - Recruiting. 2. Job hunting - United States. I. Title.
HD38.25.U6 L83 1988

Lucier, Gary. Farm income data : a historical perspective / Gary Lucier, Agnes Chesley, Mary Ahearn. Washington, DC : U. S. Dept. of Agriculture, Economic Research Service : Can be purchased from the Supt. of Docs., U. S. G.P.O., [1986] iv, 311 p. : ill. ; 28 cm. (Statistical bulletin / United States Department of Agriculture, Economic Research Service . no. 740) Cover title. "May 1986"--P.i. Bibliography: p. 8-13. LC Card 86-602022 DDC 338.1/0973 s 338.1/3/0973021 19
1. Farm income - United States - Statistics. 2. Farms - United States - Statistics. I. Chesley, Agnes. II. Ahearn, Mary C. III. Series: Statistical bulletin (United States. Dept. of Agriculture) , no. 740. IV. Title.
HD1751 .A5 no. 740 HD1769

Luck, David Johnston. Marketing research / David J. Luck, Ronald S. Rubin. 7th ed. Englewood Cliffs, NJ : Prentice-Hall, c1987. xvii, 683 p. : ill. ; 25 cm. Rev. ed. of: Marketing research / David J. Luck ... [et al.]. 6th ed. c1982. Includes bibliographical references and indexes. ISBN 0-13-557828-0 : LC Card 86-25255 DDC 658.8/3 19
1. Marketing research. I. Rubin, Ronald S. II. Title.
HF5415.2 .M3555 1987

Lucke, Robert, 1955-
Cohen, Carol E. 1983 tax capacity of the states . Washington, D.C. (1111 20th St., NW, Washington 20575) [1986] ix, 111 p. : LC Card 86-601628 DDC 336.2/013/73
HJ2385 .C59 1986

Verdier, James M. Tax expenditures . Washington, D.C. , 1982. xx, 102 p. ;
NYPL [JLF 83-663]

Lüddecke, Christa. Ost-Wirtschaftsreport Digest . Düsseldorf , Genève , 1977. 119 p. ; LC Card 84-154293
HC244 .O726 1977

Lüdeke, Rainar. Finanzsysteme, Ideal- und Realtypen . Berlin , c1983. 278 p. : ISBN 3-428-05419-9 LC Card 83-240120
HJ161 .F575 1983

LÜDERITZ REGION (NAMIBIA) - HISTORY.
Phillips, John A. S. Deutsch-englische Komödie der Irrungen um Südwestafrika . Pfaffenhofen, West Germany , 1986. 184 p., [12] p. of plates : ISBN 3-87010-105-9 LC Card 87-146587 DDC 338.4/76686366/09688 19
HD9484.G9 N366 1986

Ludger Gravel, 1864-1933 . Richer, Laurette B. [Montréal] , c1986. 170 p. : ISBN 2-9800028-1-X LC Card 87-115031
HC112.5.G73 R53 1986

Ludlow, John Malcolm Forbes, 1821-1911. Progress of the working class, 1832-1867 / J.M. Ludlow, Lloyd Jones. New York : Garland, 1984. xv, 304 p. ; 19 cm. (The World of labour) Includes bibliographical references. Reprint. Originally published: London : A. Strahan, 1867. ISBN 0-8240-5717-1 (alk. paper) : LC Card 83-48490 DDC 305.5/62/0942 19
1. Labor and laboring classes - Great Britain - History - 19th century. 2. Labor laws and legislation - Great Britain - History - 19th century. I. Jones, Lloyd, 1811-1886. II. Title. III. Series.
HD8390 .L93 1984 ***NYPL [JLC 86-387]***

Ludlow, Nicholas H. The Development Bank highways market, 1987-1991 : a practical reference guide / by Nicholas H. Ludlow and Susan Diane Ward. Washington, D.C., USA (1735 Eye St., NW, Suite 710, Washington 20006) : Development Bank Associates, c1987. 387, 2 p. : ill. ; 28 cm. Includes index. LC Card 87-71066 DDC 388.1/14 19
1. Banks and banking, International. 2. Development banks. 3. Road construction - Finance. 4. International Bank for Reconstruction and Development. I. Ward, Susan Diane. II. Development Bank Associates. III. Title.
HG3881 .L737 1987

Ludność Nadodrza, 1945-2000 /. Rauziński, Robert. Opole , 1985. 44 p. ; LC Card 86-207214
HB3608.7.O34 R38 1985

Ludowa Republika Bangladesz. see **Bangladesh.**

Ludwick, David E. The competitive position of U. S. and European Community pork and the United States and third-country markets : report to the U. S. Senate Committee on Finance on investigation no. 332-213 under Section 332 of the Tariff Act of 1930, as amended. Washington, DC : U. S. International Trade Commission, [1985] xxiii, 341 p. : ill., map ; 28 cm. (USITC publication. 1794) Cover title. Report prepared by David E. Ludwick, Judith A. Phillips, and Walker A. Pollard. "December 1985." Includes bibliographical references. LC Card 86-601366 DDC 380.1/4566492/0973 19
1. Pork industry and trade - United States. 2. Pork industry and trade - European Economic Community countries. 3. Pork industry and trade - Developing countries. 4. Competition, International. I. Phillips, Judith A. II. Pollard, Walker A. III. United States. Congress. Senate. Committee on Finance. IV. United States. International Trade Commission. V. Title.
HD9435.U52 L83 1985

LUDWIG, DANIEL KEITH, 1897-
Shields, Jerry. The invisible billionaire, Daniel Ludwig /. Boston , 1986. xii, 401 p. : ISBN 0-395-35402-1 : LC Card 86-7519 DDC 387.5/092/4 B 19
HE569.L84 S55 1986 ***NYPL [JFE 86-3861]***

Ludwig-Erhard-Preis für Wirtschaftspublizistik 1986 : Übergabe an Johannes Gross und Professor Dr. Artur Woll am 21. Februar 1986 im Hotel Königshof in Bonn. Bonn : Ludwig-Erhard-Stiftung, [1986] 45 p. : 1 ill. ; 24 cm. "ISSN 0177-0640"--P. [4] of cover. ISBN 3-88991-009-2 LC Card 87-409497 DDC 338.943 19
1. Germany, West - Economic policy. I. Gross, Johannes, 1932-. II. Woll, Artur, 1923-. III. Ludwig Erhard-Stiftung.
HC286.5 .L825 1986

Ludwig Erhard-Stiftung.
Entwicklungspolitik im Spannungsfeld von Solidarität und Eigeninteresse . Stuttgart , New York , 1986. 155 p. ; ISBN 3-437-50306-5 LC Card 87-408212 DDC 338.91/43/01724 19
HC60 .E527 1986

Kohl, Helmut, 1930- Soziale Marktwirtschaft, Fundament für morgen . Bonn [1987] 39 p. : ISBN 3-88991-011-4 LC Card 87-409383 DDC 338.943 19
HC286.5 .K565 1987

Kontinuität und Wandel in vier Jahrzehnten deutscher Wirtschaftspolitik /. Stuttgart , New York , 1986. 111 p. ; ISBN 3-437-50310-3 LC Card 87-116017 DDC 338.943 19
HC286.5 .K618 1986

Ludwig-Erhard-Preis für Wirtschaftspublizistik 1986 . Bonn [1986] 45 p. : ISBN 3-88991-009-2 LC Card 87-409497 DDC 338.943 19
HC286.5 .L825 1986

Ludwig Erhards Gesellschafts- und Wirtschaftskonzeption . Wünsche, Horst Friedrich. Stuttgart , 1986. 239 p. ; ISBN 3-87959-263-2 LC Card 86-201702
HC286.5 .W85 1986

Ludwig, Heinrich, 1942- Kirchen kämpfen mit . Mainz , 1981. 106 p. : ISBN 3-7867-0873-8 LC Card 81-188986 DDC 261.8/34562/094343 19
HD6338.2.G32 S634 1981
NYPL [JLD 86-2786]

Ludwig, Heinz. Parsche, Rüdiger. Die Belastung der Einkünfte aus nichtselbständiger Arbeit mit Einkommensteuern und Sozialabgaben in den EG-Ländern und in Schweden /. München , 1981. 2 v. ; LC Card 83-115269
HJ4719 .P37 1981

Ludwig, Heinz-Georg. Kirchen kämpfen mit . Mainz , 1981. 106 p. : ISBN 3-7867-0873-8 LC

Card 81-188986 DDC 261.8/34562/094343 19
HD6338.2.G32 S634 1981
NYPL [JLD 86-2786]

Ludwig Mond and the British alkali industry /. Lischka, J. R. (Johannes Richard), 1933- New York , 1985. 233 p. ; ISBN 0-8240-6686-3 (alk. paper) : LC Card 84-46006 DDC 338.4/7673725/0924 19
HD9660.A43 G75 1985
NYPL [JSD 86-547]

LUDWIGSHAFEN AM RHEIN (GERMANY) - COMMERCE - HISTORY.
Breunig, Willi. Vom Handelsplatz zur Industriestadt . Ludwigshafen am Rhein , 1986. 151 p. : ISBN 3-924667-13-6 LC Card 87-135540 DDC 338.0943/43 19
HC289.L95 B74 1986

LUDWIGSHAFEN AM RHEIN (GERMANY) - ECONOMIC CONDITIONS.
Breunig, Willi. Vom Handelsplatz zur Industriestadt . Ludwigshafen am Rhein , 1986. 151 p. : ISBN 3-924667-13-6 LC Card 87-135540 DDC 338.0943/43 19
HC289.L95 B74 1986

LUDWIGSHAFEN AM RHEIN (GERMANY) - INDUSTRIES - HISTORY.
Breunig, Willi. Vom Handelsplatz zur Industriestadt . Ludwigshafen am Rhein , 1986. 151 p. : ISBN 3-924667-13-6 LC Card 87-135540 DDC 338.0943/43 19
HC289.L95 B74 1986

Lübbe, Hermann. Der Wertewandel und die Arbeitsmoral / Hermann Lübbe. Köln : Arbeitgeberverband der Metallindustrie, [1984] 55 p. ; 19 cm. Bibliography of works by H. Lübbe: p. 53. ISBN 3-88575-025-2 LC Card 84-197999
1. Work ethic - Germany (West). I. Title.
HD8451 .L83 1984

Lübecker Weinhandel : Kultur- und wirtschaftsgeschichtliche Studien / herausgegeben von Elisabeth Spies-Hankammer. Lübeck : [Senat der Hansestadt Lübeck, Amt für Kultur], 1985. 260 p. : ill. ; 30 cm. (Veröffentlichungen des Senats der Hansestadt Lübeck, Amt für Kultur. Reihe B . Heft 6) Includes bibliographical references. ISBN 3-924214-27-1 LC Card 86-145675
1. Wine industry - Germany (West) - Lübeck - History. 2. Lübeck (Germany) - Economic conditions. I. Spies-Hankammer, Elisabeth. II. Series: Veröffentlichung des Senats der Hansestadt Lübeck, Amt für Kultur. Reihe B , Heft 6.
HD9383.8.L82 L82 1985

Lücke, Wolfgang, 1926- Industrielles Management . Göttingen , c1986. vi, 276 p., [1] leaf of plates : ISBN 3-525-13182-8 LC Card 87-118224 DDC 658 19
HD35 .I555 1986

LÜCKE, WOLFGANG, 1926-
Industrielles Management . Göttingen , c1986. vi, 276 p., [1] leaf of plates : ISBN 3-525-13182-8 LC Card 87-118224 DDC 658 19
HD35 .I555 1986

Luedde-Neurath, Richard. Import controls and export-oriented development : a reassessment of the South Korean case / Richard Luedde-Neurath. Boulder : Westview Press, 1986. xiv, 249 p. ; 23 cm. (Westview special studies on East Asia) Includes index. Bibliography: p. 221-240. ISBN 0-8133-7080-9 : LC Card 85-10459 DDC 382/.3/095195 19
1. Import quotas - Korea (Republic). 2. Tariff - Korea (South). 3. Nontariff trade barriers - Korea (Republic). 4. Foreign trade promotion - Korea (Republic). 5. Free trade and protection - Protection. I. Title. II. Series.
HF1602.5 .L84 1985 *NYPL [JLE 86-1557]*

Luehrmann, Arthur.
AppleWorks data bases : a hands-on guide / Arthur Luehrmann, Herbert Peckham. Gilroy, Calif. : Computer Literacy Press, c1987. viii, 159 p. : ill. ; 28 cm. Includes index. A hands-on manual on how to use the data base program of a software package called AppleWorks which, though primarily for junior high school classes, may also be used by adults. ISBN 0-941681-03-3 (pbk.) : LC Card 87-11734 DDC 005.36/9 19
1. AppleWorks (Computer program) - Juvenile literature. 2. Business - Data processing - Juvenile literature. I. Peckham, Herbert D. II. Title.
HF5548.4.A68 L838 1987

AppleWorks spreadsheets : a hands-on guide / Arthur Luehrmann, Herbert Peckham. Gilroy, Calif. : Computer Literacy Press, c1987. viii, 152 p. ; 28 cm. Includes index. A manual for using the spreadsheet program of the AppleWorks software package. ISBN 0-941681-05-X (pbk.) : LC Card 87-11745 DDC 005.36/9 19
1. AppleWorks (Computer program) - Juvenile literature. 2. Electronic spreadsheets - Juvenile literature. 3. Business - Data processing - Juvenile literature. I. Peckham, Herbert D. II. Title.
HF5548.4.A68 L847 1987

Lütkenhorst, Wilfried. Kraus, Willy. The economic development of the Pacific Basin . New York , London , 1986. x, 180 p., [1] leaf of plates : ISBN 0-312-00452-4 (alk. paper) : LC Card 86-26292 DDC 338.95 19
HF1591 .K73 1986

Lützeler, Paul Michael. Western Europe in transition . Baden-Baden , 1986. 223 p. : ISBN 3-7890-1220-3 LC Card 87-136015 DDC 341.24/22 19
HC241.25.G3 W47 1986

Luffman, George A. Business policy . Oxford, UK , New York, NY, USA , 1987. viii, 208 p. : ISBN 0-631-15545-7 : LC Card 87-722 DDC 658.4/012 19
HD30.28 .B86 1987

Lüftl, Walter. Martin, Paul C. (Paul Christoph), 1939- Die Pleite . München , c1984. 416 p. : ISBN 3-7844-7145-5 : LC Card 85-188703
HJ8011 .M36 1984

Lugano. International Foundation Humanum. see **International Foundation Humanum.**

O lugar do negro na força de trabalho /. Oliveira, Lúcia Elena Garcia de. Rio de Janeiro , 1983. 86 p. ; ISBN 85-24-00024-4 LC Card 86-129924
HD8288.5.B55 O45 1983

Lugossy, Györgyi. Szándékok és lehetőségek : Somogy megyében végzett felmérés tapasztalatai a termelőszövetkezetekben dolgozó fiatalok mozgáspályáiról / Lugossy Györgyi. Budapest : Agrárgazdasági Kutató Intézet, 1985. 85 p. : map ; 28 cm. (Agrárgazdasági Kutató Intézet, 0209-5696 . 1985/14) Bibliography: p. 81-85. ISBN 963-491-215-X LC Card 86-199350
1. Collective farms - Hungary - Somogy Megye - Officials and employees. 2. Youth - Employment - Hungary - Somogy Megye. I. Series: Agrárgazdasági Kutató Intézet (Series) , 1985/14. II. Title.
HD1492.H82 S665 1985

LUHMANN, NIKLAS.
Hermann, Ursula. Die Implementierung betrieblicher Rationalisierungshandlungen und der personelle Widerstand . Göttingen , c1984. xx, 356 p. : ISBN 3-525-12558-5 : LC Card 84-218331
HD58.8 .H48 1984

Luihn, Hans. Arbeid og samfunn : arbeidsmarkedspolitikk i Norge gjennom 100 år / Hans Luihn. [Oslo] : NKS-Forlaget, c1986. 372 p. : ill. ; 25 cm. ISBN 82-508-0574-7 : LC Card 87-157793
1. Manpower policy - Norway. 2. Labor supply - Norway. 3. Norway - Economic conditions. I. Title.
HD5800.A6 L85 1986

Lukács, Lajos. Szövetkezeti gazdálkodás elemzése / Lukács Lajos, Rákosi Miklós. Budapest : OKISZ Oktatási Központ, 1983. 155 p. : ill. ; 30 cm. (Ipari Szövetkezetek Országos Tanácsa Oktatási Központ kiadványa) ISBN 963-03-2028-2 (Magy. nemz. bibl.) LC Card 85-184472
1. Cooperative societies - Hungary - Accounting. I. Rákosi, Miklós. II. Title. III. Series.
HF5686.C67 L84 1983

Luk'ianov, V. V. Bezopasnost' dorozhnogo dvizheniia / V.V. Luk'ianov. Moskva : "Transport", 1978. 244, [4] p. ; 22 cm. Bibliography: p. [246] LC Card 81-166116
1. Transportation, Automotive - Soviet Union - Safety measures. I. Title.
HE5675.A6 L84 1978

Lula sem censura . Lula, 1945- Petrópolis [Brazil] , 1981. 101 p. ; *NYPL [JLC 86-389]*

Lula, 1945- Lula sem censura : "e aí a peãozada partiu pro pau" / edição e apresentação Altino Dantas Junior. Petrópolis [Brazil] : Editora Vozes, 1981. 101 p. ; 18 cm.
1. Lula, 1945-. 2. Trade-unions - Metal-workers - Brazil. 3. Trade-unions - Brazil. I. Dantas Junior, Altino. II. Title. *NYPL [JLC 86-389]*

LULA, 1945-
Lula, 1945- Lula sem censura . Petrópolis [Brazil] , 1981. 101 p. ; *NYPL [JLC 86-389]*

Luling, Virginia. Ethiopia's bitter medicine, settling for disaster . London , 1986. 55 p. : ISBN 0-946592-01-2 (pbk.) LC Card 86-232852 DDC 333.3/1/63
HD979.Z63 E74 1986

Lullies, Veronika. Weltz, Friedrich. Innovation im Büro . Frankfurt , New York , c1983. 343 p. ; ISBN 3-593-32724-4 LC Card 83-243001
HF5548.115 .W44 1983

LUMBER INDUSTRY AND TRADE. see **LUMBER TRADE.**

LUMBER TRADE - ALASKA.
Pierce, Brad. The timber industry in interior Alaska . [Juneau] [1986] 65 p. ; LC Card 86-621755 DDC 338.1/7498/09798 19
HD9757.A7 P54 1986

Van Patten, Jo. Alaska's commercial forest resource /. Juneau, Alaska [1986] v, 29 p. : LC Card 86-622970 DDC 333.75/09798 19
HD9757.A7 V36 1986

LUMBER TRADE - ARGENTINA - SANTIAGO DEL ESTERO (PROVINCE) - HISTORY.
Dargoltz, Raúl E. (Raúl Eduardo) La alianza anglo argentina . Buenos Aires [1983] 168 p. : LC Card 84-117468
HD9764.A73 S353 1983

LUMBER TRADE - CONGRESSES.
World trade in forest products, 2 /. Seattle , c1986. xi, 362 p. : ISBN 0-295-96337-9 LC Card 86-234388 DDC 382/.41498 19
HD9750.5 .W67 1986

LUMBER TRADE - FINLAND.
Juvonen, Risto. Sahateollisuus /. [Helsinki] . 290 p. : ISBN 951-859-690-5 LC Card 86-231276
HD9765.F4 J68 1986

LUMBER TRADE - GERMANY (WEST) - AUTOMATION.
Jordan, Reinhard, d. 1986. Holzwirtschaft im Wandel . Köln , c1986. viii, 163 p. : ISBN 3-7663-0977-3 LC Card 86-211012 DDC 338.4/5674/0943 19
HD9763.5 .J67 1986

LUMBER TRADE - IDAHO - HISTORY.
Petersen, Keith. Company town . Pullman, Wash. , Moscow, Idaho , 1987. xix, 284 p., [32] p. of plates : ISBN 0-87422-036-X (alk. paper) : LC Card 87-14980 DDC 307.7/67/0979686 19
HD9759.P63 P47 1987

LUMBER TRADE - ITALY - LECCO - HISTORY - 18TH CENTURY.
Sala, Edmondo. All'origine della borghesia lecchese . Lecco [1983] 83 p. : LC Card 85-190056
HD9765.I72 L437 1983

LUMBER TRADE - MANAGEMENT.
Sierila, Pentti, 1934- Corporate planning and strategies in forest industries /. Atlanta, GA, USA , c1987. vii, 138 p. : ISBN 0-89852-441-5 (pbk.) LC Card 87-50439 DDC 634.9/8/068 19
HD9750.5 .S54 1987

LUMBER TRADE - NEW HAMPSHIRE.
Nevel, Robert L. The timber industries of New Hampshire and Vermont . Broomall, Pa. , 1986. 56 p. : LC Card 86-601144 DDC 338.1/7498/09742 19
HD9757.N4 N48 1986

LUMBER TRADE - NEW ZEALAND - STATISTICS.

LUMBER TRADE - PLANNING.
Sierila, Pentti, 1934- Corporate planning and strategies in forest industries /. Atlanta, GA, USA , c1987. vii, 138 p. : ISBN 0-89852-441-5 (pbk.) LC Card 87-50439 DDC 634.9/8/068 19
HD9750.5 .S54 1987

LUMBER TRADE - SOUTHERN STATES.
Grupp, Monika. Entwicklung und sozio-ökonomische Bedeutung der holzverarbeitenden Industrien im Südosten der Vereinigten Staaten von Amerika /. Berlin , 1981, c1982. xii, 187, [30] p., [5] folded leaves of plates : ISBN 3-496-00301-4 LC Card

86-217598
HD9757.A13 G78 1982

LUMBER TRADE - SOUTHERN STATES - HISTORY.
Mayor, Archer H. Southern timberman . Athens , c1988. p. cm. ISBN 0-8203-0999-0 (alk. paper) LC Card 87-22897 DDC 338.7/63498/0975 19
HD9760.B83 M39 1988

LUMBER TRADE - SWITZERLAND - CANTONS - STATISTICS.
Eidgenössische Betriebszählung 1985. Bern , 1986. 108 p. ; ISBN 3-303-07007-5 LC Card 87-407623 DDC 338.1/7498/09494021 19
HD9765.S92 E37 1986

LUMBER TRADE - UNITED STATES.
Ellefson, Paul V. U. S. wood-based industry . New York , 1984. xxv, 479 p. : ISBN 0-03-063698-1 (alk. paper) : LC Card 84-8278 DDC 338.1/7498/0973 19
HD9755 .45 1984 ***NYPL [JLE 85-706]***

LUMBER TRADE - UNITED STATES - STATISTICS.
Fuller, Bernard. Treated wood update . Lexington, Mass., USA (24 Hartwell Ave., Lexington 02173) , c1985. iii, 121 p. : LC Card 86-201219 DDC 381/.45674/0973 19
HD9754 .F85 1985

LUMBER TRADE - VERMONT.
Nevel, Robert L. The timber industries of New Hampshire and Vermont . Broomall, Pa. , 1986. 56 p. : LC Card 86-601144 DDC 338.1/7498/09742 19
HD9757.N4 N48 1986

LUMBER TRADE - WASHINGTON (STATE) - HISTORY.
Ficken, Robert E. The forested land . Durham, N.C. , Seattle , c1987. xv, 324 p., [8] p. of plates : ISBN 0-295-96416-2 LC Card 87-2214 DDC 338.4/7674/09797 19
HD9757.W2 F53 1987

LUMBERMEN - WASHINGTON (STATE) - HISTORY.
Ficken, Robert E. The forested land . Durham, N.C. , Seattle , c1987. xv, 324 p., [8] p. of plates : ISBN 0-295-96416-2 LC Card 87-2214 DDC 338.4/7674/09797 19
HD9757.W2 F53 1987

Lumley, James E. A.
How to get a mortgage in 24 hours / James E.A. Lumley. New York : Wiley, c1987. xvii, 205 p. ; 22 cm. Includes index. ISBN 0-471-85249-X LC Card 86-28930 DDC 332.7/2 19
1. Mortgage loans - United States. I. Title.
HG2040.15.U5 .L85 1987

Sell it by mail : making your product the one they buy / James E.A. Lumley. New York : Wiley, c1986. xviii, 382 p. : ill. ; 24 cm. Includes index. ISBN 0-471-87908-8 : LC Card 85-16362 DDC 658.8/4 19
1. Mail-order business. 2. Direct marketing. I. Title.
HF5466 .L85 1986 ***NYPL [JLE 86-3044]***

Luna, Augusto Goicochea. see **Luna, Paco.**

Luna, David Alejandro. Manual de historia económica de El Salvador / David Alejandro Luna. 2a ed., rev. y corr. San Salvador, El Salvador : Editorial Universitaria, 1986. 230 p. : ill. ; 17 cm. (Colección El Tiempo) Includes bibliographical references. LC Card 87-127350 DDC 330.97284/053 19
1. El Salvador - Economic conditions. I. Title.
HC148 .L85 1986

Luna, Francisco Vidal. Lima, José Luiz. Estatísticas básicas do setor agrícola no Brasil /. São Paulo , 1983- v. : LC Card 83-219032 DDC 338.1/0981 19
HD9014.B82 L55 1983 ***NYPL [JLL 86-432]***

Luna, Paco. Demografía de la Alpujarra : estructura y biodinámica / Paco Luna. [Granada] : Excma. Diputación Provincial de Granada : Universidad de Granada, [1984] 301 p., [3] leaves of plates : ill. ; 22 cm. Bibliography: p. 291-298. ISBN 84-338-0205-4 LC Card 85-221373
1. Alpujarras Region (Spain) - Population. I. Title.
HB3620.A45 L85 1984

Luna, Regina Celi Miranda Reis. A terra era liberta : um estudo da luta dos posseiros pela terra no Vale do Pindaré-Ma. / Regina Celi Miranda Reis Luna. São Luís, MA : Universidade Federal do Maranhão, 1985. xxvii, 146 p. : ill. ; 22 cm. (Coleção Ciências sociais. Série Questão agrária . 1) Bibliography: p. 139-146. LC Card 87-135907 DDC 333.3/0981/21 19
1. Land tenure - Brazil - Pindaré River Valley. 2. Agriculture - Economic aspects - Brazil - Pindaré River Valley. 3. Capitalism - Brazil - Pindaré River Valley. 4. Peasantry - Brazil - Pindaré River Valley. I. Title. II. Series.
HD499.P46 L86 1985

LUNCH ROOMS. see **RESTAURANTS, LUNCH ROOMS, ETC.**

Lund, John, 1960- Neu, C. R. (Carl Richard), 1949- Toward a profile of Soviet behavior in international financial markets /. Santa Monica, CA [1987] xv, 58 p. : ISBN 0-8330-0865-X (pbk.) LC Card 87-13084 DDC 332/.042/0947 19
HG3955 .N48 1987

Lund, Reinhard. Unemployment . Berlin , New York , 1987. xx, 353 p. : ISBN 0-89925-277-X : LC Card 87-24369 DDC 331.13/7 19
HD5701.3 .U53 1987

Lund, Robert T. Keeping America at work : strategies for employing the new technologies / Robert T. Lund, John A. Hansen. New York : Wiley, c1986. xi, 260 p. : ill. ; 24 cm. Includes index. Bibliography: p. 251-255. ISBN 0-471-81563-2 LC Card 85-17900 DDC 331.12/0973 19
1. Technological innovations - United States. 2. Labor supply - United States - Effect of technological innovations on. I. Hansen, John A. II. Title.
HD45 .L86 1985 ***NYPL [JLD 86-2101]***

Lundager, Jens. Schneider, Friedrich. The development of the shadow economies for Denmark, Norway, and Sweden . Aarhus, Denmark [1986] 46 p. : LC Card 86-215193 DDC 381 19
HD2346.S29 S35 1986

Lundborg, Per, 1950- The economics of export embargoes : the case of the US-Soviet grain suspension / Per Lundborg. New York, NY : Croom Helm in association with Methuen, c1987. xi, 127 p. : ill. ; 23 cm. Bibliography: p. 119-122. Includes index. ISBN 0-7099-4151-X : LC Card 86-29370 DDC 382/.4131/0947 19
1. Grain trade - United States - Econometric models. 2. Grain trade - Soviet Union - Econometric models. 3. Embargo - Economic aspects - United States - Econometric models. 4. Economic sanctions, American - Soviet Union - Econometric models. I. Title.
HD9035 .L86 1987

Lundh, Christer. Den svenska debatten om industriell demokrati 1919-1924 / Christer Lundh. Lund : Ekonomisk-historiska föreningen, 1987- v. <1> ; 23 cm. (Skrifter utgivna av Ekonomisk-historiska föreningen . vol. 49) Summary in English. Thesis (doctoral)--Universitetet i Lund, 1987. Added t.p. with thesis statement inserted. Bibliography: p. 581-598. CONTENTS. - 1. Debatten i Sverige. ISBN 91-85611-17-4 LC Card 87-151790
1. Management - Sweden - Employee participation - History. 2. Labor and laboring classes - Sweden - History. I. Series: Skrifter utgivna av Ekonomisk-historiska föreningen i Lund , 49. II. Title.
HD5660.S9 L87 1987

Lundin, A. Rolf. Holmquist, Carin, 1948- Förhandla mer räkna mindre /. Stockholm [1984] 124 p. : ISBN 91-38-90409-8 : LC Card 84-241380
HD30.22 .H65 1984

LÜNEBURG (GERMANY) - COMMERCE - HISTORY.
Heineken, Hermann. Der Salzhandel Lüneburgs mit Lübeck bis zum Anfang des 15. Jahrhunderts /. Vaduz , 1965. 150 p. ; LC Card 86-231350
HD9213.G43 L864 1965

LÜNEBURG (PRINCIPALITY) - GENEALOGY.
Schatz- und Zinsverzeichnisse des 15. Jahrhunderts aus dem Fürstentum Lüneburg . Hildesheim , 1942. 153 p. ; LC Card 87-409521 DDC 336.2/00943/59 19
HJ2110.5.L86 S3 1942

LÜNEBURG (PRINCIPALITY) - HISTORY - SOURCES.
Schatz- und Zinsverzeichnisse des 15. Jahrhunderts aus dem Fürstentum Lüneburg . Hildesheim , 1942. 153 p. ; LC Card 87-409521 DDC 336.2/00943/59 19
HJ2110.5.L86 S3 1942

Lung, E. Bauer, Helfried. Fahrradfreundliche Verkehrspolitik in Stadt und Land . Wien , 1984. 87 p. : LC Card 85-150945
HE5739.A9 B38 1984

Lungo, Mario.
El problema de la tierra urbana : un ensayo de síntesis teórica / Mario Lungo Uclés. Ciudad Universitaria Rodrigo Facio [Costa Rica] : Confederación Universitaria Centroamericana, Secretaría General, 1986. 42 p. ; 28 cm. (Cuadernos de investigación . no. 2) Includes bibliographical references. LC Card 87-127789 DDC 333.77/13 19
1. Land use, Urban. I. Series: Cuadernos de investigación (Confederación Universitaria Centroamericana) , #2. II. Title.
HD1391 .L86 1986

El terremoto de octubre de 1986 en San Salvador y la situación habitacional de los sectores populares / Mario Lungo Uclés. Ciudad Universitaria Rodrigo Facio [Costa Rica] : Confederación Universitaria Centroamericana, Secretaría General, 1987. 26 leaves ; 28 cm. (Cuadernos de investigación . #5) Includes bibliographical references. LC Card 87-125001 DDC 363.3/495 19
1. Poor - Housing - El Salvador - San Salvador. 2. Earthquakes - Economic aspects - El Salvador - San Salvador. I. Series: Cuadernos de investigación (Confederación Universitaria Centroamericana) , #5. II. Title.
HD7287.96.S22 S265 1987

LUNGS - DUST DISEASES - GOVERNMENT POLICY - UNITED STATES.
Barth, Peter S., 1937- The tragedy of black lung . Kalamazoo, MI , 1987. xi, 292 p. ; ISBN 0-88099-044-9 (pbk.) LC Card 87-8332 DDC 368.4/1 19
HD7264 .B37 1987

LUNGS - DUST DISEASES - LAW AND LEGISLATION - UNITED STATES.
Barth, Peter S., 1937- The tragedy of black lung . Kalamazoo, MI , 1987. xi, 292 p. ; ISBN 0-88099-044-9 (pbk.) LC Card 87-8332 DDC 368.4/1 19
HD7264 .B37 1987

L'unificazione monetaria e lo SME /. Masera, R. S. Bologna , c1980. 220 p. ; LC Card 82-150717 DDC 332.4/566/094 19
HG930.5.Z8 M37 1980 ***NYPL [JLD 87-902]***

Lunsford, E. Michael.
Macros, menus, and miracles for Lotus 1-2-3 / E. Michael Lunsford. New York : Wiley, c1987. xix, 234 p. : ill. ; 25 cm. Includes index. ISBN 0-471-85996-6 (pbk.) : LC Card 87-14285 DDC 005.36/9 19
1. Lotus 1-2-3 (Computer program). 2. Macro instructions (Electronic computers). 3. Business - Data processing. I. Title.
HF5548.4.L67 L86 1987

Power user's guide to 1-2-3 / E. Michael Lunsford, Peter Antoniak. San Francisco : Sybex, c1988. xx, 367 p. : ill. ; 23 cm. Includes index. ISBN 0-89588-421-6 (pbk.) LC Card 87-61528 DDC 005.36/9 19
1. Lotus 1-2-3 (Computer program). 2. Business - Data processing. I. Antoniak, Peter. II. Title. III. Title: Power user's guide to one-two-three.
HF5548.4.L67 L87 1988

Lupande Development Workshop (1983 : Nyamaluma Wildlife Conservation Camp)
Proceedings of the Lupande Development Workshop : an integrated approach to land use management in the Luangwa Valley, Zambia, held at Nyamaluma Wildlife Conservation Camp, Lupande Game Management Area, 19-22 September 1983 / hosted by National Parks and Wildlife Service of Zambia ; editor, D.B. Dalal-Clayton ; co-editor, D.M. Lewis ; for Interim Planning Group, Luangwa Development Project, Provincial Planning Unit. Chipata, Zambia : The Project, 1984. x, 121 p. : ill. ; 30 cm. "Document no. LDP.5.83." Includes bibliographies. LC Card 84-980605 DDC 333.73/17/096894 19
1. Land use - Zambia - Congresses. 2. Land use - Luangwa River Watershed (Zambia and Mozambique) - Congresses. 3. Wildlife refuges - Luangwa River Watershed (Zambia and Mozambique) - Congresses. I.

Dalal-Clayton, D. B. (D. Barry). II. Lewis, D. M. (Dale M.). III. Zambia. National Parks and Wildlife Service. IV. Luangwa Development Project (Zambia). V. Eastern Province (Zambia). Provincial Planning Unit. Interim Planning Group. VI. Title. VII. Title: Integrated approach to land use management in the Luangwa Valley.
HD993.Z8 L835 1983 ***NYPL [JLG 87-67]***

Lupton, Tom. Achieving change : a systematic approach / Tom Lupton and Ian Tanner. Aldershots, Hants, England ; Brookfield, Vt., U. S.A. : Gower, c1987. xv, 86 p. : ill. ; 23 cm. ISBN 0-566-02526-4 : LC Card 87-17665 DDC 658.4/06 19
1. Organizational effectiveness. 2. Problem solving. I. Tanner, Ian, 1946-. II. Title.
HD58.9 .L86 1987

Luque, Carlos Antonio. Martone, Celso L. (Celso Luiz) Mercado financeiro e ajustamento macroeconômico brasileiro, 1978-1985 /. São Paulo , 1986. 82 p. : LC Card 87-120453 DDC 332.4/981 19
HG835 .M375 1986

Lur´e, I͡Uliĭ Solomonovich. Podvig na pochtovoĭ marke . Moskva , 1985. 135 p. : LC Card 86-113767
HE6183.G47 P63 1985

Lured away . Ly-Tio-Fane Pineo, Huguette. Moka, Mauritius , 1984. 261 p. :
NYPL [JLD 87-587]

Lury, D. A. Casley, D. J. Data collection in developing countries /. Oxford [Oxfordshire] , New York , 1987. p. cm. ISBN 0-19-442425-1 (pbk.) : LC Card 87-12574 DDC 001.4/222/091724 19
HA31.2 .C37 1987

Lusaka Province (Zambia). Provincial Planning Unit. Towards self sufficiency : a blueprint for agricultural development in Lusaka Province. [Lusaka, Zambia?] : Provincial Planning Unit, Lusaka Province, [1984] 100 p., [14] leaves of plates : ill., maps ; 30 cm. Report from a seminar held on the 10th of July, 1984 at Mulungushi Hall in Lusaka. Cover title: Blueprint for agricultural development in Lusaka Province. "November 1984." Bibliography: p. 97-100. LC Card 86-980293 DDC 338.1/86894 19
1. Agriculture - Economic aspects - Zambia - Lusaka Province - Planning - Congresses. 2. Agriculture - Zambia - Lusaka Province - Planning - Congresses. 3. Agricultural development projects - Zambia - Lusaka Province - Planning - Congresses. I. Title. II. Title: Blueprint for agricultural development in Lusaka Province.
HD2131.5 .L87 1984

LUSAKA (ZAMBIA) - ECONOMIC CONDITIONS.
Kamya, Andrew, 1941- Factors affecting efficiency in the informal sector in Lusaka and Kitwe /. Lusaka , 1981. iii, 40 p. ; LC Card 87-980491
HD2346.Z292 L875 1981

LUSAKA (ZAMBIA) - STATISTICS, VITAL.
Interrelationships among infant and childhood mortality, socio-economic factors and fertility in Zambia . Lusaka , Addis Ababa [1984?] 300 p. : LC Card 87-105950 DDC 304.6/32/096894 19
HB1323.I42 Z335 1984

Lush, Minnie. California real estate exam guide / Minnie Lush, John W. Reilly, Paige Bovee Vitousek. Chicago : Longman Financial Services Pub., c1987. p. cm. ISBN 0-88462-591-5 LC Card 87-3290 DDC 333.33/09794 19
1. Real estate business - California - Examinations, questions, etc. 2. Real property - California - Examinations, questions, etc. 3. Real estate agents - Licenses - California. I. Reilly, John W. II. Vitousek, Paige Bovee. III. Title.
HD266.C2 L87 1987

Luskin, Donald L. Index options & futures : the complete guide / by Donald L. Luskin ; computer research by Patrick C. Carlyle. New York : Wiley, c1987. xi, 355 p. : ill. ; 24 cm. Bibliography: p. 345-346. ISBN 0-471-85464-6 LC Card 86-28189 DDC 332.63/222 19
1. Stock index futures. I. Carlyle, Patrick C. II. Title. III. Title: Index options and futures.
HG6043 .L87 1987

Lusk's Fairfax County, Virginia assessment directory : including Fairfax City & the city of Falls Church, by street address. Washington, D.C. (1824 Jefferson Pl., NW, Washington 20036) : Rufus S. Lusk & Son, 1986. 1251, [81] p. ; 28 cm. Cover title. LC Card 87-144674 DDC 333.33/2/09755291 19
1. Real property - Virginia - Fairfax County - Directories. 2. Fairfax County (Va.) - Directories. 3. Streets - Virginia - Fairfax County - Directories. I. Rufus S. Lusk & Son. II. Title: Fairfax County, Virginia assessment directory.
HD266.V82 F24 1986

Luskutov, V. B. Ėkonomicheskie svi͡azi i sovershenstvovanie khozi͡aĭstvennogo mekhanizma . Kursk , 1985. 107 p. ; LC Card 86-235039
HC340.I57 E37 1985

Luso Consult, Gesellschaft für Agrarentwicklung und Regionalplanung. Kooperationsführer Kamerun /. Köln , 1986. 70 p. : LC Card 87-408425 DDC 330.967/1104 19
HC995 .K66 1986

Lusterman, Seymour. Trends in corporate education and training / by Seymour Lusterman. New York, N.Y. : Conference Board, c1985. vii, 23 p. ; 28 cm. (Conference Board report. no. 870) ISBN 0-8237-0311-8 (pbk.) LC Card 87-106076 DDC 331.25/92/0973 19
1. Employees, Training of - United States. 2. Employer-supported education - United States. I. Title.
HF5549.5.T7 L86 1985

Lutfi, Muchtar. Environment, agriculture, and society in the Malay world /. Kyoto, Japan , 1986. ix, 177 p. : LC Card 86-201590 DDC 338.1/09595 19
HD2080.6 .E58 1986

Luthans, Fred. Real managers / Fred Luthans, Richard M. Hodgetts, Stuart A. Rosenkrantz. Cambridge, Mass. : Ballinger, c1988. xvi, 192 p. : ill. ; 24 cm. Bibliography: p. 179-183. Includes index. ISBN 0-88730-103-7 LC Card 87-19080 DDC 658.4 19
1. Management. 2. Executives. I. Hodgetts, Richard M. II. Rosenkrantz, Stuart A. III. Title.
HD31 .L865 1988

Luther, Norman Y., 1936- Consistent correction of census and vital registration data for Thailand, 1960-80 / Norman Y. Luther, Neramit Dhanasakdi, and Fred Arnold. Honolulu, Hawaii : East-West Population Institute, East-West Center, [1986] vii, 39 p. ; 24 cm. (Papers of the East-West Population Institute . 103) "December 1986." Bibliography: p. 37-39. ISBN 0-86638-089-2 (pbk.) : LC Card 86-32807 DDC 304.6/0723 19
1. Registers of births, etc. - Thailand. 2. Thailand - Census, 1960. 3. Thailand - Census, 1970. 4. Thailand - Census, 1980. 5. Thailand - Statistical services. I. Neramit Dhanasakdi, 1946-. II. Arnold, Fred. III. Title. IV. Series.
HA39.T4 L87 1986

Luther, William M. How to develop a business plan in 15 days / William M. Luther. New York, NY : AMACOM, c1987. xiii, 241 p. : ill. ; 24 cm. Includes index. ISBN 0-8144-5874-2 LC Card 86-47854 DDC 658.4/012 19
1. Corporate planning. I. Title.
HD30.28 .L88 1987

Lüthi, Ambros, 1938- Die wirtschaftliche Ungleichheit im Rentenalter in der Schweiz / Ambros Lüthi. Freiburg/Schweiz : Universitätsverlag, 1983. 229 p. : ill. ; 23 cm. (Freiburger Studien zur Verteilung von Einkommen und Vermögen . Bd. 2) Bibliography: p. 228-229. ISBN 3-7278-0282-0 : LC Card 83-163287
1. Old age pensions - Switzerland - Statistics. 2. Pensions - Switzerland - Statistics. 3. Income distribution - Switzerland - Statistics. 4. Age distribution (Demography) - Switzerland - Statistics. I. Title. II. Series.
HD7105.35.S9 L87 1983

Luthy, David H. Cherrington, J. Owen. Cost and managerial accounting /. St. Paul , c1988. p. cm. ISBN 0-314-25327-0 : LC Card 86-24753 DDC 657/.42 19
HF5686.C8 C475 1988

Lut´i͡anova, T. Metodicheskie polozhenii͡a po prognozirovanii͡u ėkonomicheskogo i sotsial´nogo razvitii͡a soi͡uznoĭ respubliki /. Riga , 1979. 275 p. : LC Card 81-215536
HC337.L3 M35 1979

Lutinier, Bruno. Cauwet, Martine. Images économiques des entreprises . Paris [1986] 41 p. ; ISBN 2-11-064902-X : LC Card 86-229455
HD9502.F72 C38 1986

Lütkepohl, Helmut.
Lutton, Thomas. Financial condition of the U. S. electric utility industry. [Washington] [1986] xviii, 82 p. : ***NYPL [JLF 86-1386]***

Luttrell, William L. Post-capitalist industrialization : planning economic independence in Tanzania / William L. Luttrell. New York : Praeger, 1986. xv, 189 p. : maps ; 25 cm. Includes index. Bibliography: p. ISBN 0-275-92310-X : LC Card 86-9452 DDC 338.9678 19
1. Industry and state - Tanzania. 2. Industrialization. 3. Tanzania - Economic policy. 4. Tanzania - Industries. I. Title.
HD3616.T343 L88 1986
NYPL [JLE 87-351]

Lutz, Burkart, 1925- Der kurze Traum immerwährender Prosperität : eine Neuinterpretation der industriell-kapitalistischen Entwicklung im Europa des 20. Jahrhunderts / Burkart Lutz. Frankfurt/Main ; New York : Campus, c1984. 272 p. ; 21 cm. Bibliography: p. 268-272. ISBN 3-593-33418-6 LC Card 85-131822
1. Europe - Economic conditions - 20th century. 2. Europe - Industries - History - 20th century. 3. Business cycles - Europe - History - 20th century. 4. Capitalism - Europe - History - 20th century. I. Title.
HC240 .L88 1984

Lutz, Heinz Leo Müller- see **Müller-Lutz, Heinz Leo.**

Lutz, Richard John, 1947- Perspectives on methodology in consumer research /. New York , c1986. xi, 301 p. : ISBN 0-387-96238-7 : LC Card 85-26047 DDC 658.8/34 19
HF5415.3 .P464 1986 ***NYPL [JLE 86-4371]***

Lutz, Stefan. Die Körperschaftsteuer in der Europäischen Gemeinschaft : zur Harmonisierung des Satzes, des Systems und der Bemessungsgrundlage / Stefan Lutz. Pfaffenweiler : Centaurus-Verlagsgesellschaft, 1984. xii, 346 p. : ill. ; 21 cm. (Reihe Wirtschaftswissenschaften, 0177-283X . Bd. 12) Originally presented as the author's thesis (doctoral)--Johannes Gutenberg-Universität Mainz, 1984. Bibliography: p. 324-346. ISBN 3-89085-037-5 : LC Card 85-142851
1. Corporations - Taxation - European Economic Community countries. I. Series: Reihe Wirtschaftswissenschaften (Pfaffenweiler, Breisgau-Hochschwarzwald, Germany) , Bd. 12. II. Title.
HD2753.E8 L87 1984

Luukas, Ants.
[Majandi parteigrupid. Russian]
Partiĭnye gruppy v kolkhozakh i sovkhozakh / Ants Luukas ; [perevod s ėstonskogo L. Shera]. Tallin : "Eėsti raamat", 1984. 77 p., [8] p. of plates : ports. ; 17 cm. (Biblioteka sekretari͡a partorganizat͡sii) Translation of: Majandi parteigrupid. Includes bibliographical references. LC Card 87-115056
1. Collective farms - Estonia - Management. 2. State farms - Estonia - Management. 3. Party committees - Estonia. I. Title. II. Series.
HD1492.S652 E85517 1984

Luwel, A. Een economie in spanning : actuele bedenkingen / André Luwel.1e druk. Leuven : Acco, 1985. 168 p. ; 21 cm. Bibliography: p. 167-168. ISBN 90-334-1193-8 LC Card 86-123424
1. Economics. 2. Economic policy. 3. Belgium - Economic conditions. I. Title.
HB179.D8 L89 1985

Luxardo, Hervé. Rase campagne : la fin des communautés paysannes 1830-1914 / Hervé Luxardo. Paris : Aubier Montaigne, c1984. 253 p. : ill. ; 19 cm. ("Floréal," 0293-7476) Bibliography: p. 249-252. ISBN 2-7007-0376-6 : LC Card 85-101431
1. Peasantry - France - History. 2. France - Rural conditions. 3. France - Social conditions. I. Title. II. Series.
HD1536.F8 L893 1984

LUXURY.
Pinto, Isaac de, 1715-1787. [Selections. 1960.] O economista Isaac de Pinto, o seu "Tratado da circulação e do crédito," e outros escritos económicos /. Lisboa , 1960. 247 p. : LC Card 85-125396
HJ150 .P552 1960

Luzan, P. P.
Upravlenie v sisteme proizvodstvennykh otnosheniĭ /. Novosibirsk , 1974. 82 p. ; LC Card 83-120398
HD70.S63 U68 1974

Voprosy politicheskoĭ ėkonomii . Novosibirsk , 1973. 125 p. ; LC Card 81-131624
HD8526.5 .V674 1973

Luzerner historische Veröffentlichungen.
(Bd. 17) Schüpbach, Werner. Die Bevölkerung der Stadt Luzern 1850-1914 . Luzern , 1983. 323 p., [17] p. of plates : ISBN 3-7252-0432-2 LC Card 83-201416
HB3624.L8 S38 1983

LUZON (PHILIPPINES) - ECONOMIC CONDITIONS.
Cleto, Romeo B. The Ilocos and Cordillera provinces . Baguio City [Philippines] , Manila [1986] xvii, 265 p. : LC Card 87-111697 DDC 330.9599/1 19
HC457.L8 C56 1986

LUZON (PHILIPPINES) - SOCIAL CONDITIONS.
Cleto, Romeo B. The Ilocos and Cordillera provinces . Baguio City [Philippines] , Manila [1986] xvii, 265 p. : LC Card 87-111697 DDC 330.9599/1 19
HC457.L8 C56 1986

L'vov, Dmitriĭ Semenovich. Marek, A. I. (Aleksandr Isaevich) Nauchno-proizvodstvennye kompleksy . Moskva , 1985. 141, [3] p. : LC Card 86-118921
HC340.R4 M37 1985

Ly-Tio-Fane Pineo, Huguette. Lured away : the life history of Indian cane workers in Mauritius / Huguette Ly-Tio-Fane Pineo. Moka, Mauritius : Mahatma Gandhi Institute, 1984. 261 p. : ill., maps, ports. ; 22 cm. Bibliography: p. 211-261.
1. East Indians - Mauritius. 2. Sugarcane industry - Mauritius. 3. Sugar trade - Mauritius. 4. Alien labor - Mauritius. 5. Mauritius - Emigration and immigration. 6. India - Emigration and immigration. I. Title.
NYPL [JLD 87-587]

Lybeck, Johan A., 1944- Konstitutionella begränsningar i Riksdagens finansmakt : behov och tänkbara utformningar : rapport till Expertgruppen för studier i offentlig ekonomi. [Stockholm] : Finansdepartementet, [1984] 147 p. : ill. ; 21 cm. Includes bibliographies. "Ds Fi 1984:7." ISBN 91-38-08365-5 (Sve. bok.) : LC Card 84-240503
1. Finance, Public - Sweden. 2. Sweden - Economic policy. 3. Finance, Public - Law and legislation - Sweden. I. Sweden. Expertgruppen för studier i offentlig ekonomi. II. Title.
HJ1238 .L92 1984

Lydenberg, Steven D. Rating America's corporate conscience : a provocative guide to the companies behind the products you buy every day / Steven D. Lydenberg, Alice Tepper Marlin, Sean O'Brien Strub, and the Council on Economic Priorities. Reading, Mass. : Addison-Wesley, c1986. x, 499 p. : ill. ; 25 cm. Includes index. Bibliography: p. 473-480. ISBN 0-201-15886-8 : LC Card 86-8064 DDC 338.7/4/0973 19
1. Industry - Social aspects - United States. 2. Shopping - United States. I. Marlin, Alice Tepper. II. Strub, Sean O'Brien. III. Council on Economic Priorities. IV. Title.
HD60.5.U5 L93 1986
NYPL [*R-Econ. 87-1830]

Lykova, Tamara Nikolaevna. Zasluzhennyĭ rabotnik sel'skogo khoziaĭstva respubliki /. Moskva , 1986. 351 p. : LC Card 86-132613
HD1536.S65 Z37 1986

Lyn-Cook, Marlene. Marketing guidelines for Jamaica's non-traditional exports. [Miami, FL] : M. Lyn-Cook, [1986] 83 leaves : ill. ; 28 cm. Bibliography: leaves 74-83. LC Card 87-156503 DDC 382/.097292/073 19
1. Export marketing - Jamaica. 2. Jamaica - Commerce - United States. 3. United States - Commerce - Jamaica. I. Title.
HF1009.7.J25 L96 1986

Lynch, Christine M. (Christine Marie), 1962- The national directory of postcard deck media / compiled by Christine M. Lynch ; introduction and format by Edward W. Werz. Westbury, N.Y. : Asher-Gallant Press, c1987. ix, 238 p. ; 28 cm. Includes indexes. ISBN 0-87280-156-X (pbk.) LC Card 87-1071 DDC 659.13/3 19
1. Advertising, Direct-mail - United States - Directories. I. Title. II. Title: Postcard deck media.
HF5861 .L96 1987

Lynch, Gerald, 1908- Roughnecks, drillers, and tool pushers : thirty-three years in the oil fields / by Gerald Lynch ; introduction by Bobby Weaver.1st ed. Austin : University of Texas Press, 1987. xiv, 262 p. : ill. ; 24 cm. (Personal narratives of the West series) Includes index. ISBN 0-292-71553-6 LC Card 87-13857 DDC 331.7/6223382/0924 B 19
1. Lynch, Gerald, 1908-. 2. Petroleum workers - United States - Biography. 3. Petroleum industry and trade - United States - History - Sources. I. Title. II. Series.
HD8039.P42 L95 1987

LYNCH, GERALD, 1908-
Lynch, Gerald, 1908- Roughnecks, drillers, and tool pushers . Austin , 1987. xiv, 262 p. : ISBN 0-292-71553-6 LC Card 87-13857 DDC 331.7/6223382/0924 B 19
HD8039.P42 L95 1987

Lynch, John E. Economic adjustment and conversion of defense industries /. Boulder , 1987. xiv, 312 p. : ISBN 0-8133-7396-4 (pbk. : alk. paper) LC Card 87-50495 DDC 338.4/36234/0973 19
HC110.D4 E36 1987

Lynch, Terry, 1948- Kansas City Southern : route of the Southern Belle / by Terry Lynch & W.D. Caileff, Jr.1st ed. Boulder, Colo. : Pruett Pub. Co., c1987. 223 p. : ill. (some col.) ; 29 cm. Bibliography: p. 221. Includes index. ISBN 0-87108-735-9 LC Card 87-25288 DDC 385/.065/76 19
1. Kansas City Southern Railway - History. I. Caileff, W. D. (Warren D.), 1933-. II. Title.
HE2791.K17 L96 1987

Lynd, D. Picot, W. Garnett. The changing labour market for postsecondary graduates, 1975-1984 /. Ottawa , c1987. 86, 94 p. : ISBN 0-660-52896-7 (pbk.) : LC Card 87-169612 DDC 331.11/423 19
HD6278.C3 P52 1987

Lyndon Baines Johnson Library. The War on poverty, 1964-1968 [microform] . Frederick, MD , c1986- microfilm reel ISBN 0-89093-495-9 (microfilm : set) : LC Card 87-10510 DDC 338.973 19
HC110 .P63

LYNDON BAINES JOHNSON LIBRARY.
The War on poverty, 1964-1968 [microform] . Frederick, MD , c1986- microfilm reel ISBN 0-89093-495-9 (microfilm : set) : LC Card 87-10510 DDC 338.973 19
HC110 .P63

Lyndon Baines Johnson Presidential Archival Depository. see **Lyndon Baines Johnson Library.**

Lyndon, Neil. Hammer, Armand, 1897- Hammer /. New York , c1987. 544 p., [32] p. of plates : ISBN 0-399-13275-9 LC Card 86-30289 DDC 338.092/4 B 19
HC102.5.H35 A3 1987

Lynn, Leonard H. Organizing business : trade associations in America and Japan / Leonard H. Lynn, Timothy J. McKeown. Washington, D.C. : American Enterprise Institute for Public Policy Research, c1988. xviii, 191 p. ; 24 cm. (AEI studies . 459) Includes bibliographies and index. ISBN 0-8447-3629-5 (alk. paper) LC Card 87-17468 DDC 061/.3 19
1. Trade and professional associations - United States. 2. Trade and professional associations - Japan. I. McKeown, Timothy J., 1951-. II. Title. III. Series.
HD2425 .L96 1988

LYON (FRANCE) - COMMERCE - HISTORY.
Lyon, l'argent, le commerce et la soie /. Lyon , c1986. 138 p. : ISBN 2-904638-63-6 : LC Card 86-184131
HC278.L9 L96 1986

LYON (FRANCE) - ECONOMIC CONDITIONS.
Lyon, l'argent, le commerce et la soie /. Lyon , c1986. 138 p. : ISBN 2-904638-63-6 : LC Card 86-184131
HC278.L9 L96 1986

LYON (FRANCE) - HISTORY.
Lyon, l'argent, le commerce et la soie /. Lyon , c1986. 138 p. : ISBN 2-904638-63-6 : LC Card 86-184131
HC278.L9 L96 1986

Lyon, l'argent, le commerce et la soie / [direction, coordination, photographies, Albert Roguenant ; recherches et textes, Henri Hours, Olivier Zeller]. Lyon : Manufacture, c1986. 138 p. : ill. (some col.) ; 20 x 24 cm. (Archives du Lyonnais) Bibliography: p. 138. ISBN 2-904638-63-6 : LC Card 86-184131
1. Lyon (France) - Economic conditions. 2. Lyon (France) - History. 3. Banks and banking - France - Lyon - History. 4. Lyon (France) - Commerce - History. 5. Silk industry - France - Lyon - History. I. Roguenant, Albert. II. Hours, Henri. III. Zeller, Olivier. IV. Series.
HC278.L9 L96 1986

Lyon, Phil, 1948- Nearing retirement : a study of late working lives / Phil Lyon. Aldershot, Hants ; Brookfield, Vt., USA : Avebury, c1987. xix, 196 p. : ill. ; 23 cm. Bibliography: p. 186-196. ISBN 0-566-05233-4 : LC Card 86-25680 DDC 331.3/94/0941 19
1. Age and employment - Great Britain - Case studies. 2. Retirement - Great Britain - Case studies. I. Title.
HD6283.G7 L86 1987

Lyons. Centre régional de documentation pédagogique. see **Centre régional de documentation pédagogique de Lyon.**

Lyons, John, 1940- Guts : advertising from the inside out / John Lyons. New York, NY : AMACOM, c1987. viii, 317 p. : ill. ; 26 cm. ISBN 0-8144-5537-9 LC Card 86-47816 DDC 659.1 19
1. Advertising. I. Title.
HF5823 .L92 1987

Lyons, Paula. Life & health insurance : principles & practice. Chicago : Longman Financial Services Pub., c1988. xvi, 351 p. : ill. ; 28 cm. ISBN 0-88462-707-1 (pbk.) LC Card 87-18506 DDC 368.3/00973 19
1. Insurance, Life - United States - Outlines, syllabi, etc. 2. Insurance, Health - United States - Outlines, syllabi, etc. 3. Insurance, Life - Law and legislation - United States - Outlines, syllabi, etc. 4. Insurance, Health - Law and legislation - United States - Outlines, syllabi, etc. I. Title. II. Title: Life and health insurance.
HG8951 .L98 1988

Lyons, Thomas P. Economic integration and planning in Maoist China / Thomas P. Lyons. New York : Columbia University Press, 1987. xiii, 376 p. ; 25 cm. Originally presented as the author's thesis (doctoral)--Cornell, 1983. Bibliography: p. 347-367. Includes index. ISBN 0-231-06542-6 LC Card 87-5414 DDC 338.951 19
1. China - Economic conditions - 1949-. 2. China - Economic policy - 1949-. I. Title.
HC427.9 .L96 1987

Lysestøl, Peder Martin. Jugoslavia : et forsøk på sosialisme / Peder Martin Lysestøl. [Oslo] : Oktober, c1985. 179 p. : ill. ; 21 cm. Bibliography: p. 163-[165] ISBN 82-7094-421-1 LC Card 86-204691
1. Yugoslavia - Economic conditions - 1945-. 2. Socialism - Yugoslavia. I. Title.
HC407 .L97 1985

Lysikova, L. Ė. (Līūdmila Ėrazmovna) Baskin, A. I. (Arkadiĭ Isaakovich) Planirovanie potrebnosti v material'nykh resursakh na predpriiātii /. Kiev , 1983. 48 p. ; LC Card 83-243488
HD39.5 .B37 1983

Lyson, Thomas A. The changing structure of South Carolina agriculture since 1959 / by Thomas A. Lyson and Georganne L. McMullen. Clemson, S.C. : South Carolina Agricultural Experiment Station, Clemson University, [1986] 29 p. : ill. ; 22 cm. (Bulletin / South Carolina Agricultural Experiment Station . 655) "February 1986." Bibliography: p. 29. LC Card 87-620716 DDC 338.1/09757 19
1. Agriculture - Economic aspects - South Carolina. I. McMullen, Georganne L. (Georganne Louise), 1959-. II. Series: Bulletin / South Carolina Agricultural Experiment Station , 655. III. Title.
HD1775.S6 L97 1986

The M & E business studies series, 0266-4917.
Bell, G. J. (Graham J.) The business of transport /. Plymouth [Devon] , 1984. viii, 344 p. : ISBN 0-7121-2406-3 (pbk.) LC Card 84-170770 DDC 380.5 19
HE151 .B436 1984 ***NYPL [JLD 87-86]***

M & E professional studies. The Regulatory framework of accounting /. Estover, Plymouth , 1985. [12], 391 p. : ISBN 0-7121-0491-7 *NYPL [JLF 87-84]*

M. D. P. see **Magyar Dolgozók Pártja.**

M. I. C. see **Management Information Corporation.**

The M. L. Seidman memorial town hall lecture series. News and views from National Public Radio /. Memphis, Tenn. , 1989. p. cm. LC Card 87-23331 DDC 384.54/06/073 19
HE8697.P6 N48 1989

M. L. Seidman town hall lectures. see **The M. L. Seidman memorial town hall lecture series.**

M. S. ABC de la economía política / M.S. y C.C.O. Madrid : Editorial Popular, [1964] 205 p., [1] folded leaf of plates : ill. ; 17 cm. Includes bibliographical references. LC Card 85-106062
1. Economics. 2. Economic policy. 3. National income. 4. Wages. 5. Consumption (Economics). I. C. C. O. II. Title.
HB178.5 .M25 1964

M. SZ. M. P. see **Magyar Szocialista Munkáspárt.**

Maailma terveysjärjestö. see **World Health Organization.**

Maas, Kenneth M. Availability of land for mineral exploration and development in northern Alaska, 1986 / by Kenneth M. Maas. [Washington, D.C.] : U. S. Dept. of the Interior, Bureau of Mines : For sale by the Supt. of Docs., U. S. G.P.O., [1987] iv, 34 p. : ill., maps ; 28 cm. (Special publication / United States Department of the Interior, Bureau of Mines) Maps on 33 folded leaves, inserted. Bibliography: p. 13. LC Card 86-607920 DDC 333.73 19
1. Mineral lands - Alaska. 2. Mines and mineral resources - Alaska. 3. Mineral industries - Government policy - Alaska. 4. Land use - Government policy - Alaska. I. Series: Special publication (United States. Bureau of Mines). II. Title.
HD243.A3 M32 1987

Maasoumi, Esfandiar, 1950- Sargan, John Denis. Contributions to econometrics /. Cambridge , New York , 1988- p. cm. ISBN 0-521-32570-6 (v. 1) LC Card 87-6328 DDC 330/.028 19
HB139 .S37 1988

Maass, Arthur. Reuss, Martin. Interview with Professor Arthur Maass /. Fort Belvoir, Va. , 1987. p. cm. LC Card 86-32033 DDC 333.91/15/0973 19
HD1694.A5 R46 1987

Maass, Citha Doris. Indien, Nepal, Sri Lanka : Süd-Süd-Beziehungen zwischen Symmetrie und Dependenz / von Citha Doris Maass. Wiesbaden : F. Steiner, 1982. xxi, 380 p. ; 24 cm. (Beiträge zur Südasienforschung. Bd. 69) Summary in English. Bibliography: p. 362-375. ISBN 3-515-03802-7 LC Card 86-214318
1. India - Foreign economic relations - Nepal. 2. Nepal - Foreign economic relations - India. 3. India - Foreign economic relations - Sri Lanka. 4. Sri Lanka - Foreign economic relations - India. 5. Nepal - Dependency on India. 6. Sri Lanka - Dependency on India. I. Title. II. Series.
HF1590.15.N4 M33 1982

Maatschappelijke participatie van ouderen en volkshuisvesting . (3) Houben, Piet. Ouderenhuisvesting in 'n emancipatieperspectief /. Delft , 1985. 178 p. : ISBN 90-6275-118-0 : LC Card 86-149527
HD7287.92.N4 H683 1985
NYPL [JLE 86-3902]

Mabbs-Zeno, Carl. Nigeria : an export market profile / Carl Mabbs-Zeno. Washington, D.C. : U. S. Dept. of Agriculture, Economic Research Service in cooperation with the Foreign Agricultural Service : Additional copies can be purchased from the Supt. of Docs., U. S. G.P.O., [1986] vi, 54 p. : ill., map ; 28 cm. (Foreign agricultural economic report . no. 218) Cover title. "April 1986"--P. i. Bibliography: p. 42-47. Includes index. LC Card 86-601597 DDC 382/.41/09669 19
1. Produce trade - Nigeria. 2. Agriculture - Economic aspects - Nigeria. 3. Agriculture and state - Nigeria. 4. Nigeria - Commerce - United States. 5. United States - Commerce - Nigeria. I. United States. Dept. of Agriculture. Economic Research Service. II. United States. Foreign Agricultural Service. III. Title. IV. Series.
HD9017.N52 M3 1986

Mabro, Robert. The Market for North Sea crude oil /. Oxford , New York , 1986. xxxii, 341 p., [1] leaf of plates : ISBN 0-19-730001-4 LC Card 86-217261 DDC 338.2/7282/0916336 19
HD9581.N64 M37 1986

Mabud, Mohammed A. (Mohammed Abdul) Women's development, income, and fertility / Mohammed A. Mabud. Dhaka : External Evaluation Unit, Planning Commission and Canadian International Development Agency, 1985. xi, 180 p. ; 23 cm. Includes index. "March 1985." Bibliography: p. 174-178. LC Card 85-903972 DDC 305.4/09549/2 19
1. Women - Bangladesh - Social conditions. 2. Women - Employment - Bangladesh. 3. Fertility, Human - Bangladesh. I. Title.
HQ1745.6 .M33 1985 NYPL [JLD 86-2067]

Mac Lean U., Roberto. La coerción económica internacional : notas para su definición / Roberto Mac Lean U.[1a ed]. [Lima, Perú] : Centro Peruano de Estudios Internacionales, [1986] 28 p. ; 21 cm. (Documentos de trabajo . 7) Includes bibliographical references. LC Card 87-142994 DDC 337 19
1. International economic relations. I. Series: Documentos de trabajo (Centro Peruano de Estudios Internacionales) , 7. II. Title.
HF1411 .M218 1986

Mac Multiplan /. Lenfest, David. Blue Ridge Summit, Pa. , c1984. ix, 259 p. : ISBN 0-8306-0851-6 : LC Card 84-8796 DDC 001.64/25 19
HF5548.4.M74 L46 1984
NYPL [JSE 86-1870]

McAdam, Terry W.
[Careers in the nonprofit sector]
Doing well by doing good : the first complete guide to careers in the nonprofit sector / Terry W. McAdam. New York, N.Y., U. S.A. : Penguin Books, 1988, c1986. xxi, 201 p. : ill. ; 20 cm. Reprint. Originally published: Careers in the nonprofit sector. Washington, D.C. : Taft Group, c1986. Bibliograpy: p. 177-183. ISBN 0-14-046820-X (pbk.) LC Card 87-23602 DDC 650.1/4 19
1. Vocational guidance. 2. Job hunting. 3. Career changes. 4. Corporations, Nonprofit. I. Title.
HF5381 .M12 1988

McAdams, Tony. Law, business, and society / Tony McAdams ; contributing authors, Amy Gershenfeld Donnella, James Freeman. Plano, Tex. : Business Publications, 1986. xvi, 662, 52 p. : ill. ; 25 cm. Includes bibliographical references and index. ISBN 0-256-03070-7 LC Card 85-73323 DDC 346.73/065 347.30665 19
1. Business enterprises - United States. 2. Trade regulation - United States. 3. Business ethics - United States. 4. Industry - Social aspects - United States. I. Title.
KF1355 .M28 1986 NYPL [JLE 87-891]

MCADOO, WILLIAM GIBBS, 1863-1941. Shook, Dale N. William G. McAdoo and the development of national economic policy, 1913-1918 /. New York , 1987. 427 p. ; ISBN 0-8240-8092-0 (alk. paper) : LC Card 87-23766 DDC 338.973 19
HC106.2 .S55 1987

McAfee, R. Bruce. Organizational behavior : a manager's view / R. Bruce McAfee, Paul J. Champagne. St. Paul : West Pub. Co., c1987. xviii, 489 p. : ill. ; 26 cm. Includes bibliographies and index. ISBN 0-314-93201-1 : LC Card 86-24745 DDC 658.3 19
1. Organizational behavior. 2. Personnel management. I. Champagne, Paul J. II. Title.
HD58.7 .M38 1987

McAllister, John P. Orsini, Larry L. World accounting /. New York, NY (11 Penn Plaza, New York 10001) , 1987- c1986- 2 v. (loose-leaf) ; LC Card 86-73012 DDC 657 19
HF5611 .O75 1987

McAlpine, Pamela J. The air freight industry : shipper preferences and emerging trends / prepared by Pamela J. McAlpine. Menlo Park, CA (333 Ravenswood Ave., Menlo Park 94025) : SRI International, Business Intelligence Program, c1986. 12 leaves ; 28 cm. LC Card 87-402973 DDC 387.7/44/0973 19
1. Aeronautics, Commercial - United States - Freight. 2. Consumers' preferences - United States. I. Business Intelligence Program (SRI International). II. Title.
HE9788.5.U5 M37 1986

McAnelly, James R.
Business mathematics for college / James R. McAnelly, Patricia L. McAnelly. St. Paul : West Pub. Co., c1987. [584] p. : ill. ; 28 cm. Includes index. ISBN 0-314-93202-X (pbk.) LC Card 86-26670 DDC 512/.1 19
1. Business mathematics. I. McAnelly, Patricia L. II. Title.
HF5691 .M375 1987

Business mathematics for college : instructor's edition / James R. McAnelly, Patricia L. McAnelly. St. Paul : West Pub. Co., c1987. xx, 531, [30] p. : col. ill. ; 28 cm. Includes index. ISBN 0-314-26207-5 (pbk.) LC Card 86-26681 DDC 512/.1 19
1. Business mathematics. I. McAnelly, Patricia L. II. Title.
HF5691 .M375 1987b

McAnelly, Patricia L.
McAnelly, James R. Business mathematics for college . St. Paul , c1987. xx, 531, [30] p. : ISBN 0-314-26207-5 (pbk.) LC Card 86-26681 DDC 512/.1 19
HF5691 .M375 1987b

McAnelly, James R. Business mathematics for college /. St. Paul , c1987. [584] p. : ISBN 0-314-93202-X (pbk.) LC Card 86-26670 DDC 512/.1 19
HF5691 .M375 1987

MACAO - ECONOMIC CONDITIONS. Martinez, José Fernando Trindade. Recursos económicos do Ultramar Português, sua valorização e perspectivas futuras . Lisboa , 1960. 113 p. ; LC Card 86-169892
HC890 .M37 1960

Macao. Estatística, Repartição dos Serviços de. see **Macao. Repartição dos Serviços de Estatística.**

Macao. Repartição dos Serviços de Estatística. Demográficas e sociais = [Jen kuo chi she hui]. Macau : Governo de Macau, [1984] [28] p. ; 30 cm. Portuguese and Chinese. Cover title. "População, saúde, ensino, emprego, previdência, justica, cultura, tempos livres." LC Card 86-162433
1. Macao - Statistics. I. Title. II. Title: Jen kuo chi she hui.
HA4643 .M33 1984

MACAO - STATISTICS. Macao. Repartição dos Serviços de Estatística. Demográficas e sociais =. Macau [1984] [28] p. ; LC Card 86-162433
HA4643 .M33 1984

Macau. see **Macao.**

McAuliffe, Robert E. Advertising, competition, and public policy : theories and new evidence / Robert E. McAuliffe. Lexington, Mass. : Lexington Books, c1987. vi, 116 p. ; 24 cm. Includes index. Bibliography: p. [107]-112. ISBN 0-669-12391-9 (alk. paper) LC Card 85-45896 DDC 659.1/0973 19
1. Advertising - United States. 2. Competition - United States. 3. Advertising - Government policy - United States. I. Title.
HF5813.U6 M33 1987 NYPL [JLE 87-1426]

MacAvoy, Paul W. Chamber of Commerce of the United States of America. Council on Trends and Perspective. Government regulation of business . Washington, D.C. , c1979. x, 108 p. ; ISBN 0-89834-018-7(pbk.) : LC Card 79-91604 DDC 338.973
HD3616.U46 C44 1979
NYPL [JLE 80-2446]

MacBean, Alasdair I. Commodity policies : problems and prospects / Alasdair I. MacBean and D.T. Nguyen. London ; New York : Croom Helm, c1987. 438 p. : ill. ; 23 cm. (Croom Helm commodity series) "Published in the USA by Croom Helm in association with Methuen, Inc."--T.p. verso. Bibliography: p. 406-426. Includes index. ISBN 0-7099-1708-2 LC Card 87-9069 DDC 382/.3/091724 19
1. Commodity control. 2. Developing countries - Economic policy. I. Nguyen, D. T. II. Title.
HF1428 .M29 1987

MacCabe, Colin. The BBC and public service broadcasting /. Manchester , c1986. viii, 116 p. ; ISBN 0-7190-1964-8 : LC Card 86-209725

DDC 384.54/4/0941 19
HE8689.9.G7 B34 1986

McCabe, James (James M.) Leibowitz, Dennis. The cellular communications industry /. New York, N.Y. (140 Broadway, New York 10005) , c1985. ii, 67 p. : LC Card 86-201572 DDC 384.5/33/0973 19
HD9696.R363 U65 1985

McCafferty, Thomas. In-house t-e-l-e marketing : a masterplan for starting and managing a profitable telemarketing program / Thomas McCafferty. Chicago, Ill. : Probus Pub. Co., c1987. x, 337 p. : ill. ; 23 cm. Spine title: In-house telemarketing. Bibliography: p. 221-230. ISBN 0-917253-51-5 (pbk.) LC Card 86-63991 DDC 658.8/5 19
1. Telemarketing. 2. Telemarketing - Management. I. Title. II. Title: In-house telemarketing.
HF5415.1265 .M34 1987

McCalla, Douglas, 1942- Perspectives on Canadian economic history /. Toronto , c1987. 287 p. : ISBN 0-7730-4679-8 LC Card 87-168012 DDC 330.971 19
HC113 .P47 1987

McCann, Bernard. Bussière, Yves. Vieillissement de la population et demande de transport dans la région de Montréal . Montréal, Québec [1983] 83 p. : ISBN 2-89228-036-2 LC Card 84-177163
HE4509.M68 B88 1983

McCann, Michael W., 1952- Taking reform seriously : perspectives on public interest liberalism / Michael W. McCann. Ithaca : Cornell University Press, 1986. 345 p. ; 24 cm. Includes index. Bibliography: p. 321-335. ISBN 0-8014-1952-2 LC Card 86-47647 DDC 322.4/3/0973 19
1. Pressure groups - United States. 2. Public interest - United States. 3. Political participation - United States. 4. Liberalism - United States. I. Title.
JK1118 .M37 1986 ***NYPL [JLE 87-1009]***

McCann, Thomas P.
American company. McCann, Thomas P. On the inside : a story of intrique and adventure, on Wall Street, in Washington, and in the jungles of Central America / by Thomas McCann ; edited by Henry Scammell ; with a preface by Stephen Schlesinger. Boston , c1987. p. cm. ISBN 0-933341-53-9 : LC Card 87-43040 DDC 338.7/634 19
HD9249.U6 M23 1987

On the inside : a story of intrique and adventure, on Wall Street, in Washington, and in the jungles of Central America / by Thomas McCann ; edited by Henry Scammell ; with a preface by Stephen Schlesinger. Boston : Quinlan Press, c1987. p. cm. Rev. ed. of: An American company. c1976. ISBN 0-933341-53-9 : LC Card 87-43040 DDC 338.7/634 19
1. United Fruit Company. 2. Central America - History - 1951-. I. Scammell, Henry. II. McCann, Thomas P. American company. III. Title.
HD9249.U6 M23 1987

McCarthy, E. Jerome (Edmund Jerome)
Basic marketing. Readings and cases in basic marketing / edited by E. Jerome McCarthy, John F. Grashof, Andrew A. Brogowicz. 5th ed. Homewood, Ill. , 1987. ix, 365 p. : ISBN 0-256-05795-8 (pbk.) LC Card 86-83136 DDC 658.8 19
HF5415 .R334 1987

Readings and cases in basic marketing /. Homewood, Ill. , 1987. ix, 365 p. : ISBN 0-256-05795-8 (pbk.) LC Card 86-83136 DDC 658.8 19
HF5415 .R334 1987

McCarthy, Patrick, 1941- The French socialists in power, 1981-1986 /. New York , c1987. xii, 212 p. ; ISBN 0-313-25407-9 (lib. bdg. : alk. paper) LC Card 86-33569 DDC 338.944 19
HC276.2 .F699 1987

McCartin, P. J. Pryde, J. G. Survey of New Zealand farmer intentions and opinions, November 1985-January 1986 /. Canterbury, N.Z. [1986] 133 p. ; LC Card 87-107903 DDC 338.1/09931 19
HD8039.F32 N486 1986

McCartt, Anne Taylor. Dowling, Anne M. Two years of accident experience under STOP-DWI, December 1981-November 1983 /. [Albany] [1984] xiii, 67 p. : LC Card 86-622431 DDC 363.1/251 19
HE5620.D7 D68 1984

McCarty, Marilu Hurt.
Introductory economics / Marilu Hurt McCarty. Glenview, Ill. : Scott, Foresman, c1988. xxxvii, 929 p. : ill. (some col.) ; 27 cm. Includes indexes. ISBN 0-673-18320-3 : LC Card 87-23469 DDC 330 19
1. Economics. I. Title.
HB171.5 .M465 1988

Introductory economics.
McCarty, Marilu Hurt. Introductory macroeconomics / Marilu Hurt McCarty. Glenview, Ill. , c1988. xxiii, 533 p. : ISBN 0-673-18432-3 (pbk.) : LC Card 87-23434 DDC 339 19
HB172.5 .M37 1988

McCarty, Marilu Hurt. Introductory microeconomics / Marilu Hurt McCarty. Glenview, Ill. , c1988. xxiv, 550 p. : ISBN 0-673-18433-1 (pbk.) : LC Card 87-18046 DDC 338.5 19
HB172 .M385 1988

Introductory macroeconomics / Marilu Hurt McCarty. Glenview, Ill. : Scott, Foresman, c1988. xxiii, 533 p. : col. ill. ; 26 cm. Also published as part of: Introductory economics. Includes bibliographical references and indexes. ISBN 0-673-18432-3 (pbk.) : LC Card 87-23434 DDC 339 19
1. Macroeconomics. I. McCarty, Marilu Hurt. Introductory economics. II. Title.
HB172.5 .M37 1988

Introductory microeconomics / Marilu Hurt McCarty. Glenview, Ill. : Scott, Foresman, c1988. xxiv, 550 p. : col. ill. ; 26 cm. Also published as part of: Introductory economics. Includes bibliographical references and indexes. ISBN 0-673-18433-1 (pbk.) : LC Card 87-18046 DDC 338.5 19
1. Microeconomics. I. McCarty, Marilu Hurt. Introductory economics. II. Title.
HB172 .M385 1988

McCasland, William R. Transitway surveillance, communications, and control / prepared by William R. McCasland, Robert W. Stokes, John M. Mounce ; sponsored by Texas State Department of Highways and Public Transportation [and] U. S. Department of Transportation, Federal Highway Administration. College Station, Tex. : Texas Transportation Institute, the Texas A&M University System, [1986] vi, 76 p. : ill. ; 28 cm. (Research report . 425-2F (Chapter 4)) "Texas Transportation Institute [and] State Department of Highways and Public Transportation cooperative research"--Cover. Cover title: Transitway surveillance, communications, and control--manual for planning, designing and operating transitway facilities in Texas. "October 1986." "TTI-2-8/10/84-425-2F"--Cover. Bibliography: p. 71. LC Card 87-620995 DDC 380.5 s 388.3/143 19
1. High occupancy vehicle lanes. I. Stokes, Robert W. II. Mounce, John M. (John Michael). III. Texas Transportation Institute. IV. Texas. State Dept. of Highways and Public Transportation. V. Series: Research report (Texas Transportation Institute) , 425-2F. VI. Title.
HE203 .T43 no. 425-2F HE336.B8

McCaul, Colleen. Satellite in revolt : KwaNdebele : an economic and political profile / Colleen McCaul. Johannesburg, South Africa : South African Institute of Race Relations, 1987. 125 p., [11] p. of plates : ill. ; 30 cm. Bibliography: p. 112-125. ISBN 0-86982-314-0 (pbk.) LC Card 87-157406 DDC 330.9682/95063 19
1. KwaNdebele (South Africa) - Economic conditions. 2. Blacks - Employment - South Africa - KwaNdebele. 3. Blacks - South Africa - KwaNdebele - Politics and government. I. Title.
HC905.Z7 K785 1987

MacCharles, D. C. (Donald C.), 1935- Daly, D. J. (Donald James), 1922- On real wage unemployment /. Vancouver, B.C., Canada , 1986. vi, 117 p. : ISBN 0-88975-079-3 (pbk.) LC Card 87-142391 DDC 331.13/7971 19
HD4946.C3 D35 1986

MacCharles, Donald C. (Donald Clare), 1935- Daly, D. J. (Donald James), 1922- Canadian manufactured exports . Montreal, Quebec , c1986. xxviii, 180 p. ; ISBN 0-88645-025-X (pbk.) : LC Card 87-142389 DDC 382/.4567/0971 19
HF3226.5 .D26 1986

Trade among multinationals : intra-industry trade and national competitiveness / Donald C. MacCharles. London ; New York : Croom Helm, c1987. xiv, 207 p. ; 23 cm. (The Croom Helm series in international business) Bibliography: p. 190-194. Includes index. ISBN 0-7099-4618-X LC Card 87-9077 DDC 382/.3 19
1. Commercial policy. 2. Competition, International. 3. International business enterprises. 4. Canada - Commercial policy. I. Title. II. Title: Intra-industry trade and national competitiveness. III. Series.
HF1411 .M2325 1987

Macchiavelli, Niccolò di Bernardo dei. see **Machiavelli, Niccolò, 1469-1527.**

Macchitella, Carlo. Il Gigante nano . Torino , c1985. 382 p. : LC Card 86-128171 DDC 384.54/0945 19
HE8689.9.I8 G54 1985
NYPL [MWGK (Italy) 86-2853]

McClave, James T. Statistics for business and economics / James T. McClave, P. George Benson. 4th ed. San Francisco : Dellen Pub. Co., c1988. xxii, 1267 p. : ill. (some col.) ; 24 cm. Includes bibliographies and index. ISBN 0-02-379020-2 LC Card 87-20195 DDC 519.5 19
1. Commercial statistics. 2. Economics - Statistical methods. 3. Statistics. I. Benson, P. George, 1946-. II. Title.
HF1017 .M36 1988

McClellan, Keith. EAPs and the information revolution . New York , c1987. 106 p. ; ISBN 0-86656-606-6 LC Card 86-33519 DDC 331.25 19
HF5549.5.E42 E37 1987

Maccoby, Nathan, 1912- Katz, Daniel, 1903- Productivity, supervision, and morale in an office situation, part I /. New York , 1987, c1950. vii, 84 p. ; ISBN 0-8240-8211-7 (alk. paper) : LC Card 86-25804 DDC 658.3 19
HF5549 .K282 1987

McCoid, Catherine Hodge. Carrying capacities of nation-states / Catherine Hodge McCoid. New Haven, Conn. (P.O. Box 2015, Yale Station, New Haven 06520) : Human Relations Area Files, 1984. x, 198 leaves : ill. ; 23 cm. (HRAFlex books . W6-010) Cross-cultural research series Includes bibliographies. LC Card 84-152784 DDC 304.6/2 19
1. Demographic anthropology. 2. Culture. 3. Japan - Population. I. Series: HRAFlex books. Cross-cultural research series. II. Title.
GN33.5 .M38 1984 ***NYPL [JFE 86-2142]***

McCollom, James P. The Continental affair : the rise and fall of the Continental Illinois Bank / James P. McCollom.1st ed. New York : Dodd, Mead, c1987. xv, 393 p. ; 25 cm. Includes index. ISBN 0-396-08809-0 : LC Card 87-21471 DDC 332.1/223/0977311 19
1. Continental Illinois National Bank and Trust Company of Chicago. 2. Bank failures - Illinois - Chicago. I. Title.
HG2613.C44 C686 1987

McColly, Robert A. Availability of federally owned minerals for exploration and development in western states : Arizona, 1986 / by Robert A. McColly and Neal B. Anderson. [Avondale, Md.] : U. S. Dept. of the Interior, Bureau of Mines ; Washington, DC : For sale by the Supt. of Docs., U. S. G.P.O., [1987] iv, 27 p. : ill. (some col.) + 2 folded maps ; 28 cm. (Special publication) Bibliography: p. 11. LC Card 87-600086 DDC 333.8/5/09791 19
1. Mineral lands - Arizona. 2. Arizona - Public lands. I. Anderson, Neal B. II. Series: Special publication (United States. Bureau of Mines). III. Title.
HD243.A7 M36 1987

McConochie, Rodger P. Davis, Nancy Yaw. Research and consulting as a business /. Washington, D.C. , c1987. v, 41 p. : ISBN 0-913167-21-5 (pbk.) LC Card 87-20254 DDC 658.4/6 19
HD69.C6 D38 1987

McCord, Arline, 1934- McCord, William Maxwell, 1930- Paths to progress . New York , c1986. 352 p. ; ISBN 0-393-02307-9 : LC Card 85-29809 DDC 330.9172/4 19
HC59.7 .M358 1986 ***NYPL [JLD 86-3487]***

McCord, William Maxwell, 1930- Paths to progress : bread and freedom in developing societies / William McCord, with Arline McCord.1st ed. New York : Norton, c1986. 352 p. ; 22 cm. Includes bibliographical references and index. ISBN 0-393-02307-9 : LC Card 85-29809 DDC 330.9172/4 19
1. Developing countries - Economic conditions. 2. Developing countries - Economic policy. 3. Developing countries - Politics and government. I. McCord, Arline, 1934-. II. Title.
HC59.7 .M358 1986 ***NYPL [JLD 86-3487]***

McCorkle, Chester O. Economics of food processing in the United States /. San Diego , c1988. xiii, 449 p. : ISBN 0-12-482185-5 (alk. paper) LC Card 87-1245 DDC 338.4/7664/00973 19
HD9005 .E37 1988

McCormick, Regina. Davis, James E. (James Edwin), 1940- Economics . Santa Barbara, Calif. , c1988. xv, 354 p. : ISBN 0-87436-479-5 (alk. paper) LC Card 87-18670 DDC 330/.07/1273 19
HB74.5 .D39 1988

McCormick, William A. The export woodchip industry of south east NSW : major environmental issues / William A. McCormick. Barton, A.C.T. : Dept. of the Parliamentary Library, 1986. 23 p. : maps ; 30 cm. (Current issues brief, 0726-3244 . no. 2, 1986-87) At head of title: The Parliament of the Commonwealth of Australia. Bibliography: p. 21-23. LC Card 87-163674 DDC 333.75/09944 19
1. Wood chips industry - Australia - New South Wales. 2. Exports - Australia - New South Wales. I. Series: Current issues brief , 1986-87/2. II. Title.
HD9769.W383 A85 1986

McCoy, John Henry, 1912- Livestock and meat marketing / John H. McCoy and M.E. Sarhan. 3rd ed. New York : Van Nostrand Reinhold, c1988. vii, 642 p. : ill. ; 24 cm. "An AVI book." Includes bibliographies and index. ISBN 0-442-20488-4 LC Card 87-23136 DDC 381/.416/00973 19
1. Meat industry and trade - United States. I. Sarhan, M. E. II. Title.
HD9415 .M25 1988

McCracken, Grant David, 1951- Culture and consumption : new approaches to the symbolic character of consumer goods and activities / Grant McCracken. Bloomington : Indiana University Press, c1988. xv, 174 p. ; 25 cm. Bibliography: p. [147]-165. Includes index. ISBN 0-253-31526-3 LC Card 87-45394 DDC 339.4/7 19
1. Consumption (Economics) - History. 2. Culture - History. 3. Social values - History. I. Title.
HC79.C6 M385 1988

McCrea, Robert. Boxhill, Walton O. 1981 Census information on place of birth, citizenship, and immigration . Ottawa , c1986. 67, [4] p. : ISBN 0-660-52864-9 (pbk.) : LC Card 86-192857
HA741.5 1981f

McCreary, Don R. Japanese-U. S. business negotiations : a cross-cultural study / Don R. McCreary. New York : Praeger, 1986. viii, 121 p. ; 25 cm. "Praeger special studies. Praeger scientific." Includes index. Bibliography: p. 109-115. ISBN 0-275-92006-2 (alk. paper) : LC Card 86-554 DDC 658 19
1. Negotiation in business - Japan. 2. Negotiation in business - United States. 3. Japan - Commerce - United States. 4. United States - Commerce - Japan. I. Title.
HD58.6 .M38 1986 ***NYPL [JLE 86-3074]***

McCullough, Prudence.
The Wholesale-by-mail catalog. New York , 1986. iv, 364 p. ; ISBN 0-312-90379-0 (pbk.) : LC Card 87-139567 DDC 381/.2/02573 19
HF5861 .W54 1986

The Wholesale-by-mail catalog, 1987 /. New York [1987] p. cm. ISBN 0-312-00205-X (pbk.) : LC Card 86-27890 DDC 381/.2/02573 19
HF5861 .W527 1987

McCully, Al.
Clyde growth report, 1985 / for Village of Clyde by Al McCully. [Edmonton] : Alberta Municipal Affairs, [1985] iii, 66 p. : ill. ; 28 cm. "March, 1985." Bibliography: p. 65-66. LC Card 86-228996 DDC 338.97123/3 19
1. Land use - Alberta - Clyde - Planning. 2. Clyde (Alta.) - Economic policy. I. Clyde (Alta.). II. Title.
HD320.C5 M33 1985

East Prairie Metis Settlement : land use planning inventory / by Al McCully, Hugh Seaton. [Edmonton, Alta.] : Municipal Planning Section, Planning Branch, Alberta Municipal Affairs, [1982] iii, 99 p. :Bill. ; 28 cm. "March 1982." Bibliography: p. 95-97. LC Card 82-202474 DDC 333.76/17/097123 19
1. Land use - Alberta - East Prairie River Watershed - Planning. 2. Indians of North America - Canada - Mixed bloods. I. Seaton, Hugh. II. Alberta. Alberta Municipal Affairs. III. Title.
HD319.A4 M52 1982

McCusker, John J. European bills of entry and marine lists : early commercial publications and the origins of the business press / John J. McCusker. Cambridge, Mass. : Harvard University Library, 1985. 75 p. : ill. ; 26 cm. "Reprinted from the Harvard Library Bulletin, Vol. 31, No. 3, [1983], pp. 209-255, and No. 4, pp. 316-339"--P. [4]. Includes bibliographical references. LC Card 86-673685
1. Ship registers - History. 2. Ships - Cargo - Periodicals - History. 3. Commercial documents - History. 4. Journalism, Commercial - History. I. Title.
HE565.A3 M32 1985

McCutcheon, J. J. (John J.) An introduction to the mathematics of finance / J. J. McCutcheon and W.F. Scott. London : Published for the Institute of Actuaries and the Faculty of Actuaries [by] Heinemann, 1986. x, 463 p. : ill. ; 24 cm. Bibliography: p. 310-312. Includes index. ISBN 0-434-91224-7 (pbk.) : LC Card 86-219539 DDC 332/.01/51 19
1. Business mathematics. I. Scott, W. F. (William F.). II. Institute of Actuaries (Great Britain). III. Faculty of Actuaries in Scotland. IV. Title.
HF5691 .M385 1986

McDaniel, Carl D. Gitman, Lawrence J. Business world 2 /. New York , c1987. xvii, 616, [70] p. : ISBN 0-471-80596-3 LC Card 86-23441 DDC 658 19
HF5351 .G5 1987

McDaniel, Tim. Autocracy, capitalism, and the revolution in Russia / Tim McDaniel. Berkeley : University of California Press, c1987. p. cm. Bibliography: p. ISBN 0-520-05532-2 (alk. paper) LC Card 86-30790 DDC 322.4/2/0947 19
1. Labor and laboring classes - Soviet Union - History. 2. Soviet Union - Economic conditions - 1861-1917. 3. Labor policy - Soviet Union - History. I. Title.
HD8526 .M385 1987

McDonagh, Declan. Public expenditure . Dublin, Ireland , 1986. 138 p. ; ISBN 0-906980-56-9 (pbk.) : LC Card 86-143826 DDC 336.3/9 19
HJ7461 .P83 1986 ***NYPL [JLD 87-553]***

Macdonald, Donald S. Building a Canadian-American free trade area /. Washington, D.C. , c1987. xii, 217 p. ; ISBN 0-8157-2973-1 (pbk.) LC Card 87-71507 DDC 382/.0971/073 19
HF1480.15.U5 B85 1987

McDonald, Malcolm. How to sell a service : guidelines for effective selling in a service business / Malcolm H.B. McDonald with John Leppard. London : Heinemann, 1986. 149 p. : ill. ; 24 cm. (The Marketing series) Includes index. ISBN 0-434-91231-X (pbk.) : LC Card 86-212510 DDC 658.8 19
1. Selling. 2. Service industries. I. Leppard, John. II. Series: Marketing series (London, England). III. Title.
HF5438.25 .M396 1986

MacDonald, Ronald. Floating exchange rates : theories and evidence / Ronald MacDonald. London ; Boston : Allen & Unwin, 1987. p. cm. Bibliography: p. Includes index. ISBN 0-04-338134-0 (alk. paper) LC Card 87-9259 DDC 332.4/562 19
1. Foreign exchange problem. I. Title.
HG3852 .M33 1987

Macdonald, Stuart. The Trouble with technology . London , 1983. x, 224 p. : ISBN 0-86187-285-1 ***NYPL [JLE 86-1128]***

McDonald, Terrence J. The Politics of urban fiscal policy /. Beverly Hills , c1984. 176 p. : ISBN 0-8039-2373-2 LC Card 84-13431 DDC 336/.014/73 19
HJ9144 .P64 1984 ***NYPL [JLD 87-126]***

McDonnell, Edward J. Ansoff, H. Igor. The new corporate strategy /. New York , 1988. xviii, 258 p. : ISBN 0-471-62950-2 LC Card 87-23266 DDC 658.4/012 19
HD30.28 .A535 1988

McDonnell, James J. Briggs, Dwight. Journey-to-work trends . Washington, D.C. , Springfield, VA [1986] 1 v. (various pagings) : LC Card 86-602387 DDC 388.4/1314/0973 19
HE371.A3 B75 1986

MacDorman, Littleton C. Use of part-time operators / Littleton C. MacDorman. Washington, D.C. : Transportation Research Board, National Research Council, [1986] 33 p. : ill. ; 28 cm. (Synthesis of transit practice, 0732-1856 . 9) At head of title: National Cooperative Transit Research & Development Program. Bibliography: p. 22-23. ISBN 0-309-04403-0 (pbk.) LC Card 86-51175 DDC 331.25/72 19
1. Local transit - United States - Employees. 2. Part-time employment - United States. I. National Research Council (U. S.). Transportation Research Board. II. National Cooperative Transit Research & Development Program (U. S.). III. Title. IV. Series.
HD8039.S82 U65 1986

McDowell, Douglas S. Northrup, Herbert Roof, 1918- Doublebreasted operations and pre-hire agreements in construction . Philadelphia, Penn., USA , c1987. viii, 127 p. : ISBN 0-89546-067-X (pbk.) LC Card 87-81475 DDC 331.88/92 19
HD9715.U52 N67 1984 Suppl.

McDowell, M. C. (Milton C.), 1920- Math workbook for foodservice/lodging / M.C. McDowell, H.W. Crawford. 3rd ed. New York : Van Nostrand Reinhold, c1988. v, 265 p. : ill. ; 28 cm. Includes index. ISBN 0-442-21872-9 (pbk.) : LC Card 87-15960 DDC 513/.93/024642 19
1. Business mathematics - Food service - Problems, exercises, etc. 2. Business mathematics - Hotels, taverns, etc. - Problems, exercises, etc. 3. Business mathematics - Motels - Problems, exercises, etc. I. Crawford, H. W. (Hollie W.), 1919-. II. Title.
HF5695.5.F616 M317 1988

Macedo, Jorge Braga de. Custos certos, benefícios incertos . [Lisboa] [1986] 307 p. : LC Card 87-127179 DDC 341.24/22 19
HC241.25.P6 C87 1986

Macedo, Roberto Brás Matos. FGTS e a rotatividade / Roberto Brás Matos Macedo, José Paulo Z. Chahad. São Paulo-SP : Nobel ; Brasília-DF : Ministério do Trabalho, 1985. 231 p. : ill. ; 21 cm. (Coleção Estudos econômicos e sociais) "Fruto do contrato celebrado entre o Ministério do Trabalho e a Fundação Instituto de Pesquisas Econômicas para a realização da pesquisa, 'O Fundo de Garantia do Tempo de Serviço e a rotatividade da mão-de-obra'"--P. 11. Bibliography: p. 227-231. ISBN 85-21-30271-1 LC Card 85-187484
1. Insurance, Unemployment - Brazil. 2. Labor mobility - Brazil. I. Chahad, José Paulo Zeetano. II. Brazil. Ministério do Trabalho. III. Fundação Instituto de Pesquisas Econômicas (São Paulo, Brazil). IV. Title. V. Series.
HD7096.B6 M33 1985

McElroy, Jerome L. Towle, Edward L. Final report . St. Thomas, U. S.V.I. [1982] 17, 15, 4 leaves : LC Card 86-185489 DDC 333.7/097297/22 19
HC155.Z9 E56 1982

Macesich, George, 1927- Economic nationalism and stability / George Macesich. New York : Praeger, 1985. x, 163 p. ; 24 cm. (Praeger special studies. Praeger scientific) Includes bibliographical references and index. ISBN 0-03-005748-5 : LC Card 85-12342 DDC 338.9/009172/4 19
1. Economic stabilization - Developing countries. 2. Developing countries - Economic policy. I. Title.
HC59.7 .M2112 1985 ***NYPL [JLE 86-908]***

Macey, David, A. J., 1942- Government and peasant in Russia, 1861-1906 : the prehistory of the Stolypin reforms / David A.J. Macey. Dekalb, Ill. : Northern Illinois University Press, 1987. xviii, 380 p. ; 24 cm. (Studies of the Harriman Institute, Columbia University) Bibliography: p. [341]-367. Includes index. ISBN 0-87580-122-6 LC Card 87-7684 DDC 338.1/847 19
1. Agriculture - Economic aspects - Soviet Union - History - 19th century. 2. Agriculture and state - Soviet Union - History - 19th century. 3. Peasantry - Soviet Union - History - 19th century. 4. Soviet Union - Economic conditions - 1861-1917. I. Series: Studies of

the Harriman Institute. II. Title.
HD1992 .M19 1987

McFadden, John J. Retirement plans for employees / John J. McFadden. Homewood, Ill. : Irwin, 1988. xviii, 326 p. : ill. ; 25 cm. (Irwin series in insurance and economic security) The Irwin series in financial planning and insurance Includes bibliographical references and index. ISBN 0-256-05588-2 LC Card 87-81436 DDC 658.3/253 19
1. Old age pensions - United States. 2. Pensions - United States. 3. Compensation management - United States. I. Title.
HD7105.35.U6 M33 1988

McFarland, William F. New approaches to project ranking : comparisons using added capacity projects in Texas / by William F. McFarland and Jeffrey L. Memmott ; sponsored by Texas State Department of Highways and Public Transportation, in cooperation with the U. S. Department of Transportation, Federal Highway Administration. College Station, Tex. : Texas Transportation Institute, Texas A&M University System ; Springfield, Va. : Available through National Technical Information Service, [1985] xvii, 116 p. : ill. ; 28 cm. (Research report / Texas Transportation Institute, Texas A&M University System . no. 337-1F) "Research study no. 2-8-84-337." "TTI-2-8-84-337-1F"--Cover. "November 1985." Bibliography: p. 78-79. LC Card 86-622422 DDC 380.5 s 388.1/12/09764 19
1. Roads - Texas - Cost effectiveness. 2. Road construction - Texas - Cost effectiveness. I. Memmott, Jeffery L. (Jeffery Lynn). II. Texas. State Dept. of Highways and Public Transportation. III. United States. Federal Highway Administration. IV. Series: Research report (Texas Transportation Institute) , 337-1F. V. Title.
HE203 .T43 no. 337-1F HE356.T4

McFetridge, Britton. Schaefer, Andrew. CAL-OSHA routine compliance inspections . [Sacramento, CA , 1986] 25 p. ; LC Card 86-622709 DDC 363.1/164/09796 19
HD7262.5.U62 C573 1986

McFetridge, D. G., 1945-
Canadian industrial policy in action /. Toronto , Buffalo , c1985. xvii, 231 p. : ISBN 0-8020-7244-5 (pbk.) LC Card 86-672572
HD3616.C23 C36x 1985 ***NYPL [JLD 86-2871]***

Technological change in Canadian industry /. Toronto , Buffalo , c1985. xv, 233 p. ; ISBN 0-8020-7243-7 (pbk.) LC Card 86-164766 DDC 338/.06 19
HC120.T4 T42 1985 ***NYPL [JLD 87-654]***

MacGaffey, Janet. Entrepreneurs and parasites : the struggle for indigenous capitalism in Zaire / Janet MacGaffey. Cambridge [Cambridgeshire] ; New York : Cambridge University Press, 1987. xiii, 241 p. : ill. ; 24 cm. (African studies series. 57) Bibliography: p. 224-235. Includes index. ISBN 0-521-33533-7 LC Card 87-13160 DDC 338.09675/1 19
1. Capitalism - Zaire - Kisangani. 2. Capitalism - Zaire - Haut-Zaïre. 3. Capitalism - Zaire - Kivu. 4. Capitalists and financiers - Zaire - Case studies. 5. New business enterprises - Zaire - Case studies. 6. Entrepreneur. I. Title. II. Series.
HC955.Z7 K49956 1987

McGann, Anthony F. Advertising media : a managerial approach / Anthony F. McGann, J. Thomas Russell.2nd ed. Homewood, Ill. : Irwin, 1988. xii, 452 p. : ill. ; 25 cm. Includes bibliographies and index. ISBN 0-256-05988-8 LC Card 87-81340 DDC 659.1/11 19
1. Advertising media planning. I. Russell, J. Thomas. II. Title.
HF5826.5 .M36 1988

McGarry, Brad M. Jensen, Kenneth E. Utah affirmative action information, 1985. [Salt Lake City] [1986] i, 253 p. ; LC Card 86-622873 DDC 331.11/43 19
HD5725.U8 J46 1986

McGee, L. Randolph. Hultman, Charles W. An examination of issues related to multibank holding companies /. [Frankfort, Ky. , 1983] [8], 56 leaves ; LC Card 86-620545 DDC 332.1/6 19
HG2567 .H85 1983

McGee, Mark G. Human spatial abilities : sources of sex differences / Mark G. McGee. New York : Praeger, 1979. xiv, 144 p. : graphs ; 24 cm. Includes index. Bibliography: p. 117-140. ISBN 0-03-052391-5 LC Card 79-16070 DDC 153.7/52
1. Space-perception. 2. Orientation (Psychology). 3. Sex differences (Psychology). 4. Nature and nurture. I. Title.
BF469 .M3 ***NYPL [JFE 84-185]***

McGee, Robert W.
Accounting and tax aspects of computer software manufacturing / Robert W. McGee. New York : Praeger, 1987. viii, 162 p. ; 25 cm. Bibliography: p. [157]-159. Includes index. ISBN 0-275-92273-1 (alk. paper) : LC Card 87-15140 DDC 657/.73 19
1. Computer software industry - Accounting. 2. Computer software industry - Taxation - Law and legislation. I. Title.
HF5686.C54 M38 1987

Accounting for data processing costs / Robert W. McGee. New York : Quorum Books, c1988. p. cm. Bibliography: p. Includes index. ISBN 0-89930-214-9 (lib. bdg. : alk. paper) LC Card 87-24933 DDC 657/.7 19
1. Electronic data processing departments - Accounting. 2. Electronic data processing departments - Costs. I. Title.
HF5548.35 .M38 1988

Fundamentals of accounting and finance : making intelligent decisions in an unpredictable economy / Robert W. McGee. Lanham, MD : University Press of America, c1987. p. cm. Originally published: Englewood Cliffs, N.J. : Prentice-Hall, c1983. Includes index. ISBN 0-8191-6289-2 (pbk. : alk. paper) LC Card 87-21581 DDC 657 19
1. Accounting. 2. Business enterprises - Finance. I. Title.
HF5635 .M4883 1987

A model program for schools of professional accountancy / Robert W. McGee. Lanham, MD : University Press of America, c1987. xiii, 192 p. ; 23 cm. Bibliography: p. 169-192. ISBN 0-8191-6094-6 (alk. paper) : LC Card 86-28226 DDC 657/.07/1173 19
1. Accounting - Study and teaching (Graduate) - United States. I. Title.
HF5630 .M39 1987

McGill University. Centre for Developing-Area Studies. Power and poverty . Boulder , 1988. v, 186 p. ; ISBN 0-8133-7351-4 (pbk. : alk. paper) : LC Card 86-32578 DDC 338.9/009172/4 19
HC59.72.E44 P68 1988

McGonagle, John J. Vella, Carolyn M. Competitive intelligence in the computer age /. New York , 1987. xv, 189 p. ; ISBN 0-89930-169-X (lib. bdg. : alk. paper) LC Card 86-25565 DDC 651.8 19
HF5548.2 .V38 1987

McGovern, Arthur F. Cavanagh, Gerald F. Ethical dilemmas in the modern corporation /. Englewood Cliffs, NJ , c1988. x, 198 p. : ISBN 0-13-290058-0 (pbk.) LC Card 87-25726 DDC 174/.4 19
HF5387 .C38 1988

McGovern, Edmond. International trade regulation : GATT, the United States, and the European Community / Edmond McGovern.2nd ed. Exeter [Devon] : Globefield Press, 1986. xliv, 629 p. ; 24 cm. Includes index. "Preface to the second edition"--p. ix. Bibliography: p. 599-619. ISBN 0-9508463-4-1 DDC 341.7/54 19
1. Foreign trade regulation - United States. 2. Tariff - Law and legislation - United States. 3. Foreign trade regulation - European Economic Community countries. 4. Tariff - Law and legislation - European Economic Community countries. I. Title.
K3943 .M4 1982 ***NYPL [JLE 86-3637]***

McGowan, Brenda G. Trends in employee counseling programs / by Brenda G. McGowan. 1st ed. New York : Pergamon Press, c1984. 55 p. ; 28 cm. (Work in America Institute studies in productivity . 37) Bibliography: p. 49-55. ISBN 0-08-032361-8 (pbk.) : LC Card 84-22820 DDC 658.3/82 19
1. Employee counseling - United States. 2. Employee assistance programs - United States. I. Title. II. Series.
HF5549.5.C8 M34 1984
NYPL [JLM 83-380 no.37]

McGowan, Sandra.
Diet foods . Stamford, Conn., U. S.A. , c1986. xv, 195 leaves : ISBN 0-89336-487-8 (pbk.) LC Card 87-160485 DDC 381/.4166463/0973 19
HD9005 .D53 1986

The New ethnic food market . Norwalk, Conn., U. S.A. , c1986. xv, 142 leaves ; ISBN 0-89336-486-X (pbk.) LC Card 87-168111 DDC 381/.45641592/00973 19
HD9333.U62 N48 1986

New trends in food retailing /. Stamford, Conn., U. S.A. , c1985. xiii, 135 leaves : ISBN 0-89336-457-6 (soft) LC Card 87-165228 DDC 381/.45664/00973 19
HD9321.5 .N47 1985

McGranahan, David A. Social and economic characteristics of the population in metro and nonmetro counties, 1970-80 /. Washington, D.C. [1986] iv, 70 p. : LC Card 86-602790 DDC 304.6/0973 19
HC106.7 .S577 1986

McGraw, Eric. Population growth / Eric McGraw. Vero Bleach, FL : Rourke Enterprises, 1987. 46 p. : ill. (some col.) ; 27 cm. (World issues) Bibliography: p. 45. Includes index. ISBN 0-86592-276-4 LC Card 87-12729 DDC 304.6/2 19
1. Population. 2. Developing countries - Population. I. Series: World issues (Vero Beach, Fla.). II. Title.
HB871 .M325 1987

McGraw-Hill accounting 10/12 series.
Accounting, systems and procedures . New York , c1988. xv, 288 p. : ISBN 0-07-069357-9 (pbk.) LC Card 87-21936 DDC 657 19
HF5635 .A222 1988b

Accounting, systems and procedures /. New York , c1988. p. cm. ISBN 0-07-069356-0 LC Card 87-17234 DDC 657 19
HF5635 .A222 1988

The McGraw-Hill marketing series.
Parkinson, Lynn K. Using the microcomputer in marketing /. London , New York , c1987. ix, 158 p. : ISBN 0-07-084163-2 (pbk.) : LC Card 86-27364 DDC 658.8/0028/5416 19
HF5415.125 .P36 1987

McGraw-Hill Training Systems (Firm)
Customer service [motion picture] . Del Mar, CA , 1985. 1 film reel (13 min.) : ISBN 0-07-620872-9 LC Card 86-708025 DDC 658.8 11
HF5415.5

Customer service [videorecording] . Del Mar, CA , 1985. 1 videocassette (13 min.) : ISBN 0-07-109048-7 (3/4 in.) LC Card 86-708026 DDC 658.8 11
HF5415.5

Dealing with difficult customers [motion picture] /. Del Mar, CA , 1986. 1 film reel (13 min.) : ISBN 0-07-620875-3 LC Card 86-708027 DDC 658.8 11
HF5415.5

Dealing with difficult customers [videorecording] /. Del Mar, CA , 1986. 1 videocassette (13 min.) : ISBN 0-07-109068-1 (3/4 in.) LC Card 86-708028 DDC 658.8 11
HF5415.5

How to define goals and objectives [videorecording] /. Del Mar, CA , 1986. 1 videocassette (18 min.) : ISBN 0-07-109094-0 (3/4 in.) LC Card 86-700128 DDC 658.4 11
HF5549.5.G6

How to influence motivation [videorecording] /. Del Mar, CA , 1986. 1 videocassette (31 min.) : ISBN 0-07-109093-2 (3/4 in.) LC Card 86-700127 DDC 658.3 11
HF5549.5.M63

How to lead effectively [videorecording] /. Del Mar, CA , 1986. 1 videocassette (19 min.) : ISBN 0-07-109095-9 (3/4 in.) LC Card 86-700130 DDC 658.4 11
HD57.7

How to solve problems [videorecording] /. Del Mar, CA , 1986. 1 videocassette (22 min.) : ISBN 0-07-109096-7 (3/4 in.) LC Card 86-700129 DDC 658.4 11
HD30.29

An Introduction to communication on the telephone [videorecording] /. Del Mar, CA , 1987. 1 videocassette (7 min.) : LC Card 87-700082 DDC 658.8 11
HF5415.1265

The Meeting robbers [motion picture] /. Del Mar, CA , 1985. 1 film reel (20 min.) : ISBN 0-07-620874-5 LC Card 85-702616 DDC 658.4

11
HD30.3

The Meeting robbers [videorecording] /. Del Mar, CA , 1985. 1 videocassette (20 min.) : ISBN 0-07-109067-3 (3/4 in.) LC Card 85-702617 DDC 658.4 11
HD30.3

Productivity and the self-fulfilling prophecy [motion picture] . Del Mar, CA , 1987. 1 film reel (27 min.) : LC Card 87-700078 DDC 658.4 11
HF5549.5.I5

Questions and recommendations on the telephone [videorecording] /. Del Mar, CA , 1987. 1 videocassette (13 min.) : LC Card 87-700084 DDC 658.8 11
HF5415.1265

McGuigan, James R. Moyer, R. Charles, 1945- Contemporary financial management /. St. Paul , c1988. xxiv, 793, 24 p. : ISBN 0-314-64227-7 LC Card 87-24201 DDC 658.1/5 19
HG4026 .M68 1988

McGuinness, Tony. The Economics of the firm /. Oxford [Oxfordshire] , New York, NY, USA , 1987. p. cm. ISBN 0-631-14075-1 : LC Card 86-27057 DDC 338.6 19
HD2326 .E243 1987

McGuire, John. An Inquiry into the future of public and private pension plans . Winnipeg [1976] xiii, 54 p. ; LC Card 85-103269
HD7130.M36 I56 1976

McGuire, Nan. Survey of private sector work and family policy : San Francisco and Alameda counties / by Nan McGuire, Suzanne Smith, and the staff of New Ways to Work. San Francisco : New Ways to Work, c1986. 41 leaves ; 28 cm. LC Card 87-113810 DDC 331.25/72/0979461 19
1. Hours of labor - California - San Francisco. 2. Hours of labor - California - Alameda County. 3. Hours of labor, Flexible - California - San Francisco. 4. Hours of labor, Flexible - California - Alameda County. 5. Personnel management - California - San Francisco. 6. Personnel management - California - Alameda County. I. Smith, Suzanne. II. New Ways to Work (firm). III. Title.
HD5126.S4 M38 1986

McGuire, Paul F., 1907- Genesis of Oklahoma oil banking / by Paul F. McGuire. Muskogee, Okla. : Western Heritage Books, c1986. 160 p. : ill. ; 22 cm. ISBN 0-86546-068-X (pbk.) LC Card 87-118559 DDC 332.1/223/0924 B 19
1. McGuire, Paul F., 1907-. 2. Bankers - Oklahoma - Biography. 3. Banks and banking - Oklahoma. 4. Petroleum industry and trade - Oklahoma - Finance. I. Title.
HG2463.M36 A3 1986

MCGUIRE, PAUL F., 1907-
McGuire, Paul F., 1907- Genesis of Oklahoma oil banking /. Muskogee, Okla. , c1986. 160 p. : ISBN 0-86546-068-X (pbk.) LC Card 87-118559 DDC 332.1/223/0924 B 19
HG2463.M36 A3 1986

McGuire, Steven. Assessing the nuclear age . Chicago, Ill. , c1986. xvii, 382 p. ; ISBN 0-941682-07-2 LC Card 85-82511 DDC 355/.0217 19
U264 .A79 1986 *NYPL [JLE 87-11]*

Mach mich nicht an : Sexismus am Arbeitsplatz : Dokumentation einer Ausstellung / Bezirksfrauenausschuss der ÖTV Berlin (Hrsg.) ; [Katalogredaktion, Maica Evers, Virginia M. Raimundi]. Berlin : Verlag Die Arbeitswelt, c1986. [48] p. : ill. ; 30 cm. ISBN 3-88114-313-0 : LC Card 87-118837 DDC 331.4/133/0943 19
1. Sex discrimination against women - Germany, West. 2. Sexual harassment of women - Germany (West). 3. Berlin (Germany) - Exhibition. I. Evers, Maica. II. Raimundi, Virginia M. III. Gewerkschaft Öffentliche Dienste, Transport und Verkehr. Bezirksfrauenausschuss der ÖTV Berlin.
HD6060.5.G3 M33 1986

MACHADINHO (PROJECT : BRAZIL) - SOCIAL ASPECTS.
Sigaud, Lygia. Efeitos sociais de grandes projetos hidrelétricos . [Rio de Janeiro] , 1986. 116 p. ; LC Card 87-120281 DDC 333.91/4 19
HD1696.B84 S346 1986

Machado, Arlindo. Rádios livres : a reforma agrária no ar / Arlindo Machado, Caio Magri, Marcelo Masagão ; prefácio, Felix Guattari. São Paulo-SP : Brasiliense, 1986. 181 p. : ill. ; 21 cm. Bibliography: p. [180]-181. LC Card 86-157835
1. Pirate radio broadcasting. 2. Pirate radio broadcasting - Brazil. I. Magri, Caio. II. Masagão, Marcelo. III. Title.
HE8697.P57 M33 1986

Machado de Almeida, Edimilson. see **Almeida, Edimilson Machado de, 1937-**

Machado, R. C. (Raimundo de Campos), 1913- Aluminio primário no Brasil : coletanea de trabalhos, 1973-1981 / R.C. Machado. [Ouro Preto, Brasil : Fundação Gorceix], 1983. 216 p. : ill. ; 24 cm. LC Card 84-256552
1. Aluminum industry and trade - Brazil - Collected works. I. Title.
HD9539.A3 B66 1983

Machado, Vera Barrouin Crivano. O diálogo norte-sul / Vera Barrouin Crivano Machado. Brasília, DF : Ministério da Fazenda, Escola de Administração Fazendária, Centro de Pesquisa, 1983. 58 p. ; 21 cm. (Coleção Gerson Augusto da Silva . 16) LC Card 86-171831
1. International economic relations. 2. Developing countries - Foreign economic relations. I. Title. II. Series.
HF1412 .M33 1983

MACHALA SUBURBAN REGION (ECUADOR) - ECONOMIC CONDITIONS.
Maldonado Calderón, Arturo. Actividad económica del hombre del suburbio /. Machala, Ecuador , 1985. 168 p., [3] folded leaves of plates : LC Card 87-110202 DDC 330.9866/31 19
HC203.M33 M35 1985

MACHALA SUBURBAN REGION (ECUADOR) - SOCIAL CONDITIONS.
Maldonado Calderón, Arturo. Actividad económica del hombre del suburbio /. Machala, Ecuador , 1985. 168 p., [3] folded leaves of plates : LC Card 87-110202 DDC 330.9866/31 19
HC203.M33 M35 1985

MacHale, Carlos F. Vox new college Spanish and English dictionary . Lincolnwood, Ill., U. S.A. , c1984. xix, 1456, 60 p. : ISBN 0-8442-7998-6 (plain-edge ed.) : LC Card 84-61106 DDC 463/.21 19
PC4640 .V696 1984
*NYPL [*R-RGK 85-1500]*

McHale, Thomas R. Saudi oil policy and the changing world energy balance / by Thomas R. McHale. Boulder, Colo., U. S.A. : International Research Center for Energy and Economic Development, c1986. 17 p. ; 22 cm. (Occasional papers / International Research Center for Energy and Economic Development . no. 1) ISBN 0-918714-09-5 (pbk.) : LC Card 87-119219 DDC 338.2/7282/09538 19
1. Petroleum industry and trade - Government policy - Saudi Arabia. I. Series: Occasional papers / International Research Center for Energy and Economic Development , no. 1. II. Title.
HD9502.A1 O28 no. 1 HD9576.S33

Machan, Tibor R. Commerce and morality /. Totowa, N.J. , 1987. p. cm. ISBN 0-8476-7586-6 LC Card 87-16635 DDC 174/.4 19
HF5387 .C65 1987

Macharzina, Klaus.
Diskontinuitätenmanagement . Berlin , c1984. x, 320 p. : ISBN 3-503-02446-8 LC Card 85-128271
HD62.4 .D57 1984

Finanz- und bankwirtschaftliche Probleme bei internationaler Unternehmenstätigkeit /. Stuttgart , c1985. x, 267 p. : ISBN 3-7910-0394-1 LC Card 86-121195 DDC 658.1/5 19
HG4027.5 .F56 1985

McHatton, Robert J. Total telemarketing / Robert J. McHatton. New York : J. Wiley, c1988. x, 246 p. : ill. ; 23 cm. Bibliography: p. 234-235. Includes index. ISBN 0-471-62755-0 (pbk.) : LC Card 87-21547 DDC 658.8/5 19
1. Telemarketing. 2. Telephone selling. I. Title.
HF5415.1265 .M38 1988

Die Macher . Kampe, Dieter, 1953- Pfaffenweiler , 1986. 191 p. ; ISBN 3-89085-143-6 LC Card 87-133889 DDC 338.0943 19
HC286.7 .K36 1986

MACHIAVELLI, NICCOLÒ, 1469-1527 - CONTRIBUTIONS IN ECONOMICS.
Begert, Roland. Elemente einer politischen Ökonomie im Werke Machiavellis /. Bern , c1983. 224 p. : ISBN 3-258-03136-3 LC Card 83-204993
HB109.M3 B44 1983

Machiavelli zweitausend. Berner, Rudolf. Machiavelli 2000 . Zürich , c1985. 62 p. ; ISBN 3-7220-3001-3 : LC Card 86-149021
HD35 .B478 1985

Machiavelli 2000 . Berner, Rudolf. Zürich , c1985. 62 p. ; ISBN 3-7220-3001-3 : LC Card 86-149021
HD35 .B478 1985

MACHINE DATA STORAGE AND RETRIEVAL. see **INFORMATION STORAGE AND RETRIEVAL SYSTEMS.**

MACHINE INTELLIGENCE. see **ARTIFICIAL INTELLIGENCE.**

MACHINE PARTS INDUSTRY - EGYPT.
Economical study of spare parts consumption in textile industry in Egypt. Cairo, Egypt [1984?] 2 v. : LC Card 86-960234 DDC 338.4/76817677/0962 19
HD9705.5.P373 E34 1984

MACHINE PARTS INDUSTRY - KOREA (SOUTH) - DIRECTORIES.
Korean parts directory. [Seoul] , 1986. 514 p. ; LC Card 86-231593
HD9705.5.P373 K676 1986

MACHINE-TOOL INDUSTRY - BRAZIL - TECHNOLOGICAL INNOVATIONS - CASE STUDIES.
Silva, Marcos Eugênio da. Inovação tecnológica . São Paulo , 1984. 103 p. : LC Card 85-136373
HD9703.B72 S55 1984

MACHINE-TOOL INDUSTRY - BULGARIA - SOFIA.
Kostov, Miroslav. ZMM metal-working machines combine, Sofia /. Sofia , 1986. [104] p. : LC Card 87-116288 DDC 338.7/621902/0949773 19
HD9703.B94 Z384 1986

MACHINE-TOOL INDUSTRY - DEVELOPING COUNTRIES.
Machinery and economic development /. Houndmills, Basingstoke, Hampshire , 1986. xvii, 274 p. : ISBN 0-333-36391-4
NYPL [JLD 86-4380]

MACHINE-TOOL INDUSTRY - EUROPE.
Rendeiro, João Oliveira. Progresso técnico e evolução estratégica na indústria de máquinas-ferramentas . Lisboa , 1985. 111 p. : LC Card 86-189891
HD9703.E92 R45 1985

MACHINE-TOOL INDUSTRY - GERMANY (WEST) - TECHNOLOGICAL INNOVATIONS.
Zörgiebel, Wilhelm W. Technologie in der Wettbewerbsstrategie . Berlin , c1983. xv, 322 p. : ISBN 3-503-02361-5 LC Card 84-158275
HD9703.G42 Z67 1983

MACHINE-TOOL INDUSTRY - GOVERNMENT POLICY - UNITED STATES.
DiFilippo, Anthony, 1950- Military spending and industrial decline . Westport, Conn. , c1986. x, 199 p. ; ISBN 0-313-25179-7 (lib bdg. : alk. paper) LC Card 85-27144 DDC 338.4/7621902/0973 19
HD9703.U5 D54 1986
NYPL [JLD 86-2930]

MACHINE-TOOL INDUSTRY - JAPAN.
Rendeiro, João Oliveira. Progresso técnico e evolução estratégica na indústria de máquinas-ferramentas . Lisboa , 1985. 111 p. : LC Card 86-189891
HD9703.E92 R45 1985

MACHINE-TOOL INDUSTRY - PORTUGAL.
Rendeiro, João Oliveira. Progresso técnico e evolução estratégica na indústria de máquinas-ferramentas . Lisboa , 1985. 111 p. : LC Card 86-189891
HD9703.E92 R45 1985

MACHINE-TOOL INDUSTRY - SOVIET UNION - MANAGEMENT.
Khoziaĭstvennyĭ mekhanizm proizvodstvennogo ob"edineniia /. Moskva , 1985. 254 p. ; LC

Card 85-238796
HD9703.S652 K46 1985

Plaksin, V. I. (Viktor Ivanovich) Sovershenstvovanie sistem upravleniia trudom na predpriiatiiakh mashinostroeniia /. Kiev , 1986. 137, [3] p. : LC Card 85-241056
HD9703.S652 P42 1986

MACHINE-TOOL INDUSTRY - SOVIET UNION - MANAGEMENT - PROBLEMS, EXCERCISES, ETC.
Sbornik zadach i khoziaistvennykh situatsii po ėkonomike i planirovaniiu mashinostroitel'noĭ promyshlennosti /. Moskva , 1985. 246 p. ; LC Card 86-110747
HD9703.S652 S28 1985

MACHINE-TOOL INDUSTRY - SOVIET UNION - PERSONNEL MANAGEMENT.
Nauchnaia organizatsiia truda na mashinostroitel'nykh predpriiatiiakh /. Moskva , 1986. 240 p. : LC Card 86-214776
HD9703.S652 N38 1986

MACHINE-TOOL INDUSTRY - SWITZERLAND - DIRECTORIES.
Interferex 86 (Basel, Switzerland) Interferex 86, Intertable . Basel, Schweiz [1986] 284 p., [6] p. of plates : LC Card 87-409294 DDC 381/.18 19
HF5474.S92 B365 1986

MACHINE-TOOL INDUSTRY - UKRAINE.
Kryzhanovskiĭ, B. N. (Boris Nikolaevich) Spetsializatsiia zagotovitel'nogo proizvodstva /. Kiev , 1985. 125, [3] p. ; LC Card 87-112143
HD9703.S653 U474 1985

Kryzhanovskiĭ, B. N. (Boris Nikolaevich) Vspomogatel'noe proizvodstvo mashinostroeniia . Kiev , 1983. 334 p. : LC Card 83-238314
HD9703.S653 U475 1983

MACHINERY AND CIVILIZATION. see **TECHNOLOGY AND CIVILIZATION.**

Machinery and economic development / edited by Martin Fransman. Houndmills, Basingstoke, Hampshire : Macmillan, 1986. xvii, 274 p. : ill. ; 23 cm. Includes bibliographies and index. ISBN 0-333-36391-4
1. Machinery - Trade and manufacture - Developing countries. 2. Machine-tool industry - Developing countries. 3. Industrial equipment industry - Developing countries. 4. Developing countries - Industries. 5. Developing countries - Economic conditions. I. Fransman, Martin. ***NYPL [JLD 86-4380]***

MACHINERY - ECONOMIC AND SOCIAL RELATIONS. see **MACHINERY IN INDUSTRY.**

MACHINERY IN INDUSTRY - ADDRESSES, ESSAYS, LECTURES.
Microprocessors, manpower, and society . Aldershot, Hants., England , c1984. xi, 367 p. : ISBN 0-566-00631-6 ***NYPL [JLD 86-1098]***

Technischer Fortschritt und Arbeitslosigkeit /. Frankfurt/Main , New York , c1983. 372 p. : ISBN 3-593-33246-9 LC Card 84-143045
HD6331 .T39 1983 ***NYPL [JLD 87-331]***

MACHINERY IN INDUSTRY - CASE STUDIES.
Automation and industrial workers . Oxford [Oxfordshire] , New York , 1979- v. : ISBN 0-08-023339-2 (v. 1, pt. 1) : LC Card 79-40811 DDC 331
HD6331 .A93 1979 ***NYPL [JLM 82-242]***

MACHINERY IN INDUSTRY - WEST (U. S.)
Finlay, William. Work on the waterfront . Philadelphia , 1988. p. cm. ISBN 0-87722-523-0 (alk. paper) : LC Card 87-17976 DDC 331.88/11387164/0973 19
HD6515.L82 W474 1988

MACHINERY INDUSTRY - ASIA.
The Motor vehicle industry in Asia . [Singapore] [1983] xxv, 419 p. : ISBN 997-16-9057-8 LC Card 83-941793 DDC 338.4/76292/095 19
HD9710.3.A78 M67 1983
NYPL [JLE 85-1592]

MACHINERY INDUSTRY - BRAZIL - STATISTICS.
Bens de produção mecânicos . São Paulo, SP, Brasil , 1982. 386 p. : LC Card 86-150156
HD9705.B72 B46 1982

MACHINERY INDUSTRY - DIRECTORIES.
The Standard handbook of industrial distributors. Fairfield, CT, USA , c1987- v. <1-2 > ; ISBN 0-917408-02-0 (pbk. : v. 1) LC Card 86-73258 DDC 380.1/456218/025 19
HD9680.A2 S72 1987

MACHINERY INDUSTRY - FRANCE - HISTORY - 19TH CENTURY.
Edmonson, James M. From Mecanicien to ingenieur . New York, NY , 1987. x, 631 p. ; ISBN 0-8240-8036-X (alk. paper) : LC Card 87-300 DDC 338.4/76218/0944 19
HD9705.F7 E35 1987

MACHINERY INDUSTRY - GERMANY - HISTORY.
Lindenlaub, Dieter. Maschinenbauunternehmen in der Deutschen Inflation 1919-1923 . Berlin , New York , 1985. xiii, 262 p. ; ISBN 3-11-009934-9 LC Card 85-214738
HG999 .L75 1985

MACHINERY INDUSTRY - GERMANY (WEST) - CASE STUDIES.
Flexible Fertigung und Industriearbeit . Frankfurt Main , New York , c1986. v, 577, iii p. : ISBN 3-593-33648-0 LC Card 86-197535
HD5109.2.G3 F45 1986

MACHINERY INDUSTRY - GERMANY (WEST) - FORECASTING.
Baumann, Hans, 1931- Der deutsche Maschinenbau im Wandel der industriellen Output-Struktur . München , 1978. vi, 196 p. : LC Card 84-126586
HD9705.G4 B26 1978

MACHINERY INDUSTRY - MOROCCO.
Les Industries mécaniques et électriques au Maroc . Casablanca [1984] 1 v. (various pagings) ; LC Card 85-206543
HD9705.M72 I53 1984

MACHINERY INDUSTRY - NEW ZEALAND.
Gapes, R. F. (Robert Francis) The heavy engineering industry in New Zealand . [Wellington, N.Z. , 1976] 105 p. : LC Card 84-255451
HD9705.N44 G36 1976

MACHINERY INDUSTRY - PERU - FINANCE - CASE STUDIES.
Beltrán Alejos, Hugo. La situación del sector metal-mecánico en el Perú . Lima, Perú , 1985. 93, [77] p. : LC Card 86-218266
HD9506.P42 B45 1985

MACHINERY INDUSTRY - PHILIPPINES - EMPLOYEES - TRAINING OF.
Metals and engineering . Manila, Philippines , 1983. 64 p. : LC Card 87-401862 DDC 331.25/92 19
HD5716.M52 P66 1983

MACHINERY INDUSTRY - PRICES - HUNGARY - STATISTICS.
A Kohászati és a gépipari árak alakulása, 1980-1984 /. Budapest , 1986. 91 p. ; LC Card 86-202642
HD9705.H82 K64 1986

MACHINERY INDUSTRY - SOVIET UNION.
Atarov, N. Z. Regional'nyĭ aspekt mezhotraslevykh proizvodstv . Moskva , 1980. 173 p. : LC Card 81-132091
HD9705.S595 A73 1980

MACHINERY INDUSTRY - SOVIET UNION - CAPITAL INVESTMENTS.
Razvitie i razmeshchenie mashinostroeniia v investitsionnom komplekse /. Moskva , 1986. 128 p. : LC Card 86-232328
HD9705.S595 R39 1986

MACHINERY INDUSTRY - SOVIET UNION - LABOR PRODUCTIVITY.
Ėkonomicheskie funktsii upravleniia proizvoditel'nym trudom /. Kiev , 1986. 167 p. ; LC Card 87-152432
HD9705.S595 E37 1986

MACHINERY INDUSTRY - SOVIET UNION - MANAGEMENT.
IUsufovich, B. E. (Boris Efimovich) Sovershenstvovanie operativnogo upravleniia osnovnym proizvodstvom mashinostroitel'nogo predpriiatiia /. Moskva , 1982. 91 p. : LC Card 82-204954
HD9705.S595 I94 1982

MACHINERY INDUSTRY - SOVIET UNION - MANAGEMENT - MATHEMATICAL MODELS.
Modin, Anatoliĭ Andreevich. Dinamika proizvodstvennykh ob"edineniĭ i modeli planirovaniia ikh deiatel'nosti /. Moskva , 1984. 231 p. : LC Card 84-195690
HD9705.S595 M62 1984

MACHINERY INDUSTRY - VENEZUELA.
Preliminary study report on promotion of small-medium scale industries in the Republic of Venezuela. [Tokyo] [1978] ii, 27 p. : LC Card 84-249328
HD9506.V42 P74 1978

Machinery of dominance . Cockburn, Cynthia. London , Dover, N.H. , 1985. 282 p. ; ISBN 0-7453-0065-0 (pbk.) : LC Card 86-204262 DDC 331.13/3/0941 19
HD6060.5.G7 C63 1985

The machinery of greed . Henriques, Diana B. Lexington, Mass. , c1986. x, 161 p. ; ISBN 0-669-09809-4 (alk. paper) LC Card 85-23841 DDC 364.1/68 19
HD3885 .H45 1986 ***NYPL [JLE 86-2739]***

MACHINERY - PRICES - HUNGARY - STATISTICS.
A Kohászati és a gépipari árak alakulása, 1980-1984 /. Budapest , 1986. 91 p. ; LC Card 86-202642
HD9705.H82 K64 1986

MACHINERY, REPLACEMENT OF. see **REPLACEMENT OF INDUSTRIAL EQUIPMENT.**

MACHINERY - SOCIAL AND ECONOMIC ASPECTS. see **MACHINERY IN INDUSTRY.**

MACHINERY - TRADE AND MANUFACTURE - DEVELOPING COUNTRIES.
Machinery and economic development /. Houndmills, Basingstoke, Hampshire , 1986. xvii, 274 p. : ISBN 0-333-36391-4
NYPL [JLD 86-4380]

MACHINES. see **MACHINERY.**

MACHINISTS - FRANCE - HISTORY - 19TH CENTURY.
Edmonson, James M. From Mecanicien to ingenieur . New York, NY , 1987. x, 631 p. ; ISBN 0-8240-8036-X (alk. paper) : LC Card 87-300 DDC 338.4/76218/0944 19
HD9705.F7 E35 1987

MACHINISTS - RUSSIAN S.F.S.R. - RIAZAN'.
Kaplinskaia, Elena. Puteshestvie v Riazan' /. Moskva , 1978. 84 p. ; LC Card 81-155441
HD8039.M22 S654 1978

Machlup, Fritz, 1902- Lecture on international monetary issues / Fritz Machlup. Islamabad : Pakistan Institute of Development Economics, 1982. vi, 49 p. ; 25 cm. (Lectures in development economics . no. 2) LC Card 85-217227 DDC 332.4/5 19
1. International finance. I. Title. II. Series.
HG3881 .M25 1982

Machnikowska, Stefania Dzięcielska- see **Dzięcielska-Machnikowska, Stefania.**

Machowski, Heinrich. RGW-Staaten und Dritte Welt : Wirtschaftsbeziehungen und Entwicklungshilfe / Heinrich Machowski, Siegfried Schultz. Bonn : Forschungsinstitut der Deutschen Gesellschaft für Auswärtige Politik : Vertrieb, Europa Union Verlag, 1981. iii, 84 p. ; 21 cm. (Arbeitspapiere zur Internationalen Politik, 0344-9815 . 18) Bibliography: p. 64-72. ISBN 3-7713-0167-X LC Card 85-224767
1. Europe, Eastern - Foreign economic relations - Developing countries. 2. Developing countries - Foreign economic relations - Europe, Eastern. 3. Economic assistance, Communist - Developing countries. 4. Council for Mutual Economic Assistance. I. Title. II. Series.
HF1532.15.D44 M33 1981

Macht, Arbeit und Humanität . Löffler, Reiner. Göttingen , c1986. v, 563 p. ; ISBN 3-921969-12-3 LC Card 86-227215
HD6957.G3 L64 1986

Macht, Profit & Kollegen . Kusch, Franz. Stuttgart [1986] 184 p. : ISBN 3-87959-272-1 LC Card 86-182407
HD6490.C642 G35 1986

Macht, Stephen.
Contract for life, the S.A.D.D. story [motion picture] /. Los Angeles, CA , 1985. 1 film reel

(31 min.) : LC Card 85-700743 DDC 363.1 11
HE5620.D7

Contract for life, the S.A.D.D story [videorecording] /. Los Angeles, CA , 1985. 1 videocassette (31 min.) : LC Card 85-700744 DDC 363.1 11
HE5620.D7

McHugh, Cathy. Mill family : the labor systems in the southern cotton textile industry, 1880-1915 / Cathy McHugh. New York : Oxford University Press, 1988. p. cm. Bibliography: p. Includes index. ISBN 0-19-504299-9 LC Card 87-7832 DDC 331.7/67721/0975 19
1. Cotton textile industry - Southern States - Employees - History. 2. Cotton textile industry - Southern States - History. 3. Family - Southern States - History. I. Title.
HD8039.T42 U654 1988

Maciejewski, Henryk. Ekonomia polityczna kapitalizmu . Poznań , 1978. 240 p. : LC Card 81-172481
HB179.P7 E37 1978

MacInnes, John. Thatcherism at work : industrial relations and economic change / by John MacInnes. Milton Keynes, England ; Philadelphia : Open University Press, 1987. p. cm. Bibliography: p. Includes index. ISBN 0-335-15517-0 LC Card 87-24722 DDC 338.941 19
1. Industrial relations - Great Britain. 2. Great Britain - Economic policy - 1945-. 3. Great Britain - Economic conditions - 1945-. I. Title.
HD8391 .M26 1987

MACINTOSH (COMPUTER)
Adler, John R. Dynamics of MacIntosh Excel /. Homewood, Ill. , c1987. xii, 164 p. : ISBN 0-87094-907-1 (pbk.) LC Card 86-72565 DDC 005.36/9 19
HF5548.4.E93 A35 1987

MACINTOSH (COMPUTER) - PROGRAMMING.
Cavuoto, James. LaserWrite it! . Reading, Mass. , 1986. viii, 198 p. : ISBN 0-201-11327-9 : LC Card 86-3406 DDC 070.5/028/5 19
Z286.E43 C38 1986 ***NYPL [JSE 86-1226]***

Hergert, Douglas. Microsoft Excel with macros . Redmond, Wash. [New York, N.Y.] , c1986. xii, 265 p. : ISBN 0-914845-76-4 (pbk.) : LC Card 86-211548 DDC 005.36/9 19
HF5548.4.E93 H474 1986

Lenfest, David. Mac Multiplan /. Blue Ridge Summit, Pa. , c1984. ix, 259 p. : ISBN 0-8306-0851-6 : LC Card 84-8796 DDC 001.64/25 19
HF5548.4.M74 L46 1984
NYPL [JSE 86-1870]

Wolenik, Robert. MacWrite made easier /. New York , 1985. xiv, 210 p. : ISBN 0-03-001763-7 LC Card 84-19781 DDC 652/.5 19
Z52.5.M32 W64 1985 ***NYPL [JLE 85-1535]***

Wortman, Leon A. Turbo Pascal for the Mac . Blue Ridge Summit, PA , c1987. x, 274 p. : ISBN 0-8306-2927-0 (pbk.) : LC Card 87-7134 DDC 650/.028/5416 19
HF5548.5.P14 W67 1987

McIntosh, Dave. The collectors : a history of Canadian Customs and Excise / Dave McIntosh. Toronto, Ont., Canada : Published by NC Press in association with Revenue Canada, Customs and Excise and the Canadian Govt. Pub. Centre, Supply and Services Canada, c1984. 414 p. : ill. (some col.), maps ; 24 cm. Includes index. Bibliography: p. 399-406. ISBN 0-920053-29-7 LC Card 85-162089 DDC 354.710072/46/09 19
1. Customs administration - Canada - History. 2. Excise tax - Canada - History. 3. Tariff - Canada - History. 4. Smuggling - Canada - History. I. Title.
HJ6751.A6 M35 1984 ***NYPL [JLE 86-2880]***

Macintyre, Donald, 1937- Wilsher, Peter. Strike . London [1985] xiii, 284 p., [16] p. of plates : ISBN 0-233-97825-9 : LC Card 86-221981 DDC 331.89/2822334/0941 19
HD5365.M6152 1984 .W55 1985b

McIntyre, John R. The Political economy of international technology transfer /. Westport, Conn. , c1986. viii, 267 p. : ISBN 0-89930-128-2 (lib. bdg. : alk. paper) LC Card 85-28128 DDC 338.9/26 19
HD45 .P574 1986 ***NYPL [JLE 86-3313]***

McIntyre, William Stokes. 101 ways to cut your business insurance costs without sacrificing protection / William S. McIntyre, IV, Jack P. Gibson. New York : McGraw-Hill, c1988. viii, 190 p. : ill. ; 24 cm. Includes index. ISBN 0-07-045112-5 : LC Card 87-17255 DDC 368 19
1. Insurance, Business. 2. Insurance, Business - United States. I. Gibson, Jack P. II. Title. III. Title: One hundred one ways to cut your business insurance costs without sacrificing protection.
HG8059 .M38 1988

McIver, Colin, 1914- The marketing mirage : how to make it a reality / Colin McIver. New York : Nichols Pub. Co., 1987. viii, 215 p. : ill. ; 24 cm. Includes index. ISBN 0-89397-285-1 : LC Card 87-14048 DDC 658.8 19
1. Marketing. I. Title.
HF5415 .M2583 1987

Mack, Macarena. Los trabajos de las mujeres entre el campo y la ciudad, 1920-1982 : campesina, costurera, obrera de la costura, empleada doméstica, cocinera de fundo, temporera / Macarena Mack, Paulina Matta, Ximena Valdés. [Santiago, Chile] : Centro de Estudios de la Mujer, [1986] 108 p. ; 19 cm. (Biblioteca de la mujer) LC Card 86-217673
1. Women - Employment - Chile - Biography. 2. Working-class women - Chile - Biography. I. Matta, Paulina. II. Valdés, Ximena. III. Title. IV. Series.
HD6126 .M33 1986

MacKay, Donald, 1925- The Asian dream : the Pacific Rim and Canada's national railway / Donald MacKay. Vancouver : Douglas & McIntyre, c1986. 223 p. : ill., maps ; 26 cm. Maps on lining papers. Bibliography: p. 215. Includes index. ISBN 0-88894-501-9 LC Card 86-225670 DDC 385/.0971 19
1. Canadian National Railways - History. 2. Merchant marine - Canada - History. 3. Canada - Commerce - Pacific area. 4. Pacific area - Commerce - Canada. I. Title.
HE2810.C14 M33 1986

Mackay, Robert J. Public choice and regulation . Stanford, Calif. , 1987. xiii, 363 p. : ISBN 0-8179-8562-X (pbk.) : LC Card 87-3984 DDC 353.0082/6 19
HD3616.U47 P796 1987

McKee, David L. Structural change in an urban industrial region . New York , 1987. ix, 255 p. ; ISBN 0-275-92353-3 (alk. paper) : LC Card 86-30652 DDC 330.9771/3043 19
HC107.O3 S85 1987

McKell, Lynn J. A study of MAS practice and knowledge and bibliographic references for management advisory services : MASPAK / by Lynn J. McKell and Kevin D. Stocks. New York, N.Y. : American Institute of Certified Public Accountants, c1987. 100, [iv], 72 p. ; 28 cm. "An AICPA report on management consulting by CPAs." Bibliography: p. [i]-72. ISBN 0-87051-002-9 (pbk.) : LC Card 87-19491 DDC 016.6584/6 19
1. Accountants - United States. 2. Business consultants - United States. 3. Industrial management - Bibliography. I. Stocks, Kevin D. II. American Institute of Certified Public Accountants. III. Title. IV. Title: MAS practice and knowledge and bibliographic references for management advisory services. V. Title: MASPAK.
HF5616.U5 M34 1987

McKelvey, James. The debugger's handbook : UCSD and Apple Pascal / James McKelvey, Jr. Belmont, Calif. : Wadsworth Pub. Co., c1986. xvi, 138 p. : ill. ; 23 cm. Includes index. ISBN 0-534-06432-9 LC Card 85-22628 DDC 005.13/3 19
1. UCSD Pascal (Computer program language). 2. Apple computer - Programming. 3. Debugging in computer science. I. Title.
QA76.73.U25 M34 1986 ***NYPL [JSE 87-65]***

McKenna, C. J. Uncertainty and the labor market : recent developments in job-search theory / C.J. McKenna. New York : St. Martin's Press, c1985. viii, 165 p. : ill. ; 23 cm. Includes index. Bibliography: p. [155]-163. ISBN 0-312-82861-6 : LC Card 85-1988 DDC 331.11 19
1. Unemployed - Mathematical models. 2. Labor supply - Mathematical models. 3. Job hunting - Mathematical models. I. Title.
HD5707 .M39 1985 ***NYPL [JLD 86-3666]***

McKenna, John F. (John Francis), 1945- Strategy, policy, and growth : text and cases / Jack F. McKenna. Reading, Mass. : Addison-Wesley, 1988. p. cm. Includes bibliographies and index. ISBN 0-201-13987-1 : LC Card 87-1301 DDC 658.4/012 19
1. Strategic planning. I. Title.
HD30.28 .M384 1988

Mackenney, Richard. Tradesmen and traders : the world of the guilds in Venice and Europe, c. 1250-c. 1650 / Richard Mackenney. London : Croom Helm, c1987. xv, 289 p. : ill. ; 22 cm. Bibliography: p. 257-277. Includes index. ISBN 0-7099-1763-5 LC Card 87-672566
1. Guilds - Italy - Venice - History. 2. Guilds - Europe - History. I. Title.
HD6472.V4 M33x 1987b

Mackenroth, Gerhard. BEVÖLKERUNGSLEHRE.
Bevölkerungswissenschaft . Frankfurt , New York , c1985. 227 p. ; ISBN 3-593-33461-5 LC Card 85-178756
HB849 .B48 1985

Mackenroth-Symposium (1983 : Universität Bamberg) Bevölkerungswissenschaft . Frankfurt , New York , c1985. 227 p. ; ISBN 3-593-33461-5 LC Card 85-178756
HB849 .B48 1985

Mackensen, Rainer, 1927- Leben im Jahr 2000 und danach . Berlin , c1984. 213 p. : ISBN 3-7605-8571-X LC Card 85-128359
HB3595 .L43 1984

McKenzie, Dennis J., 1940- California real estate principles /. New York , c1987. ix, 364 p. : ISBN 0-471-63274-0 LC Card 87-404650 DDC 333.33/09794 19
HD266.C2 C25 1987

MACKENZIE (GUYANA) - SOCIAL CONDITIONS.
Quamina, Odida T. Mineworkers of Guyana . London , Atlantic Highlands, N.J., USA , 1987. xv, 118 p., [7] p. of plates : ISBN 0-86232-308-8 : LC Card 87-14719 DDC 305/.9622/098814 19
HD8039.A492 G9558 1987

McKenzie, Richard B. The fairness of markets : a search for justice in a free society / Richard B. McKenzie. Lexington, Mass. : Lexington Books, c1987. xiv, 235 p. : ill. ; 23 cm. Includes bibliographies and index. ISBN 0-669-14801-6 (alk. paper) LC Card 86-45958 DDC 330 19
1. Economics - Moral and ethical aspects. 2. Capitalism - Moral and ethical aspects. 3. Wealth, Ethics of. 4. Economic policy. I. Title.
HB72 .M35 1987

MacKenzie, Warren, 1927- For women only : a woman's guide to financial security / by Warren MacKenzie. Alexandria, Va. : Crystal Rainbow Pub. Co., c1986. xiii, 196 p. ; 29 cm. Bibliography: p. 187-191. Includes index. ISBN 0-938125-00-1 : LC Card 86-70681 DDC 332.024/042 19
1. Women - Finance, Personal. I. Title. II. Title: Woman's guide to financial security.
HG179 .M244 1986

McKeown, Timothy J., 1951- Lynn, Leonard H. Organizing business . Washington, D.C. , c1988. xviii, 191 p. ; ISBN 0-8447-3629-5 (alk. paper) LC Card 87-17468 DDC 061/.3 19
HD2425 .L96 1988

McKern, Bruce. The Minerals industries of ASEAN and Australia . Sydney , Boston , 1988. p. cm. ISBN 0-04-301284-1 LC Card 87-18339 DDC 338.2/0959 19
HD9506.A6592 M56 1988

McKersie, Robert B. Kochan, Thomas A. The transformation of American industrial relations /. New York , c1986. viii, 287 p. ; ISBN 0-465-08696-9 : LC Card 85-47502 DDC 331/.0973 19
HD8072 .K67 1986

Mackey, David L. Whitford, Craig A. Postmarked . Lansing, Mich. (P.O. Box 14225, Lansing 48901) , c1987. 27 p., [2] p. of plates : LC Card 87-402869 DDC 769.56/7/0977427 19
HE6185.U7 M59 1987

Mackie, Peter J., 1947- The British transport industry and the European Community : a study of regulation and modal split in the long distance and international freight market /

Peter J. Mackie, David Simon, and Anthony E. Whiteing. Aldershot, Hampshire, England ; Brookfield, Vt., U. S.A. : Gower, c1987. xvi, 184 p. : map ; 23 cm. (Institute for Transport Studies . 3) Bibliography: p. 154-159. Includes index. ISBN 0-566-05368-3 : LC Card 86-24186 DDC 380.5/24/0941 19
1. Freight and freightage - Great Britain. 2. Freight and freightage - Government policy - Great Britain. 3. Freight and freightage - Government policy - European Economic Community countries. 4. Choice of transportation. I. Simon, David, 1957-. II. Whiteing, Anthony E., 1954-. III. Series: Institute for Transport Studies (Series) , 3. IV. Title.
HE199.G5 M33 1987

McKinlay, Robert D. Global problems and world order / R.D. McKinlay and R. Little. Madison, Wis. : University of Wisconsin Press, c1986. 292 p. ; 23 cm. Includes bibliographies and index. ISBN 0-299-11384-1 (pbk.) : LC Card 86-40489 DDC 337 19
1. International economic relations. 2. Security, International. 3. International organization. I. Little, Richard. II. Title.
HF1411 .M376 1986

McKinney, Jerome B. Fraud, waste, and abuse in government . Philadelphia , c1986. x, 159 p. ; ISBN 0-89727-058-4 LC Card 86-2967 DDC 336.73 19
HJ257.2 .F72 1986 ***NYPL [JLE 86-4153]***

Mackintosh, Ian, 1927- Sunrise Europe : the dynamics of information technology / Ian Mackintosh. Oxford, UK ; New York, NY, USA : B. Blackwell, 1986. xx, 288 p. : ill. ; 24 cm. Includes index. ISBN 0-631-14406-4 : LC Card 86-6077 DDC 338.4/7004/094 19
1. Computer industry - Europe. 2. Market surveys - Europe. I. Title.
HD9696.C63 E8547 1986
NYPL [JLE 86-3364]

McKinzie, Lance. A perspective on U. S. farm problems and agricultural policy / Lance McKinzie, Timothy G. Baker, and Wallace E. Tyner. Boulder : Westview Press, 1987. xvii, 189 p. : ill. ; 23 cm. (Westview special studies in agriculture science and policy) Bibliography: p. 179-189. ISBN 0-8133-7376-X (pbk. : alk. paper) LC Card 86-51501 DDC 338.1/873 19
1. Farms, Size of - Government policy - United States. 2. Farms, Small - Government policy - United States. 3. Farms - Government policy - United States. 4. Agriculture and state - United States. 5. Agriculture - United States - Finance. I. Baker, Timothy G. II. Tyner, Wallace E. III. Title. IV. Series.
HD1470.5.U6 M35 1987

McKnight, Gerald. Gucci : a house divided / Gerald McKnight. New York : D.I. Fine, c1987. xi, 362 p. : ill. ; 24 cm. Includes index. ISBN 1-556-11037-5 (alk. paper) : LC Card 86-46390 DDC 338.7/687/0945 19
1. Gucci (Firm). 2. Clothing trade - Italy. 3. Clothing trade. I. Title.
HD9940.I84 G86 1987

Mackscheidt, K. Krischausky, D. Wohnungsgemeinnützigkeit . Köln , c1984. vi, 161 p. ; ISBN 3-452-19899-5 LC Card 84-182027
HD7339.A3 K79 1984

McLafferty, Sara L. Ghosh, Avijit. Location strategies for retail and service firms /. Lexington, Mass. , c1987. x, 212 p. : ISBN 0-669-12032-4 (alk. paper) LC Card 85-45583 DDC 658.1/1 19
HF5429.275 .G47 1987

McLaughlin, Helen E. Walking on air : an informal history of inflight service of seven U. S. airlines / by Helen E. McLaughlin. Denver, Colo. : State of the Art, c1986. vi, 210 p. : ill. ; 28 cm. Bibliography: p. 205-206. ISBN 0-930161-04-1 (pbk.) LC Card 87-115599 DDC 387.7/42/0973 19
1. Flight attendants - United States - History. I. Title.
HD8039.A432 U66 1986

McLean, Edward B. Roman Catholicism and the right to work / Edward B. McLean. Lanham : University Press of America, c1985. ix, 175 p. ; 23 cm. Bibliography: p. 167-175. ISBN 0-8191-5009-6 (alk. paper) : LC Card 85-20379 DDC 261.8/5 19
1. Catholic Church - Doctrines. 2. Open and closed shop - Religious aspects - Catholic Church. 3. Open and closed shop - United States. I. Title.
HD6338 .M436 1985 ***NYPL [JLD 86-2803]***

McLean, Ian W. The Australian economy in the long run /. Cambridge [Cambridgeshire] , New York , 1987. xi, 372 p. : ISBN 0-521-32674-5 LC Card 86-26345 DDC 330.994 19
HC605 .A7767 1987

McLean, Robert J. Exploiting opportunities in the Pacific Basin : survey results / Robert J. McLean. [Melbourne] : Committee for Economic Development of Australia, [1986] 56 p. : ill. ; 29 cm. (Monograph . no. M82) At head of title: Strategic Issues Forum. "June 1986." "CEDA study": Cover. "Registered by Australia Post-Publication No. VBP 0641": Cover. Bibliography: p. 44-45. ISBN 0-85801-162-X (pbk.) LC Card 86-203142 DDC 337.9409 19
1. Australia - Foreign economic relations - Pacific Area. 2. Pacific Area - Foreign economic relations - Australia. I. Series: Monograph series (Committee for Economic Development of Australia) , no. 82. II. Title.
HF1626.5.P33 M35 1986

McLewin, Philip J., 1939- Power and economic change : the response to emancipation in Jamaica and British Guiana, 1840-1865 / Philip J. McLewin. New York : Garland, 1987. ii, 271 p. : 1 ill. ; 24 cm. (South American and Latin American economic history) Bibliography: p. 261-271. ISBN 0-8240-1366-2 (alk. paper) : LC Card 87-8344 DDC 330.97292/04 19
1. Jamaica - Economic conditions. 2. Guyana - Economic conditions. 3. Slavery - Jamaica - Emancipation - History. 4. Slavery - Guyana - Emancipation - History. 5. Sugar workers - Jamaica - Supply and demand - History - 19th century. 6. Sugar workers - Guyana - Supply and demand - History - 19th century. 7. Jamaica - Politics and government - To 1962. 8. Guyana - Politics and government - 1803-1966. I. Title. II. Series.
HC154 .M36 1987

McLimore, J. Fred. Strategies-- successes-- senior executives speak out /. New York , c1988. xiii, 397 p. : ISBN 0-06-044354-5 (pbk.) LC Card 87-21765 DDC 658 19
HD31 .S696394 1988

McLin, Jon B. Social and economic effects of petroleum development in non-OPEC developing countries : synthesis report / Jon McLin. Geneva : International Labour Office, 1986. xiii, 104 p., [4] folded leaves of plates : ill. ; 24 cm. Bibliography: p. [99]-104. ISBN 92-2-105505-1 (pbk.) : LC Card 87-123328 DDC 338.2/782/091724 19
1. Petroleum industry and trade - Developing countries. 2. Developing countries - Economic conditions. 3. Developing countries - Social conditions. I. Title.
HD9578.D44 M396 1986

Mcloughlin, Caven S. Getting employed, staying employed : job development and training for persons with severe handicaps / edited by Caven S. Mcloughlin, J. Bradley Garner, Michael J. Callahan. Baltimore : P.H. Brookes Pub. Co., c1987. xvi, 239 p. ; 26 cm. Bibliography: p. 176-180. Includes index. ISBN 0-933716-70-2 (pbk.) : LC Card 87-13185 DDC 650.1/4/0240816 19
1. Vocational rehabilitation. 2. Handicapped - Employment. 3. Handicapped - Training of. 4. Handicapped - Vocational guidance. I. Garner, J. Bradley, 1949-. II. Callahan, Michael J. III. Title.
HD7255 .M395 1987

McLure, Charles E. The value-added tax : key to deficit reduction? / Charles E. McLure, Jr. with commentary by Mark A. Bloomfield. Washington, D.C. : American Enterprise Institute for Public Policy Research ; Lanham, MD ; xi, 184 p. : ill. ; 24 cm. (AEI studies . 450) Includes bibliographies and index. ISBN 0-8447-3613-9 (alk. paper) LC Card 86-28905 DDC 339.5/25/0973 19
1. Value-added tax - United States. 2. Budget deficits - United States. I. Bloomfield, Mark A. II. Title. III. Series.
HJ5715.U6 M364 1987

Macmillan series in information systems. Turban, Efraim. Decision support and expert systems . New York , London , c1988. xxi, 697 p. : ISBN 0-02-421650-X LC Card 87-23911 DDC 658.4/03 19
HD30.2 .T87 1988

Macmillan small business series. Small business in Europe /. Basingstoke, Hampshire , 1986. xx, 211 p. : ISBN 0-333-38405-9 : LC Card 86-673899
HD2346.E9 S62x 1986

McMillon, Bill, 1942- The old lodges & hotels of our national parks / Bill McMillon. South Bend, Ind. : Icarus Press, 1983. ix, 130 p., [32] p. of plates : ill. (some col.) ; 29 cm. ISBN 0-89651-551-6 : LC Card 83-18456 DDC 647/.947301 19
1. Hotels, taverns, etc. - United States. 2. National parks and reserves - United States. I. Title. II. Title: Old lodges and hotels of our national parks.
TX909 .M34 1983 ***NYPL [JFF 86-405]***

MacMinn, Richard D. Martin, John D., 1945- The theory of finance . Chicago , c1988. xxvi, 709 p. : ISBN 0-03-063854-2 LC Card 87-496 DDC 332/.01 19
HG173 .M353 1988

McMullen, Georganne L. (Georganne Louise), 1959- Lyson, Thomas A. The changing structure of South Carolina agriculture since 1959 /. Clemson, S.C. [1986] 29 p. : LC Card 87-620716 DDC 338.1/09757 19
HD1775.S6 L97 1986

McMullen, Kathryn Elizabeth. Betcherman, Gordon. Working with technology . [Ottawa] , 1986. 43 p. : ISBN 0-660-12174-3 (pbk.) : LC Card 86-224095 DDC 338/.06 19
HC120.A9 B47 1986

McMullen, Neil. Seeds and world agricultural progress / Neil McMullen. Washington, D.C. : National Planning Association, c1987. viii, 263 p. : ill. ; 22 cm. (NPA report . #227) ISBN 0-89068-088-4 (pbk.) : LC Card 87-60766 DDC 338.1/7 19
1. Seed industry and trade - Social aspects. 2. Seeds. 3. Agriculture - Economic aspects. I. Series. II. Series: NPA report , no. 227. III. Title.
HD9019.S43 M36 1987

Macnab, Roy Martin, 1923- Gold their touchstone : Gold Fields of South Africa, 1887-1987 : a century story / Roy Macnab. Johannesburg : J. Ball, 1987. xii, 332 p., [16] p. of plates : ill. (some col.) ; 25 cm. Includes index. ISBN 0-86850-140-9 LC Card 87-148896 DDC 338.7/6223422/09682 19
1. Gold Fields of South Africa Limited - History - 19th century. 2. Gold Fields of South Africa Limited - History - 20th century. 3. Gold industry - South Africa - History - 19th century. 4. Gold industry - South Africa - History - 20th century. 5. Gold mines and mining - South Africa - History - 19th century. 6. Gold mines and mining - South Africa - History - 20th century. I. Title.
HD9536.S64 G656 1987

McNairn, William N. The smart attorney's guide to accounting documents for discovery and evidence / William N. McNairn. 1st ed. Redondo Beach, Calif. : Quotamus Press, 1987. x, 123 p. : ill. ; 27 cm. Bibliography: p. 121-122. ISBN 0-932621-02-3 (pbk.) LC Card 86-62954 DDC 657/.024344 19
1. Accounting - United States. 2. Financial statements - United States. 3. Forensic accounting - United States. I. Title.
HF5616.U5 M346 1987

McNees, Roger W.
Noel, James S. Retention of reflective raised pavement markers /. College Station, Tex. , Springfield, Va. [1986] xiii, 170 p. : LC Card 87-620642 DDC 380.5 s 625.7/042 19
HE203 .T43 no. 322-3 TE203

State-of-the-art and objectives of reflective raised pavement markers / by Roger W. McNees and James S. Noel ; sponsored by Texas State Department of Highways and Public Transportation in cooperation with the U. S. Department of Transportation, Federal High[w]ay Administration. College Station, Tex. : Texas Transportation Institute, Texas A&M University System ; Springfield, Va. : Available through the National Technical Information Service, [1986] vii, 162 p. : ill. ; 28 cm. (Research report (Texas Transportation Institute) . 322-1) "October 1986." "Study number 2-18-3232-1." "Annotated bibliography": p. 126-155. Bibliography: p. 156-162. LC Card 87-620643 DDC 380.5 s 625.7/97 19
1. Road markings. 2. Reflectors (Safety devices). I. Noel, James S. II. Texas. State Dept. of Highways and Public Transportation. III. United States. Federal Highway Administration. IV. Series. V. Series: Research report (Texas Transportation Institute) , 322-1. VI. Title.
HE203 .T43 no. 322-1 TE203

McNeil, William C. American money and the Weimar Republic : economics and politics on the eve of the Great Depression / William C. McNeil. New York : Columbia University Press, 1986. x, 352 p. : ill. ; 24 cm. (The Political economy of international change) Includes index. Bibliography: p. [329]-344. ISBN 0-231-06236-2 LC Card 85-29962 DDC 336.3/4/0943 19
1. Loans, American - Germany - History - 20th century. 2. World War, 1914-1918 - Reparations. 3. Germany - Economic conditions - 1918-1945. 4. United States - Foreign economic relations - Germany. 5. Germany - Foreign economic relations - United States. I. Series. II. Series: Political economy of international change series. III. Title.
HG3949 .M38 1986 ***NYPL [JLE 86-3268]***

McNeill, Patrick. Research methods / Patrick McNeill. London ; New York : Tavistock Publications, 1985. 136 p. ; 21 cm. (Society now) Society now; social science paperback ; no. 300. Includes index. Bibliography: p. 129-133. ISBN 0-422-79540-2 (pbk.) LC Card 85-4656 DDC 301/.072 19
1. Sociology - Methodology. 2. Social sciences - Methodology. I. Title. II. Series.
HM24 .M37 1985 ***NYPL [JLD 86-4181]***

McNicoll, Iain H. (Iain Hugh) Gregory, P. World offshore markets . London , 1986. xiv, 215 p. ; ISBN 0-946416-06-0 (pbk.) : LC Card 86-217327 DDC 338.2/7282/0941 19
HD9571.5 .G75 1986

McNulty, Robert H., 1940- The economics of amenity : community futures and quality of life : a policy guide to urban economic development / Robert H. McNulty, Dorothy Jacobsen, R. Leo Penne, principal writer. Washington, D.C. : Partners for Livable Places, c1985. xvi, 157 p. : ill. ; 23 cm. Bibliography: p. 145-157. ISBN 0-941182-15-0 (pbk.) LC Card 85-6545 DDC 307.7/6/0973 19
1. Cities and towns - United States - Civic improvement. 2. City planning - United States. 3. Quality of life - United States. I. Jacobson, Dorothy R., 1950-. II. Penne, R. Leo, 1941-. III. Partners for Livable Places. IV. Title.
HT321 .M36 1985 ***NYPL [JLE 86-4519]***

Les Maçons de la Creuse /. Bandy de Nalèche, Louis. Limoges , 1984. 99 p., [16] p. of plates : ISBN 2-85521-059-3 : LC Card 85-169794 DDC 331.7/69321/094468 19
HB2054.C74 B36 1984

McPhee, Cosima. Brain, Peter J. The microeconomic structure of the Australian economy /. Melbourne, Australia , 1986. xxiv, 448 p. : ISBN 0-582-71502-4 (pbk.) LC Card 87-100715 DDC 330.994/063 19
HC603 .B73 1986

MACPHERSON, C. B. (CRAWFORD BROUGH), 1911- - INFLUENCE.
Israel Zipper, Ricardo. Democracia y liberalismo /. Santiago de Chile , 1984. 56 p. ; LC Card 85-197546
HB95 .I87 1984

McPherson, Edwin M. Apparel manufacturing management systems : a computer-oriented approach / by Edwin M. McPherson. Park Ridge, N.J., U. S.A. : Noyes Publications, c1987. xiv, 392 p. : ill. ; 25 cm. ISBN 0-8155-1141-8 : LC Card 87-12239 DDC 687/.068 19
1. Clothing trade - Management - Data processing. I. Title.
HD9940.A2 M42 1987

McPherson, Joseph H. Bringing innovations to market : a comprehensive approach to successful diffusion of new products and processes / Joseph H. McPherson. Menlo Park, Calif. (333 Ravenswood Ave., Menlo Park 94025-3476) : Business Intelligence Program, SRI International, c1984. 36 p. : ill. (some col.) ; 28 cm. (Report / Business Intelligence Program, SRI International . no. 704 (summer 1984)) Cover title. LC Card 87-118382 DDC 658.5/75 19
1. New products. 2. Technological innovations. I. Series: Research report (Business Intelligence Program (SRI International)) , 704. II. Title.
HF5415.153 .M35 1984

McQuaid, Ronald, 1955- The Development of high technology industries . London , New York , c1987. 363 p. : ISBN 0-7099-3942-6 LC Card 87-9086 DDC 338.4/762 19
HC79.H53 D48 1987

Macro blueprint . Sealy, Albert H. New York , 1986. viii, 407, 232 p. ; ISBN 0-89192-390-X LC Card 86-218989 DDC 338.973 19
HD2785 .S412 1986

Macro-economics /. Dornbusch, Rudiger. New York , c1987. xiv, 798 p. : ISBN 0-07-017776-7 : LC Card 86-21114 DDC 339 19
HB172.5 .D67 1987

Macro-economics in question . Sawyer, Malcolm C. [Macroeconomics in question.] Brighton, Sussex , 1982. xiii, 190 p. : ISBN 0-7108-0140-8 LC Card 86-673557
HB172.5 .S28x 1982b

MACRO INSTRUCTIONS (ELECTRONIC COMPUTERS)
Benjamin, Louis. The complete book of Excel macros /. Berkeley, Calif. , c1986. xviii, 123 p. : ISBN 0-07-881214-3 (pbk.) LC Card 86-106041 DDC 650/.028/55369 19
HF5548.4.E93 B46 1986 ***NYPL [JSE 87-239]***

Hergert, Douglas. Microsoft Excel with macros . Redmond, Wash. [New York, N.Y.] , c1986. xii, 265 p. : ISBN 0-914845-76-4 (pbk.) : LC Card 86-211548 DDC 005.36/9 19
HF5548.4.E93 H474 1986

The Lotus guide to learning Symphony macros . Reading, Mass. , c1986. viii, 243 p. : ISBN 0-201-16684-4 (pbk.) LC Card 86-213051 DDC 005.36/9 19
HF5549.4.S95 L67 1986

Lunsford, E. Michael. Macros, menus, and miracles for Lotus 1-2-3 /. New York , c1987. xix, 234 p. : ISBN 0-471-85996-6 (pbk.) : LC Card 87-14285 DDC 005.36/9 19
HF5548.4.L67 L86 1987

Shaffer, Daniel N. Macro programming for 1-2-3 . Indianapolis, Ind. , c1987. xiv, 283 p. : ISBN 0-672-46573-6 (pbk.) LC Card 86-63301 DDC 005.36/9 19
HF5548.4.L67 S48 1987

Macro programming for 1-2-3 . Shaffer, Daniel N. Indianapolis, Ind. , c1987. xiv, 283 p. : ISBN 0-672-46573-6 (pbk.) LC Card 86-63301 DDC 005.36/9 19
HF5548.4.L67 S48 1987

The macrodynamics of advanced market economies /. Eichner, Alfred S. Armonk, N.Y. , c1987. x, 945 p. : ISBN 0-87332-439-0 (pbk.) LC Card 87-9693 DDC 330.12/2 19
HB501 .E4 1987

Macroeconomic analysis . Cobham, David P. London , New York , 1987. viii, 159 p. : ISBN 0-582-29708-7 (pbk.) LC Card 86-27825 DDC 339 19
HB172.5 .C63 1987

Macroeconomic conflict and social institutions / edited by Shlomo Maital and Irwin Lipnowski. Cambridge, Mass. : Ballinger Pub. Co., c1985. xi, 249 p. : ill. ; 24 cm. Chiefly papers originating from a session on "Income policy as a social institution," at the American Economic Association's 95th Annual Meeting in New York, Dec. 28-30, 1982. Includes bibliographies and index. ISBN 0-88730-034-0 LC Card 84-24376 DDC 339.2 19
1. Income distribution - Addresses, essays, lectures. 2. Social institutions - Addresses, essays, lectures. 3. Institutional economics - Addresses, essays, lectures. 4. Macroeconomics - Addresses, essays, lectures. I. Maital, Shlomo. II. Lipnowski, Irwin. III. American Economic Association. Meeting (95th : 1982 : New York, N.Y.).
HC79.I5 M225 1985 ***NYPL [JLE 86-2562]***

Macroeconomic diplomacy in the 1980s . Henning, C. Randall. London , New York , c1987. x, 76 p. ; ISBN 0-7099-3794-6 (pbk.) LC Card 87-20041 DDC 337/.09171/3 19
HF1455 .H46 1987

Macroeconomics [i.e. Macroeconomic] impacts of energy shocks / edited by Bert G. Hickman, Hillard G. Huntington, and James L. Sweeney. Amsterdam ; New York : North-Holland ; xvi, 331 p. : ill. ; 24 cm. (Contributions to economic analysis. 163) Includes bibliographical references. ISBN 0-444-70247-4 (U. S.) LC Card 87-9035 DDC 338.4/36655/0724 19
1. Inflation (Finance) - Effect of energy costs on - Mathematical models. 2. Macroeconomics - Mathematical models. 3. Petroleum products - Prices - Mathematical models. 4. Economic policy - Mathematical models. I. Hickman, Bert G., 1924-. II. Huntington, Hillard G. III. Sweeney, James L. IV. Title: Macroeconomic impacts of energy shocks. V. Series.
HG229 .M315 1987

Macroeconomic impacts of energy shocks. Macroeconomics [i.e. Macroeconomic] impacts of energy shocks /. Amsterdam ; New York : xvi, 331 p. : ISBN 0-444-70247-4 (U. S.) LC Card 87-9035 DDC 338.4/36655/0724 19
HG229 .M315 1987

Macroeconomic medium-term models in the Nordic countries / edited by O. Bjerkholt and J. Rosted. Amsterdam ; New York : North-Holland ; x, 324 p. : ill. ; 24 cm. (Contributions to economic analysis. 164) "Based on papers that were originally presented at the "Seminar on Macroeconomic Modelling in the Nordic Countries" held at Fredriksdal, Lyngby, Denmark in October 1984"--Pref. Includes bibliographies and indexes. ISBN 0-444-70262-8 (U. S.) LC Card 87-13422 DDC 330.948/00724 19
1. Scandinavia - Economic conditions - Econometric models - Congresses. I. Bjerkholt, Olav, 1942-. II. Rosted, Jørgen. III. Seminar on Macroeconomic Modelling in the Nordic Countries (1984 : Fredriksdal, Lyngby, Denmark). IV. Series.
HC345 .M33 1987

Macroeconomic policies and adjustment in Yugoslavia . Yagci, Fahrettin, 1944- Washington, D.C. [1987] 29 p. ; ISBN 0-8213-0938-2 (pbk.) LC Card 87-16064 DDC 339.5/09497 19
HC407.Y6 Y34 1987

Macroeconomic policies, debt accumulation, and adjustment in Brazil, 1965-84 /. Martone, Celso L. (Celso Luiz) Washington, D.C. , 1987. vii, 43 p. ; ISBN 0-8213-0892-0 (pbk.) LC Card 86-1527 DDC 336.3/4/0981 19
HJ8579 .M37 1987

Macroeconomic systems /. Cuthbertson, Keith. Oxford, UK , New York, NY, USA , 1987. ix, 278 p. : ISBN 0-631-14341-6 : LC Card 87-10332 DDC 339 19
HB172.5 .C87 1987

Macroeconomic theory /. Sargent, Thomas J. Boston , c1987. xxii, 510 p. : ISBN 0-12-619751-2 (alk. paper) LC Card 86-28778 DDC 339/.01 19
HB172.5 .S27 1987

Macroeconomic uncertainty . Oxelheim, Lars. Chichester [West Sussex] , New York , c1987. xv, 251 p. : ISBN 0-471-91480-0 : LC Card 87-8333 DDC 658.1/55 19
HG3821 .O894 1987

Macroeconomics . Bach, George Leland, 1915- [Economics. Selections.] Englewood Cliffs, N.J. , c1987. xiii, 458 p. : ISBN 0-13-542887-4 (pbk.) LC Card 86-30264 DDC 339 19
HB172.5 .B33 1987

Macroeconomics /. Barro, Robert J. New York , c1987. xiv, 608 p. : ISBN 0-471-85125-6 LC Card 86-24667 DDC 339 19
HB172.5 .B36 1987

Macroeconomics . Bhaduri, Amit. Houndmills, Basingstoke, Hampshire , 1986. xii, 278 p. : ISBN 0-333-29194-8 LC Card 86-673605
HB172.5 .B48x 1986b

Macroeconomics . Bogan, Elizabeth Chapin. St. Paul, MN , c1987. xviii, 569 p. : ISBN 0-314-25867-1 : LC Card 86-24643 DDC 339 19
HB172.5 .B64 1987

Macroeconomics . Clark, J. R. (Jeff R.) San Diego , c1987. xv, 574 p. : ISBN 0-15-551226-9 (pbk.) LC Card 86-83043 DDC 339 19
HB172.5 .C585 1987

Macroeconomics . Edgmand, Michael R. Englewood Cliffs, N.J. , c1987. xvi, 495 p. : ISBN 0-13-542952-8 LC Card 86-25360 DDC 339 19
HB172.5 .E36 1987

Macroeconomics. Ekelund, Robert B. (Robert Burton), 1940- Plano, Tex. , 1987. xvi, 536 p. : ISBN 0-256-03678-0 LC Card 86-71959 DDC 339 19
HB172.5 .D44 1987

Macroeconomics /. Ekelund, Robert B. (Robert Burton), 1940- Glenview, Ill. , c1988. xxix, 592 p. : ISBN 0-673-39768-8 (pbk.) LC Card 87-23513

DDC 339 19
HB172.5 .E42 1988

Macroeconomics . Greenaway, David. Oxford, OX, UK , New York, NY, USA , 1987. p. cm. ISBN 0-631-15763-8 (pbk.) : LC Card 87-20831 DDC 339/.0941 19
HB172.5 .G75 1987

Macroeconomics /. Thompson, Allen R. Reading, Mass. , c1988. xxx, 888, [38] p. : ISBN 0-201-09684-6 (pbk.) LC Card 87-916 DDC 339 19
HB172.5 .T48 1988

Macroeconomics /. Truett, Lila J. St. Louis , 1987. xxii, 531, [44] p. : ISBN 0-8016-5158-1 (pbk.) LC Card 86-23879 DDC 339 19
HB172.5 .T78 1987

MACROECONOMICS.

Bach, George Leland, 1915- [Economics. Selections.] Macroeconomics . Englewood Cliffs, N.J. , c1987. xiii, 458 p. : ISBN 0-13-542887-4 (pbk.) LC Card 86-30264 DDC 339 19
HB172.5 .B33 1987

Barro, Robert J. Macroeconomics /. New York , c1987. xiv, 608 p. : ISBN 0-471-85125-6 LC Card 86-24667 DDC 339 19
HB172.5 .B36 1987

Beck, Horst. Auswirkungen von nicht kostenniveauneutralen Lohnänderungen auf Beschäftigung und Preisniveau . Krefeld , 1983. iii, 227 p. : ISBN 3-88358-033-3 LC Card 83-202725
HD4911 .B4 1983

Bhaduri, Amit. Macroeconomics . Houndmills, Basingstoke, Hampshire , 1986. xii, 278 p. : ISBN 0-333-29194-8 LC Card 86-673605
HB172.5 .B48x 1986b

Bober, Stanley. Modern macroeconomics . London , New York , c1988. ix, 278 p. : ISBN 0-7099-5080-2 LC Card 87-15190 DDC 339 19
HB172.5 .B62 1988

Bogan, Elizabeth Chapin. Macroeconomics . St. Paul, MN , c1987. xviii, 569 p. : ISBN 0-314-25867-1 : LC Card 86-24643 DDC 339 19
HB172.5 .B64 1987

Clark, J. R. (Jeff R.) Macroeconomics . San Diego , c1987. xv, 574 p. : ISBN 0-15-551226-9 (pbk.) LC Card 86-83043 DDC 339 19
HB172.5 .C585 1987

Cobham, David P. Macroeconomic analysis . London , New York , 1987. viii, 159 p. : ISBN 0-582-29708-7 (pbk.) LC Card 86-27825 DDC 339 19
HB172.5 .C63 1987

Cuthbertson, Keith. Macroeconomic systems /. Oxford, UK , New York, NY, USA , 1987. ix, 278 p. : ISBN 0-631-14341-6 : LC Card 87-10332 DDC 339 19
HB172.5 .C87 1987

Cysne, Rubens Penha. Política macroeconômica no Brasil, 1964/66 e 1980/84 /. Rio de Janeiro, RJ [1986?] 125 p. : LC Card 86-229936
HC187 .C983 1986

Daly, D. J. (Donald James), 1922- Managerial macroeconomics . Homewood, Ill. , 1988. xvi, 383 p. : ISBN 0-256-06000-2 LC Card 87-80950 DDC 339/.024658 19
HD30.22 .D35 1988

Dornbusch, Rudiger. Macro-economics /. New York , c1987. xiv, 798 p. : ISBN 0-07-017776-7 : LC Card 86-21114 DDC 339 19
HB172.5 .D67 1987

Edgmand, Michael R. Macroeconomics . Englewood Cliffs, N.J. , c1987. xvi, 495 p. : ISBN 0-13-542952-8 LC Card 86-25360 DDC 339 19
HB172.5 .E36 1987

Ekelund, Robert B. (Robert Burton), 1940- Macroeconomics. Plano, Tex. , 1987. xvi, 536 p. : ISBN 0-256-03678-0 LC Card 86-71959 DDC 339 19
HB172.5 .D44 1987

Ekelund, Robert B. (Robert Burton), 1940- Macroeconomics /. Glenview, Ill. , c1988. xxix, 592 p. : ISBN 0-673-39768-8 (pbk.) LC Card 87-23513 DDC 339 19
HB172.5 .E42 1988

Feucht, Martin. Theorie des Konkurrenzsozialismus . Stuttgart , New York , 1983. iv, 222 p. : ISBN 3-437-50273-5 LC Card 83-205881
HC79.S6 F48 1983

Fisher, Douglas, 1934- Monetary and fiscal policy /. New York , c1987. p. cm. ISBN 0-8147-2587-2 : LC Card 87-5478 DDC 339.5/2 19
HB172.5 .F54 1987

Fleisher, Belton M. Principles of macroeconomics /. Dubuque, Iowa , c1987. xix, 427 p. : ISBN 0-697-01035-X (pbk.) LC Card 86-72959 DDC 339 19
HB172.5 .F545 1987

Frank, Jeff. The new Keynesian economics . Brighton , 1986. xvii, 283 p. : ISBN 0-7108-0239-0 ***NYPL [JLD 86-2534]***

Gandolfo, Giancarlo. International economics II . Berlin , New York , c1987. p. cm. ISBN 0-387-17978-X (U. S.) LC Card 87-16295 DDC 332.4/5 19
HF1411 .G3363 1987

Greenaway, David. Macroeconomics . Oxford, OX, UK , New York, NY, USA , 1987. p. cm. ISBN 0-631-15763-8 (pbk.) : LC Card 87-20831 DDC 339/.0941 19
HB172.5 .G75 1987

Hahn, Frank. Equilibrium and macroeconomics /. Oxford , 1984. vi, 397 p. : ISBN 0-631-13482-4 : LC Card 87-672165
HB171 .H23x 1984b

Havrilesky, Thomas M. Introduction to modern macroeconomics /. Arlington Heights, Ill. , c1988. p. cm. ISBN 0-88295-414-8 LC Card 87-24456 DDC 339 19
HB172.5 .H38 1988

Holland, Stuart. The global economy . New York , 1987. xiv, 443 p. : ISBN 0-312-01323-X : LC Card 87-20566 DDC 339 19
HB172.5 .H655 1987

Huber, Gérard. Les conséquences à long terme de la politique macroéconomique /. Berne , 1982. 449 p. ; ISBN 3-261-04985-5 LC Card 87-672303
HB172.5 .H82x 1982

Issues in contemporary macroeconomics and distribution /. London , 1985. xxviii, 465 p. : ISBN 0-333-35483-4 : LC Card 86-673473
HB172.5 .I87x 1985b

Jäggi, Christian M. Die Makroökonomik von J.M. Keynes /. Berlin , New York , c1986. xiii, 278 p. : ISBN 0-387-16477-4 (U. S.) LC Card 86-225958
HB99.7 .J34 1986

Laidler, David E. W. Monetarist perspectives /. Deddington, Oxford , 1982. xii, 218 p. ; ISBN 0-86003-042-3 LC Card 86-673565
HG230.3 .L34x 1982b

Laroque, Guy. Fondements de l'analyse macroéconomique à court terme /. Paris , 1986. 98 p. : ISBN 2-222-03757-3 : LC Card 87-103537
HB173 .L35 1986

McCarty, Marilu Hurt. Introductory macroeconomics /. Glenview, Ill. , c1988. xxiii, 533 p. : ISBN 0-673-18432-3 (pbk.) : LC Card 87-23434 DDC 339 19
HB172.5 .M37 1988

Manohar Rao, M. J. Filtering and control of macroeconomic systems . Amsterdam ; New York : xii, 279 p. : ISBN 0-444-70188-5 (Elsevier Science Pub. Co.) LC Card 86-32928 DDC 339.5/0954 19
HC435.2 .M34 1987

Melišek, František. Ekonomický rast a štrukturálne zmeny v socialistickej ekonomike /. Bratislava , 1980. 175 p. : LC Card 82-464724 DDC 338.9 19
HD84.5 .M379 1980 ***NYPL [*QT 87-1737]***

Mistri, Maurizio. Tasso di inflazione, saggio di interesse e "nuova" macroeconomia /. Padova , 1985. x, 143 p. : LC Card 86-214490
HB539 .M54 1985

Peterson, Wallace C. Income, employment, and economic growth /. New York [c1988] xxiii, 750 p. : ISBN 0-393-95628-8 LC Card 87-17933 DDC 339 19
HB172.5 .P453 1988

Pisani-Ferry, Jean. Problèmes de macroéconomie /. Paris , 1984. 452 p. : ISBN 2-7178-0801-9 : LC Card 85-100663 DDC 339 19
HB173 .P534 1984

Prices, quantities, and expectations . Oxford [Oxfordshire] , New York , 1987. xxiv, 487 p. : ISBN 0-19-828589-2 (pbk.) : LC Card 87-7770 DDC 330.15/6 19
HB99.7 .P74 1987

Readings and cases in macroeconomics /. New York , c1987. x, 485 p. : ISBN 0-07-017779-1 (pbk.) : LC Card 86-27423 DDC 339 19
HB172.5 .D67 1987 Suppl.

Rosende Ramírez, Francisco. Consideraciones acerca del estado del debate en teoría macroeconómica /. Santiago , 1986. 51 leaves ; LC Card 87-116226 DDC 339 19
HB178.5 .R67 1986

Sargent, Thomas J. Macroeconomic theory /. Boston , c1987. xxii, 510 p. : ISBN 0-12-619751-2 (alk. paper) LC Card 86-28778 DDC 339/.01 19
HB172.5 .S27 1987

Sawyer, Malcolm C. [Macroeconomics in question.] Macro-economics in question . Brighton, Sussex , 1982. xiii, 190 p. : ISBN 0-7108-0140-8 LC Card 86-673557
HB172.5 .S28x 1982b

Slovin, Myron B. Macroeconomics for managers /. Englewood Cliffs, N.J. , c1987. xvi, 512 p. : ISBN 0-13-542937-4 LC Card 86-25199 DDC 339 19
HB172.5 .S55 1987

Social choice and public decision making /. Cambridge [Cambridgeshire] , New York , 1986. xix, 215 p. : ISBN 0-521-30454-7 LC Card 86-8580 DDC 339 19
HB846.8 .S59 1986 ***NYPL [JLE 86-4189]***

Södersten, Bo. Makroekonomi och stabiliseringspolitik /. [Malmö] , c1983. 363 p. : ISBN 91-40-05037-8 : LC Card 84-166176
HB179.S8 S63 1983

Thompson, Allen R. Macroeconomics /. Reading, Mass. , c1988. xxx, 888, [38] p. : ISBN 0-201-09684-6 (pbk.) LC Card 87-916 DDC 339 19
HB172.5 .T48 1988

Tobin, James, 1918- Essays in economics . Cambridge, Mass. , 1987. xvi, 526 p. : ISBN 0-262-20062-7 LC Card 86-21157 DDC 339 19
HB34 .T622 1987

Truett, Lila J. Macroeconomics /. St. Louis , 1987. xxii, 531, [44] p. : ISBN 0-8016-5158-1 (pbk.) LC Card 86-23879 DDC 339 19
HB172.5 .T78 1987

Whiteman, Charles H. Problems in macroeconomic theory . Boston , c1987. ix, 266 p. ; ISBN 0-12-619752-0 (pbk.) LC Card 87-17398 DDC 339 19
HB172.5 .S27 1987 Suppl. 2

Woglom, Geoffrey. Modern macroeconomics /. Glenview, Ill. , c1988. 792, 19, 14 p. : ISBN 0-673-18413-7 LC Card 87-12857 DDC 339 19
HB172.5 .W63 1988

MACROECONOMICS - ADDRESSES, ESSAYS, LECTURES.

Macroeconomic conflict and social institutions /. Cambridge, Mass. , c1985. xi, 249 p. : ISBN 0-88730-034-0 LC Card 84-24376 DDC 339.2 19
HC79.I5 M225 1985 ***NYPL [JLE 86-2562]***

MACROECONOMICS - ECONOMETRIC MODELS.

Buscher, Herbert S. Modelle der neuen klassischen Makroökonomie . München , c1986. iv, 312 p. : ISBN 3-88259-386-5 LC Card 86-230281
HB141 .B87 1986

Kendrick, David A. Feedback . Dordrecht , Boston , 1988. vi, 147 p. : ISBN 90-247-3593-9 LC Card 87-20990 DDC 339.5 19
HB172.5 .K45 1988

Lambert, Jean-Paul, 1952- Disequilibrium

macroeconomic models . Cambridge [Cambridgeshire] , New York , 1988. p. cm. ISBN 0-521-32209-X LC Card 86-24966 DDC 339.5/0724 19
HB145 .L36 1988

Pimentão, Luís Nuno de Matos. Anwendungen der Variationsrechnung auf makroökonomische Modelle /. Berlin , New York , c1986. xii, 220 p. : ISBN 0-387-16484-7 (U. S.) LC Card 86-209488
HB141 .P55 1986

Rudebusch, Glenn D., 1959- The estimation of macroeconomic disequilibrium models with regime classification information /. Berlin , New York , c1987. 128 p. : ISBN 0-387-17757-4 (U. S. : pbk.) : LC Card 87-9583 DDC 339.5 19
HB145 .R82 1987b

Vilks, Arnis. Aggregation und Kausalität im Modell des allgemeinen Konkurrenzgleichgewichts . Göttingen , c1984. 141 p. ; ISBN 3-525-11287-4 (Deut. Bibl.) LC Card 84-225754
HB842 .V55 1984

Macroeconomics for managers /. Slovin, Myron B. Englewood Cliffs, N.J. , c1987. xvi, 512 p. : ISBN 0-13-542937-4 LC Card 86-25199 DDC 339 19
HB172.5 .S55 1987

MACROECONOMICS - MATHEMATICAL MODELS.
Auerbach, Alan J. Dynamic fiscal policy /. Cambridge [Cambridgeshire] , New York , 1987. xv, 196 p. : ISBN 0-521-30041-X LC Card 86-24447 DDC 339.5/2 19
HJ131 .A94 1987

Frenkel, Michael. Ausgewählte makroökonomische Modelle offener Volkswirtschaften /. St. Gallen , 1982. 183 p. : LC Card 83-112497
HG3823 .F74 1982

Huber, Gérard. Les conséquences à long terme de la politique macroéconomique /. Berne , 1982. 449 p. ; ISBN 3-261-04985-5 LC Card 87-672303
HB172.5 .H82x 1982

Macroeconomics [i.e. Macroeconomic] impacts of energy shocks /. Amsterdam ; New York : xvi, 331 p. : ISBN 0-444-70247-4 (U. S.) LC Card 87-9035 DDC 338.4/36655/0724 19
HG229 .M315 1987

Manuelli, Rodolfo E. Exercises in dynamic macroeconomic theory /. Cambridge, Mass. , 1987. xi, 223 p. ; ISBN 0-674-27476-8 (pbk. : alk. paper) LC Card 86-25767 DDC 339/.0729 19
HB172.5 .S27 1987 Suppl.

MACROECONOMICS - MATHEMATICAL MODELS - EXAMINATIONS, QUESTIONS, ETC.
Santacoloma, Juan Francisco. Modelos macroeconómicos, ejercicios resueltos /. Bilbao , 1985. 209 p. : ISBN 84-7485-059-2 LC Card 86-201846
HB141 .S276 1985

MACROECONOMICS - MATHEMATICAL MODELS - PROBLEMS, EXERCISES.
Manuelli, Rodolfo E. Exercises in dynamic macroeconomic theory /. Cambridge, Mass. , 1987. xi, 223 p. ; ISBN 0-674-27476-8 (pbk. : alk. paper) LC Card 86-25767 DDC 339/.0729 19
HB172.5 .S27 1987 Suppl.

MACROECONOMICS - PROBLEMS, EXERCISES, ETC.
Whiteman, Charles H. Problems in macroeconomic theory . Boston , c1987. ix, 266 p. ; ISBN 0-12-619752-0 (pbk.) LC Card 87-17398 DDC 339 19
HB172.5 .S27 1987 Suppl. 2

Macromodels and forecasts of national economy : proceedings of Models and forecasts '83 and Macromodels '83 / [editor in charge, Maria Nadratowska-Kubacka]. Warszawa : Polish Scientific Publishers, 1986. 284 p. : ill. ; 24 cm. At head of title: Polska Akademia Nauk, Komitet Statystyki i Ekonometrii, Uniwersytet Łódzki, Instytut Ekonometrii i Statystyki. Includes bibliographies. ISBN 83-01-06464-1 (pbk.) : LC Card 86-226942 DDC 338.947 19
1. Central planning - Europe, Eastern - Econometric models - Congresses. 2. Europe, Eastern - Economic policy - Econometric models - Congresses. 3. Econometric models - Europe, Eastern - Congresses. I. Nadratowska-Kubacka, Maria. II. Polska Akademia Nauk. Komitet Statystyki i Ekonometrii. III. Uniwersytet Łódzki. Instytut Ekonometrii i Statystyki.
HC244 .M227 1986

MACROPROGRAMMING.
Baras, Edward M. The advanced guide to Lotus 1-2-3 /. Berkeley, Calif. , c1986. xiii, 234 p. : ISBN 0-07-881237-2 (pbk.) LC Card 86-215569 DDC 005.36/9 19
HF5548.4.L67 B36 1986

The Lotus guide to 1-2-3 advanced macro commands . Reading, Mass. [1987], c1986. x, 278 p. : ISBN 0-201-16822-7 (pbk.) : LC Card 86-32213 DDC 005.36/9 19
HF5548.4.L67 L64 1987

Macros, menus, and miracles for Lotus 1-2-3 /. Lunsford, E. Michael. New York , c1987. xix, 234 p. : ISBN 0-471-85996-6 (pbk.) : LC Card 87-14285 DDC 005.36/9 19
HF5548.4.L67 L86 1987

Mcunu, Ernest. Top level advice to aspirant black managers / Ernest Mcunu. Braamfontein : South African Institute of Management, [1985] 48 p. ; 21 cm. Cover title. LC Card 87-152084 DDC 658.4/09 19
1. Executives. 2. Executive ability. 3. Career development. 4. Blacks - Employment - South Africa. I. Title. II. Title: Black managers.
HD38.2 .M395 1985

Macve, Richard, 1940- A survey of Lloyds syndicate accounts : financial reporting at Lloyd's in 1985 / Richard Macve. Englewood Cliffs, NJ : Prentice Hall International in association with the Institute of Chartered Accountants in England and Wales, 1986. xxv, 263 p. : ill. ; 24 cm. (Research studies in accounting) Includes index. Bibliography: p. 261-262. ISBN 0-13-878273-3 : LC Card 85-12147 DDC 368/.012/094212 19
1. Lloyd's (Firm). 2. Insurance - Accounting. 3. Syndicates (Finance) - Accounting. I. Title. II. Series.
HG8039 .M33 1986 ***NYPL [JLE 87-864]***

McVoy, D. Stevens. Baldwin, Thomas F. Cable communication /. Englewood Cliffs, N.J. , c1988. p. cm. ISBN 0-13-110263-X : LC Card 87-16109 DDC 384.55/56 19
HE8700.7 .B35 1988

McWilliams, Donald B., 1936- Pinney, William E., 1941- Management science . New York , c1987. xvii, 620 p. : ISBN 0-06-045229-3 LC Card 86-22933 DDC 658.4/033 19
HD30.25 .P56 1987

MACWRITE (COMPUTER PROGRAM)
Wolenik, Robert. MacWrite made easier /. New York , 1985. xiv, 210 p. : ISBN 0-03-001763-7 LC Card 84-19781 DDC 652/.5 19
Z52.5.M32 W64 1985 ***NYPL [JLE 85-1535]***

MacWrite made easier /. Wolenik, Robert. New York , 1985. xiv, 210 p. : ISBN 0-03-001763-7 LC Card 84-19781 DDC 652/.5 19
Z52.5.M32 W64 1985 ***NYPL [JLE 85-1535]***

Madagascar : les secteurs-clés de l'économie / ce rapport économique a été préparé par le Service des études documentaires de la Lettre de l'océan Indien ; recherche et rédaction, Michèle Miech Chatenay ; direction, Maurice Botbol. Paris : Banque d'information et de documentation de l'océan Indien, 1986, c1985. 184 p. : ill. ; 30 cm. Caption title. "Liste des entreprises et organismes cités": p. 180-184. ISBN 2-905760-02-8 LC Card 87-123718
1. Economic indicators - Madagascar. 2. Madagascar - Economic conditions. 3. Madagascar - Economic policy. I. Miech Chatenay, Michèle. II. Botbol, Maurice. III. Lettre de l'océan Indien (Firm). Service des études documentaires.
HC895 .M34 1986

Madagascar.
Le Secteur non structuré d'Antsirabe . Addis-Abéba , 1985. iii, ii, 111, 24, 71 p. : ISBN 92-2-205256-0 LC Card 87-980400
HD2346.M282 A588 1985

MADAGASCAR - ECONOMIC CONDITIONS.
Madagascar . Paris , 1986, c1985. 184 p. : ISBN 2-905760-02-8 LC Card 87-123718
HC895 .M34 1986

MADAGASCAR - ECONOMIC POLICY.
Madagascar . Paris , 1986, c1985. 184 p. : ISBN 2-905760-02-8 LC Card 87-123718
HC895 .M34 1986

MADAGASCAR - POPULATION - STATISTICS.
Andrianarivelo Rafrezy, Vincent. Population de Madagascar . [Antananarivo] [1985] 154 p. : LC Card 86-981367
HA4699 .A84 1985

Mádai, Edit. Külkereskedelmi tevékenységhez kapcsolódó általános fogalommeghatározások / [összeállította, Mádai Edit]. [Budapest : s.n., 1984] (Budapest : Datorg Nyomda) 177 p. ; 21 cm. Includes index. ISBN 963-02-2359-7 LC Card 87-409581
1. Commerce - Dictionaries - Hungarian. 2. International trade - Dictionaries - Hungarian. I. Title.
HF1001 .M27 1984

Madan, B. K. (Bal Krishna), 1911- Towards monetary cooperation in South Asia / B.K. Madan. New Delhi : Concept Pub. Co., 1986, c1985. 105 p. ; 22 cm. Includes index. LC Card 86-901998 DDC 332.4/954 19
1. Monetary policy - South Asia. 2. South Asia - Commerce. 3. South Asia - Foreign economic relations. I. Title.
HG3881 .M2756 1986 ***NYPL [JLD 87-911]***

Madden, Tara Roth. Women vs. women : the uncivil business war / Tara Roth Madden. New York, NY : American Management Association, c1987. xxii, 266 p. ; 24 cm. Includes index. ISBN 0-8144-5900-5 LC Card 87-47701 DDC 658.4/095/088042 19
1. Sex role in the work environment. 2. Women - Employment. 3. Women - Psychology. 4. Interpersonal conflicts. I. Title. II. Title: Women versus women.
HD6060 .M33 1987

Madden, Thomas J. Dillon, William R. Marketing research in a marketing environment /. St. Louis , 1987. xxviii, 742, 21, 15 p. : ISBN 0-8016-1303-5 : LC Card 86-23189 DDC 658.8/3 19
HF5415.2 .D54 1987

Maddock, John, 1917- Mail for the back of beyond / John Maddock. Kenthurst : Kangaroo Press, 1986. 160 p. : ill. ; 22 cm. Bibliography: p. [159] Includes index. ISBN 0-86417-063-7 LC Card 86-207558 DDC 383/.143/0994 19
1. Trucking - Australia - History. 2. Truck drivers - Australia - History. 3. Postal service - Australia - History. I. Title.
HE5709.A6 M33 1986

Maddock, Rodney. The Australian economy in the long run /. Cambridge [Cambridgeshire] , New York , 1987. xi, 372 p. : ISBN 0-521-32674-5 LC Card 86-26345 DDC 330.994 19
HC605 .A7767 1987

Maddox, E. Nick. Anthony, William P. Envisionary management . New York , c1988. p. cm. ISBN 0-89930-257-2 (lib. bdg. : alk. paper) LC Card 87-7373 DDC 658.3 19
HD38 .A6256 1988

Maddox, R. N. (Robert Neil), 1938- Schellinck, Douglas Anton, 1949- Marketing research . New York , c1987. xii, 224 p. : ISBN 0-03-010924-8 (pbk.) LC Card 86-29029 DDC 658.8/3/0285 19
HF5415.2 .S32 1987

Maddux, Robert B. Voorhees, Lynda, A. Job performance and chemical dependency . Los Altos, Calif. , c1987. iii, 81 p. : ISBN 0-931961-27-0 (pbk.) LC Card 86-73172 DDC 658.3/82 19
HF5549.5.D7 V66 1987

Made in Japan . Morita, Akio, 1921- New York , c1986. viii, 309 p., [8] p. of plates : ISBN 0-525-24465-4 : LC Card 86-11479 DDC 338.7/6213/0924 B 19
HD9696.A3 J3658 1986
NYPL [JFE 86-5112]

Made in the U. S.A. . DiBacco, Thomas V. New York , c1987. xii, 290 p. ; ISBN 0-06-015624-4 : LC Card 86-45652 DDC 338.0973 19
HC103 .D46 1987 ***NYPL [JLD 87-1292]***

Made in the USA. DiBacco, Thomas V. Made in the U. S.A. . New York , c1987. xii, 290 p. ; ISBN 0-06-015624-4 : LC Card 86-45652 DDC 338.0973 19
HC103 .D46 1987 ***NYPL [JLD 87-1292]***

Madeira em mapas e em números. [Lisboa] :

Centro de Estudos Geográficos, Universidade de Lisboa, I.N.I.C., 1984. iii, 61 leaves : ill. ; 30 cm. (Estudos para o planeamento regional e urbano . no. 20) "2a. edição"--Leaf iii. LC Card 85-144457
1. Madeira Islands - Statistics. 2. Madeira Islands - Statistics - Maps. I. Universidade de Lisboa. Centro de Estudos Geográficos. II. Series.
HA2285 .M33 1984

MADEIRA ISLANDS - STATISTICS.
Madeira em mapas e em números. [Lisboa] , 1984. iii, 61 leaves : LC Card 85-144457
HA2285 .M33 1984

MADEIRA ISLANDS - STATISTICS - MAPS.
Madeira em mapas e em números. [Lisboa] , 1984. iii, 61 leaves : LC Card 85-144457
HA2285 .M33 1984

Madhusudhana Rao, M. Labour management relations and trade union leadership : a behavioural study of union leaders / M. Madhusudhana Rao. New Delhi : Deep & Deep Publications, c1986. 392 p. ; 23 cm. Originally presented as the author's thesis (Ph. D.--Andhra University, 1986) under title: Trade union leadership in India. Bibliography: p. [383]-390. Includes index. LC Card 86-903198 DDC 331/.0954 19
1. Trade-unions - India - Officials and employees. 2. Industrial relations - India. I. Title.
HD6812 .M23 1986

MADHYA PRADESH (INDIA) - CENSUS, 1981.
Census of India, 1981. Delhi , <[1983]-[1986]. v. in : LC Card 87-915017 DDC 304.6/0954/3021 19
HA4587.M32 C46 1983

MADHYA PRADESH, INDIA - ECONOMIC POLICY.
Madhya Pradesh (India). State Planning Board. Madhyapradeśa Sātaviṃ Pañcavarshīya Yojanā, 1985-90 evaṃ Vārshika Yojanā, 1985-86. Bhopāla [1985] 284 p. ; LC Card 87-900819
HC437.M28 M3855 1985

MADHYA PRADESH (INDIA) - SOCIAL POLICY.
Madhya Pradesh (India). State Planning Board. Madhyapradeśa Sātaviṃ Pañcavarshīya Yojanā, 1985-90 evaṃ Vārshika Yojanā, 1985-86. Bhopāla [1985] 284 p. ; LC Card 87-900819
HC437.M28 M3855 1985

Madhya Pradesh (India). State Planning Board. Madhyapradeśa Sātaviṃ Pañcavarshīya Yojanā, 1985-90 evaṃ Vārshika Yojanā, 1985-86. Bhopāla : Rājya Yojanā Maṇḍala, Madhyapradeśa Śāsana, [1985] 284 p. ; 30 cm. In Hindi. Seventh Five Year Plan of Madhya Pradesh, 1985-90; includes the Annual Plan, 1985-86. LC Card 87-900819
1. Madhya Pradesh, India - Economic policy. 2. Madhya Pradesh (India) - Social policy. I. Title.
HC437.M28 M3855 1985

Madhyapradeśa Sātaviṃ Pañcavarshīya Yojanā, 1985-90 evaṃ Vārshika Yojanā, 1985-86.
Madhya Pradesh (India). State Planning Board. Bhopāla [1985] 284 p. ; LC Card 87-900819
HC437.M28 M3855 1985

Madigan, Bob, 1949- The first-time investor / Bob Madigan, Lawrence Kasoff. Rev. ed. New York : Prentice Hall Press, c1987. xxii, 276 p. : ill. ; 24 cm. Bibliography: p. 265-267. Includes index. ISBN 0-13-942376-1 (pbk.) : LC Card 87-14399 DDC 332.6/78 19
1. Investments. I. Kasoff, Larry, 1949-. II. Title.
HG4521 .M217 1987

Mäding, Heinrich. Sparpolitik . Opladen , c1983. 152 p. ; ISBN 3-531-11659-2 LC Card 84-109103
HB241 .S675 1983

Madnick, Stuart E. The Strategic use of information technology /. New York , 1987. xiii, 206 p. : ISBN 0-19-505048-7 (alk. paper) : LC Card 87-1606 DDC 658/.05 19
HD30.2 .S79 1987

Madras Chamber of Commerce and Industry. The Madras Chamber of Commerce and Industry, 1836-1986 : 150th year commemorative directory. Madras : The Chamber, [1986] 265 p., [22] leaves of plates : ill., maps ; 29 cm. Includes index. LC Card 86-903721 DDC 380.1/06/05482 19
1. Madras (India : State) - Commerce - Directories. 2. Madras (India : State) - Industries - Directories. I. Title.
HF5239.M32 M3 1986

Tirumalai, R., 1924- The voice of enterprise . Bangalore , 1986. xxii, 464 p., [41] p. of plates : ISBN 0-333-90907-0 : LC Card 86-903465 DDC 380.1/06/05482 19
HF331.I4 T57 1986

MADRAS CHAMBER OF COMMERCE AND INDUSTRY - HISTORY.
Tirumalai, R., 1924- The voice of enterprise . Bangalore , 1986. xxii, 464 p., [41] p. of plates : ISBN 0-333-90907-0 : LC Card 86-903465 DDC 380.1/06/05482 19
HF331.I4 T57 1986

The Madras Chamber of Commerce and Industry, 1836-1986 . Madras Chamber of Commerce and Industry. Madras [1986] 265 p., [22] leaves of plates : LC Card 86-903721 DDC 380.1/06/05482 19
HF5239.M32 M3 1986

MADRAS (INDIA : STATE) - COMMERCE - DIRECTORIES.
Madras Chamber of Commerce and Industry. The Madras Chamber of Commerce and Industry, 1836-1986 . Madras [1986] 265 p., [22] leaves of plates : LC Card 86-903721 DDC 380.1/06/05482 19
HF5239.M32 M3 1986

MADRAS (INDIA : STATE) - COMMERCE - HISTORY.
Tirumalai, R., 1924- The voice of enterprise . Bangalore , 1986. xxii, 464 p., [41] p. of plates : ISBN 0-333-90907-0 : LC Card 86-903465 DDC 380.1/06/05482 19
HF331.I4 T57 1986

MADRAS (INDIA : STATE) - ECONOMIC CONDITIONS.
Tirumalai, R., 1924- The voice of enterprise . Bangalore , 1986. xxii, 464 p., [41] p. of plates : ISBN 0-333-90907-0 : LC Card 86-903465 DDC 380.1/06/05482 19
HF331.I4 T57 1986

MADRAS (INDIA : STATE) - INDUSTRIES - DIRECTORIES.
Madras Chamber of Commerce and Industry. The Madras Chamber of Commerce and Industry, 1836-1986 . Madras [1986] 265 p., [22] leaves of plates : LC Card 86-903721 DDC 380.1/06/05482 19
HF5239.M32 M3 1986

Madrick, Jeffrey G. Taking America : how we got from the first hostile takeover to megamergers, corporate raiding, and scandal / Jeff Madrick. Toronto ; New York : Bantam Books, 1987. 310 p. ; 24 cm. Bibliography: p. [298]-302. Includes index. ISBN 0-553-05229-2 LC Card 87-928 DDC 338.8/3/0973 19
1. Tender offers (Securities). 2. Consolidation and merger of corporations - United States. 3. Insider trading in securities - United States. I. Title.
HG4028.T4 M33 1987

Madrid Hurtado, Miguel de la. Message to the nation : the economic situation : National Palace, 21st of February, 1986 / Miguel de la Madrid. [Mexico City, Mexico] : Presidencia de la República, Dirección General de Comunicación Social, [1986] 15 p. : port. ; 22 cm. Cover title. LC Card 87-400574 DDC 338.972 19
1. Mexico - Economic policy 1970-. I. Title.
HC135 .M225 1986

MADRID HURTADO, MIGUEL DE LA.
Cornelius, Wayne A., 1945- The political economy of Mexico under de la Madrid . La Jolla, Calif. , 1986. 50 p. ; LC Card 87-621352 DDC 330.972/0834 19
HC135 .C7185 1986

Madrid. Instituto de Estudios Políticos. see **Instituto de Estudios Políticos (Spain)**

Madrid, Raúl L. Ferrari, Paul L. U. S. arms exports . Washington, DC , c1987. xii, 342 p. : ISBN 0-931035-12-0 (pbk.) LC Card 87-80032 DDC 382/.456234/0971 19
HD9743.U6 F47 1987

Madrid (Spain). Alcaldía. Situación de crédito, hacienda y presupuesto del Municipio de Madrid en 1907 : (presupuesto para 1908) : informe presentado al Excelentísimo Ayuntamiento / por el alcalde presidente Joaquín Sánchez de Toca. Madrid : Impr. Municipal, 1907. viii, 137 p. ; 23 cm. LC Card 85-131486
1. Finance, Public - Spain - Madrid. 2. Debts, Public - Spain - Madrid. 3. Budget - Spain - Madrid. I. Sánchez de Toca, Joaquín, 1854-1942. II. Madrid (Spain). Ayuntamiento. III. Title.
HJ9528.M38 M34 1907

Madrid (Spain). Ayuntamiento. Madrid (Spain). Alcaldía. Situación de crédito, hacienda y presupuesto del Municipio de Madrid en 1907 . Madrid , 1907. viii, 137 p. ; LC Card 85-131486
HJ9528.M38 M34 1907

Madrigal Pana, Johnny. Metodología y construcción de un indicador del ingreso familiar : aplicación a los censos nacionales de vivienda y población, 1984 / Johnny Madrigal Pana. San José, Costa Rica : Asociación Demográfica Costarricense, 1986. 43 p. ; 21 cm. Cover title. Includes bibliographical references. LC Card 87-404395 DDC 339.4/2/0972 19
1. Cost and standard of living - Mexico. 2. Income - Mexico. 3. Mexico - Census, 1984. I. Title.
HD6996 .M33 1986

Madruga, José Manuel. Azúcar y haitianos en la República Dominicana / José Manuel Madruga. Santo Domingo : Ediciones MSC, 1986. 202 p. : ill. ; 22 cm. (Senda . 1) Bibliography: p. 179-188. LC Card 87-125442 DDC 331.6/2/729407293 19
1. Sugar trade - Dominican Republic. 2. Alien labor, Haitian - Dominican Republic. 3. Sugar workers - Dominican Republic. 4. Dominican Republic - Social conditions. I. Title.
HD9114.D62 M33 1986

Madsen, Agnete Birger. Kvindeliv--hverdagsliv . Copenhagen , 1985. 111 p. : ISBN 87-00-65962-2 : LC Card 86-156606
HD6169 .K855 1985

Madsen, Jørgen Steen. Due, Jesper. Hva' nu Larsen . [Copenhagen] , c1984. 152 p. ; ISBN 87-574-4410-2 : LC Card 84-229467
HD2429.D4 D84 1984

Maeda, Narifumi, 1940- Environment, agriculture, and society in the Malay world /. Kyoto, Japan , 1986. ix, 177 p. : LC Card 86-201590 DDC 338.1/09595 19
HD2080.6 .E58 1986

Maeda, Shun'ichi. Takeuchi, Kenji, 1932- The world copper industry . Washington, D.C., U. S.A. , c1986. xxix, 179 p. : ISBN 0-8213-0852-1 LC Card 86-26554 DDC 338.2/743 19
HD9539.C6 T35 1986

Mädchen und Berufswahl : Technik alleine macht es nicht! : eine Material- und Orientierungshilfe für Lehrerinnen/Lehrer und Berufsberaterinnen/Berufsberater / herausgegeben vom Bundesminister für Bildung und Wissenschaft. Bonn : Der Bundesminister ; Bad Honnef : Vertrieb, K.H. Bock, 1986. 96 p. : ill. ; 21 cm. (Schriftenreihe Studien zu Bildung und Wissenschaft, 0175-8055 . 37) Papers of a conference sponsored by the Bundesministerium für Bildung und Wissenschaft and held in Ludwigshafen, Apr. 22-23, 1985. Bibliography: p. 94-95. ISBN 3-87066-631-5 LC Card 87-409396 DDC 331.4/2592/0943 19
1. Vocational guidance for women - Germany (West) - Congresses. 2. Occupational training for women - Germany (West) - Congresses. I. Germany (West). Bundesministerium für Bildung und Wissenschaft. II. Series.
HF5382.67.G3 M33 1986

Maedke, Wilmer O.
Information and records management. Robek, Mary F. Information and records management / Mary F. Robek, Gerald F. Brown, Wilmer O. Maedke. 3rd ed. Encino, Calif. , c1987. vi, 580 p. : ISBN 0-02-820590-1 LC Card 87-135683 DDC 651.5 19
HF5736 .R53 1987

Mägde : Lebenserinnerungen an die Dienstbotenzeit bei Bauern / herausgegeben von Therese Weber. Wien : Böhlau, 1985. 211 p. : 19 ill. ; 20 cm. (Damit es nicht verlorengeht-- . 5) Includes bibliographical references. ISBN 3-205-06154-3 LC Card 86-127196
1. Women domestics - Austria - Biography. 2. Women agricultural laborers - Austria - Biography. I. Weber, Therese. II. Series: Damit es nicht verloren geht-- . 5.
HD6072.2.A9 M34 1985

Mälich, Wolfgang. Informationstheoretische Lösung ausgewählter Entscheidungsprobleme / Wolfgang Mälich. Göttingen : Vandenhoeck & Ruprecht, c1984. vi, 269 p. : ill. ; 24 cm. (Beiträge zur ökonomischen Forschung. Bd. 15)

Bibliography: p. [265]-269. ISBN 3-525-12314-0 LC Card 84-162246
1. Information theory in economics. 2. Decision-making - Mathematical models. I. Title.
HD30.23 .M345 1984

Männer im Glashaus . Michel-Alder, Elisabeth. Zürich , c1986. 238 p. : ISBN 3-280-01561-8 LC Card 86-180438
HD38.25.S9 M52 1986

Maenner, Ulrike.
Der deutsche Software-Markt und die internationale Wettbewerbsfähigkeit deutscher Anbieter / Ulrike Maenner. Hamburg : Verlag Weltarchiv, 1986. 94 p. : ill. ; 24 cm. (Veröffentlichungen des HWWA-Institut für Wirtschaftsforschung-Hamburg) Bibliography: p. 91-94. ISBN 3-87895-320-8 LC Card 87-407404 DDC 338.4/70053/0943 19
1. Computer software industry - Germany (West). I. Title.
HD9696.C63 G446 1986

Jungnickel, Rolf. Eigenimporte der deutschen Industrie /. Hamburg , 1984. 392 p. : ISBN 3-87895-256-2 LC Card 84-247605
HF3566.5 .J86 1984

Jungnickel, Rolf. Investitionsbedingungen in der ASEAN-Region /. Hamburg , 1986. 346 p. : ISBN 3-87895-296-1 LC Card 86-192978
HG5740.8.A3 J85 1986

Maennig, Wolfgang. Die Effekte der Preisstabilisierung auf internationalen Rohstoffmärkten auf Erlöshöhe und -stabilität / von Wolfgang Maennig. Berlin : Duncker & Humblot, 1985. 168 p. : ill. ; 24 cm. (Volkswirtschaftliche Schriften. Heft 359) Bibliography: p. [150]-168. ISBN 3-428-05947-6
1. Raw materials. 2. Profit. I. Title. II. Series.
NYPL [JLE 86-1670]

Märkte und Handlungssysteme . Maring, Matthias, 1950- Frankfurt am Main , New York , c1985. ii, 228 p. : ISBN 3-8204-8285-7 LC Card 85-230052
HF5470 .M35 1985

MAFIA - UNITED STATES.
Nelli, Humbert S., 1930- The business of crime . New York , 1976. xiii, 314 p. : ISBN 0-19-502010-3 : LC Card 75-32350 DDC 364.1/06/073
HV6791 .N37 ***NYPL [JLD 86-3722]***

Magalhães, Antônio Carlos. Meu compromisso com o Nordeste : pronunciamentos, 1979 a 1983 / Antônio Carlos Magalhães. [Salvador : Casa Civil, Secretaria de Comunicação Social, 1983] 302 p. ; 23 cm. LC Card 86-233485
1. Brazil, Northeast - Economic policy. 2. Brazil, Northeast - Economic conditions. I. Title.
HC188.B7242 M34 1983

Magalhães, Antonio Rocha. Industrialização e desenvolvimento regional : a nova indústria do Nordeste / Antonio Rocha Magalhães. Brasília : Instituto de Planejamento Econômico e Social, Instituto de Planejamento, 1983. 315 p. : ill. ; 21 cm. (Serie Estudos para o planejamento. no. 24) Bibliography: p. 303-315. LC Card 84-160221 DDC 338.981/3 19
1. Industry and state - Brazil, Northeast. 2. Regional planning - Brazil, Northeast. 3. Industrial promotion - Brazil Northeast. 4. Investments - Brazil, Northeast. 5. Brazil, Northeast - Industries. I. Title. II. Series.
HD3616.B84 N676 1983
NYPL [JLD 86-3120]

Magalhães, João Paulo de Almeida. Uma política industrial para o Brasil / João Paulo de Almeida Magalhães. [Rio de Janeiro] : Edições I&P, Confederação Nacional da Indústria, [between 1985 and 1987] 161 p. ; 21 cm. (Coleção José Emírio de Moraes . 18) "Revista Indústria & Produtividade." Bibliography: p. 34-36. LC Card 87-403992 DDC 338.981 19
1. Industry and state - Brazil. 2. Brazil - Industries. I. Series: Coleção José Emírio de Moraes , vol. 18. II. Title.
HD3616.B83 M34 1985

Magallona, Merlin M. Imperialism and transnational corporations /. Quezon City , 1980. vi, 114 p. ; ***NYPL [JLD 86-2721]***

Magaña Cañas, Pedro Agustín. Una ventana a la vida : en los viejos mercados de San Salvador / Pedro Agustin Magaña Cañas. [San Salvador] : Patrocinada por la Alcaldía Municipal de San Salvador, [between 1983 and 1987] 93 p. : ill. ; 19 cm. Bibliography: p. 92. LC Card 87-400985 DDC 331.4/8138118/09728423 19
1. Women merchants - El Salvador - San Salvador. 2. Markets - El Salvador - San Salvador. I. Title.
HF3310.S26 M34 1983

MAGAZINE ADVERTISING. see **ADVERTISING, MAGAZINE.**

Magdoff, Harry. Stagnation and the financial explosion / by Harry Magdoff and Paul M. Sweezy. New York : Monthly Review Press, c1987. 208 p. : ill. ; 21 cm. Essays published in Monthly review, June 1982-June 1986. Includes bibliographical references. ISBN 0-85345-716-6 : LC Card 86-33129 DDC 330.973/0927 19
1. United States - Economic conditions - 1981-. 2. United States - Economic policy - 1981-. 3. Unemployment - United States - Effect of inflation on. 4. Capitalism - United States. 5. Marxian economics. I. Sweezy, Paul Marlor, 1910-. II. Title.
HC106.8 .M315 1987b

MAGHERA (LONDONDERRY, NORTHERN IRELAND) - HISTORY.
Clark, Wallace, 1926- Linen on the green . Belfast , 1983, c1982. xii, 183 p., [16] p. of plates : ISBN 0-9509042-0-1 LC Card 84-242010 DDC 338.4/76771164/0941629 19
HD9930.G73 N625 1983

Maghreb, 1970-1980.re de l'Afrique du nord. Bernard, Chantal. La politique de l'emploi-formation au Maghreb, 1970-1980 /. Paris , 1982. 472 p. ; ***NYPL [JLE 86-568]***

Magia e capitalismo . Rocha, Everardo P. Guimarães, 1951- São Paulo, SP , 1985. 162 p. : LC Card 85-199925
HF5827 .R58 1985

Magic formula for getting the right job. Martin, Phyllis Rodgers. Martin's magic formula for getting the right job . New York , c1987. xix, 198 p. : ISBN 0-312-01065-6 (pbk.) : LC Card 87-16302 DDC 650.1/4 19
HF5382.75.U6 M37 1987

The magic sell . Adler, Stan. Costa Mesa, Calif. , c1986. 160 p. ; ISBN 0-937359-03-3 : LC Card 87-111850 DDC 683/.83/0688 19
HF5439.H8 A36 1986

Magierska, Anna. Przywrócić Polsce : przemysł na Ziemiach Odzyskanych, 1945-1946 / Anna Magierska.Wyd. 1. Warszawa : Państwowe Wydawn. Nauk., 1986. 467 p. ; 21 cm. Bibliography: p. 439-[451]. Includes indexes. ISBN 83-01-06606-7 : LC Card 86-228089
1. Western and Northern Territories (Poland) - Industries - History. 2. Government ownership - Poland - Western and Northern Territories - History. 3. Poland - Economic policy - 1945-. I. Title.
HC340.3.Z7 W4765 1986

Magnaval, Robert. Azouaou, Alain. La Silicon Valley, un marché aux puces /. Paris , c1986. 237 p. : ISBN 2-85956-494-2 : LC Card 86-217069
HD9696.A3 U516 1986

Magni, Carlo. I mercati regionali del lavoro e il problema degli indicatori : un'analisi del caso italiano / [di] Carlo Magni ; presentazione di Siro Lombardini. Milano : F. Angeli, [1981] 133, [3] p. : ill. ; 22 cm. (Collana Università . 9) Bibliography: p. [135] ISBN 88-20-42109-7 : LC Card 81-194409
1. Labor supply - Italy. 2. Unemployment - Italy - Regional disparities. 3. Unemployment - Italy - Statistical methods. 4. Italy - Economic conditions - 1976- - Regional disparities. I. Title. II. Series.
HD5784 .M3 1981 ***NYPL [JLD 87-815]***

Magnitogorsk. Metallurgicheskiĭ kombinat. see **Magnitogorskiĭ metallurgicheskiĭ kombinat.**

MAGNITOGORSKIĬ METALLURGICHESKIĬ KOMBINAT.
Zubets, V. M. (Vasiliĭ Mikhaĭlovich) Rezervy povysheniia ėffektivnosti proizvodstva na magnitogorskom metallurgicheskom kombinate /. Cheliabinsk , 1975. 183 p. ; LC Card 81-170397
HD9525.S653 M39 1975

Magnitogorskiĭ metallurgicheskiĭ kombinat imeni Stalina. see **Magnitogorskiĭ metallurgicheskiĭ kombinat.**

Magnitogorskiĭ metallurgicheskiĭ kombinat imeni V. I. Lenina. see **Magnitogorskiĭ metallurgicheskiĭ kombinat.**

Magnitostroĭ. see **Magnitogorskiĭ metallurgicheskiĭ kombinat.**

Magnusson, Åke, 1943- Ekonomi styrning av projekt / Åke Magnusson, Lars Lemby. Stockholm : Mekan, [1984] 66 p., [3] folded leaves of plates : ill. ; 24 cm. ISBN 91-524-0729-2 LC Card 85-149256
1. Industrial project management. I. Lemby, Lars. II. Title.
HD69.P75 M34 1984

Magnusson, Lars. Isacson, Maths, 1948- Proto-industrialisation in Scandinavia . Leamington Spa, UK ; New York : p. cm. ISBN 0-85496-514-9 : LC Card 86-32062 DDC 338.09485 19
HC375 .I8 1987

Magnusson, Lars, 1941-
Isacson, Maths, 1948- Vägen till fabrikerna . [Stockholm] [Uppsala] , c1983. 195, [1] p. : ISBN 91-7021-464-6 : LC Card 84-125076
HC375 .I83 1983

Kapitalbildning i Sverige 1750-1860 : godsen / Lars Magnusson. Uppsala : Academia Ubsaliensis ; Stockholm : Distributor, Almqvist & Wiksell international, 1983. 95 p. ; 22 cm. (Acta Universitatis Upsaliensis. Uppsala studies in economic history, 0346-6493 . 25) Abstract and summary in English. Bibliography: p. 92-95. ISBN 91-554-1443-5 LC Card 83-228044
1. Sweden - Economic conditions. 2. Capital productivity - Sweden - History. 3. Agriculture - Sweden - Capital productivity - History. I. Title. II. Series.
HC374 .M34 1983

Magnusson, Sten. Södersten, Bo. Makroekonomi och stabiliseringspolitik /. [Malmö] , c1983. 363 p. : ISBN 91-40-05037-8 : LC Card 84-166176
HB179.S8 S63 1983

Magnusson, Warren, 1947- After Bennett . Vancouver, B.C. , 1986. 429 p. : ISBN 0-919573-63-0 LC Card 87-110683 DDC 338.9711 19
HC117.B8 A63 1986

Magrath, Allan J. Hardy, Kenneth G., 1941- Marketing channel management . Glenview, IL , c1988. 724 p. : ISBN 0-673-18295-9 : LC Card 87-12742 DDC 658.8/4 19
HF5415 .H229 1988

Magri, Caio. Machado, Arlindo. Rádios livres . São Paulo-SP , 1986. 181 p. : LC Card 86-157835
HE8697.P57 M33 1986

Maguire, Andrew. Bordering on trouble . Bethesda, Md. , 1986. xii, 448 p. : ISBN 0-917561-25-2 (pbk.) LC Card 86-7941 DDC 338.98 19
HC125 .B594 1986 ***NYPL [JLE 86-4501]***

Magyar Állami Földtani Intézet. Gazdaságföldtani Osztály. Összehasonlító tanulmány a világ ásványi nyersanyagainak mennyiségéről, termeléséről, ár és értékrendjeinek alakulásáról /. Budapest , 1983. 57 p. : ISBN 963-671-086-4 (Magy. nemz. bibl.) LC Card 85-130135
HD9506.A2 O85 1983

A Magyar bélyegek kézikönyve / szerkesztette, Surányi László és Visnyovszki Gábor. Budapest : Gondolat, 1986. 551 p., viii p. of plates : ill. (some col.), maps ; 24 cm. Includes bibliographies. ISBN 963-281-692-7 : LC Card 87-151573 DDC 769.569439 19
1. Postage-stamps - Hungary - History - 19th century. 2. Postage-stamps - Hungary - History - 20th century. I. Surányi, László. II. Visnyovszki, Gábor.
HE6185.H8 M32 1986

Magyar Bélyeggyűjtők Országos Szövetsége. Zlatev, István. A magyar postahivatalok, 1867-1871. években használt hely-keletbélyegzései . Budapest , 1983. 255 p. : ISBN 963-01-4848-X LC Card 86-148361
HE6980.5 .Z55 1983

MAGYAR DOLGOZÓK PÁRTJA - HISTORY.
Steinbach, Antal. A Magyar Dolgozók Pártja Központi Vezetősége 1953. júniusi határozatának agrárpolitikai előzményei /. [Budapest] , 1985. 104 p. ; ISBN 963-673-321-X LC Card 86-187055
HD1940.5.Z8 S74 1985

A Magyar Dolgozók Pártja Központi Vezetősége 1953. júniusi határozatának agrárpolitikai előzményei /. Steinbach, Antal. [Budapest] , 1985. 104 p. ; ISBN 963-673-321-X LC Card

86-187055
HD1940.5.Z8 S74 1985

Magyar Fórum (Magyarok Világszövetsége) Tanulmányok Magyarországról, magyarokról. [Budapest] [1985] 280 p. ; ISBN 963-01-7352-2 (Magy. nemz. bibl.) LC Card 87-408505
HC300.24 .T36 1985

A magyar gazdaság negyven éve /. Nyitrai, Ferencné. [Budapest] , 1985. 385 p. ; ISBN 963-09-2570-2 : LC Card 86-104105
HC300.28 .N945 1985

Magyar gazdaság 40 éve. Nyitrai, Ferencné. A magyar gazdaság negyven éve /. [Budapest] , 1985. 385 p. ; ISBN 963-09-2570-2 : LC Card 86-104105
HC300.28 .N945 1985

A Magyar háztartásstatisztikai megfigyelés módszertana / [készült a Központi Statisztikai Hivatal Közgazdasági Főosztály Háztartásstatisztikai Osztályán ; összeállitotta, Baranyai István, Nádas Magdolna]. Budapest : Központi Statisztikai Hivatal, 1986. 59 p. ; 24 cm. (Statisztikai módszertani füzetek . 20. sz.) LC Card 87-408579
1. Households - Hungary - Statistical services. I. Baranyai, István. II. Nádas, Magdolna. III. Hungary. Központi Statisztikai Hivatal. Háztartásstatisztikai Osztály. IV. Series.
HA37.H92 M34 1986

Magyar Kereskedelmi Kamara. (Old Catalog form: Hungary. Kereskedelmi Kamara) Managers in Hungary : a biographical directory of executives in [i.e. and] members of the Hungarian Chamber of Commerce / [editor, Judit Gyárfás ; associate editor, Ibolya Hepp].1st ed. [Budapest?] : Hungarian Chamber of Commerce, 1986. 368 p. ; 24 cm. ISBN 963-7073-09-4 (pbk.) LC Card 87-137498 DDC 658/.0025/439 19
1. Executives - Hungary - Directories. 2. Magyar Kereskedelmi Kamara - Directories. I. Gyárfás, Judit. II. Hepp, Ibolya. III. Title.
HD38.25.H9 M34 1986

MAGYAR KERESKEDELMI KAMARA - DIRECTORIES.
Magyar Kereskedelmi Kamara. Managers in Hungary . [Budapest?] , 1986. 368 p. ; ISBN 963-7073-09-4 (pbk.) LC Card 87-137498 DDC 658/.0025/439 19
HD38.25.H9 M34 1986

Magyar Külkereskedelmi Bank. Economic associations in Hungary with foreign participation. Budapest , 1986. 24 p. ; LC Card 87-106055 DDC 346.439/068 344.390668 19
HD62.47 .E25 1986

Magyar, Lajosné.
Jó munkát, jó közérzetet / Magyar Lajosné. [Budapest] : Magyar Nők Országos Tanácsa, [1986?] 52 p. ; 20 cm. LC Card 87-148690
1. Labor and laboring classes - Hungary. I. Title.
HD8420.5 .M33 1986

A munkaviszonyok humanizálása : zárótanulmány / [a zárótanulmányt készitette és a kutatást vezette, Magyar Lajosné]. Budapest : Szakszervezetek Elméleti Kutató Intézete, [1985] 210 p. ; 21 cm. "A téma kutatása az Intézet Gazdaság- és Életszinvonalpolitikai Részlegében folyt"--T.p. verso. "1985. mácius." Bibliography: p. 209-210. ISBN 963-608-075-5 LC Card 85-154632
1. Quality of work life. 2. Industrial relations. I. Szakszervezetek Elméleti Kutazó Intézete. Gazdaság- és Életszinvonalpolitikai Részleg. II. Title.
HD6955 .M27 1985

Magyar-Lengyel Agrárközgazdasági Konferencia (1984 : Gödöllő, Hungary) A nagyüzemek és a kisüzemek termelésének fejlődése, kapcsolatuk az iparosodó mezőgazdaságban = Development of agricultural production in small-scale and large-scale farms and their system of connections in the industrializing agriculture / Agrártudományi Egyetem Mezőgazdaságtudományi Kar Agrárgazdaságtani Tanszék ; szerkesztők, Lőkös László, Lehota József. Gödöllő : [Agrártudományi Egyetem], 1984. 174 p. ; 30 cm. Conference organized by the Gödöllői Agrártudományi Egyetem Agrárgazdaságtani Tanszék and the Akademia Rolnicza w Warszawie Katedra rolnictwa światowego and held June 11-16, 1984. Summaries in English. LC Card 86-145249
1. Agriculture - Economic aspects - Poland - Congresses. 2. Agriculture - Economic aspects - Hungary - Congresses. I. Lőkös, László. II. Lehota, József. III. Gödöllői Agrártudományi Egyetem. Agrárgazdaságtani Tanszék. IV. Akademia Rolnicza w Warszawie. Katedra rolnictwa światowego. V. Title. VI. Title: Development of agricultural production in small-scale and large-scale farms and their system of connections in the industrializing agriculture.
HD1995.7 .M32 1984

A Magyar mezőgazdaság európai összehasonlításban / [készült a Központi Statisztikai Hivatal Mezőgazdasági Statisztikai Főosztályának Módszertani és Elemzési Osztályán]. Budapest : Központi Statisztikai Hivatal, 1985. 207 p. : ill. ; 29 cm. ISBN 963-02-3856-X (Magy. nemz. bibl.) LC Card 86-157394
1. Agriculture - Economic aspects - Hungary - Statistics. 2. Agriculture - Economic aspects - Europe - Statistics. I. Hungary. Központi Statisztikai Hivatal. Mezőgazdasági Statisztikai Főosztály. Módszertani és Elemzési Osztály.
HD1940.5 .M34 1985

Magyar Nemzeti Bank. Magyar törvényes fizetőeszközök =. [Budapest] [1986?] [38] p. : LC Card 87-407726
HG970.5 .M34 1986

Magyar névtani dolgozatok, 0133-6169 .
(34) Berényi, Zsuzsanna Ágnes. A budapesti Nagyvásártelep mikrotoponímiája /. Budapest , 1983. 65 p. : ISBN 963-461-710-7 LC Card 85-167786
HF5474.H82 B83 1983

A magyar parasztság sorsfordulója, 1946-1949 /. Simon, Péter, 1926- [Budapest] , 1984. 212 p. : ISBN 963-09-2475-7 :
HD1333.H9 S57 1984 ***NYPL [JLD 86-3163]***

A magyar postahivatalok, 1867-1871. években használt hely-keletbélyegzései . Zlatev, István. Budapest , 1983. 255 p. : ISBN 963-01-4848-X LC Card 86-148361
HE6980.5 .Z55 1983

MAGYAR RÁDIÓ - HISTORY.
Lévai, Béla. Rádió-televízió anno-- /. Budapest , 1985. 94 p. : ISBN 963-223-331-X : LC Card 86-128497
HE8689.9.H8 L49 1985

A Magyar szakszervezetek feladatai a gazdaságirányítás továbbfejlesztésének segítéséban : a magyar szakszervezeteknek a XXIV. kongresszus óta végzett nemzetközi tevékenysége : a SZOT 1984. október 5-i ülése. Budapest : SZOT Kulturális, Agitációs és Propagandaosztálya, 1984. 47 p. ; 20 cm. ISBN 963-322-215-X LC Card 85-176937
1. Hungary - Economic conditions - 1968-. 2. Trade-unions - Hungary. 3. International labor activities. I. Szakszervezetek Országos Tanácsa.
HC300.28 .M3297 1984

A magyar szakszervezetek napjainkban . Györgypál, Katalin. Budapest , 1984. 128 p. ; ISBN 963-608-062-3 LC Card 85-230460
HD6680.5 .G96 1984

Magyar Szocialista Munkáspárt. Agitációs és Propaganda Osztály. Gazdasági fejlődésünk és a gazdaságirányítás továbbfejlesztése . [Budapest] , 1984. 219 p. ; ISBN 963-09-2571-0 : LC Card 85-186920
HC300.28 .G332 1984

Magyar Szocialista Munkaspart. Gazdaságpolitikai Osztály.
Gazdaságpolitikánk az élenjáró vállalatok gyakorlatában . [Budapest] , 1985. 276 p. : ISBN 963-09-2769-1 : LC Card 87-407761
HD70.H8 G39 1985

Magyar Szocialista Munkáspárt. Győr-Sopron Megyei Bizottság.
Gazdaságpolitikánk az élenjáró vállalatok gyakorlatában . [Budapest] , 1985. 276 p. : ISBN 963-09-2769-1 : LC Card 87-407761
HD70.H8 G39 1985

Munkásosztályunk fejlődése 1945-ig . Győr , 1985. 126 p. ; LC Card 86-186895
HD8420.5 .M85 1985

Magyar Szocialista Munkáspárt. Központi Bizottság. Agitációs és Propaganda Osztály.
Gazdaságpolitikánk az élenjáró vállalatok gyakorlatában . [Budapest] , 1985. 276 p. : ISBN 963-09-2769-1 : LC Card 87-407761
HD70.H8 G39 1985

A 80-as évek kapitalizmusa . [Budapest] , 1985. 406 p. ; ISBN 963-09-2696-2 : LC Card 86-186468
HB501 .A14 1985

Magyar Szocialista Munkáspárt. Marxizmus-Leninizmus Esti Egyetem. Szakositott Tagozat. A Világgazdaság fejlődésének kérdései tanulmányozásához . [Budapest] , 1981/1982. 415 p. ; LC Card 85-138909
HC59 .V489 1981

Magyar Szocialista Munkáspárt. Somogy Megyei Bizottság. A 80-as évek kapitalizmusa . [Budapest] , 1985. 406 p. ; ISBN 963-09-2696-2 : LC Card 86-186468
HB501 .A14 1985

Magyar Szocialista Munkáspárt. T͡Sentral'nyĭ Komitet. see Magyar Szocialista Munkáspárt. Központi Bizottság.

Magyar Szocialista Munkáspárt. Veszprém Megyei Bizottság. Gazdasági fejlődésünk és a gazdaságirányítás továbbfejlesztése . [Budapest] , 1984. 219 p. ; ISBN 963-09-2571-0 : LC Card 85-186920
HC300.28 .G332 1984

Magyar társadalombiztosítás az ötödik ötéves terv időszakában, 1976-1980. Fodor, András. A magyar társadalombiztosítás az V. ötéves terv időszakában, 1976-1980 /. Budapest , 1983. 147 p. ; ISBN 963-321-977-9 LC Card 85-129731
HD7172.5 .F62 1983

A magyar társadalombiztosítás az V. ötéves terv időszakában, 1976-1980 /. Fodor, András. Budapest , 1983. 147 p. ; ISBN 963-321-977-9 LC Card 85-129731
HD7172.5 .F62 1983

Magyar társadalombiztosítás az 5. ötéves terv időszakában, 1976-1980. Fodor, András. A magyar társadalombiztosítás az V. ötéves terv időszakában, 1976-1980 /. Budapest , 1983. 147 p. ; ISBN 963-321-977-9 LC Card 85-129731
HD7172.5 .F62 1983

MAGYAR TELEVÍZIÓ - HISTORY.
Lévai, Béla. Rádió-televízió anno-- /. Budapest , 1985. 94 p. : ISBN 963-223-331-X : LC Card 86-128497
HE8689.9.H8 L49 1985

Magyar Televízió. Pécsi Körzeti Stúdió.
Békés, Sándor. Az első évtized . Pécs , 1986. 221 p. : LC Card 87-148227
HE8700.9.H8 B45 1986

MAGYAR TELEVÍZIÓ. PÉCSI KÖRZETI STÚDIO - HISTORY.
Békés, Sándor. Az első évtized . Pécs , 1986. 221 p. : LC Card 87-148227
HE8700.9.H8 B45 1986

Magyar törvényes fizetőeszközök = The legal tenders of Hungary / [szerkesztette, Kapronczay Gáspár]. [Budapest] : Magyar Nemzeti Bank, [1986?] [38] p. : col. ill. ; 28 cm. Text in Hungarian, English, French, German, and Russian. Cover title. LC Card 87-407726
1. Money - Hungary. 2. Legal tender - Hungary. I. Kapronczay, Gáspár. II. Magyar Nemzeti Bank. III. Title: Legal tenders of Hungary.
HG970.5 .M34 1986

Magyar Tudományos Akadémia.
Kockázat és társadalom /. Budapest , 1987. 309 p. : ISBN 963-05-4450-4 : LC Card 87-425562
HD61 .K6 1987

Magyar Tudományos Akadémia, Budapest. Világgazdasági Kutató Intézet. Policy responses to the changing international environment . Budapest , 1981. 170 p. ; ISBN 963-301-077-2 (pbk.) LC Card 81-179118 DDC 337/.09/048 19
HC59 .P573 1981 ***NYPL [JLL 79-189 no.33]***

Magyar Tudományos Akadémia. Közgazdaságtudományi Intézet.
Activities of the Institute and Summary of the 3rd yearbook, 1960-1961. Budapest : Institute of Economics, Hungarian Academy of Sciences, 1962. 61 p. ; 24 cm. LC Card 87-146537
1. Magyar Tudományos Akadémia. Közgazdaságtudományi Intézet. 2. Economics - Research - Hungary. I. Title.
HB74.9.H9 M35 1962

Gazdaságunk helyzetéről és fejlődésünk problémáiról. [Budapest] , 1985. 239 p. : ISBN 963-09-2681-4 : LC Card 86-202400
HC300.28 .G36 1985

Soós, Károly Attila. Terv, kampány, pénz .

Budapest , 1986. 532 p. : ISBN 963-221-575-3 : LC Card 87-137237
HB3787.5 .S66 1986

MAGYAR TUDOMÁNYOS AKADÉMIA. KÖZGAZDASÁGTUDOMÁNYI INTÉZET.
Magyar Tudományos Akadémia. Közgazdaságtudományi Intézet. Activities of the Institute and Summary of the 3rd yearbook, 1960-1961. Budapest , 1962. 61 p. ; LC Card 87-146537
HB74.9.H9 M35 1962

A Magyar Tudományos Akadémia Közgazdaságtudományi Intézetének közleményei, 0460-5918 . (új sorozat, 32) Friss István emlékezete /. Budapest , 1984. 128 p. ; LC Card 86-145174
HC300.28 .F75 1984

Magyar Tudományos Akadémia. Világgazdasági Kutató Intézet. World monetary system in a time of change . Budapest [1987] 283 p. ; ISBN 963-01-7937-7 (pbk.) LC Card 87-169001 DDC 332.4/5 19
HG230.3 .W68 1987

Magyar Tudós Társaság. see **Magyar Tudományos Akadémia, Budapest.**

A magyar vegyipar fejlődése, 1945-1980 között és eredményei a magyar népgazdaság szolgálatában /. Halkovics, László. Budapest [1985] 50 p. ; ISBN 963-8191-50-3 (Magy. nmz. bibl.) LC Card 86-148561
HD9656.H92 H35 1985

Magyari-Beck, István. Alkotó teamek és alkotó módszerek . [Budapest] , 1986. 201 p. ; LC Card 87-138615
HD66 .A45 1986

Magyarország falutipusai /. Beluszky, Pál. Budapest , 1982. 167 p. : ISBN 963-7321-96-9 LC Card 84-159502
HD640.5.Z7 B44 1982

Magyarország tőkés viszonylatu gazdasági és pénzügyi kapcsolatairól /. Kiefer, Márta. [Budapest] [1985] 115 p. ; ISBN 963-608-080-1 LC Card 86-228329
HF1542.5 .K54 1985

A Magyarországi településrendszer strukturális változása / [összeállította és szerkesztette, Elekes Magdolna]. Budapest : Építésügyi és Városfejlesztési Minisztérium, Építészeti és Településfejlesztési Főosztály, 1984. 155 p., [1] folded leaf of plates : ill., maps (1 col.) ; 20 cm. (Területfejlesztési közlemények, 0139-0376 . 13. sz.) "Készült az ÉVM Építészeti és Településfejlesztési Főosztály megbízásából a Városépítési Tudományos és Tervező Intézetben kidolgozott több éves kutatómunka alapján"--T.p. verso. Bibliography: p. 149-155. ISBN 963-03-2079-7 (Magy. nemz. bibl.) LC Card 85-231254
1. Land settlement - Hungary. 2. Land use - Hungary. I. Elekes, Magdolna. II. Hungary. Építésügyi és Városfejlesztési Minisztérium. Építészeti és Településfejlesztési Főosztály. III. Városépítési Tudományos és Tervező Intézet. IV. Series.
HD640.5 .M343 1984

MAGYARÓVÁRI TIMFÖLD ÉS MŰKORUNDGYÁR (HUNGARY) - HISTORY.
Szűcs, Lajos. A Magyaróvári Timföld és Műkorundgyár története, 1934-1984. [Mosonmagyaróvár , 1984] 320 p. : ISBN 963-02-3415-7 LC Card 86-127345
HD9539.A63 H858 1984

A Magyaróvári Timföld és Műkorundgyár története, 1934-1984. Szűcs, Lajos. [Mosonmagyaróvár , 1984] 320 p. : ISBN 963-02-3415-7 LC Card 86-127345
HD9539.A63 H858 1984

Ma'had al-Takhtit al-Qawmi (Egypt) Third World countries in the international cotton economy /. [Nyon, Switzerland?] , 1979. i, 61 p. : LC Card 86-223016
HD9088.D44 T47 1979

Mahadevan, K. Infant and childhood mortality in India . Delhi, India , c1985. xiv, 120 p. : LC Card 85-905202 *NYPL [JLD 87-517]*

Mahadevan, K., 1940-
Fertility and mortality . New Delhi , Beverly Hills , 1986. 351 p. ; ISBN 0-8039-9497-4 LC Card 85-22287 DDC 304.6/3 19
HB901 .F468 1986 *NYPL [JLE 86-4122]*
Social development, cultural change, and fertility decline : a study of fertility change in India / K. Mahadevan and M. Sumangala. New Delhi ; Newbury Park, Calif. : Sage, 1987. p. cm. Bibliography: p. ISBN 0-8039-9536-9 LC Card 87-15001 DDC 304.6/32/095483 19
1. Fertility, Human - India - Kerala. 2. Kerala (India) - Social conditions. 3. Kerala, India - Economic conditions. 4. Kerala (India) - Popular culture. 5. Kerala (India) - Rural conditions. I. Sumangala, M. (Mahadevan). II. Title.
HB1050.K47 M34 1987

Mahajan, Amarjit. Problems of the aged in unorganised sector / A. Mahajan ; assisted by P.N. Mohanty, Ram Singh & Ms. Arunima. Delhi, India : Mittal Publications, 1987. viii, 106 p. ; 23 cm. Study of the Old Age Pension Scheme in Haryana. Bibliography: p. [99]-101. Includes index. LC Card 87-901315 DDC 362.6/042 19
1. Old age pensions - India - Haryana. 2. Old age assistance - India - Haryana. I. Mohanty, P. N. II. Singh, Ram. III. Arunima. IV. Title.
HD7105.35.I5 M34 1987

Mahajan, V. S., 1923- Growth of agriculture and industry in India / V.S. Mahajan. New Delhi : Deep & Deep, c1983. 176 p. ; 23 cm. Includes index. Bibliography: p. [173]-174. LC Card 83-906175 DDC 338.0954 19
1. Agriculture - Economic aspects - India. 2. Agriculture and state - India. 3. Industry and state - India. 4. India - Industries. I. Title.
HD2072 .M23 1983 *NYPL [JLD 87-671]*

Mahajan, Vijay. Innovation diffusion models of new product acceptance /. Cambridge, Mass. , 1986. xvi, 318 p. : ISBN 0-88730-076-6 LC Card 85-23300 DDC 658.8/343 19
HF5415.153 .I55 1986 *NYPL [JLE 86-3235]*

MAHALPYE DEVELOPMENT TRUST.
Gobotswang, Z. Pilot evaluation report on Mahalapye Development Trust /. Gaborone, Botswana [1982] v leaves, 61, 3 p. ; LC Card 87-122810
HD5710.85.B59 G63 1982

Mahapatro, P. C. (Poorna Chandra), 1944- Economics of cotton handloom industry in India / P.C. Mahapatro. 1st ed. New Delhi : Ashish Pub. House, 1986. xvi, 277 p. ; 22 cm. Originally presented as the author's thesis (Ph. D.--University of Bombay, 1985) under the title: Economics of cotton handloom industry in Orissa. Bibliography: p. [268]-274. Includes index. ISBN 81-7024-060-3 : LC Card 86-903087 DDC 338.4/774614/0954
1. Handloom industry - India - Orissa. 2. Cotton textile industry - India - Orissa. 3. Orissa, India - Economic conditions. I. Title.
HD9866.I63 O745 1986

Mahapatro, Prafulla Ch. Economic development of tribal India / Prafullo Chandro Mohapatro. New Delhi : Ashish Pub. House, 1987. xvi, 408 p. : maps ; 22 cm. Revision of the author's thesis (Ph. D.--Utkal University, 1983) Study relates to Koraput District, Orissa. Bibliography: p. [391]-403. Includes index. ISBN 81-7024-077-8 : LC Card 87-900212 DDC 338.954/13 19
1. Tribes - India - Koraput (District) - Economic conditions. 2. Regional planning - India - Koraput (District). 3. Koraput (India : District) - Economic conditions. I. Title.
HC437.K63 M34 1987

MAHARASHTRA (INDIA) - BIOGRAPHY.
Sāvanta, Śivāji, 1940- Laḍhata /. Pravarānagara , 1985-1986. 2 v. : LC Card 87-900715
HD9116.I415 M37 1985
Tāvare, Rāmacandra. Thāpaṭanā /. Mumbaī , 1986. 179 p. ; LC Card 87-900532
HD5820.M29 T38 1986

MAHARASHTRA (INDIA) - ECONOMIC CONDITIONS.
Pāṭīla, Narendra. Āvhāna āṇi āvāhana /. Mumbaī , 1986. 110 p., [13] p. of plates : LC Card 87-900853
HC437.M32 P38 1986

MAHARASHTRA (INDIA) - INDUSTRIES.
Desaraḍā, Eca. Ema. Śeṭī, udyoga, āṇi śikshaṇa . Auraṅgābāda , 1986. 18, 148 p. ; LC Card 87-900720
HC437.M32 D47 1986

Maharjan, Bekha L. (Bekha Lal), 1943- Small farm development problems and strategies / Bekha L. Maharjan. 1st ed. [Kathmandu] : Shiva N. Maharjan, 1984. 114 p. ; 23 cm. Bibliography: p. 107-114. LC Card 84-901301 DDC 338.1/6 19
1. Farms, Small - Nepal. 2. Agriculture - Nepal. 3. Farm management - Nepal. I. Title.
HD1476.N35 M33 1984
NYPL [JLD 86-4365]

Mahathir bin Mohamad, 1925- Dasar-dasar ekonomi Mahathir /. Kuala Lumpur , 1986. xvi, 187 p. : LC Card 86-943311
HC445.5 .D37 1986

MAHATHIR BIN MOHAMAD, 1925-
Dasar-dasar ekonomi Mahathir /. Kuala Lumpur , 1986. xvi, 187 p. : LC Card 86-943311
HC445.5 .D37 1986

Mahāwitthayālai Thammasāt.
Salam . Krung Thēp , 2525 [1982] 16, 249 p. : LC Card 82-916400
HC445.Z7 B3678 1982

Mahāwitthayālai Thammasāt. Institute of Human Resources. Thailand. Samnakngān Khana Kammakān Kansksā hǣng Chāt. Education and employment from world capitalism to the rural Thais . Bangkok, Thailand , 1985. 46 p. : LC Card 86-915875 DDC 331.13/79593 19
HD5822.55.A6 T47 1985

Maher, Michael, 1946- Butler, Stephen A. Management incentive compensation plans /. Montvale, N.J. , c1986. v, 55 p. ; ISBN 0-86641-140-2 (pbk.) LC Card 86-230062 DDC 658.4/07225 19
HD4965.5.U6 B86 1986

Mahfoozur Rahman. see **Rahman, Mahfoozur.**

Mahler, Karl-Werner, 1933- Der Waste Factor : Kritik der integrierten Unternehmensplanung aus Marketingsicht / von Karl-Werner Mahler und Hannsjörg Horseling. München-Gräfelfing : Werk-Verlag E. Banaschewski, c1983. 64 p. ; 25 cm. ISBN 3-8040-0321-4 LC Card 84-214297
1. Waste (Economics) - Germany (West). 2. Business enterprises - Germany, West. 3. Marketing - Germany, West. I. Horseling, Hannsjörg. II. Title.
HC290.5.W3 M34 1983

Mähling, Friedrich W. (Friedrich Wilhelm), 1952- Werbung, Wettbewerb und Verbraucherpolitik / Friedrich W. Mähling. München : V. Florentz, c1983. xii, 477 p. : ill. ; 21 cm. (Hochschulschriften zur Betriebswirtschaftslehre . Bd. 24) Bibliography: p. 437-474. Includes index. ISBN 3-88259-258-3 LC Card 84-144205
1. Advertising - Psychological aspects. 2. Advertising, Comparison. 3. Consumers. I. Title. II. Series.
HF5822 .M34 1983

Mahmassani, Hani S. Massimi, John J. Truck lane needs methodology . Austin , Springfield, Va. [1985] xii, 63 p. : LC Card 86-622425 DDC 388.1/3 19
HE336.T79 M37 1985

Mahon, Thomas. Charged bodies : people, power, and paradox in Silicon Valley / Thomas Mahon. New York : New American Library, c1985. 339 p. : ill. ; 23 cm. Includes index. Bibliography: p. 333-336. ISBN 0-453-00487-3 LC Card 84-18957 DDC 338.4/76213817/0979473 19
1. Microelectronics industry - California - Santa Clara County - Biography. 2. Computer industry - California - Santa Clara County - Biography. 3. Santa Clara County, Calif. - Biography. 4. Santa Clara County (Calif.) - Economic conditions. 5. Santa Clara County (Calif.) - Social conditions. I. Title.
HD9696.A3 U5666 1985
NYPL [JLD 86-1109]

Mahoney, Lawrence. The early birds : a history of Pan Am's Clipper ships / Lawrence Mahoney. Miami, FL : Pickering Press, 1987. xii, 112 p. : ill. ; 22 cm. Bibliography: p. 107-108. Includes index. ISBN 0-940495-07-4 (pbk.) LC Card 87-21974 DDC 387.7/065/73 19
1. Pan American Airways Corporation, inc. - History. 2. Seaplanes - History. I. Title.
HE9803.P36 M35 1987

Maia, Fernando M. Segurança social em Portugal : evolução e tendências / Fernando M. Maia ; prefácio de Alfredo Bruto da Costa. Lisboa : Instituto de Estudos para o Desenvolvimento, 1985. 192 p. : ill. ; 24 cm. (Caderno . 11) Includes bibliographical references. LC Card 86-149393
1. Social security - Portugal - History. 2. Social

security - Law and legislation - Portugal. I. Series: Caderno (Instituto de Estudos para o Desenvolvimento (Portugal)) , 11. II. Title.
HD7209 .M35 1985

Maĭdanchik, B. I. (Boris Iontelevich) Karpunin, M. G. (Mikhail Grigor′evich) Funktsional′no-stoimostnoĭ analiz v otraslevom upravlenii ėffektivnost′iu /. Moskva , 1983. 199 p. : LC Card 84-120682
HF5686.C8 K275 1983

Maier-Bode, F. W. Germany (West). Bundesministerium für Ernährung, Landwirtschaft und Forsten. Wissenschaftlicher Beirat. Gutachten des Wissenschaftlichen Beirats beim Bundesministerium für Ernährung, Landwirtschaft und Forsten /. Hiltrup bei Münster (Westf.) [1960?] 98 p. ; LC Card 86-185959
HD1957 .G47 1960

Maier, Charles S. In search of stability : explorations in historical political economy / Charles S. Maier. Cambridge [Cambridgeshire] ; New York : Cambridge University Press, 1987. x, 291 p. ; 24 cm. (Cambridge studies in modern political economies) Includes bibliographical references and index. ISBN 0-521-23001-2 LC Card 87-6383 DDC 338.94 19
1. Europe - Economic conditions - 20th century. 2. Europe - Economic policy. 3. Fascism - Europe - History - 20th century. 4. Representative government and representation - Europe - History - 20th century. I. Series.
HC240 .M17 1987

Maier, Ernest L. Johnson, H. Herbert Webster, 1906- How to use the business library . Cincinnati , c1984. iv, 267 p. : ISBN 0-538-05750-5 (pbk.) LC Card 83-60484 DDC 027.6/9 19
Z675.B8 J6 1984 ***NYPL [JLE 86-3971]***

Maier, Friederike. Regionalisierte Arbeitsmarkt- und Beschäftigungspolitik /. Frankfurt/Main , New York , c1983. 322 p. : ISBN 3-593-33241-8 LC Card 84-106151
HC286.7 .R44 1983

Maier, Hans E. Das Handwerk und die Berufseingliederung Jugendlicher in der Bundesrepublik Deutschland / Hans E. Maier. Berlin : Wissenschaftszentrum Berlin, [1986] 68 p. : 2 ill. ; 30 cm. (Discussion papers / IIM, Labour Market Policy, 0722-673X . IIM/LMP 86-3) "June 1986." Summary in English and German. Bibliography: p. 56-61. LC Card 86-230660
1. Occupational training - Germany, West. 2. Youth - Employment - Germany, West. 3. Apprentices - Germany, West. 4. Small business - Germany, West. 5. Occupational training - Germany (West) - Bavaria - Case studies. 6. Employees, Training of - Germany (West) - Bavaria - Case studies. I. Series: Discussion papers (International Institute of Management. Labour Market Policy) , IIM/LMP 86-3. II. Title.
HD5715.5.G4 M35 1986

Maier, Harry. Innovation und Wissenschaft . Berlin , 1985. 328 p. : LC Card 86-121669
HC290.795.T4 I56 1985

Maier, Jörg. Freizeitraum Oberstaufen : Abgrenzung und Bewertung / von Jörg Maier u. Karl Ruppert, unter Mitarbeit von E. Kerstiens-Koeberle. München : GEO-BUCH Verlag, 1976. xii, 92 p. : ill., maps ; 24 cm. (WGI-Berichte zur Regionalforschung . Heft 13) Three maps on 3 folded leaves in pocket. Bibliography: p. 89-92. ISBN 3-920397-13-4 LC Card 87-408421 DDC 330.94 380.1/45914337 19
1. Tourist trade - Germany (West) - Oberstaufen. I. Ruppert Karl. II. Title. III. Series.
HC281 .M84 Heft 13 G155.G3

Maier-Leibnitz, Heinz. Lernschock Tschernobyl / Heinz Maier-Leibnitz. Zürich : Interfrom : A. Fromm, c1986. 137 p. ; 20 cm. (Texte + Thesen. 191) ISBN 3-7201-5191-3 : LC Card 87-120438
1. Nuclear power plants - Ukraine - Chernobyl′ - Accidents - Public opinion. 2. Antinuclear movement. I. Title.
HD9698.S653 C485 1986

Maier, Lotte.
Aufbruch zum Himmel . Dortmund , c1982. 99 p. : ISBN 3-88379-328-0 : LC Card 83-125566
HE6184.A4 A84 1982

Militärmarken / Lotte Maier. Dortmund : Harenberg, 1981. 158 p. : col. ill. ; 18 cm. (Die Bibliophilen Taschenbücher . Nr. 253) Collection by Hans König. ISBN 3-88379-253-5 (kart.) : LC Card 81-180793
1. Cinderella materials (Philately) - Europe. 2. Postage-stamps - Topics - Armed Forces. I. Title. II. Series.
HE6184.S42 M35 1981

Maier, Mark. City unions : managing discontent in New York City / Mark H. Maier. New Brunswick [N.J.] : Rutgers University Press, c1987. xii, 221 p. ; 23 cm. Bibliography: p. [193]-214. Includes index. ISBN 0-8135-1229-8 (pbk.) : LC Card 86-26031 DDC 331.88/113520747/1 19
1. Trade-unions - Municipal employees - New York (N.Y.). I. Title.
HD8005.2.U53 N46 1987

Maĭer, V. F. Razvitie obshchestvennykh fondov potrebleniia na sovremennom ėtape /. Moskva , 1984. 140 p. ; LC Card 85-240059
HD7196 .R39 1984

Maierbeck, Marianne. Nutzen- und Zielprobleme privater Haushalte : e. Beitr. zur Entscheidungstheorie / von Marianne Maierbeck. Berlin : Duncker und Humblot, 1978. 203 p. : ill. : 24 cm. (Beträge zur Ökonomie von Haushalt und Verbrauch . Heft 13) Bibliography: p. [189]-203. ISBN 3-428-04220-4 : LC Card 79-356181
1. Utility theory. 2. Consumption (Economics). 3. Households - Economic aspects. I. Title.
TX7 .B4 Heft 13 HB201 ***NYPL [JLE 86-3431]***

Mail for the back of beyond /. Maddock, John, 1917- Kenthurst , 1986. 160 p. : ISBN 0-86417-063-7 LC Card 86-207558 DDC 383/.143/0994 19
HE5709.A6 M33 1986

MAIL-ORDER BUSINESS.
Bly, Robert W. Direct mail profits . Westbury, N.Y. , c1987. x, 206 p. : ISBN 0-87280-153-5 : LC Card 87-18678 DDC 659.13/3 19
HF5466 .B59 1987

Hoge, Cecil C. Mail order moonlighting /. Berkeley, Calif. , 1987. p. cm. ISBN 0-89815-222-4 LC Card 87-17953 DDC 658.8/72 19
HF5466 .H572 1987

Lumley, James E. A. Sell it by mail . New York , c1986. xviii, 382 p. : ISBN 0-471-87908-8 : LC Card 85-16362 DDC 658.8/4 19
HF5466 .L85 1986 ***NYPL [JLE 86-3044]***

Raphel, Murray, 1928- The do-it-yourself direct mail handbook /. Philadelphia, PA (402 Bethlehem Pike, Philadelphia 19118) , c1986. xix, 218 p. : LC Card 86-203353
HF5861 .R35 1986

Tepper, Ron, 1937- Secrets of a successful mail order guru . New York , c1988. ix, 230 p. : ISBN 0-471-84857-3 LC Card 87-21658 DDC 658.8/72 19
HF5466 .T36 1988

MAIL-ORDER BUSINESS - DIRECTORIES.
Goldstein, Sue, 1941- The 2nd underground shopper . Kansas City , c1985. 470 p. : ISBN 0-8362-7956-5 (pbk.) : LC Card 85-620 DDC 381/.1 19
HF5466 .G6 1985 ***NYPL [JLD 86-3080]***

Goldstein, Sue, 1941- The 3rd underground shopper . Kansas City , 1986. x, 532 p. ; ISBN 0-8362-7937-9 (pbk.) : LC Card 86-28758 DDC 381/.1 19
HF5466 .G6 1986

Wathey, Patricia Wogen. The international mail-order shopping guide /. Englewood Cliffs, N.J. , 1984. 338 p. : ISBN 0-13-473083-6 LC Card 84-8390 DDC 381/.14/025 19
HF5466 .W38 1984
NYPL [*R-Econ. 84-3915]

MAIL-ORDER BUSINESS - FRANCE.
Grémillard, Roger. 75 moyens qui ont fait leurs preuves d'augmenter vos rendements et diminuer vos coûts en publicité et en V.P.C. /. Créteil , c1982. 158 p. ; LC Card 82-238594
HF5466 .G718 1982

MAIL-ORDER BUSINESS -UNITED STATES.
Weintz, Walter. The solid gold mailbox . New York , c1987. xiv, 268 p. : ISBN 0-471-85026-8 LC Card 86-28267 DDC 658.8/72 19
HF5466 .W45 1987

MAIL-ORDER BUSINESS - UNITED STATES - DIRECTORIES.
Goldstein, Sue, 1941- The 2nd underground shopper . Kansas City , c1985. 470 p. : ISBN 0-8362-7956-5 (pbk.) : LC Card 85-620 DDC 381/.1 19
HF5466 .G6 1985 ***NYPL [JLD 86-3080]***

Goldstein, Sue, 1941- The 3rd underground shopper . Kansas City , 1986. x, 532 p. ; ISBN 0-8362-7937-9 (pbk.) : LC Card 86-28758 DDC 381/.1 19
HF5466 .G6 1986

Gottlieb, Richard. The directory of mail order catalogs /. [New York, N.Y.] , Sharon, CT , c1987. xi, 385 p. ; ISBN 0-8160-1740-9 LC Card 86-31959 DDC 016.381/14/0973 19
HF5466 .G63 1987

Palder, Edward L. The catalog of catalogs . Kensington, Md. , 1987. xxxiv, 423 p. ; ISBN 0-933149-11-5 (pbk.) : LC Card 86-51220 DDC 381/.14/029473 19
HF5466 .P35 1987

The Wholesale-by-mail catalog. New York , 1986. iv, 364 p. ; ISBN 0-312-90379-0 (pbk.) : LC Card 87-139567 DDC 381/.2/02573 19
HF5861 .W54 1986

Mail order moonlighting /. Hoge, Cecil C. Berkeley, Calif. , 1987. p. cm. ISBN 0-89815-222-4 LC Card 87-17953 DDC 658.8/72 19
HF5466 .H572 1987

MAIL STEAMERS - CARIBBEAN AREA - HISTORY.
Migliavacca, Giorgio. The Royal Mail Steam Packet Company /. [S.l.] , 1985. 41 p. : ISBN 0-934139-01-6 (pbk.) LC Card 87-149471 DDC 383/.142/09729 19
HE6939.M3 M53 1985

MAIL STEAMERS - GREAT BRITAIN - HISTORY.
Migliavacca, Giorgio. The Royal Mail Steam Packet Company /. [S.l.] , 1985. 41 p. : ISBN 0-934139-01-6 (pbk.) LC Card 87-149471 DDC 383/.142/09729 19
HE6939.M3 M53 1985

MAIL STEAMERS - NORTH ATLANTIC REGION - HISTORY.
Arnell, J. C. Steam and the North Atlantic mails . Toronto, Ont. , c1986. x, 295 p. : ISBN 0-919801-36-6 : LC Card 87-127353 DDC 383/.142/091631 19
HE6233 .A76 1986

MAIL STEAMERS - RÍO DE LA PLATA REGION (ARGENTINA AND URUGUAY) - ADMINISTRATION - HISTORY.
Marcó del Pont, José. El correo marítimo en el Río de la Plata /. Buenos Aires , 1913. 161 p. : LC Card 85-125707
HE6819.M3 M37 1913

Maillat, Denis. Held, Daniel. Marché de l'emploi . Lausanne , 1984. 205 p. : ISBN 2-88074-028-2 ***NYPL [JLE 86-679]***

Maĭminas, E. Z. (Efrem Zalmanovich), 1932- Problemy tselevoĭ orientatsii razvitiia resursnogo potentsiala /. Moskva , 1984. 205 p. : LC Card 86-143993
HC333.5 .P77 1984

Main basse sur la France /. Walter, Jean Jacques, 1932- Paris , c1984. 252 p. ; ISBN 2-7103-0188-1 LC Card 84-231340 DDC 335/.00944 19
HX264 .W36 1984 ***NYPL [JLD 86-1773]***

Main directions of agricultural development in Hungary : papers / [edited by Ádám Bisztray]. Budapest : Research Institute for Agricultural Economics, 1985. 77 p. ; 24 cm. (Bulletin, 0541-9417 . no. 61) Bibliography: p. 75-77. LC Card 86-232881 DDC 338.1 s 338.1/09439 19
1. Agriculture - Economic aspects - Hungary. I. Bisztray, Ádám. II. Agrárgazdasági Kutató Intézet. III. Series: Bulletin (Agrágazdasági Kutató Intézet) , no. 61.
HD1407 .M3 no. 61 HD1940.5

Main Hurdman (Firm) Dollars & cents of off-price shopping centers . Washington, D.C. , c1986. v, 78 p. : ISBN 0-87420-660-X (pbk.) LC Card 86-51102 DDC 381/.1 19
HF5430.3 .D65 1986

Main, V. N. (Valentin Nikolaevich) Sel′skaia intelligentsiia v gody Velikoĭ Otechestvennoĭ voĭny : ocherk partiĭnoĭ i sovetskoĭ raboty /

V.N. Main. Voronezh : Izd-vo Voronezhskogo universiteta, 1985. 158 p. ; 20 cm. Bibliography: p. 138-[157] LC Card 84-172657
1. World War, 1939-1945 - Economic aspects - Soviet Union. 2. Soviet Union - Rural conditions. 3. Professional employees - Soviet Union. 4. Kommunisticheskaia partiia Sovetskogo Soiuza - Party work. I. Title.
HC340.D4 M35 1985

Maindok, Herlinde, 1948- Frauenalltag in Männerberufen / Herlinde Maindok. Originalausg. Frankfurt am Main : Fischer Taschenbuch Verlag, 1987. 173, [2] p. ; 19 cm. (Die Frau in der Gesellschaft) Bibliography: p. [175]. ISBN 3-596-23786-6 LC Card 87-164114 DDC 331.4/81 19
1. Sexual division of labor. 2. Women in the professions. I. Title. II. Series.
HD6060.6 .M35 1987

MAINE - APPROPRIATIONS AND EXPENDITURES - STATISTICS.
Compendium of state fiscal information /. [Augusta?] [1985] 40 leaves : LC Card 86-621730 DDC 336.741/021 19
HJ2410 .C65 1985

Maine. Bureau of Banking.
The Status of Maine's financial institutions . [Augusta] [1985] 38 leaves ; LC Card 86-621914 DDC 332.1/09741 19
HG2611.M2 S73 1985

The Status of Maine's financial institutions . [Augusta] [1986] 38 leaves ; LC Card 86-621913 DDC 332.1/09741 19
HG183.M2 S7 1986

Maine. Bureau of Employment Security. Division of Economic Analysis and Research.
High technology employment . Augusta, Me. (20 Union St., Augusta 04330) [1985] iii, 23 p. : LC Card 85-623118 DDC 331.12/57/09741 19
HD5718.H542 U635 1985

Maine occupational employment in 1984 and projected to 1995 /. Auqusta, Me. (20 Union St., Augusta 04330) [1986] 32 leaves ; LC Card 87-620754 DDC 331.12/09741/021 19
HD5725.M3 M386 1986

Maine. Division of Motor Vehicles.
Pease, Allen. Appendix for the feasibility report of implementing the International Registration Plan in the State of Maine . [Augusta, Me.] [1985] 39 leaves : LC Card 85-622841 DDC 388.3/24 19
HE5633.M2 P39 1985

Pease, Allen. Report on the feasibility of implementing the International Registration Plan in the State of Maine . [Augusta, Me.] [1985] ii, 24 leaves ; LC Card 85-622840 DDC 388.3/24 19
HE5633.M2 P4 1985

MAINE - FORECASTING - STATISTICS.
Maine occupational employment in 1984 and projected to 1995 /. Auqusta, Me. (20 Union St., Augusta 04330) [1986] 32 leaves ; LC Card 87-620754 DDC 331.12/09741/021 19
HD5725.M3 M386 1986

Maine. Legislature. Office of Fiscal and Program Review. Compendium of state fiscal information /. [Augusta?] [1985] 40 leaves : LC Card 86-621730 DDC 336.741/021 19
HJ2410 .C65 1985

Maine occupational employment in 1984 and projected to 1995 / Maine Department of Labor, Bureau of Employment Security, Division of Economic Analysis and Research. Auqusta, Me. (20 Union St., Augusta 04330) : The Division, [1986] 32 leaves ; 28 cm. LC Card 87-620754 DDC 331.12/09741/021 19
1. Labor supply - Maine - Statistics. 2. Employment forecasting - Maine - Statistics. 3. Maine - Occupations - Statistics. 4. Maine - Occupations - Forecasting - Statistics. 5. Job vacancies - Maine - Statistics. 6. Job vacancies - Maine - Forecasting - Statistics. 7. Maine - Forecasting - Statistics. I. Maine. Bureau of Employment Security. Division of Economic Analysis and Research.
HD5725.M3 M386 1986

MAINE - OCCUPATIONS - FORECASTING - STATISTICS.
Maine occupational employment in 1984 and projected to 1995 /. Auqusta, Me. (20 Union St., Augusta 04330) [1986] 32 leaves ; LC Card 87-620754 DDC 331.12/09741/021 19
HD5725.M3 M386 1986

MAINE - OCCUPATIONS - STATISTICS.
Maine occupational employment in 1984 and projected to 1995 /. Auqusta, Me. (20 Union St., Augusta 04330) [1986] 32 leaves ; LC Card 87-620754 DDC 331.12/09741/021 19
HD5725.M3 M386 1986

Maine. Planning Office, State. see **Maine. State Planning Office.**

MAINE SAVINGS BANK.
Masterton, Robert R. The One Bancorp and Maine Savings Bank . New York , 1986, c1987. 22 p. : LC Card 87-60613 DDC 332.2/1/09741 19
HG2613.P794 M356 1987

Maine. State Development Office. Doing business in Maine. [Augusta, Me. , 1983] iii, 93 p. : LC Card 86-620779 DDC 346.741/07 347.41067 19
HD62.5 .D64 1983

Maine. State Planning Office. Colgan, Charles S. The natural resource industries of Maine . [Augusta, Me.] [1986] 135 p. : LC Card 87-620550 DDC 338.09741 19
HD9007.M2 C64 1986

Maingón, Thais. Kornblith, Miriam. Estado y gasto público en Venezuela, 1936-1980 /. Caracas , 1985. 287, [10] p. : LC Card 86-172043
HJ2093 .K67 1985

Mainland China economic series .
(no. 3) Chêng, Chu-yüan. The demand and supply of primary energy in mainland China /. Taipei, Taiwan, Republic of China , Seattle , c1984. viii, 178 p. ; LC Card 84-231216 DDC 333.79/11/0951 19
HD9502.C62 C49 1984 ***NYPL [JLF 87-21]***

Mainstreams in industrial organization / edited by H.W. de Jong, W.G. Shepherd. Dordrecht ; Boston : Kluwer Academic Publishers, 1986. 2 v. (x, 465 p.) ; 25 cm. (Studies in industrial organization . v. 6) "Essays and part of the discussions as presented at the Conference on Mainstreams in Industrial organization, held at the University of Amsterdam, 21-23 August 1985." -- P. v. Includes bibliographies. ISBN 90-247-3363-4 LC Card 86-12345 DDC 338.6 19
1. Industrial organization - Congresses. 2. Managerial economics - Congresses. 3. Trade regulation - Congresses. 4. Industry and state - Congresses. I. Jong, H. W. de. II. Shepherd, William G. III. Conference on Mainstreams in Industrial Organization, (1985 : University of Amsterdam).
HD29 .M25 1986 ***NYPL [JLE 87-457]***

Mainzer Beiträge zur europäischen Einigung, 0722-5466 .
(Bd. 3) Korte, Karl-Rudolf. Nippons neue Vasallen? . Bonn , c1984. 103 p. : ISBN 3-7713-0216-1 LC Card 86-230930
HF1602.15.E92 K67 1984

Mainzer ethnologische Arbeiten .
(Bd. 5) Höltz, Joachim. Kritik der Geldentstehungstheorien . Berlin , c1984. ii, 401 p. ; ISBN 3-496-00796-6 LC Card 85-147094
HG237 .H64 1984

Maione, Giuseppe, 1942- Tecnocrati e mercanti : l'industria italiana tra dirigismo e concorrenza internazionale (1945-1950) / Giuseppe Maione. Milano, Italia : SugarCo, c1986. 354 p. ; 21 cm. (Il Presente come storia) Nuova biblioteca storica Includes bibliographical references and index. LC Card 86-194293
1. Italy - Industries - History - 20th century. 2. Reconstruction (1939-1951) - Italy. 3. Technological innovations - Italy - History - 20th century. 4. Competition, International - History - 20th century. I. Title. II. Series.
HC305 .M274 1986

Mair, Colin. Midwinter, Arthur F. Rates reform . Edinburgh , 1987. 182 p. ; ISBN 1-85158-062-X : LC Card 87-167866 DDC 336/.014/41 19
HJ9421 .M53 1987

Mair, George, 1929- Inside HBO : the billion dollar war between HBO, Hollywood, and the home video revolution / George Mair.1st ed. New York : Dodd, Mead, c1988. xviii, 204 p. ; 24 cm. Includes index. ISBN 0-396-08420-6 : LC Card 87-19939 DDC 384.55/47/0973 19
1. Home Box Office (Firm). 2. Cable television - United States. 3. Motion picture industry - United States. I. Title. II. Title: HBO. III. Title: Inside Home Box Office.
HE8700.72.U6 M34 1988

Mais qui à peur du travail des femmes? /.
Maruani, Margaret. Paris , c1985. 175 p. : ISBN 2-86738-099-5 : LC Card 86-154408
HD6145 .M37 1985

Maisel, Helmut. Diversifikation und konglomerate Interdependenz : ein Beitrag zu den Wettbewerbswirkungen diagonaler Konzentration / Helmut Maisel. Frankfurt : R.G. Fischer, c1984. 237 p. : ill. ; 21 cm. Bibliography: p. 230-237. ISBN 3-88323-518-0 LC Card 84-213494
1. Diversification in industry - Germany (West) - History. 2. Conglomerate corporations - Germany, West - History. I. Title.
HD2756.2.G3 M34 1984

Maison des pays ibériques. Les Communications dans la péninsule Ibérique au Moyen-Age . Paris , 1981. 208 p. : ISBN 2-222-02922-8 : LC Card 81-213698 DDC 380.5/0946 19
HE261.A5 C65 1981 ***NYPL [JLG 86-113]***

Maison des sciences de l'homme de Strasbourg. Réformisme et révisionnisme dans les socialismes allemand, autrichien et français /. Paris , c1984. 195 p. ; ISBN 2-7351-0053-7 : LC Card 85-105830
HX273 .R39 1984 ***NYPL [JLE 86-4752]***

MAISON MENIER (NOISIEL, FRANCE)
Marrey, Bernard. Un capitalisme idéal /. Paris , c1984. 236 p., [24] p. of plates : ISBN 2-86215-060-6 : LC Card 84-252196 DDC 338.7/6413374/0944 19
HD9200.F74 M356 1984
NYPL [JLD 87-1579]

Maital, Shlomo. Macroeconomic conflict and social institutions /. Cambridge, Mass. , c1985. xi, 249 p. : ISBN 0-88730-034-0 LC Card 84-24376 DDC 339.2 19
HC79.I5 M225 1985 ***NYPL [JLE 86-2562]***

Maitron, Jean. Dictionnaire biographique du mouvement ouvrier international. Publié sous la direction de Jean Maitron et Georges Haupt ... Paris, Editions ouvrières, 1971- <c1985 > <1-2, 5 > port. 25 cm. Includes bibliographical references. CONTENTS. - 1. Autriche, par Y. Bourdet et al.--2. Japon, sous la direction de Shiota Shôbei. (v. <1 >) --[5] La Chine, sous la direction de Lucien Bianco et Yves Chevrier. ISBN 2-7082-1955-3 (v. 2) LC Card 72-333529
1. Labor and laboring classes - Biography - Dictionaries. 2. Socialists - Biography - Dictionaries. I. Haupt, Georges. II. Title.
HD4851 .M34

Majanduse Instituut (Eesti NSV Teaduste Akadeemia)
Upravlenie nauchno-tekhnicheskim progressom v soiuznykh respublikakh /. Tallin , 1986. 158 p. ; LC Card 87-123175
HC340.T4 U77 1986

Voprosy razvitiia obsluzhivaniia naseleniia . Tallin , 1985. 140 p. : LC Card 85-158428
HD9986.S683 E888 1985

MAJANDUSE INSTITUUT (EESTI NSV TEADUSTE AKADEEMIA)
Issledovaniia Instituta ėkonomiki Akademii nauk Ėstonskoĭ SSR v X piatiletke . Tallin , 1983. 233 p. ; LC Card 86-181279
HB74.9.S65 I86 1983

Majandusteaduse ABC : majandusleksikon kõigile / koostanud Uno Mereste ; [autorid, Raimund Hagelberg ... et al.]. Tallinn : "Eesti Raamat", 1985. 511 p. : ill. ; 23 cm. Title in colophon: Azbuka ėkonomicheskoĭ nauki. Includes bibliographical references and index. LC Card 85-195109
1. Economics - Dictionaries - Estonian. I. Mereste, U. (Uno). II. Hagelberg, R. III. Title: Azbuka ėkonomicheskoĭ nauki.
HB61 .M225 1985

Majd, Saman. Smirlock, Michael. Taxes and mergers . New York, N.Y. (90 Trinity Place, New York 10006) [c1986] 42 p. : LC Card 86-210061 DDC 336.24/3 19
HD2746.5 .S64 1986

Majer, Hans Georg. Osmanistische Studien zur Wirtschafts- und Sozialgeschichte . Wiesbaden , 1986. xi, 206 p., iv p. of plates : ISBN 3-477-02652-9 (Deut. Bibl.) LC Card 86-224062
HC492 .O85 1986

Majlis al-Abḥāth al-Iqtiṣādīyah wa-al-Ijtimāʻīyah. Payne, W. J. A. (William John Arthur) A preliminary report on the livestock industry in the Jonglei area /. [Khartoum?] , 1977. 1 v. (various foliations) : LC Card 81-980100
HD9427.S83 J6664 1977

al-Majlis al-Qawmī lil-Buḥūth. Economic and Social Research Council. see **Majlis al-Abḥāth al-Iqtiṣādīyah wa-al-Ijtimāʻīyah.**

Majlis al-Taʻāwun li-Duwal al-Khalīj al-ʻArabīyah.
Focus on the Gulf Co-operation Council (GCC) . London , c1984. 48 p. : LC Card 85-211534 DDC 337.53/6/041 19
HF1584.5 .F63 1984

MAJLIS AL-TAʻĀWUN LI-DUWAL AL-KHALĪJ AL-ʻARABĪYAH - CONGRESSES.
Focus on the Gulf Co-operation Council (GCC) . London , c1984. 48 p. : LC Card 85-211534 DDC 337.53/6/041 19
HF1584.5 .F63 1984

Majlis Perbandaran Pulau Pinang. Report of survey : Penang Island structure plan. [Georgetown] : Majlis Perbandaran Pulau Pinang, [1984?] xv, 193 p. : ill. (some col.) ; 30 x 31 cm. In English, with foreword in Malay. LC Card 86-945200 DDC 307/.09595/1 19
1. Pinang Island (Pinang) - Economic conditions. 2. Pinang Island (Pinang) - Social conditions. 3. Pinang Island (Pinang) - Commerce. 4. Pinang Island (Pinang) - Industries. I. Title.
HC445.Z7 P526 1984

Majmaʻ al-Lughah al-ʻArabīyah, Cairo. Lajnat al-Jughrāfiyā. al-Muʻjam al-jughrāfī / Taṣdīr wa-ishrāf Muḥammad Maḥmūd al-Ṣayyād ; iʻdād Lajnat al-Jughrāfiyā bi-al-Majmaʻ ; ikhrāj wa-tanfīdh Ibrāhīm al-Asyūṭī. 1st ed. [al-Qāhirah] : Jumhūrīyat Miṣr al-ʻArabīyah, Majmaʻ al-Lughah al-ʻArabīyah, 1974. 9,185 p. ; 27 cm. Added t.p.: A dictionary of geography. With English equivalents. Pref. in English and Arabic. Includes index. In Arabic. LC Card 77-961221
1. Geography - Dictionaries - Arabic. 2. Arabic language - Dictionaries - English. 3. English language - Dictionaries - Arabic. 4. Geography - Dictionaries. I. al-Ṣayyād, Muḥammad Maḥmūd, 1916-. II. Title. III. Title: Dictionary of geography.
G63 .M34 1974 ***NYPL [*OEO 86-3694]***

Majmūʻah ʻilmīyah .
(al-kitāb 1) Tazwīr al-mustanadāt wa-tazyīf al-ʻumlāt wa-al-asālīb al-ʻilmīyah lil-kashf ʻanhā. [Cairo] [1978] 296 p., [1] leaf of plates : ISBN 977-7049-73-0 LC Card 79-961630
HG335 .T3 1978

Majnoni, Giovanni. Euromercati e finanziamento delle esportazioni / di Giovanni Majnoni. Roma : Istituto affari internazionali ; Bologna : Il Mulino, c1981. 130 p. ; 22 cm. (Collana dello Spettatore internazionale. 53) Includes bibliographical references. LC Card 83-110156
1. Export marketing - European Economic Community countries - Finance. 2. Export marketing - Developing countries - Finance. 3. International finance. 4. International economic relations. I. Title.
HG3754.E86 M35 1981

Major bus operators . Kirk, David, 1937- Harrow Weald, Middlesex , 1985. 96 p. : ISBN 0-904711-66-8 (pbk.) : LC Card 86-214197 DDC 388.3/22/094273 19
HE5664.M34 K57 1985

Major, C.
Factors and principles determining the amount and duration of unemployment insurance cash benefits. 1980. Jonshagen, I. Employment maintenance and unemployment protection for young workers. Factors and principles determining the amount and duration of unemployment insurance cash benefits : International Social Security Association, XXth General Assembly, Manila, 28 October-6 November 1980. [Geneva , 1980] 102, 69 p. : LC Card 86-219323 DDC 368.4/4 19
HD7095 .J66 1980

Major employers in and around New York City. Hillsdale, N.J. (P.O. Box 294, Hillsdale 07642-0294) : Practical Services, c1986. iv, 112 p. ; 28 cm. LC Card 86-211679 DDC 338.7/4/025741 19
1. Job hunting - New York (N.Y.) - Directories. 2. Corporations - New York (N.Y.) - Directories. 3. Business enterprises - New York (N.Y.) - Directories.
HF5382.75.U62 N56 1986

Major fiscal issues at the 1983-1986 sessions of the General Assembly. Annapolis, Md. (90 State Cir., Annapolis 21401-1991) : Dept. of Fiscal Services, [1986] vi, 100 p. ; 28 cm. "June 1986." LC Card 86-622757 DDC 336.752 19
1. Finance, Public - Maryland. 2. Intergovernmental fiscal relations - Maryland. I. Maryland. General Assembly. Dept. of Fiscal Services.
HJ485 .M15 1986

Major import markets for builders' woodwork / International Trade Centre UNCTAD/GATT. Geneva : The Center, 1985. xiii, 180 p. : ill. ; 23 cm. LC Card 87-118537 DDC 381/.45674/094 19
1. Forest products industry - Europe. 2. Forest products industry - United States. 3. Building materials industry - Europe. 4. Building materials industry - United States. I. International Trade Centre UNCTAD/GATT.
HD9765.A2 M29 1985

Major Industrial Research Unit studies .
(no. 62) Northrup, Herbert Roof, 1918- Open shop construction revisited /. Philadelphia, Pa., U. S.A. , c1984. xxxv, 674 p. : ISBN 0-89546-047-5 : LC Card 84-48502 DDC 331.88/92 19
HD9715.U52 N67 1984 ***NYPL [TB (Pennsylvania. University. Wharton School of Finance and Commerce. Industrial Research Unit. Industrial Research Unit Study. no. 62)]***

(no. 62a) Northrup, Herbert Roof, 1918- Doublebreasted operations and pre-hire agreements in construction . Philadelphia, Penn., USA , c1987. viii, 127 p. : ISBN 0-89546-067-X (pbk.) LC Card 87-81475 DDC 331.88/92 19
HD9715.U52 N67 1984 Suppl.

Major Industrial Research Unit studies, 0083-9094 .
(no. 66) Perry, Charles R. Union corporate campaigns /. Philadelphia, Pa. , c1987. viii, 211 p. : ISBN 0-89546-065-3 : LC Card 86-82727 DDC 331.89/12 19
HD6490.O72 U665 1987

MAJOR ORDERS. see **CLERGY.**

Major report .
(no. 10) Morrison, Philip S., 1947- Data sources on residential change and the housing market . [Toronto] [1977] 76 p. : LC Card 85-158244
HD7305.T68 M67 1977

Major stages and steps in energy manpower analysis : a practical framework. Geneva : International Labour Office, 1986. viii, 80 p. : ill. ; 29 cm. Errata slips (2 p.) inserted. Bibliography: p. [74]-80. ISBN 92-2-105246-X (pbk.) : LC Card 86-222080 DDC 331.12/921042 19
1. Energy industries - Employees - Supply and demand. I. International Labour Office.
HD5718.E47 M35 1986

The majority finds its past . Lerner, Gerda, 1920- New York , 1979. xxxii, 217 p. ; ISBN 0-19-502597-0 LC Card 79-14048 DDC 301.41/2/0973
HQ1426 .L47 ***NYPL [JLD 86-3348]***

Majumder, Arun. Poverty, development, and exchange relations : a study of two Birbhum villages / Arun Majumder. New Delhi : Radiant Publishers, 1987. xiii, 141 p. : folded map ; 23 cm. ISBN 81-7027-108-8 : LC Card 87-900910
1. Bahiri (India) - Economic conditions. 2. Darpasila (India) - Economic conditions. 3. Agriculture - Economic aspects - India - Bahiri. 4. Agriculture - Economic aspects - India - Darpasila. I. Title.
HC438.B24 M35 1987

Május elseje születése /. Jemnitz, János. [Budapest] , 1986. 135, [1] p. : ISBN 963-09-2773-X : LC Card 87-408513
HD7791 .J46 1986

Makać, Antoni. Przemiany we współczesnej gospodarce światowej . Gdańsk , 1978. 360 p. ; LC Card 81-200306
HC59 .P78 1978

Makalová, Eva. Ekonomické aspekty globálních problémů lidstva / Eva Makalová. Praha : Univerzita Karlova, 1984. 97 p. ; 24 cm. (Acta Universitatis Carolinae. Oeconomica . 4-1984-20) Summary in English, German, and Russian. Bibliography: p. 79-80. LC Card 86-207353
1. Economic development - Social aspects. 2. Economic development - Environmental aspects. 3. Population - Economic aspects. I. Series: Acta Universitatis Carolinae. Oeconomica , 1984, 4/20. II. Title.
HB9 .P72a 1984, 4/20 HD75

Makarova, S. M.
Natsionalizatsiia i gossektor v razvivaiushchikhsia stranakh . Moskva , 1986. 210 p. ; LC Card 87-165820
HD4276 .N38 1986

Perspektivy resheniia prodovol'stvennoĭ problemy v razvivaiushchikhsia stranakh . Moskva , 1985. 142 p. ; LC Card 85-188217
HD9018.D44 P47 1985

"Problema neftedollarov" . Moskva , 1984. 231 p. ; LC Card 85-189000
HC498 .P75 1984

Makasheva, N. A.
Dolgovremennye tendentsii v kapitalisticheskom vosproizvodstve . Moskva , 1985. 229 p. : LC Card 86-187722
HB3711 .D62 1985

Sovremennyĭ konservatizm i krizis burzhuaznoĭ ėkonomicheskoĭ nauki . Moskva , 1986. 175 p. ; LC Card 87-165796
HB241 .S673 1986

Sovremennyĭ monetarizm i krizis burzhuaznoĭ ėkonomicheskoĭ teorii : nauchno-analiticheskiĭ obzor / [avtor obzora Makasheva N.A. ; otvetstvennyĭ redaktor Zhebrak B.A.]. Moskva : Akademiia nauk SSSR, In-t nauch. informatsii po obshchestvennym naukam, 1985. 47 p. ; 20 cm. (Seriia Problemy politicheskoĭ ėkonomii za rubezhom) Bibliography: p. 42-46. LC Card 86-187688
1. Chicago school of economics. 2. Monetary policy. I. Zhebrak, B. A. II. Title. III. Series.
HB98.3 .M35 1985

Makatjane, Tiisetso.
Internal migration and fertility in Lesotho / by Tiisetso Makatjane. [Roma, Lesotho] : Demography Unit, Dept. of Statistics, National University of Lesotho, [1985] iii, 36 leaves ; 29 cm. (Working papers in demography . working paper no. 6) "November 1985." Bibliography: leaves 31-36. LC Card 87-132347 DDC 304.6/32/096816 19
1. Fertility, Human - Lesotho. 2. Rural-urban migration - Lesotho. I. Series: Working papers in demography (National University of Lesotho. Dept. of Statistics. Demography Unit) , working paper no. 6. II. Title.
HB2123.7.A3 M35 1985

Sources of population statistics in Lesotho / by Tiisetso Makatjane. [Roma, Lesotho] : Demography Unit, Dept. of Statistics, National University of Lesotho, [1985] iii, 29 leaves ; 30 cm. (Working papers in demography . working paper no. 3) "August 1985." Bibliography: leaves 28-29. Errata slip pasted on leaf iii. LC Card 87-132320 DDC 304.6/09681/6 19
1. Lesotho - Statistical services. 2. Lesotho - Population - Statistics - Bibliography. I. Series: Working papers in demography (National University of Lesotho. Dept. of Statistics. Demography Unit) , working paper no. 3. II. Title.
HA37.L52 M35 1985

Make a fortune buying discounted mortgages /. Bel Air, Roger. Garden City, N.Y. , 1987. 152 p. : ISBN 0-385-23924-6 : LC Card 86-23949 DDC 332.63/244 19
HG5095 .B38 1987

MAKE-BUY DECISIONS. see **MAKE-OR-BUY DECISIONS.**

Make it yours! . Mucciolo, Louis. New York , c1987. xiv, 269 p. ; ISBN 0-471-62585-X (pbk.) LC Card 87-8168 DDC 658.1/141 19
HD62.7 .M79 1987

MAKE-OR-BUY DECISIONS.
Männel, Wolfgang. Die Wahl zwischen Eigenfertigung und Fremdbezug . Stuttgart , c1981. xvi, 406 p. : ISBN 3-7910-0270-8 LC Card 83-167804
HD2381 .M32 1981

Make sound decisions /. Wall, William C. Huntsville, Ala. , c1987. p. cm. ISBN 0-938745-01-8 : LC Card 87-14128 DDC 658.4/03 19
HD30.23 .W34 1987

Make them choose you . Kohlmann, James D. Englewood Cliffs, N.J. , c1988. xiv, 178 p. ; ISBN 0-13-547878-2 LC Card 87-17435 DDC 650.1/4 19
HF5549.5.I6 K58 1988

MAKE-UP (COSMETICS) see COSMETICS.

Make your job interview a success . Biegeleisen, J. I. (Jacob Israel), 1910- New York , c1987. 222 p. : ISBN 0-13-545716-5 : LC Card 87-19294 DDC 650.1/4 19
HF5549.5.I6 B5 1987

Makeev, D. A. Vneshnetorgovye svi͡azi SSSR so stranami Arabskogo Vostoka v 1922-1939 gg. / D.A. Makeev. Moskva : Moskovskiĭ gos. pedagog. in-t im. V.I. Lenina, 1983. 112 p. ; 21 cm. At head of title: Ministerstvo prosveshchenii͡a RSFSR. Moskovskiĭ ordena Lenina i ordena Trudovogo Krasnogo Znameni gosudarstvennyĭ pedagogicheskiĭ institut imeni V.I. Lenina. Includes bibliographical references. LC Card 84-189987
1. Soviet Union - Foreign economic relations - Arab countries - History. 2. Arab countries - Foreign economic relations - Soviet Union - History. 3. Soviet Union - Foreign economic relations - Egypt - History. 4. Egypt - Foreign economic relations - Soviet Union - History. I. Title.
HF1558.15.A65 M34 1983

Maker, William. Hegel on economics and freedom /. Macon, Ga. , c1987. viii, 236 p. ; ISBN 0-86554-256-2 (alk. paper) : LC Card 87-7887 DDC 330.1 19
HB107.H38 H44 1987

Mākeṭim, samasyā o sambhābanā . Jātīya Mārkeṭim Seminār̄a, 1985 (1985 : Chātra-Śikshaka Kendra, Ḍhākā Biśvabidyālaẏa) [Dhaka] , 1985. 138 p. ; LC Card 86-903411
HF5415.12.B36 J38 1985

Makhmudova, N. M. Tormysheva, T. A. (Tamara Andreevna) Okhrana truda i sotsial′noe strakhovanie trudi͡ashchikhsi͡a v Uzbekskoĭ SSR /. Tashkent , 1987. 131 p. ; LC Card 87-107413
HD7345.U93 T67 1987

Makhmutov, A. Kh. (Anas Khusainovich) Lichnoe potreblenie v usloviiākh razvitogo sotsializma / A.Kh. Makhmutov. Kazan′ : Izd-vo Kazanskogo universiteta, 1980. 249 p. ; 20 cm. Includes bibliographical references. LC Card 82-162621
1. Consumption (Economics) - Soviet Union. I. Title.
HC340.C6 M29 1980

Makhnova, V. I. (Vera Ivanovna) Teorii͡a khozi͡aĭstvennykh svi͡azeĭ / V.I. Makhnova. Moskva : Ėkonomika, 1985. 197 p. : ill. ; 22 cm. Includes bibliographical references. LC Card 86-107892
1. Soviet Union - Economic policy - 1981-. 2. Industrial procurement - Soviet Union. 3. Industrial productivity - Soviet Union. I. Title.
HC336.25 .M347 1985

Makhrov, N. V. (Nikolaĭ Vasil′evich) Modin, Anatoliĭ Andreevich. Dinamika proizvodstvennykh ob″edineniĭ i modeli planirovanii͡a ikh dei͡atel′nosti /. Moskva , 1984. 231 p. : LC Card 84-195690
HD9705.S595 M62 1984

Makin, John H.
Exchange rate targets . Washington, D.C. , c1986. ix, 59 p. ; ISBN 0-8447-3615-5 (pbk. : alk. paper) : LC Card 86-72463 DDC 332.4/5 19
HG203 .E98 1986

Trade policy and U. S. competitiveness /. Washington, D.C. , Lanham, Md. , c1987. xvi, 144 p. ; ISBN 0-8447-3633-3 (alk. paper) LC Card 87-18831 DDC 382/.3/0973 19
HF1455 .T65 1987

Mäkinen, Vesa, 1945- Yrityksen taloustieteet Tampereen yliopistossa /. Tampere , 1985. 47 leaves : ISBN 951-44-1859-X LC Card 87-107284
HD30.42.F5 Y74 1985

Making America poorer . Reynolds, Morgan O., 1942- Washington, D.C. , c1987. ix, 218 p. ; ISBN 0-932790-63-1 LC Card 87-6569 DDC 338.5/1/0973 19
HD6508 .R435 1987

Making America work again . National Commission on Jobs and Small Business (U. S.) Washington, D.C. , c1987. ix, 70 p. ; ISBN 0-9617931-0-4 (pbk.) : LC Card 86-33118 DDC 338.6/42/0973 19
HD2346.U5 N315 1987

Making and marketing arms . Kolodziej, Edward A. Princeton, N.J. , c1987. xxv, 518 p. : ISBN 0-691-07734-7 (alk. paper) : LC Card 86-30567 DDC 338.4/76234/0944 19
HD9743.F82 K64 1987

**Making cars : a history of car making in Cowley by the people who make the cars / Television History Workshop ; editors, Greg Lanning ... [et al.] ; research and interviews, Christine Peaker, Caro Webb, Richard White, with Bill Bourne ... [et al.] London ; Boston : Routledge & K. Paul, c1985. ix, 131 p. : ill. ; 24 cm. (History workshop series) Includes index. ISBN 0-7102-0272-5 : LC Card 84-13398 DDC 338.4/76292/0942574 19
1. Automobile industry workers - England - Oxford - History. 2. Automobile industry and trade - England - Oxford - History. 3. Cowley (Oxford, Eng.). I. Peaker, Christine. II. Webb, Caro. III. White, Richard. IV. Lanning, Greg. V. Television History Workshop (Great Britain).
HD8039.A82 G75 1984
NYPL [JLE 86-2303]

Making CBT happen . Gery, Gloria, 1944- Boston , 1987. xiv, 225 p. : ISBN 0-9617968-0-4 (pbk.) : LC Card 86-51671 DDC 658.3/12404 19
HF5549.5.T7 G42 1987

Making choices, making do [microform] . Helmbold, Lois Rita. 1982. vii, 385 leaves
NYPL [Sc Micro R-4672]

Making do and doing without : Kansas in the Great Depression. [Lawrence, Kan.] : Division of Continuing Education, KANU, University of Kansas, 1985, c1983. 98 p. ; 28 cm. Bibliography: p. 87-98. LC Card 86-622703 DDC 330.9781/032 19
1. Kansas - Economic conditions. 2. Depressions - 1929 - Kansas. I. University of Kansas. Division of Continuing Education.
HC107.K2 M35 1985

Making dollars and cents with dollars and sense /. Rozells, Gia L. Greensboro, N.C. , c1987. ix, 207 p. : ISBN 0-87455-101-3 (pbk.) : LC Card 87-160661 DDC 332.024/0028/55369 19
HG179 .R74 1987

Making innovation practical /. Bennett, Addison C. Chicago, Ill. , c1986. vi, 238 p. : ISBN 0-931028-79-5 LC Card 86-62191 DDC 658.4/06 19
HD58.8 .B46 1986

Making it in America /. Minkow, Barry. [Los Angeles?] , c1985. 136 p. ; LC Card 85-51822 DDC 650.1/092/4 B 19
HC102.5.M5 A3 1985

Making it on your own /. Feingold, S. Norman, 1914- Washington, D.C. , c1985. 300 p. ; ISBN 0-87491-779-4 (pbk.) : LC Card 85-7560 DDC 658/.022 19
HD62.7 .F44 1985
NYPL [*R-Econ. 85-4850]

Making mergers work . Pritchett, Price. Homewood, Ill. , c1987. xii, 108 p. ; ISBN 0-87094-980-2 LC Card 86-73001 DDC 658.1/6 19
HD2746.5 .P743 1987

Making money /. Rochette, Edward C., 1927- Frederick, CO , c1986. 107 p. : ISBN 0-939650-25-8 (pbk.) : LC Card 86-22120 DDC 364.1/33/09 19
HG335 .R63 1986

Making money with mutual funds . Renberg, Werner. New York , c1988. xviii, 217 p. : ISBN 0-471-85555-3 LC Card 87-26366 DDC 332.63/27 19
HG4530 .R46 1988

Making mortgages work for you /. Irwin, Robert, 1941- New York , c1987. viii, 185 p. : ISBN 0-07-032129-9 : LC Card 86-31270 DDC 332.7/22/0973 19
HG2040.5.U5 I75 1987

The making of a strike . Ladd, Doris M. Lincoln , c1988. x, 205 p. ; ISBN 0-8032-2876-7 (alk. paper) LC Card 87-5897 DDC 331.8/928223423/097246 19
HD5331.M72 1766 .P325 1988

The making of the AWU /. Merritt, John. Melbourne , New York , 1986. x, 432 p., [16] p. of plates : ISBN 0-19-554667-9 LC Card 86-207509 DDC 331.88/13630833/0994 19
HD8842.A874 M47 1986

The making of the Black working class in Britain /. Ramdin, Ron. Aldershot, Hants, England , Brookfield, Vt., USA , c1987. x, 626 p. ; ISBN 0-566-00943-9 LC Card 87-127153 DDC 305.5/62 19
HD8398.B55 R36 1987

The making of United States international economic policy . Cohen, Stephen D. New York , 1987. p. cm. ISBN 0-275-92334-7 (alk. paper) : LC Card 87-24082 DDC 382/.3/0973 19
HF1455 .C576 1987

Making our own way . Penvenne, Jeanne. Boston, MA (270 Bay State Rd., Boston 02215) , 1986. 20 leaves ; LC Card 87-155233 DDC 331.4/0967/91 19
HD6211.5 .P46 1986

Making performance evaluation work . Sashkin, Marshall, 1944- [Albany, N.Y.] , c1986. 57 p. : ISBN 0-8144-2326-4 (pbk.) LC Card 86-209627 DDC 658.3/125 19
HF5549.5.P35 S26 1986

Making sense of Europe /. Tugendhat, Christopher, 1937- New York , 1988. p. cm. ISBN 0-231-06682-1 (alk. paper) LC Card 87-15871 DDC 337.1/42 19
HC241.2 .T83 1988

Making seventy thousand dollars a year as a self-employed manufacturer's representative. Silliphant, Leigh. Making $70,000 a year as a self-employed manufacturer's representative /. Englewood Cliffs, N.J. , c1984. 204 p. ; ISBN 0-13-547687-9 (case) LC Card 83-16147 DDC 658.8/5 19
HF5422 .S54 1984 ***NYPL [JLE 86-2636]***

Making strategy work . Hamermesh, Richard G. New York , c1986. xiii, 245 p. : ISBN 0-471-80319-7 : LC Card 85-12456 DDC 658.4/012 19
HD30.28 .H35 1986 ***NYPL [JLE 86-2018]***

Making the grade : the development report card for the states. Washington, D.C. : Corp. for Enterprise Development, c1987. ii, 142 p. : ill. ; 28 cm. "March 1987." Bibliography: p. 117-142. ISBN 0-9605804-4-1 (pbk.) LC Card 87-70671 DDC 330.973/0927 19
1. United States - Economic conditions - 1981-. 2. Economic indicators - United States - States. 3. Index numbers (Economics). I. Corporation for Enterprise Development. II. Title.
HC106.8 .M318 1987

Making the link . Winick, Bradley H. [Washinton, D.C.] , c1986. i, 17 p. ; ISBN 0-88713-678-8 (pbk.) LC Card 87-106145 DDC 331.11/0973 19
HD5724 .W557 1986

Making the most of Medicare /. Pell, Arthur R. New York , c1987. ix, 123 p. : ISBN 0-13-547696-8 (pbk.) : LC Card 86-25160 DDC 344.73/0226 347.304226 19
HD7102.U4 P45 1987

Making the right turn : protecting the public investment in Oregon's roads and bridges / prepared for League of Oregon Cities, Association of Oregon Counties, [and] Oregon Department of Transportation ; prepared by Price Waterhouse in association with Don Barney & Associates, Inc., DeLeuw Cather and Company, [and] Government Finance Associates, Inc. [Salem? Or.] : The Department, [1986] iv, 39 p. : ill. ; 28 cm. LC Card 87-621891 DDC 388.1/14/09795 19
1. Roads - Oregon - Finance. 2. Bridges - Oregon - Finance. I. League of Oregon Cities. II. Association of Oregon Counties. III. Oregon. Dept. of Transportation. IV. Price Waterhouse (Firm).
HE356.O7 M35 1986

Making $70,000 a year as a self-employed manufacturer's representative /. Silliphant, Leigh. Englewood Cliffs, N.J. , c1984. 204 p. ; ISBN 0-13-547687-9 (case) LC Card 83-16147 DDC 658.8/5 19
HF5422 .S54 1984 ***NYPL [JLE 86-2636]***

Makó, Csaba.
Héthy, Lajos. Patterns of worker's behavior and the enterprise /. New Brunswick, U. S.A. , c1987. p. cm. ISBN 0-88738-177-4 LC Card 87-13958 DDC 331/.0471/09439 19
HD6956.M5 H47 1987

A társadalmi viszonyok erőtere, a

munkafolyamat / Makó Csaba. Budapest : Közgazdasági és Jogi Könyvkiadó, 1985. 192 p. ; 21 cm. Bibliography: p. 177-[184] Includes index. ISBN 963-221-528-1 : LC Card 86-187344
1. Personnel management. 2. Industrial sociology. 3. Personnel management - Hungary. 4. Industrial sociology - Hungary. I. Title.
HF5549 .M2953 1985

Makridakis, Spyros G. The Handbook of forecasting . New York , c1987. xviii, 638 p. : ISBN 0-471-83903-5 LC Card 86-28137 DDC 658.4/0355 19
HD30.27 .H36 1987

Hoi makrochronies exelixeis tou oikonomika mē energou plēthysmou tēs Hellados /. Phrankos, Dionysios M., 1926- Athēna , 1983. 148 p. : LC Card 85-152730
HD5811.83.A6 P47 1983

Makroekonomi och stabiliseringspolitik /. Södersten, Bo. [Malmö] , c1983. 363 p. : ISBN 91-40-05037-8 : LC Card 84-166176
HB179.S8 S63 1983

Makromodelirovanie rasshirennogo vosproizvodstva /. Kazantsev, S. V. (Sergeĭ Vladimirovich) Novosibirsk , 1980. 206, [2] p. ; LC Card 81-138742
HB139 .K39 1980

Makromodelle und Wirtschaftspolitik : Ergebnisse für die Schweiz / Herausgeber, Heidi Schelbert-Syfrig, Philipp Halbherr, Najib Harabi ; Schweizerischer Nationalfonds zur Förderung der Wissenschaftlichen Forschung. Grüsch : Rüegger, c1985. 120 p. : ill. ; 21 cm. At head of title: Nationales Forschungsprogramm Mechanismen und Entwicklung der Schweizerischen Wirtschaft. Includes bibliographies. CONTENTS. - Rationale Erwartungen und der Einfluss von wirtschaftspolitischen Massnahmen / Karl Brunner, Walter Wasserfallen -- Verbindung von zeitreihenanalytischen Methoden mit einem makroökonometrischen Strukturmodell / Christoph Koellreuter, Peter Kugler -- Einige Bemerkungen zu den ökonometrischen Methoden beider Projekte / Hermann Garbers -- Korreferat zu den Forschungsmethoden / Alexander Boeckli -- Wirtschaftspolitische Implikationen der Forschungsresultate / Heidi Schelbert-Syfrig. ISBN 3-7253-0250-2 : LC Card 85-208009
1. Switzerland - Economic policy - Econometric models. 2. Monetary policy - Switzerland - Econometric models. I. Schelbert-Syfrig, Heidi. II. Halbherr, Philipp. III. Harabi, Najib. IV. Schweizerischer Nationalfonds zur Förderung der Wissenschaftlichen Forschung. V. Nationales Forschungsprogramm Mechanismen und Entwicklung der Schweizerischen Wirtschaft.
HC397 .M26 1985

Die Makroökonomik von J.M. Keynes /. Jäggi, Christian M. Berlin , New York , c1986. xiii, 278 p. : ISBN 0-387-16477-4 (U. S.) LC Card 86-225958
HB99.7 .J34 1986

Maksimenko, Natalii͡a Mikhaĭlovna. Katalog konvertov pervogo dni͡a i kartmaksimumov, 1980-1983 /. Moskva , 1985. 221 p. : LC Card 86-102861
HE6184.F57 K38 1985

Maksimov, A. L. (Alekseĭ L'vovich) Rabochee i svobodnoe vremi͡a v uslovii͡akh razvitogo sotsializma / A.L. Maksimov. Moskva : Izd-vo "Nauka", 1981. 95 p. ; 21 cm. (Sotsializm--opyt, problemy, perspektivy) At head of title: Akademii͡a nauk SSSR. Institut ėkonomiki. Includes bibliographical references. LC Card 82-104233
1. Hours of labor - Soviet Union. 2. Leisure - Soviet Union. I. Series: Sotsializm--opyt, problemy, perspektivy (Izdatel'stvo Nauka). II. Title.
HD5195 .M34 1981

Maksimov, I͡Uriĭ Ivanovich.
Bostandzhi͡an, V. B. (Vardan Babkenovich) Optimizatsii͡a otraslevykh sistem v sostave ėkonomicheskikh programm /. Novosibirsk , 1982. 120, [1] p. : LC Card 83-107849
HC337.R852 S5234 1982

Optimizatsii͡a perspektivnykh planov razvitii͡a otraslevykh sistem . Novosibirsk , 1979. 163 p. : LC Card 81-130740
HC337.R852 S546 1979

Maksimova, M. M. (Margarita Matveevna) Burzhuaznoe gosudarstvo i vneshneėkonomicheskie svi͡azi /. Moskva , 1986. 350 p. : LC Card 86-211675
HF1411 .B79 1986

Evropeĭskoe soobshchestvo . Moskva , 1986. 270 p. : LC Card 86-202812
HC241.2 .E867 1986

Korolev, I. S. (Ivan Sergeevich) Vali͡utnye otnoshenii͡a kapitalizma . Moskva , 1986. 228 p. ; LC Card 86-232369
HG6230.3 .K66 1986

Maksoud, Henry. Os Mistérios da inflação . São Paulo , 1986. 121 p. ; LC Card 86-189815
HG835 .M57 1986

Maktabat huwāt ṭawābi' al-barīd. English. Filasṭīn fī ṭawābi' al-barīd (1865-1981). English. Palestine stamps (1865-1981) [Abdel-Wahab Elmessiri, Jean O'Hanlon, translation]. Beirut , Cairo , 1981. [80] p. : LC Card 84-960260
HE6185.P14 F5513 1981

Makten hälsan och vinsten . Nordfors, Lennart. Lund, Sweden , c1985. 195 p. : ISBN 91-44-23331-0 : LC Card 85-204849
HD7732 .N66 1985

Málaga, Juan Carlos. Ortiz, Rolando. CORDES . Lima, Perú , 1987. 96 p. ; LC Card 87-405059 DDC 338.985 19
HC227 .O73 1987

Målarettan hundra år. Böethius, Erland, 1951- Målarettan 100 år /. [Stockholm] , c1984. 448 p. : ISBN 91-7810-054-2 : LC Card 84-239262
HD6759.P26 B64 1984

Målarettan 100 år /. Böethius, Erland, 1951- [Stockholm] , c1984. 448 p. : ISBN 91-7810-054-2 : LC Card 84-239262
HD6759.P26 B64 1984

MALARIA - NIGERIA.
Nigeria . Hyattsville, Md. , 1975. iii, 35 p. ; LC Card 85-114200
HC1055 .N533 1975

Malawi : an alternative pattern of development : proceedings of a seminar held in the Centre of African Studies, University of Edinburgh, 24 and 25 May, 1984. Edinburgh : Centre of African Studies, University of Edinburgh, c1985. xviii, 642 p. : ill. ; 21 cm. (Seminar proceedings . no. 25) Includes bibliographical references. LC Card 86-100522 DDC 338.96897 19
1. Malawi - Economic conditions - Congresses. 2. Malawi - Rural conditions - Congresses. 3. Agriculture - Economic aspects - Malawi - Congresses. I. University of Edinburgh. Centre of African Studies. II. Series: Seminar proceedings (University of Edinburgh. Centre of African Studies) , no. 25.
HC935 .M36 1985

Malawi.
National rural development programme / Malawi Government. [Lilongwe, Malawi] : The Government, 1977. 7 v. : maps ; 33 cm. Documentation for proposals submitted to the African Development Fund. CONTENTS. - [1] 1978/79-1982/83 project proposals (submitted to A.D.F.) -- [2] Kawinga rural development project proposals -- [3] Lilongwe land development programme, phase IV proposals -- [4] Mzimba Rukuru-Kasitu rural development project proposals -- [5] Ntcheu rural development project proposals -- [6] Ntchisi rural development project proposals -- [7] Thiwi-Lifidzi rural development project proposals. LC Card 85-981594
1. Agriculture and state - Malawi. 2. Rural development - Government policy - Malawi. 3. Agricultural development projects - Malawi. 4. Rural development projects - Malawi. I. African Development Fund. II. Title.
HD2133.5.Z8 M35 1977

MALAWI - CENSUS, 1977.
Malaŵi population census, 1977 . Zomba [1984] 2 v. : LC Card 85-980513 DDC 304.6/096897 19
HA4707 .A4 1977b

MALAWI - COMMERCE.
Transportation of imports and exports . Lilongwe , 1984. i, 23 leaves ; LC Card 86-980329 DDC 385/.24/096897 19
HE3432 .T7 1984

MALAWI - ECONOMIC CONDITIONS - CONGRESSES.
Malawi . Edinburgh , c1985. xviii, 642 p. : LC Card 86-100522 DDC 338.96897 19
HC935 .M36 1985

Malawi. Economic Planning Division. Road transport passenger policy issues /. [Lilongwe, Malawi] [1984] i, 22 leaves : LC Card 86-980328 DDC 388.3/22/096897 19
HE5705.A6 R6 1984

Malawi. National Statistical Office. Malaŵi population census, 1977 . Zomba [1984] 2 v. : LC Card 85-980513 DDC 304.6/096897 19
HA4707 .A4 1977b

Malawi. Office of the President and Cabinet. Economic Planning Division. see **Malawi. Economic Planning Division.**

MALAWI - POLITICS AND GOVERNMENT.
Pachai, Bridglal. Land and politics in Malawi, 1875-1975 /. Kingston, Ontario, Canada , c1978. xiv, 245 p., [20] p. of plates : ISBN 0-919642-82-9 LC Card 86-673708
HD997 .P32x 1978

Malaŵi population census, 1977 : analytical report. Zomba : National Statistical Office, [1984] 2 v. : ill. ; 30 cm. Bibliography: v. 1, p. 198-199; v. 2, p. 169-171. CONTENTS. - v. 1. Population characteristics -- v. 2. Fertility, mortality, and population projections. LC Card 85-980513 DDC 304.6/096897 19
1. Malawi - Census, 1977. 2. Malawi - Population - Statistics. I. Malawi. National Statistical Office.
HA4707 .A4 1977b

MALAWI - POPULATION - STATISTICS.
Malaŵi population census, 1977 . Zomba [1984] 2 v. : LC Card 85-980513 DDC 304.6/096897 19
HA4707 .A4 1977b

MALAWI - RURAL CONDITIONS - CONGRESSES.
Malawi . Edinburgh , c1985. xviii, 642 p. : LC Card 86-100522 DDC 338.96897 19
HC935 .M36 1985

Malawi. Statistical Office, National. see **Malawi. National Statistical Office.**

Malawi. Transport Planning Unit.
Ahmad, Nisar. Locational pattern of agricultural production/purchases . Lilongwe [Malawi] , 1984. ii, 33 leaves ; LC Card 86-980325 DDC 380.1/41/096897 19
HE199.5.F3 A38 1984

Growth of road traffic densities in Malaŵi. Lilongwe , 1985. 88 leaves ; LC Card 86-980330 DDC 388.3/142/096897 19
HE367.M32 G76 1985

Inventory of designated roads in Malaŵi, 1983. [Lilongwe, Malawi] , 1984. i, 57 leaves : LC Card 86-980326 DDC 388.1/096897 19
HE367.M32 I58 1984

Transportation of imports and exports . Lilongwe , 1984. i, 23 leaves ; LC Card 86-980329 DDC 385/.24/096897 19
HE3432 .T7 1984

MALAWI UNION OF SAVINGS AND CREDIT CO-OPERATIVES - EVALUATION.
Dublin, Jack. Mid-term evaluation of the Malawi Union of Savings and Credit Co-operatives Project (612-0205) /. Lilongwe, Malawi , 1983. x, 84, [29] leaves ; LC Card 85-981350 DDC 334/.22/096897 19
HG2039.M29 D83 1983

Malaysia.
Fifth Malaysia Plan, 1986-1990. Kuala Lumpur : Printed by National Printing Dept., 1986. xxxiv, 567 p., [1] folded leaf of plates : col. ill., col. map ; 27 cm. Includes index. LC Card 86-945646 DDC 338.9595 19
1. Malaysia - Economic policy. 2. Malaysia - Social policy. 3. Malaysia - Economic conditions. I. Title.
HC445.5 .M33 1986

The Fourth Malaysia Plan, 1981-1985 and a decade of progress, 1971-1980 in brief. Kuala Lumpur : Economic Planning Unit, Prime Minister's Dept., [1981?] 50 p. : ill. ; 21 cm. LC Card 84-942047
1. Malaysia - Economic policy. I. Malaysia. Unit Perancang Ekonomi. II. Title.
HC445.5 .M33 1981a

[Ranchangan Malaysia kedua, 1971-1975. English]
Second Malaysia plan, 1971-1975. Kuala Lumpur, Printed at the Govt. Press, 1971. xv, 266 p. fold. map. 28 cm. Issued also in Malay under title: Ranchangan Malaysia kedua, 1971-1975. LC Card 76-943050 DDC 338/.09595/1 19
1. Malaysia - Economic policy. 2. Malaysia - Social

policy. I. Title.
HC445.5 .A4 1971

Malaysia and ASEAN economic cooperation /. K. A. Mohamed Ariff, 1940- Singapore , 1980, cover 1981. 177 p. ; ISBN 997-19-0207-9 LC Card 82-940035
HC441 .K18 1981

MALAYSIA - COMMERCE.
Mannur, H. G. The terms of trade and Third World countries /. Pulau Pinang , 1978. ii, 35 p. ; LC Card 84-940687
HF4055 .M36 1978

MALAYSIA - COMMERCE - HISTORY - CONGRESSES.
Kapal dan harta karam =. Kuala Lumpur , 1986. xv, 181 p. : LC Card 86-942317 DDC 387.5/09595 19
HF3800.6 .K36 1986

MALAYSIA - ECONOMIC CONDITIONS.
K. A. Mohamed Ariff, 1940- Malaysia and ASEAN economic cooperation /. Singapore , 1980, cover 1981. 177 p. ; ISBN 997-19-0207-9 LC Card 82-940035
HC441 .K18 1981

Malaysia. Fifth Malaysia Plan, 1986-1990. Kuala Lumpur , 1986. xxxiv, 567 p., [1] folded leaf of plates : LC Card 86-945646 DDC 338.9595 19
HC445.5 .M33 1986

Mehmet, Ozay. Development in Malaysia . London , Dover, N.H. , c1986. 183 p. ; ISBN 0-7099-3525-0 : LC Card 85-29079 DDC 338.9595 19
HC445.5.Z9 I51834 1986
NYPL [JLD 86-2389]

Spinanger, Dean. Industrialization policies and regional economic development in Malaysia /. Singapore , New York , 1986. xii, 197 p. : ISBN 0-19-582659-0 LC Card 86-207250 DDC 338.9595 19
HC445.5 .S68 1986

MALAYSIA - ECONOMIC CONDITIONS - BIBLIOGRAPHY.
Arief, Melanie Sritua. The Malaysian economy and politics, 1963-1983 . East Balmain, N.S.W., Australia , c1984. iv, 364 p. ; LC Card 85-942460 DDC 016.3309595/053 19
HC445.5 .A84 1984

MALAYSIA - ECONOMIC CONDITIONS - HANDBOOKS, MANUALS, ETC.
Sales & distribution guide to Malaysia /. Oxford , New York , 1988. p. cm. ISBN 0-08-034987-0 (U. S.) : LC Card 87-21043 DDC 382/.61/09595 19
HG5750.6.A3 S25 1988

MALAYSIA - ECONOMIC POLICY.
Dasar-dasar ekonomi Mahathir /. Kuala Lumpur , 1986. xvi, 187 p. : LC Card 86-943311
HC445.5 .D37 1986

Malaysia. Fifth Malaysia Plan, 1986-1990. Kuala Lumpur , 1986. xxxiv, 567 p., [1] folded leaf of plates : LC Card 86-945646 DDC 338.9595 19
HC445.5 .M33 1986

Malaysia. The Fourth Malaysia Plan, 1981-1985 and a decade of progress, 1971-1980 in brief. Kuala Lumpur [1981?] 50 p. : LC Card 84-942047
HC445.5 .M33 1981a

Malaysia. [Ranchangan Malaysia kedua, 1971-1975. English.] Second Malaysia plan, 1971-1975. Kuala Lumpur, 1971. xv, 266 p. LC Card 76-943050 DDC 338/.09595/1 19
HC445.5 .A4 1971

Spinanger, Dean. Industrialization policies and regional economic development in Malaysia /. Singapore , New York , 1986. xii, 197 p. : ISBN 0-19-582659-0 LC Card 86-207250 DDC 338.9595 19
HC445.5 .S68 1986

Malaysia - Government. see **Malaysia - Politics and government.**

MALAYSIA - INDUSTRIES.
Kimura, Fukunari. Industrial development of Malaysia . Tokyo, Japan , 1986. 25 p. : LC Card 86-232472 DDC 338.09595 19
HD9736.M32 K56 1986

Spinanger, Dean. Industrialization policies and regional economic development in Malaysia /. Singapore , New York , 1986. xii, 197 p. : ISBN 0-19-582659-0 LC Card 86-207250 DDC 338.9595 19
HC445.5 .S68 1986

Malaysia. Jabatan Perangkaan. (Old Catalog form: Malaysia. Statistics, Dept. of) Kajian semula jadual-jadual hayat mengikut jantina dan kumpulan etnik bagi Semenanjung Malaysia, 1970 dan 1980 =. Kuala Lumpur [1986] v, 27, v, 38 p. : ISBN 967-99995-2-1 (pbk.) : LC Card 87-941374
HB1474.6.A3 K35 1986

Malaysia. Kementerian Perusahaan Utama. Profile of the primary commodity sector in Malaysia. [Kuala Lumpur] [1984] 77 p. : LC Card 86-945653 DDC 338.09595 19
HD9016.M32 P76 1984

MALAYSIA - MANUFACTURES.
Kimura, Fukunari. Industrial development of Malaysia . Tokyo, Japan , 1986. 25 p. : LC Card 86-232472 DDC 338.09595 19
HD9736.M32 K56 1986

Malaysia. Ministry of Primary Industries. see **Malaysia. Kementerian Perusahaan Utama.**

Malaysia. Perangkaan, Jabatan. see **Malaysia. Jabatan Perangkaan.**

MALAYSIA - POLITICS AND GOVERNMENT - BIBLIOGRAPHY.
Arief, Melanie Sritua. The Malaysian economy and politics, 1963-1983 . East Balmain, N.S.W., Australia , c1984. iv, 364 p. ; LC Card 85-942460 DDC 016.3309595/053 19
HC445.5 .A84 1984

Malaysia. Primary Industries, Ministry of. see **Malaysia. Kementerian Perusahaan Utama.**

MALAYSIA - RURAL CONDITIONS.
Environment, agriculture, and society in the Malay world /. Kyoto, Japan , 1986. ix, 177 p. : LC Card 86-201590 DDC 338.1/09595 19
HD2080.6 .E58 1986

MALAYSIA - SOCIAL POLICY.
Malaysia. Fifth Malaysia Plan, 1986-1990. Kuala Lumpur , 1986. xxxiv, 567 p., [1] folded leaf of plates : LC Card 86-945646 DDC 338.9595 19
HC445.5 .M33 1986

Malaysia. [Ranchangan Malaysia kedua, 1971-1975. English.] Second Malaysia plan, 1971-1975. Kuala Lumpur, 1971. xv, 266 p. LC Card 76-943050 DDC 338/.09595/1 19
HC445.5 .A4 1971

MALAYSIA - STATISTICS, VITAL.
Kajian semula jadual-jadual hayat mengikut jantina dan kumpulan etnik bagi Semenanjung Malaysia, 1970 dan 1980 =. Kuala Lumpur [1986] v, 27, v, 38 p. : ISBN 967-99995-2-1 (pbk.) : LC Card 87-941374
HB1474.6.A3 K35 1986

Malaysia. Unit Perancang Ekonomi. Malaysia. The Fourth Malaysia Plan, 1981-1985 and a decade of progress, 1971-1980 in brief. Kuala Lumpur [1981?] 50 p. : LC Card 84-942047
HC445.5 .M33 1981a

Malaysia - Vital statistics. see **Malaysia - Statistics, Vital.**

The Malaysian economy and politics, 1963-1983 . Arief, Melanie Sritua. East Balmain, N.S.W., Australia , c1984. iv, 364 p. ; LC Card 85-942460 DDC 016.3309595/053 19
HC445.5 .A84 1984

Malcolm, Clark. Williams, Cecil L., 1930- The negotiable environment . Ann Arbor, Mich. , c1985. v, 82 p. : ISBN 0-936658-20-7 (pbk.) : LC Card 85-10305 DDC 658.3/82 19
HF5547.2 .W55 1985 NYPL [JLF 86-1138]

Malcolmson, Patricia E., 1944- English laundresses : a social history, 1850-1930 / Patricia E. Malcolmson. Urbana : University of Illinois Press, c1986. xv, 220 p. ; 24 cm. (The working class in European history) Includes index. Bibliography: p. [164]-209. ISBN 0-252-01293-3 LC Card 85-24599 DDC 305.4/3648/0942 19
1. Laundresses - England - Social conditions. 2. Laundresses - England - History. 3. Laundry workers - England - History. I. Title.
HD6073.L32 G75 1986
NYPL [JLE 86-4640]

MALDIVES - ECONOMIC CONDITIONS.
Haaland, Gunnar. Evolution of socio-economic dualism in the Maldives /. Bergen [1987] 30 leaves ; LC Card 87-130051 DDC 330.9549/5 19
HC596 .H33 1987

MALDIVES - SOCIAL CONDITIONS.
Haaland, Gunnar. Evolution of socio-economic dualism in the Maldives /. Bergen [1987] 30 leaves ; LC Card 87-130051 DDC 330.9549/5 19
HC596 .H33 1987

Maldonado Calderón, Arturo. Actividad económica del hombre del suburbio / Arturo Maldonado Calderón. Machala, Ecuador : El Oro, 1985. 168 p., [3] folded leaves of plates : ill., maps ; 22 cm. At head of title: Universidad Técnica de Machala, DISE. Includes bibliographical references. LC Card 87-110202 DDC 330.9866/31 19
1. Machala Suburban Region (Ecuador) - Economic conditions. 2. Machala Suburban Region (Ecuador) - Social conditions. 3. Labor supply - Ecuador - Machala Suburban Region. I. Universidad Técnica de Machala. Departamento de Investigaciones Socioeconómicas. II. Title.
HC203.M33 M35 1985

Male and female earnings in Canadian manufacturing, 1931 /. Abbott, Michael G. Kingston, Ont., Canada [1986] 82 p. ; LC Card 87-145991 DDC 331.2/87/0971 19
HD4979 .A22 1986

The male stress syndrome . Witkin-Lanoil, Georgia. New York , c1986. 246 p. ; ISBN 0-937858-59-5 LC Card 85-61815 DDC 155.9
BF575.S75 W59 1986 NYPL [JFD 86-5693]

Malecki, Donald S. Commercial liability risk management and insurance /. Malvern, Pa. , 1986. 2 v. : ISBN 0-89463-049-0 (set) LC Card 86-72708 DDC 368.8/1 19
HG8059 .C64 1986

Malek, M. Unemployment, hysteresis, and the natural rate hypothesis . Oxford, UK , New York, NY, USA , 1987. p. cm. ISBN 0-631-15688-7 : LC Card 87-14071 DDC 331.13/7 19
HD5707.5 .U555 1987

Malenter Symposion (3d : 1983) Welthandel morgen . Stuttgart , 1984. 275 p. : ISBN 3-87959-225-X LC Card 85-132786
HF4055 .W45 1984

Maletta, Héctor. Requerimientos de mano de obra en la agricultura peruana / Héctor Maletta. 1a ed. Lima, Perú : Centro de Investigación, Universidad del Pacífico, 1985. 184 p. ; 30 cm. Includes bibliographical references. LC Card 86-156077
1. Agricultural laborers - Peru. 2. Agriculture - Economic aspects - Peru. I. Title.
HD1531.P4 M34 1985

Malhotra, S. C. Puri, Vijay Kumar. Nabhi's manual for Indian residents abroad, 1985 /. New Delhi , 1985. xv, 352 p., [1] leaf of plate : LC Card 86-901951 DDC 346.54/07 345.4067 19
HG5732 .P83 1985

Malhuret, Claude. Mass deportations in Ethiopia / Claude Malhuret. [Paris] : Medecins Sans Frontieres, [1985] 65 leaves ; 30 cm. "December 1985." LC Card 86-181587 DDC 333.3/1/63 19
1. Land settlement - Ethiopia. 2. Migration, Internal - Ethiopia. I. Médecins sans frontières (Association). II. Title.
HD979 .M34 1985

Mali.
Emploi, potentialités et priorités au Mali . Addi Abeba , c1984. xix, 266 p. : ISBN 92-2-203954-8 : LC Card 85-980540
HD5847.3.A6 E47 1984
NYPL [JLE 86-484]

MALI - ECONOMIC CONDITIONS.
Dia, Mamadou. [Nations africaines et solidarité mondiale. English.] The African nations and world solidarity /. Westport, Conn. , 1987, c1961. xii, 145 p. ; ISBN 0-313-24569-X (lib. bdg. : alk. paper) LC Card 86-25734 DDC 330.96/03 19
HC800 .D5213 1987

Emploi, potentialités et priorités au Mali . Addi Abeba , c1984. xix, 266 p. : ISBN 92-2-203954-8 : LC Card 85-980540
HD5847.3.A6 E47 1984
NYPL [JLE 86-484]

Roberts, Richard L., 1949- Warriors, merchants, and slaves . Stanford, Calif. , 1987. xii, 293 p. : ISBN 0-8047-1378-2 (alk. paper) : LC Card 86-23138 DDC 330.966/23 19
HC1035 .R63 1987

MALI - ECONOMIC POLICY.
Emploi, potentialités et priorités au Mali . Addi Abeba , c1984. xix, 266 p. : ISBN 92-2-203954-8 : LC Card 85-980540
HD5847.3.A6 E47 1984
NYPL [JLE 86-484]

MALI - FOREIGN ECONOMIC RELATIONS.
Dia, Mamadou. [Nations africaines et solidarité mondiale. English.] The African nations and world solidarity /. Westport, Conn. , 1987, c1961. xii, 145 p. ; ISBN 0-313-24569-X (lib. bdg. : alk. paper) LC Card 86-25734 DDC 330.96/03 19
HC800 .D5213 1987

MALI - HISTORY.
Roberts, Richard L., 1949- Warriors, merchants, and slaves . Stanford, Calif. , 1987. xii, 293 p. : ISBN 0-8047-1378-2 (alk. paper) : LC Card 86-23138 DDC 330.966/23 19
HC1035 .R63 1987

Malik, Fredmund F. Strategie des Managements komplexer Systeme : ein Beitrag zur Management-Kybernetik evolutionärer Systeme / Fredmund F. Malik. Bern : P. Haupt, c1984. 563 p. : ill. ; 23 cm. (Schriftenreihe Unternehmung und Unternehmungsführung . Bd. 12) Enlargement of the author's Habilitationsschrift--Hochschule St. Gallen, 1978. Bibliography: p. 545-550. Includes indexes. ISBN 3-258-03306-4 : LC Card 84-178061
1. Strategic planning. 2. Cybernetics. 3. Management. I. Title. II. Series.
HD30.28 .M334 1984

Malinova, R. D. (Revekka Davydovna)
Gratsershteĭn, I. M. (Izrail' Markovich) Organizatsiia, planirovanie i upravlenie na predpriiatiiakh tsvetnoĭ metallurgii /. Moskva , 1987. 415 p. : LC Card 87-156156
HD9539.A3 S5546 1987

Malisoff, Harry. The insurance character of unemployment insurance / by Harry Malisoff. Kalamazoo, Mich. : W.E. Upjohn Institute for Employment Research, [1961] 44 p. ; 23 cm. (Unemployment insurance monographs . 3) "December 1961." Includes bibliographical references. LC Card 87-401793 DDC 368.4/4/0973 19
1. Insurance, Unemployment - United States. I. Title. II. Series.
HD7096.U5 M266 1961

Maliye ve vergi sözlüğü. Akdoğan, Abdurrahman. Açıklamalı maliye ve vergi sözlüğü /. [Ankara?] , Yenişehir, Ankara , 1986. 229 p. ; LC Card 87-968120
HJ129.T9 A43 1986

Malkin, Lawrence. The national debt / Lawrence Malkin. 1st ed. New York : Holt, c1987. ix, 309 p. ; 22 cm. Bibliography: p. 277-298. Includes index. ISBN 0-8050-0382-7 LC Card 86-27347 DDC 336.3/4/0973 19
1. Debts, Public - United States. 2. Monetary policy - United States. 3. United States - Economic policy - 1981-. 4. United States - Economic conditions - 1981-. I. Title.
HJ8119 .M34 1987

Malla, B. C. An evaluation of development activities within Sixth Plan period in Bajhang District / research team, B.C. Malla, Murari Prasad Upadhyaya, Radheshyam Acharya. Kathmandu : Centre for Economic Development and Administration, Tribhuvan University, 1985 [i.e. 1986] 76, [3] p. : map ; 30 cm. Bibliography: p. [79] LC Card 86-903487 DDC 338.9549/6 19
1. Bajhang (Nepal : District) - Economic policy - Evaluation. 2. Rural development - Nepal - Bajhang (District) - Evaluation. I. Upadhyaya, Murari Prasad. II. Acharya, Radheshyam. III. Title.
HC425.Z7 B355 1986

el Mallakh, Ragael. see **El Mallakh, Ragaei, 1925-**

Mallard, Jean-Claude, 1947- Comprendre et gérer la fiscalité de l'entreprise / Jean-Claude Mallard, avec la collaboration de Jacques Margerin, Etienne Courcoux. La Tronche : SEDIFOR ; Paris : Diffusion, Les Editions d'organisation, [1985] 255 p. : ill. (some col.) ; 27 cm. Bibliography: p. 252. Includes index. LC Card 86-166702
1. Business enterprises - Taxation - France. 2. Corporations - Taxation - France. I. Margerin, Jacques. II. Courcoux, Etienne. III. Title.
HD2753.F8 M34 1985

Maller, Steven. Mastering Omnis 3 / Steven Maller. 1st ed. Blue Ridge Summit, PA : Tab Books, 1986. xi, 207 p. : ill. ; 25 cm. Includes index. "No. 2674." ISBN 0-8306-0374-3 : LC Card 86-5758 DDC 658/.05574 19
1. Omnis 3 (Computer program). 2. Data base management. 3. Business - Data processing. I. Title. II. Title: Mastering Omnis three.
HF5548.4.O55 M35 1986
NYPL [JSE 87-264]

Mallett, Alan S. Idyll of the Kings, 1889-1979 : the story of the King Line, its ships and the men who sailed and managed them / by Alan S. Mallett. Kendal [Cumbria] : World Ship Society, 1980. 64 p. : ill., geneal. table, ports. ; 21 cm. Includes index. ISBN 0-905617-10-X (pbk.) LC Card 81-105772 DDC 387.5/065/41 19
1. King Line (Firm) - History. 2. Cargo ships - History. 3. Ship registers. I. Title.
HE945.K48 M35 1980

Mallier, A. T., 1931- Women and the economy : a comparative study of Britain and the USA / A.T. Mallier and M.J. Rosser ; foreword by Baroness Seear. Houndmills, Basingstoke, Hampshire : Macmillan, 1987. xiv, 221 p. : ill. ; 23 cm. Includes indexes. Bibliography: p. 200-211. ISBN 0-333-37938-1
1. Women - Employment - Great Britain. 2. Women - Employment - United States. 3. Women - Great Britain - Economic conditions. 4. Women - United States - Economic conditions. I. Rosser, M. J., 1949-. II. Title. ***NYPL [JLD 87-1151]***

Malloch, Theodore R. Issues in international trade and development policy / Theodore R. Malloch. New York : Praeger, 1987. ix, 178 p. ; 22 cm. Bibliography: p. [169]-170. Includes index. ISBN 0-275-92356-8 (alk. paper) : LC Card 87-11697 DDC 382/.3 19
1. Commercial policy. 2. Commerce. 3. Economic development. 4. Economic history - 1971-. I. Title.
HF1411 .M3325 1987

Mallory, Norman. Profitable no-load mutual fund trading techniques for the individual investor / by Norman Mallory. Brightwaters, N.Y. : Windsor Books, c1987. 153 p. : ill. ; 23 cm. ISBN 0-930233-11-5 (pbk.) LC Card 87-400302 DDC 332.63/27 19
1. Mutual funds. 2. Mutual funds - United States. I. Title.
HG4530 .M25 1987

Malmok, ipari és gazdasági létesitmények az első katonai felmérés térképszelvényein, 1782-1785 / Nemesné Ipoly Márta. Budapest : Hadtörténelmi Térképtár, 1982. 220 p., [1] leaf of plates : chiefly maps ; 20 cm. Summary in English, German and Russian. Includes index. ISBN 963-01-4433-6 (Magy. nemz. bibl.) LC Card 83-230040
1. Hungary - Economic conditions - 18th century - Maps. 2. Mills and mill-work - Hungary - History - 18th century - Maps. 3. Hungary - Historical geography - Maps. I. Nebesné Ipoly, Márta.
HC300.26 .M35 1982

MALNUTRITION.
(1979) American Jewish Joint Distribution Committee. [Choroba głodowa. English.] Hunger disease . New York , c1979. xiv, 261 p. : ISBN 0-471-05003-2 LC Card 78-26397 DDC 616.3/9
RC627.S7 A43 1979
NYPL [*PXV (Warsaw) 86-3505]

(1987) Kent, George, 1939- Fish, food, and hunger . Boulder , 1987. ix, 201 p. ; ISBN 0-8133-7409-X (pbk.) : LC Card 87-6066 DDC 338.3/7194 19
HD9450.5 .K46 1987

MALNUTRITION - BRAZIL.
Lima Sobrinho, Antonio Estevam de. Fome, agricultura e política no Brasil . Petrópolis , 1981. 120 p. ; LC Card 81-185801 DDC 338.1/0981 19
HD9014.B82 L56 1981
NYPL [JLD 86-3297]

MALNUTRITION - BRAZIL - SÃO PAULO (STATE) - CONGRESSES.
Seminário Nacional de Abastecimento Alimentar em Grandes Cidades--a Experiência de São Paulo (1984 : São Paulo, Brazil) Anais /. São Paulo, São Paulo, Brasil , 1984. xii, 421 p. : LC Card 87-404933 DDC 363.8/0981/61 19
HD9014.B83 S447 1984

MALNUTRITION - COLOMBIA.
Problemas agrarios colombianos /. [Bogotá, Colombia] , México, D.F. , 1986. 467 p. : ISBN 958-606-005-5 LC Card 86-221632
HD1882 .P75 1986

MALNUTRITION - DEVELOPING COUNTRIES.
Yates, Geoffrey. Food, need, greed & myopia . Ryton, Tyne and Wear , 1986. 96 p. : ISBN 0-907367-04-6 (pbk.) : LC Card 87-129951 DDC 338.1/9 19
HD9000.5 .Y38 1986

Malone, Laurence J. Smith, Adam, 1723-1790. [Selections. 1986.] The essential Adam Smith /. Oxford [Oxfordshire] , New York , 1986. p. cm. ISBN 0-19-877270-X : LC Card 86-23856 DDC 330.15/3 19
HB161 .S6522 1986b

Malone, Margaret Sahlin, 1933- Work and welfare / prepared for the Subcommittee on Employment and Productivity of the Committee on Labor and Human Resources and the Subcommittee on Social Security and Income Maintenence [sic] of the Committee on Finance, United States Senate. Washington : U. S. G.P.O. : For sale by the Supt. of Docs., Congressional Sales Office, U. S. G.P.O., 1986. ix, 162 p. ; 24 cm. (S. prt. . 99-177) At head of title: 99th Congress, 2d session, Joint committee print. Distributed to some depository libraries in microfiche. Shipping list no.: 86-749-P. "August 1986." Includes bibliographical references. Item 1043-A, 1043-B (microfiche) LC Card 86-603383 DDC 362.5/84/0973 19
1. Work Incentive Program. 2. Welfare recipients - Employment - United States. 3. Public welfare - United States. 4. United States - Politics and government - 1945-. I. United States. Congress. Senate. Committee on Labor and Human Resources. Subcommittee on Employment and Productivity. II. United States. Congress. Senate. Committee on Finance. Subcommittee on Social Security and Income Maintenance Programs. III. Title. IV. Series.
HD5715.2 .M34 1986

Maloo, Kamala, 1948- The history of famines in Rajputana, 1858-1900 A.D. / Kamala Maloo. Udaipur : Himanshu Publications, 1987. xii, 296 p. : 4 folded col. maps ; 22 cm. Bibliography: p. [271]-285. Includes index. ISBN 81-85167-00-1 : LC Card 87-901599 DDC 363.8/0954/4 19
1. Famines - India - Rajasthan - History. 2. Public welfare - India - Rajasthan - History. I. Title.
HC437.R3 M28 1987

Malpass, Peter. The Housing crisis /. London , Dover, N.H. , c1986. 243 p.: ISBN 0-7099-4605-8 : LC Card 85-31113 DDC 363.5/0941 19
HD7333.A3 H684 1986
NYPL [JLD 86-2181]

Malpica, Carlos. see **Malpica Silva Santisteban, Carlos.**

Malpica Silva Santisteban, Carlos.
La alternativa de la izquierda : presupuesto 1985 / Carlos Malpica. [Lima, Peru] : Servicios Populares, [1985] 91 p. : ill. ; 21 cm. CONTENTS. - Ley de Financiamento del Presupuesto (dictamen en minoría) -- Presupuesto general de la república, 1985 -- Anexos. LC Card 87-403544 DDC 338.985 19
1. Budget - Peru. 2. Peru - Appropriations and expenditures. 3. Peru - Economic policy. I. Title.
HJ2090 .M35 1985

El anti imperialismo del APRA y los contratos petroleros / Carlos Malpica S.S. [Lima, Peru] : Ediciones La Escena Contemporánea, [1986 or 1987] 398 p. : ill., facsims. ; 21 cm. Includes bibliographical references. LC Card 87-402097 DDC 338.2/7282/0985 19
1. Petroleum industry and trade - Government policy - Peru. 2. Partido Aprista Peruano. I. Title.
HD9574.P52 M37 1986

MALTA - ECONOMIC POLICY.
Malta. Ministry of Trade and Economic Planning. Economic Division. Development plan for Malta, 1986-1988. [Valletta, Malta] [1986] 95 p. ; LC Card 86-228319
HC310.2 .M335 1986

MALTA - FOREIGN ECONOMIC RELATIONS - LIBYA.
Mattes, Hanspeter. Aspekte der libyischen Ausseninvestitionspolitik, 1972-1985 /. Hamburg , c1985. iv, 169 p. : ISBN 3-89173-001-2 LC Card 86-173976
HG4538 .M376 1985

Malta. Ministry of Trade and Economic Planning. Economic Division. Development plan for Malta, 1986-1988. [Valletta, Malta] : Economic Division, Ministry of Trade and Economic Planning, [1986] 95 p. ; 21 cm. "... sixth development plan 1986-88 ..."--P. 2. "July 1986." Continues: Malta, guidelines for progress : development plan 1981-1985 / Malta, Office of the Prime Minister, Economic Division. [5th plan]. 1981. LC Card 86-228319
1. Malta - Economic policy. I. Malta. Office of the Prime Minister. Economic Division. Malta, guidelines for progress. II. Title.
HC310.2 .M335 1986

Malta. Office of the Prime Minister. Economic Division.
Malta, guidelines for progress. Malta. Ministry of Trade and Economic Planning. Economic Division. Development plan for Malta, 1986-1988. [Valletta, Malta] [1986] 95 p. ; LC Card 86-228319
HC310.2 .M335 1986

Malthus /. Winch, Donald. Oxford , New York , 1987. 117 p. ; ISBN 0-19-287653-8 : LC Card 87-11179 DDC 330.15/3 19
HB863 .W56 1987

Malthus, T. R. (Thomas Robert, 1766-1834.
An essay on the principle of population : the sixth edition (1826) with variant readings from the second edition (1803) / edited by E.A. Wrigley and David Souden. London : W. Pickering, 1986. 2 v. (18, xv, 711 p.) : facsims. ; 24 cm. (The Works of Thomas Robert Malthus . v. 2-3) The Pickering masters Reprint. Originally published: London : J. Murray, 1826. Bibliography: p. 701-711. Includes index. ISBN 1-85196-102-X (v. 1) LC Card 87-672118
1. Population. I. Wrigley, E. A. (Edward Anthony), 1931-. II. Souden, David. III. Series: Malthus, T. R. (Thomas Robert), 1766-1834. Works. 1986 , v. 2-3. IV. Title.
HB861 .A2x 1986 vol. 2-3

An essay on the principle of population : the first edition (1798) with introduction and bibliography / edited by E.A. Wrigley and David Souden. London : W. Pickering, 1986. 139 p. : facsim. ; 24 cm. (The Works of Thomas Robert Malthus . v. 1) The Pickering masters Reprint. Originally published: London : J. Johnson, 1798. Includes bibliographies. ISBN 1-85196-101-1 LC Card 87-672117
1. Population. I. Wrigley, E. A. (Edward Anthony), 1931-. II. Souden, David. III. Series: Malthus, T. R. (Thomas Robert), 1766-1834. Works. 1986 , v. 1. IV. Title.
HB861 .A2x 1986 vol. 1

An essay on the principle of population, or, a view of its past and present effects on human happiness : with an inquiry into our prospects respecting the future removal or mitigation of the evils which it occasions / by T. R. Malthus. Cambridge [Cambridgeshire] ; New York : Cambridge University Press, 1988. p. cm. "The version published in 1803, with the variora of 1806, 1807, 1817 and 1826, edited by Patricia James. Includes index. ISBN 0-521-24775-6 LC Card 87-9372 DDC 304.6 19
1. Population. I. James, Patricia, 1933-. II. Title.
HB861 .E7 1988

Essays on political economy / edited by E.A. Wrigley and David Souden. London : W. Pickering, 1986. 327 p. : facsims. ; 24 cm. (The Works of Thomas Robert Malthus . v. 7) The Pickering masters Reprint of works originally published 1800-1827. Bibliography: p. 325-327. ISBN 1-85196-107-0 LC Card 87-672114
1. Economics. 2. Classical school of economics. I. Wrigley, E. A. (Edward Anthony), 1931-. II. Souden, David. III. Series: Malthus, T. R. (Thomas Robert), 1766-1834. Works. 1986 , v. 7. IV. Title.
HB861 .A2x 1986 vol. 7

Essays on population / edited by E.A. Wrigley and David Souden. London : W. Pickering, 1986. 246 p. : facsims. ; 24 cm. (The Works of Thomas Robert Malthus . v. 4) The Pickering masters Reprint of works originally published 1807-1824. Bibliography: p. 245-246. ISBN 1-85196-104-6 LC Card 87-672116
1. Population. I. Wrigley, E. A. (Edward Anthony), 1931-. II. Souden, David. III. Series: Malthus, T. R. (Thomas Robert), 1766-1834. Works. 1986 , v. 4. IV. Title.
HB861 .A2x 1986 vol. 4

The measure of value stated and illustrated : with an application of it to the alterations in the value of the English currency since 1790 / T.R. Malthus. Fairfield, NJ : A.M. Kelley, 1988. p. cm. (Reprints of economic classics) ISBN 0-678-00603-2 LC Card 87-17246 DDC 332.4/1 19
1. Value. 2. Currency question - Great Britain. I. Title.
HB201 .M297 1988

Principles of political economy : the second edition (1836) with variant readings from the first edition (1820) / edited by E.A. Wrigley and David Souden. London : W. Pickering, 1986. 2 v. (18, x, 439 p.) : facsim. ; 24 cm. (The Works of Thomas Robert Malthus . v. 5-6) The Pickering masters Reprint. Originally published: London : W. Pickering, 1836. Bibliography: p. 437-439. Includes index. ISBN 1-85196-105-4 (v. 1) LC Card 87-672115
1. Economics. 2. Classical school of economics. I. Wrigley, E. A. (Edward Anthony), 1931-. II. Souden, David. III. Series: Malthus, T. R. (Thomas Robert), 1766-1834. Works. 1986 , v. 5-6. IV. Title.
HB861 .A2x 1986 vol. 5-6

Principles of political economy / T.R. Malthus. Variorum ed. / edited by John Pullen. Cambridge ; New York : Cambridge University Press, 1987. p. cm. Includes index. ISBN 0-521-32363-0 (set) LC Card 86-32742 DDC 330.15/3 19
1. Economics. 2. Classical school of economics. I. Pullen, John, 1933-. II. Title.
HB161 .M25 1987

PRINCIPLES OF POLITICAL ECONOMY.
Pullen, J. M. Lord Grenville's manuscript notes on Malthus /. [Newcastle] [1986] 94 p. ; ISBN 0-7259-0557-3 (pbk.) LC Card 87-150102 DDC 330.15/3 19
HB161.M28 P85 1986

Works. 1986 .
(v. 1) Malthus, T. R. (Thomas Robert, 1766-1834. An essay on the principle of population . London , 1986. 139 p. : ISBN 1-85196-101-1 LC Card 87-672117
HB861 .A2x 1986 vol. 1

(v. 2-3) Malthus, T. R. (Thomas Robert, 1766-1834. An essay on the principle of population . London , 1986. 2 v. (18, xv, 711 p.) : ISBN 1-85196-102-X (v. 1) LC Card 87-672118
HB861 .A2x 1986 vol. 2-3

(v. 4) Malthus, T. R. (Thomas Robert, 1766-1834. Essays on population /. London , 1986. 246 p. : ISBN 1-85196-104-6 LC Card 87-672116
HB861 .A2x 1986 vol. 4

(v. 5-6) Malthus, T. R. (Thomas Robert, 1766-1834. Principles of political economy . London , 1986. 2 v. (18, x, 439 p.) : ISBN 1-85196-105-4 (v. 1) LC Card 87-672115
HB861 .A2x 1986 vol. 5-6

(v. 7) Malthus, T. R. (Thomas Robert, 1766-1834. Essays on political economy /. London , 1986. 327 p. : ISBN 1-85196-107-0 LC Card 87-672114
HB861 .A2x 1986 vol. 7

MALTHUS, T. R. (THOMAS ROBERT, 1766-1834.
Winch, Donald. Malthus /. Oxford , New York , 1987. 117 p. ; ISBN 0-19-287653-8 : LC Card 87-11179 DDC 330.15/3 19
HB863 .W56 1987

MALTHUS, THOMAS ROBERT, 1766-1834.
Thomas Robert Malthus, critical assessments /. London , Dover, N.H. , c1986. 4 v. : ISBN 0-7099-3650-8 (set) : LC Card 85-22412 DDC 304.6/092/4 19
HB863 .T38 1986 ***NYPL [JFF 86-588]***

MALTHUSIANISM.
Jarrold, T. (Thomas), 1770-1853. Dissertations on man, philosophical, physiological, and political. London, 1806. vi p., 1 l., [9]-367, [1] p. LC Card 05-22565
HB863 .J38

Mal'tsev, V. I. (Valer'ian Ivanovich)
Ėkonomicheskie osnovy industrializatsii sel'skogo khoziaistva Severa / V.I. Mal'tsev ; otvetstvennyĭ redaktor V.P. Podoplelov. Moskva : "Nauka", 1985. 142 p. ; 20 cm. (Problemy sovetskoĭ ėkonomiki) At head of title: Akademiia nauk SSSR. Komi filial. Includes bibliographical references. LC Card 86-165352
1. Agriculture - Economic aspects - Soviet Union, Northern. 2. Farm mechanization - Soviet Union, Northern. 3. State farms - Soviet Union, Northern. I. Podoplelov, V. P. II. Title.
HD1995.N55 M34 1985

Maluku (Indonesia)
Pola dasar pembangunan daerah Propinsi Daerah Tingkat I Maluku. [Ambon] : Percetakan Negara Ambon, 1984. vii, 69 p. ; 17 cm. LC Card 86-943211
1. Maluku (Indonesia) - Economic policy. 2. Maluku (Indonesia) - Social policy. I. Title.
HC448.M34 M33 1984a

MALUKU (INDONESIA) - ECONOMIC POLICY.
Maluku (Indonesia) Pola dasar pembangunan daerah Propinsi Daerah Tingkat I Maluku. [Ambon] , 1984. vii, 69 p. ; LC Card 86-943211
HC448.M34 M33 1984a

MALUKU (INDONESIA) - SOCIAL POLICY.
Maluku (Indonesia) Pola dasar pembangunan daerah Propinsi Daerah Tingkat I Maluku. [Ambon] , 1984. vii, 69 p. ; LC Card 86-943211
HC448.M34 M33 1984a

Malvezzi, Roberto. Mil quatrocentos e sessenta dias no império do sol : 4 anos na seca e nas CEBs do sertão / Roberto Malvezzi (Gogó). São Paulo : Edições Paulinas, 1985. 197 p. : ill. ; 22 cm. (O Povo quer viver . 13) Includes bibliographical references. ISBN 85-05-00296-2 : LC Card 85-200637
1. Brazil, Northeast - Economic conditions. 2. Brazil, Northeast - Social conditions. 3. Seca. 4. Droughts - Social aspects - Brazil, Northeast. 5. Christian communities - Catholic Church - Brazil, Northeast. I. Series: Coleção O Povo quer viver , 13. II. Title.
HC188.N6 M34 1985

Malz, Friedrich. Materialien zur Vermögensbildung in Arbeitnehmerhand. Bonn [1965-<c1985. v. <1-6 > LC Card 67-123501 DDC 368.4/00943
HD7179 .M35

Mambrey, Peter. Computer und Partizipation : Ergebnisse zu Gestaltungs- und Handlungspotentialen / Peter Mambrey, Reinhard Oppermann, August Tepper. Opladen : Westdeutscher Verlag, c1986. xiv, 271 p. : ill. ; 23 cm. Bibliography: p. [252]-271. ISBN 3-531-11851-X LC Card 87-122986 DDC 650/.028/5 19
1. Business - Data processing. I. Oppermann, Reinhard, 1946-. II. Tepper, August. III. Title.
HF5548.2 .M27 1986

Mamder, Josué Sandjiman. Les effets de la crise mondiale actuelle sur l'économie et la population gabonaises / par Josué Sandjiman Mamder, Jan Vandermoortele. Addis Abéba : Bureau international du travail, Programme des emplois et des compétences techniques pour l'Afrique, c1984. 34 p. ; 30 cm. (Crise et pauvreté en Afrique : les effets de la réccession [sic] sur les économies africaines) "Le cas du Gabon"--Cover. ISBN 92-2-203795-2 LC Card 86-215256
1. Gabon - Economic conditions - 1960-. 2. Labor supply - Gabon. I. Vandermoortele, Jan. II. Jobs and Skills Programme for Africa. III. Series: Crise et pauvreté en Afrique. IV. Title.
HC975 .M36 1984

Mamis, Justin, 1929- When to sell : inside strategies for stock-market profits / Justin Mamis and Robert Mamis.Fireside ed. New York : Simon & Schuster, 1986, c1977. p. cm. Reprint. Originally published: 1st ed. New York : Farrar, Strauss and Giroux, 1977. "A Fireside book." ISBN 0-671-63605-7 LC Card 86-26971 DDC 332.6/45 19
1. Stocks. 2. Speculation. 3. Investments. I. Mamis, Robert. II. Title.
HG6041 .M34 1986

Mamis, Robert. Mamis, Justin, 1929- When to sell . New York , 1986, c1977. p. cm. ISBN 0-671-63605-7 LC Card 86-26971 DDC 332.6/45 19
HG6041 .M34 1986

al-Mamlakah al-'Arabiyah al-Sa'udiyah. see **Saudi Arabia.**

Man and work in society : a report on the symposium held on the occasion of the 50th anniversary of the original Hawthorne studies, Oakbrook, Illinois, November 10-13, 1974 / edited by Eugene Louis Cass and Frederick G. Zimmer. New York : Van Nostrand Reinhold Co., c1975. xiv, 313 p. : ill. ; 24 cm. Sponsored by Harvard University Graduate School of Business Administration and Western Electric. Includes bibliographies and index. ISBN 0-442-29359-3 LC Card 75-26866 DDC 658.3
1. Personnel management - Congresses. 2. Psychology, Industrial - Congresses. I. Cass, Eugene Louis. II. Zimmer, Frederick G. III. Western Electric Company.
HF5549 .M299 ***NYPL [JLE 76-2406]***

Man, decisions, society . Burns, Tom R. New York , c1985. xiv, 342 p. : ISBN 2-88124-004-6 (France) LC Card 84-10303 DDC 301 19
HM24 .B85 1985 ***NYPL [JLE 86-2963]***

MAN - ECONOMIC VALUE. see **HUMAN CAPITAL.**

MAN-MADE FIBERS INDUSTRY.
Boon, Gerard Karel. El mercado de tecnología . México, D.F. , 1984, c1983. 715 p. : ISBN 968-12-0252-X LC Card 85-242124
HD9929.2.A2 B66 1984

MAN-MADE FIBERS INDUSTRY - COLOMBIA.
Boon, Gerard Karel. El mercado de tecnología . México, D.F. , 1984, c1983. 715 p. : ISBN 968-12-0252-X LC Card 85-242124
HD9929.2.A2 B66 1984

MAN-MADE FIBERS INDUSTRY - MEXICO.
Boon, Gerard Karel. El mercado de tecnología . México, D.F. , 1984, c1983. 715 p. : ISBN 968-12-0252-X LC Card 85-242124
HD9929.2.A2 B66 1984

A man of influence . Attali, Jacques. [Homme d'influence. English.] London , 1986. 346 p. ; ISBN 0-297-78978-3 ***NYPL [JFE 87-583]***

A man of influence . Attali, Jacques. [Homme d'influence. English.] Bethesda, Md. , 1987, c1985. xvii, 380 p. ; ISBN 0-917561-36-8 : LC Card 86-28735 DDC 332.1/092/4 B 19
HG1552.W37 A8713 1987

Management /. Boone, Louis E. New York , c1987. xv, 677, [48] p. : ISBN 0-394-36305-1 : LC Card 86-27957 DDC 658 19
HD31 .B619 1987

Management /. Daft, Richard L. Chicago , c1988. xxv, 787 p., [1] p. of plates : ISBN 0-03-009473-9 LC Card 87-6820 DDC 658 19
HD31 .D134 1988

Management. Donnelly, James H. Fundamentals of management /. Plano, Tex. , 1987. xxviii, 827 p. : ISBN 0-256-03682-9 LC Card 86-71879 DDC 658 19
HD31 .D594 1987

Management /. Kinard, Jerry. Lexington, Mass. , c1988. xxv, 547, A58 p. : ISBN 0-669-09223-1 LC Card 87-81817 DDC 658 19
HD31 .K468 1988

Management /. Koontz, Harold, 1908- New York , c1988. xxix, 685 p. : ISBN 0-07-035552-5 : LC Card 87-21519 DDC 658.4 19
HD31 .K6 1988

Management . Mason, R. Hal (Robert Hal), 1929- Homewood, Ill. , 1987. xii, 235 p. : ISBN 0-256-05631-5 (pbk.) LC Card 86-82592 DDC 658/.049 19
HD62.4 .M373 1987

Management /. Montana, Patrick J. New York , c1987. xi, 466 p. : ISBN 0-8120-3559-3 (pbk.) : LC Card 87-1376 DDC 658 19
HD31 .M618 1987

Management accounting . Dearden, John. Englewood Cliffs, N.J. , c1988. xiv, 639 p. : ISBN 0-13-549123-1 LC Card 87-19300 DDC 658.1/511 19
HF5657.4 .D42 1988

Management accounting /. Morse, Wayne J. Reading, Mass. , c1988. xxiii, 840 p. : ISBN 0-201-15760-8 : LC Card 87-11570 DDC 658.1/511 19
HF5635 .M864 1988

Management accounting /. Mott, Graham. Aldershot, Hants, England , c1987. 231 p. : ISBN 0-566-02685-6 : LC Card 86-29615 DDC 658.1/511 19
HF5635 .M877 1987

Management accounting . Wolk, Harry I. Boston, Mass. , c1988. xiii, 754 p. : ISBN 0-534-07050-7 : LC Card 87-7348 DDC 658.1/511 19
HF5657.4 .W64 1988

MANAGEMENT ACCOUNTING. see **MANAGERIAL ACCOUNTING.**

Management Accounting in öffentlichen nichtgewinnorientierten Organisationen . Egger, Emil. Zürich , c1985. xii, 220 p. : ISBN 3-7255-2410-6 LC Card 85-132536
HF5686.N56 E33 1985

MANAGEMENT - ADDRESSES, ESSAYS, LECTURES.
Führung . Zürich , cop. 1979. 189 p. : ISBN 3-85743-841-X : LC Card 81-461814 DDC 658 19
HD35 .F8115 ***NYPL [JLE 82-593]***

Heyel, Carl, 1908- John Diebold on management. Englewood Cliffs, N.J. [1972] ix, 282 p. ISBN 0-13-510214-6 LC Card 75-170643 DDC 658
HD45 .H42 ***NYPL [JLF 73-1242]***

Systemy organizacyjne /. [Wrocław] , 1981. 75 p. : LC Card 83-161920
HB9 .B7522 nr. 188 HM131

Teoria dell'organizzazione e realtà italiana . Milano [1980] 225 p. ; ISBN 88-20-41736-7 : LC Card 80-511472 DDC 302.3/5 19
HM131 .T4 ***NYPL [JLD 81-599]***

Management advisory services . Hickman, James R. Colorado Springs, Colo. , c1987. xxiv, 510 p. : ISBN 0-07-172102-9 LC Card 87-4482 DDC 657/.068/8 19
HF5657 .H53 1987

Management advisory services manual /. Van Doren, Glenn H. Boston , c1987- 1 v. (loose-leaf) : ISBN 0-88712-505-0 (loose-leaf) LC Card 87-50240 DDC 658.4/6 19
HD69.C6 V36 1987

Management advisory services practice aid. Practice administration aid .
(3) Written communication of results in MAS engagements. New York, N.Y. (1211 Ave. of the Americas, New York 10036-8775) , c1987. 7 p. ; LC Card 87-159283 DDC 808/.066657 19
HF5719 .W74 1987

Management advisory services practice aids. Small business consulting practice aid .
(7) Personal financial planning . New York, N.Y. (1211 Ave. of the Americas, New York 10036-8775) , c1987. viii, 131 p. ; LC Card 87-142958 DDC 332.024 19
HG179 .P387 1987

(8) Valuation of a closely held business. New York, N.Y. (1211 Ave. of the Americas, New York 10036-8775) , c1987. 44 p. : LC Card 87-402129 DDC 658.1/522 19
HF5681.V3 V35 1987

Management Advisory Services (Seattle, Wash.)
Cranfill, Steven L. Small business banking . Washington, D.C. (1120 Connecticut Ave. N.W., Washington, D.C.) , c1987. ix, 78 p. : LC Card 87-135069 DDC 332.1/753 19
HG4027.7 .C7 1987

MANAGEMENT - AFRICA - ADDRESSES, ESSAYS, LECTURES.
Management problems in Africa /. London , 1986. xviii, 395 p. ; ISBN 0-333-28992-7
NYPL [Sc D 86-519]

MANAGEMENT - ALGERIA - EMPLOYEE PARTICIPATION.
Boutefnouchet, Mostefa. Le socialisme dans l'entreprise . Alger , c1978. 253 p. ; LC Card 84-207677
HD5660.A4 B68 1978

Management and cost accounting /. Drury, Colin. Workingham, Berkshire, England , 19. xv, 599 p. : ISBN 0-442-30637-7 (pbk.) LC Card 85-3266 DDC 658.1/511 19
HF5635 .D798 1986

The management and development of land and seabed resources : report of the proceedings of a CASLE regional seminar, held in Port of Spain, Trinidad on 15-18 April 1985 / Commonwealth Association of Surveying and Land Economy. London : CASLE, [1985] 139 p. : ill. ; 29 cm. Includes bibliographical references. ISBN 0-903577-29-1 (pbk.) LC Card 86-104896 DDC 333.7 19
1. Land use - Congresses. 2. Natural resources - Congresses. 3. Marine resources - Congresses. I. Commonwealth Association of Surveying and Land Economy.
HD105 .M36 1985

The Management and development of natural resources : report of the proceedings of a CASLE regional seminar held in Kuala Lumpur, Malaysia on 8-15 September 1985 / Commonwealth Association of Surveying and Land Economy. London : CASLE, [1985] 192 p. : ill. ; 29 cm. Organized by the Institution of Surveyors Malaysia. Includes bibliographical references. ISBN 0-903577-33-X (pbk.) LC Card 86-206154 DDC 333.7 19
1. Natural resources - Congresses. 2. Land use - Congresses. 3. Surveying - Congresses. I. Commonwealth Association of Surveying and Land Economy. II. Institution of Surveyors Malaysia.
HC13 .M35 1985

Management and industrial relations series .
(8) Willman, Paul. Innovation and management control . Cambridge [Cambridgeshire] , New York , 1985. viii, 215 p. ; ISBN 0-521-26802-8 LC Card 84-17481 DDC 331/.04292/0941 19
HD8039.A82 G79 1985
NYPL [JLD 85-3102]

Management and industry in China /. Pegels, C. Carl. New York , 1987. xii, 282 p. ; ISBN 0-275-92553-6 (alk. paper) : LC Card 86-25260 DDC 658/.00951 19
HD70.C5 P44 1987 ***NYPL [JLE 87-1042]***

Management & organizational behavior /. Scanlan, Burt K. Malibar, Fla. , 1987, c1983. xvi, 666 p. : ISBN 0-89464-246-4 LC Card 87-17035 DDC 658.4 19
HD31 .S3256 1987

Management and organizational behavior. Scanlan, Burt K. Management & organizational behavior /. Malibar, Fla. , 1987, c1983. xvi, 666 p. : ISBN 0-89464-246-4 LC Card 87-17035 DDC 658.4 19
HD31 .S3256 1987

The management and regulation of ground transportation at U. S. airports . Gilbert, Gorman, 1943- Washington, D.C. [1986] 153 p. : LC Card 87-600652 DDC 387.7/362 19
HE9797.4.A2 G55 1986

Management and the audit network . Kropatkin, Philip. New York , 1987. xii, 188 p. : ISBN 0-471-83286-3 LC Card 86-33983 DDC 657/.45 19
HF5667 .K74 1987

MANAGEMENT - BRAZIL - EMPLOYEE PARTICIPATION.
Ibrahim, José. O que todo cidadão precisa saber sobre comissões de fábrica /. São Paulo, SP [1986] 96 p. : ISBN 85-26-00095-0 LC Card 87-402908 DDC 338.6 19
HD5660.B7 I27 1986

MANAGEMENT - BRAZIL - EMPLOYEE PARTICIPATION - CASE STUDIES.
Comissão de fábrica . Petrópolis , 1981. 60 p. ; LC Card 86-190732
HD5660.B7 C66 1981

MANAGEMENT - BULGARIA - EMPLOYEE PARTICIPATION.
Vidinski, Lenin. Leninskite printsipi i uchastieto na trudeshtite se v upravlenieto /. Sofiia , 1982. 196 p. : LC Card 83-130010
HC403 .V495 1982

MANAGEMENT BY OBJECTIVES.
Bänsch, Axel. Operationalisierung des Unternehmenszieles, Mitgliederförderung /. Göttingen , 1983. xv, 245 p. ; ISBN 3-525-12750-2 ***NYPL [JLE 86-1770]***

Caravantes, Geraldo R. (Geraldo Ronchetti) Administração por objetivos . Porto Alegre , 1977. 191 p., [1] folded leaf of plates : LC Card 85-211209
HD30.65 .C37 1977

How to define goals and objectives [videorecording] /. Del Mar, CA , 1986. 1 videocassette (18 min.) : ISBN 0-07-109094-0

(3/4 in.) LC Card 86-700128 DDC 658.4 11
HF5549.5.G6

Odiorne, George S. The human side of management . Lexington, Mass. , c1987. xiv, 236 p. ; ISBN 0-669-15350-8 (alk. paper) LC Card 86-46314 DDC 658.3 19
HD30.65 .O35 1987

MANAGEMENT - CANADA - DECISION MAKING.
Daly, D. J. (Donald James), 1922- Managerial macroeconomics . Homewood, Ill. , 1988. xvi, 383 p. : ISBN 0-256-06000-2 LC Card 87-80950 DDC 339/.024658 19
HD30.22 .D35 1988

MANAGEMENT - CASE STUDIES.
Aguilar, Francis J. (Francis Joseph) General managers in action /. New York , 1988. viii, 498 p. : ISBN 0-19-504083-X (alk. paper) LC Card 87-12503 DDC 658.4 19
HD38.2 .A39 1987

A Casebook for systems development /. London , Baltimore, Md., USA , 1986. iv, 88, [1] p. : ISBN 0-7131-3600-6 LC Card 87-114266 DDC 658 19
HD31 .C3554 1986

Cases in business policy /. Oxford, UK , New York , 1987. ix, 538 p. : ISBN 0-631-15544-9 (pbk.) : LC Card 87-6607 DDC 658.4/012 19
HD30.28 .C379 1987

Daft, Richard L. Organization theory . St. Paul , c1987. xxviii, 338 p. : ISBN 0-314-28488-5 (pbk.) LC Card 86-28965 DDC 658.4 19
HD31 .D136 1987

Griffin, Ricky W. Instructor's manual, Practicing management, second edition /. Boston , c1987. xiii, 167 p. ; ISBN 0-395-42585-9 (pbk.) LC Card 87-400618 DDC 658 19
HD31 .G7627 1987

Griffin, Ricky W. Practicing management /. Boston , c1987. xii, 368 p. : ISBN 0-395-42584-0 (pbk.) LC Card 87-163492 DDC 658 19
HD31 .G7635 1987

MANAGEMENT - CHINA.
Chen hsing Chung-hua chih lu--kai ko ti sung ko /. Pei-ching , 1985. 4, 3, 385 p. ; LC Card 86-106324 ***NYPL [*OVY 86-3099]***

Pegels, C. Carl. Management and industry in China /. New York , 1987. xii, 282 p. ; ISBN 0-275-92553-6 (alk. paper) : LC Card 86-25260 DDC 658/.00951 19
HD70.C5 P44 1987 ***NYPL [JLE 87-1042]***

MANAGEMENT COMMITTEES.
Braiotta, Louis, 1943- The essential guide to effective corporate board committees /. Englewood Cliffs, N.J. , c1987. xiii, 178 p. ; ISBN 0-13-286139-9 LC Card 87-2265 DDC 658.4/22 19
HD2745 .B63 1987

MANAGEMENT - COMMUNICATION SYSTEMS.
Abelow, Daniel. Communications in the modern corporate environment /. Englewood Cliffs, NJ , c1986. xviii, 236 p. : ISBN 0-13-153842-X LC Card 85-16942 DDC 658/.0546 19
HF5548.2 .A24 1986 ***NYPL [JLE 86-1992]***

Business guide to communications systems /. London , 1987. x, 230 p. : ISBN 0-273-02671-2 (pbk.) : LC Card 87-147021 DDC 651.7 19
HD30.335 .B85 1987

Synnott, William R. The information weapon . New York , 1987. xi, 334 p. ; ISBN 0-471-84557-4 LC Card 86-32393 DDC 658.4/038 19
HD30.335 .S96 1987

MANAGEMENT - COMMUNICATION SYSTEMS - PLANNING.
Heldman, Robert K. Telecommunications management planning . Blue Ridge Summit, PA , c1987. xviii, 734 p. : ISBN 0-8306-2864-9 : LC Card 86-30002 DDC 658.4/038 19
HD30.335 .H45 1987

MANAGEMENT, COMPARATIVE. see **COMPARATIVE MANAGEMENT.**

MANAGEMENT - CONGRESSES.
Frontiers in creative and innovative management /. Cambridge, Mass. , 1985, c1986. xxv, 391 p. : ISBN 0-88730-057-X LC Card 85-15125 DDC 658.4 19
HD53 .F76 1986 ***NYPL [JLE 86-3614]***

Management Skills for Investment Managers Seminar (1982 : Washington, D.C.) Management Skills for Investment Managers Seminar . Charlottesville, Va. (P.O. Box 3668, Charlottesville 22903) , c1983. vi, 62 p. : LC Card 83-244808 DDC 658.1/52 19
HG4621 .M36 1982 ***NYPL [JLF 87-425]***

Management constraints of co-operatives /. Habibullah, M. Dhaka , 1986. 92 p. ; LC Card 87-900945
HD1491.B3 H34 1986

MANAGEMENT, CONSTRUCTION INDUSTRY. see **CONSTRUCTION INDUSTRY - MANAGEMENT.**

MANAGEMENT CONSULTANTS. see **BUSINESS CONSULTANTS.**

Management consulting : a guide to the profession / edited by Milan Kubr.2nd rev. ed. Geneva : International Labour Office, 1986. xv, 611 p. : ill. ; 25 cm. Bibliography: p. 587-604. Includes index. ISBN 92-2-105479-9 LC Card 87-131654 DDC 658.4/6/02373 19
1. Business consultants. I. Kubr, Milan.
HD69.C6 M36 1986

A management crisis in Natal . Mansfield, W. R. (Willard Ridgway) [Durban, South Africa] [1985 or 1986] 26 p. ; LC Card 87-400770 DDC 338.0968 19
HC905.Z9 I526 1985

MANAGEMENT - DATA PROCESSING.
Chorafas, Dimitris N. Applying expert systems in business /. New York , c1987. xii, 232 p. : ISBN 0-07-010880-3 : LC Card 86-2794 DDC 658/.05633 19
HD30.2 .C475 1987 ***NYPL [JLE 86-3893]***

Gahungu, Fidèle. Document d'initiation à l'informatique des organisations /. [Bujumbura?] [1983- v. <1 > : LC Card 86-980527
HD30.2 .G34 1983

Hertz, David Bendel, 1919- The expert executive . New York , c1988. xvi, 238 p. ; ISBN 0-471-89677-2 LC Card 87-21682 DDC 658/.05633 19
HF5548.2 .H455 1988

Huppes, T. The Western edge . Dordrecht , Boston , 1987. viii, 141 p. : ISBN 90-247-3495-9 LC Card 87-4087 DDC 338/.06 19
HD58.8 .H86 1987

Izzo, Joseph E., 1931- The embattled fortress . San Francisco , 1987. xxii, 155 p. : ISBN 1-555-42059-1 (alk. paper) LC Card 87-45429 DDC 658.4/038 19
HF5548.2 .I97 1987

Jennergren, L. Peter (Lars Peter), 1944- Discrete-events simulations models in PASCAL/MT+ on a microcomputer /. Lund, Sweden , c1984. 135 p. ; ISBN 91-44-22221-1 (pbk.) : ***NYPL [JSD 86-366]***

Kanter, Jerome. Computer essays for management /. Englewood Cliffs, N.J. , 1987, c1986. xi, 109 p. ; ISBN 0-13-165994-4 : LC Card 86-30651 DDC 658/.05 19
HD30.2 .K36 1987

Lewis, Colin David. Managing with micros . Oxford, England , 1984. 200 p. : LC Card 85-103102 DDC 658/.054 19
HF5548.2 .L425 1984 ***NYPL [JLE 86-2215]***

Maney, Tracy. A management guide to artificial intelligence /. Aldershot, Hants, England , c1986. viii, 188 p. ; ***NYPL [JLD 87-862]***

Perry, William E. Management workstations . Blue Ridge Summit, PA , c1987. vi, 186 p. : ISBN 0-8306-2833-9 : LC Card 87-1903 DDC 658/.05 19
HD30.2 .P47 1987

Sinkel, Dimitri. Computers in purchasing [microform] /. New York , c1984. 48 p. : ISBN 0-8144-2305-1 : LC Card 84-9034 DDC 658.7/2/02854 19
HF5437 .S52 1984 ***NYPL [*ZT-1565 no.12]***

The Strategic use of information technology /. New York , 1987. xiii, 206 p. : ISBN 0-19-505048-7 (alk. paper) : LC Card 87-1606 DDC 658/.05 19
HD30.2 .S79 1987

Synnott, William R. The information weapon . New York , 1987. xi, 334 p. ; ISBN 0-471-84557-4 LC Card 86-32393 DDC 658.4/038 19
HD30.335 .S96 1987

Turban, Efraim. Decision support and expert systems . New York , London , c1988. xxi, 697 p. : ISBN 0-02-421650-X LC Card 87-23911 DDC 658.4/03 19
HD30.2 .T87 1988

MANAGEMENT - DATA PROCESSING - ADDRESSES, ESSAYS, LECTURES.
Bjørn-Andersen, Niels. Managing computer impact . Norwood, N.J. , c1986. viii, 248 p. : ISBN 0-89391-358-8 LC Card 85-30754 DDC 658/.05 19
HD30.2 .B55 1986 ***NYPL [JLE 86-2806]***

MANAGEMENT - DATA PROCESSING - CONGRESSES.
Artificial intelligence in economics and management /. Amsterdam ; New York : xv, 292 p. : ISBN 0-444-87961-7 LC Card 85-31139 DDC 330/.028/563 19
HB143.5 .A78 1986 ***NYPL [JLE 86-3612]***

MANAGEMENT - DATA PROCESSING - PSYCHOLOGICAL ASPECTS.
Howard, Geoffry S. Computer anxiety and the use of microcomputers in management /. Ann Arbor, Mich. , c1986. xii, 137 p. ; ISBN 0-8357-1759-3 (alk. paper) LC Card 86-6904 DDC 658.4/0028/5 19
HD30.2 .H69 1986 ***NYPL [JLE 86-3451]***

Management decision.
(v. 24, no. 4) Meidan, Arthur, 1936- Handbook of business policy /. [Bradford, West Yorkshire, England , Birmingham, Ala.] , c1986. 123 p. : ISBN 0-86176-273-8 (pbk.) LC Card 87-150995 DDC 658.4/012 19
HD30.28 .M42 1986

MANAGEMENT - DECISION-MAKING.
Sterniczuk, Henryk. Decyzje w organizacjach gospodarczych /. Warszawa , 1980. 167 p. ; ISBN 83-208-0052-8 LC Card 81-109564
HD30.23 .S726 1980

MANAGEMENT - DECISION MAKING - CASE STUDIES.
Westin, Alan F. Managerial dilemmas . Cambridge, Mass. , 1988. p. cm. ISBN 0-88730-181-9 (pbk.) LC Card 87-22476 DDC 658.4/03 19
HD30.23 .W47 1988

Management decision support systems using fuzzy sets and possibility theory / edited by Janusz Kącprzyk and Ronald R. Yager. Köln : Verlag TÜV Rheinland, c1985. xi, 350 p. : ill. ; 24 cm. (Interdisciplinary systems research = Interdisziplinäre Systemforschung . 83) Includes bibliographies. ISBN 3-88585-143-1 (pbk.) LC Card 85-217558 DDC 658.4/033 19
1. Decision-making - Mathematical models. 2. Fuzzy sets. 3. Expert systems (Computer science). I. Kacprzyk, Janusz. II. Yager, Ronald R., 1941-.
HD30.23 .M353 1985 ***NYPL [JLE 86-4562]***

MANAGEMENT - DENMARK.
Dansk ledelse '90 i et internationalt perspektiv . [Copenhagen] , 1983. 226 p. : ISBN 87-7553-128-3 : LC Card 83-185958
HD57.7 .D38 1983

Management development series, 0074-6703 .
(no. 22) Powell, Victor. Improving public enterprise performance . Geneva , 1987. x, 226 p. : ISBN 92-2-105563-9 (pbk.) : LC Card 87-166309 DDC 350/.0092/091724 19
HD4420.8 .P68 1987

MANAGEMENT - DICTIONARIES.
Banki, Ivan S. Dictionary of administration and management . Los Angeles, Calif., USA , c1986. iv, 1369 p. ; ISBN 0-912352-08-6 LC Card 85-63870 DDC 650/.03/21 19
HD30.15 .B36 1986

Bloor, Ian G. Reference guide to management techniques and activities /. Oxford, England , New York , 1987. xi, 80 p. ; ISBN 0-08-034268-X : LC Card 86-30266 DDC 658/.003/21 19
HD30.15 .B46 1987

Johannsen, Hano. International dictionary of management /. London , c1986. 370 p. : ISBN 0-85038-970-4 ***NYPL [JLD 86-1777]***

Tixier, Maud. Dictionnaire américain-anglais-français du management /.

Paris , 1985. 381 p. ; ISBN 2-247-00647-7 : LC Card 86-160705
HD30.15 .T59 1985 ***NYPL [JLD 86-3975]***

MANAGEMENT - DICTIONARIES - FRENCH.
Tixier, Maud. Dictionnaire américain-anglais-français du management /. Paris , 1985. 381 p. ; ISBN 2-247-00647-7 : LC Card 86-160705
HD30.15 .T59 1985 ***NYPL [JLD 86-3975]***

MANAGEMENT - DICTIONARIES - ITALIAN.
Dizionario di management, matematica, statistica, R.O., logistica, produzione, personale, psicologia e sociologia del lavoro e delle organizzazioni /. Milano, Italy , c1986. 779 p. : LC Card 86-225959
HD30 .E5 vol. 30 HD30.15

MANAGEMENT - DICTIONARIES - POLYGLOT.
Angliĭsko-nemsko-frensko-rusko-bŭlgarski rechnik po upravlenie i ikonomika na promishlenostta, stroitelstvoto i transporta /. Sofiia , 1982. 764 p. ; LC Card 83-128751
HD30.15 .A43 1982 ***NYPL [*QAD 86-4204]***

Management Division history. ASME Management Division history, 1886-1980 /. New York, N.Y. (345 E. 47th St., New York 10017) , c1984. x, 169 p. : LC Card 84-206982 DDC 658/.006/073 19
HD28.A6233 A86 1984
NYPL [JLF 86-1646]

Management--emphasize your strengths [motion picture] / Sandler Institutional Films. Pasadena, CA : Barr Films, 1985, c1986. 1 film reel (22 min.) : sd., col. ; 16 mm. + 1 leader's guide. Title from data sheet. Senior high school through college students, adults, and management trainees. Issued also as videorecording. Illustrates key managerial skills, emphasizing that good managers are able to recognize what they do very well, what they do well enough, and where they need to concentrate their development efforts. LC Card 86-707743 DDC 658.4 11
1. Executive ability. I. Sandler Institutional Films. II. Barr Films.
HD38.2

Management--emphasize your strengths [videorecording] / Sandler Institutional Films. Pasadena, CA : Barr Films, 1985, c1986. 1 videocassette (22 min.) : sd., col. + 1 leader's guide. Title from data sheet. Senior high school through college students, adults, and management trainees. Issued as U-matic 3/4 in. or Beta 1/2 in. or VHS 1/2 in. Issued also as motion picture. Illustrates key managerial skills, emphasizing that good managers are able to recognize what they do very well, what they do well enough, and where they need to concentrate their development efforts. LC Card 86-707745 DDC 658.4 11
1. Executive ability. I. Sandler Institutional Films. II. Barr Films.
HD38.2

MANAGEMENT - EMPLOYEE PARTICIPATION.
Befreiung der Arbeit . Bonn , c1986. 197 p. : ISBN 3-87831-429-9 LC Card 86-194157
HD6955 .B389 1986

Die Unternehmung in der demokratischen Gesellschaft =. Berlin , New York , 1987. xiii, 390 p. : ISBN 0-89925-295-8 (U. S.) : LC Card 86-32864 DDC 658.3/152 19
HD5650 .U67 1987

Društvena reprodukcija u djelu Vladimira Bakarića /. Zagreb , 1985 printing. 204 p. ; LC Card 86-233326
HD5650 .D68 1985

Lawler, Edward E. High-involvement management /. San Francisco, Calif. , 1986. xvii, 252 p. : ISBN 0-87589-686-3 (alk. paper) LC Card 85-45909 DDC 658.3/152 19
HD5650 .L35 1986 ***NYPL [JLE 86-3096]***

Lewis, Gary A., 1927- News from somewhere . Westport, Conn. , 1986. xii, 213 p. : ISBN 0-313-24869-9 (lib. bdg. : alk. paper) LC Card 85-27269 DDC 658.3/152 19
HD5650 .L439 1986 ***NYPL [JLD 86-3587]***

L'Information et la consultation des travailleurs dans les enterprises multinationales /. [Paris] [Genève?] , 1984. 290 p. ; ISBN 2-13-038651-2 (pbk.)
HD62.4 .I53 1984 ***NYPL [JLD 87-60]***

Lora, Guillermo. Control obrero colectivo y co-gestión . La Paz, Bolivia , 1982. 45 p. ; LC Card 83-204234
HD5650 .L73 1982

Meran, Georg. Die arbeiterselbstverwaltete Firma bei Unsicherheit und asymmetrischer Information . München , c1986. ii, 134 p. : ISBN 3-88259-403-9 LC Card 87-121443 DDC 658.3/152 19
HD5650 .M397 1986

Penteado Neto, Alfredo Camargo, 1939- Organizações de trabalhadores . São Paulo , 1986. 112 p. : LC Card 87-403488 DDC 338.6 19
HD5650 .P37 1986

Varandani, Gursharan, 1946- Workers' participation in management . New Delhi , c1987. xii, 228 p. ; LC Card 87-900827 DDC 658.3/152/0954 19
HD5650 .V35 1987

Volkov, Aleksandr Ivanovich. Konfrontatsiia ili kompromiss? . Moskva , 1986. 234 p. [4] ; LC Card 86-200508 DDC 658.3/152 19
HD5650 .V65 1986

Worker participation and the politics of reform /. Philadelphia , 1987. ix, 371 p. ; ISBN 0-87722-464-1 (alk. paper) : LC Card 86-23006 DDC 658.3/152 19
HD5650 .W645 1987

MANAGEMENT - EMPLOYEE PARTICIPATION - BIBLIOGRAPHY.
Participación, cogestión y autogestión en América Latina /. Caracas , 1986. 2 v. : ISBN 980-265-396-9 (set) LC Card 87-111263
HD5660.L29 P37 1986

MANAGEMENT - EMPLOYEE PARTICIPATION - CONGRESSES.
Computers and democracy . Aldershot [Hants, England] , Brookfield [Vt.], USA , c1987. x, 434 p. : ISBN 0-566-05476-0 : LC Card 87-8398 DDC 338/.06 19
HD5650 .C65 1987

MANAGEMENT - EMPLOYEE PARTICIPATION - DICTIONARIES - SPANISH.
Participación, cogestión y autogestión en América Latina /. Caracas , 1986. 2 v. : ISBN 980-265-396-9 (set) LC Card 87-111263
HD5660.L29 P37 1986

MANAGEMENT - EMPLOYEE PARTICIPATION - HISTORY.
Ibrahim, José. O que todo cidadão precisa saber sobre comissões de fábrica /. São Paulo, SP [1986] 96 p. : ISBN 85-26-00095-0 LC Card 87-402908 DDC 338.6 19
HD5660.B7 I27 1986

MANAGEMENT - EMPLOYEE PARTICIPATION - LAW AND LEGISLATION - GERMANY (WEST)
Kroneberg, Jürgen. Die mitbestimmte selbständige Aktiengesellschaft /. Göttingen , 1982. xii, 211 p. ; ISBN 3-88415-554-7 : LC Card 83-159183 DDC 346.43/0664 344.306664 19
KK3000 .K76 1982 ***NYPL [JLD 86-1552]***

MANAGEMENT - EMPLOYEE PARTICIPATION - POLITICAL ASPECTS - YUGOSLAVIA.
Mirić, Rade. Proces samoupravne integracije . Bačka Topola , 1984. 147 p. ; LC Card 85-194104
HD5660.Y8 M57 1984

MANAGEMENT, ENGINEERING. see **ENGINEERING - MANAGEMENT.**

MANAGEMENT - EXAMINATIONS, QUESTIONS, ETC.
Jaffe, Eugene D. How to prepare for the graduate management admission test GMAT /. New York , c1987. x, 541 p. : ISBN 0-8120-3882-7 (pbk.) LC Card 87-18619 DDC 650/.076 19
HD30.413 .J33 1987

The Official guide for GMAT review /. Princeton, N.J. , c1986. 372 p. : ISBN 0-446-38435-6 (pbk.) : LC Card 86-229958 DDC 650/.076 19
HF1118 .O33 1986

MANAGEMENT - FORMS.
The AMA handbook of key management forms /. New York, NY , c1987. 732 p. : ISBN 0-8144-1144-4 LC Card 86-25955 DDC 651/.29 19
HD38 .A44 1987

MANAGEMENT - FRANCE - EMPLOYEE PARTICIPATION.
Neff, Werner, 1947- Entfremdung und Selbstverwaltung . Zürich , c1983. 322 p. : ISBN 3-85791-066-6 LC Card 87-672017
HD5660.F7 N43x 1983

The management game /. Burst, Ardis. New York, N.Y. , 1987. 274 p. : ISBN 0-670-81225-0 LC Card 86-40617 DDC 658.4/0353 19
HD30.26 .B87 1987

MANAGEMENT GAMES - DATA PROCESSING.
Löffler, Reiner, 1959- STRATEGOS . Mannheim , 1986 (Darmstadt : Copy Shop) 246, [49] p. : LC Card 87-408452 DDC 658.4/0353/0285 19
HD30.26 .L64 1986

MANAGEMENT - GERMANY (EAST) - EMPLOYEE PARTICIPATION.
Mitbestimmung in beiden deutschen Staaten /. Bonn , c1983. 66 p. ; LC Card 86-228363
HD5660.G4 M55 1983

MANAGEMENT - GERMANY (WEST) - EMPLOYEE PARTICIPATION.
Hentze, Joachim. Unternehmungsführung und Mitbestimmung /. Würzburg , 1985. 297 p. : ISBN 3-7908-0268-9 LC Card 85-186054
HD5660.G4 H43 1985

Kauer, Christian, 1951- Konfliktregelung und Mitbestimmung . Frankfurt am Main , New York , c1985. 393 p. : ISBN 3-8204-5626-0 (pbk.) LC Card 87-672045
HD5660.G4 K37x 1985

List, Stephan, 1959- Arbeitnehmerbeteiligung bei Personengesellschaften . Spardorf , c1985. v, 167 p. ; ISBN 3-922919-50-2 LC Card 86-141876
HD5660.G4 L55 1985

Mitbestimmung in beiden deutschen Staaten /. Bonn , c1983. 66 p. ; LC Card 86-228363
HD5660.G4 M55 1983

Mitbestimmung in der Krise--Krise der Mitbestimmung? . Köln , c1984. 192 p. : ISBN 3-7663-0895-5 LC Card 85-113842
HD5660.G4 M563 1984

MANAGEMENT - GREAT BRITAIN - EMPLOYEE PARTICIPATION.
Burns, Patrick. Democracy at work /. London , 1981. 164 p. : ISBN 0-330-26478-8 (pbk.) LC Card 86-673620
HD6664 .B845x 1981

A management guide to artificial intelligence /. Maney, Tracy. Aldershot, Hants, England , c1986. viii, 188 p. ; ***NYPL [JLD 87-862]***

A management guide to leveraged buyouts /. Crawford, Edward K., 1933- New York , c1987. x, 257 p. ; ISBN 0-471-83232-4 LC Card 86-32390 DDC 658.1/6 19
HD2746.5 .C7 1987

MANAGEMENT - HANDBOOKS, MANUALS, ETC.
Brownstone, David M. The manager's advisor /. New York , c1987. vii, 296 p. ; ISBN 0-8144-7682-1 (pbk.) : LC Card 87-47712 DDC 658.4 19
HD38.2 .B75 1987

Lewis, Mike. 20 activities for developing managerial effectiveness . Aldershot, Hants, England , c1986. xii, 276 p. : ISBN 0-566-02515-9 LC Card 87-147860 DDC 658.4/07124 19
HD31 .L387 1986

MANAGEMENT - HISTORY.
Alvarez Valdés, Ariel. Breve historia del pensamiento administrativo /. [Santiago del Estero, Argentina] [1985] 129 p. : LC Card 86-180293
HD30.5 .A44 1985

Hickman, Craig R. The future 500 . New York, N.Y. , c1987. xiv, 274 p. ; ISBN 0-453-00544-6 LC Card 87-15204 DDC 658 19
HD31 .H4814 1987

Management in transition . Harris, Philip R. (Philip Robert), 1926- San Francisco, Calif. ,

c1985. xxvii, 404 p. : ISBN 0-87589-660-X (alk. paper) LC Card 85-45055 DDC 658.4 19
HD58.7 .H3695 1985 ***NYPL [JLE 85-3954]***

Management incentive compensation plans /. Butler, Stephen A. Montvale, N.J. , c1986. v, 55 p. ; ISBN 0-86641-140-2 (pbk.) LC Card 86-230062 DDC 658.4/07225 19
HD4965.5.U6 B86 1986

MANAGEMENT - INDIA.
Chakraborty, S. K. Human response in organizations . Calcutta, India [1985] xv, 228 p. : LC Card 87-901782 DDC 658/.00954 19
HD58.7 .C44 1985

When the twain meet . Allahabad , 1986. vi, 170 p. ; LC Card 87-900706 DDC 658/.00954 19
HD70.I4 W54 1986

MANAGEMENT - INDIA - EMPLOYEE PARTICIPATION.
Industrial democracy in India . Saddar, Karachi, Pakistan [1985] 21 p. ; LC Card 86-222345 DDC 331/.01/12095491 19
HD7262.5.P18 I53 1985

Varandani, Gursharan, 1946- Workers' participation in management . New Delhi , c1987. xii, 228 p. ; LC Card 87-900827 DDC 658.3/152/0954 19
HD5650 .V35 1987

MANAGEMENT, INDUSTRIAL. see **INDUSTRIAL MANAGEMENT.**

Management Information Corporation. Pathways through data processing, small business systems. Cherry Hill, N.J. (140 Barclay Center, Cherry Hill 08034) , c1980. 182 p. : LC Card 81-118723 DDC 001.64/04/029473 19
HF5548.2 P295 1980 ***NYPL [JLF 86-351]***

Management information series (Monterey, Calif.)
Risk management and retention . Monterey, Calif. (1 Mission Plaza, Monterey 93940) , c1986. v, 71 p. : LC Card 86-202599 DDC 658 19
HD61 .R569 1986

MANAGEMENT INFORMATION SERVICES.
Burn, Janice. Information analysis /. London , 1987. x, 260 p. : ISBN 0-948825-50-2 (pbk.) : LC Card 87-166130 DDC 658.4/038 19
HD30.35 .B87 1987

Management information studies.
Risk management and retention . Monterey, Calif. (1 Mission Plaza, Monterey 93940) , c1986. v, 71 p. : LC Card 86-202599 DDC 658 19
HD61 .R569 1986

MANAGEMENT INFORMATION SYSTEMS.
Arn, Joseph V., 1943- Office automation . Boston, MA , c1988. xxvii, 402 p., [8] p. of plates : ISBN 0-87835-232-5 LC Card 86-28359 DDC 651.8 19
HF5547.5 .A79 1988

Bingham, John E. A handbook of systems analysis /. London , 1978. ix, 229 p. : ISBN 0-333-24198-3 : LC Card 79-309251
HF5548.2 .B47 1978b ***NYPL [JLE 80-2972]***

Gerstein, Marc Saul. The technology connection . Reading, Mass. , c1987. xiv, 194 p. : ISBN 0-201-12188-3 (pbk.) : LC Card 86-22343 DDC 658.4/012 19
HD30.28 .G47 1987

Gessford, John Evans. Modern information systems . Reading, Mass. , c1980. xii, 512 p. : ISBN 0-201-03099-3 : LC Card 78-74684 DDC 658/.05/4
HF5548.2 .G48 ***NYPL [JLE 80-1913]***

L'Information et la consultation des travailleurs dans les enterprises multinationales /. [Paris] [Genève?] , 1984. 290 p. ; ISBN 2-13-038651-2 (pbk.)
HD62.4 .I53 1984 ***NYPL [JLD 87-60]***

The Strategic use of information technology /. New York , 1987. xiii, 206 p. : ISBN 0-19-505048-7 (alk. paper) : LC Card 87-1606 DDC 658/.05 19
HD30.2 .S79 1987

MANAGEMENT INFORMATION SYSTEMS - CONGRESSES.
Information systems in Italian savings banks . Geneva , 1975. 93 p. : LC Card 84-247915
HG1939.I7 I54 1975

MANAGEMENT INFORMATION SYSTEMS - PLANNING.
Heldman, Robert K. Telecommunications management planning . Blue Ridge Summit, PA , c1987. xviii, 734 p. : ISBN 0-8306-2864-9 : LC Card 86-30002 DDC 658.4/038 19
HD30.335 .H45 1987

MANAGEMENT - JAPAN.
Fassin, Yves. Japan, management van de toekomst? /. Antwerpen , 1985. 131 p. : ISBN 90-6716-242-6 : LC Card 86-167503
HD70.J3 F37 1985

Kobayashi, Kaoru, 1931- Japan, the most misunderstood country /. Tokyo , 1984. ix, 165 p. ; ISBN 4-7890-0247-0
NYPL [JLD 86-1398]

MANAGEMENT - JAPAN - EMPLOYEE PARTICIPATION - HISTORY.
Park, Sung-Jo. U. S. labor policy in postwar Japan /. [Berlin] [c1985] 157 p. : ISBN 3-88548-424-2 LC Card 86-200166 DDC 331.11/0952 19
HD5827.A6 P37 1985

MANAGEMENT - JAPAN - MISCELLANEA.
Riccomini, Donald R., 1952- Unexpected Japan . New York , 1985. iv, 132 p. ; ISBN 0-8027-0858-7 : LC Card 85-7313 DDC 658/.00952 19
HD70.J3 R53 1985 ***NYPL [JLD 86-1348]***

MANAGEMENT - LATIN AMERICA - EMPLOYEE PARTICIPATION.
Participación, cogestión y autogestión en América Latina /. Caracas , 1986. 2 v. : ISBN 980-265-396-9 (set) LC Card 87-111263
HD5660.L29 P37 1986

MANAGEMENT, MARKETING. see **MARKETING MANAGEMENT.**

MANAGEMENT - MATHEMATICAL MODELS.
Ovsievich, Boris L'vovich. Modeli formirovaniia organizatsionnykh struktur /. Leningrad , 1979. 157, [3] p. : LC Card 81-162540
HD30.25 .O97 1979

Payne, Thomas A. Quantitative techniques for management . Reston, Va. , c1982. xii, 452 p. : ISBN 0-8359-6116-8 : LC Card 81-17818 DDC 658.4/033 19
HD30.25 .P395 1982 ***NYPL [JLE 82-399]***

Pinney, William E., 1941- Management science . New York , c1987. xvii, 620 p. : ISBN 0-06-045229-3 LC Card 86-22933 DDC 658.4/033 19
HD30.25 .P56 1987

Roy, B. (Bernard), 1934- Méthodologie multicritère d'aide à la décision /. Paris , c1985. xxii, 423 p. : ISBN 2-7178-0901-5 : LC Card 86-166619
HD30.25 .R68 1985

Tu, Pierre N. V. (Pierre Ninh Van) Introductory optimization dynamics . Berlin , New York , 1984. xiii, 387 p. : ISBN 0-387-13305-4 (U. S.)
NYPL [JSE 86-1520]

Zherebin, V. M. Proektirovanie ėkonomicheskikh informatsionnykh sistem /. Moskva , 1983. 182, [2] p., [2] folded p. of plates : LC Card 83-224346
HD30.25 .Z52 1983

MANAGEMENT - NETHERLANDS - EMPLOYEE PARTICIPATION.
Autonomie als arbeidssociologisch vraagstuk . Zeist , 1987. 237 p. : ISBN 90-6720-032-8 : LC Card 87-169950
HD5660.N4 A94 1987

MANAGEMENT - NORWAY - EMPLOYEE PARTICIPATION.
Lewis, Gary A., 1927- News from somewhere . Westport, Conn. , 1986. xii, 213 p. : ISBN 0-313-24869-9 (lib. bdg. : alk. paper) LC Card 85-27269 DDC 658.3/152 19
HD5650 .L439 1986 ***NYPL [JLD 86-3587]***

The management of change . Weiss, Joseph W. New York , 1986. xviii, 210 p. ; ISBN 0-275-92195-6 (alk. paper) : LC Card 86-9390 DDC 658.4 19
HD7256.U5 W38 1986
NYPL [JLE 86-4062]

The management of collective bargaining . Sisson, Keith. Oxford, UK , New York, NY, USA , 1987. xviii, 230 p. ; ISBN 0-631-13439-5 : LC Card 87-6642 DDC 331.89 19
HD6971.5 .S57 1987

Management of human resources in Kenya /. Wa'Weru, Murathi. Nairobi , 1984. xv, 174 p. ; LC Card 85-980435 DDC 658.3/009676/2 19
HF5549.2.K4 W39 1984b

Management of human resources in public enterprises / editors, S. Ravishankar, R.K. Mishra. New Delhi, India : Vision Books, 1985. vi, 304 p. ; 23 cm. Includes bibliographies and index. LC Card 87-402995 DDC 354.5409/2/0683 19
1. Government business enterprises - India - Personnel management. 2. Government business enterprises - Personnel management. I. Ravishankar, S., 1956-. II. Mishra, R. K., 1948-.
HD4293 .M355 1985

Management of local public works / editors, Sam M. Cristofano, William S. Foster. Washington, D.C. : Published in cooperation with the American Public Works Association by the International City Management Association, c1986. xvii, 402 p. : ill. ; 28 cm. (Municipal management series) Includes index. Bibliography: p. [381]-387. ISBN 0-87326-048-1 : LC Card 86-125 DDC 363/.068 19
1. Municipal services - Management - Addresses, essays, lectures. 2. Public works - Management - Addresses, essays, lectures. I. Cristofano, Sam M. II. Foster, William S.
HD4431 .M35 1986 ***NYPL [JLF 86-1543]***

Management of national consumption. Upravlenie na narodnoto potreblenie /. Sofiia , 1984. 235 p. : LC Card 85-212359
HC403.Z9 C628 1984

Management of organizational behavior . Hersey, Paul. Englewood Cliffs, N.J. , 1988. p. cm. ISBN 0-13-551268-9 : LC Card 87-23064 DDC 658.3 19
HD58.7 .H47 1988

Management of public budgetary institutions / [editorial board, T. Bácskai ... et al.]. Budapest : Secretariate of the Ministry of Finance, Hungary, 1986. 37 p. ; 21 cm. (Public finance in Hungary, 0230-9718 . 31) ISBN 963-03-2343-5 (pbk.) : LC Card 86-230773 DDC 336.439 19
1. Budget - Hungary. I. Bácskai, Tamás. II. Hungary. Pénzügyminisztérium. Titkárság. III. Series.
HJ2103 .M33 1986

Management of state government enterprises /. Venkatswamy, G. New Delhi, India , 1987. viii, 362 p. : ISBN 81-7051-020-1 : LC Card 87-901167 DDC 354.54/84092 19
HD4295.A5 V45 1987

The Management of strategic change / edited by Andrew M. Pettigrew. Oxford [Oxfordshire] ; New York, NY : B. Blackwell, 1988, c1987. p. cm. Based on the proceedings of an international research seminar held under the auspices of the Centre for Corporate Strategy and Change at Warwick University, Coventry, England, in May 1986. Includes bibliographies and index. ISBN 0-631-15695-X : LC Card 87-15634 DDC 658.4/012 19
1. Strategic planning - Congresses. 2. Corporate planning - Congresses. 3. Organizational change - Congresses. I. Pettigrew, Andrew M. II. University of Warwick. Centre for Corporate Strategy and Change.
HD30.28 .M344 1988

Management of the sales force /. Stanton, William J. Homewood, Ill. , 1987. xv, 704 p. : ISBN 0-256-03635-7 LC Card 86-82598 DDC 658.8/1 19
HF5438.4 .S78 1987

Management of urban services in Nairobi . Mitullah, W. V. Nairobi, Kenya , 1985. 109, 106, vi p., [6] leaves of plates : LC Card 87-116360 DDC 388.4/09676/25 19
HD4720.5.N35 M57 1985

MANAGEMENT - OPERATIONS RESEARCH. see **OPERATIONS RESEARCH.**

MANAGEMENT - PERU - EMPLOYEE PARTICIPATION - CONGRESSES.
Seminario-Taller La Autogestión Empresarial Urbana (1985 : Lima, Peru) Informe final /. [Lima, Perú] [1986 or 1987] 112 p. ; LC Card 87-404369 DDC 338.6 19
HD5660.P4 S46 1985

Management planning and control : the behavioral foundations. Rev. ed. / [edited by]

Kenneth R. Ferris, J. Leslie Livingstone. Beavercreek, Ohio : Century VII Pub. Co., c1987. xvii, 249 p. : ill. ; 23 cm. Rev. ed. of: Managerial accounting. 1975. Includes bibliographies. ISBN 0-939787-00-8 (pbk.) : LC Card 86-24930 DDC 658.1/511 19
1. Managerial accounting. 2. Organizational behavior. I. Ferris, Kenneth R. II. Livingstone, John Leslie.
HF5635 .M236 1987

Management policies in local government finance / editors, J. Richard Aronson, Eli Schwartz. 3rd ed. Washington, D.C. : Published for the ICMA Training Institute by the International City Management Association, c1987. 449 p. : ill. ; 28 cm. (Municipal management series) Includes bibliographies and index. ISBN 0-87326-075-9 : LC Card 87-2658 DDC 352.1 19
1. Local finance. 2. Municipal finance. I. Aronson, J. Richard (Jay Richard), 1937-. II. Schwartz, Eli. III. ICMA Training Institute.
HJ9105 .M3 1987

Management, principles and practices /. Holt, David H. Englewood Cliffs, N.J. , c1987. xxiv, 808 p. : ISBN 0-13-548207-0 LC Card 86-25161 DDC 658.4 19
HD31 .H6225 1987

Management problems in Africa / edited by Ukandi G. Damachi and Hans Dieter Seibel. London : MacMillan, 1986. xviii, 395 p. ; 23 cm. Includes bibliographies and index. ISBN 0-333-28992-7
1. Management - Africa - Addresses, essays, lectures. 2. Industrial relations - Africa - Addresses, essays, lectures. I. Seibel, Hans Dieter.
NYPL [Sc D 86-519]

MANAGEMENT, PRODUCT. see **PRODUCT MANAGEMENT.**

MANAGEMENT - PROGRAMMED INSTRUCTION.
Weidlein, Marianne S., 1944- Visions & business . Boulder, Colo. , 1987, c1986. 261 p. in various pagings : ISBN 0-942097-11-4 (3-ring binder ed.) : LC Card 87-7935 DDC 658/.007/7 19
HD30.4 .W43 1987

MANAGEMENT - PSYCHOLOGICAL ASPECTS.
Taetzsch, Lyn. Taking charge on the job . New York , c1978. 144 p. ; ISBN 0-917386-22-1 : LC Card 78-111025 DDC 658.4
HD38 .T17 ***NYPL [JLE 80-1910]***

MANAGEMENT - QUOTATIONS, MAXIMS, ETC.
The Last word on management /. Secaucus, N.J. , c1987. vi, 280 p. ; ISBN 0-8184-0452-3 : LC Card 87-18005 DDC 658 19
HD38 .L345 1987

Management ratios. Westwick, C. A. How to use management ratios /. Aldershot, Hants, England , 1987. xviii, 421 p. : ISBN 0-566-02425-X LC Card 87-126440 DDC 658.4/001/512924 19
HF5681.R25 W47 1987

Management reforms in China / edited by Malcolm Warner. New York : St. Martin's Press, 1987. p. cm. Bibliography: p. Includes index. ISBN 0-312-00849-X : LC Card 87-4772 DDC 658/.00951 19
1. Industrial management - China. I. Warner, Malcolm.
HD70.C5 M34 1987

Management report . Charnov, Bruce H. Westbury, N.Y. , c1987. 63 p. : ISBN 0-87280-120-9 (pbk.) : LC Card 87-24106 DDC 658.4/6 19
HD69.C6 C36 1987

MANAGEMENT RESEARCH.
Zikmund, William G. Business research methods /. Chicago , 1987, c1988. xvii, 715 p. : ISBN 0-03-012362-3 LC Card 87-5284 DDC 658.4/03/072 19
HD30.4 .Z54 1988

Management response to public issues . Buchholz, Rogene A. Englewood Cliffs, N.J. , c1985. x, 389 p. : ISBN 0-13-549940-2 (pbk.) : LC Card 84-18355 DDC 658.4/08 19
HD60 .B83 1985 ***NYPL [JLE 85-1984]***

MANAGEMENT, SALES. see **SALES MANAGEMENT.**

Management science . Pinney, William E., 1941- New York , c1987. xvii, 620 p. : ISBN 0-06-045229-3 LC Card 86-22933 DDC 658.4/033 19
HD30.25 .P56 1987

MANAGEMENT SCIENCE.
Pinney, William E., 1941- Management science . New York , c1987. xvii, 620 p. : ISBN 0-06-045229-3 LC Card 86-22933 DDC 658.4/033 19
HD30.25 .P56 1987

MANAGEMENT SCIENCE AMERICA, INC.
MSA, the software company. New York, N.Y. , c1982. v, 73 leaves : LC Card 87-143692 DDC 338.7/610053/0973 19
HD9696.C64 M355 1982

MANAGEMENT SCIENCE - DICTIONARIES - ITALIAN.
Dizionario di management, matematica, statistica, R.O., logistica, produzione, personale, psicologia e sociologia del lavoro e delle organizzazioni /. Milano, Italy , c1986. 779 p. : LC Card 86-225959
HD30 .E5 vol. 30 HD30.15

The management series /. Hubbard, L. Ron (La Fayette Ron), 1911- Los Angeles, Calif. , c1982- v. <1 > ; ISBN 0-88404-090-9 (v. 1) LC Card 82-71055 DDC 658.4
HD38 .H82 1982

MANAGEMENT - SIMULATION METHODS.
Christopher, Elizabeth M. Leadership training through gaming . New York , 1987. 187 p. : ISBN 0-89397-284-3 : LC Card 87-12362 DDC 658.4/07353 19
HD57.7 .C53 1987

Manuale delle simulazioni di gestione . Milano, Italy , 1985. 335 p. : LC Card 86-187906
HD30.26 .M36 1985

Sashkin, Marshall, 1944- Experiencing management /. Reading, Mass. , c1987. x, 234 p. : ISBN 0-201-11545-X (pbk.) : LC Card 86-28731 DDC 658.4/0352 19
HD30.26 .S27 1987

Smith, Jerald R. Airline . Englewood Cliffs, NJ , c1987. v, 115, [38] p. : ISBN 0-13-020801-9 (pbk.) LC Card 86-30488 DDC 387.7/068 19
HD30.28 .S57 1987

Management Skills for Investment Managers Seminar . Management Skills for Investment Managers Seminar (1982 : Washington, D.C.) Charlottesville, Va. (P.O. Box 3668, Charlottesville 22903) , c1983. vi, 62 p. : LC Card 83-244808 DDC 658.1/52 19
HG4621 .M36 1982 ***NYPL [JLF 87-425]***

Management Skills for Investment Managers Seminar (1982 : Washington, D.C.)
Management Skills for Investment Managers Seminar : Washington, D.C., October 26-27, 1982 / edited by James R. Vertin ; sponsored by the Institute of Chartered Financial Analysts. Charlottesville, Va. (P.O. Box 3668, Charlottesville 22903) : CFA, University of Virginia, c1983. vi, 62 p. : ill. ; 28 cm. Presentations by Richard A. Cosier, Paul F. Miller, Daniel J. Forrestal III, Harold L. Arbit, J. Richard Boylan, and Dave H. Williams. LC Card 83-244808 DDC 658.1/52 19
1. Investment advisers - Congresses. 2. Management - Congresses. I. Vertin, James R. II. Institute of Chartered Financial Analysts. III. Title.
HG4621 .M36 1982 ***NYPL [JLF 87-425]***

MANAGEMENT - SOVIET UNION.
Bakhrakh, D. N. (Dem'i͡an Nikolaevich) Osnovnye poni͡atii͡a teorii sotsial'nogo upravlenii͡a . Perm' , 1978. 100 p. ; LC Card 81-154363
HD70.S63 B35 1978

Martanus, R. V. (Ri͡urik Vital'evich) Sot͡sial'noe upravlenie . Moskva , 1986. 141 p. ; LC Card 87-156789
HD38.25.S65 M35 1986

MANAGEMENT - SOVIET UNION - EMPLOYEE PARTICIPATION - CONGRESSES.
Povyshenie trudovoĭ i obshchestvenno-politicheskoĭ aktivnosti mass kak reshai͡ushchiĭ faktor uskorenii͡a sot͡sial'no-ėkonomicheskogo progressa sotsialisticheskogo obshchestva . Kaliningrad , 1986. 382 p. ; LC Card 87-136621
HD8526.5 .P62 1986

MANAGEMENT - STATISTICAL METHODS.
Keller, Gerald. Statistics for management and economics . Belmont, Calif. , c1988. xix, 987 p. : ISBN 0-534-08622-5 LC Card 87-19845 DDC 658.4/033 19
HD30.215 .K45 1988

Payne, Thomas A. Quantitative techniques for management . Reston, Va. , c1982. xii, 452 p. : ISBN 0-8359-6116-8 : LC Card 81-17818 DDC 658.4/033 19
HD30.25 .P395 1982 ***NYPL [JLE 82-399]***

Westwick, C. A. How to use management ratios /. Aldershot, Hants, England , 1987. xviii, 421 p. : ISBN 0-566-02425-X LC Card 87-126440 DDC 658.4/001/512924 19
HF5681.R25 W47 1987

MANAGEMENT - STUDY AND TEACHING.
Limp, Wolfgang. Productivity centers . Frankfurt am Main , 1975. 64 p. ; LC Card 82-219310
HD30.4 .L55 1975

Susánszky, János. Tanulmányok a szervezésről és a vezetésről /. Budapest , 1985. 89 p. ; ISBN 963-05-4132-7 : LC Card 86-136320
HD37.H82 S857 1985

MANAGEMENT - STUDY AND TEACHING - ASIA.
Developing managers in Asia /. Singapore , Reading, Mass. , 1986. p. cm. ISBN 0-201-13653-8 : LC Card 86-28717 DDC 658/.007/15 19
HD38.25.A78 D48 1986

MANAGEMENT - STUDY AND TEACHING - FINLAND - TAMPERE.
Yrityksen taloustieteet Tampereen yliopistossa /. Tampere , 1985. 47 leaves : ISBN 951-44-1859-X LC Card 87-107284
HD30.42.F5 Y74 1985

MANAGEMENT - STUDY AND TEACHING - GREAT BRITAIN.
Hussey, D. E. (David E.) Management training and corporate strategy . Oxford [Oxfordshire] , New York , 1988. x, 201 p. : ISBN 0-08-034036-9 : LC Card 87-22075 DDC 658.4/07124 19
HD30.42.G7 H87 1988

MANAGEMENT - STUDY AND TEACHING - JAPAN.
Nötzli, Irene M. A view of Japanese management, especially management development in large business enterprises /. Zürich , c1982. ix, 281 p. : ISBN 3-7255-2191-3 (pbk.) LC Card 82-237094 DDC 658.4/07124 19
HF5549.5.T7 N638 1982 ***NYPL [TB (Zürich. Universität. Handelwissenschaftiches Seminar. Mitteilungen. Heft 156)]***

MANAGEMENT - STUDY AND TEACHING - KENYA.
Gershenberg, Irving. Multinational enterprises, transfer of managerial know-how, technology choice and employment effects . Geneva , 1983. iii, 33 p. ; ISBN 92-2-103508-5 (pbk.) LC Card 86-213574 DDC 338.8/886762 19
HD2920.5 .G47 1983

Management success secrets . Mattar, Edward Paul. Worcester, MA , 1987. p. cm. LC Card 87-15372 DDC 658.4 19
HD31 .M3375 1987

MANAGEMENT - SWEDEN - EMPLOYEE PARTICIPATION.
Ekonomisk demokrati . Stockholm [1984] ii, 169 p. : LC Card 85-108590
HD5660.S9 E38 1984

Hörte, Sven Åke. Medbestämmande . [Göteborg] , c1983. 160, [28] p. : ISBN 91-7222-576-9 LC Card 83-173622
HD5660.S9 H67 1983

Otter, Casten von, 1941- Medbestämmandeavtal i landsting . Stockholm [1984] 92 p. : LC Card 84-241542
HD5660.S9 O77 1984

MANAGEMENT - SWEDEN - EMPLOYEE PARTICIPATION - HISTORY.
Lundh, Christer. Den svenska debatten om industriell demokrati 1919-1924 /. Lund , 1987- v. <1 > ; ISBN 91-85611-17-4 LC Card 87-151790
HD5660.S9 L87 1987

Management techniques for top executives /. Parker, Frederick. Pompano Beach, Fla. , c1985. x, 194 p. : ISBN 0-682-40194-3 : LC Card 84-91085 DDC 658.4/09 19
HD38.2 .P37 1985

The Management tool box series.
Wall, William C. Prepare power-packed reports /. Huntsville, Ala. , c1987. p. cm. ISBN 0-938745-04-2 LC Card 87-13581 DDC 658.4/53 19
HF5719 .W35 1987

Management training and corporate strategy . Hussey, D. E. (David E.) Oxford [Oxfordshire] , New York , 1988. x, 201 p. : ISBN 0-08-034036-9 : LC Card 87-22075 DDC 658.4/07124 19
HD30.42.G7 H87 1988

Management Training Seminar (1982 : Joint Research Centre, Ispra, Italy) National energy planning and management in developing countries : lectures delivered at a Management Training Seminar held at the Joint Research Centre, Ispra, Italy, May 3-14, 1982 / edited by H. Neu and D. Bain. Dordrecht, Holland : D. Reidel ; Hingham, MA : Sold and distributed in the U. S.A. and Canada by Kluwer Boston, c1983. xiii, 442 p. ; 24 cm. (Ispra courses on energy systems and technology) Includes bibliographical references. ISBN 90-277-1589-0 LC Card 83-4407 DDC 333.79/09172/4 19
1. Energy policy - Developing countries - Congresses. 2. Power resources - Developing countries - Congresses. 3. Energy consumption - Developing countries - Planning - Congresses. 4. Energy consumption - Developing countries - Management - Congresses. I. Neu, H., 1920-. II. Bain, D., 1944-. III. Title. IV. Series.
HD9502.A2 M343 1982 ***NYPL [JLE 87-302]***

Management und Arbeiterschaft . Jaun, Rudolf, 1948- Zürich , c1986. 505, 10 p. ; ISBN 3-905278-08-1 LC Card 87-132013 DDC 658/.009494 19
HD70.S85 J38 1986

MANAGEMENT - UNITED STATES.
Ėpshteĭn, S. I. (Samuil Isaakovich) Burzhuaznaia nauka upravleniia i neupravliaemaia ėkonomika /. Moskva , 1986. 76 p. ; LC Card 86-201018 DDC 658/.00973 19
HD70.U5 E6 1986

Rachman, David J. Business today /. New York , c1987. xxiii, 643 p. : ISBN 0-394-35114-2 LC Card 86-24784 DDC 658 19
HF5351 .R26 1987

Upravlencheskie novovvedeniia v SShA . Moskva , 1986. 244, [3] p. : LC Card 86-231514
HD70.U5 U67 1986

MANAGEMENT - UNITED STATES - EMPLOYEE PARTICIPATION.
Wilson, Bryan David, 1954- Ownership and participation . 1985. xi, 356 ;
NYPL [JLD 87-209]

MANAGEMENT - UNITED STATES - HISTORY.
ASME Management Division history, 1886-1980 /. New York, N.Y. (345 E. 47th St., New York 10017) , c1984. x, 169 p. : LC Card 84-206982 DDC 658/.006/073 19
HD28.A6233 A86 1984
NYPL [JLF 86-1646]

MANAGEMENT - UNITED STATES - MISCELLANEA.
Riccomini, Donald R., 1952- Unexpected Japan . New York , 1985. iv, 132 p. ; ISBN 0-8027-0858-7 : LC Card 85-7313 DDC 658/.00952 19
HD70.J3 R53 1985 ***NYPL [JLD 86-1348]***

MANAGEMENT - VENEZUELA - EMPLOYEE PARTICIPATION.
Mantero, Osvaldo. Cogestión en la empresa . Caracas, Venezuela [1986] 215 p. : ISBN 0-9806771-1-3 LC Card 87-401945 DDC 658.3/152/0987 19
HD5660.V4 M36 1986

Management von Zinsänderungschancen und -risiken /. Wondrak, Bernhard. Heidelberg , c1986. xv, 254 p. : ISBN 3-7908-0341-3 LC Card 86-213976
HG6024.5 .W66 1986

Management, work, leisure : a review of research trends in western and eastern Europe = Gestion, travail, loisirs : une analyse des tendances de la recherche en Europe de l'Ouest et de l'Est / Maryse Gaudier ... [et al.]. Geneva : International Institute for Labour Studies, c1986. viii, 154 p. : ill. ; 24 cm. (Bibliography series. no. 11) English and French. Includes index. ISBN 92-9014-416-5 (pbk.) : LC Card 87-163300 DDC 306/.36/094 19
1. Work - Research - Europe. 2. Work - Research - Europe, Eastern. 3. Leisure - Research - Europe. 4. Leisure - Research - Europe, Eastern. 5. Work - Bibliography. 6. Leisure - Europe - Bibliography. 7. Leisure - Europe, Eastern - Bibliography. I. Gaudier, Maryse. II. International Institute for Labour Studies. III. Title: Gestion, travail, loisirs. IV. Series: Bibliography series (International Institute for Labour Studies) , no. 11.
HD4904.6 .M35 1986

Management workstations . Perry, William E. Blue Ridge Summit, PA , c1987. vi, 186 p. : ISBN 0-8306-2833-9 : LC Card 87-1903 DDC 658/.05 19
HD30.2 .P47 1987

MANAGEMENT - YUGOSLAVIA - EMPLOYEE PARTICIPATION.
Čelenković, Teodosije. Radna snaga u samoupravnom društvu . Beograd , 1980. 241 p. ; LC Card 82-166188
HD5811.6.A6 C45 1980

Društvena reprodukcija u djelu Vladimira Bakarića /. Zagreb , 1985 printing. 204 p. ; LC Card 86-233326
HD5650 .D68 1985

Jovanov, Neca. Dijagnoza samoupravljanja 1974-1981 /. Zagreb , 1983. 365 p. ; LC Card 84-146844
HD5660.Y8 J68 1983

Der Kapitalistische Charakter der jugoslawischen Arbeiterselbstverwaltung im Lichte des 8. Kongresses des Bundes der Kommunisten Jugoslawiens. Tirana , 1965. 54 p. ; LC Card 85-127335
HD5660.Y8 K27 1965

Milošević, Nikša. Sistem udruženog rada /. Beograd , 1985. 392 p. : LC Card 86-197428
HD5660.Y8 M55 1985

Problemi samoupravne organizacije /. Zagreb , 1981. xi, 237 p. ; LC Card 83-110609
HD5660.Y8 P675 1981

MANAGEMENT - YUGOSLAVIA - EMPLOYEE PARTICIPATION - HISTORY.
Vekić, Đuro. Samoupravljanje od ideje do stvarnosti /. Sarajevo [1983?] 263 p. ; LC Card 86-115347
HD5660.Y8 V44 1983

Management's hidden enemy . Brown, David S. (David Springer), 1915- Mt. Airy, Md. , 1987. viii, 123 p. ; ISBN 0-912338-59-8 LC Card 86-82670 DDC 658.4/5 19
HD30.3 .B76 1987

Manager in the international economy /. Vernon, Raymond, 1913- Englewood Cliffs, NJ , c1986. viii, 469 p. : ISBN 0-13-550807-X : LC Card 85-25653 DDC 658.1/8 19
HD62.4 .V48 1986 ***NYPL [JLE 86-3200]***

Managerial accounting : an introduction to concepts, methods, and uses / Sidney Davidson ... [et al.].3rd ed. Chicago : Dryden Press, c1988. xii, 926 p. : ill. ; 24 cm. Includes index. ISBN 0-03-011964-2 LC Card 87-18469 DDC 658.1/511 19
1. Managerial accounting. I. Davidson, Sidney, 1919-.
HF5635 .M2358 1988

Managerial accounting /. Dominiak, Geraldine F. Boston , c1988. xxiv, 808 p. : ISBN 0-534-07740-4 : LC Card 87-21472 DDC 658.1/5 19
HF5657.4 .D66 1988

Managerial accounting /. Engler, Calvin. Homewood, Ill. , 1987. xvi, 926 p. : ISBN 0-256-03318-8 LC Card 86-81610 . DDC 658.1/511 19
HF5657 .E54 1987

Managerial accounting /. Francia, Arthur J. Houston, Tex. , 1984. xiv, 651 p. : ISBN 0-931920-70-1 LC Card 83-72203 DDC 658.1/511 19
HF5657.4 .F72 1984

Managerial accounting /. Helmkamp, John G. New York , c1987. xxiii, 720 p. : ISBN 0-471-88910-5 LC Card 86-29021 DDC 658.1/511 19
HF5635 .H45 1987

Managerial accounting /. Smith, Jack L. New York , c1988. xxv, 717 p. : ISBN 0-07-058990-9 : LC Card 87-17223 DDC 658.1/511 19
HF5657.4 .S55 1988

MANAGERIAL ACCOUNTING - CANADA.
Ahmed, Mumtaz. Project management . Hamilton, Ont. [1986] xv, 254 p. : ISBN 0-920212-56-5 (pbk.) LC Card 87-158681 DDC 658.4/04 19
HF5635 .A26 1986

MANAGERIAL ACCOUNTING - CASE STUDIES.
Egger, Emil. Management Accounting in öffentlichen nichtgewinnorientierten Organisationen . Zürich , c1985. xii, 220 p. : ISBN 3-7255-2410-6 LC Card 85-132536
HF5686.N56 E33 1985

Managerial accounting changes for the 1990s /. Lee, John Y. Artesia, Calif., U. S.A. , c1987. iv, 87 p. : ISBN 0-9617977-0-3 (pbk.) : LC Card 87-60120 DDC 658.1/511 19
HF5657.4 .L43 1987

MANAGERIAL ACCOUNTING - CONGRESSES.
Accounting & management . Boston, Mass. , c1987. ix, 374 p. : ISBN 0-87584-186-4 (alk. paper) LC Card 87-18373 DDC 658.4/038 19
HF5657.4 .A25 1987

MANAGERIAL ACCOUNTING - DATA PROCESSING.
Gambel, Edoardo L. La valutazione, simulazione e previsione nella gestione d'impresa . Milano, Italy , c1986. 190 p. : LC Card 86-217652
HF5679 .G36 1986

Lehman, Mark W. Using the microcomputer in managerial accounting . St. Paul , c1987. x, 406 p. : ISBN 0-314-98515-8 (pbk.) LC Card 87-2194 DDC 658.1/511/02855369 19
HF5657.4 .L44 1987

Smith, Gaylord N. The Briton Manufacturing Company . New York , c1988. p. cm. ISBN 0-06-046318-X LC Card 87-15624 DDC 657/.028/55369 19
HD30.26 .S64 1988

Wells, Nancy E., 1946- Straight forward managerial accounting applications . Burlington, VT , 1987, c1986. p. cm. ISBN 0-9612704-1-1 LC Card 87-22393 DDC 658.1/511/02855369 19
HF5657.4 .W44 1987

MANAGERIAL ACCOUNTING - DECISION MAKING - PUBLIC OPINION.
A Comparative study on accounting policy between Japanese and the U. S. companies /. Tokyo, Japan , c1986. iv, 56 p. : LC Card 87-169003 DDC 657/.0952 19
HF5686.C7 C635 1986

MANAGERIAL ACCOUNTING - EXAMINATIONS, QUESTIONS, ETC.
Gleim, Irvin N. CMA examination review /. Gainesville, Fla. , c1987. 2 v. : ISBN 0-917537-21-1 (pbk. : v. 1) LC Card 87-70930 DDC 658.1/511/076 19
HF5661 .G42 1987

MANAGERIAL ACCOUNTING - HANDBOOKS, MANUALS, ETC.
Vickman, Thomas M. Handbook of model accounting reports and formats /. Englewood Cliffs, N.J. , c1987. xvii, 350 p. : ISBN 0-13-380338-4 : LC Card 86-15068 DDC 658.1/512 19
HF5635 .V53 1987 ***NYPL [JLF 87-214]***

MANAGERIAL ACCOUNTING - HISTORY.
Johnson, H. Thomas, 1938- Relevance lost . Boston, Mass. , c1987. xiii, 269 p. ; ISBN 0-87584-138-4 LC Card 86-29474 DDC 658.1/511/09 19
HF5605 .J64 1987

MANAGERIAL ACCOUNTING - PAKISTAN - CONGRESSES.
National Conference of Management Accountants (1981 : Karachi, Pakistan) National Conference of Management Accountants . [Karachi] [1981?] 141 p. in

various pagings ; LC Card 82-930763 DDC 658.1/511 19
HF5603 .N34 1981 ***NYPL [JLF 87-296]***

MANAGERIAL ACCOUNTING - PROBLEMS, EXERCISES, ETC.
Hrubec, Thomas R. The managerial accounting quizmaster /. New York , c1987. xx, 216 p. : ISBN 0-07-034472-8 (pbk.) LC Card 86-62759 DDC 658.1/511/076 19
HF5657.4 .H78 1987

The managerial accounting quizmaster /. Hrubec, Thomas R. New York , c1987. xx, 216 p. : ISBN 0-07-034472-8 (pbk.) LC Card 86-62759 DDC 658.1/511/076 19
HF5657.4 .H78 1987

MANAGERIAL ACCOUNTING - UNITED STATES - HISTORY.
Johnson, H. Thomas, 1938- Relevance lost . Boston, Mass. , c1987. xiii, 269 p. ; ISBN 0-87584-138-4 LC Card 86-29474 DDC 658.1/511/09 19
HF5605 .J64 1987

MANAGERIAL ACCUNTING - CASE STUDIES.
Dearden, John. Management accounting . Englewood Cliffs, N.J. , c1988. xiv, 639 p. : ISBN 0-13-549123-1 LC Card 87-19300 DDC 658.1/511 19
HF5657.4 .D42 1988

The managerial choice . Herzberg, Frederick. Salt Lake City, Utah , c1982. xviii, 360 p. : ISBN 0-913420-97-2 LC Card 81-85925 DDC 658.3/14 19
HF5549.5.I5 H47 1982
NYPL [JLE 86-2591]

Managerial compensation /. Nash, Allan N. Scarsdale, N.Y. , c1980. 56 p. ; ISBN 0-89361-022-4 : LC Card 80-21044 DDC 658.4/072/0973 19
HD4965.5.U6 N22
NYPL [JLM 83-380 no.15]

Managerial dictation /. Matthews, Anne L. Cincinnati , c1987. 76 p. : ISBN 0-538-07950-9 (pbk.) LC Card 86-63922 DDC 651.7/4 19
HF5547.5 .M383 1987

Managerial dilemmas . Westin, Alan F. Cambridge, Mass. , 1988. p. cm. ISBN 0-88730-181-9 (pbk.) LC Card 87-22476 DDC 658.4/03 19
HD30.23 .W47 1988

Managerial economics /. Allen, Bruce T. New York , c1988. xix, 647 p. ; ISBN 0-06-044458-4 LC Card 87-21908 DDC 338.5/024658 19
HD30.22 .A4 1988

Managerial economics . Peppers, Larry C. Englewood Cliffs, N.J. , c1987. xxii, 679 p. : ISBN 0-13-550055-9 LC Card 86-25278 DDC 338.5/024658 19
HD30.22 .P43 1987

Managerial economics /. Reekie, W. Duncan. Oxford [Oxfordshire] , Atlantic Highlands, N.J. , 1987. xi, 522 p. : ISBN 0-86003-070-9 LC Card 87-12627 DDC 338.5/024/658 19
HD30.22 .R39 1987

Managerial economics . Truett, Lila J. (Lila Jane) Cincinnati , c1988. xi, 564 p. : ISBN 0-538-08890-7 LC Card 87-60268 DDC 338.5/024658 19
HD30.22 .T78 1988

MANAGERIAL ECONOMICS - CANADA.
Daly, D. J. (Donald James), 1922- Managerial macroeconomics . Homewood, Ill. , 1988. xvi, 383 p. : ISBN 0-256-06000-2 LC Card 87-80950 DDC 339/.024658 19
HD30.22 .D35 1988

MANAGERIAL ECONOMICS - CONGRESSES.
Mainstreams in industrial organization /. Dordrecht , Boston , 1986. 2 v. (x, 465 p.) ; ISBN 90-247-3363-4 LC Card 86-12345 DDC 338.6 19
HD29 .M25 1986 ***NYPL [JLE 87-457]***

MANAGERIAL ECONOMICS - ECONOMETRIC MODELS.
Broer, D. P. Neoclassical theory and empirical models of aggregate firm behaviour /. Dordrecht , Boston , 1987. 343 p. : ISBN 90-247-3412-6 LC Card 86-23485 DDC 338.5 19
HD30.22 .B76 1987

MANAGERIAL ECONOMICS - HISTORY.
Eugen Schmalenbach . Stuttgart , 1984. xvii, 478 p. : ISBN 3-8202-0295-1 LC Card 84-215889
HF5616.G3 E93 1984

MANAGERIAL ECONOMICS - SWEDEN.
Holmquist, Carin, 1948- Förhandla mer räkna mindre /. Stockholm [1984] 124 p. : ISBN 91-38-90409-8 : LC Card 84-241380
HD30.22 .H65 1984

Managerial job change . Nicholson, Nigel. Cambridge [Cambridgeshire] , New York , 1988. xi, 274 p. : ISBN 0-521-33459-4 LC Card 87-11752 DDC 331.12/72 19
HD38.2 .N53 1988

Managerial macroeconomics . Daly, D. J. (Donald James), 1922- Homewood, Ill. , 1988. xvi, 383 p. : ISBN 0-256-06000-2 LC Card 87-80950 DDC 339/.024658 19
HD30.22 .D35 1988

Managerial marketing . Bell, Martin L. New York , c1988. xviii, 708 p. : ISBN 0-444-01215-X LC Card 87-22306 DDC 658.8 19
HF5415.13 .B434 1988

A managerial profile . Hildebrandt, Herbert William, 1931- Ann Arbor, MI , c1985. 31 p. ; ISBN 0-87712-248-2 (pbk.) LC Card 86-621187 DDC 331.4/816584/00973 19
HD6054.4.U6 H55 1985

Managerial psychology . Leavitt, Harold J. Chicago , 1988. x, 353 p. : ISBN 0-226-46973-5 : LC Card 87-16820 DDC 158.7 19
HF5548.8 .L35 1988

The manager's advisor /. Brownstone, David M. New York , c1987. vii, 296 p. ; ISBN 0-8144-7682-1 (pbk.) : LC Card 87-47712 DDC 658.4 19
HD38.2 .B75 1987

A manager's guide to productivity, quality circles, and industrial robots /. Katzan, Harry. New York , c1985. vii, 136 p. : ISBN 0-442-24823-7 LC Card 84-25739 DDC 658.5 19
HD56 .K377 1985 ***NYPL [JLE 86-4510]***

Managers in Hungary . Magyar Kereskedelmi Kamara. [Budapest?] , 1986. 368 p. ; ISBN 963-7073-09-4 (pbk.) LC Card 87-137498 DDC 658/.0025/439 19
HD38.25.H9 M34 1986

Managing a development company . Suchman, Diane R. Washington, D.C. [1987] v, 179 p. ; ISBN 0-87420-672-3 (pbk.) LC Card 87-82097 DDC 333.3/8/068 19
HD1390 .S93 1987

Managing big business : essays from the Business history review / edited by Richard S. Tedlow and Richard R. John, Jr. Boston, Mass. : Harvard Business School Press, c1986. xxvii, 425 p. ; 25 cm. Includes bibliographies and index. ISBN 0-87584-142-2 LC Card 86-7683 DDC 338.6/44/0973 19
1. Corporations - United States - History. 2. Big business - United States - Management - History. I. Tedlow, Richard S. II. John, Richard R., 1959-. III. Business history review.
HD2785 .M353 1986 ***NYPL [JLE 87-1360]***

Managing business and public policy . Aram, John D., 1942- Marshfield, Mass. , c1986. xv, 736 p. : ISBN 0-582-98830-6 LC Card 85-16955 DDC 338.973 19
HD3616.U47 A73 1985
NYPL [JLE 86-2593]

Managing business communciations . Bogert, Judith B. W., 1941- Englewood Cliffs, NJ , c1988. xiv, 434 p. : ISBN 0-13-548629-7 (pbk.) : LC Card 87-3568 DDC 658.4/5 19
HF5718 .B597 1988

Managing by the numbers . Meek, Christopher. Reading, Mass. , c1988. ix, 293 p. : ISBN 0-201-16129-X : LC Card 87-16088 DDC 338.7/4/0973 19
HD70.U5 M413 1988

Managing canal irrigation . Chambers, Robert, 1932- Cambridge [Cambridgeshire] , New York , 1988. p. cm. ISBN 0-521-34554-5 LC Card 87-16738 DDC 333.91/3/0954 19
HD1741.I29 C45 1988

Managing careers in organizations /. Feldman, Daniel C. Glenview, Ill. , c1988. 249 p. : ISBN 0-673-18562-1 (pbk.) : LC Card 87-16580 DDC 650.1/4 19
HF5549 .F386 1988

Managing cash flow /. Kelly, John M. New York , 1986. xii, 210 p. : ISBN 0-531-15509-9 LC Card 86-5657 DDC 658.1/5244 19
HG4028.C45 K453 1986
NYPL [JLE 86-4460]

Managing competitive intelligence . Morse, Diane McGinty. Menlo Park, Calif. , c1985. 36 p. : LC Card 87-404501 DDC 658.4/7 19
HD38.7 .M674 1985

Managing computer impact . Bjørn-Andersen, Niels. Norwood, N.J. , c1986. viii, 248 p. : ISBN 0-89391-358-8 LC Card 85-30754 DDC 658/.05 19
HD30.2 .B55 1986 ***NYPL [JLE 86-2806]***

Managing construction worldwide / edited by Peter R. Lansley and Peter A. Harlow. London ; New York : E. & F.N. Spon, 1987. p. cm. Includes bibliographies and indexes. CONTENTS. - v. 1. Systems for managing construction -- v. 2. Productivity and human factors in construction -- v. 3. Construction management and organisation in perspective. ISBN 0-419-14030-1 (set) LC Card 87-20545 DDC 624/.068 19
1. Construction industry - Management - Congresses. 2. Construction industry - Management - Case studies - Congresses. I. Lansley, Peter R. II. Harlow, P. A. (Peter Alan).
HD9715.A2 M296

Managing construction worldwide .
(v. 1) Systems for managing construction /. London , New York , 1987. p. cm. ISBN 0-419-14000-X LC Card 87-20546 DDC 624/.068 s 624/.068 19
HD9715.A2 M296 vol. 1

(v. 2) Productivity and human factors in construction /. London , New York , 1987. p. cm. ISBN 0-419-14010-7 LC Card 87-20547 DDC 624/.068 s 624/.068/3 19
HD9715.A2 M296 vol. 2

(v. 3) Construction management and organisation in perspective /. London , New York , 1987. p. cm. ISBN 0-419-14020-4 LC Card 87-20548 DDC 624/.068 s 624/.068 19
HD9715.A2 M296 vol. 3

Managing corporate benefit plans, 1986 /. Corporate Benefits Management Conferences (1986 : Phoenix, Ariz., etc.) Brookfield, Wis. , 1986. x, 129 p. : ISBN 0-89154-318-X (pbk.) : LC Card 87-403111 DDC 332.6/7254 19
HD7105.45.U6 C67 1986

Managing corporate data centers : COBOL restructuring. Boston, MA (200 Portland St., Boston 02114) : Yankee Group, c1987. ii, 34 p. : ill. ; 28 cm. At head of title: Communications/Information Systems. "Information systems." "April 1987." LC Card 87-148811 DDC 658/.055133 19
1. Electronic data processing departments - Management. 2. COBOL (Computer program language). I. Communications/Information Systems (Firm : Yankee Group).
HF5548.2 .M2955 1987

Managing cultural differences /. Harris, Philip R. (Philip Robert), 1926- Houston , c1987. xiii, 609 p. : ISBN 0-87201-161-5 LC Card 86-25618 DDC 658.1/8 19
HD62.4 .H37 1987

Managing economic policy change . Lamb, Geoffrey, 1944- Washington, D.C., U. S.A. [1987] x, 27 p. ; ISBN 0-8213-0921-8 (pbk.) LC Card 87-14824 DDC 338.9 19
HD87 .L36 1987

Managing export entry and expansion : concepts and practice / edited by Philip J. Rosson, Stanley D. Reid. New York : Praeger, 1987. xx, 439 p. : ill. ; 25 cm. Includes bibliographies and indexes. ISBN 0-275-92361-4 (alk. paper) : LC Card 86-30330 DDC 658.8/48 19
1. Export marketing. 2. Export sales. I. Rosson, Philip J. II. Reid, Stanley D.
HF1009.5 .M345 1987

Managing financial institutions . Gardner, Mona J. Chicago , c1988. xii, 795 p. : ISBN 0-03-005479-6 LC Card 86-32805 DDC 332.1/068/1 19
HG1615.25 .G37 1988

Managing for Uncle Sam . Reischl, Dennis K. Huntsville, Ala. , c1986. ix, 271 p. : ISBN

0-936295-01-5 (pbk.) : LC Card 87-115055 DDC 353.001/7 19
HD8005.2.U5 R45 1986

Managing human productivity . Holoviak, Stephen J. New York , 1987. xiii, 216 p. : ISBN 0-275-92481-5 (alk. paper) : LC Card 86-25247 DDC 658.3/14 19
HF5549.2.U5 H65 1987

Managing human resources . Eimicke, Victor W. Oxford [Oxfordshire] , New York , 1987. x, 211 p. : ISBN 0-08-034768-1 (U. S.) : LC Card 86-25273 DDC 658.3 19
HF5549 .E44 1987

Managing human resources in small and mid-sized companies /. Arthur, Diane. New York, NY , c1987. x, 278 p. ; ISBN 0-8144-5884-X LC Card 87-47716 DDC 658.3 19
HF5549 .A955 1987

Managing human services personnel /. Pecora, Peter J. Newbury Park, Calif. , c1987. 176 p. : ISBN 0-8039-2685-5 (pbk.) LC Card 86-27995 DDC 658.3 19
HF5549 .P36 1987

Managing industrial change in Western Europe / edited by François Duchêne and Geoffrey Shepherd. London ; New York : F. Pinter, 1987. xii, 247 p. ; 24 cm. Includes bibliographies and index. ISBN 0-86187-281-9 : LC Card 87-21875 DDC 338.94 19
1. Industry and state - Europe. I. Duchêne, François. II. Shepherd, Geoffrey, 1943-.
HD3616.E8 M36 1987

Managing industrial crises . Shrivastava, Paul. New Delhi, India , 1987. 196 p. : ISBN 81-7094-000-1 : LC Card 87-902160 DDC 363.1/79 19
HD7269.C452 I5269 1987

Managing microcomputer security . Schabeck, Timothy A. Port Jefferson Station, N.Y. (492 Old Town Rd., Port Jefferson Station 11776) , c1986. 1 v. (various pagings) : LC Card 86-216667 DDC 658.4/78 19
HF5548.37 .S33 1986

Managing new product innovations /. Souder, Wm. E. (William E.) Lexington, Mass. , c1987. xviii, 251 p. : ISBN 0-669-10809-X (alk. paper) LC Card 85-40104 DDC 658.5/75 19
HD69.N4 S634 1987

Managing new products . Kuczmarski, Thomas D., 1951- Englewood Cliffs, N.J. , c1988. xv, 304 p. : ISBN 0-13-550716-2 LC Card 87-26208 DDC 658.5/75 19
HF5415.153 .K83 1988

Managing organizational change /. Connor, Patrick E. New York , 1988. xii, 192 p. : ISBN 0-275-92335-5 (alk. paper) : LC Card 87-12475 DDC 658.4/06 19
HD58.8 .C653 1988

Managing organizational change . Fallik, Fred. Philadelphia , 1988. p. cm. ISBN 0-85066-430-6 : LC Card 87-18027 DDC 658.3 19
HF5548 .F274 1988

Managing organizational innovation . Johnson, Bonnie McDaniel, 1944- New York , 1987. xiv, 242 p. ; ISBN 0-231-06398-9 LC Card 87-307 DDC 652/.5 19
HF5548.115 .J64 1987

Managing our natural resources /. Camp, William G. Albany, N.Y. , c1988. p. cm. ISBN 0-8273-2986-5 LC Card 87-25056 DDC 333.7/0973 19
HC103.7 .C33 1988

Managing paddy-rice business of small farmers . Gaikwad, V. R., 1933- Bombay , 1986. xxiii, 239 p. : ISBN 0-86132-129-4 : LC Card 86-903247 DDC 334/.68318/0954 19
HD9066.A7 G35 1986

Managing profits, profitability & productivity in public sector banking /. Chopra, Kiran. Jalandhar , 1987. 320 p. : ISBN 81-7072-012-5 : LC Card 87-901014 DDC 332.1/0954 19
HG3284 .C56 1987

Managing projects in organizations . Frame, J. Davidson. San Francisco , 1987. xvii, 240 p. : ISBN 1-555-42031-1 (alk. paper) LC Card 86-33707 DDC 658.4/04 19
HD69.P75 F72 1987

Managing public money . Swain, David, 1942- Lanham, MD , c1987. x, 221 p. : ISBN 0-8191-6505-0 (alk. paper) : LC Card 87-14261 DDC 350.72 19
HJ141 .S93 1987

Managing public transit strategically . Fielding, Gordon J. San Francisco , 1987. xxii, 270 p. : ISBN 1-555-42068-0 (alk. paper) LC Card 87-45497 DDC 388.4/068 19
HE4301 .F54 1987

Managing quality . Garvin, David A. New York , London , c1988. xiv, 319 p. ; ISBN 0-02-911380-6 LC Card 87-15145 DDC 658.5/62 19
HF5415.157 .G37 1988

Managing real estate taxes /. Ferguson, Jerry T., 1938- Westport, Conn. , 1986. x, 185 p. ; ISBN 0-89930-106-1 (lib. bdg. : alk. paper) LC Card 85-6360 DDC 343.7305/46 347.303546 19
HJ4181 .F47 1986 ***NYPL [JLE 86-2439]***

Managing regulatory reform . Goodman, Marshall R. New York , 1987. xvi, 236 p. : ISBN 0-275-92472-5 (alk. paper) : LC Card 87-2436 DDC 338.973 19
HD3616.U47 G67 1987

Managing risk . Grose, Vernon L., 1928- Englewood Cliffs, N.J. , c1987. xii, 404 p. : ISBN 0-13-551110-0 : LC Card 87-12309 DDC 658 19
HD61 .G76 1987

Managing risk in mortgage portfolios /. Williams, Alex O., 1934- New York , c1987. xx, 161 p. : ISBN 0-89930-058-8 (lib. bdg. : alk. paper) LC Card 87-2497 DDC 332.63/244 19
HG4655 .W55 1987

Managing rural development with small farmer participation /. Bryant, Coralie. West Hartford, CT. , c1984. xiii, 79 p. : ISBN 0-931816-52-1 (pbk.) LC Card 84-4445 DDC 307.7/2 19
HD1417 .B79 1984 ***NYPL [JLE 87-1352]***

Managing rural infrastructure . Hackett, Judith C. Lexington, Ky. , c1986. iii, 36 p. : ISBN 0-87292-070-4 (pbk.) : LC Card 87-404481 DDC 363/.0973 19
HD3888 .H27 1986

Managing single-family homes /. Holland, Barbara Kamanitz. Chicago, Ill. , c1987. xiv, 155 p. ; ISBN 0-912104-92-9 (pbk.) LC Card 87-81672 DDC 333.33/8 19
HD1394 .H63 1987

Managing smart . Brief, Arthur P., 1946- Lexington, Mass. , c1987. x, 164 p. ; ISBN 0-669-12654-3 (alk. paper) LC Card 85-45978 DDC 658.3 19
HD31 .B7396 1987

Managing staff reductions in corporations /. Harrison, Clifford E., 1931- Ann Arbor, Mich. , c1986. vi, 138 p. : ISBN 0-8357-1758-5 (alk. paper) LC Card 86-11223 DDC 658.3/134 19
HF5549.5.D55 H37 1986
NYPL [JLE 86-3391]

Managing strategy in the real world . Ellis, R. Jeffery. Lexington, Mass. , c1988. xviii, 340 p. : ISBN 0-669-15898-4 (alk. paper) LC Card 87-4259 DDC 658.4/012 19
HD30.28 .E45 1988

Managing stress /. Weiss, Donald H., 1936- New York, NY , c1987. 55 p. ; ISBN 0-8144-7673-2 (pbk.) : LC Card 86-47825 DDC 158.7 19
HF5548.85 .W39 1987

Managing take-off in fast growth companies : innovation in entrepreneurial firms / edited by Raymond W. Smilor and Robert L. Kuhn. New York : Praeger, c1986. x, 191 p. : ill. ; 24 cm. (Praeger special studies. Praeger scientific) Includes bibliographies and index. ISBN 0-03-005709-4 (alk. paper) : LC Card 85-16745 DDC 658.4/2 19
1. Industrial management - Addresses, essays, lectures. 2. Leadership - Addresses, essays, lectures. I. Smilor, Raymond W. II. Kuhn, Robert Lawrence.
HD31 .T24 1986 ***NYPL [JLE 86-1303]***

Managing technological innovation /. Davis, Donald D., 1950- San Francisco , 1986. xxi, 302 p. : ISBN 1-555-42008-7 LC Card 86-15378 DDC 658.5/14 19
HD45 .D34 1986 ***NYPL [JLE 87-862]***

Managing the behavioral dynamics of internal auditing /. Wilson, James A., 1928- Altamonte Springs, Fla. [1985] xii, 112 p. : ISBN 0-89413-130-3 (pbk.) LC Card 85-169744 DDC 657/.458/019 19
HF5668.25 .W53 1985 ***NYPL [JLE 86-4318]***

Managing the changing work force . Carlson, Richard C. Menlo Park, Calif. (333 Ravenswood Ave., Menlo Park 94025-3476) , c1984. 44 p. : LC Card 86-212936 DDC 658.3 19
HD5706 .C29 1984

Managing the corporate dream . Torbert, William R., 1944- Homewood, Ill. , c1987. xxiv, 250 p. ; ISBN 0-87094-922-5 LC Card 86-72274
NYPL [JLE 87-1258]

Managing the financial function.
(no. 6) Davey, Patrick J. High interest rates and tight money. [New York, 1969] 25 p. LC Card 70-9411 DDC 332.8/0973
HB545 .D38

(report no. 6) Davey, Patrick J. High interest rates and tight money. [New York, 1969] 25 p. LC Card 70-9411 DDC 332.8/0973
HB545 .D38

Managing the media . Evans, Fred J. New York , 1987. xvii, 172 p. : ISBN 0-89930-156-8 (lib. bdg. : alk. paper) : LC Card 86-25736 DDC 659.2 19
HD59 .E93 1987

Managing the new careerists /. Derr, C. Brooklyn (Clyde Brooklyn) San Francisco , 1986. xxii, 288 p. ; ISBN 0-87589-677-4 LC Card 85-45901 DDC 658.3/02 19
HF5549.2.U5 D47 1986
NYPL [JLE 86-2427]

Managing the one-person business /. Parson, Mary Jean. New York , 1987. xii, 274 p. ; ISBN 0-396-09149-0 (pbk.) : LC Card 87-20069 DDC 658/.022 19
HD8036 .P37 1987

Managing the UK economy : current controversies / edited by Grahame Thompson, Vivienne Brown, and Rosalind Levačić. Cambridge, UK : Polity Press, 1987. xxvii, 328 p. : ill. ; 24 cm. "Based on the Open University social science course D210 Introduction to economics, first presented in 1985"--T.p. verso. "Published ... in association with Basil Blackwell"--T.p. verso. Includes bibliographies and index. ISBN 0-7456-0316-5 : LC Card 86-26860 DDC 338.941 19
1. Great Britain - Economic policy - 1945-. 2. Unemployment - Great Britain - Effect of inflation on. 3. Keynesian economics. 4. Chicago school of economics. I. Thompson, Grahame. II. Brown, Vivienne. III. Levačić, Rosalind.
HC256.5 .M392 1987

Managing through people / Dale Carnegie & Associates, Inc. ; editorial assistance, Arthur R. Pell. Newly rev. ed. Garden City, NY (1475 Franklin Ave., Garden City 11530) : The Associates, c1987. 345 p. ; 23 cm. Includes bibliographical references and index. LC Card 87-167705 DDC 658.4 19
1. Management. I. Pell, Arthur R. II. Dale Carnegie & Associates.
HD31 .M29427 1987

Managing to keep the customer . Desatnick, Robert L. San Francisco , 1987. xvi, 163 p. ; ISBN 1-555-42027-3 (alk. paper) LC Card 86-21399 DDC 658.8/12 19
HF5415.5 .D47 1987

Managing with micros . Lewis, Colin David. Oxford, England , 1984. 200 p. : LC Card 85-103102 DDC 658/.054 19
HF5548.2 .L425 1984 ***NYPL [JLE 86-2215]***

Managing with style . Rowe, Alan J. San Francisco , 1987. xviii, 225 p. : ISBN 1-555-42074-5 (alk. paper) LC Card 87-45570 DDC 658.4/03 19
HD30.28 .R676 1987

MANAGING YOUR BOSS.
Bern, Paula. How to work for a woman boss, even if you'd rather not /. New York , c1987. ix, 207 p. ; ISBN 0-396-08839-2 : LC Card 86-16735 DDC 650.1/3 19
HF5548.83 .B48 1987 ***NYPL [JLE 87-1439]***

Brahmstedt, W. T. (William T.), 1924- The courtiers of American business /. Palm Springs, Calif. , c1987. 190 p. : ISBN 0-88280-118-X (pbk.) : LC Card 86-29078 DDC 650.1/3 19
HF5386 .B777 1987

Grove, Andrew S. One-on-one with Andy Grove . New York , c1987. 235 p. ; ISBN 0-399-13250-3 : LC Card 86-30483 DDC

650.1/3 19
HF5548.83 .G77 1987

Hochheiser, Robert M., 1935- How to work for a jerk /. New York , 1987. 227 p. ; ISBN 0-394-74777-1 (pbk.) : LC Card 86-40163 DDC 650.1/3 19
HF5548.83 .H63 1987

King, Patricia, 1941- Never work for a jerk! /. New York , 1987. 356 p. ; ISBN 0-531-15522-6 LC Card 86-29014 DDC 650.1/3 19
HF5548.83 .K56 1987

Norris, Kenneth E. Winning at work . Blue Ridge Summit, PA , c1987. viii, 116 p. ; ISBN 0-8306-3077-5 : LC Card 86-27359 DDC 650.1 19
HF5548.83 .N67 1987

Managing your business with Multiplan . Witkin, Ruth K. Redmond, Wash. , 1987. xv, 525 p. ; ISBN 0-914845-94-2 (pbk.) : LC Card 87-7773 DDC 005.36/9 19
HF5548.4.M74 W57 1987

MANAGING YOUR MONEY (COMPUTER PROGRAM)
Weinberg, Mark D. Using Managing Your Money /. Indianapolis, Ind. , c1987. xviii, 422 p. : ISBN 0-88022-277-8 (pbk.) : LC Card 86-62530 DDC 332.024/0028/55369 19
HG179 .W42 1987

Managing your renovation or move to new offices /. Weber, Robert E. New York , 1987. xii, 242 p. : ISBN 0-89930-245-9 (lib. bdg. : alk. paper) LC Card 86-30583 DDC 658.2/3 19
HF5547.2 .W42 1987

Manasov, M. A. Kuba v mezhdunarodnom sotsialisticheskom razdelenii truda /. Moskva , 1986. 146 p. : LC Card 86-232928
HF1500.5.E852 K83 1986

Manatzment, hoi leitourgies tou kai ho cheirismos tou anthrōpinou paragonta . Boukēs, Sōtos D., 1933- Athēna , 1985. 58 p. : LC Card 86-160168
HF5549 .B7727 1985

MANCHE (FRANCE) - COMMERCE.
Gibon, Comte de (Paul), 1863-1929. Etudes sur le renouveau économique dans le centre et le sud de la Manche . Caen , 1919. 176 p. ; LC Card 85-666346
HC277.M26 G52x 1919

MANCHE (FRANCE) - ECONOMIC CONDITIONS.
Gibon, Comte de (Paul), 1863-1929. Etudes sur le renouveau économique dans le centre et le sud de la Manche . Caen , 1919. 176 p. ; LC Card 85-666346
HC277.M26 G52x 1919

MANCHE (FRANCE) - INDUSTRIES.
Gibon, Comte de (Paul), 1863-1929. Etudes sur le renouveau économique dans le centre et le sud de la Manche . Caen , 1919. 176 p. ; LC Card 85-666346
HC277.M26 G52x 1919

Manchester Business School (University of Manchester) Ohinata, Yo. The lending procedures of commercial banks in the United States, the United Kingdom, Japan, Germany and France /. [Manchester] [1983] 138 p. ; ISBN 0-903808-34-X (pbk.) LC Card 86-132282 DDC 332.1/753 19
HG1642.U5 O35 1983

Manchester papers on development / University of Manchester, Department of Administrative Studies, 0260-8235 . (issue no. 9 (May 1984)) Transnationals and development. Manchester, England , 1984. i, 64 p. ; ***NYPL [JLD 86-3224]***

Manchester, Paul B. Are we on the road to a balanced budget? : the budget for fiscal year 1987 and the forecasting record under the Budget Act of 1974 : a staff study / prepared for the use of the Subcommittee on Economic Resources, Competiveness [sic], and Security Economics of the Joint Economic Committee, Congress of the United States. Washington : U. S. G.P.O. : For sale by the Supt. of Docs., Congressional Sales Office, U. S. G.P.O., 1986. v, 18 p. : ill. ; 24 cm. (S. prt. . 99-180) At head of title: 99th Congress, 2d session. Joint committee print. Distributed to some depository libraries in microfiche. Shipping list no.: 86-780-P. Includes bibliographical references. Item 1000-B, 1000-C (microfiche) LC Card 86-603373 DDC 353.0072/2 19
1. Budget deficits - United States. 2. Government spending policy - United States. 3. Economic forecasting - United States. 4. United States - Economic conditions - 1981-. I. United States. Congress. Joint Economic Committee. Subcommittee on Economic Resources, Competitiveness, and Security Economics. II. Title. III. Series.
HJ2052 .M365 1986

Mancini, Andrea, 1954- La contabilità analitica dei costi : un'esperienza pilota nel comune di Roma / di Andrea Mancini. [Torino] : La Rivista trimestrale : distribuzione, C.I.D.S., 1986. 53 p. : ill. ; 24 cm. (Quaderni di AREA . 3) Cover title. "Supplemento al n. 1-2/1986 della Rivista trimestrale." ISBN 88-85851-00-2 : LC Card 87-114718
1. Cost accounting - Case studies. 2. Municipal services - Italy - Rome - Accounting - Case studies. 3. Nursery schools - Italy - Rome - Cost of operation - Accounting - Case studies. 4. School children - Food - Italy - Rome - Costs - Accounting - Case studies. I. Rivista trimestrale (Turin, Italy : 1985). N. 1-2, 1986 (Supplement). II. Title. III. Series.
HF5686.C8 M265 1986

Mancini, Giuseppe, 1940- NATO Advanced Study Institute on Intelligent Decision Support in Process Environments (1985 : San Miniato, Italy) Intelligent decision support in process environments /. Berlin , New York , c1986. xv, 524 p. : ISBN 0-387-13922-2 (U. S.) LC Card 86-6742 DDC 658.4/03 19
T57.95 .N37 1985 ***NYPL [JFE 86-4847]***

Mancuso, Joseph. How to start, finance, and manage your own small business / Joseph R. Mancuso. Rev. ed. Englewood Cliffs, N.J. : Prentice-Hall, c1984. vi, 392 p. : ill. ; 23cm. "A Spectrum book"-- Includes Bibliographical references and index. ISBN 0-13-434879-6 LC Card 84-13411 DDC 658/.022 19
1. Small business - Management. 2. Small business - Finance. I. Title.
HD62.7 .M365 1984
NYPL [*R-Econ. 84-3832]

Manczinger, Józsefné. Ajánlás a vállalatok stratégiai tervező munkájához / [Manczinger Józsefné, Rózsa Jánosné és Salamonné Huszty Anna]. [Budapest] : Ipargazdasági Intézet, [1984] 97 p. ; 29 cm. "1984. március." Includes bibliographies. LC Card 86-148677
1. Strategic planning. I. Rózsa, Jánosné. II. Salamonné Huszty, Anna. III. Title.
HD30.28 .M346 1984

Mandal, S. K. (Sushil Kumar), 1954- Regional disparities and imbalances in India's planned economic development / S.K. Mandal. New Delhi : Deep & Deep Publications, [1986], c1987. 380 p. ; 23 cm. Study of Bihar. Bibliography: p. [368]-377. Includes index. LC Card 87-900589 DDC 338.954 19
1. India - Economic conditions - Regional disparities. I. Title.
HC435.2 .M335 1987

Mandatory financial information and capital market equilibrium in Belgium /. Hawawini, Gabriel A. New York , 1987. 271 p. : ISBN 0-8240-7852-7 (alk. paper) : LC Card 87-54 DDC 332.63/222/09493 19
HG5553 .H39 1987

Mandel, Ernest.
"El capital" : cien años de controversias en torno a la obra de Karl Marx / Ernest Mandel ; [traducción de Adriana Sandoval, Stella Mastrangelo y Martí Soler].1a ed. en español. México, D.F. : Siglo Veintiuno Editores, 1985. 242 p. ; 21 cm. (Biblioteca del pensamiento socialista. Serie Estudios críticos) Includes bibliographical references. ISBN 968-231-127-6 LC Card 86-158367
1. Marx, Karl, 1818-1883. Kapital. 2. Capital. 3. Economics. I. Title. II. Series.
HB501.M37 M355 1985

La crise 1974-1982 : les faits, leur interprétation marxiste / Ernest Mandel. Paris : Flammarion, c1985. 352 p. : ill. ; 18 cm. (Champs, 0151-8089 . 151.) Includes bibliographical references. ISBN 2-08-081151-7
1. Economic history - 1971- - Addresses, essays, lectures. 2. Business cycles - History - 20th century - Addresses, essays, lectures. 3. Marxian economics - Addresses, essays, lectures. I. Title.
NYPL [JLC 86-204]

Mandela, Audrey L. Electronic mail update : intercompany networks and data communications / by Audrey L. Mandela. Boston, Mass. (200 Portland St., Boston 02114) : Yankee Group, c1986. ii, 135 p. : ill. ; 28 cm. Spine title: Data Communications. At head of title: Communications/Information Systems. "November 1986." LC Card 87-124538 DDC 384.3/4/0973 19
1. Electronic mail equipment industry - United States. 2. Market surveys - United States. I. Communications/Information Systems (Firm : Yankee Group). II. Title.
HD9696.M353 U56 1986

MANDELA, NELSON, 1918-
Mandela, Winnie. Part of my soul /. Harmondsworth , 1985. 163 p., [8] p. of plates : ***NYPL [Sc C 86-121]***

Mandela, Winnie. Part of my soul went with him /. New York , 1985, c1984. 163 p., [8] p. of plates : ISBN 0-393-02215-3 : LC Card 85-21632 DDC 968/.00496 19
DT779.955.M36 A35 1985
NYPL [JFD 86-7717]

Mandela, Winnie.
Part of my soul / Winnie Mandela ; edited by Anne Benjamin ; adapted by Mary Benson. Rev. ed. Harmondsworth : Penguin Books, 1985. 163 p., [8] p. of plates : ill., ports. ; 20 cm.
1. Mandela, Winnie. 2. Mandela, Nelson, 1918-. 3. Banned persons (South Africa) - Biography. 4. Blacks - South Africa - Politics and government. 5. Blacks - South Africa - Social conditions. 6. Civil rights movements - South Africa. I. Benjamin, Anne. II. Benson, Mary. III. Title. ***NYPL [Sc C 86-121]***

Part of my soul went with him / Winnie Mandela ; edited by Anne Benjamin and adapted by Mary Benson. 1st American ed. New York : Norton, 1985, c1984. 163 p., [8] p. of plates : ill. ; 20 cm. ISBN 0-393-02215-3 : LC Card 85-21632 DDC 968/.00496 19
1. Mandela, Winnie. 2. Mandela, Nelson, 1918-. 3. Banned persons (South Africa) - Biography. 4. Blacks - South Africa - Politics and government. 5. Blacks - South Africa - Social conditions. 6. Civil rights movements - South Africa. I. Benjamin, Anne. II. Benson, Mary. III. Title.
DT779.955.M36 A35 1985
NYPL [JFD 86-7717]

MANDELA, WINNIE.
Mandela, Winnie. Part of my soul /. Harmondsworth , 1985. 163 p., [8] p. of plates : ***NYPL [Sc C 86-121]***

Mandela, Winnie. Part of my soul went with him /. New York , 1985, c1984. 163 p., [8] p. of plates : ISBN 0-393-02215-3 : LC Card 85-21632 DDC 968/.00496 19
DT779.955.M36 A35 1985
NYPL [JFD 86-7717]

Mandeville, T. D. The Trouble with technology . London , 1983. x, 224 p. : ISBN 0-86187-285-1 ***NYPL [JLE 86-1128]***

El Manejo de los riesgos de la informática : una guía para quienes formulan las políticas de la empresa / Price Waterhouse ; traducción de la Federación Latinoamericana de Bancos. Bogotá, D.E. : La Federación : Editorial Kelly, [1984?] 61 p. : ill. ; 24 cm. (Biblioteca FELABAN. Cuadernos . 19) LC Card 85-183870
1. Business - Data processing. I. Price Waterhouse (Firm). II. Series: Cuadernos de la Biblioteca FELABAN , no. 19.
HF5548.2 .M2985 1984

Maness, Terry S. Introduction to corporate finance / Terry S. Maness. New York : McGraw-Hill, c1988. xxiii, 551 p. : ill. ; 25 cm. (McGraw-Hill series in finance) Includes indexes. ISBN 0-07-039934-4 : LC Card 87-21449 DDC 658.1/5 19
1. Corporations - Finance. I. Title.
HG4026 .M355 1988

Maney, Tracy. A management guide to artificial intelligence / Tracy Maney and Ian Reid. Aldershot, Hants, England : Gower, c1986. viii, 188 p. ; 23 cm. Includes bibliographical references and index.
1. Management - Data processing. 2. Business - Data processing. I. Reid, Ian. II. Title.
NYPL [JLD 87-862]

Manezhev, S. A. (Sergeĭ Aleksandrovich) Ėkonomicheskie otnoshenii͡a KNR so stranami

IUgo-Vostochnoĭ Azii / S.A. Manezhev. Moskva : Izd-vo "Nauka," Glav. red. vostochnoĭ lit-ry, 1980. 191 p. ; 20 cm. At head of title: Akademiia nauk SSSR. Institut Dal'nego Vostoka. Bibliography: p. 188-191. LC Card 81-130904
1. China - Foreign economic relations - Asia, Southeastern. 2. Asia, Southeastern - Foreign economic relations - China. 3. China - Commerce - Asia, Southeastern. 4. Asia, Southeastern - Commerce - China. I. Title.
HF1604.Z4 A7856 1980

Manfra, Modestino R. Formazione ed evoluzione della scienza economica / Modestino R. Manfra ; prefazione di Piero Barucci. [Firenze] : Le Monnier, [1985] viii, 163 p. ; 24 cm. (Le Monnier università . 5) Includes bibliographical references and index. ISBN 88-00-86023-0 : LC Card 86-118265
1. Economics - History. I. Title.
HB75 .M247 1985

Mangan, John. Work, leisure, and technology /. Melbourne, Australia , 1986. vi, 273 p. : ISBN 0-582-71151-7 (pbk.) LC Card 87-105477 DDC 303.4/83/0994 19
HD6331.2.A8 W67 1986

Mangham, I. L. Organization analysis and development . Chichester [West Sussex] , New York , c1987. xiii, 269 p. ; ISBN 0-471-91227-1 : LC Card 86-26713 DDC 658.4/06 19
HD58.7 .O669 1987

Mangold, Nancy R. (Nancy Rueyhwa), 1949- Changing auditors and the effect on earnings, auditors' opinions, and stock prices / by Nancy R. Mangold. Ann Arbor, Mich. : UMI Research Press, c1987. viii, 165 p. ; 24 cm. (Research for business decisions. no. 93) Revision of thesis (Ph. D.). Bibliography: p. [157]-160. Includes index. ISBN 0-8357-1786-0 (alk. paper) LC Card 87-19128 DDC 338.7/4/0973 19
1. Corporations - United States - Auditing. 2. Disclosure in accounting. 3. Corporate profits - United States - Accounting. 4. Auditors' reports - United States. 5. Stocks - Prices - United States. I. Title.
HF5686.C7 M3295 1987

Mangum, Stephen L. Hsieh, Ching-Yao, 1917- A search for synthesis in economic theory /. Armonk, N.Y. , c1985. xii, 268 p. : ISBN 0-87332-328-9 LC Card 84-29816 DDC 330.1 19
HB71 .H73 1985 *NYPL [JLE 87-315]*

Manhattan Institute for Policy Research. London Conference on Taxes and Growth (1986) London Conference on Taxes and Growth . New York, NY [1986] 61 p. ; LC Card 87-404887 DDC 339.5/25 19
HJ2279 .L655 1986

MANHATTAN (NEW YORK, N.Y.)
Baxter, Ellen. The Heights . New York, N.Y. [1986] 69 leaves : LC Card 87-401534 DDC 363.5/8 19
HD7287.96.U62 N683 1986

MANICALAND PROVINCE (ZIMBABWE) - ECONOMIC CONDITIONS - STATISTICS.
Report on demographic socio-economic survey . Harare, Zimbabwe [1984 or 1985] 18 p. : LC Card 86-980590 DDC 304.6/096891 19
HA4702.Z9 M356 1984

MANICALAND PROVINCE (ZIMBABWE) - POPULATION - STATISTICS.
Report on demographic socio-economic survey . Harare, Zimbabwe [1984 or 1985] 18 p. : LC Card 86-980590 DDC 304.6/096891 19
HA4702.Z9 M356 1984

MANICALAND PROVINCE (ZIMBABWE) - SOCIAL CONDITIONS - STATISTICS.
Report on demographic socio-economic survey . Harare, Zimbabwe [1984 or 1985] 18 p. : LC Card 86-980590 DDC 304.6/096891 19
HA4702.Z9 M356 1984

Manifest für eine Neue Europäische Linke /. Glotz, Peter, 1939- Berlin , c1985. 112, [1] p. ; ISBN 3-88680-162-4 LC Card 86-100474 DDC 320.5/31/094 19
HX238.5 .G56 1985 *NYPL [JLD 87-1162]*

Manifiesto contra el hambre en el mundo. Madrid : IEPALA : Fundamentos, c1985. 95 p. ; 20 cm. (Problemas internacionales . 11) Bibliography: p. 77-82. ISBN 84-85436-23-7 (IEPALA) LC Card 86-165078
1. Food supply - Developing countries. 2. Food relief - Developing countries. I. Instituto de Estudios Políticos para América Latina y Africa. II. Series.
HD9018.D44 M35 1985
NYPL [JLD 87-1535]

MANIFOLD BUSINESS FORMS INDUSTRY.
Formsmark II, the short-run forms market /. Arlington, VA (1730 N. Lynn St., Arlington 22209) , c1986. 107 leaves : LC Card 87-146216 DDC 381/.4565129 19
HD9800.7.A2 F67 1986

Manik Jain. see **Jain, Manik, 1938-**

MANIKINS (FASHION MODELS) see **MODELS, FASHION.**

The manipulated mind . Winn, Denise, 1950- London , c1983. 217 p. ; ISBN 0-86304-025-X LC Card 83-184383 DDC 302.3/3 19
BF632.5 .W56 1983 *NYPL [JFD 87-1158]*

MANIPUR (INDIA) - CENSUS, 1981.
Census of India, 1981. Delhi , <1985-1987. v. in : LC Card 87-915019 DDC 304.6/0954/17021 19
HA4587.M36 C46 1985

Manitoba. Economic Development Advisory Board. An Inquiry into the future of public and private pension plans . Winnipeg [1976] xiii, 54 p. ; LC Card 85-103269
HD7130.M36 I56 1976

MANITOBA - ECONOMIC POLICY.
Barber, Clarence L., 1917- Manitoba's interest in and attitude towards a proposed Canada-United States free trade area . [Winnipeg , 1985] 35 leaves : LC Card 86-175828 DDC 382/.0971/073 19
HF1479 .B37 1985

Manitoba. Manitoba Natural Resources. Five year report to the legislature on fisheries, year ending 1983-84. [Winnipeg, Man.] : Manitoba Natural Resources, [1984?] 57 p. : ill. ; 28 cm. Cover title. LC Card 87-164861 DDC 338.3/713/097127 19
1. Fisheries - Manitoba. 2. Fishery policy - Manitoba. I. Title.
HD9464.C22 M365 1984

Manitoba. Municipal Planning Branch. Rural municipality of Hanover . [Winnipeg, Man.] [1976?] iv, 55 p. : LC Card 82-219722
HC118.H34 R87 1976

Manitoba's interest in and attitude towards a proposed Canada-United States free trade area . Barber, Clarence L., 1917- [Winnipeg , 1985] 35 leaves : LC Card 86-175828 DDC 382/.0971/073 19
HF1479 .B37 1985

MANIZALES, COLOMBIA - ECONOMIC CONDITIONS.
Giraldo Zuluaga, Luisa Fernanda, 1957- La colonización antioqueña y la fundación de Manizales /. Manizales, Colombia [1983] 217 p. : LC Card 84-107745
HD519.C35 G57 1983

MANIZALES, COLOMBIA - HISTORY.
Giraldo Zuluaga, Luisa Fernanda, 1957- La colonización antioqueña y la fundación de Manizales /. Manizales, Colombia [1983] 217 p. : LC Card 84-107745
HD519.C35 G57 1983

MANJO (CAMEROON) - POPULATION.
Barbier, J. C. Migrations et développement . Paris , 1983, c1984. 372 p. : ISBN 2-7099-0711-7
NYPL [M-11 4991 no.170]

Manley, Michael, 1924- Up the down escalator : development and the international economy : a Jamaican case study / Michael Manley. Washington, D.C : Howard University Press, 1987. xv, 332 p. ; 22 cm. Bibliography: p. 295-313. Includes index. ISBN 0-88258-112-0 : LC Card 87-3872 DDC 338.97292 19
1. Jamaica - Economic conditions. 2. Jamaica - Economic policy. 3. Economic development. I. Title.
HC154 .M34 1987

Mann, H. S. (Haracharan Singh), 1922- Halting the march : eco-development in the Thar / H.S. Mann and Ishwar Prakash. [New Delhi] : Dept. of Environment, Govt. of India : Environmental Services Group, World Wildlife Fund-India, [1983] 35, [1] p., [4] p. of plates : ill. ; 27 cm. Bibliography: p. 34-[36] LC Card 86-204352 DDC 338.1/0954/4 19
1. Thar Desert (India and Pakistan) - Economic conditions. 2. Agriculture - Economic aspects - Thar Desert (India and Pakistan). 3. Agricultural productivity - Thar Desert (India and Pakistan). I. Prakash, Ishwar. II. Title.
HC437.T47 M36 1983

Mann, Hugo, 1954- Theorie und Politik der Steuerreform in der Demokratie / Hugo Mann. Frankfurt am Main ; New York : P. Lang, c1987. vi, 264 p. ; 22 cm. (Hohenheimer volkswirtschaftliche Schriften, 0721-3085 . Bd. 4) Bibliography: p. 240-264. ISBN 3-8204-9464-2 LC Card 87-407788 DDC 336.2/00943 19
1. Taxation - Germany, West. I. Title. II. Series.
HJ2687 .M3 1987

Mann, Michael. Gender and stratification /. Cambridge, CB, UK , Oxford, OX, UK , 1986. viii, 271 p. ; ISBN 0-7456-0167-7 : LC Card 85-28342 DDC 305.3 19
HQ1075 .G46 1986 *NYPL [JLE 86-2966]*

Mann, Michael, 1942- Europe and the rise of capitalism /. Oxford [Oxfordshire] , New York, NY, USA , 1987. p. cm. ISBN 0-631-15006-4 : LC Card 87-12293 DDC 330.94 19
HC240.9.C3 E97 1987

Mannarelli M., Virgilio B. Organización institucional del sector agrícola / Virgilio B. Mannarelli M. Santiago, Chile : Centro de Estudios del Desarrollo, 1985. 81, [3] p. : ill. ; 28 cm. (Materiales para discusión . no. 96) Bibliography: p. [83]-[84] LC Card 86-115545 DDC 338.1/883 19
1. Agriculture and state - Chile. 2. Agricultural administration - Chile. 3. Agriculture - Economic aspects - Chile. 4. Agriculture - Research - Chile. 5. Agricultural extension work - Chile. 6. Associations, institutions, etc. - Chile. I. Centro de Estudios del Desarrollo (Santiago, Chile). II. Title. III. Series.
HD1878 .M35 1985

Männel, Wolfgang. Die Wahl zwischen Eigenfertigung und Fremdbezug : theoretische Grundlagen, praktische Fälle / Wolfgang Männel.2., überarbeitete und erw. Aufl. Stuttgart : Poeschel, c1981. xvi, 406 p. : ill. ; 25 cm. Cover title: Eigenfertigung und Fremdbezug. Bibliography: p. [376]-390. Includes index. ISBN 3-7910-0270-8 LC Card 83-167804
1. Subcontracting. 2. Make-or-buy decisions. I. Title. II. Title: Eigenfertigung und Fremdbezug.
HD2381 .M32 1981

Mannen in een vrouwenberoep . Boon, Irene. Den Haag , 1984. 139 p. : ISBN 90-6252-426-5 : LC Card 84-243593
Z682.4.W65 B66 1984 *NYPL [JLG 87-4]*

MANNEQUINS. see **MODELS, FASHION.**

Manners, Gerald. Office policy in Britain : a review / Gerald Manners and Diana Morris. Norwich, UK : Geo Books, c1986. viii, 158 p. : ill. ; 22 cm. Includes bibliographies. ISBN 0-86094-212-0 LC Card 87-143633 DDC 338.6/042 19
1. Offices - Location - Government policy - Great Britain - History. 2. Offices - Location - Government policy - England - London Metropolitan Area - History. I. Morris, Diana. II. Title.
HF5547.25 .M36 1986

MANNHEIM (GERMANY) - HISTORY - SOURCES.
Säumt keine Minute! . Mannheim , c1986. xiii, 683 p. : ISBN 3-923003-36-6 LC Card 87-115249 DDC 331/.0943/46 19
HD8460.M35 S28 1986

Mannheimer geographiesche Arbeiten. see **Mannheimer geographische Arbeiten.**

Mannheimer Bankenforum (1985) Risikokapital über die Börse : Mannheimer Bankenforum, Symposium 25.1.1985 / herausgegeben von W. Gerke. Berlin ; New York : Springer-Verlag, c1986. x, 190 p. ; 25 cm. Papers presented at the symposium. Bibliography: p. [173]-190. ISBN 0-387-16671-8 (U. S.) LC Card 86-225903
1. Stock-exchange - Germany (West) - Congresses. 2. Capital market - Germany (West) - Congresses. 3. Risk - Germany (West) - Congresses. I. Gerke, Wolfgang. II. Title.
HG5492 .M35 1985

Mannheimer geographische Arbeiten.
(Heft 19) Miodek, Wolfgang. Innerstädtische Umzüge und Stadtentwicklung in Mannheim, 1977-1983 . Mannheim , 1986. 244 p. : ISBN 3-923750-18-8 : LC Card 86-181776
HD7288.92.G32 M355 1986

(Heft 20) Hasenfratz, Eberhard. Gemeindetypen der Pfalz . Mannheim , 1986. 197 p. : ISBN 3-923750-19-6 LC Card 86-185643
HB3596.R46 H37 1986

Manning, Brigette. Frontrunners. Chapel Hill, NC , 1987. 1 videocassette (28 min., 50 sec.) : LC Card 87-706853 DDC 338.6 11
HD9940

Manning, Willard G. Health insurance and the demand for medical care . Santa Monica, CA , 1987. p. cm. ISBN 0-8330-0864-1 LC Card 87-17587 DDC 368.3/82/00973 19
HD7102.U4 H413 1987

Mannur, H. G. The terms of trade and Third World countries / by H.G. Mannur. Pulau Pinang : School of Comparative Social Sciences, Universiti Sains Malaysia, 1978. ii, 35 p. ; 28 cm. (Discussion paper series . [no. 4] = [no. 4]) LC Card 84-940687
1. Developing countries - Commerce. 2. Malaysia - Commerce. I. Series: Discussion paper series (Universiti Sains Malaysia. Pusat Pengajian Ilmu Kemasyarakatan) , no. 4. II. Title.
HF4055 .M36 1978

Manoel, Alvaro. Política agrícola, eficiência e concentração na agricultura brasileira : um estudo do setor canavieiro paulista / Alvaro Manoel ; orientador, Roberto Mendonça de Barros. São Paulo : Instituto de Pesquisas Econômicas/USP, 1986. 180 p. : ill. ; 22 cm. (Série Ensaios econômicos . no. 54) Abstract in English. Originally presented as the author's thesis (doctoral)--Universidade de São Paulo, 1985. Bibliography: p. 171-180. LC Card 86-234338
1. Agriculture and state - Brazil. 2. Farms, Size of - Brazil. 3. Agricultural credit - Brazil. 4. Sugarcane industry - Brazil - São Paulo (State). 5. Alcohol fuel industry - Brazil - São Paulo (State). I. Series: Ensaios econômicos (Universidade de São Paulo. Instituto de Pesquisas Econômicas) , 54. II. Title.
HD1873 .M35 1986

Manohar Rao, M. J. Filtering and control of macroeconomic systems : a control system incorporating the Kalman filter for the Indian economy / M.J. Manohar Rao. Amsterdam ; New York : North-Holland ; xii, 279 p. : ill. ; 24 cm. (Contributions to economic analysis. 160) Bibliography: p. 261-271. Includes indexes. ISBN 0-444-70188-5 (Elsevier Science Pub. Co.) LC Card 86-32928 DDC 339.5/0954 19
1. India - Economic policy - 1980- - Econometric models. 2. Macroeconomics. 3. Filters (Mathematics). 4. Control theory. I. Title. II. Series.
HC435.2 .M34 1987

Manohar Singh Gill. see Gill, Manohar Singh, 1936-

Manolov, Angel. Sotsialno-ikonomicheski problemi na izpolzuvane truda na mladezhite / A. Manolov i kolektiv. Sofiia : Nauchnoizsledovatelski institut po truda, 1984. 93 p. ; 22 cm. Summary in German and Russian. Includes bibliographical references. LC Card 86-226913
1. Youth - Employment - Bulgaria. I. Nauchnoizsledovatelski institut po truda. II. Title.
HD6276.B82 M36 1984

Manolov, Manol Dimitrov. Narodnaia Respublika Bolgariia--40 let po puti sotsialisticheskogo voskhoda / [avtory M. Manolov i D. Fratev ; redaktor L. Mikhaĭlova]. [Bulgaria? : s.n., 1983?] [48] p. : col. ill. ; 22 x 24 cm. Translated from Bulgarian. Cover title: NRB--40 let po puti sotsialisticheskogo voskhoda. LC Card 85-133679
1. Bulgaria - Economic conditions - 1944-. I. Fratev, D. II. Mikhaĭlova, L. III. Title. IV. Title: Narodna Respublika Bolgariia--sorok let po puti sotsialisticheskogo voskhoda. V. Title: NRB--40 let po puti sotsialisticheskogo voskhoda.
HC403 .M36 1983

Manona, C. W. The Sullivan principles at Ford--audit a [microform] /. [s.l.] , 1981. 16 p. ;
*NYPL [*ZT-1745 no.32]*

MANORS - ESTONIA - NAMES - REGISTERS.
Eesti ala mõisate nimestik /. Tallinn , 1981. 191 p. ; LC Card 82-143283
HD1329.E75 E37 1981
NYPL [JFD 86-6806]

Manpower and migration . Seccombe, Ian J. [Durham, England] , c1981. viii, 110 p. : LC Card 84-673623
HD5812.25.A6 S42x 1981
NYPL [JLD 86-2457]

MANPOWER - BRAZIL.
Vieira, Cláudio Afonso. Urbanização e custo de reprodução da força de trabalho /. São Paulo , 1984. 175 p., [5] folded leaves of plates :

Manpower conversion in defence related industry . Wilke, Peter. Hamburg [1986] 62 p. : LC Card 86-212660 DDC 331.25/924 19
HC79.D4 W55 1986

MANPOWER DEVELOPMENT AND TRAINING. see OCCUPATIONAL TRAINING.

MANPOWER - ITALY - HISTORY.
Brunt, P. A. Italian manpower, 225 B.C.-A.D. 14 /. Oxford [Oxfordshire] , 1987, c1971. xxi, 762 p. ; ISBN 0-19-814283-8 : LC Card 87-1644 DDC 304.6/0945 19
HB3599 .B77 1987

MANPOWER PLANNING - AFRICA - CONGRESSES.
JASPA Steering Group Meeting on Priority Employment Policies and Projects for Africa (1985 : Addis Ababa, Ethiopia) Report of JASPA Steering Group Meeting on Priority Employment Policies and Projects for Africa. Addis Ababa , 1986. 43 leaves ; LC Card 87-980227 DDC 331.12/042/096 19
HD5837.A6 J37 1985

MANPOWER PLANNING - CONGRESSES.
Symposium on Strategic Human Resource Planning Applications (1985 : University of Pennsylvania, Philadelphia, Pa.) Strategic human resource planning applications /. New York , c1987. viii, 257 p. ; ISBN 0-306-42561-0 LC Card 87-11141 DDC 331.11 19
HF5549.5.M3 S95 1985

MANPOWER PLANNING - GERMANY, WEST.
Hemmers, K. (Karlheinz) Planung des Personalbedarfs in indirekten Bereichen /. Berlin , New York , 1986. viii, 141 p. : ISBN 0-387-16702-1 (U. S.) : LC Card 86-200805
HF5549.5.M3 H46 1986

MANPOWER PLANNING - GREAT BRITAIN.
UK occupation and employment trends to 1990 . London , Boston , 1986. xxiv, 249 p. : ISBN 0-408-02980-3 : LC Card 86-13617 DDC 331.12/0941 19
HD5765.A6 U38 1986 NYPL [JLE 86-4156]

MANPOWER PLANNING - INDIA.
Gangadhara Rao, M. Human resources management in Indian railways /. Delhi , 1986. xvi, 245 p. ; ISBN 81-7049-004-9 : LC Card 86-900747 DDC 385/.068/3 19
HD8039.R12 I437 1986
NYPL [JLE 86-4104]

MANPOWER PLANNING - INDIA - CONGRESSES.
Recent experiences in human resources development /. New Delhi , c1986. xvi, 448 p. ; ISBN 81-204-0120-4 : LC Card 86-902270 DDC 331.11/0954 19
HF5549.5.M3 R38 1985

Workshop on Promotion of Self-Employment in Rural Areas (1982 : Allahabad, India) Workshop on Promotion of Self-employment in Rural Areas, Allahabad, 26-30 November 1982 . New Delhi [1983] iii, 186 p. ; LC Card 83-906671 DDC 338.6/42 19
HD8037.I4 W67 1982

MANPOWER PLANNING - INDIA, NORTHEASTERN - CONGRESSES.
The Pattern & problems of population in north-east India /. New Delhi , 1986. xv, 433 p. ; ISBN 81-85024-03-0 : LC Card 86-902123 DDC 304.6/0954/1 19
HA4587.I44 P37 1986

MANPOWER PLANNING - PHILIPPINES.
Andres, Tomas Quintin D., 1942- Human resource training & development /. Quezon City , c1980. viii, 134 p. : LC Card 82-102431 DDC 658.3/12404/09599 19
HF5549.5.T7 A64 1980 NYPL [JLD 87-935]

MANPOWER PLANNING - SOUTH AFRICA.
Verslag van die Nasionale Mannekragkommissie oor indiensopleiding in die Republiek van Suid-Afrika, 1980/81 =. [Pretoria] [1984] 267 p. ; ISBN 0-621-08502-2 : LC Card 86-109914
HF5549.5.T7 V44 1984

MANPOWER PLANNING - UNITED STATES.
Committee for Economic Development. Research and Policy Committee. Work and change . New York, N.Y. , 1987 printing. iv, 76 p. : ISBN 0-87186-083-X (pbk.) : LC Card 87-694 DDC 331.12/042/0973 19
HD5724 .C6647 1987

Holoviak, Stephen J. Managing human productivity . New York , 1987. xiii, 216 p. : ISBN 0-275-92481-5 (alk. paper) : LC Card 86-25247 DDC 658.3/14 19
HF5549.2.U5 H65 1987

MANPOWER POLICY - AFRICA - COLLECTED WORKS.
Les Programmes spéciaux d'emploi et de formation de la jeunesse ... Addis Abéba , 1985- v. <1-6 > : LC Card 86-981200
HD6276.A3 P76 1985

MANPOWER POLICY - AFRICA - CONGRESSES.
JASPA Steering Group Meeting on Priority Employment Policies and Projects for Africa (1985 : Addis Ababa, Ethiopia) Report of JASPA Steering Group Meeting on Priority Employment Policies and Projects for Africa. Addis Ababa , 1986. 43 leaves ; LC Card 87-980227 DDC 331.12/042/096 19
HD5837.A6 J37 1985

MANPOWER POLICY - AFRICA, NORTH.
La Politique de l'emploi-formation au Maghreb, 1970-1980 /. Paris , 1982. 472 p. : ISBN 2-222-03122-2 LC Card 84-222103 DDC 331.11/0961 19
HD5838 .P65 1982

MANPOWER POLICY - ALGERIA.
Voss, Timm. Die algerisch-französische Arbeitsmigration . Königstein/Ts. , 1981. xiii, 193 p. : ISBN 3-7756-6937-X : LC Card 81-176949 DDC 331.6/2/65044 19
HD8438.A4 V67 1981 NYPL [JLD 86-2466]

MANPOWER POLICY - ARABIAN PENINSULA.
Osama, Abdul Rahman, 1942- The dilemma of development in the Arabian Peninsula /. London , c1987. 203 p. ; ISBN 0-7099-4240-0 : LC Card 86-29149 DDC 338.953 19
HC415.3 .O83 1987

MANPOWER POLICY - AUSTRALIA.
Aboriginal employment and training programs . Canberra , 1985. ix, 453 p. ; ISBN 0-644-00712-5 (pbk.) LC Card 87-107756 DDC 331.25/92/089011094 19
HD5850.A6 A26 1985

MANPOWER POLICY - AUSTRALIA - WESTERN AUSTRALIA.
Wiechec, Jane. Employment, the community link /. Perth, W.A. [1986] 108 p. ; LC Card 87-158082 DDC 331.12/5/09941 19
HD5850.W4 W54 1986

MANPOWER POLICY - BENIN.
Emploi d'abord . Addis Abeba , 1982. xxxviii, 499 p. ; LC Card 84-983423
hD5846.3.A6 E47 1982

MANPOWER POLICY - BRAZIL.
Campino, Antonio Carlos Coelho. Recursos e desempenhos dos programas de formação de mão-de-obra /. São Paulo, SP , Brasília, DF , 1985. 78 p. ; ISBN 85-21-30276-2 LC Card 85-187505
HD5754 .C34 1985

Emprego urgente /. Curitiba , 1984. vii, 75 p. ; LC Card 86-177208
HD5713 .E47 1984

O Mercado de trabalho no Brasil . São Paulo , 1986. 263 p. : LC Card 86-221361
HD5754 .M47 1986

MANPOWER POLICY - BRAZIL - RIO GRANDE DO NORTE.
Rio Grande do Norte (Brazil) Programas especiais do governo, 1983-1987. Natal , 1984. [83] leaves ; LC Card 87-403924 DDC 331.12/0981/32 19
HC188.R38 P76 1984

MANPOWER POLICY - BRAZIL - RIO GRANDE DO SUL.
O Emprego no Rio Grande do Sul . Porto

Alegre , 1985. 163 p. : LC Card 85-207909
HD5755.R54 E46 1985

MANPOWER POLICY - CALIFORNIA - SAN DIEGO COUNTY.
Goldman, Barbara. Final report on the San Diego job search and work experience demonstration /. New York, N.Y. (3 Park Ave., New York 10016) , c1986. xliv, 269 p. : LC Card 87-118376 DDC 331.12/042/0979498 19
HD5713.6.U542 S395 1986

MANPOWER POLICY - COLOMBIA.
Transición demográfica y oferta de fuerza de trabajo en Colombia /. [Bogotá], República de Colombia , 1986. 2 v. : ISBN 958-95096-0-6 (set) LC Card 87-113652 DDC 331.11/09861 19
HD5757.A6 T7 1986

Yepes C., Alfonso. Del caos al orden . [S.l. , 1986] ([S.l.] : Editorial Nomos) 239 p., [1] leaf of plates : LC Card 87-400255 DDC 331.1/1/09861 19
HD5757.A6 Y46 1986

MANPOWER POLICY - CONGO (BRAZZAVILLE)
N'Dzaba, Tobi. L'enseignement technique et professionnel et la satisfaction des besoins en main-d'œuvre . Paris [1983] i, 139 p. : LC Card 85-189543
HD5845.A6 N38 1983

MANPOWER POLICY - CONGRESSES.
Employment and growth . Dordrecht , Boston , 1987. xii, 310 p. : ISBN 90-247-3514-9 LC Card 87-3184 DDC 331.11 19
HD73 .E46 1987

International Conference on Employment and Training (1985 : Perth, W.A.) Full employment, uncertain futures /. [Perth, W.A.] [1985] ix, 263 p. : LC Card 86-185208 DDC 339.5 19
HD5701.3 .I55 1985

Staat und Beschäftigung . Nürnberg , 1985. 471 p. : LC Card 86-674027
HD5713 .S72x 1985

MANPOWER POLICY - CZECHOSLOVAKIA.
Adam, Jan, 1920- Employment and wage policies in Poland, Czechoslovakia, and Hungary since 1950 /. New York , 1984. xix, 251 p. ; ISBN 0-312-24457-6 : LC Card 83-40125 DDC 331.12/042/0943 19
HD5797.7.A6 A3 1984
NYPL [JLD 86-4389]

Fusko, Zoltán. Koncepcia ďalšieho rozvoja plánovitého riadenia efektívneho využívania pracovnej sily . Bratislava , 1982. 62 p. ; LC Card 83-113861
HD5772.3.A6 F87 1982

MANPOWER POLICY - DENMARK.
Jørgensen, Henning, 1949- Arbejdsmarkedsnævn i arbejdsmarkedspolitikken /. [Aalborg] [1985?]-<[1986]. v. <1-2 > : ISBN 87-88706-12-5 LC Card 87-104729
HD5799.A6 J64 1985

MANPOWER POLICY - DEVELOPING COUNTRIES.
Kahnert, Friedrich, 1929- Improving urban employment and labor productivity /. Washington, D.C. [1987] 75 p. ; ISBN 0-8213-0908-0 (pbk.) LC Card 87-10538 DDC 331.11/09172/4 19
HD5852 .K34 1987

MANPOWER POLICY - EUROPE.
Rein, Martin. Women in the social welfare labor market /. Berlin [1985] 180 p. ; LC Card 86-213535 DDC 331.4/129136294 19
HD6134 .R45 1985

MANPOWER POLICY - EUROPE - CONGRESSES.
Centre for Employment Initiatives (Great Britain) Cooperation in the field of employment . Luxembourg , Washington, DC , 1986. 55 p. ; ISBN 92-825-6086-4 (pbk.) : LC Card 87-134296 DDC 331.12/042/094 19
HD5764.A6 C45 1986

Social security and employment /. Assen, The Netherlands , 1983. 116 p. : ISBN 90-232-2011-0 (pbk.) : LC Card 83-216203 DDC 331.12/094 19
HD7164 .S594 1983 ***NYPL [JLE 86-1107]***

MANPOWER POLICY - EUROPEAN ECONOMIC COMMUNITY COUNTRIES.
Buiren, S. van. The quantitative and qualitative significance of the emergence of local initiatives for employment creation . Luxembourg , Washington, D.C. , 1986. iii, 141, 14, [12] p. : ISBN 92-825-6048-1 (pbk.) : LC Card 86-222030 DDC 331.12/042/094 19
HD5764.5.A6 B85 1986

Gizard, Xavier. Regional development and vocational training analysis and discussion of the relationship development . Berlin , Washington, DC , 1986. 49 p. ; ISBN 92-825-5911-4 (pbk.) : LC Card 87-137374 DDC 331.25/92/094 19
HD5715.5.E8 G58 1986

Wohlers, Eckhardt. Unterschiede in der Beschäftigungsentwicklung zwischen den USA, Japan und der EG . Hamburg , 1986. 294 p. : ISBN 3-87895-307-0 LC Card 86-233505
HD5724 .W57 1986

MANPOWER POLICY - FRANCE.
Comptes de l'emploi . Paris , c1984. 219 p. : ISBN 2-11-001264-1 : LC Card 85-132416
HD5775 .C5344 1984

MANPOWER POLICY - GERMANY, EAST.
Schrimpff, Wolfgang. Heterogene Koordinationsinstrumente im Beschäftigungssystem der DDR /. Münster , 1983. xv, 360 p. : ISBN 3-7923-0505-4 LC Card 85-140056
HD5780.5.A6 S37 1983

MANPOWER POLICY - GERMANY, WEST.
Seifert, Hartmut, 1944- Öffentliche Arbeitsmarktpolitik in der Bundesrepublik Deutschland . Köln [1984] ix, 288 p. ; ISBN 3-7663-0857-2 LC Card 86-127331 DDC 331.11/0943 19
HD5779 .S34 1984

Technologische Entwicklung und Beschäftigung /. Bonn [1985] 10 p. ; LC Card 86-154491
HC290.5.T4 T44 1985

Träger, Manfred Georg. Entwicklung und Funktion des britischen und deutschen Systems der Arbeitsvermittlungs- und Berufsberatungsdienste . Nürnberg , 1981. ii, 80, 48 p. ; LC Card 82-200262 DDC 331.11/0941 19
HD5765.A6 T72 1981 ***NYPL [JLD 87-905]***

MANPOWER POLICY - GREAT BRITAIN.
Coates, Ken. Trade unions and politics /. Oxford, OX, UK , New York, NY, USA , 1986. ix, 268 p. : ISBN 0-631-13752-1 : LC Card 85-22959 DDC 322/.2/0941 19
HD6667 .C63 1986 ***NYPL [JLE 86-1729]***

Standing, Guy. Unemployment and labour market flexibility . Geneva , 1986. xi, 147 p. : ISBN 92-2-105291-5 (pbk.) : LC Card 87-114658 DDC 331.13/7941 19
HD5765.A6 S72 1986

Träger, Manfred Georg. Entwicklung und Funktion des britischen und deutschen Systems der Arbeitsvermittlungs- und Berufsberatungsdienste . Nürnberg , 1981. ii, 80, 48 p. ; LC Card 82-200262 DDC 331.11/0941 19
HD5765.A6 T72 1981 ***NYPL [JLD 87-905]***

MANPOWER POLICY - GREAT BRITAIN - HISTORY - 20TH CENTURY.
Grieves, Keith. The politics of manpower, 1914-1918 /. New York, NY , 1988. vii, 241 p. ; ISBN 0-312-01320-5 LC Card 87-20511 DDC 331.12/042/0941 19
HD5765.A6 G77 1988

MANPOWER POLICY - GUINEA-BISSAU.
Ribeiro, Sérgio. Situação e perspectivas dos recursos humanos na República da Guiné-Bissau /. Addis Ababa [1984 or 1985] 49, 19 p., [8] leaves : LC Card 85-981187 DDC 331.11/0966/57 19
HD5849.A6 R53 1984

MANPOWER POLICY - HUNGARY.
Adam, Jan, 1920- Employment and wage policies in Poland, Czechoslovakia, and Hungary since 1950 /. New York , 1984. xix, 251 p. ; ISBN 0-312-24457-6 : LC Card 83-40125 DDC 331.12/042/0943 19
HD5797.7.A6 A3 1984
NYPL [JLD 86-4389]

MANPOWER POLICY - INDIA.
Chanana, Charanjit. Industrial economics in developing countries, India . New Delhi , 1983. 113 p. : LC Card 83-903832 DDC 338.0954 19
HC435.2 .C4717 1983 ***NYPL [JLD 87-674]***

Chaudhary, S. K. Planning and employment trends in India /. New Delhi , c1987. 300 p. ; LC Card 86-903543 DDC 331.11/0954/12 19
HD5819 .C47 1987

Dāśagupta, Pānnālāla, 1909- Production by the masses . Calcutta , 1983. vi, 54 p. ; LC Card 83-906787 DDC 331.11/8/0954 19
HC440.I52 D37 1983 ***NYPL [JLD 87-708]***

MANPOWER POLICY - INDIA - BIHAR.
Chaudhary, S. K. Planning and employment trends in India /. New Delhi , c1987. 300 p. ; LC Card 86-903543 DDC 331.11/0954/12 19
HD5819 .C47 1987

MANPOWER POLICY - INDIA - STATES - CASE STUDIES.
Kohli, Atul. The state and poverty in India . Cambridge [Cambridgeshire] , New York , 1987. x, 262 p. : ISBN 0-521-32008-9 LC Card 85-25554 DDC 333.3/1/54 19
HD1333.I4 K65 1986 ***NYPL [JLD 87-1517]***

MANPOWER POLICY - JAPAN.
Wohlers, Eckhardt. Unterschiede in der Beschäftigungsentwicklung zwischen den USA, Japan und der EG . Hamburg , 1986. 294 p. : ISBN 3-87895-307-0 LC Card 86-233505
HD5724 .W57 1986

MANPOWER POLICY - KANSAS.
Kansas. Legislature. Task Force on Business Training. Report of the Task Force on Business Training of the Legislative Commission on Economic Development. [Topeka, Kansas] [1986] 1 v. (various pagings) ; LC Card 87-621700 DDC 331.25/92/09781 19
HD5715.3.K2 K37 1986

MANPOWER POLICY - KENYA.
Keller, Edmond J. (Edmond Joseph), 1942- Education, manpower, and development . Nairobi , 1980. xi, 251 p. ; LC Card 81-980037 DDC 379.676/2 19
LC95.K4 K45 1980 ***NYPL [Sc D 86-948]***

Training needs for co-operative movement staff . [Nairobi?] [1984] [166] p. : LC Card 86-980729 DDC 331.12/51334/096762 19
HD3560.5.A4 T73 1984

MANPOWER POLICY - LATIN AMERICA.
Buscando la equidad. English. In search for equity . Aldershot, Hants, England , Brookfield, USA , c1987. xvi, 249 p. ; ISBN 0-566-05537-6 : LC Card 87-21225 DDC 338.98 19
HC130.B38 B8713 1987

Meller, Patricio. Una revisión de políticas de empleo para América Latina /. Santiago, Chile , 1981. 72 leaves ; LC Card 83-182110
HD5730.5.A6 M44 1981

Vargas, Ines. The NIEO and the situatuon of workers . Oslo [1985] xiv, 290 p. ; ISBN 82-7288-121-7 (pbk.) LC Card 86-205407 DDC 331/.098 19
HD6530.5 .V36 1985

MANPOWER POLICY - MALI.
Emploi, potentialités et priorités au Mali . Addi Abeba , c1984. xix, 266 p. : ISBN 92-2-203954-8 : LC Card 85-980540
HD5847.3.A6 E47 1984
NYPL [JLE 86-484]

MANPOWER POLICY - NETHERLANDS.
Arbeidsmarkt op drift . [Amsterdam] , 1986. 190 p. : ISBN 90-6287-549-1 : LC Card 86-154853
HD5792 .A72 1986 ***NYPL [JLD 86-4417]***

MANPOWER POLICY - NORWAY.
Luihn, Hans. Arbeid og samfunn . [Oslo] , c1986. 372 p. : ISBN 82-508-0574-7 : LC Card 87-157793
HD5800.A6 L85 1986

MANPOWER POLICY - PAKISTAN.
Ghafoor, Abdul. Development of human resources . Islamabad [1984] v, ii leaves, 99 p., v, ii leaves ; LC Card 85-932024 DDC 331.11/09549/1 19
HD5819 .G48 1984

MANPOWER POLICY - PERSIAN GULF STATES.
Nadwat Tanmiyat al-Mawārid al-Basharīyah fī al-Khalīj al-ʻArabī (1975 : Bahrain) Nadwat Tanmiyat al-Mawārid al-Basharīyah fī al-Khalīj al-ʻArabī . al-Kuwayt [1975?] 361, 404 p. : LC

Card 86-964662
HD5715.5.P39 N33 1975

MANPOWER POLICY - PERU.
Empleo, salarios y distribución del ingreso . [Miraflores, Lima] , 1986. 186 p. : LC Card 87-403082 DDC 331.11/0985 19
HD5761.A6 E47 1986

MANPOWER POLICY - PHILIPPINES.
International Labour Organisation. National programme for development and training of manpower for employment, Philippines . Geneva , 1979. ii, 54 p. ; LC Card 81-140367 DDC 331.25/92/09599 19
HD5825.A6 I57 1979

MANPOWER POLICY - POLAND.
Adam, Jan, 1920- Employment and wage policies in Poland, Czechoslovakia, and Hungary since 1950 /. New York , 1984. xix, 251 p. ; ISBN 0-312-24457-6 : LC Card 83-40125 DDC 331.12/042/0943 19
HD5797.7.A6 A3 1984
NYPL [JLD 86-4389]

MANPOWER POLICY - PORTUGAL.
Moura, João. Problemas e política de emprego no continente /. Lisboa , 1977. 56 p. ; LC Card 85-214189
HD5809.A6 M68 1977

MANPOWER POLICY, RURAL - BENIN.
Jobs and Skills Programme for Africa. Eléments pour une stratégie d'emploi dans les zones rurales au Bénin . Addis Abeba [1980] xii, 70, 5 p. : LC Card 87-100360
HD5846.3.A6 J63 1980

MANPOWER POLICY, RURAL - BOTSWANA.
Gobotswang, Z. Pilot evaluation report on Mahalapye Development Trust /. Gaborone, Botswana [1982] v leaves, 61, 3 p. ; LC Card 87-122810
HD5710.85.B59 G63 1982

MANPOWER POLICY, RURAL - CUBA.
MANPOWER POLICY, RURAL - INDIA - CONGRESSES.
Training of rural youth for self-employment (TRYSEM) . Hyderabad, [India] , 1981. vii, 252 p. ; LC Card 81-904606 DDC 331.3/42492/0954 19
HD5715.5.I5 T72 1981
NYPL [JLF 86-1203]

MANPOWER POLICY, RURAL - SWITZERLAND - ZÜRICH (CANTON) - HISTORY - 18TH CENTURY.
Meier, Thomas. Handwerk, Hauswerk, Heimarbeit . Zürich , c1986. 435 p., [44] p. of plates : ISBN 3-905278-07-3 LC Card 86-227651
HD2346.S92 Z875 1986

MANPOWER POLICY - RUSSIAN S.F.S.R. - MOSCOW.
Korolev, L. P. (Leonid Pavlovich) Trudovye resursy i ikh ispolʹzovanie /. Moskva , 1982. 139 p. ; LC Card 82-158161
HD5797.M66 K67 1982

MANPOWER POLICY - RUSSIAN S.F.S.R. - MOSCOW (OBLAST)
Korolev, L. P. (Leonid Pavlovich) Trudovye resursy i ikh ispolʹzovanie /. Moskva , 1982. 139 p. ; LC Card 82-158161
HD5797.M66 K67 1982

MANPOWER POLICY - SAUDI ARABIA.
Viola, Joy Winkie. Human resources development in Saudi Arabia . Boston , c1986. xxvi, 291 p. : ISBN 0-88746-070-4 (IHRDC) LC Card 85-19694 DDC 303.4/8273/0538 19
HD5812.35.A6 V56 1986
NYPL [JLE 86-2188]

MANPOWER POLICY - SINGAPORE - ADDRESSES, ESSAYS, LECTURES.
Pang, Eng Fong. Education, manpower, and development in Singapore /. Kent Ridge, Singapore , c1982. 242 p. : ISBN 997-16-9053-5 (bound) LC Card 83-941002 DDC 331.11/09595/7 19
HD5823.A6 P35 1982 NYPL [JLD 86-2364]

MANPOWER POLICY - SOUTH AFRICA.
Black advancement in the South African economy /. Braamfontein, Johannesburg , 1986. 256 p. : ISBN 0-86954-289-3 LC Card 87-119018 DDC 331.6/9968 19
HD5842.A6 B58 1986b

South Africa. National Manpower Commission. Verslag van die Nasionale Mannekragkommissie oor 'n ondersoek na die kleinsakesektor in die Republiek van Suid-Afrika, in die besonder die faktore wat die groei en ontwikkeling daarvan kan belemmer =. [Pretoria] [1983] 58 p. ; ISBN 0-620-07511-2 LC Card 85-116407 DDC 338.6/42/0968 19
HD2346.S63 S64 1983

MANPOWER POLICY - SOVIET UNION.
Granick, David. Job rights in the Soviet Union . Cambridge , New York , 1987. ix, 344 p. ; ISBN 0-521-33295-8 LC Card 86-26392 DDC 331.11/0947 19
HD5796 .G72 1987

MANPOWER POLICY - SPAIN.
Albentosa Puche, Luis. El paro en España /. Madrid , c1983. 349 p. : ISBN 84-85719-34-4 LC Card 86-121124 DDC 331.11/0946 19
HD5807 .A44 1983 NYPL [JLC 87-37]

La Reconversión industrial, la crisis y reforma agraria. [Madrid] [1984] 148 p. : ISBN 84-398-1197-7 LC Card 86-216324
HC385 .R375 1984

MANPOWER POLICY - TANZANIA.
Employment promotion in Tanzania . Addis Ababa , 1986. ii leaves, 107 p. ; LC Card 87-980150 DDC 331.11/09678 19
HD5841.3.A6 E46 1986

MANPOWER POLICY - UKRAINE.
Upravlenie trudovymi resursami . Kiev , 1986. 238 p. ; LC Card 86-233715
HD5797.U37 U67 1986

Vosproizvodstvo trudovykh resursov /. Kiev , 1984. 177, [3] p. ; LC Card 86-189052
HD5797.U37 V67 1984

MANPOWER POLICY - UNITED STATES.
Bullock, Paul. Youth training and employment from New Deal to New Federalism /. Los Angeles , c1985. xiii, 359 p. ; ISBN 0-89215-131-1 *NYPL [JLD 86-2972]*

Committee for Economic Development. Research and Policy Committee. Work and change . New York, N.Y. , 1987 printing. iv, 76 p. : ISBN 0-87186-083-X (pbk.) : LC Card 87-694 DDC 331.12/042/0973 19
HD5724 .C6647 1987

Cook, Robert F., 1943- Public service employment . Kalamazoo, Mich. , 1985. xiii, 131 p. ; ISBN 0-88099-031-7 (pbk.) LC Card 85-22495 DDC 331.13/77/0973 19
HD5713.6.U54 C66 1985
NYPL [JLE 86-3877]

Levitan, Sar A. Working but poor . Baltimore , c1987. ix, 142 p. : ISBN 0-8018-3583-6 (alk. paper) LC Card 87-16973 DDC 362.5/0973 19
HC110.I5 L468 1987

Occupations in energy-related industries [microform] . Washington, D.C. , 1981. ca. 300 p. ; *NYPL [*XME-11,557]*

Rein, Martin. Women in the social welfare labor market /. Berlin [1985] 180 p. ; LC Card 86-213535 DDC 331.4/129136294 19
HD6134 .R45 1985

Startzel, Donna C. The CETA arts and humanities experience [microform] CETA Ahead project (Arts and humanities employment analysis and documentation) /. Columbia, Md. , 1981. 197 p. ;
*NYPL [*XME-11,320]*

Startzel, Donna C. CETA (Comprehensive Employment and Training Act) and the arts and humanities [microform] . Columbia, Md. , 1981. 160 p. ; *NYPL [*XME-11,328]*

United States. Vice President's Task Force on Youth Employment. A summary report of the Vice President's Task Force on Youth Employment. Washington , 1980. 70 p. :
NYPL [JLF 86-214]

WIN handbook. [Washington, D.C.] [1984]. 1 v. (various pagings) ; *NYPL [JLF 86-372]*

Winick, Bradley H. Making the link . [Washinton, D.C.] , c1986. i, 17 p. ; ISBN 0-88713-678-8 (pbk.) LC Card 87-106145 DDC 331.11/0973 19
HD5724 .W557 1986

Wohlers, Eckhardt. Unterschiede in der Beschäftigungsentwicklung zwischen den USA, Japan und der EG . Hamburg , 1986. 294 p. : ISBN 3-87895-307-0 LC Card 86-233505
HD5724 .W57 1986

MANPOWER POLICY - UNITED STATES - ABSTRACTS.
Kotli͡arov, Vladimir Fedorovich. Bezraboti͡tsa v SShA i ee gosudarstvenno-monopolisticheskoe regulirovanie v sovremennykh usloviiakh /. Leningrad , 1977. 18 p. ; LC Card 81-166000
HD5724 .K67 1977

MANPOWER POLICY - UZBEK S.S.R.
Shister, G. A. (Grigoriĭ Aronovich) Rukovodstvo kompartii Uzbekistana podgotovkoĭ rabochikh kadrov v usloviiakh razvitogo sotsializma /. Tashkent , 1981. 274, [2] p. ; LC Card 82-204041
HD5797.U9 S54 1981

The manpower report of KEPE . LaLonde, Robert John. Athens, Greece , c1986. 122 p. ; LC Card 86-205504 DDC 331.1/09495 19
HD5811.83.A6 L3 1986

MANPOWER UTILIZATION. see **MANPOWER POLICY; PERSONNEL MANAGEMENT.**

MANPOWER UTILIZATION PLANNING. see **MANPOWER PLANNING.**

Manrakhan, J. Mauritius. Commission of Inquiry into the Sugar Industry. The human factor, the sugar industry, and Mauritius . Port Louis, Mauritius [1984] 157 p. ; LC Card 85-980119 DDC 338.1/7361/096982 19
HD9118.M45 M33 1984a

Manring, A. B. (Alvin Benjamin), 1925- Exporting from the U. S.A. : how to enter the export market / A.B. Manring.2nd ed. Vancouver : International Self-Counsel Press ; Seattle : Self-Counsel Press, c1986. xi, 114 p. : ill. ; 28 cm. (Self-counsel series) ISBN 0-88908-919-1 (pbk.) : LC Card 86-225987 DDC 658.8/48/0973 19
1. Export marketing - United States - Handbooks, manuals, etc. 2. Export sales - United States - Handbooks, manuals, etc. I. Title. II. Title: Exporting from the USA.
HF1009.5 .M356 1986

Manring, Nancy. Alternative environmental conflict management approaches . [Ann Arbor, MI] (Dana Bldg., Ann Arbor 48109-1115) [1986] 252 p. : LC Card 86-225219 DDC 363.7/058/0973 19
HC110.E5 A643 1986

Mansberg, Ruth, 1924- Carlin, Vivian F., 1919- Where can mom live? . Lexington, Mass. , c1987. viii, 206 p. : ISBN 0-669-13665-4 (alk. paper) LC Card 86-45526 DDC 363.5/9 19
HD7287.92.U54 C37 1987

Mansbridge, Jane J. Why we lost the ERA / Jane J. Mansbridge. Chicago, Ill. : University of Chicago Press, c1986. xii, 327 p. ; 23 cm. Includes bibliographical references and index. ISBN 0-226-50358-5 (pbk.) LC Card 86-6954 DDC 305.4/2/0973 19
1. Women's rights - United States. 2. Equal rights amendments - United States. 3. Feminism - United States. I. Title. II. Title: Why we lost the E.R.A.
HQ1236.5.U6 M37 1986
NYPL [JLE 86-4474]

Mansfield, Edwin. Microeconomics : theory, applications. 6th ed. New York : Norton, c1988. p. cm. Bibliography: p. Includes index. ISBN 0-393-95635-0 LC Card 87-22131 DDC 338.5 19
1. Microeconomics. I. Title.
HB172 .M36 1988

Mansfield, W. R. (Willard Ridgway) A management crisis in Natal : a question of competition / W.R. Mansfield. [Durban, South Africa] : University of Durban-Westville, [1985 or 1986] 26 p. ; 21 cm. Cover title. "Inaugural address delivered at the University of Durban-Westville on 20 August 1985." Bibliography: p. 24-26. LC Card 87-400770 DDC 338.0968 19
1. Industrial productivity - South Africa. 2. Automation - South Africa. 3. South Africa - Economic conditions - 1961-. I. Title.
HC905.Z9 I526 1985

Mansion, J. E. (Jean Edmond), 1870-1942. Harrap's new standard French and English dictionary /. London , 1980-1981. 4 v. ; ISBN 0-245-50972-0 (v.1)

Manske, Fred A., 1939- Secrets of effective leadership / Fred A. Manske, Jr. 1st ed. Memphis, TN : Leadership Education and Development, 1987. ix, 206 p. : ill. ; 25 cm. Bibliography: p. 193-198. Includes index. ISBN 0-943703-00-X LC Card 87-16870 DDC 658.4/09 19
1. Leadership. 2. Executive ability. I. Title.
HD57.7 .M37 1987

MANSLAUGHTER. see **MURDER.**

Mansner, Markku. Suomalaista yhteiskuntaa rakentamassa : Suomen Työnantajain Keskusliitto 1940-1956 / Markku Mansner. Helsinki : Teollisuuden Kustannus, [1984] 552 p., [4] p. of plates : ill. ; 26 cm. Summary in English and Swedish. Bibliography: p. 533-549. Includes index. ISBN 951-9240-75-6 LC Card 85-130291
1. Suomen Työnantajain Keskusliitto - History. 2. Industrial relations - Finland - History. 3. Labor and laboring classes - Finland - History. 4. Finland - Economic conditions. I. Suomen Työnantajain Keskusliitto. II. Title.
HD8533 .M345 1984

Manston, Peter B., 1951-
[Flea markets, antique fairs, and auctions of Britain]
Manston's flea markets, antique fairs, and auctions of Britain : including where to find markets, how to ship items, clear customs, and much more / Peter B. Manston. Sacramento, Calif., U. S.A. : Travel Keys ; New York, N.Y. : Distributed by St. Martin's Press, c1987. 277 p. : ill. ; 19 cm. "A Travel key guide." Includes index. ISBN 0-931367-10-7 (pbk. : alk. paper) : LC Card 87-16221 DDC 381/.1 19
1. Flea markets - Great Britain. 2. Antique dealers - Great Britain. 3. Auctions - Great Britain. I. Title. II. Title: Flea markets, antique fairs, and auctions of Britain.
HF5482 .M3125 1987

[Flea markets, antique fairs, and auctions of Germany]
Manston's flea markets, antique fairs, and auctions of Germany : including where to find markets, how to ship items, clear customs, and much more / Peter B. Manston. Sacramento, Calif., U. S.A. : Travel Keys ; New York, N.Y. : Distributed by St. Martin's Press, c1987. 297 p. : ill. ; 19 cm. Spine title: Manston's flea markets of Germany. "A Travel key guide." Includes index. ISBN 0-931367-08-5 (pbk.) : LC Card 86-30908 DDC 381/.1 19
1. Flea markets - Germany (West). 2. Antiques - Germany (West) - Exhibitions. 3. Auctions - Germany, West. I. Title. II. Title: Flea markets, antique fairs, and auctions of Germany. III. Title: Antique shows. IV. Title: Manston's flea markets of Germany.
HF5482 .M3135 1987

[Flea markets, antique shows, and auctions of France]
Manston's flea markets, antique shows, and auctions of France : including where to find markets, how to ship items, clear customs, and much more / by Peter B. Manston. Sacramento, Calif., U. S.A. : Travel Keys ; New York, N.Y. : Distributed by St. Martin's Press, c1987. 195 p. : ill., maps ; 19 cm. "A Travel key guide." Includes index. ISBN 0-931367-06-9 (pbk.) : LC Card 86-30909 DDC 381/.1 19
1. Flea markets - France. 2. Antiques - France - Exhibitions. 3. Auctions - France. I. Title. II. Title: Flea markets, antique shows, and auctions of France. III. Title: Antique shows.
HF5482 .M313 1987

Manston's flea markets, antique fairs, and auctions of Britain . Manston, Peter B., 1951- [Flea markets, antique fairs, and auctions of Britain.] Sacramento, Calif., U. S.A. , New York, N.Y. , c1987. 277 p. : ISBN 0-931367-10-7 (pbk. : alk. paper) : LC Card 87-16221 DDC 381/.1 19
HF5482 .M3125 1987

Manston's flea markets, antique fairs, and auctions of Germany . Manston, Peter B., 1951- [Flea markets, antique fairs, and auctions of Germany.] Sacramento, Calif., U. S.A. , New York, N.Y. , c1987. 297 p. : ISBN 0-931367-08-5 (pbk.) : LC Card 86-30908 DDC 381/.1 19
HF5482 .M3135 1987

Manston's flea markets, antique shows, and auctions of France . Manston, Peter B., 1951- [Flea markets, antique shows, and auctions of France.] Sacramento, Calif., U. S.A. , New York, N.Y. , c1987. 195 p. : ISBN 0-931367-06-9 (pbk.) : LC Card 86-30909 DDC 381/.1 19
HF5482 .M313 1987

Manston's flea markets of Germany. Manston, Peter B., 1951- [Flea markets, antique fairs, and auctions of Germany.] Manston's flea markets, antique fairs, and auctions of Germany . Sacramento, Calif., U. S.A. , New York, N.Y. , c1987. 297 p. : ISBN 0-931367-08-5 (pbk.) : LC Card 86-30908 DDC 381/.1 19
HF5482 .M3135 1987

Mantel, Ana María Martirena- see **Martirena-Mantel, Ana María.**

Mantero, Osvaldo. Cogestión en la empresa : consideraciones acerca de un modelo para Venezuela / Osvaldo Mantero.2a ed. Caracas, Venezuela : Instituto Latinoamericano de Investigaciones Sociales : Distribuido por Editorial Nueva Sociedad, [1986] 215 p. : ill. ; 22 cm. Bibliography: p. 203-215. ISBN 0-9806771-1-3 LC Card 87-401945 DDC 658.3/152/0987 19
1. Management - Venezuela - Employee participation. I. Title.
HD5660.V4 M36 1986

Mántey de Anguiano, M. G. Análisis microeconómico de los factores que determinan el valor de mercado de las empresas industriales mexicanas y su tasa de expansión / M.G. Mántey de Anguiano. [Mexico City] : Centro de Estudios Monetarios Latinoamericanos, Departamento de Investigaciones, [1986] iv, 63 leaves : ill. ; 28 cm. (Serie Cuadernos de investigación . núm. 8) Summaries also in English, French, and Portuguese. "Con la colaboración de Lourdes Pérez y Nora García." Includes bibliographical references. LC Card 87-400949 DDC 658.1/5/0972 19
1. Business enterprises - Mexico - Finance. 2. Capital investments - Mexico. I. Pérez, Lourdes. II. García, Nora. III. Series: Serie Cuadernos de investigación (Centro de Estudios Monetarios Latinoamericanos, Departamento de Investigaciones) , núm. 8. IV. Title.
HG4092 .M36 1986

Mantik, G. H. Lima tahun kepemimpinan Gubernur Kepala Daerah Tingkat I Sulawesi Utara, G.H. Mantik, 1980-1985. [Manado , 1985] 2 v. : LC Card 86-940586
HC448.S785 L55 1985

MANTIK, G. H.
Lima tahun kepemimpinan Gubernur Kepala Daerah Tingkat I Sulawesi Utara, G.H. Mantik, 1980-1985. [Manado , 1985] 2 v. : LC Card 86-940586
HC448.S785 L55 1985

Manton, Kenneth G. Health of an aging population . Hyattsville, Md. , Washington, D.C. , 1987. p. cm. ISBN 0-8406-0362-2 LC Card 86-600392 DDC 362.1/0723 s 362.1/9897/00973 19
HA37 .U1693 no. 25 RA408.A3

Manual básico do exportador. [São Paulo] : Secretaria da Indústria, Comércio, Ciência e Tecnologia do Estado de São Paulo : BANESPA, [1985] 270 p. : forms ; 28 cm. Cover title. "Total apoio à exportação." Bibliography: p. 270. LC Card 86-200367
1. Brazil - Commerce - Handbooks, manuals etc. 2. Export marketing - Brazil - Handbooks, manuals, etc. I. São Paulo (Brazil : State). Secretaria da Indústria, Comércio, Ciencia e Tecnologia.
HF3407 .M35 1985

Manual de cooperativismo estudiantil ecuatoriano /. Garzón L., Isaías. Riobamba, Ecuador [1983?] 244 p. : LC Card 86-134182
HD2965 .G38 1983

Manual de crédito industrial y agropecuario . Restrepo Correa, Alejandro. [Bogotá, D.E. , 1985] 270, 30, 4 p. : LC Card 86-110073
HG3751.9.C7 R47 1985

Manual de estadísticas básicas : sector industrial, información censal nacional. [México, D.F.] : Secretaría de Programación y Presupuesto, Coordinación General de los Servicios Nacionales de Estadística, Geografía e Informática, [1981- v. <1 > ; 21 x 28 cm. Chiefly tables. LC Card 86-225598 DDC 338.0972/021 19
1. Mexico - Industries - Statistics. I. Mexico. Coordinación General de los Servicios Nacionales de Estadística, Geografía e Informática.
HC135 .M2555 1981

Manual de guerrilha trabalhista . Lobos, Julio A. São Paulo , c1986. 142 p. : LC Card 87-130241 DDC 658.3/15/0981 19
HD6971 .L57 1986

Manual de hacienda pública . García Villarejo, Avelino. Madrid , c1985. 686 p. : ISBN 84-309-1197-9 LC Card 87-105048
HJ1244 .G37 1985

Manual de historia económica de El Salvador /. Luna, David Alejandro. San Salvador, El Salvador , 1986. 230 p. : LC Card 87-127350 DDC 330.97284/053 19
HC148 .L85 1986

Manual de interpretación de estados financieros / Instituto Chileno de Educación Cooperativa. [Santiago, Chile] : Ediciones Icecoop, [1984] 49 p. : ill. ; 19 cm. (Colección Formación. Serie Legislación cooperativa) LC Card 85-150204
1. Cooperative societies - Finance - Handbooks, manuals, etc. I. Instituto Chileno de Educación Cooperativa. II. Series.
HD2965 .M35 1984

Manual de orientação sindical urbana e rural . Sousa Neto, João Alves de. S. [i.e. São] Paulo [1980?] xviii, 190 p. : LC Card 85-200599
HD6615.S32 S68 1980

Manual de servicios municipales : ciclo de seminarios de la Diputación de Barcelona. 1a ed. Barcelona : Centre d'Estudis Urbanístics, Municipals i Territorials : Servei de Cooperació Municipal de la Diputació de Barcelona, 1982. 340 p. ; 19 cm. (CEUMT . 5) Includes bibliographical references. ISBN 84-500-5399-4 LC Card 82-214246 DDC 363/.0946 19
1. Municipal services - Spain - Congresses. 2. City planning - Spain - Congresses. I. Centre d'Estudis Urbanístics, Municipals i Territorials (Barcelona, Spain). II. Servei de Cooperació Municipal de la Diputació de Barcelona.
HD4687 .M36 1982 ***NYPL [JLC 86-139]***

Manual de sistema financiero . Cuervo García, Alvaro. Barcelona , 1987. 427 p. : ISBN 84-344-2013-9 LC Card 87-135198
HG186.S6 C84 1987

Manual for collective bargaining / National Construction Employers Council. Washington, D.C. (Suite 1040, 1101 15th St., N.W., Washington 20005) : NCEC, 1987. 1 v. (various pagings) ; 30 cm. LC Card 87-150563 DDC 331.8/90424/0973 19
1. Collective bargaining - Construction industry - United States - Handbooks, manuals, etc. I. National Construction Employers Council (U. S.).
HD6515.B9 M36 1987

Manual for Indian residents abroad, 1985. Puri, Vijay Kumar. Nabhi's manual for Indian residents abroad, 1985 /. New Delhi , 1985. xv, 352 p., [1] leaf of plate : LC Card 86-901951 DDC 346.54/07 345.4067 19
HG5732 .P83 1985

Manual for repackaging of information on population education. Unesco. Regional Office for Education in Asia and the Pacific. Bangkok , 1986. 94 p. : LC Card 86-915865 DDC 304.6/07/1 19
HB850 .U57 1986

Manual for the Career Assessment Inventory /. Johansson, Charles B. (Charles Berthil) [Minneapolis] , c1976. 93 p. : LC Card 86-219030
HF5381.5 .J64 1976

MANUAL LABOR - SOCIAL ASPECTS - CASE STUDIES.
Work in market and industrial societies /. Albany , c1984. viii, 316 p. ; ISBN 0-87395-810-1 LC Card 83-9267 DDC 306/.36 19
HD4901 .A659 1984 ***NYPL [JLE 86-4483]***

Manual--mercadeo de productos agrícolas de la Cuenca del Caribe /. Agricultural marketing handbook for Caribbean Basin products. Spanish. San José, Costa Rica . x, 434 p. : ISBN 92-9039-101-4 LC Card 86-204686
HD9014.C442 A4718 1986

Manual on fertilizer distribution / FAO, Fertilizer and Plant Nutrition Service, Land and Water Development Division. Rome : Food and Agriculture Organization of the United Nations, 1985. x, 114 p. : ill. ; 30 cm. (FAO fertilizer and plant nutrition bulletin . 8) ISBN 92-5-101433-7 (pbk.) LC Card 86-221068 DDC 668/.62/0688 19
1. Fertilizers - Marketing. 2. Fertilizers - Transportation. 3. Physical distribution of goods. I. Food and Agriculture Organization of the United Nations. Fertilizer and Plant Nutrition Service. II. Series.
HD9483.A2 M36 1985

Manual Unidad Agrícola Industrial para la Mujer. Unidad Agrícola Industrial para la Mujer /. [Mexico City] , 1981. 45 p. : LC Card 84-228117
HD6073.A29 M68 1981

Manuale delle simulazioni di gestione : didattica, progettazione ed esecuzioni dei business games / di Giorgio Eminente ... [et al.].Nuova ed. ampliata e aggiornata. Milano, Italy : F. Angeli, 1985. 335 p. : ill. ; 22 cm. (Azienda moderna. 164) Bibliography: p. 84. LC Card 86-187906
1. Management games. 2. Management - Simulation methods. I. Eminente, Giorgio.
HD30.26 .M36 1985

Manuale di ricerca sul lavoro e sulle organizzazioni / a cura di Domenico De Masi. 1a ed. Roma : NIS, 1985. 384 p. : ill. ; 23 cm. (Studi superiori NIS . 10.) Includes bibliographical references and index. LC Card 86-118313 DDC 306/.36/072 19
1. Labor and laboring classes - Research - Methodology. 2. Industrial sociology - Research - Methodology. 3. Industrial management - Research - Methodology. 4. Personnel research - Methodology. I. De Masi, Domenico. II. Series: Studi superiori NIS. Sociologia , 10.
HD4824 .M32 1985 ***NYPL [JLD 87-1160]***

Manuales Extebank. Serie Comercio exterior . (1) El Tráfico de perfeccionamiento . Madrid, España , 1983. 96 p. : ISBN 84-500-9221-3 LC Card 85-193715
HF1717.S7 T73 1983

Manuel suisse de l'industrie textile, de l'habillement et du cuir. Handbuch der schweizerischen Textil-, Bekleidungs- und Lederwirtschaft =. Zürich , 1986. 214 p. : ISBN 3-909214-07-X LC Card 86-221803
HD9940.S93 H36 1986

Manuelli, Rodolfo E. Exercises in dynamic macroeconomic theory / Rodolfo E. Manuelli and Thomas J. Sargent. Cambridge, Mass. : Harvard University Press, 1987. xi, 223 p. ; 24 cm. Contains answers to: Dynamic macroeconomic theory by Thomas J. Sargent. Includes bibliographies and index. ISBN 0-674-27476-8 (pbk. : alk. paper) LC Card 86-25767 DDC 339/.0729 19
1. Macroeconomics - Mathematical models. 2. Equilibrium (Economics) - Mathematical models. 3. Macroeconomics - Mathematical models - Problems, exercises. 4. Equilibrium (Economics) - Mathematical models - Problems, exercises, etc. I. Sargent, Thomas J. II. Sargent, Thomas J. Dynamic macroeconomic theory. III. Title.
HB172.5 .S27 1987 Suppl.

Manufactured export performance of Brazil . Nunnenkamp, Peter. Kiel [1986] v, 114 p. : LC Card 87-101193 DDC 382/.4567/0981 19
HF1513 .N86 1986

MANUFACTURERS' AGENTS - UNITED STATES.
Silliphant, Leigh. Making $70,000 a year as a self-employed manufacturer's representative /. Englewood Cliffs, N.J. , c1984. 204 p. ; ISBN 0-13-547687-9 (case) LC Card 83-16147 DDC 658.8/5 19
HF5422 .S54 1984 ***NYPL [JLE 86-2636]***

MANUFACTURERS - BRAZIL - BIOGRAPHY.
Campos Netto, José Candido de, 1880-1963. O cavvaliere Aristides Germani /. [Caxias do Sul, Brazil] [Porto Alegre] , 1978. 111 p. : LC Card 79-121861
HD9056.B62 C35 1978 ***NYPL [JLD 81-342]***

MANUFACTURES.
Industry in the 1980s . New York , 1985. xii, 228 p. : ISBN 92-1-106207-1 (pbk.) LC Card 86-227928 DDC 338.09 19
HD9720.5 .I53 1985

MANUFACTURES - AUTOMATION.
Vannini, Walter, 1958- L'automazione dei processi di produzione . Milano, Italy , c1985. 344 p. : LC Card 85-204836 DDC 338.4/54 19
HD9720.5 .V36 1985 ***NYPL [JLD 86-2523]***

MANUFACTURES - GERMANY - HISTORY.
Razvitie kapitalisticheskoĭ manufaktury v Anglii i Germanii XVI-XVII vv. . Moskva , 1981. 132 p. : LC Card 83-111684
HD9735.G32 R39 1981

MANUFACTURES - GREAT BRITAIN - HISTORY.
Razvitie kapitalisticheskoĭ manufaktury v Anglii i Germanii XVI-XVII vv. . Moskva , 1981. 132 p. : LC Card 83-111684
HD9735.G32 R39 1981

MANUFACTURES - MANAGEMENT.
Lubben, Richard T. Just-in-time manufacturing . New York , c1988. xiv, 246 p. : ISBN 0-07-038911-X LC Card 87-4058 DDC 658.5 19
HD9720.5 .L83 1988

Suzaki, Kiyoshi. The new manufacturing challenge . New York , London , c1987. xv, 255 p. : ISBN 0-02-932040-2 LC Card 86-33715 DDC 658.5 19
HD9720.5 .S98 1987

What every manager needs to know about manufacturing /. New York, NY [1987], c1983. 181 p. : ISBN 0-8144-7686-4 (pbk.) LC Card 87-47714 DDC 658 19
HD9720.5 .W38 1987

MANUFACTURES - QUALITY CONTROL.
Lubben, Richard T. Just-in-time manufacturing . New York , c1988. xiv, 246 p. : ISBN 0-07-038911-X LC Card 87-4058 DDC 658.5 19
HD9720.5 .L83 1988

MANUFACTURES - STATISTICS.
International comparative advantage in manufacturing . Vienna , 1986. xii, 226 p. : ISBN 92-1-106210-1 (pbk.) LC Card 86-214978 DDC 382.1/042 19
HF1412 .I57 1986

MANUFACTURES - TECHNOLOGICAL INNOVATIONS.
The Human side of advanced manufacturing technology /. Chichester [West Sussex] , New York , c1987. xi, 205 p. : ISBN 0-471-90867-3 : LC Card 86-32554 DDC 331.25 19
HD9720.5 .H85 1987

Suzaki, Kiyoshi. The new manufacturing challenge . New York , London , c1987. xv, 255 p. : ISBN 0-02-932040-2 LC Card 86-33715 DDC 658.5 19
HD9720.5 .S98 1987

Manufacturing Automation Planning Service. Manufacturing database management systems /. Boston, MA (89 Broad St., Boston 02110) , c1986. vii, 216 p. : LC Card 86-210661 DDC 381/.4500574/0973 19
HD9696.C63 U5226 1986

Manufacturing database management systems / Manufacturing Automation Planning Service. Boston, MA (89 Broad St., Boston 02110) : Yankee Group, c1986. vii, 216 p. : ill. ; 29 cm. (Industry research report) "June 1986." "Report no. 5, 1985"--Spine. Includes index. LC Card 86-210661 DDC 381/.4500574/0973 19
1. Computer industry - United States. 2. Computer software industry - United States. 3. United States - Manufactures - Management - Data processing. 4. Market surveys - United States. I. Manufacturing Automation Planning Service. II. Series.
HD9696.C63 U5226 1986

MANUFACTURING ENGINEERING. see **PRODUCTION ENGINEERING.**

Manufacturing establishments directory. Udyoga kāryālaya (utpādana garne) ko nāma sūcī =. [Kathmandu] [1985] 202 p. ; LC Card 87-901652
HD9736.N382 U39 1985

Manufacturing for competitive advantage . Gunn, Thomas G. Cambridge, Mass. , c1987. xvi, 221 p. ; ISBN 0-88730-154-1 LC Card 87-1093 DDC 658 19
HD9725 .G85 1987

Manufacturing in Kitchener-Waterloo : a long-term perspective / edited by David F. Walker. [Waterloo] : Dept. of Geography, University of Waterloo, c1987. xiii, 220 p. : ill. ; 23 cm. (Department of Geography publication series . no. 26) Bibliography: p. [211]-220. ISBN 0-921083-22-X (pbk.) LC Card 87-168616 DDC 338.4/767/0971344 19
1. Kitchener (Ont.) - Manufactures - Forecasting. 2. Waterloo (Ont.) - Manufactures - Forecasting. 3. Kitchener (Ont.) - Manufactures - History. 4. Waterloo (Ont.) - Manufactures - History. I. Walker, David F. II. Series.
HD9734.C3 K56 1987

Manufacturing industry in Greater London /. Weatheritt, L. London , c1975. ii, 26 p. ; ISBN 0-7168-0853-6 (pbk.) LC Card 82-213745
HD5766.L66 W43 1975

MANUFACTURING MANAGEMENT. see **PRODUCTION MANAGEMENT.**

Manufacturing matters . Cohen, Stephen S. New York , c1987. xiv, 297 p. : ISBN 0-465-04384-4 : LC Card 86-47737 DDC 338.4/767/0973 19
HD9725 .C58 1987

Manufacturing performance. [Canada] : Govt. of Canada, Industry, Trade and Commerce, [1977?] 18 p. : ill. ; 28 cm. (Discussion paper) LC Card 85-194098
1. Canada - Manufactures. I. Canada. Industry, Trade and Commerce. II. Series: Discussion paper (Canada. Industry, Trade and Commerce).
HD9734.C25 M36 1977

MANUFACTURING PROCESSES - AUTOMATION.
Computerized manufacturing automation [microform] . Washington, D.C. , 1984. 35 p. :
NYPL [*ZV-326 no.31]

The Human side of advanced manufacturing technology /. Chichester [West Sussex] , New York , c1987. xi, 205 p. : ISBN 0-471-90867-3 : LC Card 86-32554 DDC 331.25 19
HD9720.5 .H85 1987

Robots and automated manufacture /. London, U.K. , c1985. xii, 233 p. : ISBN 0-86341-053-7
NYPL [JSK 77-191 v.28]

Vannini, Walter, 1958- L'automazione dei processi di produzione . Milano, Italy , c1985. 344 p. : LC Card 85-204836 DDC 338.4/54 19
HD9720.5 .V36 1985 ***NYPL [JLD 86-2523]***

MANUFACTURING PROCESSES - CASE STUDIES.
Schonberger, Richard. World class manufacturing casebook . New York , London , c1987. xxvi, 253 p. : ISBN 0-02-929340-5 LC Card 86-25822 DDC 658 19
HD31 .S3386 1987

MANUFACTURING PROCESSES - ENERGY CONSERVATION.
Nosko, Herbert. Rationelle Energieverwendung im Industriebetrieb . Berlin , c1986. xiii, 289 p. : ISBN 3-503-02547-2 LC Card 86-192206
HD9502.A2 N67 1986

MANUFACTURING PROCESSES - ENERGY CONSERVATION - ENVIRONMENTAL ASPECTS.
Nosko, Herbert. Rationelle Energieverwendung im Industriebetrieb . Berlin , c1986. xiii, 289 p. : ISBN 3-503-02547-2 LC Card 86-192206
HD9502.A2 N67 1986

MANUFACTURING PROCESSES - TECHNOLOGICAL INNOVATIONS - MANAGEMENT.
Davis, Donald D., 1950- Managing technological innovation /. San Francisco , 1986. xxi, 302 p. : ISBN 1-555-42008-7 LC Card 86-15378 DDC 658.5/14 19
HD45 .D34 1986 ***NYPL [JLE 87-862]***

MANUFACTURING PROCESSES - UNITED STATES.
Gunn, Thomas G. Manufacturing for competitive advantage . Cambridge, Mass. , c1987. xvi, 221 p. ; ISBN 0-88730-154-1 LC Card 87-1093 DDC 658 19
HD9725 .G85 1987

MANUFACTURING PROCESSES - UNITED STATES - CONGRESSES.
Small Manufacturing and Process Industry Seminar (1985 : Las Vegas, Nev.) Small Manufacturing and Process Industry Seminar proceedings, September 18-20, 1985, Las Vegas, Nevada /. Falls Church, Va. , c1985. iv, 222 p. : ISBN 0-935406-71-9 (pbk.) LC Card 85-72347

DDC 338.6/42/0973 19
HD9725 .S55 1985 ***NYPL [JLD 86-2451]***

Manufacturing research perspectives, U. S.A.-Japan . U. S.A.-Japan Conference on Manufacturing Research (1986 : Tokyo, Japan) Amsterdam , New York , 1987. viii, 198 p. : ISBN 0-444-42868-2 LC Card 87-19851 DDC 338.4/767 19
HD9725 .U17 1986

MANUSCRIPT DEPOSITORIES. see **ARCHIVES.**

Manuscript post offices of New York State / edited by Henry Chlanda & Chester E. Wilcox. 3rd ed. [Richford, N.Y.?] : Empire State Postal History Society, 1984. xii, 54 p., [12] p. of plates : ill. ; 28 cm. Includes bibliographical references. LC Card 86-213682 DDC 383/.49747 19
1. Postal service - New York (State) - History. 2. Pen cancellations (Philately) - New York (State) - History. I. Chlanda, Henry. II. Wilcox, Chester E. III. Empire State Postal History Society.
HE6376.A1 N729 1984

Manuscript reports (International Development Research Centre (Canada)) Regional Workshop on Wood Energy in East Africa (1982 : Nairobi, Kenya) Proceedings of the Regional Workshop on Wood Energy in East Africa . Ottawa, Canada [1983] 241 p. : LC Card 86-185703 DDC 333.75 19
HD9769.F843 A367 1982

MANUSCRIPT REPOSITORIES. see **ARCHIVES.**

MANUSCRIPTS, ARABIC - EGYPT - FAYYUM.
Rāġib, Yūsuf. Marchands d'étoffes du Fayyoum au IIIe/IXe siècle d'après leurs archives (actes et lettres) /. Le Caire , 1982- v. : LC Card 83-156837 DDC 380.1/0962/2 19
HF366 .R34 1982 ***NYPL [*OFP 86-3324]***

MANUSCRIPTS - DEPOSITORIES. see **ARCHIVES.**

MANUSCRIPTS - REPOSITORIES. see **ARCHIVES.**

Manusevich, A. ÎA. (Aleksandr ÎAkovlevich) Murashko, G. P. (Galina Pavlovna) Politicheskai͡a bor′ba v Chekhoslovakii v 1944-1948 gg. i nat͡sionalizat͡sii͡a sredstv proizvodstva /. Moskva , 1986. 326, [2] p. ; LC Card 86-202951
HC270.28 .M87 1986

Manuskripte zur Altenpflege.
Seddig, Gert. Lehrbuch der Altenpflege. Hannover , c1983. 95 p. : ISBN 3-87870-204-3 LC Card 83-230557
HF5728.G3 S49 1983

Manutenzione e sostituzione : l'artigianato, i suoi modelli culturali, la città storica. Bologna : CLUEB, [1983] xviii, 227 p. : ill. (some col.) ; 23 cm. (IBC dossier . 17) At head of title: Regione Emilia-Romagna, Istituto per i beni artistici, culturali e naturali. Includes bibliographies. LC Card 84-142790
1. Artisans - Italy - Emilia-Romagna - Pictorial works. I. Istituto per i beni artistici, culturali, naturali della Regione Emilia Romagna. II. Series.
HD2346.I82 E45 1983

The many lives of Otto Kahn /. Matz, Mary Jane. New York [1984] x, 299 p., [8] p. of plates : ISBN 0-918728-36-3 : LC Card 83-26326 DDC 361.7/4/0924 B 19
HV28.K32 M37 1984 ***NYPL [JFD 86-2699]***

Many struggles . Sherwood, Marika. London , 1985, c1984. 138 p. : ISBN 0-946918-00-7 (pbk.) LC Card 86-110617 DDC 305.8/00941 19
HD8398.B55 S54 1985 ***NYPL [Sc D 86-815]***

Manzanal, Mabel. Lindenboim, Javier. Monetarismo y mercado de trabajo . Buenos Aires, Argentina , c1985. x, 471 p. : ISBN 950-9370-05-3 LC Card 87-122243 DDC 331.12/0982/73 19
HD5750.R56 L56 1985

Manzolini, Luigi. Nacamulli, Raoul C. D. La razionalità contrattata . Bologna , c1986. 166 p. : ISBN 88-15-01189-7 : LC Card 87-122104
HD6709 .N296 1986

Mão-de-obra de nível médio . Silveira, Maria Luiza Faraone. São Paulo , 1986. 239 p. : LC Card 87-143876 DDC 331.11/422 19
HD5754 .S55 1986

MAOISM. see **COMMUNISM.**

Mapelli, Barbara. Le 150 ore e la formazione professionale in azienda . Milano, Italy , c1985. 178 p. : LC Card 86-141990
HD5716.T242 I82 1985 ***NYPL [JFD 87-3739]***

MAPSIT (COMPUTER PROGRAM)
Lewis, Gordon H. Income transfer analysis /. New York , c1987. p. cm. ISBN 0-915163-01-2 LC Card 86-33744 DDC 362.5/82 19
HC110.I5 L48 1987

Maquila . Stoddard, Ellwyn R., 1927- El Paso, Tex. , c1987. ix, 91 p., [2] p. of plates : ISBN 0-87404-200-3 (pbk.) LC Card 86-51646 DDC 338.4/767/09721 19
HD9734.M42 S76 1987

Mar, Jerry. The Apple WordStar book / Jerry Mar. Glenview, Ill. : Scott, Foresman, c1984. 277 p. : ill. ; 23 cm. Includes index. ISBN 0-673-15992-2 (pbk.) : LC Card 84-5400 DDC 652 19
1. Word processing. 2. WordStar (Computer program). 3. Apple computer - Programming. I. Title.
Z52.5.W67 M37 1984 ***NYPL [JSE 86-2106]***

Marakulin, P. P. (Pavel Pavlovich)
Territorial′nai͡a organizat͡sii͡a prodovol′stvennogo kompleksa . Kiev , 1985. 163 p. ; LC Card 86-175134
HD9015.S653 U4755 1985

Maram, Sheldon L. Latin American labor organizations /. New York , 1987. xiv, 929 p. ; ISBN 0-313-22834-5 (lib. bdg. : alk. paper) LC Card 86-33613 DDC 331.88/098 19
HD6530.5 .L38 1987

MARANHÃO (BRAZIL) - APPROPRIATIONS AND EXPENDITURES.
Despesa da administração pública estadual (1965-1969) /. São Luís , 1975. 37 p. : LC Card 84-209699
HJ2080 .D47 1975

MARANHÃO (BRAZIL) - COMMERCE.
Costa Filho, João Evangelista da. Comércio externo do Maranhão /. [São Luís, Maranhão] [1982] 72 p. : LC Card 87-404935 DDC 382/.098121 19
HF3409.M3 C67 1982

Viveiros, Jerônimo de, 1884- História do comércio do Maranhão. São Luís, 1954-<1964. v. <1-3 > LC Card 55-29090
HF3409.M3 V5

MARANHÃO (BRAZIL) - ECONOMIC CONDITIONS.
Polary, José Henrique Braga. Reflexões sobre o quadro global e setorial da economia maranhense /. São Luís [Brazil] , 1981. 60 p. ; LC Card 87-404934 DDC 330.981/21063 19
HC188.M29 P65 1981

Maranhão (Brazil). Instituto de Pesquisas Econômico-Sociais e Informática. Assessoria Técnica. Despesa da administração pública estadual (1965-1969) /. São Luís , 1975. 37 p. : LC Card 84-209699
HJ2080 .D47 1975

Maranhão, Sílvio. A Questão Nordeste . Rio de Janeiro-RJ , 1984. 137 p. ; LC Card 84-191031
HC188.N6 Q47 1984

Marani, Ugo. Politica monetaria e debito pubblico . Milano, Italy , c1984. 209 p. : LC Card 85-111306 DDC 332.4/945 19
HJ8678 .P65 1984 ***NYPL [JLD 86-1207]***

Marano, Philippe. Germon, Claude. La normalisation, clé d'un nouvel essor . Paris , c1983. 156 p. ; ISBN 2-11-001026-6 : LC Card 83-217768
HD3616.F83 G47 1983

Marascuilo, Leonard A. Statistical methods for the social and behavioral sciences / Leonard A. Marascuilo, Ronald C. Serlin. New York : W.H. Freeman, c1988. xxvi, 804 p. : ill. ; 25 cm. (A Series of books in psychology) Bibliography: p. [783]-784. Includes index. ISBN 0-7167-1824-3 LC Card 87-398 DDC 519.5 19
1. Social sciences - Statistical methods. I. Serlin, Ronald C. II. Title.
HA29 .M2482 1988

Maravall, Fernando.
Economía y política industrial en España / Fernando Maravall. Madrid : Pirámide, 1987. 231 p. : ill. ; 23 cm. (Economía y administración de empresas) Includes bibliographies. ISBN 84-368-0340-X LC Card 87-121800
1. Spain - Industries. 2. Industry and state - Spain. 3. Industrial productivity - Spain. 4. European Economic Community - Spain. I. Title. II. Series.
HC385 .M2574 1987

Fanjul, Oscar. La eficiencia del sistema bancario español /. Madrid , c1985. 275 p. : ISBN 84-206-2439-X LC Card 87-111325
HG3184 .F36 1985

Marburger Arbeitskreis für Sozialrecht und Sozialpolitik. Wirtschaftsentwicklung und soziale Sicherheit . Köln , 1983. viii, 146 p. : ISBN 3-452-19567-8 LC Card 84-106615
HG9399.G32 W57 1983

Marburger, Ernst-Albrecht. Internationale Erfahrungen mit der Gurtanlegepflicht = International experience relating to compulsory seat belt use / Ernst-Albrecht Marburger, Rudolf Krupp, Herbert Löffelholz.2. Aufl. Köln : Bundesanstalt für Strassenwesen, Bereich Unfallforschung, 1982. 29, 29 p. : ill. ; 21 cm. (Forschungsberichte der Bundesanstalt für Strassenwesen, Bereich Unfallforschung, 0173-7066 . 67) English and German. LC Card 83-200842
1. Traffic safety. 2. Automobiles - Seat belts - Law and legislation. I. Krupp, Rudolf. II. Löffelholz, Herbert. III. Title. IV. Title: International experience relating to compulsory seat belt use. V. Series.
HE5614 .M288 1982

Marburger geographische Schriften, 0341-9290 . (Heft 103) Schuler, Friedrich Joachim. Struktur und Dynamik der Grosshandelsbetriebe im Ballungsraum Stuttgart /. Marburg/Lahn , 1986. xiv, 156 p. : ISBN 3-88353-027-1 LC Card 87-116934 DDC 381/.2/094347 19
HF5421.5.G4 S43 1986

Marcantonio, Roberto Silveira. Almeida, Pedro Fernando de. A indústria gaúcha de bens de capital na dinâmica da economia brasileira . Porto Alegre, RS , 1986. 257 p. ; LC Card 87-403616 DDC 338.4/76218/0981 19
HD9705.B73 R562 1986

Marcelin, Frédéric, 1848-1917. La Banque nationale d'Haïti : une page d'histoire / Frédéric Marcelin ; avec un avant-propos de Jean-Claude Sanon.2e éd. Port-au-Prince, Haïti : Editions Fardin, 1985. xi, 118 p. : ill. ; 21 cm. Reprint. Originally published: Paris : Impr. de Kugelmann, 1890. With new introd. LC Card 86-125803 DDC 332.1/1/097294 19
1. Banque nationale d'Haïti - History. 2. Banks and banking, Central - Haiti - History. 3. Banks and banking - Haiti - History. I. Title.
HG2813 .M3 1985 ***NYPL [Sc D 86-690]***

Marcelino, Aida Maria. Almedia, Maria Henriqueta de. O ganho médio do operário na indústria transformadora em Portugal e noutros países da OCDE de 1972 a 1982 /. Lisboa , 1985. 88 p. : LC Card 86-189354
HD5059 .A65 1985

Marcello, John. Desmond, Glenn M. Handbook of small business valuation formulas /. Los Angeles , c1987. 139 p. ; ISBN 0-930458-04-4 LC Card 87-402145 DDC 658.1/522 19
HG4028.V3 D478 1987

March, James G. Handbook of organizations /. New York , 1987, c1965. 2 v. (xvi, 1247 p.) : ISBN 0-8240-8215-X (set : alk. paper) : LC Card 86-25797 DDC 658.4 19
HD58.7 .H365 1987

Marchán R., Carlos (Marchán Romero)
Pensamiento agrario ecuatoriano /. Quito, Ecuador , 1986. 741 p. : LC Card 87-403503 DDC 333.3/1/866 19
HD1333.E2 P46 1986

Marchand, Bernard. Vénézuela; travailleurs et villes du pétrole. Paris, Institut des hautes études de l'Amérique latine, 1971. ix, 218 p. illus., maps (1 fold.), plates. 24 cm. (Université de Paris. Travaux et mémoires de l'Institut des hautes études de l'Amérique latine. 26) Bibliography: p. 215-216. LC Card 74-856272
1. Petroleum industry and trade - Venezuela. 2. Petroleum workers - Venezuela. I. Series: Université de Paris. Institut des hautes études de l'Amérique latine. Travaux et mémoires, 26. II. Title.
HD9574.V42 M276 ***NYPL [JLE 71-452]***

Marchands ambulants et commerçants étrangers en France et en Allemagne fédérale / coordination Gildas Simon. Poitiers : Réseau Migrinter : Dép. de géographie, 1984. 148 p. :

ill. ; 30 cm. (Études méditerranéennes. fasc. 7 (1984)) Includes bibliographies. LC Card 87-147724
1. Peddlers and peddling - France. 2. Peddlers and peddling - Germany, West. I. Simon, Gildas. II. Series. III. Series: Etudes méditerranéennes (Poitiers, France) , fasc. 7.
HF5459.F8 M37 1984

Marchands d'étoffes du Fayyoum au IIIe/IXe siècle d'après leurs archives (actes et lettres) /. Rāġib, Yūsuf. Le Caire , 1982- v. : LC Card 83-156837 DDC 380.1/0962/2 19
HF366 .R34 1982 ***NYPL [*OFP 86-3324]***

Marché de l'emploi . Held, Daniel. Lausanne , 1984. 205 p. : ISBN 2-88074-028-2
NYPL [JLE 86-679]

Le marché du call money garanti /. Mercier, Paul. Bruxelles [1983] 64 p. : LC Card 84-210204
HG1055 .M47 1983

Marchés, capital et incertitude : essais en l'honneur de Maurice Allais / sous la direction de Marcel Boiteux, Thierry de Montbrial, Bertrand Munier. Paris : Economica, c1986. 265 p. : ill. ; 24 cm. French and English. Includes bibliographies. ISBN 2-7178-1002-1 : LC Card 86-160930
1. Risk. 2. Decision-making. 3. Capital. 4. Allais, Maurice. I. Allais, Maurice. II. Boiteux, Marcel. III. Montbrial, Thierry de. IV. Munier, Bertrand.
HB615 .M37 1986

Marchés du crédit des pays d'Afrique . (17) Caselli, Clara. L'internationalisation bancaire en Egypte /. Milano [1982] 223 p. ; LC Card 83-132087 DDC 332.1/5/0962 19
HG3386.A6 C37 1982 ***NYPL [JLE 86-1969]***

Marchés nouveaux . (no 19) Sudan, the country and its market. Paris , 1979. 145 p. : LC Card 87-112726
HC835 .S83536 1979

Marchi, Valerio. Pacifici, Giorgio. Il futuro presente . Milano, Italy , c1985. 201 p. ; LC Card 86-127322 DDC 384/.0945 19
HE8174 .P33 1985

Marchini, Isa. Il Finanziamento dell'innovazione nelle imprese industriali /. Milano, Italy , c1985. 271 p. : LC Card 86-157239
HC310.T4 F55 1985

Marcilio, Maria Luiza. Caiçara : terra e população : estudo de demografia histórica e da história social de Ubatuba / Maria Luiza Marcílio. São Paulo-SP (Brasil) : Edições Paulinas : CEDHAL, c1986. 244 p. : ill. ; 21 cm. (Coleção Raizes) Includes bibliographical references. ISBN 85-05-00523-6 LC Card 87-404833 DDC 304.6/0981/61 19
1. Peasantry - Brazil - Ubatuba (São Paulo). 2. Fishers - Brazil - Ubatuba (São Paulo). 3. Poor - Brazil - Ubatuba (São Paulo). 4. Ubatuba (São Paulo, Brazil) - Population. I. Title.
HD1531.B7 M34 1986

Marciniak-Neider, Danuta. Spedycja lądowa / Danuta Neider, Janusz Neider, Bartłomiej Nowakowski. Wyd. 1. Gdańsk : Uniwersytet Gdański, 1979- v. <1 > ; 24 cm. (Skrypty uczelniane / Uniwersytet Gdański) Bibliography: v. 1, p. [191]-195. LC Card 81-181249
1. Delivery of goods - Poland. 2. Freight forwarders - Poland. I. Neider, Janusz. II. Nowakowski, Bartłomiej. III. Series: Skrypty uczelniane / Uniwersytet Gdański. IV. Title.
HF5780.P7 M37 1979

Marcinowski, Bernhard. Auswirkungen von Streckenstillegungen, dargestellt am Beispiel von Nebenbahnen in Bayern / Bernhard Marcinowski. Nürnberg : Wirtschafts- und Sozialgeographisches Institut der Friedrich-Alexander-Universität, 1983. xviii, 260 p. : ill. ; 21 cm. (Nürnberger wirtschafts- und sozialgeographische Arbeiten, 0546-9112 . Bd. 35) Summary in English and French. Originally presented as the author's thesis (doctoral--Friedrich-Alexander-Universität Erlangen-Nürnberg) Bibliography: p. 245-254. LC Card 84-162065
1. Railroads - Germany (West) - Bavaria - Passenger traffic - Case studies. I. Title. II. Series.
HE3079.B5 M28 1983

Marcó del Pont, José. El correo marítimo en el Río de la Plata / por José Marcó del Pont. Buenos Aires : Cía. Sud-Americana de Billetes de Banco, 1913. 161 p. : ill. ; 27 cm. "Publicado en la 'Revista de la Sociedad Filatélica Argentina'." Includes bibliographical references. LC Card 85-125707
1. Mail steamers - Río de la Plata Region (Argentina and Uruguay) - Administration - History. 2. Postal service - Río de la Plata Region (Argentina and Uruguay) - History. I. Title.
HE6819.M3 M37 1913

Marcon, Helmut, 1944- 150 Jahre Promotion an der Wirtschaftswissenschaftlichen Fakultät der Universität Tübingen . Stuttgart , c1984. xxxvi, 809 p. : ISBN 3-8062-0409-8 LC Card 85-140557
HB74.9.G3 A15 1984 ***NYPL [JFE 87-1673]***

Marconis, Robert. Midi-Pyrénées XIXe-XXe siècles : transports, espace, société / Robert Marconis ; préface de Bernard Kayser et Rolande Trempé. [Toulouse?] : Editions Milan, [1985?] 2 v. : ill. ; 24 cm. Two folded maps (1 col.) inserted in v. 1. Includes bibliographies. Originally presented as the author's thesis (doctoral--Université de Toulouse-Le Mirail, 1984) under the title: Les transports et l'histoire socio-spatiale de Midi-Pyrénées. CONTENTS. - t. 1. Genèse et fonctionnement de la région -- t. 2. Croissance et crise de l'agglomération toulousaine. ISBN 2-86726-084-7 (set) LC Card 87-112330
1. Midi-Pyrénées (France) - Economic conditions. 2. Toulouse Region (France) - Economic conditions. 3. Transportation - France - Toulouse Region. 4. Urban transportation - France - Toulouse Region. 5. Transportation - France - Midi-Pyrénées. I. Title.
HC277.M54 M37 1985

MARCOS, FERDINAND E. (FERDINAND EDRALIN), 1917-
Stauffer, Robert B. The Philippines under Marcos . Sydney [1986] 207 p. ; ISBN 0-908470-69-X (pbk.) LC Card 87-123266 DDC 338.9599 19
HD3616.P62 S7 1986

Marcotte, Marilee, 1960- Equal pay for work of equal value / Marilee Marcotte. Kingston, Ont., Canada : Industrial Relations Centre, Queen's University, 1987. 101 p. : ill. ; 28 cm. (School of Industrial Relations research essay series . no. 10) Bibliography: p. 99-101. ISBN 0-88886-157-5 (pbk.) LC Card 87-163236 DDC 331.2/1 19
1. Pay equity - Canada. I. Title. II. Series.
HD6061.2.C2 M37 1987

Marcus, Norman, 1934- Broadcast and cable management / Norman Marcus. Englewood Cliffs, N.J. : Prentice-Hall, c1986. xii, 308 p. : ill. ; 25 cm. Includes bibliographies and index. ISBN 0-13-083577-3 LC Card 85-3565 DDC 384.54/068 19
1. Television stations - United States - Management. 2. Radio stations - United States - Management. 3. Community antenna television - United States - Management. I. Title.
HE8700.8 .M37 1986 ***NYPL [JLE 86-3127]***

Marcus, Solomon. Modele matematice și semiotice ale dezvoltării sociale /. București , 1986. 190 p. : LC Card 86-208152
HD75.5 .M615 1986

Marcy, Sam, 1911-
Anatomy of the economic crisis / Sam Marcy. Atlanta : World View Publishers, 1982. viii, 120 p. ; 21 cm. ISBN 0-89567-077-1 (pbk.) LC Card 87-132534 DDC 330.9/048 19
1. Economic history - 1971-. 2. Marxian economics. I. Title.
HC59 .M258 1982

Anatomy of the economic crisis / Sam Marcy. Atlanta : World View Publishers, c1982. viii, 120 p. : ill. ; 21 cm. "The articles in this book appeared originally in the weekly paper Workers world"--p. viii. ISBN 0-89567-077-1 (pbk.)
1. Capitalism - Addresses, essays, lectures. 2. Economic history - 1971- - Addresses, essays, lectures. 3. Monopolies - Addresses, essays, lectures. 4. United States - Economic conditions - 1971- - Addresses, essays, lectures. I. Workers world. II. Title.
NYPL [JLD 86-1329]

MARE CLAUSUM. see **FREEDOM OF THE SEAS.**

MARE LIBERUM. see **FREEDOM OF THE SEAS.**

Marek, A. I. (Aleksandr Isaevich)
Nauchno-proizvodstvennye kompleksy : formirovanie i razvitie / A.I. Marek, A.I. Semenov ; otvetstvennyĭ redaktor D.S. L'vov. Moskva : "Nauka", 1985. 141, [3] p. : ill. ; 22 cm. (Problemy sovetskoĭ ėkonomiki) At head of title: Akademiia nauk SSSR. TSentral'nyĭ ėkonomiko-matematicheskiĭ institut. Bibliography: p. 141-[142] LC Card 86-118921
1. Research - Economic aspects - Soviet Union. 2. Technological innovations - Soviet Union. 3. Science and industry - Soviet Union. I. Semenov, A. I. II. L'vov, Dmitriĭ Semenovich. III. Title.
HC340.R4 M37 1985

Mares, David R. Penetrating the international market : theoretical considerations and a Mexican case study / David R. Mares. New York : Columbia University Press, 1987. xvi, 294 p. : ill. ; 24 cm. (The Political economy of international change) Bibliography: p. [273]-289. Includes index. ISBN 0-231-06346-6 (alk. paper) LC Card 87-6358 DDC 382/.415/097232 19
1. Produce trade - Mexico. 2. Produce trade - United States. 3. Vegetable trade - Mexico - Sinaloa (State). 4. Agriculture and state - Mexico. 5. Agriculture and state - United States. 6. Competition, International. I. Title. II. Series.
HD9014.M62 M38 1987

Maretic, Vladmir. Substituição de óleo diesel . [Brasília, Brazil] [19]84. 84 p. : LC Card 87-404960 DDC 338.4/76553 19
HD9579.D53 B737 1984

Margain, Eduardo. Seminar on Economic Integration (1982 : Inter-American Development Bank) The economic integration process of Latin America in the 1980's . Washington, D.C. [1984] 318 p. : ISBN 0-940602-17-2 (pbk.) LC Card 87-159367
HC125 .S3973 1982

MARGARINE INDUSTRY - UNITED STATES - STATISTICS.
Butter and margarine attitude & usage . Rosemont, Ill. (6300 N. River Rd., Rosemont 60018) , c1986. 234 p. : LC Card 87-404035 DDC 338.1/772/0973 19
HD9278.U4 B87 1986

Margerin, Jacques. Mallard, Jean-Claude, 1947- Comprendre et gérer la fiscalité de l'entreprise /. La Tronche , Paris [1985] 255 p. : LC Card 86-166702
HD2753.F8 M34 1985

Margin accounts. Chicago, IL : Financial Services Group, Marketing Facts, Inc., c1987. iii leaves, 59 p. : ill. ; 28 cm. LC Card 87-403672 DDC 332.64/5 19
1. Margin accounts - United States - Public opinion. 2. Public opinion - United States. I. Marketing Facts, Inc. Financial Services Group.
HG4963 .M34 1987

MARGIN ACCOUNTS - UNITED STATES - PUBLIC OPINION.
Margin accounts. Chicago, IL , c1987. iii leaves, 59 p. : LC Card 87-403672 DDC 332.64/5 19
HG4963 .M34 1987

MARGINAL PEOPLES. see **MARGINALITY, SOCIAL.**

MARGINALITY, SOCIAL - ARGENTINA - POSADAS.
Baranger, Dionisio. Migración y marginalidad en Posadas . Posadas , 1982. 53 p. : LC Card 86-205276 DDC 304.8/0982/23 19
HB2020.P67 B37 1982

MARGINALITY, SOCIAL - DEVELOPING COUNTRIES.
Oliva, Karl. Teilnahme ohne Teilhabe . Frankfurt am Main , New York , c1985. 285 p. : ISBN 3-593-33476-3 LC Card 85-147441
HC59.72.S3 O45 1985

MARGINALITY, SOCIAL - LATIN AMERICA.
Mora Forero, Jorge Rafael. Introducción a los problemas del subdesarrollo en América Latina /. Bogotá, D.E., Colombia , 1984. 96 p. ; ISBN 958-95030-9-8 LC Card 86-137776 DDC 338.98 19
HC125 .M615 1984

MARGINALITY, SOCIAL - PERU - LIMA.
Bunster, Ximena. Sellers & servants . New York , 1985. x, 258 p. : ISBN 0-03-060543-1 (alk. paper) : LC Card 85-6259 DDC 331.4/0985/25 19
HD6072.2.P42 L563 1985
NYPL [JLE 86-910]

Margiotta, Umberto. Verso un sistema di orientamento . Rimini , c1984. 290 p. : LC

Card 85-119196 DDC 370.11/3/094 19
LC5056.I8 V47 1984 NYPL [JLE 86-1555]

María Cano en el amanecer de la clase obrera /. Marín Taborda, Iván. Bogotá , 1985. 103 p. : LC Card 86-165616
HD6642 .M37 1985 NYPL [JLD 86-3540]

Maria Theresa, Empress of Austria, 1717-1780. Dickson, P. G. M. (Peter George Muir) Finance and government under Maria Theresia, 1740-1780 /. Oxford [Oxfordshire] , New York , 1987. 2 v. : ISBN 0-19-822570-9 (v. 1) : LC Card 87-1614 DDC 336.436 19
HJ1059 .D52 1987

Marian, Vasile. Elemente de teorie a valorilor economice în societatea noastră / Vasile Marian. Cluj-Napoca : Dacia, 1984. 249 p. ; 21 cm. Table of contents in English, French, Romanian, and Russian. Bibliography: p. 234-244. LC Card 85-213867
1. Value. I. Title.
HB201 .M312 1984

Mariano, Alfonso, José, Lorenzo, Manuel : migrantes, campesinos de Licto y Flores : historias de vida / recopiladas y comentadas por Hernán Carrasco, Carola Lentz. Quito, Ecuador : Ediciones Abya-Yala, 1985. 128 p., [8] leaves of plates : ill. ; 21 cm. Bibliography: p. 128. LC Card 86-136793
1. Peasantry - Ecuador - Licto - Case studies. 2. Peasantry - Ecuador - Flores (Chimborazo) - Case studies. 3. Rural-urban migration - Ecuador - Licto - Case studies. 4. Rural-urban migration - Ecuador - Flores (Chimborazo) - Case studies. 5. Migration, Internal - Ecuador - Case studies. I. Carrasco, Hernán. II. Lentz, Carola. III. Title: Migrantes, campesinos de Licto y Flores.
HD1531.E2 M37 1985

Marić, Nebojša. Nikolić, Miodrag M. Desezonizacija jugoslovenskih vremenskih serija 1971-1980 =. Beograd , 1982. 287 p. : LC Card 85-157587
HA37.Y8 A37 no. 109 HC407

Maricato, Ermínia. A Produção capitalista da casa (e da cidade) no Brasil industrial /. São Paulo , 1979. 166 p. : LC Card 80-100793
HD7323.A3 P76 1979 NYPL [JLD 80-3858]

Maricourt, Renaud de. La prévision des ventes / Renaud de Maricourt. 1re éd. Paris : Presses universitaires de France, c1985. 159 p. : ill. ; 22 cm. (Collection Gestion, 0764-2237) Bibliography: p. [152]-155. Includes index. ISBN 2-13-039013-7 : LC Card 86-138110 DDC 658.8/18 19
1. Sales forecasting. I. Series: Collection Gestion (Presses universitaires de France). II. Title.
HF5415 .M2794 1985

Marie a František Kalkusovi /. Brzoň, František. České Budějovice , 1985. 98 p., [64] p. of plates : LC Card 86-161741
HD8420.3.A1 B78 1985

Mariger, Randall P., 1954- Consumption behavior and the effects of government fiscal policies / Randall P. Mariger. Cambridge, Mass. : Harvard University Press, 1986. xi, 265 p. ; 24 cm. (Harvard economic studies. v. 158) Includes index. Bibliography: p. 257-262. ISBN 0-674-16635-3 (alk. paper) LC Card 85-17550 DDC 339.4/7/0973 19
1. Consumption (Economics) - United States. 2. Consumers - United States. I. Title. II. Series.
HC110.C6 M287 1986 NYPL [JLE 86-3315]

Marillai, Vilmos. A Szabolcs-Szatmár megyei télialma-termelés, -feldolgozás és -értékesítés rendszerének fejlesztése /. Budapest , 1985. 144 p. : ISBN 963-491-208-7 LC Card 86-196831
HD9259.A6 H87 1985

Marín Taborda, Iván. María Cano en el amanecer de la clase obrera / Iván Marín Taborda. 1a ed. Bogotá : Edita Librería Sindical Colombiana, ISMAC, 1985. 103 p. : ill. ; 22 cm. (Biblioteca Sindical ISMAC. Serie Conferencias . no. 23) Bibliography: p. 103. LC Card 86-165616
1. Cano, María, 1887-1967. 2. Trade-unions - Peru - History. 3. Trade-unions - Peru - History - Sources. I. Title. II. Series.
HD6642 .M37 1985 NYPL [JLD 86-3540]

Marinakēs, Markos, 1945- Tachydromikē historia Krētikēs Politeias, 1900-1913 / Markou Marinakē = Postal history of Cretan administration, 1900-1913 / Markou Marinaki. Athēna : M. Marinakēs, 1983. 127 p. : ill. ; 21 cm. Bibliography: p. 123. LC Card 85-151773
1. Postal service - Greece - Crete - History. 2. Postage-stamps - Greece - Crete - History. 3. Postmarks - Greece - Crete - History. I. Title. II. Title: Postal History of Cretan Administration, 1900-1913.
HE7180.5.Z7 C746 1983 NYPL [JFD 86-10347]

MARINE INSURANCE. see **INSURANCE, MARINE.**

MARINE MINERAL RESOURCES - ECONOMIC ASPECTS.
Methodologies for assessing the impact of deep sea-bed minerals on the world economy /. New York , 1986. ix, 153 p. : LC Card 87-118207 DDC 338.2 19
HD9506.A2 M47 1986

MARINE RESOURCES - CONGRESSES.
The management and development of land and seabed resources . London [1985] 139 p. : ISBN 0-903577-29-1 (pbk.) LC Card 86-104896 DDC 333.7 19
HD105 .M36 1985

Marine shrimp farming : a guide to feasibility study preparation / prepared by the International Finance Corporation ; edited and published by Aquafood Business Associates. Charleston, S.C., USA (P.O. Box 16190, Charleston 29412) : The Associates, c1987. vi, 90 leaves : ill. ; 28 cm. "April 1987." LC Card 87-404668 DDC 338.3/71543 19
1. Shrimp industry. 2. Shrimp culture - Costs. I. International Finance Corporation. II. Aquafood Business Associates (Charleston, S.C.).
HD9472.S62 M375 1987

MARINE TERMINALS - MASSACHUSETTS - BOSTON - HISTORY.
Weinbaum, Paul O. Hoosac docks . Boston, Mass. , 1985. vi, 95 p. : LC Card 85-603289 DDC 387.1/64/0974461 19
HE554.B6 W45 1985

MARINE TERMINALS - UNITED STATES - CAPITAL PRODUCTIVITY.
Improving productivity in U. S. marine container terminals /. Washington, D.C. , 1986. xiv, 205 p. : ISBN 0-309-03694-1 (pbk.) LC Card 86-62194 DDC 388.5/44/068 19
HE553 .I45 1986

MARINE TERMINALS - UNITED STATES - LABOR PRODUCTIVITY.
Improving productivity in U. S. marine container terminals /. Washington, D.C. , 1986. xiv, 205 p. : ISBN 0-309-03694-1 (pbk.) LC Card 86-62194 DDC 388.5/44/068 19
HE553 .I45 1986

MARINE TRANSPORTATION. see **SHIPPING.**

MARINERS. see **SEAMEN.**

Maring, Matthias, 1950- Märkte und Handlungssysteme : zur wissenschaftstheoretischen Analyse eines systemtheoretisch-kybernetischen Handlungsansatzes im Rahmen von idealtypischen Strukturen / Matthias Maring. Frankfurt am Main ; New York : P. Lang, c1985. ii, 228 p. : ill. ; 22 cm. (Europäische Hochschulschriften. Reihe XX, Philosophie, 0721-3417 . Bd. 179 = vol. 179 = vol. 179) Originally presented as the author's thesis (doctoral--Universität Karlsruhe (TH), 1985) Bibliography: p. 211-228. ISBN 3-8204-8285-7 LC Card 85-230052
1. Markets. 2. Commerce. 3. Cybernetics. 4. System theory. . I. Title.
HF5470 .M35 1985

Marino, John A. Pastoral economics in the Kingdom of Naples / John A. Marino. Baltimore : Johns Hopkins University Press, c1988. xii, 381 p. : ill. ; 24 cm. (The Johns Hopkins University studies in historical and political science. 106th ser., 1 (1988)) Bibliography: p. [303]-367. Includes index. ISBN 0-8018-3437-6 (alk. paper) LC Card 87-9196 DDC 338.1/763145/09457 19
1. Wool trade and industry - Government policy - Italy - Naples (Kingdom) - History. I. Series. II. Series: Johns Hopkins University studies in historical and political science , 106th ser., 1. III. Title.
HD9905.I73 N366 1988

Marion, José Carlos. A contabilidade após a reforma monetária / José Carlos Marion. 1a. ed. São Paulo : Editora Atlas, 1986. 196 p. : ill. ; 22 cm. "Demonstrações financeiras extraordinárias, conversão de cruzeiros para cruzados, os efeitos no lucro após o novo pacote, Tado a legislação contábil após o pacote, os efeitos fiscais no resultado da empresa." Annexes (p. 102-196) include legislation, etc. ISBN 85-22-40175-6 : LC Card 86-222982
1. Indexation (Economics) - Brazil. 2. Corporations - Brazil - Accounting. 3. Indexation (Economics) - Law and legislation - Brazil. 4. Corporations - Accounting - Law and legislation - Brazil. I. Title.
HG835 .M37 1986

Maris, Bernard. Eléments de politique économique : les expériences françaises d'après-guerre de 1945 à 1984 / Bernard Maris. Toulouse : Privat, c1985. 235 p. : ill. ; 24 cm. (Sociétas) Includes index. Bibliography: p. [221]-223. ISBN 2-7089-7608-7 : LC Card 85-160415 DDC 338.944 19
1. France - Economic policy - 1945-. I. Series: Societas (Privat (Firm)). II. Title.
HC276.2 .M355 1985 NYPL [JLE 87-642]

Maris, János. Ez az a munkásság-- /. Budapest , 1984. 225 p., [40] p. of plates : ISBN 963-322-103-X LC Card 85-184724
HD6680.5 .E95 1984

MARITIME AND POSTAL HAND STAMPS - HONG HONG - HISTORY - 19TH CENTURY.
Scamp, Lee C. Postal rate history of China and Hong Kong . Houston, Tex., U. S.A. , c1986. xx, 284 p. : LC Card 87-145274 DDC 383/.23/0951 19
HE7305.Z8 S33 1986

Maritime economics /. Stopford, Martin. London , Boston , 1988. p. cm. ISBN 0-04-623016-5 (alk. paper) LC Card 87-18802 DDC 387.5 19
HE735 .S76 1988

A maritime history of the United States . Bauer, K. Jack (Karl Jack), 1926- Columbia, S.C. , c1988. p. cm. ISBN 0-87249-519-1 LC Card 87-19190 DDC 387.5/0973 19
HE745 .B38 1988

MARITIME POSTAL HAND STAMPS - FRANCE - COLONIES - HISTORY.
Bergier, J. (Joseph) Marques d'entrée maritime du XVIIIème et du XIXème siècle et études diverses s'y rapportant, dont taxes et mouvements portuaires de provenance ou à destination des principaux ports d'outremer au XVIIIe s. /. Nantes [1981] 131, x p. : LC Card 82-228434
HE6986 .B47 1981

Maritime shipping in the 1980s /. Hollyer, Mark. Menlo Park, CA (333 Ravenswood Ave., Menlo Park 94025) , c1986. 18 leaves : LC Card 87-150588 DDC 387.5 19
HE735 .H57 1986

Marius, 0332-7868 .
(nr. 79) Selvig, Erling. Prosjektfinansiering i petroleumsvirksomheten /. Oslo [1983] 30, 5 p. ; LC Card 84-131887
HD9575.N62 S44 1983

Mark, D. F. W. van der. Zaïre / D.F.W. van der Mark. Zutphen : Terra, 1984. 92 p., [1] folded leaf of plates : ill. ; 25 cm. (Landendocumentatie. 1984, nr. 4) Bibliography: p. 90-91. ISBN 90-6255-523-3 LC Card 86-121676
1. Zaire - Economic conditions. I. Title.
HC955 .M37 1984

Mark (Grafschaft)
Schatzbuch der Grafschaft Mark, 1486 / bearbeitet von Willy Timm. Unna : Stadtarchiv Unna, 1986. 176 p. ; 24 cm. (Quellen zur Geschichte Unnas und der Grafschaft Mark . Bd. 1) Text in Middle High German. "Das Original der hier im Druck veröffentlichten Geschichtsquelle befindet sich im Nordrhein-Westfälischen Staatsarchiv Münster ..."--T.p. verso. Includes bibliographical references and indexes. ISBN 3-87298-042-4 LC Card 87-116701 DDC 336.2/00943/55 19
1. Taxation - Germany (West) - Mark (Grafschaft) - Lists. 2. Mark (Grafschaft) - Genealogy. 3. Mark (Grafschaft) - History - Sources. I. Timm, Willy. II. Stadtarchiv Unna (Germany). III. Nordrhein Westfälisches Staatsarchiv Münster. IV. Title. V. Series.
HJ2110.5.M36 M37 1986

MARK (GRAFSCHAFT) - GENEALOGY.
Mark (Grafschaft) Schatzbuch der Grafschaft Mark, 1486 /. Unna , 1986. 176 p. ; ISBN 3-87298-042-4 LC Card 87-116701 DDC

336.2/00943/55 19
HJ2110.5.M36 M37 1986

MARK (GRAFSCHAFT) - HISTORY - SOURCES.
Mark (Grafschaft) Schatzbuch der Grafschaft Mark, 1486 /. Unna , 1986. 176 p. ; ISBN 3-87298-042-4 LC Card 87-116701 DDC 336.2/00943/55 19
HJ2110.5.M36 M37 1986

Mark, J. Paul. The empire builders : inside the Harvard Business School / J. Paul Mark.1st ed. New York : W. Morrow, c1987. 303 p. : ports. ; 24 cm. Bibliography: p. 274-286. Includes index. ISBN 0-688-06962-2 LC Card 87-13064 DDC 650/.07/117444 19
1. Harvard University. Graduate School of Business Administration. I. Title.
HF1134.H4 M37 1987

Markanvändningen i Sverige. Stockholm : Statistiska centralbyrån : LiberFörlag, 1983. 86 p. : ill. ; 24 cm. (Sveriges officiella statistik) Title on t.p. verso: Land use in Sweden. Includes bibliographical references. ISBN 91-38-08032-X (LiberFörlag) LC Card 84-173942
1. Land use - Sweden. I. Sweden. Statistiska centralbyrån.
HD766 .M37 1983

Markar'ian, S. B. (Seda Bagdasarovna) Problemy agropromyshlennoĭ integratsii v IAponii / S.B. Markar'ian. Moskva : Izd-vo "Nauka," Glav. red. vostochnoĭ lit-ry, 1982. 286 p. ; 22 cm. At head of title: Akademiia nauk SSSR. Ordena Trudovogo Krasnogo Znameni Institut vostokovedeniia. Bibliography: p. 278-[281] Includes index. LC Card 83-143582
1. Agricultural industries - Japan. I. Title.
HD9017.J32 M37 1982

al-Markaz al-Dimūghrāfī bi-al-Qāhirah. Research monograph series.
(no. 10) Determinants of fertility in some African and Asian countries. Cairo , 1982. 698 p. : LC Card 84-960893 DDC 304.6/32 19
HB1071.7.A3 D48 1982
NYPL [JLL 73-297 no.10]

Markedsføring . Trolle, Ulf af, 1919- °slo] , 1982. 496 p. : ISBN 82-00-05931-6 : LC Card 83-184229
HF5415.12.D4 T76 1982

Marker, Kekobad Ardeshir, 1896-1984. A petal from the rose / Kekobad Ardeshir Marker. [Karachi : s.n.], 1985 (Karachi : Rosette) 2 v. : ill., facsims., geneal. tables, ports. ; 24 cm. Errata slip in each v. inserted. LC Card 85-932155
1. Marker, Kekobad Ardeshir, 1896-1984. 2. Businessmen - Pakistan - Biography. 3. Parsees - Biography. I. Title.
HC440.5.M35 A3 1985

MARKER, KEKOBAD ARDESHIR, 1896-1984.
Marker, Kekobad Ardeshir, 1896-1984. A petal from the rose /. [Karachi] 1985 (Karachi : Rosette) 2 v. : LC Card 85-932155
HC440.5.M35 A3 1985

MARKET ANALYSIS. see **MARKETING RESEARCH.**

Market and industry structure and corporate cost of capital . Sudarsanam, P. S. London [1986] 33 p. ; LC Card 86-208314 DDC 338.7/4/0941 19
HG4135 .S83 1986

Market-based public policy / edited by Richard C. Hula. New York : St. Martin's Press in association with the Policy Studies Organization, 1988. xiv, 265 p. : ill. ; 23 cm. (Policy Studies Organization series) Includes bibliographies and index. ISBN 0-312-00747-7 : LC Card 87-19703 DDC 361.6 19
1. Privatization. 2. Industry and state. 3. Decentralization in government. I. Hula, Richard C., 1947-. II. Policy Studies Organization. III. Series: Policy Studies Organization series (New York, N.Y.).
HD3612 .M36 1988

Market Databank.
Savings performance report, fourth quarter, 1985 . Los Angeles, Calif. (9100 Sunset Blvd., Suite 111, Los Angeles) , c1986- v. <1 > ; LC Card 86-202354 DDC 332.3/2/09794021 19
HG2153.C3 S287 1986

Savings performance report, fourth quarter, 1985 . Los Angeles, Calif. (9100 Sunset Blvd., Suite 111, Los Angeles) , c1986. 5 v. ; LC Card 86-213300 DDC 332.3/2/09794021 19
HG2153.C3 C288 1986

Savings performance report, second quarter, 1986 . Los Angeles, Calif. (9100 Sunset Blvd., Suite 111, Los Angeles) , c1986. 5 v. (various pagings) ; LC Card 86-224944 DDC 332.3/2/09794021 19
HG2153.C3 S284 1986

The market economy . Holland, Stuart. New York , 1987. xiv, 363 p. : ISBN 0-312-01324-8 : LC Card 87-20908 DDC 330.12/2 19
HB501 .H56 1987

The market, energy, and the environment /. Hines, Lawrence Gregory. Boston , c1988. xii, 305 p. : ISBN 0-205-10568-8 : LC Card 87-1037 DDC 333.7/0973 19
HC110.E5 H57 1988

Market Facts, Inc.
Fresh trends, 1987 . [Lincolnshire, Ill.] (400 Knightsbridge Pkwy., Lincolnshire 60069) , c1987. 4 v. ; LC Card 87-162047 DDC 381/.415/0973 19
HD9244 .F73 1987

Iced coffee taste test . Van Nuys, CA (14416 Victory Blvd. Van Nuys 91401) [1985] 132 p., 6, 6 leaves : LC Card 87-100181 DDC 381/.4566393/0973 19
HD9199.U48 I25 1985

Market Facts, Inc. Financial Services Group.
Bank services and fees. Chicago, IL (676 North St., Clair St., Chicago 60611) , 1987. 60, 8 p. ; LC Card 87-400773 DDC 332.1/7/0973 19
HG1616.C87 B36 1987

The Market for advanced business communications in the United States. New York, N.Y. : Frost & Sullivan, c1983. 2 v. (x, 365 leaves) : ill. ; 29 cm. "March 1983." "#A1142." LC Card 87-144924 DDC 384/.041 19
1. Telecommunication equipment industry - United States. 2. Telephone supplies industry - United States. 3. Data transmission equipment industry - United States. 4. Teleconferencing equipment industry - United States. 5. Telecommunication - United States. 6. Market surveys - United States. I. Frost & Sullivan.
HD9696.T443 U5465 1983

The Market for North Sea crude oil / Robert Mabro ... [et al.]. Oxford ; New York : Published by the Oxford University Press for the Oxford Institute for Energy Studies, 1986. xxxii, 341 p., [1] leaf of plates : ill. ; 24 cm. Includes bibliographical references. ISBN 0-19-730001-4 LC Card 86-217261 DDC 338.2/7282/0916336 19
1. Offshore gas industry - North Sea. 2. Offshore oil industry - North Sea. I. Mabro, Robert. II. Oxford Institute for Energy Studies.
HD9581.N64 M37 1986

The market for seafood in the United Kingdom /. Miller, Charlotte L. Terminal Island, CA , 1986. ii, 73 p. : LC Card 87-601563 DDC 382.1/4370941 19
HD9461.5 .M55 1986

Market leaders : user ratings of vendors and products / Communications/Information Systems. Boston, MA (200 Portland St., Boston 02114) : Yankee Group, c1987. v, 123 p. : ill. ; 28 cm. (Distributed systems) "May 1987." LC Card 87-402841 DDC 381/.4500416/0973 19
1. Computer industry - United States. 2. Minicomputers. 3. Consumer satisfaction - United States. I. Communications/Information Systems (Firm : Yankee Group). II. Series.
HD9696.C63 U52476 1987

Market price models for Latin America's major commodity exports /. Lord, Montague J. Washington, D.C. [1986] vii, 219 p. : LC Card 87-115208 DDC 338.5/2/098 19
HD9014.A2 L67 1986

Market reforms in health care : current issues, new directions, strategic decisions / edited by Jack A. Meyer. Washington : American Enterprise Institute for Public Policy Research, c1983. xv, 331 p. ; 23 cm. (AEI Symposia. 82F) ISBN 0-8447-2242-1 LC Card 82-22678 DDC 362.1/0973 19
1. Medical care - United States - Cost control - Congresses. 2. Medical policy - United States - Congresses. 3. Medical care, Cost of - United States - Congresses. 4. Insurance, Health - United States - Congresses. I. Meyer, Jack A.
RA410.53 .M37 1983 ***NYPL [JLC 86-373]***

Market report on scanning products & systems / Linda W. Helgerson, William Pferd III, editors. Falls Church, VA (6609 Rosecroft Pl., Falls Church 22043) : DDRI, [1986]- 1 v. (loose-leaf) ; 30 cm. LC Card 87-151419 DDC 338.7/61006424 19
1. Optical character recognition device industry. 2. Optical character recognition device industry - Directories. 3. Market surveys. I. Helgerson, Linda W. II. Pferd, William, 1922-.
HD9696.O672 M37 1986

MARKET RESEARCH. see **MARKETING RESEARCH.**

MARKET RESEARCH SOCIETY - HISTORY.
Blythe, Ian. Forty years on . Aldershot, Hants., England , Brookfield, Vt., USA , c1987. p. cm. ISBN 0-566-05005-6 : LC Card 87-8653 DDC 658.8/3/06041 19
HF5410 .B58 1987

MARKET SEGMENTATION.
Büttner, Herbert. Die segmentorientierte Marketingplanung im Einzelhandelsbetrieb /. Göttingen , 1986. 413 p. : ISBN 3-509-01424-3 LC Card 87-134581 DDC 658.8/7 19
HF5429 .B87 1986

Kiffe, Ulrich. Die Klassifizierung in der Bundesrepublik Deutschland angebotener Personenkraftwagen mit multivariaten Analysemethoden /. Münster , 1984. xx, 24, 340 p. : ISBN 3-88660-148-8 LC Card 84-208133
HD9710.G42 K48 1984

Reineke, Ulrich, 1955- Segmentationstheorien des Arbeitsmarktes und Beschäftigungsniveau . Frankfurt am Main , New York , c1986. iv, 333 p. : ISBN 3-8204-9671-8 LC Card 87-407583 DDC 331.12/0943 19
HD5706 .R43 1986

A market strategy study of the whole bean coffee market . Bruskin, R. H. [New Brunswick, N.J.] [1985] 1 v. (various pagings) : LC Card 87-100003 DDC 381/.41373/0971 19
HD9199.U48 B84 1985

Market structure and technological change /. Baldwin, William L., 1928- Chur, Switzerland , New York , c1987. viii, 170 p. ; ISBN 3-7186-0375-6 (pbk.) LC Card 86-25780 DDC 338/.06 19
HD2326 .B35 1987

MARKET SURVEY.
Specimen collection and transport market. Tustin, CA, U. S.A. (17722 Irvine Blvd., Tustin 92680) , c1987. 1 v. (various foliations) : LC Card 87-402105 DDC 380.1/45681761 19
HD9995.L32 S64 1987

MARKET SURVEYS - BIBLIOGRAPHY.
Financial Sourcebooks' sources . Naperville, Ill. , c1987. 454 p. ; ISBN 0-942061-00-4 (pbk.) : LC Card 87-8793 DDC 332/.025/73 19
HG173 .F517 1987

MARKET SURVEYS - DEVELOPING COUNTRIES.
Bicycles and components . Geneva , 1985. x, 160 p. ; LC Card 86-219298 DDC 380./456292272/091724 19
HD9993.B543 D442 1985

Surrey, John. The European power plant industry . [Brighton, Sussex] , c1981. viii, 90 p. ; ISBN 0-903422-31-X (pbk.) : LC Card 83-130609 DDC 338.4/76213121/094 19
HD9695.E92 S87 1981
NYPL [JLD 86-4078]

MARKET SURVEYS - ECONOMETRIC MODELS.
Langkamp, Peter. Die Erfassung von Carryover-Effekten im Marketing . Thun , c1984. 335 p. : ISBN 3-87144-844-3 : LC Card 85-113501
HF5415.3 .L36 1984

MARKET SURVEYS - EUROPE.
Analytical instruments markets in Europe. New York, N.Y. , c1983. xii, 253 p. ; LC Card 87-141819 DDC 380.1/45681754 19
HD9706.65.C573 E82 1983

Consumer & catering disposable products market in Europe. New York, N.Y. , c1983. [29], 386 p. ; LC Card 87-142586 DDC 380.1/4568 19
HD9971.5.T323 E853 1983

Flavors and fragrances market in Europe. New York, N.Y. , c1983. 5, 17, 8, 279 p. ; LC Card 87-141830 DDC 380.1/456645 19
HD9212.E852 F53 1983

Frozen foods market in Europe. New York, N.Y. , c1983. 2 v. (vii, 438 p.) ; LC Card 87-142593 DDC 380.1/4566402853/094 19
HD9326.A2 F76 1983

The IBM market in Europe. New York, N.Y. , c1983. 2 v. (xv, 573, 9 p.) ; LC Card 87-146364 DDC 380.1/45004/094 19
HD9696.C64 I4846 1983

Industrial hydraulics components market in Europe. New York, N.Y. , c1983. xxxvi, 338 p. ; LC Card 87-141832 DDC 381/.456212/094 19
HD9705.5.H933 E855 1983

Industrial robots market in Europe. New York, N.Y. , c1983. vi, 320 p. : LC Card 87-141842 DDC 380.1/45629892 19
HD9696.R623 E854 1983

Intravenous theraphy [sic] supplies and equipment market in Europe. New York, N.Y. , c1983. xix, 317 p. ; LC Card 87-141784 DDC 380.1/45681761 19
HD9995.I583 E854 1983

Mackintosh, Ian, 1927- Sunrise Europe . Oxford, UK , New York, NY, USA , 1986. xx, 288 p. : ISBN 0-631-14406-4 : LC Card 86-6077 DDC 338.4/7004/094 19
HD9696.C63 E8547 1986
NYPL [JLE 86-3364]

Marketing strategies for selling cosmetics & toiletries in Europe. New York, N.Y. , c1983. 381 p. ; LC Card 87-141847 DDC 380.1/456685/094 19
HD9970.5.C673 E8555 1983

Medical products packaging market in Europe. New York, N.Y. , c1983. vi, x, xi, 220 p. : LC Card 87-141779 DDC 380.1/456151 19
HD9671.A2 M43 1983

Metal working plant market in Europe. New York, N.Y. , c1983. xvi, 262 p. ; LC Card 87-141761 DDC 380.1/456817671/094 19
HD9705.E72 M48 1983

The Microprocessor based measuring instrumentation market in West European manufacturing. New York, N.Y. , c1983. [22], 262, xi p. : LC Card 87-142563
HD9706.2.E8513 M53 1983

The Microprocessor development systems market in West Europe. New York, N.Y. (106 Fulton St., New York 10038) , c1983. 2 v. : LC Card 87-401674 DDC 380.1/4500416/094 19
HD9696.C63 E765 1983

The Military tactical communications switching network market in West Europe. New York, N.Y. , c1983. xvi, 232 p. ; LC Card 87-141849
HD9744.C653 E854 1983

Mining equipment market in Europe. New York, N.Y. , c1983. xxix, 294 p. ; LC Card 87-142591 DDC 380.1/4568176/094 19
HD9506.E85 M56 1983

The Mobile radio market in Western Europe. New York, N.Y. , c1982. x, 283 p. : LC Card 87-141850 DDC 380.1/45621384165/094 19
HD9696.R363 E855 1982

The Office systems software market in Europe. New York, N.Y. , c1983. xv, 256 p. : LC Card 87-144095 DDC 380.1/450053/094 19
HD9696.C63 E8555 1983

Prepress graphic arts equipment and supplies market in Europe. New York, N.Y. , c1983. xxiii, 268 p. ; LC Card 87-141770 DDC 380.1/456816 19
HD9790.E85 P74 1983

Vinyl and acrylic latices markets in Europe. New York, N.Y. , c1983. 2 v. (xxxv, 328 leaves) : LC Card 87-143984 DDC 380.1/456684232/094 19
HD9661.E82 V55 1983

MARKET SURVEYS - EUROPEAN ECONOMIC COMMUNITY COUNTRIES.
The Rubber chemicals market in the EEC. New York, N.Y. , c1983. xxi, 303 p. ; LC Card 87-142579
HD9161.E8562 R83 1983

MARKET SURVEYS - EVALUATION.
Donius, James F. Marketplace measurement . New York, NY (155 E. 44th St., New York 11710) , c1986. xiii, 206 p. : LC Card 87-120244 DDC 659.1/11 19
HF5823 .D655 1986

MARKET SURVEYS - FRANCE.
Miller, Charlotte L. The French market for U. S. seafood products /. Terminal Island, CA , 1986. ii, 63 p. ; LC Card 86-602854 DDC 382/.4566494/0944 19
HD9462.5 .M54 1986

MARKET SURVEYS - GREAT BRITAIN.
ISBA area information, 1978 /. London , 1978. 147 p. : ISBN 0-906241-00-6 (pbk.) LC Card 83-225656 DDC 381/.1/0941021 19
HA1134 .I83 1978

Miller, Charlotte L. The market for seafood in the United Kingdom /. Terminal Island, CA , 1986. ii, 73 p. : LC Card 87-601563 DDC 382.1/4370941 19
HD9461.5 .M55 1986

U.K. consumer electronics. Norwalk, Conn., U. S.A. (6 Prowitt St., Norwalk 06855) , c1986. vi, 198 leaves ; LC Card 86-228422 DDC 381/.45621381/0941 19
HD9696.A3 G785 1986

MARKET SURVEYS - INFORMATION SERVICES - DIRECTORIES.
Financial Sourcebooks' sources . Naperville, Ill. , c1987. 454 p. ; ISBN 0-942061-00-4 (pbk.) : LC Card 87-8793 DDC 332/.025/73 19
HG173 .F517 1987

MARKET SURVEYS - ITALY.
Glücksmann, Riccardo. Telematica . Milano , 1982. xii, 273 p., [4] p. of plates : ISBN 88-7056-120-8 LC Card 84-184344
HD9696.D383 I84 1982

L'Informatica nella società italiana, 1984 . Milano [1984] 257 p. ; LC Card 84-249272 DDC 338.4/7004/0945 19
HD9696.C63 I85 1984
NYPL [JLD 86-3303]

MARKET SURVEYS - LATIN AMERICA.
Process control instrumentation in Latin America. New York, N.Y. , c1983. vi, 404 p. ; LC Card 87-141802 DDC 380.1/456817 19
HD9696.P763 L296 1983

MARKET SURVEYS - NEW YORK (STATE) - SYRACUSE.
Venkatesh, Alladi. The significance of the women's movement to marketing . New York , 1985. 209 p. ; ISBN 0-03-069588-0 (alk. paper) : LC Card 85-19106 DDC 658.8/348 19
HF5415.3 .V46 1985 ***NYPL [JLE 86-1081]***

MARKET SURVEYS - NEW ZEALAND.
Kaiser, Martin. The New Zealand software industry . Wellington, N.Z. , c1986. 1 v. (various pagings) : ISBN 0-477-06783-2 (pbk.) LC Card 86-212843 DDC 381/.450053/09931 19
HD9696.C63 N455 1986

MARKET SURVEYS - SAUDI ARABIA.
Analytical study for the market of white meat and eggs /. Jeddah [1985?] 159 p. : LC Card 85-964046 DDC 381/.4566493/09538 19
HD9437.S332 A53 1985

MARKET SURVEYS - SWEDEN.
Investering i industrirobotar . [Stockholm] [1983] 263 p. : ISBN 91-38-07833-3 LC Card 84-218538
HD9696.R623 S845 1983

MARKET SURVEYS - UNITED STATES.
Ada military & commercial markets. Norwalk, Conn., U. S.A. (6 Prowitt St., Norwalk 06855) , c1986. vii, 196 leaves ; LC Card 87-400056 DDC 381/.45005133/0973 19
HD9696.C63 U51123 1986

The Affluent market fact book . Tampa, Fla. , c1986. 83 leaves ; LC Card 86-235264 DDC 332.1/7 19
HG1616.C87 A33 1986

Aliphatic solvents market. New York, N.Y. , c1983. viii, 181 leaves : LC Card 87-142189 DDC 381/.45661807 19
HD9660.S733 U525 1983

Alternate site clinical testing. Tustin, CA, U. S.A. (17722 Irvine Blvd., Tustin 92680) , c1987. 167 leaves in various foliations : LC Card 87-402110 DDC 381/.45681761 19
HD9995.L33 U5412 1987

Artificial intelligence markets. Norwalk, Conn., U. S.A. (6 Prowitt St., Norwalk 06855) , c1986. vii, 215 leaves ; LC Card 86-227054 DDC 380.1/450063 19
HD9696.C63 U5118 1986

Attitudes toward vended coffee /. [Chicago? , 1983] 1 v. (various pagings) : LC Card 86-235525 DDC 381/.4566393 19
HD9199.U48 A88 1983

Automotive aftermarket in the U. S. New York, N.Y. , c1983. 2 v. (xiii, 435 p.) ; LC Card 87-144460
HD9710.3.U52 A93 1983

The Automotive electronics market in the U. S. New York, N.Y. , c1983. vi, 262 p. : LC Card 87-142223 DDC 381/.456292549/0973 19
HD9710.3.U52 A943 1983

Bank services and fees. Chicago, IL (676 North St., Clair St., Chicago 60611) , 1987. 60, 8 p. ; LC Card 87-400773 DDC 332.1/7/0973 19
HG1616.C87 B36 1987

Beyond private lines . Boston, MA (200 Portland St., Boston 02114) , c1987. iv, 117 p. : LC Card 87-144067 DDC 384.3/0973 19
HE7775 .B46 1987

Bruskin, R. H. A market strategy study of the whole bean coffee market . [New Brunswick, N.J.] [1985] 1 v. (various pagings) : LC Card 87-100003 DDC 381/.41373/0971 19
HD9199.U48 B84 1985

Butter and margarine attitude & usage . Rosemont, Ill. (6300 N. River Rd., Rosemont 60018) , c1986. 234 p. : LC Card 87-404035 DDC 338.1/772/0973 19
HD9278.U4 B87 1986

The Call accounting market in the United States. New York, N.Y. , c1983. x, 275 p. : LC Card 87-143500 DDC 381/.45621387 19
HD9697.T453 U522 1983

Cardiovascular surgery products markets in the U. S. New York, N.Y. , c1983. xxiii, 197 p. : LC Card 87-143453
HD9995.S93 U525 1983

Cardiovascular therapy market . Tustin, CA, U. S.A. (17722 Irvine Blvd., Tustin 92680) , c1987. 1 v. (various foliations) ; LC Card 87-402037 DDC 380.1/45681761 19
HD9995.C363 U62 1987

Catheter devices for interventional cardiology, angiography, and radiology--U. S. and international. Tustin, CA, U. S.A. (17722 Irvine Blvd., Tustin 92680) , c1987. 1 v. (various foliations) : LC Card 87-168823 DDC 381/.45681761 19
HD9995.C383 U628 1987

Caulks & sealants market. New York, N.Y. , c1983. ix, 250 p. : LC Card 87-143824
HD9999.S44453 U53 1983

CD ROM markets. Norwalk, Conn., U. S.A. (6 Prowitt St., Norwalk 06855) , c1986. v, 201 leaves : LC Card 86-227050 DDC 381/.4500456 19
HD9696.O673 U627 1986

Cholmar, Sidney. New directions in microwave ovens . Stamford, Conn., U. S.A. , c1985. x, 119 leaves ; ISBN 0-89336-459-2 (pbk.) LC Card 87-163958 DDC 381/.4568388 19
HD9971.5.S763 U53 1985

Christen, François G. Buying by mail . Menlo Park, CA (333 Ravenswood Ave., Menlo Park 94025) , c1986. v, 2, 59, 6 leaves : LC Card 86-209563 DDC 658.8/4 19
HF5415.126 .C48 1986

The Cogeneration equipment and services market in the U. S. New York, N.Y. , c1983. 2 v. (ix, 306 leaves) : LC Card 87-138703 DDC 381/.456213141 19
HD9695.U52 C64 1983

Color printer markets. Norwalk, Conn., U. S.A. (6 Prowitt St., Norwalk 06855) , c1987. vi, 188 leaves ; LC Card 87-401926 DDC 381/.456213987/0973 19
HD9696.C63 U514916 1987

The Commercial greenhouses & associated equipment & agrochemicals market. New York, N.Y. , c1983. vii, 274 leaves : LC Card 87-143480
HD9475.U52 C66 1983

Communications/Information Systems Planning Service . Boston, MA (89 Broad St., Boston

02110) , c1986. ii, 78 p. ; LC Card 86-225335 DDC 381/.45651853 19
HD9696.C63 U51492 1986

The Compact disc market--phase II . New York, N.Y. (444 Madison Ave., New York 10022) , c1986. viii, 57, [13] p. : LC Card 86-227224 DDC 381/.4562138933 19
HD9697.P563 U526 1986

A Competitive assessment of the U. S. digital central office switch industry /. Washington, D.C. , 1986. xv, 106 p. : LC Card 86-603064 DDC 382/.456321387 19
HD9696.T443 U5225 1986

Consolidated data base . San Jose, Calif. (1290 Ridder Park Dr., San Jose 95131-2398) , c1986. ii, 94 p. ; LC Card 87-108611 DDC 381/.45004/0973
HD9696.C63 U515626 1986

Consumer financial services . Boston, MA (200 Portland St., Boston 02114) , 1986. xvi, 83 p. : LC Card 86-230330 DDC 332.1/028 19
HD9696.B363 U543 1986

The Counting instrument market in the U. S. New York, N.Y. , c1983. v, 197 p. : LC Card 87-143757 DDC 381/.4568114 19
HD9696.D543 U63 1983

Crull, Anna W. New trends in gas separations . Stamford, Conn., U. S.A. , c1986. xvi, 222 leaves : ISBN 0-89336-422-3 (pbk.) LC Card 87-165549 DDC 660.2/842 19
HD9660.G372 C78 1986

Customer premises telecom equipment & the regional Bell companies. Norwalk, Conn., U. S.A. (6 Prowitt St., Norwalk 06855) , c1987. ix, 193 leaves ; LC Card 87-403216 DDC 381/.45621385 19
HD9697.T453 U5245 1987

Database management systems. Norwalk, Conn., U. S.A. (6 Prowitt St., Norwalk 06855) , c1986. iv, 149 leaves ; LC Card 86-226965 DDC 381/.4500574/0973
HD9696.C63 U515925 1986

Delson, Erwin B. The factory automation industry /. New York, N.Y. , c1985. 1 v. (various pagings) : ISBN 0-931634-16-4 (pbk.) LC Card 86-203033 DDC 338.4/76298/0973 19
HD9696.A963 U635 1985

The Diagnostic radiology market in the U. S. New York, N.Y. , c1983. xxxix, 261 p. : LC Card 87-143803 DDC 381/.45681761 19
HD9995.R333 U53 1983

Diet foods . Stamford, Conn., U. S.A. , c1986. xv, 195 leaves : ISBN 0-89336-487-8 (pbk.) LC Card 87-160485 DDC 381/.4166463/0973 19
HD9005 .D53 1986

The Digital telecommunications market. New York, N.Y. , c1983. 2 v. (vii, 269 leaves) : LC Card 87-143942 DDC 384 19
HD9697.T453 U525 1983

The Distributed digital process control systems market in the U. S. New York, N.Y. , c1983. 229 p. ; LC Card 87-141853
HD9696.P763 U527 1983

The Electronic games market in the U. S. New York, N.Y. , c1983. vii, 291 p. : LC Card 87-142142 DDC 381/.45688728 19
HD9993.E453 U622 1983

The Enhanced data network (van) market. New York, N.Y. , c1983. v, 258 p. : LC Card 87-143825
HD9696.D383 U6344 1983

The Enhanced oil recovery market, 1980-1990. New York, N.Y. , c1983. vi, 203 leaves : LC Card 87-142370 DDC 381/.45617665/0973 19
HD9565 .E53 1983

Expert systems. Boston, Mass. (89 Broad St., 14th Floor, Boston 02110) , c1985. 61 p. : LC Card 87-400871 DDC 381/.4500633/0973 19
HD9696.C63 U516435 1985

Fiber optics after long distance /. Boston, Mass. (89 Broad St., Boston 02110) , c1986. vii, 114 p. : LC Card 86-220473 DDC 381/.456213692/0973 19
HD9696.F523 U5429 1986

Flame retardants chemicals market. New York, N.Y. , c1983. vii, 315 p. : LC Card 87-143411 DDC 381/.456289223/0973 19
HD9999.F553 U64 1983

Fresh trends, 1987 . [Lincolnshire, Ill.] (400 Knightsbridge Pkwy., Lincolnshire 60069) , c1987. 4 v. ; LC Card 87-162047 DDC 381/.415/0973 19
HD9244 .F73 1987

The Future of the office products industry . Alexandria, Va. (301 N. Fairfax St., Alexandria 22314) , c1985. viii, 212, 33 p. : LC Card 86-200112 DDC 338.4/768 19
HD9800.U52 F86 1985

George, J. John. Opportunities in computer-assisted medical diagnostics . Menlo Park, Calif. (333 Ravenswood Ave., Menlo Park 94025-3476) , c1985. 32 p. : LC Card 86-232002 DDC 381/.45681761 19
HD9995.D543 U63 1985

Geriatrics OTC health aid and toiletries products market-U. S. New York, N.Y. , c1983. 2 v. (viii, 352 leaves) ; LC Card 87-144078 DDC 381/.456151/0973 19
HD9666.5 .G47 1983

Gipson, Beckilynn. Aseptic food processing and packaging . Stamford, Conn., U. S.A. , c1986. xiii, 164 leaves ; ISBN 0-89336-471-1 (pbk.) LC Card 87-405014 DDC 381/.45664028 19
HD9999.C743 U629 1986

A Guide for selecting ALM microcomputer models . Washington, D.C. (1120 Connecticut Ave., N.W., Washington 20036) , c1987. iv, 147 p. : LC Card 87-159971 DDC 332.1/028/5416 19
HG1615.25 .G85 1987

The Home computer software market. New York, N.Y. , c1983. iv, 212 p. : LC Card 87-141858 DDC 381/.45004/0973 19
HD9696.C63 U5183245 1983

Home healthcare products and services markets in the U. S. New York, N.Y. , c1983. 2 v. (x, 368 leaves) ; LC Card 87-144925 DDC 381/.45681761 19
HD9995.H563 U5436 1983

The Home terminal II . [Boston, Ma.] (89 Broad St., Boston 02110) [1986] 63 leaves : LC Card 86-211108 DDC 381/.45621396/0973 19
HD9696.C63 U518327 1986

IBM's evolving mainframes . Boston, Mass. (200 Portland St., Boston 02114) , c1986. iii, 45 p. : LC Card 86-231231 DDC 381/.4500412/0973 19
HD9696.C64 I48466 1986

Iced coffee taste test . Van Nuys, CA (14416 Victory Blvd. Van Nuys 91401) [1985] 132 p., 6, 6 leaves : LC Card 87-100181 DDC 381/.4566393/0973 19
HD9199.U48 I25 1985

Idaho Oregon Onion Promotion Committee. Sweet Spanish onion . Temple, Me. (Santa Claus Lake, Temple 04984) , 1986. ii, 46, 27 leaves : LC Card 87-120958 DDC 381/.41525/0973 19
HD9235.O62 U34 1986

The Industrial display market in the U. S. New York, N.Y. , c1983. vi, 226 leaves ; LC Card 87-142373 DDC 381/.456213985/0973 19
HD9696.I533 U54 1983

Industrial fasteners market in the U. S. New York, N.Y. , c1983. iv, 375 p. : LC Card 87-143818
HD9999.F33 U476 1983

Industrial power systems market in the U. S. New York, N.Y. , c1983. v, 312 p. ; LC Card 87-143811 DDC 381/.4562143/0973
HD9695.U52 I53 1983

Industrial robots market. New York, N.Y. , <c1983-. v. <2 > ; LC Card 87-166012 DDC 381/.45629892 19
HD9696.R623 U634 1983

The Industrial vision systems market in the U. S. New York, N.Y. , c1983. v, 246 p. : LC Card 87-143523
HD9696.I423 U5445 1983

Integral HP electric motors and asociated [sic] controls. New York, N.Y. , c1983. xii, 280 leaves ; LC Card 87-143831
HD9697.M693 U55 1983

Interactive videodisk software market. New York, N.Y. , c1983. iv, 228 leaves ; LC Card 87-143767
HD9696.C63 U518378 1983

Japanese penetration into the United States communications data processing and office equipment markets. New York, N.Y. , c1983. v, 308 p. ; LC Card 87-143908 DDC 381/.45004/0973 19
HD9696.D383 U635 1983

Leibowitz, Dennis. The cellular communications industry /. New York, N.Y. (140 Broadway, New York 10005) , c1985. ii, 67 p. : LC Card 86-201572 DDC 384.5/33/0973 19
HD9696.R363 U65 1985

Living with SNA /. Boston, MA (89 Broad St., Boston 02110) [1986] 60 p. : LC Card 86-201765 DDC 381/.4500468/0973 19
HD9696.C63 U5223 1986

Mandela, Audrey L. Electronic mail update . Boston, Mass. (200 Portland St., Boston 02114) , c1986. ii, 135 p. : LC Card 87-124538 DDC 384.3/4/0973 19
HD9696.M353 U56 1986

Manufacturing database management systems /. Boston, MA (89 Broad St., Boston 02110) , c1986. vii, 216 p. : LC Card 86-210661 DDC 381/.4500574/0973 19
HD9696.C63 U5226 1986

The Market for advanced business communications in the United States. New York, N.Y. , c1983. 2 v. (x, 365 leaves) : LC Card 87-144924 DDC 384/.041 19
HD9696.T443 U5465 1983

The Markets and competitive environment for portable computers. New York, N.Y. , c1983. xii, 356 p. : LC Card 87-143515 DDC 380.1/4500416 19
HD9696.C62 M369 1983

The Medical communications market. New York, N.Y. , c1972. vi, 163 leaves : LC Card 87-141851
HD9995.H63 U5454 1972

Metal finishing machinery market. New York, N.Y. , c1983. vii, 220 p. ; LC Card 87-141856 DDC 381/.456817671/0973 19
HD9506.U62 M38 1983

The Microwave test equipment market in the U. S. New York, N.Y. , c1983. iii, 223 p. ; LC Card 87-143814
HD9696.M533 U56 1983

The Military test equipment market in the U. S. New York, N.Y. (106 Fulton St., New York 10038) , c1983. iv, 245 p. : LC Card 87-142060 DDC 381/.45621381/0287 19
HD9743.U6 M545 1983

The Mini-microcomputer turnkey engineering systems market. New York, N.Y. , c1983. vi, 228 p. ; LC Card 87-142400 DDC 381/.4500416 19
HD9696.C63 U5262 1983

Nerve, muscle, bone stimulation, and augmentation. Tustin, CA, U. S.A. (17722 Irvine Blvd., Tustin 92680) , c1987. iv, 8, 144, [112] p. : LC Card 87-402023 DDC 338.4/7681761 19
HD9995.E43 U56 1987

The New ethnic food market . Norwalk, Conn., U. S.A. , c1986. xv, 142 leaves ; ISBN 0-89336-486-X (pbk.) LC Card 87-168111 DDC 381/.45641592/00973 19
HD9333.U62 N48 1986

New marketing strategies for office equipment. New York, N.Y. , c1983. vii, 307 p. ; LC Card 87-142201 DDC 381/.456816/0973 19
HD9801.U542 N48 1983

New specialty metals & metallurgy for high-temperature, high-strength, low-weight applications /. Norwalk, Conn., U. S.A. , c1987. 1 v. (various foliations) : ISBN 0-89336-454-1 (pbk.) LC Card 87-168123 DDC 380.1/45669/0973 19
HD9506.U62 N45 1987

New trends in food retailing /. Stamford, Conn., U. S.A. , c1985. xiii, 135 leaves : ISBN 0-89336-457-6 (soft) LC Card 87-165228 DDC 381/.45664/00973 19
HD9321.5 .N47 1985

Non-intelligent terminal market in the U. S. New York, N.Y. , c1983. vi, 197 p. : LC Card

87-143735 DDC 381/.456213985/0973 19
HD9696.C63 U52637 1983

Noninvasive cardiovascular and cardiorespiratory diagnostic devices (U. S. and international). Tustin, CA (17722 Irvine Blvd., Tustin 92680) , c1986. 1 v. (various pagings) : LC Card 87-101739 DDC 380.1/45681761 19
HD9995.C363 U65 1986

The Office automation market in the U. S. New York, N.Y. , <c1983-. v. <2 > : LC Card 87-166011 DDC 381/.456816/0973 19
HD9801.U542 O34 1983

Oilfield machinery and equipment market in the U. S. New York, N.Y. , c1983. v, 213 leaves ; LC Card 87-142516 DDC 381/.4568176 19
HD9565 .O643 1983

The Optical memory media market in the U. S. New York, N.Y. , c1983. iv, 218 leaves : LC Card 87-143513 DDC 381/.4562139767/0973 19
HD9696.C63 U52734 1983

O'Reilly, Francis J. Computer printers . Stamford, Conn., U. S.A. , c1985. iv, 103 leaves ; ISBN 0-89336-460-6 (pbk.) LC Card 87-163961 DDC 338.4/76213987 19
HD9696.C63 U52737 1985

The OTC internal medications market. New York, N.Y. (106 Fulton St., New York 10038), c1983. a-d, iii, 279 p. ; LC Card 87-142032
HD9666.5 .O8 1983

Patient monitoring disposables and equipment for critical care. Tustin, CA (17722 Irvine Blvd., Tustin 92680) , c1986. 1 v. (various foliations) : LC Card 86-203049 DDC 381/.45681761 19
HD9995.M653 U657 1986

The Personal computer hardware add-on device market. New York, N.Y. , c1983. viii, 2, 228 p. : LC Card 87-143524
HD9696.C63 U52783 1983

Petroleum products storage & distribution & information processing. New York, N.Y. , c1983. viii, 249 p. : LC Card 87-143725 DDC 381/.4566554/0973 19
HD9565 .P363 1983

The Portable compressor market. New York, N.Y. (106 Fulton St., New York 10038) , c1983. xi, 254 p. : LC Card 87-142051
HD9705.5.C643 U66 1983

Portable kitchen appliance market. New York, N.Y. , c1983. 2 v. (x, 405 p.) : LC Card 87-143951 DDC 381/.4568383/0973 19
HD9971.5.K583 U656 1983

Prepackaged kits & trays markets in the U. S. New York, N.Y. , c1983. xxiii, 188 p. : LC Card 87-142284 DDC 381/.45681761 19
HD9995.D563 U665 1983

Printed circuit board market opportunities. Norwalk, Conn., U. S.A. (6 Prowitt St., Norwalk 06855) [1986] v, 153 leaves : LC Card 86-224533 DDC 381/.4562/38174/0973 19
HD9696.P743 U66 1986

The Process control equipment market (1982-1992). New York, N.Y. , c1983. vii, 241 leaves : LC Card 87-142195 DDC 380.1/456817 19
HD9696.A963 U66 1983

Promotion strategies for household cleaning products. New York, N.Y. , c1983. 2 v. (xx, 635 p.) ; LC Card 87-142358 DDC 381/.456671/0973 19
HD9999.C4863 U56 1983

Reinforced plastics . Stamford, Conn., U. S.A. , c1986. v, 136 leaves : ISBN 0-89336-478-9 (pbk.) LC Card 87-167989 DDC 381/.45668494/0973 19
HD9662.F523 U57 1986

Report on the coffee service industry /. Columbus, Ohio [1984] 1 v. (various foliations) : LC Card 87-100404 DDC 381/.4566393 19
HD9199.U48 R47 1984

Residential heating, ventilating & cooling systems market. New York, N.Y. , c1983. iv, 269 leaves : LC Card 87-138699 DDC 381/.45697/000973 19
HD9683.U52 R47 1983

The Semiconductor assembly equipment market in the U. S. New York, N.Y. , c1983. viii, 326 p. ; LC Card 87-141854 DDC 381/.4562138152 19
HD9696.S43 U4955 1983

Shelton, Robert D. Hazardous waste management market assessment /. Menlo Park, CA (333 Ravenswood Ave., Menlo Park 94025) , c1986. 19 p. : LC Card 86-220787 DDC 338.4/7363728 19
HD9975.U52 S54 1986

Shurtleff, William, 1941- Tofutti® & other soy ice creams . Lafayette, CA , c1985. 2 v. : ISBN 0-933332-19-X (v. 1) : LC Card 85-10829 DDC 381/.4174 19
HD9330.B323 U 1985 ***NYPL [JLF 86-1035]***

Small business market factbook. Tampa, FL (P.O. Box 30168, Tampa 33630) , c1986. 106 leaves : LC Card 87-100402 DDC 338.6/42/0973 19
HG4027.7 .S64 1986

The Special surgery equipment and supplies market in the U. S. New York, N.Y. , c1983. xxiii, 332 p. : LC Card 87-142345 DDC 381/.45681761 19
HD9995.S93 U56 1983

Strategic marketing of oncology products /. Tustin, CA, U. S.A. (17722 Irvine Blvd., Tustin 92680) , c1987. 242 p. in various pagings : LC Card 87-402026 DDC 381/.45681761 19
HD9995.C353 U67 1987

Strategies for selling underground & surface mining equipment. New York, N.Y. , c1983. vii, 320 p. : LC Card 87-142333 DDC 381/.4568176/0973 19
HD9506.U62 S865 1983

Talkwriters, voice mail & speech processing in office automation. Norwalk, Conn., U. S.A. (6 Prowitt St., Norwalk 06855) , c1986. iv, 145 leaves : LC Card 86-224988 DDC 381/.45621389 19
HD9696.S643 U667 1986

Telecommunications opportunities for colleges and universities /. McLean, Va. (1355 Beverly Rd., Suite 100, McLean 22101) , c1986. 208 p. ; LC Card 86-231086 DDC 384.6/3 19
HD9696.T443 U572 1986

The Teleconferencing market. New York, N.Y. (106 Fulton St., New York 10038) , c1983. 288 p. : LC Card 87-143433
HD9696.T443 U574 1983

Third party maintenance of computers and data terminals in the United States. New York, N.Y. , c1983. vi, 269 leaves ; LC Card 87-142515 DDC 381/.4562139/0973 19
HD9696.C63 U5874 1983

Transponder supply & demand forecast. Bethesda, MD, U. S.A. , c1987. v, 150 p. : LC Card 87-403373 DDC 384.4/1 19
HE9721.U5 T73 1987

U. S. clinical testing market /. Tustin, CA, U. S.A. (17722 Irvine Blvd., Tustin 92680) , c1987. 223 leaves in various foliations ; LC Card 87-402039 DDC 381/.45681761 19
HD9995.L33 U5484 1987

The U. S. market for hazardous duty liquid pumps and valves. New York, N.Y. , c1983. 2 v. (viii, 343 leaves) : LC Card 87-401677 DDC 381/.456216 19
HD9651.5 .U16 1983

The U. S. market for intelligent terminals. New York, N.Y. , c1983. vi, 195 p. : LC Card 87-143740 DDC 381/.456213985/0973 19
HD9696.C63 U5885 1983

The U. S. mobile radio communications equipment market. New York, N.Y. , c1983. viii, 253 p. : LC Card 87-142226 DDC 384.5/3 19
HD9696.R363 U684 1983

The U. S. non telecommunications fiber optic component market in the U. S. New York, N.Y. , c1982. vi, 255 leaves : LC Card 87-143641 DDC 381/.456213692/0973 19
HD9696.F523 U557 1982

The U. S. professional/executive workstations market. New York, N.Y. , c1983. vi, 284 p. : LC Card 87-142071 DDC 381/.4500416/0973 19
HD9801.U542 U18 1983

U. S. stationary compressors market. New York, N.Y. , c1983. xi, 271 p. : LC Card 87-143527 DDC 380.1/4562153/0973 19
HD9705.5.C643 U648 1983

Understanding first-time recreation vehicle buyers . Reston, VA (P.O. Box 2999, Prepared for Recreation Vehicle Industry Association, c1986. xxvi, 80 p. ; LC Card 87-108982 DDC 381/45629226/0973 19
HD9710.37.U62 U53 1986

United States of America, tin in tinplate. London [1983] 89 p. : LC Card 84-216067 DDC 338.4/76736/0973 19
HD9529.T63 U67 1983

VHSIC . Norwalk, Conn., U. S.A. (6 Prowitt St., Norwalk 06855) , c1986. v, 219 leaves : LC Card 86-224890 DDC 381/.4562138173/0973 19
HD9696.I582 V47 1986

Video telephony markets. Norwalk, Conn., U. S.A. (6 Prowitt St., Norwalk 06855) , c1986. ii, 96 leaves : LC Card 86-224725 DDC 381/.45621386 19
HD9697.T453 U58 1986

The Videotex marketplace. Bethesda, Md. , c1984. 203 p. : ISBN 0-934960-17-8 (pbk.) : LC Card 84-201507 DDC 384 19
HD9696.D383 U638 1984
NYPL [JSF 86-430]

Virtual facsimile & PC image capture/transmission/processing. Norwalk, Conn., U. S.A. (6 Prowitt St., Norwalk 06855) , c1986. vii, 208 leaves : LC Card 86-224356 DDC 381/.4500642/0973 19
HD9696.I423 U548 1986

Welding equipment and supplies market. New York, N.Y. , c1983. 2 v. (v, 316 leaves) ; LC Card 87-143994
HD9697.W433 U548 1983

Market timing. Chua, Jess H. Gains from stock-market timing /. New York, N.Y. (90 Trinity Pl., New York 10006) [c1986] 75 p. ; LC Card 87-129798 DDC 332.63/222 19
HG4637 .C48 1986

The marketer's guide to media vehicles, methods, and options . Grossman, Ann. New York , 1987. xiv, 238 p. : ISBN 0-89930-266-1 (lib. bdg. : alk. paper) LC Card 87-2473 DDC 659.1 19
HF5826.5 .G76 1987

Marketing. Lesson 25, The green machine [videorecording] / Fountain Valley, CA : Coast Telecourses, 1985. 1 videocassette (30 min.) : sd., col. Title from data sheet. Consultants, Jack Wichert, Joseph V. Anderson. Correlated with: Contemporary marketing / Louis E. Boone, David L. Kurtz. Adults. Issued as U-matic 3/4 in. or Beta 1/2 in. or VHS 1/2 in. This segment from a telecourse illustrates how the nonprofit organization adapts the marketing mix concepts of product, price, place, and promotion to meet the organization's objectives. Points out how the nonprofit marketing manager must use different measurements to evaluate the effectiveness of nonprofit marketing. LC Card 87-705967 DDC 658.8 11

1. Marketing - Case studies. 2. Corporations, Nonprofit - Marketing - Case studies. I. Boone, Louis E. Contemporary marketing. II. Coast Community College District. III. KOCE-TV (Television station : Huntington Beach, Calif.). IV. Holt, Rinehart and Winston, inc. V. Coast Telecourses (Firm). VI. Title: Green machine.
HF5415

Marketing : introducing the Hungarian industry. [Budapest : Hungarian Institute for Market Research, 1985?] 68 p. : ill. ; 29 cm. Cover title. "Supplement of Marketing"--P. 3. LC Card 86-234770 DDC 338.7/4/09439 19

1. Hungary - Industries - Directories. 2. Business enterprises - Hungary - Directories. I. Marketing (Budapest, Hungary). Supplement.
HC300.227 .M37 1985

Marketing /. Bennett, Peter D. New York , c1988. xxvii, 763 p. : ISBN 0-07-004721-9 : LC Card 87-17335 DDC 658.8 19
HF5415 .B4293 1988

Marketing . Cateora, Philip R. Homewood, Ill. , 1987. xi, 172 p. : ISBN 0-256-05626-9 (pbk.) LC Card 86-83392 DDC 658.8/48 19
HF1009.5 .C37 1987

Marketing . Gross, Charles W. St. Paul , c1987.

xxviii, 700 p. : ISBN 0-314-85242-5 : LC Card 86-26676 DDC 658.8/02 19
HF5415.135 .G76 1987

Marketing . Hise, Richard T. Houston, Tex. , 1986. xiv, 891 p. : ISBN 0-87393-038-X LC Card 83-72200 DDC 658.8 19
HF5415 .H543 1986

Marketing . Sangiovanni, Bruno. Roma , c1986. 268 p. : LC Card 85-233830
HF5415.153 .S25 1986

Marketing . Schoell, William F. Boston , 1987. p. cm. ISBN 0-205-10569-6 LC Card 87-23178 DDC 658.8 19
HF5415 .S357 1987

Il marketing agroalimentare . Foglio, Antonio, 1940- Milano, Italy , c1985. 370 p. : LC Card 86-114259
HD9015.I8 F64 1985

Marketing and distributive education [videorecording] / produced by Rachel Stevenson for International Film Bureau Inc. Chicago, Ill. : The Bureau, 1986. 2 videocassettes (24 min. each) : sd., col. + 1 teacher's guide. Title from data sheet. Consultants, Michael Russell, Edward Harris. Originally issued as filmstrip in 1983. Junior and senior high school students. Issued as U-matic 3/4 in. or Beta 1/2 in. or VHS 1/2 in. Designed to be used in marketing studies and in career guidance programs. Presents the latest trends in sales, advertising, physical distribution, and management. CONTENTS. - Marketing as a career ; Getting a job in marketing ; Experience in selling -- Advertising and display ; The ins and outs of physical distribution ; Buying from wholesalers and managing a small shop. LC Card 86-708241 DDC 658.8 11
1. Marketing. 2. Distributive education. I. Stevenson, Rachel. II. International Film Bureau.
HF5415

Marketing Anzeigen (Firm) Meissner, Hans-Günther. Werbung und gesellschaftlicher Wandel über die kommunikativen Voraussetzungen technischen, ökonomischen und sozialen Fortschritts . [Berlin] , Hamburg [1979] 23, [4] leaves ; LC Card 84-119751
HF5802.5 .M45 1979

MARKETING - AUSTRALIA - CASE STUDIES.
Gilmour, Peter, 1942- Australian marketing casebook /. St. Lucia , c1988. p. cm. ISBN 0-7022-2091-4 (pbk.) LC Card 87-16220 DDC 658.8/00994 19
HF5415.12.A9 G54 1988

Marketing bancaire . Zollinger, Monique. [Paris] , c1985. viii, 238 p. : ISBN 2-04-016433-2 : LC Card 86-152950 DDC 332.1/068/8 19
HG1616.M3 Z65 1985

MARKETING - BANGLADESH - CONGRESSES.
Jātīya Mārketiṃ Seminārа, 1985 (1985 : Chātra-Śikshaka Kendra, Ḍhākā Biśvabidyālaẏa) Māketiṃ, samasyā o sambhābanā . [Dhaka] , 1985. 138 p. ; LC Card 86-903411
HF5415.12.B36 J38 1985

Marketing Boards für Agrarexportgüter in Entwicklungsländern /. Junginger-Dittel, K.-O. [Kiel] , 1980. iii, 48 leaves ; LC Card 85-160428
HD9018.D44 J86 1980

MARKETING - BRAZIL.
Galindo, Daniel dos Santos. Comunicação mercadológica em tempo de incertezas /. S. Paulo-SP , c1986. 167 p. : LC Card 86-224127
HF5415.12.B7 G35 1986

Neustadt, Peter. Wachstum und Strukturwandlungen Brasiliens in ihrer Bedeutung für die strategische Marketingplanung von Konsumgüterunternehmungen /. Diessenhofen , cop. 1979. ix, 463 p. : ISBN 3-7253-0092-5 : LC Card 80-469750
HF5415.12.B7 N48 1979 ***NYPL [JLD 80-3357]***

Marketing (Budapest, Hungary). Supplement.
Marketing . [Budapest , 1985?] 68 p. : LC Card 86-234770 DDC 338.7/4/09439 19
HC300.227 .M37 1985

MARKETING - CASE STUDIES.
Heller, Robert, 1932- The supermarketers . New York , c1987. xiii, 384 p. ; ISBN 0-525-24520-0 LC Card 86-23977 DDC 658.8 19
HF5415 .H374 1987

Marketing. Fountain Valley, CA , 1985. 1 videocassette (30 min.) : LC Card 87-705967 DDC 658.8 11
HF5415

Readings and cases in basic marketing /. Homewood, Ill. , 1987. ix, 365 p. : ISBN 0-256-05795-8 (pbk.) LC Card 86-83136 DDC 658.8 19
HF5415 .R334 1987

Rodgers, F. G. (Francis G.) The IBM way . New York , c1986. xiv, 235 p. ; ISBN 0-06-015522-1 : LC Card 85-45223 DDC 338.7/61004/0973 19
HD9696.C64 I4875 1986 ***NYPL [JLE 86-1374]***

Strategic marketing for nonprofit organizations . Englewood Cliffs, NJ , c1987. x, 386 p. : ISBN 0-13-851312-0 (pbk.) : LC Card 86-25262 DDC 658.8 19
HF5415 .C2854 1987

Marketing channel management . Hardy, Kenneth G., 1941- Glenview, IL , c1988. 724 p. : ISBN 0-673-18295-9 : LC Card 87-12742 DDC 658.8/4 19
HF5415 .H229 1988

Marketing channels /. Stern, Louis W., 1935- Englewood Cliffs, N.J. , c1988. xiv, 609 p. : ISBN 0-13-557158-8 : LC Card 87-17396 DDC 658.8/4 19
HF5415.129 .S75 1988

MARKETING CHANNELS.
Stern, Louis W., 1935- Marketing channels /. Englewood Cliffs, N.J. , c1988. xiv, 609 p. : ISBN 0-13-557158-8 : LC Card 87-17396 DDC 658.8/4 19
HF5415.129 .S75 1988

MARKETING CHANNELS - DIRECTORIES.
The Standard handbook of industrial distributors. Fairfield, CT, USA , c1987- v. <1-2 > ; ISBN 0-917408-02-0 (pbk. : v. 1) LC Card 86-73258 DDC 380.1/456218/025 19
HD9680.A2 S72 1987

MARKETING CHANNELS - ITALY.
Fruscio, Dario. Il sistema distributivo italiano . [Milano] , 1983. vii, 184 p. ; LC Card 83-233439 DDC 380.1/0945 19
HF5415.6 .F78 1983 ***NYPL [JLE 86-3650]***

L'Affiliazione commerciale . Milano , 1986. 100 p. : ***NYPL [JLD 87-531]***

MARKETING CHANNELS - MANAGEMENT.
Hardy, Kenneth G., 1941- Marketing channel management . Glenview, IL , c1988. 724 p. : ISBN 0-673-18295-9 : LC Card 87-12742 DDC 658.8/4 19
HF5415 .H229 1988

MARKETING CHANNELS - UNITED STATES.
Sutton, Howard, 1930- Rethinking the company's selling and distribution channels /. New York, N.Y. , c1986. v, 26 p. : ISBN 0-8237-0328-2 (pbk.) LC Card 87-404502 DDC 658.8/4 19
HF5415.129 .S87 1986

Marketing communications effectiveness to the dentist. Tustin, CA (17722 Irvine Blvd., Tustin 92680) : Biomedical Business International, c1986. 130 leaves in various foliations : ill. ; 29 cm. (Report / Biomedical Business International . #3111) LC Card 86-231569 DDC 681/.761 19
1. Dental instruments and apparatus industry - United States - Statistics. 2. Dental instruments and apparatus - United States - Marketing - Statistics. 3. Dentists - United States - Attitudes - Statistics. I. Biomedical Business International, Inc. II. Series: Report (Biomedical Business International, Inc.) , #3111.
HD9995.D43 U55 1986

MARKETING - CONGRESSES.
AMA Winter Educators' Conference (1987 : San Antonio, Tex.) 1987 AMA Winter Educators' Conference . Chicago, Ill. , c1987. viii, 411 p. : ISBN 0-87757-185-6 (pbk.) LC Card 87-944 DDC 658.8/001 19
HF5411 .A53 1987

Contemporary views on marketing practice /. Lexington, Mass. , c1987. vi, 282 p. : ISBN 0-669-15120-3 (alk. paper) LC Card 86-46218 DDC 658.8 19
HF5411 .C66 1987

Creativity in services marketing . Chicago, IL , 1986. 175 p. : ISBN 0-87757-179-1 (pbk.) LC Card 85-26785 DDC 658.8 19
HD9980.5 .C74 1986 ***NYPL [JLF 86-1783]***

Seminar on Below-the-Line and Sponsoring (1985 : Milan, Italy) Seminar on Below-the-Line and Sponsoring . Amsterdam, Netherlands [1985] vi, 270 p. : ISBN 92-831-1107-9 (pbk.) : LC Card 86-213125 DDC 658.8/2 19
HF5438.5 .S46 1985

1987 AMA educators' proceedings /. Chicago, Ill. , 1987. xiv, 287 p. ; ISBN 0-87757-182-1 LC Card 87-18680 DDC 658.8 19
HF5411 .A156 1987

MARKETING - COSTS.
Deran, Elisabeth. Low-cost marketing strategies . New York , 1987. ix, 151 p. ; ISBN 0-275-92341-X (alk. paper) : LC Card 86-30640 DDC 658.8 19
HF5415 .D458 1987

Il marketing d'acquisto . Landi, Antonio. Milano, Italy , 1986. 247 p. : ISBN 88-20-41020-6 : LC Card 86-207836
HD9680.A2 L36 1986

MARKETING - DATA PROCESSING.
Parkinson, Lynn K. Using the microcomputer in marketing /. London , New York , c1987. ix, 158 p. : ISBN 0-07-084163-2 (pbk.) : LC Card 86-27364 DDC 658.8/0028/5416 19
HF5415.125 .P36 1987

Parsons, Leonard J. Using microcomputers in marketing /. [Boston, Mass.?] , c1986. xi, 141 p. : LC Card 86-216432 DDC 658.8/0028/5416 19
HF5415.125 .P37 1986

MARKETING - DECISION MAKING.
Bell, Martin L. Managerial marketing . New York , c1988. xviii, 708 p. : ISBN 0-444-01215-X LC Card 87-22306 DDC 658.8 19
HF5415.13 .B434 1988

Benkenstein, Martin. F & E und Marketing . Wiesbaden , c1987. xvii, 319 p. ; ISBN 3-409-13327-5 LC Card 87-144515 DDC 658.8/3 19
HF5415.2 .B4563 1987

Financial dimensions of marketing . London , 1981. 2 v. : ISBN 0-333-25741-3 ***NYPL [JLL 82-44]***

Fleischer, Manfred. Organisationstheoretische Analyse von Marketing-Entscheidungsprozessen . Berlin [1977] 93 p. : LC Card 85-111320
HF5415.135 .F58 1977

Fronhoff, Bernd, 1956- Die Gestaltung von Marketingstrategien . Bergisch Gladbach , 1986. ix, 369 p. : ISBN 3-89012-067-9 LC Card 87-122913 DDC 658.8/02 19
HF5415.135 .F76 1986

Gross, Charles W. Marketing . St. Paul , c1987. xxviii, 700 p. : ISBN 0-314-85242-5 : LC Card 86-26676 DDC 658.8/02 19
HF5415.135 .G76 1987

Müller, Wolfgang, 1955- Planung von Marketing-Strategien . Frankfurt am Main , New York , c1986. xxvi, 514 p. : ISBN 3-8204-8992-4 LC Card 86-205571
HF5415.13 .M833 1986

Readings in strategic marketing . Chicago , c1988. x, 534 p. : ISBN 0-03-020864-5 (pbk.) LC Card 87-22274 DDC 658.8/02 19
HF5415.135 .R42 1988

Ringbeck, Jürgen. Qualitäts- und Werbestrategien bei Qualitätsunsicherheit der Konsumenten /. Wiesbaden , c1986. 256 p. ; ISBN 3-409-13612-6 LC Card 87-111545 DDC 658.8/02 19
HF5415.135 .R56 1986

Strategisches Marketing und Management . Bern , c1986. 205 p. : ISBN 3-258-03566-0 : LC Card 86-159360
HF5415.135 .S77 1986

Voss, Wolf-Dieter. Modellgestützte Markenpolitik . Wiesbaden , c1983. xxvi, 297 p. : ISBN 3-409-36035-2 LC Card 83-159054
HF5415.125 .V67 1983

MARKETING - DECISION MAKING - CASE STUDIES.
Bell, Martin L. Managerial marketing . New

York , c1988. xviii, 708 p. : ISBN 0-444-01215-X LC Card 87-22306 DDC 658.8 19
HF5415.13 .B434 1988

Bernhardt, Kenneth L., 1944- Cases in marketing management /. Plano, Tex. , 1985. xiii, 705 p. : ISBN 0-256-03055-3 LC Card 84-70994 DDC 658.8 19
HF5415.13 .B448 1985
NYPL [JLE 86-2513]

MARKETING - DECISION MAKING - MATHEMATICAL MODELS.
Schiller, Karla, 1955- Loglineare Modellierung mit dem Abschlusstest . München , c1986. xiii, 226 p. : ISBN 3-88259-397-0 LC Card 86-230772
HF5415.135 .S35 1986

MARKETING - DENMARK.
Trolle, Ulf af, 1919- Markedsføring . °slo] , 1982. 496 p. : ISBN 82-00-05931-6 : LC Card 83-184229
HF5415.12.D4 T76 1982

Marketing der Unternehmen des öffentlichen Personen, nahverkehrs im Spannungsfeld erwerbswirtschaftlicher und gemeinwirtschaftlicher Ziele /. Clauss, Rüdiger, 1952- Bergisch Gladbach , 1985. xiii, 308 p. : ISBN 3-89012-019-9 LC Card 85-175468
HE249 .C42 1985

MARKETING - DICTIONARIES.
Koschnick, Wolfgang J., 1942- Standard-Wörterbuch für Werbung, Massenmedien und Marketing, Deutsch-Englisch /. Berlin , New York , 1987. 590 p. ; ISBN 0-89925-293-1 (U. S.) : LC Card 87-19928 DDC 659.1/03/21 19
HF5803 .K67 1987

MARKETING - DICTIONARIES - GERMAN.
Koschnick, Wolfgang J., 1942- Standard-Lexikon für Marketing, Marktkommunikation, Markt- und Mediaforschung /. München , New York , 1987. vi, 940 p. : ISBN 3-598-10583-5 LC Card 87-143648 DDC 380.1/03/31 19
HF5415 .K617 1987

MARKETING - EUROPE - CONGRESSES.
Seminar on Retail Strategies for Profit and Growth (1986 : Brussels, Belgium) Seminar on Retail Strategies for Profit and Growth . Amsterdam, Netherlands [1986] vi, 324 p. : ISBN 92-831-1113-3 (pbk.) : LC Card 86-218316 DDC 658.8/7/0094 19
HF5429.6.E9 S45 1986

Marketing Facts, Inc. Financial Services Group.
Margin accounts. Chicago, IL , c1987. iii leaves, 59 p. : LC Card 87-403672 DDC 332.64/5 19
HG4963 .M34 1987

MARKETING - FINANCE.
Financial dimensions of marketing . London , 1981. 2 v. : ISBN 0-333-25741-3
NYPL [JLL 82-44]

MARKETING - FINLAND - CASE STUDIES.
Lindqvist, Lars-Johan. Marknadsföring till handeln . Helsingfors , 1983. 309 p. : ISBN 951-555-183-8 LC Card 84-103976
HF5421.5.F5 L56 1983

MARKETING - GERMANY, WEST.
Gebhardt, Peter. Der Markt gebrauchter Güter . Hamburg , c1986. xxvii, 250, [69] p. : ISBN 3-925630-10-4 LC Card 87-127354 DDC 381/.1 19
HF5482 .G42 1986

Krause, Hans-Ulrich. Gewinnung, Verarbeitung und Aufbereitung von Informationen für die Geschäftsfeldplanung . Giessen , c1984. xii,324 p. ; ISBN 3-922730-52-3 LC Card 85-150146
HD35 .K71215 1984

Mahler, Karl-Werner, 1933- Der Waste Factor . München-Gräfelfing , c1983. 64 p. ; ISBN 3-8040-0321-4 LC Card 84-214297
HC290.5.W3 M34 1983

MARKETING - GERMANY (WEST) - MANAGEMENT.
Ebert, Kurt, 1954- Warenwirtschaftssysteme und Warenwirtschafts-Controlling /. Frankfurt am Main , New York , c1986. xvi, 353 p. : ISBN 3-8204-9673-4 LC Card 86-218178
HF5415.15 .E24 1986

MARKETING - GREAT BRITAIN - BIBLIOGRAPHY.
Shaw, Christine. The A-Z of UK marketing information sources /. London , 1984. 233 p. ; ISBN 0-86338-048-4 (pbk.) : LC Card 84-217782 DDC 330.941/0858 19
HC256.6 .S47 1984 ***NYPL [JLD 86-2248]***

MARKETING - GREAT BRITAIN - HISTORY.
Markets and bagmen . Aldershot, Hants, England , Brookfield, Vt., USA , c1986. xii, 204 p. : ISBN 0-566-05066-8 : LC Card 86-22951 DDC 380.1/0941 19
HF5415.12.G7 M37 1986

MARKETING - GREAT BRITAIN - INFORMATION SERVICES.
Shaw, Christine. The A-Z of UK marketing information sources /. London , 1984. 233 p. ; ISBN 0-86338-048-4 (pbk.) : LC Card 84-217782 DDC 330.941/0858 19
HC256.6 .S47 1984 ***NYPL [JLD 86-2248]***

MARKETING - GREECE.
Hodēgos marketinnk Hellados, 1983 /. Athēnai [1983?] 357 p. ; LC Card 84-107807
HF5415.12.G8 H63 1983

Marketing guidelines for Jamaica's non-traditional exports. Lyn-Cook, Marlene. [Miami, FL] [1986] 83 leaves : LC Card 87-156503 DDC 382/.097292/073 19
HF1009.7.J25 L96 1986

MARKETING - HISTORY.
Bartels, Robert, 1913- The history of marketing thought /. Columbus, Ohio , c1988. p. cm. ISBN 0-942280-44-X : LC Card 87-20702 DDC 658.8/009 19
HF5415 .B36 1988

Markets and bagmen . Aldershot, Hants, England , Brookfield, Vt., USA , c1986. xii, 204 p. : ISBN 0-566-05066-8 : LC Card 86-22951 DDC 380.1/0941 19
HF5415.12.G7 M37 1986

MARKETING - HUNGARY - CONGRESSES.
A Vállalati magatartást motiváló gazdasági és társadalmi tényezők című konferencia előadásai . Pécs , 1985. 2 v. : LC Card 87-408547
HD70.H8 V334 1985

Marketing in Ghana : an analysis of operational and environmental conditions. Addis Ababa : United Nations, Economic Commission for Africa, 1984. vi, 62 p. ; 28 cm. (Research series / African Training and Research Centre for Women) Study was undertaken by the National Council of Women and Development (Ghana). "E/ECA/ATRCW/81/07." Bibliography: p. 62. LC Card 86-980249 DDC 381/.18/09667 19
1. Women merchants - Ghana. 2. Markets - Ghana. I. United Nations. Economic Commission for Africa. II. National Council of Women and Development (Ghana). III. Series: Research series / African Training and Research Centre for Women.
HD6072.6.G4 M37 1984

MARKETING - INDIA - MANAGEMENT.
Ojha, Ghanshyam Das, 1947- Organisation & management of public distribution system /. Delhi, India , 1987. x, 235 p. ; LC Card 87-900491 DDC 381/.1/0954 19
HF5415.12.I5 O44 1987

Marketing ist Philosophie. Rock, Reinhard. Marketing=Philosophie /. Frankfurt am Main , New York , c1986. 220 p. ; ISBN 3-8204-9700-5 LC Card 87-407971 DDC 658.8/001 19
HF5415 .R557 1986

MARKETING - ITALY.
Penati, Luigi. Strategie di marketing /. Milano, Italy , c1986. 332 p. : LC Card 86-217663
HF5415.12.I8 P47 1986

Marketing life insurance in a bank or thrift / edited by Jerome R. Corsi. Boulder, Colo. : Westview Press, 1986. xii, 233 p. ; 23 cm. (Westview professional handbooks on the new banking) Includes index. ISBN 0-8133-7205-4 : LC Card 86-1644 DDC 332.1/7 19
1. Banks and banking - Insurance business. 2. Insurance, Life - United States. I. Corsi, Jerome R. II. Series.
HG1616.I47 M37 1986
NYPL [JLD 86-3992]

Marketing management . Guiltinan, Joseph P. New York , c1988. xvi, 427 p. : ISBN 0-07-048929-7 : LC Card 87-23186 DDC 658.8 19
HF5415.13 .G84 1988

Marketing management . Kotler, Philip. Englewood Cliffs, NJ , 1988. p. cm. ISBN 0-13-556150-7 LC Card 87-19301 DDC 658.8 19
HF5415.13 .K64 1988

Marketing management and strategy : a reader / edited by Philip Kotler, Keith K. Cox.4th ed. Englewood Cliffs, NJ : Prentice-Hall, c1988. x, 406 p. : ill. ; 24 cm. Includes bibliographies. ISBN 0-13-558453-1 (pbk.) LC Card 87-18849 DDC 658.8 19
1. Marketing management. I. Kotler, Philip. II. Cox, Keith Kohn.
HF5415.13 .M3524 1988

MARKETING MANAGEMENT - CASE STUDIES.
Bernhardt, Kenneth L., 1944- Cases in marketing management /. Plano, Tex. , 1985. xiii, 705 p. : ISBN 0-256-03055-3 LC Card 84-70994 DDC 658.8 19
HF5415.13 .B448 1985
NYPL [JLE 86-2513]

Hartley, Robert F. Bullseyes and blunders . New York , c1987. vii, 253 p. : ISBN 0-471-84904-9 LC Card 86-23350 DDC 658 19
HD38 .H3487 1987 ***NYPL [JLE 87-1047]***

Readings and cases in marketing management /. Homewood, Ill. , 1987. xv, 443 p. : ISBN 0-256-03161-4 (pbk.) LC Card 86-82585 DDC 658.8 19
HF5415.13 .R362 1987

MARKETING MANAGEMENT - CONGRESSES.
Technology management '85 . London , c1985. 160 p. : ISBN 0-903748-61-4
NYPL [JLG 87-124]

MARKETING MANAGEMENT - DATA PROCESSING.
Voss, Wolf-Dieter. Modellgestützte Markenpolitik . Wiesbaden , c1983. xxvi, 297 p. : ISBN 3-409-36035-2 LC Card 83-159054
HF5415.125 .V67 1983

MARKETING - MANAGEMENT - DIRECTORIES.
The National directory of product publicity sources /. Westbury, N.Y. , 1987. p. cm. ISBN 0-87280-157-8 : LC Card 87-17542 DDC 338.7/616592/025 19
HD59 .N245 1987

MARKETING - MATHEMATICAL MODELS.
Bruse, Helmut. Der Absatzbereich von Unternehmen . Bonn , 1980. xiv, 323 p. : LC Card 85-164955
HF5415 .B7713 1980

Simon, Hermann. Goodwill und Marketingstrategie /. Wiesbaden , c1985. 250 p. : ISBN 3-409-13603-7 LC Card 85-232089 DDC 658.8/02 19
HF5415 .S4958 1985

MARKETING - MATHEMATICS.
Geninet, Bernard. Mathématiques et statistiques générales appliquées au marketing . Paris , c1986. 198 p. : ISBN 2-7178-1071-4 : LC Card 86-165417
HF5415 .G397 1986

The marketing mirage . McIver, Colin, 1914- New York , 1987. viii, 215 p. : ISBN 0-89397-285-1 : LC Card 87-14048 DDC 658.8 19
HF5415 .M2583 1987

MARKETING - NETHERLANDS - DECISION MAKING.
Noort, W. C. J. van, 1950- Statistiek voor marketingsbeslissingen /. Leiden , 1985. viii, 229 p. : ISBN 90-207-1351-5 : LC Card 85-214756
HF5415.2 .N66 1985

MARKETING - NIGERIA - ADO EKITI.
Adebowale, Annette, 1957- Yoruba-Märkte in Nigeria . Aachen , c1987. xxvii, 225 p. : ISBN 3-922868-64-9 LC Card 87-141899 DDC 381/.18/096692 19
HF5475.N52 A362 1987

Marketing of agricultural products /. Kohls, Richard L. New York , London , c1985. xi, 624 p. : ISBN 0-02-365670-0 LC Card 84-817 DDC 381/.41 19
HD9000.5 .K57 1985 ***NYPL [JLE 86-4145]***

MARKETING OF FARM PRODUCE. see **FARM PRODUCE - MARKETING.**

The marketing of foodstuffs in the Gambia, 1400-1980 . Barrett, Hazel R., 1955- Aldershot, Hants., England , Brookfield, Vt., U. S.A. , 1988, c1987. p. cm. ISBN 0-566-05487-6 LC Card 87-23063 DDC 381/.41/096651 19
HD9017.G262 B37 1988

Marketing of horticulture industry in India /. Sahaf, Musadiq Amin, 1958- Delhi, India , 1987. xiii, 151 p. ; LC Card 86-903833 DDC 381/.414/0954 19
HD9016.I43 J367 1987

Marketing of walnuts in India. India. Directorate of Marketing and Inspection. Faridabad , Delhi , 1986. ix, 180 p. : LC Card 86-903362
HD9259.N7 I45 1986

Marketing-oriented financial services advertising and research . Advertising Research Foundation Key Issues Workshop (1986 : Boston, Mass.) New York, NY , c1986. 119 p. : LC Card 87-404482 DDC 659.1/93321 19
HF6161.F46 A38 1986

Marketing=Philosophie /. Rock, Reinhard. Frankfurt am Main , New York , c1986. 220 p. ; ISBN 3-8204-9700-5 LC Card 87-407971 DDC 658.8/001 19
HF5415 .R557 1986

MARKETING - POLAND.
Funkcjonowanie rynku usług w Polsce /. Wrocław , 1986. 176 p. ; ISBN 83-7011-034-7 : LC Card 87-169457
HB9 .B7522 nr. 355 HD9986.P7

Marketing principles and practices /. Allvine, Fred C. San Diego , c1987. xxix, 829, 38 p. : ISBN 0-15-555101-9 LC Card 85-82622 DDC 658.8 19
HF5415 .A436 1987

Marketing public transit : a strategic approach / Christopher H. Lovelock ... [et al.]. New York : Praeger, 1987. x, 228 p. : ill. ; 24 cm. (Praeger series in public and nonprofit sector marketing) Includes bibliographies and index. ISBN 0-275-92499-8 (alk. paper) : LC Card 87-11583 DDC 388.4/068/8 19
1. Local transit - United States - Marketing. I. Lovelock, Christopher H.
HE4456 .M37 1987

Marketing real estate internationally /. Hines, Mary Alice. New York , c1988. p. cm. ISBN 0-89930-205-X (lib. bdg. : alk. paper) LC Card 87-24935 DDC 333.33/0688 19
HD1382.5 .H557 1988

Marketing research /. Kress, George. Englewood Cliffs, N.J. , c1988. p. cm. ISBN 0-13-558438-8 LC Card 87-17408 DDC 658.8/3 19
HF5415.2 .K75 1988

Marketing research /. Luck, David Johnston. Englewood Cliffs, NJ , c1987. xvii, 683 p. : ISBN 0-13-557828-0 : LC Card 86-25255 DDC 658.8/3 19
HF5415.2 .M3555 1987

Marketing research . Schellinck, Douglas Anton, 1949- New York , c1987. xii, 224 p. : ISBN 0-03-010924-8 (pbk.) LC Card 86-29029 DDC 658.8/3/0285 19
HF5415.2 .S32 1987

MARKETING RESEARCH - ADDRESSES, ESSAYS, LECTURES.
Perspectives on methodology in consumer research /. New York , c1986. xi, 301 p. : ISBN 0-387-96238-7 : LC Card 85-26047 DDC 658.8/34 19
HF5415.3 .P464 1986 ***NYPL [JLE 86-4371]***

MARKETING RESEARCH - CASE STUDIES.
Applied marketing and social research /. Chichester , New York , c1987. xvii, 488 p. : ISBN 0-471-91356-1 : LC Card 86-32447 DDC 658.8/3 19
HF5415.2 .A654 1987

MARKETING RESEARCH - CONGRESSES.
AMA Winter Educators' Conference (1987 : San Antonio, Tex.) 1987 AMA Winter Educators' Conference . Chicago, Ill. , c1987. viii, 411 p. : ISBN 0-87757-185-6 (pbk.) LC Card 87-944 DDC 658.8/001 19
HF5411 .A53 1987

1987 AMA educators' proceedings /. Chicago, Ill. , 1987. xiv, 287 p. ; ISBN 0-87757-182-1 LC Card 87-18680 DDC 658.8 19
HF5411 .A156 1987

MARKETING RESEARCH - DATA PROCESSING.
Schellinck, Douglas Anton, 1949- Marketing research . New York , c1987. xii, 224 p. : ISBN 0-03-010924-8 (pbk.) LC Card 86-29029 DDC 658.8/3/0285 19
HF5415.2 .S32 1987

MARKETING RESEARCH - GERMANY, WEST.
Windhorst, Karl-Götz. Wertewandel und Konsumentenverhalten . Münster , c1985. xxi, 299 p. : ISBN 3-7923-0520-8 LC Card 85-171929 DDC 338.5/21/0943 19
HB201 .W663 1985 ***NYPL [JLE 87-369]***

MARKETING RESEARCH - GREAT BRITAIN - CASE STUDIES.
Applied marketing and social research /. Chichester , New York , c1987. xvii, 488 p. : ISBN 0-471-91356-1 : LC Card 86-32447 DDC 658.8/3 19
HF5415.2 .A654 1987

MARKETING RESEARCH - GREAT BRITAIN - HISTORY.
Blythe, Ian. Forty years on . Aldershot, Hants., England , Brookfield, Vt., USA , c1987. p. cm. ISBN 0-566-05005-6 : LC Card 87-8653 DDC 658.8/3/06041 19
HF5410 .B58 1987

Marketing research in a marketing environment /. Dillon, William R. St. Louis , 1987. xxviii, 742, 21, 15 p. : ISBN 0-8016-1303-5 : LC Card 86-23189 DDC 658.8/3 19
HF5415.2 .D54 1987

MARKETING RESEARCH - MATHEMATICAL MODELS.
Schiller, Karla, 1955- Loglineare Modellierung mit dem Abschlusstest . München , c1986. xiii, 226 p. : ISBN 3-88259-397-0 LC Card 86-230772
HF5415.135 .S35 1986

MARKETING RESEARCH - NETHERLANDS.
Noort, W. C. J. van, 1950- Statistiek voor marketingsbeslissingen /. Leiden , 1985. viii, 229 p. : ISBN 90-207-1351-5 : LC Card 85-214756
HF5415.2 .N66 1985

MARKETING RESEARCH - STATISTICAL METHODS.
Noort, W. C. J. van, 1950- Statistiek voor marketingsbeslissingen /. Leiden , 1985. viii, 229 p. : ISBN 90-207-1351-5 : LC Card 85-214756
HF5415.2 .N66 1985

MARKETING RESEARCH - STATISTICAL METHODS - DATA PROCESSING.
Schellinck, Douglas Anton, 1949- Marketing research . New York , c1987. xii, 224 p. : ISBN 0-03-010924-8 (pbk.) LC Card 86-29029 DDC 658.8/3/0285 19
HF5415.2 .S32 1987

MARKETING RESEARCH - UNITED STATES.
ADAPSO guide to market research for the computer software and services industry. Arlington, Va. (1300 N. 17th St., Suite 300, Arlington 22209) , c1985. 71 p. ; LC Card 87-402047 DDC 005/.068/8 19
HD9696.C63 U511235 1985

MARKETING RESEARCH - UNITED STATES - HISTORY.
Blythe, Ian. Forty years on . Aldershot, Hants., England , Brookfield, Vt., USA , c1987. p. cm. ISBN 0-566-05005-6 : LC Card 87-8653 DDC 658.8/3/06041 19
HF5410 .B58 1987

MARKETING RESEARCH - UNITED STATES - TECHNOLOGICAL INNOVATIONS - CONGRESSES.
Advertising Research Foundation Key Issues Workshop (1986 : New York, N.Y.) Transcript proceedings . New York, NY (3 E. 54th St., New York 10022-3180) , c1986. 268 p. : LC Card 87-149342 DDC 658.8/3 19
HF5802.5 .A3826 1986

MARKETING - SCANDINAVIA.
Rosenlew, Andreas. Intern marknadsföring . [Helsinki] [1985] 51 p. : ISBN 951-555-227-3 LC Card 85-214635
HF5415 .R5795 1985

Marketing Science Institute.
Bloom, Paul N. Knowledge development in marketing . Lexington, Mass. , c1987. xvi, 238 p. ; ISBN 0-669-12581-4 (alk. paper) LC Card 85-45938 DDC 658.83 19
HF5415.2 .B57 1987

Nonverbal communication in advertising /. Lexington, Mass. , c1988. viii, 296 p. : ISBN 0-669-14172-0 (alk. paper) LC Card 87-17143 DDC 659.1/01/9 19
HF5822 .N66 1988

MARKETING SCIENCE INSTITUTE.
Bloom, Paul N. Knowledge development in marketing . Lexington, Mass. , c1987. xvi, 238 p. ; ISBN 0-669-12581-4 (alk. paper) LC Card 85-45938 DDC 658.83 19
HF5415.2 .B57 1987

Marketing series (London, England)
McDonald, Malcolm. How to sell a service . London , 1986. 149 p. : ISBN 0-434-91231-X (pbk.) : LC Card 86-212510 DDC 658.8 19
HF5438.25 .M396 1986

MARKETING - STATISTICAL METHODS.
Geninet, Bernard. Mathématiques et statistiques générales appliquées au marketing . Paris , c1986. 198 p. : ISBN 2-7178-1071-4 : LC Card 86-165417
HF5415 .G397 1986

Marketing-Strategie für den Detailhandel /. Moser, R. (René), 1941- Münsingen , Zürich , 1981. 159 p. : ISBN 3-85681-059-5 LC Card 83-240590
HF5429.6.S92 M67 1981

Marketing strategies for community banks /. Moran, Justin L., 1932- Boston [c1987] xiii, 199 p. ; ISBN 0-87267-105-4 LC Card 87-19280 DDC 332.1/068/8 19
HG1616.M3 M67 1987

Marketing strategies for selling cosmetics & toiletries in Europe. New York, N.Y. : Frost & Sullivan, c1983. 381 p. ; 29 cm. Spine title: Cosmetics & toiletries marketing strategies in Europe. "April, 1983." "(E605)." LC Card 87-141847 DDC 380.1/456685/094 19
1. Cosmetics - Europe - Marketing. 2. Toilet preparations - Europe - Marketing. 3. Cosmetics industry - Europe. 4. Toilet preparations industry - Europe. 5. Market surveys - Europe. I. Frost & Sullivan. II. Title: Cosmetics & toiletries marketing strategies in Europe. III. Title: Cosmetics and toiletries marketing strategies in Europe.
HD9970.5.C673 E8555 1983

Marketing strategy in action /. Tack, Alfred. Aldershot, Hants, England , c1987. v, 245 p. ; ISBN 0-566-02668-6 LC Card 86-229563 DDC 658.8 19
HF5415 .T29 1987

MARKETING - STUDY AND TEACHING.
Warmbrod, Catharine P. Skills for the changing workplace . Columbus, Ohio (1960 Kenny Rd., Columbus 43210-1090) , 1985. ix, 86 p. ; LC Card 86-205842 DDC 658.8/007/15 19
HF5415 .W3155 1985

MARKETING - STUDY AND TEACHING - CENTRAL AMERICA.
An Evaluation of ROCAP activities in marketing, 1965-71 /. Washington, D.C. (1200 18th St., N.W., Washington 20036) [1971] xvii, 82, 3 leaves, [1] leaf of plates : LC Card 81-146599
HC141 .E93 1971

MARKETING - SWEDEN.
Ledning, produktion & marknadsföring av tjänster . Malmö , c1981. 318 p. : ISBN 91-40-54058-8 : LC Card 81-174255
HD9986.S82 L43 1981

MARKETING - SWITZERLAND.
Moser, R. (René), 1941- Marketing-Strategie für den Detailhandel /. Münsingen , Zürich , 1981. 159 p. : ISBN 3-85681-059-5 LC Card 83-240590
HF5429.6.S92 M67 1981

Marketing theory. AMA Winter Educators' Conference (1987 : San Antonio, Tex.) 1987 AMA Winter Educators' Conference . Chicago, Ill. , c1987. viii, 411 p. : ISBN 0-87757-185-6 (pbk.) LC Card 87-944 DDC 658.8/001 19
HF5411 .A53 1987

Marketing to the Fortune 500 and other corporations /. Davidson, Jeffrey P. Homewood, Ill. , c1987. xv, 291 p. : ISBN 0-87094-984-5 LC Card 86-51669 DDC 658.8 19
HF5415.1 .D28 1987

Marketing to the trade. Lindqvist, Lars-Johan. Marknadsföring till handeln . Helsingfors , 1983. 309 p. : ISBN 951-555-183-8 LC Card 84-103976
HF5421.5.F5 L56 1983

Marketing today /. Rachman, David J. Chicago , c1988. xxvii, 654 p. : ISBN 0-03-013573-7 (pbk.) LC Card 87-22239 DDC 658.8 19
HF5415 .R2354 1988

MARKETING - UNITED STATES.
Davidson, Jeffrey P. Marketing to the Fortune 500 and other corporations /. Homewood, Ill. , c1987. xv, 291 p. : ISBN 0-87094-984-5 LC Card 86-51669 DDC 658.8 19
HF5415.1 .D28 1987

MARKETING - UNITED STATES - MANAGEMENT.
Cases and classics in marketing management /. San Diego , c1986. ix, 513 p. : ISBN 0-15-505775-8 LC Card 85-80071 DDC 658.8/00973 19
HF5415.13 .C28 1986 NYPL [JLE 86-3101]

MARKETING - UNITED STATES - MANAGEMENT - CASE STUDIES.
Cases and classics in marketing management /. San Diego , c1986. ix, 513 p. : ISBN 0-15-505775-8 LC Card 85-80071 DDC 658.8/00973 19
HF5415.13 .C28 1986 NYPL [JLE 86-3101]

A Collection of cases in marketing management /. St. Paul , c1987. xix, 344 p. ; ISBN 0-314-85313-8 (pbk.) LC Card 87-6072 DDC 658.8/00973 19
HF5415.13 .C64 1987

Marketing your arts & crafts . Long, Steve. Sandpoint, Idaho (9395 Rapid Lightning Rd., Sandpoint 83864) [c1987] iv, 188 p. : LC Card 87-401972 DDC 745.5/068/8 19
HF5439.H27 L66 1987

Marketing your arts and crafts. Long, Steve. Marketing your arts & crafts . Sandpoint, Idaho (9395 Rapid Lightning Rd., Sandpoint 83864) [c1987] iv, 188 p. : LC Card 87-401972 DDC 745.5/068/8 19
HF5439.H27 L66 1987

Marketing your financial planning services . Jones, H. Stanley. New York , c1988. xvi, 304 p. ; ISBN 0-471-85649-5 LC Card 87-26373 DDC 332.6/2 19
HG179.5 .J66 1988

Marketing your shopping center . Wenner, S. Albert. New York , c1987. xi, 194 p. : ISBN 0-913598-55-0 LC Card 87-2848 DDC 658.8/7 19
HF5430 .W46 1987

Marketingkommunikation in der Investitionsgüterindustrie . Weis, Hans Christian. Thun , c1983. v, 319, xxxix p. : ISBN 3-87144-741-2 : LC Card 83-159201
HF5415.123 .W45 1983

Marketplace measurement . Donius, James F. New York, NY (155 E. 44th St., New York 11710) , c1986. xiii, 206 p. : LC Card 87-120244 DDC 659.1/11 19
HF5823 .D655 1986

MARKETS.
Maring, Matthias, 1950- Märkte und Handlungssysteme . Frankfurt am Main , New York , c1985. ii, 228 p. : ISBN 3-8204-8285-7 LC Card 85-230052
HF5470 .M35 1985

MARKETS - ADDRESSES, ESSAYS, LECTURES.
Firms and markets . London , c1986. xiii, 271 p. : ISBN 0-7099-2446-1
NYPL [JLD 86-2134]

Markets and bagmen : studies in the history of marketing and British industrial performance, 1830-1939 / edited by R.P.T. Davenport-Hines. Aldershot, Hants, England ; Brookfield, Vt., USA : Gower, c1986. xii, 204 p. : ill. ; 24 cm. (Business history series) Series statement from jacket. Includes bibliographies and index. ISBN 0-566-05066-8 : LC Card 86-22951 DDC 380.1/0941 19
1. Marketing - Great Britain - History. 2. Marketing - History. I. Davenport-Hines, R. P. T. (Richard Peter Treadwell), 1953-. II. Series.
HF5415.12.G7 M37 1986

The Markets and competitive environment for portable computers. New York, N.Y. : Frost & Sullivan, c1983. xii, 356 p. : ill. ; 29 cm. Spine title: Portable computer market. "March 1983." "#A1200." LC Card 87-143515 DDC 380.1/4500416 19
1. Computer industry. 2. Computer industry - United States. 3. Microcomputers. 4. Microcomputers - United States. 5. Market surveys. 6. Market surveys - United States. I. Frost & Sullivan. II. Title: Portable computer market.
HD9696.C62 M369 1983

Markets and famines /. Ravallion, Martin. Oxford [Oxfordshire] , New York , 1987. viii, 203 p. : ISBN 0-19-828514-0 : LC Card 86-23724 DDC 381/.456413/0095492 19
HC79.F3 R38 1987

Markets and market logic /. Steidlmayer, J. Peter. Chicago , c1986. 161 p. ; ISBN 0-941275-00-0 LC Card 87-401422 DDC 332.64 19
HG6046 .S673 1986

MARKETS - BOLIVIA - LA CANCHA (COCHABAMBA)
Calderón G., Fernando. La Cancha . [Cochabamba, Bolivia] , 1984. 208 p. : LC Card 85-238895
HF5473.B62 C363 1984

MARKETS - BRAZIL - CAMPINAS (SÃO PAULO)
A Feira hippie de Campinas . Campinas, SP, Brasil , São Paulo, SP , 1986. 73 p. ; LC Card 87-404187 DDC 381/.18/098161 19
HF5473.B72 C364 1986

MARKETS - EL SALVADOR - SAN SALVADOR.
Magaña Cañas, Pedro Agustín. Una ventana a la vida . [San Salvador] [between 1983 and 1987] 93 p. : LC Card 87-400985 DDC 331.4/8138118/09728423 19
HF3310.S26 M34 1983

MARKETS - EUROPE, EASTERN.
MARKETS - GHANA.
Marketing in Ghana . Addis Ababa , 1984. vi, 62 p. ; LC Card 86-980249 DDC 381/.18/09667 19
HD6072.6.G4 M37 1984

MARKETS - GOVERNMENT POLICY - NIGERIA - EAST-CENTRAL STATE.
Anambra State, Nigeria. Government white paper on the Report of the Administrative Board of Inquiry into the Enugu Market Authority /. Enugu , 1976. 25 p. ; LC Card 86-204970
HF5475.N52 E373 1976

MARKETS - GOVERNMENT POLICY - NIGERIA - JOS.
Plateau State (Nigeria) Government views and decisions on the Report of the Panel on the Allocation of Stalls in the Three Temporary Markets in Jos . Jos [Nigeria] [1976?] 9 p. ; LC Card 87-401792 DDC 381/.18/096695 19
HF5475.N52 J66 1976

MARKETS - GUADELOUPE.
Le Lolo . Pointe-à-Pitre [1984?] 63 p. : LC Card 86-155167
HF5473.G83 L65 1984

MARKETS - HUNGARY - BUDAPEST - LANGUAGE.
Berényi, Zsuzsanna Ágnes. A budapesti Nagyvásártelep mikrotoponímiája /. Budapest , 1983. 65 p. : ISBN 963-461-710-7 LC Card 85-167786
HF5474.H82 B83 1983

MARKETS - HUNGARY - MEZŐTÚR - HISTORY.
Varga, Lajos. Túri vásár /. Mezőtúr , 1983. 188 p. ; ISBN 963-7612-04-1 LC Card 85-109670
HF5474.H82 M498 1983

MARKETS - INDIA - KENDUPATNA - CASE STUDIES.
Regulated markets in Orissa . Bhubaneswar, Orissa [1973] 56 p. ; LC Card 82-903827
HF5415.12.I5 R44 1973

MARKETS - INDIA - ORISSA - CASE STUDIES.
Regulated markets in Orissa . Bhubaneswar, Orissa [1973] 56 p. ; LC Card 82-903827
HF5415.12.I5 R44 1973

MARKETS - INDIA - SAKHI GOPAL - CASE STUDIES.
Regulated markets in Orissa . Bhubaneswar, Orissa [1973] 56 p. ; LC Card 82-903827
HF5415.12.I5 R44 1973

MARKETS - INDIA, SOUTH - HISTORY.
Bohle, Hans-Georg. Südindische Wochenmarktsysteme . Stuttgart , 1986. 290 p. : ISBN 3-515-04601-1 LC Card 87-136147 DDC 381/.18/09548 19
HF5475.I42 S682 1986

MARKETS - MALI.
Turrittin, Jane Sawyer. Men, women, and market trade in rural Mali, West Africa /. [East Lansing] , c1986. 17 p. ; LC Card 86-225178 DDC 331.4/8138118/096623 19
HD6060.65.M42 T87 1986

MARKETS - MEXICO - MEXICO CITY - HISTORY.
López Monjardín, Adriana. Hacia la ciudad del capital--México, 1790-1870 /. México, D.F. , 1985. 193 p. : LC Card 87-124857 DDC 330.972/53 19
HC138.M4 L66 1985

MARKETS - NIGERIA - ADO EKITI.
Adebowale, Annette, 1957- Yoruba-Märkte in Nigeria . Aachen , c1987. xxvii, 225 p. : ISBN 3-922868-64-9 LC Card 87-141899 DDC 381/.18/096692 19
HF5475.N52 A362 1987

The markets of Asia/Pacific--People's Republic of China /. Chen, Edward K. Y. London , Aldershot, Hants, England , c1984. 124 p., [1] leaf of plates : ISBN 0-566-02316-4 LC Card 87-672541
HC427.92 .C353x 1984b

Markets or governments . Wolf, Charles, 1924- Cambridge, Mass. , c1988. xv, 220 p. : ISBN 0-262-23134-4 LC Card 87-118516 DDC 338.9 19
HB501 .W89 1988

MARKETS - PICTORIAL WORKS.
Appuhn, Klaus D. Wohlfeil und köstlich . Dortmund , c1982. 148 p. : ISBN 3-88379-336-1 (pbk.) LC Card 87-672473
HF5470 .A66x 1982

MARKETS SURVEY - UNITED STATES.
Integrated voice/data PBXs /. Boston, MA (200 Portland St., Boston 02114) , c1987. iv, 102 p. : LC Card 87-402843 DDC 381/.45621385 19
HE8817 .I57 1987

MARKETS - WASHINGTON (STATE) - SEATTLE - PICTORIAL WORKS.
Stamets, John, 1949- Portrait of a market . Seattle , 1987. 95 p. : ISBN 0-941104-17-6 (pbk.) : LC Card 87-4746 DDC 381/.18/0979777 19
HF5472.U7 S48 1987

Markey, Ray. The trade union response to technological change in Australia / Ray Markey ; with contributions by G. Larcombe. Kensington, N.S.W. : Industrial Relations Research Centre, University of New South Wales, 1983. iii, 56 p. ; 24 cm. (Industrial Relations Research Centre monograph, 0729-2627) Includes bibliographical references.
1. Trade-unions - Australia. 2. Technological innovations - Australia. I. Larcombe, Graham. II. University of New South Wales. Industrial Relations Research Centre. III. Title. IV. Series.
NYPL [JLE 87-904]

Markgrafenland (Markgrafschaft) see **Mark (Grafschaft)**

Markham, Jerry W. The history of commodity futures trading and its regulation / Jerry W. Markham. New York : Praeger, 1987. xiv, 305 p. ; 25 cm. Includes index. Bibliography: p. 277-285. ISBN 0-275-92313-4 (alk. paper) : LC Card 86-25246 DDC 332.64/4 19
1. Commodity exchanges - United States - History. 2. Commodity exchanges - Law and legislation - United States - History. I. Title.
HG6049 .M37 1986 NYPL [JLE 87-819]

Markiewicz, Stanisław. Chrześcijaństwo a związki zawodowe / Stanisław Markiewicz. Wyd. 1. Warszawa : Instytut Wydawniczy Związków Zawodowych, 1985. 618 p. : 20 cm. Summaries and the table of contents in English, Russian, French and German. Includes index. Bibliography: p. 542-[545]

ISBN 83-202-0352-X (pbk.) :
1. Trade-unions and Christianity. 2. Trade-unions - Europe - History. 3. Trade-unions - Poland - Political activity. I. Title. ***NYPL [*QO 86-2625]***

Markkinointitutkimuksen perusteet /. Niinikoski, Risto, 1946- [Lauttakylä?] [1985] (Jyväskylässä : Gummerus) 134 p. : ISBN 951-99532-6-4 LC Card 86-122767
HF5415.2 .N54 1985

Marknadsföring av tjänster. Ledning, produktion & marknadsföring av tjänster . Malmö , c1981. 318 p. : ISBN 91-40-54058-8 : LC Card 81-174255
HD9986.S82 L43 1981

Marknadsföring till handeln . Lindqvist, Lars-Johan. Helsingfors , 1983. 309 p. : ISBN 951-555-183-8 LC Card 84-103976
HF5421.5.F5 L56 1983

Marknadsinvesteringar . Elsässer, Martin, 1957- Malmö , c1984. 168 p. : ISBN 91-38-61298-4 : LC Card 84-200312
HF1009.7.S94 E47 1984

Markov, Marko. Georgiev, I͡Ancho. Strategii͡a na kachestveni promeni /. Sofii͡a , 1986- v. <1-2 > ; LC Card 86-232319
HC403 .G465 1986

Markov, V. (Vladimir) Korchagina, A. (Aleksandra) Nagli͡adnai͡a agitatsii͡a i vstrechnye plany /. Moskva , 1978. 44 p., [16] p. of plates : LC Card 81-161419
HC340.L3 K56 1978

Markov, Walter M. Die Übergangsperiode . [Leipzig] , 1986. 80 p. ; LC Card 87-407523 DDC 338.9/009171/7 19
HC704 .U24 1986

Markova, N. L. Kadieva, D. A. Chastotnyĭ anglo-russkiĭ slovar'. Leningrad , 1986. 126 p. ; LC Card 87-146427
HB61 .K23 1986

Markowitz, Gerald E. Slaves of the Depression . Ithaca, N.Y. , 1987. x, 229 p. ; ISBN 0-8014-9464-8 (pbk. : alk. paper) LC Card 87-6671 DDC 331.25/0973 19
HD8072 .S6164 1987

Markowitz, H. (Harry), 1927- Mean-variance analysis in portfolio choice and capital markets / Harry M. Markowitz. Oxford, OX, UK ; New York, NY, USA : B. Blackwell, 1987. xi, 387 p. : ill. ; 24 cm. Bibliography: p. [369]-374. Includes index. ISBN 0-631-15381-0 : LC Card 87-2975 DDC 332.6 19
1. Portfolio management - Mathematical models. 2. Capital market - Mathematical models. I. Title.
HG4529.5 .M37 1987

Marks, Georgette A. Harrap's slang dictionary English-French/French-English / by Georgette A. Marks and Charles B. Johnson ; completely revised and edited by Jane Pratt. London : Harrap, 1984. 476 p. ; 19 cm. "Revised edition of Harrap's dictionary of slang and colloquialisms"--Pref. ISBN 0-245-54047-4
1. English language - Dictionaries - French. 2. French language - Dictionaries - English. 3. English language - Slang - Dictionaries. 4. French language - Slang - Dictionaries. I. Johnson, Charles Benjamin, 1928-. II. Pratt, Jane. III. Title. IV. Title: Slang dictionary English-French/French-English.
NYPL [JFC 86-640]

Marks, Ronald B., 1944- Personal selling : an interactive approach / Ronald B. Marks.3rd ed. Boston : Allyn and Bacon, c1988. xvi, 607 p. : ill. ; 24 cm. Includes bibliographies and index. ISBN 0-205-11087-8 LC Card 87-16098 DDC 658.8/5 19
1. Selling. 2. Selling - Psychological aspects. 3. Selling - Vocational guidance. I. Title.
HF5438.25 .M37 1988

Der Markt gebrauchter Güter . Gebhardt, Peter. Hamburg , c1986. xxvii, 250, [69] p. : ISBN 3-925630-10-4 LC Card 87-127354 DDC 381/.1 19
HF5482 .G42 1986

Markt, Staat und Solidarität bei Adam Smith / Franz-Xaver Kaufmann, Hans-Günter Krüsselberg (Hg.). Frankfurt ; New York : Campus, c1984. 238 p. ; 21 cm. Bibliography: p. 220-231. Includes indexes. CONTENTS. - Zur Vorgeschichte der wirtschaftspolitischen Vorstellungen Adam Smiths / Erich Streissler -- Ethik und Teleologie / Heinz-Dieter Kittsteiner -- Adam Smith / Andrew S. Skinner -- Adam Smith als politischer Theoretiker / Donald Winch -- Markt und Staat bei Adam Smith / Klaus Gretschmann -- Adam Smith und öffentliche Güter / Vincent Ostrom -- Solidarität als Steuerungsform / Franz-Xaver Kaufmann -- Wohlfahrt und Institutionen / Hans-Günter Krüsselberg. ISBN 3-593-33338-4 LC Card 84-202891
1. Smith, Adam, 1723-1790. 2. Economics. 3. Ethics, Modern - 18th century. 4. Political ethics. I. Kaufmann, Franz Xaver. II. Krüsselberg, Hans-Günter.
HB103.S6 M27 1984

Markt und Raum . Ipsen, Detlev. Frankfurt , New York , c1986. 250 p. : ISBN 3-593-33685-5 LC Card 87-127593 DDC 363.5/8 19
HD7339.M35 I67 1986

Der Marktanteil als Kriterium für die Produkteliminierung . Sever, Michael, 1956- Frankfurt am Main , New York , c1985. xv, 317 p. : ISBN 3-8204-8917-7 LC Card 86-111218
HF5415.15 .S39 1985

Marktchancen der Binnenschiffahrt im Container-Hinterlandverkehr der Häfen der Hamburg-Antwerpen-Range /. Mester, Bernt. Düsseldorf , 1986. xii, 304 p. ; LC Card 87-409549
HE5 .C6 Nr. 47 HE558.H3

Marktinformation.
Guinea (Revolutionäre Volksrepublik Guinea) . Köln , 1983. viii, 89 p. : LC Card 85-104313
HC1030 .G83 1983

Marktinnovationen von Universalbanken . Budde, Ramona. Berlin , c1983. xvi, 347 p. : ISBN 3-503-02192-2 LC Card 83-186914
HG1709 .B78 1983

Marktorientierte Unternehmensführung, 0178-8133 .
(Bd. 3) Müller, Wolfgang, 1955- Planung von Marketing-Strategien . Frankfurt am Main , New York , c1986. xxvi, 514 p. : ISBN 3-8204-8992-4 LC Card 86-205571
HF5415.13 .M833 1986

Marktorientierte Unternehmensführung, 0178-8183 .
(Bd. 4) Klaes, Friedhelm, 1956- Informationsverhalten kleiner und mittlerer Unternehmen der elektrotechnischen Investitionsgüterindustrie bei strategischen Entscheidungen /. Frankfurt am Main , New York , c1986. xxii, 305 p. ; ISBN 3-8204-9713-7 LC Card 87-407575 DDC 658.4/03 19
HD62.7 .K586 1986

Marktpolitik von Privatbankiers . Pott, Philipp. Frankfurt , c1983. 66 p. ; ISBN 3-88323-443-5 LC Card 84-154560
HG2021.G4 P67 1983

Marktstrategien multinationaler Pharmaunternehmen und die Arzneimittelmärkte der Dritten Welt . Wenzel, Gilbert, 1956- Frankfurt am Main , New York , c1986. 398 p. : ISBN 3-8204-9721-8 LC Card 87-407426 DDC 381/.456151/091724 19
HD9674.D44 W46 1986

Markttransparenz bei Pflanzenschutz- und Düngemitteln . Weber, Norbert. Münster-Hiltrup , 1983. xi, 247 p. : ISBN 3-7843-0277-7 : LC Card 83-234135
HD9660.P33 G328 1983

Markttransparenz in der Lebensversicherung . Stöffler, Michael. [Mainz] [1982?] vi, 248 p. : LC Card 83-202502
HG9078.Z9 S76 1982

Marktvrouwen van Bobo . Bosch, Ellie. Leiden , 1983. viii, 179 p., [18] p. of plates : LC Card 86-212595
HD6217.5.Z6 B633 1983

Der Marktwert von Produkteigenschaften /. Weber, Manfred, Dr. Berlin , c1986. xv, 335 p. : ISBN 3-428-06103-9 LC Card 87-131636 DDC 658.8 s 658.5 19
HF5415.A2 S37 Bd. 20 HF5415.157

Marktwirtschaft kontra Planwirtschaft. Zwass, Adam. Zwei Weltsysteme . Wien , c1985. 264 p. ; ISBN 3-203-50891-5 LC Card 85-240587 DDC 338.9 19
HB501 .Z93 1985 ***NYPL [JLD 87-226]***

Marktwirtschaft und Gesellschaftsordnung : Wolfgang Schmitz zum 60. Geburtstag / herausgegeben von Alfred Klose und Gerhard Merk. Berlin : Duncker & Humblot, c1983. 220 p., [1] leaf of plates : ill. ; 24 cm. "Verzeichnis der Publikationen von Wolfgang Schmitz": p. [203]-209. Includes bibliographical references and index. ISBN 3-428-05365-6 LC Card 83-191615
1. Economics - Moral and ethical aspects. 2. Capitalism - Moral and ethical aspects. 3. Economic policy - Moral and ethical aspects. 4. Social policy - Moral and ethical aspects. 5. Democracy - Moral and ethical aspects. 6. Schmitz, Wolfgang, 1923-. I. Schmitz, Wolfgang, 1923-. II. Klose, Alfred, 1928-. III. Merk, Gerhard, 1931-.
HB72 .M248 1983

Marktwirtschaft und Umwelt . Symposion "Marktwirtschaft und Umwelt" (1980 : Walter Eucken Institut) Tübingen , 1981. ix, 303 p. : ISBN 3-16-343372-3 : LC Card 81-128698 DDC 363.7/0526 19
HC79.E5 S92 1980 ***NYPL [TB (Walter Eucken Institut. Wirtschaftswissenschaftliche und wirtschaftsrechtliche Untersuchungen. Bd. 17)]***

Marktwirtschaft zweitausend. Marktwirtschaft 2000 /. Krefeld , c1983. 137 p. : ISBN 3-88289-302-8 LC Card 84-229313 DDC 338.9 19
HD75.6 .M37 1983 ***NYPL [JLD 86-3124]***

Marktwirtschaft 2000 / Matthias Wissmann, (Hrsg.). Krefeld : Sinus, c1983. 137 p. : ill. ; 21 cm. (Mitverantwortung . 2) Includes bibliographical references. CONTENTS. - Ökonomie und Ökologie / Heinz Riesenhuber -- Die Ökologie als Grundlage der Ökonomie / Herbert Gruhl -- Marktwirtschaft und Moral / Ernst Günter Vetter -- Parlamentarisches Regieren in der Krise? / Jürgen Fuchs -- Neue Medien und Kommunikationstechnologien / Roland Koch -- Die ökologische-ökonomische Herausforderung / Albrecht Geier -- Die Chancen der Technik / Ulrich Guntram -- Marktwirtschaft und Bildungssystem / Franz-Christoph Zeitler -- Arbeitsgesellschaft in der Krise / Peter Hubert Köppinger -- Eine Brücke in die Zukunft / Matthias Wissmann -- Dezentralisierung, Subsidiarität und Selbstverantwortung in der Sozialpolitik / Ulf Fink. ISBN 3-88289-302-8 LC Card 84-229313 DDC 338.9 19
1. Economic development - Environmental aspects - Addresses, essays, lectures. 2. Economic history - 1971- - Addresses, essays, lectures. 3. Social history - 1970- - Addresses, essays, lectures. 4. Economic forecasting - Addresses, essays, lectures. 5. Social prediction - Addresses, essays, lectures. I. Wissmann, Matthias, 1949-. II. Title: Marktwirtschaft zweitausend. III. Series.
HD75.6 .M37 1983 ***NYPL [JLD 86-3124]***

Márkus, László. Erdőérték- és eredményszámítás / Márkus László. Budapest : Mezőgazdasági Kiadó, 1986. 207 p. : ill. ; 20 cm. Bibliography: p. 202-204. ISBN 963-232-225-2 : LC Card 87-408586
1. Forests and forestry - Valuation. 2. Forests and forestry - Accounting. I. Title.
HF5686.F62 M37 1986

Markussen, Randi. Det fleksible køn : kvinder i butik og på kontor / Randi Markussen og Brita Foged. [Copenhagen] : Tiderne skifter, c1984. 163 p. ; 22 cm. (Kvindeforskning) Bibliography: p. 161-163. ISBN 87-7445-159-6 : LC Card 84-187146
1. Women - Employment - Denmark. 2. Part-time employment - Denmark. I. Foged, Brita. II. Title. III. Series.
HD6169 .M37 1984

Marlin, Alice Tepper.
Goldman, Benjamin A. Hazardous waste management . Washington, D.C. , c1986. xx, 316 p. : ISBN 0-933280-30-0 : LC Card 86-2748 DDC 363.7/28 19
HD9975.U52 G65 1986
NYPL [JLE 87-1159]

Lydenberg, Steven D. Rating America's corporate conscience . Reading, Mass. , c1986. x, 499 p. : ISBN 0-201-15886-8 : LC Card 86-8064 DDC 338.7/4/0973 19
HD60.5.U5 L93 1986
NYPL [*R-Econ. 87-1830]

Marmot, M. G. Immigrant mortality in England and Wales, 1970-78 : causes of death by country of birth / M.G. Marmot, A.M. Adelstein, L. Bulusu. London : H.M.S.O., 1984. xii, 144 p. : ill. ; 30 cm. (Studies on medical and population subjects. no. 47) At head of title: Office of Population Censuses and Surveys. Includes bibliographies. ISBN 0-11-691094-1 (pbk.) : LC Card 84-222968 DDC 614.4/242 19
1. Mortality - England - Statistics. 2. Mortality - Wales - Statistics. 3. England - Statistics, Vital. 4.

England - Foreign population - Statistics. 5. Wales - Statistics, Vital. 6. Wales - Foreign population - Statistics. I. Adelstein, A. M. (Abraham Manie). II. Bulusu, L. III. Title.
HB1415 .M37 1984 ***NYPL [JLG 87-55]***

Maroc. see **Morocco.**

Le Maroc face à l'endettement extérieur . Benazzou, Chaouki, 1936- [Rabat] 1986 ([Rabat] : Imprimé aux Editions maghrébines) 151 p. : LC Card 87-967050
HG3883.M8 B46 1986

Maroc, tribus, makhzen et colons . Salahdine, Mohamed. Paris , c1986. 337 p. : ISBN 2-85802-525-5 LC Card 86-159041
HC810 .S23 1986

Marois, Bernard. Klein, Jean, docteur ès sciences économiques. Gestion et stratégie financières internationales /. Paris , c1985. v, 266 p. : ISBN 2-04-015504-X : LC Card 86-192918
HG4027.5 .K58 1985

Marongiu, Paula, 1940- Thigpen, M. Elton, 1932- World demand prospects for jute /. Washington, D.C. , Rome , 1987. vi, 178 p. ; ISBN 0-8213-0867-X (pbk.) LC Card 86-32522 DDC 338.4/767713 19
HD9156.J7 T46 1987

Marot, François. Courchaure, Stéphane. Les riches . [Paris] , c1985. 261 p. ; ISBN 2-7158-0537-3 : LC Card 86-111316 DDC 305.5/234 19
HC79.C6 C68 1985 ***NYPL [JLD 86-4451]***

Maroudēs, Giōrgos.
To hēmerologio tēs peinas / Giōrgos Maroudēs ; eikonographēsē Annas Kindynē. [Athens] : Kedros, 1976. 99 p., [6] leaves of plates ; 21 cm. LC Card 84-107778
1. Famines - Greece - Athens. 2. Maroudēs, Giōrgos - Diaries. 3. Victims of famines - Greece - Diaries. 4. World War, 1939-1945 - Personal narratives, Greek. 5. World War, 1939-1945 - Greece - Athens. 6. Athens (Greece) - History - 1821-. I. Title.
HC300.F3 M37 1976

MAROUDĒS, GIŌRGOS - DIARIES.
Maroudēs, Giōrgos. To hēmerologio tēs peinas /. [Athens] , 1976. 99 p., [6] leaves of plates ; LC Card 84-107778
HC300.F3 M37 1976

Maroulis, Dimitris. Economic development and the structure of the balance of payments : the case of Greece / Dimitris Maroulis. Athens : Centre of Planning and Economic Research, 1986. 267 p. : ill. ; 25 cm. (Studies / Centre of Planning and Economic Research . 18) Thesis (Ph.D.)--University of Essex, 1984. Library's copy has misspelling in the word "case" corrected by hand. Bibliography: p. 255-265. LC Card 87-170680 DDC 382.1/7/09495 19
1. Greece - Economic conditions - 1974-. 2. Balance of payments - Greece. I. Series: Studies (Kentron Programmatismou kai Oikonomikōn Ereunōn) , 18. II. Title.
HC295 .M32 1986

Marques Cavalcante, José Cândido. see **Cavalcante, José Cândido Marques.**

Marques d'entrée maritime du XVIIIème et du XIXème siècle et études diverses s'y rapportant, dont taxes et mouvements portuaires de provenance ou à destination des principaux ports d'outremer au XVIIIe s. /. Bergier, J. (Joseph) Nantes [1981] 131, x p. : LC Card 82-228434
HE6986 .B47 1981

Marques Moreira, Marcílio. see **Moreira, Marcílio Marques.**

Marqués, Nora. Lindenboim, Javier. Monetarismo y mercado de trabajo . Buenos Aires, Argentina , c1985. x, 471 p. : ISBN 950-9370-05-3 LC Card 87-122243 DDC 331.12/0982/73 19
HD5750.R56 L56 1985

Márquez, Javier, 1909- La banca mexicana : septiembre de 1982-junio de 1985 / Javier Márquez.1a ed. [Mexico City, Mexico] : Centro de Estudios Monetarios Latinoamericanos, 1987. xi, 299 p., [3] folded leaves of plates : ill. ; 21 cm. (Estudios) Includes bibliographies. ISBN 968-615-402-7 LC Card 87-404865 DDC 332.1/0972 19
1. Banks and banking - Mexico - History. 2. Banks and banking - Government ownership - Mexico - History. I. Series: Estudios (Centro de Estudios Monetarios Latinoamericanos). II. Title.
HG2714 .M27 1987

Márquez, Pompeyo. El festín de los gemelos : dos caras de un modelo fracasado / Pompeyo Márquez. [Caracas : s.n., 1983] ([Caracas] : Industrias Sorocaima) 134 p. ; 22 cm. Includes bibliographical references. LC Card 84-195527
1. Venezuela - Economic policy. 2. Venezuela - Economic conditions - 1958-. I. Title.
HC237 .M338 1983

Marquis, Benoît, 1932- Victoire définitive sur le chômage : c'est possible / Benoît Marquis. [Montréal] : Editions de l'Heure, c1984. 176, [3] p. : ill. ; 21 cm. Bibliography: p. [177]-[179] ISBN 2-9800322-0-4 LC Card 84-191778 DDC 331.13/77 19
1. Unemployment. 2. Unemployment - Effect of inflation on. I. Title.
HD5707.5 .M37 1984 ***NYPL [JLD 86-2652]***

Marquis, M. Susan. Choice under uncertainty and the demand for health insurance / M. Susan Marquis, Martin R. Holmer ; prepared for the U. S. Department of Health and Human Services. Santa Monica, CA (P.O. Box 2138, Santa Monica 90406-2138) : Rand, [1986] ix, 50 p. ; 28 cm. (A Rand note . N-2516-HHS) "September 1986." Bibliography: p. 47-50. LC Card 87-118503 DDC 368.3/8/00973 19
1. Insurance, Health - United States - Econometric models. 2. Consumers' preferences - United States - Econometric models. 3. Risk (Insurance) - United States - Econometric models. I. Holmer, Martin R. II. United States. Dept. of Health and Human Services. III. Title. IV. Series.
HG9396 .M268 1986

Marr, Rainer, 1942-
Flexibilisierung von Arbeitszeitstrukturen : die Teilbarkeit von stellenbezogenen Aufgabenkomplexen : Zwischenbericht zum Forschungsprojekt Ma 698/2-1 der Deutschen Forschungsgemeinschaft / Rainer Marr, Gabriele Schultes-Jaskolla. [Neubiberg? : s.n., 1986] 111 leaves : 15 ill. ; 30 cm. "Neubiberg, im Mai 1986." Bibliography: leaves 106-111. LC Card 87-409556
1. Hours of labor, Flexible - Germany (West). I. Schultes-Jaskolla, Gabriele. II. Deutsche Forschungsgemeinschaft. III. Title.
HD5109.2.G3 M37 1986

Möglichkeiten und Probleme der Realisierung flexibler Arbeitszeitstrukturen in Filialen der Bayerischen Vereinsbank München /. München , 1985. 67 p. : LC Card 87-401387 DDC 331.25/72 19
HD5109.2.G32 M866 1985

MARRAKESH REGION (MOROCCO) - ECONOMIC CONDITIONS.
Pascon, Paul. [Haouz de Marrakech. English.] Capitalism and agriculture in the Haouz of Marrakesh /. London ; New York : 248 p. : ISBN 0-7103-0189-8 LC Card 87-100309 DDC 338.1/0964/6 19
HD2121.Z9 M37613 1986

Marrama, Vittorio. Programmazione e sviluppo in Unione Sovietica / Vittorio Marrama. Torino : Boringhieri, c1983. 146 p. : ill. ; 21 cm. (Serie di economia) Bibliography: p. 139-146. LC Card 85-175586
1. Soviet Union - Economic policy - 1981-. 2. Soviet Union - Economic conditions - 1976-. I. Series: Serie di economia Boringhieri. II. Title.
HC336.25 .M358 1983

Marrey, Bernard. Un capitalisme idéal / Bernard Marrey. Paris : Editions Clancier-Guénaud, c1984. 236 p., [24] p. of plates : ill. ; 21 cm. (Mémoire pour demain) Bibliography: p. 231-234. ISBN 2-86215-060-6 : LC Card 84-252196 DDC 338.7/6413374/0944 19
1. Maison Menier (Noisiel, France). 2. Chocolate industry - France - History. I. Title. II. Series.
HD9200.F74 M356 1984
NYPL [JLD 87-1579]

MARRIAGE - FINLAND - STATISTICS.
Finnäs, Fjalar. Den finlandssvenska befolkningsutvecklingen 1950-1980 . Helsingfors [1986] 216 p. : ISBN 951-9018-20-4 LC Card 86-232091
HB3608.3.A3 F56 1986

MARRIAGE - FRANCE - TERRITORIES AND POSSESSIONS - STATISTICS.
Statistique du mouvement de la population dans les D.O.M. . Paris [1985] 104 p. : ISBN 2-11-064898-8 : LC Card 86-216599
HB1003 .S73 1985

MARRIAGE - GERMANY (WEST) - STATISTICS.
Schweitzer, Walter. Heiratstafeln versus Familienstandstafeln . Wiesbaden , 1985. iii, 102 p. : LC Card 87-408703 DDC 306.8/1/0943021 19
HB1215 .S39 1985

MARRIAGE - PORTUGAL - LANHEZES - HISTORY.
Brettell, Caroline. Men who migrate, women who wait . Princeton , c1986. xv, 329 p., [8] p. of plates : ISBN 0-691-09424-1 (alk. paper) : LC Card 86-11270 DDC 304.6/09469/12 19
HB2082.L36 B74 1986 ***NYPL [JLE 87-1417]***

MARRIAGE - PORTUGAL - STATISTICS.
Carrilho, Maria José. Análise da idade média ao casamento, 1930-1978 /. Lisboa, Portugal , 1984. 27 p. : LC Card 85-124431
HB1241 .C37 1984

MARRIAGE - SPAIN - MÉRIDA - HISTORY - 17TH CENTURY - STATISTICS.
Rodríguez Grajera, Alfonso. La población de Mérida en el siglo XVII /. [Badajoz] , 1985. xv, 162 p. : ISBN 84-505-1500-9 LC Card 86-232003
HB3620.M47 R63 1985

MARRIED PEOPLE - EMPLOYMENT.
Bastress, Frances. The relocating spouse's guide to employment . Chevy Chase, Md. , c1987. xviii, 258 p. : ISBN 0-937623-01-6 (pbk.) : LC Card 87-16045 DDC 650.1/4 19
HF5382.7 .B375 1987

Krupa, Arlene. Couplepower . New York , c1987. 227 p. ; ISBN 0-396-09029-X (pbk.) : LC Card 87-20065 DDC 658.4/09 19
HD62.25 .K78 1987

Wilk, Carole. Career women and childbearing . New York , c1986. xxii, 304 p. ; ISBN 0-442-29352-6 LC Card 85-9216 DDC 306.8/743 19
HQ759 .W52 1986 ***NYPL [JLD 86-1811]***

MARRIED PEOPLE - EMPLOYMENT - SOCIAL ASPECTS - UNITED STATES.
Pleck, Joseph H. Working wives, working husbands /. Beverly Hills, Calif. , c1985. 167 p. ; ISBN 0-8039-2489-5 LC Card 85-11974 DDC 306.8/7 19
HQ536 .P59 1985 ***NYPL [JLD 86-1130]***

MARRIED PEOPLE - EMPLOYMENT - UNITED STATES.
Bastress, Frances. The relocating spouse's guide to employment . Chevy Chase, Md. , c1987. xviii, 258 p. : ISBN 0-937623-01-6 (pbk.) : LC Card 87-16045 DDC 650.1/4 19
HF5382.7 .B375 1987

Voydanoff, Patricia. Work and family life /. Newbury Park, Calif. , c1987. 136 p. ; ISBN 0-8039-2289-2 (pbk.) LC Card 87-9482 DDC 306.8/5/0973 19
HD4904.25 .V69 1987

MARRIED WOMEN - EMPLOYMENT.
Women and recession /. London , New York , 1988. xii, 294 p. ; ISBN 0-7102-0701-8 LC Card 87-20626 DDC 331.4/12 19
HD6053 .W6375 1988

MARRIED WOMEN - EMPLOYMENT - GERMANY (WEST)
Freitäger, Jürgen, 1959- Erwerb und Verwendung des Einkommens von Arbeitnehmerhaushalten mit erwerbstätiger Ehefrau /. Frankfurt am Main , New York , c1986. xix, 327 p. : ISBN 3-8204-9148-1 : LC Card 86-195223
HD9850.1 .M58 Bd. 37 HD6055.2.G3

Marrocu, Luciano. Laburismo e trade unions : l'evoluzione del movimento operaio britannico, 1867-1926 / [di] Luciano Marrocu. Bari : De Donato, 1981. 183 p. ; 21 cm. (Movimento operaio. 67) "Bibliografia ragionata" : p. 171-182. LC Card 81-137615 DDC 331.88/0941 19
1. Labour Party (Great Britain) - History. 2. Trade-unions - Great Britain - History. 3. Labor and laboring classes - Great Britain - History. 4. Trade-unions - Great Britain - Political activity - History. 5. Labor and laboring classes - Great Britain - Political activity - History. I. Title.
HD6664 .M24 ***NYPL [JLD 86-3453]***

Marsden, David. The Car industry . London , New York , 1985. viii, 210 p. : ISBN 0-422-79550-X LC Card 85-14742 DDC 331/.04292/0941 19
HD6976.A82 G72 1985
NYPL [JLD 87-403]

Marsden, Keith. Private enterprise in Africa : creating a better environment / Keith Marsden, Thérèse Bélot. Washington, D.C. : World Bank, [1987] xiii, 66 p. ; 28 cm. (World Bank discussion papers, 0259-210X . 17) Includes bibliographical references. ISBN 0-8213-0945-5 (pbk.) LC Card 87-18419 DDC 330.96/032 19
1. Africa - Economic conditions - 1960-. 2. Capitalism - Africa. 3. Africa - Economic policy. I. Bélot, Thérèse, 1947-. II. Title. III. Series.
HC800 .M353 1987

MARSEILLE (FRANCE) - BIOGRAPHY.
Castellani, Maurice. French solo /. Paris , c1985. 262 p. ; ISBN 2-86477-063-6 : LC Card 85-205040
HF5482.65.F7 C373 1985

MARSEILLE (FRANCE) - ECONOMIC CONDITIONS.
Rastoin, Pierre. Marseille, quai d'avenir /. [Paris] , c1985. 184 p. ; LC Card 86-151556
HC278.M3 R37 1985 *NYPL [JLD 87-253]*

Sanmarco, Philippe. Marseille, l'endroit du décor /. La Calade, Aix-en-Provence , 1985. 191 p. : ISBN 2-85744-219-X : LC Card 86-168990
HC278.M3 S26 1985

MARSEILLE (FRANCE) - FOREIGN POPULATION.
Sanmarco, Philippe. Marseille, l'endroit du décor /. La Calade, Aix-en-Provence , 1985. 191 p. : ISBN 2-85744-219-X : LC Card 86-168990
HC278.M3 S26 1985

MARSEILLE (FRANCE) - POLITICS AND GOVERNMENT.
Sanmarco, Philippe. Marseille, l'endroit du décor /. La Calade, Aix-en-Provence , 1985. 191 p. : ISBN 2-85744-219-X : LC Card 86-168990
HC278.M3 S26 1985

MARSEILLE (FRANCE) - SOCIAL CONDITIONS.
Sanmarco, Philippe. Marseille, l'endroit du décor /. La Calade, Aix-en-Provence , 1985. 191 p. : ISBN 2-85744-219-X : LC Card 86-168990
HC278.M3 S26 1985

Marseille, l'endroit du décor /. Sanmarco, Philippe. La Calade, Aix-en-Provence , 1985. 191 p. : ISBN 2-85744-219-X : LC Card 86-168990
HC278.M3 S26 1985

Marseille, quai d'avenir /. Rastoin, Pierre. [Paris] , c1985. 184 p. ; LC Card 86-151556
HC278.M3 R37 1985 *NYPL [JLD 87-253]*

Marsh, Arthur Ivor.
Trade union handbook : a guide and directory to the structure, membership, policy, and personnel of the British trade unions / Arthur Marsh.3d ed. Aldershot, Hants, England : Gower, 1984. x, 415 p. : ill. ; 23 cm. Bibliography: p. 393-400. ISBN 0-566-02426-8 : LC Card 84-236090 DDC 331.88/0941 19
1. Trade-unions - Great Britain - Directories. 2. Trade-unions - Great Britain - Handbooks, manuals, etc. I. Title.
HD6663 .M37 1984
*NYPL [*R-Econ. 86-3335]*

Trade union handbook : a guide and directory to the structure, membership, policy, and personnel of the British trade unions / Arthur Marsh.4th ed. Aldershot, Hants, England ; Brookfield, Vt., U. S.A. : Gower, c1988. x, 387 p. : ill. ; 23 cm. ISBN 0-566-02749-6 : LC Card 87-13408 DDC 331.88/0941 19
1. Trade-unions - Great Britain - Directories. 2. Trade-unions - Great Britain - Handbooks, manuals, etc. I. Title.
HD6663 .M37 1988

Marsh, Lawrence. Employment and technological choice of multinational enterprises in developing countries : a literature review and a case study / by Lawrence Marsh, Richard Newfarmer, and Lino Moreira. Geneva : International Labour Office, 1983. iii, 37 p. ; 30 cm. (Working papers / Multinational Enterprises Programme . working paper, no. 23) ISBN 92-2-103353-8 (pbk.) : LC Card 86-213692 DDC 338.8/8854 19
1. International business enterprises - Developing countries. 2. Appropriate technology - Developing countries. 3. Labor supply - Developing countries. I. Newfarmer, Richard S. II. Moreira, Lino. III. Series: Working papers / Multinational Enterprises Programme , working paper no. 23. IV. Title.
HD2932 .M35 1983

Marsh, Michael G., 1935- How to invest offshore successfully / Michael G. Marsh. Geneva, Switzerland : Troy Associates, c1986. 207 p. : ill. (some col.) ; 30 cm. Bibliography: p. 190-192. LC Card 86-212027 DDC 332.6/73 19
1. Investments, Foreign. 2. Investments. 3. Tax havens. 4. Banks and banking - Switzerland. 5. Precious metals. I. Title.
HG4538 .M3635 1986

Marsh, P. D. V. The art of tendering / P.D.V. Marsh. Aldershot, Hants, England : Gower Technical Press ; Brookfield, Vt. : Gower Pub. Co., c1987. ix, 171 p. ; 23 cm. Includes index. ISBN 0-291-39736-0 : LC Card 87-7429 DDC 658.7/23 19
1. Contracts, Letting of. I. Title.
HD2365 .M37 1987

Marsh, Paul (Paul R.) Dimson, Elroy, 1947- Cases in corporate finance /. Chichester [West Sussex] , New York , c1988. xxiv, 412 p. : ISBN 0-471-91764-8 : LC Card 87-6299 DDC 658.1/5 19
HG4015.5 .D56 1988

Marsh, William M. Landscape planning : environmental applications / William M. Marsh, Jeff Dozier. New York : Wiley, 1986. p. cm. Includes bibliographies and index. ISBN 0-471-85434-4 LC Card 86-28951 DDC 712 19
1. Land use - Planning - Environmental aspects. 2. Landscape architecture - Environmental aspects. 3. Landscape protection. I. Dozier, Jeff. II. Title.
HD108.6 .M37 1986

Marshak, Ronni T. Seybold, Patricia B. Integrated desk-top environments . New York , c1985. ix, 181 p. : ISBN 0-07-056324-1 (pbk.) : LC Card 84-27841 DDC 650/.028/5425 19
HF5548.4.S95 S49 1985
NYPL [JSE 86-2011]

MARSHALL, ALFRED, 1842-1924.
Reisman, David A. Alfred Marshall, progress and politics /. New York , 1987. vii, 499 p. ; ISBN 0-312-00773-6 : LC Card 87-4811 DDC 330.15/5 19
HB98.2 .R44 1987

Reisman, David A. The economics of Alfred Marshall /. New York , 1986. ix, 433 p. ; ISBN 0-312-23430-9 : LC Card 85-22321 DDC 330.15/5 19
HB98.2 .R45 1986

Marshall, Claudia. Creativity in services marketing . Chicago, IL , 1986. 175 p. : ISBN 0-87757-179-1 (pbk.) LC Card 85-26785 DDC 658.8 19
HD9980.5 .C74 1986 *NYPL [JLF 86-1783]*

Marshall, Clifford W., 1928- Solomon, Stephen S. Canadian mortgage payments /. New York , c1987. 302 p. ; ISBN 0-8120-3939-4 (pbk.) LC Card 87-13073 DDC 332.8/0212 19
HG1634 .S654 1987

Marshall, F. Ray. Unheard voices : labor and economic policy in a competitive world / Ray Marshall. New York : Basic Books, c1987. xi, 339 p. : ill. ; 22 cm. Bibliography: p. [319]-327. Includes index. ISBN 0-465-08869-4 : LC Card 83-46084 DDC 338.6 19
1. Industrial management - United States - Employee participation. 2. Employee ownership - United States. 3. Collective bargaining - United States. 4. Industrial management - Japan. 5. Competition, International. I. Title.
HD5660.U5 M36 1987

The Marshall Plan . Hogan, Michael J., 1943- Cambridge [Cambridgeshire] , New York , 1987. xiv, 482 p. ; ISBN 0-521-25140-0 LC Card 86-31773 DDC 338.91/73/04 19
HC240 .H614 1987

MARSHALL PLAN.
Donovan, Robert J. The second victory . New York , c1987. 128 p. : ISBN 0-8191-6498-4 (alk. paper) : LC Card 87-24021 DDC 338.91/73/04 19
HC240 .D65 1987

Hogan, Michael J., 1943- The Marshall Plan . Cambridge [Cambridgeshire] , New York , 1987. xiv, 482 p. ; ISBN 0-521-25140-0 LC Card 86-31773 DDC 338.91/73/04 19
HC240 .H614 1987

Kindleberger, Charles Poor, 1910- Marshall Plan days /. Boston , 1987. x, 273 p., [1] leaf of plates : ISBN 0-04-332142-9 (alk. paper) LC Card 86-32163 DDC 338.91/73/04 19
HC240 .K454 1987

Sanford, William F. The American business community and the European Recovery Program, 1947-1952 /. New York , 1987. xiv, 366 p. ; ISBN 0-8240-8091-2 (alk. paper) LC Card 87-23765 DDC 338.91/73/04 19
HC240 .S259 1987

MARSHALL PLAN - CONGRESSES.
Der Marshall-Plan und die europäische Linke /. [Frankfurt am Main] , c1986. 659 p. : ISBN 3-434-00475-0 LC Card 87-127508 DDC 338.91/73/04 19
HC240 .M2735 1986

Marshall Plan days /. Kindleberger, Charles Poor, 1910- Boston , 1987. x, 273 p., [1] leaf of plates : ISBN 0-04-332142-9 (alk. paper) LC Card 86-32163 DDC 338.91/73/04 19
HC240 .K454 1987

Der Marshall-Plan und die europäische Linke / herausgegeben von Othmar Nikola Haberl und Lutz Niethammer. [Frankfurt am Main] : Europäische Verlagsanstalt, c1986. 659 p. : ill. ; 22 cm. Bibliography: p. 615-646. Includes index. ISBN 3-434-00475-0 LC Card 87-127508 DDC 338.91/73/04 19
1. Marshall Plan - Congresses. I. Haberl, Othmar Nikola. II. Niethammer, Lutz, 1939-.
HC240 .M2735 1986

Marshall, Ray. see **Marshall, F. Ray.**

MARSHALL, TERRY.
Cantrell, Will. 101 ways to find an overseas job /. [Merrifield, VA.] [c1987] 1 v. (various pagings) ; ISBN 0-941541-00-2 (pbk.) LC Card 86-73093 DDC 650.1/4 19
HF5549.5.E45 C33 1987

Marshall-Wythe School of Law. The Environment of the workplace and human values /. New York , c1986. vii, 118 p. ; ISBN 0-8451-4205-4 LC Card 85-23908 DDC 174/.4 19
HD7260.5 .E58 1986 *NYPL [JLF 87-151]*

MARSHALLIAN ECONOMICS. see **NEOCLASSICAL SCHOOL OF ECONOMICS.**

Marshruty peredovogo opyta / [sostavitel′ N.D. Li͡aporov]. Moskva : Izd-vo polit. lit-ry, 1985. 286 p., [8] p. of plates : ill. ; 21 cm. LC Card 85-213253
1. Labor productivity - Soviet Union. 2. Industrial productivity - Soviet Union. I. Li͡aporov, Nikolaĭ Danilovich.
HC340.L3 M235 1985

Marsick, Victoria J. Learning in the workplace /. London , New York , c1987. 217 p. ; ISBN 0-7099-4659-7 LC Card 87-20062 DDC 658.3/1243 19
HF5549.5.T7 L38 1987

Marsiglia, Cecília. S/A Central Elétrica Rio Claro / Cecília Marsiglia, Maria Regina Ciparrone Mello, Nely Robles Reis Bacellar. São Paulo : Companhia Energética de São Paulo : Instituto de Estudos Brasileiros da USP, 1986. 105 p. : ill. ; 31 cm. (Fascículos da história da energia elétrica de São Paulo . no. 1) Bibliography: p. 58-59. LC Card 87-404945 DDC 363.6/2/098161 19
1. S/A Central Elétrica Rio Claro (Brazil) - History. 2. Electric utilities - Brazil - Rio Claro (São Paulo) - History. I. Mello, Maria Regina Ciparrone. II. Bacellar, Nely Robles Reis. III. Companhia Energética de São Paulo. IV. Universidade de São Paulo. Instituto de Estudos Brasileiros. V. Title. VI. Title: Sociedade Anônima Central Elétrica Rio Claro. VII. Series.
HD9685.B83 C4886 1986

Marstedt, Gerd. Psychische Belastungen in der Arbeitswelt : theoretische Ansätze, Methoden und empirische Forchungsergebnisse / Gerd Marstedt, Ulrich Mergner. Opladen : Westdeutscher Verlag, c1986. vii, 366 p. : ill. ;

23 cm. (Beiträge zur psychologischen Forschung . Bd. 9) "... die überarbeitete Fassung eines Abschlussberichts zu einem von der Deutschen Forschungsgemeinschaft geförderten theoretischen Forschungsprojekt über 'Theoretische und methodische Probleme der Erfassung psychischer Beanspruchungen'"--Pref. Bibliography: p. [345]-366. ISBN 3-531-11757-2 LC Card 87-135624
1. Psychology, Industrial. 2. Occupational diseases. I. Mergner, Ulrich. II. Deutsche Forschungsgemeinschaft. III. Title. IV. Series.
HF5548.8 .M373 1986

Martanus, R. V. (Rīurik Vital'evich) Sotsial'noe upravlenie : kadry i kadrovaia politika / R.V. Martanus. Moskva : Izd-vo Moskovskogo universiteta, 1986. 141 p. ; 20 cm. (Nauchnyĭ kommunizm) Bibliography: p. 139-141. LC Card 87-156789
1. Executives - Soviet Union. 2. Executives - Training of - Soviet Union. 3. Management - Soviet Union. 4. Soviet Union - Social policy. I. Series: Nauchnyĭ kommunizm (Izdatel'stvo Moskovskogo universiteta). II. Title.
HD38.25.S65 M35 1986

Martel, Jean-François de, 1939- Soisson, Jean Pierre, 1934- L'enjeu de la formation professionnelle /. [Paris] , c1986. iv, 315 p. : ISBN 2-213-01752-2 : LC Card 86-194690
HD5715.5.F8 S65 1986

Martens, George R. Trade unionism and politics in Niger. Lome, Togo : Regional Economic Research and Documentation Center, [1986] 93 p. ; 30 cm. Cover title. "A special issue of Labor and development, April 1986." "Erratum" slip inserted. Includes bibliographical references. LC Card 86-172446 DDC 322/.2/09669 19
1. Trade-unions - Niger - Political activity. 2. Trade-unions - Niger - History. 3. Niger - Economic conditions. I. Labor and development. Special issue. II. Title.
HD6882.Z65 M37 1986

Martín Alonso, Arturo. Invertir en Asturias / [textos Martín Alonso, Arturo, Menéndez Lastra, Constantino]. [Spain] : Servicio de Publicaciones, Comunidad Autónoma del Principado de Asturias, [1984?] 72 p. : ill. (some col.) ; 23 x 24 cm. ISBN 84-398-1662-6 LC Card 85-217277
1. Asturias (Spain) - Economic conditions. 2. Investments - Spain - Asturias. I. Menéndez Lastra, Constantino. II. Title.
HC387.A7 M37 1984

Martín, Arturo. Argüelles, Alfonso. Los Oscos y la Cuenca del Eo . [Asturias] [1984?] ix, 317 p. : ISBN 84-505-0237-3 LC Card 86-174593
HC387.A7 A74 1984

Martin, Bob, 1939- Fly there for less : 70 strategies to save money flying worldwide / Bob Martin. Kissimmee, Fla. : TeakWood Press, c1988. 136 p. ; 22 cm. Includes index. ISBN 0-937281-01-8 (pbk.) : LC Card 87-16166 DDC 387.7/12 19
1. Airlines - Rates. 2. Airlines - Reservations. 3. Air travel. I. Title.
HE9783.5 .M37 1988

Martin, Dale R. Lotus 1-2-3 applications with disk / Dale R. Martin, A. Scott Preston. Englewood Cliffs, N.J. : Prentice-Hall, c1986. viii, 120 p. : ill. ; 28 cm. "Written to supplement any intermediate accounting textbook, but it relates particularly close to the second edition of Danos and Imhoff's Intermediate accounting"--Pref. Includes disk in pocket for use on the IBM PC. ISBN 0-13-540717-6 (pbk.) LC Card 86-200542 DDC 657/.044/02855369 19
1. Accounting - Data processing. 2. Lotus 1-2-3 (Computer program). I. Preston, A. Scott. II. Danos, Paul, 1942- Intermediate accounting. III. Title.
HF5679 .M37 1986

Martin, Doris. Corporate productivity in action : how top American firms manage the competitive challenge / Doris Martin. Wailuku, Hawaii : Martin Management Books, c1987. 89 p. ; 22 cm. ISBN 0-9615541-0-X (pbk.) LC Card 85-90446 DDC 658.3/14 19
1. Industrial productivity - United States. 2. Industrial management - United States. I. Title.
HC110.I52 M37 1987

Martin, Fernand. La localisation de l'industrie pharmaceutique au Canada / par Fernand Martin. [Ottawa] : Commission d'enquête sur l'industrie pharmaceutique, c1986. 48 p. ; 28 cm. (Etude de référence) Bibliography: p. 47-48. ISBN 0-662-93544-6 LC Card 86-206756
1. Drug trade - Canada - Location. I. Canada. Commission of Inquiry on the Pharmaceutical Industry. II. Title. III. Series.
HD9670.C22 M37 1986

Martín-Guédez, Rafael, 1942-
Sistema financiero : ahorro y préstamo / Rafael Martín-Guédez. Caracas : [s.n.], [1984] (Caracas : Editorial Arte) 309 p. : ill. ; 23 cm. Date on t.p.: 1983. Bibliography: p. 305-309. LC Card 85-177967
1. Building and loan associations - Venezuela. 2. Financial institutions - Venezuela. 3. Mortgage banks - Venezuela. 4. Mortagage loans - Venezuela. 5. Saving and thrift - Venezuela. I. Title.
HG2156.V42 M37 1984

Vigencia de la multibanca : diversificación operativa de las instituciones de crédito : reforma del sistema financiero / Rafael Martín-Guédez. [Caracas? : Editora G-Nueve, 1982 or 1983] 122 p. ; 23 cm. Publisher taken from jacket. Bibliography: p. [119]-122. LC Card 83-201555
1. Banks and banking - Venezuela. 2. Inflation (Finance) - Venezuela. 3. Financial institutions - Venezuela. 4. Banks and banking - Mexico. 5. Banks and banking - United States. 6. Finance - Venezuela. I. Title.
HG2964 .M37 1982

Martin, James, 1933-
Technology's crucible : an exploration of the wxplosive impact of technology on society during the next four decades / James Martin. Englewood Cliffs, N.J. : Prentice-Hall, 1987. xii, 206 p. : ill. ; 24 cm. Includes bibliographies. ISBN 0-13-902024-1 : LC Card 86-91492 DDC 303.4/9 19
1. Twentieth century - Forecasts. 2. Twenty-first century - Forecasts. I. Title.
T20 .M348 1987 ***NYPL [JLE 87-228]***

The wired world : towards a greater understanding of the world information economy / by James Martin, Simon Grant, and the Atwater Institute. Carnforth, Lancashire, England : Savant, 1986. xiii, 140 p. : ill. ; 30 cm. Includes bibliographies. ISBN 0-906774-49-7 (pbk.) LC Card 87-157689 DDC 384 19
1. Telecommunication - International cooperation. 2. Communication and traffic. 3. Telecommunication policy. 4. Information technology. I. Grant, Simon. II. Atwater Institute. III. Title.
HE7631 .M373 1986

Martin, Janet, 1945- Treasure of the land of darkness : the fur trade and its significance for medieval Russia / Janet Martin. Cambridge [Cambridgeshire] ; New York : Cambridge University Press, 1986. x, 277 p. : ill. ; 24 cm. Includes index. Bibliography: p. 243-266. ISBN 0-521-32019-4 LC Card 86-6094 DDC 380.1/456753/0947 19
1. Fur trade - Soviet Union - History. 2. Fur trade - Political aspects - Soviet Union - History. 3. Soviet Union - Politics and government - To 1533. I. Title.
HD9944.S755 M37 1986
NYPL [JLE 87-1280]

Martin, John D., 1945- The theory of finance : evidence and applications / John D. Martin, Samuel H. Cox, Jr., and Richard D. MacMinn. Chicago : Dryden Press, c1988. xxvi, 709 p. : ill. ; 24 cm. (The Dryden Press series in finance) Includes bibliographies and index. ISBN 0-03-063854-2 LC Card 87-496 DDC 332/.01 19
1. Finance. I. Cox, Samuel H., Jr. II. MacMinn, Richard D. III. Title. IV. Series.
HG173 .M353 1988

Martin, Joseph H. Real estate license examinations : salesperson and broker / Joseph H. Martin, Eve P. Steinberg. New York, N.Y. : Prentice Hall Press, 1987. p. cm. "An Arco book." ISBN 0-668-06616-4 (pbk.) : LC Card 86-25376 DDC 333.33/076 19
1. Real estate business - United States - Examinations, questions, etc. 2. Real estate agents - Licenses - United States. I. Steinberg, Eve P. II. Title.
HD1381.5.U5 M37 1987

Martin, Linda G., 1947- The ASEAN success story . Honolulu, Hawaii , 1987. xviii, 253 p. : ISBN 0-8248-1107-0 (pbk.) : LC Card 86-29373 DDC 337.1/59 19
HC441 .A864 1987

Martin, M. Dean. Adams, John R. Professional project management . Dayton, OH (1616 Mardon Dr., Dayton 45432-2634) , c1987. viii, 154 p. : LC Card 86-51558 DDC 658.4/04 19
HD69.P75 A33 1987

Martín Martín, Victoriano. Los Rothschild y las minas de Almadén : el servicio de la deuda pública española y la comercialización del mercurio de Almadén / Victoriano Martín Martín. Madrid : Instituto de Estudios Fiscales, Ministerio de Hacienda, 1980. xiv, 639 p. ; 19 cm. Bibliography: p. 457-461. ISBN 84-7196-338-8 LC Card 83-149823
1. Debts, Public - Spain - History. 2. Debts, External - Spain - History. 3. Mercury industry and trade - Spain - Almadén - History. 4. Rothschild family - History. I. Title.
HJ8738 .M37 1980

Martín Mateo, Ramón. El Sector vivienda . Madrid , 1982. 224 p. : ISBN 84-7088-324-0 LC Card 85-219674
HD7351.A3 S43 1982

Martin, Paul C. (Paul Christoph), 1939- Die Pleite : Staatsschulden, Währungskrise und Betrug am Sparer / Paul C. Martin, Walter Lüftl. München : Wirtschaftsverlag Langen-Müller/Herbig, c1984. 416 p. : ill. ; 23 cm. Includes bibliographical references. ISBN 3-7844-7145-5 : LC Card 85-188703
1. Debts, Public. 2. Debts, External. 3. Business cycles. 4. Economic history - 1971-. I. Lüftl, Walter. II. Title.
HJ8011 .M36 1984

Martin, Peter, 1942- Inside the Bank of Canada's Weekly financial statistics : a technical guide / Peter Martin. Vancouver, B. C. : Fraser Institute, 1985. xix, 201 p. : ill. ; 28 cm. Bibliography: p. [195]-201. ISBN 0-88975-082-3
1. Bank of Canada. Weekly financial statistics. 2. Monetary policy - Canada. 3. Banks and banking - Canada. I. Fraser Institute (Vancouver, B.C.). II. Title.
NYPL [JLF 87-456]

Martin, Phyllis Rodgers. Martin's magic formula for getting the right job : 1 - 5 . 10 . 15 . 20 = the right job / by Phyllis Martin. New York : St. Martin's Press, c1987. xix, 198 p. : ill. ; 21 cm. "Resources" p. 171-192. Includes index. ISBN 0-312-01065-6 (pbk.) : LC Card 87-16302 DDC 650.1/4 19
1. Job hunting - United States. 2. Vocational guidance - United States. I. Title. II. Title: Magic formula for getting the right job.
HF5382.75.U6 M37 1987

Martín, Ramón [i.e. Ramón Martín Mateo] see Martín Mateo, Ramón.

Martín Rodríguez, Manuel. Las haciendas locales de la Provincia de Granada, 1940-1983 : un análisis económico / Manuel Martín Rodríguez, Miguel Angel Cabello Jurado. Granada : Excma. Diputación Provincial de Granada : Instituto de Desarrollo Regional de la Universidad de Granada, [1985?] 369 p. ; 25 cm. Chiefly tables. Includes bibliographical references. ISBN 84-338-0266-6 LC Card 86-230887
1. Local budgets - Spain - Granada (Province) - History - 20th century - Statistics. 2. Local finance - Spain - Granada (Province) - History - 20th century - Statistics. I. Cabello Jurado, Miguel Angel. II. Universidad de Granada. Instituto de Desarrollo Regional. III. Title.
HJ9527.G7 M37 1985

Martin, Stephen. Industrial economics : economic analysis and public policy / Stephen Martin. New York : Macmillan ; London : Collier Macmillan, c1988. xiii, 540 p. : ill. ; 25 cm. Includes bibliographical references and indexes. ISBN 0-02-376780-4 LC Card 87-24031 DDC 338.9 19
1. Industrial organization (Economic theory). 2. Industry and state. I. Title.
HD2326 .M35 1988

Martin, Stephen John, 1948- French, William B. Guide to real estate licensing examinations for salespersons and brokers /. New York , c1986. ix, 367 p. : ISBN 0-471-87754-9 : LC Card 83-23484 DDC 333.33/0973 19
HD1375 .F74 1984
NYPL [*R-Econ. 86-3475]

Martin, Susan M. Palm oil and protest : an economic history of the Ngwa region, south-eastern Nigeria, 1800-1980 / Susan M. Martin. Cambridge ; New York : Cambridge University Press, 1988. xi, 209 p. : maps ; 24

cm. (African studies series. 59) Bibliography: p. 193-203. Includes index. ISBN 0-521-34376-3 LC Card 87-17373 DDC 338.4/76643 19
1. Palm-oil industry - Nigeria - History - 20th century. 2. Igbo (African people). I. Title. II. Series.
HD9490.5.P343 N66 1988

Martin, Thomas John, 1942- Valuation reference manual : putting a price tag on a business when you're buying, when you're selling, when you're valuing. [Hicksville, N.Y. (383 S. Broadway, Hicksville 11801) : Business Owner, c1986] ix, 134 leaves ; 28 cm. LC Card 86-233027 DDC 658.1/522 19
1. Corporations - Valuation. 2. Business enterprises - Valuation. I. Title.
HG4028.V3 M33 1986

Martín Uriz, Ana María. George, Henry, 1839-1897. [Progress and poverty. Spanish.] Progreso y miseria /. [Madrid , 1985?] cxv, 384 p. : ISBN 84-7479-375-0 : LC Card 87-112201
HB171 .G276 1985

Martin Zweig's Winning on Wall Street /. Zweig, Martin E. [Winning on Wall Street.] New York , c1986. x, 293 p. : ISBN 0-446-51234-6 : LC Card 85-43167 DDC 332.63/22 19
HG6049 .Z87 1986 ***NYPL [JLE 86-2796]***

Martin Zweig's winning with new IRAs /. Zweig, Martin E. [Winning with new IRAs.] New York, NY , c1987. xvi, 207 p. : ISBN 0-446-51276-1 LC Card 86-28203 DDC 332.024/01 19
HG1660.A3 Z94 1987

Martine, Joël. L'or, la parole, l'Etat : critique marxiste des fétiches / Joël Martine. Paris : Editions Anthropos, c1983. 296 p. : ill. ; 22 cm. Includes bibliographies. ISBN 2-7157-1065-8 LC Card 83-133521
1. Capitalism. 2. Marxian economics. I. Title.
HX542 .M32 1983 ***NYPL [JLD 87-872]***

Martinell, César, 1888-1973. L'antic Gremi d'Escultors de Barcelona / Cesar Martinell. Valls : E. Castells, 1956. 68 p. ; 24 cm. Includes bibliographical references. LC Card 86-180958
1. Gremi d'Escultors de Barcelona (Spain) - History - 18th century. 2. Guilds - Spain - Barcelona - History - 18th century. 3. Sculptors - Spain - Barcelona - History - 18th century. I. Title.
HD6473.S73 B356 1956

Martinengo, Giancarlo.
Le Crisi finanziarie /. Bologna , c1985. 348 p. : ISBN 88-15-00807-1 : LC Card 85-201934 DDC 332.1 19
HG1591 .C75 1985

Lo SME e il dollaro : interdipendenza e gerarchia nei rapporti tra aree valutarie / G.C. Martinengo, P.C. Padoan. [Napoli] : Edizioni scientifiche italiane, c1983. 84 p. ; 24 cm. Bibliography: p. 79-82. LC Card 85-150597
1. European Monetary System (Organization). 2. Monetary policy - European Economic Community countries. 3. Dollar, American. I. Padoan, Pietro Carlo. II. Title.
HG930.5 .M27 1983

Martínez Alier, Juan.
[Ecologisme i l'economia. English]
Ecological economics : energy, environment, and society / Juan Martinez-Alier with Klaus Schlüpmann. Oxford [Oxfordshire] ; New York, NY, USA : Basil Blackwell, 1987. ix, 286 p. ; 24 cm. Expanded and rearranged translation of: L'ecologisme i L'economia. Bibliography: p. [248]-273. Includes index. ISBN 0-631-15739-5 : LC Card 87-14512 DDC 333.7 19
1. Economic development - Environmental aspects. 2. Environmental policy. 3. Natural resources. 4. Man - Influence on nature. I. Schlüpmann, Klaus. II. Title.
HD85.S7 M363513 1987

Martínez Alvarado, Manuel, 1914- Casas Grieve, Luis Felipe de las. Economía y frustración social . Lima, Perú [1982?] 128 p. : LC Card 83-104684
HC227 .C27 1982

Martínez, Anibal [i. e., Anibal Martínez Zuleta]. see **Martínez Zuleta, Anibal.**

Martínez Ch., Katia. Pacheco S., Janette. Situación y posibilidades alimentarias de la población urbano marginal de Arequipa /. Arequipa, Perú [1986] 38 p., 8 folded leaves of plates : LC Card 86-232480
HD9014.P53 A746 1986

Martinez, D. F. Benson, Fred C. Hot-mix pavement stability performance versus laboratory test results /. College Station, Tex. [1985] xi, 225 p. : LC Card 86-620969 DDC 380.5 s 625.8/5 19
HE203 .T43 no. 285-1 TE200

Martínez, Daniel. La Agricultura en la costa del Perú, 1978-1984 /. Lima, Perú , 1985. ca. 150 leaves : LC Card 87-403706 DDC 338.1/0985 19
HD1905.P33 A38 1985

Martínez Díaz, Nicasio. Economía y política : el reto a la juventud / Nicasio Martínez Díaz. [Asunción : s.n.], 1986 ([Asunción] : El Gráfico) 54 p. ; 20 cm. (Colección Economía paraguaya) Includes bibliographical references. LC Card 87-400204 DDC 338.9892 19
1. Paraguay - Economic policy. I. Title. II. Series.
HC222 .M38 1986

Martínez Garza, Angel. Métodos econométricos : proyecto de investigación / Angel Martínez Garza.2a ed., corr. Chapingo, Edo. de Méx. : Colegio de Postgraduados, Institución de Enseñanza e Investigación en Ciencias Agrícolas, 1982. 225 p. ; 21 cm. Bibliography: p. 223-225. LC Card 84-227751
1. Econometrics. 2. Economics - Statistical methods. I. Title.
HB139 .M385 1982

Martínez, Jesús. see **Martínez Moro, Jesús.**

Martinez, José Fernando Trindade. Recursos económicos do Ultramar Português, sua valorização e perspectivas futuras : Moçambique, Estado da India, Macau e Timor / José Fernando Trindade Martinez. Lisboa : Bertrand, 1960. 113 p. ; 22 cm. Bibliography: p. 107-113. LC Card 86-169892
1. Mozambique - Economic conditions - To 1975. 2. Goa, Daman and Diu (India) - Economic conditions. 3. Macao - Economic conditions. 4. Timor Timur (Indonesia) - Economic conditions. 5. Portugal - Colonies - Economic conditions. I. Title.
HC890 .M37 1960

Martínez Manautou, Jorge. Trabajo familiar, conducta reproductiva y estratificación social . México, D.F. , 1986. 226 p. ; ISBN 968-8241-06-7 LC Card 87-400355 DDC 304.6/32/0972 19
HB941 .T7 1986

Martínez Moro, Jesús. La tierra en la comunidad de Segovia : un proyecto señorial urbano, 1088-1500 / Jesús Martínez Moro. [Valladolid] : Universidad de Valladolid, Secretariado de Publicaciones ; [Salamanca] : Caja de Ahorros y Monte de Piedad de Salamanca, c1985. 252 p. : maps ; 24 cm. (Serie Historia y sociedad. no. 3) Includes bibliographical references. ISBN 84-86192-37-4 LC Card 86-211593
1. Land use - Spain - Segovia - History. 2. Segovia (Spain) - Population - History. 3. Segovia (Spain) - Population density - History. I. Series: Serie Historia y sociedad (Valladolid, Spain) , no. 3. II. Title.
HD780.S44 M37 1985

Martínez Nava, Juan Manuel. Conflicto estado-empresarios en los gobiernos de Cárdenas, López Mateos y Echeverría / Juan Manuel Martínez Nava. 1a ed. México : Editorial Nueva Imagen, 1984. 240 p. ; 20 cm. (Serie Testimonios) Originally presented as the author's thesis (tesis profesional del programa de licenciatura)--Colegio de México, 1982. Bibliography: p. 235-240. ISBN 968-429-411-5 LC Card 85-240016
1. Industry and state - Mexico - History - 20th century. I. Title.
HD3616.M43 M37 1984

Martínez, Nora de. Estudio de diagnóstico de la población de los barrios--Chamelecón, Suyapa, Fe y Esperanza, San Antonio, San José y San Miguel /. Tegucigalpa, D.C. [1984] 1 v. (various foliations) : LC Card 85-205996
HC145.Z7 T434 1984

Martínez Réding, Fernando. Diversos documentos y datos relativos al proyectado ferrocarril de Chamela a Aguascalientes /. Guadalajara, México , 1982. 24, iii, 98 p. : LC Card 86-115748 DDC 385/.0972 19
HE2818 .D58 1982

Martínez Sopena, Pascual. La Tierra de Campos occidental : poblamiento, poder y comunidad del siglo X al XIII / Pascual Martínez Sopena. [Valladolid] : Institución Cultural Simancas de la Diputación Provincial de Valladolid, 1985. 843 p. : ill. ; 24 cm. Originally presented as the author's thesis (doctoral--Universidad de Valladolid, 1983) Includes bibliographical references. ISBN 84-505-1390-1 LC Card 86-231937
1. Land tenure - Spain - Tierra de Campos Region - History. 2. Tierra de Campos Region (Spain) - Population - History. 3. Church lands - Spain - Tierra de Campos Region - History. 4. Social classes - Spain - Tierra de Campos Region - History. 5. Feudalism - Spain - Tierra de Campos Region - History. I. Title.
HD779.T54 M37 1985

Martínez Zuleta, Anibal. Estadística fiscal del estado . [Bogotá] , 1978. 2 v. :
NYPL [JLE 80-831]

Martinho Lenz, Matias. see **Lenz, Matias Martinho.**

Martini, Paolo. TV, sorrisi e milioni : l'avventurosa storia dei divi e della televisione italiana / Paolo Martini.1a ed. Milano : Grandi edizioni italiane : Distribuzione esclusiva Rizzoli, 1985. 243 p. ; 21 cm. Includes index. ISBN 88-345-0020-2 : LC Card 86-129631 DDC 384.55/0945 19
1. Television - Italy. 2. Television broadcasting - Italy. I. Title.
HE8700.9.I8 M37 1985

Martinique.
Plan régional de développement : région Martinique. [Fort-de-France] : Conseil régional, [1984?] 96 p. : maps ; 21 cm. "IXe plan, 1984-1988, économique, social, culturel"--Cover. LC Card 87-101613
1. Martinique - Economic policy. 2. Martinique - Social policy. I. Martinique. Conseil régional. II. Title.
HC158.6 .M36 1984

Martinique. Conseil régional. Martinique. Plan régional de développement . [Fort-de-France] [1984?] 96 p. : LC Card 87-101613
HC158.6 .M36 1984

MARTINIQUE - ECONOMIC CONDITIONS.
Blérald, Alain Ph. Histoire économique de la Guadeloupe et de la Martinique . Paris , c1986. 336 p. : ISBN 2-86537-134-4 LC Card 86-159186
HC158.5 .B54 1986

Crusol, Jean. Changer la Martinique . Paris , c1986. 91 p. : ISBN 2-903033-73-0 : LC Card 86-210884
HC158.6 .C78 1986

MARTINIQUE - ECONOMIC POLICY.
Martinique. Plan régional de développement . [Fort-de-France] [1984?] 96 p. : LC Card 87-101613
HC158.6 .M36 1984

MARTINIQUE - INDUSTRIES - DIRECTORIES.
Carnet d'adresses /. [Pointe-à-Pitre, Guadeloupe] [1986?] 64 p. : LC Card 87-152834
HG3729.G862 C37 1986

MARTINIQUE - SOCIAL POLICY.
Martinique. Plan régional de développement . [Fort-de-France] [1984?] 96 p. : LC Card 87-101613
HC158.6 .M36 1984

Martinkevich, F. S. (Feliks Stanislavovich)
Golovko, N. A. (Nikolaĭ Anatol'evich) Osnovnye neproizvodstvennye fondy kolkhozov /cN.A. Golovko ; nauchnyĭ redaktor F.S. Martinkevich. Minsk , 1984. 94, [2] p. ; LC Card 84-177536
HD1492.S652 B9237 1984

Martino, Orlando.
Mineral industries of Latin America. Mineral industries of Latin America / compiled by staff, Bureau of Mines. Washington, D.C. , 1987. p. cm. LC Card 87-600334 DDC 338.2/098 19
HD9506.L252 M37 1987

Martins Filho, Oséas de Souza. Desenvolvimento com equilíbrio social : um desafio para o Brasil / [Oséas de Souza Martins Filho]. São Luís, Ma. : [s.n.], 1985 (São Luís, MA : Serviço de Impr. e Obras Gráficas do Estado) 314 p. ; 22 cm. Bibliography: p. 303-314. LC Card 86-229862
1. Brazil - Economic policy. 2. Brazil - Social policy. 3. Equality - Brazil. I. Title.
HC187 .M33 1985

Martins, J. H.
Income and expenditure patterns of urban black

multiple households in Pretoria, 1985 / by J.H. Martins. Pretoria : Bureau of Market Research, University of South Africa, 1986. xi, 128 p. : ill. ; 30 cm. (Research report = Navorsingsverslag . no. 130.2) Previous ed.: Income and expenditure patterns of urban Black multiple households in Pretoria, 1980 / by M. Loubser, E.M.M. Nel. 1981. ISBN 0-908408-57-9 (pbk.) LC Card 86-220725 DDC 658.8/3968 s 339.4/1/0968235 19
1. Cost and standard of living - South Africa - Pretoria - Statistics. 2. Blacks - South Africa - Pretoria - Economic conditions - Statistics. 3. Households - South Africa - Pretoria - Statistics. I. Loubser, M. G. Income and expenditure patterns of urban Black multiple households in Pretoria, 1980. II. Series: Research report (University of South Africa. Bureau of Market Research) , no. 130.2. III. Title.
HC517.S7 S48 no. 130, pt. 2 HD7064.4.Z8P74

Income and expenditure patterns of urban Indian households in Pietermaritzburg, 1985 / by J.H. Martins. Pretoria : Bureau of Market Research, University of South Africa, 1986. xi, 126 p. : ill. ; 30 cm. (Research report = Navorsingsverslag . no 130.5) Includes bibliographical references. ISBN 0-908408-60-9 (pbk.) LC Card 87-140863 DDC 658.8/3968 s 339.4/1/0968475 19
1. Cost and standard of living - South Africa - Pietermaritzburg - Statistics. 2. East Indians - South Africa - Pietermaritzburg - Economic conditions - Statistics. 3. Households - South Africa - Pietermaritzburg - Statistics. I. Series: Research report (University of South Africa. Bureau of Market Research) , no. 130.5. II. Title.
HC517.S7 S48 no. 130, pt. 5 HD7064.4.Z8P54

Income and expenditure patterns of urban Indian multiple households in Durban, 1985 / by J.H. Martins. Pretoria : Bureau of Market Research, University of South Africa, 1986. xi, 126 p. : ill. ; 30 cm. (Research report = Navorsingsverslag . no 130.1) ISBN 0-908408-54-4 (pbk.) LC Card 86-208481 DDC 658.8/3968 s 339.4/1/09684 19
1. Cost and standard of living - South Africa - Durban - Statistics. 2. East Indians - South Africa - Durban - Economic conditions - Statistics. I. Series: Research report (University of South Africa. Bureau of Market Research) , no. 130.1. II. Title.
HC517.S7 S48 no. 130, pt. 1 HD7064.4.Z8D8

Martins, Luciano, 1934- Estado capitalista e burocracia no Brasil pós-64 / Luciano Martins. Rio de Janeiro, RJ : Paz e Terra, 1985. 265 p. ; 21 cm. (Coleção Estudos brasileiros. vol. 82) Includes bibliographical references. LC Card 85-232969 DDC 338.981 19
1. Capitalism - Brazil. 2. Government business enterprises - Brazil. 3. Industry and state - Brazil. 4. Bureaucracy - Brazil. 5. Brazil - Economic policy. I. Title.
*HC187 .M2947 1985 **NYPL [JLD 86-1691]***

Martin's magic formula for getting the right job . Martin, Phyllis Rodgers. New York , c1987. xix, 198 p. : ISBN 0-312-01065-6 (pbk.) : LC Card 87-16302 DDC 650.1/4 19
HF5382.75.U6 M37 1987

Martinson, Ida Marie, 1936- Women in health & illness . Philadelphia , 1986. x, 261 p. : ISBN 0-7216-2086-8 LC Card 86-6576 DDC 155.6/33 19
RC451.4.W6 W656 1986
NYPL [JLF 86-1463]

Martinussen, John. Regulations in vain? : an assessment of India's post-1974 regulations relating to activities of transnational corporations / John Martinussen. Roskilde, Denmark : International Development Studies, Roskilde University Centre, 1986. 239 p. : ill. ; 21 cm. Bibliography: p. 230-239. LC Card 87-100775 DDC 338.8/8854 19
1. International business enterprises - Government policy - India. I. Title.
HD2900 .M37 1986

Martirena-Mantel, Ana María. External debt, savings, and growth in Latin America . Washington, D.C. , Buenos Aires , 1987. xv, 207 p. ; ISBN 0-939934-95-7 (pbk.) : LC Card 87-21422 DDC 336.3/435/098 19
HJ8514.5 .E984 1987

Martishiu͡s, S. Matematicheskie metody v organizatsii sotsialisticheskogo sorevnovanii͡a . Vil'ni͡us , 1986. 238 p. : LC Card 87-130668
HC337.L53 S65 1986

Marton, Ádám. Külkereskedelmi árstatisztikai adatok, 1957-1977 /. Budapest [1978] 125 p. ; LC Card 86-196922
HB235.H8 K85 1978

Márton, Géza. A hazai energiaszerkezet-változás fontosabb regionális kérdései / Márton Géza. Budapest : Akadémiai Kiadó, 1974. 271 p. : ill. ; 25 cm. Bibliography: p. 255-264. ISBN 963-05-0062-0 LC Card 86-187425
1. Energy industries - Hungary. 2. Power resources - Hungary. I. Title.
HD9502.H92 M37 1974

Marton, Imre. Az Elmélet és a fegyverek kritikája . Budapest [1981] xxv, 509 p. ; ISBN 963-461-775-1 (Magy. nemz. bibl.) LC Card 85-139263
HC59.7 .E45 1981

Marton, Katherin. Multinationals, technology, and industrialization : implications and impact in Third World countries / Katherin Marton. Lexington, Mass. : Lexington Books, c1986. xiii, 304 p. ; 24 cm. Includes bibliographical references and index. ISBN 0-669-13209-8 (alk. paper) LC Card 86-7218 DDC 338.8/881724 19
1. International business enterprises - Developing countries. 2. Technology transfer - Developing countries. I. Title.
*HD2932 .M37 1986 **NYPL [JLE 86-3372]***

Martone, Celso L. (Celso Luiz)
Macroeconomic policies, debt accumulation, and adjustment in Brazil, 1965-84 / Celso L. Martone. Washington, D.C. : World Bank, 1987. vii, 43 p. ; 29 cm. (World Bank discussion papers . 8) Bibliography: p. 43. ISBN 0-8213-0892-0 (pbk.) LC Card 86-1527 DDC 336.3/4/0981 19
1. Debts, External - Brazil. 2. Brazil - Economic policy. I. Title. II. Series.
HJ8579 .M37 1987

Mercado financeiro e ajustamento macroeconômico brasileiro, 1978-1985 / Celso Luiz Martone, Carlos Antonio Luque, Luiz Martins Lopes. São Paulo : Instituto de Pesquisas Econômicas, 1986. 82 p. : ill. ; 23 cm. (Série Relatórios de pesquisa . no. 35) Includes bibliographical references. LC Card 87-120453 DDC 332.4/981 19
1. Monetary policy - Brazil. 2. Finance - Brazil. I. Luque, Carlos Antonio. II. Lopes, Luiz Martins. III. Title. IV. Series.
HG835 .M375 1986

Martorelli, Horacio.
Nuevo estilo de desarrollo para Uruguay : un análisis de las relaciones entre las condicionantes sociales y la dinámica poblacional en los pequeños agricultores / Horacio Martorelli, Carlos Pérez Arrarte. Montevideo, Uruguay : Centro Interdisciplinario de Estudios sobre el Desarrollo, Uruguay, 1982. 2 v. : ill. ; 28 cm. (Serie Investigaciones. no. 9) "Esta investigación contó con el apoyo de PISPAL (Programa de Investigaciones Sociales sobre Población en América Latina), de El Colegio de México. Montivideo, diciembre de 1982." Includes bibliographical references. LC Card 85-167867 DDC 338.1/09895 19
1. Agriculture - Economic aspects - Uruguay. 2. Farms, Small - Uruguay. I. Pérez Arrarte, Carlos. II. Centro Interdisciplinario de Estudios sobre el Desarrollo Uruguay. III. Series: Serie Investigaciones (Montevideo, Uruguay) , no. 9. IV. Title.
*HD1907 .M376 1982 **NYPL [JLF 86-935]***

Las relaciones de trabajos de las mujeres en zonas rurales : estudio sobre la inserción en el mercado de trabajo de las mujeres con bajos ingresos ... / Horacio Martorelli. Montevideo, Uruguay : Centro Interdisciplinario de Estudios sobre el Desarrollo, Uruguay, 1981. 264 p. : ill. ; 28 cm. (Serie Investigaciones. no. 7) Includes bibliographical references. LC Card 86-202374 DDC 331.4/83/09895 19
1. Rural women - Employment - Uruguay. I. Series: Serie Investigaciones (Montevideo, Uruguay) , no. 7. II. Title.
HD6132 .M375 1981

Marty, János. A jövedelmezőség számításának és elemzésének módszerei az ÁFÉSZEK-nél / Marty János. Budapest : Szövetkezeti Gazdaságszervezési és Számitástechnikai Iroda, 1984. 228 p. : ill. ; 29 cm. ISBN 963-7006-05-2 : LC Card 85-176220
1. Consumer cooperatives - Hungary - Finance. I. Title.
HD3492.5.A4 M37 1984

Martyni͡uk, S. M. (Stanislav Mikhaĭlovich)
Planomernost' i ėffektivnost' sotsialisticheskogo obshchestvennogo proizvodstva / S.M. Martyni͡uk. Kiev : Gol. izd-vo izdatel'skogo ob"edinenii͡a "Vyshcha shkola", 1982. 141 p. ; 21 cm. Includes bibliographical references. LC Card 83-219823
1. Soviet Union - Economic policy - 1917-. 2. Central planning - Soviet Union. I. Title.
HC335 .M3675 1982

Martynov, G. V. (Gennadiĭ Viktorovich)
Mnogootraslevye kompleksy--problemy i metody optimizatsii / G.V. Martynov ; otvetstvennyĭ redaktor L.A. Kozlov. Moskva : "Nauka", 1986. 229, [3] p. : ill. ; 22 cm. (Problemy sovetskoĭ ėkonomiki) At head of title: Akademii͡a nauk SSSR. T͡Sentral'nyĭ ėkonomiko-matematicheskiĭ institut. Bibliography: p. 226-[230] LC Card 86-232408
1. Soviet Union - Economic policy - Mathematical models. 2. Forest products industry - Soviet Union - Planning - Mathematical models. I. Kozlov, Leonard Aleksandrovich. II. Title.
HC333 .M285 1986

Maru, Rushikesh M. Beyond bureaucracy . West Hartford, Conn. , c1986. xii, 256 p. : ISBN 0-931816-44-0 LC Card 86-34420 DDC 338.9/0068 19
HC59.72.E44 B48 1986

Maruani, Margaret. Mais qui à peur du travail des femmes? / Margaret Maruani. Paris : Syros, c1985. 175 p. : ill. ; 22 cm. Bibliography: p. 169-174. ISBN 2-86738-099-5 : LC Card 86-154408
1. Women - Employment - France. I. Title.
HD6145 .M37 1985

Marucco, Dora. Fabianesimo, ghildismo, forme di democrazia industriale / Dora Marucco. Milano, Italy : F. Angeli, c1986. 82 p. ; 22 cm. (Il Pensiero politico contemporaneo . 14) Bibliography: p. 77-82. LC Card 86-194327
1. Guild socialism - History. 2. Fabian Society (Great Britain) - History. 3. Industrial management - Employee participation - History. I. Title. II. Series.
HD6479 .M37 1986

Marwege, Ulf, 1954- Neuorientierung im Westhandel der DDR? : die Wirtschaftsbeziehungen mit der Bundesrepublik Deutschland, Frankreich, Japan, und Österreich / Ulf Marwege. Bonn : Forschungsinstitut der Deutschen Gesellschaft für Auswärtige Politik : Vertrieb, Europa Union Verlag, c1984. iv, 122 p. : ill. ; 21 cm. (Arbeitspapiere zur Internationalen Politik, 0344-9815 . 30) Includes bibliographical references. ISBN 3-7713-0221-8 : LC Card 84-196602
1. Germany, East - Commerce - Germany, West. 2. Germany, West - Commerce - Germany, East. 3. Germany (East) - Commerce - France. 4. France - Commerce - Germany (East). 5. Germany (East) - Commerce - Japan. 6. Japan - Commerce - Germany (East). 7. Germany (East) - Commerce - Austria. 8. Austria - Commerce - Germany (East). I. Title. II. Title: Neuorientierung im Westhandel der D.D.R.?. III. Series.
HF3570.5.Z7 G75 1984

Marwick, Mitchell, Peat and Company. see **Peat, Marwick, Mitchell and Company.**

Marwood, Jim, 1932- Ways of working / Jim Marwood ; photographers, Jim Marwood ... [et al.]. Kenthurst : Kangaroo Press, 1986. 160 p. : ill. ; 27 cm. Bibliography: p. 158. Includes indexes. ISBN 0-86417-101-3 (pbk.) LC Card 87-105782 DDC 305.5/62/09946 19
1. Labor and laboring classes - Tasmania - Social conditions. 2. Labor and laboring classes - Tasmania - Social conditions - Pictorial works. 3. Work environment - Tasmania. 4. Work environment - Tasmania - Pictorial works. I. Title.
HD8849.T372 M37 1986

Marx and Keynes on economic recession . Sardoni, Claudio. New York , 1987. xiv, 152 p. ; ISBN 0-8147-7871-2 : LC Card 87-13749 DDC 338.5/42 19
HB3714 .S27 1987

Marx, Carl, 1818-1883. see **Marx, Karl, 1818-1883.**

Marx, G. Die Entwicklung der Wohnungsbautätigkeit in Leverkusen / [G. Marx]. Das verarbeitende Gewerbe (Industrie)

in Leverkusen / [G. Nicolini ; Herausgeber, Stadt Leverkusen, der Oberstadtdirektor, Amt für Wahlen und Meldewesen in Zusammenarbeit mit dem Kataster- und Vermessungsamt und dem Presse- und Verkehrsamt]. Leverkusen : Die Stadt, [1984] 37 p., [1] folded leaf of plates : ill., maps ; 30 cm. (Berichte zur Stadtforschung . Heft 2) Cover title. "Stadt Leverkusen, Statistik/Stadtforschung." "April 1984"--T.p. verso. Bibliography: p. 37. LC Card 84-183932
1. Construction industry - Germany (West) - Leverkusen - Statistics. 2. Housing - Germany, West - Statistics. 3. Leverkusen (Germany) - Manufactures - Statistics. 4. Leverkusen (Germany) - Industries - Statistics. I. Nicolini, G. Verarbeitende Gewerbe (Industrie) in Leverkusen. II. Leverkusen (Germany). III. Leverkusen (Germany). Amt für Wahlen und Meldewesen. IV. Title. V. Series.
HD9715.G33 L575 1984

Marx, Karl, 1818-1883.
Grundrisse der kritik der politischen Ökonomie. see Marx Karl, 1818-1883. Zur Kritik der politischen Ökonomie.

KAPITAL.
"Kapital" K. Marksa i ėkonomicheskie problemy razvitogo sotsializma /. Moskva , 1980. 260 p. ; LC Card 81-134413
HB501 .K248 1980

Kogan, A. M. (Al'bert Moiseevich) V tvorcheskoĭ laboratorii Karla Marksa . Moskva , 1983. 172, [4] p. ; LC Card 83-166605
HB501 .K57 1983

Mandel, Ernest. "El capital" . México, D.F. , 1985. 242 p. ; ISBN 968-231-127-6 LC Card 86-158367
HB501.M37 M355 1985

Pappa, Hellē. Hoi archaioi Hellēnes syngrapheis sto "Kephalaio" tou Marx /. Athēna , 1983. 112 p. ; LC Card 84-128852
HB501 .P24 1983

Porcaro, Mimmo, 1953- I difficili inizi di Karl Marx . Bari , c1986. 112 p. ; ISBN 88-22-03815-0 : LC Card 86-195836
HB501.M37 P63 1986

Wolf, Dieter, 1942- Ware und Geld . Hamburg , 1985. 405 p. ; ISBN 3-87975-301-6 LC Card 86-229352
HB501.M5 W65 1985

Wolff, Robert Paul. Moneybags must be so lucky . Amherst , c1988. p. cm. ISBN 0-87023-615-6 (alk. paper) LC Card 87-20580 DDC 335.4/1 19
HB501.M37 W64 1988

Kritik der politischen Ökonomie. see Marx Karl, 1818-1883. Zur Kritik der politischen Ökonomie.

ZUR KRITIK DER POLITISCHEN ÖKONOMIE.
Der Zweite Entwurf des "Kapitals" . Berlin , 1983. 360 p. ; LC Card 83-236586
HB175.M2585 Z86 1983

MARX, KARL, 1818-1883 - CONGRESSES.
Uchenie K. Marksa ob ėtapakh razvitiia sposoba proizvodstva i problemy zrelogo sotsializma . Leningrad , 1985. 150 p. ; LC Card 86-140577
HB97.5 .U24 1985

MARX, KARL, 1818-1883 - CONTRIBUTIONS IN ECONOMICS.
Marx, Karl, 1881-1883.
KAPITAL.
Foley, Duncan K. Understanding Capital . Cambridge, Mass. , 1986. viii, 183 p. : ISBN 0-674-92087-2 (alk. paper) LC Card 86-4736 DDC 335.4/1 19
HB501 .F644 1986 ***NYPL [JLE 86-4606]***

Marx, Roland. La vie quotidienne en Angleterre au temps de l'expérience socialiste : 1945-1951 / Roland Marx. [Paris] : Hachette littérature générale, c1983. 323 p. ; 20 cm. Includes bibliographical references. ISBN 2-01-008679-1 : LC Card 83-220426
1. Great Britain - Economic conditions - 1945-. 2. Great Britain - Social conditions - 1945-. 3. Great Britain - Politics and government - 1945-1964. 4. Socialism - Great Britain - History. I. Title.
HC256.5 .M3955 1983

Marx und Keynes /. Scherf, Harald. Frankfurt am Main , 1986. 164 p. ; ISBN 3-518-28235-2 LC Card 87-104047 DDC 330.15/6 19
HB97.5 .S283 1986

MARXIAN ECONOMICS.
Ageev, V. M. (Valentin Mikhaĭlovich) Ėkonomicheskie interesy i stimuly pri sotsializme /. Moskva , 1984. 190 p. ; LC Card 85-108645
HC336.25 .A375 1984

Bató, Sándor. Az áru mint történelmi kategória /. [Budapest] , 1985. 104 p. ; ISBN 963-673-332-5 LC Card 86-228016
HB97.5 .B3245 1985

Berg, Hermann von, 1933- Marxismus-Leninismus . Köln , 1986. 335 p. : ISBN 3-7663-0982-X ***NYPL [JLD 86-4000]***

Bowles, Samuel. Democracy and capitalism . New York , c1986. x, 244 p. ; ISBN 0-465-06052-8 : LC Card 85-47991 DDC 321.8 19
JC423 .B76 1986 ***NYPL [JLE 86-2928]***

Cazadero, Manuel. Desarrollo, crisis e ideología en la formación del capitalismo . México , 1986. 153 p. ; ISBN 968-16-2280-4 LC Card 87-403551 DDC 330.12/2 19
HB501 .C33 1986

Chao, Tzu-yuan. [Hsin lao tung chia chih li lun. German.] Neue Arbeitswerttheorie . Hamburg , 1974. x, 173 p. ; LC Card 74-351429 DDC 335.4/12 19
HD4904 .C45715

Chiang, Hsüeh-mo. She hui chu i so yu chih yen chiu /. Hang-chou , 1985. [3], 211 p. ; ***NYPL [*OVL 86-3601]***

Christoffersen, Mads. Fysisk planlægning og samfundsmæssige reproduktionsproblemer . København , 1980, c1979. 317 p. ; ISBN 87-500-1922-8 ***NYPL [JLD 86-2303]***

Classical political economy . Boston , c1988. viii, 275 p. : ISBN 0-89838-229-7 : LC Card 87-3394 DDC 330.15/3 19
HB94 .C42 1988

Clegg, Stewart. Class, politics and the economy /. London , Boston , 1986. viii, 451 p. ; ISBN 0-7102-0452-3 : LC Card 85-8369 DDC 305.5 19
HT609 .C62 1986 ***NYPL [JLD 87-459]***

Corbridge, Stuart. Capitalist world development . London , 1986. xi, 295 p. : ISBN 0-333-32405-6 ***NYPL [JLD 86-2925]***

Dämpfling, Björn, 1949- Die Marxsche Theorie der Grundrente . Hamburg , 1985. 161 p. ; ISBN 3-87975-302-4 LC Card 86-172913
HB401 .D35 1985

Dende Galicia, Marx . Sada, A Coruña [1985?] 258 p. : ISBN 84-7492-241-0 LC Card 86-215077
HB97.5 .D413 1985

Folom'ev, A. N. (Aleksandr Nikolaevich) Orudiia truda . Moskva , 1984. 107, [4] p. ; LC Card 85-138858
HC336.25 .F64 1984

La Forma-valore . Manduria , 1984. 301 p. : LC Card 86-130626 DDC 335.4/12 19
HB206 .F67 1984

Foster, John Bellamy. The theory of monopoly capitalism . New York , 1986. 280 p. ; ISBN 0-85345-688-7 : LC Card 85-32097 DDC 330.12/2 19
HB501 .F66 1986 ***NYPL [JLD 86-2415]***

Friedrich, Horst, 1935- Die Produktionsverhältnisse /. Berlin , 1981. 228 p. ; LC Card 81-175348
HC79.I52 F75 1981

García, Antonio, 1912- [Bases de la economía contemporánea.] Bases de economía política /. [Bogotá] , 1981. 283 p. ; LC Card 82-138900 DDC 330/.098 19
HB122 .G37 1981 ***NYPL [JLD 87-868]***

Grimaliuk, V. A. (Viktor Andreevich) Neposredstvenno obobshchestvlennyĭ trud /. Moskva , 1985. 110, [2] p. ; LC Card 86-111859
HD5796 .G75 1985

Ingham, Geoffrey K. Capitalism divided? . Basingstoke, Hampshire , 1984. viii, 304 p. : ISBN 0-333-30116-1 LC Card 86-673507
HC255 .I495x 1984b

International capitalism and industrial restructuring . Boston , 1987. p. cm. ISBN 0-04-338132-4 (alk. paper) LC Card 86-28870 DDC 338.7 19
HD2321 .I58 1987

Itō, Makoto, 1936- The basic theory of capitalism . Totowa, N.J. , 1987. p. cm. ISBN 0-389-20729-2 LC Card 87-905 DDC 330.12/2 19
HB97.5 .I823 1987

Koziolek, Helmut. Umfassende Intensivierung und Infrastruktur /. Berlin , 1986. 68 p. ; LC Card 86-169897
HC290.795.C3 K68 1986

Kritika antimarksistskikh ėkonomicheskikh teoriĭ v prepodavanii politicheskoĭ ėkonomii /. Moskva , 1981. 356 p. ; LC Card 82-107917
HB178 .K7 1981

Lima, Rômulo de Araújo, 1949- Em busca da dialética . Campina Grande-Paraíba , 1983. 102 p. ; LC Card 86-130003
HB97.5 .L464 1983

Liu, Shih-pai. She hui chu i so yu chih yen chiu /. Shang-hai , 1985. 2, 6, 223 p. ; ***NYPL [*OVY 86-3647]***

Liverēs, Anastasēs I. Politikē oikonomia gia holous . Athēna , 1985. 424 p. ; LC Card 86-178760
HB97.5 .L555 1985

Magdoff, Harry. Stagnation and the financial explosion /. New York , c1987. 208 p. : ISBN 0-85345-716-6 : LC Card 86-33129 DDC 330.973/0927 19
HC106.8 .M315 1987b

Marcy, Sam, 1911- Anatomy of the economic crisis /. Atlanta , 1982. viii, 120 p. ; ISBN 0-89567-077-1 (pbk.) LC Card 87-132534 DDC 330.9/048 19
HC59 .M258 1982

Martine, Joël. L'or, la parole, l'Etat . Paris , c1983. 296 p. : ISBN 2-7157-1065-8 LC Card 83-133521
HX542 .M32 1983 ***NYPL [JLD 87-872]***

Mendoza, Carlos. Teoría de la renta capitalista de la tierra ; y, Génesis de la renta capitalista de la tierra y del arrendatario /. Buenos Aires , 1985. 108 p. : ISBN 950-9478-11-3 LC Card 86-101927
HB401 .M38 1985

Mugnai, Massimo, 1947- Il mondo rovesciato . Bologna , c1984. 296 p. ; ISBN 88-15-00641-9 : LC Card 86-169123
HB206 .M84 1984

Müller, Hans-Erich, 1945- Konzentration . Hamburg , 1985. 239 p. : ISBN 3-87975-303-2 LC Card 87-110533 DDC 338.8 19
HD2757 .M85 1985

Nanitashvili, B. Stoimostnye otnosheniia v sotsialisticheskoĭ ėkonomike /. Tbilisi , 1978. 182 p. ; LC Card 81-149294
HB201 .N293 1978

Nechaev, IU. V. (IUriĭ Vasil'evich) Populiarnaia politėkonomiia /. Kiev , 1986. 246 p. : LC Card 87-169729
HC336.25 .N43 1986

Neposredstvenno-obshchestvennoe proizvodstvo v usloviiakh razvitogo sotsializma /. Leningrad , 1984. 212 p. ; LC Card 84-248045
HB97.5 .N434 1984

O'Connor, James (James R.) The meaning of crisis . Oxford, UK , New York, NY, USA , 1987. v, 197 p. ; ISBN 0-631-13819-6 (pbk.) : LC Card 86-26399 DDC 338.5/4 19
HB3714 .O24 1987

Palkin, IUriĭ Ivanovich. Ėkonomicheskie zakony i ėkonomicheskaia politika KPSS /. Kiev , 1985. 245 p. ; LC Card 87-104961
HC336.25 .P35 1985

Perelman, Michael. Marx's crises theory . New York , 1987. v, 250 p. ; ISBN 0-275-92372-X (alk. paper) : LC Card 87-6936 DDC 330.12/2 19
HB97.5 .P349 1987

Popov, Mikhail V. Planomernoe razreshenie protivorechiĭ razvitiia sotsializma kak pervoĭ fazy kommunizma /. Leningrad , 1986. 156 p. ; LC Card 87-146874
HB97.5 .P7994 1986

Renta . Moskva , 1984. 95 p. : LC Card

85-192538
HB401 .R48 1984

Resnick, Stephen A. Knowledge and class . Chicago , c1987. vii, 352 p. ; ISBN 0-226-71021-1 LC Card 86-32631 DDC 335.4 19
HB97.5 .R48 1987

Romitelli, Valerio. Critica dell'economia politica e teoria delle forze produttive /. Milano , c1982. 241 p. ; LC Card 82-200332 DDC 338.5 19
HB241 .R66 1982 ***NYPL [JLD 87-812]***

Rudolph, Günther. Karl Rodbertus (1805-1875) und die Grundrententheorie . Berlin , 1984. 332 p. ; LC Card 84-158301
HB401 .R83 1984

Sardoni, Claudio. Marx and Keynes on economic recession . New York , 1987. xiv, 152 p. ; ISBN 0-8147-7871-2 : LC Card 87-13749 DDC 338.5/42 19
HB3714 .S27 1987

Scherf, Harald. Marx und Keynes /. Frankfurt am Main , 1986. 164 p. ; ISBN 3-518-28235-2 LC Card 87-104047 DDC 330.15/6 19
HB97.5 .S283 1986

Sherman, Howard J. Foundations of radical political economy /. Armonk, N.Y. , c1987. xi, 425 p. ; ISBN 0-87332-416-1 : LC Card 86-33849 DDC 330.1 19
HB97.5 .S5117 1987

Shishkin, M. V. (Mikhail Vladislavovich) Genezis teoriĭ monopolii v marksistsko-leninskoĭ i burzhuaznoĭ literature (1840-1930-e gody) /. Leningrad , 1985. 151 p. ; LC Card 86-140591
HD2757.2 .S49 1985

Shturman, Dora, 1923- Nash novyĭ mir . Ierusalim , 1986. 464 p. : LC Card 87-114263
HB97.5 .S5155 1986

Socialist economy and economic policy /. Wien , New York , 1985. 279 p. : ISBN 0-387-81903-7 (pbk.) LC Card 86-201536
HC704 .S557 1985

Staatsgrenzen . Berlin , c1982. 183 p. ; ISBN 3-88619-089-7 LC Card 84-142799
HB90 .S75 1982

Suvorova, M. I. (Marii͡a Il'inichna) Kritika Kominternom revizionistskikh vzgli͡adov na ėkonomiku sotsializma /. Moskva , 1985. 115 p. ; LC Card 84-219550
HB97.5 .S86 1985 ***NYPL [*QIP 87-2751]***

Tetzel, Manfred. Philosophie und Ökonomie, oder, Das Exempel Bernstein /. Berlin , 1984. 187 p. : LC Card 84-166815
HB107.B52 T48 1984

Torras de la Luz, Jacinto, 1909-1963. [Selections. 1984.] Obras escogidas /. La Habana , 1984- v. <1 > : LC Card 87-125434 DDC 338.97291 19
HC152.5 .T662 1984

The Value dimension . London , New York , 1986. 239 p. ; ISBN 0-7102-0766-2 (pbk.) : LC Card 87-109334 DDC 338.5/21 19
HB203 .V33 1986

Voprosy metodologii issledovanii͡a obshchestvennogo truda pri sotsializme /. Voronezh , 1979. 163 p. ; LC Card 81-142810
HD5796 .V65 1979

Weingarten, Richard. Eine kapitaltheoretische Untersuchung zum Gesetz vom tendenziellen Fall der Profitrate einschliesslich der Bestimmung seiner empirischen Relevanz /. München , c1982. ix, 342 p. ; ISBN 3-597-10136-4 LC Card 83-134240
HB601 .W37 1982

Wolff, Richard D. Economics . Baltimore , c1987. xiv, 279 p. : ISBN 0-8018-3479-1 (alk. paper) LC Card 87-4131 DDC 330.1 19
HB90 .W65 1987

The World socialist economy. Moscow , 1986. 279 p. ; LC Card 86-231463 DDC 338.9/009171/7 19
HC704 .W67 1986

Der Zweite Entwurf des "Kapitals" . Berlin , 1983. 360 p. ; LC Card 83-236586
HB175.M2585 Z86 1983

MARXIAN ECONOMICS - ADDRESSES, ESSAYS, LECTURES.

Analytical Marxism /. Cambridge, CB ; New York : viii, 313 p. : ISBN 0-521-30025-8 LC Card 85-11697 DDC 335.4 19
HB97.5 .A487 1986 ***NYPL [JLE 86-1742]***

Couri, Sergio, 1948- Ensaios sobre a evolução dos sistemas econômicos /. Brasília-Distrito Federal [1983] 133 p. : LC Card 84-116306 DDC 330.1 19
HB97.5 .C68 1983 ***NYPL [JLE 86-3363]***

Kornai, János. [Ellentmondások és dilemmák. English.] Contradictions and dilemmas . Cambridge, Mass. , 1986, c1983. ix, 165 p. : ISBN 0-262-11107-1 LC Card 85-5168 DDC 330.9439/053 19
HC300.28 .K67213 1986 ***NYPL [JLC 86-254]***

Mandel, Ernest. La crise 1974-1982 . Paris , c1985. 352 p. : ISBN 2-08-081151-7 ***NYPL [JLC 86-204]***

MARXIAN ECONOMICS - COLLECTED WORKS.

Pătrășcanu, Lucrețiu, 1900-1954. Scrieri, articole, cuvîntări . București , 1983. 415 p. ; LC Card 84-144088
HC405 .P345 1983

Popov, I͡U. N. (I͡Uriĭ Nikolaevich), 1931- Essays in political economy /. Moscow , c1984- v. ; LC Card 84-202086 DDC 335.43 19
HB53 .P64 1984 ***NYPL [JLK 86-18]***

MARXIAN ECONOMICS - CONGRESSES.

Sheng ch'an li kuei lü yen chiu /. Pei-ching , 1985. 5, 3, 466 p. : LC Card 85-242399 DDC 335.4/12 19
HB241 .S519 1985 <Orien China> ***NYPL [*OVL 87-507]***

Sovetsko-v'etnamskiĭ simpozium na temu "Ėkonomicheskie problemy perekhoda k sotsializmu" (1984 : Moscow, R.S.F.S.R.) Ėkonomicheskie problemy perekhoda k sotsializmu stran s nerazvitoĭ ėkonomikoĭ . [Moskva , 1986. 254 p. ; LC Card 87-108102
HC444 .S69 1984

Uchenie K. Marksa ob ėtapakh razvitii͡a sposoba proizvodstva i problemy zrelogo sotsializma . Leningrad , 1985. 150 p. ; LC Card 86-140577
HB97.5 .U24 1985

MARXIAN ECONOMICS - DICTIONARIES.

Mikheev, S. Glossary of economic and social terminology in Eastern European socialist countries /. Geneva , 1986. 52, x p. ; ISBN 92-9014-413-0 : LC Card 86-214600 DDC 335.4/03/21 19
HB61 .M487 1986

MARXIAN ECONOMICS - DICTIONARIES - RUSSIAN.

Rumi͡antsev, Alekseĭ Matveevich. Instrumentariĭ ėkonomicheskoĭ nauki i praktiki . Moskva , 1985. 303 p. : LC Card 87-109217
HB61 .R86 1985

MARXIAN ECONOMICS - HISTORY - 19TH CENTURY.

Pokrytan, A. K. (Anatoliĭ Karpovich) Leninskie raboty 90-kh godov i sovremennost' /. Kiev , 1985. 159 p. ; LC Card 87-113578
HB97.5 .P538 1985

MARXIAN ECONOMICS - LATVIA - HISTORY.

Kirtovskiĭ, I. Kh. Ocherki istorii marksistsko-leninskoĭ ėkonomicheskoĭ mysli Latvii, 1920-1980 /. Riga , 1985. 199 p. ; LC Card 86-176265
HB97.5 .K542 1985

MARXIAN ECONOMICS - MATHEMATICAL MODELS.

Roemer, John E. Free to lose . Cambridge, Mass. , 1988. p. cm. ISBN 0-674-31875-7 (alk. paper) LC Card 87-12121 DDC 335.4/12 19
HB97.5 .R6167 1988

MARXIAN ECONOMICS - METHODOLOGY.

Eremin, A. M. (Al'bert Mikhaĭlovich) Metodologii͡a opredelenii͡a osnovnogo i iskhodnogo otnosheniĭ ėkonomiki sotsializma /. Kazan' , 1980. 157, [3] p. ; LC Card 81-134646
HB97.5 .E665 1980

Politicheskata ikonomii͡a kato teorii͡a i metodologii͡a /. Sofii͡a , 1986. 397 p. ; LC Card 86-210685
HB71 .M59 1986 t. 1 HB97.5

MARXIAN ECONOMICS - RESEARCH - UKRAINE - HISTORY.

Stanovlenie i razvitie sovetskoĭ ėkonomicheskoĭ nauki na Ukraine . Kiev , 1983. 285, [2] p. ; LC Card 84-120015 DDC 330/.072/04771 19
HB74.9.S65 S72 1983 ***NYPL [*QGA 87-275]***

MARXIAN ECONOMICS - STUDY AND TEACHING.

Kritika antimarksistskikh ėkonomicheskikh teoriĭ v prepodavanii politicheskoĭ ėkonomii /. Moskva , 1981. 356 p. ; LC Card 82-107917
HB178 .K7 1981

MARXIAN SCHOOL OF SOCIOLOGY.

Abercrombie, Nicholas. Class, structure, and knowledge . London , 1980. 196 p. ; ISBN 0-8147-0571-5 : ***NYPL [JLD 80-2963]***

Badaloni, Nicola. Forme della politica e teorie del cambiamento . Pisa , c1983. xxii, 264 p. ; LC Card 85-163265 DDC 306/.2 19
JA76 .B23 1983 ***NYPL [JLD 86-3306]***

Carter, Bob, 1949- Capitalism, class conflict, and the new middle class /. London , Boston , 1985. vii, 256 p., 15 p. ; ISBN 0-7100-9624-0 : LC Card 84-9956 DDC 305.5/56 19
HD8039.M39 C37 1985 ***NYPL [JLD 87-115]***

Clegg, Stewart. Class, politics and the economy /. London , Boston , 1986. viii, 451 p. ; ISBN 0-7102-0452-3 : LC Card 85-8369 DDC 305.5 19
HT609 .C62 1986 ***NYPL [JLD 87-459]***

Haug, Wolfgang Fritz. Pluraler Marxismus . Berlin , 1985- v. ; ISBN 3-88619-303-9 (Bd. 1) LC Card 86-119293 DDC 355.43/09/04 19
HX40 .H27 1985 ***NYPL [JLK 86-57]***

Mészáros, István, 1930- Philosophy, ideology, and social science . Brighton, Sussex , 1986. xix, 284 p. ; ISBN 0-85527-717-3 ***NYPL [JLD 87-1334]***

Marxian theory and the third world / edited by Diptendra Banerjee. New Delhi ; Beverly Hills : Sage Publications, 1985. 325 p. ; 25 cm. Includes bibliographical references. ISBN 0-8039-9489-3 LC Card 85-1863 DDC 335.43/09172/4 19
1. Communism - Developing countries. 2. Developing countries - Economic policy. I. Banerjee, Diptendra, 1933-.
HX517.8 .M37 1985 ***NYPL [JLE 86-3088]***

MARXISM. see **COMMUNISM; SOCIALISM.**

Marxismus aktuell .
(182) Bömer, Hermann. Die drohende Katastrophe . Frankfurt am Main , 1984. 257 p. : ISBN 3-88012-708-5 : LC Card 85-128942
HC59 .B5925 1984

Marxismus-Leninismus . Berg, Hermann von, 1933- Köln , 1986. 335 p. : ISBN 3-7663-0982-X ***NYPL [JLD 86-4000]***

Marxismus-Leninismus, eine immer junge und wissenschaftliche Lehre (Radio Program). Selections. Neue Phänomene der kapitalistischen Gesellschaft ändern nichts an ihrem Wesen : aus der Sendereihe, "Der Marxismus-Leninismus, eine immer junge und wissenschaftliche Lehre.". 2. Ausg. Wien : G. Strobl, 1976. 35 p. : ill. ; 30 cm. (Ausgewählte Sendungen von Radio Tirana . Nr. 17) Cover title. Excerpt from the program broadcasted March 26, 1972-Aug. 24, 1975. LC Card 85-144894
1. Capitalism. 2. Imperialism. 3. Social conflict. 4. Communism. I. Radio Tirana. II. Series: Ausgewählte Sendungen von Radio Tirana (Vienna, Austria) , 17. III. Title.
HB501 .M338 1976

MARXIST HISTORIOGRAPHY.

Nicholson, Linda J. Gender and history . New York , 1986. x, 238 p. ; ISBN 0-231-06220-6 (alk. paper) LC Card 85-21281 DDC 323.3/4/01 19
HQ1206 .N7 1986 ***NYPL [JLE 86-1987]***

Marxist regimes series.
Galli, Rosemary. Guinea-Bissau . London , Boulder , 1987. xvi, 217 p., [1] leaf of plates : ISBN 1-555-87025-2 (U. S. : lib. bdg.) : LC Card 86-28011 DDC 966/.5703 19
HC1080 .G35 1987

Marx's crises theory . Perelman, Michael. New York , 1987. v, 250 p. ; ISBN 0-275-92372-X (alk. paper) : LC Card 87-6936 DDC 330.12/2 19
HB97.5 .P349 1987

Die Marxsche Theorie der Grundrente . Dämpfling, Björn, 1949- Hamburg , 1985. 161 p. ; ISBN 3-87975-302-4 LC Card 86-172913
HB401 .D35 1985

Maryland. Dept. of Employment and Training. Research and Analysis Division.
Affirmative action data . Baltimore, Md. (1100 N. Eutaw St., Baltimore 21201) [1985] [17] leaves ; LC Card 86-622599 DDC 331.11/43 19
HD5725.M35 A68 1985

Zoned employment and unemployment statistics . Baltimore, Md. (1100 N. Eutaw St., Baltimore 21201) [1986] [51] p. : LC Card 86-622109 DDC 331.12/5/09752021 19
HD5725.M35 Z67 1986

Maryland. Dept. of Natural Resources. Power Plant Siting Program. see **Maryland. Power Plant Siting Program.**

Maryland Federation of Business and Professional Women's Clubs.
A history of the Maryland Federation of Business and Professional Women's Clubs, Inc., 1929-1980. [S.l.] : The Federation, c1986. iii, 206 p., [1] leaf of plates : ill. ; 23 cm. LC Card 86-206928 DDC 061/.3 19
1. Maryland Federation of Business and Professional Women's Clubs - History. I. Title.
HD6054.4.U62 M35 1986

MARYLAND FEDERATION OF BUSINESS AND PROFESSIONAL WOMEN'S CLUBS - HISTORY.
Maryland Federation of Business and Professional Women's Clubs. A history of the Maryland Federation of Business and Professional Women's Clubs, Inc., 1929-1980. [S.l.] , c1986. iii, 206 p., [1] leaf of plates : LC Card 86-206928 DDC 061/.3 19
HD6054.4.U62 M35 1986

Maryland. General Assembly. Dept. of Fiscal Services.
Major fiscal issues at the 1983-1986 sessions of the General Assembly. Annapolis, Md. (90 State Cir., Annapolis 21401-1991) [1986] vi, 100 p. ; LC Card 86-622757 DDC 336.752 19
HJ485 .M15 1986

Report on extraordinary session of the General Assembly, May 1985 . Annapolis, Md. [1985] ii, 26 leaves ; LC Card 86-622373 DDC 332.3/2/09752 19
HG2153.M3 R46 1985

Maryland. General Assembly. State Dept. of Legislative Reference. Report on extraordinary session of the General Assembly, May 1985 . Annapolis, Md. [1985] ii, 26 leaves ; LC Card 86-622373 DDC 332.3/2/09752 19
HG2153.M3 R46 1985

Maryland. Insurance Division. Directory of licensed insurers, licensed motor clubs, licensed health maintenance organizations, licensed rating organizations, registered advisory organizations . [Baltimore, Md.] (501 St. Paul Pl., Baltimore 21202) [1985] viii, 150 p. ; LC Card 86-621407 DDC 368/.0025/752 19
HG8526.M3 D59 1985

Maryland. Office of Planning Data. Employment and labor force in Maryland . Baltimore, Md. (301 W. Preston St., Baltimore) [1986] xliv, 164, [51] p. : LC Card 86-622107 DDC 331.12/5/09752 19
HD5725.M35 E43 1986

Maryland. Power Plant Siting Program. Estomin, Steven. Updated load forecast of energy and peak demand on the Delmarva Peninsula /. Bethesda, Md. (4550 Montgomery Ave., Bethesda 20814) [1986] iv, 4, 53, [18] p. : LC Card 87-620907 DDC 333.79/3212/097521 19
HD9685.U6 A123 1986

Maryland. Regional Planning Council. Census '80 . Baltimore, Md. (2225 N. Charles St., Baltimore 21218) [1983] xv, 106 leaves : LC Card 83-622347 DDC 339.2/2/097526 19
HC108.B2 C46 1983 ***NYPL [JLF 86-1594]***

März, Thomas. Interdependenzen in einem Kennzahlensystem : eine empirische Untersuchung zur Aussagefähigkeit von Kennzahlen bei der Unternehmensanalyse / Thomas März. München : Florentz, c1983. iv, 296 p. : ill. ; 21 cm. (Hochschulschriften zur Betriebswirtschaftslehre . Bd. 25) Originally presented as the author's thesis (doctoral--Technische Universität München, 1983) Bibliography: p. 284-294. Includes index. ISBN 3-88259-262-1 : LC Card 83-222369
1. Business enterprises - Valuation. 2. Corporations - Valuation. 3. Index numbers (Economics). I. Title. II. Series.
HG4028.V3 M34 1983

Marzal, Antonio, 1929- Els models d'empresa : un assaig d'aproximació històrico-analitica a la realitat social / Antoni Marzal.1a ed. Barcelona : Fundació Bofill, 1981. 241 p. : ill. ; 20 cm. (Col·lecció Temps de futur . 4) Includes bibliographical references. ISBN 84-7410-078-X LC Card 81-174362
1. Business enterprises. I. Title.
HD2736.C37 M37 1981
NYPL [JLD 87-485]

Marzelle, Fernand. Petits pavés, grands bonheurs . [Paris] , c1984. 140 p. : ISBN 2-229-01400-1 : LC Card 85-104866
HF6105.F7 P48 1984

Marzen, Walter.
Betriebswirtschaftliche Forschung und Wirtschaftspraxis : Festschrift zum 70. Geburtstag von Walter Marzen / herausgegeben von Rudolf Bratschitsch, Edmund Heinen, Carl W. Meyer. Spardorf : R.F. Wilfer, c1986. ix, 229 p. ; 21 cm. Text by Walter Marzen. Bibliography: p. [219]-227. ISBN 3-922919-82-0 LC Card 87-133392 DDC 658.4 19
1. Industrial management. 2. Marzen, Walter. I. Bratschitsch, Rudolf. II. Heinen, Edmund. III. Meyer, Carl W. (Carl Walter), 1919-. IV. Title.
HD35 .M276 1986

Ist die 35-Stunden-Woche ein Mittel zur Beseitigung der Arbeitslosigkeit? : Arbeitszeitverkürzung als technokratisches Lenkungsinstrument / Marzen, Walter. Innsbruck : Institut für Betriebswirtschaftslehre und Unternehmenspolitik, Universität Innsbruck, 1980. 29 leaves ; 30 cm. (Arbeitspapiere / Institut für Betriebswirtschaftslehre und Unternehmenspolitik, Universität Innsbruck . Heft 14) Bibliography: leaf 29. LC Card 85-170048
1. Thirty-five hour week - Austria. 2. Austria - Full employment policies. 3. Unemployment - Austria. I. Title. II. Title: Ist die fünfunddreissig-Stunden-Woche ein Mittel zur beseitigung der Arbeitslosigkeit?. III. Series: Arbeitspapiere (Universität Innsbruck. Institut für Betriebswirtschaftslehre und Unternehmenspolitik) , Heft 14.
HD5108.2.A9 M37 1980

MARZEN, WALTER.
Marzen, Walter. Betriebswirtschaftliche Forschung und Wirtschaftspraxis . Spardorf , c1986. ix, 229 p. ; ISBN 3-922919-82-0 LC Card 87-133392 DDC 658.4 19
HD35 .M276 1986

Marzo, Miguel. La conquista del espacio territorial sanjuanino / por Miguel Marzo. Mendoza : Universidad Nacional de Cuyo, Facultad de Ciencias Políticas y Sociales, Instituto de Investigaciones Políticas y Sociales, 1968. 89 p., [12] leaves of plates : ill. ; 28 cm. (Cuadernos del Instituto de Investigaciones Políticas y Sociales . no. 15.) Bibliography: p. 84-86. LC Card 82-166187
1. Land settlement - Argentina - San Juan (Province) - History. 2. Water resources development - Argentina - San Juan (Province) - History. I. Series: Cuadernos del Instituto de Investigaciones Políticas y Sociales , no. 15. II. Title.
HD479.S25 M37 1968

Más allá del salario : hacia la reforma de la propiedad de los bienes como garantía de la libertad. [Buenos Aires] : Ediciones Forum : [Distribución exclusiva, Di Litra, 1983] 30 p. ; 21 cm. (Colección Monografías) Cover title. CONTENTS. - El realismo en el ámbito socioeconómico / Mario E. Yornet -- Qué es la participación? / Roberto Pincemin y Alberto Buela -- Algunas formas de participación que han realizado el objectivo -- Los patrimonios profesionales / Roberto Pincemin. ISBN 950-9209-03-1 LC Card 84-126229
1. Property. 2. Wages. I. Series: Colección Monografías (Fundación Forum (Argentina)).
HB701 .M36 1983

MAS papers on monetary economics. Papers on monetary economics /. [Singapore] , c1981. xii, 200 p. ; ISBN 997-16-9044-6 LC Card 82-940575
HG1250.67 .P37 1981

MAS practice and knowledge and bibliographic references for management advisory services. McKell, Lynn J. A study of MAS practice and knowledge and bibliographic references for management advisory services . New York, N.Y. , c1987. 100, [iv], 72 p. ; ISBN 0-87051-002-9 (pbk.) : LC Card 87-19491 DDC 016.6584/6 19
HF5616.U5 M34 1987

Masagão, Marcelo. Machado, Arlindo. Rádios livres . São Paulo-SP , 1986. 181 p. : LC Card 86-157835
HE8697.P57 M33 1986

Masalah terdepan dalam pembangunan ekonomi Indonesia /. Juoro, Umar, 1959- Bandung , 1985. xii, 224 pp. ; LC Card 86-942991
HC447 .J86 1985

Masas, luchas, solidaridad / Elías Muñoz Vicuña [compilador]. [S.l. : s.n., 1985] ([Guayaquil] : Litografía e Impr. de la Universidad de Guayaquil) 298 p. : chiefly ill. ; 22 x 32 cm. (Colección Movimiento obrero ecuatoriano . no. 8) Bibliography: p. 286. LC Card 86-177888
1. Labor and laboring classes - Ecuador - History - 20th century. 2. Trade-unions - Ecuador - History - 20th century. I. Muñoz Vicuña, Elías. II. Series.
HD8316 .M37 1985

Masberg, Dieter. Lexikon Wirtschaftspolitik . München , c1986. 236 p. : ISBN 3-406-31302-7 LC Card 86-221788
HG151 .L45 1986

Maschinenbauunternehmen in der Deutschen Inflation 1919-1923 . Lindenlaub, Dieter. Berlin , New York , 1985. xiii, 262 p. ; ISBN 3-11-009934-9 LC Card 85-214738
HG999 .L75 1985

Masci, Raffaello. Ferragni, Fabrizio. Guida al primo lavoro /. Milano , 1986. 271 p. : ISBN 88-17-13617-4 : LC Card 86-193250
HD6276.I7 F47 1986

Masciocchi, Giuseppe. Crisi di impresa : variabili critiche e bilanci di liquidazione / Giuseppe Masciocchi. Milano : A. Giuffrè, 1983. viii, 112 p. ; 26 cm. (Studi economici e aziendali . 3) Bibliography: p. [109]-112. LC Card 84-141092 DDC 657/.73 19
1. Liquidation - Italy. 2. Business enterprises - Valuation - Italy. I. Title. II. Series.
HD2747 .M37 1983 ***NYPL [JLE 86-4053]***

Masera, R. S.
An increasing role for the ECU : a character in search of a script / Rainer Stefano Masera. Princeton, N.J. : International Finance Section, Department of Economics, Princeton University, 1987. vi, 50 p. ; 24 cm. (Essays in international finance, 0071-142X . no. 167) Bibliography: p. 31-33. ISBN 0-88165-074-9 (pbk.) : LC Card 87-3747 DDC 332/.042 s 332.4/56094 19
1. European currency unit. I. Title. II. Series.
HG136 .P7 no. 167 HG930.5

L'unificazione monetaria e lo SME / Rainer S. Masera. Bologna : Il Mulino, c1980. 220 p. ; 22 cm. (Studi e ricerche. 109) Bibliography: p. 203-211. LC Card 82-150717 DDC 332.4/566/094 19
1. European Monetary System (Organization). 2. Money - European Economic Community countries. 3. Monetary policy - European Economic Community countries. 4. Foreign exchange problem - European Economic Community countries. 5. Coinage, International. I. Title.
HG930.5.Z8 M37 1980 ***NYPL [JLD 87-902]***

Mashiakh, I͡sak. Problemi na sot͡sialisticheskata organizat͡sii͡a na truda /. Sofii͡a , 1986. 146 p. : LC Card 87-128832
HD5811.5.A6 P76 1986

Maslankowski, Willi, 1936-
Nachweis beruflicher Qualifikationen / Willi Maslankowski. 1. Ausg. Montevideo : CINTERFOR, 1979. 102 p., [2] folded leaf of plates : charts ; 24 cm. (Studien und Monographien . No. 38) LC Card 86-148766
1. Occupational training - Latin America. 2. Occupational training - Germany, West. I. Series: Estudios y monografías (CINTERFOR (Organization)) , no. 38. II. Title.
HD5715.5.L3 M37 1979

[Nachweis beruflicher Qualifikationen. Spanish. Selections]
Calificación ocupacional en la República Federal de Alemania / Willi Maslankowski.

1a ed. Montevideo : CINTERFOR, 1979. 38 p. : ill. ; 23 cm. (Estudios y monografías . no. 43) Translation of two chapters of the author's Nachweis beruflicher Qualifikationen. LC Card 86-143001
1. Occupational training - Germany, West. I. Series: Estudios y monografías (CINTERFOR (Organization)) , no. 43. II. Title.
HD5715.5.G4 M372518 1979

Mason, Andrew, 1947- HOMES : a household model for economic and social studies : reference guide for household projections, version 1.0 / Andrew Mason. Honolulu, Hawaii : East-West Population Institute, East-West Center, [1987] x, 114 p. : ill. ; 24 cm. (Papers of the East-West Population Institute, 0732-0531 . no. 106 (Aug. 1987)) Bibliography: p. 113-114. ISBN 0-86638-102-3 (pbk.) : LC Card 87-22288 DDC 304.6/028/55329 19
1. HOMES (Computer program). 2. Households - Data processing. 3. Population forecasting - Data processing. I. HOMES (Computer program). II. Series. III. Series: Papers of the East-West Population Institute , no. 106. IV. Title.
HB849.49 .M38 1987

Mason, John M. (John Michael), 1950- Operational and geometric evaluation of exclusive truck lanes / by J.M. Mason, D.R. Middleton, and H.C. Petersen ; sponsored by Texas State Department of Highways and Public Transportation, in cooperation with U. S. Department of Transportation, Federal Highway Administration. College Station, Tex. : Texas Transportation Institute, Texas A&M University System ; Springfield, Va. : Available through National Technical Information Service, [1986] vii, 156 p. : ill. ; 28 cm. (Research report / Texas Transportation Institute, Texas A&M University System . 331-3F) "Research study no. 2-18-84-331." "TTI-2-18-84-331-3F"--Cover. "May 1986." Bibliography: p. 55-56. LC Card 86-622239 DDC 380.5 s 388.3/14 19
1. Traffic flow - Texas - Evaluation. 2. Truck lanes - Texas - Evaluation. I. Middleton, D. R. (Dan R.). II. Petersen, Harry C. III. Texas. State Dept. of Highways and Public Transportation. IV. United States. Federal Highway Administration. V. Series: Research report (Texas Transportation Institute) , 331-3F. VI. Title.
HE203 .T43 no. 331-3F HE356.T4

Mason, Joseph Barry. Modern retailing : theory and practice / J. Barry Mason, Morris L. Mayer.4th ed. Plano, Tex. : Business Publications, 1987. xviii, 834 p. : ill. ; 24 cm. Includes bibliographies and indexes. ISBN 0-256-03706-X LC Card 86-71842 DDC 658.8/7 19
1. Retail trade. I. Mayer, Morris Lehman. II. Title.
HF5429 .M328 1987

MASON, LUCY RANDOLPH, 1882-1959.
Salmond, John A. Miss Lucy of the CIO . Athens , c1988. p. cm. ISBN 0-8203-0956-7 (alk. paper) LC Card 87-5822 DDC 331.88/33/0924 B 19
HD6509.M375 S25 1988

Mason, R. Hal (Robert Hal), 1929- Management : an international perspective / R. Hal Mason, Robert S. Spich. Homewood, Ill. : Irwin, 1987. xii, 235 p. : ill. ; 23 cm. (Irwin perspectives in international business) Bibliography: p. 223-228. Includes index. ISBN 0-256-05631-5 (pbk.) LC Card 86-82592 DDC 658/.049 19
1. International business enterprises - Management. I. Spich, Robert S. II. Title. III. Series.
HD62.4 .M373 1987

Mason, Richard O. Rowe, Alan J. Managing with style . San Francisco , 1987. xviii, 225 p. : ISBN 1-555-42074-5 (alk. paper) LC Card 87-45570 DDC 658.4/03 19
HD30.28 .R676 1987

Mason, Sarah R. Training Southeast Asian refugee women for employment : public policies and community programs, 1975-85 / Sarah R. Mason. Minneapolis, Minn. : Southeast Asian Refugee Studies Project, Center for Urban and Regional Affairs, University of Minnesota, 1986. viii, 142 p. : ill. ; 28 cm. (Southeast Asian Refugee Studies occasional papers . no. 4) Bibliography: p. 133-142. LC Card 86-72303 DDC 331.4/2592/08995073 19
1. Occupational training - United States. 2. Women immigrants - Employment - United States. 3. Refugees - United States. 4. Refugees - United States. I. University of Minnesota. Southeast Asian Refugee Studies Project. II. Title. III. Series.
HD5715.2 .M37 1986

Masovo-politicheskata i organizatorska rabota v usloviiata na noviia ikonomicheski mekhanizŭm. Plovdiv : Okrŭzhen kom-t na BKP : Dom za polit. prosveta, 1981. 42 p. ; 21 cm. LC Card 82-153766
1. Bulgaria - Economic policy - 1944-. 2. Bŭlgarska Komunisticheska partiia - Party work. I. Bŭlgarska komunisticheska partiia. Okrŭzhen komitet--Plovdiv. II. Dom za politicheska prosveta (Plovdiv, Bulgaria).
HC403 .M376 1981

MASPAK. McKell, Lynn J. A study of MAS practice and knowledge and bibliographic references for management advisory services . New York, N.Y. , c1987. 100, [iv], 72 p. ; ISBN 0-87051-002-9 (pbk.) : LC Card 87-19491 DDC 016.6584/6 19
HF5616.U5 M34 1987

Máspero, Emilio.
Importancia y significado de la encíclica sobre el trabajo humano del papa Juan Pablo II para el movimiento obrero latinoamericano / trabajo presentado por Emilio Máspero. [Caracas, Venezuela] : Central Latinoamericana de Trabajadores, [1984] 159 p. : ill., ports. ; 22 cm. (Colección CLAT) Cover title: El trabajo, una nueva civilización y cultura del trabajo. "Semana Social de Mar del Plata, Argentina, 6 al 9 de julio de 1984." Bibliography: p. 157-159. LC Card 87-404543 DDC 261.8/5 19
1. Catholic Church. Pope (1978- : John Paul II) Laborem exercens. 2. Church and labor. I. Title. II. Title: Trabajo, una nueva civilización y cultura del trabajo. III. Series.
HD6338 .M425 1984

Informe político y de orientación ante el VIIIo Congreso de la CLAT : Bogotá, Colombia, 7 de diciembre de 1982 / presentado por Emilio Máspero. [Caracas] : Central Latinoamericana de Trabajadores, 1983. 122 p. : ill. ; 22 cm. (Colección CLAT) Serie Documentos de base Cover title: Democracia real y renovación del movimiento de los trabajadores. LC Card 87-403072 DDC 305.5/62/098 19
1. Central Latinoamericano de Trabajadores - Congresses. 2. Labor and laboring classes - Latin America - Congresses. I. Title. II. Title: Democracia real y renovación del movimiento de los trabajadores. III. Series.
HD8110.5.A5 C466 1983

MASS COMMUNICATION. see **COMMUNICATION AND TRAFFIC; MASS MEDIA; TELECOMMUNICATION.**

Mass deportations in Ethiopia /. Malhuret, Claude. [Paris] [1985] 65 leaves ; LC Card 86-181587 DDC 333.3/1/63 19
HD979 .M34 1985

MASS FEEDING. see **FOOD SERVICE.**

MASS MEDIA AND BUSINESS - INDIA - CONGRESSES.
Government media and the public sector . New Delhi , 1983. 270 p. ; LC Card 83-907479 DDC 302.3/24/0954 19
HD59 .G62 1983 ***NYPL [JLD 86-3767]***

MASS MEDIA AND BUSINESS - UNITED STATES.
Andrunas, E. Ch. (Elena Cheslavovna) Biznes i propaganda . Moskva , 1986. 223 p. : LC Card 87-152425
HD59.6.U6 A53 1986

Blohowiak, Donald W. No comment! . New York , 1987. xvi, 221 p. ; ISBN 0-275-92820-9 (alk. paper) : LC Card 87-15831 DDC 659.2 19
HD59 .B57 1987

MASS MEDIA AND YOUTH - GERMANY (WEST)
Buschmann, Vera, 1951- Wirkungsanalyse für segmentspezifische Warentestwerbung . Frankfurt am Main , New York , c1986. xii, 270 p. : ISBN 3-8204-9275-5 LC Card 86-220570
HF5827 .B87 1986

MASS MEDIA - DICTIONARIES.
Brown, William P. The complete dictionary of media terms /. Chicago, IL , c1986. vii, 151 p. ; ISBN 0-913247-01-4 (pbk.) LC Card 86-70712 DDC 302.2/34/0321 19
HF5826.5 .B77 1986

Koschnick, Wolfgang J., 1942- Standard-Wörterbuch für Werbung, Massenmedien und Marketing, Deutsch-Englisch /. Berlin , New York , 1987. 590 p. ; ISBN 0-89925-293-1 (U. S.) : LC Card 87-19928 DDC 659.1/03/21 19
HF5803 .K67 1987

MASS MEDIA - DICTIONARIES - GERMAN.
Koschnick, Wolfgang J., 1942- Standard-Lexikon für Marketing, Marktkommunikation, Markt- und Mediaforschung /. München , New York , 1987. vi, 940 p. : ISBN 3-598-10583-5 LC Card 87-143648 DDC 380.1/03/31 19
HF5415 .K617 1987

MASS MEDIA - GREAT BRITAIN - STATISTICS.
ISBA area information, 1978 /. London , 1978. 147 p. : ISBN 0-906241-00-6 (pbk.) LC Card 83-225656 DDC 381/.1/0941021 19
HA1134 .I83 1978

MASS MEDIA - ITALY - ADDRESSES, ESSAYS, LECTURES.
Il Territorio immaginario /. Milano [1980] 106 p. ; ISBN 88-20-41848-7 : LC Card 81-123209 DDC 302.2/34/0945 19
HE8700.9.I8 T47 1980
NYPL [JFD 86-8337]

MASS MEDIA - MEXICO.
Arredondo Ramírez, Pablo. Comunicación social, poder y democracia en México /. Guadalajara, Jalisco, México , c1986. 214 p. : LC Card 86-227944
HE8689.9.M6 A77 1986

MASS MEDIA - SOCIAL ASPECTS.
Schiller, Herbert I., 1919- Information and the crisis economy /. New York , 1986. xv, 133 p. ; ISBN 0-19-520514-6 (pbk. : alk. paper) LC Card 86-2374 DDC 302.2/34 19
HE7651 .S34 1986 ***NYPL [JLD 86-3695]***

MASS MEDIA - SOCIAL ASPECTS - ADDRESSES, ESSAYS, LECTURES.
Comunicazione come dominio? /. Milano [1979] 147 p. ; ISBN 88-20-41548-8 : LC Card 79-395059 DDC 302.2/3
HM258 .C5896 ***NYPL [JLD 86-3359]***

MASS MEDIA - UNITED STATES.
United States. Congress. House. Committee on Foreign Affairs. Subcommittee on International Organizations and Movements. Modern communications and foreign policy. Washington, 1967. vii, 13R, iv, 216 p. LC Card 67-61749
E744 .U45 1967 ***NYPL [JLE 73-233]***

MASS MEDIA - UNITED STATES - AUDIENCES.
Selnow, Gary W. Planning, implementing, and evaluating targeted communication programs . New York , 1987. vi, 291 p. : ISBN 0-89930-208-4 (lib. bdg. : alk. paper) LC Card 86-30418 DDC 659.1 19
HD30.3 .S46 1987

MASS PRODUCTION - GREAT BRITAIN - HISTORY.
Lewchuk, Wayne. American technology and the British vehicle industry /. Cambridge [Cambridgeshire] , New York , 1987. viii, 304 p. : ISBN 0-521-30269-2 LC Card 86-30994 DDC 338.4/56292/0941 19
HD9710.G72 L48 1987

MASS PSYCHOLOGY. see **SOCIAL PSYCHOLOGY.**

Massa, Alison K. Housing and the environment / [by Alison K. Massa and Mark Weinberger with the assistance of Julie Castelli Nauman ... et al.]. Sacramento, CA (921 10th St., Sacramento 95814-2774) : Dept. of Housing and Community Development : For copies contact Business Services Office, The Dept., [1985?] 2 v. : ill. (some col.) ; 28 cm. Bibliography: v. 1, p. D1-D2. Includes index. CONTENTS. - v. 1. A guide to producing housing under the California Environmental Quality Act -- v. 2. Models, plans, procedures, and findings. LC Card 87-621018 DDC 363.7 19
1. Land use, Urban - California. 2. Housing policy - California. 3. Housing - Law and legislation - California. 4. Environmental law - California. I. Weinberger, Mark. II. Nauman, Julie Castelli. III. California. Dept. of Housing and Community Development. IV. Title.
HD266.C2 M37 1985

Massachusetts. Division of Employment Security. Economic Research & Analysis Service. Foley, Catherine. Massachusetts industrial employment projected changes, 1984-1995 /. [Boston] [1986] vi leaves, 37 p. : LC Card 87-620528 DDC 331.12/5/09744 19
HD5725.M4 F64 1986

Foley, Catherine. Massachusetts job outlook, occupational employment projected changes, 1984 to 1995 /. [Boston, MA] [1987] vi, 59 p. : LC Card 87-621850 DDC 331.12/5/09744021 19
HD5725.M4 F65 1987

MASSACHUSETTS - ECONOMIC CONDITIONS. Foley, Catherine. Massachusetts job outlook, occupational employment projected changes, 1984 to 1995 /. [Boston, MA] [1987] vi, 59 p. : LC Card 87-621850 DDC 331.12/5/09744021 19
HD5725.M4 F65 1987

MASSACHUSETTS - ECONOMIC CONDITIONS - STATISTICS. Foley, Catherine. Massachusetts industrial employment projected changes, 1984-1995 /. [Boston] [1986] vi leaves, 37 p. : LC Card 87-620528 DDC 331.12/5/09744 19
HD5725.M4 F64 1986

Massachusetts. General Court. Senate. Committee on Post Audit and Oversight. The Massachusetts Industrial Finance Agency . Boston, MA (Rm. 314, State House, Boston 02133) [1986] 53 p. ; LC Card 86-622280 DDC 353.97440082 19
HG3729.U6 M366 1986

Massachusetts. General Court. Senate. Post Audit and Oversight Bureau. The Massachusetts Industrial Finance Agency . Boston, MA (Rm. 314, State House, Boston 02133) [1986] 53 p. ; LC Card 86-622280 DDC 353.97440082 19
HG3729.U6 M366 1986

Massachusetts industrial employment projected changes, 1984-1995 /. Foley, Catherine. [Boston] [1986] vi leaves, 37 p. : LC Card 87-620528 DDC 331.12/5/09744 19
HD5725.M4 F64 1986

The Massachusetts Industrial Finance Agency : a performance audit : a report of the Senate Committee on Post Audit and Oversight / prepared by the Senate Post Audit and Oversight Bureau. Boston, MA (Rm. 314, State House, Boston 02133) : The Committee, [1986] 53 p. ; 29 cm. "May 20, 1986." LC Card 86-622280 DDC 353.97440082 19
1. Massachusetts Industrial Finance Agency. 2. Industrial promotion - Massachusetts. I. Massachusetts. General Court. Senate. Committee on Post Audit and Oversight. II. Massachusetts. General Court. Senate. Post Audit and Oversight Bureau.
HG3729.U6 M366 1986

MASSACHUSETTS INDUSTRIAL FINANCE AGENCY. The Massachusetts Industrial Finance Agency . Boston, MA (Rm. 314, State House, Boston 02133) [1986] 53 p. ; LC Card 86-622280 DDC 353.97440082 19
HG3729.U6 M366 1986

Massachusetts job outlook, occupational employment projected changes, 1984 to 1995 /. Foley, Catherine. [Boston, MA] [1987] vi, 59 p. : LC Card 87-621850 DDC 331.12/5/09744021 19
HD5725.M4 F65 1987

Massachusetts. Occupational Employment Statistics Unit. Occupations in services, finance, insurance, real estate, and construction, 1984 /. [Boston, MA] [1985] 185 p. : LC Card 87-621853 DDC 331.7/009744 19
HD5725.M4 O26 1985

Massachusetts. Office of the Commissioner of Banks. Cooperative bank . [Boston] [1986] p. A-G, 99, 42 p. ; LC Card 87-620912 DDC 334/.2/025744 19
HG2038.M4 C58 1986

Massad A., Carlos. Análisis de la economía dominicana /. Santo Domingo, República Dominicana , 1985. 73 p. ; LC Card 86-186259
HG3926.5 .A53 1985

Massafra, Angelo. Campagne e territorio nel Mezzogiorno fra Settecento e Ottocento / Angelo Massafra. Bari : Dedalo, c1984. 324 p. : ill. ; 21 cm. (Nuova biblioteca Dedalo . 39.) Includes bibliographical references and index. ISBN 88-22-06039-3 : LC Card 85-179303
1. Italy, Southern - Economic conditions. 2. Italy, Southern - Social conditions. I. Series: Nuova biblioteca Dedalo. Serie "Mezzogiorno, società, cultura.". II. Title.
HC307.S69 M37 1984

Massana i Llorens, Ma. Pilar. L'Hospitalet a l'inici del S. XVIII : homes i terres : cadastres de 1718 i 1724 / Ma. Pilar Massana i Llorens. L'Hospitalet de Llobregat : Centre d'Estudis de l'Hospitalet, 1985. 116 p. : facsims. ; 21 cm. (Centre d'Estudis de l'Hospitalet . 3) "Maig 1984." Bibliography: p. 49-50. LC Card 86-230458
1. Land tenure - Spain - Hospitalet de Llobregat - History - 18th century. I. Series: Centre d'Estudis de l'Hospitalet (Series) , 3. II. Title.
HD779.H67 M37 1985

Massarik, Fred. Tannenbaum, Robert. Leadership and organization . New York , 1987, c1961. xiv, 456 p. : ISBN 0-8240-8219-2 (alk. paper) : LC Card 86-27019 DDC 303.3/4 19
HD57.7 .T36 1987

Massat, Dieter. Die ökonomische Problematik von Zuweisungen an Kommunen / Dieter Massat. Thun : H. Deutsch, c1984. vii, 321 p. : ill. ; 21 cm. (Reihe Wirtschaftwissenschaften, 0253-1488 . Bd. 302) Bibliography: p. 299-321. ISBN 3-87144-792-7 LC Card 84-183709
1. Intergovernmental fiscal relations - Germany, West. 2. Grants-in-aid - Germany (West). I. Title. II. Series.
HJ1121 .M37 1984

Massenberg, Jost A., 1956- Strategie und Entwicklung deutscher Grossunternehmen : computerunterstützte Inhaltsanalyse der Hauptversammlungsansprachen der Unternehmensführung, 1966 bis 1983 / Jost A. Massenberg. Frankfurt am Main ; New York : P. Lang, c1986. xi, 398 p. : ill. ; 21 cm. (Europäische Hochschulschriften. Reihe V, Volks- und Betriebswirtschaft, 0531-7339 . Bd. 739 = vol. 739 = vol. 739) Bibliography: p. 375-398. ISBN 3-8204-9666-1 LC Card 86-220603
1. Industrial management - Germany, West. 2. Corporations - Germany (West) - Management. I. Series: Europäische Hochschulschriften. Reihe V, Volks- und Betriebswirtschaft , Bd. 739. II. Title.
HD70.G2 M37 1986

Massimi, John J. Truck lane needs methodology : a heuristic approach to solve a five option discrete network design problem / by John J. Massimi, Hani S. Mahmassani, and C. Michael Walton. Austin : Center for Transportation Research, Bureau of Engineering Research, University of Texas at Austin ; Springfield, Va. : National Technical Information Service, [distributor], [1985] xii, 63 p. : ill. ; 28 cm. (Research report . no. 356-1) "Conducted for Texas State Department of Highways and Public Transportation in cooperation with the U. S. Department of Transportation, Federal Highway Administration by Center for Transportation Research Bureau of Engineering Research, the University of Texas at Austin." "November 1985." "A study of truck lane needs; research project number 3-18-83-356." Bibliography: p. 35. LC Card 86-622425 DDC 388.1/3 19
1. Truck lanes - Texas. I. Mahmassani, Hani S. II. Walton, C. Michael. III. Texas. State Dept. of Highways and Public Transportation. IV. United States. Federal Highway Administration. V. Title. VI. Title: Study of truck lane needs. VII. Series: Research report (University of Texas at Austin. Center for Transportation Research) , no. 356-1.
HE336.T79 M37 1985

Die Massnahme-, Berichts- und Missbilligungsbeschlüsse des Parlaments im Entlastungsverfahren /. Sollmann, Axel, 1952- Frankfurt am Main , New York , c1986. 261 p. ; ISBN 3-8204-9778-1 LC Card 86-233741
HJ9925.G3 S65 1986

Masson, Jean Louis. Demain l'acier français / Jean-Louis Masson. 1re éd. Paris : Editions Cujas, c1986. 404 p. : ill. ; 24 cm. ISBN 2-254-86071-1 : LC Card 86-190326
1. Iron industry and trade - France. 2. Steel industry and trade - France. I. Title.
HD9522.5 .M37 1986

Massow, Valentin von, 1925- Dairy imports and import policy in Mali and their implications for the dairy sector in the Bamako area / Valentin H. Von Massow. Addis Ababa, Ethiopia : International Livestock Centre for Africa, [1985] v leaves, 57 p., [12] leaves ; 30 cm. (LPU working paper . no. 8) "October 1985." Bibliography: p. 55-57. LC Card 86-981009 DDC 382/.417/096623 19
1. Dairy products industry - Mali - Bamako Region. 2. Dairy products industry - Government policy - Mali. 3. Imports - Government policy - Mali. I. International Livestock Centre for Africa. II. Title. III. Series.
HD9275.M423 B366 1985

Mastenbroek, W. F. G. **[Conflicthantering en organisatie-ontwikkeling. English]** Conflict management and organization development / Willem F.G. Mastenbroek. Chichester ; New York : Wiley, c1987. x, 166 p. ; 24 cm. Translation of: Conflicthantering en organisatie-ontwikkeling. Bibliography: p. 155-162. Includes indexes. ISBN 0-471-91415-0 : LC Card 87-10463 DDC 302.3/5 19
1. Organizational change. 2. Organizational behavior. 3. Conflict management. I. Title.
HD58.8 .M32513 1987

Master forms & contracts from your copier . Burns, Robert, 1938- Tucson, AZ , c1987. 160 p. : ISBN 0-89586-513-0 (pbk.) : LC Card 86-82238 DDC 651/.29 19
HF5371 .B845 1987

Master forms and contracts from your copier. Burns, Robert, 1938- Master forms & contracts from your copier . Tucson, AZ , c1987. 160 p. : ISBN 0-89586-513-0 (pbk.) : LC Card 86-82238 DDC 651/.29 19
HF5371 .B845 1987

Master guide to field sales management tactics and techniques /. Bishop, Howard, 1938- Englewood Cliffs, N.J. , c1987. xxii, 306 p. : ISBN 0-13-559840-0 LC Card 87-17425 DDC 658.8/1 19
HF5438.4 .B57 1987

MASTER OF ARTS DEGREE. Salzman, Marian L. Wanted, liberal arts graduates . New York , 1987. xvi, 341 p. ; ISBN 0-385-24008-2 (pbk.) : LC Card 87-8846 DDC 650.1/4 19
HF5382.75.U6 S27 1987

MASTER OF BUSINESS ADMINISTRATION DEGREE. Dunfee, Thomas W. Integrating ethics into the MBA core curriculum /. [Philadelphia] , c1986. 169 leaves : LC Card 87-123702 DDC 174/.4/071173 19
HF5387 .D86 1986

MASTER OF BUSINESS ADMINISTRATION DEGREE - UNITED STATES. Lear, Robert W. How to turn your MBA into a CEO /. New York , London , c1987. xvii, 222 p. ; ISBN 0-02-569610-6 LC Card 86-28332 DDC 650/.07/1173 19
HF1131 .L39 1987

MASTER OF BUSINESS ADMINISTRATION DEGREE - UNITED STATES - DIRECTORIES. The Official guide to MBA programs /. [Los Angeles, Calif.] , Princeton, N.J. , c1986. 603 p. ; ISBN 0-446-38437-2 (pbk.) : LC Card 87-102516 DDC 658/.007/1173 19
HF1131 .O359 1986

Mastering AppleWorks /. Tymes, Elna. San Francisco , c1987. xxii, 479 p. : ISBN 0-89588-398-8 (pbk.) : LC Card 87-60799 DDC 650/.028/55369 19
HF5548.4.A68 T95 1987

Mastering Dac-Easy . Mosich, Donna M. Glenview, Ill. , c1988. p. cm. ISBN 0-673-18735-7 LC Card 87-4847 DDC 657/.028/55369 19
HF5679 .M64 1988

Mastering First Choice /. Tymes, Elna. Glenview, Ill. , c1987. ix, 301 p. : ISBN 0-673-18767-5 (pbk.) : LC Card 86-26098 DDC 650/.028/55369 19
HF5548.4.F57 T96 1987

Mastering Framework II /. Hergert, Douglas. Berkeley , c1987. xvii, 509 p. : ISBN 0-89588-390-2 (pbk.) : LC Card 86-62808 DDC 650/.028/55369 19
HF5548.4.F72 H47 1987

Mastering Lotus HAL /. Campbell, Mary V. San Francisco , c1987. xxi, 342 p. : ISBN 0-89588-422-4 (pbk.) : LC Card 87-60797 DDC 005.36/9 19
HF5548.4.L68 C35 1987

Mastering money . Lieberman, Anne M. Chicago, Ill. , Naperville, IL , c1987. xi, 267 p. : ISBN 0-88462-589-3 (pbk.) : LC Card 87-3655 DDC 332.024 19
HG179 .L486 1987

Mastering Omnis three. Maller, Steven. Mastering Omnis 3 /. Blue Ridge Summit, PA , 1986. xi, 207 p. : ISBN 0-8306-0374-3 : LC Card 86-5758 DDC 658/.05574 19
HF5548.4.O55 M35 1986
NYPL [JSE 87-264]

Mastering Omnis 3 /. Maller, Steven. Blue Ridge Summit, PA , 1986. xi, 207 p. : ISBN 0-8306-0374-3 : LC Card 86-5758 DDC 658/.05574 19
HF5548.4.O55 M35 1986
NYPL [JSE 87-264]

Mastering SuperCalc four. Harvey, Greg. Mastering SuperCalc4 /. San Francisco , c1987. xix, 311 p. : ISBN 0-89588-419-4 (pbk.) : LC Card 87-60636 DDC 005.36/9 19
HF5548.4.S87 H37 1987

Mastering SuperCalc Three. Harvey, Greg. Mastering SuperCalc3 /. Berkeley, CA , c1986. xvi, 276 p. : ISBN 0-89588-312-0 (pbk.) : LC Card 87-119243 DDC 005.36/9 19
HF5548.4.S86 H37 1986

Mastering SuperCalc 3. Harvey, Greg. Mastering SuperCalc3 /. Berkeley, CA , c1986. xvi, 276 p. : ISBN 0-89588-312-0 (pbk.) : LC Card 87-119243 DDC 005.36/9 19
HF5548.4.S86 H37 1986

Mastering SuperCalc 4. Harvey, Greg. Mastering SuperCalc4 /. San Francisco , c1987. xix, 311 p. : ISBN 0-89588-419-4 (pbk.) : LC Card 87-60636 DDC 005.36/9 19
HF5548.4.S87 H37 1987

Mastering SuperCalc3 /. Harvey, Greg. Berkeley, CA , c1986. xvi, 276 p. : ISBN 0-89588-312-0 (pbk.) : LC Card 87-119243 DDC 005.36/9 19
HF5548.4.S86 H37 1986

Mastering SuperCalc4 /. Harvey, Greg. San Francisco , c1987. xix, 311 p. : ISBN 0-89588-419-4 (pbk.) : LC Card 87-60636 DDC 005.36/9 19
HF5548.4.S87 H37 1987

Masters of tradition . Rodman, Margaret, 1947- Vancouver , 1987. 198 p. : ISBN 0-7748-0234-0 LC Card 87-158135 DDC 333.3/0993/4 19
HD1125.Z9 L657 1987

Masters, Stanley H., 1940- Reynolds, Lloyd George, 1910- Economics of labor /. Englewood Cliffs, NJ , c1987. x, 518 p. : ISBN 0-13-225772-6 LC Card 86-25149 DDC 331 19
HD4901 .R469 1987

Masterson, V. V. The Katy railroad and the last frontier / V.V. Masterson ; with a new foreword by Donovan L. Hofsommer. Columbia : University of Missouri Press, 1988. xiv, 312 p., [24] p. of plates : 46 ill., maps, ports. ; 21 cm. Originally published: Norman : University of Oklahoma Press, 1952. Bibliography: p. 291-297. Includes index. ISBN 0-8262-0668-9 (pbk. : alk. paper) LC Card 87-19146 DDC 385/.0978 19
1. Missouri-Kansas-Texas Railroad - History. 2. Southwest, Old - History. I. Title.
HE2791.M743 M37 1988

Masterton, Robert R. The One Bancorp and Maine Savings Bank : not survival, but progress / Robert R. Masterton. New York : Newcomen Society of the United States, 1986, c1987. 22 p. : ill. ; 23 cm. (Newcomen publication. no. 1282) "Address ... delivered at a '1986 Maine meeting' of the Newcomen Society of the United States held in Portland ... on December 12th, 1986"--P. 1. LC Card 87-60613 DDC 332.2/1/09741 19
1. Maine Savings Bank. I. Newcomen Society of the United States. II. Title.
HG2613.P794 M356 1987

Matarazzo Suplicy, Eduardo. see **Suplicy, Eduardo Matarazzo, 1941-**

Matarrita Mena, José Joaquín. Areas industriales de Costa Rica / José Joaquín Matarrita Mena, Reinaldo Alfaro Carvajal, Geovanni Sánchez Silesky. San José, Costa Rica, América Central : Ministerio de Industria, Energía y Minas : CONICIT, [1986] 151 p. : ill. ; 27 cm. Bibliography: p. 55-56. ISBN 997-7500-01-0 LC Card 87-404258 DDC 338.097286 19
1. Costa Rica - Industries. 2. Costa Rica - Economic conditions - 1948-. I. Alfaro Carvajal, Reinaldo. II. Sánchez Silesky, Geovanni. III. Title.
HC143 .M38 1986

Matas, Jaime. Los problemas ambientales del sistema de transporte urbano / Jaime Matas, Patricio Gross, Humberto Molina. Santiago de Chile : Instituto de Planificación del Desarrollo Urbano, 1981. 30 leaves : ill. ; 27 cm. (Documento de trabajo / Instituto de Planificación del Desarrollo Urbano . no. 123) Includes bibliographical references. LC Card 82-201768
1. Transportation - Environmental aspects - Chile - Santiago Metropolitan Area. 2. Transportation and state - Chile - Santiago Metropolitan Area. I. Gross, Patricio. II. Molina, Humberto. III. Series: Documento de trabajo (Universidad Católica de Chile. Instituto de Planificación del Desarrollo Urbano) , no. 123. IV. Title.
HE234.Z7 S355 1981

Matasar, Ann B. Corporate PACs and federal campaign financing laws : use or abuse of power? / Ann B. Matasar. New York : Quorum Books, 1986. x, 161 p. ; 24 cm. Includes index. Bibliography: p. [147]-158. ISBN 0-89930-086-3 (lib. bdg. : alk. paper)
1. Campaign funds - United States. 2. Corporations - United States - Political activity. 3. Political action committees - United States. 4. Business and politics - United States. I. Title. II. Title: Corporate P.A.C's and federal campaign financing laws.
NYPL [JLE 86-2492]

Mateev, Georgi. Georgiev, I͡Ancho. Strategii͡a na kachestveni promeni /. Sofii͡a , 1986- v. <1-2 > ; LC Card 86-232319
HC403 .G465 1986

Matejka, Harriet. Policy responses to the changing international environment . Budapest , 1981. 170 p. ; ISBN 963-301-077-2 (pbk.) LC Card 81-179118 DDC 337/.09/048 19
HC59 .P573 1981 ***NYPL [JLL 79-189 no.33]***

Matejka, J. Kenneth. Handling human performance / J. Kenneth Matejka. Richmond, Va. : R.F. Dame, c1982. v, 90 p. : ill. ; 23 cm. Bibliography: p. 83-90. ISBN 0-936328-20-7 (pbk.) LC Card 81-69197 DDC 658.3/14 19
1. Behavior modification. 2. Organizational behavior. I. Title.
HF5549.5.I5 M337 1982
NYPL [JLE 86-4361]

Matejko, Aleksander. Comparative work systems : ideologies and reality in Eastern Europe / Alexander J. Matejko. New York : Praeger, 1986. xx, 237 p. ; 25 cm. Includes index. Bibliography: p. 216-230. ISBN 0-03-004492-8 (alk. paper) : LC Card 85-6354 DDC 306/.36/0947 19
1. Industrial sociology - Europe, Eastern. 2. Labor and laboring classes - Europe, Eastern. 3. Social classes - Europe, Eastern. I. Title.
HD6957.E82 M37 1985
NYPL [JLE 86-1083]

Matejko, Alexander. The self-defeating organization : a critique of bureaucracy / by Alexander J. Matejko. New York : Praeger, 1985. xxviii, 395 p. ; 24 cm. Includes bibliographies and index. ISBN 0-03-005488-5 (alk. paper) : LC Card 85-9524 DDC 302.3/5 19
1. Organizational effectiveness. 2. Bureaucracy. I. Title.
HD58.9 .M38 1985 ***NYPL [JLE 86-2757]***

Matematicheskie metody v ėkonomike i narodnom khozi͡aĭstve : sbornik nauchnykh trudov / [redaktsionnai͡a kollegii͡a I͡U.V. Korovin (gl. redaktor) ... et al.]. Moskva : Moskovskiĭ ėkonomiko-stat. in-t, 1985. 121 p. ; 21 cm. At head of title: Ministerstvo vysshego i srednego spetsial'nogo obrazovanii͡a SSSR. Moskovskiĭ ordena Trudovogo Krasnogo Znameni ėkonomiko-statisticheskiĭ institut. Includes bibliographies. LC Card 87-152514
1. Soviet Union - Economic conditions - 1976- - Mathematical models. 2. Economics, Mathematical. I. Korovin, I͡U. V. II. Moskovskiĭ ėkonomiko-statisticheskiĭ institut.
HC336.25 M377 1985

Matematicheskie metody v organizatsii sotsialisticheskogo sorevnovanii͡a : sbornik stateĭ / pod redaktsieĭ S.I͡U. Martishi͡usa. Vil'ni͡us : Akademii͡a nauk Litovskoĭ SSR, In-t ėkonomiki, 1986. 238 p. : ill. ; 21 cm. Title in colophon: Matematiniai metodai organizuojant socialistinį lenktyniavimą. Includes bibliographies. LC Card 87-130668
1. Socialist competition - Lithuania - Statistical methods. 2. Lithuania - Industries - Statistical methods. I. Martishi͡us, S. II. Ekonomikos institutas (Lietuvos TSR Mokslų akademija). III. Title: Matematiniai metodai organizuojant socialistinį lenktyniavimą.
HC337.L53 S65 1986

Matematicheskie metody v prilozhenii k reshenii͡u ėkonomicheskikh zadach / [otvetstvennye redaktory Kh.N. Gizatullin, L.A. Istomin]. Sverdlovsk : Akademii͡a nauk SSSR, Ural'skiĭ nauchnyĭ tsentr, 1985. 116 p. : ill. ; 22 cm. Includes bibliographical references. LC Card 86-135187
1. Ural Mountains Region (R.S.F.S.R.) - Industries - Mathematical models. I. Gizatullin, Kh. N. II. Istomin, L. A. III. Akademii͡a nauk SSSR. Ural'skiĭ nauchnyĭ tsentr.
HC337.R852 U7355 1985

Matematicheskie metody v sotsial'nykh naukakh .
(vyp. 15) Nekotorye voprosy matematicheskoĭ ėkonomiki . Vil'ni͡us , 1982. 90 p. ; LC Card 83-169081
HB135 .N45 1982

Matematicheskie metody v upravlenii gorodskimi transportnymi sistemami / [otvetstvennyĭ redaktor O.G. Faĭans]. Leningrad : "Nauka," Leningradskoe otd-nie, 1979. 150 p. : ill. ; 22 cm. At head of title: Akademii͡a nauk SSSR. Institut sotsial'no-ėkonomicheskikh problem. Includes bibliographies. LC Card 81-163008
1. Transportation - Russian S.F.S.R. - Moscow - Mathematical models. 2. Urban transportation - Soviet Union - Mathematical models. I. Faĭans, O. G. (Oleg Grigor'evich). II. Institut sotsial'no-ėkonomicheskikh problem (Akademii͡a nauk SSSR).
HE311.S652 M675 1979

Matematicheskie modeli sotsialisticheskoĭ ėkonomiki . Granberg, Aleksandr Grigor'evich. Moskva , 1978. 350 p. : LC Card 81-160608
HC336.25 .G697 1978

Matematicheskiĭ analiz ėkonomicheskikh modeleĭ.
Modeli i metody reshenii͡a zadach vzaimodeĭstvii͡a ėkonomicheskikh sistem /. Novosibirsk , 1982. 160 p. : LC Card 83-164468
HB137 .M6 1982

Matematicheskiĭ i statisticheskiĭ analiz funktsii potreblenii͡a /. Val'tukh, Konstantin Kurtovich. Novosibirsk , 1986. 165, [3] p. : LC Card 86-230310
HB801 .V26 1986

Matematicheskoe modelirovanie dvizhenii͡a kadrov v organizatsii͡akh /. Romanov, A. K. (Arnol'd Konstantinovich) Moskva , 1986. 154 p. : LC Card 87-158073
HF5549.5.T8 R56 1986

Matematikos ir kibernetikos institutas (Lietuvos TSR Mokslų akademija)
Shpilevskiĭ, Ė. Printsipy dinamicheskoĭ klassifikatsii stokhasticheskikh protsessov i sistem . Vil'ni͡us , 1978. 138 p. ; LC Card 81-173567
HD38 .S715 vyp. 28 QA274

T͡Sifrovye metody i algoritmy obrabotki signalov . Vil'ni͡us , 1986. 120 p. : LC Card 86-232937
HD38 .S715 vyp. 73 TK5102.5

Matematiniai metodai organizuojant socialistinį lenktyniavimą. Matematicheskie metody v organizatsii sotsialisticheskogo sorevnovanii͡a . Vil'ni͡us , 1986. 238 p. : LC Card 87-130668
HC337.L53 S65 1986

Mateo, Ramón Martín. see **Martín Mateo, Ramón.**

MATERIAL BALANCES - ESTONIA - MATHEMATICAL MODELS.
Ėksperimental'nai͡a razrabotka natural'no-stoimostnykh mezhotraslevykh balansov soi͡uznoĭ respubliki /. Moskva , 1980. 137 p. : LC Card 85-199427
HC337.E7 E49 1980

MATERIAL BALANCES - LATVIA - MATHEMATICAL MODELS.

Ėksperimental'naia razrabotka natural'no-stoimostnykh mezhotraslevykh balansov soiuznoĭ respubliki /. Moskva , 1980. 137 p. : LC Card 85-199427
HC337.E7 E49 1980

MATERIAL BALANCES - MOLDAVIAN S.S.R.
Chertan, S. E. (Sergeĭ Evgen'evich) Sistema natural'no-stoimostnykh mezhotraslevykh balansov soiuznoĭ respubliki . Kishinev , 1984. 242, [6] p., [2] folded leaves of plates : LC Card 85-130960
HC337.M55 C46 1984

MATERIAL CULTURE - BIDASOA RIVER VALLEY (SPAIN AND FRANCE)
Garmendia Larrañaga, Juan. Artesanos de la regata del Bidasoa . San Sebastián [1983] 123 p. : ISBN 84-7148-115-4 LC Card 84-140784 DDC 331.7/94 19
HD2346.S72 B534 1983 *NYPL [3-MNE 86-3657]*

Material di ricerca (Centro studi investimenti sociali) .
(17) L'Informatica nella società italiana, 1984 . Milano [1984] 257 p. ; LC Card 84-249272 DDC 338.4/7004/0945 19
HD9696.C63 I85 1984 *NYPL [JLD 86-3303]*

Material para discusión .
(no. 12) Campero, Guillermo. El sindicalismo internacional y la redemocratización de Chile /. Santiago, Chile , 1984. 77 p. ; LC Card 86-139122 DDC 331.88/0983 19
HD6617 .C357 1984

(no. 29) Fontaine Talavera, Arturo. Pautas para la confección de una política económica . Santiago, Chile , 1984. 92 leaves : LC Card 86-177872
HC192 .F58 1984

(no. 33) Weinstein L., Jacqueline. La industria en una estrategia de desarrollo para Chile /. Santiago, Chile , 1984. 50 leaves ; LC Card 86-139143
HD3616.C52 W45 1984

(no. 85) Zúñiga R., Víctor H. La evolución de la minería no cuprífera en Chile /. Santiago, Chile , 1985. 61 leaves ; LC Card 86-115526
HD9506.C52 Z86 1985

Materiales para discusión .
(no. 85) Zúñiga R., Víctor H. La evolución de la minería no cuprífera en Chile /. Santiago, Chile , 1985. 61 leaves ; LC Card 86-115526
HD9506.C52 Z86 1985

(no. 95) Ramírez C., Valeria (Ramírez Ceballos) Desarrollo socio-económico de la Octava Región de Chile /. Santiago, Chile , 1985. i, 45 leaves ; LC Card 86-115542
HC193.B5 R35 1985

(no. 96) Mannarelli M., Virgilio B. Organización institucional del sector agrícola /. Santiago, Chile , 1985. 81, [3] p. : LC Card 86-115545 DDC 338.1/883 19
HD1878 .M35 1985

Materiali di ricerca .
(17) L'Informatica nella società italiana, 1984 . Milano [1984] 257 p. ; LC Card 84-249272 DDC 338.4/7004/0945 19
HD9696.C63 I85 1984 *NYPL [JLD 86-3303]*

(6) Reti terziarie ed economie locali . Milano, Italy , c1983. 174 p. ; LC Card 85-215649
HD9986.I83 P577 1983

Materiali lecchesi .
(3) Sala, Edmondo. All'origine della borghesia lecchese . Lecco [1983] 83 p. : LC Card 85-190056
HD9765.I72 L437 1983

Materialien aus dem Institut für Rechtswissenschaft.
Engshuber, Wolfgang. Die Auflagenpolitik des Internationalen Währungsfonds . [München] [1985?] 32 leaves ; LC Card 85-166626
HG3881.5.I58 E54 1985

Materialien aus der Bildungsforschung .
(Nr. 11) Hegelheimer, Barbara. Berufsqualifikation und Berufschancen von Frauen in der Bundesrepublik Deutschland /. Berlin , 1977. viii, 303 p. ; LC Card 85-142052
HD6059.6.G4 H428 1977

Materialien (Germany (West). Bundestag. Hauptabteilung Wissenschaftliche Dienste) .
(Nr. 98) Reform oder Revolution? . Bonn , 1987. vi, 241, A 140 p. : LC Card 87-409091 DDC 368.4/00943 19
HD7179 .R384 1987

Materialien und kleine Schriften (Ruhr-Universität Bochum. Institut für Entwicklungsforschung und Entwicklungspolitik) .
(103) Ahn, Doo-Soon. Government policy towards FDI and the reaction of foreign investors in DCs /. Bochum [1985] 23, 33 leaves ; LC Card 86-219920 DDC 332.6/73225195 19
HG5780.5.A3 A34 1985

(97) Becker, Fritz, 1947- Entwicklungseffekte durch Verkehrserschliessung in der Arabischen Republik Jemen . Bochum , 1984. 50 p. : LC Card 84-241945
HE268.7 .B4 1984 *NYPL [JLH 86-2]*

Materialien zur Arbeitsmigration und Ausländerbeschäftigung .
(Bd. 10) Hill, Paul Bernhard, 1953- Determinanten der Eingliederung von Arbeitsmigranten /. Königstein/Ts. , c1984. 228 p. : ISBN 3-7756-6939-6 LC Card 84-219137 DDC 331.6/2/0943 19
HD8458.A2 H55 1984 *NYPL [JLD 86-2467]*

(Bd. 2) Künne, Wilfried. Die Aussenwanderung jugoslawischer Arbeitskräfte . Königstein/Ts. , 1979. xii, 269 p. : ISBN 3-7756-6931-0 : LC Card 79-394439
HD8633.5 .K83 *NYPL [JLD 87-1148]*

(Bd. 5) Kremer, Manfred. Assimilation ausländischer Arbeitnehmer in der Bundesrepublik Deutschland . Königstein/Ts. , 1980. 203, 64 p. ; ISBN 3-7756-6934-5 LC Card 80-151671 DDC 303.4/8243 19
HD8458.A2 K73 1980 *NYPL [JLD 86-2549]*

(Bd. 6) Ausländerintegration in deutschen Industriebetrieben /. Königstein/Ts. , c1985. viii, 273 p. : ISBN 3-7756-6935-3 LC Card 85-194662 DDC 305.8/00943 19
HD8458.A2 A9265 1985 *NYPL [JLD 86-2193]*

(Bd. 8) Voss, Timm. Die algerisch-französische Arbeitsmigration . Königstein/Ts. , 1981. xiii, 193 p. : ISBN 3-7756-6937-X : LC Card 81-176949 DDC 331.6/2/65044 19
HD8438.A4 V67 1981 *NYPL [JLD 86-2466]*

(Bd. 9) Kontos, Maria. Verbandsstrategien zur Ausländerbeschäftigung in der Bundesrepublik . Königstein/Ts. , c1983. viii, 235 p. ; ISBN 3-7756-6938-8 LC Card 83-190064 DDC 331.6/2/0943 19
HD8458.A2 K598 1983 *NYPL [JLD 86-2465]*

Materialien zur Bevölkerungswissenschaft .
(Heft 44) Schweitzer, Walter. Heiratstafeln versus Familienstandstafeln . Wiesbaden , 1985. iii, 102 p. : LC Card 87-408703 DDC 306.8/1/0943021 19
HB1215 .S39 1985

Materialien zur Bevölkerungswissenschaft, 0178-918X .
(Bd. 49) Deutsch-Französisches Arbeitstreffen auf dem Gebiet der Demographie (1985 : Dijon, France) Referate zum Deutsch-Französischen Arbeitstreffen auf dem Gebiet der Demographie vom 30. September bis 3. Oktober 1985 in Dijon. Wiesbaden , 1986. 134 p. : LC Card 87-409287 DDC 304.6/0943 19
HB3595 .D45 1985

Materialien zur Umweltforschung .
(8) Zimmermann, Horst, 1934- Ökonomische Anreizinstrumente in einer auflagenorientierten Umweltpolitik . Stuttgart , 1983. 59 p. ; ISBN 3-17-003279-8 : LC Card 84-148886
HC110.A4 Z55 1983

Materialien zur Vermögensbildung in Arbeitnehmerhand: Thesen, Pläne, Gesetze. Bonn, Domus-Verlag [1965-<c1985 > v. <1-6 > 23 cm. (Schriftenreihe des Instituts für Städtebau, Wohnungswirtschaft und Bausparwesen. Bd 5, 16, 28, 42) Vols. <5-6 > prepared by F. Malz. Includes bibliographies. CONTENTS. - [1. Folge] 1946-1965.--2. Folge. 1965 bis 1968.--3. Folge. 1969 bis 1973.--4. Folge. 1973 bis 1977.--5. Folge. 1977 bis 1981.--6. Folge. 1981 bis 1985. LC Card 67-123501 DDC 368.4/00943
1. Social security - Germany, West. I. Malz, Friedrich. II. Series: Schriftenreihe des Instituts für Städtebau, Wohnungswirtschaft und Bausparwesen e.V. (Arnold-Knoblauch-Institut) , Bd. 5, etc.
HD7179 .M35

Material'no-tekhnicheskaia baza agropromyshlennogo kompleksa.
Material'no-tekhnichna baza ahropromyslovoho kompleksu . Kyïv , 1985. 294 p. ; LC Card 87-109155
HD9015.S653 U453 1985

Material'no-tekhnichna baza ahropromyslovoho kompleksu : rozvytok ta efektyvnist' / za redaktsiieiu I.I. Dorosha i O.M. Holovanova. Kyïv : "Urozhaĭ", 1985. 294 p. ; 21 cm. Spine title: Material'no-tekhnichna baza APK. Title in colophon: Material'no-tekhnicheskaia baza agropromyshlennogo kompleksa. Includes bibliographical references. LC Card 87-109155
1. Agricultural industries - Ukraine. 2. Agriculture - Economic aspects - Ukraine. I. Dorosh, Ivan Iosypovych. II. Golovanov, A. N. III. Title: Material'no-tekhnichna baza APK. IV. Title: Material'no-tekhnicheskaia baza agropromyshlennogo kompleksa.
HD9015.S653 U453 1985

Material'no-tekhnichna baza APK.
Material'no-tekhnichna baza ahropromyslovoho kompleksu . Kyïv , 1985. 294 p. ; LC Card 87-109155
HD9015.S653 U453 1985

Material'noe stimulirovanie v khoziaistvennom mekhanizme sotsialisticheskogo obshchestva : mezhvuzovskiĭ sbornik / pod redaktsieĭ V.I. Kotelkina, A.I. Sibireva. Leningrad : Izd-vo Leningradskogo universiteta, 1986. 152 p. ; 22 cm. At head of title: Ministerstvo vysshego i srednego spetsial'nogo obrazovaniia RSFSR. Includes bibliographical references. LC Card 86-175029
1. Incentives in industry - Soviet Union. 2. Labor productivity - Soviet Union. 3. Soviet Union - Economic policy - 1981-. I. Kotelkin, V. I. II. Sibirev, A. I.
HF5549.5.I5 M3385 1986

MATERIALS MANAGEMENT.
Woodside, Arch G. Industrial purchasing strategies . Lexington, Mass. , c1987. xiv, 223 p. : ISBN 0-669-06953-1 (alk. paper) LC Card 83-48132 DDC 658.7/2 19
HD39.5 .W66 1987

Zenz, Gary Joseph. Purchasing and the management of materials /. New York , c1981. xiii, 514 p. : ISBN 0-471-06091-7 LC Card 80-21649 DDC 658.7/2 19
HD39.5 .W47 1981 *NYPL [JLE 86-3384]*

Zenz, Gary Joseph. Purchasing and the management of materials /. New York , c1987. xvi, 542 p. : ISBN 0-471-81802-X LC Card 86-32589 DDC 658.7/2 19
HD39.5 .W47 1987

MATERIALS MANAGEMENT - UNITED STATES.
Bhote, Keki R., 1925- Supply management . New York, N.Y. , c1987. 150 p. : ISBN 0-8144-2330-2 (pbk.) : LC Card 86-28795 DDC 658.7/2/0973 19
HD39.5 .B49 1987

Materials per a l'estudi geogràfic dels pobles de l'àrea econòmica de Bellpuig / [text, Enric Vicedo i Rius i el grup de col·laboradors de l'Institut "Lo Pla d'Urgell," Bellpuig. Lleida : Institut d'Estudis Ilerdencs, Diputació Provincial de Lleida, 1985. 253 p. : ill. ; 31 cm. (Quaderns de l'I. E. I. . 2) LC Card 87-131722
1. Bellpuig Region (Spain) - Statistics. I. Vicedo i Rius, Enric. II. Institut "Lo Pla d'Urgell.". III. Series.
HA1559.B45 M38 1985

Materialsammlung des Hechaluz in Schweden .
(Nr. 7) Dies ist das Land . [Sweden] 1946 (Lund : Berlingska Boktryckeriet) 102, [1] p., [1] folded leaf of plates : LC Card 86-225837
HD850 .D54 1946

Materialy po istorii sel'skogo khoziaistva i krest'ianstva Armenii. Nyut'er Hayastani gyughatntesut'yan ev gyughats'iut'yan patmut'yan /. Erevan , 1964- v. <1 > : LC Card 86-225528
HD1995.A7 N98 1964

MATERNAL AND INFANT WELFARE - GOVERNMENT POLICY - COMMUNIST

COUNTRIES - CASE STUDIES.
Working women in socialist countries . Geneva , 1985. xvi, 234 p. : ISBN 92-2-103910-2 (pbk.) : LC Card 85-181464 DDC 304.6/32/091717 19
HB901 .W657 1985 NYPL [JLE 86-1433]

MATERNITY LEAVE - INDIA - GUJARAT.
Hirway, Indira. Denial of maternity benefits to women workers . New Delhi , c1986. iv, 151 p. ; ISBN 81-204-0154-9 : LC Card 86-903013 DDC 331.4/25763 19
HD6065.5.I4 H57 1986

MATERNITY LEAVE - LAW AND LEGISLATION - INDIA - GUJARAT.
Hirway, Indira. Denial of maternity benefits to women workers . New Delhi , c1986. iv, 151 p. ; ISBN 81-204-0154-9 : LC Card 86-903013 DDC 331.4/25763 19
HD6065.5.I4 H57 1986

Math workbook for foodservice/lodging /. McDowell, M. C. (Milton C.), 1920- New York , c1988. v, 265 p. : ISBN 0-442-21872-9 (pbk.) : LC Card 87-15960 DDC 513/.93/024642 19
HF5695.5.F616 M317 1988

Mathabane, Mark. Kaffir boy : the true story of a black youth's coming of age in apartheid South Africa / Mark Mathabane. New York : Macmillan, c1986. xii, 354 p., [8] p. of plates : ill. ; 25 cm. Includes index. ISBN 0-02-581800-7 : LC Card 86-53 DDC 968/.00496024 B 19
1. Mathabane, Mark. 2. Blacks - South Africa - Biography. 3. Apartheid - South Africa. I. Title.
DT779.95.M38 A34 1986
NYPL [Sc E 86-240]

MATHABANE, MARK.
Mathabane, Mark. Kaffir boy . New York , c1986. xii, 354 p., [8] p. of plates : ISBN 0-02-581800-7 : LC Card 86-53 DDC 968/.00496024 B 19
DT779.95.M38 A34 1986
NYPL [Sc E 86-240]

Mathematical economics /. Lancaster, Kelvin. New York , 1987, c1968. xiii, 411 p. : ISBN 0-486-65391-9 (pbk.) LC Card 87-5459 DDC 330/.01/51 19
HB135 .L355 1987

MATHEMATICAL ECONOMICS. see **ECONOMICS, MATHEMATICAL.**

MATHEMATICAL LOGIC. see **LOGIC, SYMBOLIC AND MATHEMATICAL.**

MATHEMATICAL MODELS - CONGRESSES.
IFIP Working Conference on System Modelling and Optimization (1984 : Santiago, Chile) Recent advances in system modelling and optimization . Berlin , New York , c1986. 199 p. : ISBN 0-387-17083-9 (U. S.) LC Card 86-29770 DDC 003 19
QA402 .I43 1984 NYPL [JSE 87-639]

System modelling and optimization . Berlin , New York , c1986. xii, 1046 p. : ISBN 0-387-16854-0 (U. S.) LC Card 86-15637 DDC 003 19
QA402 .S95822 1986 NYPL [JSE 86-1775]

MATHEMATICAL OPTIMIZATION - CONGRESSES.
IFIP Working Conference on System Modelling and Optimization (1984 : Santiago, Chile) Recent advances in system modelling and optimization . Berlin , New York , c1986. 199 p. : ISBN 0-387-17083-9 (U. S.) LC Card 86-29770 DDC 003 19
QA402 .I43 1984 NYPL [JSE 87-639]

IIASA (International Institute for Applied Systems Analysis) Workshop on Nondifferentiable Optimization (1984 : Sopron, Hungary) Nondifferentiable optimization . Berlin , New York , 1985. vi, 349 p. : ISBN 0-387-15979-7 (U. S.) LC Card 85-25029 DDC 658.4/03/4 19
T57.6 .I46 1984
NYPL [JLM 72-289 no.255]

Proceedings of an international conference on genetic algorithms and their applications . [S.l. , 1985] 225 p. : *NYPL [JSF 87-413]*

Stochastic optimization . Berlin , New York , c1985. x, 754 p. : ISBN 0-387-16659-9 (U. S.) LC Card 86-11865 DDC 629.8/312 19
QA402.3 .S778 1985 NYPL [JSE 86-1596]

System modelling and optimization . Berlin , New York , c1986. xii, 1046 p. : ISBN 0-387-16854-0 (U. S.) LC Card 86-15637 DDC 003 19
QA402 .S95822 1986 NYPL [JSE 86-1775]

MATHEMATICAL STATISTICS - CONGRESSES.
Steklov Seminar (1984 : Steklov Institute of Mathematics) [Statistika i upravlenie sluchaĭnykh protsessov. English.] Statistics and control of stochastic processes /. New York, N.Y. , c1985. xiii, 506 p. ; ISBN 0-911575-18-9 LC Card 85-8851 DDC 519.5 19
QA276.A1 .S7513 1984 NYPL [JSE 86-729]

Mathematical systems in economics, 0344-3302 . (72) Voeller, Joachim, 1946- Purchasing power parities for international comparisons /. Königstein/Ts. , Cambridge, Mass. , c1981. 104 p. ; ISBN 3-445-02225-9 (pbk.) LC Card 81-84382
HG3821 .V63x 1981

Mathematics and its applications (Dordrecht, Holland)
Razumikhin, Boris Sergeevich. [Fizicheskie modeli i metody teorii ravnovesiia v programmirovanii i ėkonomike. English.] Physical models and equilibrium methods in programming and economics /. Dordrecht ; Boston : xv, 351 p. : ISBN 90-277-1644-7 LC Card 83-17791 DDC 330/.0724 19
HB135 .R3913 1984 NYPL [JSD 86-491]

MATHEMATICS, BUSINESS. see **BUSINESS MATHEMATICS.**

Mathematics for business . Miller, Kathleen N. New York , c1988. iv, 252 p. : ISBN 0-07-042061-0 (pbk.) LC Card 87-23089 DDC 513/.93 19
HF5691 .M476 1988

MATHEMATICS OF FINANCE. see **BUSINESS MATHEMATICS.**

Mathematik für Wirtschaftswissenschaftler. Gál, Tomáš. Berlin , New York , c1986. xi, 160 p. : ISBN 0-387-16381-6 (U. S.) LC Card 86-208763
HB135 .G35 1986 •

Mathématiques et statistiques générales appliquées au marketing . Geninet, Bernard. Paris , c1986. 198 p. : ISBN 2-7178-1071-4 : LC Card 86-165417
HF5415 .G397 1986

Mathematische Wirtschaftstheorie . König, Heinz, 1927- Königstein/Ts. , c1986. x, 239 p. : ISBN 3-445-02393-X : LC Card 86-188816
HB135 .K66 1986

Mather, Alexander Smith. Armstrong, A. M. Land ownership and land use in the Scottish Highlands /. [Aberdeen, Grampian] , 1983. vii, 150 p. : LC Card 83-209521 DDC 333.3/09411/5 19
HD616 .A76 1983 NYPL [JLF 86-457]

Mathew, Mohan, 1931- Dimensions of dialogue / Mohan Mathew. St. Louis, Mo. : Community Wholistic Growth Center, c1984. 136 p. ; 22 cm. Bibliography: p. [129]-136. ISBN 0-918833-00-0 (pbk.) : LC Card 84-17009 DDC 302.5/44 19
1. Interpersonal communication. 2. Social values. I. Title.
HM291 .M392 1984 NYPL [JLD 86-4125]

Mathewson, G. Frank, 1942-
Competition policy and vertical exchange / G. Frank Mathewson and Ralph A. Winter. Toronto ; Buffalo : University of Toronto Press, c1985. xvii, 119 p. : ill. ; 23 cm. (The Collected research studies, 0829-2396 . vol. 7) Bibliography: p. 117-119. ISBN 0-8020-7248-8 (pbk.) LC Card 86-672936 DDC 338.6/048/0971 19
1. Competition - Government policy - Canada. 2. Vertical integration - Government policy - Canada. 3. Canada - Commercial policy. I. Winter, Ralph Albert. II. Series: Collected research papers , v. 7. III. Title.
HF1480 .M37 1985 NYPL [JLE 87-512]

New developments in the analysis of market structure . Cambridge, Mass. , 1986. xxiv, 559 p. : ISBN 0-262-19241-1 LC Card 85-4246 DDC 338.8 19
HD2326 .N43 1986 NYPL [JLD 86-3570]

Mathiasen, Karen. Corporate governance and shareholder rights : voting by institutional investors and 1986 annual meeting results / by Karen Mathiasen and Virginia Rosenbaum. Washington, DC (1755 Massachusetts Ave., N.W., Suite 600, Washington 20036) : Investor Responsibility Research Center, c1986. 96 p. ; 28 cm. (Corporate governance service) Caption title. "October 1986." LC Card 86-230362 DDC 346.73/0666 347.306666 19
1. Stockholders' voting - United States. 2. Institutional investments - United States. 3. Tender offers (Securities). I. Rosenbaum, Virginia. II. Title. III. Series.
HD2743 .M34 1986

Mathis, Franz. Festschrift für Univ.-Prof. Dr. Georg Zwanowetz anlässlich der Vollendung des 65. Lebensjahres /. [Innsbruck] , c1984. 332 p. : LC Card 84-183487
HC244 .F48 1984

Mathon, Alix.
[Haïti, un cas]
Haïti, un cas / Alix Mathon. La société des baïonnettes, un regard nouveau / Alain Turnier. [Port-au-Prince? : s.n., 1985] (Port-au-Prince, Haïti : Impr. Le Natal) 172, 271 p. ; 21 cm. Cover title. Includes index. Bibliography: p. 255-259. LC Card 86-139806 DDC 330.97294 19
1. Debts, External - Haiti - History. 2. Social classes - Haiti - History. 3. Haiti - Economic conditions. 4. Haiti - Social conditions. 5. Haiti - History - 1804-. I. Turnier, Alain. Société des baïonnettes, un regard nouveau. 1985. II. Title. III. Title: Société des baïonnettes, un regard nouveau.
HC153 .M38 1985 NYPL [Sc D 86-555]

Mathur, Iqbal. Strategies for joint ventures in the People's Republic of China / Ike Mathur and Chen Jai-Sheng. New York : Praeger, 1987. viii, 196 p. ; 22 cm. Bibliography: p. [187]-189. Includes index. ISBN 0-275-92354-1 (alk. paper) : LC Card 87-7033 DDC 338.8/8851 19
1. Joint ventures - China. 2. Investments, Foreign - China. 3. China - Economic policy - 1976-. 4. China - Commercial policy. I. Chen, Jai-Sheng. II. Title.
HD62.47 .M38 1987

Mathur, Reeta. Industrial relations in public enterprises / Reeta Mathur ; foreword by Om Prakash. 1st ed. Jaipur : Prateeksha Publications : Sole distributor, Shri Ram Books Co., 1986. vii, 226 p. ; 23 cm. Originally presented as the author's thesis (Ph. D.--University of Rajasthan, Jaipur, 1985) Bibliography: p. [221]-226. LC Card 86-902265 DDC 331/.04135454 19
1. Industrial relations - India. 2. Iron and steel workers - India. 3. Steel industry and trade - India - Personnel management. 4. Government business enterprises - India - Employees. I. Title.
HD6976.I52 M37 1986

Matiukhin, Georgiĭ Gavrilovich. Belichenko, A. N. (Al'bert Nikolaevich) Kreditnye otnosheniia mezhdu stranami-chlenami SĖV /. Moskva , 1983. 134 p. : LC Card 84-171632
HG3729.E932 B45 1983

MATLAB BĀZĀR THANA (BANGLADESH) - STATISTICS, VITAL - CASE STUDIES.
D'Souza, S. M. (Stanislaus Michael) Mortality case study, Matlab, Bangladesh /. Dhaka, Bangladesh , 1985. 80 p. : LC Card 86-902788 DDC 304.6/4/0954923 19
HB1470.6.M37 D76 1985

Matlin, Il'ia Semenovich. Opyt razrabotki i realizatsii sistemy ukrupnennykh modeleĭ perspektivnogo planirovaniia /. Moskva , 1984. 216 p. : LC Card 85-199888
HD75.5 .O69 1984

Matlock, Cora Biesele. Sixty-five years the realtor in Texas : the story of the Texas Association of Realtors, 1920-1985 / by Cora Biesele Matlock. Austin, Texas : TAR, c1986. xii, 207 p. : ill. ; 24 cm. Bibliography: p. 202-207. LC Card 86-220747 DDC 333.33/06/0764 19
1. Texas Association of Realtors - History. 2. Real estate agents - Texas - History. 3. Real estate business - Texas - History. I. Title.
HD266.T4 M38 1986

MATO GROSSO (BRAZIL : STATE) - ADMINISTRATIVE AND POLITICAL DIVISIONS.
Relatório preliminar dos municípios de Mato Grosso /. [Cuiabá] , 1984. 404 p. ; LC Card 85-202292
HC188.M3 R45 1984

Mato Grosso (Brazil : State). Gabinete de Planejamento e Coordenação. Assessoria de Informações Técnicas. Relatório preliminar dos municípios de Mato Grosso /. [Cuiabá] , 1984. 404 p. ; LC Card 85-202292
HC188.M3 R45 1984

MATO GROSSO (BRAZIL : STATE) - SOCIAL CONDITIONS.
Relatório preliminar dos municípios de Mato Grosso /. [Cuiabá] , 1984. 404 p. ; LC Card 85-202292
HC188.M3 R45 1984

MATO GROSSO, BRAZIL (STATE) - ECONOMIC CONDITIONS.
Relatório preliminar dos municípios de Mato Grosso /. [Cuiabá] , 1984. 404 p. ; LC Card 85-202292
HC188.M3 R45 1984

MATO GROSSO DO SUL (BRAZIL) - ECONOMIC POLICY.
Mato Grosso do Sul (Brazil). Fundação Instituto de Apoio ao Planejamento do Estado. O Centro-Oeste e a retomada do desenvolvimento nacional . [Campo Grande] , 1985. 113 p., [1] folded leaf : LC Card 87-404972 DDC 338.981/71 19
HC188.C46 M37 1985

Mato Grosso do Sul (Brazil). Fundação Instituto de Apoio ao Planejamento do Estado. O Centro-Oeste e a retomada do desenvolvimento nacional : proposições de Mato Grosso do Sul ao I PND/NR / Governo de Estado de Mato Grosso do Sul, Secretaria de Planejameto e Coordenação Geral, FIPLAN-MS. [Campo Grande] : FIPLAN-MS, 1985. 113 p., [1] folded leaf : ill., maps (some col.) ; 21 x 23 cm. LC Card 87-404972 DDC 338.981/71 19
1. Brazil, Central West - Economic policy. 2. Mato Grosso do Sul (Brazil) - Economic policy. I. Title.
HC188.C46 M37 1985

Matos, Ana Maria Collier. Apoio ao setor informal da economia de Pernambuco . Recife , 1985. 135 p. : LC Card 87-403615 DDC 381 19
HD2346.B72 P473 1985

MATRIMONY. see **MARRIAGE.**

Matriz de insumo-producto de la economía chilena, 1977. [Santiago] : Presidencia de la República, Oficina de Planificación Nacional, Departamento de Contabilidad Social, [1980 or 1981] 85 p. ; 33 cm. Errata slip inserted. LC Card 82-199199
1. Input-output tables - Chile. I. Chile. Oficina de Planificación Nacional. Departamento de Contabilidad Social.
HC195.I57 M37 1980

Matsiuk, A. R. (Anatoliĭ Romanovich)
Danchenko, M. I. (Mykola Ivanovych) Dystsyplina pratsi /. Kyïv , 1983. 110 p. ; LC Card 83-215106
HF5549.5.L3 D34 1983

Matsui, Konomu, 1931- R & D management systems in Japanese industry /. Amsterdam ; New York : ix, 331 p. : ISBN 0-444-86808-9 (U. S.) LC Card 83-20489 DDC 658.5/7/0952 19
HD45 .R2 1984 ***NYPL [JLD 87-107]***

Matta, Nelson da. Política habitacional / [Nelson da Matta ... et al.]. [Salvador] : Fundação Bahiana para Estudos Econômicos e Sociais, [1984] 59 p. : ports. ; 22 cm. "Conferência do Dr. Nelson da Matta, presidente do Banco Nacional da Habitação, tendo como debatedores convidados o jornalista Marco Antônio Rocha e os empresários Anibal Freitas e Rodolfo Pessoa, no auditório do Desenbanco, em 27 de julho de 1984." LC Card 87-138899 DDC 363.5/8 19
1. Housing policy - Brazil - Congresses. I. Title.
HD7323.A3 M37 1984

Matta, Paulina. Mack, Macarena. Los trabajos de las mujeres entre el campo y la ciudad, 1920-1982 . [Santiago, Chile] [1986] 108 p. ; LC Card 86-217673
HD6126 .M33 1986

Mattar, Edward Paul.
Effective management techniques : practical methods for better results / Edward Paul Mattar, III. Worcester, MA : Revere House, 1987. p. cm. To be read and used. Includes index. LC Card 87-15556 DDC 658.4 19
1. Small business - Management. 2. Executive ability. I. Title.
HD62.7 .M38 1987

Management success secrets : the people side of management / Edward Paul Mattar, III. Worcester, MA : Revere House, 1987. p. cm. Includes index. LC Card 87-15372 DDC 658.4 19
1. Management. I. Title.
HD31 .M3375 1987

Mattei, Alberto. La Politica agraria della CEE /. Torino [1986] 330 p. : LC Card 86-212028
HD1920.5.Z8 P625 1986

Mattei, Enrico. Enrico Mattei, 1945-1953 : scritti e discorsi / di Antonio Trecciola. [Matelica] : Città di Matelica, [1982] 199 p. : ill., ports. ; 24 cm. Includes bibliographical references. LC Card 84-190191
1. Ente nazionale idrocarburi. 2. Petroleum industry and trade - Government policy - Italy. 3. Italy - Politics and government - 1945-1976. I. Trecciola, Antonio. II. Title.
HD9575.I84 E585 1982

A matter of hours . Beechey, Veronica. Minneapolis, MN , c1987. 212 p. ; ISBN 0-8166-1641-8 : LC Card 87-12459 DDC 331.4/12/0942498 19
HD6136.Z6 C683 1987

Mattera, Philip. Inside U. S. business : a concise encyclopedia of leading industries / Philip Mattera. Homewood, Ill. : Dow Jones-Irwin, c1987. xiv, 424 p. ; 24 cm. Includes bibliographies and index. ISBN 0-87094-950-0 LC Card 87-70392 DDC 338.0973 19
1. United States - Industries - Handbooks, manuals, etc. I. Title. II. Title: Inside US business.
HC106.8 .M337 1987

Mattes, Hanspeter. Aspekte der libyischen Ausseninvestitionspolitik, 1972-1985 / Hanspeter Mattes. Hamburg : Deutsches Orient-Institut im Verbund der Stiftung Deutsches Übersee-Institut, c1985. iv, 169 p. : ill. ; 30 cm. (Mitteilungen des Deutschen Orient-Instituts . Nr. 26) Bibliography: p. 163-169. ISBN 3-89173-001-2 LC Card 86-173976
1. Investments, Libyan. 2. Investments, Libyan - Malta. 3. Libya - Foreign economic relations - Malta. 4. Malta - Foreign economic relations - Libya. 5. Libya - Economic policy. I. Title. II. Series.
HG4538 .M376 1985

Matteson, Michael T.
Controlling work stress : effective human resource and management strategies / Michael T. Matteson, John M. Ivancevich.1st ed. San Francisco, Calif. : Jossey-Bass, 1987. xx, 378 p. ; 24 cm. (A Joint publication in the Jossey-Bass management series, the Jossey-Bass health series, and the Jossey-Bass social and behavioral science series) Bibliography: p. 327-362. Includes indexes. ISBN 1-555-42062-1 (alk. paper) LC Card 87-45503 DDC 658.3/82 19
1. Job stress. I. Ivancevich, John M. II. Series: Jossey-Bass management series. III. Title.
HF5548.85 .M378 1987

Ivancevich, John M. Organizational behavior and management /. Plano, Tex. , 1987. xv, 780 p. : ISBN 0-256-05608-0 LC Card 86-72712 DDC 658.4 19
HD58.7 .I89 1987

Mattfeldt, Harald, 1943- Wirtschaftspolitik und Arbeitnehmerinteressen . Pönitz , 1986. 198 p. ; ISBN 3-923826-06-0 LC Card 86-162801
HB99.7 .W57 1986

MATTHAI, JOHN, 1886-
Haridasan, V., 1937- Dr. John Matthai, 1886-1959 . Cranganore, Trichur Dist., Kerala , 1986. xi, 192 p., [2] p. of plates : LC Card 86-903052 DDC 330/.092/4 B 19
HB126.I43 M374 1986

Matthew, J. Purchasing power of PTT personnel, 1965 / by J. Mat[t]hew. Trade union situation in PTT services / by Stefan Nedzynski. Brussels : Postal, Telegraph, and Telephone International, [1966] 1 v. (various pagings) ; 30 cm. English, French, German, Italian, Spanish, and Swedish. Cover title. Prepared for the 19th World Congress of the Postal, Telegraph, and Telephone Workers' International. LC Card 87-165119
1. Postal service - Employees - Salaries, etc. - Congresses. 2. Trade-unions - Postal service - Congresses. I. Nedzynski, Stefan. Trade union situation in PTT services. 1966. II. Title. III. Title: Trade union situations in PTT services.
HE6241 .M37 1966

Matthews, Anne L. Managerial dictation / Anne L. Matthews, Patricia G. Moody. 2nd ed. Cincinnati : South-Western Pub. Co., c1987. 76 p. : ill. ; 24 cm. Includes bibliographical references. "G95." ISBN 0-538-07950-9 (pbk.) LC Card 86-63922 DDC 651.7/4 19
1. Dictation (Office practice). I. Moody, Patricia G. II. Title.
HF5547.5 .M383 1987

Matthews, Carole Boggs. AppleWorks made easy / Carole Boggs Matthews. 2nd ed. Berkeley, Calif. : Osborne McGraw-Hill, c1987. xiii, 398 p. : ill. ; 24 cm. On t.p. the registered trademark symbol "TM" is superscript following "AppleWorks" in the title. Includes index. ISBN 0-07-881260-7 (pbk.) : LC Card 87-149217 DDC 005.36/9
1. AppleWorks (Computer program). 2. Apple IIe (Computer) - Programming. 3. Apple IIc (Computer) - Programming. 4. Apple IIGS (Computer) - Programming. 5. Business - Data processing. I. Title.
HF5548.4.A68 M37 1987

Matthews, Mervyn. Poverty in the Soviet Union : the life-styles of the underprivileged in recent years / Mervyn Matthews. Cambridge [Cambridgeshire] ; New York : Cambridge University Press, 1986. xv, 227 p. ; 23 cm. Includes index. Bibliography: p. 217-224. ISBN 0-521-32544-7 LC Card 86-993 DDC 305.5/69/0947 19
1. Poor - Soviet Union. 2. Cost and standard of living - Soviet Union. 3. Soviet Union - Social conditions - 1945-. I. Title.
HC340.P6 M38 1986 ***NYPL [JLD 87-262]***

Matthiasen, Leo. Informationsteknologi og arbejdsproces : teknologisk udvikling og kontorarbejdets udviklingsformer / Leo Matthiasen, Sven Nielsen, Jørgen Sauer. Roskilde : Institut for miljø, teknologi og samfund, Roskilde universitetscenter, [1983?] 339 p. : ill. ; 21 cm. Cover title. Bibliography: p. 328-339. ISBN 87-87893-19-3 LC Card 85-114664
1. Office practice - Automation. I. Nielsen, Sven. II. Sauer, Jørgen. III. Title.
HF5547.5 .M384 1983

Matthiessen, Peter. Men's lives / Peter Matthiessen. 1st Vintage Books ed. New York : Vintage Books, 1988, c1986. xvi, 335 p. ; 21 cm. Bibliography: p. [324]-335. ISBN 0-394-75560-X (pbk.) : LC Card 87-40095 DDC 338.3/72709747/21 19
1. Fishers - New York (State) - Long Island - History. 2. Seining - New York (State) - Long Island - History. 3. Long Island (N.Y.) - History. I. Title.
HD8039.F66 U5 1988

Matthöfer, Hans, 1925- Germany (West). Bundesministerium der Finanzen. Rede zur Einbringung des Bundeshaushalts 1982 . Bonn , 1982. 56 p. : LC Card 82-221425
HJ2109 .G45 1982

Mattioli, Francesco, 1947- Pirzio Ammassari, Gloria. I sindacalisti . Bari , c1982. 155 p. ; LC Card 82-131644 DDC 331.87/33/0945 19
HD6709 .P57 1982 ***NYPL [JLD 86-2840]***

Mattione, Richard P. OPEC's investments and the international financial system / Richard P. Mattione. Washington, D.C. : Brookings Institution, c1985. xi, 201 p. ; 25 cm. Includes bibliographical references and index. ISBN 0-8157-5510-4 : LC Card 84-23242 DDC 332.6/7314 19
1. Investments, Arab. 2. Petroleum industry and trade - Finance. I. Title. II. Title: O.P.E.C's investments and the international financial system.
HG4538 .M38 1985 ***NYPL [JLE 86-3698]***

Mattock, Chris. Lenchek, Tom. Superinsulated design and construction . New York , c1987. ix, 172 p. : ISBN 0-442-26051-2 : LC Card 86-7089 DDC 693.8/32 19
TJ163.5.D86 L46 1987 ***NYPL [JSF 87-235]***

Mattsson, Jan. Nationella övertaganden av utländska dotterbolag : fallstudier av några svenska koncerners åtgärder / Jan Mattsson. Stockholm : Norstedt, [1982] 213 p. : ill. ; 23 cm. Summary in English. Thesis (doctoral)--Göteborgs universitet, 1982. Extra t.p. with thesis statement and English abstract (3 p.) inserted. Bibliography: p. 206-213. ISBN 91-1-827592-3 LC Card 83-122459
1. Corporations, Swedish - Developing countries. 2. International business enterprises - Developing countries. 3. Government ownership - Developing countries. I. Title.
HD2932 .M38 1982

Mattsson, Kerstin, 1946- Yrkesvalsfågan : idéer och idétraditioner inom den statliga yrkesvägledningen för ungdom / Kerstin Mattsson. [Malmö] : CWK Gleerup, c1984. vii, 268 p. ; 21 cm. (Studies in education and psychology, 0348-291X . 13) Summary in English. Thesis (doctoral)--Stockholms universitet, 1984. Bibliography: p. 237-261. ISBN 91-40-05057-2 : LC Card 84-200481

1. Vocational guidance - Sweden. I. Series: Studies in education and psychology (Högskolan för lärarutbildning i Stockholm. Institutionen för pedagogik) , 13. II. Title.
HF5382.5.S8 M37 1984

The Maturity market : Americans 55 and over. New York, N.Y. : Find/SVP, c1985. 1 v. (various pagings) : ill. ; 29 cm. (A Business information report) ISBN 0-931634-47-4 (pbk.) LC Card 86-203045 DDC 658.8/348 19
1. Aged as consumers - United States. 2. Aged - United States - Economic conditions. I. Find/SVP (Firm). II. Series.
HC110.C6 M33 1985

Matusky, Gregory. Raab, Steven S., 1949- The blueprint for franchising a business /. New York , c1987. ix, 244 p. : ISBN 0-471-85617-7 LC Card 87-15932 DDC 658.8/7 19
HF5429.235.U5 R32 1987

Matveev, N. P. (Nikolaĭ Petrovich) Geograficheskie problemy razvitiia narodnogo khoziaistva Moskovskogo regiona /. Moskva , 1986. 104 p. : LC Card 87-135959
HC338.M6 G46 1986

Mátyás, László. Idősorok és keresztmetszeti adatok együttes felhasználása az ökonometriai vizsgálatokban / Mátyás László. Budapest : Agrárgazdasági Kutató Intézet, 1985. 119 p. ; 28 cm. (Agrárgazdasági Kutató Intézet, 0209-5696 . 1985/6) Bibliography: p. 110-119. ISBN 963-491-212-5 LC Card 86-196805
1. Econometrics. 2. Time-series analysis. I. Series: Agrárgazdasági Kutató Intézet (Series) , 1985/6. II. Title.
HB139 .M39 1985

Matz, Deborah Norelli. Hamilton, William W. Innovations in economic development . Washington, D.C. (2021 K St., Suite 711, Washington 20006) [1986] 1 v. (various foliations) : LC Card 87-620522 DDC 338.973 19
HC110.I53 H363 1986

Matz, Klaus-Jürgen. Frieden und Friedenssicherung in Vergangenheit und Gegenwart . München , 1984. 115 p. ; ISBN 3-7705-2147-1 (pbk.) :
NYPL [JFL 76-295 Bd. 7]

Matz, Manfred. Briefe aus Mittelamerika : Berichte einer Reise / von Manfred Matz. Hameln : Aktion 3. Welt Hameln e.V., Q"Antati, c1981. 59 p. : ill. ; 30 cm. Cover title. LC Card 83-204578
1. Central America - Economic conditions - 1979-. 2. Central America - Social conditions - 1979-. I. Title.
HC141 .M38 1981

Matz, Mary Jane. The many lives of Otto Kahn / by Mary Jane Matz. New York : Pendragon Press, [1984] x, 299 p., [8] p. of plates : ill. ; 23 cm. Includes index. Reprint. Originally published: 1963. ISBN 0-918728-36-3 : LC Card 83-26326 DDC 361.7/4/0924 B 19
1. Kahn, Otto Hermann, 1867-. 2. Kahn, Otto Hermann, 1867- - Art patronage. 3. Philanthropists - United States - Biography. 4. Capitalists and financiers - United States - Biography. I. Title.
HV28.K32 M37 1984 ***NYPL [JFD 86-2699]***

Matz, Viktor, 1947- Entwicklungsländer im internationalen Konjunkturzusammenhang : eine spektralanalytische Untersuchung am Beispiel der Wirkung aussenhandelsinduzierter Nachfrageveränderungen der USA auf Brasilien, Kolumbien und Mexiko / Viktor Matz. Bergisch Gladbach : J. Eul, c1986. 199, lxxvi p. ; 21 cm. Bibliography: p. [lviii]-lxxvi. ISBN 3-89012-052-0 LC Card 86-227998
1. Brazil - Commerce - United States. 2. United States - Commerce - Brazil. 3. Colombia - Commerce - United States. 4. United States - Commerce - Colombia. 5. Mexico - Commerce - United States. 6. United States - Commerce - Mexico. 7. Business cycles - Latin America. I. Title.
HF3408.U5 M37 1986

Matzner, Egon, 1938- Die Soziogenese des Staates nach Elias und Schumpeter : ihr Beitrag zu einer Theorie staatlicher Interventionen / von Egon Matzner. Berlin : Internationales Institut für Management und Verwaltung, [1979] 30, [4] p. ; 30 cm. (Discussion paper series / International Institute of Manag[e]ment . 79-57) Summary in English and German. Bibliography: p. [32]-[34] LC Card 85-135122
1. Finance, Public. 2. State, The. 3. Social policy. 4. Power (Social sciences). 5. Elias, Norbert. 6. Schumpeter, Joseph Alois, 1883-1950. I. Series: Discussion paper series (International Institute of Management) , 79-57. II. Title.
HJ105 .M37 1979

Matznetter, Josef. Beiträge zur Multiplizität wirtschaftsgeographischer Forschung . Frankfurt am Main , c1986. 151 p. : ISBN 3-89228-046-0 LC Card 87-131124 DDC 330.9 19
HC59 .B464 1986

MATZNETTER, JOSEF.
Beiträge zur Multiplizität wirtschaftsgeographischer Forschung . Frankfurt am Main , c1986. 151 p. : ISBN 3-89228-046-0 LC Card 87-131124 DDC 330.9 19
HC59 .B464 1986

MAU MAU - HISTORY.
Kanogo, Tabitha M. Squatters and the roots of Mau Mau, 1905-63 /. London , Athens , 1987. xviii, 206 p. : ISBN 0-8214-0873-9 (U.S) LC Card 87-11201 DDC 307.3/36 19
HD1538.K4 K36 1987

Throup, David. Economic & social origins of Mau Mau 1945-53 /. London , Athens , c1988. xvi, 304 p. : ISBN 0-8214-0883-6 LC Card 87-12387 DDC 307.3/36 19
HD2126.5 .T48 1988

Mauksch, Hans O. Statham, Anne. The worth of women's work . Albany , c1988. xiv, 331 p. ; ISBN 0-88706-591-0 LC Card 87-6472 DDC 331.4/0973 19
HD6095 .S73 1988

Maule, Christopher J., 1934- A survey of the economics of the retail pharmacy sector in Canada / Christopher J. Maule. [Toronto, Ont.] : Commission of Inquiry on the Pharmaceutical Industry, c1986. 42 p. ; 28 cm. (Background study) "November 1984." Bibliography: p. 41-42. ISBN 0-662-14496-1 (pbk.) LC Card 86-206188 DDC 338.4/76151/0971 19
1. Pharmaceutical industry - Canada. 2. Drugstores - Canada. I. Series: Background study (Canada. Commission of Inquiry on the Pharmaceutical Industry). II. Title.
HD9670.C22 M38 1986

Mauleón, Ignacio. Interest rates determinants and consequences for macroeconomic performance in Spain / Ignacio Mauleón, José Pérez. [Madrid] : Banco de España, Servicio de Estudios, [1984?] 65 p. : ill. ; 27 cm. (Documento de trabajo / Banco de España, Servicio de Estudios . no. 8420) Summary in Spanish. Bibliography: p. 63-65. ISBN 84-505-0648-7 (pbk.) LC Card 86-215058 DDC 332.8/2/0724 19
1. Interest rates - Spain - Econometric models. 2. Spain - Economic policy - Econometric models. I. Pérez, José. II. Series: Documento de trabajo / Banco de España, Servicio de Estudios , no. 8420. III. Title.
HG1623.S7 M38 1984

Maunders, A. R. A process of struggle : the campaign for Corby steelmaking in 1979 / Allen Maunders. Aldershot, Hampshire, England ; Brookfield, Vt., USA : Gower Pub. Co., c1987. xi, 283 p. : ill. ; 23 cm. Bibliography: p. 282-283. ISBN 0-566-05227-X : LC Card 86-25640 DDC 338.6/042 19
1. Steel industry and trade - England - Corby (Northamptonshire). 2. Iron and steel workers - England - Corby (Northamptonshire). 3. Plant shutdowns - England - Corby (Northamptonshire). I. Title.
HD9521.8.C85 M38 1987
NYPL [JLD 87-1533]

Maunz, Theodor, 1901- Stationen . Darmstadt , 1984. ix, 228 p., [1] leaf of plates : ISBN 3-534-02410-9 LC Card 85-138779
HC286.5 .S825 1984

Maurer, Jean-Luc. Modernisation agricole, développement économique et changement social : le riz, la terre et l'homme à Java / Jean-Luc Maurer ; préface de Pierre Gourou.1ère éd. Paris : Presses universitaires de France, c1986. 323 p. : maps (some col.) ; 24 cm. (Publications de l'Institut universitaire de hautes études internationales, Genève) Two folded maps inserted. Bibliography: p. 301-319. ISBN 2-13-039622-4 : LC Card 86-175394
1. Agriculture - Economic aspects - Indonesia - Bantul (Kabupaten) - Case studies. 2. Rice trade - Indonesia - Bantul (Kabupaten) - Case studies. 3. Land tenure - Indonesia - Bantul (Kabupaten) - Case studies. 4. Peasantry - Indonesia - Bantul (Kabupaten) - Case studies. I. Title. II. Series.
HD2085.B37 M38 1986

Maurer, Pierre. Loubergé, Henri. Financement et assurance des crédits à l'exportation . Genève , 1985. 502 p. : ***NYPL [JLD 86-2109]***

Mauretanië /. Heinhuis, D. Amsterdam , 's-Gravenhage , 1985. 46 p., [1] folded leaf of plates : ISBN 90-12-05188-6 LC Card 86-174578
HC1050 .H45 1985

Mauri, Arnaldo. Moneta e banca in Etiopia / Arnaldo Mauri, Clara Caselli. Milano : Finafrica, CARIPLO : Giuffrè, [1986] xi, 316 p. : ill. ; 25 cm. (I Mercati creditizi africani . 18) Bibliography: p. [301]-308. ISBN 88-14-00769-1 LC Card 86-182310
1. Banks and banking - Ethiopia. 2. Finance - Ethiopia. 3. Money - Ethiopia. I. Caselli, Clara. II. Title. III. Series.
HG3389.A6 M38 1986
NYPL [JLE 87-1721]

Mauricio Báez y la clase obrera /. Orbe, Justino José del. Santo Domingo, República Dominicana , 1981. 158 p. : LC Card 82-138627 DDC 331.88/092/4 B 19
HD6584.Z55 B346 1981
NYPL [JLE 86-3246]

MAURITANIA - ECONOMIC CONDITIONS.
Heinhuis, D. Mauretanië /. Amsterdam , 's-Gravenhage , 1985. 46 p., [1] folded leaf of plates : ISBN 90-12-05188-6 LC Card 86-174578
HC1050 .H45 1985

Mauritius Chamber of Commerce and Industry. Rules of the Mauritius Chamber of Commerce and Industry. [Mauritius?] : The Chamber, [1986?] 25 p. ; 21 cm. "Rules have been adopted at a special general meeting held on May 14, 1986"--P. 24. LC Card 87-980214 DDC 380.1/06/06982 19
1. Mauritius Chamber of Commerce and Industry.
HF339.M38 M38 1986

MAURITIUS CHAMBER OF COMMERCE AND INDUSTRY.
Mauritius Chamber of Commerce and Industry. Rules of the Mauritius Chamber of Commerce and Industry. [Mauritius?] [1986?] 25 p. ; LC Card 87-980214 DDC 380.1/06/06982 19
HF339.M38 M38 1986

MAURITIUS - COMMERCE.
Pochun, Malati J. Determinants of import prices in Mauritius /. Réduit, Mauritius , 1981. 15 p. ; LC Card 82-980680
HB235.M38 P63 1981

Mauritius. Commission of Inquiry into the Sugar Industry.
The human factor, the sugar industry, and Mauritius : a vision for the future : report / from J. Manrakhan, R. Sithanen, members of the 1982-83 Commission of Inquiry into the Sugar Industry. Port Louis, Mauritius : Govt. Printer, [1984] 157 p. ; 33 cm. Cover title: Report of the Commission of Inquiry on the Sugar Industry. At head of cover title: Mauritius. "June 1984"--Cover. Bibliography: p. 27-29. LC Card 85-980119 DDC 338.1/7361/096982 19
1. Sugar trade - Mauritius. 2. Sugar trade - Government policy - Mauritius. I. Manrakhan, J. II. Sithanen, R. III. Title. IV. Title: Report of the Commission of Inquiry on the Sugar Industry.
HD9118.M45 M33 1984a

Report of the Commission of Inquiry on the Sugar Industry. Port Louis, Mauritius : Govt. Printer, 1984. iii, 213 p. ; 32 cm. LC Card 85-980302 DDC 338.1/7361/096982 19
1. Sugar trade - Mauritius. 2. Sugar trade - Government policy - Mauritius. I. Title.
HD9118.M45 M33 1984

Mauritius. Economic Planning and Development, Ministry of. see **Mauritius. Ministry of Economic Planning and Development.**

MAURITIUS - ECONOMIC POLICY.
Mauritius. Ministry of Economic Planning and Development. Towards increasing self-reliance . Port Louis [1983] 33 p. ; LC Card 86-980675 DDC 338.969/82 19
HC597.5 .M39 1983

MAURITIUS - EMIGRATION AND IMMIGRATION.
Ly-Tio-Fane Pineo, Huguette. Lured away . Moka, Mauritius , 1984. 261 p. :
NYPL [JLD 87-587]

Mauritius. Legislative Assembly. Public Accounts Committee. Special report of the Public Accounts Committee for the 1980 session : financial and other aspects of the "sale" of Chagos Islands and the re-settlement of the displaced Ilois. Port Louis, Mauritius : L. Carl Achille, Govt. Printer, 1981. 13 p. ; 25 cm. LC Card 82-980151 DDC 333.1/6/09697 19
1. Land settlement - Mauritius. 2. Refugees - Mauritius. 3. Refugees - Chagos Islands. I. Title.
HD1030.3.Z63 M38 1981

Mauritius. Ministry of Economic Planning and Development. Towards increasing self-reliance : a development strategy paper. Port Louis : Ministry of Economic Planning and Development, [1983] 33 p. ; 25 cm. "January 1983." LC Card 86-980675 DDC 338.969/82 19
1. Mauritius - Economic policy. 2. Mauritius - Social policy. I. Title.
HC597.5 .M39 1983

MAURITIUS - SOCIAL POLICY.
Mauritius. Ministry of Economic Planning and Development. Towards increasing self-reliance . Port Louis [1983] 33 p. ; LC Card 86-980675 DDC 338.969/82 19
HC597.5 .M39 1983

Maurize, Bernard. France. Conseil économique et social. Les ports maritimes . Paris [1983] 1 v. (various pagings) : LC Card 83-186600
HE557.F8 F67 1983

Mauro, Frédéric.
[Des origines de l'inégalité entre les peuples d'Amérique. Portuguese]
Origens da desigualdade entre os povos da América / Frédéric Mauro ; tradução, Carlos Nelson Coutinho. São Paulo, SP : Brasiliense, 1986. 113 p. : ill., port. ; 21 cm. "Título original: Des origines de l'enégalité [sic] entre les peuples d'Amérique"--Verso t.p. Includes bibliographical references. LC Card 87-120229 DDC 339.2/097 19
1. Income distribution - America. 2. Poor - America. I. Title.
HC94.Z9 I56317 1986

Mauro, Garry. The Land commissioners of Texas . Austin (1700 N. Congress Ave., Austin 78701) , 1986. vii, 133 p., [2] leaves of plates : LC Card 87-620990 DDC 353.97640071/32/0922 B 19
HD243.T4 L28 1986

Maus, Rex. Harmon, Paul. Expert systems . New York , c1988. xii, 289 p. : ISBN 0-471-83950-7 (pbk.) LC Card 87-17608 DDC 650/.028/5633 19
HF5548.2 .H367 1988

Max-Planck-Institut für Bildungsforschung. Hegelheimer, Barbara. Berufsqualifikation und Berufschancen von Frauen in der Bundesrepublik Deutschland /. Berlin , 1977. viii, 303 p. ; LC Card 85-142052
HD6059.6.G4 H428 1977

Maxeiner, Dirk, 1953- Testfahrer und Autospione : Abenteuer mit geheimen Automobilen / Dirk Maxeiner, Hans G. Lehmann.1. Aufl. Stuttgart : Motorbuch Verlag, 1985. 214 p. : ill. ; 25 cm. ISBN 3-613-01022-4 : LC Card 85-170273
1. Automobile industry and trade. 2. Automobiles - Testing. 3. Trade secrets. 4. Business intelligence. 5. Competition. I. Lehmann, Hans G. (Hans Georg), 1939-. II. Title.
HD9710.A2 M385 1985

Maxeiner, James. Policy and methods in German and American antitrust law : a comparative study / James Maxeiner. New York : Praeger, 1986. xiii, 174 p. ; 25 cm. Includes index. Bibliography: p. 123-138. ISBN 0-275-92113-1 (alk. paper) : LC Card 86-8108 DDC 343/.072 342.372 19
1. Antitrust law - United States. 2. Restraint of trade - United States. 3. Antitrust law - Germany, West. 4. Restraint of trade - Germany, West. I. Title.
K3856 .M38 1986 ***NYPL [JLE 86-4413]***

Maxfield, Sylvia. Government and private sector in contemporary Mexico /. [La Jolla, Calif.] , 1987. iv, 146 p. ; LC Card 87-622060 DDC 338.972 19
HD3616.M43 G68 1987

Maximizing cash flow . Toncré, Emery. New York , c1986. ix, 210 p. : ISBN 0-471-80744-3 : LC Card 85-29643 DDC 658.1/5244 19
HG4028.C45 T66 1986
NYPL [JLE 86-3140]

Maximizing sales to hospital national accounts / Biomedical Business International. Tustin, CA, U. S.A. (17722 Irvine Blvd., Tustin 92680) : Biomedical Business International, c1987. 524 p. in various pagings : 1 ill. ; 29 cm. (Report / Biomedical Business International . #7096) "February 1987." Includes bibliography. LC Card 87-401688 DDC 681/.761/0688 19
1. Medical instruments and apparatus - United States - Marketing. 2. Drugs - United States - Marketing. 3. Multihospital systems - United States - Directories. I. Biomedical Business International, Inc. II. Series: Report (Biomedical Business International, Inc.) , #7096.
HD9994.U52 M39 1987

MAXIMUM CARDS - SOVIET UNION - CATALOGS.
Katalog konvertov pervogo dnia i kartmaksimumov, 1980-1983 /. Moskva , 1985. 221 p. : LC Card 86-102861
HE6184.F57 K38 1985

Maxton /. Brown, J. Gordon. Edinburgh , 1986. 336 p., [8] p. of plates : ISBN 1-85158-042-5
NYPL [JFE 87-30]

MAXTON, JAMES, 1885-1946.
Brown, J. Gordon. Maxton /. Edinburgh , 1986. 336 p., [8] p. of plates : ISBN 1-85158-042-5 ***NYPL [JFE 87-30]***

May, Bernhard. Reagan und die Entwicklungsländer : die Auslandshilfepolitik im amerikanischen Regierungssystem / Bernhard May. München : R. Oldenbourg, 1987. xiv, 271 p. ; 24 cm. (Schriften des Forschungsinstituts der Deutschen Gesellschaft für Auswärtige Politik e.V., Bonn. Reihe, Internationale Politik und Wirtschaft . Bd. 50) Bibliography: p. [255]-263. Includes indexes. ISBN 3-486-53981-7 LC Card 87-139481 DDC 337.730172/4 19
1. United States - Foreign economic relations - Developing countries. 2. Developing countries - Foreign economic relations - United States. 3. Military assistance, American - Developing countries. 4. Economic assistance, American - Developing countries. I. Title. II. Series.
HF1456.5.D44 M39 1987

MAY DAY (LABOR HOLIDAY) - ARGENTINA - MENDOZA (PROVINCE) - HISTORY - 20TH CENTURY.
Vélez, Roberto. Reseña histórica del 1o de mayo en Mendoza . Buenos Aires , 1983. 125 p. : LC Card 87-400123 DDC 394.2/683 19
HD7791 .V4 1983

MAY DAY (LABOR HOLIDAY) - HISTORY.
Jemnitz, János. Május elseje születése /. [Budapest] , 1986. 135, [1] p. : ISBN 963-09-2773-X : LC Card 87-408513
HD7791 .J46 1986

Roio, José Luiz del. 1o. de maio /. São Paulo , 1986. 152, [16] p. : LC Card 86-197367
HD7791 .R59 1986

MAY DAY (LABOR HOLIDAY) - HISTORY - EXHIBITIONS.
Mein Vaterland ist international . Oberhausen , 1986. 331 p. : ISBN 3-921541-62-X LC Card 86-224091
HD7791 .M45 1986

MAY DAY (LABOR HOLIDAY) - PHILIPPINES.
Labor day celebration, May, 1, 1960 . [Manila?, Philippines , 1960?] 98 p. : LC Card 85-191411
HD7791 .L17 1960

May, Gordon S. Kiger, Jack E. Accounting principles /. New York , c1987. xxvii, 1092 p. : ISBN 0-394-35482-6 : LC Card 86-29791 DDC 657 19
HF5635 .K53 1987

May, Julian.
Development planning in Transkei : the rural service centre approach / by Julian May. Durban : Development Studies Unit, University of Natal, 1985. 35 p., [5] p. ; 21 cm. (Working paper / Development Studies Unit, University of Natal . no. 15) Bibliography: p. [37]-[39] ISBN 0-86980-483-9 (pbk.) : LC Card 86-222656 DDC 338.9687/91 19
1. Transkei (South Africa) - Economic policy. 2. Rural development - South Africa - Transkei. I. Series: Working paper (University of Natal. Centre for Applied Social Sciences. Development Studies Unit) , no. 15. II. Title.
HC905.Z7 T7347 1985

Migrant labour in Transkei : cause and consequence at the village level / by Julian May. Durban : Development Studies Unit, University of Natal, 1985. 34, vii p. ; 21 cm. (Rural urban studies series . working paper no. 2) Bibliography: p. i-vii. ISBN 0-86980-467-7 (pbk.) : LC Card 86-190553 DDC 331.6/2/0968791 19
1. Migrant labor - South Africa - Transkei. 2. Migration, Internal - South Africa - Transkei. 3. Labor and laboring classes - South Africa - Transkei. I. Title. II. Series.
HD5856.S6 M39 1985

May, Leslie Steven. Evaluating business and industry training /. Boston , Norwell, MA , c1987. xv, 294 p. : ISBN 0-89838-197-5 LC Card 87-5771 DDC 658.3/12404 19
HF5549.5.T7 E88 1987

May-Strobl, Eva. Hunsdiek, Detlef. Entwicklungslinien und Entwicklungsrisiken neugegründeter Unternehmen /. Stuttgart , c1986. x, 190 p. : ISBN 3-7910-5009-5 LC Card 87-211045
HD62.5 .H86 1986

Maydell, H. J. von. Agroforstliche Landnutzung im Einzugsbereich zentraler Orte im Sahel . Köln , 1983. ix, 374 p. : ISBN 3-8039-0276-2 LC Card 87-102956 DDC 333.73/13/09663 19
HD1019.Z63 A38 1983

Mayer, C. P. (Colin P.) Edwards, J. S. S. (Jeremy S. S.) The economic analysis of accounting profitability /. Oxford , New York , 1987. 133 p. : ISBN 0-19-877241-6 : LC Card 87-5575 DDC 657/.95 19
HF5686.C7 E34 1987

Mayer, Hans, 1951- Energie für die Armen? : traditionelle Brennstoffe in Indien / Hans Mayer, Christoph Menke, Werner Siemers. Saarbrücken ; Fort Lauderdale : Breitenbach, 1984. 195 p. : ill. ; 21 cm. (ASA Studien, 0176-8433 . 2) Bibliography: p. 177-193. ISBN 3-88156-288-5 : LC Card 85-199309
1. Fuel trade - India. 2. Energy conservation - India. 3. Fuel - India. 4. Household appliances - India - Energy conservation. I. Menke, Christoph, 1956-. II. Siemers, Werner, 1956-. III. Title. IV. Series.
HD9502.I42 M38 1984

Mayer, Harold M. (Harold Melvin), 1916- Heilmann, Ronald L. Great Lakes transportation in the eighties /. Madison, WI , c1986. 100 p. : ISBN 0-936287-00-4 (pbk.) : LC Card 86-622259 DDC 386/.544/0977 19
HE398 .H45 1986

Mayer, Harold Melvin, 1916- Land uses in American cities / by Harold M. Mayer and Charles R. Hayes. Champaign, Ill. : Park Press, [c1983] vi, 176 p. : ill. ; 23 cm. Includes bibliographies and index. ISBN 0-941226-02-6 (pbk.) LC Card 82-81036 DDC 333.77/13/0973 19
1. Land use, Urban - United States. 2. City planning - United States. I. Hayes, Charles R., 1919-. II. Title.
HD257 .M39 1983 ***NYPL [JLD 86-3126]***

Mayer, Ira. The electronic mailbox / Ira Mayer. New York Wiley, 1987. p. cm. Reprint. Originally published: Hasbrouck Heights, N.J. : Hayden Book Co., c1985. Bibliography: p. Includes index. ISBN 0-471-62576-0 : LC Card 87-6250 DDC 384.3/4 19
1. Electronic mail systems. I. Title.
HE6239.E54 M39 1987

Mayer, Morris Lehman. Mason, Joseph Barry. Modern retailing . Plano, Tex. , 1987. xviii, 834 p. : ISBN 0-256-03706-X LC Card 86-71842 DDC 658.8/7 19
HF5429 .M328 1987

Mayer, Pierre. La métamorphose : essai sur le multilatéralisme et le bilatéralisme / Pierre Mayer. Paris : Economica, 1983. 110 p. : ill. ; 24 cm. (Enjeux internationaux) Bibliography: p. 107-108. ISBN 2-86592-014-3 : LC Card 84-118610
1. International economic relations. 2. Monetary policy. I. Title. II. Series.
HF1411 .M374 1983

Mayer, Ralph-Dieter. Stahl- und Leichtmetallbau, Schienenfahrzeugbau : Strukturwandlungen und Entwicklungsperspektiven / von Ralph-Dieter Mayer. Berlin : Duncker & Humblot, c1985. 352 p. : ill. ; 24 cm. (IFO-Institut für Wirtschaftsforschung. Struktur und Wachstum. Reihe

Industrie . Heft 40) ISBN 3-428-05771-6 LC Card 85-161158
1. Steel industry and trade - Germany, West. 2. Nonferrous metal industries - Germany, West. 3. Construction industry - Germany, West. 4. Railroad equipment industry - Germany (West). I. Series: Struktur und Wachstum: Reihe Industrie, Heft 40. II. Title.
HD9523.5 .M3 1985

Mayer, Richard T. Virginia alternatives for the 1990s . Fairfax, Va. , Lanham, MD , 1987. 183 p. : ISBN 0-8026-0016-6 (alk. paper) : LC Card 87-22757 DDC 338.9755 19
HC107.V8 V435 1987

Mayer, Robert Stanley. The influence of Frank A. Vanderlip and the National City Bank on American commerce and foreign policy, 1910-1920 / Robert Stanley Mayer. New York : Garland Pub., 1987. viii, 221 p. ; 23 cm. (Foreign economic policy of the United States) Originally presented as the author's thesis (Ph. D.)--Rutgers University, 1968. Bibliography: p. 201-215. ISBN 0-8240-8087-4 : LC Card 87-23793 DDC 332.1/5/097471 19
1. National City Bank of New York - History - 20th century. 2. Vanderlip, Frank A. (Frank Arthur), 1864-1937. 3. Banks and banking, American - History - 20th century. 4. United States - Commercial policy - History - 20th century. 5. United States - Foreign relations - 1909-1913. 6. United States - Foreign relations - 1913-1921. I. Title. II. Series.
HG2613.N54 N3555 1987

Mayer, Thomas. Money, banking, and the economy / Thomas Mayer, James S. Duesenberry, Robert Z. Aliber. 2nd ed. New York : Norton, c1984. xiv, 574 p. : ill. ; 24 cm. "Newsletter", v. 2, Sept. 1985 : 6 p., inserted. Includes bibliographies and index. ISBN 0-393-95313-0 LC Card 83-13498 DDC 332.1/0973 19
1. Money - United States. 2. Banks and banking - United States. 3. Monetary policy - United States. I. Duesenberry, James Stemble, 1918-. II. Aliber, Robert Z. III. Title.
HG540 .M39 1984 ***NYPL [JLE 86-2193]***

Mayer, Thomas, 1927-
Instabile Exportmärkte und wirtschaftliche Entwicklung : der Fall Kolumbien / Thomas Mayer. Tübingen : J.C.B. Mohr, c1983. vii, 181 p. : ill. ; 25 cm. (Kieler Studien, 0340-6989 . 178) Bibliography: p. 174-181. ISBN 3-16-344673-6 LC Card 83-218666
1. Export sales - Colombia - Mathematical models. 2. Colombia - Commerce - Mathematical models. 3. Prices - Colombia - Mathematical models. I. Title. II. Series.
HF3426.5 .M39 1983

Money, banking, and the economy / Thomas Mayer, James S. Duesenberry, Robert Z. Aliber. 3rd ed. New York : Norton, c1987. xiv, 488 p. : ill. ; 24 cm. Includes bibliographies and index. ISBN 0-393-95557-5 LC Card 86-33160 DDC 332.1/0973 19
1. Money - United States. 2. Banks and banking - United States. 3. Monetary policy - United States. I. Duesenberry, James Stemble, 1918-. II. Aliber, Robert Z. III. Title.
HG540 .M39 1987

Mayntz, Renate. Dokumentation und Organisation : eine vergleichende Studie zu Primär- und Sekundär-Dokumentationen in Wirtschaft, Wissenschaft und öffentlicher Verwaltung / Renate Mayntz, Norbert Szyperski.1. Aufl. Bergisch Gladbach : J. Eul, 1984. 132 p. : ill. ; 21 cm. (Reihe Planung, Information und Unternehmungsführung . Bd. 1) Bibliography: p. 127-132. ISBN 3-89012-008-3 : LC Card 85-131112
1. Communication in organizations. 2. Documentation. 3. Communication in science. 4. Science - Documentation. 5. Communication in public administration. I. Title. II. Series.
HD30.3 .M394 1984

Mayo, G. Douglas. The complete book of training : theory, principles, and techniques / G. Douglas Mayo, Philip H. DuBois. San Diego, Calif. : University Associates, c1987. ix, 217 p. : ill. ; 24 cm. Includes bibliographies and index. ISBN 0-88390-208-7 : LC Card 87-14090 DDC 658.3/124 19
1. Employees, Training of. I. DuBois, Philip H. (Philip Hunter), 1903-. II. Title.
HF5549.5.T7 M369 1987

Mayo, Herbert B. Investments : an introduction / Herbert B. Mayo.2nd ed. Chicago : Dryden Press, c1988. xx, 680 p. : ill. ; 25 cm. "This edition printed exclusively for the College for Financial Planning"--Cover. Includes bibliographies and index. ISBN 0-03-009769-X LC Card 86-29129 DDC 332.6/78 19
1. Investments. 2. Investment analysis. I. Title.
HG4521 .M37 1988

Mayor, Archer H. Southern timberman : the legacy of William Buchanan / Archer H. Mayor. Athens : University of Georgia Press, c1988. p. cm. Bibliography: p. Includes index. ISBN 0-8203-0999-0 (alk. paper) LC Card 87-22897 DDC 338.7/63498/0975 19
1. Buchanan, William, 1849-1923. 2. Businessmen - Southern States - Biography. 3. Lumber trade - Southern States - History. 4. Family corporations - Southern States - History. 5. Company towns - Southern States - History. I. Title.
HD9760.B83 M39 1988

Mayorga Acuña, Luis Fernando. Propuesta para el desarrollo de un programa de investigación sobre propiedad social con énfasis en cooperativismo /. San José, Costa Rica , 1986. ii, 70 p. : LC Card 87-125056 DDC 334/.097286 19
HD3454.A4 P76 1986

Mayorga Alba, Eleodoro. Gall, Norman. Brazil and Peru . Geneva , 1987. x, 123 p., [1] leaf of plates : ISBN 92-2-105506-X (pbk.) : LC Card 87-166425 DDC 338.2/7282/0981 19
HD9574.B82 G34 1987

Mayorga Quirós, Román. El crecimiento desigual en Centroamérica (1950-2000) / Román Mayorga Quirós. 1a ed. México, D.F. : Centro de Estudios Internacionales, Colegio de México, 1983. 125 p. : ill. ; 22 cm. Includes bibliographical references. ISBN 968-12-0238-4 LC Card 85-242511
1. Central America - Economic conditions. 2. Central America - Population. 3. Income distribution - Central America. 4. Economic forecasting - Central America. I. Title.
HC141 .M39 1983

Mayr, Alois. Heineberg, Heinz. Neue Einkaufszentren im Ruhrgebiet . Paderborn , 1986. 247 p. : ISBN 3-506-73224-2 LC Card 87-407591 DDC 381/.1/094355 19
HF5430.6.G4 H45 1986

MAZARA DEL VALLO (SICILY) - FOREIGN POPULATION - STATISTICS.
Vizzini, Sergio. Indagine socio-demografica sugli immigrati stranieri in Sicilia . Palermo [1983] 108 p. ; LC Card 86-131931
HB3600.M39 V58 1983

Maziarka, Robert F. Scott, Terrence J. Elderly housing options /. Chicago , c1987. 235 p. : ISBN 0-931028-87-6 LC Card 86-63411 DDC 363.5/9 19
HD7287.92.U54 S38 1987

Mazingira Institute. Mitullah, W. V. Management of urban services in Nairobi . Nairobi, Kenya , 1985. 109, 106, vi p., [6] leaves of plates : LC Card 87-116360 DDC 388.4/09676/25 19
HD4720.5.N35 M57 1985

Mazumdar, Dipak, 1932- Little, Ian Malcolm David. Small manufacturing enterprises . New York , 1987. x, 362 p. : ISBN 0-19-520619-3 LC Card 87-12365 DDC 338.6/42/0954 19
HD9736.I52 L57 1987

Mazurkiewicz, Eugeniusz. Podstawowe problemy polityki rolnej w PRL / Eugeniusz Mazurkiewicz. Wyd. 1. Warszawa : Książka i Wiedza, 1979. 306 p. ; 20 cm. (Ideologia a współczesność) Bibliography: p. [293]-302. LC Card 81-172693
1. Agriculture and state - Poland - History. 2. Reconstruction (1939-1951) - Poland. I. Title.
HD1995.7.Z8 M39 1979

Mazursky, Alan D., 1955- Lotus 1-2-3 : a practical learning guide / Alan D. Mazursky, Eileen Bechtold Dlugoss. Chicago : Science Research Associates, c1988. 480 p. : ill. ; 28 cm. Includes index. ISBN 0-574-18645-X (pbk.) : LC Card 87-4675 DDC 005.36/9 19
1. Lotus 1-2-3 (Computer program). 2. Business - Data processing. I. Dlugoss, Eileen Bechtold. II. Title. III. Title: Lotus One-Two-Three.
HF5548.4.L67 M32 1988

MAZUT. see **PETROLEUM PRODUCTS.**

Mazzucchelli, Vanna. Catasto e volto urbano : Milano alla metà del Settecento / Vanna Mazzucchelli. Roma : Istituto storico italiano per l'età moderna e contemporanea, 1983. 244 p. ; 26 cm. (Italia e Europa) Includes bibliographical references and index. LC Card 86-106099
1. Land tenure - Italy - Milan - History - 18th century. 2. Landowners - Italy - Milan - History - 18th century. 3. Land use, Urban - Italy - Milan - History - 18th century. 4. Cadasters - Italy - Milan - History - 18th century. I. Title. II. Series.
HD680.M54 M39 1983

MBA research paper.
Au, Norman. Selected implications for businessmen of social responsibility in South Africa . [Cape Town] [1977] ix, 141 leaves ; LC Card 81-155073
HD60.5.S7 A92 1977

MCI (FIRM) - HISTORY.
Kahaner, Larry. On the line . New York, NY , 1987, c1986. 344 p., [8] p. of plates : ISBN 0-446-38550-6 (pbk.) LC Card 87-10561 DDC 384.6/065/73 19
HE8846.M375 K34 1987

Mead, Walter J. Offshore lands . San Francisco, Calif. , c1985. xxviii, 169 p. : ISBN 0-936488-10-7 (alk. paper) : LC Card 85-63548 DDC 333.8/23/0973 19
HD242.5 .O34 1985 ***NYPL [JLE 86-2726]***

Meade, J. E. (James Edward), 1907-
[Works. 1988]
The collected papers of James Meade / edited by Susan Howson. London ; Boston : Allen & Unwin, 1988- p. cm. Includes index. CONTENTS. - v. 1. Employment and inflation. ISBN 0-04-445073-7 (v. 1. : alk. paper) LC Card 87-15288 DDC 330.1 19
1. Unemployment - Effect of inflation on - Collected works. 2. Unemployment - Great Britain - Effect of inflation on - Collected works. 3. Keynesian economics - Collected works. I. Howson, Susan, 1945-. II. Title.
HD5710 .M43 1988

Meade, James Edward, 1907- Alternative systems of business organization and of worker's remuneration / J.E. Meade. London ; Boston : Allen & Unwin, 1986. x, 144 p. : ill. ; 23 cm. Includes index. Bibliography: p. [141] ISBN 0-04-331112-1 (alk. paper) LC Card 85-26734 DDC 330/.1 19
1. Competition, Imperfect - Mathematical models. 2. Unemployment - Effect of inflation on - Mathematical models. 3. Wages - Mathematical models. I. Title.
HB238 .M4 1986 ***NYPL [JLD 86-2943]***

Meadows, Donella H. The Limits to growth. New York [1972] 205 p. ISBN 0-87663-165-0 LC Card 73-187907 DDC 330.9/04
HC59 .L54 ***NYPL [JLD 75-167]***

Meadows, W. J. The response of local authorities to central government incitement to reduce expenditure : report / prepared under the guidance of the Committee of Experts on Local and Regional Finance of the Steering Committee for Regional and Municipal Matters by W.J. Meadows, consultant. Strasbourg : Council of Europe, 1986. 33 p. ; 30 cm. (Study series, Local and regional authorities in Europe . 37) LC Card 87-135687 DDC 336.3/9/094 19
1. Local finance - Europe. 2. Government spending policy - Europe. 3. Intergovernmental fiscal relations - Europe. I. Council of Europe. Committee of Experts on Local and Regional Finance. II. Series: Study series, Local and regional authorities in Europe , 37. III. Title.
HJ9415 .M43 1986

Meals, Dennis R.
Guide to compilation and review engagements / authors, Dennis R. Meals, John R. Clay, Dan M. Guy. 8th ed. Fort Worth, Tex. : Practitioners Pub. Co., c1986- 3 v. (loose-leaf) : ill. ; 30 cm. Guy's name appears first on the earlier edition. Includes index. LC Card 86-224183 DDC 657/.3 19
1. Financial statements, Unaudited. I. Clay, John R. II. Guy, Dan M. III. Compilation and review engagements. IV. Title.
HF5667.65 .M42 1986

Guide to compilation and review engagements.
Clay, John R. Accounting for S corporations and noncorporate entities : a self-study course based upon Guide to compilation and review engagements / authors John R. Clay, Marilyn Rutledge, Barbara Gargiulo ; contributing

authors Dennis R. Meals, Dan M. Guy. Fort Worth, Tex. , c1987. 1 v. (various pagings) ; LC Card 87-163295 DDC 657/.95/076 19
HF5686.C7 C58 1987

Clay, John R. Advanced compilation and review : practice problems and solutions : a self-study course based upon Guide to compilation and review engagements / authors, John R. Clay, Marilyn Rutledge, Barbara Gargiulo ; contributing authors, Dennis R. Meals, Dan M. Guy. Fort Worth, Tex. , c1987. 1 v. (various pagings) : LC Card 87-160681 DDC 657/.3 19
HF5667.65 .M42 1986 Suppl.

The Mean season : the attack on the welfare state / Fred Block ... [et al.].1st ed. New York Pantheon Books, c1987. xvi, 205 p. ; 22 cm. Includes bibliographies and index. ISBN 0-394-55338-1 : LC Card 86-43126 DDC 361/.973 19
1. Economic assistance, Domestic - United States. 2. Public welfare - United States. 3. United States - Social policy. 4. Welfare state. I. Block, Fred L.
HC110.P63 M42 1987

Mean-variance analysis in portfolio choice and capital markets /. Markowitz, H. (Harry), 1927- Oxford, OX, UK , New York, NY, USA , 1987. xi, 387 p. : ISBN 0-631-15381-0 : LC Card 87-2975 DDC 332.6 19
HG4529.5 .M37 1987

The meaning of crisis . O'Connor, James (James R.) Oxford, UK , New York, NY, USA , 1987. v, 197 p. ; ISBN 0-631-13819-6 (pbk.) : LC Card 86-26399 DDC 338.5/4 19
HB3714 .O24 1987

Meapec studies in continuity & change in the Middle East & North Africa.
Nattagh, Nima. Agriculture & regional development in Iran /. Wisbech, Cambridgeshire, England , 1986. 105 p. : ISBN 0-906559-26-X (pbk.) : LC Card 86-230845 DDC 338.1/0955 19
HD1565.2 .N37 1986

MEASURE OF UNCERTAINTY (INFORMATION THEORY) see **UNCERTAINTY (INFORMATION THEORY)**

The measure of value stated and illustrated . Malthus, T. R. (Thomas Robert, 1766-1834. Fairfield, NJ , 1988. p. cm. ISBN 0-678-00603-2 LC Card 87-17246 DDC 332.4/1 19
HB201 .M297 1988

Measurement and analysis of socioeconomic development . McGranahan, Donald V. Geneva , 1985. xx, 504 p. :
NYPL [JLK 74-447 no.85.5]

Measurement issues and behavior of productivity variables / edited by Ali Dogramaci. Boston : Kluwer Nijhoff ; Hingham, MA, USA : Distributors for the United States and Canada, Kluwer Academic Publishers, c1986. ix, 262 p. : ill. ; 24 cm. (Studies in productivity analysis) Includes bibliographies and indexes. ISBN 0-89838-171-1 LC Card 85-8017 DDC 338/.06/0287 19
1. Industrial productivity - United States - Measurement - Addresses, essays, lectures. 2. Industrial productivity - Mathematical models - Addresses, essays, lectures. I. Dogramaci, Ali. II. Series.
HD56.25 .M43 1986 ***NYPL [JLE 86-3414]***

The measurement of supply and demand in freight transport /. Bayliss, Brian T. Aldershot, Hants, England , Brookfield, USA , 1988. p. cm. ISBN 0-566-05526-0 : LC Card 87-19817 DDC 380.5/9 19
HE199.A2 B395 1988

The measurement of tax progression /. Pfingsten, Andreas. Berlin , New York , c1986. vi, 131 p. : ISBN 0-387-16072-8 (U. S. : pbk.) LC Card 86-219663 DDC 336.2/93 19
HJ2326 .P47 1986

The measurement of the economic benefits of infrastructure services /. Diewert, W. E. (W. Erwin) Berlin , New York , c1986. 202 p. : ISBN 3-540-16810-9 : LC Card 86-22055 DDC 363 19
HC79.C3 D48 1986

Measurement of value added at constant prices in service activities / OECD, Department of Economics and Statistics = Mesure de la valeur ajoutée aux prix constants dans les activités de service / Département des affaires économiques et statistiques, OCDE. Paris : Organisation for Economic Co-operation and Development : [Washington, D.C. : v. <1 > ; 27 cm. English and French. CONTENTS. - 1. National accounts: sources and methods. ISBN 92-64-02879-X (pbk.) : LC Card 87-164470 DDC 657/.45 19
1. Service industries - Accounting. 2. Value added - Accounting. I. Organisation for Economic Co-operation and Development. Dept. of Economics and Statistics. II. Title: Mesure de la valeur ajoutée aux prix constants dans les activités de service.
HF5686.S43 M43 1987

Measures to overcome obstacles to the observance in the construction industry of ILO standards : Building, Civil Engineering, and Public Works Committee, eleventh session, Geneva, 1987. Geneva : International Labour Office, 1986. v, 89 p. : ill. ; 30 cm. "The present report has been prepared by the International Labour Office to serve as a basis for discussion of the third item on the agenda of the eleventh session of the Building, Civil Engineering, and Public Works Committee"--Introd. At head of title: International Labour Organisation, Sectoral Activities Programme. "Report III." Includes bibliographies. ISBN 92-2-105710-0 (pbk.) : LC Card 87-167948 DDC 331.25 19
1. Construction industry - Personnel management. 2. Labor laws and legislation, International. I. International Labour Office. II. International Labour Organisation. Building, Civil Engineering, and Public Works Committee. III. International Labour Organisation. Sectoral Activities Programme.
HD9715.A2 M36 1986

Measuring and analyzing levels of living in developing countries . Grootaert, Christiaan, 1950- Washington, D.C., U. S.A. , c1986. x, 139 p. : ISBN 0-8213-0758-4 (pbk.) LC Card 86-5611 DDC 339.4/7/091724 19
HD7067 .G76 1986b

Measuring and funding corporate liabilities for retiree health benefits. Washington, D.C. : Employee Benefit Research Institute, Education and Research Fund, c1987. xxxviii, 226 p. : ill. ; 23 cm. (An EBRI-ERF policy study) "This study was prepared in cooperation with the Employee Benefit Research Institute-Education and Research Fund by the staff of Milliman & Robertson, Inc." ISBN 0-86643-054-7 (pbk.) LC Card 87-24534 DDC 657/.75 19
1. Insurance, Health - United States - Accounting. 2. Postemployment benefits - United States - Accounting. 3. Liabilities (Accounting). I. Employee Benefit Research Institute (Washington, D.C.). Education and Research Fund. II. Milliman & Robertson, inc. III. Series.
HG9396 .M4 1987

Measuring changes in intra-industry competitiveness /. Menzler-Hokkanen, Ingeborg. Helsingfors [1986] 39 p. ; ISBN 951-555-247-8 (pbk.) LC Card 87-170429 DDC 338.6/048 19
HC79.I52 M46 1986

Measuring Cuban economic performance /. Pérez-López, Jorge F. Austin , 1987. xii, 202 p. : ISBN 0-292-75092-7 LC Card 86-24907 DDC 339.37291 19
HC152.5 .P47 1987

MEASURING INSTRUMENTS INDUSTRY - EUROPE.
The Microprocessor based measuring instrumentation market in West European manufacturing. New York, N.Y. , c1983. [22], 262, xi p. : LC Card 87-142563
HD9706.2.E8513 M53 1983

Measuring project impact . Cernea, Michael M. Washington, D.C., U. S.A. , c1979. vi, 93 p. ; LC Card 81-170764
HD1792 .C43 1979

Measuring tax burden in India . Shyam Nath, 1945- New Delhi , 1987. xv, 194 p. : ISBN 81-7024-072-7 : LC Card 87-900348 DDC 336.2/94/09544 19
HJ2323.I4 S59 1987

Measuring the efficiency of public programs : costs and benefits in vocational rehabilitation / edited by Monroe Berkowitz. Philadelphia : Temple University Press, 1988. p. cm. Includes index. ISBN 0-87722-527-3 (alk. paper) LC Card 87-18080 DDC 362/.0425 19
1. Vocational rehabilitation - United States - Cost effectiveness. I. Berkowitz, Monroe, 1919-.
HD7256.U5 M44 1988

Measuring the productivity of commercial banks . Mundel, Marvin Everett, 1916- White Plains, N.Y. , 1987. v, 101 p. ; ISBN 0-527-91641-2 (pbk.) LC Card 87-5034 DDC 332.1/0285/57565 19
HG1588 .M94 1987

Measuring total productivity in manufacturing organizations . Mundel, Marvin Everett, 1916- Tokyo, Japan , c1986. iv [i.e. vi], 155 p. ; ISBN 92-833-1090-4 LC Card 86-211930 DDC 658.3/14 19
HD56.25 .M87 1986

Measuring total productivity in manufacturing organizations . Mundel, Marvin Everett, 1916- White Plains, N.Y. , 1987. vi, 155 p. ; ISBN 0-527-91625-0 (pbk.) LC Card 87-5029 DDC 658.5/036 19
HD56.25 .M87 1987

MEAT INDUSTRY AND TRADE - AUSTRALIA - VICTORIA - LOCATION.
Victoria. Saleyard Working Party. Distribution of saleyards in Victoria . [Melbourne] , 1986. 69, 7, 7 p. : LC Card 87-159450 DDC 338.1/760831 19
HD9428.A83 V538 1986

MEAT INDUSTRY AND TRADE - BRAZIL - GOIÁS (STATE) - STATISTICS.
Insumos estatísticos para o diagnóstico da pecuária no Estado de Goiás /. [Goiânia-Goiás] [19]84. 156 leaves : LC Card 86-178269
HD9424.B73 G655 1984

MEAT INDUSTRY AND TRADE - BULGARIA.
Pospelowa, Galina. Schlachttier- und Fleischproduktion in Osteuropa . Giessen , Berlin , 1981. 144 p. ; ISBN 3-428-04944-6 LC Card 82-167577
HD9425.B92 P67 1981

MEAT INDUSTRY AND TRADE - DENMARK.
Kóbor, Kálmán. A hús- és a tejgazdaság jellemző vonásai Dániában /. Budapest , 1984. 111 p. : ISBN 963-491-183-8 LC Card 86-198770
HD9425.D4 K6 1984

MEAT INDUSTRY AND TRADE - IOWA - STATISTICS.
Otto, Daniel. Economic contribution and impacts of changes in Iowa's livestock and meat processing industries /. Oakdale, Iowa [1984] xi, 95 p. : LC Card 85-621899 DDC 338.1/76/009777021 19
HD9417.I8 O88 1984 ***NYPL [JLF 86-592]***

MEAT INDUSTRY AND TRADE - ITALY - PRATO REGION - HISTORY.
Nigro, Giampiero. Gli uomini dell'irco . Firenze , 1983. xxii, 184 p. : ISBN 88-00-86022-2 : LC Card 84-238769
HD9425.I83 P76 1983 ***NYPL [JLE 86-2127]***

MEAT INDUSTRY AND TRADE - SWEDEN - STOCKHOLM - CASE STUDIES.
Grenander-Nyberg, Gertrud, 1912- En charkuterifabrik med tradition . Stockholm , c1985. 207 p. : ISBN 91-38-09206-9 LC Card 86-159511
HD9145.S88 E544 1985

MEAT INDUSTRY AND TRADE - UNITED STATES.
McCoy, John Henry, 1912- Livestock and meat marketing /. New York , c1988. vii, 642 p. : ISBN 0-442-20488-4 LC Card 87-23136 DDC 381/.416/00973 19
HD9415 .M25 1988

MEAT INDUSTRY AND TRADE - UNITED STATES - HISTORY.
Skaggs, Jimmy M. Prime cut . College Station , c1986. xiii, 263 p., [8] p. of plates : ISBN 0-89096-249-9 : LC Card 85-40742 DDC 338.1/76213/0973 19
HD9415 .S58 1986 ***NYPL [JLE 86-3913]***

MEAT INDUSTRY AND TRADE - UNITED STATES - STATISTICS.
Otto, Daniel. Economic contribution and impacts of changes in Iowa's livestock and meat processing industries /. Oakdale, Iowa [1984] xi, 95 p. : LC Card 85-621899 DDC 338.1/76/009777021 19
HD9417.I8 O88 1984 ***NYPL [JLF 86-592]***

MEAT INDUSTRY AND TRADE - URUGUAY.
Uruguay, producción y comercialización de ganado y carnes. [Montevideo, Uruguay] , 1985. 90 p. : LC Card 87-403154 DDC 338.1/760883/09895 19
HD9424.U8 U783 1985

MEAT INDUSTRY AND TRADE - URUGUAY - CONGRESSES.
Taller sobre Identificación de Políticas que Permitan Dinamizar el Complejo de Producción y Comercialización de Carnes Rojas, con Enfasis en la Industria Frigorífica (1984 : Montevideo, Uruguay) Taller sobre Identificación de Políticas que Permitan Dinamizar el Complejo de Producción y Comercialización de Carnes Rojas, con Enfasis en la Industria Frigorífica. Montevideo, Uruguay [1985] 13, 18, 16 p. : LC Card 85-236237
HD9440.U82 T35 1984

MEATH - POPULATION.
Eastern Regional Development Organisation (Ireland) Eastern Region settlement strategy, 2011. Dublin [1985] viii, 21 p. : LC Card 87-672678
HB3589 .E27x 1985a

Eastern Regional Development Organisation (Ireland) Eastern Region settlement strategy, 2011. Dublin [1985] xviii, 269 p. : LC Card 87-672656
HB3589 .E27x 1985

Mécanismes et politique monétaires . Chaîneau, André. Paris , 1979, c19. 311 p. : ISBN 2-13-036227-3 *NYPL [JLD 86-2730]*

MECHANICAL BRAINS. see **CYBERNETICS.**

MECHANICAL ENGINEERS - SWITZERLAND - BIOGRAPHY.
Lang, Norbert. Johann Georg Bodmer (1786-1864) . Zürich , c1987. 92 p. : LC Card 87-134606 DDC 338/.09494 s 620/.0092/4 B 19
HC395.5.A2 S3 no. 45 TJ140.B53

MECHANICAL SPEECH RECOGNIZER. see **AUTOMATIC SPEECH RECOGNITION.**

MECHANICS' LIEN FORECLOSURE. see **FORECLOSURE.**

Mechanisation economics for individual farms. Hegrenes, Agnar. Mekaniseringsøkonomi på enkeltbruk /. Oslo , 1985. 175 p. : ISBN 82-7077-028-0 LC Card 86-180961
HD2012 .H44 1985

Mechanised food production in Tanzania . Bantje, Han. [Dar es Salaam] [1984] 3 leaves, 73 p. : LC Card 86-980118 DDC 338.1/61/09678 19
HD1471.T34 B36 1984

MECHANIZED INFORMATION STORAGE AND RETRIEVAL SYSTEMS. see **INFORMATION STORAGE AND RETRIEVAL SYSTEMS.**

Mecimore, Charles D. Woelfel, Charles J. The operating executive's guide to profit planning tools and techniques /. Chicago, Ill. , c1986. ix, 199 p. : ISBN 0-917253-24-8 : LC Card 86-3222 DDC 658.1/55 19
HF5635 .W848 1986 NYPL [JLE 86-3007]

Medbestämmande . Hörte, Sven Åke. [Göteborg] , c1983. 160, [28] p. : ISBN 91-7222-576-9 LC Card 83-173622
HD5660.S9 H67 1983

Medbestämmandeavtal i landsting . Otter, Casten von, 1941- Stockholm [1984] 92 p. : LC Card 84-241542
HD5660.S9 O77 1984

Meddelanden från Ekonomisk-historiska institutionen vid Göteborgs universitet, 0072-5080 .
(52) Jonsson, Sverker, 1941- Pressen, reklamen och konkurrensen, 1935-1978 /. Göteborg , 1982. 406 p. : ISBN 91-85196-24-X : LC Card 84-157282
HF6105.S8 J66 1982

(55) Cornell, Lasse. Arbete och arbetsformernas utveckling /. Göteborg , 1986. 161 p. : ISBN 91-85196-27-4 LC Card 86-212110
HD4851 .C67 1986

Meddelanden fran Svenska handelshögskolan .
(118) Blomqvist, H. C. (Hans-Christer), 1947- Lönebildningsforskning i Finland /. [Helsinki] [1984] 23 leaves : ISBN 951-555-207-9 LC Card 85-137027
HD5047.3 .B57 1984

(119) Edin, Per-Anders. Individuella sysselsättningskonsekvenser av nedläggningar /. Helsingfors [1984] 20 leaves ; ISBN 951-555-208-7 LC Card 85-151846
HD5803 .E33 1984

(131) Ekholm, Bo-Göran. Skattetryckets fördelning inom finländska industriföretag /. Helsingfors [1985] 39 p. ; ISBN 951-555-222-2 LC Card 85-214497
HD2753.F5 E38 1985

(132) Paul, Jan-Peter. Ekonomiska sanktioner . Helsingfors [1985] 46 p. ; ISBN 951-555-224-9 LC Card 85-212001
HF1613.5 .P38 1985

(135) Rosenlew, Andreas. Intern marknadsföring . [Helsinki] [1985] 51 p. : ISBN 951-555-227-3 LC Card 85-214635
HF5415 .R5795 1985

(149) Menzler-Hokkanen, Ingeborg. Measuring changes in intra-industry competitiveness /. Helsingfors [1986] 39 p. ; ISBN 951-555-247-8 (pbk.) LC Card 87-170429 DDC 338.6/048 19
HC79.I52 M46 1986

(5) Wahlroos, Björn. A comment on the goals and potential implications of Finnish average cost price regulation /. Helsingfors , 1978. 12, [1] leaves : ISBN 951-555-053-X LC Card 85-192907
HB236.F55 W328 1978

Meddis, Ray. Statistics using ranks : a unified approach / Ray Meddis. Oxford, OX, UK ; New York, NY, USA : B. Blackwell, 1984. vi, 449 p. : ill. ; 23 cm. Includes index. Bibliography: p. 444-446. ISBN 0-631-13788-2 (pbk.) : LC Card 84-11087 DDC 519.5 19
1. Social sciences - Statistical methods. 2. Ranking and selection (Statistics). I. Title.
HA29 .M43885 1984 NYPL [JLE 86-4708]

Médecins sans frontières (Association) Malhuret, Claude. Mass deportations in Ethiopia /. [Paris] [1985] 65 leaves ; LC Card 86-181587 DDC 333.3/1/63 19
HD979 .M34 1985

Mededeling (Landbouw-Economisch Instituut (Netherlands)) .
(351) Huizinga, W. Two lectures on the historical development of Dutch agriculture, 1600-1985 /. Den Haag [1986] 31 p. : LC Card 86-233719
HD1987 .H85 1986

Medeiros, Eduardo Raposo de. Economia internacional / Eduardo Raposo de Medeiros. Lisboa : Instituto Superior de Ciências Sociais e Políticas, 1984. 416 p., [2] folded leaves of plates : ill. ; 24 cm. "Separata de Estudos políticos e sociais, vol. XI, nos. 1-2, 1983"--T.p. verso. Bibliography: p. 388-389. LC Card 85-125328
1. Economic history - 1945-. 2. Economics. 3. Economic policy. 4. Commercial policy. 5. International agencies. 6. International economic integration. I. Title.
HC59 .M425 1984

Medellín, Carlos. Perspectivas de la economía mundial y colombiana /. Bogotá, Colombia , 1986. 106 p. ; ISBN 958-616-044-0 LC Card 87-115573 DDC 330.9861/0632 19
HC197 .P35 1986

Medi-Cal fee-for-service eligibles and prepaid health plan enrollees by age group, sex, and county--July 1983. [Sacramento] : State of California, Health and Welfare Agency, Dept. of Health Services, [1984] 21 p. : ill. ; 28 cm. (Data matters topical reports) Caption title. "Report register no: 84-03065 (April 1984)" LC Card 86-622329 DDC 362.1/04252/09794021 19
1. Medicaid - California - Statistics. 2. Health maintenance organization patients - California - Statistics. I. California. Dept. of Health Services. II. Series.
HD7102.U5 C3 1984

Medi-Cal fee-for-service eligibles and prepaid health plan enrollees by age group, sex, and county, July 1984. [Sacramento] : State of California, Health and Welfare Agency, Dept. of Health Services, [1985] 19 p. : ill. ; 28 cm. (Data matters topical reports) Caption title. At head of title: California Center for Health Statistics. "Report register no.: 85-04065 (April 1985)" LC Card 86-622330 DDC 362.1/04252/09794021 19
1. Insurance, Health - California - Statistics. I. California. Center for Health Statistics. II. Series.
HD7102.U6 C345 1985

Media debates series.
Sinclair, John, 1944- Images incorporated . London , New York , c1987. 215 p. : ISBN 0-7099-3388-6 LC Card 87-20040 DDC 659.1 19
HF5821 .S58 1987

Média et vie sociale (Association : France) Benhaïm, J.-P. (Jean-Pierre) Les radios locales privées /. Paris , c1985. 153 p. : ISBN 2-7101-0528-4 : LC Card 85-205602
HE8697.P57 B45 1985

Media Institute (Washington, D.C.) Using new communications technologies . Washington, D.C. , c1986. ix, 57 p. : ISBN 0-937790-30-3 (pbk.) : LC Card 85-63320 DDC 384 19
HF5541.T4 U75 1986

Media math . Hall, Robert W. (Robert William), 1939- Lincolnwood, Ill., U. S.A. , c1987. v, 138 p. : ISBN 0-8442-3142-8 (pbk.) : LC Card 86-62067 DDC 659.1/01/51 19
HF5826.5 .H35 1987

MEDIA PLANNING IN ADVERTISING. see **ADVERTISING MEDIA PLANNING.**

Mediaprint .
(Bd. 8) Kalte Kommunikation . Basel , c1985. 256 p. : ISBN 3-85787-134-2 LC Card 85-232413
HD9696.T463 S95 1985

(Bd. 9) "Ein Chaos wollen wir nicht" . Basel , c1985. 223 p. : ISBN 3-85787-141-5 : LC Card 86-128638
HE8689.9.S95 C57 1985

MEDIATION.
Moore, Christopher W., 1947- The mediation process . San Francisco , 1986. xxii, 348 p. ; ISBN 0-87589-673-1 (alk. paper) LC Card 85-23675 DDC 302.3 19
HM136 .M684 1986 NYPL [JLE 86-3017]

Stulberg, Joseph B. Taking charge/managing conflict /. Lexington, Mass. , c1987. xii, 175 p. ; ISBN 0-669-14014-7 (alk. paper) LC Card 86-45597 DDC 658.4 19
HD42 .S78 1987

MEDIATION AND CONCILIATION, INDUSTRIAL - INDIA.
Kher, Manik. Conciliation and adjudication today /. Pune , c1985. 99 : LC Card 85-903388 DDC 344.54/0189143 345.404189143 19
LAW NYPL [JLE 86-1567]

Sharma, B. D. (Banarsi Das), 1921- Art of conciliation and industrial unrest /. Bombay , 1985. xvi, 366 p. ; LC Card 87-902679 DDC 331.89/14/0954 19
HD5998.A3 S48 1985

The mediation process . Moore, Christopher W., 1947- San Francisco , 1986. xxii, 348 p. ; ISBN 0-87589-673-1 (alk. paper) LC Card 85-23675 DDC 302.3 19
HM136 .M684 1986 NYPL [JLE 86-3017]

Medicaid . Holahan, John. Washington, D.C. , c1986. xvii, 124 p. ; ISBN 0-87766-406-4 LC Card 86-28100 DDC 353.0084/1045 19
HD7102.U4 H59 1986

MEDICAID.
Davis, Karen, 1942- Medicare policy . Baltimore , c1986. xiii, 137 p. ; ISBN 0-8018-2874-0 (alk. paper) LC Card 85-45048 DDC 368.4/26/00973 19
HD7102.U4 D279 1986
NYPL [JLE 86-3782]

Oberg, Charles N. Medicaid, entering the third decade . Excelsior, Minn. (P.O. Box 458, Excelsior 55331-0458) , c1986. vii, 70 p. : LC Card 86-233259 DDC 362.1/0425/0973 19
HD7102.U4 O58 1986

MEDICAID - CALIFORNIA - STATISTICS.
Medi-Cal fee-for-service eligibles and prepaid health plan enrollees by age group, sex, and county--July 1983. [Sacramento] [1984] 21 p. : LC Card 86-622329 DDC 362.1/04252/09794021 19
HD7102.U5 C3 1984

MEDICAID - COST CONTROL.
Holahan, John. Medicaid . Washington, D.C. , c1986. xvii, 124 p. ; ISBN 0-87766-406-4 LC Card 86-28100 DDC 353.0084/1045 19
HD7102.U4 H59 1986

MEDICAID - COST EFFECTIVENESS.
Holahan, John. Medicaid . Washington, D.C. , c1986. xvii, 124 p. ; ISBN 0-87766-406-4 LC Card 86-28100 DDC 353.0084/1045 19
HD7102.U4 H59 1986

MEDICAID - COSTS.
Affording access to quality care . Washington, D.C. (444 N. Capitol St., N.W., Suite 250, Washington 20001) , c1986. xx, 245 p. ; LC Card 87-127057 DDC 338.4/336210452/0973 19
HD7102.U4 A66 1986

Medicaid, entering the third decade . Oberg, Charles N. Excelsior, Minn. (P.O. Box 458, Excelsior 55331-0458) , c1986. vii, 70 p. : LC Card 86-233259 DDC 362.1/0425/0973 19
HD7102.U4 O58 1986

MEDICAID - NEW YORK (STATE)
O'Connell, Julie, 1951- Medicaid reform . [Albany, N.Y.] [1983] 26 p. ; LC Card 86-620741 DDC 362.1/04252/09747 19
HD7102.U5 N668 1983

Utilization of medicaid paid health services by Medicaid recipients in New York City, Nassau, Monroe, and western central counties, 1980-1981 /. Albany, N.Y. (1 Commerce Plaza, Albany 12210) [1985] ii, 31, 17 p. : LC Card 86-622554 DDC 362.1/04252/09747 19
HD7102.U5 N684 1985

Medicaid reform . O'Connell, Julie, 1951- [Albany, N.Y.] [1983] 26 p. ; LC Card 86-620741 DDC 362.1/04252/09747 19
HD7102.U5 N668 1983

MEDICAID - UNITED STATES.
Fein, Rashi. Medical care, medical costs . Cambridge, Mass. , 1986. viii, 240 p. ; ISBN 0-674-56052-3 (alk. paper) LC Card 86-7623 DDC 368.3/82/00973 19
HG9396 .F45 1986 ***NYPL [JLE 86-3975]***

MEDICAL CARE, COST OF - UNITED STATES.
America's uninsured and underinsured . Washington , 1986. vi, 13 p. ; LC Card 86-603377 DDC 368.3/8/00973 19
HD7102.U4 A755 1986

Davis, Karen, 1942- Medicare policy . Baltimore , c1986. xiii, 137 p. ; ISBN 0-8018-2874-0 (alk. paper) LC Card 85-45048 DDC 368.4/26/00973 19
HD7102.U4 D279 1986
NYPL [JLE 86-3782]

Fein, Rashi. Medical care, medical costs . Cambridge, Mass. , 1986. viii, 240 p. ; ISBN 0-674-56052-3 (alk. paper) LC Card 86-7623 DDC 368.3/82/00973 19
HG9396 .F45 1986 ***NYPL [JLE 86-3975]***

Ginsburg, Paul B. A private health plan option strategy for Medicare /. Santa Monica, CA [1987] xvi, 116 p. ; ISBN 0-8330-0863-3 (pbk.) LC Card 87-17593 DDC 368.4/26/00973 19
HD7102.U4 G56 1987

Health insurance and the demand for medical care . Santa Monica, CA , 1987. p. cm. ISBN 0-8330-0864-1 LC Card 87-17587 DDC 368.3/82/00973 19
HD7102.U4 H413 1987

Langwell, Kathryn M. A synthesis of research on competition in the financing and delivery of health services /. Hyattsville, MD. , Springfield, VA , 1982. 85 p. ; LC Card 82-600612 DDC 338.4/73621/0973 19
RA410.53 .L36 1982 ***NYPL [JLF 86-422]***

Waller, Kal. Medicare . Cleveland , 1987. xvii, 146 p. : ISBN 0-939738-92-9 (pbk.) LC Card 87-156155 DDC 368.4/26/00973 19
HD7102.U4 W245 1987

MEDICAL CARE, COST OF - UNITED STATES - CONGRESSES.
Market reforms in health care . Washington , c1983. xv, 331 p. ; ISBN 0-8447-2242-1 LC Card 82-22678 DDC 362.1/0973 19
RA410.53 .M37 1983 ***NYPL [JLC 86-373]***

MEDICAL CARE - DEVELOPING COUNTRIES.
Bühler, Marcel. Geschäfte mit der Armut . Frankfurt/M. , c1982. 200 p. : ISBN 3-923363-02-8 (pbk.) LC Card 86-674004
HD9673.D44 B83x 1982

Uphoff, Norman Thomas. Local institutional development . West Hartford, CT , c1986. xv, 421 p. ; ISBN 0-931816-45-9 LC Card 86-15288 DDC 302.3/5 19
HC59.7 .U64 1986 ***NYPL [JLE 87-1200]***

MEDICAL CARE - ECONOMIC ASPECTS. see **MEDICAL ECONOMICS.**

Medical care, medical costs . Fein, Rashi. Cambridge, Mass. , 1986. viii, 240 p. ; ISBN 0-674-56052-3 (alk. paper) LC Card 86-7623 DDC 368.3/82/00973 19
HG9396 .F45 1986 ***NYPL [JLE 86-3975]***

MEDICAL CARE, PREPAID. see **INSURANCE, HEALTH.**

MEDICAL CARE SURVEYS - UNITED STATES.
Farley, Pamela J. Private health insurance in the United States . Rockville, MD , Springfield, VA [1986] 106 p. : LC Card 86-23618 DDC 368.3/82/00973 19
HG9396 .F3 1986

MEDICAL CARE - UNITED STATES - COST CONTROL.
Affording access to quality care . Washington, D.C. (444 N. Capitol St., N.W., Suite 250, Washington 20001) , c1986. xx, 245 p. ; LC Card 87-127057 DDC 338.4/336210452/0973 19
HD7102.U4 A66 1986

MEDICAL CARE - UNITED STATES - COST CONTROL - CONGRESSES.
Market reforms in health care . Washington , c1983. xv, 331 p. ; ISBN 0-8447-2242-1 LC Card 82-22678 DDC 362.1/0973 19
RA410.53 .M37 1983 ***NYPL [JLC 86-373]***

MEDICAL CARE - UNITED STATES - FINANCE.
Affording access to quality care . Washington, D.C. (444 N. Capitol St., N.W., Suite 250, Washington 20001) , c1986. xx, 245 p. ; LC Card 87-127057 DDC 338.4/336210452/0973 19
HD7102.U4 A66 1986

MEDICAL CARE - UNITED STATES - MARKETING.
Langwell, Kathryn M. A synthesis of research on competition in the financing and delivery of health services /. Hyattsville, MD. , Springfield, VA , 1982. 85 p. ; LC Card 82-600612 DDC 338.4/73621/0973 19
RA410.53 .L36 1982 ***NYPL [JLF 86-422]***

MEDICAL CENTERS - TEXAS - SAN ANTONIO - CONGRESSES.
A Transcription of key addresses at San Antonio's Bio-Medical Seminar /. San Antonio, TX (8961 Tesoro Dr., Suite 308, San Antonio 78217) , c1985. v, 104, [4] leaves of plates : LC Card 87-144092 DDC 338.4/7681761/09764351 19
HD9999.B443 U667 1985

The Medical communications market. New York, N.Y. : Frost & Sullivan, c1972. vi, 163 leaves : ill. ; 29 cm. "A125." LC Card 87-141851
1. Hospital communication equipment industry - United States. 2. Market surveys - United States. I. Frost & Sullivan.
HD9995.H63 U5454 1972

MEDICAL ECONOMICS - UNITED STATES.
Miller, Irwin. The health care survival curve . Homewood, Ill. , c1984. xv, 144 p. ; ISBN 0-87094-481-9 LC Card 83-73714 DDC 338.4/73621/0973 19
RA410.53 .M55 1984 ***NYPL [JLE 86-4362]***

Newhouse, Joseph P. The economics of medical care . Reading, Mass. , c1978. x, 116 p. : ISBN 0-201-08369-8 LC Card 78-52498
RA410.53 .N5 ***NYPL [JLE 79-2561]***

MEDICAL ELECTRONICS EQUIPMENT INDUSTRY - UNITED STATES.
Healthcare electronics /. Boston, MA (89 Broad St., Boston 02110) , c1986. iv, 79 p. : LC Card 86-212563 DDC 381/.45681761 19
HD9995.E43 U55 1986

MEDICAL ELECTRONICS EQUIPMENT INDUSTRY - UNITED STATES - STATISTICS.
The SBI report on the market and economics of the electromedical equipment industry. Wantagh, N.Y. , c1982. iv, 157 leaves ; LC Card 87-402136 DDC 380.1/45681761 19
HD9995.E43 U58 1982

MEDICAL EXAMINATIONS. see **DIAGNOSIS.**

MEDICAL INNOVATIONS - UNITED STATES - HISTORY.
Liebenau, Jonathan. Medical science and medical industry . Baltimore , 1987. ix, 207 p. ; ISBN 0-8018-3356-6 LC Card 86-27346 DDC 338.4/76151/0973 19
HD9666.5 .L54 1987

MEDICAL INSTRUMENTS AND APPARATUS INDUSTRY - TEXAS - SAN ANTONIO - CONGRESSES.
A Transcription of key addresses at San Antonio's Bio-Medical Seminar /. San Antonio, TX (8961 Tesoro Dr., Suite 308, San Antonio 78217) , c1985. v, 104, [4] leaves of plates : LC Card 87-144092 DDC 338.4/7681761/09764351 19
HD9999.B443 U667 1985

MEDICAL INSTRUMENTS AND APPARATUS INDUSTRY - UNITED STATES - DIRECTORIES.
Top emerging private companies. Tustin, CA, U. S.A. (17722 Irvine Blvd., Tustin 92680) , c1987. iv, 8, 144, [112] leaves : LC Card 87-402028 DDC 681/.761/029473 19
HD9994.U52 T66 1987

MEDICAL INSTRUMENTS AND APPARATUS INDUSTRY - UNITED STATES - STATISTICS.
The SBI report on the market and economics of the electromedical equipment industry. Wantagh, N.Y. , c1982. iv, 157 leaves ; LC Card 87-402136 DDC 380.1/45681761 19
HD9995.E43 U58 1982

MEDICAL INSTRUMENTS AND APPARATUS - UNITED STATES - MARKETING.
Maximizing sales to hospital national accounts /. Tustin, CA, U. S.A. (17722 Irvine Blvd., Tustin 92680) , c1987. 524 p. in various pagings : LC Card 87-401688 DDC 681/.761/0688 19
HD9994.U52 M39 1987

MEDICAL LABORATORY EQUIPMENT INDUSTRY.
Specimen collection and transport market. Tustin, CA, U. S.A. (17722 Irvine Blvd., Tustin 92680) , c1987. 1 v. (various foliations) : LC Card 87-402105 DDC 380.1/45681761 19
HD9995.L32 S64 1987

MEDICAL LABORATORY EQUIPMENT INDUSTRY - UNITED STATES.
Alternate site clinical testing. Tustin, CA, U. S.A. (17722 Irvine Blvd., Tustin 92680) , c1987. 167 leaves in various foliations : LC Card 87-402110 DDC 381/.45681761 19
HD9995.L33 U5412 1987

U. S. clinical testing market /. Tustin, CA, U. S.A. (17722 Irvine Blvd., Tustin 92680) , c1987. 223 leaves in various foliations ; LC Card 87-402039 DDC 381/.45681761 19
HD9995.L33 U5484 1987

MEDICAL OFFICES - UNITED STATES - EQUIPMENT AND SUPPLIES.
Alternate site clinical testing. Tustin, CA, U. S.A. (17722 Irvine Blvd., Tustin 92680) , c1987. 167 leaves in various foliations : LC Card 87-402110 DDC 381/.45681761 19
HD9995.L33 U5412 1987

Medical perspectives on Canadian Medicare . Taylor, Malcolm G. (Malcolm Gordon) Downsview, Ont. , 1984. vii, 201 p. : ISBN 0-919762-57-3 (pbk.) LC Card 87-673411
HD7102.C2 T34x 1984

MEDICAL POLICY - KANSAS.
Kansas policy choices . Lawrence, Kan. , c1986. x, 210 p. : ISBN 0-7006-0302-6 (pbk.) LC Card 86-204211 DDC 338.9781 19
HC107.K2 K387 1986

MEDICAL POLICY - NORWAY.
Grund, Jan. Velferdsstat i motvind /. Oslo , 1986, c1985. 139 p. : ISBN 82-00-07590-7 : LC Card 86-132818
HC365 .G78 1985 ***NYPL [JLD 86-4433]***

MEDICAL POLICY - UNITED STATES.
Miller, Irwin. The health care survival curve . Homewood, Ill. , c1984. xv, 144 p. ; ISBN 0-87094-481-9 LC Card 83-73714 DDC

338.4/73621/0973 19
RA410.53 .M55 1984 *NYPL [JLE 86-4362]*

Newhouse, Joseph P. The economics of medical care . Reading, Mass. , c1978. x, 116 p. : ISBN 0-201-08369-8 LC Card 78-52498
RA410.53 .N5 *NYPL [JLE 79-2561]*

MEDICAL POLICY - UNITED STATES - CONGRESSES.
Market reforms in health care . Washington , c1983. xv, 331 p. ; ISBN 0-8447-2242-1 LC Card 82-22678 DDC 362.1/0973 19
RA410.53 .M37 1983 *NYPL [JLC 86-373]*

Medical products packaging market in Europe. New York, N.Y. : Frost & Sullivan, c1983. vi, x, xi, 220 p. : ill. ; 28 cm. Spine title: Pharmaceutical packaging products mkt. in Europe. "July 1983." "#E566." LC Card 87-141779 DDC 380.1/456151 19
1. Drug packaging industry - Europe. 2. Market surveys - Europe. I. Frost & Sullivan. II. Title: Pharmaceutical packaging products mkt. in Europe. III. Title: Pharmaceutical packaging products market in Europe.
HD9671.A2 M43 1983

MEDICAL RECORD LINKAGE - UNITED STATES.
Statistical aspects of physician payment systems . Hyattsville, Md. [1987] vii, 33 p. : ISBN 0-8406-0357-6 LC Card 86-600375 DDC 362.1/0723 s 362.1/72 19
HA37 .U1693 no. 24 RA408.5

Medical science and medical industry . Liebenau, Jonathan. Baltimore , 1987. ix, 207 p. ; ISBN 0-8018-3356-6 LC Card 86-27346 DDC 338.4/76151/0973 19
HD9666.5 .L54 1987

MEDICAL SERVICE. see **MEDICAL CARE.**

MEDICAL SERVICE, PREPAID. see **INSURANCE, HEALTH.**

MEDICAL SOCIOLOGY. see **SOCIAL MEDICINE.**

MEDICAL SUPPLIES INDUSTRY - UNITED STATES - FINANCE - DIRECTORIES.
Pharmaceutical manufacturers of the United States /. Park Ridge, N.J., U. S.A. , 1987. vi, 300 p. ; ISBN 0-8155-1109-4 : LC Card 86-33276 DDC 338.7/616151/02573 19
HD9666.3 .P47 1987

Medicare . Waller, Kal. Cleveland , 1987. xvii, 146 p. : ISBN 0-939738-92-9 (pbk.) LC Card 87-156155 DDC 368.4/26/00973 19
HD7102.U4 W245 1987

MEDICARE.
Davis, Karen, 1942- Medicare policy . Baltimore , c1986. xiii, 137 p. ; ISBN 0-8018-2874-0 (alk. paper) LC Card 85-45048 DDC 368.4/26/00973 19
HD7102.U4 D279 1986 *NYPL [JLE 86-3782]*

Kingson, Eric R. What you must know about Social Security & Medicare /. New York , 1987. 120 p. ; ISBN 0-88687-294-4 (pbk.) : LC Card 86-62667 DDC 368.4/3/00973 19
HD7125 .K538 1987

Oberg, Charles N. Medicaid, entering the third decade . Excelsior, Minn. (P.O. Box 458, Excelsior 55331-0458) , c1986. vii, 70 p. : LC Card 86-233259 DDC 362.1/0425/0973 19
HD7102.U4 O58 1986

MEDICARE - CANADA - PUBLIC OPINION.
Taylor, Malcolm G. (Malcolm Gordon) Medical perspectives on Canadian Medicare . Downsview, Ont. , 1984. vii, 201 p. : ISBN 0-919762-57-3 (pbk.) LC Card 87-673411
HD7102.C2 T34x 1984

MEDICARE - CLAIMS ADMINISTRATION.
The American Society of Internal Medicine's carrier accountability monitoring project . Washington, DC [1986] 8 p. ; LC Card 86-219845 DDC 368.4/26/0068 19
HD7102.U4 A753 1986

Ginsburg, Paul B. A private health plan option strategy for Medicare /. Santa Monica, CA [1987] xvi, 116 p. ; ISBN 0-8330-0863-3 (pbk.) LC Card 87-17593 DDC 368.4/26/00973 19
HD7102.U4 G56 1987

MEDICARE - HANDBOOKS, MANUALS, ETC.
Getting the most from social security . Skokie, IL (3841 W. Oakton St., Skokie 60076) , c1986. 192 p. : LC Card 86-219986 DDC 344.73/023 347.30423 19
HD7125 .G43 1986

Pell, Arthur R. Making the most of Medicare /. New York , c1987. ix, 123 p. : ISBN 0-13-547696-8 (pbk.) : LC Card 86-25160 DDC 344.73/0226 347.304226 19
HD7102.U4 P45 1987

Sieforth, Jeannine Morris. Medicare savings and sense . Manzanita, Or. , c1986. xviii, 181 p. : ISBN 0-9617625-0-0 (pbk.) LC Card 86-72651 DDC 344.73/0226 347.304226 19
HD7102.U4 S525 1986

Medicare policy . Davis, Karen, 1942- Baltimore , c1986. xiii, 137 p. ; ISBN 0-8018-2874-0 (alk. paper) LC Card 85-45048 DDC 368.4/26/00973 19
HD7102.U4 D279 1986 *NYPL [JLE 86-3782]*

MEDICARE POLICY - UNITED STATES.
Ginsburg, Paul B. A private health plan option strategy for Medicare /. Santa Monica, CA [1987] xvi, 116 p. ; ISBN 0-8330-0863-3 (pbk.) LC Card 87-17593 DDC 368.4/26/00973 19
HD7102.U4 G56 1987

Medicare savings and sense . Sieforth, Jeannine Morris. Manzanita, Or. , c1986. xviii, 181 p. : ISBN 0-9617625-0-0 (pbk.) LC Card 86-72651 DDC 344.73/0226 347.304226 19
HD7102.U4 S525 1986

Medicare savings & sense. Sieforth, Jeannine Morris. Medicare savings and sense . Manzanita, Or. , c1986. xviii, 181 p. : ISBN 0-9617625-0-0 (pbk.) LC Card 86-72651 DDC 344.73/0226 347.304226 19
HD7102.U4 S525 1986

MEDICARE - UNITED STATES.
Bernstein, Merton C. Social Security . New York , c1988. xiii, 321 p. : ISBN 0-465-07916-4 : LC Card 86-47762 DDC 368.4/3/00973 19
HD7125 .B48 1988

Fein, Rashi. Medical care, medical costs . Cambridge, Mass. , 1986. viii, 240 p. ; ISBN 0-674-56052-3 (alk. paper) LC Card 86-7623 DDC 368.3/82/00973 19
HG9396 .F45 1986 *NYPL [JLE 86-3975]*

Waller, Kal. Medicare . Cleveland , 1987. xvii, 146 p. : ISBN 0-939738 92-9 (pbk.) LC Card 87-156155 DDC 368.4/26/00973 19
HD7102.U4 W245 1987

Medici Mario, 1924- La parola pubblicitaria : due secoli di storia fra slogan, ritmi e wellerismi / Mario Medici.1a ed. Pomezia : Sarin ; Venezia : Marsilio, 1986. 178 p., 40 p. of plates : ill. (some col.) ; 22 cm. (Biblioteca) Bibliography: p. 171-176. ISBN 88-317-4902-1 : LC Card 86-219876
1. Advertising - Italy - History. 2. Advertising - History. 3. Slogans. I. Title.
HF5813.I8 M43 1986

Medici, Sauro. Cremona e la sua provincia nell'Italia unita. Milano , 1984. 2 v. : ISBN 88-14-00552-4 : LC Card 86-207553
HC308.C74 C74 1984

MEDICINE AND SOCIOLOGY. see **SOCIAL MEDICINE.**

MEDICINE AND STATE. see **MEDICAL POLICY.**

MEDICINE - ECONOMIC ASPECTS. see **MEDICAL ECONOMICS.**

MEDICINE, SOCIAL. see **SOCIAL MEDICINE.**

MEDICINE - SOCIAL ASPECTS. see **SOCIAL MEDICINE.**

Mediekommissionens betænkning .
(nr. 5) Denmark. Mediekommissionen. Betænkning om et øget dansk tv-udbud. [København] , 1983. 168 p. : ISBN 87-503-4624-5 LC Card 85-128700
HE8700.9.D4 D45 1983

Medieval Iberian tradition and the development of the Mexican hacienda /. Schell, William, 1950- Syracuse, NY , 1986. 117 p. ; ISBN 0-915984-99-7 : LC Card 85-31042 DDC 307.7/2/0972 19
HD1471.M6 S34 1986 *NYPL [JLE 86-1697]*

The medieval market economy /. Day, John, 1924- Oxford, UK , New York, NY, USA , 1987. p. cm. ISBN 0-631-15479-5 : LC Card 86-26862 DDC 330.94/01 19
HC41 .D39 1987

Medieval people, 0273-3307 .
(v. 10) Ide, Arthur Frederick. The mercantile policies of Henry VII /. Irving, Tex. , 1987. v, 78 p. : ISBN 0-938659-02-2 (pbk.) : LC Card 87-4316 DDC 382/.3/0942 19
HF1533 .I34 1987

Medieval roads /. Hindle, Brian Paul. Aylesbury, Bucks, UK , 1982. 62 p. : ISBN 0-85263-600-8 (pbk.) : LC Card 83-228901 DDC 388.1/0942 19
HE363.G72 H56 1982 *NYPL [JLD 86-1755]*

MEDIGAP.
Catastrophic health insurance . Washington , 1986. iii, 278 p. : LC Card 86-603399 DDC 368.3/82/00973 19
HD7102.U4 C37 1986

The "Medigap" crisis. Catastrophic health insurance . Washington , 1986. iii, 278 p. : LC Card 86-603399 DDC 368.3/82/00973 19
HD7102.U4 C37 1986

MEDIGAP - LAW AND LEGISLATION.
Catastrophic health insurance . Washington , 1986. iii, 278 p. : LC Card 86-603399 DDC 368.3/82/00973 19
HD7102.U4 C37 1986

Medina Cervantes, José Ramón. El estado mexicano entre la inversión extranjera directa y los grupos privados de empresarios / José Ramón Medina Cervantes. 1a ed. México, D.F. : Premià, 1984. 268 p. : ill. ; 21 cm. (La Red de Jonás. México y Latinoamérica . 14) Bibliography: p. 256-267. ISBN 968-434-358-2 LC Card 86-222537
1. Investments, Foreign - Mexico - History. 2. Investment trusts - Mexico - History. I. Title. II. Series.
HG5162 .M43 1984

Medina Spangenberg, Ernesto. "Algunas consideraciones sobre el tipo real de cambio en el Uruguay, período 1.78-12.82" / Ernesto Medina Spangenberg. Montevideo, Uruguay : Universidad Mayor de la Rep. Oriental del Uruguay, Dirección General de Extensión Universitaria, División Publicaciones y Ediciones, [1984] 39 p. : ill. ; 28 cm. At head of title: Facultad de Ciencias Económicas y Administración, Instituto de Economía. LC Card 84-253583
1. Foreign exchange problem - Uruguay - Econometric models. I. Universidad de la República (Uruguay). Instituto de Economía. II. Title.
HG3940 .M43 1984

Mediobanca.
Dati cumulativi di 1356 società italiane, 1968-1983 /. [Italy , 1984] (Milano : O. Capriolo) xxvi, 258 p. ; LC Card 86-229023
HG4166 .D39 1984

Indici e dati relativi ad investimenti in titoli quotati nelle borse italiane (1985) = Indices and data on investments in listed Italian securities (1985) / a cura di "Mediobanca.". [Milano] : Mediobanca, [1985] v, 427 p. : ill. ; 25 cm. LC Card 86-210524
1. Stocks - Italy - Statistics. 2. Securities - Italy - Statistics. 3. Stock-exchange - Italy - Statistics. 4. Economic indicators - Italy. 5. Stock price indexes - Italy. I. Title. II. Title: Indices and data on investments in listed Italian securities (1985).
HG5522 .M43 1985

Medios de comunicación, hegemonía y proyectos de desarrollo. [Mexico City] : Asociación Mexicana de Investigadores de la Comunicación : Taller de Investigación en Comunicación Masiva, Universidad Autónoma Metropolitana-Xochimilco, [between 1982 and 1987] 179 p. ; 28 cm. (Cuadernos de trabajo . 1) Papers presented at the 2nd Reunión Nacional de la AMIC, held Nov. 17-19, 1982 at the Centro de Estudios Económicos y Sociales del Tercer Mundo, Mexico City. Includes bibliographies. LC Card 87-127821 DDC 338.9/007/1 19
1. Economic development - Study and teaching - Congresses. 2. Economic development - Study and teaching - Mexico - Congresses. I. Asociación Mexicana de Investigadores de la Comunicación. II. Reunión Nacional de la AMIC (2nd : 1982 : Centro de Estudios Económicos y Sociales del Tercer Mundo). III. Series: Cuadernos de trabajo (Asociación Mexicana de Investigadores de la Comunicación) , 1.
HD77 .M43 1982

Medir i Huerta, Rosa M. Les comarques gironines : aproximació a la realitat sòcio-geogràfica / elaboració, Rosa M. Medir i Huerta ; cartografia, Marta Ministral i Masgrau ; amb la supervisió del Departament de Geografia del Col·legi Universitari de Girona.1a ed. Girona : Diputació de Girona, Servei d'Estudis, Documentació i Informació, 1986. 211 p. : ill. ; 30 cm. (Col·lecció Miquel Santaló i Parvorell . 1) ISBN 84-505-3103-9 LC Card 87-101047
1. Gerona, Spain (Province) - Economic conditions. 2. Gerona (Spain : Province) - Administrative and political divisions. 3. Natural resources - Spain - Gerona (Province). 4. Infrastructure - Spain - Gerona (Province). 5. Gerona, Spain (Province) - Population. I. Ministral i Masgrau, Marta. II. Title. III. Series.
HC387.G4 M43 1986

Mediterranean Conference, HRC. IUF Mediterranean Hotel and Restaurant Workers' Conference (1978 : Palermo, Sicily) IUF Mediterranean Hotel and Restaurant Workers' Conference, Palermo, November 15-17, 1978. Petit-Lancy, Switzerland [1978?] 1 v. (various pagings) ; LC Card 83-225538
HD6475.A2 I7836 1978

MEDITERRANEAN REGION - COMMERCE - HISTORY.
Abulafia, David. Italy, Sicily, and the Mediterranean, 1100-1400 /. London , 1987. 346 p. in various pagings : ISBN 0-86078-198-4 : LC Card 87-157554 DDC 330.9182/2 19
HF3585 .A29 1987

MEDITERRANEAN REGION - ECONOMIC CONDITIONS.
Duchêne, François. The European Community and the Mediterranean /. Luxembourg , Washington, DC , 1985. 102 p. : ISBN 92-825-5326-4 (pbk.) LC Card 87-119518 DDC 337.40182/2 19
HC241.25.M4 D83 1985

Medizinisch Pharmazeutische Studiengesellschaft (Germany) Aspekte zur GKV-Strukturreform /. Stuttgart , New York , 1984. x, 102 p. ; ISBN 3-437-10918-9 LC Card 84-187001
HD7102.G3 A87 1984

Medla, Karsten, 1954- Shop-in-the-shop : ein Konzept der Angebotspräsentation im Einzelhandel / Karsten Medla. München : Florentz, c1987. xxxi, 207, 6 p. ; 21 cm. (Hochschulschriften zur Betriebswirtschaftslehre . Bd. 43) Bibliography: p. ix-xxxi. Includes index. ISBN 3-88259-428-4 LC Card 87-141864 DDC 658.8/7 19
1. Retail trade - Management. 2. Specialty stores. 3. Marketing. 4. Display of merchandise. I. Title. II. Series.
HF5429 .M36 1987

Medvedev, Zhores A., 1925- Soviet agriculture / Zhores A. Medvedev. 1st ed. New York : Norton, c1987. xiv, 464 p. ; 22 cm. Bibliography: p. 429-441. Includes index. ISBN 0-393-02472-5 LC Card 86-31119 DDC 338.1/0947 19
1. Agriculture - Economic aspects - Soviet Union - History. 2. Agriculture and state - Soviet Union - History. I. Title.
HD1992 .M385 1987

Medvedkov, S. ÎU. (Sergeĭ ÎUr'evich) Mezhdunarodnyĭ marketing amerikanskoĭ tekhnologii / S.ÎU. Medvedkov, ÎU.A. Sergeev ; otvetstvennyĭ redaktor V.A. Fedorovich. Moskva : "Nauka", 1985. 189 p. : ill. ; 20 cm. At head of title: Akademiia nauk SSSR. Institut SShA i Kanady. Includes bibliographical references. LC Card 85-187077
1. Export marketing - United States. 2. International business enterprises - United States. 3. Technology transfer - United States. I. Sergeev, ÎU. A. II. Fedorovich, V. A. (Vladimir Antonovich). III. Title.
HF1009.6 .M43 1985

Meehan, Elizabeth M. Women's rights at work : campaigns and policy in Britain and the United States / Elizabeth M. Meehan. New York : St. Martin's Press, 1985. xvii, 253 p. ; 23 cm. Includes index. Based on the author's thesis. Bibliography: p. 227-241. ISBN 0-312-88793-0 : LC Card 84-15997 DDC 331.4/133/0941 19
1. Sex discrimination in employment - Great Britain. 2. Sex discrimination in employment - United States. 3. Women - Employment - Great Britain. 4. Women - Employment - United States. I. Title.
HD6060 .M44 1984 ***NYPL [JLD 86-3580]***

Meek, Christopher.
Industrial democracy . Beverly Hills , c1985. 308 p. : ISBN 0-8039-2476-3 LC Card 85-11741 DDC 338.973/009173/2 19
HT321 .I53 1985 ***NYPL [JLD 86-3621]***

Managing by the numbers : absentee ownership and the decline of American industry / Christopher Meek, Warner Woodworth, and W. Gibb Dyer. Reading, Mass. : Addison-Wesley Pub. Co., c1988. ix, 293 p. : ill. ; 25 cm. Includes bibiographies and index. ISBN 0-201-16129-X : LC Card 87-16088 DDC 338.7/4/0973 19
1. Industrial management - United States. 2. Stock ownership - United States. 3. Consolidation and merger of corporations - United States. 4. Industrial concentration - United States. 5. Employee ownership - United States. I. Woodworth, Warner. II. Dyer, W. Gibb, 1954-. III. Title.
HD70.U5 M413 1988

Meeks, Gordon. Morandi, Larry B. Renewing resources . Denver, Colo. , 1984. vii, 133 p. ;
NYPL [JSF 86-712]

Meerhaege, Marcel Alfons Gilbert van, 1921- [Internationale economische betrekkingen en instellingen. English]
International economic institutions / M.A.G. van Meerhaeghe. 5th rev. ed. Dordrecht ; Boston : Kluwer Academic, 1987. xxviii, 368 p. ; 25 cm. Translation of: Internationale economische betrekkingen en instellingen. Includes bibliographies and indexes. ISBN 90-247-3513-0 LC Card 87-2959 DDC 337 19
1. International economic relations. 2. International economic integration. I. Title.
HF1411 .M433 1987

Mees en Chabot, twee kassiers te Rotterdam : een bijdrage tot de geschiedenis van de financiële infrastruktuur van de stad Rotterdam, 1850-1914. Delft : Eburon, c1986. 87 p. : ill. ; 24 cm. (Cahier / Centrum voor Bedrijfsgeschiedenis, Erasmus Universiteit Rotterdam . nr. 1) Bibliography: p. 83-87. ISBN 90-70879-40-9 : LC Card 86-205783
1. Banks and banking - Netherlands - Rotterdam - History. 2. Finance - Netherlands - Rotterdam - History. 3. R. Mees & Zoonen, Fa. (Rotterdam, Netherlands) - History. 4. Gebroeders Chabot, Fa. (Rotterdam, Netherlands) - History. I. Series: Cahier (Erasmus Universiteit Rotterdam. Centrum voor Bedrijfsgeschiedenis) , nr. 1.
HG3120.R62 M44 1986

Meet the members : a record of the Timber Corps of the Women's Land Army. [London?] : The Corps, [194-?] (Bristol : Bennett Bros.) 76 p., [12] p. of plates : ill. ; 19 cm. LC Card 84-190854
1. Women loggers - Great Britain - History. 2. Timber Corps (Great Britain) - History. I. Timber Corps (Great Britain).
HD6073.L92 G76 1940z

Meeting family needs . Kamerman, Sheila B. New York , c1983. 45 p. ; ISBN 0-08-030965-8 (pbk.) : LC Card 83-27159 DDC 658.3/8 19
HD4928.N62 U6355 1983
NYPL [JLM 83-380 no.33]

Meeting human needs . Troy, Kathryn. New York, NY , c1986. vii, 55 p. ; ISBN 0-8237-0323-1 (pbk.) LC Card 86-207649 DDC 658.3/8 19
HD7654 .T73 1986

The Meeting robbers [motion picture] / produced by CRM Productions, Inc. ; producers, Peter Jordan, Janice Reynolds ; director, Ron Underwood ; screenwriters, Brent Maddock, Richard Eckhaus. Del Mar, CA : McGraw-Hill Training Systems, 1985. 1 film reel (20 min.) : sd., col. ; 16 mm. + 1 leader's guide. Title from data sheet. Photographer, Virgil Harper. College students and adults. Issued also as videorecording. Illustrates how an organization's time, money, and resources are "stolen" by well-meaning employees, because they lack the skills necessary to keep their meetings results-oriented; then shows how meeting managers can plan and run productive meetings. ISBN 0-07-620874-5 LC Card 85-702616 DDC 658.4 11
1. Meetings. 2. Communication in management. I. CRM Productions. II. McGraw-Hill Training Systems (Firm).
HD30.3

The Meeting robbers [videorecording] / produced by CRM Productions, Inc. ; producers, Peter Jordan, Janice Reynolds ; director, Ron Underwood ; screenwriters, Brent Maddock, Richard Eckhaus. Del Mar, CA : McGraw-Hill Training Systems, 1985. 1 videocassette (20 min.) : sd., col. + 1 leader's guide. Title from data sheet. Photographer, Virgil Harper. College students and adults. Issued as U-matic 3/4 in. or VHS 1/2 in. Issued also as motion picture. Illustrates how an organization's time, money, and resources are "stolen" by well-meaning employees, because they lack the skills necessary to keep their meetings results-oriented; then shows how meeting managers can plan and run productive meetings. ISBN 0-07-109067-3 (3/4 in.) LC Card 85-702617 DDC 658.4 11
1. Meetings. 2. Communication in management. I. CRM Productions. II. McGraw-Hill Training Systems (Firm).
HD30.3

Meeting the challenge . New York (State). State Energy Office. Division of Policy Analysis and Planning. [Albany] [1985] 290 p. : LC Card 86-622429 DDC 333.79/3211/09747 19
HD9685.U6 N614 1985

MEGHALAYA (INDIA) - CENSUS, 1981.
Household population by religion of head of household, up to C.D. block and town level, series 14, Meghalaya . New Delhi , 1986. iii, 70 p. ; LC Card 87-901361 DDC 304.6/0954/164021 19
HA4587.M43 H68 1986

MEGHALAYA (INDIA) - ECONOMIC CONDITIONS.
Sukumaran Nair, M. K., 1948- Tribal economy in transition . New Delhi, India , 1987, c1986. 159 p. ; ISBN 81-210-0180-3 : LC Card 87-901406 DDC 330.954/164052 19
HC437.M4 S85 1987

MEGHALAYA (INDIA) - POPULATION - STATISTICS.
Household population by religion of head of household, up to C.D. block and town level, series 14, Meghalaya . New Delhi , 1986. iii, 70 p. ; LC Card 87-901361 DDC 304.6/0954/164021 19
HA4587.M43 H68 1986

MEGHALAYA (INDIA) - RELIGION - STATISTICS.
Household population by religion of head of household, up to C.D. block and town level, series 14, Meghalaya . New Delhi , 1986. iii, 70 p. ; LC Card 87-901361 DDC 304.6/0954/164021 19
HA4587.M43 H68 1986

MEGHALAYA (INDIA) - SCHEDULED TRIBES - ECONOMIC CONDITIONS.
Sukumaran Nair, M. K., 1948- Tribal economy in transition . New Delhi, India , 1987, c1986. 159 p. ; ISBN 81-210-0180-3 : LC Card 87-901406 DDC 330.954/164052 19
HC437.M4 S85 1987

Meher, Rajkishor. Kundu, Amitabh, 1948- Location of public enterprises and regional development /. New Delhi , 1986. xv, 178 p. ; LC Card 86-903373 DDC 338.954 19
HD9697.A3 I45 1986

Mehmet, Ozay. Development in Malaysia : poverty, wealth, and trusteeship / Ozay Mehmet. London ; Dover, N.H. : Croom Helm, c1986. 183 p. ; 23 cm. Includes bibliographical references and index. ISBN 0-7099-3525-0 : LC Card 85-29079 DDC 338.9595 19
1. Income distribution - Malaysia. 2. Elite (Social sciences) - Malaysia. 3. Malaysia - Economic conditions. I. Title.
HC445.5.Z9 I51834 1986
NYPL [JLD 86-2389]

Mehr, besser, billiger, aber wie? /. Reinhold, Otto. Berlin , 1985. 80 p. : LC Card 86-179312
HD70.G22 R45 1985

Mehr Flexibilität am Arbeitsmarkt /. Fels, Gerhard. Kiel , 1986. 21 p. ; ISBN 3-925357-37-8 LC Card 87-126264 DDC 331.25/72/0943 19
HD5109.2.G3 F4 1986

Mehr Technik, weniger Arbeit? : Plädoyers für sozial- und umweltverträgliche Technologien / Udo Ernst Simonis (Hrsg.). Karlsruhe : C.F. Müller, c1984. 228 p. : ill. ; 20 cm. (Alternative Konzepte . 48) Papers presented at a conference sponsored by the Georg Michael Pfaff Gedächtnisstiftung. Includes bibliographical references.

CONTENTS. - Mehr Technik, weniger Arbeit? / Udo Ernst Simonis -- Tendenzen der Entwicklung des Arbeitsmarktes und der Qualität der Arbeit / Wolfgang Klauder -- Technik und Arbeit / Otto Ullrich -- Entwicklung der Technik / Karl Friedrich Müller-Reissmann -- Ansatzpunkte sozial gesteuerter Innovation / Ulrich Klotz -- Neue Technologien und der Strukturwandel der Arbeit / Joseph Huber -- Neue Technologien und gewerkschaftliche Initiativen / Andreas Scholz -- Ökonomische Abrüstung / Burkhard Strümpel. ISBN 3-7880-9697-7 LC Card 85-108996
1. Labor supply - Effect of technological innovations on - Congresses. 2. Quality of work life - Congresses. I. Simonis, Udo Ernst. II. Georg Michael Pfaff Gedächtnisstiftung. III. Series.
HD6331 .M384 1984

Mehrjahresinvestitionsprogramm (MIP) der Landeshauptstadt Düsseldorf 1978-1982 / vom Rat der Stadt beschlossen am 14. 12. 1978. [Düsseldorf] : Oberstadtdirektor, Kämmerei, [1978?] 68, 141, 174, 5 p. ; 21 x 30 cm. All tables. Includes index. LC Card 85-141884
1. Capital budget - Germany (West) - Düsseldorf - Statistics. 2. Düsseldorf (Germany) - Appropriations and expenditures - Statistics. I. Düsseldorf (Germany). II. Düsseldorf (Germany). Rat.
HJ9494.D87 M44 1978

Mehrwert heute : der Mehrwert und seine Erscheinungsformen im Monopolkapitalismus / Autorenkollektiv DDR-UdSSR ; [verantwortliche Redaktion, Fritz Holzapfel ... et al. ; Übersetzung der Beiträge der sowjetischen Autoren, Gerda Müller]. Berlin : Verlag Die Wirtschaft, c1981. 285 p. ; 22 cm. Includes bibliographical references. LC Card 82-189316 DDC 338.5/21 19
1. Surplus value. 2. Profit. I. Holzapfel, Fritz.
HB206 .M44 1981 ***NYPL [JLD 86-2837]***

Mehta, Dileep R., 1932- Deschamps, Benoit. Chief financial officer . New York , c1988. xxvii, 582, [165] p. ; ISBN 0-471-84892-1 LC Card 87-21656 DDC 658.1/5 19
HG4026 .D48 1988

Mehta, Shirin. The peasantry and nationalism : a study of the Bardoli satyagraha / Shirin Mehta. New Delhi : Manohar, 1984. x, 215 p. : maps ; 23 cm. Based on the author's thesis (Ph. D.--Jawaharlal Nehru University) Includes index. Bibliography: p. [193]-208. LC Card 84-901701 DDC 322.4/4/095475 19
1. Peasantry - India - Bardoli Taluka - Political activity - History. 2. Nationalism - India - Bardoli Taluka - History. 3. Land tenure - India - Bardoli Taluka - History. 4. Bardoli Taluka (India) - History. I. Title.
HD1339.I4 M44 1984 ***NYPL [JLD 86-4424]***

Mehta, Suresh C. (Suresh Chandra), 1947- Agricultural credit mobilization and allocation : with special reference to District Jhabua, M.P. / Suresh C. Mehta ; foreward [sic] by A.C. Shah.1st ed. Allahabad, India : Vohra Publishers & Distributors, 1987. xv, 270 p. ; 22 cm. Revision of the author's thesis (Ph. D.--Vikram University, Ujjain) Bibliography: p. 267-270. ISBN 81-85072-06-X : LC Card 86-903677 DDC 332.7/1/09543 19
1. Agricultural credit - India - Jhābua (District). 2. Banks and banking - India - Jhābua (District). I. Title.
HG2051.I5 J466 1987

Mehta, Vadilal Lallubhai, 1903- Unemployment, inequality, parallel economy : a solution / Vadilal Lallubhai Mehta. Ahmedabad : Vimla Gram Seva Samaj Trust, 1982. viii, 141 p., [1] leaf of plates : ill. ; 22 cm. Includes bibliographical references. LC Card 82-900764 DDC 331.13/7954 19
1. Unemployment - India. 2. Underemployment - India. 3. Income distribution - India. 4. Informal sector (Economics) - India. 5. Corruption (in politics) - India. I. Title.
HD5819 .M43 1982 ***NYPL [JLD 85-2751]***

Meibom, Barbara E. Mettler- see **Mettler-Meibom, Barbara E.**

Meidan, Arthur, 1936- Handbook of business policy / by Arthur Meidan. [Bradford, West Yorkshire, England ; Birmingham, Ala.] : MCB University Press, c1986. 123 p. : ill. ; 30 cm. (Management decision, 0025-1747 . v. 24, no. 4 (1986)) Includes bibliographies and indexes. ISBN 0-86176-273-8 (pbk.) LC Card 87-150995 DDC 658.4/012 19
1. Corporate planning. I. Series: Management decision, v. 24, no. 4. II. Title.
HD30.28 .M42 1986

Meidinger, Claude. La Nouvelle économie libérale /. Paris , c1983. 280 p. : ISBN 2-7246-0487-3 : LC Card 84-140644
HB95 .N63 1983

Meidner, Rudolf. I arbetets tjänst / Rudolf Meidner. Stockholm : Tiden, 1984. 473 p. : ill. ; 22 cm. Bibliography: p. 465-473. ISBN 91-550-2932-9 : LC Card 84-229372
1. Labor policy - Sweden. 2. Trade-unions - Sweden. 3. Wages - Sweden. I. Title.
HD5803 .M45 1984

Meier, Bernd, 1952- Verbraucherpolitik in der Bundesrepublik Deutschland : theoretischer Bezugsrahmen, Bestandsaufnahme und Lückenanalyse / Bernd Meier. Frankfurt am Main ; New York : P. Lang, c1984. iii, 256 p. : ill. ; 21 cm. (Europäische Hochschulschriften. Reihe V, Volks- und Betriebswirtschaft, 0531-7339 . Bd. 578 = vol. 578 = 578) Bibliography: p. 223-250. Includes index. ISBN 3-8204-8404-3 (pbk.) LC Card 87-672663
1. Consumption (Economics) - Germany, West. 2. Consumers - Germany, West. I. Series: Europäische Hochschulschriften. Reihe V, Volks- und Betriebswirtschaft , Bd. 578. II. Title.
HC290.5.C6 M36x 1984

Meier, Christoph. Lebenszyklus und ökonomische Ungleichheit : eine Analyse der Einkommens- und Vermögensdynamik anhand von Längsschnittdaten / Christoph Meier. Freiburg, Schweiz : Universitätsverlag, 1983. 235 p. : ill. ; 23 cm. (Freiburger Studien zur Verteilung von Einkommen und Vermögen . Bd. 3) Bibliography: p. 227-235. ISBN 3-7278-0298-7 : LC Card 83-244050
1. Income - Longitudinal studies. 2. Income distribution - Longitudinal studies. I. Title. II. Series.
HB601 .M389 1983

Meier, Gerald M. Pioneers in development. New York , c1987. viii, 244 p. ; ISBN 0-19-520542-1 LC Card 86-23511 DDC 338.9 19
HD74 .P56 1987

Meier, Hans-Peter, 1944- Zwischen Zentren und Hinterland . Diessenhofen , c1982. 349 p. : ISBN 0-372-53017-9 : LC Card 83-129330
HC397 .Z88 1982

Meier, Henri B. The Swiss equity market . Westport, Conn. , 1985. xiv, 210 p. : ISBN 0-89930-147-9 (lib. bdg. : alk. paper) LC Card 85-12195 DDC 332.64/2494 19
HG5652 .M45 1985 ***NYPL [JLE 86-1965]***

Meier, Kenneth J., 1950- Applied statistics for public administration / Kenneth J. Meier, Jeffrey L. Brudney. Rev. ed. Monterey, Calif. : Brooks/Cole Pub. Co., c1987. xix, 460 p. ; 24 cm. Bibliography: p. 433-435. Includes index. LC Card 87-10342 DDC 350/.0001/5195 19
1. Statistics. 2. Public administration - Statistical methods. I. Brudney, Jeffrey L. II. Title.
HA29 .M46 1987

Meier, Kurt, Dr. Spitzenlasttarifierung, oekonomische Effizienz und Erhaltung der Eigenwirtschaftlichkeit : eine angewandte Studie der elektrizitätswirtschaftlichen Preisbildung / Kurt Meier. Bern : P. Haupt, c1983. viii, 202 p. : ill. ; 23 cm. (Berner Beiträge zur Nationalökonomie. Bd. 47) Bibliography: p. 194-202. ISBN 3-258-03322-6 : LC Card 84-108545
1. Electric utilities - Switzerland - Rates. I. Title. II. Series.
HD9685.S92 M45 1983

Meier, Thomas. Handwerk, Hauswerk, Heimarbeit : nicht-agrarische Tätigkeiten und Erwerbsformen in einem traditionellen Ackerbaugebiet des 18. Jahrhunderts (Zürcher Unterland) / Thomas Meier. Zürich : Chronos, c1986. 435 p., [44] p. of plates : ill. ; 21 cm. Originally presented as the author's thesis (doctoral)--Universität Zürich, Wintersemester 1985/85 [i.e. 1985/86] Bibliography: p. 418-433. ISBN 3-905278-07-3 LC Card 86-227651
1. Artisans - Switzerland - Zürich (Canton) - History - 18th century. 2. Zürich (Switzerland : Canton) - Occupations - History - 18th century. 3. Zürich (Switzerland : Canton) - Economic conditions. 4. Manpower policy, Rural - Switzerland - Zürich (Canton) - History - 18th century. I. Title.
HD2346.S92 Z875 1986

Meifort, J. (Joachim) Arbeitsbedingungen von Linienbus- und Strassenbahnfahrern der Dortmunder Stadtwerke Aktiengesellschaft / J. Meifort, H. Reiners, J. Schuh. Dortmund : Bundesanstalt für Arbeitsschutz und Unfallforschung, 1983. 137 p. : ill. ; 21 cm. (Schriftenreihe Arbeitsschutz . Nr. 33) Bibliography: p. 137. ISBN 3-88314-249-2 LC Card 83-204902
1. Transport workers - Germany (West) - Dortmund. 2. Dortmunder Stadtwerke AG. I. Reiners, H. (Hartmut). II. Schuh, J. (Jürgen). III. Series: Schriftenreihe Arbeitsschutz (Bundesanstalt für Arbeitsschutz und Unfallforschung) , Nr. 33.
HD8039.T72 G36 1983

Meigs, Robert F.
Meigs, Walter B. Accounting, the basis for business decisions /. New York , c1987. xxiii, 1059, 14 p. : ISBN 0-07-041640-0 : LC Card 86-21104 DDC 657 19
HF5635 .M49 1987

Meigs, Walter B. Financial accounting /. New York , c1987. xx, 738 p. : ISBN 0-07-041834-9 LC Card 87-3324 DDC 657 19
HF5635 .M492 1987

Meigs, Walter B.
Accounting, the basis for business decisions / Walter B. Meigs, Robert F. Meigs. 7th ed. New York : McGraw-Hill, c1987. xxiii, 1059, 14 p. : col. ill. ; 26 cm. Includes index. ISBN 0-07-041640-0 : LC Card 86-21104 DDC 657 19
1. Accounting. I. Meigs, Robert F. II. Title.
HF5635 .M49 1987

Financial accounting / Walter B. Meigs, Robert F. Meigs. Rev. 5th ed. New York : McGraw-Hill, c1987. xx, 738 p. : ill. (some col.) ; 25 cm. Includes index. ISBN 0-07-041834-9 LC Card 87-3324 DDC 657 19
1. Accounting. I. Meigs, Robert F. II. Title.
HF5635 .M492 1987

Principles of auditing /. Homewood, Ill. , 1987. xv, 724 p. : ISBN 0-256-03580-6 LC Card 86-82588 DDC 657/.45 19
HF5667 .P73 1987

Meijboom, Bert R., 1957-

Meijenfeldt, C. F. W. M. von. Gebruik van en alternatieven voor tropisch hout. 's-Gravenhage : Ministerie van Volkshuisvesting, Ruimtelijke Ordening en Milieubeheer : Overheidspublikaties [distributor], c1985. 207, [14] p. : ill. ; 30 cm. (Publikatiereeks milieubeheer . 85/24) Bibliography: p. [208]-[212] ISBN 90-346-0647-3 : LC Card 86-231435
1. Forest products industry - Tropics. 2. Forest products industry - Netherlands. I. Title. II. Series.
HD9750.8.T73 M45 1985

Meijer, H., 1904- De Deli Spoorweg Maatschappij : driekwart eeuw koloniaal spoor / door H. Meijer, met medewerking van F.A.J. Heckler. Zutphen : Walburg Pers, c1987. 152 p. : ill. ; 29 cm. Bibliography: p. 152. Includes index. ISBN 90-6011-540-6 : LC Card 87-157915
1. Deli Spoorweg Maatschappij - History. 2. Railroads - Sumatra - History. I. Heckler, F. A. J., 1912-. II. Title.
HE3340.D45 M45 1987

Meiklejohn Civil Liberties Institute. The Cold war against labor . Berkeley, CA , c1987. 2 v. (xxii, 915 p.) : ISBN 0-913876-19-4 (set); 0-913876-20-4 (set) : LC Card 87-18510 DDC 331.88/0973 19
HD6508 .C62 1987

MEILINK-ROELOFSZ, M. A. P. (MARIE ANTOINETTE PETRONELLA)
All of one company . Utrecht , 1986. 230 p. : ISBN 90-6194-036-2 (pbk.) : LC Card 86-203885 DDC 382/.06/01 19
HF483.E6 A65 1986

Meilink-Roelofsz, M. A. P. (Marie Antoinette Petronelle) All of one company . Utrecht , 1986. 230 p. : ISBN 90-6194-036-2 (pbk.) : LC Card 86-203885 DDC 382/.06/01 19
HF483.E6 A65 1986

Meimberg, Rudolf. Zur Vertretbarkeit von Störungen der Marktwirtschaft aus ideellen und sonstigen Gründen / von Rudolf Meimberg. Berlin : Duncker & Humblot, c1983. 62 p. ; 24 cm. (Volkswirtschaftliche Schriften. Heft 327) Includes bibliographical references. ISBN 3-428-05331-1 LC Card 83-206548 DDC 338.9 19
1. Industry and state. 2. Laissez-faire. I. Title. II. Series.
HD3611 .M42 1983

Mein Vaterland ist international : internationale

illustrierte Geschichte des 1. Mai, 1886 bis heute : Katalogbuch zur gleichnamigen Ausstellung der Neuen Gesellschaft für Bildende Kunst Berlin (NGBK) in Zusammenarbeit mit den Ruhrfestspielen Recklinghausen / Udo Achten, Matthias Reichelt, Reinhard Schultz in Zusammenarbeit mit Kai Reschke ; [Herausgeber, Neue Gesellschaft für Bildende Kunst e.V. ; Übersetzungen, Christiane Barckhausen-Canale ... et al.].1. Aufl. Oberhausen : Asso, 1986. 331 p. : ill. (some col.) ; 29 cm. Ill. on lining papers. ISBN 3-921541-62-X LC Card 86-224091
1. May Day (Labor holiday) - History - Exhibitions. I. Achten, Udo, 1943-. II. Reichelt, Matthias. III. Schultz, Reinhard. IV. Neue Gesellschaft für Bildende Kunst. V. Ruhrfestspiele Recklinghausen.
HD7791 .M45 1986

Meine Ehre ist nicht die Eure! . Tschudin, Paul, 1904- Basel , 1986. 217 p. ; ISBN 3-85990-069-2 LC Card 87-137660 DDC 331.88/092/4 B 19
HD6772.5.T74 A3 1986

Meinlschmidt, Gerhard. Statistische Methoden zur Berechnung von Preisniveauindizes integrierter Wirtschaftsräume / von Gerhard Meinlschmidt. Göttingen : Vandenhoeck & Ruprecht, c1985. 142 p. : ill. ; 25 cm. (Angewandte Statistik und Ökonometrie. Heft 28 =) Summary in English, French, and German. Bibliography: p. [129]-142. ISBN 3-525-11262-9 LC Card 85-213565
1. Index numbers (Economics). 2. Purchasing power parity - Mathematical models. 3. Price indexes. I. Series: Angewandte Statistik und Ökonometrie, Heft 28. II. Title.
HB225 .M45 1985

O meio-norte /. Melo, Mário Lacerda de. Recife , 1983. 474 p., [1] folded leaf of plates : LC Card 84-231900
HC188.N6 M45 1983

Meirelles Filho, João Carlos, 1960- Amazônia--o que fazer? / João Meirelles Filho. São Paulo : Cia. Editora Nacional, 1986. 85 p., [1] folded leaf of plates : maps ; 19 cm. (Coleção Portasabertas . v. 7) Cover title: Amazônia--o que fazer por ela? Bibliography: p. 84-85. LC Card 86-233275
1. Natural resources - Amazon River Valley Region. 2. Land settlement - Amazon River Valley Region. 3. Human ecology - Amazon River Valley Region. I. Title. II. Title: Amazônia--o que fazer por ela?.
HC187.5 .M45 1986

Meiritz, Wolfram. Eignungsorientierte Personaleinsatzplanung : ein Lösungsvorschlag auf der Basis der Theorie unscharfer Mengen und der Profilvergleichsmethode / Wolfram Meiritz. Frankfurt am Main ; New York : P. Lang, c1984. xv, 304 p. : ill. ; 21 cm. (Europäische Hochschulschriften. Reihe V, Volks- und Betriebswirtschaft, 0531-7339 . Bd. 491 = vol. 491 = vol. 491) Originally presented as the author's thesis (doctoral)--Rheinisch-Westfälische Technische Hochschule Aachen. Bibliography: p. 288-304. ISBN 3-8204-5164-1 LC Card 85-198624
1. Personnel management - Mathematical models. I. Series: Europäische Hochschulschriften. Reihe V, Volks- und Betriebswirtschaft , Bd. 491. II. Title.
HF5549 .M343 1984

Meissner, Hans-Günther.
Werbung und gesellschaftlicher Wandel über die kommunikativen Voraussetzungen technischen, ökonomischen und sozialen Fortschritts : Marketing Anzeige, Oktober, 1979 / Referent, Hans Günter Meissner. [Berlin] : Axel Springer ; Hamburg : Anzufordern bei Bild Anzeigenleitung Verkauf, [1979] 23, [4] leaves ; 30 cm. Paper of a conference of the Bild-Zeitung in cooperation with Marketing Anzeigen, presented on Oct. 9th, 1979. Bibliography: leaves [24]-[25] LC Card 84-119751
1. Advertising - Congresses. 2. Social change - Congresses. I. Marketing Anzeigen (Firm). II. Bild-Zeitung. III. Title.
HF5802.5 .M45 1979

Zukunftsaspekte der anwendungsorientierten Betriebswirtschaftslehre . Stuttgart , c1986. xii, 641 p. : ISBN 3-7910-0402-6 LC Card 86-202268
HD35 .Z84 1986

Meissner, Werner, 1937- Weiche Modelle und iterative Schätzung : eine Anwendung auf Probleme der neuen politischen Ökonomie / Werner Meissner, Marion Uhle-Fassing. Frankfurt ; New York : Campus Verlag, c1982. 114 p. : ill. ; 21 cm. (Campus Forschung. Bd. 293) "Diese Arbeit ist der Abschlussbericht zum Projekt 'Modelling in complex situations with soft information' (Az.: 11 2519)"--T.p. verso. Includes bibliographical references. ISBN 3-593-33105-5 : LC Card 83-126780
1. Econometrics. 2. Economics - Mathematical models. I. Uhle-Fassing, Marion. II. Title.
HB141 .M415 1982

Mejía, José Manuel. Promoción agraria, para quién? . Lima, Perú , 1980. 162 p. ; ***NYPL [JLD 86-3547]***

Mejía, Leonardo. Ecuador, pasado y presente /. Quito, Ecuador , 1982. 273 p. ; LC Card 83-156158
HC202 .E28 1982

Mejías, Tulio. La coordinación como consecuencia de razones y pasiones : el caso de las empresas de Guayana / Tulio Mejías, Ramón Piñango. Caracas, Venezuela : Instituto de Estudios Superiores de Administración, c1983. 37, [2] p. : ill. ; 29 cm. (Papeles de trabajo IESA . PTI-83-2) "Este trabajo fue preparado para el III Simposio sobre Desarrollo Organizacional ... 26 al 28 de octubre de 1983"--P. [iii] Bibliography: p. [39] ISBN 980-217-002-X LC Card 86-193647
1. Industrial management - Case studies. I. Piñango, Ramón. II. Title. III. Series.
HD37.S66 M37 1983

Mekaaninen metsäteollisuus .
(2) Juvonen, Risto. Sahateollisuus /. [Helsinki] . 290 p. : ISBN 951-859-690-5 LC Card 86-231276
HD9765.F4 J68 1986

Mekaniseringsøkonomi på enkeltbruk /. Hegrenes, Agnar. Oslo , 1985. 175 p. : ISBN 82-7077-028-0 LC Card 86-180961
HD2012 .H44 1985

MEL MOUNTAINS REGION (RIO GRANDE DO NORTE, BRAZIL) - RURAL CONDITIONS - CASE STUDIES.
PDRI-Serra do Mel . Natal , 1981. 52 leaves : LC Card 84-246626
HD499.M45 P37 1981

Mélanges Robert Laurent : études économiques et rurales offertes en hommage par ses collègues et anciens étudiants / P. Barral ... [et al.]. Montpellier : Centre d'histoire contemporaine du Languedoc méditerranéen et du Roussillon, Université Paul Valéry, 1980. xxi, 296 p. : port. ; 21 cm. Cover title: Hommage à Robert Laurent. "Bibliographie des travaux de Robert Laurent": p. [i]-iii. Includes bibliographical references. LC Card 83-151672
1. France - Economic conditions. 2. France - Rural conditions. 3. Laurent, Robert, 1908-. I. Laurent, Robert. II. Barral, Pierre. III. Centre d'histoire contemporaine du Languedoc méditerranéen et du Roussillon. IV. Title: Hommage à Robert Laurent.
HC273 .M43 1980

Melbourne and Metropolitan Board of Works. Statistical Division. Comparative local statistics / Melbourne Statistical Division. 2nd ed. [Melbourne] : Melbourne and Metropolitan Board of Works, [1983] 135, [2] p. : ill. ; 21 x 30 cm. "February 1983." Bibliography: p. [137] LC Card 86-228235 DDC 319.45/1 19
1. Melbourne Metropolitan Area (Vic.) - Statistics. I. Title.
HA3008.M45 M45 1983

MELBOURNE METROPOLITAN AREA (VIC.) - STATISTICS.
Melbourne and Metropolitan Board of Works. Statistical Division. Comparative local statistics /. [Melbourne] [1983] 135, [2] p. : LC Card 86-228235 DDC 319.45/1 19
HA3008.M45 M45 1983

Melby, Kari. Avdem, Anna Jorunn, 1952- Oppe først og sist i seng . Oslo , 1985. 190 p. : ISBN 82-00-07512-5 LC Card 86-175305
HD8039.H842 N82 1985

Melcher, Horst. Aufbau eines Controllingsystems für Consulting-Unternehmen / Horst Melcher. Darmstadt : Toeche-Mittler, c1982. 276 p. : ill. ; 23 cm. (Controlling-Praxis . CP 5) Bibliography: p. [251]-269. Includes index. ISBN 3-87820-052-8 LC Card 83-110639
1. Business consultants. 2. Industrial project management. 3. Strategic planning. 4. Controllership. I. Title. II. Series.
HD69.C6 M45 1982

Meleghy, Gyula, 1955- Die Vermittlerrolle der Banken bei deutschen Investitionen in Nord- und Mittelamerika bis zum Ersten Weltkrieg / vorgelegt von Gyula Meleghy. [Köln? : s.n.], 1983 (Köln : W. Kleikamp) 330 p. : ill. ; 21 cm. Thesis (doctoral)--Universität zu Köln. Bibliography: p. 310-330. LC Card 85-229675
1. Banks and banking, German - United States - History. 2. Banks and banking, German - Canada - History. 3. Banks and banking, German - Mexico - History. 4. Investments, German - United States - History. 5. Investments, German - Canada - History. 6. Investments, German - Mexico - History. I. Title.
HG3052 .M45 1983

Meletes gia tēn agrotikē oikonomia .
(14) Mēliakos, Dēm. Iōan. To exōteriko emporio portokaliōn tēs Hellados /. Athēna , 1984. 176 p. ; LC Card 86-201864
HD9259.O8 G85 1984

(15) Baltas, Nik. K. Chrēmatodotēsē ependyseōn tou agrotikou tomea . Athēna , 1984. 142 p. ; LC Card 86-201892
HD2055.5 .B35 1984

(20) Delēs, Dēmētrēs I. Hē anaptyxē tēs hellēnikēs geōrgias . Athēna , 1985. 3 v. in 2 : LC Card 86-203175
HD2055.5 .D44 1985

(9) Baltas, N. K. Empeirikē diereunēsē tēs apotamieutikēs symperiphoras kai tēs zētēsēs katatheseōn apo tous idiōtes /. Athēna [1979] 128 p. ; LC Card 86-203196
HG3250.5.A6 B34 1979

Meletes neoellēnikēs historias .
([1]) Panagiōtopoulos, Vasilēs, 1932- Plēthysmos kai oikismoi tēs Peloponnēsou . Athēna , 1985. 414 p. : LC Card 86-207132
HB3632.5.P45 P36 1985

(2) Kremmydas, Vasilēs. Hellēnikē nautilia, 1776-1835 /. Athēna , 1985-<1986. v. <1-2 > : LC Card 86-211031
HE872.5 .K74 1985

Meletes oikonomikēs historias .
(7) Papathanasopoulos, Kōnstantinos, 1950- Hellēnikē emporikē nautalia, 1833-1856 . Athēna , 1983. 470 p., [32] p. of plates : LC Card 83-237694
HE872.5 .P36 1983

Melgar, Alicia. Distribución del ingreso en el Uruguay / Alicia Melgar. Montevideo : Centro Latinoamericano de Economía Humana, 1981. 87 p. ; 28 cm. (Serie Investigaciones. no. 18) Includes bibliographical references. LC Card 86-160100
1. Income distribution - Uruguay. I. Series: Serie Investigaciones (Centro Latinoamericano de Economía Humana) , no. 18. II. Title.
HC235.I5 M448 1981

Melguizo, Angel. Junta de Andalucía. Grupo de Trabajo 14, Planificación Económica de las Corporaciones Locales y Comarcalización. Plan económico de Andalucía, 1984-1986 /. [Andalucía] , 1983. 133 p. ; ISBN 84-505-1243-3 LC Card 86-223752
HJ1249.A4 J86 1983

Melia, Jinx.
[Why Jenny can't lead]
Breaking into the boardroom : when talent and hard work aren't enough / Jinx Melia. New York : Putnam, [1987] c1986. 167 p. ; 23 cm. Reprint. Originally published under title: Why Jenny can't lead. 1986. ISBN 0-399-13326-7 LC Card 87-7007 DDC 658.4/09/024042 19
1. Women executives. 2. Sex role in the work environment. 3. Power (Social sciences). I. Title.
HD6054.3 .M45 1987

Mēliakos, Dēm. Iōan. To exōteriko emporio portokaliōn tēs Hellados / Dēm.Iōan. Mēliakou. Athēna : Agrotikē Trapeza tēs Hellados, Dieuthynsē Meletōn & Programmatismou, 1984. 176 p. ; 24 cm. (Meletes gia tēn agrotikē oikonomia . 14) Bibliography: p. 170-171. LC Card 86-201864
1. Orange industry - Greece. I. Title. II. Series.
HD9259.O8 G85 1984

Melicher, Ronald W. Unger, Maurice Albert, 1917- Real estate finance /. Cincinnati , c1984. vi, 426 p. : ISBN 0-538-19630-0 LC Card 83-61343 DDC 332.7/2 19
HG2040 .U53 1984 ***NYPL [JLE 86-4718]***

Melin, Leif. Kommunerna och näringslivet . Stockholm , c1984. 173 p. : ISBN

91-38-90331-8 : LC Card 84-253511
HC375 .K655 1984

Melišek, František. Ekonomický rast a štrukturálne zmeny v socialistickej ekonomike / František Melišek, Vladimír Mokrý. 1. vyd. Bratislava : Veda, vydavatelstvo Slovenskej akadémie vied, 1980. 175 p. : ill. ; 24 cm. Summary in French, German, and Russian. Includes index. Bibliography: p. 158-[163] LC Card 82-464724 DDC 338.9 19
1. Consumption (Economics). 2. Macroeconomics. I. Mokrý, Vladimír. II. Title.
HD84.5 .M379 1980 ***NYPL [*QT 87-1737]***

Mella Márquez, Manuel. La Izquierda europea . Barcelona , 1985. 282 p. ; ISBN 84-307-7438-6 LC Card 86-186087
HX238.5 .I97 1985 ***NYPL [JLD 86-4090]***

Mella, Piero. Contabilità delle aziende divise / Piero Mella. [Milan] : IPSOA, c1983. 281 p. : ill. ; 30 cm. (Contabilità e bilancio) IPSOA informatica Bibliography: p. 273-276. Includes index. ISBN 88-21-70036-4 LC Card 85-151879
1. Conglomerate corporations - Italy - Accounting. I. Title. II. Series.
HF5686.C7 M427 1983

Mellár, Tamás. Az érték átalakulása termelési árrá, avagy, Az un. transzformációs probléma / Mellár Tamás. Pécs : Pécsi Janus Pannonius Tudományegyetem Közgazdaságtudományi Kar, 1982. 55 p. ; 21 cm. (Dolgozatok a közgazdaságtudományok köréből, 0209-9187) Bibliography: p. 54-55. LC Card 83-179021
1. Value. 2. Prices. 3. Surplus value. I. Title. II. Title: Transzformációs probléma. III. Series.
HB203 .M44 1982

Den mellemamerikanske drøm . Lohmann, Jens. [Copenhagen] , c1984. 184 p. : ISBN 87-7456-194-4 LC Card 84-193120
HC141 .L64 1984

Meller, Patricio. Una revisión de políticas de empleo para América Latina / Patricio Meller, Alejandra Mizala. Santiago, Chile : Corporación de Investigaciones Económicas para Latinoamérica, 1981. 72 leaves ; 27 cm. (Notas técnicas . no. 46) Bibliography: leaves 67-72. LC Card 83-182110
1. Manpower policy - Latin America. 2. Wage-price policy - Latin America. I. Mizala, Alejandra. II. Title. III. Series.
HD5730.5.A6 M44 1981

Mello, Maria Regina Ciparrone. Marsiglia, Cecília. S/A Central Elétrica Rio Claro /. São Paulo , 1986. 105 p. : LC Card 87-404945 DDC 363.6/2/098161 19
HD9685.B83 C4886 1986

Mello, Zélia Maria Cardoso de. Metamorfoses da riqueza, São Paulo, 1845-1895 : contribuição ao estudo da passagem da economia mercantilescravista à economia exportadora capitalista / Zélia Maria Cardoso de Mello. São Paulo : Editora Hucitec : Prefeitura do Município de São Paulo, Secretaria Municipal de Cultura, 1985. 188 p. : ill. ; 21 cm. (Estudos históricos) Spine title: Metamorfoses da riqueza. Bibliography: p. 179-188. LC Card 85-207635
1. Wealth - Brazil - São Paulo (State) - History - 19th century. 2. Property - Brazil - São Paulo (State) - History - 19th century. 3. Landowners - Brazil - São Paulo (State) - History - 19th century. 4. Slaveholders - Brazil - São Paulo (State) - History - 19th century. I. Title. II. Title: Metamorfoses da riqueza. III. Series: Coleção Estudos históricos.
HC188.S3 M49 1985

Mellor, John Williams, 1928- Accelerating food production in Sub-Saharan Africa /. Baltimore , c1987. xix, 417 p. ; ISBN 0-8018-3390-6 (alk. paper) LC Card 86-10684 DDC 338.1/9/67 19
HD2117 .A33 1987 ***NYPL [JLE 87-1366]***

Melman, Seymour. Profits without production / Seymour Melman. Philadelphia : University of Pennsylvania Press, 1987, c1983. p. cm. Reprint. Originally published: 1st ed. New York : Knopf, 1983. Bibliography: p. Includes index. ISBN 0-8122-1258-4 (pbk.) LC Card 87-13796 DDC 338.0973 19
1. Industrial management - United States. 2. Industrial productivity - United States. 3. United States - Industries. I. Title.
HD70.U5 M425 1987

Mel'nik, B. P. (Boris Pavlovich) Baskin, A. I. (Arkadiĭ Isaakovich) Planirovanie potrebnosti v material'nykh resursakh na predpriiatii /. Kiev , 1983. 48 p. ; LC Card 83-243488
HD39.5 .B37 1983

Mel'nik, L. G. (Leonid Gerasimovich) V bitvakh za sovetskuiu Ukrainu . Kiev , 1985. 172 p. ; LC Card 85-170194
HC337.U53 D48 1985

Mel'nik, M. V. (Margarita Viktorovna) Opyt khoziaĭstvovaniia v ob"edineniiakh promyshlennosti sotsialisticheskikh stran /. Moskva , 1985. 157 p. : LC Card 87-152292
HD70.E7 O69 1985

Mel'nik, P. V. (Pavel Vasil'evich) Androsov, V. I. (Vasiliĭ Ivanovich) Effektivnost' kapital'nogo stroitel'stva v torgovle /. Moskva , 1980. 213 p. ; LC Card 81-132839
HC340.C3 A65 1980

Melo, M. Teixeira de. A economia portuguesa após o 25 de abril / M. Teixeira de Melo. Queluz [Portugal] : Literal, [1978] 149 p. ; 21 cm. LC Card 79-104785
1. Portugal - Economic conditions - 1974-. 2. Economic indicators - Portugal. I. Title.
HC392 .M45 1978

Melo, Mário Lacerda de. O meio-norte / Mário Lacerda de Melo. Recife : Ministério do Interior, Superintendência do Desenvolvimento do Nordeste, Superintendência Adjunta de Planejamento, Coordenação de Planejamento Regional, Divisão de Política Espacial, 1983. 474 p., [1] folded leaf of plates : ill. (some col.) ; 23 cm. (Série Estudos regionais . 9) Bibliography: p. 463-474. LC Card 84-231900
1. Brazil, Northeast - Economic conditions. 2. Agriculture - Economic aspects - Brazil, Northeast. I. Title. II. Series.
HC188.N6 M45 1983

Melo, Valdir Ramalho de. Seleção de agregados monetários / Valdir Ramalho de Melo, Roberto Rezende Rocha. [Brasília] : Banco Central do Brasil, [1981] 136 p. : ill. ; 21 cm. Cover title. Includes bibliographies. LC Card 85-161532
1. Monetary policy - Brazil - Econometric models. 2. Money supply - Brazil - Econometric models. 3. Demand for money - Brazil - Econometric models. 4. Economic stabilization - Brazil - Econometric models. I. Rocha, Roberto Rezende. II. Title.
HG835 .M45 1981

Melrose, Dianna. Nicaragua : the threat of a good example? / by Dianna Melrose. Oxford, U.K. : Oxfam ; Boston, MA : Distributed by Oxfam America, 1985. 68 p. : ill. ; 21 cm. "Oxfam Public Affairs Unit"--Cover. Distributor from label on p. [2] of cover. Bibliography: p. 68. ISBN 0-85598-070-2 (pbk.) : LC Card 87-116239 DDC 338.91/41/07285 19
1. Economic assistance - Nicaragua. 2. Nicaragua - Economic conditions - 1979-. 3. Nicaragua - Social conditions - 1979-. 4. Economic assistance, British - Nicaragua. 5. Oxfam America. I. Oxfam. Public Affairs Unit. II. Title.
HC146 .M45 1985

Melrose, John. BUCOMCO : a business communication simulation / John Melrose, Krisan K. Melrose.2nd ed. Chicago : Science Research Associates, c1987. vii, 187 p. : ill. ; 28 cm. ISBN 0-574-20070-3 (pbk.) : LC Card 86-31585 DDC 651.7/4 19
1. Communication in management - Simulation methods. 2. Business report writing. 3. Oral communication. I. Melrose, Krisan K. II. Title.
HF5718 .M44 1987

Melrose, Krisan K. Melrose, John. BUCOMCO . Chicago , c1987. vii, 187 p. : ISBN 0-574-20070-3 (pbk.) : LC Card 86-31585 DDC 651.7/4 19
HF5718 .M44 1987

Mel'tiukhova, N. N. (Nadezhda Nikolaevna) Odintsova, G. S. (Galina Sergeevna) Organizatsionnoe proektirovanie i planirovanie razvitiia sistem upravleniia /. Kiev , 1986. 158, [2] p. : LC Card 87-162923
HD2876 .O35 1986

Meltz, Noah M. Sharing the work : an analysis of the issues in worksharing and jobsharing / Noah M. Meltz, Frank Reid, and Gerald S. Swartz. Toronto ; Buffalo : University of Toronto Press, 1981. viii, 90 p. : ill. ; 22 cm. Bibliography: p. [89]-90. ISBN 0-8020-2383-5
1. Work sharing. 2. Job sharing. I. Reid, Frank. II. Swartz, Gerald S. III. Title. ***NYPL [JLD 82-233]***

Melzer, Manfred. The East German economy /. London , New York , c1987. 328 p. : ISBN 0-7099-1469-5 LC Card 87-17163 DDC 338.9431 19
HC290.78 .E23 1987

MÉM Mérnök- és Vezetőtovábbképző Intézet. Gyenes, Antal. Szövetkezetipolitikai, szövetkezetelméleti ismeretek /. Budapest , 1974. 217 p. ; LC Card 87-113832
HD3492.5.A4 G94 1974

Memamuluri meurneobis kapitalisturi evoluc'ia Agmosavlet' Sak'art'veloši /. Nac'vlišvili, N. T'bilisi , 1971. 107 p. ; LC Card 86-168887
HC337.G38 N33 1971

MEMBERSHIP CAMPAIGNS.
Trenbeth, Richard P. The membership mystique . Ambler, PA , c1986. xi, 280 p. : ISBN 0-930807-01-4 (pbk.) LC Card 85-70785 DDC 060/.68 19
HG177 .T74 1986

MEMBERSHIP CORPORATIONS. see **CORPORATIONS, NONPROFIT.**

The membership mystique . Trenbeth, Richard P. Ambler, PA , c1986. xi, 280 p. : ISBN 0-930807-01-4 (pbk.) LC Card 85-70785 DDC 060/.68 19
HG177 .T74 1986

Memmott, Jeffery L. (Jeffery Lynn) McFarland, William F. New approaches to project ranking . College Station, Tex. , Springfield, Va. [1985] xvii, 116 p. : LC Card 86-622422 DDC 380.5 s 388.1/12/09764 19
HE203 .T43 no. 337-1F HE356.T4

Memo (Aarhus universitet. Økonomisk institut) .
(1986-1) Schneider, Friedrich. The development of the shadow economies for Denmark, Norway, and Sweden . Aarhus, Denmark [1986] 46 p. : LC Card 86-215193 DDC 381 19
HD2346.S29 S35 1986

(1986-3) Holler, Manfred Joseph, 1946- Trading markets and entry costs /. Aarhus, Denmark [1986] 15 p. ; LC Card 86-219580 DDC 382.1 19
HD2756.5 .H64 1986

(1986-4) Paldam, Martin. How much does one percent of growth change the unemployment? . Aarhus, Denmark [1986] 35 p. : LC Card 86-221448 DDC 331.13/7 19
HD5707.5 .P34 1986

Memo (Ma'had al-Takhṭīṭ al-Qawmī (Egypt)) .
(no. 1415) Nakhla, Afaf Fouad. Update the transportation problem /. Cairo [1985- v. <1 > ; LC Card 87-401510 DDC 361.6/0962 s 380.5/24 19
HD82 .C23 no. 1415 HE199.A2

Mémoire de l'AMEEC à la Commission parlementaire sur l'énergie. "L'Energie, levier de développement économique" . [Ottawa?] [1983] 30 leaves ; LC Card 85-128816
HD9685.C3 Q4425 1983

Mémoire pour demain.
Marrey, Bernard. Un capitalisme idéal /. Paris , c1984. 236 p., [24] p. of plates : ISBN 2-86215-060-6 : LC Card 84-252196 DDC 338.7/6413374/0944 19
HD9200.F74 M356 1984
NYPL [JLD 87-1579]

Mémoire présenté à la Commission élue permanente de l'énergie et des ressources de l'Assemblée nationale du Québec /. Esso Petroleum Canada (Firm) Québec [1983] 44 leaves : LC Card 85-143347 DDC 338.2/7282/09714 19
HD9574.C23 Q43 1983

Mémoire sur le projet de la centrale Delaney. Le Projet Delaney . [St-Raymond, Québec] [1983] 76 leaves in various foliations : LC Card 84-224364
HD9685.C3 Q456 1983

Mémoires de l'Institut des hautes études chinoises .
(v. 28) Pasquet, Sylvie. L'évolution du système postal . Paris , c1986. 290 p. : ISBN 2-85757-038-4 LC Card 87-164960
HE7286.Y8 P37 1986

Les mémoires de Marcel Péroche, "sénateur" du rail /. Péroche, Marcel, 1907- Paris , c1984. 256 p., [8] p. of plates : ISBN 2-7013-0556-X : LC Card 84-206923
HD8039.R322 F87 1984

Mémoires du Centre d'études coréennes .
(v. 4) Yu, Wŏn-dong. Le déclin des marchands privilégiés en Corée . [Paris] , 1984. 104 p. : ISBN 2-905358-03-3 : LC Card 85-131336
HF3830.5 .Y78 1984

Mémoires du Cercle amical des P.T.T. de Lille, Section Histoire, 0248-9902 .
(t. 4) Histoire de la poste et des télécommunications dans la région Nord-Pas-de-Calais . [Lille] , c1983. 156 p. : LC Card 86-115052
HE6986.N67 H57 1983

MEMOIRS. see **BIOGRAPHY.**

Memoirs of Alexander Spitzmüller, Freiherr von Harmersbach (1862-1953) . Spitzmüller, Alexander, 1862-1953. Boulder , New York , 1987. xi, 327 p., [5] p. of plates : ISBN 0-88033-124-0 LC Card 87-80511 DDC 332.3/2/0924 B 19
HG1552.S65 A3 1987

Memorandum by the Minister of Public Works and Land Affairs. Memorandum deur die Minister van Openbare Werke en Grondsake . Pretoria [1985] 16 p. ; ISBN 0-621-09435-8 : LC Card 86-140379
HD4350.5 .M45 1985

Memorandum deur die Minister van Openbare Werke en Grondsake : waarin besonderhede uiteengesit word van die bouprogram vir 1985-86 ten opsigte van program 6 (geboue en strukture) van begrotingspos 11 van die Staatsinkomsterekening / Departement van Openbare Werke en Grondsake = Memorandum by the Minister of Public Works and Land Affairs : setting out particulars of the building programme for 1985-86 in respect of programme 6 (buildings and structures) of vote 11 of the State Revenue Account / Department of Public Works and Land Affairs. Pretoria : Verkrygbaar by die Staatsdrukker, [1985] 16 p. ; 30 cm. Cover title. Errata slip inserted. ISBN 0-621-09435-8 : LC Card 86-140379
1. South Africa - Public works - Finance. I. South Africa. Dept. of Public Works and Land Affairs. II. Title: Memorandum by the Minister of Public Works and Land Affairs.
HD4350.5 .M45 1985

Memorandum (Göteborgs universitet. Nationalekonomiska institutionen) .
(nr. 100) Albrecht, James W. Job search and the transition to employment . Göteborg [1986] 38 leaves ; LC Card 87-158051 DDC 331.12/8 19
HF5382.7 .A43 1986

(nr. 94) Klevmarken, N. Anders. Höj och sänk pensionsåldern /. Göteborg [1985?] 9 leaves : LC Card 86-195492
HD7203 .K57 1985

Memorandum 'vierundachtzig. Memorandum '84 . Köln , c1984. 475 p. : ISBN 3-7609-0883-7 : LC Card 85-128558
HC286.7 .M465 1984

Memorandum '84 : gegen soziale Zerstörung durch Unternehmerherrschaft : qualitatives Wachstum, 35-Stunden-Woche, Vergesellschaftung : mit den Sonderbeiträgen, Vorlauf der Akkumulation--Schwäche des Verbrauchs : zu den Ursachen der Wirtschaftskrise, Bankenpolitik in der Krise : Im Anhang das Sondermemorandum, Zerstört der Streik den Aufschwung? / Arbeitsgruppe Alternative Wirtschaftspolitik. Köln : Pahl-Rugenstein, c1984. 475 p. : 2 ill. ; 19 cm. (Kleine Bibliothek. 330) Includes bibliography. ISBN 3-7609-0883-7 : LC Card 85-128558
1. Germany, West - Economic policy - 1974-. 2. Germany, West - Full employment policies. 3. Thirty-five hour week - Germany (West). 4. Industry and state - Germany, West. 5. Industrial management - Germany (West) - Employee participation. I. Arbeitsgruppe Alternative Wirtschaftspolitik. II. Title: Memorandum 'vierundachtzig.
HC286.7 .M465 1984

Memoria. Quintas reuniones técnicas de información, evaluación y perspectivas de las empresas /. [Caracas, Venezuela] [1984?] 245 p. : LC Card 87-404408 DDC 338.8/6/09877 19
HD2843.Z75 C467 1984

Memoria /. Reunión Nacional para el Desarrollo de la Industria, el Comercio, la Distribución y Otros Servicios (1981 : Mexico City, Mexico) [Mexico City] , 1981. 428 p., [4] folded leaves of plates : LC Card 84-228700
HD3616.M42 R46 1981

Memoria al Congreso. Colombia. Ministerio de Comunicaciones. Una revolución en las comunicaciones . [Bogotá] 1986. 307 p., [5] leaves of plates : LC Card 87-401464 DDC 384/.09861 19
HE8011 .C65 1986

Memoria del ciclo de conferencias de Mesa Redonda sobre la Carta de Punta del Este /. Mesa Redonda sobre la Carta de Punta del Este (1961 : Universidad Nacional Autónoma de México) México , 1962. 224 p. : LC Card 85-105213
HC125 .M48 1961

Memoria del Seminario Estrategia de Desarrollo en Condiciones de Oferta Abundante de Energía Eléctrica . Seminario Estrategia de Desarrollo en Condiciones de Oferta Abundante de Energía Eléctrica (1980 : Asunción, Paraguay) Asunción, Paraguay [s.l.] , 1980. 165 p., [18] leaves of plates : LC Card 83-169471 DDC 363.6/2 19
HD9685.P32 S45 1980 ***NYPL [JLE 87-995]***

Memoria que la Junta Departamental del Callao eleva al Congreso de 1887. Callao : Impr. de "El Callao", 1887. 23 p. ; 22 cm. LC Card 83-191762
1. Finance, Public - Peru - Callao (Province). I. Callao (Peru : Province). Junta Departamental.
HJ979.C34 M45 1887

Memoria relativa a las cuentas generales del estado, 1935-1960 /. Spain. Tribunal de Cuentas. Madrid , 1964. 221 p. ; LC Card 85-104523
HJ1244 .S72 1964

Memorias de la Real Academia de Ciencias y Artes de Barcelona .
(31 época, núm. 801) Iglésies, Josep, 1902- El moviment de població de les comarques de la Catalunya de sobirania francesa en el curs dels segles XIX i XX /. Barcelona , 1979. 63 p. ; LC Card 81-120813
HB3620.C3 I325 1979

Memórias de um postalista /. Penteado, Jacob. São Paulo [1963] 199 p., [8] p. of plates : LC Card 85-134575
HE6834.P46 A3 1963

Memorias del Ministerio de Comunicaciones, 1982-1986. Colombia. Ministerio de Comunicaciones. Una revolución en las comunicaciones . [Bogotá] 1986. 307 p., [5] leaves of plates : LC Card 87-401464 DDC 384/.09861 19
HE8011 .C65 1986

Memorias del primer ministro obrero . Alvarez España, Waldo. La Paz, Bolivia , 1986. 300 p., [6] leaves of plates : LC Card 87-403477 DDC 331.88/0984 19
HD6608.5.A55 A3 1986

Memorias del Seminario de Operaciones Internacionales /. Seminario de Operaciones Internacionales (1981 : Quito, Ecuador) Quito, Ecuador , 1981. 156 p., [2] p. of plates : LC Card 86-174597
HF1519 .S46 1981

Memórias doces e amargas de um fabricante de açúcar /. Pimentel, José Graciliano Alves, 1903- Recife , 1980 (Recife, Pernambuco : Editora Universitária da Univ. Fed. de Pernambuco) 172 p. ; LC Card 86-158546
HD8039.S86 B755 1980

Memphis in the Great Depression /. Biles, Roger, 1950- Knoxville , c1986. 174 p. : ISBN 0-87049-497-X (alk. paper) : LC Card 85-22575 DDC 330.9768/19 19
HC108.M417 B55 1986 ***NYPL [JLD 87-34]***

MEMPHIS (TENN.) - ECONOMIC CONDITIONS.
Biles, Roger, 1950- Memphis in the Great Depression /. Knoxville , c1986. 174 p. : ISBN 0-87049-497-X (alk. paper) : LC Card 85-22575 DDC 330.9768/19 19
HC108.M417 B55 1986 ***NYPL [JLD 87-34]***

MEMPHIS (TENN.) - OFFICIALS AND EMPLOYEES.
Faist, Thomas, 1959- Soziale Schliessung in rassistisch gespaltenen Arbeitsmärkten . Frankfurt am Main , New York , c1986. 161 p. ; ISBN 3-8204-9525-8 LC Card 87-407927 DDC 331.89/28136372/0976819 19
HD5325.S2572 1968 .M46 1986

MEMPHIS (TENN.) - POLITICS AND GOVERNMENT.
Biles, Roger, 1950- Memphis in the Great Depression /. Knoxville , c1986. 174 p. : ISBN 0-87049-497-X (alk. paper) : LC Card 85-22575 DDC 330.9768/19 19
HC108.M417 B55 1986 ***NYPL [JLD 87-34]***

MEMPHIS (TENN.) - RACE RELATIONS.
Faist, Thomas, 1959- Soziale Schliessung in rassistisch gespaltenen Arbeitsmärkten . Frankfurt am Main , New York , c1986. 161 p. ; ISBN 3-8204-9525-8 LC Card 87-407927 DDC 331.89/28136372/0976819 19
HD5325.S2572 1968 .M46 1986

MEN - DISEASES - PSYCHOSOMATIC ASPECTS.
Witkin-Lanoil, Georgia. The male stress syndrome . New York , c1986. 246 p. ; ISBN 0-937858-59-5 LC Card 85-61815 DDC 155.9 19
BF575.S75 W59 1986 ***NYPL [JFD 86-5693]***

Men, money, and power . Toole, John H. Missoula, Mont. , c1986. xiv, 97 p. : ISBN 0-87842-210-2 LC Card 86-23569 DDC 332.1/224/0978685 19
HG2613.M634 F5737 1986

Men morsomt har det været /. Juncker, Flemming, 1904- [Copenhagen] , c1983. 423 p., [8] p. of plates : ISBN 87-00-54643-7 : LC Card 84-109657
HD9765.D42 J85 1983

MEN - PSYCHOLOGY.
The Psychology of men . New York , c1986. x, 310 p. ; ISBN 0-465-06718-2 LC Card 85-48022 DDC 155.3/32 19
BF692.5 .P78 1986 ***NYPL [JFE 86-2975]***

Sayers, Janet. Sexual contradictions . London , New York, NY , 1986. x, 214 p. : ISBN 0-422-78780-9 LC Card 85-27948 DDC 155.3/3 19
BF692.2 .S29 1986 ***NYPL [JFD 86-5840]***

Stechert, Kathryn B. Sweet success . New York , London , c1986. xiii, 224 p. ; ISBN 0-02-614380-1 LC Card 85-30916 DDC 650.1/024/042 19
HD6053 .S724 1986 ***NYPL [JLD 86-2435]***

Stechert, Kathryn B. [Sweet success.] On your own terms . New York , 1987, c1986. xvi, 314 p. ; ISBN 0-394-75301-1 (pbk.) : LC Card 86-40470 DDC 650.1/024042 19
HD6053 .S724 1987

Tarizzo, Domenico. Il nuovo amore di coppia /. Milano , 1982. 192 p. ; LC Card 82-141135 DDC 306.7 19
HQ21 .T338 1982 ***NYPL [JLD 87-1019]***

Witkin-Lanoil, Georgia. The male stress syndrome . New York , c1986. 246 p. ; ISBN 0-937858-59-5 LC Card 85-61815 DDC 155.9 19
BF575.S75 W59 1986 ***NYPL [JFD 86-5693]***

MEN - PSYCHOLOGY - ADDRESSES, ESSAYS, LECTURES.
The Social psychology of female-male relations . Orlando , 1986. xvi, 351 p. ; ISBN 0-12-065280-3 (alk. paper) LC Card 85-9138 DDC 305.3 19
HM132 .S569 1986 ***NYPL [JLE 86-1746]***

MEN - UNITED STATES - ATTITUDES.
Astrachan, Anthony. How men feel . Garden City, N.Y. , 1986. x, 444 p. ; ISBN 0-385-23333-7 : LC Card 85-22944 DDC 305.3/1 19
HQ1090.3 .A88 1986 ***NYPL [JLE 86-3421]***

Men who manage . Dalton, Melville. New York , 1987. xi, 318 p., [1] leaf of plates : ISBN 0-8240-8203-6 (alk. paper) : LC Card 86-25801 DDC 658.4 19
HD31 .D2 1987

Men who migrate, women who wait . Brettell, Caroline. Princeton , c1986. xv, 329 p., [8] p. of plates : ISBN 0-691-09424-1 (alk. paper) : LC Card 86-11270 DDC 304.6/09469/12 19
HB2082.L36 B74 1986 ***NYPL [JLE 87-1417]***

Men without work : a report made to the Pilgrim Trust. New York : Garland Pub., 1985. xii, 447 p. ; 21 cm. (English workers and the coming of the

welfare state, 1918-1945) Includes index. Reprint. Originally published: Cambridge : Cambridge University Press, 1938. ISBN 0-8240-7619-2 (alk. paper) : LC Card 85-13069 DDC 331.13/7941 19
1. Unemployed - Great Britain. 2. Social service - Great Britain. 3. Great Britain - Social conditions - 20th century. I. Pilgrim Trust (Great Britain). II. Series.
HD5765.A6 M46 1985
NYPL [JLD 87-1031]

Men, women, and market trade in rural Mali, West Africa /. Turrittin, Jane Sawyer. [East Lansing] , c1986. 17 p. ; LC Card 86-225178 DDC 331.4/8138118/096623 19
HD6060.65.M42 T87 1986

Men, women, and work . Blewett, Mary H. Urbana , c1988. p. cm. ISBN 0-252-01484-7 (alk. paper) LC Card 87-19039 DDC 338.4/768531/00974 19
HD8039.B72 U63 1988

Ménages débiteurs hypothécaires au Canada. Che-Alford, Janet. Mortgagor [sic] households in Canada . Ottawa , c1986. 100 p. : ISBN 0-660-52986-6 (pbk.) : LC Card 86-202749 DDC 332.7/22/0971 19
HD7287.82.C2 C48 1986

Menard, Scott W. Perspectives on population . New York , 1987. xix, 487 p. : ISBN 0-19-504092-9 (alk. paper) : LC Card 86-23652 DDC 304.6 19
HB871 .P48 1987

Menchik, Mark D. Cohen, Carol E. 1983 tax capacity of the states . Washington, D.C. (1111 20th St., NW, Washington 20575) [1986] ix, 111 p. : LC Card 86-601628 DDC 336.2/013/73
HJ2385 .C59 1986

Menck, Karl Wolfgang. Mittelstand und Entwicklungsländer : Erfahrungen mit dem Technologietransfer niedersächsischer Unternehmen / Karl-Wolfgang Menck. Hamburg : Verlag Weltarchiv, 1986. 192 p. ; 24 cm. (Veröffentlichungen des HWWA-Institut für Wirtschaftsforschung-Hamburg) Bibliography: p. 169-192. ISBN 3-87895-318-6 LC Card 87-407405 DDC 337.43/59/01724 19
1. Lower Saxony (Germany) - Foreign economic relations - Developing countries. 2. Developing countries - Foreign economic relations - Germany (West) - Lower Saxony. 3. Small business - Germany (West) - Lower Saxony. I. Title.
HF1546.19.L68 M46 1986

Mendenhall, William. A course in business statistics / William Mendenhall. 2nd ed. Boston, Mass. : PWS-KENT Pub. Co., [1988] p. cm. Bibliography: p. Includes index. ISBN 0-534-91488-8 LC Card 87-20731 DDC 519.5 19
1. Commercial statistics. I. Title.
HF1017 .M458 1988

Mendes, Margaret. Caribbean cases in auditing / by Margaret Mendes and Robertine Chaderton. Kingston, Jamaica : CFM Publications, c1986. 58 p. : ill., facsims. ; 28 cm. ISBN 976-8053-00-3 (pbk.) LC Card 87-403426 DDC 657/.45 19
1. Auditing - Caribbean Area - Case studies. I. Chaderton, Robertine. II. Title.
HF5667 .M456 1986

Méndez, Carlos. Rocca, José. Excedentes financieros y sistema bancario, Uruguay, 1974-1982 /. Montevideo, Uruguay , 1985. 39 p. : LC Card 85-213768
HC235.S3 R63 1985

Méndez Morales, José Silvestre.
México por entidades federativas / José Silvestre Méndez y Santiago Zorrilla. 1a ed. México, D.F. : Ediciones Océano, c1986. 318 p., [32] p. of plates : col. maps ; 23 cm. Cover subtitle: Orografía, hidrografía, climas, división política, historia, demografía, economía, sociedad, atlas y escudos a todo color. Bibliography: p. 316. ISBN 968-493-098-4 LC Card 87-400185 DDC 330.972/083 19
1. Mexico - Economic conditions - 1970-. 2. Mexico - Social conditions - 1970-. 3. Physical geography - Mexico - States. I. Zorrilla, Santiago. II. Title.
HC135 .M52524 1986

Zorrilla, Santiago. Diccionario de economía /. México, D.F. , c1986. 182 p. : ISBN 968-493-060-7 LC Card 87-401043 DDC 330/.03/61 19
HB61 .Z63 1986

Méndez S., José Fernando. La derrota de Andahuaylas (1974) / José Fernando Méndez S. Lima : [s.n.], 1981. 126 p. : 16 cm. (Colección Debate agrario) Bibliography: p. 104-105.
1. Peasant uprising - Peru - Andahuaylas. 2. Land reform - Peru. 3. Land reform - Law and legislation - Peru. I. Title. ***NYPL [JLB 86-27]***

Mendonça, Sonia Regina de. Estado e economia no Brasil : opções de desenvolvimento / Sonia Regina de Mendonça.1a. ed. Rio de Janeiro-RJ, Brasil : Graal, 1986. 106 p. ; 21 cm. (Biblioteca de historia. vol. no. 14) Bibliography: p. 104-106. LC Card 86-197575
1. Brazil - Economic policy. 2. Brazil - Economic conditions - 1985-. I. Series: Biblioteca de história (Edições Graal) , vol. no. 14. II. Title.
HC187 .M469 1986

MENDOZA (ARGENTINA : PROVINCE) - ECONOMIC CONDITIONS.
Fleming, William J. Region vs nation . Tempe , c1986. 82 p. ; ISBN 0-87918-066-8 LC Card 86-29919 DDC 330.982/64 19
HC177.M4 F55 1986

Fleming, William J. Regional development and transportation in Argentina . New York , 1987. ii, 218 p. : ISBN 0-8240-1360-3 (alk. paper) : LC Card 87-8401 DDC 385/.065/82 19
HE2910.G64 F54 1987

Mendoza, Carlos. Teoría de la renta capitalista de la tierra ; y, Génesis de la renta capitalista de la tierra y del arrendatario / Carlos Mendoza. Buenos Aires : Editorial Anteo, 1985. 108 p. : ill. ; 20 cm. (Colección Argentina, temas de actualidad . [13]) Papers presented at the Seminario sobre "La Cuestión Agraria en la Argentina", in 1984, at the Centro de Estudios Marxistas Leninistas Victorio Codovilla. ISBN 950-9478-11-3 LC Card 86-101927
1. Rent. 2. Marxian economics. I. Title: Teoría de la renta capitalista de la tierra. II. Title: Génesis de la renta capitalista de la tierra y del arrendatario. III. Series: Colección Argentina, temas de actualidad , 13.
HB401 .M38 1985

Mendoza, José María. Las funciones administrativas : un enfoque estratégico y táctico / José María Mendoza. Barranquilla : Ediciones Uninorte, c1985. xiv, 207 p. : ill. ; 24 cm. Includes bibliographies. ISBN 958-9105-00-9 LC Card 86-187780
1. Management. I. Title.
HD37.S66 M46 1985

Menefee Singh, Andréa. see **Singh, Andréa Menefee, 1943-**

MENÉNDEZ, JESÚS, 1911-1948.
García Galló, Gaspar M. Jorge. General de las cañas /. La Habana , 1983. 220 p., [18] p. of plates : LC Card 84-229562 DDC 331.88/13361/097291 19
HD6577.5.M46 G37 1983
NYPL [JFD 85-4783]

Menéndez Lastra, Constantino. Martín Alonso, Arturo. Invertir en Asturias /. [Spain] [1984?] 72 p. : ISBN 84-398-1662-6 LC Card 85-217277
HC387.A7 M37 1984

Ménétra, Jacques-Louis, b. 1738.
Journal de ma vie : Jacques-Louis Ménétra, compagnon vitrier au 18e siècle / présenté par Daniel Roche. Paris : Montalba, c1982. 431 p. : ill. ; 22 cm. Includes bibliographical references. ISBN 2-85870-022-2 : LC Card 82-166496 DDC 666/.1/0924 B 19
1. Ménétra, Jacques-Louis, b. 1738. 2. Glass-workers - France - History - 18th century. 3. Glass-workers - France - Biography. 4. France - Social conditions - 18th century. I. Roche, Daniel. II. Title.
HD8039.G52 F73 1982
NYPL [JFD 86-6795]

[Journal de ma vie. English]
Journal of my life / by Jacques-Louis Ménétra ; with an introduction and commentary by Daniel Roche ; translated by Arthur Goldhammer ; foreword by Robert Darnton. New York : Columbia University Press, 1986. xviii, 368 p., [1] leaf of plate : facsim. ; 24 cm. Translation of: Journal de ma vie. Bibliography: p. [359]-368. ISBN 0-231-06128-5 LC Card 85-28068 DDC 666/.1/0924 B 19
1. Ménétra, Jacques-Louis, b. 1738. 2. Glass-workers - France - History - 18th century. 3. Glass-workers - France - Biography. 4. France - Social conditions - 18th century. I. Roche, Daniel. II. Title.
HD8039.G52 F7313 1986
NYPL [JFE 86-2978]

MÉNÉTRA, JACQUES-LOUIS, B. 1738.
Ménétra, Jacques-Louis, b. 1738. Journal de ma vie . Paris , c1982. 431 p. : ISBN 2-85870-022-2 : LC Card 82-166496 DDC 666/.1/0924 B 19
HD8039.G52 F73 1982
NYPL [JFD 86-6795]

Ménétra, Jacques-Louis, b. 1738. [Journal de ma vie. English.] Journal of my life /. New York , 1986. xviii, 368 p., [1] leaf of plate : ISBN 0-231-06128-5 LC Card 85-28068 DDC 666/.1/0924 B 19
HD8039.G52 F7313 1986
NYPL [JFE 86-2978]

Menezes, Alfredo da Mota, 1944- A herança de Stroessner : Brasil-Paraguai, 1955-1980 / Alfredo da Mota Menezes. Campinas, SP : Papirus Livraria Editora, [1987] 186 p. ; 21 cm. Bibliography: p. 181-186. LC Card 87-404011 DDC 337.810892 19
1. Paraguay - Foreign economic relations - Brazil. 2. Brazil - Foreign economic relations - Paraguay. 3. Paraguay - Economic conditions - 1954-. 4. Itaipu (Power plant) - History. I. Title.
HF1524.5.B7 M46 1987

Meng, Ng Shui. see **Ng, Shui Meng.**

Mengenal administrasi dan prosedur catatan sipil pada Kantor Catatan Sipil Propinsi DKI Jakarta /. Sukarno, H., 1948- Jakarta , 1985. iii, 150 p. : LC Card 86-942212
HA37.I46 J357 1985

Menger, Carl, 1840-1921.
Carl Mengers erster Entwurf zu seinem Hauptwerk "Grundsätze" geschrieben als Anmerkungen zu den "Grundsätzen der Volkswirthschaftslehre" von Karl Heinrich Rau. Tokio : Bibliothek der Hitotsubashi Universität, 1963. xxviii, 236 p., [3] leaves of plates : facsims. ; 25 cm. Some text in English and Japanese. LC Card 85-210245
1. Economics. 2. Menger, Carl, 1840-1921. I. Menger, Carl, 1840-1921. Grundsätze der Volkswirthschaftslehre. II. Rau, Karl Heinrich. Grundsätze der Volkswirthschaftslehre. III. Hitotsubashi Daigaku. Toshokan. IV. Title.
HB175 .M47 1963

Grundsätze der Volkswirthschaftslehre.
Menger, Carl, 1840-1921. Carl Mengers erster Entwurf zu seinem Hauptwerk "Grundsätze" geschrieben als Anmerkungen zu den "Grundsätzen der Volkswirthschaftslehre" von Karl Heinrich Rau. Tokio , 1963. xxviii, 236 p., [3] leaves of plates : LC Card 85-210245
HB175 .M47 1963

MENGER, CARL, 1840-1921.
Boos, Margarete. Die Wissenschaftstheorie Carl Mengers . Wien , 1986. xiii, 252 p. ; ISBN 3-205-05044-4 LC Card 86-209140
HB101.M5 B6 1986

Höltz, Joachim. Kritik der Geldentstehungstheorien . Berlin , c1984. ii, 401 p. ; ISBN 3-496-00796-6 LC Card 85-147094
HG237 .H64 1984

Menger, Carl, 1840-1921. Carl Mengers erster Entwurf zu seinem Hauptwerk "Grundsätze" geschrieben als Anmerkungen zu den "Grundsätzen der Volkswirthschaftslehre" von Karl Heinrich Rau. Tokio , 1963. xxviii, 236 p., [3] leaves of plates : LC Card 85-210245
HB175 .M47 1963

Menke, Christoph, 1956- Mayer, Hans, 1951- Energie für die Armen? . Saarbrücken , Fort Lauderdale , 1984. 195 p. : ISBN 3-88156-288-5 : LC Card 85-199309
HD9502.I42 M38 1984

Mennenöh, Hartwig. Prognosepublizität : Vorschläge zur ungewissheitsorientierten Gestaltung einer prospektiven Berichterstattung von Unternehmen an externe Adressaten / Hartwig Mennenöh. Bochum : Studienverlag N. Brockmeyer, 1984. ii, 329 p. : ill. ; 21 cm. (Bochumer wirtschaftswissenschaftliche Studien. Nr. 101) Bibliography: p. 298-329. ISBN 3-88339-366-5 : LC Card 84-181938
1. Business forecasting. 2. Corporation reports. I. Title.
HB3730 .M396 1984

Mennes, L. B. M. European trade policies and the developing world /. London , New York , c1988. x, 368 p. ; ISBN 0-7099-4672-4 LC Card

87-8969 DDC 382/.3/094 19
HF1492 .E87 1988

Menninger Rehabilitation Research and Training Center. Hester, Edward J. Predicting which disabled employees will return to work . Topeka, Kan. (700 Jackson, 9th floor, Topeka 66603) , c1986. x, 86 p. : LC Card 86-231920 DDC 331.5/9 19
HD7256.U5 H43 1986

MENNONITES - CASE STUDIES.
Nafziger, E. Wayne. Entrepreneurship, equity, and economic development /. Greenwich, Conn. , c1986. xxiii, 308 p. : ISBN 0-89232-711-1 : LC Card 86-20151 DDC 338/.04 19
HB615 .N34 1986 ***NYPL [JLE 87-1672]***

Menon, M. S. N., 1924-
Indo-Soviet trade and economic ties / M.S.N. Menon, V.P. Morozov. New Delhi : Allied Publishers, 1986. 229 p. ; 22 cm. Covers the period up to 1986. LC Card 86-903273 DDC 337.54047 19
1. India - Foreign economic relations - Soviet Union. 2. Soviet Union - Foreign economic relations - India. I. Morozov, V. P. II. Title.
HF1590.5.S65 M46 1986

No to exploitation : the economic case of the non-aligned / M.S.N. Menon, R.K Sharma. New Delhi : Mahajan Pub. House, 1983. 163, xxxii p. ; 25 cm. Includes bibliographical references. LC Card 83-902131 DDC 337/.09172/4 19
1. Developing countries - Economic policy. 2. Developing countries - Economic conditions. I. Sharma, R. K., 1947-. II. Title.
HC59.7 .M445 1983 ***NYPL [JLE 86-4184]***

MEN'S CLOTHING INDUSTRY - SWEDEN.
Tung herrkonfektion . Stockholm , 1977. 64, [11] leaves, [1] leaf of plates : ISBN 91-38-03482-4 LC Card 84-102982
HD9940.S82 T854 1977

Men's lives /. Matthiessen, Peter. New York , 1988, c1986. xvi, 335 p. ; ISBN 0-394-75560-X (pbk.) : LC Card 87-40095 DDC 338.3/72709747/21 19
HD8039.F66 U5 1988

Mens, Rina. Aerts, Christel. Advertenties en affiches . [Wilrijk, Belgium] , 1986. 165, [7] p. : LC Card 86-222214
HF5827 .A43 1986

MEN'S SHIRT INDUSTRY.
Mercado internacional para camisas fabricadas no Ceará /. Fortaleza , 1979. 110 p. : LC Card 84-232020 DDC 338.4/7687115/098131 19
HD9969.S7 B66 1979 ***NYPL [JLD 86-4122]***

MEN'S SHIRT INDUSTRY - BRAZIL - CEARA (STATE)
Mercado internacional para camisas fabricadas no Ceará /. Fortaleza , 1979. 110 p. : LC Card 84-232020 DDC 338.4/7687115/098131 19
HD9969.S7 B66 1979 ***NYPL [JLD 86-4122]***

Mensagem apresentada á Camara Municipal /. Porto Alegre (Brazil). Mayor. Pôrto Alegre , 1936. 686 p., [7] folded leaves of plates : LC Card 85-135614
HD4635.P6 P67 1936

Mensch und Arbeit im technisch-organisatorischen Wandel .
(Bd. 3) Zangl, Hans. Durchlaufzeiten im Büro . Berlin , c1985. xvii, 365 p. : ISBN 3-503-02458-1 LC Card 85-137750
HF5549.5.C6 Z33 1985

Mensch und Luftfahrt : eine Erinnerungsschrift für Prof. Dr. Werner Guldimann, Direktor des Bundesamtes für Zivilluftfahrt, zum 65. Geburtstag und Rücktritt vom Amt, als Zeichen der Dankbarkeit / überreicht vom Bundesamt für Zivilluftfahrt. Bern : Das Bundesamt, [1981] 177 p. : ill. ; 21 cm. Contributions in German, English, French, or Italian. "Le Comité juridique de l'Organisation de l'aviation civile internationale, par Gilbert Guillaume" (9 p.) laid in. "Im Januar 1981." LC Card 83-116416
1. Aeronautics, Commercial - Switzerland. 2. Air traffic rules, International. 3. Guldimann, Werner, 1916-. I. Guldimann, Werner, 1916-. II. Switzerland. Bundesamt für Zivilluftfahrt.
HE9863.A4 M45 1981

"Die Menschen machen ihre Geschichte nicht aus freien Stücken, aber sie machen sie selbst" : Einladung zu einer Geschichte des Volkes in NRW / Hrsg., Lutz Niethammer ... [et al.] ; mit einem Vorwort von Johannes Rau ; [die Bildserien wurden erstellt von Tilman Fichter und Alexander von Plato]. Berlin : J.H.W. Dietz Nachf., [1984] 267 p. : ill. (some col.) ; 22 x 24 cm. Bibliography: p. 265-266. ISBN 3-8012-0101-5 LC Card 84-204204
1. North Rhine-Westphalia (Germany) - Economic conditions. 2. North Rhine-Westphalia (Germany) - Social conditions. 3. North Rhine-Westphalia (Germany) - Social life and customs. 4. Labor and laboring classes - Germany (West) - North Rhine-Westphalia - History - 20th century. I. Niethammer, Lutz, 1939-.
HC287.N6 M46 1984

Mensink, Ankie. De wording en verwording van de staat Marokko : een sociaal-ekonomies en histories overzicht, 1912-1972 / Ankie Mensink, Annemarie Strijbosch, Marianne Wijermars. Rotterdam : HIWAR : Verspreiding, Stichting Ordeman Distributie, 1985. 304 p. ; 21 cm. Bibliography: p. 296-302. ISBN 90-6330-109-X : LC Card 85-214935
1. Morocco - Economic conditions. 2. Morocco - Politics and government. I. Strijbosch, Annemarie. II. Wijermars, Marianne. III. Title.
HC810 .M46 1985

MENTAL CULTURE. see **MENTAL DISCIPLINE.**

MENTAL DISCIPLINE.
Scott, Gini Graham. Mind power . Englewood Cliffs, N.J. , c1987. xi, 183 p. ; ISBN 0-13-583527-5 LC Card 87-6923 DDC 650.1 19
HF5386 .S413 1987

MENTAL PHILOSOPHY. see **PHILOSOPHY; PSYCHOLOGY.**

MENTAL STEREOTYPE. see **STEREOTYPE (PSYCHOLOGY)**

Menz, Gertraud. Die Entwicklung der sowjetischen Besteuerung unter besonderer Berücksichtigung der ordnungspolitischen Funktionen / Gertraud Menz. Berlin : In Kommission bei Duncker & Humblot, 1960. 247 p. : ill. ; 25 cm. (Wirtschaftswissenschaftliche Veröffentlichungen . Bd. 13) Bibliography: p. [240]-247. LC Card 86-161289
1. Taxation - Soviet Union - History. I. Title. II. Series.
HJ2802 .M46 1960

Menzler-Hokkanen, Ingeborg. Measuring changes in intra-industry competitiveness / Ingeborg Menzler-Hokkanen. Helsingfors : Swedish School of Economics and Business Administration, [1986] 39 p. ; 30 cm. (Swedish School of Economics and Business Administration working papers, 0357-4598 = Meddelanden från Svenska handelshögskolan . 149 (1986) Bibliography: p. 29-32. ISBN 951-555-247-8 (pbk.) LC Card 87-170429 DDC 338.6/048 19
1. Industrial productivity - Mathematical models. 2. Competition, International - Mathematical models. 3. Industrial productivity - Finland - Econometric models. 4. Finland - Commerce - Econometric models. I. Series: Meddelanden fran Svenska handelshögskolan , 149. II. Title.
HC79.I52 M46 1986

Meran, Georg. Die arbeiterselbstverwaltete Firma bei Unsicherheit und asymmetrischer Information : eine vertragstheoretische Untersuchung / Georg Meran. München : V. Florentz, c1986. ii, 134 p. : ill. ; 21 cm. (Volkswirtschaftliche Forschung und Entwicklung . Bd. 27) Bibliography: p. 125-130. Includes index. ISBN 3-88259-403-9 LC Card 87-121443 DDC 658.3/152 19
1. Management - Employee participation. 2. Industrial management - Employee participation. I. Title. II. Series.
HD5650 .M397 1986

Mercadeo de productos agrícolas de la Cuenca del Caribe. Agricultural marketing handbook for Caribbean Basin products. Spanish. Manual--mercadeo de productos agrícolas de la Cuenca del Caribe /. San José, Costa Rica . x, 434 p. : ISBN 92-9039-101-4 LC Card 86-204686
HD9014.C442 A4718 1986

Mercaderes y artesanos en la Sevilla del descubrimiento /. Morell Peguero, Blanca. Sevilla , 1986. 222 p. ; ISBN 84-505-2883-6 LC Card 86-199625
HD2346.S72 S465 1986

Mercado brasileiro de celulose e papel / Ministério da Indústria e do Comércio, Conselho de Desenvolvimento Industrial, Secretaria Executiva. Brasília, D.F. : A Secretaria Ejecutiva, 1982. vii, 224 leaves : ill. ; 30 cm. "Elaborado pela Comissão Executiva para Papel e Celulose"--Pref. Photocopy. [S.l. : s.n., 1982 or 1983] LC Card 84-210712
1. Cellulose industry - Brazil. 2. Paper industry - Brazil. I. Conselho de Desenvolvimento Industrial (Brazil). Secretaria Executiva. II. Brazil. Comissão Executiva para Papel e Celulose.
HD9660.C43 B75 1982

El Mercado Común frente a la agricultura española /. Moreno Torregrosa, Pasqual. Madrid [1986?] 127 p. ; ISBN 84-86293-27-8 LC Card 86-202333
HD2022 .M67 1986

Mercado Común Latinoamericano. see **Asociación Latinoamericana de Libre Comercio.**

El Mercado de capitales como instrumento de la política económica / Catalina Rabinovich Woloshin ... [et al]. [Miraflores, Lima] : Fundación Friedrich Ebert, [1987] 111 p. ; 21 cm. (Taller de investigación . 9) Includes bibliographies. LC Card 87-169408 DDC 332.6/0985 19
1. Investments - Peru. 2. Capital market - Peru. 3. Peru - Economic policy. I. Rabinovich Woloshin, Catalina. II. Friedrich-Ebert-Stiftung. III. Series.
HG5392 .M43 1987

El mercado de deuda pública /. Sala Garrido, Ramón. [Valencia] [1984] 163 p. : ISBN 84-505-0146-6 LC Card 86-213799
HJ8739 .S25 1984

El mercado de tecnología . Boon, Gerard Karel. México, D.F. , 1984, c1983. 715 p. : ISBN 968-12-0252-X LC Card 85-242124
HD9929.2.A2 B66 1984

O mercado de terra na região metropolitana de Porto Alegre /. Clichevsky, Nora. Porto Alegre , 1982. 60 p. : LC Card 84-256219
HD500.P67 C57 1982

Mercado de trabajo rural en México . Astorga Lira, Enrique. México, D.F. , 1985. 127 p. : ISBN 968-411-139-8 LC Card 86-141300 DDC 331.7/63/0972 19
HD1531.M6 A88 1985 ***NYPL [JLC 87-68]***

Mercado de trabalho. Cadastro geral de empregados e desempregados (Lei 4,923/65) . [Brasília, Brazil] , 1985. [61] leaves ; LC Card 86-178290
HD5754 .C26 1985

O Mercado de trabalho no Brasil : aspectos teóricos e evidências empíricas / José Paulo Zeetano Chahad [organizador] São Paulo : Instituto de Pesquisas Econômicas, 1986. 263 p. : ill. ; 22 cm. (Série Relatórios de pesquisa . no. 29) Includes bibliographies. CONTENTS. - Fontes de variação de massa salarial no Brasil / Maria Helena P. Zockun -- Política salarial e inflação / Roberto Brás Matos Macedo -- Absorção de mão-de-obra industrial / Carlos Antonio Luque, José Paulo Zeetano Chahad -- A participação estrangeira no mercado de trabalho brasileiro / Ana Maria Bianchi -- Desemprego e força de trabalho / Ronaldo Lázaro Medina -- Mercado do trabalho, desemprego urbano e seguro-desemprego no Brasil / José Paulo Zeetano Chahad -- Distribuição de rendas, formas de participação na produção e setor informal / Maria Cristina Cacciamali -- O FGTS e as rescisões do contrato de trabalho / José Paulo Zeetano Chahad -- Estrutura ocupacional e rotatividade da mão-de-obra / Carlos Antonio Luque -- Recessão e emprego no setor industrial brasileiro 1980-1984 / Ivo Torres -- Setor público e emprego no Brasil / Andrea Sandro Calabi, Helio Zylberstajn. LC Card 86-221361
1. Manpower policy - Brazil. 2. Wages - Government policy - Brazil. 3. Labor supply - Brazil. 4. Alien labor - Brazil. I. Chahad, José Paulo Zeetano. II. Universidad de São Paulo. Instituto de Pesquisas Econômicas. III. Series.
HD5754 .M47 1986

Mercado financeiro e ajustamento macroeconômico brasileiro, 1978-1985 /. Martone, Celso L. (Celso Luiz) São Paulo , 1986. 82 p. : LC Card 87-120453 DDC 332.4/981 19
HG835 .M375 1986

Mercado financeiro e de capitais : curso de formação superior, grupo no. 9. [Brasília? : s.n., 1978?] 118 leaves, [25] leaves of plates : ill. ;

33 cm. Caption title. Prepared under the direction of Sérgio Augusto Cibreiros. Includes bibliography. LC Card 84-184169
1. Financial institutions - Brazil. 2. Capital market - Brazil. I. Cibreiros, Sérgio Augusto. II. Title: Curso de formação superior.
HG185.B7 M47 1978

O mercado financeiro português em 1966 /. Cavaco Silva, Aníbal A. (Aníbal António), 1939- Lisboa , 1968. xiv, 104 p. : LC Card 85-133959
HG186.P8 C38 1968

Mercado financiero, expectativas cambiarias y movimientos de capital /. Frenkel, Roberto. Buenos Aires, Argentina [1981] 46 p. : LC Card 82-236987 DDC 332/.0724 19
HG173.6.S62 F73 1981 ***NYPL [JLD 86-2636]***

O mercado habitacional no Brasil /. Lucena, José Mário Pereira de. Rio de Janeiro, RJ , 1985. v, 185 p. : LC Card 85-208372
HD7323.A3 L83 1985

El Mercado hipotecario : Madrid, 15 y 16 de noviembre de 1983 / organizado por Instituto de Empresa. Madrid : El Instituto, 1984. 162 p. ; 24 cm. Bibliography: p. 103. ISBN 84-85669-34-7 LC Card 86-211862
1. Mortgage loans - Spain - Congresses. 2. Housing - Spain - Finance - Congresses. I. Instituto de Empresa.
HG2040.5.S7 M47 1984

Mercado internacional para camisas fabricadas no Ceará / Instituto de Planejamento Econômico e Social ... [et al.]. Fortaleza : Banco do Nordeste do Brasil, 1979. 110 p. : ill. ; 21 cm. LC Card 84-232020 DDC 338.4/7687115/098131 19
1. Men's shirt industry - Brazil - Ceara (State). 2. Men's shirt industry.
HD9969.S7 B66 1979 ***NYPL [JLD 86-4122]***

El Mercado regional de frutas : una alternativa para dinamizar el mercado de frutas tropicales y sub-tropicales, 1983 / Asociación Latinoamericana de Industriales y Cámaras de la Alimentación. [Montevideo] : ALICA, 1983. 63 p. ; 29 cm. Cover title. "(FAO) Programa de Cooperación Regional y Comercio Exterior, Oficina Regional para América Latina, (ALADI) Unidad de Promoción, Complementación y Cooperación." LC Card 86-171763
1. Tropical fruit industry - Latin America. 2. Tropical fruit - Latin America - Marketing. I. Asociación Latinoamericana de Industriales y Cámaras de la Alimentación. II. Food and Agriculture Organization of the United Nations. Regional Office for Latin America. Programa de Cooperación Regional y Comercio Exterior. III. Asociación Latinoamericana de Integración. Unidad de Promoción, Complementación y Cooperación.
HD9259.T753 L295 1983

Mercado, Thomas de, d. 1575.
[Tratos y contratos de mercaderes. Selections] La economia en la Andalucia del descubrimiento / Tomás de Mercado ; prologo y selección de Antonio Acosta. Sevilla : Editoriales Andaluzas Unidas, [1985?] 276 p. ; 19 cm. (Biblioteca de la cultura andaluza . 25.) Selections from the author's Tratos y contratos de mercaderes. ISBN 84-7587-047-3 LC Card 86-151225
1. Commerce. 2. Commercial law. 3. Spain - Colonies - America - Commerce - History. 4. Andalusia (Spain : Region) - Commerce - History. I. Acosta, Antonio. II. Title.
HF1003 .M525 1985

El mercado y los precios de los productos agropecuarios /. Fragoso Gutiérrez, Juan M. México , 1983. 486 p. : LC Card 84-236815
HD9014.M62 F72 1983

Mercado y precios de productos agropecuarios. Fragoso Gutiérrez, Juan M. El mercado y los precios de los productos agropecuarios /. México , 1983. 486 p. : LC Card 84-236815
HD9014.M62 F72 1983

Mercados de capital en América Latina y el Caribe : directorio de instituciones. Caracas, Venezuela : Instituto Interamericano de Mercados de Capital, [1986] 114 p. ; 16 cm. LC Card 87-103358
1. Stock-exchange - Latin America - Directories. 2. Stock-exchange - Caribbean Area - Directories. 3. Financial institutions - Latin America - Directories. 4. Financial institutions - Caribbean Area - Directories. I. Instituto Interamericano de Mercados de Capital.
HG5160.5.A3 M47 1986

Mercados de capitales bajo inflación / Armando P. Ribas ... [et al.] ; Nicholas Bruck, editor. New York, N.Y. : Decade Media Books, c1982. xxi, 471 p. : ill. ; 24 cm. Published in cooperation with Stock Exchange of Buenos Aires, Buenos Aires, Argentina; Inter-American Development Bank, Washington, D.C. Papers presented at a conference sponsored by the Stock Exchange of Buenos Aires and the Inter-American Development Bank, in Nov. 1981. Includes bibliographical references and index. ISBN 0-910365-00-8 : LC Card 82-50965 DDC 332.64 19
1. Capital market - Congresses. 2. Inflation (Finance) - Congresses. I. Ribas, Armando P. II. Bruck, Nicholas K., 1932-. III. Buenos Aires. Bolsa de Comercio.
HG4523 .M47 1982 ***NYPL [JLE 86-3568]***

Mercados de trabajo y distribución de ingresos en cuatro centros urbanos de Argentina, 1974-1981 /. Diéguez, Héctor L. Buenos Aires, Argentina , 1984. 49 p. ; ISBN 950-621-013-6 LC Card 87-401771 DDC 331.12/982 19
HD5749 .D54 1984

Mercados financieros rurales en América Latina /. González Vega, Claudio. Santo Domingo, República Dominicana , 1986. 44 p. ; LC Card 87-400002 DDC 332.7/1/098 19
HG2051.L26 G66 1986

Mercados financieros y desarrollo /. González Vega, Claudio. Santo Domingo, República Dominicana , 1986. 73 p. : LC Card 87-102022
HG2817 .G66 1986

Mercados financieros y distribución del ingreso / James Edward Zinser, Claudio González Vega. 1a ed. Santo Domingo, República Dominicana : Centro de Estudios Monetarios y Bancarios, 1986. 117 p. : ill. ; 22 cm. (Serie Estudios) Includes bibliographies. CONTENTS. - Los mercados financieros y cambiarios regulados y no regulados y la distribución del ingreso en la República Dominicana / James Edward Zinser, Claudio González Vega -- Mercados financieros no regulados / James Edward Zinser -- El comportamiento de los prestamistas agropecuarios al racionar el crédito / Claudio González Vega -- Crédito agropecuario artificialmente barato / Claudio González Vega. LC Card 87-405027 DDC 332.1/097293 19
1. Financial institutions - Dominican Republic. 2. Credit - Dominican Republic. 3. Income distribution - Dominican Republic. I. Zinser, James Edward. II. González Vega, Claudio. III. Series: Serie Estudios (Centro de Estudios Monetarios y Bancarios (Santo Domingo, Dominican Republic)).
HG185.D65 M47 1986

Mercados mundiales de hidrocarburos : situación presente, perspectivas y tendencias futuras / Miguel S. Wionczek, coordinador.1a ed. México, D.F. : Colegio de México, Programa de Energéticos, 1983. 377 p. : ill. ; 21 cm. Includes bibliographical references. ISBN 968-12-0231-7 LC Card 84-222729
1. Petroleum industry and trade - Congresses. 2. Hydrocarbons - Congresses. 3. Gas, Natural - Congresses. I. Wionczek, Miguel S. II. Colegio de México. Programa de Energéticos.
HD9560.5 .M39 1983

Mercados y precios en la economía campesina . Cori Castro, Wilfredo. [Cuzco, Peru] , 1986. 29 p. : LC Card 86-200941
HC228.C8 C59 1986

MERCANTILE AGENCIES. see **CREDIT BUREAUS.**

MERCANTILE LAW. see **COMMERCIAL LAW.**

MERCANTILE MARINE. see **MERCHANT MARINE.**

Mercantile policies of Henry the Seventh. Ide, Arthur Frederick. The mercantile policies of Henry VII /. Irving, Tex. , 1987. v, 78 p. : ISBN 0-938659-02-2 (pbk.) : LC Card 87-4316 DDC 382/.3/0942 19
HF1533 .I34 1987

The mercantile policies of Henry VII /. Ide, Arthur Frederick. Irving, Tex. , 1987. v, 78 p. : ISBN 0-938659-02-2 (pbk.) : LC Card 87-4316 DDC 382/.3/0942 19
HF1533 .I34 1987

MERCANTILE SYSTEM.
Gomes, Leonard. Foreign trade and the national economy . New York , 1987. viii, 323 p. ; ISBN 0-312-00765-5 : LC Card 87-4674 DDC 382 19
HF1008 .G65 1987

Helmer, Hans-Josef. Merkantilismus und Kapitalismus im modernen Rationalisierungsprozess /. Frankfurt , c1986. iii, 223 p. ; ISBN 3-88323-647-0 LC Card 87-113030 DDC 330.15/13 19
HB91 .H436 1986

Justi, Johann Heinrich Gottlob von, d. 1771. Ausführliche Abhandlung von denen Steuern und Abgaben /. Wiesbaden , 1977. 202 p., [4] p. of plates : ISBN 3-409-50171-1 LC Card 84-235228
HJ2300 .J87 1977

The mercantile system and its historical significance . Schmoller, Gustav von, 1838-1917. Fairfield, NJ , 1988. p. cm. ISBN 0-678-00252-5 LC Card 87-17247 DDC 330.15/13/0943 19
HB91 .S3 1988

MERCANTILE SYSTEM - CENTRAL EUROPE - HISTORY - CONGRESSES.
Städtewesen und Merkantilismus in Mitteleuropa /. Köln , 1983. xii, 333 p. : ISBN 3-412-00382-4 LC Card 83-155285
HF1531 .S688 1983

MERCANTILE SYSTEM - DENMARK - HISTORIOGRAPHY.
Glamann, Kristof. Studier i dansk merkantilisme . [Copenhagen] , c1983. 243 p. ; ISBN 87-500-2476-0 LC Card 85-125251
HB91 .G57 1983

MERCANTILE SYSTEM - DENMARK - HISTORY - 18TH CENTURY.
Glamann, Kristof. Studier i dansk merkantilisme . [Copenhagen] , c1983. 243 p. ; ISBN 87-500-2476-0 LC Card 85-125251
HB91 .G57 1983

MERCANTILE SYSTEM - GREAT BRITAIN - HISTORY - 16TH CENTURY.
Ide, Arthur Frederick. The mercantile policies of Henry VII /. Irving, Tex. , 1987. v, 78 p. : ISBN 0-938659-02-2 (pbk.) : LC Card 87-4316 DDC 382/.3/0942 19
HF1533 .I34 1987

MERCANTILE SYSTEM - MEXICO - HISTORY - 19TH CENTURY.
Vásquez M., Luis (Vásquez Medina) El mercantilismo mexicano versus el liberalismo inglés /. México, D.F. , 1985. xiii, 215 p., [18] p. of plates : LC Card 87-403512 DDC 380.1/0972 19
HC135 .V34 1985

MERCANTILE SYSTEM - PRUSSIA (GERMANY)
Schmoller, Gustav von, 1838-1917. The mercantile system and its historical significance . Fairfield, NJ , 1988. p. cm. ISBN 0-678-00252-5 LC Card 87-17247 DDC 330.15/13/0943 19
HB91 .S3 1988

El mercantilismo mexicano versus el liberalismo inglés /. Vásquez M., Luis (Vásquez Medina) México, D.F. , 1985. xiii, 215 p., [18] p. of plates : LC Card 87-403512 DDC 380.1/0972 19
HC135 .V34 1985

Mercato comune europeo. see **European Economic Community.**

Il mercato dei segni . Frontori, Laura. Milano , c1986. xv, 186 p., [8] p. of plates : ISBN 88-7078-040-6 : LC Card 86-161029
HF5822 .F74 1986

Mercato del lavoro e politica economica . Fiorito, Riccardo, 1947- Venezia , 1984. 247 p. : ISBN 88-317-4733-9 : LC Card 86-163951
HD5701.6 .F56 1984

Mercer, David (David Steuart) IBM : how the world's most successful corporation is managed / David Mercer. London : K. Page, 1987. 306 p. ; 25 cm. Bibliography: p. 299. Includes index. ISBN 1-85091-287-4 : LC Card 87-138763 DDC 338.7/61004/0973 19
1. International Business Machines Corporation - Management - History. 2. Computer industry - Management - History. I. Title.
HD9696.C64 I4855 1987

Mercer, H. Glenn. Miller, George H. California real estate appraisal . Englewood Cliffs, N.J. ,

c1987. xiv, 348 p. : ISBN 0-13-112558-3 : LC Card 87-6956 DDC 333.33/2/09794 19
HD1387 .M545 1987

Mercer, Kent. Directory of licensed occupations and apprenticeship programs in Texas. 3rd ed. [Austin, Tex.] : Published by Information Services Division, Texas State Library for the Texas State Occupational Information Coordinating Committee, [1985] iv, 102 p. ; 28 cm. Editor: Bonnie Grobar. Rev. ed. of: Neff, Rosemary. Directory of licensed occupations and apprenticeship programs in Texas. Rev. ed. 1983. "September 1985." Bibliography: p. 101-102. LC Card 86-622006 DDC 331.7/02/09764 19
1. Vocational guidance - Texas. 2. Licenses - Texas. 3. Apprentices - Texas. 4. Texas - Occupations. I. Grobar, Bonnie. II. Neff, Rosemary. Directory of licensed occupations and apprenticeship programs in Texas. III. Texas State Library. Information Services Division. IV. Texas State Occupational Information Coordinating Committee. V. Title.
HF5382.5.U6 T45 1985

MERCHANDISE. see **COMMERCIAL PRODUCTS.**

MERCHANDISE, DISPLAY OF. see **DISPLAY OF MERCHANDISE.**

MERCHANDISING.
Bolen, William H., 1943- Contemporary retailing /. Englewood Cliffs, N.J. , c1988. xviii, 622 p. : ISBN 0-13-170309-9 LC Card 87-17514 DDC 658.8/7 19
HF5429 .B595 1988

Chapman, Edward A. Exhibit marketing . New York , c1987. x, 309 p. : ISBN 0-07-010669-X : LC Card 87-2621 DDC 659.1/52 19
HF5845 .C47 1987

Kombinationserbjudanden. Vällingby [1984] 269, [45] p. : ISBN 91-7398-243-1 LC Card 85-115578
HF5438.5 .K66 1984

MERCHANT BANKS - NIGERIA - HISTORY.
Adewunmi, Wole. Twenty five years of merchant banking in Nigeria /. Akoka , 1985. xvi, 136 p. ; ISBN 978-226-475-X : LC Card 87-142907 DDC 332.66/09669 19
HG1971.N6 A34 1985

Merchant, Kenneth A. Fraudulent and questionable financial reporting : a corporate perspective / Kenneth A. Merchant. Morristown, N.J. : Financial Executives Research Foundation, c1987. iv, 48, [36] p. ; 23 cm. Includes bibliographies. ISBN 0-910586-64-0 (pbk.) LC Card 87-80813 DDC 657/.3 19
1. Corporations - Accounting. 2. Corporations - Accounting - Corrupt practices. 3. Fraud. I. Title.
HF5686.C7 M44 1987

MERCHANT MARINE - AUSTRALIA - HISTORY.
Buckley, K. D. (Kenneth D.) South Pacific focus . Sydney , Boston , 1986. 126 p. : ISBN 0-04-909030-5 LC Card 86-71304 DDC 387.5/065/94 19
HE945.B87 B83 1986

MERCHANT MARINE - AUSTRALIA - HISTORY - PICTORIAL WORKS.
Buckley, K. D. (Kenneth D.) South Pacific focus . Sydney , Boston , 1986. 126 p. : ISBN 0-04-909030-5 LC Card 86-71304 DDC 387.5/065/94 19
HE945.B87 B83 1986

MERCHANT MARINE - BRAZIL.
Sanson, João Rogério. A política de transportes marítimos no Brasil . Rio de Janeiro , 1986. vii, 178, 5 p. : LC Card 87-403931 DDC 387.5/44/0981 19
HE597.B7 S26 1986

MERCHANT MARINE - CANADA - HISTORY.
MacKay, Donald, 1925- The Asian dream . Vancouver , c1986. 223 p. : ISBN 0-88894-501-9 LC Card 86-225670 DDC 385/.0971 19
HE2810.C14 M33 1986

MERCHANT MARINE - CARGO. see **SHIPS - CARGO.**

MERCHANT MARINE - COLOMBIA.
Hoyos Lascano, Fernando. La UNCTAD y los problemas de transporte marítimo de los países en desarrollo . Bogotá, D.E. , 1975 ([Bogotá] : Gráficas Venus) 99 p. ; LC Card 85-205214
HE807 .H69 1975

MERCHANT MARINE - EUROPE - HISTORY.
Berridge, Geoff. The politics of the South Africa run . Oxford [Oxfordshire] , New York , 1987. x, 254 p. ; ISBN 0-19-827484-X : LC Card 87-1600 DDC 387.5/094 19
HE903.4 .B47 1987

MERCHANT MARINE - GOVERNMENT POLICY.
Ademuni-Odeke, Dr. Protectionism and the future of international shipping . Dordrecht ; Boston : xxviii, 446 p. ; ISBN 90-247-2918-1 LC Card 83-25055 DDC 387.5/068 19
HE736 .A34 1984 ***NYPL [JLE 85-1539]***

MERCHANT MARINE - GOVERNMENT POLICY - BRAZIL.
Sanson, João Rogério. A política de transportes marítimos no Brasil . Rio de Janeiro , 1986. vii, 178, 5 p. : LC Card 87-403931 DDC 387.5/44/0981 19
HE597.B7 S26 1986

MERCHANT MARINE - GOVERNMENT POLICY - UNITED STATES.
Hilton, Robert, 1927- U. S. maritime industries--down for the third time? /. Washington, D.C. , c1987. vi, 60 p. : ISBN 0-89206-099-9 (pbk.) LC Card 86-31768 DDC 387.5/0973 19
HE745 .H66 1987

MERCHANT MARINE - GREECE - HISTORY.
Kremmydas, Vasilēs. Hellēnikē nautilia, 1776-1835 /. Athēna , 1985-<1986. v. <1-2 > : LC Card 86-211031
HE872.5 .K74 1985

MERCHANT MARINE - GREECE - HISTORY - 19TH CENTURY.
Papathanasopoulos, Kōnstantinos, 1950- Hellēnikē emporikē nautalia, 1833-1856 . Athēna , 1983. 470 p., [32] p. of plates : LC Card 83-237694
HE872.5 .P36 1983

MERCHANT MARINE - GREECE - MAGNESIA - HISTORY - 18TH CENTURY.
Tzamtzēs, A. I. Hē nautilia tou Pēliou stēn Tourkokratia . [Athēnai] [198-] 103 p., [20] p. of plates : LC Card 87-111965
HE872.5.Z6 T98 1980z

MERCHANT MARINE - GREECE - MAGNESIA - HISTORY - 19TH CENTURY.
Tzamtzēs, A. I. Hē nautilia tou Pēliou stēn Tourkokratia . [Athēnai] [198-] 103 p., [20] p. of plates : LC Card 87-111965
HE872.5.Z6 T98 1980z

MERCHANT MARINE - ITALY - HISTORY.
Ogliari, Francesco. Trasporti marittimi di linea /. Milano , 1975- v. : LC Card 76-507610
HE839 .O35 ***NYPL [JSK 86-35]***

MERCHANT MARINE - LATIN AMERICA.
Sepúlveda Whittle, Tomás. Los conceptos básicos del transporte marítimo y la situación de la actividad en América Latina. Santiago de Chile , Nueva York, NY , 1986. 118 p. ; ISBN 92-1-321211-9 LC Card 87-400454 DDC 387.5/098 19
HE571 .S45 1986

MERCHANT MARINE - LIST OF VESSELS. see **SHIP REGISTERS.**

MERCHANT MARINE - NEW ZEALAND - HISTORY.
Savill, David. Sail to New Zealand . London , 1986. 185 p., [20] p. of plates : ISBN 0-7090-2809-1 : LC Card 87-111329 DDC 387.5/065/41 19
HE945.S45 S28 1986

MERCHANT MARINE - NORWAY.
Nielsen, Kai. Sett fra sjøsiden . [Oslo] , c1985. 88 p. : LC Card 86-205530
HE855 .N44 1985

MERCHANT MARINE - NORWAY - BIOGRAPHY.
Jacobsen, Alf R., 1950- Eventyret Anders Jahre /. Oslo , c1982. 303 p., [16] p. of plates : ISBN 82-7094-311-8 : LC Card 83-168197
HE569.J34 J33 1982 ***NYPL [JFD 87-4754]***

MERCHANT MARINE - OCEANIA - HISTORY.
Buckley, K. D. (Kenneth D.) South Pacific focus . Sydney , Boston , 1986. 126 p. : ISBN 0-04-909030-5 LC Card 86-71304 DDC 387.5/065/94 19
HE945.B87 B83 1986

MERCHANT MARINE - OCEANIA - HISTORY - PICTORIAL WORKS.
Buckley, K. D. (Kenneth D.) South Pacific focus . Sydney , Boston , 1986. 126 p. : ISBN 0-04-909030-5 LC Card 86-71304 DDC 387.5/065/94 19
HE945.B87 B83 1986

MERCHANT MARINE - POLAND.
Kwiatkowski, Eugeniusz. Pisma o rzeczypospolitej morskiej /. Szczecin , 1985. 277 p., [24] p. of plates : ISBN 83-7007-012-4 :
NYPL [*QO 86-2539]

Sójka, Zygmunt. Polska polityka morska /. Gdańsk , 1986. 237, [1] : ISBN 83-215-1646-7(pbk.) :
NYPL [*QO 87-1818]

MERCHANT MARINE - POLAND - HISTORY - 20TH CENTURY.
Rummel, Julian. Narodziny żeglugi /. Gdańsk , 1980. 333 p., [32] leaves of plates : ISBN 83-215-3235-7 LC Card 80-147019
HE848.7 .R86 1980

MERCHANT MARINE - SOUTH AFRICA - HISTORY.
Berridge, Geoff. The politics of the South Africa run . Oxford [Oxfordshire] , New York , 1987. x, 254 p. ; ISBN 0-19-827484-X : LC Card 87-1600 DDC 387.5/094 19
HE903.4 .B47 1987

MERCHANT MARINE - SOVIET UNION - MANAGEMENT - DATA PROCESSING.
Prognozirovanie i ėffektivnost′ raboty flota . Leningrad , 1985. 104 p. : LC Card 86-170274
HE847 .P77 1985

MERCHANT MARINE - SOVIET UNION - PERSONNEL MANAGEMENT.
Mikhin, A. A. (Al′bert Afanas′evich) Povyshenie ėffektivnosti raboty morskogo transporta /. Moskva , 1985. 110, [2] p. ; LC Card 86-115398
HE848 .M55 1985

MERCHANT MARINE - UNITED STATES.
Hilton, Robert, 1927- U. S. maritime industries--down for the third time? /. Washington, D.C. , c1987. vi, 60 p. : ISBN 0-89206-099-9 (pbk.) LC Card 86-31768 DDC 387.5/0973 19
HE745 .H66 1987

Hollyer, Mark. Maritime shipping in the 1980s /. Menlo Park, CA (333 Ravenswood Ave., Menlo Park 94025) , c1986. 18 leaves : LC Card 87-150588 DDC 387.5 19
HE735 .H57 1986

Ullman, Harlan. Forecasts for U. S. maritime industries in 1989 . Washington, D.C. , c1984. ix, 42 p. : ISBN 0-89206-069-7 (pbk.) LC Card 84-27501 DDC 338.4/76238/0973 19
VM299.6 .U45 1984 ***NYPL [JLD 87-155]***

MERCHANT MARINE - UNITED STATES - BIOGRAPHY.
Shields, Jerry. The invisible billionaire, Daniel Ludwig /. Boston , 1986. xii, 401 p. : ISBN 0-395-35402-1 : LC Card 86-7519 DDC 387.5/092/4 B 19
HE569.L84 S55 1986 ***NYPL [JFE 86-3861]***

MERCHANT MARINE - UNITED STATES - HISTORY.
Bauer, K. Jack (Karl Jack), 1926- A maritime history of the United States . Columbia, S.C. , c1988. p. cm. ISBN 0-87249-519-1 LC Card 87-19190 DDC 387.5/0973 19
HE745 .B38 1988

MERCHANT SEAMEN - NEW BRUNSWICK - SAINT JOHN - HISTORY - 19TH CENTURY.
Fingard, Judith. Jack in port . Toronto , Buffalo , c1982. 292 p., [12] p. of plates : ISBN 0-8020-2458-0 LC Card 82-216821 DDC 331.7/6138754044/09715 19
HD8039.S42 C3 1982 ***NYPL [JLE 86-4038]***

MERCHANT SEAMEN - NOVA SCOTIA - HALIFAX - HISTORY - 19TH CENTURY.
Fingard, Judith. Jack in port . Toronto , Buffalo , c1982. 292 p., [12] p. of plates : ISBN 0-8020-2458-0 LC Card 82-216821 DDC

331.7/6138754044/09715 19
HD8039.S42 C3 1982 ***NYPL [JLE 86-4038]***

MERCHANT SEAMEN - QUÉBEC (PROVINCE) - QUÉBEC - HISTORY - 19TH CENTURY.
Fingard, Judith. Jack in port . Toronto , Buffalo , c1982. 292 p., [12] p. of plates : ISBN 0-8020-2458-0 LC Card 82-216821 DDC 331.7/6138754044/09715 19
HD8039.S42 C3 1982 ***NYPL [JLE 86-4038]***

MERCHANT SHIPS - CARGO. see **SHIPS - CARGO.**

MERCHANT SHIPS - GREECE.
Kapetanakē-Sēphakē, Katerina. Hē diethnopoiēsē tou kephalaiou stēn Hellada, hē periptōsē tōn diylistēriōn . Athēna , 1985. 234 p. : LC Card 86-206498
HE595.P4 K36 1985

MERCHANT SHIPS - ITALY - HISTORY.
Ogliari, Francesco. Trasporti marittimi di linea /. Milano , 1975- v. : LC Card 76-507610
HE839 .O35 ***NYPL [JSK 86-35]***

MERCHANT SHIPS - REGISTERS. see **SHIP REGISTERS.**

MERCHANT SHIPS - UNITED STATES - HISTORY.
Bauer, K. Jack (Karl Jack), 1926- A maritime history of the United States . Columbia, S.C. , c1988. p. cm. ISBN 0-87249-519-1 LC Card 87-19190 DDC 387.5/0973 19
HE745 .B38 1988

MERCHANTMEN. see **MERCHANT SHIPS.**

The merchants . Field, Michael, 1949- London , 1984. xii, 371 p., [16] p. of plates : ISBN 0-7195-4104-2 LC Card 87-672963
HC415.3 .F54x 1984

Merchants, companies, and commerce on the Coromandel Coast, 1650-1740 /. Arasaratnam, Sinnappah. Delhi , New York , 1986. x, 407 p. : ISBN 0-19-561873-4 : LC Card 86-900014 DDC 380.1/0954 19
HF3789.C67 A73 1986

MERCHANTS - EGYPT - FAYYUM - CORRESPONDENCE.
Rāġib, Yūsuf. Marchands d'étoffes du Fayyoum au IIIe/IXe siècle d'après leurs archives (actes et lettres) /. Le Caire , 1982- v. : LC Card 83-156837 DDC 380.1/0962/2 19
HF366 .R34 1982 ***NYPL [*OFP 86-3324]***

MERCHANTS - EGYPT - FAYYUM - HISTORY - SOURCES.
Rāġib, Yūsuf. Marchands d'étoffes du Fayyoum au IIIe/IXe siècle d'après leurs archives (actes et lettres) /. Le Caire , 1982- v. : LC Card 83-156837 DDC 380.1/0962/2 19
HF366 .R34 1982 ***NYPL [*OFP 86-3324]***

MERCHANTS - FRANCE - DUNKERQUE - HISTORY - 17TH CENTURY.
Pfister-Langanay, Christian. Ports, navires et négociants à Dunkerque, 1662-1792 /. Dunkerque , 1985. 677 p. : LC Card 87-115474
HD558.D85 P45 1985

MERCHANTS - FRANCE - DUNKERQUE - HISTORY - 18TH CENTURY.
Pfister-Langanay, Christian. Ports, navires et négociants à Dunkerque, 1662-1792 /. Dunkerque , 1985. 677 p. : LC Card 87-115474
HD558.D85 P45 1985

MERCHANTS - FRANCE - PARIS - POLITICAL ACTIVITY - HISTORY - 19TH CENTURY.
Nord, Philip, 1950- Paris shopkeepers and the politics of resentment /. Princeton, N.J. , c1986. xvii, 539 p. : ISBN 0-691-05454-1 : LC Card 85-42695 DDC 322/.3/0944361 19
HF5429.6.F7 N67 1986
NYPL [JLD 86-2305]

MERCHANTS - GERMANY (WEST) - SAUERLAND - HISTORY.
Höher, Peter. Heimat und Fremde . Münster , 1985. viii, 414 p., [1] p. of plates : ISBN 3-88547-290-2 LC Card 85-160726 DDC 381/.0943/42 19
HF3569.S28 H64 1985

MERCHANTS - GREECE - BIOGRAPHY.
Spēliōtakēs, K. K. Archeion Michaēl Iatrou, 1802-1893 /. Athēna , 1983. 189 p., [4] folded leaves of plates : LC Card 85-134031
HF3750.5.S64 A3 1983
NYPL [JFE 86-4131]

MERCHANTS - KOREA - BIOGRAPHY.
Cook, Harold F., 1929- Pioneer American businessman in Korea . Seoul, Korea , 1981. ix, 104 p. : LC Card 83-140523 DDC 382/.09519/0730924 B 19
HF3023.T68 C66 1981
NYPL [JFE 86-4650]

MERCHANTS - MOROCCO - ESSAOUIRA - HISTORY - 18TH CENTURY.
Schroeter, Daniel J. Merchants of Essaouira . Cambridge , New York , 1988. p. cm. ISBN 0-521-32455-6 LC Card 87-15163 DDC 330.964/6 19
HC810.Z7 E857 1988

MERCHANTS - MOROCCO - ESSAOUIRA - HISTORY - 19TH CENTURY.
Schroeter, Daniel J. Merchants of Essaouira . Cambridge , New York , 1988. p. cm. ISBN 0-521-32455-6 LC Card 87-15163 DDC 330.964/6 19
HC810.Z7 E857 1988

MERCHANTS - NETHERLANDS - BIOGRAPHY.
Wildenberg, Ivo W. (Ivo Willibrord) Johan & Pieter de la Court, 1622-1660 & 1618-1685 . Amsterdam , 1986. xiii, 180 p., [21] p. of plates : ISBN 90-302-1162-8 : LC Card 87-141484
HC322.5.A2 W55 1986

Merchants of Essaouira . Schroeter, Daniel J. Cambridge , New York , 1988. p. cm. ISBN 0-521-32455-6 LC Card 87-15163 DDC 330.964/6 19
HC810.Z7 E857 1988

MERCHANTS - PERU - LIMA.
Grompone, Romeo. Talleristas y vendedores ambulantes en Lima /. Lima , 1985. 319 p. : LC Card 85-243089
HD2346.P42 L564 1985

Merchants Record Company (Chicago, Ill.) Street fair manual . Chicago , 1907. 79 p. : LC Card 86-227641
HF5481 .S77 1907

MERCHANTS - SPAIN - SEVILLE - HISTORY - 16TH CENTURY.
Morell Peguero, Blanca. Mercaderes y artesanos en la Sevilla del descubrimiento /. Sevilla , 1986. 222 p. ; ISBN 84-505-2883-6 LC Card 86-199625
HD2346.S72 S465 1986

MERCHANTS - UNITED STATES - BIOGRAPHY.
Cook, Harold F., 1929- Pioneer American businessman in Korea . Seoul, Korea , 1981. ix, 104 p. : LC Card 83-140523 DDC 382/.09519/0730924 B 19
HF3023.T68 C66 1981
NYPL [JFE 86-4650]

Mercier, Paul. Le marché du call money garanti / Paul Mercier. Bruxelles : Centre d'études financières, [1983] 64 p. : ill. ; 24 cm. (Revue de la banque. Cahier . 24 (nov./déc. 1983) = 24) LC Card 84-210204
1. Money market - Belgium. 2. Money - Belgium. 3. Forward exchange - Belgium. I. Title. II. Title: Call money garanti. III. Series: Revue de la banque. Cahier , 24.
HG1055 .M47 1983

MERCURY INDUSTRY AND TRADE - SPAIN - ALMADÉN - HISTORY.
Martín Martín, Victoriano. Los Rothschild y las minas de Almadén . Madrid , 1980. xiv, 639 p. ; ISBN 84-7196-338-8 LC Card 83-149823
HJ8738 .M37 1980

MERCURY MINERS - SPAIN - ALMADÉN REGION - HISTORY - 16TH CENTURY.
Bleiberg, Germán, 1915- El "informe secreto" de Mateo Alemán sobre el trabajo forzoso en las minas de Almadén /. London , c1985. 150 p. ; ISBN 0-7293-0200-8 LC Card 86-178917
HD4875.S6 B58 1985

MERCURY MINES AND MINING - SPAIN - ALMADÉN REGION - HISTORY - 16TH CENTURY.
Bleiberg, Germán, 1915- El "informe secreto" de Mateo Alemán sobre el trabajo forzoso en las minas de Almadén /. London , c1985. 150 p. ; ISBN 0-7293-0200-8 LC Card 86-178917
HD4875.S6 B58 1985

Mereste, U. (Uno) Majandusteaduse ABC . Tallinn , 1985. 511 p. : LC Card 85-195109
HB61 .M225 1985

Mérey, Ildikó. Friss István emlékezete /. Budapest , 1984. 128 p. ; LC Card 86-145174
HC300.28 .F75 1984

MERGER OF CORPORATIONS. see **CONSOLIDATION AND MERGER OF CORPORATIONS.**

Mergers and acquisitions / edited by Alan J. Auerbach. Chicago : University of Chicago Press, 1988. xi, 108 p. : ill. ; 24 cm. (A National Bureau of Economic Research project report) Includes bibliographies and index. ISBN 0-226-03209-4 LC Card 87-19035 DDC 658.1/6 19
1. Consolidation and merger of corporations - Congresses. 2. Junk bonds - Congresses. 3. Consolidation and merger of corporations - Taxation - Congresses. I. Auerbach, Alan J. II. Series.
HD2746.5 .M45 1988

MERGERS, CONGLOMERATE. see **CONGLOMERATE CORPORATIONS.**

Mergers, sell-offs, and economic efficiency /. Ravenscraft, David J., 1952- Washington, D.C. , c1987. xiii, 290 p. : ISBN 0-8157-7348-X : LC Card 87-14018 DDC 338.8/3/0973 19
HD2746.5 .R38 1987

Mergers, sell-offs & economic efficiency. Ravenscraft, David J., 1952- Mergers, sell-offs, and economic efficiency /. Washington, D.C. , c1987. xiii, 290 p. : ISBN 0-8157-7348-X : LC Card 87-14018 DDC 338.8/3/0973 19
HD2746.5 .R38 1987

Mergner, Ulrich. Marstedt, Gerd. Psychische Belastungen in der Arbeitswelt . Opladen , c1986. vii, 366 p. : ISBN 3-531-11757-2 LC Card 87-135624
HF5548.8 .M373 1986

Mergos, George, 1948- Dairy development and milk cooperatives : the effects of a dairy project in India / George Mergos, Roger Slade. Washington, D.C. : World Bank, [1987] xiv, 140 p. : ill. ; 28 cm. (World Bank discussion papers, 0259-210X . 15) Bibliography: p. 135-140. ISBN 0-8213-0932-3 (pbk.) LC Card 87-15976 DDC 334/.68371/09543 19
1. Milk trade - India - Madhya Pradesh. 2. Dairying, Cooperative - India - Madhya Pradesh. I. Slade, Roger, 1941-. II. Title. III. Series.
HD9282.I53 M286 1987

MÉRIDA (SPAIN) - POPULATION - HISTORY - 17TH CENTURY - STATISTICS.
Rodríguez Grajera, Alfonso. La población de Mérida en el siglo XVII /. [Badajoz] , 1985. xv, 162 p. : ISBN 84-505-1500-9 LC Card 86-232003
HB3620.M47 R63 1985

MÉRIDA (SPAIN) - STATISTICS, VITAL - HISTORY - 17TH CENTURY.
Rodríguez Grajera, Alfonso. La población de Mérida en el siglo XVII /. [Badajoz] , 1985. xv, 162 p. : ISBN 84-505-1500-9 LC Card 86-232003
HB3620.M47 R63 1985

Meridien International Bank. Republic of Zambia, economic memorandum /. [Lusaka?] [1983?] 28 p. : LC Card 86-980289 DDC 330.96894/04 19
HC915 .R46 1983

Merk, Gerhard, 1931-
Ausgewählte Aufsätze zur Wirtschaftstheorie / Gerhard Merk. Zürich : Fraumünster-Verlag, 1986. 138 p. ; 22 cm. Includes bibliographical references. Includes index. ISBN 3-9999462-1-1 LC Card 87-409558 DDC 330.9494/073 19
1. Economics - Switzerland. 2. Inflation (Finance) - Switzerland. I. Title.
HB118.A2 M47 1986

Marktwirtschaft und Gesellschaftsordnung . Berlin , c1983. 220 p., [1] leaf of plates : ISBN 3-428-05365-6 LC Card 83-191615
HB72 .M248 1983

Merkantilismus und Kapitalismus im modernen Rationalisierungsprozess /. Helmer, Hans-Josef. Frankfurt , c1986. iii, 223 p. ; ISBN 3-88323-647-0 LC Card 87-113030 DDC 330.15/13 19
HB91 .H436 1986

Merkaz le-fituaḥ 'al-shem P. Sapir. Economic effects of the government budget /. Cambridge, Mass. , c1988. p. cm. ISBN 0-262-08172-5 LC Card 87-26187 DDC 338.9 19
HJ2005 .E25 1988

Merkaz le-ḥeker hityashvut kafrit ve-'ironit. Rural industrialization in Israel /. Boulder , 1987. xi, 193 p. ; ISBN 0-8133-7393-X (pbk. : alk. paper) : LC Card 87-2073 DDC 338.095694 19
HC415.25 .R87 1987

Merkel, Wolfgang. Ungleiche Entwicklung und Regionalpolitik in Südeuropa . Bochum , 1985. 282 p. : ISBN 3-88339-441-6 : LC Card 85-205651
HC244.5 .U48 1985

Merklein, Renate.
Die Deutschen werden ärmer : Staatsverschuldung, Geldentwertung, Markteinbussen, Arbeitsplatzverluste / Renate Merklein. Reinbek bei Hamburg : Rowohlt, 1982. 189 p. : ill. ; 19 cm. (Spiegel-Buch. 18) Includes bibliographical references and index. ISBN 3-499-33018-0 : LC Card 83-137339
1. Germany, West - Economic conditions - 1974-. I. Title.
HC286.7 .M475 1982

Die Rentenkrise / Renate Merklein. Reinbek bei Hamburg : Rowohlt, 1986. 190 p. : ill. ; 19 cm. (Spiegel-Buch. 72) Includes bibliographical references. ISBN 3-499-33072-5 : LC Card 87-100842
1. Old age pensions - Germany, West. 2. Population forecasting - Germany, West. I. Title.
HD7105.35.G3 M47 1986

Merrick, Charles M. ASME Management Division history, 1886-1980 /. New York, N.Y. (345 E. 47th St., New York 10017) , c1984. x, 169 p. : LC Card 84-206982 DDC 658/.006/073 19
HD28.A6233 A86 1984 ***NYPL [JLF 86-1646]***

Merrien, Francis. Le Renouvellement du tissu industriel . Paris [1986] 130 p. ; ISBN 2-11-001568-3 : LC Card 86-191910
HD3616.F83 R46 1986

Merrill, Lois J. Global hunger . [Evansville, Ind.] , 1986. iv, 164 p. : ISBN 0-930982-08-8 (pbk.) LC Card 87-400224 DDC 363.8/8/091724 19
HD9018.D44 G57 1986

Merrill, Ronald E. The new venture handbook : everything you need to know to start and run your own business / Ronald E. Merrill and Henry D. Sedgwick. New York, NY : American Management Association, c1987. 356 p. : ill. ; 24 cm. Bibliography: p. 339-344. Includes index. ISBN 0-8144-5895-5 LC Card 86-47818 DDC 658.1/141 19
1. New business enterprises - Management. I. Sedgwick, Henry D. II. Title.
HD62.5 .M46 1987

The Merrill series in computer information systems.
Rosen, Arnold, 1932- Office automation and information systems /. Columbus , c1987. xvi, 363 p. : ISBN 0-675-20557-3 (pbk.) LC Card 86-62495 DDC 651.8 19
HF5548 .R67 1987

Merriman, David. The control of municipal budgets : toward the effective design of tax and expenditure limitations / David Merriman. New York : Quorum Books, c1987. x, 170 p. : ill. ; 22 cm. Bibliography: p. [157]-166. Includes index. ISBN 0-89930-217-3 (lib. bdg. : alk. paper) LC Card 87-2495 DDC 352.1/2/0973 19
1. Tax and expenditure limitations - United States. 2. Municipal budgets - United States. I. Title.
HJ9157 .M47 1987

Merritt Company. Lenz, Matthew. Risk management manual /. Santa Monica, Calif. (P.O. Box 955, Santa Monica 90406) , <1972-. 3 v. (loose-leaf) : LC Card 86-209050
HG8054.5 .L46 1972

Merritt, John. The making of the AWU / John Merritt. Melbourne ; New York : Oxford University Press, 1986. x, 432 p., [16] p. of plates : ill. ; 23 cm. Bibliography: p. [416]-417. Includes index. ISBN 0-19-554667-9 LC Card 86-207509 DDC 331.88/13630833/0994 19
1. Australian Workers' Union - History. 2. Trade-unions - Australia - History. 3. Sheep shearers (Persons) - Australia - History. I. Title.
HD8842.A874 M47 1986

Mertens, Jürgen. Zur Entwicklung und zum konstellationsadäquaten Einsatz eines Beschaffungsmarketinginstrumentariums im Einzelhandel / von Jürgen Mertens. Köln : Fördergesellschaft Produkt-Marketing, 1986. 379 p. : 51 ill. ; 21 cm. (Beiträge zum Beschaffungsmarketing . Bd. 6) Cover title: Konstellationsadäquate Beschaffungspolitik im Handel. Bibliography: p. 344-376. Includes index. ISBN 3-922292-13-7 LC Card 87-143182 DDC 658.8/7 19
1. Retail trade - Equipment and supplies. 2. Retail trade - Management. I. Title. II. Title: Konstellationsadäquate Beschaffungspolitik im Handel. III. Series.
HF5429.225 .M47 1986

Merz, Joachim. Microanalytic simulation models to support social and financial policy /. Amsterdam ; New York : xvii, 553 p. : ISBN 0-444-87876-9 (U. S.) LC Card 85-25231 DDC 361.6/0724 19
HD87 .M52 1986 ***NYPL [JLD 86-3485]***

MESA PETROLEUM CO. - HISTORY.
Pickens, T. Boone (Thomas Boone) Boone /. Boston , 1987. xii, 304 p., [8] p. of plates : ISBN 0-395-41433-4 : LC Card 86-27648 DDC 338.7/6223382/0924 B 19
HD9570.P53 A3 1987

Mesa Redonda sobre la Carta de Punta del Este (1961 : Universidad Nacional Autónoma de México) Memoria del ciclo de conferencias de Mesa Redonda sobre la Carta de Punta del Este / organizado por la Sociedad de Alumnos del Doctorado en Derecho de la U.N.A.M. México : Facultad de Derecho de la U.N.A.M., 1962. 224 p. : ill., ports. ; 24 cm. Title on added t.p.: Conferencias sobre la Carta de Punta del Este. Spine title: Carta Punta del Este. LC Card 85-105213
1. Alliance for progress - Congresses. 2. Economic assistance - Latin America - Congresses. 3. Latin America - Economic conditions - 1945- - Congresses. I. Sociedad de Alumnos del Doctorado en Derecho de la U.N.A.M. II. Universidad Nacional Autónoma de México. Facultad de Derecho. III. Title. IV. Title: Conferencias sobre la Carta de Punta del Este. V. Title: Carta Punta del Este.
HC125 .M48 1961

Mescon, Michael H. Rachman, David J. Business today /. New York , c1987. xxiii, 643 p. : ISBN 0-394-35114-2 LC Card 86-24784 DDC 658 19
HF5351 .R26 1987

Mescon, Timothy S. Cases in strategic management : an industry approach / Timothy S. Mescon, George S. Vozikis. New York : Harper & Row, c1988. ix, 725 p. : ill. ; 24 cm. Includes bibliographies. ISBN 0-06-044465-7 (pbk.) LC Card 87-25141 DDC 658.4/012 19
1. Corporate planning - United States - Case studies. I. Vozikis, George S. (George Soterios), 1948-. II. Title.
HD30.28 .M46 1988

Mesfin Gabre Michael. Labour-management relations in public enterprises in Africa. Geneva, Switzerland : International Labour Office, 1983. 84 p. ; 24 cm. (Labour-management relations series, 0538-8325 . 60) Includes bibliographical references. CONTENTS. - Labour-management relations in public enterprises in Africa / [Mesfin Gabre Michael] -- Labour-management relations in public enterprises in Africa : the Nigerian case / by T.M. Yesufu -- Labour-management relations in Tunisian public enterprises / by N. Ladhari. ISBN 92-2-103009-1 (pbk.) LC Card 86-213649 DDC 658.3 s 331/.04135/000096 19
1. Industrial relations - Africa. 2. Industrial relations - Nigeria. 3. Industrial relations - Tunisia. 4. Government business enterprises - Africa. 5. Government business enterprises - Nigeria. 6. Government business enterprises - Tunisia. I. Yesufu, T. M. (Tijani M.) Labour-management relations in public enterprises in Africa. 1983. II. Ladhari, Noë. Labour-management relations in Tunisian public enterprises. 1983. III. Title. IV. Series.
HD6961.A1 I73 no. 60 HD8776.5

Meskhii͡a, I͡A. E. (I͡Akov Egnatovich) Voprosy metodologii regional'nogo ėkonomicheskogo prognozirovanii͡a / I͡A.E. Meskhii͡a. Moskva : Izd-vo "Nauka", 1983. 183 p. : ill. ; 20 cm. (Problemy sovetskoĭ ėkonomiki) At head of title: Akademii͡a nauk SSSR. T͡Sentral'nyĭ ėkonomiko-matematicheskiĭ institut. Nauchnyĭ sovet po kompleksnoĭ probleme "Optimal'noe planirovanie i upravlenie narodnym khozi͡aĭstvom." Includes bibliographical references. LC Card 84-141931
1. Economic forecasting - Georgian S.S.R. 2. Georgian S.S.R. - Economic conditions - Econometric models. I. Title.
HC337.G38 M43 1983

La mesocracia de Costa Rica, 1821-1926 /. Villalobos Vega, Bernardo. San José , c1986. 309 p. ; ISBN 997-7232-15-6 LC Card 86-231140
HC143.Z9 S38 1986

Hē mesogeiakē politikē tēs EOK . Arampatzēs, E. Thessalonikē , 1983. 268 p. ; LC Card 84-185339
HC241.25.M4 A73 1983

Mesropian, André. Les relations du Liban avec la Communauté économique européenne / André Mesropian. Beyrouth, Liban : Ministère de l'information, [between 1972 and 1984] 65 p. ; 22 cm. (Etudes et documents du Centre de diffusion libanais) LC Card 84-196415
1. Lebanon - Foreign economic relations - European Economic Community countries. 2. European Economic Community countries - Foreign economic relations - Lebanon. 3. Lebanon - Commerce - European Economic Community countries. 4. European Economic Community countries - Commerce - Lebanon. I. Title. II. Series.
HF1583.9.Z4 E865 1972

Message to the nation . Madrid Hurtado, Miguel de la. [Mexico City, Mexico] [1986] 15 p. : LC Card 87-400574 DDC 338.972 19
HC135 .M225 1986

Messen und Ausstellungen als Mittel der Absatzpolitik mittelständischer Herstellerbetriebe /. Mortsiefer, Joachim. Göttingen , 1986. 534 p. : ISBN 3-509-01399-9 : LC Card 86-210320 DDC 381/.18 19
HF5470 .M583 1986

Messick, David M. Experimental social dilemmas /. Frankfurt am Main , New York , c1986. vi, 234 p. : ISBN 3-8204-8574-0 (pbk.) : LC Card 86-10307 DDC 302 19
HM132 .E96 1986 ***NYPL [JLD 87-1177]***

Messier, Suzanne. Perspectives d'emploi pour les Québécoises dans la décennie 1980 : document approuvé par le Comité sur les questions économiques le 12 août 1983 / Suzanne Messier. Québec : Gouvernement du Québec, Conseil du statut de la femme, [1983] vi, 73 p. ; 28 cm. Bibliography: p. [71]-73. ISBN 2-550-10439-0 LC Card 84-221697
1. Women - Employment - Québec (Province). 2. Employment forecasting - Québec (Province). I. Québec (Province). Comité sur les questions économiques. II. Québec (Province). Conseil du statut de la femme. III. Title.
HD6100.Q4 M47 1983

Messinger, Heinz. Klatt, Edmund. Langenscheidt's standard German dictionary /. New York , 1983-1984. 1341 p. ; ***NYPL [JFC 86-781]***

Messner, Stephen D. Real estate market analysis . New York , 1988. xvii, 350 p. : ISBN 0-275-92414-9 (alk. paper) : LC Card 87-15832 DDC 333.33/22 19
HD1382.5 .R396 1988

Messprobleme öffentlicher Aktivitäten . Gantner, Manfried. Baden-Baden , 1984. 353 p. ; ISBN 3-7890-0989-X : LC Card 84-252950
HJ2005 .G35 1984

Die Messung der Arbeitslosigkeit /. Riese, Martin. Berlin , c1986. 199 p. : ISBN 3-428-06034-2 LC Card 86-215265 DDC 331.12/0724 19
HD5707.5 .R54 1986

Messwerte der Informationsnachfrage in komplexen Beurteilungsprozessen /. Knorr, Peter. Kiel , 1986. xvi, 241 p. : ISBN 3-922553-77-X LC Card 86-149044
HB133 .K59 1986

Mester, Bernt. Marktchancen der Binnenschiffahrt im Container-Hinterlandverkehr der Häfen der Hamburg-Antwerpen-Range / von Bernt Mester. Düsseldorf : Verkehrs-Verlag J. Fischer, 1986. xii, 304 p. ; 24 cm. (Buchreihe des Instituts für Verkehrswissenschaft an der Universität zu Köln, 0341-5767 . Nr. 47) Includes added t.p. with thesis statement. Originally presented as the author's thesis

(doctoral)--Universität zu Köln, 1986. Bibliography: p. 289-304. LC Card 87-409549
1. Harbors - Germany (West) - Hamburg - Management. 2. Harbors - Belgium - Antwerp - Management. 3. Containerization - Germany (West) - Hamburg Region. 4. Containerization - Belgium - Antwerp. I. Title. II. Series.
HE5 .C6 Nr. 47 HE558.H3

Un Mestiere e un paese : i sabionanti di Sottomarina / a cura di Fabrizio Boscolo, Cinzio Gibin, Piergiorgio Tiozzo.1a ed. Venezia : Marsilio, 1986. 172 p. : ill. (some col.) ; 24 cm. (Itinerari culturali del comune di Chioggia . n. 4) Bibliography: p. 169-172. ISBN 88-317-4893-9 LC Card 86-219883
1. Sand and gravel industry - Italy - Sottomarina Region - Employees. 2. Sand and gravel industry - Italy - Sottomarina Region. 3. Sand - Italy - Sottomarina Region. 4. Dredging - Italy - Sottomarina Region. I. Boscolo, Fabrizio. II. Gibin, Cinzio. III. Tiozzo, Piergiorgio. IV. Title. V. Series.
HD8039.S252 I85 1986

Il mestiere politico del sindacato /. Carrieri, Mimmo. Roma , 1986. 218 p. ; ISBN 88-359-2930-X : LC Card 86-200898
HD8485 .C37 1986

Mestmäcker, Ernst Joachim. Vereinbarkeit von Preisregelungen auf dem Arzneimittelmarkt mit dem Recht der Europäischen Wirtschaftsgemeinschaft / Ernst-Joachim Mestmäcker. 1. Aufl. Baden-Baden : Nomos-Verlagsgesellschaft, 1979. 83 p. ; 23 cm. (Schriftenreihe Europäische Wirtschaft. Bd. 97) Preface and summary also in English and French. Includes bibliographical references. ISBN 3-7890-0444-8 : LC Card 80-515375
1. Price regulation - Germany, West. 2. Drugs - Prices - European Economic Community countries. 3. Drugs - Prices - Germany, West. I. Title.
KK6444.D78 M47 ***NYPL [JLD 81-684]***

Mesure de la valeur ajoutée aux prix constants dans les activités de service. Measurement of value added at constant prices in service activities /. Paris . v. <1 > ; ISBN 92-64-02879-X (pbk.) : LC Card 87-164470 DDC 657/.45 19
HF5686.S43 M43 1987

Mesure des ressources humaines et gestion de l'entreprise /. Vatteville, Éric. Paris , c1985. 286 p. : ISBN 2-7178-0969-4 : LC Card 86-137038 DDC 658.3 19
HF5549 .V382 1985

Mesure et incidence des dépenses fiscales au Québec /. Jobin, Jacques. Montréal [1984] 27 p. ; LC Card 85-169988
HB3 .C3 vol. 8511 HJ4662.A45

Mészáros, István, 1930- Philosophy, ideology, and social science : essays in negation and affirmation / István Mészáros. Brighton, Sussex : Wheatsheaf, 1986. xix, 284 p. ; 23 cm. Includes index. Bibliography: p. [269]-281. ISBN 0-85527-717-3
1. Political sociology. 2. Marxian school of sociology. I. Title. ***NYPL [JLD 87-1334]***

Mészáros, Sándor.
Borszéki, Éva. Élelmiszer-gazdaságunk versenyképessége . Budapest , 1986. 284, [1] p. : ISBN 963-221-590-7 : LC Card 87-148751
HD1940.5 .B66 1986

Borszéki, Éva. Élelmiszergazdaságunk versenyképessége . Budapest , 1985. 147 p. ; ISBN 963-491-213-3 LC Card 86-199073
HD1940.5 .B67 1985

Felügyelőbizottságok az ÁFÉSZ-ekben / Mészáros Sándor. [Budapest] : SZÖVOSZ Szövetkezetpolitikai Főosztálya és a Szövetkezeti Kutató Intézet Közös Kiadványa, [1976] 58 p. ; 21 cm. (Közlemények . 110) "Budapest, 1976. január." LC Card 86-187734
1. Consumer cooperatives - Hungary - Auditing. I. Series: Közlemények / Szövetkezeti Kutató Intézet, 110. II. Title.
HD3332.5.A5 M47 1976

A világ műtrágyatermelésének és -felhasználásának előrejelzése / Mészáros Sándor. Budapest : Akadémiai Kiadó, 1985. 143 p. : ill. ; 19 cm. (A Nagyüzemi gazdálkodás kérdései, 0077-2658) Bibliography: p. 129-130. ISBN 963-05-3670-6 : LC Card 86-136326
1. Fertilizer industry - Forecasting - Econometric models. I. Title. II. Series.
HD9483.A2 M47 1985

Meszéna, György. Módszerek a beruházási tevékenység kvantitatív elemzéséhez /. Budapest , 1985. 207 p. : ISBN 963-05-3607-2 : LC Card 86-100399
HG4028.C4 M57 1985

Meszticzky, András. Termelőszövetkezeti szakemberek munkahelyváltoztatása : vezetői fluktuáció 187 gazdaságban / Meszticzky András. [Budapest] : Szövetkezeti Kutató Intézet, 1985. 165 p. : ill. ; 29 cm. (Közlemények, 0133-4905 . 189) Bibliography: p. 158. LC Card 86-218526
1. Collective farms - Hungary - Officials and employees. 2. Labor turnover - Hungary. I. Series: Közlemények (Szövetkezeti Kutató Intézet) ;v189. II. Title.
HD1492.H8 M37 1985

Meta-analysis . Wolf, Fredric M. (Fredric Marc) Beverly Hills , c1986. 65 p. : ISBN 0-8039-2756-8 LC Card 85-52372
NYPL [JLK 77-39 no.59]

META-ANALYSIS.
The Psychology of gender . Baltimore , c1986. vii, 293 p. : ISBN 0-8018-2974-7 (alk. paper) LC Card 85-19822 DDC 155.3/3 19
BF692.2 .P76 1986 ***NYPL [JFE 86-2969]***

Wolf, Fredric M. (Fredric Marc) Meta-analysis . Beverly Hills , c1986. 65 p. : ISBN 0-8039-2756-8 LC Card 85-52372
NYPL [JLK 77-39 no.59]

Metaeconomic conceptualization and social criteria of development /. Buračas, A. (Antanas) Vilnius , 1987 [i.e. 1986] 60, [4] p. ; LC Card 87-672211
HB131 .B87x 1986

Metais de Minas Gerais, S.A. Programa pegmatitos. 2a. ed. rev. Belo Horizonte : METAMIG, 1981. 95 p. : ill. ; 24 cm. At head of title: Governo de Estado de Minas Gerais, Secretaria de Indústria, Comércio e Turismo. On cover: Administração de recursos minerais, 1980/83. LC Card 83-220720
1. Mineral industries - Brazil. 2. Economic development projects - Brazil. 3. Pegmatites - Brazil. I. Title.
HD9506.B72 M48 1981

METAL CASTINGS INDUSTRY - AUSTRALIA - WESTERN AUSTRALIA.
A Study of the Western Australian casting and forging industry. [Perth] [1984?]-[1985] 2 v. ; LC Card 86-207984 DDC 388.4/7671/09941 19
HD9506.A8 W385 1984

METAL-CUTTING - DICTIONARIES.
Kleiber, Achim W. Fachwörterbuch, Schweissen, Schneiden und verwandte Verfahren /. Düsseldorf , 1986- , c1985- v. ; ISBN 3-87155-707-2 (Bd. 1) LC Card 86-149500 DDC 671.5/2/0331 19
TS227.5 .K54 1986 ***NYPL [JSK 86-83]***

METAL-CUTTING - DICTIONARIES - GERMAN.
Kleiber, Achim W. Fachwörterbuch, Schweissen, Schneiden und verwandte Verfahren /. Düsseldorf , 1986- , c1985- v. ; ISBN 3-87155-707-2 (Bd. 1) LC Card 86-149500 DDC 671.5/2/0331 19
TS227.5 .K54 1986 ***NYPL [JSK 86-83]***

METAL FINISHING EQUIPMENT INDUSTRY - UNITED STATES.
Metal finishing machinery market. New York, N.Y. , c1983. vii, 220 p. ; LC Card 87-141856 DDC 381/.456817671/0973 19
HD9506.U62 M38 1983

Metal finishing machinery market. New York, N.Y. : Frost & Sullivan, c1983. vii, 220 p. ; 29 cm. "A990." "April 1983." LC Card 87-141856 DDC 381/.456817671/0973 19
1. Metal finishing equipment industry - United States. 2. Market surveys - United States. I. Frost & Sullivan.
HD9506.U62 M38 1983

METAL INDUSTRIES. see **METAL-WORK; MINERAL INDUSTRIES.**

METAL OXIDE SEMICONDUCTORS, COMPLEMENTARY.
Annaratone, Marco. Digital CMOS circuit design /. Boston , c1986. xv, 344 p. : ISBN 0-89838-224-6 LC Card 86-10646 DDC 621.395 19
TK7871.99.M44 A56 1986
NYPL [JSE 87-634]

METAL TRADE - FINLAND - HISTORY.
Metsänkylä, Antti. Metallityön tallennus . Helsinki , 1986. 77 p. : ISBN 951-9074-93-7 LC Card 87-101629
HD9506.F52 M43 1986

METAL TRADE - FINLAND - MUSEUMS.
Metsänkylä, Antti. Metallityön tallennus . Helsinki , 1986. 77 p. : ISBN 951-9074-93-7 LC Card 87-101629
HD9506.F52 M43 1986

METAL TRADE - PORTUGAL - HISTORY.
Mónica, Maria Filomena, 1943- Artesãos e operários . Lisboa [1986] 228 p., [24] p. of plates : LC Card 86-229921
HD8596 .M65 1986

METAL TRADE - SENEGAL.
ECA/UNIDO Basic Metals and Engineering Industries Development Programme Mission. Rapport de la Mission sur le programme de développement des industries métallurgiques de base et mécaniques en République du Sénégal. [S.l.] [1979] 41, 3 p. (2 fold.) ; LC Card 80-981173
HD9506.S42 E33 1979

METAL TRADE - SWEDEN - STATISTICS.
Svensk gjuteriindustri . Stockholm , 1982. 62 p. : ISBN 91-38-07151-7 LC Card 83-220920
HD9506.S82 S92 1982

METAL TRADE - UNITED STATES.
The Competitiveness of American metal mining and processing . Washington , 1986. x, 186 p. ; LC Card 86-603391 DDC 338.2/74/0973 19
HD9506.U62 C63 1986

New specialty metals & metallurgy for high-temperature, high-strength, low-weight applications /. Norwalk, Conn., U. S.A. , c1987. 1 v. (various foliations) : ISBN 0-89336-454-1 (pbk.) LC Card 87-168123 DDC 380.1/45669/0973 19
HD9506.U62 N45 1987

METAL-WORK - AUSTRALIA - WESTERN AUSTRALIA.
A Study of the Western Australian casting and forging industry. [Perth] [1984?]-[1985] 2 v. ; LC Card 86-207984 DDC 388.4/7671/09941 19
HD9506.A8 W385 1984

METAL-WORK - AUSTRIA.
Kramer, Helmut, 1939- Industrielle Strukturprobleme Österreichs . Wien , 1980. 112 p. ; LC Card 81-103725 DDC 338.4/76691/09436 19
HD9525.A82 K73 1980
NYPL [JLD 86-1237]

METAL-WORK - GERMANY (WEST) - NORTH RHINE-WESTPHALIA - STATISTICS.
Zensus im Bergbau und verarbeitenden Gewerbe Nordrhein-Westfalen 1979 . Düsseldorf [1983] 109 p. ; LC Card 87-407314 DDC 943/.55 s 338.2/0943/55021 19
HA1320.N6 A32 Heft 497 HD9506.G23N6

METAL-WORK - GREAT BRITAIN - PERSONNEL MANAGEMENT.
Jaques, Elliott. The changing culture of a factory /. New York , 1987. xvii, 341 p. ; ISBN 0-8240-8212-5 (alk. paper) : LC Card 86-25815 DDC 671/.068 19
HD8039.M5 J37 1987

METAL-WORK - PERU - FINANCE - CASE STUDIES.
Beltrán Alejos, Hugo. La situación del sector metal-mecánico en el Perú . Lima, Perú , 1985. 93, [77] p. : LC Card 86-218266
HD9506.P42 B45 1985

METAL-WORK - UNITED STATES - AUTOMATION.
Hicks, Donald A. Automation technology and industrial renewal . Washington, D.C. [1985], c1986. xiii, 160 p. ; ISBN 0-8447-3598-1 LC Card 85-31568 DDC 671 19
HD9506.U62 H53 1986
NYPL [JSE 86-1901]

METAL-WORK - UNITED STATES - TECHNOLOGICAL INNOVATIONS.
Hicks, Donald A. Automation technology and industrial renewal . Washington, D.C. [1985], c1986. xiii, 160 p. ; ISBN 0-8447-3598-1 LC Card 85-31568 DDC 671 19
HD9506.U62 H53 1986
NYPL [JSE 86-1901]

METAL-WORK - VENEZUELA.
Preliminary study report on promotion of small-medium scale industries in the Republic of Venezuela. [Tokyo] [1978] ii, 27 p. : LC Card 84-249328
HD9506.V42 P74 1978

METAL-WORKERS - BULGARIA - BIOGRAPHY.
Trudova slava /. Sofiīā , <1986-. v. <4 > : LC Card 86-228746
HD8039.M62 B88 1986

METAL-WORKERS - FINLAND - HISTORY.
Metsänkylä, Antti. Metallityön tallennus . Helsinki , 1986. 77 p. : ISBN 951-9074-93-7 LC Card 87-101629
HD9506.F52 M43 1986

METAL-WORKERS - GREAT BRITAIN.
Jaques, Elliott. The changing culture of a factory /. New York , 1987. xvii, 341 p. ; ISBN 0-8240-8212-5 (alk. paper) : LC Card 86-25815 DDC 671/.068 19
HD8039.M5 J37 1987

METAL-WORKERS - HUNGARY - CASE STUDIES.
Héthy, Lajos. Patterns of worker's behavior and the enterprise /. New Brunswick, U. S.A. , c1987. p. cm. ISBN 0-88738-177-4 LC Card 87-13958 DDC 331/.0471/09439 19
HD6956.M5 H47 1987

METAL-WORKERS - PERU.
Parodi Solari, Jorge. Ser obrero es algo relativo-- . Lima [1986] 184 p. ; LC Card 87-405297 DDC 331.7/671/0985 19
HD8039.M52 P46 1986

METAL-WORKERS - PHILIPPINES - TRAINING OF.
Metals and engineering . Manila, Philippines , 1983. 64 p. : LC Card 87-401862 DDC 331.25/92 19
HD5716.M52 P66 1983

METAL-WORKERS - ROMANIA - TRANSYLVANIA - HISTORY.
Vajda, Lajos. Erdélyi bányák, kohók, emberek, századok . Bukarest , 1981. 544 p. : LC Card 83-124763
HD8039.M61 R68 1981

METAL-WORKERS' STRIKE, U. S., 1935 - HISTORY.
Suggs, George G., 1929- Union busting in the Tri-State . Norman , 1986. xiv, 282 p. : ISBN 0-8061-2012-6 (alk. paper) LC Card 86-6910 DDC 331.89/2871/0973 19
HD5325.M52 1935 .S84 1986
NYPL [JLD 86-3971]

METAL-WORKING MACHINERY INDUSTRY - EUROPE.
Metal working plant market in Europe. New York, N.Y. , c1983. xvi, 262 p. ; LC Card 87-141761 DDC 380.1/456817671/094 19
HD9705.E72 M48 1983

Metal working plant market in Europe. New York, N.Y. : Frost & Sullivan, c1983. xvi, 262 p. ; 28 cm. "July 1983." LC Card 87-141761 DDC 380.1/456817671/094 19
1. Metal-working machinery industry - Europe. 2. Market surveys - Europe. I. Frost & Sullivan.
HD9705.E72 M48 1983

Metallgewerkschaften in Südafrika / Eugen Loderer (Hrsg.). [Köln] : Bund-Verlag, c1983. 217 p. ; 21 cm. (Schriftenreihe der Otto Brenner Stiftung . 34) Includes bibliographical references. CONTENTS. - Für den friedlichen Wandel in Südafrika / Eugen Loderer -- Gewerkschaften in Südafrika / Helmut Bley -- Die nicht-rassische Gewerkschaftsbewegung Südafrikas 1973 bis 1982 / Gottfried Wellmer -- Der IMB und die Metallgewerkschaften in Südafrika 1951 bis 1982 / Herman Rebhan, Werner Thönnissen / Reform oder Kontrolle? / Fred Sauls -- Die Reaktion der weissen Gewerkschaften auf die Arbeitrechtsreform von 1979 / Ike van der Watt / Arbeitnehmer und Gewerkschaften in Südafrika / Siegfried Ehlers -- Der Mann des Jahres. ISBN 3-7663-0530-1 LC Card 85-232412 DDC 331.88/171/0968 19
1. Trade-unions - Metal-workers - South Africa - Addresses, essays, lectures. 2. Trade-unions - South Africa - Addresses, essays, lectures. I. Loderer, Eugen. II. Otto Brenner Stiftung. III. Series. IV. Series: Otto Brenner Stiftung. Schriftenreihe, 34.
HD6870.5.Z7 M54 1983
NYPL [JLD 87-1964]

Metallityön tallennus . Metsänkylä, Antti. Helsinki , 1986. 77 p. : ISBN 951-9074-93-7 LC Card 87-101629
HD9506.F52 M43 1986

Metallurgicheski kombinat, Magnitogorsk. see **Magnitogorskiĭ metallurgicheskiĭ kombinat.**

METALLURGY - SPAIN - ALMERÍA (PROVINCE)
Sánchez Picón, Andrés. La minería del Levante almeriense, 1838-1930 . Almería [1983] 308 p., [14] leaves of plates : ISBN 84-85219-49-X LC Card 85-126928
HD9506.S762 A457 1983

Metals and engineering : NMYC-World Bank Vocational Training Project sector specific plan, 1982-85. Manila, Philippines : The Project, 1983. 64 p. : ill. (some col.) ; 28 cm. Includes bibliographical references. LC Card 87-401862 DDC 331.25/92 19
1. Metal-workers - Philippines - Training of. 2. Machinery industry - Philippines - Employees - Training of. 3. Occupational training - Philippines. I. NMYC-World Bank Vocational Training Project.
HD5716.M52 P66 1983

METALS AS AN INVESTMENT.
Persons, Robert H., 1922- The investor's encyclopedia of gold, silver, and other precious metals. [New York, 1974] x, 316 p. ISBN 0-394-49597-7 LC Card 74-14860 DDC 332.6/328
HG5073 .P38 *NYPL [JLF 86-388]*

METALS AT HIGH TEMPERATURES.
(1987) New specialty metals & metallurgy for high-temperature, high-strength, low-weight applications /. Norwalk, Conn., U. S.A. , c1987. 1 v. (various foliations) : ISBN 0-89336-454-1 (pbk.) LC Card 87-168123 DDC 380.1/45669/0973 19
HD9506.U62 N45 1987

METALS - PRICES - HUNGARY - STATISTICS.
A Kohászati és a gépipari árak alakulása, 1980-1984 /. Budapest , 1986. 91 p. ; LC Card 86-202642
HD9705.H82 K64 1986

METALWORK. see **METAL-WORK.**

Metamorfoses da riqueza. Mello, Zélia Maria Cardoso de. Metamorfoses da riqueza, São Paulo, 1845-1895 . São Paulo , 1985. 188 p. : LC Card 85-207635
HC188.S3 M49 1985

Metamorfoses da riqueza, São Paulo, 1845-1895 . Mello, Zélia Maria Cardoso de. São Paulo , 1985. 188 p. : LC Card 85-207635
HC188.S3 M49 1985

La métamorphose . Mayer, Pierre. Paris , 1983. 110 p. : ISBN 2-86592-014-3 : LC Card 84-118610
HF1411 .M374 1983

Il metano in Italia . Ascari, Sergio. Milano, Italy , c1985. 292 p. : LC Card 86-135353
HD9579.M43 I82 1985

MÉTAYER SYSTEM - BRAZIL - SÃO PAULO (STATE) - HISTORY - 19TH CENTURY - CASE STUDIES.
Witter, José Sebastião. A Revolta dos Parceiros /. São Paulo, SP , 1986. 77 p. : LC Card 87-102716
HD4875.B8 W58 1986

MÉTAYER SYSTEM - GAMBIA.
Robertson, A. F. The dynamics of productive relationships . Cambridge [Cambridgeshire] , New York , 1987. xix, 321 p. : ISBN 0-521-32834-9 LC Card 86-11801 DDC 333.33/5 19
HD1478.A35 R63 1987
NYPL [JLE 87-1299]

MÉTAYER SYSTEM - GHANA.
Robertson, A. F. The dynamics of productive relationships . Cambridge [Cambridgeshire] , New York , 1987. xix, 321 p. : ISBN 0-521-32834-9 LC Card 86-11801 DDC 333.33/5 19
HD1478.A35 R63 1987
NYPL [JLE 87-1299]

MÉTAYER SYSTEM - INDIA.
Ghosh, Tushar Kanti. Operation Barga and land reforms . Delhi , New Delhi, India , 1986. vii, 200 p. ; ISBN 81-7018-315-4 : LC Card 86-900505 DDC 333.3/1/54 19
HD1478.I5 G48 1986 *NYPL [JLD 86-4347]*

MÉTAYER SYSTEM - LESOTHO.
Robertson, A. F. The dynamics of productive relationships . Cambridge [Cambridgeshire] , New York , 1987. xix, 321 p. : ISBN 0-521-32834-9 LC Card 86-11801 DDC 333.33/5 19
HD1478.A35 R63 1987
NYPL [JLE 87-1299]

MÉTAYER SYSTEM - PORTUGAL.
Almeida, João Ferreira de. Classes sociais nos campos . Lisboa [1986] 544 p. : LC Card 87-400121 DDC 305.5/63 19
HD1536.P77 A44 1986

MÉTAYER SYSTEM - SENEGAL.
Robertson, A. F. The dynamics of productive relationships . Cambridge [Cambridgeshire] , New York , 1987. xix, 321 p. : ISBN 0-521-32834-9 LC Card 86-11801 DDC 333.33/5 19
HD1478.A35 R63 1987
NYPL [JLE 87-1299]

MÉTAYER SYSTEM - SUDAN.
Robertson, A. F. The dynamics of productive relationships . Cambridge [Cambridgeshire] , New York , 1987. xix, 321 p. : ISBN 0-521-32834-9 LC Card 86-11801 DDC 333.33/5 19
HD1478.A35 R63 1987
NYPL [JLE 87-1299]

Metcalfe, Stan. Hartley, Jill. New electronic information services . Aldershot, Hants, England , Brookfield, Vt., USA , c1987. 147 p. : ISBN 0-566-05489-2 (pbk.) : LC Card 87-23600 DDC 338.4/700574/0941 19
HD9696.D364 G74 1987

Métellus, Champagne. La doctrine coopérative / Champagne Métellus. Port-au-Prince, Haïti : [s.n., 1984] (Port-au-Prince, Haïti : Impr. La Phalange) 94 p. : ill. ; 21 cm. LC Card 85-168867 DDC 334 19
1. Cooperative societies. 2. Cooperation. I. Title.
HD2971 .M47 1984

METHANE INDUSTRY - ITALY.
Ascari, Sergio. Il metano in Italia . Milano, Italy , c1985. 292 p. : LC Card 86-135353
HD9579.M43 I82 1985

METHANOL INDUSTRY - DELAWARE RIVER VALLEY (N.Y.-DEL. AND N.J.) - HISTORY.
Myers, Frank Daniel. The wood chemical industry in the Delaware Valley /. Middletown, N.Y. , 1986. [160] p. : LC Card 87-108267
HD9660.M573 U616 1986

METHOD OF WORK. see **WORK.**

Methoden der Politikberatung im wirtschaftspolitischen Bereich / Beirat für Wirtschafts- und Sozialfragen ; [Mitglieder, Hermann Blaha ... et al.]. Wien : C. Ueberreuter, 1984. 116 p. ; 24 cm. Papers presented at a symposium held Nov. 17-18, 1983 in Vienna, sponsored by the Beirat für Wirtschafts- und Sozialfragen. Includes bibliographical references. CONTENTS. - Sachverständigenrat zur Begutachtung der gesamtwirtschaftlichen Entwicklung / Gerhard Fels -- Konjunkturbeauftragter des Bundesrates / Waldemar Jucker -- Beirat für Wirtschafts- und Sozialfragen / Herbert Tumpel -- Österreichs sozialpartnerschaftliches System im internationalen Vergleich / Gerhard Lehmbruch. LC Card 84-222756
1. Austria - Economic policy - 1945- - Congresses. 2. Austria - Economic conditions - 1945- - Congresses. 3. Central Europe - Economic conditions - Congresses. I. Blaha, Hermann. II. Fels, Gerhard. III. Beirat für Wirtschafts- und Sozialfragen.
HC265 .M39 1984

Methoden und Kriterien zur Überprüfung des Erfolgs von Aufklärungskampagnen : Handbuch zur Durchführung von Wirksamkeitsanalysen / Martin Pfaff ... [et al.] ; unter Mitarbeit von Stefan Empter und Gerhard Fuchs ; Internationales Institut für Empirische Sozialökonomie (INIFES). Köln : Bundesanstalt für Strassenwesen, Bereich Unfallforschung, 1982. 99, [93] p. : ill. ; 21 cm. (Forschungsberichte der Bundesanstalt für Strassenwesen, Bereich Unfallforschung, 0173-7066 . 69) Title on spine: Überprüfung von Aufklärungskampagnen. "Bericht zum Forschungsprojekt 7824 der Bundesanstalt für Strassenwesen, Bereich Unfallforschung." Includes bibliography. LC Card 83-178796
1. Traffic safety - Study and teaching - Germany (West). I. Pfaff, Martin. II. Internationales Institut für

Empirische Sozialökonomie. III. Bundesanstalt für Strassenwesen (Germany). Bereich Unfallforschung. IV. Title: Überprüfung von Aufklärungskampagnen. V. Series.
HE5614.5.G3 M37 1982

Methoden zur Prognose des Wohnungsmarktgeschehens auf regionaler Ebene . Hornung, Daniel. Diessenhofen , 1983. xvi, 251 p. : ISBN 3-7253-0214-6 LC Card 86-114266
HD7353.A3 H66 1983

Méthodes de consolidation des comptes dans les pays de l'OCDE. Consolidation policies in OECD countries . Paris , 1987. 60, 63 p. ; ISBN 92-64-02876-5 : LC Card 87-168671 DDC 657/.3 19
HF5681.B2 C593 1987

Methodologia tou isozygiou plērōmōn tēs Helladas = Balance of payments methodology of Greece = Méthodologie de la balance des paiements de la Grèce / [Eurostat]. Luxembourg : Office des publications officielles des Communautés européennes, 1986, c1985. 155 p. ; 23 cm. Greek, English, and French. ISBN 92-825-5642-5 : LC Card 86-176326
1. Balance of payments - Greece - Statistical methods. I. Statistical Office of the European Communities. II. Title: Balance of payments methodology of Greece.
HG3883.G6 S72 1986

Methodologie der EG-Agrarpreisindizes (Output und Input) = Methodology of EC agricultural price indices (output and input). Luxembourg : Office des publications officielles des Communautés européennes ; Washington, DC : [Distributor], European Community Information Service, 1985. 228 p. ; 30 cm. Issued by the Statistical Office of the European Communities. English, French, German, and Italian. On cover: Eurostat. ISBN 92-825-5463-5 : LC Card 87-107275 DDC 338.1/3/094021 19
1. Agricultural prices - European Economic Community countries - Statistical methods. 2. Input-output analysis - European Economic Community countries. 3. Price indexes. 4. Agricultural prices - European Economic Community Countries - Statistics. I. Statistical Office of the European Communities. II. Eurostat. III. Title: Methodology of EC agricultural price indices (output and input).
HD1920.5 .M47 1985

Méthodologie multicritère d'aide à la décision /. Roy, B. (Bernard), 1934- Paris , c1985. xxii, 423 p. : ISBN 2-7178-0901-5 : LC Card 86-166619
HD30.25 .R68 1985

Methodologies for assessing the impact of deep sea-bed minerals on the world economy / Department of International Economic and Social Affairs. New York : United Nations, 1986. ix, 153 p. : ill. ; 28 cm. Bibliography: p. 143-153. LC Card 87-118207 DDC 338.2 19
1. Mineral industries. 2. Mineral resources in submerged lands - Economic aspects. 3. Marine mineral resources - Economic aspects. I. United Nations. Dept. of International Economic and Social Affairs.
HD9506.A2 M47 1986

Methodologies for the collection and analysis of mortality data : proceedings of a seminar at Dakar, Senegal, July 7-10, 1981 / sponsored by Committee on Factors Affecting Mortality and the Length of Life, International Union for the Scientific Study of Population, and Direction de la statistique, Senegal ; Jacques Vallin, John H. Pollard, and Larry Heligman, editors. Liège, Belgium : Ordina Editions, 1984. vi, 510 p. : ill. ; 24 cm. Summaries in French. Includes bibliographical references and index. ISBN 2-87040-032-2 (pbk.) LC Card 86-205582 DDC 304.6/4/072 19
1. Mortality - Research - Methodology - Congresses. I. Vallin, Jacques. II. Pollard, J. H. III. Heligman, Larry. IV. International Union for the Scientific Study of Population. Committee on Factors Affecting Mortality and Length of Life. V. Senegal. Direction de la statistique.
HB1321 .M48 1984

Methodologische Betrachtungen der Annahmen zum menschlichen Verhalten aus der Sicht der Volkswirtschaftslehre . Bökenkamp, Joachim. Göttingen , c1985. v, 446 p. ; ISBN 3-925391-01-0 LC Card 87-121278 DDC 330/.01/9 19
HB74.P8 B59 1985

A methodology for determining the socially optimum uses of estuarine resources . Stauth, Roy. Rondebosch, South Africa [1982] v, 119 leaves : LC Card 86-210152
HC905.Z7 G87 1982

Methodology of EC agricultural price indices (output and input) Methodologie der EG-Agrarpreisindizes (Output und Input) =. Luxembourg , Washington, DC , 1985. 228 p. ; ISBN 92-825-5463-5 : LC Card 87-107275 DDC 338.1/3/094021 19
HD1920.5 .M47 1985

The Methuen EEC series.
Weyman-Jones, Thomas G., 1947- Energy in Europe . London , New York , 1986. xii, 176 p. : ISBN 0-416-36590-6 LC Card 86-18169 DDC 333.79/094 19
TJ163.25.E85 W48 1986
NYPL [JLD 87-1305]

Methuen introductions to development.
Cole, J. P. (John Peter), 1928- Development and underdevelopment . London , New York , 1987. vi, 104 p. : ISBN 0-416-92080-2 (pbk.) LC Card 86-23758 DDC 338.9/009172/4 19
HC59.7 .C59 1987

Findlay, Allan M. Population and development in the Third World /. London , New York , 1987. xii, 84 p. : ISBN 0-416-91950-2 (pbk.) : LC Card 86-31094 DDC 304.6/09172/4 19
HB884 .F56 1987

METHYL ISOCYANATE - ENVIROMENTAL ASPECTS - INDIA - BHOPAL.
Everest, Larry. Behind the poison cloud . Chicago , 1986. 192 p. : ISBN 0-916650-26-X : LC Card 85-26863 DDC 363.1/79 19
HD7269.C452 I524 1986
NYPL [JSD 86-425]

METHYL ISOCYANATE - ENVIRONMENTAL ASPECTS - INDIA - BHOPAL.
Chishti, Anees, 1941- Dateline Bhopal . New Delhi , 1986. 160 p. ; LC Card 86-901993 DDC 363.1/79
HD7269.C452 I5225 1986
NYPL [JLD 87-1050]

Kurzman, Dan. A killing wind . New York , c1987. xvi, 297 p., [16] p. of plates : ISBN 0-07-035687-4 LC Card 87-3398 DDC 363.1/79 19
HD7269.C452 I525 1987

Sufrin, Sidney C., 1910- Bhopal, its setting, responsibility, and challenge /. Delhi , 1985. 98 p. ; ISBN 81-202-0135-3 : LC Card 85-903246 DDC 363.1/79 19
HD7269.C452 I527 1985
NYPL [JLD 86-1321]

METHYL ISOCYANATE - TOXICOLOGY - INDIA - BHOPAL.
Shrivastava, Paul. Bhopal . Cambridge, Mass. , c1987. xvi, 184 p. : ISBN 0-88730-084-7 LC Card 86-26575 DDC 363.1/79 19
HD7269.C452 I5268 1987

Shrivastava, Paul. Managing industrial crises . New Delhi, India , 1987. 196 p. : ISBN 81-7094-000-1 : LC Card 87-902160 DDC 363.1/79 19
HD7269.C452 I5269 1987

Les métiers de la publicité /. Placier, Anne. Paris , c1984. 247 p., [15] p. of plates : ISBN 2-86745-019-5 LC Card 85-118630
HF5828.4 .P58 1984

Metin Heper. see **Heper, Metin.**

METIS. see **INDIANS OF NORTH AMERICA - CANADA - MIXED BLOODS.**

Metode matematice în problematica dezvoltării. Modele matematice și semiotice ale dezvoltării sociale /. București , 1986. 190 p. : LC Card 86-208152
HD75.5 .M615 1986

Metodicheskie osnovy analiza i prognozirovaniia fondootdachi . Shevchuk, L. V. (Liudmila Vladimirovna) Minsk , 1983. 118 p. : LC Card 84-118665
HD9715.S73 B9465 1983

Metodicheskie polozheniia po prognozirovaniiu ėkonomicheskogo i sotsial'nogo razvitiia soiuznoĭ respubliki / [redaktor T. Lut'ianova]. Riga : "Zinatne", 1979. 275 p. : ill. ; 20 cm. At head of title: Akademiia nauk Latviĭskoĭ SSR. Institut ėkonomiki. Bibliography: p. [269]-275. LC Card 81-215536
1. Economic forecasting - Latvia. 2. Latvia - Economic conditions - Econometric models. I. Lut'ianova, T. II. Ekonomikas institūts (Latvijas PSR Zinātņu akadēmija).
HC337.L3 M35 1979

Metodicheskie rekomendatsii po issledovaniiu proizvodstvennoĭ infrastruktury territorial'no-proizvodstvennykh kompleksov i promyshlennykh uzlov / [otvetstvennye redaktory A.I. Demenev, V.I. Shipilov]. Sverdlovsk : Akademiia nauk SSSR, Ural'skiĭ nauch. tsentr, In-t ėkonomiki, 1983. 79 p. (some folded) ; 21 cm. LC Card 86-113572
1. Infrastructure (Economics) - Soviet Union - Methodology. 2. Territorial production complexes - Soviet Union - Methodology. I. Demenev, Anatoliĭ Iosifovich. II. Shipilov, V. I. III. Institut ėkonomiki (Akademiia nauk SSSR. Ural'skiĭ nauchnyĭ tsentr).
HC340.C3 M416 1983

Metodicheskie ukazaniia k razrabotke planov ėkonomicheskogo i sotsial'nogo razvitiia RSFSR /. Gosplan RSFSR. Moskva , 1985. 462 p. ; LC Card 85-232541
HC337.R85 G67 1985

Metodiki opredeleniia ėkonomicheskoĭ ėffektivnosti kapital'nykh vlozheniĭ v sotsialisticheskikh stranakh : referativnyĭ sbornik / [redaktsionnaia kollegiia sbornika Kazakevich V.P., Tovmosian M.E. (otvetstvennyĭ za vypusk), Khachaturov T.S. (nauchnyĭ redaktor) ; materialy sbornika podgotovili V.V. Klykovym i A.M. Mirenkovym]. Moskva : Akademiia nauk SSSR, In-t nauch. informatsii po obshchestvennym naukam, 1981. 101 p. ; 20 cm. (Seriia Aktual'nye problemy razvitogo sotsializma) Includes bibliographical references. LC Card 82-204402
1. Capital productivity - Europe, Eastern. 2. Capital productivity - Communist countries. I. Kazakevich, V. P. II. Tovmosian, M. E. III. Khachaturov, T. S. (Tigran Sergeevich), 1906-. IV. Klykov, V. V. V. Mirenkov, A. M. VI. Institut nauchnoĭ informatsii po obshchestvennym naukam (Akademiia nauk SSSR). VII. Series.
HC244.Z9 C35 1981

El método de los componentes demográficos para realizar proyecciones de población. Camposortega Cruz, Sergio. México, D.F. [1984] 35 p. : LC Card 85-164750
HB849.53 .C36 1984

O método dos modelos e a análise económica da exploração agrícola /. Pereira, Mário. Lisboa , 1962. 233 p. : LC Card 85-221042
HD2027 .M415 1962

Metodologi for Danmarks betalingsbalance = Balance of payments methodology of Denmark. Luxembourg : Kontoret for de europæiske fællesskabers officielle publikationer ; Washington, D.C. : European Community Information Service [distributor], 1985. 181 p. ; 23 cm. Danish, English, and French. Prepared by Danmarks statistik in cooperation with the Statistical Office of the European Communities. ISBN 92-825-4927-5 : LC Card 86-122287
1. Balance of payments - Denmark. 2. Balance of payments - Denmark - Statistical services. I. Danmarks statistik. II. Statistical Office of the European Communities. III. Title: Balance of payments methodology of Denmark.
HG3883.D4 M48 1985

Metodología de evaluación y programación de sistemas de producción y consumo, MEPS / [autores, Pierre Vigier Dubois, coordinador del proyecto; Javier Tantaleán Arbulú, experto planificación; Beniamin Zacharias, experto en modelos]. Lima, Perú : Grupo de Política Tecnológica, Junta Acuerdo de Cartagena, [1985]- v. <1 > : ill. ; 29 cm. LC Card 86-215609
1. Economic development - Graphic methods. 2. Economics - Graphic methods. 3. Economic policy - Evaluation - Forms. 4. Economic development projects - Evaluation - Forms. 5. Technology assessment - Forms. I. Vigier Dubois, Pierre. II. Tantaleán Arbulú, Javier. III. Zacharias, Beniamin. IV. Board of the Cartagen Agreement. Grupo de Política Tecnológica.
HD75 .M48 1985

Metodología de la encuesta nacional de hogares. Bogotá, D.E., Colombia : República de Colombia, Departamento Administrativo

Nacional de Estadística, [1985] 64 p. : ill. ; 24 cm. (Documentos / República de Colombia, Departamento Administrativo Nacional de Estadística, DANE) Includes bibliographical references. LC Card 85-240042
1. Household surveys - Colombia. I. Colombia. Departamento Administrativo Nacional de Estadística. II. Series: Documentos (Colombia. Departamento Administrativo Nacional de Estadística).
HB849.49 .M48 1985

Metodología de las cuentas nacionales de Colombia. Bogotá, D.E. : Departamento Administrativo Nacional de Estadística, [1986] 291 p. ; 24 cm. (Colección Documentos, 0120-7423 . 3) At head of title: "Resolución no. 00017 minigobierno"--P. 1 of cover. Includes bibliographical references. LC Card 87-403848 DDC 339.3861 19
1. National income - Colombia - Accounting. I. Colombia. Departamento Administrativo Nacional de Estadística. II. Series: Colección Documentos (Colombia. Departamento Administrativo Nacional de Estadística) , 3.
HC200.I5 M47 1986

Metodología y construcción de un indicador del ingreso familiar . Madrigal Pana, Johnny. San José, Costa Rica , 1986. 43 p. ; LC Card 87-404395 DDC 339.4/2/0972 19
HD6996 .M33 1986

Metodologicheski vŭprosi na politicheskata ikonomiia v pet toma .
(t. 1) Politicheskata ikonomiia kato teoriia i metodologiia /. Sofiia , 1986. 397 p. ; LC Card 86-210685
HB71 .M59 1986 t. 1 HB97.5

Metodologicheskie polozheniia razrabotki krupnykh territorial'nykh programm / otvetstvennye redaktory A.G. Aganbegian, R.I. Shniper. Novosibirsk : Izd-vo "Nauka," Sibirskoe otd-nie, 1986. 303 p. : ill. ; 21 cm. At head of title: Akademiia nauk SSSR. Sibirskoe otdelenie. Institut ėkonomiki i organizatsii promyshlennogo proizvodstva. Includes bibliographical references. LC Card 86-211369
1. Siberia (R.S.F.S.R.) - Industries - Location. 2. Territorial production complexes - Russian S.F.S.R. - Siberia. 3. Siberia (R.S.F.S.R.) - Economic policy. I. Aganbegian, Abel Gezevich. II. Shniper, R. I. (Ruvin Isaakovich). III. Institut ėkonomiki i organizatsii promyshlennogo proizvodstva (Akademiia nauk SSSR).
HC337.R853 D56 1986

Metodologicheskie problemy analiza dolgosrochnykh sotsial'no-ėkonomicheskikh protsessov / [Otvetstvennye redaktory V.G. Grebennikov ; A.A. Ryvkin]. Moskva : Vses. nauch.-issl. in-t sistemnykh issledovaniĭ, 1979. 116 p. : ill. ; 26 cm. (Sbornik trudov . 1979, vyp. 9) Includes bibliographies. LC Card 87-462037
1. Economic policy. 2. Economic development - Social aspects. I. Grebennikov, Valeriĭ Grigor'evich. II. Ryvkin, Al'bert Anatol'evich. III. Series: Sbornik trudov (Vsesoiuznyĭ nauchno-issledovatel'skiĭ institut sistemnykh issledovaniĭ) , 1979, vyp. 9.
HD87 .M48 1979

Metodologicheskie problemy formirovaniia territorial'no-proizvodstvennykh kompleksov / pod redaktsieĭ V.P. Gukova. Novosibirsk : Akademiia nauk SSSR, Sibirskoe otd-nie, In-t ėkonomiki i organizatsii promyshlennogo proizvodstva, 1980. 162 p. : ill. ; 20 cm. (Sbornik nauchnykh trudov) Cover title: Metodologicheskie problemy formirovaniia TPK. Includes bibliographies. LC Card 82-106930
1. Territorial production complexes - Soviet Union. 2. Territorial production complexes - Russian S.F.S.R. - Siberia. I. Gukov, Vladimir Pavlovich. II. Title: Metodologicheskie problemy formirovaniia TPK. III. Series: Sbornik nauchnykh trudov (Institut ėkonomiki i organizatsii promyshlennogo proizvodstva (Akademiia nauk SSSR)).
HC336.25 .M46 1980

Metodologicheskie problemy formirovaniia TPK. Metodologicheskie problemy formirovaniia territorial'no-proizvodstvennykh kompleksov /. Novosibirsk , 1980. 162 p. : LC Card 82-106930
HC336.25 .M46 1980

Metodologiia opredeleniia osnovnogo i iskhodnogo otnosheniĭ ėkonomiki sotsializma /. Eremin, A. M. (Al'bert Mikhaĭlovich) Kazan' , 1980. 157, [3] p. ; LC Card 81-134646
HB97.5 .E665 1980

Metodologiia prognozirovaniia vosproizvodstva i ispol'zovaniia resursov v ėkonomike SSSR / [otvetstvennye redaktory V.K. Fal'tsman, A.I. Gladyshevskiĭ]. Moskva : Akademiia nauk SSSR, TSentr. ėkonomiko-matematicheskiĭ in-t, 1984. 201 p. : ill. ; 21 cm. Includes bibliographies. LC Card 85-199435
1. Industrial productivity - Soviet Union - Forecasting - Mathematical models. I. Fal'tsman, Vladimir Konstantinovich. II. Gladyshevskiĭ, Alekseĭ Igorevich. III. TSentral'nyĭ ėkonomiko-matematicheskiĭ institut (Akademiia nauk SSSR).
HC340.I52 M485 1984

Métodos de estimación de la economía oculta . Ruesga Benito, Santos, 1953- Madrid [1985?] 55 p. : ISBN 88-470-7531-18 LC Card 87-111661
HD2346.S7 R84 1985

Métodos econométricos . Martínez Garza, Angel. Chapingo, Edo. de Méx. , 1982. 225 p. ; LC Card 84-227751
HB139 .M385 1982

Métodos para la aplicación de las series metódicas ocupacionales /. Alcántara, Alcides de. Montevideo , 1978. 73 p. : LC Card 86-142696
HD5715 .A44 1978

Metody i modeli razvitiia regional'nykh ėkonomicheskikh sistem : sbornik nauchnykh trudov / pod redaktsieĭ I.N. Voevody. Novosibirsk : IĖiOPP SO AN SSSR, 1985. 165 p. : ill. ; 20 cm. At head of title: Akademiia nauk SSSR. Sibirskoe otdelenie. Institut ėkonomiki i organizatsii promyshlennogo proizvodstva. Includes bibliographies. LC Card 86-219402
1. Siberia (R.S.F.S.R.) - Economic conditions - Mathematical models. 2. Siberia (R.S.F.S.R.) - Economic conditions - Forecasting. 3. Siberia (R.S.F.S.R.) - Industries - Planning - Mathematical models. I. Voevoda, Ivan Nikiforovich. II. Institut ėkonomiki i organizatsii promyshlennogo proizvodstva (Akademiia nauk SSSR).
HC337.R852 S52545 1985

Metody sochetaniia otraslevogo i territorial'nogo planirovaniia /. Chistiakov, E. G. (Evgeniĭ Gavrilovich) Moskva , 1982. 147, [3] p. : LC Card 82-189489
HC336.25 .C516 1982

METRO AUTOMOBILE.
Willman, Paul. Innovation and management control . Cambridge [Cambridgeshire] , New York , 1985. viii, 215 p. ; ISBN 0-521-26802-8 LC Card 84-17481 DDC 331/.04292/0941 19
HD8039.A82 G79 1985
NYPL [JLD 85-3102]

Metropoli e agricoltura / G. Beltrame ... [et al.] ; a cura di P. Bolchini e D. Lorandi. Milano : F. Angeli, c1982. 319 p. : ill. ; 22 cm. (CDRL : Centro documentazione e ricerche per la Lombardia . 4) Includes bibliographical references. LC Card 82-246692 DDC 333.76/13/094521 19
1. Land use, Rural - Government policy - Italy - Milan Region. 2. Environmental policy - Italy - Milan Region. 3. Conservation of natural resources - Government policy - Italy - Milan Region. 4. Urbanization - Italy - Milan Region. 5. Regional planning - Italy - Milan Region. 6. Agriculture - Economic aspects - Italy - Milan Region. I. Beltrame, G. (Gianni). II. Bolchini, Piero, 1935-. III. Lorandi, D. (Daniela).
HD680.M54 M47 1982
NYPL [JLD 86-3678]

METROPOLITAN AREAS - FRANCE - CONGRESSES.
Colloque Les Périphéries urbaines (1984 : Angers, France) Actes du Colloque Les Périphéries urbaines . Caen , c1985. 270 p. : ISBN 2-905461-03-9 : LC Card 86-173712
HB2263 .C65 1984

METROPOLITAN AREAS - UNITED STATES.
Sheets, Robert G. The impact of service industries on underemployment in metropolitan economies /. Lexington, Mass. , c1987. xii, 185 p. ; ISBN 0-669-14575-0 (alk. paper) LC Card 86-45884 DDC 331.13 19
HD5709.2.U6 S54 1987

Strategic real estate submarkets . Denver, Colo. (1009 Grant St., Suite 304, Denver 80203) , c1986. 195 p. : LC Card 86-228061 DDC 333.33/22/0973 19
HD255 .S77 1986

METROPOLITAN EDISON COMPANY.
Impacts of hazardous technology . Albany , c1987. x, 233 p. : ISBN 0-88706-332-2 LC Card 86-1943 DDC 363.1/79 19
HD9698.U54 M475 1987
NYPL [JLE 87-1233]

METROPOLITAN TRANSPORTATION. see **URBAN TRANSPORTATION.**

Metropolitan Washington Council of Governments.
Growth trends to the year 2010. Washington, D.C. , c1986. i, 32 p. : LC Card 87-129483 DDC 304.6/2/09753021 19
HA305 .G76 1986

Kaufmann, Elizabeth Irwin. Traffic growth resulting from future development . Washington, D.C. (1875 Eye St., N.W., Washington 20006-5454) , c1987. ix, 53, 15 p. : LC Card 87-161086 DDC 388.4/13142/09753 19
HE356.5.W3 K38 1987

Metropolitan Washington Council of Governments. Dept. of Metropolitan Development and Information Resources.
Growth trends to the year 2010. Washington, D.C. , c1986. i, 9 p. : LC Card 87-153125 DDC 304.6/2/09753021 19
HA305 .G77 1986

Langford, Jay. Economic trends in metropolitan Washington, 1980-1985 ; [author, Jay Langford, Vetoria S. Alston]. Washington, D.C. (1875 Eye St., NW., Suite 200, Washington 20006) , c1986. viii, 68 p. : LC Card 87-105032 DDC 330.9753/04 19
HC108.W3 L36 1986

METROPOLITIAN AREAS - GOVERNMENT POLICY - INDIA.
Contribution to national and regional planning problems /. Calcutta , 1983. vii, 174 p., [2] leaves of plates (some folded) : LC Card 83-907550 DDC 338.954 19
HC435.2 .C63 1983 ***NYPL [JLD 86-3868]***

Metsä- ja uittotöiden työtapaturmat vuonna 1982 = Olycksfall i skogs- och flottningsarbete ar 1982 = Occupational accidents in forestry, year 1982. Tampere : Työsuojeluhallitus ; Helsinki : Myy Valtion painatuskeskus, 1984. 50 p. : ill. ; 30 cm. (Tilastotiedotus / Työsuojeluhallitus, 0357-234X = Statistisk rapport / Arbetarskyddsstyrelsen . 2/84) Text in Finnish and Swedish, with summary in English; table of contents and appendices also in English. ISBN 951-46-7685-8 LC Card 85-149625
1. Forests and forestry - Finland - Accidents. I. Title: Olycksfall i skogs- och flottningsarbete år 1982. II. Title: Occupational accidents in forestry, year 1982. III. Series: Tilastotiedotus (Finland. Työsuojeluhallitus) , 84/2.
HD7269.F7262 F56 1984

Metsänkylä, Antti. Metallityön tallennus : selvitys ammattialaan kohdistuvasta museaalisesta tallennuksesta / Antti Metsänkylä. Helsinki : Museovirasto, Tutkimusosasto, 1986. 77 p. : 50 ill. ; 30 cm. (Työväenkulttuuriprojektin julkaisu . 4) Summary in English. Bibliography: p. 70-74. ISBN 951-9074-93-7 LC Card 87-101629
1. Metal trade - Finland - Museums. 2. Metal trade - Finland - History. 3. Metal-workers - Finland - History. I. Title. II. Series.
HD9506.F52 M43 1986

Metszetek az agrártársadalom struktúrájából /. Simó, Tibor. Budapest , 1985. 167 p. ; ISBN 963-7700-25-0 : LC Card 86-232606
HD1536.H9 S56 1985

Mettler-Meibom, Barbara E.
Breitbandtechnologie : über die Chancen sozialer Vernunft in technologiepolitischen Entscheidungsprozessen / Barbara Mettler-Meibom. Opladen : Westdeutscher Verlag, c1986. xxiv, 477, [60] p. : ill. ; 23 cm. (Beiträge zur sozialwissenschaftlichen Forschung, 0175-615X . Bd. 79) Includes bibliography. ISBN 3-531-11782-3 LC Card 86-184911
1. Telecommunication - Social aspects - Germany (West). 2. Television broadcasting - Germany, West. I. Title. II. Series.
HE8154 .M47 1986

Metz, Lance E. Sherman's guide to Hugh Moore Park / written and researched by Lance E. Metz. 1st ed. Easton, PA : Center for Canal History and Technology, 1988. p. cm. ISBN

0-930973-07-0 (pbk.) : LC Card 87-25622 DDC 338.09748/22 19
1. Canals - Pennsylvania - Easton Region - History - 19th century. 2. Transportation - Pennsylvania - Easton Region - History - 19th century. 3. Iron industry and trade - Pennsylvania - Easton Region - History - 19 century. 4. Easton Region (Pa.) - Industries - History - 19th century. 5. Easton Region (Pa.) - History - 19th century. 6. Hugh Moore Park (Easton, Pa.) - Guide-books. I. Sherman, Theodore A., 1899-1980. II. Title. III. Title: Guide to Hugh Moore Park.
HE395 .P43 1988

Metz, Matthias. Kundenfreundliches Verhalten : als qualitatives Instrument des Bankbetriebs / von Matthias Metz. Frankfurt am Main : F. Knapp, c1985. xxi, 349 p. : ill. ; 21 cm. Bibliography: p. 294-349. ISBN 3-7819-0326-5 LC Card 85-202352
1. Public relations - Germany (West) - Banks and banking. 2. Customer relations. 3. Banks and banking - Germany (West) - Quality control. I. Title.
HG1616.P8 M47 1985

Metzelaar, Lawrence C. Learning to use Lotus 1-2-3 / Lawrence C. Metzelaar, Marianne B. Fox. Menlo Park, Calif. : Benjamin/Cummings Pub. Co., c1987. xi, 286 p. : ill. ; 28 cm. Includes index. ISBN 0-8053-6736-5 (pbk.) LC Card 86-214400 DDC 005.36/9 19
1. Lotus 1-2-3 (Computer program). 2. Business - Data processing. I. Fox, Marianne B. II. Title.
HF5548.4.L67 M47 1987

Metzger, Bertram L. Profit sharing in 38 large companies : piece of the action for 1,000,000 participants / by Bert L. Metzger. Evanston, Ill. : Profit Sharing Research Foundation, 1975-78. 2 v. : ill. ; 28 cm. Includes bibliographical references and index. ISBN 0-911192-25-5 : LC Card 75-39379 DDC 658.32/25
1. Profit-sharing - United States. 2. Corporations - United States - Finance - Directories. I. Profit-Sharing Research Foundation. II. Title.
HD2984 .M47 ***NYPL [JLF 86-389]***

Meu compromisso com o Nordeste . Magalhães, Antônio Carlos. [Salvador , 1983] 302 p. ; LC Card 86-233485
HC188.B7242 M34 1983

Le Meuble : état de la situation : document de réflexion / déposé par le Secrétariat permanent des conférences socio-économiques à la Conférence sur l'industrie du meuble tenue à Montréal, le 28 et le 29 juin 1983.2e éd. corr. [Québec] : Secrétariat permanent des conférences socio-économiques du Québec, [1983] xiii, 109 p. : ill. ; 28 cm. (Les Conférences socio-économiques du Québec) ISBN 2-550-10196-0 LC Card 85-124226
1. Furniture industry and trade - Québec (Province). I. Québec (Province). Secrétariat des conférences socio-économiques. II. Series.
HD9773.C23 Q425 1983

Meuleman, Johan H. Le Constantinois entre les deux guerres mondiales : l'évolution économique et sociale de la population rurale / Johan H. Meuleman. Assen, Pays-Bas : Van Gorcum, 1985. 296 p., [1] folded leaf of plates : ill. ; 24 cm. Summary in Arabic. Bibliography: p. 268-280. ISBN 90-232-2093-5 : LC Card 86-119662
1. Constantine (Algeria : Wilāyah) - Economic conditions. 2. Constantine (Algeria : Wilāyah) - Rural conditions. 3. Agriculture - Economic aspects - Algeria - Constantine (Province). 4. Rural development - Algeria - Constantine (Province). I. Title.
HC815.Z7 C666 1985

Meulen, Harm van der. Vakbeweging in verandering . Deventer , 1986. 191 p. : ISBN 90-267-1082-8 : LC Card 86-224831
HD6727 .V29 1986

MEULEN, HARM VAN DER.
Vakbeweging in verandering . Deventer , 1986. 191 p. : ISBN 90-267-1082-8 : LC Card 86-224831
HD6727 .V29 1986

Meurer, Cornelia. Leibfritz, Willi. Steuerliche Investitionsförderung im internationalen Vergleich /. Berlin , c1985. 255 p. : ISBN 3-428-05776-7 LC Card 85-161706
HJ4631 .L38 1985

Meurer, Heinrich W., 1950-
Wirtschaftsgeologische Aspekte bei der privaten Investition in Öl- und Gasbohrvorhaben in den USA / vorgelegt von Heinrich W. Meurer. [Cologne? : s.n., 1982] (Aachen : Fotodruck J. Mainz) vi, 163 p., [3] folded leaves of plates : ill. ; 21 cm. Thesis--Universität zu Köln. Bibliography: p. 158-163. LC Card 84-200100
1. Petroleum industry and trade - United States - Finance. 2. Gas industry - United States - Finance. 3. Prospecting - Economic aspects - United States. 4. Petroleum - Geology - United States. 5. Gas, Natural - Geology - United States. I. Title.
HD9565 .M48 1982

Meurling, Kim. Aktiv butikk / Kim Meurling. Oslo : Bedriftsøkonomens forlag, 1980. 186 p. : ill. ; 22 cm. (Aktuell økonomi for detaljhandelen) ISBN 82-7037-129-7 : LC Card 81-174134
1. Stores, Retail - Management. 2. Stores, Retail - Norway - Management. I. Title. II. Series.
HF5429 .M44 1980

MEXICAN-AMERICAN BORDER REGION - COMMERCE.
González-Aréchiga, Bernardo. Vinculación fronteriza a Estados Unidos y su cambio con la crisis /. Tijuana, Baja California , 1985. 54 p. ; ISBN 968-607-500-3 LC Card 86-187758
HF3239.M49 G66 1985

MEXICAN-AMERICAN BORDER REGION - ECONOMIC CONDITIONS.
Bilbao, Elena. La frontera de San Ysidro . Tijuana, Baja California , 1986. 27 p. ; ISBN 968-607-513-5 LC Card 87-125801 DDC 330.9794/98 19
HC108.S65 B55 1986

The U. S.-Mexico border region . [El Paso] , 1984, c1982. viii, 446 p. : ISBN 0-87404-091-4 (pbk.) LC Card 87-401861 DDC 333.7/0972/1 19
HC137.M46 U17 1984

MEXICAN-AMERICAN BORDER REGION - ECONOMIC CONDITIONS - RESEARCH.
Espinoza Jaramillo, Frida. El estado de la investigación nacional acerca de la frontera norte de México /. [México] , 1985. 47 leaves ; LC Card 87-402765 DDC 330.972/10834 19
HC137.M46 E76 1985

MEXICAN-AMERICAN BORDER REGION - ECONOMIC POLICY.
The U. S.-Mexico border region . [El Paso] , 1984, c1982. viii, 446 p. : ISBN 0-87404-091-4 (pbk.) LC Card 87-401861 DDC 333.7/0972/1 19
HC137.M46 U17 1984

MEXICAN AMERICAN BORDER REGION - INDUSTRIES.
Stoddard, Ellwyn R., 1927- Maquila . El Paso, Tex. , c1987. ix, 91 p., [2] p. of plates : ISBN 0-87404-200-3 (pbk.) LC Card 86-51646 DDC 338.4/767/09721 19
HD9734.M42 S76 1987

Trabis, Roland. Industrie et politique à la frontière Mexique-U. S.A. . Paris , c1985. 241 p., [1] p. of plates : ISBN 2-222-03772-7 : LC Card 86-175728
HC138.N84 T73 1985

MEXICAN AMERICAN WOMEN - CALIFORNIA - HISTORY - CASE STUDIES.
Ruíz, Vicki. Cannery women, cannery lives . Albuquerque , c1987. xviii, 194 p. : ISBN 0-8263-1006-0 LC Card 87-13878 DDC 331.88/1640282/09794 19
HD6515.F72 U547 1987

MEXICAN AMERICAN WOMEN - EMPLOYMENT - CALIFORNIA - SANTA CLARA RIVER VALLEY.
Zavella, Patricia, 1949- Women's work and Chicano families . Ithaca , 1987. xviii, 191 p. ; ISBN 0-8014-1730-9 (pbk. : alk. paper) LC Card 87-5245 DDC 305.4/3664 19
HD6073.C272 U596 1987

MEXICAN AMERICANS - COLORADO - HISTORY.
Land, water, and culture . Albuquerque , c1987. ix, 422 p. : ISBN 0-8263-0989-5 (pbk.) LC Card 87-10957 DDC 333.1/6/09788 19
HD243.N5 L36 1987

MEXICAN AMERICANS - NEW MEXICO - HISTORY.
Land, water, and culture . Albuquerque , c1987. ix, 422 p. : ISBN 0-8263-0989-5 (pbk.) LC Card 87-10957 DDC 333.1/6/09788 19
HD243.N5 L36 1987

The Mexican colonial copper industry /. Barrett, Elinore M. Albuquerque , c1987. xi, 143 p. : ISBN 0-8263-0929-1 LC Card 86-24991 DDC 338.2/743/0972 19
HD9539.C7 M417 1987

MEXICAN INDIANS. see **INDIANS OF MEXICO.**

The Mexican Left, the popular movements, and the politics of austerity / edited by Barry Carr and Ricardo Anzaldúa Montoya ; translations by Sandra del Castillo. La Jolla, Calif. : Center for U. S.-Mexican Studies, University of California, San Diego, 1986. vi, 96 p. ; 23 cm. (Monograph series / Center for U. S.-Mexican Studies, University of California, San Diego . 18) Includes bibliographical references. CONTENTS. - The Mexican Left, the popular movements, and the politics of austerity, 1982-1985 / Barry Carr -- The Mexican Left and the economic crisis / Enrique Semo -- Wages and economic crisis in Mexico / Jeffrey Bortz -- Crisis in Mexico : impacts on the working class and the labor movement / Alejandro Alvarez -- The SNTE and the teachers' movement, 1982-1984 / Luis Hernández -- Mexico's national coordinadoras in a context of economic crisis / Ana María Prieto. LC Card 87-621353 DDC 322/.2/0972 19
1. Mexico - Economic conditions - 1970-. 2. Socialism - Mexico. 3. Trade-unions - Mexico - Political activity. 4. Popular fronts - Mexico. 5. Right and left (Political science). I. Carr, Barry. II. Anzaldúa Montoya, Ricardo. III. Series: Monograph series (University of California, San Diego. Center for U. S.-Mexican Studies) , 18.
HC135 .M525535 1986

Mexican petroleum and United States-Mexican relations, 1919-1923 /. Baldridge, Donald C. (Donald Carl) New York , 1987. 255 p. ; ISBN 0-8240-8070-X (alk. paper) LC Card 87-23817 DDC 338.2/7282/0972 19
HD9574.M6 B324 1987

The Mexican rescue /. Kraft, Joseph. New York , 1984. 66 p. ; LC Card 84-10354 DDC 336.3/4/0972 19
HJ8519 .K73 1984 ***NYPL [JLE 86-2931]***

A Mexican response /. Rubio F., Luis. New York , 1987. vi, 72 p. ; ISBN 0-87078-215-0 (pbk.) LC Card 87-162458 DDC 336.3/4/0972 19
HJ8519 .R83 1987

The Mexican time bomb /. Bailey, Norman A. New York , 1987. vi, 61 p. ; ISBN 0-87078-209-6 (pbk.) : LC Card 87-400092 DDC 336.3/4/0972 19
HJ8519 .B26 1987

Mexican topics : questions involving Mexico that have aroused international public interest. [México, D.F.] : Presidencia de la República, Dirección General de Comunicación Social, [1986] 2 portfolios : ill. (some col.) ; 29 cm. Cover title. CONTENTS. - [1] Introduction. Democracy in Mexico. Undocumented Mexican migration to the U. S.A. Foreign debt. Public sector participation in Mexico's economy. Thesis and action during the three years of Presidente Miguel de la Madrid's administration. Permanent campaign against drug trafficking -- 2. Mexican foreign policy. Education policy. Moral renovation. Foreign trade. Ecology. The 1985 earthquake. Tourism activities. LC Card 86-221843 DDC 972.08/3 19
1. Mexico - Economic policy 1970-. 2. Mexico - Politics and government - 1970-. 3. Mexico - Emigration and immigration. 4. United States - Emigration and immigration. 5. Debts, External - Mexico. 6. Government business enterprises - Mexico. 7. Narcotics, Control of - Mexico. 8. Mexico - Foreign relations - 1970-. 9. Education and state - Mexico. 10. Earthquakes - Mexico - Mexico City Region. 11. Corruption (in politics) - Mexico. 12. Environmental policy - Mexico. I. Mexico. Dirección General de Comunicación Social.
HC135 .M52554 1986

MEXICANS - CALIFORNIA - LA JOLLA (SAN DIEGO)
De Murguía, Valdemar. Capital flight and economic crisis . La Jolla, Calif. , 1986. 27 p. ; LC Card 87-621351 DDC 332/.042 19
HG3916 .D4 1986

Mexico, a synoptic view. 2nd ed. México, D.F. : Instituto Nacional de Estadística, Geografía e Informática, 1986. 46 p. : col. ill. ; 23 cm. Includes bibliographical references. LC Card 87-105428 DDC 330.972/0834 19
1. Mexico - Economic conditions - 1970- - Statistics. I. Instituto Nacional de Estadística, Geografía e

Informática (Mexico).
HC135 .M54527 1986

MEXICO - APPROPRIATIONS AND EXPENDITURES.

Mexico - Archives. see **Archives - Mexico.**

MEXICO - CENSUS.
Fernández, Sonia. Análisis comparativo de la información sobre población ocupada . México, D.F. [1977] 28 p. ; LC Card 84-227473
HD5731.A6 F46 1977

MEXICO - CENSUS, 1970.
Pedrero, Mercedes. Indicadores para el estudio de la población económicamente activa basados en la información censal de 1970 /. México, D.F. [1977] 495 p. ; LC Card 85-202779
HA765 .P43 1977

MEXICO - CENSUS, 1980.
X censo general de población y vivienda, 1980 . México, D.F. , c1985- v. <1-6 > : ISBN 968-8099-30-9 (v. 1) LC Card 86-226718
HA761.5 1980d

MEXICO - CENSUS, 1984.
Madrigal Pana, Johnny. Metodología y construcción de un indicador del ingreso familiar . San José, Costa Rica , 1986. 43 p. ; LC Card 87-404395 DDC 339.4/2/0972 19
HD6996 .M33 1986

Mexico (City) Centro de Estudios Monetarios Latinoamericanos. see **Centro de Estudios Monetarios Latinoamericanos.**

MEXICO (CITY) - COMMERCE - HISTORY.
Kicza, John E., 1947- Colonial entrepreneurs, families and business in Bourbon Mexico City /. Albuquerque , c1983. 1 v. : ISBN 0-8263-0655-1 (v. 1) LC Card 82-21962 DDC 305.5/54/097253 19
HF3240.M5 K52 1983 NYPL [JLL 83-164]

Mexico (City). Instituto Mexicano del Seguro Social. see **Instituto Mexicano del Seguro Social.**

MEXICO (CITY) - MANUFACTURES - HISTORY.
Kicza, John E., 1947- Colonial entrepreneurs, families and business in Bourbon Mexico City /. Albuquerque , c1983. 1 v. : ISBN 0-8263-0655-1 (v. 1) LC Card 82-21962 DDC 305.5/54/097253 19
HF3240.M5 K52 1983 NYPL [JLL 83-164]

MEXICO CITY (MEXICO) - ECONOMIC CONDITIONS.
López Monjardín, Adriana. Hacia la ciudad del capital--México, 1790-1870 /. México, D.F. , 1985. 193 p. : LC Card 87-124857 DDC 330.972/53 19
HC138.M4 L66 1985

Mexico (City). Nacional Financiera, S. A. see **Nacional Financiera, S. A., Mexico.**

Mexico. Comisión de Estudios del Territorio Nacional. Departamento de Estudios Interdisciplinarios. Proyecto EI-5-3 . México, D.F. [1977] ca. 150 p. : LC Card 82-119251
HC137.Q5 P76 1977

Mexico. Comisión Nacional de Alimentación. Elementos para la programación del desarrollo de la industria de aceites y pastas vegetales en México. México , 1985. 306 p. : ISBN 968-665-105-5 LC Card 86-232449
HD9490.M62 E44 1985

MEXICO - COMMERCE.
Business Mexico /. México, D.F. , 1978. 343 p. : LC Card 87-405299 DDC 332.1/732272 19
HF3237 .B87 1978

Información básica sobre el GATT y el desarrollo industrial y comercial de México. México , c1985. 79, 62 p. ; LC Card 87-400559 DDC 338.0972 19
HC135 .I53 1985

MEXICO - COMMERCE - UNITED STATES.
Matz, Viktor, 1947- Entwicklungsländer im internationalen Konjunkturzusammenhang . Bergisch Gladbach , c1986. 199, lxxvi p. ; ISBN 3-89012-052-0 LC Card 86-227998
HF3408.U5 M37 1986

MEXICO - COMMERCE - UNITED STATES - CONGRESSES.
U. S.-Mexico relations . Stanford, Calif. , c1987. xii, 401 p. ; ISBN 0-8047-1319-7 (alk. paper) LC Card 86-23103 DDC 338.1/872 19
HD1792 .U19 1987

MEXICO - COMMERCIAL POLICY.
Kate, Adriaan ten. La política de protección en el desarrollo económico de México /. México , 1979. 376 p. ; ISBN 968-16-0352-4 LC Card 87-672671
HF1775 .K37x 1979

Mexico. Congreso. Cámara de Senadores. Consulta sobre el GATT . México , c1986. v, 540 p. ; LC Card 87-114865 DDC 382/.0972 19
HF1481 .M45 1986

México, una economía en transición /. México, D.F. , 1984-1985. 3 v. ; ISBN 968-18-1900-4 (v. 1) LC Card 86-235462
HC135 .M549 1985

MEXICO - COMMERCIAL POLICY - CONGRESSES.
Reunión Nacional para el Desarrollo de la Industria, el Comercio, la Distribución y Otros Servicios (1981 : Mexico City, Mexico) Memoria /. [Mexico City] , 1981. 428 p., [4] folded leaves of plates : LC Card 84-228700
HD3616.M42 R46 1981

MEXICO - COMMMERCE - HISTORY - 19TH CENTURY.
Alvarado Gómez, Armando. Principales productos del comercio exterior mexicano del siglo XIX /. México, D.F. , 1985. v. <1 > ; LC Card 87-401206 DDC 382/.0972 19
HF3236 .A5 1985

Mexico. Congreso. Cámara de Senadores. Consulta sobre el GATT : memoria. México : Dirección de Publicaciones de la Coordinación de Información y Relaciones Públicas del Senado de la República, c1986. v, 540 p. ; 21 cm. (Cuadernos del Senado . 59) On cover: LIII Legislatura, Senado de la República. LC Card 87-114865 DDC 382/.0972 19
1. Mexico - Commercial policy. 2. Tariff - Mexico. 3. General Agreement on Tariffs and Trade (Organization). I. Title. II. Series.
HF1481 .M45 1986

Información básica sobre el GATT y el desarrollo industrial y comercial de México. México , c1985. 79, 62 p. ; LC Card 87-400559 DDC 338.0972 19
HC135 .I53 1985

Mexico. Congreso. Cámara e Senadores. Sección de Estadística y Anales de Jurisprudencia. El Petróleo . México, D.F. , 1923. vi, 352 p. ; LC Card 85-220440
HD9574.M6 P4475 1923

Mexico. Coordinación General de los Servicios Nacionales de Estadística, Geografía e Informática. Manual de estadísticas básicas . [México, D.F.] [1981- v. <1 > ; LC Card 86-225598 DDC 338.0972/021 19
HC135 .M2555 1981

MEXICO - CULTURAL POLICY.
Esparza Oteo T., Luis. La política cultural del estado mexicano y el desarrollo de la T.V. /. México, D.F. , 1984. 116 p. ; LC Card 87-404017 DDC 384.55/4/0972 19
HE8700.9.M6 E84 1984

Mexico. Dirección General de Comunicación Social. Mexican topics . [México, D.F.] [1986] 2 portfolios : LC Card 86-221843 DDC 972.08/3 19
HC135 .M52554 1986

MEXICO - ECONOMIC CONDITIONS - 19TH CENTURY.
Vásquez M., Luis (Vásquez Medina) El mercantilismo mexicano versus el liberalismo inglés /. México, D.F. , 1985. xiii, 215 p., [18] p. of plates : LC Card 87-403512 DDC 380.1/0972 19
HC135 .V34 1985

MEXICO - ECONOMIC CONDITIONS - 1918-
Nacional Financiera, 1934-1984 . México, D.F. , 1985. 310 p. ; ISBN 968-665-107-1 LC Card 87-400288 DDC 332.2 19
HG2718.N33 N33 1985

Ramírez L., Fernando (Ramírez López) Estado y crisis del desarrollo nacional . México, D.F. , 1983. 242 p. ; LC Card 86-220975
HC135 .R234 1983

Serrano Illescas, Alfonso. Pobre patria! /. México, D.F. , 1982. 132 p. ; ISBN 968-409-161-3 LC Card 85-122377
HC135 .S368 1982

MEXICO - ECONOMIC CONDITIONS - 1970-
Bilbao, Elena. La frontera de San Ysidro . Tijuana, Baja California , 1986. 27 p. ; ISBN 968-607-513-5 LC Card 87-125801 DDC 330.9794/98 19
HC108.S65 B55 1986

Buen L., Néstor de (Buen Lozano) Sindicatos, democracia y crisis /. México , 1985. xii, 122 p. ; ISBN 968-452-054-9 LC Card 86-209080
HD6532 .B84 1985

Business Mexico /. México, D.F. , 1978. 343 p. : LC Card 87-405299 DDC 332.1/732272 19
HF3237 .B87 1978

Cernea, Michael M. Measuring project impact . Washington, D.C., U. S.A. , c1979. vi, 93 p. ; LC Card 81-170764
HD1792 .C43 1979

Cornelius, Wayne A., 1945- The political economy of Mexico under de la Madrid . La Jolla, Calif. , 1986. 50 p. ; LC Card 87-621352 DDC 330.972/0834 19
HC135 .C7185 1986

Dávila Flores, Alejandro, 1956- La crisis financiera en México /. [Mexico City, Mexico] , 1986. 228 p. : LC Card 87-401258 DDC 330.972/0834 19
HG185.M6 D33 1986

Domitra, Michael. Mexiko . Bonn [1984] 24 p. ; LC Card 85-134274 DDC 330.972/0834 19
HC135 .D65 1984

Huerta González, Arturo. Economía mexicana . [Mexico City, Mexico] , 1986. 246 p. : LC Card 87-404065 DDC 330.972/0834 19
HC135 .H84 1986

López Díaz, Pedro. Crítica de la economía y la política /. México , 1985. 255 p. ; ISBN 968-590-060-4 LC Card 86-156378
HB501 .L856 1985

Méndez Morales, José Silvestre. México por entidades federativas /. México, D.F. , c1986. 318 p., [32] p. of plates : ISBN 968-493-098-4 LC Card 87-400185 DDC 330.972/083 19
HC135 .M52524 1986

The Mexican Left, the popular movements, and the politics of austerity /. La Jolla, Calif. , 1986. vi, 96 p. ; LC Card 87-621353 DDC 322/.2/0972 19
HC135 .M525535 1986

México, una economía en transición /. México, D.F. , 1984-1985. 3 v. ; ISBN 968-18-1900-4 (v. 1) LC Card 86-235462
HC135 .M549 1985

Pinal Verges, Jorge. México es mágico . México , c1986. 92 p. ; ISBN 968-409-352-7 LC Card 87-401447 DDC 338.972 19
HC135 .P54 1986

Rivera Ríos, Miguel Angel. Crisis y reorganización del capitalismo mexicano, 1960-1985 /. México, D.F. , 1986. 227 p. : ISBN 968-411-149-5 LC Card 87-401541 DDC 330.972/083 19
HC135 .R435 1986

Sacristán, Antonio. La situación económica mundial y México . México, D.F. [1980] 72 p. ; LC Card 87-400921 DDC 330.972/0834 19
HC59 .S3122 1980

MEXICO - ECONOMIC CONDITIONS - 1970- - CONGRESSES.
Mexiko . Bonn [1983?] 127, [2] p. ; LC Card 85-206583
HC135 .M585 1983

MEXICO - ECONOMIC CONDITIONS - 1970- - REGIONAL DISPARITIES.
Acevedo Conde, María Luisa. Pobreza y riqueza en 378 municipios de México /. México, D.F. , 1984. 281 p. : LC Card 86-219445
HC140.P6 A25 1984

MEXICO - ECONOMIC CONDITIONS - 1970- - RESEARCH.
Espinoza Jaramillo, Frida. El estado de la investigación nacional acerca de la frontera norte de México /. [México] , 1985. 47 leaves ; LC Card 87-402765 DDC 330.972/10834 19
HC137.M46 E76 1985

MEXICO - ECONOMIC CONDITIONS - 1970- - STATISTICS.

Mexico, a synoptic view. México, D.F. , 1986. 46 p. : LC Card 87-105428 DDC 330.972/0834 19
HC135 .M54527 1986

MEXICO - ECONOMIC POLICY.
Austin, Ruben Vargas, 1915- The development of economic policy in Mexico with special reference to economic doctrines, 1600-1958 /. New York , 1987. 336 p. ; ISBN 0-8240-1354-9 (alk. paper) : LC Card 87-8569 DDC 338.972 19
HC135 .A84 1987

García Alba Iduñate, Pascual, 1948- [Financial aspects of macroeconomic management in Mexico. Spanish.] Causas y efectos de la crisis económica en México /. México, D.F. , 1984. 124 p. : ISBN 968-12-0285-6 LC Card 86-138030
HC135 .G29818 1984

Gies, Christoph. Die Spielregeln für Kapitalanlagen in Mexiko . Frankfurt , c1986. ix, 314 p. : ISBN 3-88323-603-9 LC Card 86-231145
HG5162 .G48 1986

Hellman, Judith Adler. Notes on the failure of reformist capitalism in Mexico /. Toronto, Ont., Canada [1976] 24 p ; LC Card 85-155317 DDC 338.972 19
HC135 .H38 1976

Kate, Adriaan ten. La política de protección en el desarrollo económico de México /. México , 1979. 376 p. ; ISBN 968-16-0352-4 LC Card 87-672671
HF1775 .K37x 1979

Orozco, Jesús. Ideología y programa de gobierno en los discursos de toma de posesión de los presidentes de México, 1928-1982 /. Guadalajara, Jal., México , c1983. 47 p. ; ISBN 968-511-003-4 LC Card 83-191579
HC135 .O66 1983

Ramírez L., Fernando (Ramírez López) Estado y crisis del desarrollo nacional . México, D.F. , 1983. 242 p. ; LC Card 86-220975
HC135 .R234 1983

Solís M., Leopoldo. Alternativas para el desarrollo /. México, D.F. , 1985, c1980. 155 p. ; ISBN 968-270-487-1 LC Card 86-222497
HC135 .S636 1985

MEXICO - ECONOMIC POLICY 1970-
Bennett, Mark. Public policy and industrial development . Boulder, Colo. , 1986. xii, 134 p. : ISBN 0-86531-821-2 : LC Card 83-23456 DDC 338.4/76292/0972 19
HD9710.3.M42 B46 1986 ***NYPL [JLE 86-2581]***

Cornelius, Wayne A., 1945- The political economy of Mexico under de la Madrid . La Jolla, Calif. , 1986. 50 p. ; LC Card 87-621352 DDC 330.972/0834 19
HC135 .C7185 1986

Flores Domínguez, David. Queremos hechos /. México, D.F. , c1982. 154 p. ; ISBN 968-7163-01-1 LC Card 83-142817
HC135 .F54 1982

Hampson, Fen Osler. Forming economic policy . London , 1986. x, 161 p. : ISBN 0-86187-628-8 ***NYPL [JLE 86-3813]***

Huerta González, Arturo. Economía mexicana . [Mexico City, Mexico] , 1986. 246 p. : LC Card 87-404065 DDC 330.972/0834 19
HC135 .H84 1986

Kraft, Joseph. The Mexican rescue /. New York , 1984. 66 p. ; LC Card 84-10354 DDC 336.3/4/0972 19
HJ8519 .K73 1984 ***NYPL [JLE 86-2931]***

Madrid Hurtado, Miguel de la. Message to the nation . [Mexico City, Mexico] [1986] 15 p. : LC Card 87-400574 DDC 338.972 19
HC135 .M225 1986

Mexican topics . [México, D.F.] [1986] 2 portfolios : LC Card 86-221843 DDC 972.08/3 19
HC135 .M52554 1986

Pinal Verges, Jorge. México es mágico . México , c1986. 92 p. ; ISBN 968-409-352-7 LC Card 87-401447 DDC 338.972 19
HC135 .P54 1986

Rivera Ríos, Miguel Angel. Crisis y reorganización del capitalismo mexicano, 1960-1985 /. México, D.F. , 1986. 227 p. : ISBN 968-411-149-5 LC Card 87-401541 DDC 330.972/083 19
HC135 .R435 1986

Rizzo, Sócrates. Opciones de política económica, 1979-1982 /. México, D.F. [1983] 133 p. : LC Card 86-205260 DDC 338.972 19
HC135 .R44 1983

Teichman, Judith A., 1947- Policymaking in Mexico . Boston , c1988. p. cm. ISBN 0-04-445033-8 : LC Card 87-18704 DDC 338.2/7282/0972 19
HD9574.M6 T45 1988

MEXICO - ECONOMIC POLICY - 1970- - CONGRESSES.
Mexiko . Bonn [1983?] 127, [2] p. ; LC Card 85-206583
HC135 .M585 1983

MEXICO - ECONOMIC POLICY - 1971-
Gómez de Reyes, María Teresa. Experiencias de políticas de estabilización . México, D.F. , 1985. iv, 66 leaves ; LC Card 87-122042 DDC 338.982 19
HC125 .G57 1985

MEXICO - ECONOMIC POLICY - CONGRESSES.
Reunión Nacional para el Desarrollo de la Industria, el Comercio, la Distribución y Otros Servicios (1981 : Mexico City, Mexico) Memoria /. [Mexico City] , 1981. 428 p., [4] folded leaves of plates : LC Card 84-228700
HD3616.M42 R46 1981

MEXICO - EMIGRATION AMD IMMIGRATION.
López Castro, Gustavo. La casa dividida . Zamora, Mich. [i.e. Michoacán] [S.l.] , 1986. 169 p. : ISBN 968-7230-19-3 LC Card 87-400954 DDC 304.8/73/07237 19
HB3532.G66 L66 1986

MEXICO - EMIGRATION AND IMMIGRATION.
Gregory, Peter. The myth of market failure . Baltimore , 1986. viii, 299 p. ; ISBN 0-8018-3343-4 : LC Card 85-45927 DDC 331.12/0972 19
HD5731.A6 G74 1986 ***NYPL [JLE 86-3065]***

Mexican topics . [México, D.F.] [1986] 2 portfolios : LC Card 86-221843 DDC 972.08/3 19
HC135 .M52554 1986

MEXICO - EMIGRATION AND IMMIGRATION - ADDRESSES, ESSAYS, LECTURES.
Los Factores del cambio demográfico en México /. México, D.F. , 1984. 422 p. : ISBN 968-231-281-7 LC Card 85-231767
HB1361 .F33 1984 ***NYPL [JLE 87-753]***

MEXICO - EMIGRATION AND IMMIGRATION - STATISTICS.
Indicadores de la migración en México. México, D.F. , 1985. ix, 161 p. ; ISBN 968-89200-3-7 LC Card 86-217222
HB1991 .I55 1985

México es mágico . Pinal Verges, Jorge. México , c1986. 92 p. ; ISBN 968-409-352-7 LC Card 87-401447 DDC 338.972 19
HC135 .P54 1986

MEXICO - EXECUTIVE DEPARTMENTS.
Flores Domínguez, David. Queremos hechos /. México, D.F. , c1982. 154 p. ; ISBN 968-7163-01-1 LC Card 83-142817
HC135 .F54 1982

MEXICO - FOREIGN ECONOMIC RELATIONS.
Aschentrupp Toledo, Hermann. La dimensión política de la crisis y renegociación de la deuda externa mexicana /. México, D.F. [1985] 229 p. ; LC Card 87-401754 DDC 336.3/4/0972 19
HJ8519 .A8 1985

MEXICO - FOREIGN ECONOMIC RELATIONS - UNITED STATES.
Baldridge, Donald C. (Donald Carl) Mexican petroleum and United States-Mexican relations, 1919-1923 /. New York , 1987. 255 p. ; ISBN 0-8240-8070-X (alk. paper) LC Card 87-23817 DDC 338.2/7282/0972 19
HD9574.M6 B324 1987

Beelen, George D. Harding and Mexico . New York , 1987. xiii, 200 p., [16] p. of plates : ISBN 0-8240-8073-4 (alk. paper) LC Card 87-23724 DDC 337.72073 19
HF1456.5.M6 B44 1987

Bodayla, Stephen D. Financial diplomacy . New York , 1987. x, 216 p. ; ISBN 0-8240-8074-2 (alk. paper) LC Card 87-23790 DDC 337.73072 19
HF1456.5.M6 B63 1987

González-Aréchiga, Bernardo. Vinculación fronteriza a Estados Unidos y su cambio con la crisis /. Tijuana, Baja California , 1985. 54 p. ; ISBN 968-607-500-3 LC Card 86-187758
HF3239.M49 G66 1985

Hirst, Mônica. As relações dos Estados Unidos com as potências médias na América Latina, México e Brasil /. [Rio de Janeiro] , 1985. 48 leaves ; LC Card 87-143873 DDC 337.73072 19
HF1456.5.M6 H57 1985

MEXICO - FOREIGN RELATIONS - 1910-1946.
Bodayla, Stephen D. Financial diplomacy . New York , 1987. x, 216 p. ; ISBN 0-8240-8074-2 (alk. paper) LC Card 87-23790 DDC 337.73072 19
HF1456.5.M6 B63 1987

MEXICO - FOREIGN RELATIONS - 1970-
Mexican topics . [México, D.F.] [1986] 2 portfolios : LC Card 86-221843 DDC 972.08/3 19
HC135 .M52554 1986

Mexico - Government. see **Mexico - Politics and government.**

MEXICO - HISTORY - SPANISH COLONY, 1540-1810.
Barrett, Elinore M. The Mexican colonial copper industry /. Albuquerque , c1987. xi, 143 p. : ISBN 0-8263-0929-1 LC Card 86-24991 DDC 338.2/743/0972 19
HD9539.C7 M417 1987

MEXICO - HISTORY - 1867-1910.
Keremitsis, Dawn, 1921- The cotton textile industry in Porfiriato, Mexico, 1870-1910 /. New York , 1987. 232 p. : ISBN 0-8240-1364-6 (alk. paper) : LC Card 87-7619 DDC 338.4/767721/0972 19
HD9884.M42 K47 1987

MEXICO - HISTORY - 1910-1946.
Cárdenas, Lázaro, 1895-1970. Los ejidos de Yucatán y el henequén . [Mexico City, Mexico] , c1984. 79 p. : LC Card 87-403579 DDC 333.3/1/7265 19
HD1333.M62 Y823 1984

Mexico - History, Economic. see **Mexico - Economic conditions.**

MEXICO - INDUSTRIES.
Gies, Christoph. Die Spielregeln für Kapitalanlagen in Mexiko . Frankfurt , c1986. ix, 314 p. : ISBN 3-88323-603-9 LC Card 86-231145
HG5162 .G48 1986

Información básica sobre el GATT y el desarrollo industrial y comercial de México. México , c1985. 79, 62 p. ; LC Card 87-400559 DDC 338.0972 19
HC135 .I53 1985

México, una economía en transición /. México, D.F. , 1984-1985. 3 v. ; ISBN 968-18-1900-4 (v. 1) LC Card 86-235462
HC135 .M549 1985

MEXICO - INDUSTRIES - STATISTICS.
Manual de estadísticas básicas . [México, D.F.] [1981- v. <1 > ; LC Card 86-225598 DDC 338.0972/021 19
HC135 .M2555 1981

MEXICO - MANUFACTURES.
Huerta González, Arturo. Economía mexicana . [Mexico City, Mexico] , 1986. 246 p. : LC Card 87-404065 DDC 330.972/0834 19
HC135 .H84 1986

MEXICO (MEXICO) - INDUSTRIES - HISTORY.
García Luna O., Margarita (García Luna Ortega) El movimiento obrero en el Estado de México . Toluca, Estado de México , 1984. 302 p. : ISBN 968-514-014-6 LC Card 86-173738
HC137.M473 G37 1984

MEXICO - OCCUPATIONS - STATISTICS.
Pedrero, Mercedes. Indicadores para el estudio de la población económicamente activa basados en la información censal de 1970 /. México, D.F. [1977] 495 p. ; LC Card 85-202779
HA765 .P43 1977

MEXICO - POLITICS AND GOVERNMENT - 1821-1861.
Tenenbaum, Barbara, 1946- The politics of

penury . Albuquerque , c1986. xviii, 250 p. ; ISBN 0-8263-0890-2 : LC Card 86-16027 DDC 336.72 19
HJ802 .T46 1986 ***NYPL [JLE 87-482]***

MEXICO - POLITICS AND GOVERNMENT - 20TH CENTURY.
Orozco, Jesús. Ideología y programa de gobierno en los discursos de toma de posesión de los presidentes de México, 1928-1982 /. Guadalajara, Jal., México , c1983. 47 p. ; ISBN 968-511-003-4 LC Card 83-191579
HC135 .O66 1983

MEXICO - POLITICS AND GOVERNMENT - 1970-
Domitra, Michael. Mexiko . Bonn [1984] 24 p. ; LC Card 85-134274 DDC 330.972/0834 19
HC135 .D65 1984

Leduc, Renato. Los diablos del petróleo /. [Mexico City, Mexico] [1986] 131 p. ; LC Card 86-219535 DDC 338.2/7282/0972 19
HD9574.M62 P3745 1986

Mexican topics . [México, D.F.] [1986] 2 portfolios : LC Card 86-221843 DDC 972.08/3 19
HC135 .M52554 1986

MEXICO - POLITICS AND GOVERNMENT - 1970- - CONGRESSES.
Mexiko . Bonn [1983?] 127, [2] p. ; LC Card 85-206583
HC135 .M585 1983

MEXICO - POPULATION.
Planeación familiar y cambio demográfico. México, D.F. [1983], c1982. 554 p. : ISBN 968-8241-63-6 LC Card 84-227488 DDC 304.6/0972 19
HB3531 .P57 1983 ***NYPL [JLE 86-3248]***

MEXICO - POPULATION - ECONOMIC ASPECTS - STATISTICS.
Pedrero, Mercedes. Indicadores para el estudio de la población económicamente activa basados en la información censal de 1970 /. México, D.F. [1977] 495 p. ; LC Card 85-202779
HA765 .P43 1977

MEXICO - POPULATION, RURAL - HISTORY - 20TH CENTURY.

MEXICO - POPULATION - STATES - STATISTICS.
X censo general de población y vivienda, 1980 . México, D.F. , c1985- v. <1-6 > : ISBN 968-8099-30-9 (v. 1) LC Card 86-226718
HA761.5 1980d

MEXICO - POPULATION - STATISTICS.
Proyecciones de la población de México y de las entidades federativas, 1980-2010. México, D.F. , c1985. xiii, 134 p. ; ISBN 968-8097-66-7 LC Card 86-223751
HB3531 .P78 1985

X censo general de población y vivienda, 1980 . México, D.F. , c1985- v. <1-6 > : ISBN 968-8099-30-9 (v. 1) LC Card 86-226718
HA761.5 1980d

México por entidades federativas /. Méndez Morales, José Silvestre. México, D.F. , c1986. 318 p., [32] p. of plates : ISBN 968-493-098-4 LC Card 87-400185 DDC 330.972/083 19
HC135 .M52524 1986

MEXICO - RURAL CONDITIONS.
Acevedo Conde, María Luisa. Pobreza y riqueza en 378 municipios de México /. México, D.F. , 1984. 281 p. : LC Card 86-219445
HC140.P6 A25 1984

Cernea, Michael M. Measuring project impact . Washington, D.C., U. S.A. , c1979. vi, 93 p. ; LC Card 81-170764
HD1792 .C43 1979

Trabajo familiar, conducta reproductiva y estratificación social . México, D.F. , 1986. 226 p. ; ISBN 968-8241-06-7 LC Card 87-400355 DDC 304.6/32/0972 19
HB941 .T7 1986

Vivienda rural, México. [Mexico City] [1982?] 40 p. : LC Card 86-174056
HD7289.M6 V58 1982

Mexico. Secretaría de Asentamientos Humanos y Obras Públicas. Vivienda rural, México. [Mexico City] [1982?] 40 p. : LC Card 86-174056
HD7289.M6 V58 1982

Mexico. Secretaría de Energía, Minas e Industria Paraestatal. Directorio del sector energía, minas e industria paraestatal, 1984. [Mexico City] : Secretaría de Energía, Minas e Industria Paraestatal, 1984. 497 p. ; 21 x 28 cm. Includes index. ISBN 968-86000-4-0 LC Card 87-404794 DDC 333.79/0972 19
1. Energy industries - Mexico - Directories. 2. Mineral industries - Mexico - Directories. 3. Government business enterprises - Mexico - Directories. I. Title.
HD9502.M62 M49 1984

Mexico. Secretaría de Hacienda y Crédito Público. Pequeña y mediana empresa. [Mexico City, Mexico] [1983] 220 p. ; ISBN 968-8060-29-01 LC Card 86-144218
HD2346.M4 P47 1983

Mexico. Secretaría de la Reforma Agraria. El Proceso de la capacitación . [Mexico City] [1982] 194 p. : LC Card 84-220474
HD326 .P76 1982

MEXICO. SECRETARÍA DE LA REFORMA AGRARIA - OFFICIALS AND EMPLOYEES - IN-SERVICE TRAINING.
El Proceso de la capacitación . [Mexico City] [1982] 194 p. : LC Card 84-220474
HD326 .P76 1982

Mexico. Secretaría de Pesca. Nociones básicas sobre cooperativismo pesquero. [Mexico City, Mexico] , 1985. 313 p. : ISBN 968-8170-25-9 LC Card 86-217319 DDC 334/.6892/0972 19
HD9464.B72 N63 1985

Mexico. Seguro Social, Instituto del. see **Instituto Mexicano del Seguro Social.**

MEXICO - SOCIAL CONDITIONS - 1970-
Méndez Morales, José Silvestre. México por entidades federativas /. México, D.F. , c1986. 318 p., [32] p. of plates : ISBN 968-493-098-4 LC Card 87-400185 DDC 330.972/083 19
HC135 .M52524 1986

México, una economía en transición /. México, D.F. , 1984-1985. 3 v. ; ISBN 968-18-1900-4 (v. 1) LC Card 86-235462
HC135 .M549 1985

MEXICO - SOCIAL POLICY.
Flores Domínguez, David. Queremos hechos /. México, D.F. , c1982. 154 p. ; ISBN 968-7163-01-1 LC Card 83-142817
HC135 .F54 1982

Orozco, Jesús. Ideología y programa de gobierno en los discursos de toma de posesión de los presidentes de México, 1928-1982 /. Guadalajara, Jal., México , c1983. 47 p. ; ISBN 968-511-003-4 LC Card 83-191579
HC135 .O66 1983

Mexico. Subcoordinación de Análisis y Política Laboral. La Mujer y el trabajo en México . México , 1986. 346 p. : ISBN 968-8132-48-9 LC Card 87-101329
HD6101 .M86 1986

Mexico. Subcoordinación de Programas Institucionales y Documentación. La Mujer y el trabajo en México . México , 1986. 346 p. : ISBN 968-8132-48-9 LC Card 87-101329
HD6101 .M86 1986

México, una economía en transición / coordinadores, Alejandro Violante, Roberto Dávila. 1a ed. México, D.F. : Editorial Limusa, 1984-1985. 3 v. ; 23 cm. Articles presented at a meeting of social science researchers at the Colegio Nacional de Economistas, 1982. Includes bibliographical references. CONTENTS. - v. 1. Política monetaria y fiscal -- v. 2. Industria y comercio exterior -- v. 3. Problemas socioeconómicos. ISBN 968-18-1900-4 (v. 1) LC Card 86-235462
1. Mexico - Economic conditions - 1970-. 2. Mexico - Social conditions - 1970-. 3. Mexico - Industries. 4. Mexico - Commercial policy. 5. Industry and state - Mexico. 6. Monetary policy - Mexico. 7. Investments, Foreign - Mexico. I. Violante, Alejandro. II. Dávila, Roberto. III. Colegio Nacional de Economistas (Mexico).
HC135 .M549 1985

Mexiko : Krise, Austeritätspolitik und politische Stabilität : Expertengespräch in Bonn, 16. Juni 1983. Bonn : Forschungsinstitut der Friedrich-Ebert-Stiftung, [1983?] 127, [2] p. ; 21 cm. (Analysen aus der Abteilung Entwicklungsländerforschung, 0174-5190 . Nr. 111/112) Papers presented at a workshop sponsored by the Friedrich-Ebert-Stiftung. Bibliography: p. 123-[127] CONTENTS. - Mexiko, der Weg in die Krise / Michael Ehrke -- Bemerkungen zur mexikanischen Verschuldungskrise / Jürgen Westphalen -- Mexiko, Wachstumspotential und Entwicklungsstrategie in den 80er Jahren / Klaus Esser -- Was bleibt von Mexikos politischer Stabilität in den achtziger Jahren / Manfred Mols -- Die Wirtschaftspolitik der Regierung Miguel de la Madrid / Rainer Godau. LC Card 85-206583
1. Mexico - Economic conditions - 1970- - Congresses. 2. Mexico - Economic policy - 1970- - Congresses. 3. Debts, External - Mexico - Congresses. 4. Mexico - Politics and government - 1970- - Congresses. I. Friedrich-Ebert-Stiftung. II. Series.
HC135 .M585 1983

Mexiko . Domitra, Michael. Bonn [1984] 24 p. ; LC Card 85-134274 DDC 330.972/0834 19
HC135 .D65 1984

Mey, Harald. Wirtschaftsreformen und neue Entwicklungsstrategien in der Volksrepublik China /. Frankfurt am Main , New York , c1986. 185 p. ; ISBN 3-8204-9101-5 LC Card 86-220822
HC427.92 .W56 1986

Meyer-Abich, Klaus Michael, 1936- Die Grenzen der Atomwirtschaft : die Zukunft von Energie, Wirtschaft und Gesellschaft / Klaus Michael Meyer-Abich, Bertram Schefold ; Einleitung von Carl Friedrich von Weizsäcker ; mit einer Stellungnahme der Studiengruppe der Vereinigung Deutscher Wissenschaftler. München : C.H. Beck, c1986. 230 p. : ill. ; 23 cm. (Die Sozialverträglichkeit von Energiesystemen . Bd. 8) Bibliography: p. [225]-230. ISBN 3-406-31317-5 LC Card 86-192439
1. Nuclear industry - Social aspects. I. Schefold, Bertram, 1943-. II. Vereinigung Deutscher Wissenschaftler. III. Title. IV. Series.
HD9698.A2 M49 1986

Meyer, Anton. Zukunftsorientiertes Marketing für Theorie und Praxis . Berlin , c1984. 340 p., [1] leaf of plates : ISBN 3-428-05651-5 LC Card 85-115141
HF5415 .Z85 1984

Meyer, August. Das Syndikat : Reichswerke "Hermann Göring" / August Meyer. Braunschweig : Steinweg-Verlag, c1986. 348 p. ; 21 cm. "Quellen und Literatur": p. 312-320. Includes index. ISBN 3-925151-18-4 LC Card 87-129940 DDC 338.2/73/0943 19
1. Reichswerke Aktiengesellschaft für Erzbergbau und Eisenhütten "Hermann Göring" - History. 2. Iron industry and trade - Germany - History. 3. Conglomerate corporations - Germany - History. 4. Government business enterprises - Germany - History. 5. Germany - Economic policy - 1933-1945. 6. Germany - Industries - History. I. Title.
HD9523.9.R45 M49 1986

Meyer, Carl W. (Carl Walter), 1919- Marzen, Walter. Betriebswirtschaftliche Forschung und Wirtschaftspraxis . Spardorf , c1986. ix, 229 p. ; ISBN 3-922919-82-0 LC Card 87-133392 DDC 658.4 19
HD35 .M276 1986

Meyer, Charles W. Social security . Lexington, Mass. , c1987. x, 153 p. : ISBN 0-669-14518-1 (alk. paper) LC Card 86-45891 DDC 368.4/3/00973 19
HD7125 .S593 1987 ***NYPL [JLE 87-1286]***

Meyer, Conrad. Die Bankbilanz als finanzielles Führungsinstrument : unter besonderer Berücksichtigung aufsichtsrechtlicher Bestimmungen im In- und Ausland / von Conrad Meyer. Bern : P. Haupt, c1986. x, 655 p. : ill. ; 23 cm. (Bankwirtschaftliche Forschungen. Bd. 96) "Die vorliegende Publikation wurde von den Erziehungsbehörden des Kantons Zürich im Jahre 1985 als Habilitationsschrift angenommen"--P. i. Bibliography: p. 637-655. ISBN 3-258-03587-3 LC Card 86-199541
1. Banks and banking - Switzerland - State supervision. 2. Banks and banking - Switzerland - Accounting. I. Title. II. Series.
HG1526 .B27 Bd. 96 HG1778.S9

Meyer-Cording, Claus, 1953- Die Auswirkungen kreditfinanzierter Staatsausgaben auf das Volkseinkommen : ein makroökonomische Untersuchung / Claus Meyer-Cording. Frankfurt am Main ; New York : P. Lang, c1986. v, 256 p. : ill. ; 21 cm. (Europäische Hochschulschriften. Reihe V, Volks- und Betriebswirtschaft, 0531-7339 . Bd. 722 = vol. 722 = vol. 722) Includes bibliographical references. ISBN

3-8204-9634-3 LC Card 86-204989
1. National income - Accounting - Mathematical models. 2. Monetary policy - Mathematical models. 3. Debts, Public - Mathematical models. I. Series: Europäische Hochschulschriften. Reihe V, Volks- und Betriebswirtschaft , Bd. 722. II. Title.
HB141.5 .M49 1986

Meyer, Herbert E., 1945- Real-world intelligence : organized information for executives / Herbert E. Meyer.1st ed. New York : Weidenfeld & Nicolson, c1987. 102 p. ; 22 cm. ISBN 1-555-84147-3 LC Card 87-20787 DDC 658.4/7 19
1. Business intelligence. I. Title.
HD38.7 .M47 1987

Meyer, Jack A. Market reforms in health care . Washington , c1983. xv, 331 p. ; ISBN 0-8447-2242-1 LC Card 82-22678 DDC 362.1/0973 19
RA410.53 .M37 1983 ***NYPL [JLC 86-373]***

Meyer, Jean, 1924- Le poids de l'Etat / Jean Meyer ; préface de Pierre Chaunu. Paris : Presses universitaires de, c1983. 304 p. : ill. ; 23 cm. (Histoires, 0246-6120) Bibliography: p. [299]-304. ISBN 2-13-037770-X : LC Card 83-175028
1. War - Economic aspects - France. 2. War - Economic aspects - Europe. 3. France - Economic conditions - 19th century. 4. France - Economic conditions - 20th century. 5. Europe - Economic conditions - 19th century. 6. Europe - Economic conditions - 20th century. I. Title. II. Series.
HC280.D4 M49 1983

Meyer, Jean, 1926- Gestion budgétaire / Jean Meyer. 9e éd. actualisée. [Paris] : Dunod, 1984. xvi, 283, 191 p. : ill. ; 24 cm. (Gestion "module") Bibliography: p. [280]-283. ISBN 2-04-015608-9 : LC Card 85-166398 DDC 658.1/54 19
1. Budget in business. I. Title. II. Series.
HG4026 .M49 1984

Meyer, Jean Claude. Lefebvre, André, docteur en droit. Planification et aménagement des communes, des départements et des régions /. Paris , c1985. 335 p. : ISBN 2-7013-0620-5 : LC Card 86-113657 DDC 338.944 19
HT395.F7 L43 1985 ***NYPL [JLD 87-1577]***

Meyer, John Robert.
Deregulation and the future of intercity passenger travel / John R. Meyer and Clinton V. Oster, Jr., with John S. Strong ... [et al.]. Cambridge, Mass. : MIT Press, c1987. xviii, 294 p. : ill. ; 24 cm. (MIT Press series on the regulation of economic activity . 15) Bibliography: p. [261]-286. Includes index. ISBN 0-262-13225-7 LC Card 86-27308 DDC 387.7/42/0973 19
1. Aeronautics, Commercial - United States - Deregulation. 2. Transportation - United States - Passenger traffic. I. Oster, Clinton V. II. Title. III. Series.
HE9803.A35 M49 1987
Entrepreneurship . Wien , New York , 1984, c1983. 218 p. ; ISBN 0-387-81830-8 (U. S.) LC Card 84-26677 DDC 338/.04 19
HB615 .E635 1984 ***NYPL [JLE 85-1253]***

Meyer, N. Dean. The information edge / N. Dean Meyer, Mary E. Boone. New York : McGraw-Hill Bk. Co., c1987. xvii, 333 p. ; 24 cm. (The Converging technologies series) Includes bibliographies and indexes. ISBN 0-07-041782-2 LC Card 86-222546 DDC 651.8 19
1. Office practice - Automation. I. Boone, Mary E. II. Title. III. Series.
HF5547.5 .M495 1987

MEYER, PAUL J.
Strain, Lois S. (Lois Smith) The story of Paul J. Meyer . Hollywood, Fla. , c1986. xii, 193 p. : ISBN 0-8119-0720-1 : LC Card 86-29525 DDC 338/.04/0924 B 19
HF5386 .S8832 1986

Meyer, Paul Werner. Zukunftsorientiertes Marketing für Theorie und Praxis . Berlin , c1984. 340 p., [1] leaf of plates : ISBN 3-428-05651-5 LC Card 85-115141
HF5415 .Z85 1984

MEYER, PAUL WERNER.
Zukunftsorientiertes Marketing für Theorie und Praxis . Berlin , c1984. 340 p., [1] leaf of plates : ISBN 3-428-05651-5 LC Card 85-115141
HF5415 .Z85 1984

Meyer, Peter. Die Bedeutung wichtiger Typen von Produktionsfunktionen für die Input-Output-Analyse / Peter Meyer. Frankfurt : R.G. Fischer, c1983. 109 p. : ill. ; 21 cm. (Schriften zur quantitativen Wirtschaftsforschung . Bd. 8) Spine title: Bedeutung von Produktionsfunktionen für die Input-Output-Analyse. Bibliography: p. 106-109. ISBN 3-88323-438-9 LC Card 83-206578
1. Production functions (Economic theory). 2. Input-output analysis. I. Title. II. Title: Bedeutung von Produktionsfunktionen für die Input-Output-Analyse. III. Series.
HB241 .M49 1983

Meyer, Petra. Die Entwicklung der Organisationswissenschaft im deutschsprachigen Raum : eine dogmengeschichtliche Analyse und integrative Bestandsaufnahme / Petra Meyer. München : Müller + Botermann, c1985. 309 p. : ill. ; 21 cm. (Reihe Planung, Organisation, Unternehmensführung . Bd. 1) Bibliography: p. 271-305. Includes index. ISBN 3-924361-10-X LC Card 87-114143
1. Industrial organization - Europe, German-speaking. I. Title. II. Series.
HD70.E8 M48 1985

Meyer, Rolf. Die Entsorgungswirtschaft einer Wirtschaftsregion : eine ökonomische Analyse am Beispiel der Sonderabfallbeseitigung in Hamburg / Rolf Meyer. Schwarzenbek : R. Martienss, 1983. 400 p. : ill. ; 21 cm. Date of publication and ISBN from label on verso of t.p. Bibliography: p. 370-395. "Nachtrag zum Literaturverzeichnis": p. 399. ISBN 3-921757-20-7 LC Card 84-103993
1. Recycling industry - Germany (West) - Hamburg. I. Title.
HD9975.G43 H355 1983

Meyer, Rolf, 1957- Integration der Informationsverarbeitung im Büro : konzeptionelle und empirische Ansätze zur organisatorischen Gestaltung der betrieblichen Informationsverarbeitung / Rolf Meyer ; mit einem Geleitwort von Norbert Szyperski. Bergisch Gladbach : Eul, c1986. xiv, 327 p. : ill. ; 21 cm. (BIFOA-Monographien . Bd. 26) Based on the author's thesis (doctoral)--Universität zu Köln, 1986. Bibliography: p. 295-327. ISBN 3-89012-062-8 LC Card 87-104032 DDC 651.8 19
1. Office practice - Automation. 2. Office practice - Automation - Psychological aspects. 3. Business - Data processing. 4. Office management. I. Title. II. Series.
HF5547.5 .M497 1986

Meyer, Willm Rolf. Ressourcenumverteilung zugunsten von Problemregionen : das Beispiel Ruhrgebiet / Willm Rolf Meyer. Frankfurt/Main ; New York : Campus, c1982. 262 p. : ill. ; 21 cm. (Campus Forschung. Bd. 250) Bibliography: p. 248-262. ISBN 3-593-33036-9 LC Card 82-161064 DDC 336.1/85 19
1. Intergovernmental fiscal relations - Germany (West) - Ruhr (Region). 2. Transfer payments - Germany (West) - Ruhr (Region). 3. Germany (West) - Economic conditions - 1974- - Regional disparities. 4. Ruhr (Germany : Region) - Economic conditions. I. Title.
HJ1121 .M49 1982 ***NYPL [JLD 86-3292]***

Meyerhuber, Carl I., 1940- Less than forever : the rise and decline of union solidarity in western Pennsylvania, 1914-1948 / Carl I. Meyerhuber, Jr. Selinsgrove : Susquehanna University Press ; London : Associated University Presses, c1987. 235 p. ; 25 cm. Bibliography: p. [224]-229. Includes index. ISBN 0-941664-27-9 (alk. paper) LC Card 86-62504 DDC 331.88/09748 19
1. Trade-unions - Pennsylvania - History - 20th century. I. Title.
HD6517.P4 M49 1987

Meyerowitz, Joanne J. (Joanne Jay) Women adrift : independent wage earners in Chicago, 1880-1930 / Joanne J. Meyerowitz. Chicago : University of Chicago Press, 1988. p. cm. (Women in culture and society) Bibliography: p. Includes index. ISBN 0-226-52197-4 LC Card 87-22449 DDC 331.4/09773/11 19
1. Women - Employment - Illinois - Chicago - History. 2. Women - Illinois - Chicago - Social conditions. I. Title. II. Series.
HD6096.C4 M49 1988

Meyers, Edward M. Rebuilding America's cities : a policy analysis of the U. S. Conference of Mayors / prepared under the leadership of Ernest N. Morial, Mayor of New Orleans and President, U. S. Conference of Mayors ; and Marion Barry, Jr., Mayor of Washington, D.C. and Chair, Special Committee on a National Urban Policy by Edward M. Meyers, Project Director. Cambridge, Mass. : Ballinger Pub. Co., c1986. xxi, 290 p. : ill. ; 24 cm. Includes bibliographical references and index. ISBN 0-88730-051-0 LC Card 85-30780 DDC 307.3/4/0973 19
1. Urban renewal - United States. 2. Urban policy - United States. 3. Community development, Urban - United States. I. Barry, Marion, 1936-. II. Morial, Ernest N. III. United States Conference of Mayors. IV. Title.
HT175 .U59 1986 ***NYPL [JLE 86-2874]***

Meyers, Frederic.
Job equity and other studies in industrial relations . Los Angeles , c1982. 274 p. : LC Card 82-621216 DDC 331/.0973 19
HD5708.45.U6 J6 1982 ***NYPL [JLD 87-273]***

MEYERS, FREDERIC - ADDRESSES, ESSAYS, LECTURES.
Job equity and other studies in industrial relations . Los Angeles , c1982. 274 p. : LC Card 82-621216 DDC 331/.0973 19
HD5708.45.U6 J6 1982 ***NYPL [JLD 87-273]***

Meyers, Joan.
Buying and selling a home in today's market. The Kiplinger/Changing times guide to buying and selling a home / by the editors of Changing times magazine. Washington, DC , New York, NY , c1987. iii, 311 p. : ISBN 0-938721-02-X (pbk.) : LC Card 87-167806 DDC 643/.12 19
HD1379 .K52 1987

Meyerson, Ann, 1949- Critical perspectives on housing /. Philadelphia , 1986. xxi, 686 p. : ISBN 0-87722-395-5 LC Card 85-17274 DDC 363.5/0973 19
HD7293 .C738 1986 ***NYPL [JLE 86-3639]***

Mezhdunaroden sŭvet za novi initsiativi v sŭtrudnichestvoto Iztok--Zapad (Bulgaria)
Varna Forum II "Tŭrgoviiata Iztok--Zapad" . [Sofia] , 1985. 248 p. ; LC Card 86-196109
HF1411 .V37 1985

Mezhdunarodnaia organizatsiia truda. see **International Labor Organization.**

Mezhdunarodnaia valiutnaia sistema stran--chlenov SEV /. Konstantinov, IU. A. (IUriĭ Anatol'evich) Moskva , 1982. 231 p. ; LC Card 82-210094
HG3942 .K67 1982

Mezhdunarodni ikonomicheski otnosheniia pri sotsializma . Vŭlkovski, Georgi Danov. Sofiia , 1985 [i.e. 1986] 151 p. ; LC Card 87-134453
HC244 .V84 1986

Mezhdunarodnite pŭtnicheski prevozi i tekhnite valutno-finansovi problemi /. Petrov, Milan, k.i.n. Sofiia , 1984. 95, [1] p. ; LC Card 85-167160
HE265.A2 P48 1984

Mezhdunarodnoe rabochee dvizhenie : spravochnik / [otvetstvennye redaktory, V.V. Zagladin, B.I. Koval']. Moskva : Izd-vo polit. lit-ry, 1980. 412 p. ; 21 cm. At head of title: Institut mezhdunarodnogo rabochego dvizheniia. Akademiia nauk SSSR. Includes bibliographical references. LC Card 81-143888
1. Labor and laboring classes - History - 20th century. 2. Trade-unions - History - 20th century. 3. Trade-unions and communism - History - 20th century. 4. Communism - 1945-. I. Zagladin, V. V. II. Koval', Boris Iosifovich. III. Institut mezhdunarodnogo rabochego dvizheniia (Akademiia nauk SSSR).
HD4854 .M474 1980

Mezhdunarodnye korporatsii i sotsial'no-ėkonomicheskie problemy razvivaiushchikhsia stran /. Karagodin, N. A. Moskva , 1981. 196, [3] p. ; LC Card 82-162679
HC59.7 .K28 1981

Mezhdunarodnye monopolii . Ershov, Stal' Aleksandrovich. Moskva , 1980. 125 p. : LC Card 81-135534
HD2755.5 .E77 1980

Mezhdunarodnye organizatsii vo vneshneėkonomicheskoĭ politike imperializma /. Prokhorova, Galina Nikolaevna. Moskva , 1986. 183 p. ; LC Card 86-232949
HF1411 .P692 1986

Mezhdunarodnye transportnye tarify /. Konovalova, N. A. (Nina Alekseevna) Moskva ,

1985. 278 p. ; LC Card 86-127719
HE195.5.E852 K65 1985

Mezhdunarodnyĭ bank dli͡a rekonstrukt͡si i razvitii͡a. see **International Bank for Reconstruction and Development.**

Mezhdunarodnyĭ institut ėkonomicheskikh problem mirovoĭ sot͡sialisticheskoĭ sistemy. SĖV -- osnovnye napravlenii͡a sotrudnichestva . Moskva , 1984. 203 p. ; LC Card 85-177814
HC243.5 .S48 1984

Mezhdunarodnyĭ komitet registratsii chastot. see **International Frequency Registration Board.**

Mezhdunarodnyĭ kredit i vneshnii͡a zadolzhennost′ razvivai͡ushchikhsi͡a stran /. Katash, S. S. Moskva , 1984. 43 p. ; LC Card 87-100185
HG3877 .K37 1984

Mezhdunarodnyĭ marketing amerikanskoĭ tekhnologii /. Medvedkov, S. I͡U. (Sergeĭ I͡Ur′evich) Moskva , 1985. 189 p. : LC Card 85-187077
HF1009.6 .M43 1985

Mezhdunarodnyĭ vali͡utnyĭ fond v uslovii͡akh sovremennogo kapitalizma /. Tan′kov, A. V. Moskva , 1984. 85 p. ; LC Card 87-100183
HG3881.5.I58 T35 1984

Mezhduokrŭzhna partiĭna shkola (Sofia, Bulgaria) Sbornik ot lekt͡sii po aktualni problemi na sotsialno-ikonomicheskata politika na partii͡ata. Sofii͡a , 1985. 203 p. ; LC Card 86-140158
HC403 .S27 1985

Mezhotraslevye balansy kapitalisticheskikh stran . Klimenko, B. I. Moskva , 1986. 150 p. ; LC Card 86-231527
HC110.I57 K65 1986

Mezhotraslevye kompleksy v sisteme modeleĭ / pod redaktsieĭ N.P. Fedorenko i Ė.F. Baranova. Moskva : Izd-vo "Nauka", 1983. 319 p. : ill. ; 21 cm. (Voprosy optimal′nogo planirovanii͡a i upravlenii͡a sot͡sialisticheskoĭ ėkonomikoĭ) On leaf preceding t.p.: Akademii͡a nauk SSSR. T͡Sentral′nyĭ ėkonomiko-matematicheskiĭ institut. Includes bibliographies. LC Card 83-236937
1. Soviet Union - Economic conditions - 1976- - Econometric models. I. Fedorenko, Nikolaĭ Prokof′evich. II. T͡Sentral′nyĭ ėkonomiko-matematicheskiĭ institut (Akademii͡a nauk SSSR). III. Series.
HC336.25 .M49 1983

Mezhotraslevye svi͡azi v I͡Akutskoĭ ASSR : sbornik nauchnykh trudov / [otvetstvennyĭ redaktor A.D. Kirillin]. I͡Akutsk : I͡Akutskiĭ filial SO AN SSSR, 1985. 80 p. ; 20 cm. At head of title: Akademii͡a nauk SSSR. Ordena Lenina Sibirskoe otdelenie. I͡Akutskiĭ filial. Otdel ėkonomiki. Includes bibliographies. LC Card 86-193902
1. Input-output analysis - Russian S.F.S.R. - I͡Akutskai͡a A.S.S.R. 2. I͡Akutskai͡a A.S.S.R. (R.S.F.S.R.) - Industries. I. Kirillin, A. D. (Andreĭ Dmitrievich). II. Akademii͡a nauk SSSR. I͡Akutskiĭ filial. Otdel ėkonomiki.
HC337.I23 I576 1985

Mezhregional′nye mezhotraslevye balansy / otvetstvennyĭ redaktor M.K. Bandman ; [Aleksandr Grigor′evich Granberg ... et al.]. Novosibirsk : Izd-vo "Nauka," Sibirskoe otd-nie, 1983. 220 p. : ill. ; 22 cm. (Optimizat͡sii͡a territorial′nykh sistem) At head of title: Akademii͡a nauk SSSR. Sibirskoe otdelenie. Institut ėkonomiki i organizat͡sii promyshlennogo proizvodstva. Includes bibliographical references. LC Card 84-172934
1. Soviet Union - Commerce - Mathematical models. 2. Russian S.F.S.R. - Commerce - Mathematical models. 3. Transcaucasia - Commerce - Mathematical models. I. Bandman, Mark Konstantinovich. II. Granberg, Aleksandr Grigor′evich. III. Institut ėkonomiki i organizat͡sii promyshlennogo proizvodstva (Akademii͡a nauk SSSR). IV. Series.
HF3626.5 .M49 1983

Mezinárodní socialistická ekonomická integrace a předmětné sféry specializace národohospodářského komplexu ČSSR /. Fingerland, Jaroslav. Praha , 1985. 169 p. ; LC Card 86-215200
HF1542.3.Z4 C654 1985

A mezőgazdaság nemzetközi összehasonlításának módszerei . Szász, Kálmán. Budapest , 1986. 96 p. ; ISBN 963-02-4381-4 LC Card 87-419792
HD1425 .S95 1986

A Mezőgazdasági és az erdőgazdálkodási árstatisztika módszere / [készült a Központi Statisztikai Hivatal Mezőgazdasági Statisztikai Főosztályán]. Budapest : Központi Statisztikai Hivatal, 1986. 81 p. ; 24 cm. (Statisztikai módszertani füzetek . 19. sz.) LC Card 87-408580
1. Agricultural prices - Hungary - Statistical services. 2. Forest prices - Prices - Hungary - Statistical services. I. Hungary. Központi Statisztikai Hivatal. Mezőgazdasági Statisztikai Főosztály. II. Series.
HD9015.H82 M486 1986

Mezőgazdasági és Élelmezésügyi Minisztérium Statisztikai és Gazdaságelemző Központ (Series) . (1985/1) A Szocialista nagyüzemek főbb ágazatainak költség- és jövedelemhelyzete 1984-ben /. Budapest , 1985. 35, [46] p. ; LC Card 85-177804
HD1492.H8 S93 1985

Mezőgazdasági és élelmiszeripari adattár a felszabadulástól napjainkig / [összeállította Sütő Kálmánné, Bungai Mária ; szerkesztette, Gajdosné, Németh Olga]. Budapest : Mezőgazdasági és Élelmezésügyi Minisztérium Statisztikai és Gazdaságelemző Központ, 1985. 152 p. ; 24 cm. Tables. ISBN 963-502-393-6 LC Card 86-202515
1. Agriculture - Economic aspects - Hungary - Statistics. 2. Food industry and trade - Hungary - Statistics. I. Sütő, Kálmánné. II. Bungai, Mária. III. Gajdosné Németh, Olga. IV. Hungary. Statisztikai és Gazdaságelemző Központ.
HD1940.5 .M497 1985

Mezőgazdasági és élelmiszeripari adattár a felszabadulástól napjainkig. English. Collection of data of agriculture and food industry from the liberation till now / [collected by Sütő Kálmánné, Bungai Mária ; edited by Gajdosné Németh Olga]. Budapest : Ministry of Agriculture and Food Centre of Statistics and Economic Analysis, 1985. 85 p. ; 23 cm. Statistical data lacking in this edition. For complete statistical data see Hungarian edition. ISBN 963-502-393-6 LC Card 86-230345
1. Agriculture - Economic aspects - Hungary - Statistics. 2. Food industry and trade - Hungary - Statistics. I. Sütő, Kálmánné. II. Bungai, Mária. III. Gajdosné Németh, Olga. IV. Hungary. Statisztika és Gazdaságelemző Központ. V. Title.
HD1940.5 .M49713 1985

Mezőgazdasági és élelmiszeripari termékeink a külpiaci versenyben /. Éliás, András. Budapest , 1985. 197 p. ; ISBN 963-232-064-6 : LC Card 86-185883
HD9015.H82 E59 1985

A Mezőgazdasági és élelmiszeripari vállalatok gazdálkodása / szerkesztette, Csete László ; [írta Barcza Gabriella ... et al.]. Budapest : Mezőgazdasági Kiadó, 1984. 315, [1] p. : ill. ; 20 cm. Bibliography: p. 311-[316] ISBN 963-231-968-0 : LC Card 85-230887
1. State farms - Hungary - Management. 2. Food industry and trade - Hungary - Management. I. Csete, László. II. Barcza, Gabriella.
HD1493.H8 M48 1984

A mezőgazdasági ipar, ellenfél vagy partner? /. Papp, Sándor. [Budapest] , 1985. 154 p. : ISBN 963-09-2547-8 : LC Card 85-230966
HD9015.H82 P36 1985

A mezőgazdasági nagyüzemek pénz- és hitelrendszere /. Kis, Pál. Budapest , 1985. 261 p. ; ISBN 963-232-050-6 : LC Card 85-230947
HD1440.H9 K57 1985

Mezőgazdasági szövetkezetek Pest megyében, 1985 : szövetkezeti és közös vállalati kislexikon / szerkesztette, Lakatos Ernő. Budapest : Pest Megyei TESZÖV Elnöksége, 1985. 442 p. : ill. ; 25 cm. Summary in German and Russian. Includes bibliographical references and indexes. ISBN 963-02-4206-0 LC Card 87-137365
1. Collective farms - Hungary - Pest Megye. 2. Agriculture, Cooperative - Hungary - Pest Megye. I. Lakatos, Ernő. II. Pest Megye (Hungary).
HD1492.H82 P475 1985

A Mezőgazdasági szövetkezetek szabályozó rendszere / [szerzők, Haás László ... et al. ; szerkesztette, Huszár József]. [Budapest] : Termelőszövetkezetek Országos Tanácsa, 1979. 119 p. ; 20 cm. (TOT füzetek . 4) Includes index. LC Card 86-187443
1. Collective farms - Hungary. 2. Collective farms - Law and legislation - Hungary. I. Haás, László. II. Huszár, József. III. Series.
HD1492.H8 M417 1979

Mezőgazdasági szövetkezeti mozgalom érdekképviselete Csongrád megyében (1967-1987) Két évtized . Szeged , 1987. 116 p., [67] p. of plates : LC Card 87-407665
HD1492.H82 C765 1987

A Mezőgazdasági termelés ár- és költségviszonyai nemzetközi összehasonlításban / [készült a Központi Statisztikai Hivatal Mezőgazdasági Statisztikai Főosztályának Módszertani és Elemzési Osztályán]. Budapest : Központi Statisztikai Hivatal, 1986. 89 p. : ill. ; 29 cm. Chiefly tables. "Források jegyzéke": p. 89. LC Card 87-407682
1. Agricultural prices - Statistics. I. Hungary. Központi Statisztikai Hivatal. Mezőgazdasági Statisztikai Főosztály. Módszertani és Elemzési Osztály.
HD1447 .M49 1986

A mezőgazdasági vállalati szervezet fejlődésének és fejlesztésének törvényszerűségei /. Vályi, Éva. Budapest , 1985. 107, [1] p. : ISBN 963-05-3468-1 : LC Card 86-137169
HD1492.H8 V33 1985

MEZŐTÚR (HUNGARY) - HISTORY.
Varga, Lajos. Túri vásár /. Mezőtúr , 1983. 188 p. ; ISBN 963-7612-04-1 LC Card 85-109670
HF5474.H82 M498 1983

Mezőtúri helytörténeti füzetek, 0134-0727 . (5) Varga, Lajos. Túri vásár /. Mezőtúr , 1983. 188 p. ; ISBN 963-7612-04-1 LC Card 85-109670
HF5474.H82 M498 1983

Mezzino, Antonio, 1950- Favaretto, Ilario, 1945- L'impresa artigiana tra economia e territorio . Milano, Italy , c1986. 212 p. : LC Card 86-193238
HD2346.I82 P464 1986

Mezzogiorno : studierapport om Syditalien i forbindelse med jordskælvet ved Napoli 1980 / Institut 3D HH. [S.l. : s.n., 1980?] (København : Kunstakademiets trykkeri) 78 p. : ill. ; 21 x 30 cm. Cover title. Bibliography: p. 77-78. LC Card 85-128057
1. Italy, Southern - Economic conditions - 1945-. 2. Italy, Southern - Politics and government. 3. Buildings - Italy, Southern - Earthquake effects. 4. Earthquakes - Italy, Southern. 5. Disaster relief - Italy, Southern. I. Kunstakademiet (Denmark). Arkitektskolen.
HC307.S6 M49 1980

Mezzogiorno e demografia nel entésimoquinto secolo. Cozzetto, Fausto. Mezzogiorno e demografia nel XV secolo /. Soveria M.lli, CZ , c1986. ix, 202 p. ; LC Card 86-213782
HB3600.N37 C69 1986

Mezzogiorno e demografia nel XV secolo /. Cozzetto, Fausto. Soveria M.lli, CZ , c1986. ix, 202 p. ; LC Card 86-213782
HB3600.N37 C69 1986

Mezzogiorno e demografia nel 15$_0$ secolo. Cozzetto, Fausto. Mezzogiorno e demografia nel XV secolo /. Soveria M.lli, CZ , c1986. ix, 202 p. ; LC Card 86-213782
HB3600.N37 C69 1986

Mezzogiorno e modernizzazione . Barone, Giuseppe, 1947- Torino , c1986. xii, 408 p. ; ISBN 88-06-59238-6 : LC Card 86-219130
HC307.S69 B37 1986

Il Mezzogiorno sussidiato . Boccella, Nicola Maria, 1952- Milano, Italy , c1982. 264 p. : LC Card 85-163271
HD7185.S68 B62 1982

MF tanulmányok. Tanulmányok Magyarországról, magyarokról. [Budapest] [1985] 280 p. ; ISBN 963-01-7352-2 (Magy. nemz. bibl.) LC Card 87-408505
HC300.24 .T36 1985

MHAISAL (INDIA) - ECONOMIC CONDITIONS.
Deshpande, V. D. (Vasant Dattatraya), 1930- The Mhaisal untouchables /. Pune , 1983. xi, 168 p. ; LC Card 83-906084 DDC 338.954/792 19
HC438.M45 D48 1983

NYPL [JLD 87-1139]

The Mhaisal untouchables /. Deshpande, V. D. (Vasant Dattatraya), 1930- Pune , 1983. xi, 168 p. ; LC Card 83-906084 DDC 338.954/792 19
HC438.M45 D48 1983

NYPL [JLD 87-1139]

Mhlanga, Constance C. Slum and squatter settlements in Sub-Saharan Africa . New York , 1988. p. cm. ISBN 0-275-92309-6 (alk. paper) : LC Card 87-11705 DDC 307.3/36 19
HD7287.96.A438 S57 1988

MI-Wirtschaftswissenschaften.
Schaefer, Felix, 1950- Muster-Stichproben-Pläne für Bevölkerungs-Stichproben in der Bundesrepublik Deutschland und West-Berlin /. München , c1979. 160 p. : ISBN 3-478-39760-X; 3-478-39760-1 LC Card 84-135457
HB3595 .S29 1979

Miaėl'tsemeės, S. V. Voprosy razvitiia obsluzhivaniia naseleniia . Tallin , 1985. 140 p. : LC Card 85-158428
HD9986.S683 E888 1985

Miakota, IU. K. Orlov, V. A. (Vasiliĭ Adamovich) Khudozhestvennye markirovannye konverty SSSR . Moskva , 1984. 120 p. : LC Card 84-168398
HE6185.S652 O75 1984

MIAMI (FLA.) - ECONOMIC CONDITIONS.
Botifoll, Luis J. How Miami's new image was created /. Coral Gables, Fla. [1985?] 16 p. ; LC Card 87-124138
HC108.M5 B68 1985

MIAMI (FLA.) - ECONOMIC POLICY.
Botifoll, Luis J. How Miami's new image was created /. Coral Gables, Fla. [1985?] 16 p. ; LC Card 87-124138
HC108.M5 B68 1985

Miami, Fla. Florida International University. see **Florida International University.**

MIC. see **Management Information Corporation.**

MIC 1986 motorcycle retail outlet profile survey.
1986 motorcycle retail outlet profile survey. Costa Mesa, CA (3151 Airway Ave., Bldg. P-1, Costa Mesa 92626) , c1987. 33 p. : LC Card 87-401918 DDC 381/.456292275/0973021 19
HD9710.5.U52 A15 1987

Michael Hardy Productions.
You need me [filmstrip] . Pleasantville, NY , 1986. 2 filmstrips (71 fr. each) : LC Card 86-700183 DDC 650.1 11
HF382.7

You need me [videorecording] . Pleasantville, NY , 1986. 1 videocassette (30 min.) : LC Card 87-705080 DDC 650.1 11
HF5382.7

Your job [filmstrip] . Pleasantville, NY , 1986. 2 filmstrips (ca. 74 fr. each) : LC Card 86-700184 DDC 650.1 11
HF5549.5.C35

Your job [videorecording] . Pleasantville, NY , 1986. 1 videocassette (30 min.) : LC Card 87-705039 DDC 650.1 11
HF5549.5.C35

MICHAEL HENLEY AND SON - HISTORY.
Ville, Simon P. English shipowning during the industrial revolution . Manchester, UK , Wolfeboro, NH, USA , c1987. x, 192 p. : ISBN 0-7190-1714-9 LC Card 87-11043 DDC 387.5/065/41 19
HE945.M49 V55 1987

Michael M. Kaiser Associates. How to find information about companies in the telecommunications, data processing, and office automation industries /. Washington, DC , c1987. ii, 130 p. ; ISBN 0-934940-48-7 (pbk.) LC Card 86-51630 DDC 338.7/61004/072073 19
HD9696.A3 U559 1987

Michaels, Susan. Points, a guide to frequent flyer bonus programs / Susan Michaels and Taylor MilSal. New York : Hippocrene Books, c1987. 161 p. : ill. ; 18 cm. ISBN 0-87052-375-9 (pbk.) : LC Card 87-8681 DDC 387.7/1 19
1. Frequent flyer programs - United States. 2. Advertising - Airlines - United States. 3. Airlines - United States - Rates. 4. Air travel - United States. I. MilSal, Taylor. II. Title.
HF6161.A38 M53 1987

Michaelson, Gerald A. Winning the marketing war : a field manual for business leaders / Gerald A. Michaelson with contributions by Sun Tzu ... [et al.]. Lanham, MD : Madison Books ; [Cambridge, Mass.] : Abt Books, c1987. xv, 270 p. : ill. ; 24 cm. Bibliography: p. 263-267. ISBN 0-8191-5781-3 (alk. paper) : LC Card 87-11115 DDC 658.8 19
1. Marketing. I. Title.
HF5415 .M527 1987

Michalet, Charles Albert. Le capitalisme mondial / Charles-Albert Michalet. 2e éd. entièrement ref. Paris : Presses universitaires de France, [c1985], c1976. 368 p. : ill. ; 22 cm. (Economie en liberté, 0768-0988) Includes bibliographical references. ISBN 2-13-039215-6 : LC Card 86-137294 DDC 338.8/8 19
1. International business enterprises. 2. International economic integration. I. Title. II. Series.
HD2755.5 .M52 1985

Michel-Alder, Elisabeth. Männer im Glashaus : von der Macht über Geist, Geld und Güter : 12 Gespräche / Elisabeth Michel-Alder. Zürich : Orell Füssli, c1986. 238 p. : ports. ; 23 cm. ISBN 3-280-01561-8 LC Card 86-180438
1. Executives - Switzerland - Biography. 2. Success - Switzerland. 3. Elite (Social sciences) - Switzerland - Biography. I. Title.
HD38.25.S9 M52 1986

Michel, Allen, 1945- Takeover madness : corporate America fights back / Allen Michel, Israel Shaked. New York : Wiley, c1986. xii, 397 p. : ill. ; 24 cm. Includes indexes. ISBN 0-471-01079-0 LC Card 85-32315 DDC 658.1/8 19
1. Consolidation and merger of corporations - United States - Prevention - Case studies. 2. Tender offers (Securities) - Case studies. I. Shaked, Israel, 1948-. II. Title.
HD2746.5 .M53 1986 ***NYPL [JLE 86-2989]***

Michel, Mark. The beginner's guide to real estate wealth / by Mark Michel. Greensboro, N.C. : Omnibus Press, c1986. xiv, 177 p. : ill. ; 23 cm. Bibliography: p. 18. Includes index. ISBN 0-939383-04-7 (pbk.) : LC Card 86-218980 DDC 332.63/24 19
1. Real estate investment. I. Title.
HD1382.5 .M52 1986

Michel, Nelson Emílio. Evolução dos índices do número e do valor de cheques compensados no Rio Grande do Sul, período de 1960-7, e sua análise estatística / Nelson Emílio Michel. Porto Alegre : Universidade Federal do Rio Grande do Sul, Faculdade de Ciências Econômicas, Centro de Estudos e Pesquisas Econômicas (IEPE), 1976. 79 leaves : ill. ; 33 cm. (Estudos e trabalhos mimeografados . no. 32) Includes bibliographical references. LC Card 82-159893
1. Checks - Brazil - Rio Grande do Sul. I. Universidade Federal do Rio Grande do Sul. Centro de Estudos e Pesquisas Econômicas. II. Title. III. Series.
HG1692 .M53 1976

Michel, Pierre A.
European equity markets . New York , 1984. 470 p. : ISBN 0-8240-6307-4 (alk. paper) : LC Card 83-49440 DDC 332.64/094
HG5430.5.A3 E84 1984
NYPL [JLE 86-4508]

Hawawini, Gabriel A. Mandatory financial information and capital market equilibrium in Belgium /. New York , 1987. 271 p. : ISBN 0-8240-7852-7 (alk. paper) : LC Card 87-54 DDC 332.63/222/09493 19
HG5553 .H39 1987

Michel Privatpostkarten-Katalog Deutschland (Ganzsachen auf Privatbestellung) : Deutsches Reich, 1873-1945. München : Schwaneberger, c1984. 368 p. : ill. ; 20 cm. Includes index. ISBN 3-87858-418-0 LC Card 86-167804
1. Postage-stamps, Local - Germany - Catalogs. 2. Postage-stamps - Germany - Catalogs.
HE6185.G62 M48 1984

Michel, Victor Joseph Jules, 1915-1982. Victor Michel . Bruxelles , c1985. 263 p., [8] p. of plates : ISBN 2-87003-189-0 : LC Card 86-163882
HD6722.5.M52 V52 1985

MICHEL, VICTOR JOSEPH JULES, 1915-1982.
Victor Michel . Bruxelles , c1985. 263 p., [8] p. of plates : ISBN 2-87003-189-0 : LC Card 86-163882
HD6722.5.M52 V52 1985

Michelbach, Roger. Probleme der Sanierung der Deutschen Bundesbahn durch die Änderung institutioneller Rahmenbedingungen / Roger Michelbach. Thun : H. Deutsch, c1984. xi, 450 p. : ill. ; 21 cm. (Reihe Wirtschaftswissenschaften, 0253-1488 . Bd. 323) Bibliography: p. 402-446. ISBN 3-87144-865-6 LC Card 85-137676
1. Deutsche Bundesbahn - Finance. 2. Transportation - Germany, West - Passenger traffic. 3. Transportation and state - Germany, West. I. Title. II. Series.
HE3080.D4 M53 1984

Micheletti, Michele. Organizing interest and organized protest : difficulties of member representation for the Swedish Central Organization of Salaried Employees (TCO) / Michele Micheletti. [Stockholm] : Dept. of Political Science, University of Stockholm, 1985. vii, 253 p. ; 25 cm. (Stockholm studies in politics, 0346-6620 . 29) Thesis (doctoral)--University of Stockholm. Errata sheet inserted. Abstract, 1 p., inserted. Bibliography: p. 217-253. ISBN 91-7146-451-4 (pbk.) LC Card 86-145828 DDC 322/.2/09481 19
1. Trade-unions - Professional employees - Sweden. 2. Pressure groups - Sweden. 3. Corporate state - Sweden. 4. Sweden - Politics and government - 1973-. I. Title. II. Series.
HD8572.T5 M53 1985
NYPL [JLL 74-316 no.29]

Michelin . Barrière, Antoine. Nonette , 1983. 289 p. ; ISBN 2-902894-20-1
NYPL [JLD 86-4467]

Michels, Winfried. Burberg, Paul-Helmuth. Zielgruppenorientierte kommunale Wirtschaftsförderung . Münster , c1983. xi, 207, 16 p. : ISBN 3-88497-042-9 LC Card 84-173863
HC289.M9 B87 1983

MICHELSEN URIBE, JAIME.
Donadío, Alberto, 1953- Por qué cayó Jaime Michelsen? /. Bogotá , c1984. 142 p. : ISBN 84-89209-42-1 LC Card 85-122262
HG2908.C65 D66 1984

Michelsons, Angelo. Tre incognite per lo sviluppo . Milano, Italy , c1986. 383 p. : LC Card 86-198933
HC310.I53 T74 1986

Michie, Jonathan. Wages in the business cycle : an empirical and methodological analysis / Jonathan Michie. London : F. Pinter, 1987. vii, 194 p. : ill. ; 23 cm. Bibliography: p. [178]-190. Includes indexes. ISBN 0-86187-686-5 LC Card 87-148946 DDC 331.2/1 19
1. Wages - Econometric models. 2. Business cycles - Econometric models. I. Title.
HD4906 .M43 1987

Michie, R. C., 1949- The London and New York stock exchanges, 1850-1914 / R.C. Michie. London ; Boston : Allen & Unwin, 1987. xv, 312 p. ; 23 cm. Bibliography: p. 285-303. Includes index. ISBN 0-04-332117-8 (alk. paper) LC Card 87-1394 DDC 332.64/241 19
1. Stock Exchange (London, England) - History. 2. New York Stock Exchange - History. I. Title.
HG4577 .M52 1987

MICHIGAN - APPROPRIATIONS AND EXPENDITURES - STATISTICS.
Allocation of state spending by county . Lansing, MI (P.O. Box 30036, Lansing 48909) [1986] 124 p. : LC Card 87-620967 DDC 336.3/9/09774 19
HJ2053.M5 A554 1986

Michigan beyond 2000 /. Johnston, William B., 1945- Lanham , Indianapolis, IN , c1987. xxv, 161 p. : ISBN 0-8191-6462-3 (alk. paper) LC Card 87-10725 DDC 338.9774 19
HC107.M5 J64 1987

MICHIGAN. BUREAU OF COMMUNITY SERVICES.
Michigan. Dept. of Labor. An assessment of the effectiveness of the Bureau of Community Services, Michigan Economic and Social Opportunity Commission, and community action agencies /. [Lansing, Mich.] [1986] 56 p. : LC Card 87-620767 DDC 362/.9774 19
HC107.M53 P6333 1986

MICHIGAN - CAPITAL AND CAPITOL - HISTORY - 19TH CENTURY.
Whitford, Craig A. Postmarked . Lansing, Mich. (P.O. Box 14225, Lansing 48901) , c1987. 27 p., [2] p. of plates : LC Card 87-402869 DDC 769.56/7/0977427 19
HE6185.U7 M59 1987

Michigan. Dept. of Labor. An assessment of the effectiveness of the Bureau of Community Services, Michigan Economic and Social Opportunity Commission, and community action agencies / Michigan Department of

Labor. [Lansing, Mich.] : The Department, [1986] 56 p. : ill. ; 28 cm. Cover title. "April 1986." Bibliography: p. 13. LC Card 87-620767 DDC 362/.9774 19
1. Michigan. Bureau of Community Services. 2. Michigan Economic and Social Opportunity Commission. 3. Economic assistance, Domestic - Michigan. 4. Community development corporations - Michigan. I. Title.
HC107.M53 P6333 1986

MICHIGAN ECONOMIC AND SOCIAL OPPORTUNITY COMMISSION.
Michigan. Dept. of Labor. An assessment of the effectiveness of the Bureau of Community Services, Michigan Economic and Social Opportunity Commission, and community action agencies /. [Lansing, Mich.] [1986] 56 p. : LC Card 87-620767 DDC 362/.9774 19
HC107.M53 P6333 1986

MICHIGAN - ECONOMIC CONDITIONS.
Johnston, William B., 1945- Michigan beyond 2000 /. Lanham , Indianapolis, IN , c1987. xxv, 161 p. : ISBN 0-8191-6462-3 (alk. paper) LC Card 87-10725 DDC 338.9774 19
HC107.M5 J64 1987

MICHIGAN - ECONOMIC POLICY.
Johnston, William B., 1945- Michigan beyond 2000 /. Lanham , Indianapolis, IN , c1987. xxv, 161 p. : ISBN 0-8191-6462-3 (alk. paper) LC Card 87-10725 DDC 338.9774 19
HC107.M5 J64 1987

MICHIGAN - INDUSTRIES - LOCATION - CASE STUDIES.
Jones, Bryan D. The sustaining hand . Lawrence, Kan. , c1986. xii, 247 p. : ISBN 0-7006-0278-X : LC Card 85-24631 DDC 338.4/76292/09774 19
HD9710.U53 M433 1986 ***NYPL [JLE 86-2386]***

Michigan Infrastructure Coalition. Michigan's infrastructure : priorities for the future : a report of the Michigan Infrastructure Coalition. [Lansing, Mich.] (P.O. Box 13023, Lansing 48901) : The Coalition, [1986] iii, 31, [5] p. : ill. ; 28 cm. LC Card 86-622635 DDC 363/.09774 19
1. Infrastructure (Economics) - Michigan. I. Title.
HC107.M53 C36 1986

Michigan League for Human Services. Helping handbook /. Lansing, MI (300 N. Washington Square, Suite 401, Lansing 48933) , 1986. v, 101 p. ; LC Card 87-110874 DDC 361.6/025/774 19
HC107.M53 P633 1986

Michigan. Legislature. House of Representatives. Special House Committee to Study Consumers Power Company. Report of the Special House Committee to Study Consumers Power Company : Michigan House of Representatives, 83rd Legislature, regular session of 1985. Lansing, Mich. (The Capitol, Lansing 48909) : The Committee, [1985] iv leaves, 57 p. ; 28 cm. "November 19, 1985." Includes bibliographical references. LC Card 86-622638 DDC 338.7/6136362/09774 19
1. Consumers Power Company. 2. Electric utilities - Michigan. 3. Gas industry - Michigan. I. Title.
HD9685.U7 C785 1985

Michigan. Legislature. Senate. Fiscal Agency. Allocation of state spending by county . Lansing, MI (P.O. Box 30036, Lansing 48909) [1986] 124 p. : LC Card 87-620967 DDC 336.3/9/09774 19
HJ2053.M5 A554 1986

Michigan management and executive development studies .
(#4) Hildebrandt, Herbert William, 1931- A managerial profile . Ann Arbor, MI , c1985. 31 p. ; ISBN 0-87712-248-2 (pbk.) LC Card 86-621187 DDC 331.4/816584/00973 19
HD6054.4.U6 H55 1985

Michigan, Mich., 1847-1848. Whitford, Craig A. Postmarked . Lansing, Mich. (P.O. Box 14225, Lansing 48901) , c1987. 27 p., [2] p. of plates : LC Card 87-402869 DDC 769.56/7/0977427 19
HE6185.U7 M59 1987

Michigan papers in Japanese studies .
(no. 15) The Japanese competition . Ann Arbor, MI , 1987. xii, 124 p. ; ISBN 0-939512-30-0 LC Card 86-31756 DDC 338.4/76292/0952 19
HD9710.J32 J374 1987
NYPL [JFL 81-188 no.15]

Michigan study manual for life and accident and health insurance. Chicago : R&R Newkirk, c1987. v, 56 p. ; 28 cm. ISBN 0-88462-729-2 (unb.) LC Card 87-18552 DDC 368.3/009774 19
1. Insurance - Michigan - Examinations, questions, etc. 2. Insurance law - Michigan - Examinations, questions, etc. I. R & R Newkirk.
HG8101.M5 M53 1987

Michigan. University. Institute for Social Research. Survey Research Center. see **Michigan. University. Survey Research Center.**

Michigan. University. Survey Research Center. Research on the quality of life /. Ann Arbor, Mich. , 1986. xiv, 365 p. ; ISBN 0-87944-308-1 : LC Card 86-15179 DDC 305/.0973 19
HN60 .R47 1986 ***NYPL [JLE 86-3621]***

Michigan. University. Survey Research Center. Economic Behavior Program. For publications, see: **Michigan. University. Survey Research Center.**

Michigan's infrastructure . Michigan Infrastructure Coalition. [Lansing, Mich.] (P.O. Box 13023, Lansing 48901) [1986] iii, 31, [5] p. : LC Card 86-622635 DDC 363/.09774 19
HC107.M53 C36 1986

Michulka, Jean H. Let's talk business / Jean H. Michulka. 3rd ed. Cincinnati, Ohio : South-Western Pub. Co., c1988. x, 370 p. : ill. ; 28 cm. Includes index. ISBN 0-538-05920-6 (pbk.) LC Card 86-63174 DDC 658.4/52 19
1. Business communication. 2. Oral communication. I. Title.
HF5718 .M5 1988

MICRO COMPUTERS. see **MICROCOMPUTERS.**

Micro e macroeconomia . Silva, Fábio Gomes da. Petrópolis , 1983. 125 p. : LC Card 83-202597
HD2757.3 .S55 1983

Micro-economics and the public economy. Cullis, John C. Microeconomics and the public economy . Oxford, OX, UK , New York, NY, USA , 1987. xx, 251 p. : ISBN 0-631-15552-X : LC Card 87-5169 DDC 338.5 19
HB172 .C85 1987

Micro-electronics and clothing . Hoffman, Kurt. New York , 1988. xxxii, 253 p. ; ISBN 0-275-92798-9 (alk. paper) : LC Card 87-25736 DDC 338.4/5687 19
HD9940.A2 H63 1988

Micro-electronics and employment revisited . Kaplinsky, Raphael. Geneva , 1987. xiv, 181 p. : ISBN 92-2-105611-2 (pbk.) : LC Card 87-163570 DDC 331.7/6213817 19
HD9696.A2 K37 1987

Micro to mainframe links /. Kopeck, Ronald F. Berkeley, Calif. , c1986. xviii, 286 p. : ISBN 0-07-881228-3 (pbk.) LC Card 86-210460 DDC 004.6 19
HF5548.2 .K628 1986

Microanalytic simulation models to support social and financial policy / edited by Guy Orcutt, Joachim Merz, Hermann Quinke. Amsterdam ; New York : North-Holland ; xvii, 553 p. : ill. ; 23 cm. (Information research and resource reports . v. 7) Includes index. Bibliography: p. 519-546. ISBN 0-444-87876-9 (U. S.) LC Card 85-25231 DDC 361.6/0724 19
1. Economic policy - Evaluation - Mathematical models - Addresses, essays, lectures. 2. Social policy - Evaluation - Mathematical models - Addresses, essays, lectures. I. Orcutt, Guy. II. Merz, Joachim. III. Quinke, Hermann. IV. Series.
HD87 .M52 1986 ***NYPL [JLD 86-3485]***

MICROBIAL ENERGY CONVERSION. see **BIOMASS ENERGY.**

Microcomputer applications for CPAs /. Bien, Frederick A. New York, NY , c1986. 8, 34, 34, 65 p. : LC Card 87-121259 DDC 657/.028/5536 19
HF5679 .B54 1986

Microcomputer applications within the urban transportation environment . National Conference on Microcomputers in Urban Transportation (1985 : San Diego, Calif.) New York, N.Y. , c1985. 824 p. : ISBN 0-87262-508-7 (pbk.) LC Card 85-73250 DDC 388.4/028/5416 19
HE305 .N33 1985 ***NYPL [JSD 86-535]***

Microcomputer software in economics. Walstad, William B. An annotated catalog of microcomputer software in economics /. New York, NY (2 Park Ave., New York 10016) , c1986. viii, 160 p. ; LC Card 86-210285 DDC 330/.028/5536 19
HB74.8 .W34 1986

Microcomputer systems design and debugging. Wray, William C. What every engineer should know about microcomputer systems design and debugging /. New York, N.Y. , c1984. ix, 183 p. : ISBN 0-8247-7160-5 LC Card 83-25204 DDC 001.64 19
QA76.6 .W73 1984 ***NYPL [JSE 86-1632]***

MICROCOMPUTERS - ACCESS CONTROL.
Schabeck, Timothy A. Managing microcomputer security . Port Jefferson Station, N.Y. (492 Old Town Rd., Port Jefferson Station 11776) , c1986. 1 v. (various pagings) : LC Card 86-216667 DDC 658.4/78 19
HF5548.37 .S33 1986

Microcomputers and productivity . Fleming, Maureen. White Plains, NY , c1984. iii, 125 p. ; ISBN 0-86729-109-5 (pbk.) LC Card 84-164284 DDC 650/.028/54 19
HF5548.2 .F49 1984 ***NYPL [JLf 87-8]***

MICROCOMPUTERS - CATALOGS.
Bowker's complete sourcebook of personal computing 1985. New York , c1984. lxviii, 1050 p. ; ISBN 0-8352-1931-3 (pbk.) : LC Card 84-20460 DDC 001.64 19
QA76.5 .B669 1984 ***NYPL [JSE 86-443]***

MICROCOMPUTERS - CONGRESSES.
National Conference on Microcomputers in Urban Transportation (1985 : San Diego, Calif.) Microcomputer applications within the urban transportation environment . New York, N.Y. , c1985. 824 p. : ISBN 0-87262-508-7 (pbk.) LC Card 85-73250 DDC 388.4/028/5416 19
HE305 .N33 1985 ***NYPL [JSD 86-535]***

MICROCOMPUTERS - DESIGN AND CONSTRUCTION.
Wray, William C. What every engineer should know about microcomputer systems design and debugging /. New York, N.Y. , c1984. ix, 183 p. : ISBN 0-8247-7160-5 LC Card 83-25204 DDC 001.64 19
QA76.6 .W73 1984 ***NYPL [JSE 86-1632]***

MICROCOMPUTERS - ECONOMIC ASPECTS - UNITED STATES.
A Competitive assessment of the United States microcomputer industry . Washington, D.C. [1986] xiv, 123 p. : ***NYPL [JLF 87-251]***

Microcomputers for financial planning /. Drew, Rodney. Aldershot, Hampshire, England , Brookfield, Vt., U. S.A. , c1987. x, 105 p. : ISBN 0-566-02579-5 (pbk.) : LC Card 87-8405 DDC 658.1/5/0285416 19
HG4012.5 .D73 1987

Microcomputers in business . Spence, J. Wayne. St. Louis , 1987. vii, 224 p. : ISBN 0-8016-5030-5 (pbk.) LC Card 86-30013 DDC 650/.028/5536 19
HF5548.2 .S728 1987

MICROCOMPUTERS - PROGRAMMING.
Berry, Dick. Forecasting sales with the personal computer . New York , c1988. p. cm. ISBN 0-89930-329-3 (lib. bdg. : alk. paper) : LC Card 87-7284 DDC 658.8/18/0285416 19
HF5415.2 .B458 1988

Bhaskar, Krish N. The impact of microprocessors on the small accounting practice /. Englewood Cliffs, N.J. , c1986. xvi, 167 p. ; ISBN 0-13-453291-0 (pbk.) LC Card 85-25764 DDC 657/.028/5416 19
HF5679 .B45 1986 ***NYPL [JLE 86-4067]***

Collins, Rip, 1947- Double your sales commission using a personal computer /. Dubuque, Iowa , c1986. ix, 155 p. ; ISBN 0-697-00802-9 (pbk.) : LC Card 85-71486 DDC 658.8/1/00285536 19
HF5438.35 .C65 1986 ***NYPL [JLE 86-1773]***

Edwards, Chris, 1947- Developing microcomputer-based business systems /. Englewood Cliffs, N.J. , 1983, c1982. x, 202 p. : ISBN 0-13-204545-1 (pbk.) LC Card 83-60581

DDC 658/.054 19
HF5548.2 .E293 1983 ***NYPL [JLE 87-1181]***

Fleming, Maureen. Microcomputers and productivity . White Plains, NY , c1984. iii, 125 p. ; ISBN 0-86729-109-5 (pbk.) LC Card 84-164284 DDC 650/.028/54 19
HF5548.2 .F49 1984 ***NYPL [JLf 87-8]***

Gambel, Edoardo L. La valutazione, simulazione e previsione nella gestione d'impresa . Milano, Italy , c1986. 190 p. : LC Card 86-217652
HF5679 .G36 1986

Hicks, Sam A. The use of microcomputers in accounting /. St. Paul , c1985. xx, 349 p. : ISBN 0-314-87064-4 (pbk.) LC Card 85-8950 DDC 657/.028/54 19
HF5679 .H535 1985 ***NYPL [JLF 86-1720]***

Holliday, Paul, 1938- A handbook of software development and operating procedures for microcomputers /. New York , c1985. xix, 181 p. : ISBN 0-02-949510-5 : LC Card 84-19384 DDC 001.64/2 19
QA76.6 .H645 1985 ***NYPL [JSE 87-332]***

Holtz, Herman. How to make money with your micro /. New York , c1984. xiv, 324 p. : ISBN 0-471-88455-3 (pbk.) : LC Card 84-3589 DDC 001.64 19
HF5548.2 .H5925 1984
NYPL [JLE 86-2074]

Huff, Kathryn. Developing and using microcomputer business systems /. St. Paul , c1987. xvi, 224, [29] p. : ISBN 0-314-34730-5 (pbk.) LC Card 87-2184 DDC 658/.05416 19
HF5548.2 .H785 1987

Lewis, Colin David. Managing with micros . Oxford, England , 1984. 200 p. : LC Card 85-103102 DDC 658/.054 19
HF5548.2 .L425 1984 ***NYPL [JLE 86-2215]***

Prague, Cary N. Programming with dBase III /. Blue Ridge Summit, Pa. , 1985. ix, 292 p. ; ISBN 0-8306-0976-8 : LC Card 84-23979 DDC 001.64/2 19
QA76.9.D3 P728 1985 ***NYPL [JSE 87-75]***

Prague, N. Cary. Programming with dBASE III PLUS /. Blue Ridge Summit, PA , c1986. vi, 375 p. : ISBN 0-8306-0326-3 : LC Card 86-5736 DDC 005.74 19
QA76.9.D3 P729 1986 ***NYPL [JSE 87-539]***

Simpson, Henry. Programming the IBM PC user interface /. New York , c1985. vii, 228 p. : ISBN 0-07-057297-6 (pbk.) : LC Card 85-7924 DDC 005.265 19
QA76.8.I2594 S575 1985
NYPL [JSE 86-1154]

Wolverton, Van, 1939- Running MS DOS . Bellevue, Wash. [New York, NY] , c1985. xv, 423 p. : ISBN 0-914845-68-3 LC Card 85-18951 DDC 005.4/469 19
QA76.76.O63 W65 1985
NYPL [JSE 86-1760]

Wray, William C. What every engineer should know about microcomputer systems design and debugging /. New York, N.Y. , c1984. ix, 183 p. : ISBN 0-8247-7160-5 LC Card 83-25204 DDC 001.64 19
QA76.6 .W73 1984 ***NYPL [JSE 86-1632]***

Zimmerman, Steven M. Understanding and using microcomputers /. St. Paul , c1988. xxvi, 371 p. : ISBN 0-314-60096-5 (pbk.) LC Card 87-19044 DDC 650/.028/5416 19
HF5548.2 .Z58 1988

MICROCOMPUTERS - PURCHASING.
Grieb, William E. The small business computer today and tomorrow /. New York, N.Y. , c1984. 287 p. : ISBN 0-671-55907-9 (pbk.) : LC Card 86-207213 DDC 658/.05416 19
HF5548.2 .G733 1984

MICROCOMPUTERS - UNITED STATES.
A Competitive assessment of the United States microcomputer industry . Washington, D.C. [1986] xiv, 123 p. : LC Card 86-602781 DDC 338.4/700416/0973 19
HD9696.C63 U514937 1986

The Markets and competitive environment for portable computers. New York, N.Y. , c1983. xii, 356 p. : LC Card 87-143515 DDC 380.1/4500416 19
HD9696.C62 M369 1983

The Personal computer hardware add-on device market. New York, N.Y. , c1983. viii, 2, 228 p. : LC Card 87-143524
HD9696.C63 U52783 1983

MICROCOMPUTERS - UNITED STATES - PROGRAMMING.
The Mini-microcomputer turnkey engineering systems market. New York, N.Y. , c1983. vi, 228 p. ; LC Card 87-142400 DDC 381/.4500416 19
HD9696.C63 U5262 1983

MICROCOMPUTERS - UNITED STATES - STATISTICS.
The Home terminal II . [Boston, Ma.] (89 Broad St., Boston 02110) [1986] 63 leaves : LC Card 86-211108 DDC 381/.45621396/0973 19
HD9696.C63 U518327 1986

Microcomputing in accounting series.
Lehman, Mark W. Using the microcomputer in cost accounting . St. Paul , c1988. x, 396 p. : ISBN 0-314-34729-1 (pbk.) LC Card 87-10632 DDC 657/.42/02855369 19
HF5686.C8 L34 1988

Lehman, Mark W. Using the microcomputer in managerial accounting . St. Paul , c1987. x, 406 p. : ISBN 0-314-98515-8 (pbk.) LC Card 87-2194 DDC 658.1/511/02855369 19
HF5657.4 .L44 1987

The Microcomputing series.
Allegretti, Enzo V. Understanding and using Symphony /. St. Paul, MN , c1987. xvii, 226, [31] p., [4] p. of plates : ISBN 0-314-34640-6 (pbk.) LC Card 87-4986 DDC 005.36/9 19
HF5548.4.S95 A45 1987

Huff, Kathryn. Developing and using microcomputer business systems /. St. Paul , c1987. xvi, 224, [29] p. : ISBN 0-314-34730-5 (pbk.) LC Card 87-2184 DDC 658/.05416 19
HF5548.2 .H785 1987

Ross, Steven C. Understanding and using Lotus 1-2-3 . St. Paul , c1987. xv, 232, [34] p. : ISBN 0-314-34741-0 (pbk.) LC Card 86-33964 DDC 650/.028/55369 19
HF5548.4.L67 R673 1987

Ross, Steven C. Understanding and using SuperCalc 3 /. St. Paul , c1987. xiii, 184, [27] p. : ISBN 0-314-30123-2 (pbk.) LC Card 86-32548 DDC 005.36/9 19
HF5548.4.S86 R67 1987

Varnon, M. S. Developing and using office applications with AppleWorks . St. Paul , c1987. xi, 366 p. : ISBN 0-314-34129-3 (pbk.) : LC Card 86-24696 DDC 651.8/5369 19
HF5548.4.A68 V37 1987

Zimmerman, Steven M. Understanding and using microcomputers /. St. Paul , c1988. xxvi, 371 p. : ISBN 0-314-60096-5 (pbk.) LC Card 87-19044 DDC 650/.028/5416 19
HF5548.2 .Z58 1988

Microeconomia--teoria, modelos econométricos e aplicações à economia brasileira /. Barbosa, Fernando de Holanda. Rio de Janeiro , 1985. 534 p. : LC Card 87-118555 DDC 338.5 19
HB179.P75 B37 1985

The microeconomic structure of the Australian economy /. Brain, Peter J. Melbourne, Australia , 1986. xxiv, 448 p. : ISBN 0-582-71502-4 (pbk.) LC Card 87-100715 DDC 330.994/063 19
HC603 .B73 1986

Microeconomic theory /. Ōtani, Yoshihiko, 1938- Berlin , New York , c1987. xiii, 274 p. : ISBN 0-387-17994-1 (U. S. : pbk.) LC Card 87-20628 DDC 338.5 19
HB172 .O83 1987

Microeconomics . Amos, Orley M., 1954- Belmont, Calif. , c1987. xxi, 768 p. : ISBN 0-534-06951-7 (pbk.) LC Card 87-110402 DDC 338.5 19
HB172 .A64 1987

Microeconomics . Bach, George Leland, 1915- [Economics. Selections.] Englewood Cliffs, N.J. , c1987. p. cm. ISBN 0-13-580408-6 LC Card 86-25577 DDC 338.5 19
HB172 .B2325 1987

Microeconomics . Clark, J. R. (Jeff R.) San Diego , c1987. xii, 454 p. : ISBN 0-15-551225-0 (pbk.) LC Card 86-83044 DDC 338.5 19
HB172 .C543 1987

Microeconomics /. Eaton, Buford Curtis, 1943- New York, N.Y. , c1988. xv, 471 p. : ISBN 0-7167-1818-9 LC Card 87-15034 DDC 338.5 19
HB172 .E23 1988

Microeconomics /. Ekelund, Robert B. (Robert Burton), 1940- Glenview, Ill. , c1988. xxx, 619 p. : ISBN 0-673-39769-6 (pbk.) LC Card 87-23514 DDC 338.5 19
HB172 .E39 1988

Microeconomics /. Heyne, Paul T. Chicago , c1988. xiv, 411 p. : ISBN 0-574-19485-1 (pbk.) : LC Card 87-22194 DDC 338.5 19
HB172 .H525 1988

Microeconomics . Mansfield, Edwin. New York , c1988. p. cm. ISBN 0-393-95635-0 LC Card 87-22131 DDC 338.5 19
HB172 .M36 1988

Microeconomics /. Thompson, Allen R. Reading, Mass. , c1988. xxx, 888, [35] p. : ISBN 0-201-09683-8 (pbk.) LC Card 87-910 DDC 338.5 19
HB172 .T49 1988

Microeconomics /. Truett, Lila J. (Lila Jane) St. Louis , 1987. xx, 533, [33] p. : ISBN 0-8016-5151-4 (pbk.) LC Card 86-30029 DDC 338.5 19
HB172 .T784 1987

Microeconomics and the public economy . Cullis, John C. Oxford, OX, UK , New York, NY, USA , 1987. xx, 251 p. : ISBN 0-631-15552-X : LC Card 87-5169 DDC 338.5 19
HB172 .C85 1987

Microeconomics & the public economy. Cullis, John C. Microeconomics and the public economy . Oxford, OX, UK , New York, NY, USA , 1987. xx, 251 p. : ISBN 0-631-15552-X : LC Card 87-5169 DDC 338.5 19
HB172 .C85 1987

MICROECONOMICS - ECONOMETRIC MODELS.
Vilks, Arnis. Aggregation und Kausalität im Modell des allgemeinen Konkurrenzgleichgewichts . Göttingen , c1984. 141 p. ; ISBN 3-525-11287-4 (Deut. Bibl.) LC Card 84-225754
HB842 .V55 1984

MICROECONOMICS - MATHEMATICAL MODELS.
Pohmer, Karlheinz. Mikroökonomische Theorie der personellen Einkommens- und Vermögensverteilung . Berlin , New York , c1985. ix, 214 p. : ISBN 0-387-15174-5 (U. S.) LC Card 85-164096
HB523 .P64 1985

Microeconomics with business applications /. Blair, Roger D. New York , c1987. xvii, 514 p. : ISBN 0-471-88304-2 LC Card 86-26770 DDC 338.5 19
HB172 .B5413 1987

Microeconomics with calculus /. Binger, Brian R. Glenview, Ill. , c1988. 609 p. : ISBN 0-673-18002-6 LC Card 87-12132 DDC 338.5/01/515 19
HB172 .B52 1988

La microelectrónica, la tecnología de la información y sus efectos en los países en vía de desarrollo /. Rada, Juan F. México, D.F. , c1983. 158 p. ; ISBN 968-12-0214-7 LC Card 85-243097
HD9696.A3 D447 1983

MICROELECTRONICS - ADDRESSES, ESSAYS, LECTURES.
(1984) Neue Technologien und Arbeitswelt . Köln , c1984. 197 p. : ISBN 3-7663-0893-9 LC Card 85-160745
HD6331.2.G28 N475 1984
NYPL [JLD 86-3861]

Microelectronics, automation, and employment in the automobile industry / edited by Susumu Watanabe ; preface by Ajit S. Bhalla ; foreword by Aubrey Silberston. Chichester [West Sussex] ; New York : Wiley, c1987. xix, 203 p. : ill. ; 24 cm. "A Study prepared for the International Labour Office within the framework of the World Employment Programme." Includes bibliographies and index. ISBN 0-471-91484-3 : LC Card 86-32532 DDC 331.7/6292 19
1. Automobile industry workers - Effect of technological innovations on. 2. Automobile industry

and trade - Technological innovations. I. Watanabe, Susumu. II. International Labour Office. III. World Employment Programme.
HD8039.A8 M52 1987

MICROELECTRONICS - GERMANY (EAST)
Ökonomische und soziale Wirksamkeit des wissenschaftlich-technischen Fortschritts /. Berlin , 1986. 314 p. ; ISBN 3-320-00713-0 LC Card 87-100866 DDC 338/.06 19
HC290.795.T4 O38 1986

MICROELECTRONICS INDUSTRY - CALIFORNIA - SANTA CLARA COUNTY.
Azouaou, Alain. La Silicon Valley, un marché aux puces /. Paris , c1986. 237 p. : ISBN 2-85956-494-2 : LC Card 86-217069
HD9696.A3 U516 1986

MICROELECTRONICS INDUSTRY - CALIFORNIA - SANTA CLARA COUNTY - BIOGRAPHY.
Mahon, Thomas. Charged bodies . New York , c1985. 339 p. : ISBN 0-453-00487-3 LC Card 84-18957 DDC 338.4/76213817/0979473 19
HD9696.A3 U5666 1985
NYPL [JLD 86-1109]

MICROELECTRONICS INDUSTRY - CALIFORNIA - SANTA CLARA COUNTY - HISTORY.
Caddes, Carolyn, 1935- Portraits of success . Palo Alto, Calif. , 1986. viii, 138 p. : ISBN 0-935382-56-9 : LC Card 86-40032 DDC 338.4/7621/0979473 19
HD9696.A3 U53173 1986
NYPL [MFX (Caddes) 87-542]

MICROELECTRONICS INDUSTRY - EUROPE.
The Microprocessor based measuring instrumentation market in West European manufacturing. New York, N.Y. , c1983. [22], 262, xi p. : LC Card 87-142563
HD9706.2.E8513 M53 1983

MICROELECTRONICS INDUSTRY - ITALY - CONGRESSES.
Convegno nazionale del PCI (1982 : Milan, Italy) Le nuove frontiere dello sviluppo . Milano, Italy , c1983. 368 p. ; LC Card 85-174697
HD9696.A3 I727 1982

MICROELECTRONICS INDUSTRY - RESEARCH.
Boehme, Joachim. Innovationsförderung durch Kooperation . Berlin , c1986. 227 p. ; ISBN 3-503-02618-5 LC Card 87-133032 DDC 338.4/762 19
HD9696.A2 B64 1986

MICROELECTRONICS INDUSTRY - TECHNOLOGICAL INNOVATIONS.
Boehme, Joachim. Innovationsförderung durch Kooperation . Berlin , c1986. 227 p. ; ISBN 3-503-02618-5 LC Card 87-133032 DDC 338.4/762 19
HD9696.A2 B64 1986

Kaplinsky, Raphael. Micro-electronics and employment revisited . Geneva , 1987. xiv, 181 p. : ISBN 92-2-105611-2 (pbk.) : LC Card 87-163570 DDC 331.7/6213817 19
HD9696.A2 K37 1987

MICROELECTRONICS - INFORMATION SERVICES - GERMAN-SPEAKING COUNTRIES.
Gensior, Sabine. Mikroelektronik-Anwendung und ihre Bedeutung für die Qualifikationen . Berlin , 1986. 39, 118 p. ; LC Card 87-409403 DDC 338/.06 19
HD6331.2.G27 G46 1986

MICROELECTRONICS - RESEARCH.
Boehme, Joachim. Innovationsförderung durch Kooperation . Berlin , c1986. 227 p. ; ISBN 3-503-02618-5 LC Card 87-133032 DDC 338.4/762 19
HD9696.A2 B64 1986

MICROELECTRONICS - SOCIAL ASPECTS.
Kofler, Leo. Beherrscht uns die Technik? . Hamburg , 1983. 160 p. ; ISBN 3-87975-249-4 LC Card 84-181044
HD6331 .K685 1983

National Research Council (U. S.). Committee on Women's Employment and Related Social Issues. Panel on Technology and Women's Employment. Computer chips and paper clips . Washington, D.C. , 1986. v. : ISBN 0-309-03688-7 (v. 1) LC Card 86-18113 DDC 331.4/8165137/0973 19
HD6331.18.M39 N38 1986
NYPL [JLL 87-129]

New technology and women's employment. Bruxelles , New York [1983] 78 p. ; LC Card 85-160627 DDC 331.4/2 19
HD6331 .N49 1983 ***NYPL [JLD 86-1807]***

Soziale Aspekte der Mikroelektronik /. Berlin , 1985. 122 p. ; LC Card 87-409418 DDC 306/.46 19
HD6331 .S683 1985

MICROELECTRONICS - SOCIAL ASPECTS - ADDRESSES, ESSAYS, LECTURES.
Microprocessors, manpower, and society . Aldershot, Hants., England , c1984. xi, 367 p. : ISBN 0-566-00631-6 ***NYPL [JLD 86-1098]***

MICROELECTRONICS - SOCIAL ASPECTS - CONGRESSES.
Arbeitsplätze morgen /. Stuttgart , c1986. 431 p. : ISBN 3-519-02446-2 LC Card 86-171663
HD6331 .A695 1986

MICROELECTRONICS - SOCIAL ASPECTS - GERMAN-SPEAKING COUNTRIES.
Gensior, Sabine. Mikroelektronik-Anwendung und ihre Bedeutung für die Qualifikationen . Berlin , 1986. 39, 118 p. ; LC Card 87-409403 DDC 338/.06 19
HD6331.2.G27 G46 1986

MICROELECTRONICS - SOCIAL ASPECTS - GERMANY (WEST)
Poppe, Jürgen. Mikroelektronik, Jobkiller oder Jobknüller? . Pfaffenweiler , 1984. 93 p. : ISBN 3-89085-027-8 : LC Card 85-129494
HD6331.2.G28 P66 1984

Welsch, Johann. Gewerkschaften und Strukturwandel . Köln , c1986. iii, 114 p. ; ISBN 3-7663-3011-X LC Card 86-223645 DDC 331.13/704 19
HD6694 .W37 1986

Widersprüche der Automationsarbeit . West-Berlin , c1987. 228 p. ; ISBN 3-88619-362-4 LC Card 87-145099 DDC 331.12/0943 19
HD6331.2.G28 W55 1987

Micromanaging . Geis, George T. Englewood Cliffs, NJ , c1987. xiv, 233 p. ; ISBN 0-13-581901-6 (pbk.) LC Card 86-30470 DDC 658/.05416 19
HD30.2 .G44 1987

MICROMINIATURE ELECTRONIC EQUIPMENT. see **MICROELECTRONICS.**

MICROMINIATURIZATION (ELECTRONICS) see **MICROELECTRONICS.**

Micropower series.
Hoenig, Alan. Framework with applications for the IBM PC /. Dubuque, Iowa , c1985. xiii, 213 p. : ISBN 0-697-00725-1 (pbk.) : LC Card 85-60013 DDC 005.3/69 19
HF5548.4.F7 H64 1985
NYPL [JSE 86-2110]

The Microprocessor based measuring instrumentation market in West European manufacturing. New York, N.Y. : Frost & Sullivan, c1983. [22], 262, xi p. : ill. ; 29 cm. Spine title: Microprocessor-based mfg. instru. in Europe. "February 1983." "(#E625)" LC Card 87-142563
1. Measuring instruments industry - Europe. 2. Microelectronics industry - Europe. 3. Market surveys - Europe. I. Frost & Sullivan. II. Title: Microprocessor-based mfg. instru. in Europe.
HD9706.2.E8513 M53 1983

Microprocessor-based mfg. instru. in Europe. The Microprocessor based measuring instrumentation market in West European manufacturing. New York, N.Y. , c1983. [22], 262, xi p. : LC Card 87-142563
HD9706.2.E8513 M53 1983

Microprocessor development systems in Europe. The Microprocessor development systems market in West Europe. New York, N.Y. (106 Fulton St., New York 10038) , c1983. 2 v. : LC Card 87-401674 DDC 380.1/4500416/094 19
HD9696.C63 E765 1983

The Microprocessor development systems market in West Europe. New York, N.Y. (106 Fulton St., New York 10038) : Frost & Sullivan, c1983. 2 v. : ill. ; 29 cm. Spine title: Microprocessor development systems in Europe. "March 1983." "#E645." LC Card 87-401674 DDC 380.1/4500416/094 19
1. Computer industry - Europe. 2. Microprocessors - Economic aspects - Europe. 3. Market surveys - Europe. I. Frost & Sullivan. II. Title: Microprocessor development systems in Europe.
HD9696.C63 E765 1983

MICROPROCESSORS - ECONOMIC ASPECTS - EUROPE.
The Microprocessor development systems market in West Europe. New York, N.Y. (106 Fulton St., New York 10038) , c1983. 2 v. : LC Card 87-401674 DDC 380.1/4500416/094 19
HD9696.C63 E765 1983

Microprocessors, manpower, and society : a comparative, cross-national approach / edited by Malcolm Warner. Aldershot, Hants., England : Gower, c1984. xi, 367 p. : ill. ; 23 cm. Includes bibliographies and index. ISBN 0-566-00631-6
1. Machinery in industry - Addresses, essays, lectures. 2. Automation - Addresses, essays, lectures. 3. Microelectronics - Social aspects - Addresses, essays, lectures. 4. Industrial relations - Addresses, essays, lectures. I. Warner, Malcolm.
NYPL [JLD 86-1098]

MICROSOFT EXCEL (COMPUTER PROGRAM)
Adler, John R. Dynamics of MacIntosh Excel /. Homewood, Ill. , c1987. xii, 164 p. : ISBN 0-87094-907-1 (pbk.) LC Card 86-72565 DDC 005.36/9 19
HF5548.4.E93 A35 1987

Microsoft Excel with macros . Hergert, Douglas. Redmond, Wash. [New York, N.Y.] , c1986. xii, 265 p. : ISBN 0-914845-76-4 (pbk.) : LC Card 86-211548 DDC 005.36/9 19
HF5548.4.E93 H474 1986

The Microstructure of securities markets / Kalman J. Cohen ... [et al.]. Englewood Cliffs, N.J. : Prentice-Hall, c1986. ix, 254 p. ; 24 cm. Includes index. Bibliography: p. 233-243. ISBN 0-13-581794-3 LC Card 85-28265 DDC 332.64 19
1. Securities - United States. 2. Stock-exchange - United States. I. Cohen, Kalman J.
HG4661 .M53 1986 ***NYPL [JLE 86-2001]***

Microtheory . Baumol, William J. Brighton, Sussex , 1986. xxvii, 286 p. : ISBN 0-7450-0110-6 LC Card 86-673554
HB171 .B326x 1986b

Microtheory . Baumol, William J. Brighton, Sussex , c1986. xxvii, 286 p. : ISBN 0-7450-0110-6 ***NYPL [JLF 86-1374]***

MICROWAVE EQUIPMENT INDUSTRY - UNITED STATES.
The Microwave test equipment market in the U. S. New York, N.Y. , c1983. iii, 223 p. ; LC Card 87-143814
HD9696.M533 U56 1983

Microwave equipment market in the U. S. The Microwave test equipment market in the U. S. New York, N.Y. , c1983. iii, 223 p. ; LC Card 87-143814
HD9696.M533 U56 1983

MICROWAVE MEASUREMENTS.
The Microwave test equipment market in the U. S. New York, N.Y. , c1983. iii, 223 p. ; LC Card 87-143814
HD9696.M533 U56 1983

MICROWAVE OVEN INDUSTRY - UNITED STATES.
Cholmar, Sidney. New directions in microwave ovens . Stamford, Conn., U. S.A. , c1985. x, 119 leaves ; ISBN 0-89336-459-2 (pbk.) LC Card 87-163958 DDC 381/.4568388 19
HD9971.5.S763 U53 1985

The Microwave test equipment market in the U. S. New York, N.Y. : Frost & Sullivan, c1983. iii, 223 p. ; 29 cm. Spine title: Microwave equipment market in the U. S. "July 1983." "#A1216." LC Card 87-143814
1. Microwave equipment industry - United States. 2. Testing equipment industry - United States. 3. Electronic apparatus and appliances - Testing - Equipment and supplies. 4. Microwave measurements. 5. Market surveys - United States. I. Frost & Sullivan.

II. Title: Microwave equipment market in the U. S.
HD9696.M533 U56 1983

Mid career crisis /. Selles, G. (Gert) Deventer [1985?] 135 p. : ISBN 90-6001-934-2 LC Card 86-163138
HF5384 .S45 1985

Mid year review of the economy, 1986-87 /. Adiseshiah, Malcolm S. New Delhi , 1987. 193 p. : ISBN 81-7062-016-3 : LC Card 87-900477 DDC 330.954/052 19
HC435.2 .A648 1987

The midas touch . Train, John. New York , c1987. xi, 207 p. ; ISBN 0-06-015643-0 : LC Card 86-45157 DDC 332.6/092/4 B 19
HG172.B84 T72 1987

The Mid-Atlantic region in transition . Fuller, Theodore, 1929- Washington, D.C. [1986] v, 13 p. : LC Card 86-602014 DDC 331.12/0974 19
HD5725.A12 F85 1986

MIDDLE AGE AND EMPLOYMENT. see **AGE AND EMPLOYMENT.**

MIDDLE AGE - PSYCHOLOGICAL ASPECTS.
Selles, G. (Gert) Mid career crisis /. Deventer [1985?] 135 p. : ISBN 90-6001-934-2 LC Card 86-163138
HF5384 .S45 1985

MIDDLE AGED MEN - PORTUGAL - STATISTICS.
Carrilho, Maria José. Análise da idade média ao casamento, 1930-1978 /. Lisboa, Portugal , 1984. 27 p. : LC Card 85-124431
HB1241 .C37 1984

MIDDLE AGED WOMEN - PORTUGAL - STATISTICS.
Carrilho, Maria José. Análise da idade média ao casamento, 1930-1978 /. Lisboa, Portugal , 1984. 27 p. : LC Card 85-124431
HB1241 .C37 1984

MIDDLE AGED WORKERS. see **AGE AND EMPLOYMENT.**

MIDDLE AGES.
Abulafia, David. Italy, Sicily, and the Mediterranean, 1100-1400 /. London , 1987. 346 p. in various pagings : ISBN 0-86078-198-4 : LC Card 87-157554 DDC 330.9182/2 19
HF3585 .A29 1987

MIDDLE CLASSES - EUROPE - HISTORY - 19TH CENTURY - CONGRESSES.
Arbeiter und Bürger im 19. Jahrhundert . München , 1986. xiv, 342 p. ; ISBN 3-486-52871-8 LC Card 86-212379
HD8376 .A72 1986

MIDDLE CLASSES - GERMANY - HISTORY.
Vereinswesen und bürgerliche Gesellschaft in Deutschland /. München , 1984. 180 p. ; ISBN 3-486-52081-4 LC Card 84-205111
HD2429.G3 V46 1984

MIDDLE CLASSES - GERMANY (WEST) - BAVARIA - HISTORY.
Hesselmann, Hans. Das Wirtschaftsbürgertum in Bayern 1890-1914 . [Stuttgart] , 1985. 419 p. : ISBN 3-515-04565-1 LC Card 86-127555
HC287.B3 H46 1985

MIDDLE CLASSES - HISTORY - 19TH CENTURY.
Jones, Charles A., 1949- International business in the nineteenth century . New York , c1987. xi, 260 p. ; ISBN 0-8147-4172-X : LC Card 87-11321 DDC 338.8/8/09034 19
HF497 .J66 1987

MIDDLE CLASSES - ITALY - HISTORY - 20TH CENTURY.
D'Angelo, Lucio. Ceti medi e ricostruzione . [Milano] , 1981. vi, 287 p. ; LC Card 81-213297
JN5657.D45 D36 1981
NYPL [JLE 86-3459]

MIDDLE CLASSES - SPAIN - VALENCIA - HISTORY - 18TH CENTURY.
Franch Benavent, Ricardo, 1956- Crecimiento comercial y enriquecimiento burgués en la Valencia del siglo XVIII /. Valencia [1986?] 340 p. : ISBN 84-505-4154-9 LC Card 87-110614
HF3690.V3 F7 1986

MIDDLE CLASSES - UNITED STATES.
Davidson, James Dale. The squeeze /. New York , c1980. 281 p. ; ISBN 0-671-40084-3 LC Card 79-28411 DDC 330.973
HC106.7 .D38 ***NYPL [JLE 80-1960]***

Haley, Charles T. To do good and do well [microform] . 1980. x, 233 leaves ;
NYPL [Sc Micro R-4654]

MIDDLE CLASSES - VENEZUELA - HISTORY - 20TH CENTURY.
Brito Figueroa, Federico. La aristocracia del dinero en Venezuela actual, 1945-1985 /. Barquisimeto, Venezuela , 1986- v. <1 > ; ISBN 980-608-700-3 (v. 1) : LC Card 87-404343 DDC 305.5/234/0987 19
HG185.V4 B75 1986

MIDDLE EAST - COMMERCE - EUROPE - HISTORY.
Ashtor, Eliyahu, 1914- East-West trade in the medieval Mediterranean /. London , 1986. [344] p. ; ISBN 0-86078-193-3 LC Card 87-134358 DDC 382/.094/056 19
HF3756.Z7 E92 1986

MIDDLE EAST - ECONOMIC CONDITIONS - 19TH CENTURY.
The Fertile Crescent, 1800-1914 . New York , 1987. p. cm. ISBN 0-19-504951-9 LC Card 86-33275 DDC 330.956 19
HC415.15 .F47 1987

MIDDLE EAST - FOREIGN ECONOMIC RELATIONS - EUROPE.
Ashtor, Eliyahu, 1914- East-West trade in the medieval Mediterranean /. London , 1986. [344] p. ; ISBN 0-86078-193-3 LC Card 87-134358 DDC 382/.094/056 19
HF3756.Z7 E92 1986

MIDDLE EAST - FOREIGN ECONOMIC RELATIONS - JAPAN.
Shimizu, Hiroshi. Introduction to Japan's economic and political relations with the Middle East in the inter-war period . Kent Ridge, Singapore [1985] v, 47 leaves ; LC Card 87-110444 DDC 337.52056 19
HF1602.15.M626 S56 1985

MIDDLE EAST - FOREIGN ECONOMIC RELATIONS - UNITED STATES.
Godfried, Nathan. Bridging the gap between rich and poor . New York , 1987. xii, 225 p. ; ISBN 0-313-25648-9 (lib. bdg. : alk. paper) LC Card 87-8471 DDC 338.91/73/056 19
HC415.15 .G63 1987

Painter, David S. [Oil and the American century.] Private power and public policy . London , c1986. xii, 302 p. : ISBN 1-85043-021-7 LC Card 87-673320
HD9566 .P24x 1986b

MIDDLE EAST - FOREIGN RELATIONS - JAPAN.
Shimizu, Hiroshi. Introduction to Japan's economic and political relations with the Middle East in the inter-war period . Kent Ridge, Singapore [1985] v, 47 leaves ; LC Card 87-110444 DDC 337.52056 19
HF1602.15.M626 S56 1985

MIDDLE EAST - HISTORY - TO 622.
Labor in the ancient Near East /. New Haven, Conn. , 1987. xiv, 289 p. : ISBN 0-940490-68-4 LC Card 86-32227 DDC 305.5/62/09394 19
HD8656 .L33 1987 ***NYPL [*OAC (American Oriental series)]***

MIDDLE EAST - HISTORY - 1517-
The Fertile Crescent, 1800-1914 . New York , 1987. p. cm. ISBN 0-19-504951-9 LC Card 86-33275 DDC 330.956 19
HC415.15 .F47 1987

The Middle East in the world economy, 1800-1914 /. Owen, Edward Roger John. London , New York , 1987, c1981. xix, 378 p. : ISBN 0-416-03272-9 (pbk.) LC Card 86-24385 DDC 330.956 19
HC415.15 .O94 1987

MIDDLE EAST - POLITICS AND GOVERNMENT - 1945-

MIDDLE EAST - RELATIONS - UNITED STATES.
Laufer, Leopold Yehuda. U. S. aid to the West Bank and Gaza . [Jerusalem] [1985] 54 p. ; LC Card 87-400340 DDC 338.91/73/056951 19
HC415.25.Z7 W4735 1985

Middle East science policy studies .
(no. 11) Commander, Simon. The state and agricultural development in Egypt since 1973 /. London , Atlantic Highlands, NJ , 1988. p. cm. ISBN 0-86372-080-3 LC Card 87-3616 DDC 338.1/862 19
HD2123.Z8 C66 1988

(no. 7) Agricultural policy in Jordan /. London ; Atlantic Highlands, NJ : 147 p. : ISBN 0-86372-070-6 LC Card 86-21480 DDC 338.1/85695 19
HD2059.Z8 A34 1986

MIDDLE EAST - STRATEGIC ASPECTS.

MIDDLE-LEVEL MANAGERS. see **MIDDLE MANAGERS.**

MIDDLE MANAGERS - GERMANY (WEST)
Fricke, Werner. Beteiligung im Industriebetrieb . Frankfurt/Main , New York , c1985. 291 p. ; ISBN 3-593-32735-X LC Card 85-202742
HD5660.G4 F73 1985

MIDDLE MANAGERS - ITALY - CONGRESSES.
Tecnici, ricercatori, quadri e sindacato /. Roma , 1985. 126 p. : LC Card 86-169979
HD8038.I8 T43 1985

MIDDLE MANAGERS - SALARIES, PENSIONS, ETC. - UNITED STATES.
Nash, Allan N. Managerial compensation /. Scarsdale, N.Y. , c1980. 56 p. ; ISBN 0-89361-022-4 : LC Card 80-21044 DDC 658.4/072/0973 19
HD4965.5.U6 N22
NYPL [JLM 83-380 no.15]

MIDDLE MANAGERS - TRAINING OF - JAPAN.
Nötzli, Irene M. A view of Japanese management, especially management development in large business enterprises /. Zürich , c1982. ix, 281 p. : ISBN 3-7255-2191-3 (pbk.) LC Card 82-237094 DDC 658.4/07124 19
HF5549.5.T7 N638 1982 ***NYPL [TB (Zürich. Universität. Handelwissenschafticthes Seminar. Mitteilungen. Heft 156)]***

MIDDLE MANAGERS - UNITED STATES.
Tomasko, Robert M. Downsizing . New York , c1987. p. cm. ISBN 0-8144-5907-2 LC Card 87-47709 DDC 338.6/4 19
HD69.S5 T59 1987

MIDDLE MANAGERS - UNITED STATES - DISMISSAL OF.
Brandt, Ed. Fifty and fired . Bedford, Mass. , c1987. xii, 242 p. ; ISBN 0-938179-07-1 : LC Card 87-12150 DDC 650.1/4/0240564 19
HD38.25.U6 B7 1987

MIDDLE WEST - ECONOMIC CONDITIONS.
Stinson, Thomas F., 1942- Governing the heartland . Washington , 1986. xii, 159 p. : LC Card 86-603376 DDC 336/.014/77 19
HJ9181 .S75 1986

MIDDLE WEST - HISTORY.
Fite, Gilbert Courtland, 1918- The farmers' frontier, 1865-1900 /. Norman [1987], c1966. xiv, 272 p. : ISBN 0-8061-2063-0 (pbk.) LC Card 86-40534 DDC 338.1/0977 19
HD8039.F3 U643 1987

MIDDLE WEST - RURAL CONDITIONS - CONGRESSES.
Agricultural distress in the Midwest, past & present /. Iowa City , 1986. ix, 111 p. : ISBN 0-87414-049-8 : LC Card 86-29932 DDC 338.1/0977 19
HD1773.A3 A37 1986

Middlebrooks, David J. Lehr, Richard I. The new unionism . New York, N.Y. , c1987. 114 p. ; ISBN 0-88057-672-3 (pbk.) LC Card 86-82864 DDC 331.88/0973 19
HD6508 .L427 1987

Middlebury Conference on Economic Affairs (1984) Incentive-based incomes policies . Cambridge, Mass. , c1986. xxi, 263 p. : ISBN 0-88730-082-0 LC Card 85-20090 DDC 331.2/9 19
HC79.W24 I465 1986 ***NYPL [JLE 86-3724]***

Middleton, D. R. (Dan R.) Mason, John M. (John Michael), 1950- Operational and geometric evaluation of exclusive truck lanes /. College Station, Tex. , Springfield, Va. [1986] vii, 156 p. : LC Card 86-622239 DDC 380.5 s 388.3/14 19
HE203 .T43 no. 331-3F HE356.T4

Midgley, James. Social security, inequality, and the Third world / James Midgley. Chichester, [Sussex] ; New York : Wiley, c1984. x, 225 p. ; 24 cm. (Social development in the Third World) Includes index. Bibliography: p. 211-220. ISBN 0-471-90061-3 LC Card 84-5188 DDC 368.4/009172/4 19
1. Social security - Developing countries. 2. Income distribution - Developing countries. I. Title. II. Series.
HD7252 .M52 1984 ***NYPL [JLE 86-2165]***

MIDI-PYRÉNÉES (FRANCE) - ECONOMIC CONDITIONS.
Marconis, Robert. Midi-Pyrénées XIXe-XXe siècles . [Toulouse?] [1985?] 2 v. : ISBN 2-86726-084-7 (set) LC Card 87-112330
HC277.M54 M37 1985

Midi-Pyrénées XIXe-XXe siècles . Marconis, Robert. [Toulouse?] [1985?] 2 v. : ISBN 2-86726-084-7 (set) LC Card 87-112330
HC277.M54 M37 1985

Mid-term evaluation of the Malawi Union of Savings and Credit Co-operatives Project (612-0205) /. Dublin, Jack. Lilongwe, Malawi , 1983. x, 84, [29] leaves ; LC Card 85-981350 DDC 334/.22/096897 19
HG2039.M29 D83 1983

Midttun, Atle, 1952- The Politics of energy forecasting . Oxford [Oxfordshire] , New York , 1987. xiii, 314 p. : ISBN 0-19-828547-7 : LC Card 86-23885 DDC 333.79 19
HD9502.A2 P66 1987

Midwinter, Arthur F. Rates reform : issues, arguments & evidence / Arthur Midwinter & Colin Mair. Edinburgh : Mainstream Pub., 1987. 182 p. ; 25 cm. Includes bibliographies and index. ISBN 1-85158-062-X : LC Card 87-167866 DDC 336/.014/41 19
1. Local finance - Great Britain. I. Mair, Colin. II. Title.
HJ9421 .M53 1987

Miech Chatenay, Michèle.
Madagascar . Paris , 1986, c1985. 184 p. : ISBN 2-905760-02-8 LC Card 87-123718
HC895 .M34 1986

Somalia, productive sectors of the economy /. Paris , 1985. 115 leaves : ISBN 2-905760-00-1 (pbk.) LC Card 87-124493 DDC 338.967/73 19
HC850 .S658 1985

Miegel, Meinhard. Die verkannte Revolution / Meinhard Miegel, unter Mitarbeit von Mark Baier, Stefanie Wahl ; mit einem Vorwort von Kurt H. Biedenkopf. 1. Aufl. Stuttgart : Bonn Aktuell, 1983- v. : ill. ; 20 cm. (IWG Impulse . Bd. 5) Includes bibliographical references and index. CONTENTS. - 1. Einkommen und Vermögen der privaten Haushalte. ISBN 3-87959-196-2 (Bd. 1) LC Card 83-206487 DDC 330.943/087 19
1. Income - Germany, West. 2. Wealth - Germany, West. 3. Germany, West - Economic conditions - 1974-. I. Baier, Mark. II. Wahl, Stefanie. III. Series: Institut für Wirtschafts-und Gesellschaftspolitik. IWG Impulse, Bd. 5. IV. Title.
HC286.7 .M53 1983 ***NYPL [JLK 86-154]***

Miegge, Mario. Vocazione e lavoro : due trattati puritani, William Perkins e Richard Steele / Mario Miegge. [Bologna] : I. Bovolenta : N. Zanichelli [distributor], c1985. 97 p. : ill. ; 20 cm. (Pugillaria . 7) Includes bibliographical references and index. LC Card 87-131793
1. Vocational guidance - Great Britain - History - 17th century. 2. Perkins, William, 1558-1602. Treatise of the vocations. 3. Steele, Richard, 1629-1692. Tradesman's calling. I. Title.
HF5382.5.G7 M52 1985

Mielke, Robert B. Live births by estimated marital status of mother, California, 1981. [Sacramento] : State of California, Health and Welfare Agency, Dept. of Health Services, [1984] 22 p. : ill. ; 28 cm. (Data matters topical reports) Caption title. "Report register no. 84-01080 (February 1984)" Bibliography: p. 22. LC Card 86-622328 DDC 304.6/32/09794 19
1. Childbirth - California - Statistics. 2. California - Statistics, Vital. I. California. Dept. of Health Services. II. Title. III. Series.
HB935.C2 M54 1984

Miernyk, William H. The coalmining industry in the United States / William H. Miernyk. Geneva : International Institute for Labour Studies, 1986. 53, ix p. : ill., map ; 24 cm. (Research series . no. 83) At head of title: Strategic factors in industrial relations systems. Bibliography: p. 50-53. ISBN 92-9014-409-2 (pbk.)
1. Collective bargaining - Coal mining industry - United States. 2. Coal-miners - United States. I. Title. II. Title: Strategic factors in industrial relations systems. III. Series: Geneva. International Institute for Labour Studies. Research series, no. 83.
NYPL [JLE 87-1534]

Mies, Maria.
Indian women in subsistence and agricultural labour / Maria Mies, assisted by Lalita K. and Krishna Kumari. Geneva : International Labour Office, 1986. x, 158 p. ; 24 cm. (Women, work, and development, 0253-2042 . 12) Includes bibliographies. ISBN 92-2-105397-0 (pbk.) : LC Card 87-114124 DDC 331.4/83/0954 19
1. Women in agriculture - India. 2. Women in rural development - India. I. Kumari, Lalita K. II. Kumari, Krishna, 1951-. III. Title. IV. Series.
HD6073.A292 I46 1986

Patriarchy and accumulation on a world scale : women in the international division of labour / Maria Mies. London ; Atlantic Highlands, NJ : Zed Books, 1986. 251 p. ; 23 cm. (Third World books) Includes index. Bibliography: p. 236-246. ISBN 0-86232-341-X LC Card 86-18916 DDC 305.4 19
1. Sexual division of labor. 2. Women - History. 3. Women - Social conditions. I. Title. II. Series.
HD6060.6 .M54 1986 ***NYPL [JLD 86-3206]***

MIESBACH (GERMANY : LANDKREIS) - ECONOMIC CONDITIONS.
Gräf, Peter. Zur Raumrelevanz infrastruktureller Massnahmen . Kallmünz/Regensburg , 1978. xxxvii, 259 p., [9] leaves of plates (7 folded) : ISBN 3-7847-6518-1 LC Card 85-205909
HC281 .M8 Bd. 18 HC288.M53

Mieth, Dietmar. Christian ethics and economics . Edinburgh , New York , c1980. xii, 114 p. ; ISBN 0-8164-2282-6 (Seabury Press : pbk.) LC Card 80-50892
HF1411 .C422 1980

Mieth, Dietmar Marie. Unemployment and the right to work /. Edinburgh , New York , c1982. x, 98 p. ; ISBN 0-8164-2391-1 (Seabury Press : pbk.) LC Card 87-150638
HD5707.5 .U544 1982

Mig i vechnost′ rekorda. Myt′ i vichnist′ rekordu . Kyïv , 1985. 124 p., [24] p. of plates : LC Card 86-178641
HC340.S6 M97 1985

Migliaro, Al. An Executive's guide to econometric forecasting . Flushing, N.Y. , c1983. 74 p. : ISBN 0-932126-10-3 (pbk.) LC Card 82-90726 DDC 330/.028 19
HB3730 .E978 1983 ***NYPL [JLF 86-1166]***

Migliaro, Luis Razeto. see **Razeto M., Luis, 1945-**

Migliavacca, Giorgio.
The postal history of Lombardy under Austrian rule, 1707-1796 : a fascinating saga / by Giorgio Migliavacca. [S.l.] : Laurel Publications International, 1985. [40] p. : ill. ; 22 cm. "Reprinted from February-June 1983 Postal history journal." Bibliography: p. [40]. ISBN 0-934139-03-2 (pbk.) LC Card 87-149625 DDC 383/.49452 19
1. Postal service - Italy - Lombardy - History - 18th century. 2. Postal service - Austria - History - 18th century. 3. Lombardy (Italy) - History - Austrian rule, 1714-1796. I. Title. II. Title: Postal history journal.
HE7016.L66 M54 1985

The Royal Mail Steam Packet Company / by Giorgio Migliavacca. [S.l.] : Laurel Publications International, 1985. 41 p. : ill. ; 22 cm. Bibliography: p. 12. Includes Tables of routes for the packets of the Royal Mail Steam Packet Company, commencing from Southampton, March, 1860. ISBN 0-934139-01-6 (pbk.) LC Card 87-149471 DDC 383/.142/09729 19
1. Royal Mail Steam Packet Company - History. 2. Mail steamers - Great Britain - History. 3. Mail steamers - Caribbean Area - History. I. Title.
HE6939.M3 M53 1985

Migración y marginalidad en Posadas . Baranger, Dionisio. Posadas , 1982. 53 p. : LC Card 86-205276 DDC 304.8/0982/23 19
HB2020.P67 B37 1982

Migraciones laborales en el Perú : su significación y tendencias actuales. [Monterrico] : Universidad de Lima, Centro de Investigaciones Económicas y Sociales, [c1984] 47 p. : ill. ; 30 cm. (Serie Avances de investigación no. 4) "Documento elaborado por el equipo de Migraciones Laborales, en el marco del Proyecto DGE-OIT PER/79/PO8." Includes bibliographical references. LC Card 84-235623 DDC 331.12/7985 19
1. Labor supply - Peru. 2. Labor supply - Peru - Lima Metropolitan Area. 3. Migration, Internal - Peru. 4. Cost and standard of living - Peru - Departments. 5. Peru - Census. I. Universidad de Lima. Centro de Investigaciones Económicas y Sociales.
HD5761 .M53 1984 ***NYPL [JLF 86-799]***

Migracja siły roboczej do krajów EWG i jej konsekwencje społeczno-gospodarcze /. Rymarczyk, Jan. [Wrocław] , 1982. 239 p., [4] folded leaves ; LC Card 83-153742
HB9 .B7522 nr. 218 HD8378.5.A2

Migracje a ruchliwość społeczna ludności w Polsce /. Witkowski, Janusz. Warszawa , 1985. 168 p. : LC Card 86-175948
HB2068.7.A3 W58 1985

Migracje wewnętrzne ludności : stan w 1970 r. według podziału administracyjnego z 1975 r. / [temat zrealizowany przez zespół w składzie Mikołaj Latuch (kierownik zespołu) ; Zbigniew Strzelecki (sekretarz zespołu), Wiesław Turos ; redakcja naukowa Maria Namysłowska].Wyd. 1. Warszawa : Szkoła Główna Planowania i Statystyki, Instytut Gospodarstwa Społecznego, 1980. xvi, 389 p. ; 25 cm. (Monografie i opracowania. 87. 2) Chiefly tables. Includes bibliographical references. LC Card 86-215694
1. Migration, Internal - Poland - Statistics. 2. Poland - Population - Statistics. I. Latuch, Mikołaj. II. Strzelecki, Zbigniew. III. Turos, Wiesław. IV. Namysłowska, Maria. V. Series: Monografie i opracowania (Szkoła Główna Planowania i Statystyki (Warsaw, Poland)) , 87.
HB2068.7.A3 M54 1980

MIGRANT AGRICULTURAL LABORERS - FLORIDA.
The Hands that feed us . Washington, D.C. , c1986. iii leaves, 150, 2 p., [3] leaves of plates : ISBN 0-86566-039-5 (pbk.) : LC Card 87-154337 DDC 331.5/44/09759 19
HD1527.F6 H36 1986

MIGRANT AGRICULTURAL LABORERS - HOUSING - OREGON.
The Dilema of farmworker housing . [Portland, Or.] [1986] 78, [112] p. : LC Card 86-622584 DDC 363.5/9 19
HD7289.U7 O73 1986

MIGRANT AGRICULTURAL LABORERS - JORDAN.
Seccombe, Ian J. Manpower and migration . [Durham, England] , c1981. viii, 110 p. : LC Card 84-673623
HD5812.25.A6 S42x 1981
NYPL [JLD 86-2457]

MIGRANT AGRICULTURAL LABORERS - KENYA - HISTORY - 20TH CENTURY.
Kanogo, Tabitha M. Squatters and the roots of Mau Mau, 1905-63 /. London , Athens , 1987. xviii, 206 p. : ISBN 0-8214-0873-9 (U.S) LC Card 87-11201 DDC 307.3/36 19
HD1538.K4 K36 1987

MIGRANT LABOR - BRAZIL.
Incao, Maria da Conceição d'. A questão do bóia-fria /. São Paulo-Brasil , 1984. 93 p. : LC Card 85-187274
HD5856.B6 I53 1984

MIGRANT LABOR - BRAZIL - POLITICAL ACTIVITY.

MIGRANT LABOR - BRAZIL - SERVICES FOR.
Brazil. Ministério do Interior. Secretaria de Planejamento. Programa nacional de apoio às migrações internas /. Brasília , 1980. 42 p. ; LC Card 86-203543 DDC 362.8/5 19
HB2023 .B73 1980

MIGRANT LABOR - DEVELOPING COUNTRIES.
Palmer, Ingrid. The impact of male out-migration on women in farming /. West Hartford, Conn. , c1985. xviii, 78 p. ; ISBN 0-931816-22-X (pbk.) LC Card 85-5240 DDC 331.4/83/091724 19
HD6073.A292 D4472 1985
NYPL [JLF 86-1626]

MIGRANT LABOR - DEVELOPING COUNTRIES - ADDRESSES, ESSAYS, LECTURES.
Labour circulation and the labour process /. London [England] , Dover, N.H. , c1985. xvi, 416 p. : ISBN 0-7099-3342-8 : LC Card 84-14306 DDC 331.12/791 19
HD5856.D44 L33 1984
NYPL [JLD 86-2532]

MIGRANT LABOR - DEVELOPING COUNTRIES - CONGRESSES.
ASA Conference, Migrants, Workers, and the Social Order (1986 : University of Kent) Migrants, workers, and the social order /. London , New York , 1987. p. cm. ISBN 0-422-61680-X (pbk.) LC Card 87-10253
HD5856.D44 A72 1986

MIGRANT LABOR - GERMANY - HISTORY.
Population, labour, and migration in 19th- and 20th-century Germany /. Leamington Spa [UK] ; New York : xii, 200 p. : ISBN 0-85496-503-3 : LC Card 86-24470 DDC 331.6/2/0943 19
HD5856.G3 P66 1987

MIGRANT LABOR - HUNGARY - CONGRESSES.
Árucsere és migráció . Miskolc , 1986. 237 p. : ISBN 963-01-6995-9 : LC Card 87-409685
HD5856.H9 A78 1986

MIGRANT LABOR - INDIA.
Pande, Sunanda. Trends in occupational mobility among migrants /. Jaipur , 1986. xii, 232 p. ; ISBN 81-7033-023-8 : LC Card 86-902816 DDC 331.5/44/0954 19
HD5856.I4 P36 1986

Ray, S. N., M.A. Migrant women workers . Ranchi [1982] iii, 92 p., [3] leaves of plates : LC Card 85-903727 DDC 331.4/0954 19
HD6189 .R39 1982 *NYPL [JLD 86-3370]*

MIGRANT LABOR - INDIA - CONGRESSES.
Migrant labour and related issues /. New Delhi , c1987. xii, 334 p. : ISBN 81-204-0199-9 : LC Card 87-901172
HD5856.I4 M54 1985

MIGRANT LABOR - IRELAND.
Rottman, David B. The population structure and living circumstances of Irish travellers . Dublin , 1986. 134 p. : ISBN 0-7070-0084-X (pbk.) : LC Card 86-215759 DDC 330.9417 s 305.5/68 19
HC257.I6 E3 no. 131 DX217

MIGRANT LABOR - RUSSIAN S.F.S.R. - NON-CHERNOZEM REGION.
Vasil´ev, Ivan Afanas´evich. Korennye i priezzhie /. Moskva , 1980. 86 p. ; LC Card 81-178115
HD1536.S65 V375 1980

MIGRANT LABOR - SOUTH AFRICA.
Jeeves, Alan. Migrant labour in South Africa's mining economy . Kingston, Canada , 1985. xiv, 323 p. ; ISBN 0-7735-0420-6 DDC 331.7'6223422 *NYPL [JLE 85-3148]*

MIGRANT LABOR - SOUTH AFRICA - TRANSKEI.
May, Julian. Migrant labour in Transkei . Durban , 1985. 34, vii p. ; ISBN 0-86980-467-7 (pbk.) : LC Card 86-190553 DDC 331.6/2/0968791 19
HD5856.S6 M39 1985

MIGRANT LABOR - SOUTH ASIA.
Gilani, Ijaz. Citizens slaves, guest-workers . Islamabad, Pakistan , c1985. 84 p. ; LC Card 85-931825 DDC 331.6/2/54 19
HD5856.S64 G55 1985

MIGRANT LABOR - TOGO.
Dovi-Sodemekou, Folly B. (Folly Bebey) Emploi et éducation dans le 2e plan de développement économique et social du Togo /. Lomé, Togo [1985] 89, 52, 9, 2 p. : LC Card 87-131183
HD5846.5.A6 D68 1985

Migrant labour and related issues / editor, Vidyut Joshi. New Delhi : Oxford & IBH Pub. Co., c1987. xii, 334 p. : ill. ; 22 cm. Revised papers presented at the National Seminar on Migrant Labour and Related Issues, held at Gandhi Labour Institute, Ahmedabad, India, in October 1985. Includes bibliographies and index. ISBN 81-204-0199-9 : LC Card 87-901172
1. Migrant labor - India - Congresses. 2. Rural-urban migration - India - Congresses. I. Joshi, Vidyuta. II. Gandhi Labour Institute, Ahmedabad. III. National Seminar on Migrant Labour and Related Issues (1985 : Gandhi Labour Institute, Ahmedabad).
HD5856.I4 M54 1985

Migrant labour in South Africa's mining economy . Jeeves, Alan. Kingston, Canada , 1985. xiv, 323 p. ; ISBN 0-7735-0420-6 DDC 331.7'6223422 *NYPL [JLE 85-3148]*

Migrant labour in Transkei . May, Julian. Durban , 1985. 34, vii p. ; ISBN 0-86980-467-7 (pbk.) : LC Card 86-190553 DDC 331.6/2/0968791 19
HD5856.S6 M39 1985

MIGRANT REMITTANCES - KENYA.
Mukras, M. S. Recent findings on the determinants of urban-rural income transfers in Kenya /. [Nairobi?] , 1985. ii, 33 leaves : LC Card 85-980600
HC865.Z9 I516 1985

Migrant women workers . Ray, S. N., M.A. Ranchi [1982] iii, 92 p., [3] leaves of plates : LC Card 85-903727 DDC 331.4/0954 19
HD6189 .R39 1982 *NYPL [JLD 86-3370]*

Migrantes, campesinos de Licto y Flores. Mariano, Alfonso, José, Lorenzo, Manuel . Quito, Ecuador , 1985. 128 p., [8] leaves of plates : LC Card 86-136793
HD1531.E2 M37 1985

Migrants, workers, and the social order /. ASA Conference, Migrants, Workers, and the Social Order (1986 : University of Kent) London , New York , 1987. p. cm. ISBN 0-422-61680-X (pbk.) LC Card 87-10253
HD5856.D44 A72 1986

Migrasi / editor, Mukhlis, Kathryn Robinson. Cet. 1. Ujung Pandang : Lembaga Penerbitan, Universitas Hasanuddin, 1985. xi, 205 p. : maps ; 23 cm. Includes bibliographies. CONTENTS. - Kalola, sebuah desa yang pernah ditinggalkan banyak penghuninya / Cik Hasan Bisri -- Kebudayaan masyarakat perantau / Mudjahirin Thohir -- Perantau Flores Timur di kotamadya Ujungpandang / Elias Kopong. LC Card 87-940461
1. Migration, Internal - Indonesia - Sulawesi Selatan. I. Mukhlis, 1948-. II. Robinson, Kathryn Mae, 1949-.
HB2108.S8 M54 1985

Migratie en arbeidsmarkt /. Dijk, Jouke van. Assen , 1986. 239 p. : ISBN 90-232-2213-X : LC Card 86-215033
HB2065 .D54 1986

Migration /. Jackson, J. A. (John Archer), 1929- London , New York , 1986. 91 p. : ISBN 0-582-48052-3 LC Card 85-13098 DDC 304.8/0941 19
HB2043 .M54 1986 *NYPL [JLD 86-2119]*

MIGRATION. see **MIGRATION, INTERNAL.**

Migration and employment in the tea estates of Nepal /. Kansakar, Vidya Bir Singh. Kathmandu , 1985. vii, 87, iv, xvii p. ; LC Card 86-903522 DDC 331.12/5372/095496 19
HD8039.T182 N355 1985

Migration and settlement : a multiregional comparative study / edited by Andrei Rogers and Frans J. Willekens. Dordrecht ; Boston : D. Reidel ; xix, 496 p. ; 25 cm. (GeoJournal library) Includes indexes. Bibliography: p. 475-489. ISBN 90-277-2119-X LC Card 85-25626 DDC 304.8 19
1. Migration, Internal - Cross-cultural studies. 2. Migration, Internal - Case studies. 3. Demography - Cross-cultural studies. I. Rogers, Andrei. II. Willekens, Frans. III. Series.
HB1952 .M539 1986 *NYPL [JLE 86-4091]*

Migration and uneven rural development in Africa . Chilivumbo, Alifeyo. Lanham, MD , c1985. xx, 118 p. : ISBN 0-8191-4929-2 (alk. paper) : LC Card 85-17908 DDC 307.2 19
HB2123.6.A3 C47 1985
NYPL [JLD 86-1953]

MIGRATION, INTERNAL - ADDRESSES, ESSAYS, LECTURES.
Multiregional demography . Laxenburg, Austria , c1984. v, 81 p. : LC Card 84-218929 DDC 304.6 19
HB1951 .M85 1983 *NYPL [JLE 86-583]*

MIGRATION, INTERNAL - AFRICA - ADDRESSES, ESSAYS, LECTURES.
Population and development projects in Africa /. Cambridge [Cambridgeshire] , New York , 1985. xvi, 329 p. : ISBN 0-521-30527-6 LC Card 84-29323 DDC 304.6/096 19
HB2121.A3 P67 1985 *NYPL [JLF 86-186]*

MIGRATION, INTERNAL - AFRICA, EASTERN - CONGRESSES.
Proceedings of the workshop on the "Interrelationship between agricultural settlement, agricultural development, and population change" in selected Eastern Africa Countries, Ethiopia, Kenya, Sudan, and Tanzania, held at the Population Studies and Research Institute, University of Nairobi, April 13-16, 1981. Nairobi [1981] 304 p. : LC Card 85-980248 DDC 338.1/09676 19
HD982.Z63 P76 1981

MIGRATION, INTERNAL - ANDES REGION.
Salazar, Ernesto, 1946- Pioneros de la selva . Quito, Ecuador , 1986. 228 p., [11] leaves of plates : LC Card 87-400290 DDC 338.1/09866/43 19
HD1516.E25 S25 1986

MIGRATION, INTERNAL - ARGENTINA.
Baranger, Dionisio. Migración y marginalidad en Posadas . Posadas , 1982. 53 p. : LC Card 86-205276 DDC 304.8/0982/23 19
HB2020.P67 B37 1982

Lindenboim, Javier. La terciarización del empleo en la Argentina. Buenos Aires , 1985. vi, 59, 50, 3 p. ; LC Card 87-122527 DDC 381 19
HD2346.A73 L56 1985

MIGRATION, INTERNAL - ASIA, SOUTHEASTERN - CONGRESSES.
Seminar on the Effect of Internal Migration, Urbanization, and Resettlement in the IGCC Region on its Population/Family Planning Programmes (1980 : Jakarta, Indonesia) Seminar on the Effect of Internal Migration, Urbanization, and Resettlement in the IGCC Region on its Population/Family Planning Programmes . Kuala Lumpur, Malaysia [1980?] 131 p. : LC Card 81-941408
HB2101 .S45 1980

MIGRATION, INTERNAL - BOLIVIA.
Wiggins, Steve. Colonización en Bolivia /. Sucre, Bolivia [1976?] iv, 112 p. : LC Card 83-203672
HD486 .W54 1976

MIGRATION, INTERNAL - BRAZIL.
Milone, Paulo Cesar. População, migração e desenvolvimento econômico . São Paulo , 1986. 150 p. : LC Card 87-118486 DDC 304.6/0981 19
HB3563 .M45 1986

Spindel, Cheywa R. Espaços de socialização e exploração do menor assalariado . São Paulo, SP , 1986. 254 p. ; LC Card 87-405001 DDC 331.3/1/0981 19
HD6276.B72 S67 1986

MIGRATION, INTERNAL - BRAZIL - RONDÔNIA (STATE)
5 anos de migração em Rondônia, 1979/83 /. Porto Velho , 1984. 7, [19] leaves : LC Card 87-151286 DDC 304.8/0981/75 19
HB2024.R65 A12 1984

MIGRATION, INTERNAL - CAMEROON.
Barbier, J. C. Migrations et développement . Paris , 1983, c1984. 372 p. : ISBN 2-7099-0711-7
NYPL [M-11 4991 no.170]

MIGRATION, INTERNAL - CASE STUDIES.
Migration and settlement . Dordrecht ; Boston : xix, 496 p. ; ISBN 90-277-2119-X LC Card 85-25626 DDC 304.8 19
HB1952 .M539 1986 *NYPL [JLE 86-4091]*

MIGRATION, INTERNAL - CHILE.
Lira, Luis Felipe. Estructura agraria, crecimiento de la población y migraciones . Santiago, Chile , 1976. 90 p. ; LC Card 83-169710
HB2025 .L57 1976

MIGRATION, INTERNAL - COLOMBIA.
Reproducción de fuerza de trabajo, educación y migración en el sector rural colombiano /. Bogotá, Colombia , 1985. 98, [52] p. : LC Card 87-402979 DDC 331.1/09861 19
HD5757.A6 R46 1985

MIGRATION, INTERNAL - COLOMBIA - NARIÑO (DEPT.)
Cerón Solarte, Benhur. Contexto socioeconómico de las migraciones internas en Nariño /. Pasto [Colombia] , 1985. i, 276, 51

p. : LC Card 87-102199
HB2028.N37 C47 1985

MIGRATION, INTERNAL - CONGRESSES.
The Future of migration. Paris , Washington, D.C. , 1987. 319 p. : ISBN 92-64-12949-9 (pbk.) : LC Card 87-163484 DDC 304.8/094 19
HB1952 .F88 1987

Policies of population redistribution /. Oulu , 1981. 199 p. : ISBN 951-675-071-0 (pbk.) LC Card 83-148782 DDC 304.8 19
HB1952 .P65 1981

Projecting migration for integrated rural and urban development planning. Liege, Belgium , c1980. 46 p. ; LC Card 84-221919 DDC 304.8 19
HB1952 .P76 1980
NYPL [JLL 77-289 no. 16]

MIGRATION, INTERNAL - CROSS-CULTURAL STUDIES.
Migration and settlement . Dordrecht ; Boston : xix, 496 p. ; ISBN 90-277-2119-X LC Card 85-25626 DDC 304.8 19
HB1952 .M539 1986 ***NYPL [JLE 86-4091]***

MIGRATION, INTERNAL - DEVELOPING COUNTRIES - ADDRESSES, ESSAYS, LECTURES.
Labour circulation and the labour process /. London [England] , Dover, N.H. , c1985. xvi, 416 p. : ISBN 0-7099-3342-8 : LC Card 84-14306 DDC 331.12/791 19
HD5856.D44 L33 1984
NYPL [JLD 86-2532]

MIGRATION, INTERNAL - DEVELOPING COUNTRIES - CONGRESSES.
ASA Conference, Migrants, Workers, and the Social Order (1986 : University of Kent) Migrants, workers, and the social order /. London , New York , 1987. p. cm. ISBN 0-422-61680-X (pbk.) LC Card 87-10253
HD5856.D44 A72 1986

MIGRATION, INTERNAL - ECUADOR.
Salazar, Ernesto, 1946- Pioneros de la selva . Quito, Ecuador , 1986. 228 p., [11] leaves of plates : LC Card 87-400290 DDC 338.1/09866/43 19
HD1516.E25 S25 1986

MIGRATION, INTERNAL - ECUADOR - CASE STUDIES.
Mariano, Alfonso, José, Lorenzo, Manuel . Quito, Ecuador , 1985. 128 p., [8] leaves of plates : LC Card 86-136793
HD1531.E2 M37 1985

MIGRATION, INTERNAL - EGYPT.
Ibrahim, Saad Eddin. Internal migration in Egypt . Cairo, Egypt [1982] 86, viii p. : LC Card 84-960007 DDC 304.8/0962 19
HB2121.7.A3 I27 1982

MIGRATION, INTERNAL - ETHIOPIA.
Malhuret, Claude. Mass deportations in Ethiopia /. [Paris] [1985] 65 leaves ; LC Card 86-181587 DDC 333.3/1/63 19
HD979 .M34 1985

Niggli, Peter, 1950- [Äthiopien, Deportationen und Zwangsarbeitslager. English.] Ethiopia, deportations and forced-labour camps . [Berlin , 1986] 86 p., [1] leaf of plates : LC Card 87-131977 DDC 333.3/1/63 19
HD979 .N3413 1986

MIGRATION, INTERNAL - EUROPE - CONGRESSES.
The Future of migration. Paris , Washington, D.C. , 1987. 319 p. : ISBN 92-64-12949-9 (pbk.) : LC Card 87-163484 DDC 304.8/094 19
HB1952 .F88 1987

MIGRATION, INTERNAL - EUROPE, EASTERN.
Migrace a osídlení v socialistických zemích =. Praha , 1984- v. <1 > : LC Card 87-160334
HB2041 .M526 1984

Rakovskiĭ, S. N. (Sergeĭ Nikolaevich) Migrat͡sii naselenii͡a v zarubezhnykh sotsialisticheskikh stranakh Evropy . Moskva , 1983. 152 p. ; LC Card 85-181642
HB2041 .R35 1983

MIGRATION, INTERNAL - EUROPE - HISTORY - 19TH CENTURY.
Labor migration in the Atlantic economies . Westport, Conn. , 1985. xvi, 491 p. : ISBN 0-313-24637-8 (lib. bdg. : alk. paper) LC Card 85-7975 DDC 331.12/7 19
HD8375 .L33 1985 ***NYPL [JLE 86-1127]***

MIGRATION, INTERNAL - EUROPE, SOUTHERN - CONGRESSES.
The Future of migration. Paris , Washington, D.C. , 1987. 319 p. : ISBN 92-64-12949-9 (pbk.) : LC Card 87-163484 DDC 304.8/094 19
HB1952 .F88 1987

MIGRATION, INTERNAL - FRANCE - CONGRESSES.
Colloque Les Périphéries urbaines (1984 : Angers, France) Actes du Colloque Les Périphéries urbaines . Caen , c1985. 270 p. : ISBN 2-905461-03-9 : LC Card 86-173712
HB2263 .C65 1984

MIGRATION, INTERNAL - FRANCE - ROUSSILLON (PROVINCE) - HISTORY.
Iglésies, Josep, 1902- El moviment de població de les comarques de la Catalunya de sobirania francesa en el curs dels segles XIX i XX /. Barcelona , 1979. 63 p. ; LC Card 81-120813
HB3620.C3 I325 1979

MIGRATION, INTERNAL - GERMANY - HISTORY.
Population, labour, and migration in 19th- and 20th-century Germany /. Leamington Spa [UK] ; New York : xii, 200 p. : ISBN 0-85496-503-3 : LC Card 86-24470 DDC 331.6/2/0943 19
HD5856.G3 P66 1987

MIGRATION, INTERNAL - GERMANY (WEST)
Fuchs, Gerhard, 1939- Die Bundesrepublik Deutschland . Stuttgart , 1983. 296 p. : ISBN 3-12-922191-3 LC Card 83-166769 DDC 330.943/087 19
HD656 .F8 1983 ***NYPL [JLE 86-578]***

MIGRATION, INTERNAL - GERMANY (WEST) - NECKAR RIVER (REGION)
Heinzmann, Ute. Umzugsverhalten der Bevölkerung in ausgewählten ländlichen Teilräumen am Beispiel der Region Neckar-Alb . Tübingen , 1985. 69, [4] p. : LC Card 86-195573
HB2056.N43 H45 1985

MIGRATION, INTERNAL - GERMANY (WEST) - RHINELAND-PALATINATE - HISTORY.
Migration und Dorfkultur . Stuttgart , 1984. viii, 429 p. : ISBN 3-515-04199-0 LC Card 85-131269
HB2056.R53 M54 1984

MIGRATION, INTERNAL - GERMANY (WEST) - RUHR (REGION)
Nahwanderungen im Ruhrgebiet, 1976-1984 /. Essen , c1986. 61 p. : ISBN 3-923494-67-X LC Card 87-408772 DDC 330.943/55 19
HC288.R8 N34 1986

MIGRATION, INTERNAL - GHANA.
Arhin, Kwame. The expansion of cocoa production in Ghana . [Ghana] [1985] xiii, 137 p., [5] p. of plates : LC Card 86-222543 DDC 338.1/7374/09667 19
HD8039.C6362 G42 1985

MIGRATION, INTERNAL - GOVERNMENT POLICY - BRAZIL.
Brazil. Ministério do Interior. Secretaria de Planejamento. Programa nacional de apoio às migrações internas /. Brasília , 1980. 42 p. ; LC Card 86-203543 DDC 362.8/5 19
HB2023 .B73 1980

MIGRATION, INTERNAL - GOVERNMENT POLICY - INDONESIA - HISTORY - 20TH CENTURY.
Otten, Mariël. Transmigrasi . Copenhagen , c1986. 254 p. : LC Card 87-144670 DDC 333.3/1/598 19
HD896 .O88 1986

MIGRATION, INTERNAL - GREAT BRITAIN.
Jackson, J. A. (John Archer), 1929- Migration /. London , New York , 1986. 91 p. : ISBN 0-582-48052-3 LC Card 85-13098 DDC 304.8/0941 19
HB2043 .M54 1986 ***NYPL [JLD 86-2119]***

MIGRATION, INTERNAL - GREECE - HISTORY - 17TH CENTURY.
Dokos, Kōnstantinos. Hē Sterea Hellas kata ton Henetotourkikon polemon, 1684-1699 kai ho Salōnōn Philotheos /. Athēnai , 1985. 255 p. ; LC Card 86-211599
HB2092.5.A3 D64 1985

MIGRATION, INTERNAL - HUNGARY - CONGRESSES.
Árucsere és migráció . Miskolc , 1986. 237 p. : ISBN 963-01-6995-9 : LC Card 87-409685
HD5856.H9 A78 1986

MIGRATION, INTERNAL - HUNGARY - STATISTICS.
Harcsa, István. Vándorlás, mobilitás, keresetalakulás . Budapest , 1987. 86 p. ; ISBN 963-340-812-1 : LC Card 87-409641
HB2052.5.A3 H37 1987

MIGRATION, INTERNAL - INDIA.
Khan, Najma. Studies in human migration /. New Delhi , 1983. vi, 275 p. ; LC Card 83-907120 DDC 304.8/0954 19
HB3639 .K48 1983 ***NYPL [JLD 86-4136]***

Studies in migration . Delhi , 1986. x, 400 p. : ISBN 81-85054-08-8 : LC Card 86-902753 DDC 304.8/0954 19
HB2099 .S78 1986

MIGRATION, INTERNAL - INDIA - BIBLIOGRAPHY.
Khan, Najma. Studies in human migration /. New Delhi , 1983. vi, 275 p. ; LC Card 83-907120 DDC 304.8/0954 19
HB3639 .K48 1983 ***NYPL [JLD 86-4136]***

MIGRATION, INTERNAL - INDIA - KARNATAKA.
Prabhakara, N. R. Internal migration and population redistribution in India . New Delhi , 1986, c1985. xi, 117 p. ; LC Card 86-902406 DDC 304.8/0954/87 19
HB2100.K37 P73 1985

MIGRATION, INTERNAL - INDIA - STATISTICS.
Hobbs, Frank. Demographic estimates, projections, and selected social characteristics of the population of India /. Washington, D.C. [1986] vii, 148 p. : LC Card 87-601294 DDC 304.6/0954/021 19
HA4585 .H63 1986

MIGRATION, INTERNAL - INDONESIA.
Kebschull, Dietrich. Transmigration in Indonesia . Hamburg , 1984. xxiv, 134 p. ; LC Card 86-223779 DDC 304.8/09598 19
HB2107 .K4 1984

MIGRATION, INTERNAL - INDONESIA - SULAWESI SELATAN.
Migrasi /. Ujung Pandang , 1985. xi, 205 p. : LC Card 87-940461
HB2108.S8 M54 1985

MIGRATION, INTERNAL - IRELAND.
Rottman, David B. The population structure and living circumstances of Irish travellers . Dublin , 1986. 134 p. : ISBN 0-7070-0084-X (pbk.) : LC Card 86-215759 DDC 330.9417 s 305.5/68 19
HC257.I6 E3 no. 131 DX217

MIGRATION, INTERNAL - LATIN AMERICA - CONGRESSES.
Fachtagung "Bevölkerungsentwicklung, Bevölkerungswanderung und Urbanisierung in Lateinamerika" (1984 : Eichstätt, Germany) Desarrollo demográfico, migraciones y urbanización en América Latina . Regensburg , c1986. 432 p. : LC Card 86-181152
HB3530.5.A3 F33 1984

MIGRATION, INTERNAL - LIBYA.
Khalaf Allāh, Ramaḍān ʻUraybī. Ḥarakat al-quwá al-ʻāmilah wa-al-tanmiyah al-iqlīmiyah fī Lībiyā /. Ṭarābulus, al-Jamāhīrīyah al-ʻArabīyah al-Lībīyah al-Shaʻbīyah al-Ishtirākīyah , 1984. 279 p. : LC Card 86-965535
HB2121.6.A3 K47 1984

MIGRATION, INTERNAL - MATHEMATICAL MODELS.
Raschke, Freddy, 1950- Bevölkerungsstruktur, Mobilität und Lohn . Frankfurt am Main , New York , c1985. vi, 194 p. : ISBN 3-8204-5697-X LC Card 85-221450
HD4911 .R37 1985

MIGRATION, INTERNAL - MEXICO.
Gregory, Peter. The myth of market failure . Baltimore , 1986. viii, 299 p. ; ISBN 0-8018-3343-4 : LC Card 85-45927 DDC 331.12/0972 19
HD5731.A6 G74 1986 ***NYPL [JLE 86-3065]***

Mora, Teresa. La Mixteca baja, su migración . México, D.F. , 1982. 129, [84] leaves ; LC

Card 87-122391 DDC 304.6/0972/74 19
HB3532.O18 M67 1982

MIGRATION, INTERNAL - MEXICO - ADDRESSES, ESSAYS, LECTURES.
Los Factores del cambio demográfico en México /. México, D.F. , 1984. 422 p. : ISBN 968-231-281-7 LC Card 85-231767
HB1361 .F33 1984 ***NYPL [JLE 87-753]***

MIGRATION, INTERNAL - MEXICO - STATISTICS.
Indicadores de la migración en México. México, D.F. , 1985. ix, 161 p. ; ISBN 968-89200-3-7 LC Card 86-217222
HB1991 .I55 1985

MIGRATION, INTERNAL - MEXICO - YUCATAN.
Villanueva, Eric. Crisis henequenera y movimientos campesinos en Yucatán, 1966-1983 /. México, D.F. , 1985. 220 p., [10] p. of plates : ISBN 968-603-803-5 LC Card 86-118134 DDC 304.8/0972/65 19
HD9156.H463 M67 1985
NYPL [JLD 87-342]

MIGRATION, INTERNAL - NEPAL.
Kansakar, Vidya Bir Singh. Migration and employment in the tea estates of Nepal /. Kathmandu , 1985. vii, 87, iv, xvii p. ; LC Card 86-903522 DDC 331.12/5372/095496 19
HD8039.T182 N355 1985

MIGRATION, INTERNAL - NETHERLANDS.
Dijk, Jouke van. Migratie en arbeidsmarkt /. Assen , 1986. 239 p. : ISBN 90-232-2213-X : LC Card 86-215033
HB2065 .D54 1986

MIGRATION, INTERNAL - NIGERIA - ILORIN.
Watts, Susan J. Population mobility and multilocality in Ilorin, Kwara State, Nigeria /. [Liverpool , 1981-] v. <1 > : LC Card 86-226489 DDC 304.8/09669/5 19
HB2126.7.I46 W37 1981

MIGRATION, INTERNAL - PARAGUAY.
El Fenómeno migratorio en el Paraguay /. Asunción, Paraguay [1985] 258 p. : LC Card 86-100044
HB2033 .F45 1985

MIGRATION, INTERNAL - PERU.
Migraciones laborales en el Perú . [Monterrico] [c1984] 47 p. : LC Card 84-235623 DDC 331.12/7985 19
HD5761 .M53 1984 ***NYPL [JLF 86-799]***

MIGRATION, INTERNAL - PHILIPPINES.
Nguiagain, Titus, 1953- Trends and patterns of internal migration in the Philippines, 1970-1980 /. [Quezon] [1986] 41 p. ; LC Card 87-120929 DDC 304.8/09599 19
HB2109 .N48 1986

MIGRATION, INTERNAL - PHILIPPINES - ILOCOS NORTE - CASE STUDIES.
Findley, Sally E. Rural development and migration . Boulder , 1987. xxiii, 308 p. : ISBN 0-8133-7326-3 (pbk. : alk. paper) : LC Card 86-33987 DDC 304.8/09599 19
HB2110.I43 F56 1987

MIGRATION, INTERNAL - POLAND.
Witkowski, Janusz. Migracje a ruchliwość społeczna ludności w Polsce /. Warszawa , 1985. 168 p. : LC Card 86-175948
HB2068.7.A3 W58 1985

MIGRATION, INTERNAL - POLAND - STATISTICS.
Migracje wewnętrzne ludności . Warszawa , 1980. xvi, 389 p. ; LC Card 86-215694
HB2068.7.A3 M54 1980

MIGRATION, INTERNAL - PORTUGAL.
A População de Portugal /. [Lisbon] , 1976. 116 p., [1] folded leaf of plates : LC Card 85-204353
HB3621 .P67 1976

MIGRATION, INTERNAL - PRINCE EDWARD ISLAND.
Prince Edward Island's migration patterns . [Charlottetown, P.E.I.] [1986] 40 leaves : LC Card 87-165892 DDC 304.8/09717 19
HB1990.P74 P75 1986

MIGRATION, INTERNAL - SOUTH AFRICA.
Kok, P. C. Black migration to the PWV complex . Pretoria , 1985. viii, 79 p. : ISBN 0-7969-0313-1 (pbk.) : LC Card 86-232836 DDC 304.8/0968 19
HB2123.4.P68 K65 1985

MIGRATION, INTERNAL - SOUTH AFRICA - TRANSKEI.
May, Julian. Migrant labour in Transkei . Durban , 1985. 34, vii p. ; ISBN 0-86980-467-7 (pbk.) : LC Card 86-190553 DDC 331.6/2/0968791 19
HD5856.S6 M39 1985

MIGRATION, INTERNAL - SOUTH ASIA - ADDRESSES, ESSAYS, LECTURES.
Population redistribution and development in South Asia /. Dordrecht , Boston , 1985. 243 p. : ISBN 90-277-1938-1 : LC Card 84-26260 DDC 304.8/0959 19
HB2096.5 .P66 1985 ***NYPL [JLE 86-3852]***

MIGRATION, INTERNAL - SPAIN.
Emigración y retorno . [Madrid] , 1981. 325 p., [2] folded leaves of plates : ISBN 84-500-5097-9 LC Card 82-145134 DDC 325.46 19
JV8251 .E49 1981 ***NYPL [JLE 86-3179]***

MIGRATION, INTERNAL - SPAIN - CATALONIA - HISTORY.
Iglésies, Josep, 1902- El moviment de població de les comarques de la Catalunya de sobirania francesa en el curs dels segles XIX i XX /. Barcelona , 1979. 63 p. ; LC Card 81-120813
HB3620.C3 I325 1979

MIGRATION, INTERNAL - SRI LANKA - STATISTICS.
Sri Lanka census of population and housing, 1981. [Colombo] , 1985. 3 v. in 1 ; LC Card 86-903509 DDC 304.6/09549/3021 19
HA4570.8 .A4 1981b

MIGRATION, INTERNAL - SWITZERLAND.
Interregionale Wanderungen in der Schweiz . Zürich , c1978. 2 v. : LC Card 85-215084
HB2083 .I57 1978

MIGRATION, INTERNAL - THAILAND.
Goldstein, Sidney, 1927- Urban-rural migration differentials in Thailand /. [Bangkok] , 1974. 49 p. ; LC Card 78-301310 DDC 301.36/1
HB2104.55.A3 G64
NYPL [JLM 83-719 no.12]

MIGRATION, INTERNAL - THAILAND - BANGKOK REGION.
Kānsamrūat kānyāithin kh [Bangkok] [1986] 57, 165 p. ; LC Card 87-915769
HB2104.55.B36 K35 1986

MIGRATION, INTERNAL - THAILAND - BANGKOK REGION - STATISTICS.
Kānsamrūat kānyāithin kh [Bangkok] [1986] 57, 165 p. ; LC Card 87-915769
HB2104.55.B36 K35 1986

MIGRATION, INTERNAL - THAILAND - KHON KAEN (PROVINCE)
Kānsamrūat kānyāithin kh [Bangkok] [1986] 57, 165 p. ; LC Card 87-915769
HB2104.55.B36 K35 1986

MIGRATION, INTERNAL - THAILAND - KHON KAEN (PROVINCE) - STATISTICS.
Kānsamrūat kānyāithin kh [Bangkok] [1986] 57, 165 p. ; LC Card 87-915769
HB2104.55.B36 K35 1986

MIGRATION, INTERNAL - TOGO.
Akakpo-Ahianyo, Anani. Contribution à l'étude des migrations au Togo /. Lomé , 1976. 108 p., [5] p. of plates : LC Card 87-150756
HB2125.8.A3 A38 1976

MIGRATION, INTERNAL - UNITED STATES.
Forecasting interstate migration with limited data . Iowa City , 1982. 37 p. :
NYPL [*ZT-1564 no.33]

Rogerson, Peter. Job turnover and interregional migration [microform] /. Iowa City , 1981. 25 p. : ***NYPL [*ZT-1564 no.31]***

MIGRATION, INTERNAL - UNITED STATES - HISTORY - 19TH CENTURY.
Schapiro, Morton Owen. Filling up America . Greenwich, Conn. , c1986. xiii, 149 p. : ISBN 0-89232-675-1 : LC Card 86-2771 DDC 304.6/0973 19
HB3505 .S33 1986 ***NYPL [JLE 86-3386]***

MIGRATION, INTERNAL - UNITED STATES - STATISTICS.
Goreham, Gary. South Dakotans on the move . Brookings, S.D. [1984] 24 p. : LC Card 85-620511 DDC 304.8/09783/021 19
HB1985.S8 G67 1984

MIGRATION, INTERNAL - ZAMBIA.
Stepwise migration. Lusaka [1981] 34, 3, 2 p. : LC Card 85-980416
HB2123.6.A3 S74 1981

Migration of Asian workers to the Arab world / edited by Godfrey Gunatilleke. Tokyo, Japan : United Nations University, c1986. v, 358 p. ; 24 cm. Includes bibliographies. ISBN 92-808-0555-X (pbk.) LC Card 87-131112 DDC 331.6/2/50174927 19
1. Alien labor, Asian - Arab countries. 2. Emigrant remittances - Asia. I. Gunatilleke, Godfrey.
HD8656 .M53 1986

Migration of Sudanese . Abu Gabal, Sayed Ahmed. [Khartoum] , 1984. 18, [14] p. ; LC Card 86-980176 DDC 331.6/2/6240174927 19
HD8766 .A65 1984

Migration und Dorfkultur : Untersuchungen in Abwanderungsregionen des Landes Rheinland-Pfalz / herausgegeben von Herbert Schwedt. Stuttgart : F. Steiner Verlag Wiesbaden, 1984. viii, 429 p. : ill. ; 24 cm. (Mainzer Studien zur Sprach- und Volksforschung. 7) "Die Arbeit von Almut Hoffmann-Hempler wurde vom Fachbereich 13 Philologie I der Johannes Gutenberg-Universität zu Mainz 1984 als Dissertation zur Erlangung des akademischen Grades des Doktors der Philosophie (Dr. phil.) angenommen." Bibliography: p. 395-420. CONTENTS. - Abwanderung und Dorfkultur / Herbert Schwedt -- Infrastruktur / Peter Bahn -- Fremdenverkehr in einem Abwanderungsgebiet / Almut Hoffmann-Hempler. ISBN 3-515-04199-0 LC Card 85-131269
1. Rural-urban migration - Germany (West) - Rhineland-Palatinate - History. 2. Migration, Internal - Germany (West) - Rhineland-Palatinate - History. 3. Rhineland-Palatinate (Germany) - Rural conditions. I. Schwedt, Herbert.
HB2056.R53 M54 1984

Migration und ihre sozialen Folgen . Korte, Hermann, 1937- Göttingen , c1983. 170 p. ; ISBN 3-525-85366-1 LC Card 84-150019
HD8458.A2 K65 1983

Migration und psychische Belastung . Busch, Angelika. Berlin , 1983. 351 p. ; ISBN 3-496-00733-8 LC Card 83-193476
HD8458.I8 B87 1983

Migrations des explusés du Nigéria. Dovi-Sodemekou, Folly B. (Folly Bebey) Emploi et éducation dans le 2e plan de développement économique et social du Togo /. Lomé, Togo [1985] 89, 52, 9, 2 p. : LC Card 87-131183
HD5846.5.A6 D68 1985

Migrations et développement . Barbier, J. C. Paris , 1983, c1984. 372 p. : ISBN 2-7099-0711-7
NYPL [M-11 4991 no.170]

Migrations rurales et urbanisation en République populaire du Congo. Addis Ababa : Bureau international du travail, Programme des emplois et des compétences techniques pour l'Afrique, 1984. x, 168 p. : ill. ; 29 cm. "Version provisoire." Bibliography: p. 113-120. LC Card 84-980878
1. Rural-urban migration - Congo (Brazzaville). 2. Urbanization - Congo (Brazzaville). 3. Congo (Brazzaville) - Population, Rural. 4. Congo (Brazzaville) - Economic conditions. I. Jobs and Skills Programme for Africa.
HB2125.A3 M54 1984

MIGRATORY WORKERS. see **MIGRANT LABOR.**

Migrat͡sii naselenii͡a v zarubezhnykh sot͡sialisticheskikh stranakh Evropy . Rakovskiĭ, S. N. (Sergeĭ Nikolaevich) Moskva , 1983. 152 p. ; LC Card 85-181642
HB2041 .R35 1983

Migrat͡sii͡a i rasselenie v sot͡sialisticheskikh stranakh. Migrace a osídlení v socialistických zemích =. Praha , 1984- v. <1 > : LC Card 87-160334
HB2041 .M526 1984

Mihalik, István. Tanulmányok az anyagi érdekeltség, jövedelemszabályozás témaköréből /. [Budapest] , 1985. 126 p. : ISBN 963-673-308-2 LC Card 86-147619
HD5022.5 .T37 1985

Mihçiyazgan, Ursula. Wir haben uns vergessen : ein intrakultureller Vergleich türkischer

Lebensgeschichten / Ursula Mihçiyazgan. Hamburg : E.B.-Verlag Rissen, c1986. 428 p. ; 21 cm. (Pädagogische Beiträge zur Kulturbegegnung . Bd. 4) Bibliography: p. 422-428. ISBN 3-923002-30-0 : LC Card 87-104026
1. Alien labor, Turkish - Germany (West) - Cross-cultural studies. 2. Sociology - Biographical methods. I. Title. II. Series.
HD8458.T9 M54 1986

Mihelič, Darja. Neagrarno gospodarstvo Pirana od 1280 do 1340 = La produzione non rurale di Pirano dal 1280 al 1340 / Darja Mihelič. Ljubljana : Slovenska akademija znanosti in umetnosti, 1985. 244 p., [12] p. on folded leaves : ill. ; 24 cm. (Dela / Slovenska akademija znanosti in umetnosti, Razred za zgodovinske in družbene vede. Zgodovinski inštitut Milka Kosa = Opera / Academia Scientiarum et Artium Slovenica, Classis I, Historia et Sociologia . 27. 8) Summary in Italian. Bibliography: p. [9]-13. Includes indexes. LC Card 86-202646
1. Piran (Slovenia) - Economic conditions. I. Title. II. Title: Produzione non rurale di Pirano dal 1280 al 1340. III. Series: Dela (Slovenska akademija znanosti in umetnosti. Razred za zgodovinske in družbene vede) , 27.
HC407.Z7 P576 1985

Mikesell, Raymond Frech.
The global copper industry : problems and prospects / Raymond F. Mikesell. London ; New York : Croom Helm, c1988. p. cm. (Croom Helm commodity series) Bibliography: p. Includes index. ISBN 0-7099-3508-0 LC Card 87-23073 DDC 338.2/743 19
1. Copper industry and trade. I. Title.
HD9539.C6 M53 1988

Nonfuel minerals : foreign dependence and national security / Raymond F. Mikesell. Ann Arbor : University of Michigan Press, c1987. xii, 257 p. : ill. ; 24 cm. "A Twentieth Century Fund book." Bibliography: p. 215-243. Includes index. ISBN 0-472-10083-1 : LC Card 86-27247 DDC 333.8/5/0973 19
1. Nonfuel minerals industry - United States. 2. Nonfuel minerals industry - Government policy - United States. 3. Strategic materials - Government policy - United States. I. Title.
HD9506.U62 M42 1987

The world mining industry : investment strategy and public policy / Raymond F. Mikesell, John W. Whitney. Boston : Allen & Unwin, 1987. p. cm. (World industry studies . 6) Bibliography: p. Includes index. ISBN 0-04-338120-0 (alk. paper) LC Card 87-1763 DDC 338.2 19
1. Mineral industries - Finance. 2. Mineral industries - Government policy. I. Whitney, John W. (John Wallis). II. Title. III. Series.
HD9506.A2 M525 1987

Mikhaĭlin, I. V. (Igor′ Viktorovich) Baranova, T. N. (Tat′i͡ana Nikolaevna) Rabochiĭ klass Ispanii boretsi͡a . Moskva , 1978. 151 p. ; LC Card 81-147187
HD8586.5 .B37 1978

Mikhaĭlov, I. V. (Ivan Vasil′evich)
Ėkonomicheskie interesy i uskorenie nauchno-tekhnicheskogo progressa . Leningrad , 1984. 157 p. ; LC Card 86-186728
HC340.T4 E36 1984

Mikhaĭlov, V. V. (Vram Vagramovich) Tarify i rezhimy ėlektropotreblenii͡a / V.V. Mikhaĭlov. 2-e izd., perer. i dop. Moskva : Ėnergoatomizdat, 1986. 214 p. : ill. ; 21 cm. (Ėkonomii͡a topliva i ėlektroėnergii) Bibliography: p. 212-[213] LC Card 86-108009
1. Electric utilities - Soviet Union - Rates. I. Series: Ėkonomii͡a topliva i ėlektroėnergii (Ėnergoatomizdat (Firm)). II. Title.
HD9685.S762 M55 1986

Mikhaĭlova, L. Manolov, Manol Dimitrov. Narodnai͡a Respublika Bolgarii͡a--40 let po puti sotsialisticheskogo voskhoda /. [Bulgaria? , 1983?] [48] p. : LC Card 85-133679
HC403 .M36 1983

Mikhaĭlova, Tati͡ana. Zhecheva, Marii͡a. Informatsionno osiguri͡avane na profsi͡uiuznite organi . Sofii͡a , 1985. 138 p. : LC Card 86-192068
HD6782 .Z44 1985

Mikheev, S.
Glossary of economic and social terminology in Eastern European socialist countries / S. Mikheev, R. Ray. Geneva : International Institute for Labour Studies, 1986. 52, x p. ; 24 cm. (Research series . no. 85) At head of title: Quality of working life. Bibliography: p. 52. ISBN 92-9014-413-0 : LC Card 86-214600 DDC 335.4/03/21 19
1. Economics - Dictionaries. 2. Europe, Eastern - Economic policy - Dictionaries. 3. Marxian economics - Dictionaries. I. Ray, R. II. Title. III. Title: Quality of working life. IV. Series: Research series (International Institute for Labour Studies) , no. 85.
HB61 .M487 1986

Remuneration in Eastern European countries / S. Mikheev, R. Ray. Geneva : International Institute for Labour Studies, 1985. vi, 45, ix p. ; 24 cm. (Research series (International Institute for Labour Studies) . no. 82) At head of title: Quality of working life. Bibliography: p. 42-45. ISBN 92-9014-408-4 (pbk.) : LC Card 86-216036 DDC 331.2/947 19
1. Wages - Europe, Eastern. 2. Bonus system - Europe, Eastern. 3. National income - Europe, Eastern. I. Ray, R. II. Title. III. Title: Quality of working life. IV. Series. V. Series: Research series (International Institute for Labour Studies) , no. 82.
HD5014 .M55 1985

Mikhin, A. A. (Al′bert Afanas′evich) Povyshenie ėffektivnosti raboty morskogo transporta / A.A. Mikhin. Moskva : "Transport", 1985. 110, [2] p. ; 22 cm. Bibliography: p. [111] LC Card 86-115398
1. Merchant marine - Soviet Union - Personnel management. I. Title.
HE848 .M55 1985

Mikkelsen, Britha. Kongstad, Per. Industri, fagbevægelse og lønarbejde i Kenya . Roskilde [1983] 76 p. ; LC Card 85-238103
HC865 .K66 1983

Mikl-Horke, Gertraude, 1944- Organisierte Arbeit : Einführung in die Arbeitssoziologie / von Gertraude Mikl-Horke. München : R. Oldenbourg, c1984. vii, 230 p. : ill. ; 24 cm. Bibliography: p. [227]-228. Includes index. ISBN 3-486-28481-9 (pbk.) LC Card 87-672757
1. Industrial sociology. I. Title.
HD6955 .M54x 1984

Mikolaschek, Cornelia. Freizeit als Gegenstand der Politik : Konzepte der Parteien und Verbände / Cornelia Mikolaschek, Peter Mikolaschek. Frankfurt [am Main] ; New York : Campus, c1984. 202 p. : ill. ; 21 cm. (Campus Forschung. Bd. 370) Bibliography: p. 193-202. ISBN 3-593-33346-5 LC Card 84-175844
1. Labor and laboring classes - Germany, West - Recreation. 2. Leisure - Germany, West. I. Mikolaschek, Peter. II. Title.
HD7395.R4 M55 1984

Mikolaschek, Peter. Mikolaschek, Cornelia. Freizeit als Gegenstand der Politik . Frankfurt [am Main] , New York , c1984. 202 p. : ISBN 3-593-33346-5 LC Card 84-175844
HD7395.R4 M55 1984

Mikroelektronik-Anwendung und ihre Bedeutung für die Qualifikationen . Gensior, Sabine. Berlin , 1986. 39, 118 p. ; LC Card 87-409403 DDC 338/.06 19
HD6331.2.G27 G46 1986

Mikroelektronik, Jobkiller oder Jobknüller? . Poppe, Jürgen. Pfaffenweiler , 1984. 93 p. : ISBN 3-89085-027-8 : LC Card 85-129494
HD6331.2.G28 P66 1984

Mikromesaies kai megales epicheirēseis stēn Hellēnikē viomēchania. Athēna : ICAP, 1982. 32 p. ; 28 cm. Includes bibliographical references. LC Card 85-152476
1. Industries, Size of - Greece. I. ICAP Hellas, S.A.
HD69.S5 M54 1982

Mikroökonomische Theorie der personellen Einkommens- und Vermögensverteilung . Pohmer, Karlheinz. Berlin , New York , c1985. ix, 214 p. : ISBN 0-387-15174-5 (U. S.) LC Card 85-164096
HB523 .P64 1985

Mikroökonomische Modelle des städtischen Verkehrs . Pauck, Reinhard. Baden-Baden , 1983. 295 p. : ISBN 3-7890-0779-X LC Card 83-157997 DDC 388.4/0724 19
HE305 .P39 1983 ***NYPL [JLD 87-977]***

Mikułowski-Pomorski, Jerzy. Prace z zakresu socjologii /. Kraków , 1979. 137 p. ; LC Card 80-129964
HB9 .K53 nr. 117 HC340.3.Z7K7

Mikul′skiĭ, Konstantin Ivanovich.
Problema tempov ėkonomicheskogo rosta v sovremennom mire /. Moskva , 1986. 383 p. : LC Card 87-124359
HC244 .P747 1986

Tromlakova, E. M. (Elena Mikhaĭlovna) Ėffektivnost′ proizvodstva v evropeĭskikh stranakh SĖV /. Moskva , 1986. 157 p. ; LC Card 86-233225
HC244.Z9 I5188 1986

Mikus, Werner. Struktur- und Entwicklungsprobleme der Industrie Perus /. Heidelberg , c1985. 338 p. : ISBN 3-88326-165-3 LC Card 86-108518 DDC 338.0985 19
HC227 .S77 1985

Las mil caras del movimiento social boliviano /. Sandoval, Godofredo. La Paz, Bolivia [1986] 132 p. : LC Card 86-227792
HD6608.5 .S25 1986

Mil quatrocentos e sessenta dias no império do sol . Malvezzi, Roberto. São Paulo , 1985. 197 p. : ISBN 85-05-00296-2 : LC Card 85-200637
HC188.N6 M34 1985

El milagro y la crisis . Bacha, Edmar Lisboa. México , 1986. 468 p. : ISBN 968-16-2152-2 LC Card 87-400019 DDC 338.981 19
HC187 .B128 1986

Milanesi, Marica, 1947- Commercio in Lombardia /. Milano , c1986- v. <1 > : LC Card 87-158732
HF3589.L65 C65 1986

Milano, Carol.
Lewis, William, 1946- The Prentice-Hall directory of executive search firms /. New York , c1986. v, 328 p. ; ISBN 0-671-55518-9 (pbk.) LC Card 85-30190 DDC 658.4/07111/02573 19
HD38.25.U6 L49 1986 ***NYPL [*R-Econ. 87-1586]***

Lewis, William, 1946- Profitable careers in nonprofit /. New York , c1987. vi, 202 p. ; ISBN 0-471-83699-0 (pbk.) : LC Card 87-6102 DDC 331.7/02 19
HF5382.5.U5 L44 1987

Milano, centro finanziario internazionale /. Sury, Paul de. [Milano] [1984] viii, 138 p. : ISBN 88-14-00312-2 : LC Card 86-114645
HG3090.M52 S87 1984

Milanović, Branko. Jugoslovenska privreda između stagnacije i razvoja /. Beograd , 1986. viii, 298 p. : LC Card 87-151260
HC407 .J83 1986

Milcherzeugnis-Nachfrage unter veränderten Marktbedingungen . Schmidt, Erich, 1941- Münster-Hiltrup , 1985. vii, 89 p. : ISBN 3-7843-0320-X : LC Card 87-408713 DDC 338.1/8 19
HD9282.G2 S29 1985

Milei, Lajos. Gazdaságpolitikánk az élenjáró vállalatok gyakorlatában . [Budapest] , 1985. 276 p. : ISBN 963-09-2769-1 : LC Card 87-407761
HD70.H8 G39 1985

Miles, Don G. Systems economics . Ames , 1987. xvii, 252 p. : ISBN 0-8138-1738-2 LC Card 86-27586 DDC 330 19
HB171 .S99 1987

Miles, Mike E. Wurtzebach, Charles H. Modern real estate /. New York , c1987. xii, 772 p. : ISBN 0-471-84890-5 LC Card 86-23412 DDC 333.33/0973 19
HD1375 .W873 1987

Miles, Robert, 1950- Capitalism and unfree labour : anomaly or necessity? / Robert Miles. London ; New York : Tavistock Publications ; 250 p. : ill. ; 24 cm. Bibliography: p. [226]-247. Includes index. ISBN 0-422-61730-X LC Card 87-3599 DDC 331.11/734 19
1. Capitalism. 2. Wages. 3. Labor policy. 4. Slave labor - Cross-cultural studies. 5. Labor and laboring classes. I. Title. II. Title: Capitalism and unfree labor.
HB501 .M654 1987

Milgate, Murray. The New Palgrave . New York , c1987. p. cm. ISBN 0-935859-10-1 (set) : LC Card 87-1946 DDC 330/.03/21 19
HB61 .N49 1987

Milhano, Vicente. Problemas sociais e económicos : concentração? ou descentralização? : ecos do II Congresso da Indústria e dos Economistas : 1957-1958 /

Vicente Milhano. Covilhã : Livraria Nacional, 1958. 185 p. ; 22 cm. LC Card 86-126181 DDC 338.09469 19
1. Portugal - Industries - Congresses. 2. Portugal - Industries - Location - Congresses. I. Title.
HC392 .M58 1958

Milhouse, Virginia Hall, 1950- Henderson, George, 1932- International business and cultures . New York, NY , 1987. p. cm. ISBN 0-943025-03-6 : LC Card 87-24378 DDC 658/.049 19
HF1008 .H46 1987

Milieubeleidsplan Noord-Holland 1982-1988 . North Holland (Netherlands) [Haarlem] [1987] 60 p. ; LC Card 87-159912
HC327.N6 N67 1987

Milieuvervuiling en milieubeleid economisch bekeken /. Kock, Suzan de, 1949- Antwerpen [1977] 140 p. ; ISBN 90-289-0313-1 : LC Card 78-384758
HC320.E5 K6 *NYPL [JLD 80-3195]*

Milimo, J. T. Rural small enterprises in Zambia : results of a country-wide survey / by J.T. Milimo, Yacob Fisseha. [Lusaka] : University of Zambia, Rural Development Studies Bureau, [1985] 71 p. ; 29 cm. (Report / University of Zambia, Rural Development Studies Bureau . no. 25) "September 1985." Bibliography: p. 70-71. LC Card 87-980231 DDC 338.6/42/096894 19
1. Small business - Zambia. 2. Rural industry - Zambia. I. Fisseha, Yacob. II. University of Zambia. Rural Development Studies Bureau. III. Series: Report / University of Zambia, Rural Development Studies Bureau , no. 25. IV. Title.
HD2346.Z29 M55 1985

Militärmarken /. Maier, Lotte. Dortmund , 1981. 158 p. : ISBN 3-88379-253-5 (kart.) : LC Card 81-180793
HE6184.S42 M35 1981

"Militant" library series .

The militant worker . Lash, Scott. London , 1984. vii, 264 p. ; ISBN 0-435-82516-X LC Card 87-673366
HD8076 .L37x 1984b

Militär, Rüstung, Sicherheit .
(Bd. 29) Müller, Erwin, 1947- Rüstungspolitik und Rüstungsdynamik . Baden-Baden , 1985. 378 p. ; ISBN 3-7890-1076-6 LC Card 85-154502
HC110.D4 M85 1985

(Bd. 32) Entwicklung und Rüstung . Baden-Baden , 1984. 303 p. ; ISBN 3-7890-1068-5 LC Card 85-175510
HC79.D4 E58 1984

(Bd. 37) Zivile Alternativen für die Rüstungsindustrie /. Baden-Baden , 1986. 174 p. ; ISBN 3-7890-1262-9 LC Card 87-108651 DDC 338.4/76234/0943 19
HD9743.G48 Z58 1986

MILITARISM, ANTI. see **MILITARISM.**

MILITARISM - ECONOMIC ASPECTS.
Vlas'evich, IU. E. (IUriĭ Evlampievich) Ėkonomicheskoe bremia militarizma /. Moskva , 1980. 181 p. ; LC Card 81-134793
HC79.D4 V58 1980

MILITARY AERONAUTICS EQUIPMENT INDUSTRY.
Military electro-optics markets. Norwalk, Conn., U. S.A. (6 Prowitt St., Norwalk 06855) , c1986. vi, 238 leaves : LC Card 86-226982 DDC 380.1/456234 19
HD9744.P732 M55 1986

MILITARY ASSISTANCE, AMERICAN.
Ferrari, Paul L. U. S. arms exports . Washington, DC , c1987. xii, 342 p. : ISBN 0-931035-12-0 (pbk.) LC Card 87-80032 DDC 382/.456234/0971 19
HD9743.U6 F47 1987

Trends in foreign aid, 1977-86 . Washington , 1986. vii, 21 p. : LC Card 87-601358 DDC 338.91/73 19
HC60 .T69 1986

MILITARY ASSISTANCE, AMERICAN - ASIA, SOUTHEASTERN - CONGRESSES.
U. S. ASEAN relations . Washington, D.C. , 1987. xxii, 222 p. ; ISBN 0-943057-00-0 (pbk.) LC Card 87-50526 DDC 337.59073 19
HF1456.5.A7 U72 1987

MILITARY ASSISTANCE, AMERICAN - DEVELOPING COUNTRIES.
May, Bernhard. Reagan und die Entwicklungsländer . München , 1987. xiv, 271 p. ; ISBN 3-486-53981-7 LC Card 87-139481 DDC 337.730172/4 19
HF1456.5.D44 M39 1987

MILITARY ASSISTANCE, AMERICAN - POLITICAL ASPECTS - DEVELOPING COUNTRIES.
Guess, George M. The politics of United States foreign aid /. New York , 1987. 297 p. ; ISBN 0-312-00448-6 : LC Card 86-26301 DDC 338.91/09172/4 19
HC60 .G7383 1987

MILITARY ASSISTANCE, FRENCH.
Kolodziej, Edward A. Making and marketing arms . Princeton, N.J. , c1987. xxv, 518 p. : ISBN 0-691-07734-7 (alk. paper) : LC Card 86-30567 DDC 338.4/76234/0944 19
HD9743.F82 K64 1987

MILITARY AUTOMATIC CHECKOUT EQUIPMENT INDUSTRY - UNITED STATES.
The Military test equipment market in the U. S. New York, N.Y. (106 Fulton St., New York 10038) , c1983. iv, 245 p. : LC Card 87-142060 DDC 381/.45621381/0287 19
HD9743.U6 M545 1983

MILITARY-CIVIL RELATIONS. see **MILITARISM.**

MILITARY COMMUNICATION EQUIPMENT INDUSTRY - EUROPE.
The Military tactical communications switching network market in West Europe. New York, N.Y. , c1983. xvi, 232 p. ; LC Card 87-141849
HD9744.C653 E854 1983

Military electro-optics markets. Norwalk, Conn., U. S.A. (6 Prowitt St., Norwalk 06855) : International Resource Development Inc., c1986. vi, 238 leaves : ill. ; 28 cm. (Report / International Resource Development Inc. . #711) "October 1986." LC Card 86-226982 DDC 380.1/456234 19
1. Precision guided munitions industry. 2. Military aeronautics equipment industry. 3. Market surveys. I. International Resource Development, inc. II. Series: Report / International Resource Development Inc. , #711.
HD9744.P732 M55 1986

MILITARY GOVERNMENT - LATIN AMERICA - ADDRESSES, ESSAYS, LECTURES.
Petras, James F., 1937- Latin America . Totowa, N.J. , 1986. xi, 187 p. ; ISBN 0-8476-7505-X : LC Card 86-1885 DDC 337.8 19
HC125 .P4643 1986 *NYPL [JLE 86-4366]*

Military Government of Germany (U. S.) see **Germany (Territory under Allied Occupation, 1945-1955. U. S. Zone). Office of Military Government.**

MILITARY HISTORY, MODERN - 20TH CENTURY.
Escalation and intervention . Boulder, Colo. , 1986. x, 181 p. ; ISBN 0-8133-7200-3 : LC Card 86-4020 DDC 327.1/6 19
U104 .E83 1986 *NYPL [JLE 86-4131]*

MILITARY PLANNING.
Williams, Geoffrey Lee. Global defence . New Delhi , c1984. xlvi, 366 p. ; ISBN 0-7069-2478-9 : LC Card 84-900260 DDC 355/.0335 19
UA11 .W55 1984 *NYPL [JLD 86-3709]*

MILITARY POLICY.
Nuclear winter and national security . Maxwell Air Force Base, Ala. , Washington, D.C. , 1986. xiii, 76 p. ; LC Card 86-7967 DDC 355/.0217 19
U263 .N845 1986 *NYPL [JFE 87-751]*

Rumble, Greville. The politics of nuclear defence . Cambridge [Cambridgeshire] , 1985. xi, 285 p. ; ISBN 0-7456-0194-4 : LC Card 85-18643 DDC 355/.0217 19
U263 .R86 1985 *NYPL [JLD 86-1092]*

Shepherd, William G. The ultimate deterrent . New York , 1986. x, 137 p. ; ISBN 0-275-92368-1 (alk. paper) : LC Card 86-20486 DDC 355/.03 19
UA10.5 .S524 1986 *NYPL [JLE 87-884]*

Williams, Geoffrey Lee. Global defence . New Delhi , c1984. xlvi, 366 p. ; ISBN 0-7069-2478-9 : LC Card 84-900260 DDC 355/.0335 19
UA11 .W55 1984 *NYPL [JLD 86-3709]*

MILITARY POWER. see **DISARMAMENT.**

MILITARY RESEARCH - EUROPE.
Greenwood, David. The SDI and Europe /. Aberdeen, Scotland [1985] 64 p. ; LC Card 86-150232 DDC 355/.07/094 19
U395.E85 G73 1985 *NYPL [JFG 87-57]*

MILITARY SERVICE, COMPULSORY - GREAT BRITAIN - HISTORY - 20TH CENTURY.
Grieves, Keith. The politics of manpower, 1914-1918 /. New York, NY , 1988. vii, 241 p. ; ISBN 0-312-01320-5 LC Card 87-20511 DDC 331.12/042/0941 19
HD5765.A6 G77 1988

MILITARY SOCIOLOGY. see **SOCIOLOGY, MILITARY.**

Military spending and industrial decline . DiFilippo, Anthony, 1950- Westport, Conn. , c1986. x, 199 p. ; ISBN 0-313-25179-7 (lib bdg. : alk. paper) LC Card 85-27144 DDC 338.4/7621902/0973 19
HD9703.U5 D54 1986
NYPL [JLD 86-2930]

The Military tactical communications switching network market in West Europe. New York, N.Y. : Frost & Sullivan, c1983. xvi, 232 p. ; 29 cm. Spine title: Tactical military communications in Europe. "April 1983." "#E512." LC Card 87-141849
1. Military communication equipment industry - Europe. 2. Telecommunication swtiching systems equipment industry - Europe. 3. Market surveys - Europe. I. Frost & Sullivan. II. Title: Tactical military communications in Europe.
HD9744.C653 E854 1983

The Military test equipment market in the U. S. New York, N.Y. (106 Fulton St., New York 10038) : Frost & Sullivan, c1983. iv, 245 p. : ill. ; 29 cm. "August 1983." "#A1213." LC Card 87-142060 DDC 381/.45621381/0287 19
1. Military automatic checkout equipment industry - United States. 2. Market surveys - United States. I. Frost & Sullivan.
HD9743.U6 M545 1983

Militer autrement /. Tozzi, Michel. Bruxelles, Belgique , Lyon, France [1985] 162 p. ; ISBN 2-85008-067-5 : LC Card 86-178750
HD6684 .T66 1985

Milivojević, Marko, 1957- The debt rescheduling process / Marko Milivojević. London : F. Pinter, 1985. xvi, 240 p. : ill. ; 23 cm. Bibliography: p. 222-231. Includes index. ISBN 0-86187-575-3 LC Card 87-672863
1. Loans, Foreign - Developing countries. 2. Debts, External - Developing countries. I. Title.
HG3891.5 .M55x 1985b

Miljøstatistik og lidt forureningsøkonomi . Møllmann Boye, Erik. [Århus] , 1978. 53 leaves : LC Card 86-460199
HC79.P55 M65 1978

Milk, meat biscuits, and the terraqueous machine . Wade, Mary Dodson. Austin, Tex. , c1987. 49 p. : ISBN 0-89015-605-0 : LC Card 87-6813 DDC 338.7/664/00924 B 92 19
HD9010.B65 W33 1987

MILK - PRICES - GOVERNMENT POLICY - GERMANY (WEST)
Schmidt, Erich, 1941- Milcherzeugnis-Nachfrage unter veränderten Marktbedingungen . Münster-Hiltrup , 1985. vii, 89 p. : ISBN 3-7843-0320-X : LC Card 87-408713 DDC 338.1/8 19
HD9282.G2 S29 1985

MILK - PRICES - GOVERNMENT POLICY - UNITED STATES.
State milk regulation . [Washington, D.C.] (1301 New York Ave., N.W., Washington 20005-4788) [1986] viii, 62 p. ; LC Card 86-602413 DDC 338.1/771/0973 19
HD9282.U4 S72 1986

MILK TRADE - AZORES.
Casaca, José Paulo Martins. O papel do sector leiteiro no desenvolvimento económico dos Açores . Ponta Delgada , 1985. 260, [16] p., [1] leaf of plates : LC Card 86-167454
HD9282.A962 C37 1985

MILK TRADE - BRAZIL.
Souza, Francisco Araújo Salles de. O estado e o cartel do leite no Brasil /. Brasília, Distrito

Federal , 1981. 130 p. : LC Card 81-217015
HD9282.B72 S65 1981 *NYPL [JLD 86-3366]*

MILK TRADE - BRAZIL - GOIÁS (STATE) - STATISTICS.
Insumos estatísticos para o diagnóstico da pecuária no Estado de Goiás /. [Goiânia-Goiás] [19]84. 156 leaves : LC Card 86-178269
HD9424.B73 G655 1984

MILK TRADE - BRAZIL - PARANÁ (STATE) - COSTS.
Custo de produção . Curitiba, Paraná , 1987. 88 p. ; LC Card 87-405296 DDC 338.1/371/098162 19
HD9282.B73 P3435 1987

MILK TRADE - GOVERNMENT POLICY - AZORES.
Casaca, José Paulo Martins. O papel do sector leiteiro no desenvolvimento económico dos Açores . Ponta Delgada , 1985. 260, [16] p., [1] leaf of plates : LC Card 86-167454
HD9282.A962 C37 1985

MILK TRADE - GOVERNMENT POLICY - UNITED STATES.
Federal milk marketing orders . [Ames, Iowa] [1986] 50 p. : LC Card 86-229061 DDC 338.1/771/0973 19
HD9282.U4 F43 1986

State milk regulation . [Washington, D.C.] (1301 New York Ave., N.W., Washington 20005-4788) [1986] viii, 62 p. ; LC Card 86-602413 DDC 338.1/771/0973 19
HD9282.U4 S72 1986

MILK TRADE - GOVERNMENT POLICY - URUGUAY.
Forteza, Alvaro. Efectos de la política económica en el mercado de leche fluida /. Montevideo, Uruguay [1986] 126 p. : LC Card 87-121158
HD9282.U72 F67 1986

MILK TRADE - HUNGARY.
Csatorday, Géza. A szállítási rendszer fejlesztési lehetőségeinek vizsgálata a tejiparban /. Budapest , 1985. 94 p. : ISBN 963-491-216-8 LC Card 86-199210
HE199.5.M5 C73 1985

MILK TRADE - INDIA - MADHYA PRADESH.
Mergos, George, 1948- Dairy development and milk cooperatives . Washington, D.C. [1987] xiv, 140 p. : ISBN 0-8213-0932-3 (pbk.) LC Card 87-15976 DDC 334/.68371/09543 19
HD9282.I53 M286 1987

MILK - TRANSPORTATION.
Csatorday, Géza. A szállítási rendszer fejlesztési lehetőségeinek vizsgálata a tejiparban /. Budapest , 1985. 94 p. : ISBN 963-491-216-8 LC Card 86-199210
HE199.5.M5 C73 1985

Milke, Harry. Auf sicherem Kurs . [Berlin] [1976] 80 leaves (some folded) : LC Card 85-190579
HC290.78 .A84 1976

Milkin, Petŭr. 40 brigadirski leta /. Sofiia , 1986. 173 p., [12] p. of plates : LC Card 87-103049
HD4870.B9 A15 1986

Milkovich, George T. Compensation / George T. Milkovich, Jerry M. Newman. 2nd ed. Plano, Tex. : Business Publications, 1987. xiv, 655 p. : ill., forms ; 24 cm. Ill. on lining papers. Includes bibliographical references and indexes. ISBN 0-256-03709-4 LC Card 86-72247 DDC 658.3/2 19
1. Compensation management. I. Newman, Jerry M. II. Title.
HF5549.5.C67 M54 1987

Mill family . McHugh, Cathy. New York , 1988. p. cm. ISBN 0-19-504299-9 LC Card 87-7832 DDC 331.7/67721/0975 19
HD8039.T42 U654 1988

Mill, John Stuart, 1806-1873. Principles of political economy : with some of their applications to social philosophy / by John Stuart Mill ; edited with an introduction by Sir William Ashley. Fairfield, NJ : A.M. Kelley, 1987. liii, 1013 p. ; 21 cm. (Reprints of economic classics) Reprint. Originally published: London ; New York : Longmans, Green, 1909. Bibliography: p. [981]-1004. Includes index. ISBN 0-678-00073-5 LC Card 86-21290 DDC 330 19
1. Economics. I. Ashley, W. J. (William James), Sir, 1860-1927. II. Title.
HB161 .M6 1987

MILL, JOHN STUART, 1806-1873.
Hollander, Samuel. The economics of John Stuart Mill /. Oxford, U.K. , 1985. 2 v. (xx, 1037 p.) ; ISBN 0-631-14045-X (set) LC Card 86-673535
HB103.M7 H64x 1985 *NYPL [JLE 87-951]*

Riley, Jonathan, 1955- Liberal utilitarianism . Cambridge [Cambridgeshire] , New York , 1987. p. cm. ISBN 0-521-30692-2 LC Card 87-6598 DDC 302/.13 19
HB846.8 .R55 1987

Mill, Ulrich. Organisation als soziales System . Berlin , c1986. 219 p. ; ISBN 3-924859-22-1 LC Card 87-137969 DDC 302.3/5 19
HD58.7 .O6687 1986

MILLARD, BILL.
Littman, Jonathan, 1958- Once upon a time in ComputerLand . Tucson, AZ , c1987. xiii, 296 p., [8] p. of plates : ISBN 0-89586-502-5 : LC Card 87-3823 DDC 381/.4500416/0973 19
HD9696.C64 C655 1987

Millard, Patricia. Trade associations and professional bodies of the United Kingdom /. Oxford , New York , 1987. vii, 513 p. ; ISBN 0-08-033390-7 LC Card 87-132682 DDC 062/.025 19
HD2429.G7 T73 1987

Mille villages socialistes en Algérie. Lesbet, Djaffar. Les 1000 villages socialistes en Algérie /. Alger , Paris , c1983. 335 p. : ISBN 2-86738-008-1 : LC Card 84-156989 DDC 335/.00965 19
HX441.5.A6 L47 1983 *NYPL [JLD 87-236]*

MILLENNIALISM - ARGENTINA.
Fogel, Ramón B. Movimientos campesinos en el Paraguay /. Asunción, Paraguay , 1986. 230 p., [1] leaf of plates : LC Card 86-189517
HD1531.P3 F64 1986

MILLENNIALISM - PARAGUAY.
Fogel, Ramón B. Movimientos campesinos en el Paraguay /. Asunción, Paraguay , 1986. 230 p., [1] leaf of plates : LC Card 86-189517
HD1531.P3 F64 1986

Millennium management . Lareau, William. Piscataway, NJ [1986]. ix, 214 p. : ISBN 0-8329-0431-7 : LC Card 86-18247 DDC 658.4/06 19
HD58.8 .L37 1986 *NYPL [JLE 87-1139]*

Miller, Arthur I.
Imagery in scientific thought : creating 20th-century physics / Arthur I. Miller. Boston : Birkhäuser, c1984. xiv, 355 p. : ill. ; 25 cm. "A Pro scientia viva title." Includes index. Bibliography: p. [315]-338. ISBN 0-8176-3196-8 LC Card 83-26649 DDC 502.8 19
1. Science - History. 2. Creative thinking. I. Title.
Q175 .M628 1984 *NYPL [JSE 86-1114]*

Imagery in scientific thought : creating 20th-century physics / Arthur I. Miller.1st MIT Press ed. Cambridge, Mass. : MIT Press, 1986, c1984. xiv, 355 p. : ill. ; 24 cm. Includes index. Bibliography: p. [315]-338. ISBN 0-262-63104-0 (pbk.) : LC Card 85-23212 DDC 502.8 19
1. Science - History. 2. Creative thinking. I. Title.
Q175 .M628 1986 *NYPL [JSE 87-67]*

Miller, Charlotte L.
The French market for U. S. seafood products / Charlotte Miller. Terminal Island, CA : National Marine Fisheries Service, Southwest Region, 1986. ii, 63 p. ; 28 cm. (Administrative report . SWR-86-7) Distributed to depository libraries in microfiche. "June 1986." Bibliography: p. 16. Item 609-C-8 (microfiche) LC Card 86-602854 DDC 382/.4566494/0944 19
1. Fish trade - France. 2. Fish trade - United States. 3. Fish trade - France - Directories. 4. Market surveys - France. I. United States. National Marine Fisheries Service. Southwest Region. II. Series: Administrative report (United States. National Marine Fisheries Service. Southwest Region) , SWR-86-7. III. Title.
HD9462.5 .M54 1986

The market for seafood in the United Kingdom / Charlotte Miller. Terminal Island, CA : National Marine Fisheries Service, Southwest Region, 1986. ii, 73 p. : 1 ill., 1 map ; 28 cm. (Administrative report . SWR-86-8) Distributed to depository libraries in microfiche. "June 1986." Bibliography: p. 17-18. Item 609-C-8 (microfiche) LC Card 87-601563 DDC 382.1/4370941 19
1. Fish trade - Great Britain. 2. Fish trade - United States. 3. Shellfish trade - Great Britain. 4. Shellfish trade - United States. 5. Fish trade - Great Britain - Directories. 6. Shellfish trade - Great Britain - Directories. 7. Market surveys - Great Britain. I. United States. National Marine Fisheries Service. Southwest Region. II. Series: Administrative report (United States. National Marine Fisheries Service. Southwest Region) , SWR-86-8. III. Title.
HD9461.5 .M55 1986

Miller, D. B. Peasants and politics . Melbourne , c1978. 218 p. : ISBN 0-7267-2027-5
NYPL [JLE 81-1456]

Miller, Danny. Kets de Vries, Manfred F. R. Unstable at the top . New York , 1988, c1987. xiv, 221 p. ; ISBN 0-453-00562-4 LC Card 87-23182 DDC 158.7 19
HD58.7 .K475 1988

Miller, Edwin Leroy, 1929- Hildebrandt, Herbert William, 1931- A managerial profile . Ann Arbor, MI , c1985. 31 p. ; ISBN 0-87712-248-2 (pbk.) LC Card 86-621187 DDC 331.4/816584/00973 19
HD6054.4.U6 H55 1985

Miller, Eleanor M., 1948- Statham, Anne. The worth of women's work . Albany , c1988. xiv, 331 p. ; ISBN 0-88706-591-0 LC Card 87-6472 DDC 331.4/0973 19
HD6095 .S73 1988

Miller, Ernest C. (Ernest Conrad), 1912-
Pennsylvania's oil industry / by Ernest C. Miller. 3rd ed., rev. and enlarged. Gettysburg, PA. : Pennsylvania Historical Association, 1974, c1954. iii, 69 p. : ill. ; 23 cm. (Pennsylvania history studies . no. 4) Bibliography: p. 63-68. LC Card 87-100839
1. Petroleum industry and trade - Pennsylvania - History. I. Title. II. Series.
HD9567.P4 M5 1974

Miller, George H.
California real estate appraisal : residential properties / George H. Miller, H. Glenn Mercer, Kenneth W. Gilbeau.3rd ed. Englewood Cliffs, N.J. : Prentice-Hall, c1987. xiv, 348 p. : ill. ; 29 cm. Includes index. ISBN 0-13-112558-3 : LC Card 87-6956 DDC 333.33/2/09794 19
1. Real property - Valuation. 2. Real property - Valuation - California. 3. Dwellings - Valuation. 4. Dwellings - Valuation - California. I. Mercer, H. Glenn. II. Gilbeau, Kenneth W. III. Title.
HD1387 .M545 1987

Residential real estate appraisal : an introduction to real estate appraising / George H. Miller, Kenneth W. Gilbeau.2nd ed. Englewood Cliffs, N.J. : Prentice Hall, c1988. xiv, 336 p. : ill. ; 28 cm. Includes index. ISBN 0-13-762428-X (pbk.) : LC Card 87-6960 DDC 333.33/2 19
1. Real property - Valuation. 2. Dwellings - Valuation. I. Gilbeau, Kenneth W. II. Title.
HD1387 .M547 1988

Miller, Irwin. The health care survival curve : competition and cooperation in the marketplace / Irwin Miller. Homewood, Ill. : Dow Jones-Irwin, c1984. xv, 144 p. ; 24 cm. Includes index. Bibliography: p. 130-137. ISBN 0-87094-481-9 LC Card 83-73714 DDC 338.4/73621/0973 19
1. Medical economics - United States. 2. Health maintenance organizations - United States. 3. Medical policy - United States. 4. Voluntarism - United States. 5. Competition - United States. I. Title.
RA410.53 .M55 1984 *NYPL [JLE 86-4362]*

Miller, James C., III. Spending and deficits / James C. Miller III. Washington, D.C. : American Enterprise Institute for Public Policy Research, c1987. 18 p. ; 23 cm. (The G. Warren Nutter lectures in political economy) Includes bibliographical references. ISBN 0-8447-1382-1 (pbk.) LC Card 87-134671 DDC 339.5/23/0973 19
1. Budget deficits - United States. 2. Government spending policy - United States. I. Title. II. Series.
HJ2052 .M54 1987

Miller, James Clifford. Public choice and regulation . Stanford, Calif. , 1987. xiii, 363 p. ; ISBN 0-8179-8562-X (pbk.) : LC Card 87-3984 DDC 353.0082/6 19
HD3616.U47 P796 1987

Miller, Janice James.
Issues for managers : an international perspective / Janice James Miller, John A. Kilpatrick. Homewood, Ill. : Irwin, 1987. xii, 139 p. : ill. ; 23 cm. (Irwin perspectives in international business) Includes bibliographies and index. ISBN 0-256-05630-7 (pbk.) LC Card 87-80633 DDC 658/.049 19
1. International business enterprises - Management. I. Kilpatrick, John A., 1942-. II. Title. III. Series.
HD62.4 .M54 1987

Miller, Robert R., 1929- Introduction to business . Homewood, Ill. , 1987. x, 138 p. : ISBN 0-256-05628-5 (pbk.) LC Card 86-82593 DDC 658/.049 19
HD62.4 .M55 1987

Miller, Jill. You can't kill the spirit : women in a Welsh mining village / Jill Miller. London : Women's Press, c1986. 142 p. : ill. ; 20 cm. (Women's studies politics) ISBN 0-7043-4021-6 (pbk.) : LC Card 87-100804 DDC 305.4/2/0942995 19
1. Coal Strike, Great Britain, 1984-1985. 2. Coal miners' wives - Wales - Abertillery (Gwent) - Biography. I. Title. II. Series.
HD5365.M6152 1984 .W345 1986

Miller, Kathleen N. Mathematics for business : college course / Kathleen N. Miller.6th ed. New York : Gregg Division, McGraw-Hill, c1988. iv, 252 p. : ill. (some col.) ; 28 cm. Includes index. ISBN 0-07-042061-0 (pbk.) LC Card 87-23089 DDC 513/.93 19
1. Business mathematics. I. Title.
HF5691 .M476 1988

Miller, Lowell. The Wholesale-by-mail catalog, 1987 /. New York [1987] p. cm. ISBN 0-312-00205-X (pbk.) : LC Card 86-27890 DDC 381/.2/02573 19
HF5861 .W527 1987

Miller, Lynn Orr. Consumer guide : best rated mutual funds / author, Lynn Orr Miller. [Skokie, IL] : Publications International, c1986. 64 p. ; 28 cm. (Consumer guide magazine investment series . no. 7) Includes index. LC Card 86-219152 DDC 332.63/27 19
1. Mutual funds. I. Series: Consumer guide investment series , no. 3. II. Title.
HG4530 .M56 1986

Miller, M. H. (Marcus H.) Williamson, John, 1937- Targets and indicators . Washington, DC , 1987. xii, 108 p. : ISBN 0-88132-064-1 LC Card 87-22724 DDC 332.4/5 19
HG3881 .W4936 1987

Miller, Marc L. Social science in natural resource management systems /. Boulder , 1987. xii, 265 p. : ISBN 0-8133-7485-5 (pbk. : alk. paper) LC Card 87-23138 DDC 333.7/0973 19
HC103.7 .S62 1987

Miller, Mark J. Employer sanctions in Western Europe / by Mark J. Miller. Staten Island, N.Y. : Center for Migration Studies of New York, 1987. viii, 67 p. ; 28 cm. (CMS occasional papers and documentation) "A report submitted to the German Marshall Fund of the United States." Bibliography: p. [62]-67. ISBN 0-934733-20-1 (pbk.) : LC Card 86-31739 DDC 331.6/2/094 19
1. Alien labor - Europe. 2. Aliens, Illegal - Europe. 3. Sanctions, Administrative - Europe. I. German Marshall Fund of the United States. II. Title. III. Series.
HD8378.5.A2 M5395 1987

Miller, Norma R. Feingold, S. Norman, 1914- Emerging careers . Garrett Park, Md. , c1983- v. ; ISBN 0-912048-32-8 (pbk.) : LC Card 83-80074 DDC 331.7/02 19
HF5382 .F44 1983 ***NYPL [JLL 86-205]***

Miller, Norman, 1933- Yeager, Rodger. Wildlife, wild death . Albany, NY , c1986. xvi, 173 p. : ISBN 0-88706-168-0 LC Card 86-5791 DDC 333.95/16/09676 19
QL84.6.K4 Y43 1986 ***NYPL [JLE 86-3870]***

Miller, Paul B. W. The FASB : the people, the process, and the politics / Paul B.W. Miller, Rodney J. Redding. Homewood, Ill. : Irwin, 1986. xvi, 145 p. : ill. ; 23 cm. (The Robert N. Anthony/Willard J. Graham series in accounting) Includes bibliographies and indexes. ISBN 0-256-03520-2 LC Card 85-82340
1. Accounting - Standards - United States. I. Redding, Rodney J. II. Title. III. Title: F.A.S.B. IV. Series.
NYPL [JLE 87-872]

Miller, Peter G. The common-sense mortgage : how to cut the cost of home ownership by $100,000 or more / Peter G. Miller.3rd ed. New York : Perennial Library, c1987. xvi, 285 p. ; 22 cm. Includes index. ISBN 0-06-055081-3 : LC Card 86-46265 DDC 332.7/22 19
1. Mortgages. 2. Mortgage loans. 3. Housing - Finance. I. Title.
HG2040 .M54 1987

Miller, Richard Edgar, 1947- EAPs and the information revolution . New York , c1987. 106 p. ; ISBN 0-86656-606-6 LC Card 86-33519 DDC 331.25 19
HF5549.5.E42 E37 1987

Miller, Richard Kendall, 1946- Color machine vision : a market forecast and applications assessment / written by Richard K. Miller. Madison, GA : SEAI Technical Publications, [c1986] 174 leaves : ill. ; 28 cm. Includes bibliographies. ISBN 0-89671-079-3 (pbk.) LC Card 87-116822 DDC 380.1/4500637 19
1. Computer industry. 2. Robot vision. 3. Computer vision. 4. Market surveys. I. Title.
HD9696.C62 M55 1986

Miller, Robert B. (Robert Bruce), 1931-
Conceptual selling : the revolutionary system for face-to-face selling used by America's best companies / Robert B. Miller and Stephen E. Heiman with Tad Tuleja.1st ed. Berkeley, Calif. : Miller-Heiman ; New York, N.Y. : Distributed by H. Holt, c1987. 320 p. : ill. ; 25 cm. Includes index. ISBN 0-8050-0410-6 LC Card 86-29428 DDC 658.8/5 19
1. Selling. I. Heiman, Stephen E. II. Tuleja, Tad, 1944-. III. Title.
HF5438.25 .M566 1987

Miller, Robert B. (Robert Burnham), 1942-
Minitab handbook for business and economics / Robert B. Miller. Boston : PWS-Kent Pub. Co., c1988. x, 331 p. : ill. ; 24 cm. (The Duxbury series in statistics and decision sciences) "Portion of this book previously appeared in Minitab handbook, second edition by Ryan/Joiner/Ryan"--T.p. verso. Bibliography: p. 326. Includes index. ISBN 0-87150-092-2 (pbk.) LC Card 86-32830 DDC 519.5/02855369 19
1. Minitab (Computer system) - Handbooks, manuals, etc. 2. Commercial statistics - Data processing - Handbooks, manuals, etc. 3. Statistics - Data processing - Handbooks, manuals, etc. I. Title. II. Series.
HF1017 .M494 1988

Miller, Robert E. How to compete successfully in a public accounting practice / Robert E. Miller, Jr. Englewood Cliffs, N.J. : Prentice-Hall, c1987. xx, 250 p. ; 25 cm. Includes index. ISBN 0-13-402157-6 LC Card 87-18677 DDC 657/.068 19
1. Accounting firms - Management. I. Title.
HF5627 .M54 1987

Miller, Robert R., 1929- Introduction to business : an international perspective / Robert R. Miller, Janice James Miller. Homewood, Ill. : Irwin, 1987. x, 138 p. : ill. ; 23 cm. (Irwin perspectives in international business) Includes bibliographies and index. ISBN 0-256-05628-5 (pbk.) LC Card 86-82593 DDC 658/.049 19
1. International business enterprises - Management. 2. International economic relations. I. Miller, Janice James. II. Title. III. Series.
HD62.4 .M55 1987

Miller, Roger LeRoy.
Economic issues for consumers / Roger Leroy Miller. 5th ed. St. Paul : West Pub. Co., c1987. xxxv, 526 p. : ill. ; 27 cm. Includes bibliographies and index. ISBN 0-314-30391-X (alk. paper) LC Card 86-24722 DDC 332.024 19
1. Finance, Personal. 2. Consumer education. I. Title.
HG179 .M48 1987

Economics today / Roger LeRoy Miller. 6th ed. New York : Harper & Row, c1988. xxix, 893, [50] p. : ill. ; 28 cm. Includes bibliographies and indexes. ISBN 0-06-044489-4 LC Card 87-18453 DDC 330 19
1. Economics. I. Title.
HB171.5 .M642 1988

North, Douglass Cecil. The economics of public issues /. New York , c1987. ix, 214 p. ; ISBN 0-06-044832-6 (pbk.) LC Card 86-33627 DDC 330.973/092 19
HB34 .N6 1987

Miller, Rory. Region and class in modern Peruvian history /. [Liverpool] , 1987. 207 p. : ISBN 0-902806-20-3 LC Card 87-148309 DDC 330.985/0633 19
HC227 .R386 1987

Miller, Russell.
The house of Getty / Russell Miller. London : M. Joseph, 1985 361 p., [32] p. of plates : ill. ; 24 cm. Includes index. ISBN 0-7181-2601-7 : LC Card 86-222703 DDC 332/.092/4 B 19
1. Getty, J. Paul (Jean Paul), 1892-1976. 2. Getty family. 3. Businessmen - United States - Biography. 4. Millionaires - United States - Biography. 5. Petroleum industry and trade - United States - History. I. Title.
HD9570.G4 M55 1986b

The house of Getty / Russell Miller. Large print ed. South Yarmouth, Ma. : J. Curley, [1987], c1985. 669 p. [16] p. of plates : ill., ports. ; 22 cm. ISBN 1-555-04230-9 LC Card 86-24259 DDC 332/.092/4 B 19
1. Getty, J. Paul (Jean Paul), 1892-1976. 2. Getty family. 3. Businessmen - United States - Biography. 4. Millionaires - United States - Biography. 5. Petroleum industry and trade - United States - History. I. Title.
HD9570.G4 M55 1987

Miller, Shirley. Trade unions in South Africa, 1970-1980 : a directory and statistics / Shirley Miller. Cape Town : Southern Africa Labour and Development Research Unit, 1982. xxxxv, 278 p. ; 30 cm. (Saldru working paper . no. 45) Includes index. ISBN 0-7992-0469-2
1. Trade unions - South Africa - Directories. 2. Trade unions - South Africa - Statistics. I. Title. II. Series.
NYPL [Sc F 86-217]

Miller, Stanley S. Competitive manufacturing : using production as a management tool / Stanley S. Miller. New York : Van Nostrand Reinhold, c1988. ix, 245 p. : ill. ; 24 cm. Bibliography: p. 236-237 Includes index. ISBN 0-442-26395-3 LC Card 87-10484 DDC 658.5/03 19
1. Strategic planning. 2. Production management. I. Title.
HD30.28 .M52 1988

Miller, Thomas C.
Construction lending for income-producing property. Construction lending for income-producing properties : real estate mortgage lending for bankers. Washington, D.C. (1120 Connecticut Ave., N.W. Washington 20036) , c1986. xiv, 163 p. : LC Card 86-209027 DDC 332.1/753 19
HG2040.5.U5 M49 1986

Miller-Tiedeman, Anna, 1934- Lifecareer : the quantum leap into a process theory of career / by Anna Miller-Tiedeman. Vista, CA : Lifecareer Foundation, c1988. v, 65 p. ; 22 cm. Bibliography: p. 59-63. Includes index. ISBN 0-9613436-3-X (pbk.) LC Card 87-17298 DDC 331.7/02 19
1. Vocational guidance. 2. Career development. I. Title.
HF5381 .M496 1988

Miller, William D. (William Dennis), 1953- Bank pricing and valuation / William D. Miller. New York, N.Y. : Executive Enterprises Publications Co., c1988. xiv, 279 p. : ill. ; 28 cm. Bibliography: p. 271-279. ISBN 0-88057-806-8 (pbk.) LC Card 87-81070 DDC 332.1/068/1 19
1. Banks and banking - Valuation. I. Title.
HG1708 .M55 1988

Milliarden für den Geier, oder, Der Fall des Friedrich Flick /. Ohlsen, Manfred. Berlin , 1985. 458 p. : LC Card 86-149056
HC282.5.F54 O35 1985

Millikin, Michael D. Seybold, Patricia B. Integrated desk-top environments . New York , c1985. ix, 181 p. : ISBN 0-07-056324-1 (pbk.) : LC Card 84-27841 DDC 650/.028/5425 19
HF5548.4.S95 S49 1985
NYPL [JSE 86-2011]

Milliman & Robertson, inc. Measuring and funding corporate liabilities for retiree health benefits. Washington, D.C. , c1987. xxxviii, 226 p. : ISBN 0-86643-054-7 (pbk.) LC Card 87-24534 DDC 657/.75 19
HG9396 .M4 1987

Milling, Bryan E. Banking strategies for businesses : a guide for the independent manager / Bryan E. Milling. Radnor, PA : Chilton Book, c1987. viii, 231 p. : ill. ; 24 cm. Includes index. ISBN 0-8019-7651-0 (pbk.) : LC Card 86-47959 DDC 658.1/592 19
1. Small business - Finance. 2. Bank loans. 3.

Investments. 4. Banks and banking. I. Title. II. Title: Guide for the independent manager.
HG4027.7 .M55 1987

Million Dollar Round Table (Des Plaines, Ill.). Bottom Line Task Force. In search of profitability -- agent's business plan /. Des Plaines, Ill.] , c1986. 124 p. : LC Card 87-167903 DDC 368/.0068 19
HG8877 .I49 1986

MILLIONAIRES.
Courchaure, Stéphane. Les riches . [Paris] , c1985. 261 p. ; ISBN 2-7158-0537-3 : LC Card 86-111316 DDC 305.5/234 19
HC79.C6 C68 1985 ***NYPL [JLD 86-4451]***

Heller, Robert, 1932- The age of the common millionaire /. New York , c1987. p. cm. ISBN 0-525-24588-X LC Card 87-19973 DDC 305.5/234 19
HC79.W4 H45 1987

MILLIONAIRES - CANADA.
Francis, Diane. Controlling interest . Toronto, Ont., Canada , c1986. 352 p. ; ISBN 0-7715-9744-4 LC Card 86-218086 DDC 338.8/0971 19
HD2809 .F73 1986

MILLIONAIRES - RESEARCH.
Bergan, Helen, 1937- Where the money is . Alexandria, Va. , c1985. 101 p. : ISBN 0-9615277-0-6 (pbk.) : LC Card 85-72141 DDC 361.7 19
HG177 .B48 1985 ***NYPL [JLD 87-844]***

MILLIONAIRES - UNITED STATES.
Allen, Michael Patrick. The founding fortunes . New York , c1987. p. cm. LC Card 87-9912 DDC 332/.0973 19
HC110.W4 A44 1987

Lapham, Lewis H. Money and class in America . New York , 1988, c1987. p. cm. ISBN 1-555-84109-0 LC Card 87-22515 DDC 305.5/234/0973 19
HC110.W4 L24 1988

Wagman, Robert J. Instant millionaires . [Kensington, Md.] , 1986. 298 p. ; ISBN 0-933149-05-0 (pbk.) : LC Card 86-50285 DDC 795.3/092/2 19
HG6126 .W27 1986

MILLIONAIRES - UNITED STATES - BIOGRAPHY.
Miller, Russell. The house of Getty /. London , 19. 361 p., [32] p. of plates : ISBN 0-7181-2601-7 : LC Card 86-222703 DDC 332/.092/4 B 19
HD9570.G4 M55 1986b

Miller, Russell. The house of Getty /. South Yarmouth, Ma. [1987], c1985. 669 p. [16] p. of plates : ISBN 1-555-04230-9 LC Card 86-24259 DDC 332/.092/4 B 19
HD9570.G4 M55 1987

Shields, Jerry. The invisible billionaire, Daniel Ludwig /. Boston , 1986. xii, 401 p. : ISBN 0-395-35402-1 : LC Card 86-7519 DDC 387.5/092/4 B 19
HE569.L84 S55 1986 ***NYPL [JFE 86-3861]***

MILLIONAIRESSES - RESEARCH.
Bergan, Helen, 1937- Where the money is . Alexandria, Va. , c1985. 101 p. : ISBN 0-9615277-0-6 (pbk.) : LC Card 85-72141 DDC 361.7 19
HG177 .B48 1985 ***NYPL [JLD 87-844]***

Millions in poverty grip . Varma, S. C. New Delhi , 1984. xv, 172 p. ; LC Card 84-900600 DDC 331.12/042/0954 19
HD5710.85.I4 V37 1984
NYPL [JLD 86-4236]

MILLS AND MILL-WORK - HUNGARY - HISTORY - 18TH CENTURY - MAPS.
Malmok, ipari és gazdasági létesítmények az első katonai felmérés térképszelvényein, 1782-1785 /. Budapest , 1982. 220 p., [1] leaf of plates : ISBN 963-01-4433-6 (Magy. nemz. bibl.) LC Card 83-230040
HC300.26 .M35 1982

Mills, Dixie L. Gardner, Mona J. Managing financial institutions . Chicago , c1988. xii, 795 p. : ISBN 0-03-005479-6 LC Card 86-32805 DDC 332.1/068/1 19
HG1615.25 .G37 1988

Mills, Edwin S. Studies in Indian urban development / Edwin S. Mills, Charles M. Becker ; with a contribution by Satyendra Verma. New York : Published for the World Bank [by] Oxford University Press, 1986. viii, 214 p. ; 25 cm. (A World Bank research publication) Includes bibliographies and index. ISBN 0-19-520507-3 : LC Card 86-2489 DDC 307.1/4/0954 19
1. Cities and towns - India - Growth. 2. City planning - India. I. Becker, Charles M., 1954-. II. Verma, Satyendra. III. Title.
HT147.I5 M56 1986 ***NYPL [JLE 86-3750]***

Mills, J. C. (Joseph C.) Price responses of Malawi smallholder farmers--fast, slow or none? [microform] / by J.C. Mills. [Zomba] : Dept. of Economics, University of Malawi, [1975] 42, [2] p. ; 32 cm. (Occasional paper / Dept. of Economics, Chancellor College . no. 2) Cover title. Bibliography: p. [43]-[44] Microfilm. New York : New York Public Library, 1986. 1 microfilm reel ; 35 mm. (MN *ZZ-25,866) LC Card 80-980238 DDC 338.1/3/096897 19
1. Farms, Small - Malawi. 2. Acreage allotments - Malawi. 3. Food prices - Malawi. I. Series: Occasional paper (Chancellor College. Dept. of Economics) , no. 2. 2. II. Title.
HD1476.M33 M54 1975
NYPL [*ZT-1646 no.53]

Mills, John. Gould, Bryan. Monetarism or prosperity? /. London , 1981. x, 222 p. : ISBN 0-333-30782-8 LC Card 86-673392
HG939.5 .G65x 1981

Mills, William R. West, Gary, 1947- Dac-Easy accounting and payroll made easy /. Blue Ridge Summit, PA , c1987. ix, 261 p. : ISBN 0-8306-2914-9 (pbk.) : LC Card 87-10056 DDC 657/.028/55369 19
HF5679 .W47 1987

Millward, Neil. British workplace industrial relations, 1980-1984 : the DE/ESRC/PSI/ACAS surveys / Neil Millward and Mark Stevens. Aldershot, England ; Brookfield, Vt. : Gower Pub. Co., c1986. xxi, 341 p. ; 22 cm. Includes bibliographical references and index. ISBN 0-566-05391-8 : LC Card 86-25625 DDC 331/.0941 19
1. Industrial relations - Great Britain. I. Stevens, Mark, 1947-. II. Title.
HD8391 .M55 1986 ***NYPL [JLD 87-1287]***

Millwood, David. Good aid : a study of quality in small projects / by David Millwood & Helena Gezelius. Stockholm, Sweden : Swedish International Development Authority, c1985. 246 p. : ill. ; 25 cm. Includes bibliographical references. ISBN 91-586-7059-9 (pbk.) : LC Card 87-142767 DDC 338.91/485 19
1. Economic development projects - Nepal. 2. Economic development projects - Tunisia. 3. Economic development projects - Kenya. 4. Economic assistance, Swedish - Nepal. 5. Economic assistance, Swedish - Tunisia. 6. Economic assistance, Swedish - Kenya. I. Gezelius, Helena. II. Title.
HC425.Z9 E446 1985

Milne, Robert D. Broader perspectives on the interest of pension plan participants /. Charlottesville, Va. (P.O. Box 3665, Charlottesville 22903) , c1985. vii, 43 p. : LC Card 85-196669 DDC 332.6/7254 19
HD7105.45.U6 B76 1985
NYPL [JLL 81-133 no. 22]

Mil'ner, Bentsion Zakharovich. Sistemnyĭ podkhod k organizatsii upravleniia / B.Z. Mil'ner, L.I. Evenko, V.S. Rapoport. Moskva : "Ėkonomika", 1983. 223 p. : ill. ; 22 cm. Bibliography: p. 220-[222] LC Card 83-229946
1. Industrial management - Soviet Union. I. Evenko, Leonid Ivanovich. II. Rapoport, Vladimir Samuilovich. III. Title.
HD70.S63 M54 1983

Milner, Chris. Williamson, John, 1937- Political economy and international money . New York , 1987. xii, 292 p. ; ISBN 0-8147-5434-1 : LC Card 86-23484 DDC 332.4/5 19
HG3881 .W4934 1987

Milon munaḥim be-khalkalah ve-nihul 'asaḳim /. Yaḳir, E. (Eli), 1929- Tel-Aviv , 1986. 414, 38 p. : LC Card 87-162041
HB61 .Y25 1986

Milone, Paulo Cesar. População, migração e desenvolvimento econômico : evidências do caso brasileiro / Paulo Cesar Milone. São Paulo : Instituto de Pesquisas Econômicas, 1986. 150 p. : ill. ; 23 cm. (Série Relatórios de pesquisa . no. 34) Bibliography: p. 147-150. LC Card 87-118486 DDC 304.6/0981 19
1. Brazil - Population. 2. Migration, Internal - Brazil. 3. Brazil - Economic policy. I. Title. II. Series.
HB3563 .M45 1986

Milošević, Nikša. Sistem udruženog rada / Nikša Milošević. Beograd : NIO Poslovna politika, 1985. 392 p. : ill. ; 24 cm. (Biblioteka Udžbenici i skripta) In Serbo-Croatian (roman) Bibliography: p. 371-385. LC Card 86-197428
1. Management - Yugoslavia - Employee participation. 2. Yugoslavia - Economic policy - 1945-. 3. Yugoslavia - Politics and government - 1945-. I. Title. II. Series.
HD5660.Y8 M55 1985

MilSal, Taylor. Michaels, Susan. Points, a guide to frequent flyer bonus programs /. New York , c1987. 161 p. : ISBN 0-87052-375-9 (pbk.) : LC Card 87-8681 DDC 387.7/1 19
HF6161.A38 M53 1987

Milton, Arthur, 1922- Milton on America : taking the economic pulse of the U. S.A. / by Arthur Milton. Secaucus, N.J. : Citadel Press, 1987. 192 p., [8] p. of plates : ports. ; 24 cm. ISBN 0-8065-1039-0 : LC Card 87-401577 DDC 330.973/0927 19
1. United States - Economic conditions - 1981-. I. Title.
HC106.8 .M55 1987

Milton Friedman . Butler, Eamonn. Aldershot, Hants, England , c1985. 272 p. : ISBN 0-85117-261-X : ***NYPL [JLD 86-1090]***

Milton on America . Milton, Arthur, 1922- Secaucus, N.J. , 1987. 192 p., [8] p. of plates : ISBN 0-8065-1039-0 : LC Card 87-401577 DDC 330.973/0927 19
HC106.8 .M55 1987

Milwid, Beth, 1948- What you get when you go for it / Beth Milwid. 1st ed. New York : Dodd, Mead, c1987. 248 p. ; 25 cm. Includes index. ISBN 0-396-08905-4 LC Card 86-29084 DDC 331.4/81/000973 19
1. Women in the professions - United States. I. Title.
HD6054.2.U6 M55 1987

Le mimétisme technologique des Tiers-Mondes . Lambert, Denis Clair. Paris , 1983. 223 p. : ISBN 2-7178-0597-4 : LC Card 83-233513
HC59.72.T4 L35 1983

Min, Pyong Gap, 1942- Ethnic business enterprise : the case of Korean small business in Atlanta / by Pyong Gap Min.1st ed. Staten Island, N.Y. : Center for Migration Studies of New York, 1988. p. cm. Bibliography: p. Includes index. ISBN 0-934733-15-5 : LC Card 86-33366 DDC 338.6/422/0899570758231 19
1. Korean American business enterprises - Georgia - Atlanta. I. Title.
HD2346.U52 A845 1988

Mina de Morro Velho . Grossi, Yonne de Souza. Rio de Janeiro, RJ , 1981. 265 p. : LC Card 81-216799 DDC 338.7/6223422/098151 19
HD8039.M74 B65 1981
NYPL [JLD 86-3591]

Mina Swaminathan, 1933- Who cares? : a study of child care facilities for low-income working women in India / Mina Swaminathan. New Delhi : Centre for Women's Development Studies, 1985. xi, 159 p. : ill. ; 23 cm. Bibliography: p. 155-159. LC Card 86-900126
1. Day care centers - India. 2. Women - Employment - India. 3. Poor - India. I. Title.
HV861.I4 M56 1985 ***NYPL [JLD 86-3265]***

La mina vista desde el guardatojo . Escóbar, Filemón, 1936- La Paz, Bolivia , 1986. 77 p. ; LC Card 87-118481 DDC 331.7/622/0984 19
HD8039.M61 B57 1986

Minami, Ryōshin, 1933-
[Nihon no keizai hatten. English]
The economic development of Japan : a quantitative study / Ryōshin Minami ; translated by Ralph Thompson and Ryōshin Minami with assistance from David Merriman. Basingstoke, Hampshire : Macmillan, 1986. xxvi, 487 p. : ill. ; 23 cm. (Studies in the modern Japanese economy) Translation of: Nihon no keizai hatten. Bibliography: p. 460-477. Includes index. ISBN 0-333-38582-9 LC Card 87-672411
1. Japan - Economic conditions. - 1868-. 2. Japan - Economic policy. I. Title. II. Series.
HC462.7 .M47513x 1986b

Minas Geraes, Brazil. see **Minas Gerais, Brazil.**

Minas Gerais, Brazil.
IV plano mineiro de desenvolvimento econômico e social : diretrizes. [Belo Horizonte] : Estado de Minas Gerais, [1983] 347 p. : maps ; 23 cm. LC Card 86-201630
1. Minas Gerais, Brazil - Economic policy. 2. Minas Gerais (Brazil) - Social policy. I. Title. II. Title: Quatro plano mineiro de desenvolvimento econômico e social. III. Title: 4o. plano mineiro de desenvolvimento econômico e social.
HC188.M6 M48 1983

Minas Gerais (Brazil). Conselho Estadual de Energia. Uso de energia na indústria de cimento em Minas Gerais, 1980-1983. [Belo Horizonte] , 1985. 146 p. : LC Card 86-152639
HD9622.B73 M569 1985

MINAS GERAIS, BRAZIL - ECONOMIC CONDITIONS.
Dornas Filho, João. O ouro das Gerais e a civilização da Capitania /. São Paulo , 1957. 238 p., [8] leaves of plates : LC Card 84-215039
HC187 .D72 1957

MINAS GERAIS, BRAZIL - ECONOMIC POLICY.
Banco de Desenvolvimento de Minas Gerais. Perspectivas para a ação do BDMG no período 1983-85. Belo Horizonte, MG, Brasil [1983] 67 p. : LC Card 83-207712
HG2889.M55 B37 1983

Haddad, Paulo Roberto. Dimensões do planejamento estadual no Brasil . Rio de Janeiro , 1985. 188 p. : LC Card 86-195636
HC188.M6 H33 1985

Minas Gerais, Brazil. IV plano mineiro de desenvolvimento econômico e social . [Belo Horizonte] [1983] 347 p. : LC Card 86-201630
HC188.M6 M48 1983

Minas Gerais (Brazil). Grupo de Trabalho de Energia de Biomassa. Seminário de Energia de Biomassa (1985? : Belo Horizonte, Brazil?) Seminário de Energia de Biomassa . [Belo Horizonte?] , <[1986?-. v. <[1-2] > : LC Card 87-107998
HD9502.5.B543 B67 1985

MINAS GERAIS (BRAZIL) - INDUSTRIES - CONGRESSES.
Seminários sobre Perspectivas dos Setores Produtivos de Minas Gerais (1986 : Belo Horizonte, Brazil) Seminários sobre Perspectivas dos Setores Produtivos de Minas Gerais . Belo Horizonte , 1986. 124 leaves ; LC Card 87-108000 DDC 338.0981/51 19
HC188.M6 S46 1986

Minas Gerais (Brazil). Secretaria de Estado da Fazenda.
Secretaria de Estado da Fazenda : políticas e diretrizes. Belo Horizonte : A Secretaria, [1983] 48 p. ; 22 cm. Cover title. LC Card 85-207912
1. Minas Gerais (Brazil). Secretaria de Estado da Fazenda. 2. Finance, Public - Brazil - Minas Gerais. I. Title.
HJ929.M52 M55 1983

MINAS GERAIS (BRAZIL). SECRETARIA DE ESTADO DA FAZENDA.
Minas Gerais (Brazil). Secretaria de Estado da Fazenda. Secretaria de Estado da Fazenda . Belo Horizonte [1983] 48 p. ; LC Card 85-207912
HJ929.M52 M55 1983

Minas Gerais (Brazil). Secretaria de Estado da Fazenda. Assessoria Econômica e Tributária. Economia mineira e o financiamento do setor público . Belo Horizonte , 1985. 126 p. : LC Card 85-207952
HJ2529.M5 E26 1985

MINAS GERAIS (BRAZIL) - SOCIAL POLICY.
Minas Gerais, Brazil. IV plano mineiro de desenvolvimento econômico e social . [Belo Horizonte] [1983] 347 p. : LC Card 86-201630
HC188.M6 M48 1983

Minayo, Maria Cecília de Souza. Os homens de ferro : estudo sobre os trabalhadores da indústria extrativa de minério de ferro da Companhia Vale do Rio Doce em Itabira, Minas Gerais / Maria Cecília de Souza Minayo. Rio de Janeiro : Dois Pontos Editora, 1986. 244 p. : ill. ; 22 cm. Bibliography p. 235-244. LC Card 87-129149 DDC 331.7/622341/098151 19
1. Iron miners - Brazil - Itabira. 2. Iron miners - Brazil - Doce River Valley (Minas Gerais and Espírito Santo). 3. Companhia Vale do Rio Doce - Employees. I. Title.
HD8039.M72 B86 1986

Minbaev, B. M. Sovershenstvovanie khoziaĭstvennogo mekhanizma v usloviiakh razvitogo sotsializma /. Tashkent , 1985. 142, [2] p. ; LC Card 86-220208
HC337.U96 S68 1985

Minc, Alain. L'avenir en face / Alain Minc. Paris : Editions du Seuil, c1984. 255 p. ; 24 cm. (L'Histoire immédiate) Includes bibliographical references. ISBN 2-02-006828-1 : LC Card 84-218171
1. France - Economic policy - 20th century. 2. France - Economic conditions - 20th century. I. Title.
HC276 .M6126 1984 ***NYPL [JLE 87-2165]***

MIND. see **PSYCHOLOGY.**

Mind managers and defiled doordarshan /. Bhat, Vighnesh N., 1951- Jalandhar , 1987. 208 p. ; ISBN 81-7072-011-7 : LC Card 87-900504 DDC 302.2/345/0954 19
HE8700.9.I5 B53 1987

Mind over money . Forman, Norm. Toronto, Ont. , Garden City, N.Y. , 1987. xi, 248 p. ; ISBN 0-385-25104-1 LC Card 86-32814 DDC 332.024 19
HG222.3 .F67 1987

Mind power . Scott, Gini Graham. Englewood Cliffs, N.J. , c1987. xi, 183 p. ; ISBN 0-13-583527-5 LC Card 87-6923 DDC 650.1 19
HF5386 .S413 1987

Mind your own business . Warner, Alice Sizer. New York , c1987. xii, 165 p. ; ISBN 1-555-70014-4 : LC Card 86-23641 DDC 658.1/1 19
HD62.5 .W37 1987

MINDANAO ISLAND (PHILIPPINES) - ECONOMIC CONDITIONS - STATISTICS.
Socio economic factbook of Mindanao. Davao City, Philippines [1985] 568 p. ; LC Card 85-234433
HA4617.M56 S63 1985

MINDANAO ISLAND (PHILIPPINES) - STATISTICS.
Socio economic factbook of Mindanao. Davao City, Philippines [1985] 568 p. ; LC Card 85-234433
HA4617.M56 S63 1985

MINDEN REGION (NORTH RHINE-WESTPHALIA, GERMANY) - ECONOMIC CONDITIONS.
Henning, Friedrich-Wilhelm. Vorindustrielles Gewerbe und wirtschaftlicher Wandel im Paderborner Land im 19. Jahrhundert /. Dortmund , 1983. 67 p. ; LC Card 83-198581
HC288.P27 H46 1983

Minding the public's business. [Ottawa] : Economic Council of Canada, 1986. xii, 180 p. : ill. ; 27 cm. Bibliography: p. [165]-176. ISBN 0-660-12217-0 (pbk.) : LC Card 87-127219 DDC 338.971 19
1. Government business enterprises - Canada. 2. Canada - Economic policy. I. Economic Council of Canada.
HD4005 .M53 1986

MINE ACCIDENTS - GERMANY - HISTORY - SOURCES.
Bis vor die Stufen des Throns . München , c1986. 530 p. : ISBN 3-406-31297-7 LC Card 87-103686 DDC 331.7/622334/0943 19
HD8039.M61 G32 1986

MINE ACCIDENTS - MEXICO - BARROTERÁN.
Arenal, Sandra. Barroterán! . [Mexico City?] , c1984. 116 p. ; ISBN 968-495-016-0 LC Card 85-195552
HD8039.M62 M63 1984

La mine d'argile est notre champ /. Traoré, Aminata. [Abidjan?] [1985] (Abidjan : Société d'impr. ivoirienne) [36] p. : LC Card 86-200373
HD6073.P82 I967 1985

Mine, mill & microchip . Flynt, J. Wayne, 1940- Northridge, Calif. , 1987. 376 p. : ISBN 0-89781-215-8 LC Card 87-9192 DDC 338.09761 19
HC107.A4 F57 1987

Mine, mill, and microchip. Flynt, J. Wayne, 1940- Mine, mill & microchip . Northridge, Calif. , 1987. 376 p. : ISBN 0-89781-215-8 LC Card 87-9192 DDC 338.09761 19
HC107.A4 F57 1987

Mineração meio-ambiente e o planejamento municipal. São Paulo : Associação Brasileira de Geologia de Engenharia, [1982] 24 leaves : ill. ; 30 cm. At head of title: XXVI Congresso dos Municípios do Estado de São Paulo, patrocinio da Associação Paulista dos Municípios e Prefeitura Municipal da Praia Grande, São Paulo, abril 1982. Bibliography: leaves 21-22. LC Card 85-210329
1. Mineral industries - Environmental aspects - Brazil - São Paulo (State). 2. Mining law - Brazil - São Paulo (State). 3. Environmental protection - Brazil - São Paulo (State). I. Associação Brasileira de Geologia de Engenharia.
HD9506.B73 S3664 1982

Mineral bulletin .
(MR 179) Whillans, Robert T. Mineral exploration expenditures in Canada, 1969-1975 /. [Ottawa] , c1978. vi, 13 p. : LC Card 85-182002 DDC 338.2/3 19
HD9506.C2 W45 1978

Mineral development in Bihar, 1979-80 to 1988-89 /. Kalra, G. D. New Delhi , 1983. 2 v. : LC Card 83-905955 DDC 338.2/0954/12 19
HD9506.I43 B545 1983
NYPL [JLE 86-4727]

Mineral exploration expenditures in Canada, 1969-1975 /. Whillans, Robert T. [Ottawa] , c1978. vi, 13 p. : LC Card 85-182002 DDC 338.2/3 19
HD9506.C2 W45 1978

MINERAL INDUSTRIES - ALASKA - RED DOG CREEK WATERSHED.
Alaska. Office of Mineral Development. Red Dog project analysis /. [Juneau?] [1984] 300 p. in various pagings : LC Card 84-622211 DDC 333.8/5/097986 19
HD9506.U63 R422 1984

MINERAL INDUSTRIES - ANTARCTIC REGIONS.
Mitchell, Barbara. Frozen stakes . London , Washington, D.C. , c1983. iii, 135 p. : ISBN 0-905347-45-5 (pbk.) : LC Card 84-173206 DDC 333.8/5/09989 19
HD9506.A585 M57 1983
NYPL [JLD 86-3548]

MINERAL INDUSTRIES - ASIA, SOUTHEASTERN.
The Minerals industries of ASEAN and Australia . Sydney , Boston , 1988. p. cm. ISBN 0-04-301284-1 LC Card 87-18339 DDC 338.2/0959 19
HD9506.A6592 M56 1988

The Pacific challenge in international business /. Ann Arbor, Mich. , 1987. viii, 342 p. ; ISBN 0-8357-1620-1 (alk. paper) LC Card 87-5008 DDC 338.09182/3 19
HC460.5 .P32 1987

MINERAL INDUSTRIES - AUSTRALIA.
The Minerals industries of ASEAN and Australia . Sydney , Boston , 1988. p. cm. ISBN 0-04-301284-1 LC Card 87-18339 DDC 338.2/0959 19
HD9506.A6592 M56 1988

MINERAL INDUSTRIES - BOLIVIA.
Lazarte, Jorge. Crisis de identidad y centralidad minera . [La Paz, Bolivia] [1986] 37 p. : LC Card 87-401455 DDC 331.88/122/0984 19
HD8039.M61 B586 1986

MINERAL INDUSTRIES - BRAZIL.
Análise econômico-financeira da indústria de mineração, 1978-1982 /. Brasília , 1984. viii, 105 p. : LC Card 86-146667
HD9506.B72 A65 1984

Metais de Minas Gerais, S.A. Programa pegmatitos. Belo Horizonte , 1981. 95 p. : LC Card 83-220720
HD9506.B72 M48 1981

Silva, Roberto Gama e. São mesmo nossos os minerais não-energéticos? /. Rio de Janeiro, RJ , 1985. 164 p. : LC Card 86-153246
HD9506.B72 S55 1985

MINERAL INDUSTRIES - BRAZIL - HISTORY.

Dornas Filho, João. O ouro das Gerais e a civilização da Capitania /. São Paulo , 1957. 238 p., [8] leaves of plates : LC Card 84-215039
HC187 .D72 1957

MINERAL INDUSTRIES - CANADA.
Selected readings in mineral economics /. New York , c1987. ix, 399 p. : ISBN 0-08-035864-0 : LC Card 87-8237 DDC 338.2/0971 19
HD9506.C22 S44 1987

MINERAL INDUSTRIES - CHILE.
Zúñiga R., Víctor H. La evolución de la minería no cuprífera en Chile /. Santiago, Chile , 1985. 61 leaves ; LC Card 86-115526
HD9506.C52 Z86 1985

MINERAL INDUSTRIES - DEVELOPING COUNTRIES.
Nwoke, Chibuzo. Third World minerals and global pricing . London [Atlantic Highlands] N.J. , 1987. x, 229 p. : ISBN 0-86232-441-6 : LC Card 87-12621 DDC 338.2/3 19
HD9506.D452 N86 1986

MINERAL INDUSTRIES - DIRECTORIES.
Don Nelson's Mining & mining equipment/service companies world wide . Barnet, Herts., U.K. [1982] 562 p. ; ISBN 946-0-04005-X *NYPL [JSD 86-337]*

MINERAL INDUSTRIES - EAST ASIA.
The Pacific challenge in international business /. Ann Arbor, Mich. , 1987. viii, 342 p. ; ISBN 0-8357-1620-1 (alk. paper) LC Card 87-5008 DDC 338.09182/3 19
HC460.5 .P32 1987

MINERAL INDUSTRIES - ENVIRONMENTAL ASPECTS - BRAZIL - SÃO PAULO (STATE)
Mineração meio-ambiente e o planejamento municipal. São Paulo [1982] 24 leaves : LC Card 85-210329
HD9506.B73 S3664 1982

MINERAL INDUSTRIES - EUROPE - HISTORY - 20TH CENTURY.
Egea Bruno, Pedro María. La minería cartagenera en torno a la primera guerra mundial, 1909-1923 /. [Murcia] , 1983. 76 p. : ISBN 84-86031-30-3 LC Card 85-199662
HD9506.S762 C374 1983

MINERAL INDUSTRIES - FINANCE.
Mikesell, Raymond Frech. The world mining industry . Boston , 1987. p. cm. ISBN 0-04-338120-0 (alk. paper) LC Card 87-1763 DDC 338.2 19
HD9506.A2 M525 1987

MINERAL INDUSTRIES - GERMANY (WEST) - MANAGEMENT - EMPLOYEE PARTICIPATION.
Kauer, Christian, 1951- Konfliktregelung und Mitbestimmung . Frankfurt am Main , New York , c1985. 393 p. : ISBN 3-8204-5626-0 (pbk.) LC Card 87-672045
HD5660.G4 K37x 1985

MINERAL INDUSTRIES - GERMANY (WEST) - NORTH RHINE-WESTPHALIA - STATISTICS-
Zensus im Bergbau und verarbeitenden Gewerbe Nordrhein-Westfalen 1979 . Düsseldorf [1983] 109 p. ; LC Card 87-407314 DDC 943/.55 s 338.2/0943/55021 19
HA1320.N6 A32 Heft 497 HD9506.G23N6

MINERAL INDUSTRIES - GOVERNMENT OWNERSHIP - BOLIVIA.
Diagnóstico general de la Corporación Minera de Bolivia, 1985 . La Paz, Bolivia , 1986. 2 v. ; LC Card 87-401587 DDC 338.2/0984 19
HD9506.B64 C646 1986

MINERAL INDUSTRIES - GOVERNMENT OWNERSHIP - BOLIVIA - HISTORY.
Tórrez G. O., José Guillermo (Torrez Gómez Ortega) Minería e integración boliviana /. La Paz, Bolivia , 1986. 181 p., [8] leaves of plates : LC Card 87-400195 DDC 338.2/0984 19
HD9506.B64 C67 1986

MINERAL INDUSTRIES - GOVERNMENT OWNERSHIP - PERU.
Aste Daffos, Juan. Minería peruana . Lima , 1986. 102 p. ; LC Card 87-143088 DDC 338.2/0985 19
HD9506.P42 A827 1986

MINERAL INDUSTRIES - GOVERNMENT POLICY.
Mikesell, Raymond Frech. The world mining industry . Boston , 1987. p. cm. ISBN 0-04-338120-0 (alk. paper) LC Card 87-1763 DDC 338.2 19
HD9506.A2 M525 1987

MINERAL INDUSTRIES - GOVERNMENT POLICY - ALASKA.
Maas, Kenneth M. Availability of land for mineral exploration and development in northern Alaska, 1986 /. [Washington, D.C.] [1987] iv, 34 p. : LC Card 86-607920 DDC 333.73 19
HD243.A3 M32 1987

MINERAL INDUSTRIES - GOVERNMENT POLICY - BOLIVIA.
Diagnóstico general de la Corporación Minera de Bolivia, 1985 . La Paz, Bolivia , 1986. 2 v. ; LC Card 87-401587 DDC 338.2/0984 19
HD9506.B64 C646 1986

MINERAL INDUSTRIES - GOVERNMENT POLICY - BRAZIL.
Silva, Roberto Gama e. São mesmo nossos os minerais não-energéticos? /. Rio de Janeiro, RJ , 1985. 164 p. : LC Card 86-153246
HD9506.B72 S55 1985

MINERAL INDUSTRIES - GOVERNMENT POLICY - CANADA, NORTHERN.
The Northern mineral sector . Ottawa [1985] 37, 37 p. : ISBN 0-662-53700-9 (pbk.) LC Card 85-162718 DDC 338.2/0971 19
HD9506.C23 N6758 1985
NYPL [JLF 86-175]

MINERAL INDUSTRIES - GOVERNMENT POLICY - SPAIN - ANDALUSIA.
Plan económico para Andalucía, 1984-1986 /. Andalucía [1985?] 164 p. ; ISBN 84-505-0611-5 LC Card 86-205786
HD3616.S495 A536 1985

MINERAL INDUSTRIES - HISTORY.
Harvey, Charles E. The Rio Tinto Company . Penzance, Cornwall , 1981. xiv, 390 p. : ISBN 0-906720-03-6 : LC Card 82-127720 DDC 338.8/87 19
HD9506.G74 R564 1981
NYPL [JLD 86-2605]

MINERAL INDUSTRIES - HUNGARY - CONGRESSES.
A Bányászat műszaki, gazdasági szakembereinek II. ágazati tanácskozása . [Budapest , 1979] (Szolnok : NKFV Nyomda) 83 p. ; LC Card 82-205242
HD9506.H92 B36 1979

MINERAL INDUSTRIES - INDIA - ANDHRA PRADESH.
Saibaba, G. Labour conditions in the mining industry of Andhra Pradesh . Tirupati [1985?] v, 314 p. ; LC Card 86-901021 DDC 331/.0422/095484 19
HD8039.M61 I47 1985
NYPL [JLD 87-1057]

MINERAL INDUSTRIES - INDIA - BIHAR.
Kalra, G. D. Mineral development in Bihar, 1979-80 to 1988-89 /. New Delhi , 1983. 2 v. : LC Card 83-905955 DDC 338.2/0954/12 19
HD9506.I43 B545 1983
NYPL [JLE 86-4727]

MINERAL INDUSTRIES - ITALY - MONTEMASSI - HISTORY.
Pertempi, Silvia. Montemassi . Torino , 1986. 238 p. ; ISBN 88-7011-250-0 : LC Card 87-134525
HD9506.I83 M656 1986

MINERAL INDUSTRIES - ITALY - STATISTICS.
Wagner, Hermann, Dr. Italien /. Hannover , Stuttgart , 1982. xv, 190 p., 4 folded leaves of plates : LC Card 83-235644
HD9506.I82 W34 1982

MINERAL INDUSTRIES - LATIN AMERICA.
Mineral industries of Latin America /. Washington, D.C. , 1987. p. cm. LC Card 87-600334 DDC 338.2/098 19
HD9506.L252 M37 1987

Zorn, Stephen. Minería y elaboración de minerales . Buenos Aires , 1986. ii, 84 p. ; LC Card 87-402781 DDC 338.2/098 19
HD9506.L252 Z67 1986

MINERAL INDUSTRIES - MEXICO - DIRECTORIES.
Mexico. Secretaría de Energía, Minas e Industria Paraestatal. Directorio del sector energía, minas e industria paraestatal, 1984. [Mexico City] , 1984. 497 p. ; ISBN 968-86000-4-0 LC Card 87-404794 DDC 333.79/0972 19
HD9502.M62 M49 1984

MINERAL INDUSTRIES - MEXICO - STATISTICS - HISTORY - 19TH CENTURY.
Flores Clair, Eduardo. Estadísticas mineras de México en el siglo XIX /. México, D.F. , 1985. 181 p. ; LC Card 87-401718 DDC 338.2/0972 19
HD9506.M62 F57 1985

MINERAL INDUSTRIES - MOROCCO.
Les Industries mécaniques et électriques au Maroc . Casablanca [1984] 1 v. (various pagings) ; LC Card 85-206543
HD9705.M72 I53 1984

MINERAL INDUSTRIES - NORTH DAKOTA - EMPLOYEES - STATISTICS.
Mining, second quarter, 1984 /. Bismarck, N.D. (1000 E. Divide, Bismarck 58502) [1986] 43 p. : LC Card 86-623004 DDC 331.12/522/09784 19
HD8039.M5982 N675 1986

MINERAL INDUSTRIES - NORWAY.
Norway. Utvalg for delutredning om industrielle mineraler. Industrimineraler . Oslo [1982] 134 p. : ISBN 82-00-70754-7 LC Card 83-123304
HD9506.N72 N67 1982

MINERAL INDUSTRIES - NORWAY - HISTORY - 19TH CENTURY.
Drivenes, Einar-Arne. Fiskarbonde og gruveslusk /. Oslo , c1985. 161, [1] p. : ISBN 82-00-07480-3 LC Card 86-204801
HD9506.N72 D75 1985

Mineral industries of Latin America / compiled by staff, Bureau of Mines. Washington, D.C. : U. S. Dept. of the Interior, Bureau of Mines, 1987. p. cm. (Mineral perspectives) Updated ed. of: Mineral industries of Latin America / Orlando Martino. 1981. Bibliography: p. LC Card 87-600334 DDC 338.2/098 19
1. Mineral industries - Latin America. I. United States. Bureau of Mines. II. Martino, Orlando. Mineral industries of Latin America. III. Series.
HD9506.L252 M37 1987

MINERAL INDUSTRIES - PERU.
Cisneros Orna, Manuel H. Minería, riqueza y pobreza del Perú /. [Lima, Peru] [1986] 205 p. : LC Card 87-100765
HD9506.P42 C57 1986

MINERAL INDUSTRIES - PERU - CERRO DE PASCO - HISTORY.
DeWind, Josh. Peasants become miners . New York , 1987. vii, 421 p. : ISBN 0-8240-1358-1 (alk. paper) LC Card 87-8361 DDC 338.2/0985/23 19
HD8039.M61 P44 1987

MINERAL INDUSTRIES - PERU - HISTORY.
Ríos Burga, Jaime R. Ciclos productivos en el espacio peruano colonial, siglos XVI-XIX . Lima, Perú , 1986. 70 p. : LC Card 87-401070 DDC 338.5/42/0983 19
HC227 .R456 1986

MINERAL INDUSTRIES - PERU - HISTORY - 20TH CENTURY.
Dore, Elizabeth. Acumulación y crisis en la minería peruana, 1900-1977 /. [Lima] [1986] 168 p. : LC Card 86-235232
HD9506.P42 D66 1986

MINERAL INDUSTRIES - POLITICAL ASPECTS - GERMANY - HISTORY - 20TH CENTURY.
Hayes, Peter, 1946- Industry and ideology . Cambridge [Cambridgeshire] , New York , 1987. xxviii, 411 p. : ISBN 0-521-32948-5 LC Card 86-28388 DDC 338.7/66/00943 19
HD9654.9.I5 H39 1987

MINERAL INDUSTRIES - QUÉBEC (PROVINCE) - ROUYN.
Berthiaume, Nicole, 1952- Rouyn-Noranda . Rouyn [Québec] , 1981. xiii, 169 p. : ISBN 2-89073-103-0 LC Card 83-132846
HD9524.C23 R683 1981

MINERAL INDUSTRIES - RUSSIAN S.F.S.R. - SIBERIA.
De-Gennin, Vil′gel′m, 1676-1750. [Opisanie ural′skikh i sibirskikh zavodov 1735. English.] Description of Ural and Siberian factories in 1735 /. [Washington, D.C.] , 1987. p. cm. LC

Card 87-600052 DDC 338.0947/87 19
HC337.R852 U733613 1987

MINERAL INDUSTRIES - RUSSIAN S.F.S.R. - SOVIET FAR EAST - FORECASTING.
Nikitin, V. S. (Vadim Semenovich) Prognozirovanie razvitiia regional'nogo gorno-promyshlennogo kompleksa /. Moskva , 1982. 141, [3] p. : LC Card 83-154711
HD9506.S7473 S656 1982

MINERAL INDUSTRIES - RUSSIAN S.F.S.R. - URAL MOUNTAINS REGION.
De-Gennin, Vil'gel'm, 1676-1750. [Opisanie ural'skikh i sibirskikh zavodov 1735. English.] Description of Ural and Siberian factories in 1735 /. [Washington, D.C.] , 1987. p. cm. LC Card 87-600052 DDC 338.0947/87 19
HC337.R852 U733613 1987

MINERAL INDUSTRIES - SOCIAL ASPECTS - INDIA - CHOTA NAGPUR.
Prasad, Maheshwari, 1944- Social aspects of mining towns of the tribal region /. New Delhi , 1986- v. <1- > ; LC Card 86-902979 DDC 307.7/66/095412 19
HD9506.I43 C486 1986

MINERAL INDUSTRIES - SOUTH AFRICA.
South Africa. Commission of Inquiry into the Possible Introduction of a Five-Day Working Week in the Mining Industry. Report of the Commission of Inquiry into the Possible Introduction of a Five-Day Working Week in the Mining Industry of the Republic of South Africa. [Pretoria] , 1977. iii, 194 p. : LC Card 85-148007
HD5119.M5982 S68 1977

MINERAL INDUSTRIES - SOVIET UNION.
Mineral'noe syr'e i ėkonomiia material'nykh i ėnergeticheskikh resursov /. Moskva , 1986. 333, [3] p. : LC Card 87-119481
HD9502.S652 M56 1986

MINERAL INDUSTRIES - SOVIET UNION - CAPITAL PRODUCTIVITY.
Osnovnye fondy i proizvodstvennye moshchnosti v gornoĭ promyshlennosti /. Moskva , 1984. 207 p. : LC Card 85-138074
HD9506.S7472 O86 1984

MINERAL INDUSTRIES - SOVIET UNION - PLANNING.
Gol'd, G. S. (Grigoriĭ Solomonovich) Optimizatsiia dolgosrochnogo planirovaniia razvitiia mineral'no-syr'evykh otrasleĭ /. Moskva , 1985. 148 p. : LC Card 86-118644
HD9506.S7472 G65 1985

MINERAL INDUSTRIES - SPAIN - ALMERÍA (PROVINCE)
Sánchez Picón, Andrés. La minería del Levante almeriense, 1838-1930 . Almería [1983] 308 p., [14] leaves of plates : ISBN 84-85219-49-X LC Card 85-126928
HD9506.S762 A457 1983

MINERAL INDUSTRIES - SPAIN - CARTAGENA CITY REGION - HISTORY - 20TH CENTURY.
Egea Bruno, Pedro María. La minería cartagenera en torno a la primera guerra mundial, 1909-1923 /. [Murcia] , 1983. 76 p. : ISBN 84-86031-30-3 LC Card 85-199662
HD9506.S762 C374 1983

MINERAL INDUSTRIES - STATISTICS.
Összehasonlító tanulmány a világ ásványi nyersanyagainak mennyiségéről, termeléséről, ár és értékrendjeinek alakulásáról /. Budapest , 1983. 57 p. : ISBN 963-671-086-4 (Magy. nemz. bibl.) LC Card 85-130135
HD9506.A2 O85 1983

MINERAL INDUSTRIES - SWEDEN.
Sweden. Malmfältsutredningen. Framtid i malmfälten . [Stockholm] [1984] 155, 5 p. : ISBN 91-38-08283-7 LC Card 86-111519
HD9506.S82 S94 1984

MINERAL INDUSTRIES - TAXATION - NEVADA - STATISTICS.
1982-83 net proceeds of mines /. Carson City, Nev. [1983] 17 leaves ; LC Card 87-620959 DDC 336.2/78622/09793021 19
HJ4242.M56 A14 1983

MINERAL INDUSTRIES - UNITED STATES.
The Competitiveness of American metal mining and processing . Washington , 1986. x, 186 p. ; LC Card 86-603391 DDC 338.2/74/0973 19
HD9506.U62 C63 1986

MINERAL INDUSTRIES - UNITED STATES - EMPLOYEES - STATISTICS.
Occupational employment in mining, construction, finance, and services. Washington, D.C. [1986] vi, 141 p. ; LC Card 86-603149 DDC 331.12/51/000973021 19
HD9506.U62 O23 1986

MINERAL INDUSTRIES - UNITED STATES - MANAGEMENT - CASE STUDIES.
Gavin, James. Organization development in the mining industry . New York , 1986. viii, 247 p. : ISBN 0-275-92061-5 (alk. paper) : LC Card 85-24400 DDC 622/.068 19
HD9506.U62 G38 1986
NYPL [JLE 86-3024]

MINERAL LANDS - ALASKA.
Maas, Kenneth M. Availability of land for mineral exploration and development in northern Alaska, 1986 /. [Washington, D.C.] [1987] iv, 34 p. : LC Card 86-607920 DDC 333.73 19
HD243.A3 M32 1987

MINERAL LANDS - ARIZONA.
McColly, Robert A. Availability of federally owned minerals for exploration and development in western states . [Avondale, Md.] , Washington, DC [1987] iv, 27 p. : LC Card 87-600086 DDC 333.8/5/09791 19
HD243.A7 M36 1987

Mineral perspectives.
Mineral industries of Latin America /. Washington, D.C. , 1987. p. cm. LC Card 87-600334 DDC 338.2/098 19
HD9506.L252 M37 1987

Mineral policy background paper, 0706-103X .
(no. 20) Mohide, Thomas Patrick. Silver /. Toronto, Ont. [1985] xiv, 406 p. : ISBN 0-7743-9897-3 (pbk.) LC Card 85-165981 DDC 338.2/7421/0971 19
HD9536.C22 M64 1985
NYPL [JLG 86-145]

Mineral policy background paper, 0706-1034 .
(no. 23) Hwang, Hae-Shin. Dominant firm price leadership . Toronto, Ont. [1986] 40 p. : ISBN 0-7729-2122-9 : LC Card 87-161006 DDC 338.2/3 19
HD9539.N5 H93 1986

MINERAL RESOURCES IN SUBMERGED LANDS - ECONOMIC ASPECTS.
Methodologies for assessing the impact of deep sea-bed minerals on the world economy /. New York , 1986. ix, 153 p. : LC Card 87-118207 DDC 338.2 19
HD9506.A2 M47 1986

MINERAL RESOURCES, MARINE. see **MARINE MINERAL RESOURCES.**

MINERAL RESOURCES - TAXATION - BRAZIL - MINAS GERAIS.
Economia mineira e o financiamento do setor público . Belo Horizonte , 1985. 126 p. : LC Card 85-207952
HJ2529.M5 E26 1985

Mineral'noe syr'e i ėkonomiia material'nykh i ėnergeticheskikh resursov / pod redaktsieĭ A.S. Astakhova. Moskva : "Nedra", 1986. 333, [3] p. : ill. ; 23 cm. Bibliography: p. 333-[334] LC Card 87-119481
1. Power resources - Economic aspects - Soviet Union. 2. Mineral industries - Soviet Union. I. Astakhov, A. S. (Aleksandr Semenovich).
HD9502.S652 M56 1986

MINERALS. see **MINES AND MINERAL RESOURCES.**

The Minerals industries of ASEAN and Australia : problems and prospects / edited by Bruce McKern and Praipol Koomsup. Sydney ; Boston : Allen & Unwin, 1988. p. cm. Bibliography: p. Includes index. ISBN 0-04-301284-1 LC Card 87-18339 DDC 338.2/0959 19
1. Mineral industries - Asia, Southeastern. 2. Mineral industries - Australia. I. McKern, Bruce. II. Praiphol Koomsup. III. ASEAN.
HD9506.A6592 M56 1988

La minería cartagenera en torno a la primera guerra mundial, 1909-1923 /. Egea Bruno, Pedro María. [Murcia] , 1983. 76 p. : ISBN 84-86031-30-3 LC Card 85-199662
HD9506.S762 C374 1983

La minería del Levante almeriense, 1838-1930 . Sánchez Picón, Andrés. Almería [1983] 308 p., [14] leaves of plates : ISBN 84-85219-49-X LC Card 85-126928
HD9506.S762 A457 1983

Minería e integración boliviana /. Tórrez G. O., José Guillermo (Torrez Gómez Ortega) La Paz, Bolivia , 1986. 181 p., [8] leaves of plates : LC Card 87-400195 DDC 338.2/0984 19
HD9506.B64 C67 1986

Minería peruana . Aste Daffos, Juan. Lima , 1986. 102 p. ; LC Card 87-143088 DDC 338.2/0985 19
HD9506.P42 A827 1986

Minería, riqueza y pobreza del Perú /. Cisneros Orna, Manuel H. [Lima, Peru] [1986] 205 p. : LC Card 87-100765
HD9506.P42 C57 1986

Minería y elaboración de minerales . Zorn, Stephen. Buenos Aires , 1986. ii, 84 p. ; LC Card 87-402781 DDC 338.2/098 19
HD9506.L252 Z67 1986

Mineros de ayer y de hoy. Lazarte, Jorge. Crisis de identidad y centralidad minera . [La Paz, Bolivia] [1986] 37 p. : LC Card 87-401455 DDC 331.88/122/0984 19
HD8039.M61 B586 1986

MINERS - AUSTRALIA - HISTORY.
Payton, Philip, 1953- The Cornish miner in Australia . Trewolsta, Trewirgie, Kernow [Cornwall] , 1984. xi, 242 p. : ISBN 0-907566-51-0 : LC Card 85-202456 DDC 305.8/9167094 19
HD8039.M62 A87 1984
NYPL [JLD 86-4079]

MINERS - BOLIVIA.
Escóbar, Filemón, 1936- La mina vista desde el guardatojo . La Paz, Bolivia , 1986. 77 p. ; LC Card 87-118481 DDC 331.7/622/0984 19
HD8039.M61 B57 1986

Poppe, René. Interior mina . La Paz, Bolivia , 1986. 236 p. ; LC Card 87-400962 DDC 331.7/622/0984 19
HD8039.M61 B634 1986

MINERS - BULGARIA - BIOGRAPHY.
Trudova slava /. Sofiia , <1986-. v. <4 > : LC Card 86-228746
HD8039.M62 B88 1986

MINERS - COLORADO - HISTORY.
Neuschatz, Michael. The golden sword . New York , 1986. xii, 301 p. ; ISBN 0-313-25104-5 (lib. bdg. : alk. Paper) LC Card 85-27026 DDC 331.88/122334/09788 19
HD8039.M61 U48 1986
NYPL [JLE 87-766]

MINERS - GERMANY - HISTORY - SOURCES.
Bis vor die Stufen des Throns . München , c1986. 530 p. : ISBN 3-406-31297-7 LC Card 87-103686 DDC 331.7/622334/0943 19
HD8039.M61 G32 1986

MINERS - GERMANY (WEST) - RUHR (REGION) - HISTORY.
Günter, Janne, 1937- Mündliche Geschichtsschreibung . Mülheim/Ruhr , 1982. 142, [1] p. : ISBN 3-923456-00-X LC Card 85-146144
HD8039.M61 G343 1982

MINERS - GERMANY (WEST) - RUHR (REGION) - INTERVIEWS.
Günter, Janne, 1937- Mündliche Geschichtsschreibung . Mülheim/Ruhr , 1982. 142, [1] p. : ISBN 3-923456-00-X LC Card 85-146144
HD8039.M61 G343 1982

MINERS - GERMANY (WEST) - SAARLAND - ECONOMIC CONDITIONS.
Steffens, Horst. Autorität und Revolte . Weingarten , c1987. 419 p. : ISBN 3-924027-47-1 LC Card 87-141439 DDC 331/.0422334/094342 19
HD8039.M61 G383 1987

MINERS - HEALTH AND HYGIENE - GERMANY - HISTORY - SOURCES.
Bis vor die Stufen des Throns . München , c1986. 530 p. : ISBN 3-406-31297-7 LC Card 87-103686 DDC 331.7/622334/0943 19
HD8039.M61 G32 1986

MINERS - INDIA - ANDHRA PRADESH.
Saibaba, G. Labour conditions in the mining industry of Andhra Pradesh . Tirupati [1985?]

v, 314 p. ; LC Card 86-901021 DDC 331/.0422/095484 19
HD8039.M61 I47 1985
NYPL [JLD 87-1057]

MINERS - INDIA - CHOTA NĀGPUR.
Prasad, Maheshwari, 1944- Social aspects of mining towns of the tribal region /. New Delhi , 1986- v. <1- > ; LC Card 86-902979 DDC 307.7/66/095412 19
HD9506.I43 C486 1986

MINERS - PERU - CERRO DE PASCO - HISTORY.
DeWind, Josh. Peasants become miners . New York , 1987. vii, 421 p. : ISBN 0-8240-1358-1 (alk. paper) LC Card 87-8361 DDC 338.2/0985/23 19
HD8039.M61 P44 1987

MINERS - ROMANIA - TRANSYLVANIA - HISTORY.
Vajda, Lajos. Erdélyi bányák, kohók, emberek, századok . Bukarest , 1981. 544 p. : LC Card 83-124763
HD8039.M61 R68 1981

MINERS' STRIKE, MINERAL DEL MONTE, MEXICO, 1766.
Ladd, Doris M. The making of a strike . Lincoln , c1988. x, 205 p. ; ISBN 0-8032-2876-7 (alk. paper) LC Card 87-5897 DDC 331.8/928223423/097246 19
HD5331.M72 1766 .P325 1988

MINERS - THAILAND, SOUTHERN.
Saphāp læ ʻōkāt nai kānthamngān nai kitčhakān m [Bangkok] [2509 i.e. 1966] 2, 35 p., [5] leaves of plates : LC Card 80-911179
HD8039.M72 T527 1966

MINERS - THAILAND, SOUTHERN - SUPPLY AND DEMAND.
Saphāp læ ʻōkāt nai kānthamngān nai kitčhakān m [Bangkok] [2509 i.e. 1966] 2, 35 p., [5] leaves of plates : LC Card 80-911179
HD8039.M72 T527 1966

MINERS - UNITED STATES - HISTORY.
Jones, Mother, 1843?-1930. [Selections. 1988.] The speeches and writings of Mother Jones /. Pittsburgh, Pa. , 1988. p. cm. ISBN 0-8229-3575-9 LC Card 87-25192 DDC 331.88/0973 19
HD8072 .J7832 1988

MINERS' WIVES - PERU - CANARIA - POLITICAL ACTIVITY.
Hernández, Zoila. El coraje de las mineras . Lima, Perú , 1986. 184 p. : LC Card 86-232046
HD5361.Z9 C35 1986

Minerva-Fachserie Wirtschafts- und Sozialwissenschaften.
Hauff, Hanns Joachim Paul. Aufstieg zur Macht . München , c1983. 85 p. : ISBN 3-597-10422-3 LC Card 83-136638
HD38.2 .H38 1983

Möller, Wolf-Peter. Der Erfolg von Unternehmenszusammenschlüssen . München , c1983. 403 p. : ISBN 3-597-10456-8 LC Card 83-227517
HD2746.5 .M65 1983

Riechey, Gunter. Möglichkeiten und Grenzen der Beeinflussung der Preissetzungsmöglichkeiten der Unternehmen /. München , c1982. 286 p. : ISBN 3-597-10144-5 LC Card 83-160762
HC290.5.W24 R54 1982

Schertler, Walter. Attraktivitätsanalyse von Dienstleistungen . München , c1983. 183 p. : ISBN 3-597-10420-7 LC Card 83-140207
HD9984.5 .S25 1983

Weingarten, Richard. Eine kapitaltheoretische Untersuchung zum Gesetz vom tendenziellen Fall der Profitrate einschliesslich der Bestimmung seiner empirischen Relevanz /. München , c1982. ix, 342 p. ; ISBN 3-597-10136-4 LC Card 83-134240
HB601 .W37 1982

Minervin, I. G. Podgotovka upravlencheskikh kadrov--opyt, problemy, perspektivy (po zarubezhnym materialam) . Moskva , 1984. 188 p. ; LC Card 85-188986
HD30.4 .P6 1984

MINES AND MINERAL RESOURCES - ALASKA.
Maas, Kenneth M. Availability of land for mineral exploration and development in northern Alaska, 1986 /. [Washington, D.C.] [1987] iv, 34 p. : LC Card 86-607920 DDC 333.73 19
HD243.A3 M32 1987

MINES AND MINERAL RESOURCES - ALASKA - RED DOG CREEK WATERSHED.
Alaska. Office of Mineral Development. Red Dog project analysis /. [Juneau?] [1984] 300 p. in various pagings : LC Card 84-622211 DDC 333.8/5/097986 19
HD9506.U63 R422 1984

MINES AND MINERAL RESOURCES - ANTARCTIC REGIONS.
Mitchell, Barbara. Frozen stakes . London , Washington, D.C. , c1983. iii, 135 p. : ISBN 0-905347-45-5 (pbk.) : LC Card 84-173206 DDC 333.8/5/09989 19
HD9506.A585 M57 1983
NYPL [JLD 86-3548]

MINES AND MINERAL RESOURCES - CHILE - COQUIMBO (PROVINCE)
Chouteau, Eujenio. Informe sobre la provincia de Coquimbo /. Santiago de Chile , 1887. 262 p. ; LC Card 85-165581
HC193.C64 C46 1887

MINES AND MINERAL RESOURCES - INDIA - BIHAR.
Kalra, G. D. Mineral development in Bihar, 1979-80 to 1988-89 /. New Delhi , 1983. 2 v. : LC Card 83-905955 DDC 338.2/0954/12 19
HD9506.I43 B545 1983
NYPL [JLE 86-4727]

MINES AND MINERAL RESOURCES - ITALY - STATISTICS.
Wagner, Hermann, Dr. Italien /. Hannover , Stuttgart , 1982. xv, 190 p., 4 folded leaves of plates : LC Card 83-235644
HD9506.I82 W34 1982

MINES AND MINERAL RESOURCES - SPAIN - ALMERÍA (PROVINCE)
Sánchez Picón, Andrés. La minería del Levante almeriense, 1838-1930 . Almería [1983] 308 p., [14] leaves of plates : ISBN 84-85219-49-X LC Card 85-126928
HD9506.S762 A457 1983

MINES AND MINERAL RESOURCES - STATISTICS.
Összehasonlító tanulmány a világ ásványi nyersanyagainak mennyiségéről, termeléséről, ár és értékrendjeinek alakulásáról /. Budapest , 1983. 57 p. : ISBN 963-671-086-4 (Magy. nemz. bibl.) LC Card 85-130135
HD9506.A2 O85 1983

MINES AND MINERAL RESOURCES - TAXATION - LAW AND LEGISLATION - MINNESOTA.
Minnesota mining tax guide. Eveleth, MN (612 Pierce St., Eveleth 55743) [1984] 42 p. : LC Card 86-620843 DDC 343.77605/582 347.76035582 19
HJ4232.M56 M56 1984

MINES AND MINERAL RESOURCES - TAXATION - MINNESOTA.
Minnesota mining tax guide. Eveleth, MN (612 Pierce St., Eveleth 55743) [1984] 42 p. : LC Card 86-620843 DDC 343.77605/582 347.76035582 19
HJ4232.M56 M56 1984

MINES AND MINERAL RESOURCES - TAXATION - NEVADA - STATISTICS.
Net proceeds of mines, 1985-86 /. Carson City, Nev. [1986] 18 leaves ; LC Card 87-620610 DDC 336.2/78622/09793021 19
HJ4242.M56 N47 1986

1982-83 net proceeds of mines /. Carson City, Nev. [1983] 17 leaves ; LC Card 87-620959 DDC 336.2/78622/09793021 19
HJ4242.M56 A14 1983

MINES AND MINERAL RESOURCES - UNITED STATES.
An Appraisal of minerals availability for 34 commodities /. [Pittsburgh, Pa.] , 1987. iii, 300 p. : LC Card 87-600244 DDC 333.8/5 19
HD9506.A2 A72 1987

MINES AND MINING. see **MINERAL INDUSTRIES; MINES AND MINERAL RESOURCES.**

MINES AND MINING - MACHINERY. see **MINING MACHINERY.**

Minev, Miroslav, 1928- Zadachite na DKMS vŭv VUZ za povishavane na ikonomicheskata podgotovka na studentite i mladite khora ot drugite otri͡adi na mladezhta . Svishtov , 1985. 91 p. ; LC Card 86-159994
HB74.9.B9 Z33 1985

Mineworkers of Guyana . Quamina, Odida T. London , Atlantic Highlands, N.J., USA , 1987. xv, 118 p., [7] p. of plates : ISBN 0-86232-308-8 : LC Card 87-14719 DDC 305/.9622/098814 19
HD8039.A492 G9558 1987

Minford, Patrick. Unemployment : cause and cure / Patrick Minford with Paul Ashton ... [et al.].2nd ed. Oxford, UK ; New York, NY, USA : B. Blackwell, 1985. x, 214 p. : ill. ; 24 cm. Includes index. Bibliography: p. [202]-205. ISBN 0-631-14506-0 : LC Card 85-13511 DDC 331.13/7941 19
1. Unemployment - Great Britain. 2. Insurance, Unemployment - Great Britain. 3. Industrial relations - Great Britain. 4. Unemployment - European Economic Community countries. I. Ashton, Paul. II. Title.
HD5765.A6 M55 1985
NYPL [JLE 86-2297]

Mingé, M. Ronald. Bowman, Thomas F. Finding your best place to live in America /. New York , c1981. xiii, 337 p. : ISBN 0-940162-00-8 (pbk.) : LC Card 81-51506 DDC 973.927 19
HT123 .B665 ***NYPL [Pub. Cat. 86-574]***

MINHO (PORTUGAL) - ECONOMIC CONDITIONS.
Perspectivas sobre o norte de Portugal. Porto , 1981. 242 p. : LC Card 83-163948
HC393.M55 P47 1981

MINHO (PORTUGAL) - SOCIAL CONDITIONS.
Perspectivas sobre o norte de Portugal. Porto , 1981. 242 p. : LC Card 83-163948
HC393.M55 P47 1981

Minhoue, Alphonse. Albagli, Claude. Le rôle économique et social du paysan africain et l'autosuffisance alimentaire /. Abidjan , c1984. 70 p. : ISBN 2-7236-0648-1 LC Card 85-179020
HD9017.S82 A43 1984

MINI COMPUTERS. see **MINICOMPUTERS.**

Mini micro turnkey engineering systems. The Mini-microcomputer turnkey engineering systems market. New York, N.Y. , c1983. vi, 228 p. ; LC Card 87-142400 DDC 381/.4500416 19
HD9696.C63 U5262 1983

The Mini-microcomputer turnkey engineering systems market. New York, N.Y. : Frost & Sullivan, c1983. vi, 228 p. ; 29 cm. Title on spine: Mini micro turnkey engineering systems. "January 1983." "#A1208." LC Card 87-142400 DDC 381/.4500416 19
1. Computer industry - United States. 2. Computer software industry - United States. 3. Minicomputers - United States - Programming. 4. Microcomputers - United States - Programming. 5. Engineering - United States - Data processing - Equipment and supplies. 6. Turnkey computer systems - United States. 7. Market surveys - United States. I. Frost & Sullivan. II. Title: Mini micro turnkey engineering systems.
HD9696.C63 U5262 1983

MINIATURE COMPUTERS. see **MINICOMPUTERS.**

MINICOMPUTERS - PROGRAMMING.
Bhaskar, Krish N. The impact of microprocessors on the small accounting practice /. Englewood Cliffs, N.J. , c1986. xvi, 167 p. ; ISBN 0-13-453291-0 (pbk.) LC Card 85-25764 DDC 657/.028/5416 19
HF5679 .B45 1986 ***NYPL [JLE 86-4067]***

MINICOMPUTERS - PURCHASING.
Pathways through data processing, small business systems. Cherry Hill, N.J. (140 Barclay Center, Cherry Hill 08034) , c1980. 182 p. : LC Card 81-118723 DDC 001.64/04/029473 19
HF5548.2 P295 1980 ***NYPL [JLF 86-351]***

MINICOMPUTERS - UNITED STATES.
The Personal computer hardware add-on device market. New York, N.Y. , c1983. viii, 2, 228 p. : LC Card 87-143524
HD9696.C63 U52783 1983

MINICOMPUTERS - UNITED STATES - PROGRAMMING.
The Mini-microcomputer turnkey engineering

systems market. New York, N.Y. , c1983. vi, 228 p. ; LC Card 87-142400 DDC 381/.4500416 19
HD9696.C63 U5262 1983

Minier, Vincent. Politiques vivrières, dépendances alimentaires et développement /. [Paris] , c1984. iv, 129 p. : ISBN 2-86844-000-2 : LC Card 84-248912
HD9017.S152 P65 1984

Minimills and integrated mills . Hogan, William Thomas, 1919- Lexington, Mass. , c1987. 148 p. : ISBN 0-669-14021-X (alk. paper) LC Card 86-45605 DDC 338.4/7669142/0973 19
HD9515 .H599 1987

The minimum cost of living in Nebraska /. Love, Douglas O. [Lincoln] [1986] 2 v. : LC Card 87-620964 DDC 339.4/2/09782 19
HD6993.N4 L68 1986

MINIMUM INCOME. see **INCOME MAINTENANCE PROGRAMS.**

A minimum tax for Canada . Wilson, Michael H. (Michael Holcombe), 1937- [Ottawa] [1985] iii, 15, 15, iii p. ; LC Card 86-202601 DDC 336.24/2 19
HJ4661 .W55 1985

A minimum tax for Canada /. Wilson, Michael H. (Michael Holcombe), 1937- [Ottawa] [1985] vi, 52, 56, vi p. ; LC Card 86-202606 DDC 336.24/2 19
HJ4661 .W54 1985

MINIMUM WAGE. see **WAGES - MINIMUM WAGE.**

MINING. see **MINERAL INDUSTRIES; MINES AND MINERAL RESOURCES.**

Mining & mining equipment/service companies worldwide. Don Nelson's Mining & mining equipment/service companies world wide . Barnet, Herts., U.K. [1982] 562 p. ; ISBN 946-0-04005-X ***NYPL [JSD 86-337]***

MINING ACCIDENTS. see **MINE ACCIDENTS.**

Mining and mining equipment/service companies worldwide, 1982-83. Don Nelson's Mining & mining equipment/service companies world wide . Barnet, Herts., U.K. [1982] 562 p. ; ISBN 946-0-04005-X ***NYPL [JSD 86-337]***

Mining equipment market in Europe. New York, N.Y. : Frost & Sullivan, c1983. xxix, 294 p. ; 29 cm. "November 1983." "(#E633)." LC Card 87-142591 DDC 380.1/4568176/094 19
1. Mining machinery industry - Europe. 2. Market surveys - Europe. I. Frost & Sullivan.
HD9506.E85 M56 1983

MINING LAW - BRAZIL - SÃO PAULO (STATE)
Mineração meio-ambiente e o planejamento municipal. São Paulo [1982] 24 leaves : LC Card 85-210329
HD9506.B73 S3664 1982

MINING MACHINERY INDUSTRY - DIRECTORIES.
Don Nelson's Mining & mining equipment/service companies world wide . Barnet, Herts., U.K. [1982] 562 p. ; ISBN 946-0-04005-X ***NYPL [JSD 86-337]***

MINING MACHINERY INDUSTRY - EUROPE.
Mining equipment market in Europe. New York, N.Y. , c1983. xxix, 294 p. ; LC Card 87-142591 DDC 380.1/4568176/094 19
HD9506.E85 M56 1983

MINING MACHINERY INDUSTRY - UNITED STATES.
Strategies for selling underground & surface mining equipment. New York, N.Y. , c1983. vii, 320 p. : LC Card 87-142333 DDC 381/.4568176/0973 19
HD9506.U62 S865 1983

MINING MACHINERY - MARKETING.
Strategies for selling underground & surface mining equipment. New York, N.Y. , c1983. vii, 320 p. : LC Card 87-142333 DDC 381/.4568176/0973 19
HD9506.U62 S865 1983

Mining, second quarter, 1984 / prepared by Research and Statistics. Bismarck, N.D. (1000 E. Divide, Bismarck 58502) : Job Service North Dakota, [1986] 43 p. : ill. ; 28 cm. (North Dakota occupational profiles) "April 1986." "OES 1-3." LC Card 86-623004 DDC 331.12/522/09784 19
1. Mineral industries - North Dakota - Employees - Statistics. I. Job Service North Dakota. Research and Statistics Section. II. Series.
HD8039.M5982 N675 1986

MINISTERS OF THE GOSPEL. see **CLERGY.**

Ministral i Masgrau, Marta. Medir i Huerta, Rosa M. Les comarques gironines . Girona , 1986. 211 p. : ISBN 84-505-3103-9 LC Card 87-101047
HC387.G4 M43 1986

MINITAB (COMPUTER SYSTEM)
Bond, Kenneth M. Essential business statistics . Boston , c1988. xiii, 332 p. : ISBN 0-534-91530-2 LC Card 87-25652 DDC 519.5/028/55369 19
HF1017 .B63 1988

Levine, David M., 1946- Using Minitab with Basic business statistics /. Englewood Cliffs, N.J. , c1986. viii, 160 p. : ISBN 0-13-057779-0 (pbk.) LC Card 87-400304 DDC 519.5/028/55369 19
HF1017 .L425 1986

MINITAB (COMPUTER SYSTEM) - HANDBOOKS, MANUALS, ETC.
Miller, Robert B. (Robert Burnham), 1942- Minitab handbook for business and economics /. Boston , c1988. x, 331 p. : ISBN 0-87150-092-2 (pbk.) LC Card 86-32830 DDC 519.5/02855369 19
HF1017 .M494 1988

Minitab handbook for business and economics /. Miller, Robert B. (Robert Burnham), 1942- Boston , c1988. x, 331 p. : ISBN 0-87150-092-2 (pbk.) LC Card 86-32830 DDC 519.5/02855369 19
HF1017 .M494 1988

MINK . Bergan, Roar. Oslo , 1984. 71 p. : ISBN 82-537-2138-2 : LC Card 85-178061
HC365 .B388 1984

Mink, Barbara P., 1945- Mink, Oscar G. Groups at work /. Englewood Cliffs, N.J. , c1987. xiii, 279 p. : ISBN 0-87778-196-6 LC Card 87-9081 DDC 658.4/036 19
HD66 .M55 1987

Mink, Oscar G. Groups at work / Oscar G. Mink, Barbara P. Mink, Keith Q. Owen ; with contributions from Phil Jones ... [et al.]. Englewood Cliffs, N.J. : Educational Technology Publications, c1987. xiii, 279 p. : ill. ; 25 cm. (Techniques in training and performance development series) Bibliography: p. 261-270. Includes index. ISBN 0-87778-196-6 LC Card 87-9081 DDC 658.4/036 19
1. Work groups. 2. Group relations training. I. Mink, Barbara P., 1945-. II. Owen, Keith Q. III. Title. IV. Series.
HD66 .M55 1987

Minkes, A. L. Business behaviour & management structure / A.L. Minkes and C.S. Nuttall. London : Croom Helm, c1985. 224 p. ; 23 cm. Includes bibliographical references and index. ISBN 0-7099-1795-3
1. Industrial management - Great Britain. 2. Industrial management - Great Britain - Case studies. I. Nuttall, C. S., 1920-. II. Title. III. Title: Business behaviour and management structure. ***NYPL [JLD 87-1113]***

Minkow, Barry. Making it in America / by Barry Minkow. [Los Angeles?] : B. Minkow, c1985. 136 p. ; 21 cm. LC Card 85-51822 DDC 650.1/092/4 B 19
1. Minkow, Barry. 2. Businessmen - United States - Biography. 3. Success in business - United States. I. Title.
HC102.5.M5 A3 1985

MINKOW, BARRY.
Minkow, Barry. Making it in America /. [Los Angeles?] , c1985. 136 p. ; LC Card 85-51822 DDC 650.1/092/4 B 19
HC102.5.M5 A3 1985

Minneapolis Chamber of Commerce. Ninth Federal Reserve District Farm Forum (1965 : Minneapolis, Minn.) Farm Forum of the Ninth Federal Reserve District . Hopkins, Minn. [1965] 99 p. : LC Card 87-110732
HD9007.A14 N56 1965

Minneapolis. InterStudy (Center) see **InterStudy (Center)**

Minnerly, W. Lee. 1986 membership profile /. Chicago, Ill. , c1986. ix, 44 p. : ISBN 0-911780-85-8 (pbk.) LC Card 87-144205 DDC 333.33/2/0973 19
HD251 .A17 1986

Minnesota.
Financial and compliance report on federally assisted programs for the year ended June 30, 1985 / prepared through a cooperative agreement between Department of Finance ... [et al.]. [Saint Paul, Minn.] : State of Minnesota, [1986] x, 92 p. ; 28 cm. LC Card 87-620971 DDC 353.97760072/52 19
1. Grants-in-aid - Minnesota - Accounting. 2. Intergovernmental fiscal relations - Minnesota - Accounting. I. Minnesota. Dept. of Finance. II. Title.
HJ515 .M55 1986

Minnesota. Dept. of Finance.
Cash flow report. [St. Paul] : Dept. of Finance, [1986] 26, [4] leaves : ill. ; 28 cm. Cover title. "January 1986." LC Card 86-622795 DDC 336.776 19
1. Finance, Public - Minnesota. 2. Cash flow - Minnesota. I. Title.
HJ515 .M56 1986

Minnesota. Financial and compliance report on federally assisted programs for the year ended June 30, 1985 /. [Saint Paul, Minn.] [1986] x, 92 p. ; LC Card 87-620971 DDC 353.97760072/52 19
HJ515 .M55 1986

Minnesota. Dept. of Revenue.
Minnesota mining tax guide. Eveleth, MN (612 Pierce St., Eveleth 55743) [1984] 42 p. : LC Card 86-620843 DDC 343.77605/582 347.76035582 19
HJ4232.M56 M56 1984

Railroads--methods of valuing operating property and the amounts of tax payments . [Minneapolis] [1986] 18 leaves : LC Card 87-620974 DDC 336.22/5 19
HE1075.M6 R35 1986

Minnesota. Dept. of Revenue. Research Office.
Minnesota tax handbook . [St. Paul] [1985] iii, 70 p. ; LC Card 86-620842 DDC 343.77604 347.76034 19
HJ2415 .M49 1985

Minnesota. Finance, Dept. of. see **Minnesota. Dept. of Finance.**

Minnesota. Legislature. Railroads--methods of valuing operating property and the amounts of tax payments . [Minneapolis] [1986] 18 leaves : LC Card 87-620974 DDC 336.22/5 19
HE1075.M6 R35 1986

Minnesota. Local Government Aids & Analysis Division. Property tax delinquency in Minnesota . St. Paul, Minn. [1984?] iv, 84 p. : LC Card 86-622652 DDC 336.22 19
HJ4232.A25 P76 1984

Minnesota mining tax guide. Eveleth, MN (612 Pierce St., Eveleth 55743) : Dept. of Revenue, Minerals Tax Division, [1984] 42 p. : ill. ; 28 cm. Cover title. "December 1984." "1884-1984 Minnesota's iron mining centennial." LC Card 86-620843 DDC 343.77605/582 347.76035582 19
1. Mines and mineral resources - Taxation - Minnesota. 2. Mines and mineral resources - Taxation - Law and legislation - Minnesota. I. Minnesota. Dept. of Revenue.
HJ4232.M56 M56 1984

Minnesota. Office of the Legislative Auditor. Program Evaluation Division. Tax increment financing. Saint Paul, Minn. (Veterans Service Bldg., Saint Paul 55155) : Program Evaluation Division, Office of the Legislative Auditor, State of Minnesota, 1986. xix, 138 p. : ill. ; 28 cm. (Studies of the Program Evaluation Division . 56) "January 1986." Includes bibliographical references. LC Card 86-623133 DDC 336.22/09776 19
1. Tax increment financing - Minnesota. 2. Tax increment financing - Law and legislation - Minnesota. 3. Urban renewal - Minnesota. I. Title. II. Series.
HJ9261 .M55 1986

Minnesota. Revenue, Dept. of. see **Minnesota. Dept. of Revenue.**

Minnesota studies in macroeconomics .
(v. 1) Contractual arrangements for intertemporal trade /. Minneapolis, MN , c1987. p. cm. ISBN 0-8166-1533-0 : LC Card

86-24888 DDC 332.64/4/0724 19
HB801 .C629 1987

Minnesota tax handbook : a profile of state and local taxes in Minnesota. 1984 ed. [St. Paul] : Minnesota Dept. of Revenue, Research Office, [1985] iii, 70 p. ; 22 cm. Cover title. "January, 1985." LC Card 86-620842 DDC 343.77604 347.76034 19
1. Taxation - Minnesota. 2. Local taxation - Minnesota. I. Minnesota. Dept. of Revenue. Research Office.
HJ2415 .M49 1985

MINORITIES - EMPLOYMENT - CANADA.
Ornstein, Michael D. The work experience of immigrants to Canada [microform] . Downsview, Ont. , 1983. 48 leaves ; *NYPL [*ZT-1732 no.16]*

MINORITIES - EMPLOYMENT - GREAT BRITAIN.
Verma, Gajendra K. Race, training, and employment /. London , New York , 1987. vi, 134 p. : ISBN 1-85000-243-6 : LC Card 87-15470 DDC 331.3/46/0941 19
HD5715.5.G7 V47 1987

MINORITIES - EMPLOYMENT - MARYLAND - STATISTICS.
Affirmative action data . Baltimore, Md. (1100 N. Eutaw St., Baltimore 21201) [1985] [17] leaves ; LC Card 86-622599 DDC 331.11/43 19
HD5725.M35 A68 1985

MINORITIES - EMPLOYMENT - SOVIET UNION, NORTHERN.
Sotsial'nye problemy truda u narodnosteĭ Severa /. Novosibirsk , 1986. 213 p. ; LC Card 87-164784
HD5797.N75 S67 1986

MINORITIES - EMPLOYMENT - UNITED STATES.
Bailey, Thomas Raymond. Immigrant and native workers . Boulder , 1987. xvi, 168 p. : ISBN 0-8133-7349-2 : LC Card 86-28205 DDC 331.6/2/0973 19
HD8081.A5 B35 1987

Occupations in energy-related industries [microform] . Washington, D.C. , 1981. ca. 300 p. ; *NYPL [*XME-11,557]*

Selected affirmative action topics in employment and business set-asides . Washington, D.C. , 1985- v. <1 > : LC Card 85-603434 DDC 331.13/3/0973 19
HF5549.5.A34 S45 1985

MINORITIES - EMPLOYMENT - UTAH - STATISTICS.
Jensen, Kenneth E. Utah affirmative action information, 1985. [Salt Lake City] [1986] i, 253 p. ; LC Card 86-622873 DDC 331.11/43 19
HD5725.U8 J46 1986

MINORITIES - GERMANY, WEST.
Ausländerintegration in deutschen Industriebetrieben /. Königstein/Ts. , c1985. viii, 273 p. : ISBN 3-7756-6935-3 LC Card 85-194662 DDC 305.8/00943 19
HD8458.A2 A9265 1985
NYPL [JLD 86-2193]

MINORITIES - GREAT BRITAIN.
Little, Alan. Loading the law . London , 1982. 67 p. ; ISBN 0-902355-98-8 (pbk.)
NYPL [JLD 87-1941]

MINORITIES - HOUSING - ENGLAND - BIRMINGHAM (WEST MIDLANDS)
Henderson, J. W. (Jeffrey William), 1947- Race, class, and state housing . Aldershot, Hants, England ;Brookfield, Vt. , c1987. xxiii, 331 p. : ISBN 0-566-00785-1 :
NYPL [JLD 87-1476]

MINORITIES - HOUSING - GOVERNMENT POLICY - GREAT BRITAIN.
Henderson, J. W. (Jeffrey William), 1947- Race, class, and state housing . Aldershot, Hants, England ;Brookfield, Vt. , c1987. xxiii, 331 p. : ISBN 0-566-00785-1 :
NYPL [JLD 87-1476]

MINORITIES - HOUSING - GOVERNMENT POLICY - UNITED STATES.
Race, ethnicity, and minority housing in the United States /. New York , 1986. xxv, 224 p. ; ISBN 0-313-24848-6 (lib. bdg. : alk. paper) LC Card 86-9971 DDC 363.5/9 19
HD7288.72.U5 R33 1986
NYPL [JLE 87-946]

MINORITIES - HOUSING - GREAT BRITAIN.
Henderson, J. W. (Jeffrey William), 1947- Race, class, and state housing . Aldershot, Hants, England ;Brookfield, Vt. , c1987. xxiii, 331 p. : ISBN 0-566-00785-1 :
NYPL [JLD 87-1476]

MINORITIES - HOUSING - UNITED STATES.
The Fair Housing Assistance Program evaluation /. Washington, D.C. [1985] 1 v. (various pagings) : *NYPL [JLF 87-17]*

Race, ethnicity, and minority housing in the United States /. New York , 1986. xxv, 224 p. ; ISBN 0-313-24848-6 (lib. bdg. : alk. paper) LC Card 86-9971 DDC 363.5/9 19
HD7288.72.U5 R33 1986
NYPL [JLE 87-946]

MINORITIES - RUSSIAN S.F.S.R. - LENINGRAD - HISTORY - 19TH CENTURY.
I͡Ukhneva, N. V. Ėtnicheskiĭ sostav i ėtnosotsial'nai͡a struktura naselenii͡a Peterburga . Leningrad , 1984. 220 p., [1] folded leaf of plates : LC Card 85-116858
HB3608.L4 I94 1984 *NYPL [*QGK 87-925]*

MINORITIES - SOVIET UNION, NORTHERN - SOCIAL CONDITIONS.
Sotsial'nye problemy truda u narodnosteĭ Severa /. Novosibirsk , 1986. 213 p. ; LC Card 87-164784
HD5797.N75 S67 1986

MINORITIES - UNITED STATES - POLITICAL ACTIVITY.
LeMay, Michael C., 1941- The struggle for influence . Lanham , c1985. xv, 452 p. : ISBN 0-8191-4653-6 (alk. paper) : LC Card 85-6105 DDC 323.1/73 19
E184.A1 L44 1985 *NYPL [IE 85-3562]*

Minority business advisor. [Great Falls, Mont.] (1101 15th St. N., Great Falls 59401) : [Minority Business Advisors, c1985- 1 v. (loose-leaf) : ill. ; 30 cm. Cover title. LC Card 86-200612 DDC 338.973 19
1. Minority business enterprises - Government policy - United States. 2. Minority business enterprises - Law and legislation - United States. 3. Government purchasing - United States - Directories. I. Minority Business Advisors (Firm).
HD2346.U5 M55 1985

Minority Business Advisors (Firm) Minority business advisor. [Great Falls, Mont.] (1101 15th St. N., Great Falls 59401) [c1985- 1 v. (loose-leaf) : LC Card 86-200612 DDC 338.973 19
HD2346.U5 M55 1985

MINORITY BUSINESS ENTERPRISES - GOVERNMENT POLICY - UNITED STATES.
Minority business advisor. [Great Falls, Mont.] (1101 15th St. N., Great Falls 59401) [c1985- 1 v. (loose-leaf) : LC Card 86-200612 DDC 338.973 19
HD2346.U5 M55 1985

MINORITY BUSINESS ENTERPRISES - LAW AND LEGISLATION - UNITED STATES.
Minority business advisor. [Great Falls, Mont.] (1101 15th St. N., Great Falls 59401) [c1985- 1 v. (loose-leaf) : LC Card 86-200612 DDC 338.973 19
HD2346.U5 M55 1985

MINORITY BUSINESS ENTERPRISES - UNITED STATES.
Selected affirmative action topics in employment and business set-asides . Washington, D.C. , 1985- v. <1 > : LC Card 85-603434 DDC 331.13/3/0973 19
HF5549.5.A34 S45 1985

United States. Small Business Administration. Office of Procurement and Technical Assistance. Report to the Administrator on the analysis of the management and administration of the Procurement and Technical Assistance programs /. [Washington, D.C.] , 1984. 1 v. (various pagings) : *NYPL [JLF 86-1066]*

MINORITY GROUPS. see MINORITIES.

MINORITY WOMEN - EMPLOYMENT - SOUTH AFRICA.
Van der Walt, Sunette. Die vrou in die werksituasie in die RSA . Pretoria , 1986. vii, 156 p. : ISBN 0-7969-0373-5 LC Card 87-121977
HD6212 .V363 1986

MINORITY YOUTH - EMPLOYMENT - UNITED STATES.
Bullock, Paul. Youth training and employment from New Deal to New Federalism /. Los Angeles , c1985. xiii, 359 p. ; ISBN 0-89215-131-1 *NYPL [JLD 86-2972]*

Minőségfejlesztés az élelmiszer-termelésben . Kopcsó, István. Budapest , 1984. 253 p. : ISBN 963-231-707-6 : LC Card 85-183244
HD9000.5 .K644 1984

Minssen, Heiner. Fischer, Joachim, 1948- Neue Leistungspolitik in der Bekleidungsindustrie . Frankfurt/Main , New York , c1986. 264 p. : ISBN 3-593-33635-9 LC Card 86-197222
HD9940.G32 F57 1986

Minting, monetary circulation and exchange rates. International Congress on Economic History (8th : 1982 : Budapest, Hungary) Münzprägung, Geldumlauf und Wechselkurse . Trier , 1984. 421 p. : ISBN 3-923087-06-3 (pbk.)
HG205 1982 .I53 *NYPL [JLE 86-3176]*

Minton, Michael H. What is a wife worth? : the leading expert places a high dollar value on homemaking / Michael H. Minton with Jean Libman Block.1st McGraw-Hill pbk. ed. New York : McGraw-Hill, 1984, c1983. 192 p. ; 20 cm. Includes index. Bibliography: p. [181]-185. Reprint. Originally published : New York : Morrow, 1983. ISBN 0-07-042414-4 (pbk.) : LC Card 84-11221 DDC 331.4/28164/0973 19
1. Wages - Housewives - United States. 2. Housewives - United States - Economic conditions. I. Block, Jean Libman. II. Title.
HD4966.H842 U65 1984
NYPL [JLD 87-12]

MINTS - GEORGIA - DAHLONEGA - HISTORY - 19TH CENTURY.
Head, Sylvia. The neighborhood mint . Macon, Ga. , c1986. xviii, 206 p. : ISBN 0-86554-240-6 (alk. paper) : LC Card 86-23500 DDC 737.49758/273 19
HG461.D342 H4 1986

MINTS - MEXICO - MEXICO CITY - HISTORY - 18TH CENTURY.
Cortina Portilla, Manuel. Algo sobre la plata en México en el siglo XVIII /. México , 1986. 48 p., [1] folded leaf of plates : LC Card 87-404604 DDC 332.4/042/097253 19
HG661 .C67 1986

MINTS - UNITED STATES - HISTORY.
Wolman, Paul. The U. S. Mint /. New York , c1987. 92 p. : ISBN 0-87754-829-3 (lib. bdg.) : LC Card 86-31720 DDC 353.0082/2 19
HG459 .W65 1987

Mintzberg, Henry. Quinn, James Brian, 1928- The strategy process . Englewood Cliffs, N.J. , c1988. p. cm. ISBN 0-13-850892-5 LC Card 87-1160 DDC 658.4/012 19
HD30.28 .Q53 1988

Minujin Z., Alberto. Los Factores del cambio demográfico en México /. México, D.F. , 1984. 422 p. : ISBN 968-231-281-7 LC Card 85-231767
HB1361 .F33 1984 *NYPL [JLE 87-753]*

Minutas das exposições de motivos e portarias dos programas . Brazil. Ministério do Interior. Subsecretaria de Programas Regionais. [Brasília] [1983?] [40] leaves ; LC Card 87-400579 DDC 333.91/15/0981 19
HD1696.B8 B75 1983

Miodek, Wolfgang. Innerstädtische Umzüge und Stadtentwicklung in Mannheim, 1977-1983 : ein verhaltensbezogener Analyseansatz des Wohnstandortwahlverhaltens mobiler Haushalte / von Wolfgang Miodek. Mannheim : Im Selbstverlag des Geographischen Instituts der Universität, 1986. 244 p. : ill. ; 21 cm. (Mannheimer geographische Arbeiten. Heft 19) Originally presented as the author's thesis (doctoral)--Universität Mannheim, 1985. Summary in English and German. Bibliography: p. 210-223. ISBN 3-923750-18-8 : LC Card 86-181776
1. Residential mobility - Germany, West - Mannheim. 2. Housing - Germany, West - Mannheim. I. Title. II. Series.
HD7288.92.G32 M355 1986

Miracle, Gordon E. Voluntary regulation of advertising : a comparative analysis of the

United Kingdom and the United States / Gordon E. Miracle, Terence Nevett. Lexington, Mass. : Lexington Books, c1987. xxvi, 322 p. : ill. ; 24 cm. Includes bibliographies and index. ISBN 0-669-13135-0 (alk. paper) LC Card 86-45294 DDC 338.4/76591/0941 19
1. Advertising - United States - Self-regulation. 2. Advertising - Great Britain - Self-regulation. 3. Advertising laws - United States. 4. Advertising laws - Great Britain. I. Nevett, T. R. (Terence R.). II. Title.
HF5834 .M57 1987

Mirakhor, Abbas.
Iqbal, Zubair. Islamic banking /. Washington, D.C. , 1987. v, 62 p. ; ISBN 0-939934-82-5 (pbk.) : LC Card 87-4166 DDC 332.1/0917/671 19
HG3270.2.A6 I67 1987

Theoretical studies in Islamic banking and finance /. Houston, Tex. , 1987. xvi, 245 p. : ISBN 0-932625-07-X : LC Card 86-83221 DDC 332.1/0917/4927 19
HG3368.A6 T47 1987

Miranda Neto, Manoel José de. O dilema da Amazônia / Miranda Neto. 2a. ed. Belém, Pará : Edições CEJUP, [1986] 154 p. ; 23 cm. Bibliography: p. 141-154. LC Card 87-119394 DDC 330.981/1063 19
1. Amazon River Region - Economic conditions. 2. Brazil - Economic conditions. 3. Regional planning - Amazon River Region. I. Title.
HC188.A5 M57 1986

Mirenkov, A. M. Metodiki opredeleniia ėkonomicheskoĭ ėffektivnosti kapital'nykh vlozheniĭ v sotsialisticheskikh stranakh . Moskva , 1981. 101 p. ; LC Card 82-204402
HC244.Z9 C35 1981

Mirer, Thad W. Economic statistics and econometrics / Thad W. Mirer. 2nd ed. New York : Macmillan ; London : Collier Macmillan, c1988. xvi, 400 p. : ill. ; 24 cm. Bibliography: p. 389-392. Includes index. ISBN 0-02-381821-2 LC Card 87-24027 DDC 330/.028 19
1. Economics - Statistical methods. 2. Econometrics. I. Title.
HB137 .M57 1988

Mirić, Rade. Proces samoupravne integracije : studija slučaja (politikološki aspekt) / Rade Mirić. Bačka Topola : Centar za kulturu, obrazovanje i informisanje--Izdavačka delatnost, 1984. 147 p. ; 21 cm. (Biblioteka Naša praksa) In Serbo-Croatian (roman) Bibliography: p. 140-145. LC Card 85-194104
1. Management - Employee participation - Political aspects - Yugoslavia. 2. Yugoslavia - Economic policy - 1945-. I. Title. II. Series.
HD5660.Y8 M57 1984

Mirimanian, Khachatur Pogosovich. Nyut'er Hayastani gyughatntesut'yan ev gyughats'iut'yan patmut'yan /. Erevan , 1964- v. <1 > : LC Card 86-225528
HD1995.A7 N98 1964

Mirkes, Adolf, 1913- Simon, Josef, 1865-1949. Josef Simon, Schuhmacher, Gewerkschafter, Sozialist mit Ecken und Kanten /. Köln , c1985. 465 p. : ISBN 3-7663-0923-4 LC Card 85-186450
HD6695.S55 A3 1985

Mirkin, B. G. (Boris Grigor'evich) Modelirovanie sotsial'nykh faktorov v ėkonomiko-matematicheskikh issledovaniiakh /. Moskva , 1984. 148 p. : LC Card 87-125299
HC336.25. .M636 1984

Mironosetskiĭ, Nikolaĭ Borisovich. Imitatsionnoe modelirovanie proizvodstvennykh protsessov . Novosibirsk , 1979. 152 p. : LC Card 81-132238
HD70.S63 I44 1979

Mirovaia prodovol'stvennaia problema i naselenie . Oskolkova, O. B. (Ol'ga Borisovna) Moskva , 1982. 77 p. ; LC Card 82-198944
HD9000.5 .O84 1982

Mirovoe kapitalisticheskoe khoziaĭstvo v vos'midesiatye gody. Mirovoe kapitalisticheskoe khoziaĭstvo v 80-e gody . Moskva , 1985. 220 p. ; LC Card 87-166175
HC59 .M549 1985

Mirovoe kapitalisticheskoe khoziaĭstvo v 80-e gody : obostrenie protivorechiĭ : referativnyĭ sbornik / [sostavitel' i redaktor sbornika Zubchenko L.A.]. Moskva : Akademiia nauk SSSR, In-t nauch. informatsii po obshchestvennym naukam, 1985. 220 p. ; 20 cm. (Seriia Problemy mezhdunarodnykh ėkonomicheskikh otnosheniĭ) Includes bibliographies. LC Card 87-166175
1. Economic history - 1971-. 2. Economic policy. 3. Capitalism. I. Zubchenko, L. A. II. Title: Mirovoe kapitalisticheskoe khoziaĭstvo v vos'midesiatye gody. III. Series.
HC59 .M549 1985

Mirovoe sotsialisticheskoe khoziaĭstvo. The World socialist economy. Moscow , 1986. 279 p. ; LC Card 86-231463 DDC 338.9/009171/7 19
HC704 .W67 1986

Mirowski, Philip, 1951- Against mechanism : why economics needs protection from science / Philip Mirowski. Totowa, N.J. : Rowman & Littlefield, 1987. p. cm. Bibliography: p. Includes index. ISBN 0-8476-7436-3 : LC Card 87-21925 DDC 330/.09 19
1. Economics - History. 2. Science - History. I. Title.
HB71 .M635 1987

MISCARRIAGE. see **ABORTION.**

Miscellaneous casualty insurance in Japan. 3rd ed. Tokyo, Japan : Non-Life Insurance Institute of Japan, [1986] xi, 315 p. ; 28 cm. (Japanese practices of non-life insurance series . v. 3) LC Card 87-103937 DDC 368.5/00952 19
1. Insurance, Casualty - Japan. I. Songai Hoken Jigyō Kenkyūjo (Japan).
HG8705.A6 M57 1986

Miscellaneous lace records /. University of Nottingham. Dept. of Manuscripts. [Nottingham] [c1985] 12 p. ; LC Card 87-116493 DDC 016.3384/7677653/0942527 19
HD9933.G73 N688 1985

Miscellaneous publication (University of Minnesota. Agricultural Experiment Station)
(1986-37) Alexander von Humboldt Award Colloquium (1984) Technology, human capital, and the world food problem /. St. Paul, MN , 1986. x, 167 p. : LC Card 86-622216 DDC 338.1/9/1724 19
HD9018.D44 A44 1984

Miscellany II . Workshop: Middle Management and the Fisc. (1983 : Lahore, Pakistan) Lahore [1984?] 251 p. : LC Card 86-930242 DDC 354.549/10072 19
HJ3611.5 .W67 1983

MISCONDUCT OF OFFICE - MALAYSIA.
Lim, Kit Siang. BMF, scandal of scandals /. Petaling Jaya [1986] ix, 68 p. : LC Card 86-943248 DDC 364.1/68/09595 19
HG3300.6.A6 L553 1986

Misczynski, Dean J. Barbaria, Janet. The growth revolt . Sacramento, Calif. [1980] 66 p. : LC Card 81-620644 DDC 336.794 19
HJ4191 .B37 1980 ***NYPL [JLF 86-369]***

Mishkin, Frederic S. Current readings on money, banking, and financial markets /. Boston , c1987. xii, 356 p. : ISBN 0-316-94020-8 (pbk.) LC Card 87-4116 DDC 332 19
HG175 .C87 1987

Mishra, Bhagabat, 1940- Economics of public distribution system in food-grains / by Bhagabat Mishra. New Delhi : Ashish Pub. House, 1985. xviii, 306 p. (some folded) ; 22 cm. Revision of the author's thesis (Ph. D.--Utkal University, 1982) Includes index. Bibliography: p. 285-304. LC Card 85-902748 DDC 381/.4131/095413 19
1. Rice trade - Government policy - India - Orissa. 2. Grain trade - Government policy - India - Orissa. 3. Food supply - Government policy - India - Orissa. I. Title.
HD9066.I63 O756 1982
NYPL [JLD 86-1149]

Mishra, G. P. Village industries and agriculture in changing agrarian situation / G.P. Mishra, Ravi P. Rai, Brijesh K. Bajpai. New Delhi : Ashish Pub. House, c1985. 120 p. ; 23 cm. Includes bibliographies and index. ISBN 81-7024-010-7 LC Card 85-904926 DDC 338.6/34/0954 19
1. Cottage industries - India. 2. Agriculture - Social aspects - India. 3. India - Social conditions. I. Rai, Ravi Prakash. II. Bajpai, Brijesh K. III. Title.
HD2346.15 M49 1985 ***NYPL [JLD 86-3746]***

Mishra, M. N. (Maha Narain), 1945- Appraisal of credit facilities provided by banking institutions in rural development / M.N. Mishra. 1st ed. Meerut, U.P., India : Pragati Prakashan, [1987?] x, 251, ii p. ; 23 cm. "A research project financed by the U.G.C." Study conducted in a village in Uttar Pradesh. Bibliography: p. [i]-ii (3rd group) LC Card 87-900918 DDC 332.2 19
1. Development banks - India - Uttar Pradesh. 2. Small business - India - Uttar Pradesh - Finance. 3. Rural development - India - Uttar Pradesh - Finance. I. India. University Grants Commission. II. Title.
HG3284 .M49 1987

Mishra, R. K., 1948-
Management of human resources in public enterprises /. New Delhi, India , 1985. vi, 304 p. ; LC Card 87-402995 DDC 354.5409/2/0683 19
HD4293 .M355 1985

Public enterprises in India . Bombay , 1983. xxii, 524 p. ; LC Card 83-905617 DDC 354.5409/2 19
HD4293 .P793 1983 ***NYPL [JLD 87-723]***

Misi, Sándor. Soós, Gábor, 1922- Mit kell tudni a magyar agrártermelésről? /. [Budapest] , 1984. 218 p. ; ISBN 963-09-2474-9 : LC Card 85-154641
HD1940.5 .S66 1984

Misiaszek, Zbigniew. Prace z zakresu ekonomiki i organizacji przedsiębiorstw handlowych /. Kraków , 1978. 176 p. ; LC Card 81-200309
HB9 .K53 nr. 101 HF5429.6.P6

Miskell, Jack T. Holography, new commercial opportunities /. Stamford, Conn. , c1985. vii, 149 leaves : ISBN 0-89336-480-0 (soft) LC Card 87-165251 DDC 380.1/456213675 19
HD9707.5.H342 H64 1985

Misko, K. M. (Konstantin Mikhaĭlovich) Lipko, A. G. (Alekseĭ Gennad'evich) Proizvodstvo i potreblenie v regione /. Moskva , 1986. 142 p. : LC Card 86-211374
HC336.25 .L56 1986

A Miskolci Herman Ottó Múzeum néprajzi kiadványai, 0544-4233 .
(18) Árucsere és migráció . Miskolc , 1986. 237 p. : ISBN 963-01-6995-9 : LC Card 87-409685
HD5856.H9 A78 1986

Misr. see **Egypt.**

Misra, Girish Kumar, 1941- Kundu, Amitabh, 1948- Location of public enterprises and regional development /. New Delhi , 1986. xv, 178 p. ; LC Card 86-903373 DDC 338.954 19
HD9697.A3 I45 1986

Misra, Rameshwar Prasad, 1930- Development issues of our time / R.P. Misra. New Delhi : Concept Pub. Co., 1985. xi, 368 p. : ill. ; 25 cm. Includes bibliographies and index. LC Card 85-903754 DDC 338.9/009172/4 19
1. Economic development - Addresses, essays, lectures. 2. Developing countries - Economic policy - Addresses, essays, lectures. I. Title.
HC59.7 .M5334 1985 ***NYPL [JLE 86-1375]***

MISREPRESENTATION (LAW) see **FRAUD.**

Miss Lucy of the CIO . Salmond, John A. Athens , c1988. p. cm. ISBN 0-8203-0956-7 (alk. paper) LC Card 87-5822 DDC 331.88/33/0924 B 19
HD6509.M375 S25 1988

Missione impresariale del Governo dello Stato di São Paulo in Italia.
Industria dei pezzi per autoveicoli /. [São Paulo] , 1973. 1 v. (various pagings), [12] leaves of plates : LC Card 86-146007
HD9710.3.B72 I53 1973

Industria petrolchimica /. [São Paulo] , 1973. 1 v. (various pagings), [22] leaves of plates : LC Card 86-146014
HD9579.C33 B7417 1973

MISSISSIPPI - ECONOMIC CONDITIONS.
Moore, John Hebron. The emergence of the Cotton Kingdom in the Old Southwest . Baton Rouge , c1988. xii, 323 p. : ISBN 0-8071-1404-9 (pbk.) LC Card 87-2803 DDC 330.9762 19
HC107.M7 M66 1988

Misslbeck, Johannes, 1954- Der Österreichische Gewerkschaftsbund : Analyse einer korporatistischen Gewerkschaft / Johannes Misslbeck. Frankfurt/M. : Wisslit, [1983] iii, 197 p. : ill. ; 21 cm. Bibliography: p. 179-197. ISBN 3-89038-000-X (pbk.) LC Card 84-191049
1. Österreichischer Gewerkschaftsbund - History. 2. Trade-unions - Austria - Political activity - History. I. Title.
HD8403 .M57 1983

MISSOURI - APPROPRIATIONS AND EXPENDITURES - STATISTICS.
Missouri. General Assembly. Senate. Appropriations Committee. FY 87 budget summary . [Jefferson City, Mo.] [1986] 66 leaves : LC Card 87-620981 DDC 353.97780072/253 19
HJ2053.M8 M57 1986

Missouri. General Assembly. Senate. Appropriations Committee. FY 87 budget summary : 83rd General Assembly, 2nd regular session / prepared by Senate Appropriations staff. [Jefferson City, Mo.] : The Committee, [1986] 66 leaves : ill. ; 28 cm. Cover title. LC Card 87-620981 DDC 353.97780072/253 19
1. Budget - Missouri - Statistics. 2. Missouri - Appropriations and expenditures - Statistics. I. Title.
HJ2053.M8 M57 1986

MISSOURI-KANSAS-TEXAS RAILROAD - HISTORY.
Masterson, V. V. The Katy railroad and the last frontier /. Columbia , 1988. xiv, 312 p., [24] p. of plates : ISBN 0-8262-0668-9 (pbk. : alk. paper) LC Card 87-19146 DDC 385/.0978 19
HE2791.M743 M37 1988

Mistakable French . Thody, Philip Malcolm Waller, 1928- New York , 1985. 224 p. ; ISBN 0-684-18324-2 : LC Card 84-51853 DDC 443/.21 19
PC2593 .T46 1985 *NYPL [JFD 86-5781]*

Os Mistérios da inflação : idéias e propostas discutidas em Visão / artigos de Henry Maksoud e entrevistas com Francisco Lafaiete Lopes ... [et al.]. São Paulo : Editora Visão, 1986. 121 p. ; 21 cm. LC Card 86-189815
1. Inflation (Finance) - Brazil. 2. Brazil - Economic conditions - 1964-1985. 3. Brazil - Economic conditions - 1985-. I. Maksoud, Henry. II. Visão.
HG835 .M57 1986

Misthoi kai eisodēmata stēn Hellada, 1842-1923 . Pizanias, Petros. Athēna , 1985. 324 p., [20] p. of plates : LC Card 87-111106
HG3250.5.A7 P59 1985

Mistral, Jacques. La Crise de l'endettement international . Paris , c1986. 410 p. : ISBN 2-7178-1127-3 : LC Card 86-222862
HJ8017 .C74 1986

Mistri, Maurizio. Tasso di inflazione, saggio di interesse e "nuova" macroeconomia / Maurizio Mistri. Padova : CEDAM, 1985. x, 143 p. : ill. ; 25 cm. Includes bibliographies. LC Card 86-214490
1. Interest rates - Effect of inflation on. 2. Macroeconomics. I. Title.
HB539 .M54 1985

Miszewski, Bronisław. Borcz, Leszek. Przewodnik metodyczny do ekonomii politycznej dla doktorantów nieekonomistów /. Gliwice , 1979. 79 p. ; LC Card 81-182800
HB74.5 .B67 1979

Miszlivetz, Ferenc. Az Elmélet és a fegyverek kritikája . Budapest [1981] xxv, 509 p. ; ISBN 963-461-775-1 (Magy. nemz. bibl.) LC Card 85-139263
HC59.7 .E45 1981

Mit kell tudni a hetedik ötéves tervről? /. Bagota, Béla. [Budapest] , 1986. 238 p. ; ISBN 963-09-2815-9 : LC Card 86-210804
HC300.28 .B319 1986

Mit kell tudni a KGST-ről? /. Szelecki, György. [Budapest] , 1986. 126, [5] p. : ISBN 963-09-2731-4 : LC Card 86-210839
HC243.5 .S94 1986

Mit kell tudni a magyar agrártermelésről? /. Soós, Gábor, 1922- [Budapest] , 1984. 218 p. ; ISBN 963-09-2474-9 : LC Card 85-154641
HD1940.5 .S66 1984

Mit kell tudni a világ szakszervezeteiről? /. Pécsi, Anna. [Budapest] , 1972. 237 p. ; LC Card 85-178719
HD6476 .P29 1972

Mit kell tudni a 7. ötéves tervről? Bagota, Béla. Mit kell tudni a hetedik ötéves tervről? /. [Budapest] , 1986. 238 p. ; ISBN 963-09-2815-9 : LC Card 86-210804
HC300.28 .B319 1986

Mit kell tudni az 1987. évi népgazdasági tervről? /. Bagota, Béla. [Budapest] , 1987. 239 p. ; ISBN 963-09-3110-9 : LC Card 87-151787
HC300.28 .B329 1987

Mit kell tudni, 0324-7813.
Bagota, Béla. Mit kell tudni a hetedik ötéves tervről? /. [Budapest] , 1986. 238 p. ; ISBN 963-09-2815-9 : LC Card 86-210804
HC300.28 .B319 1986

Bagota, Béla. Mit kell tudni az 1987. évi népgazdasági tervről? /. [Budapest] , 1987. 239 p. ; ISBN 963-09-3110-9 : LC Card 87-151787
HC300.28 .B329 1987

Soós, Gábor, 1922- Mit kell tudni a magyar agrártermelésről? /. [Budapest] , 1984. 218 p. ; ISBN 963-09-2474-9 : LC Card 85-154641
HD1940.5 .S66 1984

Szelecki, György. Mit kell tudni a KGST-ről? /. [Budapest] , 1986. 126, [5] p. : ISBN 963-09-2731-4 : LC Card 86-210839
HC243.5 .S94 1986

MIT Press series on organization studies .
(8) Hirschhorn, Larry. The workplace within . Cambridge, Mass. , c1988. x, 265 p. ; ISBN 0-262-08169-5 LC Card 87-20144 DDC 158.7 19
HF5548.8 .H493 1988

MIT Press series on the regulation of economic activity .
(12) Perspectives on safe & sound banking . Cambridge, Mass. , 1986. xxi, 358 p. ; ISBN 0-262-02246-X LC Card 85-23882 DDC 332.1/0973 19
HG2481 .P47 1986 *NYPL [JLE 86-2960]*

(14) Public regulation . Cambridge, Mass. , c1987. xiv, 404 p. ; ISBN 0-262-02258-3 LC Card 86-21302 DDC 338.973 19
HD3616.U47 P83 1987

(15) Meyer, John Robert. Deregulation and the future of intercity passenger travel /. Cambridge, Mass. , c1987. xviii, 294 p. : ISBN 0-262-13225-7 LC Card 86-27308 DDC 387.7/42/0973 19
HE9803.A35 M49 1987

Mit qualitativ neuen Schritten zu höchsten Leistungen : Seminar des Zentralkomitees der SED mit den Generaldirektoren der Kombinate und den Parteiorganisatoren des ZK am 13. und 14. März 1986 in Leipzig : Brief der Teilnehmer des Seminars an den Generalsekretär des ZK der SED und Vorsitzenden des Staatsrates der DDR, Genossen Erich Honecker : aus dem Referat und aus dem Schlusswort des Mitglieds des Politbüros und Sekretärs des ZK der SED, Genossen Günter Mittag. Berlin : Dietz, 1986. 80 p. ; 20 cm. ISBN 3-320-00807-2 LC Card 87-144292 DDC 338.9431 19
1. Central planning - Germany (East). 2. Germany, East - Economic policy. I. Honecker, Erich. II. Mittag, Günter, 1926-. III. Sozialistische Einheitspartei Deutschlands. Zentralkomitee.
HC290.78 .M567 1986

Mitarbeiter-Kapitalbeteiligung in der Wirtschaft Niedersachsens . Schanz, Günther, 1943- Spardorf , c1984. 228 p. : ISBN 3-922919-26-X : LC Card 84-162288
HD5660.G412 L687 1984

Mitarbeiterbeteiligung und Mitbestimmung im Unternehmen / herausgegeben von Felix R. FitzRoy und Kornelius Kraft. Berlin ; New York : W. de Gruyter, 1987, c1986. ix, 351 p. : ill. ; 24 cm. Includes bibliographies. ISBN 3-11-010668-X LC Card 87-137953 DDC 658.3/152/0943 19
1. Industrial management - Germany (West) - Employee participation. 2. Industrial management - Germany (West) - Employee participation - Law and legislation. I. FitzRoy, Felix. II. Kraft, Kornelius.
HD5660.G4 M53 1987

Der mitbestimmte Aktiengesellschaftskonzern . Richter, Bernd, 1954- Köln , c1983. ix, 394 p. : ISBN 3-7663-0820-3 LC Card 83-215341
HD5660.G4 R53 1983

Mitbestimmung (Düsseldorf, Germany) Neue Technologien und Arbeitswelt . Köln , c1984. 197 p. : ISBN 3-7663-0893-9 LC Card 85-160745
HD6331.2.G28 N475 1984
NYPL [JLD 86-3861]

Mitbestimmung in der Krise--Krise der Mitbestimmung? : Gespräche mit Betroffenen / geführt von Heribert Kohl und Bernd Schütt ; mit einem Vorwort von Ernst Breit. Köln : Bund-Verlag, c1984. 192 p. : ill. ; 21 cm. (Schriftenreihe der Hans-Böckler-Stiftung . 11) ISBN 3-7663-0895-5 LC Card 85-113842
1. Management - Germany (West) - Employee participation. I. Kohl, Heribert, 1940-. II. Schütt, Bernd. III. Breit, Ernst. IV. Series: Schriftenreihe (Hans-Böckler-Stiftung) , 11.
HD5660.G4 M563 1984

Mitbestimmung, Norm und Wirklichkeit : Fallstudie aus einem Grossbetrieb der Automobilindustrie / Hans Diefenbacher ... [et al.], unter Mitarbeit von Ulrich Schasse. Frankfurt ; New York : Campus, c1984. 369 p. ; 21 cm. (Campus Forschung. Bd. 384) Bibliography: p. 263-270. ISBN 3-593-33325-2 LC Card 85-128882
1. Automobile industry and trade - Germany (West) - Management - Employee participation - Case studies. 2. Industrial management - Germany (West) - Employee participation - Case studies. I. Diefenbacher, Hans. II. Schasse, Ulrich.
HD5658.A82 G35 1984

Mitchell, B. R. (Brian R.) British historical statistics / by B.R. Mitchell. Cambridge [Cambridgeshire] ; New York : Cambridge University Press, 1988. p. cm. Includes index. ISBN 0-521-33008-4 LC Card 86-24513 DDC 314.1 19
1. Great Britain - Statistics - History. I. Title.
HA1134 .M58 1988

Mitchell, Barbara. Frozen stakes : the future of Antarctic minerals / by Barbara Mitchell. London ; Washington, D.C. : International Institute for Environment and Development, c1983. iii, 135 p. : ill. ; 21 cm. Includes bibliographies. ISBN 0-905347-45-5 (pbk.) : LC Card 84-173206 DDC 333.8/5/09989 19
1. Mineral industries - Antarctic regions. 2. Mines and mineral resources - Antarctic regions. 3. Antarctic regions - International status. I. Title.
HD9506.A585 M57 1983
NYPL [JLD 86-3548]

Mitchell, Bridger M.
Park, Rolla Edward. Optimal peak-load pricing for local telephone calls /. Santa Monica, CA , 1986. xiii, 37 p. : ISBN 0-8330-0741-6 (pbk.) LC Card 86-204468 DDC 384.6/3 19
HE8825 .P369 1986

Park, Rolla Edward. Optimal peak-load pricing for local telephone calls . Santa Monica, CA , c1986. x, 72 p. : ISBN 0-8330-0747-5 (pbk.) LC Card 86-203146 DDC 384.6/3 19
HE8825 .P369 1986 Suppl.

Park, Rolla Edward. Optimal peak-load pricing for local telephone calls . Santa Monica, CA , c1987. x, 75 p. : ISBN 0-8330-0857-9 (pbk.) LC Card 87-154411 DDC 384.6/3 19
HE8825 .P37 1987

Park, Rolla Edward. Optimal peak-load pricing for local telephone calls /. Santa Monica, CA , c1987. xiii, 41 p. : ISBN 0-8330-0856-X (pbk.) LC Card 87-410013 DDC 384.6/3 19
HE8825 .P369 1987

Mitchell, Garry. The trainer's handbook : the AMA guide to effective training / Garry Mitchell. New York : AMACOM, c1987. ix, 351 p. : ill. ; 26 cm. Bibliography: p. 336-338. Includes index. ISBN 0-8144-5875-0 LC Card 86-47819 DDC 658.3/124 19
1. Employees, Training of. I. Title.
HF5549.5.T7 M58 1987

Mitchell-Lama housing mortgage delinquencies . New York (State). Legislature. Legislative Commission on Expenditure Review. Albany, N.Y. (111 Washington Ave., Albany 12210-2277) [1985] 5, ii, 44 p. : LC Card 86-620632 DDC 353.97470086/5045 19
HD7303.N7 N394 1985 *NYPL [JLF 87-104]*

Mitchell, Nikola. Trinidad and Tobago : a social studies course for secondary schools / Nikola Mitchell. London : Macmillan Caribbean, 1981 92 p. : ill., maps ; 25 cm. Bibliography: p. 92. ISBN 0-333-31482-4 (pbk.) LC Card 85-187281 DDC 300/.7/1272983 19
1. Trinidad and Tobago - Economic conditions - Study and teaching (Secondary) - Trinidad and Tobago. 2. Trinidad and Tobago - Social conditions - Study and teaching (Secondary) - Trinidad and Tobago. I. Title.
HC157.T83 M58 1985

Mitchell, Robert B., 1952- Tedesco, Eleanor Hollis. Administrative office systems management /. New York , c1987. xii, 736 p. : ISBN 0-471-01201-7 LC Card 86-26800 DDC

651.3 19
HF5547 .T37 1987

Mitchell, Theodore R. Political education in the Southern Farmers' Alliance, 1887-1900 / Theodore R. Mitchell. Madison, Wis. : University of Wisconsin Press, 1987. xiv, 242 p. : ill. ; 24 cm. Bibliography: p. 209-236. Includes index. ISBN 0-299-11470-8 : LC Card 87-40141 DDC 338.1/06/075 19
1. National Farmers' Alliance and Industrial Union - History. 2. Farmers - Southern States - Political activity - History - 19th century. 3. Farmers - Education - Southern States - History - 19th century. 4. Civics - Study and teaching - Southern States - History - 19th century. 5. Populism - Southern States - History - 19th century. I. Title.
HD1485.N35 M58 1987

Mitgliedererwartungen in Bankgenossenschaften . Bakonyi, Emmerich. Stuttgart , c1983. 389 p. : ISBN 3-8001-8188-6 LC Card 84-106778
HG2035 .B28 1983

Mitgliederförderndes Kooperations- und Konkurrenzmanagement in genossenschaftlichen Systemen /. Lipfert, Helmut. Göttingen , c1986. xvii, 302 p. : ISBN 3-525-12754-5 LC Card 86-235180 DDC 334/.068 19
HD3498 .L53 1986

Mitgliederförderung in Strassenverkehrsgenossenschaften /. Berger, Axel. Münster , 1985. 455 p. ; ISBN 3-7923-0537-2 (Deut. Bibl.) LC Card 86-148185
HD6698.T72 B863 1985

Mitgliederversammlungen und Willensbildung in Genossenschaften /. Deppenkemper, Bernhard. Gelsenkirchen , 1984. 316 p. : ISBN 3-88485-473-9 LC Card 85-114636
HG2039.G4 D45 1984

Mitre, Antonio. El monedero de los Andes : región económica y moneda boliviana en el siglo XIX / Antonio Mitre. La Paz : Hisbol, 1986. 134 p. ; 28 cm. Bibliography: p. 123-133. LC Card 87-403038 DDC 332.4/98 19
1. Monetary policy - Andes Region - History - 19th century. 2. Andes Region - Commerce - History - 19th century. 3. Silver industry - Bolivia - Potosí - History - 19th century. 4. Monetary policy - Bolivia - History - 19th century. I. Title.
HG803 .M57 1986

Mitrofanova, L. V. Puti razvitiia infrastruktury regiona /. Ufa , 1984. 117 p. : LC Card 85-199949
HE255.Z7 B377 1984

Mitroff, Ian I. Business not as usual : rethinking our individual, corporate, and industrial strategies for global competition / Ian I. Mitroff, in collaboration with Susan A. Mohrman and Geoffrey Little.1st ed. San Francisco : Jossey-Bass Publishers, 1987. xxi, 194 p. : ill. ; 24 cm. (The Jossey-Bass management series) Bibliography: p. 181-187. Includes index. ISBN 1-555-42030-3 (alk. paper) LC Card 86-46333 DDC 338.9 19
1. Industrial management - United States. 2. Organizational change - United States. 3. Industrial organization - United States. 4. Competition, International. I. Mohrman, Susan Albers. II. Little, Geoffrey, 1956-. III. Title. IV. Series.
HD70.U5 M52 1987

Mitschke, Joachim. Steuer- und Transferordnung aus einem Guss : Entwurf einer Neugestaltung der direkten Steuern und Sozialtransfers in der Bundesrepublik Deutschland / Joachim Mitschke.1. Aufl. Baden-Baden : Nomos, 1985. 274 p. : ill. ; 23 cm. (Schriften zur Ordnungspolitik . Bd. 2) Bibliography: p. 245-250. Includes index. ISBN 3-7890-1097-9 LC Card 85-235532
1. Taxation - Germany, West. 2. Taxation - Law and legislation - Germany, West. 3. Transfer payments - Germany, West. 4. Negative income tax - Germany (West). I. Title. II. Series.
HJ2687 .M57 1985

Mitsotaki, Alexandra Gourdain. Public development finance corporations : their role in the new forms of investment in developing countries / by Alexandra Gourdain Mitsotaki. Paris : Development Centre of the Organisation for Economic Co-operation and Development, 1986. 40 p. ; 23 cm. (Development Centre papers) Includes bibliographical references. LC Card 86-221546 DDC 332.6/734/01724 19
1. Investments, West German - Developing countries. 2. Investments, British - Developing countries. 3. Investments, French - Developing countries. I. Title. II. Series.
HG5993 .M57 1986

Mittag, Günter, 1926- Mit qualitativ neuen Schritten zu höchsten Leistungen . Berlin , 1986. 80 p. ; ISBN 3-320-00807-2 LC Card 87-144292 DDC 338.9431 19
HC290.78 .M567 1986

Mittal, Satya Narayan, 1947- Central taxation of income in India since 1951 : a critical and suggestive study / Satya Narayan Mittal. Delhi : B.R. Pub. Corp. ; New Delhi : Distributed by D.K. Publishers' Distributors, 1986. 321 p. ; 23 cm. Bibliography: p. [309]-316. Includes index. ISBN 81-7018-327-8 : LC Card 86-902918 DDC 336.24/0954 19
1. Income tax - India. I. Title.
HJ4766 .M58 1986

Mitteilung der Staatlichen Zentralverwaltung für Statistik der DDR über die Durchführung des Volkswirtschaftsplanes 1982. Berlin : Panorama DDR, 1983. 46 p. ; 20 cm. (Dokumente zur Politik der Deutschen Demokratischen Republik . 1/1983) LC Card 85-145182
1. Germany, East - Economic conditions. 2. Germany, East - Economic policy. 3. Germany, East - Industries. I. Germany (East). Staatliche Zentralverwaltung für Statistik. II. Series: Dokumente zur Politik der Deutschen Demokratischen Republik , 1983/1.
HC290.78 .M58 1983

Mitteilungen aus dem Handelswissenschaftlichen Seminar der Universität Zürich .
(Heft 156) Nötzli, Irene M. A view of Japanese management, especially management development in large business enterprises /. Zürich , c1982. ix, 281 p. : ISBN 3-7255-2191-3 (pbk.) LC Card 82-237094 DDC 658.4/07124 19
HF5549.5.T7 N638 1982 ***NYPL [TB (Zürich. Universität. Handelwissenschaftiches Seminar. Mitteilungen. Heft 156)]***

(Heft 163) Egger, Emil. Management Accounting in öffentlichen nichtgewinnorientierten Organisationen . Zürich , c1985. xii, 220 p. : ISBN 3-7255-2410-6 LC Card 85-132536
HF5686.N56 E33 1985

Mitteilungen des Deutschen Orient-Instituts .
(Nr. 25) Philipp, Hans-Jürgen. Die landwirtschaftliche Modernisierung Saudi-Arabiens im 20. Jahrhundert /. Hamburg , c1984. 132 p. : LC Card 85-166668
HD2060.Z8 P48 1984

(Nr. 26) Mattes, Hanspeter. Aspekte der libyischen Ausseninvestitionspolitik, 1972-1985 /. Hamburg , c1985. iv, 169 p. : ISBN 3-89173-001-2 LC Card 86-173976
HG4538 .M376 1985

Mittelbetriebe und Entwicklungsländer . Moosmann, Bernfried, 1957- Frankfurt am Main , New York , c1986. x, 290 p. ; ISBN 3-8204-9518-5 LC Card 86-232976
HF3569.B2 M66 1986

Mitteleuropa und die Länder am unteren Donaulauf im 18. und 19. Jahrhundert. Paskaleva-Zakharieva, Virzhiniia. Sredna Evropa i zemite po Dolniia Dunav prez XVIII-XIX v. . Sofiia , 1986. 317 p. : LC Card 86-219994
HC244 .P29 1986

Mittelman, James H. Out from underdevelopment : prospects for the Third World / James H. Mittelman. New York : St. Martin's Press, 1988. p. cm. Bibliography: p. Includes index. ISBN 0-312-01188-1 : LC Card 87-22927 DDC 338.9/009172/4 19
1. Developing countries - Economic policy. 2. Developing countries - Economic conditions. I. Title.
HC59.7 .M5337 1988

Mittelstädt, Axel. Klau, Friedrich. Labour market flexibility and external price shocks /. Paris, France , c1985. 60 p. : LC Card 86-205164 DDC 331.12 19
HD5707 .K54 1985

Die mittelständische Unternehmung . Hinderer, Michael. München , c1984. xix, 435 p. : ISBN 3-88259-328-8 LC Card 85-152951
HD2341 .H56 1984

Mittelstand, Träger der Marktwirtschaft . Hamer, Eberhard. Minden , c1984- v. ; ISBN 3-7907-3056-4 (Bd. 1) LC Card 85-175274 DDC 338.6/42/0943 19
HD2346.G3 H215 1984 ***NYPL [JLK 86-61]***

Mittelstand und Entwicklungsländer . Menck, Karl Wolfgang. Hamburg , 1986. 192 p. ; ISBN 3-87895-318-6 LC Card 87-407405 DDC 337.43/59/01724 19
HF1546.19.L68 M46 1986

Mitter, Swasti, 1939- Common fate, common bond : women in the global economy / Swasti Mitter. London ; Wolfeboro, N.H., USA : Pluto Press, 1986. 184 p. : ill. ; 20 cm. Bibliography: p. [175]-177. Includes index. ISBN 0-7453-0026-X (pbk.) : LC Card 87-101525 DDC 331.4/2 19
1. Women - Employment. I. Title.
HD6053 .M54 1986

The Mitterrand and Reagan economic experiments . Saint-Etienne, Christian, 1951- [Stanford, Calif.] , c1986. 36 p ; ISBN 0-8179-5082-6 (pbk.) LC Card 86-27776 DDC 338.944 19
HC276.2 .S24 1986

Mitulescu, Sorin. Cazacu, Honorina. Democraţia socialistă în acţiune . Bucureşti , 1985. 192 p. : LC Card 86-216024
HD5660.R6 C39 1985

Mitullah, W. V. Management of urban services in Nairobi : focus on matatu mode of public transport / W.V. Mitullah. Nairobi, Kenya : Mazingira Institute, 1985. 109, 106, vi p., [6] leaves of plates : maps ; 30 cm. "Part of a comparative research project 'Urban Growth and Management of Urban Reform' of the Institute of Environmental Studies (IES) of the University of Toronto"--Acknowledgments. "June 1985." Bibliography: p. [i]-vi. LC Card 87-116360 DDC 388.4/09676/25 19
1. Municipal services - Kenya - Nairobi. 2. Transportation - Kenya - Nairobi. 3. Informal sector (Economics) - Kenya - Nairobi. I. Mazingira Institute. II. University of Toronto. Institute of Environmental Studies. III. Title.
HD4720.5.N35 M57 1985

Mitverantwortung .
(2) Marktwirtschaft 2000 /. Krefeld , c1983. 137 p. : ISBN 3-88289-302-8 LC Card 84-229313 DDC 338.9 19
HD75.6 .M37 1983 ***NYPL [JLD 86-3124]***

MIXED ECONOMY - CONGRESSES.
Reassessing the role of government in the mixed economy /. Boulder , 1987. p. cm. ISBN 0-8133-0598-5 : LC Card 87-20142 DDC 338.9 19
HD73 .R43 1987

Mixed-use development handbook /. Schwanke, Dean. Washington, D.C. , 1987. xv, 364 p. : ISBN 0-08-742665-0 LC Card 86-51443 DDC 333.3/8 19
HD1390 .S38 1987

MIXTEC INDIANS - POPULATION.
Mora, Teresa. La Mixteca baja, su migración . México, D.F. , 1982. 129, [84] leaves ; LC Card 87-122391 DDC 304.6/0972/74 19
HB3532.O18 M67 1982

La Mixteca baja, su migración . Mora, Teresa. México, D.F. , 1982. 129, [84] leaves ; LC Card 87-122391 DDC 304.6/0972/74 19
HB3532.O18 M67 1982

Miyao, Takahiro. Urban dynamics and urban externalities / Takahiro Miyao and Yoshitsugu Kanemoto. Chur, Switzerland ; New York : Harwood Academic Publishers, c1987. viii, 107 p. : ill. ; 22 cm. (Fundamentals of pure and applied economics, 0191-1708 . vol. 11.) Includes bibliographies and index. ISBN 3-7186-0333-0 (pbk.) LC Card 86-25629 DDC 330.9173/2 19
1. Population density. 2. Externalities (Economics). 3. Urban economics. I. Kanemoto, Yoshitsugu. II. Series: Fundamentals of pure and applied economics , v. 11. III. Title.
HB2161 .M595 1987

Mizala, Alejandra. Meller, Patricio. Una revisión de políticas de empleo para América Latina /. Santiago, Chile , 1981. 72 leaves ; LC Card 83-182110
HD5730.5.A6 M44 1981

MIZORAM (INDIA) - CENSUS, 1981.
Household population by religion of head of household, upto C.D. block and town level,

series 31, Mizoram . Delhi , 1986. xiii, 17 p. ; LC Card 87-900232 DDC 304.6/0954/166021 19
HA4587.M58 H68 1986

MIZORAM (INDIA) - POPULATION - STATISITCS.
Household population by religion of head of household, upto C.D. block and town level, series 31, Mizoram . Delhi , 1986. xiii, 17 p. ; LC Card 87-900232 DDC 304.6/0954/166021 19
HA4587.M58 H68 1986

MIZORAM (INDIA) - RELIGION - STATISTICS.
Household population by religion of head of household, upto C.D. block and town level, series 31, Mizoram . Delhi , 1986. xiii, 17 p. ; LC Card 87-900232 DDC 304.6/0954/166021 19
HA4587.M58 H68 1986

Mizruchi, Mark S. Intercorporate relations . Cambridge [Cambridgeshire] , New York , 1987. x, 330 p. : ISBN 0-521-33503-5 LC Card 87-6388 DDC 338.7 19
HD2741 .I585 1987

Mjella, Ali. Salomon, Robert. Ruvuma region . Dar es Salaam , 1981. 32 leaves : LC Card 85-981451
HD7289.T352 R897 1981

Mkrtchīan, G. M. (Gagik Mkrtichevich) Bostandzhīan, V. B. (Vardan Babkenovich) Optimizatsiia otraslevykh sistem v sostave ėkonomicheskikh programm /. Novosibirsk , 1982. 120, [1] p. : LC Card 83-107849
HC337.R852 S5234 1982

Mkwawa, D. A. Y. A review of aerodrome statistics in Tanzania, 1970-1982. Dar es Salaam : Aerodromes Division, Ministry of Works, [1984] xix, 143 p. : ill. ; 27 cm. At head of title: The United Republic of Tanzania. "March 1984." LC Card 87-403351 DDC 387.7/36/09678021 19
1. Airports - Tanzania - Statistics. 2. Aeronautics, Commercial - Tanzania - Statistics. I. Tanzania. Aerodromes Division. II. Title.
HE9797.5.T34 M58 1984

Mladenov, Vŭlko P. Zhamin, V. A. (Vitaliĭ Alekseevich) Sotsialisticheskaia ėkonomicheskaia integratsiia--faktor povysheniia ėffektivnosti proizvodstva stran SĖV /. Moskva , Varna , 1978. 93 p. ; LC Card 81-149558
HC244 .Z46 1978

MNB Közgazdasági Főosztály közleményei, 0231-259X .
(13) Langmár, Andrásné. A Német Szövetségi Köztársaság bankrendszere /. Budapest [1987] 71 p. : ISBN 963-7103-59-7 LC Card 87-409642
HG3048 .L47 1987

MNC's in Nigeria . Onimode, Bade. Ibadan , 1983. ix, 144 p. ; ISBN 978-231-800-0 (pbk.) LC Card 86-195403 DDC 338.8/88669 19
HD2928 .O55 1983

Mnogootraslevye kompleksy--problemy i metody optimizatsii /. Martynov, G. V. (Gennadiĭ Viktorovich) Moskva , 1986. 229, [3] p. : LC Card 86-232408
HC333 .M285 1986

Moar, L. Gregory, P. World offshore markets . London , 1986. xiv, 215 p. ; ISBN 0-946416-06-0 (pbk.) : LC Card 86-217327 DDC 338.2/7282/0941 19
HD9571.5 .G75 1986

Moavenzadeh, Fred, 1935- The construction industry in developing countries. Nairobi : United Nations Centre for Human Settlements (Habitat), 1984. 2 v. ; 30 cm. "Report is an abridged version ... study prepared for the United Nations Centre for Human Settlements by Professor Fred Moavenzadeh"--P. ii. "HS/32/8 (v. 1); HS/35/84/E (v. 2)"--T.p. verso. Includes bibliographies. CONTENTS. - v. 1. Contributions to socio-economic growth -- v. 2. Profile of the industry in selected countries. LC Card 85-980242 DDC 338.4/767/091724 19
1. Construction industry - Developing countries. I. United Nations Centre for Human Settlements. II. Title.
HD9715.D44 M63 1984

Moberg, Krister, 1950- Dahlgren, Bo, 1924- Nyckeln til styrelserummet . Stockholm [1983] 182 p. : ISBN 91-1-837051-9 : LC Card 83-210185
HD2883 .D34 1983

Mobil in South Africa : the challenge. [Cape Town] : Public Affairs Dept. of Mobil Oil Southern Africa, [1986] 64 p. : ill. (some col.) ; 29 cm. Cover title. "Issued by the Public Affairs Department of Mobil Oil Southern Africa (Pty) Ltd., edited and produced by International Research and Information Services (IRIS), Cape Town"--P. 4 of cover. ISBN 0-620-09921-6 (pbk.) LC Card 87-126457 DDC 338.7/6223382/0968 19
1. Mobil Oil Southern Africa, pty., ltd. 2. Petroleum industry and trade - South Africa. I. International Research and Information Services (Cape Town, South Africa). II. Mobil Oil Southern Africa, pty., ltd. Public Affairs Dept.
HD9577.S64 M636 1986

MOBIL OIL SOUTHERN AFRICA, PTY., LTD.
Mobil in South Africa . [Cape Town] [1986] 64 p. : ISBN 0-620-09921-6 (pbk.) LC Card 87-126457 DDC 338.7/6223382/0968 19
HD9577.S64 M636 1986

Mobil Oil Southern Africa, pty., ltd. Public Affairs Dept. Mobil in South Africa . [Cape Town] [1986] 64 p. : ISBN 0-620-09921-6 (pbk.) LC Card 87-126457 DDC 338.7/6223382/0968 19
HD9577.S64 M636 1986

MOBILE COMMUNICATION SYSTEMS - EUROPE.
The Mobile radio market in Western Europe. New York, N.Y. , c1982. x, 283 p. : LC Card 87-141850 DDC 380.1/45621384165/094 19
HD9696.R363 E855 1982

MOBILE HOME PARKS - GOVERNMENT POLICY - CALIFORNIA.
Local government mobilehome and mobilehome park policies in California . [Sacramento, Calif.] [1986] iii, 70 p. ; LC Card 86-622920 DDC 333.33/8 19
HD7289.62.U6 L63 1986

MOBILE HOMES - GOVERNMENT POLICY - CALIFORNIA.
Local government mobilehome and mobilehome park policies in California . [Sacramento, Calif.] [1986] iii, 70 p. ; LC Card 86-622920 DDC 333.33/8 19
HD7289.62.U6 L63 1986

Mobile Lebensformgruppen Südost-Arabiens im Wandel . Asche, H. (Hartmut) Berlin , 1981, c1982. xii, 344 p. : ISBN 3-496-00302-2 LC Card 86-217612
HD8039.F652 O522 1982

The Mobile radio market in Western Europe. New York, N.Y. : Frost & Sullivan, c1982. x, 283 p. : ill. ; 29 cm. "December 1982." "#E462." LC Card 87-141850 DDC 380.1/45621384165/094 19
1. Radio supplies industry - Europe. 2. Cellular radio equipment industry - Europe. 3. Mobile communication systems - Europe. 4. Market surveys - Europe. I. Frost & Sullivan.
HD9696.R363 E855 1982

Mobilität und Beruf . Koll, Hermann Josef. Opladen , 1981. xviii, 564 p. ; ISBN 3-531-11551-0 : LC Card 81-158683
HD5717.5.G3 K64 1981

Mobilités professionnelles et géographiques au Québec, 1954-64-74 /. Garon-Audy, Muriel. Montréal , 1980. 61 p. ; LC Card 81-105620 DDC 331.12/7971 19
HD5717.5.C22 Q44 1980
NYPL [JLM 79-970 no.22]

MOBILITY. see LABOR MOBILITY; MIGRATION, INTERNAL; RESIDENTIAL MOBILITY; SOCIAL MOBILITY.

Mobility and employment in urban Southeast Asia . Costello, Michael A. Boulder , 1987. xvi, 190 p. : ISBN 0-8133-7352-2 (pbk. : alk. paper) : LC Card 87-10649 DDC 307.2 19
HB2107 .C67 1987

The mobility of labor and capital . Sassen, Saskia. Cambridge [Cambridgeshire] , New York , 1988. p. cm. ISBN 0-521-32227-8 LC Card 87-14586 DDC 331.12/791 19
HD6300 .S37 1988

MOBILIZATION, INDUSTRIAL. see INDUSTRIAL MOBILIZATION.

Mobilization of the private sector in Burkina Faso . Berg, Elliot. [Burkina Faso? , 1985] 21 p. ; LC Card 87-116357 DDC 338.966/25 19
HC1040 .B47 1985

Mobilizing bank lending to debtor countries /. Cline, William R. Washington, DC , 1987. viii, 92 p. : ISBN 0-88132-062-5 (pbk.) LC Card 87-16857 DDC 332.1/5 19
HG3891.5 .C58 1987

Mobilizing invisible assets /. Itami, Hiroyuki, 1945- Cambridge, Mass. , 1987. xi, 186 p. : ISBN 0-674-57770-1 (alk. paper) LC Card 86-26972 DDC 658.4/012 19
HD30.28 .I85 1987

Mobilizing the peasantry for rural development [microform] . Fassil G. Kiros. [Addis Ababa , 1982] 20 leaves ; LC Card 82-980723 DDC 334/.683/0963 19
HD1538.E7 F37 1982
NYPL [*Z-3952 no.39]

Moçambique. see Mozambique.

Mock Cedeño, Ariel. Las empresas públicas en Panamá : tres tesis políticas / Ariel Mock Cedeño, Rufino Fernández. Panamá, Rep. de Panamá : Ediciones Conaisa, 1986. vi, 89, [5] p. ; 21 cm. (Cuadernos administrativos . 1) Errata slip inserted. Bibliography: p. [90]-[93]. LC Card 87-400433 DDC 338.97287 19
1. Government business enterprises - Panama. 2. Panama - Economic policy. I. Fernández, Rufino. II. Title. III. Series.
HD4043 .M63 1986

MODAL CHOICE IN TRANSPORTATION. see CHOICE OF TRANSPORTATION.

MODAL SPLIT (TRANSPORTATION) see CHOICE OF TRANSPORTATION.

MODDERNO, FRANCINE.
Cantrell, Will. 101 ways to find an overseas job /. [Merrifield, VA.] [c1987] 1 v. (various pagings) ; ISBN 0-941541-00-2 (pbk.) LC Card 86-73093 DDC 650.1/4 19
HF5549.5.E45 C33 1987

MODEL CITIES. see CITY PLANNING.

A model for joint public sector/private sector participation in core area housing development and core area revitalization /. Levin, Earl A. [Winnipeg, Man., Canada] , 1985. ix leaves, 93 p. ; LC Card 86-137674 DDC 363.5/8 19
HD7305.M3 L48 1985 ***NYPL [JLF 86-1313]***

A model for the study of international trade politics . Kolarik, William F. New York , 1987. 613 p. : ISBN 0-8240-8086-6 (alk. paper) : LC Card 87-23788 DDC 382/.0947/0730724 19
HF3105 .K64 1987

Model housing from the great exhibition to the festival of Britain /. Gaskell, S. Martin. London , New York , 1986. x, 180 p. : ISBN 0-7201-1834-4 : LC Card 86-23775 DDC 363.5/0941 19
HD7333.A3 G37 1986

Model of an Islamic bank /. Ṣiddiqi, Muḥammad Iqbal. Lahore, Pakistan , 1986. 90 p. ; LC Card 87-931018 DDC 332.1/0917/671 19
HG3368.A6 S54 1986

A model program for schools of professional accountancy /. McGee, Robert W. Lanham, MD , c1987. xiii, 192 p. ; ISBN 0-8191-6094-6 (alk. paper) : LC Card 86-28226 DDC 657/.07/1173 19
HF5630 .M39 1987

A model to predict urban influenced land prices /. Weideman, Donald James. [Edmonton, Alta.] [1986] xi, 294 p. : ISBN 0-88654-148-4 (pbk.) LC Card 86-231786 DDC 333.33/7 19
HD319.A4 W45 1986

Le modèle centre-périphérique appliqué à l'est du Québec . Gagnon, Alain. Rimouski , c19. ix, 154 p. ; LC Card 80-143484
HC117.G37 G33 1980

Modele matematice şi semiotice ale dezvoltării sociale / sub redacţia, Solomon Marcus. Bucureşti : Editura Academiei Republicii Socialiste România, 1986. 190 p. : ill. ; 24 cm. At head of title: Academia Republicii Socialiste România, Comisia "Revoluţia Ştiinţifică şi Tehnică." "Volumul de faţă este o continuare a lucrării colective 'Metode matematice în problematica dezvoltării'"--Pref. Table of contents in English, Romanian, and Russian. Includes bibliographies. LC Card 86-208152

1. Economic development - Mathematical models. 2. Economic policy - Mathematical models. I. Marcus, Solomon. II. Academia Republicii Socialiste România. Comisia Revoluția Științifică și Tehnică. III. Metode matematice în problematica dezvoltării.
HD75.5 .M615 1986

Les Modèles de consommation et les politiques alimentaires dans les pays du Maghreb : séminaire international, 17-19 décembre 1984, Alger / Centre de recherche en économie appliquée (C.R.E.A.) [et] Organisation des Nations Unies pour l'alimentation et l'agriculture (F.A.O.) [et] Centre international de hautes études agronomiques méditerranéennes, Institut agronomique méditerranéen de Montpellier. Alger : C.R.E.A., [1985?] 401 p. : ill. ; 30 cm. Includes bibliographical references. LC Card 87-132818
1. Food consumption - Africa, North - Congresses. 2. Food supply - Africa, North - Congresses. I. Centre de recherches en économie appliquée (Algiers, Algeria). II. Food and Agriculture Organization of the United Nations. III. Institut agronomique méditerranéen de Montpellier.
HD9017.A24 M63 1985

Les modèles scandinaves et la détermination des ententes salariales des industries manufacturières canadiennes . Dussault, François. Montréal [1982] 21, [11] p. ; LC Card 82-196710
HD4979 .D875 1982

Modeli formirovaniia organizatsionnykh struktur /. Ovsievich, Boris L'vovich. Leningrad , 1979. 157, [3] p. : LC Card 81-162540
HD30.25 .O97 1979

Modeli i metody resheniia zadach vzaimodeĭstviia ėkonomicheskikh sistem / otvetstvennye redaktory E.L. Berliand, V.V. Radchenko. Novosibirsk : Izd-vo "Nauka," Sibirskoe otd-nie, 1982. 160 p. : ill. ; 22 cm. (Matematicheskiĭ analiz ėkonomicheskikh modeleĭ) At head of title: Akademiia nauk SSSR. Sibirskoe otdelenie. Institut ėkonomiki i organizatsii promyshlennogo proizvodstva. Includes bibliographies. LC Card 83-164468
1. Economics - Statistical methods. I. Berliand, Efim L'vovich. II. Radchenko, V. V. (Viktor Vladimirovich). III. Institut ėkonomiki i organizatsii promyshlennogo proizvodstva (Akademiia nauk SSSR). IV. Series.
HB137 .M6 1982

Modeling metropolitan economies for forecasting and policy analysis /. Drennan, Matthew P., 1937- New York , 1985. x, 242 p. ; ISBN 0-8147-1781-0 (alk. paper) : LC Card 85-13784 DDC 330.9173/2 19
HT321 .D74 1985 ***NYPL [JLE 86-1102]***

Modelirovanie ėkonomicheskogo povedeniia sotsialisticheskogo predpriiatiia / [otvetstvennye redaktory Petrakov N.IA., Voronovitskiĭ, M.M.]. Moskva : Akademiia nauk SSSR, TSentr. ėkonomiko-matematicheskiĭ in-t, 1984. 131 p. : ill. ; 20 cm. Includes bibliographies. LC Card 86-144437
1. Industrial management - Mathematical models. 2. Industrial management - Soviet Union. I. Petrakov, Nikolaĭ IAkovlevich. II. Voronovitskiĭ, M. M. III. TSentral'nyĭ ėkonomiko-matematicheskiĭ institut (Akademiia nauk SSSR).
HD30.25 .M623 1984

Modelirovanie i optimizatsionnye raschety : primenitel'no k agropromyshlennym formirovaniiam / [avtory V.A. Tochilin ... et al. ; redaktsionnaia kollegiia A.M. Onishchenko (otvetstvennyĭ redaktor) ... et al.]. Kiev : Nauk. dumka, 1986. 222, [2] p. : ill. ; 21 cm. At head of title: Akademiia nauk Ukrainskoĭ SSR. Institut ėkonomiki. Bibliography: p. 218-[223]. LC Card 86-233713
1. Agricultural industries - Soviet Union - Management - Mathematical models. I. Tochilin, Viktor Aleksandrovich. II. Onishchenko, Alekseĭ Moiseevich. III. Instytut ekonomiky (Akademiia nauk Ukraïns'koï RSR).
HD9015.S652 M62 1986

Modelirovanie i prognozirovanie ėlementov uslovno-chistoĭ produktsii i finansovykh potokov / [otvetstvennye redaktory IUriĭ Pavlovich Solov'ev, Alekseĭ Igorevich Gladyshevskiĭ]. Moskva : Akademiia nauk SSSR, TSentr. ėkonomiko-matematicheskiĭ in-t, 1981. 180 p. : ill. ; 20 cm. Includes bibliographies. LC Card 83-171742
1. Production functions (Economic theory). I. Solov'ev, IU. P. IUriĭ Pavlovich). II. Gladyshevskiĭ, Alekseĭ Igorevich. III. TSentral'nyĭ ėkonomiko-matematicheskiĭ institut (Akademiia nauk SSSR).
HD30.25 .M635 1981

Modelirovanie mezhotraslevykh vzaimodeĭstviĭ / [otvetstvennyĭ redaktor IU.V. IAremenko]. Moskva : Izd-vo "Nauka", 1984. 277 p. : ill. ; 23 cm. (Problemy sovetskoĭ ėkonomiki) At head of title: Akademiia nauk SSSR. TSentral'nyĭ ėkonomiko-matematicheskiĭ institut. Bibliography: p. 272-[275] LC Card 84-175111
1. Soviet Union - Economic conditions - 1976- - Econometric models. 2. Economic forecasting - Soviet Union. I. IAremenko, IUriĭ Vasil'evich. II. TSentral'nyĭ ėkonomiko-matematicheskiĭ institut (Akademiia nauk SSSR).
HC336.25 .M6314 1984

Modelirovanie razvitiia mezhotraslevyh kompleksov Latviĭskoĭ SSR : sbornik nauchnykh trudov / [redaktsionnaia kollegiia, L. Frolova (otv. redaktor), Ė. Vasermanis, A. Spilbergs]. Riga : Latviĭskiĭ gos. universitet im. P. Stuchki, 1985. 106 p. : ill. ; 21 cm. At head of title: Ministerstvo vysshego i srednego spetsial'nogo obrazovaniia Latviĭskoĭ SSR. Latviĭskiĭ ordena Trudovogo Krasnogo Znameni gosudarstvennyĭ universitet imeni Petra Stuchki. Kafedra ėkonomicheskoĭ kibernetiki. Includes bibliographies. LC Card 86-177817
1. Agricultural industries - Latvia - Mathematical models. 2. Service industries - Latvia - Mathematical models. I. Frolova, L. II. Vasermanis, Ė. III. Spilbergs, A. IV. Pētera Stučkas Latvijas Valsts universitāte. Ekonomiskās kibernētikas katedra.
HD9015.S653 L376 1985

Modelirovanie sbalansirovannosti i soglasovaniia planovykh resheniĭ v sfere narodnogo blagosostoianiia /. Sheviakov, Alekseĭ IUr'evich. Moskva , 1986. 211 p. : LC Card 86-177908
HC336.25 .S525 1986

Modelirovanie sotsial'nykh faktorov v ėkonomiko-matematicheskikh issledovaniiakh / [otvetstvennye redaktory Gavrilets IU.N., Mirkin B.G.]. Moskva : Akademiia nauk SSSR, TSentr. ėkonomiko-matematicheskiĭ in-t, 1984. 148 p. : ill. ; 21 cm. Includes bibliographies. LC Card 87-125299
1. Soviet Union - Economic conditions - 1976- - Mathematical models. 2. Social surveys - Soviet Union - Methodology. I. Gavrilets, IU. N. (IUriĭ Nikolaevich). II. Mirkin, B. G. (Boris Grigor'evich). III. TSentral'nyĭ ėkonomiko-matematicheskiĭ institut (Akademiia nauk SSSR).
HC336.25. .M636 1984

Modelirovanie v obshchestvennykh naukakh . Karakozova, Ė. V. (Ėl'vira Viktorovna) Moskva , 1986. 101 p. ;
NYPL [*QI 87-3444]

Modelización de sistemas financieros mediante dinámica de sistemas . Domínguez Machuca, J. A. (José Antonio) [Sevilla] , 1983. 269 p. : ISBN 84-500-3164-8 LC Card 85-138246
HG186.S6 D65 1983

Das Modell der Ausgleichslösung . Bürkle, Roland. München , c1983. 210 p. : ISBN 3-88259-255-9 LC Card 83-222868
HD30.23 .B865 1983

Modelle der neuen klassischen Makroökonomie . Buscher, Herbert S. München , c1986. iv, 312 p. : ISBN 3-88259-386-5 LC Card 86-230281
HB141 .B87 1986

Modellgestützte Markenpolitik . Voss, Wolf-Dieter. Wiesbaden , c1983. xxvi, 297 p. : ISBN 3-409-36035-2 LC Card 83-159054
HF5415.125 .V67 1983

Modelli di programmazione matematica per la pianificazione aziendale /. Cantore, Corrado M., 1948- Milano [1978] 295 p. ; LC Card 79-338281
HD30.28 .C36 ***NYPL [JLD 80-3558]***

Modelling household formation and dissolution / edited by Nico Keilman, Anton Kuijsten, Ad Vossen. Oxford [Oxfordshire] ; New York : Oxford University Press, c1987. p. cm. Includes indexes. ISBN 0-19-829500-6 : LC Card 87-18581 DDC 306.8/5/0724 19
1. Households - Mathematicals models. I. Keilman, Nico. II. Kuijsten, Anton. III. Vossen, Ad.
HB849.49 .M63 1987

Modelling, policy and economics of energy and power systems. IASTED Symposia on Modelling, Policy and Economics of Energy and Power Systems, and Alternative Energy Sources and Technology (1981 : San Francisco, Calif.) Proceedings of the IASTED Energy Symposia : Modelling, Policy and Economics of Energy and Power Systems [and] Alternative Energy Sources and Technology, May 20-22, 1981, San Francisco, U. S.A. /. Anaheim, Calif. [1981?] 209 p. : ISBN 0-88986-027-0
NYPL [JSF 86-1103]

Modelling the labor market. Modelling the labour market /. London , New York , 1988. p. cm. ISBN 0-412-28830-3 LC Card 87-23084 DDC 331.12/0724 19
HD5765.A6 M63 1988

Modelling the labour market / edited by Michael Beenstock. London ; New York : Chapman and Hall, 1988. p. cm. (International studies in economic modelling) Includes bibliographies and index. ISBN 0-412-28830-3 LC Card 87-23084 DDC 331.12/0724 19
1. Labor supply - Great Britain - Econometric models. I. Beenstock, Michael, 1946-. II. Title: Modelling the labor market. III. Series.
HD5765.A6 M63 1988

Un modello interpretativo dell'import-export italiano, 1970-1983 /. Bertelè, Umberto. Bologna , c1985. 172 p. : ISBN 88-15-00919-1 : LC Card 86-176592
HF3586.5 .B47 1985

Modello padano, localismo e modernizzazione : società e politica nella pianura occidentale bolognese / a cura di Fausto Anderlini ; introduzione di Mauro Zani ; contributi di Fausto Anderlini ... [et al.]. Bologna : Il Mulino, c1986. 470 p. : ill. ; 22 cm. Bibliography: p. 250-254. ISBN 88-15-01220-6 : LC Card 87-103653
1. Bologna (Italy : Province) - Economic policy. 2. Bologna (Italy : Province) - Social policy. 3. Regional planning - Italy - Bologna (Province).
HC307.B57 M63 1986

Un modelo de análisis monetario y de programación financiera /. Brovedani, Bruno. [Mexico City, Mexico] , 1984. ii, 203 p. : LC Card 86-158393
HG660.5 .B7 1984

Modelo económico chileno : trayectoria de una crítica / José Pablo Arellano ... [et al.].1a ed. Santiago, Chile : Editorial Aconcagua, [1982] 606 p. ; 18 cm. (Colección lautaro) Includes bibliographical references. LC Card 83-201307
1. Chile - Economic policy. 2. Chile - Economic conditions - 1973-. 3. Chicago school of economics. I. Arellano, José Pablo. II. Title: Trayectoria de una crítica.
HC192 .M63 1982

Modelo energético de tránsito /. Comisión Energía y Recursos de AEPDEN-Amigos de la Tierra. Madrid [1979?] 136 p. ; ISBN 84-85639-02-2 LC Card 79-126051
HD9502.S662 C66 1979 ***NYPL [JLC 87-71]***

Modelo estocástico para a estimação do produto potencial "IPEA/Depto. de Economia-UnB.". Castro, Paulo Furtado de. [Brasília, Brazil] [1981] 12, [16] : LC Card 85-210547
HC190.I5 C37 1981

Modelos de televisión y radio y su influencia en la génesis cultural. Fuenzalida, Valerio. Modelos de TV y radio y su influencia en la génesis cultural /. [Santiago, Chile] , 1980. 16 leaves ; LC Card 85-209582
HE8689.9.C5 F84 1980

Modelos de TV y radio y su influencia en la génesis cultural /. Fuenzalida, Valerio. [Santiago, Chile] , 1980. 16 leaves ; LC Card 85-209582
HE8689.9.C5 F84 1980

Modelos de valoración de acciones y metodos de constrastación /. Grande Esteban, Ildefonso. Bilbao [1985?] 319 p. : ISBN 84-7585-025-1 LC Card 87-111240
HG4636 .G88 1985

Modelos macroeconómicos, ejercicios resueltos /. Santacoloma, Juan Francisco. Bilbao , 1985. 209 p. : ISBN 84-7485-059-2 LC Card 86-201846
HB141 .S276 1985

Modelos macroeconómicos en economías abiertas /. Santacoloma, Juan Francisco. Bilbao , 1983. 3 v. : ISBN 84-7485-037-1 (set) LC Card

84-168556 DDC 339/.0724 19
HB141 .S28 1983 ***NYPL [JLL 86-351]***

MODELS, CLOTHING. see **MODELS, FASHION.**

MODELS, FASHION.
Addams, Jon, 1941- How to become a professional model /. Philadelphia, PA , c1987. p. cm. ISBN 0-943331-01-3 : LC Card 87-20656 DDC 659.1/52 19
HD6073.M77 A33 1987

MODELS, FASHION - NORWAY - DIARIES.
Stai, Anette. Crazy business . Oslo , c1984. 146 p., [48] p. of plates : ISBN 82-09-10210-9 LC Card 85-160098
HD6073.M772 N677 1984

MODELS, FASHION - UNITED STATES.
Hartman, Tori. Specialty modeling /. New York , c1988. x, 128 p. ; ISBN 0-525-48356-X LC Card 87-22470 DDC 659.1/52 19
HD6073.M772 U55 1988

Orenstein, Vik, 1960- How to break into modeling /. Cincinnati, Ohio , c1987. 169 p. : ISBN 0-89879-282-7 (pbk.) : LC Card 87-21703 DDC 659.1/52 19
HD6073.M772 U56 1987

Models for investment and disinvestment decision making under uncertainty [microform] / prepared by Michigan State University, Dept. of Agricultural Economics, East Lansing ... ; edited by L. J. Robison, M. H. Abkin ; prepared for Electric Power Research Institute, Palo Alto, Calif. ; Demand and Conservation Program, Energy Analysis and Environment Division. East Lansing : Michigan State University, Dept. of Agricultural Economics, 1982. 173 p. : ill. ; 28 cm. EPRI-EA-2204. Final report, January 1982. Bibliography: p. 169-172. Microfiche. Springfield, Va. : NTIS, 1982. 3 microfiches : negative ; 11 x 15 cm. (DE82902068)
1. Energy consumption - United States. 2. Energy policy - Economic aspects - United States. I. Robison L. J. II. Abkin, M. H. III. Electric Power Research Institute. Demand and Conservation Program.
NYPL [*XME-11,286]

MODELS, MATHEMATICAL. see **MATHEMATICAL MODELS.**

Modern advanced accounting /. Larsen, E. John. New York , c1988. xx, 1002 p. ; ISBN 0-07-036508-3 : LC Card 87-22621 DDC 657/.046 19
HF5635 .M8756 1988

MODERN ARCHITECTURE. see **ARCHITECTURE, MODERN.**

Modern banking . Austin, Douglas V. Boston , c1985. x, 406 p. : ISBN 0-87267-053-8 LC Card 84-21754 DDC 332.1/068 19
HG1615 .A98 1985 ***NYPL [JLE 85-3956]***

Modern Bulgaria in figures and facts : statistical reference book. [Sofia] : Bulgarian Association of Tourism and Recreation, [1984?] 48 p. : col. ill. ; 22 cm. LC Card 87-101850 DDC 314.97/7 19
1. Bulgaria - Economic conditions - 1944- - Statistics. 2. Bulgaria - Statistics. I. Bŭlgarska asotsiatsiia za turizŭm i otdikh.
HC403 .M63 1984

Modern business financing . Colman, Robert Douglas. Englewood Cliffs, N.J. , c1986. xxi, 281 p. : ISBN 0-13-589060-8 LC Card 85-20490 DDC 658.1/5 19
HG4027.3 .C64 1986 ***NYPL [JLF 86-616]***

Modern business reports.
Andover, James J. Credit and collections problem solver . New York, NY, U. S.A. , c1987. x, 175 p. : ISBN 0-86604-219-9 (pbk.) LC Card 87-156416 DDC 658.8/8 19
HG3751 .A53 1987

Effective cash flow management. New York, N.Y., U. S.A. , c1985. x, 223 p. : ISBN 0-86604-176-1 (pbk.) LC Card 86-205438 DDC 658.1/5244 19
HG4028.C45 E34 1985

Moore, Carl L. Profitable ratio analysis techniques /. New York, N.Y., U. S.A. , c1986. ix leaves, 201 p. : ISBN 0-86604-206-7 (pbk.) LC Card 86-208178 DDC 658.4/033 19
HF5681.R25 M58 1986

Sales motivation . New York, N.Y., U. S.A. , c1985. viii, 131 leaves ; ISBN 0-86604-150-8 (pbk.) LC Card 86-232974 DDC 658.3/14 19
HF5438.25 .S253 1985

Structured hiring . New York, NY, U. S.A. , c1987. viii leaves, 144 p. : ISBN 0-86604-221-0 (pbk.) LC Card 87-156398 DDC 658.3/112 19
HF5549.5.R44 S83 1987

Modern capitalism .
(v. 1) Capitalism and equality in America /. Lanham [New York] , c1987. ix, 306 p. : ISBN 0-8191-5572-1 (v. 1 : alk. paper) : LC Card 86-24739 DDC 330.12/2 19
HB501 .C2423 1987

(v. 2) Capitalism and equality in the Third World /. Lanham [New York] , c1987. 375 p. ; ISBN 0-8191-5574-8 (v. 2 : alk. paper) : LC Card 86-24749 DDC 330.12/2 19
HB501 .C24234 1987

MODERN CIVILIZATION. see **CIVILIZATION, MODERN.**

Modern communications and foreign policy.
United States. Congress. House. Committee on Foreign Affairs. Subcommittee on International Organizations and Movements. Washington, 1967. vii, 13R, iv, 216 p. LC Card 67-61749
E744 .U45 1967 ***NYPL [JLE 73-233]***

Modern developments in public finance : essays in honor of Arnold Harberger / edited by Michael J. Boskin. Oxford, UK ; New York, NY, USA : B. Blackwell, 1987. xii, 259 p. : ill. ; 24 cm. Includes bibliographies and index. ISBN 0-631-15595-3 : LC Card 87-6568 DDC 336 19
1. Finance, Public. 2. Harberger, Arnold C. I. Harberger, Arnold C. II. Boskin, Michael J.
HJ141 .M59 1987

Modern economics . Browne, M. Neil, 1944- Englewood Cliffs, N.J. , c1987. xvi, 464 p. : ISBN 0-13-587940-X (pbk.) LC Card 86-25256 DDC 330 19
HB171.5 .B724 1987

MODERN ETHICS. see **ETHICS, MODERN.**

Modern European history.
Edmonson, James M. From Mecanicien to ingenieur . New York, NY , 1987. x, 631 p. ; ISBN 0-8240-8036-X (alk. paper) : LC Card 87-300 DDC 338.4/76218/0944 19
HD9705.F7 E35 1987

Griffiths, A. R. G., 1940- The Irish Board of Works, 1831-1878 /. New York , 1987. iii, 214 p. ; ISBN 0-8240-7810-1 (alk. paper) : LC Card 87-24495 DDC 363/.09415 19
HD4150.3 .G75 1987

Morrison, Daniel, 1945- "Trading peasants" and urbanization in eighteenth-century Russia . New York , 1987. 415 p. ; ISBN 0-8240-8059-9 (alk. paper) : LC Card 87-7425 DDC 307.2 19
HB2068.S65 M67 1987

Segal, Paul Harold, 1946- The French state and French private investment in Czechoslovakia, 1918-1938 . New York , 1987. vi, 379 p. ; ISBN 0-8240-8041-6 (alk. paper) : LC Card 87-252 DDC 332.6/7344/0437 19
HG5470.3.A3 S44 1987

Share, Michael. The Central Workers' Circle of St. Petersburg, 1889-1894 . New York , 1987. xi, 396 p., [6] p. of plates : ISBN 0-8240-8063-7 (alk. paper) : LC Card 87-374 DDC 305.5/62/0947453 19
HD8522.T753 S53 1987

Stein, Margot B. (Margot Ballou), 1945- The social origins of a labor elite . New York , 1987. xxiv, 515 p. : ISBN 0-8240-8043-2 (alk. paper) : LC Card 87-6913 DDC 305/.9385 19
HD8039.R322 F88 1987

Modern information systems . Gessford, John Evans. Reading, Mass. , c1980. xii, 512 p. : ISBN 0-201-03099-3 : LC Card 78-74684 DDC 658/.05/4
HF5548.2 .G48 ***NYPL [JLE 80-1913]***

Modern international economics /. Ethier, Wilfred. New York , c1988. xx, 556, 62 p. : ISBN 0-393-95556-7 LC Card 87-21762 DDC 337 19
HF1411 .E824 1988

Modern job safety and health / Wayne T. Brooks, technical consultant ; Prentice Hall Information Services editorial staff contributors, Rich Arthurs, supervisory editor ... [et al.]. Paramus, N.J. : Prentice Hall Information Services, c1987- 1 v. (loose-leaf) : ill. ; 30 cm. Includes index. LC Card 87-403957 DDC 363.1/1/068 19
1. Industrial safety - United States - Management. 2. Industrial hygiene - United States - Management. 3. Industrial accidents - United States. 4. Workers' compensation - United States. I. Prentice-Hall, inc. Information Services Division.
HD6067.2.U6 M63 1987

Modern labor economics . Ehrenberg, Ronald G. Glenview, Ill. [1987], c1988. 721 p. : ISBN 0-673-18964-3 LC Card 87-9789 DDC 331 19
HD4901 .E34 1988

Modern macroeconomics . Bober, Stanley. London , New York , c1988. ix, 278 p. : ISBN 0-7099-5080-2 LC Card 87-15190 DDC 339 19
HB172.5 .B62 1988

Modern macroeconomics /. Woglom, Geoffrey. Glenview, Ill. , c1988. 792, 19, 14 p. : ISBN 0-673-18413-7 LC Card 87-12857 DDC 339 19
HB172.5 .W63 1988

Modern organiseren en menselijker werken / onder redactie van Herman Steensma, René v. d. Vlist en Jacques Allegro. 's-Gravenhage : VUGA, 1985. 198 p. : ill. ; 24 cm. Includes bibliographies and index. ISBN 90-6095-314-2 : LC Card 85-214437
1. Psychology, Industrial. 2. Psychology, Industrial - Netherlands. 3. Organizational change. I. Steensma, Herman. II. Vlist, R. van der. III. Allegro, Jacques.
HF5548.8 .M55 1985

Modern organization theory : a symposium of the Foundation for Research on Human Behavior / edited by Mason Haire. New York : Garland Pub., 1987, c1959. x, 324 p. : ill. ; 23 cm. (Continuity in administrative science) Reprint. Originally published: New York : Wiley, c1959. Includes bibliographies and index. ISBN 0-8240-8208-7 (alk. paper) : LC Card 86-27072 DDC 658 19
1. Organization. 2. Organizational behavior. I. Haire, Mason. II. Foundation for Research on Human Behavior. III. Series.
HD31 .M614 1987

Modern portfolio theory, the capital asset pricing model, and arbitrage pricing theory . Harrington, Diana R., 1940- Englewood Cliffs, N.J. , c1987. x, 229 p. : ISBN 0-13-597261-2 (pbk.) LC Card 86-22693 DDC 332.6 19
HG4637 .H37 1987

Modern real estate /. Wurtzebach, Charles H. New York , c1987. xii, 772 p. : ISBN 0-471-84890-5 LC Card 86-23412 DDC 333.33/0973 19
HD1375 .W873 1987

Modern retailing . Mason, Joseph Barry. Plano, Tex. , 1987. xviii, 834 p. : ISBN 0-256-03706-X LC Card 86-71842 DDC 658.8/7 19
HF5429 .M328 1987

Modern sexism . Benokraitis, Nijole V. (Nijole Vaicaitis) Englewood Cliffs , c1986. xiii, 187 p. ; ISBN 0-13-597634-0 LC Card 85-28256
HQ1426 .B428 1986 ***NYPL [JLE 86-4225]***

Modern South Wales : essays in economic history / edited by Colin Baber and L.J. Williams. Cardiff : University of Wales Press ; Atlantic Highlands, N.J. : Distributed in the U. S.A. and Canada by Humanities Press, 1986. ix, 324 p. : ill. ; 23 cm. Distributor statement from label on t.p. Bibliography: p. [279]-312. Includes index. ISBN 0-7083-0943-7 LC Card 86-226166 DDC 330.9429/4085 19
1. Wales, South - Economic conditions. 2. Wales, South - Industries - History. I. Baber, Colin. II. Williams, L. J.
HC257.W3 M63 1986

Modern Soviet economic performance /. Buck, Trevor. New York, NY , 1987. viii, 192 p. ; ISBN 0-631-14417-X : LC Card 86-24457 DDC 330.947/085 19
HC336.25 .B826 1987

Modern Spanish and English dictionary. Vox Modern Spanish and English dictionary . Lincolnwood, Ill. , c1986. xxxiv, 487, 45, 484 p. : ISBN 0-8442-7990-0 LC Card 86-61160
NYPL [*R-RGK 86-7059]

Modern tramcars of Basle (Switzerland) Basler Verkehrs-Betriebe (BVB) . Villigen AG,

Schweiz , c1984. 56 p., [188] p. of plates, xv p. : ISBN 3-85649-045-0 : LC Card 84-160209
HE4919.B37 B37 1984

Modern work and human meaning /. Raines, John C. Philadelphia , c1986. 150 p. ; ISBN 0-664-24703-2 (pbk.) LC Card 85-26370 DDC 241/.64 19
BJ1498 .R335 1986 ***NYPL [JLD 86-2382]***

Modernisation agricole, développement économique et changement social . Maurer, Jean-Luc. Paris , c1986. 323 p. : ISBN 2-13-039622-4 : LC Card 86-175394
HD2085.B37 M38 1986

La modernisation des banques françaises . Pastré, Olivier. Paris [1985] 234 p. : ISBN 2-11-001537-3 : LC Card 86-179536
HG3026 .P37 1985

Modernización de la agricultura y pobreza rural en Guatemala /. Hintermeister, Alberto. [Santiago, Chile] , 1982. 59 leaves : LC Card 87-403247 DDC 338.1/6/097281 19
HC144.Z9 P624 1982

La Modernización económica de España, 1830-1930 / compilación de Nicolás Sánchez-Albornoz. Madrid : Alianza, c1985. 343 p. : ill. ; 20 cm. (Alianza Universidad. 431) Includes bibliographies. ISBN 84-206-2431-4 LC Card 87-111312
1. Spain - Economic conditions - 19th century. 2. Spain - Economic conditions - 1918-1975. 3. Spain - Economic conditions - Regional disparities. I. Sánchez-Albornoz, Nicolás.
HC385 .M623 1985

Modernización económica de España, 1830-1930. English. The economic modernization of Spain, 1830-1930 / edited by Nicolás Sánchez-Albornoz ; translated by Karen Powers and Manuel Sañudo. New York : New York University Press, c1987. xv, 295 p. : ill. ; 24 cm. Translation of: La modernización económica de España, 1830-1930. Includes bibliographies and index. ISBN 0-8147-7861-5 : LC Card 87-5535 DDC 330.946/07 19
1. Spain - Economic conditions. 2. Spain - History - 19th century. 3. Spain - History - 20th century. I. Sánchez-Albornoz, Nicolás. II. Title.
HC385 .M62313 1987

Modernization of agriculture in developing countries . Arnon, Itzhak, 1909- Chichester [West Sussex] , New York , c1987. xxiii, 626 p. : ISBN 0-471-91586-6 : LC Card 87-6288 DDC 338.1/09172/4 19
HD1417 .A76 1987

Modernization of Punjab agriculture /. Kahlon, A. S., 1923- New Delhi , 1984. vi, 145 p. ; LC Card 84-902491 DDC 338.1/0954/5 19
S471.I32 P845 1984 ***NYPL [JLD 86-4410]***

The modernization of the Louisiana sugar industry, 1830-1910 /. Heitmann, John Alfred. Baton Rouge , c1987. xii, 298 p. : ISBN 0-8071-1324-7 LC Card 86-27639 DDC 338.4/56641/09763 19
HD9107.L8 H45 1987

Modiano, Eduardo Marco.
Da inflação ao cruzado : a política econômica no primeiro ano da Nova República / Eduardo Modiano. Rio de Janeiro : Editora Campus, c1986. 126 p. : ill. ; 21 cm. Includes bibliographical references. ISBN 85-7001-362-0 : LC Card 87-102624
1. Brazil - Economic policy. 2. Inflation (Finance) - Brazil. 3. Brazil - Economic conditions - 1985-. I. Title.
HC187 .M593 1986

Salários, preços e câmbio : os multiplicadores dos choques numa economia indexada / Eduardo Marco Modiano. Rio de Janeiro, RJ : Pontifícia Universidade Católica do Rio de Janeiro, Departamento de Economia, 1984. 55, [5] leaves ; 30 cm. (Texto para discussão . no. 70) "Publicada com a colaboração da ANPEC e o apoio financeiro do PNPE"--P. [60] Bibliography: Leaf [60] LC Card 84-234066
1. Wages - Brazil - Econometric models. 2. Prices - Brazil - Econometric models. 3. Indexation (Economics) - Brazil - Econometric models. I. Series: Texto para discussão (Pontifícia Universidade Católica do Rio de Janeiro. Departamento de Economia) , no. 70. II. Title.
HD5004 .M56 1984

MODICA (SICILY) - DESCRIPTION.
Vernuccio, Pietro, 1947- Una città in cerca d'identità . Modica , 1984. 201 p., [12] p. of plates : LC Card 86-164886
HC308.M53 V47 1984

MODICA (SICILY) - ECONOMIC CONDITIONS.
Vernuccio, Pietro, 1947- Una città in cerca d'identità . Modica , 1984. 201 p., [12] p. of plates : LC Card 86-164886
HC308.M53 V47 1984

MODICA (SICILY) - INDUSTRIES.
Vernuccio, Pietro, 1947- Una città in cerca d'identità . Modica , 1984. 201 p., [12] p. of plates : LC Card 86-164886
HC308.M53 V47 1984

MODICA, SICILY - SOCIAL CONDITIONS.
Vernuccio, Pietro, 1947- Una città in cerca d'identità . Modica , 1984. 201 p., [12] p. of plates : LC Card 86-164886
HC308.M53 V47 1984

Modifikat͡sii teorii "poleznosti" /. Potapov, V. V. (Viktor Vladimirovich) Moskva , 1984. 132 p. ; LC Card 84-247447
HB201 .P65 1984

Modigliani, Franco. The Debate over stabilization policy /. Cambridge [Cambridgeshire] , New York , 1986. xiv, 270 p. : ISBN 0-521-26790-0 LC Card 84-21366 DDC 338.9 19
HB3732 .D43 1986 ***NYPL [JLF 86-1945]***

Modin, Anatoliĭ Andreevich. Dinamika proizvodstvennykh ob″edineniĭ i modeli planirovanii͡a ikh deiātel′nosti / A.A. Modin, N.V. Makhrov, V.I. Danilin ; otvetstvennyĭ redaktor N.I͡A. Petrakov. Moskva : Izd-vo "Nauka", 1984. 231 p. : ill. ; 22 cm. (Problemy sovetskoĭ ėkonomiki) At head of title: Akademii͡a nauk SSSR. T͡Sentral′nyĭ ėkonomiko-matematicheskiĭ institut. Bibliography: p. 227-[230] LC Card 84-195690
1. Machinery industry - Soviet Union - Management - Mathematical models. I. Makhrov, N. V. (Nikolaĭ Vasil′evich). II. Danilin, Vi͡acheslav Ivanovich. III. Petrakov, Nikolaĭ I͡Akovlevich. IV. Title.
HD9705.S595 M62 1984

MODIS IV . Bjerkholt, Olav, 1942- Oslo , 1980. 189 p. : ISBN 82-537-1014-3 (pbk.) LC Card 81-120697 DDC 330.9481/00724 19
HC365 .B46 1980

Módszerek a beruházási tevékenység kvantitatív elemzéséhez / szerkesztette Meszéna György ; [a kötet szerzői, Bakonyi Árpád ... et al.]. Budapest : Akadémiai Kiadó, 1985. 207 p. : ill. ; 25 cm. ISBN 963-05-3607-2 : LC Card 86-100399
1. Capital investments - Mathematical models. 2. Capital investments - Hungary - Mathematical models. I. Meszéna, György. II. Bakonyi, Árpád.
HG4028.C4 M57 1985

Módszertani kiadványsorozat, 0230-7278 . (1986/2) Gáti, Gábor. A munkahely-racionalizálás korszerű megközelítési módjai az élelmiszeriparban /. Budapest , 1986. 106 p. : ISBN 963-02-4171-4 LC Card 87-137979
HD9000.5 .G336 1986

MODULAR BUILDING. see **MODULAR CONSTRUCTION.**

MODULAR CONSTRUCTION.
Bianchi, Roberto, 1954- Le tecniche esecutive nell'edilizia residenziale degli anni '80 . Milano, Italy , c1986. 144 p. : LC Card 87-126093
HD9715.5.I83 L653 1986

MODULAR CONSTRUCTION INDUSTRY - ITALY - LOMBARDY.
Bianchi, Roberto, 1954- Le tecniche esecutive nell'edilizia residenziale degli anni '80 . Milano, Italy , c1986. 144 p. : LC Card 87-126093
HD9715.5.I83 L653 1986

MODULAR CONSTRUCTION INDUSTRY - QUÉBEC (PROVINCE)
Duchaine, Paul. Bâtiments préfabriqués résidentiels et industriels à ossature de bois . [Québec] , c1985. 36 p. : ISBN 2-550-12116-3 LC Card 86-133426
HD9715.5.C23 Q43 1985

MODULAR CONSTRUCTION INDUSTRY - SWEDEN.
Sweden. Exportstödsutredningen. Ökad trähusexport . [Stockholm] [1984] 51 p. ; ISBN 91-38-08165-2 LC Card 84-219457
HD9715.5.S82 S94 1984

MODULAR PROGRAMMING.
Wolff, Bruno B. Modular programming routines for the Apple II+/IIe/IIc /. Blue Ridge Summit, PA , 1985. x, 243 p. : ISBN 0-8306-0732-3 : LC Card 85-17331 DDC 005.265 19
QA76.8.A66 W65 1985 ***NYPL [JSE 86-1017]***

Modular programming routines for the Apple II+/IIe/IIc /. Wolff, Bruno B. Blue Ridge Summit, PA , 1985. x, 243 p. : ISBN 0-8306-0732-3 : LC Card 85-17331 DDC 005.265 19
QA76.8.A66 W65 1985 ***NYPL [JSE 86-1017]***

MODULAR STRUCTURES. see **MODULAR CONSTRUCTION.**

Los módulos de servicios . Gómez-Samper, Henry. Caracas , c1984. 48, 3 [i.e. 4] leaves ; ISBN 980-217-005-4 LC Card 86-193565
HD4343 .G65 1984

Modwel, Suman Kumar, 1936- Export effort of India / Suman Kumar Modwel, M.L. Varma. New Delhi : Indian Institute of Foreign Trade, 1986. ix, 83, [1] p. ; 25 cm. Bibliography: p. [84] LC Card 86-903364 DDC 382/.6/0954 19
1. India - Commercial policy. I. Varma, M. L. II. Indian Institute of Foreign Trade. III. Title.
HF1589 .M63 1986

Möbis, Harry. Ordnung, Disziplin, Sicherheit : Aufgaben und Erfahrungen / Harry Möbis.2. Aufl. Berlin : Staatsverlag der Deutschen Demokratischen Republik, 1983. 95 p. ; 22 cm. (Der Sozialistische Staat) Bibliography: p. 83. LC Card 83-186990
1. Labor discipline - Germany, East. 2. Employee rules - Germany (East). 3. Employee morale - Germany (East). I. Title.
HF5549.5.L3 M63 1983

Moebs, Eva. Moebs, G. Michael. Pricing financial services /. Homewood, Ill. , c1986. xviii, 246 p. : ISBN 0-87094-594-7 LC Card 85-73688
NYPL [JLE 86-2817]

Moebs, G. Michael. Pricing financial services / G. Michael Moebs, Eva Moebs. Homewood, Ill. : Dow Jones-Irwin, c1986. xviii, 246 p. : ill. ; 24 cm. Includes statistical tables and index. Bibliography:231-232. ISBN 0-87094-594-7 LC Card 85-73688
1. Financial institutions - United States. 2. Financial institutions - Accounting. I. Moebs, Eva. II. Title.
NYPL [JLE 86-2817]

Mögliche globale Wirtschaftsstrategie im dritten Jahrtausend. Pousset, Henri, 1914- Mögliche globale Wirtschaftsstrategie im 3. Jahrtausend /. Frankfurt am Main , c1986. 190 p. : ISBN 3-88129-956-4 LC Card 86-160350
HD84 .P65 1986

Mögliche globale Wirtschaftsstrategie im 3. Jahrtausend /. Pousset, Henri, 1914- Frankfurt am Main , c1986. 190 p. : ISBN 3-88129-956-4 LC Card 86-160350
HD84 .P65 1986

Möglichkeiten betriebswirtschaftlicher Beurteilung privater Kapitalanlagen . Jaap, Christiane. Berlin , c1986. xxiii, 322 p. : ISBN 3-428-06008-3 LC Card 86-189069
HG4028.C4 J28 1986

Möglichkeiten des Berufswechsels von Haupterwerbslandwirten unter besonderer Berücksichtigung von Agrarstruktur und Arbeitsmarkt /. Kretschmann, Rolf. Göttingen , 1986. xi, 109 p. : LC Card 87-408871 DDC 331.25/924 19
HD1536.G3 K746 1986

Möglichkeiten und Grenzen der Aussagefähigkeit von Teilkonzernabschlüssen /. Kohlmann, Ulrike, 1954- München , c1986. viii, 180 p. ; ISBN 3-88259-419-5 LC Card 87-121768 DDC 657/.95/0943 19
HF5686.C7 K644 1986

Möglichkeiten und Grenzen der Beeinflussung der Preissetzungsmöglichkeiten der Unternehmen /. Riechey, Gunter. München , c1982. 286 p. : ISBN 3-597-10144-5 LC Card 83-160762
HC290.5.W24 R54 1982

Möglichkeiten und Probleme der Realisierung flexibler Arbeitszeitstrukturen in Filialen der Bayerischen Vereinsbank München / bearbeitet von Rainer Marr, Sebastian Schuh. München : Fachbereich Wirtschafts- und

Organisationswissenschaften, Universität der Bundeswehr, 1985. 67 p. : ill. ; 30 cm. (Studienprojekte der Professur für Entscheidungs- und Organisationsforschung, Personalwesen) Includes bibliographical references. LC Card 87-401387 DDC 331.25/72 19
1. Hours of labor, Flexible - Germany (West) - Munich. 2. Bank employees - Germany (West) - Munich. 3. Bayerische Vereinsbank. I. Marr, Rainer, 1942-. II. Schuh, Sebastian. III. Series.
HD5109.2.G32 M866 1985

Möglichkeiten zur Fortsetzung der Gemeindefinanzreform. Zeidler, Achim, 1952- Frankfurt am Main , New York , c1985. xx, 301 p. : ISBN 3-8204-8534-1 LC Card 86-125215 DDC 336/.014/43 19
HJ9473 .Z4 1985

Moeller, Robert G. Peasants and lords in modern Germany . Boston , 1986. 267 p. ; ISBN 0-04-943037-8 (alk. paper) LC Card 85-6113 DDC 305.5/63 19
HD655 .P34 1986 ***NYPL [JLE 86-1702]***

Moen, Elizabeth. Perspectives on population . New York , 1987. xix, 487 p. : ISBN 0-19-504092-9 (alk. paper) : LC Card 86-23652 DDC 304.6 19
HB871 .P48 1987

Mönchen-Gladbach, Ger. Katholische Sozialwissenschaftliche Zentralstelle. see **Katholische Sozialwissenschaftliche Zentralstelle, Mönchen-Gladbach, Ger.**

Moffatt, Thomas L.
Land that job! / Thomas L. Moffatt. Madison, Wis. : Science Tech Publishers, 1987, c1982. vii, 152 p. : ill. ; 24 cm. Reprint. Originally published: New York : Harper & Row, c1982. Includes index. ISBN 0-910239-09-6 (pbk.) LC Card 87-4319 DDC 650.1/4 19
1. Job hunting. I. Title.
HF5382.7 .M63 1987

Selection interviewing for managers / Thomas L. Moffatt. Madison, Wis. : Science Tech Publishers, c1987. x, 196 : ill. ; 25 cm. Originally published : Harper & Row, 1979. Includes index. ISBN 0-910239-08-8 : LC Card 86-26313 DDC 658.3/112 19
1. Employment interviewing. I. Title.
HF5549.5.I6 M64 1987

Mogel, William A. Transportation and marketing of natural gas. Update '86 / by William A. Mogel. New York, N.Y. : Executive Enterprises Publications, c1986. iii, 165 p. : ill. ; 28 cm. Includes bibliographical references. ISBN 0-88057-466-6 (pbk.) LC Card 86-220986 DDC 388.5 19
1. Gas, Natural - Law and legislation - United States. 2. Gas, Natural - Pipe lines - Law and legislation - United States. I. Title.
HD9580.U5 M64 1985 Suppl.

Mogensen, Margit, 1946- Godsejerrøster . København , 1984. 320 p. : ISBN 87-7526-018-2 : LC Card 84-224395
HD1333.D42 R674 1984

Mogg, William Rees- see **Rees-Mogg, William, 1928-**

Mogridge, M. C. Project identification : preliminary study : technical appendix no. 6--transportation / M.C. Mogridge. Nairobi : Nairobi Urban Study Group, [1971] 81 leaves in various pagings : 17 maps ; 30 cm. "31 July 1971." LC Card 87-118674
1. Transportation - Kenya - Nairobi. 2. Transportation and state - Kenya - Nairobi. I. Nairobi Urban Study Group. II. Title.
HE283.5.Z7 N456 1971

Mohácsi, Kálmán. Kartali, János. A friss és feldolgozott zöldségek, gyümölcsök bel- és külkereskedelmi forgalmazásának aktuális problémái /. Budapest , 1985. 108 p. ; ISBN 963-491-203-6 LC Card 86-195487
HD9220.H82 K37 1985

Mohamad Riad el Ghonemy. see **El Ghonemy, Mohamad Riad, 1924-**

Mohamed, Yagoub Abdalla. The North Kordofan rural water supply baseline survey / prepared by the Institute of Environmental Studies, University of Khartoum, for the Cooperative American Relief Everywhere (CARE) by Yagoub Abdalla Mohamed, Mohamed Osman El Sammani, Mohamed Zein Shadad. Khartoum : The Institute, 1982. xv, 152 p. : ill., maps ; 23 cm. At head of title: The Democratic Republic of the Sudan. "Published ... in cooperation with Program for International Development, Clark University, Worcester, Massachusetts 01610"--T.p. verso. Bibliography: p. 152. LC Card 85-981166
1. Water-supply, Rural - Economic aspects - Sudan - Kurdufān al-Shamālīyah. 2. Water-supply, Rural - Environmental aspects - Sudan - Kurdufān al-Shamālīyah. I. El Sammani, Mohammed Osman. II. Shadad, Mohamed Zein. III. Jāmi'at al-Kharṭūm. Ma'had al-Dirāsāt al-Bī'īyah. IV. CARE (Firm). V. Sudan. VI. Clark University (Worcester, Mass.). Program for International Development. VII. Title.
HD1699.S82 K875 1982

Mohammed Ghanem, Shukri. see **Ghanem, Shukri Mohammed.**

MOHAMMEDANISM. see **ISLAM.**

Mohan Lall Nigam, Brij. see **Nigam, Brij Mohan Lall, 1935-**

Mohan Mathew. see **Mathew, Mohan, 1931-**

Mohanty, P. N. Mahajan, Amarjit. Problems of the aged in unorganised sector /. Delhi, India , 1987. viii, 106 p. ; LC Card 87-901315 DDC 362.6/042 19
HD7105.35.I5 M34 1987

Mohd. Hamdan Adnan. Public relations . Kuala Lumpur , 1986. 259 p. : LC Card 86-944684 DDC 659.2/09595 19
HD59.6.M4 P83 1986

Mohide, Thomas Patrick. Silver / Thomas Patrick Mohide. Toronto, Ont. : Ministry of Natural Resources, [1985] xiv, 406 p. : ill. ; 30 cm. (Mineral policy background paper, 0706-103X . no. 20) Bibliography: p. 397-403. ISBN 0-7743-9897-3 (pbk.) LC Card 85-165981 DDC 338.2/7421/0971 19
1. Silver industry - Canada. 2. Silver industry. I. Title. II. Series.
HD9536.C22 M64 1985 ***NYPL [JLG 86-145]***

Mohrman, Susan Albers. Mitroff, Ian I. Business not as usual . San Francisco , 1987. xxi, 194 p. : ISBN 1-555-42030-3 (alk. paper) LC Card 86-46333 DDC 338.9 19
HD70.U5 M52 1987

Mohs, Ralf-Matthias. Exporte, komparative Vorteile und wirtschaftliche Entwicklung in den Schwellenländern : der Erklärungsbeitrag des Faktorproportionentheorems / von Ralf-Matthias Mohs. Göttingen : Schwartz, [1983] 236 p. : ill. ; 23 cm. (Arbeitsberichte des Ibero-Amerika-Instituts für Wirtschaftsforschung der Universität Göttingen . Heft 21) Bibliography: p. 221-236. ISBN 3-509-01345-X LC Card 84-126961
1. Developing countries - Commerce - Econometric models. 2. Factor proportions - Developing countries. 3. Comparative advantage (Commerce). I. Title. II. Series.
HF4055 .M64 1983

Moĭnov, Moĭno. Zadachite na DKMS vŭv VUZ za povishavane na ikonomicheskata podgotovka na studentite i mladite khora ot drugite otri͡adi na mladezhta . Svishtov , 1985. 91 p. ; LC Card 86-159994
HB74.9.B9 Z33 1985

Moiseenko, Nikolaĭ Andreevich. Dolgosrochnoe sotsial'no-ėkonomicheskoe planirovanie /. Leningrad , 1986. 165 p. : LC Card 87-146872
HC338.T5 D65 1986

Moiseev, Anatoliĭ Vasil'evich.
Ėkonomicheskiĭ slovar'-spravochnik : posobie dli͡a uchashchikhsi͡a / A.V. Moiseev, K.T͡S. Petrosi͡an, N.N. Pilipenko ; pod redaktsieĭ A.V. Moiseeva. Moskva : "Prosveshchenie", 1978. 239 p. ; 21 cm. Includes index. LC Card 81-165938
1. Economics - Dictionaries - Russian. 2. Soviet Union - Economic policy - Dictionaries - Russian. I. Petrosi͡an, K. T͡S. (Karmlen T͡Saturovich). II. Pilipenko, Nikolaĭ Nikolaevich. III. Title.
HB61 .M56 1978

Osnovy ėkonomiki vazhneĭshikh otrasleĭ narodnogo khozi͡aĭstva SSSR : kniga dli͡a uchiteli͡a / A.V. Moiseev, K.T͡S. Petrosi͡an ; pod redaktsieĭ A.V. Moiseeva. Moskva : "Prosveshchenie", 1984. 191 p. : ill. ; 23 cm. Includes bibliographical references. LC Card 85-113764
1. Soviet Union - Economic policy - 1981-. 2. Soviet Union - Economic conditions - 1976-. I. Petrosi͡an, K. T͡S. (Karmlen T͡Saturovich). II. Title.
HC336.25 .M654 1984

MOJOCOYA (BOLIVIA) - ECONOMIC CONDITIONS.
Estudio cultural y socio económico de Mojocoya--Redención Pampa. Estudio cultural socio económico, Mojocoya y Redención Pampa. Sucre, Bolivia , 1979. 266 p. : LC Card 83-204567
HC183.M65 E77 1979

MOJOCOYA (BOLIVIA) - SOCIAL CONDITIONS.
Estudio cultural y socio económico de Mojocoya--Redención Pampa. Estudio cultural socio económico, Mojocoya y Redención Pampa. Sucre, Bolivia , 1979. 266 p. : LC Card 83-204567
HC183.M65 E77 1979

Mojocoya y Redención Pampa. Estudio cultural y socio económico de Mojocoya--Redención Pampa. Estudio cultural socio económico, Mojocoya y Redención Pampa. Sucre, Bolivia , 1979. 266 p. : LC Card 83-204567
HC183.M65 E77 1979

Mokan, Ivan Il'ich.
Ot͡senka ėffektivnosti proizvodstva i rezervy ee rosta . Kishinev , 1982. 130 p. : LC Card 83-179279
HD9015.S653 M6454 1982

Sovershenstvovanie planirovani͡a i usilenie khozi͡aĭstvennogo mekhanizma . Kishinev , 1983. 134 p. ; LC Card 84-231201
HC336.25 .S6736 1983

Mokitimi, None. Swallow, Brent M. Cattle marketing in Lesotho /. Maseru, Lesotho [1986] iv, 75 leaves : LC Card 87-132309 DDC 381/.416213/096816 19
HD9433.L452 S9 1986

Mokri͡ak, V. I. (Vladimir Il'ich) Todyka, I͡Uriĭ Nikolaevich. Gosudarstvennyĭ apparat i problemy okhrany prirody v uslovii͡akh APK /. Kishinev , 1986. 179, [5] p. ; LC Card 86-141430
HD1995.M5 T63 1986

Mokry, Benjamin W. Entrepreneurship and public policy : can government stimulate business startups? / Benjamin W. Mokry. New York : Quorum Books, c1988. p. cm. Bibliography: p. Includes index. ISBN 0-89930-239-4 (lib. bdg. : alk. paper) LC Card 87-24934 DDC 338.9 19
1. Entrepreneurship. 2. New business enterprises. I. Title.
HB615 .M65 1988

Mokrý, Vladimír. Melišek, František. Ekonomický rast a štrukturálne zmeny v socialistickej ekonomike /. Bratislava , 1980. 175 p. : LC Card 82-464724 DDC 338.9 19
HD84.5 .M379 1980 ***NYPL [*QT 87-1737]***

Molano, Alfredo. Selva adentro : una historia oral de la colonización del Guaviare / Alfredo Molano.1a ed. Bogotá : Ancora Editores, 1987. 142 p. : map ; 20 cm. Includes bibliographical references. ISBN 958-9012-02-7 LC Card 87-404301 DDC 986.1/65 19
1. Land settlement - Colombia - Guaviare - History. 2. Guaviare (Colombia) - History. 3. Guaviare (Colombia) - Social conditions. 4. Narcotics, Control of - Colombia - Guaviare - History - 20th century. 5. Guaviare (Colombia) - Economic conditions. 6. Oral history. I. Title.
HD519.G8 M65 1987

Molano Gragera, Juan Carlos. Introducción a la historia del movimiento obrero en Montijo . [Montijo?] [1982?] 103 p., 48 p. of plates : ISBN 84-300-6966-6 LC Card 85-177027
HD8590.M65 I57 1982

Moldau, Juan Hersztajn. Custo dos recursos domésticos / Juan Hersztajn Moldau, Eli Roberto Pelin. Rio de Janeiro : IPEA/INPES, 1985. 94, 4 p. ; 30 cm. (Série Estudos de política industrial e comércio exterior . no. 3) Bibliography: p. 93-94. LC Card 86-200395
1. Costs, Industrial - Brazil. 2. Foreign trade promotion - Brazil. 3. Comparatives advantage (Commerce). 4. Competition, International. I. Pelin, Eli Roberto, 1946-. II. Title. III. Series.
HC190.C7 M64 1985

Moldavia, U.S.S.R. see **Moldavian S. S. R.**

Moldavian Soviet Socialist Republic. see **Moldavian S. S. R.**

MOLDAVIAN S.S.R. - ECONOMIC POLICY.
Chertan, S. E. (Sergeĭ Evgen′evich) Sistema natural′no-stoimostnykh mezhotraslevykh balansov soi͡uznoĭ respubliki . Kishinev , 1984. 242, [6] p., [2] folded leaves of plates : LC Card 85-130960
HC337.M55 C46 1984

MOLDAVIAN S.S.R. - ECONOMIC POLICY- - MATHEMATICAL MODELS.
Optimal′noe planirovanie /. Kishinev , 1982. 166 p. : LC Card 83-149332
HD9015.S653 M64526 1982

MOLDAVIAN S.S.R. - INDUSTRIES - HISTORY.
Shornikov, P. M. (Petr Mikhaĭlovich) Promyshlennost′ i rabochiĭ klass Moldavskoĭ SSR v gody Velikoĭ Otechestvennoĭ voĭny /. Kishinev , 1986. 148, [4] p. ; LC Card 86-141169
HC337.M553 D47 1986

MOLDING (CLAY, PLASTER, ETC.) see **PROSTHESIS.**

Mole, R. H. (Richard H.) BASIC business analysis and operations research / R.H. Mole. London ; Boston : Butterworths, 1987. 136 p. : ill. ; 22 cm. (Butterworths BASIC series) Includes bibliographies and index. ISBN 0-408-01590-X (pbk.) : LC Card 86-26398 DDC 658.4/034/0285526 19
1. Industrial management - Mathematical models. 2. Operations research - Data processing. 3. Basic (Computer program language). I. Title. II. Series.
HD30.25 .M66 1987

Molina Chocano, Guillermo. Estado liberal y desarrollo capitalista en Honduras / Guillermo Molina Chocano. 3a ed. Tegucigalpa, Honduras : Universidad Nacional Autónoma de Honduras, Editorial Universitaria, 1985. 136 p. : ill. ; 20 cm. (Colección Realidad nacional . no. 4) Bibliography: p. 131-136. LC Card 86-233622
1. Investments, Foreign - Honduras - History - 19th century. 2. Honduras - Economic conditions. 3. Honduras - Economic policy. I. Series: Colección Realidad nacional (Tegucigalpa, Honduras) , no. 4. II. Title.
HG5202 .M65 1985

Molina, Guillermo [i.e. Guillermo Molina Chocano] see **Molina Chocano, Guillermo.**

Molina, Humberto. Matas, Jaime. Los problemas ambientales del sistema de transporte urbano /. Santiago de Chile , 1981. 30 leaves : LC Card 82-201768
HE234.Z7 S355 1981

Molina Ibáñez, Mercedes. Capitalismo y socialismo : economía y espacio / Mercedes Molina Ibáñez. Madrid : Cincel, c1984. 128 p. : ill. ; 21 cm. (Cuadernos de estudio. Serie Geografía . 16) Bibliography: p. 127-128. ISBN 84-7046-358-6 LC Card 85-135836
1. Capitalism. 2. Socialism. 3. Industry - Location. I. Title. II. Series.
HB501 .M694 1984

Molina Jiménez, Iván. Acuña Ortega, Víctor H. El desarrollo económico y social de Costa Rica . [San José, Costa Rica] , 1986. vi, 135 p. ; ISBN 997-7440-08-5 LC Card 87-100815
HC143 .A54 1986

Molina Osegueda, Carlos Alberto. Acumulación agrícola y agroindustrial / [Carlos Alberto Molina Osequeda]. [1a ed.]. [San Salvador, El Salvador, C.A. : Editorial Universitaria, 1980] 187 p. : ill. ; 23 cm. Originally presented as the author's thesis (licenciado en economía) Bibliography: p. 185-187. LC Card 86-174381
1. Agriculture - Economic aspects - El Salvador - History. 2. El Salvador - Economic conditions. I. Title.
HD1827 .M65 1980

Molinaro, Remo. Gesundheitswesen und Kostendämpfung in der Bundesrepublik : Beschreibung und Analyse aus schweizerischer Sicht / Remo Molinaro. Berlin ; New York : Springer-Verlag, c1986. xvi, 108 p. ; 25 cm. (Gesundheitssystemforschung) Bibliography: p. [103]-108. ISBN 0-387-16648-3 (U. S.) LC Card 86-200720
1. Insurance, Health - Germany (West) - Cost control. I. Title. II. Series.
HD7102.G3 M58 1986

MOLISE (ITALY) - ECONOMIC CONDITIONS.
Quintano, Claudio. Il sistema industriale del Molise /. Bologna , c1986. 106 p. : ISBN 88-15-01163-3 : LC Card 86-214879
HC307.M64 Q56 1986

MOLISE (ITALY) - INDUSTRIES.
Quintano, Claudio. Il sistema industriale del Molise /. Bologna , c1986. 106 p. : ISBN 88-15-01163-3 : LC Card 86-214879
HC307.M64 Q56 1986

Molitor, Monika. Auswirkungen von Computeranwendungen auf die Leistungsstruktur von Unternehmensorganisationen / Monika Molitor. Frankfurt am Main : Haag + Herchen, c1984. 278 p. : ill. ; 21 cm. Originally presented as the author's thesis (doctoral--Universität Frankfurt am Main, 1984) Bibliography: p. 276-278. ISBN 3-88129-808-8 : LC Card 85-140214
1. Industrial management - Germany (West) - Data processing. I. Title.
HD70.G23 M64 1984

Möller, Ferdinand, 1955- Agrarstruktur und Agrarstrukturpolitik in Spanien, eine Analyse vor dem Hintergrund der Erweiterung der Europäischen Gemeinschaft / Ferdinand Möller. Frankfurt am Main ; New York : P.Lang, c1986. ix, 255 p. ; 21 cm. (Europäische Hochschulschriften. Reihe XXXI, Politikwissenschaft, 0721-3654 . Bd. 95 = vol. 95 = vol. 95) Bibliography: p. 222-238. ISBN 3-8204-9529-0 LC Card 87-407540 DDC 338.1/846 19
1. Agriculture - Economic aspects - Spain. 2. Agriculture and state - Spain. 3. European Economic Community - Spain. I. Series: Europäische Hochschulschriften. Reihe XXXI, Politikwissenschaft , Bd. 95. II. Title.
HD2023 .M65 1986

Möller, Hans Peter. Bilanzkennzahlen und Ertragsrisiken des Kapitalmarktes : eine empirische Untersuchung des Ertragsrisiko-Informationsgehaltes von Bilanzkennzahlen deutscher Aktiengesellschaften / Hans Peter Möller. Stuttgart : C.E. Poeschel, 1986. xii, 240 p. : ill. ; 24 cm. (Betriebswirtschaftliche Abhandlungen . n.F., Bd. 62) The author's Habilitationsschrift--Universität Augsburg, 1985. Bibliography: p. 230-237. ISBN 3-7910-0382-8 LC Card 86-149711
1. Accounting - Germany, West. 2. Capital market - Germany, West. 3. Risk. I. Title. II. Series.
HF5681.C25 M64 1986

Möller, Wolf-Peter. Der Erfolg von Unternehmenszusammenschlüssen : eine empirische Untersuchung / Wolf-Peter Möller. München : Minerva Publikation, c1983. 403 p. : ill. ; 21 cm. (Minerva-Fachserie Wirtschafts- und Sozialwissenschaften) Originally presented as the author's thesis (doctoral)--Universität des Saarlandes, 1982. Bibliography: p. 374-403. ISBN 3-597-10456-8 LC Card 83-227517
1. Consolidation and merger of corporations - Germany, West. 2. Executives - Germany (West) - Interviews. I. Title. II. Series.
HD2746.5 .M65 1983

Møllmann Boye, Erik.
Beskrivende økonomi /. [Copenhagen] , c1985-c1986. 2 v. (810 p.) : ISBN 87-574-4652-0 (set) LC Card 86-159064
HB179.D8 B47 1986

Miljøstatistik og lidt forureningsøkonomi : en materialeorienteret oversigt / af Erik Møllmann Bøye. [Århus] : Institut for erhvervs- og samfundsbeskrivelse, 1978. 53 leaves : ill. ; 24 cm. (Kompendium C . nr. 9) Bibliography: leaves 52-53. LC Card 86-460199
1. Pollution - Economic aspects. 2. Environmental policy. I. Title. II. Series.
HC79.P55 M65 1978

Molloy, John T. How to work the competition into the ground and have fun doing it : a proven program to raise your personal productivity / John T. Molloy. New York, NY : Warner Books, 1987. xiii, 206 p. ; 21 cm. Includes index. ISBN 0-446-38499-2 (pbk.) : LC Card 86-24761 DDC 650.1 19
1. Success in business. 2. Performance. I. Title.
HF5386 .M72 1987

Molnár, Edit S.
Pataki, Judit. Közvéleménykutatás népesedési kérdésekről /. Budapest , c1985. 75 p. ; LC Card 86-166976
HA1201 .A64 no. 60 HB3592.5.A3

Pongrácz, Tiborné. A terhességmegszakításon átesett 18 éven aluli hajadonok társadalmi-demográfiai jellemzői /. Budapest , c1986. 115 p. ; LC Card 87-409645
HA1201 .A64 no. 62 HQ767.5.H8

Molnár, László. Budapesti pedagógusok közlekedési oktatási és nevelési konferenciája . [Budapest , 1978] ([Budapest] :fKészült az MTI Sokszorosító Üzemében) 100 p. ; LC Card 82-204792
HE5614 .B78 1978

Molodezh′ i udarnyĭ kommunisticheskiĭ trud . Chanturii͡a, V. K. (Vladimir Kapitonovich) Moskva , 1981. 205 p. : LC Card 82-178361
HD6276.S592 C46 1981

Molodezh′--problemy i perspektivy.
Popov, V. D. (Vladimir Dmitrievich) Ėkonomika plius pedagogika . Moskva , 1986. 288 p. ; LC Card 86-103180
HB74.9.S65 P66 1986

Molodost′, trud, romantika : fotoal′bom o vsesoi͡uznom studencheskom otri͡ade / [pod obshcheĭ redaktsieĭ Pristupko Viktora Aleksandrovicha ; tekst Korsakovoĭ Tat′i͡any Aleksandrovny]. Moskva : Izd-vo "Planeta", 1985. 183 p., [8] p. of plates : chiefly col. ill., ports. ; 26 cm. LC Card 86-113851
1. Labor service - Soviet Union - Pictorial works. 2. Students - Employment - Soviet Union - Pictorial works. 3. Youth - Employment - Soviet Union - Pictorial works. I. Pristupko, Viktor Aleksandrovich. II. Korsakova, Tat′i͡ana Aleksandrovna.
HD4870.S65 M65 1985

Molot, Maureen Appel, 1941- Laux, Jeanne Kirk, 1942- State capitalism . Ithaca , 1988. ix, 250 p. ; ISBN 0-8014-2079-2 (alk. paper) LC Card 87-47600 DDC 338.6/2/0971 19
HD4005 .L38 1988

Molozhavenko, Vladimir. Zharkoe solnt͡se Surkhana / Vladimir Molozhavenko. Moskva : "Mysl′", 1982. 189 p., [16] p. of plates : ill. ; 20 cm. LC Card 82-177858
1. Surkhandar′inskai͡a oblast′ (Uzbek S.S.R.) - Economic conditions. 2. Agricultural industries - Uzbek S.S.R. - Surkhandar′inskai͡a oblast′. I. Title.
HC337.U962 S975 1982

Molt, Walter, 1932- Technik von gestern für die Ziele von morgen? . Opladen , c1986. 153 p. ; ISBN 3-531-11713-0 LC Card 86-230906
HD9502.A2 T43 1986

Momeni, Jamshid A., 1938- Race, ethnicity, and minority housing in the United States /. New York , 1986. xxv, 224 p. ; ISBN 0-313-24848-6 (lib. bdg. : alk. paper) LC Card 86-9971 DDC 363.5/9 19
HD7288.72.U5 R33 1986
NYPL [JLE 87-946]

Moments of truth /. Carlzon, Jan. Cambridge, Mass. , c1987. xiii, 135 p. ; ISBN 0-88730-200-9 LC Card 87-1070 DDC 387.7/065/485 19
HE9860.S28 C37 1987

Momoh, Mike. Yearwood, John. Storage facilities in the chiefdoms of Bo and Pujehun District /. Bo [1983] vi, 31 leaves : LC Card 87-110214 DDC 338.1/6 19
HD9017.S53 B599 1983

Monarch's clear & simple filing and records management. Taylor, Mary Sue, 1938- Clear & simple filing and records management /. New York, NY , c1987. 171 p. : ISBN 0-671-62397-4 (pbk.) : LC Card 86-28534 DDC 651.5 19
HF5736 .T388 1987

Monash University. Centre of Southeast Asian Studies. Mortimer, Rex, 1926-1979. Stubborn survivors . [Clayton, Vic.] , 1984. xvii, 180 p. : ISBN 0-86746-299-X (pbk.) LC Card 87-672646
HC59.7 .M593x 1984

MONASTERIES - ITALY - SIENA REGION - HISTORY.
Epstein, Stephan R., 1960- Alle origini della fattoria toscana . Firenze , c1986. 315 p. : LC Card 87-104355
HD1470.5.I82 S544 1986

Monbeig, Pierre. Les Phénomènes de "frontière" dans les pays tropicaux . Paris , 1981. vii, 456 p. : LC Card 83-122397
HD1131 .P47 1981

MONBEIG, PIERRE.
Les Phénomènes de "frontière" dans les pays tropicaux . Paris , 1981. vii, 456 p. : LC Card

83-122397
HD1131 .P47 1981

Mönchengladbacher Gespräche .
(2) Soziallehre der Kirche und katholische Verbände /. Köln , 1980. 244 p. ; ISBN 3-7616-0568-4 (pbk.) : LC Card 81-122896 DDC 306/.6/0943 19
HN39.G3 S693 ***NYPL [JLC 86-231]***
(4) Alternative Ökonomie? /. Köln , 1982. 244 p. ; ISBN 3-7616-0671-0 (pbk.) LC Card 84-109717 DDC 338.9 19
HD88 .A48 1982 ***NYPL [JLC 86-230]***

MOND, LUDWIG.
Lischka, J. R. (Johannes Richard), 1933- Ludwig Mond and the British alkali industry /. New York , 1985. 233 p. ; ISBN 0-8240-6686-3 (alk. paper) : LC Card 84-46006 DDC 338.4/7673725/0924 19
HD9660.A43 G75 1985
NYPL [JSD 86-547]

Monday, H. R. Proposals for the establishment of an African Institute of Chartered Accountants. [New York?] : United Nations Economic and Social Council, Economic Commission for Africa, [1984] 10 p. ; 28 cm. A paper prepared by H.R. Monday, Jnr prepared for the Fifth Biennial Training Development Conference of the African Association for Training and Development, Addis Ababa, Ethiopia, 19-29 November 1984. Cover title. LC Card 86-122510 DDC 657/.06/06 19
1. African Institute of Chartered Accountants. 2. Accountants - Africa. I. United Nations. Economic Commission for Africa. II. Title.
HF5616.A35 M65 1984

Un monde méditerranéen . Bresc, Henri. [Roma] , 1986. 2 v. (981 p.) : ISBN 2-7283-0103-4 (set) LC Card 87-139949
HC307.S5 B74 1986

Il Mondo oggi : politica, guerre, economia, società in 90 tavole. Milano : Europeo, <[1986]- >, <c1983- > v. <2 > : col. ill., col. maps ; 25 cm. "Supplemento al n. 21 di Europeo"--T.p. verso. ISBN 0-330-28132-1 LC Card 87-103039
1. Economic history - 1971- - Statistics. I. Europeo. N. 21 (Supplement).
HC59 .M596 1986

Il mondo rovesciato . Mugnai, Massimo, 1947- Bologna , c1984. 296 p. ; ISBN 88-15-00641-9 : LC Card 86-169123
HB206 .M84 1984

Mondragón, Rubén. Consejo Superior de Planificación Económica (Honduras) Situación actual y perspectivas económicas, 1972 . Tegucigalpa, D.C., Honduras, C.A. , 1972. 38, [18] leaves ; LC Card 86-158684
HC145 .C66 1972

Mondy, R. Wayne, 1940- Caruth, Donald L. Staffing the contemporary organization . New York , 1988. xii, 309 p. : ISBN 0-89930-236-X (lib. bdg. : alk. paper) LC Card 87-13092 DDC 658.3 19
HF5549 .C296 1988

Mone, Edward M. London, Manuel. Career management and survival in the workplace . San Francisco , 1987. xviii, 226 p. ; ISBN 1-555-42043-5 (alk. paper) LC Card 86-46334 DDC 658.3/14 19
HF5549.5.C35 L65 1987

El monedero de los Andes . Mitre, Antonio. La Paz , 1986. 134 p. ; LC Card 87-403038 DDC 332.4/98 19
HG803 .M57 1986

Moneta e banca in Etiopia /. Mauri, Arnaldo. Milano [1986] xi, 316 p. : ISBN 88-14-00769-1 LC Card 86-182310
HG3389.A6 M38 1986
NYPL [JLE 87-1721]

Monetäre Steuerungsprobleme in sozialistischen Planwirtschaften /. Hartwig, Karl-Hans. Stuttgart , New York , 1987. vi, 146 p. ; ISBN 3-437-50295-6 LC Card 87-136038 DDC 339.5/3/0947 19
HG925 .H37 1987

Monetarism and liberalization . Edwards, Sebastián. Cambridge, MA , c1987. xxi, 233 p. : ISBN 0-88730-105-3 LC Card 86-25959 DDC 338.983 19
HC192 .E249 1987 ***NYPL [JLE 87-1485]***

Monetarism or prosperity? /. Gould, Bryan. London , 1981. x, 222 p. : ISBN 0-333-30782-8 LC Card 86-673392
HG939.5 .G65x 1981

Monetarisme og økonomisk politik /. Brink, Helge. [Copenhagen] , c1984. 125 p. ; ISBN 87-574-4380-7 : LC Card 84-253099
HG1092 .B75 1984

Monetarismo y mercado de trabajo . Lindenboim, Javier. Buenos Aires, Argentina , c1985. x, 471 p. : ISBN 950-9370-05-3 LC Card 87-122243 DDC 331.12/0982/73 19
HD5750.R56 L56 1985

Monetarist perspectives /. Laidler, David E. W. Deddington, Oxford , 1982. xii, 218 p. ; ISBN 0-86003-042-3 LC Card 86-673565
HG230.3 .L34x 1982b

Monetary aggregates as targets . Freedman, Charles. [Ottawa] , 1981. vii, 49 p. ; LC Card 81-198954 DDC 332.4/6/0724 19
HG230.3 .F74 1981
NYPL [JLM 75-1420 no.27]

The monetary and banking development of Singapore and Malaysia /. Lee, S. Y. (Sheng-Yi) Singapore , 1986. 298 p. : ISBN 997-16-9098-5 (pbk.) LC Card 86-943034 DDC 332.4/9595 19
HG1250.67 .L43 1986

Monetary and financial relations within the system of contemporary state monopoly capitalism. Parichno-kreditni i finansovi otnosheniia v sistemata na sŭvremenniia dŭrzhavno-monopolisticheski kapitalizŭm /. Sofiia , 1985. 245 p. : LC Card 86-153156
HG3881 .P2936 1985

Monetary and fiscal policy /. Fisher, Douglas, 1934- New York , c1987. p. cm. ISBN 0-8147-2587-2 : LC Card 87-5478 DDC 339.5/2 19
HB172.5 .F54 1987

Monetary Authority of Singapore.
Papers on monetary economics /. [Singapore] , c1981. xii, 200 p. ; ISBN 997-16-9044-6 LC Card 82-940575
HG1250.67 .P37 1981

Monetary Authority of Singapore. Economics Dept. Papers on monetary economics /. [Singapore] , c1981. xii, 200 p. ; ISBN 997-16-9044-6 LC Card 82-940575
HG1250.67 .P37 1981

Monetary chaos in Europe . Brown, Brendan, 1951- London , New York , c1987. p. cm. ISBN 0-7099-5035-7 : LC Card 87-23059 DDC 332.4/5/094 19
HG186.A2 B76 1987

MONETARY CORRECTION. see **INDEXATION (ECONOMICS)**

Monetary economics /. Beecham, B. Julian, 1927- London , New York , 1988. p. cm. ISBN 0-582-02042-5 LC Card 87-17142 DDC 332.4 19
HG221 .B424 1988

Monetary integration . Hildebrand, John R. Bristol, Ind., U. S.A. , c1987. viii, 81 p. ; ISBN 1-556-05004-6 (pbk.) LC Card 87-50033 DDC 332.4/6 19
HG230.3 .H535 1987

MONETARY MANAGEMENT. see **MONETARY POLICY.**

Monetary nationalism and international stability /. Hayek, Friedrich A. von (Friedrich August), 1899- Fairfield, NJ , 1988. p. cm. ISBN 0-678-00047-6 LC Card 87-17244 DDC 332.4 19
HG221 .H345 1988

Monetary policy : review of the Sukhamoy Chakravarty report / Sukhamoy Chakravarty ... [et al.]. New Delhi : India International Centre, c1986. 70 p. ; 24 cm. (IIC monograph series . no. 10) Review of the Report of the Committee to Review the Working of the Monetary System, also known as the Chakravarty report. LC Card 87-900210 DDC 332.4/954 19
1. Monetary policy - India. I. Chakravarty, Sukhamoy. II. India. Committee to Review the Working of the Monetary System. III. Series.
HG1235 .M66 1986

MONETARY POLICY - AFRICA, SUB-SAHARAN.
Green, Reginald Herbold. The IMF and stabilisation in sub-Saharan Africa . Brighton, England [1986] ii, 70 p. ; LC Card 86-208478 DDC 332.1/52 19
HC800 .G72 1986

Monetary policy and the financial system /. Horvitz, Paul M. Englewood Cliffs, N.J. , c1987. xii, 532 p. : ISBN 0-13-599861-1 LC Card 86-25447 DDC 332.4/973 19
HG540 .H67 1987

Monetary policy and the international diffusion of interest rates /. Brimmer, Andrew F. Miami, Fla. [1982] iii, 47 p. : LC Card 86-204514 DDC 332.4/973 19
HG540 .B75 1982

Monetary policy and uncertainty : collected papers from the 1982-1984 Konstanz Seminars / Manfred J.M. Neumann, ed. ; with contributions by, R.J. Barro ... [et al.].1. Aufl. Baden-Baden : Nomos Verlagsgesellschaft, 1986. 262 p. : ill. ; 23 cm. (Schriften zur monetären Ökonomie. Bd. 23) Includes bibliographies. ISBN 3-7890-1257-2 (pbk.) LC Card 86-225786 DDC 332.4/0724 19
1. Monetary policy - Mathematical models - Congresses. 2. Uncertainty - Mathematical models - Congresses. 3. Rational expectations (Economic theory) - Congresses. I. Neumann, Manfred J. M. (Manfred Johann Michael), 1940-. II. Barro, Robert J.
HG230.3 .M655 1986

MONETARY POLICY - ANDES REGION - HISTORY - 19TH CENTURY.
Mitre, Antonio. El monedero de los Andes . La Paz , 1986. 134 p. ; LC Card 87-403038 DDC 332.4/98 19
HG803 .M57 1986

MONETARY POLICY - ARGENTINA.
Argentina 1984 . [Buenos Aires?] [1984] 95 p. ; LC Card 85-132860
HJ8569 .A75 1984

Canitrot, Adolfo. Orden social y monetarismo /. Buenos Aires, Argentina [1982 or 1983] 50 p. ; LC Card 83-213595
HC173 .C35 1982

Conesa, Eduardo R. Bases y puntos de partida para la recuperación de la economía argentina . Buenos Aires, Argentina , c1986. 178 p. : ISBN 950-53-7109-8 LC Card 87-400257 DDC 338.982 19
HC175 .C6145 1986

Lindenboim, Javier. Monetarismo y mercado de trabajo . Buenos Aires, Argentina , c1985. x, 471 p. : ISBN 950-9370-05-3 LC Card 87-122243 DDC 331.12/0982/73 19
HD5750.R56 L56 1985

Oría, Gerardo J. (Gerardo Juan) Teoría y práctica de la indexación . Buenos Aires , 1985. 216 p. ; ISBN 950-9209-28-7 LC Card 86-151154
HG815 .O75 1985

Peláez, Carlos Manuel. O cruzado e o austral . São Paulo , 1986. 174 p. : ISBN 85-22-40173-X LC Card 87-102770 DDC 332.4/981 19
HG835 .P43 1986

Pereira, Luiz Carlos Bresser. [Inflação e recessão. English.] The theory of inertial inflation . Boulder, Colo. , 1987. xiii, 206 p. : ISBN 1-555-87007-4 (alk. paper) : LC Card 86-29832 DDC 332.4/1/0981 19
HG835 .P4413 1987

Rosales Díaz, Ramón. Programas de reactivación económica y sistemas financieros . [Lima] , 1986. 68 p. : LC Card 87-400247 DDC 332.4/982 19
HG815 .R67 1986

MONETARY POLICY - ARGENTINA - HISTORY - 20TH CENTURY.
García, Valeriano F. A critical inquiry into Argentine economic history, 1946-1970 /. New York , 1987. vi, 127 p. : ISBN 0-8240-1361-1 (alk. paper) : LC Card 87-7620 DDC 330.982/062 19
HG815 .G27 1987

MONETARY POLICY - BOLIVIA - HISTORY - 19TH CENTURY.
Mitre, Antonio. El monedero de los Andes . La Paz , 1986. 134 p. ; LC Card 87-403038 DDC 332.4/98 19
HG803 .M57 1986

MONETARY POLICY - BRAZIL.
Assis, José Carlos de. A sombra do cruzado . Rio de Janeiro , 1986. 137 p. : LC Card

87-128261 DDC 332.4/981 19
HG835 .A88 1986

Braga, Roberto Saturnino. Saturnino, o momento histórico do Congresso Nacional. Brasília , 1983. 58 p. ; LC Card 83-202638
HC187 .B76 1983

Bulhões, Octávio Gouveia de. Desdobramentos inflacionários. [Salvador] [1984] 43 p. : LC Card 86-861354 DDC 332.4/1/0981 19
HG835 .B85 1984

Fischer, Bernhard, fl. 1979- Brasilien ohne Inflation? . Kiel [1986] 28 p. ; LC Card 87-120443 DDC 330 s 332.4/1/0981 19
HB44 .K45 no. 124 HG835

Galvêas, Ernane. Sistema financeiro e mercado de capitais /. Rio de Janeiro , 1985. 171 p. : LC Card 85-208367
HG185.B7 G35 1985

Langoni, Carlos Geraldo. A crise do desenvolvimento, uma estratégia para o futuro /. Rio de Janeiro , 1985. xix, 176 p. : ISBN 85-03-00001-6 : LC Card 85-151246 DDC 338.981 19
HG835 .L36 1985 ***NYPL [JLD 86-288]***

Lemgruber, Antonio Carlos. O controle da base monetária e as flutuações dos multiplicadores monetários e creditícios /. [Brasília] [1981?] 118 p. : LC Card 85-154853
HG835 .L35 1981

Martone, Celso L. (Celso Luiz) Mercado financeiro e ajustamento macroeconômico brasileiro, 1978-1985 /. São Paulo , 1986. 82 p. : LC Card 87-120453 DDC 332.4/981 19
HG835 .M375 1986

National Monetary Council (Brazil) Brazil--money and credit programming in 1983 /. Brazil [1982] 38 p. ; LC Card 87-131446
HG835 .N36 1982

Ness, Walter L. A influência da correção monetária no sistema financeiro /. Rio de Janeiro , 1977. 205 p. : LC Card 85-206096
HG229 .N385 1977

Peláez, Carlos Manuel. O cruzado e o austral . São Paulo , 1986. 174 p. : ISBN 85-22-40173-X LC Card 87-102770 DDC 332.4/981 19
HG835 .P43 1986

Pereira, Luiz Carlos Bresser. [Inflação e recessão. English.] The theory of inertial inflation . Boulder, Colo. , 1987. xiii, 206 p. : ISBN 1-555-87007-4 (alk. paper) : LC Card 86-29832 DDC 332.4/1/0981 19
HG835 .P4413 1987

Vianna, Pedro Jorge Ramos. Inflação vs. indexação, uma contribuição ao tema /. Fortaleza-Ceará [19]84. 121 p. : LC Card 86-130092
HG835 .V53 1984

MONETARY POLICY - BRAZIL - ECONOMETRIC MODELS.
Melo, Valdir Ramalho de. Seleção de agregados monetários /. [Brasília] [1981] 136 p. : LC Card 85-161532
HG835 .M45 1981

MONETARY POLICY - BRAZIL - HISTORY.
Cardoso, Eliana A. Inflation, growth and the real exchange rate . New York , 1987. 98 p. : ISBN 0-8240-1356-5 (alk. paper) : LC Card 87-8570 DDC 330.981 19
HC187 .C218 1987

MONETARY POLICY - BRAZIL - HISTORY - 20TH CENTURY.
Vianna, Maria Lúcia Teixeira Werneck. A administração do "milagre" . Petrópolis , 1987. 180 p. ; LC Card 87-403982 DDC 332.4/981 19
HG835 .V527 1987

MONETARY POLICY - BRAZIL - MATHEMATICAL MODELS.
Harris, John Andrew de Oliveira. Evolução e definição da moeda /. Rio de Janeiro, RJ , 1985. 90 p. : LC Card 87-135878 DDC 332.4/981 19
HG835 .H37 1985

MONETARY POLICY - CANADA.
Fiscal and monetary policy /. Toronto , Buffalo , c1986. xviii, 339 p. : ISBN 0-8020-7263-1 (pbk.) LC Card 86-672943 DDC 336.3/0971 19
HJ793 .F55 1986 ***NYPL [JLE 87-511]***

Howitt, Peter, 1946- Monetary policy in transition . Toronto , Scarborough, Ont. [1986] viii, 140 p. : ISBN 0-88806-136-6 (pbk.) LC Card 86-229489 DDC 332.1/12/0971 19
HG655 .H69 1986

MONETARY POLICY - CARIBBEAN AREA.
Calderón González, Arnoldo. América Latina y el Caribe . México, D.F. , 1985. 51, [25] leaves ; LC Card 87-121714 DDC 332.4/98 19
HG660.5 .C35 1985

Jones-Hendrickson, S. B. (Simon B.) Public finance and monetary policy in open economies . [Kingston, Jamaica] , 19. 172 p. ;
NYPL [Sc D 86-830]

MONETARY POLICY - CHILE.
Edwards, Sebastián. Monetarism and liberalization . Cambridge, MA , c1987. xxi, 233 p. : ISBN 0-88730-105-3 LC Card 86-25959 DDC 338.983 19
HC192 .E249 1987 ***NYPL [JLE 87-1485]***

Gatica, Jaime. Deindustrialization in Chile /. Boulder , 1988. p. cm. ISBN 0-8133-7392-1 : LC Card 86-32513 DDC 338.983 19
HD9734.C52 G37 1988

Gutiérrez Urrutia, Mario. Reflexiones sobre apertura financiera . Santiago , 1982. 36 p. : LC Card 82-203323
HG845 .G87 1982

Nowak, Felicitas. Financial liberalization revisited . Göttingen [1986] 49 p. : LC Card 87-121206 DDC 332/.0983 19
HG185.C5 N69 1986

MONETARY POLICY - CONGRESSES.
Directions for reform . New Delhi [1984] x, 78 p. ; ISBN 0-7069-2692-7 : LC Card 84-903168 DDC 332/.042 19
HG3881 .D57 1984 ***NYPL [JLD 86-4409]***

Financial innovation and monetary policy . [Tokyo] , c1986. ix, 339 p. : ISBN 4-13-047029-9 : LC Card 86-222823 DDC 332/.095 19
HG187.E37 F55 1986

Geldwertstabilität und Wirtschaftswachstum . Göttingen , c1984. xii, 230 p. : ISBN 3-525-13169-0 LC Card 84-232466
HG203 .G46 1984

Inflation in the world economy /. Manchester [Eng.] , 1976. xvii, 334 p. : ISBN 0-7190-0630-9 LC Card 76-356701
HG229 .I453 1976 ***NYPL [JLD 78-401]***

Monetary theory and economic institutions . New York , 1987. ix, 349 p. : ISBN 0-312-00407-9 : LC Card 86-26069 DDC 332.4/01 19
HG203 .M68 1987

The Monetary versus fiscal policy debate . Totowa, N.J. , 1986. 171 p. : ISBN 0-8476-7454-1 : LC Card 85-11912 DDC 339.5/2 19
HG230.3 .M64 1986 ***NYPL [JLE 86-4720]***

Symposium on Monetary Theory (1986 : Institute of Economics, Academia Sinica) Symposium on Monetary Theory, January 3-8, 1986 =. Taipei, Taiwan, Republic of China [1986?] 2 v. (iv, 630 p.) : LC Card 87-152394 DDC 332.4 19
HG203 .S96 1986

World monetary system in a time of change . Budapest [1987] 283 p. ; ISBN 963-01-7937-7 (pbk.) LC Card 87-169001 DDC 332.4/5 19
HG230.3 .W68 1987

MONETARY POLICY - COSTA RICA - HISTORY.
Daremblum, Jaime. Del cacao al colón . San José, Costa Rica [1977?- v. <1- > ; LC Card 87-402194 DDC 332.4/97286 19
HG682 .D37 1977

MONETARY POLICY - DENMARK.
Brink, Helge. Monetarisme og økonomisk politik /. [Copenhagen] , c1984. 125 p. ; ISBN 87-574-4380-7 : LC Card 84-253099
HG1092 .B75 1984

MONETARY POLICY - DEVELOPING COUNTRIES.
Damanik, Konta I. Kurs mata uang sebagai alat kebijakan di negara sedang berkembang (NSB) /. Salatiga , 1980. ii, 21 leaves ; LC Card 85-941470
HG1496 .D35 1980

MONETARY POLICY - DEVELOPING COUNTRIES - CONGRESSES.
Directions for reform . New Delhi [1984] x, 78 p. ; ISBN 0-7069-2692-7 : LC Card 84-903168 DDC 332/.042 19
HG3881 .D57 1984 ***NYPL [JLD 86-4409]***

Economic liberalization in developing countries /. Oxford [Oxfordshire] , New York , 1986. vi, 278 p. : ISBN 0-631-15023-4 : LC Card 86-6153 DDC 338.9/009172/4 19
HC59.7 .E3116 1986 ***NYPL [JLE 86-4644]***

MONETARY POLICY - EAST ASIA - CONGRESSES.
Financial innovation and monetary policy . [Tokyo] , c1986. ix, 339 p. : ISBN 4-13-047029-9 : LC Card 86-222823 DDC 332/.095 19
HG187.E37 F55 1986

MONETARY POLICY - ECONOMETRIC MODELS.
Adolph, Brigitte. Rationale Erwartungen, Arbeitsverträge und Wirtschaftspolitik /. München , c1986. ii, 127 p. : ISBN 3-88259-346-6 LC Card 87-104701 DDC 330/.01/9 19
HB175 .A26 1986

Rasche, Robert H. Controlling the growth of monetary aggregates /. Boston , c1987. xviii, 212 p. : ISBN 0-89838-226-2 : LC Card 87-3737 DDC 332.4/6 19
HG230.3 .R37 1987

Rötheli, Tobias F. Das Volkseinkommen und die internationalen Kapitalbewegungen /. Bern , c1986. 128 p. ; ISBN 3-258-03669-1 LC Card 87-110633 DDC 332.4/5/0724 19
HG3891 .R67 1986

MONETARY POLICY - ECUADOR.
Abril-Ojeda, Galo. Política monetaria y desarrollo industrial en el Ecuador, 1970-1983 /. Quito , 1985. 118 p. : ISBN 91-85894-10-9 LC Card 86-103812
HG865 .A27 1985

MONETARY POLICY - EUROPE.
Geld- und Währungsordnung /. Berlin , c1983. 249 p. : ISBN 3-428-05530-6 LC Card 84-141547
HG999.5 .G4556 1983

MONETARY POLICY - EUROPE, EASTERN.
Brabant, Jozef M. van. Adjustment, structural change, and economic efficiency . Cambridge [Cambridgeshire] , New York , 1987. xviii, 480 p. ; ISBN 0-521-33455-1 LC Card 87-785 DDC 332.4/947 19
HG186.E82 B7 1987

Hartwig, Karl-Hans. Monetäre Steuerungsprobleme in sozialistischen Planwirtschaften /. Stuttgart , New York , 1987. vi, 146 p. ; ISBN 3-437-50295-6 LC Card 87-136038 DDC 339.5/3/0947 19
HG925 .H37 1987

MONETARY POLICY - EUROPE - HISTORY - 20TH CENTURY.
Brown, Brendan, 1951- Monetary chaos in Europe . London , New York , c1987. p. cm. ISBN 0-7099-5035-7 : LC Card 87-23059 DDC 332.4/5/094 19
HG186.A2 B76 1987

MONETARY POLICY - EUROPEAN ECONOMIC COMMUNITY COUNTRIES.
Gil, Gonzalo. Aspectos financieros y monetarios de la integración española en la Comunidad Económica Europea /. [Madrid] [1985] 187 p. : ISBN 84-505-2233-1 LC Card 87-101729
HC241.25.S6 G55 1985

Martinengo, Giancarlo. Lo SME e il dollaro . [Napoli] , c1983. 84 p. ; LC Card 85-150597
HG930.5 .M27 1983

Masera, R. S. L'unificazione monetaria e lo SME /. Bologna , c1980. 220 p. ; LC Card 82-150717 DDC 332.4/566/094 19
HG930.5.Z8 M37 1980 ***NYPL [JLD 87-902]***

Die Währungspolitik in den Ländern der Europäischen Wirtschaftsgemeinschaft . Luxembourg , Washington, D.C. , 1972. 451 p. ; LC Card 85-116654
HG930.5 .W34 1972

MONETARY POLICY - EUROPEAN ECONOMIC COMMUNITY COUNTRIES - CONGRESSES.
International monetary and financial integration . Dordrecht , Boston , c1988. xii,

403 p. : ISBN 90-247-3563-7 LC Card 87-3622 DDC 332.4/94 19
HG930.5 .I586 1988

Problemy valiutnogo soiuza stran-chlenov Evropeiskogo ėkonomicheskogo soobshchestva i razvitie mezhdunarodnoĭ valiutnoĭ sistemy kapitalizma . Sofiia , 1984. 151 p. ; LC Card 85-224144
HG3942.8 .P76 1984

MONETARY POLICY - FRANCE.
Chaîneau, André. Mécanismes et politique monétaires . Paris , 1979, c19. 311 p. : ISBN 2-13-036227-3 *NYPL [JLD 86-2730]*

MONETARY POLICY - GERMANY - HISTORY.
Otruba, Gustav. A. Hitler's "Tausend-Mark-Sperre" und die Folgen für Österreichs Fremdenverkehr (1933-1938) /. Linz , c1983. iii, 205 p. ; ISBN 3-85320-308-6 LC Card 84-213145
HG999 .O87 1983

MONETARY POLICY - GERMANY - HISTORY - 20TH CENTURY.
The Adaptation to inflation /. Berlin , New York , 1986. xvi, 512 p. : ISBN 0-89925-287-7 (U. S.) LC Card 86-29134 DDC 338.943 19
HC286.2 .A62 1986

MONETARY POLICY - GERMANY, WEST.
Eschenbaum, Gerhard. Krisenbevorratung von Rohstoffen unter spezieller Berücksichtigung einer Finanzierung aus Währungsreserven der Deutschen Bundesbank /. Bochum , 1983. xix, 464 p. : ISBN 3-88339-314-2 : LC Card 83-218426
HF1054.G4 E83 1983

Geld- und Währungsordnung /. Berlin , c1983. 249 p. : ISBN 3-428-05530-6 LC Card 84-141547
HG999.5 .G4556 1983

Öffentliche Finanzen, Kredit und Kapital . Berlin , c1985. xvi, 618 p., [1] leaf of plates : ISBN 3-428-05737-6 LC Card 85-164173
HJ161 .O33 1985

Panek, Hans-Thomas. Die Währungskrisen vom November 1968 bis Mai 1971 im politischen Prozess der Bundesrepublik Deutschland /. Köln , 1977. 293 p. ; ISBN 3-921471-29-X LC Card 86-184843
HG999.5 .P35 1977

Probleme monetärer und finanzwirtschaftlicher Steuerung im Systemvergleich /. Duisburg , c1986. 175 p. : ISBN 3-921473-43-8 LC Card 86-211745
HC286.6 .P754 1986

Runge, Harry. Haushaltsfinanzierung durch Notendruck /. Berlin , c1986. 69 p. ; ISBN 3-428-05984-0 LC Card 86-165742
HG1004 .R75 1986

Seja, Jürgen, 1953- Selektive Effekte der global orientierten Geldpolitik der Deutschen Bundesbank auf die Marktstruktur im Bankensektor /. Frankfurt am Main , New York , c1983. xiii, 370 p. ; ISBN 3-8204-5282-6 LC Card 86-119382
HG3055 .S5 1983

Vomfelde, Werner. Abschied von Keynes? . Frankfurt am Main , New York , c1985. 205 p. : ISBN 3-593-33567-0 LC Card 86-159600
HB99.7 .V65 1985

MONETARY POLICY - GERMANY (WEST) - ECONOMETRIC MODELS.
Kudiss, Reinhard, 1952- Die Bestimmung des Produktionspotentials in Theorie und Empirie . Frankfurt am Main , New York , c1984. xvi, 198 p. : ISBN 3-8204-5579-5 LC Card 85-189908
HB3730 .K766 1984

MONETARY POLICY - GREAT BRITAIN.
Beecham, B. Julian, 1927- Monetary economics /. London , New York , 1988. p. cm. ISBN 0-582-02042-5 LC Card 87-17142 DDC 332.4 19
HG221 .B424 1988

Blake, Hubert, 1893- Currency and credit before and since 1914 [microform] /. London , 1923. viii, 91 p. ; *NYPL [*ZT-1736 no.1]*

Gould, Bryan. Monetarism or prosperity? /. London , 1981. x, 222 p. : ISBN 0-333-30782-8 LC Card 86-673392
HG939.5 .G65x 1981

Kaldor, Nicholas, 1908- The scourge of monetarism /. Oxford , New York , 1986. xxv, 112 p. : ISBN 0-19-877248-3 *NYPL [JLD 86-2212]*

Ricardo, David, 1772-1823. Scritti monetari /. Roma [1985] 495 p. ; LC Card 86-207988
HG938 .R63 1985

MONETARY POLICY - GREAT BRITAIN - HISTORY.
Kunz, Diane B., 1952- The battle for Britain's gold standard in 1931 /. London , New York , c1987. viii, 207 p. ; ISBN 0-7099-3120-4 LC Card 87-9065 DDC 332.4/222/0941 19
HG939 .K85 1987

MONETARY POLICY - HISTORY.
Butler, Eamonn. Milton Friedman . Aldershot, Hants, England , c1985. 272 p. : ISBN 0-85117-261-X : *NYPL [JLD 86-1090]*

Rousseas, Stephen William. Post Keynesian monetary economics /. Armonk, N.Y. , c1986. x, 126 p.; ISBN 0-87332-355-6 LC Card 85-14181 DDC 332.4/6 19
HG230.3 .R68 1986 *NYPL [JLE 86-4326]*

Schwartz, Anna Jacobson. Money in historical perspective /. Chicago , 1987. xvii, 442 p. : ISBN 0-226-74228-8 : LC Card 87-5973 DDC 332.4/9 19
HG538 .S354 1987

Monetary policy in transition . Howitt, Peter, 1946- Toronto , Scarborough, Ont. [1986] viii, 140 p. : ISBN 0-88806-136-6 (pbk.) LC Card 86-229489 DDC 332.1/12/0971 19
HG655 .H69 1986

MONETARY POLICY - INDIA.
Monetary policy . New Delhi , c1986. 70 p. ; LC Card 87-900210 DDC 332.4/954 19
HG1235 .M66 1986

Reserve Bank of India. Committee to Review the Working of the Monetary System. Report of the Committee to Review the Working of the Monetary System. Bombay [1985] vii, 371 p. ; LC Card 87-902447 DDC 332.4/954 19
HG1235 .R47 1985

Thaker, B. C. Fiscal policy, monetary analysis, and debt management . New Delhi , 1985. xvi, 356 p. : LC Card 85-903636 DDC 339.5/2/0954 19
HG230.3 .T46 1985 *NYPL [JLD 86-1324]*

MONETARY POLICY - INDIA - HISTORY.
Ambirajan, S. Political economy and monetary management . Madras , c1984. viii, 203 p. ; LC Card 87-900241 DDC 332.4/954 19
HC433 .A42 1984

MONETARY POLICY - ISLAMIC COUNTRIES.
Ṣiddīqī, Muḥammad Nejātullah, 1931- Banking and monetary polic[i]es in Islamic economics /. Khartoum [between 1983 and 1986] 40 p. ; LC Card 86-980021 DDC 332.1/0917/671 19
HG3368.A6 S53 1986

MONETARY POLICY - ITALY.
Oltre la crisi . Bologna , c1986. x, 745 p. : ISBN 88-15-01249-4 : LC Card 87-149887
HC305 .O45 1986

Politica monetaria e politica dell'occupazione in Italia, in un contesto di innovazione finanziaria /. Milano , c1984. 166 p. ; LC Card 84-245111 DDC 332/.0945 19
HG1029.5 .P63 1984

Tasgian, Astrig. L'imposta e il deposito previo sugli acquisti di valuta e la crisi della lira del 1976 . Milano , c1983. 139 p. : LC Card 83-187693 DDC 332.4/945 19
HG1029.5 .T37 1983 *NYPL [JLD 87-813]*

MONETARY POLICY - ITALY - CONGRESSES.
Politica monetaria e debito pubblico . Milano, Italy , c1984. 209 p. : LC Card 85-111306 DDC 332.4/945 19
HJ8678 .P65 1984 *NYPL [JLD 86-1207]*

MONETARY POLICY - ITALY - HISTORY - 20TH CENTURY.
Ciocca, Pierluigi, 1941- Interesse e profitto . Bologna , c1982. 245 p. : LC Card 84-139966 DDC 332/.0945 19
HG186.I8 C56 1982

MONETARY POLICY - JAPAN.
Japan's response to crisis and change in the world economy /. Armonk, N.Y. , c1986. xiii, 309 p. : ISBN 0-87332-405-6 LC Card 86-21907 DDC 338.952 19
HC462.9 .J355 1986 *NYPL [JLE 87-1199]*

Suzuki, Yoshio, 1931- [Nihon kin'yū keizairon. English.] Money, finance, and macroeconomic performance in Japan /. New Haven , c1986. xvii, 218, p. : ISBN 0-300-03387-7 LC Card 85-26375 DDC 332/.0952 19
HG187.J3 S96 1986 *NYPL [JLE 86-2788]*

MONETARY POLICY - KOREA (SOUTH)
Korea . Washington, D.C., U. S.A. [1987] 2 v. : ISBN 0-8213-0887-4 (pbk. : v. 1) LC Card 87-2213 DDC 338.9519/5 19
HD3616.K853 K67 1987

MONETARY POLICY - LATIN AMERICA.
Brovedani, Bruno. Un modelo de análisis monetario y de programación financiera /. [Mexico City, Mexico] , 1984. ii, 203 p. : LC Card 86-158393
HG660.5 .B7 1984

Calderón González, Arnoldo. América Latina y el Caribe . México, D.F. , 1985. 51, [25] leaves ; LC Card 87-121714 DDC 332.4/98 19
HG660.5 .C35 1985

Echegaray, Alfredo. Evolución y perspectivas de la cooperación financiera en América Latina /. Buenos Aires , 1982. 147 p. ; LC Card 86-198731
HG185.L3 E25 1982

Economic reform and stabilization in Latin America /. New York , c1986. xxiii, 348 p. : ISBN 0-275-92307-X (alk. paper) : LC Card 86-9405 DDC 338.98 19
HC125 .E374 1986 *NYPL [JLE 87-1073]*

Langoni, Carlos Geraldo. A crise do desenvolvimento, uma estratégia para o futuro /. Rio de Janeiro , 1985. xix, 176 p. : ISBN 85-03-00001-6 : LC Card 85-151246 DDC 338.981 19
HG835 .L36 1985 *NYPL [JLD 86-288]*

Pastor, Manuel. The International Monetary Fund and Latin America . Boulder, Colo. , 1987. xvi, 228 p. : ISBN 0-8133-7373-5 (pbk. : alk. paper) : LC Card 86-32575 DDC 332.4/98 19
HG660.5 .P33 1987

Políticas macro-económicas . Santiago de Chile [1986] 409 p. : LC Card 87-403669 DDC 338.98 19
HC125 .P657 1986

Tamagna, Frank M. [Banca central en América Latina. English.] Central banking in Latin America /. México , 1965. xii, 285 p. ; LC Card 87-403322 DDC 332.1/1/098 19
HG2710.5.A7 T3513 1965

MONETARY POLICY - LATIN AMERICA - MATHEMATICAL MODELS.
Canto, Victor A. Currency substitution . Boston , c1987. viii, 196 p. ; ISBN 0-89838-195-9 LC Card 86-27747 DDC 332.4/56/098 19
HG3823 .C36 1987

MONETARY POLICY - MATHEMATICAL MODELS.
Blang, Hans-Georg, 1953- Die Variabilität relativer Preisänderungen und die Varianz monetärer Aggregate /. Frankfurt am Main , New York , c1986. xxvii, 338 p. : ISBN 3-8204-9074-4 LC Card 86-156110
HG229 .B555 1986

Borgmeier, Bernd, 1955- Der Einfluss verschiedener Preisbildungsmechanismen auf die gesamtwirtschfliche Beschäftigung /. Frankfurt am Main , New York , c1984. 362 p. : ISBN 3-8204-5601-5 : LC Card 85-198888
HB221 .B592 1984

Eichberger, Jürgen, 1952- Geld und Kredit in einer Ökonomie mit festen Preisen . Frankfurt am Main , New York , c1984. 152 p. : ISBN 3-8204-5441-1 LC Card 85-191492
HG230.3 .E53 1984

Freedman, Charles. Monetary aggregates as targets . [Ottawa] , 1981. vii, 49 p. ; LC Card 81-198954 DDC 332.4/6/0724 19
HG230.3 .F74 1981
NYPL [JLM 75-1420 no.27]

Grössl, Ingrid. Der Zusammenhang von finanz- und realwirtschaftlichem Sektor einer offenen, stationären Volkswirtschaft . Berlin , c1986. 162 p. : ISBN 3-428-05986-7 LC Card 86-206327
HG3882 .G76 1986

Harris, John Andrew de Oliveira. Evolução e definição da moeda /. Rio de Janeiro, RJ , 1985. 90 p. : LC Card 87-135878 DDC 332.4/981 19
HG835 .H37 1985

Herberg, Horst. Stagflation as a consequence of an expansionary monetary or fiscal policy under flexible exchange rates /. Stockholm, Sweden [1978] 34 leaves ; LC Card 81-116937
HD5710 .H47 1978

Kostiainen, Seppo. Capital controls under alternative exchange rate and monetary policy regimes /. Joensuu , 1986. 27 p. ; ISBN 951-696-619-5 (pbk.) LC Card 87-100851 DDC 332.4/5 19
HG3823 .K673 1986

Kudiss, Reinhard, 1952- Die Bestimmung des Produktionspotentials in Theorie und Empirie . Frankfurt am Main , New York , c1984. xvi, 198 p. : ISBN 3-8204-5579-5 LC Card 85-189908
HB3730 .K766 1984

Meyer-Cording, Claus, 1953- Die Auswirkungen kreditfinanzierter Staatsausgaben auf das Volkseinkommen . Frankfurt am Main , New York , c1986. v, 256 p. : ISBN 3-8204-9634-3 LC Card 86-204989
HB141.5 .M49 1986

Spreter, Jürgen. Theoretische und empirische Analyse der Determinanten des Geldschöpfungsmultiplikators /. Krefeld , 1983. v, 221 p. : ISBN 3-88358-029-5 LC Card 83-154608
HG226.3 .S67 1983

Steingräber, Carola, 1956- Geld- und Fiskalpolitik in Portfolio-orientierten Modellen kleiner offener Volkswirtschaften . Rheinfelden , c1986. ix, 219 p. : ISBN 3-87718-532-0 LC Card 86-182509
HG230.3 .S74 1986

Vollmer, Friedrich Uwe, 1958- Informations- und Veränderungskosten in makroökonomischen Transmissionsmodellen /. Frankfurt am Main , New York , c1986. 169 p. : ISBN 3-8204-9142-2 LC Card 86-194476
HB221 .V64 1986

MONETARY POLICY - MATHEMATICAL MODELS - CONGRESSES.
Monetary policy and uncertainty . Baden-Baden , 1986. 262 p. : ISBN 3-7890-1257-2 (pbk.) LC Card 86-225786 DDC 332.4/0724 19
HG230.3 .M655 1986

MONETARY POLICY - MEXICO.
México, una economía en transición /. México, D.F. , 1984-1985. 3 v. ; ISBN 968-18-1900-4 (v. 1) LC Card 86-235462
HC135 .M549 1985

MONETARY POLICY - NEPAL.
Sharma, Gunanidhi. Monetary structure of the Nepalese economy . New Delhi , c1987. xiv, 243 p. : ISBN 81-7003-076-5 : LC Card 87-900309 DDC 332.4/95493 19
HG1220.9 .S52 1987

MONETARY POLICY - NETHERLANDS.
Zijlstra, J. Gematigd monetarisme . Leiden , 1985. ix, 330 p. : ISBN 90-207-1382-5 : LC Card 85-201189
HG1065 .Z55 1985 ***NYPL [JLE 87-379]***

MONETARY POLICY - NEW ZEALAND.
Dickens, Rodney. Overseas experience with "strict" monetary targetry and its implications for New Zealand /. Wellington [1986] iii, 24 leaves ; LC Card 87-137038 DDC 332.4/9931 19
HG230.3 .D53 1986

Holmes, Frank Wakefield, Sir, 1924- Recent developments in monetary policy . [Wellington] [1976] 5 p. ; LC Card 82-216052
HG1480.5 .H65 1976

MONETARY POLICY - PARAGUAY.
Andrada, René. Reforma estructural de nuestra economía /. [Asunción , 1986] (Asunción, Paraguay : Ediciones y Arte) 150 p. : LC Card 86-227031
HG885 .A85 1986

Palacios, Eulalio R. Reflexiones sobre economia nacional e internacional /. [S.l.] 1986 (Asunción, Paraguay : Tall. Gráf. de la Impr. Nacional) 333 p. ; LC Card 86-226634
HC222 .P36 1986

MONETARY POLICY - PERU.
Rosales Díaz, Ramón. Programas de reactivación económica y sistemas financieros . [Lima] , 1986. 68 p. : LC Card 87-400247 DDC 332.4/982 19
HG815 .R67 1986

MONETARY POLICY - POLAND.
Probleme monetärer und finanzwirtschaftlicher Steuerung im Systemvergleich /. Duisburg , c1986. 175 p. : ISBN 3-921473-43-8 LC Card 86-211745
HC286.6 .P754 1986

MONETARY POLICY - SINGAPORE.
Papers on monetary economics /. [Singapore] , c1981. xii, 200 p. ; ISBN 997-16-9044-6 LC Card 82-940575
HG1250.67 .P37 1981

MONETARY POLICY - SOUTH ASIA.
Madan, B. K. (Bal Krishna), 1911- Towards monetary cooperation in South Asia /. New Delhi , 1986, c1985. 105 p. ; LC Card 86-901998 DDC 332.4/954 19
HG3881 .M2756 1986 ***NYPL [JLD 87-911]***

MONETARY POLICY - SOUTHERN STATES - HISTORY.
Schweikart, Larry. Banking in the American South from the age of Jackson to Reconstruction /. Baton Rouge , c1987. xiv, 367 p. : ISBN 0-8071-1403-0 LC Card 87-12784 DDC 332.1/0975 19
HG2604 .S39 1987

MONETARY POLICY - SPAIN.
Cuervo García, Alvaro. Manual de sistema financiero . Barcelona , 1987. 427 p. : ISBN 84-344-2013-9 LC Card 87-135198
HG186.S6 C84 1987

MONETARY POLICY - SPAIN - HISTORY - 17TH CENTURY - SOURCES.
Ebersole, Alva Vernon. Dos documentos de 1627 sobre la economía de España /. Valencia [1986?] 49 p. ; ISBN 84-7274-144-3 LC Card 87-107711
HG1133 .E24 1986

MONETARY POLICY - SPAIN - HISTORY - 20TH CENTURY.
Fanjul Martín, Enrique. La evolución de la política monetaria española (1940-1978) . [Madrid] , 1979. 164 p. ; LC Card 85-202991
HG1135 .F35 1979

MONETARY POLICY - SWITZERLAND.
Baltensperger, Ernst. Geldmengenpolitik und Inflationskontrolle . Diessenhofen , c1984. 132 p. : ISBN 3-7253-0224-3 : LC Card 84-178054 DDC 332.4/9494 19
HG1155 .B345 1984 ***NYPL [JLD 87-168]***

Geld- und Währungsordnung /. Berlin , c1983. 249 p. : ISBN 3-428-05530-6 LC Card 84-141547
HG999.5 .G4556 1983

Genberg, Hans. External influences on the Swiss economy under fixed and flexible exchange rates /. Grüsch , c1985. ii, 182 p. : ISBN 3-7253-0249-9 (pbk.) LC Card 86-156330
HG3963 .G45 1985 ***NYPL [JLD 87-539]***

Genberg, Hans. Influences externes sur l'économie suisse en changes fixes et flottants /. Genève , c1985. ii, 202 p. : ISBN 2-8257-0127-0 : LC Card 85-235579 DDC 332.4/5609494 19
HG3963 .G46 1985 ***NYPL [JLD 86-2381]***

Heri, Erwin W. Die Geldnachfrage . Berlin , New York , c1986. 226 p. : ISBN 0-387-17157-6 (U. S.) LC Card 86-232268
HG226.5 .H47 1986

MONETARY POLICY - SWITZERLAND - ECONOMETRIC MODELS.
Makromodelle und Wirtschaftspolitik . Grüsch , c1985. 120 p. : ISBN 3-7253-0250-2 : LC Card 85-208009
HC397 .M26 1985

MONETARY POLICY - SWITZERLAND - HISTORY - 20TH CENTURY.
Tanner, Jakob. Bundeshaushalt, Währung und Kriegswirtschaft . Zürich , c1986. 438 p. : ISBN 3-85791-100-X : LC Card 86-199729
HJ1258 .T35 1986

MONETARY POLICY - TANZANIA.
Green, Reginald Herbold. The IMF and stabilisation in sub-Saharan Africa . Brighton, England [1986] ii, 70 p. ; LC Card 86-208478 DDC 332.1/52 19
HC800 .G72 1986

MONETARY POLICY - TURKEY.
Ataç, Beyhan. Kuramda ve Türkiye'de istikrar politikası açısından parasal ve mali işlemler /. Eskişehir [1979?] iv, 173 p. ; LC Card 82-245649
HG1206.5 .A79 1979

MONETARY POLICY - UNITED STATES.
Anderson, Hugold. Government without taxation /. Warwick, R.I. , c1987. 52 p. ; LC Card 87-133116 DDC 336.2/00973 19
HJ2381 .A76 1987

Brimmer, Andrew F. Monetary policy and the international diffusion of interest rates /. Miami, Fla. [1982] iii, 47 p. : LC Card 86-204514 DDC 332.4/973 19
HG540 .B75 1982

Central bankers, bureaucratic incentives, and monetary policy /. Dordrecht ; Boston : xiv, 251 p. : ISBN 90-247-3366-9 LC Card 86-12572 DDC 332.1/12/0973 19
HG2565 .C33 1986 ***NYPL [JLE 87-394]***

Economic choices . Arlington, Va. , c1987. 73 p. : ISBN 0-932765-08-4 (pbk.) : LC Card 87-686 DDC 338.973 19
HC106 .E24 1987

Foltyn, Ferenc. Inflációelméletek és az amerikai monetáris politika /. Budapest , 1985. 126 p. ; ISBN 963-05-3905-5 : LC Card 85-191099
HG229 .F642 1985

Geld- und Währungsordnung /. Berlin , c1983. 249 p. : ISBN 3-428-05530-6 LC Card 84-141547
HG999.5 .G4556 1983

Horvitz, Paul M. Monetary policy and the financial system /. Englewood Cliffs, N.J. , c1987. xii, 532 p. : ISBN 0-13-599861-1 LC Card 86-25447 DDC 332.4/973 19
HG540 .H67 1987

Hutchinson, Harry D. Money, banking, and the United States economy /. Englewood Cliffs, NJ , 1988. p. cm. ISBN 0-13-600156-4 LC Card 87-19299 DDC 332.1/0973 19
HG2491 .H8 1988

Klein, John J., 1929- Money and the economy /. San Diego , c1986. xi, 560 p. : ISBN 0-15-564007-0 LC Card 85-80078 DDC 332.4/973 19
HG540 .K57 1986 ***NYPL [JLE 86-3392]***

Malkin, Lawrence. The national debt /. New York , c1987. ix, 309 p. ; ISBN 0-8050-0382-7 LC Card 86-27347 DDC 336.3/4/0973 19
HJ8119 .M34 1987

Mayer, Thomas. Money, banking, and the economy /. New York , c1984. xiv, 574 p. : ISBN 0-393-95313-0 LC Card 83-13498 DDC 332.1/0973 19
HG540 .M39 1984 ***NYPL [JLE 86-2193]***

Mayer, Thomas, 1927- Money, banking, and the economy /. New York , c1987. xiv, 488 p. : ISBN 0-393-95557-5 LC Card 86-33160 DDC 332.1/0973 19
HG540 .M39 1987

Öffentliche Finanzen, Kredit und Kapital . Berlin , c1985. xvi, 618 p., [1] leaf of plates : ISBN 3-428-05737-6 LC Card 85-164173
HJ161 .O33 1985

The Prospects for economic recovery. Washington, D.C. , 1982. xx, 120 p. :
NYPL [JLF 86-1215]

The Search for stable money . Chicago , 1987. xvii, 408 p. ; ISBN 0-226-15829-2 LC Card 86-25654 DDC 332.4/973 19
HG540 .S38 1987

Streit, Joachim. Finanzinnovationen, Deregulierung und Geldmengensteuerung in den USA /. Tübingen , c1986. xi, 188 p. : ISBN 3-16-345156-X (pbk.) LC Card 87-408200 DDC 332/.0973 19
HG181 .S825 1986

Wanniski, Jude, 1936- The political economy in perspective [microform] . Morristown, N.J. (66 Macculloch Ave., Morristown 07960) [1983] 5 p. ; LC Card 83-239685 DDC 332.4/973 19
HG540 .W36 1983 ***NYPL [*ZT-1708 no.21]***

MONETARY POLICY - UNITED STATES - HISTORY.
Degen, Robert A. The American monetary

system . Lexington, Mass. , c1987. x, 242 p. ; ISBN 0-669-15827-5 (alk. paper) LC Card 86-46363 DDC 332.4/973 19
HG501 .D44 1987

MONETARY POLICY - UNITED STATES - HISTORY - 20TH CENTURY.
Greider, William. Secrets of the temple . New York , c1987. 798 p. ; ISBN 0-671-47989-X : LC Card 87-16712 DDC 332.1/1/0973 19
HG2563 .G72 1987

MONETARY POLICY - VENEZUELA.
Cantó, Leandro. La caída del bolívar /. Caracas, Venezuela [1983 or 1984] 223 p. ; LC Card 84-186552 DDC 332.4/987 19
HG915 .C36 1983 ***NYPL [JLD 87-2426]***

MONETARY QUESTION. see **CURRENCY QUESTION; MONEY.**

MONETARY STABILIZATION. see **MONETARY POLICY.**

Monetary structure of the Nepalese economy . Sharma, Gunanidhi. New Delhi , c1987. xiv, 243 p. : ISBN 81-7003-076-5 : LC Card 87-900309 DDC 332.4/95493 19
HG1220.9 .S52 1987

Monetary theory and economic institutions : proceedings of a conference held by the International Economic Association at Fiesole, Florence, Italy / edited by Marcello de Cecco and Jean-Paul Fitoussi. New York : St. Martin's Press, 1987. ix, 349 p. : ill. ; 23 cm. Includes bibliographies and indexes. ISBN 0-312-00407-9 : LC Card 86-26069 DDC 332.4/01 19
1. Money - Congresses. 2. Financial institutions - Congresses. 3. Monetary policy - Congresses. I. De Cecco, Marcello. II. Fitoussi, Jean Paul. III. International Economic Association.
HG203 .M68 1987

MONETARY UNIONS - CONGRESSES.
Problemy valiutnogo soiuza stran-chlenov Evropeĭskogo ėkonomicheskogo soobshchestva i razvitie mezhdunarodnoĭ valiutnoĭ sistemy kapitalizma . Sofiia , 1984. 151 p. ; LC Card 85-224144
HG3942.8 .P76 1984

The Monetary versus fiscal policy debate : lessons from two decades / edited by R.W. Hafer. Totowa, N.J. : Rowman & Allanheld, 1986. 171 p. : ill. ; 24 cm. Papers presented at the ninth annual economic policy conference held Oct. 12-13, 1984, sponsored by the Federal Reserve Bank of St. Louis. Includes bibliographies and index. ISBN 0-8476-7454-1 : LC Card 85-11912 DDC 339.5/2 19
1. Monetary policy - Congresses. 2. Fiscal policy - Congresses. I. Hafer, R. W. (Rick W.). II. Federal Reserve Bank of St. Louis.
HG230.3 .M64 1986 ***NYPL [JLE 86-4720]***

Monetkina, L. N. (Lidiia Nikolaevna) IUsufovich, B. E. (Boris Efimovich) Sovershenstvovanie operativnogo upravleniia osnovnym proizvodstvom mashinostroitel'nogo predpriiatiia /. Moskva , 1982. 91 p. : LC Card 82-204954
HD9705.S595 I94 1982

Money . Moore, Carl H., 1916- Jefferson, N.C. , c1987. xi, 164 p. : ISBN 0-89950-272-5 (lib. bdg.) : LC Card 87-42515 DDC 332.4/9 19
HG231 .M63 1987

Money . Smalis, I. A., 1918- Santa Fe, NM, USA , 1987. 87 p. : ISBN 0-86534-100-1 : LC Card 87-6439 DDC 650.1 19
HF5386 .S637 1987

MONEY - AFRICA.
Seidman, Ann Willcox, 1926- Money, banking, and public finance in Africa /. London , Atlantic Highlands, N.J., USA , 1986. xv, 363 p. : ISBN 0-86232-429-7 LC Card 87-111822 DDC 332.1/096 19
HG187.5.A2 S45 1986

Money and banking . Johnson, Ivan C. Chicago , c1988. xix, 604 p. : ISBN 0-03-012518-9 LC Card 87-15002 DDC 332.1 19
HG221 .J667 1988

Money and banking in medieval and Renaissance Venice /. Lane Frederic Chapin, 1900- Baltimore , c1985- v. : ISBN 0-8018-3157-1 (v. 1) LC Card 84-47947 DDC 332.1/0945/31 19
HG1040.V46 L36 1985 ***NYPL [JLL 86-121]***

Money and banking in Nigeria /. Uzoaga, William Okefie. Enugu, Nigeria , 1981. xiv, 304 p. ; ISBN 978-15-6175-0 ***NYPL [Sc D 84-373]***

Money and capital markets in Nigeria . Shahi, M. A. (Muslehuddin Akhil) Bombay , 1983. xi [i.e. x], 60 p. ; LC Card 83-905358 DDC 332/.0412/09669 19
HG187.5.N6 S5 1983 ***NYPL [JLE 87-691]***

Money and capital markets in the Gambia and United Kingdom, and the problem of economic management at central bank level . Faal, A. A. [S.l. , 198-] 27 leaves ; LC Card 87-400415 DDC 332.1/0966/51 19
HG187.5.G25 F3 1980z

Money and class in America . Lapham, Lewis H. New York , 1988, c1987. p. cm. ISBN 1-555-84109-0 LC Card 87-22515 DDC 305.5/234/0973 19
HC110.W4 L24 1988

Money and finance in Zimbabwe. Whitsun Foundation. Project 1.09 . Harare, Zimbabwe [1983?] ix, 260 p. : ISBN 0-7974-0607-7 (pbk.) LC Card 87-402552 DDC 332.1/096891 19
HG1352 .W48 1983

Money and liberty in modern Europe . Reddy, William M. Cambridge [Cambridgeshire] , New York , 1987. xii, 264 p. ; ISBN 0-521-30445-8 LC Card 86-11709 DDC 332.4/94 19
HG922 .R43 1987 ***NYPL [JLE 87-1346]***

Money and the economy /. Klein, John J., 1929- San Diego , c1986. xi, 560 p. : ISBN 0-15-564007-0 LC Card 85-80078 DDC 332.4/973 19
HG540 .K57 1986 ***NYPL [JLE 86-3392]***

MONEY - ASIA - HISTORY.
Thierry, François. Monnaies d'Extrême Orient /. Paris , <[1986- v. <2 > : ISBN 2-11-080873-X (v. 2) : LC Card 86-218568
HG1250.5 .T45 1986

MONEY - AUSTRALIA - HISTORY.
Butlin, S. J. (Sydney James), d. 1977. The Australian monetary system, 1851 to 1914 /. [s.l] , 1986. 404 p. : ISBN 1-86252-307-X (pbk.) LC Card 87-154610 DDC 332.4/994 19
HG1394 .B87 1986

Money, banking, and financial markets /. Auerbach, Robert D. New York , London , c1988. p. cm. ISBN 0-02-305040-3 LC Card 87-11173 DDC 332.1 19
HG221 .A914 1988

Money, banking, and monetary policy /. Campbell, Colin Dearborn, 1917- Chicago , c1988. xx, 617 p. : ISBN 0-03-009494-1 LC Card 87-6890 DDC 332.1 19
HG221 .C245 1988

Money, banking, and public finance in Africa /. Seidman, Ann Willcox, 1926- London , Atlantic Highlands, N.J., USA , 1986. xv, 363 p. : ISBN 0-86232-429-7 LC Card 87-111822 DDC 332.1/096 19
HG187.5.A2 S45 1986

Money, banking, and the economy /. Mayer, Thomas. New York , c1984. xiv, 574 p. : ISBN 0-393-95313-0 LC Card 83-13498 DDC 332.1/0973 19
HG540 .M39 1984 ***NYPL [JLE 86-2193]***

Money, banking, and the economy /. Mayer, Thomas, 1927- New York , c1987. xiv, 488 p. : ISBN 0-393-95557-5 LC Card 86-33160 DDC 332.1/0973 19
HG540 .M39 1987

Money, banking, and the United States economy /. Hutchinson, Harry D. Englewood Cliffs, NJ , 1988. p. cm. ISBN 0-13-600156-4 LC Card 87-19299 DDC 332.1/0973 19
HG2491 .H8 1988

MONEY - BELGIUM.
Mercier, Paul. Le marché du call money garanti /. Bruxelles [1983] 64 p. : LC Card 84-210204
HG1055 .M47 1983

Verheirstraeten, A. Geld, krediet en intrest in de Belgische financiële sector /. Leuven , 1977. xxii, 337 p. : LC Card 78-345984
HG1055 .V47 ***NYPL [JLM 86-1310 nr.23]***

Money (Birmingham, Ala.) Winning with mutual funds /. Birmingham, Ala. , c1987. 224 p. : ISBN 0-8487-0722-2 LC Card 87-61719 DDC 332.63/27 19
HG4930 .W56 1987

The Money book of money . Klein, Robert J. Boston , c1987. xvii, 522 p. ; ISBN 0-316-49840-8 : LC Card 86-33777 DDC 332.024 19
HG179 .K57 1987

MONEY - BRAZIL - HISTORY.
Cavalcanti, Amaro, 1849-1922. O meio circulante nacional . Brasília-Distrito Federal , 1983- v. : LC Card 84-160002
HG833 .C38 1983 ***NYPL [JLL 85-246]***

MONEY - BRAZIL - MATHEMATICAL MODELS.
Harris, John Andrew de Oliveira. Evolução e definição da moeda /. Rio de Janeiro, RJ , 1985. 90 p. : LC Card 87-135878 DDC 332.4/981 19
HG835 .H37 1985

MONEY - BYZANTINE EMPIRE - HISTORY - SOURCES.
Euangelatou-Notara, Phlōrentia. "Sēmeiōmata" Hellēnikōn kōdikōn hōs pēgē dia tēn ereunan tou oikonomikou kai koinōnikou viou tou Vyzantiou, apo tou 9ou aiōnos mechri tou etous 1204 /. Athēnai , 1982. 296 p. ; LC Card 86-212063
HC294 .E9 1982

Money (Chicago, Ill.)
Klein, Robert J. The Money book of money . Boston , c1987. xvii, 522 p. ; ISBN 0-316-49840-8 : LC Card 86-33777 DDC 332.024 19
HG179 .K57 1987

Money guide . Kansas City, Mo. , c1987. vii, 128 p. : ISBN 0-8362-2210-5 (pbk.) : LC Card 87-1200 DDC 332.63/22 19
HG4921 .M68 1987

MONEY - CHINA - HISTORY.
Chung-kuo li tai huo pi. English. A History of Chinese currency . [Peking] , Kowloon, Hong Kong , 1983. 220 p. : ISBN 962-7094-01-3 LC Card 86-233155 DDC 769.5/5951 19
HG1282 .C4913 1983

MONEY - COLOMBIA.
Villar Borrero, Eduardo. El dinero y el sector financiero a su alcance /. Bogotá, Colombia , c1984. 64 p. : ISBN 84-8276-321-0 LC Card 84-241500
HG855 .V54 1984

MONEY - CONGRESSES.
International Congress on Economic History (8th : 1982 : Budapest, Hungary) Münzprägung, Geldumlauf und Wechselkurse . Trier , 1984. 421 p. : ISBN 3-923087-06-3 (pbk.)
HG205 1982 .I53 ***NYPL [JLE 86-3176]***

Monetary theory and economic institutions . New York , 1987. ix, 349 p. : ISBN 0-312-00407-9 : LC Card 86-26069 DDC 332.4/01 19
HG203 .M68 1987

Symposium on Monetary Theory (1986 : Institute of Economics, Academia Sinica) Symposium on Monetary Theory, January 3-8, 1986 =. Taipei, Taiwan, Republic of China [1986?] 2 v. (iv, 630 p.) : LC Card 87-152394 DDC 332.4 19
HG203 .S96 1986

MONEY - COSTA RICA - HISTORY.
Daremblum, Jaime. Del cacao al colón . San José, Costa Rica [1977?- v. <1- > ; LC Card 87-402194 DDC 332.4/97286 19
HG682 .D37 1977

MONEY - DICTIONARIES.
Kay, William. A-Z guide to money /. London , 1986, c1983. 281 p. : ISBN 0-09-467160-5 : LC Card 86-224824 DDC 332/.03/21 19
HG216 .K39 1986

MONEY - ECUADOR.
Pensamiento monetario y financiero /. Quito, Ecuador , 1986. 2 v. : LC Card 87-150740 DDC 332.4/9866 19
HG862 .P46 1986

MONEY - EGYPT - HISTORY.
Höltz, Joachim. Kritik der Geldentstehungstheorien . Berlin , c1984. ii, 401 p. ; ISBN 3-496-00796-6 LC Card 85-147094
HG237 .H64 1984

Money, employment, and interest . Fujino, Shozaburo, 1927- Tokyo, Japan , New York, NY [1987] xii, 220 p. : ISBN 4-314-00464-9 :

LC Card 87-165395 DDC 330.15/6 19
HB99.7 .F85 1987

MONEY - ETHIOPIA.
Mauri, Arnaldo. Moneta e banca in Etiopia /. Milano [1986] xi, 316 p. : ISBN 88-14-00769-1 LC Card 86-182310
HG3389.A6 M38 1986 *NYPL [JLE 87-1721]*

MONEY - EUROPE, EASTERN.
Bokros, Lajos. Piac és pénz a modern gazdaságban /. Budapest , 1985. 340, [1] p. ; ISBN 963-221-551-6 : LC Card 86-185991
HB95 .B65 1985

MONEY - EUROPE - HISTORY.
Reddy, William M. Money and liberty in modern Europe . Cambridge [Cambridgeshire] , New York , 1987. xii, 264 p. ; ISBN 0-521-30445-8 LC Card 86-11709 DDC 332.4/94 19
HG922 .R43 1987 *NYPL [JLE 87-1346]*

Spufford, Peter. Handbook of medieval exchange /. London : Woodbridge, Suffolk ; xcii, 376 p., [3] leaves of plates (1 folded) : ISBN 0-86193-105-X LC Card 86-673816
HG3942 .S68x 1986

Spufford, Peter. Handbook of medieval exchange /. London : Woodbridge, Suffolk ; xcii, 376, [3] p., [1] fold. leaf : ISBN 0-86193-105-X *NYPL [JLE 86-4344]*

MONEY - EUROPE - HISTORY - CONGRESSES.
International Congress on Economic History (8th : 1982 : Budapest, Hungary) Münzprägung, Geldumlauf und Wechselkurse . Trier , 1984. 421 p. : ISBN 3-923087-06-3 (pbk.)
HG205 1982 .I53 *NYPL [JLE 86-3176]*

MONEY - EUROPE - HISTORY - EXHIBITIONS - CATALOGS.
Coin and conscience . [Boston, Mass.] , 1986. [28] p. : LC Card 86-203197 DDC 332.4/94 19
HG925 .C65 1986

MONEY - EUROPEAN ECONOMIC COMMUNITY COUNTRIES.
Coffey, Peter. The European monetary system--past, present, and future /. Dordrecht ; Boston : p. cm. ISBN 90-247-3446-0 LC Card 86-23833 DDC 332.4/5/094 19
HG930.5 .C63 1987

The European monetary system . Washington, D.C. , c1986. vii, 75 p. : ISBN 0-939934-79-5 (pbk.) : LC Card 86-21432 DDC 332.4/5/094 19
HG930.5 .E86863 1986

Grauwe, Paul de. Exchange rates, money, and output . New York , 1985. xii, 240 p. : ISBN 0-312-27403-3 : LC Card 84-11692 DDC 339/.094 19
HC241.2 .G69 1985 *NYPL [JLD 86-3007]*

Masera, R. S. L'unificazione monetaria e lo SME /. Bologna , c1980. 220 p. ; LC Card 82-150717 DDC 332.4/566/094 19
HG930.5.Z8 M37 1980 *NYPL [JLD 87-902]*

Murtazina, E. N. Problemy valiutnoĭ integratsii v Evropeĭskom soobshchestve . Moskva , 1985. 75 p. ; LC Card 85-224384
HG3942.8 .M87 1985

MONEY - EXAMINATIONS, QUESTIONS, ETC.
Beecham, B. Julian, 1927- Monetary economics /. London , New York , 1988. p. cm. ISBN 0-582-02042-5 LC Card 87-17142 DDC 332.4 19
HG221 .B424 1988

Money, finance, and macroeconomic performance in Japan /. Suzuki, Yoshio, 1931- [Nihon kin'yū keizairon. English.] New Haven , c1986. xvii, 218, p. : ISBN 0-300-03387-7 LC Card 85-26375 DDC 332/.0952 19
HG187.J3 S96 1986 *NYPL [JLE 86-2788]*

Money, financial institutions, and economic activity /. Dalgaard, Bruce R. Glenview, Ill. , c1987. 560 p. : ISBN 0-673-15876-4 LC Card 87-4851 DDC 332.1 19
HG173 .D28 1987

MONEY - FRANCE.
Chaîneau, André. Mécanismes et politique monétaires . Paris , 1979, c19. 311 p. : ISBN 2-13-036227-3 *NYPL [JLD 86-2730]*

MONEY - FRANCE - HISTORY - 20TH CENTURY.
Néré, Jacques. Le problème du mur d'argent . Paris , c1985. 159 p. ; ISBN 2-214-06264-5 : LC Card 86-149791
HG979 .N47 1985

The money game in old New York . Browder, Clifford, 1928- Lexington, KY , c1986. viii, 319 p., [8] p. of plates : ISBN 0-8131-1573-6 LC Card 85-17938 DDC 332/.092/4 B 19
HG172.D74 B76 1986 *NYPL [JFE 86-1911]*

MONEY - GERMANY (WEST)
Boeck, Klaus. Die DM als internationale Reservewährung . Hamburg , 1974. 75 p. ; LC Card 75-550711 *NYPL [JLE 80-744]*

MONEY - GERMANY (WEST) - BREMEN - HISTORY.
Förster, Walter, 1914- Das Haus am Wall . Bremen , c1983. 159 p. : ISBN 3-920699-45-9 LC Card 84-155521
HG1010.B7 F67 1983

MONEY - GERMANY (WEST) - HAMBURG - HISTORY - 17TH CENTURY.
Schneider, Konrad. "Banco, Species und Courant" . Koblenz , c1986. 136 p. : ISBN 3-923708-03-3 LC Card 87-134369 DDC 332.1/0943/515 19
HG1010.H24 S36 1986

MONEY - GERMANY (WEST) - HAMBURG - HISTORY - 18TH CENTURY.
Schneider, Konrad. "Banco, Species und Courant" . Koblenz , c1986. 136 p. : ISBN 3-923708-03-3 LC Card 87-134369 DDC 332.1/0943/515 19
HG1010.H24 S36 1986

MONEY - GREAT BRITAIN.
Beecham, B. Julian, 1927- Monetary economics /. London , New York , 1988. p. cm. ISBN 0-582-02042-5 LC Card 87-17142 DDC 332.4 19
HG221 .B424 1988

Great Britain. Decimal Currency Board. Conversion of accounting records. London, 1969. [1], 33 p. ISBN 0-11-700407-3 : LC Card 77-489376 DDC 657
HF5635 .G777

Locke, John, 1632-1704. Several papers relating to money, interest and trade, &c. /. Fairfield, NJ , 1988. p. cm. ISBN 0-678-00334-3 LC Card 87-17243 DDC 332.4/941 19
HG937 .L74 1988

Ricardo, David, 1772-1823. Scritti monetari /. Roma [1985] 495 p. ; LC Card 86-207988
HG938 .R63 1985

MONEY - GREAT BRITAIN - HISTORY.
Schwartz, Anna Jacobson. Money in historical perspective /. Chicago , 1987. xvii, 442 p. : ISBN 0-226-74228-8 : LC Card 87-5973 DDC 332.4/9 19
HG538 .S354 1987

Money, growth, and stability /. Hahn, Frank. Oxford, U.K. , 1985. viii, 392 p. : ISBN 0-631-14354-8 LC Card 87-672166
HG221.3 .H28x 1985b

Money guide : the stock market / by the editors of Money. Kansas City, Mo. : Andrews, McMeel & Parker, c1987. vii, 128 p. : ill. ; 22 cm. "Previously published in magazine format as Money guide: the stock market by Money magazine"--T.p. verso. ISBN 0-8362-2210-5 (pbk.) : LC Card 87-1200 DDC 332.63/22 19
1. Stocks - United States. 2. Investments - United States. 3. Stock-exchange - United States. I. Money (Chicago, Ill.). II. Title: Stock market.
HG4921 .M68 1987

MONEY - HISTORY.
Heinsohn, Gunnar. Privateigentum, Patriarchat, Geldwirtschaft . Frankfurt am Main , 1984. 218 p. ; ISBN 3-518-28055-4 : LC Card 84-150578
HC31 .H45 1984

Lopez, Robert Sabatino. The shape of medieval monetary history /. London , 1986. 330 p. 1 v. (various pagings) : ISBN 0-86078-195-X LC Card 87-133292 DDC 332.4/94 19
HG243 .L67 1986

Moore, Carl H., 1916- Money . Jefferson, N.C. , c1987. xi, 164 p. : ISBN 0-89950-272-5 (lib. bdg.) : LC Card 87-42515 DDC 332.4/9 19
HG231 .M63 1987

Rice, Jonathan. How to survive and profit from the coming currency recall /. Chicago , c1986. xiii, 258 p. : ISBN 0-8092-4998-7 : LC Card 86-6215 DDC 332.4/973 19
HG540 .R53 1986 *NYPL [JLE 86-3508]*

Rochette, Edward C., 1927- Making money /. Frederick, CO , c1986. 107 p. : ISBN 0-939650-25-8 (pbk.) : LC Card 86-22120 DDC 364.1/33/09 19
HG335 .R63 1986

MONEY - HISTORY - JUVENILE LITERATURE.
Drobot, Eve. Amazing investigations . New York , 1988. p. cm. ISBN 0-13-023714-0 LC Card 87-18661 DDC 332.4/9 19
HG173.8 .D76 1988

MONEY - HUNGARY.
Magyar törvényes fizetőeszközök =. [Budapest] [1986?] [38] p. : LC Card 87-407726
HG970.5 .M34 1986

Soós, Károly Attila. Terv, kampány, pénz . Budapest , 1986. 532 p. : ISBN 963-221-575-3 : LC Card 87-137237
HB3787.5 .S66 1986

Money in historical perspective /. Schwartz, Anna Jacobson. Chicago , 1987. xvii, 442 p. : ISBN 0-226-74228-8 : LC Card 87-5973 DDC 332.4/9 19
HG538 .S354 1987

MONEY IN LITERATURE.
Brera, Paolo. Denaro . [Brescia] [1984] 110 p. ; LC Card 86-102925
HB49 .B74 1984

Money in the family . Wilson, Gail. Aldershot, Hants., England , Brookfield, USA , c1987. ix, 271 p. ; ISBN 0-566-05389-6 : LC Card 87-7402 DDC 339.2/2 19
HG179 .W53517 1987

Money in the ground . Orban, John. Oklahoma City , 1985. xv, 216 p. : ISBN 0-9615776-0-6 (pbk.) : LC Card 86-120440 DDC 332.63 19
HG6047.P47 O73 1985

Money, income, and time . Cencini, Alvaro. London , New York , 1988. p. cm. ISBN 0-86187-943-0 : LC Card 87-7279 DDC 332.4 19
HG221 .C39 1988

MONEY - INDIA.
Explanatory notes on current statistics. Bombay [1978] iii, 74 p. ; LC Card 85-229381
HG187.I4 E98 1978

MONEY - INDIA - HISTORY.
Goswami, Prodyot Kumar, 1940- Indian currency and exchange, 1835-1940 /. New Delhi , 1983. viii, 134 p. ; LC Card 83-903565 DDC 332.4/560954 19
HG1234 .G67 1983 *NYPL [JLD 87-673]*

MONEY, INTERNATIONAL. see **COINAGE, INTERNATIONAL.**

MONEY - IRAQ - HISTORY.
Höltz, Joachim. Kritik der Geldentstehungstheorien . Berlin , c1984. ii, 401 p. ; ISBN 3-496-00796-6 LC Card 85-147094
HG237 .H64 1984

MONEY - ITALY - VENICE - HISTORY.
Lane Frederic Chapin, 1900- Money and banking in medieval and Renaissance Venice /. Baltimore , c1985- v. : ISBN 0-8018-3157-1 (v. 1) LC Card 84-47947 DDC 332.1/0945/31 19
HG1040.V46 L36 1985 *NYPL [JLL 86-121]*

MONEY LAUNDERING.
Naylor, R. T., 1945- Hot money and the politics of debt /. New York, N.Y. , 1987. 463 p. ; ISBN 0-671-62319-2 LC Card 86-33739 DDC 364.1/68 19
HG3891 .N39 1987

MONEY LAUNDERING - AUSTRALIA.
Kwitny, Jonathan. The crimes of patriots . New York , c1987. 424 p., [8] p. of plates : ISBN 0-393-02387-7 : LC Card 87-22032 DDC 364.1/0994 19
HG3448.N846 K95 1987

MONEY - LAW AND LEGISLATION - BRAZIL.
Nassif, Luís. O cruzado . São Paulo/SP , 1986. 255 p. : LC Card 86-224110
HG835 .N37 1986

MONEY - LAW AND LEGISLATION - BRAZIL - HISTORY.
Cavalcanti, Amaro, 1849-1922. O meio circulante nacional . Brasília-Distrito Federal , 1983- v. : LC Card 84-160002
HG833 .C38 1983 *NYPL [JLL 85-246]*

MONEY - LAW AND LEGISLATION - ECUADOR.
Pensamiento monetario y financiero /. Quito, Ecuador , 1986. 2 v. : LC Card 87-150740 DDC 332.4/9866 19
HG862 .P46 1986

Money making money . Kennedy, David W. New York , 1987. 215 p. ; ISBN 0-88687-296-0 : LC Card 86-62737 DDC 332.6/78 19
HG4921 .K44 1987

Money-making real estate . Janik, Carolyn. New York, NY , 1988. 306 p. : ISBN 0-670-81137-8 : LC Card 87-23103 DDC 332.63/24 19
HD1382.5 .J35 1988

MONEY - MALAYSIA.
Lee, S. Y. (Sheng-Yi) The monetary and banking development of Singapore and Malaysia /. Singapore , 1986. 298 p. : ISBN 997-16-9098-5 (pbk.) LC Card 86-943034 DDC 332.4/9595 19
HG1250.67 .L43 1986

The money manager /. Brown, Carolann D. (Carolann Doherty), 1946- Norfolk, Va. , c1987. p. cm. ISBN 0-89865-531-5 : LC Card 87-5456 DDC 332.024 19
HG4527 .B675 1987

MONEY MARKET.
El ABC de la Bolsa. Barcelona [1983?] 93 p. : ISBN 84-383-0028-6 LC Card 86-139799
HG4521 .A213 1983

Käsmeier, Josef H. Euromärkte und nationale Finanzmärkte . Berlin , c1984. 179 p. : ISBN 3-428-05595-0 : LC Card 86-134582 DDC 332.4/5 19
HG3897 .K375 1984
NYPL [JLL 74-61 Bd.117]

Stigum, Marcia L. The Dow Jones-Irwin guide to bond and money market investments /. Homewood, Ill. , c1987. xiii, 298 p. : ISBN 0-87094-892-X : LC Card 86-71921
*NYPL [*R-Econ. 87-1260]*

MONEY MARKET - BELGIUM.
Mercier, Paul. Le marché du call money garanti /. Bruxelles [1983] 64 p. : LC Card 84-210204
HG1055 .M47 1983

MONEY MARKET - CANADA.
Hunter, W. T. Canadian financial markets /. Peterborough, Canada , c1986. 193 p. : ISBN 0-921149-01-8 (pbk.) LC Card 86-206029 DDC 332.6/0973 19
HG185.C2 H86 1986

MONEY MARKET - CONGRESSES.
Shifting frontiers in financial markets /. Dordrecht ; Boston : xii, 360 p. : ISBN 90-247-3225-5 LC Card 85-18821 DDC 332 19
HG4523 .S54 1986 *NYPL [JLE 86-2694]*

MONEY MARKET - EUROPE - CONGRESSES.
L'Information financière . Bruxelles , 1983. 220 p. ; ISBN 2-8027-0298-X LC Card 84-104169
HG151.5 .I56 1983

MONEY MARKET FUNDS - HANDBOOKS, MANUALS, ETC.
The Handbook of fixed income securities /. Homewood, Ill. , 1987. xxx, 1376 p. : ISBN 0-87094-745-1 LC Card 86-50815
NYPL [JLE 87-939]

MONEY MARKET FUNDS - UNITED STATES.
Seligman, Barnard. Choosing an investment company /. Cambridge, Mass. , c1987. xvii, 174 p. : ISBN 0-88730-094-4 LC Card 87-1437 DDC 332.6 19
HG4930 .S45 1987

MONEY MARKET FUNDS - UNITED STATES - HANDBOOKS, MANUALS, ETC.
Stigum, Marcia L. After the trade . Homewood, Ill. , c1988. xvii, 303 p. : ISBN 0-87094-937-3 LC Card 87-50773 DDC 332.63/232/0973 19
HG4941 .S75 1988

MONEY MARKET - HANDBOOKS, MANUALS, ETC.
Darst, David M., 1947- The handbook of the bond and money markets /. New York , c1981. xv, 461 p. : ISBN 0-07-015401-5 LC Card 80-36816 DDC 332.63/23
HG4527 .D37 *NYPL [JLE 87-568]*

Kemp, L. J. (Lynette J.) The Wardley guide to world money and securities markets /. London , 1984. xvii, 472 p. ; ISBN 0-903121-66-2 *NYPL [JLG 86-203]*

MONEY MARKET - ITALY.
Bagella, Michele. Gli istituti di credito speciale e il mercato finanziario, 1947-1962 /. Milano, Italy , c1986. 289 p. ; LC Card 86-232526
HG3729.I7 B34 1986

MONEY MARKET - MATHEMATICAL MODELS.
Ohlson, James A. The theory of financial markets and information /. New York , c1987. xiii, 181 p. ; ISBN 0-444-01161-7 LC Card 87-9100 DDC 332.6 19
HG173 .O34 1987

MONEY MARKET - NIGERIA.
Shahi, M. A. (Muslehuddin Akhil) Money and capital markets in Nigeria . Bombay , 1983. xi [i.e. x], 60 p. ; LC Card 83-905358 DDC 332/.0412/09669 19
HG187.5.N6 S5 1983 *NYPL [JLE 87-691]*

MONEY MARKET - UNITED STATES.
Gart, Alan. Handbook of the money and capital markets /. New York , c1988. p. cm. ISBN 0-89930-270-X (lib. bdg. : alk. paper) LC Card 87-24938 DDC 332.63/2/0973 19
HG181 .G367 1988

Henning, Charles N. Financial markets and the economy /. Englewood Cliffs, N.J. , c1988. xvi, 638 p. : ISBN 0-13-316894-8 LC Card 87-24413 DDC 332/.0973 19
HG181 .H37 1988

MONEY - MATHEMATICAL MODELS.
Blang, Hans-Georg, 1953- Die Variabilität relativer Preisänderungen und die Varianz monetärer Aggregate /. Frankfurt am Main , New York , c1986. xxvii, 338 p. : ISBN 3-8204-9074-4 LC Card 86-156110
HG229 .B555 1986

Harris, John Andrew de Oliveira. Evolução e definição da moeda /. Rio de Janeiro, RJ , 1985. 90 p. : LC Card 87-135878 DDC 332.4/981 19
HG835 .H37 1985

Illing, Gerhard. Geld und asymmetrische Information /. Berlin , New York , 1985. vi, 148 p. : ISBN 0-387-13999-0 (U. S.) LC Card 85-142939
HG220.A2 I55 1985

Owen, Dorian, 1953- Money, wealth, and expenditure . Cambridge [Cambridgeshire] , New York , 1986. xi, 210 p. ; ISBN 0-521-26761-7 LC Card 85-19009 DDC 339.4/7/0724 19
HB820 .O94 1986 *NYPL [JLE 87-1594]*

Puumanen, Kari. Three essays on money, wealth, and the exchange rate /. Helsinki , 1986. 143 p. : ISBN 951-686-119-9 (pbk.) LC Card 86-235460 DDC 332.4/0724 19
HG221 .P97 1986

Serra, Daniel. Monnaie, inflation et croissance /. Paris , 1982. xi, 306 p. : ISBN 2-7178-0478-1 : LC Card 82-153767 DDC 332.4/0724 19
HG221 .S485 1982 *NYPL [JLE 86-1903]*

Money minutes /. Loeb, Marshall. Boston , c1987. ix, 210 p. ; ISBN 0-316-53058-1 (pbk.) : LC Card 87-10245 DDC 332.024 19
HG179 .L553 1987

The money moguls . Goobey, Alastair Ross. Cambridge [Cambridgeshire] , Wolfeboro, N.H. , 1987. viii, 19 p. : ISBN 0-85941-391-8 (U. S.) : LC Card 86-26669 DDC 332.6 19
HG4521 .G5558 1986 *NYPL [JLE 87-826]*

MONEY - MORAL AND ETHICAL ASPECTS.
Wagner, Falk. Geld oder Gott? . Stuttgart , c1984. 162 p. ; ISBN 3-608-91389-0 LC Card 86-121379
HG221.3 .W255 1984

MONEY - NIGERIA.
Uzoaga, William Okefie. Money and banking in Nigeria /. Enugu, Nigeria , 1981. xiv, 304 p. ; ISBN 978-15-6175-0 *NYPL [Sc D 84-373]*

MONEY, PAPER. see **PAPER MONEY.**

MONEY - PENNSYLVANIA - HISTORY - 18TH CENTURY.
Schweitzer, Mary M. Custom and contract . New York , 1987. xii, 271 p. : ISBN 0-231-06288-5 LC Card 87-8003 DDC 338.9748 19
HC107.P4 S417 1987

MONEY - POLAND - HISTORY.
Cywiński, Henryk. Dziesięć wieków pieniądza polskiego 980-1980 /. Warszawa , 1982. 243 p., [24] p. of plates : ISBN 83-205-3413-5 LC Card 83-119732
HG1087 .C98 1982

MONEY - PORTUGAL.
Girão, José António. Salários, inflação e moeda . Lisboa , 1984. 50 p. : LC Card 85-157764
HG1145 .G57 1984

Money problems /. Perry, Richard D. Elgin, Ill. , c1987. 111 p. ; ISBN 1-555-13797-0 (pbk.) LC Card 86-73209 DDC 332.024 19
HG179 .P367 1987

MONEY - PSYCHOLOGICAL ASPECTS.
Brera, Paolo. Denaro . [Brescia] [1984] 110 p. ; LC Card 86-102925
HB49 .B74 1984

Forman, Norm. Mind over money . Toronto, Ont. , Garden City, N.Y. , 1987. xi, 248 p. ; ISBN 0-385-25104-1 LC Card 86-32814 DDC 332.024 19
HG222.3 .F67 1987

Gurney, Kathleen. Your money personality . New York , 1988. p. cm. ISBN 0-385-24254-9 LC Card 87-24449 DDC 332.4/01/9 19
HG222.3 .G87 1988

Lieberman, Annette. Unbalanced accounts . New York , c1987. xx, 281 p. ; ISBN 0-87113-141-2 LC Card 86-28845 DDC 332.4/01/9 19
HG179 .L49 1987

MONEY, QUANTITY THEORY OF. see **QUANTITY THEORY OF MONEY.**

MONEY RAISING. see **FUND RAISING.**

MONEY - ROME.
Greene, Kevin. The archaeology of the Roman economy /. London , 1986. 192 p. : ISBN 0-7134-4593-9 : LC Card 86-226151 DDC 330.937/06 19
HC39 .G72 1986

MONEY - SENEGAL.
Répertoire financier et monétaire du Sénégal, 1985. Le Vésinet, France [1985?] ii, 98 leaves ; LC Card 86-202435
HJ2184.5 .R46 1985

Money sense . Nichols, Harwood, 1942- Washington, DC , 1987. p. cm. ISBN 0-87491-871-5 (pbk.) : LC Card 87-24129 DDC 332.024/007 19
HG179 .N53 1987

MONEY - SINGAPORE.
Lee, S. Y. (Sheng-Yi) The monetary and banking development of Singapore and Malaysia /. Singapore , 1986. 298 p. : ISBN 997-16-9098-5 (pbk.) LC Card 86-943034 DDC 332.4/9595 19
HG1250.67 .L43 1986

MONEY - SOVIET UNION.
Denezhnoe obrashchenie i kredit SSSR /. Moskva , 1986. 374 p. : LC Card 87-157773
HG3729.S632 D46 1986

Konnik, I. I. (Iosif Isaakovich) Denezhnoe obrashchenie v protsesse rasshirennogo sotsialisticheskogo vosproizvodstva /. Moskva , 1982. 269 p. ; LC Card 83-165373
HG186.S55 K65 1982

Organizatsiia i planirovanie kredita i denezhnogo obrashcheniia /. Moskva , 1984. 350 p. ; LC Card 85-108172
HG3729.S632 O74 1984

MONEY STOCK. see **MONEY SUPPLY.**

MONEY SUPPLY - BRAZIL.
Lemgruber, Antonio Carlos. O controle da base monetária e as flutuações dos multiplicadores monetários e creditícios /. [Brasília] [1981?]

118 p. : LC Card 85-154853
HG835 .L35 1981

MONEY SUPPLY - BRAZIL - ECONOMETRIC MODELS.
Melo, Valdir Ramalho de. Seleção de agregados monetários /. [Brasília] [1981] 136 p. : LC Card 85-161532
HG835 .M45 1981

MONEY SUPPLY - CARIBBEAN AREA.
Calderón González, Arnoldo. América Latina y el Caribe . México, D.F. , 1985. 51, [25] leaves ; LC Card 87-121714 DDC 332.4/98 19
HG660.5 .C35 1985

MONEY SUPPLY - DENMARK.
Brink, Helge. Monetarisme og økonomisk politik /. [Copenhagen] , c1984. 125 p. ; ISBN 87-574-4380-7 : LC Card 84-253099
HG1092 .B75 1984

MONEY SUPPLY - ECONOMETRIC MODELS.
Bordo, Michael D. The long-run behavior of the velocity of circulation . Cambridge [Cambridgeshire] , New York , 1987. xiv, 181 p. : ISBN 0-521-32633-8 LC Card 86-32628 DDC 332.4/14 19
HG226.6 .B67 1987

Rasche, Robert H. Controlling the growth of monetary aggregates /. Boston , c1987. xviii, 212 p. : ISBN 0-89838-226-2 : LC Card 87-3737 DDC 332.4/6 19
HG230.3 .R37 1987

MONEY SUPPLY - FRANCE - ECONOMETRIC MODELS.
Gubitz, Andrea. Geldmärkte und Europäisches Währungssystem . Idstein , 1985. vii, 201 p. : ISBN 3-925196-00-5 LC Card 86-230130
HG3949 .G82 1985

MONEY SUPPLY - GERMANY (WEST) - ECONOMETRIC MODELS.
Gubitz, Andrea. Geldmärkte und Europäisches Währungssystem . Idstein , 1985. vii, 201 p. : ISBN 3-925196-00-5 LC Card 86-230130
HG3949 .G82 1985

MONEY SUPPLY - INDIA.
Reserve Bank of India. Committee to Review the Working of the Monetary System. Report of the Committee to Review the Working of the Monetary System. Bombay [1985] vii, 371 p. ; LC Card 87-902447 DDC 332.4/954 19
HG1235 .R47 1985

MONEY SUPPLY - JAPAN.
Suzuki, Yoshio, 1931- [Nihon kin'yū keizairon. English.] Money, finance, and macroeconomic performance in Japan /. New Haven , c1986. xvii, 218, p. : ISBN 0-300-03387-7 LC Card 85-26375 DDC 332/.0952 19
HG187.J3 S96 1986 ***NYPL [JLE 86-2788]***

MONEY SUPPLY - LATIN AMERICA.
Calderón González, Arnoldo. América Latina y el Caribe . México, D.F. , 1985. 51, [25] leaves ; LC Card 87-121714 DDC 332.4/98 19
HG660.5 .C35 1985

MONEY SUPPLY - LATIN AMERICA - MATHEMATICAL MODELS.
Canto, Victor A. Currency substitution . Boston , c1987. viii, 196 p. ; ISBN 0-89838-195-9 LC Card 86-27747 DDC 332.4/56/098 19
HG3823 .C36 1987

MONEY SUPPLY - MATHEMATICAL MODELS.
Freedman, Charles. Monetary aggregates as targets . [Ottawa] , 1981. vii, 49 p. ; LC Card 81-198954 DDC 332.4/6/0724 19
HG230.3 .F74 1981
NYPL [JLM 75-1420 no.27]

Illing, Gerhard. Geld und asymmetrische Information /. Berlin , New York , 1985. vi, 148 p. : ISBN 0-387-13999-0 (U. S.) LC Card 85-142939
HG220.A2 I55 1985

Spreter, Jürgen. Theoretische und empirische Analyse der Determinanten des Geldschöpfungsmultiplikators /. Krefeld , 1983. v, 221 p. : ISBN 3-88358-029-5 LC Card 83-154608
HG226.3 .S67 1983

MONEY SUPPLY - SWITZERLAND.
Baltensperger, Ernst. Geldmengenpolitik und Inflationskontrolle . Diessenhofen , c1984. 132 p. : ISBN 3-7253-0224-3 : LC Card 84-178054 DDC 332.4/9494 19
HG1155 .B345 1984 ***NYPL [JLD 87-168]***

MONEY - SWITZERLAND.
Zenger, Christoph. Kursschwankungen des Schweizerfrankens in ihren Auswirkungen auf Produktion, Export, Import und Fremdenverkehr . Bern , c1982. vi, 263 p. : ISBN 3-258-03172-X : LC Card 83-242397 DDC 332.4/9494 19
HG1155 .Z46 1982

MONEY - SWITZERLAND - BASEL-STADT - HISTORY.
Rosen, Josef. Verwaltung und Ungeld in Basel, 1360-1535 . Stuttgart , 1986. 231 p. ; ISBN 3-515-03348-3 : LC Card 86-184510
HG1160.B37 R67 1986

Money talks . Lant, Jeffrey L. Cambridge, Mass. , c1985. vii, 302 p. : ISBN 0-940374-08-0 (pbk.) LC Card 87-105725 DDC 001 19
HD69.C6 L27 1985

MONEY - UNITED STATES.
Hutchinson, Harry D. Money, banking, and the United States economy /. Englewood Cliffs, NJ , 1988. p. cm. ISBN 0-13-600156-4 LC Card 87-19299 DDC 332.1/0973 19
HG2491 .H8 1988

Klein, John J., 1929- Money and the economy /. San Diego , c1986. xi, 560 p. : ISBN 0-15-564007-0 LC Card 85-80078 DDC 332.4/973 19
HG540 .K57 1986 ***NYPL [JLE 86-3392]***

Lapham, Lewis H. Money and class in America . New York , 1988, c1987. p. cm. ISBN 1-555-84109-0 LC Card 87-22515 DDC 305.5/234/0973 19
HC110.W4 L24 1988

Mayer, Thomas. Money, banking, and the economy /. New York , c1984. xiv, 574 p. : ISBN 0-393-95313-0 LC Card 83-13498 DDC 332.1/0973 19
HG540 .M39 1984 ***NYPL [JLE 86-2193]***

Mayer, Thomas, 1927- Money, banking, and the economy /. New York , c1987. xiv, 488 p. : ISBN 0-393-95557-5 LC Card 86-33160 DDC 332.1/0973 19
HG540 .M39 1987

MONEY - UNITED STATES - CRIMINAL PROVISIONS.
United States. President's Commission on Organized Crime. Organized crime and money laundering . Washington, D.C. [1985]. vi, 189 p. : ***NYPL [JLE 86-1282]***

MONEY - UNITED STATES - HISTORY.
Degen, Robert A. The American monetary system . Lexington, Mass. , c1987. x, 242 p. ; ISBN 0-669-15827-5 (alk. paper) LC Card 86-46363 DDC 332.4/973 19
HG501 .D44 1987

Livingston, James, 1949- Origins of the Federal Reserve System . Ithaca , 1986. 250 p. ; ISBN 0-8014-1844-5 (alk. paper) LC Card 85-48199 DDC 332.1/1/0973 19
HG2563 .L58 1986 ***NYPL [JLE 86-2522]***

Moore, Carl H., 1916- Money . Jefferson, N.C. , c1987. xi, 164 p. : ISBN 0-89950-272-5 (lib. bdg.) : LC Card 87-42515 DDC 332.4/9 19
HG231 .M63 1987

Pick, Franz. The U. S. dollar . Bethel, CT , c1986. xvi, 103 p., [1] folded leaf of plates : ISBN 0-916373-04-5 (pbk.): LC Card 86-210094 DDC 332.4/973 19
HG539 .P5 1986

Schwartz, Anna Jacobson. Money in historical perspective /. Chicago , 1987. xvii, 442 p. : ISBN 0-226-74228-8 : LC Card 87-5973 DDC 332.4/9 19
HG538 .S354 1987

MONEY - VENEZUELA.
Cantó, Leandro. La caída del bolívar /. Caracas, Venezuela [1983 or 1984] 223 p. ; LC Card 84-186552 DDC 332.4/987 19
HG915 .C36 1983 ***NYPL [JLD 87-2426]***

Money, wealth, and expenditure . Owen, Dorian, 1953- Cambridge [Cambridgeshire] , New York , 1986. xi, 210 p. ; ISBN 0-521-26761-7 LC Card 85-19009 DDC 339.4/7/0724 19
HB820 .O94 1986 ***NYPL [JLE 87-1594]***

MONEY - YUGOSLAVIA.
Soós, Károly Attila. Terv, kampány, pénz . Budapest , 1986. 532 p. : ISBN 963-221-575-3 : LC Card 87-137237
HB3787.5 .S66 1986

MONEY - ZIMBABWE.
Whitsun Foundation. Project 1.09 . Harare, Zimbabwe [1983?] ix, 260 p. : ISBN 0-7974-0607-7 (pbk.) LC Card 87-402552 DDC 332.1/096891 19
HG1352 .W48 1983

Moneybags must be so lucky . Wolff, Robert Paul. Amherst , c1988. p. cm. ISBN 0-87023-615-6 (alk. paper) LC Card 87-20580 DDC 335.4/1 19
HB501.M37 W64 1988

MONEYXHISTORY.
Höltz, Joachim. Kritik der Geldentstehungstheorien . Berlin , c1984. ii, 401 p. ; ISBN 3-496-00796-6 LC Card 85-147094
HG237 .H64 1984

Mongiello, Joseph.
Advanced composites . Stamford, Conn. , c1985. x, 206 leaves : ISBN 0-89336-442-8 (soft) LC Card 87-166023 DDC 338.4/7620118 19
HD9999.C7152 A38 1985

Reinforced plastics . Stamford, Conn., U. S.A. , c1986. v, 136 leaves : ISBN 0-89336-478-9 (pbk.) LC Card 87-167989 DDC 381/.45668494/0973 19
HD9662.F523 U57 1986

MONGOLIA - ECONOMIC CONDITIONS.
Opyt stroitel'stva sotsialisticheskoĭ ėkonomiki v stranakh Azii /. Moskva , 1986. 290 p. ; LC Card 87-126301
HC412 .O675 1986

MONGOLIA - RURAL CONDITIONS.
Graĭvoronskiĭ, Vladimir Viktorovich. Kooperirovannoe aratstvo MNR--izmeneniia v urovne zhizni, 1960-1980 /. Moskva , 1982. 213 p. : LC Card 82-213253
HD1491.M55 G73 1982

Monheim, Felix. Die Entwicklung der peruanischen Agrarreform 1969-1979 und ihre Durchführung im Departement Puno [microform] / von Felix Monheim. Wiesbaden : F. Steiner, 1981. 37 p. ; 24 cm. (Erdkundliches Wissen. Heft 55) "Geographische Zeitschrift. Beihefte."--Series t.p. Bibliography: p. [36]-37. Microfilm. New York : New York Public Library, 1986. 1 microfilm reel ; 35 mm. (MN *ZZ-25,803) ISBN 3-515-03629-6 : LC Card 82-113404 DDC 333.3/1/8536 19
1. Land reform - Peru - Puno (Dept.). 2. Land reform - Peru. I. Geographische Zeitschrift. Supplement. II. Title.
HD1333.P42 P955 1981
NYPL [*ZT-1647 no.11]

Mónica, Maria Filomena, 1943- Artesãos e operários : indústria, capitalismo e classe operária em Portugal (1870-1934) / Maria Filomena Mónica. Lisboa : Instituto de Ciências Sociais da Universidade de Lisboa, [1986] 228 p., [24] p. of plates : ill. ; 22 cm. (Colecção Teses e teorias . 1) Bibliography: p. [219]-228. LC Card 86-229921
1. Labor and laboring classes - Portugal - History. 2. Hat trade - Portugal - History. 3. Glass trade - Portugal - History. 4. Metal trade - Portugal - History. 5. Textile industry - Portugal - History. I. Title. II. Series.
HD8596 .M65 1986

Monitoring and evaluating small business projects : a step by step guide for private development organizations / by members of the Small Enterprise Evaluation Project and Shirley Buzzard and Elaine Edgcomb, editors. [New York, NY] : PACT, c1987. ix, 262 p. : ill. ; 29 cm. Bibliography: p. 259-262. LC Card 87-6945 DDC 361.7 19
1. Small business - Developing countries - Evaluation. 2. Economic development projects - Evaluation. 3. Non-governmental organizations. I. Buzzard, Shirley. II. Edgcomb, Elaine. III. Small Enterprise Evaluation Project.
HD2346.5 .M65 1987

Monitoring the competition . Fuld, Leonard M. New York, N.Y. , c1988. xiii, 204 p. ; ISBN 0-471-85261-9 LC Card 87-21607 DDC 658.4/7 19
HD38.7 .F86 1988

Monk, Sarah. Fothergill, Steve. Property and industrial development /. London , Wolfeboro, N.H. , 1987. 187 p. : ISBN 0-09-170741-2 (pbk.) : LC Card 87-2627 DDC 333.3/8/0941 19
HD598 .F68 1987

Mönkemeyer, Karl, 1916- Krelle, Wilhelm. Wachstum bei Erschöpfbaren Ressourcen, gibt es das? . Münster , c1982. 59 p. : ISBN 3-402-04434-X LC Card 83-215135
HC55 .K74 1982

MÖNKEMEYER, KARL, 1916-
Krelle, Wilhelm. Wachstum bei Erschöpfbaren Ressourcen, gibt es das? . Münster , c1982. 59 p. : ISBN 3-402-04434-X LC Card 83-215135
HC55 .K74 1982

Monnaie, inflation et croissance /. Serra, Daniel. Paris , 1982. xi, 306 p. : ISBN 2-7178-0478-1 : LC Card 82-153767 DDC 332.4/0724 19
HG221 .S485 1982 ***NYPL [JLE 86-1903]***

Monnaies d'Extrême Orient /. Thierry, François. Paris , <[1986- v. <2 > : ISBN 2-11-080873-X (v. 2) : LC Card 86-218568
HG1250.5 .T45 1986

Monnier, Lionel. Escarmelle, Jean-François. L'Etat industriel dans les politiques de sortie de crise . Louvain-la-Neuve , 1986. 237 p. : ISBN 2-87077-301-3 : LC Card 86-229137
HD3616.B43 E84 1986

Monografi sumber daya ekonomi di bidang kehutanan Kalimantan Timur : laporan / dalam rangka kerja sama antara Proyek Penelitian Sumber Daya Ekonomi, Lembaga Ilmu Pengetahuan Indonesia dengan Fakultas Kehutanan, Institut Pertanian Bogor. Bogor : Fakultas Kehutanan, Institut Pertanian Bogor, 1975. ix, 67 leaves : map ; 28 cm. (SDE . 8) Folded map in pocket. Includes bibliographical references. LC Card 80-941771
1. Forest products industry - Indonesia - Kalimantan Timur. I. Institut Pertanian Bogor. Fakultas Kehutanan. II. Proyek Sumber Daya Ekonomi (Indonesia). III. Series.
HD9766.I73 K356 1975

Monografía de la República de El Salvador /. Calderón Chacón, Godofredo. San Salvador, El Salvador , 1986. iv, 132 p. : LC Card 87-401545 DDC 330.97284/052 19
HC148 .C35 1986

Monografía del café /. Fabián, Miguel Angel. [San Salvador] , 1984. 39 leaves : LC Card 86-177543
HD9199.S142 F33 1984

Monografía del café. Fabián, Miguel Angel. Monografía del café /. [San Salvador] , 1984. 39 leaves : LC Card 86-177543
HD9199.S142 F33 1984

Monografías (Castilla-La Mancha (Spain). Junta de Comunidades) .
(7) Sánchez Sánchez, Isidro. Castilla-La Mancha en la época contemporánea, 1808-1939 /. [Castilla-La Mancha] [1986] iii, 204 p. : ISBN 84-505-3538-7 LC Card 87-122049
HC387.C245 S36 1986

Monografías (Instituto de Estudios Financieros (Spain)) .
(no. 23) Los Problemas financieros en el Estado regionalizado /. Madrid , 1983. 207 leaves ; LC Card 85-177739
HJ1120 .P75 1983

Monografías (Instituto de Estudios Fiscales (Spain)) .
(no. 15) Sevilla Segura, Jorge. El proceso de implantación del IVA . [Madrid] [1982?] iii, 182 p. ; LC Card 85-201954
HJ5715.G7 S4 1982

(no. 3) Morón Bécquer, Pedro. El ahorro vinculado a la adquisición de viviendas . Madrid [1984?] 35 p. : ISBN 84-7196-476-7 : LC Card 85-201073
HG2156.S72 M67 1984

(no. 30) González Blanch, Francisco. Implantación en España de un sistema de tarificación por el uso de la infraestructura viaria /. Madrid [1984?] 204 p. ; ISBN 84-7196-470-8 : LC Card 85-201965
HJ5956.E86 G66 1984

(no. 4) Cuenca García, Eduardo. Las intervenciones financieras comunitarias /. Madrid [1985?] 53 p. ; ISBN 84-7196-523-2 LC Card 85-200493
HJ2094.5 .C84 1985

(núm. 1) Zurdo y Ruiz-Ayúcar, Juan. Algunas ideas sobre tributación federal de la renta en Estados Unidos /. [Madrid] [1978?] 53, [17] leaves ; LC Card 85-203311
HJ4652 .Z87 1978

(núm. 7) Fanjul Martín, Enrique. La evolución de la política monetaria española (1940-1978) . [Madrid] , 1979. 164 p. ; LC Card 85-202991
HG1135 .F35 1979

Monografias (Instituto de Estudos Econômicos, Sociais e Políticos de São Paulo) .
(1) Muszynski, Maria Judith de Brito. O impacto político das migrações internas . São Paulo , 1986. 169 p. : LC Card 86-234794
HB2023 .M87 1986

(2) Spindel, Cheywa R. Espaços de socialização e exploração do menor assalariado . São Paulo, SP , 1986. 254 p. ; LC Card 87-405001 DDC 331.3/1/0981 19
HD6276.B72 S67 1986

Monografie i opracowania (Szkoła Główna Planowania i Statystyki (Warsaw, Poland)) .
(134) Wyższa Szkoła Handlowa, Szkoła Główna Handlowa, Miejska Szkoła Handlowa, 1906-1945 /. Warszawa , 1984. 180 p. : LC Card 85-241871
HB74.9.P7 W98 1984

(196) Witkowski, Janusz. Migracje a ruchliwość społeczna ludności w Polsce /. Warszawa , 1985. 168 p. : LC Card 86-175948
HB2068.7.A3 W58 1985

(65) Sulmicki, Jan. Transfer postępu naukowo-technicznego przez przedsiębiorstwa międzynarodowe a długookresowe zmiany w przedsiębiorstwa międzynarodowe a długookresowe zmiany w międzynarodowym podziale pracy /. Warszawa , 1978. 288 p. ; LC Card 81-205742
HF1411 .S876 1978

(87) Migracje wewnętrzne ludności . Warszawa , 1980. xvi, 389 p. ; LC Card 86-215694
HB2068.7.A3 M54 1980

Monografier utgivna av Sociologiska institutionen vid Göteborgs universitet .
(nr. 28) Hörte, Sven Åke. Medbestämmande . [Göteborg] , c1983. 160, [28] p. : ISBN 91-7222-576-9 LC Card 83-173622
HD5660.S9 H67 1983

Monografies d'estudis locals. Història .
(1) Torrent, Emili. Evolució del transport a Salt /. [Salt, Spain] [1984] 32 p. : ISBN 84-85946-59-6 LC Card 87-161246
HE311.S72 S257 1984

Monograph (Academy of Accounting Historians) .
(2) Previts, Gary John. John Raymond Wildman . University, Ala. , 1978. viii, 84 p. ; LC Card 86-224716
HF5604.5.W55 P74 1978

(4) Selected papers from the Charles Waldo Haskins accounting history seminars /. [University, Ala.] , 1983. iv, 172 p. ; LC Card 86-224698 DDC 657/.09 19
HF5611 .S45 1983

(5) Parker, R. H. (Robert Henry) The development of the accountancy profession in Britain to the early twentieth century /. [University, Ala.] , 1986. ix, 74 p. ; LC Card 86-226162 DDC 657/.09 19
HF5616.G7 P36 1986

Monograph and research series (University of California, Los Angeles. Institute of Industrial Relations) .
(43) Bullock, Paul. Youth training and employment from New Deal to New Federalism /. Los Angeles , c1985. xiii, 359 p. ; ISBN 0-89215-131-1 ***NYPL [JLD 86-2972]***

(30) Job equity and other studies in industrial relations . Los Angeles , c1982. 274 p. : LC Card 82-621216 DDC 331/.0973 19
HD5708.45.U6 J6 1982 ***NYPL [JLD 87-273]***

(32) Sex role stereotyping and affirmative action policy /. Los Angeles, Calif. , c1982. 227 p. : LC Card 82-623259 DDC 331.4/133 19
HD6060 .S49 1982 ***NYPL [JLD 87-275]***

(35) How mighty a force? . Los Angeles , c1983. ix, 369 p. ; ***NYPL [JLD 87-277]***

(45) The Future directions of employee relations /. Los Angeles, Calif. , c1985. xiv, 418 p. ; ISBN 0-89215-132-3 ***NYPL [JLD 86-3596]***

(45) The Future directions of employee relations /. Los Angeles, Calif. , c1985. xiv, 418 p. : ISBN 0-89215-132-3 (pbk.) LC Card 86-622936 DDC 331/.0973 19
HD8072.5 .F87 1985

Monograph (Financial Analysts Research Foundation) .
(no. 21) Atchison, Michael D. New financial instruments . Charlottesville, Va. (P.O. Box 3665, Charlottesville 22903) , c1985. viii, 108 p. ; LC Card 85-195578 DDC 332.63 19
HG6024.3 .A83 1985 ***NYPL [JLL 81-133 no.21]***

(no. 22) Broader perspectives on the interest of pension plan participants /. Charlottesville, Va. (P.O. Box 3665, Charlottesville 22903) , c1985. vii, 43 p. : LC Card 85-196669 DDC 332.6/7254 19
HD7105.45.U6 B76 1985 ***NYPL [JLL 81-133 no. 22]***

Monograph (Kōbe Daigaku. Keiei Gakubu) .
(no. 4) Futatsugi, Yūsaku, 1935- [Gendai Nihon no kigyō shūdan. English.] Japanese enterprise groups /. [Kobe] , 1986. 179 p. : LC Card 86-220427 DDC 338.8/0952 19
HD2756.2.J3 F8813 1986

A monograph on access planning as an essay on explorations in alternatives /. Ramana, D. V. Kuala Lumpur [1982] 86 p. : LC Card 84-940306 DDC 338.954 19
HD75 .R36 1982

Monograph series (Committee for Economic Development of Australia) .
(no. 82) McLean, Robert J. Exploiting opportunities in the Pacific Basin . [Melbourne] [1986] 56 p. : ISBN 0-85801-162-X (pbk.) LC Card 86-203142 DDC 337.9409 19
HF1626.5.P33 M35 1986

Monograph series in finance and economics .
(monograph 1985-2) Stoll, Hans R. The stock exchange specialist system . New York, N.Y. (90 Trinity Place, New York 10006) [c1985] 53 p. : LC Card 86-210049 DDC 332.64/273 19
HG4572 .S856 1985

(monograph 1985-3) Smirlock, Michael. Taxes and mergers . New York, N.Y. (90 Trinity Place, New York 10006) [c1986] 42 p. : LC Card 86-210061 DDC 336.24/3 19
HD2746.5 .S64 1986

(monograph 1986-1) Black, Deborah G. Success and failure of futures contracts . New York, N.Y. (90 Trinity Pl., New York 10006) [c1986] 70 p. ; LC Card 87-129777 DDC 332.64/4 19
HG6046 .B52 1986

(monograph 1986-2) Chua, Jess H. Gains from stock-market timing /. New York, N.Y. (90 Trinity Pl., New York 10006) [c1986] 75 p. ; LC Card 87-129798 DDC 332.63/222 19
HG4637 .C48 1986

Monograph series (Jāmi'at al-Kharṭūm. Markaz al-Dirāsāt wa-al-Buḥūth al-Inmā'īyah) .
(no. 24) Jalāl al-Dīn, Muḥammad al-'Awaḍ. Some aspects of Sudanese migration to the oil-producing Arab countries, during the 1970's /. [Khartoum] [1985] 52 p. ; LC Card 86-980666 DDC 331.6/2/62409174927 19
HD8766 .J35 1985

Monograph series of the David M. Kennedy Center for International Studies at Brigham Young University .
(v. 1) Hickman, Martin Berkeley, 1925- David Matthew Kennedy . Salt Lake City, Utah , c1987. xi, 403 p. : ISBN 0-87579-093-3 : LC Card 87-19898 DDC 332.1/092/4 B 19
HG2463.K46 H53 1987

Monograph series on Soviet Union.
Adirim, I. G. (Itskhok Girshevich) Stagflation in the USSR /. Falls Church, VA (7700 Leesburg Pike, #212, Falls Church 22043) [1983] xi, 122 leaves ; LC Card 84-162596 DDC 332.4/1/0947 19
HC340.I5 A44 1983 ***NYPL [JLF 86-1839]***

Kogan, Ninel. New standards for evaluating

technological innovation in the USSR . Falls Church, VA (7700 Leesburg Pike, #250, Falls Church 22043) , c1986. xii, 103 leaves (some folded) : LC Card 87-151964 DDC 338.4/7681766/0947 19
HD9579.C33 S654 1986

Tesler, Edward. Soviet economic planning . Falls Church, VA (7700 Leesburg Pike, #250, Falls Church 22043) , c1986. ix, 88 leaves : LC Card 87-403383 DDC 338.947 19
HC335 .T425 1986

Monograph series (University of California, San Diego. Center for U. S.-Mexican Studies) .
(18) The Mexican Left, the popular movements, and the politics of austerity /. La Jolla, Calif. , 1986. vi, 96 p. ; LC Card 87-621353 DDC 322/.2/0972 19
HC135 .M525535 1986

(20) Government and private sector in contemporary Mexico /. [La Jolla, Calif.] , 1987. iv, 146 p. ; LC Card 87-622060 DDC 338.972 19
HD3616.M43 G68 1987

Monograph (University of Michigan. Natural Resources Sociology Research Lab) .
(2) West, Patrick C. Natural resource bureaucracy and rural poverty . Ann Arbor, MI , c1982. xiii, 168 p. : LC Card 83-102928 DDC 333.7/16/0973 19
HD1761 .W423 1982 ***NYPL [JLE 86-4095]***

Monograph (University of the West Indies (Mona, Jamaica). Dept. of Economics) .
(#1) The Debt problem in Jamaica . Mona, Jamaica , c1986. viii, 125 p. : ISBN 976-410-002-3 (pbk.) LC Card 87-403413 DDC 336.3/4/097292 19
HJ8552 .D43 1986

(#2) The State in Caribbean society /. Mona, Jamaica , c1986. vii, 157 p. ; ISBN 976-410-001-5 (pbk.) LC Card 87-403404 DDC 330.9729/052 19
HC151 .S73 1986

Monographic publications.
Twierdochlebow, W. J. Solidarność . Menlo Park, CA , 1985. 72, v leaves ; LC Card 86-221919 DDC 331.89/28238204/094382 19
HD5397.7.S512 1980 .G358 1985

Monographie d'unités domestiques. Bahizi, Joseph. [Bujumbura] [1985] 41 leaves ; LC Card 86-980542
HC880.Z7 M843 1985

Monographies d'économétrie.
Laroque, Guy. Fondements de l'analyse macroéconomique à court terme /. Paris , 1986. 98 p. : ISBN 2-222-03757-3 : LC Card 87-103537
HB173 .L35 1986

Monographs and theoretical studies in sociology and anthropology in honour of Nels Anderson, 0169-9202 .
(publication 22) Sixel, Friedrich W. Crisis and critique . Leiden , New York , 1987. p. cm. ISBN 90-04-08284-0 (pbk.) : LC Card 87-17217 DDC 330.12/2 19
HB501 .S618 1987

Monographs in comparative public policy.
Economics and politics of industrial policy . Boulder , 1986. xi, 120 p. ; ISBN 0-8133-7140-6 (pbk. : alk. paper) : LC Card 85-26478 DDC 338.94 19
HD3616.U47 E34 1986
NYPL [JLE 86-4353]

Monographs in development anthropology.
Lands at risk in the Third World . Boulder , 1987. xiii, 416 p. : ISBN 0-8133-7311-5 (pbk. : alk. paper) : LC Card 86-51423 DDC 333.73/13 19
HD1131 .L37 1987

Monographs in economic anthropology .
(no. 2) Entrepreneurship and social change /. Lanham, MD [S.l.] , c1986. 275 p. : ISBN 0-8191-5165-3 (alk. paper) : LC Card 85-26533 DDC 338/.04 19
HB615 .E629 1986 ***NYPL [JLD 86-3073]***

Monographs in international studies. Latin America series .
(no. 12) Wallace, Brian F. Ownership and development . Athens, Ohio , 1987. ix, 176 p. ; ISBN 0-89680-145-4 (pbk.) LC Card 86-33255 DDC 332.6/7322861 19
HD9734.C62 W35 1987

Monographs in International studies. Southeast Asia series .
(no. 80) Nguyen, Anh Tuan. South Vietnam, trial and experience . Athens, Ohio , 1987. 461 p. : ISBN 0-89680-141-1 (pbk.) : LC Card 86-23532 DDC 338.9597 19
HC444 .N43 1987

Monographs in organizational behavior and industrial relations .
(v. 6) Bain, Joe Staten, 1912- Industrial organization . Greenwich, Conn. , c1987. 2 v. ; ISBN 0-89232-702-2 (set) LC Card 87-2618 DDC 338.6 19
HD2326 .B34 1987

Monographs series in finance and economics .
(monograph 1985-4/5) Benston, George J. An analysis of the causes of savings and loan association failures /. New York, N.Y. (90 Trinity Place, New York 10006) [1985] 182 p. : LC Card 86-209942 DDC 332.3/2/0973 19
HG2151 .B46 1985

Monopole, Profite, Ausbeutung /. Tammer, Hans. Berlin , 1983. 237 p. : LC Card 84-142912
HD2757.2 .T35 1983

MONOPOLIES - ADDRESSES, ESSAYS, LECTURES.
Firms and markets . London , c1986. xiii, 271 p. : ISBN 0-7099-2446-1
NYPL [JLD 86-2134]

Marcy, Sam, 1911- Anatomy of the economic crisis /. Atlanta , c1982. viii, 120 p. : ISBN 0-89567-077-1 (pbk.) ***NYPL [JLD 86-1329]***

MONOPOLIES - AUSTRIA.
Morawetz, Inge, 1955- Die verborgene Macht . Frankfurt , New York , c1986. 200 p. : ISBN 3-593-33662-6 LC Card 86-223864
HG3008 .M67 1986

MONOPOLIES - CONGRESSES.
The Economics of market dominance /. Oxford, UK , New York, NY, USA , 1987. p. cm. ISBN 0-631-14784-5 : LC Card 86-26416 DDC 338.8/2 19
HD2326 .E24 1987

Probleme der staatsmonopolistischen Wirtschaftsregulierung . Rostock , 1981. 35 p. ; LC Card 86-211250
HB501 .P694 1981

MONOPOLIES - ECUADOR.
Los Grupos monopólicos en el Ecuador . Quito, Ecuador , 1986. 208 p. : LC Card 87-404236 DDC 338.8/2/09866 19
HD2838 .G78 1986

MONOPOLIES - GERMANY - HISTORY.
Proizvoditel'nye sily i monopolisticheskiĭ kapital v Rossii i Germanii v kontse XIX-nachale XX vv. /. Moskva , 1986. 223 p. ; LC Card 87-159751
HD2859 .P76 1986

MONOPOLIES, GOVERNMENT. see **GOVERNMENT MONOPOLIES.**

MONOPOLIES - GOVERNMENT POLICY - MATHEMATICAL MODELS.
Besanko, David, 1955- Designing regulatory policy with limited information /. Chur, Switzerland , New York , c1987. viii, 80 p. : ISBN 3-7186-0385-3 (pbk.) LC Card 87-277 DDC 351.82/6 19
HD3612 .B47 1987

MONOPOLIES - MATHEMATICAL MODELS.
Besanko, David, 1955- Designing regulatory policy with limited information /. Chur, Switzerland , New York , c1987. viii, 80 p. : ISBN 3-7186-0385-3 (pbk.) LC Card 87-277 DDC 351.82/6 19
HD3612 .B47 1987

Thomée, Friedrich, 1920- Dynamische Preisbildungsprozesse in Monopol /. Wiesbaden , c1983. 247 p. : ISBN 3-409-13035-7 : LC Card 84-116637
HB221 .T465 1983

MONOPOLIES, PARTIAL. see **OLIGOPOLIES.**

MONOPOLIES - SOVIET UNION - HISTORY.
Proizvoditel'nye sily i monopolisticheskiĭ kapital v Rossii i Germanii v kontse XIX-nachale XX vv. /. Moskva , 1986. 223 p. ; LC Card 87-159751
HD2859 .P76 1986

MONOPOLIES - UNITED STATES.
Asch, Peter. Economic theory and the antitrust dilemma /. Malabar, Fla. , 1984, c1970. x, 414 p. : ISBN 0-89874-699-X LC Card 83-19947 DDC 338.8/0973 19
HD2785 .A78 1984 ***NYPL [JLE 86-4132]***

Kozlova, K. B. Institutsionalizm v amerikanskoĭ politėkonomii . Moskva , 1987. 214, [2] p. ; LC Card 87-159642
HB99.5 .K69 1987

Primeaux, Walter J. Direct electric utility competition . New York, NY, USA , 1986. xiii, 297 p. ; ISBN 0-03-004858-3 (alk. paper) : LC Card 85-20487 DDC 338.8/26136362/0973 19
HD9685.U5 P74 1985 ***NYPL [JLE 86-4075]***

Monopoliia i imperiia . Parfenov, I. D. (Igor' Danilovich) Saratov , 1980. 191, [1] p. ; LC Card 81-142784
HD2845 .P36 1980

MONOPSONIES.
Bontrup, Heinz-J. Preisbildung bei Rüstungsgütern /. Köln , c1986. 247 p. ; ISBN 3-8046-8677-X LC Card 87-122749 DDC 338.4/36234 19
HD9743.A2 B59 1986

Köhler, Helmut, 1944- Nachfragewettbewerb und Marktbeherrschung /. Tübingen , 1986. 121 p. ; ISBN 3-16-345124-1 (Deut. Bibl.) LC Card 86-223313
HD2757.4 .K64 1986

Monro, Kate M. Taintor, Sarah Augusta. The secretary's handbook /. New York , London , c1988. p. cm. ISBN 0-02-008830-2 LC Card 87-24960 DDC 651.7/402 19
HF5547.5 .T29 1988

Monsell, William, 1812-1894. On some of the impediments to Irish manufacturing industry / by William Monsell. Dublin : J.F. Fowler, 1865. 48 p. ; 25 cm. "Containing I. A lecture given at the Limerick Athenaeum, on Tuesday, the 31st of January, 1865; and II. A speech made in the House of Commons on Friday, the 7th of April, 1865, in support of a motion that government should inquire into the Irish railway system." LC Card 85-666368
1. Ireland - Industries. 2. Railroads - Ireland. I. Title.
HC260.5 .M66x 1865

MONSOONS - ECONOMIC ASPECTS - ASIA.
Oshima, Harry T. (Harry Tatsumi) The transition to an industrial economy in monsoon Asia /. Manila, Philippines , c1983. 111 p. ; LC Card 87-105003 DDC 338.095 19
HC412 .O694 1983

Montador, Robert Bruce. Chouraqui, Jean Claude. Public debt in a medium-term context and its implications for fiscal policy /. [Paris, France] , c1986. 67 p. : LC Card 86-218210 DDC 339.5 19
HJ8030 .C48 1986

Montags biste sowieso geschafft : Frauen am Fliessband erzählen / Verena Born (Hrsg.).1. Aufl. Hamburg : Junius, 1982. 167 p. : ill. ; 21 cm. ISBN 3-88506-118-X (pbk.) LC Card 87-673006
1. Working class women - Germany (West) - Interviews. 2. Assembly-line methods. I. Born, Verena.
HD6068.2.G3 M66x 1982

Montana. Dept. of Labor and Industry. Research and Analysis Bureau. Montana industry and occupational employment outlook, 1984-1990 /. Helena, MT (P.O. Box 1728, Helena 59624) [1986] 100 p. : LC Card 86-622364 DDC 331.12/09786/021 19
HD5725.M9 M665 1986

MONTANA - ECONOMIC CONDITIONS.
Brower, John C. The economic impact of coal mining in Montana /. Missoula, Mont. [1985] 31 p. : LC Card 87-620608 DDC 338.2/724/09786 19
HD9547.M6 B76 1985

House, Verne W. Trends in the Montana economy and taxation /. Bozeman [1986] 19 p. : LC Card 87-620963 DDC 330.9786/033 19
HC107.M9 H68 1986

Montana industry and occupational employment outlook, 1984-1990 / State of Montana, Department of Labor and Industry, Research and Analysis Bureau. Helena, MT (P.O. Box

1728, Helena 59624) : The Bureau, [1986] 100 p. : ill. ; 28 cm. "June 1986." LC Card 86-622364 DDC 331.12/09786/021 19
1. Employment forecasting - Montana - Statistics. 2. Montana - Occupations - Forecasting - Statistics. I. Montana. Dept. of Labor and Industry. Research and Analysis Bureau.
HD5725.M9 M665 1986

Montana. Labor Market Information Section. Occupational employment statistics . Helena, Mont. (P.O. Box 1728, Helena 59624) [1986] ii, 93 p. : LC Card 86-622803 DDC 331.12/51/0009786021 19
HD5725.M9 O256 1986

MONTANA - OCCUPATIONS - FORECASTING - STATISTICS.
Montana industry and occupational employment outlook, 1984-1990 /. Helena, MT (P.O. Box 1728, Helena 59624) [1986] 100 p. : LC Card 86-622364 DDC 331.12/09786/021 19
HD5725.M9 M665 1986

MONTANA - OCCUPATIONS - STATISTICS.
Occupational employment statistics . Helena, Mont. (P.O. Box 1728, Helena 59624) [1986] ii, 93 p. : LC Card 86-622803 DDC 331.12/51/0009786021 19
HD5725.M9 O256 1986

Montana, Patrick J. Management / by Patrick Montana and Bruce Charnov. New York : Barron's, c1987. xi, 466 p. : ill. ; 23 cm. (Barron's business review series) Includes index. ISBN 0-8120-3559-3 (pbk.) : LC Card 87-1376 DDC 658 19
1. Management. I. Charnov, Bruce H. II. Title. III. Series.
HD31 .M618 1987

Montanari, Augusto, b. 1843. Nicolò Copernico ed il suo libro De monetae cudendae ratione : studio / del Augusto Montanari.2. ed. coll'aggiunta di una memoria del Dott. Arturo Wolynski premessa alla traduzione polacca di questo studio (Varsavia 1876). Padova : Minerva, 1877. 70 p. ; 17 cm. Includes bibliographical references. LC Card 85-666421
1. Copernicus, Nicolaus, 1473-1543. De monetae cudendae ratione. I. Title.
HG220.P6 C636x 1877

Montbrial, Thierry de. Marchés, capital et incertitude . Paris , c1986. 265 p. : ISBN 2-7178-1002-1 : LC Card 86-160930
HB615 .M37 1986

Monteiro, Jorge Vianna. Cavalcanti, Bianor Scelza. Administração da política industrial no Brasil . Rio de Janeiro , 1986. ii, 87, 10 p. : LC Card 87-102756 DDC 338.981 19
HD3616.B83 C28 1986

Montel, Werner, 1947- Fokkink, Manfred, 1955- Denk ja nicht, Du bist selber schuld . Gelsenkirchen-Buer , 1980. 180 p. : LC Card 82-114713
HD6276.G4 F6 1980 ***NYPL [JLE 86-1457]***

Monteleone, Franco, 1938- La Radio . Torino , c1984. 126 p., [41] p. of plates : LC Card 86-201755
HE8699.I8 R335 1984

Montemassi . Pertempi, Silvia. Torino , 1986. 238 p. ; ISBN 88-7011-250-0 : LC Card 87-134525
HD9506.I83 M656 1986

MONTEMASSI (ITALY) - ECONOMIC CONDITIONS.
Pertempi, Silvia. Montemassi . Torino , 1986. 238 p. ; ISBN 88-7011-250-0 : LC Card 87-134525
HD9506.I83 M656 1986

MONTEMASSI (ITALY) - SOCIAL CONDITIONS.
Pertempi, Silvia. Montemassi . Torino , 1986. 238 p. ; ISBN 88-7011-250-0 : LC Card 87-134525
HD9506.I83 M656 1986

Montero H., Martín. Cléves S., Rodrigo. Rendimientos de beneficiado de café . San José, Costa Rica , 1986. 35 leaves : LC Card 87-403521 DDC 338.1/6 19
HD9199.C82 C57 1986

The Monterrey elite and the Mexican State, 1880-1940 /. Saragoza, Alex. Austin , c1988. p. cm. ISBN 0-292-71113-1 LC Card 87-23779 DDC 305.5/234/097213 19
HG185.M6 S27 1988

MONTERREY (MEXICO) - INDUSTRIES - HISTORY.
Cerutti, Mario. Burguesía y capitalismo en Monterrey, 1850-1910 /. México, D.F. , 1983. 214 p. ; ISBN 968-8430-10-2 LC Card 86-221932
HC138.M6 C47 1983

Saragoza, Alex. The Monterrey elite and the Mexican State, 1880-1940 /. Austin , c1988. p. cm. ISBN 0-292-71113-1 LC Card 87-23779 DDC 305.5/234/097213 19
HG185.M6 S27 1988

Los montes de Toledo en el siglo XVIII . Sánchez González, Ramón. Toledo , 1984. 222 p. : ISBN 84-00-05873-9 LC Card 87-105458
HB3620.T62 S26 1984

Montes, José María. Los Problemas del conocimiento y la perspectiva ambiental del desarrollo /. México, D.F. , 1986. 476 p., [1] folded leaf of plates : ISBN 968-231-372-4 LC Card 87-119336 DDC 363.7/0098 19
HD75.6 .P76 1986

Montevideo (Uruguay). Intendencia Municipal. Vicario, Luis B. Algunas características del inventario de vivienda . [Montevideo] , 1985. 42 p. : LC Card 86-152477
HD7330.M64 V53 1985

Vicario, Luis B. Lineamientos básicos del Programa Habitacional de Emergencia, 1985-86 /. [Montevideo] , 1985. 25 p. : LC Card 87-122422 DDC 363.5/8 19
HD7287.96.U82 M668 1985

Montgomery County census update survey : summary report, 1984. [Silver Spring, Md.] (8787 Georgia Ave., Silver Spring 20907) : Montgomery County Planning Board, [1985] 59 p. : ill. ; 28 cm. "August 1985." LC Card 86-622600 DDC 304.6/09752/84 19
1. Montgomery County (Md.) - Population - Statistics. 2. Population forecasting - Maryland - Montgomery County - Statistics. I. Montgomery County Planning Board.
HA427.M65 M66 1985

MONTGOMERY COUNTY (MD.) - POPULATION - STATISTICS.
Montgomery County census update survey . [Silver Spring, Md.] (8787 Georgia Ave., Silver Spring 20907) [1985] 59 p. : LC Card 86-622600 DDC 304.6/09752/84 19
HA427.M65 M66 1985

Montgomery County Planning Board. Montgomery County census update survey . [Silver Spring, Md.] (8787 Georgia Ave., Silver Spring 20907) [1985] 59 p. : LC Card 86-622600 DDC 304.6/09752/84 19
HA427.M65 M66 1985

Montgomery, Robert Hiester, 1872-1953. [Auditing]
Montgomery's Auditing. 10th ed., Rev. college version / Philip L. Defliese ... [et al.]. New York : Wiley, c1987. xxv, 896 p. : ill. ; 25 cm. Includes bibliographical references and index. ISBN 0-471-85423-9 LC Card 86-28938 DDC 657/.45 19
1. Auditing. I. Defliese, Philip L. II. Title. III. Title: Auditing.
HF5667 .M7 1987

Montgomery, Stephen L. Profitable pricing strategies / Stephen L. Montgomery. New York : McGraw-Hill, c1988. xiii, 174 p. : ill. ; 24 cm. Bibliography: p. 161-162. Includes index. ISBN 0-07-042860-3 : LC Card 87-4089 DDC 658.8/16 19
1. Pricing. I. Title.
HF5416.5 .M67 1988

MONTGOMERY WARD - HISTORY.
Hoge, Cecil C. The first 100 years are the toughest /. Berkeley, Calif. , 1987. p. cm. ISBN 0-89815-221-6 LC Card 87-7077 DDC 380.1/45000/6073 19
HF5467.S4 H64 1987

Montgomery's Auditing. Montgomery, Robert Hiester, 1872-1953. [Auditing.] New York , c1987. xxv, 896 p. : ISBN 0-471-85423-9 LC Card 86-28938 DDC 657/.45 19
HF5667 .M7 1987

Monti, Aldino. Alle origini della borghesia urbana : la proprietà immobiliare a Bologna, 1797-1810 / Aldino Monti. Bologna : Società editrice il Mulino, c1985. 469 p. : ill. ; 22 cm. (Cultura e vita civile nel Settecento) Includes bibliographical references and index. ISBN 88-15-00833-0 : LC Card 86-110136 DDC 333.3/0945/41 19
1. Land tenure - Italy - Bologna - History. 2. Land reform - Italy - Bologna - History. 3. Social classes - Italy - Bologna - History. I. Title. II. Series.
HD680.B65 M66 1985 ***NYPL [JLD 87-481]***

Monticone, Alberto. La Storia dei poveri . Roma , c1985. xii, 300 p. ; ISBN 88-382-3530-9 : LC Card 86-198943
HC240.9.P6 S76 1985

Montoro, André Franco. São Paulo (Brazil : State). Governor (1982- : Montoro) O orçamento de São Paulo para 1984 /. São Paulo , 1983. 24 p. ; LC Card 87-130676 DDC 354.81/6100722 19
HJ2080.5.S3 S26 1983

Montoro Romero, Ricardo. La inserción en la actividad económica, empleo y paro juvenil / Ricardo Montoro Romero. 1a ed. Barcelona : Publicaciones de Juventud y Sociedad ; Madrid : Ministerio de Cultura, Instituto de la Juventud, c1985. 191 p. ; 21 cm. (Informe juventud en España . 6) Bibliography: p. 189-191. ISBN 84-86434-11-4 LC Card 86-186530
1. Youth - Employment - Spain. 2. Strikes and lockouts - Spain. I. Title. II. Series.
HD6276.S672 M65 1985

Montpellier, France. Centre d'histoire contemporaine du Languedoc méditerranéen et du Roussillon. see Centre d'histoire contemporaine du Languedoc méditerranéen et du Roussillon.

Montpellier, France. Institut agronomique méditerranéen. see Institut agronomique méditerranéen de Montpellier.

Montréal, Québec. McGill University. see McGill University.

Monza, Alfredo. Sraffa y sus usos / Alfredo Monza. 1a ed. Buenos Aires : Ediciones del IDES, 1985. 102 p. : ill. ; 18 cm. (Ediciones del IDES, 0326-6133 . 7.) Includes bibliographical references. ISBN 950-43-0654-3 LC Card 86-172226
1. Sraffa, Piero. 2. Economics. I. Series: Ediciones del IDES , 7. II. Title.
HB117.S73 M66 1985

Moock, Joyce Lewinger. Understanding Africa's rural households and farming systems /. Boulder , 1986. xiv, 234 p. : ISBN 0-8133-7175-9 : LC Card 85-32318 DDC 338.1/0967 19
HD1476.A357 U53 1986
NYPL [JLE 86-4336]

Moody, Fran. Bard, Ray. Breaking in . New York , 1985. 256 p. ; ISBN 0-688-05893-0 (pbk.) LC Card 85-6571 DDC 331.25/92/02573 19
HF5549.5.T7 B29 1985
NYPL [*R-Econ. 86-248]

Moody, Patricia G. Matthews, Anne L. Managerial dictation /. Cincinnati , c1987. 76 p. : ISBN 0-538-07950-9 (pbk.) LC Card 86-63922 DDC 651.7/4 19
HF5547.5 .M383 1987

Mookerji, Radhakumud, 1884-1964. Indian land-system : ancient, mediaeval, and modern, with special reference to Bengal / by Radha Kumud Mookerji. Alipore, Bengal : Supt., Govt. Print., Bengal Govt. Press, 1940. 112, v p. ; 26 cm. At head of title: Government of Bengal. Land Revenue Commission. Includes index. LC Card 87-123602
1. Land tenure - India - Bengal - History. I. Bengal (India). Land Revenue Commission. II. Title.
HD879.B4 M63 1940

Mooney, James E. (James Edward) Liability risk retention : choices, chances, and challenges : a review of the 1986 federal act and its prospects / by James E. Mooney. Springfield, N.J. (262 Mountain Ave., P.O. Box 50, Springfield 07081) : J.E. Mooney, c1987. i, 53 p. ; 28 cm. Cover title. LC Card 87-90408 DDC 368.5/00973 19
1. Insurance, Liability - United States. 2. Insurance, Products liability - United States. I. Title.
HG9990.3 .M66 1987

Mooney, Peter.
The Changing passenger car markets . Stamford, Conn., U. S.A. , c1985. viii, 227 leaves : ISBN 0-89336-479-7 (pbk.) LC Card 87-404429 DDC 381/.4566849 19
HD9710.U52 C385 1985

Plastics EMI shielding : state of the art, state of

the industry / Peter J. Mooney, project analyst. Stamford, Conn., U. S.A. : Business Communications Co., c1985. xxii, 297 leaves : ill. ; 29 cm. (Business opportunity report . GB-066R) "August 1985"--T.p. verso. ISBN 0-89336-409-6 (soft) LC Card 87-168832 DDC 338.4/76684 19
1. Plastics industry and trade - United States - Electric equipment. 2. Plastics in electric engineering - United States. 3. Shielding (Electricity). 4. Electromagnetic interference. I. Title. II. Series.
HD9661.U62 M654 1985

Plastics in business machines . Stamford, Conn. , c1986. vii, 215 leaves : ISBN 0-89336-433-6 (soft) : LC Card 87-165036 DDC 380.1/456684 19
HD9801.A2 P56 1986

Mooney, Sean, 1945- Basic concepts of accounting and taxation of property/casualty insurance companies /. New York, N.Y. , c1984. 66 p. : ISBN 0-932387-01-2 :
NYPL [JLE 86-2615]

Moonis Raza. see **Raza, Moonis.**

MOONLIGHTING. see **SUPPLEMENTARY EMPLOYMENT.**

Moore, Carl H., 1916- Money : its origin, development, and modern use / by Carl H. Moore and Alvin E. Russell. Jefferson, N.C. : McFarland, c1987. xi, 164 p. : ill. ; 24 cm. Bibliography: p. 157-158. Includes index. ISBN 0-89950-272-5 (lib. bdg.) : LC Card 87-42515 DDC 332.4/9 19
1. Money - History. 2. Money - United States - History. I. Russell, Alvin E. II. Title.
HG231 .M63 1987

Moore, Carl L. Profitable ratio analysis techniques / by Carl L. Moore. New York, N.Y., U. S.A. : Alexander Hamilton Institute, c1986. ix leaves, 201 p. : ill. ; 28 cm. (Modern business reports) ISBN 0-86604-206-7 (pbk.) LC Card 86-208178 DDC 658.4/033 19
1. Ratio analysis. 2. Industrial management. I. Title. II. Series.
HF5681.R25 M58 1986

Moore, Carol Ann. Evaluating business and industry training /. Boston , Norwell, MA , c1987. xv, 294 p. : ISBN 0-89838-197-5 LC Card 87-5771 DDC 658.3/12404 19
HF5549.5.T7 E88 1987

Moore, Christopher W., 1947- The mediation process : practical strategies for resolving conflict / Christopher W. Moore.1st ed. San Francisco : Jossey-Bass, 1986. xxii, 348 p. ; 24 cm. (Jossey-Bass social and behavioral science series) Includes index. Bibliography: p. 321-336. ISBN 0-87589-673-1 (alk. paper) LC Card 85-23675 DDC 302.3 19
1. Mediation. 2. Conflict management. I. Title.
HM136 .M684 1986 NYPL [JLE 86-3017]

Moore, F. Richard. Programming in C with a bit of UNIX / F. Richard Moore. Englewood Cliffs, NJ : Prentice-Hall, 1985. vii, 193 p. : ill. ; 24 cm. Includes index. Chapter 7 is devoted entirely to the discussion of bibliographical references. ISBN 0-13-730102-2 : LC Card 84-26642 DDC 001.64/24 19
1. C (Computer program language). 2. UNIX (Computer operating system). I. Title.
QA76.73.C15 M66 1985
NYPL [JSE 86-1377]

Moore, Gary A. Labor and the economy : an introduction to analysis, issues, and institutions / Gary A. Moore, Randyl D. Elkin. Cincinnati : South-Western Pub. Co., c1983. viii, 502 p. : ill. ; 24 cm. "H75." Includes bibliographies and index. ISBN 0-538-08750-1 LC Card 81-85863 DDC 331/.0973 19
1. Labor economics. 2. Labor and laboring classes - United States. I. Elkin, Randyl D. II. Title.
HD4901 .M825 1983 NYPL [JLE 87-831]

Moore, George S. (George Stevens), 1905- The banker's life / George S. Moore. 1st ed. New York : Norton, c1987. 328 p., [20] p. of plates : ill. ; 24 cm. Erratum slip inserted. Includes index. ISBN 0-393-02458-X LC Card 86-31123 DDC 332.1/092/4 B 19
1. Moore, George S. (George Stevens), 1905-. 2. Bankers - New York (N.Y.) - Biography. I. Title.
HG2463.M59 A3 1987

MOORE, GEORGE S. (GEORGE STEVENS), 1905-
Moore, George S. (George Stevens), 1905- The banker's life /. New York , c1987. 328 p., [20] p. of plates : ISBN 0-393-02458-X LC Card 86-31123 DDC 332.1/092/4 B 19
HG2463.M59 A3 1987

Moore, James M. (James Mendon), 1925- An engineers guide to spreadsheets, word processors & data base managers / James M. Moore and William E. Hammer, Jr. Norcross, GA : Institute of Industrial Engineers : Copies may be obtained from Industrial Engineering and Management Press, c1986. xi, 154 p. : ill. ; 23 cm. Includes bibliographies and index. ISBN 0-89806-081-8 (pbk.) LC Card 87-157586 DDC 620/.0028/553 19
1. Electronic spreadsheets. 2. Word processors. 3. Data base management. I. Hammer, William E. II. Title.
HF5548 .M566 1986

Moore, Janice D. Thorne. A step toward independence: economic self sufficiency : a manual for domestic violence programs developing, employment training, and small business projects / prepared by Janice D. Thorne Moore for the National Coalition Against Domestic Violence, Employment Training and Small Business Project. Washington, D.C. : The Project, c1986. iii, 117 p. : ill. ; 28 cm. Bibliography: p. 110-111. LC Card 86-209069 DDC 362.8/3 19
1. Occupational training for women - United States. 2. Small business - United States. 3. New business enterprises - United States. 4. Abused women - Employment - United States. I. National Coalition Against Domestic Violence (U. S.). Employment Training and Small Business Project. II. Title.
HD6059.6.U6 M66 1986

Moore, Jim. Trends in the disposable incomes of Australian families, 1964-65 to 1985-86 / Jim Moore and Peter Whiteford. Woden, ACT : Social Security Review, Dept. of Social Security, [1986] vii, 103 p. ; 30 cm. (Research paper . no. 31) Background/discussion paper ; no. 11 Bibliography: p. 35-37. ISBN 0-642-51700-2 (pbk.) LC Card 87-154435 DDC 339.394 19
1. Income - Australia - Statistics. 2. Social security - Australia - Statistics. I. Whiteford, Peter. II. Series: Research paper (Australia. Dept. of Social Security. Development Division) , no. 31. III. Title.
HC610.I5 M66 1986

Moore, John Hebron. The emergence of the Cotton Kingdom in the Old Southwest : Mississippi, 1770-1860 / John Hebron Moore. Baton Rouge : Louisiana State University Press, c1988. xii, 323 p. : map ; 23 cm. Bibliography: p. [299]-313. Includes index. ISBN 0-8071-1404-9 (pbk.) LC Card 87-2803 DDC 330.9762 19
1. Mississippi - Economic conditions. 2. Cotton trade - Mississippi - History. 3. Plantation life - Mississippi - History. 4. Slavery - Mississippi - History. I. Title.
HC107.M7 M66 1988

Moore, L. K. S. (Linda K. S.) Videotext and home banking services in France. New York, NY (654 Madison Ave., New York 10021) : Research Co. of America, c1986. 59, 3 leaves : ill. ; 21 x 31 cm. (Electronic banking abroad) LC Card 86-203144 DDC 332.1/028 19
1. Home banking services - France. 2. Videotex (Data transmission system) - France. I. Title. II. Series.
HG1711 .M66 1986

Moore, Lynda L. Not as far as you think : the realities of working women / Lynda L. Moore. Lexington, Mass. : Lexington Books, c1986. xii, 201 p. ; 24 cm. Includes bibliographical references. ISBN 0-669-10836-7 : LC Card 85-40109 DDC 331.4/0973 19
1. Women - Employment - United States - Addresses, essays, lectures. 2. Sex discrimination in employment - United States - Addresses, essays, lectures. 3. Women - United States - Psychology - Addresses, essays, lectures. I. Title.
HD6095 .M66 1986 NYPL [JLE 86-1878]

Moore, Mark Harrison. Inspectors-general : junkyard dogs or man's best friend / by Mark H. Moore and Margaret Jane Gates. New York : Russell Sage Foundation, c1986. 120 p. ; 24 cm. (Social research perspectives : occasional reports on current topics . 13) Includes bibliographical references. ISBN 0-87154-605-1 : LC Card 86-6728 DDC 353.0072/32 19
1. Finance, Public - United States - Accounting. 2. Administrative agencies - United States - Auditing. 3. United States - Executive departments - Auditing. I. Gates, Margaret Jane. II. Series: Social research perspectives , 13. III. Title.
HJ9801 .M66 1987 NYPL [JLE 87-1762]

Moore, Richard H. Japanese agriculture : patterns of rural development / by Richard H. Moore. Boulder : Westview Press, 1987. p. cm. (Westview special studies on Asia) Bibliography: p. ISBN 0-8133-7406-5 LC Card 87-13553 DDC 338.1/0952/115 19
1. Land tenure - Japan - Nakada-chō (Miyagi-ken). 2. Agriculture and state - Japan - Nakada-chō (Miyagi-ken). 3. Rural development - Japan - Nakada-chō (Miyagi-ken). 4. Rice - Japan - Nakada-chō (Miyagi-ken). I. Title. II. Series.
HD920.N33 M65 1987

Moore, Sarah J. Lambert, Richard D. The transformation of an Indian labor market . Amsterdam , Philadelphia , 1986. ix, 249 p. ; ISBN 0-915027-63-1 (alk. paper) : LC Card 86-26900 DDC 331.11/0954/792 19
HD5820.P78 L36 1986

Moore, Sylvia F.
Langwell, Kathryn M. A synthesis of research on competition in the financing and delivery of health services /. Hyattsville, MD. , Springfield, VA , 1982. 85 p. ; LC Card 82-600612 DDC 338.4/73621/0973 19
RA410.53 .L36 1982 NYPL [JLF 86-422]

The short-term effects of marital disruption on the labor supply behavior of young women / Sylvia F. Moore. Columbus, Ohio (Suite 585, 1375 Perry St., Columbus, Ohio, 43201) : Center for Human Resource Research, College of Administrative Science, Ohio State University. 1979. v, 133 p. ; ill. ; 28 cm. "October 1979." "Prepared under a contract with the employment and Training Administration, U. S. Dept of Labor, under authority of The Comprehensive employment and training act." Bibliography: p. 130-133.
1. Women - Employment - United States. 2. Labor supply - United States. I. Ohio. State University, Columbus. Center for Human Resource Research. II. Title. *NYPL [JLF 86-649]*

Moorsom, Richard. The scope for sanctions : economic measures against South Africa / Richard Moorsom. London : Catholic Institute for International Relations, 1986. 102 p. ; 21 cm. Bibliography: p. 87-91. ISBN 0-946848-66-1 (pbk.) : LC Card 86-226230 DDC 337.41068 19
1. Economic sanctions - South Africa. 2. Great Britain - Foreign economic relations - South Africa. 3. South Africa - Foreign economic relations - Great Britain. I. Title.
HF1613.4 .M66 1986

Moosmann, Bernfried, 1957- Mittelbetriebe und Entwicklungsländer : zur Auslandstätigkeit mittelständischer Unternehmen aus Baden-Württemberg im Bereich der Entwicklungsländer / Bernfried Moosmann. Frankfurt am Main ; New York : P. Lang, c1986. x, 290 p. ; 21 cm. (Europäische Hochschulschriften. Reihe V, Volks- und Betriebswirtschaft, 0531-7339 . Bd. 747 = vol. 747 = vol. 747) Originally presented as the author's thesis (doctoral)--Universität Konstanz, 1986. Bibliography: p. 261-290. ISBN 3-8204-9518-5 LC Card 86-232976
1. Baden-Württemberg (Germany) - Commerce - Developing countries. 2. Developing countries - Commerce - Germany (West) - Baden-Württemberg. 3. Small business - Germany (West) - Baden-Württemberg. I. Series: Europäische Hochschulschriften. Reihe V, Volks- und Betriebswirtschaft , Bd. 747. II. Title.
HF3569.B2 M66 1986

Mora Forero, Jorge Rafael. Introducción a los problemas del subdesarrollo en América Latina / por Jorge R. Mora Forero. 2a ed. Bogotá, D.E., Colombia : Universidad Pedagógica Nacional, Departamento Ciencias Sociales, 1984. 96 p. ; 22 cm. Bibliography: p. 89-95. ISBN 958-95030-9-8 LC Card 86-137776 DDC 338.98 19
1. Latin America - Economic conditions - 1945-. 2. Marginality, Social - Latin America. 3. Economic development. I. Title.
HC125 .M615 1984

Mora, Teresa. La Mixteca baja, su migración : Nieves Ixpantepec y San Nicolás Hidalgo, Oax. / Teresa Mora Vázquez. México, D.F. : Instituto Nacional de Antropología e Historia, Departamento de Etnología y Antropología Social, 1982. 129, [84] leaves ; 28 cm. (Cuadernos / DEAS-INAH . 30) Bibliography: leaves 125-129. LC Card 87-122391 DDC 304.6/0972/74

19
1. Oaxaca (Mexico) - Population. 2. Migration, Internal - Mexico. 3. Mixtec Indians - Population. 4. Indians of Mexico - Population. 5. Oaxaca (Mexico) - Economic conditions. I. Series: Cuadernos de trabajo (Instituto Nacional de Antropología e Historia (Mexico). Departamento de Etnología y Antropología Social) , 30. II. Title.
HB3532.O18 M67 1982

Moradiellos, Enrique. El Sindicato de los obreros mineros de Asturias, 1910-1930 / Enrique Moradiellos. Oviedo : Universidad de Oviedo, Servicio de Publicaciones, 1986. 158 p. : ill. ; 22 cm. Bibliography: p. 155-158. ISBN 84-7468-111-1 LC Card 86-212987
1. Sindicato de los Obreros Mineros de Asturias - History. 2. Trade-unions - Miners - Spain - Asturias - History. I. Title.
HD6764.M62 O375 1986

Moraes, Olacyr Francisco de. História empresarial vivida /. São Paulo , 1986-<1987. v. <1-3 > ; LC Card 86-226035
HD70.B7 H57 1986

Morais, Benedict. Public relations . Kuala Lumpur , 1986. 259 p. : LC Card 86-944684 DDC 659.2/09595 19
HD59.6.M4 P83 1986

MORAL PHILOSOPHY. see **ETHICS.**

Moral rights in the workplace / edited by Gertrude Ezorsky ; James W. Nickel, advisory editor. Albany : State University of New York Press, c1987. xii, 312 p. ; 24 cm. "Published under the sponsorship of the National Society for Philosophy and Public Affairs." Includes bibliographies. ISBN 0-88706-362-4 LC Card 86-6949 DDC 331.25 19
1. Quality of work life - United States. 2. Civil rights - United States. 3. Industrial relations - United States. I. Ezorsky, Gertrude, 1926-. II. Nickel, James W.
HD6957.U6 M67 1987 *NYPL [JLE 87-1197]*

Morale e morali /. Sichirollo, Livio. Roma , 1985. 179 p. ; ISBN 88-359-2798-6 : LC Card 85-233121 DDC 170/.9 19
BJ74 .S53 1985 *NYPL [JFD 87-941]*

MORALE, EMPLOYEE. see **EMPLOYEE MORALE.**

Morales Anaya, Rolando. Morales, Juan Antonio. Coyuntura económica /. La Paz , 1987. 99 p. : LC Card 87-403036 DDC 330.984/052 19
HC182 .M66 1987

Morales, Argemiro. Flórez Nieto, Carmen Elisa. The existence of a Latin American mortality pattern . Bogotá, Colombia , 1985. 153 p. : LC Card 87-145922
HB1397 .F56 1985

Morales C., Pedro A. Política industrial y adquisición de tecnología en la actividad química en Costa Rica / Pedro A. Morales C. [San José, Costa Rica] : Universidad de Costa Rica, Instituto de Investigaciones en Ciencias Económicas, [1984] ii, 55 p. ; 28 cm. (Documentos de trabajo . no. 71) Bibliography: p. 55. LC Card 86-199221
1. Chemical industry - Government policy - Costa Rica. 2. Chemical industry - Costa Rica - Technological innovations. I. Series: Documentos de trabajo (Universidad de Costa Rica. Instituto de Investigaciones en Ciencias Económicas) , no. 71. II. Title.
HD9655.C82 M67 1984

Morales, Cesáreo. Aún tiembla . México , c1986. 332 p., [8] p. of plates : ISBN 968-419-620-2 LC Card 87-403523 DDC 363.3/495/097253 19
HC138.M43 A95 1986

Morales, Juan Antonio. Coyuntura económica / Juan Antonio Morales, Rolando Morales ; responsable, Samuel Doria Medina. La Paz : ILDIS : Econométrica, 1987. 99 p. : col. ill. ; 21 cm. Bibliography: p. 92-99. LC Card 87-403036 DDC 330.984/052 19
1. Bolivia - Economic conditions - 1982-. 2. Bolivia - Economic policy. I. Morales Anaya, Rolando. II. Doria Medina, Samuel, 1958-. III. Title.
HC182 .M66 1987

Morales, Nelson. Gómez-Samper, Henry. Los módulos de servicios . Caracas , c1984. 48, 3 [i.e. 4] leaves ; ISBN 980-217-005-4 LC Card 86-193565
HD4343 .G65 1984

MORALITY. see **ETHICS.**

Morality and economics . Vanberg, Viktor. New Brunswick [N.J.] , 1987. p. cm ISBN 0-912051-19-1 (pbk.) LC Card 87-19213 DDC 174/.26 19
HB72 .V268 1987

Morality of the market : religious and economic perspectives / contributors include Kenneth E. Boulding ... [et al.] ; edited by Walter Block, Geoffrey Brennan, Kenneth Elzinga. Vancouver, B.C., Canada : Fraser Institute, c1985. xxv, 601 p. ; 22 cm. "Proceedings of an International Symposium on Religion, Economics, and Social Thought, held August 9-11, 1982 in Vancouver, British Columbia"--Verso t.p. Includes bibliographies and index. ISBN 0-88975-074-2 (pbk.) : LC Card 86-158049 DDC 174/.4 19
1. Economics - Religious aspects - Congresses. 2. Religion and politics - Congresses. 3. Religion and sociology - Congresses. 4. Capitalism - Religious aspects - Congresses. 5. Socialism and religion. I. Boulding, Kenneth Ewart, 1910-. II. Block, Walter, 1941-. III. Brennan, H. Geoffrey, 1944-. IV. Elzinga, Kenneth G. V. International Symposium on Religion, Economics, and Social Thought (1982 : Vancouver, B.C.). VI. Fraser Institute (Vancouver, B.C.).
HB72 .M56 1985

MORALS. see **ETHICS.**

Moran, Justin L., 1932- Marketing strategies for community banks / Justin L. Moran. Boston : Bankers, [c1987] xiii, 199 p. ; 24 cm. ISBN 0-87267-105-4 LC Card 87-19280 DDC 332.1/068/8 19
1. Bank marketing. I. Title.
HG1616.M3 M67 1987

Moran, Robert, 1928- Converging voice/data/video technologies at the workstation /. Stamford, Conn., U. S.A. , c1986. v, 119 leaves ; ISBN 0-89336-466-5 (pbk.) LC Card 87-168057 DDC 380.1/45004 19
HD9801.A2 C66 1986

Moran, Robert T., 1938- Harris, Philip R. (Philip Robert), 1926- Managing cultural differences /. Houston , c1987. xiii, 609 p. : ISBN 0-87201-161-5 LC Card 86-25618 DDC 658.1/8 19
HD62.4 .H37 1987

Moran, Thomas J. Stapleton, Charles O. California real estate principles /. Chicago , c1987. xvi, 428, 8 p. : ISBN 0-88462-569-9 (pbk.) LC Card 86-24870 DDC 333.33/09794 19
HD266.C2 S73 1987

Morandi, Larry B. Renewing resources : a critique of the issues / by Larry Morandi, Gordon Meeks, Jr., Douglas M. Sacarto. Denver, Colo. : National Conference of State Legislatures, 1984. vii, 133 p. ; 28 cm. Bibliography: p. 127-133.
1. Renewable natural resources - United States. 2. Water-supply - United States. 3. Water - Pollution - United States. 4. Air - Pollution - United States. 5. Forest policy - United States. I. Meeks, Gordon. II. Sacarto, Douglas M. III. Title.
NYPL [JSF 86-712]

Morata, Pedro Costa. see **Costa Morata, Pedro.**

Moratória com diretas já . Luca, Walmor de. Brasília , 1984. 69 p. ; LC Card 86-152773
HC188.S26 L83 1984

Morawetz, Inge, 1955-
Stahl und Eisen bricht . Wien [1986] xi, 202 p. : ISBN 3-900351-62-7 LC Card 87-140293 DDC 330.9436/053 19
HC265 .S736 1986

Die verborgene Macht : personelle Verflechtungen zwischen Grossbanken, Industrie und Unternehmerverbänden in Österreich / Inge Morawetz. Frankfurt ; New York : Campus, c1986. 200 p. : ill. ; 21 cm. (Campus Forschung. Bd. 499) Bibliography: p. 176-185. ISBN 3-593-33662-6 LC Card 86-223864
1. Banks and banking - Austria. 2. Corporations - Austria. 3. Employers' associations - Austria. 4. Monopolies - Austria. 5. Capitalism - Austria. I. Title.
HG3008 .M67 1986

Mørch, Henning. Befolkningsbeskrivelse : noter til befolkningsgeografi / Henning Mørch.2. udg. [Copenhagen] : Laboratorium for kulturøkologi og landbrugsgeografi ; Brenderup : I kommission hos Geografforlaget, 1982. 160 p. : ill. ; 30 cm. Bibliography: p. 126-127. ISBN 87-87601-58-1 LC Card 83-195528
1. Population. 2. Population geography. 3. Denmark - Population. I. Title.
HB871 .M27 1982

Morche, S. Soziale Aspekte der Mikroelektronik /. Berlin , 1985. 122 p. ; LC Card 87-409418 DDC 306/.46 19
HD6331 .S683 1985

Mordasova, L. A. (Lidiía Andrianovna) Trudovye resursy v torgovle / L.A. Mordasova. Moskva : Ėkonomika, 1985. 128 p. ; 20 cm. Includes bibliographical references. LC Card 86-158800
1. Labor and laboring classes - Soviet Union. 2. Labor supply - Soviet Union. 3. Soviet Union - Commerce. I. Title.
HD8526.5 .M54 1985

Mordey, R. (Richard) Planning control . London , Wolfeboro, N.H. , c1987. 234 p. ; ISBN 0-7099-3790-3 : LC Card 86-24079 DDC 333.73/17/0941 19
HD596 .P53 1987 *NYPL [JLD 87-803]*

MORDOVSKAÍA A.S.S.R. (R.S.F.S.R.) - ECONOMIC CONDITIONS - STATISTICS.
Narodnoe khoziaĭstvo Mordovskoĭ ASSR za gody odinnadtsatoĭ piatiletki, 1981-1985 gg. . Saransk , 1986. 198 p. ; LC Card 87-120800
HA1448.M59 N33 1986

MORDOVSKAÍA A.S.S.R. (R.S.F.S.R.) - STATISTICS.
Narodnoe khoziaĭstvo Mordovskoĭ ASSR za gody odinnadtsatoĭ piatiletki, 1981-1985 gg. . Saransk , 1986. 198 p. ; LC Card 87-120800
HA1448.M59 N33 1986

More children of better quality? . Kälvemark, Ann-Sofie, 1941- Uppsala , Stockholm , 1980. 160 p. : ISBN 91-554-1094-4 LC Card 81-114081
HB3617 .K34 1980

More profit from your retail business . Husack, Glen A. [S.l.] , c1977. 84 p. : ISBN 0-88896-066-2 (pbk.) LC Card 85-174558
HF5429 .H85 1977

More words of Wall Street . Pessin, Allan H. Homewood, Ill. , 1986. v, 269 p. ; ISBN 0-87094-701-X LC Card 86-70777
NYPL [JLE 86-4060]

Moreau, David H. Snyder, Thomas (Thomas P.) Paying for growth . Washington, D.C. , 1986. x, 133 p. : ISBN 0-87420-663-4 (pbk.) LC Card 86-51156 DDC 338.4/3363/0973 19
HJ9156 .S69 1986

Moreau, François. Le développement international des banques canadiennes : croissance, expansion, concentration / François Moreau. Montréal, Québec : Editions Saint-Martin, c1985. 159 p. ; 23 cm. (Collection "Interventions économiques") Bibliography: p. [153]-159. ISBN 2-89035-120-3 LC Card 86-186883
1. Banks and banking, Canadian. 2. Banks and banking, International. I. Series: Collection "Interventions économiques". II. Title.
HG2704 .M67 1985

Moreira, Lino. Marsh, Lawrence. Employment and technological choice of multinational enterprises in developing countries . Geneva , 1983. iii, 37 p. ; ISBN 92-2-103353-8 (pbk.) : LC Card 86-213692 DDC 338.8/8854 19
HD2932 .M35 1983

Moreira, Marcílio Marques. The Brazilian quandary / by Marcílio Marques Moreira. New York : Priority Press Publications, 1986. vi, 87 p. : ill. ; 23 cm. "A Twentieth Century Fund paper." Bibliography: p. 75-87. ISBN 0-87078-171-5 (pbk.) : LC Card 86-210942 DDC 332.3/4/0981 19
1. Debts, External - Brazil. 2. Brazil - Economic conditions - 1945-1964. 3. Brazil - Economic conditions - 1964-1985. I. Title.
HJ8579 .M66 1986

Moreira, Maria Neuman Ribeiro. Fernandes, Adelita Neto Carleial. Condições de vida nos bairros de Fortaleza, nov/84 a mar/85 . Fortaleza , 1986. 92 p. : LC Card 86-196902
HC189.F67 F47 1986

Morel, Bernard. Sanmarco, Philippe. Marseille, l'endroit du décor /. La Calade, Aix-en-Provence , 1985. 191 p. : ISBN 2-85744-219-X : LC Card 86-168990
HC278.M3 S26 1985

Morell Peguero, Blanca. Mercaderes y artesanos en la Sevilla del descubrimiento / Blanca Morell Peguero. Sevilla : Diputación Provincial, 1986. 222 p. ; 25 cm. (Publicaciones de la Excma.

Diputación Provincial de Sevilla. Sección Historia . ser. 1a, no. 29) Bibliography: p. [219]-222. ISBN 84-505-2883-6 LC Card 86-199625
1. Artisans - Spain - Seville - History - 16th century. 2. Merchants - Spain - Seville - History - 16th century. 3. Seville (Spain) - Economic conditions. 4. Seville (Spain) - Social conditions. I. Title. II. Series.
HD2346.S72 S465 1986

Morelos, José B. Fernández, Sonia. Análisis comparativo de la información sobre población ocupada . México, D.F. [1977] 28 p. ; LC Card 84-227473
HD5731.A6 F46 1977

Moreno Torregrosa, Pasqual. El Mercado Común frente a la agricultura española / por Pasqual Moreno Torregrosa. Madrid : Ediciones "Vanguardia Obrera", [1986?] 127 p. ; 20 cm. (Serie Documentos) Bibliography: p. 125-127. ISBN 84-86293-27-8 LC Card 86-202333
1. Agriculture - Economic aspects - Spain - History - 20th century. 2. European Economic Community - Spain. I. Title.
HD2022 .M67 1986

Morgan, Ann D. British imports of consumer goods : a study of import penetration 1974-85 / Ann D. Morgan. Cambridge [Cambridgeshire] ; New York : Cambridge University Press, 1988. xi, 129 p. ; 24 cm. (Occasional papers / the National Institute of Economic and Social Research . 42) Bibliography: p. 125-127. Includes index. ISBN 0-521-35349-1 LC Card 87-25662 DDC 382/.5/0941 19
1. Great Britain - Commerce. I. Series: Occasional papers (National Institute of Economic and Social Research) , 42. II. Title.
HF3506.5 .M67 1988

Morgan, David R. Intergovernmental relations and public policy /. New York , 1986. viii, 224 p. : ISBN 0-313-25443-5 (lib. bdg. : alk. paper) LC Card 86-3155 DDC 353.9/29 19
JK325 .I575 1986 ***NYPL [JLE 87-749]***

Morgan, Eleanor. Corporate taxation and investment : the implication of the 1984 tax reform / Eleanor J. Morgan. Haldershot, Hants Gull, England ; Brookfield, Vt., USA : Gower Pub. Co., c1986. x, 220 p. ; 22 cm. Bibliography: p. 214-216. ISBN 0-566-05265-2 : LC Card 86-25642 DDC 336.24/3/0941 19
1. Corporations - Taxation - Great Britain - Case studies. 2. Investments - Taxation - Great Britain - Case studies. 3. Tax incentives - Great Britain - Case studies. I. Title.
HJ4708.A7 M63 1986

Morgan-Gérard, Florence. Equal opportunities and vocational training : catalogue of training innovations in the EC member states / Florence Morgan-Gérard. Berlin : European Centre for the Development of Vocational Training, [1982] 69 p. ; 20 cm. "Results of a survey conducted in the member states of the European Communities by the European Centre for the Development of Vocational Training (CEDEFOP), Berlin, 1980." ISBN 92-825-2489-2
1. Occupational training - European Economic Community countries. 2. Labor supply - European Economic Community countries. I. European Centre for the Development of Vocational Training. II. Title.
NYPL [JLD 87-1318]

Morgan-Grenville, Fern. The Green alternative . London , 1987. xv, 368 p. : ISBN 0-413-60280-X : LC Card 87-143624 DDC 333.7/2 19
HC260.E5 G736 1987

Morgan, James N. Burpee, C. Gaye. 1985 household survey of Grenada . Ann Arbor, Mich. , 1986. 168 p. : ISBN 0-87944-317-0 (pbk.) LC Card 86-217405 DDC 339.4/1/0723 19
HD7009.9.Z8 G843 1986

Morgan, Jane. Conflict and order : the police and labour disputes in England and Wales, 1900-1939 / Jane Morgan. Oxford [Oxfordshire] ; New York : Clarendon Press, c1987. p. cm. Bibliography: p. Includes index. ISBN 0-19-820128-1 : LC Card 87-11027 DDC 331.89/2942 19
1. Labor disputes - England - History - 20th century. 2. Labor disputes - Wales - History - 20th century. 3. Police - England - History - 20th century. 4. Police - Wales - History - 20th century. I. Title.
HD5366.A6 M67 1987

Morgan Management Systems, Inc.
Startzel, Donna C. The CETA arts and humanities experience [microform] CETA Ahead project (Arts and humanities employment analysis and documentation) /. Columbia, Md. , 1981. 197 p. ;
NYPL [*XME-11,320]

Startzel, Donna C. CETA (Comprehensive Employment and Training Act) and the arts and humanities [microform] . Columbia, Md. , 1981. 160 p. ; ***NYPL [*XME-11,328]***

Morgunov, ÎU. G. (ÎUriĭ Grigor´evich) Pochtovye marki . Moskva , 1984. 223 p. : LC Card 85-185295
HE6185.C92 P63 1984

Mori, Joseph E. Pahler, Arnold J. Advanced accounting . San Diego , c1988. xxi, 1208 p. : ISBN 0-15-501827-2 LC Card 87-81162 DDC 657/.046 19
HF5635 .P215 1988

Morial, Ernest N. Meyers, Edward M. Rebuilding America's cities . Cambridge, Mass. , c1986. xxi, 290 p. : ISBN 0-88730-051-0 LC Card 85-30780 DDC 307.3/4/0973 19
HT175 .U59 1986 ***NYPL [JLE 86-2874]***

Morin, André, analyste en rémunération.
Analyse de l'évolution des principaux indicateurs économiques au Québec, en Ontario, au Canada et aux Etats-Unis : 1965-1980. [Québec] : Gouvernement du Québec, Conseil du trésor, Bureau de recherche sur la rémunération, [1982] 209 p. ; 28 cm. Cover title. Chiefly tables. "Préparé par messieurs André Morin et Jean Nadeau ... sous la direction de monsieur Jacques Chouinard"--P. [3] ISBN 2-551-04641-6 LC Card 83-103355
1. Economic indicators - Québec (Province). 2. Economic indicators - Ontario. 3. Economic indicators - United States. 4. Economic indicators - Canada. 5. Québec (Province) - Economic conditions - Statistics. 6. Ontario - Economic conditions - Statistics. 7. Canada - Economic conditions - 1945- - Statistics. 8. United States - Economic conditions - 1961- - Statistics. I. Nadeau, Jean. II. Chouinard, Jacques, 1944-. III. Québec (Province). Conseil du trésor. Bureau de la recherche sur la rémunération. IV. Title.
HC117.Q4 M66 1982

Nadeau, Jean. Les indicateurs globaux de la productivité . Québec [1982] 41 p. : ISBN 2-551-05072-3 LC Card 83-221751
HC120.I52 N33 1982

Morin, Jean, 1875-1969. Souvenirs d'un banquier français : 1875-1947 / Jean Morin. Paris : Denoël, c1983. 326 p., [8] p. of plates : ill. ; 23 cm. ISBN 2-207-22988-2 : LC Card 84-172168
1. Morin, Jean, 1875-1969. 2. Bankers - France - Biography. 3. Banks and banking - France - History. 4. Crédit lyonnais - History. I. Title.
HG1552.M67 A3 1983

MORIN, JEAN, 1875-1969.
Morin, Jean, 1875-1969. Souvenirs d'un banquier français . Paris , c1983. 326 p., [8] p. of plates : ISBN 2-207-22988-2 : LC Card 84-172168
HG1552.M67 A3 1983

Morineau, Michel.
Incroyables gazettes et fabuleux métaux : les retours des trésors américains d'après les gazettes hollandaises (XVIe-XVIIIe siècles) / Michel Morineau. London ; New York : Cambridge University Press ; 687 p. : ill. ; 24 cm. (Studies in modern capitalism = Etudes sur le capitalisme moderne) Bibliography: p. [656]-679. ISBN 0-521-25384-5 : LC Card 83-7177 DDC 330.94/022 19
1. Precious metals - Europe - History. 2. Precious metals - Spain - History. 3. Precious metals - Portugal - History. 4. Precious metals - America - History. 5. Europe - Economic conditions. I. Title. II. Title: Gazettes hollandaises.
HC240 .M73 1985 ***NYPL [JLE 85-1587]***

Pour une histoire économique vraie / Michel Morineau. [Lille] : Presses universitaires de Lille, c1985. 512 p. : ill. ; 25 cm. (Economies et sociétés) Includes bibliographical references. ISBN 2-85939-234-3 : LC Card 86-142388 DDC 330.9 19
1. Economic history. I. Series: Economies et sociétés (Lille, France). II. Title.
HC51 .M64 1985

Morínigo, José N. Las artesanías de cuero y tejido en el Paraguay : estructura y dinámica del mercado en la región central / José Nicolás Morínigo, Antonio Valenzuela C. Pecci. Asunción : Comité de Iglesias, 1979. 106, [1] p. : ill. ; 27 cm. (Cuadernos de investigación . doc. no. 3) "Mayo 1979." Bibliography: p. [107] LC Card 83-219583
1. Leather industry and trade - Paraguay - Asunción Region. 2. Leather industry and trade - Paraguay. 3. Textile industry - Paraguay - Asunción Region. 4. Textile industry - Paraguay. I. Valenzuela C. Pecci, Antonio. II. Title.
HD9780.P373 A866 1979
NYPL [JLF 86-1810]

Morita, Akio, 1921- Made in Japan : Akio Morita and Sony / Akio Morita with Edwin M. Reingold and Mitsuko Shimomura.1st ed. New York : Dutton, c1986. viii, 309 p., [8] p. of plates : ill., ports. ; 25 cm. ISBN 0-525-24465-4 : LC Card 86-11479 DDC 338.7/6213/0924 B 19
1. Morita, Akio, 1921-. 2. Sonī Kabushiki Kaisha - History. 3. Industrialists - Japan - Biography. 4. Electronic industries - Japan - History. I. Reingold, Edwin M. II. Shimomura, Mitsuko, 1938-. III. Title.
HD9696.A3 J3658 1986
NYPL [JFE 86-5112]

MORITA, AKIO, 1921-
Morita, Akio, 1921- Made in Japan . New York , c1986. viii, 309 p., [8] p. of plates : ISBN 0-525-24465-4 : LC Card 86-11479 DDC 338.7/6213/0924 B 19
HD9696.A3 J3658 1986
NYPL [JFE 86-5112]

Moriya, Hiroshi, 1932- Kyōsha no kanrigaku Kanpishi / Moriya Hiroshi. 880-03 Dai 1-han. Kyōto-shi : PHP Kenkyūjo, 1984. 273 p. ; 20 cm. In Japanese. ISBN 4-569-21374-X : LC Card 85-142427
1. Han, Fei, d. 233 B.C. Han Fei tzu. 2. Executives - Conduct of life. 3. Leadership. 4. Strategic planning. I. Han, Fei, d. 233 B.C. Han Fei-tzu. Japanese & Chinese. Selections. 1984. II. Title. III. Title: Kanpishi.
HF5387 .M67 1984 <Orien Japan>
NYPL [*OSM 87-1463]

Morley, C. D. Planning in turbulence /. Jerusalem , 1986. xii, 158 p. : ISBN 965-223-657-8 (pbk.) LC Card 87-163701 DDC 658.4/012 19
HD87.5 .P5 1986

MORNEAU, MICHEL, 1895- - INTERVIEWS.
Lemieux-Pépin, Madeleine. P'tit train va loin . Ottawa , 1985. vii, 191 p. ; LC Card 86-177382
HE2808.1 .L45 1985

Mörner, Magnus. Compraventas de tierras en el Cuzco, 1825-1869 / por Magnus Mörner, con la asistencia de George Calafut, Elizabeth Kuon Arce, Francisco Martínez Díaz. Estocolmo : Instituto de Estudios Latinoamericanos de Estocolmo, 1984. 66 p. : ill. ; 30 cm. (Estudios históricos sobre estructuras agrarias andinas . nr 1) Includes bibliographies. LC Card 87-403757 DDC 333.3/0985/37 19
1. Land tenure - Peru - Cuzco (Dept.) - History - 19th century. I. Title. II. Series.
HD559.C87 M67 1984

Moro, Beniamino, 1945- Programmazione lineare e teoria dell'impresa / Beniamino Moro. Milano : F. Angeli, [1980] 182 p. : ill. ; 22 cm. (Collana Università . 4) Bibliography: p. [181]-182. ISBN 88-20-41708-1 : LC Card 80-489699
1. Linear programming. 2. Industrial management - Linear programming. I. Title. II. Series.
T57.74 .M67 ***NYPL [JLD 87-792]***

Moro, Domenico. Crisi e ristrutturazione dell'industria siderurgica italiana / Domenico Moro. [Milano] : Giuffrè, [1984] 256 p. : ill. ; 25 cm. (Collana di diritto ed economia . 4) At head of title: Università degli studi di Pavia, Dipartimento di ricerche aziendali. Includes bibliographical references. LC Card 84-181172 DDC 338.4/76691/0945 19
1. Steel industry and trade - Italy. 2. Iron industry and trade - Italy. I. Title. II. Series.
HD9525.I82 M67 1984
NYPL [JLE 86-3649]

Moro, Jesús Martínez. see **Martínez Moro, Jesús.**

Moroccan mirages . Swearingen, Will D. (Will Davis), 1946- Princeton, N.J. , c1987. xvii, 217 p., [9] p. of plates : ISBN 0-691-05505-X (alk. paper) : LC Card 87-6981 DDC 338.1/0964 19
HD2121 .S94 1987

MOROCCANS - NETHERLANDS.
Bel Ghazi, Hassan. Van soek naar

arbeidsmarkt . [Bussum] , 1986. 176 p. ; ISBN 90-293-0638-6 : LC Card 86-234591
HD8518.5.M6 B45 1986

MOROCCO - CENSUS, 1960.
Morocco. Maṣlaḥah al-Markazīyah lil-Iḥṣā'īyāt. Résultats préliminaires du recensement de 1960 . [Rabat] [1964?] 43 leaves ; LC Card 82-960641
HD7372.3.A3 M67 1964

MOROCCO - COMMERCE - EUROPEAN ECONOMIC COMMUNITY COUNTRIES.
Qarouach, Mostafa. L'agriculture marocaine face au deuxième élargissement de la CEE /. [S.l.] 1983 (Casablanca : Editions maghrébines) 117 p. ; LC Card 83-192279 DDC 382/.41/0964 19
HD9017.M82 Q37 1983 ***NYPL [JLD 86-4326]***

MOROCCO - ECONOMIC CONDITIONS.
Mensink, Ankie. De wording en verwording van de staat Marokko . Rotterdam , 1985. 304 p. ; ISBN 90-6330-109-X : LC Card 85-214935
HC810 .M46 1985

Pourquoi, où et comment investir /. Casablanca, Maroc [1985] 126 p. ; LC Card 86-198948
HG5832.A3 P68 1985

Salahdine, Mohamed. Maroc, tribus, makhzen et colons . Paris , c1986. 337 p. : ISBN 2-85802-525-5 LC Card 86-159041
HC810 .S23 1986

MOROCCO - ECONOMIC POLICY.
Pourquoi, où et comment investir /. Casablanca, Maroc [1985] 126 p. ; LC Card 86-198948
HG5832.A3 P68 1985

MOROCCO - FOREIGN ECONOMIC RELATIONS.
Pourquoi, où et comment investir /. Casablanca, Maroc [1985] 126 p. ; LC Card 86-198948
HG5832.A3 P68 1985

MOROCCO - INDUSTRIES.
Les Industries mécaniques et électriques au Maroc . Casablanca [1984] 1 v. (various pagings) ; LC Card 85-206543
HD9705.M72 I53 1984

Morocco. Maṣlaḥah al-Markazīyah lil-Iḥṣā'īyāt. Résultats préliminaires du recensement de 1960 : logements / [Royaume du Maroc, Cabinet royal, Délégation générale à la promotion nationale et au plan, Service central des statistiques]. [Rabat] : Le Service, [1964?] 43 leaves ; 31 cm. LC Card 82-960641
1. Housing - Morocco - Statistics. 2. Morocco - Census, 1960. I. Title.
HD7372.3.A3 M67 1964

MOROCCO - SOCIAL CONDITIONS.
Bel Ghazi, Hassan. Van soek naar arbeidsmarkt . [Bussum] , 1986. 176 p. ; ISBN 90-293-0638-6 : LC Card 86-234591
HD8518.5.M6 B45 1986

Salahdine, Mohamed. Maroc, tribus, makhzen et colons . Paris , c1986. 337 p. : ISBN 2-85802-525-5 LC Card 86-159041
HC810 .S23 1986

Morocco (1956-) see Morocco.

Morón Bécquer, Pedro. El ahorro vinculado a la adquisición de viviendas : incentivos financieros y fiscales / Pedro Morón Becquer, Juan San Román Rodríguez. Madrid : Ministerio de Economía y Hacienda, Instituto de Estudios Fiscales, [1984?] 35 p. : ill. ; 24 cm. (Monografía / Instituto de Estudios Fiscales . no. 3.) Includes bibliographical references. ISBN 84-7196-476-7 : LC Card 85-201073
1. Building and loan associations - Spain. 2. Saving and investment - Spain. I. San Román Rodríguez, Juan. II. Series: Monografías (Instituto de Estudios Fiscales (Spain)) , no. 3. III. Title.
HG2156.S72 M67 1984

Morozov, V. P.
Menon, M. S. N., 1924- Indo-Soviet trade and economic ties /. New Delhi , 1986. 229 p. ; LC Card 86-903273 DDC 337.54047 19
HF1590.5.S65 M46 1986

Zherebin, V. M. Proektirovanie ėkonomicheskikh informatsionnykh sistem /. Moskva , 1983. 182, [2] p., [2] folded p. of plates : LC Card 83-224346
HD30.25 .Z52 1983

Morozova, M. IU. (Marina IUr'evna)
Sovremennaia pakistanskaia derevnia : osobennosti sotsial'no-ėkonomicheskoĭ ėvoliutsii / M.IU. Morozova. Moskva : Izd-vo "Nauka," Glav. red. vostochnoĭ lit-ry, 1986. 172 p. ; 20 cm. At head of title: Akademiia nauk SSSR. Ordena Trudovogo Krasnogo Znameni Institut vostokovedeniia. Summary in English. Bibliography: p. 160-[171] LC Card 86-174352
1. Agriculture - Economic aspects - Pakistan. 2. Pakistan - Rural conditions. I. Title.
HD2075.5 .M67 1986

Morozzo Della Rocca, Roberto, 1955- La Storia dei poveri . Roma , c1985. xii, 300 p. ; ISBN 88-382-3530-9 : LC Card 86-198943
HC240.9.P6 S76 1985

Morris, Cynthia Taft. Comparative patterns of economic development, 1850-1914 / Cynthia Taft Morris, Irma Adelman. Baltimore : Johns Hopkins University Press, c1988. xi, 575 p. ; 24 cm. (Johns Hopkins studies in development) Bibliography: p. 479-569. Includes index. ISBN 0-8018-3507-0 (alk. paper) LC Card 87-45480 DDC 338.9/009 19
1. Economic history - 1750-1918. 2. Economic development - History. I. Adelman, Irma. II. Title. III. Series.
HC51 .M645 1988

Morris, D. S.
The Guardian book of the General Strike /. Aldershot, Hants, England , Brookfield, Vt. , 1987. p. cm. ISBN 0-7045-3081-3 : LC Card 87-25287 DDC 331.89/25/0941 19
HD5365.A6 G8 1987

Haigh, R. H. Soviet foreign policy, the League of Nations and Europe, 1917-39 /. Aldershot, Hants , 1986. x, 138 p. ; ***NYPL [JFD 86-5778]***

Morris, Daniel E. Lomax, Timothy J. Guidelines for estimating the cost effectiveness of high-occupancy vehicle lanes /. College Station, Tex. , Springfield, Va. [1985] xiii, 55 p. : LC Card 86-622240 DDC 380.5 s 388.3/142 19
HE203 .T43 no. 339-5 HE356.T4

Morris, David J.
Garbage disposal economics : a statistical snapshot / by David Morris and Brenda Platt. Washington, DC : Institute for Local Self-Reliance, [1987] v, 101 p. : ill. ; 28 cm. "February 1987." Bibliography: p. 97-101. ISBN 0-917582-44-6 (pbk.) : LC Card 87-4182 DDC 338.4/3363728/0973 19
1. Refuse and refuse disposal - Economic aspects - United States - Case studies. 2. Recycling (Waste, etc.) - Economic aspects - United States - Case studies. I. Platt, Brenda. II. Institute for Local Self-Reliance.
HD4483 .G37 1987

Substituting agricultural materials for petroleum based industrial products / by David Morris, Tom Abeles. Washington, D.C. : Institute for Local Self-Reliance, c1986. i, 33 p. ; 28 cm. "A technical report"--Cover. "October 1986." Bibliography: p. 31-33. ISBN 0-917582-46-2 (pbk.) : LC Card 86-21350 DDC 338.4/76628 19
1. Biomass energy industries - United States. 2. Biomass chemicals industry - United States. I. Abeles, Tom P. II. Institute for Local Self-Reliance. III. Title.
HD9502.5.B543 U654 1986

Morris, Derek. Strategic behaviour and industrial competition /. Oxford [Oxfordshire] , New York , 1986. 243 p. ; ISBN 0-19-828562-0 (pbk.) : LC Card 86-28535 DDC 338.6 19
HD2326 .S786 1986

Morris, Diana. Manners, Gerald. Office policy in Britain . Norwich, UK , c1986. viii, 158 p. : ISBN 0-86094-212-0 LC Card 87-143633 DDC 338.6/042 19
HF5547.25 .M36 1986

Morris Goldseker Foundation (Baltimore, Md.) Szanton, Peter L. Baltimore 2000 . [Baltimore, Md.] , c1986. v, 51 p. : LC Card 87-125975 DDC 330.9752/71043 19
HC108.B2 S9 1986

Morris, Jenny, 1950- Women workers and the sweated trades : the origins of minimum wage legislation / Jenny Morris. Aldershot, Hants, England ; Brookfield, Vt., USA : Gower, c1986. 248 p. ; 22 cm. Bibliography: p. 239-248. ISBN 0-566-05188-5 : LC Card 86-9850 DDC 331.4/23 19
1. Sweating system - Great Britain - History. 2. Women - Employment - Great Britain - History. 3. Labor policy - Great Britain - History. 4. Wages - Minimum wage - Law and legislation - Great Britain. 5. Wages - Women - Law and legislation - Great Britain. I. Title.
HD2339.G7 M67 1986 ***NYPL [JLD 86-4089]***

Morris, Joseph M., 1949- Joint ventures : an accounting, tax, and administrative guide / Joseph M. Morris ; contributing author, Charles A. Hawes. New York : Wiley, c1987. xii, 324 p. ; 24 cm. Includes index. ISBN 0-471-01170-3 LC Card 86-28083 DDC 658/.044 19
1. Joint ventures - Management. 2. Joint ventures - Accounting. 3. Joint ventures - Finance. 4. Joint ventures - Taxation - United States. I. Hawes, Charles A. II. Title.
HD62.47 .M67 1987

Morris, Michael, 1949- Poverty and public policy : an analysis of federal intervention efforts / Michael Morris and John B. Williamson. Westport, Conn. : Greenwood Press, 1986. xii, 236 p. ; 22 cm. (Studies in social welfare policies and programs, 8755-5360 . no. 3) Includes index. Bibliography: p. [191]-224. ISBN 0-313-24942-3 (lib. bdg. : alk. paper) LC Card 86-398 DDC 361.6/1/0973 19
1. Public welfare - United States. 2. Poor - United States. 3. United States - Social policy. I. Williamson, John B. II. Title. III. Series.
HV95 .M67 1986 ***NYPL [JLD 87-510]***

Morris, Peter W. G. The anatomy of major projects : a study of the reality of project management / Peter W.G. Morris and George H. Hough. Chichester ; New York : Wiley, c1987. p. cm. Bibliography: p. Includes index. ISBN 0-471-91551-3 : LC Card 87-8176 DDC 658.4/04 19
1. Industrial project management. I. Hough, George H. II. Title.
HD69.P75 M674 1987

Morris, Sandra. Horner, Ken. Guide to computer installations in southern California . Palo Alto, Calif. , c1986. iv, 750 p. : LC Card 87-134229 DDC 004/.025/7949 19
HD9696.C63 U518343 1986

Morris, Timothy, 1953- Innovations in banking : business strategies and employee relations / Timothy Morris. London ; Wolfeboro, N.H. : Croom Helm, c1986. 137 p. : ill. ; 23 cm. "Loosely derived from my Ph. D. thesis"--Pref. Includes index. Bibliography: p. 128-132. ISBN 0-7099-4607-4 : LC Card 86-13400 DDC 332.1/068/3 19
1. Bank management - Great Britain. 2. Trade-unions - Bank employees - Great Britain. 3. Banks and banking - Great Britain - Personnel management. 4. Industrial relations - Great Britain. I. Title.
HG2988 .M675 1986 ***NYPL [JLD 87-81]***

Morris, William C. (William Clinton), 1928- Sashkin, Marshall, 1944- Experiencing management /. Reading, Mass. , c1987. x, 234 p. : ISBN 0-201-11545-X (pbk.) : LC Card 86-28731 DDC 658.4/0352 19
HD30.26 .S27 1987

Morris, William H., Jr. Disability insurance : a complete handbook on today's most needed financial benefits / by William H. Morris, Jr. Lexington, Ky. (98 Dennis Dr., Lexington 40503) : Lexington House, c1986. x, 93 p. : ill., forms, port. ; 22 cm. LC Card 87-402218 DDC 368.3/86/00973 19
1. Insurance, Disability - United States. I. Title.
HD7105.25.U6 M67 1986

Morrisey, George L.
Below, Patrick J. The executive guide to strategic planning /. San Francisco, Calif. , c1987. xxiii, 136 p. : ISBN 1-555-42032-X (alk. paper) LC Card 86-27863 DDC 658.4/012 19
HD30.28 .B45 1987

The executive guide to operational planning / George L. Morrisey, Patrick J. Below, Betty L. Acomb. 1st ed. San Francisco : Jossey-Bass, 1988. xxvii, 130 p. : ill. ; 24 cm. (The Jossey-Bass management series) Bibliography: p. 121-125. Includes index. ISBN 1-555-42064-8 (alk. paper) LC Card 87-45508 DDC 658.4/012 19
1. Corporate planning. 2. Strategic planning. I. Below, Patrick J. II. Acomb, Betty L. III. Title. IV. Series.
HD30.28 .M65 1988

Performance appraisals in the public sector : key to effective supervision / George L.

Morrisey. Reading, Mass. : Addison-Wesley, 1983. xiii, 172 p. ; 24 cm. Bibliography: p. 169-172. ISBN 0-201-04847-7 (pbk.) : LC Card 83-6049 DDC 353.001/42 19
1. Employees, Rating of - United States. 2. Civil service - United States - Personnel management. 3. United States - Officials and employees - Rating of. I. Title.
JK766.6 .M67 1983 ***NYPL [JLE 83-3164]***

Morrison, Ann M. Breaking the glass ceiling : can women reach the top of America's largest corporations? / Ann M. Morrison, Randall P. White, Ellen Van Velsor, and the Center for Creative Leadership. Reading, Mass. : Addison-Wesley Pub. Co., c1987. ix, 229 p. : ill. ; 22 cm. Bibliography: p. 219-224. Includes index. ISBN 0-201-15787-X : LC Card 87-1853 DDC 658.4/09/024042 19
1. Women executives - United States. 2. Success in business - United States. I. White, Randall P. II. Van Velsor, Ellen. III. Center for Creative Leadership. IV. Title.
HD6054.4.U6 M67 1987

Morrison, Charles Edward, 1944- Asia-Pacific report, 1987-88 . Honolulu, Hawaii , 1987. p. cm. ISBN 0-86638-098-1 : LC Card 87-20074 DDC 909/.098230828 19
HC412 .A72415 1987

Morrison, Daniel, 1945- "Trading peasants" and urbanization in eighteenth-century Russia : the Central Industrial Region / Daniel Morrison. New York : Garland Pub., 1987. 415 p. ; 24 cm. (Modern European history) Originally presented as the author's thesis (Ph. D.--Columbia University, 1981) Bibliography: p. 401-415. ISBN 0-8240-8059-9 (alk. paper) : LC Card 87-7425 DDC 307.2 19
1. Rural-urban migration - Russian S.F.S.R. - History - 18th century. 2. Urbanization - Russian S.F.S.R. - History - 18th century. 3. Cities and towns - Russian S.F.S.R. - History - 18th century. I. Title. II. Title: Central Industrial Region. III. Series.
HB2068.S65 M67 1987

Morrison, Elizabeth, 1959- U. S. agriculture & Third World development . Boulder , 1987. xi, 258 p. ; ISBN 1-555-87011-2 (lib. bdg.) : LC Card 86-29860 DDC 338.1/09172/4 19
HD1765 .U15 1987

Morrison, Malcolm H. The transition to retirement : the employer's perspective / by Malcolm H. Morrison. Washington, D.C. (1990 M St., N.W., Washington 20036) : Bureau of Social Science Research, c1985. 85 p. : ill. ; 23 cm. Bibliography: p. 69-70. LC Card 85-169472 DDC 306/.38/0973 19
1. Retirement - United States. 2. Retirement - United States - Planning. 3. Age and employment - United States. I. Title.
HQ1062 .M64 1985 ***NYPL [JLE 86-2236]***

Morrison, Philip S., 1947- Data sources on residential change and the housing market : a guide to contemporary sources and tests of bias in residential property data in metropolitan Toronto / Philip S. Morrison. [Toronto] : Centre for Urban and Community Studies, University of Toronto, [1977] 76 p. : ill. ; 28 cm. (Major report . no. 10) "March 1977." Bibliography: p. 66-68. LC Card 85-158244
1. Dwellings - Prices - Ontario - Toronto Metropolitan Area - Information services - Ontario - Toronto Metropolitan Area. 2. Dwellings - Prices - Ontario - Toronto Metropolitan Area - Statistical methods. 3. Statistical hypothesis testing. I. Title. II. Series.
HD7305.T68 M67 1977

Morrison, Richard J. Lewis, Gordon H. Income transfer analysis /. New York , c1987. p. cm. ISBN 0-915163-01-2 LC Card 86-33744 DDC 362.5/82 19
HC110.I5 L48 1987

Morrison, Rodney J., 1934- Henry C. Carey and American economic development / Rodney J. Morrison. Philadelphia : American Philosophical Society, 1986. ix, 91 p. : port. ; 26 cm. (Transactions of the American Philosophical Society, 0065-9746 . v. 76, pt. 3) Bibliography: p. 84-89. Includes index. ISBN 0-87169-763-7 (pbk.) LC Card 86-71420 DDC 338.973/0092/4 19
1. Carey, Henry Charles, 1793-1879 - Contributions in Economics. 2. Free trade and protection. 3. United States - Economic policy - To 1933. 4. Economic development. I. Title. II. Series.
HB119.C3 M67 1986

Morrison, Steven A., 1951- The economic effects of airline deregulation / Steven Morrison, Clifford Winston. Washington, D.C. : Brookings Institution, c1986. xi, 84 : ill. ; 23 cm. (Studies in the regulation of economic activity) Includes bibliographical references and index. ISBN 0-8157-5845-6 (pbk.) : LC Card 85-48202 DDC 387.7/1 19
1. Aeronautics and state - United States. 2. Air lines - United States. I. Winston, Clifford, 1952-. II. Title.
HE9803.A4 M67 1986 ***NYPL [JLE 86-3309]***

Morrissey, Elizabeth S. Characteristics of poverty in nonmetro counties / Elizabeth S. Morrissey. Washington, D.C. : U. S. Dept. of Agriculture, Economic Research Service : Supt. of Docs., U. S. G.P.O., distributor, 1985. iv, 10 p. : ill., 1 map ; 28 cm. (Rural development research report . no. 52) Distributed to depository libraries in microfiche. "July 1985"--p. iii. Bibliography: p. 10. Cover title. S/N 001-019-00400-2 Item 24-G-2 (microfiche) LC Card 86-602555 DDC 362.5/0973 19
1. Poverty research - United States. 2. Rural poor - United States. I. United States. Dept. of Agriculture. Economic Research Service. II. Title. III. Series.
HC110.P6 M67 1985

Morrissey, William. Harmon, Paul. Expert systems . New York , c1988. xii, 289 p. : ISBN 0-471-83950-7 (pbk.) LC Card 87-17608 DDC 650/.028/5633 19
HF5548.2 .H367 1988

Morrisson, Christian.
Lecaillon, Jacques. Economic policies and agricultural performance . Paris , 1985. 158 p. ; LC Card 86-216027 DDC 338.1/86625 19
HD2144 .L42 1985

Lecaillon, Jacques. Economic policies and agricultural performance . Paris , 1986. 174 p. ; LC Card 87-158595 DDC 338.1/86623 19
HD2143.5.Z8 L43 1986

Mors, Matthias. Planung und Erwartungsbildung in der Investitionsentscheidung : eine empirisch orientierte Analyse an Hand von Befragungsdaten / Matthias Mors. Frankfurt am Main : Haag + Herchen, c1983. 190 p. : ill. ; 21 cm. Bibliography: p. 173-187. ISBN 3-88129-619-0 LC Card 83-174677
1. Capital investments - Mathematical models. 2. Decision-making - Mathematical models. I. Title.
HG4028.C4 M65 1983

Morse, Diane McGinty.
Carlson, Richard C. Managing the changing work force . Menlo Park, Calif. (333 Ravenswood Ave., Menlo Park 94025-3476) , c1984. 44 p. : LC Card 86-212936 DDC 658.3 19
HD5706 .C29 1984

Involving managers in competitive analysis / Diane McGinty Morse. Menlo Park, CA (333 Ravenswood Ave., Menlo Park 94025) : SRI International, Business Intelligence Program, c1986. 11 leaves : ill. ; 28 cm. (Datalog file . no. 86-1025) LC Card 86-220559 DDC 658.4/012 19
1. Business intelligence. 2. Strategic planning. I. Business Intelligence Program (SRI International). II. Title. III. Series.
HD38.7 .M67 1986

Managing competitive intelligence : techniques and tools for effectively analyzing the competitive environment / Diane McGinty Morse. Menlo Park, Calif. : SRI International, Business Intelligence Program, c1985. 36 p. : ill. (some col.) ; 28 cm. (Report / Business Intelligence Program . no. 718 (Spring 1985)) LC Card 87-404501 DDC 658.4/7 19
1. Business intelligence. 2. Strategic planning. 3. Competition. I. Series: Research report (Business Intelligence Program (SRI International)) , 718. II. Title.
HD38.7 .M674 1985

Morse, Leon William. Practical handbook of industrial traffic management / Leon Wm. Morse. 7th ed. Washington : Traffic Service Corp., 1987. xiii, 642 p. : ill. ; 24 cm. Includes index. ISBN 0-87408-039-8 LC Card 86-51249 DDC 658.7/882 19
1. Shipment of goods. I. Title. II. Title: Industrial traffic management.
HF5761 .M74 1987

Morse, Nancy C., 1920- Katz, Daniel, 1903- Productivity, supervision, and morale in an office situation, part I /. New York , 1987, c1950. vii, 84 p. ; ISBN 0-8240-8211-7 (alk. paper) : LC Card 86-25804 DDC 658.3 19
HF5549 .K282 1987

Morse, Roberta. The Black female professional / by Roberta Morse. Washington, D.C. : Mental Health Research and Development Center, Institute for Urban Affairs and Research, Howard University, [1983] i, 48 p. ; 28 cm. (Occasional paper / Mental Health Research and Development Center, Institute for Urban Affairs and Research, Howard University . no. 21) Bibliography: p. 46-48. LC Card 83-80187 DDC 305.4/8896073 19
1. Women in the professions - United States. 2. Sex discrimination against women - United States. 3. Sex discrimination in employment - United States. 4. Racism - United States. 5. Afro-American women - Attitudes. 6. Women in the professions - United States - Attitudes. I. Series: Occasional paper (Howard University. Institute for Urban Affairs and Research) , no. 21. II. Title.
HQ1426 .M88 1983 ***NYPL [Sc F 86-230]***

Morse, Wayne J. Management accounting / Wayne J. Morse, James R. Davis, Al L. Hartgraves. 2nd ed. Reading, Mass. : Addison-Wesley, c1988. xxiii, 840 p. : ill. ; 24 cm. Includes bibliographical references and index. ISBN 0-201-15760-8 : LC Card 87-11570 DDC 658.1/511 19
1. Managerial accounting. I. Davis, James Richard, 1947-. II. Hartgraves, Al L. III. Title.
HF5635 .M864 1988

Morska vrata na rodinata : 80 godini pristanishte Varna / sŭstavitel Temenuzhka Li͡ubenova.1. izd., porŭchano. Varna : Kn-vo "Georgi Bakalov", 1986. 146 p., [32] p. of plates : ill. ; 20 cm. Includes bibliographical references. LC Card 86-233471
1. Harbors - Bulgaria - Varna - History. 2. Varna (Bulgaria) - Commerce - History. I. Li͡ubenova, Temenuzhka.
HE557.B9 M67 1986

MORTAGAGE LOANS - VENEZUELA.
Martín-Guédez, Rafael, 1942- Sistema financiero . Caracas [1984] (Caracas : Editorial Arte) 309 p. : LC Card 85-177967
HG2156.V42 M37 1984

Mortalidad infantil y clases sociales . García Molina, Carlos. [Medellín, Colombia] [1986] 103 p. : ISBN 958-9127-05-3 LC Card 87-400685 DDC 304.6/4/0880542 19
HB1323.I42 C74 1986

MORTALITY - ADDRESSES, ESSAYS, LECTURES.
Fertility and mortality . New Delhi , Beverly Hills , 1986. 351 p. ; ISBN 0-8039-9497-4 LC Card 85-22287 DDC 304.6/3 19
HB901 .F468 1986 ***NYPL [JLE 86-4122]***

MORTALITY - AFRICA - CONGRESSES.
Expert Group Meeting on Fertility and Mortality Levels and Trends in Africa and Their Policy Implications (1979 : Monrovia, Liberia) Population dynamics . [Addis Ababa] [1981] ix, 581 p. : LC Card 82-980086 DDC 304.6/3/096 19
HB3661.A3 E9 1979 ***NYPL [JLF 83-591]***

MORTALITY - BANGLADESH - CASE STUDIES.
D'Souza, S. M. (Stanislaus Michael) Mortality case study, Matlab, Bangladesh /. Dhaka, Bangladesh , 1985. 80 p. : LC Card 86-902788 DDC 304.6/4/0954923 19
HB1470.6.M37 D76 1985

MORTALITY - BANGLADESH - MATLAB BAZAR THANA - CASE STUDIES.
D'Souza, S. M. (Stanislaus Michael) Mortality case study, Matlab, Bangladesh /. Dhaka, Bangladesh , 1985. 80 p. : LC Card 86-902788 DDC 304.6/4/0954923 19
HB1470.6.M37 D76 1985

Mortality by occupation and socio-economic group in Norway, 1970-1980. Borgan, Jens-Kristian. Dødelighet i yrker og sosioøkonomiske grupper 1970-1980 /. Oslo , 1986. 217 p. : ISBN 82-537-2339-3 : LC Card 86-231576
HB1445 .B66 1986

MORTALITY - CANADA - TABLES.
Nagnur, D. N. Longevity and historical life tables . Ottawa , c1986. 215 p. : ISBN 0-660-52882-7 (pbk.) : LC Card 86-215300
HB1359.N34 1986

Mortality case study, Matlab, Bangladesh /.

D'Souza, S. M. (Stanislaus Michael) Dhaka, Bangladesh , 1985. 80 p. : LC Card 86-902788 DDC 304.6/4/0954923 19
HB1470.6.M37 D76 1985

MORTALITY - COLOMBIA.
Flórez Nieto, Carmen Elisa. The existence of a Latin American mortality pattern . Bogotá, Colombia , 1985. 153 p. : LC Card 87-145922
HB1397 .F56 1985

MORTALITY - DENMARK - STATISTICS.
Regionale dødelighedsforskelle i Danmark 1971-79. København , 1983. 136 p. : ISBN 87-501-0582-5 : LC Card 84-169325
HA1473 .A35 nr. 39 HB1441

MORTALITY - DEVELOPING COUNTRIES.
Tabutin, Dominique. Les transitions de mortalité dans le Tiersmonde . Louvain-la-Neuve, Belgique [1985] 33 p. : LC Card 86-178578
HB1528 .T33 1985

MORTALITY - DEVELOPING COUNTRIES - TABLES.
Age structure of mortality in developing countries . New York , 1986. vi, 267 p. : LC Card 87-401611 DDC 304.6/4 19
HB1528 .A36 1986

MORTALITY - DOMINICA.
Ebanks, G. E. Mortality, fertility, and family planning . Santiago, Chile [1985] 123 p. ; LC Card 87-131697 DDC 304.6/2/09729841 19
HB1376.D65 E32 1985

MORTALITY - ECONOMIC ASPECTS - ASIA, SOUTHEASTERN - CONGRESSES.
Workshop on Socio-economic Correlates of Mortality Differentials in Japan and ASEAN (1984 : Singapore) Socio-economic correlates of mortality in Japan and ASEAN /. Singapore , c1986. xxi, 295 p. : LC Card 86-945167 DDC 304.6/4/0952 19
HB1481 .W67 1984

MORTALITY - ECONOMIC ASPECTS - JAPAN - CONGRESSES.
Workshop on Socio-economic Correlates of Mortality Differentials in Japan and ASEAN (1984 : Singapore) Socio-economic correlates of mortality in Japan and ASEAN /. Singapore , c1986. xxi, 295 p. : LC Card 86-945167 DDC 304.6/4/0952 19
HB1481 .W67 1984

MORTALITY - ENGLAND - STATISTICS.
Marmot, M. G. Immigrant mortality in England and Wales, 1970-78 . London , 1984. xii, 144 p. : ISBN 0-11-691094-1 (pbk.) : LC Card 84-222968 DDC 614.4/242 19
HB1415 .M37 1984 ***NYPL [JLG 87-55]***

Mortality, expectation of life, and the Hungarian experience /. Pollard, J. H. [North Ryde, N.S.W.] [1986] 59 p. ; ISBN 0-85837-578-8 (pbk.) LC Card 87-110257 DDC 304.6/4/09439 19
HB1422.5.A3 P65 1986

Mortality, fertility, and family planning . Ebanks, G. E. Santiago, Chile [1985] 123 p. ; LC Card 87-131697 DDC 304.6/2/09729841 19
HB1376.D65 E32 1985

MORTALITY - FRANCE - TERRITORIES AND POSSESSIONS - STATISTICS.
Statistique du mouvement de la population dans les D.O.M. . Paris [1985] 104 p. : ISBN 2-11-064898-8 : LC Card 86-216599
HB1003 .S73 1985

MORTALITY - GERMANY (WEST) - STATISTICS.
Rohde, Horst. Sterbetafeln für Personenkraftwagen und Kombinationskraftwagen . Essen , 1981. 64 p. ; LC Card 87-408032 DDC 363.1/252/0943021 19
HE5614.5.G3 R64 1981

MORTALITY - GREAT BRITAIN.
Class and health . London , New York , 1986. x, 223 p. : ISBN 0-422-60360-0 : LC Card 86-5972 DDC 362.1/0941 19
RA418.3.G7 C56 1986 ***NYPL [JLE 87-505]***

MORTALITY - GREAT BRITAIN - LONGITUDINAL STUDIES.
Class and health . London , New York , 1986. x, 223 p. : ISBN 0-422-60360-0 : LC Card 86-5972 DDC 362.1/0941 19
RA418.3.G7 C56 1986 ***NYPL [JLE 87-505]***

MORTALITY - HUNGARY - MATHEMATICAL MODELS.
Pollard, J. H. Mortality, expectation of life, and the Hungarian experience /. [North Ryde, N.S.W.] [1986] 59 p. ; ISBN 0-85837-578-8 (pbk.) LC Card 87-110257 DDC 304.6/4/09439 19
HB1422.5.A3 P65 1986

MORTALITY - INDONESIA.
Recent trends in fertility and mortality in Indonesia /. Honolulu, Hawaii , 1987. xvi, 96 p. : ISBN 0-86638-092-2 (pbk.) : LC Card 87-11178 DDC 304.6/32/09598 19
HB1057 .R43 1987

MORTALITY - IVORY COAST.
Enquête démographique à passages répétés, 1978-1979 . [Abidjan] [1980?] 270 p. : LC Card 85-213692 DDC 304.6/09666/8 19
HB3666.A3 E57 1980 ***NYPL [JLF 86-1023]***

MORTALITY - KENYA.

MORTALITY - MALAYSIA - STATISTICS.
Kajian semula jadual-jadual hayat mengikut jantina dan kumpulan etnik bagi Semenanjung Malaysia, 1970 dan 1980 =. Kuala Lumpur [1986] v, 27, v, 38 p. : ISBN 967-99995-2-1 (pbk.) : LC Card 87-941374
HB1474.6.A3 K35 1986

MORTALITY - MATHEMATICAL MODELS.
Arretx, Carmen. Cuatro lecciones de William Brass . Santiago de Chile , 1977. 88 p. : LC Card 83-169600
HB1321.B73 A77 1977

MORTALITY - MEXICO.
Planeación familiar y cambio demográfico. México, D.F. [1983], c1982. 554 p. : ISBN 968-8241-63-6 LC Card 84-227488 DDC 304.6/0972 19
HB3531 .P57 1983 ***NYPL [JLE 86-3248]***

MORTALITY - MEXICO - ADDRESSES, ESSAYS, LECTURES.
Los Factores del cambio demográfico en México /. México, D.F. , 1984. 422 p. : ISBN 968-231-281-7 LC Card 85-231767
HB1361 .F33 1984 ***NYPL [JLE 87-753]***

MORTALITY - NEBRASKA - TABLES.
Nebraska abridged life expectancy tables, 1960-1980 /. [Lincoln, Neb.] [1985?] 40, 78, 3 leaves : LC Card 86-622212 DDC 304.6/09782021 19
HB1355.N42 N43 1985

MORTALITY - NORWAY - STATISTICS.
Borgan, Jens-Kristian. Dødelighet i yrker og sosioøkonomiske grupper 1970-1980 /. Oslo , 1986. 217 p. : ISBN 82-537-2339-3 : LC Card 86-231576
HB1445 .B66 1986

MORTALITY - RESEARCH - METHODOLOGY - CONGRESSES.
Methodologies for the collection and analysis of mortality data . Liège, Belgium , 1984. vi, 510 p. : ISBN 2-87040-032-2 (pbk.) LC Card 86-205582 DDC 304.6/4/072 19
HB1321 .M48 1984

MORTALITY - SAINT LUCIA.
Ebanks, G. E. Mortality, fertility, and family planning . Santiago, Chile [1985] 123 p. ; LC Card 87-131697 DDC 304.6/2/09729841 19
HB1376.D65 E32 1985

MORTALITY - SOCIAL ASPECTS - ASIA, SOUTHEASTERN - CONGRESSES.
Workshop on Socio-economic Correlates of Mortality Differentials in Japan and ASEAN (1984 : Singapore) Socio-economic correlates of mortality in Japan and ASEAN /. Singapore , c1986. xxi, 295 p. : LC Card 86-945167 DDC 304.6/4/0952 19
HB1481 .W67 1984

MORTALITY - SOCIAL ASPECTS - JAPAN - CONGRESSES.
Workshop on Socio-economic Correlates of Mortality Differentials in Japan and ASEAN (1984 : Singapore) Socio-economic correlates of mortality in Japan and ASEAN /. Singapore , c1986. xxi, 295 p. : LC Card 86-945167 DDC 304.6/4/0952 19
HB1481 .W67 1984

MORTALITY - SPAIN - MÉRIDA - HISTORY - 17TH CENTURY - STATISTICS.
Rodríguez Grajera, Alfonso. La población de Mérida en el siglo XVII /. [Badajoz] , 1985. xv, 162 p. : ISBN 84-505-1500-9 LC Card 86-232003
HB3620.M47 R63 1985

MORTALITY - STATISTICAL METHODS.
London, Dick, 1943- Survival models and their estimation /. Winsted, Conn. , c1986 (1987 printing) xii, 282 p. : ISBN 0-936031-01-8 (pbk.) LC Card 87-402847 DDC 304.6/4/015195 19
HG8782 .L57 1987

Mortality statistics : perinatal and infant : social and biological factors : review of the Registar General on deaths in England and Wales, 1984. London : H.M.S.O., 1986. viii, 49 p. ; 30 cm. (Series DH3, 0266-3589 . no. 17) At head of title: Office of Population Censuses and Surveys. Bibliography: p. viii. ISBN 0-11-691069-0 (pbk.) : LC Card 87-147154 DDC 614.5/992 19
1. Perinatal mortality - England - Statistics. 2. Infants - England - Mortality - Statistics. 3. Perinatal mortality - Wales - Statistics. 4. Infants - Wales - Mortality - Statistics. I. Great Britain. Office of Population Censuses and Surveys. II. Series.
HB1323.I42 G764 1984

MORTALITY - SWITZERLAND - TABLES.
Schweizerische Volkssterbetafeln . Bern , 1955. 70 leaves ; LC Card 85-144744
HB1453 .S38 1955

MORTALITY - TANZANIA.

MORTALITY - THAILAND.
Sanœ 'Intharasuksī. Khonrao tāi dai kī withī /. Krung Thēp , 2526 [1983] 620 p. ; LC Card 83-916563
HB1474.55.A3 S36 1983

MORTALITY - TOGO.
Locoh, Thérèse. La fécondité en Afrique noire /. Lomé [1985] 36, 22 leaves : LC Card 87-126644
HB1071 .L63 1985

MORTALITY - UNITED STATES - STATES - TABLES - COLLECTED WORKS.
U. S. decennial life tables for 1979-81. Hyattsville, Md. , Washington, D.C. , 1985-<1986. v. ; LC Card 85-600190 DDC 304.6/4/0973021 19
HB1335 .U17 1985 ***NYPL [JLM 86-491]***

MORTALITY - UNITED STATES - TABLES - COLLECTED WORKS.
U. S. decennial life tables for 1979-81. Hyattsville, Md. , Washington, D.C. , 1985-<1986. v. ; LC Card 85-600190 DDC 304.6/4/0973021 19
HB1335 .U17 1985 ***NYPL [JLM 86-491]***

MORTALITY - UNITED STATES - TABLES - METHODOLOGY - COLLECTED WORKS.
U. S. decennial life tables for 1979-81. Hyattsville, Md. , Washington, D.C. , 1985-<1986. v. ; LC Card 85-600190 DDC 304.6/4/0973021 19
HB1335 .U17 1985 ***NYPL [JLM 86-491]***

MORTALITY - VENEZUELA.
Flórez Nieto, Carmen Elisa. The existence of a Latin American mortality pattern . Bogotá, Colombia , 1985. 153 p. : LC Card 87-145922
HB1397 .F56 1985

MORTALITY - WALES - STATISTICS.
Marmot, M. G. Immigrant mortality in England and Wales, 1970-78 . London , 1984. xii, 144 p. : ISBN 0-11-691094-1 (pbk.) : LC Card 84-222968 DDC 614.4/242 19
HB1415 .M37 1984 ***NYPL [JLG 87-55]***

Mortgage-backed securities : new strategies, applications, and research / edited by Frank J. Fabozzi. Chicago, Ill. : Probus Pub. Co., c1987. xi, 474 p. : ill. ; 24 cm. Includes index. ISBN 0-917253-47-7 : LC Card 86-15087 DDC 332.63/232 19
1. Mortgage bonds - United States. 2. Securities - United States. 3. Portfolio management - United States. 4. Secondary mortgage market - United States. I. Fabozzi, Frank J.
HG4655 .M65 1987 ***NYPL [JLE 87-783]***

Mortgage Bankers Association of America.
Income and cost for origination and servicing of 1 to 4 unit residential loans, 1985. Washington, D.C. (1125 15th St., N.W., Washington 20005-2766) , c1986. 32 p. ; LC Card 87-106156 DDC 332.3/2/0973021 19
HG2040.5.U5 I535 1986

MORTGAGE BANKS - GERMANY, WEST.
Dieckhöner, Bruno. Rentabilitätsrisiken aus dem Hypothekargeschäft von Kreditinstituten in Zeiten der Geldentwertung /. Wiesbaden , c1984. xi, 395 p. : ISBN 3-409-14002-6 : LC Card 85-119494
HG2040.5.G4 D53 1984

Goedecke, Wolfgang. Realkredit . Frankfurt am Main , c1982. 120 p. ; ISBN 3-7819-0275-7 LC Card 83-139826
HG2040.5.G4 G64 1982

Schubäus, Klaus. Das Hypothekenbankgeschäft in den Niederlanden und in der Bundesrepublik Deutschland /. Berlin , c1984. 251 p. : ISBN 3-428-05569-1 LC Card 84-250906
HG2040.5.N37 S38 1984

MORTGAGE BANKS - NETHERLANDS.
Schubäus, Klaus. Das Hypothekenbankgeschäft in den Niederlanden und in der Bundesrepublik Deutschland /. Berlin , c1984. 251 p. : ISBN 3-428-05569-1 LC Card 84-250906
HG2040.5.N37 S38 1984

MORTGAGE BANKS - UNITED STATES - STATISTICS.
Income and cost for origination and servicing of 1 to 4 unit residential loans, 1985. Washington, D.C. (1125 15th St., N.W., Washington 20005-2766) , c1986. 32 p. ; LC Card 87-106156 DDC 332.3/2/0973021 19
HG2040.5.U5 I535 1986

MORTGAGE BANKS - VENEZUELA.
Martín-Guédez, Rafael, 1942- Sistema financiero . Caracas [1984] (Caracas : Editorial Arte) 309 p. : LC Card 85-177967
HG2156.V42 M37 1984

MORTGAGE BONDS - UNITED STATES.
Mortgage-backed securities . Chicago, Ill. , c1987. xi, 474 p. : ISBN 0-917253-47-7 : LC Card 86-15087 DDC 332.63/232 19
HG4655 .M65 1987 ***NYPL [JLE 87-783]***

MORTGAGE CLOSING COSTS. see **SETTLEMENT COSTS.**

MORTGAGE COMPANIES. see **MORTGAGE BANKS.**

MORTGAGE FORECLOSURE. see **FORECLOSURE.**

The mortgage kit . Steinmetz, Thomas C. Chicago, IL , c1987. ix, 188 p. : ISBN 0-88462-658-X (pbk.) : LC Card 87-3693 DDC 332.7/22 19
HG2040.5.U5 S72 1987

MORTGAGE LENDING. see **MORTGAGE LOANS.**

MORTGAGE LOANS - CANADA.
Che-Alford, Janet. Mortgagor [sic] households in Canada . Ottawa , c1986. 100 p. : ISBN 0-660-52986-6 (pbk.) : LC Card 86-202749 DDC 332.7/22/0971 19
HD7287.82.C2 C48 1986

MORTGAGE LOANS - CANADA - TABLES.
Solomon, Stephen S. Canadian mortgage payments /. New York , c1987. 302 p. ; ISBN 0-8120-3939-4 (pbk.) LC Card 87-13073 DDC 332.8/0212 19
HG1634 .S654 1987

MORTGAGE LOANS - COMPUTER PROGRAMS - CATALOGS.
Guide to real estate and mortgage banking software /. Washington, D.C. , 1986. 3 v. ; ISBN 0-917935-14-4 (pbk. : set) LC Card 86-63061 DDC 333.3/028/553 19
HD1380 .G85 1986a

MORTGAGE LOANS - GREAT BRITAIN.
Boléat, Mark. The mortgage market /. London , Boston , 1987. x, 176 p. ; ISBN 0-04-334011-3 (alk. paper) LC Card 86-28875 DDC 332.7/22 19
HG2040.5.G7 B65 1987

MORTGAGE LOANS - SPAIN.
Trilla i Bellart, Carme. La financiación del acceso a la vivienda de España, 1976-1981 /. [Barcelona] [1984] 56 p. : LC Card 86-160004
HD7351.A4 T75 1984

MORTGAGE LOANS - SPAIN - CATALONIA.
Trilla i Bellart, Carme. Finançament del l'accés a l'habitatge a Catalunya en els darrers anys /. [Barcelona] [1984] 58 p. : LC Card 86-160332
HD7351.C37 T75 1984

MORTGAGE LOANS - SPAIN - CONGRESSES.
El Mercado hipotecario . Madrid , 1984. 162 p. ; ISBN 84-85669-34-7 LC Card 86-211862
HG2040.5.S7 M47 1984

MORTGAGE LOANS - TEXAS.
Texas real estate finance /. New York , c1987. xviii, 365 p. : ISBN 0-471-82300-7 (pbk.) LC Card 86-29004 DDC 332.7/2/09764 19
HD266.T4 T5 1987

MORTGAGE LOANS - UNITED STATES.
Bass, Gary J. A practical and simple guide to a home mortgage /. Irving, Tex. , c1987. v, 66 p. : ISBN 0-944319-00-9 (pbk.) LC Card 87-82025 DDC 332.7/22/0973 19
HG2040.5.U5 B367 1987

Construction lending for income-producing properties . Washington, D.C. (1120 Connecticut Ave., N.W. Washington 20036) , c1986. xiv, 163 p. : LC Card 86-209027 DDC 332.1/753 19
HG2040.5.U5 M49 1986

DeBat, Don. The mortgage manual . Chicago , c1986. ix, 154 p. ; ISBN 0-8092-4890-5 (pbk.) : LC Card 86-23972 DDC 332.7/22 19
HG2040.5.U5 D423 1986

Financing land acquisition and development /. Washington, D.C. , c1987. 134 p. : ISBN 0-86718-281-4 (pbk.) LC Card 87-61069 DDC 332.7/2/0973 19
HD1390 .F56 1987

G-Yohannes, Arefaine. The professional's desktop guide to real estate finance /. Chicago, Ill. , c1988. p. cm. ISBN 0-917253-93-0 : LC Card 87-17918 DDC 332.7/2 19
HG2040.5.U5 G125 1988

Hiller, Michael D. How to get the 1 hour real estate loan . Encino, CA (16161 Ventura Blvd., #C-719, Encino 91436) , c1987. 170 p. : LC Card 87-154252 DDC 332.7/22/0973 19
HG2040.5.U5 H53 1987

Hines, Mary Alice. Real estate debt financing /. New York , c1987. xviii, 405 p. ; ISBN 0-471-85493-X LC Card 87-6200 DDC 332.7/2/0973 19
HG2040.5.U5 H55 1987

Irwin, Robert, 1941- Making mortgages work for you /. New York , c1987. viii, 185 p. : ISBN 0-07-032129-9 : LC Card 86-31270 DDC 332.7/22/0973 19
HG2040.5.U5 I75 1987

Knox, Albert H. What homebuyers should know about buying a home /. New York , c1987. vii, 192 p. : ISBN 0-533-06883-5 : LC Card 85-91377 DDC 643/.12 19
HD1379 .K656 1987

Lumley, James E. A. How to get a mortgage in 24 hours /. New York , c1987. xvii, 205 p. ; ISBN 0-471-85249-X LC Card 86-28930 DDC 332.7/2 19
HG2040.15.U5 .L85 1987

Stevenson, Eric. The secondary market and securitization for income property mortgages /. Washington, D.C. (1125 15th St., N.W., Washington 20005) , c1986. xiii, 129 p. : LC Card 87-153518 DDC 332.1/753 19
HG2040.5.U5 S73 1986

United States. Office of Urban Rehabilitation and Community Reinvestment. FHA Title I property improvement loan insurance [microform] . Washington , 1978. 19 p. ;
NYPL [*ZT-1564 no.11]

Wiedemer, John P., 1918- Real estate finance /. Englewood Cliffs, N.J. , c1987. xvi, 396 p. : ISBN 0-13-762774-2 LC Card 86-30471 DDC 332.7/2/0973 19
HG2040.5.U5 W54 1987

MORTGAGE LOANS - UNITED STATES - HANDBOOKS, MANUALS, ETC.
Friedman, Janet T. (Janet Teri), 1957- Safecracking the mortgage secrets . Houston, Tex. , c1987. 141 p. : ISBN 0-942037-00-6 (pbk.) : LC Card 87-13357 DDC 332.7/22/0973 19
HG2040.5.U5 F75 1987

Steinmetz, Thomas C. The mortgage kit . Chicago, IL , c1987. ix, 188 p. : ISBN 0-88462-658-X (pbk.) : LC Card 87-3693 DDC 332.7/22 19
HG2040.5.U5 S72 1987

MORTGAGE LOANS - UNITED STATES - STATISTICS.
Gramley, Lyle E. Real estate finance and housing . Washington, D.C. (1125 15th St., N.W., Washington 20005) , c1987. vii, 132 p. : LC Card 87-124264 DDC 332.7/2/0973021 19
HG2040.5.U5 G73 1987

Income and cost for origination and servicing of 1 to 4 unit residential loans, 1985. Washington, D.C. (1125 15th St., N.W., Washington 20005-2766) , c1986. 32 p. ; LC Card 87-106156 DDC 332.3/2/0973021 19
HG2040.5.U5 I535 1986

MORTGAGE LOANS, VARIABLE RATE - TABLES.
Financial comprehensive ARM payment tables /. Boston, Mass. , Philadelphia, PA , c1985. 255 p. ; ISBN 0-89471-379-5 (pbk.) : LC Card 85-206951 DDC 332.8/2/021 19
HG1634 .F44 1985

Friedman, Jack P. Adjustable rate mortgages /. New York , c1987. viii, 293 p. ; ISBN 0-8120-3764-2 (soft) : LC Card 86-28852 DDC 332.8/2 19
HG1634 .F75 1987

MORTGAGE LOANS, VARIABLE RATE - UNITED STATES.
Irwin, Robert, 1941- Making mortgages work for you /. New York , c1987. viii, 185 p. : ISBN 0-07-032129-9 : LC Card 86-31270 DDC 332.7/22/0973 19
HG2040.5.U5 I75 1987

The mortgage manual . DeBat, Don. Chicago , c1986. ix, 154 p. ; ISBN 0-8092-4890-5 (pbk.) : LC Card 86-23972 DDC 332.7/22 19
HG2040.5.U5 D423 1986

The mortgage market /. Boléat, Mark. London , Boston , 1987. x, 176 p. ; ISBN 0-04-334011-3 (alk. paper) LC Card 86-28875 DDC 332.7/22 19
HG2040.5.G7 B65 1987

MORTGAGES - NEW YORK (STATE)
New York (State). Legislature. Legislative Commission on Expenditure Review. Mitchell-Lama housing mortgage delinquencies . Albany, N.Y. (111 Washington Ave., Albany 12210-2277) [1985] 5, ii, 44 p. : LC Card 86-620632 DDC 353.97470086/5045 19
HD7303.N7 N394 1985 ***NYPL [JLF 87-104]***

MORTGAGES - PENNSYLVANIA.
A Sunset performance audit of the Pennsylvania Housing Finance Agency pursuant to Act 1981-142 /. Harrisburg, Pa. (Rm. 400, Finance Bldg., Harrisburg 17120) [1985] ii, 75 p. ; LC Card 85-623018 DDC 353.97480086/5045 19
HD7303.P4 P425 1985
NYPL [JLF 86-1807]

MORTGAGES - UNITED STATES.
Bel Air, Roger. Make a fortune buying discounted mortgages /. Garden City, N.Y. , 1987. 152 p. : ISBN 0-385-23924-6 : LC Card 86-23949 DDC 332.63/244 19
HG5095 .B38 1987

Economic development and real estate financing /. N[ew] Y[ork], N.Y. (41 E. 42nd St., N[ew] Y[ork] 10017) [c1985] iii, 203 p. : LC Card 86-221586 DDC 332.7/2/0973 19
HD255 .E26 1985

Hiller, Michael D. How to get the 1 hour real estate loan . Encino, CA (16161 Ventura Blvd., #C-719, Encino 91436) , c1987. 170 p. : LC Card 87-154252 DDC 332.7/22/0973 19
HG2040.5.U5 H53 1987

Hines, Mary Alice. Financing real estate with securities /. New York , c1988. p. cm. ISBN 0-471-62813-1 LC Card 87-26336 DDC 332.7/2 19
HG4655 .H56 1988

Mortgagor [sic] households in Canada . Che-Alford, Janet. Ottawa , c1986. 100 p. : ISBN 0-660-52986-6 (pbk.) : LC Card 86-202749 DDC 332.7/22/0971 19
HD7287.82.C2 C48 1986

Mortimer, Jeylan T., 1943- Work, family, and personality : transition to adulthood / Jeylan T. Mortimer, Jon Lorence, Donald S. Kumka. Norwood, N.J. : Ablex Pub. Corp., c1986. viii, 267 p. : ill. ; 24 cm. (Modern sociology) Includes

indexes. Bibliography: p. 231-255. ISBN 0-89391-293-X LC Card 85-20951 DDC 306/.36/09774 19
1. Work and family - Michigan - Longitudinal studies. 2. Personality and occupation - Michigan - Longitudinal studies. 3. Adulthood - Michigan - Psychological aspects - Longitudinal studies. I. Lorence, Jon. II. Kumka, Donald S. III. Title.
HD4904.25 .M67 1986 ***NYPL [JLE 87-869]***

Mortimer, Rex, 1926-1979. Stubborn survivors : dissenting essays on peasants and Third World development / Rex Mortimer ; edited by Herbert Feith and Rodney Tiffen. [Clayton, Vic.] : Centre of Southeast Asian Studies, Monash University, 1984. xvii, 180 p. : port. ; 21 cm. (Monash paper on Southeast Asia, 0727-6680 . no. 10) "Bibliography of works by Rex Mortimer": p. 175-179. Includes bibliographies. ISBN 0-86746-299-X (pbk.) LC Card 87-672646
1. Developing countries. 2. Peasantry - Developing countries. I. Feith, Herbert. II. Tiffen, Rodney. III. Monash University. Centre of Southeast Asian Studies. IV. Series: Monash papers on Southeast Asia, no. 10. V. Title.
HC59.7 .M593x 1984

Mortimore, Michael. Devlin, Robert. External debt in Bolivia /. Boulder, Colo. , 1987. p. cm. ISBN 0-8133-7366-2 : LC Card 87-2088 DDC 336.3/4/0984 19
HJ8574 .D48 1987

Morton, Clive, 1931- Burrows, Geoff, 1941- The canecutters /. Carlton, Vic. , 1986. xvi, 288 p. : ISBN 0-522-84304-2 LC Card 86-215188 DDC 331.7/6361/0994 19
HD8039.S86 A83 1986

Mortsiefer, Joachim. Messen und Ausstellungen als Mittel der Absatzpolitik mittelständischer Herstellerbetriebe / von Joachim Mortsiefer. Göttingen : O. Schwartz, 1986. 534 p. : ill. ; 23 cm. (Schriften zur Handelsforschung. Nr. 69) Bibliography: p. 476-521. ISBN 3-509-01399-9 : LC Card 86-210320 DDC 381/.18 19
1. Fairs. 2. Exhibitions. 3. Small business - Germany, West. I. Title.
HF5470 .M583 1986

MORTUARY STATISTICS. see **MORTALITY.**

Moschis, George P., 1944- Consumer socialization : a life cycle perspective / George P. Moschis. Lexington, Mass. : Lexington Books, 1987. xiii, 353 p. ; 24 cm. Includes index. Bibliography: p. [297]-339. ISBN 0-669-11244-5 (alk. paper) LC Card 85-45165 DDC 658.8/342 19
1. Consumers. I. Title.
HF5415.3 .M66 1987 ***NYPL [JLE 87-1666]***

Moscoso Pacheco, Arturo C. Con la vida a cuestas : testimonio de cargadores alcohólicos en Cochabamba / Arturo C. Moscoso Pacheco. Oruro, Bolivia : Centro de Investigación y Servicio Popular, 1987. 122 p. : ill. ; 21 cm. Bibliography: p. 119-120. LC Card 87-403838 DDC 362.2/922/088388 19
1. Porters - Bolivia - Cochabamba - Alcohol use. I. Title.
HD8039.P66 B56 1987

Moscove, Stephen A. Accounting information systems : concepts and practice for effective decision making / Stephen A. Moscove, Mark G. Simkin.3rd ed. New York : Wiley, c1987. xxi, 824 p. : ill. ; 25 cm. Includes bibliographies and index. ISBN 0-471-84033-5 LC Card 86-32387 DDC 657/.028/5 19
1. Accounting - Data processing. 2. Information storage and retrieval systems - Accounting. I. Simkin, Mark G. II. Title.
HF5679 .M62 1987

Moscow. Academy of Sciences. see **Akademiia nauk SSSR.**

Moscow challenges the world /. Ratiu, Ion. London , 1986. 410 p. ; ISBN 0-907671-23-5
NYPL [JLE 87-1665]

Moscow. Gosudarstvennyĭ bank. SSSR. see **Gosudarstvennyĭ bank SSSR.**

MOSCOW REGION (R.S.F.S.R.) - ECONOMIC CONDITIONS.
Geograficheskie problemy razvitiia narodnogo khoziaĭstva Moskovskogo regiona /. Moskva , 1986. 104 p. : LC Card 87-135959
HC338.M6 G46 1986

MOSCOW (R.S.F.S.R.) - ECONOMIC CONDITIONS.
Khoziaĭstvovat' umelo i ėffektivno /. Moskva , 1985. 267, [5] p. ; LC Card 85-148146
HC338.M6 K47 1985

MOSCOW (R.S.F.S.R.) - ECONOMIC POLICY.
Khoziaĭstvovat' umelo i ėffektivno /. Moskva , 1985. 267, [5] p. ; LC Card 85-148146
HC338.M6 K47 1985

Moser, Beat. Konflikt und Kooperation der Dritten Welt mit Industrieländern / Beat Moser. Diessenhofen : Rüegger, c1985. xi, 352 p. : ill. ; 21 cm. (Zürcher Beiträge zür politischen Wissenschaft. Bd. 9) Bibliography: p. 330-341. ISBN 3-7253-0236-7 : LC Card 85-139491
1. Developing countries - Foreign economic relations. 2. Dependency. 3. International cooperation. I. Title.
HF1413 .M66 1985

Moser, Colletta H., 1940- Reynolds, Lloyd George, 1910- Economics of labor /. Englewood Cliffs, NJ , c1987. x, 518 p. : ISBN 0-13-225772-6 LC Card 86-25149 DDC 331 19
HD4901 .R469 1987

Moser, R. (René), 1941- Marketing-Strategie für den Detailhandel / R. Moser. Münsingen : Buchverlag Fischer ; Zürich : SIB Schweizerisches Institut für Betriebsökonomie und höhere kaufmännische Bildung, 1981. 159 p. : ill. ; 21 cm. (Schriftenreihe SIB) Bibliography: p. [160] ISBN 3-85681-059-5 LC Card 83-240590
1. Retail trade - Switzerland. 2. Marketing - Switzerland. I. Title. II. Series.
HF5429.6.S92 M67 1981

Moser, Reinhard.
Exportmarketing / von Reinhard Moser. 2., verb. und erw. Aufl. [Linz : Johannes Kepler Universität Linz, 1979?] 120 leaves : 26 ill. ; 30 cm. "Universitätslehrgang zur Ausbildung von Exportkaufleuten an der Sozial- und Wirtschaftswissenschaftlichen Fakultät der Universität Linz"--Cover. Bibliography: leaf 120. LC Card 84-183280
1. Export marketing. I. Johannes Kepler Universität Linz. Sozial- und Wirtschaftswissenschaftliche Fakultät. II. Title.
HF1009.5 .M67 1979

Topritzhofer, Edgar, 1944- Das Exportgeschäft . Wien , 1984. 250 p. : ISBN 3-85428-025-4 LC Card 84-232997
HF1009.5 .T665 1984

MOSHAVIM.
Schwartz, Moshe. Non-agricultural employment for moshav youth in the Galilee /. Rehovot, Israel , c1985. 36, [2] p. ; LC Card 86-115596 DDC 331.3/4/0956945 19
HD6276.I66 G347 1985

Mosich, A. N.
Larsen, E. John. Modern advanced accounting /. New York , c1988. xx, 1002 p. ; ISBN 0-07-036508-3 : LC Card 87-22621 DDC 657/.046 19
HF5635 .M8756 1988

Modern advanced accounting. Larsen, E. John. Modern advanced accounting / E. John Larsen, A.N. Mosich. 4th ed. New York , c1988. xx, 1002 p. ; ISBN 0-07-036508-3 : LC Card 87-22621 DDC 657/.046 19
HF5635 .M8756 1988

Mosich, Donna M. Mastering Dac-Easy : accounting and payroll solutions / Donna M. Mosich, Robert W. Chamberlain. Glenview, Ill. : Scott, Foresman, c1988. p. cm. Includes index. ISBN 0-673-18735-7 LC Card 87-4847 DDC 657/.028/55369 19
1. Dac-Easy Accounting (Computer program). 2. Dac-Easy Payroll (Computer program). 3. Accounting - Data processing. 4. Payrolls - Data processing. I. Chamberlain, Robert W. II. Title.
HF5679 .M64 1988

Mosin, V. P. Ėkonomicheskie sviazi i sovershenstvovanie khoziaĭstvennogo mekhanizma . Kursk , 1985. 107 p. ; LC Card 86-235039
HC340.I57 E37 1985

Moskau, 1917-35 . Kreis, Barbara, 1947- [Germany] , c1985. 243 p., [3] p. of plates : ISBN 3-921420-26-1 : LC Card 86-170426
HD7345.M6 K73 1985

Moskovskiĭ ėkonomiko-statisticheskiĭ institut. Matematicheskie metody v ėkonomike i narodnom khoziaĭstve . Moskva , 1985. 121 p. ; LC Card 87-152514
HC336.25 M377 1985

Moskovskiĭ finansovyĭ institut. Rol' finansovo-kreditnogo mekhanizma v povyshenii ėffektivnosti obshchestvennykh zatrat . Moskva , 1984. 153 p. ; LC Card 86-113408
HG186.S55 R64 1984

Moskovskiĭ gosudarstvennyĭ pedagogicheskiĭ institut imeni V.I. Lenina. Razvitie kapitalisticheskoĭ manufaktury v Anglii i Germanii XVI-XVII vv. . Moskva , 1981. 132 p. : LC Card 83-111684
HD9735.G32 R39 1981

Moskovskiĭ, I. D. (Igor' Dmitrievich) Finansy i khoziaĭstvennyĭ raschet v usloviiakh ėkonomicheskogo ėksperimenta / I.D. Moskovskiĭ. Moskva : "Finansy i statistika", 1984. 60 p. ; 20 cm. (Predpriiatie--samostoiatel'nost' i otvetstvennost') Includes bibliographical references. LC Card 87-100142
1. Electric industries - Soviet Union - Finance - Management. I. Series. II. Series: Predpriiatie--samostoiatel'nost' i otvetstvennost' ("Finansy i statistika" (Firm)). III. Title.
HD9697.A3 S656 1984

Moskovtsev, I. S. (Ivan Sergeevich) Sovremennyĭ imperializm, antogonizmy i krizisy / I.S. Moskovtsev. Moskva : "Ėkonomika", 1985. 67 p. : ill. ; 20 cm. LC Card 85-232554
1. Capitalism - Social aspects. I. Title.
HB501 .M7219 1985

Moskow, Michael H. Working women . Washington, D.C. , c1987. xxii, 419 p. ; ISBN 0-87179-547-7 LC Card 87-9410 DDC 331.4/0973 19
HD6095 .W742 1987

Moskowitz, Herbert. Tsai, Hsien-Tang. A 3-interval polynomial approximation for continuous univariate distribution functions /. West Lafayette, Ind. [1986] 7, 14 p. : LC Card 86-622753 DDC 658/.001/9 s 519/.2 19
HD6483 .P8 no. 898 QA273.6

Moskowitz, Milton. The global marketplace : 102 of the most influential companies outside America / Milton Moskowitz. New York : Macmillan, c1987. xi, 708 p. : ill. ; 25 cm. Bibliography: p. 691-694. Includes index. ISBN 0-02-587590-6 LC Card 87-15897 DDC 338.8/8 19
1. International business enterprises - Case studies. I. Title.
HD2755.5 .M675 1987

Mosley, Paul. Foreign aid, its defense and reform / Paul Mosley. Lexington, Ky. : University Press of Kentucky, c1987. xiv, 264 p. ; 24 cm. Bibliography: p. 243-257. Includes index. ISBN 0-8131-1608-2 : LC Card 86-23400 DDC 338.91/09172/4 19
1. Economic assistance - Developing countries. I. Title.
HC60 .M67 1987

Mosley, W. Henry (Wiley Henry), 1933- The dynamics of birth spacing and marital fertility in Kenya / W. Henry Mosley, Linda H. Werner, Stanley Becker. [Nairobi? : s.n., 1981] 63 leaves : ill. ; 30 cm. "Revised April 1981." Bibliography: leaves 53-56. LC Card 85-980189
1. Fertility, Human - Kenya. 2. Birth intervals - Kenya. I. Werner, Linda H. II. Becker, Stan. III. Title.
HB1072.5.A3 M66 1981

Mosquera, Gilma. see **Mosquera Torres, Gilma.**

Mosquera Torres, Gilma. Clases, segregación y barrios / Gilma Mosquera Torres, Jacques Aprile-Gniset. Cali, Colombia : Universidad del Valle, 1984. 126 p. : ill. ; 22 cm. Includes bibliographies. LC Card 86-218143
1. Housing - Social aspects - Colombia - Valle del Cauca. 2. Discrimination in housing - Colombia - Valle del Cauca. 3. Land use, Urban - Colombia - Valle del Cauca. I. Aprile-Gniset, Jacques. II. Title.
HD7325.V35 M67 1984

Moss, Alison. Ladbrook, Denis A. Disadvantaged youth in an isolated region . [Pilbara, W.A.] [1985] ix, 125 p. : LC Card 87-121044 DDC 331.3/4/099413 19
HD6276.A83 P555 1985

Moss, Bernard H.
[Origins of the French labor movement, 1830-1914. French]
Aux origines du mouvement ouvrier français :

le socialisme des ouvriers de métier, 1830-1914 / Bernard H. Moss ; traduit de l'anglais par Michel Cordillot ; préface de Jacques Rougerie. Paris : Belles lettres, 1985. xi, 236 p. ; 24 cm... (Annales littéraires de l'Université de Besançon . 326) Translation of: Origins of the French labor movement, 1830-1914. Includes indexes. "Essai bibliographique": p. 209-224. ISBN 2-251-60326-3
1. Socialism - France - History. 2. Skilled labor - France - Political activity - History. 3. Trade-unions - France - Political activity - History. I. Series: Besançon, France. Université. Annales littéraires, 326. II. Title.
NYPL [M-10 6410 n.326]

Moss, Nicholas. BBC TV presents : a fiftieth anniversary celebration : TV50 / Nicholas Moss ; foreword by Bill Cotton. London : BBC Data Publications, 1986. 120 p. : ill. (some col.) ; 28 cm. Includes index. ISBN 0-946358-29-X LC Card 87-146728 DDC 384.55/4/06041 19
1. British Broadcasting Corporation. Television Service - History. 2. Television broadcasting - Great Britain - History. I. Title.
HE8700.9.G7 M67 1986

Mossavar-Rahmani, Bijan. Natural gas trade in transition /. Cambridge, MA , c1987. 91 p. ; ISBN 0-942781-00-7 (pbk.) LC Card 87-81051 DDC 338.2/7285 19
HD9581.A2 N38 1987

Mossman, Jennifer. Encyclopedia of geographic information sources, international volume . Detroit, Mich. , c1988. 479 p. ; ISBN 0-8103-0410-4 : LC Card 87-23777 DDC 016.33 19
HF5341 .E53 1988

Mostyn, Barbara. Motivational research : passing fad or permanent feature? / by Barbara Mostyn. Bradford : MCB, 1977. [6], 44 p. ; 30 cm. (Motivational research series. no. 1) Bibliography: p. 41-44. ISBN 0-905440-28-5 : LC Card 79-311507
1. Motivation research (Marketing). 2. Motivation (Psychology). I. Title.
HF5415.3 .M67 ***NYPL [JLF 79-1442]***

Mot strømmen . Bjørklund, Tor, 1947- Oslo , c1982. 396 p. : ISBN 82-00-06338-0 : LC Card 83-134961
HC241.25.N7 B56 1982

Motamen, Sima. International debt and central banking in the 1980s /. New York , 1987. viii, 234 p. ; ISBN 0-312-00530-X : LC Card 87-4300 DDC 336.3/435/091724 19
HJ8899 .I574 1987

MOTELS - ACCOUNTING.
Cote, Raymond. Understanding hospitality accounting I /. East Lansing, Mich. , c1987. p. cm. ISBN 0-86612-035-1 : LC Card 87-15724 DDC 657/.837 19
HF5686.H75 C63 1987

Mothé-Gautrat, Daniel, 1924- Pour une nouvelle culture d'entreprise / Daniel Mothé-Gautrat. Paris : Editions La Découverte, 1986. 173 p. ; 22 cm. (Cahiers libres. 415) Bibliography: p. 167-169. ISBN 2-7071-1596-7 : LC Card 86-185142
1. Industrial relations - France. 2. Collective bargaining - France. 3. Corporate culture - France. 4. Trade-unions - France. I. Title.
HD8431 .M63 1986

MOTHERHOOD.
Wilk, Carole. Career women and childbearing . New York , c1986. xxii, 304 p. ; ISBN 0-442-29352-6 LC Card 85-9216 DDC 306.8/743 19
HQ759 .W52 1986 ***NYPL [JLD 86-1811]***

MOTHERS - EMPLOYMENT - AUSTRALIA.
Frey, Dianne. Survey of sole parent pensioners' workforce barriers /. Woden, ACT [1986] 40 p. : ISBN 0-642-51708-8 LC Card 87-154429 DDC 331.4/4 19
HD6220 .F74 1986

MOTHERS - EMPLOYMENT - POLAND - ŁÓDŹ.
Praca zawodowa a życie rodzinne kobiet /. [Łódź] , 1979. 120 p. ; LC Card 81-109965
HD6054.2.P72 L636 1979

MOTHERS' PENSIONS - UNITED STATES.
Lopata, Helena Znaniecka, 1925- Widows and dependent wives . New York , 1986. xxi, 242 p. ; ISBN 0-03-046301-7 (alk. paper) : LC Card 85-16753 DDC 362.8/382 19
HV699 .L67 1985 ***NYPL [JLE 86-2182]***

Motion and time study . Mundel, Marvin Everett, 1916- Englewood Cliffs, N.J. , c1985. xvi, 752 p. : ISBN 0-13-603044-0 LC Card 84-18173 DDC 658.5/42 19
T60.7 .M86 1985 ***NYPL [JSE 86-2187]***

MOTION PICTURE INDUSTRY - SOVIET UNION - STATISTICAL METHODS.
Mukhin, P. A. (Pavel Aleksandrovich) Statistika kinematografii . Moskva , 1984. 103 p. : LC Card 85-203673
HA29.5.R9 M85 1984

MOTION PICTURE INDUSTRY - UNITED STATES.
Mair, George, 1929- Inside HBO . New York , c1988. xviii, 204 p. ; ISBN 0-396-08420-6 : LC Card 87-19939 DDC 384.55/47/0973 19
HE8700.72.U6 M34 1988

MOTION PICTURES - SOCIAL ASPECTS - STATISTICAL METHODS.
Mukhin, P. A. (Pavel Aleksandrovich) Statistika kinematografii . Moskva , 1984. 103 p. : LC Card 85-203673
HA29.5.R9 M85 1984

MOTION STUDY.
Mundel, Marvin Everett, 1916- Motion and time study . Englewood Cliffs, N.J. , c1985. xvi, 752 p. : ISBN 0-13-603044-0 LC Card 84-18173 DDC 658.5/42 19
T60.7 .M86 1985 ***NYPL [JSE 86-2187]***

Why the office staff scared of time and motion study? . Saddar, Karachi, Pakistan [1985] 1 v. (various pagings) leaves ; LC Card 86-146552
HD5070.5 .W49 1985

MOTIVATION.
Applied behavioral science for plant managers /. Columbia, Md. , c1987. vii, 102 p. : ISBN 0-87683-830-1 (pbk.) LC Card 86-31926 DDC 658.3 19
HF5548.8 .A715 1987

Motivation and work behavior / [compiled by] Richard M. Steers, Lyman W. Porter. 4th ed. New York : McGraw-Hill, c1987. xii, 595 p. : ill. ; 24 cm. (McGraw-Hill series in management) Includes bibliographies and indexes. ISBN 0-07-060948-9 : LC Card 86-27865 DDC 658.3/14 19
1. Employee motivation. 2. Psychology, Industrial. I. Steers, Richard M. II. Porter, Lyman W.
HF5549.5.M63 M667 1987

MOTIVATION IN INDUSTRY. see **EMPLOYEE MOTIVATION.**

Motivation, planning, and action . Nuttin, Jozef, 1909- [Théorie de la motivation humaine. English.] Leuven, Belgium , Hillsdale, N.J. , c1984. viii, 251 p. ; ISBN 0-89859-332-8 (L. Erlbaum) LC Card 83-16416 DDC 153.8 19
BF503 .N8713 1984 ***NYPL [JFE 86-2315]***

MOTIVATION (PSYCHOLOGY)
Habtamu Wondimu. Some factors which affect peasant motivation to work in the Ethiopian agricultural producers cooperatives /. [Addis Ababa] [1983] 60 leaves : LC Card 84-980911 DDC 334/.683/0963 19
HD1491.E83 H3 1983b ***NYPL [JLG 86-163]***

Handbook of motivation and cognition . New York , c1986. x, 610 p. : ISBN 0-89862-667-6 LC Card 85-24916 DDC 153.8 19
BF503 .H36 1986 ***NYPL [JFE 86-2410]***

Mostyn, Barbara. Motivational research . Bradford , 1977. [6], 44 p. ; ISBN 0-905440-28-5 : LC Card 79-311507
HF5415.3 .M67 ***NYPL [JLF 79-1442]***

Nuttin, Jozef, 1909- [Théorie de la motivation humaine. English.] Motivation, planning, and action . Leuven, Belgium , Hillsdale, N.J. , c1984. viii, 251 p. ; ISBN 0-89859-332-8 (L. Erlbaum) LC Card 83-16416 DDC 153.8 19
BF503 .N8713 1984 ***NYPL [JFE 86-2315]***

Sales motivation . New York, N.Y., U. S.A. , c1985. viii, 131 leaves ; ISBN 0-86604-150-8 (pbk.) LC Card 86-232974 DDC 658.3/14 19
HF5438.25 .S253 1985

Sanders, Mary. R.P.M. realize your power to motivate /. Farmington Hills, Mich. , c1986. 153 p., [2] p. of plates : ISBN 0-9616833-0-9 (pbk.) LC Card 87-111586 DDC 658.3/14 19
HF5549.5.M63 S26 1986

Vroom, Victor Harold, 1932- Some personality determinants of the effects of participation /. New York , 1987, c1960. x, 91 p. ; ISBN 0-8240-8225-7 (alk. paper) : LC Card 86-27081 DDC 158.7 19
HF5548.8 .V695 1987

Wünschmann, Andreas, 1942- Unbewusst dagegen . Stuttgart , 1984, c1980. 177 p. : ISBN 3-87959-214-4 (pbk.) LC Card 87-673462
HD9698.A2 W86x 1984

MOTIVATION (PSYCHOLOGY) - ADDRESSES, ESSAYS, LECTURES.
Herzberg, Frederick. The managerial choice . Salt Lake City, Utah , c1982. xviii, 360 p. : ISBN 0-913420-97-2 LC Card 81-85925 DDC 658.3/14 19
HF5549.5.I5 H47 1982
NYPL [JLE 86-2591]

MOTIVATION RESEARCH (MARKETING)
Assael, Henry. Consumer behavior and marketing action /. Boston, Mass. , c1987. xix, 700 p., [8] p. of plates : ISBN 0-534-07530-4 : LC Card 86-21336 DDC 658.8/342 19
HF5415.3 .A83 1987

The Climate of persuasion . [Richmond, VA.] , 1959. 58 p. : ***NYPL [JLF 86-1150]***

Mostyn, Barbara. Motivational research . Bradford , 1977. [6], 44 p. ; ISBN 0-905440-28-5 : LC Card 79-311507
HF5415.3 .M67 ***NYPL [JLF 79-1442]***

Runyon, Kenneth E. Consumer behavior and the practice of marketing /. Columbus , c1987. xv, 776 p. : ISBN 0-675-20463-1 LC Card 86-62987 DDC 658.8/342 19
HF5415.3 .R86 1987

Schiffman, Leon G. Consumer behavior /. Englewood Cliffs, N.J. , c1987. xviii, 724 p. : ISBN 0-13-169020-5 LC Card 86-25224 DDC 658.8/342 19
HF5415.3 .S29 1987

Zaltman, Gerald. Consumer behavior . Malabar, Fla. , 1987, c1983. p. cm. ISBN 0-89874-989-1 LC Card 86-21297 DDC 658.8/342 19
HF5415.3 .Z28 1987

MOTIVATION RESEARCH (MARKETING) - ADDRESSES, ESSAYS, LECTURES.
Perspectives on methodology in consumer research /. New York , c1986. xi, 301 p. : ISBN 0-387-96238-7 : LC Card 85-26047 DDC 658.8/34 19
HF5415.3 .P464 1986 ***NYPL [JLE 86-4371]***

MOTIVATION RESEARCH (MARKETING) - MATHEMATICAL MODELS.
Horn, Christel-Margret. Feldtheorie und Konsumverhalten /. Freiburg im Breisgau , c1983. 121 p. : ISBN 3-448-01293-9 LC Card 84-136042
HF5415.3 .H65 1983

Die Motivation von Arbeitnehmern im Innen- und Aussendienst des Vertriebs . Huellen, Karl Konrad. Münster [1986] iv, 245 p. : ISBN 3-88660-356-3 (Deut. Bibl.) LC Card 87-114821 DDC 658.3/14 19
HF5549.5.M63 H84 1986

Motivational research . Mostyn, Barbara. Bradford , 1977. [6], 44 p. ; ISBN 0-905440-28-5 : LC Card 79-311507
HF5415.3 .M67 ***NYPL [JLF 79-1442]***

Motivations to remit . Lucas, Robert E. B. [Tel Aviv] [1985] 27 leaves ; LC Card 86-177234
HG3984.9 .L83 1985

Motkin, G. A. Ėkonomicheskie problemy prirodopolʹzovaniia /. Moskva , 1985. 137 p. : LC Card 86-119089
HC340.E5 E395 1985

MOTOR-CARS. see **AUTOMOBILES.**

MOTOR FUELS - TAXATION - UNITED STATES.
Oppenheimer, Ernest J., 1924- Gasoline tax advantages /. New York, N.Y. , c1987. 88 p. ; ISBN 0-9603982-5-2 (pbk.) : LC Card 86-862507 DDC 336.2/7866553827 19
HD9579.G5 U5732 1987

The Motor vehicle industry in Asia : a study of ancillary firm development / edited by Konosuke Odaka. [Singapore] : Published for Council for Asian Manpower Studies by Singapore University Press, [1983] xxv, 419 p. : ill. ; 24 cm. Includes bibliographies. ISBN 997-16-9057-8 LC Card 83-941793 DDC 338.4/76292/095 19

1. Automobile supplies industry - Asia. 2. Automobile industry and trade - Asia. 3. Machinery industry - Asia. I. Odaka, Kōnosuke, 1935-. II. Council for Asian Manpower Studies. III. Title.
HD9710.3.A78 M67 1983 *NYPL [JLE 85-1592]*

MOTOR VEHICLES - MAINTENANCE AND REPAIR - ECONOMIC ASPECTS - SOUTH AFRICA - STATISTICS.
Sensus van motorhandel en hersteldienste, 1977 =. Pretoria [1982?] xiv, 166 p. : ISBN 0-621-07034-3 : LC Card 82-240419
HD9710.S72 S46 1982

MOTOR VEHICLES - WASHINGTON METROPOLITAN AREA - STATISTICS.
1986 Beltway cordon count of vehicular and passenger volumes. [Washington, D.C.] [1986] iv, 35 p., [109] p. : LC Card 87-119314 DDC 388.4/1314/09753021 19
HE5634.W3 A17 1986

Motorcycle accident facts, 1984. [Springfield, Ill.] : Illinois Dept. of Transportation, 1984. 15 p. : ill. ; 22 cm. Cover title. LC Card 86-622490 DDC 363.1/259 19
1. Traffic accidents - Illinois - Statistics. 2. Motorcycles - Illinois - Accidents - Statistics. I. Illinois. Dept. of Transportation.
HE5614.3.I4 M674 1984

MOTORCYCLE INDUSTRY - SOUTH AFRICA - STATISTICS.
Sensus van motorhandel en hersteldienste, 1977 =. Pretoria [1982?] xiv, 166 p. : ISBN 0-621-07034-3 : LC Card 82-240419
HD9710.S72 S46 1982

MOTORCYCLE INDUSTRY - UNITED STATES.
1986 motorcycle retail outlet profile survey. Costa Mesa, CA (3151 Airway Ave., Bldg. P-1, Costa Mesa 92626) , c1987. 33 p. : LC Card 87-401918 DDC 381/.456292275/0973021 19
HD9710.5.U52 A15 1987

MOTORCYCLE INDUSTRY - UNITED STATES - HISTORY.
Wright, David, 1943- The Harley-Davidson Motor Company . Osceola, Wis., USA , c1987. 288 p. : ISBN 0-87938-245-7 : LC Card 87-5519 DDC 338.7/6292275/0973 19
HD9710.5.U54 H378 1987

MOTORCYCLE RACING - HISTORY.
Wright, David, 1943- The Harley-Davidson Motor Company . Osceola, Wis., USA , c1987. 288 p. : ISBN 0-87938-245-7 : LC Card 87-5519 DDC 338.7/6292275/0973 19
HD9710.5.U54 H378 1987

Motorcycle retail outlet profile survey. 1986 motorcycle retail outlet profile survey. Costa Mesa, CA (3151 Airway Ave., Bldg. P-1, Costa Mesa 92626) , c1987. 33 p. : LC Card 87-401918 DDC 381/.456292275/0973021 19
HD9710.5.U52 A15 1987

MOTORCYCLE SUPPLIES INDUSTRY - SOUTH AFRICA - STATISTICS.
Sensus van motorhandel en hersteldienste, 1977 =. Pretoria [1982?] xiv, 166 p. : ISBN 0-621-07034-3 : LC Card 82-240419
HD9710.S72 S46 1982

MOTORCYCLES - GERMANY (WEST) - SAFETY MEASURES.
Grosse-Berndt, Gisela. Wirksamkeitsuntersuchung zum ADAC-Motorrad-Sicherheitstraining. Köln [1983] iii, 160, ii, 112, 27 p. : LC Card 84-147564
HE5614.5.G3 G75 1983

MOTORCYCLES - ILLINOIS - ACCIDENTS - STATISTICS.
Motorcycle accident facts, 1984. [Springfield, Ill.] , 1984. 15 p. : LC Card 86-622490 DDC 363.1/259 19
HE5614.3.I4 M674 1984

MOTORCYCLES - NETHERLANDS - STATISTICS.
Het Bezit en gebruik van motorfietsen, 1984 /. 's-Gravenhage , 1985. 26 p. : ISBN 90-357-0397-9 : LC Card 86-218867
HE5616.5 .B49 1985

MOTORCYCLING - NETHERLANDS - STATISTICS.
Het Bezit en gebruik van motorfietsen, 1984 /. 's-Gravenhage , 1985. 26 p. : ISBN 90-357-0397-9 : LC Card 86-218867
HE5616.5 .B49 1985

The motorization of American cities /. St. Clair, David James, 1950- New York , 1986. xi, 192 p. ; ISBN 0-275-92126-3 (alk. paper) : LC Card 86-523 DDC 388.4/1321/0973 19
HE5623 .S617 1986 *NYPL [JLE 86-3608]*

Mott, Graham. Management accounting / Graham Mott. Aldershot, Hants, England ; Brookfield, Vt., U. S.A. : Gower, c1987. 231 p. : ill. ; 22 cm. Includes index. ISBN 0-566-02685-6 : LC Card 86-29615 DDC 658.1/511 19
1. Managerial accounting. I. Title.
HF5635 .M877 1987

Mott, Luiz R. B. (Luiz Roberto de Barros) Piauí colonial : população, economia e sociedade / Luiz R.B. Mott. [Teresina] : Projeto Petrônio Portella, [1985] 142 p. : map ; 22 cm. Includes bibliographies. LC Card 86-131892
1. Piauí (Brazil) - Economic conditions. 2. Piauí (Brazil) - Social conditions. 3. Piauí (Brazil) - Population - History. 4. Plantations - Brazil - Piauí - History. 5. Piauí, Brazil - History. I. Title.
HC188.P5 M67 1985

Mott, Peter. Aufbereitung von Ergebnissen der Stadtverkehrsforschung . Hof/Saale , 1986. 2 v. : LC Card 87-408335 DDC 388.4/0943 19
HE4774 .A94 1986

Motta, Fernando C. Prestes. Burocracia e autogestão : a proposta de Proudhon / Fernando C. Prestes Motta. São Paulo, Brasil : Brasiliense, 1981. 170 p. ; 21 cm. Bibliography: p. [168]-170. LC Card 82-106136
1. Proudhon, P.-J. (Pierre-Joseph), 1809-1865 - Contributions in mutualism. 2. Proudhon, P.-J. (Pierre-Joseph), 1809-1865 - Contributions in bureaucracy. 3. Mutualism. 4. Bureaucracy. I. Title.
HD2961 .M658 1981

Mottura, Paolo. La Gestione degli istituti di credito industriale /. Milano [1985] xviii, 868 p. : ISBN 88-14-00665-2 : LC Card 86-170383
HG3726 .G47 1985

Motylev, Veniamin Vol′fovich. Rol′ bankov v usilenii gospodstva finansovogo kapitala /. Moskva , 1985. 206 p. ; LC Card 86-102078
HG3881 .R615 1985

Mouat, Frederic J. (Frederic John), 1816-1897. The death tribute of England to India : being an examination of the deaths and invaliding of officers of H.M. British Forces serving in India, from 1861 to 1870 inclusive, considered with special reference to the question of the present value of European life in India / by Frederic J. Mouat. London : Charles and Edwin Layton, 1875. 14 p. ; 21 cm. Cover title: Death tribute. LC Card 87-168950
1. British - India - Death. I. Title. II. Title: Death tribute.
HB1469 .M67 1875

MOULAGE. see **PROSTHESIS.**

Mould, Maurice C., 1925- Financial information for management of a development finance institution : some guidelines / Maurice C. Mould with Martin I. Stoller, John B. Morse, Jr., and Diane Glynis McNaughton. Washington, D.C. : World Bank, [1987] 1 v. (various pagings) : forms ; 28 cm. (Industry and finance series, 0256-2235 . v. 21) World Bank technical paper, 0253-7494 ; no. 63 ISBN 0-8213-0913-7 (pbk.) LC Card 87-15989 DDC 332.2 19
1. Development credit corporations - Management. 2. Development banks - Management. I. Title. II. Series.
HG3726 .M68 1987

Mounbaga, Emmanuel Seidou, 1957- Finanzpolitik und Wirtschaftsentwicklung in der Dritten Welt : Einsatz und Wirkungen finanzpolitischer Instrumente im Entwicklungsprozess / von Emmanuel Seidou Mounbaga. München : Ifo-Institut für Wirtschaftsforschung, c1986. 265 p. ; 21 cm. (Ifo Forschungsberichte der Abteilung Entwicklungsländer . 67) Bibliography: p. 241-265. ISBN 3-8039-0341-6 LC Card 86-233152
1. Finance, Public - Developing countries. 2. Developing countries - Economic policy. 3. Developing countries - Economic conditions. I. Title. II. Series.
HJ1620 .M68 1986

Mounce, John M. (John Michael) McCasland, William R. Transitway surveillance, communications, and control /. College Station, Tex. [1986] vi, 76 p. : LC Card 87-620995 DDC 380.5 s 388.3/143 19
HE203 .T43 no. 425-2F HE336.B8

Mount, Joan. Cook, W. Rupert. Canadian statistical data . [Canada] [1985?] vi, 218 p. : LC Card 87-118992 DDC 354.710081/9 19
HA37.C26 C66 1985

MOUNTAINS - ITALY - PARMA (PROVINCE) - CONGRESSES.
Economia e società della montagna parmense . [Italy , 1984?] (Parma : Officina grafica artigiana) 115 p. ; LC Card 85-156635
HC307.P33 E27 1984

Mountains of butter, lakes of milk . Pfeiffer, Gabrielle. Genève , 1986. 78, [4] p. : LC Card 87-109400 DDC 382/.417 19
HD9275.A2 P48 1986

Mountjoy, Alan B. Africa, geography and development / Alan B. Mountjoy, David Hilling. Totowa, NJ : Barnes & Noble, 1987. p. cm. Bibliography: p. Includes index. ISBN 0-389-20722-5 LC Card 87-1306 DDC 330.96/0328 19
1. Africa - Economic conditions - 1960-. 2. Africa - Description and travel - 1977-. I. Hilling, David. II. Title.
HC800 .M68 1987

Moura, Gerson. A campanha do petróleo / Gerson Moura. São Paulo-SP : Brasiliense, 1986. 92 p. : ill. ; 16 cm. (Tudo é história . 109) Bibliography: p. [91]-92. LC Card 86-190721
1. Petróleo Brasileiro, S.A. - History. 2. Petroleum industry and trade - Brazil - History. I. Title. II. Series.
HD9574.B84 P445 1986

Moura, Hélio A. de (Hélio Augusto) Dinâmica demográfica recente dos estados e microrregiões do Nordeste, 1960/1980 / Hélio Augusto de Moura, Taís de Freitas Santos. Recife [Brazil] : Divisão de Estudos Populacionais, Departamento de Estatística Aplicada, Instituto de Pesquisas Sociais, Fundação Joaquim Nabuco, 1986. 95 p., [6] folded p. of plates : ill. ; 22 cm. Bibliography: p. 46-47. LC Card 87-131106 DDC 304.6/0981/3 19
1. Brazil, Northeast - Population. I. Santos, Taís de Freitas. II. Title.
HB3564.N66 M68 1986

Moura, João. Problemas e política de emprego no continente / João Moura. Lisboa : Gabinete de Estudos, Planeamento e Organização, Ministério do Trabalho, 1977. 56 p. ; 23 cm. (Série Estudos . 36) Summary in English and French. "Este texto foi apresentado na Conferência sobre a Economia Portuguesa que se efectuou em Lisboa, de 11 a 13 de Outubro de 1976, promovida pelo Fundo German Marshall dos Estados Unidos e pela Fundação Gulbenkian"--P. 5. Includes bibliographical references. LC Card 85-214189
1. Labor supply - Portugal. 2. Manpower policy - Portugal. I. Series: Série Estudos (Portugal. Ministério do Trabalho. Gabinete de Estudos, Planeamento e Organização) , 36. II. Title.
HD5809.A6 M68 1977

Moura, Margarida Maria. Camponeses / Margarida Maria Moura. São Paulo : Editora Atica, 1986. 78 p. ; 18 cm. (Série Princípios . 52) Bibliography: p. [75]-78. ISBN 85-08-01089-3 LC Card 86-230194
1. Peasantry - Brazil - History. 2. Peasantry - History. I. Title.
HD1531.B7 M68 1986

Mouriaux, René.
Bon, Frédéric, 1943- Résultats des élections aux conseils de prud'hommes par département . St. Martin d'Hères [France] [1982] 303 p. ; LC Card 84-152037
HD5555 .B65 1982

Syndicalisme et politique / René Mouriaux. Paris : Editions ouvrières, c1985. 212 p. : ill. ; 22 cm. (Collection "Portes ouvertes," 0757-9365) Bibliography: p. 191-195. LC Card 86-159539
1. Trade-unions - France - Political activity. 2. Political parties - France. I. Title.
HD6687 .M68 1985

Mousiopoulou, Kalliopē Papathanasē- see **Papathanasē-Mousiopoulou, Kalliopē.**

Mousourou, Loukia M. Gynaikeia apascholēsē kai oikogeneia stēn Hellada kai allou / Loukias M. Mousourou ; prologos D.G. Tsaousē. Athēna : Vivliopōleion tēs "Hestias", c1985. 220 p. : ill. ; 21 cm. (Hellēnikē koinōnia . 3) Bibliography: p.

197-217. Includes index. LC Card 86-205975
1. Wives - Employment - Greece. 2. Wives - Employment. 3. Family - Greece. 4. Family. I. Title. II. Series.
HD6181.83 .M68 1985

Moustakas, Dion. E. Hai ploutoparagōgikai dynameis tēs nēsou Androu / hypo Dion. E. Moustaka. En Athēnais : Hellēnikē Geōgraphikē Hetaireia, 1924. 25 p. : ill. ; 23 cm. (Dēmosieuma / Hellēnikē Geōgraphikē Hetaireia . 4) LC Card 87-100195
1. Andros Island (Greece) - Economic conditions. I. Hellēnikē Geōgraphikē Hetaireia (Athens, Greece). II. Series: Dēmosieuma (Hellēnikē Geōgraphikē Hetaireia (Athens, Greece)) , 4. III. Title.
HC297.A53 M68 1924

Mouton, Jane Srygley. Blake, Robert Rogers, 1918- Spectacular teamwork . New York , c1987. viii, 219 p. : ISBN 0-471-85311-9 LC Card 86-28123 DDC 658.4/036 19
HD66 .B54 1987

Mouvement national démocratique (Guinea) Où allons nous?. [Conakry] [1986?] 92 p. ; LC Card 87-115579
HC1030 .O89 1986

Le mouvement syndical à l'île Maurice /. Allgoo, Rajpalsingh. Port Louis, Ile Maurice , 1985. 110 p., [14] leaves of plates : LC Card 87-119075
HD8840.3.A5 A7825 1985

Mouvements (Paris, France) .
(2) Touraine, Alain. Le mouvement ouvrier /. [Paris] , c1984. 438 p. : ISBN 2-213-01361-6 : LC Card 84-202370 DDC 322/.2/0944 19
HD6684 .T655 1984 ***NYPL [JLE 86-279]***

Movement for a no poverty society : transactions of an expert group meeting appointed by the United Nations / edited by Sugata Dasgupta. Calcutta : Institute of Social Change and Social Welfare, 1980. 78 p. ; 23 cm. Includes bibliographical references. LC Card 81-902107
1. Poverty - Asia - Congresses. 2. Poverty - Pacific Area - Congresses. 3. Rural development - Asia - Congresses. 4. Rural development - Pacific Area - Congresses. 5. Asia - Social conditions - Congresses. 6. Pacific area - Social conditions - Congresses. I. Dasgupta, Sugata, 1926-. II. Social Welfare Development Centre for Asia and the Pacific. III. Institute of Social Change and Social Welfare (Calcutta, India).
HC415.P6 M68 1980

El moviment de població de les comarques de la Catalunya de sobirania francesa en el curs dels segles XIX i XX /. Iglésies, Josep, 1902- Barcelona , 1979. 63 p. ; LC Card 81-120813
HB3620.C3 I325 1979

Il movimento cooperativo in Italia nel primo dopoguerra (1918-1925) /. Caroleo, Anna, 1948- Milano, Italy , c1986. 376 p. ; LC Card 86-192160
HD3503 .C36 1986

Movimento demográfico da matriz de Vila Viçosa nos séculos XVI e XVII /. Pestana, M. Inácio. [Vila Viçosa, Portugal , 1985] 32 p. : LC Card 86-199468
HB3622.V55 P47 1985

O movimento operário em Lourenço Marques, 1898-1927 /. Capela, José. [Porto?] [1981?] 281, [1] p. ; LC Card 87-401260 DDC 331.88/0967/9 19
HD6869.Z8 M363 1981

O movimento sindical metalúrgico em Santa Luzia /. Franco, José Ronaldo de Mello. [Santa Luzia, Minas Gerais, Brazil?] 1985. 111 p. ; LC Card 87-404244 DDC 331.88/171/098151 19
HD6614.M5 F73 1985

O Movimento sindical no interior : o caso dos trabalhadores metalúrgicos e têxteis. Piracicaba, SP : Editora UNIMEP, [19]84. 38, [10] p. : ill. ; 21 cm. (Cadernos do mestrado. Série "História do trabalho" . no. 1) Includes bibliographical references. LC Card 86-200279
1. Trade-unions - Textile workers - Brazil - São Paulo (State) - History - 20th century. 2. Trade-unions - Metal-workers - Brazil - São Paulo (State) - History - 20th century. I. Series.
HD6615.S32 M68 1984

Movimiento obrero del Ecuador, 1970-1979 : documentos / [recopilados] por Elías Muñoz Vicuña y Leonardo Vicuña Izquierdo. Guayaquil, Ecuador : Librería y Distribuidora Continental, [1985] 300 p. ; 22 cm. (Colección Movimiento obrero ecuatoriano . no. 7) Imprint stamped on p. [1]. Includes bibliographical references. LC Card 86-105256 DDC 331.88/09866 19
1. Trade-unions - Ecuador - History - Sources. 2. Labor and laboring classes - Ecuador - History - Sources. I. Muñoz Vicuña, Elías. II. Vicuña Izquierdo, Leonardo. III. Series.
HD6627 .M68 1985 ***NYPL [JLD 86-3140]***

El movimiento obrero en Cantabria (1955-1977) /. Argos Villar, José Carlos. [Santander?] [1982?] 227 p. ; ISBN 84-300-6979-8 LC Card 86-203186
HD8589.C3 A74 1982

El movimiento obrero en el Estado de México . García Luna O., Margarita (García Luna Ortega) Toluca, Estado de México , 1984. 302 p. : ISBN 968-514-014-6 LC Card 86-173738
HC137.M473 G37 1984

Movimiento obrero en Jalisco, período 1925-1930 /. Gutiérrez Zermeño, Rodolfo, 1953- Guadalajara, Jalisco, México , 1985. 64 p. ; ISBN 968-8322-01-6 LC Card 86-208368
HD6535.J35 G88 1985

El movimiento obrero en Nicaragua . Pérez Bermúdez, Carlos. [S.l. , 1985] ([Managua, Nicaragua?] : Editorial "El Amanecer") 2 v. in 1 : LC Card 86-174663
HD6557 .P473 1985

El movimiento obrero en Valladolid durante la II República, 1931-1936 /. Prado Moura, Angel de. [Castilla y León] , 1985. 234 p. : ISBN 84-505-2341-9 LC Card 86-214605
HD8119.V34 P72 1985

Movimiento obrero, estado y modernización capitalista en el Ecuador, 1960-1983 /. Ycaza, Patricio. Ecuador [1985 or 1986] 38 p. ; LC Card 86-171415
HC202 .Y35 1985

Movimientos campesinos en el Paraguay /. Fogel, Ramón B. Asunción, Paraguay , 1986. 230 p., [1] leaf of plates : LC Card 86-189517
HD1531.P3 F64 1986

Movimientos sociales en el noroeste de México / [Rubén Burgos, coordinación]. 1a ed. de la UAS. México : Universidad Autónoma de Sinaloa, 1985. 282 p. ; 21 cm. (Realidad nacional . 19) Papers from the Seminario Regional Movimientos Sociales en el Noroeste de México, held in Culiacán, Sinaloa, March 30-31, 1984, sponsored by the Instituto de Investigaciones Sociales, (UNAM), and the United Nations University. Bibliography: p. 222-223. ISBN 968-590-072-8 LC Card 87-102068
1. Peasantry - Mexico - Political activity - Congresses. 2. Social movements - Mexico - Congresses. 3. Students - Mexico - Political activity - Congresses. 4. Labor and laboring classes - Mexico - Political activity - Congresses. 5. Trade-unions - Mexico - Congresses. I. Burgos, Rubén. II. Seminario Regional Movimientos Sociales en el Noroeste de México (1984 : Culiacán, Mexico). III. Universidad Nacional Autónoma de México. Instituto de Investigaciones Sociales. IV. United Nations University. V. Series: Realidad nacional (Culiacán, Mexico) , 19.
HD1531.M6 M684 1985

Moving ahead together. Cooperative League of the U. S. A. How to organize a co-op . Washington , 1969. 53 p. :
NYPL [JLF 86-590]

MOVING, HOUSEHOLD - UNITED STATES - STATISTICS.
Transportation fact book. Alexandria, VA (1611 Duke St., Alexandria 22314-3482) , c1987. iii, 75 p. : LC Card 87-155218 DDC 388.3/2/0973021 19
HE5623 .T67 1987

MOVING-PICTURE INDUSTRY - EUROPE.
Tydeman, John. New media in Europe . London , New York , c1986. xii, 260 p. : ISBN 0-07-084799-1 : LC Card 85-19839 DDC 384.55/094 19
HE8700.9.E8 T93 1986
NYPL [JLE 86-3209]

Moving towards the year 2000 : global problems and the future. Moscow : "Social Sciences Today" Editorial Board, 1987. 204 p. ; 21 cm. ("Philosophical and social aspects of science and technology" series . 1) "At head of title: USSR Academy of Sciences, the Scientific Council for Philosophical and Social Aspects of Science and Technology." Bibliography: p. 199-[203] LC Card 87-163642 DDC 333.7 19
1. Environmental policy. 2. Natural resources. 3. Food supply. 4. Economic forecasting. 5. Socialism. I. Nauchnyĭ sovet po filosofskim i sotsial'nym problemam nauki i tekhniki (Akademiia nauk SSSR). II. Series.
HC79.E5 M69 1987

Moving up . Mrkvicka, Edward F. New York , 1985. 193 p. ; ISBN 0-688-02427-0 : LC Card 84-27272 DDC 650.1/4 19
HF5382.7 .M75 1985 ***NYPL [JLD 86-4148]***

Mower, A. Glenn (Alfred Glenn) International cooperation for social justice : global and regional protection of economic/social rights / A. Glenn Mower, Jr. Westport, Conn. : Greenwood Press, c1985. x, 271 p. ; 22 cm. (Studies in human rights, 0146-3586 . no. 6) Includes index. Bibliography: p. [263]-267. ISBN 0-313-24702-1 (lib. bdg.) LC Card 84-27954 DDC 341.4/81 19
1. International covenant on economic, social, and cultural rights. 2. Civil rights (International law). 3. Social justice. I. Title. II. Series.
K3240.4 .M676 1985 ***NYPL [JLD 85-3575]***

Mowery, David C.
Alliance politics and economics : multinational joint ventures in commercial aircraft / David C. Mowery. Cambridge, Mass. : Ballinger Pub. Co., c1987. xi, 194 p. : ill. ; 24 cm. "American Enterprise Institute/Ballinger publication." Bibliography: p. 171-183. Includes index. ISBN 0-88730-213-0 LC Card 86-32178 DDC 338.8/87 19
1. Aircraft industry - International cooperation. 2. Aircraft industry - United States. 3. Joint ventures. 4. Technology transfer. 5. Competition, International. 6. International economic relations. I. American Enterprise Institute for Public Policy Research. II. Title.
HD9711.A2 M68 1987

Technology and employment . Washington, D.C. , 1987. xiii, 225 p. : ISBN 0-309-03744-1 (pbk.) : LC Card 87-42807 DDC 331.12/0973 19
HD6331.2.U5 T43 1987

Moya Rodríguez, Jorge. Rojas Rojas, Edgar. Indices de eficiencia económica para la industria beneficiadora de café . San José, Costa Rica , 1986. 14 leaves : LC Card 87-403520 DDC 338.1/6 19
HD9199.C82 R65 1986

Le Moyen Age pour quoi faire? /. Pernoud, Régine, 1909- [Paris] , c1986. 315 p. : ISBN 2-234-01940-0 : LC Card 86-189820
HC41 .P46 1986

Moyer, R. Charles, 1945- Contemporary financial management / R. Charles Moyer, James R. McGuigan, William J. Kretlow. Rev. 3rd ed., 3rd ed. rev. print. St. Paul : West Pub. Co., c1988. xxiv, 793, 24 p. : ill. ; 27 cm. Includes bibliographies and indexes. ISBN 0-314-64227-7 LC Card 87-24201 DDC 658.1/5 19
1. Corporations - Finance. 2. Business enterprises - Finance. I. McGuigan, James R. II. Kretlow, William J. III. Title.
HG4026 .M68 1988

Moynihan, Daniel P. (Daniel Patrick), 1927- The politics of a guaranteed income; the Nixon administration and the Family assistance plan [by] Daniel P. Moynihan.[1st ed.] New York, Random House [1973] xiii, 579 p. 25 cm. Includes bibliographical references. ISBN 0-394-46354-4 LC Card 77-37069 DDC 362.5
1. Guaranteed annual income - United States. 2. Public welfare - United States. 3. United States - Social policy. I. Title.
HC110.I5 M65 ***NYPL [JLE 74-384]***

MOZAMBIQUE - ECONOMIC CONDITIONS - TO 1975.
Martinez, José Fernando Trindade. Recursos económicos do Ultramar Português, sua valorização e perspectivas futuras . Lisboa , 1960. 113 p. ; LC Card 86-169892
HC890 .M37 1960

MOZAMBIQUE - ECONOMIC CONDITIONS - 1975- - STATISTICS.
Os Distritos em números /. [Maputo?] [1983-1985] 10 v. ; LC Card 86-980977 DDC 330.67/905021 19
HC890 .D57 1983

Mozambique, food and agriculture sector /. Caballero, Lorenzo. Uppsala , 1984. 223, [30] p. : ISBN 91-576-2129-2 (pbk.) LC Card 86-218958

DDC 338.1/0967/9 19
HD9017.M86 C33 1984

Mozambique Institute of Scientific Research. see **Lourenço Marquez (City). Instituto de Investigação Cientifica de Moçambique.**

MOZAMBIQUE - RURAL CONDITIONS.
Wuyts, Marc. Camponeses e economia rural em Moçambique [microform] /. Maputo , 1978. 31, A1-A6 p. ; LC Card 80-980386 DDC 338.1/0967/9 19
HD2129 .W89 1978
NYPL [*ZT-1564 no.14]

MOZAMBIQUE - SOCIAL CONDITIONS - 1975- - STATISTICS.
Os Distritos em números /. [Maputo?] [1983-1985] 10 v. ; LC Card 86-980977 DDC 330.67/905021 19
HC890 .D57 1983

Mozhin, V. P.
Ėkonomicheskoe razvitie Sibiri i Dal′nego Vostoka /. Moskva , 1980. 263 p. ; LC Card 81-143669
HC337.R852 S5242 1980

Gosudarstvenno-monopolisticheskiĭ kapitalizm i razmeshchenie proizvoditel′nykh sil /. Moskva , 1984. 182 p. ; LC Card 84-239188
HC240 .G565 1984

Teoreticheskie i metodologicheskie problemy regional′noĭ ėkonomiki . Moskva , 1983. 158 p. : LC Card 87-100005
HC340.D5 T437 1983

M.P.G.I. (Guadeloupe) A.B.C. de l'économie guadeloupéene /. [Basse-Terre, Guadeloupe , 1986] 200 p., [27] leaves of plates : LC Card 87-125723
HC158.5 .A52 1986

MR/Censa series on the Americas.
Transition and development . New York, NY [Berkeley, Calif.] , c1986. 352 p. ; ISBN 0-85345-705-0 (pbk.) : LC Card 86-12579 DDC 335.43/09172/4 19
HX517.8 .T73 1986 ***NYPL [JLD 86-3907]***

Mrkvicka, Edward F. Moving up : proven strategies for career success / Edward F. Mrkvicka, Jr.1st ed. New York : W. Morrow, 1985. 193 p. ; 22 cm. Includes index. ISBN 0-688-02427-0 : LC Card 84-27272 DDC 650.1/4 19
1. Job hunting. 2. Job security. 3. Promotions. I. Title.
HF5382.7 .M75 1985 ***NYPL [JLD 86-4148]***

MRPC (Series) .
(no. 11) India. Directorate of Marketing and Inspection. Marketing of walnuts in India. Faridabad , Delhi , 1986. ix, 180 p. : LC Card 86-903362
HD9259.N7 I45 1986

(no. 19) Report on the marketing of sandalwood in India. Faridabad , 1986. viii, 196 p. : LC Card 86-903266 DDC 381/.41497394/0954 19
HD9769.S33 I47 1986

MRS. FIELDS COOKIES (FIRM)
Fields, Debbi. "One smart cookie" . New York , c1987. 173 p., [16] p. of plates : ISBN 0-671-61838-5 LC Card 87-15172 DDC 338.7/6647525/0924 B 19
HD9058.C65 F544 1987

MS-DOS (COMPUTER OPERATING SYSTEM)
Wolverton, Van, 1939- Running MS DOS . Bellevue, Wash. [New York, NY] , c1985. xv, 423 p. : ISBN 0-914845-68-3 LC Card 85-18951 DDC 005.4/469 19
QA76.76.O63 W65 1985
NYPL [JSE 86-1760]

MSA, the software company. New York, N.Y. : Frost & Sullivan, c1982. v, 73 leaves : ill. ; 29 cm. "December 1982." "#A1157." LC Card 87-143692 DDC 338.7/610053/0973 19
1. Management Science America, Inc. 2. Computer software industry - United States. 3. Computer service industry - United States. I. Frost & Sullivan.
HD9696.C64 M355 1982

Msambichaka, L. A. (Lucian A.) Food grain shortfalls in Tanzania, 1961-1981 : a retrospective assessment / by L.A. Msambichaka. Dar es Salaam, Tanzania : Economic Research Bureau, University of Dar es Salaam, c1982. 38 p. ; 30 cm. (E.R.B. paper . 82.3) Bibliography: p. 37-38. LC Card 85-980863 DDC 338.1/9/678 19
1. Grain trade - Tanzania. 2. Food supply - Tanzania. I. Title. II. Series.
HD9047.T32 M726 1982

MTI Film & Video.
Real inside [motion picture] /. Deerfield, IL , 1985. 1 film reel (12 min.) : LC Card 87-705522 DDC 791.43 11
HF5549.5.I6

Real inside [videorecording] /. Deerfield, IL, 1985. 1 videocassette (12 min.) : LC Card 87-705515 DDC 791.43 11
HF5549.5.I6

Mubyarto. Kredit pedesaan di Indonesia /. Yogyakarta , 1986. xii, 160 p. ; LC Card 86-943011
HG2051.I65 K74 1986

Mucciolo, Louis. Make it yours! : How to own your own business, buy a business, start a business, franchise a business / Louis Mucciolo. New York : Wiley, c1987. xiv, 269 p. ; 24 cm. Includes index. ISBN 0-471-62585-X (pbk.) LC Card 87-8168 DDC 658.1/141 19
1. Small business - Management. I. Title.
HD62.7 .M79 1987

Muchinsky, Paul M. Psychology applied to work : an introduction to industrial and organizational psychology / Paul M. Muchinsky.2nd ed. Chicago, Ill. : Dorsey Press, c1987. xxvi, 712, xix p. : ill. ; 24 cm. Includes bibliographies and indexes. ISBN 0-256-03671-3 LC Card 86-81818 DDC 158.7 19
1. Psychology, Industrial. 2. Organizational behavior. I. Title.
HF5548.8 .M756 1987

Mudahar, Mohinder S. Fertilizer marketing systems and policies in the developing world / by Mohinder S. Mudahar and Edwin C. Kapusta. Muscle Shoals, Ala. : International Fertilizer Development Center, 1987. 43 p. : ill. ; 29 cm. (Technical bulletin IFDC . T-33) Bibliography: p. 38-41. ISBN 0-88090-059-8 (pbk.) LC Card 87-3152 DDC 381/.4566862/091724 19
1. Fertilizers - Developing countries - Marketing. 2. Fertilizer industry - Government policy - Developing countries. I. Kapusta, E. C., 1925-. II. Series: Technical bulletin (International Fertilizer Development Center) , T-33. III. Title.
HD9483.D44 K36 1987

Mudança social no Nordeste . Corrêa, Rossini. São Luís , 1986. 176 p., [6] p. of plates : LC Card 87-152221 DDC 322/.2/098121 19
HD8289.M37 C67 1986

Muegge, Herman, 1935- International economic restructuring and the regional community /. Aldershot, Hants, England , Brookfield, Vt., USA , c1987. x, 404 p. : ISBN 0-566-05478-7 : LC Card 87-11841 DDC 330.9 19
HF1412 .I574 1987

Mühlfeld, Claus, 1940- Konflikt und Kooperation in Arbeitgeberverbänden / Claus Mühlfeld, Friedrich Schönweiss, Matthias Engler. Augsburg : Maro Verlag, 1985. 403 p. ; 21 cm. (Reihe Wissenschaftliche Texte. Bd. 38) Augsburger Schriften zur Wirtschaftssoziologie Bibliography: p. 395-403. ISBN 3-87512-138-4 : LC Card 86-152717
1. Trade and professional associations - Germany, West. I. Schönweiss, Friedrich. II. Engler, Matthias. III. Title.
HD2429.G3 M84 1985

Müller, Alfred. Die schweizerischen Bahnpoststempel : mit Linienangabe von Beginn bis heute / Alfred Müller. Bern : Zumstein, 1977. 28 p. : ill. ; 25 cm. Bibliography: p. 27. Includes index. LC Card 85-138287
1. Railway mail service - Switzerland. 2. Postmarks - Switzerland. I. Title.
HE7139.R2 M85 1977

Mueller, Charles Curt.
Das oligarquias agrárias ao predomínio urbano-industrial : um estudo do processo de formação de políticas agrícolas no Brasil / Charles C. Mueller. Rio de Janeiro : Instituto de Planejamento Econômico e Social, Programa Nacional de Pequisa Econômica, 1983. 363 p. ; 21 cm. (Série PNPE . 9) Bibliography: p. 355-363. LC Card 87-403875 DDC 305.5/232/0981 19
1. Brazil - Economic conditions - 19th century. 2. Brazil - Economic conditions - 1918-. 3. Agriculture and state - Brazil - History. 4. Elite (Social sciences) - Brazil - History. I. Title. II. Series.
HC187 .M76 1983

Expansão da fronteira agrícola e meio-ambiente : a experiência recente do Brasil / Charles C. Mueller. [S.l. : s.n., between 1979 and 1985] 38, [4] leaves, [1] leaf of plates : ill. ; 30 cm. "Este trabalho baseia-se na monografia 'Expansão da fronteira agrícola e meio-ambiente no Brasil: o Sul do Centro-Oeste e a Amazônia,' preparada pelo autor como contribuição ao projeto CEPAL/PNUMA, Estilos de Desenvolvimento e Meio-Ambiente na América Latina"--P. [1] Bibliography: leaves [39]-[42] LC Card 86-197353
1. Land settlement - Environmental aspects - Brazil, Central West. 2. Land settlement - Environmental aspects - Amazon River Region. I. Title.
HD499.C45 M83 1979

Müller, Friedemann. Wirtschaftssanktionen im Ost-West-Verhältnis . Baden-Baden , 1983. 234 p. : ISBN 3-7890-0963-6 LC Card 84-132150
HF1413.5 .W57 1983

Müller, Geraldo. Alimentação e agricultura no Brasil : subsídios para o estudo da evolução alimentar-nutricional nas metrópoles brasileiras no período 1960/75 / Geraldo Muller. [São Paulo] : CEBRAP, 1984. 64 p. : ill. ; 28 cm. (Cadernos CEBRAP . nova sér., 3) Bibliography: p. 51-53. LC Card 86-132127
1. Agriculture - Economic aspects - Brazil. 2. Farm mechanization - Brazil. 3. Food supply - Brazil. I. Centro Brasileiro de Análise e Planejamento. II. Series: Caderno CEBRAP , nova sér., 3. III. Title.
HD1872 .M85 1984

Mueller, H. Dieter (Heinz Dieter), 1952-
Berufswahlfreiheit und Kultur : Grundlegung einer kulturtheoretisch orientierten Berufswahlforschung / H. Dieter Mueller. München : Profil, c1986. 276, [46] p. ; 21 cm. (Reihe Wissenschaft) Bibliography: p. [17]-[46] (2d group). ISBN 3-89019-166-5 LC Card 87-124783 DDC 331.11/72/0943 19
1. Free choice of employment - Germany, West. 2. Free choice of employment. I. Title.
HD4903.5.G4 M84 1986

Müller-Lutz, Heinz Leo.
Versicherungswirtschaftliches Studienwerk /. Wiesbaden , c1981. v. <8-10 > ; LC Card 86-171689
HG8618 .V47 1981

Mueller, Reinhold C.
Lane Frederic Chapin, 1900- Money and banking in medieval and Renaissance Venice /. Baltimore , c1985- v. : ISBN 0-8018-3157-1 (v. 1) LC Card 84-47947 DDC 332.1/0945/31 19
HG1040.V46 L36 1985 ***NYPL [JLL 86-121]***

Lane Frederic Chapin, 1900- Studies in Venetian social and economic history /. London , 1987. 346 p. in various pagings : ISBN 0-86078-202-6 LC Card 87-160893 DDC 945/.31 19
HC308.V4 L36 1987

Müller, Ronald E. National economic growth and stabilization policy in the age of multinational corporations : the challenge of our postmarket economy / Ronald E. Müller. [Sydney] : Transnational Corporations Research Project, University of Sydney, 1979. vi, 45 p. : ill. ; 21 cm. (Occasional paper / Transnational Corporations Research Project, University of Sydney . no. 3 (Jan. 1979)) "Originally published ... in U. S. Economic Growth from 1976 to 1986: Prospects, Problems and Patterns, U. S. Government Printing Office, Washington 1977"--T.p. verso. Includes bibliographical references. ISBN 0-908470-00-2 (pbk.) LC Card 87-672345
1. United States - Economic policy - 1971-1981. 2. Economic stabilization - United States. 3. International business enterprises. I. Series: Occasional paper / Transnational Corporations Research Project, University of Sydney , no. 3. II. Title.
HC106.7 .M84x 1979

Müller, Thomas.
Friedrich, R. (Rainer) Energie und Umwelt . Stuttgart [1985] 115 p. : LC Card 87-409534 DDC 333.79/0943/46 19
HD9502.G43 B324 1985

Friedrich, R. (Rainer) Energie und Umwelt . Stuttgart [1985] 124 p. : LC Card 87-409533 DDC 333.79/0943/46 19
HD9502.G43 B3238 1985

Müllverwertung und -Beseitigung in Baden-Württemberg . Koch, Thilo. Stuttgart ,

1984. ii, 177 p. : LC Card 84-158868
HD4485.G32 B335 1984

München als Industriestadt /. Fritz, Carl, b. 1890. Berlin , 1913. 163 p. ; LC Card 85-666347
HC289.M86 F74x 1913

Münchner Studien zur Sozial- und Wirtschaftsgeographie. For additional listing of contents, see Old Catalog.
(Bd. 18) Gräf, Peter. Zur Raumrelevanz infrastruktureller Massnahmen . Kallmünz/Regensburg , 1978. xxxvii, 259 p., [9] leaves of plates (7 folded) : ISBN 3-7847-6518-1 LC Card 85-205909
HC281 .M8 Bd. 18 HC288.M53
(Bd. 25) Decker, Hedwig. Standortverlagerungen der Industrie in der Region München /. Kallmünz/Regensburg , 1984. xxvi, 92 p. : ISBN 3-7847-6525-4 LC Card 86-136483 DDC 304.2/0943 s 338.6/042/094336 19
HC281 .M8 Bd. 25 HC289.M86

Mündliche Geschichtsschreibung . Günter, Janne, 1937- Mülheim/Ruhr , 1982. 142, [1] p. : ISBN 3-923456-00-X LC Card 85-146144
HD8039.M61 G343 1982

Die Münzenberg-Legende . Surmann, Rolf. Köln , c1983. 307 p. : ISBN 3-922009-53-0 LC Card 83-155325
HD8450 .S87 1983

MÜNZENBERG, WILLI.
Surmann, Rolf. Die Münzenberg-Legende . Köln , c1983. 307 p. : ISBN 3-922009-53-0 LC Card 83-155325
HD8450 .S87 1983

Mueses, Danilo A. Seebeck : héroe o villano? / Danilo A. Mueses. [S.l.] : Federación Interamericana de Filatelía ; República Dominicana : SFD, [1986?] 170, [5] p. : ill. ; 22 cm. (Publicación Emilio Obregón) Bibliography: p. [171]-[173] LC Card 86-177691
1. Postage-stamps - Latin America - History - 19th century. 2. Postage-stamp printing - History - 19th century. 3. Postage-stamp design - History - 19th century. 4. Seebeck, Nicholas F., 1857-1899. I. Title. II. Series.
HE6185.L29 M84 1986

Muet, Pierre-Alain. Artus, Patrick. Investissement et emploi /. Paris , c1986. 260 p. : ISBN 2-7178-1196-6 : LC Card 87-125878
HG4028.C4 A74 1986

Mugged on Wall Street . Chase, C. David. New York , c1987. 349 p. : ISBN 0-671-62706-6 LC Card 87-4707 DDC 332.6/78 19
HG4910 .C52 1987

Muggli, Christoph. Flückiger, Hans. Siedlungsstruktur . Bern , c1985. 118 p. : ISBN 3-258-03529-6 : LC Card 86-134805
HN603.5 .F58 1985 *NYPL [JLE 86-3789]*

Mugglin, Markus. Exportrisikogarantie, internationale Verschuldung und schweizerische Entwicklungspolitik / Markus Mugglin. 1. Aufl. Adliswil : Institut für Sozialethik des SEK, Entwicklungsstudien, 1985. 56 p. : ill. ; 21 cm. (Entwicklungspolitische Diskussionsbeiträge . 26) Includes bibliographical references. ISBN 3-7229-4036-X LC Card 85-148130
1. Switzerland - Foreign economic relations - Developing countries. 2. Developing countries - Foreign economic relations - Switzerland. 3. Risk - Developing countries. 4. Switzerland - Economic policy. 5. Debts, External - Developing countries. 6. Insurance, Export credit - Developing countries. I. Title. II. Series.
HF1574.5.D44 M84 1985

MUGINA (BURUNDI : COMMUNE) - ECONOMIC CONDITIONS.
Bahizi, Joseph. Monographie d'unités domestiques. [Bujumbura] [1985] 41 leaves ; LC Card 86-980542
HC880.Z7 M843 1985

MUGINA (BURUNDI : COMMUNE) - SOCIAL CONDITIONS.
Bahizi, Joseph. Monographie d'unités domestiques. [Bujumbura] [1985] 41 leaves ; LC Card 86-980542
HC880.Z7 M843 1985

Mugnai, Massimo, 1947- Il mondo rovesciato : contraddizione e "valore" in Marx / Massimo Mugnai. Bologna : Il Mulino, c1984. 296 p. ; 22 cm. (Saggi. 280) Includes bibliographical references and index. ISBN 88-15-00641-9 : LC Card 86-169123
1. Surplus value. 2. Marxian economics. I. Title.
HB206 .M84 1984

Muhammad Nejatullah Siddiqi. see **Ṣiddīqī, Muḥammad Nejātullah, 1931-**

Muḥammad Raḍwān, Samīr. see **Raḍwān, Samīr Muḥammad.**

MUHAMMADANISM. see **ISLAM.**

Mühlbayer, Michael, 1955- Prospektive Erfolgsanalyse und Unternehmensbonität / Michael Mühlbayer. Frankfurt am Main ; New York : P. Lang, c1986. vii, 388 p. : ill. ; 21 cm. (Europäische Hochschulschriften. Reihe V, Volks- und Betriebswirtschaft, 0531-7339 . Bd. 699 = vol. 699 = vol. 699) Bibliography: p. 347-388. ISBN 3-8204-9462-6 LC Card 86-190036
1. Business enterprises - Germany, West - Finance. I. Series: Europäische Hochschulschriften. Reihe V, Volks- und Betriebswirtschaft , Bd. 699. II. Title.
HG4156 .M84 1986

Mühlberg, Dietrich. Proletariat . Wien , 1986. 275 p. : ISBN 3-205-00561-9 LC Card 86-673962
HD4853 .P76x 1986

Muhlstein, Anka. James de Rothschild : Francfort, 1792-Paris, 1868 : une métamorphose, une légende / Anka Muhlstein. [Paris] : Gallimard, c1981. 242 p., [16] p. of plates : ill. ; 21 cm. Includes bibliographical references. LC Card 82-149581 DDC 332.1/092/4 B 19
1. Rothschild, James, baron de, 1792-1868. 2. Bankers - France - Biography. 3. Jews - France - Biography. I. Title.
HG1552.R816 M84 1981
*NYPL [*PWZ (Rothschild, J.) 86-6471]*

Mujer trabajadora. Condiciones socioeconómicas de la mujer trabajadora en la República Dominicana /. Santo Domingo, República Dominicana , 1986. 150 p. ; LC Card 86-208584
HD6112.5 .C65 1986

Mujer, trabajo y empleo / Maruja Barrig, editora. Lima, Perú : Asociación de Defensa y Capacitación Legal, [1985] 294 p. ; 21 cm. Includes bibliographies. LC Card 86-121871 DDC 331.4/0985 19
1. Women - Employment - Peru - Congresses. 2. Working class women - Peru - Congresses. I. Barrig, Maruja. II. Asociación de Defensa y Capacitación Legal (Peru).
HD6131 .M85 1985 *NYPL [JLD 87-492]*

La Mujer y el trabajo en México : antología. 1a ed. México : Secretaría del Trabajo y Previsíon Social, Subsecretaría B, Unidad Coordinadora de Políticas, Estudios y Estadísticas del Trabajo, Subcoordinacíon de Análisis y Política Laboral [y] Subcoordinacíon de Programas Institucionales y Documentación, 1986. 346 p. : ill. ; 23 cm. (Cuadernos laborales . 31) Includes bibliographies. ISBN 968-8132-48-9 LC Card 87-101329
1. Women - Employment - Mexico - Case studies. 2. Offshore assembly industry - Mexican-American Border Region. I. Mexico. Subcoordinación de Análisis y Política Laboral. II. Mexico. Subcoordinación de Programas Institucionales y Documentación. III. Series: Cuadernos laborales (Mexico City, Mexico) , 31.
HD6101 .M86 1986

Mujeres en Desarrollo, Inc. (Dominican Republic) Campesinas y políticos, 1986 . Santo Domingo, República Dominicana , 1986. 83 p. : LC Card 87-102259
HD6073.A292 D653 1986

Mujeres fronterizas en la industria maquiladora /. Carrillo V., Jorge (Carrillo Viveros) [Mexico City] , Tijuana, B.C.N. , 1985. 216 p. : ISBN 968-290-389-0 LC Card 87-400964 DDC 331.4 19
HD6073.O332 M483 1985

Mukerjee, Dilip.
Lessons from Korea's industrial experience / Dilip Mukerjee. Kuala Lumpur, Malaysia : Institute of Strategic and International Studies, Malaysia, c1986. vi, 81 p. ; 23 cm. Bibliography: p. [79]-81. ISBN 967-94701-3-X (pbk.) LC Card 86-944002 DDC 338.09519/5 19
1. Korea (South) - Economic conditions - 1960-. 2. Korea (South) - Industries. I. Title.
HC467 .M84 1986

Lessons from the Caribbean Basin initiative / Dilip Mukerjee. Kuala Lumpur, Malaysia : Institute of Strategic and International Studies, c1985. 36 p. ; 21 cm. (ISIS research note) Bibliography: p. 33-36. ISBN 967-99974-6-4 (pbk.) LC Card 87-101396 DDC 338.91/73/0729 19
1. Caribbean Basin Initiative, 1983-. 2. United States - Commercial policy. 3. United States - Commerce - Caribbean Area. 4. Caribbean Area - Commerce - United States. 5. United States - Commerce - Central America. 6. Central America - Commerce - United States. I. Title.
HF1456.5.C27 M85 1985

Primary commodities : from concern to complacency / Dilip Mukerjee. Kuala Lumpur, Malaysia : Institute of Strategic and International Studies, c1985. 39 p. ; 21 cm. (ISIS research note) Bibliography: p. 37-39. ISBN 967-99974-7-2 (pbk.) : LC Card 87-105669 DDC 338/.02 19
1. Commercial products. 2. Raw materials. I. Institute of Strategic and International Studies (Malaysia). II. Title.
HF1040.7 .M85 1985

Mukerji Ray, Renuka. see **Ray, Renuka Mukerji, 1903-**

Mukerji, Sukumar, 1931- Student research abstracts in population studies /. Bombay , 1986, c1985. xi, 434 p. ; LC Card 86-902278 DDC 304.6/095 19
HA4553 .S78 1986

Mukherjee, Sakti Pada. Bose, P. K. Graduate employment and higher education in West Bengal /. Paris , New Delhi , 1983. vi, 288, [1] p. : ISBN 0-85226-078-4 (pbk.) LC Card 83-163900 DDC 331.11/423 19
HD6278.I52 W473 1983
NYPL [JLD 86-2269]

Mukhin, P. A. (Pavel Aleksandrovich) Statistika kinematografii : uchebnoe posobie / P.A. Mukhin, V.ÎA. Orlova. Moskva : Vses. gos. in-t kinematografii Goskino SSSR, 1984. 103 p. : ill. ; 22 cm. At head of title: Goskino SSSR. Vsesoiuznyĭ gosudarstvennyĭ ordena Trudovogo Krasnogo Znameni institut kinematografii. Kafedra ėkonomiki i organizatsii kinoproizvodstva. Includes bibliographical references. LC Card 85-203673
1. Social sciences - Statistical methods. 2. Motion pictures - Social aspects - Statistical methods. 3. Motion picture industry - Soviet Union - Statistical methods. I. Orlova, V. ÎA. (Valentina ÎAkovlevna). II. Title.
HA29.5.R9 M85 1984

Mukhlif, Hādī Aḥmad. al-Tawzīʻ al-jughrāfī li-mazāriʻ al-dawlah fī al-ʻIrāq wa-atharihā fī al-tanmiyah al-iqtiṣādīyah / ta'līf Hādī Aḥmad Mukhlif. al-Ṭabʻah 1. [Baghdad] : Sā'adat Jāmiʻat Baghdād ʻalá ṭabʻih, 1985. 2 v. (607 p., 3 leaves of plates) : ill., maps ; 24 cm. Bibliography: v. 2, p. 566-604. LC Card 86-963500
1. State farms - Iraq - Income distribution. 2. Agriculture and state - Iraq. 3. Agriculture - Economic aspects - Iraq. I. Title.
HD1493.I72 M85 1985

Mukhlis, 1948- Migrasi /. Ujung Pandang , 1985. xi, 205 p. : LC Card 87-940461
HB2108.S8 M54 1985

Mukhopadhyay, Subhas Chandra, 1938- The agrarian policy of the British in Bengal : the formative period, 1698-1772 / Subhas Chandra Mukhopadhyay. Allahabad, India : Chugh Publications, 1987. xi, 195 p. ; 22 cm. Bibliography: p. [185]-195. ISBN 81-85076-11-1 : LC Card 87-900481 DDC 338.1/85414 19
1. Land value taxation - India - Bengal - History. 2. India - History - 18th century. 3. East India Company. I. Title.
HJ4392.I4 M85 1987

Mukhopadhyay, Subodh Kumar, 1942- Bāṃlāra ārthika itihāsa, ashṭādaśa śatābdī / Subodha Kumāra Mukhopādhyāẏa. Kalakātā : Ke.Pi. Bāgacī, 1985. 214 p. ; 22 cm. In Bengali. Bibliography: p. [207]-210. Includes index. LC Card 85-903918
1. Bengal (India) - Economic conditions. I. Title.
HC437.B43 M85 1985

Működési forma, belső mechanizmus : tanulmány és esettanulmányok az általános fogyasztási és értékesítő szövetkezetekről. Budapest : Szövetkezeti Kutató Intézet, 1985. 208 p. : ill. ; 29 cm. (Közlemények, 0113-4905 . 191) Bibliography: p. 201-202. CONTENTS. - A belső mechanizmus, szervezeti és önelszámolási rendszer továbbfejlesztése / Bándli Imre -- Korszerű vezetési módszerek és eszközök a vezetői gyakorlatban / Boda József -- Megújulás a

Tata és Vidéke ÁFÉSZ-nél / Hegedűs István -- A belső mechanizmus korszerűsítése a Szolnok és Vidéke ÁFÉSZ-nél / Hegedűs Miklósné -- Az általános fogyasztási és értékesítő szövetkezetek működési formája, belső mechanizmusa (összefoglaló tanulmány) / Domokos József. LC Card 87-408582
1. Consumer cooperatives - Hungary. I. Bándli, Imre. II. Series: Közlemények / Szövetkezeti Kutató Intézet, 191.
HD3332.5.A4 M85 1985

Mukras, M. S. Recent findings on the determinants of urban-rural income transfers in Kenya / by M.S. Mukras. [Nairobi?] : Tekuza Research Institute, 1985. ii, 33 leaves : ill. ; 29 cm. (Research paper series . no. 2) Bibliography: p. 29-32. LC Card 85-980600
1. Migrant remittances - Kenya. I. Title. II. Series.
HC865.Z9 I516 1985

Mulakhkhaṣ kitāb Naẓrah taḥlīlīyah fī mushkilat al-ghidhā' fī al-buldān al-'Arabīyah /. Qāsim, Ṣubḥī, 1934- [Jordan?] , 1982. 103 p. ; LC Card 86-203782
HD9018.A55 Q269 1982

Mülder, Wilhelm. Organisatorische Implementierung von computergestützten Personalinformationssystemen : Einführungsprobleme und Lösungsansätze / Wilhelm Mülder. Berlin ; New York : Springer, 1984. xix, 257 p. : ill. ; 24 cm. (Betriebs- und Wirtschaftsinformatik . 11) Originally presented as the author's thesis (doctoral)--Universität Essen, 1982. Bibliography: p. [241]-257. ISBN 0-387-13360-7 (U. S.) LC Card 84-238144
1. Personnel management - Data processing. I. Title. II. Series.
HF5549.5.D37 M85 1984

A mulher na agricultura portuguesa . Cavaco, Carminda. [Lisbon] , 1981. 34 leaves : LC Card 85-216534
HD6073.F32 P83 1981

A mulher na cultura brasileira /. Horta, Elisabeth Vorcaro. Belo Horizonte , 1975. 122 p. ; LC Card 75-511579
HQ1542 .H66 ***NYPL [Sc D 86-811]***

A Mulher rural e mudanças no processo de produção agrícola : estudos sobre a América Latina / organizadoras, Cheywa Spindel, Jane Jaquette, Mabel Cordini. [Brasília] : Instituto Interamericano de Cooperação para a Agricultura, [1984] i, 161 p. ; 30 cm. (Série Proposições, resultados e recomendações de eventos técnicos, 0253-4746 . no. 337) "Julho/84." Includes bibliographies. LC Card 86-150197
1. Women in agriculture - Latin America. 2. Women farmers - Latin America. 3. Women agricultural laborers - Latin America. 4. Farmers' wives - Latin America. I. Spindel, Cheywa R. II. Jaquette, Jane S., 1942-. III. Cordini, Mabel. IV. Inter-American Institute for Cooperation on Agriculture. V. Series: Serie Resultados, ponencias y recomendaciones de eventos técnicos , no. 337.
HD6073.A292 L295 1984

Mulheres e trabalhadoras . Pena, Maria Valéria Junho. Rio de Janeiro, RJ , 1981. iii, 227 p. ; LC Card 81-216820 DDC 331.4/0981 19
HD6124 .P46 1981 ***NYPL [JLD 86-1557]***

As mulheres nas organizações profissionais /. Dabat, Christine. Recife , 1985. 21 p. ; LC Card 86-177927
HD2429.B6 D33 1985

Mulkh Raj. Employment, income, and housing / Mulkh Raj. New Delhi : Ess Ess Publications, 1987. viii, 130 p. : ill. ; 23 cm. Study on housing projects in Andhra Pradesh, Gujarat, Karnataka, and Maharashtra. Bibliography: p. 87-88. Includes index. ISBN 81-7000-025-4 : LC Card 87-901029 DDC 331.12/5/0954 19
1. Housing - India. 2. Labor supply - India. 3. Income - India. I. Title.
HD7361.A3 M85 1987

Mullan, Bob. Taylor, Laurie, 1935- Uninvited guests . London , 1986. 218 p. : ISBN 0-7011-2973-5 : LC Card 86-183414 DDC 791.44/75/0941 19
HE8689.7.A8 T39 1986

Mullard, Maurice, 1946- The politics of public expenditure / Maurice Mullard. London ; New York : Croom Helm, c1987. 220 p. : ill. ; 22 cm. Bibliography: p. 208-220. ISBN 0-7099-4674-0 : LC Card 87-6777 DDC 336.3/9/0941 19
1. Great Britain - Appropriations and expenditures. 2. Government spending policy - Great Britain. I. Title.
HJ7764 .M85 1987

Mullen, Brian. The psychology of consumer behavior / Brian Mullen. Hillsdale, N.J. : L. Erlbaum, 1988. p. cm. Includes index. ISBN 0-89859-857-5 LC Card 87-15601 DDC 658.8/342 19
1. Consumers. I. Title.
HF5415.3 .M85 1988

Müller-Armack, Andreas, 1941- Vollbeschäftigung, eine Utopie? /. Bern , c1986. 330 p. : ISBN 3-258-03567-9 LC Card 86-224133
HD5779 .V64 1986

Müller, Christoph, 1957- Organisatorische Gestaltung des Job Sharing in der Unternehmung : ein Konzept zur Strukturierung von Job-Sharing-Arbeitsplätzen in der Bundesrepublik Deutschland / Christoph Müller. Köln : Müller-Botermann, c1986. xiii, 404 p. ; 21 cm. (Reihe Personalwesen, Organisation, Unternehmungsführung . Bd. 1) Bibliography: p. 354-404. ISBN 3-924361-12-6 LC Card 87-114139 DDC 331.25/72 19
1. Job sharing - Germany (West). 2. Hours of labor, Flexible - Germany (West). I. Title. II. Series.
HD5110.2.G3 M85 1986

Müller, Erwin, 1947- Rüstungspolitik und Rüstungsdynamik : Fall USA : zur Analyse der Rüstungsmotive einer Weltmacht und zur Theorie moderner Rüstungsdynamik / Erwin Müller.1. Aufl. Baden-Baden : Nomos Verlagsgesellschaft, 1985. 378 p. ; 23 cm. (Militär, Rüstung, Sicherheit . Bd. 29) Revision of thesis (doctoral)--Universität Tübingen. Bibliography: p. 357-378. ISBN 3-7890-1076-6 LC Card 85-154502
1. Armaments - Economic aspects - United States. 2. Munitions - Economic aspects - United States. I. Title. II. Series.
HC110.D4 M85 1985

Müller, Fr. (Friedrich), Dr. Ferdinand von Steinbeis : sein Leben und Wirken 1807-1893 : eine Gedenkschrift / von Dr. Fr. Müller ; mit einem biographischen Begleitwork von Dr. R. Piloty. Tübingen : H. Laupp'schen Buchhandlung, 1907. vi, 215 p. : ports. ; 23 cm. Includes bibliographical references. LC Card 85-666358
1. Steinbeis, Ferdinand von, 1807-1893. 2. Industrialists - Germany - Biography. I. Piloty, Robert, 1863-1926. II. Title.
HC282.5.S67 M85x 1907

Müller, Frieder, 1944- Volkswirtschaftliche Gesamtrechnung und Preisveränderungen : Untersuchungen auf der Basis einer Neufassung des Aggregatbegriffs, mit einem preisbereinigten Kontensystem für die Bundesrepublik Deutschland (UT) / Frieder Müller. Königstein/Ts. : Verlagsgruppe Athenäum, Hain, Hanstein, 1984. xx, 414 p. : ill. ; 23 cm. (Hain Ökonomie . Bd. 7) Originally presented as the author's Habilitationsschrift, Tübingen, 1982. Includes index. Bibliography: p. 352-373. ISBN 3-445-02378-6 LC Card 85-142948 DDC 339.343 19
1. National income - Germany, West - Accounting. 2. Gross national product - Germany, West. I. Title. II. Series.
HC79.I5 M85 1984 ***NYPL [JLE 86-3225]***

Müller-Godeffroy, Heinrich. Der Neue Protektionismus . Bonn , c1983. 195 p. : ISBN 3-87831-370-5 LC Card 83-198686
HF1756 .N58 1983

Müller, Hans-Erich, 1945- Konzentration : die Marxsche Theorie wirtschaftlicher Macht / Hans-Erich Müller. Hamburg : VSA-Verlag, 1985. 239 p. : ill. ; 24 cm. Bibliography: p. 233-239. ISBN 3-87975-303-2 LC Card 87-110533 DDC 338.8 19
1. Industrial concentration. 2. Monopolies. 3. Saving and investment. 4. Marxian economics. I. Title.
HD2757 .M85 1985

Müller, Heinz, Dipl.-Kfm. Dr. Die Warenplazierung als absatzpolitisches Instrument im Selbstbedienungseinzelhandel / von Heinz Müller. Göttingen : O. Schwartz, 1982. 479 p. : ill. ; 24 cm. (Schriften zur Handelsforschung. Nr. 66) Bibliography: p. 413-479. ISBN 3-509-01287-9 LC Card 84-174456
1. Display of merchandise. 2. Self-sercie stores. I. Title.
HF5845 .M964 1982

Müller, Herbert, 1948- Die Umrechnung der Jahresabschlüsse ausländischer Konzernunternehmen und die Verrechnung der daraus resultierenden Umrechnungsdifferenzen : der Versuch einer Weiterentwicklung durch das Prinzip der Wertäquivalenz / Herbert Müller. Bochum : N. Brockmeyer, 1986. x, 348 p. ; 21 cm. (Bochumer wirtschaftswissenschaftliche Studien. Nr. 113) Bibliography: p. 314-348. ISBN 3-88339-547-1 LC Card 87-143252 DDC 657/.48 19
1. Foreign exchange - Accounting. 2. International business enterprises - Accounting. I. Title.
HG3853.7 .M84 1986

Müller, Jürg. Brasilien / Jürg Müller. 1. Aufl. Stuttgart : E. Klett, 1984. 278 p. : ill., maps ; 23 cm. (Länderprofile, geographische Strukturen, Daten, Entwicklungen) Bibliography: p. 270-275. ISBN 3-12-928881-3 (pbk.) LC Card 87-673406
1. Brazil - Economic conditions - 1964-1985. 2. Brazil - Social conditions - 1964-. I. Title.
HC187 .M79x 1984

Müller, Jürgen, 1943- Sektorale Struktur und Entwicklung der industriellen Beschäftigung in den Regionen der Bundesrepublik Deutschland / von Jürgen Müller. Berlin : Duncker & Humblot, c1983. xiii, 200 p. : ill. ; 24 cm. (Beiträge zur angewandten Wirtschaftsforschung. Bd. 12) Bibliography: p. 164-[175] ISBN 3-428-05449-0 LC Card 84-109872
1. Germany (West) - Economic conditions - 1974- - Regional disparities - Econometric models. 2. Germany (West) - Industries - Location - Econometric models. 3. Labor supply - Germany (West) - Econometric models. I. Title.
HC286.7 .M8 1983

Müller, K. (Karl), 1953- Auf dem Weg in die Freiheit . Graz , 1984. 356 p. : LC Card 87-672377
HD8419.S82 A93x 1984

Müller, Karl-Wilhelm, 1953- Die Theorie erschöpfbarer natürlicher Ressourcen bei wachsender Bevölkerung / Karl-Wilhelm Müller. Frankfurt am Main ; New York : P. Lang, c1984. 191 p. : ill. ; 21 cm. (Europäische Hochschulschriften. Reihe V, Volks- und Betriebswirtschaft, 0531-7339 . Bd. 507 = vol. 507 = vol. 507) Originally presented as the author's thesis (doctoral)--Universität Oldenburg, 1983. Bibliography: p. 181-191. ISBN 3-8204-5315-6 LC Card 85-197540
1. Economic development - Environmental aspects - Mathematical models. 2. Nonrenewable natural resources - Management - Mathematical models. 3. Population - Mathematical models. I. Series: Europäische Hochschulschriften. Reihe V, Volks- und Betriebswirtschaft , Bd. 507. II. Title.
HD75.6 .M85 1984

Müller, Karlhans, 1938- Vom Tauschhandel zur Weltwirtschaft : Märkte, Mächte, Monopole / Karlhans Müller. Reutlingen : Ensslin & Laiblin, c1984. 320 p. : ill. ; 24 cm. Includes index. ISBN 3-7709-0564-4 LC Card 87-673138
1. Economic history. 2. Commerce - History. I. Title.
HC21 .M85x 1984

Müller, Lajos. Halmos, Csaba. A szakszervezetek és a tervezés /. Budapest , 1983. 178 p. ; ISBN 963-608-052-6 LC Card 85-108502
HD6680.5 .H34 1983

Müller, Lothar. Die Bedeutung der Lohn-Leistungsrelation : eine empirische Analyse bei gewerblichen Arbeitnehmern im industriellen Bereich in Anlehnung an equity-theoretische Modellvorstellungen / von Lothar Müller. Karlsruhe : M. Wahl, c1983. iii, 272 p. : ill. ; 21 cm. (Wissenschaftliche Beiträge Karlsruhe . Nr. 11) Bibliography: p. 252-272. ISBN 3-88147-014-X LC Card 84-174174
1. Wages and labor productivity - Econometric models. I. Title. II. Series.
HD4945 .M84 1983

Müller-Luckner, Elisabeth. Arbeiter und Bürger im 19. Jahrhundert . München , 1986. xiv, 342 p. ; ISBN 3-486-52871-8 LC Card 86-212379
HD8376 .A72 1986

Müller, Michael, 1948- Befreiung der Arbeit . Bonn , c1986. 197 p. : ISBN 3-87831-429-9 LC Card 86-194157
HD6955 .B389 1986

Muller, N. D. Unemployment and the search for work in Transkei : aspects of a survey of workseekers in Transkei conducted in September 1982 / by N.D. Muller. Umtata, Transkei : Institute for Management and Development Studies, University of Transkei, [1982] 19 leaves ; 30 cm. (I.M.D.S. fact paper . no.

5, 1982) Bibliography: leaf 19. LC Card 86-206957 DDC 331.13/7968791 19
1. Unemployment - South Africa - Transkei. 2. Labor supply - South Africa - Transkei. I. Series: I.M.D.S. fact paper, no. 5. II. Title.
HD5842.T73 M85 1982

Muller, Pierre. Le technocrate et le paysan : essai sur la politique française de modernisation de l'agriculture de 1945 à nos jours / Pierre Muller. Paris : Editions Economie et humanisme : Editions ouvrières, c1984. 173 p. ; 21 cm. (Collection Développement et civilisations) Includes bibliographical references. ISBN 2-7082-2347-X : LC Card 84-171796 DDC 338.1/6 19
1. Agriculture and state - France. 2. Agriculture - Economic aspects - France. 3. Agricultural innovations - France. I. Title.
HD1947 .M85 1984 ***NYPL [JLD 86-3738]***

Müller, Rainer, 1953- Krisenmanagement in der Unternehmung : Vorgehen, Massnahmen und Organisation / Rainer Müller.2., überarbeitete und erw. Aufl. Frankfurt am Main ; New York : P. Lang, c1986. xxvii, 773 p. : 113 ill. ; 21 cm. (Kölner Schriften zur Betriebswirtschaft und Organisation, 0721-3123 . Bd. 5) Based on the author's thesis (doctoral)--Universität zu Köln, 1981/1982. Summary in English. Bibliography: p. 648-743. Includes indexes. ISBN 3-8204-7479-X LC Card 87-409055 DDC 658.4 19
1. Crisis management - Germany (West). I. Title. II. Series.
HD49 .M84 1986

Muller, S. Besluitvorming . Deventer , 1986. 151 p. : ISBN 90-267-1065-8 LC Card 86-201119
HD30.23 .B476 1986

Müller, Stefan, 1955- Schweizerische Sozialpolitik : Probleme und Lösungswege / Stefan Müller. Bern ; New York : P. Lang, c1984. 204 p. : ill. ; 21 cm. (Europäische Hochschulschriften. Reihe XXXI, Politikwissenschaft . Bd. 58 = v. 58 = v. 58) Bibliography: p. 199-204. ISBN 3-261-03410-6 LC Card 85-189979
1. Social security - Switzerland. I. Series: Europäische Hochschulschriften. Reihe XXXI, Politikwissenschaft , Bd. 58. II. Title.
HD7210 .M85 1984

Muller, Thomas, 1933- The fourth wave : California's newest immigrants / Thomas Muller, Thomas J. Espenshade, with Donald Manson ... [et al.]. Washington : Urban Institute Press, c1985. xvii, 217 p. ; 23 cm. Bibliography: p. 207-217. ISBN 0-87766-349-1 LC Card 85-22646 DDC 331.6/2/720794 19
1. Alien labor, Mexican - California - History. 2. Alien labor, Asian - California - History. 3. United States - Emigration and immigration - History. 4. California - Foreign population - History. I. Espenshade, Thomas J. II. Title.
HD8081.M6 M85 1985
NYPL [JLE 86-3014]

Müller, Ursula, 1949- Arbeitsmarkterfahrungen und Berufsorientierungen Jugendlicher . München , c1983. 177 p. : ISBN 3-87966-202-9 LC Card 84-170074
HD6276.G4 A73 1983

Müller-Vogg, Hugo. Die Krise der deutschen Gewerkschaften : ziellos, ratlos, machtlos? / Hugo Müller-Vogg. Stuttgart : Bonn Aktuell, c1986. 96 p. ; 19 cm. Includes index. ISBN 3-87959-284-5 LC Card 87-104011
1. Trade-unions - Germany, West. I. Title.
HD6694 .M847 1986

Müller, Wolfgang, 1955- Planung von Marketing-Strategien : die Entwicklung von Marketing-Strategien im strategischen Marketing-Planungsprozess : eine theoretische Analyse unter besonderer Berücksichtigung eines markenbezogenen Produktpositionierungs-Modells / Wolfgang Müller. Frankfurt am Main ; New York : Lang, c1986. xxvi, 514 p. : ill. ; 23 cm. (Marktorientierte Unternehmensführung, 0178-8133 . Bd. 3) Bibliography: p. 455-510. Includes index. ISBN 3-8204-8992-4 LC Card 86-205571
1. Marketing management. 2. Marketing - Decision making. I. Title. II. Series.
HF5415.13 .M833 1986

Muller y Machicado Asociados.
Acuerdos y documentos de la nueva política económica, 1986 /. [La Paz, Bolivia?] [1987] 134 p. ; LC Card 87-403664 DDC 338.984 19
HC182 .A585 1987

Evaluación económica, 1986 . [La Paz, Bolivia] [1986] 278 p. ; LC Card 87-403510 DDC 330.884/052 19
HC182 .E95 1986

Mullineux, A. W.
International banking and financial systems : a comparison / Andrew Mullineux. London ; Boston : Graham & Trotman, c1987. 243 p. ; 25 cm. Bibliography: p. 235-239. Includes index. ISBN 0-86010-916-X : LC Card 87-23605 DDC 332.1 19
1. Banks and banking. 2. Banks and banking, International. 3. Finance. 4. International finance. I. Title.
HG1573 .M84 1987

International money and banking : the creation of a new order / A.W. Mullineux. New York : New York University Press, 1987. xii, 207 p. ; 23 cm. Bibliography: p. 193-200. Includes index. ISBN 0-8147-5436-8 : LC Card 87-12393 DDC 332.1/5 19
1. Banks and banking, International. 2. International finance. I. Title.
HG3881 .M815 1987

U.K. banking after deregulation / A.W. Mullineux. London ; New York : Croom Helm, c1987. 180 p. ; 22 cm. "Published in the USA by Croom Helm in association with Methuen ... New York, NY"--T.p. verso. Bibliography: p. 166-171. Includes index. ISBN 0-7099-4689-9 LC Card 87-6742 DDC 332.1/0941 19
1. Banks and banking - Great Britain. 2. Banks and banking - Great Britain - Deregulation. I. Title. II. Title: UK banking after deregulation.
HG2988 .M85 1987

Mulquin, Marie Eve.
Empalme del índice de precios al consumidor : una nota aclaratoria / Marie Eve Mulquin. [San José] : Universidad de Costa Rica, Instituto de Investigaciones en Ciencias Económicas, 1981. 15 leaves ; 29 cm. (Documentos de trabajo (Universidad de Costa Rica. Instituto de Investigaciones en Ciencias Económicas) . no. 25) Includes bibliographical references. LC Card 81-216387
1. Consumer price indexes. 2. Consumer price indexes - Costa Rica. I. Series. II. Series: Documentos de trabajo (Universidad de Costa Rica. Instituto de Investigaciones en Ciencias Económicas) , no. 25. III. Title.
HB221 .M774 1981

Las estadísticas del sector construcción en Costa Rica : evaluación para su utilización en el análisis de coyuntura económica / Marie Eve Mulquin. [San José] : Universidad de Costa Rica, Instituto de Investigaciones en Ciencias Económicas, 1981. 39 p. ; 28 cm. (Documentos de trabajo . no. 26) Includes bibliographical references. LC Card 81-216965
1. Construction industry - Costa Rica - Statistics. I. Series: Documentos de trabajo (Universidad de Costa Rica. Instituto de Investigaciones en Ciencias Económicas) , no. 26. II. Title.
HD9715.C82 M85 1981

Múlt, jelen, jövő a műszaki haladás szolgálatában : az 1985. évi megyei tudományos hetek előadásainak tanulmánykötete / [szerkesztők, Dányi Pál, Bujdosó Attila]. Pécs : Műszaki és Természettudományi Egyesületek Szövetsége Baranya Megyei Szervezete, 1985. 305 p. : ill. ; 29 cm. Includes bibliographies. LC Card 87-408539
1. Baranya Megye (Hungary) - Economic conditions - Congresses. 2. Technological innovations - Hungary - Baranya Megye - Congresses. I. Danyi, Pál. II. Bujdosó, Attila. III. Műszaki és Természettudományi Egyesületek Szövetsége. Baranya Megyei Szervezet.
HC300.29.B37 M86 1985

Multi-agency financial investigative task forces [microform] Rev. 10/31/83 Washington, D.C. : Office of Investigations, Criminal Investigation Division, Internal Revenue Service, [1983] 1 v. (various pagings) : ill. ; 28 cm. Cover title. Microfilm. New York : New York Public Library, 1986. 1 microfilm reel ; 35 mm. (MN *ZZ-26,374)
1. Administrative agencies - United States. 2. Finance - United States. I. United States. Internal Revenue Service. Office of Investigations. II. Title: Financial investigative task forces.
NYPL [*ZT-1708 no.61]

Multi-level marketing. Cunningham, Jan. All about multi-level marketing . Denver, CO (1020 15th St., Suite 41C, Denver 80202) , c1986. 173 p. : LC Card 86-213072 DDC 658.8/4 19
HF5415.126 .C85 1986

Multidisciplinary-Multidonor Mission (United Nations Development Programme)
Development programme of the Kagera Basin . [Kigali] [1982] viii, 73 leaves : LC Card 85-980886 DDC 338.967 19
HC860.Z9 E444 1982

Multifarm use of agricultural machinery. Rome : Food and Agriculture Organization of the United Nations ; Ann Arbor, MI : UNIPUB [distributor], 1985. viii, 63 p. ; 23 cm. (FAO agriculture series . no. 17) Bibliography: p. [48] ISBN 92-5-101469-8 (pbk.) LC Card 86-217873 DDC 631.3/09172/4 19
1. Farm mechanization, Cooperative - Developing countries. I. Series.
HD1417 .M85 1985

Multifund investing . Hirsch, Michael D. Homewood, Ill. , c1987. xx, 237 p. : ISBN 0-87094-912-8 LC Card 86-71215 DDC 332.63/27 19
HG4530 .H57 1987

MULTIHOSPITAL SYSTEMS - UNITED STATES - DIRECTORIES.
Maximizing sales to hospital national accounts /. Tustin, CA, U. S.A. (17722 Irvine Blvd., Tustin 92680) , c1987. 524 p. in various pagings : LC Card 87-401688 DDC 681/.761/0688 19
HD9994.U52 M39 1987

Multilateral co-operation in southern Africa, 1984 : a report / by the Multilateral Development Council of Ministers, issued by directive of the Republics of South Africa, Transkei, Bophuthatswana, Venda, Ciskei. Pretoria : Publications Division of the Dept. of Foreign Affairs, 1984. 20 p. : ill. ; 21 cm. Based on a summit meeting of the heads of states of the above mentioned Republics November 11, 1982 in Pretoria. ISBN 0-621-09124-3 (pbk.) LC Card 86-209427 DDC 338.968 19
1. South Africa - Economic policy. I. Multilateral Development Council of Ministers (South Africa).
HC905 .M85 1984

Multilateral Development Council of Ministers (South Africa) Multilateral co-operation in southern Africa, 1984 . Pretoria , 1984. 20 p. : ISBN 0-621-09124-3 (pbk.) LC Card 86-209427 DDC 338.968 19
HC905 .M85 1984

Multilevel marketing. Harden, Michael P. (Michael Patrick), 1952- The handbook of multilevel marketing . Carrollton, TX , c1987. 138 p. : ISBN 0-938703-10-2 (pbk.) : LC Card 86-25439 DDC 658.8/4 19
HF5415.126 .H37 1987

MULTILEVEL MARKETING.
Cunningham, Jan. All about multi-level marketing . Denver, CO (1020 15th St., Suite 41C, Denver 80202) , c1986. 173 p. : LC Card 86-213072 DDC 658.8/4 19
HF5415.126 .C85 1986

Harden, Michael P. (Michael Patrick), 1952- The handbook of multilevel marketing . Carrollton, TX , c1987. 138 p. : ISBN 0-938703-10-2 (pbk.) : LC Card 86-25439 DDC 658.8/4 19
HF5415.126 .H37 1987

Robinson, Dean L. Network marketing /. Salt Lake City, Utah , c1983. 137 p. : LC Card 86-202974 DDC 658.8/4 19
HF5415.126 .R63 1983

Les multinacionals a Catalunya /. Cabana, Francesc, 1934- Barcelona , 1986. 154 p. ; ISBN 84-7410-162-X LC Card 86-222016
HD2888.5.C38 C33 1986

Multinational accounting . Prodhan, B. London , Dover, N.H. , c1986. xi, 399 p. : ISBN 0-7099-4010-6 : LC Card 86-4521 DDC 657/.95 19
HF5686.I56 P76 1986 ***NYPL [JLD 86-2595]***

The multinational bank . Scheer, Harold. Genève , 1987. 131, [6] p. : LC Card 87-155370 DDC 332.1/5 19
HG3881 .S338 1987

Multinational banking /. Grubel, Herbert G. Singapore , 1985. iii, 21 p. ; ISBN 997-19-8817-8

(pbk.) LC Card 86-940563 DDC 332.1/6 19
HG3881 .G747 1985

The multinational construction industry /. Seymour, Howard, 1961- London , New York , c1987. 295 p. ; ISBN 0-7099-5438-7 LC Card 87-21720 DDC 338.8/87 19
HD9715.A2 S49 1987

MULTINATIONAL CORPORATIONS. see **INTERNATIONAL BUSINESS ENTERPRISES.**

Multinational corporations : Operations and finance.
International Industrial Conference, 1st, San Francisco, 1957. Private investment /. New York , 1980, c1958. xi, 282 p. ; ISBN 0-405-13355-3 LC Card 80-606 DDC 332.6/7314
HG4538 .I537 1957d ***NYPL [JLD 81-249]***

Multinational corporations in India. Johri, Lalit M. Business strategies of multinational corporations in India . New Delhi , 1983. v, 172 p. ; LC Card 83-906128 DDC 338.8/87 19
HD9672.I52 J63 1983 ***NYPL [JLD 86-4081]***

Multinational corporations in Nigeria. Onimode, Bade. MNC's in Nigeria . Ibadan , 1983. ix, 144 p. ; ISBN 978-231-800-0 (pbk.) LC Card 86-195403 DDC 338.8/88669 19
HD2928 .O55 1983

Multinational corporations, OPEC, cartels, foreign investment, and technology transfer [microform] : special studies, 1982-1985 / edited by Michael Davis. Frederick, MD : University Publications of America, 1987. microfilm reel Accompanied by a printed reel guide, compiled by Mike Acquaviva. ISBN 0-89093-552-1 (microfilm) : LC Card 87-6249 DDC 338.8 19
1. International business enterprises. 2. Organization of Petroleum Exporting Countries. 3. Investments, Foreign - United States. 4. Mineral industries. 5. Technology transfer - Soviet Union. 6. Technology transfer - United States. I. Davis, Michael C., 1953-. II. Acquaviva, Mike. III. University Publications of America, Inc.
HD2755.5

Multinational corporations, the environment and development. Pearson, Charles S. Down to business . Washington, DC (1735 New York Ave., NW, Washington, DC 20006) , c1985. vii, 107 p. ; ISBN 0-915825-04-X (pbk.) : LC Card 84-52795
HD69.P6 P42 1985 ***NYPL [JLE 86-3186]***

Multinational enterprise and world competition . Clegg, Jeremy, 1955- New York , 1987. xiv, 206 p. : ISBN 0-312-00852-X : LC Card 87-4735 DDC 338.8/8 19
HD2755.5 .C54 1987

Multinational enterprises : information and consultation concerning their manpower plans. Geneva : International Labour Office, 1985. xii, 195 p. ; 24 cm. Includes bibliographies. ISBN 92-2-105094-7 (pbk.) : LC Card 86-210138 DDC 331.25 19
1. Manpower planning. 2. International business enterprises. 3. Industrial relations. I. International Labour Office.
HF5549.5.M3 M85 1985

Multinational enterprises, transfer of managerial know-how, technology choice and employment effects . Gershenberg, Irving. Geneva , 1983. iii, 33 p. ; ISBN 92-2-103508-5 (pbk.) LC Card 86-213574 DDC 338.8/886762 19
HD2920.5 .G47 1983

Multinational finance /. Buckley, Adrian. Deddington, Oxford , Atlantic Highlands, N.J. , 1986. x, 398 p. : ISBN 0-86003-542-5 LC Card 86-226038 DDC 658.1/599 19
HG4027.5 .B83 1986

Multinational managers and host government interactions / Lee A. Tavis, editor. Notre Dame, Ind. : University of Notre Dame Press, c1987. p. cm. ISBN 0-268-01364-0 : LC Card 86-40590 DDC 658.4/08/091724 19
1. International business enterprises - Social aspects - Developing countries. I. Tavis, Lee A.
HD2932 .M847 1987

Multinational marketing management : cases and readings / [compiled by] Robert D. Buzzell, John A. Quelch. Reading, Mass. : Addison-Wesley, c1988. x, 500 p. : ill. ; 24 cm. Bibliography: p. 499-500. Includes index. ISBN 0-201-07996-8 (pbk.) : LC Card 87-12599 DDC 658.8/48 19
1. Export marketing - Management. I. Buzzell, Robert D. (Robert Dow), 1933-. II. Quelch, John A.
HF1009.5 .M85 1988

The multinational mission . Prahalad, C. K. New York , London , c1987. ix, 290 p. : ISBN 0-02-925050-1 LC Card 87-11970 DDC 658/.049 19
HD62.4 .P69 1987

Multinational risk assessment and management . Ting, Wenlee. New York , c1987. p. cm. ISBN 0-89930-175-4 (lib. bdg. : alk. paper) LC Card 87-5970 DDC 658 19
HD61 .T56 1987

Multinationale Bankenverflechtungen . Brosset, Michel. Bern , c1983. vii, 245 p. : ISBN 3-258-03275-0 : LC Card 83-178197
HG1526 .B27 Bd. 79 HG3881

Multinationale Konzerne : ihr Einfluss auf die Lage der Beschäftigten : dokumentiert am Beispiel der Bundesrepublik Deutschland und unter besonderer Berücksichtigung gewerkschaftlicher Probleme / Klaus Peter Kisker ... [et al.]. Köln : Bund, c1982. 478 p. : ill. ; 21 cm. (Schriftenreihe der Otto Brenner Stiftung . 25) Bibliography: p. 475-478. ISBN 3-7663-0506-9 LC Card 82-196963 DDC 332.6/73/0943 19
1. Investments, Foreign, and employment - Germany (West) - Addresses, essays, lectures. 2. Corporations, West German - Addresses, essays, lectures. I. Kisker, Klaus Peter. II. Series. III. Series: Otto Brenner Stiftung. Schriftenreihe, 25.
HD5710.75.G3 M84 1982 ***NYPL [JLD 86-2753]***

Multinationals and employment in a West African sub-region . Iyanda, Olukunle. Geneva , 1984. iv, 49 p. ; ISBN 92-2-103623-5 (pbk.) : LC Card 86-213585 DDC 388.8/88664 19
HD2928.8 .I92 1984

Multinationals and maldevelopment . Alschuler, Lawrence R., 1941- New York , 1988. xii, 218 p. : ISBN 0-312-00531-8 : LC Card 87-4307 DDC 338.9 19
HD82 .A5493 1988

Multinationals and the restructuring of the world economy / edited by Michael Taylor and Nigel Thrift. London ; Dover, N.H. : Croom Helm, c1986- viii, 389 p. : ill., maps ; 23 cm. (Croom Helm series in geography and environment) Includes indexes. Forms v. 2 of: The Geography of multinationals, edited by Michael Taylor and Nigel Thrift. Bibliography: p. 360-378. CONTENTS. - -- v. 2. The geography of multinationals. ISBN 0-7099-2457-7 (v. 2) : LC Card 85-29081 DDC 338.8/81 19
1. International business enterprises - Addresses, essays, lectures. 2. International economic relations - Addresses, essays, lectures. I. Taylor, Michael, 1946-. II. Thrift, N. J. III. Geography of multinationals. v. 2.
HD2755.5 .M8442 1986 ***NYPL [JLD 86-2089]***

Multinationals and world trade . Casson, Mark, 1945- London , Boston , 1986. xi, 401 p. : ISBN 0-04-338125-1 (alk. paper) LC Card 85-15734 DDC 338.8/8 19
HD2748 .C37 1986 ***NYPL [JLD 86-1224]***

Multinationals as mutual invaders : intra-industry direct foriegn [sic] investment / edited by Asim Erdilek. London : Croom Helm, c1985. 217 p. : ill. ; 23 cm. "Contains six papers and twelve comments that were commissioned for and presented at a US National Science Foundation workshop ... on 21 April 1983, in Washington, DC"--P. 1. Bibliography: p. 193-203. Includes index. ISBN 0-7099-0935-7 : LC Card 86-673843
1. Investments, Foreign - Congresses. 2. International business enterprises - Congresses. I. Erdilek, Asim.
HG4538 .M85x 1985b

Multinationals from the Third World . Lall, Rajiv B. Delhi , New York , 1986. 100 p. : ISBN 0-19-561895-5 : LC Card 86-900021 DDC 338.8/8954 19
HG4538 .L274 1986

Multinationals, technology, and industrialization . Marton, Katherin. Lexington, Mass. , c1986. xiii, 304 p. ; ISBN 0-669-13209-8 (alk. paper) LC Card 86-7218 DDC 338.8/881724 19
HD2932 .M37 1986 ***NYPL [JLE 86-3372]***

Multinationals, the state, and control of the Nigerian economy /. Biersteker, Thomas J. Princeton, N.J. , c1987. xvii, 344 p. : ISBN 0-691-07728-2 (alk. paper) : LC Card 86-25214 DDC 338.8/88669 19
HG5881.A3 B54 1987

Multinationals--theory and history / edited by Peter Hertner and Geoffrey Jones. Aldershot, Hants, England ; Brookfield, Vt., USA : Gower, c1986. vii, 200 p. : 23 cm. Papers originally presented at a conference held at the European University Institute, Florence, during 19-21 Sept. 1983 and sponsored by the European Science Foundation. Includes bibliographical references and index. ISBN 0-566-05078-1 : LC Card 85-24955 DDC 338.8/8 19
1. International business enterprises - Congresses. 2. International business enterprises - Europe - Congresses. I. Hertner, Peter. II. Jones, Geoffrey. III. European Science Foundation.
HD2755.5 .M86 1986 ***NYPL [JLD 86-1575]***

Multinationella förtag : en utmaning för ekonomisk forskning / Lars Engwall & Jan-Erik Vahlne, red. Lund : Doxa, 1985. 196 p. : ill. ; 21 cm. (Doxa ekonomi) Bibliography: p. 183-192. Includes indexes. CONTENTS. - Direktinvesteringskommitténs strategi och erfarenheter för fortsatt forskning om multinationella företag / av Jan-Erik Vahlne -- Allmän välfärd och ekonomisk politik / av Hans-Fredrik Samuelsson -- Om internationella företag och behovet av ett historiskt synsätt / av Håkan Lindgren -- De multinationella företagen, organisationesteorin och den institutionella ekonomiska teorin / av Bengt Abrahamsson -- Varför studera multinationella företag? / av Per Heum -- Multinationella företag och internationell ekonomisk politik / av Göte Hansson -- Transnationella företag och industripolitik / av Mats Forsgren & Anders Larsson -- Lokalisering av FoU i svenska multinationella företag / av Fredrik Bergholm & Jan-Erik Vahlne -- Multinationella företag och internationella investeringar / av Jan Johanson & Lars-Gunnar Mattsson. ISBN 91-578-0210-6 : LC Card 86-216456
1. International business enterprises. 2. International business enterprises - Sweden. I. Engwall, Lars. II. Vahlne, Jan-Erik, 1941-.
HD2755.5 .M864 1985

MULTIPLAN (COMPUTER PROGRAM)
Lenfest, David. Mac Multiplan /. Blue Ridge Summit, Pa. , c1984. ix, 259 p. : ISBN 0-8306-0851-6 : LC Card 84-8796 DDC 001.64/25 19
HF5548.4.M74 L46 1984 ***NYPL [JSE 86-1870]***

Witkin, Ruth K. Managing your business with Multiplan . Redmond, Wash. , 1987. xv, 525 p. ; ISBN 0-914845-94-2 (pbk.) : LC Card 87-7773 DDC 005.36/9 19
HF5548.4.M74 W57 1987

MULTIPLE EMPLOYMENT. see **SUPPLEMENTARY EMPLOYMENT.**

Multiple imputation for nonresponse in surveys /. Rubin, Donald B. New York , c1987. xxix, 258 p. : ISBN 0-471-08705-X : LC Card 86-28935 DDC 001.4/225 19
HA31.2 .R83 1987

MULTIPLE IMPUTATION (STATISTICS)
Rubin, Donald B. Multiple imputation for nonresponse in surveys /. New York , c1987. xxix, 258 p. : ISBN 0-471-08705-X : LC Card 86-28935 DDC 001.4/225 19
HA31.2 .R83 1987

MULTIPLE USE OF FOREST LANDS. see **FORESTS AND FORESTRY - UNITED STATES - MULTIPLE USE.**

MULTIPLIER (ECONOMICS)
Sell, Friedrich L. Der Konsumcharakter der Einkommensentstehung . Freiburg im Breisgau , c1982. 221 p. : ISBN 3-448-01269-6 LC Card 82-233541 DDC 339.4/7/0724 19
HB820 .S44 1982 ***NYPL [JLD 87-1580]***

Multiregional demography : four essays / Andrei Rogers, editor. Laxenburg, Austria : International Institute for Applied Systems Analysis, c1984. v, 81 p. : ill. ; 24 cm. (Research reports / International Institute for Applied Systems Analysis . RR 84-2) "February 1984." Includes bibliographies. LC Card 84-218929 DDC 304.6 19
1. Population geography - Addresses, essays, lectures. 2. Migration, Internal - Addresses, essays, lectures. I. Rogers, Andrei. II. Series: Research reports (Interntional Institute for Applied Systems Analysis) .

RR84-2.
HB1951 .M85 1983 *NYPL [JLE 86-583]*

Mumford, Alan. Handbook of management development /. Aldershot, Hants, England , Brookfield, Vt., U. S.A. , c1986. xxiii, 452 p. : ISBN 0-566-02563-9 LC Card 86-226592 DDC 658.4/07124 19
HD38.2 .H36 1986

Mummery, A. F. (Albert Frederick), 1855-1895. The physiology of industry : being an exposure of certain fallacies in existing theories of economics / by A.F. Mummery and J.A. Hobson. Fairfield, NJ : A.M. Kelley, 1988. p. cm. (Reprints of economic classics) Reprint. Originally published: London : J. Murray, 1889. ISBN 0-678-00673-3 LC Card 87-17943 DDC 330.1 19
1. Economics. 2. Industry. 3. Production (Economic theory). I. Hobson, J. A. (John Atkinson), 1858-1940. II. Title.
HB171 .M95 1988

Mumpower, Jeryl, 1949- New York State in the year 2000 /. Albany, N.Y. , 1988. 572 p. : ISBN 0-88706-602-X LC Card 87-6486 DDC 338.5/443/09747 19
HC107.N7 N447 1988

Munasinghe, Mohan, 1945- Rural electrification for development : policy analysis and applications / Mohan Munasinghe. Boulder : Westview Press, 1987. xxiii, 440 p. : ill. ; 23 cm. (Westview special studies in natural resources and energy management) "Published in cooperation with the Institute for Technology Policy in Development, State University of New York, Stony Brook." Bibliography: p. 419-430. ISBN 0-8133-0088-6 (pbk.) LC Card 87-50130 DDC 333.79/32/091724 19
1. Rural electrification - Developing countries. 2. Rural electrification - Government policy - Developing countries. 3. Rural development - Government policy - Developing countries. I. State University of New York at Stony Brook. Institute for Technology Policy in Development. II. Title.
HD9688.D44 M85 1987

Münch, Erwin. Technik auf dem Prüfstand . Essen , Gräfelfing [1982] 183 p. : ISBN 3-7736-0340-1 LC Card 83-187518
HD9698.G42 T43 1982

Münch, Manfred. Glogowski, Erhard. Neue Finanzdienstleistungen . Wiesbaden , c1986. 305 p. : ISBN 3-409-14101-4 LC Card 87-131647 DDC 332.1/0943 19
HG3048 .G57 1986

Münch, Paul, 1913-
Gesellschaft für Öffentliche Wirtschaft und Gemeinwirtschaft. Wissenschaftlicher Beirat. Zum Problem der Aufgabenverlagerung auf öffentliche Unternehmen . Baden-Baden , 1984. 73 p. ; ISBN 3-7890-1048-0 LC Card 85-143795
HD4177 .G47 1984

Öffentliche Unternehmen in Rezession und Aufschwung . Berlin , 1977. 165 p. : LC Card 85-180964
HD3845 .G43 Heft 14 HD3842

Münchener geographische Hefte .
(Nr. 50) Beiträge zur empirischen Bürostandortforschung /. Kallmünz , 1983. 167 p. : ISBN 3-7847-6050-3 : LC Card 84-176770
HF5547.25 .B45 1983

Mundel, Marvin Everett, 1916-
BASIC, a personal computer language for improving productivity / Marvin E. Mundel and David Danner. Tokyo, Japan : Asian Productivity Organization, c1986. v, 322 p. ; 26 cm. Includes index. ISBN 92-833-1089-0 LC Card 86-211814 DDC 005.26 19
1. Basic (Computer program language). 2. Business mathematics - Data processing. I. Danner, David, 1948-. II. Title.
HF5548.5.B3 M86 1986

Measuring the productivity of commercial banks : algorithms and PC programs / Marvin E. Mundel. White Plains, N.Y. : UNIPUB/Kraus International Publications, 1987. v, 101 p. ; 26 cm. + diskette. Diskette enclosed inside pocket. Includes index. ISBN 0-527-91641-2 (pbk.) LC Card 87-5034 DDC 332.1/0285/57565 19
1. Banks and banking - Labor productivity - Measurement - Data processing. 2. Algorithms. I. Title.
HG1588 .M94 1987

Measuring total productivity in manufacturing organizations : algorithms and P-C programs / Marvin E. Mundel. Tokyo, Japan : Asian Productivity Organization, c1986. iv [i.e. vi], 155 p. ; 26 cm. Includes index. ISBN 92-833-1090-4 LC Card 86-211930 DDC 658.3/14 19
1. Industrial productivity - Measurement - Data processing. 2. Industrial productivity - Measurement - Computer programs. 3. Algorithms. I. Asian Productivity Organization. II. Title.
HD56.25 .M87 1986

Measuring total productivity in manufacturing organizations : algorithms and PC programs / Marvin E. Mundel. White Plains, N.Y. : UNIPUB/Kraus International Publications, 1987. vi, 155 p. ; 26 cm. + diskette. Diskette enclosed inside pocket. Includes index. ISBN 0-527-91625-0 (pbk.) LC Card 87-5029 DDC 658.5/036 19
1. Industrial productivity - Measurement - Data processing. 2. Algorithms. I. Title.
HD56.25 .M87 1987

Motion and time study : improving productivity / Marvin E. Mundel.6th ed. Englewood Cliffs, N.J. : Prentice-Hall, c1985. xvi, 752 p. : ill. ; 24 cm. (Prentice-Hall international series in industrial and systems engineering) Includes bibliographical references and index. ISBN 0-13-603044-0 LC Card 84-18173 DDC 658.5/42 19
1. Motion study. 2. Time study. I. Title.
T60.7 .M86 1985 *NYPL [JSE 86-2187]*

El mundo del trabajo . Encuentro Latinoamericano de Pastoral Social (1986 : Bogotá, Colombia) Bogotá , 1986. 92 p. ; ISBN 958-625-053-9 LC Card 87-400623 DDC 261.8/5 19
HD6338 .C277 1981 Suppl.

Mundo del trabajo urbano. Falcón, Ricardo. El mundo del trabajo urbano, 1890-1914 /. Buenos Aires , c1986. 141 p. ; ISBN 950-25-1414-2 : LC Card 87-101423
HD8266 .F35 1986

El mundo del trabajo urbano, 1890-1914 /. Falcón, Ricardo. Buenos Aires , c1986. 141 p. ; ISBN 950-25-1414-2 : LC Card 87-101423
HD8266 .F35 1986

Munet, Elisée. France. Conseil économique et social. Le développement de l'élevage des équidés en France . [Paris] [1986] 166 p. in various pagings : LC Card 86-133487
HD9434.F72 F73 1986

MUNGO (CAMEROON)
Barbier, J. C. Migrations et développement . Paris , 1983, c1984. 372 p. : ISBN 2-7099-0711-7
NYPL [M-11 4991 no.170]

MUNICH (GERMANY) - INDUSTRIES.
Fritz, Carl, b. 1890. München als Industriestadt /. Berlin , 1913. 163 p. ; LC Card 85-666347
HC289.M86 F74x 1913

MUNICH (GERMANY) - INDUSTRIES - LOCATION.
Decker, Hedwig. Standortverlagerungen der Industrie in der Region München /. Kallmünz/Regensburg , 1984. xxvi, 92 p. : ISBN 3-7847-6525-4 LC Card 86-136483 DDC 304.2/0943 s 338.6/042/094336 19
HC281 .M8 Bd. 25 HC289.M86

Munich. Gesellschaft für Strahlen- und Umweltforschung. see **Gesellschaft für Strahlen- und Umweltforschung.**

MUNICIPAL ACCOUNTING. see **MUNICIPAL FINANCE - ACCOUNTING.**

Municipal accounting for developing countries /. Jones, David C., 1935- London , Washington, D.C. , c1984. xii, 896 p. : ISBN 0-8213-0350-3 : LC Card 84-3623 DDC 352.1/71/091724 19
HJ9773 .J66 1984 *NYPL [JLF 86-1628]*

MUNICIPAL ADMINISTRATION. see **MUNICIPAL GOVERNMENT.**

Municipal bonds /. Lamb, Robert. New York , c1987. xx, 327 p. ; ISBN 0-07-036084-7 : LC Card 86-27539 DDC 336.3/1 19
HJ9145 .L35 1987

MUNICIPAL BONDS - RATINGS - NEW YORK (STATE)
Ishmael, Cheryl. Ratemaking . [Albany, N.Y.] [1984] xi, 152 p. : *NYPL [JLF 86-598]*

MUNICIPAL BONDS - RATINGS - UNITED STATES.
Ishmael, Cheryl. Ratemaking . [Albany, N.Y.] [1984] xi, 152 p. : *NYPL [JLF 86-598]*

MUNICIPAL BONDS - UNITED STATES.
Cooner, James J. Investing in municipal bonds . New York , c1987. xvi, 233 p. : ISBN 0-471-84941-3 LC Card 86-28911 DDC 332.63/233/0973 19
HG4952 .C66 1987

Howell, Dean M., 1932- How to buy tax free bonds . Denver, Colo. , 1987. 165 p. ; LC Card 86-91807 DDC 332.63/233/0973 19
HG4952 .H68 1987

Lamb, Robert. Municipal bonds /. New York , c1987. xx, 327 p. ; ISBN 0-07-036084-7 : LC Card 86-27539 DDC 336.3/1 19
HJ9145 .L35 1987

MUNICIPAL BUDGETS - GERMANY, WEST.
Gemeindehaushalte zur Haushaltswirtschaft der Städte Hannover, Düsseldorf, Köln, Frankfurt, Stuttgart, München. Bonn am Rhein , 1964. 148 p. ; LC Card 87-408349 DDC 336/.014/43 19
HJ9473 .G46 1964

MUNICIPAL BUDGETS - UNITED STATES.
Merriman, David. The control of municipal budgets . New York , c1987. x, 170 p. : ISBN 0-89930-217-3 (lib. bdg. : alk. paper) LC Card 87-2495 DDC 352.1/2/0973 19
HJ9157 .M47 1987

MUNICIPAL CONTRACTS. see **PUBLIC CONTRACTS.**

MUNICIPAL CORPORATIONS - TAXATION - SPAIN - ANDALUSIA.
Junta de Andalucía. Grupo de Trabajo 14, Planificación Económica de las Corporaciones Locales y Comarcalización. Plan económico de Andalucía, 1984-1986 /. [Andalucía] , 1983. 133 p. ; ISBN 84-505-1243-3 LC Card 86-223752
HJ1249.A4 J86 1983

MUNICIPAL FINANCE.
Management policies in local government finance /. Washington, D.C. , c1987. 449 p. : ISBN 0-87326-075-9 : LC Card 87-2658 DDC 352.1 19
HJ9105 .M3 1987

MUNICIPAL FINANCE - ACCOUNTING.
Jones, David C., 1935- Municipal accounting for developing countries /. London , Washington, D.C. , c1984. xii, 896 p. : ISBN 0-8213-0350-3 : LC Card 84-3623 DDC 352.1/71/091724 19
HJ9773 .J66 1984 *NYPL [JLF 86-1628]*

MUNICIPAL FINANCE - BRAZIL - SAO PAULO (STATE)
Nalin, Irineu. Finanças municipais no Estado de São Paulo . São Paulo , 1985. 88 p. : LC Card 86-233330
HJ9388.A2 S286 1985

MUNICIPAL FINANCE - DEVELOPING COUNTRIES - ACCOUNTING.
Jones, David C., 1935- Municipal accounting for developing countries /. London , Washington, D.C. , c1984. xii, 896 p. : ISBN 0-8213-0350-3 : LC Card 84-3623 DDC 352.1/71/091724 19
HJ9773 .J66 1984 *NYPL [JLF 86-1628]*

MUNICIPAL FINANCE - GERMANY, WEST.
Gemeindehaushalte zur Haushaltswirtschaft der Städte Hannover, Düsseldorf, Köln, Frankfurt, Stuttgart, München. Bonn am Rhein , 1964. 148 p. ; LC Card 87-408349 DDC 336/.014/43 19
HJ9473 .G46 1964

MUNICIPAL FINANCE - GERMANY (WEST) - NORTH RHINE-WESTPHALIA.
Kops, Manfred. Die regionalen Verteilungswirkungen des kommunalen Finanzausgleichs . Thun , c1983. xvii, 537, 259 p. : ISBN 3-87144-728-5 : LC Card 83-159176
HJ9493.5.N6 K66 1983

MUNICIPAL FINANCE - GERMANY (WEST) - NORTH RHINE-WESTPHALIA - ACCOUNTING.
Kops, Manfred. Die regionalen Verteilungswirkungen des kommunalen Finanzausgleichs . Thun , c1983. xvii, 537, 259 p. : ISBN 3-87144-728-5 : LC Card 83-159176
HJ9493.5.N6 K66 1983

Municipal finance in India . Rajagopal Rao, Narayanamurthy, 1925- New Delhi, India , 1986. xix, 411 p. ; ISBN 81-210-0067-X : LC

Card 86-901947 DDC 336/.014/54 19
HJ9565 .R35 1986

Municipal finance in the metropolitan cities of India. Jai Bhagwan, 1948- New Delhi , 1983. xii, 249 p. ; LC Card 83-906365 DDC 352.1/0954 19
HJ9065.D4 A14 1983 NYPL [JLD 87-890]

MUNICIPAL FINANCE - INDIA.
Rajagopal Rao, Narayanamurthy, 1925- Municipal finance in India . New Delhi, India , 1986. xix, 411 p. ; ISBN 81-210-0067-X : LC Card 86-901947 DDC 336/.014/54 19
HJ9565 .R35 1986

MUNICIPAL FINANCE - INDIA - CASE STUDIES.
Jai Bhagwan, 1948- Municipal finance in the metropolitan cities of India . New Delhi , 1983. xii, 249 p. ; LC Card 83-906365 DDC 352.1/0954 19
HJ9065.D4 A14 1983 NYPL [JLD 87-890]

MUNICIPAL FINANCE - INDIA - DELHI.
Jai Bhagwan, 1948- Municipal finance in the metropolitan cities of India . New Delhi , 1983. xii, 249 p. ; LC Card 83-906365 DDC 352.1/0954 19
HJ9065.D4 A14 1983 NYPL [JLD 87-890]

MUNICIPAL FINANCE - MIDDLE WEST.
Stinson, Thomas F., 1942- Governing the heartland . Washington , 1986. xii, 159 p. : LC Card 86-603376 DDC 336/.014/77 19
HJ9181 .S75 1986

MUNICIPAL FINANCE - NETHERLANDS.
Bakker, G. J. Op arbeid bezuinigd? . 's-Gravenhage , 1986. 116 p. ; ISBN 90-12-05321-8 LC Card 87-108889
HJ9507 .B35 1986

MUNICIPAL FINANCE - SPAIN - HISTORY - 18TH CENTURY.
Romeo Mateo, María Cruz, 1960- Realengo y municipio . Alicante , 1986. 171 p. : ISBN 84-505-3131-4 LC Card 87-137181
HD780.A435 R66 1986

MUNICIPAL FINANCE - UNITED STATES.
Changing the course . Washington , 1986. xvii, 142 p. : LC Card 86-603365 DDC 336.1/85 19
HJ275 .C455 1986

Lamb, Robert. Municipal bonds /. New York , c1987. xx, 327 p. ; ISBN 0-07-036084-7 : LC Card 86-27539 DDC 336.3/1 19
HJ9145 .L35 1987

Pagano, Michael A. How the public works . Washington, D.C. , c1986. ix, 68, 6 p. : ISBN 0-933729-13-8 (pbk.) : LC Card 87-129719 DDC 338.4/3363/0973 19
HJ9145 .P343 1986

MUNICIPAL FINANCE - UNITED STATES - HISTORY - ADDRESSES, ESSAYS, LECTURES.
The Politics of urban fiscal policy /. Beverly Hills , c1984. 176 p. : ISBN 0-8039-2373-2 LC Card 84-13431 DDC 336/.014/73 19
HJ9144 .P64 1984 NYPL [JLD 87-126]

MUNICIPAL GOVERNMENT - BRAZIL - BAHIA (STATE) - STATISTICS.
Catálogo de informações sócio-econômicas dos municípios, Bahia /. Salvador, BA [1984] 354 p. ; LC Card 86-210868
HA988.B3 C38 1984

MUNICIPAL GOVERNMENT - BRAZIL - CONGRESSES.
Encontro de Trabalho sobre Descentralização dos Serviços Municipais (1983 : Rio de Janeiro, Brazil) Relatório final /. [Rio de Janeiro] [1983] 60 leaves ; LC Card 84-160735
HD4634 .E53 1983

MUNICIPAL GOVERNMENT - INDIA.
Public administration in India . Allahabad , 1983. xii, 308 p. ; LC Card 83-907416 DDC 354.54 19
JQ224 .P75 1983 NYPL [JLE 86-4197]

MUNICIPAL GOVERNMENT - LAW AND LEGISLATION. see MUNICIPAL CORPORATIONS.

MUNICIPAL GOVERNMENT - SPAIN - HISTORY - 18TH CENTURY.
Romeo Mateo, María Cruz, 1960- Realengo y municipio . Alicante , 1986. 171 p. : ISBN 84-505-3131-4 LC Card 87-137181
HD780.A435 R66 1986

MUNICIPAL GOVERNMENT - SWEDEN - PUBLIC OPINION.
Sannerstedt, Anders, 1945- Attityder till kommunal service /. [Stockholm] [1981] vi, 166 p. : ISBN 91-38-06586-X LC Card 82-244101
HD4485.S8 S26 1981

MUNICIPAL GOVERNMENT - UNITED STATES.
Abney, Glenn. The politics of state and city administration /. Albany, N.Y. , c1986. xvi, 260 p. ; ISBN 0-88706-255-5 LC Card 85-14873 DDC 353.9 19
JK2408 .A26 1986 NYPL [JLE 86-3711]

Stone, Clarence N. (Clarence Nathan), 1935- Urban policy and politics in a bureaucratic age /. Englewood Cliffs, N.J. , c1986. xv, 397 p. ; ISBN 0-13-939562-8 LC Card 85-6481 DDC 320.8/0973 19
JS331 .S76 1986 NYPL [JLE 86-3158]

MUNICIPAL GOVERNMENT - UNITED STATES - HISTORY - ADDRESSES, ESSAYS, LECTURES.
The Politics of urban fiscal policy /. Beverly Hills , c1984. 176 p. : ISBN 0-8039-2373-2 LC Card 84-13431 DDC 336/.014/73 19
HJ9144 .P64 1984 NYPL [JLD 87-126]

MUNICIPAL LAW (MUNICIPAL CORPORATIONS) see MUNICIPAL CORPORATIONS.

MUNICIPAL OFFICIALS AND EMPLOYEES - UNITED STATES.
Stone, Clarence N. (Clarence Nathan), 1935- Urban policy and politics in a bureaucratic age /. Englewood Cliffs, N.J. , c1986. xv, 397 p. ; ISBN 0-13-939562-8 LC Card 85-6481 DDC 320.8/0973 19
JS331 .S76 1986 NYPL [JLE 86-3158]

MUNICIPAL OWNERSHIP - GERMANY, WEST.
Sander, Otfried. Kommunale Wirtschaftsunternehmen /. Köln , 1982. xiv, 144 p. : ISBN 3-555-00464-6 LC Card 81-192097
HD4659 .S26 1982

Municipal ownership in the electric utility industry. Schap, David. New York , 1986. xiii, 128 p. ; ISBN 0-03-006347-7 : LC Card 85-19418 DDC 363.6/2/0973 19
HD9685.U5 S3 1986 NYPL [JLE 86-3180]

MUNICIPAL OWNERSHIP - UNITED STATES - HISTORY.
Schap, David. Municipal ownership in the electric utility industry . New York , 1986. xiii, 128 p. ; ISBN 0-03-006347-7 : LC Card 85-19418 DDC 363.6/2/0973 19
HD9685.U5 S3 1986 NYPL [JLE 86-3180]

MUNICIPAL REVENUE - MIDDLE WEST.
Stinson, Thomas F., 1942- Governing the heartland . Washington , 1986. xii, 159 p. : LC Card 86-603376 DDC 336/.014/77 19
HJ9181 .S75 1986

MUNICIPAL SERVICES - ARGENTINA - CASE STUDIES.
Funciones y servicios de competencia municipal /. Córdoba, República Argentina , 1984. 94 leaves ; LC Card 87-121632 DDC 352.082 19
HD4629 .F86 1984

MUNICIPAL SERVICES - AUSTRIA - CONGRESSES.
Linzer Kommunalwissenschaftliche Tagung (1978) Privatisierung kommunaler Aufgaben? . Linz , c1978. 62 p. ; ISBN 3-7141-7871-6 LC Card 85-185084
HD4651 .L56 1978

MUNICIPAL SERVICES - BRAZIL - CONGRESSES.
Encontro de Trabalho sobre Descentralização dos Serviços Municipais (1983 : Rio de Janeiro, Brazil) Relatório final /. [Rio de Janeiro] [1983] 60 leaves ; LC Card 84-160735
HD4634 .E53 1983

MUNICIPAL SERVICES - BRAZIL - DISTRITO FEDERAL.
Souza Filho, José Ornellas de. Exposição do governador do Distrito Federal, José Ornellas de Souza Filho, na ADESG, em 02/09/83. [Brasília , 1983 or 1984] 40, [31 leaves] : LC Card 85-148272
HC188.D57 S68 1983

MUNICIPAL SERVICES - BRAZIL - FORTALEZA.
Fernandes, Adelita Neto Carleial. Condições de vida nos bairros de Fortaleza, nov/84 a mar/85 . Fortaleza , 1986. 92 p. : LC Card 86-196902
HC189.F67 F47 1986

MUNICIPAL SERVICES - BRAZIL - PORTO ALEGRE.
Porto Alegre (Brazil). Mayor. Mensagem apresentada á Camara Municipal /. Pôrto Alegre , 1936. 686 p., [7] folded leaves of plates : LC Card 85-135614
HD4635.P6 P67 1936

MUNICIPAL SERVICES - BRAZIL - RIO GRANDE DO SUL.
Rio Grande do Sul (Brazil) Relatorios provinciaes. [1850-1859] 19 pamphlets in 1 v. ; LC Card 84-217966
HD4635.R54 R56 1850

MUNICIPAL SERVICES - BRAZIL - SANTA CATARINA (STATE) - STATISTICS.
Sinopse de informações dos municípios catarinenses. Florianópolis, SC , 1986. 155 leaves : LC Card 87-403943 DDC 330.981/64063 19
HC188.S26 S555 1986

MUNICIPAL SERVICES - COLOMBIA.
Buenahora Febres-Cordero, Norma. Cúcuta y sus servicios públicos básicos /. Bogotá, D.E. , 1984. 136 p. ; LC Card 85-205425
HD4637.A5 B84 1984

MUNICIPAL SERVICES - COLOMBIA - CÚCUTA.
Buenahora Febres-Cordero, Norma. Cúcuta y sus servicios públicos básicos /. Bogotá, D.E. , 1984. 136 p. ; LC Card 85-205425
HD4637.A5 B84 1984

MUNICIPAL SERVICES - FINANCE.
Rizzieri, Juarez Alexandre Baldini. Desenvolvimento econômico e urbanização . São Paulo , 1982. 219 p. : LC Card 83-150574 DDC 330.9173/2 19
HT321 .R59 1982 NYPL [JLD 86-3817]

MUNICIPAL SERVICES - FLORIDA - PLANNING.
Florida. Public Facilities Financing Commission. Florida 2000, meeting the challenge . [Tallahassee] [1984] v, 44 p. ; LC Card 86-623234 DDC 363/.09759 19
HC107.F63 C345 1984

MUNICIPAL SERVICES - GERMANY - HISTORY - 20TH CENTURY.
Ambrosius, Gerold. Die öffentliche Wirtschaft in der Weimarer Republik . Baden-Baden , 1984. 306 p. ; ISBN 3-7890-0912-1 LC Card 84-230508
HD4175 .A626 1984

MUNICIPAL SERVICES - ITALY - ROME - ACCOUNTING - CASE STUDIES.
Mancini, Andrea, 1954- La contabilità analitica dei costi . [Torino] , 1986. 53 p. : ISBN 88-85851-00-2 : LC Card 87-114718
HF5686.C8 M265 1986

MUNICIPAL SERVICES - KENYA - NAIROBI.
Mitullah, W. V. Management of urban services in Nairobi . Nairobi, Kenya , 1985. 109, 106, vi p., [6] leaves of plates : LC Card 87-116360 DDC 388.4/09676/25 19
HD4720.5.N35 M57 1985

MUNICIPAL SERVICES - MANAGEMENT - ADDRESSES, ESSAYS, LECTURES.
Management of local public works /. Washington, D.C. , c1986. xvii, 402 p. : ISBN 0-87326-048-1 : LC Card 86-125 DDC 363/.068 19
HD4431 .M35 1986 NYPL [JLF 86-1543]

MUNICIPAL SERVICES - SPAIN - CONGRESSES.
Manual de servicios municipales . Barcelona , 1982. 340 p. ; ISBN 84-500-5399-4 LC Card 82-214246 DDC 363/.0946 19
HD4687 .M36 1982 NYPL [JLC 86-139]

MUNICIPAL SERVICES - SPAIN - GARROTXA REGION.
La Garrotxa . [Barcelona , c1983. xv, 323 p. : ISBN 84-7231-912-1 LC Card 85-184803
HC387.G34 G37 1983

MUNICIPAL SERVICES - SWEDEN - PUBLIC OPINION.
Sannerstedt, Anders, 1945- Attityder till

kommunal service /. [Stockholm] [1981] vi, 166 p. : ISBN 91-38-06586-X LC Card 82-244101
HD4485.S8 S26 1981

MUNICIPAL SERVICES - UNITED STATES.
Stone, Clarence N. (Clarence Nathan), 1935- Urban policy and politics in a bureaucratic age /. Englewood Cliffs, N.J. , c1986. xv, 397 p. ; ISBN 0-13-939562-8 LC Card 85-6481 DDC 320.8/0973 19
JS331 .S76 1986 ***NYPL [JLE 86-3158]***

MUNICIPAL SERVICES - VENEZUELA - CARACAS - CASE STUDIES.
Gómez-Samper, Henry. Los módulos de servicios . Caracas , c1984. 48, 3 [i.e. 4] leaves ; ISBN 980-217-005-4 LC Card 86-193565
HD4343 .G65 1984

MUNICIPAL SERVICES WITHIN CORPORATE LIMITS. see **MUNICIPAL GOVERNMENT; MUNICIPAL SERVICES.**

Municipal tax policy in New York City . Citizens Budget Commission (New York, N.Y.) New York, N.Y. (110 E. 42nd St., New York 10017) [1986] iii leaves, 25 p. ; LC Card 87-110053 DDC 336.2/0097471 19
HJ9289.N4 C54 1986

MUNICIPAL TRANSIT. see **LOCAL TRANSIT.**

MUNICIPAL TRANSPORTATION. see **URBAN TRANSPORTATION.**

MUNICIPAL WATER SUPPLY - AUSTRALIA - CONGRESSES.
National Workshop on Urban Water Demand Management (1986 : Alexander Library, Perth Cultural Centre) Working papers for the National Workshop on Urban Water Demand Management . Leederville, WA [1986] xii, 657 p. : LC Card 87-119946 DDC 333.91/2/0994 19
HD4465.A8 N37 1986

MUNICIPAL WATER SUPPLY - AUSTRALIA - WESTERN AUSTRALIA - FINANCE.
Water Authority of Western Australia. Water Authority of Western Australia Corporate plan, 1986-1991. Appendix C, asset investment program /. Leederville, W.A. [1986] 42 p. ; LC Card 87-158833 DDC 354.9410082/325 19
HD1700.W4 W38 1986

MUNICIPAL WATER SUPPLY - DENMARK - RATES.
Denmark. Udvalget til undersøgelse af vandforsyningernes økonomiske baggrund. Vandpriser . København [1983] 108 p. ; ISBN 87-503-4559-1 LC Card 84-169901
HD4465.D4 D46 1983

Lauritzen, Niels, 1947- Rapporter /. København [1983] 59 p. : ISBN 87-503-4574-5 LC Card 84-169893
HD4465.D4 L38 1983

Rapporter udarbejdet af Forvaltningshøjskolen og Miljøstyrelsens økonomifunktion. København [1983] 59 p. : ISBN 87-503-4574-5 LC Card 85-150558
HD4465.D4 R36 1983

Teknisk-økonomisk-organisatorisk analyse /. København [1983] 131 p. : ISBN 87-503-4561-3 LC Card 84-169883
HD4465.D4 T44 1983

MUNICIPAL WATER SUPPLY - DEVELOPING COUNTRIES - PLANNING.
Okun, Daniel Alexander. Community piped water supply systems in developing countries . Washington, D.C. , 1987. xi, 249 p. : ISBN 0-8213-0896-3 (pbk.) LC Card 87-8161 DDC 363.6/1/091724 19
HD4465.D44 O38 1987

MUNICIPAL WATER SUPPLY - DEVELOPING COUNTRIES - PLANNING - CITIZEN PARTICIPATION - PLANNING.
Whyte, Anne V. T. Guidelines for planning community participation activities in water supply and sanitation projects /. Geneva , Albany, NY , 1986. 53 p. : ISBN 92-4-170096-3 (pbk.) : LC Card 87-137091 DDC 333.91/009172/4 19
HD4465.D44 W49 1986

MUNICIPAL WATER SUPPLY - FINANCE.
Herrington, Paul. Pricing of water services /. Paris , Washington, D.C. , 1987. 145 p. : ISBN 92-64-12921-9 (pbk.) : LC Card 87-167536 DDC 338.4/336361 19
HD4456 .H47 1987

MUNICIPAL WATER SUPPLY - RATES.
Herrington, Paul. Pricing of water services /. Paris , Washington, D.C. , 1987. 145 p. : ISBN 92-64-12921-9 (pbk.) : LC Card 87-167536 DDC 338.4/336361 19
HD4456 .H47 1987

MUNICIPAL WATER SUPPLY - UNITED STATES - CONGRESSES.
AWWA Seminar on the Rate Making Process: Going Beyond the Cost of Service (1986 : Denver, Colo.) Proceedings /. Denver, CO , c1986. vi, 58 p. ; ISBN 0-89867-368-2 (pbk.) LC Card 87-107641 DDC 338.4/336361/0973 19
HD4461 .A915 1986

MUNICIPAL WATER SUPPLY - UNITED STATES - RATES - CONGRESSES.
AWWA Seminar on the Rate Making Process: Going Beyond the Cost of Service (1986 : Denver, Colo.) Proceedings /. Denver, CO , c1986. vi, 58 p. ; ISBN 0-89867-368-2 (pbk.) LC Card 87-107641 DDC 338.4/336361/0973 19
HD4461 .A915 1986

MUNICIPALITIES. see **CITIES AND TOWNS; MUNICIPAL GOVERNMENT.**

Municipio de Poncitlán. Guadalajara, Jal., México : Instituto de Geografía y Estadística, Universidad de Guadalajara, [1979] 71 p. : ill., maps ; 22 cm. LC Card 86-188934
1. Poncitlán (Mexico) - Economic conditions - Statistics. I. Universidad de Guadalajara. Instituto de Geografía y Estadística.
HC138.P63 M85 1979

Os Municípios do Rio Grande do Sul : informações históricas, sócio-econômicas e políticas / Estado do Rio Grande do Sul, Assembléia Legislativa, Comissão de Estudos Municipais. [Porto Alegre] : A Comissão, 1985. 250, [7] p. : maps ; 23 cm. Chiefly tables. Bibliography: p. [257]. LC Card 87-401216 DDC 318.1/65 19
1. Rio Grande do Sul (Brazil) - Statistics. 2. Cities and towns - Brazil - Rio Grande do Sul - Statistics. I. Rio Grande do Sul (Brazil). Comissão de Estudos Municipais.
HA988.R8 M86 1985

Munier, Bertrand. Marchés, capital et incertitude . Paris , c1986. 265 p. : ISBN 2-7178-1002-1 : LC Card 86-160930
HB615 .M37 1986

MUNITIONS - BRAZIL.
Tavares, José, 1949- Indústria bélica brasileira . Brasília , 1983. 44 p. ; LC Card 84-235004
HC187 .T2943 1983

Wöhlcke, Manfred, 1942- Brasilien als Produzent und Exporteur von Rüstungsgütern /. Baden-Baden , 1987. 176 p. : ISBN 3-7890-1355-2 LC Card 87-135627 DDC 338.4/36234/0981 19
HD9743.B682 W64 1987

MUNITIONS - DEVELOPING COUNTRIES.
Brzoska, Michael. Arms transfers to the Third World, 1971-85 /. Oxford , New York , 1987. xv, 383 p. : ISBN 0-19-829116-7 : LC Card 87-5579 DDC 382/.456234/091724 19
HD9743.D442 B79 1987

Defence, security, and development /. New York , 1987. xiii, 219 p. : ISBN 0-312-01243-8 : LC Card 87-12129 DDC 338.4/76234/091724 19
HC59.72.D4 D436 1987

MUNITIONS - DEVELOPING COUNTRIES - MORAL AND ETHICAL ASPECTS - EXHIBITIONS.
Rüstungsexport, ein todsicheres Geschäft . Idstein/Ts. , 1984. 1 v. (various pagings) : LC Card 86-152420
HD9743.D442 R87 1984

MUNITIONS - ECONOMIC ASPECTS - CONGRESSES.
Peace, defence, and economic analysis . New York , 1987. xxxiii, 450 p. : ISBN 0-312-01321-3 : LC Card 87-19708 DDC 338.4/7355 19
HC79.D4 P43 1987

MUNITIONS - ECONOMIC ASPECTS - HISTORY - 20TH CENTURY.
Rosecrance, Richard N. The rise of the trading state . New York , c1986. xiii, 268 p. : ISBN 0-465-07035-3 : LC Card 85-47558 DDC 382/.09/04 19
HF1007 .R549 1985 ***NYPL [JLE 86-951]***

MUNITIONS - ECONOMIC ASPECTS - UNITED STATES.
Braun, Axel. Rüstungskonversionsbemühungen in den USA in den 70iger Jahren . Frankfurt am Main , c1984. x, 379 p. : ISBN 3-88129-856-8 LC Card 85-154003
HC110.D4 B72 1984

Fernández Tabío, Luis René. Los intereses económicos en la producción militar de los Estados Unidos /. La Habana , 1982. ii, 87 p. : LC Card 87-400639 DDC 338.4/76234/0973 19
HD9743.U6 F46 1982

Müller, Erwin, 1947- Rüstungspolitik und Rüstungsdynamik . Baden-Baden , 1985. 378 p. ; ISBN 3-7890-1076-6 LC Card 85-154502
HC110.D4 M85 1985

Weida, William J. The political economy of national defense /. Boulder , 1987. xvii, 230 p. ; ISBN 0-8133-0432-6 (alk. paper) : LC Card 86-19015 DDC 355.6/22/0973 19
UA23 .W3694 1987 ***NYPL [JLE 87-1043]***

MUNITIONS - EUROPE.
Greenwood, David. The SDI and Europe /. Aberdeen, Scotland [1985] 64 p. ; LC Card 86-150232 DDC 355/.07/094 19
U395.E85 G73 1985 ***NYPL [JFG 87-57]***

MUNITIONS - FRANCE.
Dussauge, Pierre. L'industrie française de l'armement . Paris , c1985. xi, 179 p. : ISBN 2-7178-0999-6 : LC Card 86-216731
HD9743.F82 D87 1985

Kolodziej, Edward A. Making and marketing arms . Princeton, N.J. , c1987. xxv, 518 p. : ISBN 0-691-07734-7 (alk. paper) : LC Card 86-30567 DDC 338.4/76234/0944 19
HD9743.F82 K64 1987

MUNITIONS - FRANCE - TECHNOLOGICAL INNOVATIONS.
Dussauge, Pierre. L'industrie française de l'armement . Paris , c1985. xi, 179 p. : ISBN 2-7178-0999-6 : LC Card 86-216731
HD9743.F82 D87 1985

MUNITIONS - GERMANY - HISTORY - 20TH CENTURY.
Siegfried, Klaus-Jörg, 1940- Rüstungsproduktion und Zwangsarbeit im Volkswagenwerk, 1939-1945 . Frankfurt , New York , c1986. 239 p. : ISBN 3-593-33765-7 LC Card 87-133375 DDC 338.4/76234/0943 19
HD9743.G48 S56 1986

MUNITIONS - GERMANY, WEST.
Zivile Alternativen für die Rüstungsindustrie /. Baden-Baden , 1986. 174 p. ; ISBN 3-7890-1262-9 LC Card 87-108651 DDC 338.4/76234/0943 19
HD9743.G48 Z58 1986

MUNITIONS - GOVERNMENT POLICY - UNITED STATES.
Ferrari, Paul L. U. S. arms exports . Washington, DC , c1987. xii, 342 p. : ISBN 0-931035-12-0 (pbk.) LC Card 87-80032 DDC 382/.456234/0971 19
HD9743.U6 F47 1987

MUNITIONS - GREAT BRITAIN.
Shein, A. I. (Aleksandr Ivanovich) Voenno-promyshlennyĭ kompleks Velikobritanii /. Moskva , 1985. 165 p. : LC Card 84-219560
HC260.D4 S54 1985 ***NYPL [*QGR 87-2278]***

MUNITIONS - ITALY - HISTORY.
Frumento, Armando. Le repubbliche cisalpina e italiana . Milano , 1985. xii, 608 p. ; LC Card 86-215881
HD9525.I82 F72 1985

MUNITIONS - POLITICAL ASPECTS - SWEDEN.
Hagelin, Björn, 1947- Kulorna rullar . Stockholm , 1985. 186 p. : ISBN 91-7324-253-5 LC Card 86-124793
HD9743.S82 H34 1985

MUNITIONS - PRICES.
Bontrup, Heinz-J. Preisbildung bei Rüstungsgütern /. Köln , c1986. 247 p. ; ISBN 3-8046-8677-X LC Card 87-122749 DDC 338.4/36234 19
HD9743.A2 B59 1986

MUNITIONS - SOUTH AFRICA.
Automating apartheid . Philadelphia , c19. ix, 107 p. : ISBN 0-910082-00-6 (pbk.) : LC Card 86-201384 DDC 382/.45004/0968 19
HD9696.C63 S62 1984

MUNITIONS - SWEDEN.
Hagelin, Björn, 1947- Kulorna rullar . Stockholm , 1985. 186 p. : ISBN 91-7324-253-5 LC Card 86-124793
HD9743.S82 H34 1985

MUNITIONS TRADE. see **MUNITIONS.**

MUNITIONS - UNITED STATES.
Automating apartheid . Philadelphia , c19. ix, 107 p. : ISBN 0-910082-00-6 (pbk.) : LC Card 86-201384 DDC 382/.45004/0968 19
HD9696.C63 S62 1984

Ferrari, Paul L. U. S. arms exports . Washington, DC , c1987. xii, 342 p. : ISBN 0-931035-12-0 (pbk.) LC Card 87-80032 DDC 382/.456234/0971 19
HD9743.U6 F47 1987

Weida, William J. The political economy of national defense /. Boulder , 1987. xvii, 230 p. ; ISBN 0-8133-0432-6 (alk. paper) : LC Card 86-19015 DDC 355.6/22/0973 19
UA23 .W3694 1987 ***NYPL [JLE 87-1043]***

MUNITIONS - UNITED STATES - DIRECTORIES.
Top 500 RDT&E companies /. Greenwich, CT, U. S.A. (100 Northfield St., Greenwich 06830) , c1986. 721, [50] p. : LC Card 87-120786 DDC 338.7/6234/02573 19
HD9743.U6 T66 1986

MUNITIONS - UNITED STATES - PRICES.
Vasi͡utovich, V. P. (Vladimir Petrovich) T͡Senoobrazovanie v voennom proizvodstve SShA /. Moskva , 1980. 221 p. ; LC Card 81-143903
HD9743.U6 V37 1980

Munkaerőhelyzet és kereseti viszonyok az állami gazdaságokban, kombinátokban és a mezőgazdasági termelőszövetkezetekben, 1980-1985 / [készült a Központi Statisztikai Hivatal Mezőgazdasági Statisztikai Főosztályának Gépesitési és Munkaügyi Osztályán]. Budapest : Központi Statisztikai Hivatal, 1987. 45 p. ; 29 cm. LC Card 87-419798
1. Agricultural laborers - Hungary - Statistics. 2. Agricultural wages - Hungary - Statistics. I. Hungary. Központi Statisztikai Hivatal. Gépesitési és Munkaügyi Osztály.
HD1536.H9 M85 1987

A munkahely-racionalizálás korszerű megközelítési módjai az élelmiszeriparban /. Gáti, Gábor. Budapest , 1986. 106 p. : ISBN 963-02-4171-4 LC Card 87-137979
HD9000.5 .G336 1986

A munkásosztály szolgálatában /. Gáspár, Sándor. [Budapest] , c1983. 326 p., [26] p. of plates : ISBN 963-322-025-4 : LC Card 84-129952
HD6680.5.Z55 G375 1983

Munkásosztályunk fejlődése 1945-ig : tudományos tanácskozás Győrben, 1984. január 26-27 / [szerkesztette, Sipos Levente]. Győr : Győr Megyei Lapkiadó, 1985. 126 p. ; 20 cm. Conference organized by Magyar Történelmi Társulat and MSZMP Győr-Sopron Megyei Bizottsága. LC Card 86-186895
1. Labor and laboring classes - Hungary - History. I. Sipos, Levente. II. Magyar Történelmi Társulat. III. Magyar Szocialista Munkáspárt. Győr-Sopron Megyei Bizottság.
HD8420.5 .M85 1985

Munkaszervezet és termelékenység a magyar parasztságnál a XIX-XX. században /. Szabó, László. Szolnok , 1968 (Debrecen : Szabadság Lapnyomda) 167 p. : LC Card 86-188720
HD1536.H9 S89 1968

Munkaügy a belkereskedelemben / szerkesztette, Koszó Károly ; [írták, Bartókné Erdődi Ibolya ... et al.]. [Budapest] : Belkereskedelmi Továbbképző Intézet, 1986. 272 p. ; 24 cm. (Szakmai kiskönyvtár) Bibliography: p. 272. ISBN 963-01-7513-4 : LC Card 87-148137
1. Personnel management - Hungary. 2. Retail trade - Hungary - Personnel management. 3. Hungary - Commercial policy. I. Koszó, Károly. II. Bartókné Erdődi, Ibolya. III. Series.
HF5549.2.H85 M86 1986

Munkaügyi elemzések .
(9) Németh, Ernő. A bér- és keresetszabályozás müködése 1983-ban /. [Budapest] [1984] 245 p. : ISBN 963-02-3277-4 LC Card 85-231744
HD5022.5 .N46 1984

Munkaügyi Információs Központ (Hungary). Munkaügyi Információs és Gazdaságelemző Főosztály. Németh, Ernő. A bér- és keresetszabályozás müködése 1983-ban /. [Budapest] [1984] 245 p. : ISBN 963-02-3277-4 LC Card 85-231744
HD5022.5 .N46 1984

Munkaügyi statisztikai és módszertani ismeretek / [irták, Huszár Ernőné ... et al. ; szerkesztette, Légár János]. Átdolg. bőv. új kiad. Budapest : Állami Bér- és Munkaügyi Hivatal Munkaügyi Kutatóintézete, 1985. 323 p. : ill. ; 22 cm. (Munkaügyi szakkönyv) ISBN 963-10-6513-8 : LC Card 83-228566
1. Labor and laboring classes - Statistical methods. 2. Labor supply - statistical methods. I. Huszár, Ernőné. II. Légár, János. III. Series.
HD4826.5 .M86 1985

Munkaügyi szakkönyv.
Munkaügyi statisztikai és módszertani ismeretek /. Budapest , 1985. 323 p. : ISBN 963-10-6513-8 : LC Card 83-228566
HD4826.5 .M86 1985

A Munkavédelem agitációs és propaganda rendszere / [összeállította Bonifert György]. Budapest : Fogyasztási Szövetkezetek Országos Tanácsa, 1983. 51 p. : ill. ; 19 cm. (Munkavédelem, szociálpolitika, 0231-1933) ISBN 963-7006-04-4 LC Card 85-110318
1. Industrial hygiene - Hungary. 2. Industrial safety - Hungary. 3. Propaganda, Communist - Hungary. I. Bonifert, György. II. Series.
HD7702.5 .M85 1983

Munkavédelem, szociálpolitika, 0231-1933.
A Munkavédelem agitációs és propaganda rendszere /. Budapest , 1983. 51 p. : ISBN 963-7006-04-4 LC Card 85-110318
HD7702.5 .M85 1983

A munkaviszonyok humanizálása . Magyar, Lajosné. Budapest [1985] 210 p. ; ISBN 963-608-075-5 LC Card 85-154632
HD6955 .M27 1985

Munkholt, Peer. The Soviet economy : protection of the military sector in case of protracted deterioration / Peer Munkholt. Köln : Bundesinstitut für Ostwissenschaftliche und Internationale Studien, 1985. iii, 79 p. ; 29 cm. (Sonderveröffentlichung des Bundesinstituts für Ostwissenschaftliche und Internationale Studien) Cover title. Bibliography: p. 66-75. LC Card 86-673837
1. Soviet Union - Defenses - Economic aspects. 2. Soviet Union - Economic policy - 1981-. 3. Soviet Union - Military policy - Economic aspects. I. Title. II. Series.
HC340.D4 M86x 1985

Munna, Raymond J., 1941- Franchise selection : separating fact from fiction : a guide for entrepreneurs, investors, attorneys, accountants, and management/marketing advisors : handbook for franchisees / by Raymond J. Munna.1st ed. Kenner, La. : A Granite Publishers, c1987. 215 p. ; 28 cm. Includes bibliographies and index. ISBN 0-935669-12-4 (pbk.) : LC Card 87-25039 DDC 658.8/708 19
1. Franchises (Retail trade) - United States. I. Title.
HF5429.235.U5 M86 1987

Muñoz, Arturo Guillermo. El Táchira fronterizo : el aislamiento regional y la integración nacional en el caso de los Andes (1881-1899) / Arturo Guillermo Muñoz. Caracas : Biblioteca de Autores y Temas Tachirenses, 1985. 315 p. ; 22 cm. (Biblioteca de autores y temas tachirenses. 86) Bibliography: p. 301-315. ISBN 980-265-178-8 LC Card 87-402928 DDC 330.987/120633 19
1. Táchira (Venezuela) - Economic conditions. 2. Regionalism - Venezuela - Táchira - History - 19th century. 3. Los Andes (Venezuela) - History - 19th century. I. Series: Biblioteca de Autores y Temas Tachirenses (Series) , 86. II. Title.
HC238.T3 M86 1985

Muñoz Vicuña, Elías.
Masas, luchas, solidaridad /. [S.l. , 1985] ([Guayaquil] : Litografía e Impr. de la Universidad de Guayaquil) 298 p. : LC Card 86-177888
HD8316 .M37 1985

Movimiento obrero del Ecuador, 1970-1979 . Guayaquil, Ecuador [1985] 300 p. ; LC Card 86-105256 DDC 331.88/09866 19
HD6627 .M68 1985 ***NYPL [JLD 86-3140]***

Munro, J. Forbes. Britain in tropical Africa, 1880-1960 : economic relationships and impact / J. Forbes Munro. London : Macmillan, 1984. 89 p. : map ; 22 cm. (Studies in economic and social history) Bibliography: p. 73-85. Includes index. ISBN 0-333-32330-0 LC Card 87-672364
1. Africa, Sub-Saharan - Economic conditions. 2. Great Britain - Colonies - Africa - Economic policy. 3. Great Britain - Colonies - Africa - Economic conditions. I. Title.
HC800 .M86x 1984

Munson, Patricia. The Online commercial database business /. Stamford, Conn., U. S.A. , c1985. xxi, 230 leaves : ISBN 0-89336-320-0 (pbk.) LC Card 87-40457 DDC 381/.4500574/0973 19
HD9696.D363 U66 1985

Münster in Westfalen (Germany)
Burberg, Paul-Helmuth. Zielgruppenorientierte kommunale Wirtschaftsförderung . Münster , c1983. xi, 207, 16 p. : ISBN 3-88497-042-9 LC Card 84-173863
HC289.M9 B87 1983

MÜNSTER IN WESTFALEN (GERMANY) - ECONOMIC CONDITIONS.
Burberg, Paul-Helmuth. Zielgruppenorientierte kommunale Wirtschaftsförderung . Münster , c1983. xi, 207, 16 p. : ISBN 3-88497-042-9 LC Card 84-173863
HC289.M9 B87 1983

MÜNSTER IN WESTFALEN (GERMANY) - HISTORY.
Weidner, Marcus, 1964- Nur Gräber als Spuren . Münster , c1984. 134 p. : ISBN 3-924550-02-6 LC Card 86-116688 DDC 331.11/732/094355 19
HD4875.G4 W45 1984

MÜNSTER IN WESTFALEN (GERMANY) - INDUSTRIES.
Burberg, Paul-Helmuth. Zielgruppenorientierte kommunale Wirtschaftsförderung . Münster , c1983. xi, 207, 16 p. : ISBN 3-88497-042-9 LC Card 84-173863
HC289.M9 B87 1983

Münstersche geographische Arbeiten .
(Heft 4) Periphere Räume . Paderborn , 1979. 183 p. : ISBN 3-506-73204-8 LC Card 85-209554
HC240 .P38 1979

Münstersche geographische Arbeiten, 0176-1064 .
(Heft 24) Heineberg, Heinz. Neue Einkaufszentren im Ruhrgebiet . Paderborn , 1986. 247 p. : ISBN 3-506-73224-2 LC Card 87-407591 DDC 381/.1/094355 19
HF5430.6.G4 H45 1986

(Heft 25) Rönick, Volker. Regionale Entwicklungspolitik und Massenarmut im ländlichen Raum Nordost-Brasiliens . Paderborn , 1986. 136 p. : ISBN 3-506-73225-0 LC Card 87-407836 DDC 338.981/3 19
HC188.N6 R66 1986

Münzprägung, Geldumlauf und Wechselkurse .
International Congress on Economic History (8th : 1982 : Budapest, Hungary) Trier , 1984. 421 p. : ISBN 3-923087-06-3 (pbk.)
HG205 1982 .I53 ***NYPL [JLE 86-3176]***

Muqtada, M. Social and economic formations in Bangladesh agriculture : a historical perspective / M. Muqtada. Dacca, Bangladesh : Bureau of Economic Research, Dhaka University, 1986. 68 p. ; 29 cm. (Research report . new ser. no. 3) Bibliography: p. 61-63. LC Card 86-902421 DDC 338.1/09549/2 19
1. Agriculture - Economic aspects - Bangladesh. 2. Agriculture - Social aspects - Bangladesh. I. Series: Research report (University of Dhaka, Bureau of Economic Research) , new ser. no. 3. II. Title.
HD2075.6 .M86 1986

Mur, Ana María. Cobriza, Cobriza, 1971 /. [Lima? Peru] , 1981. 136 p. ; LC Card 83-106108
HD5361 .M612 1971

Murakami, Yasusuke, 1931-
The Political economy of Japan. Stanford, Calif. , 1987- v. <1 > : ISBN 0-8047-1380-4 (v. 1 : alk. paper) : LC Card 86-30037 DDC

338.952 19
HC462.9 .P57 1987

Round Table Discussions on Japan in the Global Community. Japan in the global community . [Tokyo] , c1986. 129, [38] p. : ISBN 4-13-057014-5 : LC Card 87-129161 DDC 337.52 19
HF1601 .R68 1986

Murashko, G. P. (Galina Pavlovna) Politicheskai͡a bor'ba v Chekhoslovakii v 1944-1948 gg. i natsionalizatsii͡a sredstv proizvodstva / G.P. Murashko ; otvetstvennyĭ redaktor A.I͡A. Manusevich. Moskva : "Nauka", 1986. 326, [2] p. ; 21 cm. At head of title: Akademii͡a nauk SSSR. Institut slavi͡anovedenii͡a i balkanistiki. Bibliography: p. 297-[327]. LC Card 86-202951
1. Czechoslovakia - Economic policy - 1945-. 2. Government ownership - Czechoslovakia - History. 3. Czechoslovakia - Politics and government - 1945-. I. Manusevich, A. I͡A. (Aleksandr I͡Akovlevich). II. Title.
HC270.28 .M87 1986

Murashko, V. M. (Vasiliĭ Maksimovich) Kontrol' i analiz dei͡atel'nosti predprii͡atiĭ po zagotovkam sel'skokhozi͡aĭstvennoĭ produktsii / V.M. Murashko. Moskva : "Finansy i statistika", 1981. 144 p. ; 22 cm. LC Card 82-177216
1. Agriculture - Ukraine - Accounting. 2. Agriculture - Ukraine - Auditing. I. Title.
HF5686.A36 M87 1981

Murata, Alice. (joint author) Liu, William Thomas, 1930- Transition to nowhere . Nashville , c1979. 214 p., [2] leaves of plates : ISBN 0-8202-0189-8 : LC Card 78-21129 DDC 361.5/3/09597
HV640.5.V5 L58 ***NYPL [JLD 87-670]***

Murata, Yasuo, 1931- Optimal control methods for linear discrete-time economic systems / Yasuo Murata. New York : Springer-Verlag, c1982. x, 202 p. ; 25 cm. Includes bibliographies and indexes. ISBN 0-387-90709-2 LC Card 82-19137 DDC 338.9/00724 19
1. Economic policy - Mathematical models. 2. Economic stabilization - Mathematical models. 3. Control theory. I. Title.
HD75.5 .M87 1982 ***NYPL [JLE 87-95]***

Murav'eva, I. I͡U. Kaplan, L. M. (Lev Moiseevich) Ėkonomicheskie problemy upravlenii͡a stroitel'nym proizvodstvom na Severe /. Leningrad , 1983. 167 p. : LC Card 84-113191
HD9715.S73 N675 1983

MURAVLENKO, V. I. (VIKTOR IVANOVICH) I͡Urasova, M. Neft͡anik . Moskva , 1981. 254 p. : LC Card 82-111110
HD8039.P42 S654 1981

MURCIA (SPAIN : PROVINCE) - POPULATION - HISTORY.
Chacón Jiménez, Francisco. Murcia, un modelo económico en el mundo mediterráneo durante el siglo XVI /. [Murcia] , 1978. 29 p., [7] folded leaves of plates : ISBN 84-600-1243-3 LC Card 86-133743
HC387.M8 C48 1978

MURCIA (SPAIN : REGION) - POPULATION - STATISTICS.
Bel Adell, María del Carmen. Datos básicos para el estudio de la población en la región de Murcia /. [Murcia] , c1985. 223 p. ; ISBN 84-600-3907-2 LC Card 86-218876
HA1558.M8 B44 1985

MURCIA (SPAIN : REGION) - SOCIAL CONDITIONS - STATISTICS.
Bel Adell, María del Carmen. Datos básicos para el estudio de la población en la región de Murcia /. [Murcia] , c1985. 223 p. ; ISBN 84-600-3907-2 LC Card 86-218876
HA1558.M8 B44 1985

MURCIA, SPAIN (PROVINCE) - ECONOMIC CONDITIONS.
Chacón Jiménez, Francisco. Murcia, un modelo económico en el mundo mediterráneo durante el siglo XVI /. [Murcia] , 1978. 29 p., [7] folded leaves of plates : ISBN 84-600-1243-3 LC Card 86-133743
HC387.M8 C48 1978

MURCIA, SPAIN (PROVINCE) - HISTORY.
Chacón Jiménez, Francisco. Murcia, un modelo económico en el mundo mediterráneo durante el siglo XVI /. [Murcia] , 1978. 29 p., [7] folded leaves of plates : ISBN 84-600-1243-3 LC Card 86-133743
HC387.M8 C48 1978

Murcia, un modelo económico en el mundo mediterráneo durante el siglo XVI /. Chacón Jiménez, Francisco. [Murcia] , 1978. 29 p., [7] folded leaves of plates : ISBN 84-600-1243-3 LC Card 86-133743
HC387.M8 C48 1978

MURDER - AUSTRALIA.
Kwitny, Jonathan. The crimes of patriots . New York , c1987. 424 p., [8] p. of plates : ISBN 0-393-02387-7 : LC Card 87-22032 DDC 364.1/0994 19
HG3448.N846 K95 1987

Murdock, Steven H. The Farm financial crisis . Boulder , 1988. xvi, 205 p. : ISBN 0-8133-7186-4 (pbk. : alk. paper) : LC Card 86-32601 DDC 338.1/3/0973 19
HD1761 .F295 1988

Murga Frassinetti, Antonio.

Murillo Toro, Manuel, 1816-1880. Escritos económicos / Manuel Murillo Toro. 2a ed. Bogotá, Colombia : Editorial Incunables, 1985. 120 p. ; 23 cm. LC Card 86-165762
1. Colombia. Ministerio de Hacienda. 2. Finance, Public - Colombia. I. Title.
HJ943 .M87 1985

Murilo Pessoa, Dirceu. see **Pessoa, Dirceu Murilo.**

Murin, William J. Stone, Clarence N. (Clarence Nathan), 1935- Urban policy and politics in a bureaucratic age /. Englewood Cliffs, N.J. , c1986. xv, 397 p. ; ISBN 0-13-939562-8 LC Card 85-6481 DDC 320.8/0973 19
JS331 .S76 1986 ***NYPL [JLE 86-3158]***

MURMANSKAI͡A ZHELEZNAI͡A DOROGA - HISTORY.
Kharitonov, S. F. (Sergeĭ Fedorovich) Rasskaz o velikom severnom puti /. Petrozavodsk , 1984. 143 p. : LC Card 84-247171
HE3140.M87 K46 1984

Murphy, Barbara (Barbara Anne) New York State property valuation trends by class : 1974-1980 / Barbara A. Murphy. Albany, N.Y. : State Board of Equalization and Assessment, [1986] viii, 47 p. : ill. ; 28 cm. "October 1986"--Cover. LC Card 86-623052 DDC 336.22/2 19
1. Real property tax - New York (State). I. New York (State). State Board of Equalization and Assessment. II. Title.
HJ4249 .M87 1986

Murphy, Herta A. Effective business communications / Herta A. Murphy, Herbert W. Hildebrandt. 5th ed. New York : McGraw-Hill, c1988. xx, 730 p. : col. ill. ; 25 cm. Includes bibliographical references and index. ISBN 0-07-044094-8 LC Card 87-17330 DDC 651.7 19
1. Commercial correspondence. 2. Business report writing. 3. Business communication. I. Hildebrandt, Herbert William, 1931-. II. Title.
HF5721 .M85 1988

Murphy Institute studies in political economy. The Boundaries of economics /. Cambridge , New York , 1988. xi, 122 p. ; ISBN 0-521-34450-6 LC Card 87-17772 DDC 330 19
HB33 .B68 1988

Murphy, John J.
Study guide for Technical analysis of the futures markets : a self-training manual / John J. Murphy. New York, NY : New York Institute of Finance : Prentice-Hall, c1987. x, 142 p. : ill. ; 24 cm. Designed to be used exclusively with the author's Technical analysis of the futures markets. ISBN 0-13-858747-7 (pbk.) : LC Card 87-10991 DDC 332.64/4 19
1. Commodity exchanges. I. Murphy, John J. Technical analysis of the futures markets. II. Title.
HG6046 .M87 1986 Suppl.

Technical analysis of the futures markets. Murphy, John J. Study guide for Technical analysis of the futures markets : a self-training manual / John J. Murphy. New York, NY , c1987. x, 142 p. : ISBN 0-13-858747-7 (pbk.) : LC Card 87-10991 DDC 332.64/4 19
HG6046 .M87 1986 Suppl.

Murphy, John M., 1944- Branding . New York , 1987. xii, 192 p., [12] p. of plates : ISBN 0-07-044055-7 : LC Card 86-27797 DDC 658.8/27 19
HD69.B7 B73 1987

Murphy, Kevin J., 1950- Effective listening : hearing what people say and putting it to work for you / Kevin J. Murphy. Toronto ; New York : Bantam Books, 1987. ix, 179 p. ; 22 cm. ISBN 0-553-05212-8 LC Card 86-47893 DDC 658.4/52 19
1. Communication in management. 2. Listening. I. Title.
HD30.3 .M87 1987

Murphy, Laura. Murphy, Michael, 1927- Ferryliner vacations in North America . New York , c1988. ix, 277 p. : ISBN 0-525-48355-1 (pbk.) : LC Card 87-13640 DDC 910/.2/02 19
HE5772.A3 M87 1988

Murphy, Michael, 1927- Ferryliner vacations in North America : ocean travel and inland cruising / Michael and Laura Murphy.1st ed. New York : E.P. Dutton, c1988. ix, 277 p. : ill. ; 21 cm. Bibliography: p. 275-277. ISBN 0-525-48355-1 (pbk.) : LC Card 87-13640 DDC 910/.2/02 19
1. Ferries - North America. 2. Ocean travel. 3. Cruise ships - North America. I. Murphy, Laura. II. Title.
HE5772.A3 M87 1988

Murphy, Patricia A. Introduction to ACH corporate payments /. Washington, D.C. (1901 L St., N.W., Suite 640, Washington 20036) [c1986] 90 p. : LC Card 86-222675 DDC 332.1/028 19
HG1710 .I58 1986

Murray, Andy. Fridjhon, Michael. Conspiracy of giants . Johannesburg , c1986. xii, 419 p. : ISBN 0-947012-34-6 LC Card 87-139111 DDC 338.4/76631/0968 19
HD9367.S7 F75 1986

Murray, John D. Kuszczak, John. A VAR analysis of economic interdependence . [Ottawa] [1987] ii, 55 p. : LC Card 87-167407 DDC 338.5/42/0971 19
HB3755 .K87 1987

MURRAY, PHILIP, 1886-1952 - CONGRESSES.
Forging a union of steel . Ithaca, N.Y. , c1987. vii, 153 p. : ISBN 0-87546-135-2 (pbk.) LC Card 87-21508 DDC 331.88/169142/0973 19
HD6515.I5 F58 1987

Murray, Roger. Sparks, Donald L. Namibia's future . London, U.K. , New York, N.Y., USA , c1985. 96 p., [4] p. of plates : LC Card 87-132083 DDC 330.9688/03 19
HC940 .S62 1985

Murray, Roger F. Graham, Benjamin, 1894- [Security analysis.] Graham and Dodd's security analysis. New York , c1988. xiii, 656 p. : ISBN 0-07-013235-6 : LC Card 87-19990 DDC 332.63/2 19
HG4529 .G7 1988

Murtazina, E. N. Problemy vali͡utnoĭ integrat͡sii v Evropeĭskom soobshchestve : nauchno-analiticheskiĭ obzor / [avtor obzora, E.N. Murtazina ; otvetstvennyĭ redaktor, I͡U.A. Borko]. Moskva : INION AN SSSR, 1985. 75 p. ; 20 cm. (Serii͡a Problemy integrat͡sii stran Zapadnoĭ Evropy) "Obzor"--cover. At head of title: Akademii͡a nauk SSSR. Institut nauchnoĭ informat͡sii po obshchestvennym naukam. Bibliography: p. 70-75. LC Card 85-224384
1. Foreign exchange problem - European Economic Community countries. 2. Money - European Economic Community countries. 3. Monetary unions. I. Borko, I͡Uriĭ Antonovich. II. Title. III. Series.
HG3942.8 .M87 1985

Musaĭev, M. Sămădzadă, Z. (Ziĭad) Onunju beshillikdă Sovet Azărbaĭjanynyn igtisadi vă sosial inkishafy /. Baky , 1981. 237 p. ; LC Card 82-153126
HC337.A9 S32 1981

Musalén, Elba. Gómez, Carmen. Población y energía en la República Dominicana, 1990-2000. Santo Domingo, República Dominicana [1985] vi, 86 p. : LC Card 86-176044
HD9502.D652 G65 1985

Muscheid, Jutta. Die Steuerpolitik in der Bundesrepublik Deutschland, 1949-1982 / von Jutta Muscheid. Berlin : Duncker & Humblot,

c1986. 212 p. : ill. ; 24 cm. (Volkswirtschaftliche Schriften. Heft 365) Bibliography: p. [203]-212. ISBN 3-428-06004-0 LC Card 86-206446
1. Taxation - Germany, West - History. 2. Fiscal policy - Germany (West) - History. I. Title. II. Series.
HJ2687 .M84 1986

Musée Carnavalet. Atget, Géniaux, Vert . Paris [1984] 63, [1] p. : ISBN 2-901414-09-5 : LC Card 86-137985
HF5459.F8 A87 1984 NYPL [MFW 87-159]

Museo della zona del cuoio. Il Pappagallo giallo . [Pisa] , Firenze , c1986. 194 p., [1] leaf of plates : LC Card 86-212573
HD9780.I82 P37 1986

Museo provinciale Sigismondo Castromediano. La Questione demaniale in Terra d'Otranto nel XIX secolo . [Roma] [Lecce] [1985?] 183 p., [6] leaves of plates : LC Card 86-180857
HD680.O87 Q47 1985

Museu CMTC dos Transportes Públicos (São Paulo, Brazil) Lopes, Miriam B. P. Oelsner (Miriam Bettina Paulina Oelsner) Pequena história dos transportes públicos de São Paulo. São Paulo [1985] 91 p. : LC Card 86-158179
HE5653.Z7 C675 1985

Museu da Fazenda Federal. Ciclo da mineração /. Rio de Janeiro-RJ , 1984. 95 p. : LC Card 85-186500
HD9536.B82 C56 1984

Museum für Kunst und Kulturgeschichte der Stadt Dortmund. Leben mit Gneisenau, hundert Jahre-- . Dortmund , Essen [1986?] 317 p. : ISBN 3-88474-323-6 LC Card 87-408388 DDC 331.7/622334/094355 19
HD8039.M62 G335 1986

Mushtaqur Rahman. see **Rahman, Mushtaqur.**

MUSIC AND STATE.
Perris, Arnold. Music as propaganda . Westport, Conn. , c1985. x, 247 p. ; ISBN 0-313-24505-3 (lib. bdg.) LC Card 84-27969 DDC 781/.15 19
ML3838 .P43 1985 NYPL [JMD 86-149]

Music as propaganda . Perris, Arnold. Westport, Conn. , c1985. x, 247 p. ; ISBN 0-313-24505-3 (lib. bdg.) LC Card 84-27969 DDC 781/.15 19
ML3838 .P43 1985 NYPL [JMD 86-149]

MUSIC, POPULAR (SONGS, ETC.) - UNITED STATES.
Wacholtz, Larry E. Inside country music /. New York , 1986. 254 p. ; ISBN 0-8230-7532-X (pbk. : alk. paper) LC Card 86-4234 DDC 784.5/2/002373 19
ML3790 .W24 1986 NYPL [JNE 86-18]

MUSIC - PSYCHOLOGY.
Perris, Arnold. Music as propaganda . Westport, Conn. , c1985. x, 247 p. ; ISBN 0-313-24505-3 (lib. bdg.) LC Card 84-27969 DDC 781/.15 19
ML3838 .P43 1985 NYPL [JMD 86-149]

MUSIC TRADE - UNITED STATES.
Wacholtz, Larry E. Inside country music /. New York , 1986. 254 p. ; ISBN 0-8230-7532-X (pbk. : alk. paper) LC Card 86-4234 DDC 784.5/2/002373 19
ML3790 .W24 1986 NYPL [JNE 86-18]

MUSICAL INSTRUMENT INDUSTRY - GERMANY (WEST)
Breitenacher, Michael. Strukturwandlungen und Entwicklungsperspektiven im Musikinstrumentenbau, in der Spielwaren- und Sportgeräteherstellung und in der Schmuckindustrie /. Berlin , c1984. 188 p. : ISBN 3-428-05566-7 LC Card 84-186644
HD9999.M83 G32 1984

MUSICAL INSTRUMENTS - INDUSTRY AND TRADE. see **MUSIC TRADE.**

Musioł, Magdalena. Buk, Halina. Analiza ekonomiczna przedsiębiorstw przemsłowych /. Katowice , 1977. 285 p. ; LC Card 82-102080
HD36 .B775 1977

Muslim Commercial Bank. Research & Planning Division. Seminar on Growth of Pakistani Banking at Home & Abroad (1982 : Peshawar, Pakistan) Growth of Pakistani banking . Karachi , 1982. 26 p. ; LC Card 83-931177 DDC 332.1/09549/1 19
HG3290.5.A6 S46 1982
NYPL [JLE 86-4582]

Muslim countries. see **Islamic countries.**

Muslim Empire. see **Islamic Empire.**

MUSLIM WOMEN. see **WOMEN, MUSLIM.**

Muslim world : geography and development / edited by Mushtaqur Rahman. Lanham, MD : University Press of America, c1987. viii, 190 p. : ill., maps ; 24 cm. Includes bibliographies and index. ISBN 0-8191-6558-1 (alk. paper) : LC Card 87-14087 DDC 330.917/671 19
1. Islamic countries - Economic conditions. 2. Agriculture - Islamic countries. 3. Urbanization - Islamic countries. 4. Economic development - Religious aspects - Islam. 5. Islam - 20th century. I. Rahman, Mushtaqur.
HC499 .M875 1987

MUSLIMISM. see **ISLAM.**

MUSLIMS - WOMEN. see **WOMEN, MUSLIM.**

Musnik, Isabelle. Tapie, les secrets de sa réussite / Isabelle Musnik. Paris : Plon, c1986. 261 p. : ill. ; 24 cm. Includes bibliographical references. ISBN 2-259-01546-8 : LC Card 87-167974
1. Tapie, Bernard, 1943-. 2. Businessmen - France - Biography. 3. Entrepreneurship - France. I. Title.
HC272.5.T3 M87 1986

--Muss kommen, aber nix von Herzen . Rosen, Rita. Opladen , 1986. 262 p. : ISBN 3-8100-0572-X LC Card 87-112784
HD6149 .R67 1986

Musschenga, A. W. Zelfzorg en verzorging . Kampen [1985] 237 p. ; ISBN 90-242-4072-7 : LC Card 86-175292
HC325 .Z43 1985

Mussil, Felix. Schwarz, Heino, 1936- Katholisch, proletarisch und in der Einheitsgewerkschaft /. Mainz , c1983. 141 p. : ISBN 3-7867-1046-5 LC Card 83-193395 DDC 331.88/0943 19
HD6694 .S34 1983 NYPL [JLD 86-2783]

MUSSULMANISM. see **ISLAM.**

Muster-Stichproben-Pläne für Bevölkerungs-Stichproben in der Bundesrepublik Deutschland und West-Berlin /. Schaefer, Felix, 1950- München , c1979. 160 p. : ISBN 3-478-39760-X; 3-478-39760-1 LC Card 84-135457
HB3595 .S29 1979

Műszaki és Természettudományi Egyesületek Szövetsége. Baranya Megyei Szervezet. Múlt, jelen, jövő a műszaki haladás szolgálatában . Pécs , 1985. 305 p. : LC Card 87-408539
HC300.29.B37 M86 1985

Műszaki fejlesztés, versenyképesség /. Szekér, Gyula. [Budapest] , 1984. 136 p. ; ISBN 963-09-2534-6 : LC Card 85-177507
HC300.295.T4 S97 1984

Muszynski, Bernhard.
Bemerkungen zur "Krise der Arbeitsgesellschaft. " Ahrens, Gerhard, 1939- Staatsverschuldung ohne Ende? / Gerhard Ahrens. Bemerkungen zur "Krise der Arbeitsgesellschaft" / Bernhard Muszynski. Hamburg [1984] 37 leaves ; LC Card 85-166341
HJ8650 .A37 1984

Muszynski, Maria Judith de Brito. O impacto político das migrações internas : o caso de São Paulo (1945-1982) / Maria Judith de Brito Muszynski. São Paulo : Instituto de Estudos Econômicos, Sociais e Políticos de São Paulo, 1986. 169 p. : ill. ; 21 cm. (Monografias. 1) Bibliography: p. 163-169. LC Card 86-234794
1. Rural-urban migration - Brazil. 2. Rural-urban migration - Brazil - Sao Paulo. 3. Brazil - Politics and government - 20th century. 4. São Paulo (Brazil) - Politics and government. I. Series: Monografias (Instituto de Estudos Econômicos, Sociais e Políticos de São Paulo) , 1. II. Title.
HB2023 .M87 1986

Muszynski, Maurice.
Les assignats de la Révolution française / Maurice Muszynski ; préface de Albert Soboul. Bruyères-le-Châtel : Editions Le Landit, c1981. 163 p. : ill., facsims. ; 26 cm. (Collection "Histoire du papier monnaie français" . v. 2) Bibliography: p. 160-161. LC Card 87-672912
1. Assignats. 2. Paper money - France - History - 18th century. I. Series. II. Series: Collection "Histoire du papier monnaie français" , 2. III. Title.
HG978 .M87x 1981

Les billets de la Banque de France ; Les émissions du Trésor / Maurice Muszynski ; préface de la première édition par Henri Guitard ; préface de la deuxième édition par Maurice Kolsky. 3e éd. Bruyères-le-Châtel : Edition Le Landit, 1985. 160 p. : ill. ; 26 cm. (Collection "Histoire du papier monnaie français" . 1) Bibliography: p. 160. LC Card 83-132282
1. Banque de France. 2. Bank notes - France - Catalogs. I. Title. II. Series.
HG985 .M88 1985

Mutharayappa, R. Hanumantha Rayappa, P. (Pullikunta), 1938- Backwardness and welfare of scheduled castes and scheduled tribes in India /. New Delhi , 1986. xi, 121 p. ; ISBN 81-7024-059-X : LC Card 86-902970
HC437.K27 H36 1986

Muthesius, Peter, 1930- Bankmitarbeiter und die neuen Informationstechniken . Frankfurt am Main , c1986. 240 p. ; ISBN 3-7819-0341-9 LC Card 86-228992
HG1709 .B355 1986

Muttalib, M. A. Public housing /. Hyderabad, A.P. , c1983. xx, 345 p. ; LC Card 85-903848 DDC 363.5/8 19
HD7288.78.I4 P83 1983
NYPL [JLF 86-1782]

Mutual Economic Aid Council. see **Sovet ėkonomicheskoĭ vzaimopomoshchi.**

Mutual forebearance behavior and price-cost margins. Strickland, Allyn D. Firm diversification, mutual forbearance behavior and price-cost margins /. New York , 1984. 155 p. ; ISBN 0-8240-4159-3 (alk. paper) LC Card 79-53209 DDC 338.8/3/0973
HD2756.U5 S76 1984 NYPL [JLE 86-3907]

MUTUAL FUNDS.
Hirsch, Michael D. Multifund investing . Homewood, Ill. , c1987. xx, 237 p. : ISBN 0-87094-912-8 LC Card 86-71215 DDC 332.63/27 19
HG4530 .H57 1987

Mallory, Norman. Profitable no-load mutual fund trading techniques for the individual investor /. Brightwaters, N.Y. , c1987. 153 p. : ISBN 0-930233-11-5 (pbk.) LC Card 87-400302 DDC 332.63/27 19
HG4530 .M25 1987

Miller, Lynn Orr. Consumer guide . [Skokie, IL] , c1986. 64 p. ; LC Card 86-219152 DDC 332.63/27 19
HG4530 .M56 1986

Renberg, Werner. Making money with mutual funds . New York , c1988. xviii, 217 p. : ISBN 0-471-85555-3 LC Card 87-26366 DDC 332.63/27 19
HG4530 .R46 1988

MUTUAL FUNDS - BRAZIL - DIRECTORIES.
Guia ação . RJ [i.e. Rio de Janeiro] [1985 or 1986] 285 p. ; LC Card 87-405004 DDC 332.6/78/0981 19
HG5334.5 .G85 1985

MUTUAL FUNDS - EUROPE.
Charro Valls, José María. Sociedades de garantía recíproca . Salamanca, España , 1985. 73 p. ; ISBN 84-7481-349-2 LC Card 87-133330
HG5634.5 .C47 1985

MUTUAL FUNDS - ITALY - CONGRESSES.
I Fondi comuni di investimento . Napoli , c1985. 183 p. ; LC Card 86-193326
HG5526 .F66 1985

MUTUAL FUNDS - JAPAN.
Charro Valls, José María. Sociedades de garantía recíproca . Salamanca, España , 1985. 73 p. ; ISBN 84-7481-349-2 LC Card 87-133330
HG5634.5 .C47 1985

MUTUAL FUNDS - SPAIN.
Charro Valls, José María. Sociedades de garantía recíproca . Salamanca, España , 1985. 73 p. ; ISBN 84-7481-349-2 LC Card 87-133330
HG5634.5 .C47 1985

MUTUAL FUNDS - UNITED STATES.
Mallory, Norman. Profitable no-load mutual fund trading techniques for the individual investor /. Brightwaters, N.Y. , c1987. 153 p. : ISBN 0-930233-11-5 (pbk.) LC Card 87-400302 DDC 332.63/27 19
HG4530 .M25 1987

Seligman, Barnard. Choosing an investment company /. Cambridge, Mass. , c1987. xvii, 174

p. : ISBN 0-88730-094-4 LC Card 87-1437 DDC 332.6 19
HG4930 .S45 1987

Winning with mutual funds /. Birmingham, Ala. , c1987. 224 p. : ISBN 0-8487-0722-2 LC Card 87-61719 DDC 332.63/27 19
HG4930 .W56 1987

MUTUAL FUNDS - UNITED STATES - DIRECTORIES.
Directory of no-load mutual funds. Boca Raton, FL (P.O. Box 3007, Boca Raton 33431-0907) , c1986. 19 p. ; LC Card 86-231040 DDC 332.63/27 19
HG4930 .D57 1986

MUTUAL FUNDS - UNITED STATES - STATISTICS.
Winning with mutual funds /. Birmingham, Ala. , c1987. 224 p. : ISBN 0-8487-0722-2 LC Card 87-61719 DDC 332.63/27 19
HG4930 .W56 1987

Mutual gains . Cohen-Rosenthal, Edward. New York , 1987. xv, 287 p. : ISBN 0-275-92204-9 (alk. paper) : LC Card 86-25249 DDC 331/.01/12 19
HD6490.L33 C64 1987

MUTUAL INSURANCE. see INSURANCE.

MUTUALISM.
Motta, Fernando C. Prestes. Burocracia e autogestão . São Paulo, Brasil , 1981. 170 p. ; LC Card 82-106136
HD2961 .M658 1981

MUTUALISM - FRANCE.
Boursier, François, 1947- L'économie sociale, mythes et réalités /. Lyon [1984] 108 p. : ISBN 2-85008-045-4 : LC Card 84-154709 DDC 334/.0944 19
HD3494 .B63 1984 ***NYPL [JLD 87-330]***

MUTUALISM - FRANCE - HISTORY.
Boursier, François, 1947- L'économie sociale, mythes et réalités /. Lyon [1984] 108 p. : ISBN 2-85008-045-4 : LC Card 84-154709 DDC 334/.0944 19
HD3494 .B63 1984 ***NYPL [JLD 87-330]***

Muysken, J. Economische wetenschappen . Maastricht , Assen , 1985. 224 p. ; ISBN 90-232-2148-6 LC Card 86-111599
HB21 .E248 1985

Muzhitskikh, V. V. (Viktor Vasil'evich) Finansirovanie i kreditovanie kapital'nogo stroitel'stva v usloviiakh ėkonomicheskogo ėksperimenta / V.V. Muzhitskikh. Moskva : "Finansy i statistika", 1985. 157 p. ; 20 cm. (Predpriiatie--samostoiatel'nost' i otvetstvennost') Includes bibliographical references. LC Card 86-169842
1. Construction industry - Soviet Union - Finance. 2. Construction industry - Soviet Union - Capital productivity. I. Series. II. Series: Predpriiatie--samostoiatel'nost' i otvetstvennost' ("Finansy i statistika" (Firm)). III. Title.
HD9715.S72 M894 1985

Muzyria, Aleksandra Alekseevna. Synov'iam v nasledstvo /. Moskva , 1986. 204 p. : LC Card 86-132407
HD8529.M62 S97 1986

Mwanza Mujila. La gestion planifiée de l'entreprise commerciale de détail : problèmes de marketing et de management / Mwanza Mujila. Lubumbashi [Zaire] : Cyondo, 1984. 287 p. : ill. ; 21 cm. LC Card 85-177323
1. Retail trade. 2. Marketing. 3. Retail trade - Management. I. Title.
HF5429 .M88 1984

Mwendwa, H. Agatsiva, J. L. Land use mapping of Kenya using remote sensing techniques /. [Nairobi] , 1982. iv, 39 p. : LC Card 84-980919 DDC 333.73/13/028 19
HD983.Z7 A38 1982

My--khoziaeva proizvodstva : sbornik ocherkov / [zav. redaktsieĭ G.F. Skuratova]. Moskva : Profizdat, 1984. 261 p. : ill. ; 18 cm. LC Card 85-107808
1. Works councils - Soviet Union. 2. Industrial management - Soviet Union - Employee participation. I. Skuratova, G. F.
HD5660.S65 M9 1984

My reminiscences . Ray, Renuka Mukerji, 1903- New Delhi , 1982. ix, 294 p., [5] p. of plates : LC Card 82-905707 DDC 954.03/5 19
DS481.R33 A38 1982 ***NYPL [JFD 85-9372]***

My tale of two worlds . Harris, Lement, 1904- New York , 1986. 289 p. : ISBN 0-7178-0645-6 : LC Card 86-10671 DDC 338.1/092/4 B 19
S417.H35 A36 1986 ***NYPL [JLD 87-1376]***

My tale of 2 worlds. Harris, Lement, 1904- My tale of two worlds . New York , 1986. 289 p. : ISBN 0-7178-0645-6 : LC Card 86-10671 DDC 338.1/092/4 B 19
S417.H35 A36 1986 ***NYPL [JLD 87-1376]***

Myers, Donald W. Employee problem prevention and counseling . Westport, Conn. , 1985. xii, 338 p. ; ISBN 0-89930-084-7 (lib. bdg.) LC Card 84-26499 DDC 658.3/85 19
HF5549.5.C8 E47 1985
NYPL [JLE 86-1105]

Myers, Frank Daniel. The wood chemical industry in the Delaware Valley / written and compiled by Frank Daniel Myers III. Middletown, N.Y. : Prior King Press, 1986. [160] p. : ill. ; 28 cm. + 1 map (55 x 61 cm. folded to 20 x 28 cm.) (An Observer publication) Published also as v. 20, no. 9-10/v. 21, no. 1-8 of the Observer. Includes bibliography. LC Card 87-108267
1. Methanol industry - Delaware River Valley (N.Y.-Del. and N.J.) - History. 2. Chemical industry - Delaware River Valley (N.Y.-Del. and N.J.) - History. 3. Charcoal industry - Delaware River Valley (N.Y.-Del. and N.J.) - History. 4. Forest products industry - Delaware River Valley (N.Y.-Del. and N.J.) - History. 5. Wood distillation - History. I. Title. II. Series.
HD9660.M573 U616 1986

Myers, Norman. Not far afield : U. S. interests and the global environment / Norman Myers. Washington, DC : World Resources Institute, c1987. vi, 73 p. : ill. ; 28 cm. (World Resources Institute report, 0880-2582) "June 1987." Bibliography: p. 59-73. ISBN 0-915825-24-4 (pbk.): LC Card 87-50723 DDC 333.7/09172/4 19
1. Environmental policy - Economic aspects - Developing countries. 2. Environmental policy - Economic aspects - United States. I. Title. II. Series.
HC59.72.E5 M93 1987

Myers, Richard A. Gómez-Samper, Henry. Los módulos de servicios . Caracas , c1984. 48, 3 [i.e. 4] leaves ; ISBN 980-217-005-4 LC Card 86-193565
HD4343 .G65 1984

Myers, Stanley E., 1926- Structured COBOL with business applications / Stanley E. Myers. Englewood Cliffs, NJ : Prentice-Hall, c1988. xi, 772 p. : ill. ; 28 cm. Includes index. ISBN 0-13-854167-1 (pbk.) : LC Card 86-30646 DDC 005.13/3 19
1. COBOL (Computer program language). 2. Structured programming. 3. Business - Data processing. I. Title.
HF5548.5.C2 M94 1988

Mylius, Ralph, 1945- The illustrated Lotus 1-2-3 : (release 2.01) book / Ralph Mylius. Dallas : Wordware Pub., c1987. vi, 381 p. ; 25 cm. Includes index. ISBN 0-915381-67-2 (pbk.) LC Card 86-28217 DDC 005.36/9 19
1. Lotus 1-2-3 (Computer program). 2. Business - Data processing. I. Title. II. Title: Illustrated Lotus one-two-three.
HF5548.4.L67 M95 1987

Mylov, V. V. Gazovyĭ most . Sverdlovsk , 1985. 206 p. : LC Card 86-186324
HD9581.S653 S54 1985

Mymrina, L. I. Simpozium "Nauchno-tekhnicheskiĭ progress i intensifikatsiia obshchestvennogo proizvodstva" (1984 : Podol'sk, Moscow, R.S.F.S.R.) Formy i metody vzaimodeĭstviia nauki i proizvodstva /. Moskva , 1984. 237 p. ; LC Card 85-240380
HC340.T4 S48 1984

Myrdal, Gunnar, 1898- Increasing interdependence between states but failure of international cooperation / Gunnar Myrdal. Göteborg : Gothenburg University, 1978. 53 p. ; 21 cm. (Félix Neubergh lecture. 1) Lecture delivered at Gothenburg University in Oct. 1977. ISBN 91-7360-052-0 LC Card 80-511073 DDC 327.1/7 19
1. International cooperation - Addresses, essays, lectures. 2. International relations - Addresses, essays, lectures. I. Series: Félix Neubergh lecture, 1st. II. Title.
JX1954 .M94 ***NYPL [JLD 81-302]***

Myrdal, M. Erwee, Johannes Albertus. Trends in the construction of dwelling units in the Port Elizabeth/Uitenhage and East London/King William's town regions, 1970-1984, including additions and alterations /. Port Elizabeth [South Africa] [1985] 44 leaves : ISBN 0-86988-244-9 (pbk.) LC Card 86-229280 DDC 363.5/1/096875 19
HD7374.4.P6 E735 1985

Myrell, Günter, 1952- Arbeit, Arbeit über alles? . Köln , 1985. 160 p. : ISBN 3-8025-2167-6 LC Card 86-148728
HD4854 .A725 1985

Mystery man of high finance. How, Douglas. [Very private person.] Canada's mystery man of high finance . Hantsport, N.S. , 1986. 173 p. : ISBN 0-88999-305-X (pbk.) LC Card 86-207291 DDC 338.092/2 B 19
HG172.K55 H68 1986

Myt' i vichnist' rekordu : dokumental'ni opovidi / [sostavitel' Aleksandr Petrovich Rakin]. Kyïv : Vyd-vo TSK LKSMU "Molod'", 1985. 124 p., [24] p. of plates : ill. ; 17 cm. Title in colophon: Mig i vechnost' rekorda. LC Card 86-178641
1. Socialist competition - Soviet Union. I. Rakin, Aleksandr Petrovich. II. Title: Mig i vechnost' rekorda.
HC340.S6 M97 1985

The myth of market failure . Gregory, Peter. Baltimore , 1986. viii, 299 p. ; ISBN 0-8018-3343-4 : LC Card 85-45927 DDC 331.12/0972 19
HD5731.A6 G74 1986 ***NYPL [JLE 86-3065]***

Mythen . Bel Ghazi, Hassan. Amsterdam [1985] 111 p. ; ISBN 90-6617-024-7 LC Card 86-145232
HD8518.5.A2 B44 1985

Myths and reality of external constraints on development /. Riedel, James. Aldershot, Hampshire, U.K. , Brookfield, Vt., USA , 1987. xvi, 111 p. : ISBN 0-566-05336-5 (pbk.) : LC Card 86-31801 DDC 330.9172/4 19
HC59.7 .R494 1987

N. A. A. see National Association of Accountants.

N. A. S. D. see National Association of Securities Dealers.

N. A. T. O. see North Atlantic Treaty Organization.

N. C. A. E. R. see National Council of Applied Economic Research.

N. C. G. E. see National Council for Geographic Education.

N. C. T. C. O. G. see North Central Texas Council of Governments.

N. E. D. O. see National Economic Development Office.

N. L. K. P. see Kommunisticheskaia partiia Sovetskogo Soiuza.

N. M. A. see National Micrographics Association.

N. O. W. see National Organization for Women.

N. P. C. see National Productivity Council (India)

N. R. I. see Nomura Sōgō Kenkyūjo.

N. R. M. A. see National Retail Merchants Association.

N. S. D. A. P. see Nationalsozialistische Deutsche Arbeiter-Partei.

N. U. P. I. see Oslo. Norsk utenrikspolitisk institutt.

N-US.
Barrett, John (John J.) The industrial work model . Menomonie, Wis. , c1987. v, 143 p. : ISBN 0-916671-73-9 (pbk.) LC Card 87-403218 DDC 362.0425 19
HD7256.U5 B37 1987

N. Z. Institute of Economic Research. see New Zealand Institute of Economic Research.

Na planovom fronte /. Strumilin, S. G. (Stanislav Gustavovich), 1877-1974. Moskva , 1980. 463 p. ; LC Card 81-135522
HC335.2 .S83 1980

Na putu ka visoko industrijalizovanom socijalizmu /. Stojanović, Radmila. Beograd , 1984. 208 p. ; LC Card 85-194079
HD3611 .S77 1984

Naaber, V. Eesti ala mõisate nimestik /. Tallinn , 1981. 191 p. ; LC Card 82-143283
HD1329.E75 E37 1981
NYPL [JFD 86-6806]

Naar groter eenheid . Hueting, Ernest. Amsterdam , 1983, c1982. 432 p. : ISBN 90-6012-531-2 : LC Card 83-184649
HD6727 .H83 1983 ***NYPL [JLG 87-188]***

Nabhi's manual for Indian residents abroad, 1985 /. Puri, Vijay Kumar. New Delhi , 1985. xv, 352 p., [1] leaf of plate : LC Card 86-901951 DDC 346.54/07 345.4067 19
HG5732 .P83 1985

Nabije-Oostenreeks.
Bel Ghazi, Hassan. Van soek naar arbeidsmarkt . [Bussum] , 1986. 176 p. ; ISBN 90-293-0638-6 : LC Card 86-234591
HD8518.5.M6 B45 1986

Nabli, Mustapha K. Grauwe, Paul de. Exchange rates, money, and output . New York , 1985. xii, 240 p. : ISBN 0-312-27403-3 : LC Card 84-11692 DDC 339/.094 19
HC241.2 .G69 1985 ***NYPL [JLD 86-3007]***

Nacamulli, Raoul C. D. La razionalità contrattata : imprese, sindacati e contesto economico / Raoul C.D. Nacamulli, Giovanni Costa, Luigi Manzolini. Bologna : Il Mulino, c1986. 166 p. : ill. ; 22 cm. (Studi e ricerche. 214) Bibliography: p. 157-166. ISBN 88-15-01189-7 : LC Card 87-122104
1. Collective bargaining - Italy. 2. Collective labor agreements - Italy. 3. Trade-unions - Italy. 4. Industrial relations - Italy. I. Costa, G. (Giovanni). II. Manzolini, Luigi. III. Title.
HD6709 .N296 1986

Nach fünfundzwanzig Jahren : Beiträge zur Geschichte und Gegenwart des WDR / herausgegeben von Walter Först. Köln : Kohlhammer-Grote, 1980. 399 p. : ill., maps, ports. (some col.) ; 23 cm. (Annalen des Westdeutschen Rundfunks. Bd. 4) Includes index. ISBN 3-7745-6465-5
1. Westdeutscher Rundfunk - History. 2. Radio broadcasting - Germany, West. 3. Television broadcasting - Germany, West. I. Först, Walter, 1920-. II. Series: Westdeutscher Rundfunk. Annalen, Bd. 4. 4.
NYPL [MWGK (Germany) 74-75 Bd.4]

Die Nachfrage nach Ausrüstungsinvestitionen in der Schweiz 1963-1980 . Karas, Thomas H. Frankfurt am Main , c1984. v, 91 p. : ISBN 3-88129-798-7 : LC Card 84-208150
HC400.D4 K37 1984

Nachfragewettbewerb und Marktbeherrschung /. Köhler, Helmut, 1944- Tübingen , 1986. 121 p. ; ISBN 3-16-345124-1 (Deut. Bibl.) LC Card 86-223313
HD2757.4 .K64 1986

Nachrichtendiffusion in Grossunternehmen . Braehmer, Uwe. Münster [1983?] 271 p. : ISBN 3-88660-090-0 LC Card 83-206152
HD30.3 .B69 1983

Nachrichtentechnische Gesellschaft im VDE. NTG-Fachtagung (1986 : Nuremberg, Germany) Von der Nachrichtentechnik zur Informationstechnik . Berlin , c1986. 104 p. : ISBN 3-8007-1485-X LC Card 87-136748 DDC 384 19
HE7604 .N74 1986

Nachschlagewerke Arbeitsschutz.
Dienststellenverzeichnis Arbeitsschutz . Dortmund , Bremerhaven , 1983. 217 p. ; ISBN 3-88314-274-3 LC Card 83-196051
HD7708 .D55 1983

Nachtkamp, Hans Heinrich. Finanzsysteme, Ideal- und Realtypen . Berlin , c1983. 278 p. : ISBN 3-428-05419-9 LC Card 83-240120
HJ161 .F575 1983

Nachweis beruflicher Qualifikationen /. Maslankowski, Willi, 1936- Montevideo , 1979. 102 p., [2] folded leaf of plates : LC Card 86-148766
HD5715.5.L3 M37 1979

El nacimiento de América . García, Miguel Angel. México, D.F. , 1984. 284 p. : ISBN 968-415-089-X LC Card 87-403199 DDC 332/.0415/091812 19
HC94.Z9 S34 1984

NACIONAL FINANCIERA, S.A. (MEXICO) - HISTORY.
Nacional Financiera, 1934-1984 . México, D.F. , 1985. 310 p. ; ISBN 968-665-107-1 LC Card 87-400288 DDC 332.2 19
HG2718.N33 N33 1985

Nacional Financiera, 1934-1984 : medio siglo de banca de desarrollo : testimonio de sus directores generales. 1a ed. México, D.F. : Nacional Financiera, 1985. 310 p. ; 21 cm. Includes bibliographical references. ISBN 968-665-107-1 LC Card 87-400288 DDC 332.2 19
1. Nacional Financiera, S.A. (Mexico) - History. 2. Development banks - Mexico - History. 3. Mexico - Economic conditions - 1918-. 4. Economic development projects - Mexico - Finance - History. I. Nacional Financiera, S. A., Mexico.
HG2718.N33 N33 1985

Naciones Unidas. see United Nations.

A NACPA position paper.
Just treatment for those who work for the church. Cincinnati, OH (100 E. 8th St., Cincinnati 45202) , c1986. ix, 21 p. ; LC Card 86-228672 DDC 254/.0068/3 19
HF5549 .J87 1986

NACS convenience store customer purchasing patterns research report / conducted for the National Association of Convenience Stores ; co-sponsored by Coca-Cola USA ... [et al.] ; conducted by Research Triangle Institute ; project coordination by Workable Systems, Inc. [Falls Church, Va. : NACS, 1985?] vi, 76 p. : ill. ; 28 cm. Cover title. LC Card 86-157648 DDC 381/.1 19
1. Convenience stores - United States. 2. Retail trade surveys - United States. I. National Association of Convenience Stores (U. S.). II. Research Triangle Institute.
HF5469.55.U62 N33 1985
NYPL [JLF 87-810]

Nac'vlišvili, N. Memamuluri meurneobis kapitalisturi evoluc'ia Aġmosavlet' Sak'art'veloši / N. Nac'vlišvili. T'bilisi : Gamomc'emloba "Mec'niereba", 1971. 107 p. ; 22 cm. In Georgian. Title in colophon: Kapitalisticheskaia ėvoliutsiia pomeshchich'ego khoziaistva v Vostochnoĭ Gruzii. At head of title: Sak'art'velos mec'nierebat'a akademia. Iv. Javaxišvilis saxelobis istoriis, ark'eologiisa da et'nograp'iis instituti. Summary in Russian. Includes bibliographical references. LC Card 86-168887
1. Capitalism - Georgian S.S.R. - History - 19th century. 2. Georgian S.S.R. - Economic conditions. 3. Georgian S.S.R. - Commerce - History - 19th century. I. Title. II. Title: Kapitalisticheskaia ėvoliutsiia pomeshchich'ego khoziaistva v Vostochnoĭ Gruzii.
HC337.G38 N33 1971

Nádas, Magdolna. A Magyar háztartásstatisztikai megfigyelés módszertana /. Budapest , 1986. 59 p. ; LC Card 87-408579
HA37.H92 M34 1986

Nadeau, Jean.
Les indicateurs globaux de la productivité : méthodologie et statistiques, 1971-1981. Québec : Gouvernement du Québec, Conseil du trésor, Bureau de recherche sur la rémunération, [1982] 41 p. : ill. ; 28 cm. "Préparé par ... Jean Nadeau et André Morin ... sous la direction de ... Jacques Chouinard"--P. [3] ISBN 2-551-05072-3 LC Card 83-221751
1. Industrial productivity - Canada. 2. Industrial productivity - Québec (Province). 3. Industrial productivity - United States. 4. Industrial productivity - Ontario. I. Morin, André, analyste en rémunération. II. Chouinard, Jacques, 1944-. III. Québec (Province). Conseil du trésor. Bureau de la recherche sur la rémunération. IV. Title.
HC120.I52 N33 1982

Morin, André, analyste en rémunération. Analyse de l'évolution des principaux indicateurs économiques au Québec, en Ontario, au Canada et aux Etats-Unis . [Québec] [1982] 209 p. ; ISBN 2-551-04641-6 LC Card 83-103355
HC117.Q4 M66 1982

Nadel, Jack. Cracking the global market : how to do business around the corner and around the world / Jack Nadel. New York, NY : American Management Association, c1987. ix, 246 p. ; 24 cm. Includes index. ISBN 0-8144-5911-0 LC Card 87-47703 DDC 658.8/48 19
1. Commerce. 2. Export sales. 3. United States - Commerce. 4. Export sales - United States. 5. Competition, International. I. Title.
HF1008 .N33 1987

Nader, Ralph. The big boys : power and position in American business / Ralph Nader and William Taylor.1st ed. New York : Pantheon Books, c1986. xix, 571 p. ; 24 cm. Includes index. Bibliography: p. 523-553. ISBN 0-394-53338-0 : LC Card 85-25979 DDC 338.6/44/0973 19
1. Big business - United States. 2. Businessmen - United States. I. Taylor, William, 1959-. II. Title.
HD2785 .N33 1986 ***NYPL [JLE 86-2421]***

Nadler, David. Strategic organization design : concepts, tools & processes / David Nadler, Michael Tushman. Glenview, Ill. : Scott, Foresman, c1988. 209 p. : ill. ; 24 cm. (Management applications series) Includes bibliographies and indexes. ISBN 0-673-15860-8 (pbk.) LC Card 87-9832 DDC 658.4/012 19
1. Organizational behavior. 2. Organization. I. Tushman, Michael. II. Title.
HD58.7 .N33 1988

Nadler, Stephen D. Van Doren, Glenn H. Management advisory services manual /. Boston , c1987- 1 v. (loose-leaf) : ISBN 0-88712-505-0 (loose-leaf) LC Card 87-50240 DDC 658.4/6 19
HD69.C6 V36 1987

Nadratowska-Kubacka, Maria. Macromodels and forecasts of national economy . Warszawa , 1986. 284 p. : ISBN 83-01-06464-1 (pbk.) : LC Card 86-226942 DDC 338.947 19
HC244 .M227 1986

Nadvornik, Wolfgang. Konzernrechnungslegung in Österreich : Begründung und Grundsätze für ihre Reform / Wolfgang Nadvornik. Linz : Trauner, c1985. ii, 109 p. ; 21 cm. Spine title: Konzernrechnungslegung. Bibliography: p. 100-109. ISBN 3-85320-341-8 : LC Card 85-218757
1. Corporations - Austria - Accounting. 2. Corporations - Accounting - Law and legislation - Austria. I. Title. II. Title: Konzernrechnungslegung.
HF5686.C7 N27 1985

Nadwat Tanmiyat al-Mawārid al-Basharīyah fī al-Khalīj al-'Arabī . Nadwat Tanmiyat al-Mawārid al-Basharīyah fī al-Khalīj al-'Arabī (1975 : Bahrain) al-Kuwayt [1975?] 361, 404 p. : LC Card 86-964662
HD5715.5.P39 N33 1975

Nadwat Tanmiyat al-Mawārid al-Basharīyah fī al-Khalīj al-'Arabī (1975 : Bahrain) Nadwat Tanmiyat al-Mawārid al-Basharīyah fī al-Khalīj al-'Arabī : al-Baḥrayn, 15-18 Fabrāyir 1975. al-Kuwayt : al-Ma'had al-'Arabī lil-Takhṭīṭ, [1975?] 361, 404 p. : ill. ; 24 cm. Arabic and English. Cover title. Title on added t.p.: Seminar on Human Resources Development in the Arabian Gulf States. Includes bibliographies. LC Card 86-964662
1. Occupational training - Government policy - Persian Gulf States. 2. Vocational training - Government policy - Persian Gulf States. 3. Manpower policy - Persian Gulf States. 4. Labor supply - Persian Gulf States. I. Arab Planning Institute. II. Title. III. Title: Seminar on Human Resources Development in the Arabian Gulf States.
HD5715.5.P39 N33 1975

Næringslivets utviklingsmuligheter i innlandet / fra et utvalg oppnevnt ved kongelig resolusjon av 21. august 1981. Oslo : Universitetsforlaget, [1983] 291 p. : ill. ; 28 cm. (Norges offentlige utredninger . 1983:21) ISBN 82-00-70803-9 LC Card 83-237323
1. Norway - Economic conditions - 1945-. 2. Regional planning - Norway. I. Series.
HC365 .N32 1983

Nafees Baig. see Baig, Nafees, 1941-

Naffah, Najah, 1945- Ellis, Clarence Arthur, 1943- Design of office information systems /. Berlin , New York , c1987. vi, 248 p. : ISBN 0-387-17810-4 (U. S.) : LC Card 87-9582 DDC 651.8 19
HF5548.2 .E445 1987

Nafziger, E. Wayne.
Entrepreneurship, equity, and economic development / by E. Wayne Nafziger. Greenwich, Conn. : JAI Press, c1986. xxiii, 308 p. : ill., map ;c24 cm. (Contemporary studies in economic and financial analysis. v. 53) Includes index. Bibliography: p. 283-295. ISBN 0-89232-711-1 : LC Card 86-20151 DDC 338/.04 19
1. Businessmen - India - Case studies. 2. Businessmen - Nigeria - Case studies. 3. Mennonites - Case studies. I. Title.
HB615 .N34 1986 ***NYPL [JLE 87-1672]***

Inequality in Africa : political elites, proletariat, peasants, and the poor / E. Wayne Nafziger. Cambridge [Cambridgeshire] ; New York : Cambridge University Press, c1988. p. cm. (African society today) Bibliography: p. Includes index. ISBN 0-521-26881-8 LC Card 87-24263 DDC 339.2/096 19
1. Income distribution - Africa. 2. Poor - Africa. 3. Peasantry - Africa. 4. Elite (Social sciences) - Africa. 5. Africa - Economic conditions. I. Title. II. Series.
HC800.Z9 I5136 1988

Nag Chowdhury-Zilly, Aditee. The vagrant peasant : agrarian distress and desertion in Bengal, 1770-1830 / von Aditee Nag Chowdhury-Zilly. Wiesbaden : F. Steiner, 1982. xv, 196 p. : ill. ; 24 cm. (Beiträge zur Südasienforschung. Bd. 71) Extra t.p. with thesis statement inserted. Thesis (doktorgrades)--Karl-Ruprecht-Universität, Heidelberg, 1982. Bibliography: p. 180-196. ISBN 3-515-03855-8 (pbk.) LC Card 86-214350
1. Agricultural laborers - India - Bengal - History. 2. Land tenure - India - Bengal - History. 3. Famines - India - Bengal - History. 4. Bengal (India) - Rural conditions. 5. Peasantry - India - Bengal - History. I. Title. II. Series.
HD1537.I4 N327 1982

Nag, Prithvish. Census mapping survey /. New Delhi , 1984. xxiii, 299 p. : LC Card 84-902653 DDC 304.6 19
HA31.25 .C46 1984 ***NYPL [JLE 85-3881]***

NAGALAND (INDIA) - CENSUS, 1981.
Census of India, 1981. Delhi , <1983-1985. v. in : LC Card 87-915021 DDC 304.6/0954/165021 19
HA4587.N33 C46 1983

Nagarsekara, Sureśa. Pāṭīla, Narendra. Āvhāna āṇi āvāhana /. Mumbaī , 1986. 110 p., [13] p. of plates : LC Card 87-900853
HC437.M32 P38 1986

Nagdiev, S. A. (Seĭfulakh Ataevich) Ispol'zovanie ėkonomicheskikh zakonov v upravlenii sotsialisticheskim proizvodstvom / S.A. Nagdiev. Leningrad : Izd-vo Leningradskogo universiteta, 1983. 87 p. ; 22 cm. At head of title: Ministerstvo vysshego i srednego spetsial'nogo obrazovaniia RSFSR. Includes bibliographical references. LC Card 84-197365
1. Industrial productivity - Soviet Union. 2. Industrial management - Soviet Union. I. Title.
HD56 .N34 1983

Nagliadnaia agitatsiia i vstrechnye plany /. Korchagina, A. (Aleksandra) Moskva , 1978. 44 p., [16] p. of plates : LC Card 81-161419
HC340.L3 K56 1978

Nagnur, D. N. Longevity and historical life tables : 1921-1981 (abridged), Canada and the provinces / by Dhruva Nagnur = Longévité et tables de mortalité chronologiques (abrégées) : 1921-1981, Canada et provinces / par Dhruva Nagnur. Ottawa : Statistics Canada, c1986. 215 p. : ill. ; 28 cm. Chiefly tables. Bibliography: p. [37]. ISBN 0-660-52882-7 (pbk.) : LC Card 86-215300
1. Mortality - Canada - Tables. 2. Canada - Statistics, Vital. I. Title. II. Title: Longévité et tables de mortalité chronologiques (abrégées).
HB1359.N34 1986

Nagy, Istvánné. Budapest és a jelentősebb városok napi munkaerővonzási körzete népességének főbb jellemzői, 1980. január 1. /. Budapest , 1986. 106 p. : ISBN 963-02-4578-7 LC Card 87-407674
HA1205 .B83 1986

Nagy, József. Kovács, Kálmán. Tervezési szintek érdekeltségének összehangolása gazdaságszabályozási eszközökkel . Budapest , 1984. 50 p. : ISBN 963-491-189-7 LC Card 86-198789
HD1940.5.Z8 K68 1984

Nagy, Lajos, 1926- A Gazdaság és társadalom viszonya a szocializmus építésének jelenlegi időszakában . Szeged , 1985. 181 p. ; LC Card 86-207975
HC300.28 .G27 1985

Nagy, László, 1914- Szövetkezetelmélet, szövetkezetpolitika, szövetkezeti jog / Nagy László. Budapest : Közgazdasági és Jogi Könyvkiadó, 1986. 299, [1] p. ; 19 cm. Bibliography: p. 297-[300]. ISBN 963-221-904-X : LC Card 87-138020 DDC 334/.09439 19
1. Cooperation - Hungary - History. 2. Cooperative societies - Law and legislation - Hungary. 3. Cooperation - History. I. Title.
HD3492.5.A4 N34 1986

Nagyné Szauter, Edit. A gazdaságilag elmaradott térségek társadalmi-gazdasági jellemzői / [készült a Központi Statisztikai Hivatal Területi Statisztikai Főosztályán ; szerkesztette, Kovács Tibor ; összeállították, Nagyné Szauter Edit, Soós Lőrinc]. Budapest : Központi Statisztikai Hivatal, 1986. 41 p. : map ; 29 cm. LC Card 86-215345
1. Hungary - Economic conditions - 1968- - Regional disparities - Statistics. 2. Hungary - Social conditions - 1945- - Statistics. 3. Regional planning - Hungary - Statistics. I. Kovács, Tibor. II. Soós, Lőrinc. III. Hungary. Központi Statisztikai Hivatal. Területi Statisztikai Főosztály.
HC300.28 .N26 1986

A nagyüzemek és a kisüzemek termelésének fejlődése, kapcsolatuk az iparosodó mezőgazdaságban =. Magyar-Lengyel Agrárközgazdasági Konferencia (1984 : Gödöllő, Hungary) Gödöllő , 1984. 174 p. ; LC Card 86-145249
HD1995.7 .M32 1984

A Nagyüzemi gazdálkodás kérdései, 0077-2658. Mészáros, Sándor. A világ műtrágyatermelésének és -felhasználásának előrejelzése /. Budapest , 1985. 143 p. : ISBN 963-05-3670-6 : LC Card 86-136326
HD9483.A2 M47 1985

Vályi, Éva. A mezőgazdasági vállalati szervezet fejlődésének és fejlesztésének törvényszerűségei /. Budapest , 1985. 107, [1] p. : ISBN 963-05-3468-1 : LC Card 86-137169
HD1492.H8 V33 1985

A nagyvállalatok helyzetéről /. Dévai, Katalin. [Budapest] , 1984. 68 p. ; ISBN 963-673-293-0 LC Card 85-175237
HD2852.5 .D48 1984

NAGYVÁSÁRTELEP (BUDAPEST, HUNGARY) - LANGUAGE.
Berényi, Zsuzsanna Ágnes. A budapesti Nagyvásártelep mikrotoponímiája /. Budapest , 1983. 65 p. : ISBN 963-461-710-7 LC Card 85-167786
HF5474.H82 B83 1983

Nah- und Mittelost-Verein (Germany) Zweite wissenschaftliche Regionaltagung über Nah- und Mittelost . Berlin , 1963. vi, 177 p. ; LC Card 85-167419
HC59.7 .D385 no. 62/93 HC415.15

Nahuatzen, agricultura y comercio en una comunidad serrana /. García López, Lucía. Zamora, Mich. , México, D.F. , c1984. 115 p. : ISBN 968-7230-03-7 LC Card 85-154045 DDC 338.1/0972/37 19
HD1795.N34 G37 1984 ***NYPL [JLD 87-16]***

NAHUATZEN REGION (MEXICO) - COMMERCE.
García López, Lucía. Nahuatzen, agricultura y comercio en una comunidad serrana /. Zamora, Mich. , México, D.F. , c1984. 115 p. : ISBN 968-7230-03-7 LC Card 85-154045 DDC 338.1/0972/37 19
HD1795.N34 G37 1984 ***NYPL [JLD 87-16]***

Nahwanderungen im Ruhrgebiet, 1976-1984 / Herausgeber, Kommunalverband Ruhrgebiet, Abteilung Öffentlichkeitsarbeit ; Bearbeitung, Kommunalverband Ruhrgebiet, Abteilung Wirtschaftsstruktur, EDV, Statistik ; Autoren, Rainer Burisch ... [et al.]. Essen : Der Kommunalverband, c1986. 61 p. : ill. ; 30 cm. (Arbeitshefte Ruhrgebiet) Includes bibliographical references. ISBN 3-923494-67-X LC Card 87-408772 DDC 330.943/55 19
1. Ruhr (Germany : Region) - Economic conditions. 2. Ruhr (Germany : Region) - Population. 3. Migration, Internal - Germany (West) - Ruhr (Region). I. Burisch, Rainer. II. Kommunalverband Ruhrgebiet. Abteilung Öffentlichkeitsarbeit. III. Kommunalverband Ruhrgebiet. Abteilung Wirtschaftsstruktur, EDV, Statistik. IV. Series.
HC288.R8 N34 1986

Naĭdenov, Naĭden, Kh. (Naĭden Khristov) Bulgarian chemical industry / [author of the text and compiler Naiden Naidenov ; translator, Vladimir Kotchev]. Sofia : Reklama Pub. House, 1985. 59 p. : col. ill. ; 33 cm. Cover title: Bulgarian chemical industry directory. LC Card 86-218952 DDC 338.7/66/00254977 19
1. Chemical industry - Bulgaria - Directories. I. Title. II. Title: Bulgarian chemical industry directory.
HD9656.B82 N35 1985

Naidu, D. A. Fertility and mortality . New Delhi , Beverly Hills , 1986. 351 p. ; ISBN 0-8039-9497-4 LC Card 85-22287 DDC 304.6/3 19
HB901 .F468 1986 ***NYPL [JLE 86-4122]***

Naidu, Usha Sidana, 1947- Child labour and health . Bombay , c1985. xi, 287 p. ; LC Card 86-900928 DDC 331.3/1/0956 19
HD6250.I42 C46 1985
NYPL [JLD 87-1553]

Naím, Moisés. Posibilidades y limitaciones del funcionamiento de los mercados en los países menos desarrollados : una aplicación del enfoque de mercados y jerarquías al caso de Venezuela / Moisés Naím. Caracas : Ediciones IESA, c1985. 88 p. : ill. ; 29 cm. (Papeles de trabajo IESA . PTI 84-6) Bibliography: p. 86-88. ISBN 980-217-006-2 LC Card 86-193990
1. Capitalism. 2. Capitalism - Developing countries. I. Title. II. Series.
HB501 .N255 1985

Nairobi. Environment Liaison Centre. see **Environment Liaison Centre.**

NAIROBI (KENYA). CITY COUNCIL - AUDITING.
Kenya. Public Accounts Committee. Report of the Public Accounts Committee on the Special report of the Controller and Auditor-General on the City Council of Nairobi. Nairobi [1981] i, 23 p. ; LC Card 85-980597
HJ9620.5.Z9 N344 1981

Nairobi Urban Study Group. Mogridge, M. C. Project identification . Nairobi [1971] 81 leaves in various pagings : LC Card 87-118674
HE283.5.Z7 N456 1971

Naisbitt Group. Naisbitt, John. The year ahead, 1986 . New York, NY , c1985. 168 p. ; ISBN 0-446-38330-9 LC Card 85-17909 DDC 338.5/443/0973 19
HC106.8 .N35 1985 ***NYPL [JLD 86-2987]***

Naisbitt, John. The year ahead, 1986 : ten powerful trends shaping your future / John Naisbitt and the Naisbitt Group. New York, NY : Warner Books, c1985. 168 p. ; 21 cm. "Mostly from the data base and publications of the Naisbitt Group"--T.p. verso. Includes index. ISBN 0-446-38330-9 LC Card 85-17909 DDC 338.5/443/0973 19
1. Industry - Social aspects - United States. 2. Social prediction - United States. 3. United States - Economic conditions - 1981-. I. Naisbitt Group. II. Title.
HC106.8 .N35 1985 ***NYPL [JLD 86-2987]***

Naison, Mark, 1946- The Tenant movement in New York City, 1904-1984 /. New Brunswick, N.J. , c1986. xiv, 289 p. : ISBN 0-8135-1203-4 (pbk.) : LC Card 85-27894 DDC 333.33/8 19
HD7288.85.U62 N58 1986
NYPL [JLE 86-4565]

Naissance d'une région, rue Esprit-des-lois . Savary, Gilles. [Bordeaux] [1986] 274 p. : ISBN 2-904506-06-5 : LC Card 86-165118
HC277.A6 S28 1986

Najri, José Antonio, 1948- Crisis, producción y desarrollo : (discursos y ponencias) / José Antonio Najri. Santo Domingo, Repúblic Dominicana : [s.n.], 1986 (Santo Domingo, República Dominicana : Editora Corripio) ix, 248 p. ; 23 cm. LC Card 87-102092
1. Dominican Republic - Commercial policy. 2. Industry and state - Dominican Republic. 3. Industrial promotion - Dominican Republic. 4. Investments, Foreign - Dominican Republic. 5. Dominican Republic - Industries. I. Title.
HF1502 .N34 1986

Nakae, Katsumi, 1935- Edo no shokunin : dentō no waza ni ikiru / Nakae Katsumi. Tōkyō : Tairyūsha, 1986. 229 p. : ill., ports. ; 20 cm. In Japanese. ISBN 4-88470-522-X : LC Card 86-184888
1. Artisans - Japan. 2. Handicraft - Japan. I. Title.
HD2346.J3 N26 1986 <Orien Japan>
NYPL [*OSM 87-1217]

Nakamura, Masanori, 1935- Gijutsu kakushin to joshi rōdō /. Tōkyō , 1985. x, 219 p. : ISBN 4-13-051068-1 ***NYPL [*OSL 87-1658]***

Nakano, Yoshiaki, 1944-
Pereira, Luiz Carlos Bresser. [Inflação e recessão. English.] The theory of inertial inflation . Boulder, Colo. , 1987. xiii, 206 p. : ISBN 1-555-87007-4 (alk. paper) : LC Card 86-29832 DDC 332.4/1/0981 19
HG835 .P4413 1987

Nakev, Ĭordan V. (Ĭordan Vladimirov)
Intenzifikatsiia i efektivno izpolzuvane na osnovnite fondove / Ĭordan V. Nakev. 1. izd. Sofiia : Dŭrzh. izd-vo "Tekhnika", 1985. 203 p. ; 20 cm. Includes bibliographical references. LC Card 85-243258
1. Capital productivity - Bulgaria. I. Title.
HC403.Z9 C356 1985

Nakhisa, Sellah A. Parking boys in the city of Kenya "Nairobi" / presented by Sellah A. Nakhisa. [Nairobi : s.n., 1981?] ii, 27 leaves ; 30 cm. Bibliography: p. 27. "Index no. 13741." LC Card 82-980697 DDC 331.3/1 19
1. Parking lots - Kenya - Nairobi - Employees - Social conditions. 2. Children - Employment - Kenya - Nairobi. 3. Kikuyu (African people) - Social conditions. I. Title.
HE367.K43 P376 1981

Nakhla, Afaf Fouad. Update the transportation problem / by Afaf Fouad Nakhla and Rafat Riad Riskalla. Cairo : Institute of National Planning, [1985- v. <1 > ; 28 cm. (Memo / the Institute of National Planning . no. 1415) Cover title. "Oct. 1985"--V. 1. Bibliography: v. 1, p. 35. LC Card 87-401510 DDC 361.6/0962 s 380.5/24 19
1. Freight and freightage - Mathematical models. 2. Freight and freightage - Linear programming - Data processing. 3. Algorithms. I. Riskalla, Rafat Riad. II. Series: Memo (Ma'had al-Takhṭīṭ al-Qawmī (Egypt)) , no. 1415. III. Title.
HD82 .C23 no. 1415 HE199.A2

Nakoplenie i ego rol′ v obshchestvennom vosproizvodstve Uzbekskoĭ SSR /. Chumanova, N. I. Tashkent , 1982. 116 p. ; LC Card 83-193447
HC337.U963 S33 1982

NAL Merchant Bank.
Adewunmi, Wole. Twenty five years of merchant banking in Nigeria /. Akoka , 1985. xvi, 136 p. ; ISBN 978-226-475-X : LC Card 87-142907 DDC 332.66/09669 19
HG1971.N6 A34 1985

NAL MERCHANT BANK - HISTORY.
Adewunmi, Wole. Twenty five years of merchant banking in Nigeria /. Akoka , 1985. xvi, 136 p. ; ISBN 978-226-475-X : LC Card 87-142907 DDC 332.66/09669 19
HG1971.N6 A34 1985

Nalbantian, Haig R. Incentives, cooperation, and risk sharing . Totowa, N.J. , 1987. xvi, 239 p. : ISBN 0-8476-7464-9 LC Card 87-4558 DDC 658.3/22 19
HF5549.5.C67 I56 1987

Nalin, Irineu. Finanças municipais no Estado de São Paulo : avaliação recente, subsídios à reforma tributária / Irineu Nalin. São Paulo : Governo do Estado de São Paulo, Secretaria do Interior, Fundação Prefeito Faria Lima, Centro de Estudos e Pesquisas de Administração Municipal, 1985. 88 p. : ill. ; 21 cm. LC Card 86-233330
1. Municipal finance - Brazil - Sao Paulo (State). I. Title.
HJ9388.A2 S286 1985

Nallet, Jean François.
Comité d'entreprise et formation / Jean-François Nallet ; [publié par] Centre INFFO. Paris-La Défense (Tour Europe, 92080 cedex 07) : Centre INFFO, 1977. 140 p. (1 fold.) ; 30 cm. LC Card 78-358400
1. Works councils - France. 2. Occupational training - France. I. Title.
HD5660.F7 N34

Comité d'entreprise et formation / ... réalisé par Jean-François Nallet. Paris-la-Défense : Centre INFFO, 1979. 181 p. ; 30 cm. (Guides techniques / Centre INFFO) "Novembre 1979."
1. Works councils - France. 2. Occupational training - France. I. Title. ***NYPL [JLF 81-80]***

Nam, Charles B. Think about our population : the changing face of America / Charles B. Nam. New York City, NY : Walker, 1988. viii, 117 p. : ill. ; 22 cm. (The Think series) Bibliography: p. 111-113. Includes index. ISBN 0-8027-6753-2 LC Card 87-21601 DDC 304.6/0973 19
1. United States - Population. 2. Population. I. Title. II. Series.
HB3505 .N29 1988

Nambudiri, C. N. S. Third World multinationals : technology choice and employment generation in Nigeria / by C.N.S. Nambudiri. Geneva : International Labour Office, 1983. iv, 41 p. ; 30 cm. (Working papers / Multinational Enterprises Programme . working paper no. 25) "Research on employment effects of multinational enterprises." Bibliography: p. 36-38. ISBN 92-2-103386-4 (pbk.) LC Card 86-213622 DDC 338.8/88669 19
1. International business enterprises - Nigeria. 2. Technology - Nigeria. 3. Labor supply - Nigeria. I. Series: Working papers / Multinational Enterprises Programme , working paper no. 25. II. Title.
HD2928 .N35 1983

Namdar, Shamim A. Employment implications of agricultural growth / by Shamim A. Namdar. Lahore : Economic Research Institute, Lahore, 1980. 82 leaves : charts ; 29 cm. (Occasional study) Publication / Economic Research Institute ; no. 179 Bibliography: leaves 81-82. LC Card 84-930891 DDC 331.12/93/0954914 19
1. Agricultural laborers - Pakistan - Punjab. 2. Agricultural innovations - Pakistan - Punjab. 3. Green Revolution - Pakistan - Punjab. I. Series: Occasional study (Punjab Economic Research Institute, Lahore). II. Title.
HD1537.P2 N36 1980 ***NYPL [JLF 86-1956]***

The [Name of community] nonprofit sector in a time of government retrenchment. Washington, D.C. : Urban Institute Press, c1984-<c1986 > v. <1-2, 5-6, 9-11, 13-15 > : ill. ; 28 cm. At head of title: The Nonprofit Sector Project. Some vols. issued by Urban Institute in series: An Urban Institute research report. Companion reports issued under title: Government spending and the nonprofit sector in [name of community]. CONTENTS. - [1] New York -- [2] Pittsburgh -- [5] Chicago -- [6] Twin cities -- [9] Dallas/Fort Worth -- [10] Atlanta -- [11] Jackson -- [13] San Francisco Bay area -- [14] Phoenix -- [15] Boise. LC Card 87-167661 DDC 338.7/4/0973 19
1. Corporations, Nonprofit - United States - Finance. I. Nonprofit Sector Project (Urban Institute). II. Series: Urban Institute research report.
HG4061 .N36 1984

NAMIBIA - ECONOMIC CONDITIONS.
Sparks, Donald L. Namibia's future . London, U.K. , New York, N.Y., USA , c1985. 96 p., [4] p. of plates : LC Card 87-132083 DDC 330.9688/03 19
HC940 .S62 1985

Namibia - Government. see **Namibia - Politics and government.**

NAMIBIA - HISTORY - 1884-1915.
Phillips, John A. S. Deutsch-englische Komödie der Irrungen um Südwestafrika . Pfaffenhofen, West Germany , 1986. 184 p., [12] p. of plates : ISBN 3-87010-105-9 LC Card 87-146587 DDC 338.4/76686366/09688 19
HD9484.G9 N366 1986

NAMIBIA - INTERNATIONAL STATUS.
Shell out of Namibia and South Africa . London [1986] 19 . : LC Card 87-138719 DDC 338.8/87 19
HD9571.9.S45 S54 1986

NAMIBIA - POLITICS AND GOVERNMENT - 1946-
Sparks, Donald L. Namibia's future . London, U.K. , New York, N.Y., USA , c1985. 96 p., [4] p. of plates : LC Card 87-132083 DDC 330.9688/03 19
HC940 .S62 1985

Namibia's future . Sparks, Donald L. London, U.K. , New York, N.Y., USA , c1985. 96 p., [4] p. of plates : LC Card 87-132083 DDC 330.9688/03 19
HC940 .S62 1985

Namysłowska, Maria. Migracje wewnętrzne ludności . Warszawa , 1980. xvi, 389 p. ; LC Card 86-215694
HB2068.7.A3 M54 1980

Nangia, Parveen. Child labour : cause-effect syndrome / Parveen Nangia. New Delhi : Janak Publishers, c1987. ix, 295 p. : ill., 1 folded map ; 23 cm. Demographic and socioeconomic aspects of child workers in India. Includes bibliographical references. ISBN 81-85146-00-4 : LC Card 86-903812 DDC 331.3/1/0954 19
1. Children - Employment - India. I. Title.
HD6250.I42 N35 1987

Nanitashvili, B. Stoimostnye otnosheniia v sotsialisticheskoĭ ėkonomike / B. Nanitashvili. Tbilisi : Izd-vo "Sabchota Sakartvelo", 1978. 182 p. ; 21 cm. Title on t.p. verso: Girebulebit'i urt'iert'obani soc'ialistur ekonomikaši. Includes bibliographical references. LC Card 81-149294
1. Value. 2. Marxian economics. I. Title. II. Title: Girebulebit'i urt'iert'obani soc'ialistur ekonomikaši.
HB201 .N293 1978

Nanjundappa, D. M., 1930- Area planning and rural development / D.M. Nanjundappa. New Delhi : Associated, c1981. viii, 52 p. ; 22 cm. Includes index. LC Card 81-903723 DDC 307/.12/0954 19
1. Rural development - India. 2. Regional planning - India. I. Title.
HN690.Z9 C6649 1981
NYPL [JLD 86-2687]

NAPA bulletin .
(2) Baba, Marietta L. Business and industrial anthropology . Washington, D.C. , c1986. vii, 48 p. ; ISBN 0-913167-16-9 (pbk.) : LC Card 86-26602 DDC 302.3/5 19
HD58.7 .B33 1986

(4) Davis, Nancy Yaw. Research and consulting as a business /. Washington, D.C. , c1987. v, 41 p. : ISBN 0-913167-21-5 (pbk.) LC Card 87-20254 DDC 658.4/6 19
HD69.C6 D38 1987

NAPAL - ECONOMIC POLICY.

NAPLES (ITALY) - EARTHQUAKE, 1980.
Terremoto e crisi urbana . Napoli , 1981. 207 p. ; ***NYPL [JLE 86-4532]***

NAPLES (KINGDOM) - POPULATION - HISTORY - SOURCES.
Cozzetto, Fausto. Mezzogiorno e demografia nel XV secolo /. Soveria M.lli, CZ , c1986. ix, 202 p. ; LC Card 86-213782
HB3600.N37 C69 1986

NAPLES (KINGDOM) - SOCIAL CONDITIONS.
Rao, Anna Maria, 1949- L'"Amaro della feudalità" . Napoli , c1984. 382 p. ; ISBN 88-7042-265-8 : LC Card 85-200705
HD1333.I82 N367 1984

NAPOLEONIC WARS. see **FRANCE - HISTORY - REVOLUTION, 1789-1799.**

The Napoleonic wars and their impact on factor returns and output growth in England, 1793-1815 /. Hueckel, Glenn R. (Glenn Russell), 1945- New York , 1985. lvi, 212 p. ; ISBN 0-8240-6683-9 : LC Card 84-46003 DDC 330.941/073 19
HC254.5 .H78 1985 ***NYPL [JLE 86-4294]***

NAPOLEONIC WARS, 1800-1814 - ECONOMIC ASPECTS - GREAT BRITAIN.
Hueckel, Glenn R. (Glenn Russell), 1945- The Napoleonic wars and their impact on factor returns and output growth in England, 1793-1815 /. New York , 1985. lvi, 212 p. ; ISBN 0-8240-6683-9 : LC Card 84-46003 DDC 330.941/073 19
HC254.5 .H78 1985 ***NYPL [JLE 86-4294]***

Napoles, Veronica, 1951- Corporate identity design / Veronica Napoles. New York : Van Nostrand Reinhold, c1988. 144 p. : ill. ; 24 cm. Bibliography: p. 139-141. Includes index. ISBN 0-442-26844-0 (pbk.) : LC Card 87-6190 DDC 659.2/85 19
1. Corporate image. 2. Industrial design coordination. 3. Trademarks. 4. Logotype. I. Title.
HD59.2 .N36 1988

Napravleniia i formy realizatsii obshchenarodnoĭ sobstvennosti / pod redaktsieĭ O.V. Katikhina. Moskva : Akademiia nauk SSSR, In-t ėkonomiki, Sektor sotsialist. sobstvennosti, 1986. 171 p. ; 20 cm. Includes bibliographical references. LC Card 87-163156
1. Government ownership - Soviet Union. 2. Socialist property - Soviet Union. I. Katikhin, O. V. (Oleg Vladimirovich). II. Institut ėkonomiki (Akademiia nauk SSSR). Sektor sotsialisticheskoĭ sobstvennosti.
HD4213 .N36 1986

Naranjo M., José R. La artesanía del queso larense / José R. Naranjo M. Caracas : Fundación para el Desarrollo Social de la

Región Capital, 1985. 202 p., [16] p. of plates : ill. (some col.), maps ; 23 cm. (Serie Testimonios artesanales de Venezuela) Bibliography: p. [197]-202. ISBN 980-265-223-7 LC Card 87-403552 DDC 338.1/773/098725 19
1. Cheese industry - Venezuela - Lara. 2. Cheesemakers - Venezuela - Lara. I. Title. II. Series.
HD9280.V43 L376 1985

NARATHIWAT (THAILAND : PROVINCE) - STATISTICS.
Samut sathiti rāi pī, 2509 . [Bangkok] [19]69. 35 p., [1] leaf of plates : LC Card 83-921129
HA4600.55.Z9 N3737 1969

Narayan Prasad, P. S. C.D. Deshmukh, his contribution to monetary and economic policy / P.S. Narayan Prasad. New Delhi : Lancer International in association with India International Centre, c1985. xiv, 54 p., [1] leaf of plates : port. ; 22 cm. Includes bibliographical references. LC Card 85-905075 DDC 338.954 19
1. Deshmukh, Chintaman Dwarkanath, 1896-. 2. Finance - India. 3. Economists - India - Biography. 4. India - Economic conditions - 1947-. 5. India - Economic policy. I. Title.
HC432.5.D47 N37 1985
NYPL [JLD 86-3239]

Narayanan, S. Demand-supply gap and public distribution of foodgrains in India / S. Narayanan. New Delhi : Agricole Pub. Academy, 1986. xii, 166 p. ; 23 cm. Revision of the author's thesis (Ph. D.--Gujarat University) Bibliography: p. 160-163. Includes index. ISBN 81-85005-00-1 : LC Card 86-902667 DDC 338.1/731/0954 19
1. Grain trade - India. I. Title.
HD9046.I4 N28 1986

NARBONNE REGION (FRANCE) - ANTIQUITIES, ROMAN.
Roman, Yves. De Narbonne à Bordeaux . Lyon , c1983. 333 p. : ISBN 2-7297-0200-8 : LC Card 84-179554
HF377 .R65 1983

NARCOTIC LAWS - UNITED STATES.
United States. President's Commission on Organized Crime. America's habit . Washington, D.C. , 1986. 486, [312] p. ;
NYPL [JLE 86-3348]

NARCOTIC TRADE. see **NARCOTICS, CONTROL OF.**

NARCOTIC TRAFFIC. see **NARCOTICS, CONTROL OF.**

NARCOTICS, CONTROL OF - COLOMBIA - GUAVIARE - HISTORY - 20TH CENTURY.
Molano, Alfredo. Selva adentro . Bogotá , 1987. 142 p. : ISBN 958-9012-02-7 LC Card 87-404301 DDC 986.1/65 19
HD519.G8 M65 1987

NARCOTICS, CONTROL OF - MEXICO.
Mexican topics . [México, D.F.] [1986] 2 portfolios : LC Card 86-221843 DDC 972.08/3 19
HC135 .M52554 1986

NARCOTICS, CONTROL OF - UNITED STATES.
United States. President's Commission on Organized Crime. America's habit . Washington, D.C. , 1986. 486, [312] p. ;
NYPL [JLE 86-3348]

NARCOTICS, CONTROL OF - VENEZUELA.
Ojeda, Roseliano. Cómo se desangra un país-- ! . Valencia [Venezuela] , c1987. 241 p. ; ISBN 980-212-037-5 LC Card 87-169695 DDC 330.987/0633 19
HC237 .O365 1987

NARCOTICS - JURISPRUDENCE. see **NARCOTIC LAWS.**

Narodna Republika Bŭlgarii͡a. T͡Sarevski, Nesho Vŭlev. The People's Republic of Bulgaria . Sofia , 1986. 102 p. ; LC Card 87-123346 DDC 337.1/4977 19
HC403 .T748 1986

Narodna Respublika Bolgarii͡a--sorok let po puti sotsialisticheskogo voskhoda. Manolov, Manol Dimitrov. Narodnai͡a Respublika Bolgarii͡a--40 let po puti sotsialisticheskogo voskhoda /. [Bulgaria? , 1983?] [48] p. : LC Card 85-133679
HC403 .M36 1983

Narodnai͡a DemokraticheskaiA Respublika Iemen . Burmistrov, V. N. (Vladimir Nikolaevich) Moskva , 1981. 173, [3] p. ; LC Card 82-107303
HC415.342 .B87 1981

Narodnai͡a Respublika Bolgarii͡a--40 let po puti sotsialisticheskogo voskhoda /. Manolov, Manol Dimitrov. [Bulgaria? , 1983?] [48] p. : LC Card 85-133679
HC403 .M36 1983

Narodnata Mladezh v Bŭlgarii͡a. see **Dimitrovski komunisticheski mladezhki sŭi͡uz.**

Národní technické muzeum v Praze. Album der Industrie des Reichenberger Handelskammer-Bezirks. [Praha] , 1981. 2 v. in 1 : LC Card 84-190839
HC270.292.L52 A42 1981

Narodno-khozi͡aĭstvennye proport͡sii, ikh planirovanie i prognozirovanie / redakt͡sionnai͡a kollegii͡a A.S. Emel'i͡anov (otvetstvennyĭ redaktor) ... [et al.]. Kiev : Nauk. dumka, 1985. 318 p. : ill. ; 21 cm. (Planovoe upravlenie ėkonomikoĭ razvitogo sotsializma . t. 1) On p. preceding t.p.: Nauchno-issledovatel'skiĭ ėkonomicheskiĭ institut Gosplana USSR. Bibliography: p. 311-[314]. Includes index. LC Card 86-210651
1. Ukraine - Economic conditions - 1945-. 2. Economic forecasting - Ukraine. I. Emel'i͡anov, Aleksandr Sergeevich. II. Naukovo-doslidnyĭ ekonomichnyĭ instytut. III. Series.
HC337.U5 P5 1985 t. 1

Narodnoe khozi͡aĭstvo Bashkirskoĭ ASSR za gody odinnadt͡satoĭ pi͡atiletki, 1981-1985 gg. : statisticheskiĭ sbornik / [redaktor L.A. Vilenchik]. Ufa : Bashkirskoe knizhnoe izd-vo, 1986. 254 p. ; 18 cm. LC Card 87-165386
1. Bashkirskai͡a A.S.S.R. (R.S.F.S.R.) - Economic conditions - Statistics. 2. Bashkirskai͡a A.S.S.R. (R.S.F.S.R.) - Statistics. I. Vilenchik, L. A.
HC337.B28 N37 1986

Narodnoe khozi͡aĭstvo Karel'skoĭ ASSR : statisticheskiĭ sbornik / T͡SSU RSFSR, Statisticheskoe upravlenie Karel'skoĭ ASSR. Petrozavodsk : "Karelii͡a", 1985. 94 p. ; 23 cm. Chiefly tables. LC Card 86-124957
1. Karel'skai͡a A.S.S.R. (R.S.F.S.R.) - Statistics. 2. Karel'skaia A.S.S.R. (R.S.F.S.R.) - Economic conditions - Statistics. I. Russian S.F.S.R. T͡Sentral'noe statisticheskoe upravlenie. II. Statisticheskoe upravlenie Karel'skoĭ ASSR.
HA1448.K32 N37 1985

Narodnoe khozi͡aĭstvo Kirovskoĭ oblasti v desi͡atoĭ pi͡atiletke, 1976-1980 gg. : statisticheskiĭ sbornik / [obshchai͡a redakt͡sii͡a sbornika osushchestvlena P.S. Kas'i͡anovym]. Kirov : Volgo-Vi͡atskoe knizhnoe izd-vo, Kirovskoe otd-nie, 1981. 95 p. ; 21 cm. At head of title: T͡SSU RSFSR. Statisticheskoe upravlenie Kirovskoĭ oblasti. LC Card 82-146329
1. Kirovskai͡a oblast' (R.S.F.S.R.) - Statistics. 2. Kirovskai͡a oblast' (R.S.F.S.R.) - Economic conditions - Statistics. I. Kas'i͡anov, P. S. II. Statisticheskoe upravlenie Kirovskoĭ oblasti.
HC337.R852 K576 1981

Narodnoe khozi͡aĭstvo Mordovskoĭ ASSR za gody odinnadt͡satoĭ pi͡atiletki, 1981-1985 gg. : statisticheskiĭ sbornik / [sostavitel' A.O. Strezhnev]. Saransk : Mordovskoe knizhnoe izd-vo, 1986. 198 p. ; 18 cm. At head of title: T͡SSU RSFSR. Statisticheskoe upravlenie Mordovskoĭ ASSR. LC Card 87-120800
1. Mordovskai͡a A.S.S.R. (R.S.F.S.R.) - Statistics. 2. Mordovskai͡a A.S.S.R. (R.S.F.S.R.) - Economic conditions - Statistics. I. Strezhnev, A. O. II. Russian S.F.S.R. T͡Sentral'noe statisticheskoe upravlenie. III. Statisticheskoe upravlenie Mordovskoĭ ASSR.
HA1448.M59 N33 1986

Narodnoe khozi͡aĭstvo Tadzhikistana v gody Velikoĭ Otechestvennoĭ voĭny : 1941-1945 gg. / otvet. redaktor Kh.M. Saidmuradov. Dushanbe : "Donish", 1980. 169, [3] p. ; 20 cm. At head of title: Akademii͡a nauk Tadzhikskoĭ SSR. Institut ėkonomiki. Bibliography: p. 163-[170] LC Card 81-130944
1. World War, 1939-1945 - Economic aspects - Tajik S.S.R. 2. Tajik S.S.R. - Economic conditions. I. Saidmuradov, Khabibullo Muradovich. II. Institut ėkonomiki (Akademii͡a fanhoi RSS Tojikiston).
HC337.T233 D45 1980

Narodnokhozi͡aĭstvennai͡a ėffektivnost'--pokazateli, metody ot͡senki / [redaktor toma A.S. Astakhov]. Moskva : "Ėkonomika", 1984. 247 p. : ill. ; 23 cm. (Ėkonomika i upravlenie) At head of title: Akademii͡a narodnogo khozi͡aĭstva pri Sovete Ministrov SSSR. Includes bibliographical references. LC Card 84-188306
1. Efficiency, Industrial - Soviet Union. 2. Industrial productivity - Soviet Union. I. Astakhov, A. S. II. Akademii͡a narodnogo khozi͡aĭstva SSSR. III. Series.
HC336.25 .N3515 1984

Narodnyĭ universitet. Fakul'tet pravovykh znaniĭ. Avak'i͡an, Suren Adibekovich. Sovety i rukovodstvo ėkonomikoĭ . Moskva , 1985. 110 p. ; LC Card 87-118114
HC336.25 .A87 1985

Narodonaselenie.
(vyp. 17) Nechernozem'e . Moskva , 1977. 94 p. ; LC Card 82-107146
HB3608.N57 N43 1977

Narodonaselenie i sot͡sial' no-ėkonomicheskoe razvitie. Population and socioeconomic development /. Moscow , 1986. 186 p. ; LC Card 86-226273 DDC 304.6/09172/4 19
HB849.41 .P644 1986

Narodziny żeglugi /. Rummel, Julian. Gdańsk , 1980. 333 p., [32] leaves of plates : ISBN 83-215-3235-7 LC Card 80-147019
HE848.7 .R86 1980

Narong Phetprasœt.
Rængngān dek læ sōphēnī nai rabop sētthakit kānm Rængngān Thai. Krung Thēp , 2528 [1985] 53 p. ; LC Card 86-915944
HD5822.55.A6 R35 1985

Narŭchnik na profsŭi͡uznii͡a aktivist : kachestvoto--chelen opit i init͡siativi / [sŭstaviteli Vasil Spasov, Licho Lichev. [Sofia?] : Profizdat, 1985. 264 p. ; 21 cm. Includes bibliographical references. LC Card 85-216969
1. Labor productivity - Bulgaria. 2. Industrial productivity - Bulgaria. 3. Quality of products - Bulgaria. I. Spasov, Vasil. II. Lichev, Licho.
HC403.Z9 L366 1985

Narŭchnik na profsŭi͡uznii͡a aktivist po proizvodstveno-masovata rabota / [sŭstavitel Licho Lichev]. Sofii͡a : Profizdat, 1986. 200 p. ; 21 cm. Bibliography: p. 156-167. LC Card 86-197739
1. Socialist competition - Bulgaria - Handbooks, manuals, etc. 2. Employee motivation - Bulgaria - Handbooks, manuals, etc. I. Lichev, Licho.
HC403.Z9 S658 1986

NARYNSKAI͡A OBLAST' (KIRGHIZ S.S.R.) - ECONOMIC CONDITIONS.
Israilov, A. (Asangazy) Razmeshchenie proizvoditel'nykh sil v Narynskoĭ oblasti /. Frunze , 1978. 56 p. ; LC Card 81-147534
HC337.K5452 N375 1978

NARYNSKAI͡A OBLAST' (KIRGHIZ S.S.R.) - INDUSTRIES - LOCATION.
Israilov, A. (Asangazy) Razmeshchenie proizvoditel'nykh sil v Narynskoĭ oblasti /. Frunze , 1978. 56 p. ; LC Card 81-147534
HC337.K5452 N375 1978

The NASDAQ handbook : the stock market of tomorrow--today. Chicago, Ill. : Probus Pub. Co., c1987. vii, 577 p. : ill. ; 24 cm. "A complete reference for investors, registered representatives, company executives, researchers, the financial press, and students of finance." Bibliography: p. 573-577. Includes index. ISBN 0-917253-54-X : LC Card 87-12378 DDC 332.64/3/0973 19
1. NASDAQ Market System. 2. Stocks - Prices - Data bases. 3. Stock-exchange. I. National Association of Securities Dealers.
HG4551 .N37 1987

NASDAQ MARKET SYSTEM.
The NASDAQ handbook . Chicago, Ill. , c1987. vii, 577 p. : ISBN 0-917253-54-X : LC Card 87-12378 DDC 332.64/3/0973 19
HG4551 .N37 1987

Naselenie i tovarooborot . Beli͡aevskiĭ, I. K. (Igor' Konstantinovich) Moskva , 1980. 144 p. : LC Card 81-135180
HB801 .B377 1980

Naselenie Leningrada / [redakt͡sionnai͡a kollegii͡a Ė.K. Vasil'eva (glavnyĭ redaktor) ... et al. ; redaktor-sostavitel' Ė.K. Vasil'eva]. Moskva : "Finansy i statistika", 1981. 94 p. : ill. ; 20 cm. (Serii͡a Popul͡iarnai͡a demografii͡a . vyp. 3) Includes bibliographical references. LC Card 82-118662
1. Leningrad (R.S.F.S.R.) - Population. I. Vasil'eva, Ė. K. II. Series.
HB2278.L46 N37 1981

Nash, Allan N. Managerial compensation / by Allan Nash. 1st ed. Scarsdale, N.Y. : Work in America Institute, c1980. 56 p. ; 28 cm. (Work in America Institute studies in productivity . 15) Includes bibliographies. ISBN 0-89361-022-4 : LC Card 80-21044 DDC 658.4/072/0973 19
1. Executives - Salaries, pensions, etc. - United States. 2. Middle managers - Salaries, pensions, etc. - United States. I. Title. II. Series.
HD4965.5.U6 N22
NYPL [JLM 83-380 no.15]

Nash novyĭ mir . Shturman, Dora, 1923- Ierusalim , 1986. 464 p. : LC Card 87-114263
HB97.5 .S5155 1986

Nasha ėkonomika . Guber, A. A. (Aleksandr Andreevich) Moskva , 1986. 157 p. ; LC Card 87-132459 DDC 330.947/085/3 19
HC336.25 .G82 1986

Näsi, Juha. Yrityksen taloustieteet Tampereen yliopistossa /. Tampere , 1985. 47 leaves : ISBN 951-44-1859-X LC Card 87-107284
HD30.42.F5 Y74 1985

Nasoki za usŭvŭrshenstvuvane na sistemata za upravlenie na truda /. Lekov, Kostadin. Sofiia , 1985. 103 p. ; LC Card 86-230344
HF5549.2.B9 L46 1985

The Nassau understanding : structural adjustment and closer integration for accelerated development in the Caribbean community. [Nassau, Bahamas : s.n., 1984] 7 p. : ill. (some col.) ; 28 cm. Cover title. LC Card 87-109663 DDC 338.9729 19
1. Caribbean area - Economic policy - Congresses. 2. Caribbean area - Economic integration - Congresses. 3. Caribbean Community - Congresses.
HC151 .N37 1984

Nassif, Luís. O cruzado : por dentro do choque / Luís Nassif.1a. ed. São Paulo/SP : Livraria Cultura Editora, 1986. 255 p. : ill. ; 21 cm. (Coleção Fonte de informação) "Legislação" (p. [206]-255) contains decrees, regulations, etc. LC Card 86-224110
1. Inflation (Finance) - Brazil. 2. Inflation (Finance) - Argentina. 3. Brazil - Economic conditions - 1964-1985. 4. Brazil - Economic conditions - 1985-. 5. Argentina - Economic conditions - 1983-. 6. Brazil - Economic policy. 7. Argentina - Economic policy. 8. Money - Law and legislation - Brazil. I. Title. II. Series.
HG835 .N37 1986

NASSTRAC (Firm) NASSTRAC's 1986 small shipments and parcels guidelines to the cost-effective selection of UPS/USPS/LTL domestic ground services (and other services). Washington, D.C. (1750 Pa. Ave., NW, Suite 1105, Washington 20006-4502) , 1986. 82 p. : LC Card 87-127320 DDC 380.5/24/0973 19
HE597.U6 N37 1986

NASSTRAC's 1986 small shipments and parcels guidelines to the cost-effective selection of UPS/USPS/LTL domestic ground services (and other services). Washington, D.C. (1750 Pa. Ave., NW, Suite 1105, Washington 20006-4502) : National Small Shipments Traffic Conference, 1986. 82 p. : ill. ; 21 cm. Pages 78-82 blank for "Notes." LC Card 87-127320 DDC 380.5/24/0973 19
1. Freight and freightage - United States - Rates. I. NASSTRAC (Firm). II. Title: Small shipments and parcels guidelines to the cost-effective selection of UPS/USPS/LTL domestic ground services (and other services).
HE597.U6 N37 1986

Nastoiashchee i budushchee sovkhoza. Babaev, Akmyrat. Sovkhozyn̄g shu gùni ve geljegi /. Ashgabat , 1982. 55 p. : LC Card 84-126905
HD1493.S652 T873 1982

NATAL (SOUTH AFRICA) - ECONOMIC CONDITIONS.
Natal (South Africa). South Coast Regional Planning Committee. Draft regional plan for the South Coast. Pietermaritzburg, Natal, South Africa , 1974. 144 p., [2] folded leaves of plates : ISBN 0-909232-03-2 (pbk.) LC Card 84-246771
HC517.N3 A44 vol. 29 HC905.Z7N37

NATAL (SOUTH AFRICA) - ECONOMIC POLICY.
Spies, P. H. Perspectives on the future of Natal/KwaZulu /. Pietermaritzburg , 1986. 149 p. : ISBN 0-909232-59-8 (pbk.) : LC Card 87-166530 DDC 361.2/5/09684 s 361.6/1/09684 19
HC517.N3 A44 vol. 69 JQ2224

Natal (South Africa). South Coast Regional Planning Committee. Draft regional plan for the South Coast. Pietermaritzburg, Natal, South Africa : Town and Regional Planning Commission, Natal, 1974. 144 p., [2] folded leaves of plates : ill. (some col.) ; 30 cm. (Natal town and regional planning reports . v. 29) Cover title: Natal South Coast. Bibliography: p. 136-139. ISBN 0-909232-03-2 (pbk.) LC Card 84-246771
1. Natal (South Africa) - Economic conditions. 2. Physical geography - South Africa - Natal. I. Natal (South Africa). Town and Regional Planning Commission. II. Title. III. Title: Natal South Coast. IV. Series.
HC517.N3 A44 vol. 29 HC905.Z7N37

Natal (South Africa). Town and Regional Planning Commission.
Natal (South Africa). South Coast Regional Planning Committee. Draft regional plan for the South Coast. Pietermaritzburg, Natal, South Africa , 1974. 144 p., [2] folded leaves of plates : ISBN 0-909232-03-2 (pbk.) LC Card 84-246771
HC517.N3 A44 vol. 29 HC905.Z7N37

Stretch, C. The effectiveness of town planning in Natal . Pietermaritzburg, Natal, South Africa , 1986. 35 p. ; LC Card 86-159747 DDC 361.2/5/09684 s 307.1/2/096845 19
HC517.N3 A44 vol. 64 HT169.S62P56

Natal South Coast. Natal (South Africa). South Coast Regional Planning Committee. Draft regional plan for the South Coast. Pietermaritzburg, Natal, South Africa , 1974. 144 p., [2] folded leaves of plates : ISBN 0-909232-03-2 (pbk.) LC Card 84-246771
HC517.N3 A44 vol. 29 HC905.Z7N37

Natal town and regional planning report .
(v. 64) Stretch, C. The effectiveness of town planning in Natal . Pietermaritzburg, Natal, South Africa , 1986. 35 p. ; LC Card 86-159747 DDC 361.2/5/09684 s 307.1/2/096845 19
HC517.N3 A44 vol. 64 HT169.S62P56

(v. 69) Spies, P. H. Perspectives on the future of Natal/KwaZulu /. Pietermaritzburg , 1986. 149 p. : ISBN 0-909232-59-8 (pbk.) : LC Card 87-166530 DDC 361.2/5/09684 s 361.6/1/09684 19
HC517.N3 A44 vol. 69 JQ2224

Natal town and regional planning reports .
(v. 29) Natal (South Africa). South Coast Regional Planning Committee. Draft regional plan for the South Coast. Pietermaritzburg, Natal, South Africa , 1974. 144 p., [2] folded leaves of plates : ISBN 0-909232-03-2 (pbk.) LC Card 84-246771
HC517.N3 A44 vol. 29 HC905.Z7N37

(v. 69) Spies, P. H. Perspectives on the future of Natal/KwaZulu /. Pietermaritzburg , 1986. 149 p. : ISBN 0-909232-59-8 (pbk.) : LC Card 87-166530 DDC 361.2/5/09684 s 361.6/1/09684 19
HC517.N3 A44 vol. 69 JQ2224

Natal town and regional planning supplementary report .
(v. 18) Nattrass, Jill. Informal Black business in Durban . Pietermaritzburg, Natal, South Africa , 1986. xviii, 138 p. : ISBN 0-909232-58-X (pbk.) : LC Card 87-112836 DDC 381 19
HD2346.S632 D86 1986

Natale, Samuel M. Ethics and morals in business / Samuel M. Natale. 2nd ed. rev. and enl. Birmingham, Ala. : Religious Education Press, c1987. 209 p. ; 23 cm. Includes bibliographies and index. ISBN 0-89135-036-5 LC Card 87-9424 DDC 174/.4 19
1. Business ethics. I. Title.
HF5387 .N36 1987

Nath, Kamla. Labor-saving techniques in food processing : rural women and technological change in the Gambia / by Kamla Nath. Boston, MA (270 Bay State Rd., Boston 02215) : African Studies Center, Boston University, 1985. 26 leaves ; 28 cm. (Working papers / African Studies Center, Boston University . no. 108) Bibliography: leaf 25. LC Card 87-155092 DDC 331.4/25 19
1. Women agricultural laborers - Gambia. 2. Sexual division of labor - Gambia. 3. Agricultural innovations - Social aspects - Gambia. I. Boston University. African Studies Center. II. Series: Working papers (Boston University. African Studies Center) , no. 108. III. Title.
HD6073.A292 G256 1985

Nath, Raghu. Comparative management . Cambridge, Mass. , c1988. xv, 321 p. : ISBN 0-88730-136-3 LC Card 87-17459 DDC 658 19
HD30.55 .C656 1988

Nath, Uma Ram. Smoking, Third World alert / Uma Ram Nath. Oxford [Oxfordshire] ; New York : Oxford University Press, 1986. x, 291 p. : ill. ; 23 cm. (Oxford medical publications) "Published with assistance from the Swedish International Development Authority and the World Health Organization." Includes index. Bibliography: p. [278]-279. ISBN 0-19-261402-9 : LC Card 86-5201 DDC 363.1/9 19
1. Tobacco industry - Developing countries. 2. Tobacco habit - Developing countries. 3. Advertising - Cigarettes - Developing countries. 4. Public health - Developing countries. I. Title.
HD9148.D44 N37 1986
NYPL [JLD 87-992]

Nathan, Richard P. Reagan and the States / Richard P. Nathan, Fred C. Doolittle, and associates. Princeton, N.J. : Princeton University Press, c1987. xv, 375 p. : ill. ; 25 cm. Includes bibliographical references and index. ISBN 0-691-07748-7 (alk. paper) : LC Card 87-45529 DDC 353.0072/5 19
1. Budget - United States. 2. Grants-in-aid - United States. 3. Intergovernmental fiscal relations - United States. 4. United States - Economic policy - 1981-. 5. Finance, Public - United States - States - Case studies. 6. Local finance - United States - Case studies. I. Doolittle, Fred C. II. Title.
HJ2051 .N167 1987

Nathorst-Böös, Ernst, 1918- Lagerqvist, Lars O. Vad kostade det? . Stockholm , c18. 115 p. : ISBN 91-36-02399-X : LC Card 86-158743
HD7040 .L34 1985

Nation (Bangkok, Thailand) New era of professional banking . [Bangkok] , 1986. 51 p. : LC Card 86-200653 DDC 332.1/025/593 19
HG3300.55.A8 B366 1986

Nation building . Alexander, Carlton. Kingston, Jamaica , c1983. 100 p. : LC Card 84-172595 DDC 338.97293 19
HC154 .A79 1983

A Nation in debt : economists debate the federal budget deficit / edited by Richard H. Fink and Jack C. High. Frederick, Md. : University Publications of America, c1987. p. cm. ISBN 0-89093-963-2 : LC Card 86-28254 DDC 339.5/23/0973 19
1. Budget deficits - United States. 2. Debts, Public - United States. 3. Budget - Law and legislation - United States. I. Fink, Richard H. II. High, Jack C.
HJ2052 .N36 1987

National Academy of Engineering. Technology and global industry . Washington, D.C. , 1987. vi, 272 p. : ISBN 0-309-03736-0 (pbk.) LC Card 87-7765 DDC 338/.06 19
HC79.T4 T438 1987

National Academy of Public Administration. Nonprofit organizations, a government management tool /. New York , 1980. xxi, 173 p. ; ISBN 0-03-053966-8 : LC Card 79-23632 DDC 350 19
JK468.R45 N66 ***NYPL [JLE 80-1874]***

National Academy of Sciences, Washington, D. C. National Academy of Engineering. see **National Academy of Engineering.**

The National accountancy examination scheme . Bodi ya Taifa ya Wahasibu na Wakaguzi Hesabu Tanzania. Dar es Salaam [1983] xxviii leaves, 269 p. ; LC Card 87-118290
HF5616.T34 B63 1983

The National accountancy examination scheme . Bodi ya Taifa ya Wahasibu na Wakaguzi Hesabu Tanzania. Dar es Salaam , 1985. ii, 41 leaves ; LC Card 86-980364
HF5616.T34 B63 1985

The National accountancy examination scheme . Bodi ya Taifa ya Wahasibu na Wakaguzi Hesabu Tanzania. Dar es Salaam [1985] xxiii leaves, 275 p. ; LC Card 86-980376 DDC 657/.09678 19
HF1176.T34 B64 1985

NATIONAL ACCOUNTING. see **NATIONAL INCOME - ACCOUNTING.**

National accounts statistics, 1977-1984. St. John's Antigua : Statistical Office, Ministry of Finance, [1985] 44 leaves : ill. ; 28 cm. LC Card 86-221979 DDC 339.37297/4 19
1. National income - Antiqua - Accounting - Statistics. I. Antiqua. Ministry of Finance. Statistics Division.
HC155.5.Z7 A576 1985

National Action/Research on the Military-Industrial Complex. Automating apartheid . Philadelphia , c19. ix, 107 p. : ISBN 0-910082-00-6 (pbk.) : LC Card 86-201384 DDC 382/.45004/0968 19
HD9696.C63 S62 1984

National Agricultural Outlook Conference (U. S.) (1976 : Washington, D.C.) 1977 U. S. agricultural outlook : papers presented at the National Agricultural Outlook Conference / sponsored by the U. S. Department of Agriculture, held in Washington, D.C., November 15-18, 1976 ; prepared for the Committee on Agriculture and Forestry, United States Senate. Washington : U. S. G.P.O. : For sale by the Supt. of Docs., U. S. G.P.O., 1976. vi, 445 p. : ill. ; 24 cm. At head of title: 94th Congress, 2d session, committee print. "December 10, 1976. Includes bibliographical references. LC Card 86-602345
1. Agriculture - Economic aspects - United States. I. United States. Dept. of Agriculture. II. United States. Senate. Committee on Agriculture and Forestry. III. Title. IV. Title: 1977 US agricultural outlook.
HD1765 .N37 1976

NATIONAL AGRICULTURE AND FOOD CORPORATION.
Bantje, Han. Mechanised food production in Tanzania . [Dar es Salaam] [1984] 3 leaves, 73 p. : LC Card 86-980118 DDC 338.1/61/09678 19
HD1471.T34 B36 1984

National Alliance of Business.
Employment policies . Washington, D.C. , 1986. 16, [2] p. ; ISBN 0-88713-611-7 (pbk.) LC Card 87-127759 DDC 331.12/042/0973 19
HD5724 .E449 1986

Winick, Bradley H. Making the link . [Washinton, D.C.] , c1986. i, 17 p. ; ISBN 0-88713-678-8 (pbk.) LC Card 87-106145 DDC 331.11/0973 19
HD5724 .W557 1986

National Association for Campus Activities (U. S.) Future perfect . Columbia, S.C. (P.O. Box 6828, Columbia 29260) , c1987. x, 104 p. : LC Card 87-143129 DDC 650.1 19
HF5549.5.C35 F87 1987

National Association for the Practice of Anthropology (U. S.) Baba, Marietta L. Business and industrial anthropology . Washington, D.C. , c1986. vii, 48 p. ; ISBN 0-913167-16-9 (pbk.) : LC Card 86-26602 DDC 302.3/5 19
HD58.7 .B33 1986

NATIONAL ASSOCIATION (GREAT BRITAIN)
Working Men's Association, the first convention, and the National Association. New York , 1986. 1 v. (various pagings) : ISBN 0-8240-5586-1 : LC Card 86-33479 DDC 322/.2/0942 19
HD8396 .W67 1986

National Association of Accountants. Butler, Stephen A. Management incentive compensation plans /. Montvale, N.J. , c1986. v, 55 p. ; ISBN 0-86641-140-2 (pbk.) LC Card 86-230062 DDC 658.4/07225 19
HD4965.5.U6 B86 1986

National Association of Church Personnel Administrators (U. S.) Just treatment for those who work for the church. Cincinnati, OH (100 E. 8th St., Cincinnati 45202) , c1986. ix, 21 p. ; LC Card 86-228672 DDC 254/.0068/3 19
HF5549 .J87 1986

National Association of Convenience Stores (U. S.)
NACS convenience store customer purchasing patterns research report /. [Falls Church, Va. , 1985?] vi, 76 p. : LC Card 86-157648 DDC 381/.1 19
HF5469.55.U62 N33 1985
NYPL [JLF 87-810]

Survey of automation in the convenience store industry /. Alexandria, Va. (1605 King St., Alexandria 22314-2792) , c1986. vii, 39, 9 p. : LC Card 87-147614 DDC 381/.1 19
HF5469.55.U62 S87 1986

National Association of Cost Accountants. see **National Association of Accountants.**

National Association of Exterminators and Fumigators. see **National Pest Control Association.**

National Association of Home Builders (U. S.)
Financing land acquisition and development /. Washington, D.C. , c1987. 134 p. : ISBN 0-86718-281-4 (pbk.) LC Card 87-61069 DDC 332.7/2/0973 19
HD1390 .F56 1987

Higher density housing . Washington, D.C. , c1986. 155 p. : ISBN 0-86718-271-7 (pbk.) LC Card 86-63356 DDC 690/.83 19
HD1390.5 .H545 1986

National Association of Manufactures (U. S.)
Combating takeover attempts. Washington, D.C. , c1986. xi, 12 p. : LC Card 86-224303 DDC 658.1/6 19
HD2746.5 .C645 1986

National Association of Office and Industrial Parks. San Antonio Chapter. A Transcription of key addresses at San Antonio's Bio-Medical Seminar /. San Antonio, TX (8961 Tesoro Dr., Suite 308, San Antonio 78217) , c1985. v, 104, [4] leaves of plates : LC Card 87-144092 DDC 338.4/7681761/09764351 19
HD9999.B443 U667 1985

National Association of Real Estate Boards. American Institute of Real Estate Appraisers. see **American Institute of Real Estate Appraisers.**

National Association of Rotary Clubs of America. see **Rotary International.**

National Association of Securities Dealers. The NASDAQ handbook . Chicago, Ill. , c1987. vii, 577 p. : ISBN 0-917253-54-X : LC Card 87-12378 DDC 332.64/3/0973 19
HG4551 .N37 1987

National Association of State Units on Aging.
Tiven, Marjorie. State initiatives in elderly housing . Washington, DC , c1987. xviii, 79 p. ; LC Card 87-154352 DDC 363.5/9 19
HD7287.92.U54 T58 1987

National Audiovisual Center.
The Business of caring [videorecording] /. Washington, DC , 1984. 1 videocassette (23 min.) : LC Card 84-707513 DDC 362.7 11
HF5549.5.D39

Under the influence [motion picture] /. Washington, DC , 1983. 1 film reel (25 min.) : LC Card 84-700613 DDC 362.2 11
HE5620.D7

Under the influence [videorecording] /. Washington, DC , 1983. 1 videocassette (25 min.) : LC Card 84-706720 DDC 362.2 11
HE5620.D7

National Automated Clearing House Association.
ACH marketing handbook. [Washington, DC] (1901 L St., NW, Suite 640, Washington 20036) [c1987] 123, [24] p. ; LC Card 87-130512 DDC 332.1/028 19
HG4028.C45 A28 1987

ACH receivers handbook. Washington, D.C. (1901 L St., N.W., Suite 640, Washington 20036) , c1986. 104 p. : LC Card 87-112783 DDC 332.1/028 19
HG2306 .A25 1986

Guide to ACH processor selection & evaluation . Washington, D.C. (Suite 640, 1901 L St., N.W., Washington 20036) , c1987. v, 199 p. ; LC Card 87-402621 DDC 332.1/028 19
HG2322 .G85 1987

Introduction to ACH corporate payments /. Washington, D.C. (1901 L St., N.W., Suite 640, Washington 20036) [c1986] 90 p. : LC Card 86-222675 DDC 332.1/028 19
HG1710 .I58 1986

National Aviation Facilities Experimental Center (U. S.) Airport transportation . Arlington, Va. , Washington, D.C. [1961] vii, 289, 42 leaves : LC Card 84-132332
HE9797.4.A2 A38 1961

NATIONAL BANK NOTES - UNITED STATES - CATALOGS.
Prather, Dewitt G. United States national bank notes and their seals /. Charlotte, NC , c1986. xvi, 200 p., 16 p. of plates : ISBN 0-9616836-0-0 LC Card 86-90441 DDC 769.5/5973 19
HG607 .P73 1986

NATIONAL BANK OF COMMERCE (TANZANIA)
Nsekela, Amon J. (Amon James), 1930- The NBC, a profile of a public enterprise commercial bank . [Dar es Salaam] , 1983. 57 p. : LC Card 85-981339 DDC 332.1/2/09678 19
HG3397.A8 N375 1983

National Bank of Cuba. see **Banco Nacional de Cuba (Founded 1948)**

National Bank of Hungary. see **Magyar Nemzeti Bank.**

National Bank of Switzerland. see **Schweizerische Nationalbank.**

National broadcasting under siege .
Etzioni-Halevy, Eva. New York , 1987. xii, 228 p. ; ISBN 0-312-00772-8 : LC Card 87-4702 DDC 384.54 19
HE8689.6 .E89 1987

National Bureau of Economic Research Conference on Current Trade Policy Issues (1985 : Cambridge, Mass.) Current U. S. trade policy . Cambridge, Mass. (1050 Massachusetts Ave., Cambridge 02138) , 1986. iii, 128 p. ; LC Card 86-201110 DDC 382/.3/0973 19
HF1455 .C87 1986

A National Bureau of Economic Research monograph.
Schwartz, Anna Jacobson. Money in historical perspective /. Chicago , 1987. xvii, 442 p. : ISBN 0-226-74228-8 : LC Card 87-5973 DDC 332.4/9 19
HG538 .S354 1987

A National Bureau of Economic Research project report.
The Black youth employment crisis /. Chicago , 1986. viii, 469 p. : ISBN 0-226-26164-6 LC Card 85-20989 DDC 331.3/46396073 19
HD6273 .B57 1986 ***NYPL [JLE 86-3726]***

The Effects of taxation on capital accumulation /. Chicago , 1987. ix, 490 p. : ISBN 0-226-24088-6 : LC Card 86-25025 DDC 332/.0415 19
HJ2305 .E29 1987

Mergers and acquisitions /. Chicago , 1988. xi, 108 p. : ISBN 0-226-03209-4 LC Card 87-19035 DDC 658.1/6 19
HD2746.5 .M45 1988

Pensions in the U. S. economy /. Chicago , 1988. ix, 200 p. : ISBN 0-226-06285-6 LC Card 87-19987 DDC 331.25/2/0973 19
HD7105.45.U6 P46 1988

Taxes and capital formation /. Chicago , 1987. xii, 118 p. : ISBN 0-226-24079-7 LC Card 87-5898 DDC 336.2/00973 19
HJ2381 .T395 1987

National Capital Region Transportation Planning Board.
Kaufmann, Elizabeth Irwin. Traffic growth resulting from future development . Washington, D.C. (1875 Eye St., N.W., Washington 20006-5454) , c1987. ix, 53, 15 p. : LC Card 87-161086 DDC 388.4/13142/09753 19
HE356.5.W3 K38 1987

1986 Beltway cordon count of vehicular and passenger volumes. [Washington, D.C.] [1986] iv, 35 p., [109] p. : LC Card 87-119314 DDC 388.4/1314/09753021 19
HE5634.W3 A17 1986

1986 D.C. Core Cordon Count of vehicular and passenger volumes /. [Washington, D.C.] , c1986. iv, 34 p., [66] p. : LC Card 87-105302 DDC 388.4/13142/09753 19
HE372.W3 A15 1986

National Center for Food and Agricultural Policy (U. S.) Agriculture and the environment /. Washington, D.C. , c1986. xvii, 298 p. : ISBN 0-915707-33-0 (pbk.) : LC Card 87-43010 DDC 363.7/31 19
HD1755 .P47 1986

National Center for Health Services Research. Langwell, Kathryn M. A synthesis of research on competition in the financing and delivery of health services /. Hyattsville, MD. , Springfield, VA , 1982. 85 p. ; LC Card 82-600612 DDC 338.4/73621/0973 19
RA410.53 .L36 1982 NYPL [JLF 86-422]

National Center for Health Services Research and Health Care Technology Assessment (U. S.) Farley, Pamela J. Private health insurance in the United States . Rockville, MD , Springfield, VA [1986] 106 p. : LC Card 86-23618 DDC 368.3/82/00973 19
HG9396 .F3 1986

National Center for Health Statistics (U. S.) Centers for Disease Control suicide surveillance . Atlanta, GA [1985] ii, 33 p. : LC Card 86-602520 DDC 362.2 19
HB1323.S82 U53 1985

Health of an aging population . Hyattsville, Md. , Washington, D.C. , 1987. p. cm. ISBN 0-8406-0362-2 LC Card 86-600392 DDC 362.1/0723 s 362.1/9897/00973 19
HA37 .U1693 no. 25 RA408.A3

Statistical aspects of physician payment systems . Hyattsville, Md. [1987] vii, 33 p. : ISBN 0-8406-0357-6 LC Card 86-600375 DDC 362.1/0723 s 362.1/72 19
HA37 .U1693 no. 24 RA408.5

U. S. decennial life tables for 1979-81. Hyattsville, Md. , Washington, D.C. , 1985-<1986. v. ; LC Card 85-600190 DDC 304.6/4/0973021 19
HB1335 .U17 1985 NYPL [JLM 86-491]

National Center for Productivity and Quality of Working Life. Starting a labor-management committee in your organization : some pointers for action. Washington : National Center for Productivity and Quality of Working Life : for sale by the Supt. of Docs., U. S. Govt. Print. Off., 1978. 55 p. ; 27 cm. Bibliography: p. 47-50. LC Card 78-603560 DDC 658.31/5
1. Labor-management committees - United States. 2. Industrial productivity - United States. I. Title.
HD6490.L33 N37 1978 NYPL [JLF 81-235]

National Center for Research in Vocational Education (U. S.)
A National entrepreneurship education agenda for action / Novella Ross ... [et al.]. Columbus, Ohio : National Center for Research in Vocational Education, Ohio State University, 1984. xiv, 114 p. : ill. ; 28 cm. (Leadership training series . no. 66) Bibliography: p. 113-114. LC Card 86-201272 DDC 658.4/2 19
1. Business education - United States. 2. Entrepreneur - Study and teaching - United States. I. Ross, Novella. II. Series: Leadership training series (Columbus, Ohio) , no. 66. III. Title.
HF1131 .N28 1984

Risks & rewards of entrepreneurship /. Saint Paul, Minn. , c1988. 123 p. : ISBN 0-8219-0323-3 (pbk.) LC Card 87-21787 DDC 338/.04 19
HB615 .R56 1988

Warmbrod, Catharine P. Skills for the changing workplace . Columbus, Ohio (1960 Kenny Rd., Columbus 43210-1090) , 1985. ix, 93 p. ; LC Card 86-205907 DDC 651/.07/15 19
HF1106 .W36 1985

Warmbrod, Catharine P. Skills for the changing workplace . Columbus, Ohio (1960 Kenny Rd., Columbus 43210-1090) , 1985. ix, 86 p. ; LC Card 86-205842 DDC 658.8/007/15 19
HF5415 .W3155 1985

A National Chamber Foundation report. Burgess, Paul L. An incentives approach to improving the unemployment compensation system /. Kalamazoo, Mich. , 1987. xv, 273 p. : ISBN 0-88099-048-1 (pbk.) LC Card 87-23128 DDC 368.4/4/00973 19
HD7096.U5 B87 1987

NATIONAL CHARACTERISTICS, AMERICAN - HISTORY.
White, Colin (Colin M.) Russia and America . London , New York , c1987. 268 p. ; ISBN 0-7099-5246-5 LC Card 87-13646 DDC 330.947 19
HC333 .W46 1987

NATIONAL CHARACTERISTICS, RUSSIAN - HISTORY.
White, Colin (Colin M.) Russia and America . London , New York , c1987. 268 p. ; ISBN 0-7099-5246-5 LC Card 87-13646 DDC 330.947 19
HC333 .W46 1987

NATIONAL CITY BANK OF NEW YORK - HISTORY - 20TH CENTURY.
Mayer, Robert Stanley. The influence of Frank A. Vanderlip and the National City Bank on American commerce and foreign policy, 1910-1920 /. New York , 1987. viii, 221 p. ; ISBN 0-8240-8087-4 : LC Card 87-23793 DDC 332.1/5/097471 19
HG2613.N54 N3555 1987

National Coalition Against Domestic Violence (U. S.). Employment Training and Small Business Project. Moore, Janice D. Thorne. A step toward independence: economic self sufficiency . Washington, D.C. , c1986. iii, 117 p. : LC Card 86-209069 DDC 362.8/3 19
HD6059.6.U6 M66 1986

National Commission on Fraudulent Financial Reporting (U. S.) The Institute of Internal Auditors reports on fraud . Altamonte Springs, Fla. , c1987. xv, 74 p. : ISBN 0-89413-164-8 (pbk.) LC Card 87-401942 DDC 657/.3 19
HF5686.C7 I53 1987

National Commission on Jobs and Small Business (U. S.) Making America work again : jobs, small business, and the international challenge / [the National Commission on Jobs and Small Business]. Washington, D.C. : The Commission, c1987. ix, 70 p. ; 23 cm. ISBN 0-9617931-0-4 (pbk.) : LC Card 86-33118 DDC 338.6/42/0973 19
1. Small business - United States. 2. Competition, International. I. Title.
HD2346.U5 N315 1987

National Commission on Working Women. DeGooyer, Janice. Women's work, undervalued, underpaid . Washington, D.C. , 1984, c1982. 27, [4] leaves : *NYPL [*ZT-1708 no.39]*

National Committee for Research on the 1980 Census. Levy, Frank, 1941- Dollars and dreams . New York , 1987. p. cm. ISBN 0-87154-523-3 : LC Card 86-42952 DDC 339.2/0973 19
HC110.I5 L47 1987

National Conference of Management Accountants . National Conference of Management Accountants (1981 : Karachi, Pakistan) [Karachi] [1981?] 141 p. in various pagings ; LC Card 82-930763 DDC 658.1/511 19
HF5603 .N34 1981 NYPL [JLF 87-296]

National Conference of Management Accountants (1981 : Karachi, Pakistan) National Conference of Management Accountants : management accounting, challenges, and prospects / organised by Institute of Cost & Management Accountants of Pakistan. [Karachi] : The Institute, [1981?] 141 p. in various pagings ; 28 cm. Cover title. Includes bibliographical references. LC Card 82-930763 DDC 658.1/511 19
1. Managerial accounting - Pakistan - Congresses. 2. Accounting - Pakistan - Congresses. I. Institute of Cost & Management Accountants of Pakistan. II. Title.
HF5603 .N34 1981 NYPL [JLF 87-296]

National Conference on Microcomputers in Urban Transportation (1985 : San Diego, Calif.) Microcomputer applications within the urban transportation environment : proceedings of the National Conference on Microcomputers in Urban Transportation / sponsored by the Urban Transportation Division of the American Society of Civil Engineers, San Diego, California, June 19-21, 1985 ; Mark D. Abkowitz, editor ; Robert Stammer, Jr., associate editor. New York, N.Y. : The Society, c1985. 824 p. : ill., maps ; 22 cm. Includes bibliographies and indexes. ISBN 0-87262-508-7 (pbk.) LC Card 85-73250 DDC 388.4/028/5416 19
1. Urban transportation - Data processing - Congresses. 2. Microcomputers - Congresses. I. Abkowitz, Mark David. II. Stammer, Robert. III. American Society of Civil Engineers. Urban Transportation Division. IV. Title.
HE305 .N33 1985 NYPL [JSD 86-535]

National Conference on Public Expenditure: the Kay Issues (1985 : Dublin, Dublin) Public expenditure . Dublin, Ireland , 1986. 138 p. ; ISBN 0-906980-56-9 (pbk.) : LC Card 86-143826 DDC 336.3/9 19
HJ7461 .P83 1986 NYPL [JLD 87-553]

National Conference on Rural Development, Des Moines, 1973. Proceedings. Prepared for the Subcommittee on Rural Development of the Committee on Agriculture and Forestry, United States Senate. Washington, U. S. Govt. Print. Off., 1974. iii, 108 p. illus. 24 cm. At head of title: 93d Congress, 1st session. Committee print. LC Card 74-600918 DDC 309.2/63/0973
1. Community development - United States - Congresses. 2. Agricultural education - United States - Congresses. 3. United States - Rural conditions - Congresses. I. United States. Congress. Senate. Committee on Agriculture and Forestry. Subcommittee on Rural Development. II. Title: Proceedings of a National Conference on Rural Development.
HN65 .N35 1973 NYPL [JLE 81-564 no.2]

NATIONAL CONSCIOUSNESS. see **NATIONALISM.**

National Construction Employers Council (U. S.) Manual for collective bargaining /. Washington, D.C. (Suite 1040, 1101 15th St., N.W., Washington 20005) , 1987. 1 v. (various pagings) ; LC Card 87-150563 DDC 331.8/90424/0973 19
HD6515.B9 M36 1987

National Cooperative Transit Research & Development Program (U. S.) MacDorman, Littleton C. Use of part-time operators /. Washington, D.C. [1986] 33 p. : ISBN 0-309-04403-0 (pbk.) LC Card 86-51175 DDC 331.25/72 19
HD8039.S82 U65 1986

National Cotton Council of America. Horne, M. K. (McDonald Kelso), 1909- The economic outlook for U. S. cotton . Memphis, Tenn. , 1962. 32 p. : LC Card 86-162675
HD9075 .H73 1962

National Council for Cement and Building Materials (India) National Workshop on Productivity Enhancement in Indian Cement Industry-- a Pragmatic Approach to Modernisation (1986 : New Delhi, India) National Workshop on Productivity Enhancement in Indian Cement Industry-- a Pragmatic Approach to Modernisation, 19-20 March 1986 . New Delhi [1986] 42 p. : LC Card 87-901966 DDC 338.4/766694/0954 19
HD9622.I52 N34 1986

National Council for Geographic Education. Science/earth science on stamps and banknotes [slide] /. Lincoln, Neb. , 1984. 30 slides : LC Card 85-702119 DDC 551 11
HE6183.S36

National Council for Industrial Defense. see **National Safety Council.**

National Council for Industrial Safety. see **National Safety Council.**

National Council for Urban Economic Development. Winick, Bradley H. Making the link . [Washinton, D.C.] , c1986. i, 17 p. ; ISBN 0-88713-678-8 (pbk.) LC Card 87-106145 DDC 331.11/0973 19
HD5724 .W557 1986

National Council of Applied Economic Research. Kalra, G. D. Mineral development in Bihar, 1979-80 to 1988-89 /. New Delhi , 1983. 2 v. : LC Card 83-905955 DDC 338.2/0954/12 19
HD9506.I43 B545 1983
NYPL [JLE 86-4727]

National Council of Educational Research and Training (India) Parakh, B. S. Population education . New Delhi , 1985. xxviii, 355 p. ; LC Card 86-903303 DDC 304.6/07/1054 19
HB850.5.I4 P37 1985

National Council of Geography Teachers. see **National Council for Geographic Education.**

National Council of Women and Development (Ghana) Marketing in Ghana . Addis Ababa , 1984. vi, 62 p. ; LC Card 86-980249 DDC 381/.18/09667 19
HD6072.6.G4 M37 1984

National Council on Employment Policy. Job generation . Salt Lake City, Utah , c1986. xiv, 138 p. ; ISBN 0-913420-89-1 (pbk.) LC Card 86-31285 DDC 331.12/094 19
HD5724 .J63 1986

National Council on Family Relations. Pleck, Joseph H. Working wives, working husbands /. Beverly Hills, Calif. , c1985. 167 p. ; ISBN 0-8039-2489-5 LC Card 85-11974 DDC 306.8/7 19
HQ536 .P59 1985 ***NYPL [JLD 86-1130]***

National CPE curriculum : a pathway to excellence / prepared by the national curriculum task forces of the Continuing Professional Education Division of the American Institute of Certified Public Accountants. New York, N.Y. : National Curriculum Project, Continuing Professional Education Division, AICPA, c1987- 1 v. (loose-leaf) : ill. ; 30 cm. Includes index. ISBN 0-87051-001-0 (loose-leaf : CIP data sheet) : LC Card 87-18832 DDC 657/.07/15 19
1. Accounting - Outlines, syllabi, etc. 2. Professional education. 3. Continuing education. I. American Institute of Certified Public Accountants. Continuing Professional Education Division. II. National Curriculum Project (American Institute of Certified Public Accountants).
HF5635 .N25 1987

National Curriculum Project (American Institute of Certified Public Accountants) National CPE curriculum . New York, N.Y. , c1987- 1 v. (loose-leaf) : ISBN 0-87051-001-0 (loose-leaf : CIP data sheet) : LC Card 87-18832 DDC 657/.07/15 19
HF5635 .N25 1987

The national debt /. Davis, Bertha, 1910- New York , c1987. 112 p. ; ISBN 0-531-10415-X LC Card 87-10441 DDC 336.3/4/0973 19
HJ2052 .D38 1987

The national debt /. Malkin, Lawrence. New York , c1987. ix, 309 p. ; ISBN 0-8050-0382-7 LC Card 86-27347 DDC 336.3/4/0973 19
HJ8119 .M34 1987

The national debt and economic policy in the medium term /. FitzGerald, John D. Dublin , c1986. 62 p. : ISBN 0-7070-0089-0 (pbk.) : LC Card 87-110464 DDC 336.3/4/09417 19
HJ8630.A2 F58 1986

NATIONAL DEBTS. see **DEBTS, PUBLIC.**

National Development Bank (Portugal) see **Banco de Fomento Nacional.**

National Development Council (U. S.) Economic development and real estate financing /. N[ew] Y[ork], N.Y. (41 E. 42nd St., N[ew] Y[ork] 10017) [c1985] iii, 203 p. : LC Card 86-221586 DDC 332.7/2/0973 19
HD255 .E26 1985

National development strategy and programme /. Somalia. Ministry of National Planning. Mogadishu [1985] vi, 199 p. ; LC Card 86-980272 DDC 338.967/73 19
HC850 .S653 1985

The national directory of postcard deck media /. Lynch, Christine M. (Christine Marie), 1962- Westbury, N.Y. , c1987. ix, 238 p. ; ISBN 0-87280-156-X (pbk.) LC Card 87-1071 DDC 659.13/3 19
HF5861 .L96 1987

The National directory of product publicity sources / compiled by Patricia DiPrima-LeConche ; introduction by Ronald E. Roel. Westbury, N.Y. : Asher-Gallant Press, 1987. p. cm. Includes index. ISBN 0-87280-157-8 : LC Card 87-17542 DDC 338.7/616592/025 19
1. Public relations - Directories. 2. Marketing - Management - Directories. I. DiPrima-LeConche, Patricia, 1958-. II. Title: Product publicity sources.
HD59 .N245 1987

National directory, training and employment programs for Americans with disabilities / sponsored by Department of Health & Human Services and the Department of Education. Washington, D.C. : U. S. Dept. of Health and Human Services, [1985] vii, 374 p. : ill. ; 28 cm. Cover title. "September 11, 1985"--P. i. LC Card 85-602984 DDC 362.4/0484/02573 19
1. Handicapped - Employment - United States - States - Directories. 2. Vocational rehabilitation - United States - States - Directories. 3. Handicapped - Services for - United States - States - Directories. I. Title: Training and employment programs for Americans with disabilities.
HD7256.U5 N335 1985 ***NYPL [JLF 87-466]***

National Economic Development Office. (Old Catalog form: Great Britain. National Economic Development Office.)
Value added tax: a report by the National Economic Development Office. 2d ed. London, H.M.S.O., 1971. vi, 113 p. forms. 25 cm. Includes bibliographical references. ISBN 0-11-700550-9 LC Card 72-180346 DDC 336.2/71
1. Value-added tax - Great Britain. 2. Value-added tax - Europe.
HJ5715.G7 N36 1971 ***NYPL [JLE 74-313]***

National economic growth and stabilization policy in the age of multinational corporations . Müller, Ronald E. [Sydney] , 1979. vi, 45 p. : ISBN 0-908470-00-2 (pbk.) LC Card 87-672345
HC106.7 .M84x 1979

National emerging industries resourceguide / Dileep Rao, editor. Minneapolis, MN : Amacom, c1986. 368, 124 p. ; 28 cm. ISBN 0-8144-5851-3 LC Card 85-82163 DDC 338.7/61/0002573 19
1. New business enterprises - Management. 2. New business enterprises - Finance. 3. New business enterprises - Location. 4. Business consultants - Directories. I. Rao, Dileep.
HD62.5 .N38 1986 ***NYPL [JLF 86-1717]***

National emerging industries site selection guide / Dileep Rao, editor. Minneapolis, MN : InterFinance Corp., c1986. 124 p. ; 28 cm. (Growth-track business guidebooks, 0886-6732) On. t.p. the registered trademark symbol "TM" is superscript following "Growth-track" in the series statement. CONTENTS. - Locational determinants for emerging industry / Robert M. Ady -- Emerging communities offer excellent opportunities / Robert Zdenek -- States & countries strategies for emerging industries growth -- Real estate developers -- Research & development parks -- Incubator buildings -- Industrial/office/mixed park. LC Card 86-231272 DDC 338.6/042/02573 19
1. United States - Industries - Location - Directories. 2. Industrial sites - United States - Location. 3. Small business - United States - Location - Directories. 4. Industrial districts - United States - Location. 5. New business enterprises - United States - Location - Directories. I. Rao, Dileep. II. InterFinance Corporation. III. Series.
HC110.D5 N38 1986

National energy data systems : proceedings of an international workshop / edited by Dilip R. Ahuja, R.K. Pachauri, N.K. Gopalakrishnan. New Delhi : Concept, 1984, c1983. xxvi, 511 p. ; 23 cm. Proceedings of the International Workshop on National Energy Data Systems, organized by the Tata Energy Research Institute, and held at New Delhi, Dec. 15-18, 1982. Includes bibliographical references and indexes. LC Card 84-901310 DDC 333.79/09172/4 19
1. Power resources - Information services - Developing countries - Congresses. 2. Energy policy - Information services - Developing countries - Congresses. I. Ahuja, Dilip R. II. Pachauri, R. K. III. Gopalakrishnan, N. K. IV. Tata Energy Research Institute. V. International Workshop on National Energy Data Systems (1982 : New Delhi, India).
HD9502.D442 N37 1984
NYPL [JLD 86-4320]

The national energy plan, 1985-2000 /. Sudan. National Energy Plan Committee. Khartoum, Sudan , 1985. iii, iii, 158 p. : LC Card 86-980496 DDC 333.79/09624 19
HD9502.S732 S83 1985a

National energy planning and management in developing countries . Management Training Seminar (1982 : Joint Research Centre, Ispra, Italy) Dordrecht, Holland , Hingham, MA , c1983. xiii, 442 p. ; ISBN 90-277-1589-0 LC Card 83-4407 DDC 333.79/09172/4 19
HD9502.A2 M343 1982
NYPL [JLE 87-302]

National energy policy. New Delhi : Lok Sabha Secretariat, 1986. v, 67 p. ; 26 cm. Study based on published sources and discussions in the Parliament, intended to serve as a background material for the members of Parliament, India. Bibliography: p. 64. "Corrigenda"--Slip tipped in. "PRIS-(Bro.-5)/86"--T.p. verso. LC Card 87-900181
1. Energy policy - India. I. India. Parliament. Lok Sabha. Secretariat.
HD9502.I42 N36 1986

National energy policy plan projections to 2010 . United States. Dept. of Energy. Office of Policy, Planning, and Analysis. Washington, D.C. [1985] 1 v. (various pagings) : LC Card 86-601637 DDC 333.79/0973 19
HD9502.U52 U5125 1985

National energy program, 1986-1990. Metro Manila, Philippines : Ministry of Energy, [1986] 64 p. : ill. ; 28 cm. LC Card 86-207642 DDC 333.79/09599 19
1. Energy policy - Philippines. 2. Philippines. Ministry of Energy.
HD9502.P62 N373 1986

A National entrepreneurship education agenda for action /. National Center for Research in Vocational Education (U. S.) Columbus, Ohio , 1984. xiv, 114 p. : LC Card 86-201272 DDC 658.4/2 19
HF1131 .N28 1984

National Examinations Board for Supervisory Studies (Great Britain) Cost reduction. Oxford , New York , 1986. ix, 65 p. : ISBN 0-08-034177-2 (pbk.) LC Card 87-100499 DDC 658.1/552 19
HD47.3 .C67 1986

NATIONAL FARMERS' ALLIANCE AND INDUSTRIAL UNION - HISTORY. Mitchell, Theodore R. Political education in the Southern Farmers' Alliance, 1887-1900 /. Madison, Wis. , 1987. xiv, 242 p. : ISBN 0-299-11470-8 : LC Card 87-40141 DDC 338.1/06/075 19
HD1485.N35 M58 1987

National Farmers' Union Development Trust (Great Britain) Gasson, Ruth M. Labour sharing in agriculture /. [London] [1979] 117 p. ; ISBN 0-901859-82-6 (pbk.) LC Card 83-226074 DDC 331.25/72 19
HD5119.A292 G744 1979

National Film Board of Canada.
National industrial relations film catalogue. [Ottawa, Ont.] , c1986. 31, 21 p. ; ISBN 0-662-54352-1 (pbk.) LC Card 86-203066 DDC 016.331 19
HD6971 .N24 1986

Real inside [motion picture] /. Deerfield, IL , 1985. 1 film reel (12 min.) : LC Card 87-705522 DDC 791.43 11
HF5549.5.I6

Real inside [videorecording] /. Deerfield, IL, 1985. 1 videocassette (12 min.) : LC Card 87-705515 DDC 791.43 11
HF5549.5.I6

National financial policies and capital formation in Africa : proceedings of a symposium, Cairo, Egypt. Dakar, Senegal : Association of African Central Banks, African Centre for Monetary Studies, [1986] iii, 205 p. ; 25 cm. Proceedings of the Symposium on National Financial Policies and Capital Formation in Africa, held July 13-20, 1984, sponsored by the African Centre for Monetary Studies and the Central Bank of Egypt. "February 1986." Includes bibliographies. LC Card 87-404123 DDC 332/.096 19
1. Saving and investment - Government policy - Africa - Congresses. 2. Banks and banking, Cooperative - Government policy - Africa - Congresses. 3. Investments, Foreign - Government policy - Africa - Congresses. I. African Centre for Monetary Studies. II. Symposium on National Financial Policies and Capital Formation in Africa (1985 : Cairo, Egypt). III. Bank al-Markazī al-Miṣrī.
HG5822 .N38 1986

NATIONAL FORESTS. see **FOREST RESERVES.**

National Forum on Issues in Vocational Assessment (2nd : 1986 : Dallas, Tex.) Second National Forum on Issues in Vocational Assessment : the issues papers : papers presented at the Second National Forum on Issues in Vocational Assessment, March 12-15, 1986, at the Ramada Hotel/Market Center, Dallas, Texas / edited by Ronald Fry. Menomonie, Wis. : Materials Development Center, Stout Vocational Rehabilitation Institute, School of Education and Human Services, University of Wisconsin-Stout, c1985. vii, 236 p. : ill. ; 28 cm. Cover title: The issues papers. Includes bibliographies. ISBN 0-916671-71-2 (pbk.) LC Card 86-217148 DDC 362/.0425 19
1. Vocational rehabilitation - United States - Congresses. 2. Vocational education - United States -

Evaluation - Congresses. I. Fry, Ronald. II. Stout Vocational Rehabilitation Institute. Materials Development Center. III. Title. IV. Title: Issues papers.
HD7256.U5 N336 1986

National Foundation for the Study of Equal Employment Policy. Walsh, J. Michael (Joseph Michael), 1943- Drug and alcohol abuse in the workplace . Washington, D.C. , 1987. xiv, 149 p. ; ISBN 0-916559-08-4 (pbk.) LC Card 87-60167 DDC 658.3/822 19
HF5549.5.E42 W35 1987

National Foundation for the Study of Equal Employment Policy (U. S.) Responding to comparable worth in today's environment . [Washington, D.C.] , c1986. xi, 160 leaves ; ISBN 0-916559-07-6 (loose-leaf) : LC Card 86-63777 DDC 658.3/2 19
HD6061.2.U6 R47 1986

National Governors' Association. Guide to state capital formation incentives and innovations /. [Washington, D.C. , 1983] vii, 154 p. ; LC Card 86-673432
HC110.153 G84x 1983

National Governors' Association. Center for Policy Research. Affording access to quality care . Washington, D.C. (444 N. Capitol St., N.W., Suite 250, Washington 20001) , c1986. xx, 245 p. ; LC Card 87-127057 DDC 338.4/336210452/0973 19
HD7102.U4 A66 1986

National Governors' Association. Policy Research, Center for. see **National Governors' Association. Center for Policy Research.**

National health insurance in Canada and Australia . Brown, Malcolm C. (Malcolm Clarence), 1941- Canberra , 1983. vii, 108 p. ; ISBN 0-86784-281-4 (pbk.) LC Card 86-214526 DDC 368.4/2/00971 19
HD7102.A8 B75 1983

NATIONAL INCOME - ACCOUNTING - HANDBOOKS, MANUALS, ETC.
Handbook of national accounting . New York , 1986. xi, 180 p. : ISBN 92-1-161264-0 (pbk.) LC Card 87-106896 DDC 339.3/2 19
HC79.I5 H36 1986

NATIONAL INCOME - ACCOUNTING - MATHEMATICAL MODELS.
Meyer-Cording, Claus, 1953- Die Auswirkungen kreditfinanzierter Staatsausgaben auf das Volkseinkommen . Frankfurt am Main , New York , c1986. v, 256 p. : ISBN 3-8204-9634-3 LC Card 86-204989
HB141.5 .M49 1986

NATIONAL INCOME - ALGERIA - ACCOUNTING.
Labidi, M. (Mourad) Comptabilité nationale /. Alger , 1982. 381 p. : LC Card 84-237940
HC815.Z9 I515 1982

National income and economic progress : essays in honour of Colin Clark / edited by Duncan Ironmonger, J.O.N. Perkins, Tran Van Hoa. New York : St. Martin's Press, 1988. p. cm. Bibliography: p. Includes index. ISBN 0-312-01566-6 : LC Card 87-24063 DDC 339.3 19
1. National income - Accounting. 2. Economics - Statistical methods. 3. Clark, Colin, 1905-. I. Clark, Colin, 1905-. II. Ironmonger, D. S. III. Perkins, J. O. N. (James Oliver Newton), 1924-. IV. Tran, Van Hoa.
HB141.5 .N375 1988

NATIONAL INCOME - ANTIQUA - ACCOUNTING - STATISTICS.
National accounts statistics, 1977-1984. St. John's Antigua [1985] 44 leaves : LC Card 86-221979 DDC 339.37297/4 19
HC155.5.Z7 A576 1985

NATIONAL INCOME - ARGENTINA - ACCOUNTING - EFFECT OF INFLATION ON.
Oferta y demanda global a precios corrientes /. [Buenos Aires, Argentina] , 1982. 115 leaves ; LC Card 87-402103 DDC 339.382 19
HC180.I5 O38 1982

NATIONAL INCOME - AUSTRIA - ACCOUNTING - HISTORY - 19TH CENTURY.
Wagner, Adolph, 1835-1917. Die Ordnung des österreichischen Staatshaushaltes--1863 /. Wien , c1984. 308 p. ; ISBN 3-85447-086-X LC Card 85-223615
HJ1065 .W34 1984

NATIONAL INCOME - BRAZIL - RIO GRANDE DO SUL - ACCOUNTING - STATISTICS.
Areas estatísticamente comparáveis do Rio Grande do Sul, 1940-80 . Porto Alegre, RS , 1986. 186 p. : LC Card 87-403481 DDC 339.381/65 19
HC188.R4 A73 1986

NATIONAL INCOME - COLOMBIA - ACCOUNTING.
Cortés de Pinzón, Magdalena. Bases de contabilidad nacional /. [Bogotá, Colombia] [1982] 96 p. : LC Card 82-216044
HC79.I5 C675 1982

Metodología de las cuentas nacionales de Colombia. Bogotá, D.E. [1986] 291 p. ; LC Card 87-403848 DDC 339.3861 19
HC200.I5 M47 1986

NATIONAL INCOME - CUBA - ACCOUNTING.
Pérez-López, Jorge F. Measuring Cuban economic performance /. Austin , 1987. xii, 202 p. : ISBN 0-292-75092-7 LC Card 86-24907 DDC 339.37291 19
HC152.5 .P47 1987

NATIONAL INCOME - ECONOMETRIC MODELS.
Rötheli, Tobias F. Das Volkseinkommen und die internationalen Kapitalbewegungen /. Bern , c1986. 128 p. ; ISBN 3-258-03669-1 LC Card 87-110633 DDC 332.4/5/0724 19
HG3891 .R67 1986

NATIONAL INCOME - EUROPE, EASTERN.
Mikheev, S. Remuneration in Eastern European countries /. Geneva , 1985. vi, 45, ix p. ; ISBN 92-9014-408-4 (pbk.) : LC Card 86-216036 DDC 331.2/947 19
HD5014 .M55 1985

Tromlakova, E. M. (Elena Mikhaĭlovna) Ėffektivnost′ proizvodstva v evropeĭskikh stranakh SĖV /. Moskva , 1986. 157 p. ; LC Card 86-233225
HC244.Z9 I5188 1986

NATIONAL INCOME - EUROPEAN ECONOMIC COMMUNITY COUNTRIES - ACCOUNTING - STATISTICS.
Regnskaber og statistikker for den offentlige sektor 1970-1981 =. Luxembourg , Washington, DC , 1983. clxxii, 279 p. ; ISBN 92-825-4066-9 LC Card 84-174459
HC240.9.I5 R45 1983

NATIONAL INCOME - FRANCE - ACCOUNTING.
Sources et méthodes d'élaboration des comptes nationaux. [Paris] [1983] 481 p. ; LC Card 84-161813
HC271 .A218 no. 440-441 HJ9925.F8

NATIONAL INCOME - GAMBIA - STATISTICS.
Estimates of national income at constant prices in the Gambia. [Banjul] [1985] 49 leaves ; LC Card 87-120773 DDC 339.366/51 19
HC1070.Z9 I54 1985

Sources and methods of estimation of national income at current prices in the Gambia. [Banjul, Gambia] [1985] vi, 151 p. ; LC Card 87-116289 DDC 339.366/51 19
HC1070.Z9 I57 1985

NATIONAL INCOME - GERMANY, WEST - ACCOUNTING.
Müller, Frieder, 1944- Volkswirtschaftliche Gesamtrechnung und Preisveränderungen . Königstein/Ts. , 1984. xx, 414 p. : ISBN 3-445-02378-6 LC Card 85-142948 DDC 339.343 19
HC79.I5 M85 1984 ***NYPL [JLE 86-3225]***

Revidierte Ergebnisse, 1960 bis 1984 /. Stuttgart , 1985. 468 p. ; LC Card 86-204499 DDC 339.343 19
HC290.5.I5 R48 1985

NATIONAL INCOME - GERMANY (WEST) - ACCOUNTING - ECONOMETRIC MODELS.
Busch, Wilfried, 1948- Staatsausgaben, Produktion und Beschäftigung . Frankfurt am Main , New York , c1984. viii, 304 p. : ISBN 3-8204-5352-0 LC Card 85-199154
HJ7792 .B87 1984

NATIONAL INCOME - GREAT BRITAIN - ACCOUNTING - ECONOMETRIC MODELS.
The Cambridge multisectoral dynamic model of the British economy /. Cambridge [Cambridgeshire] , New York , 1988. p. cm. ISBN 0-521-33004-1 LC Card 86-33375 DDC 330.941/00724 19
HC256.6 .C29 1988

NATIONAL INCOME - MEXICO - ACCOUNTING - STATISTICS - STATES.
Estructura económica del Estado de [name of state] . México, D.F. [s.l.] , c1985-<c1987. v. <[1-7] > : ISBN 968-89202-6-6 (v. [1]) LC Card 86-229829
HC140.I5 E88 1985

NATIONAL INCOME - NORWAY - ACCOUNTING.
Kvartalsvis nasjonalregnskap 1978-1983 =. Oslo , 1984. 99 p. ; ISBN 82-537-2143-9 : LC Card 85-223735
HA1501 B, nr. 510 HC370.I5

The National income of Trinidad & Tobago, 1966-1985. Port of Spain : Republic of Trinidad & Tobago, Central Statistical Office, c1987. vi, 281 p. : ill. ; 28 cm. Cover title. Includes bibliographical references. LC Card 87-403406 DDC 339.37298/3 19
1. National income - Trinidad and Tobago. I. Trinidad and Tobago. Central Statistical Office. II. Title: National income of Trinidad and Tobago, 1966-1985.
HC157.Z9 I516 1987

National income of Trinidad and Tobago, 1966-1985. The National income of Trinidad & Tobago, 1966-1985. Port of Spain , c1987. vi, 281 p. : LC Card 87-403406 DDC 339.37298/3 19
HC157.Z9 I516 1987

A National income-related pension scheme. Dublin : Stationery Office : To be purchased from the Govt. Publications Sale Office, G.P.O., [1976] viii, 195 p. ; 24 cm. LC Card 82-127069
1. Social security - Ireland. I. Ireland. Dept. of Social Welfare.
HD7168 .N39 1976

NATIONAL INCOME - RÉUNION - STATISTICS.
Abramovici, G. Comptes économiques de la Réunion, série 1975-1980 . Ste Clotilde, [Réunion] [1983?] 133 p. ; LC Card 86-980541
HC598 .A37 1983

NATIONAL INCOME - SLOVENIA - STATISTICS.
Flajs, Andrej. Družbeno bogastvo SR Slovenije ob koncu 1980. leta /. Ljubljana , 1986. 75 p. ; ISBN 86-81141-04-X LC Card 86-216767
HA1634.S58 F54 1986

NATIONAL INCOME - SOVIET UNION.
Adirim, I. G. (Itskhok Girshevich) Stagflation in the USSR /. Falls Church, VA (7700 Leesburg Pike, #212, Falls Church 22043) [1983] xi, 122 leaves ; LC Card 84-162596 DDC 332.4/1/0947 19
HC340.I5 A44 1983 ***NYPL [JLF 86-1839]***

Lazurenko, S. G. (Serafima Grigor′evna) Izmerenie vli͡ianii͡a nauchno-tekhnicheskogo progressa na rost nat͡sional′nogo dokhoda /. Moskva , 1981. 127 p. ; LC Card 82-115905
HC340.T4 L39 1981

NATIONAL INCOME - SPAIN - ACCOUNTING.
Ruesga Benito, Santos, 1953- Métodos de estimación de la economía oculta . Madrid [1985?] 55 p. : ISBN 88-470-7531-18 LC Card 87-111661
HD2346.S7 R84 1985

NATIONAL INCOME - TRINIDAD AND TOBAGO.
The National income of Trinidad & Tobago, 1966-1985. Port of Spain , c1987. vi, 281 p. : LC Card 87-403406 DDC 339.37298/3 19
HC157.Z9 I516 1987

NATIONAL INCOME - UNITED STATES - ACCOUNTING - CONGRESSES.
Carson, Carol S. The use of national income and product accounts for public policy . Washington, D.C. , 1986. 26 p. : LC Card 86-601338 DDC 339.5/0973 19
HC110.I5 C37 1986

National industrial relations film catalogue. [Ottawa, Ont.] : National Film Board of

Canada, c1986. 31, 21 p. ; 28 cm. Title on added t.p.: Le catalogue de la Cinémathèque nationale des relations industrielles. Includes index. ISBN 0-662-54352-1 (pbk.) LC Card 86-203066 DDC 016.331 19
1. Industrial relations - Film catalogs. 2. Personnel management - Film catalogs. I. National Film Board of Canada. II. Title: Catalogue de la Cinémathèque national des relations industrielles.
HD6971 .N24 1986

National Institute of Economics and Social Research.
Occasional papers .
(38) Utton, Michael A. Profits and stability of monopoly /. Cambridge [Cambridgeshire] , New York , 1986. vii, 96 p. ; ISBN 0-521-32550-1 LC Card 86-4226 DDC 338.8/2/0941 19
HD2757.3 .U88 1986 ***NYPL [TB (National Institute of Economic and Social Research. Occasional papers. v.38)]***

National Institute of Educational Planning and Administration (India) Education and the new international order /. New Delhi , 1983, c1982. xx, 147 p. ; LC Card 83-902560 DDC 370/.11/5 19
HF1411 .E28 1983 ***NYPL [JLD 86-3707]***

National Institute of Labour Science (Korea) International Labour Organisation. National Institute of Labour Science (NILS) (preparatory assistance), Republic of Korea . Geneva , 1976. 43 p. ; ISBN 92-2-101617-X (pbk.) LC Card 84-145790
HD7758 .I58 1976

NATIONAL INSTITUTE OF LABOUR SCIENCE (KOREA)
International Labour Organisation. National Institute of Labour Science (NILS) (preparatory assistance), Republic of Korea . Geneva , 1976. 43 p. ; ISBN 92-2-101617-X (pbk.) LC Card 84-145790
HD7758 .I58 1976

National Institute of Labour Science (NILS) (preparatory assistance), Republic of Korea . International Labour Organisation. Geneva , 1976. 43 p. ; ISBN 92-2-101617-X (pbk.) LC Card 84-145790
HD7758 .I58 1976

National Institute of Labour Studies (Australia) Structured chaos . Melbourne , New York , 1985. viii, 111 p. : ISBN 0-19-554687-3 LC Card 86-222312 DDC 338/.06/0994 19
HC610.I52 S77 1985

National Institute of Public Finance and Policy (India) Kabra, Kamal Nayan. Black money . New Delhi , 1985. 47 p. ; LC Card 87-900898 DDC 381 19
HJ2348.5 .K32 1985

National Instrument Society of America. see **Instrument Society of America.**

National issues forums.
The Trade gap . Dayton, Ohio (100 Commons Rd., Dayton 45459-2777) , c1987. 35 p. : LC Card 87-71294 DDC 382.1/7/0973 19
HF3031 .T7 1987

National League of Cities. Barnes, William R. Employment problems and America's cities /. [Washington, D.C.] , 1984. xiii, 66, 33 p. ;
NYPL [JLF 86-1]

NATIONAL LIBERATION MOVEMENTS.
Az Elmélet és a fegyverek kritikája . Budapest [1981] xxv, 509 p. ; ISBN 963-461-775-1 (Magy. nemz. bibl.) LC Card 85-139263
HC59.7 .E45 1981

NATIONAL LIBERATION MOVEMENTS - DEVELOPING COUNTRIES.
Kruijer, G. J. (Gerardus Johannes), 1919- Development through liberation . Atlantic Highlands, NJ , 1987. x, 257 p. ; ISBN 0-391-03538-X LC Card 87-3710 DDC 338.9/009172/4 19
HC59.72.P6 K78 1987

National management of the international economy /. Panić, M. New York , 1988. p. cm. ISBN 0-312-01294-2 : LC Card 87-18764 DDC 337 19
HF1411 .P2935 1988

National Meeting on Productivity of U. S. Marine Terminals (1986 : Long Beach, Calif.) Improving productivity in U. S. marine container terminals /. Washington, D.C. , 1986. xiv, 205 p. : ISBN 0-309-03694-1 (pbk.) LC Card 86-62194 DDC 388.5/44/068 19
HE553 .I45 1986

National Micrographics Association. Saffady, William, 1944- The automated office . Silver Spring, Md. , c1981. viii, 241 p. : ISBN 0-89258-072-0 LC Card 81-208697 DDC 651.8/4 19
HF5548.2 .S165 ***NYPL [JLE 86-3919]***

National Monetary Council (Brazil) Brazil-- money and credit programming in 1983 / National Monetary Council. Brazil : Central Bank of Brazil, Administration Department of Material Resources, Printing Division, [1982] 38 p. ; 30 cm. "December 16, 1982." LC Card 87-131446
1. Monetary policy - Brazil. 2. Credit - Brazil. I. Title.
HG835 .N36 1982

National Office Products Association. The Future of the office products industry . Alexandria, Va. (301 N. Fairfax St., Alexandria 22314) , c1985. viii, 212, 33 p. : LC Card 86-200112 DDC 338.4/768 19
HD9800.U52 F86 1985

NATIONAL ORGANIZATION FOR WOMEN.
Hawkes, Ellen. Feminism on trial . New York , c1986. 420 p. ; ISBN 0-688-04850-1 : LC Card 85-31968 DDC 305.4/2/0973 19
HQ1413.F63 H39 1986
NYPL [JLE 86-2863]

NATIONAL PARKS AND RESERVES - ALASKA.
Roberts, Malcolm B. Senate Transportation Committee, RS 2477 Task Force report /. [Anchorage, Alaska] [1986] 121 leaves, 27 p. : LC Card 86-622718 DDC 333.78/09798 19
HE356.A4 R63 1986

NATIONAL PARKS AND RESERVES - ALASKA - MANAGEMENT.
Skilbred, Amy. The Watt/Clark record . Washington, D.C. (1901 Pennsylvania Ave., N.W., Washington 20006) , c1984. iii, 63, [18] p. : LC Card 86-206945 DDC 363.7/009798 19
HC107.A47 E57 1984

NATIONAL PARKS AND RESERVES - ALASKA - PLANNING.
Skilbred, Amy. The Watt/Clark record . Washington, D.C. (1901 Pennsylvania Ave., N.W., Washington 20006) , c1984. iii, 63, [18] p. : LC Card 86-206945 DDC 363.7/009798 19
HC107.A47 E57 1984

NATIONAL PARKS AND RESERVES - UNITED STATES.
McMillon, Bill, 1942- The old lodges & hotels of our national parks /. South Bend, Ind. , 1983. ix, 130 p., [32] p. of plates : ISBN 0-89651-551-6 : LC Card 83-18456 DDC 647/.947301 19
TX909 .M34 1983 ***NYPL [JFF 86-405]***

National Pest Control Association. Pinto, Lawrence J. The structural pest control industry . Vienna, Va. (8150 Leesburg Pike, Suite 1100, Vienna 22180) , 1981. 26, [10] p. : LC Card 86-214768 DDC 338.4/762896/0973 19
HD9718.5.P473 U663 1981

NATIONAL PLANNING. see **ECONOMIC POLICY; SOCIAL POLICY.**

National policies for developing high technology industries : international comparisons / edited by Francis W. Rushing and Carole Ganz Brown. Boulder, Colo. : Westview Press, c1986. xiv, 247 p. : ill. ; 23 cm. (Westview special studies in science, technology and public policy) Includes bibliographies. ISBN 0-8133-7280-1 (soft : alk. paper) LC Card 86-50530 DDC 338.4/762 19
1. High technology industries - Government policy - Case studies. 2. Industry and state - Case studies. 3. Technology and state - Case studies. I. Rushing, Francis W. II. Brown, Carole Ganz.
HC79.H53 N38 1986 ***NYPL [JLE 86-4504]***

A national policy for organized free trade . Hodin, Michael W. New York , 1987. 481 p. ; ISBN 0-8240-8085-8 (alk. paper) : LC Card 87-23719 DDC 382/.45669142/0973 19
HD9515 .H59 1987

NATIONAL PRODUCT, GROSS. see **GROSS NATIONAL PRODUCT.**

National Productivity Council (India) National Workshop on Productivity Enhancement in Indian Cement Industry-- a Pragmatic Approach to Modernisation (1986 : New Delhi, India) National Workshop on Productivity Enhancement in Indian Cement Industry-- a Pragmatic Approach to Modernisation, 19-20 March 1986 . New Delhi [1986] 42 p. : LC Card 87-901966 DDC 338.4/766694/0954 19
HD9622.I52 N34 1986

National Productivity Council of India. see **National Productivity Council (India)**

A National productivity review reprint series. Inside productivity . New York, N.Y. , c1987. iv, 156 p. : ISBN 0-88057-671-5 (pbk.) LC Card 86-82865 DDC 338/.06 19
HD56 .I528 1987

National programme for development and training of manpower for employment, Philippines . International Labour Organisation. Geneva , 1979. ii, 54 p. ; LC Card 81-140367 DDC 331.25/92/09599 19
HD5825.A6 I57 1979

National Programme on Worker's Participation and Development (1983 : Mauritius) Report on the National Programme on Worker's Participation and Development, 3-14 October, 1983, Mauritius. [Mauritius? : s.n., between 1983 and 1985] 33 p. ; 23 cm. Corrigendum slip inserted. LC Card 86-980341 DDC 658.3/152/096982 19
1. Trade-unions - Officials and employees - Training of - Mauritius - Congresses. 2. Industrial management - Mauritius - Employee participation - Congresses. I. Title.
HD6890.5 .N37 1983

National Public Radio (U. S.) News and views from National Public Radio /. Memphis, Tenn. , 1989. p. cm. LC Card 87-23331 DDC 384.54/06/073 19
HE8697.P6 N48 1989

NATIONAL PUBLIC RADIO (U. S.)
News and views from National Public Radio /. Memphis, Tenn. , 1989. p. cm. LC Card 87-23331 DDC 384.54/06/073 19
HE8697.P6 N48 1989

National Railroad Passenger Corporation. see **Amtrak.**

The national recorder /. Williams, 1949- Denver, CO , c1983. ii, 456 p. ; LC Card 87-106311 DDC 353.9/382326/025 19
HD255 .W54 1983

The national register of advertising slogans & headlines /. Grinnell, J. D., 1944- Westbury, N.Y. , 1987. p. cm. ISBN 0-87280-159-4 : LC Card 87-17577 DDC 659.13/22 19
HF6135 .G74 1987

National Research Council Commission on Behavioral and Social Sciences and Education. Women's work, men's work . Washington, D.C. , 1986. xii, 173 p. : ISBN 0-309-03429-9 (pbk.) LC Card 85-11541 DDC 331.1/33/0973 19
HD6060.5.U5 W66 1986
NYPL [JLF 86-1430]

National Research Council Committee on Women's Employment and Related Social Issues. Women's work, men's work . Washington, D.C. , 1986. xii, 173 p. : ISBN 0-309-03429-9 (pbk.) LC Card 85-11541 DDC 331.1/33/0973 19
HD6060.5.U5 W66 1986
NYPL [JLF 86-1430]

National Research Council (U. S.). Committee on Population. Population growth and economic development . Madison, Wis. , 1987. xiii, 702 p. ; ISBN 0-299-11130-X : LC Card 86-40447 DDC 338.9/009172/4 19
HB884 .P66547 1987

National Research Council (U. S.). Committee on Population and Demography. Panel on Indonesia. Recent trends in fertility and mortality in Indonesia /. Honolulu, Hawaii , 1987. xvi, 96 p. : ISBN 0-86638-092-2 (pbk.) : LC Card 87-11178 DDC 304.6/32/09598 19
HB1057 .R43 1987

National Research Council (U. S.). Committee on Productivity of Marine Terminals. Improving productivity in U. S. marine container terminals /. Washington, D.C. , 1986. xiv, 205 p. : ISBN 0-309-03694-1 (pbk.) LC Card 86-62194 DDC 388.5/44/068 19
HE553 .I45 1986

National Research Council (U. S.). Committee on Women's Employment and Related Social Issues. Panel on Technology and Women's Employment.
Computer chips and paper clips : technology and women's employment / Heidi I. Hartmann, Robert E. Kraut, and Louise A. Tilly, editors ; Panel on Technology and Women's Employment, Committee on Women's Employment and Related Social Issues, Commission on Behavioral and Social Sciences and Education, National Research Council. Washington, D.C. : National Academy Press, 1986. v. : ill. ; 23 cm. Includes index. Bibliography: v. 1, p. 183-199. CONTENTS. - v. 1. [without special title] ISBN 0-309-03688-7 (v. 1) LC Card 86-18113 DDC 331.4/8165137/0973 19
1. Women white collar workers - Effect of technological innovations on. 2. Office practice - Automation. 3. Microelectronics - Social aspects. 4. Women - Employment - Government policy - United States. I. Hartmann, Heidi I. II. Kraut, Robert E. III. Tilly, Louise. IV. Title.
HD6331.18.M39 N38 1986
NYPL [JLL 87-129]

Women, clerical work, and office automation . Washington, D.C. , 1986. vi, 64 p. ; LC Card 86-602559 DDC 331.4/8165137/0973 19
HD6095 .W685 1986

National Research Council (U. S.). Transportation Research Board.
MacDorman, Littleton C. Use of part-time operators /. Washington, D.C. [1986] 33 p. : ISBN 0-309-04403-0 (pbk.) LC Card 86-51175 DDC 331.25/72 19
HD8039.S82 U65 1986

National Research Council (U. S.). Working Group on Population Growth and Economic Development. Population growth and economic development . Madison, Wis. , 1987. xiii, 702 p. ; ISBN 0-299-11130-X : LC Card 86-40447 DDC 338.9/009172/4 19
HB884 .P66547 1987

National Research Council. Working Group on Population Growth and Economic Development. Population growth and economic development . Washington, D.C. , 1986. ix, 108 p. ; ISBN 0-309-03641-0 (pbk.) LC Card 86-862 DDC 304.6/09172/4 19
HB884 .P6655 1986 ***NYPL [JLE 86-3533]***

NATIONAL RESOURCES. see NATURAL RESOURCES.

National Retail Merchants Association.
Cash, R. Patrick. Improving apparel shop profits] [New York, N.Y.] [c1986] 285 p. : ISBN 0-87102-131-5 LC Card 86-61313 DDC 687/.068/8 19
HD9940.A2 C37 1986

National Retail Merchants Association. Visual Merchandising Board of Directors.
International display and visual merchandising /. Glen Cove, N.Y. , 1987. p. cm. ISBN 0-86636-052-2 : LC Card 87-61166 DDC 659.1/5 19
HF5845 .I73 1987

National rural development programme /. Malawi. [Lilongwe, Malawi] , 1977. 7 v. : LC Card 85-981594
HD2133.5.Z8 M35 1977

National Rural Electric Cooperative Association. Small Decentralized Hydropower (SDH) Program. Evaluating electrification experience . Washington, D.C. , 1982- v. <1 > : LC Card 86-176385 DDC 333.91/4 19
HD9688.D44 E9 1982

NATIONAL RURAL EMPLOYMENT PROGRAMME (INDIA)
Hirway, Indira. Wage employment programmes in rural development . New Delhi , c1986. vi, 112 p. ; ISBN 81-204-0072-0 : LC Card 86-903398 DDC 331.2/95475 19
HD5070.G85 H57 1986

National Safety Council. Introduction to occupational health and safety /. Chicago, Ill. , c1986. xvii, 519 p. : ISBN 0-87912-133-5 LC Card 84-61216 DDC 658.3/82 19
HD7261 .I68 1986

NATIONAL SECURITY.
The future for European energy security /. London , 1985. 177 p. : ISBN 0-86187-573-7
NYPL [JLE 86-1018]

Johansen, Robert C. Toward an alternative security system . New York, N.Y. , c1983. 57 p. ; ISBN 0-911646-12-5 (pbk.) : LC Card 83-215670 DDC 355/.03 19
UA10.5 .J64 1983

Shepherd, William G. The ultimate deterrent . New York , 1986. x, 137 p. ; ISBN 0-275-92368-1 (alk. paper) : LC Card 86-20486 DDC 355/.03 19
UA10.5 .S524 1986 ***NYPL [JLE 87-884]***

Stern, Jonathan P. Soviet oil and gas exports to the West . Aldershot, Hants, England , Brookfield, Vt., USA , c1987. xi, 123 p. : ISBN 0-566-05124-9 : LC Card 86-32772 DDC 382/.4228/0947 19
HD9575.S652 S74 1987

Tinbergen, Jan, 1903- Warfare and welfare . Brighton, Sussex , New York , 1987. xiv, 189 p. ; ISBN 0-312-00957-7 (St. Martin's) : LC Card 87-9625 DDC 361.6/1 19
HB846 .T55 1987

National Seminar of Senior Research Workers on Public Enterprise (1982 : Hyderabad, India) Public enterprises in India . Bombay , 1983. xxii, 524 p. ; LC Card 83-905617 DDC 354.5409/2 19
HD4293 .P793 1983 ***NYPL [JLD 87-723]***

National Seminar on Migrant Labour and Related Issues (1985 : Gandhi Labour Institute, Ahmedabad) Migrant labour and related issues /. New Delhi , c1987. xii, 334 p. : ISBN 81-204-0199-9 : LC Card 87-901172
HD5856.I4 M54 1985

National Seminar on Population, Employment, and Development Planning in Sierra Leone (1980 : Freetown, Sierra Leone) Contributed papers to the National Seminar on Population, Employment, and Development Planning in Sierra Leone : held in Freetown from 28th April to 1st May 1980 / organized jointly by the International Labour Organization and the Government of Sierra Leone. Freetown, Sierra Leone : Population Section, Central Planning Unit, Ministry of Development and Economic Planning, <[1980- > v. <2 > : ill. ; 30 cm. "September 1980." Includes bibliographies. LC Card 87-163849 DDC 304.6/0966/4 19
1. Sierra Leone - Population - Congresses. 2. Sierra Leone - Economic conditions - 1961- - Congresses. 3. Sierra Leone - Social conditions - 1961- - Congresses. I. International Labour Organisation. II. Sierra Leone. Ministry of Development and Economic Planning. Population Section. III. Title.
HB3666.9.A3 N38 1980

National Seminar on the Mid-Year Review of the Economy 1986-87 (1986 : India International Centre) Adiseshiah, Malcolm S. Mid year review of the economy, 1986-87 /. New Delhi , 1987. 193 p. : ISBN 81-7062-016-3 : LC Card 87-900477 DDC 330.954/052 19
HC435.2 .A648 1987

NATIONAL SERVICE - BRAZIL.
Fundação Projeto Rondon. Diretrizes de planejamento . [Brasília , 1982] [21] leaves ; LC Card 85-186578
HD4870.B6 F86 1982

NATIONAL SERVICE - GERMANY, WEST.
Wer fürchtet sich vor'm schwarzen Mann? niemand! und wenn er kommt? dann lesen wir . Velbert , c1985. 95 p. : ISBN 3-922319-08-4 : LC Card 86-206116 DDC 355.2/2363/0943 19
HD4870.G3 W47 1985

NATIONAL SERVICE - GUYANA.

NATIONAL SERVICE - QUÉBEC (PROVINCE)
Bisaillon, Guy. Service national du Québec . Québec [1981] 54, [4] leaves ; LC Card 82-212578
HD4870.C2 B57 1981

NATIONAL SOCIALISTS - BIOGRAPHY.
Smelser, Ronald, 1942- Robert Ley, Hitler's labor leader /. New York , 1988. p. cm. ISBN 0-85496-161-5 : LC Card 87-20960 DDC 331/.092/4 B 19
HD8453.L49 S64 1988

National styles of regulation . Vogel, David, 1947- Ithaca, N.Y. , 1986. 325 p. ; ISBN 0-8014-1658-2 LC Card 85-21332 DDC 363.7/056/0941 19
HC260.E5 V64 1986 ***NYPL [JLE 86-2434]***

National survey of entrepreneurial education.
National Survey of entreprenuerial [sic] education /. [Washington, D.C.?] . v. : LC Card 86-603453 DDC 658/.022/071173 19
HF1131 .N325 1986

National Survey of entreprenuerial [sic] education / edited by George T. Solomon. 3rd ed. [Washington, D.C.?] : U. S. Small Business Administration : National Center for Research in Vocational Education : v. : ill., forms ; 28 cm. Description based on vol. 4. Distributed to depository libraries in microfiche. Includes bibliographies. Item 901-B (microfiche) CONTENTS. - v. 4. Nebraska, New Hampshire, New Jersey, New Mexico, New York, Nevada, North Carolina, North Dakota. LC Card 86-603453 DDC 658/.022/071173 19
1. Business education - United States - Curricula. 2. Small business - Management - Study and teaching - United States. 3. Business enterprises - Study and teaching - United States. 4. Entrepreneurship - Study and teaching - United States. I. Solomon, George T. II. United States. Small Business Administration. III. Title: National survey of entrepreneurial education.
HF1131 .N325 1986

National Symposium on the Prevention of Leading Work-related Diseases and Injuries (1985 : Atlanta, Ga.) Proposed national strategies for the prevention of leading work-related diseases and injuries. [Washington, D.C.] , 1986- v. <1 > ; LC Card 87-111984 DDC 363.1/17/0973 19
HD7262.5.U6 P75 1986

National Telemarketing Center. Telemarketing . [S.l.] , c1987. [64] p. ; LC Card 87-154058 DDC 658.8/5 19
HF5415.1265 .T44 1987

National Textbook Company.
Vox Modern Spanish and English dictionary . Lincolnwood, Ill. , c1986. xxxiv, 487, 45, 484 p. : ISBN 0-8442-7990-0 LC Card 86-61160
NYPL [*R-RGK 86-7059]

Vox new college Spanish and English dictionary . Lincolnwood, Ill., U. S.A. , c1984. xix, 1456, 60 p. : ISBN 0-8442-7998-6 (plain-edge ed.) : LC Card 84-61106 DDC 463/.21 19
PC4640 .V696 1984
NYPL [*R-RGK 85-1500]

National Textbook language dictionaries.
Vox new college Spanish and English dictionary . Lincolnwood, Ill., U. S.A. , c1984. xix, 1456, 60 p. : ISBN 0-8442-7998-6 (plain-edge ed.) : LC Card 84-61106 DDC 463/.21 19
PC4640 .V696 1984
NYPL [*R-RGK 85-1500]

NATIONAL WOMEN'S TRADE UNION LEAGUE OF AMERICA - HISTORY.
Payne, Elizabeth Anne, 1943- Reform, labor, and feminism . Urbana , c1988. p. cm. ISBN 0-252-01445-6 (alk. paper) LC Card 87-10794 DDC 331.88/092/4 B 19
HD6079.2.U5 P38 1988

National Workshop on Productivity Enhancement in Indian Cement Industry-- a Pragmatic Approach to Modernisation, 19-20 March 1986 . National Workshop on Productivity Enhancement in Indian Cement Industry-- a Pragmatic Approach to Modernisation (1986 : New Delhi, India) New Delhi [1986] 42 p. : LC Card 87-901966 DDC 338.4/766694/0954 19
HD9622.I52 N34 1986

National Workshop on Productivity Enhancement in Indian Cement Industry-- a Pragmatic Approach to Modernisation (1986 : New Delhi, India) National Workshop on Productivity Enhancement in Indian Cement Industry-- a Pragmatic Approach to Modernisation, 19-20 March 1986 : proceedings. New Delhi : National Council for Cement and Building Materials, [1986] 42 p. : ill. ; 30 cm. "Organised by National Council for Cement and Building Materials (NCB) jointly with National Productivity Council; cosponsored

by Cement Manufacturers' Association"--T.p. verso. "Productivity Board for Cement Industry"--Cover. LC Card 87-901966 DDC 338.4/766694/0954 19
1. Cement industries - India - Congresses. 2. Industrial productivity - India - Congresses. I. National Council for Cement and Building Materials (India). II. National Productivity Council (India). III. Cement Manufacturers' Association (India). IV. Title.
HD9622.I52 N34 1986

National Workshop on Project Evaluation (1984 : National Institute for Public Administration, Lusaka, Zambia) Collected papers of the National Workshop on Project Evaluation, held at the National Institute for Public Administration, 10-14 December, 1984. [Lusaka] : University Workshop on Project Evaluation, 1985. 1 v. in various pagings ; 29 cm. Cover title. At head of title: The University of Zambia. Organized by the University of Zambia. "February 1985." Includes bibliographies. LC Card 85-981123 DDC 338.96894/0068 19
1. Economic development projects - Zambia - Evaluation - Congresses. 2. Agricultural development projects - Zambia - Evaluation - Congresses. I. University of Zambia. II. Title.
HC915.Z9 E446 1984

National Workshop on Rural Development (1979 : Mogadishu, Somalia) Somalia's rural development strategy, 1981-1990. Mogadishu, Somalia [1981?] vii, 45, [49] leaves : LC Card 83-980772 DDC 338.1/86773 19
HD2125.Z8 S65 1981 ***NYPL [JLG 86-58]***

National Workshop on Self Reliance and Self Sufficiency in the Nigerian Economy (1978 : University of Ibadan) Self-reliance and self-sufficiency : papers presented at the National Workshop on Self Reliance and Self Sufficiency in the Nigerian Economy. [Ibadan, Nigeria] : Nigerian Institute of Social and Economic Research and the Federal Ministry of Finance, 1979. 156 p. : ill. ; 22 cm. Workshop held between Sept. 10 and 13, 1978, at the University of Ibadan. Bibliography: p. 75. LC Card 87-402546 DDC 338.9669 19
1. Nigeria - Economic policy - Congresses. 2. Nigeria - Economic conditions - 1970- - Congresses. 3. Agriculture - Economic aspects - Nigeria - Congresses. 4. Nigeria - Foreign economic relations - Congresses. I. Nigerian Institute of Social and Economic Research. II. Nigeria. Federal Ministry of Finance. III. Title.
HC1055 .N386 1978

National Workshop on Urban Water Demand Management (1986 : Alexander Library, Perth Cultural Centre) Working papers for the National Workshop on Urban Water Demand Management : Alexander Library, Perth Cultural Centre / National Workshop on Urban Water Demand Management, Perth, Western Australia, 29 April to 1 May 1986 ; sponsored by Australian Water Resources Council, Western Australian Water Resources Council in co-operation with CSIRO, Division of Groundwater Research, [and] major urban water and sewerage authorities of Australia. Leederville, WA : Western Australian Water Resources Council, [1986] xii, 657 p. : ill. ; 30 cm. Includes bibliographies. LC Card 87-119946 DDC 333.91/2/0994 19
1. Municipal water supply - Australia - Congresses. I. Australian Water Resources Council. II. Western Australian Water Resources Council. III. Commonwealth Scientific and Industrial Research Organization (Australia). Division of Groundwater Research. IV. Title.
HD4465.A8 N37 1986

The national world of local government /. Rhodes, R. A. W. London , Boston , 1986. xviii, 441 p. ; ISBN 0-04-320170-9 (alk. paper) LC Card 85-15103 DDC 352.041 19
JS3137 .R49 1986 ***NYPL [JLD 86-1931]***

Nationale Wege der Inflationsbekämpfung / von Hartmut Berg ... [et al.] ; herausgegeben von Josua Werner. Berlin : Duncker & Humblot, c1986. 223 p. : ill. ; 24 cm. (Schriften des Vereins für Socialpolitik, Gesellschaft für Wirtschafts- und Sozialwissenschaften . n.F., Bd. 157) Includes one article in English. Papers presented at meetings of the Wirtschaftspolitischer Ausschuss held in Innsbruck in 1983 and Freiburg i. Br. in 1984. Includes bibliographies. CONTENTS. - Inflation and counter-inflation policies in the Netherlands / by Pieter Korteweg -- Zur Problematik der niederländischen Strategie der Inflationsbekämpfung / von Hartmut Berg -- Der österreichische Weg der Inflationsbekämpfung / von Hans Seidel -- Kritische Anmerkungen zur österreichischen Strategie der Inflationsbekämpfung / von Hans-Rudolf Peters -- Inflation und Inflationsbekämpfung in Grossbritannien / von Klaus H. Hennings -- Inflation und Inflationsbekämpfung im internationalen Vergleich / von Werner Zohlnhöfer -- Die französische Stabilisierungspolitik (1945-1985) / von François Bilger -- Stabilitätspolitische Charakteristika im Ländervergleich Frankreich-Deutschland / von Joachim Klaus. ISBN 3-428-06077-6 LC Card 87-132310 DDC 332.4/1/094 19
1. Economic stabilization - Europe - Congresses. 2. Europe - Economic policy - Congresses. 3. Inflation (Finance) - Europe - Congresses. 4. Europe - Economic conditions - 1945- - Congresses. I. Berg, Hartmut. II. Werner, Josua. III. Gesellschaft für Wirtschafts- und Sozialwissenschaft, Verein für Socialpolitik. Wirtschaftspolitischer Ausschuss. IV. Series.
HC240 .N315 1986

Nationales Forschungsprogramm Mechanismen und Entwicklung der Schweizerischen Wirts chaft. Nydegger, Alfred. Investitionen und Innovationen in kleineren Industriebetrieben . Diessenhofen , c1983. viii, 317 p. : ISBN 3-7253-0196-4 LC Card 83-224277 DDC 658.1/592 19
HG4027.7 .N93 1983 ***NYPL [JLD 87-633]***

Nationales Forschungsprogramm Mechanismen und Entwicklung der Schweizerischen Wirtschaft.
Genberg, Hans. Influences externes sur l'économie suisse en changes fixes et flottants /. Genève , c1985. ii, 202 p. : ISBN 2-8257-0127-0 : LC Card 85-235579 DDC 332.4/5609494 19
HG3963 .G46 1985 ***NYPL [JLD 86-2381]***

Makromodelle und Wirtschaftspolitik . Grüsch , c1985. 120 p. : ISBN 3-7253-0250-2 : LC Card 85-208009
HC397 .M26 1985

Oberhänsli, Urs. Altersvorsorge, Kapitalschwemme oder Kapitalmangel? . Bern , c1986. xii, 222 p. : ISBN 3-258-03578-4 : LC Card 86-149614
HD7105.35.S9 O24 1986

Nationalisation of Guyana's bauxite . Shahabuddeen, M., 1931- Georgetown, Guyana , 1981. xvii, 306 p. ; LC Card 82-145233 DDC 338.2/74926 19
HD9539.A63 G888 1981
NYPL [Sc E 86-189]

NATIONALISM - AFRICA.
Dia, Mamadou. [Nations africaines et solidarité mondiale. English.] The African nations and world solidarity /. Westport, Conn. , 1987, c1961. xii, 145 p. ; ISBN 0-313-24569-X (lib. bdg. : alk. paper) LC Card 86-25734 DDC 330.96/03 19
HC800 .D5213 1987

NATIONALISM AND NATIONALITY. see **NATIONALISM.**

NATIONALISM - EGYPT - HISTORY.
Beinin, Joel, 1948- Workers on the Nile . Princeton, N.J. , c1987. xix, 488 p. : ISBN 0-691-05506-8 (alk. paper) : LC Card 87-45510 DDC 305.5/62/0962 19
HD8786 .B45 1987

NATIONALISM - INDIA - BARDOLI TALUKA - HISTORY.
Mehta, Shirin. The peasantry and nationalism . New Delhi , 1984. x, 215 p. : LC Card 84-901701 DDC 322.4/4/095475 19
HD1339.I4 M44 1984 ***NYPL [JLD 86-4424]***

NATIONALISM - INDIA - HISTORY.
Chatterji, Rakhahari, 1943- Working class and the nationalist movement in India . New Delhi , c1984. ix, 215 p. ; LC Card 84-902674 DDC 322.4/4/0954 19
HD8686 .C47 1984 ***NYPL [JLD 87-709]***

NATIONALISM - IRELAND.
Russell, George William, 1867-1935. Co-operation and nationality . Dublin , c1982. 103 p. ; ISBN 0-7165-0335-2 (pbk.) LC Card 82-192895 DDC 334/.683/09417 19
HD1491.I6 R87 1982 ***NYPL [JLD 86-2358]***

NATIONALISM - MEXICO.
Serrano Illescas, Alfonso. Pobre patria! /. México, D.F. , 1982. 132 p. ; ISBN 968-409-161-3 LC Card 85-122377
HC135 .S368 1982

NATIONALISM - PORTUGAL - HISTORY.
Ferreira, António Fonseca. A acumulação capitalista em Portugal . Porto , 1977. 156 p. ; LC Card 85-194898
HF3696 .F47 1977

The Nationality structure of the international banking market and the role of interbank operations. Basle : Bank for International Settlements, Monetary and Economic Dept., [1985] 12 leaves ; 30 cm. Cover title. "May 1985." LC Card 86-139771 DDC 332.1/5 19
1. Banks and banking, International. 2. Banks and banking, Foreign. I. Bank for International Settlements. Monetary and Economic Dept.
HG3881 .N33 1985

NATIONALIZATION. see **GOVERNMENT OWNERSHIP.**

Nationalökonomie und Realität . Dichmann, Werner. Berlin , c1983. 488 p. ; ISBN 3-428-05517-9 LC Card 84-172295
HB71 .D48 1983

Nationalsozialistische Arbeiter-Partei. see **Nationalsozialistische Deutsche Arbeiter-Partei.**

NATIONALSOZIALISTISCHE DEUTSCHE ARBEITER-PARTEI - HISTORY.
Hayes, Peter, 1946- Industry and ideology . Cambridge [Cambridgeshire] , New York , 1987. xxviii, 411 p. : ISBN 0-521-32948-5 LC Card 86-28388 DDC 338.7/66/00943 19
HD9654.9.I5 H39 1987

Nationalsozialistische deutsche Arbeiterpartei. see **Nationalsozialistische Deutsche Arbeiter-Partei.**

Nationalstrafe. Studer, Stefan. Nationalstrasse, Nationalstrafe, oder, Die Demokratie bleibt auf der Strecke /. Zürich , 1985. 191 p. : ISBN 3-85869-037-6 : LC Card 86-129406
HE363.S92 S83 1985

Nationalstrasse, Nationalstrafe. Studer, Stefan. Nationalstrasse, Nationalstrafe, oder, Die Demokratie bleibt auf der Strecke /. Zürich , 1985. 191 p. : ISBN 3-85869-037-6 : LC Card 86-129406
HE363.S92 S83 1985

Nationalstrasse, Nationalstrafe, oder, Die Demokratie bleibt auf der Strecke /. Studer, Stefan. Zürich , 1985. 191 p. : ISBN 3-85869-037-6 : LC Card 86-129406
HE363.S92 S83 1985

Nationella övertaganden av utländska dotterbolag . Mattsson, Jan. Stockholm [1982] 213 p. : ISBN 91-1-827592-3 LC Card 83-122459
HD2932 .M38 1982

NATIONS, SMALL. see **STATES, SMALL.**

Nations Unies. see **United Nations.**

NATIVE RACES.
Schmidt, Aurel, 1935- Der Fremde bin ich selber . Basel , c1982. 261 p. : ISBN 3-85787-103-2 : LC Card 83-109021
HC79.E5 S284 1982

NATO. see **North Atlantic Treaty Organization.**

NATO Advanced Study Institute on Intelligent Decision Support in Process Environments (1985 : San Miniato, Italy) Intelligent decision support in process environments / edited by Erik Hollnagel, Giuseppe Mancini, David D. Woods. Berlin ; New York : Published in cooperation with NATO Scientific Affairs Division [by] Springer-Verlag, c1986. xv, 524 p. : ill. ; 25 cm. (NATO ASI series. Series F, Computer and systems sciences . v. 21) "Proceedings of the NATO Advanced Study Institute on Intelligent Decision Support in Process Environments held in San Miniato, Italy, September 16-27, 1985"--T.p. verso. Bibliography: p. [469]-506. ISBN 0-387-13922-2 (U. S.) LC Card 86-6742 DDC 658.4/03 19
1. Decision-making - Congresses. 2. Artificial intelligence - Congresses. I. Hollnagel, Erik, 1941-. II. Mancini, Giuseppe, 1940-. III. Woods, David D., 1952-. IV. North Atlantic Treaty Organization. Scientific Affairs Division. V. Title.
T57.95 .N37 1985 ***NYPL [JFE 86-4847]***

Nats͡ionalizats͡iia i gossektor v razvivai͡ushchikhsi͡a stranakh : referativnyĭ sbornik / [otvetstvennyĭ redaktor sbornika Makarova S.M.]. Moskva : Akademii͡a nauk

SSSR, In-t nauch. informatsii po obshchestvennym naukam, 1986. 210 p. ; 20 cm. (Seriia Ekonomika razvivaiushchikhsia stran Azii i Afriki) Includes bibliographies. LC Card 87-165820
1. Government ownership - Asia. 2. Government business enterprises - Asia. 3. Government ownership - Developing countries. 4. Government business enterprises - Developing countries. I. Makarova, S. M. II. Series.
HD4276 .N38 1986

Natsional'nyi komitet SSSR po avtomaticheskomu upravleniiu. Litovskaia territorial'naia gruppa.
Razrabotka i issledovanie algoritmov dinamicheskoi klassifikatsii protsessov . Vil'nius , 1979. 93 p. : LC Card 82-150323
HD38 .S715 vyp. 37 T57.83

Shpilevskii, E. Printsipy dinamicheskoi klassifikatsii stokhasticheskikh protsessov i sistem . Vil'nius , 1978. 138 p. ; LC Card 81-173567
HD38 .S715 vyp. 28 QA274

Sistema raspoznavaniia ritmogramm serdtsa . Vil'nius , 1980. 55 p. : LC Card 81-194159
HD38 .S715 vyp. 49 QP112.5.C3

TSifrovye metody i algoritmy obrabotki signalov . Vil'nius , 1986. 120 p. : LC Card 86-232937
HD38 .S715 vyp. 73 TK5102.5

Nattagh, Nima. Agriculture & regional development in Iran / by Nima Nattagh. Wisbech, Cambridgeshire, England : Middle East & North African Studies Press, 1986. 105 p. : ill., maps ; 21 cm. (Menas studies in continuity & change in the Middle East and North Africa) Bibliography: p. 97-102. Includes index. ISBN 0-906559-26-X (pbk.) : LC Card 86-230845 DDC 338.1/0955 19
1. Agriculture - Economic aspects - Iran. 2. Agriculture and state - Iran. 3. Regional planning - Iran. 4. Iran - Population, Rural. I. Title. II. Title: Agriculture and regional development in Iran. III. Series: Meapec studies in continuity & change in the Middle East & North Africa.
HD1565.2 .N37 1986

Nattrass, Jill. Informal Black business in Durban : a socio-economic study of informal business in Inanda and Clermont / by Jill Nattrass, Humphrey Glass. Pietermaritzburg, Natal, South Africa : Natal Town and Regional Planning Commission, 1986. xviii, 138 p. : ill. ; 30 cm. (Natal town and regional planning supplementary report . v. 18) Bibliography: p. 136-138. ISBN 0-909232-58-X (pbk.) : LC Card 87-112836 DDC 381 19
1. Black business enterprises - South Africa - Durban. 2. Informal sector (Economics) - South Africa - Durban. 3. Blacks - Employment - South Africa - Durban. I. Glass, Humphrey. II. Title. III. Series.
HD2346.S632 D86 1986

NATURAL BEAUTY CONSERVATION. see **LANDSCAPE PROTECTION.**

NATURAL CALAMITIES. see **NATURAL DISASTERS.**

NATURAL DISASTERS - ECONOMIC ASPECTS.
Hirshleifer, Jack. Economic behaviour in adversity /. Chicago , 1987. ix, 310 p. ; ISBN 0-226-34282-4 : LC Card 87-19846 DDC 330.9 19
HC79.D45 H57 1987

NATURAL FOOD. see **FOOD, NATURAL.**

NATURAL FOODS INDUSTRY - QUÉBEC (PROVINCE)
Fortin, Andrée. Le Rézo . Québec, Québec , 1985. 282 p. : ISBN 2-89224-052-2 LC Card 86-225353
HD3290.A3 Q435 1985

NATURAL FOODS INDUSTRY - UNITED STATES.
Diet foods . Stamford, Conn., U. S.A. , c1986. xv, 195 leaves : ISBN 0-89336-487-8 (pbk.) LC Card 87-160485 DDC 381/.4166463/0973 19
HD9005 .D53 1986

NATURAL GAS. see **GAS, NATURAL.**

Natural gas liquids and the Soviet gas processing industry /. Sagers, Matthew J. Washington, D.C. [1986] viii, 72, 2 p. : LC Card 87-601287 DDC 338.4/766573 19
HD9581.2.L573 S657 1986

Natural gas markets and contracts / edited by Rolf Golombek, Michael Hoel, and Jon Vislie. Amsterdam ; New York : North-Holland ; x, 320 p. : ill. ; 24 cm. (Contributions to economic analysis. 161) Includes bibliographies and indexes. ISBN 0-444-70206-7 (U. S.) LC Card 87-5061 DDC 380.1/42285/094 19
1. Gas industry - Europe. 2. Gas industry. I. Golombek, Rolf, 1959-. II. Hoel, Michael. III. Vislie, Jon, 1946-. IV. Series.
HD9581.E82 N37 1987 ***NYPL [TB (Contributions to economic analysis. v.161)]***

Natural gas trade in transition / Bijan Mossavar-Rahmani, editor. Cambridge, MA : Energy and Environmental Policy Center, Harvard University, c1987. 91 p. ; 23 cm. (Harvard international energy studies . no. 1) Includes bibliographical references. ISBN 0-942781-00-7 (pbk.) LC Card 87-81051 DDC 338.2/7285 19
1. Gas industry. I. Mossavar-Rahmani, Bijan. II. Series.
HD9581.A2 N38 1987

NATURAL GAS WELLS. see **GAS WELLS.**

Natural resource bureaucracy and rural poverty . West, Patrick C. Ann Arbor, MI , c1982. xiii, 168 p. : LC Card 83-102928 DDC 333.7/16/0973 19
HD1761 .W423 1982 ***NYPL [JLE 86-4095]***

Natural resource economics : policy problems and contemporary analysis / edited by Daniel W. Bromley. Boston : Kluwer-Nijhoff : Distributors for the U. S. and Canada, Kluwer Academic Publishers, c1986. xiv, 234 p. : ill. ; 24 cm. (Recent economic thought series) Includes bibliographies and index. ISBN 0-89838-203-3 LC Card 85-24215 DDC 333.7 19
1. Natural resources - Addresses, essays, lectures. 2. Economic policy - Addresses, essays, lectures. 3. Externalities (Economics) - Addresses, essays, lectures. I. Bromley, Daniel W., 1940-. II. Series.
HC59 .N318 1986 ***NYPL [JLE 86-3471]***

Natural resource economics . Conrad, Jon M. Cambridge [Cambridgeshire] , New York , 1987. x, 231 p. : ISBN 0-521-33188-9 LC Card 87-11582 DDC 333.7 19
HC59 .C693 1987

The natural resource industries of Maine . Colgan, Charles S. [Augusta, Me.] [1986] 135 p. : LC Card 87-620550 DDC 338.09741 19
HD9007.M2 C64 1986

Natural resource policy and income distribution /. Rose, Adam Zachery. Baltimore , c1988. xvi, 139 p. : ISBN 0-8018-3523-2 (alk. paper) LC Card 87-2788 DDC 333.7/0973 19
HC103.7 .R67 1988

NATURAL RESOURCES - ADDRESSES, ESSAYS, LECTURES.
Natural resource economics . Boston , c1986. xiv, 234 p. : ISBN 0-89838-203-3 LC Card 85-24215 DDC 333.7 19
HC59 .N318 1986 ***NYPL [JLE 86-3471]***

NATURAL RESOURCES - AFRICA.
Lewis, Lawrence. African environments and resources /. Boston , 1987. p. cm. ISBN 0-04-916010-9 (alk. paper) LC Card 87-16751 DDC 333.7/096 19
HC800 .L48 1987

Natural resources and the human environment for food and agriculture in Africa. Rome , 1986. iv, 83 p. : ISBN 92-5-102354-9 (pbk.) LC Card 86-222103 DDC 338.1/096 19
HC800 .N34 1986

NATURAL RESOURCES - AFRICA, SUB-SAHARAN - MANAGEMENT.
United States. Congress. House. Committee on Science and Technology. Prospects for sustainable development in Sub-Saharan Africa . Washington , 1986. vii, 88 p. ; LC Card 86-603140 DDC 338.967 19
HD2117 .U48 1986

NATURAL RESOURCES - AMAZON RIVER VALLEY REGION.
Meirelles Filho, João Carlos, 1960- Amazônia--o que fazer? /. São Paulo , 1986. 85 p., [1] folded leaf of plates : LC Card 86-233275
HC187.5 .M45 1986

Natural resources and economic development in Central America . Leonard, H. Jeffrey. New Brunswick, N.J., U. S.A. , c1987. xxii, 279 p. : ISBN 0-88738-722-5 (pbk.) LC Card 87-10871 DDC 333.7/09728 19
HC141 .L44 1987

Natural resources and the human environment for food and agriculture in Africa. Rome : Food and Agriculture Organization of the United Nations, 1986. iv, 83 p. : ill. ; 30 cm. (FAO environment and energy paper . 6) Includes bibliographical references. ISBN 92-5-102354-9 (pbk.) LC Card 86-222103 DDC 338.1/096 19
1. Natural resources - Africa. 2. Food supply - Africa. 3. Agriculture - Economic aspects - Africa. I. Food and Agriculture Organization of the United Nations. II. Series.
HC800 .N34 1986

Natural resources and the macroeconomy / edited by J. Peter Neary and Sweder van Wijnbergen. Oxford, UK : B. Blackwell, 1986. xvi, 352 p. : ill. ; 24 cm. "Proceedings of the conference 'Natural Resources and the Macroeconomy,' organized by the Centre for Economic Policy Research, London, on June 10-11, 1985"--Pref. Includes bibliographies and index. ISBN 0-631-15087-0 LC Card 86-673943
1. Nonrenewable natural resources - Congresses. 2. Petroleum industry and trade - Economic aspects - Congresses. I. Neary, J. Peter. II. Wijnbergen, Sweder van, 1951-. III. Centre for Economic Policy Research (Great Britain).
HC59 .N3194x 1986b

NATURAL RESOURCES - ASIA.
Asia-Pacific report . Honolulu, Hawaii , 1986. x, 104 p. : ISBN 0-86638-071-X (pbk.) LC Card 85-27538 DDC 909/.09823/0828 19
HC412 .A7242 1986 ***NYPL [JLF 87-143]***

NATURAL RESOURCES - AUSTRALIA - STATISTICS.
Australian resources in a world context . Canberra , 1982. iv, 87 p. : ISBN 0-642-05273-5 (pbk.) LC Card 86-673749
HF3941.5 .A97x 1982

NATURAL RESOURCES - BELIZE.
Belize . Belize City, Belize , 1984. xvi, 151 p. : LC Card 86-136310 DDC 333.7/097282 19
HC142 .B447 1984 ***NYPL [JLF 87-170]***

NATURAL RESOURCES - BRAZIL - BRASÍLIA REGION.
Franz, Paulo Renato Ferreira. Região geoeconômica de Brasília . Planaltina-DF [Brazil] , 1985. 70 p. : LC Card 87-143606 DDC 338.1/3/098174 19
HD1875.B7 F7 1985

NATURAL RESOURCES - BRAZIL - PARANÁ RIVER VALLEY (GOIÁS)
Projeto de Desenvolvimento Integrado da Bacia do Araguaia-Tocantins. Plano de desenvolvimento da área-programa do Vale do Paraná /. Brasília , 1985. 128 p., [8] folded leaves of plates : LC Card 86-199833
HC188.P36 P76 1985

NATURAL RESOURCES - BRITISH COLUMBIA - MANAGEMENT.
Dorcey, Anthony H. J., 1944- Bargaining in the governance of Pacific coastal resources . Vancouver, B.C. , c1986. xvi, 219 p. : ISBN 0-920146-34-1 (pbk.) LC Card 86-222720 DDC 333.91/7/09711 19
HC117.B8 D67 1986

NATURAL RESOURCES - BRITISH COLUMBIA - SLOCAN RIVER VALLEY.
Biophysical resources of the Slocan Valley /. Victoria, B.C. , 1982. ix, 102 p. : ISBN 0-7718-8310-2 (pbk.) LC Card 84-117204 DDC 333.7/09711/43 19
HC117.B8 B46 1982

NATURAL RESOURCES - CANADA.
Canada's environment . [Ottawa] , 1986. 20 p. : ISBN 0-662-14571-2 (pbk.) LC Card 86-222737 DDC 333.7/0971 19
HC120.E5 C345 1986

NATURAL RESOURCES - CANADA, NORTHERN.
Saltykovskaia, L. V. (Liliia Veniaminovna) Blizhnii Sever Kanady . Moskva , 1983. 78, [2] p. : LC Card 83-196848
HC117.N48 S25 1983

NATURAL RESOURCES - CENTRAL AMERICA.
Leonard, H. Jeffrey. Natural resources and economic development in Central America . New Brunswick, N.J., U. S.A. , c1987. xxii, 279 p. : ISBN 0-88738-722-5 (pbk.) LC Card 87-10871

DDC 333.7/09728 19
HC141 .L44 1987

NATURAL RESOURCES - COLOMBIA.
Patiño, Víctor Manuel. Los recursos naturales de Colombia . Bogotá , 1980. 149 p. : ISBN 84-8277-057-8 LC Card 86-208425 DDC 333.7/09861 19
HC197.5 .P3 1980

NATURAL RESOURCES - CONGRESSES.
Demands on rural lands . Boulder, Colo. , 1987. xvi, 336 p. : ISBN 0-8133-7361-1 (pbk. : alk. paper) LC Card 87-50751 DDC 333.76/13 19
HD105 .D43 1987

The management and development of land and seabed resources . London [1985] 139 p. : ISBN 0-903577-29-1 (pbk.) LC Card 86-104896 DDC 333.7 19
HD105 .M36 1985

The Management and development of natural resources . London [1985] 192 p. : ISBN 0-903577-33-X (pbk.) LC Card 86-206154 DDC 333.7 19
HC13 .M35 1985

NATURAL RESOURCES - CONSERVATION.
see **CONSERVATION OF NATURAL RESOURCES.**

NATURAL RESOURCES - COSTA RICA.
Bonilla, Alexander. Situación ambiental de Costa Rica /. [San José] [1985] 271 p. : ISBN 997-7590-57-5 LC Card 86-156609
HC143.Z9 E52 1985

NATURAL RESOURCES - DEVELOPING COUNTRIES.
Hagemann, Hermann. Die Formierung der rohstoffpolitischen Forderungen der Entwicklungsländer auf der Ebene der Vereinten Nationen bis zur ersten Konferenz für Handel und Entwicklung (UNCTAD 1) 1946 /. Münster , 1983. xix, 384, [14], 42 p. : ISBN 3-923676-11-5 LC Card 84-172079
HC59.7 .H27 1983

Population growth and economic development . Madison, Wis. , 1987. xiii, 702 p. ; ISBN 0-299-11130-X : LC Card 86-40447 DDC 338.9/009172/4 19
HB884 .P66547 1987

NATURAL RESOURCES - DEVELOPING COUNTRIES - MANAGEMENT.
Sustainable resource development in the Third World /. Boulder , 1987. vi, 177 p. : ISBN 0-8133-7522-3 (alk. paper) LC Card 87-20137 DDC 333.7/15/091724 19
HC59.7 .S8826 1987

Uphoff, Norman Thomas. Local institutional development . West Hartford, CT , c1986. xv, 421 p. ; ISBN 0-931816-45-9 LC Card 86-15288 DDC 302.3/5 19
HC59.7 .U64 1986 ***NYPL [JLE 87-1200]***

NATURAL RESOURCES - DOMINICAN REPUBLIC.
La República Dominicana . McLean, Va. , 1981. xii, 134 p. : LC Card 86-218146
HC153.5 .R45 1981

NATURAL RESOURCES - ECONOMIC ASPECTS.
Bartov, Vladimir Fotievich. Kont͡septsii vzaimodeĭstvii͡a ėkonomiki i prirody /. Moskva , 1984. 157 p. ; LC Card 84-225876
HC79.E5 B369 1984

NATURAL RESOURCES - FINLAND - MANAGEMENT.
Environmental policies in Finland . [Helsinki] [1986] 542 p. : ISBN 951-46-9823-1 LC Card 87-100734 DDC 363.7/056/094897 19
HC340.2.Z9 E52 1986

NATURAL RESOURCES - FLORIDA - MANAGEMENT.
The Saddlebrook papers . [Fort Lauderdale] [Tallahassee] [1985] v leaves, 177 p. : LC Card 86-621089 DDC 338.9759 19
HC107.F63 E547 1985

NATURAL RESOURCES - GERMANY (WEST)
Gesamtkonzeption nachwachsende Rohstoffe des Bundesministeriums für Ernährung, Landwirtschaft und Forsten . Münster-Hiltrup , 1983. vi, 196 p. : ISBN 3-7843-0202-5 : LC Card 84-126491
HD9502.G42 G47 1983

NATURAL RESOURCES - GOVERNMENT POLICY.
Tietenberg, Thomas H. Environmental and natural resource economics /. Glenview, Ill. , c1988. 559 p. : ISBN 0-673-18945-7 LC Card 87-23250 DDC 333.7 19
HC79.E5 T525 1988

NATURAL RESOURCES - GOVERNMENT POLICY - AFRICA.
Lewis, Lawrence. African environments and resources /. Boston , 1987. p. cm. ISBN 0-04-916010-9 (alk. paper) LC Card 87-16751 DDC 333.7/096 19
HC800 .L48 1987

NATURAL RESOURCES - GOVERNMENT POLICY - INDIA.
Sukhwal, B. L., 1929- India . New York , 1987. viii, 200 p. : ISBN 0-938719-13-0 LC Card 86-81410 DDC 333.7/0954 19
HC433.5 .S85 1987

NATURAL RESOURCES - GOVERNMENT POLICY - SWEDEN.
Höglund, Bengt. Spelet om resurserna i den svenska blandekonomin /. Lund , c1984. 227 p. : ISBN 91-7504-041-7 : LC Card 84-200450
HC373.5 .H64 1984

NATURAL RESOURCES - HONDURAS.
Imagen de la estructura económica-social y explotación de los recursos naturales /. Tegucigalpa, D.C., Honduras, C.A. , 1973. viii, 334 p. : LC Card 86-177356
HC145 .I52 1973

NATURAL RESOURCES - INDIA.
Sukhwal, B. L., 1929- India . New York , 1987. viii, 200 p. : ISBN 0-938719-13-0 LC Card 86-81410 DDC 333.7/0954 19
HC433.5 .S85 1987

NATURAL RESOURCES - INDIA - SULTANPUR.
Resource analysis for integrated development, Sultanpur District, Uttar Pradesh. New Delhi , 1986. xii, 436 p. : LC Card 87-902515
HC437.S85 R47 1986

NATURAL RESOURCES - JUVENILE FILMS.
What's a natural resource? [motion picture] /. Los Angeles, Calif. , 1986, c1987. 1 film reel (15 1/2 min.) : LC Card 86-708242 DDC 333.7 11
HC59

What's a natural resource? [videorecording] /. Los Angeles, Calif. , 1986, c1987. 1 videocassette (15 1/2 min.) : LC Card 86-708243 DDC 333.7 11
HC59

NATURAL RESOURCES - KAZAKH S.S.R.
Ėkonomicheskai͡a ot͡senka i prognozirovanie ispolʹzovanii͡a prirodnykh resursov Kazakhstana /. Alma-Ata , 1980. 161 p. ; LC Card 82-106708
HC337.K3 E34 1980

NATURAL RESOURCES - KIRGHIZ S.S.R. - CONGRESSES.
Sipozium "Geografii͡a v Kirgizii" (1980 : Frunze, Kirghiz S.S.R.) Sovremennye problemy geografii Kirgizii . Frunze , 1980. 167 p. : LC Card 82-121674
HC337.K545 S56 1980

NATURAL RESOURCES - MANAGEMENT.
Repetto, Robert C. World enough and time . New Haven , c1986. xiv, 147 p. ; ISBN 0-300-03648-5 LC Card 85-20180 DDC 333.7 19
HC59 .R43 1986 ***NYPL [JLD 86-1434]***

NATURAL RESOURCES - MANAGEMENT - MATHEMATICAL MODELS.
Economic-ecological modeling /. Amsterdam ; New York : x, 329 p. : ISBN 0-444-70298-9 LC Card 87-20048 DDC 333.7/0724 19
HC79.E5 E267 1987

NATURAL RESOURCES - MATHEMATICAL MODELS.
Faber, Malte Michael. Entropie, Umweltschutz und Rohstoffverbrauch . Berlin , New York , 1983. ix, 181 p. : ISBN 0-387-12297-4 (U. S.) LC Card 83-193381
HC79.E5 F23 1983

NATURAL RESOURCES - MEXICAN-AMERICAN BORDER REGION.
The U. S.-Mexico border region . [El Paso] , 1984, c1982. viii, 446 p. : ISBN 0-87404-091-4 (pbk.) LC Card 87-401861 DDC 333.7/0972/1 19
HC137.M46 U17 1984

NATURAL RESOURCES - MINNESOTA.
Waters, Thomas F. The Superior North Shore /. Minneapolis , c1987. xix, 361 p. : ISBN 0-8166-1613-2 : LC Card 87-13585 DDC 333.7/09776/7 19
HC107.M6 W38 1987

NATURAL RESOURCES - NAVAJO INDIAN RESERVATION.
Resource studies of the Navajo Indian Reservation . [Denver? Colo.] , 1986. 187 p. in various pagings : LC Card 86-603130 DDC 333.7/09791/3 19
HC107.A165 R47 1986

NATURAL RESOURCES - NORWAY.
Naturressurser og miljø 1983 . Oslo , 1984. 100 p. : ISBN 82-537-1993-0 : LC Card 84-161695
HC363.5 .N38 1984

Ressursregnskap og ressursbudsjett /. [Oslo] [1984?] 28 p. : LC Card 85-239023
HC363.5 .R46 1984

NATURAL RESOURCES - NORWAY - STATISTICS.
Naturressurser 1982 . Oslo , 1983. 62 p. : ISBN 82-537-1837-3 : LC Card 83-174054
HC363.5 .N372 1983

NATURAL RESOURCES - ONTARIO.
Waters, Thomas F. The Superior North Shore /. Minneapolis , c1987. xix, 361 p. : ISBN 0-8166-1613-2 : LC Card 87-13585 DDC 333.7/09776/7 19
HC107.M6 W38 1987

NATURAL RESOURCES - PACIFIC AREA.
Asia-Pacific report . Honolulu, Hawaii , 1986. x, 104 p. : ISBN 0-86638-071-X (pbk.) LC Card 85-27538 DDC 909/.09823/0828 19
HC412 .A7242 1986 ***NYPL [JLF 87-143]***

NATURAL RESOURCES - PERU - CHANDLES RIVER VALLEY.
Inventario, evaluación e integración de los recursos naturales de la zona Esperanza-Chandles-Yaco /. Lima, Perú , 1980. v, xi, 229, 24, [12] p. of plates : LC Card 84-155289
HC228.E86 I58 1980

NATURAL RESOURCES - PERU - ESPERANZA REGION (LORETO)
Inventario, evaluación e integración de los recursos naturales de la zona Esperanza-Chandles-Yaco /. Lima, Perú , 1980. v, xi, 229, 24, [12] p. of plates : LC Card 84-155289
HC228.E86 I58 1980

NATURAL RESOURCES - PERU - YACO RIVER VALLEY.
Inventario, evaluación e integración de los recursos naturales de la zona Esperanza-Chandles-Yaco /. Lima, Perú , 1980. v, xi, 229, 24, [12] p. of plates : LC Card 84-155289
HC228.E86 I58 1980

NATURAL RESOURCES - RESEARCH - BRITISH COLUMBIA.
Dorcey, Anthony H. J., 1944- Bargaining in the governance of Pacific coastal resources . Vancouver, B.C. , c1986. xvi, 219 p. : ISBN 0-920146-34-1 (pbk.) LC Card 86-222720 DDC 333.91/7/09711 19
HC117.B8 D67 1986

NATURAL RESOURCES - RUSSIAN S.F.S.R. - DAGESTANSKAI͡A A.S.S.R.
Sovershenstvovanie khozi͡aĭstvennogo mekhanizma i ratsionalʹnoe ispolʹzovanie resursov . Makhachkala , 1985. 190 p. : LC Card 87-136485
HC337.D3 S655 1985

NATURAL RESOURCES - RUSSIAN S.F.S.R. - SIBERIA.
Adzhiev, M. Ė. (Murad Ėskanderovich) Sibirʹ--XX vek /. Moskva , 1983. 252 p., [24] p. of plates : LC Card 83-161484
HC337.R852 S522 1983

Regionalʹnye osobennosti rat͡sionalizat͡sii prirodopolʹzovanii͡a i okhrany sredy /. Irkutsk , 1980. 177 p. ; LC Card 82-111826
HC337.R852 S5266 1980

NATURAL RESOURCES - RUSSIAN S.F.S.R. - SOVIET FAR EAST.

Regional'nye osobennosti ratsionalizatsii prirodopol'zovaniia i okhrany sredy /. Irkutsk , 1980. 177 p. ; LC Card 82-111826
HC337.R852 S5266 1980

NATURAL RESOURCES - RUSSIAN S.F.S.R. - URAL MOUNTAINS REGION.
Aktual'nye problemy prirodopol'zovaniia v promyshlennom regione /. Sverdlovsk , 1985. 151 p. : LC Card 86-126638
HC337.R852 U732 1985

Problemy osvoeniia prirodnykh resursov Ural'skogo Severa /. Sverdlovsk , 1985. 70 p. : LC Card 86-195834
HC337.R852 U7359 1985

NATURAL RESOURCES - SOCIAL ASPECTS - UNITED STATES.
Social science in natural resource management systems /. Boulder , 1987. xii, 265 p. : ISBN 0-8133-7485-5 (pbk. : alk. paper) LC Card 87-23138 DDC 333.7/0973 19
HC103.7 .S62 1987

NATURAL RESOURCES - SOVIET UNION.
Ėkonomicheskie problemy prirodopol'zovaniia /. Moskva , 1985. 137 p. : LC Card 86-119089
HC340.E5 E395 1985

Kompleksnye problemy obespecheniia ėkonomiki mineral'nym syr'em /. Moskva , 1984. 115 p. : LC Card 85-192528
HF1051 .K64 1984

Novikov, Ė. A. (Ėnergiĭ Alekseevich) Gorod i prirodopol'zovanie /. Leningrad , 1984. 143 p. ; LC Card 85-125032
HC333.5 .N68 1984

Tupytsia, IUriĭ IUr'evich. Ėkologo-ėkonomicheskaia ėffektivnost' prirodopol'zovaniia /. Moskva , 1980. 165 p. ; LC Card 81-146449
HC333.5 .T86 1980

NATURAL RESOURCES - SOVIET UNION - FORECASTING.
Problemy tselevoĭ orientatsii razvitiia resursnogo potentsiala /. Moskva , 1984. 205 p. : LC Card 86-143993
HC333.5 .P77 1984

NATURAL RESOURCES - SOVIET UNION, NORTHERN.
Krasnopol'skiĭ, B. Kh. (Boris Khananovich) Infrastruktura v sisteme regional'nogo khoziaĭstvennogo kompleksa Severa . Moskva , 1980. 143, [2] p. ; LC Card 81-131391
HC336.9.N65 K73 1980

Problemy osvoeniia prirodnykh resursov Ural'skogo Severa /. Sverdlovsk , 1985. 70 p. : LC Card 86-195834
HC337.R852 U7359 1985

NATURAL RESOURCES - SPAIN - GERONA (PROVINCE)
Medir i Huerta, Rosa M. Les comarques gironines . Girona , 1986. 211 p. : ISBN 84-505-3103-9 LC Card 87-101047
HC387.G4 M43 1986

NATURAL RESOURCES - STUDY AND TEACHING - CONGRESSES.
Land, water, and mineral resources in science education /. Oxford , New York , 1987. xii, 312 p. : ISBN 0-08-033915-8 : LC Card 86-30527 DDC 333.7/07/101724 19
HC28 .L27 1987

NATURAL RESOURCES - STUDY AND TEACHING - DEVELOPING COUNTRIES - CONGRESSES.
Land, water, and mineral resources in science education /. Oxford , New York , 1987. xii, 312 p. : ISBN 0-08-033915-8 : LC Card 86-30527 DDC 333.7/07/101724 19
HC28 .L27 1987

NATURAL RESOURCES - SUDAN - MANAGEMENT.
Atta el Moula, Mutasim el Amin. On the problem of resource management in the Sudan /. [Khartoum] , 1985. 131 leaves : LC Card 86-980662 DDC 333.7/09624 19
HC835 .A85 1985

NATURAL RESOURCES - TANZANIA.
Ole Saibull, Solomon, 1935- Hotuba ya Ndugu S.A. ole Saibull, mbunge, waziri wa maliasili na utalii . Dar es Salaam, Tanzania , 1979. 56 p. ; LC Card 83-244807
HC885 .O44 1979

NATURAL RESOURCES - UKRAINE.
Kompleksnoe ispol'zovanie prirodnykh resursov . Kiev , 1985. 174 p. ; LC Card 86-175133
HC337.U5 K6372 1985

Resursy narodnogo khoziaĭstva . Kiev , 1985. 308 p. : LC Card 86-226867
HC337.U5 P5 1985 t. 2 HC337.U53I52

NATURAL RESOURCES - UNITED STATES.
Rose, Adam Zachery. Natural resource policy and income distribution /. Baltimore , c1988. xvi, 139 p. : ISBN 0-8018-3523-2 (alk. paper) LC Card 87-2788 DDC 333.7/0973 19
HC103.7 .R67 1988

NATURAL RESOURCES - UNITED STATES - MANAGEMENT - JUVENILE LITERATURE.
Camp, William G. Managing our natural resources /. Albany, N.Y. , c1988. p. cm. ISBN 0-8273-2986-5 LC Card 87-25056 DDC 333.7/0973 19
HC103.7 .C33 1988

NATURAL RESOURCES - VENEZUELA - GUAYANA REGION - ADDRESSES, ESSAYS, LECTURES.
Exploración de la Guayana /. [Caracas] [1983] 158 p., [20] p. of plates : LC Card 85-178221 DDC 333.7/0988/1 19
HC238.G8 E98 1983 ***NYPL [JSF 86-461]***

NATURAL SCIENCE. see SCIENCE.

Natural value /. Wieser, Friedrich, Freiherr von, 1851-1926. [Natürliche Werth. English.] Fairfield, NJ , 1988. p. cm. ISBN 0-678-00821-3 LC Card 87-17245 DDC 338.5/21 19
HB201 .W65 1988

NATURE AND NURTURE.
McGee, Mark G. Human spatial abilities . New York , 1979. xiv, 144 p. : ISBN 0-03-052391-5 LC Card 79-16070 DDC 153.7/52
BF469 .M3 ***NYPL [JFE 84-185]***

The nature of leadership . Gardner, John William, 1912- Washington, D.C. (1828 L St., N.W., Washington 20036) , c1986. 20 p. ; LC Card 87-167132 DDC 303.3/4 19
HD57.7 .G37 1986

The Nature of public enterprise /. Ramanadham, Venkata Vemuri, 1920- New York , 1984. 302 p. : ISBN 0-312-86778-6 : LC Card 83-40570
NYPL [JLD 86-1037]

Naturressurser og miljø 1983 : foreløpige nøkkeltall fra ressursregnskapene for miljø, energi, mineraler, skog, fisk og areal. Oslo : Statistisk sentralbyrå : I kommisjon hos H. Aschehoug og Universitetsforlaget, 1984. 100 p. : ill. ; 30 cm. (Rapporter fra Statistisk sentralbyrå, 0332-8422 . 84/1) ISBN 82-537-1993-0 : LC Card 84-161695
1. Natural resources - Norway. 2. Environmental policy - Norway. I. Norway. Statistisk sentralbyrå. II. Series.
HC363.5 .N38 1984

Naturressurser 1982 : foreløpige nøkkeltall fra ressursregnskapene for energi, mineraler, skog, fisk og areal. Oslo : Statistisk sentralbyrå : I kommisjon hos H. Aschehoug og Universitetsforlaget, 1983. 62 p. : ill. ; 29 cm. (Rapporter fra Statistisk sentralbyrå, 0332-8422 . 83/1) ISBN 82-537-1837-3 : LC Card 83-174054
1. Natural resources - Norway - Statistics. I. Norway. Statistisk sentralbyrå. II. Series.
HC363.5 .N372 1983

Nauchen tsentūr po ikonomika, organizatsiia i upravlenie na naukata i teknicheskiia progres (Bulgaria). Klub za teknichesko i nauchno tvorchestvo na mladezhta. Aktivizirane na mladezhkoto nauchno i tekhnichesko tvorchestvo /. Sofiia , 1985. 135 p. : LC Card 86-220354
HC403.Z9 T419 1985

Nauchnaia konferentsiia po teme "Zakon povysheniia proizvoditel'nosti truda i rol' finansov i kredita v ego ispol'zovanii v stroitel'stve kommunizma" (1983 : Moskovskiĭ finansovyĭ institut) Rol' finansovo-kreditnogo mekhanizma v povyshenii ėffektivnosti obshchestvennykh zatrat . Moskva , 1984. 153 p. ; LC Card 86-113408
HG186.S55 R64 1984

Nauchnaia konferentsiia "Uchenie K. Marksa ob ėtapakh razvitiia sposoba proizvodstva i kontseptsiia razvitogo sotsializma" (1983 : Leningrad, R.S.F.S.R.) Uchenie K. Marksa ob ėtapakh razvitiia sposoba proizvodstva i problemy zrelogo sotsializma . Leningrad , 1985. 150 p. ; LC Card 86-140577
HB97.5 .U24 1985

Nauchnaia organizatsiia truda na mashinostroitel'nykh predpriiatiiakh / pod obshcheĭ redaktsieĭ V.P. Radukina ; [V.P. Radukin ... et al.]. Moskva : "Mashinostroenie", 1986. 240 p. : ill. ; 23 cm. (Dlia vuzov) Authorized for instructional purposes. Includes index. Bibliography: p. 237. LC Card 86-214776
1. Machine-tool industry - Soviet Union - Personnel management. I. Radukin, V. P. (Viktor Pavlovich). II. Series.
HD9703.S652 N38 1986

Nauchnaia organizatsiia truda v dorozhnom khoziaĭstve /. Busurin, K. A. Moskva , 1981. 159 p. ; LC Card 87-461013
HD9717.5.R63 S653 1981

Nauchnaia organizatsiia truda v promyshlennosti / [redaktsionnaia kollegiia S.S. Novozhilov (glavnyĭ redaktor) ... et al.]. 2-e izd., perer. i dop. Moskva : "Ėkonomika", 1986. 414 p. : ill. ; 23 cm. At head of title: Nauchno-issledovatel'skiĭ institut truda i Vsesoiuznyĭ nauchno-metodicheskiĭ tsentr po organizatsii truda i upravleniia proizvodstvom Gosudarstvennogo komiteta SSSR po trudu i sotsial'nym voprosam. Includes bibliographical references. LC Card 86-218434
1. Industrial management - Soviet Union. 2. Personnel management - Soviet Union. 3. Labor and laboring classes - Soviet Union. I. Novozhilov, Sergeĭ Nikolaevich. II. Nauchno-issledovatel'skiĭ institut truda (Soviet Union). III. Vsesoiuznyĭ nauchno-metodicheskiĭ tsentr po organizatsii truda i upravleniia proizvodstvom (Soviet Union).
HD36 .N323 1986

Nauchno-issledovatel'kiĭ institut planirovaniia (Moldavian S.S.R.) Optimal'noe planirovanie /. Kishinev , 1982. 166 p. : LC Card 83-149332
HD9015.S653 M64526 1982

Nauchno-issledovatel'skiĭ institut avtomatizirovannykh sistem planirovaniia i upravleniia narodnym khoziaĭstvom (Byelorussian S.S.R.) OĖkonomicheskie problemy razvitiia narodnogo khoziaĭstva i povyshenie ėffektivnosti obshchestvennogo proizvodstva /. Minsk , 1984. 148 p. : LC Card 85-147020
HC337.B93 E45 1984

Nauchno-issledovatel'skiĭ institut planirovaniia (Moldavian S.S.R.) Planirovanie ėkonomiki Moldavskoĭ SSR /. Kishinev , 1986. 161 p. ; LC Card 86-203680
HD9015.S653 M6457 1986

Nauchno-issledovatel'skiĭ institut sel'skogo khoziaĭstva Kraĭnego Severa (Noril'sk, R.S.F.S.R.) Sistema vedeniia sel'skogo i promyslovogo khoziaĭstva na Eniseĭskom Severe . Novosibirsk , 1986. 211 p. ; LC Card 86-227282
HD1995.K73 S57 1986

Nauchno-issledovatel'skiĭ institut truda (Soviet Union)
Nauchnaia organizatsiia truda v promyshlennosti /. Moskva , 1986. 414 p. : LC Card 86-218434
HD36 .N323 1986

Organizatsiia i stimulirovanie truda rabotnikov transportnykh uzlov . Moskva , 1984. 96 p. ; LC Card 87-100191
HD8039.T72 S656 1984

Nauchno-populiarnaia literatura (Naukova dumka (Firm))
Akopov, Mykhaĭlo Arutiunovych. Dukhovnyĭ mir sovetskogo cheloveka /. Kiev , 1985. 124, [3] p. ; LC Card 86-139846
JN6581 .A64 1985 ***NYPL [*QIK 87-3448]***

Nauchno-prakticheska konferentsiia po podobriavane na kachestvoto na razrabotvaneto na chast "Bezopasnost, khigiena na truda i pozharna bezopasnost" (BKhTPB) kūm proektite za obektite po kapitalnoto stroitelstvo s proizvodstveno prednaznachenie . Nauchno-prakticheska konferentsiia po podobriavane na kachestvoto na razrabotvaneto na chast "Bezopasnost, khigiena na truda i pozharna bezopasnost" (BKhTPB) kūm proektite za obektite po kapitalnoto stroitelstvo s

proizvodstveno prednaznachenie (1984) [Bulgaria] [1984?] 56 p. ; LC Card 86-102624
HD7741.5 .N39 1984

Nauchno-prakticheska konferentsiia po podobriavane na kachestvoto na razrabotvaneto na chast "Bezopasnost, khigiena na truda i pozharna bezopasnost" (BKhTPB) kŭm proektite za obektite po kapitalnoto stroitelstvo s proizvodstveno prednaznachenie (1984)
Nauchno-prakticheska konferentsiia po podobriavane na kachestvoto na razrabotvaneto na chast "Bezopasnost, khigiena na truda i pozharna bezopasnost" (BKhTPB) kŭm proektite za obektite po kapitalnoto stroitelstvo s proizvodstveno prednaznachenie : dokladi : 28 noemvri 1984 godina. [Bulgaria] : Nauchno-prakticheski sŭiuzi v Bŭlgariia, [1984?] 56 p. ; 22 cm. At head of title: Komitet po truda i sotsialnoto delo ... LC Card 86-102624
1. Industrial hygiene - Bulgaria - Congresses. I. Nauchno-prakticheski sŭiuzi v Bŭlgariia. II. Bulgaria. Komitet po truda i sotsialnoto delo. III. Title.
HD7741.5 .N39 1984

Nauchno-prakticheska konferentsiia "Prebroiavane na naselenieto i zhilishtniia fond--teoriia i praktika," 9-11 oktomvri 1986 g., Slŭnchev briag /. Nauchno-prakticheska konferentsiia "Prebroiavane na naselenieto i zhilishtniia fond--teoriia i praktika" (1986 : Slŭnchev briag, Bulgaria) Sofiia , 1986- v. <1 > : LC Card 87-156528
HA1621.5 1985

Nauchno-prakticheska konferentsiia "Prebroiavane na naselenieto i zhilishtniia fond--teoriia i praktika" (1986 : Slŭnchev briag, Bulgaria) Nauchno-prakticheska konferentsiia "Prebroiavane na naselenieto i zhilishtniia fond--teoriia i praktika," 9-11 oktomvri 1986 g., Slŭnchev briag / [avtorite Dano Balevski ... et al.]. Sofiia : TSentr. stat. upr., 1986- v. <1 > : ill. ; 23 cm. At head of title v. 1- : TSentralno statistichesko upravlenie pri Ministerskiia sŭvet. Programno-tselevi kolektiv "Prebroiavane na naselenieto i zhilishtniia fond." Includes bibliographical references. LC Card 87-156528
1. Bulgaria - Census, 1985 - Congresses. 2. Housing - Bulgaria - Congresses. I. Balevski, Dano. II. Bulgaria. Tsentralno statistichesko upravlenie. III. Programno-tselevi kolektiv "Prebroiavane na naselenieto i zhilishtniia fond" (Bulgaria). IV. Title.
HA1621.5 1985

Nauchno-prakticheski sŭiuzi v Bŭlgariia.
Nauchno-prakticheska konferentsiia po podobriavane na kachestvoto na razrabotvaneto na chast "Bezopasnost, khigiena na truda i pozharna bezopasnost" (BKhTPB) kŭm proektite za obektite po kapitalnoto stroitelstvo s proizvodstveno prednaznachenie (1984) Nauchno-prakticheska konferentsiia po podobriavane na kachestvoto na razrabotvaneto na chast "Bezopasnost, khigiena na truda i pozharna bezopasnost" (BKhTPB) kŭm proektite za obektite po kapitalnoto stroitelstvo s proizvodstveno prednaznachenie . [Bulgaria] [1984?] 56 p. ; LC Card 86-102624
HD7741.5 .N39 1984

Nauchno-proizvodstvennye kompleksy . Marek, A. I. (Aleksandr Isaevich) Moskva , 1985. 141, [3] p. : LC Card 86-118921
HC340.R4 M37 1985

Nauchno-tekhnicheskaia revoliutsiia i rabochiĭ klass pri kapitalizme . Vasil'chuk, IU. A. Moskva , 1980. 295 p. : LC Card 81-130590
HD6331 .V22 1980

Nauchno-tekhnicheskata revoliutsiia--zakonomernost na uskoreno razvitie na sotsialisticheskoto obshtestvo /. Trendafilov, Toncho. Sofiia , 1985. 93 p. : LC Card 86-163246
HC403.Z9 T477 1985

Nauchno-tekhnicheskiĭ progress i strukturnye sdvigi v ėkonomike sovremennogo kapitalizma : referativnyĭ sbornik / [otvetstvennyĭ redaktor i sostavitel' sbornika B.A. Gorokhov]. Moskva : Akademiia nauk SSSR, In-t nauch. informatsii po obshchestvennym naukam, 1987. 168 p. ; 20 cm. (Seriia "Sotsial'no-ėkonomicheskie i ideologicheskie problemy NTR") LC Card 87-165811
1. Technological innovations - Economic aspects - Europe. 2. Research, Industrial - Europe. 3. Technological innovations - Economic aspects - United States. 4. Research, Industrial - United States. I. Gorokhov, B. A. II. Series: Seriia "Sotsial'no-ėkonomicheskie i ideologicheskie problemy NTR".
HC240.9.T4 N38 1987

Nauchno-tekhnicheskiĭ progress i tiazhelaia promyshlennost' IAponii /. Skorov, Mikhail Sergeevich. Moskva , 1980. 213, [3] p. ; LC Card 81-130564
HC465.T4 S56 1980

Nauchno-tekhnicheskiiat progres i problemite na truda : po materiali ot nauchno-prakticheska konferentsiia na tezi tema, sŭstoiala se v Sofiia na 10 maĭ 1985 g. / [sŭstavitel i nauchen rŭkovoditel Dimitŭr Shopov]. Sofiia : Profizdat, 1986. 297 p. : ill. ; 20 cm. Includes bibliographical references. LC Card 86-196075
1. Labor supply - Bulgaria - Effect of technological innovations on - Congresses. I. Shopov, Dimitŭr.
HD6331.2.B9 N38 1986

Nauchno-tekhnicheskiiat progress--delo na vsichki. Varna : [s.n.], 1985. 187 p. : ill. ; 20 cm. (Biblioteka "V pomosht na propagandista i agitatora" . no. 5-1985 g.) At head of title: Okrŭzhen komitet na BKP--Varna. Dom za politicheska prosveta. Includes bibliographical references. LC Card 86-198872
1. Technological innovations - Bulgaria. I. Bŭlgarska komunisticheska partiia. Okrŭzhen komitet (Varnenski okrŭg). II. Dom za politicheska prosveta (Varna, Bulgaria). III. Series: Biblioteka "V pomosht na propagandista i agitatora" , 1985, 5.
HC403.Z9 T46 1985

Nauchnoizsledovatelski institut po profesionalno obrazovanie (Bulgaria) Izsledvane roliata na proizvodstvenata sreda, trudovite kolektivi i nastavnitsite za formirane na komunistichesko otnoshenie kŭm truda u podrastvashchtite /. Sofiia , 1984. 150 p. ; LC Card 85-166784
HD6276.B82 I97 1984

Nauchnoizsledovatelski institut po profsŭiuzni problemi Georgi Dimitrov.
Aktualni ikonomicheski problemi . Sofiia , 1985. 227 p. ; LC Card 86-205815
HC403 .A67 1985

Profsŭiuzno stroitelstvo . Sofiia , 1985. 310 p. : LC Card 86-209854
HD6782 .P78 1985

Nauchnoizsledovatelski institut po truda.
Manolov, Angel. Sotsialno-ikonomicheski problemi na izpolzuvane truda na mladezhite /. Sofiia , 1984. 93 p. ; LC Card 86-226913
HD6276.B82 M36 1984

Nauchnye trudy (Nauchno-issledovatel'skiĭ ėkonomicheskiĭ institut (Soviet Union))
Problemy ėffektivnosti ispol'zovaniia trudovykh resursov /. Moskva , 1981. 147 p. ; LC Card 82-150334
HC340.L3 P64 1981

Nauchnyĭ kommunizm (Izdatel'stvo Moskovskogo universiteta)
Martanus, R. V. (Riurik Vital'evich) Sotsial'noe upravlenie . Moskva , 1986. 141 p. ; LC Card 87-156789
HD38.25.S65 M35 1986

Nauchnyĭ sovet AN SSSR "Ėkonomicheskie zakonomernosti razvitiia sotsializma i sorevnovanie dvukh sistem." Problema tempov ėkonomicheskogo rosta v sovremennom mire /. Moskva , 1986. 383 p. : LC Card 87-124359
HC244 .P747 1986

Nauchnyĭ sovet AN SSSR po ėkonomicheskim problemam nauchno-tekhnicheskoĭ revoliutsii.
Simpozium "Nauchno-tekhnicheskiĭ progress i intensifikatsiia obshchestvennogo proizvodstva" (1984 : Podol'sk, Moscow, R.S.F.S.R.) Formy i metody vzaimodeĭstviia nauki i proizvodstva /. Moskva , 1984. 237 p. ; LC Card 85-240380
HC340.T4 S48 1984

Upravlenie nauchno-tekhnicheskim progressom v soiuznykh respublikakh /. Tallin , 1986. 158 p. ; LC Card 87-123175
HC340.T4 U77 1986

Nauchnyĭ sovet "Ėkonomicheskie zakonomernosti razvitiia sotsializma i ego pererastaniia v kommunizm" (Akademiia nauk SSSR)
"Kapital" K. Marksa i ėkonomicheskie problemy razvitogo sotsializma /. Moskva , 1980. 260 p. ; LC Card 81-134413
HB501 .K248 1980

Nauchnyĭ sovet "Mirovaia sotsialisticheskaia sistema." (Akademiia nauk SSSR) Problema tempov ėkonomicheskogo rosta v sovremennom mire /. Moskva , 1986. 383 p. : LC Card 87-124359
HC244 .P747 1986

Nauchnyĭ sovet po ėkonomicheskim, sotsial'nym i pravovym problemam APK (Akademiia nauk SSSR) Relaciones agrarias en el socialismo. Moscú , 1986. 223 p. ; LC Card 87-126164
HD9015.S652 R45 1986

Nauchnyĭ sovet po filosofskim i sotsial'nym problemam nauki i tekhniki (Akademiia nauk SSSR) Moving towards the year 2000 . Moscow , 1987. 204 p. ; LC Card 87-163642 DDC 333.7 19
HC79.E5 M69 1987

Nauchnyĭ sovet po kompleksnoĭ probleme edinoĭ transportnoĭ sistemy SSSR.
Sovershenstvovanie khoziaĭstvennogo mekhanizma na transporte /. Moskva , 1983. 223 p. : LC Card 85-199829
HE255.A2 S68 1983

Nauchnyĭ sovet po kompleksnoĭ probleme "Optimal'noe planirovanie i upravlenie narodnym khoziaĭstvom" (Akademiia nauk SSSR)
Khoziaĭstvennyĭ mekhanizm i povyshenie ėffektivnosti proizvodstva /. Moskva , 1986. 252 p. ; LC Card 86-232347
HC340.I52 K49 1986

Programmno-tselevoĭ metod v planirovanii /. Moskva , 1982. 150 p. : LC Card 83-162853
HC336.25 .P6577 1982

Nauchnyĭ sovet po probleme "Ėkonomicheskaia ėffektivnost' osnovnykh fondov, kapital'nykh vlozheniĭ i novoĭ tekhniki" (Akademiia nauk SSSR) Problemy povysheniia ėkonomicheskoĭ ėffektivnosti kapital'nykh vlozheniĭ v territorial'nye promyshlennye kompleksy. Moskva , 1983. 170 p. : LC Card 84-202808
HC340.C3 P747 1983

Nauchnyĭ sovet "Sotsial'no-ėkonomicheskie problemy narodonaseleniia" (Akademiia nauk SSSR)
Demograficheskaia politika sotsialisticheskogo obshchestva /. Moskva , 1986. 190 p. : LC Card 87-120466
HB3607 .D425 1986

Demograficheskaia politika sotsialisticheskogo obshchestva /. Moskva , 1986. 190 p. ;
NYPL [*QIP 87-2842]

Naučnoistraživački i razvojni rad u organizacijama udruženog rada /. Čubra, Nikola. Beograd , 1982. 165 p. : LC Card 82-166181
HD30 .C83 1982

Naukkarinen, Arvo. Policies of population redistribution /. Oulu , 1981. 199 p. : ISBN 951-675-071-0 (pbk.) LC Card 83-148782 DDC 304.8 19
HB1952 .P65 1981

Naukova rada z kibernetyky (Akademiia nauk Ukraïns'koï RSR) Problemy modelirovaniia makroėkonomicheskikh sistem . Kiev , 1982. 100 p. ; LC Card 83-144893
HB139 .P755 1982

Naukovi zapysky (Ukraïns'kyĭ tekhnichno-hospodars'kyĭ instytut (Munich, Germany)) . (ch. 21) Vytanovych, Illia. Sotsial'no-ekonomichni ideï v zmahanniakh halyts'kykh ukraïntsiv na perelomi XIX-XX vv. /. Miunkhen , 1970. 74 p. ; LC Card 86-214348
HC337.U52 G358 1970

Naukovo-doslidnyĭ ekonomichnyĭ instytut.
Agropromyshlennyĭ kompleks i problemy obespecheniia naseleniia prodovol'stviem . Kiev , 1983. 190 p. : LC Card 86-139699
HD9015.S653 U4295 1983

Naukovo-doslidnyĭ ekonomichnyĭ instytut.
Narodno-khoziaĭstvennye proportsii, ikh planirovanie i prognozirovanie /. Kiev , 1985. 318 p. : LC Card 86-210651
HC337.U5 P5 1985 t. 1

Resursy narodnogo khoziaĭstva . Kiev , 1985. 308 p. : LC Card 86-226867
HC337.U5 P5 1985 t. 2 HC337.U53I52

Nauman, Julie Castelli. Massa, Alison K. Housing and the environment /. Sacramento, CA (921 10th St., Sacramento 95814-2774) [1985?] 2 v. : LC Card 87-621018 DDC 363.7 19
HD266.C2 M37 1985

Naumann, Thomas. Stadtbahn für Würzburg : Wege aus der Krise im Stadtverkehr : Fakten, Argumente, Lösungen / Thomas Naumann, Christian Langenheim. Würzburg : Eigendruck im Selbstverlag, 1985. 237 p., [3] leaves of plates : ill. ; 21 cm. Includes bibliographies. LC Card 86-166915
1. Street-railroads - Germany (West) - Würzburg. 2. Street-railroads. I. Langenheim, Christian. II. Title.
HE4779.W84 N38 1985

Naur, Maja. Political mobilization and industry in Libya / Maja Maur. [Uppsala] : Akademisk Forlag, c1986. 268 p. : ill. ; 22 cm. Bibliography: p. 231-243. ISBN 87-500-2648-8 (pbk.) : LC Card 87-141231 DDC 338.961/2 19
1. Industry and state - Libya. I. Title.
HD3616.L752 N38 1986

Naust, Hermann. Direkte Steuern und intertemporale Allokation : eine wohlfahrtsökonomische Betrachtung / von Hermann Naust. Köln : C. Heymanns Verlag, c1983. xiv, 374 p. : ill. ; 21 cm. (Annales Universitatis Saraviensis. Rechts- und Wirtschaftswissenschaftliche Abteilung . Bd. 108) Originally presented as the author's thesis (doctoral)--Universität Saarland, 1981. Bibliography: p. [363]-372. ISBN 3-452-19402-7 : LC Card 83-163600 DDC 336.2 19
1. Taxation. 2. Taxation - Effect of inflation on. 3. Income tax. 4. Taxation of articles of consumption. I. Title. II. Series.
HJ3851 .N38 1983

NAUT-rapport .
(1983:8) Den Offentliga sektorns sysselsättningsutveckling i Norden under 1970-talet =. [Oslo] [Solna] 1983. iiii, 150 p. : ISBN 91-38-07556-3 LC Card 85-184428
HD8013.S344 O35 1983

Hē nautilia tou Pēliou stēn Tourkokratia . Tzamtzēs, A. I. [Athēnai] [198-] 103 p., [20] p. of plates : LC Card 87-111965
HE872.5.Z6 T98 1980z

NAVAL ADMINISTRATION. see **UNITED STATES. NAVY.**

NAVAL POWER. see **UNITED STATES. NAVY.**

Navarro, Hugo. La vivienda de interés social en Panamá : (una metodología para su investigación) / Hugo Navarro. Panamá : Editorial Universitaria, 1975. 288 p. : ill. ; 21 cm. "Traducción de Prof. Rafael Moscote E."--P. [5] Originally presented as the author's thesis (Grado de M. Sc.--University of Manchester) under the title: An approach to research organization for low cost housing in Panama. Bibliography: p. 273-288. LC Card 84-100873
1. Housing - Research - Panama. 2. Public housing - Great Britain. I. Title.
HD7312.A3 N38 1975

Navarro, José Cantón. see **Cantón Navarro, José, 1925-**

Navarro, Susan S. Dynamic effects of exchange rate changes in the Philippines in 1970-1980 / by Susan S. Navarro. [Quezon] : University of the Philippines, School of Economics, [1986] 25 p. ; 28 cm. (Discussion paper / University of the Philippines, School of Economics . no. 8603) "February 1986." Includes bibliographical references. LC Card 87-120911 DDC 332.4/5609599 19
1. Devaluation of currency - Philippines. 2. Foreign exchange problem - Philippines. I. Series: Discussion paper / University of the Philippines, School of Economics , 8603. II. Title.
HG1265 .N38 1986

Naveau, Jacques, docteur en droit. L'Europe et le transport aérien / Jacques Naveau. Bruxelles : Bruylant, 1983. 346 p. ; 24 cm. Bibliography: p. [335]-339. ISBN 2-8027-0304-8 LC Card 85-114595
1. Aeronautics, Commercial - Europe. 2. Aeronautics, Commercial - Government policy - Europe. 3. Aeronautics, Commercial - Law and legislation. I. Title.
HE9842.A4 N38 1983

NAVIGATION, INLAND. see **INLAND NAVIGATION.**

NAVIGATION - MISSISSIPPI RIVER - HISTORY.
White, Bob. The child of an eagle . [Cape Girardeau, Mo. , c1980] v, 78 p. : LC Card 87-405068 DDC 386/.22436 19
HE630.M6 W48 1980

NAVIGATORS. see **SEAMEN.**

Naville, Pierre. La maîtrise du salariat / Pierre Naville. Paris : Anthropos, c1984. 153 p. ; 22 cm. Bibliography: p. [151]-153. ISBN 2-7157-1099-2 : LC Card 85-100916
1. Industrial sociology - France. 2. Labor and laboring classes - France. 3. Socialism - France. 4. France - Economic conditions - 1945-. I. Title.
HD6957.F8 N38 1984 ***NYPL [JLD 87-333]***

Navin Chandra Joshi. see **Joshi, Navin Chandra.**

Navis, A. A. Ning, Hasjim, 1916- Pasang surut pengusaha pejuang . Jakarta , 1986. x, 392 p., [1] leaf of plates : LC Card 86-944750
HC446.5.N56 A3 1986

NAVVIES. see **LABOR AND LABORING CLASSES.**

Nawaz Dawood. see **Dawood, Nawaz.**

Naylor, R. T., 1945- Hot money and the politics of debt / R.T. Naylor. New York, N.Y. : Linden Press/Simon and Schuster, 1987. 463 p. ; 25 cm. Bibliography: p. 381-384. Includes index. ISBN 0-671-62319-2 LC Card 86-33739 DDC 364.1/68 19
1. Money laundering. 2. International finance. 3. Debts, External - Developing countries. I. Title.
HG3891 .N39 1987

Nazarov, Mikhail Georgievich. Proizvoditel′nost′ truda v razvitom sotsialisticheskom obshchestve /. Moskva , 1982. 214 p. ; LC Card 83-166417
HC340.L3 P687 1982

Nazarova, N. S. (Nina Semenovna) Voprosy razvitiia torgovli v Tadzhikistane / N.S. Nazarova. Dushanbe : Izd-vo "Irfon", 1978. 172 p. ; 20 cm. Includes bibliographical references. LC Card 81-146150
1. Tajik S.S.R. - Commerce. 2. Tajik S.S.R. - Economic conditions. I. Title.
HF3629.T35 N39 1978

Nazi Party. see **Nationalsozialistische Deutsche Arbeiter-Partei.**

The NBC, a profile of a public enterprise commercial bank . Nsekela, Amon J. (Amon James), 1930- [Dar es Salaam] , 1983. 57 p. : LC Card 85-981339 DDC 332.1/2/09678 19
HG3397.A8 N375 1983

NBER conference report.
Current U. S. trade policy . Cambridge, Mass. (1050 Massachusetts Ave., Cambridge 02138) , 1986. iii, 128 p. ; LC Card 86-201110 DDC 382/.3/0973 19
HF1455 .C87 1986

NBER summary report.
Conference on the Effects of Taxation on Capital Formation (1986 : Palm Beach, Fla.) Taxes and capital formation. Cambridge, Mass. (1050 Massachusetts Ave., Cambridge 02138) , 1986. 40 p. ; LC Card 87-101954 DDC 336.2/00973 19
HJ2381 .C6974 1986

NCHSR research report series.
Langwell, Kathryn M. A synthesis of research on competition in the financing and delivery of health services /. Hyattsville, MD. , Springfield, VA , 1982. 85 p. ; LC Card 82-600612 DDC 338.4/73621/0973 19
RA410.53 .L36 1982 ***NYPL [JLF 86-422]***

Ncube, Patrick Donsi. Harbans Singh, 1940- Conceptual and methodological issues on agricultural marketing research in Zambia /. [Lusaka, Zambia] [1979?] 19, [2] leaves ; LC Card 85-980091
HD9017.Z32 H37 1979

Ndabahagamye, Illuminata. Inventaire du secteur parapublic au Burundi, 1960-1984 / par Illuminata Ndabahagamye ; postface de J.P. Ollivier. Bujumbura, Burundi : Editions du Centre de perfectionnement et de formation en cours d'emploi, c1986. 211 p. : ill. ; 32 cm. "Mars 1986." Includes bibliographical references. LC Card 86-981403
1. Government business enterprises - Burundi. I. Title.
HD4348 .N3 1986

Ndeshyo Rurihose. La stratégie de l'Organisation de l'unité africaine pour le développement : le cadre institutionnel / par Ndeshyo Rurihose, Ntumba Luaba. [Kinshasa] : Presses universitaires du Zaïre, 1981. 80 p. : ill. ; 24 cm. At head of title: Université nationale du Zaïre, Faculté de droit. Bibliography: p. 79-80. LC Card 83-161631
1. Africa - Economic conditions. 2. African cooperation. 3. Organization of African Unity. I. Ntumba Luaba. II. Title.
HC800 .N393 1981

Ndlela, Daniel Boda. Dualism in the Rhodesian colonial economy / Daniel Boda Ndlela. [Lund] : Distributor, Dept. of Economics, University of Lund, [1981] vi, 241 p. : ill., maps ; 23 cm. (Lund economic studies. 22) Extra t.p. with thesis statement inserted. Originally presented as the author's thesis (doctoral--University of Lund, 1981). Bibliography: p. 231-241. LC Card 86-673434
1. Zimbabwe - Economic conditions - To 1965. 2. Zimbabwe - Economic policy. 3. Great Britain - Colonies - Economic policy. I. Title.
HC910 .N34x 1981

N'Dzaba, Tobi. L'enseignement technique et professionnel et la satisfaction des besoins en main-d'œuvre : le cas de la République populaire du Congo / Tobi N'Dzaba. Paris : Unesco, Institut international de planification de l'éducation, [1983] i, 139 p. : ill. ; 30 cm. (Cahiers de l'IIPE . no 68) Includes bibliographical references. LC Card 85-189543
1. Manpower policy - Congo (Brazzaville). 2. Education - Congo (Brazzaville). I. Title. II. Series.
HD5845.A6 N38 1983

Ne pole pereĭti-- /. Krasnenkov, Vladimir. Moskva , 1986. 174 p. ; LC Card 86-132520
HD1995.N515 K73 1986

Neagrarno gospodarstvo Pirana od 1280 do 1340 =. Mihelič, Darja. Ljubljana , 1985. 244 p., [12] p. on folded leaves : LC Card 86-202646
HC407.Z7 P576 1985

NEAR EAST - COMMERCE.
Emery, James J. Technology trade with the Middle East /. Boulder , 1986. xvii, 302 p. : ISBN 0-8133-7043-4 : LC Card 85-3215 DDC 338.9/26 19
HC415.15.Z9 H533 1986 ***NYPL [JLE 86-2460]***

Ilgen, Thomas L. Trading technology . New York , 1987. x, 203 p. ; ISBN 0-275-92483-1 (alk. paper) : LC Card 86-21197 DDC 338.94/06 19
HC415.15 .I45 1986 ***NYPL [JLE 87-832]***

NEAR EAST - ECONOMIC CONDITIONS.
Owen, Edward Roger John. The Middle East in the world economy, 1800-1914 /. London , New York , 1987, c1981. xix, 378 p. : ISBN 0-416-03272-9 (pbk.) LC Card 86-24385 DDC 330.956 19
HC415.15 .O94 1987

NEAR EAST - ECONOMIC CONDITIONS - RESEARCH - CONGRESSES.
Zweite wissenschaftliche Regionaltagung über Nah- und Mittelost . Berlin , 1963. vi, 177 p. ; LC Card 85-167419
HC59.7 .D385 no. 62/93 HC415.15

Near East - Government. see **Near East - Politics and government.**

NEAR EAST - POLITICS AND GOVERNMENT - RESEARCH - CONGRESSES.
Zweite wissenschaftliche Regionaltagung über Nah- und Mittelost . Berlin , 1963. vi, 177 p. ; LC Card 85-167419
HC59.7 .D385 no. 62/93 HC415.15

NEAR EAST - SOCIAL CONDITIONS - RESEARCH - CONGRESSES.
Zweite wissenschaftliche Regionaltagung über Nah- und Mittelost . Berlin , 1963. vi, 177 p. ; LC Card 85-167419
HC59.7 .D385 no. 62/93 HC415.15

Nearing retirement . Lyon, Phil, 1948- Aldershot, Hants , Brookfield, Vt., USA , c1987. xix, 196 p. : ISBN 0-566-05233-4 : LC Card 86-25680 DDC 331.3/94/0941 19
HD6283.G7 L86 1987

Neary, J. Peter. Natural resources and the macroeconomy /. Oxford, UK , 1986. xvi, 352 p. : ISBN 0-631-15087-0 LC Card 86-673943
HC59 .N3194x 1986b

Neate, F. W. The Developing global securities market /. London ; Boston : viii, 192 p. ; ISBN 0-86010-979-8 LC Card 87-19086 DDC 332.6/5 19
HG4508 .D48 1987

Nebbeling, Susanne Wied- see **Wied-Nebbeling, Susanne.**

Nebelung, Michael, 1958- Bangladesh im Schatten der Macht /. Aachen , c1986. vi, 328, 57 p. : ISBN 3-922868-31-2 LC Card 86-228249
HC440.8 .B358 1986

Nebesné Ipoly, Márta. Malmok, ipari és gazdasági létesitmények az első katonai felmérés térképszelvényein, 1782-1785 /. Budapest , 1982. 220 p., [1] leaf of plates : ISBN 963-01-4433-6 (Magy. nemz. bibl.) LC Card 83-230040
HC300.26 .M35 1982

Nebraska abridged life expectancy tables, 1960-1980 / prepared by Nebraska Department of Health, Division of Health Data and Statistical Research. [Lincoln, Neb.] : The Division, [1985?] 40, 78, 3 leaves : ill. ; 28 cm. Errata slip inserted. LC Card 86-622212 DDC 304.6/09782021 19
1. Mortality - Nebraska - Tables. 2. Nebraska - Statistics, Vital. I. Nebraska. Division of Health Data and Statistical Research.
HB1355.N42 N43 1985

NEBRASKA - APPROPRIATIONS AND EXPENDITURES - STATISTICS.
Nebraska. Legislature. Appropriations and revenues, fiscal year 1985-86 . [Lincoln] [1985] i, 49 leaves ; LC Card 85-623111 DDC 336.782 19
HJ2053.N34 A66 1985

Nebraska can work /. Stauss, Connie. [Lincoln , 1986- v. <1 > : LC Card 86-622362 DDC 363/.09782 19
HC107.N23 C37 1986

Nebraska Commission on the Status of Women. Women in numbers . Lincoln, Neb. (Box 94600, Lincoln 68509-4600) , 1985. iii, 168 p. : LC Card 86-622214 DDC 331.4/125/09782 19
HD6096.N3 W66 1985

Nebraska. Dept. of Labor. (Old Catalog form: Nebraska. Labor Dept.)
Women in numbers . Lincoln, Neb. (Box 94600, Lincoln 68509-4600) , 1985. iii, 168 p. : LC Card 86-622214 DDC 331.4/125/09782 19
HD6096.N3 W66 1985

Nebraska. Dept. of Revenue. Tax expenditure report for sales and use tax--Nebraska and local option, property tax, individual income tax, fiduciary income tax, corporation income tax, miscellaneous taxes . Lincoln, Neb. [1985] 245 p. ; LC Card 86-622058 DDC 343.78204 347.8204 19
HJ2419 .T39 1985

Nebraska. Division of Health Data and Statistical Research. Nebraska abridged life expectancy tables, 1960-1980 /. [Lincoln, Neb.] [1985?] 40, 78, 3 leaves : LC Card 86-622212 DDC 304.6/09782021 19
HB1355.N42 N43 1985

Nebraska Energy Office. Community energy management as an economic development strategy . [Lincoln, Neb.] (Box 95085, Lincoln 68509-5085) [1984 or 1985] iv, 396 p. : LC Card 86-622211 DDC 333.79/0973 19
HD9502.U52 C656 1984

[Nebraska job prospects] 1983-1988. [Lincoln, Neb. (550 South 16th St., Lincoln 68509) : Nebraska Occupational Information Coordinating Committee, <1985- >] v. <1, 5-9 > : ill. ; 22 x 28 cm. "August 1985"--First prelim. p., v. <4 > CONTENTS. - [v. 1 without special title] -- [v. 5] Panhandle job prospects -- [v. 6] Central region job prospects -- [v. 7] Mid-Plains job prospects -- [v. 8] Southeast job prospects -- [v. 9] Northeast job prospects. LC Card 86-622062 DDC 331.12/09782/021 19
1. Employment forecasting - Nebraska - Statistics. 2. Job vacancies - Nebraska - Statistics. 3. Nebraska - Occupations - Statistics. I. Nebraska Occupational Information Coordinating Committee.
HD5725.N2 N474 1985

Nebraska. Labor, Dept. of. see **Nebraska. Dept. of Labor.**

Nebraska. Legislature.
Appropriations and revenues, fiscal year 1985-86 : summary of actions taken during the 1985 legislative session. [Lincoln] : Legislative Fiscal Office, [1985] i, 49 leaves ; 28 cm. "July 1985." LC Card 85-623111 DDC 336.782 19
1. Nebraska - Appropriations and expenditures - Statistics. 2. Revenue - Nebraska - Statistics. I. Nebraska. Legislature. Legislative Fiscal Office. II. Title.
HJ2053.N34 A66 1985

Nebraska. Legislature. Legislative Fiscal Office. Nebraska. Legislature. Appropriations and revenues, fiscal year 1985-86 . [Lincoln] [1985] i, 49 leaves ; LC Card 85-623111 DDC 336.782 19
HJ2053.N34 A66 1985

Nebraska Occupational Information Coordinating Committee.
Greater Nebraska job prospects, 1983-1988 /. [Lincoln, Neb.] [1985] ii, 54 p. : LC Card 86-622213 DDC 331.12/09781/021 19
HD5725.N2 G74 1985

[Nebraska job prospects] 1983-1988. [Lincoln, Neb. (550 South 16th St., Lincoln 68509) , <1985- >] v. <1, 5-9 > : LC Card 86-622062 DDC 331.12/09782/021 19
HD5725.N2 N474 1985

NEBRASKA - OCCUPATIONS - STATISTICS.
[Nebraska job prospects] 1983-1988. [Lincoln, Neb. (550 South 16th St., Lincoln 68509) , <1985- >] v. <1, 5-9 > : LC Card 86-622062 DDC 331.12/09782/021 19
HD5725.N2 N474 1985

NEBRASKA - POPULATION - STATISTICS.
Women in numbers . Lincoln, Neb. (Box 94600, Lincoln 68509-4600) , 1985. iii, 168 p. : LC Card 86-622214 DDC 331.4/125/09782 19
HD6096.N3 W66 1985

Nebraska. Revenue, Dept. of. see **Nebraska. Dept. of Revenue.**

Nebraska. Secretary of State. Tax expenditure report for sales and use tax--Nebraska and local option, property tax, individual income tax, fiduciary income tax, corporation income tax, miscellaneous taxes . Lincoln, Neb. [1985] 245 p. ; LC Card 86-622058 DDC 343.78204 347.8204 19
HJ2419 .T39 1985

NEBRASKA - STATISTICS, VITAL.
Nebraska abridged life expectancy tables, 1960-1980 /. [Lincoln, Neb.] [1985?] 40, 78, 3 leaves : LC Card 86-622212 DDC 304.6/09782021 19
HB1355.N42 N43 1985

Nechaev, ĪU. V. (ĪUriĭ Vasil′evich) Populiārnaiā politėkonomiiā / ĪU.V. Nechaev, ĪU.I. Palkin. Kiev : Izd-vo polit. lit-ry Ukrainy, 1986. 246 p. : ill. (some col.) ; 18 cm. Includes bibliographical references. LC Card 87-169729
1. Soviet Union - Economic policy - 1981-. 2. Soviet Union - Economic conditions - 1976-. 3. Marxian economics. I. Palkin, ĪUriĭ Ivanovich. II. Title.
HC336.25 .N43 1986

Nechernozem′e : demograficheskie protsessy / [redaktsionnaiā kollegiiā D.I. Valenteĭ (glavnyĭ redaktor) ... et al. ; redaktory-sostaviteli N.T. Agafonov, B.S. Khorev]. Moskva : "Statistika", 1977. 94 p. ; 21 cm. (Narodonaselenie. vyp. 17) At head of title: Ministerstvo vysshego i srednego spetsial′nogo obrazovaniiā SSSR. Nauchno-tekhnicheskiĭ sovet. Sektsiiā narodonaseleniiā. Includes bibliographical references. LC Card 82-107146
1. Non-Chernozem Region (R.S.F.S.R.) - Population. 2. Non-Chernozem Region (R.S.F.S.R.) - Population, Rural. I. Valenteĭ, D. I. (Dmitriĭ Ignat′evich). II. Agafonov, Nikolaĭ Timofeevich. III. Khorev, Boris Sergeevich. IV. Series.
HB3608.N57 N43 1977

Serie Bank- en effectenbedrijf. see **Serie Bank- en effectenbedrijf.**

NEDERLANDS VERBOND VAN VAKVERENIGINGEN - HISTORY - 20TH CENTURY.
Hueting, Ernest. Naar groter eenheid . Amsterdam , 1983, c1982. 432 p. : ISBN 90-6012-531-2 : LC Card 83-184649
HD6727 .H83 1983 ***NYPL [JLG 87-188]***

Nederlandsche Bank (Amsterdam, Netherlands)
Zijlstra, J. Gematigd monetarisme . Leiden , 1985. ix, 330 p. : ISBN 90-207-1382-5 : LC Card 85-201189
HG1065 .Z55 1985 ***NYPL [JLE 87-379]***

NEDERLANDSCHE OOST-INDISCHE COMPAGNIE - HISTORY.
All of one company . Utrecht , 1986. 230 p. : ISBN 90-6194-036-2 (pbk.) : LC Card 86-203885 DDC 382/.06/01 19
HF483.E6 A65 1986

NEDERLANDSE AARDOLIE MAATSCHAPPIJ - HISTORY.
Jong, H. J. de (Herman J.) Schoonebeek, olierijk in Zuidoost-Drenthe /. [Zuidwolde] , 1986. 232 p. : ISBN 90-6509-902-6 : LC Card 86-175279
HD9575.N43 N435 1986

Nederlandse overheidsuitgaven /. Drees, W. 's-Gravenhage , 1985. 270 p. ; ISBN 90-6095-330-4 : LC Card 85-197601
HJ1200 .D74 1985

Nederlandse Vereniging van Erkende Reclame Adviesbureaux. Effectiviteit in de reclame . Alphen aan den Rijn , 1986. 125 p. : ISBN 90-14-03587-X : LC Card 86-205967
HF5813.N4 E35 1986

Nederlandse woontheorieën /. Priemus, Hugo. Delft , 1984. vi, 92 p. : ISBN 90-6275-126-1 : LC Card 84-226472
HD7344.A3 P67 1984 ***NYPL [JLE 86-2510]***

Nedlog, D'Lanor. Insider's guide to antique bazaars in Japan / by D'Lanor Nedlog. Tokyo, Japan : GoldSprint Ltd., c1986. 124 p. : ill. ; 21 cm. (Encounter file series) ISBN 4-906231-00-4 LC Card 87-123282 DDC 381/.18 19
1. Fairs - Japan - Directories. 2. Bazaars, Oriental - Directories. 3. Antique dealers - Japan - Directories. I. Title. II. Series.
HF5475.J3 N43 1986

Nedo. see **National Economic Development Office.**

Nedorezov, A. I. (Aleksandr Ivanovich) Rabochiĭ klass i stroitel′stvo sotsializma v stranakh TSentral′noĭ i ĪUgo-Vostochnoĭ Evropy /. Moskva , 1977. 382 p. ; LC Card 81-174150
HD8376.5 .R33 1977

Nedzynski, Stefan.
Trade union situation in PTT services. 1966.
Matthew, J. Purchasing power of PTT personnel, 1965 / by J. Mat[t]hew. Trade union situation in PTT services / by Stefan Nedzynski. Brussels [1966] 1 v. (various pagings) ; LC Card 87-165119
HE6241 .M37 1966

Needles, Belverd E.
The Complete CPA examination review, auduiing, 1986-1987 /. Boston , c1986. 42, 237, 177, 12 p. : ISBN 0-395-41132-7 (pbk.) LC Card 86-80561 DDC 657/.45/076 19
HF5667 .C5852 1986

Principles of accounting / Belverd E. Needles, Henry R. Anderson, James C. Caldwell. 3rd ed. Boston, MA : Houghton Mifflin Co., c1987. xx, 1100, [38] p. : ill. (some col.) ; 26 cm. Includes bibliographical references and index. ISBN 0-395-35702-0 LC Card 86-80401 DDC 657 19
1. Accounting. I. Anderson, Henry R., 1939-. II. Caldwell, James C. III. Title.
HF5635 .N35 1987

Neeley, L. Paden. Accounting principles and practices / L. Paden Neeley, Frank J. Imke. 3rd ed. Cincinnati : South-Western Pub. Co., c1987. xx, 1052 p. : ill. (some col.) ; 24 cm. Includes index. ISBN 0-538-01631-0 LC Card 86-63073 DDC 657 19
1. Accounting. I. Imke, Frank J. II. Title.
HF5635 .N38 1987b

Neeley, Ralph E. Kerns, Allen F. Dictionary of worker traits /. Philadelphia, PA , 1987- p. cm. ISBN 0-9618599-9-7 LC Card 87-12478 DDC 331.7/02/0973 19
HB2595 .K43 1987

Neeser, Ph. Pour un rôle actif de la Communauté économique européenne sur la scène agricole internationale . Paris , c1986. 184 p. ; ISBN 2-11-001582-9 : LC Card 86-174918
HD1431 .P68 1986

Neff, Rosemary.
Directory of licensed occupations and apprenticeship programs in Texas. Mercer, Kent. Directory of licensed occupations and apprenticeship programs in Texas. 3rd ed. [Austin, Tex.] [1985] iv, 102 p. ; LC Card 86-622006 DDC 331.7/02/09764 19
HF5382.5.U6 T45 1985

Neff, Werner, 1947- Entfremdung und Selbstverwaltung : Gespräche und Fallstudien zur "autogestion" in Frankreich / Werner Neff. Zürich : Limmat c1983. 322 p. : ill. ; 21 cm. (Reihe W) Abridged and rev. ed. of the author's thesis (doctoral--Freie Universität Berlin, Berlin-Dahlem). Bibliography: p. 317-322. ISBN 3-85791-066-6 LC Card 87-672017
1. Management - France - Employee participation. 2. Alienation (Social psychology) - France. I. Title.
HD5660.F7 N43x 1983

Neffa, Julio César. La participación de los trabajadores en la gestión empresarial en la República del Perú, 1968-1980 / Julio César Neffa. 1a ed. Ginebra, Suiza : Instituto Internacional de Estudios Laborales, 1986. vi, 112, x p. : ill. ; 24 cm. (Serie de investigación . no. 84) Includes bibliographies. ISBN 92-9014-410-6 LC Card 87-400930 DDC 658.3/152/0985 19
1. Industrial management - Peru - Employee participation - History - 20th century. I. Series: Research series (International Institute for Labour Studies) , no. 84. II. Title.
HD5660.P4 N44 1986

Neft' i razvitie, Liviia, Alzhir /. Kukushkin, Vladimir IUr'evich. Moskva , 1985. 227 p. ; LC Card 85-180876
HD9577.L52 K85 1985
*NYPL [*QIP 87-3410]*

Neftianik . IUrasova, M. Moskva , 1981. 254 p. : LC Card 82-111110
HD8039.P42 S654 1981

NEGATIVE INCOME TAX - GERMANY (WEST)
Mitschke, Joachim. Steuer- und Transferordnung aus einem Guss . Baden-Baden , 1985. 274 p. : ISBN 3-7890-1097-9 LC Card 85-235532
HJ2687 .M57 1985

NEGATIVE INCOME TAX - GREAT BRITAIN.
Lenkowsky, Leslie, 1946- Politics, economics, and welfare reform . Lanham, MD [Washington, D.C.] , c1986. vii, 207 p. ; ISBN 0-8191-5215-3 (alk. paper) : LC Card 85-29456 DDC 362.5/82 19
HC260.I5 L46 1986 *NYPL [JLE 86-2801]*

NEGATIVE INCOME TAX - UNITED STATES.
Lenkowsky, Leslie, 1946- Politics, economics, and welfare reform . Lanham, MD [Washington, D.C.] , c1986. vii, 207 p. ; ISBN 0-8191-5215-3 (alk. paper) : LC Card 85-29456 DDC 362.5/82 19
HC260.I5 L46 1986 *NYPL [JLE 86-2801]*

Negishi, Takashi, 1933- Itō, Motoshige, 1951- Disequilibrium trade theories /. Chur, Switzerland , New York , c1987. viii, 100 p. : ISBN 3-7186-0412-4 LC Card 87-11834 DDC 380.1 19
HF1008 .I855 1987

Négociants et chargeurs . Chalmin, Philippe. Paris , 1985. 299 p. : ISBN 2-7178-0851-5 : LC Card 85-149921 DDC 333.7 19
HF1051 .C42 1985

The negotiable environment . Williams, Cecil L., 1930- Ann Arbor, Mich. , c1985. v, 82 p. : ISBN 0-936658-20-7 (pbk.) : LC Card 85-10305 DDC 658.3/82 19
HF5547.2 .W55 1985 *NYPL [JLF 86-1138]*

NEGOTIABLE INSTRUMENTS.
Baross, Jenő. A kereskedelmi hitel és a váltó gyakorlata /. Budapest , 1985. 123 p. ; LC Card 86-228454
HG3754.5.H9 B37 1985

NEGOTIABLE INSTRUMENTS - HUNGARY.
Baross, Jenő. A kereskedelmi hitel és a váltó gyakorlata /. Budapest , 1985. 123 p. ; LC Card 86-228454
HG3754.5.H9 B37 1985

NEGOTIABLE INSTRUMENTS - UNITED STATES.
Story, Joseph, 1779-1845. Commentaries on the law of promissory notes [microform]. Boston, 1868. xliv, 739 p. LC Card 12-34848
*NYPL [*ZT-1734]*

Venedikian, Harry M. Export-import financing /. New York , c1986. xvii, 456 p. : ISBN 0-471-82449-6 : LC Card 85-29566 DDC 332.7/42 19
HG3754.U5 V46 1986 *NYPL [JLE 86-2998]*

Negotiate your way to financial success /. Posluns, Ronald J. New York , c1987. 176 p. ; ISBN 0-399-13239-2 LC Card 87-2408 DDC 658.1/5 19
HD58.6 .P67 1987

Negotiating Lome III . Stevens, Christopher. Sussex [1986] 23 p. : LC Card 86-222421 DDC 337.406 19
HC241.25.D44 S74 1986

Negotiating Lome Three. Stevens, Christopher. Negotiating Lome III . Sussex [1986] 23 p. : LC Card 86-222421 DDC 337.406 19
HC241.25.D44 S74 1986

Negotiating Lome 3. Stevens, Christopher. Negotiating Lome III . Sussex [1986] 23 p. : LC Card 86-222421 DDC 337.406 19
HC241.25.D44 S74 1986

NEGOTIATION - CONGRESSES.
Bargaining behavior /. Tübingen , 1978. x, 383 p. : ISBN 3-16-340972-5 LC Card 86-227549 DDC 330 s 658.4 19
HB41 .B29 1967 Bd. 7 HD58.6

Coalition forming behavior /. Tübingen , 1978. viii, 375 p. : ISBN 3-16-340982-2 LC Card 86-227555 DDC 330 s 658.4 19
HB41 .B29 1967 vol. 8 HD58.6

NEGOTIATION IN BUSINESS.
Chapman, Jack, 1945- How to make $1,000 a minute . Berkeley, Calif. , c1987. xii, 90 p. : ISBN 0-89815-191-0 (pbk.) : LC Card 86-23099 DDC 650.1/4 19
HF5549.5.P7 C48 1987

Kennedy, Gavin. Doing business abroad /. New York , c1985. 268 p. ; ISBN 0-671-55484-0 : LC Card 85-14416 DDC 658.4 19
HD58.6 .K45 1985 *NYPL [JLD 86-2339]*

Kennedy, Gavin. Pocket negotiator /. Oxford, OX, UK ; New York, NY, USA : xi, 264 p. : ISBN 0-631-15451-5 : LC Card 87-6302 DDC 658 19
HD58.6 .K47 1987

Kuhn, Robert Lawrence. Dealmaker . New York , c1988. xi, 316 p. : ISBN 0-471-62465-9 LC Card 87-21543 DDC 658 19
HD58.6 .K84 1988

Posluns, Ronald J. Negotiate your way to financial success /. New York , c1987. 176 p. ; ISBN 0-399-13239-2 LC Card 87-2408 DDC 658.1/5 19
HD58.6 .P67 1987

Smith, Homer B., 1915- Selling through negotiation . Alexandria, VA , c1987. 192 p. ; ISBN 0-9618228-1-3 (soft) : LC Card 87-10998 DDC 658.8/1 19
HF5438.25 .S64 1987

Snowdon, Sondra. The global edge . New York , c1986. 431 p. ; ISBN 0-671-60122-9 : LC Card 86-3990 DDC 395/.22 19
HF5387 .S59 1986 *NYPL [JLE 86-3489]*

Stumm, David Arthur. Developing negotiation skills in sales personnel . New York , 1987. xiv, 148 p. ; ISBN 0-89930-279-3 (alk. paper) LC Card 87-11260 DDC 658.8/1/00683 19
HF5438.25 .S773 1987

NEGOTIATION IN BUSINESS - CHINA.
Campbell, Nigel. China strategies . [Manchester, Greater Manchester] [Hong Kong] , c1986. xxiv, 161 p. : ISBN 0-903808-51-X (pbk.) LC Card 86-235360 DDC 332.6/7314/0951 19
HD2910 .C36 1986

NEGOTIATION IN BUSINESS - CONGRESSES.
Bargaining behavior /. Tübingen , 1978. x, 383 p. : ISBN 3-16-340972-5 LC Card 86-227549 DDC 330 s 658.4 19
HB41 .B29 1967 Bd. 7 HD58.6

Coalition forming behavior /. Tübingen , 1978. viii, 375 p. : ISBN 3-16-340982-2 LC Card 86-227555 DDC 330 s 658.4 19
HB41 .B29 1967 vol. 8 HD58.6

NEGOTIATION IN BUSINESS - GERMANY (WEST)
Kauer, Christian, 1951- Konfliktregelung und Mitbestimmung . Frankfurt am Main , New York , c1985. 393 p. : ISBN 3-8204-5626-0 (pbk.) LC Card 87-672045
HD5660.G4 K37x 1985

NEGOTIATION IN BUSINESS - GHANA.
Essays from the Ghana-Valco renegotiations, 1982-85 /. [Accra, Ghana] 1986 (Accra : Printed by the Ghana Pub. Corp.) viii, 163 p. ; ISBN 996-490-120-8 (pbk.) LC Card 87-127499 DDC 338.8/87 19
HD9539.A63 G44 1986

NEGOTIATION IN BUSINESS - JAPAN.
McCreary, Don R. Japanese-U. S. business negotiations . New York , 1986. viii, 121 p. ; ISBN 0-275-92006-2 (alk. paper) : LC Card 86-554 DDC 658 19
HD58.6 .M38 1986 *NYPL [JLE 86-3074]*

NEGOTIATION IN BUSINESS - UNITED STATES.
McCreary, Don R. Japanese-U. S. business negotiations . New York , 1986. viii, 121 p. ; ISBN 0-275-92006-2 (alk. paper) : LC Card 86-554 DDC 658 19
HD58.6 .M38 1986 *NYPL [JLE 86-3074]*

NEGROES (NON-UNITED STATES) see **BLACKS.**

NEGROES (UNITED STATES) see **AFRO-AMERICANS.**

Négy évtizede új úton a magyar mezőgazdaság /. Almási, István. [Budapest] [1985] 159 p. : ISBN 963-7252-41-X LC Card 86-228893
HD1940.5 .A85 1985

Neider, Janusz. Marciniak-Neider, Danuta. Spedycja lądowa /. Gdańsk , 1979- v. <1 > ; LC Card 81-181249
HF5780.P7 M37 1979

NEIGHBORHOOD.
Galster, George C., 1948- Homeowners and neighborhood reinvestment /. Durham , 1987. xii, 354 p. ; ISBN 0-8223-0725-1 LC Card 87-13448 DDC 307.3/36 19
HD1387 .G34 1987

Housing and neighborhoods . New York , 1987. xii, 319 p. : ISBN 0-313-25459-1 (lib. bdg. : alk. paper) LC Card 87-7527 DDC 307.3/36 19
HD7287.5 .H47 1987

United States. National Commission on Neighborhoods. People, building neighborhoods . [Washington?] , Washington [1979] xi, 358 p. : LC Card 79-602955 DDC 307.7/6/0973
HN90.C6 U66 1979 *NYPL [JLM 81-194]*

NEIGHBORHOOD GOVERNMENT - UNITED STATES.
Zimmerman, Joseph Francis, 1928- Participatory democracy . New York , 1986. xi, 229 p. ; ISBN 0-275-92132-8 (alk. paper) : LC Card 86-8129 DDC 323/.042/0973 19
JF493.U6 Z56 1986 *NYPL [JLE 86-3632]*

The neighborhood mint . Head, Sylvia. Macon, Ga. , c1986. xviii, 206 p. : ISBN 0-86554-240-6 (alk. paper) : LC Card 86-23500 DDC 737.49758/273 19
HG461.D342 H4 1986

NEIGHBORHOOD - UNITED STATES.
Varady, David P. Neighborhood upgrading . Albany , c1986. x, 184 p. : ISBN 0-88706-299-7 LC Card 85-30392 DDC 307.3/362/0973 19
HT175 .V37 1986 *NYPL [JLE 87-373]*

Neighborhood upgrading . Varady, David P. Albany , c1986. x, 184 p. : ISBN 0-88706-299-7 LC Card 85-30392 DDC 307.3/362/0973 19
HT175 .V37 1986 *NYPL [JLE 87-373]*

Neij, Rob. Hueting, Ernest. Naar groter eenheid . Amsterdam , 1983, c1982. 432 p. : ISBN 90-6012-531-2 : LC Card 83-184649
HD6727 .H83 1983 *NYPL [JLG 87-188]*

Neikirk, William. Volcker, portrait of the money man / William R. Neikirk. New York : Congdon & Weed ; Chicago, Ill. : Distributed by Contemporary Books, c1987. xvi, 222 p. ; 24 cm. Bibliography: p. 221-222. ISBN 0-86553-178-1 LC Card 87-19953 DDC 332.1/1/0924 B 19
1. Volcker, Paul A. 2. Economists - United States -

Biography. 3. Board of Governors of the Federal Reserve System (U. S.) - Officials and employees - Biography. 4. United States - Economic policy - 1971-1981. 5. United States - Economic policy - 1981-. I. Title.
HB119.V6 N45 1987

Neilimo, Kari, 1944- Hinnanasetanta, toiminta-analyyttinen tutkimus pienyrityksistä / Kari Neilimo. Tampere : Tampereen yliopisto, 1984 90, [8] leaves : ill. ; 30 cm. (Tampereen yliopiston Yrityksen taloustieteen ja yksityisoikeuden laitoksen julkaisuja. A:2, 0357-5365 . 38) Summary in English. Bibliography: leaves [94]-[95] ISBN 951-44-1729-1 LC Card 86-140431
1. Price policy - Finland. 2. Small business - Finland. I. Title.
HF5416.5 .N45 1985

Neill, Robert Hitt. How to lose your farm in ten easy lessons and cope with it / Robert Hitt Neill and James R. Baugh. Leland, Miss. : Mississippi River Pub. Co., c1987. xi, 138 p. ; 21 cm. ISBN 0-9617591-1-9 (pbk.) : LC Card 87-14176 DDC 338.1/3/097624 19
1. Family farms - Mississippi River - Delta - Finance. 2. Bankruptcy - Psychological aspects. I. Baugh, James R. II. Title.
HD1476.U6 A156 1987

Neiman, Max. Energy efficiency . Washington, D.C. , 1987, c1986. 333 p. : ISBN 0-918249-05-8 (pbk.) LC Card 86-28817 DDC 333.79/16/0973 19
HD9502.U52 E4883 1987

Neinstein, Murray.
Barron's regents exams and answers. Bookkeeping. Kornbluh, Elaine H. Barron's regents exams and answers. Bookkeeping-accounting / Elaine H. Kornbluh. Woodbury, N.Y. , c1987. 318 p. in various pagings ; ISBN 0-8120-3185-7 (pbk.) : LC Card 87-403397 DDC 657/2/076 19
HF5661 .N4 1987

Neirynck, Jacques. Le Consommateur averti / Jacques Neirynck. Lausanne : P. M. Favre, 1979. 173 p. ; 21 cm. (En question) Bibliography: p. 169. ISBN 2-8289-0029-X : LC Card 79-394845 DDC 381/.34
1. Consumer protection. 2. Consumers. I. Title.
HC79.C63 N43 ***NYPL [JLD 86-2606]***

Nejatullah Siddiqi, Muhammad. see **Ṣiddīqī, Muḥammad Nejātullah, 1931-**

Nekotorye problemy internatsional'nogo vospitaniia v mnogonatsional'nom trudovom kollektive / [redkollegiia sbornika Dzhunusov M.S., otvetstvennyĭ redaktor, Kovalev IU.A]. Moskva : In-t sotsiologicheskikh issledovaniĭ AN SSSR, 1985. 135 p. ; 20 cm. At head of title: Akademiia nauk SSSR. Institut sotsiologicheskikh issledovaniĭ. Sovetskaia sotsiologicheskaia assotsiatsiia. Includes bibliographical references. LC Card 86-233779
1. Work groups - Soviet Union. 2. Personnel management - Soviet Union. 3. Soviet Union - Ethnic relations. 4. Labor mobility - Soviet Union. I. Dzhunusov, M. (Maskhud). II. Kovalev, IU. A. III. Institut sotsiologicheskikh issledovaniĭ (Akademiia nauk SSSR). IV. Sovetskaia sotsiologicheskaia assotsiatsiia.
HD8526.5 .N45 1985

Nekotorye problemy ispol'zovaniia trudovykh rezervov v Ėstonskoĭ SSR. Tööjõu kasutamise probleeme Eesti NSV-s /. Tallinn , 1986. 179 p. ; LC Card 87-107003
HD5797.E75 T66 1986

Nekotorye voprosy matematicheskoĭ ėkonomiki : materialy k seminaru pri Institute matematiki i kibernetiki AN Litovskoĭ SSR "Matematicheskie metody v sotsial'nykh naukakh" / pod redaktsieĭ Ė. Vilkasa i Ch. Shimialisa. Vil'nius : In-t matematiki i kibernetiki Akademii nauk Litovskoĭ SSR, 1982. 90 p. ; 20 cm. (Matematicheskie metody v sotsial'nykh naukakh . vyp. 15) Titles on added t.p.: Kai kurie matematinės ekonomikos klausimai; On some problems of mathematical economics. At head of title: Institut matematiki i kibernetiki Akademii nauk Litovskoĭ SSR. Summaries in English and Lithuanian. Inclues bibliographies. LC Card 83-169081
1. Economics, Mathematical - Congresses. I. Vilkas, Ė., 1935-. II. Shimialis, Ch. III. Title: Kai kurie matematinės ekonomikos klausimai. IV. Title: On some problems of mathematical economics. V. Series.
HB135 .N45 1982

Nekrasov, M. D. Valentik, I. IA. (Ivan IAkovlevich) Ėkonomicheskie osnovy intensifikatsii lesnogo khoziaĭstva Karel'skoĭ ASSR /. Leningrad , 1986. 135, [1] p. : LC Card 87-125199
HD9765.S653 K378 1986

Nekrasov, Nikolai Nikolaevich.
Gosudarstvenno-monopolisticheskiĭ kapitalizm i razmeshchenie proizvoditel'nykh sil /. Moskva , 1984. 182 p. ; LC Card 84-239188
HC240 .G565 1984

Osobennosti i problemy razmeshcheniia proizvoditel'nykh sil SSSR v period razvitogo sotsializma /. Moskva , 1980. 273 p. ; LC Card 81-143866
HC340.D5 O86 1980

Nel, P. A. The BM industrial register and its application in industrial marketing / by P.A. Nel. Pretoria : Bureau of Market Research, University of South Africa, 1977. iii, 29, [34] p. ; 30 cm. (Research report / Bureau of Market Research, University of South Africa = Navorsingsverslag / Buro vir Marknavorsing, Universiteit van Suid-Afrika . no. 59) Includes bibliographical references. ISBN 0-949951-74-9 (pbk.) LC Card 85-127469
1. Industry - Classification. 2. South Africa - Industries - Classification. 3. Industrial marketing - South Africa. I. Series. II. Series: Research report (University of South Africa. Bureau of Market Research) , no. 59. III. Title.
HC905 .N45 1977

Nell, Edward J. Prosperity and public spending : transformational growth and the role of government / Edward Nell. Boston : Allen & Unwin, 1987. p. cm. (Studies in international political economy. 1) Bibliography: p. Includes index. ISBN 0-04-339044-7 (alk. paper) LC Card 87-1383 DDC 339.5/22 19
1. Expenditures, Public. 2. Economic development. I. Series. II. Series: Studies in international political economy (Boston, Mass.) , 1. III. Title.
HJ7451 .N44 1987

Nellevad, Per. Larsson, Folke. Varuhandeln. [Stockholm] [1981] 137 p. : ISBN 91-38-06014-0 LC Card 84-120411
HF5429.6.S9 L368 1981

Nelli, Humbert S., 1930- The business of crime : Italians and syndicate crime in the United States / Humbert S. Nelli. New York : Oxford University Press, 1976. xiii, 314 p. : ill. ; 22 cm. Includes index. Bibliography: p. [303]-306. ISBN 0-19-502010-3 : LC Card 75-32350 DDC 364.1/06/073
1. Organized crime - United States. 2. Mafia - United States. I. Title.
HV6791 .N37 ***NYPL [JLD 86-3722]***

Nellis, John R. Public enterprises in Sub-Saharan Africa / John R. Nellis. Washington, D.C., U. S.A. : World Bank, [1986] vii, 66 p. : ill. ; 28 cm. (World Bank discussion papers, 0259-210X . 1) Bibliography: p. 66. ISBN 0-8213-0845-9 (pbk.) LC Card 86-24756 DDC 338.7/4/0967 19
1. Government business enterprises - Africa, Sub-Saharan. I. Title. II. Series.
HD4338 .N45 1986

Nelson, Bergen A. Fielder, Lonnie L. Agricultural statistics and prices for Louisiana, 1909-1985 /. [Baton Rouge, LA] [1986] iv, [122] p. : LC Card 87-620749 DDC 338.1/09763 s 338.1/09763/021 19
HD1775.L8 L7 no. 659

Nelson, Charles R. The investor's guide to economic indicators / Charles R. Nelson. New York : Wiley, c1987. viii, 193 p. : ill. ; 24 cm. Includes index. ISBN 0-471-85902-8 LC Card 87-2134 DDC 330.973/0927 19
1. Economic indicators - United States. 2. Investments - United States. I. Title.
HC106.8 .N38 1987

Nelson, Don. Don Nelson's Mining & mining equipment/service companies world wide . Barnet, Herts., U.K. [1982] 562 p. ; ISBN 946-0-04005-X ***NYPL [JSD 86-337]***

Nelson, John R., 1952- Liberty and property : political economy and policymaking in the new nation, 1789-1812 / John R. Nelson, Jr. Baltimore : Johns Hopkins University Press, c1987. xv, 221 p. : ill. ; 24 cm. (The Johns Hopkins University studies in historical and political science. 105th ser., 2) Bibliography: p. 187-212. Includes index. ISBN 0-8018-3440-6 (alk. paper) LC Card 86-21373 DDC 338.973 19
1. United States - Economic policy - To 1933. 2. United States - Politics and government - 1789-1815. 3. Liberalism - United States - History. 4. Laissez-faire - History. I. Title. II. Series.
HC105 .N45 1987

Nelson, Kay Yarborough. Using Lotus Manuscript / Kay Yarborough Nelson and William Fletcher. Berkeley, Calif. : Osborne McGraw-Hill, c1987. xvii, 410 p. : ill. ; 24 cm. Includes index. ISBN 0-07-881003-5 (pbk.) : LC Card 87-401628 DDC 652/.5 19
1. Lotus Manuscript (Computer program). 2. Word processing. I. Fletcher, Bill, 1957-. II. Lotus Manuscript (Computer program). III. Title.
HF5548.115 .N45 1987

Nelson, Michael, 1966- Golden tokens . Roxbury, Conn. , c1987. p. cm. ISBN 0-941067-00-9 LC Card 86-27826 DDC 388.4/28 19
HE4211 .G58 1987

Nelson, Nadine, 1919- Nelson, Selmer, 1917- Grossenburg's fifty years with John Deere /. Freeman, S.D. , c1987. viii, 167 p. : LC Card 87-80826 DDC 338.7/681763/0978361 19
HD9486.U6 G766 1987

Nelson, Richard Alan, 1947- Heath, Robert L. (Robert Lawrence), 1941- Issues management . Beverly Hills , c1986. 288 p. ; ISBN 0-8039-2535-2 LC Card 85-14547 DDC 659.2 19
HD59 .H33 1986 ***NYPL [JLD 87-19]***

Nelson, Richard R. Understanding technical change as an evolutionary process / Richard R. Nelson. Amsterdam ; New York : North-Holland ; viii, 125 p. ; 20 cm. (Professor Dr. F. de Vries lectures in economics . v. 8) Bibliography: p. 123-125. Includes index. ISBN 0-444-70207-5 (pbk.) LC Card 87-9109 DDC 338/.06 19
1. Technological innovations - Economic aspects. 2. Technology and state. I. Title. II. Series.
HC79.T4 N45 1987

Nelson, Robert B. Decision point : a business game book / Robert B. Nelson. New York, NY : AMACOM, American Management Association, c1987. x, 278 p. : ill. ; 23 cm. ISBN 0-8144-7659-7 (pbk.) : LC Card 86-47820 DDC 658.4/03 19
1. Decision-making - Case studies. I. Title.
HD30.23 .N44 1987

Nelson, Selmer, 1917- Grossenburg's fifty years with John Deere / by Selmer Nelson, Nadine Nelson. 1st ed. Freeman, S.D. : Printed by Pine Hill Press, c1987. viii, 167 p. : ill. ; 29 cm. "Privately printed." Includes index. LC Card 87-80826 DDC 338.7/681763/0978361 19
1. Grossenburg Implement, Inc. - History. 2. Deere & Company - History. 3. Agricultural machinery industry - United States - History. 4. Agricultural machinery industry - South Dakota - Winner - History. I. Nelson, Nadine, 1919-. II. Title. III. Title: Grossenburg's 50 years with John Deere.
HD9486.U6 G766 1987

Nemchinov, Sergeĭ Valentinovich. Pochtovye marki . Moskva , 1984. 223 p. : LC Card 85-185295
HE6185.C92 P63 1984

A Német Szövetségi Köztársaság bankrendszere /. Langmár, Andrásné. Budapest [1987] 71 p. : ISBN 963-7103-59-7 LC Card 87-409642
HG3048 .L47 1987

Németh, Ernő. A bér- és keresetszabályozás működése 1983-ban / [készitette, Németh Ernő, Tolvaly Anikó]. [Budapest] : Állami Bér és Munkaügyi Hivatal, Munkaügyi Információs Központ, [1984] 245 p. : ill. ; 24 cm. (Munkaügyi elemzések . 9) "Készült az ÁBMH Munkaügyi Információs Központ Munkaügyi Információs és Gazdaságelemző Főosztályán"--T.p. verso. Chiefly tables. ISBN 963-02-3277-4 LC Card 85-231744
1. Wages - Hungary. I. Tolvaly, Anikó. II. Munkaügyi Információs Központ (Hungary). Munkaügyi Információs és Gazdaságelemző Főosztály. III. Title. IV. Series.
HD5022.5 .N46 1984

Németi, László.
Hatékonyság és fejlesztési lehetőségek a mai magyar mezőgazdaságban / Németi László. Budapest : Mezőgazdasági Kiadó, 1986. 189 p. : ill. ; 20 cm. Bibliography: p. 186-[188]. ISBN

963-232-238-X : LC Card 87-407758
1. Agriculture - Economic aspects - Hungary. 2. Agricultural productivity - Hungary. I. Title.
HD1940.5 .N46 1986

A személyzeti munka gyakorlati kérdései a mezőgazdasági termelőszövetkezetekben / [szerző, Németi László]. [Budapest] : Termelőszövetkezetek Országos Tanácsa, 1984. 243 p. ; 20 cm. (TOT füzetek, 0139-4851 . 16) Bibliography: p. 131-138. ISBN 963-502-370-7 LC Card 86-147870
1. Collective farms - Hungary - Personnel management. I. Title. II. Series.
HD1492.H8 N43 1984

Nemetz, Peter N., 1944- The Pacific rim . Vancouver , 1987, c1986. ix, 319 p. : ISBN 0-7748-0266-9 (pbk.) LC Card 87-140238 DDC 330.99 19
HF4030.7 .P33 1987

Nemoto, Masao.
[TQC to toppu bu-kachō no yakuwari. English] Total quality control for management : strategies and techniques from Toyota and Toyoda Gosei / by Masao Nemoto ; translated and edited by David Lu. Englewood Cliffs, N.J. : Prentice Hall, Inc., c1987. xix, 238 p. : ill. ; 24 cm. Translation of: TQC to toppu bu-kachō no yakuwari. Includes index. ISBN 0-13-925637-7 : LC Card 87-2329 DDC 658.4/036 19
1. Quality circles. 2. Quality control. I. Lu, David John, 1928-. II. Title.
HD66 .N4613 1987

Nemtsev, F. L. (Fedor Logvinovich) Upravlenie trudom v usloviiakh nauchno-tekhnicheskogo progressa / F.L. Nemtsev. Minsk : "Belarus'", 1985. 125 p. ; 20 cm. Bibliography: p. 125. LC Card 85-231066
1. Personnel management - Soviet Union. 2. Labor productivity - Soviet Union. I. Title.
HF5549.2.S65 N45 1985

Nemzedéki vonások a mezőgazdasági kistermelésben /. Halász, Péter. Budapest , 1984. 72 p. ; ISBN 963-491-192-7 LC Card 86-198744
HD1476.H8 H252 1984

A Nemzeti vagyon és az állóeszközállomány 1970-1978 / [készült a Központi Statisztikai Hivatal Közgazdasági Főosztályán ; főmunkatársak Darabont Árpád, Pozsonyi Pál]. [Budapest] : Központi Statiszikai Hivatal, [1979] 140 p. ; 29 cm. (Statisztikai időszaki közlemények . 448. köt.) "1979. április 9/10." LC Card 82-193609
1. Wealth - Hungary - Statistics. 2. Gross national product - Hungary - Statistics. 3. Capital - Hungary - Statistics. I. Darabont, Árpád. II. Pozsonyi, Pál. III. Hungary. Központi Statisztikai Hivatal. Közgazdasági Főosztály. IV. Series.
HC300.295.W4 N454 1979

Nemzetközi biztosítás a külkereskedelem szolgálatában /. Pálfi, Sándor. [Budapest] [1986] 63 p. ; ISBN 963-02-4369-5 LC Card 87-425585
HG8059 .P35 1986

A nemzetközi pénzügyek és a külkereskedelmi fizetések gyakorlata /. Szilvássy, Erika. Budapest , 1985. 286 p. ; ISBN 963-221-529-X : LC Card 86-190902
HG3881 .S95 1985

Nemzetközi szervezetek statisztikai tevékenységéből .
(69. sz) Az Ipari robotok termelésének és felhasználásának trendjei /. Budapest , 1985. 63 p. : LC Card 86-199458
HD9696.R623 H852 1985

Nemzetközi tőkemozgások és a KGST /. Sinkovics, Alfréd. Budapest , 1986, c1985. 336, [1] p. : ISBN 963-221-493-5 : LC Card 87-408509
HG3891 .S57 1986

NEOCLASSICAL SCHOOL OF ECONOMICS - ADDRESSES, ESSAYS, LECTURES.
Post Keynesian economic theory . Sussex , Armonk, N.Y. , 1985. xii, 235 p. ; ISBN 0-87332-318-1 LC Card 84-23615 DDC 330/.09/04 19
HB87 .P62 1985 *NYPL [JLD 87-1155]*

Neoclassical theory and empirical models of aggregate firm behaviour /. Broer, D. P. Dordrecht , Boston , 1987. 343 p. : ISBN 90-247-3412-6 LC Card 86-23485 DDC 338.5 19
HD30.22 .B76 1987

NEO-FASCISM. see **FASCISM.**

Neoh, Soon Kean. Stock market investment in Malaysia and Singapore / Neoh Soon Kean. Kuala Lumpur : Berita Publishing, 1986. vii, 312 p. : ill. ; 23 cm. ISBN 967-96906-6-0 (pbk.) LC Card 86-943422 DDC 332.63/22/09595 19
1. Stocks - Malaysia. 2. Stocks - Singapore. I. Title.
HG5750.6.A5 N46 1986

Neomercantilism. Koot, Gerard M. English historical economics, 1870-1926 . Cambridge [Cambridgeshire] , New York , 1987. viii, 277 p. ; ISBN 0-521-32854-3 LC Card 87-11592 DDC 330/.0941 19
HB103.A2 K65 1987

NEO-NAZISM. see **FASCISM.**

Neoricardianische Modelle zur Theorie des internationalen Handels und ihre Kritik der neoklassischen Aussenhandelstheorie . Kattermann, Dieter. Bremen , 1981. 135, A-G p. : ISBN 3-88722-039-0 LC Card 82-177622 DDC 337/.0724 19
HF1412 .K37 1981 *NYPL [JLD 86-2740]*

Nepal, a state of poverty /. Seddon, David. New Delhi , c1987. xxii, 288 p. ; ISBN 0-7069-3414-8 : LC Card 87-900823 DDC 330.9549/6 19
HC425 .S43 1987

NEPAL - CENSUS.
A Study on the improvement of the national sample censuses of agriculture in Nepal. Kathmandu , 1986. 67 p. : LC Card 87-900372 DDC 338.1/09549/6 19
HD2065.9 .S78 1986

NEPAL - CENSUS, 1981.
Population census, 1981--Nepal. Kathmandu, Nepal , 1984- <v. 1, pt. 1-4, 5-7; v. 2; v. 3 in 9 > ; LC Card 85-904528
HA4570.9 .A4 1981c

NEPAL - COMMERCE - INDIA.
Dahal, Kishor. Indo-Nepal trade . Kathmandu, Nepal , c1987. x, 66, [9] p. ; LC Card 87-902005 DDC 382/.0954/05496 19
HF3788.N45 D34 1987

NEPAL - DEPENDENCY ON INDIA.
Maass, Citha Doris. Indien, Nepal, Sri Lanka . Wiesbaden , 1982. xxi, 380 p. ; ISBN 3-515-03802-7 LC Card 86-214318
HF1590.15.N4 M33 1982

NEPAL - ECONOMIC CONDITIONS.
Seddon, David. Nepal, a state of poverty /. New Delhi , c1987. xxii, 288 p. ; ISBN 0-7069-3414-8 : LC Card 87-900823 DDC 330.9549/6 19
HC425 .S43 1987

NEPAL - ECONOMIC POLICY.
NEPAL - ECONOMIC POLICY - CONGRESSES.
Cooperative development and basic needs /. Kathmandu, Nepal , 1985. iii, 238 p. ; LC Card 86-900318 DDC 338.9549/3 19
HC425 .C66 1985

Nepal Family Planning and Maternal Health Project. Nepal fertility survey, 1976. Kathmandu, Nepal [1977] xi, 347 p. : LC Card 87-915005
HB1046.9.A3 N464 1977

Nepal fertility survey, 1976. First report. Kathmandu, Nepal : H.M. Govt., Health Ministry, Nepal Family Planning and Maternal Child Health Project Central Office, [1977] xi, 347 p. : ill. ; 30 cm. At head of title: World Fertility Survey. "August 1977." Includes bibliography. LC Card 87-915005
1. Fertility, Human - Nepal - Statistics. I. World Fertility Survey. II. Nepal Family Planning and Maternal Health Project.
HB1046.9.A3 N464 1977

NEPAL - FOREIGN ECONOMIC RELATIONS - INDIA.
Maass, Citha Doris. Indien, Nepal, Sri Lanka . Wiesbaden , 1982. xxi, 380 p. ; ISBN 3-515-03802-7 LC Card 86-214318
HF1590.15.N4 M33 1982

NEPAL - INDUSTRIES - DIRECTORIES.
Udyoga kāryālaya (utpādana garne) ko nāma sūci =. [Kathmandu] [1985] 202 p. ; LC Card 87-901652
HD9736.N382 U39 1985

Nepal. Kendrīya Tathyāṅka Vibhāga.
Population census, 1981--Nepal. Kathmandu, Nepal , 1984- <v. 1, pt. 1-4, 5-7; v. 2; v. 3 in 9 > ; LC Card 85-904528
HA4570.9 .A4 1981c

A Study on the improvement of the national sample censuses of agriculture in Nepal. Kathmandu , 1986. 67 p. : LC Card 87-900372 DDC 338.1/09549/6 19
HD2065.9 .S78 1986

Udyoga kāryālaya (utpādana garne) ko nāma sūci =. [Kathmandu] [1985] 202 p. ; LC Card 87-901652
HD9736.N382 U39 1985

NEPAL - MANUFACTURES - DIRECTORIES.
Udyoga kāryālaya (utpādana garne) ko nāma sūci =. [Kathmandu] [1985] 202 p. ; LC Card 87-901652
HD9736.N382 U39 1985

Nepal National Committee for Man and the Biosphere.
NEPAL - POPULATION - STATISTICS.
Population census, 1981--Nepal. Kathmandu, Nepal , 1984- <v. 1, pt. 1-4, 5-7; v. 2; v. 3 in 9 > ; LC Card 85-904528
HA4570.9 .A4 1981c

Nepal. Rāshṭriya Janasaṅkhyā Āyoga. Nepālamā janasaṅkhyā śikshā. Kāṭhamāḍauṃ, Nepāla , 2042 [1985] 195 p. ; LC Card 87-902146
HB850.5.N35 N46 1985

NEPAL - SOCIAL CONDITIONS.
Seddon, David. Nepal, a state of poverty /. New Delhi , c1987. xxii, 288 p. ; ISBN 0-7069-3414-8 : LC Card 87-900823 DDC 330.9549/6 19
HC425 .S43 1987

Nepālamā janasaṅkhyā śikshā. Kāṭhamāḍauṃ, Nepāla : Śrī 5 ko Sarakāra, Rāshṭriya Janasaṅkhyā Āyogako Sacivālaya, 2042 [1985] 195 p. ; 25 cm. In Nepali. On population education in Nepal. Includes bibliographies. LC Card 87-902146
1. Population - Study and teaching - Nepal. I. Nepal. Rāshṭriya Janasaṅkhyā Āyoga.
HB850.5.N35 N46 1985

A népgazdasági szintü gazdaságpolitikai döntések végrehajtását segitő szakszervezeti munka . Juhász, Ottó. [Budapest] [1984] 136 p. ; ISBN 963-608-064-X LC Card 86-126615
HD6680.5 .J84 1984

A Népmozgalmi statisztika fejlődése Magyarországon. Budapest : Központi Statisztikai Hivatal Népességtudományi Kutató Intézet, 1985- v. <1 > ; 29 cm. (A Központi Statisztikai Hivatal Népességtudományi Kutató Intézetének történeti demográfiai füzetei . 1-) Summary in English and Russian. Bibliography: v. 1, p. 43. CONTENTS. - 1. A hivatalos népmozgalmi statisztika fejlődése Magyarországon a statisztikai szolgálat megalakulásától a polgári anyakönyvezés elrendeléséig (1867-1894) / írta, Kármán Tamásné. LC Card 86-190535
1. Hungary - Statistical services - History. 2. Hungary - Statistics, Vital - History. 3. Registers of births, etc. - Hungary - History. I. Kármán, Tamásné. II. Series: Központi Statisztikai Hivatal Népességtudományi Kutató Intézetének történeti demográfiai füzetei , 1, etc.
HA37.H92 N46 1985

Neposredstvenno obobshchestvlennyĭ trud /. Grimaliuk, V. A. (Viktor Andreevich) Moskva , 1985. 110, [2] p. ; LC Card 86-111859
HD5796 .G75 1985

Neposredstvenno-obshchestvennoe proizvodstvo v usloviiakh razvitogo sotsializma / pod redaktsieĭ N.D. Kolesova. Leningrad : Izd-vo Leningradskogo universiteta, 1984. 212 p. ; 22 cm. At head of title: Leningradskiĭ ordena Lenina i ordena Trudovogo Krasnogo Znameni gosudarstvennyĭ universitet imeni A.A. Zhdanova. Includes bibliographical references. LC Card 84-248045
1. Marxian economics. I. Kolesov, Nikolai Dmitrievich. II. Leningradskiĭ gosudarstvennyĭ universitet imeni A.A. Zhdanova.
HB97.5 .N434 1984

Neppl, Rainer. Zur Wahrnehmung und Bewertung der Gerechtigkeit der Einkommens-Verteilung / Rainer Neppl. Regensburg : S. Roderer, 1986. 310 p. : ill. ; 21 cm. (Theorie und Forschung . Bd 14. Bd. 6) Bibliography: p. 248-260. ISBN

3-89073-362-X LC Card 87-121773 DDC 339.2 19
1. Income distribution. 2. Distributive justice. 3. Equality. 4. Social psychology. I. Series: Theorie und Forschung , Bd. 14. II. Title.
HB523 .N47 1986

Neramit Dhanasakdi, 1946- Luther, Norman Y., 1936- Consistent correction of census and vital registration data for Thailand, 1960-80 /. Honolulu, Hawaii [1986] vii, 39 p. ; ISBN 0-86638-089-2 (pbk.) : LC Card 86-32807 DDC 304.6/0723 19
HA39.T4 L87 1986

Néré, Jacques. Le problème du mur d'argent : les crises du franc (1924-1926) / Jacques Néré. Paris : Pensée universelle, c1985. 159 p. ; 19 cm. Bibliography: p. [150]-155. ISBN 2-214-06264-5 : LC Card 86-149791
1. Money - France - History - 20th century. 2. Finance - France - History - 20th century. 3. France - Economic conditions - 1918-1945. I. Title.
HG979 .N47 1985

Nerlove, Marc, 1933-
Household and economy : welfare economics of endogenous fertility / Marc Nerlove, Assaf Razin, Efraim Sadka. Boston : Academic Press, 1987. xiii, 155 p. : ill. ; 24 cm. (Economic theory, econometrics, and mathematical economics) Includes bibliographies and indexes. ISBN 0-12-515752-5 LC Card 86-10764 DDC 304.6/32 19
1. Fertility, Human. 2. Population policy. I. Razin, Assaf. II. Sadka, Efraim. III. Title.
HB901 .N47 1987 ***NYPL [JLE 87-1715]***

Population policy and individual choice : a theoretical investigation / Marc Nerlove, Assaf Razin, and Efraim Sadka. Washington, D.C., U. S.A. : International Food Policy Research Institute, 1987. 52 p. : ill. ; 26 cm. (Research report (International Food Policy Research Institute) . 60) Bibliography: p. 51-52. ISBN 0-89629-062-X (pbk.) LC Card 87-16802 DDC 363.9 19
1. Fertility, Human - Mathematical models. 2. Population policy - Mathematical models. 3. Economic development - Mathematical models. I. Razin, Assaf. II. Sadka, Efraim. III. Series. IV. Series: Research report (International Food Policy Research Institute) , 60. V. Title.
HB901 .N474 1987

Nerve, muscle, bone stimulation, and augmentation. Revision 3. Tustin, CA, U. S.A. (17722 Irvine Blvd., Tustin 92680) : Biomedical Business International, c1987. iv, 8, 144, [112] p. : ill. ; 29 cm. (Report / Biomedical Business International . #7026) "April 1987." LC Card 87-402023 DDC 338.4/7681761 19
1. Electrotherapeutic equipment industry - United States. 2. Market surveys - United States. I. Biomedical Business International, Inc. II. Series: Report (Biomedical Business International, Inc.) , #7026.
HD9995.E43 U56 1987

Nery, Sebastiáo. Crime e castigo da dívida externa / Sebastião Nery, Alencar Furtado. Brasília-Distrito Federal : Dom Quixote, [1986] 170 p. ; 23 cm. Includes bibliographical references. LC Card 86-208917
1. Debts, External - Brazil. I. Furtado, Alencar. II. Title.
HJ8579 .N47 1986

Nesher, Ariela. Rural industrialization in Israel /. Boulder , 1987. xi, 193 p. ; ISBN 0-8133-7393-X (pbk. : alk. paper) : LC Card 87-2073 DDC 338.095694 19
HC415.25 .R87 1987

Ness, Leland S. Precision guided munitions . Greenwich, CT., U. S.A. (P.O. Box 4585, Greenwich 06830) , c1986. 606, 4 p. ; LC Card 86-207047 DDC 380.1/456234 19
HD9744.P732 P74 1986

Ness, Walter L. A influência da correção monetária no sistema financeiro / Walter L. Ness, Jr. Rio de Janeiro : Instituto Brasileiro de Mercado de Capitais, 1977. 205 p. : ill. ; 21 cm. (Série Estudos especiais . 5) Bibliography: p. [199]-205. LC Card 85-206096
1. Indexation (Economics) - Brazil. 2. Inflation (Finance) - Brazil. 3. Interest rates - Brazil. 4. Monetary policy - Brazil. I. Title. II. Series.
HG229 .N385 1977

Nest egg investing . Sheen, Brian J., 1952- New York , c1987. 224 p. : ISBN 0-399-13185-X : LC Card 87-2268 DDC 332.6/78 19
HG179 .S455 1987

Nesterov, V. G. (Vladimir Gavrilovich) Andrianov, V. V. Za slovom--delo /. Moskva , 1985. 124 p. ; LC Card 85-213388
HC338.S87 A53 1985

Nestone, Alberto. Protektionismus : Plädoyer für ein Tabu / ALberto Nestone. München : Profil, c1984. 76 p. : ill. ; 21 cm. (Reihe Wissenschaft) ISBN 3-89019-108-8 LC Card 85-127389
1. Free trade and protection - Protection. 2. Foreign exchange problem. I. Series: Reihe Wissenschaft (Munich, Germany). II. Title.
HF1713 .N38 1984

NET NATIONAL PRODUCT. see **NATIONAL INCOME.**

Net proceeds of mines, 1985-86 / prepared by Division of Assessment Standards for certification by the Nevada Tax Commission. Carson City, Nev. : Dept. of Taxation, [1986] 18 leaves ; 28 cm. Cover title. Tables. "May 27, 1986." LC Card 87-620610 DDC 336.2/78622/09793021 19
1. Mines and mineral resources - Taxation - Nevada - Statistics. I. Nevada. Division of Assessment Standards.
HJ4242.M56 N47 1986

NETHERLANDIC LANGUAGE. see **DUTCH LANGUAGE.**

NETHERLANDS ANTILLES - ECONOMIC CONDITIONS.
Nos futuro . Curaçao, NA , Zutphen , c1986. 496 p. : ISBN 90-6011-512-0 : LC Card 86-220862
HC157.5 .N67 1986

NETHERLANDS ANTILLES - SOCIAL CONDITIONS.
Nos futuro . Curaçao, NA , Zutphen , c1986. 496 p. : ISBN 90-6011-512-0 : LC Card 86-220862
HC157.5 .N67 1986

NETHERLANDS - APPROPRIATIONS AND EXPENDITURES.
Drees, W. Nederlandse overheidsuitgaven /. 's-Gravenhage , 1985. 270 p. ; ISBN 90-6095-330-4 : LC Card 85-197601
HJ1200 .D74 1985

Netherlands. Centraal Bureau voor de Statistiek. Hoofdafdeling Bevolkingsstatistieken.
Nouwt, P. Vruchtbaarheid van geboortegeneraties gebaseerd op waarnemingen over de periode 1950-1983 /. 's-Gravenhage , 1985. 95 p. ; ISBN 90-357-0197-6 : LC Card 86-218161
HB1015 .N68 1985

Netherlands. Centraal Bureau voor de Statistiek. Hoofdafdeling Economische Basistellingen.
Vierde algemene bedrijfstelling 1978 /. 's-Gravenhage , 1985-<1986. <3 v.; in 11 > ; ISBN 90-357-0319-7 (d. 2, A) : LC Card 86-202940
HC323 .V54 1985

Netherlands. Centraal Bureau voor de Statistiek. Hoofdafdeling Sociaal-Culturele Statistieken.
Beek, P. van. De leefsituatie van Surinamers en Antillianen in Nederland, 1985 /. 's-Gravenhage , 1986- v. <1 > : ISBN 90-357-0558-0 : LC Card 87-120083
HD8518.5.S87 B44 1986

De Leefsituatie van Turken en Marokkanen in Nederland 1984 /. 's-Gravenhage , 1985-<1987. v. <1-3 > : ISBN 90-357-0457-6 : LC Card 86-234067
HD8518.5.T87 L44 1985

Netherlands. Centraal Bureau voor de Statistiek. Hoofdafdeling Sociale Rekeningen. Flevoland statistisch bezien . 's-Gravenhage , 1986. 50 p. : ISBN 90-357-0466-5 : LC Card 86-208188
HA1387.F48 F56 1986

Netherlands. Centraal Bureau voor de Statistiek. Hoofdafdeling Statistieken van Verkeer en Vervoer. Het Bezit en gebruik van motorfietsen, 1984 /. 's-Gravenhage , 1985. 26 p. : ISBN 90-357-0397-9 : LC Card 86-218867
HE5616.5 .B49 1985

NETHERLANDS - COMMERCE.
Exportnota. [Hague , 1982] 60 p. ; ISBN 90-12-04106-6 LC Card 83-197657
HF3616.5 .E9 1982

NETHERLANDS - COMMERCE - JAPAN.
Puyenbroek, R. (Rien) Exportgids Japan /. Amsterdam , 1985. 149 p. : ISBN 90-10-05277-X LC Card 85-236503
HF3618.J33 P89 1985

NETHERLANDS - COMMERCE - UNITED STATES.
Puyenbroek, R. (Rien) Exportgids Verenigde Staten /. Amsterdam , 1985. 140 p. : ISBN 90-10-05276-1 LC Card 85-236520
HF3618.U6 P89 1985

NETHERLANDS - COMMERCIAL POLICY.
Exportnota. [Hague , 1982] 60 p. ; ISBN 90-12-04106-6 LC Card 83-197657
HF3616.5 .E9 1982

NETHERLANDS - ECONOMIC CONDITIONS.
Handel en wandel in de dertiende eeuw /. Amsterdam , c1986. 139 p. : ISBN 90-6707-112-9 LC Card 86-199144
HC324 .H36 1986

NETHERLANDS - ECONOMIC CONDITIONS - 1918-1945.
Kloosterman, Robert. Werkloosheid in Nederland, 1920-1939 . Utrecht , 1985. xiv, 351 p. : ISBN 90-6194-315-9 : LC Card 86-150980
HD5792 .K56 1985 ***NYPL [JLD 86-3407]***

NETHERLANDS - ECONOMIC CONDITIONS - 1945-
Sociaal-Economische Raad. Advies inzake het sociaal-economisch beleid op middellange termijn 1986-1990 /. Den Haag [1986] 142, 150 p. ; ISBN 90-6587-248-5 LC Card 86-234847
HC321 .S63 1986, nr. 10 HC325

De Verzorgingsstaat, slopen of renoveren? /. Assen , 1986. 152 p. : ISBN 90-232-2180-X : LC Card 86-186673
HC325 .V45 1986

Zelfzorg en verzorging . Kampen [1985] 237 p. ; ISBN 90-242-4072-7 : LC Card 86-175292
HC325 .Z43 1985

NETHERLANDS - ECONOMIC POLICY.
Renshaw, Geoffrey. Adjustment and economic performance in industrialised countries . Geneva , 1986. xiv, 180 p. ; ISBN 92-2-105510-8 (pbk.) : LC Card 87-123435 DDC 338.9/009172/2 19
HC286.7 .R46 1986

Schouten, D. B. J. Het wankele evenwicht in de economie . Leiden , 1986. xiv, 189 p. ; ISBN 90-207-1436-8 : LC Card 86-167831
HD85.D8 S36 1986

Sociaal-Economische Raad. Advies inzake het sociaal-economisch beleid op middellange termijn 1986-1990 /. Den Haag [1986] 142, 150 p. ; ISBN 90-6587-248-5 LC Card 86-234847
HC321 .S63 1986, nr. 10 HC325

NETHERLANDS - EMIGRATION AND IMMIGRATION.
Aalberts, Monique M. J. Gezinsvorming door jonge migranten . 's-Gravenhage , 1985. 93 p. : ISBN 90-12-04999-7 LC Card 85-235621
HD8518.5.A2 A24 1985

NETHERLANDS - FOREIGN ECONOMIC RELATIONS.
Kox, Henk. Kapitaal-export vanuit Nederland . Amsterdam , 1985. 136 p. : ISBN 90-71284-01-8 LC Card 85-237950
HG5562 .K69 1985

Netherlands - Government. see **Netherlands - Politics and government.**

NETHERLANDS - INDUSTRIES - CONGRESSES.
Failed transitions to modern industrial society . Montreal , c1975. vii, 105 p. : ISBN 0-919958-00-1 LC Card 80-510009 DDC 303.4/094 19
HM101 .F26 ***NYPL [JLE 81-166]***

NETHERLANDS - INDUSTRIES - STATISTICS.
Vierde algemene bedrijfstelling 1978 /. 's-Gravenhage , 1985-<1986. <3 v.; in 11 > ; ISBN 90-357-0319-7 (d. 2, A) : LC Card 86-202940
HC323 .V54 1985

NETHERLANDS - INDUSTRIES - TECHNOLOGICAL INNOVATIONS - CASE STUDIES.
Ondernemen en vernieuwen . Delft, Netherlands , 1985. 240 p. : ISBN 90-6275-189-X LC Card 86-113900
HD2346.N4 O53 1985

Netherlands (Kingdom, 1815-). Centraal Bureau voor de Statistiek.

Statistische onderzoekingen: M.
(9) Netherlands (Kingdom, 1815-). Centraal Bureau voor de Statistiek. Hoofdafdeling Bevolkingsstatistieken. De gehuwde vrouw en haar kindertal anno 1975 /. 's-Gravenhage , 1980. 78 p. : LC Card 81-100844
HB1015 .N47 1980
NYPL [JLM 78-1515 nr.9]

Netherlands (Kingdom, 1815-). Centraal Bureau voor de Statistiek. Hoofdafdeling Bevolkingsstatistieken. De gehuwde vrouw en haar kindertal anno 1975 / Centraal Bureau voor de Statistiek, Hoofdafdeling Bevolkingsstatistieken. 's-Gravenhage : Staatsuitgeverij, 1980. 78 p. : ill. ; 30 cm. (Statistische onderzoekingen . M9) Summary in English. Bibliography: p. 50-51. LC Card 81-100844
1. Fertility, Human - Netherlands - Statistics. 2. Wives - Netherlands - Statistics. I. Series. II. Series: Netherlands (Kingdom, 1815-). Centraal Bureau voor de Statistiek. Statistische onderzoekingen: M., 9. III. Title.
HB1015 .N47 1980
NYPL [JLM 78-1515 nr.9]

Netherlands (Kingdom, 1815-) Sociaal-Economische Raad. see **Sociaal-Economische Raad.**

Netherlands. Ministerie van Buitenlandse Zaken. Voorlichtingsdienst Ontwikkelingssamenwerking. Wereldbevolking groeiend ontwikkelingsprobleem. Den Haag [1975] 66 p. : LC Card 87-118557
HB883.5 .W47 1975

Netherlands. Ministerie van Economische Zaken. Exportnota. [Hague , 1982] 60 p. ; ISBN 90-12-04106-6 LC Card 83-197657
HF3616.5 .E9 1982

Netherlands. Ministerie van Financiën. Fraudenota. [Hague , 1982] 42 p. ; ISBN 90-12-04091-4 LC Card 83-197641
HJ2348.5 .F72 1982

Netherlands. Ministerie van Financiën. Afdeling Beleidsanalyse. Evaluatiemethoden, een introductie . 's-Gravenhage [1984] v, 188 p. : ISBN 90-12-04825-7 LC Card 85-196500
HD58.9 .E93 1984

Netherlands. Nationale Advies Raad voor Ontwikkelingssamenwerking.
Advies minimum internationale arbeidsnormen / Nationale Advies Raad voor Ontwikkelingssamenwerking. 's-Gravenhage : Staatsuitgeverij, [1984] 97 p. ; 24 cm. (Publikaties van de Nationale Advies Raad voor Ontwikkelingssamenwerking . 84) "November 1984." Includes bibliographical references. ISBN 90-12-04950-4 LC Card 86-193168
1. Labor laws and legislation, International. I. Title. II. Series.
HC60 .N465 no. 84a K1705.4

Advies vrouwen en ontwikkeling / Nationale Advies Raad voor Ontwikkelingssamenwerking. [The Hague : Staatsuitgeverij, 1985] 53 p. ; 24 cm. (Publikaties van de Nationale Advies Raad voor Ontwikkelingssamenwerking . 85) Includes bibliographical references. ISBN 90-12-04985-7 LC Card 86-198854
1. Women in development. I. Title. II. Series.
HC60 .N465 no. 85 HQ1240

NETHERLANDS - POLITICS AND GOVERNMENT - 1648-1715.
Wildenberg, Ivo W. (Ivo Willibrord) Johan & Pieter de la Court, 1622-1660 & 1618-1685 . Amsterdam , 1986. xiii, 180 p., [21] p. of plates : ISBN 90-302-1162-8 : LC Card 87-141484
HC322.5.A2 W55 1986

NETHERLANDS - POPULATION.
Fulpen, Hans van. Volkshuisvesting in demografisch en economisch perspectief /. 's-Gravenhage , 1985. 354 p. : ISBN 90-12-05159-2 LC Card 86-169936
HD7344.A3 F85 1985

NETHERLANDS - POPULATION - STATISTICS.
Nouwt, P. Vruchtbaarheid van geboortegeneraties gebaseerd op waarnemingen over de periode 1950-1983 /. 's-Gravenhage , 1985. 95 p. ; ISBN 90-357-0197-6 : LC Card 86-218161
HB1015 .N68 1985

NETHERLANDS. REGERINGSCOMMISSARIAAT VOOR DE BUITENLANDSE AGRARISCHE AANGELEGENHEDEN - ARCHIVES.
Plas, W. Inventaris van het archief van Regeringscommissariaat voor de Buitenlandse Agrarische Aangelegenheden (RECOBAA), 1946-1950 /. [Hague] [1985] 111 p. ; LC Card 87-101964
HD9015.N42 P55 1985

Netherlands. Rijksnijverheidsdienst. Ondernemen en vernieuwen . Delft, Netherlands , 1985. 240 p. : ISBN 90-6275-189-X LC Card 86-113900
HD2346.N4 O53 1985

NETHERLANDS. RIJKSNIJVERHEIDSDIENST.
Ondernemen en vernieuwen . Delft, Netherlands , 1985. 240 p. : ISBN 90-6275-189-X LC Card 86-113900
HD2346.N4 O53 1985

NETHERLANDS - SOCIAL CONDITIONS.
Handel en wandel in de dertiende eeuw /. Amsterdam , c1986. 139 p. : ISBN 90-6707-112-9 LC Card 86-199144
HC324 .H36 1986

NETHERLANDS - SOCIAL CONDITIONS - 1945-
Zelfzorg en verzorging . Kampen [1985] 237 p. ; ISBN 90-242-4072-7 : LC Card 86-175292
HC325 .Z43 1985

NETHERLANDS - SOCIAL POLICY.
Bel Ghazi, Hassan. Mythen . Amsterdam [1985] 111 p. ; ISBN 90-6617-024-7 LC Card 86-145232
HD8518.5.A2 B44 1985

Netherlands. Staten-Generaal. Eerste Kamer. Interparlamentarische Konferenz über die Rheinverschmutzung (1977 : Den Haag, Netherlands) Interparlamentarische Konferenz über die Rheinverschmutzung . 's Gravenhage , 1977. 62 p. ; ISBN 90-12-01782-3 LC Card 86-149213
HC240.9.E5 I77 1977

Netherlands. Staten-Generaal. Tweede Kamer. Interparlamentarische Konferenz über die Rheinverschmutzung (1977 : Den Haag, Netherlands) Interparlamentarische Konferenz über die Rheinverschmutzung . 's Gravenhage , 1977. 62 p. ; ISBN 90-12-01782-3 LC Card 86-149213
HC240.9.E5 I77 1977

NETHERLANDS - STATISTICAL SERVICES.
Litz, Hans Peter. Amtliche Statistik in marktwirtschaftlich organisierten Industriegesellschaften . Frankfurt , New York , c1986. xii, 312 p. : ISBN 3-593-33752-5 LC Card 87-108767 DDC 350.81/9 19
HA37.G3 L58 1986

Netherlands. Statistiek, Centraal Bureau voor de. see **Netherlands. Centraal Bureau voor de Statistiek.**

Netherlands West Indies. see **Netherlands Antilles.**

Neto, Manoel José de Miranda. see **Miranda Neto, Manoel José de.**

Netto, José Candido de Campos. see **Campos Netto, José Candido de, 1880-1963.**

Nettolohn? Recktenwald, Werner. Wie errechne ich meinen Nettolohn? . Saarbrücken [1985?] 112 p. ; ISBN 3-88968-029-1 LC Card 85-171297 DDC 343.4305/242 344.3035242 19
HJ4720.A7 R42 1985

Network marketing /. Robinson, Dean L. Salt Lake City, Utah , c1983. 137 p. : LC Card 86-202974 DDC 658.8/4 19
HF5415.126 .R63 1983

NETWORK THEORY. see **SYSTEM ANALYSIS.**

Networking with the I.B.M. Network and Cluster. Hurwicz, Michael. Networking with the IBM Network & Cluster /. Blue Ridge Summit, Pa. , 1985. x, 518 p. : ISBN 0-8306-0929-6 : LC Card 85-4639 DDC 001.64/404 19
TK5105.7 .H87 1985 *NYPL [JSE 86-1975]*

Networking with the IBM Network & Cluster /. Hurwicz, Michael. Blue Ridge Summit, Pa. , 1985. x, 518 p. : ISBN 0-8306-0929-6 : LC Card 85-4639 DDC 001.64/404 19
TK5105.7 .H87 1985 *NYPL [JSE 86-1975]*

Networks and electronic office systems . International Conference on Networks and Electronic Office Systems (1983 : University of Reading) London , c1983. 240 p. : ISBN 0-903748-52-5 *NYPL [JSG 86-298]*

Networks and electronic office systems . International Conference on Networks and Electronic Office Systems (1985 : London, England) London , c1985. 166 p. : ISBN 0-903748-60-6 *NYPL [JSG 86-264]*

NETWORKS, COMPUTER. see **COMPUTER NETWORKS.**

NETWORKS, INFORMATION. see **INFORMATION NETWORKS.**

Neu, Axel Dietmar, 1942- Entkoppelung von Wirtschaftswachstum und Energieverbrauch : eine Strategie der Energiepolitik? / von Axel D. Neu. Kiel : Institut für Weltwirtschaft Kiel, [1978] 91 p. : ill. ; 30 cm. (Kieler Diskussionsbeiträge, 0455-0420 = Kiel discussion papers . 52) Cover title. "Februar 1978." Bibliography: p. 85-91. LC Card 85-174721
1. Energy policy - Germany, West. 2. Germany (West) - Industries - Energy conservation. I. Series: Kieler Diskussionsbeiträge , 52. II. Title.
HB44 .K45 no. 52 HD9502.G42

Neu, C. R. (Carl Richard), 1949- Toward a profile of Soviet behavior in international financial markets / C.R. Neu, John Lund. Santa Monica, CA : Rand, [1987] xv, 58 p. : ill. ; 23 cm. "Prepared for the Office of the Under Secretary of Defense for Policy." "August 1987." "R-3524-USDP." Includes bibliographical references. ISBN 0-8330-0865-X (pbk.) LC Card 87-13084 DDC 332/.042/0947 19
1. Foreign exchange problem - Soviet Union. 2. Balance of payments - Soviet Union. 3. Loans, Foreign - Soviet Union. 4. Capital movements - Soviet Union. I. Lund, John, 1960-. II. Rand Corporation. III. United States. Office of the Under Secretary of Defense for Policy. IV. Title.
HG3955 .N48 1987

Neu, H., 1920- Management Training Seminar (1982 : Joint Research Centre, Ispra, Italy) National energy planning and management in developing countries . Dordrecht, Holland , Hingham, MA , c1983. xiii, 442 p. ; ISBN 90-277-1589-0 LC Card 83-4407 DDC 333.79/09172/4 19
HD9502.A2 M343 1982
NYPL [JLE 87-302]

Neudecker, Heinz. The Practice of econometrics . Dordrecht , Boston , 1987. xii, 273 p. : ISBN 90-247-3502-5 LC Card 87-4054 DDC 330/.028 19
HB139 .P7 1987

Neue Arbeits- und Tätigkeitsformen : Colloquium, Brussels, 25. 4. 1986 : Dokumentation = New forms of work and activity : documentation / herausgegeben von Ralf Dahrendorf, Eberhard Köhler, Françoise Piotet. Dublin, Ireland : Europäische Stiftung zur Verbesserung der Lebens- und Arbeitsbedingungen ; [Washington, D.C. : European Community Information Service, distributor], c1986. xvi, 339 p. ; 24 cm. German, English, and French. Papers presented at the Colloquium on New Forms of Work and Activity, sponsored by the European Foundation for the Improvement of Living and Working Conditions, Apr. 25, 1986, in Brussels. CONTENTS. - Employment flexibility and internal and external labour markets / John Atkinson -- Issues in job sharing / Joyce Epstein -- Telework / Rosalyn Moran and Jean Tansey -- Les consequences des formes nouvelles d'emploi sur la vie familiale et l'organsation / Françoise Piotet -- Auswirkungen von neuen Arbeitsformen aus betriebspsychologischer Sicht / Otto Renda & Hans-Jürgen Reuter -- Legal and contractual limitations to working time / Roger Blanpain -- Les consequences des formes nouvelles d'emploi sur le droit du travail et de la securité sociale / Yota Kravaritou-Manitakis -- Neue Wege der Arbeitsorganisation / Lothar Gretsch -- Lifestyle, economic structure and time use / Jonathan Gershuny. ISBN 92-825-6418-5 LC Card 87-408469 DDC 306/.36/094 19
1. Work - Social aspects - European Economic Community countries - Congresses. 2. Work environment - European Economic Community countries - Congresses. 3. Job sharing - European Economic Community countries - Congreesses. 4.

Hours of labor, Flexible - European Economic Community countries - Congresses. I. Dahrendorf, Ralf. II. Köhler, Eberhard. III. Piotet, F. (Françoise). IV. European Foundation for the Improvement of Living and Working Conditions. V. Colloquium on New Forms of Work and Activity (1986 : Brussels, Belgium). VI. Title: New forms of work and activity.
HD6957.E86 N48 1986

Neue Arbeitswerttheorie . Chao, Tzu-yuan. [Hsin lao tung chia chih li lun. German.] Hamburg , 1974. x, 173 p. ; LC Card 74-351429 DDC 335.4/12 19
HD4904 .C45715

Neue betriebswirtschaftliche Forschung .
(Bd. 22) Kremeyer, Heinz. Eigenfertigung und Fremdbezug unter finanzwirtschaftlichen Aspekten /. Wiesbaden , c1982. 330 p. : ISBN 3-409-37340-3 LC Card 83-148058
HD2748 .K74 1982

(Bd. 34) Werder, Axel von. Organisationsstruktur und Rechtsnorm . Wiesbaden , c1986. 564 p. : ISBN 3-409-13107-8 LC Card 86-224483
HD58.7 .W35 1986

(22) Kremeyer, Heinz. Eigenfertigung und Fremdbezug unter finanzwirtschaftlichen Aspekten /. Wiesbaden , c1982. 330 p. : ISBN 3-409-37340-3 LC Card 83-148058
HD2748 .K74 1982

(27) Fritz, Wolfgang, Dipl.-Kfm. Warentest und Konsumgüter-Marketing . Wiesbaden , c1984. 596 p. : ISBN 3-409-13600-2 LC Card 84-207784
HF5415.2 .F75 1984

(33) Ebers, Mark. Organisationskultur, ein neues Forschungsprogramm? /. Wiesbaden , c1985. 223 p. ; ISBN 3-409-13105-1 LC Card 86-135588
HD58.8 .E24 1985

(34) Werder, Axel von. Organisationsstruktur und Rechtsnorm . Wiesbaden , c1986. 564 p. : ISBN 3-409-13107-8 LC Card 86-224483
HD58.7 .W35 1986

Neue Einkaufszentren im Ruhrgebiet . Heineberg, Heinz. Paderborn , 1986. 247 p. : ISBN 3-506-73224-2 LC Card 87-407591 DDC 381/.1/094355 19
HF5430.6.G4 H45 1986

Neue Entwicklungen bei Arbeit, Entgelt und Führung / herausgegeben von Heinz Knebel und Ernst Zander ; mit Beiträgen von Heinrich Axer ... [et al.]. Freiburg im Breisgau : R. Haufe, c1984. 169 p. : ill. ; 21 cm. Papers from a meeting sponsored by CONSULECTRA Unternehmungsberatung and REFA-Verband in Hamburg. ISBN 3-448-01480-X : LC Card 84-249237
1. Personnel management - Germany, West - Congresses. 2. Compensation management - Germany (West) - Congresses. 3. Labor supply - Germany (West) - Effect of automation on - Congresses. I. Knebel, Heinz. II. Zander, Ernst. III. CONSULECTRA Unternehmungsberatung. IV. REFA-Verband (Hamburg, Germany).
HF5549.2.G3 N48 1984

Neue Finanzdienstleistungen . Glogowski, Erhard. Wiesbaden , c1986. 305 p. : ISBN 3-409-14101-4 LC Card 87-131647 DDC 332.1/0943 19
HG3048 .G57 1986

Neue Formen des Auslandengagements . Hämisegger, Kuno, 1956- Bern , New York , c1986. 292 p. : ISBN 3-261-03598-6 LC Card 86-208515
HF1411 .H253 1986

Neue Gesellschaft für Bildende Kunst. Mein Vaterland ist international . Oberhausen , 1986. 331 p. : ISBN 3-921541-62-X LC Card 86-224091
HD7791 .M45 1986

Neue Heimat : Gewerkschaften und Wohnungspolitik / Manfred Fuhrich ... [et al.]. Hamburg : VSA-Verlag, 1983. 231 p. : ill. ; 21 cm. Includes bibliographical references. ISBN 3-87975-238-9 LC Card 83-150360
1. Neue Heimat (Firm : Hamburg, Germany). 2. Housing - Germany, West - Hamburg. 3. Business enterprises, Trade-union - Germany (West) - Hamburg. 4. Corruption (in politics) - Germany (West) - Hamburg. I. Fuhrich, Manfred, 1950-.
HD7339.H3 N48 1983

NEUE HEIMAT (FIRM : HAMBURG, GERMANY)
Neue Heimat . Hamburg , 1983. 231 p. : ISBN 3-87975-238-9 LC Card 83-150360
HD7339.H3 N48 1983

Neue historische Bibliothek.
Abelshauser, Werner. Wirtschaftsgeschichte der Bundesrepublik Deutschland (1945-1980) /. Frankfurt am Main , 1983. 186 p. : ISBN 3-518-11241-4 : LC Card 83-180531
HC286.7 .A26 1983

Neue Industriepolitik oder Stärkung der Marktkräfte? : strukturpolitische Konzeptionen im internationalen Vergleich / Hans-Hagen Härtel ... [et al.]. Hamburg : Verlag Weltarchiv, 1986. xiii, 221 p. ; 24 cm. (Spezialuntersuchung 1 im Rahmen der HWWA-Strukturberichterstattung 1987) Veröffentlichungen des HWWA-Institut für Wirtschaftsforschung-Hamburg Issued by the HWWA-Institut für Wirtschaftsforschung-Hamburg. Bibliography: p. 209-215. Includes index. ISBN 3-87895-315-1 LC Card 87-408234 DDC 338.9 19
1. Industry and state - Germany, West. 2. Industry and state - United States. 3. Industry and state - Japan. 4. Industry and state - Austria. 5. Industry and state - Great Britain. 6. Industry and state - Italy. I. Härtel, Hans-Hagen. II. HWWA-Institut für Wirtschaftsforschung-Hamburg. III. Series: Spezialuntersuchung ... im Rahmen der HWWA-Strukturberichterstattung 1987 , 1.
HD3616.G4 N48 1986

Neue Leistungspolitik in der Bekleidungsindustrie . Fischer, Joachim, 1948- Frankfurt/Main , New York , c1986. 264 p. : ISBN 3-593-33635-9 LC Card 86-197222
HD9940.G32 F57 1986

Neue Phänomene der kapitalistischen Gesellschaft ändern nichts an ihrem Wesen . Marxismus-Leninismus, eine immer junge und wissenschaftliche Lehre (Radio Program). Selections. Wien , 1976. 35 p. : LC Card 85-144894
HB501 .M338 1976

Der Neue Protektionismus : zur politischen Ökonomie von Handelsbeschränkungen gegenüber Fertigwarenexporten aus Entwicklungsländern / Heinrich Müller-Godeffroy ... [et al.]. Bonn : Verlag Neue Gesellschaft, c1983. 195 p. : ill. ; 22 cm. (Reihe Weltwirtschaft) Bibliography: p. 183-193. ISBN 3-87831-370-5 LC Card 83-198686
1. United States - Commercial policy. 2. Germany, West - Commercial policy. 3. United States - Commerce - Developing countries. 4. Developing countries - Commerce - United States. 5. Germany (West) - Commerce - Developing countries. 6. Developing countries - Commerce - Germany (West). 7. Free trade and protection - Protection. I. Müller-Godeffroy, Heinrich. II. Series: Reihe Weltwirtschaft (Bonn, Germany).
HF1756 .N58 1983

Der Neue Protektionismus / herausgegeben von Armin Gutowski. Hamburg : Verlag Weltarchiv, 1984. 149 p. ; 24 cm. (Veröffentlichungen des HWWA-Institut für Wirtschaftsforschung-Hamburg) Papers originally presented at a symposium organized by the HWWA-Institut für Wirtschaftsforschung-Hamburg, October 1983. Includes bibliographical references. CONTENTS. - Protektionismus im historischen Rückblick / Knut Borchardt -- Nationale Währungspolitik in einem internationalen Kapitalmarkt / Jürg Niehans -- Ist das Freihandelskonzept noch zeitgemäss? Hans-Eckart Scharrer -- Entwicklungsländer und Protektionismus / Dietrich Kebschull -- Der neue Protektionismus aus der Sicht der politischen Ökonomie / Werner Zohlnhöfer -- Protektionismus ist kein Null-Summenspiel / F. Wilhelm Christians -- Protektionismus führt zur Bürokratisierung / Carl Heinz Illies -- Begleiterscheinung der nationalen Krisenüberwindungsstrategie / Rudolf Henschel -- Der "neue Protektionismus" aus der Sicht der EG / Eberhard Rhein -- Für eine neue GATT-Runde / Klaus Kautzor-Schröder. ISBN 3-87895-251-1 LC Card 84-222112
1. Free trade and protection - Congresses. I. Gutowski, Armin. II. HWWA-Institut für Wirtschaftsforschung-Hamburg.
HF1703 .N48 1984

Die neue Sicht der Dinge . Biedenkopf, Kurt H. München , c1985. 458 p. ; ISBN 3-492-02813-6 LC Card 86-105815
HB95 .B53 1985

Neue Technologien und Arbeitswelt : was erwartet die Arbeitnehmer? / Heribert Kohl, Bernd Schütt (Hrsg.) ; mit einem Vorwort von Siegfried Bleicher. Köln : Bund-Verlag, c1984. 197 p. : ill. ; 21 cm. (Wissenschaft im Arbeitnehmerinteresse . Bd. 4) Selected articles from the periodical "Die Mitbestimmung." Includes bibliographies. ISBN 3-7663-0893-9 LC Card 85-160745
1. Labor supply - Germany (West) - Effect of technological innovations on - Addresses, essays, lectures. 2. Microelectronics - Addresses, essays, lectures. 3. Robotics - Germany (West) - Addresses, essays, lectures. I. Kohl, Heribert, 1940-. II. Schütt, Bernd. III. Mitbestimmung (Düsseldorf, Germany). IV. Series.
HD6331.2.G28 N475 1984 ***NYPL [JLD 86-3861]***

Neue Zahlungsverkehrsinstrumente . Christians, Volker C. Frankfurt am Main , 1985. 216 p. ; ISBN 3-922182-17-8 : LC Card 86-100407
HG1710 .C48 1985

Neue Zukunft. Leben im Jahr 2000 und danach . Berlin , c1984. 213 p. : ISBN 3-7605-8571-X LC Card 85-128359
HB3595 .L43 1984

Die neuere Diskussion über den Zusammenhang von Wechselkursflexibilität und Inflation /. Kotios, Angelos, 1957- Köln , 1986. 384 p. ; ISBN 3-921471-58-3 LC Card 87-407838 DDC 332.4/5 19
HG3821 .K67 1986

Neuere Entwicklungen in der Unternehmenstheorie : Erich Gutenberg zum 85. Geburtstag / herausgegeben von Helmut Koch ; unter Mitwirkung von Horst Albach ... [et al.]. Wiesbaden : Gabler, c1982. xiii, 290 p. : ill. ; 25 cm. Includes bibliographies. ISBN 3-409-39810-4 LC Card 87-672661
1. Industrial management. 2. Gutenberg, Erich, 1897-. I. Gutenberg, Erich, 1897-. II. Koch, Helmut, 1919-. III. Albach, Horst.
HD35 .N4814x 1982

Neuerungen in den Aussenwirtschafts- und Devisenvorschriften Jugoslawiens /. Kovač, Josef. Hamburg , c1985. 100 p. : ISBN 3-9800762-9-6 LC Card 86-160924
HG3965.5 .K68 1985

Neufeld, Rose. Exploring nontraditional jobs for women / by Rose Neufeld ; photographs by William Neufeld. 1st ed. New York : Rosen Pub. Group, c1987. x, 149 p. : ill. ; 23 cm. Includes index. ISBN 0-8239-0698-1 : LC Card 86-29827 DDC 331.7/02/024042 19
1. Vocational guidance for women - United States. I. Title.
HF5382.65 .N48 1987

Neuman, W. Russell. The paradox of mass politics : knowledge and opinion in the American electorate / W. Russell Neuman. Cambridge, Mass. : Harvard University Press, 1986. 241 p. : ill. ; 25 cm. Includes index. Bibliography: p. [222]-236. ISBN 0-674-65455-2 (alk. paper) LC Card 86-288 DDC 324.973 19
1. Voting - United States. 2. Public opinion - United States. 3. Elite (Social sciences) - United States. 4. United States - Politics and government - 1945-. I. Title.
JK1967 .N48 1986 ***NYPL [JLE 86-4140]***

Neumann, Carl Wolfgang. Historische Entwicklung und heutiger Stand der Wettbewerbstheorie : kritische Bestandsaufnahme zum Disput zwischen "funktionsfähigem Wettbewerb" und "neuklassischem/freiem Wettbewerb" um ein angemessenes Wettbewerbskonzept, einschliesslich der dogmenhistorischen Wurzeln / Carl Wolfgang Neumann. Königstein/Ts. : Athenäum, 1982. 318 p. ; 22 cm. (Schriften zum Wirtschafts-, Arbeits- und Sozialrecht . Bd. 19) Originally presented as the author's thesis (doctoral)--Freie Universität Berlin, 1982. Bibliography: p. 309-318. ISBN 3-7610-6362-8 : LC Card 83-154547
1. Competition. 2. Competition, International. I. Title. II. Series.
HB238 .N48 1982

Neumann, Günther, 1945- Probleme monetärer und finanzwirtschaftlicher Steuerung im Systemvergleich /. Duisburg , c1986. 175 p. : ISBN 3-921473-43-8 LC Card 86-211745
HC286.6 .P754 1986

Neumann János Számitógéptudományu Társaság. System modelling and optimization . Berlin , New York , c1986. xii, 1046 p. : ISBN 0-387-16854-0 (U. S.) LC Card 86-15637 DDC 003 19
QA402 .S95822 1986 *NYPL [JSE 86-1775]*

Neumann, Karl-Heinz. Gebührenpolitik im Telekommunikationsbereich / Karl-Heinz Neumann. 1. Aufl. Baden-Baden : Nomos Verlagsgesellschaft, 1984. 348 p. : ill. ; 23 cm. (Wirtschaftsrecht und Wirtschaftspolitik. Bd. 79) Originally presented as the author's thesis (doctoral--Universität Bonn, 1984) Bibliography: p. 332-348. ISBN 3-7890-1049-9 : LC Card 86-166218
1. Telecommunication - Germany (West) - Rates. 2. Telecommunication policy - Germany (West). 3. Telephone - Germany (West) - Rates. I. Title.
HE8157 .N48 1984

Neumann, Manfred J. M. (Manfred Johann Michael), 1940- Monetary policy and uncertainty . Baden-Baden , 1986. 262 p. : ISBN 3-7890-1257-2 (pbk.) LC Card 86-225786 DDC 332.4/0724 19
HG230.3 .M655 1986

Neumann, Michael, 1950- König, Heinz, 1927- Mathematische Wirtschaftstheorie . Königstein/Ts. , c1986. x, 239 p. : ISBN 3-445-02393-X : LC Card 86-188816
HB135 .K66 1986

Neumann, Walter. Krahl, Hans-Jürgen. Vom Ende der abstrakten Arbeit . Frankfurt , 1984. 209 p. ; ISBN 3-88535-075-0 LC Card 84-188656
HD4904 .K6915 1984

Neumark, Fritz, 1900- Studien zur Entwicklung der ökonomischen Theorie /. Berlin , c1981- v. ; ISBN 3-428-04862-8 (v. 1) : LC Card 81-154218 DDC 330/.09 19
HB75 .S787 1981
NYPL [JLL 73-186 Bd.115]

Neun, Hansjörg, 1953- Projektübergabe bei der technischen Zusammenarbeit mit Entwicklungsländer / Hansjörg Neun. Augsburg : Maro Verlag, [1985] viii, 315 p. : ill. ; 21 cm. (Augsburger Schriften zur Wirtschaftssoziologie) Reihe Wissenschaftliche Texte ; Bd. 35 Originally presented as the author's thesis (doctoral--Augsburg) under the title: Bedeutung und Probleme der Projektübergabe für die Planung und Durchführung der Technischen Zusammenarbeit mit Entwichlungsländern. Bibliography: p. 301-315. ISBN 3-87512-135-X : LC Card 86-228570
1. Economic development projects - Developing countries - Management. 2. Technical assistance - Developing countries - Management. I. Title. II. Series.
HD84 .N43 1985

Neundörfer, Konrad. Wir und die Dritte Welt : Probleme der Entwicklungs- und Handelspolitik / Konrad Neundörfer. Köln : C. Heymann, c1985. x, 214 p. ; 21 cm. Bibliography: p. vii-x. ISBN 3-452-20304-2 LC Card 85-164555
1. Developing countries - Economic policy. 2. Developing countries - Economic conditions. 3. Developing countries - Commerce. 4. Economic assistance, West German - Developing countries. 5. Technical assistance, West German - Developing countries. 6. Economic assistance - Developing countries. 7. Technical assistance - Developing countries. I. Title.
HC59.7 .N375 1985

Neuorientierung des Wettbewerbsschutzes : Jubiläumsschrift 25 Jahre FIW. Köln : C. Heymann, 1986. viii, 231 p. ; 23 cm. (FIW-Schriftenreihe, 0429-9485 . Heft 120) Contains papers from the 19. Innsbrucker Symposion which was held in 1985. Includes bibliographical references. PARTIAL CONTENTS. - Neue Ansätze des dynamischen Wettbewerbs aus der Sicht des Sachverständigenrates / Ernst Helmstädter -- Neuorientierung in der deutschen Wettbewerbspolitik? / Otto Schlecht -- Marktstruktur und volkswirtschaftliche Effizienz / Wolfgang Kartte -- Entwicklung der deutschen Rechtspraxis in der Bestimmung von Macht / Gerd Pfeiffer -- Die Politik der Gemeinschaft zur Stärkung der Stellung des Innovators / Fernand Braun -- Innovatorischer und imitatorischer Wettbewerb in der Wirtschaftsordnung / Horst Albach -- Wettbewerb und Ethik / Joseph Kardinal Höffner -- Zur Bedeutung von Marktstruktur und -verhalten in der materiellen Fusionskontrolle des GWB / Kurt Markert -- Ressourcenstärke und Abschreckungswirkung in der Fusionskontrolle / Manfred Dirrheimer -- Preismissbrauchsaufsicht gegenüber innovativen Unternehmen / Horst-Manfred Schellhaass -- Ist die Freiheit ein Schutzgut des Kartellrechts und der Wettbewerbspolitik? / Robert Knöpfle. ISBN 3-452-20666-1 : LC Card 87-138003
1. Restraint of trade - Germany (West) - Congresses. 2. Antitrust law - Germany (West) - Congresses. 3. Restraint of trade - European Economic Community countries - Congresses. 4. Antitrust law - European Economic Community countries - Congresses. I. Forschungsinstitut für Wirtschaftsverfassung und Wettbewerb (Cologne, Germany). II. Innsbrucker Symposion (19th : 1985). III. Series.
HB41 .F22 Heft 120 KK6456

Neuorientierung im Westhandel der D.D.R.? Marwege, Ulf, 1954- Neuorientierung im Westhandel der DDR? . Bonn , c1984. iv, 122 p. : ISBN 3-7713-0221-8 : LC Card 84-196602
HF3570.5.Z7 G75 1984

Neuorientierung im Westhandel der DDR? . Marwege, Ulf, 1954- Bonn , c1984. iv, 122 p. : ISBN 3-7713-0221-8 : LC Card 84-196602
HF3570.5.Z7 G75 1984

Neuschäffer, Hubertus. Engelhardt, Hans Dieter von. Die Livländische Gemeinnützige und Ökonomische Sozietät (1792-1939) . Köln , 1983. ix, 215 p., [3] leaves of plates : ISBN 3-412-04282-X LC Card 84-117318
HD1486.S65 E54 1983

Neuschatz, Michael. The golden sword : the coming of capitalism to the Colorado mining frontier / Michael Neuschatz. New York : Greenwood Press, 1986. xii, 301 p. ; 25 cm. (Contributions in American studies, 0084-9227 . no. 84) Includes index. Bibliography: p. [293]-297. ISBN 0-313-25104-5 (lib. bdg. : alk. Paper) LC Card 85-27026 DDC 331.88/122334/09788 19
1. Miners - Colorado - History. 2. Trade-unions - Miners - Colorado - History. 3. Capitalism - Colorado - History. 4. Colorado - Economic conditions. I. Title. II. Series.
HD8039.M61 U48 1986
NYPL [JLE 87-766]

NEUSS (GERMANY) - HISTORY.
Kiefer, Rolf. Sozialdemokratische Arbeiterbewegung in der Stadt Neuss vom Sozialistengesetz bis zum Ersten Weltkrieg /. Reinbek , c1982. iv, 159 p. ; ISBN 3-88756-025-6 LC Card 83-186919
HD8460.N48 K54 1982

Neustadt, Peter. Wachstum und Strukturwandlungen Brasiliens in ihrer Bedeutung für die strategische Marketingplanung von Konsumgüterunternehmungen / Peter Neustadt. Diessenhofen : Rüegger, cop. 1979. ix, 463 p. : ill. ; 23 cm. (Lateinamerikanisches Institut ander Hochschule St. Gallen für Wirtschafts- und Sozialwissenschaften ; Bd. 16) Originally presented as the author's thesis, Hochschule für Wirtschafts- und Sozialwissenschaften, St. Gall, Switzerland. Bibliography: p. 411-420. ISBN 3-7253-0092-5 : LC Card 80-469750
1. Marketing - Brazil. 2. Commercial products - Brazil. 3. Consumers - Brazil. I. Series: St. Gall, Switzerland. Hochschule für Wirtschafts- und Sozialwissenschaften. Lateinamerikanisches Institut. Buchreihe, Bd. 16. II. Title.
HF5415.12.B7 N48 1979
NYPL [JLD 80-3357]

Neustadt, Richard E. Richard E. Neustadt lecture, May 13, 1986. Seattle, WA : Institute of Public Policy and Management, Graduate School of Public Affairs, University of Washington, [1986] 35 p. : port. ; 23 cm. (Brewster C. Denny lecture series) Cover title. Bibliography: p. 33-35. LC Card 87-402984 DDC 339.5/2/0973 19
1. Fiscal policy - United States. 2. Budget - United States. I. Title. II. Series.
HJ257.2 .N48 1986

NEUVILLE-SUR-SEINE (FRANCE) - ECONOMIC CONDITIONS.
Dautriat, Pierre. Vignes et vignerons d'autrefois dans le Barséquanais . Saint-Seine-l'Abbaye , c1984. 70 p. : ISBN 2-86701-018-7 : LC Card 85-117852
HD9385.F82 N483 1984

Neuvostoliiton-kauppa Suomen kansantaloudessa / Kari Alho ... [et al.]. Helsinki : Elinkeinoelämän Tutkimuslaitos, 1986. 220 p. : ill. ; 25 cm. (Sarja B / Elinkeinoelämän, 0356-7443 = Series B / The Research Institute of the Finnish Economy . 50) Summary in English. Bibliography: p. 169-172. ISBN 951-9206-18-3 LC Card 87-127628
1. Finland - Commerce - Soviet Union. 2. Soviet Union - Commerce - Finland. 3. Finland - Economic conditions - 1945-. I. Alho, Kari.
HF3633.S65 N48 1986

Nevada. Dept. of Transportation. Planning Division. Log of the federal-aid interstate system comprising the Nevada primary state highway system, 1985 /. Carson City, Nev. [Washington] [1985] 41 leaves ; LC Card 86-622234 DDC 388.1/09793 19
HE356.N37 L632 1985

Nevada. Dept. of Transportation. Research Division.
Log of the federal-aid interstate system comprising the Nevada primary state highway system, 1985 /. Carson City, Nev. [Washington] [1985] 41 leaves ; LC Card 86-622234 DDC 388.1/09793 19
HE356.N37 L632 1985

1985 log, federal-aid urban routes /. Carson City, Nev. [1984] iii leaves, 165 p. ; LC Card 86-622235 DDC 388.4/042 19
HE356.N37 A17 1984

Nevada. Division of Assessment Standards.
Net proceeds of mines, 1985-86 /. Carson City, Nev. [1986] 18 leaves ; LC Card 87-620610 DDC 336.2/78622/09793021 19
HJ4242.M56 N47 1986

1982-83 net proceeds of mines /. Carson City, Nev. [1983] 17 leaves ; LC Card 87-620959 DDC 336.2/78622/09793021 19
HJ4242.M56 A14 1983

NEVADA - ECONOMIC CONDITIONS.
Passi, Michael M. Poverty in the State of Nevada . Carson City, Nev. (1100 E. William St., Suite 117, Carson City 89710) [1986] [11] leaves, 69, 16 p., [1] leaf of plates : LC Card 86-622269 DDC 330.9793/033/08806942 19
HC107.N33 P623 1986

Nevada. Employment Security Dept. Employment Security Research Section. see **Nevada. Employment Security Research Section.**

Nevada. Employment Security Research Section.
Nevada occupational information system . [Carson City, Nev.] (505 E. King St., Carson City 89710) [1986] vii, 385 p. : LC Card 86-622271 DDC 331.12/09793/021 19
HD5725.N3 N45843 1986

Nevada. Legislature. Legislative Commission.
Study of the fees and taxes which produce revenue for the construction and maintenance of the highways. [Carson City, Nev.] : Legislative Commission of the Legislative Counsel Bureau, State of Nevada, [1986] viii, 74 p. ; 28 cm. (Bulletin / Legislative Commission of the Legislative Counsel Bureau, State of Nevada . no. 87-23) "August 1986." LC Card 86-623141 DDC 388.1/14/09793 19
1. Roads - Nevada - Finance. 2. Fees, Administrative - Nevada. 3. Taxation - Nevada. I. Series: Bulletin (Nevada. Legislature. Legislative Counsel Bureau) , no. 87-23. II. Title.
HE356.N37 N42 1986

Nevada occupational information system : labor supply/demand report, 1986 / prepared for Nevada State Occupational Information Coordinating Committee (SOICC) by Nevada Employment Security Department, Employment Security Research Section. [Carson City, Nev.] (505 E. King St., Carson City 89710) : SOICC, [1986] vii, 385 p. : map ; 28 cm. "Seventh edition"--Letter of transmittal. "February 1986." LC Card 86-622271 DDC 331.12/09793/021 19
1. Labor supply - Nevada - Statistics. 2. Employment forecasting - Nevada - Statistics. 3. Nevada - Occupations - Statistics. I. Nevada. Employment Security Research Section. II. Nevada. State Occupational Information Coordinating Committee.
HD5725.N3 N45843 1986

NEVADA - OCCUPATIONS - STATISTICS.
Nevada occupational information system . [Carson City, Nev.] (505 E. King St., Carson City 89710) [1986] vii, 385 p. : LC Card 86-622271 DDC 331.12/09793/021 19
HD5725.N3 N45843 1986

Nevada. Office of Community Services. Passi, Michael M. Poverty in the State of Nevada . Carson City, Nev. (1100 E. William St., Suite 117, Carson City 89710) [1986] [11] leaves,

69, 16 p., [1] leaf of plates : LC Card 86-622269 DDC 330.9793/033/08806942 19
HC107.N33 P623 1986

NEVADA - POPULATION.
Passi, Michael M. Poverty in the State of Nevada . Carson City, Nev. (1100 E. William St., Suite 117, Carson City 89710) [1986] [11] leaves, 69, 16 p., [1] leaf of plates : LC Card 86-622269 DDC 330.9793/033/08806942 19
HC107.N33 P623 1986

Nevada Small Business Development Center. A Basic guide to exporting /. [Reno, Nev.] [198-] 68 leaves ; LC Card 86-622819
HF3035 .B37 1980z

Nevada. State Occupational Information Coordinating Committee. Nevada occupational information system . [Carson City, Nev.] (505 E. King St., Carson City 89710) [1986] vii, 385 p. : LC Card 86-622271 DDC 331.12/09793/021 19
HD5725.N3 N45843 1986

Nevaer, Louis E. V. Corporate financial planning and management in a deficit economy / Louis E.V. Nevaer and Steven A. Deck. New York : Quorum Books, 1987. 171 p. : ill. ; 25 cm. Includes bibliographical references and index. ISBN 0-89930-202-5 (lib. bdg. : alk. paper) LC Card 86-25582 DDC 658.1/145 19
1. Corporations - United States - Finance. 2. Corporate planning - United States. 3. Budget deficits - United States. 4. United States - Economic conditions - 1981-. I. Deck, Steven A. II. Title.
HG4063 .N48 1987

Nevel, Robert L. The timber industries of New Hampshire and Vermont : a periodic assessment of timber output / Robert L. Nevel, Jr., Nicolas Engalichev, William G. Gove. Broomall, Pa. : U. S. Dept. of Agriculture, Forest Service, Northeastern Station, 1986. 56 p. : ill. ; 28 cm. (Resource bulletin NE . 89) Includes bibliographical references and index. LC Card 86-601144 DDC 338.1/7498/09742 19
1. Lumber trade - New Hampshire. 2. Lumber trade - Vermont. 3. Forest products industry - New Hampshire. 4. Forest products industry - Vermont. 5. Timber - New Hampshire. 6. Timber - Vermont. I. Engalichev, Nicolas. II. Gove, William G. III. Title. IV. Series.
HD9757.N4 N48 1986

Neven, Peter, 1953- Arbeits- und Freizeitpädagogik : eine intra- und interdisziplinäre Konzeptualisierung erziehungswissenschaftlicher Teildisziplinen / Peter Neven. Düsseldorf : Verlagsanstalt Handwerk, [1982?] 424 p. ; 24 cm. (Wirtschafts-, Berufs- und Sozialpädagogische Texte . Bd. 2) Bibliography: p. 401-424. ISBN 3-87864-087-0 LC Card 84-119072
1. Work. 2. Leisure. 3. Rest periods. 4. Adult education. I. Title. II. Series.
HD4901 .N47 1982

Never work for a jerk! /. King, Patricia, 1941- New York , 1987. 356 p. ; ISBN 0-531-15522-6 LC Card 86-29014 DDC 650.1/3 19
HF5548.83 .K56 1987

Nevermann, Helga. Venture Capital : ein betriebswirtschaftlicher und steuerlicher Vergleich zwischen den USA und der Bundesrepublik Deutschland / Helga Nevermann, Dieter Falk.1. Aufl. Baden-Baden : Nomos, 1986. 146 p. ; 23 cm. (Schriften des Instituts für Ausländisches und Internationales Finanz- und Steuerwesen der Universität Hamburg . Bd. 10) Bibliography: p. 143-146. ISBN 3-7890-1263-7 LC Card 87-121846 DDC 332/.0415/0943 19
1. Venture capital - Germany (West). 2. Venture capital - United States. I. Falk, Dieter. II. Title. III. Series.
HG5492 .N48 1986

Neves, Tancredo, 1910- Tancredo Neves na defesa do consumidor / palestra proferida pelo Exmo. Sr. Doutor Tancredo de Almeida Neves, em 21 de novembro de 1984, na Comissão de Defesa do Consumidor. Brasília : Câmara dos Deputados, Centro de Documentação e Informação, Coordenação de Publicações, 1985. 48 p. : 1 port. ; 23 cm. LC Card 86-129214
1. Consumer protection - Brazil. I. Brazil. Congresso Nacional. Câmara dos Deputados. Comissão de Defesa do Consumidor. II. Title.
HC190.C63 N48 1985

Nevett, T. R. (Terence R.) Miracle, Gordon E. Voluntary regulation of advertising . Lexington, Mass. , c1987. xxvi, 322 p. : ISBN 0-669-13135-0 (alk. paper) LC Card 86-45294 DDC 338.4/76591/0941 19
HF5834 .M57 1987

Neville-Rolfe, Edmund. Stanton, B. F. (Bernard Freeland), 1925- The cereals dilemma . Ithaca, N.Y. [1986] 50 p. : LC Card 86-622419 DDC 338.1/731/094 19
HD9045.A2 S7 1986

Neville Sepala Karunatilake. see **Karunatilake, H. N. S.**

Nevison, John M. The elements of spreadsheet style / John M. Nevison. New York : Prentice Hall Press, c1987. xiv, 197 p. : ill. ; 24 cm. "A Brady book." Bibliography: p. 187-188. Includes index. ISBN 0-13-080565-3 (pbk.) : LC Card 87-6922 DDC 005.3 19
1. Electronic spreadsheets. 2. Business - Data processing. I. Title.
HF5548.2 .N416 1987

Nevitt, Peter K. Equipment leasing for commercial bankers / Peter K. Nevitt, Frank J. Fabozzi, Edmond J. Seifried. Philadelphia, Pa. : R. Morris Associates, c1987. x, 123 p. ; 23 cm. Includes index. ISBN 0-936742-37-2 (pbk.) : LC Card 87-5532 DDC 332.1/068/5 19
1. Industrial equipment leases - United States. 2. Banks and banking - United States. I. Fabozzi, Frank J. II. Seifried, Edmond J. III. Title.
HD39.4 .N485 1987

Nevitte, Neil. Ethnic preference and public policy in developing states /. Boulder, Colo. , 1986. ix, 203 p. ; ISBN 0-931477-89-1 : LC Card 86-13505 DDC 323.1/09172/4 19
JF1063.D44 E87 1986 NYPL [JLE 86-4694]

New American boom. Kiplinger forecasts . Washington, DC , New York, NY , c1986. vi, 330 p. ; ISBN 0-938721-01-1 (pbk.) : LC Card 86-203273 DDC 338.5/443/0973 19
HC106.8 .K56 1986

A new approach to capital budgeting for city and county governments /. Wacht, Richard F. Atlanta, Ga. , 1987. ix, 149 p. : ISBN 0-88406-190-6 (pbk.) : LC Card 87-21157 DDC 352.1/2 19
HJ9147 .W33 1987

New approach to vocational training / by G. Hosomi ... [et al.] ; translated from the Japanese by N. Tagaya ; in collaboration with the Human Resourses Development Bureau, Ministry of Labour, Japan. Islamabad, Pakistan : Asian and Pacific Skill Development Programme, International Labour Office, 1985-1986. 2 v. : ill. ; 22 cm. ISBN 92-2-105078-5 (pbk. : v. 1) LC Card 86-221389 DDC 331.25/92/0952 19
1. Occupational training - Japan. 2. Vocational education - Japan. I. Hosomi, Gen, 1929-. II. Japan. Shokugyō Nōryoku Kaihatsukyoku. III. Asian and Pacific Skill Development Programme.
HD5715.5.J3 N48 1985

New approaches to project ranking . McFarland, William F. College Station, Tex. , Springfield, Va. [1985] xvii, 116 p. : LC Card 86-622422 DDC 380.5 s 388.1/12/09764 19
HE203 .T43 no. 337-1F HE356.T4

New approaches to social science history .
(v. 4) Soviet quantitative history /. Beverly Hills , c1984. 216 p. : ISBN 0-8039-2082-2 LC Card 83-19196 DDC 306/.072047 19
HD715 .S5956 1984 NYPL [JLD 87-841]

(v. 5) The Politics of urban fiscal policy /. Beverly Hills , c1984. 176 p. : ISBN 0-8039-2373-2 LC Card 84-13431 DDC 336/.014/73 19
HJ9144 .P64 1984 NYPL [JLD 87-126]

New biotechnology comes to market / Philip Rotheim, project analyst. Stamford, Conn., U. S.A. : Business Communications Co., c1985. viii, 205 leaves : ill. ; 29 cm. (Business opportunity report . C-032R) "July 1985"--T.p. verso. ISBN 0-89336-436-3 (soft) LC Card 87-167067 DDC 381/.456606 19
1. Biotechnology industries. 2. Market surveys. I. Rotheim, Philip. II. Business Communications Co. III. Series.
HD9999.B442 N48 1985

NEW BUSINESS ENTERPRISES - CASE STUDIES.
Kuriloff, Arthur H. Starting and managing the small business /. New York , c1988. xxi, 663 p. : ISBN 0-07-035665-3 : LC Card 87-3832 DDC 658/.022 19
HD62.5 .K87 1988

NEW BUSINESS ENTERPRISES - DEVELOPING COUNTRIES - HANDBOOKS, MANUALS, ETC.
Doing a feasibility study . Washington, D.C. , c1987. 173 p. : ISBN 0-912917-07-5 (pbk.) : LC Card 86-61951 DDC 658/.022/091724 19
HD62.5 .D63 1987

NEW BUSINESS ENTERPRISES - EUROPE - ADDRESSES, ESSAYS, LECTURES.
New firms and regional development in Europe /. London , Dover, N.H. , c1986. 322 p. : ISBN 0-7099-1577-2 : LC Card 85-28372 DDC 338.7/1/094 19
HD2346.E9 N48 1986 NYPL [JLD 86-1597]

NEW BUSINESS ENTERPRISES - FINANCE.
Durkacz, Victor Edward. Financial planning for new businesses /. Chichester [West Sussex] , New York , c1985. 257 p. : ISBN 0-471-90843-6 (pbk.) : LC Card 85-17927 DDC 658.1/5 19
HG4027.6 .D87 1985 NYPL [JLE 86-929]

National emerging industries resourceguide /. Minneapolis, MN , c1986. 368, 124 p. ; ISBN 0-8144-5851-3 LC Card 85-82163 DDC 338.7/61/0002573 19
HD62.5 .N38 1986 NYPL [JLF 86-1717]

NEW BUSINESS ENTERPRISES - FINANCE - CONGRESSES.
Financing new technology . London , 1984. 124 p. : ISBN 0-903887-126-5 (pbk.) LC Card 86-117401 DDC 338.6/041 19
HG4027.6 .F55 1984 NYPL [JLD 87-1346]

NEW BUSINESS ENTERPRISES - FRANCE.
Bourg, Claude, 1935- J'ai créé mon entreprise . [Paris] , c1986. 223 p. ; LC Card 86-159708
HD62.5 .B68 1986

NEW BUSINESS ENTERPRISES - GERMANY (WEST)
Hunsdiek, Detlef. Entwicklungslinien und Entwicklungsrisiken neugegründeter Unternehmen /. Stuttgart , c1986. x, 190 p. : ISBN 3-7910-5009-5 LC Card 87-211045
HD62.5 .H86 1986

NEW BUSINESS ENTERPRISES - GOVERNMENT POLICY - EUROPE.
D'Angelillo, Massimo, 1956- Job creation . Milano, Italy , c1985. 231 p. ; LC Card 86-156936
HD5764.A6 D418 1985
NYPL [JLD 86-3248]

NEW BUSINESS ENTERPRISES - GREAT BRITAIN.
Small firms growth and development /. Aldershot, Hampshire, England , Brookfield, Vt., U. S.A. , c1986. xix, 325 p. : ISBN 0-566-00811-4 *NYPL [JLD 86-3474]*

NEW BUSINESS ENTERPRISES - GREAT BRITAIN - CASE STUDIES.
Chisnall, Peter M. Small firms in action . London , New York , c1987. vii, 149 p. ; ISBN 0-07-084180-2 (pbk.) : LC Card 87-21518 DDC 658/.022 19
HD2346.G7 C55 1987

NEW BUSINESS ENTERPRISES - GREAT BRITAIN - FINANCE.
Durkacz, Victor Edward. Financial planning for new businesses /. Chichester [West Sussex] , New York , c1985. 257 p. : ISBN 0-471-90843-6 (pbk.) : LC Card 85-17927 DDC 658.1/5 19
HG4027.6 .D87 1985 NYPL [JLE 86-929]

NEW BUSINESS ENTERPRISES - HUNGARY.
Dévai, Katalin. A nagyvállalatok helyzetéről /. [Budapest] , 1984. 68 p. ; ISBN 963-673-293-0 LC Card 85-175237
HD2852.5 .D48 1984

NEW BUSINESS ENTERPRISES - INFORMATION SERVICES - UNITED STATES.
Price, Courtney H. The entrepreneur's resource handbook /. Denver, Colo. , 1987. 178 p. : ISBN 0-944303-00-5 (pbk.) LC Card 87-62190
HD62.5 .P65 1987

NEW BUSINESS ENTERPRISES - JUVENILE LITERATURE.
Risks & rewards of entrepreneurship /. Saint Paul, Minn. , c1988. 123 p. : ISBN

0-8219-0323-3 (pbk.) LC Card 87-21787 DDC 338/.04 19
HB615 .R56 1988

NEW BUSINESS ENTERPRISES - LOCATION.
National emerging industries resourceguide /. Minneapolis, MN , c1986. 368, 124 p. ; ISBN 0-8144-5851-3 LC Card 85-82163 DDC 338.7/61/0002573 19
HD62.5 .N38 1986 ***NYPL [JLF 86-1717]***

NEW BUSINESS ENTERPRISES - MAINE - HANDBOOKS, MANUALS, ETC.
Doing business in Maine. [Augusta, Me. , 1983] iii, 93 p. : LC Card 86-620779 DDC 346.741/07 347.41067 19
HD62.5 .D64 1983

NEW BUSINESS ENTERPRISES - MANAGEMENT.
Delany, George. The #1 home business book . Blue Ridge Summit, PA [1987] 168 p. : ISBN 0-8306-3022-8 (pbk.) : LC Card 87-2936 DDC 658/.041 19
HD8036 .D44 1987

Hawken, Paul. Growing a business /. New York , c1987. 251 p. ; ISBN 0-671-64457-2 LC Card 87-16431 DDC 658.1/141 19
HD62.5 .H38 1987

Kamoroff, Bernard. Small time operator . Laytonville, Calif. , c1986. 190 p. : ISBN 0-917510-06-2 (pbk.) : LC Card 84-73438
NYPL [JLF 86-947]

Merrill, Ronald E. The new venture handbook . New York, NY , c1987. 356 p. : ISBN 0-8144-5895-5 LC Card 86-47818 DDC 658.1/141 19
HD62.5 .M46 1987

National emerging industries resourceguide /. Minneapolis, MN , c1986. 368, 124 p. ; ISBN 0-8144-5851-3 LC Card 85-82163 DDC 338.7/61/0002573 19
HD62.5 .N38 1986 ***NYPL [JLF 86-1717]***

Schöllhammer, Hans, 1933- Entrepreneurship and small business management /. Malabar, Fla. , 1988. xvi, 608 p. : ISBN 0-89464-235-9 LC Card 87-14818 DDC 658/.022 19
HD62.5 .S354 1988

Taylor, Charlotte. The entrepreneurial workbook . New York, N.Y. , c1985. ix, 148 p. : ISBN 0-452-25660-7 : LC Card 84-29439 DDC 658/.022 19
HD62.5 .T39 1985 ***NYPL [JLF 86-795]***

NEW BUSINESS ENTERPRISES - QUÉBEC (PROVINCE)
Se lancer en affaires . [Quebec] , c1986. 450 p. : ISBN 2-551-09144-6 LC Card 86-138587 DDC 658.1/1 19
HD62.5 .S4 1986

NEW BUSINESS ENTERPRISES - TENNESSEE - MANAGEMENT.
Yates, M. M. (Maurice M.) How to start and manage a business of your own in Tennessee. Greeneville, Tenn. , c1986. ii, 66 p. : LC Card 86-209197 DDC 658.1/141/09768 19
HD62.5 .Y28 1986

NEW BUSINESS ENTERPRISES - TEXAS.
Doing business in Texas. [Austin, Tex.] [1986], c1985. 52, [64] p. : LC Card 87-621557 DDC 332.6/7322764 19
HC107.T4 D65 1986

NEW BUSINESS ENTERPRISES - UNITED STATES.
Hutchinson, Van. College cash . San Diego , 1987. p. cm. ISBN 0-15-619150-4 (pbk.) : LC Card 87-8666 DDC 658.4/2 19
HD62.5 .H88 1987

Moore, Janice D. Thorne. A step toward independence: economic self sufficiency . Washington, D.C. , c1986. iii, 117 p. : LC Card 86-209069 DDC 362.8/3 19
HD6059.6.U6 M66 1986

Waymon, Lynne. Starting and managing a business from your home /. Washington, D.C. , 1986. vi, 48 p. ; LC Card 86-602842 DDC 658/.041 19
HD62.5 .W395 1986

Williams, Bruce, 1932- The Bruce Williams book . New York , 1987. p. cm. ISBN 0-8128-3119-5 : LC Card 86-42692 DDC 658/022 19
HD62.5 .W49 1987

NEW BUSINESS ENTERPRISES - UNITED STATES - CASE STUDIES.
Perri, Colleen, 1936- Entrepreneurial women. Kenosha, WI , c1988. p. cm. ISBN 0-941579-02-6 LC Card 87-7370 DDC 338/.04/088042 19
HD2346.U5 P43 1988

Smith, Geoffrey N. Sweat equity . New York , c1986. 254 p. : ISBN 0-671-55210-4 LC Card 86-6622 DDC 658/.022 19
HD62.5 .S625 1986 ***NYPL [JLD 86-3014]***

NEW BUSINESS ENTERPRISES - UNITED STATES - LOCATION - DIRECTORIES.
National emerging industries site selection guide /. Minneapolis, MN , c1986. 124 p. ; LC Card 86-231272 DDC 338.6/042/02573 19
HC110.D5 N38 1986

NEW BUSINESS ENTERPRISES - UNITED STATES - MANAGEMENT.
Davidson, Jeffrey P. Look before you leap . New York , 1988. p. cm. ISBN 0-8027-1012-3 LC Card 87-23274 DDC 658.4/2 19
HD62.5 .D38 1988

Kingstone, Brett. The dynamos . New York , c1987. xx, 256 p. : ISBN 0-471-85827-7 LC Card 87-1754 DDC 338/.04/0922 B 19
HC102.5.A2 K56 1987

Schaefer, Robert A. Starting and managing a small service business /. Washington, D.C. , 1986. v, 57 p. ; LC Card 86-603435 DDC 658/.022 19
HD9981.5 .S32 1986

NEW BUSINESS ENTERPRISES - UNITED STATES - STATES.
Corporation for Enterprise Development. Building the new economy . Washington, D.C. , 1986. iv, 178 p. ; ISBN 0-9605804-2-5 (pbk.) LC Card 86-61273 DDC 338.973 19
HC110.I53 C67 1986

NEW BUSINESS ENTERPRISES - VIRGINIA - MANAGEMENT.
Virginia, a guide to establishing a manufacturing business. Richmond, Va. [1986] iv, 30 p. ; LC Card 86-622659 DDC 343.755/07 347.55037 19
HD9727.V8 V573 1986

NEW BUSINESS ENTERPRISES - WISCONSIN - KENOSHA - CASE STUDIES.
Perri, Colleen, 1936- Entrepreneurial women /. Kenosha, WI , c1987. 140 p. : ISBN 0-941579-00-X (pbk.) LC Card 87-154216 DDC 338/.04/088042 19
HD2346.U52 K376 1987b

Perri, Colleen, 1936- Entrepreneurial women /. Kenosha, WI , c1988. p. cm. ISBN 0-941579-28-X LC Card 87-7380 DDC 338/.04/088042 19
HD2346.U52 K376 1988

NEW BUSINESS ENTERPRISES - ZAIRE - CASE STUDIES.
MacGaffey, Janet. Entrepreneurs and parasites . Cambridge [Cambridgeshire] , New York , 1987. xiii, 241 p. : ISBN 0-521-33533-7 LC Card 87-13160 DDC 338.09675/1 19
HC955.Z7 K49956 1987

New businesses and the structure of telecommunications utilities. California. Public Utilities Commission. Report to the Legislature . [San Francisco] [1984] 40 leaves ; LC Card 86-622236 DDC 384.6/09794 19
HE8840.C2 C35 1984

New Canadian readings.
Perspectives on Canadian economic history /. Toronto , c1987. 287 p. : ISBN 0-7730-4679-8 LC Card 87-168012 DDC 330.971 19
HC113 .P47 1987

New cargo-handling techniques . Couper, A. D. Geneva , 1986. xii, 172 p., [1] folded leaf of plates : ISBN 92-2-105419-5 (pbk.) : LC Card 87-117776 DDC 331.7/61387164 19
HD6331.18.L65 C68 1986

The new case for silver /. Rosenthal, Daniel M. Lafayette, CA , c1986. ix, 157 p. : ISBN 0-9615814-1-7 (pbk.): LC Card 86-208965 DDC 332.63/28 19
HG305 .R67 1986

The new China . Rabushka, Alvin. San Francisco , Boulder, Colo. , 1987. xii, 254 p. ; ISBN 0-936488-15-8 (pbk. : alk. paper) LC Card 87-10574 DDC 338.951 19
HC427.92 .R33 1987

New class politics . Cannon, William B., 1920- Washington, D.C. , c1986. 137 p. ; ISBN 0-89758-042-7 (pbk.) : LC Card 86-27511 DDC 336.73 19
HJ2051 .C35 1986

The new commodity trading systems and methods /. Kaufman, Perry J. New York , c1987. xvi, 521 p. : ISBN 0-471-87879-0 LC Card 87-6073 DDC 332.64/4 19
HG6036 .K38 1987

The New Communist Third World : an essay in political economy / edited by Peter Wiles. London : Croom Helm, c1982. 392 p. ; 23 cm. Bibliography: p. 378-386. Includes index. ISBN 0-7099-2709-6 LC Card 86-673518
1. Developing countries - Commerce. 2. Communist countries - Commerce. I. Wiles, Peter John de la Fosse.
HF1413 .N495x 1982b

New communities for urban squatters . Choguill, Charles L. New York , c1987. xiv, 213 p. : ISBN 0-306-42545-9 LC Card 86-30501 DDC 307.3/36 19
HD7361.6.D57 C46 1987

The new corporate strategy /. Ansoff, H. Igor. New York , 1988. xviii, 258 p. : ISBN 0-471-62950-2 LC Card 87-23266 DDC 658.4/012 19
HD30.28 .A535 1988

New courses for the Colorado River : major issues for the next century / edited by Gary D. Weatherford and F. Lee Brown.1st ed. Albuquerque : University of New Mexico Press, c1986. xx, 253 p. : ill., maps ; 24 cm. Based on proceedings of the Colorado River Working Symposium held at Bishop's Lodge, Santa Fe, New Mexico, May 23-26, 1983. Includes bibliographies and index. ISBN 0-8263-0854-6 LC Card 85-24577 DDC 333.91/009791/3 19
1. Water consumption - Colorado River Watershed (Colo.-Mexico) - Congresses. 2. Water quality management - Colorado River Watershed (Colo.-Mexico) - Congresses. 3. Water-supply - Navajo Indian Reservation - Congresses. 4. Colorado River - Water-rights - Congresses. I. Weatherford, Gary D. II. Brown, Franklin Lee. III. Colorado River Working Symposium (1983 : Santa Fe, N.M.).
HD1695.C7 N49 1986 ***NYPL [JLE 86-1736]***

New Deal labor policy and the American industrial economy /. Vittoz, Stanley. Chapel Hill , c1987. 241 p. ; ISBN 0-8078-1729-5 LC Card 86-24911 DDC 331/.0973 19
HD8072 .V715 1987

New deal labor policy and the southern cotton textile industry, 1933-1941 /. Hodges, James A., 1932- Knoxville , c1986. xii, 252 p. : ISBN 0-87049-496-1 (alk. paper) : LC Card 85-20368 DDC 338.4/767721/0975 19
HD8039.T42 U652 1986
NYPL [JLE 86-3477]

NEW DEAL, 1933-1939.
Biles, Roger, 1950- Memphis in the Great Depression /. Knoxville , c1986. 174 p. : ISBN 0-87049-497-X (alk. paper) : LC Card 85-22575 DDC 330.9768/19 19
HC108.M417 B55 1986 ***NYPL [JLD 87-34]***

Olson, James Stuart, 1946- Saving capitalism . Princeton, N.J. , c1988. p. cm. ISBN 0-691-04749-9 (alk. paper) : LC Card 87-7275 DDC 353.0082/5/09 19
HG3729.U5 O47 1988

Vittoz, Stanley. New Deal labor policy and the American industrial economy /. Chapel Hill , c1987. 241 p. ; ISBN 0-8078-1729-5 LC Card 86-24911 DDC 331/.0973 19
HD8072 .V715 1987

NEW DEAL, 1933-1939 - SOUTHERN STATES - HISTORY.
Hodges, James A., 1932- New deal labor policy and the southern cotton textile industry, 1933-1941 /. Knoxville , c1986. xii, 252 p. : ISBN 0-87049-496-1 (alk. paper) : LC Card 85-20368 DDC 338.4/767721/0975 19
HD8039.T42 U652 1986
NYPL [JLE 86-3477]

New developments in the analysis of market structure : proceedings of a conference held by

the International Economic Association in Ottawa, Canada / edited by Joseph E. Stiglitz and G. Frank Mathewson. Cambridge, Mass. : MIT Press, 1986. xxiv, 559 p. : ill. ; 23 cm. Includes bibliographies and index. ISBN 0-262-19241-1 LC Card 85-4246 DDC 338.8 19
1. Industrial organization (Economic theory) - Congresses. 2. Vertical integration - Congresses. 3. Oligopolies - Congresses. 4. Competition - Congresses. I. Stiglitz, Joseph E. II. Mathewson, G. Frank, 1942-.
HD2326 .N43 1986 ***NYPL [JLD 86-3570]***

The new Dietz Confederate States catalog and handbook /. Skinner, Hubert C. Miami, Fla. (1007 Kane Concourse, Bay Harbor Islands 33154) , 1986. viii, 270 p. : LC Card 86-206685 DDC 769.56975/075/0973 19
HE6500 .S58 1986

New dimensions in foreign economic policy : industrial -- oil -- banking : three symposia, National industrial policy (Japan -- France -- Korea -- Brazil); Ten years after the first oil shock; The future of internationa banking / edited by Ernest H. Preeg and Diane B. Bendahmane ; with an introduction by Ambassador Preeg. Washington, DC : Center for the Study of Foreign Affairs, Foreign Service Institute, U. S. Dept. of State : For sale by the Supt. of Docs., U. S. G.P.O., 1986. xiii, 118 p. ; 24 cm. Shipping list no.: 86-643-P. "Released April 1986"--T.p. verso. Bibliography: p. 115-117. Item 872-A S/N 044-000-02131-5 LC Card 86-600514 DDC 337.73 19
1. International economic relations - Congresses. 2. International finance - Congresses. 3. Energy policy - Congresses. 4. Industry and state - Congresses. I. Preeg, Ernest H. II. Bendahmane, Diane B. III. Center for the Study of Foreign Affairs (U. S.).
HF1410.5 .N488 1986

New directions in budget theory / edited by Irene Rubin. Albany, N.Y. : State University of New York Press, 1987, c1988. p. cm. (SUNY series in public administration) Includes index. ISBN 0-88706-624-0 LC Card 87-9977 DDC 350.72/2 19
1. Budget. I. Rubin, Irene. II. Series.
HJ2005 .N48 1987

New directions in human resources . Cook, Mary F., 1937- Englewood Cliffs, N.J. , c1987. xxx, 466 p. : ISBN 0-13-612433-X LC Card 87-1286 DDC 658.3 19
HF5549 .C7244 1987

New directions in microwave ovens . Cholmar, Sidney. Stamford, Conn., U. S.A. , c1985. x, 119 leaves ; ISBN 0-89336-459-2 (pbk.) LC Card 87-163958 DDC 381/.4568388 19
HD9971.5.S763 U53 1985

The New economic role of American states : strategies in a competitive world economy / edited by R. Scott Fosler (Committee for Economic Development). New York : Oxford University Press, 1988. x, 370 p. ; 24 cm. Bibliography: p. 343-358. Includes index. ISBN 0-19-505003-7 LC Card 87-12499 DDC 338.973 19
1. United States - Economic policy - 1981-. 2. Industry and state - United States - States. I. Fosler, R. Scott. II. Committee for Economic Development.
HC106.8 .N495 1988

New electronic information services . Hartley, Jill. Aldershot, Hants, England , Brookfield, Vt., USA , c1987. 147 p. : ISBN 0-566-05489-2 (pbk.) : LC Card 87-23600 DDC 338.4/700574/0941 19
HD9696.D364 G74 1987

NEW ENGLAND - ECONOMIC CONDITIONS.
Blewett, Mary H. Men, women, and work . Urbana , c1988. p. cm. ISBN 0-252-01484-7 (alk. paper) LC Card 87-19039 DDC 338.4/768531/00974 19
HD8039.B72 U63 1988

New English-Croatian and Croatian-English dictionary. Bogadek, F. A. (Francis Aloysius), 1882- [New English-Croatian and Croatian-English dictionary.] Cassell's New English-Croatian and Croatian-English dictionary /. New York [c1985] vii, 531, 497, 46, 7 p. ; ISBN 0-02-512140-5 LC Card 85-23140 DDC 491.8/2321 19
PG1377 .B72 1985 ***NYPL [*QAD 87-600]***

The new environment in international accounting . Belkaoui, Ahmed, 1943- New York , c1988. p. cm. ISBN 0-89930-267-X (lib. bdg. : alk. paper) LC Card 87-7252 DDC 657/.95 19
HF5686.I56 B45 1988

New ERA occasional paper .
(no. 002) Gurung, Harka B. Food systems and society in Nepal . Kathmandu, Nepal , 1981. 53, iii p. : LC Card 83-901141 DDC 338.1/9/5496 19
HD9016.N42 G87 1981 ***NYPL [JLG 86-71]***

New era of professional banking : who's who in Bangkok Bank Limited. [Bangkok] : The Nation, 1986. 51 p. : col. ill. ; 30 cm. Cover title. Includes [31] pages of advertising matter. LC Card 86-200653 DDC 332.1/025/593 19
1. Bangkok Bank Limited. 2. Bangkok Bank Limited - Directories. I. Nation (Bangkok, Thailand).
HG3300.55.A8 B366 1986

The New ethnic food market : product developments, marketing strategies, processing technologies / Sandra McGowan, project analyst. Norwalk, Conn., U. S.A. : Business Communications Co., c1986. xv, 142 leaves ; 29 cm. (Business opportunity report . GA-057) ISBN 0-89336-486-X (pbk.) LC Card 87-168111 DDC 381/.45641592/00973 19
1. Ethnic food industry - United States. 2. Ethnic food industry. 3. Market surveys - United States. I. McGowan, Sandra. II. Business Communications Co. III. Series.
HD9333.U62 N48 1986

The new expatriates . Tung, Rosalie L. (Rosalie Lam), 1948- Cambridge, Mass. , c1988. xiii, 200 p. : ISBN 0-88730-133-9 LC Card 87-17835 DDC 658.3/1 19
HF5549 .T82 1988

New farm technology and income distribution /. Stanislaus, M. Sebastian. New Delhi , c1984. viii, 76 p. : LC Card 84-902272 DDC 338.1/3/095482 19
HD2075.T57 S73 1984 ***NYPL [JLD 87-669]***

New financial instruments . Atchison, Michael D. Charlottesville, Va. (P.O. Box 3665, Charlottesville 22903) , c1985. viii, 108 p. ; LC Card 85-195578 DDC 332.63 19
HG6024.3 .A83 1985
NYPL [JLL 81-133 no.21]

The new financial planner . Bertot, Cathey H. Homewood, Ill. , c1986. xvi, 266 p. : ISBN 0-87094-587-4 LC Card 85-52442 DDC 332.024/01 19
HG179 .B458 1986 ***NYPL [JLE 87-537]***

New firms and regional development in Europe / edited by David Keeble & Egbert Wever. London ; Dover, N.H. : Croom Helm, c1986. 322 p. : ill., maps ; 23 cm. Includes bibliographies and index. ISBN 0-7099-1577-2 : LC Card 85-28372 DDC 338.7/1/094 19
1. Small business - Europe - Addresses, essays, lectures. 2. New business enterprises - Europe - Addresses, essays, lectures. 3. Europe - Industries - Location - Addresses, essays, lectures. I. Keeble, David. II. Wever, E.
HD2346.E9 N48 1986 ***NYPL [JLD 86-1597]***

The New foreign exchange and foreign trade regime of Yugoslavia /. Novi devizni i spoljnotrgovinski režim SFRJ. English. Belgrade , 1986. 217 p. ; ISBN 86-7145-007-4 LC Card 87-148102 DDC 332.4/5609497 19
HG3965.5 .N6813 1986

New forms of work and activity. Neue Arbeits- und Tätigkeitsformen . Dublin, Ireland [Washington, D.C.] c1986. xvi, 339 p. ; ISBN 92-825-6418-5 LC Card 87-408469 DDC 306/.36/094 19
HD6957.E86 N48 1986

The new game on Wall Street /. Sobel, Robert, 1931 (Feb. 19)- New York , c1987. xii, 244 p. : ISBN 0-471-84527-2 LC Card 86-33986 DDC 332.6/78 19
HG4921 .S6156 1987

A new global tea model . Akiyama, T. (Takamasa), 1944- Washington, D.C. , 1987. vi, 130 p. ; ISBN 0-8213-0868-8 LC Card 87-6238 DDC 382/.41372 19
HD9198.A2 A424 1987

New Granada (Republic, 1842-1858) see **Colombia.**

New Granada (State, 1831-1842) see **Colombia.**

New Haven. Collegiate School. see **Yale University.**

New Haven. Yale University. see **Yale University.**

The new helots . Cohen, Robin. Aldershot, Hants, England , Brookfield, Vt., USA , c1987. xiii, 290 p. : ISBN 0-566-00932-3 : LC Card 87-19807 DDC 331.6/2 19
HD6304 .C64 1987

New ideas in environmental education / edited by Sâlvano Briceño and David C. Pitt. London ; New York : Croom Helm, c1988. xiv, 219 p. ; 23 cm. "Published in the USA by Croom Helm in association with Methuen, Inc."--T.p. verso. Includes bibliographies and index. ISBN 0-7099-5042-X LC Card 87-15696 DDC 363.7/007/1 19
1. Environmental policy - Study and teaching. 2. Environmental protection - Study and teaching. I. Briceño, Sâlvano. II. Pitt, David C.
HC79.E5 N45 1988

The new industrial economics . Ricketts, Martin J. New York , 1987. xii, 306 p. : ISBN 0-312-00458-3 : LC Card 86-27918 DDC 338.6 19
HD2326 .R53 1987

The new industrial organization . Jacquemin, Alexis. Oxford [Oxfordshire] ; New York : p. cm. ISBN 0-19-828568-X : LC Card 86-23816 DDC 338.6 19
HD2326 .J29 1987

New international economic order / [managing editor, S. Pshennikov]. Moscow : USSR Academy of Sciences : "Social Sciences Today" Editorial Board, 1984. 196 p. ; 22 cm. (The Developing countries, problems and perspectives . no. 4) Title from colophon: Novyĭ mezhdunarodnyĭ ėkonomicheskiĭ pori͡adok. Bibliography: p. 184-[188] LC Card 85-151148 DDC 337/.09/047 19
1. International economic relations - Addresses, essays, lectures. 2. Developing countries - Economic policy - Addresses, essays, lectures. I. Pshennikov, S. II. Title: Novyĭ mezhdunarodnyĭ ėkonomicheskiĭ pori͡adok. III. Series.
HF1411 .N398 1984 ***NYPL [JLD 86-2664]***

The new IRA handbook . Sacks, Frank. Chicago [1987], c1986. 126 p. : ISBN 0-911445-05-6 (pbk.) : LC Card 87-130659 DDC 332.024/01 19
HG1660.U5 S23 1987

New Jersey . Johnson, James P., 1937- Northridge, Calif. , 1987. 624 p. : ISBN 0-89781-206-9 LC Card 87-8247 DDC 338.09749 19
HC107.N5 J64 1987

New Jersey. Agriculture Department. see **New Jersey. Dept. of Agriculture.**

New Jersey. Bureau of Urban Strategies. Proposed solutions to local fiscal resource disparities in the state of New Jersey : Division of Local Government Services' policy analysis report. Trenton, N.J. : New Jersey Dept. of Community Affairs, Division of Local Government Services, Bureau of Urban Strategies, [1980] vi, 353 p. ; 29 cm. "Prepared by the Division of Local Government Services' Bureau of Urban Strategies"--P. vi. Bibliography: p. 351-353. LC Card 81-622089 DDC 336.02/749 19
1. Intergovernmental fiscal relations - New Jersey. 2. Property tax - New Jersey. 3. Revenue sharing - New Jersey. I. Title.
HJ585 .N38 1980 ***NYPL [JLF 86-1372]***

NEW JERSEY - CENSUS, 1980.
Crowley, Charles. Income and poverty in New Jersey [microform] . Trenton, N.J. [1982] 32 p. ; LC Card 83-620831 DDC 339.2/2/09749 19
HC107.N53 I5113 1982
NYPL [*ZT-1712 no.31]

New Jersey. Dept. of Agriculture. (Old Catalog form: New Jersey. Agriculture Department) Grassroots, an agriculture retention and development program for New Jersey. [Trenton, N.J.] : New Jersey Dept. of Agriculture : New Jersey Dept. of Environmental Protection, [1980] 65 p. : maps ; 28 cm. "October 31, 1980." LC Card 81-621630 DDC 333.76/17/09749 19
1. Land use, Rural - Government policy - New Jersey. 2. Agriculture and state - New Jersey. I. Title.
HD211.N5 N47 1980 ***NYPL [JLF 86-1575]***

New Jersey. Dept. of Commerce and Economic Development. Office of Economic Research. County business growth. Trenton, N.J. (CN 824, Trenton 08625-0824) [1987] 2 v. : LC Card 87-404521 DDC 331.12/09749/021 19
HD5725.N5 C68 1987

New Jersey. Division of Coastal Resources. Hudson Waterfront Walkway plan and design guidelines /. [Trenton, N.J.] , 1984] 136 p. : *NYPL [JLF 87-913]*

New Jersey. Division of Criminal Justice. Rebovich, Donald. Understanding hazardous waste crime . [Trenton?] [1986] viii, 70 p. : LC Card 86-622805 DDC 364.1/42 19
HD9975.U53 A1157 1986

NEW JERSEY - ECONOMIC CONDITIONS. Johnson, James P., 1937- New Jersey . Northridge, Calif. , 1987. 624 p. : ISBN 0-89781-206-9 LC Card 87-8247 DDC 338.09749 19
HC107.N5 J64 1987

NEW JERSEY - ECONOMIC CONDITIONS - STATISTICS. County business growth. Trenton, N.J. (CN 824, Trenton 08625-0824) [1987] 2 v. : LC Card 87-404521 DDC 331.12/09749/021 19
HD5725.N5 C68 1987

New Jersey ethnic life series . (7) Wright, Giles R. Work /. Trenton , c1987. 82 p. : ISBN 0-89743-072-7 (pbk.) LC Card 87-1573 DDC 331.6/2/09749 19
HD8083.N4 W75 1987

New Jersey Historical Commission. Wright, Giles R. Work /. Trenton , c1987. 82 p. : ISBN 0-89743-072-7 (pbk.) LC Card 87-1573 DDC 331.6/2/09749 19
HD8083.N4 W75 1987

NEW JERSEY - INDUSTRIES - HISTORY. Johnson, James P., 1937- New Jersey . Northridge, Calif. , 1987. 624 p. : ISBN 0-89781-206-9 LC Card 87-8247 DDC 338.09749 19
HC107.N5 J64 1987

NEW JERSEY - INDUSTRIES - STATISTICS. County business growth. Trenton, N.J. (CN 824, Trenton 08625-0824) [1987] 2 v. : LC Card 87-404521 DDC 331.12/09749/021 19
HD5725.N5 C68 1987

New Jersey Institute for Continuing Legal Education. Chalfin, Robert J. Seminar material for understanding and using financial statements /. Newark, N.J. (15 Washington St., Newark 07102) , c1987. 95, [43] leaves ; LC Card 87-402010 DDC 657/.33/024344 19
HF5681.B2 C415 1987

New Jersey. Legislature. Emergency Response System Study Commission. Public hearing before Emergency Response System Study Commission on implementation of a statewide enhanced 911 service : September 10, 1986, Camden County College, Blackwood, New Jersey / public hearing recorded and transcribed by Office of Legislative Services, Public Information Office, Hearing Unit. [Trenton, N.J.] : The Commission, [1986] 49 p. ; 28 cm. Cover title. LC Card 87-621252 DDC 384.6/42 19
1. Telephone - New Jersey - Emergency reporting systems. 2. Emergency communication systems - New Jersey. I. New Jersey. Legislature. Office of Legislative Services. Public Information Office. Hearing Unit. II. Title.
HE8840.N5 N48 1986

New Jersey. Legislature. General Assembly. Transportation, Communications & High Technology Committee. Public hearing before the Assembly Transportation, Communications & High Technology Committee on transportation infrastructure : April 24, 1986, State House Annex, Room 403, Trenton, New Jersey. [Trenton, N.J.] : The Committee, [1986]. 95 p. ; 28 cm. Cover title.
1. Transportation - New Jersey. 2. Roads - New Jersey. 3. Infrastructure (Economics) - New Jersey.
NYPL [JLF 86-1583]

New Jersey. Legislature. Office of Legislative Services. Public Information Office. Hearing Unit. New Jersey. Legislature. Emergency Response System Study Commission. Public hearing before Emergency Response System Study Commission on implementation of a statewide enhanced 911 service . [Trenton, N.J.] [1986] 49 p. ; LC Card 87-621252 DDC 384.6/42 19
HE8840.N5 N48 1986

NEW JERSEY - OCCUPATIONS - STATISTICS. Sheppard, Thomas M. Occupational outlook for New Jersey and JTPA labor market areas, 1982-1990 [microform]. Trenton, N.J. [1984] ii leaves, 50 p. ; LC Card 84-623480 DDC 331.12/09749 19
HD5725.N5 S47 1984
*NYPL [*ZT-1745 no.24]*

NEW JERSEY - POPULATION - STATISTICS. Population projections for New Jersey and counties . Trenton, N.J. , 1985. 2 v. ; LC Card 86-622231 DDC 304.6/2/09749021 19
HA525 .P66 1985

New Jersey State Data Center. Crowley, Charles. Income and poverty in New Jersey [microform] . Trenton, N.J. [1982] 32 p. ; LC Card 83-620831 DDC 339.2/2/09749 19
HC107.N53 I5113 1982
*NYPL [*ZT-1712 no.31]*

New Jersey study manual for life and accident and health insurance. Chicago : R & R Newkirk, c1987. p. cm. ISBN 0-88462-726-8 LC Card 87-13103 DDC 368.3/009749 19
1. Insurance - New Jersey - Examinations, questions, etc. 2. Insurance law - New Jersey - Examinations, questions, etc. I. R & R Newkirk.
HG8101.N48 N47 1987

The new Keynesian economics . Frank, Jeff. Brighton , 1986. xvii, 283 p. : ISBN 0-7108-0239-0 *NYPL [JLD 86-2534]*

The new manufacturing challenge . Suzaki, Kiyoshi. New York , London , c1987. xv, 255 p. : ISBN 0-02-932040-2 LC Card 86-33715 DDC 658.5 19
HD9720.5 .S98 1987

New marketing strategies for office equipment. New York, N.Y. : Frost & Sullivan, c1983. vii, 307 p. ; 29 cm. "July 1983." "#A1093." LC Card 87-142201 DDC 381/.456816/0973 19
1. Electronic office machine industry - United States. 2. Electronic office machines - Marketing. 3. Market surveys - United States. I. Frost & Sullivan.
HD9801.U542 N48 1983

New materials for new semiconductors / Philip Rotheim, project analyst. Stamford, Conn., U. S.A. : Business Communications Co., c1986. xii, 198 leaves : ill. ; 29 cm. (Business opportunity report . GB-080) "April 1986"--T.p. verso. ISBN 0-89336-475-4 (soft) LC Card 87-404262 DDC 381/.4562138152/0973 19
1. Semiconductor industry - United States. 2. Integrated circuits industry - United States. 3. Semiconductors. I. Rotheim, Philip. II. Series.
HD9696.S43 U492 1986

New media in Europe . Tydeman, John. London , New York , c1986. xii, 260 p. : ISBN 0-07-084799-1 : LC Card 85-19839 DDC 384.55/094 19
HE8700.9.E8 T93 1986
NYPL [JLE 86-3209]

New Mexico. Bureau of Economic Research and Analysis. New Mexico youth in the labor force. [Albuquerque, N.M.] (P.O. Box 1928, Albuquerque 87103) [1986] v leaves, 74 p. : LC Card 87-620614 DDC 331.3/4/09789 19
HD6274.N6 N49 1986

New Mexico Labor and Industrial Commission. Office of the Labor Commissioner. Characteristics of occupational injuries and illnesses in New Mexico, 1983 /. Santa Fe, N.M. [1983] 47 p. : LC Card 86-620786 DDC 363.1/12/09789021 19
HD7262.5.U62 N626 1983

New Mexico land grant series. Land, water, and culture . Albuquerque , c1987. ix, 422 p. : ISBN 0-8263-0989-5 (pbk.) LC Card 87-10957 DDC 333.1/6/09788 19
HD243.N5 L36 1987

New Mexico. Occupational Health and Safety Bureau. Data Management Section. Characteristics of occupational injuries and illnesses in New Mexico, 1982 /. Santa Fe, N.M. [1983?] 43 p. : LC Card 86-621034 DDC 363.1/12/09789021 19
HD7262.5.U62 N625 1983

Characteristics of occupational injuries and illnesses in New Mexico, 1983 /. Santa Fe, N.M. [1983] 47 p. : LC Card 86-620786 DDC 363.1/12/09789021 19
HD7262.5.U62 N626 1983

New Mexico. Traffic Safety Bureau. Highway safety plan, fiscal year 1987 / State of New Mexico. Santa Fe, N.M. (P.O. Box 1028, Santa Fe 87504-1028) : State of New Mexico, Transportation Dept., Traffic Safety Bureau, [1986] 190 leaves : ill. ; 28 cm. Cover title: Highway safety plan and alcohol plan, fiscal year 1987. Bibliography: leaf 94. LC Card 86-622688 DDC 363.1/256/09789 19
1. Traffic safety - New Mexico. I. Title. II. Title: Highway safety plan and alcohol plan, fiscal year 1987.
HE5614.3.N47 N49 1986

New Mexico youth in the labor force. [Albuquerque, N.M.] (P.O. Box 1928, Albuquerque 87103) : [New Mexico Employment Security Dept., Bureau of Economic Research and Analysis, 1986] v leaves, 74 p. : ill. ; 28 cm. Cover title. LC Card 87-620614 DDC 331.3/4/09789 19
1. Youth - Employment - New Mexico - Statistics. 2. Labor supply - New Mexico - Statistics. I. New Mexico. Bureau of Economic Research and Analysis.
HD6274.N6 N49 1986

New office information technology . Long, Richard J. London , New York , c1987. xix, 333 p. : ISBN 0-7099-4103-X (jacket); 0-7099-4130-X LC Card 87-3601 DDC 651.8 19
HF5547.5 .L65 1987

New opportunities for entrepreneurship / edited by Herbert Giersch. Boulder : Westview Press, 1987. p. cm. (Publications of the Institute of World Economics, University of Kiel) ISBN 0-8133-0597-7 LC Card 87-20143 DDC 338/.04 19
1. New business enterprises. 2. Small business. 3. Entrepreneurship. I. Giersch, Herbert. II. Series.
HD62.5 .N48 1987

New opportunities to purchase natural gas /. Williams, Anna Fay, 1935- Lilburn, Ga. , c1988. xiv, 372 p. : ISBN 0-88173-034-3 : LC Card 86-46134 DDC 665.7/44/068 19
HD9581.U5 W54 1988

The new options market /. Ansbacher, Max G. New York , c1987. xvii, 280 p. : ISBN 0-8027-7308-7 (pbk.) : LC Card 87-18892 DDC 332.64/52 19
HG6042 .A57 1987

New Orleans dockworkers . Rosenberg, Daniel, 1953- Albany , c1988. x, 233 p. ; ISBN 0-88706-649-6 LC Card 87-10156 DDC 331.7/61387164/0976335 19
HD8039.L82 U664 1988

NEW ORLEANS (LA.) - RACE RELATIONS. Rosenberg, Daniel, 1953- New Orleans dockworkers . Albany , c1988. x, 233 p. ; ISBN 0-88706-649-6 LC Card 87-10156 DDC 331.7/61387164/0976335 19
HD8039.L82 U664 1988

The New Palgrave : a dictionary of economics / edited by John Eatwell, Murray Milgate, Peter Newman. New York : Stockton Press, c1987. p. cm. Sequel to: Dictionary of political economy /Robert Harry Inglis Palgrave. 1910. Bibliography: p. Includes index. ISBN 0-935859-10-1 (set) : LC Card 87-1946 DDC 330/.03/21 19
1. Economics - Dictionaries. I. Eatwell, John. II. Milgate, Murray. III. Newman, Peter K., 1928-. IV. Palgrave, Robert Harry Inglis, Sir, 1827-1919. Dictionary of political economy.
HB61 .N49 1987

New patterns in employment . (no. 5) Social security and employment /. Assen, The Netherlands , 1983. 116 p. : ISBN 90-232-2011-0 (pbk.) : LC Card 83-216203 DDC 331.12/094 19
HD7164 .S594 1983 *NYPL [JLE 86-1107]*

New patterns of management /. Likert, Rensis, 1903- New York , 1987. vii, 279 p. : ISBN 0-8240-8214-1 (alk. paper) : LC Card 86-25800 DDC 658.4 19
HD31 .L43 1987

New perspectives on compensation / editors, David B. Balkin, Luis R. Gomez-Mejia.

Englewood Cliffs, N.J. : Prentice-Hall, c1987. xviii, 363 p. : ill. ; 24 cm. Includes bibliographies. ISBN 0-13-615212-0 (pbk.) LC Card 86-25534 DDC 658.3/2 19
1. Compensation management. 2. Wages. I. Balkin, David B., 1948-. II. Gomez-Mejia, Luis R.
HF5549.5.C67 N49 1987

New perspectives on the financial system / edited by Laurence Harris ... [et al.] ; with an introductory essay by Michael Meacher. London ; New York : Croom Helm, c1988. 410 p. : ill. ; 23 cm. "Published in the USA by Croom Helm in association with Metheun, Inc."--T.p. verso. Includes bibliographies and index. ISBN 0-7099-3741-5 LC Card 87-15723 DDC 332/.0941 19
1. Finance - Great Britain. I. Harris, Laurence.
HG186.G7 N44 1988

The new politics of the budgetary process /. Wildavsky, Aaron B. Glenview, Ill. , c1988. xxiv, 468 p. : ISBN 0-673-39754-8 (pbk.) LC Card 87-23391 DDC 353.0072/2 19
HJ2051 .W483 1988

New priorities in public spending / edited by M.S. Levitt. Brookfield, VT : Gower, 1987. 129 p. ; 23 cm. (Joint studies in public policy . 13) Papers from a conference held July 9-10, 1986, organized by the National Institute of Economic and Social Research. Bibliography: p. [124]-126. Includes index. ISBN 0-566-05386-1 : LC Card 86-22946 DDC 336.3/9/0941 19
1. Government spending policy - Great Britain - Congresses. 2. Great Britain - Appropriations and expenditures - Congresses. 3. Fiscal policy - Great Britain - Congresses. I. Levitt, M. S., 1938-. II. National Institute of Economic and Social Research. III. Series: Joint studies in public policy (National Institute of Economic and Social Research) , 13.
HJ7764 .N49 1987

NEW PRODUCT ANNOUNCEMENTS (DATA BASE)
New Product Announcements (NPA) user's guide. Cleveland, Ohio (11001 Cedar Ave., Cleveland 44106) , 1986- 1 v. (loose-leaf) ; LC Card 86-220025 DDC 025/.0633802 19
HF5415.153 .N46 1986

New Product Announcements (NPA) user's guide. Cleveland, Ohio (11001 Cedar Ave., Cleveland 44106) : Predicasts, 1986- 1 v. (loose-leaf) ; 30 cm. Spine title: NPA user's guide. On t.p. the registered trademark symbol "TM" is superscript following "New Product Announcements" in the title. Includes index. LC Card 86-220025 DDC 025/.0633802 19
1. New Product Announcements (Data base). I. Predicasts, inc. II. Title: NPA user's guide.
HF5415.153 .N46 1986

NEW PRODUCTS - HISTORY - 20TH CENTURY.
I'll buy that! . New York , c1986. 240 p. : ISBN 0-89043-046-2 LC Card 86-1281 DDC 303.4/83 19
HF5415.153 .I45 1986 ***NYPL [JLG 87-125]***

NEW PRODUCTS - ENVIRONMENTAL ASPECTS.
Thomé, Gotthardt, 1949- Produktgestaltung und Ökologie /. München , c1981. xii, 212 p. : ISBN 3-88259-086-6 : LC Card 81-146058
HD69.N4 T54 1981 ***NYPL [JLD 86-2800]***

NEW PRODUCTS - JAPAN - AWARDS.
The Best of Japan. Tokyo , New York, N.Y., U. S.A. , 1987. 288, xiv p. : ISBN 0-87011-801-3 (U. S. : pbk.) : LC Card 86-40432 DDC 338.4/7/000952 19
HF5415.153 .B47 1987

NEW PRODUCTS - MANAGEMENT.
Souder, Wm. E. (William E.) Managing new product innovations /. Lexington, Mass. , c1987. xviii, 251 p. : ISBN 0-669-10809-X (alk. paper) LC Card 85-40104 DDC 658.5/75 19
HD69.N4 S634 1987

Van Nest, Dean G. (Dean Gillette), 1923- Developing global new products . Ann Arbor, Mich. , c1987. viii, 123 p. : ISBN 0-8357-1793-3 (alk. paper) LC Card 87-5844 DDC 658.5/75/0973 19
HD69.N4 V36 1987

NEW PRODUCTS - MARKETING.
Bauer, Hans H. Die Entscheidung des Handels über die Aufnahme neuer Produkte . Berlin , c1980. xxiii, 479 p. ; ISBN 3-428-04702-8 LC Card 87-408771 DDC 658.8 s 658.8/343 19
HF5415.A2 S37 Bd. 10 HF5415.153

Sangiovanni, Bruno. Marketing . Roma , c1986. 268 p. : LC Card 85-233830
HF5415.153 .S25 1986

NEW PRODUCTS - MARKETING - MATHEMATICAL MODELS - CONGRESSES.
Innovation diffusion models of new product acceptance /. Cambridge, Mass. , 1986. xvi, 318 p. : ISBN 0-88730-076-6 LC Card 85-23300 DDC 658.8/343 19
HF5415.153 .I55 1986 ***NYPL [JLE 86-3235]***

New profits in gold, silver, strategic metals . Cavelti, Peter C., 1947- New York , 1984, c1985. 221 p. : ISBN 0-07-010288-0 LC Card 84-12268 DDC 332.63 19
HG261 .C38 1985 ***NYPL [JLE 84-2956]***

The new quick job-hunting map /. Bolles, Richard Nelson. Berkeley, Calif. , c1985. 63 p. : ISBN 0-89815-151-1 (pbk.) : LC Card 86-220490 DDC 650.1/4
HF5382.7 .B63 1985

The new real estate game . Norton, Hollis. Chicago , c1987. 233 p. : ISBN 0-8092-4794-1 : LC Card 86-32902 DDC 346.7304/37 347.306437 19
HD1382.5 .N675 1987

New RHC strategies /
Communications/Information Systems. Boston, MA (200 Portland St., Boston 02114) : Yankee Group, c1987. iii, 117 p. ; 28 cm. (Communications Systems & Services) "March 1987." LC Card 87-147694 DDC 384.6/065/73 19
1. American Telephone and Telegraph Company - Reorganization. 2. Telecommunication systems - United States. 3. Telephone - United States. I. Communications/Information Systems (Firm : Yankee Group). II. Series: Communications Systems & Services (Series).
HE8846.A55 N497 1987

NEW SPAIN - ECONOMIC POLICY.
Austin, Ruben Vargas, 1915- The development of economic policy in Mexico with special reference to economic doctrines, 1600-1958 /. New York , 1987. 336 p. ; ISBN 0-8240-1354-9 (alk. paper) : LC Card 87-8569 DDC 338.972 19
HC135 .A84 1987

NEW SPAIN - MANUFACTURES - HISTORY - 18TH CENTURY.
Velázquez, María del Carmen. Notas sobre sirvientes de las Californias y proyecto de obraje en Nuevo México /. México, D.F. [1985], c1984. 246 p. ; ISBN 968-12-0298-8 LC Card 85-243085
HD2346.U52 C294 1985

New specialty metals & metallurgy for high-temperature, high-strength, low-weight applications / Richard W. Bryant, project analyst. Norwalk, Conn., U. S.A. : Business Communications Co., c1987. 1 v. (various foliations) : ill. ; 29 cm. (Business opportunity report . GB-085) ISBN 0-89336-454-1 (pbk.) LC Card 87-168123 DDC 380.1/45669/0973 19
1. Metal trade - United States. 2. Metals at high temperatures. 3. Metals - Fracture. 4. Market surveys - United States. I. Bryant, Richard W. II. Business Communications Co. III. Series.
HD9506.U62 N45 1987

New standards for evaluating technological innovation in the USSR . Kogan, Ninel. Falls Church, VA (7700 Leesburg Pike, #250, Falls Church 22043) , c1986. xii, 103 leaves (some folded) : LC Card 87-151964 DDC 338.4/7681766/0947 19
HD9579.C33 S654 1986

New statistical procedures for the social sciences . Wilcox, Rand R. Hillsdale, N.J. , 1987. p. cm. ISBN 0-89859-936-9 : LC Card 87-9001 DDC 300/.1/5195 19
HA29 .W522 1987

New technology and public relations : a guide for public relations and public affairs practitioners / edited by Kalman B. Druck, project chairman, Merton Fiur, editor-in-chief, Don Bates, project director. New York, NY (310 Madison Ave., New York 10017) : Foundation for Public Relations Research and Education, c1986. xviii, 170 p. : ill. ; 28 cm. LC Card 87-105313 DDC 659.2/028/5 19
1. Public relations - Data processing. I. Druck, Kalman B. II. Fiur, Merton. III. Bates, Don. IV. Foundation for Public Relations Research and Education (U. S.).
HD59 .N44 1986

New technology and regional development / edited by Bert van der Knapp [sic] and Egbert Wever. London ; Wolfeboro, N.H. : C. Helm, c1987. 188 p. : ill. ; 23 cm. Includes bibliographies and index. ISBN 0-7099-3106-9 : LC Card 86-23983 DDC 338.9/26 19
1. Technological innovations. 2. Regional planning. 3. Research, Industrial. I. Knaap, G. A. van der. II. Wever, E.
HC79.T4 N48 1987

New technology and the process of labour regulation / Eric Batstone ... [et al.]. Oxford [Oxfordshire] ; New York : Oxford University Press, 1987. p. cm. Includes bibliographies. ISBN 0-19-827274-X : LC Card 87-11146 DDC 331/.0941 19
1. Industrial relations - Great Britain - Effect of technological innovations on - Case studies. I. Batstone, Eric.
HD6331.2.G7 N48 1987

New technology and women's employment. Bruxelles ; New York : International Confederation of Free Trade Unions, [1983] 78 p. ; 21 cm. Cover title. "D/1983/0403/7"--p. [2] of cover. Bibliography: p. 77-78. LC Card 85-160627 DDC 331.4/2 19
1. Women white collar workers - Effect of automation on. 2. Office practice - Automation. 3. Microelectronics - Social aspects.
HD6331 .N49 1983 ***NYPL [JLD 86-1807]***

New technology as organizational innovation : the development and diffusion of microelectronics / edited by Johannes M. Pennings and Arend Buitendam. Cambridge, Mass. : Ballinger Pub. Co., c1987. xvi, 308 p. : ill. ; 24 cm. (Ballinger series on the management of innovation and change) Includes bibliographies and index. ISBN 0-88730-186-X LC Card 86-32110 DDC 658.5/14 19
1. Technological innovations - Management. 2. Organizational change. I. Pennings, Johannes M. II. Buitendam, Arend. III. Series.
HD45 .N43 1987

New technology at work /. Francis, Arthur. Oxford [Oxfordshire] , New York , 1986. vi, 216 p. ; ISBN 0-19-878016-8 : LC Card 86-12705 DDC 338/.06 19
HD6331 .F66 1987 ***NYPL [JLD 87-912]***

New technology in the office environment /. Armour, Hazel. Aldershot, Hampshire, England , Brookfield, Vt., USA , c1986. viii, 138 p. : ISBN 0-566-05031-5 LC Card 86-215701 DDC 338.4/561651 19
HF5547.5 .A786 1986

New theories of the multinational enterprise / edited by Alan M. Rugman. London : Croom Helm, c1982. 303 p. : ill. ; 23 cm. "Proceedings of a conference held in October 1981 at Dalhousie University, Canada ... sponsored by the Centre for International Business Studies ..."--Pref. Bibliography: p. 280-293. Includes indexes. ISBN 0-7099-2224-8 LC Card 86-673671
1. International business enterprises - Congresses. I. Rugman, Alan M. II. Dalhousie University. Centre for International Business Studies.
HD2755.5 .N485x 1982

New tides in the Pacific : Pacific Basin Cooperation and the Big Four (Japan, PRC, USA, USSR) / edited by Roy Kim and Hilary Conroy. New York : Greenwood Press, 1987. xiii, 216 p. ; 22 cm. (Contributions in political science, 0147-1066 . no. 188) Bibliography: p. [201]-203. Includes index. ISBN 0-313-25625-X (lib. bdg. : alk. paper) LC Card 87-8406 DDC 337.1/9 19
1. Pacific Area - Economic integration. 2. Pacific Area cooperation. 3. Pacific Area - National security. I. Kim, Roy U. T. II. Conroy, Hilary, 1919-. III. Series.
HC681 .N48 1987

NEW TOWNS - RUSSIAN S.F.S.R. - SIBERIA, EASTERN.
Sotsial′noe razvitie molodezhi v trudovykh kollektivakh novykh gorodov Sibiri . Irkutsk , 1980. 158 p. ; LC Card 82-110658
HD6276.S593 S527 1980

New trends in food retailing / Sandra McGowan, project analyst. Stamford, Conn., U. S.A. : Business Communications Co., c1985. xiii, 135

leaves : ill. ; 29 cm. (Business opportunity report . GA-045R) "July 1985"--T.p. verso. ISBN 0-89336-457-6 (soft) LC Card 87-165228 DDC 381/.45664/00973 19
1. Grocery trade - United States. 2. Market surveys - United States. I. McGowan, Sandra. II. Business Communications Co. III. Series.
HD9321.5 .N47 1985

New trends in gas separations . Crull, Anna W. Stamford, Conn., U. S.A. , c1986. xvi, 222 leaves : ISBN 0-89336-422-3 (pbk.) LC Card 87-165549 DDC 660.2/842 19
HD9660.G372 C78 1986

The new unionism . Lehr, Richard I. New York, N.Y. , c1987. 114 p. ; ISBN 0-88057-672-3 (pbk.) LC Card 86-82864 DDC 331.88/0973 19
HD6508 .L427 1987

The new venture handbook . Merrill, Ronald E. New York, NY , c1987. 356 p. : ISBN 0-8144-5895-5 LC Card 86-47818 DDC 658.1/141 19
HD62.5 .M46 1987

New Ways to Work (firm) McGuire, Nan. Survey of private sector work and family policy . San Francisco , c1986. 41 leaves ; LC Card 87-113810 DDC 331.25/72/0979461 19
HD5126.S4 M38 1986

The new world of commercial banking /. Compton, Eric N., 1925- Lexington, Mass. , c1987. xvi, 316 p. : ISBN 0-669-14017-1 (alk. paper) LC Card 86-45002 DDC 332.1/2/068 19
HG2491 .C646 1987

New York Chamber of Commerce and Industry. New York City Partnership. The Partnership. New York, N.Y. , c1986. 44 p. : LC Card 86-223138 DDC 380.1/06/07471 19
HF296.N4 N48 1986

NEW YORK CHAMBER OF COMMERCE AND INDUSTRY.
New York City Partnership. The Partnership. New York, N.Y. , c1986. 44 p. : LC Card 86-223138 DDC 380.1/06/07471 19
HF296.N4 N48 1986

New York (City). Advertising Research Foundation. see **Advertising Research Foundation.**

New York (City) American Society of Mechanical Engineers. see **American Society of Mechanical Engineers.**

New York (City) Committee for Economic Development. see **Committee for Economic Development.**

NEW YORK (CITY) - ECONOMIC CONDITIONS - ECONOMETRIC MODELS.
Drennan, Matthew P., 1937- Modeling metropolitan economies for forecasting and policy analysis /. New York , 1985. x, 242 p. ; ISBN 0-8147-1781-0 (alk. paper) : LC Card 85-13784 DDC 330.9173/2 19
HT321 .D74 1985 ***NYPL [JLE 86-1102]***

New York City Partnership.
Going for it [motion picture] /. New York, NY , 1987. 1 film reel (12 min.) : LC Card 87-705727 DDC 331.3 11
HD6275

Going for it [videorecording] /. New York, NY , 1987. 1 videocassette (12 min.) : LC Card 87-705728 DDC 331.3 11
HD6275

The Partnership. New York, N.Y. : New York City Partnership : New York Chamber of Commerce and Industry, c1986. 44 p. : ill. ; 30 cm. Cover title. LC Card 86-223138 DDC 380.1/06/07471 19
1. New York Chamber of Commerce and Industry. 2. New York City Partnership. 3. Industrial promotion - New York (N.Y.). 4. Urban renewal - New York (N.Y.). 5. Community development - New York (N.Y.). I. New York Chamber of Commerce and Industry. II. Title.
HF296.N4 N48 1986

NEW YORK CITY PARTNERSHIP.
New York City Partnership. The Partnership. New York, N.Y. , c1986. 44 p. : LC Card 86-223138 DDC 380.1/06/07471 19
HF296.N4 N48 1986

New York (City) Population Council. see **Population Council, New York.**

New York City's capital program . Citizens Budget Commission (New York, N.Y.) New York, N.Y. (110 E. 42nd St., New York 10017) [1986] 17 leaves ; LC Card 87-110059 DDC 336.3/9/097471 19
HJ9289.N4 C54 1986a

New York Institute of Finance.
The New York Institute of Finance guide to investing. New York, N.Y. , c1987. xi, 296 p. : ISBN 0-13-620436-8 (pbk.) : LC Card 87-11323 DDC 332.6/78 19
HG4921 .N53 1987

Stocks, bonds, options, futures . New York, N.Y. [Englewood Cliffs, N.J.] , c1987. 332 p. : ISBN 0-13-846718-8 : LC Card 87-11324 DDC 332.6/78 19
HG4921 .S7945 1987

Study guide for After the trade is made . New York, NY , c1987. ix, 217 p. : ISBN 0-13-858721-3 (pbk.) : LC Card 87-14155 DDC 332.64/273 19
HG4910 .W365 1986 Suppl.

The Successful sales assistant's handbook. New York, N.Y. , c1987. xi, 268 p. : ISBN 0-13-860305-7 (pbk.) : LC Card 87-11322 DDC 332.6/2/0688 19
HG4621 .S84 1987

Weiss, David M., 1938- After the trade is made . New York, N.Y. , c1986. xii, 436 p. : ISBN 0-13-018581-7 : LC Card 85-30997 DDC 332.64/273 19
HG4910 .W365 1986 ***NYPL [JLE 86-4304]***

The New York Institute of Finance guide to investing. New York, N.Y. : The Institute, c1987. xi, 296 p. : ill. ; 23 cm. Spine title: Guide to investing. Bibliography: p. 256-257. Includes index. ISBN 0-13-620436-8 (pbk.) : LC Card 87-11323 DDC 332.6/78 19
1. Investments - United States. 2. Securities - United States. 3. Brokers - United States. I. New York Institute of Finance. II. Title: Guide to investing.
HG4921 .N53 1987

New York Mercantile Exchange guide . New York Mercantile Exchange (N.Y.) Chicago, Ill. (4025 W. Peterson Ave., Chicago 60646) , c1986- 1 v. (loose-leaf) ; LC Card 86-216683
HG6049 .N48 1986

New York Mercantile Exchange (N.Y.) New York Mercantile Exchange guide : exchange officials, membership directory, by-laws and rules. Chicago, Ill. (4025 W. Peterson Ave., Chicago 60646) : Published for the New York Mercantile Exchange by Commerce Clearing House, c1986- 1 v. (loose-leaf) ; 26 cm. Includes index. LC Card 86-216683
1. New York Mercantile Exchange (N.Y.). I. Title.
HG6049 .N48 1986

NEW YORK MERCANTILE EXCHANGE (N. Y.)
New York Mercantile Exchange (N.Y.) New York Mercantile Exchange guide . Chicago, Ill. (4025 W. Peterson Ave., Chicago 60646) , c1986- 1 v. (loose-leaf) ; LC Card 86-216683
HG6049 .N48 1986

New York Mercantile Exchange (U. S.) The Domestic U. S. oil industry and low oil prices . [Cambridge, Mass.] , c1987. v, 61 leaves : LC Card 87-402219 DDC 338.2/7282/0973 19
HD9574.U62 D66 1987

New York nonprofit organizations . Altschuler, David M. Washington, D.C. (2100 M St., N.W., Washington 20037) , c1987. vii, 43 p. : LC Card 87-159600 DDC 658.1/5 19
HD2769.2.U6 A48 1987

NEW YORK (N.Y.) - ECONOMIC CONDITIONS.
Stansell, Christine. City of women . Urbana , 1987, c1986. xiv, 301 p. ; ISBN 0-252-01481-2 (pbk.) LC Card 87-16163 DDC 305.4/2/097471 19
HD6096.N6 S8 1987

NEW YORK (N.Y.) - OCCUPATIONS.
Stafford, Walter W. Closed labor markets . New York, N.Y. (105 E. 22nd St., New York 10010) , c1985. xvi, 203, 3, [2] p. ; LC Card 85-186853 DDC 331.12/09747/1 19
HD5726.N5 S73 1985 ***NYPL [Sc F 86-274]***

NEW YORK (N.Y.) - PUBLIC WORKS - FINANCE.
Citizens Budget Commission (New York, N.Y.) New York City's capital program . New York, N.Y. (110 E. 42nd St., New York 10017) [1986] 17 leaves ; LC Card 87-110059 DDC 336.3/9/097471 19
HJ9289.N4 C54 1986a

NEW YORK (N.Y.) - SOCIAL CONDITIONS.
Stansell, Christine. City of women . Urbana , 1987, c1986. xiv, 301 p. ; ISBN 0-252-01481-2 (pbk.) LC Card 87-16163 DDC 305.4/2/097471 19
HD6096.N6 S8 1987

The Tenant movement in New York City, 1904-1984 /. New Brunswick, N.J. , c1986. xiv, 289 p. : ISBN 0-8135-1203-4 (pbk.) : LC Card 85-27894 DDC 333.33/8 19
HD7288.85.U62 N58 1986
NYPL [JLE 86-4565]

NEW YORK (STATE) - APPROPRIATIONS AND EXPENDITURES.
Altschuler, David M. New York nonprofit organizations . Washington, D.C. (2100 M St., N.W., Washington 20037) , c1987. vii, 43 p. : LC Card 87-159600 DDC 658.1/5 19
HD2769.2.U6 A48 1987

New York (State). Assembly. see **New York (State). Legislature. Assembly.**

New York (State). Budget, Division of the. see **New York (State). Division of the Budget.**

New York (State). Bureau of Labor Market Information. County profiles . Albany, N.Y. [1984-<1985. v. : LC Card 84-623501 DDC 330.9747/043 19
HC107.N7 C64 1984

New York State College of Agriculture and Life Sciences. Agricultural Economics, Dept. of. see **New York State College of Agriculture and Life Sciences. Dept. of Agricultural Economics.**

New York State College of Agriculture and Life Sciences. Dept. of Agricultural Economics. The Farm credit crisis policy options and consequences /. Ithaca, N.Y. [1986] ii, 57 p. : LC Card 86-621935 DDC 338.1 s 332.7/1/0973 19
HD1775.N8 C6 no. 86-3 HG2051.U6

New York State Conference of Mayors and Other Municipal Officials. Baynes, Peter A. Distribution of local sales tax revenue . Albany, N.Y. (119 Washington Ave., Albany 12210) [1986] 13 p. : LC Card 87-106773 DDC 336.2/713/09747 19
HJ5715.U62 N72 1986

New York (State). Council on Health Care Financing. Subcommittee on Health Insurance. Health insurance : public policy in New York : a report from the Subcommittee on Health Insurance, Council on Health Care Financing. Albany, N.Y. : The Council, [1985?] 1 v. (various pagings) : ill. ; 28 cm. Includes bibliographies. LC Card 86-622080 DDC 368.3/82/009747 19
1. Insurance, Health - New York (State). 2. Insurance, Health - Government policy - New York (State). I. Title.
HD7102.U5 N655 1985

New York (State). Dept. of Labor. (Old Catalog form: New York (State). Labor Dept.) Statistics relative to the New York State Unemployment Insurance Fund, 1936-1984. Albany, N.Y. [1985] vii, 66 p. ; LC Card 86-622164 DDC 368.4/4/009747021 19
HD7096.U6 N793 1985

New York (State). Dept. of Labor. Bureau of Labor Market Information. see **New York (State). Bureau of Labor Market Information.**

New York (State). Dept. of Labor. Division of Research and Statistics. Bureau of Labor Market Information. see **New York (State). Bureau of Labor Market Information.**

New York (State). Dept. of Law. Environmental Protection Bureau. Jaffe, Susan. Toxic chemical accidents in New York State . New York, N.Y. (2 World Trade Center, New York 10047) [1986] 27, 13, 33 p. ; LC Card 86-622820 DDC 363.1/79 19
HD7269.C452 U54 1986

New York (State). Dept. of Motor Vehicles. (Old Catalog form: New York (State). Motor Vehicles, Dept. of)
Dowling, Anne M. Two years of accident experience under STOP-DWI, December 1981-November 1983 /. [Albany] [1984] xiii, 67 p. : LC Card 86-622431 DDC 363.1/251 19
HE5620.D7 D68 1984

New York (State). Dept. of Social Services. (Old Catalog form: New York (State). Social Services, Dept. of)

New York (State). Dept. of Social Services. Division of Medical Assistance.
O'Connell, Julie, 1951- Medicaid reform . [Albany, N.Y.] [1983] 26 p. ; LC Card 86-620741 DDC 362.1/04252/09747 19
HD7102.U5 N668 1983

Utilization of medicaid paid health services by Medicaid recipients in New York City, Nassau, Monroe, and western central counties, 1980-1981 /. Albany, N.Y. (1 Commerce Plaza, Albany 12210) [1985] ii, 31, 17 p. : LC Card 86-622554 DDC 362.1/04252/09747 19
HD7102.U5 N684 1985

New York (State). Dept. of Taxation and Finance. (Old Catalog form: New York (State). Taxation and Finance Dept.)
The President's tax reform proposal . [Albany, N.Y.] [1985] 48 leaves : LC Card 86-622434 DDC 336.2/009747 19
HJ2424 .P84 1985

The United States Senate's tax reform proposal . [Albany, N.Y.?] [1986] 18, 6, 2 leaves ; LC Card 87-620727 DDC 336.2/009747 19
HJ2424 .U55 1986

New York (State). Division of Equalization and Assessment. Understanding the equalization rate /. Albany, N.Y. (Governor Nelson A. Rockefeller Empire State Plaza, Albany 12223) [1986] 28 p. : LC Card 87-620729 DDC 336.22/2 19
HJ4249 .U53 1986

New York (State). Division of Housing and Community Renewal.
Nolon, John R. Housing rehabilitation under the Community Development Block Grant Program . [New York, N.Y.] [1984] 150 p. in various pagings ; LC Card 86-622826 DDC 363.5/8 19
HD7303.N7 N65 1984

Special needs housing demonstration program report. New York, N.Y. (2 World Trade Center, New York 10047) : New York State Division of Housing and Community Renewal, [1984] 1 v. (various foliations) : ill. ; 29 cm. Cover title. "January 1984." LC Card 86-622827 DDC 363.5/8 19
1. Rental housing - Government policy - New York (State). 2. Public housing - Government policy - New York (State). I. Title.
HD7288.85.U62 N754 1984

New York (State). Division of the Budget. (Old Catalog form: New York (State). Executive Dept. Budget Division)
The President's tax reform proposal . [Albany, N.Y.] [1985] 48 leaves : LC Card 86-622434 DDC 336.2/009747 19
HJ2424 .P84 1985

The United States Senate's tax reform proposal . [Albany, N.Y.?] [1986] 18, 6, 2 leaves ; LC Card 87-620727 DDC 336.2/009747 19
HJ2424 .U55 1986

NEW YORK (STATE) - ECONOMIC CONDITIONS.
County profiles . Albany, N.Y. [1984-<1985. v. : LC Card 84-623501 DDC 330.9747/043 19
HC107.N7 C64 1984

New York State in the year 2000 /. Albany, N.Y. , 1988. 572 p. : ISBN 0-88706-602-X LC Card 87-6486 DDC 338.5/443/09747 19
HC107.N7 N447 1988

Tese, Vincent. Rebuilding New York--the next phase, from recovery to resurgence . [New York, NY (1515 Broadway, New York 10036) , 1985] 74 leaves ; LC Card 86-622413 DDC 338.9747 19
HC107.N7 T47 1985

NEW YORK (STATE) - ECONOMIC POLICY.
New York (State). Legislature. Legislative Commission on Public-Private Cooperation. Legislative Commission on Public-Private Cooperation second report . [Albany] [1984] 57 p. ; LC Card 86-622576 DDC 338.9747 19
HC107.N7 N3743 1984

New York (State). Legislature. Legislative Commission on Public-Private Cooperation. Working together for New York's economy . [Albany] [1983] 57 p. ; LC Card 86-622577 DDC 338.9747 19
HC107.N7 N3743 1983

Tese, Vincent. Rebuilding New York--the next phase, from recovery to resurgence . [New York, NY (1515 Broadway, New York 10036) , 1985] 74 leaves ; LC Card 86-622413 DDC 338.9747 19
HC107.N7 T47 1985

New York State Financial Control Board.
Staff report on modification no. 86-13 to New York City's FYs 1986-1989 financial plan, February 1986 /. [Albany, N.Y.] [1986] 128 leaves ; LC Card 86-622416 DDC 352.1/09747/1 19
HJ9289.N4 S734 1986

Staff report on modification no. 86-8 to New York City's FYs 1986-1989 financial plan. [Albany] [1985] 92 leaves ; LC Card 86-622159 DDC 336.747/1 19
HJ9289.N4 S73 1985

Staff report on proposed modification no. 86-12 to New York City's financial plan relating to the New York City Transit Authority and Staten Island Rapid Transit Operating Authority. [Albany] [1986] 27 leaves ; LC Card 86-622415 DDC 388.4/042 19
HE4491.N65 S7 1986

New York (State). Governor's Office of Employee Relations. Sashkin, Marshall, 1944- Making performance evaluation work . [Albany, N.Y.] , c1986. 57 p. : ISBN 0-8144-2326-4 (pbk.) LC Card 86-209627 DDC 658.3/125 19
HF5549.5.P35 S26 1986

New York State in the year 2000 / edited by Jeryl L. Mumpower and Warren F. Ilchman. Albany, N.Y. : State University of New York Press, 1988. 572 p. : ill. ; 26 cm. Bibliography: p. 561-563. Includes index. ISBN 0-88706-602-X LC Card 87-6486 DDC 338.5/443/09747 19
1. Economic forecasting - New York (State). 2. New York (State) - Economic conditions. I. Mumpower, Jeryl, 1949-. II. Ilchman, Warren Frederick.
HC107.N7 N447 1988

NEW YORK (STATE) - INDUSTRIES - LOCATION.
New York (State). Legislature. Legislative Commission on the Modernization and Simplification of Tax Administration and the Tax Law. Interstate business locational decisions and the effect of the state's tax structure on after-tax rates-of-return of manufacturing firms . [Albany] [1984] 121 p. : LC Card 86-621116 DDC 336.2/07 19
HJ4655.N54 N55 1984

New York (State). Labor, Dept. of. see **New York (State). Dept. of Labor.**

New York (State). Labor Market Information, Bureau of. see **New York (State). Bureau of Labor Market Information.**

New York (State). Legislature.
New York (State). Legislature. Legislative Commission on Critical Transportation Choices. CHIPS, the Consolidated Local Street and Highway Improvement Program . [Albany, N.Y.] [1986] i, 18 leaves ; LC Card 87-620568 DDC 388.1/12 19
HE356.N7 N37 1986

New York (State). Legislature. Assembly. (Old Catalog Form: New York (State). Assembly)

New York (State). Legislature. Assembly. Committee on Local Governments. Lost revenue . [Albany, N.Y.?] [1986] 13, 22 leaves ; LC Card 87-620567 DDC 336.2/009747 19
HJ3324 .L67 1986

New York (State). Legislature. Assembly. Standing Committee on Housing. Seligson, Wendy. Rural housing in N.Y.S. /. [Albany, N.Y.] [1979] [61] p. : LC Card 82-621690 DDC 363.5/8/09747 19
HD7289.U7 N77 1979 ***NYPL [JLF 86-765]***

New York (State). Legislature. Assembly. Standing Committee on Labor. A report on the plight of the collective bargaining system / New York State Assembly Standing Committee on Labor. [Albany] : The Committee, [1984] 64 p. ; 28 cm. Cover title. Bibliography: p. 60-64. LC Card 86-622572 DDC 331.89/0973 19
1. "January 1984.". 2. Collective bargaining - United States. 3. Personnel management - United States. 4. Trade-unions - United States - Organizing. I. Title.
HD6508 .N49 1984

New York (State). Legislature. Legislative Commission on Critical Transportation Choices.
CHIPS, the Consolidated Local Street and Highway Improvement Program : time for an increase! : a report to the Legislature / by the Legislative Commission on Critical Transportation Choices. [Albany, N.Y.] : The Commission, [1986] i, 18 leaves ; 28 cm. Cover title. "February 1986." Includes bibliographical references. LC Card 87-620568 DDC 388.1/12 19
1. Roads - Government policy - New York (State). 2. Roads - Maintenance and repair - Government policy - New York (State). I. New York (State). Legislature. II. Title.
HE356.N7 N37 1986

Conrail : past, present, and future? : the advancements & protection of New York State's "interests" in the proposed sale of Conrail to Norfolk Southern : an informational report / by the New York State Legislative Commission on Critical Transportation Choices ; Norman J. Levy, chairman. [Albany] : The Commission, [1986] i, 134 p. ; 28 cm. "January 1986." Includes bibliographical references. LC Card 87-620569 DDC 385/.065/73 19
1. Conrail. 2. Norfolk Southern Corporation. 3. Railroads - New York (State). I. Levy, Norman J. II. Title.
HE2791.C899 N48 1986

New York (State). Legislature. Legislative Commission on Expenditure Review.
Federal rural transportation assistance : program audit / Legislative Commission on Expenditure Review. Albany, N.Y. (111 Washington Ave., Albany 12210-2277) : The Commission, [1986] 5, ii, 64 p. : ill. ; 28 cm. Cover title. "March 1986." Bibliography: p. 35-41. LC Card 86-622160 DDC 353.0087/5/009747 19
1. Rural transit - New York (State). 2. Rural transit - Government policy - New York (State). 3. Federal aid to transportation - New York (State). I. Title.
HE5633.N7 N53 1986

Mitchell-Lama housing mortgage delinquencies : program audit / Legislative Commission on Expenditure Review. Albany, N.Y. (111 Washington Ave., Albany 12210-2277) : The Commission, [1985] 5, ii, 44 p. : ill. ; 28 cm. Cover title. "August 1985." Bibliography: p. 37. LC Card 86-620632 DDC 353.97470086/5045 19
1. Housing - New York (State) - Finance. 2. Mortgages - New York (State). I. Title.
HD7303.N7 N394 1985 ***NYPL [JLF 87-104]***

New York (State). Legislature. Legislative Commission on Public-Private Cooperation.
Legislative Commission on Public-Private Cooperation second report : the Local Development Amendment / Joseph R. Pisani, chairman ; commission members, Lawrence Bennett ... [et al.]. [Albany] : The Commission, [1984] 57 p. ; 28 cm. "March 31, 1984." LC Card 86-622576 DDC 338.9747 19
1. New York (State). Legislature. Legislative Commission on Public-Private Cooperation. 2. New York (State) - Economic policy. 3. Industry and state - New York (State). 4. Tax incentives - New York (State). 5. Industrial promotion - New York (State). 6. Business and politics - New York (State). I. Title.
HC107.N7 N3743 1984

Working together for New York's economy : the preliminary report of the Legislative Commission on Public-Private Cooperation / Joseph R. Pisani, chairman, commission members, Lawrence Bennett ... [et al.]. [Albany] : The Commission, [1983] 57 p. ; 28 cm. "March 31, 1983." LC Card 86-622577 DDC 338.9747 19
1. New York (State) - Economic policy. 2. Industry and state - New York (State). 3. Tax incentives - New York

(State). 4. Industrial promotion - New York (State). 5. Business and politics - New York (State). I. Title.
HC107.N7 N3743 1983

NEW YORK (STATE). LEGISLATURE. LEGISLATIVE COMMISSION ON PUBLIC-PRIVATE COOPERATION.
New York (State). Legislature. Legislative Commission on Public-Private Cooperation. Legislative Commission on Public-Private Cooperation second report . [Albany] [1984] 57 p. ; LC Card 86-622576 DDC 338.9747 19
HC107.N7 N3743 1984

New York (State). Legislature. Legislative Commission on Science & Technology. Conference on Cable Television (1981 : Brooklyn College Student Union) Proceedings /. [Albany, N.Y.] (P.O. Box 167, Albany 12248) [1982] 77 p. ; LC Card 86-622177 DDC 384.55/47/09747 19
HE8700.72.U6 C66 1981

New York (State). Legislature. Legislative Commission on State-Local Relations. Feigenbaum, Todd R. New York's highway system . Albany, N.Y. (150 State St., Albany 12207) [1986] 2, iv, 130 p. : LC Card 87-620939 DDC 388.1/09747 19
HE356.N7 F45 1986

New York's highway system . Albany, N.Y. , 1986. S-2, iv, 130 p. : ***NYPL [JLD 86-2346]***

New York (State). Legislature. Legislative Commission on the Modernization and Simplification of Tax Administration and the Tax Law.
An evaluation of the sales tax audit program of the New York State Department of Taxation and Finance. [Albany] [1985] 2, 75 p. : LC Card 86-621117 DDC 353.97470072/47 19
HJ5715.U6 E83 1985

Interstate business locational decisions and the effect of the state's tax structure on after-tax rates-of-return of manufacturing firms : a working paper / prepared by the staff of the Legislative Commission on the Modernization and Simplification of Tax Administration and the Tax Law. [Albany] : The Commission, [1984] 121 p. : ill. ; 28 cm. Cover title. "December 31, 1984." Bibliography: p. 116-121. LC Card 86-621116 DDC 336.2/07 19
1. Tax incentives - New York (State). 2. Tax credits - New York (State). 3. Business enterprises - Taxation - New York (State). 4. New York (State) - Industries - Location. 5. New York (State) - Manufactures. I. Title.
HJ4655.N54 N55 1984

Interstate tax comparisons . [Albany, N.Y.] [1985] 106 p. ; LC Card 86-621354 DDC 336.2/009747 19
HJ2424 .I57 1985

Who pays New York taxes? . [Albany, N.Y.] [1985] 2, 101 p. : LC Card 86-621353 DDC 336.2/94/09747 19
HJ2322.N7 W48 1985

New York (State). Legislature. Senate. Finance Committe. Ishmael, Cheryl. Ratemaking . [Albany, N.Y.] [1984] xi, 152 p. : ***NYPL [JLF 86-598]***

New York (State). Lieutenant Governor's Task Force on Plant Closings. Final report / Lieutenant Governor's Task Force on Plant Closings. [Albany] : The Task Force, [1985] 1 v. (various foliations) ; 28 cm. "March 1985." LC Card 86-622454 DDC 338.6/042 19
1. Plant shutdowns - New York (State). 2. Plant shutdowns - Government policy - New York (State). I. Title.
HD5708.55.U62 N76 1985

NEW YORK (STATE) - MANUFACTURES.
New York (State). Legislature. Legislative Commission on the Modernization and Simplification of Tax Administration and the Tax Law. Interstate business locational decisions and the effect of the state's tax structure on after-tax rates-of-return of manufacturing firms . [Albany] [1984] 121 p. : LC Card 86-621116 DDC 336.2/07 19
HJ4655.N54 N55 1984

New York (State). Motor vehicle, Dept. of. see **New York (State). Dept. of Motor Vehicles.**

New York (State). Office of Economic Development. Tese, Vincent. Rebuilding New York--the next phase, from recovery to resurgence . [New York, NY (1515 Broadway, New York 10036) , 1985] 74 leaves ; LC Card 86-622413 DDC 338.9747 19
HC107.N7 T47 1985

New York (State). Office of the Special Deputy Comptroller for the City of New York. Reforming the contract process in New York City / Office of the New York State Comptroller. [Albany] : The Comptroller, [1986] 13 leaves ; 28 cm. "September 11, 1986." "Report 17-87." LC Card 86-623049
1. Public contracts - New York (N.Y.). 2. Public contracts - New York (N.Y.) - Management. I. Title.
HD3861.U6 N48 1986

NEW YORK (STATE) - POPULATION - STATISTICS - HISTORY.
Shupe, Barbara, 1941- New York State population, 1790-1980 . New York , c1987. xxvii, 333 p. : ISBN 1-555-70009-8 : LC Card 86-28487 DDC 304.6/2/09747 19
HA545 .S58 1987

New York State population, 1790-1980 . Shupe, Barbara, 1941- New York , c1987. xxvii, 333 p. : ISBN 1-555-70009-8 : LC Card 86-28487 DDC 304.6/2/09747 19
HA545 .S58 1987

New York State property valuation trends by class . Murphy, Barbara (Barbara Anne) Albany, N.Y. [1986] viii, 47 p. : LC Card 86-623052 DDC 336.22/2 19
HJ4249 .M87 1986

New York State School of Industrial and Labor Relations. Collective bargaining in American industry . Lexington, Mass. , c1987. ix, 351 p. ; ISBN 0-669-12594-6 (alk. paper) LC Card 85-45936 DDC 331.89/0973 19
HD6508 .C656 1987

NEW YORK (STATE) - SOCIAL CONDITIONS.
County profiles . Albany, N.Y. [1984-<1985. v. : LC Card 84-623501 DDC 330.9747/043 19
HC107.N7 C64 1984

New York (State). Social Services, Dept. of. see **New York (State). Dept. of Social Services.**

New York (State). State Board of Equalization and Assessment. Murphy, Barbara (Barbara Anne) New York State property valuation trends by class . Albany, N.Y. [1986] viii, 47 p. : LC Card 86-623052 DDC 336.22/2 19
HJ4249 .M87 1986

New York (State). State College of Agriculture and Life Sciences. see **New York State College of Agriculture and Life Sciences.**

New York (State). State Energy Office. Division of Policy Analysis and Planning. Meeting the challenge : an analysis of electricity supply options for New York State / prepared by Division of Policy Analysis & Planning, New York State Energy Office. [Albany] : The Office, [1985] 290 p. : ill. ; 28 cm. "December 1985." Includes bibliographical references. LC Card 86-622429 DDC 333.79/3211/09747 19
1. Electric utilities - New York (State) - Planning. 2. Electric power consumption - New York (State) - Forecasting. I. Title.
HD9685.U6 N614 1985

New York (State). Taxation and Finance, Dept. of. see **New York (State). Dept. of Taxation and Finance.**

New York (State.) Urban Development Corporation. see **Urban Development Corporation.**

NEW YORK STOCK EXCHANGE.
Stoll, Hans R. The stock exchange specialist system . New York, N.Y. (90 Trinity Place, New York 10006) [c1985] 53 p. : LC Card 86-210049 DDC 332.64/273 19
HG4572 .S856 1985

NEW YORK STOCK EXCHANGE - HISTORY.
Michie, R. C., 1949- The London and New York stock exchanges, 1850-1914 /. London , Boston , 1987. xv, 312 p. ; ISBN 0-04-332117-8 (alk. paper) LC Card 87-1394 DDC 332.64/241 19
HG4577 .M52 1987

New York study manual for life and accident and health insurance. Chicago : R & R Newkirk, c1987. p. cm. ISBN 0-88462-725-X LC Card 87-13102 DDC 368.3/009747 19
1. Insurance - New York (State) - Examinations, questions, etc. 2. Insurance law - New York (State) - Examinations, questions, etc. I. R & R Newkirk.
HG8101.N49 N47 1987

New York times. Fowler, Elizabeth M. The New York times career planner /. New York , 1987. p. cm. ISBN 0-8129-1212-8 : LC Card 87-9964 DDC 650.1/4 19
HF5382.75.U6 F68 1987

The New York times career planner /. Fowler, Elizabeth M. New York , 1987. p. cm. ISBN 0-8129-1212-8 : LC Card 87-9964 DDC 650.1/4 19
HF5382.75.U6 F68 1987

New York Times (Firm). Marketing Research Dept. Auto outlook IV /. [New York] , c1986. 60 leaves ; LC Card 86-231268 DDC 381/.456292/0973 19
HD9710.U52 A76 1986

New York University. Graduate School of Business Administration. Salomon Brothers Center for the Study of Financial Institutions. see **Salomon Brothers Center for the Study of Financial Institutions.**

New York University. Salomon Brothers Center for the Study of Financial Institutions. see **Salomon Brothers Center for the Study of Financial Institutions.**

New York's highway system : a vital economic asset / an interim report of the New York State Legislative Commission on State-Local Relations. Albany, N.Y. : The Commission, 1986. S-2, iv, 130 p. : ill. ; 23 cm. Title from cover. "February, 1986." Bibliography: p. 121-130.
1. Roads - New York (State) - Finance. 2. Infrastructure (Economics) - New York (State). 3. Intergovernmental fiscal relations - New York (State). I. New York (State). Legislature. Legislative Commission on State-Local Relations. ***NYPL [JLD 86-2346]***

New York's highway system . Feigenbaum, Todd R. Albany, N.Y. (150 State St., Albany 12207) [1986] 2, iv, 130 p. : LC Card 87-620939 DDC 388.1/09747 19
HE356.N7 F45 1986

New Zealand. Advisory Committee on the Heavy Engineering Industry. Gapes, R. F. (Robert Francis) The heavy engineering industry in New Zealand . [Wellington, N.Z. , 1976] 105 p. : LC Card 84-255451
HD9705.N44 G36 1976

NEW ZEALAND - COMMERCE - HAWAII - STATISTICS.
Hawaii's trade with New Zealand, 1976-1985 /. Honolulu, Hawaii (P.O. Box 2359, Honolulu 96804) [1986] 14 p. : LC Card 87-620878 DDC 382/.09931/0969021 19
HF3161.H3 H3878 1986

New Zealand. Dept. of Justice. (Old Catalog form: New Zealand. Justice, Dept. of)
New Zealand. Working Party on Liquor. The sale of liquor in New Zealand . [Wellington, N.Z. , 1986] 212, [1] p. : LC Card 87-147518 DDC 338.4/76631/09931 19
HD9390.N452 N49 1986

New Zealand. Dept. of Labour. Research and Planning Division. Towards forecasting manpower requirements. Wellington [N.Z.] [1977] 90 p. : LC Card 85-184797
HD5850.4.A6 T69 1977

New Zealand. Dept. of Lands and Survey. (Old Catalog form: New Zealand. Lands and Survey Dept.)
The Remarkables and Hector mountains, Otago, New Zealand . Dunedin, N.Z. , 1977. 215 p., [9] leaves of plates (some folded) : LC Card 85-115616
HD1120.5.Z8 R457 1977

New Zealand Dept. of Trade and Industry. Gapes, R. F. (Robert Francis) The heavy engineering industry in New Zealand . [Wellington, N.Z. , 1976] 105 p. : LC Card 84-255451
HD9705.N44 G36 1976

NEW ZEALAND - ECONOMIC CONDITIONS - 1945- - ECONOMETRIC MODELS.
Clements, R. T. The Reserve Bank econometric model of the New Zealand economy . Wellington [1986] 62 p., [2] leaves of plates : LC Card 87-142103 DDC 330.9931/00724 19
HC665 .C54 1986

New Zealand Institute of Economic Research. (Old Catalog form: N. Z. Institute of Economic Research) Holmes, Frank Wakefield, Sir, 1924- Recent developments in monetary policy . [Wellington] [1976] 5 p. ; LC Card 82-216052
HG1480.5 .H65 1976

New Zealand. Justice, Dept. of. see **New Zealand. Dept. of Justice.**

New Zealand. Land Settlement Board. The Remarkables and Hector mountains, Otago, New Zealand . Dunedin, N.Z. , 1977. 215 p., [9] leaves of plates (some folded) : LC Card 85-115616
HD1120.5.Z8 R457 1977

New Zealand. Lands and Survey, Dept. of. see **New Zealand. Dept. of Lands and Survey.**

NEW ZEALAND - MANUFACTURES. Gapes, R. F. (Robert Francis) The heavy engineering industry in New Zealand . [Wellington, N.Z. , 1976] 105 p. : LC Card 84-255451
HD9705.N44 G36 1976

New Zealand. National Housing Commission. The Private residential landlord and tenant in Christchurch . Wellington, N.Z. [1986] viii, 105 p. : ISBN 0-477-03810-7 (pbk.) LC Card 87-147647 DDC 333.33/8 19
HD7288.85.N452 C576 1986

NEW ZEALAND - POPULATION - STATISTICS. Trends and patterns in New Zealand fertility, 1912-1983. Wellington, N.Z. , 1986. 77 p. : ISBN 0-477-06453-1 (pbk.) : LC Card 86-219193 DDC 304.6/32/09931021 19
HB1102.5.A3 T74 1986

The New Zealand software industry . Kaiser, Martin. Wellington, N.Z. , c1986. 110 p. : ISBN 0-477-06781-6 (pbk.) LC Card 86-212814 DDC 338.4/70053/09931 19
HD9696.C63 N454 1986

The New Zealand software industry . Kaiser, Martin. Wellington, N.Z. , c1986. 1 v. (various pagings) : ISBN 0-477-06783-2 (pbk.) LC Card 86-212843 DDC 381/.450053/09931 19
HD9696.C63 N455 1986

New Zealand. Trade and Industry, Dept. of. see **New Zealand Dept. of Trade and Industry.**

New Zealand. Working Party on Liquor. The sale of liquor in New Zealand : report of the Working Party on Liquor : presented to the Minister of Justice Geoffrey Palmer / with a foreword by the Minister of Justice. [Wellington, N.Z. : V.R. Ward, Govt. Printer, 1986] 212, [1] p. : ill. ; 30 cm. Bibliography: p. 212-[213] LC Card 87-147518 DDC 338.4/76631/09931 19
1. Alcoholic beverage industry - Government policy - New Zealand. 2. Liquor industry - Government policy - New Zealand. 3. License system - New Zealand. I. New Zealand. Dept. of Justice. II. Title.
HD9390.N452 N49 1986

New Zealand's overseas development assistance : proceedings of a seminar held on 22 and 23 November 1985 in Wellington. Wellington : New Zealand Institute of International Affairs, [1985] 79 p. ; 30 cm. (Pamphlet, 0112-1057 . no. 48) CONTENTS. - New directions for New Zealand's foreign aid / Helen Clark -- The national government's record & future plans / Doug Graham -- Trends, issues & directions in New Zealand's development assistance / David Stone -- The administration of aid / Colin Bell -- Commercial participation / Roger Gudgeon -- Disaster relief and emergency aid / Mary Sinclair -- Training programmes, foreign students, on-the-job training, development education / James Irving -- Private sector participation in development assistance / John Groome -- Voluntary agencies panel -- Summing up / Rod Alley. LC Card 86-210636 DDC 338.91/931/01724 19
1. Economic assistance, New Zealand - Developing countries. I. New Zealand Institute of International Affairs. II. Series: Pamphlet (New Zealand Institute of International Affairs) , no. 48.
HC60 .N478 1985

Newbery, David M. G. The Theory of taxation for developing countries /. New York , c1987. xvi, 694 p. ; ISBN 0-19-520498-0 LC Card 87-11106 DDC 336.2/009172/4 19
HJ2351.7 .T47 1987

Newbold, Paul. Statistics for business and economics / Paul Newbold. 2nd ed. Englewood Cliffs, N.J. : Prentice Hall, c1988. xiii, 866 p. : ill. (some col.) ; 25 cm. Includes bibliographical references and index. ISBN 0-13-845173-7 LC Card 87-14363 DDC 519.5 19
1. Commercial statistics. 2. Economics - Statistical methods. 3. Statistics. I. Title.
HF1017 .N48 1988

Newcomen Society of the United States. Larson, Elwin S. Brooklyn Union Gas . New York , 1987. 23 p. : LC Card 87-60614 DDC 338.7/6657/0974723 19
HD9581.U53 B765 1987

Masterton, Robert R. The One Bancorp and Maine Savings Bank . New York , 1986, c1987. 22 p. : LC Card 87-60613 DDC 332.2/1/09741 19
HG2613.P794 M356 1987

Newell, M. J.
Organisation. The Organisation in its environment / I.A. Todd ... [et al.]. 2nd ed. London , 1984. xiii, 624 p. : ISBN 0-421-32290-X (pbk.) : LC Card 84-242095 DDC 302.3/5 19
HD31 .O7217 1984 ***NYPL [JLD 86-2539]***

Newfarmer, Richard S. Marsh, Lawrence. Employment and technological choice of multinational enterprises in developing countries . Geneva , 1983. iii, 37 p. ; ISBN 92-2-103353-8 (pbk.) : LC Card 86-213692 DDC 338.8/8854 19
HD2932 .M35 1983

Newfoundland.
Submission to the Federal Commission of Inquiry on Unemployment Insurance / Government of Newfoundland and Labrador. [St. John's] : Province of Newfoundland, Canada, [1985] 63, vi p. : ill. ; 29 cm. "November 1985." Errata slip inserted. LC Card 86-215851 DDC 368.4/4/009718 19
1. Insurance, Unemployment - Canada. 2. Insurance, Unemployment - Newfoundland. 3. Newfoundland - Economic conditions. I. Canada. Commission of Inquiry on Unemployment Insurance. II. Title.
HD7096.C2 N48 1985

Newfoundland air mails . Harmer, C. H. C. (Cyril Henry Carrington) Cinnaminson, N.J., U. S.A. , 1984. x, 181 p. : LC Card 87-147693 DDC 383/.144/09718 19
HE6185.C23 N475 1984

Newfoundland and Labrador. see **Newfoundland.**

NEWFOUNDLAND - ECONOMIC CONDITIONS. Newfoundland. Submission to the Federal Commission of Inquiry on Unemployment Insurance /. [St. John's] [1985] 63, vi p. : LC Card 86-215851 DDC 368.4/4/009718 19
HD7096.C2 N48 1985

Newhouse, Joseph P. The economics of medical care : a policy perspective / Joseph P. Newhouse. Reading, Mass. : Addison-Wesley Pub. Co., c1978. x, 116 p. : graphs ; 24 cm. (Perspectives on economics series) Includes bibliographical references and index. ISBN 0-201-08369-8 LC Card 78-52498
1. Medical economics - United States. 2. Medical policy - United States. I. Title.
RA410.53 .N5 ***NYPL [JLE 79-2561]***

Newitt, Jane. Johnston, William B., 1945- Michigan beyond 2000 /. Lanham , Indianapolis, IN , c1987. xxv, 161 p. : ISBN 0-8191-6462-3 (alk. paper) LC Card 87-10725 DDC 338.9774 19
HC107.M5 J64 1987

Newly industrializing countries and the political economy of south-south relations / edited by Jerker Carlsson and Timothy M. Shaw. New York : St. Martin's Press, 1988. p. cm. Bibliography: p. Includes index. ISBN 0-312-01180-6 : LC Card 87-23476 DDC 337/.09172/4 19
1. Developing countries - Foreign economic relations - Case studies. 2. International economic relations - Case studies. 3. Industry and state - Developing countries - Case studies. I. Carlsson, Jerker, 1950-. II. Shaw, Timothy M.
HF1413 .N497 1988

Newman & Hermanson Company. Evaluation of the small cities component of the community development block grant program [microform] : compliance program / [prepared by] Newman and Hermanson Co. ; [Constance B. Newman, overall responsibility.] Cambridge, Mass. : Urban Systems Research and Engineering, Inc., 1981. viii, xvii, 147 p. ; 28 cm. "Feb., 1981." "HUD-0002762." "Contract H-5075." "Prepared for Department of Housing and Urban Development, Office of Policy Development and Research." Microfiche. Springfield, Va. : NTIS, 1983. 2 microfiches : negative ; 11 x 15 cm. (PB83-185983)
1. Federal aid to community development - United States. 2. Community development, Urban - United States. 3. Block grants - United States. I. Newman, Constance B. II. Urban Systems Research & Engineering. III. Title. ***NYPL [*XME-11,274]***

Newman, Anne, 1951- Foreign investment in South Africa and Namibia : a directory of U. S., Canadian, and British corporations operating in South Africa and Namibia ; with a survey of the 100 largest U. S. bank holding companies and their practices and policies on lending to South Africa / by Anne Newman and Cathy Bowers. Washington, D.C. : Investor Responsibility Research Center, [1984] ii, 279 p. ; 28 cm. "December 1984." Includes index. ISBN 0-931035-00-7 (pbk.) LC Card 85-130985 DDC 332.6/73/0968 19
1. Investments, Foreign - South Africa - Directories. 2. Corporations, Foreign - South Africa - Directories. 3. Investments, American - South Africa - Directories. 4. Corporations, American - South Africa - Directories. 5. Banks and banking, American - South Africa - Directories. I. Bowers, Cathy. II. Title.
HG5851.A3 N49 1984 ***NYPL [Sc F 85-173]***

Newman, Constance B. Newman & Hermanson Company. Evaluation of the small cities component of the community development block grant program [microform] . Cambridge, Mass. , 1981. viii, xvii, 147 p. ;
NYPL [*XME-11,274]

Newman, Geoffrey R. (Geoffrey Richard), 1933- The Bickerdike machine papers / by Geoffrey R. Newman. Toronto : Unitrade Press, c1986. 144 p. : ill. ; 23 cm. Bibliography: p. 143-144. ISBN 0-919801-51-X (pbk.) : LC Card 87-167878 DDC 681/.7676 19
1. Postal service - Equipment and supplies - History. I. Title.
HE6237 .N48 1986

Newman, Jerry M. Milkovich, George T. Compensation /. Plano, Tex. , 1987. xiv, 655 p. : ISBN 0-256-03709-4 LC Card 86-72247 DDC 658.3/2 19
HF5549.5.C67 M54 1987

Newman, Karin. The selling of British Telecom / Karin Newman. London ; New York : Holt, Rinehart and Winston, c1986. viii, 176 p. : ill. ; 25 cm. Includes index. ISBN 0-03-910639-X
1. British Telecom. 2. Telecommunication - Great Britain. 3. Privatization - Great Britain - Case studies. I. Title. ***NYPL [JLF 86-853]***

Newman, Marie Mastin. The vital link : electric transmission and the public interest / by Marie Mastin Newman and Bruce S. Edelston ; edited by Susan E. Clark. Washington, DC : Edison Electric Institute, c1986. vii, 48 p. : ill. (some col.) ; 23 cm. (Decisionmakers bookshelf) ISBN 0-931032-21-0 (pbk.) LC Card 86-200991 DDC 363.6/2/0973 19
1. Electric utilities - Government policy - United States. I. Edelston, Bruce S. II. Clark, Susan E. III. Title. IV. Series.
HD9685.U5 N493 1986

Newman, Peter K., 1928- The New Palgrave . New York , c1987. p. cm. ISBN 0-935859-10-1 (set) : LC Card 87-1946 DDC 330/.03/21 19
HB61 .N49 1987

News and views from National Public Radio / edited by Mel G. Grinspan. Memphis, Tenn. : Rhodes College, 1989. p. cm. (The M. L. Seidman memorial town hall lecture series) LC Card 87-23331 DDC 384.54/06/073 19
1. Radio in politics - United States. 2. Radio journalism - United States. 3. National Public Radio (U. S.). I. Grinspan, Mel G. II. National Public Radio (U. S.). III. Series.
HE8697.P6 N48 1989

NEWS BROADCASTS. see **RADIO JOURNALISM.**

News from somewhere . Lewis, Gary A., 1927- Westport, Conn. , 1986. xii, 213 p. : ISBN 0-313-24869-9 (lib. bdg. : alk. paper) LC Card 85-27269 DDC 658.3/152 19
HD5650 .L439 1986 ***NYPL [JLD 86-3587]***

Newsletter Management Corporation. Directory of no-load mutual funds. Boca Raton, FL (P.O. Box 3007, Boca Raton 33431-0907) , c1986. 19 p. ; LC Card 86-231040 DDC 332.63/27 19
HG4930 .D57 1986

NEWSPAPER ADVERTISING. see **ADVERTISING, NEWSPAPER.**

Newsweek, inc.
The Compact disc market--phase II . New York, N.Y. (444 Madison Ave., New York 10022) , c1986. viii, 57, [13] p. : LC Card 86-227224 DDC 381/.4562138933 19
HD9697.P563 U526 1986

1986 buyers of new cars . New York, N.Y. (444 Madison Ave., New York 10022) , c1986. 2 v. : LC Card 86-229142 DDC 381/.456292/0973021 19
HD9710.U52 A17 1986

Newton Dunn, Bill. Greater in Europe / by Bill Newton Dunn. London : Regency Press, c1985. 85 p. ; 20 cm. Includes index. ISBN 0-7212-0731-6 (pbk.) : LC Card 87-146946 DDC 341.24/22 19
1. European Economic Community - Great Britain. I. Title.
HC241.25.G7 N48 1985

Newton, P. W. (Peter Wesley), 1948- The Spatial impact of technological change /. Totowa, NJ , 1987. p. cm. ISBN 0-389-20753-5 LC Card 87-11460 DDC 338/.06 19
HC79.T4 S77 1987

Newton, Peter W. Burke, Terry, 1942- A roof over their heads . Melbourne , 1984. xiv, 178 p. : ISBN 0-642-87172-8
NYPL [JLD 86-2639]

The Next oil shock : a planning guide for world energy markets. Bala Cynwyd, PA (150 Monument Rd., Bala Cynwyd 19004) : Chase Econometrics, 1986. 2 v. : ill. (some col.) ; 29 cm. Vol. 2 has special title: Reference tables. LC Card 87-109243 DDC 333.82/32 19
1. Petroleum industry and trade - Forecasting. I. Chase Econometrics (Firm).
HD9560.5 .N47 1986

The next ten years in British social and economic policy /. Cole, George Douglas Howard, 1889-1959. New York , 1985. xxi, 459 p. ; ISBN 0-8240-7607-9 (alk. paper) : LC Card 85-13055 DDC 338.941 19
HC256.3 .C6 1985 ***NYPL [JLD 86-3300]***

Neyman, Jerzy, 1894- Lectures and conferences on mathematical statistics and probability. 2d ed., rev. and enl. Washington, Graduate School, U. S. Dept. of Agriculture, 1952. vii, 274 p. illus. 24 cm. Original mimeographed ed. published in 1938 under title: Lectures and conferences on mathematical statistics. "References": p. 253-254. LC Card Agr52-278 DDC 311.2
1. Mathematical statistics. I. Graduate School, USDA. II. Title.
HA29 .N48 1952

Neymeyer, Robert J. Agricultural distress in the Midwest, past & present /. Iowa City , 1986. ix, 111 p. : ISBN 0-87414-049-8 : LC Card 86-29932 DDC 338.1/0977 19
HD1773.A3 A37 1986

Nezavisimye strany Afriki : finansovo-kreditnyĭ mekhanizm razvitii͡a / [otvetstvennyĭ redaktor I͡U.M. Osipov]. Moskva : Izd-vo "Nauka," Glav. red. vostochnoĭ lit-ry, 1986. 276 p. ; 23 cm. At head of title: Akademii͡a nauk SSSR. Institut Afriki. Summary in English. Bibliography: p. 265-[271] Includes index. LC Card 87-110032
1. Finance - Africa. 2. Finance - Developing countries. I. Osipov, I͡Uriĭ Mikhaĭlovich. II. Institut Afriki (Akademii͡a nauk SSSR).
HG187.5.A2 N49 1986

Nezēs, Giōrgos P. Hodēgos exagōgikōn diadikasiōn /. [Athēna] [1983] 184 p. : LC Card 86-170148
HF1009.7.E86 H63 1983

Ng, Shui Meng. Workshop on Socio-economic Correlates of Mortality Differentials in Japan and ASEAN (1984 : Singapore) Socio-economic correlates of mortality in Japan and ASEAN /. Singapore , c1986. xxi, 295 p. : LC Card 86-945167 DDC 304.6/4/0952 19
HB1481 .W67 1984

Ngirabatware, Augustin. Les taux de change flottants et les pays souscapitalisés : théories du change, choix des régimes de change et les nouvelles stratégies monétaires / par Augustin Ngirabatware. Fribourg, Suisse : Editions universitaires, c1986. 340 p. : ill. ; 21 cm. (Documents économiques . 28) Bibliography: p. 323-340. ISBN 2-8271-0330-3 : LC Card 86-170584
1. Foreign exchange problem - Developing countries. 2. Foreign exchange. I. Title. II. Series.
HG3877 .N48 1986

Ngoppramān phǣndin phǣn mai . Čhanthiphā Sukhumālachāt. [Bangkok?] 2521 [1978] 173 (some folded), [3] leaves : LC Card 81-917611
HJ2162.55 .C47 1978

Nguiagain, Titus, 1953- Trends and patterns of internal migration in the Philippines, 1970-1980 / by Titus Nguiagain. [Quezon] : University of the Philippines, School of Economics, [1986] 41 p. ; 29 cm. (Discussion paper / University of the Philippines, School of Economics . no. 8606) "June 1986." Bibliography: p. 40-41. LC Card 87-120929 DDC 304.8/09599 19
1. Migration, Internal - Philippines. I. Series: Discussion paper / University of the Philippines, School of Economics , 8606. II. Title.
HB2109 .N48 1986

Nguyen, Anh Tuan. South Vietnam, trial and experience : a challenge for development / by Nguyen Anh Tuan. Athens, Ohio : Ohio University Center for International Studies, Center for Southeast Asian Studies, 1987. 461 p. : map ; 22 cm. (Monographs in International studies. Southeast Asia series . no. 80) Bibliography: p. 458-461. ISBN 0-89680-141-1 (pbk.) : LC Card 86-23532 DDC 338.9597 19
1. Vietnam - Economic policy. 2. Vietnam - Economic conditions. 3. Vietnam - Politics and government - 1945-1975. I. Title. II. Series.
HC444 .N43 1987

Nguyen, D. T. MacBean, Alasdair I. Commodity policies . London , New York , c1987. 438 p. : ISBN 0-7099-1708-2 LC Card 87-9069 DDC 382/.3/091724 19
HF1428 .M29 1987

Nguyen, Tim K. Applied 1-2-3 : creating spreadsheet systems for others / Tim K. Nguyen and Joseph R. Little. New York, N.Y. : Prentice Hall Press, c1987. p. cm. "A Brady book." Includes index. ISBN 0-13-729542-1 : LC Card 87-11390 DDC 005.36/9 19
1. Lotus 1-2-3 (Computer program). 2. Electronic spreadsheets. 3. Business - Data processing. I. Little, Joseph R. II. Title. III. Title: Applied one-two-three.
HF5548.4.L67 N48 1987

Nibhon Debavalya. Knodel, John E. Thailand's reproductive revolution . Madison, Wis. , c1987. xiii, 251 p. : ISBN 0-299-11050-8 LC Card 87-8172 DDC 304.6/32/09593 19
HB1054.55.A3 K576 1987

Niblock, Tim. Symposium on the Energy Economy (1984 : Durham, Durham) Prospects for the world oil industry . London , Dover, N.H. , c1985. 131 p. : ISBN 0-7099-4104-8 : LC Card 85-4186 DDC 338.2/7282 19
HD9560.5 .S96 1985 ***NYPL [JLD 85-2430]***

Nicanovich, Marta Beatriz. The role fulfilled by the International Trade Centre UNCTAD/GATT within the framework of the United Nations development policy / par Marta Beatriz Nicanovich. Genève : Institut universitaire de hautes études internationales, 1986. xii, 248, 103, xix p. : ill. ; 30 cm. Thesis (diplôme)--Institut universitaire de hautes études internationales. Bibliography: p. i-xix. LC Card 86-225702 DDC 382/.06/01 19
1. Foreign trade promotion - Developing countries. I. International Trade Centre UNCTAD/GATT. II. Title.
HF1417.5 .N52 1986

Nicaragua : Texte und Fragen / [Redaktion, Viola Schmid in Zusammenarbeit mit Günter Dulon ... et al.]. Hamburg : [Missionshilfe Verlag, 1986] 95 p. : ill. ; 24 cm. (Studienheft Nr. 15 des Missionshilfe Verlages, Hamburg) Cover title. Includes bibliographical references. ISBN 3-921620-32-5 LC Card 86-191836 DDC 330.97285/053 19
1. Nicaragua - Economic conditions - 1979-. 2. Nicaragua - Social conditions - 1979-. 3. Nicaragua - Politics and government - 1979-. I. Schmid, Viola. II. Dulon, Günter. III. Series: Studienheft des Missionshilfe Verlages , Nr. 15.
HC146 .N56 1986

Nicaragua . Melrose, Dianna. Oxford, U.K. , Boston, MA , 1985. 68 p. : ISBN 0-85598-070-2 (pbk.) : LC Card 87-116239 DDC 338.91/41/07285 19
HC146 .M45 1985

NICARAGUA CANAL (NICARAGUA)
United States. Congress. House. Committee on Foreign Affairs. Discussion of the Nicaragua ship canal and the Tehuantepec ship railway schemes before the Committee on Foreign Affairs of the House of Representatives. [Washington] [1882?] 80 p. ; LC Card 82-602443
HE536 .U55 1882

NICARAGUA - ECONOMIC CONDITIONS - 1979-
Haugstveit, Nils. The Nicaraguan development process, 1979-85 . Oslo [1987] 148 p. : ISBN 82-7288-136-5 (pbk.) LC Card 87-164230 DDC 338.97285 19
HC146 .H38 1987

Melrose, Dianna. Nicaragua . Oxford, U.K. , Boston, MA , 1985. 68 p. : ISBN 0-85598-070-2 (pbk.) : LC Card 87-116239 DDC 338.91/41/07285 19
HC146 .M45 1985

Nicaragua . Hamburg [1986] 95 p. : ISBN 3-921620-32-5 LC Card 86-191836 DDC 330.97285/053 19
HC146 .N56 1986

Wheelock, Jaime. Entre la crisis y la agresión . Managua, Nicaragua [1985] 148 p. : LC Card 85-241401 DDC 333.3/1/7285 19
HD1333.N5 W48 1985 ***NYPL [JLC 86-312]***

NICARAGUA - ECONOMIC POLICY.
Bereciuk, Román M. Introducción en la teoría de la planificación de la economía nacional /. [Managua] , 1986. 93 leaves ; LC Card 87-403888 DDC 338.97285 19
HC146 .B47 1986

Haugstveit, Nils. The Nicaraguan development process, 1979-85 . Oslo [1987] 148 p. : ISBN 82-7288-136-5 (pbk.) LC Card 87-164230 DDC 338.97285 19
HC146 .H38 1987

Nicaragua - Government. see **Nicaragua - Politics and government.**

NICARAGUA - POLITICS AND GOVERNMENT - 1979-
Colburn, Forrest D. Post-revolutionary Nicaragua . Berkeley , c1986. xi, 145 p. : ISBN 0-520-05524-1 LC Card 85-5798 DDC 338.1/097285 19
HD1817 .C63 1986 ***NYPL [JLD 86-2414]***

Nicaragua . Hamburg [1986] 95 p. : ISBN 3-921620-32-5 LC Card 86-191836 DDC 330.97285/053 19
HC146 .N56 1986

Vilas, Carlos María. Democracia y participación obrera en la Revolución Sandinista /. Morelia, Michoacán , 1985. 44 p., [6] p. of plates : LC Card 87-128110 DDC 322/.2/097285 19
HD8168 .V55 1985

NICARAGUA - RURAL CONDITIONS.
Colburn, Forrest D. Post-revolutionary Nicaragua . Berkeley , c1986. xi, 145 p. : ISBN 0-520-05524-1 LC Card 85-5798 DDC 338.1/097285 19
HD1817 .C63 1986 ***NYPL [JLD 86-2414]***

NICARAGUA - SOCIAL CONDITIONS - 1979-
Melrose, Dianna. Nicaragua . Oxford, U.K. , Boston, MA , 1985. 68 p. : ISBN 0-85598-070-2 (pbk.) : LC Card 87-116239 DDC 338.91/41/07285 19
HC146 .M45 1985

Nicaragua . Hamburg [1986] 95 p. : ISBN 3-921620-32-5 LC Card 86-191836 DDC 330.97285/053 19
HC146 .N56 1986

The Nicaraguan development process, 1979-85 . Haugstveit, Nils. Oslo [1987] 148 p. : ISBN 82-7288-136-5 (pbk.) LC Card 87-164230 DDC 338.97285 19
HC146 .H38 1987

Niccodemi, Gino. Economia tra teoria e politica /. Milano , c1984. 295 p. ; LC Card 84-171327 DDC 330/.09 19
HB75 .E28 1984 ***NYPL [JLD 87-819]***

Nichol, Judith. Jones, Geoffrey. The history of the British Bank of the Middle East /. Cambridge [Cambridgeshire] , New York , 1986- v. : ISBN 0-521-32322-3 (v. 1) LC Card 85-31359 DDC 332.1/5/0955 19
HG3270.2.A8 B755 1986 NYPL [JLL 87-87]

Nicholas, Don. Benjamin, Louis. The complete book of Excel macros /. Berkeley, Calif. , c1986. xviii, 123 p. : ISBN 0-07-881214-3 (pbk.) LC Card 86-106041 DDC 650/.028/55369 19
HF5548.4.E93 B46 1986 NYPL [JSE 87-239]

Nicholas Kaldor /. Thirlwall, A. P. Washington Square, NY , 1987. xvii, 360 p., [8] pages of plates : ISBN 0-8147-8177-2 : LC Card 87-22065 DDC 330/.092/4 B 19
HB103.K36 T45 1987

Nichols, Harwood, 1942- Money sense : teach your child about money / Harwood Nichols. Washington, DC : Acropolis Books, 1987. p. cm. Includes index. ISBN 0-87491-871-5 (pbk.) : LC Card 87-24129 DDC 332.024/007 19
1. Finance, Personal - Study and teaching. 2. Children - Finance, Personal - Study and teaching. 3. Consumer education. I. Title.
HG179 .N53 1987

Nichols, John Spicer. Soley, Lawrence C. Clandestine radio broadcasting . New York , 1987. xiv, 384 p. ; ISBN 0-275-92259-6 (alk. paper) : LC Card 86-21169 DDC 384.54 19
HE8697.P6 S59 1986 NYPL [MWGH 87-1678]

Nicholson, D. J. Bruton, Michael J. Local planning in practice /. London , 1987. 452 p. : ISBN 0-09-165381-9 *NYPL [JLE 87-1201]*

Nicholson, Linda J. Gender and history : the limits of social theory in the age of the family / Linda J. Nicholson. New York : Columbia University Press, 1986. x, 238 p. ; 24 cm. Includes bibliographical references and index. ISBN 0-231-06220-6 (alk. paper) LC Card 85-21281 DDC 323.3/4/01 19
1. Feminism - Philosophy. 2. Feminism - United States - History. 3. Liberalism. 4. Marxist historiography. I. Title.
HQ1206 .N7 1986 NYPL [JLE 86-1987]

Nicholson, Marjorie. The TUC overseas : the roots of policy / Marjorie Nicholson. London ; Boston : Allen & Unwin, c1986. xvi, 329 p. ; 23 cm. Includes index. Bibliography: p. [305]-312. ISBN 0-04-331103-2 (alk. paper) LC Card 85-28607 DDC 331.88/0941 19
1. Trades Union Congress - History - 20th century. 2. Labour Party (Great Britain) - History - 20th century. 3. Trade-unions - Great Britain - Colonies - History - 20th century. 4. International labor activities - History - 20th century. I. Title. II. Title: T.U.C. overseas.
HD8383 .N52 1986 NYPL [JLD 86-2932]

Nicholson, Nigel. Managerial job change : men and women in transition / Nigel Nicholson and Michael A. West. Cambridge [Cambridgeshire] ; New York : Cambridge University Press, 1988. xi, 274 p. : ill. ; 24 cm. Bibliography: p. 254-264. Includes indexes. ISBN 0-521-33459-4 LC Card 87-11752 DDC 331.12/72 19
1. Executives. 2. Career changes. 3. Organizational change. I. West, Michael. II. Title.
HD38.2 .N53 1988

Nicholson, Norm. The individual investor's microcomputer resource guide / Norm Nicholson. 4th ed. Chicago : American Association of Individual Investors : Investment Information Services Press, c1986. viii, 216 p. ; 23 cm. Includes indexes. ISBN 0-930369-17-3 (pbk.) LC Card 86-204335 DDC 332.6/028/553 19
1. Investments - Data processing. 2. Investment analysis - Data processing. 3. Computer programs - Directories. 4. Investment analysis - Data processing - Information services - United States - Directories. I. American Association of Individual Investors. II. Title.
HG4515.5 .N53 1986

Nicht-sequentielle Suche, Preiswerbung und Marktgleichgewicht /. Le Vaillant de Folleville, Patrice, 1954- Frankfurt am Main , New York , c1986. 198 p. : ISBN 3-8204-9058-2 LC Card 86-153194
HB221 .L42 1986

Nicht-tarifäre Instrumente der Agrarhandelspolitik . Jaeschke, Hans-Dieter. Münster-Hiltrup , 1986. 187 p. ; ISBN 3-7843-0326-9 LC Card 87-408954 DDC 382/.3 19
HD9000.5 .J33 1986

Nichtkapitalistische Produktionsverhältnisse und Konkurrenz . Heipel, Gerd. Pfaffenweiler , 1986. vii, 459 p. ; ISBN 3-89085-116-9 LC Card 86-171832
HD9199.B8 S22 1986

Nick, Harry. Ökonomische und soziale Wirksamkeit des wissenschaftlich-technischen Fortschritts /. Berlin , 1986. 314 p. ; ISBN 3-320-00713-0 LC Card 87-100866 DDC 338/.06 19
HC290.795.T4 O38 1986

NICKEL INDUSTRY - INDONESIA - SAROAKO.
Robinson, Kathryn May, 1949- Stepchildren of progress . Albany, N.Y. , c1986. xvi, 315 p. : ISBN 0-88706-119-2 LC Card 86-5847 DDC 307.7/66/095984 19
HD9539.N52 I547 1986 NYPL [JLE 86-4126]

Nickel, James E. The Productivity sourcebook /. Amherst, Mass. [1987] x, 467 p. : ISBN 0-87425-075-7 (pbk.) LC Card 87-404037 DDC 658.3/14 19
HD57 .P7114 1987

Nickel, James W. Moral rights in the workplace /. Albany , c1987. xii, 312 p. ; ISBN 0-88706-362-4 LC Card 86-6949 DDC 331.25 19
HD6957.U6 M67 1987 NYPL [JLE 87-1197]

NICKEL - PRICES - ECONOMETRIC MODELS.
Hwang, Hae-Shin. Dominant firm price leadership . Toronto, Ont. [1986] 40 p. : ISBN 0-7729-2122-9 : LC Card 87-161006 DDC 338.2/3 19
HD9539.N5 H93 1986

Nickell, S. J. The Rise in unemployment /. Oxford, UK , New York, NY, USA , 1987, c1986. 382 p. : ISBN 0-631-15419-1 (pbk.) : LC Card 87-699 DDC 331.13/7 19
HD5707.5 .R57 1987

Nickels, William G. Understanding business / William G. Nickels. St. Louis : Times Mirror/Mosby College Pub., 1987. xxix, 721, 115, 2 p. : col. ill. ; 26 cm. Includes bibliographical references and index. ISBN 0-8016-3627-2 LC Card 86-23080 DDC 650 19
1. Business. 2. Business - Vocational guidance. I. Title.
HF5351 .N53 1987

Nickelsburg, Gerald. Canto, Victor A. Currency substitution . Boston , c1987. viii, 196 p. ; ISBN 0-89838-195-9 LC Card 86-27747 DDC 332.4/56/098 19
HG3823 .C36 1987

Nickerson, Lloyd C. Barlow, Raymond E. The glass industry in Sandwich /. Windham, N.H. , c1983- v. : ISBN 0-9610166-0-4 (v. 4) LC Card 82-73582 DDC 338.4/76661/0974492 19
HD9623.U46 S263 1983 NYPL [3-MPW+ 84-1016]

Nicolas, Jean-Pierre, 1941- La pauvreté intolérable : biographie sociale d'une famille assistée / Jean-Pierre Nicolas ; préface de Jacques Beauchard. Toulouse : Erès, [1984] 208 p. : ill. ; 24 cm. (Stratégie et communications sociales) Includes bibliographical references. ISBN 2-86586-026-4 : LC Card 85-118841
1. Poor - France - Case studies. 2. Social service - France - Case studies. 3. Social workers - France - Case studies. I. Title. II. Series.
HC280.P6 N53 1984

Nicoletti, Bernardo.
I circoli di qualità : concetti base ed esperienze italiane / Bernardo Nicoletti. Milano, Italy : F. Angeli, c1986. 249 p. ; 22 cm. (Azienda moderna. 189) Bibliography: p. [245]-249. LC Card 86-207976
1. Quality circles. 2. Quality circles - Italy - Case studies. I. Title.
HD66 .N53 1986

Eminente, Giorgio. Strategia aziendale e sviluppo tecnologico . Bologna , c1985. 253 p. : ISBN 88-15-00917-5 : LC Card 86-176732
HD9696.A3 I733 1985

Nicolini, G.
Verarbeitende Gewerbe (Industrie) in Leverkusen. Marx, G. Die Entwicklung der Wohnungsbautätigkeit in Leverkusen / [G. Marx]. Das verarbeitende Gewerbe (Industrie) in Leverkusen / [G. Nicolini ; Herausgeber, Stadt Leverkusen, der Oberstadtdirektor, Amt für Wahlen und Meldewesen in Zusammenarbeit mit dem Kataster- und Vermessungsamt und dem Presse- und Verkehrsamt]. Leverkusen [1984] 37 p., [1] folded leaf of plates : LC Card 84-183932
HD9715.G33 L575 1984

Nicolò Copernico ed il suo libro De monetae cudendae ratione . Montanari, Augusto, b. 1843. Padova , 1877. 70 p. ; LC Card 85-666421
HG220.P6 C636x 1877

Nicot, Bernard Henri. Darbéra, Richard. Le planificateur et le cyclopousse . Caen , 1986. xiii, 190 p. : ISBN 2-86878-015-6 : LC Card 86-192929
HE311.I4 D36 1986

Nicourt, Christian. Conditions de travail en agriculture : bilan des recherches et propositions / C. Nicourt, N. Sée. Paris : Institut national de la recherche agronomique, <1985- > v. <2 > : ill. ; 30 cm. (Economie et sociologie rurales / INRA) Cover title. Numbering of v. 2 given on cover as 5. CONTENTS. - -- [2] Synthèse. ISBN 2-85340-585-0 (v. 2) LC Card 86-218948
1. Agricultural laborers - France. 2. Agricultural wages - France. I. Sée, N. (Norbert). II. Institut national de la recherche agronomique (France). III. Series: Série Economie et sociologie rurales. IV. Title.
HD1536.F8 N53 1985

Niederfeld, Reinhard, 1961- Wolffsohn, Michael. Politik als Investitionsmotor? . Frankfurt am Main , New York , c1985. 141 p. : ISBN 3-8204-7487-0 (pbk.) LC Card 87-672289
HD2810.5 W64x 1985

Die niederösterreichische Grundherrschaft . Feigl, Helmuth. [Wien] , 1964. 379 p. ; LC Card 85-127367
HD639.L6 F45 1964

Der niederrheinische Wirtschaftsraum . Schanz, Hermann J. Stuttgart , c1986. xxii, 466 p. ; ISBN 3-7910-5014-1 LC Card 87-135757 DDC 330.943/55 19
HC289.D755 S32 1986

Niedersächsische Landeszentrale für Politische Bildung. Frauen und neue Technologien /. Hannover , 1986. 112 p. ; LC Card 87-407392 DDC 331.4/0943 19
HD6059.G3 F74 1986

Niedersächsisches Landesverwaltungsamt. Statistik.
Agrarberichterstattung 1983 . Hannover , 1985. viii, 143 p., [3] p. of plates : LC Card 86-222908
HD1960.L68 A38 1985

Landwirtschaftszählung 1979, Gartenbauerhebung 1981/82 . Hannover , 1983. xv, 132 p. ; LC Card 85-117833
HD9013.7.L68 L37 1983

Niederschriften der Europäischen Reisezugfahrplankonferenz für die Jahre 1985/87. Conférence européenne des horaires des trains de voyageurs (1984 : Paris, France) Procès-verbaux de la Conférence européenne des horaires des trains de voyageurs pour les années 1985/87 . Paris , 1984. 619 p. ; LC Card 85-152699
HE3004 .C64 1984

Niehaus, Richard J. Symposium on Strategic Human Resource Planning Applications (1985 : University of Pennsylvania, Philadelphia, Pa.) Strategic human resource planning applications /. New York , c1987. viii, 257 p. ; ISBN 0-306-42561-0 LC Card 87-11141 DDC 331.11 19
HF5549.5.M3 S95 1985

Nielsen, Bue. Stålindustri, kriseregioner og fagbevægelse . [Copenhagen] , 1983. 217 p. : LC Card 84-169019
HD9525.E752 S73 1983

Nielsen, Jens Petter. Hovda, Gudmund. Dagbok frå bondekongressen i Moskva, oktober 1923 /. Oslo , 1984. 46 p. ; ISBN 82-902503-1-2 LC Card 85-190754
HD1405 .H68 1984

Nielsen, Johan, 1948- Lauritzen, Niels, 1947- Rapporter /. København [1983] 59 p. : ISBN 87-503-4574-5 LC Card 84-169893
HD4465.D4 L38 1983

Nielsen, Kai. Sett fra sjøsiden : om arbeidsforholdene i handelsflåten / Kai Nielsen. [Oslo] : Falken, c1985. 88 p. : ill. ; 21 cm. LC Card 86-205530
1. Merchant marine - Norway. I. Title.
HE855 .N44 1985

Nielsen, Margit, 1950- Udenrigsøkonomi i Østeuropa : tilpasning eller krise? / Margit Nielsen. Esbjerg : Sydjysk universitetsforlag, 1985. 99 p. ; 22 cm. (Handelsserie fra Institut for øst-vest forskning, 0108-5387 . 6) Bibliography: p. 89-91. ISBN 87-88521-19-2 LC Card 85-227937
1. Europe, Eastern - Foreign economic relations. 2. Europe, Eastern - Economic policy. I. Title. II. Series.
HF1531 .N54 1985

Nielsen, Ruth, 1946- Strategies for integrating women into the labour market /. Copenhagen, Denmark , 1982. 347 p. : ISBN 87-88209-08-3 (pbk.) LC Card 86-673782
HD6052 .S77x 1982

Nielsen, Sven. Matthiasen, Leo. Informationsteknologi og arbejdsproces . Roskilde [1983?] 339 p. : ISBN 87-87893-19-3 LC Card 85-114664
HF5547.5 .M384 1983

Niemeier, Joachim, 1955- Wettbewerbsumwelt und interne Konfigurationen : theoretische Ansätze und empirische Prüfung / Joachim Niemeier. Frankfurt am Main ; New York : P. Lang, c1986. xv, 412 p. : ill. ; 21 cm. (Europäische Hochschulschriften. Reihe V, Volks- und Betriebswirtschaft, 0531-7339 . Bd. 758 = vol. 758 = vol. 758) Originally presented as the author's thesis (doctoral)--Universität Stuttgart, Wintersemester 1986/87. Bibliography: p. 355-384. ISBN 3-8204-9541-X LC Card 87-407931 DDC 338.6/048 19
1. Competition. 2. Industrial management. I. Series: Europäische Hochschulschriften. Reihe V, Volks- und Betriebswirtschaft , Bd. 758. II. Title.
HD41 .N54 1986

Niemes, Horst. Faber, Malte Michael. Entropie, Umweltschutz und Rohstoffverbrauch . Berlin , New York , 1983. ix, 181 p. : ISBN 0-387-12297-4 (U. S.) LC Card 83-193381
HC79.E5 F23 1983

Niemeyer, Gerhard. Eine automatentheoretische Baumkonstruktion zur Simulation hierarchischer Management-Strukturen / G. Niemeyer. [Regensburg] : Universität Regensburg, Wirtschaftswissenschaftliche Fakultät, [1984] 64 p. : ill. ; 30 cm. (Regensburger Diskussionsbeiträge zur Wirtschaftswissenschaft . Nr. 172) "Februar 1984." LC Card 84-181485
1. Organization charts. I. Title. II. Series.
HD38 .N513 1984

Niemi, Albert W. U. S. economic history / Albert W. Niemi, Jr. Lanham, MD : University Press of America, [1987], c1980. xiii, 475 p. : ill. ; 23 cm. Reprint. Originally published: 2nd ed. Chicago : Rand McNally College Pub., c1980. Bibliography: p. 431-457. Includes indexes. ISBN 0-8191-6335-X (pbk. : alk. paper) : LC Card 87-10730 DDC 330.973 19
1. United States - Economic conditions. 2. United States - Economic policy. I. Title. II. Title: US economic history.
HC103 .N5 1987

Nienhaus, Volker. Kontroversen um Markt und Plan : sozialistische Wirtschaftsrechnung, indikative Planung, Konvergenzthese, überbetriebliche Investitionsplanung / Volker Nienhaus. Darmstadt : Wissenschaftliche Buchgesellschaft, 1984. vi, 171 p. ; 20 cm. (Erträge der Forschung, 0174-0695 . Bd. 205) Bibliography: p. 153-167. Includes index. ISBN 3-534-08700-3 LC Card 84-181049
1. Laissez-faire. 2. Industry and state. 3. Germany, West - Economic policy. I. Title. II. Series.
HB95 .N47 1984

The NIEO and the situatuon of workers . Vargas, Ines. Oslo [1985] xiv, 290 p. ; ISBN 82-7288-121-7 (pbk.) LC Card 86-205407 DDC 331/.098 19
HD6530.5 .V36 1985

Niepce, Janine. Les Femmes au travail 1882-1982 /. Paris , 1982. [70] leaves : LC Card 86-161448
HD6145 .F44 1982

Nierhaus, Herbert. Relations between the European Community and the member states of the Association of South-East Asian Nations /. Brussels [1986] 55 p. : LC Card 87-135576 DDC 337.4059 19
HF1532.5 .R46 1986

Nierman, G. Caris, J. Fuseren in non-profit organisaties . Nijmegen , 1986. 107 p. : ISBN 90-255-0018-8 : LC Card 86-205531
HD2746.5 .C35 1986

Niesen, Katrin. Grosse-Berndt, Gisela. Wirksamkeitsuntersuchung zum ADAC-Motorrad-Sicherheitstraining. Köln [1983] iii, 160, ii, 112, 27 p. : LC Card 84-147564
HE5614.5.G3 G75 1983

Niess-Mache, Charlotte. Demontage des Sozialstaats . Köln , 1986. 177 p. ; ISBN 3-8161-0107-0 LC Card 87-104505 DDC 338.943 19
HC286.7 .D455 1986

Niessen, Hans-Joachim. Schattenwirtschaft in der Bundesrepublik : eine empirische Bestandsaufnahme der sozialen und räumlichen Verteilung schattenwirtschaftlicher Aktivitäten / Hans-Joachim Niessen, Rainer Ollmann. Opladen : Leske + Budrich, 1987. 246 p. : ill. ; 21 cm. Bibliography: p. 230-245. ISBN 3-8100-0592-4 LC Card 87-131108
1. Informal sector (Economics) - Germany (West). I. Ollmann, Rainer. II. Title.
HD2346.G3 N545 1987

Niessen, Jan. Emancipatie in internationaal perspectief : het organiseren van Marokkaanse arbeiders in Nederland / door Jan Niessen. Amsterdam : VU, 1987. 282 p. ; 24 cm. Summary in Arabic and French. Thesis (doctoral)--Vrije Universiteit te Amsterdam, 1987. Bibliography: p. 255-269. ISBN 90-6256-460-7 : LC Card 87-158046
1. Alien labor, Moroccan - Netherlands. 2. Trade-unions - Netherlands. I. Title.
HD8518.5.M6 N54 1987

Niethammer, Lutz, 1939-
Der Marshall-Plan und die europäische Linke /. [Frankfurt am Main] , c1986. 659 p. : ISBN 3-434-00475-0 LC Card 87-127508 DDC 338.91/73/04 19
HC240 .M2735 1986

"Die Menschen machen ihre Geschichte nicht aus freien Stücken, aber sie machen sie selbst" . Berlin [1984] 267 p. : ISBN 3-8012-0101-5 LC Card 84-204204
HC287.N6 M46 1984

Nieto, Antonio López. see **López Nieto, Antonio.**

Nieto de Alba, Ubaldo, 1931- De la dictadura al socialismo democrático : análisis sobre el cambio de modelo socioeconómico en España / Ubaldo Nieto de Alba. Madrid : Unión Editorial, c1984. 269 p. ; 22 cm. Includes bibliographical references. ISBN 84-7209-177-5 LC Card 86-146735 DDC 338.946 19
1. Dictators - Spain - History - 20th century. 2. Socialism - Spain - History - 20th century. 3. Spain - Economic policy. 4. Spain - Social policy. 5. Spain - Economic conditions - 1918-1975. 6. Spain - Economic conditions - 1975-. I. Title.
HC385 .N49 1984 ***NYPL [JLD 86-2390]***

Nieuwenhuizen, René. Bakker, G. J. Op arbeid bezuinigd? . 's-Gravenhage , 1986. 116 p. ; ISBN 90-12-05321-8 LC Card 87-108889
HJ9507 .B35 1986

Nieuwenhuysen, A. van (Andrée) Les finances du duc de Bourgogne, Philippe le Hardi (1384-1404) : économie et politique / A. van Nieuwenhuysen. Bruxelles, Belgique : Editions de l'Université de Bruxelles, 1984. 556 p. ; 24 cm. (Université libre de Bruxelles, Faculté de philosophie et lettres . 90) Bibliography: p. [13]-43. ISBN 2-8004-0838-3 : LC Card 85-160639
1. Finance, Public - France - Burgundy - History. 2. Philip, Duke of Burgundy, 1342-1404. I. Series: Université libre de Bruxelles, Faculté de philosophie et lettres (Series) , 90. II. Title.
HJ1099.B85 N54 1984

Nieuwenhuysen, J. P. Hall, Richard, 1937- The Prices Surveillance Authority /. Melbourne [1987] 24 p. ; ISBN 0-85801-167-0 (pbk.) LC Card 87-156317 DDC 338.5/26/0994 19
HB236.A8 H35 1987

Nigam, Brij Mohan Lall, 1935- Banking and economic growth; with special reference to India, by B. M. L. Nigam.[1st ed.] Bombay, Vora [1967] xii, 207 p. 22 cm. "Approved for the Ph.D. degree of the Lucknow University." Bibliography: p. [203] LC Card SA68-4077 DDC 332.1/0954
1. Banks and banking - India. 2. Development banks - India. I. Title.
HG3284 .N5 ***NYPL [JLD 74-2222]***

Nigam, Raj Kumar, 1923-
Banking in India in the eighties . New Delhi , 1986. 533 p. in various pagings ; LC Card 86-903123 DDC 332.1/068 19
HG3284 .B267 1986

Towards a viable and vibrant public sector in India . New Delhi , 1986. xiii, 188, 163, 8, 103 p. ; LC Card 86-903205 DDC 338.6/2/0954
HD4293 .T667 1986

Niger.
Dynamique de l'emploi dans un système sahélien, le Niger . Addis Abéba , 1980. lxxii, 301 p. ; ISBN 92-2-202351-X : LC Card 82-980599
HD5846.7.A6 D95 1980

Joint program assessment of grain marketing in Niger . [Niamey, Niger] [1983] 2 v. : LC Card 87-114421 DDC 381/.4131/096626 19
HD9049.N552 J65 1983

NIGER - CENSUS, 1977.
Recensement général de la population 1977 . Niamey , 1985-<1986. v. <1-3 > : LC Card 87-157638
HA4724 .A4 1977

Niger. Direction de la statistique et de l'informatique. Recensement général de la population 1977 . Niamey , 1985-<1986. v. <1-3 > : LC Card 87-157638
HA4724 .A4 1977

NIGER - ECONOMIC CONDITIONS.
Martens, George R. Trade unionism and politics in Niger. Lome, Togo [1986] 93 p. ; LC Card 86-172446 DDC 322/.2/09669 19
HD6882.Z65 M37 1986

NIGER - ECONOMIC CONDITIONS - 1970-
Dynamique de l'emploi dans un système sahélien, le Niger . Addis Abéba , 1980. lxxii, 301 p. ; ISBN 92-2-202351-X : LC Card 82-980599
HD5846.7.A6 D95 1980

NIGER - ECONOMIC POLICY.
Dynamique de l'emploi dans un système sahélien, le Niger . Addis Abéba , 1980. lxxii, 301 p. ; ISBN 92-2-202351-X : LC Card 82-980599
HD5846.7.A6 D95 1980

Niger. Ministère du plan. Plan quinquennal de développement économique et social, 1979-1983 /. [Niamey] [1980] 666 p. : LC Card 86-138814
HC1020 .N535 1980

Niger. Ministère du plan. Plan quinquennal de développement économique et social, 1979-1983 / Ministère du plan. [Niamey] : République du Niger, Ministère du plan : Diffusion, Secrétariat général du Gouvernement, [1980] 666 p. : ill. ; 30 cm. "Erratum": [4] p. inserted. LC Card 86-138814
1. Niger - Economic policy. 2. Niger - Social policy. I. Title.
HC1020 .N535 1980

NIGER - POPULATION - STATISTICS.
Recensement général de la population 1977 . Niamey , 1985-<1986. v. <1-3 > : LC Card 87-157638
HA4724 .A4 1977

NIGER RIVER VALLEY - ECONOMIC CONDITIONS.
Roberts, Richard L., 1949- Warriors, merchants, and slaves . Stanford, Calif. , 1987. xii, 293 p. : ISBN 0-8047-1378-2 (alk. paper) : LC Card 86-23138 DDC 330.966/23 19
HC1035 .R63 1987

NIGER - SOCIAL POLICY.
Niger. Ministère du plan. Plan quinquennal de développement économique et social, 1979-1983 /. [Niamey] [1980] 666 p. : LC Card 86-138814
HC1020 .N535 1980

Nigeria : economic, education, and health themes / by HEERN Consultants Inc. Hyattsville, Md. : HEERN Consultants, 1975. iii, 35 p. ; 22 cm. Erratum slip inserted. Includes bibliographies. CONTENTS. - The importance of research and data base in economic development in Nigeria / by Daniel U. Akpan -- Nigerian investment in education / by Edet M. Ekereke -- Malaria--a life-long problem / by

Paul A. Akpan. LC Card 85-114200
1. Nigeria - Economic conditions - 1970-. 2. Education - Nigeria. 3. Malaria - Nigeria. I. Akpan, Daniel U. Importance of research and data base in economic development in Nigeria. 1975. II. Ekereke, Edet M. Nigerian investment in education. 1975. III. Akpan, Paul A. Malaria--a life-long problem. 1975. IV. HEERN Consultants.
HC1055 .N533 1975

Nigeria . Mabbs-Zeno, Carl. Washington, D.C. [1986] vi, 54 p. : LC Card 86-601597 DDC 382/.41/09669 19
HD9017.N52 M3 1986

Nigeria and the international capitalist system / edited by Toyin Falola and Julius O. Ihonvbere. Boulder, Colo. : L. Rienner Publishers, 1988. v, 154 p. ; 24 cm. (GSIS monograph series in world affairs) Bibliography: p. 129-148. Includes index.
ISBN 1-555-87087-2 (alk. paper) : LC Card 87-23183 DDC 337.669 19
1. Nigeria - Foreign economic relations. 2. Nigeria - Economic conditions - 1960-. 3. Nigeria - Foreign relations. 4. Nigeria - Dependency on foreign countries. 5. Petroleum industry and trade - Nigeria. I. Falola, Toyin. II. Ihonvbere, Julius Omozuanvbo. III. Series.
HF1616.7 .N54 1988

NIGERIA - COLONIAL INFLUENCE.
Anyansi-Archibong, Chi. B., 1949- Strategy and structure of enterprise in a developing country /. Aldershots, Hants, England , Brookfield, Vt., USA , c1988. xvii, 274 p. : ISBN 0-566-05471-X : LC Card 87-12020 DDC 658/.009669 19
HD70.N43 A59 1988

NIGERIA - COMMERCE - UNITED STATES.
Mabbs-Zeno, Carl. Nigeria . Washington, D.C. [1986] vi, 54 p. : LC Card 86-601597 DDC 382/.41/09669 19
HD9017.N52 M3 1986

NIGERIA - COMMERCIAL POLICY.
Oyejide, T. Ademola. The effects of trade and exchange rate policies on agriculture in Nigeria /. Washington, D.C., USA , c1986. 61 p. : ISBN 0-89629-056-5 (pbk.) LC Card 86-21309 DDC 338.1/09669 19
HD2145.5 .O94 1986

NIGERIA CONSTRUCTION AND FURNITURE COMPANY.
East-Central State, Nigeria. Government white paper on the report of the Administrative Board of Inquiry into the Nigeria Construction and Furniture Company Limited /. [Enugu, Nigeria] [1976] 19 p. ; LC Card 86-205140
HD9773.N54 N543 1976

NIGERIA - DEPENDENCY ON FOREIGN COUNTRIES.
Nigeria and the international capitalist system /. Boulder, Colo. , 1988. v, 154 p. ; ISBN 1-555-87087-2 (alk. paper) : LC Card 87-23183 DDC 337.669 19
HF1616.7 .N54 1988

Nigeria, East-Central State. see **East-Central State, Nigeria.**

NIGERIA - ECONOMIC CONDITIONS - TO 1960.
Britain and Nigeria . London ; Atlantic Highlands, New Jersey : vi, 250 p. ; ISBN 0-86232-303-7 : LC Card 86-232062 DDC 337.410669 19
HF1534.5.N6 B75 1987

NIGERIA - ECONOMIC CONDITIONS - 1960-
Adedeji, Adebayo. Some reflections on Nigeria's economic performance since independence, and thoughts on future prospects /. Addis Ababa [1985] 57 p. ; LC Card 86-980957 DDC 330.9669/05 19
HC1055 .A546 1985

Nigeria and the international capitalist system /. Boulder, Colo. , 1988. v, 154 p. ; ISBN 1-555-87087-2 (alk. paper) : LC Card 87-23183 DDC 337.669 19
HF1616.7 .N54 1988

NIGERIA - ECONOMIC CONDITIONS - 1970-
Heinecke, P. Development administration in Nigeria . [Nigeria , 1985?] 201 p. ; LC Card 86-207544 DDC 338.9669 19
HC1055 .H446 1985

Heinecke, P. Freedom in the grave . [Zaria, Nigeria] [1985] 178 p. ; LC Card 86-153310 DDC 337.66906 19
HC1055 .H45 1985

Nigeria . Hyattsville, Md. , 1975. iii, 35 p. ; LC Card 85-114200
HC1055 .N533 1975

Okongwu, Chu S. P., 1934- The Nigerian economy . Enugu, Nigeria , 1986. vi, 453 p. : ISBN 978-15-6038-X (pbk.) : LC Card 87-132237 DDC 330.9669/05 19
HC1055 .O39 1986

Uzoaga, William Okefie. Money and banking in Nigeria /. Enugu, Nigeria , 1981. xiv, 304 p. ; ISBN 978-15-6175-0 ***NYPL [Sc D 84-373]***

NIGERIA - ECONOMIC CONDITIONS - 1970- - CONGRESSES.
National Workshop on Self Reliance and Self Sufficiency in the Nigerian Economy (1978 : University of Ibadan) Self-reliance and self-sufficiency . [Ibadan, Nigeria] , 1979. 156 p. : LC Card 87-402546 DDC 338.9669 19
HC1055 .N386 1978

NIGERIA - ECONOMIC POLICY.
Biersteker, Thomas J. Multinationals, the state, and control of the Nigerian economy /. Princeton, N.J. , c1987. xvii, 344 p. : ISBN 0-691-07728-2 (alk. paper) : LC Card 86-25214 DDC 338.8/88669 19
HG5881.A3 B54 1987

Fadahunsi, Akin. The development process and technology . Uppsala , 1986. 41 p. ; ISBN 91-7106-257-2 (pbk.) LC Card 87-119156 DDC 338.9669/07 19
HC1055.Z9 T43 1986

Heinecke, P. Development administration in Nigeria . [Nigeria , 1985?] 201 p. ; LC Card 86-207544 DDC 338.9669 19
HC1055 .H446 1985

Ogunba, C. K. An ailing African economy and the IMF medicine /. Ile-Ife [Nigeria] [1985] 40, [1] p. ; LC Card 86-207586 DDC 332.1/52 19
HG3881.5.I58 O37 1985

Okongwu, Chu S. P., 1934- The Nigerian economy . Enugu, Nigeria , 1986. vi, 453 p. : ISBN 978-15-6038-X (pbk.) : LC Card 87-132237 DDC 330.9669/05 19
HC1055 .O39 1986

Oyejide, T. Ademola. The effects of trade and exchange rate policies on agriculture in Nigeria /. Washington, D.C., USA , c1986. 61 p. : ISBN 0-89629-056-5 (pbk.) LC Card 86-21309 DDC 338.1/09669 19
HD2145.5 .O94 1986

State, oil, and agriculture in Nigeria /. Berkeley , c1987. xiv, 327 p. : ISBN 0-87725-166-5 (pbk.) : LC Card 87-2941 DDC 338.1/8669 19
HD2145.5 .S73 1987

NIGERIA - ECONOMIC POLICY - 1970-
Biersteker, Thomas J. Multinationals, the state, and control of the Nigerian economy /. Princeton, N.J. , c1987. xvii, 344 p. : ISBN 0-691-07728-2 (alk. paper) : LC Card 86-25214 DDC 338.8/88669 19
HG5881.A3 B54 1987

NIGERIA - ECONOMIC POLICY - CONGRESSES.
National Workshop on Self Reliance and Self Sufficiency in the Nigerian Economy (1978 : University of Ibadan) Self-reliance and self-sufficiency . [Ibadan, Nigeria] , 1979. 156 p. : LC Card 87-402546 DDC 338.9669 19
HC1055 .N386 1978

Physical planning inputs in national and state development plans . Ibadan [1984?] v, 312 p. : LC Card 87-400745 DDC 338.9669 19
HC1055 .P488 1984

Nigeria. Federal Ministry of Finance. National Workshop on Self Reliance and Self Sufficiency in the Nigerian Economy (1978 : University of Ibadan) Self-reliance and self-sufficiency . [Ibadan, Nigeria] , 1979. 156 p. : LC Card 87-402546 DDC 338.9669 19
HC1055 .N386 1978

NIGERIA - FOREIGN ECONOMIC RELATIONS.
Nigeria and the international capitalist system /. Boulder, Colo. , 1988. v, 154 p. ; ISBN 1-555-87087-2 (alk. paper) : LC Card 87-23183 DDC 337.669 19
HF1616.7 .N54 1988

NIGERIA - FOREIGN ECONOMIC RELATIONS - CONGRESSES.
National Workshop on Self Reliance and Self Sufficiency in the Nigerian Economy (1978 : University of Ibadan) Self-reliance and self-sufficiency . [Ibadan, Nigeria] , 1979. 156 p. : LC Card 87-402546 DDC 338.9669 19
HC1055 .N386 1978

Nigeria's external relations . Ibadan , 1986. 577 p. ; LC Card 87-132060 DDC 337.669 19
HF1616.7 .N55 1986

NIGERIA - FOREIGN ECONOMIC RELATIONS - EUROPE, EASTERN - CONGRESSES.
Economic co-operation between Nigeria and the socialist countries of Eastern Europe /. Lagos , 1986, c1984. 210 p. : ISBN 978-13-2828-2 (pbk.) LC Card 87-155295 DDC 337.669047 19
HF1616.7.Z4 E8523 1986

NIGERIA - FOREIGN ECONOMIC RELATIONS - GREAT BRITAIN.
Britain and Nigeria . London ; Atlantic Highlands, New Jersey : vi, 250 p. ; ISBN 0-86232-303-7 : LC Card 86-232062 DDC 337.410669 19
HF1534.5.N6 B75 1987

NIGERIA - FOREIGN RELATIONS.
Nigeria and the international capitalist system /. Boulder, Colo. , 1988. v, 154 p. ; ISBN 1-555-87087-2 (alk. paper) : LC Card 87-23183 DDC 337.669 19
HF1616.7 .N54 1988

NIGERIA - FOREIGN RELATIONS - 1960- - CONGRESSES.
Nigeria's external relations . Ibadan , 1986. 577 p. ; LC Card 87-132060 DDC 337.669 19
HF1616.7 .N55 1986

Nigeria - Government. see **Nigeria - Politics and government.**

NIGERIA - MANUFACTURES - COSTS - ECONOMETRIC MODELS.
Iyare, S. International cost differences in developing countries . Durham, England [1983] 14, [9] leaves : LC Card 86-207078 DDC 338.4/367/09667 19
HD9737.G52 I97 1983

NIGERIA - POLITICS AND GOVERNMENT - 1960- - CONGRESSES.
Nigeria's external relations . Ibadan , 1986. 577 p. ; LC Card 87-132060 DDC 337.669 19
HF1616.7 .N55 1986

NIGERIA - POLITICS AND GOVERNMENT - 1979-
Heinecke, P. Freedom in the grave . [Zaria, Nigeria] [1985] 178 p. ; LC Card 86-153310 DDC 337.66906 19
HC1055 .H45 1985

Nigeria. Presidential Commission on Parastatals. REPORT OF THE PRESIDENTIAL COMMISSION ON PARASTATALS.

Nigeria. Presidential Commission on Revenue Allocation.

NIGERIA. REPORT OF THE PRESIDENTIAL COMMISSION ON REVENUE ALLOCATION.

NIGERIA - RURAL CONDITIONS.
Jackson, Cecile, 1953- The Kano River Irrigation Project /. West Hartford, Conn. , 1985. xviii, 66 p. ; ISBN 0-931816-19-X LC Card 85-5242 DDC 331.4/83/09669 19
HD6073.F32 N64 1985
NYPL [JLF 86-1634]

Spiro, Heather M. The Ilora farm settlement in Nigeria /. West Hartford, Conn. , 1985. xvii, 50 p. : ISBN 0-931816-20-3 LC Card 85-5230 DDC 331.4/83/089963 19
HD6073.F3 N667 1985
NYPL [JLF 86-1629]

NIGERIA - SOCIAL CONDITIONS - 1960-
Heinecke, P. Freedom in the grave . [Zaria, Nigeria] [1985] 178 p. ; LC Card 86-153310 DDC 337.66906 19
HC1055 .H45 1985

Okongwu, Chu S. P., 1934- The Nigerian economy . Enugu, Nigeria , 1986. vi, 453 p. : ISBN 978-15-6038-X (pbk.) : LC Card 87-132237 DDC 330.9669/05 19
HC1055 .O39 1986

NIGERIA - SOCIAL POLICY.
Okongwu, Chu S. P., 1934- The Nigerian economy . Enugu, Nigeria , 1986. vi, 453 p. : ISBN 978-15-6038-X (pbk.) : LC Card 87-132237 DDC 330.9669/05 19
HC1055 .O39 1986

NIGERIA - SOCIAL POLICY - CONGRESSES.
Physical planning inputs in national and state development plans . Ibadan [1984?] v, 312 p. : LC Card 87-400745 DDC 338.9669 19
HC1055 .P488 1984

The Nigerian economy . Okongwu, Chu S. P., 1934- Enugu, Nigeria , 1986. vi, 453 p. : ISBN 978-15-6038-X (pbk.) : LC Card 87-132237 DDC 330.9669/05 19
HC1055 .O39 1986

Nigerian Institute of International Affairs.
Economic co-operation between Nigeria and the socialist countries of Eastern Europe /. Lagos , 1986, c1984. 210 p. : ISBN 978-13-2828-2 (pbk.) LC Card 87-155295 DDC 337.669047 19
HF1616.7.Z4 E8523 1986

Nigeria's external relations . Ibadan , 1986. 577 p. ; LC Card 87-132060 DDC 337.669 19
HF1616.7 .N55 1986

Nigerian Institute of Management. Management Research Unit. Report on survey of job evaluation practices in some Nigerian organisations /. Lagos [1981] 2, 59, [1] leaves ; LC Card 87-110199 DDC 331.25 19
HF5549.5.J62 R46 1981

Nigerian Institute of Social and Economic Research.
A Critical appraisal of the economic and social conditions in the west African subregion /. [Lagos , 1979-1980] 10 v. : LC Card 87-159535 DDC 330.966 19
HC1000 .C75 1979

National Workshop on Self Reliance and Self Sufficiency in the Nigerian Economy (1978 : University of Ibadan) Self-reliance and self-sufficiency . [Ibadan, Nigeria] , 1979. 156 p. : LC Card 87-402546 DDC 338.9669 19
HC1055 .N386 1978

Towards an African economic community . [Ibadan, Nigeria] , 1986. 401 p. ; ISBN 978-18-1040-8 LC Card 87-143033 DDC 337.1/66 19
HC1000 .T69 1986

Transportation in Nigerian national development . Ibadan , c1981. xi, 602 p. : ISBN 978-18-1010-6 (pbk.) LC Card 82-196087 DDC 380.5/09669 19
HE287.7 .T72 1981 ***NYPL [Sc E 86-178]***

Nigerian Institute of Social and Economic Research. Physical Planning Division.
Physical planning inputs in national and state development plans . Ibadan [1984?] v, 312 p. : LC Card 87-400745 DDC 338.9669 19
HC1055 .P488 1984

Nigerian small farmers : problems and prospects in integrated rural development / edited by S. Olajuwon Olayide, J.A. Eweka, V.E. Bello-Osagie. Benin-City, Bendel State, Nigeria : Published by Centre for Agricultural Rural and Development [i.e. Centre for Agricultural and Rural Development] (CARD), University of Ibadan, Nigeria, for Benin-Owena River Basin Development Authority, 1980. xv, 315 p. ; 23 cm. Includes bibliographical references. LC Card 82-206979 DDC 338.1/6 19
1. Farms, Small - Nigeria - Addresses, essays, lectures. 2. Peasantry - Nigeria - Addresses, essays, lectures. 3. Agriculture - Economic aspects - Nigeria - Addresses, essays, lectures. 4. Rural development - Nigeria - Addresses, essays, lectures. I. Olayide, S. Olajuwon. II. Eweka, J. A. (Julius A.). III. Bello-Osagie, V. E. IV. University of Ibadan. Centre for Agricultural and Rural Development. V. Benin-Owena River Basin Development Authority.
HD1339.N5 N54 1980 ***NYPL [Sc D 86-883]***

Nigerian Stock Exchange. Alile, H. I. The Nigerian stock market in operation /. [Lagos, Nigeria] 1986 (Lagos, Nigeria : Jeromelaiho & Associates) 194, v p. : LC Card 87-143647 DDC 332.64/2669 19
HG5881.N6 A43 1986

NIGERIAN STOCK EXCHANGE.
Alile, H. I. The Nigerian stock market in operation /. [Lagos, Nigeria] 1986 (Lagos, Nigeria : Jeromelaiho & Associates) 194, v p. : LC Card 87-143647 DDC 332.64/2669 19
HG5881.N6 A43 1986

The Nigerian stock market in operation /. Alile, H. I. [Lagos, Nigeria] 1986 (Lagos, Nigeria : Jeromelaiho & Associates) 194, v p. : LC Card 87-143647 DDC 332.64/2669 19
HG5881.N6 A43 1986

NIGERIANS - TOGO.
Dovi-Sodemekou, Folly B. (Folly Bebey) Emploi et éducation dans le 2e plan de développement économique et social du Togo /. Lomé, Togo [1985] 89, 52, 9, 2 p. : LC Card 87-131183
HD5846.5.A6 D68 1985

Nigeria's external relations : the first twenty-five years / [edited by] G.O. Olusanya and R.A. Akindele. Ibadan : University Press Ltd., 1986. 577 p. ; 24 cm. Papers from a 1985 conference on "25 years of Nigeria's foreign policy" organized by the Nigerian Institute of International Affairs. "Twenty-five years of Nigeria's foreign policy : a select bibliography / edited by R.T. Okotore": p. [477]-504. Includes bibliographies and index. LC Card 87-132060 DDC 337.669 19
1. Nigeria - Foreign economic relations - Congresses. 2. Nigeria - Foreign relations - 1960- - Congresses. 3. Nigeria - Politics and government - 1960- - Congresses. I. Olusanya, G. O. (Gabriel Olakunde). II. Akindele, R. A. 1939-. III. Nigerian Institute of International Affairs.
HF1616.7 .N55 1986

Nigerija. see **Nigeria.**

Niggli, Peter, 1950-
[Athiopien, Deportationen und Zwangsarbeitslager. English]
Ethiopia, deportations and forced-labour camps : a study / by Peter Niggli, Switzerland on behalf of the Berliner Missionswerk. [Berlin : Berliner Missionswerk, 1986] 86 p., [1] leaf of plates : ill. ; 30 cm. Cover title. Translation of: Äthiopien, Deportationen und Zwangsarbeitslager. LC Card 87-131977 DDC 333.3/1/63 19
1. Land settlement - Ethiopia. 2. Migration, Internal - Ethiopia. 3. Refugees - Ethiopia - Interviews. I. Title.
HD979 .N3413 1986

NIGHT WORK - EUROPEAN ECONOMIC COMMUNITY COUNTRIES.
Copsey, S. M. Shiftwork review . Luxembourg , Washington, DC , 1986. xi, 122 p. : ISBN 92-825-6419-3 (pbk.) : LC Card 87-137298 DDC 331.25/72 19
HD5111.6.E86 C66 1986

Nightmare . Perry, Susan. New York , c1985. xvii, 261 p. ; ISBN 0-02-595930-1 : LC Card 85-13710 DDC 338.7/616139435 19
HD9995.C64 A236 1985
NYPL [JLE 85-3950]

Nigro, Giampiero. Gli uomini dell'irco : indagine sui consumi di carne nel basso Medioevo : Prato alla fine del '300 / Giampiero Nigro. Firenze : Le Monnier, 1983. xxii, 184 p. : ill. ; 24 cm. (Le Monnier università . 4) Bibliography: p. xviii-xxii. ISBN 88-00-86022-2 : LC Card 84-238769
1. Meat industry and trade - Italy - Prato Region - History. 2. Animal industry - Italy - Prato Region - History. 3. Slaughtering and slaughter-houses - Italy - Prato Region - History. 4. Butchers - Italy - Prato Region - History. 5. Food consumption - Italy - Prato Region - History. I. Title.
HD9425.I83 P76 1983 ***NYPL [JLE 86-2127]***

Nihei, Yasumitsu, 1933- Stewart, Charles T., 1922- Technology transfer and human factors /. Lexington, Mass. , 1987. xiii, 200 p. ; ISBN 0-669-14251-4 (alk. paper) LC Card 86-45751 DDC 338.9/26 19
T174.3 .S74 1987 ***NYPL [JLE 87-634]***

Nihon. see **Japan.**

Nihon Daigaku. Keizai Gakubu. International Symposium on the Role of the Asia-Pacific Region in World Economic Development (1984 : Tokyo, Japan) Proceedings of the International Symposium on the Role of the Asia-Pacific Region in World Economic Development . Tokyo , c1985. iv, 325 p. : LC Card 87-108109 DDC 337.9 19
HC681 .I58 1984

Nihon Ginkō. Kin'yū Kenkyūjo. Financial innovation and monetary policy . [Tokyo] , c1986. ix, 339 p. : ISBN 4-13-047029-9 : LC Card 86-222823 DDC 332/.095 19
HG187.E37 F55 1986

Nihon kōkigyō no saisei / Shigemori Akira hen. 880-02 Shohan. Kyōto-shi : Hōritsu Bunkasha, 1986. 4, 8, 289 p. : ill. ; 19 cm. Errata slip inserted. In Japanese. Includes bibliographical references. ISBN 4-589-01273-1 : LC Card 86-216062
1. Government business enterprises - Japan. 2. Government business enterprises - Japan - Finance. 3. Transportation and state - Japan. I. Shigemori, Akira, 1942-.
HD4313 .N46 1986 <Orien Japan>
NYPL [*OSM 87-2537]

Nihon no enerugī kaihatsu seisaku /. Suzuki, Shigeru, 1949- Kyōto-shi , 1985. vii, 274 p. : ISBN 4-623-01582-3 : LC Card 85-221878
HD9502.J32 S89 1985 <Orien Japan>
NYPL [*OSM 86-3954]

Nihon Nōritsu Kyōkai. Kyanon no seisan kakushin. English. Canon production system . Stamford, Conn. , c1987. xxi, 230 p. : ISBN 0-915299-06-2 : LC Card 85-63498 DDC 681/.418/0683 19
HD9708.5.C354 K92513 1987

Nihon Rōdō Kyōkai. Labor unions and labor-management relations. Tokyo, Japan , 1986. 48 p. : ISBN 4-538-74002-0 : LC Card 86-220438 DDC 331/.0952 19
HD8726.5 .L33 1986

Niinikoski, Risto, 1946- Markkinointitutkimuksen perusteet / Risto Niinikoski. 5. painos. [Lauttakylä?] : Satakonsultit, [1985] (Jyväskylässä : Gummerus) 134 p. : ill. ; 25 cm. Bibliography: p. 133-134. ISBN 951-99532-6-4 LC Card 86-122767
1. Marketing research. I. Title.
HF5415.2 .N54 1985

Nijkamp, Peter.
International Symposium on Technological Change and Employment: Urban and Regional Dimensions (1985 : Zandvoort, Netherlands) Technological change, employment, and spatial dynamics . Berlin , New York , c1986. vii, 466 p. : ISBN 0-387-16478-2 (U. S. : pbk.) LC Card 86-10081 DDC 331.12 19
HD6331 .I6 1985
NYPL [JLM 72-289 v.270]

Regional labour markets . Amsterdam ; New York : xvii, 500 p. : ISBN 0-444-70323-3 LC Card 87-22200 DDC 331.12 19
HD5707 .R37 1987

Nikiforov, A. V. (Andreĭ Vladimirovich) Agrarnye preobrazovanii͡a v stranakh Afriki na sovremennom ėtape /. Moskva , 1982. 227 p. ; LC Card 83-143645
HD2117 .A347 1982

Nikiforov, L. V. Kuznet͡sova, T. E. Proizvodstvennai͡a sfera sovremennogo sela /. Moskva , 1986. 199 p. ; LC Card 86-164902
HD9015.S652 K89 1986

Nikiphoroff, Basilio, 1945- Campos, Luis A. (Luis Alberto), 1949- Pequeños campesinos y su incertidumbre . Asunción, Paraguay [1986] 224 p. : LC Card 87-400281 DDC 305.5/63 19
HD1531.P3 C36 1986

Nikitin, Sergeĭ Mikhaĭlovich. Indeksy t͡sen i produktsii v kapitalisticheskikh stranakh / S.M. Nikitin, E.P. Shpakovskai͡a. Moskva : Izd-vo "Nauka," 1981. 255 p. ; 20 cm. At head of title: Akademii͡a nauk SSSR. Ordena Trudovogo krasnogo znameni Institut mirovoĭ ėkonomiki i mezhdunarodnykh otnosheniĭ. Includes bibliographical references. LC Card 86-460234
1. Price indexes. I. Shpakovskai͡a, E. P. (Elena Petrovna). II. Title.
HB225 .N52 1981

Nikitin, V. S. (Vadim Semenovich)
Prognozirovanie razvitii͡a regionalʹnogo gorno-promyshlennogo kompleksa / V.S. Nikitin. Moskva : Izd-vo "Nauka", 1982. 141, [3] p. : ill. ; 20 cm. (Problemy sovetskoĭ ėkonomiki) At head of title: Akademii͡a nauk SSSR. Dalʹnevostochnyĭ nauchnyĭ t͡sentr. Severo-Vostochnyĭ kompleksnyĭ nauchno-issledovatelʹskiĭ institut. Bibliography: p. 133-[142] LC Card 83-154711
1. Mineral industries - Russian S.F.S.R. - Soviet Far East - Forecasting. 2. Economic forecasting - Russian S.F.S.R. - Soviet Far East. 3. Soviet Far East (R.S.F.S.R.) - Economic policy. I. Title.
HD9506.S7473 S656 1982

Nikitin, V. V. (Vasiliĭ Vasil'evich) Goriuchee--frontu, 1941-1945 / V.V. Nikitin. Moskva : Voen. izd-vo, 1984. 203 p. : ill. ; 23 cm. Includes bibliographical references. LC Card 85-152473
1. Petroleum industry and trade - Soviet Union - History. 2. World War - Soviet Union - Equipment and supplies. 3. Soviet Union - Armed Forces - Fuel. I. Title.
HD9575.S652 N55 1984

Nikitina, V. Z. (Valentina Zakharovna) Ėksperimental'naia razrabotka natural'no-stoimostnykh mezhotraslevykh balansov soiuznoĭ respubliki /. Moskva , 1980. 137 p. : LC Card 85-199427
HC337.E7 E49 1980

Nikolaev, Ivan. Izrabotvane na kolektivnite reshenia / Ivan Nikolaev. Sofiia : Nauchnoizsledovatelski in-t po profsiuzni problemi "G. Dimitrov" pri TSK na BPS, 1985. 69 p. ; 20 cm. Summary in English and Russian. Includes bibliographical references. LC Card 86-174800
1. Industrial management - Bulgaria - Decision making. 2. Work groups - Bulgaria. 3. Decision making, Group - Bulgaria. I. Title.
HD30.23 .N55 1985

Nikolić, Miodrag M. Desezonizacija jugoslovenskih vremenskih serija 1971-1980 = Seasonal adjustment of Yugoslav time series 1971-1980 / Miodrag Nikolić, Nebojša Marić. Beograd : Savezni zavod za statistiku, 1982. 287 p. : ill. ; 24 cm. (Studije, analize i prikazi . 109) In Serbo-Croatian (roman) Tables. Errata slip inserted. Summary in English. Bibliography: p. 286. LC Card 85-157587
1. Seasonal variations (Economics) - Yugoslavia. 2. Time-series analysis. I. Marić, Nebojša. II. Title. III. Title: Seasonal adjustment of Yugoslav time series 1971-1980. IV. Series.
HA37.Y8 A37 no. 109 HC407

NIL po problemam prodovol'stvennogo kompleksa (Bŭlgarska akademiia na naukite) Rol'mezhdunarodnykh monopoliĭ v prodovol'stvennoĭ sisteme /. Sofiia , 1985. 113 p. ; LC Card 86-109190
HD9000.5 .R62 1985

Niland, John R.
Alternatives to arbitration /. Sydney , Boston , 1986. x, 468 p. ; ISBN 0-86861-857-8 (pbk.) LC Card 85-81482 DDC 331/.0994 19
HD5630.A6 A47 1986

Control, consensus, or chaos? : managers and industrial relations reform / John Niland and Dennis Turner. Sydney ; Boston : Allen & Unwin, 1985. xiv, 330 p. : ill. ; 22 cm. (Research study (Committee for Economic Development of Australia) . P25) "CEDA study"--Cover. On t.p.: Committee for Economic Development of Australia. Includes index. Bibliography: p. 313-322. ISBN 0-86861-447-5 (pbk.) LC Card 85-70461 DDC 331.89/0994 19
1. Industrial relations - Australia. 2. Collective bargaining - Australia. I. Turner, Dennis E. II. Committee for Economic Development of Australia. III. Series. IV. Series: Research study (Committee for Economic Development of Australia) , P25. V. Title.
HD8846.5 .N55 1985 ***NYPL [JLD 87-354]***

Nilson, Bengt, 1952- Handelspolitik under skärpt konkurrens : England och Sverige 1929-39 / Bengt Nilson. Lund : Gleerup : Liber, c1983. 217 p. ; 23 cm. (Bibliotheca historica Lundensis. 58) ACQ MSG: E 49-140. Extra t.p. with thesis statement and English abstract inserted. Thesis (doctoral)--Universitetet i Lund, 1983. Summary in English. Bibliography: p. 196-209. Includes indexes. ISBN 91-40-04894-2 : LC Card 84-144528
1. Sweden - Commercial policy. 2. Sweden - Foreign economic relations - Great Britain. 3. Great Britain - Foreign economic relations - Sweden. I. Title.
HF1567 .N55 1983

Nilsson, Roy. Kitui water resources development study : phase I reconnaissance survey / prepared by Roy Nilsson. Nairobi, Kenya : Louis Berger International, [1982] 13, [31] leaves : ill., maps ; 30 cm. At head of title: Ministry of Economic Planning and Development, Arid and Semi Arid Lands Development Project. "May 1982." Two maps on 2 folded leaves in pocket. LC Card 85-980998 DDC 333.91/009676/24 19
1. Water-supply - Kenya - Kitui (District). 2. Water resources development - Kenya - Kitui (District). I. Louis Berger International, inc. II. Arid and Semi Arid Lands Development Project (Kenya). III. Title.
HD1699.K42 K586 1982

Nilsson, William P. Achieving strategic goals through executive development / William P. Nilsson. Reading, Mass. : Addison-Wesley, c1987. xv, 266 p. : ill. ; 25 cm. Bibliography: p. 257-258. Includes index. ISBN 0-201-12751-2 : LC Card 86-32201 DDC 658.4/012 19
1. Executives, Training of. 2. Strategic planning. I. Title.
HD38.2 .N54 1987

Nimmergut, Jörg, 1939- Werben mit Sex / Jörg Nimmergut. Originalausg. München : W. Heyne, c1982. 383 p. : ill. ; 18 cm. (Kompaktwissen. Nr. 119) Includes index. ISBN 3-453-53132-9 (pbk.) LC Card 86-673618
1. Sex in advertising. I. Title.
HF5827 .N45x 1982

Ning, Hasjim, 1916- Pasang surut pengusaha pejuang : otobiografi Hasjim Ning / seperti dituturkan kepada A.A. Navis.Cet. 1. Jakarta : Grafitipers, 1986. x, 392 p., [1] leaf of plates : ill., ports. ; 21 cm. Includes index. LC Card 86-944750
1. Ning, Hasjim, 1916-. 2. Businessmen - Indonesia - Biography. I. Navis, A. A. II. Title.
HC446.5.N56 A3 1986

NING, HASJIM, 1916-
Ning, Hasjim, 1916- Pasang surut pengusaha pejuang . Jakarta , 1986. x, 392 p., [1] leaf of plates : LC Card 86-944750
HC446.5.N56 A3 1986

Ninth Federal Reserve District Farm Forum (1965 : Minneapolis, Minn.) Farm Forum of the Ninth Federal Reserve District : report of proceedings of the Farm Forum / sponsored by the Minneapolis Chamber of Commerce, 8 March 1965, Minneapolis, Minnesota, U. S.A. Hopkins, Minn. : Distributed by Minneapolis-Moline, [1965] 99 p. : ill. ; 29 cm. Cover title. "Theme: Agribusiness marketing here and abroad." LC Card 87-110732
1. Produce trade - Government policy - Middle West - Congresses. 2. Farm produce - Middle West - Marketing - Congresses. 3. Agriculture and state - Middle West - Congresses. 4. Produce trade - Government policy - United States - Congresses. 5. Farm produce - United States - Marketing - Congresses. 6. Agriculture and state - United States - Congresses. I. Minneapolis Chamber of Commerce. II. Title.
HD9007.A14 N56 1965

Niopek, Wolfgang. Ehinger, Jürgen. Erfahrungen mit der Mitbestimmung in kommunalen Unternehmen . Baden-Baden , 1986. 147 p. ; ISBN 3-7890-1289-0 LC Card 87-118963 DDC 350.87/00943 19
HD2768.G44 E38 1986

Nippon. see **Japan.**

Nippons neue Vasallen? . Korte, Karl-Rudolf. Bonn , c1984. 103 p. : ISBN 3-7713-0216-1 LC Card 86-230930
HF1602.15.E92 K67 1984

Nissen, Bruce, 1948- Theories of the labor movement /. Detroit, Mich. , 1987. xi, 395 p. ; ISBN 0-8143-1815-0 : LC Card 86-32414 DDC 331.88/09 19
HD6476 .T47 1987

NITROGEN.
Sheldrick, William F. World nitrogen survey /. Washington, D.C. , 1987. xxv, 227 p. : ISBN 0-8213-0895-5 LC Card 87-6203 DDC 338.4/7668624 19
HD9660.N7 S55 1987

NITROGEN INDUSTRIES.
Sheldrick, William F. World nitrogen survey /. Washington, D.C. , 1987. xxv, 227 p. : ISBN 0-8213-0895-5 LC Card 87-6203 DDC 338.4/7668624 19
HD9660.N7 S55 1987

Niven, John. The American President Lines and its forebears, 1848-1984 : from paddlewheelers to containerships / John Niven. Newark : University of Delaware Press, c1987. 327 p. : ill. ; 25 cm. Includes bibliographies and index. ISBN 0-87413-299-1 (alk. paper) LC Card 85-40660 DDC 387.5/06573 19
1. American President Lines, Ltd. - History. I. Title.
HE753.A465 N58 1987

Nivens, Beatryce. The Black woman's career guide / Beatryce Nivens. Rev. ed. New York : Anchor Press/Doubleday, 1987. xvi, 362 p. ; 21 cm. Includes bibliographical references and index. ISBN 0-385-24161-5 (pbk.) : LC Card 87-1193 DDC 650.1/4/088042 19
1. Vocational guidance for women - United States. 2. Afro-American women - Employment. I. Title.
HF5382.5.U5 N5 1987

Nivola, Pietro S. The politics of energy conservation / Pietro S. Nivola. Washington, D.C. : Brookings Institution, c1986. x, 294 p. ; 24 cm. Includes bibliographical references and index. ISBN 0-8157-6088-4 : LC Card 85-48265 DDC 333.79/16/0973 19
1. Energy conservation - United States. 2. Energy policy - United States. I. Brookings Institution, Washington, D. C. II. Title.
TJ163.4.U6 N58 1986 ***NYPL [JLE 86-2515]***

Niẓām al-iʻānah fī al-iqtiṣād al-Saʻūdī /. Shaykh, Riyāḍ ʻAbd al-Ḥafīẓ. al-Mamlakah al-ʻArabīyah al-Suʻūdīyah , 1985. 77 p. : LC Card 86-208281
HC415.33.Z9 E447 1985

N'Kaloulou, Bernard, 1952- Dynamique paysanne et développement rural au Congo / Bernard N'Kaloulou. Paris : L'Harmattan, c1984. 260 p. : ill. ; 22 cm. (Collection Alternatives paysannes) Bibliography: p. 251-258. ISBN 2-85802-416-X LC Card 84-246506 DDC 305.5/63 19
1. Peasantry - Congo (Brazzaville). 2. Rural development - Congo (Brazzaville). 3. Congo (Brazzaville) - Rural conditions. 4. Congo (Brazzaville) - Economic conditions - Regional disparities. I. Title. II. Series.
HD1006 .N57 1984 ***NYPL [JLD 87-304]***

NMYC-World Bank Vocational Training Project. Metals and engineering . Manila, Philippines , 1983. 64 p. : LC Card 87-401862 DDC 331.25/92 19
HD5716.M52 P66 1983

No comment! . Blohowiak, Donald W. New York , 1987. xvi, 221 p. ; ISBN 0-275-92820-9 (alk. paper) : LC Card 87-15831 DDC 659.2 19
HD59 .B57 1987

No cost/low cost investing /. Currier, Chet. New York , 1987. 240 p. ; ISBN 0-531-15527-7 LC Card 87-13690 DDC 332.6/78 19
HG4910 .C86 1987

No one need apply . Bowes, Lee, 1951- Boston, Mass. , c1987. xiv, 268 p. ; ISBN 0-87584-149-X (alk. paper) LC Card 86-29512 DDC 658.3/11 19
HF5549.5.R44 B69 1987

No to exploitation . Menon, M. S. N., 1924- New Delhi , 1983. 163, xxxii p. ; LC Card 83-902131 DDC 337/.09172/4 19
HC59.7 .M445 1983 ***NYPL [JLE 86-4184]***

NOBEL PRIZES - BIOGRAPHY.
Lives of the laureates . Cambridge, Mass. , c1986. xii, 135 p. : ISBN 0-262-02255-9 LC Card 86-2919 DDC 330/.092/2 B 19
HB76 .L58 1986 ***NYPL [JFD 86-9827]***

Nobel Symposium on "Population Growth and World Development: a Fifty-year Perspective" (1981 : Noresund, Norway) Population and the world economy in the 21st century /. Oxford , 1982. viii, 264 p. : ISBN 0-631-12964-2 LC Card 86-673281
HC59 .P638x 1982b

Nöbel, T. Internationale Wirtschaft und revolutionärer Weltprozess /. [Berlin] , 1983. 390 p. ; LC Card 84-167604
HF1410.5 .I592 1983

Noble, Charles, 1948- Liberalism at work : the rise and fall of OSHA / Charles Noble. Philadelphia : Temple University Press, 1986. x, 292 p. : ill. ; 24 cm. (Labor and social change) Includes bibliographical references and index. ISBN 0-87722-421-8 (alk. paper) : LC Card 86-1766 DDC 353.0083/0289 19
1. Industrial hygiene - United States. 2. Industrial safety - United States. 3. Capitalism. 4. Liberalism. 5. Industry and state - United States. 6. United States - Social policy. I. Temple University Press. II. Title. III. Series.
HD7654 .N63 1986 ***NYPL [JLE 86-4426]***

NOBLE METALS. see **PRECIOUS METALS.**

Nochevnyĭ, V. A. (Vladimir Antonovich) Sovetskaia Belorussiia v 11-ĭ piatiletke . Minsk , 1986. 117 p. : LC Card 87-128043
HC337.B93 S677 1986

Nociones básicas sobre cooperativismo pesquero.

1a ed. [Mexico City, Mexico] : Secretaría de Pesca, 1985. 313 p. : forms ; 23 cm. (Serie Técnica. Administración . N 1) Cover subtitle: Manual de capacitación pesquera. ISBN 968-8170-25-9 LC Card 86-217319 DDC 334/.6892/0972 19
1. Fish trade - Mexico. 2. Fisheries, Cooperative - Mexico. I. Mexico. Secretaría de Pesca. II. Series.
HD9464.B72 N63 1985

Nocks, Elaine C., 1945- Einstein, Gilles O., 1950- Learning to use SPSSx /. Englewood Cliffs, N.J. , c1987. viii, 183 p. : ISBN 0-13-528050-8 (pbk.) LC Card 86-30263 DDC 005.3/29 19
HA32 .E45 1987

Noe, Robert M. Caruth, Donald L. Staffing the contemporary organization . New York , 1988. xii, 309 p. : ISBN 0-89930-236-X (lib. bdg. : alk. paper) LC Card 87-13092 DDC 658.3 19
HF5549 .C296 1988

Noel, James S.
McNees, Roger W. State-of-the-art and objectives of reflective raised pavement markers /. College Station, Tex. , Springfield, Va. [1986] vii, 162 p. : LC Card 87-620643 DDC 380.5 s 625.7/97 19
HE203 .T43 no. 322-1 TE203

Retention of reflective raised pavement markers / by James S. Noel and Roger W. McNees ; sponsored by the State Department of Highways and Public Transportation in cooperation with the U. S. Department of Transportation, Federal Highway Administration. College Station, Tex. : Texas Transportation Institute, Texas A&M University System ; Springfield, Va. : Available through the National Technical Information Service, [1986] xiii, 170 p. : ill. ; 28 cm. (Research report / Texas Transportation Institute, Texas A&M University System . 322-3) "October 1986." Bibliography: p. 118. "TTI-2-18-82-322-3"--Cover. LC Card 87-620642 DDC 380.5 s 625.7/042 19
1. Road markings. 2. Reflectors (Safety devices). I. McNees, Roger W. II. Texas. State Dept. of Highways and Public Transportation. III. United States. Federal Highway Administration. IV. Title. V. Title: Reflective raised pavement markers. VI. Series: Research report (Texas Transportation Institute) , 322-3.
HE203 .T43 no. 322-3 TE203

Noellert, William A. Howell, Thomas R., 1949- The EEC and the third Multifiber Arrangement . Washington, DC , 1986. [14], 126, [12] p. : LC Card 86-224652 DDC 382/.45677/0094 19
HD9865.E852 H68 1986

Nössler, Bernd. Der Widerstand geht weiter . Freiburg i. Br. , 1982. 261 p. : ISBN 3-921472-30-X LC Card 82-192690
HD9698.G43 W937 1982

Nofal, Maria Beatriz. Absentee entrepreneurship and the dynamics of the motor vehicle industry in Argentina / Maria Beatriz Nofal. New York : Praeger, 1987. p. cm. Bibliography: p. Includes index. ISBN 0-275-92607-9 (alk. paper) : LC Card 87-15159 DDC 629.2/0982 19
1. Automobile industry and trade - Argentina. I. Title.
HD9710.A72 N64 1987

Noga, George. The outlook for almonds, 1986 / by George Noga. Altamonte Springs, FL (1180 Spring Centre S. Blvd., Altamonte Springs 32714) : Certified Financial Services, [c1986] 36 p. : ill. ; 21 cm. Cover title. LC Card 86-220553 DDC 338.1/7455/0973 19
1. Almond industry - United States. I. Title.
HD9259.A47 U56 1986

Nogaĭ, A. I. (Anatoliĭ Il'ich) Ėkonomicheskiĭ analiz raboty predpriiatiĭ legkoĭ promyshlennosti / A.I. Nogaĭ. Moskva : "Legkaia i pishchevaia promyshl.", 1982. 175 p. : ill. ; 20 cm. Includes bibliographical references. LC Card 83-142136
1. Textile industry - Soviet Union - Management. I. Title.
HD9865.S652 N64 1982

Nogami, Otto. Campino, Antonio Carlos Coelho. Recursos e desempenhos dos programas de formação de mão-de-obra /. São Paulo, SP , Brasília, DF , 1985. 78 p. ; ISBN 85-21-30276-2 LC Card 85-187505
HD5754 .C34 1985

Nogueira, Antonio de Pádua Ferraz, 1933- Aspectos econômicos, jurídicos e sociais da Reforma Agrária /. São Paulo-SP Brasil [1985] 75 p. ; LC Card 86-220237
HD1333.B6 A85 1985

Nogueira, Mauro R. O brasileiro não é viável-- : uma avaliação diferente da situação política, econômica e social do Brasil / Mauro R. Nogueira. São Paulo : Instituto Brasileiro de Marketing, c1984. 253 p. : ill. ; 22 cm. Bibliography: p. 253. LC Card 84-256564
1. Brazil - Economic conditions - 1964-1985. 2. Brazil - Social conditions - 1964-. 3. Brazil - Politics and government - 1964-1985. I. Title.
HC187 .N57 1984

Nohlen, Dieter. Ungleiche Entwicklung und Regionalpolitik in Südeuropa . Bochum , 1985. 282 p. : ISBN 3-88339-441-6 : LC Card 85-205651
HC244.5 .U48 1985

Noir, Michel, 1944- 1988 : le grand rendez-vous / Michel Noir. [Paris] : J.C. Lattès, c1984. 263 p. : ill. ; 23 cm. Bibliography: p. 257-[262] LC Card 84-169744
1. High technology industries - France. 2. France - Economic policy - 1945-. 3. France - Politics and government - 1981-. I. Title. II. Title: Grand rendez-vous.
HC280.H53 N65 1984 ***NYPL [JLE 87-2052]***

Nokov, Khristo. Problemy valiutnogo soiuza stran-chlenov Evropeĭskogo ėkonomicheskogo soobshchestva i razvitie mezhdunarodnoĭ valiutnoĭ sistemy kapitalizma . Sofiia , 1984. 151 p. ; LC Card 85-224144
HG3942.8 .P76 1984

Nolan, Brian. Income distribution and the macroeconomy / Brian Nolan. Cambridge [Cambridgeshire] ; New York : Cambridge University Press, 1987. xii, 208 p. : ill. ; 24 cm. Bibliography: p. [198]-204. Includes indexes. ISBN 0-521-32612-5 LC Card 87-6606 DDC 339.2/0941 19
1. Income distribution - Great Britain. 2. Great Britain - Economic conditions - 1945-. 3. Great Britain - Economic policy - 1945-. I. Title.
HC260.I5 N65 1987

Nolan, Janet. Palmer, Michele. Catalogue of interviews . [Storrs, Conn.] , 1983. ii, 79 p. ; LC Card 86-621476 DDC 331.12/09746 19
HD6331.2.U52 C86 1983

Nold, Wolfgang. Die Kosten der Gesetze und Verordnungen in Staat, Wirtschaft und Gesellschaft / Wolfgang Nold. 2. Aufl. Konstanz : W. Hartung-Gorre, 1983. xii, 237 p. : ill. ; 21 cm. Bibliography: p. 226-237. ISBN 3-923200-07-2 LC Card 83-195590
1. Industry and state - Germany, West. 2. Industrial laws and legislation - Germany (West) - Compliance costs. I. Title.
HD3616.G4 N65 1983

Noll, Wulf. Lokales Informationssystem Arbeitsmarkt (LISA) / Autoren, Wulf Noll, Bernhard Rechmann. Essen : Kommunalverband Ruhrgebiet, 1986. 262 p. ; 30 cm. (Arbeitshefte Ruhrgebiet) Chiefly tables. Includes bibliographical references. ISBN 3-923494-64-5 LC Card 87-409105 DDC 331.12/5/094355 19
1. Labor supply - Germany (West) - Ruhr (Region) - Statistics. 2. Ruhr (Germany : Region) - Occupations - Statistics. I. Rechmann, Bernhard. II. Kommunalverband Ruhrgebiet. III. Title. IV. Series.
HD5780.R82 N65 1986

Nolon, John R. Housing rehabilitation under the Community Development Block Grant Program : materials for local officials of New York's smaller communities / New York State Division of Housing and Community Renewal. [New York, N.Y.] : The Division, [1984] 150 p. in various pagings ; 28 cm. "April 1984." Includes bibliographies. LC Card 86-622826 DDC 363.5/8 19
1. Housing rehabilitation - New York (State). I. Community Development Block Grant Program (U. S.). II. New York (State). Division of Housing and Community Renewal. III. Title.
HD7303.N7 N65 1984

Nomadism versus sedenterization . Amin, Nasr El Din Osman. [Khartoum?] Sudan , 1986. 105 leaves : LC Card 86-981112
HD977 .A65 1986

NOMADS - SUDAN - CASE STUDIES.
Amin, Nasr El Din Osman. Nomadism versus sedenterization . [Khartoum?] Sudan , 1986. 105 leaves : LC Card 86-981112
HD977 .A65 1986

NOMADS - SUDAN - SEDENTARISATION - CASE STUDIES.
Amin, Nasr El Din Osman. Nomadism versus sedenterization . [Khartoum?] Sudan , 1986. 105 leaves : LC Card 86-981112
HD977 .A65 1986

Noman, Ayesha. Status of women and fertility in Bangladesh / Ayesha Noman. Dhaka, Bangladesh : University Press, c1983. xv, 91 p. ; 23 cm. (UPL monograph series . 1) Bibliography: p. [87]-91. LC Card 83-905271 DDC 305.4/2/095492 19
1. Fertility, Human - Bangladesh. 2. Women - Bangladesh - Social conditions. 3. Bangladesh - Population policy. I. Title.
HB1050.6.A3 N65 1983
NYPL [JLD 86-2056]

Nomenclador de centros poblados. [Caracas] : República de Venezuela, Presidencia de la República, Oficina Central de Estadística e Informática, [1986-1987] 7 v. : maps (some col.) ; 23 cm. "XI censo general de población y vivienda." Chiefly tables. Errata slip inserted in v. 2. CONTENTS. - [1] Región capital -- [2] Región central -- [3] Región Los Andes -- [4] Región de Los Llanos -- [5] Región Zuliana -- [6] Región Centro-Occidental -- [7] Total nacional. LC Card 87-119549
1. Census districts - Venezuela. 2. Venezuela - Census, 1981. I. Venezuela. Oficina Central de Estadística e Informática.
HA1091.5 1981a

Nomenclature des marchandises. Tarifs routiers de marchandises. Paris [1986] 201 p. ; ISBN 2-7212-0295-2 LC Card 87-123802
HE5668.A6 T37 1986

Nomenclature des marchandises, route. Tarifs routiers de marchandises. Paris [1986] 201 p. ; ISBN 2-7212-0295-2 LC Card 87-123802
HE5668.A6 T37 1986

Nomenklatura artykułów i usług do badania spożycia (NAS). Wyd. 2., uzup. Warszawa : Zarząd Wydawnictw Statystycznych i Drukarni, 1980. 87 p. ; 24 cm. (Zeszyty metodyczne . nr. 34) At head of title: Główny Urząd Statystyczny. LC Card 81-109132
1. Commercial products - Poland - Classification. 2. Poland - Industries - Classification. I. Poland. Główny Urząd Statystyczny. II. Series.
HF1044.P6 N66 1980

Nominallohnentwicklung in der Bundesrepublik Deutschland . Ibler, Josef. Regensburg , c1986. 256 p. : ISBN 3-924956-18-9 LC Card 87-118941 DDC 331.2/943 19
HD5029 .I2 1986

Nomura Research Institute of Technology. see **Nomura Sōgō Kenkyūjo.**

Nomura Sōgō Kenkyūjo. The World economy and financial markets in 1995 . Kamakura-shi, Kanagawa-ken, Japan , 1986. 183 p. : LC Card 86-201317 DDC 332.1 19
HG3881 .W597 1986

Non aux économistes. Walbert, F. Non aux économistes, ou, Les ravages du dogmatisme /. Paris , c1984. 170 p. ; LC Card 87-152097
HB173 .W15 1984

Non aux économistes, ou, Les ravages du dogmatisme /. Walbert, F. Paris , c1984. 170 p. ; LC Card 87-152097
HB173 .W15 1984

Non entertainment automotive electronics. The Automotive electronics market in the U. S. New York, N.Y. , c1983. vi, 262 p. : LC Card 87-142223 DDC 381/.456292549/0973 19
HD9710.3.U52 A943 1983

Non resident Indians . Dhawan, O. P. New Delhi , 1984. xvi, 428 p. ; LC Card 85-900577 DDC 346.54/07 345.4067 19
HG5732 .D43 1984 ***NYPL [JLE 86-1363]***

Non-agricultural employment for moshav youth in the Galilee /. Schwartz, Moshe. Rehovot, Israel , c1985. 36, [2] p. ; LC Card 86-115596 DDC 331.3/4/0956945 19
HD6276.I66 G347 1985

NONALIGNMENT.
Vohra, Dewan C. Economic relevance of non-alignment /. New Delhi , 1983. xv, 387 p. ; LC Card 83-901770 DDC 338.9/009172/4 19
HC59.7 .V63 1983 ***NYPL [JLD 86-3799]***

NONALIGNMENT - CONGRESSES.
Issues before non-alignment . New Delhi , 1983. 190 p. ; LC Card 83-903478 DDC 327/.09171/6 19
JX1393.N54 I87 1983 ***NYPL [JLE 86-4176]***

NON-CHERNOZEM REGION (R.S.F.S.R.) - POPULATION.
Nechernozem'e . Moskva , 1977. 94 p. ; LC Card 82-107146
HB3608.N57 N43 1977

NON-CHERNOZEM REGION (R.S.F.S.R.) - POPULATION, RURAL.
Nechernozem'e . Moskva , 1977. 94 p. ; LC Card 82-107146
HB3608.N57 N43 1977

NON-CHERNOZEM REGION (R.S.F.S.R.) - RURAL CONDITIONS.
Krasnenkov, Vladimir. Ne pole pereĭti-- /. Moskva , 1986. 174 p. ; LC Card 86-132520
HD1995.N515 K73 1986

NONCONFORMISTS. see **DISSENTERS.**

NONCONFORMITY. see **CONFORMITY.**

Nondifferentiable optimization . IIASA (International Institute for Applied Systems Analysis) Workshop on Nondifferentiable Optimization (1984 : Sopron, Hungary) Berlin , New York , 1985. vi, 349 p. : ISBN 0-387-15979-7 (U. S.) LC Card 85-25029 DDC 658.4/03/4 19
T57.6 .I46 1984
NYPL [JLM 72-289 no.255]

Nonfederal housing programs . Stegman, Michael A. Washington, D.C. , 1987. viii, 231 p. ; ISBN 0-87420-673-1 LC Card 87-51080 DDC 363.5/8 19
HD7293.Z9 S75 1987

NONFERROUS METAL INDUSTRIES - GERMANY, WEST.
Mayer, Ralph-Dieter. Stahl- und Leichtmetallbau, Schienenfahrzeugbau . Berlin , c1985. 352 p. : ISBN 3-428-05771-6 LC Card 85-161158
HD9523.5 .M3 1985

NONFERROUS METAL INDUSTRIES - GREAT BRITAIN - HISTORY.
Toomey, Robert R., 1949- Vivian and Sons, 1809-1924 . New York , 1985. 427 p. ; ISBN 0-8240-6692-8 (alk. paper) : LC Card 84-46012 DDC 338.7/622343/0941 19
HD9539.C7 G778 1985
NYPL [JLE 86-4440]

NONFERROUS METAL INDUSTRIES - SOVIET UNION - MANAGEMENT.
Gratsershteĭn, I. M. (Izrail' Markovich) Organizatsiia, planirovanie i upravlenie na predpriiatiiakh tsvetnoĭ metallurgii /. Moskva , 1987. 415 p. : LC Card 87-156156
HD9539.A3 S5546 1987

NONFERROUS METAL INDUSTRIES - UNITED STATES.
The End-use markets for 13 nonferrous metals /. Washington, D.C. [1986] vii, 52 p. ; LC Card 86-602419 DDC 381/.45673/0973 19
HD9539.A3 U44 1986

Nonfuel minerals . Mikesell, Raymond Frech. Ann Arbor , c1987. xii, 257 p. : ISBN 0-472-10083-1 : LC Card 86-27247 DDC 333.8/5/0973 19
HD9506.U62 M42 1987

NONFUEL MINERALS INDUSTRIES - DEVELOPING COUNTRIES - FINANCE.
Financing foreign development of non-fuel mineral resources . [Washington, D.C.] [1986] 308 p. : LC Card 86-602175 DDC 332.1/5 19
HD9506.D452 F56 1986

NONFUEL MINERALS INDUSTRY.
An Appraisal of minerals availability for 34 commodities /. [Pittsburgh, Pa.] , 1987. iii, 300 p. : LC Card 87-600244 DDC 333.8/5 19
HD9506.A2 A72 1987

NONFUEL MINERALS INDUSTRY - GOVERNMENT POLICY - UNITED STATES.
Mikesell, Raymond Frech. Nonfuel minerals . Ann Arbor , c1987. xii, 257 p. : ISBN 0-472-10083-1 : LC Card 86-27247 DDC 333.8/5/0973 19
HD9506.U62 M42 1987

NONFUEL MINERALS INDUSTRY - UNITED STATES.
An Appraisal of minerals availability for 34 commodities /. [Pittsburgh, Pa.] , 1987. iii, 300 p. : LC Card 87-600244 DDC 333.8/5 19
HD9506.A2 A72 1987

Mikesell, Raymond Frech. Nonfuel minerals . Ann Arbor , c1987. xii, 257 p. : ISBN 0-472-10083-1 : LC Card 86-27247 DDC 333.8/5/0973 19
HD9506.U62 M42 1987

NON-GOVERNMENTAL ORGANIZATIONS.
Monitoring and evaluating small business projects . [New York, NY] , c1987. ix, 262 p. : LC Card 87-6945 DDC 361.7 19
HD2346.5 .M65 1987

NON-GOVERNMENTAL ORGANIZATIONS - AFRICA.
Diversity in development . New York, NY , c1985. 49 p. : ISBN 0-932140-06-8 (pbk.) LC Card 86-231753 DDC 361.7/096 19
HC800.Z9 E444 1985

NON-GOVERNMENTAL ORGANIZATIONS - AFRICA - DIRECTORIES.
Diversity in development . New York, NY , c1986. xvii, 620 p. : ISBN 0-932140-07-6 (pbk.) LC Card 86-231757 DDC 361.7/025/73 19
HC800.Z9 E444 1986

NON-GOVERNMENTAL ORGANIZATIONS - CONGRESSES.
Global Meeting on Environment and Development for Non-governmental Organisations (1985 : Nairobi, Kenya) Sustainable development . [Nairobi, Kenya] [1985 or 1986] 109 p. : LC Card 86-981176 DDC 363.7/057 19
HC79.E5 G595 1985

NON-GOVERNMENTAL ORGANIZATIONS - DEVELOPING COUNTRIES.
Hellinger, Steve. Aid for just development . Washington, D.C. (1010 Vermont Ave., N.W., Suite 521, Washington 20005) , c1987. vii, 191 p. ; LC Card 87-404422 DDC 338.91/09172/4 19
HC60 .H38516 1987

Schneider, Bertrand. La révolution aux pieds nus . Paris , c1985. 344 p. ; ISBN 2-213-01684-4 : LC Card 86-179661
HC60 .S314 1985

NON-GOVERNMENTAL ORGANIZATIONS - GERMANY (WEST)
Kress, Roland, 1961- Die politischen Stiftungen in der Entwicklungspolitik . Bochum , 1985. iv, 224 p. ; ISBN 3-88339-426-2 : LC Card 85-175519
HC60 .K727 1985

Non-intelligent terminal market in the U. S. New York, N.Y. : Frost & Sullivan, c1983. vi, 197 p. : ill. ; 29 cm. "February 1983." "#A1160." LC Card 87-143735 DDC 381/.456213985/0973 19
1. Computer industry - United States. 2. Computer terminals. 3. Market surveys - United States. I. Frost & Sullivan.
HD9696.C63 U52637 1983

Noninvasive cardiovascular and cardiorespiratory diagnostic devices (U. S. and international). 1st revision. Tustin, CA (17722 Irvine Blvd., Tustin 92680) : Biomedical Business International, c1986. 1 v. (various pagings) : ill. ; 29 cm. (Report / Biomedical Business International . #7045) "August 1986." LC Card 87-101739 DDC 380.1/45681761 19
1. Cardiovascular equipment industry - United States. 2. Cardiovascular equipment industry. 3. Market surveys - United States. 4. Market surveys. I. Series: Report (Biomedical Business International, Inc.) , #7045.
HD9995.C363 U65 1986

Nonlinear economic dynamics / edited by Jean-Michel Grandmont. Boston : Academic Press, c1987. xiii, 195 p. : ill. ; 24 cm. (Economic theory, econometrics, and mathematical economics) "Presented or circulated at a conference held in Paris in June 1985 and were first published as an issue of the Journal of economic theory, vol. 40, no. 1, October 1986, pages 1-196"--Pref. Includes bibliographies. ISBN 0-12-295140-9 (alk. paper) LC Card 86-32129 DDC 338.5/442/0151 19
1. Business cycles - Mathematical models - Congresses. 2. Economics - Mathematical models - Congresses. I. Grandmont, Jean-Michel.
HB3711 .N655 1987

Non-manipulative selling /. Alessandra, Anthony J. New York , c1987. x, 262 p. : ISBN 0-13-623307-4 (pbk.) : LC Card 86-43174 DDC 658.8/5 19
HF5438.25 .A43 1987

Nonmanipulative selling. Alessandra, Anthony J. Non-manipulative selling [sound recording] . Chicago, Ill. , p1985. 6 sound cassettes : LC Card 86-754983
HF5438.25

Non-manipulative selling [sound recording] . Alessandra, Anthony J. Chicago, Ill. , p1985. 6 sound cassettes : LC Card 86-754983
HF5438.25

Nonmanufacturing Arkansas staffing patterns. Occupational employment statistics program . [Little Rock, Ark.] (P.O. Box 2981, Little Rock 72203) [1986] v leaves, 223 p. ; LC Card 87-620868 DDC 331.12/51/0009767021 19
HD5725.A8 O264 1986

Nono recenseamento geral do Brasil--1980. Inquéritos especiais /. Rio de Janeiro, Brasil , 1984. 4 v. in 5. ; ***NYPL [JLF 86-202]***

NONPRESCRIPTION DRUG INDUSTRY - UNITED STATES.
Geriatrics OTC health aid and toiletries products market-U. S. New York, N.Y. , c1983. 2 v. (viii, 352 leaves) ; LC Card 87-144078 DDC 381/.456151/0973 19
HD9666.5 .G47 1983

The OTC internal medications market. New York, N.Y. (106 Fulton St., New York 10038), c1983. a-d, iii, 279 p. ; LC Card 87-142032
HD9666.5 .O8 1983

NONPROFIT CORPORATIONS. see **CORPORATIONS, NONPROFIT.**

The nonprofit economy /. Weisbrod, Burton Allen, 1931- Cambridge, Mass. , 1988. p. cm. ISBN 0-674-62625-7 (alk. paper) LC Card 87-23718 DDC 338.7/4 19
HD2769.2.U6 W45 1988

Nonprofit organizational effectiveness study : early stage discussion paper. Washington, D.C. (1828 L St., N.W., Washington 20036) : Independent Sector, c1986. v, 125 p. ; 28 cm. "A study being conducted by the Effective Sector Leadership/Management Program of Independent Sector"--Cover. "October 1986." Bibliography: p. 109-125. LC Card 87-141542 DDC 658/.048 19
1. Organizational effectiveness. 2. Corporations, Nonprofit - Management. I. Independent Sector (Firm). Effective Sector Leadership/Management Program.
HD31 .N57 1986

Nonprofit organizations, a government management tool / edited by Harold Orlans ; foreword by George H. Esser ; contributors, Martha Derthick ... [et al.]. New York : Praeger, 1980. xxi, 173 p. ; 24 cm. Papers from a conference sponsored by the National Academy of Public Administration. Includes bibliographical references and index. ISBN 0-03-053966-8 : LC Card 79-23632 DDC 350 19
1. Research and development contracts, Government - United States. 2. Social sciences - Research - United States. 3. Corporations, Nonprofit - United States. I. Orlans, Harold, 1921-. II. Derthick, Martha. III. National Academy of Public Administration.
JK468.R45 N66 ***NYPL [JLE 80-1874]***

The nonprofit sector and the new federal budget /. Abramson, Alan J. Washington, D.C. , c1986. xviii, 138 p. : ISBN 0-87766-401-3 (pbk.) : LC Card 87-154012 DDC 361.7/63/0973 19
HJ2052 .A54 1986

Nonprofit Sector Project (Urban Institute)
Abramson, Alan J. The nonprofit sector and the new federal budget /. Washington, D.C. , c1986. xviii, 138 p. : ISBN 0-87766-401-3 (pbk.) : LC Card 87-154012 DDC 361.7/63/0973 19
HJ2052 .A54 1986

Altschuler, David M. New York nonprofit organizations . Washington, D.C. (2100 M St., N.W., Washington 20037) , c1987. vii, 43 p. : LC Card 87-159600 DDC 658.1/5 19
HD2769.2.U6 A48 1987

Government spending and the nonprofit sector in [name of community]. Washington, D.C. , <c1984-c1985. v. <1-11 > ; LC Card 87-168173 DDC 339.5/22/0973 19
HJ2052 .G67 1984

The [Name of community] nonprofit sector in a time of government retrenchment. Washington,

D.C. , c1984-<c1986. v. <1-2, 5-6, 9-11, 13-15 > : LC Card 87-167661 DDC 338.7/4/0973 19
HG4061 .N36 1984

Salamon, Lester M. Rhode Island nonprofit organizations . Washington, D.C. , Providence, RI , c1987. vii, 40 p. : LC Card 87-148803 DDC 338.7/4/09745 19
HD2769.2.U6 S25 1987

Salamon, Lester M. San Francisco Bay Area nonprofit organizations . Washington, D.C. (2100 M St., N.W., Washington 20037) , c1987. vi, 26 p. : LC Card 87-403000 DDC 338.7/4/0979461 19
HJ9205.S3 S34 1987

NONPROLIFERATION, NUCLEAR. see **NUCLEAR NONPROLIFERATION.**

NONRENEWABLE NATURAL RESOURCES.
Randall, Alan, 1944- Resource economics . New York , c1987. xiii, 434 p. ; ISBN 0-471-87468-X LC Card 87-4988 DDC 333.7 19
HC59 .R256 1987

Sauermann, Heinz. Theorie und Politik nichtregenerierbarer natürlicher Ressourcen /. Frankfurt am Main , c1982. viii, 251 p. : ISBN 3-88129-573-9 : LC Card 83-126048
HC55 .S26 1982

NONRENEWABLE NATURAL RESOURCES - CONGRESSES.
Natural resources and the macroeconomy /. Oxford, UK , 1986. xvi, 352 p. : ISBN 0-631-15087-0 LC Card 86-673943
HC59 .N3194x 1986b

NONRENEWABLE NATURAL RESOURCES - ECONOMETRIC MODELS.
Schäfer, Martin, 1951- Resource extraction and market structure /. Berlin , New York , c1986. ix, 154 p. : ISBN 0-387-16081-7 (U. S.) LC Card 86-1786 DDC 333.7/0973 19
HC59 .S344 1986 ***NYPL [JLM 72-289 no.263]***

NONRENEWABLE NATURAL RESOURCES - MANAGEMENT - MATHEMATICAL MODELS.
Müller, Karl-Wilhelm, 1953- Die Theorie erschöpfbarer natürlicher Ressourcen bei wachsender Bevölkerung /. Frankfurt am Main , New York , c1984. 191 p. : ISBN 3-8204-5315-6 LC Card 85-197540
HD75.6 .M85 1984

NONRENEWABLE NATURAL RESOURCES - MATHEMATICAL MODELS.
Angebotsentwicklung und Preisbildung natürlicher Ressourcen /. München , 1986. vii, 148, 10 p. : ISBN 3-486-26171-1 LC Card 86-182074
HC59 .A794 1986

Ströbele, Wolfgang. Wirtschaftswachstum bei begrenzten Energieressourcen /. Berlin , c1984. 173 p. : ISBN 3-428-05541-1 LC Card 84-176734
HD84 .S747 1984

Thimrén, Claes. Imperfectly competitive markets for exhaustible resources . Stockholm, Sweden [1986] 94 p. : ISBN 91-7258-212-X (pbk.) LC Card 87-151530 DDC 333.7/0724 19
HB238 .T54 1986

Toward a new Iron Age? . Cambridge, Mass. , 1987. vi, 173 p. : ISBN 0-674-89818-4 (alk. paper) LC Card 86-22923 DDC 333.8/5 19
HC59 .T63 1987

Withagen, Cees, 1950- Economic theory and international trade in natural exhaustible resources /. Berlin , New York , 1985. vi, 172 p. : ISBN 0-387-15970-3 LC Card 85-22101 DDC 333.7 19
HC59 .W55 1985 ***NYPL [JLM 72-289 no.253]***

Nontariff barriers . Oppenheimer, Michael F. Boulder , 1987. xiii, 203 p. ; ISBN 0-8133-7403-0 (pbk. : alk. paper) LC Card 87-50073 DDC 338.4/762/000973 19
HC110.H53 O66 1987

NONTARIFF DISTORTIONS OF TRADE. see **NONTARIFF TRADE BARRIERS.**

NONTARIFF TRADE BARRIERS.
Foreign regulations affecting U. S. textile/apparel exports. [Washington, D.C.] [1986] 283 p. ; LC Card 86-601588
HF2651.T42 F67 1986

Jaeschke, Hans-Dieter. Nicht-tarifäre Instrumente der Agrarhandelspolitik . Münster-Hiltrup , 1986. 187 p. ; ISBN 3-7843-0326-9 LC Card 87-408954 DDC 382/.3 19
HD9000.5 .J33 1986

NONTARIFF TRADE BARRIERS - BRAZIL.
Green, Ronald D. Brazilian government support for the aerospace industry /. [Washington, D.C.?] [1987] xi, 44 p. ; LC Card 87-601479 DDC 338.4/76291/0981 19
HD9711.B72 G74 1987

NONTARIFF TRADE BARRIERS - CASE STUDIES.
Oppenheimer, Michael F. Nontariff barriers . Boulder , 1987. xiii, 203 p. ; ISBN 0-8133-7403-0 (pbk. : alk. paper) LC Card 87-50073 DDC 338.4/762/000973 19
HC110.H53 O66 1987

NONTARIFF TRADE BARRIERS - DEVELOPING COUNTRIES.
Ohlinger, Hans A., 1954- Die Relevanz nicht-tarifärer Handelshemmnisse im internationalen Handel und ihre Wirkungen auf die Integration der Entwicklungsländer in die Weltwirtschaft /. Frankfurt am Main , New York , c1986. iii, 400 p. : ISBN 3-8204-8344-6 LC Card 87-407585 DDC 382/.5/091724 19
HF1430 .O38 1986

NONTARIFF TRADE BARRIERS - EAST ASIA.
Unfair foreign trade practices . Washington , 1986. v, 27 p. ; LC Card 86-603374 DDC 382/.0973/05 19
HF3126.5 .U53 1986

NONTARIFF TRADE BARRIERS - KOREA (REPUBLIC)
Luedde-Neurath, Richard. Import controls and export-oriented development . Boulder , 1986. xiv, 249 p. ; ISBN 0-8133-7080-9 : LC Card 85-10459 DDC 382/.3/095195 19
HF1602.5 .L84 1985 ***NYPL [JLE 86-1557]***

Nonverbal communication in advertising / edited by Sid Hecker, David W. Stewart. Lexington, Mass. : Lexington Books, c1988. viii, 296 p. : ill. ; 24 cm. Papers from a conference held in New York in May 1986 and jointly by the Division of Consumer Psychology, American Psychological Association, the Marketing Science Institute, and Young and Rubicam. Bibliography: p. [265]-290. ISBN 0-669-14172-0 (alk. paper) LC Card 87-17143 DDC 659.1/01/9 19
1. Advertising - Psychological aspects. 2. Nonverbal communication (Psychology). I. Hecker, Sid. II. Stewart, David W. III. American Psychological Association. Division of Consumer Psychology. IV. Marketing Science Institute. V. Young and Rubicam.
HF5822 .N66 1988

NONWOVEN FABRICS INDUSTRY.
Boon, Gerard Karel. El mercado de tecnología . México, D.F. , 1984, c1983. 715 p. : ISBN 968-12-0252-X LC Card 85-242124
HD9929.2.A2 B66 1984

Noonan, Amanda. Hartley, Jill. New electronic information services . Aldershot, Hants, England , Brookfield, Vt., USA , c1987. 147 p. : ISBN 0-566-05489-2 (pbk.) : LC Card 87-23600 DDC 338.4/700574/0941 19
HD9696.D364 G74 1987

Noort, W. C. J. van, 1950- Statistiek voor marketingsbeslissingen / W.C.J. van Noort. Leiden : Stenfert Kroese, 1985. viii, 229 p. : ill. ; 23 cm. Includes index. ISBN 90-207-1351-5 : LC Card 85-214756
1. Marketing research - Statistical methods. 2. Marketing research - Netherlands. 3. Marketing - Netherlands - Decision making. 4. Commercial statistics. I. Title.
HF5415.2 .N66 1985

Norback, Craig T. VGM's careers encyclopedia /. Lincolnwood, Ill., U. S.A. , c1988. xi, 484 p. ; ISBN 0-8442-6132-7 LC Card 87-62404 DDC 331.7/02/0973 19
HF5382.5.U5 C337 1988

Norbye, Ole David Koht, 1919- Chowdhury, Ashraf U. Norway's commodity assistance and import support to Bangladesh . [Oslo, Norway] [1986] 83 p. : LC Card 87-150872 DDC 338.91/481/05492 19
HC440.8 .C48 1986

Nord-Atlantik-Pakt-Organisation. see **North Atlantic Treaty Organization.**

Nord, Philip, 1950- Paris shopkeepers and the politics of resentment / Philip G. Nord. Princeton, N.J. : Princeton University Press, c1986. xvii, 539 p. : ill. ; 23 cm. Includes index. Bibliography: p. 497-518. ISBN 0-691-05454-1 : LC Card 85-42695 DDC 322/.3/0944361 19
1. Merchants - France - Paris - Political activity - History - 19th century. 2. Stores, Retail - France - Paris - History - 19th century. 3. Paris - Politics and government. I. Title.
HF5429.6.F7 N67 1986 ***NYPL [JLD 86-2305]***

Nord-Rüdiger, Dietlinde. Kraak, Bernhard. Berufliche Motivation und berufliches Verhalten . Göttingen , c1984. i, 145 p. ; ISBN 3-8017-0218-9 LC Card 85-100278
HF5549.5.M63 K73 1984

Nord, Stephen. Sheets, Robert G. The impact of service industries on underemployment in metropolitan economies /. Lexington, Mass. , c1987. xii, 185 p. ; ISBN 0-669-14575-0 (alk. paper) LC Card 86-45884 DDC 331.13 19
HD5709.2.U6 S54 1987

Norden, Gilbert. Einkommensgerechtigkeit, was darunter verstanden wird : eine Erkundungsstudie / Gilbert Norden. Wien : H. Böhlau, 1985. 304 p. : ill. ; 21 cm. (Studien zur qualitativen Sozialforschung . Bd. 5) Bibliography: p. 265-277. ISBN 3-205-06324-4 LC Card 86-196913
1. Distributive justice. 2. Income distribution - Austria. I. Title. II. Series.
HB523 .N67 1985

Nordeste/Bahia. Avena Filho, Armando. Nordeste e Bahia . Salvador , 1986. 196 p. ; LC Card 87-403867 DDC 338.981/42 19
HC188.B3 A94 1986

Nordeste e Bahia . Avena Filho, Armando. Salvador , 1986. 196 p. ; LC Card 87-403867 DDC 338.981/42 19
HC188.B3 A94 1986

Nordeste, estatísticas. [S.l.] : Escritório Técnico de Estudos Econômicos do Nordeste, Banco do Nordeste do Brasil, [195-] iv, 50 leaves : ill. ; 28 cm. (Banco do Nordeste do Brasil S.A. . 4) Cover title. Chiefly tables. Includes bibliographical references. LC Card 85-127235
1. Brazil, Northeast - Economic conditions - Statistics. 2. Brazil, Northeast - Social conditions - Statistics. I. Banco do Nordeste do Brasil. Escritório Técnico de Estudos Econômicos do Nordeste. II. Series.
HC188.N6 N69 1950z

Nordfors, Lennart. Makten hälsan och vinsten : politik från arbetarskydd till arbetsmiljö / Lennart Nordfors. Lund, Sweden : Studentlitteratur, c1985. 195 p. : ill. ; 23 cm. (Politik som rationellt handlande . 10) Politisk orientering Summary in English. Bibliography: p. 189-195. ISBN 91-44-23331-0 : LC Card 85-204849
1. Industrial safety - Sweden. 2. Industrial safety - Law and legislation - Sweden. 3. Work environment - Government policy - Sweden. I. Title. II. Series.
HD7732 .N66 1985

Nordia .
(v. 15, no. 2) Policies of population redistribution /. Oulu , 1981. 199 p. : ISBN 951-675-071-0 (pbk.) LC Card 83-148782 DDC 304.8 19
HB1952 .P65 1981

Nordisk arealklassifikation / Nordiska utskottet för miljöstatistik. København : Nordisk statistisk sekretariat, [1985] 19 p. ; 25 cm. (Tekniske rapporter, 0106-9039 . 39) ISBN 87-88083-23-3 LC Card 86-162708
1. Land use - Scandinavia - Classification. I. Nordiska utskottet för miljöstatistik. II. Series.
HD730 .N67 1985

Nordiska Afrikainstitutet.
Research report.
(no. 65. 65) Sano, Hans-Otto. The political economy of food in Nigeria 1960-1982 . Uppsala , 1983. 108 p. : ISBN 91-7106-210-6
NYPL [JLD 84-860]

Nordiska ämbetsmannakommittén för transportfrågor. Arbejdsgruppen vedrørende cykeltrafik. Cykeltrafik i nordiske byer /. København , 1982. 207 p. : ISBN 87-7303-045-7

LC Card 83-242616
HE5739.S34 C94 1982

Nordiska utskottet för miljöstatistik. Nordisk arealklassifikation /. København [1985] 19 p. ; ISBN 87-88083-23-3 LC Card 86-162708
HD730 .N67 1985

Nordkalottens produktregister, utbudskatalog : Norrbottens län. Luleå : Nordkalottens handelskonsult, [1982] 90 p. ; 30 cm. (Nordkalottkommitténs publikationsserie, 0348-8608 . 14a) Cover title. LC Card 83-227269
1. Norrbottens län (Sweden) - Commerce - Directories. I. Nordkalottkommittén. II. Series.
HF5206.N67 N67 1982

Nordkalottkommittén. Nordkalottens produktregister, utbudskatalog . Luleå [1982] 90 p. ; LC Card 83-227269
HF5206.N67 N67 1982

Nordkalottkommitténs publikationsserie, 0348-8608 .
(14a) Nordkalottens produktregister, utbudskatalog . Luleå [1982] 90 p. ; LC Card 83-227269
HF5206.N67 N67 1982

Nordlie, Peter G. Airport transportation . Arlington, Va. , Washington, D.C. [1961] vii, 289, 42 leaves : LC Card 84-132332
HE9797.4.A2 A38 1961

Nordmann-Werner, Karin, 1945- Kompetenzvermittlung durch Sachliteratur : Probleme der Wissenschaftsvermittlung untersucht am Beispiel von Wirtschaftssachbuchtexten / Karin Nordmann-Werner. Frankfurt am Main ; New York : Lang, c1984. 391 p. ; 21 cm. (Europäische Hochschulschriften. Reihe XXI, Linguistik, 0721-3352 . Bd. 23 = vol. 23 = vol. 23) Bibliography: p. 379-382. ISBN 3-8204-5278-8 LC Card 85-193184
1. Economics - Germany (West) - Textbooks. 2. Economics - Study and teaching - Germany, West. I. Title.
HB74.9.G3 N67 1984

Nordrhein Westfälisches Staatsarchiv Münster. Mark (Grafschaft) Schatzbuch der Grafschaft Mark, 1486 /. Unna , 1986. 176 p. ; ISBN 3-87298-042-4 LC Card 87-116701 DDC 336.2/00943/55 19
HJ2110.5.M36 M37 1986

Nörenberg, Günther. Planwirtschaft im Zerrspiegel des Linksradikalismus / Günther Nörenberg. Berlin : Verlag Die Wirtschaft, 1984. 108 p. ; 22 cm. (Beiträge zur kritik der bürgerlichen Ideologie und des Revisionismus) Includes bibliographical references. LC Card 84-196372
1. Economic policy. 2. Central planning. 3. Radicalism. 4. Communism. 5. Socialism. I. Title.
HC59 .N652 1984

NORFOLK SOUTHERN CORPORATION. New York (State). Legislature. Legislative Commission on Critical Transportation Choices. Conrail . [Albany] [1986] i, 134 p. ; LC Card 87-620569 DDC 385/.065/73 19
HE2791.C899 N48 1986

Norge. see **Norway.**

Norge--E.F., økonomisk samarbeid. Norge--EF, økonomisk samarbeid. [Oslo] [1981] 45 p. ; ISBN 82-7177-111-6 LC Card 84-167865
HC241.25.N7 N55 1981

Norge--EF, økonomisk samarbeid. [Oslo] : Kongelige Utenriksdepartement, [1981] 45 p. ; 22 cm. (Aktuelle utenrikspolitiske spørsmål . nr. 8 (des. 1981)) ISBN 82-7177-111-6 LC Card 84-167865
1. European Economic Community - Norway. I. Norway. Kgl. Utenriksdepartement. II. Title: Norge--E.F., økonomisk samarbeid. III. Series. IV. Series: Aktuelle utenrikspolitiske spørsmål , nr. 8.
HC241.25.N7 N55 1981

Norge mot Europa? . Jørgensen, Nils-Johan. København , 1982. 250 p. ; ISBN 87-87733-30-7 : LC Card 82-172919
HC241.25.N7 J67 1982

Norges offentlige utredninger .
(1982:24) Norway. Utvalg for delutredning om industrielle mineraler. Industrimineraler . Oslo [1982] 134 p. : ISBN 82-00-70754-7 LC Card 83-123304
HD9506.N72 N67 1982
(1983:16) Organiseringen av statens deltagelse i petroleumsvirksomheten /. Oslo [1983] 44 p. : ISBN 82-00-70798-9 LC Card 83-244370
HD9575.N62 O74 1983
(1983:21) Næringslivets utviklingsmuligheter i innlandet /. Oslo [1983] 291 p. : ISBN 82-00-70803-9 LC Card 83-237323
HC365 .N32 1983
(1983:27) Norway. "Tempo-utvalget." Petroleumsvirksomhetens framtid . Oslo [1983] 167 p. : ISBN 82-00-70810-1 LC Card 83-235609
HD9575.N62 N6855 1983
(1983:52) Forsikring i Norge /. Oslo [1983] 226 p. ; ISBN 82-00-70870-5 LC Card 84-158459
HG8668.5 .F67 1983

Norges offisielle statistikk .
(B 510) Kvartalsvis nasjonalregnskap 1978-1983 =. Oslo , 1984. 99 p. ; ISBN 82-537-2143-9 : LC Card 85-223735
HA1501 B, nr. 510 HC370.I5

Norges teknisk-naturvitenskapelige forskningsråd. (Old Catalog form: Norway. Det Teknisk-naturvitenskapelige forskningsråd)
Killi, Egil.
Transportproblemer, -politikk, -forskning og -undervisning i USA. Slemdal, 1968. 65, 3, 5 l. LC Card 75-408744
HE203 .K5 ***NYPL [JLF 86-617]***

Norkett, P. T. C. Guide to company information in Great Britain / Paul Norkett. Burnt Mill, Harlow, Essex, U.K. : Longman Group in association with ICC Information Group, c1986. xi, 208 p. : ill. ; 24 cm. ISBN 0-582-97820-3 (pbk.) : LC Card 86-220140 DDC 338.7/4/072041 19
1. Corporations - Great Britain - Information services. I. Title.
HD2845 .N67 1986

Norlin, Bo. Bjørklund, Tor, 1947- Mot strømmen . Oslo , c1982. 396 p. : ISBN 82-00-06338-0 : LC Card 83-134961
HC241.25.N7 B56 1982

La normalisation, clé d'un nouvel essor . Germon, Claude. Paris , c1983. 156 p. ; ISBN 2-11-001026-6 : LC Card 83-217768
HD3616.F83 G47 1983

Norman, George, 1946- Greenhut, Melvin L. The economics of imperfect competition . Cambridge [Cambridgeshire] , New York , 1987. xix, 408 p. : ISBN 0-521-30552-7 LC Card 86-11707 DDC 338.6/048 19
HB238 .G74 1987 ***NYPL [JLE 87-1413]***

Norman, Neville R. The economics of personal tax escalation in Australia / Neville R. Norman. [Sydney] : Committee for Economic Development of Australia ; Sydney ; xii, 173 p. : ill. ; 22 cm. (Research study . P24) "CEDA study." Includes index. Bibliography: p. 164-166. ISBN 0-86861-652-4 (pbk.) LC Card 84-72057 DDC 336.24/2/0994 19
1. Income tax - Australia. 2. Fiscal policy - Australia. I. Series: Research study (Committee for Economic Development of Australia) , P24. II. Title.
HJ4802 .N67 1985 ***NYPL [JLD 86-1906]***

Normante y Carcavilla, Lorenzo.
Discurso sobre la utilidad de los conocimientos económico-políticos y la necesidad de su estudio metódico ; Proposiciones de economía civil y comercio ; Espíritu del señor Melón en su ensayo político sobre el comercio / Lorenzo Normante y Carcavilla ; edición a cargo de Antonio Peiró Arroyo. [Aragón] : Diputación General de Aragón, Departamento de Economía y Hacienda : Diputación General de Aragón, Departamento de Cultura y Educación, [1984?] 1 v. (various pagings) ; 20 cm. (Colección Biblioteca economistas aragoneses . 1) Includes bibliographical references and indexes. ISBN 84-505-0473-2 LC Card 87-104302
1. Spain - Economic policy - Study and teaching - History - 18th century. 2. Spain - Commercial policy - Study and teaching - History - 18th century. 3. Economics - Spain - History - 18th century. 4. Spain - Commerce - History - 18th century. I. Normante y Carcavilla, Lorenzo. Proposiciones de economía civil y comercio. 1984. II. Normante y Carcavilla, Lorenzo. Espíritu del señor Melón en su ensayo político sobre el comercio. 1984. III. Peiró Arroyo, Antonio. IV. Title. V. Title: Discurso sobre la utilidad de los conocimientos económico-políticos y la necesidad de su estudio metódico. VI. Title: Proposiciones de economía civil y comercio. VII. Title: Espíritu del señor Melón en su ensayo político sobre el comercio. VIII. Series.
HC385 .N57 1984

Espíritu del señor Melón en su ensayo político sobre el comercio. 1984. Normante y Carcavilla, Lorenzo. Discurso sobre la utilidad de los conocimientos económico-políticos y la necesidad de su estudio metódico ; Proposiciones de economía civil y comercio ; Espíritu del señor Melón en su ensayo político sobre el comercio / Lorenzo Normante y Carcavilla ; edición a cargo de Antonio Peiró Arroyo. [Aragón] [1984?] 1 v. (various pagings) ; ISBN 84-505-0473-2 LC Card 87-104302
HC385 .N57 1984

Proposiciones de economía civil y comercio. 1984. Normante y Carcavilla, Lorenzo. Discurso sobre la utilidad de los conocimientos económico-políticos y la necesidad de su estudio metódico ; Proposiciones de economía civil y comercio ; Espíritu del señor Melón en su ensayo político sobre el comercio / Lorenzo Normante y Carcavilla ; edición a cargo de Antonio Peiró Arroyo. [Aragón] [1984?] 1 v. (various pagings) ; ISBN 84-505-0473-2 LC Card 87-104302
HC385 .N57 1984

Normen voor nieuwwaarde en afschrijving van slijtende duurzame produktiemiddelen in de fruitteelt alsmede voor de grondwaarde : prijspeil 1984 en 1985. Den Haag : Landbouw-Economisch Instituut, [1986] 67 p. ; 30 cm. (Interne nota / Landbouw-Economisch Instituut . 330) "Augustus 1986." LC Card 86-234475
1. Fruit trade - Netherlands - Accounting. 2. Depreciation. 3. Economic life (of economic goods). I. Landbouw-Economisch Instituut (Netherlands). II. Series: Interne nota , 330.
HF5686.F7 N67 1986

Normengeleitetes Verhalten in den Sozialwissenschaften / von Dietrich Dörner ... [et al.] ; herausgegeben von Horst Todt. Berlin : Duncker & Humblot, c1984. 199 p. ; 24 cm. (Schriften des Vereins für Socialpolitik, Gesellschaft für Wirtschafts- und Sozialwissenschaften . n.F., Bd. 141) Papers presented at two meetings of the Sozialwissenschaftlicher Ausschuss of the Gesellschaft für Wirtschafts- und Sozialwissenschaften (Verein für Socialpolitik) held in 1982 and 1983. Includes bibliographies and indexes. CONTENTS. - Formale Konzepte eingeschränkt rationalen Verhaltens / von Angela Klopstech und Reinhard Selten -- Egoismus und Altruismus / von Werner Güth -- Cognitive dissonance in economics / von Ekkehart Schlicht -- Normen, Altruismus und politische Partizipation / von Karl-Dieter Opp -- "Unsichtbare-Hand Erklärung" und soziale Normen / von Viktor Vanberg -- Die Regulation von Unbestimmtheit und die Dynamik von Loyalitätsbeziehungen / von Dietrich Dörner -- Normen und die Allokation sozialer Wertschätzung / von Siegwart Lindenberg. ISBN 3-428-05622-1 LC Card 86-140299
1. Economics - Psychological aspects - Congresses. 2. Sociology - Congresses. I. Dörner, Dietrich. II. Todt, Horst. III. Gesellschaft für Wirtschafts- und Sozialwissenschaften, Verein für Socialpolitik. Sozialwissenschaftlicher Ausschuss. IV. Series.
HB74.P8 N67 1984

Normungsprobleme der Dritten Welt / O. Sturen ... [et al.]. Dortmund : Rhein-Ruhr Druck Sander, 1979. 98 p. ; 25 cm. (Arbeitsgemeinschaft für Rationalisierung des Landes Nordrhein-Westfalen, 0402-8066 . 201) Papers and discussions held at a working session of the Arbeitsgruppe Vereinheitlichung, Mar. 23, 1979. LC Card 85-239680
1. Standardization - Developing countries - Congresses. I. Sturen, O. (Ole). II. Arbeitsgemeinschaft für Rationalisierung des Landes Nordrhein-Westfalen. Arbeitsgruppe Vereinheitlichung. III. Series: Arbeitsgemeinschaft für Rationalisierung des Landes Nordrhein-Westfalen (Series) , 201.
HD30 .A7 Heft 201 T59.A1

Noroeste de México .
(no. 5) Radding, Cynthia. [Acumulación originaria de capital agrario en Sonora.] La acumulación originaria de capital agrario en Sonora ; Registro de los archivos del Estado de Sonora /. [Hermosillo, Sonora] , 1981. 90 p. : LC Card 82-118209
HD329.S6 R33 1981

Norpoth, Helmut. Iversen, Gudmund R. Analysis of variance /. Newbury Park , c1987. 94 p. : ISBN 0-8039-3001-1 (pbk.) LC Card 87-61276 DDC 519.5/35 19
HA31.35 .I85 1987

NORRBOTTENS LÄN (SWEDEN) - COMMERCE - DIRECTORIES.
Nordkalottens produktregister, utbudskatalog . Luleå [1982] 90 p. ; LC Card 83-227269
HF5206.N67 N67 1982

Norris, Kenneth E. Winning at work : the road to career success / Kenneth E. Norris.1st ed. Blue Ridge Summit, PA : Liberty House, c1987. viii, 116 p. ; 22 cm. Includes index. ISBN 0-8306-3077-5 : LC Card 86-27359 DDC 650.1 19
1. Managing your boss. 2. Interpersonal relations. 3. Career development. 4. Success. I. Title.
HF5548.83 .N67 1987

NORRIS, WILLIAM C., 1911-
Worthy, James C. William C. Norris . Cambridge, Mass. , c1987. xiv, 259 p. : ISBN 0-88730-087-1 LC Card 87-1808 DDC 338.7/61004/0924 B 19
HD9696.C62 N689 1987

Nørrung, Per. The producing commune / Per Nørrung, Jens Kjeldsen, Martin Schultz. Aalborg Ø., Denmark : Forlaget Alfuff, 1985. 39 p. ; 22 cm. (Skrift / Forlaget Alfuff . nr. 2) ISBN 87-88353-11-7 (pbk.) LC Card 87-100060 DDC 334/.6/09489 19
1. Producer cooperatives - Denmark. 2. Communal living - Denmark. I. Kjeldsen, Jens. II. Schultz, Martin, 1950-. III. Series: Skrift (Forlaget Alfuff (Ålborg, Denmark)) , nr. 2. IV. Title.
HD3209.A4 N67 1985

NORSEMEN. see **NORTHMEN.**

Norsk boreriggeierforening. Norske vilkår for kaskoforsikring av borefartøyer og forsikring av utstyr og forsyninger til borefartøyer, med motiver. English. Norwegian conditions for hull insurance of drilling vessels and insurance of equipment and supplies for drilling vessels, with comments /. [Bergen] , 1977. 107 p. ; LC Card 84-199054
HE964.5.N6 N6713 1977

Norsk industris internasjonalisering, rettet mot utviklingslandene : industriseminar ved Chr. Michelsens institutt, 26. april 1982 / Kjell J. Havnevik og Arve Ofstad (red.). Bergen : Chr. Michelsens institutt, [1982] vi, 57 p. ; 30 cm. (DERAP publications = DERAP publikasjoner . nr. 149) CONTENTS. - Noen hovedtrekk i utviklingen av en ny internasjonal arbeidsdeling og erfaringer med norske industri-etableringer i u-land / Bjørn Pedersen Saga -- Hvilke rammebetingelser arbeides det med i FN og andre internasjonale organisasjoner, og kan disse få konsekvenser for norske bedrifters internasjonalisering? / Ole David Koht Norbye -- Hvilke tiltak kan og bør fagbevegelsen gjennomføre for å styre utviklingen av norsk industris internasjonalisering / Knut Sanden -- Internasjonalisering av norsk industri rettet mot utviklingslandene / Kjell-Martin Frederiksen -- Norske industrietableringer i utviklingsland / Kjell J. Havnevik og Arve Ofsted. LC Card 83-139811
1. Corporations, Norwegian - Developing countries - Congresses. I. Havnevik, Kjell J. II. Ofstad, Arve. III. Chr. Michelsens institutt. IV. Series: DERAP publications , no. 149.
HD2932 .N67 1982

Norsk oljeforsikringspool. Norske vilkår for kaskoforsikring av borefartøyer og forsikring av utstyr og forsyninger til borefartøyer, med motiver. English. Norwegian conditions for hull insurance of drilling vessels and insurance of equipment and supplies for drilling vessels, with comments /. [Bergen] , 1977. 107 p. ; LC Card 84-199054
HE964.5.N6 N6713 1977

Norsk produktivitetsinstitutt. Industrimakten Japan . Oslo , 1982. 151 p. : ISBN 82-518-1630-0 : LC Card 84-126986
HD70.J3 I549 1982

Norsk utenrikspolitisk institutt, Oslo. see **Oslo. Norsk utenrikspolitisk institutt.**

Den Norske kvinnerevolusjonen : kvinners arbeid 1975-85 / Kari Skrede og Kristin Tornes (red.). Oslo : Universitetsforlaget, c1986. 166 p. : ill. ; 22 cm. (Arbeid i 80-åra) Bibliography: p. 160-165. CONTENTS. - Kvinners plass i offentlig arbeidsmarkedspolitikk / av Kristin Tornes -- Velferdsstaten--det er kvinnene / av Randi Kjeldstad -- Velferd og lokal sysselsetting / av Anne Marie Stokken -- Si meg hvor du bor / av Olaf Foss -- Kjerringa mot strømmen og gutta i røyken / av Birgit Helene Jevnaker -- Fra formidling av arbeid til sertifisering for trygd / av Anne-Kathrine Broch-Due -- Roller i endring / av Gunvor Iversen. ISBN 82-00-18318-1 LC Card 87-155462
1. Women - Employment - Norway. 2. Feminism - Norway. I. Skrede, Kari. II. Tornes, Kristin. III. Series.
HD6170 .N68 1986

Norske vilkår for kaskoforsikring av borefartøyer og forsikring av utstyr og forsyninger til borefartøyer, med motiver. English.
Norwegian conditions for hull insurance of drilling vessels and insurance of equipment and supplies for drilling vessels, with comments / [prepared by a working group appointed by the Norwegian Association of Drilling Contractors and the Norwegian Oil Risk Pool]. [Bergen] : Norwegian Oil Risk Pool, 1977. 107 p. ; 28 cm. LC Card 84-199054
1. Insurance, Marine - Norway. 2. Insurance, Marine - Norway - Policies. I. Norsk boreriggeierforening. II. Norsk oljeforsikringspool.
HE964.5.N6 N6713 1977

O Norte cearense / Marlene Maria da Silva, coordenadora. Recife : Ministério do Interior, Superintendência do Desenvolvimento do Nordeste, Superintendência Adjunta de Planejamento, Coordenação de Planejamento Regional, Divisão de Política Espacial, 1985. 303 p. : ill., maps (some col.) ; 24 cm. (Série Estudos regionais . 12) Bibliography: p. 293-299. LC Card 86-209022
1. Agriculture - Economic aspects - Brazil - Ceará (State). 2. Agricultural geography - Brazil - Ceará (State). 3. Ceará (Brazil : State) - Population. 4. Land use, Rural - Brazil - Ceará (State). 5. Cities and towns - Brazil - Ceará (State). 6. Ceará, Brazil (State) - Industries. I. Silva, Marlene Maria da. II. Series.
HD1875.C4 N67 1985

NORTH AMERICA - ECONOMIC CONDITIONS - CONGRESSES.
Current economic and financial issues of the North American and Caribbean countries /. Mexico, D.F. , 1983. 390 p. : LC Card 87-106905 DDC 330.97/00539 19
HC95 .C87 1983

North American Economics and Finance Association. Current economic and financial issues of the North American and Caribbean countries /. Mexico, D.F. , 1983. 390 p. : LC Card 87-106905 DDC 330.97/00539 19
HC95 .C87 1983

NORTH AMERICAN INDIANS. see **INDIANS OF NORTH AMERICA.**

North American Telecommunications Association. Industry basics . Washington, D.C. (2000 M St., N.W., Suite 550, Washington 20036) , c1986. 53 p. : LC Card 86-208618 DDC 384.6/0973 19
HE8731 .I53 1986

North Atlantic Treaty Organization. Scientific Affairs Division. NATO Advanced Study Institute on Intelligent Decision Support in Process Environments (1985 : San Miniato, Italy) Intelligent decision support in process environments /. Berlin , New York , c1986. xv, 524 p. : ISBN 0-387-13922-2 (U. S.) LC Card 86-6742 DDC 658.4/03 19
T57.95 .N37 1985 ***NYPL [JFE 86-4847]***

North Brabant (Netherlands)
Begroting 1986 . ['s-Hertogenbosch] [1985] 91 p. ; LC Card 86-136324
HJ2128.5.N6 B44 1985

Prognose van het budget van de Provincie op middellange termijn (zgn. meerjarenramingen) behorende bij de Ontwerp-Provinciale Begroting 1982. ['s-Hertogenbosch] [1982?] 7, [52] p. ; LC Card 86-232148
HJ2128.5.N6 P76 1982

NORTH BRABANT (NETHERLANDS) - APPROPRIATIONS AND EXPENDITURES - FORECASTING.
Begroting 1986 . ['s-Hertogenbosch] [1985] 91 p. ; LC Card 86-136324
HJ2128.5.N6 B44 1985

Prognose van het budget van de Provincie op middellange termijn (zgn. meerjarenramingen) behorende bij de Ontwerp-Provinciale Begroting 1982. ['s-Hertogenbosch] [1982?] 7, [52] p. ; LC Card 86-232148
HJ2128.5.N6 P76 1982

NORTH CAROLINA - APPROPRIATIONS AND EXPENDITURES.
North Carolina. General Assembly. Fiscal Research Division. Overview, fiscal and budgetary actions . Raleigh, N.C. (Legislative Office Bldg., Raleigh 27611) [1986]. 248 p. : LC Card 87-620950 DDC 353.97560072/2 19
HJ2053.N8 N668 1986

NORTH CAROLINA - ECONOMIC CONDITIONS.
Piedmont Carolinas, where wealth awaits you. Charlotte, N.C. [1930?] 47 p. : LC Card 85-666462
HC107.N8 P53x 1930

North Carolina. General Assembly. Fiscal Research Division.
Fiscal facts / North Carolina General Assembly, Fiscal Research Division. [Raleigh] : The Division, 1986. 51 p. : ill. ; 23 cm. Cover title. LC Card 87-620951 DDC 336.756 19
1. Finance, Public - North Carolina - Statistics. I. Title.
HJ615 .N65 1986

Overview, fiscal and budgetary actions : North Carolina General Assembly 1986 session / prepared by the Fiscal Research Division of the North Carolina General Assembly. Raleigh, N.C. (Legislative Office Bldg., Raleigh 27611) : The Division, [1986]. 248 p. : ill. ; 29 cm. LC Card 87-620950 DDC 353.97560072/2 19
1. Budget - North Carolina. 2. North Carolina - Appropriations and expenditures. I. Title.
HJ2053.N8 N668 1986

North Central Texas Council of Governments. Transportation data book . Arlington, Tex. (P.O. Drawer COG, Arlington 76005-5888) , c1987. 101 leaves in various foliations : LC Card 87-152338 DDC 380.5/09764/2812 19
HE310.D25 T73 1987

NORTH DAKOTA - ECONOMIC CONDITIONS.
Coon, Randal C. North Dakota lignite industry's contribution to the state economy /. Fargo, N.D. [1986] v, 40 p. : LC Card 86-623006 DDC 338.2/722/09784 19
HD9559.L6 U5525 1986

North Dakota employment and wages, 1984 / prepared by Research and Statistics ; Dale R. Dehlin, primary researcher. Bismarck, N.D. (1000 E. Divide, Bismarck 58501) : Job Service North Dakota, [1985] [3], 13, 13 leaves ; 28 cm. "December 1985." LC Card 86-623005 DDC 331.12/5/09784021 19
1. Labor supply - North Dakota - Statistics. 2. Wages - North Dakota - Statistics. I. Dehlin, Dale R. II. Job Service North Dakota. Research and Statistics Section.
HD5725.N84 N73 1985

North Dakota lignite industry's contribution to the state economy /. Coon, Randal C. Fargo, N.D. [1986] v, 40 p. : LC Card 86-623006 DDC 338.2/722/09784 19
HD9559.L6 U5525 1986

North Dakota occupational profiles.
Finance, insurance, and real estate . Bismarck, N.D. (1000 E. Divide, Bismarck 58502) [1986] 55 p. : LC Card 86-623003 DDC 332.12/51/0009784 19
HD5718.B262 U64 1986

Mining, second quarter, 1984 /. Bismarck, N.D. (1000 E. Divide, Bismarck 58502) [1986] 43 p. : LC Card 86-623004 DDC 331.12/522/09784 19
HD8039.M5982 N675 1986

North Dakota. State Highway Dept. Planning Division. Federal, state, and local highway financing /. Bismarck, N.D. [1986] 33 leaves : LC Card 87-620924 DDC 388.1/14/09784 19
HE356.N9 F42 1986

North, Douglass Cecil. The economics of public issues / Douglass C. North, Roger LeRoy Miller. 7th ed. New York : Harper & Row, c1987. ix, 214 p. ; 21 cm. Includes bibliographical references and index. ISBN 0-06-044832-6 (pbk.) LC Card 86-33627 DDC 330.973/092 19
1. Economics. 2. Industry and state. 3. Economic policy. I. Miller, Roger LeRoy. II. Title.
HB34 .N6 1987

North-East India Council for Social Science Research.
Land reforms and peasant movement . New Delhi , Guwahati , c1986. xix, 232 p. ; LC Card 86-902255 DDC 333.3/1/541 19
HD1333.I42 N65 1986

The Pattern & problems of population in north-east India /. New Delhi , 1986. xv, 433 p. ; ISBN 81-85024-03-0 : LC Card 86-902123 DDC 304.6/0954/1 19
HA4587.I44 P37 1986

NORTH-EASTERN STATE (NIGERIA) - ECONOMIC CONDITIONS.
The North-Eastern State of Nigeria. [Nigeria? , 1968?] (Zaria : Gaskiya Corp.) 83 p. : LC Card 86-235207
HC1055.Z9 N676 1968

NORTH-EASTERN STATE (NIGERIA) - SOCIAL CONDITIONS.
The North-Eastern State of Nigeria. [Nigeria? , 1968?] (Zaria : Gaskiya Corp.) 83 p. : LC Card 86-235207
HC1055.Z9 N676 1968

The North-Eastern State of Nigeria. [Nigeria? : s.n., 1968?] (Zaria : Gaskiya Corp.) 83 p. : ill. (some col.), ports., col. map ; 22 cm. Cover title: This is the North Eastern State of Nigeria. LC Card 86-235207
1. North-Eastern State (Nigeria) - Economic conditions. 2. North-Eastern State (Nigeria) - Social conditions. I. Title: This is the North Eastern State of Nigeria.
HC1055.Z9 N676 1968

NORTH EASTERN TRADING ESTATES LTD.
Loebl, Herbert. Government factories and the origins of British regional policy, 1934-1948 . Aldershot, Hants, England , Brookfield, Vt., USA , c1987. p. cm. ISBN 0-566-05343-8 LC Card 87-23075 DDC 338.6/2/0941 19
HD4145 .L64 1987

North Holland (Netherlands) Milieubeleidsplan Noord-Holland 1982-1988 : evaluatie van activiteiten over 1985 en 1986 : prioriteitstelling geplande activiteiten 1987 tot 1991. [Haarlem] : Provincie Noord-Holland, [1987] 60 p. ; 30 cm. (Voordracht / Provinciale Staten van Noord-Holland . 69) "Begroting 1987." LC Card 87-159912
1. Environmental policy - Netherlands - North Holland. 2. Environmental protection - Netherlands - North Holland. I. Series: Voordracht , 69. II. Title.
HC327.N6 N67 1987

The North Kordofan rural water supply baseline survey /. Mohamed, Yagoub Abdalla. Khartoum , 1982. xv, 152 p. : LC Card 85-981166
HD1699.S82 K875 1982

NORTH RHINE-WESTPHALIA (GERMANY) - ECONOMIC CONDITIONS.
Kleinebeckel, Arno. Unternehmen Braunkohle . Köln , 1986. 287 p. : ISBN 3-7743-0225-1 LC Card 86-193426
HD9559.L6 G36 1986

"Die Menschen machen ihre Geschichte nicht aus freien Stücken, aber sie machen sie selbst" . Berlin [1984] 267 p. : ISBN 3-8012-0101-5 LC Card 84-204204
HC287.N6 M46 1984

Weimar, Robert. Die Umweltvorsorge im Rahmen der Landesplanung Nordrhein-Westfalen . Frankfurt am Main , New York , c1983. xxiii, 313 p. : ISBN 3-8204-7669-5 LC Card 83-206670
HC287.N6 W44 1983

NORTH RHINE-WESTPHALIA (GERMANY) - ECONOMIC CONDITIONS - CASE STUDIES.
Dick, Walter, 1949- Die ökonomische Bedeutung der Qualität des Schienengüterverkehrs . Berlin , c1980. xi, 331 p. : ISBN 3-428-04731-1 LC Card 84-130833
HE2446.N67 D52 1980

NORTH RHINE-WESTPHALIA (GERMANY) - ECONOMIC POLICY.
Landesentwicklungsplan VI . [Düsseldorf] [1977] [4] p., [17] leaves of plates : LC Card 86-105018
HC287.N6 L28 1977

NORTH RHINE-WESTPHALIA (GERMANY) - ECONOMIC POLICY - MAPS.
Landesentwicklungsplan VI . [Düsseldorf] [1977] [4] p., [17] leaves of plates : LC Card 86-105018
HC287.N6 L28 1977

North Rhine-Westphalia (Germany). Finanzministerium. Finanzplanung des Landes Nordrhein-Westfalen 1986 bis 1990. Stand: August 1986. Düsseldorf : Finanzminister des Landes Nordrhein-Westfalen, [1986] iii, 27, [28] p. ; 30 cm. "Landtag Nordrhein-Westfalen, 10. Wahlperiode." LC Card 86-233121
1. Finance, Public - Germany (West) - North Rhine-Westphalia. I. North-Rhine-Westphalia (Germany). Landtag. II. Title.
HJ1150.N62 N62 1986

NORTH RHINE-WESTPHALIA (GERMANY) - INDUSTRIES - HISTORY.
Kleinebeckel, Arno. Unternehmen Braunkohle . Köln , 1986. 287 p. : ISBN 3-7743-0225-1 LC Card 86-193426
HD9559.L6 G36 1986

NORTH RHINE-WESTPHALIA (GERMANY) - INDUSTRIES - STATISTICS.
Zensus im Bergbau und verarbeitenden Gewerbe Nordrhein-Westfalen 1979 . Düsseldorf [1983] 109 p. ; LC Card 87-407314 DDC 943/.55 s 338.2/0943/55021 19
HA1320.N6 A32 Heft 497 HD9506.G23N6

North Rhine-Westphalia (Germany). Landesplanungsbehörde.
Landesentwicklungsplan VI . [Düsseldorf] [1977] [4] p., [17] leaves of plates : LC Card 86-105018
HC287.N6 L28 1977

North-Rhine-Westphalia (Germany). Landtag. North Rhine-Westphalia (Germany). Finanzministerium. Finanzplanung des Landes Nordrhein-Westfalen 1986 bis 1990. Düsseldorf [1986] iii, 27, [28] p. ; LC Card 86-233121
HJ1150.N62 N62 1986

NORTH RHINE-WESTPHALIA (GERMANY) - MANUFACTURES - STATISTICS.
Zensus im Bergbau und verarbeitenden Gewerbe Nordrhein-Westfalen 1979 . Düsseldorf [1983] 109 p. ; LC Card 87-407314 DDC 943/.55 s 338.2/0943/55021 19
HA1320.N6 A32 Heft 497 HD9506.G23N6

North Rhine-Westphalia (Germany). Ministerium für Arbeit, Gesundheit und Soziales. Jansen, Paul Günter. Arbeitsmarktatlas . [Düsseldorf] [1977] 206, A19 p. : LC Card 85-173256
HD5780.A76 J36 1977

North Rhine-Westphalia (Germany). Ministerium für Landes- und Stadtentwicklung. Ruhender Verkehr in Wohngebieten /. Dortmund , c1983, [1982] 121 p. : LC Card 83-236251
HE363.G32 P377 1983

NORTH RHINE-WESTPHALIA (GERMANY) - POPULATION - STATISTICS.
Vorausberechnung der Bevölkerung in den kreisfreien Städten und Kreisen Nordrhein-Westfalens . Düsseldorf [1983] 103 p. : LC Card 86-202728
HA1320.N6 A32 Heft 500

NORTH RHINE-WESTPHALIA (GERMANY) - SOCIAL CONDITIONS.
"Die Menschen machen ihre Geschichte nicht aus freien Stücken, aber sie machen sie selbst" . Berlin [1984] 267 p. : ISBN 3-8012-0101-5 LC Card 84-204204
HC287.N6 M46 1984

NORTH RHINE-WESTPHALIA (GERMANY) - SOCIAL LIFE AND CUSTOMS.
"Die Menschen machen ihre Geschichte nicht aus freien Stücken, aber sie machen sie selbst" . Berlin [1984] 267 p. : ISBN 3-8012-0101-5 LC Card 84-204204
HC287.N6 M46 1984

North Rhine-Westphalia. Institut für Landes- und Stadtentwicklungsforschung. see **Institut für Landes- und Stadtentwicklungsforschung des Landes Nordrhein-Westfalen.**

North Sea Oil Panel occasional paper .
(no. 12 12) Way of life . London [1980?] 84 p. ; ISBN 0-86226-076-0 (pbk.) LC Card 82-218547 DDC 304.8 19
HD9571.7.S36 W39 1980
NYPL [JLD 85-427]

North/south countertrade . Jones, Stephen F. London , c1984. 97 p. : LC Card 85-239985 DDC 382/.091722/01724 19
HF1414.3 .J65 1984

North-South dialogue at the beginning of the 1980's. Der Nord-Süd-Dialog zu Beginn der 80er Jahre =. Baden-Baden , 1982. 99 p. ; ISBN 3-7890-0774-9 ***NYPL [JLE 87-1282]***

NORTH-WEST PROVINCE (CAMEROON) - COMMERCE.
Discover the North West of Cameroon . [Bamenda? , 1984] 197 p., [2] p. of plates : LC Card 87-101117 DDC 330.967/11204 19
HC995.Z7 N673 1984

NORTH-WEST PROVINCE (CAMEROON) - ECONOMIC CONDITIONS.
Discover the North West of Cameroon . [Bamenda? , 1984] 197 p., [2] p. of plates : LC Card 87-101117 DDC 330.967/11204 19
HC995.Z7 N673 1984

Northcott, Jim. Knetsch, Werner. Die industrielle Anwendung der Mikroelektronik in der Bundesrepublik Deutschland, Frankreich, Grossbritannien . Haar bei München , c1985. 142 p. : ISBN 3-89090-121-2 : LC Card 86-106735
HC290.5.A9 K5 1985

Northeast Hazardous Waste Project (U. S.) Rebovich, Donald. Understanding hazardous waste crime . [Trenton?] [1986] viii, 70 p. : LC Card 86-622805 DDC 364.1/42 19
HD9975.U53 A1157 1986

Northeast-Midwest Research Institute. Coalition of Northeast Governors. Policy Research Center. A case of inequity [microform] . [New York] , 1977. 39 p. ;
NYPL [*ZT-1564 no.21]

Northeastern Forest Experiment Station (Broomall, Pa.) Widmann, Richard H. Ohio timber products output--1983 /. Broomall, PA [1986] 29 p. : LC Card 86-603412 DDC 338.1/7498/09771021 19
HD9757.O3 W53 1986

NORTHEASTERN STATES - ECONOMIC CONDITIONS.
Domestic pottery of the northeastern United States, 1625-1850 /. Orlando , 1985. xxi, 319 p. : ISBN 0-12-703870-1 (alk. paper) LC Card 85-9038 DDC 338.4/76663974 19
HD9611.7.A115 D66 1985
NYPL [3-MPH 86-2845]

Northern Alberta Development Council. W.J. Page & Associates. Telecommunications in Northern Alberta /. [Edmonton, Alta. , 1986?] 39, [96] p. : LC Card 86-235313 DDC 384/.068 19
HE7819.A43 W15 1986

Northern enterprise . Bliss, Michael. Toronto, Ont. , c1987. 640 p. : ISBN 0-7710-1577-1 : LC Card 87-151013 DDC 380.1/0971 19
HF3224 .B65 1987

The Northern mineral sector : a framework for discussion. Ottawa : Indian and Northern Affairs Canada, [1985] 37, 37 p. : ill. ; 28 cm. English and French. Title on added t.p.: Le secteur minier dans le Nord. "March, 1985." ISBN 0-662-53700-9 (pbk.) LC Card 85-162718 DDC 338.2/0971 19
1. Mineral industries - Government policy - Canada, Northern. 2. Industrial promotion - Canada, Northern. 3. Canada, Northern - Economic policy. I. Canada. Indian and Northern Affairs Canada. II. Title: Secteur minier dans le Nord.
HD9506.C23 N6758 1985
NYPL [JLF 86-175]

NORTHERN PACIFIC RAILROAD COMPANY - HISTORY - 19TH CENTURY.
Lewty, Peter J., 1934- To the Columbia gateway . Pullman, Wash. , 1987. p. cm. ISBN 0-87422-030-0 (alk. paper) : LC Card 87-21041 DDC 385/.09795 19
HE2791.N855 L48 1987

NORTHERN PACIFIC RAILWAY COMPANY - HISTORY.
Curtis, Jane, 1918- Frederick Billings, Vermonter, pioneer lawyer, business man, conservationist . Woodstock, VT , c1986. 135 p. : ISBN 0-930985-04-4 (pbk.) : LC Card 86-28103 DDC 385/.092/4 B 19
HE2754.B5 C87 1986

Northern Regional Management Centre (Great Britain) Cost reduction. Oxford , New York , 1986. ix, 65 p. : ISBN 0-08-034177-2 (pbk.) LC Card 87-100499 DDC 658.1/552 19
HD47.3 .C67 1986

NORTHERN TERRITORY - ECONOMIC CONDITIONS - CONGRESSES.
Economy and people in the north /. Darwin , 1985. v, 294 p. : ISBN 0-86784-591-0 (pbk.) : LC Card 86-159263 DDC 330.9719/03 19
HC607.N6 E27 1985

NORTHERN TERRITORY - INDUSTRIES - CONGRESSES.
Economy and people in the north /. Darwin , 1985. v, 294 p. : ISBN 0-86784-591-0 (pbk.) : LC Card 86-159263 DDC 330.9719/03 19
HC607.N6 E27 1985

NORTHLAND BANK.
Estey, Willard Z. Report of the inquiry into the collapse of the CCB and Northland Bank /. Ottawa, Canada , c1986. xiii, 641 p. : ISBN 0-660-12171-9 (pbk.) : LC Card 87-134617 DDC 332.1/2/0971 19
HG2708.C36 E89 1986

Johnson, Arthur, 1951- Breaking the banks /. Toronto, Canada , c1986. xi, 256 p. ; ISBN 0-88619-072-X LC Card 87-120151 DDC 332.1/2/0971 19
HG2708.C36 J64 1986

NORTHMEN.
Wilson, David McKenzie. Economic aspects of the Vikings in the West-the archaeological basis /. Göteborg , 1980. 36 p. ; ISBN 91-7360-075-X (pbk.) LC Card 81-154587 DDC 330.94 19
HC41 .W55 1980

Northrup, David O. Northrup, Herbert Roof, 1918- Open shop construction revisited /. Philadelphia, Pa., U. S.A. , c1984. xxxv, 674 p. : ISBN 0-89546-047-5 : LC Card 84-48502 DDC 331.88/92 19
HD9715.U52 N67 1984 ***NYPL [TB (Pennsylvania. University. Wharton School of Finance and Commerce. Industrial Research Unit. Industrial Research Unit Study. no. 62)]***

Northrup, Herbert Roof, 1918-
Doublebreasted operations and pre-hire agreements in construction : the facts and the law : a supplement to Open shop construction revisited / by Herbert R. Northrup, Robert E. Williams, and Douglas S. McDowell. Philadelphia, Penn., USA : Industrial Research Unit, Wharton School, University of Pennsylvania, c1987. viii, 127 p. : ill. ; 23 cm. (Major Industrial Research Unit series . no. 62a) Includes index. ISBN 0-89546-067-X (pbk.) LC Card 87-81475 DDC 331.88/92 19
1. Trade-unions - Construction workers - Law and legislation - United States. 2. Construction workers - Legal status, laws, etc. - United States. 3. Open and closed shop - Law and legislation - United States. 4. Construction industry - United States - Personnel management. 5. Open and closed shop - United States. I. Williams, Robert E., 1942-. II. McDowell, Douglas S. III. Northrup, Herbert Roof, 1918- Open shop construction revisited. IV. Title. V. Title: Double-breasted operations and prehire agreements in construction. VI. Series: Major Industrial Research Unit studies , no. 62a.
HD9715.U52 N67 1984 Suppl.

Open shop construction revisited / by Herbert R. Northrup with the assistance of David O. Northrup. Philadelphia, Pa., U. S.A. : Industrial Research Unit, Wharton School, University of Pennsylvania, c1984. xxxv, 674 p. : ill. ; 24 cm. (Major Industrial Research Unit studies . no. 62) Includes index. Bibliography: p. 659. ISBN 0-89546-047-5 : LC Card 84-48502 DDC 331.88/92 19
1. Construction industry - United States - Personnel management. 2. Open and closed shop - United States. I. Northrup, David O. II. Series. III. Series: Pennsylvania. University. Wharton School of Finance and Commerce. Industrial Research Unit. Industrial Research Unit study, no. 62. IV. Title.
HD9715.U52 N67 1984 ***NYPL [TB (Pennsylvania. University. Wharton School of Finance and Commerce. Industrial Research Unit. Industrial Research Unit Study. no. 62)]***

Open shop construction revisited. Northrup, Herbert Roof, 1918- Doublebreasted operations and pre-hire agreements in construction : the facts and the law : a supplement to Open shop construction revisited / by Herbert R. Northrup, Robert E. Williams, and Douglas S. McDowell. Philadelphia, Penn., USA , c1987. viii, 127 p. : ISBN 0-89546-067-X (pbk.) LC Card 87-81475 DDC 331.88/92 19
HD9715.U52 N67 1984 Suppl.

NORTHWESTERN BELL TELEPHONE COMPANY.
Chronicles of corporate change . Lexington, Mass. , c1987. xiv, 254 p. : ISBN 0-669-13685-9 (alk. paper) LC Card 86-45555 DDC 384.6/065/73 19
HE8846.A55 C47 1987

Norton, Hollis.
How to make it when you're cash poor / Hollis Norton. Rev. and updated, 1st Fireside ed. New York : Simon & Schuster, 1986. 232 p. ; 22 cm. "A Fireside book." Includes index. ISBN 0-671-62803-8 (pbk.) LC Card 86-26174 DDC 332.63/24 19
1. Real estate investment. 2. Success in business. I. Title.
HD1382.5 .N67 1986

The new real estate game : building wealth under the new tax laws / Hollis Norton. Chicago : Contemporary Books, c1987. 233 p. : ill. ; 24 cm. Includes index. ISBN 0-8092-4794-1 : LC Card 86-32902 DDC 346.7304/37 347.306437 19
1. Real estate investment. 2. Real property and taxation - United States. I. Title.
HD1382.5 .N675 1987

Norton, Mary Beth. "To toil the livelong day" . Ithaca, N.Y. , 1987. xi, 312 p. ; ISBN 0-8014-1847-X (alk. paper) LC Card 86-47975 DDC 331.4/0973 19
HD6095 .T6 1987

Norton, W. E. Australian economic statistics, 1949-50 to 1984-85 / W.E. Norton, P.J. Kennedy. [Sydney] : Reserve Bank of Australia, [1985] 2 v. : ill. ; 28 cm. (Occasional paper / Reserve Bank of Australia . no. 8A-8B) "November 1985"--V. 1, t.p. Includes bibliographical references and indexes. CONTENTS. - 1. Tables -- 2. Graphs. ISBN 0-642-09904-9 (pbk. : v. 1) LC Card 86-222671 DDC 330.994/05/021 19
1. Australia - Economic conditions - 1945 - Statistics. I. Kennedy, P. J. II. Series: Occasional paper / Reserve Bank of Australia , no. 8A-8B. III. Title.
HC605 .N6326 1985

Norušis, M. J. (Marija J.), 1948-
The SPSS guide to data analysis for SPSS with additional instructions for SPSS/PC / Marija J. Norušis. Chicago, IL : SPSS, c1987. xiii, 428 p. : ill. ; 24 cm. Bibliography: p. 420. Includes index. ISBN 0-918469-42-2 (pbk.) LC Card 87-60776 DDC 001.4/22 19
1. SPSS X (Computer system). 2. Social sciences - Data processing. 3. Social sciences - Statistical methods. I. SPSS Inc. II. Title. III. Title: Data analysis.
HA32 .N6519 1987

SPSS/PC+ Advanced Statistics V2.0 for the IBM PC/XT/AT and PS/2 / Marija J. Norusis. Chicago, Ill. : SPSS Inc., c1988. 1 v. (various pagings) : ill. ; 28 cm. Bibliography: p. B-213-B-214. Includes index. ISBN 0-918469-57-0 (pbk.) LC Card 87-62355 DDC 005.36/9 19
1. SPSS/PC Plus (Computer system). 2. Social sciences - Data processing. I. SPSS Inc. II. Title.
HA32 .N6634 1988

SPSS/PC+ V2.0 base manual for the IBM PC/XT/AT and PS/2 / [Marija J. Norusis]. Chicago, Ill. : SPSS Inc., c1988. 606 p. in various pagings : ill. ; 28 cm. + reference card. Includes bibliography and index. ISBN 0-918469-55-4 (pbk.) LC Card 87-62353 DDC 300/.28/5416 19
1. SPSS/PC+ (Computer system). 2. Social sciences - Data processing. I. SPSS Inc. II. Title: SPSS/PC plus version 2.0 base manual for the IBM PC/XT/AT and PS/2. III. Title: SPSS/PC V 2.0 base manual for the IBM PC/XT/AT and PS/2.
HA32 .N6674 1988

Norway. Arbeidsdirektoratet. Undersøkelse av personer som var med i en del av arbeidsmarkedsetatens tiltak pr. 31. mars 1978. Oslo , 1979. iv, 68, 4 p. ; LC Card 83-109890
HD5800.A6 U53 1979

Norway. Central Bureau of Statistics. see **Norway. Statistisk sentralbyrå.**

NORWAY - COMMERCE - DEVELOPING COUNTRIES.
Kristiansen, Stein. U-hjelp og handel . Bergen [1982] iv, 325 p. : LC Card 83-139901
HC60 .K76 1982

NORWAY - COMMERCE - HANSEATIC LEAGUE - HISTORY.
Schelzel, Manfred. Hanseschiffahrt mit Norwegen /. Bergen , 1979. 33 leaves ; LC Card 85-174193
HF458 .S34 1979

Norway. Departementet for utviklingshjelp.
Bangladesh . Fantoft, Norway , 1986. xxxiii, 353 p. : ISBN 82-905840-8-3 (pbk.) LC Card 87-128545 DDC 330.9549/205 19
HC440.8 .B352 1986

Chowdhury, Ashraf U. Norway's commodity assistance and import support to Bangladesh . [Oslo, Norway] [1986] 83 p. : LC Card 87-150872 DDC 338.91/481/05492 19
HC440.8 .C48 1986

NORWAY - ECONOMIC CONDITIONS.
Bergh, Trond, 1946- Vitenskap og politikk . Oslo , 1984. 269 p. : ISBN 82-03-11342-7 : LC Card 84-184253
HB116.3.A2 B47 1984

Drivenes, Einar-Arne. Fiskarbonde og gruveslusk /. Oslo , c1985. 161, [1] p. : ISBN 82-00-07480-3 LC Card 86-204801
HD9506.N72 D75 1985

Luihn, Hans. Arbeid og samfunn . [Oslo] , c1986. 372 p. : ISBN 82-508-0574-7 : LC Card 87-157793
HD5800.A6 L85 1986

NORWAY - ECONOMIC CONDITIONS - 1945-
Aarrestad, Jostein. Oljen og norsk økonomi /. [Oslo] , c1984. 118 p. : ISBN 82-508-0285-3 LC Card 86-207964
HD9575.N62 A5 1984

Ertresvåg, Per-Aslak, 1931- Ekko av fremtiden /. Oslo , c1986. 163 p. : ISBN 82-504-0815-2 LC Card 86-217931
HC365 .E77 1986

Næringslivets utviklingsmuligheter i innlandet /. Oslo [1983] 291 p. : ISBN 82-00-70803-9 LC Card 83-237323
HC365 .N32 1983

Vannebo, Olav. De tjenesteytende næringer i 80-åra /. Oslo , 1981. iii, 178 p. : ISBN 82-518-1573-8 : LC Card 83-194969
HD9986.N82 V36 1981

NORWAY - ECONOMIC CONDITIONS - 1945- - ECONOMETRIC MODELS.
Bergan, Roar. MINK . Oslo , 1984. 71 p. : ISBN 82-537-2138-2 : LC Card 85-178061
HC365 .B388 1984

Bjerkholt, Olav, 1942- MODIS IV . Oslo , 1980. 189 p. : ISBN 82-537-1014-3 (pbk.) LC Card 81-120697 DDC 330.9481/00724 19
HC365 .B46 1980

NORWAY - ECONOMIC POLICY.
Grund, Jan. Velferdsstat i motvind /. Oslo , 1986, c1985. 139 p. : ISBN 82-00-07590-7 : LC Card 86-132818
HC365 .G78 1985 ***NYPL [JLD 86-4433]***

NORWAY - FOREIGN RELATIONS - EUROPE.
Jørgensen, Nils-Johan. Norge mot Europa? . København , 1982. 250 p. ; ISBN 87-87733-30-7 : LC Card 82-172919
HC241.25.N7 J67 1982

Norway. Kgl. Utenriksdepartement. Norge--EF, økonomisk samarbeid. [Oslo] [1981] 45 p. ; ISBN 82-7177-111-6 LC Card 84-167865
HC241.25.N7 N55 1981

Norway. Miljøverndepartementet.
Ressursregnskap og ressursbudsjett /. [Oslo] [1984?] 28 p. : LC Card 85-239023
HC363.5 .R46 1984

Norway number one . Tuffs, V. York, England , c1983. 52 p. : ISBN 0-906845-26-2 (pbk.) LC Card 87-100273 DDC 769.569481 19
HE6183.K56 T83 1983

NORWAY - SOCIAL CONDITIONS - 1945-
Ertresvåg, Per-Aslak, 1931- Ekko av fremtiden

/. Oslo , c1986. 163 p. : ISBN 82-504-0815-2 LC Card 86-217931
HC365 .E77 1986

NORWAY - SOCIAL POLICY.
Grund, Jan. Velferdsstat i motvind /. Oslo , 1986, c1985. 139 p. : ISBN 82-00-07590-7 : LC Card 86-132818
HC365 .G78 1985 ***NYPL [JLD 86-4433]***

NORWAY - STATISTICS, VITAL.
Borgan, Jens-Kristian. Dødelighet i yrker og sosioøkonomiske grupper 1970-1980 /. Oslo , 1986. 217 p. : ISBN 82-537-2339-3 : LC Card 86-231576
HB1445 .B66 1986

Siring, Erling. To notater om sammenlikning av data fra fruktbarhetsundersøkelsen 1977 med data fra registre /. Oslo , 1983. 43 p. : ISBN 82-537-2006-8 : LC Card 84-161768
HB1025 .S57 1983

Norway. Statistisk centralbyraa. see **Norway. Statistisk sentralbyrå.**

Norway. Statistisk sentralbyrå. (Old Catalog form: Norway. Statistisk centralbyraa)
Attidues to Norwegian development assistance, 1974. Oslo , 1975. 57 p. ; LC Card 86-460167
HA1503 .A18 nr. 34 HC60

Bjerkholt, Olav, 1942- MODIS IV . Oslo , 1980. 189 p. : ISBN 82-537-1014-3 (pbk.) LC Card 81-120697 DDC 330.9481/00724 19
HC365 .B46 1980

Engrosprisstatistikk . Oslo , 1982. 120 p. ; ISBN 82-537-1833-0 : LC Card 83-139816
HB235.N6 E54 1982

Kvartalsvis nasjonalregnskap 1978-1983 =. Oslo , 1984. 99 p. ; ISBN 82-537-2143-9 : LC Card 85-223735
HA1501 B, nr. 510 HC370.I5

Naturressurser og miljø 1983 . Oslo , 1984. 100 p. : ISBN 82-537-1993-0 : LC Card 84-161695
HC363.5 .N38 1984

Naturressurser 1982 . Oslo , 1983. 62 p. : ISBN 82-537-1837-3 : LC Card 83-174054
HC363.5 .N372 1983

Ressursregnskap for fisk. Oslo , 1982. 53 p. : ISBN 82-537-1765-2 : LC Card 82-229877
HD9465.N62 R47 1982

Norway. "Tempo-utvalget."
Petroleumsvirksomhetens framtid : det framtidige omfanget av petroleumsvirksomheten på norsk sokkel / fra et utvalg ("Tempo-utvalget") oppnevnt ved kongelig resolusjon 5. mars 1982. Oslo : Universitetsforlaget, [1983] 167 p. : ill. ; 28 cm. (Norges offentlige utredninger . 1983:27) "Avgitt til Olje- og energidepartementet 20. april 1983." Summary in English. ISBN 82-00-70810-1 LC Card 83-235609
1. Petroleum industry and trade - Norway. 2. Petroleum industry and trade - Government policy - Norway. I. Title. II. Series.
HD9575.N62 N6855 1983

Norway. Utvalg for delutredning om industrielle mineraler. Industrimineraler : industrimineraler, naturstein og pukk : produksjon, forbruk, prospektering, forskning, forvaltning og lovgivning : delutredning / fra et utvalg oppnevnt av Industridepartementet 30. juli 1979. Oslo : Universitetsforlaget, [1982] 134 p. : ill. ; 28 cm. (Norges offentlige utredninger . 1982:24) ISBN 82-00-70754-7 LC Card 83-123304
1. Mineral industries - Norway. 2. Industrial minerals - Norway. I. Title. II. Series.
HD9506.N72 N67 1982

Norway's commodity assistance and import support to Bangladesh . Chowdhury, Ashraf U. [Oslo, Norway] [1986] 83 p. : LC Card 87-150872 DDC 338.91/481/05492 19
HC440.8 .C48 1986

Norwegian Institute of International Affairs, Oslo. see **Oslo. Norsk utenrikspolitisk institutt.**

Nos futuro : wegen naar een toekomst voor de Nederlandse Antillen. Curaçao, NA : Universiteit van de Nederlandse Antillen ; Zutphen : Walburg Pers, c1986. 496 p. : ill. ; 24 cm. By K.E.M. Bongenaar and others. Dutch and English. Includes bibliographies. ISBN 90-6011-512-0 : LC Card 86-220862
1. Netherlands Antilles - Economic conditions. 2. Netherlands Antilles - Social conditions. 3. Netherlands Antilles - Politics and government. I. Bongenaar, Karel E. M. II. Universiteit van de Nederlandse Antillen.
HC157.5 .N67 1986

Nosko, Herbert. Rationelle Energieverwendung im Industriebetrieb : technisch-organisatorische, ökonomische und ökologische Grundlagen unternehmerischer Energiepolitik / von Herbert Nosko. Berlin : E. Schmidt, c1986. xiii, 289 p. : ill. ; 25 cm. (Technological economics . Bd. 16) Originally presented as the author's thesis (doctoral)--Freie Universität Berlin. Bibliography: p. 244-284. ISBN 3-503-02547-2 LC Card 86-192206
1. Industry - Energy conservation. 2. Manufacturing processes - Energy conservation. 3. Industry - Energy conservation - Environmental aspects. 4. Manufacturing processes - Energy conservation - Environmental aspects. I. Title. II. Series.
HD9502.A2 N67 1986

Nosov, Nikolaĭ Evgen´evich. Kopanev, A. I. (Aleksandr Il´ich) Krest´ i͡ane Russkogo Severa v XVII v. /. Leningrad , 1984. 242 p. ; LC Card 84-170666
HD719.R88 K67 1984 ***NYPL [*QG 86-3646]***

Nossiter, Bernard D. The global struggle for more : Third World conflicts with rich nations / Bernard D. Nossiter.1st ed. New York : Harper & Row, c1987. xvi, 254 p. ; 22 cm. "A Twentieth Century Fund essay." Bibliography: p. 217-245. Includes index. ISBN 0-06-435851-8 : LC Card 86-45762 DDC 337/.09172/4 19
1. Developing countries - Economic policy. 2. Developing countries - Economic conditions. 3. Debts, External - Developing countries. 4. Developing countries - Foreign economic relations. I. Title.
HC59.7 .N676 1987

Not as far as you think . Moore, Lynda L. Lexington, Mass. , c1986. xii, 201 p. ; ISBN 0-669-10836-7 : LC Card 85-40109 DDC 331.4/0973 19
HD6095 .M66 1986 ***NYPL [JLE 86-1878]***

Not far afield . Myers, Norman. Washington, DC , c1987. vi, 73 p. : ISBN 0-915825-24-4 (pbk.): LC Card 87-50723 DDC 333.7/09172/4 19
HC59.72.E5 M93 1987

Not heard on the street . Joy, Maurice. Chicago, Ill. , c1986. viii, 133 p. ; ISBN 0-917253-40-X : LC Card 86-3213 DDC 332.6/0207 19
HG4513 .J69 1986 ***NYPL [JLD 86-2885]***

Not in front of the servants . Dawes, Frank Victor. London , 1984. 178 p., [16] p. of plates : ISBN 0-09-155291-5 (pbk.) : LC Card 84-195925 DDC 640/.46/0942 19
HD8039.D52 G718 1984
NYPL [JLD 86-1944]

Notas críticas sobre el plan Reagan para la cuenca del Caribe / Juan Valdés Paz ... [et al.]. La Habana : Centro de Estudios sobre América, 1982. 84 p. ; 27 cm. (Avances de investigación . no. 13) Cover title: Notas críticas sobre el plan Reagan para Centroamérica y el Caribe. Bibliography: p. 79-84. LC Card 87-400638 DDC 337.729073 19
1. United States - Foreign economic relations - Caribbean area. 2. Caribbean area - Foreign economic relations - United States. 3. Caribbean Basin Initiative, 1983-. 4. Caribbean Area - Economic conditions - 1945-. I. Valdés Paz, Juan. II. Centro de Estudios sobre América. III. Series: Avances de investigación (Havana, Cuba) , no. 13.
HF1456.5.C27 N67 1982

Notas para una discusión sobre política económica y la experiencia latinoamericana. Vuscovic, Pedro. Montevideo, Uruguay [1983] 29 p. ; LC Card 86-160128
HC125 .V87 1983

Notas sobre sirvientes de las Californias y proyecto de obraje en Nuevo México /. Velázquez, María del Carmen. México, D.F. [1985], c1984. 246 p. ; ISBN 968-12-0298-8 LC Card 85-243085
HD2346.U52 C294 1985

Notas técnicas .
(no. 31) Ffrench-Davis, Ricardo. Origen y destino de las exportaciones chilenas, 1965-80 /. Santiago, Chile , 1981. 22, 6, [27] leaves ; LC Card 83-182100
HF3416.5 .F46 1981b

(no. 46) Meller, Patricio. Una revisión de políticas de empleo para América Latina /. Santiago, Chile , 1981. 72 leaves ; LC Card 83-182110
HD5730.5.A6 M44 1981

Notas y material de estudio sobre el desarrollo y el sindicalismo realizado en el Instituto Americano para el Desarrollo del Sindicalismo Libre /. Solterer, Josef, 1897- Lima, Perú [1986] xv, 76, [5] p. : LC Card 86-235556
HD85.S7 S65 1986

Notat (Aarhus universitet. Geografisk institut) .
(36) Dansk industripolitik . [Århus] , 1983. 143 p. : LC Card 84-164502
HD3616.D43 D35 1983

(37) Sadolin, Pia. Regional udvikling i Danmark /. [Aarhus] , 1983. 92 p. : LC Card 84-164625
HC355 .S26 1983

Notat (Aarhus universitet. Økonomisk institut) .
(1981-2) Skou, Niels Holger. Teknologipolitik /. Aarhus [1981] 52 p. ; LC Card 82-194649
HC59.72.T4 S56 1981

(1981-2) Skou, Niels Holger. Teknologipolitik /. Aarhus [1981] 52 p. ; LC Card 82-194649
HC59.72.T4 S56 1981

(1986-1) Laursen, Karsten. Udviklingslandenes økonomi /. Århus [1986] ii, 203 p. : LC Card 86-215996
HC59.7 .L3243 1986

Note e relazioni, 0535-9856 .
(anno 1986, n. 3) Indagine sulla lettura e su altri aspetti dell'impiego del tempo libero . [Roma] , 1986. 140 p., [5] p. of plates : LC Card 87-165864
HA1363 .A27 no. 3 Z1003.5.I8

Note modification agreement. Hiller, Michael D. How to get the 1 hour real estate loan . Encino, CA (16161 Ventura Blvd., #C-719, Encino 91436) , c1987. 170 p. : LC Card 87-154252 DDC 332.7/22/0973 19
HG2040.5.U5 H53 1987

Note technique (Institut des sciences agronomiques du Burundi)
Bergen, D. Étude socio-économique sur la culture du riz irrigué dans le périmètre de Mugerero (S.R.D. Imbo) /. Bujumbura , 1985. 96 leaves : LC Card 86-980581
HD9066.B952 B47 1985

Noter over dansk landbrugshistorie. Greve Strand : Landbrugets informationskontor, 1982. 53 p. : ill. ; 30 cm. Cover title. ISBN 87-7470-314-5 : LC Card 83-170741
1. Agriculture - Economic aspects - Denmark - History. 2. Farmers - Denmark - Political activity - History. I. Landbrugets informationskontor.
HD2002 .N67 1982

Notes on some definitions of the multinational enterprise. Ottawa : Foreign Investment Division, Research and Analysis Branch, Foreign Investment Review Agency, [1971] 31 leaves ; 36 cm. Cover title. "First printed, August 1971." Bibliography: leaves 24-31. LC Card 82-210581
1. International business enterprises. I. Canada. Foreign Investment Review Agency. Foreign Investment Division.
HD2755.5 .N68 1971

Notes on the failure of reformist capitalism in Mexico /. Hellman, Judith Adler. Toronto, Ont., Canada [1976] 24 p ; LC Card 85-155317 DDC 338.972 19
HC135 .H38 1976

NOTES, PROMISSORY. see **PROMISSORY NOTES.**

NOTICE OF DISMISSAL. see **EMPLOYEES, DISMISSAL OF.**

Noticia de Andalucía /. Comín, Alfonso C. Sevilla [1985] 338 p. ; ISBN 84-7587-037-6 LC Card 86-219377
HC387.A64 C62 1985

Noticiari econòmic internacional, 1980 / [Banca Catalana, Banc Industrial de Catalunya]. [Barcelona] : Catalana d'Estudis Econòmics, [1981?] 116 p. : ill. ; 21 cm. LC Card 82-144538
1. International economic relations. I. Banca Catalana. II. Banco Industrial de Catalunya.
HF1411 .N6745 1981

Notícias publicadas, de março de 1977 a janeiro de 1979. [Brasília] : SEPLAN/GDF, [198-?] 116 leaves : ill. ; 33 cm. "Convênio SEPLAN/GDF." LC Card 85-108219
1. Brasília Region (Brazil) - Economic policy. 2. Distrito Federal (Brazil) - Economic policy. I.

SEPLAN/GDF (Organization).
HC189.B7 N68 1980z

Notre projet de société pour Haïti /. Ronceray, Hubert de. [Port-au-Prince?] [1986?] 52 p. : LC Card 86-210570
HC153 .R66 1986

Nottbohm, Klaus, 1927-
Hamer, Eberhard. Mittelstand, Träger der Marktwirtschaft . Minden , c1984- v. ; ISBN 3-7907-3056-4 (Bd. 1) LC Card 85-175274 DDC 338.6/42/0943 19
HD2346.G3 H215 1984 ***NYPL [JLK 86-61]***

NOTTBOHM, KLAUS, 1927- - ADDRESSES, ESSAYS, LECTURES.
Hamer, Eberhard. Mittelstand, Träger der Marktwirtschaft . Minden , c1984- v. ; ISBN 3-7907-3056-4 (Bd. 1) LC Card 85-175274 DDC 338.6/42/0943 19
HD2346.G3 H215 1984 ***NYPL [JLK 86-61]***

The Nottingham labour movement, 1880-1939 /. Wyncoll, Peter, 1939-1982. London , Atlantic Highlands, N.J. , 1985. 256 p. ; ISBN 0-85315-613-1 (pbk.) : LC Card 86-213667 DDC 331.88/09425/27 19
HD6669.N68 W96 1985

Die Notwendige Hilfe : Grundlagen, Leitlinien und Instrumente der Entwicklungszusammenarbeit / mit Beiträgen von Dieter W. Benecke ... [et al.] ; [Günther Rüther (Hrsg.)]. Melle : E. Knoth, [1986] 207 p. : ill. ; 24 cm. (Forschungsbericht (Konrad-Adenauer-Stiftung) . 48) "Die Konzeption dieser Veröffentlichung geht hervor aus den Beiträgen der entwicklungspolitischen Fachtagungen, die das Bildungswerk der Konrad-Adenauer-Stiftung jährlich in Schloss Eichholz durchführt"--T.p. verso. Bibliography: p. 200-204. Includes index. ISBN 3-88368-111-3 : LC Card 86-197696
1. Economic assistance, West German - Developing countries. 2. Technical assistance, West German - Developing countries. I. Benecke, Dieter W. II. Rüther, Günther. III. Konrad-Adenauer-Stiftung. Bildungswerk. IV. Series. V. Series: Forschungsbericht (Konrad-Adenauer-Stiftung) , 48.
HC60 .N69 1986

Nötzli, Irene M. A view of Japanese management, especially management development in large business enterprises / von Irene M. Nötzli. Zürich : Schulthess Polygraphischer Verlag, c1982. ix, 281 p. : ill. ; 23 cm. (Mitteilungen aus dem Handelswissenschaftlichen Seminar der Universität Zürich . Heft 156) Bibliography: p. 275-281. ISBN 3-7255-2191-3 (pbk.) LC Card 82-237094 DDC 658.4/07124 19
1. Executives - Training of - Japan. 2. Middle managers - Training of - Japan. 3. Management - Study and teaching - Japan. 4. Personnel management - Japan. I. Title. II. Series.
HF5549.5.T7 N638 1982 ***NYPL [TB (Zürich. Universität. Handelwissenschafticlies Seminar. Mitteilungen. Heft 156)]***

Nougaret, Pierre. Charbon, Paul. Le facteur et ses métamorphoses /. Barembach , c1984. 266 p., [24] p. of plates : ISBN 2-902912-40-4 LC Card 85-118656 DDC 383/.4944 19
HE6989.P4 C48 1984 ***NYPL [JLG 86-165]***

Nõukogude Liidu Kommunistlik Partei. see **Kommunisticheskaia partiia Sovetskogo Soiuza.**

Nourrir les villes en Afrique sub-saharienne / la réalisation de cet ouvrage a été coordonnée par N. Bricas ... [et al.]. Paris : L'Harmattan, c1985. 421 p. : ill. ; 24 cm. (Collection "Villes et entreprises") At head of title: ALTERSIAL, ENSIA-GRET, CERED, CERNEA, M.S.A., ORSTOM. "Contributions de Cl. Arditi [et al.]"--T.p. verso. Bibliography: p. 413-415. ISBN 2-85802-562-X LC Card 86-222243
1. Food supply - Africa, Sub-Saharan. 2. Urbanization - Africa, Sub-Saharan. I. Arditi, Claude. II. Bricas, N. (Nicolas). III. Series.
HD9017.S82 N68 1985

La Nouvelle économie libérale / sous la direction de Claude Meidinger. Paris : Presses de la Fondation nationale des sciences politiques, c1983. 280 p. : ill. ; 22 cm. Includes bibliographies and index. ISBN 2-7246-0487-3 : LC Card 84-140644
1. Laissez-faire. 2. Chicago school of economics. 3. Supply-side economics. I. Meidinger, Claude.
HB95 .N63 1983

Nouvelles technologies et enjeux sociaux : recherche coopérative France-R.D.A. / sous la direction de Y. Bouchut, J.-H. Jacot, S. Latchinian. Lyon : Presses universitaires de Lyon, c1986. 230 p. : ill. ; 24 cm. (Economie des changements technologiques) Summaries in French and German. Includes bibliographies. CONTENTS. - Nouvelles technologies, crise et mutations du mode de production capitaliste / par Y. Bouchut, J.H. Jacot -- Automatisation et robotique en économie socialiste / par H. Gläss -- Progrès scientifique et technique, plus-value et profit dans le capitalisme contemporain / par F. Holzapfel, H. Klemm, G. Köhler -- Changements techniques, sortie de crise et réformulation du rapport salarial / par C. Le Bas -- Les transferts de technologie de l'ouest vers l'est / par Marie Lavigne -- Défi du progrès scientifique et technique aux pays en voie de développement et possibilités de sa maîtrise / par S. Latchinian -- Coopération et "Co-développement" enjeux et perspectives / par D. Dufourt, R. Sandretto. ISBN 2-7297-0279-2 : LC Card 86-187357
1. Technological innovations - Economic aspects. 2. Technological innovations - Social aspects. 3. Technology - International cooperation. 4. Labor supply - Effect of technological innovations on. 5. Capitalism. 6. Socialism. I. Bouchut, Y. (Yves). II. Jacot, Jacques-Henri. III. Latchinian, Sarkis. IV. Series.
HC79.T4 N68 1986

Nouwt, P. Vruchtbaarheid van geboortegeneraties gebaseerd op waarnemingen over de periode 1950-1983 / [P. Nouwt] ; Centraal Bureau voor de Statistiek, Hoofdafdeling Bevolkingsstatistieken. 's-Gravenhage : Staatsuitgeverij/CBS-publikaties, 1985. 95 p. ; 30 cm. (Statistische onderzoekingen . M25) Dutch and English. ISBN 90-357-0197-6 : LC Card 86-218161
1. Fertility, Human - Netherlands - Statistics. 2. Netherlands - Population - Statistics. 3. Netherlands - Statistics, Vital. I. Netherlands. Centraal Bureau voor de Statistiek. Hoofdafdeling Bevolkingsstatistieken. II. Title. III. Series.
HB1015 .N68 1985

A nova ordem econômica internacional e suas consequências no Brasil . Simonsen, Mário Henrique. Salvador , 1983. 60 p. ; LC Card 87-144638 DDC 337.81 19
HF1513 .S55 1983

A nova política salarial e as negociações coletivas de trabalho no Brasil, 1979-1982 . Sousa, Amaury de. [Brazil?] 1983. 109 leaves ; LC Card 87-404781 DDC 331.2/981 19
HD5004 .S675 1983

Novaes, Paulo, 1913- Organización y recursos humanos / Paulo Novaes. 1a ed. Montevideo : CINTERFOR, 1976, 1977 printing. 122 p. : ill. ; 25 cm. (Estudios y monografías . no. 21) LC Card 86-139048
1. Manpower policy. 2. Occupational training. I. Series: Estudios y monografías (CINTERFOR (Organization)) , no. 21. II. Title.
HD5713 .N68 1977

Novak, Mijo. Problemi samoupravne organizacije /. Zagreb , 1981. xi, 237 p. ; LC Card 83-110609
HD5660.Y8 P675 1981

Novas buscas em comunicação .
(v. 2) Lima, Gerson Moreira, 1952- Releasemania, uma contribuição para o estudo do press-release no Brasil /. São Paulo, SP , c1985. 114 p. : LC Card 85-184576 DDC 659.2 19
HM263 .L478 1985 ***NYPL [JFD 86-2728]***

Nove, Alec. The Soviet economy on the brink of reform . Boston , 1988. p. cm. ISBN 0-04-335063-1 (alk. paper) LC Card 87-19514 DDC 338.947 19
HC335 .C626 1988

NOVE, ALEC.
The Soviet economy on the brink of reform . Boston , 1988. p. cm. ISBN 0-04-335063-1 (alk. paper) LC Card 87-19514 DDC 338.947 19
HC335 .C626 1988

NOVELISTS, AMERICAN - 20TH CENTURY - BIOGRAPHY.
Davis, Burke, 1913- War bird . Chapel Hill , c1987. viii, 267 p., [26] p. of plates : ISBN 0-8078-1752-X (alk. paper) LC Card 87-5934 DDC 338.7/67721/0924 B 19
HD9880.S67 D38 1987

Noves aportacions sobre la repoblació de Verdú en el centenari de la seva carta de Franquesa (1184-1984) /. Bertran i Roigé, Prim. Lleida , 1984. 23 p., [1] leaf of plates : ISBN 84-00-05783-X LC Card 86-140657
HD780.V44 B47 1984

Novi devizni i spoljnotrgovinski režim SFRJ. English. The New foreign exchange and foreign trade regime of Yugoslavia / Radojko Filipović ... [et al.]. Belgrade : Exportpress, 1986. 217 p. ; 23 cm. Translation of: Novi devizni i spoljnotrgovinski režim SFRJ. ISBN 86-7145-007-4 LC Card 87-148102 DDC 332.4/5609497 19
1. Foreign exchange administration - Yugoslavia. 2. Yugoslavia - Commerce. 3. Foreign exchange - Law and legislation - Yugoslavia. I. Filipović, Radojko. II. Title.
HG3965.5 .N6813 1986

Novi englesko-hrvatski i hrvatsko-engleski rječnik. Bogadek, F. A. (Francis Aloysius), 1882- [New English-Croatian and Croatian-English dictionary.] Cassell's New English-Croatian and Croatian-English dictionary /. New York [c1985] vii, 531, 497, 46, 7 p. ; ISBN 0-02-512140-5 LC Card 85-23140 DDC 491.8/2321 19
PG1377 .B72 1985 ***NYPL [*QAD 87-600]***

Novikov, A. A. (Anatoliĭ Aleksandrovich) Steklov Seminar (1984 : Steklov Institute of Mathematics) [Statistika i upravlenie sluchaĭnykh protsessov. English.] Statistics and control of stochastic processes /. New York, N.Y. , c1985. xiii, 506 p. ; ISBN 0-911575-18-9 LC Card 85-8851 DDC 519.5 19
QA276.A1 .S7513 1984 ***NYPL [JSE 86-729]***

Novikov, Ė. A. (Ėnergiĭ Alekseevich) Gorod i prirodopolʹzovanie / Ė.A. Novikov ; otvetstvennyĭ redaktor N.T. Agafonov. Leningrad : Izd-vo "Nauka," Leningradskoe otd-nie, 1984. 143 p. ; 20 cm. At head of title: Akademiia nauk SSSR. Institut sotsialʹno-ėkonomicheskikh problem. Includes bibliographical references. LC Card 85-125032
1. Natural resources - Soviet Union. 2. City planning - Soviet Union. 3. Environmental policy - Soviet Union. I. Agafonov, Nikolaĭ Timofeevich. II. Title.
HC333.5 .N68 1984

Novikov, V. N. (Valeriĭ Nikolaevich) Sovershenstvovanie ėkonomicheskogo mekhanizma v neproizvodstvennoĭ sfere : voprosy teorii i praktiki / V.N. Novikov. Kiev : Nauk. dumka, 1986. 195 p. ; 20 cm. At head of title: Akademiia nauk Ukrainskoĭ SSR. Institut ėkonomiki. Includes bibliographical references. LC Card 86-233718
1. Service industries - Ukraine. I. Title.
HD9986.S683 U3855 1986

Novitskiĭ, N. A. (Nikolaĭ Aleksandrovich) Faktornyĭ analiz ėffektivnosti razmeshcheniia proizvodstva / N.A. Novitskiĭ. Moskva : Izd-vo "Nauka", 1982. 126 p. : ill. ; 22 cm. (Problemy sovetskoĭ ėkonomiki) At head of title: Akademiia nauk SSSR. Gosplan SSSR. Sovet po izucheniiu proizvoditelʹnykh sil. Includes bibliographical references. LC Card 83-193429
1. Soviet Union - Industries - Location. 2. Regional planning - Soviet Union. 3. Factor analysis. I. Title.
HC340.D5 N68 1982

Novo federalismo. Serra, José. [Novo federalismo.] Um novo federalismo ; O sistema tributário "diagnóstico e reforma" /. São Paulo , 1984. 43 p. ; LC Card 87-124038 DDC 336.2/00981 19
HJ3424.A4 S47 1984

Novosibirskiĭ gosudarstvennyĭ pedagogicheskiĭ institut. Upravlenie v sisteme proizvodstvennykh otnosheniĭ /. Novosibirsk , 1974. 82 p. ; LC Card 83-120398
HD70.S63 U68 1974

Novosibirskiĭ gosudarstvennyĭ universitet. Rabochie Sibiri v borʹbe za sotsialisticheskuiu revoliutsiiu i postroenie sotsializma . Novosibirsk , 1975. 119 p. ; LC Card 85-187793
HD8529.S652 R283 1975

Novozhilov, Sergeĭ Nikolaevich. Nauchnaia organizatsiia truda v promyshlennosti /. Moskva , 1986. 414 p. : LC Card 86-218434
HD36 .N323 1986

Novy, Klaus.
Anders leben . Berlin , 1985. 231 p. : ISBN 3-8012-0107-4 LC Card 85-189669
HD7287.72.G32 N6725 1985

Genossenschafts-Bewegung : zur Geschichte und Zukunft der Wohnreform / Klaus Novy. Berlin : Transit, c1983. 176 p. : ill. ; 21 cm. Includes bibliographical references. ISBN 3-88747-017-6 LC Card 84-190729
1. Housing, Cooperative - Germany - History. 2. Housing, Cooperative - Austria - History. 3. Housing, Cooperative - Switzerland - History. I. Title.
HD7287.72.G3 N68 1983

Illustrierte Geschichte der Gemeinwirtschaft : wirtschaftliche Selbsthilfe in der Arbeiterbewegung von den Anfängen bis 1945 / Klaus Novy, Michael Prinz. Berlin : Dietz, c1985. 239 p. : ill. (some col.) ; 22 x 25 cm. Bibliography: p. 239. ISBN 3-8012-0111-2 LC Card 86-122604
1. Cooperation - Germany. 2. Business enterprises, Trade-union - Germany - History. I. Prinz, Michael, 1952-. II. Title.
HD3498 .N68 1985

Novyĭ mezhdunarodnyĭ ėkonomicheskiĭ poriadok. New international economic order /. Moscow , 1984. 196 p. ; LC Card 85-151148 DDC 337/.09/047 19
HF1411 .N398 1984 NYPL [JLD 86-2664]

NOW. see **National Organization for Women.**

Nowak, Felicitas.
The allocation of bank credit and the efficiency of investment / Felicitas Nowak. Göttingen, Rep. Fed. de Alemania : Ibero-Amerika Institut für Wirtschaftsforschung, Universität Göttingen, [1986] 23 p. : ill. ; 30 cm. (Diskussionsbeiträge / Ibero-Amerika Institut für Wirtschaftsforschung, Universität Göttingen . Nr. 41 =) "October 1986." Bibliography: p. 23. LC Card 87-121215 DDC 332.7/0724 19
1. Bank loans - Mathematical models. 2. Credit - Mathematical models. 3. Interest rates - Mathematical models. 4. Investments - Mathematical models. I. Series: Diskussionsbeiträge (Universität Göttingen. Ibero-Amerika Institut für Wirtschaftsforschung) , no. 41. II. Title.
HG1641 .N68 1986

Financial liberalization revisited : the case of Chile (1973-83) / Felicitas Nowak. Göttingen : Ibero-Amerika Institut für Wirtschaftsforschung, Universität Göttingen, [1986] 49 p. : ill. ; 30 cm. (Diskussionsbeiträge . Nr. 40 =) "October 1986." Bibliography: p. 48-49. LC Card 87-121206 DDC 332/.0983 19
1. Finance - Chile. 2. Monetary policy - Chile. 3. Chile - Economic policy. I. Series: Diskussionsbeiträge (Universität Göttingen. Ibero-Amerika Institut für Wirtschaftsforschung) , no. 40. II. Title.
HG185.C5 N69 1986

Nowak, Leszek. Teoria ekonomiczna . Poznań , 1978. 147 p. : LC Card 81-206275
HB54 .P6 nr. 76 HB179.P7

Nowakowski, Bartłomiej. Marciniak-Neider, Danuta. Spedycja lądowa /. Gdańsk , 1979- v. <1 > ; LC Card 81-181249
HF5780.P7 M37 1979

Nowotny, Hans-Joachim Hoffmann- see **Hoffmann-Nowotny, Hans-Joachim.**

Nowotny, Helga. Social concerns for the 1980s . Wien , c1984. 359 p. ; ISBN 3-900376-18-2 (pbk.)
NYPL [JLE 86-2856]

Noyes, Alexander Dana, 1862-1945. Financial chapters of the war [microform], by Alexander Dana Noyes. New York, Scribner, 1916. xi, 255 p. 20 cm. Microfilm. New York : New York Public Library, 1986. 1 microfilm reel ; 35 mm. (MN *ZZ-26,416). LC Card 16-19959
1. World War, 1914-1918 - Finance. 2. World War, 1914-1918 - Economic aspects. I. Title.
*D635 .N6 NYPL [*ZT-1735 no.5]*

Noyes Data Corporation. Pharmaceutical manufacturers of the United States /. Park Ridge, N.J., U. S.A. , 1987. vi, 300 p. ; ISBN 0-8155-1109-4 : LC Card 86-33276 DDC 338.7/616151/02573 19
HD9666.3 .P47 1987

Nozette, Stewart, 1957- Commercializing SDI technologies /. New York , 1987. xvi, 246 p. : ISBN 0-275-92332-0 (alk. paper) : LC Card 87-18333 DDC 338.4/762 19
HC110.H53 C65 1987

NPA Committee on Food and Agriculture. Sumner, Daniel A. (Daniel Alan), 1950- Removal of price supports and supply controls for U. S. tobacco . Demoines, Iowa , Washington, D.C. , c1985. viii, 64 p. ; ISBN 0-89068-084-1 LC Card 85-63194
NYPL [JLF 86-1014]

U. S. agriculture and Third World economic development . Washington, D.C. , c1987. xv, 103 p. : ISBN 0-89068-086-8 (pbk.): LC Card 86-62757 DDC 338.9/009172/4 19
HD1755 .U173 1987

NPA report .
(#227) McMullen, Neil. Seeds and world agricultural progress /. Washington, D.C. , c1987. viii, 263 p. : ISBN 0-89068-088-4 (pbk.) : LC Card 87-60766 DDC 338.1/7 19
HD9019.S43 M36 1987

(no. 220) Sumner, Daniel A. (Daniel Alan), 1950- Removal of price supports and supply controls for U. S. tobacco . Demoines, Iowa , Washington, D.C. , c1985. viii, 64 p. ; ISBN 0-89068-084-1 LC Card 85-63194
NYPL [JLF 86-1014]

(no. 227) McMullen, Neil. Seeds and world agricultural progress /. Washington, D.C. , c1987. viii, 263 p. : ISBN 0-89068-088-4 (pbk.) : LC Card 87-60766 DDC 338.1/7 19
HD9019.S43 M36 1987

NPA user's guide. New Product Announcements (NPA) user's guide. Cleveland, Ohio (11001 Cedar Ave., Cleveland 44106) , 1986- 1 v. (loose-leaf) ; LC Card 86-220025 DDC 025/.0633802 19
HF5415.153 .N46 1986

NRB--40 let po puti sotsialisticheskogo voskhoda. Manolov, Manol Dimitrov. Narodnaia Respublika Bolgariia--40 let po puti sotsialisticheskogo voskhoda /. [Bulgaria? , 1983?] [48] p. : LC Card 85-133679
HC403 .M36 1983

Nsekela, Amon J. (Amon James), 1930-
The NBC, a profile of a public enterprise commercial bank : selected speeches / by Amon J. Nsekela. [Dar es Salaam] : NBC House, 1983. 57 p. : ill., ports. ; 21 cm. LC Card 85-981339 DDC 332.1/2/09678 19
1. National Bank of Commerce (Tanzania). I. Title.
HG3397.A8 N375 1983

A time to act : liberation and development in a Tanzanian context / Amon J. Nsekela. Dar es Salaam : Dar es Salaam University Press, c1984. xxi, 142 p. ; 21 cm. ISBN 997-660-025-9 LC Card 86-981097 DDC 338.9678 19
1. Tanzania - Economic policy. 2. Tanzania - Social policy. 3. Tanzania - Politics and government - 1964-. I. Title.
HC885 .N86 1984

Az NSZK a változó világgazdaságban /. Inotai, András. Budapest , 1986, c1985. 259 p. ; ISBN 963-221-584-2 : LC Card 87-136644
HC286.7 .I56 1986

NSZZ "SOLIDARNOŚĆ" (LABOR ORGANIZATION)
A Lengyel földindulás /. Malakoff , New York , 1980. 150 p. ; LC Card 81-177379
HD8537.N783 L45 1980 NYPL [JLB 86-24]

Wałęsa, Lech, 1943- [Chemin d'espoir. English.] A way of hope /. New York , c1987. 325 p., [17] p. of plates : ISBN 0-8050-0668-0 LC Card 87-21194 DDC 322/.2/0924 B 19
HD6735.7.Z55 W34813 1987

NSZZ "SOLIDARNOŚĆ" (LABOR ORGANIZATION) - ABSTRACTS.
Twierdochlebow, W. J. Solidarność . Menlo Park, CA , 1985. 72, v leaves ; LC Card 86-221919 DDC 331.89/28238204/094382 19
HD5397.7.S512 1980 .G358 1985

NSZZ "SOLIDARNOŚĆ" (LABOR ORGANIZATION) - HISTORY.
Stelmach, Waldemar. Drugie oblicze "Solidarności" /. Warszawa , 1985. 222 p. : ISBN 83-202-0391-0 : LC Card 86-208212
HD8537.N783 S74 1985

NTG-Fachberichte .
(Bd. 97) NTG-Fachtagung (1986 : Nuremberg, Germany) Von der Nachrichtentechnik zur Informationstechnik . Berlin , c1986. 104 p. : ISBN 3-8007-1485-X LC Card 87-136748 DDC 384 19
HE7604 .N74 1986

NTG-Fachberichte, 0341-0196 .
(97) NTG-Fachtagung (1986 : Nuremberg, Germany) Von der Nachrichtentechnik zur Informationstechnik . Berlin , c1986. 104 p. : ISBN 3-8007-1485-X LC Card 87-136748 DDC 384 19
HE7604 .N74 1986

NTG-Fachtagung (1986 : Nuremberg, Germany) Von der Nachrichtentechnik zur Informationstechnik : Vorträge der NTG-Fachtagung anlässlich des VDE-Kongresses '86 am 14. und 15. Oktober 1986 in Nürnberg / wissenschaftliche Tagungsleitung, P. Bocker ; Veranstalter, Nachrichtentechnische Gesellschaft im VDE (NTG) ; [Redaktion, Roland Werner]. Berlin : VDE-Verlag, c1986. 104 p. : ill. ; 30 cm. (NTG-Fachberichte, 0341-0196 . 97) Includes bibliographies. CONTENTS. - Zusammenwachsen von Nachrichten- und Datenverarbeitungstechnik in der Informationstechnik / Ronald Dingeldey -- Nachrichtenformen als Elemente der Kommunikation / K.-L. Plank -- Endgeräte für das ISDN-Diensteangebot / W. Andexser -- Das universelle Kommunikationsnetz / G. Wiest -- Rechnerarchitektur / W.K. Giloi -- Softwaretechnologie / R. Lutze -- Rechnernetze / J. Swoboda -- Wissensbasierte Systeme in der Industrie / D. Schütt -- Diensteintegration und Netzevolution / P. Kahl -- Gegenwärtiger Stand und zukünftige Entwicklung der Architektur für offene Kommunikation / H. Kunze -- Zukunftsträchtige Anwendungen der Kommunikationstechnik am Arbeitsplatz, zu Hause und unterwegs / W. Preger. ISBN 3-8007-1485-X LC Card 87-136748 DDC 384 19
1. Telecommunications - Congresses. I. Bocker, P., 1933-. II. Werner, Roland, Dipl.-Ing. III. VDE-Kongress '86 (1986 : Nuremberg, Germany). IV. Nachrichtentechnische Gesellschaft im VDE. V. Series. VI. Series: NTG-Fachberichte , Bd. 97. VII. Title.
HE7604 .N74 1986

Ntumazah, Ndeh. France's satrapy in Kamerun is safe / by Ndeh Ntumazah. [London, England : Union des populations du Cameroun, 1985] 22 leaves ; 28 cm. Cover title. "September 1985." LC Card 87-138988 DDC 337.6711044 19
1. Cameroon - Dependency on foreign countries. 2. Cameroon - Politics and government - 1960-. 3. Cameroon - Foreign economic relations - France. 4. France - Foreign economic relations - Cameroon. I. Title.
HC995 .N78 1985

Ntumba Luaba. Ndeshyo Rurihose. La stratégie de l'Organisation de l'unité africaine pour le développement . [Kinshasa] , 1981. 80 p. : LC Card 83-161631
HC800 .N393 1981

Nu-Markets Associates. International telecommunications markets, production & trade /. New York, N.Y. , 1986. 317 p. : ISBN 0-935859-11-X (pbk.) LC Card 86-23052 DDC 338.7/62138 19
HD9696.T442 I578 1986

Nuccio, Oscar. Il pensiero economico italiano / Oscar Nuccio. [Sassari] : Gallizzi, 1984-<1985 > <v. 1, t. 1-2; in 2 > ; 25 cm. Includes bibliographies. CONTENTS. - 1. Le fonti (1050-1450). L'etica laica e la formazione dello spirito economico <t. 1-2 > LC Card 87-110173
1. Economics - Italy - History. I. Title.
HB109.A2 N833 1984

Nuclear arms and the human race . Jaipal, Rikhi, 1916- New Delhi , 1986. xix, 306 p. ; ISBN 81-7023-074-8 : LC Card 86-901813 DDC 355/.0217 19
U263 .J35 1986 NYPL [JLD 87-960]

NUCLEAR ARMS CONTROL.
World peace and the developing countries . Basingstoke, Hampshire , 1986. xix, 272 p. ; ISBN 0-333-43636-9 *NYPL [JLD 87-1192]*

The Nuclear connection : a reassessment of nuclear power and nuclear proliferation / edited by Alvin Weinberg, Marcelo Alonso, Jack N. Barkenbus. New York : Paragon House Publishers, 1985. 295 p. : ill. ; 23 cm. "A Washington Institute book." Includes bibliographical references and index. ISBN 0-88702-204-9 : LC Card 84-26786 DDC 333.79/24 19
1. Nuclear industry - Addresses, essays, lectures. 2. Nuclear nonproliferation - Addresses, essays, lectures. I. Weinberg, Alvin Martin, 1915-. II. Alonso, Marcelo. III. Barkenbus, Jack N. IV. Washington Institute for Values in Public Policy.
HD9698.A2 N77 1985 NYPL [JLE 86-1546]

Nuclear defence. Rumble, Greville. The politics of

nuclear defence . Cambridge [Cambridgeshire] , 1985. xi, 285 p. ; ISBN 0-7456-0194-4 : LC Card 85-18643 DDC 355/.0217 19
U263 .R86 1985 ***NYPL [JLD 86-1092]***

NUCLEAR DISARMAMENT.
Aguirre, Mariano A. De Hiroshima a los euromisiles /. Madrid , c1984. 254 p. : ISBN 84-309-1062-X LC Card 85-215587
U264 .A39 1984 ***NYPL [JFC 86-1643]***

Assessing the nuclear age . Chicago, Ill. , c1986. xvii, 382 p. ; ISBN 0-941682-07-2 LC Card 85-82511 DDC 355/.0217 19
U264 .A79 1986 ***NYPL [JLE 87-11]***

Cook, Alice. Greenham women everywhere . Boston, Mass. , 1984, c1983. 127, [1] p. : ISBN 0-89608-199-0 ***NYPL [JLD 87-215]***

Fehér, Ferenc, 1933- Doomsday or deterrence? . Armonk, N.Y. , c1986. 154 p. ; ISBN 0-87332-368-8 : LC Card 86-10074 DDC 327.1/74 19
JX1974.7 .F38 1986 ***NYPL [JLE 86-4319]***

Jaipal, Rikhi, 1916- Nuclear arms and the human race . New Delhi , 1986. xix, 306 p. ; ISBN 81-7023-074-8 : LC Card 86-901813 DDC 355/.0217 19
U263 .J35 1986 ***NYPL [JLD 87-960]***

La Amenaza de guerra nuclear /. Madrid , 1985. 129 p. ; ISBN 84-7477-027-0 LC Card 86-100273 DDC 355/.0217 19
U263 .A44 1985 ***NYPL [JLD 86-2519]***

Loeb, Paul Rogat, 1952- Hope in hard times . Lexington, Mass. , c1987. ix, 322 p. : ISBN 0-669-12929-1 LC Card 85-46044 DDC 327.1/74 19
JX1974.7 .L63 1986 ***NYPL [JLE 86-4051]***

Poklad, B. I. (Boris Iosifovich) Real′nosti sovremennogo mira i politika konfrontatsii /. Moskva , 1985. 157 p. ; LC Card 85-170137
JX1974.7 .P585 1985 ***NYPL [*QIK 87-1550]***

NUCLEAR ENERGY.
Assessing the nuclear age . Chicago, Ill. , c1986. xvii, 382 p. ; ISBN 0-941682-07-2 LC Card 85-82511 DDC 355/.0217 19
U264 .A79 1986 ***NYPL [JLE 87-11]***

NUCLEAR ENERGY - GOVERNMENT POLICY - GERMANY (WEST)
Der Sofortige Ausstieg ist möglich . Bonn [1986] 35 cm : LC Card 87-409511 DDC 333.79/24/0943 19
HD9698.G42 S64 1986

NUCLEAR ENERGY - GOVERNMENT POLICY - INDIA.
The Indian atom . New Delhi , c1986. v, 166 p. ; LC Card 87-900288 DDC 333.79/24/0954 19
HD9698.I52 I52 1986

NUCLEAR ENERGY - GOVERNMENT POLICY - UNITED STATES - HISTORY.
Helmreich, Jonathan E. Gathering rare ores . Princeton, N.J. , c1986. xiv, 303 p. : ISBN 0-691-04738-3 (alk. paper) : LC Card 86-4862 DDC 327.1/11 19
HD9698.U52 H45 1986
NYPL [JLE 86-4584]

Nuclear energy in Britain / [prepared by Reference Services, Publications Division Central Office of Information, London]. 7th ed. London : H.M.S.O., 1981. 31, [1] p. : ill. ; 21 cm. (Central Office of Information reference pamphlet. 28) Bibliography: p. [32] ISBN 0-11-701011-1 (pbk.) LC Card 81-165924 DDC 333.79/24/0941 19
1. Nuclear industry - Great Britain. 2. Nuclear power plants - Great Britain. I. Great Britain. Central Office of Information. Reference Services.
HD9698.G72 N83 1981

NUCLEAR ENERGY - LAW AND LEGISLATION - UNITED STATES.
Kohn, Stephen M. (Stephen Martin) Protecting environmental & nuclear whistleblowers . Washington, D.C. , c1985. xiii, 346 p. : ISBN 0-9615323-0-0 (pbk.) LC Card 85-61844 DDC 342.73/0684 347.302684 19
KF5342 .K64 1985 ***NYPL [JLE 86-1787]***

NUCLEAR ENERGY - POLITICAL ASPECTS - GERMANY (WEST)
Tschernobyl hat unser Leben verändert . Reinbek bei Hamburg , 1986. 203 p. : ISBN 3-499-15922-8 : LC Card 87-123041 DDC 363.1/79 19
HD9698.G42 T73 1986

NUCLEAR ENERGY - PUBLIC OPINION - PSYCHOLOGICAL ASPECTS.
Wünschmann, Andreas, 1942- Unbewusst dagegen . Stuttgart , 1984, c1980. 177 p. : ISBN 3-87959-214-4 (pbk.) LC Card 87-673462
HD9698.A2 W86x 1984

NUCLEAR ENGINEERING - UNITED STATES - CONGRESSES.
Transition in the nuclear industry . New York, N.Y. , c1985. iii, 233 p. : ISBN 0-87262-443-9 (pbk.) LC Card 85-70499 DDC 338.4/762148/0973 19
HD9698.U52 T73 1985 ***NYPL [JSD 86-173]***

NUCLEAR EXPORTS. see **NUCLEAR NONPROLIFERATION.**

Nuclear imperatives and public trust . Carter, Luther J. Washington, D.C. [Baltimore, Md.] , c1987. xii, 473 p. ; ISBN 0-915707-29-2 : LC Card 87-4706 DDC 363.7/28 19
HC110.E5 C358 1987

NUCLEAR INDUSTRY.
Nuclear power . Chichester , New York , c1987. xvii, 416 p. : ISBN 0-471-90732-4 : LC Card 86-26714 DDC 333.79/24 19
HD9698.A2 N79 1987

Thomas, S. D. (Steve D.) The realities of nuclear power . Cambridge , New York , 1988. p. cm. ISBN 0-521-32750-4 LC Card 87-22488 DDC 338.4/7621483 19
HD9698.A2 T53 1988

NUCLEAR INDUSTRY - ADDRESSES, ESSAYS, LECTURES.
The Nuclear connection . New York , 1985. 295 p. : ISBN 0-88702-204-9 : LC Card 84-26786 DDC 333.79/24 19
HD9698.A2 N77 1985 ***NYPL [JLE 86-1546]***

NUCLEAR INDUSTRY - ENVIRONMENTAL ASPECTS - GERMANY (WEST)
Wer WAA sät wird Widerstand ernten! /. Hamburg [1979] 31 p. : LC Card 85-171252
HD9698.G42 W47 1979

NUCLEAR INDUSTRY - ENVIRONMENTAL ASPECTS - GERMANY (WEST) - CONGRESSES.
Technik auf dem Prüfstand . Essen , Gräfelfing [1982] 183 p. : ISBN 3-7736-0340-1 LC Card 83-187518
HD9698.G42 T43 1982

NUCLEAR INDUSTRY - GERMANY (WEST)
Der Sofortige Ausstieg ist möglich . Bonn [1986] 35 cm : LC Card 87-409511 DDC 333.79/24/0943 19
HD9698.G42 S64 1986

Wer WAA sät wird Widerstand ernten! /. Hamburg [1979] 31 p. : LC Card 85-171252
HD9698.G42 W47 1979

NUCLEAR INDUSTRY - GERMANY (WEST) - CONGRESSES.
Technik auf dem Prüfstand . Essen , Gräfelfing [1982] 183 p. : ISBN 3-7736-0340-1 LC Card 83-187518
HD9698.G42 T43 1982

NUCLEAR INDUSTRY - GOVERNMENT POLICY.
Gruhl, Herbert, 1921- Der atomare Selbstmord /. München , c1986. 190 p. : ISBN 3-7766-1448-X LC Card 86-226120
HD9698.A2 G74 1986

NUCLEAR INDUSTRY - GOVERNMENT POLICY - CASE STUDIES.
Nuclear power . Chichester , New York , c1987. xvii, 416 p. : ISBN 0-471-90732-4 : LC Card 86-26714 DDC 333.79/24 19
HD9698.A2 N79 1987

Nuclear power in crisis . New York , 1987. 327 p. : ISBN 0-89397-267-3 : LC Card 86-23710 DDC 333.79/24/0941 19
HD9698.G72 N85 1987

NUCLEAR INDUSTRY - GOVERNMENT POLICY - EUROPE.
Hatch, Michael T., 1945- Politics and nuclear power . Lexington, KY , 1986. xi, 219 p. ; ISBN 0-8131-1583-3 : LC Card 85-29545 DDC 333.79/24/094 19
HD9698.E82 H38 1986
NYPL [JLD 86-2137]

NUCLEAR INDUSTRY - GOVERNMENT POLICY - GREAT BRITAIN.
Closing the door on a nuclear future . [Harbour View, Bantry, Co. Cork , 1986] [7] leaves : LC Card 87-111333 DDC 333.79/27/0941 19
HD9698.G72 C56 1986

Nuclear power in crisis . New York , 1987. 327 p. : ISBN 0-89397-267-3 : LC Card 86-23710 DDC 333.79/24/0941 19
HD9698.G72 N85 1987

NUCLEAR INDUSTRY - GOVERNMENT POLICY - UNITED STATES.
NUCLEAR INDUSTRY - GREAT BRITAIN.
Nuclear energy in Britain /. London , 1981. 31, [1] p. : ISBN 0-11-701011-1 (pbk.) LC Card 81-165924 DDC 333.79/24/0941 19
HD9698.G72 N83 1981

NUCLEAR INDUSTRY - POLITICAL ASPECTS - HISTORY.
Helmreich, Jonathan E. Gathering rare ores . Princeton, N.J. , c1986. xiv, 303 p. : ISBN 0-691-04738-3 (alk. paper) : LC Card 86-4862 DDC 327.1/11 19
HD9698.U52 H45 1986
NYPL [JLE 86-4584]

NUCLEAR INDUSTRY - SAFETY MEASURES - GOVERNMENT POLICY - INTERNATIONAL COOPERATION.
IAEA safeguards, 1980-1985 . Vienna , 1986. 15 p. ; LC Card 87-114776 DDC 363.1/79 19
HD9698.5 .I24 1986

NUCLEAR INDUSTRY - SOCIAL ASPECTS.
Meyer-Abich, Klaus Michael, 1936- Die Grenzen der Atomwirtschaft . München , c1986. 230 p. : ISBN 3-406-31317-5 LC Card 86-192439
HD9698.A2 M49 1986

NUCLEAR INDUSTRY - SWEDEN.
Bergquist, Sven, 1926- De heta åren /. [Stockholm] , 1985. 319 p. : ISBN 91-7566-089-X LC Card 85-233735
HD9698.S84 S923 1985

Regionala effekter av en kärnkraftsavveckling . [Stockholm] [1979] 254 p. : ISBN 91-38-05243-1 LC Card 82-219566
HD9698.S82 O42 1979b Suppl.

Samhällsekonomiska effekter av en kärnkraftsavveckling . [Stockholm] [1979] 149 p. ; ISBN 91-38-05244-X LC Card 82-219542
HD9698.S82 O42 1979

NUCLEAR INDUSTRY - UNITED STATES - CONGRESSES.
Transition in the nuclear industry . New York, N.Y. , c1985. iii, 233 p. : ISBN 0-87262-443-9 (pbk.) LC Card 85-70499 DDC 338.4/762148/0973 19
HD9698.U52 T73 1985 ***NYPL [JSD 86-173]***

NUCLEAR NONPROLIFERATION - ADDRESSES, ESSAYS, LECTURES.
The Nuclear connection . New York , 1985. 295 p. : ISBN 0-88702-204-9 : LC Card 84-26786 DDC 333.79/24 19
HD9698.A2 N77 1985 ***NYPL [JLE 86-1546]***

Nuclear proliferation and international security /. New Delhi , 1985-86 [i.e. 1985] 310 p. ; ISBN 1-85127-058-4 : LC Card 85-904278 DDC 327.1/74 19
JX1974.73 .N814 1985
NYPL [JLD 86-1334]

NUCLEAR POLICY - UNITED STATES - HISTORY.
Holl, Jack M. United States civilian nuclear power policy, 1954-1984 . Washington, D.C. , Springfield, Va. [1986] 46 p., [1] leaf of plates : LC Card 86-601137 DDC 333.79/24 19
HD9698.U52 H65 1986

NUCLEAR POLLUTION. see **RADIOACTIVE POLLUTION.**

Nuclear power : policy and prospects / edited by P.M.S. Jones. Chichester ; New York : Wiley, c1987. xvii, 416 p. : ill. ; 26 cm. (World energy options) "A Wiley-Interscience publication." Includes bibliographies and index. ISBN 0-471-90732-4 : LC Card 86-26714 DDC 333.79/24 19
1. Nuclear industry. 2. Nuclear power plants - Environmental aspects. 3. Nuclear power plants - Waste disposal - Environmental aspects. 4. Nuclear industry - Government policy - Case studies. I. Jones, P. M. S. II. Series.
HD9698.A2 N79 1987

Nuclear power . Openshaw, Stan. London , Boston , 1986. xiv, 348 p. : ISBN 0-7102-0183-4 : LC Card 85-8202 DDC

363.1/79 19
TK9153 .O64 1986 **NYPL [JSD 87-128]**

Nuclear power in crisis : politics and planning for the nuclear state / edited by Andrew Blowers and David Pepper. New York : Nichols Pub. Co., 1987. 327 p. : ill. ; 24 cm. Includes bibliographies and index. ISBN 0-89397-267-3 : LC Card 86-23710 DDC 333.79/24/0941 19
1. Nuclear industry - Government policy - Great Britain. 2. Nuclear industry - Government policy - Case studies. I. Blowers, Andrew. II. Pepper, David.
HD9698.G72 N85 1987

NUCLEAR POWER INDUSTRY - SPAIN.
Costa Morata, Pedro. Centrales nucleares en España . Madrid [1987?] 51 p. : ISBN 84-398-8834-1 LC Card 87-165955
HD9698.S72 C62 1987

NUCLEAR POWER PLANTS - ACCIDENTS - ECONOMIC ASPECTS - PENNSYLVANIA.
Impacts of hazardous technology . Albany , c1987. x, 233 p. : ISBN 0-88706-332-2 LC Card 86-1943 DDC 363.1/79 19
HD9698.U54 M475 1987
NYPL [JLE 87-1233]

NUCLEAR POWER PLANTS - ACCIDENTS - SOCIAL ASPECTS - PENNSYLVANIA.
Impacts of hazardous technology . Albany , c1987. x, 233 p. : ISBN 0-88706-332-2 LC Card 86-1943 DDC 363.1/79 19
HD9698.U54 M475 1987
NYPL [JLE 87-1233]

NUCLEAR POWER PLANTS - ENVIRONMENTAL ASPECTS.
Atomkraft am Ende? /. Göttingen , 1986. 191 p. ; ISBN 3-923478-16-X LC Card 86-228667
HD9698.A2 A795 1986

Nuclear power . Chichester , New York , c1987. xvii, 416 p. : ISBN 0-471-90732-4 : LC Card 86-26714 DDC 333.79/24 19
HD9698.A2 N79 1987

NUCLEAR POWER PLANTS - ENVIRONMENTAL ASPECTS - GREAT BRITAIN.
Closing the door on a nuclear future . [Harbour View, Bantry, Co. Cork , 1986] [7] leaves : LC Card 87-111333 DDC 333.79/27/0941 19
HD9698.G72 C56 1986

NUCLEAR POWER PLANTS - ENVIRONMENTAL ASPECTS - IRELAND.
Closing the door on a nuclear future . [Harbour View, Bantry, Co. Cork , 1986] [7] leaves : LC Card 87-111333 DDC 333.79/27/0941 19
HD9698.G72 C56 1986

NUCLEAR POWER PLANTS - ENVIRONMENTAL ASPECTS - SPAIN - CATALONIA.
Vilanova, Santiago, 1947- L'econacionalisme . Barcelona , 1981. 142 p. ; ISBN 84-7031-281-2 LC Card 81-212886
HC387.C25 V527 1981

NUCLEAR POWER PLANTS - GOVERNMENT POLICY.
Atomkraft am Ende? /. Göttingen , 1986. 191 p. ; ISBN 3-923478-16-X LC Card 86-228667
HD9698.A2 A795 1986

NUCLEAR POWER PLANTS - GOVERNMENT POLICY - EUROPE.
Hatch, Michael T., 1945- Politics and nuclear power . Lexington, KY , 1986. xi, 219 p. ; ISBN 0-8131-1583-3 : LC Card 85-29545 DDC 333.79/24/094 19
HD9698.E82 H38 1986
NYPL [JLD 86-2137]

NUCLEAR POWER PLANTS - GOVERNMENT POLICY - GERMANY (WEST)
Zukünftige Energiepolitik . München , 1985. 189 p. : ISBN 3-89147-002-9 LC Card 87-104306
HD9698.G42 Z85 1985

NUCLEAR POWER PLANTS - GOVERNMENT POLICY - UNITED STATES - HISTORY.
Holl, Jack M. United States civilian nuclear power policy, 1954-1984 . Washington, D.C. , Springfield, Va. [1986] 46 p., [1] leaf of plates : LC Card 86-601137 DDC 333.79/24 19
HD9698.U52 H65 1986

NUCLEAR POWER PLANTS - GREAT BRITAIN.
Nuclear energy in Britain /. London , 1981. 31, [1] p. : ISBN 0-11-701011-1 (pbk.) LC Card 81-165924 DDC 333.79/24/0941 19
HD9698.G72 N83 1981

NUCLEAR POWER PLANTS - LAW AND LEGISLATION - UNITED STATES.
NUCLEAR POWER PLANTS - LOCATION.
Openshaw, Stan. Nuclear power . London , Boston , 1986. xiv, 348 p. : ISBN 0-7102-0183-4 : LC Card 85-8202 DDC 363.1/79 19
TK9153 .O64 1986 **NYPL [JSD 87-128]**

NUCLEAR POWER PLANTS - SAFETY MEASURES.
Openshaw, Stan. Nuclear power . London , Boston , 1986. xiv, 348 p. : ISBN 0-7102-0183-4 : LC Card 85-8202 DDC 363.1/79 19
TK9153 .O64 1986 **NYPL [JSD 87-128]**

NUCLEAR POWER PLANTS - UKRAINE - CHERNOBYL´ - ACCIDENTS - PUBLIC OPINION.
Maier-Leibnitz, Heinz. Lernschock Tschernobyl /. Zürich , c1986. 137 p. ; ISBN 3-7201-5191-3 : LC Card 87-120438
HD9698.S653 C485 1986

NUCLEAR POWER PLANTS - UNITED STATES - LOCATION - PLANNING - CONGRESSES.
Facility location and land use . New York, N.Y. , c1986. vii, 40 p. : ISBN 0-87262-574-5 (pbk.) LC Card 86-25926 DDC 338.6/042 19
HD171.A15 F33 1986

NUCLEAR POWER PLANTS - WASTE DISPOSAL - ENVIRONMENTAL ASPECTS.
Nuclear power . Chichester , New York , c1987. xvii, 416 p. : ISBN 0-471-90732-4 : LC Card 86-26714 DDC 333.79/24 19
HD9698.A2 N79 1987

NUCLEAR POWER PLANTS - WASTE DISPOSAL - GOVERNMENT POLICY - UNITED STATES.
NUCLEAR PROLIFERATION. see **NUCLEAR NONPROLIFERATION.**

Nuclear proliferation and international security / edited by K. Subrahmanyam. New Delhi : Lancer International in association with Institute for Defence Studies and Analyses, 1985-86 [i.e. 1985] 310 p. ; 22 cm. Includes bibliographical references and index. ISBN 1-85127-058-4 : LC Card 85-904278 DDC 327.1/74 19
1. Nuclear nonproliferation - Addresses, essays, lectures. 2. Security, International - Addresses, essays, lectures. I. Subrahmanyam, K. II. Institute for Defence Studies and Analyses.
JX1974.73 .N814 1985
NYPL [JLD 86-1334]

NUCLEAR WARFARE.
Aguirre, Mariano A. De Hiroshima a los euromisiles /. Madrid , c1984. 254 p. : ISBN 84-309-1062-X LC Card 85-215587
U264 .A39 1984 **NYPL [JFC 86-1643]**

Assessing the nuclear age . Chicago, Ill. , c1986. xvii, 382 p. ; ISBN 0-941682-07-2 LC Card 85-82511 DDC 355/.0217 19
U264 .A79 1986 **NYPL [JLE 87-11]**

Goldman, Peter Louis, 1933- The end of the world that was . New York , c1986. xiv, 129 p., [8] p. of plates : ISBN 0-525-24428-X LC Card 85-31223 DDC 920/.073 19
CT220 .G6 1986 **NYPL [JFD 86-6015]**

Jaipal, Rikhi, 1916- Nuclear arms and the human race . New Delhi , 1986. xix, 306 p. ; ISBN 81-7023-074-8 : LC Card 86-901813 DDC 355/.0217 19
U263 .J35 1986 **NYPL [JLD 87-960]**

La Amenaza de guerra nuclear /. Madrid , 1985. 129 p. ; ISBN 84-7477-027-0 LC Card 86-100273 DDC 355/.0217 19
U263 .A44 1985 **NYPL [JLD 86-2519]**

Nuclear winter and national security . Maxwell Air Force Base, Ala. , Washington, D.C. , 1986. xiii, 76 p. ; LC Card 86-7967 DDC 355/.0217 19
U263 .N845 1986 **NYPL [JFE 87-751]**

Rumble, Greville. The politics of nuclear defence . Cambridge [Cambridgeshire] , 1985. xi, 285 p. ; ISBN 0-7456-0194-4 : LC Card 85-18643 DDC 355/.0217 19
U263 .R86 1985 **NYPL [JLD 86-1092]**

NUCLEAR WEAPONS.
Aguirre, Mariano A. De Hiroshima a los euromisiles /. Madrid , c1984. 254 p. : ISBN 84-309-1062-X LC Card 85-215587
U264 .A39 1984 **NYPL [JFC 86-1643]**

Assessing the nuclear age . Chicago, Ill. , c1986. xvii, 382 p. ; ISBN 0-941682-07-2 LC Card 85-82511 DDC 355/.0217 19
U264 .A79 1986 **NYPL [JLE 87-11]**

Rumble, Greville. The politics of nuclear defence . Cambridge [Cambridgeshire] , 1985. xi, 285 p. ; ISBN 0-7456-0194-4 : LC Card 85-18643 DDC 355/.0217 19
U263 .R86 1985 **NYPL [JLD 86-1092]**

NUCLEAR WINTER.
Nuclear winter and national security . Maxwell Air Force Base, Ala. , Washington, D.C. , 1986. xiii, 76 p. ; LC Card 86-7967 DDC 355/.0217 19
U263 .N845 1986 **NYPL [JFE 87-751]**

Nuclear winter and national security : implications for future policy / study director, Dennis M. Drew ; with contributions from Fred J. Reule ... [et al.]. Maxwell Air Force Base, Ala. : Air University Press ; Washington, D.C. : For sale by the Supt. of Docs., U. S. G.P.O., 1986. xiii, 76 p. ; 23 cm. At head of title: Center for Aerospace Doctrine, Research, and Education. "July 1986." LC Card 86-7967 DDC 355/.0217 19
1. Nuclear warfare. 2. Nuclear winter. 3. Military policy. I. Drew, Dennis M. II. Reule, Fred J. III. Air University (U. S.). Center for Aerospace Doctrine, Research, and Education.
U263 .N845 1986 **NYPL [JFE 87-751]**

Núcleo de Assistência Industrial (Paraíba) Setor exportador paraibano . João Pessoa , 1976. 72 leaves : LC Card 84-239455
HF3409.P32 S47 1976

Nürnberger wirtschafts- und sozialgeographische Arbeiten. For other vols. in this series, see Old Catalog
(Bd. 37, etc) Arabian gulf studies /. Nürnberg , 1985- v. <1 > : LC Card 86-205380 DDC 330.953/053 19
HC415.3 .A7 1985

Nueva alternativa para el desarrollo . Poveda Ramos, Gabriel. Bogotá , 1974. 249 p. : LC Card 78-345029
HD1883 1974 .P68 **NYPL [JLE 80-482]**

Nueva biblioteca colombiana de cultura. Serie breve. Historia.
Pombo, José Ignacio de, 1761-1815. Comercio y contrabando en Cartagena de Indias, 2 de junio de 1800 /. Bogotá, Colombia , 1986. 124 p. ; LC Card 87-107126
HJ6864 .P66 1986

Nueva forma de funcionamiento del capitalismo.
Caputo, Orlando. Notas metodológicas para el análisis de la nueva forma de funcionamiento del capitalismo . Cochabamba [1980] 33 leaves ; LC Card 83-204246
HC192 .C216 1980

Nueva Granada (Republic, 1842-1858) see **Colombia.**

Nueva Granada (State, 1831-1842) see **Colombia.**

La Nueva política económica : a quiénes beneficia? / CEPROMIN, Centro de Promoción Minera. La Paz, Bolivia : CEPROMIN, 1986. 57 p. : ill. ; 21 cm. (Cuaderno de formación . no. 6) Cover title. Bibliography: p. 57. LC Card 87-403839 DDC 338.984 19
1. Bolivia - Economic policy. 2. Debts, Public - United States. 3. Bolivia - Dependency on the United States. 4. Bolivia - Foreign economic relations - United States. 5. United States - Foreign economic relations - Bolivia. 6. International economic relations. I. Centro de Promoción Minera (Bolivia). II. Series.
HC182 .N84 1986

Nuevas tecnologías, economía y sociedad en España / Manuel Castells ... [et al.] ; prólogo de Felipe González. Madrid : Alianza, c1986. 2 v. (xvi, 1056 p.) : ill. ; 23 cm. Bibliography: v. 2, p. [1047]-1056. ISBN 84-206-9495-9 (set) LC Card 86-205429
1. Technological innovations - Economic aspects - Spain. 2. Spain - Economic conditions - 1975-. 3. Spain - Social conditions - 1975-. 4. Spain - Industries. 5. High technology industries - Spain. 6. Quality of

life - Spain. I. Castells, Manuel.
HC390.T4 N84 1986

El nuevo Estado fiscal español . Gimeno Ullastres, Juan Antonio. Madrid , 1981. xx, 315 p. : ISBN 84-7214-219-1 LC Card 85-176738
HJ1249.A1 G56 1981

Nuevo estilo de desarrollo para Uruguay . Martorelli, Horacio. Montevideo, Uruguay , 1982. 2 v. : LC Card 85-167867 DDC 338.1/09895 19
HD1907 .M376 1982 NYPL [JLF 86-935]

NUEVO LAREDO (MEXICO) - ECONOMIC CONDITIONS.
Trabis, Roland. Industrie et politique à la frontière Mexique-U. S.A. . Paris , c1985. 241 p., [1] p. of plates : ISBN 2-222-03772-7 : LC Card 86-175728
HC138.N84 T73 1985

Nuevo León (Mexico : State). Archivo General del Estado. Permisos y concesiones, 1890-1912 / Archivo General del Estado, Nuevo León. [Monterrey, Mexico] : El Archivo, [1981] 43 leaves ; 29 cm. (Serie Indices y catálogos) Cover title. Includes bibliographical references and indexes. LC Card 81-216459
1. Industry and state - Mexico - Nuevo León (State). 2. Concessions - Mexico - Nuevo León (State). 3. Licenses - Mexico - Nuevo León (State). I. Title. II. Series.
HD3616.M44 N866 1981

NUGAN HAND BANK - CORRUPT PRACTICES.
Kwitny, Jonathan. The crimes of patriots . New York , c1987. 424 p., [8] p. of plates : ISBN 0-393-02387-7 : LC Card 87-22032 DDC 364.1/0994 19
HG3448.N846 K95 1987

The number of Egyptian workers in the Arab oil countries, 1974-1983 . Feiler, Gil. Tel Aviv , c1986. i, 30 leaves ; LC Card 87-404430 DDC 331.6/2/620536 19
HD8662 .F45 1986

Number one home business book. Delany, George. The #1 home business book . Blue Ridge Summit, PA [1987] 168 p. : ISBN 0-8306-3022-8 (pbk.) : LC Card 87-2936 DDC 658/.041 19
HD8036 .D44 1987

The number one real estate investment no one talks about /. Hornwood, Sanford W. Englewood Cliffs, N.J. , c1987. xv, 239 p. : ISBN 0-13-626482-4 : LC Card 86-25482 DDC 332.63/244 19
HG4655 .H67 1987

Number 1 real estate investment no one talks about. Hornwood, Sanford W. The number one real estate investment no one talks about /. Englewood Cliffs, N.J. , c1987. xv, 239 p. : ISBN 0-13-626482-4 : LC Card 86-25482 DDC 332.63/244 19
HG4655 .H67 1987

NUMBERS, INDEX. see **INDEX NUMBERS (ECONOMICS)**

Numeracion general de todas las personas de ambos sexos, edades y calidades q[ue] se hà hecho en esta ciudad de Lima, año de 1700 / estudio introductorio por Noble David Cook. Lima : Oficina de Asuntos Culturales de la Corporación Financiera de Desarrollo, 1985. xv, 358 p. : col. port. ; 18 x 21 cm. "Realizado ... por orden del virrey don Melchor Portocarrero, conde de la Monclova"--P. vii. Photoreproduction of the ms. now in the Biblioteca Nacional, Madrid. LC Card 87-400680
1. Lima (Peru) - Population - Statistics. 2. Lima (Peru) - Census, 1700. I. Cook, Noble David. II. Portocarrero Lasso de la Vega, Melchor, conde de la Monclova, 1636-1705. III. Corporación Financiera de Desarrollo (Peru). Oficina de Asuntos Culturales. IV. Spain. Biblioteca Nacional.
HA1069.L7 N86 1985

NUMERACY - DICTIONARIES.
Targett, David. The Pocket guide to business numeracy /. Oxford, OX ; New York, NY, USA : x, 184 p. : ISBN 0-631-15124-9 : LC Card 86-31032 DDC 513/.93/0321 19
HF5695 .T34 1987

Numéros de relations. Tarifs routiers de marchandises. Paris [1986] 956 p. ; ISBN 2-7212-0297-9 LC Card 87-119821
HE5668.A6 T38 1986

Numéros de relations, route. Tarifs routiers de marchandises. Paris [1986] 956 p. ; ISBN 2-7212-0297-9 LC Card 87-119821
HE5668.A6 T38 1986

NUMISMATICS - ASIA - CATALOGS.
Thierry, François. Monnaies d'Extrême Orient /. Paris , <[1986- v. <2 > : ISBN 2-11-080873-X (v. 2) : LC Card 86-218568
HG1250.5 .T45 1986

Nunes, Edson de Oliveira. State and society in Brazil . Boulder , 1987. x, 349 p. ; ISBN 0-8133-7401-4 (pbk. : alk. paper) : LC Card 87-2160 DDC 981/.063 19
HC187 .S78 1987

Nunes, Helvídio. Reforma tributária : reivindicação permanente do Nordeste / Helvídio Nunes. Brasília : [s.n.], 1982. 108 p. ; 23 cm. LC Card 86-128083
1. Taxation - Brazil. 2. Brazil - Economic policy. 3. Brazil, Northeast - Economic policy. 4. Brazil - Politics and government - 1964-1985. I. Title.
HJ2527 .N85 1982

Nunes, Morris A., 1949- Balance sheet management : squeezing extra profits and cash from your company / Morris A. Nunes. New York : Wiley, c1987. xvi, 288 p. : ill. ; 28 cm. Includes index. ISBN 0-471-62956-1 (pbk.) LC Card 87-23093 DDC 658.1/51 19
1. Financial statements. 2. Corporate profits. 3. Cash management. I. Title.
HF5681.B2 N86 1987

Núñez del Arco, José. Seminar on Economic Integration (1982 : Inter-American Development Bank) The economic integration process of Latin America in the 1980's . Washington, D.C. [1984] 318 p. : ISBN 0-940602-17-2 (pbk.) LC Card 87-159367
HC125 .S3973 1982

Núñez, Francisco J. Orozco, Jesús. Ideología y programa de gobierno en los discursos de toma de posesión de los presidentes de México, 1928-1982 /. Guadalajara, Jal., México , c1983. 47 p. ; ISBN 968-511-003-4 LC Card 83-191579
HC135 .O66 1983

Nungesser, Lisa G. Bullard, Diane L. Texas public transit reference manual /. College Station, Tex. [1985] xv, 279 p. : LC Card 86-623065 DDC 388.4/09764 19
HE4426.T4 B84 1985

Nunnelee, Randolph. Trends in Kenyan short wave listening . Nairobi, Kenya , c1979. vii, 87 [26] leaves : LC Card 85-980967 DDC 384.54/3 19
HE8697.A8 T74 1979

Nunnenkamp, Peter.
The international debt crisis of the Third World : causes and consequences for the world economy / Peter Nunnenkamp. New York : St. Martin's Press, 1986. xvi, 205 p. ; 23 cm. Includes indexes. Bibliography: p. 187-197. ISBN 0-312-42003-X : LC Card 85-2008 DDC 336.3/435/091724 19
1. Debts, External - Developing countries. 2. Developing countries - Foreign economic relations. I. Title.
HJ8899 .N86 1985 NYPL [JLD 86-2529]

Manufactured export performance of Brazil : analysis of determinants and prospects / by Peter Nunnenkamp and Ugo Fasano-Filho. Kiel : Kiel Institute of World Economics, Dept. IV, [1986] v, 114 p. : ill. ; 30 cm. (Kiel working paper, 0341-0787 . no. 269) Bibliography: p. 111-114. LC Card 87-101193 DDC 382/.4567/0981 19
1. Foreign trade promotion - Brazil. 2. Brazil - Manufactures - Statistics. 3. Brazil - Commerce - Statistics. I. Fasano-Filho, Ugo, 1956-. II. Series: Kieler Arbeitspapiere , Arbeitspapier Nr. 269. III. Title.
HF1513 .N86 1986

Die Rolle öffentlicher Industrieunternehmen im Exportsektor Indiens / Peter Nunnenkamp. Hamburg : Weltarchiv, 1985. xiv, 268 p. : ill. ; 23 cm. (Schriften des Zentrums für Regionale Entwicklungsforschung der Justus-Liebig-Universität Giessen, 0170-1614 . Bd. 30) Thesis (doctoral)--Justus-Liebig-Universität Giessen. Bibliography: p. 243-268. ISBN 3-87895-285-6 : LC Card 87-111454
1. Government business enterprises - India. 2. Foreign trade promotion - India. 3. Export trading companies - India. I. Title. II. Series.
HD4293 .N85 1985

NUORO (SARDINIA : PROVINCE) - INDUSTRIES.
L'Osservatorio provinciale sul lavoro e sulle professioni . Milano, Italy , c1984. 143 p. : LC Card 84-190423
HD5785.N86 O87 1984 NYPL [JLD 86-1275]

NUORO (SARDINIA : PROVINCE) - OCCUPATIONS.
L'Osservatorio provinciale sul lavoro e sulle professioni . Milano, Italy , c1984. 143 p. : LC Card 84-190423
HD5785.N86 O87 1984 NYPL [JLD 86-1275]

Nuova biblioteca Dedalo. Serie "Mezzogiorno, società, cultura."
Massafra, Angelo. Campagne e territorio nel Mezzogiorno fra Settecento e Ottocento /. Bari , c1984. 324 p. : ISBN 88-22-06039-3 : LC Card 85-179303
HC307.S69 M37 1984

Le nuove frontiere dello sviluppo . Convegno nazionale del PCI (1982 : Milan, Italy) Milano, Italy , c1983. 368 p. ; LC Card 85-174697
HD9696.A3 I727 1982

Nuove politiche di finanziamento degli enti locali in Italia . Romagnoli, Gian Cesare, 1948- Milano, Italy , c1985. 260 p. : LC Card 86-169439
HJ9497 .R65 1985

I nuovi colletti bianchi . Guala Duca, Riccardo, 1935- Milano, Italy , c1985. 164 p. : LC Card 86-128292 DDC 331.7/92/0945 19
HD8039.M4 I854 1985

NUPE (ORGANIZATION) - HISTORY.
Dix, Bernard. Serving the public, building the union . London , 1987- v. <1 > : ISBN 0-85315-645-X (v. 1) : LC Card 87-169851 DDC 331.88/09421 19
HD8005.2.G7 D59 1987

Nupi. see **Oslo. Norsk utenrikspolitisk institutt.**

NUPI rapport .
(nr. 97) Austvik, Ole Gunnar. Søkelys på mekanismene i oljemarkedet /. Oslo [1986?] 66 p. : LC Card 86-197742
HD9560.5 .A75 1986

Nur Gräber als Spuren . Weidner, Marcus, 1964- Münster , c1984. 134 p. : ISBN 3-924550-02-6 LC Card 86-116688 DDC 331.11/732/094355 19
HD4875.G4 W45 1984

Nuremberg thimblemakers /. Greif, Helmut. [Des Moines, Iowa] , c1986. 30 p. : LC Card 86-209810 DDC 338.4/76878 19
HD8039.T522 G34 1986

Nurgalieva, E. N. Problemy ukrepleniia trudovoĭ distsipliny i predotvrashcheniia tekuchesti kadrov na predpriiatiiakh TSentral'nogo Kazakhstana . Karaganda , 1982. 126 p. ; LC Card 84-226131
HF5549.5.L3 P76 1982

Nürnberger wirtschafts- und sozialgeographische Arbeiten, 0546-9112 .
(Bd. 35) Marcinowski, Bernhard. Auswirkungen von Streckenstillegungen, dargestellt am Beispiel von Nebenbahnen in Bayern /. Nürnberg , 1983. xviii, 260 p. : LC Card 84-162065
HE3079.B5 M28 1983

(Bd. 38) Ritter, Wigand. Qatar, ein arabisches Erdölemirat /. Nürnberg , 1985. 201 p. : LC Card 86-205396
HC415.37 .R58 1985

(Bd. 39) Reichert, Thomas. Andorra, eine Landeskunde . Nürnberg , 1986. xviii, 320 p. : LC Card 87-131037 DDC 330.946/79083 19
HC390.5 .R45 1986

NURSERY SCHOOLS - ITALY - ROME - COST OF OPERATION - ACCOUNTING - CASE STUDIES.
Mancini, Andrea, 1954- La contabilità analitica dei costi . [Torino] , 1986. 53 p. : ISBN 88-85851-00-2 : LC Card 87-114718
HF5686.C8 M265 1986

Nurturing advanced technology enterprises . Allen, David N. New York , c1986. xvi, 268 p. ; ISBN 0-275-92136-0 (alk. paper) : LC Card 86-9411 DDC 338.4/762/0009748 19
HC107.P43 H533 1986 NYPL [JLE 86-3609]

Nusbaumer, Jacques, économiste.
Services in the global market / edited by Jacques Nusbaumer. Boston : Kluwer Academic Publishers, c1987. ix, 245 p. ; 25 cm. Bibliography: p. 231-242. Includes index. ISBN 0-89838-198-3 LC Card 87-4053 DDC 338.4/6 19
1. Service industries. I. Title.
HD9980.5 .N88 1987

[Services, nouvelle donne de l'économie. English]
The services economy : lever to growth / Jacques Nusbaumer. Boston : Kluwer Academic, c1987. 116 p. ; 24 cm. Translation of: Services, nouvelle donne de l'économie. Bibliography: p. 109-112. Includes index. ISBN 0-89838-192-4 LC Card 86-21397 DDC 338.4/6 19
1. Service industries. I. Title.
HD9980.5 .N8713 1987

Nuscheler, Franz. Die Entwicklungspolitik der Regierung Thatcher : wie konservativ ist die Overseas Aid-Politik der britischen Konservativen? / von Franz Nuscheler. [Bonn] : Friedrich Ebert Stiftung, [1986] 93 p. : ill. ; 21 cm. (Analysen aus der Abteilung Entwicklungsländerforschung, 0174-5190 . Nr. 122) "Januar 1986." Bibliography: p. 85-89. LC Card 86-186261
1. Economic assistance, British - Developing countries. 2. Great Britain - Economic policy - 1945-. 3. Investments, British - Developing countries. 4. Conservatism - Great Britain. 5. Conservatism - United States. I. Title. II. Series.
HC60 .N87 1986

Nussbaum, Helga. Proizvoditel'nye sily i monopolisticheskiĭ kapital v Rossii i Germanii v kontse XIX-nachale XX vv. /. Moskva , 1986. 223 p. ; LC Card 87-159751
HD2859 .P76 1986

NUTRITION AND STATE. see **NUTRITION POLICY.**

NUTRITION - CHILE.
Hardy, Clarisa. Hambre + dignidad=ollas comunes /. [Santiago, Chile] , 1986. 282 p., [16] p. of plates : *NYPL [JLD 87-334]*

NUTRITION - DEVELOPING COUNTRIES - HANDBOOKS, MANUALS, ETC.
Handbuch der Landwirtschaft und Ernährung in den Entwicklungsländern /. Stuttgart , c1982- v. : ISBN 3-8001-3059-9 (Bd. 1) LC Card 84-155503 DDC 338.1/09172/4 19
HD1417 .H24 1982 NYPL [JLL 86-257]

NUTRITION EXTENSION WORK - UNITED STATES.
Obert, Jessie Craig, 1911- Community nutrition /. New York , c1986. xviii, 478 p. : ISBN 0-471-82187-X LC Card 85-16910 DDC 363.8/8/0973 19
HV696.F6 O23 1986 NYPL [JLE 86-1398]

Nutrition in agriculture .
(no. 2) Integrating nutrition into agricultural and rural development projects . Rome , 1984. ix, 132 p. : ISBN 92-5-102150-3
NYPL [JLG 86-181]

NUTRITION POLICY - ASIA - CONGRESSES.
An Integrated approach to population, food, and nutrition policies and programmes for national development . Bangkok, Thailand [1979 or 1980] 39 p. ; LC Card 82-169080
HA4553 .I58 1979

NUTRITION POLICY - BOLIVIA.
Proyecto harinas compuestas . La Paz, Bolivia , 1982. 272, [2], 3 p., [9] p. of plates : LC Card 83-195592
HD9044.B52 P76 1982

NUTRITION POLICY - BRAZIL.
Avaliação global do programa de nutrição Brasil-BIRD . [São Paulo, SP] [Brasília] , 1981- v. <1 > : LC Card 87-123819 DDC 363.8/56/0981 19
HD9014.B82 A82 1981

NUTRITION POLICY - DEVELOPING COUNTRIES.
Food policy . Baltimore , c1987. xiv, 567 p. : ISBN 0-8018-3500-3 (pbk.) : LC Card 86-27613 DDC 363.8/56/091724 19
HD9018.D44 F665 1987

Integrating nutrition into agricultural and rural development projects . Rome , 1984. ix, 132 p. : ISBN 92-5-102150-3 *NYPL [JLG 86-181]*

Perspektivy reshenii͡a prodovol'stvennoĭ problemy v razvivai͡ushchikhsi͡a stranakh . Moskva , 1985. 142 p. ; LC Card 85-188217
HD9018.D44 P47 1985

NUTRITION POLICY - INDIA.
Dogra, Bharat. Empty stomachs and packed godowns . New Delhi , 1987. viii, 126 p. ; LC Card 87-900472 DDC 338.1/9/54 19
HD9016.I42 D64 1987

NUTRITION POLICY - MEXICO - ADDRESSES, ESSAYS, LECTURES.
Por una nueva política alimentaria /. [México, D.F.] , 1984. 114 p. ; LC Card 85-131176 DDC 338.1/9/72 19
HD9014.M62 P67 1984 NYPL [JLC 86-348]

NUTRITION POLICY - PHILIPPINES.
Leviste, Jose P., 1945- Food for thought . Los Baños, Laguna, Philippines , c1985. 150 p. : LC Card 86-193278 DDC 338.1/8599 19
HD2088 .L48 1985

NUTRITION POLICY - STUDY AND TEACHING (SECONDARY)
Williams, Sonja, 1953- Exploding the hunger myths . San Francisco , c1987. xv, 173 p. : ISBN 0-935028-23-4 (pbk.) : LC Card 87-3360 DDC 363.8/07/1273 19
HD9000.5 .W476 1987

NUTRITION POLICY - UNITED STATES.
Dirt rich, dirt poor . New York , 1986. xii, 188 p. ; ISBN 0-7102-0378-0 LC Card 85-8274 DDC 338.1/9/73 19
HD1761 .D55 1986 NYPL [JLD 87-821]

Obert, Jessie Craig, 1911- Community nutrition /. New York , c1986. xviii, 478 p. : ISBN 0-471-82187-X LC Card 85-16910 DDC 363.8/8/0973 19
HV696.F6 O23 1986 NYPL [JLE 86-1398]

United States. Congress. Senate. Committee on Agriculture, Nutrition, and Forestry. Review of the implementation of the Food Security Act of 1985 . Washington , 1987. iv, 180 p. : LC Card 87-601199 DDC 338.1/9/73 19
HD1761 .U515 1987

NUTRITION - STUDY AND TEACHING (ELEMENTARY)
Rubin, Laurie, 1956- Food first curriculum /. San Francisco, CA , c1984. viii, 146 p. : ISBN 0-935028-17-X : LC Card 84-8986 DDC 372.8/3 19
HD9000.5 .R73 1984 NYPL [JLF 86-1436]

NUTRITION SURVEYS.
Review of food consumption surveys-1985 . Rome , 1986. xxiv, 212 p. ; ISBN 92-5-102375-1 (pbk.) LC Card 86-222995 DDC 339.4/8664 19
HD9000.4 .R483 1986

NUTRITION SURVEYS - MEXICO - DISTRITO FEDERAL.
Restrepo, Iván. La basura . México, D.F. , 1985. 193 p. : LC Card 86-209151
HD9014.M63 M47 1985

Nuttall, C. S., 1920- Minkes, A. L. Business behaviour & management structure /. London , c1985. 224 p. ; ISBN 0-7099-1795-3
NYPL [JLD 87-1113]

Nuttin, Jozef, 1909-
[Théorie de la motivation humaine. English]
Motivation, planning, and action : a relational theory of behavior dynamics / Joseph Nuttin ; translated by Raymond P. Lorion and Jean E. Dumas. Leuven, Belgium : Leuven University Press ; Hillsdale, N.J. : L. Erlbaum Associates, c1984. viii, 251 p. ; 24 cm. (Louvain psychology series studia psychologica) Rev. and enl. translation of: Théorie de la motivation humaine. Includes indexes. Bibliography: p. 217-234. ISBN 0-89859-332-8 (L. Erlbaum) LC Card 83-16416 DDC 153.8 19
1. Motivation (Psychology). 2. Psychology - Philosophy. 3. Cognition. I. Title. II. Series.
BF503 .N8713 1984 NYPL [JFE 86-2315]

Nutzen- und Zielprobleme privater Haushalte .
Maierbeck, Marianne. Berlin , 1978. 203 p. : ISBN 3-428-04220-4 : LC Card 79-356181
TX7 .B4 Heft 13 HB201
NYPL [JLE 86-3431]

Nutzung ökonomisch-mathematischer Methoden und der elektronischen Rechentechnik zur Erhöhung der Reaktionsfähigkeit der Industriekombinate gegenüber der Bedarfsdynamik. Wissenschaftliche Tagung "Nutzung Ökonomisch-Mathematischer Methoden und der Elektronischen Rechentechnik zur Erhöhung der Reaktionsfähigkeit der Industriekombinate gegenüber der Bedarfsdynamik" (1983 : Technische Hochschule Karl-Marx Stadt) Wissenschaftliche Tagung "Nutzung Ökonomisch-Mathematischer Methoden und der Elektronischen Rechentechnik zur Erhöhung der Reaktionsfähigkeit der Industriekombinate gegenüber der Bedarfsdynamik," 8. Juni 1983 . Karl-Marx-Stadt [1983] iii, 56 p. ; LC Card 84-117572
HD30.25 .W56 1983

Nutzung von anonymisierten Einzelangaben aus Daten der amtlichen Statistik : Bedingungen und Möglichkeiten / Herausgeber, Statistisches Bundesamt, Wiesbaden. Stuttgart : W. Kohlhammer, 1987. 200 p. : ill. ; 24 cm. (Band 5 der Schriftenreihe Forum der Bundesstatistik) German and English. Includes bibliographies. ISBN 3-17-003338-7 LC Card 87-401358
1. Social sciences - Statistics - Research - Methodology. I. Germany (West). Statistisches Bundesamt. II. Series: Schriftenreihe Forum der Bundesstatistik , Bd. 5.
HA29.5.G4 N88 1987

NUWARA ELIYA (SRI LANKA : DISTRICT) - POPULATION - STATISTICS.
Population profile, Nuwara Eliya District. [Colombo] [1985?] viii, 35 p. : LC Card 86-902529 DDC 304.6/09549/3 19
HA4570.8.Z9 N886 1985

NWB-Schriften für die internationale Steuerpraxis.
Ausländische Investitionen in U. S.-Grundvermögen /. Herne , 1984, c1983. 86 p. ; ISBN 3-482-69041-3 LC Card 84-203818 DDC 346.43/07 344.3067 19
K3830.4 .A97 1984 NYPL [JLD 86-2326]

Nweihed, Kaldone G., 1929- Bolívar y el Tercer Mundo : la devolución de un anticipo revalorizado / Kaldone G. Nweihed. Caracas, Venezuela : Comité Ejecutivo del Bicentenario de Simón Bolívar, c1984. 400 p. : col. maps ; 23 cm. (Colección Bicentenario. no. 4) Includes bibliographical references and indexes. ISBN 84-499-7056-3 LC Card 85-136718
1. Bolívar, Simón, 1783-1830 - Views on colonies. 2. Colonies. 3. Decolonization. 4. Developing countries. I. Series: Colección Bicentenario (Caracas, Venezuela). II. Title.
F2235.3 .N98 1984 NYPL [JFE 86-1176]

Nwoke, Chibuzo. Third World minerals and global pricing : a new theory / Chibuzo Nwoke. London ; [Atlantic Highlands] N.J. : Zed Books, 1987. x, 229 p. : ill. ; 23 cm. Bibliography: p. 214-225. Includes index. ISBN 0-86232-441-6 : LC Card 87-12621 DDC 338.2/3 19
1. Mineral industries - Developing countries. I. Title.
HD9506.D452 N86 1986

Ny teknik för elproduktion, elanvändning : utredning för 1981 års energikommitté. Stockholm : Energiforskningsnämnden, [1983] 172 p. : ill. ; 24 cm. (Efn-rapport, 0281-0301 . nr 4) "Ds I 1983:21." LC Card 84-108404
1. Electric utilities - Sweden. 2. Electric power consumption - Sweden. 3. Energy policy - Sweden. 4. Electric power - Sweden - Conservation. I. Sweden. 1981 års energikommitté. II. Sweden. Energiforskningsnämnden. III. Series.
HD9685.S852 N9 1983

Den nya given . Bergman, Åke. Stockholm [1986] 157 p. ; ISBN 91-550-3244-3 : LC Card 86-235012
HD70.S8 B48 1986

Nyanteng, V. K.
Local food prices : trends and factors affecting them / by V.K. Nyanteng. [Ghana] : Institute of Statistical, Social, and Economic Research, University of Ghana, 1978. 37 p. : ill. ; 32 cm. (Discussion paper / Institute of Statistical, Social, and Economic Research, University of Ghana . no. 5) "May 1978." Bibliography: p. 31-32. LC Card 87-403379 DDC 338.4/3664/009667 19
1. Food prices - Ghana. I. Series: Discussion paper (University of Ghana. Institute of Statistical, Social, and

Economic Research) , no. 5. II. Title.
HD9017.G452 N92 1978

Supplementary occupations and incomes of cocoa farmers in the Suhum agricultural district of Ghana / by V.K. Nyanteng. Legon : Institute of Statistical, Social, and Economic Research, University of Ghana, 1979. 17 p. ; 33 cm. (Discussion paper . no. 8) Bibliography: p. 17. LC Card 87-402747 DDC 331.7/63374/09667 19
1. Cocoa farmers - Ghana - Supplementary employment - Case studies. I. Series: Discussion paper (University of Ghana. Institute of Statistical, Social, and Economic Research) , no. 8. II. Title.
HD8039.C6362 G46 1979

Yam production, marketing, and prices in Ghana / Victor Kwame Nyanteng. Legon : Institute of Statistical, Social, and Economic Research, University of Ghana, 1978. vii leaves, 159 p. : ill. ; 29 cm. "Essentially the work the author submitted to the University of Ghana for an M.Sc. degree in agricultural economics in 1969"--Pref. Includes bibliographies. LC Card 87-400731 DDC 338.1/7523/09667 19
1. Yam industry - Ghana. 2. Yams - Ghana. I. University of Ghana. Institute of Statistical, Social, and Economic Research. II. Title.
HD9235.S92 G46 1978

Nyberg, Peter. On the choice of optimal central bank currency baskets / by Peter Nyberg. Åbo : Åbo akademi, 1982. 24 p. ; 21 cm. (Meddelanden från ekonomisk-statsvetenskapliga fakulteten. Serie A. 181) Bibliography: p. 24.
1. Foreign exchange problem - Mathematical models. 2. Currency question - Mathematical models. I. Series: Turku, Finland. Akademi (1918-). Statsvetenskapliga facultaten. Meddelanden. Serie A. , 181. II. Title.
NYPL [JLL 77-251 no. 181]

Nyckeln til styrelserummet . Dahlgren, Bo, 1924- Stockholm [1983] 182 p. : ISBN 91-1-837051-9 : LC Card 83-210185
HD2883 .D34 1983

NYCOM municipal management series . (no. 4) Baynes, Peter A. Distribution of local sales tax revenue . Albany, N.Y. (119 Washington Ave., Albany 12210) [1986] 13 p. : LC Card 87-106773 DDC 336.2/713/09747 19
HJ5715.U62 N72 1986

Nydegger, Alfred. Investitionen und Innovationen in kleineren Industriebetrieben : eine Ursachenanalyse mit besonderer Betonung des Risikoverhaltens : Ergebnisse einer Befragung / Alfred Nydegger, Herbert Oberhänsli, Reinhold Harringer. Diessenhofen : Rüegger, c1983. viii, 317 p. : ill. ; 23 cm. (Schweizerisches Institut für Aussenwirtschafts-, Struktur- und Regionalforschung an der Hochschule St. Gallen . Bd. 5) "Nationales Forschungsprogramm 9: Mechanismen und Entwicklung der Schweizerischen Wirtschaft und deren soziale Auswirkungen. Projekt Nr. 4.366-0.79.09: Risikoaversion als Bestimmungsfaktor des Investitionsverhaltens, besonders bei Innovationsinvestitionen"--T.p. verso. Bibliography: p. 311-317. ISBN 3-7253-0196-4 LC Card 83-224277 DDC 658.1/592 19
1. Small business - Switzerland - Finance. 2. Venture capital - Switzerland. I. Oberhänsli, Herbert. II. Harringer, Reinhold. III. Nationales Forschungsprogramm Mechanismen und Entwicklung der Schweizerischen Wirts chaft. IV. Series: Schweizerisches Institut für Aussenwirtschafts-, Struktur- und Regionalforschung an der Hochschule St. Gallen (Series) , Bd. 5. V. Title.
HG4027.7 .N93 1983 ***NYPL [JLD 87-633]***

Nygaard, Kristen, 1926- Computers and democracy . Aldershot [Hants, England] , Brookfield [Vt.], USA , c1987. x, 434 p. : ISBN 0-566-05476-0 : LC Card 87-8398 DDC 338/.06 19
HD5650 .C65 1987

Nyitrai, Ferencné.
A magyar gazdaság negyven éve / Nyitrai Ferencné. [Budapest] : Kossuth, 1985. 385 p. ; 21 cm. Bibliography: p. 385. ISBN 963-09-2570-2 : LC Card 86-104105
1. Hungary - Economic conditions - 1945-. I. Title. II. Title: Magyar gazdaság 40 éve.
HC300.28 .N945 1985

Prioritások gazdaságunk fejlesztésében / Nyitrai Ferencné. [Budapest] : Kossuth, 1986. 270 p. ; 20 cm. ISBN 963-09-2782-9 : LC Card 87-408568
1. Hungary - Economic policy - 1968-. 2. Central planning - Hungary. I. Title.
HC300.28 .N954 1986

Nyolcvanas évek kapitalizmusa. A 80-as évek kapitalizmusa . [Budapest] , 1985. 406 p. ; ISBN 963-09-2696-2 : LC Card 86-186468
HB501 .A14 1985

De Nyuddannedes indplacering på arbejdsmarkedet 1981-1983 : Undervisningsministeriets projekt vedrørende en løbende registrering af beskæftigelsesudviklingen for nyuddannede. [Copenhagen : Undervisningsministeriets Økonomisk-statistiske konsulent, 1986] 1 v. (various pagings) : ill. ; 21 cm. (Uddannelses analyser . 1986, nr. 1 (Juni 1986)) ISBN 87-503-6320-4 LC Card 87-127126
1. College graduates - Employment - Denmark - Statistics. 2. Labor supply - Denmark - Effect of education on - Statistics. I. Series: Uddannelses analyser , 1986, nr. 1.
HD6278.D4 N98 1986

A nyúlhústermelés és export gazdasági problémái /. Szajkó, Pál. Budapest , 1985. 57 p. : ISBN 963-491-207-9 LC Card 86-196798
HD9438.R4 H97 1985

Nyut'er Hayastani gyughatntesut'yan ev gyughats'iut'yan patmut'yan / [khmbagrakan kolegia, S.T. Eremyan ... et al. ; Kh.P. Mirimanyan, glkh. khmbagir]. Erevan : Haykakan SSR Gitut'yunneri Akademiayi Hratarakch'ut'yun, 1964- v. <1 > : ill. ; 23 cm. Armenian and Russian. Title on added t.p.: Materialy po istorii sel′skogo khoziaistva i krest′ianstva Armenii. At head of title: Haykakan SSR Gitut'yunneri Akademia, Patmut'yan Instituti Gyughatntesut'yan ev Gyughats'iut'yan Patmut'yan Handznazhoghov. "Suyn zhoghovatsuum amp'op'vats ē Handznazhoghovi I ev II gitakan sesianerum kardats'vats zekuts'umneri nshanakalits' masě"--T.p. verso. Includes bibliographical references. LC Card 86-225528
1. Agriculture - Economic aspects - Armenian S.S.R. - History - Congresses. 2. Agriculture - Armenian S.S.R. - History - Congresses. 3. Peasantry - Armenian S.S.R. - History - Congresses. I. Mirimanian, Khachatur Pogosovich. II. Patmut'yan Institut (Haykakan SSR Gitut'yunneri Akademia). Gyughatntesut'yan ev Gyughats'iut'yan Patmut'yan Handznazhoghov. III. Title: Materialy po istorii sel′skogo khoziaistva i krest′ianstva Armenii.
HD1995.A7 N98 1964

OAA. see **Food and Agriculture Organization of the United Nations.**

O. A. G. [i. e. Ostasien-Gesellschaft] see **Deutsche Gesellschaft für Natur- und Völkerkunde Ostasiens.**

O. A. S. see **Organization of American States.**

O. A. U. For corporate body referred to by these initials, see: **Organization of African Unity.**

O. C. D. E. see **Organization for Economic Cooperation and Development.**

O cavvaliere Aristides Germani /. Campos Netto, José Candido de, 1880-1963. [Caxias do Sul, Brazil] [Porto Alegre] , 1978. 111 p. : LC Card 79-121861
HD9056.B62 C35 1978 ***NYPL [JLD 81-342]***

O Comércio e suas profissões : imagens, Brasil 1500/1946 / editoração, texto e projeto gráfico, Arthur Bosisio Júnior ; pesquisa, Jaury Nepomuceno de Oliveira e A. Bosisio Jr. Rio de Janeiro : Serviço Nacional de Aprendizagem Comercial, Departamento Nacional, Divisão de Planejamento, Coordenadoria de Divulgação e Promoções, 1983. 127, [5] p. : ill. ; 23 x 27 cm. Bibliography: p. [130] LC Card 84-161651
1. Peddlers and peddling - Brazil - History. 2. Retail trade - Brazil - History. 3. Business education - Brazil - History. I. Bosísio Júnior, Arthur. II. Oliveira, Jaury Nepumuceno de.
HF5459.B7 C65 1983 ***NYPL [JLF 86-1408]***

O dawaniu /. Garczyński, Stefan. Warszawa , 1985. 172 p. ; ISBN 83-10-08676-8
NYPL [*QO 87-1235]

O desencontro marcado . Alves, Denise. Petrópolis , 1985. 169 p. ; LC Card 85-226159
HQ1075 .A44 1985 ***NYPL [JFD 86-7232]***

O. E. A. see **Organization of American States.**

O. E. C. D. see **Organization for Economic Cooperation and Development.**

O. E. O. see **United States. Office of Economic Opportunity.**

O economista Isaac de Pinto, o seu "Tratado da circulação e do crédito," e outros escritos económicos /. Pinto, Isaac de, 1715-1787. [Selections. 1960.] Lisboa , 1960. 247 p. : LC Card 85-125396
HJ150 .P552 1960

O estado e o cartel do leite no Brasil /. Souza, Francisco Araújo Salles de. Brasília, Distrito Federal , 1981. 130 p. : LC Card 81-217015
HD9282.B72 S65 1981
NYPL [JLD 86-3366]

O Gosudarstvennom bi͡udzhete SSSR na 1986 god i ob ispolnenii Gosudarstvennogo bi͡udzheta SSSR za 1984 god . Dementsev, V. V. (Viktor Vladimirovich) Moskva , 1985. 28 p. ; LC Card 86-203425
HJ2129 .D46 1985

O Gosudarstvennom plane ėkonomicheskogo i sotsial′nogo razvitii͡a SSSR na 1981-1985 gody ... . Baĭbakov, Nikolaĭ Konstantinovich. Moskva , 1981. 44 p. ; LC Card 82-200045
HC336.25 .B33945 1981

O. I. T. see **International Labor Organization.**

OMGUS. see **Germany (Territory under Allied Occupation, 1945-1955. U. S. Zone). Office of Military Government.**

O. M. S. see **World Health Organization.**

O. M. T. see **World Tourism Organization.**

O meio circulante nacional . Cavalcanti, Amaro, 1849-1922. Brasília-Distrito Federal , 1983- v. : LC Card 84-160002
HG833 .C38 1983 ***NYPL [JLL 85-246]***

O. P. E. C. see **Organization of Petroleum Exporting Countries.**

O.P.E.C.'s investments and the international financial system. Mattione, Richard P. OPEC's investments and the international financial system /. Washington, D.C. , c1985. xi, 201 p. ; ISBN 0-8157-5510-4 : LC Card 84-23242 DDC 332.6/7314 19
HG4538 .M38 1985 ***NYPL [JLE 86-3698]***

O. T. A. N. see **North Atlantic Treaty Organization.**

O. U. A. For corporate body referred to by these initials, see: **Organization of African Unity.**

Oakley, Allen. Lowe, Adolph, 1893- Essays in political economics . New York , 1987. 257 p. ; ISBN 0-8147-6168-2 LC Card 87-11219 DDC 338.9 19
HD82 .L693 1987

Oates, Wallace E. Baumol, William J. The theory of environmental policy /. Cambridge [Cambridgeshire] , New York , 1988. x, 299 p. : ISBN 0-521-32224-3 LC Card 87-24975 DDC 363.7/001 19
HC79.E5 B375 1988

OAXACA (MEXICO) - ECONOMIC CONDITIONS.
Mora, Teresa. La Mixteca baja, su migración . México, D.F. , 1982. 129, [84] leaves ; LC Card 87-122391 DDC 304.6/0972/74 19
HB3532.O18 M67 1982

OAXACA (MEXICO) - POPULATION.
Mora, Teresa. La Mixteca baja, su migración . México, D.F. , 1982. 129, [84] leaves ; LC Card 87-122391 DDC 304.6/0972/74 19
HB3532.O18 M67 1982

Ob approksimat͡sii makroėkonomicheskikh zavisimosteĭ posredstvom tablichnykh i splaĭnovykh proizvodstvennykh funkt͡siĭ /. Zoidov, K. Kh. Moskva , 1985. 25, [3] p. : LC Card 86-162091
HB142 .Z65 1985

Obando S., Marta. Encuesta residencial de consumo energético / elaborado por Marta Obando S. ; revisado por Gloria Villa ; aprobado por Jorge Blanco Roldán. San José, Costa Rica : Dirección Sectorial de Energía, 1985. iv, 56, [71] p. : ill. ; 28 cm. "United States of America, Agencia para el Desarrollo Internacional"--Cover. Errata slip inserted. Bibliography: p. [71] LC Card 86-219603
1. Dwellings - Costa Rica - Energy consumption. I. Villa, Gloria. II. Costa Rica. Dirección Sectorial de Energía. III. Title.
HD9502.C82 O23 1985

Obdachlosenhilfe im Sozialstaat . Drygala, Anke, 1950- Weinheim , 1986. 154 p. ; ISBN

3-407-58292-7 LC Card 87-103682 DDC 362.5/83 19
HD7287.96.G3 D79 1986

Obel, Børge. Innovation and entrepreneurship in organizations . Amsterdam ; New York : vii, 207 p. : ISBN 0-444-42716-3 (U. S.) : LC Card 86-24207 DDC 658.4/012 19
HD41 .I56 1986

Oberai, A. S. Land settlement policies and population redistribution in developing countries . New York , 1988. xiv, 395 p. ; ISBN 0-275-92799-7 (alk. paper) LC Card 87-15837 DDC 333.3/1/1724 19
HD1131 .L364 1988

Oberbeck, Herbert. Baethge, Martin. Zukunft der Angestellten . Frankfurt , New York , c1986. 460 p. : ISBN 3-593-33368-6 (pbk.) LC Card 87-673317
HD5707 .B28x 1986

Oberfranken (Germany). Bezirksplanungsstelle. Regionalbericht Region Oberfranken-West /. [München] , 1976. 83 p. : LC Card 86-231827
HC288.O16 R44 1976

OBERFRANKEN (GERMANY) - ECONOMIC CONDITIONS.
Regionalbericht Region Oberfranken-West /. [München] , 1976. 83 p. : LC Card 86-231827
HC288.O16 R44 1976

OBERFRANKEN (GERMANY) - POPULATION.
Regionalbericht Region Oberfranken-West /. [München] , 1976. 83 p. : LC Card 86-231827
HC288.O16 R44 1976

OBERFRANKEN (GERMANY) - SOCIAL CONDITIONS.
Regionalbericht Region Oberfranken-West /. [München] , 1976. 83 p. : LC Card 86-231827
HC288.O16 R44 1976

Oberg, Charles N. Medicaid, entering the third decade : enrollment in HMOs and alternative health systems / Charles N. Oberg, Cynthia Longseth Polich. Excelsior, Minn. (P.O. Box 458, Excelsior 55331-0458) : InterStudy, c1986. vii, 70 p. : ill. ; 28 cm. Bibliography: p. 68-70. LC Card 86-233259 DDC 362.1/0425/0973 19
1. Medicaid. 2. Medicare. 3. Poor - Medical care - United States. 4. Health maintenance organizations. I. Polich, Cynthia Longseth. II. InterStudy (Center). III. Title.
HD7102.U4 O58 1986

OBERGURGL (AUSTRIA) - ECONOMIC CONDITIONS - MATHEMATICAL MODELS.
Alpine Areas Workshop (1974 : Schloss Laxenburg) Alpine Areas Workshop, May 13-17, 1974 /. Laxenburg [1974] 80 p. : LC Card 82-212849
HC268.O25 A46 1974

Oberhänsli, Herbert. Nydegger, Alfred. Investitionen und Innovationen in kleineren Industriebetrieben . Diessenhofen , c1983. viii, 317 p. : ISBN 3-7253-0196-4 LC Card 83-224277 DDC 658.1/592 19
HG4027.7 .N93 1983 ***NYPL [JLD 87-633]***

Oberhänsli, Urs. Altersvorsorge, Kapitalschwemme oder Kapitalmangel? : Untersuchung über das Spar- und Erwerbsverhalten der Rentner in der Schweiz / Urs Oberhänsli, Robert Fluder, Serge Gaillard. Bern : P. Haupt, c1986. xii, 222 p. : ill. ; 21 cm. "Nationales Forschungsprogramm Nr. 9 Mechanismen und Entwicklung der Schweizerischen Wirtschaft"--Cover. Bibliography: p. 125-127. ISBN 3-258-03578-4 : LC Card 86-149614
1. Old age pensions - Switzerland. I. Fluder, Robert. II. Gaillard, Serge. III. Nationales Forschungsprogramm Mechanismen und Entwicklung der Schweizerischen Wirtschaft. IV. Title.
HD7105.35.S9 O24 1986

Oberndörfer, Dieter.
Die Wirtschaft der Vereinigten Staaten und der Bundesrepublik Deutschland . Bonn , c1977. 106 p. ; ISBN 3-87198-079-X LC Card 86-104673
HC106.7 .W57 1977

Wirtschaftlicher Wandel, religiöser Wandel und Wertwandel . Berlin , c1985. 411 p. : ISBN 3-428-05784-8 LC Card 85-218417
HC286.7 .W58 1985

Oberreit, Wolfgang. Peru, Kolonisation und Abhängigkeit . Saarbrücken , Fort Lauderdale , 1981. 192 p. : ISBN 3-88156-165-X : LC Card 82-104103
HD1905.O75 P47 1981

Oberschelp, Reinhard.
Beiträge zur niedersächsischen Preisgeschichte des 16. bis 19. Jahrhunderts /. Hildesheim , 1986. lxiii, 541 p. ; ISBN 3-7848-3874-X LC Card 87-407399 DDC 338.1/331/094359 19
HD9043.4 .B45 1986

Werbegraphik 1830-1870, aus niedersächsischen Zeitungen /. [Hannover] , Hildesheim , 1986. xv, 280 p. : ISBN 3-7848-3875-8 LC Card 87-408153 DDC 659.13/2/094359 19
HF5996.L68 W47 1986

Obert, Jessie Craig, 1911- Community nutrition / Jessie Craig Obert. 2nd ed. New York : Wiley, c1986. xviii, 478 p. : ill. ; 24 cm. Includes bibliographies and index. ISBN 0-471-82187-X LC Card 85-16910 DDC 363.8/8/0973 19
1. Food relief - United States. 2. Nutrition policy - United States. 3. Nutrition extension work - United States. I. Title.
HV696.F6 O23 1986 ***NYPL [JLE 86-1398]***

L'obiettivo occupazione nell'esperienza italiana /. Faustini, Gino, 1930- Torino , c1984. 265 p. ; LC Card 86-168096
HD5784 .F38 1984

Obnaruzhenie izmeneniĭ svoĭstv sluchaĭnykh protsessov : materialy k seminaru pri Institute matematiki i kibernetiki AN Litovskoĭ SSR "Statisticheskie problemy upravleniia" / pod redaktsieĭ L. Tel'ksnis. Vil'nius : In-t matematiki i kibernetiki Akademii nauk Litovskoĭ SSR, 1984. 243 p. : ill. ; 20 cm. (Statisticheskie problemy upravleniia, 0132-5302 . vyp. 65) Titles on added t.p.: Atsitiktinių procesų savybių pasikeitimo suradimas. Detection of changes in the properties of random processes. At head of title: Institut matematiki i kibernetiki AN Litovskoĭ SSR ... Summaries in English and Lithuanian. Includes bibliographies. LC Card 84-168819
1. Stochastic processes - Congresses. I. Tel'ksnis, L. II. Atstiktinių procesų savybių pasikeitimo seminaras (1st : 1984 : Palanga, Lithuania). III. Title: Atsitiktinių procesų savybių pasikeitimo suradimas. IV. Title: Detection of changes in the properties of random processes. V. Series.
HD38 .S715 vyp. 65 QA274.A1

Obobshchestvlenie i ėkonomicheskie interesy v sotsialisticheskom obshchestve / B.IA. Gershkovich, V.I. Livshits, S.S. Slepakov ; pod redaktsieĭ B.IA. Gershkovicha. Moskva : "Vysshaia shkola", 1983. 127 p. ; 22 cm. Includes bibliographical references. LC Card 84-204638
1. Government ownership - Soviet Union. 2. Incentives in industry - Soviet Union. I. Gershkovich, B. IA. (Boris IAkovlevich). II. Livshits, V. I. (Vadim Isaevich). III. Slepakov, S. S. (Sergeĭ Semenovich).
HD3856.R9 O26 1983

Obobshchestvlenie sel'skokhoziaĭstvennogo proizvodstva / otvetstvennyĭ redaktor V.A. Tikhonov. Moskva : "Nauka", 1986. 159 p. ; 20 cm. (Problemy sovetskoĭ ėkonomiki) At head of title: Akademiia nauk SSSR. Ordena Trudovogo Krasnogo Znameni Institut ėkonomiki. Includes bibliographical references. LC Card 86-177899
1. Agricultural industries - Soviet Union. I. Tikhonov, Vladimir Aleksandrovich. II. Institut ėkonomiki (Akademiia nauk SSSR).
HD9015.S652 O26 1986

Oborne, Michael West. China's special economic zones / by Michael Oborne. Paris : Development Centre of the Organisation for Economic Co-operation and Development ; [Washington, D.C. : OECD Publications and Information Centre, distributor], 1986. 185 p. : ill. ; 23 cm. (Development Centre studies) Bibliography: p. 160-173. ISBN 92-64-12801-8 (pbk.) : LC Card 86-217671 DDC 338.6/042/0951 19
1. Industrial districts - China. 2. Investments, Foreign - China. 3. China - Economic policy - 1976-. 4. Free ports and zones - China. 5. China - Foreign economic relations. I. Title.
HC427.92 .O27 1986

Una Obra cooperativa / Departamento Administrativo Nacional de Cooperativas. Bogotá, Colombia : DANCOOP, [1982] 276 p. ; 23 cm. LC Card 86-226857
1. Cooperative societies - Colombia. 2. Colombia. Departmento Administrativo Nacional de Cooperativas. 3. Cooperative societies - Government policy - Colombia. I. Colombia. Departmento Administrativo Nacional de Cooperativas.
HD3477.A4 O27 1982

Obrajes. Salvucci, Richard J., 1951- Textiles and capitalism in Mexico . Princeton, N.J. , c1987. p. cm. ISBN 0-691-07749-5 (alk. paper) : LC Card 87-45535 DDC 338.4/767702824/0972 19
HD9864.M62 S25 1987

Obras escogidas /. Torras de la Luz, Jacinto, 1909-1963. [Selections. 1984.] La Habana , 1984- v. <1 > : LC Card 87-125434 DDC 338.97291 19
HC152.5 .T662 1984

Obras hidroeléctricas binacionales en América Latina. [Buenos Aires, Argentina] : Banco Interamericano de Desarrollo, Instituto para la Integración de América Latina, 1985. vii leaves, 385 p., 3 leaves of plates : ill. ; 29 cm. (Publ. . no. 237) "Distr. especial, BID.INTAL/DP.284/85." Includes bibliographical references. LC Card 86-180644
1. Water resources development - Rio de la Plata Region (Argentina and Uruguay). 2. Hydroelectric power plants - Rio de la Plata Region (Argentina and Uruguay). 3. Itaipu (Power plant). 4. Entidad Binacional Yacyretá. 5. Comisión Técnica Mixta de Salto Grande. 6. Water resources development - Uruguay River Region. 7. Water resources development - Paraná River Region (Brazil-Argentina). I. Institute for Latin American Integration. II. Series: Publ. (Institute for Latin American Integration) , no. 237.
HD1696.A7 O27 1985

Obras selectas /. López, Alejandro, 1876-1940. [Selections. 1983.] Bogotá, D.E. , 1983. xiii, 458 p. ; LC Card 86-233252
HC197 .L6172 1983

Obrers a Catalunya . Huertas, Josep Maria. Barcelona , 1982. 409 p. : ISBN 84-85905-06-7 LC Card 83-101512
HD8589.C32 H83 1982 ***NYPL [JLD 86-3659]***

Obretenov, Borcho Vasilev. 40 brigadirski leta /. Sofiia , 1986. 173 p., [12] p. of plates : LC Card 87-103049
HD4870.B9 A15 1986

O'Brien, Jacqueline Wasserman. Financial planners and planning organizations directory . Detroit, Mich. , c1987. viii, 605 p. ; ISBN 0-8103-4397-5 : LC Card 87-21259 DDC 332.6/2 19
HG179.5 .F56 1987

O'Brien, Patrick Karl. The economic effects of the American Civil War / prepared for the Economic History Society by Patrick K. O'Brien. Atlantic Highlands, NJ : Humanities Press International, 1988. p. cm. (Studies in economic and social history) Bibliography: p. Includes index. ISBN 0-391-03561-4 : LC Card 87-18631 DDC 330.973/07 19
1. United States - History - Civil War, 1861-1865 - Economic aspects. I. Economic History Society. II. Title.
HC105.6 .O27 1988

Observation, 0826-9947 .
(no. 29) Courchene, Thomas J. Ontario's proposals for the Canadian securities industry /. Toronto , Scarborough, Ont. [1986] 39 p. : ISBN 0-88806-137-4 (pbk.) LC Card 87-133168 DDC 332.63/2 19
HG5158 .C68 1986

(no. 30) Canadian-Japanese economic relations in a triangular perspective /. Toronto , Scarborough, Ont. [1987] vi, 54 p. : ISBN 0-88806-139-0 (pbk.) LC Card 87-169818 DDC 337.52071 19
HF1480.15.J3 C35 1987

Observations on the commerce of the American states. Sheffield, John Holroyd, Earl of, 1735-1821. London, 1784. 2 p.l., xlvii, 345, [21] p., 1 l. LC Card 06-17319
HF3025 .S58

Observatoire économique et statistique des transports (France) Villette, Jean. Transports, décentralisation 9o plan /. Paris , c1986. 161 p. : ISBN 2-11-001549-7 : LC Card 86-181094
HE248.A2 V55 1986

An Observer publication.
Myers, Frank Daniel. The wood chemical industry in the Delaware Valley /. Middletown, N.Y. , 1986. [160] p. : LC Card 87-108267
HD9660.M573 U616 1986

Observing interaction . Bakeman, Roger. Cambridge [Cambridgeshire] , New York , 1986. ix, 221 p. : ISBN 0-521-25632-1 LC Card 85-22362 DDC 300/.1/51954 19
H62 .B284 1986 ***NYPL [JLD 86-3069]***

Obshchestvennyĭ kharakter proizvodstva i sotsialisticheskaia sobstvennost′ / pod obshcheĭ redaktsieĭ V.N. Cherkovtsa ; [redkollegiia knigi V.V Radaev--otv. redaktor knigi ... et al.]. Moskva : Ėkonomika, 1985. 286 p. ; 23 cm. Includes bibliographical references. LC Card 85-173513
1. Industrial productivity - Soviet Union. 2. Socialist property - Soviet Union. I. Cherkovets, Viktor Nikitich. II. Radaev, Valeriĭ Viktorovich.
HC340.I52 O27 1985

Obshtestvenata sobstvenost pri sotsializma /. Kostov, Ivan Dimitrov. Sofiia , 1985. 111 p. ; LC Card 86-122395
HD4263 .K67 1985

OBSOLESCENCE (ACCOUNTING) see **DEPRECIATION.**

Obstfeld, Maurice. Krugman, Paul R. International economics . Glenview, Ill. , 1987. xxvii, 656, [35] p. : ISBN 0-316-50475-0 LC Card 87-17229 DDC 337 19
HF1411 .K74 1987

Obtaining venture financing . Henderson, James W. Lexington, Mass. , c1988. xii, 366 p. : ISBN 0-669-10931-2 (alk. paper) LC Card 85-40234 DDC 658.1/5224 19
HG4963 .H44 1988

Obudho, Robert A. Slum and squatter settlements in Sub-Saharan Africa . New York , 1988. p. cm. ISBN 0-275-92309-6 (alk. paper) : LC Card 87-11705 DDC 307.3/36 19
HD7287.96.A438 S57 1988

Obukhov, V. N. (Valeriĭ Nikolaevich) Organizatsiia i provedenie vnutrivedomstvennykh reviziĭ na promyshlennykh predpriiatiiakh / V.N. Obukhov. Moskva : Finansy, 1978. 75 p. ; 20 cm. Includes bibliographical references. LC Card 81-153891
1. Government business enterprises - Soviet Union - Management. 2. Government business enterprises - Soviet Union - Accounting. I. Title.
HD4213 .O28 1978

Obul Reddy, D. (Donthi Reddy), 1946- Co-operative agricultural development banks : a case study of Andhra Pradesh / D. Obul Reddy. Delhi : B.R. Pub. Corp. ; New Delhi : Distributed by D.K. Publishers' Distributors, 1986. 429 p. ; 23 cm. Includes index. Bibliography: p. [410]-421. ISBN 81-7018-378-2 : LC Card 86-902655 DDC 334/.2 19
1. Agricultural cooperative credit associations - India - Andhra Pradesh - Case studies. 2. Agricultural cooperative credit associations - India - Case studies. I. Title.
HG2051.I5 A646 1986
NYPL [JLD 87-1527]

Ocampo, Silvia. El equilibrio de los sexos : análisis de la problemática femenina / Silvia Vera Ocampo. Buenos Aires : [s.n.], 1980 (Buenos Aires : Audivert) 302 p. ; 23 cm. Includes bibliographical references.
1. Women - Social conditions. 2. Women - Psychology. I. Title. ***NYPL [JLD 86-913]***

Occasional paper (American Agricultural Economics Association) .
(no. 1) Agricultural trade research and information needs . [Ames, Iowa] [1985] 32 p. : LC Card 86-229053 DDC 380.1/41/072073 19
HD1410.6.U5 A39 1985

Occasional paper (Australian Institute of International Affairs) .
(no. 2) Lougheed, A. L. Trends in international trade and Australia's performance /. Canberra, Australia , 1986. 16, [4] p. : ISBN 0-909992-18-5 (pbk.) LC Card 87-107912 DDC 382/.0994 19
HF3946.5 .L68 1986

Occasional paper (Chancellor College. Dept. of Economics) .
(no. 2. 2) Mills, J. C. (Joseph C.) Price responses of Malawi smallholder farmers--fast, slow or none? [microform] /. [Zomba] [1975] 42, [2] p. ; LC Card 80-980238 DDC 338.1/3/096897 19
HD1476.M33 M54 1975
NYPL [*ZT-1646 no.53]

Occasional paper (Commonwealth Foundation (British Commonwealth)) .
(no. 39) Industrial management education in the Commonwealth . London, England [1976] 38 p. ; LC Card 85-100411 DDC 658/.007/11171241 19
HD70.D44 I5 1976

Occasional paper (Credit Research Foundation) Walia, Tirlochan S. Credit policy of the firm and issues in cost of financing accounts receivable . Lake Success, N.Y. (3000 Marcus Ave., Lake Success 11042) , c1986. [16] p. : LC Card 86-212977 DDC 658.1/5244 19
HG3752.3 .W35 1986

Occasional paper (George Washington University. Center for Washington Area Studies) .
(no. 4) Gale, Dennis E. Black and white urban-to-suburban outmigrants . Washington, D.C. [1986] 46 p. : LC Card 87-404424 DDC 307.2 19
HB1987.W34 G35 1986

Occasional paper (Howard University. Institute for Urban Affairs and Research) .
(no. 21) Morse, Roberta. The Black female professional /. Washington, D.C. [1983] i, 48 p. ; LC Card 83-80187 DDC 305.4/8896073 19
HQ1426 .M88 1983 ***NYPL [Sc F 86-230]***

Occasional paper (International Monetary Fund) .
(no. 48) The European monetary system . Washington, D.C. , c1986. vii, 75 p. : ISBN 0-939934-79-5 (pbk.) : LC Card 86-21432 DDC 332.4/5/094 19
HG930.5 .E86863 1986

(no. 48) The European monetary system . Washington, D.C. , c1986. vii, 75 p. : ISBN 0-939934-79-5 (pbk.) : LC Card 86-21432 DDC 332.4/5/094 19
HG930.5 .E86863 1986

(no. 49) Iqbal, Zubair. Islamic banking /. Washington, D.C. , 1987. v, 62 p. ; ISBN 0-939934-82-5 (pbk.) : LC Card 87-4166 DDC 332.1/0917/671 19
HG3270.2.A6 I67 1987

(no. 50) Crockett, Andrew. Strengthening the international monetary system . Washington, D.C. , c1987. vii, 84 p. ; LC Card 86-33750 DDC 332.4/5 19
HG3881 .C694 1987

(no. 50) Crockett, Andrew. Strengthening the international monetary system . Washington, D.C. , c1987. vii, 84 p. ; LC Card 86-33750 DDC 332.4/5 19
HG3881 .C694 1987

(no. 51) The Role of the SDR in the international monetary system . Washington, D.C. , 1987. vii, 62 p. : ISBN 0-939934-81-7 (pbk.) : LC Card 87-4184 DDC 332.4/5 19
HG3898 .R65 1987

(no. 52) Kopits, George. Structural reform, stabilization, and growth in Turkey /. Washington, D.C. , c1987. v, 46 p. : ISBN 0-939934-84-1 (pbk.) : LC Card 87-3583 DDC 338.9561 19
HC492 .K67 1987

(no. 53) Floating exchange rates in developing countries . Washington, D.C. , 1987. v, 43 p. : ISBN 0-939934-89-2 (pbk.) : LC Card 87-3025 DDC 332.4/56/091724 19
HG3877 .F58 1987

(no. 54) Corden, W. M. (Warner Max) Protection and liberalization . Washington, D.C. , c1987. v, 28 p. ; ISBN 0-939934-95-7 (pbk.) : LC Card 87-16932 DDC 382.7 19
HF1411 .C5954 1987

Occasional paper (Massey University. Dept. of Business Studies) .
(no. 23) Lal, Mohan. Financing small businesses /. Palmerston North, N.Z. [1977] 25, [2] p. ; LC Card 85-151230
HG4027.7 .L35 1977

Occasional paper (Regional Employment Program for Latin America and the Caribbean) .
(44) Tokman, Víctor E. Desarrollo desigual y absorción de empleo . [Santiago, Chile] , 1982. 34 p. ; LC Card 87-403246 DDC 330.98/0038 19
HC125 .T57 1982

(45) Hintermeister, Alberto. Modernización de la agricultura y pobreza rural en Guatemala /. [Santiago, Chile] , 1982. 59 leaves : LC Card 87-403247 DDC 338.1/6/097281 19
HC144.Z9 P624 1982

(46) Hintermeister, Alberto. El empleo agrícola en una estructra en transformación . [Santiago, Chile] , 1982. 27 p. ; LC Card 87-403249 DDC 331.7/63/097285 19
HD1531.N5 H56 1982

(48) García, Norberto E. Absorción creciente con subempleo persistente (América Latina, 1950-80) /. [Santiago, Chile] , 1982. 35 p. ; LC Card 87-403250 DDC 331.12/098 19
HD5730.5.A6 G355 1982

(49) García, Norberto E. Industria manufacturera y empleo . [Santiago, Chile] , 1982. 51 p. ; LC Card 87-403251 DDC 338.4/767/098 19
HD9734.L32 G36 1982

Occasional paper series in regional and urban planning .
(occasional paper no. 22) Wise, Gregory J. The effect of tax exempt forestland on town property tax revenues . Madison [1986] 40 leaves : LC Card 86-623093 DDC 336.22/09775 19
HJ4284.A3 W59 1986

Occasional paper series (National University of Singapore. Dept. of Japanese Studies) .
(no. 2) Shimizu, Hiroshi. Introduction to Japan's economic and political relations with the Middle East in the inter-war period . Kent Ridge, Singapore [1985] v, 47 leaves ; LC Card 87-110444 DDC 337.52056 19
HF1602.15.M626 S56 1985

Occasional paper (Third World Forum) .
(no. 11) Hall, Kenneth O. The Group of 77 . Nyon, Switzerland , 1979. 48 p. ; LC Card 86-202645
HF1413 .H27 1979

(no. 11) Hall, Kenneth O. The Group of 77 . Nyon, Switzerland , 1979. 48 p. ; LC Card 86-202645
HF1413 .H27 1979

(no. 3) Oteiza, Enrique. Technical co-operation among Third World countries and the international order /. Mexico, D.F. , 1978. 72 p. ; LC Card 86-223022 DDC 338.9/26 19
HC60 .O838 1978

(no. 6) Third World countries in the international cotton economy /. [Nyon, Switzerland?] , 1979. i, 61 p. : LC Card 86-223016
HD9088.D44 T47 1979

(no. 7) Ahmad, Qazi Kholiquzzaman, 1943- World trade in a primary commodity . Nyon, Switzerland , 1979. i, 83 p. ; LC Card 86-202627
HD9156.J7 A38 1979

Occasional paper (University of Durban-Westville. Institute for Social and Economic Research) .
(no. 14) Padayachee, Vishnu. An analysis of some aspects of employment and unemployment in the African townships of Umlazi and Lamontville . Durban [South Africa] [1985] iii, 49 p. ; ISBN 0-949947-75-X (pbk.) LC Card 87-404149 DDC 331.12/5/0968455 19
HD5842.D87 P33 1985

Occasional paper (University of Zambia. Business & Economics Association) .
(no. 15) A Study into the evolution and performance of the transport sector in Zambia with particular reference to the operations of the ZIMCO group of transport companies /. [Lusaka?] [1980?] 89 p. : LC Card 86-981420
HE284.6 .S78 1980

(no. 3) Harbans Singh, 1940- Conceptual and methodological issues on agricultural marketing research in Zambia /. [Lusaka, Zambia] [1979?] 19, [2] leaves ; LC Card 85-980091
HD9017.Z32 H37 1979

Occasional papers (India. Vital Statistics Division) .
(1985, no. 1) SRS based abridged life tables, 1976-80. New Delhi , 1986. v, 37 p. : LC Card 87-901200
HB1470 .S77 1986

Occasional papers (Kent-Koop (Society)) .
(1) Boratav, Korkut. Housing yearbook /. Ankara, Turkey , 1985. 32, [2] p. ; LC Card

87-403323 DDC 363.5/09561 19
HD7358.25.A3 B67 1985

Occasional papers (Mekhon Shiloaḥ le-ḥeḳer) ha-Mizraḥ ha-tikhon ṿe-Afriḳah) .
(96) Feiler, Gil. The number of Egyptian workers in the Arab oil countries, 1974-1983 . Tel Aviv , c1986. i, 30 leaves ; LC Card 87-404430 DDC 331.6/2/620536 19
HD8662 .F45 1986

Occasional papers (National Institute of Economic and Social Research) .
(41) Levitt, M. S., 1938- The growth and efficiency of public spending /. Cambridge [Cambridgeshire] , New York , 1987. xiv, 201 p. : ISBN 0-521-34621-5 (U. S.) LC Card 87-11636 DDC 339.5/22/0941 19
HJ7764 .L475 1987

(42) Morgan, Ann D. British imports of consumer goods . Cambridge [Cambridgeshire] , New York , 1988. xi, 129 p. ; ISBN 0-521-35349-1 LC Card 87-25662 DDC 382/.5/0941 19
HF3506.5 .M67 1988

(43) Hart, P. E. (Peter Edward) Youth unemployment in Great Britain /. Cambridge [Cambridgeshire] , New York, NY, USA , 1988. p. cm. ISBN 0-521-35348-3 LC Card 87-25597 DDC 331.3/4137941 19
HD6276.G72 H37 1988

Occasional papers (Rabindra Bharati University. Dept. of Economics) .
(1981) Problems of urban unemployment. Calcutta , 1981. ix, 114 p. ; LC Card 83-907262 DDC 331.13/77/0954 19
HD5819 .P76 1981 ***NYPL [JLF 86-1766]***

Occasional papers series (Florida International University. Latin American and Caribbean Center) .
(#8) Rama, Ruth. Las relaciones económicas México-Estados Unidos . Miami, FL (Tamiami Trail, Miami 33199) [1984] 55 p. ; LC Card 85-226824
HD9014.M62 R36 1984

Occasional papers series (University of Durham. Centre for Middle Eastern and Islamic Studies) .
(no. 31) The Gulf in the early 20th century . [Durham] , c1986. 215 p., [1] leaf of plates : LC Card 87-100795 DDC 330.953/6 19
HC415.3 .G85 1986

Occasional papers series (University of Illinois at Urbana-Champaign. African Studies Program) .
(no. 2) Bunker, Stephen G., 1944- Double dependency and constraints on class formation in Bugisu, Uganda /. Urbana, Ill. , 1983. v, 88 p. : LC Card 86-229748 DDC 303.3/09676/1 19
HD1538.U43 B86 1983

Occasional papers series (University of Massachusetts at Amherst. Program in Latin American Studies) .
(no. 18) Wiarda, Howard J., 1939- Population, internal unrest, and U. S. security in Latin America /. [Amherst] , 1986. 50 p. ; LC Card 87-621399 DDC 304.6/098 19
HB3530.5.A3 W5 1986

(no. 19) Deere, Carmen Diana. The peasantry in political economy . [Amherst, MA] , 1987. 76 p. ; LC Card 87-404080 DDC 305.5/63 19
HD1531.L3 D44 1987

Occasional papers (University of Miami. Institute of Interamerican Studies) .
(no. 1984-1) Jorge, Antonio, 1931- An evaluation of Cuba's post-revolutionary socioeconomic models /. Coral Gables, Fla. [1984?] 26 p. ; LC Card 87-124135 DDC 330.97291/064 19
HC152.5 .J66 1984

(no. 1985-1) Botifoll, Luis J. How Miami's new image was created /. Coral Gables, Fla. [1985?] 16 p. ; LC Card 87-124138
HC108.M5 B68 1985

Urquidi, Víctor L. Basic issues in Latin American development prospects /. Coral Gables, Fla. [between 1983 and 1986] 27 p. ; LC Card 87-118247 DDC 338.98 19
HC125 .U765 1983

Occasional papers (University of the West Indies (Saint Augustine, Trinidad and Tobago). Institute of Social and Economic Research). Human resources .
(4) Abdulah, Norma. The availability and utilization of skills in Guyana /. St. Augustine, Trinidad [1981] xv, 105 p. ; LC Card 84-146702 DDC 331.11/422 19
HD5759.3.A6 A24 1981
NYPL [JLE 86-4442]

Occasional papers (University of the West Indies (St. Augustine, Trinidad and Tobago). Institute of Social and Economic Research). General .
(3) Joefield-Napier, Wallace. Financial integration and interest rate linkages between North Atlantic and Caribbean economies, January 1968 to December 1976 /. St. Augustine, Trinidad [1980] vii, 82 p. : LC Card 81-132125 DDC 332.8/2/0724 19
HG1623.C27 J64 1980 ***NYPL [Sc E 86-329]***

Occasional papers (University of Zambia. Rural Development Studies Bureau) .
(no. 21) Strengthening women's participation in food and agricultural marketing . [Lusaka] [1984] 78 p. ; LC Card 86-980282 DDC 331.4/83/096894 19
HD6073.A292 Z3374 1984

Occasional publication (University of Cambridge. Centre of Latin American Studies) .
(no. 3) Land, people, and planning in contemporary Amazonia /. [Cambridge, Cambridgeshire] , 1980. xvi, 313 p. : LC Card 87-672189
HC167.A42 L36x 1980

Occasional study (Punjab Economic Research Institute, Lahore)
Namdar, Shamim A. Employment implications of agricultural growth /. Lahore , 1980. 82 leaves : LC Card 84-930891 DDC 331.12/93/0954914 19
HD1537.P2 N36 1980 ***NYPL [JLF 86-1956]***

OCCIDENTAL CIVILIZATION. see **CIVILIZATION, OCCIDENTAL.**

OCCUPATION AND PERSONALITY. see **PERSONALITY AND OCCUPATION.**

OCCUPATION, CHOICE OF. see **VOCATIONAL GUIDANCE.**

OCCUPATION DISEASES. see **OCCUPATIONAL DISEASES.**

OCCUPATION, FREE CHOICE OF. see **FREE CHOICE OF EMPLOYMENT.**

OCCUPATIONAL ACCIDENTS. see **INDUSTRIAL ACCIDENTS.**

Occupational accidents and diseases : a review of data sources : consolidated report. Dublin, Ireland : European Foundation for the Improvement of Living and Working Conditions ; Washington, DC : European Community Information Service [distributor], 1986. 116 p. ; 30 cm. (Research report) Bibliography: p. 65-82. ISBN 92-825-6426-6 LC Card 87-135635 DDC 363.1/1/094 19
1. Industrial hygiene - European Economic Community countries. 2. Industrial accidents - European Economic Community countries. 3. Workers' compensation - European Economic Community countries. I. European Foundation for the Improvement of Living and Working Conditions. II. Series: Research report / European Foundation for the Improvement of Living and Working Conditions.
HD7694.5 .O33 1986

Occupational accidents in forestry, year 1982. Metsä- ja uittotöiden työtapaturmat vuonna 1982 =. Tampere , Helsinki , 1984. 50 p. : ISBN 951-46-7685-8 LC Card 85-149625
HD7269.F7262 F56 1984

OCCUPATIONAL APTITUDE TESTS.
Baehr, Melany E. Experience and background questionnaire . [Park Ridge, Ill.] (1550 Northwest Highway, Park Ridge 60068) , c1986. 20 p. ; LC Card 87-404268 DDC 658.3/1125 19
HF5381.7 .B327 1986

OCCUPATIONAL ASPIRATIONS. see **VOCATIONAL INTERESTS.**

Occupational briefs. Chronicle occupational briefs and occupational reprints. Moravia, NY [1986- 4 v. (loose-leaf) : LC Card 86-231523 DDC 331.7/02/0973 19
HF5382.5.U5 C49 1986

Occupational briefs. Chronicle occupational briefs and occupational reprints. Moravia, NY [1987]- 4 v. (loose-leaf) : LC Card 87-403954 DDC 331.7/02/0973 19
HF5382.5.U5 C49 1987

Occupational characteristics of disabled workers, 1975-1976 : analysis of social security disability benefit allowances to workers during 1975-1976 / Thomas J. Fischbach ... [et al.]. Cincinnati, Ohio (4676 Columbia Pkwy., Cincinnati 45226) : U. S. Dept. of Health and Human Services, Public Health Service, Centers for Disease Control, National Institute for Occupational Safety and Health, Division of Surveillance, Hazard Evaluations, and Field Studies, [1986] xix, 187 p. ; 28 cm. (DHHS (NIOSH) publication. no. 86-106) "April 1986." Bibliography: p. 149-150. LC Card 86-602391 DDC 363.1/12/0973 19
1. Insurance, Disability - United States. 2. Industrial hygiene - United States. I. Fischbach, Thomas. II. Series: DHHS publication, no. (PHS) 86-106.
HD7105.25.U6 O23 1986

OCCUPATIONAL DISEASES - BRAZIL.
De que adoecem e morrem os trabalhadores /. São Paulo , 1985. 236 p. ; LC Card 85-231487
HD7683 .D4 1985

OCCUPATIONAL DISEASES - CANADA - STATISTICS.
Employment injuries and occupational illnesses . Ottawa, Ont. , c1986. 92 p. ; ISBN 0-662-54738-1 (pbk.) LC Card 87-147113 DDC 363.1/12/0971 19
HD7262.5.C3 E463 1986

OCCUPATIONAL DISEASES - CONGRESSES.
Brancoli, Mario. The financial aspects of insurance against employment accidents /. Geneva , 1974. 42 p. ; LC Card 84-247775
HD7260.5 .B73 1974

OCCUPATIONAL DISEASES - GERMANY (WEST)
Köchling, Annegret, 1944- Bildschirmarbeit . Köln , c1985. 212 p. : ISBN 3-7663-0853-X
NYPL [JLD 87-392]

Ochs, Peter. Analyse und Bewertung ausgewählter sozialwissenschaftlichen Forschungen /. Dortmund , Bremerhaven , 1983. 102 p. ; ISBN 3-88314-245-X LC Card 83-207278
HD7708 .O28 1983

OCCUPATIONAL DISEASES - MEXICO.
Enfermedades de trabajo. México, D.F. , c1983. 403 p. : ISBN 968-8242-08-X LC Card 85-216152
HD7262.5.M6 E54 1983

OCCUPATIONAL DISEASES - NEW MEXICO - STATISTICS.
Characteristics of occupational injuries and illnesses in New Mexico, 1982 /. Santa Fe, N.M. [1983?] 43 p. : LC Card 86-621034 DDC 363.1/12/09789021 19
HD7262.5.U62 N625 1983

Characteristics of occupational injuries and illnesses in New Mexico, 1983 /. Santa Fe, N.M. [1983] 47 p. : LC Card 86-620786 DDC 363.1/12/09789021 19
HD7262.5.U62 N626 1983

Occupational employment in mining, construction, finance, and services. Washington, D.C. : U. S. Dept. of Labor, Bureau of Labor Statistics : For sale by the Supt. of Docs., U. S. G.P.O., [1986] vi, 141 p. ; 28 cm. (Bulletin . 2264) Shipping list no.: 86-836-P. "September 1986." S/N 029-001-02911-0 Item 768-A-1 LC Card 86-603149 DDC 331.12/51/000973021 19
1. Mineral industries - United States - Employees - Statistics. 2. Construction industry - United States - Employees - Statistics. 3. Financial institutions - United States - Employees - Statistics. 4. Service industries workers - United States - Statistics. I. United States. Bureau of Labor Statistics. II. Series: Bulletin (United States. Bureau of Labor Statistics) , 2264.
HD9506.U62 O23 1986

Occupational employment statistics : 1985 statewide survey of transportation, communication & utilities, wholesale & retail trade, education, state & local government. Helena, Mont. (P.O. Box 1728, Helena 59624) : Montana Dept. of Labor & Industry, Research & Analysis Bureau, Labor Market Information Section, [1986] ii, 93 p. : ill. ; 28 cm. Cover title: Occupational employment statistics of

Montana, 1985. LC Card 86-622803 DDC 331.12/51/0009786021 19
1. Labor supply - Montana - Statistics. 2. Montana - Occupations - Statistics. I. Montana. Labor Market Information Section. II. Title: Occupational employment statistics of Montana, 1985.
HD5725.M9 O256 1986

Occupational employment statistics of Montana, 1985. Occupational employment statistics . Helena, Mont. (P.O. Box 1728, Helena 59624) [1986] ii, 93 p. : LC Card 86-622803 DDC 331.12/51/0009786021 19
HD5725.M9 O256 1986

Occupational employment statistics program : staffing patterns for selected nonmanufacturing industries in Arkansas, 1984. [Little Rock, Ark.] (P.O. Box 2981, Little Rock 72203) : Research and Analysis Section, Employment Security Division, [1986] v leaves, 223 p. ; 28 cm. Cover title: Nonmanufacturing Arkansas staffing patterns. "Released July 1986." LC Card 87-620868 DDC 331.12/51/0009767021 19
1. Labor Supply - Arkansas - Statistics. 2. Arkansas - Occupations - Statistics. I. Arkansas. Employment Security Division. Research and Analysis Section. II. Title: Nonmanufacturing Arkansas staffing patterns.
HD5725.A8 O264 1986

Occupational Employment Statistics Program (Ark.) Staffing patterns for manufacturing industries and hospitals /. Little Rock, Ark. [1983?] vi leaves, 249 p. ; LC Card 86-623216 DDC 331.12/57/09767 19
HD5725.A8 S79 1983

OCCUPATIONAL FORECASTING. see **EMPLOYMENT FORECASTING.**

Occupational groups in ancient India. Rāya, Śaśikānta, 1957- Prācīna Bhārata meṃ vyāvasāyika samudāya, 600 Ī. Pū. se 200 Ī. taka =. Naī Dillī , 1986. 176 p. ; LC Card 87-902475
HB3639 .R39 1986

Occupational mobility among Blacks in South Africa /. Schneier, Steffen. Cape Town [1983] vi, 219 p. : ISBN 0-7992-0567-2 (pbk.) LC Card 84-197038 DDC 331.12/72/089968 19
HD8801 .S34 1983 NYPL [JLG 86-123]

OCCUPATIONAL MOBILITY - BERLIN (GERMANY) - STATISTICS.
Ergebnisse der Personalstrukturerhebung in Berlin (West) am 2. Oktober 1968 /. Berlin [1971] 75 p. ; LC Card 85-171250
HA1330.B6 B45 Heft 174 HD5717.5.G32B47

OCCUPATIONAL MOBILITY - BRAZIL.
Força de trabalho no Brasil . Rio de Janeiro , 1982. 73 p. : ISBN 85-24-00002-3 LC Card 87-403683 DDC 331.12/72/0981 19
HD5717.5.B6 F67 1982

OCCUPATIONAL MOBILITY - GERMANY, WEST.
Allehoff, Wolfgang H., 1949- Berufswahl und berufliche Interessen /. Göttingen , c1985. 177 p. : ISBN 3-8017-0217-0 LC Card 85-235199
HF5381.5 .A45 1985

Koll, Hermann Josef. Mobilität und Beruf . Opladen , 1981. xviii, 564 p. ; ISBN 3-531-11551-0 : LC Card 81-158683
HD5717.5.G3 K64 1981

OCCUPATIONAL MOBILITY - MATHEMATICAL MODELS.
Sahin, Izzet. Job mobility and private pensions /. Brookfield, Wis. , c1986. xv, 49 p. ; ISBN 0-89154-305-8 (pbk.) LC Card 87-129468 DDC 331.25/2/0724 19
HD7105 .S229 1986

OCCUPATIONAL MOBILITY - QUÉBEC (PROVINCE)
Garon-Audy, Muriel. Mobilités professionnelles et géographiques au Québec, 1954-64-74 /. Montréal , 1980. 61 p. ; LC Card 81-105620 DDC 331.12/7971 19
HD5717.5.C22 Q44 1980
NYPL [JLM 79-970 no.22]

OCCUPATIONAL MOBILITY - SOUTH AFRICA.
Schneier, Steffen. Occupational mobility among Blacks in South Africa /. Cape Town [1983] vi, 219 p. : ISBN 0-7992-0567-2 (pbk.) LC Card 84-197038 DDC 331.12/72/089968 19
HD8801 .S34 1983 NYPL [JLG 86-123]

OCCUPATIONAL MOBILITY - SWITZERLAND.
Leibundgut, Hansjörg, 1947- Die Bedeutung der beruflichen Mobilität als arbeitsmarktlicher Ausgleichsprozess . Bern , New York , c1986. ix, 235 p. : ISBN 3-261-03630-3 LC Card 87-122350 DDC 331.12/79494 19
HD5717.5.S9 L45 1986

OCCUPATIONAL MORTALITY - DENMARK.
Rønne, Henning. Dødelighed og førtidspensionering blandt ansatte på danske kraftværker /. København , 1985. 73 p. : ISBN 87-7359-155-6 LC Card 85-228083
HD7262.5.D4 R66 1985

OCCUPATIONAL MORTALITY - NORWAY - STATISTICS.
Borgan, Jens-Kristian. Dødelighet i yrker og sosioøkonomiske grupper 1970-1980 /. Oslo , 1986. 217 p. : ISBN 82-537-2339-3 : LC Card 86-231576
HB1445 .B66 1986

Occupational outlook for New Jersey and JTPA labor market areas, 1982-1990 [microform]. Sheppard, Thomas M. Trenton, N.J. [1984] ii leaves, 50 p. ; LC Card 84-623480 DDC 331.12/09749 19
HD5725.N5 S47 1984
*NYPL [*ZT-1745 no.24]*

OCCUPATIONAL PRESTIGE - POLAND.
U nas dole i niedole /. Warszawa , 1978. 283 p. ; LC Card 81-208722
HD8038.P6 U25 1978

OCCUPATIONAL PRESTIGE - UNITED STATES.
Bose, Christine E. Jobs and gender . New York , 1985. xiv, 206 p. ; ISBN 0-03-071692-6 (alk. paper) : LC Card 85-6305 DDC 305.4/3/00973 19
HD6058 .B67 1985 NYPL [JLE 86-3694]

The velvet ghetto . San Francisco , 1986. 147 leaves in various foliations : LC Card 86-161157 DDC 331.4/816592/0973 19
HD6054.2.U6 V45 1986

Occupational projections, 1984-1995 : service delivery area 1-[16] / Labor Market Information Unit, Iowa Department of Job Service, in cooperation with the Iowa State Occupational Information Coordinating Committee and the Office of Planning and Programming. [Des Moines?] : The Unit, [1985] 16 v. in 1 ; 28 cm. "April 1985." LC Card 86-621925 DDC 331.12/09777/021 19
1. Labor supply - Iowa - Statistics. 2. Employment forecasting - Iowa - Statistics. I. Iowa. Labor Market Information Unit. II. Iowa State Occupational Information Coordinating Committee. III. Iowa. Office for Planning and Programming.
HD5725.I8 O26 1985

OCCUPATIONAL RETRAINING - BERLIN (GERMANY) - STATISTICS.
Gaulke, Klaus-Peter. Lehre und Berufsausübung . Berlin , 1986. 122 p. ; ISBN 3-428-06000-8 LC Card 86-166545
HC281 .B33 Heft 89 HD5715.5.G42B47

OCCUPATIONAL RETRAINING - CANADA.
Saunders, Ronald. Aid to workers in declining industries /. [Toronto, Ont.] , c1984. 72 p. : ISBN 0-7743-9007-7 (pbk.) LC Card 84-174952 DDC 331.13/77/0971 19
HD6331.2.C2 S28 1984
NYPL [JLD 86-1287]

OCCUPATIONAL RETRAINING - EUROPEAN ECONOMIC COMMUNITY COUNTRIES.
L'Association des travailleurs aux choix technologiques . Luxembourg , Washington, D.C. , 1986. 45 p. : ISBN 92-825-5880-0 : LC Card 86-179382
HD6331.2.E86 A88 1986

La Formation des syndicalistes aux nouvelles technologies de l'information et à leur introduction dans les entreprises . Luxembourg , Washington, D.C. , 1986. 52, 13, 7 p. : ISBN 92-825-5881-9 : LC Card 86-179989
HD6331.2.E86 F67 1986

OCCUPATIONAL RETRAINING - GERMANY, WEST.
Kretschmann, Rolf. Möglichkeiten des Berufswechsels von Haupterwerbslandwirten unter besonderer Berücksichtigung von Agrarstruktur und Arbeitsmarkt /. Göttingen , 1986. xi, 109 p. : LC Card 87-408871 DDC 331.25/924 19
HD1536.G3 K746 1986

OCCUPATIONAL RETRAINING - ITALY.
Rapporto ISFOL 1985 . Milano, Italy , c1985. 533 p. : LC Card 86-156267
HD5715.5.I8 R393 1985

OCCUPATIONAL RETRAINING - KANSAS.
Kansas. Legislature. Task Force on Business Training. Report of the Task Force on Business Training of the Legislative Commission on Economic Development. [Topeka, Kansas] [1986] 1 v. (various pagings) ; LC Card 87-621700 DDC 331.25/92/09781 19
HD5715.3.K2 K37 1986

OCCUPATIONAL RETRAINING - POLAND.
Kowtun, Józef. Rola, funkcje i zadania mistrza w systemie dokształcania i wychowania robotników /. Warszawa , 1979. 151, [1] p. ; LC Card 81-180277
HF5549.5.T7 K687 1979

OCCUPATIONAL RETRAINING - UNITED STATES.
Goldstein, Harold. Training for work in the computer age . Washington, D.C. , 1986. iv, 109 p. ; LC Card 86-601422 DDC 331.25/92 19
HD5715.2 .G63 1986

OCCUPATIONAL RETRAINING - UNITED STATES - FINANCE.
Howe, Mike. Accessing private industry council funding . [Northridge, CA] (17624 Romar St., Northridge 91325) [1987?] 24, [15] leaves ; LC Card 87-401761 DDC 362.8/5 19
HD5715.2 .H69 1987

Occupational safety and health (Marcel Dekker, Inc.) .
(v. 13) Hendrick, Kingsley. Investigating accidents with STEP /. New York , c1987. xviii, 454 p. : ISBN 0-8247-7510-4 LC Card 86-24165 DDC 363.1/065 19
HD7262.25 .H46 1987

Occupational safety and health series .
(54) Andreoni, Diego. The cost of occupational accidents and diseases /. Geneva , c1986. viii, 142 p. : ISBN 92-2-103758-4 (pbk.) : LC Card 87-119442 DDC 338.4/336311 19
HD7262 .A73 1986

Occupational sex-typing. Cohn, Samuel, 1954- The process of occupational sex-typing . Philadelphia , 1985. viii, 279 p. ; ISBN 0-87722-402-1 : LC Card 85-14864 DDC 331.4/8165137/0941 19
HD6060.65.G7 C64 1985
NYPL [JLE 86-917]

Occupational social work . Googins, Bradley, 1944- Silver Spring, MD , 1987. p. cm. ISBN 0-87101-151-4 LC Card 87-20414 DDC 362.8/5 19
HD7261 .G66 1987b

Occupational social work /. Googins, Bradley, 1944- Englewood Cliffs, N.J. , c1987. xii, 227 p. : ISBN 0-13-629445-6 : LC Card 86-25514 DDC 658.3/82 19
HD7261 .G66 1987

Occupational stress and organizational effectiveness / edited by Anne W. Riley and Stephen J. Zaccaro. New York : Praeger, c1987. xii, 285 p. : ill. ; 24 cm. Papers presented at the 7th Annual Applied Behavioral Science Symposium, sponsored by the Dept. of Psychology at Virginia Polytechnic Institute and State University, held in 1984. Includes bibliographies. Includes index. ISBN 0-275-92281-2 (alk. paper) : LC Card 86-25250 DDC 158.7 19
1. Job stress - Congresses. 2. Employee assistance programs - Congresses. 3. Personnel management - Congresses. 4. Organizational effectiveness - Congresses. I. Riley, Anne W. II. Zaccaro, Stephen J. III. Virginia Tech Symposium on Applied Behavioral Science (7th : 1984). IV. Virginia Polytechnic Institute and State University. Psychology Dept.
HF5548.85 .O24 1987

OCCUPATIONAL TRAINING.
Alcántara, Alcides de. Métodos para la aplicación de las series metódicas ocupacionales /. Montevideo , 1978. 73 p. : LC Card 86-142696
HD5715 .A44 1978

Novaes, Paulo, 1913- Organización y recursos humanos /. Montevideo , 1976, 1977 printing.

122 p. : LC Card 86-139048
HD5713 .N68 1977

Retuerto, Enrique. Determinación de necesidades de formación profesional . Montevideo , 1983. 110 p. ; LC Card 86-149551
HD5715 .R47 1983

Richter, Lothar. Training needs . Geneva , 1986. viii, 83 p. : ISBN 92-2-105458-6 (pbk.) : LC Card 86-222104 DDC 331.25/92 19
HD5715 .R53 1986

Weibel, Bernd, 1951- Differenzierung der Berufsausbildung . Heidelberg , 1984. iv, 326, 6 p. : ISBN 3-88326-138-6 LC Card 85-189624
HF5381 .W43 1984

OCCUPATIONAL TRAINING - AFRICA.
Livingstone, Ian. Youth employment & youth employment programmes in Africa . Addis Ababa , 1986. 7 v. : ISBN 92-2-105527-2 (pbk. : v. 1) LC Card 87-980143 DDC 331.3/4/096 19
HD6276.A32 L58 1986

OCCUPATIONAL TRAINING - AFRICA, NORTH.
La Politique de l'emploi-formation au Maghreb, 1970-1980 /. Paris , 1982. 472 p. : ISBN 2-222-03122-2 LC Card 84-222103 DDC 331.11/0961 19
HD5838 .P65 1982

OCCUPATIONAL TRAINING - ASIA, SOUTHEASTERN.
Vente, Rolf E. Education and training for industrial development in Singapore and other ASEAN countries . Baden-Baden , Singapore , 1984. 175 p. : ISBN 3-7890-0941-5 LC Card 84-186381 DDC 331.25/92/0959 19
HD5715.5.S55 V46 1984
NYPL [JLD 86-2773]

OCCUPATIONAL TRAINING - AUSTRIA.
Amanshauser, Wilfried. Jugendarbeitsmarktförderung in Österreich /. Wien [1985] ii, 71, 3 p. ; LC Card 86-165982
HD6276.A9 A43 1985

OCCUPATIONAL TRAINING - BERLIN (GERMANY) - STATISTICS.
Gaulke, Klaus-Peter. Lehre und Berufsausübung . Berlin , 1986. 122 p. ; ISBN 3-428-06000-8 LC Card 86-166545
HC281 .B33 Heft 89 HD5715.5.G42B47

OCCUPATIONAL TRAINING - BOLIVIA - ORURO - CASE STUDIES.
Alaix, Ramón. Experiencias de educación y producción de fe y alegría en Oruro y Santa Cruz . La Paz, Bolivia , 1986. 191 p. ; LC Card 86-208411 DDC 331.25/92/098413 19
HD5715.5.B52 S262 1986

OCCUPATIONAL TRAINING - BOLIVIA - SANTA CRUZ - CASE STUDIES.
Alaix, Ramón. Experiencias de educación y producción de fe y alegría en Oruro y Santa Cruz . La Paz, Bolivia , 1986. 191 p. ; LC Card 86-208411 DDC 331.25/92/098413 19
HD5715.5.B52 S262 1986

OCCUPATIONAL TRAINING - BRAZIL.
Fontes, Lauro (Lauro Barreto) Formação profissional & produtividade no desempenho humano /. [Rio de Janeiro] , 1985. 119, [2] p. ; LC Card 85-221895
HD5715.5.B68 F66 1985

Silva, Angela Inês Gandra e. Os acordos SENAI/empresa . Rio de Janeiro-RJ-Brasil , 1985. xvii, 97 p. ; LC Card 86-176735
HD5715.5.B68 S55 1985

Silveira, Maria Luiza Faraone. Mão-de-obra de nível médio . São Paulo , 1986. 239 p. : LC Card 87-143876 DDC 331.11/422 19
HD5754 .S55 1986

OCCUPATIONAL TRAINING - BRAZIL - PARAÍBA (STATE)
Azevedo, Edilza Araújo. Causas de evasão. [Campina Grande, Brasil] , 1984. 104 leaves : LC Card 85-203901
HD5715.5.B69 P335 1984

OCCUPATIONAL TRAINING - BURUNDI.
Formation des adultes . [Bujumbura] [1984- v. <1 > : LC Card 86-980941
HD5715.5.B94 F67 1984

OCCUPATIONAL TRAINING - CALIFORNIA - SAN DIEGO COUNTY.
Goldman, Barbara. Final report on the San Diego job search and work experience demonstration /. New York, N.Y. (3 Park Ave., New York 10016) , c1986. xliv, 269 p. : LC Card 87-118376 DDC 331.12/042/0979498 19
HD5713.6.U542 S395 1986

OCCUPATIONAL TRAINING - CHILE - SANTIAGO.
Corvalán Vásquez, Oscar E., 1947- Empleo y capacitación en los talleres informales de Santiago /. Montevideo , 1984. 150 p. ; LC Card 86-127324
HD2346.C54 S263 1984

OCCUPATIONAL TRAINING - COMPUTER-ASSISTED INSTRUCTION.
Technology-based training. Oxford , New York , c1986. ix, 357 p. : ISBN 0-08-034097-0 LC Card 87-160178 DDC 658.3/12404 19
HF5549.5.T7 T39 1986

OCCUPATIONAL TRAINING - CONGRESSES.
International Conference on Employment and Training (1985 : Perth, W.A.) Full employment, uncertain futures /. [Perth, W.A.] [1985] ix, 263 p. : LC Card 86-185208 DDC 339.5 19
HD5701.3 .I55 1985

OCCUPATIONAL TRAINING - DEVELOPING COUNTRIES - CONGRESSES.
Seminar "Planung des Berufsausbildungswesens in Entwicklungsländern" (1965 : Berlin, Germany) Seminar "Planung des Berufsausbildungswesens in Entwicklungsländern" vom 22. Juli bis 17. August 1965 /. Berlin-Tegel [1965?] 1 portfolio ; LC Card 87-407604
HD5715.5.D44 S46 1965

OCCUPATIONAL TRAINING - EQUIPMENT AND SUPPLIES.
Industrial training products & services markets. Norwalk, Conn., U. S.A. (6 Prowitt St., Norwalk 06855) , c1987. vi, 174 leaves ; LC Card 87-153554 DDC 381/.45658312404 19
HD9811.A2 I53 1987

OCCUPATIONAL TRAINING - EUROPEAN ECONOMIC COMMUNITY COUNTRIES.
Gizard, Xavier. Regional development and vocational training analysis and discussion of the relationship development . Berlin , Washington, DC , 1986. 49 p. ; ISBN 92-825-5911-4 (pbk.) : LC Card 87-137374 DDC 331.25/92/094 19
HD5715.5.E8 G58 1986

Morgan-Gérard, Florence. Equal opportunities and vocational training . Berlin [1982] 69 p. ; ISBN 92-825-2489-2 ***NYPL [JLD 87-1318]***

OCCUPATIONAL TRAINING - EUROPEAN ECONOMIC COMMUNITY COUNTRIES - CONGRESSES.
Drexel, Ingrid. Vocational training problems in small and medium-sized enterprises . Luxembourg , Washington, DC , 1986. 279 p. : ISBN 92-825-5707-3 (pbk.) LC Card 86-213476 DDC 331.25/92/094 19
HD5715.5.E8 D74 1986

OCCUPATIONAL TRAINING FOR WOMEN - GERMANY (WEST)
Frauen und Beruf, zwischen Wunsch und Realität . Bonn , Bad Honnef , 1986. 142 p. ; ISBN 3-87066-629-3 : LC Card 87-409372 DDC 331.4/0943 19
HD6149 .F719 1986

Hegelheimer, Armin. Gleichwertigkeit von allgemeiner und beruflicher Bildung /. Bonn , Bad Honnef , 1986. v, 74 p. ; ISBN 3-87066-628-5 : LC Card 87-409371 DDC 331.4/2592/0943 19
HD6059.6.G4 H42 1986

Hegelheimer, Barbara. Berufsqualifikation und Berufschancen von Frauen in der Bundesrepublik Deutschland /. Berlin , 1977. viii, 303 p. ; LC Card 85-142052
HD6059.6.G4 H428 1977

Selk, Michael, 1943- Geschlecht und Berufswahl . Frankfurt am Main , New York , c1984. 289 p. : ISBN 3-8204-5375-X LC Card 85-193055
HD6059.6.G4 S45 1984

OCCUPATIONAL TRAINING FOR WOMEN - GERMANY (WEST) - CONGRESSES.
Mädchen und Berufswahl . Bonn , Bad Honnef , 1986. 96 p. : ISBN 3-87066-631-5 LC Card 87-409396 DDC 331.4/2592/0943 19
HF5382.67.G3 M33 1986

Workshop "Berufswege von Frauen" (1984 : Berlin, Germany) Berufsverläufe von Frauen . München , Weinheim , c1986. 291 p. : ISBN 3-87966-253-3 LC Card 87-407975 DDC 331.7/02/024042 19
HF5382.67.G3 W67 1984

OCCUPATIONAL TRAINING FOR WOMEN - GREAT BRITAIN.
Wickham, Ann. Women and training /. Milton Keynes, England , Philadelphia, PA, USA , c1986. x, 147 p. ; ISBN 0-335-15119-1 LC Card 86-5176 DDC 331.4/2592/0941 19
HD6059.6.G7 W52 1986
NYPL [JLD 86-3495]

OCCUPATIONAL TRAINING FOR WOMEN - KENYA - CONGRESSES.
Exhibition and income generation for women . [Nairobi?] [1985] 17, 11 p. ; LC Card 85-981503 DDC 331.4/09676/2 19
HD6210.5 .E94 1985

OCCUPATIONAL TRAINING FOR WOMEN - UNITED STATES.
Moore, Janice D. Thorne. A step toward independence: economic self sufficiency . Washington, D.C. , c1986. iii, 117 p. : LC Card 86-209069 DDC 362.8/3 19
HD6059.6.U6 M66 1986

OCCUPATIONAL TRAINING - FRANCE.
Nallet, Jean François. Comité d'entreprise et formation /. Paris-La Défense (Tour Europe, 92080 cedex 07) , 1977. 140 p. (1 fold.) ; LC Card 78-358400
HD5660.F7 N34

Nallet, Jean François. Comité d'entreprise et formation /. Paris-la-Défense , 1979. 181 p. ;
NYPL [JLF 81-80]

Soisson, Jean Pierre, 1934- L'enjeu de la formation professionnelle /. [Paris] , c1986. iv, 315 p. : ISBN 2-213-01752-2 : LC Card 86-194690
HD5715.5.F8 S65 1986

OCCUPATIONAL TRAINING - GERMANY, WEST.
Feuerstein, Thomas. Humanisierung der Arbeit und Reform der beruflichen Bildung . München , c1983. 221 p. ; ISBN 3-87966-184-7 LC Card 83-222687
HD5715.5.G4 F48 1983

Klause, Dieter. Wegweiser zur Weiterbildung . Bonn , 1982. 101 p. ; LC Card 83-206662
HF5549.5.T7 K58 1982

Kornblum, Hans-Joachim. Therapie in der Berufsschule? . München , c1984. x, 458 p. : ISBN 3-597-10503-3 : LC Card 85-105593
HD5715.5.G4 K67 1984

Maier, Hans E. Das Handwerk und die Berufseingliederung Jugendlicher in der Bundesrepublik Deutschland /. Berlin [1986] 68 p. : LC Card 86-230660
HD5715.5.G4 M35 1986

Maslankowski, Willi, 1936- Nachweis beruflicher Qualifikationen /. Montevideo , 1979. 102 p., [2] folded leaf of plates : LC Card 86-148766
HD5715.5.L3 M37 1979

Maslankowski, Willi, 1936- [Nachweis beruflicher Qualifikationen. Spanish. Selections.] Calificación ocupacional en la República Federal de Alemania /. Montevideo , 1979. 38 p. : LC Card 86-143001
HD5715.5.G4 M372518 1979

Sardei-Biermann, Sabine. Jugendliche zwischen Schule und Arbeitswelt . München , c1984. v, 318 p. ; ISBN 3-87966-219-3 LC Card 84-240405
HD5715.5.G4 S27 1984

Wagner, Karin. Relation between education, employment, and productivity and their impact on education and labour market policies . Berlin , Washington, DC , 1986. ix, 80 p. ; ISBN 92-825-6371-5 : LC Card 87-136255 DDC 331.12/042/0941 19
HD5715.5.G4 W35 1986

Ziefuss, Horst. Jugendliche in der gewerblich-technischen Ausbildung in Industrie und Handwerk . Kiel , c1986. 352 p. : ISBN 3-89088-011-8 LC Card 87-407898 DDC

331.3/42592/0943 19
HD5715.5.G4 Z54 1986

OCCUPATIONAL TRAINING - GERMANY (WEST) - BAVARIA - CASE STUDIES.
Maier, Hans E. Das Handwerk und die Berufseingliederung Jugendlicher in der Bundesrepublik Deutschland /. Berlin [1986] 68 p. : LC Card 86-230660
HD5715.5.G4 M35 1986

OCCUPATIONAL TRAINING - GERMANY (WEST) - HESSE - CASE STUDIES.
Dobischat, Rolf, 1950- Berufliche Weiterbildung, Arbeitsmarkt und Region . Frankfurt am Main , New York , c1985. 691 p. : ISBN 3-8204-5673-2 LC Card 86-158931
HD5715.5.G42 H473 1985

OCCUPATIONAL TRAINING - GERMANY (WEST) - NORTH RHINE-WESTPHALIA - CASE STUDIES.
Dobischat, Rolf, 1950- Berufliche Weiterbildung, Arbeitsmarkt und Region . Frankfurt am Main , New York , c1985. 691 p. : ISBN 3-8204-5673-2 LC Card 86-158931
HD5715.5.G42 H473 1985

OCCUPATIONAL TRAINING - GOVERNMENT POLICY - EUROPE.
Promotion of cooperation amongst research and development organizations in the field of vocational training . Berlin , Washington, DC , 1986. 111 p. ; ISBN 92-825-6570-X (pbk.) : LC Card 87-133749 DDC 331.25/92/094
HD5715.5.E78 P77 1986

OCCUPATIONAL TRAINING - GOVERNMENT POLICY - PERSIAN GULF STATES.
Nadwat Tanmiyat al-Mawārid al-Basharīyah fī al-Khalīj al-ʻArabī (1975 : Bahrain) Nadwat Tanmiyat al-Mawārid al-Basharīyah fī al-Khalīj al-ʻArabī . al-Kuwayt [1975?] 361, 404 p. : LC Card 86-964662
HD5715.5.P39 N33 1975

OCCUPATIONAL TRAINING - GOVERNMENT POLICY - UNITED STATES.
Job training under the new federalism . [Chicago?] , 1986. ii, 299 p. : LC Card 86-203209 DDC 331.25/92/0973 19
HD5715.2 .J63 1986

OCCUPATIONAL TRAINING - GREAT BRITAIN.
Chapman, Paul G., 1952- The youth training scheme in the United Kingdom /. Aldershot, Hants, England , Brookfield, Vt., U. S.A. , c1987. x, 124 p. ; ISBN 0-566-05360-8 : LC Card 86-29604 DDC 331.3/42592/0941 19
HD5715.5.G7 C47 1987

Verma, Gajendra K. Race, training, and employment /. London , New York , 1987. vi, 134 p. : ISBN 1-85000-243-6 : LC Card 87-15470 DDC 331.3/46/0941 19
HD5715.5.G7 V47 1987

Wagner, Karin. Relation between education, employment, and productivity and their impact on education and labour market policies . Berlin , Washington, DC , 1986. ix, 80 p. ; ISBN 92-825-6371-5 : LC Card 87-136255 DDC 331.12/042/0941 19
HD5715.5.G4 W35 1986

OCCUPATIONAL TRAINING - GREAT BRITAIN - HISTORY.
Sheldrake, John, 1944- The history of industrial training in Britain /. Aldershot Hants, England , Brookfield, Vt., USA , c1987. v, 75 p. ; ISBN 0-566-05294-6 : LC Card 86-29601 DDC 331.25/92 19
HD5715.5.G7 S54 1987

OCCUPATIONAL TRAINING - GUYANA.
Abdulah, Norma. The availability and utilization of skills in Guyana /. St. Augustine, Trinidad [1981] xv, 105 p. ; LC Card 84-146702 DDC 331.11/422 19
HD5759.3.A6 A24 1981
NYPL [JLE 86-4442]

OCCUPATIONAL TRAINING - HAITI.
International Labour Organisation. Institut national de formation professionnelle (INFP) . Genève , 1982. ii, 69 p. : ISBN 92-2-203229-2 LC Card 83-234817
HD5715.5.H2 I57 1982

OCCUPATIONAL TRAINING - HISTORY.
Breve reseña histórica de la formación profesional y del trabajo /. Bogotá [1973] 29, [1] leaves ; LC Card 85-208500
HD5715 .B74 1973

Koeder, Kurt W. Berufsbegleitendes Studium . Grafenau/Württ. , c1983. 286 p. : ISBN 3-88508-901-7 LC Card 84-185882
HD5715 .K63 1983

OCCUPATIONAL TRAINING - HONDURAS.
International Labour Organisation. Desarrollo de la formación profesional rural . Ginebra , 1982. ii, 30 p. : ISBN 92-2-303048-X LC Card 84-113985
HD5715.5.H8 I58 1982

OCCUPATIONAL TRAINING - INDIA.
Bihar (India). Rural Development Dept. Trysem . [Paṭanā] , 1980. 41 p. ; LC Card 80-908290
HD6276.I42 B54 1980

OCCUPATIONAL TRAINING - INDIA - CONGRESSES.
Training of rural youth for self-employment (TRYSEM) . Hyderabad, [India] , 1981. vii, 252 p. ; LC Card 81-904606 DDC 331.3/42492/0954 19
HD5715.5.I5 T72 1981
NYPL [JLF 86-1203]

OCCUPATIONAL TRAINING - ITALY.
Organizzazione del lavoro, mobilità e aspetti formativi nella contrattazione . Milano, Italy , c1982. 172 p. ; LC Card 83-106874
HD6709 .O73 1982

Rapporto ISFOL 1985 . Milano, Italy , c1985. 533 p. : LC Card 86-156267
HD5715.5.I8 R393 1985

OCCUPATIONAL TRAINING - ITALY - NUORO (SARDINIA : PROVINCE)
L'Osservatorio provinciale sul lavoro e sulle professioni . Milano, Italy , c1984. 143 p. : LC Card 84-190423
HD5785.N86 O87 1984
NYPL [JLD 86-1275]

OCCUPATIONAL TRAINING - IVORY COAST.
Gboizo, J. Emplois et qualifications dans le secteur métaux-mécanique-électricité en Côte d'Ivoire /. [Abidjan] , 1981. 93 leaves ; LC Card 83-234024
HD5846.9.A6 G36 1981

OCCUPATIONAL TRAINING - JAPAN.
New approach to vocational training /. Islamabad, Pakistan , 1985-1986. 2 v. : ISBN 92-2-105078-5 (pbk. : v. 1) LC Card 86-221389 DDC 331.25/92/0952 19
HD5715.5.J3 N48 1985

OCCUPATIONAL TRAINING - KANSAS.
Kansas. Legislature. Task Force on Business Training. Report of the Task Force on Business Training of the Legislative Commission on Economic Development. [Topeka, Kansas] [1986] 1 v. (various pagings) ; LC Card 87-621700 DDC 331.25/92/09781 19
HD5715.3.K2 K37 1986

OCCUPATIONAL TRAINING - LATIN AMERICA.
Agudelo Mejía, Santiago. Lineamientos para la implantación de un servicio de certificación ocupacional /. Montevideo , 1983. 67 p. : LC Card 86-142627
HD5715.5.L3 A348 1983

Certificación ocupacional . Ciudad de México , 1981. 76 p. ; ISBN 968-8290-30-0 LC Card 86-142976
HD5715.5.L3 C47 1981

Ducci, María Angélica. Formación profesional . Montevideo , 1983. 102 p. ; LC Card 86-142632
HD5715.5.L29 D83 1983

Maslankowski, Willi, 1936- Nachweis beruflicher Qualifikationen /. Montevideo , 1979. 102 p., [2] folded leaf of plates : LC Card 86-148766
HD5715.5.L3 M37 1979

OCCUPATIONAL TRAINING - LATIN AMERICA - CONGRESSES.
La Formación profesional ante las exigencias del desarrollo. Montevideo , 1980. 98 p. ; LC Card 86-139077
HD5715.5.L3 F664 1980

OCCUPATIONAL TRAINING - LATIN AMERICA - PLANNING.
Concepto y aplicación del enfoque de sistemas en los procesos y técnicas de instrucción. Montevideo , 1980. 283 p. : LC Card 86-143811
HD5715.5.L29 C66 1980

OCCUPATIONAL TRAINING - LAW AND LEGISLATION - BRAZIL.
Silva, Angela Inês Gandra e. Os acordos SENAI/empresa . Rio de Janeiro-RJ-Brasil , 1985. xvii, 97 p. ; LC Card 86-176735
HD5715.5.B68 S55 1985

OCCUPATIONAL TRAINING - MALAWI.
Ettema, Wim. Small-scale industry in Malawi . Zomba [1983] iv, 50, [9] leaves, 9 p. : LC Card 84-980489 DDC 338.6/42/096897 19
HD2356.M3 E88 1983

OCCUPATIONAL TRAINING - PANAMA.
International Labour Organisation. Fortalecimiento del sistema de formación profesional . Ginebra , 1982. 47 p. ; ISBN 92-2-303194-X LC Card 84-113933
HD5715.5.P3 I57 1982

OCCUPATIONAL TRAINING - PHILIPPINES.
International Labour Organisation. National programme for development and training of manpower for employment, Philippines . Geneva , 1979. ii, 54 p. ; LC Card 81-140367 DDC 331.25/92/09599 19
HD5825.A6 I57 1979

Metals and engineering . Manila, Philippines , 1983. 64 p. : LC Card 87-401862 DDC 331.25/92 19
HD5716.M52 P66 1983

OCCUPATIONAL TRAINING - PORTUGAL.
Silva, Manuela. A igualdade de oportunidades de formação profissional para as mulheres /. Lisboa , 1983. 51, [1] p. : LC Card 84-238349
HD6179 .S56 1983

OCCUPATIONAL TRAINING - RESEARCH - LATIN AMERICA.
Certificación ocupacional . Ciudad de México , 1981. 76 p. ; ISBN 968-8290-30-0 LC Card 86-142976
HD5715.5.L3 C47 1981

OCCUPATIONAL TRAINING - SINGAPORE.
Vente, Rolf E. Education and training for industrial development in Singapore and other ASEAN countries . Baden-Baden , Singapore , 1984. 175 p. : ISBN 3-7890-0941-5 LC Card 84-186381 DDC 331.25/92/0959 19
HD5715.5.S55 V46 1984
NYPL [JLD 86-2773]

OCCUPATIONAL TRAINING - SOUTH AFRICA.
Black advancement in the South African economy /. Braamfontein, Johannesburg , 1986. 256 p. : ISBN 0-86954-289-3 LC Card 87-119018 DDC 331.6/9968 19
HD5842.A6 B58 1986b

OCCUPATIONAL TRAINING - SPAIN.
Triadú, Joaquim, 1959- Les professions del futur /. Barcelona , 1986. 186 p. : ISBN 84-86421-20-9 LC Card 86-214981
HF5382.5.S7 T75 1986

OCCUPATIONAL TRAINING - TERMINOLOGY.
Vocational training . Geneva , 1986. vii, 132 p. ; ISBN 92-2-105457-8 (pbk.) : LC Card 87-123102 DDC 331.25/92/0321 19
HD5715 .V63 1986

OCCUPATIONAL TRAINING - UNITED STATES.
Breakthrough for disadvantaged youth. [Washington] 1969. iii, 256 p. LC Card 79-604757 DDC 331.3/4/0973
HD6273 .B7 ***NYPL [JLF 86-435]***

Bushnell, David S. Training for new technology /. New York , c1983. 41 p. ; ISBN 0-08-029508-8 : LC Card 83-17341 DDC 658.3/124 19
HD5715.2 .B87 1983
NYPL [JLM 83-380 no.27]

Cook, Robert F., 1943- Public service employment . Kalamazoo, Mich. , 1985. xiii, 131 p. ; ISBN 0-88099-031-7 (pbk.) LC Card 85-22495 DDC 331.13/77/0973 19
HD5713.6.U54 C66 1985
NYPL [JLE 86-3877]

Education and training for older persons . [Washington, D.C.?] , 1981. iii, 64 p. :
NYPL [JLF 86-1274]

Job training under the new federalism . [Chicago?] , 1986. ii, 299 p. : LC Card 86-203209 DDC 331.25/92/0973 19
HD5715.2 .J63 1986

Mason, Sarah R. Training Southeast Asian refugee women for employment . Minneapolis, Minn. , 1986. viii, 142 p. : LC Card 86-72303 DDC 331.4/2592/08995073 19
HD5715.2 .M37 1986

Paradis, Adrian A. Opportunities in vocational & technical careers /. Lincolnwood, Ill., U. S.A. , c1987. xi, 147 p. : ISBN 0-8442-6018-5 LC Card 87-60104 DDC 371.4/25/02373 19
HF5382.5.U5 P28 1987

Startzel, Donna C. The CETA arts and humanities experience [microform] CETA Ahead project (Arts and humanities employment analysis and documentation) /. Columbia, Md. , 1981. 197 p. ;
*NYPL [*XME-11,320]*

Startzel, Donna C. CETA (Comprehensive Employment and Training Act) and the arts and humanities [microform] . Columbia, Md. , 1981. 160 p. ; *NYPL [*XME-11,328]*

United States. Employment and Training Administration. Office of Youth Program. Completing the youth agenda . Washington , 1979. 73 p. ; *NYPL [JLF 86-454]*

OCCUPATIONAL TRAINING - UNITED STATES - FINANCE.
Howe, Mike. Accessing private industry council funding . [Northridge, CA] (17624 Romar St., Northridge 91325) [1987?] 24, [15] leaves ; LC Card 87-401761 DDC 362.8/5 19
HD5715.2 .H69 1987

OCCUPATIONAL TRAINING - URUGUAY.
Estimación de las necesidades de formación profesional en el Uruguay . Montevideo , 1981. 98 leaves ; LC Card 86-174016
HD5715.5.U8 E86 1981

Occupational trends, nineteen eighty-two--nineteen ninety-five. Occupational trends, 1982-1995. Little Rock, AR (P.O. Box 2981, Little Rock, AR 72203) [1986]- v. ;
NYPL [JLM 87-353]

Occupational trends, 1982-1995. Little Rock, AR (P.O. Box 2981, Little Rock, AR 72203) : Research and Analysis Section, Arkansas Employment Security Division, [1986]- v. ; 28 cm. Includes bibliographical references. CONTENTS. - [1]. City of Little Rock service delivery area -- [2] Southwest service delivery area -- [3] West Central service delivery area -- [4] Western service delivery area.
1. Labor Supply - Arkansas. 2. Employment forecasting - Arkansas. 3. Arkansas - Occupations. I. Arkansas. Employment Security Division. Research and Analysis Section. II. Title: Occupational trends, nineteen eighty-two--nineteen ninety-five.
NYPL [JLM 87-353]

OCCUPATIONS - CHOICE. see **VOCATIONAL GUIDANCE.**

OCCUPATIONS - CLASSIFICATION.
Dictionary of occupational titles /. [Washington] , 1977. xli, 1371 p. ; LC Card 78-601723 DDC 331.7/003
HB2595 .U543 1977
*NYPL [*R-TMH 78-1740]*

Gottfredson, Gary D. Dictionary of Holland occupational codes /. Palo Alto, CA , c1982. xviii, 500 p. ; ISBN 0-89106-020-X
NYPL [JLE 86-3992]

Kerns, Allen F. Dictionary of worker traits /. Philadelphia, PA , 1987- p. cm. ISBN 0-9618599-9-7 LC Card 87-12478 DDC 331.7/02/0973 19
HB2595 .K43 1987

OCCUPATIONS - COLLECTED WORKS.
Feingold, S. Norman, 1914- Emerging careers . Garrett Park, Md. , c1983- v. ; ISBN 0-912048-32-8 (pbk.) : LC Card 83-80074 DDC 331.7/02 19
HF5382 .F44 1983 *NYPL [JLL 86-205]*

OCCUPATIONS - DICTIONARIES.
Dictionary of occupational titles /. [Washington] , 1977. xli, 1371 p. ; LC Card 78-601723 DDC 331.7/003
HB2595 .U543 1977
*NYPL [*R-TMH 78-1740]*

Gottfredson, Gary D. Dictionary of Holland occupational codes /. Palo Alto, CA , c1982. xviii, 500 p. ; ISBN 0-89106-020-X
NYPL [JLE 86-3992]

Kerns, Allen F. Dictionary of worker traits /. Philadelphia, PA , 1987- p. cm. ISBN 0-9618599-9-7 LC Card 87-12478 DDC 331.7/02/0973 19
HB2595 .K43 1987

OCCUPATIONS - DISEASES. see **OCCUPATIONAL DISEASES.**

OCCUPATIONS - FORECASTING.
Jobs for the '90s [videorecording] /. Pleasantville, NY , 1987. 1 videocassette (48 min.) : LC Card 87-705264 DDC 331.7 11
HF5382

OCCUPATIONS - HISTORY - JUVENILE LITERATURE.
Franck, Irene M. Helpers and aides /. New York, N.Y. , c1987. x, 182 p. : ISBN 0-8160-1445-0 LC Card 86-24370 DDC 331.7 19
HF5381.2 .F68 1987

OCCUPATIONS - HYGIENIC ASPECTS. see **INDUSTRIAL HYGIENE.**

Occupations in energy-related industries [microform] : opportunities for minority youth : submitted to ... Office of Minority Economic Impact, U. S. Dept. of Energy / by Resouces, Inc. Washington, D.C. : The Company, 1981. ca. 300 p. ; 28 cm. "DOE/MI/01004-T5." "March 19, 1981." Includes bibliographical references. Microfiche. Springfield, Va. : NTIS 1982. 4 microfiches : negative ; 11 x 15 cm. (DE 82 010433)
1. Minorities - Employment - United States. 2. Youth - Employment - United States. 3. Manpower policy - United States. I. United States. Dept. of Energy. Office of Minority Economic Impact. II. Resources, Inc.
*NYPL [*XME-11,557]*

Occupations in services, finance, insurance, real estate, and construction, 1984 / prepared by Massachusetts Division of Employment Security, Economic Research & Analysis Service, Occupational Employment Statistics Unit. [Boston, MA] : Commonwealth of Massachusetts, Division of Employment Security, [1985] 185 p. : ill. ; 28 cm. "November 1985." LC Card 87-621853 DDC 331.7/009744 19
1. Labor supply - Massachusetts - Statistics. 2. Wages - Massachusetts - Statistics. I. Massachusetts. Occupational Employment Statistics Unit.
HD5725.M4 O26 1985

OCCUPATIONS - JUVENILE LITERATURE.
Blacker, Terence. If I could work /. New York , c1988. p. cm. ISBN 0-397-32245-3 : LC Card 87-3972 DDC 331.7/02 19
HF5381.2 .B55 1988

OCCUPATIONS - PICTORIAL WORKS - JUVENILE LITERATURE.
100 words about working /. San Diego , c1988. p. cm. ISBN 0-15-200553-6 LC Card 87-8363 DDC 331.7/02 19
HF5382 .A13 1988

Occupations Study Group (Great Britain)
Rajan, Amin, 1942- Services--the second industrial revolution? . London , Boston , 1987. xviii, 257 p. : ISBN 0-408-02003-2 LC Card 86-32739 DDC 331.12/9042 19
HD9982.5 .R34 1987

UK occupation and employment trends to 1990 . London , Boston , 1986. xxiv, 249 p. : ISBN 0-408-02980-3 : LC Card 86-13617 DDC 331.12/0941 19
HD5765.A6 U38 1986 *NYPL [JLE 86-4156]*

OCCUPATIONS - WEST VIRGINIA - STATISTICS.
State of West Virginia Job Training Partnership Act . Charleston, W.Va. (112 California Ave., Charleston 25305-0112) [1986] vi, 233 p. ; LC Card 86-622901 DDC 331.1/09754/021 19
HD5725.W4 S7 1986

OCEAN - ECONOMIC ASPECTS. see **MARINE RESOURCES; SHIPPING.**

OCEAN LINERS - HISTORY.
Ogliari, Francesco. Trasporti marittimi di linea /. Milano , 1975- v. : LC Card 76-507610
HE839 .O35 *NYPL [JSK 86-35]*

OCEAN MINERAL RESOURCES. see **MARINE MINERAL RESOURCES.**

OCEAN ROUTES. see **TRADE ROUTES.**

OCEAN TRANSPORTATION. see **SHIPPING.**

Ochel, Wolfgang, 1943-
Laumer, Helmut. Strukturpolitik für traditionelle Industriezweige in Japan /. Berlin , c1985. 173 p. : ISBN 3-428-05920-4 LC Card 86-151482
HD3616.J32 L38 1985

Service economies in Europe : opportunities for growth / by Wolfgang Ochel and Manfred Wegner. Boulder : Westview Press, 1987. p. cm. Bibliography: p. ISBN 0-8133-0580-2 : LC Card 87-21690 DDC 338.4/6/094 19
1. Service industries - Europe. I. Wegner, Manfred. II. Title.
HD9986.A2 O28 1987

Ocherki ėkonomicheskoĭ istorii Shri Lanki . Ivanov, L. G. (Leonid Grigor′evich) Moskva , 1978. 222 p. ; LC Card 81-153039
HC424 .I95 1978

Ocherki istorii marksistsko-leninskoĭ ėkonomicheskoĭ mysli Latvii, 1920-1980 /. Kirtovskiĭ, I. Kh. Riga , 1985. 199 p. ; LC Card 86-176265
HB97.5 .K542 1985

Ochs, Peter. Analyse und Bewertung ausgewählter sozialwissenschaftlichen Forschungen / P. Ochs. Dortmund : Bundesanstalt für Arbeitsschutz und Unfallforschung ; Bremerhaven : Wirtschaftsverlag NW, 1983. 102 p. ; 21 cm. (Forschungsbericht / Bundesanstalt für Arbeitsschutz und Unfallforschung . Nr. 327) Summary in English and German. Bibliography: p. 95-102. ISBN 3-88314-245-X LC Card 83-207278
1. Industrial safety - Germany, West. 2. Occupational diseases - Germany (West). 3. Job stress - Germany (West). 4. Stress (Psychology). I. Series: Forschungsbericht / Bundesanstalt für Arbeitsschutz und Unfallforschung , Nr. 327. II. Title.
HD7708 .O28 1983

Ochsenanspannung in Westafrika . Kirk, Michael, 1955- Göttingen , c1984. iv, 220 p. ; ISBN 3-88694-057-8 LC Card 86-202167 DDC 338.1/09688 19
HD2134 .K57 1984

Ochsner, Neal. Common sense real estate / Neal Ochsner. 1st ed. New York : Holt, c1987. xi, 239 p. : ill. ; 22 cm. Includes index. ISBN 0-8050-0509-9 LC Card 87-8420 DDC 332.63/24 19
1. Real estate investment. 2. Real estate business. I. Title.
HD1382.5 .O36 1987

O'Connell, Julie, 1951- Medicaid reform : a policy discussion / prepared by New York State Department of Social Services, Division of Medical Assistance. [Albany, N.Y.] : The Division, [1983] 26 p. ; 28 cm. "Prepared by Julie O'Connell and Barbara Frankel"--Prelim. leaf 2. "March 1983"--Cover. LC Card 86-620741 DDC 362.1/04252/09747 19
1. Medicaid - New York (State). I. Frankel, Barbara, 1950-. II. New York (State). Dept. of Social Services. Division of Medical Assistance. III. Title.
HD7102.U5 N668 1983

O'Connell, Richard T. Bowerman, Bruce L. Computer modeling for business and industry /. New York , c1984. vii, 219 p. : ISBN 0-8247-7296-2 LC Card 84-17063 DDC 519.5/0285425 19
HF1017 .B655 1984 *NYPL [JSE 86-623]*

O'Connor, Brian. Palmer, Michele. Catalogue of interviews . [Storrs, Conn.] , 1983. ii, 79 p. ; LC Card 86-621476 DDC 331.12/09746 19
HD6331.2.U52 C86 1983

O'Connor, Feargus, 1794-1855. Feargus O'Connor, attack and defense. New York , 1986. 1 v. (various pagings) ; ISBN 0-8240-5592-6 (alk. paper) : LC Card 86-27131 DDC 322/.2/0924 19
HD8396 .F43 1986

O'Connor, Harvey, 1897-1987. O'Connor, Jessie Lloyd, 1904- Harvey and Jessie . Philadelphia , 1988. p. cm. ISBN 0-87722-519-2 (alk. paper) LC Card 87-21737 DDC 322/.2/0922 B 19
HD8073.A1 O25 1988

O'CONNOR, HARVEY, 1897-1987.
O'Connor, Jessie Lloyd, 1904- Harvey and Jessie . Philadelphia , 1988. p. cm. ISBN 0-87722-519-2 (alk. paper) LC Card 87-21737 DDC 322/.2/0922 B 19
HD8073.A1 O25 1988

O'Connor, James (James R.) The meaning of crisis : a theoretical introduction / James O'Connor. Oxford, UK ; New York, NY, USA : B. Blackwell, 1987. v, 197 p. ; 23 cm. Includes bibliographical references and index. ISBN 0-631-13819-6 (pbk.) : LC Card 86-26399 DDC 338.5/4 19
1. Depressions. 2. Business cycles. 3. Marxian economics. I. Title.
HB3714 .O24 1987

O'Connor, Jessie Lloyd, 1904- Harvey and Jessie : a couple of radicals / Jessie Lloyd O'Connor, Harvey O'Connor, and Susan M. Bowler. Philadelphia : Temple University Press, 1988. p. cm. Includes bibliographical references and index. ISBN 0-87722-519-2 (alk. paper) LC Card 87-21737 DDC 322/.2/0922 B 19
1. O'Connor, Jessie Lloyd, 1904-. 2. O'Connor, Harvey, 1897-1987. 3. Labor and laboring classes - United States - Biography. 4. Radicals - United States - Biography. I. O'Connor, Harvey, 1897-1987. II. Bowler, Susan M. III. Title.
HD8073.A1 O25 1988

O'CONNOR, JESSIE LLOYD, 1904-
O'Connor, Jessie Lloyd, 1904- Harvey and Jessie . Philadelphia , 1988. p. cm. ISBN 0-87722-519-2 (alk. paper) LC Card 87-21737 DDC 322/.2/0922 B 19
HD8073.A1 O25 1988

O'Connor, Melvin C. Chasteen, Lanny G., 1942- Intermediate accounting /. New York , c1987. xxviii, 1328 p. : ISBN 0-394-35802-3 : LC Card 86-29865 DDC 657/.044 19
HF5635 .C474 1987

O'Connor, Nuala. Jobsuss : the enterprise file / Nuala O'Connor Cork : Published in collaboration with Radio Telefís Éireann by The Mercier Press, cl985. 96 p. ; 21 cm. ISBN 0-85342-748-8 (pbk.) : LC Card 86-220513 DDC 658/.022/09417 19
1. Small business - Management. 2. Small business - Ireland - Management - Case studies. I. Radio Telefís Éireann. II. Title.
HD62.7 .O36 1985

OCS report .
Webster, Frank L. Pacific OCS lease sale, October 1, 1964, Oregon and Washington /. [Washington] [1985] iii, 36 p. : LC Card 86-601138 DDC 333.33/9 19
HD243.A18 W43 1985

La Ocupación y su remuneración en las empresas petroleras en Colombia, 1977-1984. Bogotá, D.E. : Departamento Administrativo Nacional de Estadística, [1986] 37 p. : ill. ; 24 cm. (Colección Temas, 0120-7431) Includes bibliographical references. LC Card 87-402964 DDC 331.12/5223382/09861 19
1. Petroleum workers - Colombia. 2. Wages - Petroleum workers - Colombia. 3. Trade-unions - Petroleum workers - Colombia. I. Colombia. Departamento Administrativo Nacional de Estadística. II. Series: Colección Temas (Bogotá, Colombia).
HD8039.P42 V446 1986

Odagiri, Hiroyuki, 1946- A study of company profit-rate time series : new results for Japan and International comparison / Hiroyuki Odagiri, Hideki Yamawaki. Berlin : Wissenschaftszentrum Berlin, [1986] 15, 5 p. ; 30 cm. (Discussion papers / IIMV/Strukturpolitik--IIM/Industrial Policy, Wissenschattszentrum Berlin, 0722-6748 . IIM/IP 86-3) "February 1986." Summary in English and German. Bibliography: p. 5. LC Card 87-165037 DDC 338.7/4/0952 19
1. Corporate profits - Japan - Mathematical models. 2. Corporate profits - Mathematical models. I. Yamawaki, Hideki. II. Series: Discussion papers (International Institute of Management. Industrial Policy) , IIM/IP 86-3. III. Title.
HG4028.P7 O33 1986

Odaka, Kōnosuke, 1935- The Motor vehicle industry in Asia . [Singapore] [1983] xxv, 419 p. : ISBN 997-16-9057-8 LC Card 83-941793 DDC 338.4/76292/095 19
HD9710.3.A78 M67 1983 *NYPL [JLE 85-1592]*

Odbudowa podstaw gospodarki Śląska Opolskiego na przykładzie przemysłu, 1945-1949 /. Lis, Michał. [Opole] , 1978. 254 p. : LC Card 81-201084
HC340.Z7 O665 1978

O'Dell, Carla S., 1950- Grayson, C. Jackson (Charles Jackson), 1923- American business, a two-minute warning . New York , London , c1988. xvii, 368 p. : ISBN 0-02-912680-0 LC Card 87-19391 DDC 658/.00973 19
HD70.U5 G69 1988

O'Dell, Jerry W. BASIC statistics, an introduction to problem solving with your personal computer / by Jerry W. O'Dell. 1st ed. Blue Ridge Summit, PA : Tab Books, c1984. vii, 452 p. : ill. ; 21 cm. Includes index. Bibliography: p. 447. ISBN 0-8306-0759-5 : LC Card 84-8804 DDC 519.5/028/542 19
1. Statistics - Data processing. 2. Electronic digital computers - Programming. I. Title.
QA276.4 .O34 1984 *NYPL [JSD 86-378]*

Odell, John S., 1945- Destler, I. M. Anti-protection . Washington, DC , c1987. xii, 204 p. ; ISBN 0-88132-065-X (pbk.) LC Card 87-22545 DDC 382/.3/0973 19
HF1455 .D482 1987

O'Dell memorial monograph, 0141-1454 .
(no. 13) Armstrong, A. M. Land ownership and land use in the Scottish Highlands /. [Aberdeen, Grampian] , 1983. vii, 150 p. : LC Card 83-209521 DDC 333.3/09411/5 19
HD616 .A76 1983 *NYPL [JLF 86-457]*

Odén, Bertil, 1939- Sydafrika i södra Afrika / av Bertil Odén. Uppsala : SIDA : Distribueras av Nordiska Afrikainstitutet, 1985. 181 p. : ill. ; 25 cm. Bibliography: p. 157-162. ISBN 91-7106-236-X LC Card 85-221741
1. Regional economics. 2. South Africa - Economic conditions. 3. Africa, Southern - Economic conditions. I. Title.
HC905 .O34 1985 *NYPL [Sc E 86-483]*

ODER RIVER REGION - POPULATION.
Rauziński, Robert. Ludność Nadodrza, 1945-2000 /. Opole , 1985. 44 p. ; LC Card 86-207214
HB3608.7.O34 R38 1985

Odink, J. G. Inkomensherverdeling : enkele aspecten van de inkomensherverdeling door de overheid in Nederland / J.G. Odink. Groningen : Wolters-Noordhoff, c1985. 254 p. : ill. ; 24 cm. Summary in English. Thesis (doctoral)--Technische Hogeschool Twente te Enschede, 1985. Bibliography: p. 231-240. ISBN 90-01-66101-7 : LC Card 86-149572
1. Income distribution - Netherlands. 2. Distribution (Economic theory). I. Title.
HC329.5.I5 O35 1985

Odint͡sova, G. S. (Galina Sergeevna)
Organizat͡sionnoe proektirovanie i planirovanie razvitii͡a sistem upravlenii͡a / G.S. Odint͡sova, A.I. Kovalev, N.N. Mel′tiukhova. Kiev : Nauk. dumka, 1986. 158, [2] p. : ill. ; 20 cm. At head of title: Akademii͡a nauk Ukrainskoĭ SSR. Khar′kovskoe otdelenie Instituta ėkonomiki. Bibliography: p. 154-[159] LC Card 87-162923
1. Business enterprises - Soviet Union - Management. 2. Industrial management - Soviet Union. I. Kovalev, A. I. (Anatoliĭ Ivanovich). II. Mel′tiukhova, N. N. (Nadezhda Nikolaevna). III. Title.
HD2876 .O35 1986

Odiorne, George S. The human side of management : management by integration and self-control / George S. Odiorne. Lexington, Mass. : Lexington Books, in association with University Associates, Inc., San Diego, Calif., c1987. xiv, 236 p. ; 24 cm. Bibliography: p. [221]-223. Includes index. ISBN 0-669-15350-8 (alk. paper) LC Card 86-46314 DDC 658.3 19
1. Management by objectives. 2. Personnel management. 3. Employees, Training of. 4. Job enrichment. I. Title.
HD30.65 .O35 1987

O'Donnell, Carol.
The basis of the bargain : gender, schooling, and jobs / Carol O'Donnell. Sydney ; Boston : G. Allen & Unwin, 1984. 186 p. ; 23 cm. Originally presented as thesis (Ph. D.)--Macquarie University. Includes index. Bibliography: p. 171-183. ISBN 0-86861-497-1 LC Card 84-70146 DDC 331.4/133/0994 19
1. Sex discrimination in employment - Australia. 2. Women - Employment - Australia. 3. Education of women - Australia. 4. Sex discrimination in education - Australia. I. Title.
HD6060.5.A8 O36 1984 *NYPL [JLD 86-2017]*

Getting equal : labour market regulation and women's work / Carol O'Donnell and Philippa Hall. Sidney ; Boston : Allen & Unwin, 1988. p. cm. Bibliography: p. Includes index. ISBN 0-04-302005-4 LC Card 87-22302 DDC 331.2/1 19
1. Equal pay for equal work - Australia. 2. Equal pay for equal work - Law and legislation - Australia. 3. Equal pay for equal work - United States. 4. Equal pay for equal work - Law and legislation - United States. 5. Equal pay for equal work - Sweden. 6. Equal pay for equal work - Law and legislation - Sweden. I. Hall, Philippa. II. Title.
HD6060.5.A8 O365 1988

O'Dowd, John. Cody, Seamus. The Parliament of labour . Dublin, Ireland , 1986. 253 p. : LC Card 87-102467 DDC 331.88/09418/35 19
HD8400.3.A5 D833 1986

Odra i Nadodrze.
Rauziński, Robert. Ludność Nadodrza, 1945-2000 /. Opole , 1985. 44 p. ; LC Card 86-207214
HB3608.7.O34 R38 1985

Odyssey . Sculley, John. New York , c1987. xiv, 450 p., [16] p. of plates : ISBN 0-06-015780-1 : LC Card 87-45142 DDC 331.7/61004165/0924 B 19
HD9696.C62 S38 1987

The OECD Compatible Trade and Production data base, 1970-1983 /. Brodin, Anders. [Paris, France] , c1986. ii, 81 p. ; LC Card 86-213116 DDC 382/.021 19
HF1016 .B68 1986

OECD Group of Financial Statisticians. Bank profitability . Paris , Washington, D.C. , 1987. 235 p. ; ISBN 92-64-12915-4 (pbk.) : LC Card 87-164235 DDC 332.1/021 19
HG1708 .B29 1987

OECD road safety research : a synthesis : report / prepared by an OECD scientific experts group. Paris : Organisation for Economic Co-operation and Development ; [Washington, D.C. : OECD Publications and Information Centre, distributor], 1986. 106 p. : ill. ; 27 cm. (Road transport research) ISBN 92-64-12814-X (pbk.) : LC Card 86-212506 DDC 363.1/25 19
1. Traffic safety - Research. I. Organisation for Economic Co-operation and Development. II. Series.
HE5614 .O34 1986

Oechsler, Ronald G. Statistical abstract of East-West trade and finance : staff report / prepared by Ronald G. Oechsler, Leyla Woods. Washington, D.C. : Office of Trade and Investment Analysis, International Trade Administration, U. S. Dept. of Commerce : For sale by the Supt. of Docs., U. S. G.P.O., [1986]. vi, 43 p. : ill. ; 28 cm. Shipping list no.: 86-369-P. "#March 1986." "Project DIE-47-86." S/N 003-009-00475-6 Item 231-B-1 LC Card 86-601999 DDC 382/.091713/01717021 19
1. East-West trade (1945-) - Statistics. 2. Balance of payments - Statistics. I. Woods, Leyla. II. United States. International Trade Administration. Office of Trade and Investment Analysis. III. Title.
HF1411 .O3455 1986

OECOLOGY. see **ECOLOGY.**

OEF International. Doing a feasibility study . Washington, D.C. , c1987. 173 p. : ISBN 0-912917-07-5 (pbk.) : LC Card 86-61951 DDC 658/.022/091724 19
HD62.5 .D63 1987

Öffentliche Arbeitsmarktpolitik in der Bundesrepublik Deutschland . Seifert, Hartmut, 1944- Köln [1984] ix, 288 p. ; ISBN 3-7663-0857-2 LC Card 86-127331 DDC 331.11/0943 19
HD5779 .S34 1984

Öffentliche Finanzen, Kredit und Kapital : Festschrift für Werner Ehrlicher zur Vollendung des 65. Lebensjahres / herausgegeben von Dieter Cansier und Dietmar Kath ; mit Beiträgen von Günter Ashauer ... [et al.]. Berlin : Duncker & Humblot, c1985. xvi, 618 p., [1] leaf of plates : ill. ; 24 cm. Three contributions in English. "Verzeichnis der Veröffentlichungen von Werner Ehrlicher": p. [609]-616. Includes bibliographies. ISBN 3-428-05737-6 LC

Card 85-164173
1. Finance, Public. 2. Finance, Public - Germany, West. 3. Finance, Public - United States. 4. Monetary policy. 5. Monetary policy - Germany, West. 6. Monetary policy - United States. 7. Ehrlicher, Werner. I. Ehrlicher, Werner. II. Cansier, Dieter. III. Kath, Dietmar. IV. Ashauer, Günter.
HJ161 .O33 1985

Öffentliche Finanzwirtschaft in Westdeutschland, 1944-1948 . Scherpenberg, Jens van. Frankfurt am Main , c1984. 544 p. : ISBN 3-88323-502-4 LC Card 84-182435
HJ1120 .S317 1984

Öffentliche Güter und der Öffentlichkeitsgrad von Gütern /. Bonus, Holger. Konstanz [1979] 39, 3 p. ; LC Card 85-171986
HB846.5 .B66 1979

Öffentliche Unternehmen in Rezession und Aufschwung : eine Diskussion im Wissenschaftlichen Beirat der Gesellschaft für Öffentliche Wirtschaft und Gemeinwirtschaft / [Herausgeber, Gesellschaft für Öffentliche Wirtschaft und Gemeinwirtschaft e.V., Berlin ; Redaktion, Karl Kühne, Paul Münch, Theo Thiemeyer]. Berlin : Die Gesellschaft, 1977. 165 p. : ill. ; 21 cm. (Schriftenreihe der Gesellschaft für Öffentliche Wirtschaft und Gemeinwirtschaft e.V. . Heft 14) Papers from a meeting of the Wissenschaftlicher Beirat, Gesellschaft für Öffentliche Wirtschaft und Gemeinwirtschaft held 1976 in Emmershausen. Includes bibliographical references. LC Card 85-180964
1. Government business enterprises - Congresses. 2. Economic stabilization - Congresses. 3. Economic history - 1971- - Congresses. I. Kühne, Karl. II. Münch, Paul, 1913-. III. Thiemeyer, Theo. IV. Series.
HD3845 .G43 Heft 14 HD3842

Die öffentliche Wirtschaft in der Weimarer Republik . Ambrosius, Gerold. Baden-Baden , 1984. 306 p. ; ISBN 3-7890-0912-1 LC Card 84-230508
HD4175 .A626 1984

Öffentlichkeitsarbeit Dritte Welt in Österreich. Jäggle, Martin. Öffentlichkeitsarbeit 3. Welt in Österreich /. Wien , 1975- v. <1 > ; LC Card 86-234031
HC60 .J344 1975

Öffentlichkeitsarbeit 3. Welt in Österreich /. Jäggle, Martin. Wien , 1975- v. <1 > ; LC Card 86-234031
HC60 .J344 1975

Oehrig, Robert J. Trends in Kenyan short wave listening . Nairobi, Kenya , c1979. vii, 87 [26] leaves : LC Card 85-980967 DDC 384.54/3 19
HE8697.A8 T74 1979

Der ÖKO-Plan . Brunowsky, Ralf-Dieter, 1949- München , c1984. 236, [1] p. ; ISBN 3-492-02922-1 LC Card 84-251156
HC290.5.E5 B78 1984

Ökologie und Sozialismus : Perspektiven einer umweltfreundlichen Politik / Norbert W. Kunz (Hrsg.). Köln : Bund-Verlag, c1986. 369 p. ; 21 cm. Includes bibliographical references. ISBN 3-7663-0983-8 LC Card 87-107373 DDC 363.7/056/0943 19
1. Environmental policy - Germany, West. 2. Socialism - Germany, West. 3. Sozialdemokratische Partei Deutschlands. 4. Grünen (Political party). I. Kunz, Norbert, 1958-.
HC290.E5 O39 1986

Ökologische Unternehmenspolitik / Reinhard Pfriem (Hg.). Frankfurt ; New York : Campus, c1986. 280 p. ; 21 cm. "Eine Publikation des Instituts für Ökologische Wirtschaftsforschung (IÖW) GmbH, Berlin"--T.p. verso. Bibliography: p. 265-280. ISBN 3-593-33580-8 LC Card 87-407999 DDC 363.7 19
1. Economic development - Environmental aspects. 2. Economic policy. 3. Environmental policy. I. Pfriem, Reinhard. II. Institut für Ökologische Wirtschaftsforschung.
HD75.6 .O347 1986

Die ökologische Wirtschaft . Fornallaz, Pierre. Aarau , c1986. 128 p. : ISBN 3-85502-252-6 : LC Card 86-180445
HC79.E5 F62 1986

Ökonometrie als Instrument der Interessenpolitik . Hasse, Rolf. Köln , 1985. ii, 109 p. : ISBN 3-921471-52-4 : LC Card 85-216061
HF1733.D44 H37 1985

Ökonometrische Systeme mit variablen Strukturen . Röhling, Wolfgang. Freiburg im Breisgau , c1983. x, 263 p. : ISBN 3-448-01353-6 LC Card 84-132199
HB139 .R63 1983

Ein ökonometrischer Ansatz zur Erklärung des Bausparens /. Schulze, Konrad. Bonn , c1985. xii, 150 p. : ISBN 3-87169-319-7 LC Card 86-231621
HC290.5.S3 S38 1985

OÉkonomicheskie problemy razvitiia narodnogo khoziaistva i povyshenie ėffektivnosti obshchestvennogo proizvodstva / [nauchnye redaktory F.A. Dronov, Ė.I. Petrovich]. Minsk : Nauchno-issl. in-t avtomatizirovannykh sistem planirovaniia i upravleniia nar. khoziaistvom Gosplana Belorusskoĭ SSR, 1984. 148 p. : ill. ; 20 cm. Includes bibliographical references. LC Card 85-147020
1. Byelorussian S.S.R. - Economic policy. I. Dronov, Fedor Amosovich. II. Petrovich, Ė. I. III. Nauchno-issledovatel'skiĭ institut avtomatizirovannykh sistem planirovaniia i upravleniia narodnym khoziaistvom (Byelorussian S.S.R.).
HC337.B93 E45 1984

Ökonomie, Politik und Krise . Hahn, Jörg. Würzburg , 1984. 137 p. ; ISBN 3-88479-183-4 LC Card 85-113948
HB3732 .H34 1984

Ökonomie und Autonomie . Köhler, Holm-Detlev, 1956- Frankfurt , c1986. 213 p. ; ISBN 3-925798-24-2 LC Card 87-108165 DDC 334/.0943 19
HD3498 .K63 1986

Ökonomie und Ethik . Waibl, Elmar. Stuttgart-Bad Cannstatt , c1984. 429 p. ; ISBN 3-7728-0892-1 LC Card 85-130712
HB501 .W28 1984

Ökonomie und Gesellschaft an der Wende von der Antike zum Mittelalter . Herrmann, Joachim, 1932- Berlin , 1979. 72 p. : LC Card 85-209249
HC31 .H47 1979

Ökonomische Analyse dinglicher Sicherheiten . Duttle, Josef. Krefeld , 1986. xvii, 417 p. : ISBN 3-88358-062-7 LC Card 87-104300
HG3711.G3 D87 1986

Ökonomische Analyse von Streik und Aussperrung im Rahmen einer marktwirtschaftlichen Ordnung /. Klemm, Günther. Köln , 1983. viii, 214 p. : ISBN 3-921471-43-5 : LC Card 83-216635 DDC 331.89/2 19
HD5306 .K55 1983

Ökonomische Anreizinstrumente in einer auflagenorientierten Umweltpolitik . Zimmermann, Horst, 1934- Stuttgart , 1983. 59 p. ; ISBN 3-17-003279-8 : LC Card 84-148886
HC110.A4 Z55 1983

Ökonomische Ansätze zur Analyse des Energieverbrauchs der Haushalte für Rauwärmzwecke /. Suding, Paul H. München , 1984. ix, 252, 10 p. : ISBN 3-486-28661-7 LC Card 84-209002
HD9502.G42 S8 1984

Die ökonomische Bedeutung der Qualität des Schienengüterverkehrs . Dick, Walter, 1949- Berlin , c1980. xi, 331 p. : ISBN 3-428-04731-1 LC Card 84-130833
HE2446.N67 D52 1980

Ökonomische Institutionenanalyse . Elsner, Wolfram. Berlin , c1986. xv, 469 p. : ISBN 3-428-06035-0 LC Card 86-206447
HB99.5 .E47 1986

Ökonomische Instrumente der Umweltpolitik . Umweltpolitisches Gespräch (1983 : Bad Godesberg, Bonn, Germany) Berlin , c1984. 108 p. ; ISBN 3-503-02401-8 LC Card 86-152141
HC290.5.E5 U625 1983

Die ökonomische Problematik von Zuweisungen an Kommunen /. Massat, Dieter. Thun , c1984. vii, 321 p. : ISBN 3-87144-792-7 LC Card 84-183709
HJ1121 .M37 1984

"Ökonomische Probleme der bedarfsorientierten Produktionsdurchführung" : 5. und 6. September 1984 : Thesen und Kurzfassungen ausgewählter Diskussionsbeiträge / Technische Hochschule Karl-Marx-Stadt, Sektion Wirtschaftswissenschaften ; [Redaktion, W. Schuster]. Karl-Marx-Stadt : Der Rektor der Technischen Hochschule Karl-Marx-Stadt, 1984. 139 p. : ill. ; 21 cm. (Tagungsberichte (Technische Hochschule Karl-Marx-Stadt) . Heft 9) Wissenschaftliche Tagung LC Card 84-245348
1. Industrial management - Germany (East) - Congresses. 2. Consumption (Economics) - Germany (East) - Congresses. I. Schuster. II. Technische Hochschule Karl-Marx-Stadt. Sektion Wirtschaftswissenschaften. III. Series. IV. Series: Tagungsberichte (Technische Hochschule Karl-Marx-Stadt) , Heft 9.
HD70.G22 O35 1984

Ökonomische Sicherungspolitik /. Forster, Edgar. Berlin , c1983. 280 p. : ISBN 3-428-05366-4 LC Card 83-220475
HD7101 .F67 1983

Ökonomische Strategie der achtziger Jahre und Effektivität des Wirtschaftsrechts. Ökonomische Strategie der 80er Jahre und Effektivität des Wirtschaftsrechts /. Berlin , 1984. 48 p. ; LC Card 84-159925
HC290.78 .O36 1984

Ökonomische Strategie der 80er Jahre und Effektivität des Wirtschaftsrechts / [verantwortlich für dieses Heft, Gerhard Schüssler]. Berlin : Akademie-Verlag, 1984. 48 p. ; 24 cm. (Abhandlungen der Akademie der Wissenschaften der DDR. Abteilung Veröffentlichung der Wissenschaftlichen Räte, 0302-8054 . Jahrg. 1983, Nr. W 3) Papers of a meeting held by the Rat für Staats- und Rechtwissenschaftliche Forschung of the Akademie der Wissenschaften der DDR on 6/25/1982. Includes bibliographical references. CONTENTS. - Die Wirtschaftsstrategie des X. Parteitages und die Erhöhung der Wirksamkeit des Wirtschaftsrechts / Uwe-Jens Heuer -- Das neue Vertragsgesetz und die Vervollkommnung des Wirtschaftsrechts / Gerhard Walter -- Die Erhöhung der Wirksamkeit des Wirtschaftsrechts im Prozess der Rechtsetzung und Rechtsverwirklichung / Siegfried Bergmann -- Die Erhöhung der Effektivität des wissenschaftlich-technischen Rechtsschutzes / Ernst Winklbauer -- Zum Verhältnis von Recht und Ökonomie / Gerhard Haney. LC Card 84-159925
1. Germany East - Economic policy - Congresses. I. Schüssler, Gerhard. II. Akademie der Wissenschaften der DDR. Rat für Staats- und Rechtswissenschaftliche Forschung. III. Title: Ökonomische Strategie der achtziger Jahre und Effektivität des Wirtschaftsrechts. IV. Series: Abhandlungen der Akademie der Wissenschaften der DDR , Jahrg. 1983, Nr. W 3.
HC290.78 .O36 1984

Ökonomische Strategie und Vervollkommnung der staatlichen Leitung / [Autorenkollektiv, Hans Hofmann (Leitung)]. Potsdam-Babelsberg : Akademie für Staats- und Rechtswissenschaft der DDR, Sektion Marxismus-Leninismus, 1983. 64 p. ; 21 cm. (Aktuelle Beiträge der Staats- und Rechtswissenschaft, 0568-7551 . Heft 285) Bibliography: p. 60-64. LC Card 84-180104
1. Germany, East - Economic policy. I. Hofmann, Hans, Dr. habil. II. Series.
HC290.78 .O387 1983

Ökonomische Strategie und volkswirtschaftliche Masseninitiative /. Otto, Wolfgang, Diplom-Staatswissenschaftler. Berlin , 1984. 61 p. : LC Card 85-189271
HC290.78 .O88 1984

Ökonomische und ökologische Perspektiven der Agrarpolitik . Ahn, Lothar. Köln , 1983. 98 p. : ISBN 3-7609-5124-4 LC Card 83-155478
HD1920.5 .A627 1983

Ökonomische und soziale Wirksamkeit des wissenschaftlich-technischen Fortschritts / [Akademie für Gesellschaftswissenschaften beim ZK der SED ; Autorenkollektiv, Michael Büchner, Harry Nick (Leiter) ... et al. ; Mitarbeit, Rainer Beier ... et al.]. Berlin : Dietz, 1986. 314 p. ; 23 cm. Includes bibliographical references and index. ISBN 3-320-00713-0 LC Card 87-100866 DDC 338/.06 19
1. Technological innovations - Germany, East. 2. Microelectronics - Germany (East). 3. Communism and technology - Germany (East). I. Büchner, Michael. II. Nick, Harry. III. Akademie für Gesellschaftswissenschaften beim ZK der SED.
HC290.795.T4 O38 1986

Ökonomisches Denken und soziale Ordnung : Festschrift für Erik Boettcher / herausgegeben von Hans Albert. Tübingen : J.C.B. Mohr, 1984. viii, 293 p. ; 24 cm. List of works by Erik Boettcher: p. [275]-284. Includes bibliographies and

indexes. ISBN 3-16-344777-5 (Deut. Bibl.) LC Card 84-193300
1. Economics. 2. Boettcher, Erik. I. Boettcher, Erik. II. Albert, Hans, 1921-.
HB175 .O46 1984

Ökonomisches Risiko und Versicherung in sozialistischen Volkswirtschaften . Schönfelder, Bruno. Berlin , c1986. 284 p. : ISBN 3-428-05968-9 LC Card 86-185328
HD7180.5 .S36 1986

Ölangebotsmodelle . Fertig, Klaus. Hamburg , 1986. 236 p. : ISBN 3-87895-302-X LC Card 86-225350
HD9502.A2 F46 1986

Oelke, Eckhard. Territoriale Probleme der ökonomischen Integration der EG-Länder / Eckhard Oelke. 1. Aufl. Gotha : H. Haack, 1986. 118 p. : ill. ; 22 cm. Bibliography: p. 113-118. ISBN 3-7301-0872-7 LC Card 87-118872 DDC 337.1/42 19
1. European Economic Community. 2. Europe - Economic integration. I. Title.
HC241.2 .O32 1986

Oelkers, Claus, 1952- Entscheidungsorganisation : Versuch einer Integration von Elementen der Organisation, der EDV und des Rechnungswesens unter wissenschaftstheoretischen Aspekten / Claus Oelkers. Frankfurt am Main ; New York : P. Lang, c1986. 263 p. : ill. ; 21 cm. (Europäische Hochschulschriften. Reihe V, Volks- und Betriebswirtschaft, 0531-7339 . Bd. 733 = vol. 733 = vol. 733) Bibliography: p. 248-263. ISBN 3-8204-9396-4 LC Card 86-221177
1. Industrial organization (Economic theory). 2. Business enterprises - Decision making. 3. Business enterprises - Data processing. 4. Business enterprises - Accounting. I. Series: Europäische Hochschulschriften. Reihe V, Volks- und Betriebswirtschaft , Bd. 733. II. Title.
HD2326 .O35 1986

Örtliche Versorgungswirtschaft . Bartsch, Heinz. Potsdam-Babelsberg , 1985. 79 p. : LC Card 86-121253
HD2768.G4 B27 1985

Der Österreichische Baupreisindex 1971-1985 / bearbeitet im Österreichischen Statistischen Zentralamt. Wien : Das Zentralamt, 1986. 107 p. ; 30 cm. (Beiträge zur österreichischen Statistik . 810. Heft) LC Card 87-409417 DDC 314.36 s 338.4/3691/09436 19
1. Building materials - Prices - Austria - Statistics. I. Österreichisches Statistisches Zentralamt. II. Series.
HA1173 .A27 Heft 810 HD9715.8.A92

Österreichische Entwicklungshilfe, 1970-1983 . Höll, Otmar. Wien , Laxenburg, Austria , c1986. 187 p. : ISBN 3-7003-0659-8 LC Card 86-192362
HC60 .H6643 1986

Das österreichische Foreign Debt Management, 1956-1983 . Speiser, Harald. Regensburg , c1985. 120 p. : ISBN 3-924956-06-5 LC Card 86-222064
HJ8636 .S66 1985

Die Österreichische Gemeinwirtschaft im Jahre 1976 : eine Sonderauswertung der nichtlandwirtschaftlichen Bereichszählungen / bearbeitet im Österreichischen Statistischen Zentralamt. Wien : Kommissionsverlag, C. Ueberreuter : Auslieferung, R. Lechner, 1980. 102 p. ; 30 cm. (Beiträge zur österreichischen Statistik . 563. Heft) Chiefly tables. LC Card 85-208409
1. Austria - Economic conditions - 1945- - Statistics. 2. Austria - Industries - Statistics. I. Österreichisches Statistisches Zentralamt. II. Series.
HA1173 .A27 Heft 563 HC265

Österreichische Gesellschaft für Raumforschung und Raumplanung. Grasberger, Helmut, 1941- Die Untersuchung des Wohnwertes von Wohngebieten /. Wien , New York , 1983. 108 p., [15] folded leaves of plates : ISBN 0-387-81752-2 (U. S.) LC Card 84-142695
HD7337.A3 G73 1983

Der Österreichische Gewerkschaftsbund . Misslbeck, Johannes, 1954- Frankfurt/M. [1983] iii, 197 p. : ISBN 3-89038-000-X (pbk.) LC Card 84-191049
HD8403 .M57 1983

Österreichische Nationalbank. (Old Catalog form: Österreichische Nationalbank, Vienna) Geldwertstabilität und Wirtschaftswachstum . Göttingen , c1984. xii, 230 p. : ISBN 3-525-13169-0 LC Card 84-232466
HG203 .G46 1984

ÖSTERREICHISCHE VOLKSPARTEI - HISTORY.
Vodopivec, Alexander. 40 Jahre Wirtschaftsbund . Wien [1985?] 107 p. ; LC Card 86-169299
HC265 .V589 1985

ÖSTERREICHISCHER GEWERKSCHAFTSBUND - HISTORY.
Misslbeck, Johannes, 1954- Der Österreichische Gewerkschaftsbund . Frankfurt/M. [1983] iii, 197 p. : ISBN 3-89038-000-X (pbk.) LC Card 84-191049
HD8403 .M57 1983

Schriftenreihe für Agrarpolitik und Agrarsoziologie. see **Schriftenreihe für Agrarpolitik und Agrarsoziologie.**

Oettinger, Anthony G. Weinhaus, Carol L. Behind the telephone debates /. Norwood, N.J. , 1987. p. cm. ISBN 0-89391-452-5 LC Card 87-19459 DDC 384.6/0973 19
HE8815 .W45 1987

Oettinger, Craig Milton, 1945- The politics of excluded groups : Black mobilization in a sample of 77 northern cities [microform] / by Craig M. Oettinger. 1978. xvi, 454 leaves : ill. ; 28 cm. Thesis (Ph. D.)--Brown University, 1978. Vita. Bibliography: leaves 439-454. Microfilm of typescript. Ann Arbor, Mich. : University Microfilms International, 1979. 1 microfilm reel ; 35 mm.
1. Community power. 2. Political participation - United States. 3. Afro-Americans - Politics and suffrage.
NYPL [Sc Micro R-4615]

Oettle, Karl.
Flexible Arbeitszeit gegen starre Sozialsysteme /. Baden-Baden , 1986. 254 p. ; ISBN 3-7890-1213-0 LC Card 87-101055 DDC 331.25/72/0943 19
HD5109.2.G3 F43 1986

Ökonomische Probleme des öffentlichen Verkehrs : ausgewählte Beiträge zu wirtschaftlichen Gegenwarts- und Zukunftsfragen öffentlicher Verkehrsbetriebe und Verkehrsverwaltungen / Karl Oettle.1. Aufl. Baden-Baden : Nomos Verlagsgesellschaft, 1981. 373 p. ; 23 cm. (Schriften zur öffentlichen Verwaltung und öffentlichen Wirtschaft. Bd. 28) Summary in English, French, German, and Russian. Includes indexes. Bibliography: p. 341-354. ISBN 3-7890-0568-1 : LC Card 82-159141 DDC 380.5/068 19
1. Transportation - Germany, West. 2. Transportation and state - Germany, West. I. Title.
HE249 .O33 1981 ***NYPL [JLD 86-2588]***

O'Fee, J. H. The input of labour on farms in Northern Ireland / J.H. O'Fee. Belfast : Economics and Statistics Division, Dept. of Agriculture, 1986. i, 41 leaves ; 30 cm. LC Card 86-218985 DDC 331.11/8 19
1. Agricultural laborers - Northern Ireland. 2. Agricultural productivity - Northern Ireland. I. Title.
HD1535.N675 O47 1986

La ofensiva empresarial contra la intervención del estado /. Rey Romay, Benito. México , 1984. 160 p. ; ISBN 968-231-283-3 LC Card 86-151140
HD4013 .R49 1984

Oferta y demanda global a precios corrientes / preparado por Departamentos de Cuentas Nacionales ... [et al.]. [Buenos Aires, Argentina] : Gerencia de Investigaciones y Estadísticas Económicas del Banco Central de la República Argentina, 1982. 115 leaves ; 29 cm. (Serie de trabajos metodológicos y sectoriales . no. 20) LC Card 87-402103 DDC 339.382 19
1. National income - Argentina - Accounting - Effect of inflation on. I. Banco Central de la República Argentina. Departamento de Cuentas Nacionales. II. Series.
HC180.I5 O38 1982

La oferta y la demanda de empleos . Pérez P., María José. Bogotá, Colombia , c1984. 64 p. ; ISBN 84-8276-322-9 LC Card 84-241503
HD5757.A6 P47 1984

Off camera . Levinson, Richard. New York, N.Y. , c1986. 279 p. ; ISBN 0-452-25873-1 LC Card 86-18089 DDC 384.55/023/73 19
HE8700.4 .L48 1986
NYPL [MWGR 87-881]

The off-farm labour supply of padi farmers in Kelantan, Malaysia [microform] /. Chew, T. A. [Canberra] , c1984. 19 p. ; ISBN 0-86784-513-9 (pbk.) LC Card 85-670027 DDC 331.12/93318/095951 19
HD5854.55.M4 C47 1984
NYPL [*ZF-1745 no.58]

Off-price shopping centers. Dollars & cents of off-price shopping centers . Washington, D.C. , c1986. v, 78 p. : ISBN 0-87420-660-X (pbk.) LC Card 86-51102 DDC 381/.1 19
HF5430.3 .D65 1986

Offant, Pierre. Adaptation structurelle de l'économie française à la limitation de la consommation d'énergie / Pierre Offant. Dijon : Institut de mathématiques économiques : Diffuseur, Libr. de l'Université, c1984. 224, iii p. : ill. ; 21 cm. (Collection de l'I.M.E. . no 27) Bibliography: p. 223-224. ISBN 2-85975-026-6 LC Card 85-205959
1. Energy consumption - France. 2. France - Economic policy - 1981-. 3. Energy policy - France. I. Title. II. Series.
HD9502.F72 O33 1984

Offene Jugendarbeit im Arbeiterviertel : Erfahrungen und Analysen / Erwin Bienewald . . . [et al.] ; mit Karikaturen von Jari Cuypers. Bensheim : Päd. Extra Buchverlag, 1978. 229 p. : ill. ; 20 cm. Bibliography and filmography: p. 225-229. ISBN 3-921450-57-8 LC Card 84-120278
1. Youth - Employment - Germany, West. 2. Youth - Social aspects - Germany (West). I. Bienewald, Erwin, 1950-.
HD6276.G4 O38 1978

Offene und verdeckte Arbeitslosigkeit in der Bundesrepublik . Schmidt, Rainer, Dr. Tübingen , c1986. viii, 124 p. : ISBN 3-16-345158-6 LC Card 87-126258 DDC 331.13/7943 19
HD5779 .S2495 1986

OFFENSES AFFECTING THE PUBLIC TRADE. see **COMMERCIAL CRIMES.**

OFFENSES AGAINST SOCIALIST PROPERTY - LAW AND LEGISLATION - SOVIET UNION.
Ėvel′son, Evgeniia. Sudebnye protsessy po ėkonomicheskim delam v SSSR . London , 1986. 370 p. ; ***NYPL [*QIX 87-4024]***

Den Offentliga sektorns sysselsättningsutveckling i Norden under 1970-talet = Julkisen sektorin työllisyyskehitys pohjoismaissa 1970-luvun aikana. [Oslo] : Nordiska arbetsmarknadsutskottet ; [Solna : Arbetsmarknadsstyrelsen, distributor], 1983. iiii, 150 p. : ill. ; 25 cm. (NAUT-rapport . 1983:8) Summary in English and Finnish. Includes bibliographical references. ISBN 91-38-07556-3 LC Card 85-184428
1. Scandinavia - Officials and employees. 2. Labor supply - Scandinavia. I. Title: Julkisen sektorin työllisyyskehitys pohjoismaissa 1970-luvun aikana. II. Series.
HD8013.S344 O35 1983

OFFER TO PURCHASE (SECURITIES) see **TENDER OFFERS (SECURITIES)**

Offergeld, Johannes. Spezialisierung des Verkehrsangebotes und Strukturwandel in der verladenden Wirtschaft : dargestellt am Beispiel von Strukturwandlungen in der Flachglasindustrie und ihren Auswirkungen auf den Verkehrssektor / Johannes Offergeld. Göttingen : Vandenhoeck & Ruprecht, 1984. 185 p. : ill. ; 24 cm. (Beiträge aus dem Institut für Verkehrswissenschaft an der Universität Münster . Heft 102) Bibliography: p. 180-185. ISBN 3-525-85690-3 (Deut. Bibl.) LC Card 84-197725
1. Transportation - Germany, West. 2. Transportation and state - Germany, West. 3. Glass trade - Germany (West) - Case studies. I. Title. II. Series.
HE131 .M8 Heft 102 HE249

Offermann, Andreas. Projekt-Controlling bei der Entwicklung neuer Produkte / Andreas Offermann. Thun : H. Deutsch, c1985. 524 p. : ill. ; 21 cm. (Reihe Wirtschaftswissenschaften, 0253-1488 . Bd. 329) Bibliography: p. 476-524. ISBN 3-87144-885-0 LC Card 85-208022
1. New products. 2. Industrial project management. I.

Title. II. Series.
HD69.N4 O36 1985

The office, a facility based on change /. Propst, Robert. Zeeland, MI , 1986 printing, c1968. 71 p. : ISBN 0-936658-01-0 (pbk.) : LC Card 86-23653 DDC 651.3 19
HF5547 .P76 1986

OFFICE ADMINISTRATION. see **OFFICE MANAGEMENT.**

Office automation . Arn, Joseph V., 1943- Boston, MA , c1988. xxvii, 402 p., [8] p. of plates : ISBN 0-87835-232-5 LC Card 86-28359 DDC 651.8 19
HF5547.5 .A79 1988

Office automation . Wagoner, Kathleen P. New York , c1987. xvii, 432 p. : ISBN 0-471-84505-1 (pbk.) LC Card 86-26775 DDC 651.8 19
HF5547.5 .W33 1987

Office automation and information systems /. Rosen, Arnold, 1932- Columbus , c1987. xvi, 363 p. : ISBN 0-675-20557-3 (pbk.) LC Card 86-62495 DDC 651.8 19
HF5548 .R67 1987

Office automation and the implications for office development /. Dowall, David E. [Berkeley] [1986] 171 p. ; LC Card 86-622512 DDC 651.8 19
HF5547.5 .D64 1986

The Office automation market in the U. S. New York, N.Y. : Frost & Sullivan, <c1983- > v. <2 > : ill. ; 29 cm. "January 1983." LC Card 87-166011 DDC 381/.456816/0973 19
1. Electronic office machine industry - United States. 2. Computer industry - United States. 3. Office practice - Automation. 4. Market surveys - United States. I. Frost & Sullivan.
HD9801.U542 O34 1983

Office automation systems handbook /. Lord, Kenniston W. Blue Ridge Summit, PA. , 1988. p. cm. ISBN 0-8306-2899-1 : LC Card 87-7112 DDC 650/.028/5 19
HF5548.2 .L589 1988

Office automation using the IBM personal computer systems . Burgess, Ross. London , 1986. 180 p. : ISBN 0-00-383104-3 (pbk.) : LC Card 86-220136 DDC 651.8/4165 19
HF5548.2 .B783 1986

OFFICE BUILDINGS - CALIFORNIA - SAN FRANCISCO.
Dowall, David E. Back-offices and San Francisco's office development growth cap /. [Berkeley] [1986] 23 p. : LC Card 86-622513 DDC 333.77/17/0979461 19
HD268.S4 D68 1986

OFFICE BUILDINGS - CALIFORNIA - SAN FRANCISCO BAY AREA - LOCATION.
Dowall, David E. Back-offices and San Francisco's office development growth cap /. [Berkeley] [1986] 23 p. : LC Card 86-622513 DDC 333.77/17/0979461 19
HD268.S4 D68 1986

OFFICE BUILDINGS - SOCIAL ASPECTS - NEW YORK (STATE) - ROCHESTER - ANECDOTES, FACETIAE, SATIRE, ETC.
Jackson, Mason, 1926- The building /. Interlaken, N.Y. , 1987. 128 p. : ISBN 0-932334-90-3 LC Card 86-24115 DDC 974.7/89043 19
HD8039.M4 U54 1987

Office Coffee Development Group. Attitudes toward vended coffee /. [Chicago? , 1983] 1 v. (various pagings) : LC Card 86-235525 DDC 381/.4566393 19
HD9199.U48 A88 1983

OFFICE DE LA CONSTRUCTION DU QUÉBEC - AUDITING.
Québec (Province). Bureau du vérificateur général. Vérification spéciale . [Québec] [1978-<1987? >] v. <1-3 > ; LC Card 82-212701
HD9715.C33 Q45 1978

Office de la construction du Québec. Service de la recherche. Les Accidents du travail dans la construction au Québec /. [Quebec] [1983] vii, 256 p. : ISBN 2-550-10554-0 LC Card 85-100967
HD9715.C33 Q42 1983

OFFICE EQUIPMENT. see **OFFICE EQUIPMENT AND SUPPLIES.**

OFFICE EQUIPMENT AND SUPPLIES - DICTIONARIES - POLYGLOT.
Schramm, Herbert F. W. Burghagen Fachwörterbuch . Hamburg , c1964. 160 p. ; LC Card 84-256680
HF5548 .S37 1964

OFFICE EQUIPMENT AND SUPPLIES INDUSTRY - GERMANY (WEST)
Büromaschinen, Datenverarbeitungsgeräte und -einrichtungen . Berlin [1984] xxi, 400 p. : ISBN 3-428-05740-6 LC Card 86-139011
HC281 .B33 Heft 82 HD9800.G3

OFFICE EQUIPMENT AND SUPPLIES INDUSTRY - UNITED STATES.
The Future of the office products industry . Alexandria, Va. (301 N. Fairfax St., Alexandria 22314) , c1985. viii, 212, 33 p. : LC Card 86-200112 DDC 338.4/768 19
HD9800.U52 F86 1985

OFFICE EQUIPMENT AND SUPPLIES - INFORMATION SERVICES - UNITED STATES - DIRECTORIES.
How to find information about companies in the telecommunications, data processing, and office automation industries /. Washington, DC , c1987. ii, 130 p. ; ISBN 0-934940-48-7 (pbk.) LC Card 86-51630 DDC 338.7/61004/072073 19
HD9696.A3 U559 1987

OFFICE EQUIPMENT LEASES.
Weber, Robert E. Managing your renovation or move to new offices /. New York , 1987. xii, 242 p. : ISBN 0-89930-245-9 (lib. bdg. : alk. paper) LC Card 86-30583 DDC 658.2/3 19
HF5547.2 .W42 1987

OFFICE ETIQUETTE. see **BUSINESS ETIQUETTE.**

Office information technology . Goldfield, Randy J. New York , 1986. xiv, 226 p. : ISBN 0-89930-108-8 (lib. bdg. : alk. paper) LC Card 86-614 DDC 651.8 19
HF5547.5 .G65 1986 ***NYPL [JLE 87-1107]***

OFFICE LANDSCAPING. see **OFFICE LAYOUT.**

OFFICE LAYOUT - PSYCHOLOGICAL ASPECTS.
Williams, Cecil L., 1930- The negotiable environment . Ann Arbor, Mich. , c1985. v, 82 p. : ISBN 0-936658-20-7 (pbk.) : LC Card 85-10305 DDC 658.3/82 19
HF5547.2 .W55 1985 ***NYPL [JLF 86-1138]***

OFFICE MACHINES. see **OFFICE EQUIPMENT AND SUPPLIES.**

OFFICE MAIL PROCEDURES - GERMANY (WEST)
Schumann, Matthias. Eingangspostbearbeitung in Bürokommunikationssystemen . Berlin , New York , c1987. xi, 156 p. ; ISBN 0-387-17369-2 (U. S.) LC Card 87-133887 DDC 651.7/59 19
HF5547 .S457 1987

OFFICE MANAGEMENT.
Arn, Joseph V., 1943- Office automation . Boston, MA , c1988. xxvii, 402 p., [8] p. of plates : ISBN 0-87835-232-5 LC Card 86-28359 DDC 651.8 19
HF5547.5 .A79 1988

Kallaus, Norman Francis, 1924- Administrative office management /. Cincinnati , c1987. ix, 774 p. : ISBN 0-538-07560-0 LC Card 85-61633 DDC 651.3 19
HF5547 .K43 1987

Katz, Daniel, 1903- Productivity, supervision, and morale in an office situation, part I /. New York , 1987, c1950. vii, 84 p. ; ISBN 0-8240-8211-7 (alk. paper) : LC Card 86-25804 DDC 658.3 19
HF5549 .K282 1987

Long, Richard J. New office information technology . London , New York , c1987. xix, 333 p. : ISBN 0-7099-4103-X (jacket); 0-7099-4130-X LC Card 87-3601 DDC 651.8 19
HF5547.5 .L65 1987

Meyer, Rolf, 1957- Integration der Informationsverarbeitung im Büro . Bergisch Gladbach , c1986. xiv, 327 p. : ISBN 3-89012-062-8 LC Card 87-104032 DDC 651.8 19
HF5547.5 .M497 1986

Propst, Robert. The office, a facility based on change /. Zeeland, MI , 1986 printing, c1968. 71 p. : ISBN 0-936658-01-0 (pbk.) : LC Card 86-23653 DDC 651.3 19
HF5547 .P76 1986

Smith, Harold T., 1932- The Administrative manager . Chicago , c1987. xii, 548 p. : ISBN 0-574-20065-7 : LC Card 86-24881 DDC 651.8 19
HF5547 .S577 1987

Tedesco, Eleanor Hollis. Administrative office systems management /. New York , c1987. xii, 736 p. : ISBN 0-471-01201-7 LC Card 86-26800 DDC 651.3 19
HF5547 .T37 1987

Wagoner, Kathleen P. Integrated office systems . New York , c1987. xxi, 734 p., [4] p. of plates : ISBN 0-471-01195-9 LC Card 86-26793 DDC 651.8 19
HF5547 .W26 1987

Weltz, Friedrich. Innovation im Büro . Frankfurt , New York , c1983. 343 p. ; ISBN 3-593-32724-4 LC Card 83-243001
HF5548.115 .W44 1983

Zangl, Hans. Durchlaufzeiten im Büro . Berlin , c1985. xvii, 365 p. : ISBN 3-503-02458-1 LC Card 85-137750
HF5549.5.C6 Z33 1985

OFFICE MANAGEMENT - HYGIENIC ASPECTS.
Köchling, Annegret, 1944- Bildschirmarbeit . Köln , c1985. 212 p. : ISBN 3-7663-0853-X
NYPL [JLD 87-392]

Office of Military Government for Germany (U. S.) see **Germany (Territory under Allied Occupation, 1945-1955. U. S. Zone). Office of Military Government.**

OFFICE ORGANIZATION AND MANAGEMENT. see **OFFICE MANAGEMENT.**

OFFICE PLANNING. see **OFFICE LAYOUT.**

Office policy in Britain . Manners, Gerald. Norwich, UK , c1986. viii, 158 p. : ISBN 0-86094-212-0 LC Card 87-143633 DDC 338.6/042 19
HF5547.25 .M36 1986

OFFICE POLITICS.
Davis, William, 1933- The corporate infighter's handbook . London , 1984. 144 p. : ISBN 0-283-99133-X (pbk.) : LC Card 85-240558 DDC 650.1 19
HF5386 .D325 1984 ***NYPL [JLE 87-618]***

Dollé, Anne. Ça va comme un lundi . [Paris] , c1984. 237 p. ; ISBN 2-01-010177-4 : LC Card 85-143058 DDC 650.1/3 19
HF5386 .D63 1984

OFFICE POLITICS - UNITED STATES.
Fernandez, John P., 1941- Survival in the corporate fishbowl . Lexington, Mass. , c1987. xiii, 314 p. : ISBN 0-669-10336-5 (alk. paper) LC Card 85-40021 DDC 302.3/5 19
HD6957.U6 F47 1987

Office practice. Fulton, Patsy J. General office procedures for colleges /. Cincinnati , c1988. viii, 399 p. : ISBN 0-538-11732-X (pbk.) LC Card 86-63580 DDC 651 19
HF5547.5 .F84 1988

OFFICE PRACTICE - AUTOMATION.
Armour, Hazel. New technology in the office environment /. Aldershot, Hampshire, England , Brookfield, Vt., USA , c1986. viii, 138 p. : ISBN 0-566-05031-5 LC Card 86-215701 DDC 338.4/561651 19
HF5547.5 .A786 1986

Arn, Joseph V., 1943- Office automation . Boston, MA , c1988. xxvii, 402 p., [8] p. of plates : ISBN 0-87835-232-5 LC Card 86-28359 DDC 651.8 19
HF5547.5 .A79 1988

Automazione d'ufficio . Roma [1985] 248 p. : LC Card 86-213829
HF1152.P28 A95 1985

Baethge, Martin. Zukunft der Angestellten . Frankfurt , New York , c1986. 460 p. : ISBN 3-593-33368-6 (pbk.) LC Card 87-673317
HD5707 .B28x 1986

Bergerud, Marly, 1942- Introduction to office systems . New York , c1987. xvi, 440 p., [12]

p. of plates : ISBN 0-471-85532-4 (pbk.) LC Card 86-28188 DDC 652/.5 19
HF5548.115 .B462 1987

Bergerud, Marly, 1942- Word and information processing . New York , c1987. xvi, 578 p. : ISBN 0-471-84504-3 LC Card 86-24748 DDC 652/.5 19
HF5548.115 .B46 1987

Burgess, Ross. Office automation using the IBM personal computer systems . London , 1986. 180 p. : ISBN 0-00-383104-3 (pbk.) : LC Card 86-220136 DDC 651.8/4165 19
HF5548.2 .B783 1986

Communications/Information Systems Planning Service . Boston, MA (89 Broad St., Boston 02110) , c1986. ii, 78 p. ; LC Card 86-225335 DDC 381/.45651853 19
HD9696.C63 U51492 1986

Dordick, Herbert S., 1925- Innovative management using telecommunications . New York , c1986. x, 226 p. : ISBN 0-471-81296-X : LC Card 86-7797 DDC 658.4/5 19
HF5541.T4 D67 1986 ***NYPL [JLE 86-4425]***

Dowall, David E. Office automation and the implications for office development /. [Berkeley] [1986] 17I p. ; LC Card 86-622512 DDC 651.8 19
HF5547.5 .D64 1986

Ellis, Clarence Arthur, 1943- Design of office information systems /. Berlin , New York , c1987. vi, 248 p. : ISBN 0-387-17810-4 (U. S.) : LC Card 87-9582 DDC 651.8 19
HF5548.2 .E445 1987

Fischer, Barbara S. Office systems integration . New York , 1987. xxi, 215 p. : ISBN 0-89930-109-6 (lib. bdg. : alk. paper) LC Card 87-2498 DDC 651.8 19
HF5547.5 .F56 1987

Goldfield, Randy J. Office information technology . New York , 1986. xiv, 226 p. : ISBN 0-89930-108-8 (lib. bdg. : alk. paper) LC Card 86-614 DDC 651.8 19
HF5547.5 .G65 1986 ***NYPL [JLE 87-1107]***

Harvey, David. The electronic office in the smaller business /. Aldershot, Hants, England , Brookfield, Vt., U. S.A. , c1986. vii, 214 p. : ISBN 0-566-02578-7 LC Card 86-225568 DDC 651.8/416 19
HF5547.5 .H365 1986

Hunt, H. Allan. Clerical employment and technological change /. Kalamazoo, Mich. , 1986. x, 296 p. : ISBN 0-88099-042-2 (pbk.) LC Card 86-26556 DDC 331.12/5165137/0973 19
HD5718.M392 U65 1986

Image processing in office automation. Norwalk, Conn., U. S.A. (6 Prowitt St., Norwalk 06855) , c1986. vii, 220 leaves ; LC Card 86-228429 DDC 381/.4500642 19
HD9696.I422 I44 1986

Johnson, Bonnie McDaniel, 1944- Managing organizational innovation . New York , 1987. xiv, 242 p. ; ISBN 0-231-06398-9 LC Card 87-307 DDC 652/.5 19
HF5548.115 .J64 1987

Kupsh, Joyce. The electronic office /. Mission Hills, Calif. , c1987. x, 307 p. : ISBN 0-02-803510-0 (pbk.) LC Card 87-402084 DDC 651.8 19
HF5548 .K85 1987

Long, Richard J. New office information technology . London , New York , c1987. xix, 333 p. : ISBN 0-7099-4103-X (jacket); 0-7099-4130-X LC Card 87-3601 DDC 651.8 19
HF5547.5 .L65 1987

Lord, Kenniston W. Office automation systems handbook /. Blue Ridge Summit, PA. , 1988. p. cm. ISBN 0-8306-2899-1 : LC Card 87-7112 DDC 650/.028/5 19
HF5548.2 .L589 1988

Matthiasen, Leo. Informationsteknologi og arbejdsproces . Roskilde [1983?] 339 p. : ISBN 87-87893-19-3 LC Card 85-114664
HF5547.5 .M384 1983

Meyer, N. Dean. The information edge /. New York , c1987. xvii, 333 p. ; ISBN 0-07-041782-2 LC Card 86-222546 DDC 651.8 19
HF5547.5 .M495 1987

Meyer, Rolf, 1957- Integration der Informationsverarbeitung im Büro . Bergisch Gladbach , c1986. xiv, 327 p. : ISBN 3-89012-062-8 LC Card 87-104032 DDC 651.8 19
HF5547.5 .M497 1986

National Research Council (U. S.). Committee on Women's Employment and Related Social Issues. Panel on Technology and Women's Employment. Computer chips and paper clips . Washington, D.C. , 1986. v. : ISBN 0-309-03688-7 (v. 1) LC Card 86-18113 DDC 331.4/8165137/0973 19
HD6331.18.M39 N38 1986
NYPL [JLL 87-129]

New technology and women's employment. Bruxelles , New York [1983] 78 p. ; LC Card 85-160627 DDC 331.4/2 19
HD6331 .N49 1983 ***NYPL [JLD 86-1807]***

The Office automation market in the U. S. New York, N.Y. , <c1983-. v. <2 > : LC Card 87-166011 DDC 381/.456816/0973 19
HD9801.U542 O34 1983

Popyk, Marilyn K., 1945- Word processing and information systems . New York , c1986. xx, 345 p., [15] p. of plates : ISBN 0-07-050594-2 (pbk.) : LC Card 85-23813 DDC 652/.5 19
HF5548.115 .P66 1986 ***NYPL [JSE 87-273]***

Roessner, J. David. The Impact of office automation on clerical employment, 1985-2000 . Westport, Conn. , 1985. xii, 297 p. : ISBN 0-89930-119-3 (lib. bdg. : alk. paper) LC Card 85-6523 DDC 331.12/9165137 19
HD8039.B27 U548 1986
NYPL [JLE 86-1424]

Rosen, Arnold, 1932- Office automation and information systems /. Columbus , c1987. xvi, 363 p. : ISBN 0-675-20557-3 (pbk.) LC Card 86-62495 DDC 651.8 19
HF5548 .R67 1987

Saffady, William, 1944- The automated office . Silver Spring, Md. , c1981. viii, 241 p. : ISBN 0-89258-072-0 LC Card 81-208697 DDC 651.8/4 19
HF5548.2 .S165 ***NYPL [JLE 86-3919]***

Schumann, Matthias. Eingangspostbearbeitung in Bürokommunikationssystemen . Berlin , New York , c1987. xi, 156 p. ; ISBN 0-387-17369-2 (U. S.) LC Card 87-133887 DDC 651.7/59 19
HF5547 .S457 1987

Smith, Harold T., 1932- The Administrative manager . Chicago , c1987. xii, 548 p. : ISBN 0-574-20065-7 : LC Card 86-24881 DDC 651.8 19
HF5547 .S577 1987

Tedesco, Eleanor Hollis. Administrative office systems management /. New York , c1987. xii, 736 p. : ISBN 0-471-01201-7 LC Card 86-26800 DDC 651.3 19
HF5547 .T37 1987

Varnon, M. S. Developing and using office applications with AppleWorks . St. Paul , c1987. xi, 366 p. : ISBN 0-314-34129-3 (pbk.) : LC Card 86-24696 DDC 651.8/5369 19
HF5548.4.A68 V37 1987

Wagoner, Kathleen P. Integrated office systems . New York , c1987. xxi, 734 p., [4] p. of plates : ISBN 0-471-01195-9 LC Card 86-26793 DDC 651.8 19
HF5547 .W26 1987

Wagoner, Kathleen P. Office automation . New York , c1987. xvii, 432 p. : ISBN 0-471-84505-1 (pbk.) LC Card 86-26775 DDC 651.8 19
HF5547.5 .W33 1987

Walbrück, Hans-Jürgen, 1956- Entwicklung von branchen-spezifischen integrierten Bürokommunikationssystemen . Bergisch Gladbach , c1986. 368 p. : ISBN 3-89012-044-X : LC Card 86-174155
HF5547.5 .W345 1986

Women, clerical work, and office automation . Washington, D.C. , 1986. vi, 64 p. ; LC Card 86-602559 DDC 331.4/8165137/0973 19
HD6095 .W685 1986

Zangl, Hans. Durchlaufzeiten im Büro . Berlin , c1985. xvii, 365 p. : ISBN 3-503-02458-1 LC Card 85-137750
HF5549.5.C6 Z33 1985

OFFICE PRACTICE - AUTOMATION - ADDRESSES, ESSAYS, LECTURES.

Human aspects in office automation /. Amsterdam , New York , 1984. xv, 322 p. : ISBN 0-444-42327-3 : LC Card 84-5917 DDC 363.1/19651 19
HF5547.5 .H85 1984 ***NYPL [JLF 86-892]***

OFFICE PRACTICE - AUTOMATION - CONGRESSES.

IEEE Computer Society Office Automation Symposium (1987 : National Bureau of Standards) IEEE Computer Society Office Automation Symposium, National Bureau of Standards, Gaithersburg, MD, 27-29 April 1987. Washington, D.C. , Los Angeles, CA , c1987. xi, 319 p. : ISBN 0-8186-0770-X (pbk.) LC Card 86-83315 DDC 651.8 19
HF5548 .I44 1987

IFIP TC 8 Working Conference on Office Systems (1985 : Helsinki, Finland) Office systems . Amsterdam ; New York : vii, 199 p. : ISBN 0-444-70105-2 (Elsevier Science Pub. Co.) LC Card 86-16841 DDC 651.8 19
HF5547.5 .I345 1985 ***NYPL [JLD 87-1264]***

IFIP TC 8/WG 8.4 Working Conference on Methods and Tools for Office Systems (1986 : Pisa, Italy) Office systems . Amsterdam ; New York : xi, 347 p. : ISBN 0-444-70241-5 (U. S.) LC Card 87-8916 DDC 651.8 19
HF5548.2 .I285 1986

International Conference on Networks and Electronic Office Systems (1983 : University of Reading) Networks and electronic office systems . London , c1983. 240 p. : ISBN 0-903748-52-5 ***NYPL [JSG 86-298]***

International Conference on Networks and Electronic Office Systems (1985 : London, England) Networks and electronic office systems . London , c1985. 166 p. : ISBN 0-903748-60-6 ***NYPL [JSG 86-264]***

Technology and the transformation of white-collar work /. Hillsdale, N.J. , 1987. x, 281 p. : ISBN 0-89859-633-5 : LC Card 86-29039 DDC 331.7/92/0973 19
HD8039.M4 U577 1987

OFFICE PRACTICE - AUTOMATION - INFORMATION SERVICES - UNITED STATES - DIRECTORIES.

How to find information about companies in the telecommunications, data processing, and office automation industries /. Washington, DC , c1987. ii, 130 p. ; ISBN 0-934940-48-7 (pbk.) LC Card 86-51630 DDC 338.7/61004/072073 19
HD9696.A3 U559 1987

OFFICE PRACTICE - AUTOMATION - MANAGEMENT.

Head, Robert V. Planning and implementing information resource centers for end-user computing /. Wellesley, MA , c1985. viii, 186 p. : ISBN 0-89435-123-0 : LC Card 84-61536
NYPL [JLE 86-2117]

Weltz, Friedrich. Innovation im Büro . Frankfurt , New York , c1983. 343 p. ; ISBN 3-593-32724-4 LC Card 83-243001
HF5548.115 .W44 1983

OFFICE PRACTICE - AUTOMATION - PSYCHOLOGICAL ASPECTS.

Dy, Fe Josefina F. Visual display units . Geneva , 1985. ix, 138 p. : ISBN 92-2-105083-1 (pbk.) : LC Card 86-214267 DDC 651.8 19
HF5547.5 .D9 1985

Long, Richard J. New office information technology . London , New York , c1987. xix, 333 p. : ISBN 0-7099-4103-X (jacket); 0-7099-4130-X LC Card 87-3601 DDC 651.8 19
HF5547.5 .L65 1987

Meyer, Rolf, 1957- Integration der Informationsverarbeitung im Büro . Bergisch Gladbach , c1986. xiv, 327 p. : ISBN 3-89012-062-8 LC Card 87-104032 DDC 651.8 19
HF5547.5 .M497 1986

OFFICE PRACTICE - AUTOMATION - PSYCHOLOGICAL ASPECTS - CASE STUDIES.

Fallik, Fred. Managing organizational change . Philadelphia , 1988. p. cm. ISBN 0-85066-430-6 :

LC Card 87-18027 DDC 658.3 19
HF5548 .F274 1988

OFFICE PRACTICE - AUTOMATION - STUDY AND TEACHING - UNITED STATES.
Goldfield, Randy J. Training in the automated office . New York , 1987. ix, 190 p. ; ISBN 0-89930-112-6 (lib. bdg. : alk. paper) LC Card 86-30605 DDC 658.3/1245 19
HF5547.5 .G655 1987

OFFICE PRACTICE - DENMARK - PSYCHOLOGICAL ASPECTS.
Agervold, Mogens. Kontorarbejde . [Copenhagen] , c1983. 126 p. ; ISBN 87-500-2489-2 : LC Card 84-126389
HF5547.5 .A43 1983

OFFICE PRACTICE - EXAMINATIONS, QUESTIONS, ETC.
Czukor, John C. Beginning office worker /. New York , c1988. 291 p. ; ISBN 0-13-072018-6 (pbk.) : LC Card 87-20740 DDC 651.3/7/076 19
HF5547.5 .B414 1988

Lindsell, Sheryl L. CPS®--Certified Professional Secretary® examination /. New York, N.Y. , c1987. xxx, 286 p. : ISBN 0-13-122805-6 (pbk.) : LC Card 87-11381 DDC 651.3/741/076 19
HF5547.5 .L554 1987

OFFICE PRACTICE - GERMANY (WEST) - AUTOMATION.
Schmidt-Prestin, Barbara, 1953- Bildschirmtext in Unternehmen . Bergisch Gladbach , c1986. xvi, 308 p. : ISBN 3-89012-064-4 LC Card 87-129114 DDC 651.8/0943 19
HD9696.T463 G365 1986

OFFICE PRACTICE - HANDBOOKS, MANUALS, ETC.
Dorrell, Jean, 1926- The answer book . Los Angeles, CA , c1987. ix, 358 p. : ISBN 0-935732-12-8 (pbk.) : LC Card 87-23408 DDC 651 19
HF5547.5 .D63 1987

OFFICE PRACTICE - PROBLEMS, EXERCISES, ETC.
Certified professional secretary examination review series. [Kansas City, Mo.?] , New York , c1986- v. <1, 6 > : ISBN 0-471-84353-9 (pbk. : v. 1) LC Card 87-100577 DDC 651.3/74/076 19
HF5547.5 .C44 1986

OFFICE PRACTICE - STUDY AND TEACHING.
Warmbrod, Catharine P. Skills for the changing workplace . Columbus, Ohio (1960 Kenny Rd., Columbus 43210-1090) , 1985. ix, 93 p. ; LC Card 86-205907 DDC 651/.07/15 19
HF1106 .W36 1985

OFFICE PRACTICE - VOCATIONAL GUIDANCE.
Filbert, Judith Ann. Homemaking skills go to the office . Bozeman, Mont. (P.O. Box 6244, Bozeman 59771) , c1986. 46 p. ; LC Card 86-218123 DDC 651.3/741/02373 19
HF5547.5 .F53 1986

OFFICE RECORDS. see **BUSINESS RECORDS.**

OFFICE SUPPLIES. see **OFFICE EQUIPMENT AND SUPPLIES.**

Office systems . IFIP TC 8 Working Conference on Office Systems (1985 : Helsinki, Finland) Amsterdam ; New York : vii, 199 p. : ISBN 0-444-70105-2 (Elsevier Science Pub. Co.) LC Card 86-16841 DDC 651.8 19
HF5547.5 .I345 1985 ***NYPL [JLD 87-1264]***

Office systems . IFIP TC 8/WG 8.4 Working Conference on Methods and Tools for Office Systems (1986 : Pisa, Italy) Amsterdam ; New York : xi, 347 p. : ISBN 0-444-70241-5 (U. S.) LC Card 87-8916 DDC 651.8 19
HF5548.2 .I285 1986

Office systems integration . Fischer, Barbara S. New York , 1987. xxi, 215 p. : ISBN 0-89930-109-6 (lib. bdg. : alk. paper) LC Card 87-2498 DDC 651.8 19
HF5547.5 .F56 1987

Office systems software.
Communications/Information Systems Planning Service . Boston, MA (89 Broad St., Boston 02110) , c1986. ii, 78 p. ; LC Card 86-225335 DDC 381/.45651853 19
HD9696.C63 U51492 1986

The Office systems software market in Europe. New York, N.Y. : Frost & Sullivan, c1983. xv, 256 p. : ill. ; 29 cm. "#E599." "January 1983." LC Card 87-144095 DDC 380.1/450053/094 19
1. Computer software industry - Europe. 2. Market surveys - Europe. I. Frost & Sullivan.
HD9696.C63 E8555 1983

OFFICE, TENURE OF. see **CIVIL SERVICE.**

Officer, Lawrence H. International economics /. Boston , c1987. x, 274 p. : ISBN 0-89838-196-7 LC Card 86-33776 DDC 337 19
HF1411 .I51725 1987

OFFICES - LOCATION - GERMANY (WEST)
Standorte und Einzugsbereiche tertiärer Einrichtungen . Damrstadt , 1985. vi, 403 p., [1] folded leaf of plates : ISBN 3-534-08402-0 LC Card 86-228150
HF5547.25 .S73 1985

Standorte von Büros im Urteil der Beschäftigten und sonstiger Nutzer /. Stuttgart , 1983. 140 p. : LC Card 83-220559
HF5547.25 .S74 1983

OFFICES - LOCATION - GERMANY (WEST) - CONGRESSES.
Beiträge zur empirischen Bürostandortforschung /. Kallmünz , 1983. 167 p. : ISBN 3-7847-6050-3 : LC Card 84-176770
HF5547.25 .B45 1983

OFFICES - LOCATION - GERMANY (WEST) - MUNICH - CONGRESSES.
Beiträge zur empirischen Bürostandortforschung /. Kallmünz , 1983. 167 p. : ISBN 3-7847-6050-3 : LC Card 84-176770
HF5547.25 .B45 1983

OFFICES - LOCATION - GOVERNMENT POLICY - ENGLAND - LONDON METROPOLITAN AREA - HISTORY.
Manners, Gerald. Office policy in Britain . Norwich, UK , c1986. viii, 158 p. : ISBN 0-86094-212-0 LC Card 87-143633 DDC 338.6/042 19
HF5547.25 .M36 1986

OFFICES - LOCATION - GOVERNMENT POLICY - GREAT BRITAIN - HISTORY.
Manners, Gerald. Office policy in Britain . Norwich, UK , c1986. viii, 158 p. : ISBN 0-86094-212-0 LC Card 87-143633 DDC 338.6/042 19
HF5547.25 .M36 1986

The Official guide for GMAT review / prepared for the Graduate Management Admission Council by Educational Testing Service. Princeton, N.J. : ETS, c1986. 372 p. : ill. ; 28 cm. Rev. ed. of: The Official guide to GMAT. c1984. ISBN 0-446-38435-6 (pbk.) : LC Card 86-229958 DDC 650/.076 19
1. Graduate Management Admission Test - Study guides. 2. Management - Examinations, questions, etc. 3. Business - Examinations, questions, etc. I. Graduate Management Admission Council. II. Educational Testing Service. III. Official guide to GMAT. IV. Title: GMAT review.
HF1118 .O33 1986

Official guide to GMAT. The Official guide for GMAT review /. Princeton, N.J. , c1986. 372 p. : ISBN 0-446-38435-6 (pbk.) : LC Card 86-229958 DDC 650/.076 19
HF1118 .O33 1986

The Official guide to MBA programs / edited by Charlotte Kurst. [Los Angeles, Calif.] : Graduate Management Admission Council ; Princeton, N.J. : Inquiries to GMAT Program Direction Office, Educational Testing Service, c1986. 603 p. ; 28 cm. "In association with Warner Books"--T.p. verso. ISBN 0-446-38437-2 (pbk.) : LC Card 87-102516 DDC 658/.007/1173 19
1. Master of business administration degree - United States - Directories. 2. Business education - United States - Directories. I. Kurst, Charlotte. II. Graduate Management Admission Council.
HF1131 .O359 1986

Official U. S. Customs Service Guide to importing into the United States. Importing into the United States. Rocklin, Calif. , c1987. 83 p. : ISBN 0-914629-35-2 (pbk.) : LC Card 87-16931 DDC 343.73/087 347.30387 19
HF3055 .I46 1987

Offiong, Daniel A. Organised labour and political development in Nigeria / by D.A. Offiong. Calabar, Nigeria : Centaur Press, 1983. x, 362 p. ; 24 cm. Cover title: Organised labour & political development in Nigeria. Bibliography: p. 339-351. Includes index. ISBN 978-231-601-6 (pbk.) LC Card 86-173440 DDC 322/.2/09669 19
1. Trade-unions - Nigeria - Political activity - History. 2. Nigeria - Politics and government. I. Title. II. Title: Organised labour & political development in Nigeria.
HD6885.5.Z65 O36 1983

Offizieller Jubiläumsband der Deutschen Bundesbahn : 150 Jahre deutsche Eisenbahnen / Toni Liebl ... [et al.].2. Aufl. München : Eisenbahn-Lehrbuch Verlagsgesellschaft, 1985. 239 p. : ill. (some col.) ; 25 cm. Bibliography: p. 234-238. ISBN 3-923967-03-9 LC Card 86-168073
1. Deutsche Bundesbahn - History. 2. Railroads - Germany - History. I. Liebl, Anton J.
HE3078 .O44 1985b

OFFSHORE ASSEMBLY INDUSTRY - COSTA RICA.
Las Exportaciones y la incidencia del sector externo en el desarrollo económico. [San José] , 1984. 32, [8], [7], 4 leaves ; LC Card 87-115490 DDC 338.1/097286 19
HD9014.C772 E95 1984

OFFSHORE ASSEMBLY INDUSTRY - EMPLOYEES - HEALTH AND HYGIENE - MEXICO.
Arenal, Sandra. Sangre joven . México, D.F. , 1986. 130 p., [2] p. of plates : ISBN 968-427-128-X LC Card 87-139058 DDC 331.4/87/0972 19
HD6073.O332 M4953 1986

OFFSHORE ASSEMBLY INDUSTRY - MEXICAN-AMERICAN BORDER REGION.
La Mujer y el trabajo en México . México , 1986. 346 p. : ISBN 968-8132-48-9 LC Card 87-101329
HD6101 .M86 1986

OFFSHORE ASSEMBLY INDUSTRY - MEXICO.
Stoddard, Ellwyn R., 1927- Maquila . El Paso, Tex. , c1987. ix, 91 p., [2] p. of plates : ISBN 0-87404-200-3 (pbk.) LC Card 86-51646 DDC 338.4/767/09721 19
HD9734.M42 S76 1987

OFFSHORE GAS INDUSTRY - GOVERNMENT POLICY - UNITED STATES.
Offshore lands . San Francisco, Calif. , c1985. xxviii, 169 p. : ISBN 0-936488-10-7 (alk. paper) : LC Card 85-63548 DDC 333.8/23/0973 19
HD242.5 .O34 1985 ***NYPL [JLE 86-2726]***

OFFSHORE GAS INDUSTRY - NORTH SEA.
The Market for North Sea crude oil /. Oxford , New York , 1986. xxxii, 341 p., [1] leaf of plates : ISBN 0-19-730001-4 LC Card 86-217261 DDC 338.2/7282/0916336 19
HD9581.N64 M37 1986

OFFSHORE GAS INDUSTRY - PACIFIC COAST (U. S.)
Webster, Frank L. Pacific OCS lease sale, October 1, 1964, Oregon and Washington /. [Washington] [1985] iii, 36 p. : LC Card 86-601138 DDC 333.33/9 19
HD243.A18 W43 1985

Offshore lands : oil and gas leasing and conservation on the outer continental shelf / Walter J. Mead ... [et al.] ; foreword by Stephen L. McDonald. San Francisco, Calif. : Pacific Institute for Public Policy Research, c1985. xxviii, 169 p. : ill. ; 24 cm. (Pacific studies in public policy) Includes index. Bibliography: p. 157-166. ISBN 0-936488-10-7 (alk. paper) : LC Card 85-63548 DDC 333.8/23/0973 19
1. Oil and gas leases - United States. 2. Continental shelf - United States. 3. Offshore oil industry - Government policy - United States. 4. Offshore gas industry - Government policy - United States. I. Mead, Walter J.
HD242.5 .O34 1985 ***NYPL [JLE 86-2726]***

OFFSHORE OIL INDUSTRY.
Gregory, P. World offshore markets . London , 1986. xiv, 215 p. ; ISBN 0-946416-06-0 (pbk.) : LC Card 86-217327 DDC 338.2/7282/0941 19
HD9571.5 .G75 1986

OFFSHORE OIL INDUSTRY - GOVERNMENT POLICY - GREAT

BRITAIN.
Hann, Danny. Government and North Sea oil /. Basingstoke, Hampshire , c1986. ix, 175 p. : ISBN 0-333-39436-4 ***NYPL [JLD 86-2581]***

OFFSHORE OIL INDUSTRY - GOVERNMENT POLICY - UNITED STATES.
Offshore lands . San Francisco, Calif. , c1985. xxviii, 169 p. : ISBN 0-936488-10-7 (alk. paper) : LC Card 85-63548 DDC 333.8/23/0973 19
HD242.5 .O34 1985 ***NYPL [JLE 86-2726]***

OFFSHORE OIL INDUSTRY - GREAT BRITAIN.
Gregory, P. World offshore markets . London , 1986. xiv, 215 p. ; ISBN 0-946416-06-0 (pbk.) : LC Card 86-217327 DDC 338.2/7282/0941 19
HD9571.5 .G75 1986

OFFSHORE OIL INDUSTRY - NORTH SEA.
Hann, Danny. Government and North Sea oil /. Basingstoke, Hampshire , c1986. ix, 175 p. : ISBN 0-333-39436-4 ***NYPL [JLD 86-2581]***

The Market for North Sea crude oil /. Oxford , New York , 1986. xxxii, 341 p., [1] leaf of plates : ISBN 0-19-730001-4 LC Card 86-217261 DDC 338.2/7282/0916336 19
HD9581.N64 M37 1986

OFFSHORE OIL INDUSTRY - PACIFIC COAST (U. S.)
Webster, Frank L. Pacific OCS lease sale, October 1, 1964, Oregon and Washington /. [Washington] [1985] iii, 36 p. : LC Card 86-601138 DDC 333.33/9 19
HD243.A18 W43 1985

OFFSHORE OIL INDUSTRY - SOCIAL ASPECTS - CONGRESSES.
Women, work, and family in the British, Canadian, and Norwegian oilfields /. New York , 1987. p. cm. ISBN 0-312-00528-8 : LC Card 86-31393 DDC 305.4/3665 19
HD9560.5 .W66 1987

OFFSHORE OIL INDUSTRY - SOCIAL ASPECTS - DENMARK - ESBJERG (KOMMUN)
Søgaard, Villy. Offshoreaktiviteter i Nordsøen og basebyen Esbjerg /. [Århus] , 1983. 200 p. : ISBN 87-88615-02-2 : LC Card 84-164755
HD9575.N62 S64 1983

OFFSHORE OIL INDUSTRY - SOCIAL ASPECTS - SCOTLAND.
Way of life . London [1980?] 84 p. ; ISBN 0-86226-076-0 (pbk.) LC Card 82-218547 DDC 304.8 19
HD9571.7.S36 W39 1980 ***NYPL [JLD 85-427]***

OFFSHORE OIL INDUSTRY - UNITED STATES.
Hartung, Hans. Verfahren zur Nutzung erschöpfbarer Ressourcen . Tübingen , 1986. ix, 172 p. : ISBN 3-16-345126-8 (Deut. Bibl. : pbk.) LC Card 86-233079
HD9565 .H36 1986

Offshoreaktiviteter i Nordsøen og basebyen Esbjerg /. Søgaard, Villy. [Århus] , 1983. 200 p. : ISBN 87-88615-02-2 : LC Card 84-164755
HD9575.N62 S64 1983

Oficina Internacional de Trabajo. see **International Labor Office.**

Ofstad, Arve. Norsk industris internasjonalisering, rettet mot utviklingslandene . Bergen [1982] vi, 57 p. ; LC Card 83-139811
HD2932 .N67 1982

Ogawa, Deborah Kimiko. Gottfredson, Gary D. Dictionary of Holland occupational codes /. Palo Alto, CA , c1982. xviii, 500 p. ; ISBN 0-89106-020-X ***NYPL [JLE 86-3992]***

Ogg, Clayton W. Webb, Shwu-Eng. Idling erodible cropland . Washington, D.C. [1986] iii, 31 p. : LC Card 86-601632 DDC 338.1 s 338.1/62 19
HD1751 .A91854 no. 550 HD256

Ogien, Ruwen. Théories ordinaires de la pauvreté / Ruwen Ogien. 1re éd. Paris : Presses universitaires de France, 1983. 176 p. ; 21 cm. (Le Sociologue. 51) Bibliography: p. [172]-176. ISBN 2-13-037937-0 : LC Card 84-151584
1. Poverty. I. Title.
HC79.P6 O47 1983

Ogier, Walter C. Poon, Raymond S. Biotechnology instrumentation . Menlo Park, Calif. (333 Ravenswood Ave., Menlo Park 94025-3476) , c1985. 32 p. : LC Card 87-160671 DDC 338.4/766063 19
HD9706.65.B552 P66 1985

Ogilvy, David, 1911- The unpublished David Ogilvy / David Ogilvy ; edited by Joel Raphaelson. 1st rev. ed. New York : Crown, c1986. 178 p., [6] p. of plates : ill., ports. ; 22 cm. ISBN 0-517-56609-5 : LC Card 87-13583 DDC 659.1/092/4 B 19
1. Ogilvy, David, 1911-. 2. Advertising - United States - Biography. I. Raphaelson, Joel. II. Title.
HF5810.O34 A3 1986

OGILVY, DAVID, 1911-
Ogilvy, David, 1911- The unpublished David Ogilvy /. New York , c1986. 178 p., [6] p. of plates : ISBN 0-517-56609-5 : LC Card 87-13583 DDC 659.1/092/4 B 19
HF5810.O34 A3 1986

Ogled o privrednom sistemu Jugoslavije /. Popović, Strašimir, 1916- Beograd [1983?] 165 p. ; LC Card 86-197560
HC407 .P65 1983

Ogliari, Francesco. Trasporti marittimi di linea / Francesco Ogliari, Lamberto Radogna. Milano : Cavallotti, 1975- v. : ill. ; 30 cm. Includes bibliographies. CONTENTS. - v. 1. Dal Ferdinando I oltre l'oceano.--v. 2. Dall'Adriatico destinazione Oriente e Americhe.--v. 3. La navigazione generale italiana: le sue eredi, le minori.--v. 4. Dal clipper a elica al "Conte di Savoia".--v. 5. Dallo smoking alla divisa, la marina mercantile italiana dal 1932 al 1945.--v. 6. Gli anni della fenice- il Grupo Finmare e le compagnie sovvenzionate dal 1945 al 1985. LC Card 76-507610
1. Merchant marine - Italy - History. 2. Merchant ships - Italy - History. 3. Ocean liners - History. I. Radogna, Lamberto. II. Title.
HE839 .O35 ***NYPL [JSK 86-35]***

O'glove, Thornton L. Quality of earnings : the investor's guide to how much money a company is really making / Thornton L. O'glove with Robert Sobel. New York : Free Press, c1987. xviii, 204 p. : ill. ; 25 cm. Bibliography: p. 189-196. Includes index. ISBN 0-02-922630-9 LC Card 86-25631 DDC 657/.33 19
1. Financial statements. 2. Business enterprises - Finance. 3. Accounting. I. Sobel, Robert, 1931 (Feb. 19)-. II. Title.
HG4028.B2 O35 1987

Ogorodnik, M. A. (Mikhail Antonovich) Androsov, V. I. (Vasiliĭ Ivanovich) Ėffektivnost′ kapital′nogo stroitel′stva v torgovle /. Moskva , 1980. 213 p. ; LC Card 81-132839
HC340.C3 A65 1980

Ogunba, C. K. An ailing African economy and the IMF medicine / by C.K. Ogunba. Ile-Ife [Nigeria] : C.K. Ogunba, [1985] 40, [1] p. ; 18 cm. Cover title. Page [41] is p. 3 of cover. Bibliography: p. [41]. LC Card 86-207586 DDC 332.1/52 19
1. International Monetary Fund - Nigeria. 2. Loans, Foreign - Nigeria. 3. Nigeria - Economic policy. I. Title.
HG3881.5.I58 O37 1985

Ogwude, Innocent C. (Innocent Chuka) Industrial demand for freight transport in Kaduna State / Innocent C. Ogwude. Zaria [Nigeria] : Centre for Social and Economic Research, Ahmadu Bello University, [1984] 101 p. : ill. ; 25 cm. (C.S.E.R. research report . no. 11) "May 1984." Bibliography: p. 84-86. LC Card 86-152627 DDC 380.5/24/096695 19
1. Transportation - Nigeria - Kaduna State. 2. Kaduna State (Nigeria) - Industries. 3. Freight and freightage - Nigeria - Kaduna State. I. Ahmadu Bello University. Centre for Social and Economic Research. II. Series: C.S.E.R. research series , 11. III. Title.
HE287.7.Z7 K336 1984

Oh, Sungjung. Kim, Chungsoo. Effects of neo-protectionism on the Korean exports /. [Seoul] , 1986. 203 p. : LC Card 86-234427 DDC 382/.095195/073 19
HF3830.5.Z7 U54 1986

O'Hara, Patrick, 1946- Iaconetti, Joan. First-time manager /. New York , London , 1987, c1985. xii, 290 p. : ISBN 0-02-085730-6 (pbk.) : LC Card 86-24454 DDC 658.4 19
HD38.2 .I19 1987

O'Hare, William P. Wealth and economic status : a perspective on racial inequity / William P. O'Hare. Washington, D.C. : Joint Center for Political Studies, 1983. vii, 33 p. : graphs ; 23 cm. Bibliography: p. 31-33. ISBN 0-941410-35-8 (pbk.) : LC Card 83-22171 DDC 339.2/2/0973 19
1. Wealth - United States. 2. Afro-Americans - Economic conditions. I. Title.
HC110.W4 O33 1983 ***NYPL [JLE 86-2065]***

Ohinata, Yo. The lending procedures of commercial banks in the United States, the United Kingdom, Japan, Germany and France / by Yo Ohinata ; editor, Melanie Rydings. [Manchester] : Centre for Business Research in association with Manchester Business School, University of Manchester, [1983] 138 p. ; 30 cm. (Banking and financial services reports, 0264-200X) "November, 1983." Bibliography: p. 138. ISBN 0-903808-34-X (pbk.) LC Card 86-132282 DDC 332.1/753 19
1. Bank loans - United States. 2. Bank loans - Great Britain. 3. Bank loans - Japan. 4. Bank loans - Germany (West). 5. Bank loans - France. I. Rydings, Melanie. II. Centre for Business Research (Manchester, Greater Manchester). III. Manchester Business School (University of Manchester). IV. Title. V. Series.
HG1642.U5 O35 1983

Ohio canal era . Scheiber, Harry N. Athens , 1987. xxvi, 430 p. ; ISBN 0-8214-0048-7 LC Card 86-23800 DDC 386/.48/09771 19
HE395.O34 S34 1987

OHIO - ECONOMIC CONDITIONS.
Scheiber, Harry N. Ohio canal era . Athens , 1987. xxvi, 430 p. ; ISBN 0-8214-0048-7 LC Card 86-23800 DDC 386/.48/09771 19
HE395.O34 S34 1987

OHIO - ECONOMIC CONDITIONS - CONGRESSES.
Structural change in an urban industrial region . New York , 1987. ix, 255 p. ; ISBN 0-275-92353-3 (alk. paper) : LC Card 86-30652 DDC 330.9771/3043 19
HC107.O3 S85 1987

OHIO - ECONOMIC CONDITIONS - STATISTICS.
Ohio poverty indicators. Cleveland, Ohio (668 Euclid Ave, Suite 700, Cleveland 44114) , c1986-<c1987. v. <1-2 > : LC Card 87-107608 DDC 362.5/2/09771 19
HC107.O323 P6355 1986

OHIO - ECONOMIC POLICY - CONGRESSES.
Structural change in an urban industrial region . New York , 1987. ix, 255 p. ; ISBN 0-275-92353-3 (alk. paper) : LC Card 86-30652 DDC 330.9771/3043 19
HC107.O3 S85 1987

Ohio poverty indicators. Cleveland, Ohio (668 Euclid Ave, Suite 700, Cleveland 44114) : Council for Economic Opportun[i]ties in Greater Cleveland, c1986-<c1987 > v. <1-2 > : ill. ; 28 cm. Cover title. CONTENTS. - v. 1. Trends, 1980-1986 -- v. 2. Trends, 1970-1987. LC Card 87-107608 DDC 362.5/2/09771 19
1. Poor - Ohio - Statistics. 2. Ohio - Economic conditions - Statistics. I. Council for Economic Opportunities in Greater Cleveland (Cleveland, Ohio).
HC107.O323 P6355 1986

Ohio. State University, Columbus. Center for Human Resource Research. Moore, Sylvia F. The short-term effects of marital disruption on the labor supply behavior of young women /. Columbus, Ohio (Suite 585, 1375 Perry St., Columbus, Ohio, 43201) , 1979. v, 133 p. ; ***NYPL [JLF 86-649]***

Ohio. State University, Columbus. Human Resource Research, Center for. see **Ohio. State University, Columbus. Center for Human Resource Research.**

Ohio timber products output--1983 /. Widmann, Richard H. Broomall, PA [1986] 29 p. : LC Card 86-603412 DDC 338.1/7498/09771021 19
HD9757.O3 W53 1986

Ohiorhenuan, John F. E. Onimode, Bade. MNC's in Nigeria . Ibadan , 1983. ix, 144 p. ; ISBN 978-231-800-0 (pbk.) LC Card 86-195403 DDC 338.8/88669 19
HD2928 .O55 1983

Ohlinger, Hans A., 1954- Die Relevanz nicht-tarifärer Handelshemmnisse im internationalen Handel und ihre Wirkungen auf die Integration der Entwicklungsländer in die

Weltwirtschaft / Hans A. Ohlinger. Frankfurt am Main ; New York : P. Lang, c1986. iii, 400 p. : ill. ; 21 cm. (Europäische Hochschulschriften. Reihe V, Volks- und Betriebswirtschaft, 0531-7339 . Bd. 741 = vol. 741 = vol. 741) Bibliography: p. 378-400. ISBN 3-8204-8344-6 LC Card 87-407585 DDC 382/.5/091724 19
1. Nontariff trade barriers - Developing countries. 2. Foreign trade and employment. 3. Import quotas. 4. Export marketing - Developing countries. I. Series: Europäische Hochschulschriften. Reihe V, Volks- und Betriebswirtschaft , Bd. 741. II. Title.
HF1430 .O38 1986

Ohlmeyer, Dietrich. Selbsthilfe zum Beispiel . Hannover , 1984. 264 p. : ISBN 3-921951-18-6 LC Card 85-233577
HD3190.A3 L687 1984

Ohlsen, Manfred. Milliarden für den Geier, oder, Der Fall des Friedrich Flick / Manfred Ohlsen. 3., erw. Aufl. Berlin : Verlag der Nation, 1985. 458 p. : ill. ; 21 cm. Bibliography: p. 453-454. LC Card 86-149056
1. Flick, Friedrich, 1883-. 2. Businessmen - Germany - Biography. 3. Germany - Industries - History - 20th century. I. Title.
HC282.5.F54 O35 1985

Ohlsen, Ralph-Rainer, 1955- Der deutsche Export nach Grossbritannien von 1923 bis 1933 : seine Veränderung und seine Bedeutung / Ralph-Rainer Ohlsen ; mit einem Geleitwort von Friedrich-Wilhelm Henning. Bergisch Gladbach : Eul, c1986. ii, 256 p. : ill. ; 21 cm. Originally presented as the author's thesis (doctoral)--Universität zu Köln, 1985. Bibliography: p. 227-254. ISBN 3-89012-043-1 LC Card 86-160346
1. Germany - Commerce - Great Britain. 2. Great Britain - Commerce - Germany. I. Title.
HF1546.5.G7 O37 1986

Ohlson, James A. The theory of financial markets and information / James A. Ohlson. New York : North Holland, c1987. xiii, 181 p. ; 24 cm. Bibliography: p. 173-175. Includes index. ISBN 0-444-01161-7 LC Card 87-9100 DDC 332.6 19
1. Finance - Mathematical models. 2. Capital market - Mathematical models. 3. Money market - Mathematical models. I. Title.
HG173 .O34 1987

Ohlson, M. K. Economics of price and income / M.K. Ohlson. Dubuque, Iowa : Kendall/Hunt, c1986. vi, 126 p. : ill. ; 23 cm. Bibliography: p. 125-126. ISBN 0-8403-4173-3 (pbk.); 0-8403-4173-4 LC Card 86-82292 DDC 338.5/2 19
1. Prices. 2. Income. 3. Supply and demand. I. Title.
HB221 .O38 1986

Ohlson, Thomas. Brzoska, Michael. Arms transfers to the Third World, 1971-85 /. Oxford , New York , 1987. xv, 383 p. : ISBN 0-19-829116-7 : LC Card 87-5579 DDC 382/.456234/091724 19
HD9743.D442 B79 1987

Ohlweiler, Otto Alcides. Evolução sócio-econômica do Brasil / Otto Alcides Ohlweiler. Porto Alegre-RS, Brasil : Tchê, [1986?] 209 p. ; 22 cm. Includes bibliographies. LC Card 86-229515
1. Brazil - Economic conditions. 2. Brazil - Politics and government. 3. Brazil - History - To 1821. 4. Brazil - History - 1822-. I. Title.
HC187 .O43 1986

Öhman, Berndt, 1940- Kommunerna och sysselsättningspolitiken : om arbetsfördelningen mellan kommunerna och arbetsmarknadsverket : en studie i offentlig förvaltning : rapport från AMS-kommittén / Berndt Öhman. [Stockholm] : Arbetsmarknadsdepartementet : Liber, [1985] 212 p. ; 21 cm. "Ds A 1985:2." Bibliography: p. 171-178. ISBN 91-38-08745-6 LC Card 86-114034
1. Labor supply - Sweden. 2. Labor policy - Sweden. 3. Decentralization in government - Sweden. I. Title.
HD5803 .O36 1985

Ohne Arbeit geh'ste kaputt : Reportagen aus dem Innenleben der Krise / Werner Balsen ... [et al.]. Köln : Pahl-Rugenstein, c1983. 183 p. : ill. ; 20 cm. (Kleine Bibliothek. 302) ISBN 3-7609-0798-9 LC Card 84-176249
1. Unemployment - Germany (West) - Psychological aspects - Interviews. I. Balsen, Werner, 1953-.
HD5779 .O355 1983

Ohr, Renate. Internationale Interdependenz nationaler Geld- und Gütermärkte bei flexiblen Wechselkursen / Renate Ohr. Hamburg : Weltarchiv, 1980. 217 p. : ill. ; 24 cm. (Veröffentlichungen des HWWA-Institut für Wirtschaftsforschung-Hamburg) Bibliography: p. 205-217. ISBN 3-87895-194-9 LC Card 84-120800
1. Foreign exchange problem - Mathematical models. I. Title.
HG3823 .O47 1980

Ohta, H. (Hiroshi), 1940- Spatial price theory of imperfect competition / by H. Ohta. 1st ed. College Station : Texas A&M University Press, c1988. p. cm. (Texas A & M University economic series . no. 8) Bibliography: p. Includes index. ISBN 0-89096-372-X : LC Card 87-22333 DDC 338.5/2 19
1. Prices. 2. Space in economics. 3. Competition, Imperfect. I. Title. II. Series.
HB221 .O385 1988

Oikonomikē kai koinōnikē anaptyxis Anat. Makedonias kai Thrakēs : geōrgia, ktēnotrophia, dasē, alieia : hyphistamenē katastasis / [Hē ergasia hautē exeponēthē hypo tou Grapheiou Prōtogenous paragōgēs tou Tmmatos Programmatos tēs VII HYSAP, apoteloumenou ek tōn Kasapē Stergiou ... et al.]. Kavalla : Periphereiakē Dioikēsis Anat. Makedonias-Thrakēs, [1973-] v. <1 > : ill. ; 34 cm. "VII YSAPO4"--cover. LC Card 87-125407
1. Agriculture - Economic aspects - Greece - Statistics. I. Kasapēs, Stergios. II. Greece. Periphereiakē Dioikēsis Anat. Makedonias-Thrakēs. VII Hypēresia Syntonismou Anaptyxeōs Periphereias. Grapheion Prōtogenous Paragōgēs.
HD2055.5 .O54 1973

Oikonomikē politikē /. Gianniōtēs, Alexandros. Thessalonikē [1984?] 298 p. : LC Card 86-184634
HD85.G7 G53 1984

Oikonomikes metamorphōseis tēs agrotikēs Helladas . Karapostolēs, Vasilēs. Athēna , 1981. 52 [1] p. : LC Card 86-194022
HD2055.5 .K36 1981

Oil . Hamilton, Adrian, 1944- London , 1986. 191 p., [16] p. of plates : ISBN 0-7181-2783-8 : LC Card 87-106290 DDC 338.2/7282/09 19
HD9560.5 .H25 1986

OIL. see **PETROLEUM.**

Oil & gas databook for developing countries . Fee, Derek. London , 1985. 215 p. : ISBN 0-86010-617-9 : LC Card 85-208594 DDC 333.8/23/091724 19
HD9578.D44 F44 1985 *NYPL [JLE 86-3684]*

Oil and diplomacy . Casillas, Rex J. New York , 1987. p. cm. ISBN 0-8240-8078-5 : LC Card 87-23769 DDC 337.730538 19
HF1456.5.S33 C37 1987

Oil and gas databook for developing countries. Fee, Derek. Oil & gas databook for developing countries . London , 1985. 215 p. : ISBN 0-86010-617-9 : LC Card 85-208594 DDC 333.8/23/091724 19
HD9578.D44 F44 1985 *NYPL [JLE 86-3684]*

Oil and gas in a nutshell /. Lowe, John S., 1941- St. Paul, Minn. , 1983. xlvii, 443 p. ; ISBN 0-314-73469-4 LC Card 83-6811 DDC 346.7304/6823 347.30646823 19
KF1850 .L68 1983 *NYPL [JLC 86-226]*

OIL AND GAS LEASES - CANADA - PROVINCES.
Pasay, Janice L. The effect of the western accord and recent provincial royalty changes on petroleum industry capital expenditures /. Calgary, Alta. , 1986. iv, 27, 4 leaves ; LC Card 86-203742 DDC 338.2/3 19
HD9574.C22 P37 1986

OIL AND GAS LEASES - LOUISIANA.
Lam, Manuel. Louisiana crude oil and natural gas report and severance and royalty sensitivity to price, second half 1985 /. Baton Rouge, La (P.O. Box 44156, Baton Rouge 70804-4156) [1986] iii, 31 p. : LC Card 86-621907 DDC 338.2/728/09763 19
HD9560.8.U53 L65 1986

OIL AND GAS LEASES - OKLAHOMA - STATISTICS.
Oklahoma casinghead gas production report. [Denver, Colo.] (P.O. Box 2612, Denver 80201) , <[c1986-. v. <1-2 > ; LC Card 86-219814 DDC 338.2/7285/09766021 19
HD9581.U52 O56 1986

OIL AND GAS LEASES - PACIFIC COAST (U. S.)
Webster, Frank L. Pacific OCS lease sale, October 1, 1964, Oregon and Washington /. [Washington] [1985] iii, 36 p. : LC Card 86-601138 DDC 333.33/9 19
HD243.A18 W43 1985

OIL AND GAS LEASES - UNITED STATES.
Hartung, Hans. Verfahren zur Nutzung erschöpfbarer Ressourcen . Tübingen , 1986. ix, 172 p. : ISBN 3-16-345126-8 (Deut. Bibl. : pbk.) LC Card 86-233079
HD9565 .H36 1986

Kloepfer, Deanne. The Watt record . Washington, D.C. [1983] ii, 66, 9, 3 p. : LC Card 86-232533 DDC 333.1/0973 19
HD183.L3 K58 1983

Offshore lands . San Francisco, Calif. , c1985. xxviii, 169 p. : ISBN 0-936488-10-7 (alk. paper) : LC Card 85-63548 DDC 333.8/23/0973 19
HD242.5 .O34 1985 *NYPL [JLE 86-2726]*

The oil and gas Publishing /. Welker, Anthony J. Tulsa , c1985. xii, 258 p. : ISBN 0-87814-279-7 (pbk.) : LC Card 85-2096 DDC 338.2/728/0973 19
HD9565 .W46 1985 *NYPL [JLD 86-4010]*

Oil & honor . Petzinger, Thomas. New York , c1987. 495 p., [8] p. of plates : ISBN 0-399-13276-7 LC Card 87-2255 DDC 338.8/3622338/0973 19
HD9569.T4 P48 1987

Oil and honor. Petzinger, Thomas. Oil & honor . New York , c1987. 495 p., [8] p. of plates : ISBN 0-399-13276-7 LC Card 87-2255 DDC 338.8/3622338/0973 19
HD9569.T4 P48 1987

Oil and natural gas industries in Canada, 1978. [Ottawa] : Energy, Mines, and Resources Canada, c1978. viii, 104 p. : ill. ; 28 cm. (Report / Energy, Mines, and Resources Canada . ER 78-2) Abstract in English and French. LC Card 85-187299
1. Petroleum industry and trade - Canada. 2. Gas industry - Canada. I. Canada. Energy, Mines and Resources Canada. II. Series: Report (Canada. Energy, Mines and Resources Canada) , ER78-2.
HD9574.C22 O39 1978

Oil and other multinationals in India /. Patwardhan, M. S., 1927- Bombay , 1986. xvi, 171 p. : LC Card 87-900107 DDC 338.8/87 19
HD9576.I42 P37 1986

OIL CONSERVATION. see **PETROLEUM CONSERVATION.**

An Oil daily report.
Paulson, S. Lawrence. Reagan on energy . New York, NY (850 3rd Ave., New York 10022) , 1981. 248 p. in various pagings ; LC Card 82-111477 DDC 333.79/0973 19
HD9502.U52 P38 *NYPL [JLF 87-368]*

Oil diplomacy in the twentieth century /. Venn, Fiona. Basingstoke, Hampshire , c1986. xii, 228 p. : ISBN 0-333-35781-7
NYPL [JLD 86-3415]

OIL FIELD CHEMICALS INDUSTRY - UNITED STATES.
The Enhanced oil recovery market, 1980-1990. New York, N.Y. , c1983. vi, 203 leaves : LC Card 87-142370 DDC 381/.45617665/0973 19
HD9565 .E53 1983

OIL FIELD EQUIPMENT AND SUPPLIES INDUSTRY - UNITED STATES.
The Enhanced oil recovery market, 1980-1990. New York, N.Y. , c1983. vi, 203 leaves : LC Card 87-142370 DDC 381/.45617665/0973 19
HD9565 .E53 1983

Oilfield machinery and equipment market in the U. S. New York, N.Y. , c1983. v, 213 leaves ; LC Card 87-142516 DDC 381/.4568176 19
HD9565 .O643 1983

OIL FIELDS - ALASKA.
Livey, Jay. The effect of state income tax policy on the development of marginal oil fields . [Juneau] [1986] vii leaves, 52 p., [17] leaves : LC Card 86-622190 DDC 333.8/232/09798 19
HD9560.8.U53 A445 1986

OIL FIELDS - REPRESSURING. see **SECONDARY RECOVERY OF OIL.**

OIL FIELDS - SECONDARY RECOVERY OPERATIONS. see **SECONDARY RECOVERY OF OIL.**

OIL INDUSTRIES - AUSTRIA.
Landwirtschaftliche Produktionsalternativen am Beispiel Ethanol, Ölsaaten und Eiweissfutterpflanzen /. Wien , 1985. 141 p. : LC Card 86-108149 DDC 338.1/09436 19
HD1935 .L33 1985

OIL INDUSTRIES - GOVERNMENT POLICY - UNITED STATES.
Grigsby, S. Elaine. Alternative export strategies and U. S. agricultural policies for grains and oilseeds, 1950-83 /. [Washington, D.C.] , 1986. v., 37 p. : LC Card 86-602816 DDC 382/.4131/0973 19
HD9036 .G83 1986

OIL INDUSTRIES - MEXICO.
Elementos para la programación del desarrollo de la industria de aceites y pastas vegetales en México. México , 1985. 306 p. : ISBN 968-665-105-5 LC Card 86-232449
HD9490.M62 E44 1985

OIL INDUSTRY WORKERS - FAMILY RELATIONSHIPS - CONGRESSES.
Women, work, and family in the British, Canadian, and Norwegian oilfields /. New York , 1987. p. cm. ISBN 0-312-00528-8 : LC Card 86-31393 DDC 305.4/3665 19
HD9560.5 .W66 1987

OIL LANDS. see **OIL FIELDS.**

OIL-PALM - BRAZIL.
Substituição de óleo diesel . [Brasília, Brazil] [19]84. 84 p. : LC Card 87-404960 DDC 338.4/76553 19
HD9579.D53 B737 1984

OIL POOLS. see **OIL FIELDS.**

OIL REFINERIES. see **PETROLEUM REFINERIES.**

OIL SANDS INDUSTRY - GOVERNMENT POLICY - ALBERTA - WOLF LAKE REGION.
Eglington, Peter. An economic analysis of oilsands policy in Canada . Ottawa, Ont. [1984] 1 v. (various pagings) : LC Card 84-213823 DDC 333.8/232 19
HD9574.C23 W654 1984

OIL SANDS INDUSTRY - GOVERNMENT POLICY - CANADA.
Eglington, Peter. An economic analysis of oilsands policy in Canada . Ottawa, Ont. [1984] 1 v. (various pagings) : LC Card 84-213823 DDC 333.8/232 19
HD9574.C23 W654 1984

The oil scouts . Tennent, James C. [Pennsylvania? , 1986] 85 p. : LC Card 87-404148 DDC 338.2/7282/09748 19
HD9567.P4 T46 1986

Oil tanker databook, 1985 /. Champness, Michael. London ; New York : vii, 347 p. ; ISBN 0-85334-311-X LC Card 86-217414 DDC 387.5/448 19
HE566.T3 C42 1985

OIL TANKERS. see **TANKERS.**

Oil tankers to South Africa, 1980-1981. Amsterdam : Shipping Research Bureau, c1982. vi, 99 p. : map ; 30 cm. "June 1982." Bibliography: p. 93-94. Includes indexes. ISBN 90-70331-05-5 (pbk.) LC Card 86-213340 DDC 387.5/448 19
1. Petroleum - South Africa - Transportation. 2. Tankers. 3. Embargo. I. Shipping Research Bureau (Amsterdam, Netherlands).
HE595.P4 O37 1982

OIL WELL BORING. see **OIL WELL DRILLING.**

OIL WELL DRILLING.
(1985) Orban, John. Money in the ground . Oklahoma City , 1985. xv, 216 p. : ISBN 0-9615776-0-6 (pbk.) : LC Card 86-120440 DDC 332.63 19
HG6047.P47 O73 1985

OIL WELLS - CALIFORNIA - STATISTICS.
California crude oil production, 1960-1985. Los Angeles, Calif. (417 S. Hill St., Suite 930, Los Angeles 90013) , c1986. 149 p., [1] folded leaf of plates : LC Card 87-150171 DDC 338.2/7282/09794021 19
HD9567.C2 C385 1986

OIL WELLS - PENNSYLVANIA - HISTORY - 19TH CENTURY.
Tennent, James C. The oil scouts . [Pennsylvania? , 1986] 85 p. : LC Card 87-404148 DDC 338.2/7282/09748 19
HD9567.P4 T46 1986

OIL WELLS - WYOMING - STATISTICS.
Wyoming oil and gas production by county /. Casper, Wyo. (P.O. Box 2640, Casper 82602) [1986] [40] p. : LC Card 86-622904 DDC 338.2/728/09787021 19
HD9567.W8 W94 1986

Wyoming oil and gas, 1985 /. Casper, Wyo. (P.O. Box 2640, Casper 82602) [1986?] 50 p. ; LC Card 86-622903 DDC 338.2/728/09787021 19
HD9567.W8 W96 1986

Oilfield machinery and equipment market in the U. S. New York, N.Y. : Frost & Sullivan, c1983. v, 213 leaves ; 29 cm. "January, 1983." "A1154." LC Card 87-142516 DDC 381/.4568176 19
1. Oil field equipment and supplies industry - United States. 2. Market surveys - United States. I. Frost & Sullivan.
HD9565 .O643 1983

OILSEEDS - AUSTRIA.
Landwirtschaftliche Produktionsalternativen am Beispiel Ethanol, Ölsaaten und Eiweissfutterpflanzen /. Wien , 1985. 141 p. : LC Card 86-108149 DDC 338.1/09436 19
HD1935 .L33 1985

Ojeda, Roseliano. Cómo se desangra un país-- ! : qué hacer-- ? / Roseliano Ojeda. Valencia [Venezuela] : Vadell Hnos. Editores, c1987. 241 p. ; 22 cm. Cover subtitle: Endeudamiento, refinanciamiento, fuga de capitales, corrupción, drogas, desunión. "Recetario, 21 febrero, sábado, 1987"--P. 1 of cover. ISBN 980-212-037-5 LC Card 87-169695 DDC 330.987/0633 19
1. Venezuela - Economic conditions - 1958-. 2. Debt - Venezuela. 3. Capital movements - Venezuela. 4. Corruption (in politics) - Venezuela. 5. Narcotics, Control of - Venezuela. I. Title.
HC237 .O365 1987

Ojha, Ghanshyam Das, 1947- Organisation & management of public distribution system / Ojha Ghanshyam Das ; foreword by G. Ram Reddy. Delhi, India : Mittal Publications, 1987. x, 235 p. ; 22 cm. In the context of India. Bibliography: p. [219]-230. Includes index. LC Card 87-900491 DDC 381/.1/0954 19
1. Physical distribution of goods - Government policy - India. 2. Food supply - Government policy - India. 3. Marketing - India - Management. I. Title. II. Title: Organisation and Management of public distribution system.
HF5415.12.I5 O44 1987

Ökad eldning med skogsråvara . Sweden. Statens industriverk. Stockholm , 1980. 203 p. : ISBN 91-38-05361-6 LC Card 82-236954
HD9769.F843 S87 1980

Ökad export av svensk energiteknik--ett handlingsprogram . Sweden. Utredningen rörande export av teknik inom energisektorn. [Stockholm] [1983] 171, [64] p. : ISBN 91-38-08037-0 LC Card 84-219591
HD9502.S82 S974 1983

Ökad trähusexport . Sweden. Exportstödsutredningen. [Stockholm] [1984] 51 p. ; ISBN 91-38-08165-2 LC Card 84-219457
HD9715.5.S82 S94 1984

Okai, Matthew. Rural poverty and alleviation measures in Sierra Leone / by Matthew Okai. [Rome] : Food and Agriculture Organization of the United Nations, 1983. 91 p. : maps ; 30 cm. (Series of in-depth studies on rural poverty alleviation = Série d'études approfondies sur la lutte contre la pauvreté rurale . no. 6) Bibliography: p. 43-44. LC Card 87-400417 DDC 338.1/8/664 19
1. Rural poor - Sierra Leone. 2. Agricultural development projects - Sierra Leone. 3. Rural development projects - Sierra Leone. 4. Sierra Leone - Rural conditions. I. Series: Serie de estudios profundos , no. 6. II. Title.
HC1065.Z9 P66 1983

OKBT Tudományos Kutatási Szakbizottság (Hungary) Az OKBT Tudományos Kutatási Szakbizottság kezdeményezése, illetve megbízása alapján készült kutatások, 1973-1983 /. [Budapest] , 1983. 124 p. : ISBN 963-02-3169-7 (Magy. nemz. bibl.) LC Card 85-126922
HE5614.5.H8 O38 1983
NYPL [JLD 87-1181]

O'Keefe, Hsu Yuet Heung. A crise do petróleo e a economia brasileira / Hsu Yuet Heung O'Keefe. São Paulo : Instituto de Pesquisas Econômicas, 1984. 137 p. : ill. ; 21 cm. (Série Ensaios econômicos . 32) Originally presented as the author's thesis (doctoral--Universidade de São Paulo, 1983) under title: Crise do petróleo e impactos nos preços relativos e no consumo das famílias brasileiras. Bibliography: p. 133-137. LC Card 85-143617 DDC 338.2/3 19
1. Petroleum products - Prices - Brazil. 2. Petroleum products - Prices - Brazil - Econometric models. 3. Dwellings - Brazil - Energy consumption. 4. Brazil - Industries - Energy conservation. I. Series: Ensaios econômicos (Universidade de São Paulo. Instituto de Pesquisas Econômicas) , 32. II. Title.
HD9574.B82 O43 1984
NYPL [JLD 86-2712]

O'Keeffe, Linda. Statistical packages for the IBM PC family / written by Linda O'Keeffe, Jay Klagge. New York : McGraw-Hill, c1986. x, 162 p. : ill. ; 24 cm. (The Seybold series on professional computing) Includes index. ISBN 0-07-056320-9 : LC Card 85-18213 DDC 658/.055365 19
1. Commercial statistics - Computer programs. 2. IBM Personal Computer XT - Programming. I. Klagge, Jay. II. Title. III. Series.
HF1017 .O39 1986 ***NYPL [JSE 86-1876]***

Okhrana truda i sots͡ial'noe strakhovanie trudi͡ashchikhs͡ia v Uzbekskoĭ SSR /. Tormysheva, T. A. (Tamara Andreevna) Tashkent , 1987. 131 p. ; LC Card 87-107413
HD7345.U93 T67 1987

Okhrana truda v trubnom proizvodstve / [L.V. Lenskai͡a ... et al.]. Proizvodstvennoe izd. Moskva : "Metallurgii͡a", 1986. 151, [1] p. : ill. ; 21 cm. Bibliography: p. [152]-p. [3] of cover. LC Card 85-163240
1. Pipe industry - Soviet Union - Safety measures. I. Lenskai͡a, L. V. (Lilii͡a Vasil'evna).
HD9529.P53 S686 1986

Okimoto, Daniel I., 1942- Inside the Japanese system . Stanford, Calif. , c1988. xiii, 286 p. : ISBN 0-8047-1425-8 (alk. paper) LC Card 87-18820 DDC 330.952/04 19
HC462.9 .I587 1988

Oklahoma casinghead gas production report. [Denver, Colo.] (P.O. Box 2612, Denver 80201) : Petroleum Information Corp., <[c1986- > v. <1-2 > ; 28 cm. Cover title. CONTENTS. - [1] Statewide -- [2] Northeast. LC Card 86-219814 DDC 338.2/7285/09766021 19
1. Gas industry - Oklahoma - Statistics. 2. Gas wells - Oklahoma - Statistics. 3. Oil and gas leases - Oklahoma - Statistics. I. Petroleum Information Corporation.
HD9581.U52 O56 1986

Oklahoma farmers and ranchers. Plaxico, James Sam, 1924- Financial status of Oklahoma farmers and ranchers, 1985 . [Stillwater] [1986] 42 p. ; LC Card 86-622478 DDC 338.1/3/09766021 19
HD1775.O5 P57 1986

OKLAHOMA STATE UNIVERSITY. COLLEGE OF BUSINESS ADMINISTRATION - HISTORY.
Kincaid, William M. A history of the Oklahoma State University, College of Business Administration /. Stillwater, Okla. , c1987. x, 227 p. : ISBN 0-914956-31-0 LC Card 87-11046 DDC 650/.07/1176634 19
HF1134.O57 K55 1987

Okolo, Julius Emeka. West Africa--regional cooperation and development /. Boulder , 1988. p. cm. ISBN 0-8133-7354-9 : LC Card 87-9290 DDC 338.966 19
HC1000 .W47 1988

Okongwu, Chu S. P., 1934- The Nigerian economy : being an anatomy of a traumatized economy with some proposals for stabilization / by Chu S.P. Okongwu. Enugu, Nigeria : Fourth Dimension Pub. Co., 1986. vi, 453 p. : ill. ; 23 cm. (Issues in Nigerian development series) Bibliography: p. 451-453. Includes index. ISBN 978-15-6038-X (pbk.) : LC Card 87-132237 DDC 330.9669/05 19
1. Nigeria - Economic conditions - 1970-. 2. Nigeria -

Social conditions - 1960-. 3. Nigeria - Economic policy. 4. Nigeria - Social policy. I. Title. II. Series.
HC1055 .O39 1986

Ökonomie aktuell.
Reinhold, Otto. Mehr, besser, billiger, aber wie? /. Berlin , 1985. 80 p. : LC Card 86-179312
HD70.G22 R45 1985

Ökonomische Probleme des öffentlichen Verkehrs . Oettle, Karl. Baden-Baden , 1981. 373 p. ; ISBN 3-7890-0568-1 : LC Card 82-159141 DDC 380.5/068 19
HE249 .O33 1981 ***NYPL [JLD 86-2588]***

Okonomische und soziale Wirksamkeit des wissenschaftlich-technischen Fortschritts / [Autoren-kollektiv; Michael Bücher ... et al.]. Berlin : Dietz, 1986. 314 p. : ill. ; 22 cm. Some articles translated from the Russian. Includes bibliographical references and indexes. ISBN 3-320-00713-0
1. Technological innovations - Addresses, essays, lectures. 2. Industrial productivity - Addresses, essays, lectures. 3. Labor productivity - Addresses, essays, lectures. I. Büchner, Michael.
NYPL [JLD 86-4381]

Økonomisk oversigt. Danish economic survey. [Copenhagen] [1984] 72 p. : LC Card 86-220598 DDC 330.9489/058 19
HC355 .D226 1984

Økonomisk politik i en åben økonomi /. Sørensen, Peter Birch. København , 1985. vi, 179 p. : LC Card 86-135751
HB135 .S575 1985

Økonomiske forhold ved generasjonsskifte i landbruket =. Knapskog, Kåre. Oslo , 1986. 95 p. : ISBN 82-7077-032-9 LC Card 86-231818
HD2012 .K6 1986

Ökopesszimizmus, technooptimizmus és korunk globális problémái /. Görög, Tibor. [Budapest] , 1984. 85 p. : ISBN 963-673-290-6 LC Card 85-130717
HC59 .G6226 1984

Okruzhaiushchaia sreda i problemy planirovaniia /. Raiatskas, R. L. (Raimundas Leonovich), 1937- Moskva , 1981. 272 p. ; LC Card 87-462039
HD75.6 .R35 1981

Okrŭzhen komitet na BKP--IAmbol. Godini na vŭzkhod . IAmbol , 1986. 87 p., [40] p. of plates : LC Card 87-103737
HC403.Z7 I64 1986

Okrŭzhen komitet na BKP--Vratsa. Deistvena organizatorska i ideino-vŭzpitatelna rabota za izpŭlnenie resheniiata na Fevruarskiia plenum na TSK na BKP /. Vratsa , 1985. 56 p. : LC Card 86-172762
HC403 .D45 1985

Okrŭzhen naroden sŭvet--IAmbol. Godini na vŭzkhod . IAmbol , 1986. 87 p., [40] p. of plates : LC Card 87-103737
HC403.Z7 I64 1986

Oksenberg, Michel, 1938- Lieberthal, Kenneth. Bureaucratic politics and Chinese energy development /. [Washington, D.C.] [1986] xii, 405 p. ; LC Card 86-602422 DDC 333.79/0951 19
HD9502.C62 L54 1986

Ökten, Rita. Die Bedeutung des Umweltschutzes für die Wirtschaft der DDR / Rita Ökten. Berlin : A. Spitz, c1986. 87 p. : ill. ; 21 cm. Bibliography: p. 83-87. ISBN 3-87061-311-4 LC Card 86-194057
1. Environmental policy - Germany, East. 2. Environmental protection - Germany, East. I. Title.
HC290.795.E5 O38 1986

Okun, Daniel Alexander. Community piped water supply systems in developing countries : a planning manual / Daniel A. Okun and Walter R. Ernst. Washington, D.C. : World Bank, 1987. xi, 249 p. : ill. ; 27 cm. (World Bank technical paper, 0253-7494 . no. 60) Bibliography: p. 212-222. ISBN 0-8213-0896-3 (pbk.) LC Card 87-8161 DDC 363.6/1/091724 19
1. Municipal water supply - Developing countries - Planning. 2. Waterworks - Developing countries - Planning. 3. Water-supply engineering - Developing countries. I. Ernst, Walter R., 1929-. II. Title. III. Series.
HD4465.D44 O38 1987

Okun, Mitchell. Fair play in the marketplace : the first battle for pure food and drugs / Mitchell Okun. Dekalb, Ill. : Northern Illinois University Press, 1986. xii, 345 p. : ill. ; 23 cm. Includes index. Bibliography: p. [307]-323. ISBN 0-87580-115-3 LC Card 85-25921 DDC 363.1/926/0973 19
1. Food adulteration and inspection - United States - History - 19th century. 2. Food adulteration and inspection - Law and legislation - United States - History - 19th century. 3. Food adulteration and inspection - New York (State) - History - 19th century. 4. Food adulteration and inspection - Law and legislation - New York (State) - History - 19th century. I. Title.
HD9000.9.U5 O39 1986
NYPL [JLD 86-2513]

Ōkurashō Zaisei Kin'yū Kenkyūjo (Japan) Japan and the United States today . New York , 1986, c1987. vii, 234 p. : ISBN 0-231-06575-2 LC Card 86-32640 DDC 332/.042/0952 19
HG3903 .J35 1987

Olayide, S. Olajuwon.
Eweka, J. A. (Julius A.) Village development . Ibadan, Nigeria , 1979. xvi, 194 p. ; LC Card 86-172121 DDC 338.1/9/669 19
HD2145.5 .E94 1979

Nigerian small farmers . Benin-City, Bendel State, Nigeria , 1980. xv, 315 p. ; LC Card 82-206979 DDC 338.1/6 19
HD1339.N5 N54 1980 ***NYPL [Sc D 86-883]***

Ölçen, Ali Nejat. Türken und Rückkehr : eine Untersuchung in Duisburg über die Rückkehrneigung türkischer Arbeitnehmer als Funktion ökonomischer und sozialer Faktoren / Ali Nejat Ölçen.1. Aufl. Frankfurt a.M. : Dağyeli, 1986. 132 p. ; 30 cm. (Studien und Arbeiten . 1) ISBN 3-924320-51-9 LC Card 87-138316 DDC 331.6/2/56104355 19
1. Alien labor, Turkish - Germany (West) - Duisburg. 2. Return migration - Turkey. 3. Saving and thrift - Germany (West) - Duisburg. 4. Cost and standard of living - Germany (West) - Duisburg. I. Title. II. Series.
HD8458.T9 O43 1986

OLD AGE ASSISTANCE - EUROPE.
Schmitz, Heinz. Vermeidung von Armut im Alter . München , c1983. 267 p. : ISBN 3-89019-099-5 LC Card 84-197886
HD7164 .S29 1983

OLD AGE ASSISTANCE - INDIA - HARYANA.
Mahajan, Amarjit. Problems of the aged in unorganised sector /. Delhi, India , 1987. viii, 106 p. ; LC Card 87-901315 DDC 362.6/042 19
HD7105.35.I5 M34 1987

OLD AGE HOMES - GERMANY (WEST) - MANAGEMENT.
Seddig, Gert. Lehrbuch der Altenpflege. Hannover , c1983. 95 p. : ISBN 3-87870-204-3 LC Card 83-230557
HF5728.G3 S49 1983

OLD AGE PENSIONS.
Demographische Entwicklung und kapitalbildende Altersversorgungssysteme /. Bergisch Gladbach , 1984. iii, 67 p. ; LC Card 85-154174
HD7091 .D46 1984

Retirement income provisions overseas. [Canberra] [1984] 162 p. ; ISBN 0-642-51580-8 (pbk.) LC Card 84-252861 DDC 331.25/22 19
HD7105.3 .R46 1984

Soler Bordetas, Francisco Javier. Fondos de pensiones /. Bilbao [1985?] 152 p. : ISBN 84-234-0575-3 LC Card 86-166028
HD7105.45.S7 S57 1985

OLD AGE PENSIONS - ACCOUNTING.
Amble, Joan Lordi. A guide to implementation of Statement 87 on employer's accounting for pensions . Stamford, Conn. (High Ridge Park, P.O. Box 3821, Stamford 06905-0821) , c1986. vii, 106 p. : LC Card 87-133173 DDC 657/.75
HF5686.O5 A56 1986

Public record . Stamford, Conn. (P.O. Box 3821, Stamford 06905-0821) [1986] 424 p. ; LC Card 86-81700 DDC 657/.75 19
HF5686.O5 P83 1986

OLD AGE PENSIONS - DENMARK.
Vesterø Jensen, Carsten. Det tvedelte pensionssystem /. Roskilde [1984] 284 p. ; LC Card 84-181865
HD7105.35.D4 J45 1984

OLD AGE PENSIONS - DEVELOPING COUNTRIES.
Partsch, Manfred. Prinzipien und Formen sozialer Sicherung in nicht-industriellen Gesellschaften /. Berlin , c1983. 168 p. ; ISBN 3-428-05484-9 LC Card 84-148527 DDC 368.4/009172/4 19
HD7252 .P37 1983 ***NYPL [JLE 85-1238]***

OLD AGE PENSIONS - EUROPE.
Quadagno, Jill S. The transformation of old age security . Chicago , 1988. p. cm. ISBN 0-226-69923-4 : LC Card 87-18754 DDC 368.4/00973 19
HD7125 .Q46 1988

OLD AGE PENSIONS - GERMANY, EAST.
Püschel, Herbert. Die Rentenversorgung der Arbeiter und Angestellten in der DDR /. Berlin , c1986. 206 p. ; ISBN 3-7303-0068-7 LC Card 87-408895 DDC 331.25/2/09431 19
HD7180.5 .P87 1986

OLD AGE PENSIONS - GERMANY, WEST.
Genosko, Joachim. Arbeitsangebot und Alterssicherung /. Regensburg , c1985. vii, 287 p. : ISBN 3-924956-05-7 LC Card 86-230675
HD7105.35.G3 G46 1985

Haueisen, Peter, 1955- Unmittelbare Versorgungszusage und Direktversicherung als Gestaltungsformen der betrieblichen Altersversorgung /. Frankfurt am Main , New York , c1983. xx, 297 p. : ISBN 3-8204-7592-3 LC Card 86-107083 DDC 331.25/2/0943 19
HD7105.35.G3 H38 1983

Infratest Sozialforschung. Datenlage zur Alterssicherung . Bonn , 1984. 330 p. : LC Card 86-132439 DDC 331.25/2/0943 19
HD7105.35.G3 I54 1984

Merklein, Renate. Die Rentenkrise /. Reinbek bei Hamburg , 1986. 190 p. : ISBN 3-499-33072-5 : LC Card 87-100842
HD7105.35.G3 M47 1986

Schmidt, Axel. Betriebliche Altersversorgung in mittelständischen Unternehmen /. Stuttgart , c1985. xiii, 213 p. : ISBN 3-7910-5004-4 : LC Card 86-164220
HD7105.35.G3 S35 1985
NYPL [JLL 73-505 Nr. 3]

Sicherung der Altersvorsorge durch Aufgabenteilung zwischen Individualversicherung und gesetzlicher Rentenversicherung . München , 1986. xi, 242 p. : ISBN 3-88512-017-8 : LC Card 86-163171
HD7105.35.G3 S53 1986

OLD AGE PENSIONS - GERMANY (WEST) - CONGRESSES.
Renten 2000 . München , c1985. 124 p. : ISBN 3-7892-7267-1 LC Card 87-118239 DDC 331.25/2/0943 19
HD7105.35.G3 R46 1985

OLD AGE PENSIONS - GERMANY (WEST) - MATHEMATICAL MODELS.
Helberger, Christof. Beitragsäquivalenz oder interpersonelle Umverteilung in der gesetzlichen Rentenversicherung? . Berlin , 1981. 96 p. ; LC Card 81-201422 DDC 331.25/2/0943 19
HD7105.35.G3 H44 1981
NYPL [JLM 81-818 v.63]

OLD AGE PENSIONS - GOVERNMENT POLICY - UNITED STATES.
Wendling, Wayne. The regulatory impact on pensions /. Brookfield, Wis. , 1986. xiii, 91 p. : ISBN 0-89154-314-7 (pbk.) : LC Card 87-129712 DDC 331.25/2/0973 19
HD7105.35.U6 W46 1986

OLD AGE PENSIONS - GREAT BRITAIN.
Paterson, Martin, 1927- Pensions . Cambridge, England , Wolfeboro, N.H., USA, , 1988. p. cm. ISBN 0-85941-380-2 : LC Card 87-8324 DDC 331.25/2/0941 19
HD7105.35.G7 P38 1988

Pensions . London , Boston , 1987. xvi, 249 p. : ISBN 0-04-332127-5 (alk. paper) LC Card 86-32086 DDC 331.25/2/0941 19
HD7165 .P46 1987

OLD AGE PENSIONS - INDIA - HARYANA.
Mahajan, Amarjit. Problems of the aged in unorganised sector /. Delhi, India , 1987. viii, 106 p. ; LC Card 87-901315 DDC 362.6/042 19
HD7105.35.I5 M34 1987

OLD AGE PENSIONS - LAW AND LEGISLATION - ECONOMIC ASPECTS - QUÉBEC (PROVINCE)
Régie des rentes du Québec. Régime de rentes

du Québec . Québec [1983] 45 leaves : LC Card 85-131814
HD7130.Z8 Q47 1983

OLD AGE PENSIONS - LAW AND LEGISLATION - GERMANY (EAST)
Püschel, Herbert. Die Rentenversorgung der Arbeiter und Angestellten in der DDR /. Berlin , c1986. 206 p. ; ISBN 3-7303-0068-7 LC Card 87-408895 DDC 331.25/2/09431 19
HD7180.5 .P87 1986

OLD AGE PENSIONS - LAW AND LEGISLATION - GERMANY (WEST)
Schmidt, Axel. Betriebliche Altersversorgung in mittelständischen Unternehmen /. Stuttgart , c1985. xiii, 213 p. : ISBN 3-7910-5004-4 : LC Card 86-164220
HD7105.35.G3 S35 1985 ***NYPL [JLL 73-505 Nr. 3]***

OLD AGE PENSIONS - LAW AND LEGISLATION - GREAT BRITAIN.
Paterson, Martin, 1927- Pensions . Cambridge, England , Wolfeboro, N.H., USA, , 1988. p. cm. ISBN 0-85941-380-2 : LC Card 87-8324 DDC 331.25/2/0941 19
HD7105.35.G7 P38 1988

OLD AGE PENSIONS - QUÉBEC (PROVINCE)
Régie des rentes du Québec. Régime de rentes du Québec . Québec [1983] 45 leaves : LC Card 85-131814
HD7130.Z8 Q47 1983

OLD AGE PENSIONS - SPAIN.
Soler Bordetas, Francisco Javier. Fondos de pensiones /. Bilbao [1985?] 152 p. : ISBN 84-234-0575-3 LC Card 86-166028
HD7105.45.S7 S57 1985

OLD AGE PENSIONS - SWITZERLAND.
Oberhänsli, Urs. Altersvorsorge, Kapitalschwemme oder Kapitalmangel? . Bern , c1986. xii, 222 p. : ISBN 3-258-03578-4 : LC Card 86-149614
HD7105.35.S9 O24 1986

OLD AGE PENSIONS - SWITZERLAND - STATISTICS.
Lüthi, Ambros, 1938- Die wirtschaftliche Ungleichheit im Rentenalter in der Schweiz /. Freiburg/Schweiz , 1983. 229 p. : ISBN 3-7278-0282-0 : LC Card 83-163287
HD7105.35.S9 L87 1983

OLD AGE PENSIONS - TAXATION - GERMANY, WEST.
Weise, Herbert. Rentenfinanzierung und Rentenbesteuerung . Kiel , 1978. iii, 64 leaves ; LC Card 85-188549
HJ4720.A7 W45 1978

OLD AGE PENSIONS - TAXATION - LAW AND LEGISLATION - GERMANY (WEST)
Weise, Herbert. Rentenfinanzierung und Rentenbesteuerung . Kiel , 1978. iii, 64 leaves ; LC Card 85-188549
HJ4720.A7 W45 1978

OLD AGE PENSIONS - UNITED STATES.
McFadden, John J. Retirement plans for employees /. Homewood, Ill. , 1988. xviii, 326 p. : ISBN 0-256-05588-2 LC Card 87-81436 DDC 658.3/253 19
HD7105.35.U6 M33 1988

Pension integration . Washington, D.C. [1986] 28 p. : LC Card 86-603093 DDC 331.25/2/0973 19
HD7125 .P392 1986

Pensions & profit sharing. [Chicago, Ill.] , c1987- xiii, 351 p. ; ISBN 0-88462-650-4 (pbk.) LC Card 87-1608 DDC 658/.3/25 19
HD7105.35.U6 P45 1987

Quadagno, Jill S. The transformation of old age security . Chicago , 1988. p. cm. ISBN 0-226-69923-4 : LC Card 87-18754 DDC 368.4/00973 19
HD7125 .Q46 1988

Wolff, Nancy, 1955- Income redistribution and the Social Security program /. Ann Arbor , c1987. vi, 181 p. : ISBN 0-8357-1807-7 LC Card 87-10791 DDC 368.4/3/00973 19
HD7105.35.U6 W65 1987

OLD AGE PENSIONS - UNITED STATES - ACCOUNTING.
Clark, Hal G. Illustrations of accounting for pensions and for settlements and curtailments of defined benefit pension plans . New York, N.Y. (1211 Ave. of the Americas, New York 10036-8775) , c1987. 34 p. ; LC Card 87-401762 DDC 657/.75 19
HF5686.O5 C56 1987

OLD AGE PENSIONS - UNITED STATES - FORECASTING.
Andrews, George H., 1932- Actuarial projections for the old-age, survivors, and disability insurance program of social security in the United States of America /. Itasca, Ill., U. S.A. , c1987. viii, 188 p. : LC Card 87-1101 DDC 368.4/301/0973 19
HC106.8 .A56 1987

OLD AGE, SURVIVORS AND DISABILITY INSURANCE. see **SOCIAL SECURITY.**

The old lodges & hotels of our national parks /. McMillon, Bill, 1942- South Bend, Ind. , 1983. ix, 130 p., [32] p. of plates : ISBN 0-89651-551-6 : LC Card 83-18456 DDC 647/.947301 19
TX909 .M34 1983 ***NYPL [JFF 86-405]***

Old lodges and hotels of our national parks. McMillon, Bill, 1942- The old lodges & hotels of our national parks /. South Bend, Ind. , 1983. ix, 130 p., [32] p. of plates : ISBN 0-89651-551-6 : LC Card 83-18456 DDC 647/.947301 19
TX909 .M34 1983 ***NYPL [JFF 86-405]***

Old Mutual income tax guide, 1986/87 /. Divaris, Costa. [S.l.] c1987 (Cape Town : Old Mutual Print. Works) xvi, 261 p. : LC Card 87-152138 DDC 343.6805/2 346.80352 19
HJ4790.4 .D58 1987

Older persons and their homes, today and tomorrow . Blank, Thomas O., 1947- [Harrisburg] [1986] 60 leaves : LC Card 86-623023 DDC 363.5/9 19
HD7287.92.U54 B55 1986

Older persons and their housing, today and tomorrow /. Blank, Thomas O., 1947- Springfield, Ill., U. S.A. , c1988. xviii, 304 p. ; ISBN 0-398-05377-4 LC Card 87-16827 DDC 363.5/9 19
HD7287.92.U54 B554 1988

OLDER WORKERS. see **AGED - EMPLOYMENT.**

Ole Saibull, Solomon, 1935- Hotuba ya Ndugu S.A. ole Saibull, mbunge, waziri wa maliasili na utalii : bajeti ya 1979/80. Dar es Salaam, Tanzania : Mpigachapa wa Serikali, 1979. 56 p. ; 21 cm. In Swahili. Cover title. LC Card 83-244807
1. Tanzania. Wizara ya Maliasilli na Utalii - Appropriations and expenditures. 2. Natural resources - Tanzania. 3. Tourist trade - Tanzania. I. Title.
HC885 .O44 1979

Olearnik, Janusz. Funkcjonowanie rynku usług w Polsce /. Wrocław , 1986. 176 p. ; ISBN 83-7011-034-7 : LC Card 87-169457
HB9 .B7522 nr. 355 HD9986.P7

Oleksy, Walter G., 1930- Kozlowski, Joseph G. Complete guide to cost-effective employee benefit programs /. Englewood Cliffs, N.J. , c1987. xix, 276 p. : ISBN 0-13-160037-0 LC Card 87-11816 DDC 658.3/25 19
HD4928.N62 U636 1987

Olesen, Morten Weise. Sadolin, Pia. Regional udvikling i Danmark /. [Aarhus] , 1983. 92 p. : LC Card 84-164625
HC355 .S26 1983

OLIGARCHY - ECUADOR - CHIMBORAZO - HISTORY.
Sylva Charvet, Paola. Gamonalismo y lucha campesina . [Quito] , 1986. 250 p., [3] leaves of plates : LC Card 87-101122
HD529.C47 S95 1986

OLIGOPOLIES - CASE STUDIES.
Welzmüller, Rudolf. Preispolitik und Akkumulation . Köln , c1982. 283 p. : ISBN 3-7663-0522-0 : LC Card 82-140922 DDC 338.8/266/00943 19
HD9654.5 .W44 1982 ***NYPL [JLD 86-2908]***

OLIGOPOLIES - CONGRESSES.
New developments in the analysis of market structure . Cambridge, Mass. , 1986. xxiv, 559 p. : ISBN 0-262-19241-1 LC Card 85-4246 DDC 338.8 19
HD2326 .N43 1986 ***NYPL [JLD 86-3570]***

Oligopoly, competition, and welfare /. Oxford, OX, UK , New York, NY, USA , 1985. 191 p. : ISBN 0-631-14479-X (pbk.) LC Card 85-11200 DDC 338.8/2 19
HD2757.3 .O44 1985 ***NYPL [JLE 86-1961]***

OLIGOPOLIES - ECONOMETRIC MODELS.
Schäfer, Martin, 1951- Resource extraction and market structure /. Berlin , New York , c1986. ix, 154 p. : ISBN 0-387-16081-7 (U. S.) LC Card 86-1786 DDC 333.7/0973 19
HC59 .S344 1986 ***NYPL [JLM 72-289 no.263]***

OLIGOPOLIES - GREAT BRITAIN.
Utton, Michael A. Profits and stability of monopoly /. Cambridge [Cambridgeshire] , New York , 1986. vii, 96 p. ; ISBN 0-521-32550-1 LC Card 86-4226 DDC 338.8/2/0941 19
HD2757.3 .U88 1986 ***NYPL [TB (National Institute of Economic and Social Research. Occasional papers. v.38)]***

OLIGOPOLIES - MATHEMATICAL MODELS.
Hwang, Hae-Shin. Dominant firm price leadership . Toronto, Ont. [1986] 40 p. : ISBN 0-7729-2122-9 : LC Card 87-161006 DDC 338.2/3 19
HD9539.N5 H93 1986

Schoch, Hans. Size and price in oligopoly /. Königstein, Ts. , Cambridge, Mass. , 1981. viii, 151 p. : ISBN 3-445-12157-5 LC Card 80-84489 DDC 338.8/2/0724 19
HD2757.3 .S36 1981

Oligopoly, competition, and welfare / edited by P.A. Geroski, L. Phlips, A. Ulph. Oxford, OX, UK ; New York, NY, USA : B. Blackwell, 1985. 191 p. : ill. ; 23 cm. Proceedings of a joint meeting of the E.S.R.C. Industrial Economics Study Group and the E.S.R.C. Economic Theory Study Group. "Published in cooperation with The journal of industrial economics." Includes indexes. Bibliography: p. 173-183. ISBN 0-631-14479-X (pbk.) LC Card 85-11200 DDC 338.8/2 19
1. Oligopolies - Congresses. 2. Competition, Unfair - Congresses. 3. Welfare economics - Congresses. I. Geroski, Paul. II. Phlips, Louis. III. Ulph, Alistair. IV. E.S.R.C. Industrial Economics Study Group. V. E.S.R.C. Economic Theory Study Group.
HD2757.3 .O44 1985 ***NYPL [JLE 86-1961]***

Olin, Harold Bennett. Realty brokerage operations by savings institutions / Harold B. Olin. Chicago, IL (111 E. Wacker Dr., Chicago 60601) : United States League of Savings Institutions, c1986. 38, [96] p. : ill. ; 28 cm. Bibliography: p. [77]-[80] LC Card 86-212493 DDC 332.3/2 19
1. Real estate business - United States. 2. Building and loan associations - United States. I. Title.
HD255 .O45 1986

Oliu, Walter E. Brusaw, Charles T. The business writer's handbook /. New York , c1987. xxviii, 764 p. : ISBN 0-312-00571-7 : LC Card 87-4361 DDC 651.7/5 19
HF5726 .B874 1987

Oliva, Karl. Teilnahme ohne Teilhabe : Kritik und Integration soziologischer Literatur zur Marginalität in der Weltgesellschaft / Karl Oliva. Frankfurt am Main ; New York : Campus, c1985. 285 p. : ill. ; 21 cm. (Campus Forschung. Bd. 427) Originally presented as the author's thesis (doctoral)--Universität Zürich, 1983/84. Bibliography: p. 269-285. ISBN 3-593-33476-3 LC Card 85-147441
1. Saving and investment - Developing countries. 2. Marginality, Social - Developing countries. I. Title.
HC59.72.S3 O45 1985

OLIVE-OIL INDUSTRY.
Políticas oleícolas nacionales /. [S.l.] [1985] 130 p. in various pagings ; LC Card 86-131977 DDC 338.4/7664362 19
HD9490.5.O462 P65 1985

OLIVE-OIL INDUSTRY - GOVERNMENT POLICY.
Políticas oleícolas nacionales /. [S.l.] [1985] 130 p. in various pagings ; LC Card 86-131977 DDC 338.4/7664362 19
HD9490.5.O462 P65 1985

OLIVE-OIL INDUSTRY - ITALY - TUSCANY.
Vino e olio in Toscana =. Firenze , c1985. 386 p. : LC Card 86-138958 DDC 338.4/76632/009455

19
HD9385.I82 T858 1985 ***NYPL [JSF 87-35]***

OLIVE-OIL INDUSTRY - ITALY - TUSCANY - DIRECTORIES.
Vino e olio in Toscana =. Firenze , c1985. 386 p. : LC Card 86-138958 DDC 338.4/76632/009455 19
HD9385.I82 T858 1985 ***NYPL [JSF 87-35]***

Oliveira Andrade, Manuel Correia de. see **Andrade, Manuel Correia de Oliveira.**

Oliveira, César. Goodolphim, Costa, 1842-1910. A associação . Lisboa, Portugal , 1974. 206 p. ; LC Card 87-401116 DDC 334/.09494 19
HD3529.A4 G66 1974

Oliveira, Georgina. Dabat, Christine. As mulheres nas organizações profissionais /. Recife , 1985. 21 p. ; LC Card 86-177927
HD2429.B6 D33 1985

Oliveira, Geraldo Sabino de. História do sindicalismo no Rio Grande do Norte / Geraldo Sabino de Oliveira. 1a. ed. Natal [Brazil] : CLIMA, 1985. 68 p., [6] leaves of plates : ill. ; 21 cm. (Coleção Edições CLIMA . vol. 40) LC Card 87-403987 DDC 331.88/0981/32 19
1. Trade-unions - Brazil - Rio Grande do Norte - History - 20th century. I. Title.
HD6615.R54 O45 1985

Oliveira, Jaury Nepumuceno de. O Comércio e suas profissões . Rio de Janeiro , 1983. 127, [5] p. : LC Card 84-161651
HF5459.B7 C65 1983 ***NYPL [JLF 86-1408]***

Oliveira, Lúcia Elena Garcia de. O lugar do negro na força de trabalho / [Lúcia Elena Garcia de Oliveira, Rosa Maria Porcaro, Tereza Cristina N. Araújo Costa]. Rio de Janeiro : Secretaria de Planejamento da Presidência da República, Fundação Instituto Brasileiro de Geografia e Estatística, 1983. 86 p. ; 23 cm. Bibliography: p. 83-86. ISBN 85-24-00024-4 LC Card 86-129924
1. Blacks - Employment - Brazil. 2. Labor supply - Brazil. 3. Discrimination in employment - Brazil. 4. Social mobility - Brazil. I. Porcaro, Rosa Maria. II. Costa, Tereza Cristina N. Araújo. III. Title.
HD8288.5.B55 O45 1983

Oliveira, Maria Chambarelli de. Achegas à história do rodoviarismo no Brasil / Maria Chambarelli de Oliveira. Rio de Janeiro-RJ : Memórias Futuras Edições, c1986. 137 p., [1] leaf of plates : ill. ; 21 cm. Includes bibliographies. LC Card 86-232581
1. Roads - Brazil - History. 2. Automóvel Club do Brasil - History. I. Title.
HE359.B7 O45 1986

Oliveira, Nélson V. de. Companhia de Viação São Paulo-Mato Grosso. Ante-projeto do núcleo de colonização "Presidente Kennedy" /. Mato Grosso, Brasil , 1962. 40 p., [15] leaves of plates : LC Card 85-135105
HD1516.B8 C64 1962

Oliveira, Plinio Corrêa de, 1908- A propriedade privada e a livre iniciativa no tufão agro-reformista / Plinio Corrêa de Oliveira, Carlos Patricio del Campo. [São Paulo] : Editora Vera Cruz, [1985] xvi, 174 p., [16] p. of plates : ill. ; 29 cm. Cover title: A reforma agrária socialista e confiscatória. "TFP"--Spine. Bibliography: p. 165-174. LC Card 87-104428
1. Land reform - Brazil. I. Campo, Carlos Patricio del. II. Sociedade Brasileira de Defesa da Tradição, Família e Propriedade. III. Title. IV. Title: Reforma agrária socialista e confiscatória.
HD1333.B6 O385 1985

Oliveira, Victor J. Distribution of rural employment growth by race : a case study / Victor J. Oliveira. Washington, D.C. : U. S. Dept. of Agriculture, Economic Research Service : Copies from the Supt. of Docs., U. S. G.P.O., [1986] vii, 17 p. : ill. ; 28 cm. (Rural development research report . no. 54) Cover title. "January 1986"--P. iii. Bibliography: p. 16-17. LC Card 86-601118 DDC 331.6/09758 19
1. Labor supply - Georgia. 2. Afro-Americans - Employment - Georgia. 3. Rural development - Georgia. I. Title. II. Series.
HD5725.G4 O56 1986

Oliver, E. Eugene. Cost accounting : a practical approach / E. Eugene Oliver. Englewood Cliffs, NJ : Prentice-Hall, c1987. xv, 352 p. : ill. ; 25 cm. Includes index. ISBN 0-13-179979-7 LC Card 86-25225 DDC 657/.42 19
1. Cost accounting. I. Title.
HF5686.C8 O45 1987

Oliver, Thomas, 1950-
The real Coke, the real story / Thomas Oliver. 1st ed. New York : Random House, 1986. 195 p. ; 24 cm. ISBN 0-394-55273-3 : LC Card 86-10151 DDC 338.7/66362/0973 19
1. Coca-Cola Company. 2. Coca-Cola Company - History. 3. Soft drink industry - United States. 4. Soft drink industry - United States - History. I. Title.
HD9349.S634 C67 1986
NYPL [JLE 86-4489]

The real Coke, the real story / Thomas Oliver. New York : Penguin Books, 1987, c1986. 234 p., [9] p. of plates : ill., ports. ; 18 cm. Bibliography: p. [231]-234. ISBN 0-14-010408-9 (pbk.) LC Card 87-11836 DDC 338.7/66362/0973 19
1. Coca-Cola Company. 2. Coca-Cola Company - History. 3. Soft drink industry - United States. 4. Soft drink industry - United States - History. I. Title.
HD9349.S634 C67 1987

Oliveros, Gumersindo. Dillon, K. Burke. Recent experience with multilateral official debt rescheduling /. Washington, D.C. , c1987. v, 22 p. : LC Card 87-2633 DDC 336.3/435 19
HG3891.5 .D55 1987

OLIVETTI M-24 (COMPUTER) - PROGRAMMING.
Aloi, Felice. Il budget con il personal computer . Milano, Italy , c1984. 226 p. : LC Card 84-250395 DDC 658.1/54/02854165 19
HG4028.B8 A46 1984

Oljeersättningsprogrammet i ett samhällsekonomiskt perspektiv. Stockholm : Statens industriverk, 1983. 39, 67, 54, 71 p. : ill. ; 30 cm. (SIND PM, 0346-573X . 1983:6) Includes bibliographical references. ISBN 91-38-07618-7 LC Card 83-232276
1. Energy policy - Sweden. 2. Petroleum conservation - Sweden. 3. Sweden - Economic conditions - 1945-. I. Sweden. Statens industriverk. II. Series.
HD9502.S82 O55 1983

Oljen og norsk økonomi /. Aarrestad, Jostein. [Oslo] , c1984. 118 p. : ISBN 82-508-0285-3 LC Card 86-207964
HD9575.N62 A5 1984

Ol'khovaia͡, L. V. Ural i problemy regional'noĭ istoriografii. Sverdlovsk , 1986. 83 p. ; LC Card 87-159699
HC337.R852 U73853 1986

Ollerenshaw, Philip, 1953- Banking in nineteenth-century Ireland : the Belfast banks, 1825-1914 / Philip Ollerenshaw. Manchester, UK ; Wolfeboro, NH, USA : Manchester University Press, c1987. 263 p. : map ; 23 cm. Based on the author's thesis (Ph. D.)--University of Sheffield, 1982. Bibliography: p. 203-255. Includes index. ISBN 0-7190-2276-2 : LC Card 87-11113 DDC 332.1/09416/7 19
1. Banks and banking - Northern Ireland - Belfast - History. 2. Banks and banking - Ireland - History. 3. Banks and banking - Great Britain - History. 4. Great Britain - Economic conditions. 5. Ireland - Economic conditions. I. Title. II. Title: Banking in 19th century Ireland.
HG950.B45 O55 1987

Ollmann, Rainer. Niessen, Hans-Joachim. Schattenwirtschaft in der Bundesrepublik . Opladen , 1987. 246 p. : ISBN 3-8100-0592-4 LC Card 87-131108
HD2346.G3 N545 1987

Olnek, Jay I. The invisible hand : how free trade is choking the life out of America / Jay I. Olnek.2nd ed. Riverdale, N.Y. : North Stonington Press, c1984. 176 p. : ill. ; 24 cm. Includes index. Bibliography: p. 167-170. ISBN 0-938538-01-2 LC Card 82-24634 DDC 382.7/1/0973 19
1. Free trade and protection - Protection - History. 2. Inflation (Finance) - United States - History. 3. Foreign trade and employment - United States - History. 4. United States - Commercial policy - History. I. Title.
HF1455 .O49 1984 ***NYPL [JLE 87-21]***

Olofsson, Christer.
Kommunala bolag med industriutvecklings uppgifter : en kartläggning och analys / av Christer Olofsson. Stockholm : LiberFörlag : Statens industriverk, [1984] 82 p. ; 25 cm. (Kommunal näringspolitik) SIND, 0346-5748 ; 1984:1 Bibliography: p. 81-82. ISBN 91-38-08114-8 LC Card 85-106731
1. Industry and state - Sweden. 2. Economic development projects - Sweden. 3. Subsidies - Sweden. I. Title. II. Series.
HD3616.S53 O46 1984

De regionala utvecklingsbolagen : instrument för industriell utveckling? / Christer Olofsson. Stockholm : LiberFörlag, [1983] 118 p. ; 24 cm. (SIND, 0346-5748 . 1983:4) Bibliography: p. 115-118. ISBN 91-38-07479-6 LC Card 83-234309
1. Industrial promotion - Sweden. 2. Economic development projects - Sweden. 3. Sweden - Economic conditions - 1945-. I. Title. II. Series.
HC380.I53 O46 1983

Olózaga, Hernán Echavarría. see **Echavarría Olózaga, Hernán.**

Olsen, Poul Erik, 1952- Godsejerrøster . København , 1984. 320 p. : ISBN 87-7526-018-2 : LC Card 84-224395
HD1333.D42 R674 1984

Ol'sevich, I͡U. I͡A. (I͡Uriĭ I͡Akovlevich) Kritika antimarksistskikh vzgli͡adov po problemam NTR /. Moskva , 1987. 157 p. ; LC Card 87-164887
HC340.T4 K75 1987

Olson, James Stuart, 1946- Saving capitalism : the Reconstruction Finance Corporation and the New Deal, 1933-1940 / James S. Olson. Princeton, N.J. : Princeton University Press, c1988. p. cm. Bibliography: p. Includes index. ISBN 0-691-04749-9 (alk. paper) : LC Card 87-7275 DDC 353.0082/5/09 19
1. Reconstruction Finance Corporation - History. 2. New Deal, 1933-1939. 3. United States - Economic policy - 1933-1945. I. Title.
HG3729.U5 O47 1988

Olson, Jerry C. (Jerry Corrie), 1944- Peter, J. Paul. Consumer behavior . Homewood, Ill. , 1987. xvii, 698 p., [16] p. of plates : ISBN 0-256-03177-0 LC Card 86-81801 DDC 658.8/342 19
HF5415.3 .P468 1987

Olson Research Associates. Community bank guide to asset/liability management policies /. Washington, D.C. (1120 Connecticut Ave., N.W., Washington 20036) , c1987. v, 241 p. : LC Card 87-167068 DDC 332.1/2/0681 19
HG1615.25 .C65 1987

Olsson, Hans. Industrins lönsamhet, finansiering och investeringar under 1970-talet : LU80, bilaga 9. [Stockholm] : LiberFörlag, [1981] 58 p. : ill. ; 22 cm. "Rapport ... av Hans Olsson"--P. 1. "Ds E 1981:8." Includes bibliographical references. ISBN 91-38-06530-4 LC Card 84-120594
1. Corporations - Sweden - Finance. 2. Corporate profits - Sweden. 3. Capital investments - Sweden. I. Sweden. Ekonomidepartementet. Långtidsutredningen 1980. II. Title.
HG4211 .O45 1981

Oltmann, Joachim. Kalter Krieg und kommunale Integration : Arbeiterbewegung im Stadtteil Bremen-Vegesack, 1945-1956 / Joachim Oltmann. Marburg : Verlag Arbeiterbewegung und Gesellschaftswissenschaft, c1987. 500 p. ; 21 cm. (Schriftenreihe der Studiengesellschaft für Sozialgeschichte und Arbeiterbewegung . Bd. 63) Bibliography: p. 485-500. ISBN 3-921630-71-1 LC Card 87-142718 DDC 331.88/0943/52 19
1. Trade-unions - Germany (West) - Bremen - History - 20th century. 2. Vegesack (Bremen, Germany). I. Title. II. Series.
HD6699.B7 O48 1987

Oltre la crisi : le prospettive di sviluppo dell'economia italiana e il contributo del sistema finanziario / Ente per gli studi monetari, bancari e finanziari "Luigi Einaudi". Bologna : Il Mulino, c1986. x, 745 p. : ill. ; 22 cm. (Temi e discussioni) Includes bibliographical references. ISBN 88-15-01249-4 : LC Card 87-149887
1. Italy - Economic policy. 2. Monetary policy - Italy. 3. Italy - Full employment policies. 4. Economic stabilization - Italy. I. Ente per gli studi monetari, bancari e finanziari Luigi Einaudi.
HC305 .O45 1986

Olusanya, G. O. (Gabriel Olakunde) Nigeria's external relations . Ibadan , 1986. 577 p. ; LC Card 87-132060 DDC 337.669 19
HF1616.7 .N55 1986

Olycksfall i skogs- och flottningsarbete år 1982. Metsä- ja uittotöiden työtapaturmat vuonna 1982 =. Tampere , Helsinki , 1984. 50 p. : ISBN 951-46-7685-8 LC Card 85-149625
HD7269.F7262 F56 1984

Olyniec, James H. Transition in the nuclear industry . New York, N.Y. , c1985. iii, 233 p. : ISBN 0-87262-443-9 (pbk.) LC Card 85-70499 DDC 338.4/762148/0973 19
HD9698.U52 T73 1985 ***NYPL [JSD 86-173]***

Om E.F. Iversen, John, 1954- Om EF . København , 1984. 143 p. : ISBN 87-412-3775-7 : LC Card 84-186203
HC241.2 .I84 1984

Om EF . Iversen, John, 1954- København , 1984. 143 p. : ISBN 87-412-3775-7 : LC Card 84-186203
HC241.2 .I84 1984

Om het behoud van een explosieve stad : werk en welvaart in en om Amsterdam 1961-1985 / P.E. de Hen ... [et al.]. Muiderberg : Coutinho, 1986. 298 p. : ill. ; 26 cm. Bibliography: p. 294-298. ISBN 90-6283-661-5 : LC Card 86-205071
1. Amsterdam (Netherlands) - Economic conditions - 1945-. 2. Amsterdam (Netherlands) - Industries. 3. Kamer van Koophandel en Fabrieken voor Amsterdam. I. Hen, Paul de.
HC328.A5 O4 1986

Om Kumar, 1944- Sites and services in urban housing in India / Om Kumar. New Delhi : Ess Ess Publications, 1987. xii, 86 p. : maps ; 22 cm. Spine title: Sites & services in urban housing in India. With special reference to the Madras Urban Development Project I. Bibliography: p. [82]-86. Includes index. ISBN 81-7000-026-2 : LC Card 87-900362 DDC 363.5/0954 19
1. Housing - India. 2. Housing - India - Location. I. Title. II. Title: Sites & services in urban housing in India.
HD7361.A3 O5 1987

Om kvindearbejdets igangværende udvikling og perspektiver, i relation til den teknologiske udvikling /. Vedel, Gitte. Roskilde , 1982. 103 leaves : LC Card 83-172895
HD6060.65.D4 V42 1982

Om lönearbete : en bok i arbetssociologi / Jan Ch. Karlsson (red) ... [et al.]. [Stockholm] : Norstedt, [1983] 260 p. : ill. ; 21 cm. Bibliography: p. 250-260. Includes index. ISBN 91-1-833281-1 : LC Card 84-165851
1. Industrial sociology - Sweden. I. Karlsson, Jan, 1948-.
HD6957.S8 O42 1983

Om Prakash, 1916- Economy and food in ancient India / Om Prakash. Delhi : Bharatiya Vidya Prakashan, 1987- v. <1- > ; 28 cm. Bibliography: v. 1, p. [161]-172. Includes index. CONTENTS. - pt. 1. Economy. ISBN 81-217-0027-2 : LC Card 87-902484 DDC 338.1/9/34 19
1. India - Economic conditions - To 1000. 2. Agriculture and state - India - History. 3. Food supply - India - History. I. Title.
HC434 .O45 1987

Ōmae, Ken'ichi, 1943- Beyond national borders : reflections on Japan and the world / Kenichi Ohmae. Homewood, Ill. : Dow Jones-Irwin, c1987. xi, 128 p. : ill. ; 24 cm. Includes bibliographical references. ISBN 1-556-23017-6 LC Card 86-72864 DDC 337.52 19
1. Japan - Foreign economic relations - United States. 2. United States - Foreign economic relations - Japan. 3. International economic relations. 4. Japan - Economic conditions - 1945-. 5. Communication in foreign trade. I. Title.
HF1602.15.U6 O4 1987

Omel′chenko, O. A. Chanturiia, V. K. (Vladimir Kapitonovich) Molodezh′ i udarnyĭ kommunisticheskiĭ trud . Moskva , 1981. 205 p. : LC Card 82-178361
HD6276.S592 C46 1981

Omfattning och erfarenheter : huvudrapport. Stockholm : Liber : Statens industriverk, [1984] 127 p. : ill. ; 25 cm. (Kommunal näringspolitik) SIND, 0346-5748 ; 1984:8 Bibliography: p. 117-119. ISBN 91-38-08319-1 LC Card 85-106802
1. Sweden - Industries. 2. Industrial promotion - Sweden. 3. Regional planning - Sweden. I. Sweden. Statens industriverk. II. Series.
HC375 .O39 1984

Omgeving, doelstellingen en organisatie : visies uit theorie en praktijk : aangeboden aan Prof. Dr. H.O. Goldschmidt, hoogleraar aan de Katholieke Hogeschool te Tilburg, op 24 april 1986, ter gelegenheid van zijn emeritaat / redactie, J.A.C. de Haan, J.A.M. Oonincx, P. Ribbers. Assen : Van Gorcum, 1986. viii, 464 p. : ill., 1 port. ; 24 cm. Includes bibliographies. ISBN 90-232-2208-3 : LC Card 86-182876
1. Corporations - Netherlands - Finance. 2. Organization. 3. Goldschmidt, H. O. I. Goldschmidt, H. O. II. Haan, J. A. C. de. III. Oonincx, J. A. M. IV. Ribbers, P.
HG4181 .O44 1986

The omnipresence of Walter Bagehot /. St. John-Stevas, Norman. Oxford [Oxfordshire] , New York , 1987. p. cm. ISBN 0-19-951554-9 (pbk.) : LC Card 87-13923 DDC 330/.092/4 19
HB103.B2 S29 1987

OMNIS 3 (COMPUTER PROGRAM)
Maller, Steven. Mastering Omnis 3 /. Blue Ridge Summit, PA , 1986. xi, 207 p. : ISBN 0-8306-0374-3 : LC Card 86-5758 DDC 658/.05574 19
HF5548.4.O55 M35 1986 ***NYPL [JSE 87-264]***

On edge . Goldberg, Ellen S. New York , 1987. ix, 116 p. ; ISBN 0-275-92604-4 (alk. paper) : LC Card 86-25324 DDC 332.1/5 19
HG3881 .G6142 1987

On-line database services markets. Norwalk, Conn., U. S.A. (6 Prowitt St., Norwalk 06855) : International Resource Development, c1984. v, 207 leaves ; 29 cm. (Report / International Resource Development Inc. . #591) "February 1984." LC Card 86-233709 DDC 381/.4502504/0973 19
1. Computer service industry. 2. Information services. 3. Market surveys. I. International Resource Development, inc. II. Series: Report / International Resource Development Inc. , #591.
HD9696.C62 O66 1984

On-line information . Walsh, Brendan P., 1955- Oxford, [Oxfordshire] , New York, NY, USA , 1987. xli, 327 p. : ISBN 0-631-15543-0 : LC Card 87-13154 DDC 025/.04/02465 19
HF5548.2 .W294 1987

On real wage unemployment /. Daly, D. J. (Donald James), 1922- Vancouver, B.C., Canada , 1986. vi, 117 p. : ISBN 0-88975-079-3 (pbk.) LC Card 87-142391 DDC 331.13/7971 19
HD4946.C3 D35 1986

On rolls the green revolution / [editor, Su Wenming ; contributors, Yao Lin ... et al. ; art, Zhang Oingsheng]. Beijing, China : Beijing Review : Distributed by China International Book Trading Corp., [1984] 142 p., [36] p. of plates : ill. ; 19 cm. (China today . 9) Colophon title in Chinese: Lü se ko ming. CONTENTS. - A word to our readers -- Exegesis of a revolution -- Flexible policy -- Rural poverty can be licked -- Science pays dividends -- The road to prosperity -- Greening the mountainous regions -- Reform of the managerial system -- China's rural economic policy -- The goal of modernized farming. LC Card 86-115054 DDC 338.1/0951 19
1. Agriculture - Economic aspects - China. 2. Rural development - China. 3. Green Revolution - China. 4. Agriculture and state - China. I. Su, Wenming. II. Yao, Lin. III. Title: Lü se ko ming. IV. Series. V. Series: China today (Peking, China) , 9.
HD2097 .O5 1984 ***NYPL [JLK 83-122 no.9]***

On some of the impediments to Irish manufacturing industry /. Monsell, William, 1812-1894. Dublin , 1865. 48 p. ; LC Card 85-666368
HC260.5 .M66x 1865

On some problems of mathematical economics. Nekotorye voprosy matematicheskoĭ ėkonomiki . Vil′nius , 1982. 90 p. ; LC Card 83-169081
HB135 .N45 1982

On the choice of optimal central bank currency baskets /. Nyberg, Peter. Åbo , 1982. 24 p. ;
NYPL [JLL 77-251 no. 181]

On the inside . McCann, Thomas P. Boston , c1987. p. cm. ISBN 0-933341-53-9 : LC Card 87-43040 DDC 338.7/634 19
HD9249.U6 M23 1987

On the line . Kahaner, Larry. New York, NY , 1987, c1986. 344 p., [8] p. of plates : ISBN 0-446-38550-6 (pbk.) LC Card 87-10561 DDC 384.6/065/73 19
HE8846.M375 K34 1987

On the problem of resource management in the Sudan /. Atta el Moula, Mutasim el Amin. [Khartoum] , 1985. 131 leaves : LC Card 86-980662 DDC 333.7/09624 19
HC835 .A85 1985

On the question of mechanisation of Mozambican agriculture today . Wuyts, Marc. [Maputo, Mozambique] , 1979. 22 p. : LC Card 83-207389
HD2129 .W893 1979

On the use of Ventcel-Freidlin estimates in approximating the probability of ruin /. Ruohonen, Matti. Vaasa , 1979. 27 p. : ISBN 951-683-103-6 (pbk.) LC Card 83-223364
HG8054.5 .R86 1979

On your own terms . Stechert, Kathryn B. [Sweet success.] New York , 1987, c1986. xvi, 314 p. ; ISBN 0-394-75301-1 (pbk.) : LC Card 86-40470 DDC 650.1/024042 19
HD6053 .S724 1987

Onado, Marco. I Conti finanziari dell'Emilia-Romagna /. [Bologna] , c1984. 157 p. : ISBN 88-15-00522-6 : LC Card 84-235593 DDC 332.1/0945/4 19
HG3089.E45 C66 1984 ***NYPL [JLE 86-3198]***

Onakomaiya, S. O. Transportation in Nigerian national development . Ibadan , c1981. xi, 602 p. : ISBN 978-18-1010-6 (pbk.) LC Card 82-196087 DDC 380.5/09669 19
HE287.7 .T72 1981 ***NYPL [Sc E 86-178]***

Az önálló vállalattá szervezés elméleti és módszertani megalapozása /. Palicz, András. Budapest , 1984. 81 p. : ISBN 963-02-3351-7 : LC Card 86-126838
HD70.H8 P35 1984

Once upon a time in ComputerLand . Littman, Jonathan, 1958- Tucson, AZ , c1987. xiii, 296 p., [8] p. of plates : ISBN 0-89586-502-5 : LC Card 87-3823 DDC 381/.4500416/0973 19
HD9696.C64 C655 1987

ONCHOCERCIASIS - GHANA - VOLTA RIVER REGION.
Ewusi, Kodwo. The development and resettlement of oncho-freed zones in the Volta River Basin of West Africa . [Legon, Ghana] [1985] 89 p. ; LC Card 87-127503 DDC 333.3/1/667 19
HD1022.Z8 V654 1985

ONCHOCERIASIS - BENIN - CASE STUDIES.
Ewusi, Kodwo. The development and resettlement of oncho-freed zones in the Volta River Basin of West Africa . [Legon, Ghana] [1985] 89 p. ; LC Card 87-127503 DDC 333.3/1/667 19
HD1022.Z8 V654 1985

ONCHOCERIASIS - BURKINA FASO - CASE STUDIES.
Ewusi, Kodwo. The development and resettlement of oncho-freed zones in the Volta River Basin of West Africa . [Legon, Ghana] [1985] 89 p. ; LC Card 87-127503 DDC 333.3/1/667 19
HD1022.Z8 V654 1985

ONCOLOGISTS - UNITED STATES - ATTITUDES.
Strategic marketing of oncology products /. Tustin, CA, U. S.A. (17722 Irvine Blvd., Tustin 92680) , c1987. 242 p. in various pagings : LC Card 87-402026 DDC 381/.45681761 19
HD9995.C353 U67 1987

Ondernemen en vernieuwen : hommage aan de kleine en middelgrote industrie naar aanleiding van 75 jaar Rijksnijverheidsdienst / redactie, J. Eekels (eindredactie), H.H.C.M. Christiaans, R.H. Kaasschieter. Delft, Netherlands : Delftse Universitaire Pers, 1985. 240 p. : ill. ; 24 cm. ISBN 90-6275-189-X LC Card 86-113900
1. Small business - Netherlands - Technological innovations - Case studies. 2. Netherlands - Industries - Technological innovations - Case studies. 3. Netherlands. Rijksnijverheidsdienst. I. Eekels, J. II. Christiaans, H. H. C. M. III. Kaasschieter, R. H. IV. Netherlands. Rijksnijverheidsdienst.
HD2346.N4 O53 1985

Ondernemende vrouwen /. Houweling, Marjolein. Amsterdam , c1985. 128 p. : ISBN 90-6834-018-2 : LC Card 86-166264
HD2346.N4 H68 1985

Ondernemingsstrategie, theorie en praktijk :

bundel opstellen aangeboden aan prof. dr. J. Kreiken ter gelegenheid van zijn afscheid als hoogleraar aan de Afdeling der Bedrijfskunde van de Technische Hogeschool Twente / onder redactie van J. Bilderbeek, J.M.L. Janssen, G.W.R. Vijge. Leiden : Stenfert Kroese, c1986. xi, 346 p. : ill., 1 port. ; 25 cm. "Lijst van intekenaars": [3] p. inserted. Includes bibliographies. Bibliography of works by J. Kreiken: p. [344]-346. ISBN 90-207-1424-4 : LC Card 86-199689
1. Corporate planning. 2. Corporate planning - Netherlands. 3. Kreiken, J., 1925-. I. Kreiken, J., 1925-. II. Bilderbeek, J. III. Janssen, J. M. L. (Johannes Marinus Lodevicus), 1918-. IV. Vijge, G. W. A., 1942-.
HD37.D8 O54 1986

Onderzoek naar werkgelegenheid, inkomen en de structuur van de stedelijke economie van Paramaribo : de informele en de formele sector in Paramaribo : onderzoeksontwerp / Instituut voor Economische en Sociaal Onderzoek. Paramaribo, Suriname : Faculteit der Sociaal-Economische Wetenschappen, Universiteit van Suriname, [1978] 69 leaves : ill. ; 30 cm. "Augustus 1978." LC Card 87-115836
1. Labor supply - Surinam - Paramaribo. 2. Paramaribo (Surinam) - Economic conditions. 3. Informal sector (Economics) - Surinam - Paramaribo. I. Universiteit van Suriname. Instituut voor Economisch en Sociaal Onderzoek.
HD5759.5.P37 O53 1978

Onderzoeksmemorandum .
(no. 17) Investeren in Nederland /. 's-Gravenhage [1986] 122 p. : LC Card 86-231212
HG5562 .I58 1986
(no. 23) Stoffel, R. A. Internationale vergelijking loonstructuur /. 's-Gravenhage [1986] 20 p. : LC Card 86-231311
HD5014 .S76 1986

The One Bancorp and Maine Savings Bank . Masterton, Robert R. New York , 1986, c1987. 22 p. : LC Card 87-60613 DDC 332.2/1/09741 19
HG2613.P794 M356 1987

One hundred and one ways to find an overseas job. Cantrell, Will. 101 ways to find an overseas job /. [Merrifield, VA.] [c1987] 1 v. (various pagings) ; ISBN 0-941541-00-2 (pbk.) LC Card 86-73093 DDC 650.1/4 19
HF5549.5.E45 C33 1987

One hundred one best performing companies in America. Paul, Ronald N. The 101 best performing companies in America /. Chicago, Ill. , c1986. vii, 382 p. ; ISBN 0-917253-39-6 : LC Card 86-4947 DDC 338.7/4/0973 19
HD2785 .P38 1986 ***NYPL [JLE 86-3151]***

One hundred one ways to cut your business insurance costs without sacrificing protection. McIntyre, William Stokes. 101 ways to cut your business insurance costs without sacrificing protection /. New York , c1988. viii, 190 p. : ISBN 0-07-045112-5 : LC Card 87-17255 DDC 368 19
HG8059 .M38 1988

One hundred one ways to find an overseas job. Cantrell, Will. 101 ways to find an overseas job /. [Merrifield, VA.] [c1987] 1 v. (various pagings) ; ISBN 0-941541-00-2 (pbk.) LC Card 86-73093 DDC 650.1/4 19
HF5549.5.E45 C33 1987

One hundred predictions for the baby boom. Russell, Cheryl, 1953- 100 predictions for the baby boom . New York , c1987. 249 p. ; ISBN 0-306-42527-0 LC Card 87-2443 DDC 338.5/443/0973 19
HC106.8 .R87 1987

One hundred words about working. 100 words about working /. San Diego , c1988. p. cm. ISBN 0-15-200553-6 LC Card 87-8363 DDC 331.7/02 19
HF5382 .A13 1988

The one minute maniac /. Book, Jeffrey. Kansas City, Mo. , c1987. 140 p. : ISBN 0-8362-1260-6 (pbk.) : LC Card 87-914 DDC 658.4/093 19
HD69.T54 B66 1987

The one minute organizing secret . Parikh, Girish, 1934- Chicago, IL , c1986. 60, 2 p. ; ISBN 0-932888-37-2 (pbk.) : LC Card 85-62926 DDC 650.1 19
HF5736 .P34 1986

One-on-one with Andy Grove . Grove, Andrew S. New York , c1987. 235 p. ; ISBN 0-399-13250-3 : LC Card 86-30483 DDC 650.1/3 19
HF5548.83 .G77 1987

"One smart cookie" . Fields, Debbi. New York , c1987. 173 p., [16] p. of plates : ISBN 0-671-61838-5 LC Card 87-15172 DDC 338.7/6647525/0924 B 19
HD9058.C65 F544 1987

One thousand five hundred ninety-four Evans Drive, Southwest. Brown, Edmund D. 1594 Evans Drive, S.W. . Atlanta, Ga. (1594 Evans Dr., S.W., Atlanta 30310) , c1983. 213 p. : LC Card 82-62570 DDC 338.7/62193 19
HD9529.S294 A842 1983
NYPL [JLF 86-1803]

One thousand one advertising cuts from the twenties and thirties. 1,001 advertising cuts from the twenties and thirties /. New York , 1987. 103 p. : ISBN 0-486-25490-9 (pbk.) LC Card 87-15546 DDC 659.13/2/0973 19
HF5813.U6 A525 1987

One-two-three, the complete reference. Campbell, Mary V. 1-2-3, the complete reference /. Berkeley, Calif. , c1986. xii, 892 p. : ISBN 0-07-881005-1 (pbk.) : LC Card 86-230048 DDC 005.36/9 19
HF5548.4.L67 C35 1986

O'Neil, Mike. Burn, Janice. Information analysis /. London , 1987. x, 260 p. : ISBN 0-948825-50-2 (pbk.) : LC Card 87-166130 DDC 658.4/038 19
HD30.35 .B87 1987

O'Neill, Ken, 1944- Small business development . Aldershot, Hampshire , Brookfield, Vt., U. S.A. , c1987. xix, 276 p. : ISBN 0-566-05382-9 : LC Card 87-22386 DDC 338.6/42/0941 19
HD2346.G7 S58 1987

O'Neill, Richard P. An Economic analysis of natural gas resources and supply /. Washington, D.C. [1986] xx, 179 p. : LC Card 86-603066 DDC 338.2/7285/0973 19
HD9581.U5 E26 1986

Az önelszámoló rendszer alkalmazásának, a kistermelők integrálásának és a kihelyezett részlegeknek a hatása a mezőgazdasági vállalatok szervezeti felépitésére, s annak müködésére /. Pilling, András. Budapest , 1985. 89 p. ; ISBN 963-491-206-0 LC Card 86-196755
HD1492.H8 P55 1985

Onikienko, V. V. (Vladimir Vasil'evich) Vosproizvodstvo trudovykh resursov /. Kiev , 1984. 177, [3] p. ; LC Card 86-189052
HD5797.U37 V67 1984

Onimode, Bade. MNC's in Nigeria : multinational corporations in Nigeria / Bade Onimode, John Ohiorhenuan, Tunde Adeniran. Ibadan : L. Shyraden Nigeria, 1983. ix, 144 p. ; 21 cm. Bibliography: p. 137-144. ISBN 978-231-800-0 (pbk.) LC Card 86-195403 DDC 338.8/88669 19
1. International business enterprises - Nigeria. 2. Corporations, Foreign - Nigeria. 3. Investments, Foreign - Nigeria. I. Ohiorhenuan, John F. E. II. Adeniran, Tunde. III. Title. IV. Title: Multinational corporations in Nigeria.
HD2928 .O55 1983

ONION INDUSTRY - IDAHO.
Idaho Oregon Onion Promotion Committee. Sweet Spanish onion . Temple, Me. (Santa Claus Lake, Temple 04984) , 1986. ii, 46, 27 leaves : LC Card 87-120958 DDC 381/.41525/0973 19
HD9235.O62 U34 1986

ONION INDUSTRY - OREGON.
Idaho Oregon Onion Promotion Committee. Sweet Spanish onion . Temple, Me. (Santa Claus Lake, Temple 04984) , 1986. ii, 46, 27 leaves : LC Card 87-120958 DDC 381/.41525/0973 19
HD9235.O62 U34 1986

ONION INDUSTRY - UNITED STATES.
Idaho Oregon Onion Promotion Committee. Sweet Spanish onion . Temple, Me. (Santa Claus Lake, Temple 04984) , 1986. ii, 46, 27 leaves : LC Card 87-120958 DDC 381/.41525/0973 19
HD9235.O62 U34 1986

Onishchenko, Alekseĭ Moiseevich. Modelirovanie i optimizatsionnye raschety . Kiev , 1986. 222, [2] p. : LC Card 86-233713
HD9015.S652 M62 1986

Onken, Werner, 1953- Perspektiven einer ökologischen Ökonomie /. Hann. [i.e. Hannoversch] Münden , c1983. 91 p. ; ISBN 3-87998-402-6 : LC Card 83-180506
HC290.5.E5 P47 1983

Online business databases 1987. Staud, Josef L. Online Wirtschaftsdatenbanken 1987 . Frankfurt am Main , New York , 1987. 2 v. (953 p.) : ISBN 3-8204-9457-X LC Card 87-401300 DDC 025/.0633/025 19
HF5548.2 .S7737 1987

The Online commercial database business / Patricia Munson, project analyst. Stamford, Conn., U. S.A. : Business Communications Co., c1985. xxi, 230 leaves : ill. ; 29 cm. (Business opportunity report . G-068) ISBN 0-89336-320-0 (pbk.) LC Card 87-40457 DDC 381/.4500574/0973 19
1. Data base industry - United States. 2. Computer networks - United States. 3. Data transmission equipment industry - United States. I. Munson, Patricia. II. Business Communications Co. III. Series.
HD9696.D363 U66 1985

Online databases in the securities and financial markets. New York, N.Y. : Cuadra/Elsevier, c1987. xxii, 322 p. ; 26 cm. "Subset of ... January (main) and April (supplement) 1987 issues of the Cuadra/Elsevier Directory of online databases, plus major changes identified through June 1987"--Pref. Includes indexes. ISBN 0-444-01276-1 (pbk.) LC Card 87-19954 DDC 025/.0633/0025 19
1. Finance - Data bases - Directories. 2. Securities - Data bases - Directories. 3. Business - Data bases - Directories. I. Directory of online data bases.
HG174 .O44 1987

Online-Kostenrechnung für die CIM-Planung . Knoop, Jens. Berlin , c1986. 242 p. : ISBN 3-503-02569-3 LC Card 86-227596
HF5686.C8 K5835 1986

Online Wirtschaftsdatenbanken 1987 . Staud, Josef L. Frankfurt am Main , New York , 1987. 2 v. (953 p.) : ISBN 3-8204-9457-X LC Card 87-401300 DDC 025/.0633/025 19
HF5548.2 .S7737 1987

The only other investment guide you'll ever need /. Tobias, Andrew P. New York , c1987. 271 p. ; ISBN 0-671-64166-2 LC Card 87-20494 DDC 332.6/78 19
HG4521 .T6 1987

Ontario.
Foodland preservation : a proposed policy statement of the Government of Ontario issued for public review. Toronto, Ont. : Ministry of Agriculture & Food, Foodland Preservation Branch : Ministry of Municipal Affairs, Office of Local Planning Policy, [1986?] 16 p. : maps ; 30 cm. Cover title. LC Card 86-226909 DDC 333.76/16/09713 19
1. Land use, Rural - Government policy - Ontario. 2. Agricultural conservation - Government policy - Ontario. I. Ontario. Ministry of Agriculture and Food. II. Ontario. Ministry of Municipal Affairs. III. Title.
HD319.O5 O5 1986

Ontario Agricultural Commission. Canadian farming . Toronto , 1881. 432 p., [4] folded leaves of plates : LC Card 85-666092
HD1783 .C3x 1881

Ontario. Agriculture and Food, Ministry of. see **Ontario. Ministry of Agriculture and Food.**

Ontario. Community Renewal Branch. Peter Barnard Associates. An evaluation of the Ontario Home Renewal Program . [Toronto] , 1976. x, 43, [28] p. : LC Card 85-192287
HD7305.O6 P47 1976

Ontario. Consultation Panel on Pay Equity. Report of the Consultation Panel on Pay Equity. Toronto, Ont., Canada [1986] 123 p. ; ISBN 0-7729-1657-8 (pbk.) LC Card 87-117472 DDC 331.2/1 19
HD6061.2.C22 O577 1986

ONTARIO - ECONOMIC CONDITIONS.
Economic and fiscal review . Toronto, Ont. [1986] i, 89 p. : ISBN 0-7729-1950-X (pbk.) LC Card 87-169450 DDC 330.9713/04 19
HJ2460.O5 E28 1986

ONTARIO - ECONOMIC CONDITIONS - STATISTICS.
Morin, André, analyste en rémunération.

Analyse de l'évolution des principaux indicateurs économiques au Québec, en Ontario, au Canada et aux Etats-Unis . [Québec] [1982] 209 p. ; ISBN 2-551-04641-6 LC Card 83-103355
HC117.Q4 M66 1982

Ontario. Interministerial Task Force on Agricultural Finance. Report of the Interministerial Task Force on Agricultural Finance. [Toronto, Ont. : Ministry of Agriculture and Food, 1986] vii, 65, [42] p. : ill. ; 31 cm. "May 1986." Cover title. Includes bibliographical references. LC Card 87-127476 DDC 332.7/1/09713 19
1. Agriculture - Ontario - Finance. 2. Agricultural credit - Ontario. I. Ontario. Ministry of Agriculture and Food. II. Title.
HD1790.O6 O573 1986

Ontario. Legislative Assembly. Select Committee on Highway Safety. Select Committee on Highway Safety : final report / Fred Young, chairman. [Ontario, Canada] : The Committee, [1977] 1 v. in various pagings : ill. ; 28 cm. Cover title. LC Card 85-184813
1. Traffic safety - Ontario. I. Young, Fred. II. Title.
HE5614.5.C2 O5 1977

Ontario. Ministry of Agriculture and Food. Ontario. Foodland preservation . Toronto, Ont. [1986?] 16 p. : LC Card 86-226909 DDC 333.76/16/09713 19
HD319.O5 O5 1986

Ontario. Interministerial Task Force on Agricultural Finance. Report of the Interministerial Task Force on Agricultural Finance. [Toronto, Ont. , 1986] vii, 65, [42] p. : LC Card 87-127476 DDC 332.7/1/09713 19
HD1790.O6 O573 1986

Ontario. Ministry of Labour. Research Branch. Historical trends in job vacancies by major occupation groups . Toronto, Ont. [1976] 26 p. : LC Card 82-213963 DDC 331.2 s 331.12/4/09713021 19
HD5729.O6 E46 no. 16

Ontario. Ministry of Municipal Affairs. Ontario. Foodland preservation . Toronto, Ont. [1986?] 16 p. : LC Card 86-226909 DDC 333.76/16/09713 19
HD319.O5 O5 1986

Ontario. Ministry of Treasury and Economics. Economic and fiscal review . Toronto, Ont. [1986] i, 89 p. : ISBN 0-7729-1950-X (pbk.) LC Card 87-169450 DDC 330.9713/04 19
HJ2460.O5 E28 1986

Ontario study of the service sector . [Toronto] [1986] 479 p. : ISBN 0-7729-2049-4 LC Card 87-136763 DDC 338.4/7/0009713 19
HD9985.C33 O67 1986

ONTARIO - OCCUPATIONS - STATISTICS. Historical trends in job vacancies by major occupation groups . Toronto, Ont. [1976] 26 p. : LC Card 82-213963 DDC 331.2 s 331.12/4/09713021 19
HD5729.O6 E46 no. 16

ONTARIO - OFFICIALS AND EMPLOYEES - SALARIES, ETC. - ECONOMETRIC MODELS.
Abbott, Michael G. Alternative estimates of union-nonunion and public-private wage differentials in Ontario, 1981 /. Kingston, Ont., Canada , 1987. ii, 47 p. ; ISBN 0-88886-166-4 (pbk.) LC Card 87-170767 DDC 331.2/2/09713 19
HD4980.O5 A64 1987

Ontario study of the service sector : background papers. [Toronto] : Ministry of Treasury and Economics, [1986] 479 p. : ill. ; 30 cm. "December 1986." Includes bibliographical references. ISBN 0-7729-2049-4 LC Card 87-136763 DDC 338.4/7/0009713 19
1. Service industries - Ontario. I. Ontario. Ministry of Treasury and Economics.
HD9985.C33 O67 1986

Ontario's proposals for the Canadian securities industry /. Courchene, Thomas J. Toronto , Scarborough, Ont. [1986] 39 p. : ISBN 0-88806-137-4 (pbk.) LC Card 87-133168 DDC 332.63/2 19
HG5158 .C68 1986

Ontiveros, Suzanne R. Corporate social responsibility . Santa Barbara, Calif. , c1986. xv, 229 p. ; ISBN 0-87436-469-8 (alk. paper) : LC Card 86-3416 DDC 658.4/08 19
HD60 .C693 1986 ***NYPL [JLE 86-3089]***

Ontleding van genoteerde maatskappye JEB industriële afdelingsgemiddeldes : gelees te word saam met verslag A 5 A (H), 1974-1983 = Analysis of quoted companies JSE industrial sectional averages : to be read together with report A 5 E (R), 1974-1983. Pretoria : Buro vir Finansiële Analise, Universiteit van Pretoria, 1984. iv, 163 p. ; 26 cm. (Verslag / Buro vir Finansiële Analise, Universiteit van Pretoria = Report / Bureau of Financial Analysis, University of Pretoria . no. C75) ISBN 0-86979-588-0 LC Card 85-156278
1. Corporations - South Africa. I. University of Pretoria. Bureau of Financial Analysis. II. Title: Analysis of quoted companies JSE industrial sectional averages.
HD2922 .O57 1984

De ontwikkeling van de paprikateelt . Goudswaard, A. Den Haag [1986] 60 p. : LC Card 86-233094
HD9211.P353 N424 1986

Onufriev, ÎU. G. Prodovol'stvennaîa problema i sel'skoe khoziaîstvo stran Latinskoĭ Ameriki /. Moskva , 1981. 311 p. ; LC Card 82-108167
HD9014.L32 P76 1981

Onunju beshillikdă Sovet Azărbaĭjanynyn igtisadi vă sosial inkishafy /. Sămădzadă, Z. (Ziîad) Baky , 1981. 237 p. ; LC Card 82-153126
HC337.A9 S32 1981

Oommen, M. A., 1932- Issues in teaching of economics in Indian universities /. New Delhi , c1987. vii, 145 p. ; ISBN 81-204-0203-0 : LC Card 87-901784 DDC 330/.07/1154 19
HB74.9.I4 I88 1987

Ooninex, J. A. M. Omgeving, doelstellingen en organisatie . Assen , 1986. viii, 464 p. : ISBN 90-232-2208-3 : LC Card 86-182876
HG4181 .O44 1986

Oost-Indische Compagnie. see **Nederlandsche Oost-Indische Compagnie.**

Oosterhof, Hanneke. Henkes, Barbara. Kaatje, ben je boven? . Nijmegen , c1985. 192 p. : ISBN 90-6168-242-8 : LC Card 85-237937
HD6072.2.N4 H46 1985

Oostindische vereenigde maatschappij. see **Nederlandsche Oost-Indische Compagnie.**

Op arbeid bezuinigd? . Bakker, G. J. 's-Gravenhage , 1986. 116 p. ; ISBN 90-12-05321-8 LC Card 87-108889
HJ9507 .B35 1986

Op een beteren weg : schetsen uit de geschiedenis van de arbeidersbeweging aangeboden aan mevrouw dr. J.M. Welcker / redactie, Mies Campfens, Margreet Schrevel, Fritjof Tichelman. Amsterdam : Van Gennep, 1985. 239 p. : ill. ; 22 cm. (Nederlandse arbeidersbeweging. 16) Bibliography of works by J.M. Welcker: p. [223]-227. Includes bibliographies and index. ISBN 90-6012-654-8 : LC Card 85-236523
1. Welcker, J. M. 2. Labor and laboring classes - Netherlands - History - 1849-. 3. Socialism - Netherlands - History - 1849-. I. Welcker, J. M. II. Campfens, Mies. III. Schrevel, Margreet, 1951-. IV. Tichelman, Fritjof.
HD8516 .O6 1985 ***NYPL [JLD 86-3427]***

Op het spoor van de Körver . Bläsing, J. F. E. (Joachim F. E.), 1940- Leiden , 1986. xvi, 396 p. : ISBN 90-247-8065-9 : LC Card 86-214829
HD9052.N44 H453 1986

La Opción preferencial por los pobres : de la teoría a la práctica / Marcelo Astoreca ... [et al.] ; editores, Raúl Urzúa F., Patricio Dooner D. [Santiago] : CISOC Bellarmino, [1987] 360 p. : ill. ; 21 cm. Papers from the Seminario "La Opción Preferencial por los Pobres: de la Teoría a la Práctica," held Sept. 1986, and sponsored by the Centro de Investigaciones Socioculturales Roberto Bellarmino. Includes bibliographies. LC Card 87-403060 DDC 362.5/098 19
1. Poor - Latin America - Congresses. 2. Poor - Government policy - Latin America - Congresses. I. Astoreca, Marcelo. II. Urzúa, Raúl. III. Dooner, Patricio. IV. CISOC Bellarmino. V. Seminario "La Opción Preferencial por los Pobres: de la Teoría a la Práctica" (1986 : Santiago, Chile?).
HC130.P6 O63 1987

Las opciones de política económica en Uruguay /. Bensión, Alberto. Montevideo, Uruguay , 1986. 106 p., [48] leaves ; LC Card 87-121223 DDC 338.9895 19
HC232 .B44 1986

Opciones de política económica, 1979-1982 /. Rizzo, Sócrates. México, D.F. [1983] 133 p. : LC Card 86-205260 DDC 338.972 19
HC135 .R44 1983

Opciones para la evaluación de las empresas públicas /. Kelly de Escobar, Janet. Caracas , c1985. 36 p. ; ISBN 980-217-008-9 LC Card 86-201812
HD62.35 .K45 1985

Opciones y experiencias . (no. 4) Dubly, Alain. La organización campesina . Quito, Ecuador , 1985. 37 p. : LC Card 87-404544 DDC 322/.2/09866 19
HD1531.E2 D83 1985

Opções de política econômica /. Coelho, Carlos Nayro de Azevedo. Brasília , 1986. 137 p. ; LC Card 87-403318 DDC 338.981 19
HC187 .C565 1986

Opções energéticas : memória da terceira sessão e trabalhos, 1979-1982 / Programa de Contribuições ao Estudo de Problemas Mineiros. Belo Horizonte, MG : Impr. Oficial de Minas Gerais, 1983. 328 p., [30] leaves of plates : ill. ; 25 cm. LC Card 83-205480
1. Power resources - Brazil - Congresses. 2. Renewable energy sources - Brazil - Congresses. I. Programa de Contribuições ao Estudo de Problemas Mineiros (Minas Gerais, Brazil).
HD9502.B72 O63 1983

OPEC. see **Organization of Petroleum Exporting Countries.**

OPEC aid and the challenge of development / edited by Abdelkader Benamara and Sam Ifeagwu. London ; New York : Croom Helm, c1987. x, 130 p. ; 23 cm. "Proceedings of the seminar to mark the 10th anniversary of the OPEC Fund for International Development, held in Vienna, Austria, 23 June 1986"--Half t.p. Published in the USA in association with Methuen, Inc., New York, NY. Bibliography: p. 100. ISBN 0-7099-1969-7 LC Card 87-9160 DDC 338.91/09172/4 19
1. OPEC Fund for International Development - Congresses. 2. Economic assistance - Developing countries - Congresses. I. Abdelkader, Benamara. II. Ifeagwu, Sam. III. OPEC Fund for International Development.
HC60 .O5754 1987

OPEC Fund for International Development. OPEC aid and the challenge of development /. London , New York , c1987. x, 130 p. ; ISBN 0-7099-1969-7 LC Card 87-9160 DDC 338.91/09172/4 19
HC60 .O5754 1987

OPEC FUND FOR INTERNATIONAL DEVELOPMENT - CONGRESSES. OPEC aid and the challenge of development /. London , New York , c1987. x, 130 p. ; ISBN 0-7099-1969-7 LC Card 87-9160 DDC 338.91/09172/4 19
HC60 .O5754 1987

OPEC, the rise and fall of an exclusive club /. Ghanem, Shukri Mohammed. London ; New York : x, 233 p. ; ISBN 0-7103-0175-8 LC Card 87-131574 DDC 341.7/5472282 19
HD9560.1.O66 G55 1986

OPEC's investments and the international financial system /. Mattione, Richard P. Washington, D.C. , c1985. xi, 201 p. ; ISBN 0-8157-5510-4 : LC Card 84-23242 DDC 332.6/7314 19
HG4538 .M38 1985 ***NYPL [JLE 86-3698]***

OPEN AND CLOSED SHOP - GREAT BRITAIN.
Dunn, Stephen. The closed shop in British industry /. London , 1984. xii, 181 p. ; ISBN 0-333-26202-6 LC Card 87-673181
HD6488.2.G7 D86x 1984

OPEN AND CLOSED SHOP - LAW AND LEGISLATION - UNITED STATES.
Northrup, Herbert Roof, 1918- Doublebreasted operations and pre-hire agreements in construction . Philadelphia, Penn., USA , c1987. viii, 127 p. : ISBN 0-89546-067-X (pbk.) LC Card 87-81475 DDC 331.88/92 19
HD9715.U52 N67 1984 Suppl.

OPEN AND CLOSED SHOP - RELIGIOUS ASPECTS - CATHOLIC CHURCH.
McLean, Edward B. Roman Catholicism and

the right to work /. Lanham , c1985. ix, 175 p. ; ISBN 0-8191-5009-6 (alk. paper) : LC Card 85-20379 DDC 261.8/5 19
HD6338 .M436 1985 NYPL [JLD 86-2803]

OPEN AND CLOSED SHOP - UNITED STATES.
McLean, Edward B. Roman Catholicism and the right to work /. Lanham , c1985. ix, 175 p. ; ISBN 0-8191-5009-6 (alk. paper) : LC Card 85-20379 DDC 261.8/5 19
HD6338 .M436 1985 NYPL [JLD 86-2803]

Northrup, Herbert Roof, 1918- Doublebreasted operations and pre-hire agreements in construction . Philadelphia, Penn., USA , c1987. viii, 127 p. : ISBN 0-89546-067-X (pbk.) LC Card 87-81475 DDC 331.88/92 19
HD9715.U52 N67 1984 Suppl.

Northrup, Herbert Roof, 1918- Open shop construction revisited /. Philadelphia, Pa., U. S.A. , c1984. xxxv, 674 p. : ISBN 0-89546-047-5 : LC Card 84-48502 DDC 331.88/92 19
HD9715.U52 N67 1984 NYPL [TB (Pennsylvania. University. Wharton School of Finance and Commerce. Industrial Research Unit. Industrial Research Unit Study. no. 62)]

Open file report (United States. Bureau of Mines) .
(86-52) Financing foreign development of non-fuel mineral resources . [Washington, D.C.] [1986] 308 p. : LC Card 86-602175 DDC 332.1/5 19
HD9506.D452 F56 1986

The Open policy at work / [editor, Su Wenming]. Beijing, China : Beijing Review Publications : Distributed by China International Book Trading Corp. (Guoji Shudian), [1985] 281 p. ; 19 cm. (China today . 10) Colophon and spine title: Chung-kuo tui wai ching chi kuan hsi erh shih liu t'iao. LC Card 86-219666 DDC 337.51 19
1. China - Foreign economic relations. 2. Investments, Foreign - China. 3. Joint ventures - China. 4. China - Commerce. I. Su, Wenming. II. Title: Chung-kuo tui wai ching chi kuan hsi erh shih liu t'iao. III. Series.
HF1604 .O63 1985

Open-range management and property rights in pastoral Africa . Behnke, Roy H., 1947- London [1985] 29 p. : LC Card 86-209817 DDC 333.2 19
HD977.Z63 B44 1985

Open road . Patton, Phil. New York , c1986. 304 p. : ISBN 0-671-53021-6 : LC Card 86-1832 DDC 388.1/0973 19
HE355 .P38 1986 NYPL [JLE 86-2812]

OPEN SEA (MARE LIBERUM) see **FREEDOM OF THE SEAS.**

Open shop construction revisited /. Northrup, Herbert Roof, 1918- Philadelphia, Pa., U. S.A. , c1984. xxxv, 674 p. : ISBN 0-89546-047-5 : LC Card 84-48502 DDC 331.88/92 19
HD9715.U52 N67 1984 NYPL [TB (Pennsylvania. University. Wharton School of Finance and Commerce. Industrial Research Unit. Industrial Research Unit Study. no. 62)]

Open the box . Root, Jane. London , 1986. 126 p. : ISBN 0-906890-78-0 (pbk.) : LC Card 86-206072 DDC 302.2/345/0941 19
HE8700.9.G7 R66 1986

Open University Press. Developing local economic strategies . Milton Keynes [England] , Philadelphia , 1987. p. cm. ISBN 0-335-15522-7 LC Card 87-22681 DDC 338.941 19
HC256.6 .D48 1987

Openshaw, Stan. Nuclear power : siting and safety / Stan Openshaw. London ; Boston : Routledge & K. Paul, 1986. xiv, 348 p. : ill., maps ; 23 cm. Includes index. Bibliography: p. 325-337. ISBN 0-7102-0183-4 : LC Card 85-8202 DDC 363.1/79 19
1. Nuclear power plants - Location. 2. Nuclear power plants - Safety measures. I. Title.
TK9153 .O64 1986 NYPL [JSD 87-128]

Operai e scelte politiche : il caso delle zone bianche a economia diffusa del Veneto / F. Anderlini ... [et al.] ; a cura di Fausto Anderlini e Cesco Chinello ; introduzione di Umberto Curi ; con 45 fotografie di Uliano Lucas. Milano, Italy : F. Angeli, c1986. 267 p., 45 p. of plates : ports. ; 22 cm. Includes bibliographical references. LC Card 86-169148
1. Labor and laboring classes - Italy - Veneto - Attitudes. 2. Party affiliation - Italy - Veneto. I. Anderlini, Fausto. II. Chinello, Cesco.
HD8439.V462 O64 1986

Les opérateurs français du commerce international agro-alimentaire /. Pezet, P. (Pierre) Paris , c1984. 85 p. : ISBN 2-279-52812-6 LC Card 85-136648 DDC 382/.456413/00944 19
HD9012.5 .P43 1984

The operating executive's guide to profit planning tools and techniques /. Woelfel, Charles J. Chicago, Ill. , c1986. ix, 199 p. : ISBN 0-917253-24-8 : LC Card 86-3222 DDC 658.1/55 19
HF5635 .W848 1986 NYPL [JLE 86-3007]

Operating results of independent supermarkets, 1984. Washington, D.C. (1750 K St., N.W., Washington 20006) : Research Dept., Food Marketing Institute, c1985. 137 p. : ill. ; 28 cm. LC Card 86-218675 DDC 381/.456413/00973 19
1. Supermarkets - United States - Finance - Statistics. 2. Grocery trade - United States - Finance - Statistics. I. Food Marketing Institute. Research Dept.
HF5469.23.U62 O643 1985

Operating results of independent supermarkets, 1985. Washington, D.C. (1750 K St., Washington 20006) : Research Dept., Food Marketing Institute, c1986. ix, 141 p. : ill. ; 28 cm. LC Card 86-225218 DDC 381/.456413/00973021 19
1. Supermarkets - United States - Statistics. 2. Grocery trade - United States - Statistics. I. Food Marketing Institute. Research Dept.
HF5469.23.U62 O64 1986

OPERATING STATEMENTS. see **FINANCIAL STATEMENTS.**

Operation Barga and land reforms . Ghosh, Tushar Kanti. Delhi , New Delhi, India , 1986. vii, 200 p. ; ISBN 81-7018-315-4 : LC Card 86-900505 DDC 333.3/1/54 19
HD1478.I5 G48 1986 NYPL [JLD 86-4347]

OPERATIONAL ANALYSIS. see **OPERATIONS RESEARCH.**

Operational and geometric evaluation of exclusive truck lanes /. Mason, John M. (John Michael), 1950- College Station, Tex. , Springfield, Va. [1986] vii, 156 p. : LC Card 86-622239 DDC 380.5 s 388.3/14 19
HE203 .T43 no. 331-3F HE356.T4

Operational auditing. Kowalczyk, David S., 1946- Cadmus' operational auditing /. New York , c1987. x, 422 p. ; ISBN 0-471-82660-X LC Card 87-23267 DDC 657/.458 19
HF5668.25 .K696 1987

OPERATIONAL RESEARCH. see **OPERATIONS RESEARCH.**

Operationalisierung des Unternehmenszieles Mitgliederförderung /. Bänsch, Axel. Göttingen , c1983. xv, 245 p. ; ISBN 3-525-12750-2 LC Card 83-199427
HD3498 .B35 1983

Operationalisierung des Unternehmenszieles, Mitgliederförderung /. Bänsch, Axel. Göttingen , 1983. xv, 245 p. ; ISBN 3-525-12750-2 *NYPL [JLE 86-1770]*

Operations report (Mortgage Bankers Association of America) .
(no. 8) Income and cost for origination and servicing of 1 to 4 unit residential loans, 1985. Washington, D.C. (1125 15th St., N.W., Washington 20005-2766) , c1986. 32 p. ; LC Card 87-106156 DDC 332.3/2/0973021 19
HG2040.5.U5 I535 1986

OPERATIONS RESEARCH - ADDRESSES, ESSAYS, LECTURES.
Der Praktische Nutzen empirischer Forschung /. Tübingen , 1981. viii, 324 p. ; ISBN 3-16-344392-3 : LC Card 81-197515 DDC 658.4/03 19
HD30.4 .P7 1981 NYPL [JLE 86-1360]

OPERATIONS RESEARCH - CONGRESSES.
IIASA (International Institute for Applied Systems Analysis) Workshop on Nondifferentiable Optimization (1984 : Sopron, Hungary) Nondifferentiable optimization . Berlin , New York , 1985. vi, 349 p. : ISBN 0-387-15979-7 (U. S.) LC Card 85-25029 DDC 658.4/03/4 19
T57.6 .I46 1984 NYPL [JLM 72-289 no.255]

OPERATIONS RESEARCH - DATA PROCESSING.
Mole, R. H. (Richard H.) BASIC business analysis and operations research /. London , Boston , 1987. 136 p. : ISBN 0-408-01590-X (pbk.) : LC Card 86-26398 DDC 658.4/034/0285526 19
HD30.25 .M66 1987

Operativnaia frakhtovaia deiatel'nost' na morskom transporte /. Rakhovetskiĭ, A. N. (Anatoliĭ Nikolaevich) Moskva , 1986. 159 p. : LC Card 86-115637
HE597.S615 R36 1986

Opie, John, 1934- The law of the land : two hundred years of American farmland policy / John Opie. Lincoln : University of Nebraska Press, c1987. xxi, 231 p. : maps ; 24 cm. Bibliography: p. [201]-223. Includes index. ISBN 0-8032-3553-4 (alk. paper) LC Card 86-30860 DDC 338.1/873 19
1. Agriculture and state - United States - History. I. Title.
HD1761 .O65 1987

OPINION, PUBLIC. see **PUBLIC OPINION.**

Opinion Research Corporation (U. S.). Financial Services Group. How consumers view credit unions . New York, NY (1 Penn Plaza, Suite 1631, New York 10119) , c1986. 37, 7 leaves, [166] p. ; LC Card 87-111937 DDC 334/.22/0973 19
HG2037 .H68 1986

Opitz, Otto.
Die EDV als Wettbewerbsinstrument des Handels / Otto Opitz, Leo Schubert. Augsburg : Institut für Statistik und Mathematische Wirtschaftstheorie der Universität Augsburg, [1986] 37 leaves : ill. ; 30 cm. (Arbeitspapiere zur mathematischen Wirtschaftsforschung . Heft 85) Bibliography: leaf 37. LC Card 87-407366 DDC 650/.028/5416 19
1. Business - Data processing. I. Schubert, Leo. II. Title.
HF5548.2 .O656 1986

Zur Analyse des Personal Computer Marktes 1985 : Fragen der Datengewinnung und Datenauswertung / Otto Opitz, Jürgen Hansohm, Hermann Locarek. Augsburg : Institut für Statistik und Mathematische Wirtschaftstheorie der Universität Augsburg, [1986] 35 leaves : ill. ; 30 cm. (Arbeitspapiere zur mathematischen Wirtschaftsforschung . Heft 84) Bibliography: leaf 35. LC Card 87-407365 DDC 380.1/4500416 19
1. Computer industry. 2. Microcomputers. I. Hansohm, Jürgen. II. Locarek, Hermann. III. Title.
HD9696.C62 O664 1986

Oplata truda v sel'skom khoziaĭstve . Sazonov, S. N. (Sergeĭ Nikolaevich) Moskva , 1984. 268 p. ; LC Card 84-244595
HD4966.A292 S6574 1984

OPOLE (POLAND : VOIVODESHIP) - INDUSTRIES - HISTORY.
Lis, Michał. Odbudowa podstaw gospodarki Śląska Opolskiego na przykładzie przemysłu, 1945-1949 /. [Opole] , 1978. 254 p. : LC Card 81-201084
HC340.Z7 O665 1978

Oposição Sindical Metalúrgica (São Paulo, Brazil) Comissão de fábrica . Petrópolis , 1981. 60 p. ; LC Card 86-190732
HD5660.B7 C66 1981

Oppe først og sist i seng . Avdem, Anna Jorunn, 1952- Oslo , 1985. 190 p. : ISBN 82-00-07512-5 LC Card 86-175305
HD8039.H842 N82 1985

Oppen, Maria. Informationstechnologie im Dienstleistungsbereich . Berlin , c1985. 258 p. : ISBN 3-924859-15-9 : LC Card 86-220033 DDC 338.4/561 19
HD9980.5 .I54 1985

Oppenheim, Eve.
Local area networks . Stamford, Conn., U. S.A. , c1986. xvi, 186 leaves : ISBN 0-89336-438-X (pbk.) LC Card 87-404428 DDC 381/.4500468/0973 19
HD9696.C63 U52253 1986

Packet switching equipment markets /.

Stamford, Conn., U. S.A. , c1985. v, 205 leaves : ISBN 0-89336-465-7 (pbk.) LC Card 87-403884 DDC 381/.456213878 19
HD9696.T443 U556 1985

Voice compression technology . Stamford, Conn., U. S.A. , c1985. xii, 146 leaves ; ISBN 0-89336-430-4 (soft) LC Card 87-165256 DDC 380.1/45621389 19
HD9696.T442 V65 1985

Oppenheim, Peter K. International banking / Peter K. Oppenheim. 5th ed. Washington, D.C. (1120 Connecticut Ave., N.W., Washington 20036) : Education Policy & Development, American Bankers Association, 1987. xii, 398 p. : ill. ; 25 cm. Bibliography: p. 301-302. Includes index. LC Card 87-403739 DDC 332.1/5 19
1. Banks and banking, International. I. Title.
HG3881 .O6 1987

Oppenheimer, Ernest J., 1924- Gasoline tax advantages / by Ernest J. Oppenheimer. New York, N.Y. : Pen & Podium, c1987. 88 p. ; 22 cm. Includes index. ISBN 0-9603982-5-2 (pbk.) : LC Card 86-862507 DDC 336.2/7866553827 19
1. Motor fuels - Taxation - United States. I. Title.
HD9579.G5 U5732 1987

Oppenheimer, Max Stul. Chips! : strategic issues in computer industry negotiation / Max Stul Oppenheimer. Homewood, Ill. : Dow Jones-Irwin, c1987. xii, 203 p. : ill. ; 24 cm. Includes index. ISBN 0-87094-942-X (pbk.) LC Card 86-72272 DDC 004/.068/7 19
1. Computers - Purchasing. 2. Computer programs - Purchasing. 3. Data processing service centers. 4. Computer service industry. 5. Computer industry. I. Title.
HD9696.C62 O665 1987

Oppenheimer, Michael F.
Emery, James J. Technology trade with the Middle East /. Boulder , 1986. xvii, 302 p. : ISBN 0-8133-7043-4 : LC Card 85-3215 DDC 338.9/26 19
HC415.15.Z9 H533 1986 ***NYPL [JLE 86-2460]***

Nontariff barriers : the effects on corporate strategy in high-technology sectors / Michael F. Oppenheimer and Donna M. Tuths. Boulder : Westview Press, 1987. xiii, 203 p. ; 22 cm. (Westview special studies in international economics and business) Bibliography: p. 199-201. ISBN 0-8133-7403-0 (pbk. : alk. paper) LC Card 87-50073 DDC 338.4/762/000973 19
1. High technology industries - United States - Case studies. 2. Nontariff trade barriers - Case studies. 3. Exports - United States - Case studies. 4. Small business - United States - Case studies. 5. Competition, Unfair - Case studies. I. Tuths, Donna M. II. Title.
HC110.H53 O66 1987

Oppermann, Reinhard, 1946- Mambrey, Peter. Computer und Partizipation . Opladen , c1986. xiv, 271 p. : ISBN 3-531-11851-X LC Card 87-122986 DDC 650/.028/5 19
HF5548.2 .M27 1986

Opportunities for Indo-British economic cooperation . Assocham Trade Mission to UK, 1984. New Delhi [1985] 43, xiii p., [4] p. of plates : LC Card 87-902558 DDC 337.54041 19
HF3788.G7 A87 1985

Opportunities in computer-assisted medical diagnostics . George, J. John. Menlo Park, Calif. (333 Ravenswood Ave., Menlo Park 94025-3476) , c1985. 32 p. : LC Card 86-232002 DDC 381/.45681761 19
HD9995.D543 U63 1985

Opportunities in insurance careers /. Schrayer, Robert M. Lincolnwood, Ill., U. S.A. , c1987. xi, 145 p. : ISBN 0-8442-6008-8 LC Card 87-60102 DDC 368/.0023/73 19
HG8531 .S37 1987

Opportunities in vocational & technical careers /. Paradis, Adrian A. Lincolnwood, Ill., U. S.A. , c1987. xi, 147 p. : ISBN 0-8442-6018-5 LC Card 87-60104 DDC 371.4/25/02373 19
HF5382.5.U5 P28 1987

Opportunities in vocational and technical careers. Paradis, Adrian A. Opportunities in vocational & technical careers /. Lincolnwood, Ill., U. S.A. , c1987. xi, 147 p. : ISBN 0-8442-6018-5 LC Card 87-60104 DDC 371.4/25/02373 19
HF5382.5.U5 P28 1987

Optical & "smart" cards. Norwalk, Conn., U. S.A (6 Prowitt St., Norwalk 06855) : International Resource Development, Inc., c1986. vi, 271 leaves : ill. ; 28 cm. (Report / International Resource Development Inc. . #696) "May 1986." LC Card 86-226974 DDC 381/.45621399 19
1. Optical character recognition device industry. 2. Optical data processing. 3. Market surveys. I. International Resource Development, inc. II. Title: Optical and "smart" cards. III. Series: Report / International Resource Development Inc. , #696.
HD9696.O672 O65 1986

Optical and "smart" cards. Optical & "smart" cards. Norwalk, Conn., U. S.A. (6 Prowitt St., Norwalk 06855) , c1986. vi, 271 leaves : LC Card 86-226974 DDC 381/.45621399 19
HD9696.O672 O65 1986

OPTICAL CHARACTER RECOGNITION DEVICE INDUSTRY.
Market report on scanning products & systems /. Falls Church, VA (6609 Rosecroft Pl., Falls Church 22043) [1986]- 1 v. (loose-leaf) ; LC Card 87-151419 DDC 338.7/61006424 19
HD9696.O672 M37 1986

Optical & "smart" cards. Norwalk, Conn., U. S.A. (6 Prowitt St., Norwalk 06855) , c1986. vi, 271 leaves : LC Card 86-226974 DDC 381/.45621399 19
HD9696.O672 O65 1986

O'Reilly, Francis J. The "smart card" . Stamford, Conn., U. S.A. [1986] xii, 106 leaves ; ISBN 0-89336-470-3 (soft) : LC Card 87-163972 DDC 380.1/4568 19
HD9696.O672 O74 1986

OPTICAL CHARACTER RECOGNITION DEVICE INDUSTRY - DIRECTORIES.
Market report on scanning products & systems /. Falls Church, VA (6609 Rosecroft Pl., Falls Church 22043) [1986]- 1 v. (loose-leaf) ; LC Card 87-151419 DDC 338.7/61006424 19
HD9696.O672 M37 1986

OPTICAL DATA PROCESSING.
(1986) Optical & "smart" cards. Norwalk, Conn., U. S.A. (6 Prowitt St., Norwalk 06855) , c1986. vi, 271 leaves : LC Card 86-226974 DDC 381/.45621399 19
HD9696.O672 O65 1986

Optical disk document storage and retrieval systems. Norwalk, Conn., U. S.A. (6 Prowitt St., Norwalk 06855) : International Resource Development, c1987. vii, 188 leaves ; 29 cm. (Report / International Resource Development . #730) "March 1987." LC Card 87-146516 DDC 380.1/4562139767 19
1. Optical storage device industry. 2. Market surveys. I. International Resource Development, inc. II. Series: Report / International Resource Development Inc. , #730.
HD9696.O672 O673 1987

Optical fiber in the local loop. Norwalk, Conn. (6 Prowitt St., Norwalk 06855) : International Resource Development Inc., c1986. iv, 208 leaves : ill. ; 29 cm. (Report / International Resource Development Inc. . #718) "November 1986." LC Card 87-127281 DDC 381/.456213692/0973 19
1. Fiber optics industry. 2. Telephone supplies industry. 3. Market surveys. I. International Resource Development, inc. II. Series: Report / International Resource Development Inc. , #718.
HD9696.F522 O67 1986

OPTICAL INDUSTRY - UNITED STATES - HISTORY.
Fahy, Thomas P. Richard Scott Perkin and the Perkin-Elmer Corporation /. [United States] c1987. xv, 271 p. : ISBN 0-9618075-0-4 LC Card 86-63869 DDC 338.7/666156/0973 19
HD9707.U62 P474 1987

The Optical memory media market in the U. S. New York, N.Y. : Frost & Sullivan, c1983. iv, 218 leaves : ill. ; 29 cm. Spine title: Optical memory media markets in the U. S. "#A1215." "August 1983." LC Card 87-143513 DDC 381/.4562139767/0973 19
1. Computer industry - United States. 2. Optical storage device industry - United States. 3. Market surveys - United States. I. Frost & Sullivan. II. Title: Optical memory media markets in the U. S.
HD9696.C63 U52734 1983

Optical memory media markets in the U. S. The Optical memory media market in the U. S. New York, N.Y. , c1983. iv, 218 leaves : LC Card 87-143513 DDC 381/.4562139767/0973 19
HD9696.C63 U52734 1983

OPTICAL SCANNERS.
Agi, Michael. Optische Beleg- und Seitenleser . Bonn , c1976. 96 p. ; LC Card 85-112068
HF5548.4.O6 A34 1976

OPTICAL STORAGE DEVICE INDUSTRY.
Optical disk document storage and retrieval systems. Norwalk, Conn., U. S.A. (6 Prowitt St., Norwalk 06855) , c1987. vii, 188 leaves ; LC Card 87-146516 DDC 380.1/4562139767 19
HD9696.O672 O673 1987

OPTICAL STORAGE DEVICE INDUSTRY - UNITED STATES.
The Optical memory media market in the U. S. New York, N.Y. , c1983. iv, 218 leaves : LC Card 87-143513 DDC 381/.4562139767/0973 19
HD9696.C63 U52734 1983

Optimal capacity planning under stagnating demand /. Kleindorfer, Paul R. Berlin [1985] 18, 4 leaves : LC Card 86-205882
HD69.C3 K49 1985

Optimal control methods for linear discrete-time economic systems /. Murata, Yasuo, 1931- New York , c1982. x, 202 p. ; ISBN 0-387-90709-2 LC Card 82-19137 DDC 338.9/00724 19
HD75.5 .M87 1982 ***NYPL [JLE 87-95]***

Optimal control theory with economic applications /. Seierstad, Atle. Amsterdam ; New York : xvi, 445 p. : ISBN 0-444-87923-4 (Elsevier Science Pub. Co.) LC Card 86-16504 DDC 629.8/312 19
QA402.3 .S4 1986 ***NYPL [JLE 87-1123]***

Optimal decisions under uncertainty . Sengupta, Jatikumar. Berlin , New York , 1985. 286 p. ; ISBN 0-387-15032-3 (U. S.) LC Card 84-26683 DDC 658.4/033 19
HD30.23 .S46 1985 ***NYPL [JLE 86-4652]***

Optimal financing policy of the firm . Tuovila, Olavi. Vaasa , 1983. 127 p. : ISBN 951-683-199-0 (pbk.) LC Card 84-204398
HG4012 .T86 1983

Optimal peak-load pricing for local telephone calls /. Park, Rolla Edward. Santa Monica, CA , 1986. xiii, 37 p. : ISBN 0-8330-0741-6 (pbk.) LC Card 86-204468 DDC 384.6/3 19
HE8825 .P369 1986

Optimal peak-load pricing for local telephone calls . Park, Rolla Edward. Santa Monica, CA , c1986. x, 72 p. : ISBN 0-8330-0747-5 (pbk.) LC Card 86-203146 DDC 384.6/3 19
HE8825 .P369 1986 Suppl.

Optimal peak-load pricing for local telephone calls /. Park, Rolla Edward. Santa Monica, CA , c1987. xiii, 41 p. : ISBN 0-8330-0856-X (pbk.) LC Card 87-410013 DDC 384.6/3 19
HE8825 .P369 1987

Optimal peak-load pricing for local telephone calls . Park, Rolla Edward. Santa Monica, CA , c1987. x, 75 p. : ISBN 0-8330-0857-9 (pbk.) LC Card 87-154411 DDC 384.6/3 19
HE8825 .P37 1987

Optimale Entscheidungen in Organisationen /. Fandel, G. (Günter), 1943- Berlin , New York , 1979. vi, 143 p. : ISBN 0-387-09109-2 (U. S.) LC Card 83-161352
HD58.8 .F35 1979

Optimale Liquidität . Suhr, Dieter. Frankfurt am Main , c1986. 155 p. ; ISBN 3-7819-0349-4 LC Card 86-228333
HG178 .S84 1986

Die optimale Organisationsstruktur eines mittleren Bankbetriebes . Bolliger, Peter. Bern , c1984. xiii, 234 p. : ISBN 3-258-03358-7 : LC Card 84-174443
HG1526 .B27 Bd. 86 HG1616.B7

Optimale valutaområder /. Heinrich, Hans, 1952- [Odense] , 1984. 142 p. : ISBN 87-981541-2-5 : LC Card 85-129406
HG3957 .H45 1984

Die optimale Versicherungsentscheidung als risikopolitisches Problem . Dimmer, Klaus. Karlsruhe , c1986. xiv, 320 p. : LC Card 87-114755 DDC 368/.0072 19
HG8054.5 .D555 1986

Die optimale Wahl steuerbegünstigter Kapitalanlagen unter Berücksichtigung der Einkommensteuerprogression . Hummeltenberg, Rita. Berlin , c1984. xi, 276 p. : ISBN 3-503-02437-9 LC Card 85-227381
HJ4719 .H86 1984

Optimal'noe planirovanie / [redaktsionnaia kollegiia P.S. Soltan (otvetstvennyĭ redaktor) ... et al.]. Kishinev : "Shtiintsa", 1982. 166 p. : ill. ; 22 cm. At head of title: Gosplan Moldavskoĭ SSR. Nauchno-issledovatel'skiĭ institut planirovaniia. Includes bibliographies. LC Card 83-149332
1. Agricultural industries - Moldavian S.S.R. - Planning - Mathematical models. 2. Moldavian S.S.R. - Economic policy- - Mathematical models. I. Soltan, Petr Semenovich. II. Nauchno-issledovatel'kiĭ institut planirovaniia (Moldavian S.S.R.).
HD9015.S653 M64526 1982

Optimal'noe planirovanie gruzopotokov /. Galaburda, V. G. Moskva , 1985. 255 p. : LC Card 85-243810
HE2457 .G35 1985

Optimiser les ressources humaines dans l'entreprise . Gruère, Jean-Pierre. Paris , c1984. 69, 42 p. : ISBN 2-7101-0462-8 : LC Card 84-217427
HF5549.5.A78 G78 1984

OPTIMIZATION (MATHEMATICS) see **MATHEMATICAL OPTIMIZATION.**

OPTIMIZATION TECHNIQUES. see **MATHEMATICAL OPTIMIZATION.**

OPTIMIZATION THEORY. see **MATHEMATICAL OPTIMIZATION.**

Optimizatsiia dolgosrochnogo planirovaniia razvitiia mineral'no-syr'evykh otrasleĭ /. Gol'd, G. S. (Grigoriĭ Solomonovich) Moskva , 1985. 148 p. : LC Card 86-118644
HD9506.S7472 G65 1985

Optimizatsiia otraslevykh sistem. Optimizatsiia perspektivnykh planov razvitiia otraslevykh sistem . Novosibirsk , 1979. 163 p. : LC Card 81-130740
HC337.R852 S546 1979

Optimizatsiia otraslevykh sistem v sostave ėkonomicheskikh programm /. Bostandzhian, V. B. (Vardan Babkenovich) Novosibirsk , 1982. 120, [1] p. : LC Card 83-107849
HC337.R852 S5234 1982

Optimizatsiia perspektivnykh planov razvitiia otraslevykh sistem : sbornik nauchnykh trudov / pod redaktsieĭ A.M. Alekseeva i IU.I. Maksimova. Novosibirsk : IĖiOPP SO AN SSSR, 1979. 163 p. : ill. ; 20 cm. (Optimizatsiia otraslevykh sistem) At head of title: Akademiia nauk SSSR. Sibirskoe otdelenie. Institut ėkonomiki i organizatsii promyshlennogo proizvodstva. Includes bibliographies and index. LC Card 81-130740
1. Siberia, Western (R.S.F.S.R.) - Industries - Planning. 2. Industrial management - Russian S.F.S.R. - Siberia, Western. I. Alekseev, Anatoliĭ Mikhaĭlovich. II. Maksimov, IUriĭ Ivanovich. III. Institut ėkonomiki i organizatsii promyshlennogo proizvodstva (Akademiia nauk SSSR). IV. Series.
HC337.R852 S546 1979

Optimizatsiia planirovaniia polimerno-neftekhimicheskogo kompleksa / [otvetstvennyĭ redaktor B.P. Suvorov]. Moskva : Akademiia nauk SSSR, TSentr. ėkonomiko-matematicheskiĭ in-t, 1984. 141 p. : ill. ; 21 cm. Includes bibliographies. LC Card 86-143987
1. Petroleum chemicals industry - Soviet Union - Forecasting. 2. Petroleum products - Soviet Union - Forecasting. I. Suvorov, B. P. (Boris Pavlovich). II. TSentral'nyĭ ėkonomiko-matematicheskiĭ institut (Akademiia nauk SSSR).
HD9579.C33 S655 1984

Optimizatsiia struktur upravleniia /. Baĭriev, B. S. Ashkhabad , 1985. 169, [23] p. : LC Card 86-196466
HC337.T23 B35 1985

Optimizatsiia territorial'nykh sistem. Mezhregional'nye mezhotraslevye balansy /. Novosibirsk , 1983. 220 p. : LC Card 84-172934
HF3626.5 .M49 1983

OPTIMUM CURRENCY AREAS. see **MONETARY UNIONS.**

OPTION (CONTRACT)
Andersen, Torben Juul. Currency and interest rate hedging . New York, N.Y. , c1987. viii, 272 p. : ISBN 0-13-195645-0 LC Card 87-7758 DDC 332.64/5 19
HG3853 .A53 1987

Koziol, Joseph D. A handbook for professional futures and options traders /. New York , c1987. xvi, 325 p. : ISBN 0-471-87423-X : LC Card 87-8180 DDC 332.64/4 19
HG6024.A3 K68 1987

OPTION (CONTRACT) - GERMANY (WEST)
Janssen, Friedrich, 1948- Bedeutung und Ausstattung von Wandel- und Optionsanleihen /. Göttingen , 1982. 279 p. : ISBN 3-509-01319-0 LC Card 83-240528
HG5501 .J35 1982

OPTION (CONTRACT) - INDIA.
OPTION (CONTRACT) - UNITED STATES.
Angell, George. Agricultural options . New York, NY , c1986. ix, 230 p. : ISBN 0-8144-5822-X LC Card 85-48215 DDC 332.64/25 19
HG6047.G8 A54 1986 ***NYPL [JLE 86-2854]***

Atchison, Michael D. New financial instruments . Charlottesville, Va. (P.O. Box 3665, Charlottesville 22903) , c1985. viii, 108 p. ; LC Card 85-195578 DDC 332.63 19
HG6024.3 .A83 1985
NYPL [JLL 81-133 no.21]

Option pricing & investment strategies /. Bookstaber, Richard M., 1950- Chicago, Ill. , c1987. x, 233 p. : ISBN 0-917253-81-7 : LC Card 87-17919 DDC 332.64/52 19
HG6042 .B65 1987

Option pricing and investment strategies. Bookstaber, Richard M., 1950- Option pricing & investment strategies /. Chicago, Ill. , c1987. x, 233 p. : ISBN 0-917253-81-7 : LC Card 87-17919 DDC 332.64/52 19
HG6042 .B65 1987

Option strategies . Smith, Courtney. New York , c1987. viii, 256 p. : ISBN 0-471-84367-9 LC Card 87-6174 DDC 332.64/52 19
HG6024.3 .S55 1987

Options . Ritchken, Peter. Glenview, Ill. , c1987. xiii, 414 p. : ISBN 0-673-18307-6 (pbk.) LC Card 86-29721 DDC 332.64/52 19
HG6042 .R57 1987

Options for Malaysian agriculture . Seminar "Malaysian Agriculture--What Next?" (1985 : Kuala Lumpur, Malaysia) [Kuala Lumpur] , 1986. xxiv, 203 p. : ISBN 967-99982-0-7 (pbk.) LC Card 86-943314 DDC 338.1/8595 19
HD2080.6.Z8 S45 1985

Options for U. S. fisheries investment in the Pacific Islands region /. Doulman, David J., 1950- Honolulu, Hawaii, U. S.A. , 1987. vi, 30 p. ; ISBN 0-86638-097-3 (pbk.) LC Card 87-9198 DDC 338.3/72758 19
HD9469.T83 I743 1987

Options for US fisheries investment in the Pacific Islands region. Doulman, David J., 1950- Options for U. S. fisheries investment in the Pacific Islands region /. Honolulu, Hawaii, U. S.A. , 1987. vi, 30 p. ; ISBN 0-86638-097-3 (pbk.) LC Card 87-9198 DDC 338.3/72758 19
HD9469.T83 I743 1987

The options strategy spectrum /. Yates, James W. Homewood, Ill. , c1987. x, 214 p. : ISBN 0-87094-961-6 LC Card 87-70393 DDC 332.64/52 19
HG6042 .Y38 1987

Optische Beleg- und Seitenleser . Agi, Michael. Bonn , c1976. 96 p. ; LC Card 85-112068
HF5548.4.O6 A34 1976

Opyt khoziaĭstvovaniia v ob"edineniiakh promyshlennosti sotsialisticheskikh stran / [avtory predisloviia i nauchnye redaktory S.E. Kamenitser, M.V. Mel'nik]. Moskva : "Ėkonomika", 1985. 157 p. : ill. ; 21 cm. Includes bibliographical references. LC Card 87-152292
1. Industrial management - Europe, Eastern. 2. Industrial organization - Europe, Eastern. 3. Industrial management - Bulgaria. 4. Technological innovations - Germany (East) - Management. I. Kamenitser, Solomon Efremovich. II. Mel'nik, M. V. (Margarita Viktorovna).
HD70.E7 O69 1985

Opyt razrabotki i realizatsii sistemy ukrupnennykh modeleĭ perspektivnogo planirovaniia / [otvetstvennye redaktory, I.S. Matlin, A.A. Bardina, IU.P. Solov'ev]. Moskva : Akademiia nauk SSSR, TSentr. ėkonomiko-matematicheskiĭ in-t, 1984. 216 p. : ill. ; 21 cm. Includes bibliographies. LC Card 85-199888
1. Economic policy - Mathematical models. 2. Central planning - Mathematical models. I. Matlin, Il'ia Semenovich. II. Bardina, A. A. III. Solov'ev, IU. P. (IUriĭ Pavlovich). IV. TSentral'nyĭ ėkonomiko-matematicheskiĭ institut (Akademiia nauk SSSR).
HD75.5 .O69 1984

Opyt stroitel'stva sotsialisticheskoĭ ėkonomiki v stranakh Azii / [redkollegiia G.V. Griaznov (otvetstvennyĭ redaktor), I.S. Kazakevich, S.K. Roshchin]. Moskva : Izd-vo "Nauka," Glav. red. vostochnoĭ lit-ry, 1986. 290 p. ; 23 cm. At head of title: Akademiia nauk SSSR. Ordena Trudovogo Krasnogo Znameni Institut vostokovedeniia. Summary in English. Bibliography: p. 283-289. LC Card 87-126301
1. Asia - Economic conditions - 1945-. 2. Mongolia - Economic conditions. 3. Vietnam - Economic conditions. 4. Korea (North) - Economic conditions. 5. Laos - Economic conditions. I. Griaznov, Gennadiĭ Viktorovich. II. Kazakevich, I. S. (Igor' Stepanovich). III. Roshchin, S. K. (Stanislav Kuz'mich). IV. Institut vostokovedeniia (Akademiia nauk SSSR).
HC412 .O675 1986

L'or de la Dombes . Benoît, Bruno. Trévoux [1983] 120 p. : ISBN 2-85698-025-2 LC Card 83-229770
HD9536.F83 T743 1983

ORAL BIOGRAPHY.
Günter, Janne, 1937- Mündliche Geschichtsschreibung . Mülheim/Ruhr , 1982. 142, [1] p. : ISBN 3-923456-00-X LC Card 85-146144
HD8039.M61 G343 1982

ORAL HISTORY.
Molano, Alfredo. Selva adentro . Bogotá , 1987. 142 p. : ISBN 958-9012-02-7 LC Card 87-404301 DDC 986.1/65 19
HD519.G8 M65 1987

ORANGE INDUSTRY - GREECE.
Mēliakos, Dēm. Iōan. To exōteriko emporio portokaliōn tēs Hellados /. Athēna , 1984. 176 p. ; LC Card 86-201864
HD9259.O8 G85 1984

ORANGE TRADE.
Dean, Gerald W. World trade in fresh oranges . Berkeley, Calif. [1967] 70 p. : LC Card 87-401008 DDC 338.1/09794 s 382/.41431 19
HD1407 .C27 no. 18 HD9259.O7

Orback, Jens. Agriculture and incentives, the Tanzanian case : a report on agricultural price policy in Tanzania and its effects on production pattern and market development : report from a minor research task / Jens Orback. Uppsala : Swedish University of Agricultural Sciences, International Rural Development Centre, 1985. 37, [2] leaves, [1] leaf of plates : ill. ; 30 cm. (Working paper / Swedish University of Agricultural Sciences, International Rural Development Centre, 0280-4301 = Arbetsrapport / U-landsavdelningen . 32) Bibliography: leaf 38-leaf 39. LC Card 86-215091 DDC 338.1/8 19
1. Agricultural price supports - Tanzania. 2. Agricultural prices - Tanzania. 3. Agriculture - Economic aspects - Tanzania. I. Series: Arbetsrapport (Sveriges lantbruksuniversitet. U-landsavdelningen) , 32. II. Title.
HD2128.5 .O73 1985

Orban, John. Money in the ground : oil & gas investments explained / by John Orban III.1st ed. Oklahoma City : Meridian Press, 1985. xv, 216 p. : ill. ; 23 cm. Bibliography: p. [157]-160. Includes index. ISBN 0-9615776-0-6 (pbk.) : LC Card 86-120440 DDC 332.63 19
1. Petroleum industry and trade - Finance. 2. Investments. 3. Oil well drilling. 4. Gas well drilling. I. Title.
HG6047.P47 O73 1985

Orbánné Nagy, Mária.
Az élelmiszerfogyasztás várható tendenciái hosszabb távon / Orbánné Nagy Mária. Budapest : Agrárgazdasági Kutató Intézet, 1983. 98 p. ; 29 cm. (Agrárgazdasági Kutató Intézet, 0209-5696 . 1983/17) Bibliography: p. 59-62. ISBN 963-491-166-8 LC Card 85-219700
1. Food consumption - Hungary - Forecasting. 2. Food consumption forecasting. I. Series: Agrárgazdasági Kutató Intézet (Series) , 1983/17. II. Title.
HD9015.H82 O73 1983

Kartali, János. A friss és feldolgozott zöldségek, gyümölcsök bel- és külkereskedelmi forgalmazásának aktuális problémái /. Budapest , 1985. 108 p. ; ISBN 963-491-203-6 LC Card 86-195487
HD9220.H82 K37 1985

Orbe, Justino José del. Mauricio Báez y la clase obrera / Justino José del Orbe. [1a ed.] Santo Domingo, República Dominicana : Taller, 1981. 158 p. : ill. ; 23 cm. (Biblioteca Taller. no. 128) LC Card 82-138627 DDC 331.88/092/4 B 19
1. Báez, Mauricio, 1910-1950. 2. Trade-unions - Dominican Republic - Officials and employees - Biography. 3. Trade-unions - Dominican Republic - History. 4. Labor and laboring classes - Dominican Republic - History. I. Title.
HD6584.Z55 B346 1981
NYPL [JLE 86-3246]

Orbell, John. A guide to tracing the history of a business / John Orbell. Aldershot, Hants, Eng. ; Brookfield, Vt., USA : Gower, c1987. p. cm. Bibliography: p. ISBN 0-566-05591-0 : LC Card 87-15505 DDC 338.7/072 19
1. Business enterprises - History - Handbooks, manuals, etc. 2. Business enterprises - Historiography. 3. Business enterprises - Great Britain - History - Handbooks, manuals, etc. 4. Business enterprises - Great Britain - Historiography. I. Title.
HD2321 .O7 1987

Orbital management . Lehr, Jay H., 1936- Lanham, MD [Cambridge, MA] , c1987. xvi, 104 p. : ISBN 0-8191-6264-7 (alk. paper) : LC Card 87-143 DDC 658.4/02 19
HD50 .L44 1987

O orçamento de São Paulo para 1984 /. São Paulo (Brazil : State). Governor (1982- : Montoro) São Paulo , 1983. 24 p. ; LC Card 87-130676 DDC 354.81/6100722 19
HJ2080.5.S3 S26 1983

ORCHARDS - ENGLAND.
Rendell, John. An economic survey of intensive bush cider orchards, 1972-1981 . [Reading, Berks.] [1984] 24 p. : ISBN 0-7049-0814-X (pbk.) : LC Card 85-111963 DDC 338.1/74117 19
HD9398.G83 E57 1984

ORCHARDS - GERMANY (WEST) - LOWER SAXONY - STATISTICS.
Landwirtschaftszählung 1979, Gartenbauerhebung 1981/82 . Hannover , 1983. xv, 132 p. ; LC Card 85-117833
HD9013.7.L68 L37 1983

Orcutt, Guy. Microanalytic simulation models to support social and financial policy /. Amsterdam ; New York : xvii, 553 p. : ISBN 0-444-87876-9 (U. S.) LC Card 85-25231 DDC 361.6/0724 19
HD87 .M52 1986 ***NYPL [JLD 86-3485]***

Orczyk, Józef. Determinanty polityki kadrowej w przedsiębiorstwie . Poznań , 1984. 142 p. : LC Card 86-194984
HB54 .P6 nr. 129 HF5549.2.P6

Ordem dos Economistas de São Paulo. O Perfil do economista. [São Paulo, Brazil] [1984?] 60 p. : LC Card 87-402012 DDC 330/.092/2 19
HB123.B8 P47 1984

Orden social y monetarismo /. Canitrot, Adolfo. Buenos Aires, Argentina [1982 or 1983] 50 p. ; LC Card 83-213595
HC173 .C35 1982

Order, freedom, and the polity : critical essays on the open society / George W. Carey, editor. Lanham, MD : University Press of America ; [Bryn Mawr, Pa.] : Intercollegiate Studies Institute, c1986. x, 184 p. ; 24 cm. Essays given at a conference on the open society, held at Georgetown University in 1982, sponsored by the Georgetown University Government Deoartment and the Intercollogiate Studies Institute. Includes bibliographies. ISBN 0-8191-5155-6 (alk. paper) : LC Card 85-26438 DDC 323.44 19
1. Liberty - Congresses. 2. Democracy - Congresses. I. Carey, George Wescott, 1933-. II. Georgetown University, Washington, D.C. Dept. of Government. III. Intercollegiate Studies Institute.
JC571 .O77 1986 ***NYPL [JLE 86-3182]***

ORDERS, MAJOR. see **CLERGY.**

Ordinary life insurance reference manual. 1986 ordinary life insurance reference manual . Hartford, Conn. (101 Pearl St., Hartford 06103) [1986] 88 p. ; LC Card 87-163896 DDC 368/.006/073 19
HG8955 .A56 1986

Ordnung der Wirtschaft durch Wettbewerb . Holzwarth, Fritz. Freiburg im Breisgau , c1985. 217 p. ; ISBN 3-448-01510-5 LC Card 86-109043
HB95 .H65 1985

Die Ordnung des österreichischen Staatshaushaltes--1863 /. Wagner, Adolph, 1835-1917. Wien , c1984. 308 p. ; ISBN 3-85447-086-X LC Card 85-223615
HJ1065 .W34 1984

Ordnung, Disziplin, Sicherheit . Möbis, Harry. Berlin , 1983. 95 p. ; LC Card 83-186990
HF5549.5.L3 M63 1983

Ordnungstheorie und ökonomische Wissenschaft . Recktenwald, Horst Claus. Erlangen , 1985. 65 p. : ISBN 3-922135-40-4 LC Card 85-234440
HB175 .R35 1985

Ordo Politicus. For other vols. in this series, see Old Catalog.
(Bd. 25) Wirtschaftlicher Wandel, religiöser Wandel und Wertwandel . Berlin , c1985. 411 p. : ISBN 3-428-05784-8 LC Card 85-218417
HC286.7 .W58 1985

Ordoliberalismus und christliche Soziallehre . Bossle, Lothar. [Ordoliberalismus und christliche Soziallehre.] München , c1983. 63 p. ; ISBN 3-485-03085-6 LC Card 84-174227
HC55 .B64 1983

Ordóñez G., Myriam. Población y familia rural en Colombia / Myriam Ordóñez G. Bogotá : Pontificia Universidad Javeriana, Facultad de Estudios Interdisciplinarios, Programa de Población, 1986. 179 p. : ill. ; 20 cm. "Investigación realizada para el Ministerio de Agricultura"--Label on t.p. Bibliography: p. 143-146. LC Card 86-208940
1. Colombia - Population, Rural. 2. Rural families - Colombia. I. Title.
HB2447 .O73 1986

Ordre des experts comptables et des comptables agréés (France). Conseil supérieur. Le Contrôle de qualité . [Paris] [1983] 297 p. : ISBN 2-900670-20-9 : LC Card 85-106388
HF5616.F7 C66 1983

Ordzhonikidze, É. A. (Éteri Aleksandrovna) Vačroba da vačart'a p'ena rep'ormamdeli xanis Sak'art'veloši / E. Orjonikiże. T'bilisi : Gamomc'emloba "Mec'niereba", 1974. 158 p. ; 22 cm. In Georgian. Title in colophon: Torgovlia i kupechestvo v doreformennoĭ Gruzii. At head of title: Sak'art'velos SSR mec'nierebat'a akademia. Iv. Javaxišvilis saxelobis istoriis, ark'eologiisa da et'nograp'iis instituti. Summary in Russian. Includes bibliographical references. LC Card 86-168874
1. Georgian S.S.R. - Commerce - History - 19th century. I. Title. II. Title: Torgovlia i kupechestvo v doreformennoĭ Gruzii.
HF3629.G4 O73 1974

O'Regan, Fred. Hellinger, Steve. Aid for just development . Washington, D.C. (1010 Vermont Ave., N.W., Suite 521, Washington 20005) , c1987. vii, 191 p. ; LC Card 87-404422 DDC 338.91/09172/4 19
HC60 .H38516 1987

Oregon. Bureau of Labor Industries. The Dilema of farmworker housing . [Portland, Or.] [1986] 78, [112] p. : LC Card 86-622584 DDC 363.5/9 19
HD7289.U7 O73 1986

Oregon Center for Health Statistics. Suicides and homicides, Oregon residents, 1979 to 1981. Portland, OR (1400 S.W. 5th Ave., Portland 97201) [1986] 39 p. : LC Card 87-620589 DDC 614.5/985844/09795 19
HB1323.S82 U57 1986

Oregon county finances, fiscal 1984. Eugene, OR : Bureau of Governmental Research and Service, University of Oregon, [1985] 17, [12] p. ; 29 cm. (BGRS . no. 85-8) "August 1985." "PC#5"--T.p. verso. LC Card 86-622281 DDC 336/.014/795 19
1. Local finance - Oregon. I. University of Oregon. Bureau of Governmental Research and Service. II. Series: BGRS (Series) , no. 85-8.
HJ9302 .O725 1985

Oregon. Dept. of Transportation. Making the right turn . [Salem? Or.] [1986] iv, 39 p. : LC Card 87-621891 DDC 388.1/14/09795 19
HE356.O7 M35 1986

Oregon express companies /. Forster, Dale E. Eugene, Ore. , c1985. vi, 231 p. : LC Card 87-121202 DDC 383/.143/09795 19
HE6376.A1 O735 1985

OREGON PACIFIC & EASTERN RAILWAY - HISTORY - 19TH CENTURY.
Lewty, Peter J., 1934- To the Columbia gateway . Pullman, Wash. , 1987. p. cm. ISBN 0-87422-030-0 (alk. paper) : LC Card 87-21041 DDC 385/.09795 19
HE2791.N855 L48 1987

Oregon. Task Force on State Compensation and Classification Equity. Final report and recommendations of the Task Force on State Compensation and Classification Equity to the Sixty third Legislative Assembly. [Salem OR] (338 State Capitol, Salem 97310) : The Task Force, [1985] 51 p. : ill. ; 28 cm. Cover title. "March 1985." LC Card 86-622414 DDC 331.2/1 19
1. Equal pay for equal work - Government policy - Oregon. I. Title.
HD6061.2.U62 O75 1985

Oregon. Transportation, Dept. of. see **Oregon. Dept. of Transportation.**

O'Reilly, Francis J.
Computer printers : directions, trends, markets, technologies / Fran O'Reilly. Stamford, Conn., U. S.A. : Business Communications Co., c1985. iv, 103 leaves ; 29 cm. (Business opportunity report . G-091) "August 1985"--T.p. verso. ISBN 0-89336-460-6 (pbk.) LC Card 87-163961 DDC 338.4/76213987 19
1. Computer printer supplies industry - United States. 2. Market surveys - United States. I. Title. II. Series.
HD9696.C63 U52737 1985

The "smart card" : projected markets and technological developments / Francis O'Reilly. Stamford, Conn., U. S.A. : Business Communications Co., [1986] xii, 106 leaves ; 29 cm. (Business opportunity report . G-100) ISBN 0-89336-470-3 (soft) : LC Card 87-163972 DDC 380.1/4568 19
1. Optical character recognition device industry. 2. Personal identification products industry. 3. Market surveys. I. Title. II. Series.
HD9696.O672 O74 1986

O'Reilly, James T., 1947- Unions' rights to company information / by James T. O'Reilly, with the assistance of Jodi C. Aronson. Rev. ed. Philadelphia, Pa. : Industrial Research Unit, the Wharton School, c1987. xiii, 312 p. ; 23 cm. (Labor relations and public policy series, 0075-7470 . no. 21) Includes bibliographical references. ISBN 0-89546-060-2 LC Card 85-82257
1. Trade-unions - United States. 2. Freedom of information - United States. 3. Corporations - United States. I. Aronson, Jodi C. II. Title. III. Series.
NYPL [JLL 74-174 no.21]

Oren, Ditza L. Preventing dishonest behavior in the electronics industry : confidential report based on personal interviews with 79 executives and managers from 65 Silicon Valley and Bay Area electronics companies / by Ditza L. Oren. [United States : D.L. Oren, 1985] vii, 115 leaves : col. ill. ; 28 cm. "Conducted jointly by Ditza L. Oren and Hedva Porat." "March 1985." LC Card 86-224386 DDC 621.381/068/3 19
1. Electronic industry workers - California - Attitudes. 2. Employee theft - California. 3. Alcoholism and employment - California. 4. Employee morale - California. I. Title.
HD8039.E38 U65 1985

ORENSE (SPAIN : PROVINCE) - EMIGRATION AND IMMIGRATION.
Azcárate, Blanca, 1954- Ursachen, Umfang und Auswirkungen der Abwanderung im ländlichen Bereich Galiciens am Beispiel der Provinz Orense /. Frankfurt am Main , New York , c1985. 213 p. : ISBN 3-8204-8166-4 LC Card 85-190546
HD8589.O74 A92 1985

ORENSE (SPAIN : PROVINCE) - POPULATION, RURAL.
Azcárate, Blanca, 1954- Ursachen, Umfang und Auswirkungen der Abwanderung im ländlichen Bereich Galiciens am Beispiel der Provinz Orense /. Frankfurt am Main , New York , c1985. 213 p. : ISBN 3-8204-8166-4 LC Card

85-190546
HD8589.O74 A92 1985

Orenstein, Vik, 1960- How to break into modeling / Vik Orenstein. 1st ed. Cincinnati, Ohio : Writer's Digest Books, c1987. 169 p. : ill. ; 26 cm. Includes index. ISBN 0-89879-282-7 (pbk.) : LC Card 87-21703 DDC 659.1/52 19
1. Models, Fashion - United States. I. Title.
HD6073.M772 U56 1987

Oreshkin, V. V. (Vasiliĭ Vladimirovich) Sovershenstvovanie sistemy narodnokhoziaĭstvennogo upravleniia v sotsialisticheskikh stranakh . Moskva , 1986. 196 p. ; LC Card 87-163453
HC244 .S595115 1986

Öresundsförbindelser : översyn 1983. [Stockholm] : Liber, [1983] 196 p. : ill. ; 21 cm. At head of title: Kommunikationsdepartementet. "Ds K 1983:2." Includes bibliographical references. ISBN 91-38-08123-7 LC Card 84-218397
1. Transportation - Sound, The (Denmark and Sweden). I. Sweden. Kommunikationsdepartementet.
HE256.Z7 S665 1983

Orfield, Gary. Job training under the new federalism . [Chicago?] , 1986. ii, 299 p. : LC Card 86-203209 DDC 331.25/92/0973 19
HD5715.2 .J63 1986

Organ, Dennis W. The Applied psychology of work behavior . Plano, Tex. , 1987. ix, 501 p. : ISBN 0-256-03431-1 (pbk.) LC Card 86-72246 DDC 158.7 19
HF5548.8 .A72 1987

ORGAN TRADE. see **MUSIC TRADE.**

De organisatie-aspecten van de automatisering /. Völlmar, H. Leiden , 1985. xiv, 316 p. : ISBN 90-207-1347-7 : LC Card 85-220224
HD45.2 .V65 1985

Organisation als soziales System : Kontrolle und Kommunikationstechnologie in Arbeitsorganisationen / Rüdiger Seltz, Ulrich Mill, Eckart Hildebrandt (Hg.). Berlin : Edition Sigma, c1986. 219 p. ; 21 cm. "Wissenschaftszentrum Berlin für Sozialforschung. Forschungsschwerpunkt Arbeitspolitik"--P. facing t.p. Includes bibliographies. ISBN 3-924859-22-1 LC Card 87-137969 DDC 302.3/5 19
1. Organizational behavior. 2. Organizational development. 3. Industry - Social aspects. I. Seltz, Rüdiger. II. Mill, Ulrich. III. Hildebrandt, Eckart.
HD58.7 .O6687 1986

Organisation & management of public distribution system /. Ojha, Ghanshyam Das, 1947- Delhi, India , 1987. x, 235 p. ; LC Card 87-900491 DDC 381/.1/0954 19
HF5415.12.I5 O44 1987

Organisation and Management of public distribution system. Ojha, Ghanshyam Das, 1947- Organisation & management of public distribution system /. Delhi, India , 1987. x, 235 p. ; LC Card 87-900491 DDC 381/.1/0954 19
HF5415.12.I5 O44 1987

Organisation asienne de productivité. see **Asia Productivity Organization.**

Organisation commune des régions sahariennes (France). Bureau des études statistiques, économiques et sociales. L'Energie électrique au Sahara. [Paris] [196-?] 19 p. : LC Card 83-123000
HD9685.A52 E54 1960z

Organisation coopérative et développement rural /. Lombeya Bosongo L. [Kinshasa] , 1985. 173 p. ; LC Card 86-185252
HD1491.5 .L66 1985

Organisation de coopèration et de développement économiques. see **Organization for Economic Cooperation and Development.**

Organisation de l'Institut national de formation et de perfectionnement professionnels de Bangui (INFPP) . International Labour Organisation. Genève , 1980. 14 p. ; ISBN 92-2-202448-6 LC Card 82-214934
HD5716.M342 C335 1980

Organisation de l'unité africaine. see **Organization of African Unity.**

Die Organisation der Gewerkschaften der Sowjetunion /. Reznikov, Iosif Emmanuilovich. Moskau , 1927. 76 p. ; LC Card 86-231829
HD6732 .R398 1927

Organisation der strategischen Planung . Link, Jörg. Heidelberg , c1985. xvii, 178 p. : ISBN 3-7908-0333-2 LC Card 86-160239 DDC 658.4/012 19
HD30.28 .L545 1985

Organisation des Etats américains. see **Organization of American States.**

Organisation des Nations Unies. see **United Nations.**

Organisation des Nations Unies pour l'alimentation et l'agriculture. see **Food and Agriculture Organization of the United Nations.**

Organisation du Traité de l'Atlantique-Nord. see **North Atlantic Treaty Organization.**

Organisation for Economic Cooperation and Development. see **Organization for Economic Cooperation and Development.**

Organisation for Economic Co-operation and Development.
Bank profitability . Paris , Washington, D.C. , 1987. 235 p. ; ISBN 92-64-12915-4 (pbk.) : LC Card 87-164235 DDC 332.1/021 19
HG1708 .B29 1987

Berg, Elliot. Absorptive capacity in the Sahel countries. [Paris] [Ouagadougou, Burkina Faso] [1983] xi, 133 p. ; LC Card 87-402541 DDC 338.91/0966 19
HC1002 .B47 1983

Coal . Paris [Washington, D.C.] 1987. 108 p. ; ISBN 92-64-12909-X (pbk.) : LC Card 87-163847 DDC 363.7/31 19
HD9540.6 .C63 1987

Co-ordinated urban transport pricing . Paris [Washington, D.C.] 1985. 151 p. : ISBN 92-64-12692-9 (pbk.) : LC Card 86-125699 DDC 388.4/042 19
HE305 .C58 1985

Dubarle, Patrick. The space industry . Paris, France [Washington, D.C.] c1985. 92 p. : ISBN 92-64-12772-0 : LC Card 86-210154 DDC 338.4/76291 19
HD9711.5.A2 D83 1985

Effectiveness of road safety education programmes . Paris [Washington, D.C.] 1986. 134 p. : ISBN 92-64-12881-6 : LC Card 87-119891 DDC 363.1/2575/07 19
HE5613.5 .E33 1986

The Future of migration. Paris , Washington, D.C. , 1987. 319 p. : ISBN 92-64-12949-9 (pbk.) : LC Card 87-163484 DDC 304.8/094 19
HB1952 .F88 1987

Harmonization of accounting standards . Paris , Washington, D.C. , 1986. 147 p. ; ISBN 92-64-12895-6 (pbk.) : LC Card 87-124490 DDC 657/.0218 19
HF5611 .H37 1986

Information technology and economic prospects. Paris , Washington, D.C. , 1987. 221 p. : ISBN 92-64-12927-8 (pbk.) : LC Card 87-163173 DDC 331.1 19
HD9696.A2 I54 1987

Innovation policy . Paris , Washington, D.C. , 1987. 75 p. ; ISBN 92-64-12918-9 (pbk.) : LC Card 87-164488 DDC 338/.06 19
HC260.5.Z9 T45 1987

International trade in services. Paris , Washington, D.C. , 1986. 46 p. ; ISBN 92-64-12860-3 (pbk.) : LC Card 87-122911 DDC 382/.45621380282 19
HD9697.A842 I58 1986

Labour market flexibility . Paris , Washington, D.C. , 1986. 23 p. ; LC Card 86-215799 DDC 331.12 19
HD5707 .L28 1986

OECD road safety research . Paris [Washington, D.C.] 1986. 106 p. : ISBN 92-64-12814-X (pbk.) : LC Card 86-212506 DDC 363.1/25 19
HE5614 .O34 1986

Petro chemical industry . Paris, France [Washington, D.C.] 1985. 161 p. : ISBN 92-64-12683-X (pbk.) : LC Card 85-177511 DDC 338.4/7661804 19
HD9579.C32 P48 1985

Productivity in industry . Paris , 1986. 108 p. ; ISBN 92-64-12816-6 (pbk.) : LC Card 86-213264 DDC 338/.06 19
HC79.I52 P78 1986

The role of large firms in local job creation . Paris [Washington, D.C.] c1986. 31 p. ; LC Card 87-130519 DDC 331.12/4 19
HD5710.5 .R65 1986

Statistics on external indebtedness . Paris , 1985. 27 p. ; LC Card 86-204760 DDC 336.3/435/091724 19
HJ8899 .S7 1985

Structural adjustment and multinational enterprises. Paris [Washington, D.C.] 1985. 68 p. ; ISBN 92-64-12770-4 (pbk.) : LC Card 86-214254 DDC 338.8/8 19
HD2755.5 .S85 1985

Trends of change in telecommunications policy. Paris , Washington, D.C. , 1987. 353 p. : ISBN 92-64-12940-5 (pbk.) : LC Card 87-163585 DDC 384/.068 19
HE7645 .T74 1987

Venture capital . Paris , Washington, D.C. , 1986. 65 p. : ISBN 92-64-12901-4 (pbk.) : LC Card 87-124464 DDC 332/.0415 19
HG4751 .V46 1986

Wienert, Helgard. East-West technology transfer. The trade and economic aspects /. Paris , c1986. 453 p. : ISBN 92-64-12817-4
NYPL [JLE 87-1561]

ORGANISATION FOR ECONOMIC CO-OPERATION AND DEVELOPMENT.
Blades, Derek W. Discrepancies between imports and exports in OECD foreign trade statistics /. Paris, France , c1984. i, 42 p. ; LC Card 86-205155 DDC 382/.021 19
HF1016 .B569 1984

Consolidation policies in OECD countries . Paris , 1987. 60, 63 p. ; ISBN 92-64-02876-5 : LC Card 87-168671 DDC 657/.3 19
HF5681.B2 C593 1987

Harmonization of accounting standards . Paris , Washington, D.C. , 1986. 147 p. ; ISBN 92-64-12895-6 (pbk.) : LC Card 87-124490 DDC 657/.0218 19
HF5611 .H37 1986

Public sector deficits in OECD countries . New York , 1987. p. cm. ISBN 0-312-00533-4 : LC Card 87-11876 DDC 339.5/23/091724 19
HJ2043 .P8 1987

Venture capital . Paris , Washington, D.C. , 1986. 65 p. : ISBN 92-64-12901-4 (pbk.) : LC Card 87-124464 DDC 332/.0415 19
HG4751 .V46 1986

Organisation for Economic Co-operation and Development. Committee for Fisheries. Problems of trade in fishery products. Paris, France , Washington, D.C. , c1985. 384 p. : ISBN 92-64-12775-5 (pbk.) : LC Card 86-203595 DDC 382/.437 19
HD9450.5 .P76 1985

Organisation for Economic Co-operation and Development. Committee of Experts on Restrictive Business Practices. Competition policy and deregulation . Paris , 1986. 35 p. ; LC Card 86-217040 DDC 338.6/048 19
HD3612 .C65 1986

Organisation for Economic Co-operation and Development. Committee on Consumer Policy. Consumers and life insurance / report by the OECD Committee on Consumer Policy. Paris : Organisation for Economic Co-operation and Development ; Washington, D.C. : OECD Publications and Information Centre [distributor], 1987. 79 p. ; 23 cm. Bibliography: p. 76-79. ISBN 92-64-12920-0 (pbk.) : LC Card 87-163859 DDC 368.3/2 19
1. Insurance, Life. 2. Consumers - Attitudes. 3. Insurance, Life - Government policy. I. Title.
HG8771 .O73 1987

Organisation for Economic Co-operation and Development. Committee on Fiscal Affairs. Taxation in developed countries . Paris , Washington, D.C. , 1987. 99 p. ; ISBN 92-64-12929-4 (pbk.) : LC Card 87-163512 DDC 336.24 19
HJ4621 .T28 1987

ORGANISATION FOR ECONOMIC CO-OPERATION AND DEVELOPMENT - CONGRESSES.
Le Iniziative locali per l'occupazione . Milano,

Italy , c1985. 244 p. : LC Card 85-221711 DDC 331 s 331.12/042 19
HD85.I7 I68 no. 75 HD5713.5
NYPL [JLD 87-446]

Organisation for Economic Co-operation and Development. Dept. of Economics and Statistics.
Measurement of value added at constant prices in service activities /. Paris . v. <1 > ; ISBN 92-64-02879-X (pbk.) : LC Card 87-164470 DDC 657/.45 19
HF5686.S43 M43 1987

Standardised unemployment rates . Paris, France [Washington, D.C.] 1985. 93 p. ; LC Card 86-143095 DDC 331.13/7/072 19
HD5711 .S77 1985 NYPL [JLF 86-1743]

Organisation for Economic Co-operation and Development. Development Centre.
Inventaire . Paris [Washington, D.C.] 1986. xxvii, 262 p. ; ISBN 92-64-02871-4 : LC Card 87-129509
HD77.5.A34 I58 1986

Répertoire : projets de recherche en matière de développement en Afrique / Centre de développement de l'OCDE [et] Conseil pour le développement de la recherche économique et sociale en Afrique = Register : development research projects in Africa / OECD Development Center [and] Council for the Development of Economic and Social Research in Africa. Paris : Organisation for Economic Co-operation and Development ; Washington, D.C. : OECD Publications and Information Centre, [distributor], 1986. xxiv, 523 p. ; 27 cm. French and English. ISBN 92-64-02872-2 : LC Card 87-146730
1. Economic development - Research - Africa - Directories. 2. Social sciences - Research - Africa - Directories. I. Codesria. II. Title. III. Title: Register.
HD77.5.A34 O75 1986

Research and other activities of the Development Centre, 1983-1985. Paris, France , 1985. 50 p. ; LC Card 86-213499 DDC 338.9 19
HD77 .R47 1985

Wellons, Philip A. Banks and specialised financial intermediaries in development /. Paris , Washington, D.C. , 1986. 150 p. : ISBN 92-64-12867-0 (pbk.) : LC Card 87-114506 DDC 332.1/09172/4 19
HG3550 .W45 1986

Zorn, Stephen. Minería y elaboración de minerales . Buenos Aires , 1986. ii, 84 p. ; LC Card 87-402781 DDC 338.2/098 19
HD9506.L252 Z67 1986

Organisation for Economic Co-operation and Development. Environment Committee.
Environmental policies in Yugoslavia . Paris [Washington, D.C.] c1986. 160 p., [2] p. of plates : ISBN 92-64-12866-2 (pbk.) : LC Card 87-120078 DDC 363.7/056/09497 19
HC407.Z9 E555 1986

Organisation for Economic Co-operation and Development. Library.
Bibliographie spécialisée analytique .
(48) Organisation for Economic Co-operation and Development. Library. L'emploi des jeunes =. [Paris] , 1980. [6], 119 p. ; LC Card 81-122004 DDC 016.3313/4 19
HD6270 .O72 1980

L'emploi des jeunes = Youth employment. [Paris] : Organisation de coopération et de développement économiques, 1980. [6], 119 p. ; 27 cm. (Bibliographie spécialisée analytique = Special annotated bibliography . 48, 1980) English and French. "The French abstracts in the bibliography where [sic] prepared by Mrs Forest and the English ones by Mrs Tracey"--3rd prelim. page. "EXD/BIB (80) 9." LC Card 81-122004 DDC 016.3313/4 19
1. Youth - Employment - Abstracts. I. Forest, Mrs. II. Tracey, Mrs. III. Title. IV. Title: Youth employment. V. Series: Organisation for Economic Co-operation and Development. Library. Bibliographie spécialisée analytique , 48.
HD6270 .O72 1980

Organisation for Economic Co-operation and Development. Secretariat. Flexibility in the labour market . Paris [Washington, D.C.] 1986. 146 p. ; ISBN 92-64-12892-1 (pbk.) LC Card 87-123763 DDC 331.12 19
HD5707 .F59 1986

Organisation for Economic Co-operation and Development. Working Group on Accounting Standards. Consolidation policies in OECD countries . Paris , 1987. 60, 63 p. ; ISBN 92-64-02876-5 : LC Card 87-168671 DDC 657/.3 19
HF5681.B2 C593 1987

Organisation for European Economic Co-operation. Terminologie des échanges et paiements internationaux et de la comptabilité nationale; français-anglais, anglais-français: glossaire et définitions. Terms used in international trade and payments and national accounts; English-French, French-English; glossary and definitions. Paris [1958] 146, [6] p. 27 cm. Bibliography: p. [151] LC Card 58-47135 DDC 382.03
1. Commerce - Dictionaries. 2. Commerce - Dictionaries - French. 3. English language - Dictionaries - French. 4. French language - Dictionaries - English. I. Title.
HF1002 .O7 NYPL [JLF 87-128]

The Organisation in its environment / I.A. Todd ... [et al.]. 2nd ed. London : Sweet & Maxwell, 1984. xiii, 624 p. : ill. ; 22 cm. Rev. ed. of: The organization / M.J. Newell. 1979. Includes indexes. ISBN 0-421-32290-X (pbk.) : LC Card 84-242095 DDC 302.3/5 19
1. Industrial organization - Great Britain. 2. Organization. I. Todd, I. A. II. Newell, M. J. Organisation.
HD31 .O7217 1984 NYPL [JLD 86-2539]

Organisation Internationale du Travail. see **International Labor Organization.**

Organisation mondiale de la santé. see **World Health Organization.**

Organisation Mondiale du Tourisme. see **World Tourism Organization.**

Organisation of African Trade Union Unity.
Turner, Terisa. Trade union action to stop oil to South Africa /. Port Harcourt , c1985. v, 35 p. ; LC Card 87-673464
HF1613.4 .T87x 1985

Organisational design . Rowbottom, Ralph William. Aldershot, Hants, England , Brookfield, Vt., USA , 1987. 165 p. : ISBN 0-566-05408-6 : LC Card 86-31946 DDC 658.4/02 19
HD50 .R68 1987

Organisationsänderung in Unternehmungen . Dieterle, W. (Willi) Göttingen , 1986. iii, 169 p. : ISBN 3-509-01425-1 LC Card 87-131121 DDC 338/.06 19
HD58.8 .D54 1986

Organisationskultur, ein neues Forschungsprogramm? /. Ebers, Mark. Wiesbaden , c1985. 223 p. ; ISBN 3-409-13105-1 LC Card 86-135588
HD58.8 .E24 1985

Organisationsstruktur und Rechtsnorm . Werder, Axel von. Wiesbaden , c1986. 564 p. : ISBN 3-409-13107-8 LC Card 86-224483
HD58.7 .W35 1986

Organisationstheoretische Analyse von Marketing-Entscheidungsprozessen . Fleischer, Manfred. Berlin [1977] 93 p. : LC Card 85-111320
HF5415.135 .F58 1977

Organisatorische Gestaltung des Job Sharing in der Unternehmung . Müller, Christoph, 1957- Köln , c1986. xiii, 404 p. ; ISBN 3-924361-12-6 LC Card 87-114139 DDC 331.25/72 19
HD5110.2.G3 M85 1986

Organisatorische Implementierung von computergestützten Personalinformationssystemen . Mülder, Wilhelm. Berlin , New York , 1984. xix, 257 p. : ISBN 0-387-13360-7 (U. S.) LC Card 84-238144
HF5549.5.D37 M85 1984

Organised labour and political development in Nigeria /. Offiong, Daniel A. Calabar, Nigeria , 1983. x, 362 p. ; ISBN 978-231-601-6 (pbk.) LC Card 86-173440 DDC 322/.2/09669 19
HD6885.5.Z65 O36 1983

Organised labour & political development in Nigeria. Offiong, Daniel A. Organised labour and political development in Nigeria /. Calabar, Nigeria , 1983. x, 362 p. ; ISBN 978-231-601-6 (pbk.) LC Card 86-173440 DDC 322/.2/09669 19
HD6885.5.Z65 O36 1983

Organiseringen av statens deltagelse i petroleumsvirksomheten / fra et utvalg oppnevnt ved kongelig resolusjon 5. mars 1982. Oslo : Universitetsforlaget, [1983] 44 p. : ill. ; 28 cm. (Norges offentlige utredninger . 1983:16) "Avgitt til Olje- og energidepartementet 21. februar 1983." ISBN 82-00-70798-9 LC Card 83-244370
1. Petroleum industry and trade - Government policy - Norway. 2. Petroleum industry and trade - Government ownership - Norway. I. Norway. II. Series.
HD9575.N62 O74 1983

Organisierte Arbeit . Mikl-Horke, Gertraude, 1944- München , c1984. vii, 230 p. : ISBN 3-486-28481-9 (pbk.) LC Card 87-672757
HD6955 .M54x 1984

Organismos Proōthēseōs Exagōgōn (Greece)
Boukēs, Sōtos D., 1933- Manatzment, hoi leitourgies tou kai ho cheirismos tou anthrōpinou paragonta . Athēna , 1985. 58 p. : LC Card 86-160168
HF5549 .B7727 1985

Organismos Proōthēseōs Exagōgōn (Greece). Dieuthynsē Eidikōn Meletōn-E.O.K.
Hodēgos exagōgikōn diadikasiōn /. [Athēna] [1983] 184 p. : LC Card 86-170148
HF1009.7.E86 H63 1983

Organismos Proōthēseōs Exagōgōn (Greece). Dieuthynsē Ereunas Agoras. Hypodēmata. Athēna , 1985. 86 p. : LC Card 86-194391
HD9787.G62 H96 1985

Organização das Cooperativas Brasileiras.
Propostas cooperativistas /. Curitiba , 1986. 56 p. : LC Card 87-403655 DDC 334 19
HD2953 .P76 1986

Organização das Cooperativas Brasileiras. Depto. Econômico. As Cooperativas na balança comercial brasileira . [Brasília] [1986] 98 p. : LC Card 87-403826 DDC 334/.63/0981021 19
HF3401.5 .C66 1986

Organização das Cooperativas do Estado do Paraná.
Custo de produção . Curitiba, Paraná , 1987. 88 p. ; LC Card 87-405296 DDC 338.1/371/098162 19
HD9282.B73 P3435 1987

Custo de produção de café /. Curitiba-Paraná [19]84. 47 p. ; LC Card 85-211612
HD9199.B7 C93 1984

Encontro Estadual de Cooperativismo (1979 : Curitiba, Brazil) Anais /. [Curitiba] [1979] 41 leaves : LC Card 84-223142
HD3475.A3 P364 1979

Propostas cooperativistas /. Curitiba , 1986. 56 p. : LC Card 87-403655 DDC 334 19
HD2953 .P76 1986

Organização de Cooperação e de Desenvolvimento Económicos. see **Organization for Economic Cooperation and Development.**

A organização do trabalho na lavoura algodoeira paulista /. Fleury, Maria Tereza Leme. [São Paulo, Brasil] 1984. 208 p. : LC Card 85-145302 DDC 338.1/7351/098161 19
HD9084.B62 S264 1984
NYPL [JLE 86-1740]

Organização dos Estados Americanos. see **Organization of American States.**

Organización andina, drama y posibilidad /. Sánchez Enríquez, Rodrigo. Huancayo, Perú [1987] xxii, 219 p. : LC Card 87-404025 DDC 330.98/0038 19
HC167.A5 S26 1987

La organización campesina . Dubly, Alain. Quito, Ecuador , 1985. 37 p. : LC Card 87-404544 DDC 322/.2/09866 19
HD1531.E2 D83 1985

Organización campesina . Gianotten, Vera. Amsterdam , Cinnaminson, N.J. , c1985. ix, 531 p., [4] p. of plates : ISBN 90-6765-162-1 LC Card 85-200688
HD1531.P4 G5 1985

Organización Campesina Muisne-Esmeraldas.
Campesinado y organización en Esmeraldas /. [Quito, Ecuador?] [1986] 213 p. : LC Card 86-171561
HD1531.E2 C36 1986

Organización de cooperación y desarrollo económicos. see **Organization for Economic Cooperation and Development.**

Organización de la estadística en Cuba /. Silva Fernández, Ricardo. Playa, Ciudad de La Habana , 1985 printing, c1980. 136 p. : LC Card 87-115269 DDC 354.72910081/9 19
HA37.C866 S55 1985

Organización de las Naciones Unidas para la Agricultura y la Alimentación. see **Food and Agriculture Organization of the United Nations.**

Organización de los Estados Americanos. see **Organization of American States.**

Organización institucional del sector agrícola /. Mannarelli M., Virgilio B. Santiago, Chile , 1985. 81, [3] p. : LC Card 86-115545 DDC 338.1/883 19
HD1878 .M35 1985

Organizacion Internacional del Trabajo. see **International Labor Office.**

Organización Mundial de la Salud. see **World Health Organization.**

Organización y recursos humanos /. Novaes, Paulo, 1913- Montevideo , 1976, 1977 printing. 122 p. : LC Card 86-139048
HD5713 .N68 1977

Las organizaciones económicas populares en la nueva coyuntura económica /. Razeto M., Luis, 1945- Santiago, Chile , 1984. 23 p. ; LC Card 84-227565
HD2346.C53 R39 1984

Organizaciones obreras cristianas en la oposición al franquismo (1951-1975) . Domínguez, Javier. Bilbao [1985?] 479 p. ; ISBN 84-271-1431-1 LC Card 87-153234
HD6481.2.S7 D65 1985

Las organizaciones sindicales, obreras y burocráticas contemporáneas en México /. Freyre Rubio, Javier. Azcapotzalco [Mexico] , c1983. 265 p. : ISBN 968-597-500-0 LC Card 86-218318
HD6532 .F74 1983

Organizacja i technika handlu zagranicznego . Dmowski, Zygmunt. Gdańsk , 1979. 201 p. ; LC Card 81-181043
HF1558.7 .D59 1979

Organizacja i technika portów morskich / Andrzej Grzelakowski ... [et al.]. Wyd. 1. Gdańsk : Wydawn. Uniwersytetu Gdańskiego, 1978. 292 p. : ill. ; 25 cm. (Skrypty uczelniane / Uniwersytet Gdański) Includes bibliographies. LC Card 81-200313
1. Harbors - Poland. I. Grzelakowski, Andrzej. II. Series: Skrypty uczelniane / Uniwersytet Gdański.
HE557.P58 O73 1978

Organizacja produkcji w przemyśle / [redaktor zeszytu Zygmunt Gładzicki]. Wrocław : Państwowe Wydawn. Nauk., 1970. 64 p. : ill. ; 24 cm. (Prace naukowe Instytutu Organizacji i Ekonomiki Politechniki Wrocławskiej . nr. 2. 1) Summaries in English and Russian. Includes bibliographies. CONTENTS. - O roli nauki organizacji i zarządzania w rozwoju postępu techniczno-organizacyjnego / Leszek Krzyżanowski -- Metody organizacji niezsynchronizowanych linii potokowych / Tadeusz Czarny -- Metody ustalania danych wyjściowych dla obliczania taktu potokowych linii montażowych / Tadeusz Czarny -- Zagadnienie wyznaczania liczby robotników rezerwowych w potokowych liniach produkcyjnych / Zbigniew Kulaś, Marek Piałucha. LC Card 87-137344
1. Industrial organization - Poland - Mathematical models. I. Gładzicki, Zygmunt. II. Series: Prace naukowe Instytutu Organizacji i Ekonomiki Politechniki Wrocławskiej , nr. 2.
HD70.P6 O745 1970

Organizacja transportu samochodowego /. Krasucka, Alicja. Gdańsk , 1984. 181 p., [8] leaves of plates (7 folded) : ISBN 83-7017-058-7 : LC Card 86-173836
HE5675.7.A6 K7 1984

Organizačně institucionální soustava řízení MSEI /. Stránská, Ludmila. Praha , 1985. 167 p. : LC Card 86-215270
HC243.5 .S88 1985

Organizações de trabalhadores . Penteado Neto, Alfredo Camargo, 1939- São Paulo , 1986. 112 p. : LC Card 87-403488 DDC 338.6 19
HD5650 .P37 1986

ORGANIZATION.
Bozeman, Barry. All organizations are public . San Francisco , 1987. xix, 184 p. : ISBN 1-555-42036-2 (alk. paper) LC Card 86-27699 DDC 302.3/5 19
HD58.9 .B69 1987

Davis, Stanley M. Future perfect /. Reading, Mass. , c1987. 243 p. : ISBN 0-201-11513-1 : LC Card 87-18669 DDC 658 19
HD31 .D325 1987

Fleischer, Manfred. Organisationstheoretische Analyse von Marketing-Entscheidungsprozessen . Berlin [1977] 93 p. : LC Card 85-111320
HF5415.135 .F58 1977

Ford, Robert Clayton, 1945- Organization theory . New York , c1988. xxii, 482 p. : ISBN 0-06-042124-X LC Card 87-23796 DDC 302.3/5 19
HD31 .F5726 1988

Grandori, Anna. Teorie dell'organizzazione . [Milano] , 1984. xxiii, 213 p. : ISBN 88-14-00411-0 : LC Card 85-162760
HD37.I8 G73 1984

Grandori, Anna. [Teorie dell'organizzazione. English.] Perspectives on organization theory /. Cambridge, Mass. , c1987. xxvi, 199 p. : ISBN 0-88730-214-9 LC Card 87-11359 DDC 302.3/5 19
HD37.I8 G7313 1987

Handbook of organizations /. New York , 1987, c1965. 2 v. (xvi, 1247 p.) : ISBN 0-8240-8215-X (set : alk. paper) : LC Card 86-25797 DDC 658.4 19
HD58.7 .H365 1987

Jagoe, A. L. (Armiger L.), 1921- The winning corporation . Washington, D.C. , c1987. xviii, 232 p. ; ISBN 0-87491-858-9 : LC Card 87-1766 DDC 658.4 19
HD31 .J245 1987

Johns, Gary, 1946- Organizational behavior . Glenview, Ill. , c1988. xxii, 676 p. : ISBN 0-673-18418-0 (p. 4 of cover); 0-673-18418-8 LC Card 87-23296 DDC 658.3 19
HD58.7 .J6 1988

Modern organization theory . New York , 1987, c1959. x, 324 p. : ISBN 0-8240-8208-7 (alk. paper) : LC Card 86-27072 DDC 658 19
HD31 .M614 1987

Nadler, David. Strategic organization design . Glenview, Ill. , c1988. 209 p. : ISBN 0-673-15860-8 (pbk.) LC Card 87-9832 DDC 658.4/012 19
HD58.7 .N33 1988

Omgeving, doelstellingen en organisatie . Assen , 1986. viii, 464 p. : ISBN 90-232-2208-3 : LC Card 86-182876
HG4181 .O44 1986

The Organisation in its environment /. London , 1984. xiii, 624 p. : ISBN 0-421-32290-X (pbk.) : LC Card 84-242095 DDC 302.3/5 19
HD31 .O7217 1984 ***NYPL [JLD 86-2539]***

Organizing industrial development /. Berlin , New York , 1986. xi, 391 p. : ISBN 0-89925-168-4 (U. S.) LC Card 86-24074 DDC 338.9 19
HD31 .O783 1986 ***NYPL [JLE 87-789]***

Puxty, Anthony G. Organization and management . London , 1986. viii, 280 p. ; ISBN 0-273-02138-9 (pbk.) : LC Card 87-122002 DDC 658 19
HD31 .P88 1986

Rowbottom, Ralph William. Organisational design . Aldershot, Hants, England , Brookfield, Vt., USA , 1987. 165 p. : ISBN 0-566-05408-6 : LC Card 86-31946 DDC 658.4/02 19
HD50 .R68 1987

Susánszky, János. Tanulmányok a szervezésről és a vezetésről /. Budapest , 1985. 89 p. ; ISBN 963-05-4132-7 : LC Card 86-136320
HD37.H82 S857 1985

Takahashi, Nobuo, 1957- Design of adaptive organizations . Berlin , New York , c1987. vi, 140 p. : ISBN 0-387-17834-1 (U. S.) : LC Card 87-9834 DDC 658.4/06 19
HD58.8 .T35 1987

Tannenbaum, Robert. Leadership and organization . New York , 1987, c1961. xiv, 456 p. : ISBN 0-8240-8219-2 (alk. paper) : LC Card 86-27019 DDC 303.3/4 19
HD57.7 .T36 1987

Volkmann, Helmut, 1936- Der Informationsmarkt . München , c1985. 366 p. : ISBN 3-89003-016-5 LC Card 85-195750
HD35 .V596 1985

ORGANIZATION - ADDRESSES, ESSAYS, LECTURES.
Organization--communication . Norwood, N.J. , c1986- v. : ISBN 0-89391-274-3 (v. 1) LC Card 85-6159 DDC 302.3/5 19
HD31 .O727 1986 ***NYPL [JLL 86-382]***

Organizational theory and public policy /. Beverly Hills, Calif. , c1983. 304 p. : ISBN 0-8039-2006-7 LC Card 83-9704 DDC 302.3/5 19
HD38 .O75 1983 ***NYPL [JLD 87-1123]***

People and organisations . Aldershot, Hants. , c1982. ix, 143 p. : ISBN 0-566-00373-2 LC Card 82-189914 DDC 658.3/124 19
HD31 .P375 1982 ***NYPL [JLD 86-2775]***

Systemy organizacyjne /. [Wrocław] , 1981. 75 p. : LC Card 83-161920
HB9 .B7522 nr. 188 HM131

Teoria dell'organizzazione e realtà italiana . Milano [1980] 225 p. ; ISBN 88-20-41736-7 : LC Card 80-511472 DDC 302.3/5 19
HM131 .T4 ***NYPL [JLD 81-599]***

Organization analysis and development : a social construction of organizational behaviour / edited by Iain L. Mangham. Chichester [West Sussex] ; New York : Wiley, c1987. xiii, 269 p. ; 24 cm. (Industrial psychology and organizational behaviour) Bibliography: p. 251-265. Includes index. ISBN 0-471-91227-1 : LC Card 86-26713 DDC 658.4/06 19
1. Organizational behavior. 2. Organizational change. I. Mangham, I. L. II. Series.
HD58.7 .O669 1987

Organization and management . Puxty, Anthony G. London , 1986. viii, 280 p. ; ISBN 0-273-02138-9 (pbk.) : LC Card 87-122002 DDC 658 19
HD31 .P88 1986

ORGANIZATION - CASE STUDIES.
Daft, Richard L. Organization theory . St. Paul , c1987. xxviii, 338 p. : ISBN 0-314-28488-5 (pbk.) LC Card 86-28965 DDC 658.4 19
HD31 .D136 1987

ORGANIZATION CHARTS.
Niemeyer, Gerhard. Eine automatentheoretische Baumkonstruktion zur Simulation hierarchischer Management-Strukturen /. [Regensburg] [1984] 64 p. : LC Card 84-181485
HD38 .N513 1984

Organization--communication : emerging perspectives / Lee Thayer, editor. Norwood, N.J. : Ablex Pub. Corp., c1986- v. : ill. ; 24 cm. (People, communication, organization) Includes bibliographies and indexes. ISBN 0-89391-274-3 (v. 1) LC Card 85-6159 DDC 302.3/5 19
1. Organization - Addresses, essays, lectures. 2. Communication in organizations - Addresses, essays, lectures. I. Thayer, Lee O. II. Series.
HD31 .O727 1986 ***NYPL [JLL 86-382]***

ORGANIZATION - CONGRESSES.
Organizational theory and inquiry . Beverly Hills , c1985. 231 p. ; ISBN 0-8039-2494-1 LC Card 85-8137 DDC 302/.072 19
HM131 .O683 1985 ***NYPL [JLD 86-3567]***

Organization development . Burke, W. Warner (Wyatt Warner), 1935- Reading, Mass. , c1987. xiv, 189 p. : ISBN 0-201-10697-3 : LC Card 86-26474 DDC 658.4/06 19
HD58.8 .B878 1987

Organization development in the mining industry . Gavin, James. New York , 1986. viii, 247 p. : ISBN 0-275-92061-5 (alk. paper) : LC Card 85-24400 DDC 622/.068 19
HD9506.U62 G38 1986
NYPL [JLE 86-3024]

ORGANIZATION - DICTIONARIES.
Banki, Ivan S. Dictionary of administration and management . Los Angeles, Calif., USA ,

c1986. iv, 1369 p. ; ISBN 0-912352-08-6 LC Card 85-63870 DDC 650/.03/21 19
HD30.15 .B36 1986

ORGANIZATION EFFECTIVENESS.
Hauff, Hanns Joachim Paul. Aufstieg zur Macht . München , c1983. 85 p. : ISBN 3-597-10422-3 LC Card 83-136638
HD38.2 .H38 1983

Lareau, William. Millennium management . Piscataway, NJ [1986]. ix, 214 p. : ISBN 0-8329-0431-7 : LC Card 86-18247 DDC 658.4/06 19
HD58.8 .L37 1986 ***NYPL [JLE 87-1139]***

ORGANIZATION - EVALUATION.
Evaluatiemethoden, een introductie . 's-Gravenhage [1984] v, 188 p. : ISBN 90-12-04825-7 LC Card 85-196500
HD58.9 .E93 1984

Organization for Economic Co-operation and Development.

Organization for Economic Cooperation and Development.
Agricultural trade with developing countries. Paris [Washington, D.C.] 1984. 113 p. ; ISBN 92-64-12579-5 (pbk.) LC Card 84-221780 DDC 382/.41/091724 19
HD9018.D44 A37 1984
NYPL [JLE 86-3906]

The Export credit financing systems in OECD member countries. Paris , Washington, D.C. , 1987. 285 p. : ISBN 92-64-12947-2 (pbk.) : LC Card 87-170161 DDC 351.82/76 19
HG3753 .E88 1987

Information activities, electronics, and telecommunications technologies . Paris , Washington, D.C.] 1981- v. : ISBN 92-64-12241-9 (pbk. : v. 1) LC Card 81-211344 DDC 338.4/700151 19
HD9696.C62 I53 ***NYPL [JLL 86-393]***

International trade and the consumer . Paris [Washington, D.C. , 1986. 296 p. ; ISBN 92-64-12813-1 (pbk.) : LC Card 86-216097 DDC 382/.3 19
HF1410.5 .I585 1986 ***NYPL [JLE 87-1541]***

ORGANIZATION - INDIA.
When the twain meet . Allahabad , 1986. vi, 170 p. ; LC Card 87-900706 DDC 658/.00954 19
HD70.I4 W54 1986

ORGANIZATION, INDUSTRIAL. see **INDUSTRIAL ORGANIZATION.**

ORGANIZATION OF AFRICAN UNITY.
Ndeshyo Rurihose. La stratégie de l'Organisation de l'unité africaine pour le développement . [Kinshasa] , 1981. 80 p. : LC Card 83-161631
HC800 .N393 1981

Organization of American States. Council. Inter-American Economic and Social Council. see **Inter-American Economic and Social Council.**

Organization of American States. Departamento de Desarrollo Regional. see **Organization of American States. Dept. of Regional Development.**

Organization of American States. Dept. of Regional Development.
River Transportation Seminar (1986 : Iquitos, Peru) Tratado de cooperación amazónica . Washington, D.C. , 1986. iii, 110 p. ; ISBN 0-8270-2473-8 (pbk.) LC Card 87-115058
HE387.A6 R58 1986

Tratado de cooperación amazónica . Washington, D.C. , 1986. iii, 101 p. ; ISBN 0-8270-2304-9 (pbk.) LC Card 86-152493
HE359.A5 T73 1986

Organization of American States. Executive Secretariat for Economic and Social Affairs.
The Economy of Latin America and the Caribbean . Washington, D.C. [1986] v, 30 p. ; ISBN 0-8270-2333-2 (pbk.) : LC Card 86-203268 DDC 336.3/435/09729 19
HJ8514.5 .E34 1986

Organization of American States. General Secretariat. Dept. of Regional Development. see **Organization of American States. Dept. of Regional Development.**

Organization of American States. Inter-American Committee for Agricultural Development. see **Inter-American Committee for Agricultural Development.**

Organization of American States. Regional Development, Dept. of. see **Organization of American States. Dept. of Regional Development.**

Organization of American States. Secretariá Ejecutiva para Asuntos Económicos y Sociales. see **Organization of American States. Executive Secretariat for Economic and Social Affairs.**

Organization of innovation : east-west perspectives / editors, John Child, Paul Bate. Berlin ; New York : W. de Gruyter, 1987. x, 238 p. : ill. ; 24 cm. (De Gruyter studies in organization . 11) "Based on a selection of papers delivered at the third in a series of Workshops on Capitalist-Socialist Organizations, held in Helsinki in August 1984"--P. [v] Includes bibliographies. ISBN 0-89925-167-6 (U. S.) : LC Card 87-19936 DDC 658.4/06 19
1. Technological innovations - Management - Congresses. 2. Technological innovations - Communist countries - Management - Congresses. 3. Technology and state - Congresses. 4. Technology and state - Communist countries - Congresses. 5. Comparative management - Congresses. I. Child, John, 1940-. II. Bate, Paul. III. Workshop on Capitalist-Socialist Organizations (3rd : 1984 : Helsinki, Finland). IV. Series.
HD45 .O73 1987

ORGANIZATION OF PETROLEUM EXPORTING COUNTRIES - ADDRESSES, ESSAYS, LECTURES.
Calderón Berti, Humberto. Petróleo y opinión pública /. [Caracas?] [1983?] 455 p. : LC Card 85-119987 DDC 338.2/72/0987 19
HD9574.V42 C364 1983
NYPL [JLE 86-535]

ORGANIZATION OF PETROLEUM EXPORTING COUNTRIES - STATISTICS.
Facts and figures . Vienna , 1984? 45 p. :
NYPL [JLD 86-2319]

ORGANIZATION - RESEARCH - ADDRESSES, ESSAYS, LECTURES.
Tagiuri, Renato. Organizational climate. Boston, 1968. viii, 246 p. LC Card 68-8418 DDC 301.4
HM131 .T27 ***NYPL [JLD 86-684]***

ORGANIZATION - RESEARCH - CONGRESSES.
Organizational theory and inquiry . Beverly Hills , c1985. 231 p. ; ISBN 0-8039-2494-1 LC Card 85-8137 DDC 302/.072 19
HM131 .O683 1985 ***NYPL [JLD 86-3567]***

ORGANIZATION, SOCIAL. see **SOCIAL STRUCTURE.**

Organization theory . Daft, Richard L. St. Paul , c1987. xxviii, 338 p. : ISBN 0-314-28488-5 (pbk.) LC Card 86-28965 DDC 658.4 19
HD31 .D136 1987

Organization theory . Ford, Robert Clayton, 1945- New York , c1988. xxii, 482 p. : ISBN 0-06-042124-X LC Card 87-23796 DDC 302.3/5 19
HD31 .F5726 1988

Organization theory and technocratic consciousness . Alvesson, Mats, 1956- [Organisationsteori och teknokratiskt medvetande. English.] Berlin , New York , 1987. ix, 286 p. : ISBN 0-89925-165-X : LC Card 86-24057 DDC 306/.36 19
HD6955 .A44313 1987

The organization woman . Highman, Edith L. New York, N.Y. , c1985. 204 p. ; ISBN 0-89885-237-4 LC Card 84-27775 DDC 658.4/09/024042 19
HD6054.3 .H54 1985 ***NYPL [JLD 86-1930]***

Organizational behavior . Johns, Gary, 1946- Glenview, Ill. , c1988. xxii, 676 p. : ISBN 0-673-18418-0 (p. 4 of cover); 0-673-18418-8 LC Card 87-23296 DDC 658.3 19
HD58.7 .J6 1988

Organizational behavior . McAfee, R. Bruce. St. Paul , c1987. xviii, 489 p. : ISBN 0-314-93201-1 : LC Card 86-24745 DDC 658.3 19
HD58.7 .M38 1987

Organizational behavior /. Vecchio, Robert P. Chicago [1987], c1988. xv, 576 p. : ISBN 0-03-000853-0 LC Card 86-29262 DDC 658.3 19
HD58.7 .V43 1988

ORGANIZATIONAL BEHAVIOR.
Advances in organizational psychology . Newbury Park , c1987. 314 p. ; ISBN 0-8039-2802-5 LC Card 87-9484 DDC 158.7 19
HF5548.8 .A58 1987

The Applied psychology of work behavior . Plano, Tex. , 1987. ix, 501 p. : ISBN 0-256-03431-1 (pbk.) LC Card 86-72246 DDC 158.7 19
HF5548.8 .A72 1987

Argyris, Chris, 1923- Personality and organization . New York , 1987, c1957. xiii, 291 p. ; ISBN 0-8240-8200-1 (alk. paper) : LC Card 86-27054 DDC 658.4 19
HD58.7 .A75 1987

Behaviour in organisations . Johannesburg , New York , 1986, c1983. 924 p. : ISBN 0-07-450690-0 (pbk.) : LC Card 87-113321 DDC 158.7/0968 19
HD58.7 .B426 1986

Brief, Arthur P., 1946- Managing smart . Lexington, Mass. , c1987. x, 164 p. ; ISBN 0-669-12654-3 (alk. paper) LC Card 85-45978 DDC 658.3 19
HD31 .B7396 1987

Carrion, Rosinha Machado. Participação ou manipulação . Porto Alegre, RS , 1984. 111 p. : LC Card 84-209842 DDC 658 19
HD37.P63 C29 1984 ***NYPL [JLE 86-2263]***

Chakraborty, S. K. Human response in organizations . Calcutta, India [1985] xv, 228 p. : LC Card 87-901782 DDC 658/.00954 19
HD58.7 .C44 1985

Dailey, Robert C. Understanding people in organizations /. St. Paul, MN , c1988. xviii, 525 p. : ISBN 0-314-24254-6 LC Card 86-32460 DDC 658.4 19
HD58.7 .D34 1988

DeMarco, Tom. Peopleware . New York, NY , c1987. x, 188 p. : ISBN 0-932633-05-6 (pbk.) : LC Card 87-22293 DDC 658.3/14 19
HD31 .D42185 1987

Dyllick, Thomas. Gesellschaftliche Instabilität und Unternehmungsführung . Bern , c1982. xiv, 394 p. : ISBN 3-258-03212-2 LC Card 83-115754
HD58.7 .D94 1982

Effective behavior in organizations . Homewood, Ill. , 1988. xxvi, 959 p. : ISBN 0-256-05967-5 LC Card 87-82176 DDC 658.4 19
HD58.7 .E35 1988

Flohr, Bernd. Fungibilität und Elastizität von Personal /. Göttingen , c1984. xvi, 439 p. ; ISBN 3-525-12665-4 LC Card 85-125026
HF5549 .F584 1984

Grandori, Anna. Teorie dell'organizzazione . [Milano] , 1984. xxiii, 213 p. : ISBN 88-14-00411-0 : LC Card 85-162760
HD37.I8 G73 1984

Grandori, Anna. [Teorie dell'organizzazione. English.] Perspectives on organization theory /. Cambridge, Mass. , c1987. xxvi, 199 p. : ISBN 0-88730-214-9 LC Card 87-11359 DDC 302.3/5 19
HD37.I8 G7313 1987

The Great writings in management and organizational behavior /. New York , c1987. p. cm. ISBN 0-394-36099-0 LC Card 86-33900 DDC 658 19
HD31 .G74 1987

Greif, Siegfried. Konzepte der Organisationspsychologie . Bern , c1983. 320 p. : ISBN 3-456-81262-0 LC Card 83-240680
HD58.7 .G72 1983

Halloran, Jack, 1931- Applied human relations . Englewood Cliffs, N.J. , c1987. xvi, 528 p. : ISBN 0-13-040742-9 LC Card 86-25336 DDC 658.3 19
HD58.7 .H34 1987

Hampton, David R. Organizational behavior and the practice of management /. Glenview, Ill. , c1987. 876 p. : ISBN 0-673-18303-3 LC Card 86-24798 DDC 658.4 19
HD58.7 .H35 1987

Handbook of organizations /. New York , 1987,

c1965. 2 v. (xvi, 1247 p.) : ISBN 0-8240-8215-X (set : alk. paper) : LC Card 86-25797 DDC 658.4 19
HD58.7 .H365 1987

Hermann, Ursula. Die Implementierung betrieblicher Rationalisierungshandlungen und der personelle Widerstand . Göttingen , c1984. xx, 356 p. : ISBN 3-525-12558-5 : LC Card 84-218331
HD58.8 .H48 1984

Hersey, Paul. Management of organizational behavior . Englewood Cliffs, N.J. , 1988. p. cm. ISBN 0-13-551268-9 : LC Card 87-23064 DDC 658.3 19
HD58.7 .H47 1988

Higgins, James M. Human relations . New York , c1987. xvi, 479 p. : ISBN 0-394-35112-6 : LC Card 86-31450 DDC 658.3/145 19
HF5549 .H474 1987

Hirschhorn, Larry. The workplace within . Cambridge, Mass. , c1988. x, 265 p. ; ISBN 0-262-08169-5 LC Card 87-20144 DDC 158.7 19
HF5548.8 .H493 1988

Hollingsworth, J. Rogers (Joseph Rogers), 1932- The governance of the American economy . Berlin [1985] 60 p. ; LC Card 86-205784 DDC 330.973 19
HC106.8 .H635 1985

Ivancevich, John M. Organizational behavior and management /. Plano, Tex. , 1987. xv, 780 p. : ISBN 0-256-05608-0 LC Card 86-72712 DDC 658.4 19
HD58.7 .I89 1987

Johns, Gary, 1946- Organizational behavior . Glenview, Ill. , c1988. xxii, 676 p. : ISBN 0-673-18418-0 (p. 4 of cover); 0-673-18418-8 LC Card 87-23296 DDC 658.3 19
HD58.7 .J6 1988

Kets de Vries, Manfred F. R. Unstable at the top . New York , 1988, c1987. xiv, 221 p. ; ISBN 0-453-00562-4 LC Card 87-23182 DDC 158.7 19
HD58.7 .K475 1988

Korteweg, Hans. Helen of delen . Amsterdam , 1986, c1985. 222 p. ; ISBN 90-254-6652-4 : LC Card 86-182872
HD58.8 .K66 1986

Kovach, Barbara E. Survival on the fast track /. New York , c1988. xv, 240 p. ; ISBN 0-396-09027-3 LC Card 87-19940 DDC 658.4/092 19
HD57.7 .K69 1988

Lattmann, Charles. Die verhaltenswissenschaftlichen Grundlagen der Führung des Mitarbeiters /. Bern , c1981. 565 p. : ISBN 3-258-03094-4 : LC Card 82-163528 DDC 658.3 19
HD58.7 .L36 1981 ***NYPL [JLE 86-1595]***

McAfee, R. Bruce. Organizational behavior . St. Paul , c1987. xviii, 489 p. : ISBN 0-314-93201-1 : LC Card 86-24745 DDC 658.3 19
HD58.7 .M38 1987

Management planning and control . Beavercreek, Ohio , c1987. xvii, 249 p. : ISBN 0-939787-00-8 (pbk.) : LC Card 86-24930 DDC 658.1/511 19
HF5635 .M236 1987

Mastenbroek, W. F. G. [Conflicthantering en organisatie-ontwikkeling. English.] Conflict management and organization development /. Chichester , New York , c1987. x, 166 p. ; ISBN 0-471-91415-0 : LC Card 87-10463 DDC 302.3/5 19
HD58.8 .M32513 1987

Matejka, J. Kenneth. Handling human performance /. Richmond, Va. , c1982. v, 90 p. : ISBN 0-936328-20-7 (pbk.) LC Card 81-69197 DDC 658.3/14 19
HF5549.5.I5 M337 1982
NYPL [JLE 86-4361]

Modern organization theory . New York , 1987, c1959. x, 324 p. : ISBN 0-8240-8208-7 (alk. paper) : LC Card 86-27072 DDC 658 19
HD31 .M614 1987

Muchinsky, Paul M. Psychology applied to work . Chicago, Ill. , c1987. xxvi, 712, xix p. : ISBN 0-256-03671-3 LC Card 86-81818 DDC 158.7 19
HF5548.8 .M756 1987

Nadler, David. Strategic organization design . Glenview, Ill. , c1988. 209 p. : ISBN 0-673-15860-8 (pbk.) LC Card 87-9832 DDC 658.4/012 19
HD58.7 .N33 1988

Organisation als soziales System . Berlin , c1986. 219 p. ; ISBN 3-924859-22-1 LC Card 87-137969 DDC 302.3/5 19
HD58.7 .O6687 1986

Organization analysis and development . Chichester [West Sussex] , New York , c1987. xiii, 269 p. ; ISBN 0-471-91227-1 : LC Card 86-26713 DDC 658.4/06 19
HD58.7 .O669 1987

Robbins, Stephen P., 1943- Essentials of organizational behavior /. Englewood Cliffs, N.J. , c1988. p. cm. ISBN 0-13-286485-1 LC Card 87-19876 DDC 658.3 19
HD58.7 .R6 1988

Sauter, Franz, 1956- Transaktionskostentheorie der Organisation /. München , c1985. iv, 187, 2 p. : ISBN 3-89003-013-0 LC Card 85-194969
HB846.3 .S28 1985

Scanlan, Burt K. Management & organizational behavior /. Malibar, Fla. , 1987, c1983. xvi, 666 p. : ISBN 0-89464-246-4 LC Card 87-17035 DDC 658.4 19
HD31 .S3256 1987

Schuster, Fred E. The Schuster report . New York , c1986. xvi, 200 p. : ISBN 0-471-83293-6 : LC Card 86-9190 DDC 658.3/14 19
HD58.8 .S38 1986 ***NYPL [JLE 86-3973]***

Sims, Henry P., 1939- The thinking organization /. San Francisco , 1986. xxvii, 375 p. : ISBN 0-87589-690-1 LC Card 85-45913 DDC 302.3/5 19
HD58.7 .S584 1986 ***NYPL [JLE 86-2921]***

Social science approaches to business behavior /. New York , 1987. vii, 183 p. : ISBN 0-8240-8201-X (alk. paper) : LC Card 86-25802 DDC 658.4 19
HD58.7 .S66 1987

The Social science of organization[s] . New York , 1987. ix, 182 p. : ISBN 0-8240-8213-3 (alk. paper) : LC Card 86-27069 DDC 658.4/03 19
HD58.7 .S67 1987

Staudinger, Hans-Joachim, 1957- Die Überwachung der Geschäftsführung, eine betriebswirtschaftliche Betrachtung . München , c1986. lxxxvi, 340 p. ; ISBN 3-88259-412-8 LC Card 87-125378 DDC 663/.3/0685 19
HD35 .S6745 1986

Szilagyi, Andrew D. Organizational behavior and performance /. Glenview, Ill. , c1987. 742 p. : ISBN 0-673-16664-3 : LC Card 86-26087 DDC 658.4 19
HD58.7 .S97 1987

Tubbs, Stewart L., 1943- A systems approach to small group interaction /. New York , 1987. p. cm. ISBN 0-394-36539-9 : LC Card 87-23394 DDC 302.3/4 19
HD66 .T82 1987

Umstot, Denis D. Understanding organizational behavior /. St. Paul , c1988. xviii, 532 p. : ISBN 0-314-62488-0 LC Card 87-25255 DDC 658.3 19
HD58.7 .U47 1988

Vecchio, Robert P. Organizational behavior /. Chicago [1987], c1988. xv, 576 p. : ISBN 0-03-000853-0 LC Card 86-29262 DDC 658.3 19
HD58.7 .V43 1988

Werder, Axel von. Organisationsstruktur und Rechtsnorm . Wiesbaden , c1986. 564 p. : ISBN 3-409-13107-8 LC Card 86-224483
HD58.7 .W35 1986

Wersebe, Hilmar von, 1943- Struktureller und funktionaler Pluralismus in der öffentlichen Verwaltung /. Frankfurt am Main , New York , c1986. 100 p. : ISBN 3-8204-9136-8 LC Card 86-229888
HD58.7 .W36 1986

Wickham, Alexandre. Les carriéristes . Paris , c1983. 358 p. ; ISBN 2-85956-348-2 : LC Card 84-122542 DDC 650.1/4 19
HF5386 .W494 1983 ***NYPL [JLE 86-4124]***

Williams, Cecil L., 1930- The negotiable environment . Ann Arbor, Mich. , c1985. v, 82 p. : ISBN 0-936658-20-7 (pbk.) : LC Card 85-10305 DDC 658.3/82 19
HF5547.2 .W55 1985 ***NYPL [JLF 86-1138]***

Wilson, Gerald L., 1943- Organizational communication /. New York , c1986. xiv, 322 p. : ISBN 0-06-042387-0 LC Card 85-8723 DDC 658.4/5 19
HD58.7 .W55 1986 ***NYPL [JLE 86-2600]***

ORGANIZATIONAL BEHAVIOR - ADDRESSES, ESSAYS, LECTURES.
Handbook of industrial and organizational psychology /. New York , c1983. xxvii, 1740 p. : ISBN 0-471-88642-4 LC Card 83-42702 DDC 158.7 19
HF5548.8 .H265 1983 ***NYPL [JLE 86-1120]***

Organizational behavior and management /. Ivancevich, John M. Plano, Tex. , 1987. xv, 780 p. : ISBN 0-256-05608-0 LC Card 86-72712 DDC 658.4 19
HD58.7 .I89 1987

Organizational behavior and performance /. Szilagyi, Andrew D. Glenview, Ill. , c1987. 742 p. : ISBN 0-673-16664-3 : LC Card 86-26087 DDC 658.4 19
HD58.7 .S97 1987

Organizational behavior and psychology series. Feldman, Daniel C. Managing careers in organizations /. Glenview, Ill. , c1988. 249 p. : ISBN 0-673-18562-1 (pbk.) : LC Card 87-16580 DDC 650.1/4 19
HF5549 .F386 1988

Organizational behavior and the practice of management /. Hampton, David R. Glenview, Ill. , c1987. 876 p. : ISBN 0-673-18303-3 LC Card 86-24798 DDC 658.4 19
HD58.7 .H35 1987

ORGANIZATIONAL BEHAVIOR - CASE STUDIES.
Egan, Gerard. Change agent skills in helping and human service settings /. Monterey, Calif. , c1985. xi, 306 p. : ISBN 0-534-03624-4 : LC Card 84-7804 DDC 361.3/07 19
HV11 .E43 1985 ***NYPL [JLE 86-1963]***

Organizational capital . Tomer, John F. New York , 1987. xvi, 188 p. : ISBN 0-275-92582-X (alk. paper) : LC Card 87-16828 DDC 338.5 19
HD31 .T635 1987

ORGANIZATIONAL CHANGE - ADDRESSES, ESSAYS, LECTURES.
Kirkpatrick, Donald L. How to manage change effectively /. San Francisco , 1985. xxii, 280 p. : ISBN 0-87589-659-6 LC Card 85-45060 DDC 658.4/06 19
HD58.8 .K52 1985 ***NYPL [JLE 87-1191]***

People and organisations . Aldershot, Hants. , c1982. ix, 143 p. : ISBN 0-566-00373-2 LC Card 82-189914 DDC 658.3/124 19
HD31 .P375 1982 ***NYPL [JLD 86-2775]***

Organizational change and the Third World . Jedlicka, Allen D. New York , 1987. xii, 141 p. ; ISBN 0-275-92317-7 (alk. paper) : LC Card 87-13252 DDC 658.4/06/091724 19
HC59.72.E44 J43 1987

Organizational change as a development strategy . Hage, Jerald, 1932- Boulder, Colo. , 1987. xvi, 293 p. ; ISBN 1-555-87012-0 (lib. bdg. : alk. paper) : LC Card 87-12730 DDC 338.9/0068 19
HC59.72.E44 H34 1987

ORGANIZATIONAL CHANGE - CASE STUDIES.
Archier, Georges. [Entreprise du 3e type. English.] The type 3 company /. New York , 1987. xiv, 123 p. ; ISBN 0-89397-282-7 : LC Card 87-11203 DDC 658/.00973 19
HD58.9 .A7313 1987

Potts, Mark. The leading edge . New York , c1987. iv, 220 p. ; ISBN 0-07-050599-3 LC Card 86-10567 DDC 658.4/06 19
HD58.8 .P68 1987 ***NYPL [JLE 87-33]***

ORGANIZATIONAL CHANGE - CONGRESSES.
Frontiers in creative and innovative management /. Cambridge, Mass. , 1985,

c1986. xxv, 391 p. : ISBN 0-88730-057-X LC Card 85-15125 DDC 658.4 19
HD53 .F76 1986 ***NYPL [JLE 86-3614]***

The Management of strategic change /. Oxford [Oxfordshire] , New York, NY , 1988, c1987. p. cm. ISBN 0-631-15695-X : LC Card 87-15634 DDC 658.4/012 19
HD30.28 .M344 1988

ORGANIZATIONAL CHANGE - DEVELOPING COUNTRIES.
Hage, Jerald, 1932- Organizational change as a development strategy . Boulder, Colo. , 1987. xvi, 293 p. ; ISBN 1-555-87012-0 (lib. bdg. : alk. paper) : LC Card 87-12730 DDC 338.9/0068 19
HC59.72.E44 H34 1987

Jedlicka, Allen D. Organizational change and the Third World . New York , 1987. xii, 141 p. ; ISBN 0-275-92317-7 (alk. paper) : LC Card 87-13252 DDC 658.4/06/091724 19
HC59.72.E44 J43 1987

ORGANIZATIONAL CHANGE - GERMANY (WEST)
Arbeitsgestaltung in der Serienfertigung . Frankfurt [am Main] , New York , c1984. 315 p. : ISBN 3-593-32733-3 LC Card 84-230390
HD58.8 .A73 1984

Geiser, Josef. Wachstumshemmnisse mittelständischer Industriebetriebe /. Göttingen , 1983. xi, 385 p. : ISBN 3-509-01353-0 LC Card 84-221327
HD2346.G3 G372 1983

Kempf, Thomas. Umsetzung organisatorischer Neuerungen . Berlin , 1986. 237 p. : ISBN 3-88118-133-4 LC Card 87-114986
HD58.8 .K46 1986

ORGANIZATIONAL CHANGE - GERMANY (WEST) - CASE STUDIES.
Dieterle, W. (Willi) Organisationsänderung in Unternehmungen . Göttingen , 1986. iii, 169 p. : ISBN 3-509-01425-1 LC Card 87-131121 DDC 338/.06 19
HD58.8 .D54 1986

ORGANIZATIONAL CHANGE - HUNGARY.
Antal, Iván. Vállalatok környezete, céljai, szervezete /. Budapest , 1986. 270 p. : ISBN 963-221-567-2 : LC Card 87-149512
HD70.H8 A536 1986

ORGANIZATIONAL CHANGE - JAPAN - HISTORY - CASE STUDIES.
Westney, D. Eleanor. Imitation and innovation . Cambridge, Mass. , 1987. viii, 252 p. : ISBN 0-674-44437-X (alk. paper) LC Card 87-273 DDC 338.6/0952 19
HD70.J3 W47 1987

ORGANIZATIONAL CHANGE - NETHERLANDS.
During, W. E. Innovatieproblematiek in kleine industriële bedrijven /. Assen , 1986. 242 p. : ISBN 90-232-2196-6 : LC Card 86-186964
HD2346.N4 D87 1986

Korteweg, Hans. Helen of delen . Amsterdam , 1986, c1985. 222 p. ; ISBN 90-254-6652-4 : LC Card 86-182872
HD58.8 .K66 1986

ORGANIZATIONAL CHANGE - UNITED STATES.
Change master companies [videorecording] . Chicago, IL , 1987. 1 videocassette (42 min.) : LC Card 87-705608 DDC 658.3 11
HD45

Mitroff, Ian I. Business not as usual . San Francisco , 1987. xxi, 194 p. : ISBN 1-555-42030-3 (alk. paper) LC Card 86-46333 DDC 338.9 19
HD70.U5 M52 1987

ORGANIZATIONAL CHANGE - UNITED STATES - CASE STUDIES.
Gavin, James. Organization development in the mining industry . New York , 1986. viii, 247 p. : ISBN 0-275-92061-5 (alk. paper) : LC Card 85-24400 DDC 622/.068 19
HD9506.U62 G38 1986
NYPL [JLE 86-3024]

Organizational climate. Tagiuri, Renato. Boston, 1968. viii, 246 p. LC Card 68-8418 DDC 301.4
HM131 .T27 ***NYPL [JLD 86-684]***

Organizational communication / edited by Sherry Devereaux Ferguson and Stewart Ferguson. 2nd ed. New Brunswick, N.J., U. S.A. : Transaction Books, c1987. p. cm. ISBN 0-88738-164-2 : LC Card 87-13856 DDC 658.4/5 19
1. Communication in organizations. 2. Communication in management. I. Ferguson, Sherry. II. Ferguson, Stewart.
HD30.3 .O72 1987

Organizational communication /. Wilson, Gerald L., 1943- New York , c1986. xiv, 322 p. : ISBN 0-06-042387-0 LC Card 85-8723 DDC 658.4/5 19
HD58.7 .W55 1986 ***NYPL [JLE 86-2600]***

ORGANIZATIONAL DEVELOPMENT.
Organisation als soziales System . Berlin , c1986. 219 p. ; ISBN 3-924859-22-1 LC Card 87-137969 DDC 302.3/5 19
HD58.7 .O6687 1986

ORGANIZATIONAL EFFECTIVENESS.
The Art of managing human resources /. New York , 1987. xii, 307 p. : ISBN 0-19-504882-2 (alk. paper) LC Card 86-31107 DDC 658.3/01 19
HF5549.5.M3 A78 1987

Bozeman, Barry. All organizations are public . San Francisco , 1987. xix, 184 p. : ISBN 1-555-42036-2 (alk. paper) LC Card 86-27699 DDC 302.3/5 19
HD58.9 .B69 1987

Brightman, Harvey J. Group problem solving . Atlanta, Ga. , 1987. p. cm. ISBN 0-88406-201-5 : LC Card 87-21876 DDC 658.4/036 19
HD30.29 .B735 1987

Chronicles of corporate change . Lexington, Mass. , c1987. xiv, 254 p. : ISBN 0-669-13685-9 (alk. paper) LC Card 86-45555 DDC 384.6/065/73 19
HE8846.A55 C47 1987

Cornyn-Selby, Alyce, 1946- Take your hands off my attitude! . Portland, Or. , 1987. p. cm. ISBN 0-941383-02-4 : LC Card 87-15074 DDC 158.7 19
HD58.9 .C67 1987

Czander, William M. The application of social systems thinking to organizational consulting /. Lanham , c1986. 243 p. ; ISBN 0-8191-5183-1 (alk. paper) : LC Card 85-29508 DDC 658.4/6 19
HD69.C6 C9 1986 ***NYPL [JLE 86-3269]***

Davis, Marvin A. Turn-around . Chicago , c1987. 194 p. ; ISBN 0-8092-4780-1 : LC Card 86-29285 DDC 658.4/06 19
HD58.8 .D38 1987

DeMarco, Tom. Peopleware . New York, NY , c1987. x, 188 p. : ISBN 0-932633-05-6 (pbk.) : LC Card 87-22293 DDC 658.3/14 19
HD31 .D42185 1987

Dieterle, W. (Willi) Organisationsänderung in Unternehmungen . Göttingen , 1986. iii, 169 p. : ISBN 3-509-01425-1 LC Card 87-131121 DDC 338/.06 19
HD58.8 .D54 1986

Evaluatiemethoden, een introductie . 's-Gravenhage [1984] v, 188 p. : ISBN 90-12-04825-7 LC Card 85-196500
HD58.9 .E93 1984

Finkin, Eugene F. Successful corporate turnarounds . New York , 1987. xviii, 211 p. : ISBN 0-89930-232-7 (lib. bdg. : alk. paper) : LC Card 86-25280 DDC 658.4/063 19
HD58.8 .F52 1987

Friedman, Stewart D. Leadership succession systems and corporate performance /. New York, N.Y. (316 Uris Hall, New York 10027) , c1985. ix, 141 p. ; LC Card 86-162460 DDC 331.25/96 19
HD38.2 .F73 1985

Friedman, Stewart D. Leadership succession systems and corporate performance /. New York, N.Y. (316 Uris Hall, New York, N.Y. 10027) , c1985. ix, 141 p. :
NYPL [JLF 87-255]

Greinke, Helmut, 1957- Entscheidungsverlauf und Entscheidungseffizienz . Krefeld , 1986. viii, 249 p. : ISBN 3-88358-057-0 LC Card 86-172311
HD30.23 .G74 1986

Harman, Willis W. Creativity and intuition in business . Menlo Park, Calif. (333 Ravenswood Ave., Menlo Park 94025-3476) , c1985. 28 p. : LC Card 86-232128 DDC 658.4/09 19
HD53 .H37 1985

Hickman, Craig R. The future 500 . New York, N.Y. , c1987. xiv, 274 p. ; ISBN 0-453-00544-6 LC Card 87-15204 DDC 658 19
HD31 .H4814 1987

Hobbs, James B. Corporate staying power . Lexington, Mass. , c1987. xi, 178 p. ; ISBN 0-669-11153-8 (alk. paper) LC Card 85-45096 DDC 338.7/4/0973 19
HD58.9 .H62 1987 ***NYPL [JLE 87-1125]***

Kantrow, Alan M., 1947- The constraints of corporate tradition . New York , c1987. xvii, 216 p. ; ISBN 0-06-015753-4 : LC Card 86-46075 DDC 302.3/5 19
HD58.7 .K375 1987

Künzli, Ernst. Forschungs- und Entwicklungsplanung . Bern , c1984. 292 p. : ISBN 3-258-03351-X : LC Card 84-178059
HD30.4 .K86 1984

Lichtarski, Jan. Kryteria i metody oceny efektywności przedsięwzięć organizatorskich w przedsiębiorstwie /. [Wrocław] , 1982. 197 p. : LC Card 83-153426
HB9 .B7522 nr. 216 HD58.9

Lupton, Tom. Achieving change . Aldershots, Hants, England , Brookfield, Vt., U. S.A. , c1987. xv, 86 p. : ISBN 0-566-02526-4 : LC Card 87-17665 DDC 658.4/06 19
HD58.9 .L86 1987

Matejko, Alexander. The self-defeating organization . New York , 1985. xxviii, 395 p. ; ISBN 0-03-005488-5 (alk. paper) : LC Card 85-9524 DDC 302.3/5 19
HD58.9 .M38 1985 ***NYPL [JLE 86-2757]***

Nonprofit organizational effectiveness study . Washington, D.C. (1828 L St., N.W., Washington 20036) , c1986. v, 125 p. ; LC Card 87-141542 DDC 658/.048 19
HD31 .N57 1986

Owen, Harrison, 1936- Spirit . Potomac, Md. , 1987. viii, 245 p. : ISBN 0-9618205-0-0 (pbk.) LC Card 87-70469 DDC 658.4/06 19
HD58.8 .O94 1987

Pecora, Peter J. Managing human services personnel /. Newbury Park, Calif. , c1987. 176 p. : ISBN 0-8039-2685-5 (pbk.) LC Card 86-27995 DDC 658.3 19
HF5549 .P36 1987

Quality, productivity, and innovation . New York , c1987. xx, 427 p. : ISBN 0-444-01194-3 LC Card 87-6815 DDC 658.5 19
HD58.9 .Q35 1987

Robert, Michel, 1941- The strategist CEO . New York , 1988. viii, 140 p. : ISBN 0-89930-268-8 (lib. bdg. : alk. paper) LC Card 87-10945 DDC 658.4/012 19
HD30.28 .R63 1988

Schlesinger, James R. Organizational structures and planning /. [Santa Monica, Calif. , 1966] iii, 45 p. : LC Card 87-404140 DDC 353.6 19
HD58.9 .S35 1966

Shea, Gordon F., 1925- Company loyalty . New York, N.Y. , c1987. 86 p. : ISBN 0-8144-2331-0 (pbk.) : LC Card 86-28883 DDC 650.1 19
HD58.9 .S48 1987

Sloma, Richard S. Getting it to the bottom line . New York , London , c1987. ix, 196 p. : ISBN 0-02-929540-8 LC Card 87-411 DDC 658.4/063 19
HD58.9 .S56 1987

ORGANIZATIONAL EFFECTIVENESS - ADDRESSES, ESSAYS, LECTURES.
Kirkpatrick, Donald L. How to manage change effectively /. San Francisco , 1985. xxii, 280 p. : ISBN 0-87589-659-6 LC Card 85-45060 DDC 658.4/06 19
HD58.8 .K52 1985 ***NYPL [JLE 87-1191]***

ORGANIZATIONAL EFFECTIVENESS - CASE STUDIES.
Archier, Georges. [Entreprise du 3e type. English.] The type 3 company /. New York , 1987. xiv, 123 p. : ISBN 0-89397-282-7 : LC Card 87-11203 DDC 658/.00973 19
HD58.9 .A7313 1987

Hobbs, James B. Corporate staying power . Lexington, Mass. , c1987. xi, 178 p. ; ISBN 0-669-11153-8 (alk. paper) LC Card 85-45096

DDC 338.7/4/0973 19
HD58.9 .H62 1987 **NYPL [JLE 87-1125]**

Paul, Ronald N. The 101 best performing companies in America /. Chicago, Ill. , c1986. vii, 382 p. ; ISBN 0-917253-39-6 : LC Card 86-4947 DDC 338.7/4/0973 19
HD2785 .P38 1986 **NYPL [JLE 86-3151]**

ORGANIZATIONAL EFFECTIVENESS - CONGRESSES.
Ginzberg, Eli, 1911- Resizing for organizational effectiveness . New York, N.Y. (316 Uris Hall, New York 10027) , c1985. vii, 43 p. ; LC Card 86-162474 DDC 658.1/6 19
HD58.9 .G56 1985

Occupational stress and organizational effectiveness /. New York , c1987. xii, 285 p. : ISBN 0-275-92281-2 (alk. paper) : LC Card 86-25250 DDC 158.7 19
HF5548.85 .O24 1987

ORGANIZATIONAL INNOVATION. see **ORGANIZATIONAL CHANGE.**

Organizational set-up of road transport . Subrahmanyam, P., 1934- Delhi , New Delhi , 1987. xi, 233 [i.e. 333] p. : ISBN 81-7018-398-7 : LC Card 86-903830 DDC 354.54/8400878/09 19
HE365.I42 S83 1987

Organizational structures and planning /. Schlesinger, James R. [Santa Monica, Calif. , 1966] iii, 45 p. : LC Card 87-404140 DDC 353.6 19
HD58.9 .S35 1966

Organizational theory and inquiry : the paradigm revolution / edited by Yvonna S. Lincoln. Beverly Hills : Sage Publications, c1985. 231 p. ; 23 cm. (Sage focus editions. v. 75) Based on papers presented at a conference held at the University of Kansas in November 1983. Includes bibliographies. ISBN 0-8039-2494-1 LC Card 85-8137 DDC 302/.072 19
1. Organization - Congresses. 2. Organization - Research - Congresses. 3. Paradigms (Social sciences) - Congresses. I. Lincoln, Yvonna S.
HM131 .O683 1985 **NYPL [JLD 86-3567]**

Organizational theory and public policy / edited by Richard H. Hall and Robert E. Quinn. Beverly Hills, Calif. : Sage Publications, c1983. 304 p. : ill. ; 23 cm. (Sage focus editions. 63) Includes bibliographies. ISBN 0-8039-2006-7 LC Card 83-9704 DDC 302.3/5 19
1. Organization - Addresses, essays, lectures. 2. Policy sciences - Addresses, essays, lectures. I. Hall, Richard H., 1934-. II. Quinn, Robert E.
HD38 .O75 1983 **NYPL [JLD 87-1123]**

Organizational transitions . Beckhard, Richard, 1918- Reading, Mass. , c1987. xii, 117 p. : ISBN 0-201-10887-9 (pbk.) : LC Card 86-25863 DDC 658.4/06 19
HD58.8 .B4 1987

ORGANIZATIONS. see **ASSOCIATIONS, INSTITUTIONS, ETC.**

Organizat͡sii͡a i planirovanie kredita i denezhnogo obrashchenii͡a / pod redaktsieĭ A.I͡A. Rotleĭdera ; [A.I͡A. Rotleĭder ... et al.]. Moskva : "Vysshai͡a shkola", 1984. 350 p. ; 21 cm. Authorized for instructional purposes. Includes index. LC Card 85-108172
1. Credit - Soviet Union. 2. Money - Soviet Union. 3. Gosudarstvennyĭ bank SSSR. I. Rotleĭder, A. I͡A. (Arkadiĭ I͡Akovlevich).
HG3729.S632 O74 1984

Organizat͡sii͡a i provedenie vnutrivedomstvennykh reviziĭ na promyshlennykh predprii͡atii͡akh /. Obukhov, V. N. (Valeriĭ Nikolaevich) Moskva , 1978. 75 p. ; LC Card 81-153891
HD4213 .O28 1978

Organizat͡sii͡a i stimulirovanie truda rabotnikov transportnykh uzlov : sbornik nauchnykh trudov / [redakt͡sionnai͡a kollegii͡a N.A. Safronov i A.F. Zubkova]. Moskva : Nauchno-issl. in-t truda Gos. kom-ta SSSR po trudu i sots. voprosam, 1984. 96 p. ; 21 cm. Includes bibliographical references. LC Card 87-100191
1. Transport workers - Soviet Union - Labor productivity. I. Safronov, N. A. II. Zubkova, A. F. (Antonina Fedorovna). III. Nauchno-issledovatel'skiĭ institut truda (Soviet Union).
HD8039.T72 S656 1984

Organizat͡sii͡a, planirovanie i upravlenie na predprii͡atii͡akh tsvetnoĭ metallurgii /. Gratsershteĭn, I. M. (Izrail' Markovich) Moskva , 1987. 415 p. : LC Card 87-156156
HD9539.A3 S5546 1987

Organizat͡sii͡a sorevnovanii͡a i sovershenstvovanie khozi͡aĭstvennogo mekhanizma / pod redaktsieĭ Kapustina E.I., Voeĭkova M.I., Torkanovskogo E.P. Moskva : Profizdat, 1982. 206 p. ; 20 cm. Includes bibliographical references. LC Card 82-202826
1. Socialist competition - Soviet Union. 2. Industrial management - Soviet Union. I. Kapustin, E. I. II. Voeĭkov, M. I. (Mikhail Illarionovich). III. Torkanovskiĭ, E. P. (Evgeniĭ Petrovich).
HC340.S6 O684 1982

Organizat͡sionno-ėkonomicheskie problemy sovershenstvovanii͡a funkt͡sionirovanii͡a transportnykh sistem / [otvetstvennyĭ redaktor Tikhomirov E.F.]. Moskva : Akademii͡a nauk SSSR, T͡Sentr. ėkonomiko-matematicheskiĭ in-t, 1984. 144 p. : ill. ; 21 cm. Includes bibliographies. LC Card 85-199422
1. Transportation, Automotive - Soviet Union - Management - Mathematical models. I. Tikhomirov, E. F. II. T͡Sentral'nyĭ ėkonomiko-matematicheskiĭ institut (Akademii͡a nauk SSSR).
HE5675.A6 O765 1984

Organizat͡sionnoe proektirovanie i planirovanie razvitii͡a sistem upravlenii͡a /. Odintsova, G. S. (Galina Sergeevna) Kiev , 1986. 158, [2] p. : LC Card 87-162923
HD2876 .O35 1986

Organizat͡sionnye formy i metody upravlenii͡a proizvodstvom : na materialakh Moldavskoĭ SSR / [redakt͡sionnai͡a kollegii͡a A.I. Belous (otvetstvennyĭ redaktor) ... et al.]. Kishinev : "Shtiintsa", 1980. 130 p. ; 21 cm. At head of title: Akademii͡a nauk Moldavskoĭ SSR. Institut ėkonomiki. Includes bibliographical references. LC Card 81-140768
1. Agricultural industries - Moldavian S.S.R. - Management. 2. Industrial management - Moldavian S.S.R. I. Belous, A. I. (Anatoliĭ Ivanovich). II. Institutul de Ekonomie (Akademii͡a de Shtiintse a RSSM).
HD9015.S653 M6453 1980

Organized crime . United States. President's Commission on Organized Crime. Washington, D.C. , 1983. vi, 159 p. :
NYPL [JLE 86-1587]

Organized crime and money laundering . United States. President's Commission on Organized Crime. Washington, D.C. [1985]. vi, 189 p. :
NYPL [JLE 86-1282]

Organized crime, business, and labor unions. United States. President's Commission on Organized Crime. The edge . Washington, D.C. , 1985. 356 p. ; **NYPL [JLE 87-41]**

Organized crime, business and labor unions. United States. President's Commission on Organized Crime. The edge . Washington, D.C. , 1986. xxii, 393 p. ;
NYPL [JLE 86-2671]

ORGANIZED CRIME - NORTHEASTERN STATES.
Rebovich, Donald. Understanding hazardous waste crime . [Trenton?] [1986] viii, 70 p. : LC Card 86-622805 DDC 364.1/42 19
HD9975.U53 A1157 1986

ORGANIZED CRIME - UNITED STATES.
Block, Alan A. Organizing crime /. New York, N.Y. , c1981. 238 p. ; ISBN 0-444-99079-8 LC Card 80-25099 DDC 364.1/06 19
HV6030 .B55 **NYPL [JLE 86-4076]**

Nelli, Humbert S., 1930- The business of crime . New York , 1976. xiii, 314 p. : ISBN 0-19-502010-3 : LC Card 75-32350 DDC 364.1/06/073
HV6791 .N37 **NYPL [JLD 86-3722]**

United States. President's Commission on Organized Crime. America's habit . Washington, D.C. , 1986. 486, [312] p. ;
NYPL [JLE 86-3348]

United States. President's Commission on Organized Crime. The edge . Washington, D.C. , 1985. 356 p. ; **NYPL [JLE 87-41]**

United States. President's Commission on Organized Crime. The edge . Washington, D.C. , 1986. xxii, 393 p. ;
NYPL [JLE 86-2671]

United States. President's Commission on Organized Crime. Organized crime . Washington, D.C. , 1983. vi, 159 p. :
NYPL [JLE 86-1587]

United States. President's Commission on Organized Crime. Organized crime and money laundering . Washington, D.C. [1985]. vi, 189 p. : **NYPL [JLE 86-1282]**

Organizing business . Lynn, Leonard H. Washington, D.C. , c1988. xviii, 191 p. ; ISBN 0-8447-3629-5 (alk. paper) LC Card 87-17468 DDC 061/.3 19
HD2425 .L96 1988

Organizing crime /. Block, Alan A. New York, N.Y. , c1981. 238 p. ; ISBN 0-444-99079-8 LC Card 80-25099 DDC 364.1/06 19
HV6030 .B55 **NYPL [JLE 86-4076]**

Organizing industrial development / editor, Rolf Wolff. Berlin ; New York : W. de Gruyter, 1986. xi, 391 p. : ill. ; 24 cm. (De Gruyter studies in organization . 7) Includes bibliographies. ISBN 0-89925-168-4 (U. S.) LC Card 86-24074 DDC 338.9 19
1. Organization. I. Wolff, Rolf, 1953-. II. Series.
HD31 .O783 1986 **NYPL [JLE 87-789]**

Organizing interest and organized protest . Micheletti, Michele. [Stockholm] , 1985. vii, 253 p. ; ISBN 91-7146-451-4 (pbk.) LC Card 86-145828 DDC 322/.2/09481 19
HD8572.T5 M53 1985
NYPL [JLL 74-316 no.29]

Organizzare l'azienda. Settore marketing. Sangiovanni, Bruno. Marketing . Roma , c1986. 268 p. : LC Card 85-233830
HF5415.153 .S25 1986

Organizzazione del lavoro, mobilità e aspetti formativi nella contrattazione : spoglio di contratti collettivi nazionali e di accordi integrativi aziendali, 1978-1981 / ISFOL in collaborazione con la Fondazione Giacomo Brodolini ; introduzione di Antonella Attanasio. Milano, Italy : F. Angeli, c1982. 172 p. ; 22 cm. (Strumenti e ricerche . 3) LC Card 83-106874
1. Collective labor agreements - Italy. 2. Industrial organization - Italy. 3. Promotions - Italy. 4. Occupational training - Italy. I. Istituto per lo sviluppo della formazione professionale dei lavoratori. II. Fondazione Giacomo Brodolini. III. Series.
HD6709 .O73 1982

Organizzazione del Trattato dell'Atlantico del Nord. see **North Atlantic Treaty Organization.**

Organizzazione del Trattato Nord Atlantico. see **North Atlantic Treaty Organization.**

Organizzazione dell'unità africana. see **Organization of African Unity.**

Oría, Gerardo J. (Gerardo Juan) Teoría y práctica de la indexación : el caso argentino / Gerardo J. Oría. Buenos Aires : Ediciones Forum, 1985. 216 p. ; 20 cm. Bibliography: p. 208-209. ISBN 950-9209-28-7 LC Card 86-151154
1. Indexation (Economics) - Argentina. 2. Indexation (Economics). 3. Monetary policy - Argentina. I. Title.
HG815 .O75 1985

The Oriental challenge : investigations on business opportunities in Thailand, Singapore, and Indonesia / O.L.J. Lauwerier & A.D. Schermer (editors). Delft, the Netherlands : Eburon, 1987. 281 p. : ill. ; 24 cm. Includes bibliographies. ISBN 90-70879-62-X (pbk.) LC Card 87-170212 DDC 332.6/732259 19
1. Thailand - Economic conditions. 2. Singapore - Economic conditions. 3. Indonesia - Economic conditions. 4. Investments, Foreign - Thailand. 5. Investments, Foreign - Singapore. 6. Investments, Foreign - Indonesia. I. Lauwerier, O. L. J. (O. L. Jeroen). II. Schermer, A. D. (Abram D.).
HC445 .O75 1987

ORIENTATION (PSYCHOLOGY)
McGee, Mark G. Human spatial abilities . New York , 1979. xiv, 144 p. : ISBN 0-03-052391-5 LC Card 79-16070 DDC 153.7/52
BF469 .M3 **NYPL [JFE 84-185]**

ORIENTE (PERU) - ECONOMIC CONDITIONS.
Peru, Kolonisation und Abhängigkeit . Saarbrücken , Fort Lauderdale , 1981. 192 p. : ISBN 3-88156-165-X : LC Card 82-104103
HD1905.O75 P47 1981

Origen de una empresa pública . Chumacero,

Antonio. Tepic, Nayarit , 1985 [i.e. 1986] xviii, 279 p. : LC Card 87-145432 DDC 338.7/6371/0972 19
HD9144.M44 T333 1986

Origen y destino de las exportaciones chilenas, 1965-80 /. Ffrench-Davis, Ricardo. Santiago, Chile , 1981. 22, 6, [27] leaves ; LC Card 83-182100
HF3416.5 .F46 1981b

Los orígenes conflictivos de la seguridad social argentina /. Isuani, Ernesto A. (Ernesto Aldo) Buenos Aires , c1985. 140 p. ; ISBN 950-25-0128-4 : LC Card 86-174656
HD7149 .I88 1985

Los orígenes de la clase obrera en Costa Rica . Acuña Ortega, Víctor H. San José [1986] 85 p. : LC Card 87-402904 DDC 331/.097286 19
HD8136 .A28 1986

Los orígenes económicos de la crisis en Centroamérica /. López, Roberto. San José, Costa Rica [1986] 134 p. : LC Card 87-106423
HC141 .L67 1986

Origens da desigualdade entre os povos da América /. Mauro, Frédéric. [Des origines de l'inégalité entre les peuples d'Amérique. Portuguese.] São Paulo, SP , 1986. 113 p. : LC Card 87-120229 DDC 339.2/097 19
HC94.Z9 I56317 1986

The origin of rights /. Salhany, Roger E. Toronto , 1986. viii, 175 p. ; ISBN 0-459-38750-2 LC Card 86-177651 DDC 342.71/085 347.10285 19
KDZ574 .S25 1986 ***NYPL [JLE 87-1679]***

Original papers (Bowling Green State University. Social Philosophy & Policy Center) . (no. 7) Vanberg, Viktor. Morality and economics . New Brunswick [N.J.] , 1987. p. cm ISBN 0-912051-19-1 (pbk.) LC Card 87-19213 DDC 174/.26 19
HB72 .V268 1987

Le origini dell'industria /. Guarracino, Scipione, 1943- Milano, Italy , c1985. 83 p. : LC Card 86-157399
HD2321 .G78 1985

Origins of the Federal Reserve System . Livingston, James, 1949- Ithaca , 1986. 250 p. ; ISBN 0-8014-1844-5 (alk. paper) LC Card 85-48199 DDC 332.1/1/0973 19
HG2563 .L58 1986 ***NYPL [JLE 86-2522]***

ORINOCO RIVER REGION (VENEZUELA) - ADMINISTRATIVE AND POLITICAL DIVISIONS.
Esquema de ordenamiento territorial de la faja petrolífera del Orinoco . Caracas , 1982. 46 p. : LC Card 86-162734
HC238.O75 E87 1982

ORINOCO RIVER REGION (VENEZUELA) - ECONOMIC CONDITIONS.
Esquema de ordenamiento territorial de la faja petrolífera del Orinoco . Caracas , 1982. 46 p. : LC Card 86-162734
HC238.O75 E87 1982

ORINOCO RIVER REGION (VENEZUELA) - SOCIAL CONDITIONS.
Esquema de ordenamiento territorial de la faja petrolífera del Orinoco . Caracas , 1982. 46 p. : LC Card 86-162734
HC238.O75 E87 1982

Orissa, India. Bureau of Statistics and Economics. (Old Catalog form: Orissa. Statistics and Economics, Bureau of)
A Report on index numbers of parity between prices received and prices paid by the farmers in the state of Orissa /. Bhubaneswar, Orissa [1985] 11 p. : LC Card 87-401032 DDC 338.1/3/095413 19
HD2075.O7 R46 1985

ORISSA (INDIA) - CENSUS, 1981.
Census of India, 1981. Delhi , <[1982]-1986. v. in : LC Card 87-915022 DDC 315.4/13 19
HA4587.O74 C46 1982

ORISSA, INDIA - ECONOMIC CONDITIONS.
Mahapatro, P. C. (Poorna Chandra), 1944- Economics of cotton handloom industry in India /. New Delhi , 1986. xvi, 277 p. ; ISBN 81-7024-060-3 : LC Card 86-903087 DDC 338.4/774614/0954
HD9866.I63 O745 1986

ORISSA, INDIA - INDUSTRIES.
Sahu, Promod K. (Promod Kumar), 1942- Industrial economy of Orissa /. Delhi , New Delhi , 1986. viii, 152 p. ; ISBN 81-7018-401-0 : LC Card 86-903551 DDC 338.0954/13 19
HC437.O7 S24 1986

Orissa, India. Statistics and Economics, Bureau of. see **Orissa, India. Bureau of Statistics and Economics.**

Orkin, Mark. Disinvestment, the struggle, and the future : what black South Africans really think / Mark Orkin. Johannesburg : Ravan Press, 1986. xii, 78 p. : ill. ; 21 cm. A CASE/IBR study. Includes bibliographies and index. ISBN 0-86975-305-3 (pbk.) LC Card 87-100474 DDC 332.6/73/0968 19
1. Disinvestments - South Africa. 2. Blacks - South Africa - Economic conditions. 3. Disinvestments - South Africa - Public opinion. 4. Public opinion - South Africa. I. Community Agency for Social Enquiry (South Africa). II. Institute for Black Research (Durban, South Africa). III. Title.
HG5851.A3 O47 1986

Orlans, Harold, 1921- Nonprofit organizations, a government management tool /. New York , 1980. xxi, 173 p. ; ISBN 0-03-053966-8 : LC Card 79-23632 DDC 350 19
JK468.R45 N66 ***NYPL [JLE 80-1874]***

Orlebeke, Charles J. Federal aid to Chicago / Charles J. Orlebeke. Washington, D.C. : Brookings Institution, c1983. xvii, 80 p. ; 23 cm. Includes bibliographical references. ISBN 0-8157-6649-1 (pbk.) LC Card 82-74097 DDC 336.1/85 19
1. Grants-in-aid - Illinois - Chicago. 2. Federal-city relations - Illinois - Chicago. I. Title.
HJ9229.C5 O74 1983 ***NYPL [JLE 86-4696]***

Orlov, A. V. (Aleksandr Vasil'evich) Ėkonomika SSSR--edinyĭ narodnokhozi͡aĭstvennyĭ kompleks /. Moskva , 1981. 143 p. : LC Card 82-111112
HC336.25 .E39 1981

Orlov, Boris Pavlovich. Khozi͡aĭstvennoe osvoenie novykh raĭonov i ėkonomicheskiĭ rost Sibiri . Novosibirsk , 1980. 173 p. : LC Card 83-182452
HC337.R852 S5247 1980

Orlov, I. N. (Igor' Nikolaevich) Khlystova, E. A. (Evgenii͡a Andreevna) Sever i Sibir' zovut molodykh /. Moskva , 1985. 109 p. : LC Card 86-153085
HF5549.5.I5 K452 1985

Orlov, N. V. (Nikolaĭ Vasil'evich) Orlov, V. A. (Vasiliĭ Adamovich) Khudozhestvennye markirovannye konverty SSSR . Moskva , 1984. 120 p. : LC Card 84-168398
HE6185.S652 O75 1984

Orlov, V. A. (Vasiliĭ Adamovich)
Khudozhestvennye markirovannye konverty SSSR : 1980-1981 gg. : katalog-spravochnik / [avt.-sost., V.A. Orlov, N.V Orlov ; otvetstvennyĭ redaktor, I͡U.K. Mi͡akota]. Moskva : "Radio i svi͡az'", 1984. 120 p. : ill. ; 22 cm. At head of title: Vsesoi͡uznoe obshchestvo filatelistov. LC Card 84-168398
1. Stamped envelopes - Soviet Union - Catalogs. I. Orlov, N. V. (Nikolaĭ Vasil'evich). II. Mi͡akota, I͡U. K. III. Vsesoi͡uznoe obshchestvo filatelistov (Soviet Union). IV. Title.
HE6185.S652 O75 1984

Orlova, M. I. (Marii͡a Ivanovna) Sbornik zadach i khozi͡aĭstvennykh situatsiĭ po ėkonomike i planirovanii͡u mashinostroitel'noĭ promyshlennosti /. Moskva , 1985. 246 p. ; LC Card 86-110747
HD9703.S652 S28 1985

Orlova, V. I͡A. (Valentina I͡Akovlevna) Mukhin, P. A. (Pavel Aleksandrovich) Statistika kinematografii . Moskva , 1984. 103 p. : LC Card 85-203673
HA29.5.R9 M85 1984

Orlova, Zhanna. Dobroe imi͡a / Zhanna Orlova. Moskva : Moskovskiĭ rabochiĭ, 1986. 124 p. ; 20 cm. (Vremi͡a i my) LC Card 86-131980
1. Labor and laboring classes - Russian S.F.S.R. - Moscow. I. Title. II. Series.
HD8530.M62 O75 1986

Örning, Birgitta. Solidaritetsarbete : inblickar i fackets, folkrörelsernas och andra intresseorganisationers arbete / Birgitta Örning. Stockholm : Socialstyrelsen, [1978?] 66 p. : ill. ; 30 cm. (SM delrapport . 7) Cover title. Includes bibliographical references. LC Card 81-140576
1. Welfare work in industry - Sweden. 2. Social service - Sweden. I. Sweden. Socialstyrelsen. II. Title. III. Series.
HD7728 .O75 1978

Ornstein, Michael D. The work experience of immigrants to Canada [microform] : 1969-1976 / Michael D. Ornstein. Downsview, Ont. : Institute for Behavioural Research, York University, 1983. 48 leaves ; 28 cm. "Report submitted to the Department of Employment and Immigration, Ottawa, January 1982." Includes bibliographical references. Microfilm. New York : New York Public Library, 1986. 1 microfilm reel ; 35 mm. (MN *ZZ-26,610)
1. Alien labor - Canada. 2. Minorities - Employment - Canada. 3. Labor supply - Canada. I. Title.
NYPL [*ZT-1732 no.16]

OROGRAPHY. see **MOUNTAINS.**

OROLOGY. see **MOUNTAINS.**

Orozco Cadena, José. Contabilidad general : teoría y práctica aplicada a la legislación nacional : una visión objetiva y de conjunto para empresarios, profesionales y estudiantes / por José Orozco Cadena.1a ed. Quito, Ecuador : Productora de Publicaciones, 1986. xii, 551, [1] p. : ill. ; 22 cm. Bibliography: p. [552]. LC Card 86-218544 DDC 657/.09866 19
1. Accounting - Ecuador. 2. Accounting - Law and legislation - Ecuador. I. Title.
HF5616.E2 O76 1986

Orozco, Jesús. Ideología y programa de gobierno en los discursos de toma de posesión de los presidentes de México, 1928-1982 / Jesús Orozco y Francisco J. Núñez. Guadalajara, Jal., México : ITESO, c1983. 47 p. ; 21 cm. (Huella, cuadernos de divulgación académica . 3) ISBN 968-511-003-4 LC Card 83-191579
1. Mexico - Economic policy. 2. Mexico - Social policy. 3. Mexico - Politics and government - 20th century. I. Núñez, Francisco J. II. Title. III. Series.
HC135 .O66 1983

Orrman, Eljas. Bebyggelsen i Pargas, S:t Mårtens och Vemo socknar i egentliga Finland under senmedeltiden och på 1500-talet / Eljas Orrman. Helsingfors : SHS, 1986. 293 p. : ill. ; 21 cm. (Historiallisia tutkimuksia, 0073-2559 . 131) Summary in German. Bibliography: p. 269-276. ISBN 951-9254-73-0 LC Card 86-199875
1. Land settlement - Finland - Turun ja Porin lääni - History. 2. Finland - History - 1523-1611. I. Title. II. Series.
HD723 .O77 1986

Orsini, Larry L. World accounting / by Larry L. Orsini, John P. McAllister, Rajeev N. Parikh ; contributing editor, Ernst & Whinney. New York, NY (11 Penn Plaza, New York 10001) : M. Bender, 1987- c1986- 2 v. (loose-leaf) ; 26 cm. (Accounting series) Includes index. LC Card 86-73012 DDC 657 19
1. Comparative accounting. 2. Accounting. I. McAllister, John P. II. Parikh, Rajeev N. III. Ernst & Whinney. IV. Series: Accounting series (Matthew Bender (Firm)). V. Title.
HF5611 .O75 1987

O.R.S.T.O.M. (Agency : France) Investigación agraria y crisis . Quito , 1986. 498 p. : LC Card 87-400125 DDC 338.1/098 19
HD1860.A53 I58 1986

Az Ország közuthálózatának müszaki minősítése és nyilvántartása / [szerkesztette, Törőcsik Frigyes]. [Budapest] : Közlekedési Minisztérium Közuti Főosztály, 1983. 2 v. : ill. (some col.), maps ; 29 cm. Includes bibliographies. LC Card 84-253458
1. Roads - Hungary. 2. Roads - Hungary - Evaluation. 3. Information storage and retrieval systems - Roads. 4. Traffic engineering - Hungary. I. Törőcsik, Frigyes. II. Hungary. Közlekedési Minisztérium. Közuti Főosztály.
HE363.H82 O76 1983

Országos Forditó és Forditáshitelesitő Iroda (Budapest, Hungary) Tanulmányok a vezetők minősítéséről és a személyi értékelés rendszeréről. Budapest , 1985. 211 p. ; ISBN 963-02-3494-7 (Magy. nemz. bibl.) LC Card 85-193396
HF5549.5.R3 T35 1985

Ortega Campos, Pedro. Una década de la economía jiennense, 1969-1979 / Pedro Ortega Campos. [Jaén] : Cámara Oficial de Comercio e Industria de la Provincia de Jaén, [1984] 122

leaves : ill. ; 31 cm. Bibliography: leaves 117-121. ISBN 84-505-0662-X LC Card 86-187312
1. Jaén, Spain (Province) - Economic conditions. 2. Jaén, Spain (Province) - Population. 3. Education - Spain - Jaén (Province). I. Title.
HC387.J3 O76 1984

Ortega, Gonzalo Guzmán. see **Guzmán Ortega, Gonzalo.**

ORTES, GIAMMARIA, 1713-1790.
De Franchis, Carlo. Giammaria Ortes . Napoli , 1930. 165 p. ; LC Card 87-139766
HB109.O68 D4 1930

Ortíz, Alvaro [i. e., Alvaro Ortíz Saravia] see **Ortíz Saravia, Alvaro.**

Ortiz de Montellano, Ana. Tecnologías pesqueras en el trópico húmedo de México / Ana Ortiz de Montellano. 1a ed. México, D.F. : Centro de Ecodesarrollo, 1985. 146 p. : map ; 20 cm. Includes bibliographical references. LC Card 86-208331
1. Fish trade - Mexico. 2. Fish trade - Mexico - Technological innovations. 3. Fishers - Mexico. I. Centro de Ecodesarrollo. II. Title.
HD9464.M42 O77 1985

Ortiz, Edgar. Current economic and financial issues of the North American and Caribbean countries /. Mexico, D.F. , 1983. 390 p. : LC Card 87-106905 DDC 330.97/00539 19
HC95 .C87 1983

Ortiz, Rafael Illescas. see **Illescas Ortiz, Rafael.**

Ortiz, Rolando. CORDES : gestión y transitoriedad hacia el gobierno regional / Rolando Ortiz, Rafael García Euribe, Juan Carlos Málaga. Lima, Perú : Centro Peruano de Estudios para el Desarrollo Regional, 1987. 96 p. ; 21 cm. LC Card 87-405059 DDC 338.985 19
1. Peru - Economic policy. 2. Regional planning - Peru. I. García Euribe, Rafael. II. Málaga, Juan Carlos. III. Title.
HC227 .O73 1987

Ortíz Saravia, Alvaro. Estrategias para el desarrollo de la Sierra /. Cusco , c1986. 418 p. : LC Card 86-199393
HC228.A54 E87 1986

Ortmeyer, August. Bremicker, Burckhardt. Analyse der Arbeitslosigkeit in den Regionen Nordrhein-Westfalens . Bochum , 1984. xx, 381 p. : ISBN 3-88339-362-2 LC Card 84-196621 DDC 331.13/794355 19
HD5780.N6 B74 1984 ***NYPL [JLD 86-2367]***

Ortoleva, Peppino. La Radio . Torino , c1984. 126 p., [41] p. of plates : LC Card 86-201755
HE8699.I8 R335 1984

Ortona, Egidio. Anni d'America / Egidio Ortona. Bologna : Il Mulino, c1984- v. ; 22 cm. (Storia/memoria) Includes indexes. CONTENTS. - 1. La ricostruzione, 1944-1951 -- 2. La diplomazia, 1953-1961. ISBN 88-15-00531-5 (v. 1) : LC Card 84-240652 DDC 338.91/73/045 19
1. Economic assistance, American - Italy. 2. Reconstruction (1939-1951) - Italy. 3. Italy - Foreign relations - United States. 4. United States - Foreign relations - Italy. I. Title.
HC305 .O78 1984 ***NYPL [JLL 86-503]***

Ortscheidt, Pierre. L'entreprise face au nouveau droit de travail / Pierre Ortscheidt. Paris : Economica, c1985. 221 p. ; 24 cm. (Le Point sur) Includes bibliographical references and index. ISBN 2-7178-0915-5 : LC Card 85-191518
1. Labor laws and legislation - France. 2. Trade-unions - Law and legislation - France. 3. Business enterprises - France. I. Title.
KJV3399 .O78 1985 ***NYPL [JLE 87-358]***

Orudiia truda . Folom'ev, A. N. (Aleksandr Nikolaevich) Moskva , 1984. 107, [4] p. ; LC Card 85-138858
HC336.25 .F64 1984

ORURO (BOLIVIA) - INDUSTRIES - HISTORY.
González-Aramayo Z., Vicente (González-Aramayo Zuleta) Breve historia de la industria orureña /. Oruro, Bolivia [1983] 199 p. ; LC Card 85-144157
HC183.O7 G66 1983

Oruzbaev, A. U. Sovershenstvovanie ėkonomicheskikh metodov upravleniia sel'skokhoziaĭstvennym proizvodstvom /. Frunze , 1982. 158 p. ; LC Card 83-196563
HD9015.S653 K577 1982

Osadchaia, Irina Mikhaĭlovna. Kozlova, K. B. Institutsionalizm v amerikanskoĭ politėkonomii . Moskva , 1987. 214, [2] p. ; LC Card 87-159642
HB99.5 .K69 1987

Osama, Abdul Rahman, 1942- The dilemma of development in the Arabian Peninsula / Abdul Rahman Osama. London ; Wolfeboro, N.H. : Croom Helm, c1987. 203 p. ; 22 cm. Bibliography: p. 187-195. Includes index. ISBN 0-7099-4240-0 : LC Card 86-29149 DDC 338.953 19
1. Arabian Peninsula - Economic policy. 2. Manpower policy - Arabian Peninsula. 3. Arabian Peninsula - Politics and government. 4. Arabian Peninsula - Social conditions. 5. Arabian Peninsula - Economic conditions. I. Title.
HC415.3 .O83 1987

Osaze, Bob. Es. Readings and cases in Nigerian corporate policy and strategy / by Bob.Es. Osaze. [Benin City, Nigeria] : Distributed by the Benin University Bookshop, [between 1982 and 1984] vi, 185, 17, 23 p. : ill. ; 25 cm. Includes bibliographies. LC Card 84-237026 DDC 658.4/012/09669 19
1. Industrial management - Nigeria - Case studies. I. Title.
HD70.N43 O83 1982

Osborne, Stephen. Social credit for beginners : an armchair guide / by J.S. Osborne & J.T. Osborne. Vancouver, Canada : Pulp Press Book Publishers, c1986. 229, [1] p. : ill. ; 22 cm. Bibliography: p. [230] ISBN 0-88978-175-3 (pbk.) LC Card 87-122126 DDC 332.5/6/0971 19
1. Social credit - History - 20th century. 2. Social credit - Canada - History - 20th century. 3. Canada - Politics and government - 20th century. I. Osborne, Tom, 1949-. II. Title.
HG355 .O83 1986

Osborne, Tom, 1949- Osborne, Stephen. Social credit for beginners . Vancouver, Canada , c1986. 229, [1] p. : ISBN 0-88978-175-3 (pbk.) LC Card 87-122126 DDC 332.5/6/0971 19
HG355 .O83 1986

Los Oscos y la Cuenca del Eo . Argüelles, Alfonso. [Asturias] [1984?] ix, 317 p. : ISBN 84-505-0237-3 LC Card 86-174593
HC387.A7 A74 1984

O'Shea, Arthur J. Guide for occupational exploration /. [Washington, D.C.] , Circle Pines, Minn. , c1984. vii, 984 p. : LC Card 87-402857 DDC 331.7/02/0973 19
HF5382.5.U5 G83 1984

Osher, Bill. The blue-chip graduate : a four-year college plan for career success / Bill Osher & Sioux Henley Campbell. Atlanta, Ga. : Peachtree Publishers, c1987. 238 p. : ill. ; 24 cm. Bibliography: p. 234-238. ISBN 0-934601-19-4 (pbk.) : LC Card 86-63534 DDC 650.1/4/024375 19
1. Vocational guidance. 2. Career development. 3. Job hunting. 4. College graduates - Employment. I. Campbell, Sioux Henley. II. Title.
HF5381 .O889 1987

Oshima, Harry T. (Harry Tatsumi) The transition to an industrial economy in monsoon Asia / by Harry T. Oshima. Manila, Philippines : Asian Development Bank, c1983. 111 p. ; 28 cm. (Asian Development Bank economic staff paper . no. 20) "October 1983"--Cover. Bibliography: p. 101-111. LC Card 87-105003 DDC 338.095 19
1. Asia - Industries. 2. Asia - Manufactures. 3. Agriculture - Economic aspects - Asia. 4. Monsoons - Economic aspects - Asia. I. Asian Development Bank. II. Title. III. Series.
HC412 .O694 1983

Osiatyński, Wiktor, 1945- Współczesny konserwatyzm i liberalizm amerykański / Wiktor Osiatyński. Wyd. 1. Warszawa : Państwowe Wydawn. Naukowe, 1984. 552 p. ; 21 cm. (Współczesne doktryny polityczno-prawne USA) Summaries in Russian and English. Bibliography: p. 483-[500] ISBN 83-01-04929-4 (pbk.) :
1. Political science - United States - History. 2. Conservatism - United States. 3. Liberalism - United States. I. Title. ***NYPL [*QO 86-3450]***

Osigweh, Chimezie A. B., 1955- Communicating employee responsibilities and rights . New York, c1987. xiv, 254 p. ; ISBN 0-89930-200-9 (lib. bdg. : alk. paper) LC Card 86-25281 DDC 658.3/15 19
HF5549.5.C6 C5825 1987

Osipov, A. S. (Aleksandr Sergeevich) "Chastitsa serdtsa moego--" . Leningrad , 1981. 331 p. : LC Card 82-179000
HD8530.L5 C42 1981

Osipov, IUriĭ Mikhaĭlovich. Nezavisimye strany Afriki . Moskva , 1986. 276 p. ; LC Card 87-110032
HG187.5.A2 N49 1986

Oskolkova, O. B. (Ol'ga Borisovna) Mirovaia prodovol'stvennaia problema i naselenie : nauchno-analiticheskiĭ obzor / [avtor obzora O.B. Oskolkova ; otvetstvennyĭ redaktor IU.A. Borko]. Moskva : Akademiia nauk SSSR, In-t nauch. informatsii po obshchestvennym naukam, 1982. 77 p. ; 20 cm. (Seriia Mezhdunarodnye ėkonomicheskie otnosheniia) "Obzor"--Cover. Bibliography: p. 73-77. LC Card 82-198944
1. Food supply. 2. Population. I. Borko, IUriĭ Antonovich. II. Title. III. Series.
HD9000.5 .O84 1982

Oslo. Norsk utenrikspolitisk institutt. (Old Catalog form: Norsk utenrikspolitisk institutt, Oslo.)
NUPI-rapport.
(nr. 88) Braathu, Jan. Diversification strategies and security-of-supply . Oslo [1984?] 74 p. ; LC Card 85-129223 DDC 382/.42285/094 19
HD9581.E8552 B7 1984
NYPL [JLM 78-136 no.88]

Osmanistische Studien zur Wirtschafts- und Sozialgeschichte : in memoriam Vančo Boškov / herausgegeben von Hans Georg Majer. Wiesbaden : O. Harrassowitz, 1986. xi, 206 p., iv p. of plates : ill. ; 24 cm. English and German. Includes bibliographical references. ISBN 3-477-02652-9 (Deut. Bibl.) LC Card 86-224062
1. Turkey - Economic conditions - Congresses. 2. Turkey - History - 1453-1683 - Congresses. 3. Bokov, Vanco, 1934-1984 - Congresses. I. Boškov, Vančo, 1934-1984. II. Majer, Hans Georg.
HC492 .O85 1986

Osmers, Dieter. Entwicklungspolitische Erwachsenenbildung in der Bundesrepublik mit Hilfe kommunaler Konfliktfelder / Dieter Osmers. Frankfurt am Main : Haag + Herchen, c1983. 161 p., [2] folded leaves of plates : ill. ; 21 cm. (Beiträge zur Entwicklungspädagogik . Bd. 2) Bibliography: p. 157-161. ISBN 3-88129-669-7 LC Card 84-135387
1. Economic development - Study and teaching - Germany (West). 2. Adult education - Germany, West. I. Title. II. Series.
HD77.5.G3 O85 1983

Osmond, John. Work in the future : alternatives to unemployment / John Osmond. Wellingborough, Northamptonshire ; Rochester, Vt. : Thorsons Pub. Group, 1986. 144 p. : ill. ; 22 cm. Includes bibliographies and index. ISBN 0-7225-1245-7 (pbk.) : LC Card 87-100557 DDC 306/.36 19
1. Work. 2. Unemployment. I. Title.
HD5707.5 .O84 1986

Os'mova, Markiana Nikolaevna.
Cheshsko-russkiĭ ėkonomicheskiĭ slovar' . Moskva , Praga , 1986. 300 p. ; LC Card 85-146401
HB61 .C453 1986 ***NYPL [*QAD 87-1680]***

Vneshneėkonomicheskie otnosheniia sotsialisticheskikh stran v usloviiakh NTR /. Moskva , 1985. 215 p. ; LC Card 84-219529
HF1531 .V62 1985 ***NYPL [*QIP 87-2072]***

Osnove dugoročnog razvoja SR Hrvatske--svodna studija / [autori i redaktori Zvonimir Baletić ... et al.]. Zagreb : Republička zajednica za znanstveni rad SR Hrvatske, Republički zavod za društveno planiranje SR Hrvatske, 1984. 437 p. ; 24 cm. (Znanstvene osnove dugoročnog razvoja SR Hrvatske do 2000. godine . 1) In Serbo-Croatian (roman). Includes bibliographical references. LC Card 87-151188
1. Croatia - Economic policy. 2. Economic forecasting - Yugoslavia - Croatia. I. Baletić, Zvonimir. II. Republički zavod za društveno planiranje SR Hrvatske. III. Series.
HC407.Z7 C7647 1984

Osnovi na sotsialnoto osiguriavane /. Penkov, Petŭr. Sofiia , 1984. 191 p. : LC Card 86-104011
HD7091 .P335 1984

Osnovni prichini i usloviia za vŭznikvane na PTP s tezhki posledstviia, pŭtishta i metodi za tiakhnoto otstraniavane /. Osnovnye prichiny i

usloviia vozniknoveniia PTP s tiazhelymi posledstviiami, puti i metody ikh ustraneniia. Bulgarian. Sofiia , 1985. 95 p. : LC Card 87-101607
HF5614.5.S62 O7516 1985

Osnovnye faktory rosta proizvoditel'nosti truda v sel'skom khoziaistve / otvetstvennyi redaktor Rukosuev P.N. Moskva : In-t ėkonomiki AN SSSR, 1986. 158 p. ; 20 cm. Includes bibliographical references. LC Card 87-163422
1. Agricultural industries - Soviet Union - Labor productivity. I. Rukosuev, P. N. (Platon Nikolaevich). II. Institut ėkonomiki (Akademiia nauk SSSR).
HD9015.S652 O85 1986

Osnovnye fondy i proizvodstvennye moshchnosti v gornoi promyshlennosti / [avtory, N.I. Ivanov ... et al.]. Moskva : "Nedra", 1984. 207 p. : ill. ; 22 cm. Includes bibliographical references. LC Card 85-138074
1. Mineral industries - Soviet Union - Capital productivity. I. Ivanov, N. I. (Nikolai Ivanovich).
HD9506.S7472 O86 1984

Osnovnye idei piatiletki /. Kirichenko, Vadim Nikitich. Moskva , 1981. 92 p. : LC Card 82-123953
HC336.25 .K569 1981

Osnovnye kategorii krest'ian v period pozdnego feodalizma, XVII--pervaia polovina XIX vv. : mezhvuzovskii sbornik nauchnykh trudov / [redaktsionnaia kollegiia D.I. Budaev, A.E. Kondratenkov (otvetstvennye redaktory) ... et al.]. Smolensk : Smolenskii gos. pedagog. in-t im. Karla Marksa, 1985. 134 p., [1] leaf of plates : port. ; 20 cm. At head of title: Ministerstvvo prosveshcheniia RSFSR ... "K 70-letiiu zasluzhennogo deiatelia nauki RSFSR, doktora istoricheskikh nauk, professora Alekseia Alekseevicha Kondrashenkova"--t.p. "Spisok nauchnykh rabot professora A.A. Kondrashenkova": p. 128. Includes bibliographical references. LC Card 86-120158
1. Peasantry - Russian S.F.S.R. - History. 2. Serfdom - Russian S.F.S.R. - History. I. Budaev, Dmitrii Ivanovich. II. Kondratenkov, A. E. (Aleksandr Erofeevich). III. Kondrashenkov, Aleksei Alekseevich. IV. Smolenskii gosudarstvennyi pedagogicheskii institut imeni Karla Marksa.
HD1536.S65 O86 1985

Osnovnye neproizvodstvennye fondy kolkhozov /cN.A. Golovko ; nauchnyi redaktor F.S. Martinkevich. Golovko, N. A. (Nikolai Anatol'evich) Minsk , 1984. 94, [2] p. ; LC Card 84-177536
HD1492.S652 B9237 1984

Osnovnye poniatiia teorii sotsial'nogo upravleniia . Bakhrakh, D. N. (Dem'ian Nikolaevich) Perm' , 1978. 100 p. ; LC Card 81-154363
HD70.S63 B35 1978

Osnovnye prichiny i usloviia vozniknoveniia PTP s tiazhelymi posledstviiami, puti i metody ikh ustraneniia. Bulgarian. Osnovni prichini i usloviia za vŭznikvane na PTP s tezhki posledstviia, pŭtishta i metodi za tiakhnoto otstraniavane / [preveli ot ruski Konstantin Kosev, Chavdar Borisov]. Sofiia : TSentr. komisiia po bezopasnostta na dvizhenieto, 1985. 95 p. : ill. ; 21 cm. (Za bezopasnost i kultura na dvizhenieto . 27) Translation of: Osnovnye prichiny i usloviia vozniknoveniia PTP s tiazhelymi posledstviiami, puti i metody ikh ustraneniia. LC Card 87-101607
1. Traffic accidents - Russian S.F.S.R. 2. Traffic safety - Russian S.F.S.R. 3. Drinking and traffic accidents - Russian S.F.S.R. 4. Transportation, Automotive - Russian S.F.S.R. - Safety measures. I. Kosev, Konstantin. II. Borisov, Chavdar. III. Bulgaria. TSentralna komisiia po bezopasnostta na dvizhenieto. IV. Title. V. Series.
HF5614.5.S62 O7516 1985

Osnovy ėkonomiki i upravleniia stroitel'nym proizvodstvom / [P.B. Gorbushin ... et al.]. Moskva : Stroiizdat, 1978. 285 p. ; 21 cm. (Ėkonomicheskie znaniia--stroiteliu, srednee zveno) Includes bibliographical references. LC Card 81-171493
1. Construction industry - Soviet Union - Management. I. Gorbushin, Petr Borisovich. II. Series.
HD9715.S72 O86 1978

Osnovy ėkonomiki vazhneishikh otraslei narodnogo khoziaisva SSSR . Moiseev, Anatolii Vasil'evich. Moskva , 1984. 191 p. : LC Card 85-113764
HC336.25 .M654 1984

Osnovy teorii narodonaseleniia / pod redaktsiei D.I. Valenteia ; [D.I. Valentei ... et al.]. Izd. 3-e, perer. i dop. Moskva : "Vysshaia shkola", 1986. 374 p. : ill. ; 21 cm. Authorized for instructional purposes. Bibliography: p. [365]-369. Includes index. LC Card 86-218424
1. Population. 2. Soviet Union - Population. I. Valentei, D. I. (Dmitrii Ignat'evich).
HB851 .O82 1986

Osobennosti i problemy razmeshcheniia proizvoditel'nykh sil SSSR v period razvitogo sotsializma / [redaktsionnaia kollegiia N.N. Nekrasov (otvetstvennyi redaktor) ... et al.]. Moskva : Izd-vo "Nauka", 1980. 273 p. ; 21 cm. (Problemy sovetskoi ėkonomiki) At head of title: Akademiia nauk SSSR. Gosplan SSSR. Sovet po izucheniiu proizvoditel'nykh sil. Includes bibliographical references. LC Card 81-143866
1. Soviet Union - Industries - Location. I. Nekrasov, Nikolai Nikolaevich. II. Sovet po izucheniiu proizvoditel'nykh sil (Soviet Union).
HC340.D5 O86 1980

Osobennosti khoziaistvennogo mekhanizma v zarubezhnykh stranakh--chlenakh SĖV : uchebnoe posobie / pod red. N.A. Cherkasova. Leningrad : Leningradskii universitet, 1984. 54 p. ; 20 cm. At head of title: Ministerstvo vysshego i srednego spetsial'nogo obrazovaniia RSFSR. Leningradskii ordena Lenina i ordena Trudovogo Krasnogo Znameni gosudarstvennyi universitet imeni A.A. Zhdanova. Ėkonomicheskii fakul'tet. Includes bibliographies. LC Card 85-153742
1. Europe, Eastern - Economic policy. 2. Europe, Eastern - Economic conditions - 1945-. I. Cherkasov, N. A. II. Leningradskii gosudarstvennyi universitet imeni A.A. Zhdanova. Ėkonomicheskii fakul'tet.
HC244 .O723 1984

Osobennosti popolneniia osnovnykh otriadov intelligentsii / [sostaviteli M.Kh. Titma, I.A. Aimre ; otvetstvennyi redaktor R.N. Pullat]. Tallin : Akademiia nauk Ėstonskoi SSR, In-t istorii, 1981. 131 p. : ill. ; 19 cm. (Sotsial'naia struktura) Includes bibliographical references. LC Card 82-125732
1. Professional employees - Estonia. 2. College graduates - Estonia. 3. Estonia - Occupations. I. Titma, M. Kh. II. Aimre, I. A. III. Pullat, Raimo. IV. Ajaloo Instituut (Eesti NSV Teaduste Akadeemia). V. Series.
HD8038.S652 E775 1981

Osobennosti razvitiia i puti povysheniia ėffektivnosti proizvoditel'nykh sil regiona / [otvetstvennye redaktory A.F. Bliudenov, G.V. Znamenskii]. Sverdlovsk : Akademiia nauk SSSR, Ural'skii nauch. tsentr, 1984. 141 p. ; 22 cm. Includes bibliographical references. LC Card 86-135171
1. Cheliabinskaia oblast' (R.S.F.S.R.) - Industries. 2. Industrial productivity - Russian S.F.S.R. - Cheliabinskaia oblast'. I. Bliudenov, A. F. (Anatolii Fedorovich). II. Znamenskii, G. V. III. Akademiia nauk SSSR. Ural'skii nauchnyi tsentr.
HC337.R852 C456 1984

Osobowość a przystosowanie zawodowe marynarza /. Borucki, Zenon. Wrocław , 1986. 174 p. : ISBN 83-04-02007-6 : LC Card 86-221057
HD8039.S4 B67 1986

Osorio, Sergio Reyes. see **Reyes Osorio, Sergio.**

OSPEDALE DELLA SCALA DI SIENA - HISTORY.
Epstein, Stephan R., 1960- Alle origini della fattoria toscana . Firenze , c1986. 315 p. : LC Card 87-104355
HD1470.5.I82 S544 1986

Ospina, Enrique. Gunderson, Ralph O. Agricultural and socioeconomic perspectives of Arkansas . Morrilton, AR , 1987. p. cm. ISBN 0-933595-13-1 : LC Card 87-24146 DDC 338.1/09767 19
HD1775.A8 G85 1987

Osservatorio sui processi di internazionalizzazione (Università commerciale Luigi Bocconi) Italia multinazionale . Milano , 1986. 2 v. : LC Card 87-158571
HD2864 .I82 1986

Osswald, Richard, 1917- Lebendige Arbeitswelt : die Sozialgeschichte der Daimler-Benz AG von 1945 bis 1985 / Richard Osswald. Stuttgart : Deutsche Verlags-Anstalt, c1986. 394 p. : ill. ; 23 cm. ISBN 3-421-06309-5 LC Card 86-148169
1. Daimler-Benz Aktiengesellschaft. 2. Automobile industry and trade - Germany, West. 3. Industrial management - Germany (West) - Employee participation. 4. Labor disputes - Germany, West. I. Title.
HD9710.G44 D385 1986

Összefoglalás, Szolnok megye agroökológiai potenciálja az ezredfordulón / [szerkesztette és a munkát vezette, Csete László ; irták, Balogh Sándor ... et al.]. Budapest : Agrárgazdasági Kutató Intézet, 1984. 115 p. : map ; 29 cm. (Agrárgazdasági Kutató Intézet, 0209-5696 . 1984/12) ISBN 963-491-193-5 LC Card 86-198809
1. Agriculture - Economic aspects - Hungary - Szolnok Megye. 2. Agricultural ecology - Hungary - Szolnok Megye. I. Csete, László. II. Balogh, Sándor, Dr. III. Series: Agrárgazdasági Kutató Intézet (Series) , 1984/12.
HD1940.5.Z9 S966 1984

Összehasonlító tanulmány a világ ásványi nyersanyagainak mennyiségéről, termeléséről, ár és értékrendjeinek alakulásáról / [a tanulmány összeállítói, Ság László ... et al.]. Budapest : Magyar Állami Földtani Intézet, Gazdaságföldtani Osztály, 1983. 57 p. : ill. ; 25 cm. Bibliography: p. 38. ISBN 963-671-086-4 (Magy. nemz. bibl.) LC Card 85-130135
1. Mineral industries - Statistics. 2. Mines and mineral resources - Statistics. I. Ság, László. II. Magyar Állami Földtani Intézet. Gazdaságföldtani Osztály.
HD9506.A2 O85 1983

Ost-Wirtschafts Report Digest.
Ost-Wirtschaftsreport Digest . Düsseldorf , Genève , 1977. 119 p. ; LC Card 84-154293
HC244 .O726 1977

Ost-Wirtschaftsreport Digest : die wichtigsten Informationen über das Ost-Geschäft / [Chefredaktion, Julius B. Struminski ; technische Redaktion, Christa Lüddecke]. Düsseldorf : Handelsblatt GmbH ; Genève : Business International, 1977. 119 p. ; 30 cm. Cover title. LC Card 84-154293
1. Europe, Eastern - Economic conditions. 2. Europe, Eastern - Commerce. 3. Europe, Eastern - Industries. 4. Europe, Eastern - Foreign economic relations. I. Struminski, Julius B. II. Lüddecke, Christa. III. Title: Ost-Wirtschafts Report Digest.
HC244 .O726 1977

Ostal'tseva, Alevtina Fedorovna. Parfënov, I. D. (Igor' Danilovich) Monopoliia i imperiia . Saratov , 1980. 191, [1] p. ; LC Card 81-142784
HD2845 .P36 1980

Oster, Clinton V. Meyer, John Robert. Deregulation and the future of intercity passenger travel /. Cambridge, Mass. , c1987. xviii, 294 p. : ISBN 0-262-13225-7 LC Card 86-27308 DDC 387.7/42/0973 19
HE9803.A35 M49 1987

Oster, Sharon. The strategic use of regulatory investment by industry sub-groups [microform] : [part one] / Sharon Oster. New Haven, Ct. : Dept. of Economics, Yale University, 1980. 39 p. ; 28 cm. Final report. "Sept. 1980" on t.p., "Nov. 80" on "Report documentation page". Sponsored by Office of Economic Research / Advocacy, Small Business Administration. Microfiche. Springfield, Va. : NTIS, 1983. 1 microfiche : negative ; 11 x 15 cm. (PB83-181842)
1. Trade regulation - United States. 2. Competition, Unfair - United States. I. United States. Small Business Administration. Office of Economic Research / Advocacy. II. Yale University. Dept. of Economics. III. Title. ***NYPL [*XME-11,347]***

ÖSTERGOTLANDS LÄN (SWEDEN) - RURAL CONDITIONS.
Bäck, Kalle, 1949- Bondeopposition och bondeinflytande under frihetstiden . Stockholm , c1984. 326 p. : ISBN 91-36-02263-2 : LC Card 84-252422
HD1536.S8 B33 1984

Osterkamp, Rigmar.
Österreichische Texte zur Gesellschaftskritik . (Bd. 28) Stahl und Eisen bricht . Wien [1986] xi, 202 p. : ISBN 3-900351-62-7 LC Card 87-140293 DDC 330.9436/053 19
HC265 .S736 1986

Österreichisches Institut für Wirtschaftsforschung.
Strukturpolitik als Dimension der Vollbeschäftigungspolitik /. Stuttgart , c1983. 103 p. : ISBN 3-437-50276-X : LC Card 83-233394
HD5706 .S82 1983

Vom Nachzügler zum Vorbild(?) . Stuttgart , c1985. 183 p. : ISBN 3-437-50303-0 LC Card 86-200243
HC265 .V65 1985

Österreichisches MaB-Hochgebirgsprogramm. Alpine Areas Workshop (1974 : Schloss Laxenburg) Alpine Areas Workshop, May 13-17, 1974 /. Laxenburg [1974] 80 p. : LC Card 82-212849
HC268.O25 A46 1974

Österreichisches Statistisches Zentralamt. Ergebnisse der nichtlandwirtschaftlichen Betriebszählung vom 1. September 1954 /. Wien , 1958. 84 p. ; LC Card 84-252994
HD5779 .E74 1958

Handel, Lagerung 1983 /. Wien , 1986- v. <1-> ; LC Card 87-408429 DDC 314.36 s 380.1/09436/021 19
HA1173 .A27 Heft 793 HF3541.5

Lenkerberechtigungen im Jahre 1977 /. Wien , 1978. 69 p. ; LC Card 86-196229
HA1173 .A27 Heft 490 HE5667.A6

Lohn- und Einkommensteuerstatistik 1979 . Wien , 1985. xxxv, 59 p. : LC Card 86-233093
HJ4713.A7 L64 1985

Der Österreichische Baupreisindex 1971-1985 /. Wien , 1986. 107 p. ; LC Card 87-409417 DDC 314.36 s 338.4/3691/09436 19
HA1173 .A27 Heft 810 HD9715.8.A92

Die Österreichische Gemeinwirtschaft im Jahre 1976 . Wien , 1980. 102 p. ; LC Card 85-208409
HA1173 .A27 Heft 563 HC265

Statistik der gewerblichen Wirtschaft . Wien , 1986. 2 v. ; LC Card 87-409345 DDC 314.36 s 338.09436/021 19
HA1173 .A27 Heft 790 HC265

Strassenverkehrszählung 1980 auf Bundesstrassen im gesamten Bundesgebiet der Republik Österreich /. Wien , 1985. 288 p. : LC Card 86-170848
HA1173 .A27 Heft 750 HE363.A93T7

Osteuropa im Blickpunkt : 30 Jahre Gesellschaft für Ost- und Südostkunde / [Herausgeber und Redaktion, H.J. Uibopuu, Franz Templ, Irmgard Holaschke]. Linz : Gesellschaft für Ost- und Südostkunde, [1985?] 168 p. ; 21 cm. Bibliography of works published by the Gesellschaft für Ost- und Südostkunde: p. 141-156. LC Card 87-142952 DDC 382/.091713/01717 19
1. East-West trade (1945-). 2. Europe, Eastern - Foreign economic relations. I. Uibopuu, Henn-Jüri, 1929-. II. Templ, Franz. III. Holaschke, Irmgard. IV. Gesellschaft für Ost- und Südostkunde (Linz, Austria).
HF1411 .O687 1985

Osteuropaforschung .
(Bd. 17) Sibirien, ein russisches und sowjetisches Entwicklungsproblem /. Berlin , c1986. 274 p. : ISBN 3-87061-260-6 LC Card 86-229174
HC336.9.S53 S53 1986

OSTHOLSTEIN (GERMANY) - POLITICS AND GOVERNMENT.
Rüdel, Holger. Landarbeiter und Sozialdemokratie in Ostholstein, 1872 bis 1878 . Neumünster , 1986. 581 p. ; ISBN 3-529-02909-2 LC Card 87-119718 DDC 331.88/13/0943512 19
HD6699.O88 R83 1986

Ostorozhno--"Nemetskaia volna" . Ostrogorskiĭ, V. M. (Vladimir Mikhaĭlovich) Moskva , 1985. 254 p. ; LC Card 85-197423
HE8699.G3 O86 1985

Ostrogorskiĭ, V. M. (Vladimir Mikhaĭlovich) Ostorozhno--"Nemetskaia volna" : istoki i istoriia zapadnogermanskogo inoveshchaniia / V. Ostrogorskiĭ. Moskva : "Iskusstvo", 1985. 254 p. ; 20 cm. (Imperializm--sobytiia, fakty, dokumenty) Bibliography: p. [249]-252. LC Card 85-197423
1. Deutsche Welle. 2. Radio broadcasting - Germany, West. 3. Radio audiences - Soviet Union. I. Series: Imperializm--sobytiia, fakty, dokumenty ("Iskusstvo" (Firm)). II. Title.
HE8699.G3 O86 1985

Ostsee-Jahrbuch, 0720-4868 .
(1983) Handelshäfen im Ostseeraum /. [Lübeck] [1983] 232 p. : LC Card 84-192969
HE557.A3 H36 1983

Ostwald, Werner. Koziolek, Helmut. Reproduktion und Infrastruktur /. Berlin , c1986. 224 p. : ISBN 3-349-00017-7 LC Card 87-130782 DDC 363/.09431 19
HC290.795.C3 K675 1986

Osubor, John Uche. Business finance and banking in Nigeria / John Uche Osubor. Owerri, Imo State, Nigeria : New Africa Pub. Co., 1984. vii, 209 p. : ill. ; 21 cm. Bibliography: p. 207-209. ISBN 978-235-700-13 (pbk.) LC Card 86-207599 DDC 332.1/09669 19
1. Banks and banking - Nigeria. 2. Financial institutions - Nigeria. 3. Business enterprises - Nigeria - Finance. 4. Corporations - Nigeria - Finance. I. Title.
HG3431.A6 O85 1984

O'Sullivan, Patrick. Geographical economics / Patrick O'Sullivan. London : Macmillan, 1981. 199 p. : ill. ; 23 cm. Includes index. ISBN 0-333-31854-4 LC Card 86-673424
1. Geography, Economic. I. Title.
HF1025 .O86x 1981b

Osushchestvlenie ėkonomicheskoĭ politiki Kommunisticheskoĭ partii v usloviiakh Evropeĭskogo Severa RSFSR, 1917-1925 gg. /. Rapoport, IU. M. (IUriĭ Mikhaĭlovich) Leningrad , 1984. 216 p. ; LC Card 84-217989
HC336.9.N65 R36 1984

Osvobodivshiesia strany . Illarionov, Sergeĭ Ivanovich. Moskva , 1987. 260, [4] p. ; LC Card 87-118170
HF1413 .I54 1987

Osvoenie Severa Sovetskogo Soiuza /. Slavin, S. V. (Samuil Venediktovich) Moskva , 1982. 206 p. : LC Card 83-137884
HC336.9.N65 S56 1982

Oswald, Sharon L. Phillips, Jack J., 1945- Recruiting, training, and retaining new employees . San Francisco , 1987. xxii, 324 p. ; ISBN 1-555-42042-7 (alk. paper) LC Card 86-46332 DDC 658.3/14 19
HF5549.5.R44 P49 1987

Oswalt, Beverly J., 1948- Arn, Joseph V., 1943- Office automation . Boston, MA , c1988. xxvii, 402 p., [8] p. of plates : ISBN 0-87835-232-5 LC Card 86-28359 DDC 651.8 19
HF5547.5 .A79 1988

Ot Stalingrada do Berlina /. Chuĭkov, V. I. (Vasiliĭ Ivanovich), 1900- Moskva , 1985. 699 p. : ***NYPL [*QGR 87-2179]***

OTA reports.
Computerized manufacturing automation [microform] . Washington, D.C. , 1984. 35 p. : ***NYPL [*ZV-326 no.31]***

Otani, Yoshihiko, 1938- Microeconomic theory / Yoshihiko Otani, Mohamed El-Hodiri. Berlin ; New York : Springer-Verlag, c1987. xiii, 274 p. : ill. ; 24 cm. Bibliography: p. [268]-272. Includes index. ISBN 0-387-17994-1 (U. S. : pbk.) LC Card 87-20628 DDC 338.5 19
1. Microeconomics. I. El-Hodiri, Mohamed A. II. Title.
HB172 .O83 1987

The OTC internal medications market. New York, N.Y. (106 Fulton St., New York 10038): Frost & Sullivan, c1983. a-d, iii, 279 p. ; 29 cm. "December 1983." "A1232." LC Card 87-142032
1. Nonprescription drug industry - United States. 2. Market surveys - United States. I. Frost & Sullivan. II. Title: Over-the-counter medications market.
HD9666.5 .O8 1983

Otechestven front. Okrŭzhen komitet (IAmbolski okrŭg, Bulgaria) Godini na vŭzkhod . IAmbol , 1986. 87 p., [40] p. of plates : LC Card 87-103737
HC403.Z7 I64 1986

Oteiza, Enrique.
Autoafirmación colectiva . México , 1983. 327 p. ; ISBN 968-16-1335-X LC Card 86-159023
HC59.7 .A92 1983

Technical co-operation among Third World countries and the international order / by Enrique Oteiza and Anisur Rahman ; edited by Leelananda de Silva. Mexico, D.F. : Third World Forum, 1978. 72 p. ; 22 cm. (Third World Forum occasional paper . no. 3) Includes bibliographical references. LC Card 86-223022 DDC 338.9/26 19
1. Technical assistance - Developing countries. 2. International cooperation. I. Rahman, Anisur, 1950-. II. De Silva, Leelananda. III. Series: Occasional paper (Third World Forum) , no. 3. IV. Title.
HC60 .O838 1978

Other comprehensive bases of accounting / Lawrence Lindenberg, technical manager ; Margaret Monaghan, senior technical advisor ; Susan Sgromo, technical manager. New York, N.Y. (1211 Ave. of the Americas, New York 10036-8775) : American Institute of Certified Public Accountants, c1986. vii, 52 p. ; 23 cm. (Technical information for practitioners series . 1) LC Card 86-206776 DDC 657/.0218 19
1. Accounting - Standards - United States. I. American Institute of Certified Public Accountants. II. Series.
HF5616.U5 O88 1986

Otorita Pengembangan Daerah Industri Pulau Batam. A Guide for investors. [Jakarta] [1984] 112 p. : LC Card 86-942985 DDC 332.6/73225981 19
HC448.B38 G85 1984

Otraslevaia sistema planirovaniia . Stukolov, P. M. (Petr Mikhaĭlovich) Moskva , 1985. 71 p. : LC Card 85-196558
HD9696.A3 S697 1985

El otro sendero . Soto, Hernando de, 1941- [Lima] , 1986. xxxvi, 317 p. : LC Card 87-400476 DDC 381 19
HD2346.P4 S67 1986

Otruba, Gustav.
A. Hitler's "Tausend-Mark-Sperre" und die Folgen für Österreichs Fremdenverkehr (1933-1938) / Gustav Otruba. Linz : Trauner, c1983. iii, 205 p. ; 24 cm. (Linzer Schriften zur Sozial- u. Wirtschaftsgeschichte . Bd. 9) Bibliography: p. 184-199. Includes indexes. ISBN 3-85320-308-6 LC Card 84-213145
1. Monetary policy - Germany - History. 2. Germany - Foreign economic relations - Austria. 3. Austria - Foreign economic relations - Germany. 4. Tourist trade - Austria - History. I. Title. II. Series.
HG999 .O87 1983

Prokopp, Ludwig Ferdinand. Europäische Commerzreisen um die Mitte des 18. Jahrhunderts /. Linz , c1982. xiii, 446 p., [1] folded leaf of plates : ISBN 3-85320-296-1 LC Card 83-150921
HF3548.C36 P76 1982

Otsenka ėffektivnosti proizvodstva i rezervy ee rosta : ėkonomicheskie voprosy narodnogo khoziaĭstva : mezhvuzovskiĭ sbornik / [redaktsionnaia kollegiia I.I. Mokan (otvetstvennyĭ redaktor) ... et al.]. Kishinev : "Shtiintsa", 1982. 130 p. : ill. ; 22 cm. At head of title: Ministerstvo vysshego i srednego spetsial'nogo obrazovaniia Moldavskoĭ SSR. Kishinevskiĭ ordena Trudovogo Krasnogo Znameni gosudarstvennyĭ universitet imeni V.I. Lenina. Includes bibliographical references. LC Card 83-179279
1. Agricultural industries - Moldavian S.S.R. - Industrial capacity. I. Mokan, Ivan Il'ich. II. Universitatia de Stat "V.I. Lenin.".
HD9015.S653 M6454 1982

Otsuka, Keijiro. Comparative technology choice in development : the Indian and Japanese cotton textile industries / Keijiro Otsuka, Gustav Ranis, and G. Saxonhouse. New York : St. Martin's, 1988. viii, 247 p. : ill. ; 23 cm. Bibliography: p. 231-241. Includes index. ISBN 0-312-00516-4 : LC Card 86-29666 DDC 338.4/567721/0952 19
1. Cotton textile industry - India. 2. Cotton textile industry - Japan. 3. Cotton textile industry - India - Technological innovations. 4. Cotton textile industry - Japan - Technological innovations. I. Ranis, Gustav. II. Saxonhouse, Gary R. III. Title.
HD9886.I42 O87 1988

Ott, Alfred Eugen. Technologischer Wandel, Analyse und Fakten /. Tübingen , 1986. ix, 330 p. ; ISBN 3-16-345132-2 LC Card 87-109808 DDC 338/.06 19
HC79.T4 T4355 1986

Ott, György. A vállalati bértarifarendszer / Ott György. [Budapest] : Népszava, 1984. 110 p. ; 20 cm. (Vállalatunk, 0230-9173) Bibliography: p. 107. ISBN 963-322-158-7 : LC Card 85-176915
1. Wages - Hungary. 2. Compensation management - Hungary. I. Title.
HD5022.5 .O77 1984

Ott, Lyman. Hildebrand, David K., 1940- Statistical thinking for managers /. Boston, Mass. , c1987. xvii, 894 p. : ISBN 0-87150-036-1 LC Card 86-29222 DDC 519.5/024658 19
HD30.215 .H54 1987

Ottavi, Antonio. Franchini, Augusto. Le aziende di credito . Bologna , <1986-. v. <2 > ; LC Card 87-170318
HG3751 .F73 1986

Otten, Mariël. Transmigrasi : myths and realities : Indonesian resettlement policy, 1965-1985 / by Mariël Otten. Copenhagen : International Work Group for Indigenous Affairs, c1986. 254 p. : ill. ; 21 cm. (IWGIA document, 0105-4503 . no. 57) Spine title: Indonesia. Bibliography: p. 248-251. LC Card 87-144670 DDC 333.3/1/598 19
1. Land settlement - Government policy - Indonesia - History - 20th century. 2. Migration, Internal - Government policy - Indonesia - History - 20th century. I. Title. II. Title: Indonesia. III. Series: IWGIA document , 57.
HD896 .O88 1986

Otter, Casten von, 1941- Medbestämmandeavtal i landsting : det rör sig, men går det framåt / Casten von Otter, Annika Jederström. Stockholm : Arbetslivscentrum : Brevskolan, distributor, [1984] 92 p. : ill. ; 21 cm. (Varia, 0280-8293 . nr. 20) Includes bibliographical references. LC Card 84-241542
1. Management - Sweden - Employee participation. 2. Local government - Sweden. I. Jederström, Annika. II. Title.
HD5660.S9 O77 1984

Otto Brenner Stiftung.
Metallgewerkschaften in Südafrika /. [Köln] , c1983. 217 p. ; ISBN 3-7663-0530-1 LC Card 85-232412 DDC 331.88/171/0968 19
HD6870.5.Z7 M54 1983
NYPL [JLD 87-1964]

Schriftenreihe.
(25) Multinationale Konzerne . Köln , c1982. 478 p. : ISBN 3-7663-0506-9 LC Card 82-196963 DDC 332.6/73/0943 19
HD5710.75.G3 M84 1982
NYPL [JLD 86-2753]

(34) Metallgewerkschaften in Südafrika /. [Köln] , c1983. 217 p. ; ISBN 3-7663-0530-1 LC Card 85-232412 DDC 331.88/171/0968 19
HD6870.5.Z7 M54 1983
NYPL [JLD 87-1964]

Otto, Daniel. Economic contribution and impacts of changes in Iowa's livestock and meat processing industries / Daniel Otto, Gene Futrell. Oakdale, Iowa : Legislative Extended Assistance Group, University of Iowa, [1984] xi, 95 p. : ill. ; 28 cm. "Project commissioned by the Legislative Extended Assistance Group." "January 1984." Bibliography: p. 95. LC Card 85-621899 DDC 338.1/76/009777021 19
1. Animal industry - Iowa - Statistics. 2. Meat industry and trade - Iowa - Statistics. 3. Animal industry - United States - Statistics. 4. Meat industry and trade - United States - Statistics. I. Futrell, Gene A., 1928-. II. Iowa. General Assembly. Legislative Extended Assistance Group. III. Title.
HD9417.I8 O88 1984 ***NYPL [JLF 86-592]***

Die Otto-Gruppe . Otto, Werner, 1909- Düsseldorf , 1983, c1982. 319 p., [32] p. of plates : ISBN 3-430-17322-1 : LC Card 83-199344
HD2860.O77 O78 1982

Otto, Klaus-Friedrich. Ein Zuhause für Menschen . Frankfurt am Main , c1986. 204 p. : ISBN 3-921722-03-9 LC Card 87-133035
HD7339.A3 Z78 1986

Otto, Manfred. Abiturienten und Hochschulabsolventen beim Übergang vom Studium in den Beruf . Nürnberg , 1983. 407 p. : LC Card 84-140881
HD6278.G4 A25 1983

OTTO VERSAND (FIRM : HAMBURG, GERMANY)
Otto, Werner, 1909- Die Otto-Gruppe . Düsseldorf , 1983, c1982. 319 p., [32] p. of plates : ISBN 3-430-17322-1 : LC Card 83-199344
HD2860.O77 O78 1982

Otto, Werner, 1909- Die Otto-Gruppe : der Weg zum Grossunternehmen / Werner Otto.1. Aufl. Düsseldorf : Econ, 1983, c1982. 319 p., [32] p. of plates : ill. (some col.) ; 22 cm. ISBN 3-430-17322-1 : LC Card 83-199344
1. Otto Versand (Firm : Hamburg, Germany). 2. Leadership. 3. Industrial management. 4. Businessmen - Germany, West. 5. Executive ability. I. Title.
HD2860.O77 O78 1982

Otto, Wolfgang, Diplom-Staatswissenschaftler. Ökonomische Strategie und volkswirtschaftliche Masseninitiative / Wolfgang Otto. 1. Aufl. Berlin : Staatsverlag der Deutschen Demokratischen Republik, 1984. 61 p. : ill. ; 22 cm. (Der Sozialistische Staat) Includes bibliographical references. LC Card 85-189271
1. Central planning - Germany (East). 2. Germany, East - Economic policy. 3. Democratic centralism - Germany (East). I. Title.
HC290.78 .O88 1984

Ottoman agriculture in 16th century Anatolia . İslamoğlu-İnan, Huri, 1947- Berlin [1982] 45, [21] p. : LC Card 86-674028
HD2056.7 .I84x 1982

The Ottoman empire and European capitalism, 1820-1913 . Pamuk, Şevket. Cambridge [Cambridgeshire] , New York , 1987. xii, 278 p. : ISBN 0-521-33194-3 LC Card 86-28386 DDC 330.956/01 19
HF1583.4 .P36 1987

Où allons nous?. [Conakry] : Mouvement national démocratique, [1986?] 92 p. ; 17 cm. Cover title: Guinée, où allons nous? LC Card 87-115579
1. Guinea - Economic conditions - 1984-. 2. Guinea - Politics and government - 1958-. I. Mouvement national démocratique (Guinea). II. Title: Guinée, où allons nous?.
HC1030 .O89 1986

Où vas-tu paysan? Keddeman, Willem. Emploi et revenus dans le secteur agricole traditionnel au Bénin /. Addis Abéba , 1982. 64 p. ; LC Card 87-980402
HD2141 .K43 1982

Ouderenhuisvesting in 'n emancipatieperspectief /. Houben, Piet. Delft , 1985. 178 p. : ISBN 90-6275-118-0 : LC Card 86-149527
HD7287.92.N4 H683 1985
NYPL [JLE 86-3902]

Our common future / World Commission on Environment and Development. Oxford ; New York : Oxford University Press, 1987. xv, 383 p. ; 21 cm. (Oxford paperbacks) Includes bibliographies. ISBN 0-19-282080-X (pbk.) : LC Card 87-7853 DDC 363.7 19
1. Economic development - Environmental aspects. 2. Man - Influence on nature. 3. Environmental policy. 4. Human ecology. I. World Commission on Environment and Development.
HD75.6 .O97 1987

Our demographically divided world /. Brown, Lester Russell, 1934- Washington, D.C. , c1986. 54 p. : ISBN 0-916468-75-5 (pbk.) LC Card 86-51475 DDC 304.6 19
HB871 .B744 1986

Our work, our lives, our words : women's history and women's work / edited by Leonore Davidoff and Belinda Westover. Basingstoke, Hampshire : Macmillan, 1986. xiii, 189 p. : ill. ; 23 cm. (Women in society) Includes index. Bibliography: p. 182-185. ISBN 0-333-36598-4
1. Women - Employment - Great Britain - History - 20th century. 2. Work and family - Great Britain - History - 20th century. I. Davidoff, Leonore. II. Westover, Belinda. III. Series. IV. Series: Women in society (London, England).
NYPL [JLD 86-4220]

O ouro das Gerais e a civilização da Capitania /. Dornas Filho, João. São Paulo , 1957. 238 p., [8] leaves of plates : LC Card 84-215039
HC187 .D72 1957

Ouro Preto, Affonso Celso de Assis Figueiredo, Visconde de, 1836-1912. Década republicana /. Brasília, Distrito Federal , c1986. 2 v. ; ISBN 85-23-00062-3 (set) LC Card 86-211423
HJ923 .D38 1986

Out from underdevelopment . Mittelman, James H. New York , 1988. p. cm. ISBN 0-312-01188-1 : LC Card 87-22927 DDC 338.9/009172/4 19
HC59.7 .M5337 1988

Out of the cage . Braybon, Gail. London , New York , 1987. xiii, 330 p. : ISBN 0-86358-046-7 : LC Card 87-13510 DDC 305.4/0941 19
HD6135 .B7 1987

Out of the crucible . Dickerson, Dennis C., 1949- Albany , c1986. xiv, 323 p. : ISBN 0-88706-305-5 LC Card 85-30450 DDC 331.6/3/960730748 19
HD8039.I52 U535 1986
NYPL [JLE 86-4411]

OUTDOOR ADVERTISING. see **ADVERTISING, OUTDOOR.**

OUTDOOR RELIEF. see **PUBLIC WELFARE; CHARITIES.**

The outer city /. Herington, John. London , New York , 1984. 205 p. : ISBN 0-06-318237-8
NYPL [JLE 86-1465]

Outer Seven. see **European Free Trade Association.**

Outes Ruso, Xosé Luis, 1943- Introducción a la teoría del crecimiento económico / Xosé Luis Outes Ruso. Sada, A Coruña : Ediciós do Castro, 1984. 359 p. : ill. ; 18 cm. (Serie Liminar. Economía) Bibliography: p. 351-359. ISBN 84-7492-320-4 LC Card 87-105223
1. Economic development. I. Title. II. Series.
HD75.5 .O97 1984

Outlaws in the promised land . Cockcroft, James D. New York , 1986. 306 p. ; ISBN 0-394-54592-3 : LC Card 84-73206 DDC 331.6/2/72073 19
HD8081.M6 C63 1986
NYPL [JLE 86-2776]

Outlet shopper /. Benson, Carolyn Vogel. Arlington, Va. , c1985. x, 172 p. ; ISBN 0-915168-00-6 (pbk.) LC Card 86-229410 DDC 381/.1 19
HF5429.215.U6 B46 1985

OUTLET STORES - MARYLAND - DIRECTORIES.
Benson, Carolyn Vogel. Outlet shopper /. Arlington, Va. , c1985. x, 172 p. ; ISBN 0-915168-00-6 (pbk.) LC Card 86-229410 DDC 381/.1 19
HF5429.215.U6 B46 1985

OUTLET STORES - PENNSYLVANIA - DIRECTORIES.
Benson, Carolyn Vogel. Outlet shopper /. Arlington, Va. , c1985. x, 172 p. ; ISBN 0-915168-00-6 (pbk.) LC Card 86-229410 DDC 381/.1 19
HF5429.215.U6 B46 1985

OUTLET STORES - UNITED STATES.
Dollars & cents of off-price shopping centers . Washington, D.C. , c1986. v, 78 p. : ISBN 0-87420-660-X (pbk.) LC Card 86-51102 DDC 381/.1 19
HF5430.3 .D65 1986

OUTLET STORES - VIRGINIA - DIRECTORIES.
Benson, Carolyn Vogel. Outlet shopper /. Arlington, Va. , c1985. x, 172 p. ; ISBN 0-915168-00-6 (pbk.) LC Card 86-229410 DDC 381/.1 19
HF5429.215.U6 B46 1985

OUTLET STORES - WASHINGTON METROPOLITAN AREA - DIRECTORIES.
Benson, Carolyn Vogel. Outlet shopper /. Arlington, Va. , c1985. x, 172 p. ; ISBN 0-915168-00-6 (pbk.) LC Card 86-229410 DDC 381/.1 19
HF5429.215.U6 B46 1985

An Outline of Japanese tax administration. [Tokyo], Japan : National Tax Administration, 1985. 85 p., [1] leaf of plates : ill. ; 26 cm. LC Card 86-209172 DDC 354.520072/4 19
1. Tax administration and procedure - Japan. 2. Taxation - Japan. I. Japan. Kokuzeichō.
HJ3627 .O87 1985

The outlook for almonds, 1986 /. Noga, George. Altamonte Springs, FL (1180 Spring Centre S. Blvd., Altamonte Springs 32714) [c1986] 36 p. : LC Card 86-220553 DDC 338.1/7455/0973 19
HD9259.A47 U56 1986

The Outlook for gas demand in new markets, 1986-2010 : a report of the A.G.A. Gas Demand Committee / prepared by the Planning and Analysis Group. Arlington, Va. (1515 Wilson Blvd., Arlington 22209) : American Gas Association, c1986. 54 p. : ill. (some col.) ; 28 cm. "August 1986." Includes bibliographies. "Catalog no. F00778." LC Card 87-403083 DDC 333.8/23312 19
1. Gas industry - United States - Forecasting. I. A.G.A. Gas Demand Committee. II. American Gas Association.

Planning and Analysis Group.
HD9581.U5 O95 1986

Outlook for state spending and revenues in the late '80s . Hamilton, Billy. College Station, Tex. , c1985. 14 p. : ISBN 0-86599-055-7 (pbk.) LC Card 86-622256 DDC 336.764 19
HJ2053.T5 H36 1985

Um outro Nordeste . Takeya, Denise Monteiro. Fortaleza , 1985. 137 p. : LC Card 86-232681
HD9084.B62 R568 1985

OUTSIDE BROKERS. see **BROKERS.**

Outside Moscow . Bahry, Donna. New York , 1987. 236 p. : ISBN 0-231-06290-7 LC Card 87-8020 DDC 336.47 19
HJ2130 .B35 1987

Outstanding dissertations in economics. Barbosa, Manuel P. (Manuel Pinto), 1944- Growth, migration, and the balance of payments in a small open economy, Portugal /. New York , 1984. xv, 212 p. : ISBN 0-8240-4169-0 : LC Card 79-53646 DDC 382.1/7/0724 19
HD5809.A6 B37 1984 ***NYPL [JLE 86-4171]***

Strickland, Allyn D. Firm diversification, mutual forbearance behavior and price-cost margins /. New York , 1984. 155 p. ; ISBN 0-8240-4159-3 (alk. paper) LC Card 79-53209 DDC 338.8/3/0973
HD2756.U5 S76 1984 ***NYPL [JLE 86-3907]***

Ovando, Jorge. El tributo indígena en las finanzas bolivianas del siglo XIX / Jorge Ovando Sanz. 1a ed. La Paz, Bolivia : Comité Ejecutivo de la Universidad Boliviana, [1985] 565 p. : ill. ; 19 cm. Bibliography: p. 537-543.
1. Indians of South America - Bolivia - Land tenure. 2. Encomiendas (Latin America). 3. Land tenure - Bolivia. 4. Taxation - Bolivia. 5. Bolivia - Economic conditions. I. Title. ***NYPL [JLC 86-407]***

Ovando Sanz, Jorge. see **Ovando, Jorge.**

Ovchinnikov, V. P. (Veniamin Petrovich) Arkhangel'skiĭ avtograf / V.P. Ovchinnikov. Arkhangel'sk : Severo-Zapadnoe knizhnoe izd-vo, 1983. 94 p. : ill. ; 15 cm. (Rukopozhatie druzeĭ--Arkhangel'sk-Vologda) LC Card 84-173501
1. Arkhangelskaia oblast' (R.S.F.S.R.) - Economic conditions. I. Title. II. Series.
HC337.R852 A746 1983

OVER-THE-COUNTER MARKETS - GREAT BRITAIN.
Wilmot, Tom (Tom G.) Inside the over-the-counter market in the UK /. Westport, Conn. , 1985. xiii, 119 p. ; ISBN 0-89930-166-5 LC Card 85-24431 DDC 332.64/3/0941 19
HG5432 .W55 1985 ***NYPL [JLD 86-3625]***

OVER-THE-COUNTER MARKETS - UNITED STATES.
Gross, LeRoy. The stockbroker's guide to put and call option strategies. [New York, 1974] viii, 116 p. ISBN 0-13-846741-9 LC Card 74-166476 DDC 332.6/45
HG6041 .G75 ***NYPL [JLE 87-573]***

Wilmot, Tom (Tom G.) Inside the over-the-counter market in the UK /. Westport, Conn. , 1985. xiii, 119 p. ; ISBN 0-89930-166-5 LC Card 85-24431 DDC 332.64/3/0941 19
HG5432 .W55 1985 ***NYPL [JLD 86-3625]***

Over-the-counter medications market. The OTC internal medications market. New York, N.Y. (106 Fulton St., New York 10038), c1983. a-d, iii, 279 p. ; LC Card 87-142032
HD9666.5 .O8 1983

Overbeek, Johannes. Röpke, Wilhelm, 1899-1966. [Problem of economic order.] 2 essays /. Lanham, MD , c1987. x, 103 p. ; ISBN 0-8191-6125-X (alk. paper) : LC Card 86-33982 DDC 338.9 19
HD82 .R682 1987

The overburdened economy . Dumas, Lloyd J. Berkeley , c1986. xiv, 297 p. ; ISBN 0-520-05686-8 (alk. paper) LC Card 85-20856 DDC 331.13/7973 19
HD5724 .D775 1986 ***NYPL [JLD 86-2582]***

Overgangen fra uddannelse til erhverv . Westergård-Nielsen, Niels C. Aarhus [Copenhagen] [1983] iii, 41 p. : LC Card 84-125491
HD5701.6 .W47 1983

Overseas aid and the transfer of technology . Burch, David, 1942 Jan. 16- Aldershot, [Hants, England] , Brookfield [Vt.], USA , c1987. xiv, 370 p. ; ISBN 0-566-00480-1 : LC Card 87-237 DDC 338.1/81 19
HD1431 .B87 1987

Overseas Development Council. Committee on African Development Strategies (U. S.) Compact for African development . Berkeley, CA (2120 Berkeley Way, Berkeley 94720) [1985] 24 p. : LC Card 86-200473 DDC 338.967 19
HC800 .C645 1985

Overseas Development Institute (London, England) Commander, Simon. The state and agricultural development in Egypt since 1973 /. London , Atlantic Highlands, NJ , 1988. p. cm. ISBN 0-86372-080-3 LC Card 87-3616 DDC 338.1/862 19
HD2123.Z8 C66 1988

Overseas experience with "strict" monetary targetry and its implications for New Zealand /. Dickens, Rodney. Wellington [1986] iii, 24 leaves ; LC Card 87-137038 DDC 332.4/9931 19
HG230.3 .D53 1986

Översyn av vissa frågor rörande jordbruksprisregleringen / Jordbruksdepartementet. [Stockholm] : LiberFörlag, [1981] iii, 104, 13, 22, 2, 9, 14 p. : ill. ; 21 cm. "Ds Jo 1981:10." ISBN 91-38-06616-5 LC Card 83-245209
1. Agricultural price supports - Sweden. 2. Agriculture and state - Sweden. I. Sweden. Jordbruksdepartementet.
HD2018 .O94 1981

Overview, fiscal and budgetary actions . North Carolina. General Assembly. Fiscal Research Division. Raleigh, N.C. (Legislative Office Bldg., Raleigh 27611) [1986]. 248 p. : LC Card 87-620950 DDC 353.97560072/2 19
HJ2053.N8 N668 1986

Overview of current issues relating to single-employer defined benefit pension plans and Pension Benefit Guaranty Corporation (PBGC) premiums : scheduled for hearings before the Subcommittee on Oversight of the Committee on Ways and Means on April 7 and 9, 1987 / prepared by the staff of the Joint Committee on Taxation. Washington : U. S. G.P.O., 1987. iii, 49 p. ; 24 cm. At head of title: Joint committee print. Distributed to some depository libraries in microfiche. Shipping list no.: 87-226-P. "April 6, 1987." Includes bibliographical references. Item 1002-A, 1002-B (microfiche) LC Card 87-601357 DDC 331.25/2/0973 19
1. Pensions - United States. 2. Pension Benefit Guaranty Corporation. 3. Self-employed - Pensions - United States. I. United States. Congress. House. Committee on Ways and Means. Subcommittee on Oversight. II. United States. Congress. Joint Committee on Taxation.
HD7125 .O88 1987

Ovezov, Batyr Balyshevich. Baĭriev, B. S. Optimizatsiia struktur upravleniia /. Ashkhabad , 1985. 169, [23] p. : LC Card 86-196466
HC337.T23 B35 1985

Ovsepian, R. L. (Rudik Levonovich) Karapetian, S. A. Regional'nye osobennosti sotsial'no-demograficheskogo razvitiia Armianskoĭ SSR /. Erevan , 1986. 215 p. ; LC Card 87-118556
HB3608.A75 K37 1986

Ovsienko, IU. V. Sistemnyĭ podkhod v reshenii nekotorykh problem sotsial'no-ekonomicheskogo optimuma /. Moskva , 1984. 88 p. ; LC Card 86-144288
HC340.I52 S57 1984

Ovsievich, Boris L'vovich. Modeli formirovaniia organizatsionnykh struktur / B.L. Ovsievich. Leningrad : "Nauka," Leningradskoe otd-nie, 1979. 157, [3] p. : ill. ; 20 cm. At head of title: Akademiia nauk SSSR. Institut sotsial'no-ėkonomicheskikh problem. Bibliography: p. 153-[158] LC Card 81-162540
1. Management - Mathematical models. 2. Industrial organization - Mathematical models. I. Title.
HD30.25 .O97 1979

Ovsiienko, O. F. Krakh zubatovshchyny na Ukraïni / O.F. Ovsiienko. Kyïv : Nauk. dumka, 1987. 137, [3] p. ; 20 cm. Title in colophon: Krakh zubatovshchiny na Ukraine. Bibliography: p. 117-[138] LC Card 87-161669
1. Labor policy - Ukraine - History - 20th century. 2. Zubatov, Sergeĭ Vasil'evich, 1864-1917. 3. Strikes and lockouts - Ukraine - History - 20th century. 4. Trade-unions - Police - Ukraine - History - 20th century. I. Title. II. Title: Krakh zubatovshchiny na Ukraine.
HD8529.U43 O97 1987

Oweiss, Ibrahim M. What gold investors need to know about the collapse of the oil cartel / by Ibrahim M. Oweiss. Bethel, CT : Silver & Gold Report, c1986. 37 leaves : ill. ; 28 cm. "Special situation report"--P. 1 of cover. LC Card 86-209518 DDC 332.63 19
1. Gold. 2. Investments. 3. Petroleum industry and trade. 4. Organization of Petroleum Exporting Countries. I. Silver & gold report. II. Title.
HG293 .O84 1986

Owen, Dorian, 1953- Money, wealth, and expenditure : integrated modelling of consumption and portfolio behaviour / Dorian Owen. Cambridge [Cambridgeshire] ; New York : Cambridge University Press, 1986. xi, 210 p. ; 24 cm. Includes indexes. Bibliography: p. 176-196. ISBN 0-521-26761-7 LC Card 85-19009 DDC 339.4/7/0724 19
1. Consumption (Economics) - Mathematical models. 2. Wealth - Mathematical models. 3. Money - Mathematical models. I. Title.
HB820 .O94 1986 ***NYPL [JLE 87-1594]***

Owen, Edward Roger John. The Middle East in the world economy, 1800-1914 / Roger Owen. London ; New York : Methuen, 1987, c1981. xix, 378 p. : maps ; 24 cm. (University paperbacks. 952) Bibliography: p. 346-370. Includes index. ISBN 0-416-03272-9 (pbk.) LC Card 86-24385 DDC 330.956 19
1. Near East - Economic conditions. I. Title.
HC415.15 .O94 1987

Owen, Gail T. Residential property sales in Maryland : fiscal years 1983 and 1984 / [author[s], Gail Owen, Robert Lefenfeld]. Baltimore, Md. (2225 N. Charles St., Baltimore 21218-5767) : Regional Planning Council, [1985] iv, 79 leaves : maps ; 28 cm. "March, 1985." "85-06"--Cover. LC Card 86-622370 DDC 333.33/8 19
1. House selling - Maryland - Statistics. 2. Real estate business - Maryland - Statistics. I. Lefenfeld, Robert M. II. Regional Planning Council (Md.). III. Title.
HD266.M3 O9 1985

Owen, Harrison, 1936- Spirit : transformation and development in organizations / Harrison Owen. Potomac, Md. : Abbott Pub., 1987. viii, 245 p. : ill. ; 24 cm. Bibliography: p. 243-245. ISBN 0-9618205-0-0 (pbk.) LC Card 87-70469 DDC 658.4/06 19
1. Organizational change. 2. Organizational effectiveness. 3. Communication in organization. I. Title.
HD58.8 .O94 1987

Owen, Keith Q. Mink, Oscar G. Groups at work /. Englewood Cliffs, N.J. , c1987. xiii, 279 p. : ISBN 0-87778-196-6 LC Card 87-9081 DDC 658.4/036 19
HD66 .M55 1987

Owen, Robert R. (Robert Randolph) Arthur Young guide to financing for growth : ten alternatives for raising capital / Robert R. Owen, Daniel R. Garner, Dennis S. Bunder. New York : Wiley, c1986. xiv, 298 p. ; 24 cm. ISBN 0-471-81946-8 : LC Card 86-1612 DDC 658.1/522 19
1. Small business - Finance. 2. Business enterprises - Finance. 3. Capital. I. Garner, Daniel R. II. Bunder, Dennis S. III. Title.
HG4027.7 .O94 1986 ***NYPL [JLE 86-2667]***

Owen, Wilfred. Transportation and world development / Wilfred Owen. Baltimore : Johns Hopkins University Press, c1987. xiv, 156 p. : ill. ; 24 cm. Bibliography: p. 149. Includes index. ISBN 0-8018-3495-3 (alk. paper) LC Card 87-4154 DDC 380.5 19
1. Transportation. 2. Economic development. I. Title.
HE151 .O94 1987

Owens, John. Keane, John, 1949- After full employment /. London , Dover, N.H., USA , 1986. 198 p. ; ISBN 0-09-164091-1 (pbk.) : LC Card 86-213691 DDC 339.5/0941 19
HD5765.A6 K42 1986

Own your own franchise . Bard, Ray. Reading, Mass. , 1987. vii, 455 p. ; ISBN 0-201-11439-9 (pbk.) : LC Card 87-14389 DDC 658.8/708 19
HF5429.235.U5 B37 1987

Owners and power in Sweden's listed companies 1985. Sundqvist, Sven-Ivan, 1939- Ägarna och makten i Sveriges börsföretag 1985 =. [Stockholm] [1985] 318 p. : ISBN 91-7588-085-7 : LC Card 86-105378
HG186.S85 S86 1985 ***NYPL [JLE 86-3810]***

OWNERSHIP. see **PROPERTY.**

Ownership and development . Wallace, Brian F. Athens, Ohio , 1987. ix, 176 p. ; ISBN 0-89680-145-4 (pbk.) LC Card 86-33255 DDC 332.6/7322861 19
HD9734.C62 W35 1987

Ownership and participation . Wilson, Bryan David, 1954- 1985. xi, 356 ;
NYPL [JLD 87-209]

Ownership and use of motor-cycles 1984. Het Bezit en gebruik van motorfietsen, 1984 /. 's-Gravenhage , 1985. 26 p. : ISBN 90-357-0397-9 : LC Card 86-218867
HE5616.5 .B49 1985

Owosekun, Akinola Adeniyi. Towards an African economic community . [Ibadan, Nigeria] , 1986. 401 p. ; ISBN 978-18-1040-8 LC Card 87-143033 DDC 337.1/66 19
HC1000 .T69 1986

OX DRIVING - ZAMBIA - EASTERN PROVINCE.
Rajeswaran, K. A feasibility study on the ox-driven scotch cart project . Lusaka, Zambia [1985] vii leaves, 66 p., [3] leaves of plates : LC Card 87-980373 DDC 388.3/41/096894 19
HE153 .R35 1985

OX INDUSTRY - ZAMBIA - EASTERN PROVINCE.
Rajeswaran, K. A feasibility study on the ox-driven scotch cart project . Lusaka, Zambia [1985] vii leaves, 66 p., [3] leaves of plates : LC Card 87-980373 DDC 388.3/41/096894 19
HE153 .R35 1985

Oxelheim, Lars. Macroeconomic uncertainty : international risks and opportunities for the corporation / Lars Oxelheim and Clas Wihlborg. Chichester [West Sussex] ; New York : Wiley, c1987. xv, 251 p. : ill. ; 24 cm. Bibliography: p. 239-242. Includes indexes. ISBN 0-471-91480-0 : LC Card 87-8333 DDC 658.1/55 19
1. Foreign exchange. 2. Hedging (Finance). 3. Risk management. 4. Country risk. I. Wihlborg, Clas. II. Title.
HG3821 .O894 1987

Oxenbøll, Erik. Glamann, Kristof. Studier i dansk merkantilisme . [Copenhagen] , c1983. 243 p. ; ISBN 87-500-2476-0 LC Card 85-125251
HB91 .G57 1983

Oxfam America. Seidman, Ann Willcox, 1926- The roots of crisis in southern Africa /. Trenton, N.J. [1985] xvii, 209 p. : ISBN 0-86543-026-8 (pbk.) : LC Card 85-72995 DDC 968.06/3 19
E183.8.S6 S45 1985 ***NYPL [Sc E 86-368]***

OXFAM AMERICA.
Melrose, Dianna. Nicaragua . Oxford, U.K. , Boston, MA , 1985. 68 p. : ISBN 0-85598-070-2 (pbk.) : LC Card 87-116239 DDC 338.91/41/07285 19
HC146 .M45 1985

Oxfam. Public Affairs Unit. Melrose, Dianna. Nicaragua . Oxford, U.K. , Boston, MA , 1985. 68 p. : ISBN 0-85598-070-2 (pbk.) : LC Card 87-116239 DDC 338.91/41/07285 19
HC146 .M45 1985

Oxford Committee for Famine Relief. see **Oxfam.**

Oxford Institute for Energy Studies. The Market for North Sea crude oil /. Oxford , New York , 1986. xxxii, 341 p., [1] leaf of plates : ISBN 0-19-730001-4 LC Card 86-217261 DDC 338.2/7282/0916336 19
HD9581.N64 M37 1986

Oxley, Alan. Barton / Alan Oxley. Glossop, Derbyshire : Transport Pub. Co., c1983- v. <1 > : ill. ; 21 x 26 cm. Bibliography: pt, 1, p. 135. CONTENTS. - pt. 1. 1908-1949. ISBN 0-903839-64-4 (v. 1) LC Card 86-219518 DDC 388.3/22/09425 19
1. Barton Transport - History. 2. Barton, Thomas Henry, 1866-1946. 3. Bus lines - Great Britain - History. 4. Bus industry - Great Britain - History. I. Title.
HE5663.Z7 B376 1983

Oxman V., Verónica. Gálvez, Thelma. Yo trabajo así-- en casa particular /. Santiago, Chile , 1985. 113 p. : LC Card 86-208887
HD6072.2.C5 G35 1985

Oxygène pour tous les cerveaux /. Le Guen, René. Paris , c1985. 204 p. : ISBN 2-209-05743-4 : LC Card 86-117864 DDC 331.7/12/0944 19
HD8038.F7 L4 1985

Oyarce Pérez, Luis. Sistema de remuneraciones en la empresa / Luis Oyarce Pérez. Santiago, Chile : Universidad de Chile, Facultad de Ciencias Económicas y Administrativas, Instituto de Estudios de Relaciones de Trabajo y Organización, 1982. ix, 174 p. : ill. ; 22 cm. (Serie Estudios y monografías) Limited edition of 500 copies. Bibliography: p. 171-174. LC Card 84-228804
1. Wages. I. Title. II. Series.
HD4906 .O98 1982

Oye, Kenneth A., 1949- Cooperation under anarchy /. Princeton, N.J. , 1986. 260 p. ; ISBN 0-691-07695-2 : LC Card 85-42936 DDC 327.1/1 19
D445 .C736 1986 ***NYPL [JLE 86-1938]***

Oyejide, T. Ademola. The effects of trade and exchange rate policies on agriculture in Nigeria / T. Ademola Oyejide. Washington, D.C., USA : International Food Policy Research Institute, c1986. 61 p. : ill. ; 26 cm. (Research report . 55) "October 1986." Bibliography: p. 59-61. ISBN 0-89629-056-5 (pbk.) LC Card 86-21309 DDC 338.1/09669 19
1. Agriculture and state - Nigeria. 2. Nigeria - Commercial policy. 3. Foreign exchange administration - Nigeria. 4. Nigeria - Economic policy. I. Series: Research report (International Food Policy Research Institute) , 55. II. Title.
HD2145.5 .O94 1986

Oyo State (Nigeria). Ministry of Trade, Industries & Co-operatives. Investment opportunities in the field of small scale industries in Oyo State of Nigeria. Ibadan, Oyo State of Nigeria [1977?] v, 94 p., [15] p. of plates : LC Card 86-173553 DDC 658.1/592/096692 19
HD2346.N52 O965 1977

Oza, Nikhil M.

Ozadovskiĭ, A. A. (Andreĭ Andreevich) Uoll-strit protiv Afriki / A.A. Ozadovskiĭ. Kiev : Izd-vo polit. lit-ry Ukrainy, 1985. 228, [4] p. ; 20 cm. Bibliography: p. 226-[229]. LC Card 86-219442
1. Africa, Sub-Saharan - Foreign economic relations - United States. 2. United States - Foreign economic relations - Africa, Sub-Saharan. 3. Africa, Sub-Saharan - Dependency on United States. 4. International business enterprises - United States. 5. International business enterprises - Africa, Sub-Saharan. 6. Africa, Sub-Saharan - Strategic aspects. I. Title.
HF1611.Z4 U556 1985

Özer, İlhan. Kamu alacaklarının tahsili teorisi ve Türkiye'de uygulaması / İlhan Özer. Ankara : Türkiye ve Orta Doğu Amme İdaresi Enstitüsü, 1979. xv, 236 p. ; 24 cm. (Türkiye ve Orta-Doğu Âmme İdaresi Enstitüsü. Yayınları. no. 187) Bibliography: p. 229-236. LC Card 85-968002
1. Taxation - Turkey. 2. Taxation. I. Title. II. Series.
HJ2906.5 .O93 1979

Ozerov, V. K. (Viktor Konstantinovich) Analiz dinamiki sotsialisticheskogo rasshirennogo vosproizvodstva / V.K. Ozerov ; otvetstvennyĭ redaktor A.G. Aganbegi͡an. Novosibirsk : Izd-vo "Nauka," Sibirskoe otd-nie, 1984. 263 p. ; 21 cm. At head of title: Akademii͡a nauk SSSR. Sibirskoe otdelenie. Institut ėkonomiki i organizat͡sii promyshlennogo proizvodstva. Includes bibliographical references. LC Card 85-151291
1. Industrial productivity - Soviet Union - Statistics. 2. Economic indicators - Soviet Union. I. Aganbegi͡an, Abel Gezevich. II. Title.
HC340.I52 O97 1984

Özol, Ertuğrul İhsan. The Turkish economy, 1981. Istanbul [1981] 256 p. : LC Card 87-404163 DDC 330.9561/038 19
HC492 .T876 1981

ISSN 0360-2702

BIBLIOGRAPHIC GUIDE TO
BUSINESS AND ECONOMICS
1987

Volume 3
P—Z

G.K. HALL & CO.
70 Lincoln Street, Boston, Massachusetts

Manufactured in the United States of America.
ISBN 0-8161-7086-X

P & F charts . Lerbinger, Paul, 1955- Niederglatt , c1984. 231 p. : ISBN 3-85684-031-1 : LC Card 84-119357
HG6041 .L47 1984

P. A. N. see **Polska Akademia Nauk.**

P. B. G. C. see **Pension Benefit Guaranty Corporation.**

P. C. E. see **Partido Comunista de España.**

P. C. F. see **Parti communiste français.**

P. C. I. see **Partito comunista italiano.**

P. E. W. S. see **American Sociological Association. Section on Political Economy of the World System.**

P.M.E., ayudas, estímulos e instituciones especializadas en la C.E.E. : propuestas para las P.M.E. españolas. [Madrid] : Cámara de Comercio e Industria de Madrid, [1983?] 141 p. ; 22 cm. Bibliography: p. 139-141. ISBN 84-500-8571-3 LC Card 85-135456
1. Small business - European Economic Community countries. I. Cámara Ofical de Comercio e Industria de Madrid. II. Title: PME, ayudas, estímulos e instituciones especializadas en la C.E.E.
HD2346.E93 P16 1983

P. S. A. see **Pakistan Sociological Association.**

Paarlberg, Robert L. Fixing farm trade : policy options for the United States / Robert L. Paarlberg. Cambridge, Mass. : Ballinger, c1988. xiv, 159 p. ; 24 cm. (The Council on Foreign Relations series on international trade) "A Council on Foreign Relations book."--Jacket. Includes bibliographies and index. ISBN 0-88730-196-7 LC Card 87-24118 DDC 382/.41/0973 19
1. Produce trade - Government policy - United States. 2. Agriculture and state - United States. 3. United States - Commercial policy. 4. Agriculture - Economic aspects - United States. I. Title. II. Series.
HD9006 .P27 1988

Paauwe, J., 1953- Vakbeweging in verandering . Deventer , 1986. 191 p. : ISBN 90-267-1082-8 : LC Card 86-224831
HD6727 .V29 1986

Pacanins A., Guillermo (Pacanins Acevedo) La aviación comercial en Venezuela, de la carreta al avión / Guillermo Pacanins A. Caracas : [G. Pacanins A.], 1985. 159 p. : ill. ; 23 cm. Bibliography: p. 156. LC Card 85-184048
1. Aeronautics, Commercial - Venezuela - History. I. Title.
HE9841.A3 P33 1985

Pace, Edmond E. Developing a basic loan training program / Edmond E. Pace, Donald G. Simonson, Duane C. Gilkey. 2nd ed. Philadelphia, Pa. : Robert Morris Associates, c1987. 108 p. ; 23 cm. ISBN 0-936742-41-0 (pbk.) : LC Card 87-7936 DDC 332.1/753/0683 19
1. Commercial loans - Study and teaching - United States. 2. Bank loans - Study and teaching - United States. 3. Loan officers - United States - Training of. I. Simonson, Donald G. II. Gilkey, Duane C. III. Robert Morris Associates. IV. Title.
HG1642.U5 P33 1987

Pace University. Institute of International Banking.
International banking and global financing . New York, NY , c1983. xiv, 257 p. : ISBN 0-88239-015-5 (pbk.) : LC Card 84-60076 DDC 332.1/5 19
HG205 .I54 1983

International banking and world economic growth . New York , 1987. xviii, 183 p. : ISBN 0-275-92669-9 (alk. paper) : LC Card 87-7353 DDC 332.1/5 19
HG3881 .I575133 1987

Pachai, Bridglal. Land and politics in Malawi, 1875-1975 / by Bridglal Pachai. Kingston, Ontario, Canada : Limestone Press, c1978. xiv, 245 p., [20] p. of plates : ill., maps ; 24 cm. (Modern Africa . no. 2) Includes bibliographical references and index. ISBN 0-919642-82-9 LC Card 86-673708
1. Land use - Malawi. 2. Agriculture - Economic aspects - Malawi. 3. Malawi - Politics and government. I. Series: Modern Africa series, no. 2. II. Title.
HD997 .P32x 1978

Pachauri, R. K.
Energy policy issues . New Delhi , c1987. 146 p. : LC Card 87-900625 DDC 333.79/0954 19
HD9502.I42 E536 1987

Global energy interactions /. Ahmedabad , 1987. xxxi, 1290 p. : LC Card 87-902497 DDC 333.79 19
HD9502.A2 G545 1987b

National energy data systems . New Delhi , 1984, c1983. xxvi, 511 p. ; LC Card 84-901310 DDC 333.79/09172/4 19
HD9502.D442 N37 1984
NYPL [JLD 86-4320]

The political economy of global energy / R.K. Pachauri. Delhi ; New York : Oxford University Press, 1985. xiii, 191 p. : ill. ; 25 cm. Bibliography: p. 179-187. Includes index. LC Card 85-900034 DDC 333.79 19
1. Energy industries. 2. Energy policy. I. Title.
HD9502.A2 P32 1985

Pacheco B., Gabriel (Pacheco Bustamante) Apuntes sobre el problema parcelario en la Provincia de Chancay / Gabriel Pacheco B. Huacho, Perú : Universidad Nacional José F. Sánchez Carrión, Facultad de Sociología, 1984. 49 p. ; 21 cm. Based on field work done July-Sept. 1984 in the Huaura and Pativilca valleys in Peru and presented at the Taller Agrario in Oct. 1984. On cover: 5. LC Card 86-124478
1. Agriculture, Cooperative - Peru - Chancay (Province). I. Universidad Nacional "José Faustino Sánchez Carrión." Facultad de Sociología. II. Title.
HD1491.P42 C56 1984

Pacheco D., Rubén. Industria de la construcción : vivienda para panameños de escasos recursos? / preparado por Rubén Pacheco D. ; colaboradores, Eladio Araúz, José Baíz. [Panamá] : Ministerio de Vivienda, Dirección General de Desarrollo Urbano, 1974. 17, [1] leaves, [4] leaves of plates : ill. ; 28 cm. Bibliography: leaf [18]. LC Card 87-400643
1. Construction industry - Panama - Panama (District). 2. Housing - Panama - Panama (District). 3. Poor - Housing - Government policy - Panama. I. Araúz, Eladio. II. Baíz, José. III. Panama. Dirección General de Desarrollo Urbano. IV. Title. V. Title: Vivienda para panameños de escasos recursos?.
HD9715.P223 P367 1974

Pacheco, Lucas. La política económica en el Ecuador : una vison [i.e. visión] histórica / Lucas Pacheco. Quito, Ecuador : Publicaciones Tercer Mundo : CIPAD, 1985. 219 p. ; 22 cm. (Colección Pensamiento social) Originally presented as the author's thesis (grado de maestro)--Universidad Nacional Autónoma de México, 1978. Includes bibliographies. LC Card 87-400294 DDC 338.9866 19
1. Ecuador - Economic policy. 2. Ecuador - Economic conditions - 1972-. 3. Latin America - Economic policy. I. Series: Colección Pensamiento social (Quito, Ecuador). II. Title.
HC202 .P26 1985

Pacheco O., Amparo. Préstamo del BID al sector pesquero : el fracaso de un programa de desarrollo / Amparo Pacheco O., Alicia Bermúdez M. [San José] : Instituto de Investigaciones en Ciencias Económicas, Universidad de Costa Rica, 1984. 50 p. : ill. ; 28 cm. (Documentos de trabajo . no. 77) Bibliography: p. 50. LC Card 86-185463
1. Fish trade - Government policy - Latin America. 2. Inter-American Development Bank. I. Bermúdez M., Alicia. II. Universidad de Costa Rica. Instituto de Investigaciones en Ciencias Económicas. III. Series: Documentos de trabajo (Universidad de Costa Rica. Instituto de Investigaciones en Ciencias Económicas) , no. 77. IV. Title.
HD9464.A2 P33 1984

Pacheco, Rufino Gil. see **Gil Pacheco, Rufino.**

Pacheco S., Janette.
Región sur, problemática y perspectivas /. Arequipa [1986?] 164 p. ; LC Card 87-404224 DDC 330.984/052 19
HC182 .R39 1986

Situación y posibilidades alimentarias de la población urbano marginal de Arequipa / Janette Pacheco S., Katia Martínez Ch. Arequipa, Perú : CECYCAP, [1986] 38 p., 8 folded leaves of plates : ill. ; 21 cm. (Documentos / CECYCAP) Includes bibliographical references. LC Card 86-232480
1. Food consumption - Peru - Arequipa. 2. Poor - Peru - Arequipa - Nutrition. 3. Food crops - Peru - Arequipa. I. Martínez Ch., Katia. II. Series: Documentos (Centro de Estudios Cristianos y Capacitación Popular (Peru)). III. Title.
HD9014.P53 A746 1986

Pachev, Tasho. Elitnite i͡adra v trudovite kolektivi . [Sofia] [1985] 105 p. ; LC Card 86-104039
HD66 .E42 1985

PACIFIC AREA - COMMERCE.
Anderson, Kym. Australia's trade growth with developing countries /. Canberra, Australia , 1983. iv, 55 p. ; ISBN 0-86413-001-5 (pbk.) LC Card 86-673748
HF3948.D44 A52x 1983

The Pacific rim . Vancouver , 1987, c1986. ix, 319 p. : ISBN 0-7748-0266-9 (pbk.) LC Card 87-140238 DDC 330.99 19
HF4030.7 .P33 1987

PACIFIC AREA - COMMERCE - CANADA.
MacKay, Donald, 1925- The Asian dream . Vancouver , c1986. 223 p. : ISBN 0-88894-501-9 LC Card 86-225670 DDC 385/.0971 19
HE2810.C14 M33 1986

PACIFIC AREA - COMMERCE - UNITED STATES.
U. S. trade relations in the Pacific Rim . Washington , 1987. v, 57 p. ; LC Card 87-601361 DDC 382/.0973/09 19
HF3126.5 .U17 1987

PACIFIC AREA COOPERATION.
Das Dreieck Europa-Amerika-Asien /. [Diessenhofen] , 1986. 154 p. : ISBN 3-7253-0272-3 LC Card 86-231548
HC412 .D7 1986

Kovrigin, E. B. (Evgeniĭ Borisovich) Protivorechii͡a i perspektivy formirovanii͡a "Tikhookeanskogo soobshchestva" /. Moskva , 1986. 173, [3] p. ; LC Card 86-200677
HC681 .K68 1986

New tides in the Pacific . New York , 1987. xiii, 216 p. ; ISBN 0-313-25625-X (lib. bdg. : alk. paper) LC Card 87-8406 DDC 337.1/9 19
HC681 .N48 1987

PACIFIC AREA COOPERATION - CONGRESSES.
International Symposium on the Role of the Asia-Pacific Region in World Economic Development (1984 : Tokyo, Japan) Proceedings of the International Symposium on the Role of the Asia-Pacific Region in World Economic Development . Tokyo , c1985. iv, 325 p. : LC Card 87-108109 DDC 337.9 19
HC681 .I58 1984

PACIFIC AREA - ECONOMIC CONDITIONS.
Asia-Pacific report . Honolulu, Hawaii , 1986. x, 104 p. : ISBN 0-86638-071-X (pbk.) LC Card 85-27538 DDC 909/.09823/0828 19
HC412 .A7242 1986 ***NYPL [JLF 87-143]***

Asia-Pacific report, 1987-88 . Honolulu, Hawaii , 1987. p. cm. ISBN 0-86638-098-1 : LC Card 87-20074 DDC 909/.098230828 19
HC412 .A72415 1987

The Pacific rim . Vancouver , 1987, c1986. ix, 319 p. : ISBN 0-7748-0266-9 (pbk.) LC Card 87-140238 DDC 330.99 19
HF4030.7 .P33 1987

Woodward, Maria Lourdes. Business issues for the Asia-Pacific region /. Menlo Park, CA (333 Ravenswood Ave., Menlo Park 94025) , c1986. 14 p. ; LC Card 86-220779 DDC 330.95/0428
HC413.A78 W66 1986

PACIFIC AREA - ECONOMIC INTEGRATION.
Kovrigin, E. B. (Evgeniĭ Borisovich) Protivorechii͡a i perspektivy formirovanii͡a "Tikhookeanskogo soobshchestva" /. Moskva , 1986. 173, [3] p. ; LC Card 86-200677
HC681 .K68 1986

New tides in the Pacific . New York , 1987. xiii, 216 p. ; ISBN 0-313-25625-X (lib. bdg. : alk. paper) LC Card 87-8406 DDC 337.1/9 19
HC681 .N48 1987

The Pacific lake . Manila, Philippines , c1986. xvi, 248 p. : LC Card 87-111641 DDC 337.1/9 19
HF1600.15.P16 P33 1986

PACIFIC AREA - ECONOMIC POLICY - CONGRESSES.
International Symposium on the Role of the Asia-Pacific Region in World Economic Development (1984 : Tokyo, Japan)

Proceedings of the International Symposium on the Role of the Asia-Pacific Region in World Economic Development . Tokyo , c1985. iv, 325 p. : LC Card 87-108109 DDC 337.9 19
HC681 .I58 1984

PACIFIC AREA - FOREIGN ECONOMIC RELATIONS - AUSTRALIA.
McLean, Robert J. Exploiting opportunities in the Pacific Basin . [Melbourne] [1986] 56 p. : ISBN 0-85801-162-X (pbk.) LC Card 86-203142 DDC 337.9409 19
HF1626.5.P33 M35 1986

PACIFIC AREA - FOREIGN ECONOMIC RELATIONS - CONGRESSES.
International Symposium on the Role of the Asia-Pacific Region in World Economic Development (1984 : Tokyo, Japan) Proceedings of the International Symposium on the Role of the Asia-Pacific Region in World Economic Development . Tokyo , c1985. iv, 325 p. : LC Card 87-108109 DDC 337.9 19
HC681 .I58 1984

PACIFIC AREA - FOREIGN ECONOMIC RELATIONS - PHILIPPINES.
The Pacific lake . Manila, Philippines , c1986. xvi, 248 p. : LC Card 87-111641 DDC 337.1/9 19
HF1600.15.P16 P33 1986

PACIFIC AREA - FOREIGN RELATIONS.
Asia-Pacific report, 1987-88 . Honolulu, Hawaii , 1987. p. cm. ISBN 0-86638-098-1 : LC Card 87-20074 DDC 909/.098230828 19
HC412 .A72415 1987

PACIFIC AREA - INDUSTRIES - CONGRESSES.
The Industrial future of the Pacific basin /. Boulder , 1984. xvi, 285 p. : ISBN 0-86531-685-6 LC Card 83-51653 DDC 338.9/009182/3 19
HC681 .I53 1984 ***NYPL [JLD 86-3100]***

PACIFIC AREA - NATIONAL SECURITY.
New tides in the Pacific . New York , 1987. xiii, 216 p. ; ISBN 0-313-25625-X (lib. bdg. : alk. paper) LC Card 87-8406 DDC 337.1/9 19
HC681 .N48 1987

PACIFIC AREA - POLITICS AND GOVERNMENT.
Asia-Pacific report . Honolulu, Hawaii , 1986. x, 104 p. : ISBN 0-86638-071-X (pbk.) LC Card 85-27538 DDC 909/.09823/0828 19
HC412 .A7242 1986 ***NYPL [JLF 87-143]***

Asia-Pacific report, 1987-88 . Honolulu, Hawaii , 1987. p. cm. ISBN 0-86638-098-1 : LC Card 87-20074 DDC 909/.098230828 19
HC412 .A72415 1987

Woodward, Maria Lourdes. Business issues for the Asia-Pacific region /. Menlo Park, CA (333 Ravenswood Ave., Menlo Park 94025) , c1986. 14 p. ; LC Card 86-220779 DDC 330.95/0428
HC413.A78 W66 1986

PACIFIC AREA - POPULATION.
Asia-Pacific report . Honolulu, Hawaii , 1986. x, 104 p. : ISBN 0-86638-071-X (pbk.) LC Card 85-27538 DDC 909/.09823/0828 19
HC412 .A7242 1986 ***NYPL [JLF 87-143]***

PACIFIC AREA - POPULATION - ABSTRACTS.
Student research abstracts in population studies /. Bombay , 1986, c1985. xi, 434 p. ; LC Card 86-902278 DDC 304.6/095 19
HA4553 .S78 1986

PACIFIC AREA - SOCIAL CONDITIONS - CONGRESSES.
Movement for a no poverty society . Calcutta , 1980. 78 p. ; LC Card 81-902107
HC415.P6 M68 1980

PACIFIC AREA - STRATEGIC ASPECTS.
Sea lane security studies . Taipei, Taiwan, Republic of China , 1986. 100 p. ; LC Card 87-133640 DDC 359/.03 19
HE327 .S435 1986

Pacific basin project .
(no. 2) The Industrial future of the Pacific basin /. Boulder , 1984. xvi, 285 p. : ISBN 0-86531-685-6 LC Card 83-51653 DDC 338.9/009182/3 19
HC681 .I53 1984 ***NYPL [JLD 86-3100]***

Pacific Bell Directory (Firm) A Tribute to small business . [Washington, D.C.] , San Francisco , c1987. 72 p. : LC Card 87-403591 DDC 338.6/42 19
HD2346.U5 T75 1987

The Pacific challenge in international business / edited by W. Chan Kim and Philip K.Y. Young ; with a foreword by Vern Terpstra. Ann Arbor, Mich. : UMI Research Press, 1987. viii, 342 p. ; 25 cm. (Research for business decisions. no. 72) Includes bibliographies and index. ISBN 0-8357-1620-1 (alk. paper) LC Card 87-5008 DDC 338.09182/3 19
1. East Asia - Industries. 2. Asia, Southeastern - Industries. 3. Mineral industries - East Asia. 4. Mineral industries - Asia, Southeastern. 5. East Asia - Manufactures. 6. Asia, Southeastern - Manufactures. 7. Service industries - East Asia. 8. Service industries - Asia, Southeastern. I. Kim, W. Chan. II. Young, Philip K. Y.
HC460.5 .P32 1987

PACIFIC COAST REGION (PERU) - ECONOMIC CONDITIONS - STATISTICS.
La Agricultura en la costa del Perú, 1978-1984 /. Lima, Perú , 1985. ca. 150 leaves : LC Card 87-403706 DDC 338.1/0985 19
HD1905.P33 A38 1985

Pacific economic papers.
Anderson, Kym. Australia's trade growth with developing countries /. Canberra, Australia , 1983. iv, 55 p. ; ISBN 0-86413-001-5 (pbk.) LC Card 86-673748
HF3948.D44 A52x 1983

Pacific Institute for Public Policy Research.
Friedman, Milton, 1912- Politics and tyranny . San Francisco, Calif. , c1984. 68 p. ; ISBN 0-936488-00-X (pbk.) : LC Card 84-61364 DDC 330 19
HB98.3 .F75 1984 ***NYPL [JLE 87-857]***

The Pacific lake : Philippine perspectives on a Pacific community / edited by Jose P. Leviste, Jr. Manila, Philippines : Philippine Council for Foreign Relations in cooperation with SGV Foundation, c1986. xvi, 248 p. : ill. ; 24 cm. Includes bibliographies. LC Card 87-111641 DDC 337.1/9 19
1. Philippines - Foreign economic relations - Pacific Area. 2. Pacific Area - Foreign economic relations - Philippines. 3. Pacific Area - Economic integration. I. Leviste, Jose P., 1945-.
HF1600.15.P16 P33 1986

Pacific OCS lease sale, October 1, 1964, Oregon and Washington /. Webster, Frank L. [Washington] [1985] iii, 36 p. : LC Card 86-601138 DDC 333.33/9 19
HD243.A18 W43 1985

Pacific Research Institute for Public Policy.
Rabushka, Alvin. The new China . San Francisco , Boulder, Colo. , 1987. xii, 254 p. ; ISBN 0-936488-15-8 (pbk. : alk. paper) LC Card 87-10574 DDC 338.951 19
HC427.92 .R33 1987

Pacific research monograph.
(13) Philp, Norman E. The cash incentive . Canberra , 1986. xii, 135 p. : ISBN 0-86784-984-3 (pbk.) LC Card 87-150813
HD2346.P37 P46 1986

Pacific research monograph, 0155-9060 .
(12) Daniel, Philip. Foreign investment in Papua New Guinea . Canberra , 1986. x, 144 p. : ISBN 0-86784-761-1 (pbk.) LC Card 87-151193 DDC 332.6/7322953 19
HG5982.A3 D36 1986

The Pacific rim : investment, development, and trade / edited by Peter N. Nemetz. Vancouver : University of British Columbia Press, 1987, c1986. ix, 319 p. : ill. ; 23 cm. Includes bibliographies. ISBN 0-7748-0266-9 (pbk.) LC Card 87-140238 DDC 330.99 19
1. Pacific area - Commerce. 2. Pacific area - Economic conditions. 3. Investments, Foreign - Pacific area. 4. Power resources - Pacific area. I. Nemetz, Peter N., 1944-.
HF4030.7 .P33 1987

Pacific Science Association. Environment and resources in the Pacific /. Geneva, Switzerland , 1985. iv, 294 p. : LC Card 86-217776 DDC 333.7/2/099 19
HC681.3.E5 E58 1985

Pacific Science Congress (15th : 1983 : Dunedin, N.Z.) Environment and resources in the Pacific /. Geneva, Switzerland , 1985. iv, 294 p. : LC Card 86-217776 DDC 333.7/2/099 19
HC681.3.E5 E58 1985

Pacifica Radio Archive.
The Farmer is the man [sound recording]. Los Angeles, Calif. , p1983. 1 sound cassette (58 min.) : LC Card 87-751678
HD8039.F3

Honeymoon uranium mine occupation [sound recording]. Los Angeles, Calif. , p1983. 1 sound cassette (53 min.) : LC Card 87-752867
HD9539.U72

Pacifici, Giorgio. Il futuro presente : comunicazione, tecnologia e lavoro in una società che cambia / Giorgio Pacifici, Roberto Giua, Valerio Marchi ; presentazione di Giuseppe de Vergottini. Milano, Italy : F. Angeli, c1985. 201 p. ; 22 cm. (Sociologia. 87) Includes bibliographies. LC Card 86-127322 DDC 384/.0945 19
1. Telecommunication - Italy. 2. Telecommunication - Social aspects - Italy. 3. Communication in management - Italy. 4. Electronic data processing - Social aspects - Italy. I. Giua, Roberto. II. Marchi, Valerio. III. Series: Sociologia (Franco Angeli editore) , 87. IV. Title.
HE8174 .P33 1985

PACIFICORP - HISTORY.
Frisbee, Don C. The PacifiCorp story . New York , 1985. 27 p. : LC Card 85-60699 DDC 338.7/6136362/09787 19
HD9685.U7 P344 1985

The PacifiCorp story . Frisbee, Don C. New York , 1985. 27 p. : LC Card 85-60699 DDC 338.7/6136362/09787 19
HD9685.U7 P344 1985

Pacione, Michael. Population geography . London , Dover, N.H. , c1986. 322 p. : ISBN 0-7099-4045-9 : LC Card 86-6210 DDC 304.6 19
HB1951 .P653 1986 ***NYPL [JLD 86-3692]***

Pack, Edgar. Städte und Steuern in der Politik Julians : Untersuchungen zu den Quellen eines Kaiserbildes / Edgar Pack. Bruxelles : Latomus, 1986. 420 p. ; 25 cm. (Collection Latomus. v. 194) Revision of the author's thesis (doctoral--Universität zu Köln, 1983) originally presented under the title: Studien zur Gesetzgebung des Kaisers Julian. Bibliography: p. [387]-395. Includes indexes. ISBN 2-87031-134-6 LC Card 87-105922 DDC 336.2/014/37 19
1. Local taxation - Rome. 2. Local taxation - Law and legislation - Rome. 3. Rome - History - Julian, 361-363. I. Title. II. Series.
HJ9497.A3 P33 1986

Pack, Howard.
Fostering the capital-goods sector in LDCS : a survey of evidence and requirements / prepared by Howard Pack. Washington, D.C. (1818 H St., N.W., Washington 20433) : World Bank, [1980] v, 59. 2 leaves ; 28 cm. (World Bank staff working paper . no. 376) Cover title. "March 1980." Bibliography: leaves 57-59. LC Card 80-121299
1. Industrial equipment industry - Developing countries. I. Title. II. Series.
HD9680.D44 P33 1980

Productivity, technology, and industrial development : a case study in textiles / Howard Pack. New York : Oxford University Press, c1987. x, 193 p. : ill. ; 25 cm. (A World Bank research publication) "Published for the World Bank." Bibliography: p. 179-185. Includes index. ISBN 0-19-520543-X : LC Card 86-33271 DDC 331.11/8 19
1. Cotton textile industry - Labor productivity - Case studies. I. Title.
HD9870.5 .P25 1987

Pack, Ludwig. Betriebswirtschaftliche Entscheidungen bei Stagnation . Wiesbaden , c1984. xvi, 327 p. : ISBN 3-409-13303-8 LC Card 84-197990
HD30.23 .B486 1984

Pack your own parachute . Hirsch, Paul Morris. Reading, Mass. , c1987. xix, 197 p. ; ISBN 0-201-12205-7 (pbk.) : LC Card 87-14388 DDC 658.4/09 19
HD38.25.U6 H578 1987

PACKAGED BUILDINGS. see **BUILDINGS, PREFABRICATED.**

PACKAGED HOUSES. see **PREFABRICATED HOUSES.**

PACKAGING.
(1986) Sacharow, Stanley. Packaging, an introduction /. Cleveland, OH , c1986. p. cm.

ISBN 0-15-004486-0 LC Card 87-8362 DDC 658.5/64 19
HF5770 .S274 1986

Packaging, an introduction /. Sacharow, Stanley. Cleveland, OH , c1986. p. cm. ISBN 0-15-004486-0 LC Card 87-8362 DDC 658.5/64 19
HF5770 .S274 1986

Packard, Peter, 1924- Slater, John, 1936- The skills of appraisal /. Aldershot, Hants, England , Brookfield, Vt., U. S.A. , c1988. p. cm. ISBN 0-566-02729-1 LC Card 87-22388 DDC 658.3/125 19
HF5549.5.R3 S57 1988

Packard, William V. Sea-trading / William V. Packard. London : Fairplay Publications, c1984-c1986. 3 v. : ill ; 24 cm. Includes indexes. CONTENTS. - v. 1. The ships -- v. 2. Cargoes -- v. 3. Trading. ISBN 0-905045-64-5 (pbk.) LC Card 86-204836 DDC 387.5/44 19
1. Shipping. 2. Ships. 3. Ships - Cargo. I. Title.
HE571 .P26 1984

Packer. Fresh trends, 1987 . [Lincolnshire, Ill.] (400 Knightsbridge Pkwy., Lincolnshire 60069) , c1987. 4 v. ; LC Card 87-162047 DDC 381/.415/0973 19
HD9244 .F73 1987

Packer, Arnold E. Johnston, William B., 1945- Workforce 2000 . Indianapolis, Ind. [Washington, D.C.?] , 1987. xxvii, 117 p. : LC Card 87-601910 DDC 331.12/5/0973 19
HD8072.5 .J64 1987

PACKET SWITCHING (DATA TRANSMISSION)
Packet switching equipment markets /. Stamford, Conn., U. S.A. , c1985. v, 205 leaves : ISBN 0-89336-465-7 (pbk.) LC Card 87-403884 DDC 381/.456213878 19
HD9696.T443 U556 1985

Packet switching equipment markets / Eve Oppenheim, project analyst. Stamford, Conn., U. S.A. : Business Communications Co., c1985. v, 205 leaves : ill. ; 29 cm. (Business opportunity report . G-093) "November 1985"--T.p. verso. ISBN 0-89336-465-7 (pbk.) LC Card 87-403884 DDC 381/.456213878 19
1. Telecommunication switching systems equipment industry - United States. 2. Data transmission equipment industry - United States. 3. Packet switching (Data transmission). I. Oppenheim, Eve. II. Business Communications Co. III. Series.
HD9696.T443 U556 1985

PACKING. see **PACKAGING.**

PACKING-HOUSES - UNITED STATES - HISTORY.
Skaggs, Jimmy M. Prime cut . College Station , c1986. xiii, 263 p., [8] p. of plates : ISBN 0-89096-249-9 : LC Card 85-40742 DDC 338.1/76213/0973 19
HD9415 .S58 1986 ***NYPL [JLE 86-3913]***

Pacsy, Vivian A. Hoffman, Frank. Accounting fundamentals . New York , c1987. vi, 229 p. : ISBN 0-07-029210-8 (pbk.) : LC Card 86-27352 DDC 657 19
HF5635 .H678 1987

Pacto Andino. see **Acuerdo de Cartagena.**

El pacto y la democracia sociales /. López-Orihuela, Alcides, 1926- Caracas, Venezuela [1986] (Caracas : Editorial Greco) xvi, 129 p. ; ISBN 90-826548-5-X LC Card 87-402941 DDC 338.987 19
HC237 .L667 1986

Pädagogische Aspekte entwicklungspolitischer Öffentlichkeitsarbeit /. Krämer, Georg. Frankfurt/Main , 1980. 233 p. : ISBN 3-88129-332-9 LC Card 81-466304
HC59.7 .K687 ***NYPL [JLD 87-528]***

Pädagogische Beiträge zur Kulturbegegnung . (Bd. 4) Mihçiyazgan, Ursula. Wir haben uns vergessen . Hamburg , c1986. 428 p. ; ISBN 3-923002-30-0 : LC Card 87-104026
HD8458.T9 M54 1986

Padaki, V. (Vijay)
Industrial sickness . Ahmedabad , c1984. xv, 459 p. ; LC Card 87-902007 DDC 363.1/19677/00954 19
HD9866.I63 A385 1984

Issues in modernization of the textile industry . Ahmedabad , 1985. 87 p. : LC Card 87-902140 DDC 338.4/7677/00954 19
HD9866.I62 I58 1985

Padayachee, Vishnu. An analysis of some aspects of employment and unemployment in the African townships of Umlazi and Lamontville : a preliminary investigation / Vishnu Padayachee. Durban [South Africa] : Institute for Social and Economic Research, University of Durban-Westville, [1985] iii, 49 p. ; 21 cm. (Occasional paper / Institute for Social and Economic Research, University of Durban-Westville . no. 14) "December 1985." Bibliography: p. 45-49. ISBN 0-949947-75-X (pbk.) LC Card 87-404149 DDC 331.12/5/0968455 19
1. Labor supply - South Africa - Durban. 2. Unemployment - South Africa - Durban. 3. Income - South Africa - Durban. I. Series: Occasional paper (University of Durban-Westville. Institute for Social and Economic Research) , no. 14. II. Title.
HD5842.D87 P33 1985

PADDY FIELD CULTURE. see **IRRIGATION FARMING.**

PADERBORN REGION (GERMANY) - ECONOMIC CONDITIONS.
Henning, Friedrich-Wilhelm. Vorindustrielles Gewerbe und wirtschaftlicher Wandel im Paderborner Land im 19. Jahrhundert /. Dortmund , 1983. 67 p. ; LC Card 83-198581
HC288.P27 H46 1983

Padilla, Hilario J. Cleto, Romeo B. The Ilocos and Cordillera provinces . Baguio City [Philippines] , Manila [1986] xvii, 265 p. : LC Card 87-111697 DDC 330.9599/1 19
HC457.L8 C56 1986

Padoa, Fabio. L'assicurazione internazionale : il mercato dei rischi, problemi della domanda e problemi dell'offerta, perché l'assicurazione italiana è sottosviluppata, l'ambiente macroeconomico, la conduzione dell'impresa, l'assicurazione e il potere, le nuove frontiere / Fabio Padoa. Milano : U. Hoepli, c1983. 140 p. : ill. ; 21 cm. Bibliography: p. 139-140. ISBN 88-20-31384-7 LC Card 85-189997
1. Insurance, Business. 2. Risk (Insurance). 3. Insurance, Business - Italy. 4. Risk (Insurance) - Italy. I. Title.
HG8059 .P33 1983

Padoan, Pietro Carlo.
Le Crisi finanziarie /. Bologna , c1985. 348 p. : ISBN 88-15-00807-1 : LC Card 85-201934 DDC 332.1 19
HG1591 .C75 1985

Martinengo, Giancarlo. Lo SME e il dollaro . [Napoli] , c1983. 84 p. ; LC Card 85-150597
HG930.5 .M27 1983

Arbeiterbewegung in den Rheinlanden. see **Die Arbeiterbewegung in den Rheinlanden.**

Paelinck, Jean H. P. Human behaviour in geographical space . Aldershot, Hants, England , Brookfield, Vt., U. S.A. , c1986. x, 328 p. : ISBN 0-566-00807-6 : LC Card 85-5528 DDC 338.9 19
HT391 .H785 1986 ***NYPL [JLD 86-1630]***

Paepe, Michel de. La Verrerie champenoise, Charbonneaux-B.S.N. Reims, de 1870 à nos jours /. Die , c1984. 279 p. : ISBN 2-904638-12-1 : LC Card 84-247744
HD9623.F8 V47 1984

Un Paese che cambia / a cura di Basilio M. Biucchi. Locarno : A. Dadò, 1985. 293 p. : ill. ; 26 cm. Bibliography: p. 291-292. CONTENTS. - Cambia tutto e cambia poco / Silvano Toppi -- Il Ticino come volontà e rappresentanza / Roberto Bianchi -- Svizzeri di lingua italiana / Sandro Bianconi -- Agricoltura e forze idriche / Basilio M. Biucchi -- Il ruolo delle vie di communicazione e dei trasporti nel Ticino del secondo dopoguerra / Remigio Ratti -- Da un paese di piccoli proprietari ad un paese di inquilini / Angela Rossi -- Dal più Stato al meno Stato / Martino Rossi -- Una popolazione che cambia / Dania Suckow-Poretti -- Domanda di educazione e politica scolastica 1940-1980 / Elio Venturelli. LC Card 85-195116 DDC 330.9494/7 19
1. Ticino (Switzerland) - Economic conditions. 2. Ticino (Switzerland) - Social conditions. I. Biucchi, Basilio M. (Basilio Mario), 1908-1983.
HC398.T5 P34 1985

Pagano, Michael A. How the public works : major issues in infrastructure finance / Michael A. Pagano. Washington, D.C. : National League of Cities, c1986. ix, 68, 6 p. : ill. ; 28 cm. (A Policy working paper of the National League of Cities) "September 1986." ISBN 0-933729-13-8 (pbk.) : LC Card 87-129719 DDC 338.4/3363/0973 19
1. Municipal finance - United States. 2. Capital investments - United States. 3. Infrastructure (Economics) - United States - Finance. 4. Grants-in-aid - United States. 5. Urban policy - United States. I. Title. II. Series.
HJ9145 .P343 1986

Page, G. Terry. Johannsen, Hano. International dictionary of management /. London , c1986. 370 p. : ISBN 0-85038-970-4
NYPL [JLD 86-1777]

Page, John M., 1949- Little, Ian Malcolm David. Small manufacturing enterprises . New York , 1987. x, 362 p. : ISBN 0-19-520619-3 LC Card 87-12365 DDC 338.6/42/0954 19
HD9736.I52 L57 1987

Page, John R., 1949- Accounting and information systems / John Page, Paul Hooper. 3rd ed. Englewood Cliffs, N.J. : Prentice-Hall, c1987. xiii, 738 p. : ill. ; 25 cm. Includes index. ISBN 0-13-002361-2 LC Card 86-25429 DDC 657/.028/5 19
1. Accounting - Data processing. 2. Information storage and retrieval systems - Accounting. I. Hooper, H. Paul. II. Title.
HF5679 .P25 1987

Page, Olivia. How to find information about foreign firms /. Washington, D.C. , c1987. 93 p. ; ISBN 0-934940-46-0 (pbk.) : LC Card 86-51568 DDC 016.3388/8873 19
HD2785 .H69 1987

Page, Robert M. Stigma / Robert M. Page. London ; Boston : Routledge & Kegan Paul, 1984. xii, 207 p. ; 22 cm. (Concepts in social policy . 2) Includes index. Bibliography: p. 184-201. ISBN 0-7100-9786-7 : LC Card 83-24638 DDC 302/.12 19
1. Stigma (Social psychology). 2. Social service - Great Britain. 3. Unmarried mothers - Great Britain - Case studies. 4. Great Britain - Social policy. I. Title. II. Series.
HM291 .P25 1984 ***NYPL [JLD 86-3113]***

Paggi, Mechel S. Impact of agricultural exports for Texas / Mechel S. Paggi. College Station, Tex. : Dept. of Agricultural Economics, Texas A&M University, [1986] 20 leaves, [1] leaf of plates : ill. ; 29 cm. (Faculty paper series / Department of Agricultural Economics, Texas A&M University . FP 86-12) "October 1986." LC Card 87-620821 DDC 382/.41/09764 19
1. Agriculture - Economic aspects - Texas. 2. Texas - Commerce. 3. Texas - Economic conditions. I. Series: Faculty paper series , FP 86-12. II. Title.
HD1775.T4 P34 1986

Pagini din gîndirea economică militară românească / studiu introductiv, selectarea textelor și adnotări de Gheorghe Anghel, Gheorghe Tudor ; cuvînt înainte de Ivanciu Nicolae-Văleanu. București : Editura Militară, 1983. 219 p. ; 21 cm. Collection of articles from various publications. Includes bibliographical references. LC Card 84-116220
1. Armaments - Economic aspects - Romania. 2. Romania - Defenses - Economic aspects. 3. War - Economic aspects - Romania. I. Anghel, Gheorghe. II. Tudor, Gheorghe.
HC405.Z9 D443 1983

Pahl-Rugenstein Hochschulschriften Gesellschafts- und Naturwissenschaften .
(124) Ahn, Lothar. Ökonomische und ökologische Perspektiven der Agrarpolitik . Köln , 1983. 98 p. : ISBN 3-7609-5124-4 LC Card 83-155478
HD1920.5 .A627 1983

(181) Kurthen, Hermann. Politische Ökonomie und Persönlichkeitstheorie . Köln , 1985. 245 p. ; ISBN 3-7609-5181-3 LC Card 85-155083
HB74.P8 K87 1985

(220) Schwohnke, Andreas. Teleheimarbeit als neue Rationalisierungsstrategie . Köln , 1986. vii, 237, [14] p. : ISBN 3-7609-5220-8 LC Card 86-224163
HD2336.G3 S38 1986

Pahler, Arnold J. Advanced accounting : concepts and practice / Arnold J. Pahler, Joseph E. Mori.3rd ed. San Diego : Harcourt Brace Jovanovich, c1988. xxi, 1208 p. : ill. ; 25 cm. Includes bibliographical references and index. ISBN 0-15-501827-2 LC Card 87-81162 DDC 657/.046 19

1. Accounting. I. Mori, Joseph E. II. Title.
HF5635 .P215 1988

Pai Panandiker, V. A., 1935- Development bureaucracy / V.A. Pai Panandiker, R.N. Bishnoi, O.P. Sharma. New Delhi : Oxford & IBH, c1983. ix, 252 p. ; 23 cm. "Under the auspices of Centre for Policy Research." Includes index. LC Card 83-902420 DDC 352.94/233/09542 19
1. Agriculture and state - India - Karnal (District). 2. Agriculture and state - India - Gorakhpur (District). 3. Bureaucracy - India - Karnal (District). 4. Bureaucracy - India - Gorakhpur (District). I. Bishnoi, R. N. II. Sharma, O. P. III. Title.
HD2075.K359 P34 1983 ***NYPL [JLD 86-3762]***

PAI, T. A. (TONSE ANANTH), 1922-1981. Kamath, M. V., 1921- The innovative banker, T.A. Pai, his life and times /. Manipal , Bombay , 1983. x, 247 p., [9] p. of plates : LC Card 83-904531 DDC 332.1/2/0924 B 19
HG1552.P4 K36 1983 ***NYPL [JFE 87-879]***

Paillet, Marc. Le grand inventaire : socialisme ou libéralisme / Marc Paillet Paris : Denoël, c1985. 176 p. ; 23 cm. Includes bibliographical references. ISBN 2-207-23172-0 : LC Card 86-127029 DDC 338.944 19
1. Government ownership - France. 2. Privatization - France. 3. Privatization. I. Title.
HD4168 .P35 1985 ***NYPL [JLE 87-1232]***

Paim, Gilberto. Computador faz política / Gilberto Paim. Rio de Janeiro, RJ-Brasil : Associação Promotora de Estudos de Economia, [1985] 164 p. ; 21 cm. Includes bibliographical references. LC Card 86-128056
1. Computer industry - Brazil. 2. Electronic data processing - Government policy - Brazil. I. Title.
HD9696.C63 B75 1985

Paine, Suzanne. Fforde, Adam. The limits of national liberation . London , New York , c1987. 246 p. ; ISBN 0-7099-1036-3 LC Card 87-8977 DDC 338.9597 19
HC444 .F46 1987

PAINT INDUSTRY AND TRADE - UNITED STATES - FORECASTING.
Special analysis and outlook for E.I. Du Pont De Nemours & Company (Inc.), Chemicals and Pigments Department. Boston, Mass. (7 Liberty Sq., Boston 02109) [1986] 17, [6] p. : LC Card 86-205857 DDC 338.4/766/00973 19
HD9660.P253 U672 1986

Painter, David S.
[Oil and the American century]
Private power and public policy : multinational oil companies and U. S. foreign policy, 1941-1954 / David S. Painter. London : I.B. Taurus, c1986. xii, 302 p. : maps ; 23 cm. American ed. published as: Oil and the American century: the political economy of U. S. foreign oil policy, 1941-1954. Bibliography: p. 271-294. Includes index. ISBN 1-85043-021-7 LC Card 87-673320
1. Petroleum industry and trade - Government policy - United States - History - 20th century. 2. Petroleum industry and trade - Middle East - History - 20th century. 3. United States - Foreign economic relations - Middle East. 4. Middle East - Foreign economic relations - United States. I. Title.
HD9566 .P24x 1986b

Painting and Drywall Work Preservation Fund. A Practical guide to investigating public works violations /. Oakland, CA (520 3rd St., Suite 204, Oakland 94607) , 1986. 73 p., [3] leaves of plates : LC Card 86-209657 DDC 363.2/5 19
HD3890.C2 P7 1986

Pais, H. Poverty alleviation programmes : feedback from Jhabua / H. Pais, C.S.K. Singh. New Delhi : National Labour Institute, 1986. xii, 48, [3] p. (some folded) : ill. ; 25 cm. Cover title: Feedback from Jhabua. LC Card 86-903597 DDC 362.5/8/09543 19
1. Poor - India - Jhābua (District). 2. Jhābua (India : District) - Economic conditions. 3. Economic development projects - India - Jhābua (District). 4. Economic assistance, Domestic - India - Jhābua (District). I. Singh, C. S. K. II. Title. III. Title: Feedback from Jhabua.
HC437.J43 P35 1986

País Vasco (Spain). Gabinete de Prospección Sociológica. Kaiero Uria, Andoni. Las elecciones sindicales en Euskadi, representación de los trabajadores en la empresa e implantación de los sindicatos . Vitoria , 1985. 629 p. : ISBN 84-7542-199-7 LC Card 87-146467
HD6490.R42 S74 1985

El paisaje de montaña en Extremadura . Gurría Gascón, José Luis. Cáceres [1985?] 273 p. : ISBN 84-600-3949-8 LC Card 87-111451
HC387.E7 G87 1985

Paiūodis, A. Problemy razvitii͡a i sovershenstvovanii͡a material'no-tekhnicheskoĭ bazy torgovli i obshchestvennogo pitanii͡a v dvenadtsatoĭ pi͡atiletke . Vil'ni͡us , 1985. 169 p. ; LC Card 86-102743
HF3629.L5 P76 1985

Paiva, Francisco Ismar Martins. Projeto Pesca Industrial à Vela. [Natal, Brazil] : Estado do Rio Grande do Norte, Companhia de Desenvolvimento Industrial, [1982 or 1983] 91 p. : ill. ; 21 x 33 cm. Cover title. "Equipe de Elaboração, Francisco Ismar Martins Paiva, Antónia Maria de Araújo Fernandes, Zizeuda Souza Gomes"--P. 3. Includes bibliographical references. LC Card 85-102872
1. Fish trade - Brazil - Rio Grande do Norte. 2. Economic development projects - Brazil - Rio Grande do Norte. 3. Shark fisheries - Brazil - Rio Grande do Norte. 4. Light fishing. I. Fernandes, Antónia Maria de Araújo. II. Gomes, Zizeuda Souza. III. Rio Grande do Norte (Brazil). Companhia de Desenvolvimento Industrial. IV. Title.
HD9464.B73 R487 1982

Pajestka, Jozef. Gospodarka w procesie reformowania /. Warszawa , 1986. 423 p. : ISBN 83-208-0514-7 : LC Card 87-102275
HC340.3 .G68 1986

Pak, U-hŭi. Enos, John L. (John Lawrence), 1924- The adoption and diffusion of imported technology . New York , c1988. 272 p. : ISBN 0-7099-2030-X LC Card 87-19894 DDC 338.9519/506 19
HC470.T4 E56 1987

Pakhomov, V. P. (Vi͡acheslav Petrovich) Problemy osvoenii͡a prirodnykh resursov Ural'skogo Severa /. Sverdlovsk , 1985. 70 p. : LC Card 86-195834
HC337.R852 U7359 1985

Pakistan : country study and Norwegian aid review / Alf Morten Jerve, ed. Fantoft, Norway : Chr. Michelsen Institute, Dept. of Social Science and Development, [1985] xvii, 414 p. : ill. ; 21 cm. "October 1985." Bibliography: p. 367-399. Includes indexes. ISBN 82-905840-4-0 (pbk.) LC Card 86-235254 DDC 338.91/481/05491 19
1. Economic assistance, Norwegian - Pakistan. 2. Pakistan - Economic conditions. I. Jerve, Alf Morten.
HC440.5 .P26 1985

Pakistan . Galal, M. F. Rome [i.e. Multan] , 1978. vii, 36 p. ; LC Card 83-931176
HD9086.P32 G35 1978

Pakistan Council for Science and Technology. Growth of R & D manpower and expenditure in Pakistan. Islamabad , 1985. 66 p. ; LC Card 85-932022 DDC 331.12/510014/095491021 19
HC440.5.Z9 R44 1985

Pakistan. Directorate of Communication Strategy. Journalist Workshop on Population and Development Reporting (1981 : Islāmābād, Pakistan) Journalist Workshop on Population and Development Reporting, Oct. 31-Nov. 5, 1981, Islamabad /. [Pakistan , 1982? (Lahore : Directorate of Production and Publication) 63, 12 p. ; LC Card 83-930293 DDC 304.6 19
HB849 .J67 1981

Pakistan. Directorate of Training Income Tax. Workshop: Middle Management and the Fisc. (1983 : Lahore, Pakistan) Miscellany II . Lahore [1984?] 251 p. : LC Card 86-930242 DDC 354.549/10072 19
HJ3611.5 .W67 1983

PAKISTAN - ECONOMIC CONDITIONS.
Ahrens, Heinz-Dietmar. Towards reducing the dependence on capital imports . Wiesbaden , 1982. xvi, 337 p. : ISBN 3-515-03853-1 (pbk.) LC Card 86-214363 DDC 338.9549/1 19
HC440.5 .A726 1982

Employment, distribution, and basic needs in Pakistan . Lahore , 1986. xxxiv, 408 p., [1] leaf of plates : LC Card 86-930280 DDC 330.9549/1 19
HD5820.5.A6 E47 1986

Illarionov, Sergeĭ Ivanovich. Rol' gosudarstva v razvitii ėkonomiki Pakistana . Moskva , 1981. 196, [3] p. ; LC Card 82-112505
HC440.5 .I39 1981

Kibria, Ghulam. Development options . Karachi , 1984. xi, 267 p. ; LC Card 84-931764 DDC 338.9549/1 19
HC440.5 .K53 1984

Pakistan . Fantoft, Norway [1985] xvii, 414 p. : ISBN 82-905840-4-0 (pbk.) LC Card 86-235254 DDC 338.91/481/05491 19
HC440.5 .P26 1985

PAKISTAN - ECONOMIC CONDITIONS - CONGRESSES.
Population, human and national resources in Pakistan /. [Karachi , 198-?] 19 p. ; LC Card 85-931341
HA4590.5 .P66 1980z

PAKISTAN - ECONOMIC POLICY.
Ahrens, Heinz-Dietmar. Towards reducing the dependence on capital imports . Wiesbaden , 1982. xvi, 337 p. : ISBN 3-515-03853-1 (pbk.) LC Card 86-214363 DDC 338.9549/1 19
HC440.5 .A726 1982

Evaluation of the Fifth Five Year Plan, 1978-83. Islamabad [1983] 54 p. ; LC Card 84-931227 DDC 338.9549/1 19
HC440.5 .E86 1983

Illarionov, Sergeĭ Ivanovich. Rol' gosudarstva v razvitii ėkonomiki Pakistana . Moskva , 1981. 196, [3] p. ; LC Card 82-112505
HC440.5 .I39 1981

Pakistan's development priorities . Karachi , 1984. 390 p. ; LC Card 85-930745 DDC 338.9549/1 19
HC440.5 .P3624 1984b

Pakistan Engineering Congress. Ghias-ud-Din, Mian. Role of management, training & research in railroad operations /. [Pakistan , 1983?] (Lahore : Caxton Printing Press) 98 p., A-C folded leaves of plates : LC Card 86-903113 DDC 385/.068 19
HE3300.5 .G48 1983

Pakistan. Federal Bureau of Statistics. Consumer price index numbers of Pakistan, 1980-81 =. Karachi [1985] 118 p. ; LC Card 86-930250 DDC 338.5/28/095491 19
HB235.P25 C65 1985

Pakistan. Industrial Credit & Investment Corporation. Economics & Research Dept. Financial performance of PICIC assisted companies ... [Karachi] [198-?] v. <1 > ; LC Card 85-931756
HG4244.5 .F56 1980z

Pakistan International Airlines. Pī.Ā'ī.Ae. ṭayyāre kā ighvā, dahshat gardī kī intihā, 'amle aur musāfiroṇ ke ta'aṣṣurāt, Pishāvar, 18 Mārc, 1981. Islāmābād [1981] 27 p. ; LC Card 82-930104
HE9871.5.Z7 H56 1981

Pakistan. Ministry of Food, Agriculture & Cooperatives. Water Management Wing. Water users associations in Pakistan. Islamabad , 1984. 108 p. ; LC Card 85-930345 DDC 333.91/3/095491 19
HD1741.P13 W37 1984

Pakistan. Planning Commission.
Evaluation of the Fifth Five Year Plan, 1978-83. Islamabad [1983] 54 p. ; LC Card 84-931227 DDC 338.9549/1 19
HC440.5 .E86 1983

The Sixth Five Year National Energy Plan, 1983-88. [Islamabad] : The Commission, [1983 or 1984] 88 p. ; 24 cm. LC Card 84-932174 DDC 333.79/09549/1 19
1. Energy policy - Pakistan. I. Title.
HD9502.P272 P33 1983

PAKISTAN - POPULATION - CONGRESSES.
Population, human and national resources in Pakistan /. [Karachi , 198-?] 19 p. ; LC Card 85-931341
HA4590.5 .P66 1980z

Pakistan Population Planning Council.
Population, human and national resources in Pakistan /. [Karachi , 198-?] 19 p. ; LC Card 85-931341
HA4590.5 .P66 1980z

PAKISTAN - POPULATION POLICY - CONGRESSES.
Population, human and national resources in

Pakistan /. [Karachi , 198-?] 19 p. ; LC Card 85-931341
HA4590.5 .P66 1980z

PAKISTAN - RURAL CONDITIONS.
Morozova, M. IU. (Marina IUr'evna) Sovremennaia pakistanskaia derevnia . Moskva , 1986. 172 p. ; LC Card 86-174352
HD2075.5 .M67 1986

Pakistan Sociological Association. Population, human and national resources in Pakistan /. [Karachi , 198-?] 19 p. ; LC Card 85-931341
HA4590.5 .P66 1980z

Pakistan's development priorities : choices for the future / edited by Shaid Javed Burki and Robert LaPorte, Jr. Karachi : Oxford University Press, 1984. 390 p. ; 22 cm. (UGC monograph series in economics) Includes index. LC Card 85-930745 DDC 338.9549/1 19
1. Pakistan - Economic policy. I. Burki, Shaid Javed. II. Laporte, Robert. III. Series.
HC440.5 .P3624 1984b

Pakistan's energy policy . Rashed, Saeed Ahmed. Islamabad, Pakistan , 1983. iv, 102 p. : LC Card 83-930777 DDC 333.79/09549/1 19
HD9502.P272 R373 1983 *NYPL [JLD 86-3857]*

Pál, József, Dr. Erdei Ferenc agrárgazdasági és szövetkezetelméleti munkásságáról . Budapest [1986] 39 p. ; LC Card 87-408584
HD1940.5.E72 E73 1986

Pál, László. Bőhm, Antal. Társadalmunk ingázói, az ingázók társadalma /. [Budapest] , 1985. 166, [I] p. ; ISBN 963-09-2654-7 : LC Card 86-185996
HD5717.5.H9 B64 1985

Palacios, Eulalio R. Reflexiones sobre economia nacional e internacional / Eulalio R. Palacios. [S.l. : s.n.], 1986 (Asunción, Paraguay : Tall. Gráf. de la Impr. Nacional) 333 p. ; 24 cm. LC Card 86-226634
1. Paraguay - Economic conditions - 1954-. 2. Paraguay - Economic policy. 3. Monetary policy - Paraguay. 4. Debts, External - Paraguay. 5. Paraguay - Commercial policy. I. Title.
HC222 .P36 1986

Palamarchuk, Aleksandr Semenovich.
Rekonstruktsiia predpriiatiĭ i ėffektivnost' proizvodstva / A.S. Palamarchuk. Moskva : Izd-vo "Znanie," 1981. 62, [2] p. ; 20 cm. (Novoe v zhizni, nauke, tekhnike. Seriia "Ėkonomika i organizatsiia proizvodstva" . no. 4, 1981 g.) Bibliography: p. [63]-[64] LC Card 81-179552
1. Industrial equipment - Soviet Union. 2. Capital investments - Soviet Union. I. Series: Novoe v zhizni, nauke, tekhnike. Seriia "Ėkonomika i organizatsiia proizvodstva" , 1981, no. 4. II. Title.
HD39.3 .P34 1981

Palánkai, Tibor.
Evropeĭskoe soobshchestvo . Moskva , 1986. 270 p. : LC Card 86-202812
HC241.2 .E867 1986

Gazdasági hadviselés a kölcsönös függés korszakában / Palánkai Tibor. [Budapest] : Kossuth, 1985. 88 p. ; 19 cm. Includes bibliographical references. ISBN 963-09-2633-4 : LC Card 86-128423
1. Economic sanctions. 2. East-West trade (1945-). 3. International economic relations. 4. World politics - 1945-. I. Title.
HF1413.5 .P35 1985

Palau, Tomás. El cultivo del algodón y la soya en el Paraguay y sus derivaciones sociales. 1a ed. Santiago de Chile : Naciones Unidas, 1986. 148 p. ; 23 cm. (Estudios e informes de la CEPAL, 0256-9795 . 58) "Preparado por el señor Tomás Palau ... con la colaboración del señor Ramón Fogel y de la señora M. Victoria Heikel"--T.p. verso. "LC/G.1414. Marzo de 1986"--T.p. verso. "Publicación de las Naciones Unidas. Número de venta: S.86.II.G.8"--T.p. verso. Bibliography: p. 139-141. ISBN 92-1-321207-0 LC Card 87-400251 DDC 338.1/7351/09892 19
1. Cotton trade - Paraguay. 2. Soybean industry - Paraguay. 3. Agriculture and state - Paraguay. I. Title. II. Series.
HD9084.P25 P35 1986

Palazzi, Paolo. Domanda di lavoro e produttività nell'industria italiana / Paolo Palazzi, Paolo Piacentini. Bologna : Il Mulino, c1980. 177 p. ; 22 cm. (Studi e ricerche. 111) Includes bibliographical references. LC Card 82-156294 DDC 331.13/7945 19
1. Unemployment - Italy. 2. Labor supply - Italy. 3. Industrial productivity - Italy. 4. Italy - Full employment policies. I. Piacentini, Paolo, 1948-. II. Title.
HD5784 .P28 1980 *NYPL [JLD 86-2811]*

Paldam, Martin. How much does one percent of growth change the unemployment? : a study of 17 OECD countries, 1948-1980 / Martin Paldam. Aarhus, Denmark : Institute of Economics, University of Aarhus, [1986] 35 p. : ill. ; 21 cm. (Memo . 1986-4) Bibliography: p. 34-35. LC Card 86-221448 DDC 331.13/7 19
1. Unemployment - Econometric models. 2. Production functions (Economic theory). 3. Economic development - Econometric models. I. Series: Memo (Aarhus universitet. Økonomisk institut) , 1986-4. II. Title.
HD5707.5 .P34 1986

Palder, Edward L. The catalog of catalogs : where to get information about almost anything for almost nothing / by Edward L. Palder. Kensington, Md. : Woodbine House, 1987. xxxiv, 423 p. ; 21 cm. Includes index. ISBN 0-933149-11-5 (pbk.) : LC Card 86-51220 DDC 381/.14/029473 19
1. Catalogs, Commercial - Directories. 2. Mail-order business - United States - Directories. I. Title.
HF5466 .P35 1987

Palestine Mandate issues, 1921-1948 . Collins, Norman J. [New York] , c1987. 52 p. : LC Card 87-400470 DDC 383/.495694 19
HE7186 .C65 1987

PALESTINE PROBLEM, 1917- see JEWISH-ARAB RELATIONS.

Palestine Zionist Executive. Dept. of Agricultural Colonisation. Bericht der Exekutive der Zionistischen Organisation an den XV. Zionisten-Kongress. Jerusalem , 1927 (Jerusalem : Azriel) 110 p., [1] folded leaf of plates : LC Card 86-122608
HD1516.P18 B525 1927

PALESTINE ZIONIST EXECUTIVE. DEPT. OF AGRICULTURAL COLONISATION.
Bericht der Exekutive der Zionistischen Organisation an den XV. Zionisten-Kongress. Jerusalem , 1927 (Jerusalem : Azriel) 110 p., [1] folded leaf of plates : LC Card 86-122608
HD1516.P18 B525 1927

PALESTINIAN ARABS - EMPLOYMENT - ISRAEL.
Semyonov, Moshe. Hewers of wood and drawers of water . Ithaca, NY , c1987. xii, 152 p. : ISBN 0-87546-133-6 (pbk. : alk. paper) LC Card 87-2682 DDC 331.6/99275695 19
HD8660 .S45 1987

PALESTINIAN ARABS - GAZA STRIP.
Semyonov, Moshe. Hewers of wood and drawers of water . Ithaca, NY , c1987. xii, 152 p. : ISBN 0-87546-133-6 (pbk. : alk. paper) LC Card 87-2682 DDC 331.6/99275695 19
HD8660 .S45 1987

PALESTINIAN ARABS - GOVERNEMNT POLICY - UNITED STATES.
Laufer, Leopold Yehuda. U. S. aid to the West Bank and Gaza . [Jerusalem] [1985] 54 p. ; LC Card 87-400340 DDC 338.91/73/056951 19
HC415.25.Z7 W4735 1985

PALESTINIAN ARABS - GOVERNMENT POLICY - ISRAEL.
Laufer, Leopold Yehuda. U. S. aid to the West Bank and Gaza . [Jerusalem] [1985] 54 p. ; LC Card 87-400340 DDC 338.91/73/056951 19
HC415.25.Z7 W4735 1985

PALESTINIAN ARABS - WEST BANK.
Semyonov, Moshe. Hewers of wood and drawers of water . Ithaca, NY , c1987. xii, 152 p. : ISBN 0-87546-133-6 (pbk. : alk. paper) LC Card 87-2682 DDC 331.6/99275695 19
HD8660 .S45 1987

PALESTINIANS. see PALESTINIAN ARABS.

PALEY, WILLIAM S. (WILLIAM SAMUEL), 1901-
Paper, Lewis J. Empire . New York , 1987. x, 384 p., [16] p. of plates : ISBN 0-312-00591-1 : LC Card 87-4368 DDC 384.54/092/4 B 19
HE8689.8.P34 P36 1987

Pálfi, Sándor. Nemzetközi biztosítás a külkereskedelem szolgálatában / [készitette, Pálfi Sándor ; szerkesztette, Ferenczi András]. [Budapest] : DATORG Külkereskedelmi Adatfeldolgozó és Szervező Rt., [1986] 63 p. ; 29 cm. "Lezárva: 1986. április 15"--T.p. verso. "Megjelenik: a DATORG Tanácsadó Iroda Tanácsadó Szolgálata keretében"--T.p. verso. ISBN 963-02-4369-5 LC Card 87-425585
1. Insurance, Business. 2. Insurance, Export credit. 3. International trade. I. DATORG Tanácsadó Iroda. Tanácsadó Szolgálat. II. Title.
HG8059 .P35 1986

Palgrave, Robert Harry Inglis, Sir, 1827-1919. Dictionary of political economy. The New Palgrave : a dictionary of economics / edited by John Eatwell, Murray Milgate, Peter Newman. New York , c1987. p. cm. ISBN 0-935859-10-1 (set) : LC Card 87-1946 DDC 330/.03/21 19
HB61 .N49 1987

Palicz, András. Az önálló vállalattá szervezés elméleti és módszertani megalapozása / Palicz András. Budapest : System Szervezési Vállalat, 1984. 81 p. : ill. ; 29 cm. (Szervezési módszerek, 0139-262X . 45. köt.) Bibliography: p. 79. ISBN 963-02-3351-7 : LC Card 86-126838
1. Industrial management - Hungary. 2. Business enterprises - Hungary. I. Title. II. Series.
HD70.H8 P35 1984

Paliĭ, V. F. (Vitaliĭ Fedorovich) Khoziaĭstvennyĭ mekhanizm proizvodstvennogo ob"edineniia /. Moskva , 1985. 254 p. ; LC Card 85-238796
HD9703.S652 K46 1985

Palikhe, Komal Prasad. Cottage industries in Nepal / by Komal Prasad Palikhe. 1st ed. Kathmandu, Nepal : Bhagirathi Palikhe, 1986. 93 p. ; 22 cm. Bibliography: p. 90-91. LC Card 86-903473 DDC 338.6/34/095493 19
1. Cottage industries - Nepal. I. Title.
HD2346.N36 P35 1986

Paliwoda, Stanley J. Research in international marketing /. London , Dover, N.H. , c1986. 376 p. : ISBN 0-7099-4313-X : LC Card 85-29052 DDC 382/.6 19
HF1009.5 .R46 1986 *NYPL [JLD 86-2264]*

Palkin, IUriĭ Ivanovich.
Ėkonomicheskie zakony i ėkonomicheskaia politika KPSS / IU.I. Palkin, P.S. Eshchenko. Kiev : Gol. izd-vo izdatel'skogo ob"edineniia "Vyshcha shkola", 1985. 245 p. ; 21 cm. Includes bibliographical references. LC Card 87-104961
1. Soviet Union - Economic policy - 1981-. 2. Marxian economics. I. Eshchenko, P. S. (Petr Stepanovich). II. Title.
HC336.25 .P35 1985

Nechaev, IU. V. (IUriĭ Vasil'evich) Populiarnaia politėkonomiia /. Kiev , 1986. 246 p. : LC Card 87-169729
HC336.25 .N43 1986

Pallais, Don. Guide to forecasts and projections / authors, Don Pallais, Stephen D. Holton ; contributing author, Marilyn Rutledge. 1st ed. Fort Worth, Tex. : Practitioners Pub. Co., 1986. 2 v. (loose-leaf) : ill. ; 30 cm. Includes bibliographical references. CONTENTS. - v. 1. Text -- v. 2. Authoritative literature. LC Card 87-108778 DDC 657/.3 19
1. Financial statements - Standards - United States. I. Holton, Stephen D. II. Rutledge, Marilyn. III. Title.
HF5681.B2 P15 1986

Pallaschke, Diethard. IIASA (International Institute for Applied Systems Analysis) Workshop on Nondifferentiable Optimization (1984 : Sopron, Hungary) Nondifferentiable optimization . Berlin , New York , 1985. vi, 349 p. : ISBN 0-387-15979-7 (U. S.) LC Card 85-25029 DDC 658.4/03/4 19
T57.6 .I46 1984
NYPL [JLM 72-289 no.255]

PALLETIZED CARGO SYSTEMS. see UNITIZED CARGO SYSTEMS.

Pallotta, Luigi, 1951- Tecnici, ricercatori, quadri e sindacato /. Roma , 1985. 126 p. : LC Card 86-169979
HD8038.I8 T43 1985

Palm oil and protest . Martin, Susan M. Cambridge , New York , 1988. xi, 209 p. : ISBN 0-521-34376-3 LC Card 87-17373 DDC 338.4/76643 19
HD9490.5.P343 N66 1988

PALM-OIL INDUSTRY - NIGERIA - HISTORY - 20TH CENTURY.

Martin, Susan M. Palm oil and protest . Cambridge , New York , 1988. xi, 209 p. : ISBN 0-521-34376-3 LC Card 87-17373 DDC 338.4/76643 19
HD9490.5.P343 N66 1988

Palmer, Ingrid.
The impact of agrarian reform on women / Ingrid Palmer ; prepared under the auspices of the Population Council. West Hartford, Conn. : Kumarian Press, c1985. xiv, 55 p. ; 28 cm. (Women's roles & gender differences in development . 6) Kumarian Press case studies series Bibliography: p. 52-55. ISBN 0-931816-21-1 (pbk.) LC Card 85-5250 DDC 331.4/83/091724 19
1. Women in agriculture - Developing countries. 2. Land reform - Developing countries. 3. Rural women - Developing countries. I. Population Council, New York. II. Title. III. Series.
HD6073.A292 D447 1985 ***NYPL [JLF 86-1633]***

The impact of male out-migration on women in farming / Ingrid Palmer ; prepared under the auspices of the Population Council. West Hartford, Conn. : Kumarian Press, c1985. xviii, 78 p. ; 28 cm. (Women's roles & gender differences in development . 7) Kumarian Press case studies series Bibliography: p. 76-78. ISBN 0-931816-22-X (pbk.) LC Card 85-5240 DDC 331.4/83/091724 19
1. Women in agriculture - Developing countries. 2. Migrant labor - Developing countries. 3. Rural women - Developing countries. I. Population Council, New York. II. Title. III. Series.
HD6073.A292 D4472 1985 ***NYPL [JLF 86-1626]***

Palmer, Michele. Catalogue of interviews : Connecticut workers and a half century of technological change, 1930-1980, oral history project / compiled and edited by Michele Palmer with the assistance of Janet Nolan and Brian O'Connor. [Storrs, Conn.] : Center for Oral History at the University of Connecticut, 1983. ii, 79 p. ; 23 cm. Includes index. LC Card 86-621476 DDC 331.12/09746 19
1. Labor supply - Connecticut - Effect of technological innovations on - History - 20th century - Sources. 2. Labor and laboring classes - Connecticut - Interviews. I. Nolan, Janet. II. O'Connor, Brian. III. University of Connecticut. Center for Oral History. IV. Title. V. Title: Connecticut workers and a half century of technological change, 1930-1980, oral history project.
HD6331.2.U52 C86 1983

Palmer, Russell E. Handbook of accounting and auditing /. Boston , c1981. 1 v. (various pagings) ; ISBN 0-88712-221-3 (Update 1985) LC Card 80-53166 DDC 657/.02/02 19
HF5635.H22 ***NYPL [*R-Econ. 85-31]***

PALOUSE RIVER VALLEY (IDAHO AND WASH.) - HISTORY, LOCAL.
Prevost, Nancy M., 1953- Paradise in the Palouse . Fairfield, Wash. , c1985. 35 p. : ISBN 0-87770-365-5 (pbk.) LC Card 85-17842 DDC 338.1/09797/39 19
HD1775.W2 P74 1985 ***NYPL [JFF 86-559]***

PALOUSE RIVER VALLEY (IDAHO AND WASH.) - SOCIAL LIFE AND CUSTOMS.
Prevost, Nancy M., 1953- Paradise in the Palouse . Fairfield, Wash. , c1985. 35 p. : ISBN 0-87770-365-5 (pbk.) LC Card 85-17842 DDC 338.1/09797/39 19
HD1775.W2 P74 1985 ***NYPL [JFF 86-559]***

A pályafejlődés vizsgálatának módszertani lehetőségei a felsőoktatásban /. Szilágyi, Klára J. Budapest , 1985. 110 p. ; ISBN 963-404-020-9 LC Card 86-174899
HF5429.6.H8 S95 1985

Pamiati Abrama IUr'evicha Dobrago. Pamiati Abrama IUr'evicha Dobrogo. Parizh , 1939. 101 p., [1] leaf of plates : LC Card 83-136332
HG185.S65 P36 1939

Pamiati Abrama IUr'evicha Dobrogo. Pamiati Abrama IUr'evicha Dobrago. Parizh : Sobrano i izdano kruzhkom druzeĭ Abrama IUr'evicha Dobrago, 1939. 101 p., [1] leaf of plates : port. ; 20 cm. Russian and French. LC Card 83-136332
1. Dobryĭ, Abram IUr'evich, 1867-1936. 2. Capitalists and financiers - Ukraine - Biography. 3. Sugar trade - Ukraine - Biography. I. Title.
HG185.S65 P36 1939

Pammesberger, Hans-Peter.
Ausländerbeschäftigung als dauerhafter Angebotsfaktor auf dem Arbeitsmarkt der Bundesrepublik Deutschland / Hans-Peter Pammesberger. Hamburg : Kovač, c1986. xii, 297 p. : ill. ; 21 cm. Bibliography: p. 286-297. ISBN 3-925630-06-6 LC Card 86-227741
1. Alien labor - Germany, West. I. Title.
HD8458.A2 P35 1986

Pamphlet (New Zealand Institute of International Affairs) .
(no. 48) New Zealand's overseas development assistance . Wellington [1985] 79 p. ; LC Card 86-210636 DDC 338.91/931/01724 19
HC60 .N478 1985

Pamphlet series (International Monetary Fund) .
(no. 43) International Monetary Fund. Technical assistance and training services of the International Monetary Fund. Washington, D.C. , 1985. iii, 31 p. : LC Card 86-202820 DDC 332.1/52 19
HG3881.5.I58 I568 1985

PAMPHLETS.
Bly, Robert W. Create the perfect sales piece . New York , c1985. xii, 242 p. : ISBN 0-471-82525-5 (pbk.) : LC Card 85-12457 DDC 659.13/2 19
HF5823 .B635 1985 ***NYPL [JLE 86-3454]***

Pamuk, Şevket. The Ottoman empire and European capitalism, 1820-1913 : trade, investment, and production / Şevket Pamuk. Cambridge [Cambridgeshire] ; New York : Cambridge University Press, 1987. xii, 278 p. : ill. ; 24 cm. (Cambridge Middle East library) Bibliography: p. 259-273. Includes index. ISBN 0-521-33194-3 LC Card 86-28386 DDC 330.956/01 19
1. Turkey - Foreign economic relations. 2. Turkey - Commerce - History - 19th century. 3. Investments, European - Turkey - History - 19th century. 4. Turkey - Industries - History - 19th century. 5. Capitalism - Turkey - History - 19th century. I. Title. II. Series.
HF1583.4 .P36 1987

Pamukchiev, Minko Stoĭchev. Intelektualizatsiia na truda i proizvodstvoto / Minko Pamukchiev. Sofiia : Profizdat, 1982. 48 p. ; 20 cm. (Poreditsa "Ikonomicheski znaniia" . 1982, 1) Biblioteka na Druzhestvo "Georgi Kirkov" Includes bibliographical references. LC Card 82-183037
1. Psychology, Industrial. 2. Labor productivity - Bulgaria. I. Title. II. Series.
HF5548.8 .P255 1982

Pan Am . Davies, R. E. G. (Ronald Edward George) New York , c1987. vi, 90 p. : ISBN 0-517-56639-7 : LC Card 87-5581 DDC 387.7/065/73 19
HE9803.P36 D38 1987

Pan American Airways. see Pan American World Airways, inc.

PAN AMERICAN AIRWAYS CORPORATION, INC. - HISTORY.
Mahoney, Lawrence. The early birds . Miami, FL , 1987. xii, 112 p. : ISBN 0-940495-07-4 (pbk.) LC Card 87-21974 DDC 387.7/065/73 19
HE9803.P36 M35 1987

Pan American Union. Inter-American Economic and Social Council. see Inter-American Economic and Social Council.

PAN AMERICAN WORLD AIRWAYS, INC. - HISTORY.
Davies, R. E. G. (Ronald Edward George) Pan Am . New York , c1987. vi, 90 p. : ISBN 0-517-56639-7 : LC Card 87-5581 DDC 387.7/065/73 19
HE9803.P36 D38 1987

PAN EUROPA MOVEMENT. see EUROPEAN FEDERATION.

Pan trade union studies.
Aldred, Chris. Women at work /. London , 1981. 173 p. : ISBN 0-330-26479-6 (pbk.) LC Card 86-673456
HD6135 .A79x 1981

Burns, Patrick. Democracy at work /. London , 1981. 164 p. : ISBN 0-330-26478-8 (pbk.) LC Card 86-673620
HD6664 .B845x 1981

Panagiōtopoulos, Vasilēs, 1932- Plēthysmos kai oikismoi tēs Peloponnēsou : 13os-18os aiōnas / Vasilēs Panagiōtopoulos. Athēna : Historiko Archeio, Emporikē Trapeza tēs Hellados, 1985. 414 p. : maps ; 24 cm. (Meletes neoellēnikēs historias . [1]) Originally presented as the author's thesis (doctoral--Panepistēmio Paris IV) under the title: "Le peuplement du Péloponnèse (XIIIe-XVIIIe siècles)" Bibliography: p. 375-384. Includes index. LC Card 86-207132
1. Peloponnesus (Greece) - Population - History. I. Title. II. Series.
HB3632.5.P45 P36 1985

Panama : structural change and growth prospects / Latin America and the Caribbean Regional Office. Washington, D.C., U. S.A. : World Bank, c1985. xxv, 307 p., [8] p., [1] leaf of plates : ill., 1 folded map (col.), form ; 27 cm. (A World Bank country study) "Report no. 5236-PAN." "February 28, 1985." ISBN 0-8213-0580-8 LC Card 85-12420 DDC 338.97287 19
1. Finance, Public - Panama. 2. Labor supply - Panama. 3. Agriculture and state - Panama. 4. Industry and state - Panama. 5. Panama - Economic policy. 6. Panama - Economic conditions - 1979-. I. International Bank for Reconstruction and Development. Latin America and the Caribbean Regional Office. II. Series.
HC147 .P43 1985 ***NYPL [JLF 86-1919]***

Panama.
International Labour Organisation. Fortalecimiento del sistema de formación profesional . Ginebra , 1982. 47 p. ; ISBN 92-2-303194-X LC Card 84-113933
HD5715.5.P3 I57 1982

PANAMA CANAL (PANAMA) - RATES AND TOLLS.
El Efecto que tendrían los aumentos de los peajes del Canal de Panamá sobre países seleccionados de América Latina y el Caribe . Washington, D.C. [1982] iii, 76 p. ; LC Card 85-176637
HE538.R3 E34 1982

Panama. Contraloría General de la República.
Informe sobre la administración fiscal correspondiente a 1971 / República de Panamá, Contraloría General de la República. [Panama, Panama] : La Contraloría, 1972. iii, 31 p. ; 27 cm. LC Card 83-183287
1. Finance, Public - Panama - Accounting - Statistics. I. Title.
HJ9923.P28 P35 1972

Panama. Dirección General de Desarrollo Urbano. Pacheco D., Rubén. Industria de la construcción . [Panamá] , 1974. 17, [1] leaves, [4] leaves of plates : LC Card 87-400643
HD9715.P223 P367 1974

PANAMA - ECONOMIC CONDITIONS.
Zúñiga, Mauro. El drama de Panamá . [Panama? , 1986] 44 p. ; LC Card 86-232667
HC147 .Z57 1986

PANAMA - ECONOMIC CONDITIONS - 1979-
Gómez Pérez, José Antonio, 1950- Desarrollo, crisis, deuda y política económica en Panamá . Panamá , 1985. vii, 168 p. : LC Card 86-122320 DDC 338.97287 19
HC147 .G66 1985 ***NYPL [JLD 86-2899]***

Panama . Washington, D.C., U. S.A. , c1985. xxv, 307 p., [8] p., [1] leaf of plates : ISBN 0-8213-0580-8 LC Card 85-12420 DDC 338.97287 19
HC147 .P43 1985 ***NYPL [JLF 86-1919]***

PANAMA - ECONOMIC POLICY.
Gómez Pérez, José Antonio, 1950- Desarrollo, crisis, deuda y política económica en Panamá . Panamá , 1985. vii, 168 p. : LC Card 86-122320 DDC 338.97287 19
HC147 .G66 1985 ***NYPL [JLD 86-2899]***

Mock Cedeño, Ariel. Las empresas públicas en Panamá . Panamá, Rep. de Panamá , 1986. vi, 89, [5] p. ; LC Card 87-400433 DDC 338.97287 19
HD4043 .M63 1986

Panama . Washington, D.C., U. S.A. , c1985. xxv, 307 p., [8] p., [1] leaf of plates : ISBN 0-8213-0580-8 LC Card 85-12420 DDC 338.97287 19
HC147 .P43 1985 ***NYPL [JLF 86-1919]***

PANAMA - ECONOMIC POLICY - CASE STUDIES.
Cartas, José María. Precondiciones para la implementación de la economía social de mercado en América Latina . Buenos Aires, República Argentina , c1985. 80 p. ; LC Card 87-101628
HC125 .C374 1985

PANAMA - INDUSTRIES.
Correa V., Virgilio (Correa Vásquez) Centelleo de la industria en Panamá /. [Panama?] 1986 ([Panama, Panama] : Tall. Gráf. del Centro de Impresión Educativa) 279 p., [6] p. of plates : LC Card 87-404562 DDC 338.097287 19
HC147 .C67 1986

Panama. Ministerio de Vivienda.
Redeterminación de usos del suelo en Ancón y redelimitación del sitio de defensa de Albrook / Ministerio de Vivienda. [Panama, Panama] : El Ministerio, [between 1981 and 1987] [15] leaves : map ; 28 cm. Caption title. LC Card 87-403861 DDC 333.73/17/097287 19
1. Land use - Panama - Albrook - Planning. I. Title.
HD385.A4 P36 1981

Panama (Republic) see **Panama.**

Panandikar, V. A. Pai. see **Pai Panandiker, V. A., 1935-**

PANCHAYAT - INDIA - KURNOOL (DISTRICT) - CASE STUDIES.
Wade, Robert. Village republics . Cambridge [Cambridgeshire] , New York , 1988. p. cm. ISBN 0-521-30146-7 LC Card 86-33389 DDC 334/.683/095484 19
HD1491.I392 K878 1988

Panchenko, A. I.
Perspektivnoe planirovanie razvitii͡a agrarno-promyshlennogo kompleksa /. Novosibirsk , 1979. 159 p. : LC Card 81-143730
HD9015.S652 P47 1979

Problemy formirovanii͡a i upravlenii͡a agrarno-promyshlennym kompleksom . Novosibirsk , 1979. 157 p. : LC Card 81-143766
HD9015.S652 P73 1979

Rukosuev, P. N. (Platon Nikolaevich) Ėkonomicheskai͡a ėffektivnost′ zhivotnovodstva v sisteme APK /. Moskva , 1985. 127 p. ; LC Card 86-133226
HD9425.S652 R86 1985

Panda, Jagannath, 1952- Sahu, Promod K. (Promod Kumar), 1942- Industrial economy of Orissa /. Delhi , New Delhi , 1986. viii, 152 p. ; ISBN 81-7018-401-0 : LC Card 86-903551 DDC 338.0954/13 19
HC437.O7 S24 1986

Pande, Sunanda. Trends in occupational mobility among migrants / by Sunanda Pande ; forward [sic] by C. Lakshmanna. 1st ed. Jaipur : Rawat Publications, 1986. xii, 232 p. ; 23 cm. Bibliography: p. [219]-227. Includes index. ISBN 81-7033-023-8 : LC Card 86-902816 DDC 331.5/44/0954 19
1. Migrant labor - India. 2. Labor mobility - India. I. Title.
HD5856.I4 P36 1986

Pāṇḍeya, Āśā. Hindī vijñāpanoṃ kī bhāshā / Āśā Pāṇḍeya. 1. saṃskaraṇa. Bambaī : Blekī eṇḍa Sana Pabliśarsa, 1986. xv, 105, [3] p. ; 22 cm. In Hindi. Study of Hindi used in advertising. Bibliography: p. [107]-108. LC Card 87-901590
1. Advertising copy. 2. Hindi language. I. Title.
HF5827 .P36 1986

Pandit, Jyoti. Shupe, Barbara, 1941- New York State population, 1790-1980 . New York , c1987. xxvii, 333 p. : ISBN 1-555-70009-8 : LC Card 86-28487 DDC 304.6/2/09747 19
HA545 .S58 1987

Pandora Press history.
Braybon, Gail. Out of the cage . London , New York , 1987. xiii, 330 p. : ISBN 0-86358-046-7 : LC Card 87-13510 DDC 305.4/0941 19
HD6135 .B7 1987

Panek, Hans-Thomas. Die Währungskrisen vom November 1968 bis Mai 1971 im politischen Prozess der Bundesrepublik Deutschland / Hans-Thomas Panek. Köln : Institut für Wirtschaftspolitik an der Universität zu Köln, 1977. 293 p. ; 24 cm. (Untersuchungen / Institut für Wirtschaftspolitik an der Universität zu Köln . 41) Bibliography: p. 280-293. ISBN 3-921471-29-X LC Card 86-184843
1. Monetary policy - Germany, West. 2. Germany, West - Economic conditions. 3. Germany, West - Politics and government. I. Series: Untersuchungen (Universität zu Köln. Institut für Wirtschaftspolitik) , 41. II. Title.
HG999.5 .P35 1977

A Panel Advisory Service report.
Bedford Properties, Lenexa, Kansas . Washington, D.C. (1090 Vermont Ave., N.W., Washington 20005) [1986?] 37 p. : LC Card 87-141440 DDC 333.3/8/09781675 19
HD268.L46 B43 1986

Urban Land Institute. R.S. Wallace Station, East Peoria, Illinois . Washington, D.C. (1090 Vermont Ave., N.W., Washington 20005) , c1986. 36 p. : LC Card 86-216045 DDC 333.77/17/0977352 19
HD268.E26 U73 1986

Panettieri, José. Argentina : historia de un país periférico, 1860-1914 / José Panettieri. [Buenos Aires] : Centro Editor de América Latina, c1986. 219 p. ; 21 cm. (Bibliotecas universitarias. Historia) Includes bibliographical references. ISBN 950-25-1317-7 LC Card 86-226796
1. Argentina - Economic policy. 2. Argentina - Politics and government - 1860-1910. 3. Argentina - Politics and government - 1910-1943. 4. Argentina - Social conditions. I. Title. II. Series.
HC175 .P334 1986

PANEUROPEAN FEDERATION. see **EUROPEAN FEDERATION.**

Panevina, M. N. (Mai͡a Nikolaevna) Kirtovskiĭ, I. Kh. Ocherki istorii marksistsko-leninskoĭ ėkonomicheskoĭ mysli Latvii, 1920-1980 /. Riga , 1985. 199 p. ; LC Card 86-176265
HB97.5 .K542 1985

Pang, Eng Fong. Education, manpower, and development in Singapore / Pang Eng Fong. Kent Ridge, Singapore : Singapore University Press, c1982. 242 p. : ill. ; 23 cm. Includes index. Bibliography: p. 237-240. ISBN 997-16-9053-5 (bound) LC Card 83-941002 DDC 331.11/09595/7 19
1. Labor supply - Singapore - Effect of education on - Addresses, essays, lectures. 2. Manpower policy - Singapore - Addresses, essays, lectures. I. Title.
HD5823.A6 P35 1982 NYPL [JLD 86-2364]

Panhā bāng prakān kīeokap mai læ kānpramœ̄n phon kānkhūapkhum kānsong mai læ mai prǣrūp ' Thailand. Krom Sǣtthakit Kānphānit. Rāingān phon kānsksā wičhai . [Krung Thēp Mahā Nakh 2521 [1978] 24, [7] folded p., [7] p. of plates : LC Card 81-183926
HD9766.T52 T47 1978

Pani, Narendar, 1954- Reforms to pre-empt change : land legislation in Karnataka / Narendar Pani. New Delhi : Concept Pub. Co., 1983. ix, 122 p. ; 22 cm. Includes index. Bibliography: p. [116]-119. LC Card 83-902691 DDC 333.3/1/5487 19
1. Land reform - India - Karnataka - History. 2. Land reform - Law and legislation - India - Karnataka - History. 3. Pre-emption - India - Karnataka - History. I. Title.
HD1333.I42 K376 1983
NYPL [JLD 86-3841]

Panić, M. National management of the international economy / M. Panić. New York : St. Martin's Press, 1988. p. cm. Bibliography: p. Includes index. ISBN 0-312-01294-2 : LC Card 87-18764 DDC 337 19
1. International economic relations. 2. International economic integration. 3. Energy policy. I. Title.
HF1411 .P2935 1988

The panic of 1857 and the coming of the Civil War /. Huston, James L., 1947- Baton Rouge , c1987. xviii, 315 p. ; ISBN 0-8071-1368-9 LC Card 87-2705 DDC 338.5/42 19
HB3717 1857 .H87 1987

PANICS. see **DEPRESSIONS.**

Panin, I͡U. I. Prognozirovanie i ėffektivnost′ raboty flota . Leningrad , 1985. 104 p. : LC Card 86-170274
HE847 .P77 1985

Panjab University. Dept. of Sociology.
Development, socio-cultural dimensions /. Jaipur , 1986. xxi, 264 p. ; ISBN 81-7033-020-3 : LC Card 86-902849 DDC 306/.0954 19
HC435.2 .D478 1986

Pankova, E. A. (Evgenii͡a Afanas′evna)
Vneshneėkonomicheskie svi͡azi razvivai͡ushchikhsi͡a stran : sovremennye problemy gosudarstvennogo regulirovanii͡a / E.A. Pankova, V.V. Serzhenko. Moskva : Izd-vo "Nauka," Glav. red. vostochnoĭ lit-ry, 1985. 158 p. ; 20 cm. At head of title: Akademii͡a nauk SSSR. Ordena Trudovogo Krasnogo Znameni Institut vostokovedenii͡a. Summary in English. Bibliography: p. 150-[157] LC Card 86-130427
1. Developing countries - Foreign economic relations. 2. Investments, Foreign - Developing countries. 3. Loans, Foreign - Developing countries. I. Serzhenko, V. V. (Viktor Vasil′evich). II. Title.
HF1413 .P36 1985

Pankow, Michael. Untersuchungen zur Verbesserung der betrieblichen Arbeitssituation unter Verwendung der Akzeptanz im Rahmen von Arbeitsanalyse und Arbeitsentwicklung / Michael Pankow. Hamburg : Kovač, c1986. 1 v. (various pagings) ; 21 cm. Includes bibliography. ISBN 3-925630-13-9 LC Card 87-146606 DDC 658.3/14 19
1. Job satisfaction. 2. Employee motivation. I. Title.
HF5549.5.J63 P345 1986

Panorama del Departamento ... / Banco de Crédito del Perú. [Lima?] : El Banco, 1984-<1987 > v. <1-8 > : ill. ; 28 cm. Cover title. CONTENTS. - [1] Del Cuzco -- [2] De Tacna -- [3] De La Libertad -- [4] Del Santa -- [5] De Loreto -- [6] Del Distrito Financiero Sur-Oriente -- [7] Del Distrito Financiero del Oriente -- [8] Del Distrito Financiero del Centro. LC Card 86-202585
1. Peru - Economic conditions - 1968-. 2. Finance - Peru - Departments. I. Banco de Crédito del Perú.
HC227 .P354 1984

Panov, Ogni͡an. Trendafilov, Toncho. Nauchno-tekhnicheskata revoli͡ut͡sii͡a--zakonomernost na uskorenoto razvitie na sot͡sialisticheskoto obshtestvo /. Sofii͡a , 1985. 93 p. : LC Card 86-163246
HC403.Z9 T477 1985

Panshev, L. V. Vologodskiĭ razbeg / L.V. Panshev. Arkhangel′sk : Severo-Zapadnoe knizhnoe izd-vo, 1983. 93 p. : ill. ; 15 cm. (Rukopozhatie druzeĭ--Arkhangel′sk-Vologda) LC Card 86-195235
1. Vologda (R.S.F.S.R.) - Economic conditions. I. Title. II. Series.
HC338.V58 P35 1983

Panteleev, Vladimir Dmitrievich. Kompleksnyĭ ėkonomicheskiĭ analiz v. ASUP / V.D. Panteleev. Leningrad : "Sudostroenie", 1981. 176 p. ; 22 cm. Bibliography: p. 171-[174] LC Card 87-462046
1. Industrial management - Data processing. I. Title. II. Title: Kompleksnyĭ ėkonomicheskiĭ analiz v. A.S.U.P.
HD30.2 .P365 1981

Pantelides, Edith A. El hogar como unidad de análisis de los datos censales : importancia y posibilidades / Edith Alejandra Pantelides. Santiago de Chile : Centro Latinoamericano de Demografía, 1972. ii, 48 p. : ill. ; 28 cm. (Serie C / CELADE . no. 147) Bibliography: p. 48. LC Card 83-169482
1. Household surveys. 2. Household surveys - Costa Rica - Grecia. 3. Costa Rica - Census, 1968. 4. Household surveys - Argentina - Belén (Catamarca). 5. Argentina - Census, 1969. I. Series: Serie C (CELADE (Organization)) , no. 147. II. Title.
HA755 .U53 no. 147 HB849.49

Pany, Raj Kishor. Institutional credit for agriculture in India / Raj Kishor Pany. New Delhi : Ashish Pub. House, 1985. xxi, 483 p. : ill., maps ; 23 cm. Originally presented as the author's thesis (Ph. D.--Utkal University, 1984) Bibliography: p. [461]-477. Includes index. ISBN 81-7024-009-3 : LC Card 85-904046 DDC 332.7/1/095413 19
1. Agricultural credit - India - Orissa. 2. Agriculture - India - Orissa - Finance. I. Title.
HD2075.O7 P36 1985

Papachristodoulou, Christos. Inventions, innovations, and economic growth in Sweden : an appraisal of the Schumpeterian theory / by Christos Papachristodoulou. Uppsala : Uppsala University, Dept. of Economics, c1986. iv, 187 p. : ill. ; 21 cm. Thesis (doctoral)--Uppsala University, 1986. Bibliography: p. 176-187. LC Card 87-672434
1. Technological innovations - Sweden. 2. Sweden - Economic conditions - 1945-. 3. Schumpeter, Joseph Alois, 1883-1950. 4. Inventions - Sweden. I. Title.
HC380.T4 P36x 1986

Papageorgiou, Demetris. Economic liberalization in developing countries /. Oxford [Oxfordshire] , New York , 1986. vi, 278 p. : ISBN 0-631-15023-4 : LC Card 86-6153 DDC 338.9/009172/4 19
HC59.7 .E3116 1986 NYPL [JLE 86-4644]

Papageōrgiou, Giōrgos. Hoi syntechnies sta Giannena kata ton 19o kai tis arches tou 20ou aiōna (arches 19ou ai. hōs 1912) / Giōrgou Papageōrgiou. Iōannina : Panepistēmio Iōanninōn ; Athēna : Ekdosē kai diathesē : 454 p. ; 25 cm. (Seira epistēmonikōn diatrivōn tēs philosophikēs scholēs . 4) Originally presented as the author's thesis (doctoral--Panepistēmion Iōanninōn, Philosophikē Scholē, 1982) Bibliography: p. [399]-417. Includes index. LC Card 84-137611
1. Guilds - Greece - Iōannina - History - 19th century. 2. Guilds - Greece - Iōannina - History - 20th century. I. Title. II. Series.
HD2346.G752 I566 1982

Papalekas, J. Chr. (Johannes Chr.) Strukturwandel des Ausländerproblems . Bochum , c1986. 309 p. : ISBN 3-88339-529-3 LC Card 87-121913 DDC 331.6/2/0943 19
HD8458.A2 S786 1986

Papandreou, Nicholas C. LaLonde, Robert John. The manpower report of KEPE . Athens, Greece , c1986. 122 p. ; LC Card 86-205504 DDC 331.1/09495 19
HD5811.83.A6 L3 1986

Papandropoulos, Athan. Hodēgos marketinnk Hellados, 1983 /. Athēnai [1983?] 357 p. ; LC Card 84-107807
HF5415.12.G8 H63 1983

Papanek, Gábor. Botos, Balázs. Kérdőjelek iparunk fejlesztésében /. Budapest , 1984. 391, [1] p. ; ISBN 963-221-392-0 : LC Card 85-156613
HC300.28 .B69 1984

Papanek, Gustav Fritz. The Indian economy . Boulder, Colo. , 1988. ix, 374 p. : ISBN 0-8133-7505-3 (pbk. : alk. paper) LC Card 87-22472 DDC 330.954/05 19
HC435.2 .I555 1988

Paparoni, Luigi. Immagini di industria in Italia . Roma , c1985. [128] p. : LC Card 86-145396
HC305 .I46 1985

Papastamkos, G. (Geōrgios) Arampatzēs, E. Hē mesogeiakē politikē tēs EOK . Thessalonikē , 1983. 268 p. ; LC Card 84-185339
HC241.25.M4 A73 1983

Papathanasē-Mousiopoulou, Kalliopē. Syntechnies & epangelmata stē Thrakē, . 1685-1920 / K. Papathanasē Mousiopoulou. Athēna : Pitsilos, 1985. 247 p. : ill. ; 22 cm. Bibliography: p. 11-16. Includes index. LC Card 86-208086
1. Trade-unions - Thrace - History. 2. Thrace - Occupations - History. I. Title. II. Title: Syntechnies kai epangelmata stē Thrakē, 1685-1920.
HD6795.5.Z8 T56 1985

Papathanasopoulos, Kōnstantinos, 1950- Hellēnikē emporikē nautalia, 1833-1856 : exelixē kai anaprosarmogē / Kōnstantinou Papathanasopoulou. Athēna : Morphōtiko Hidryma Ethnikēs Trapezēs, 1983. 470 p., [32] p. of plates : ill. ; 23 cm. (Meletes oikonomikēs historias . 7) Bibliography: p. 431-442. Includes indexes. LC Card 83-237694
1. Merchant marine - Greece - History - 19th century. I. Title. II. Series.
HE872.5 .P36 1983

O papel do sector leiteiro no desenvolvimento económico dos Açores . Casaca, José Paulo Martins. Ponta Delgada , 1985. 260, [16] p., [1] leaf of plates : LC Card 86-167454
HD9282.A962 C37 1985

O Papel-moeda em Portugal. [Lisbon] : Banco de Portugal, [1985?] 502 p. : ill. (some col.) ; 33 cm. LC Card 86-226586
1. Paper money - Portugal - History. 2. Bank notes - Portugal - History. I. Banco de Portugal.
HG1147 .P36 1985

Papeles de trabajo IESA .
(PTI 84-6) Naím, Moisés. Posibilidades y limitaciones del funcionamiento de los mercados en los países menos desarrollados . Caracas , c1985. 88 p. : ISBN 980-217-006-2 LC Card 86-193990
HB501 .N255 1985

(PTI-83-2) Mejías, Tulio. La coordinación como consecuencia de razones y pasiones . Caracas, Venezuela , c1983. 37, [2] p. : ISBN 980-217-002-X LC Card 86-193647
HD37.S66 M37 1983

(PTI-83-3) Kelly de Escobar, Janet. Del actor racional al cesto de basura . Caracas, Venezuela , c1983. 31 p., 3 leaves : ISBN 980-217-003-8 LC Card 86-201788
HD30.23 .K363 1983

(PTI-84-5) Gómez-Samper, Henry. Los módulos de servicios . Caracas , c1984. 48, 3 [i.e. 4] leaves ; ISBN 980-217-005-4 LC Card 86-193565
HD4343 .G65 1984

(PTI-85-9) Kelly de Escobar, Janet. Opciones para la evaluación de las empresas públicas /. Caracas , c1985. 36 p. ; ISBN 980-217-008-9 LC Card 86-201812
HD62.35 .K45 1985

Papeles de trabajo para la gerencia.
Castillo, Julián. La amortización de deudas en Colombia . Bogotá, Colombia , 1985. 162 leaves ; LC Card 86-204058 DDC 332.7/09861 19
HG4028.A5 C37 1985

Paper (Canadian Centre for Folk Culture Studies) .
(no. 55) Lemieux-Pépin, Madeleine. P'tit train va loin . Ottawa , 1985. vii, 191 p. ; LC Card 86-177382
HE2808.1 .L45 1985

Paper (Economic and Social Research Institute) .
(no. 131) Rottman, David B. The population structure and living circumstances of Irish travellers . Dublin , 1986. 134 p. : ISBN 0-7070-0084-X (pbk.) : LC Card 86-215759 DDC 330.9417 s 305.5/68 19
HC257.I6 E3 no. 131 DX217

PAPER GOLD. see **SPECIAL DRAWING RIGHTS.**

PAPER - HISTORY.
Entwurff und Beschreibung von der Papiermacherey, worinnen der Ursprung des Papiermachens, der Fortgang, wie heutiges Tages das Papier gemachet wird, wie solches viele Mühe und Arbeit hat, benebst denen bey den Papiermachern befindlichen Wörtern, denen Kayserlichen Verordnungen und andern dahin einschlagenden Dingen /. [Mainz , 1962] (Darmstadt : E. Roether) 1 v. (various pagings) : LC Card 87-107659
HD9820.5 .E57 1962

PAPER INDUSTRY.
Grefermann, Klaus. Papier- und Pappeverarbeitung . Berlin , c1986. 209 p. : ISBN 3-428-06050-4 LC Card 86-233133
HD9833.5 .G73 1986

PAPER INDUSTRY - BRAZIL.
Mercado brasileiro de celulose e papel /. Brasília, D.F. , 1982. vii, 224 leaves : LC Card 84-210712
HD9660.C43 B75 1982

PAPER INDUSTRY - CANADA - ENERGY CONSERVATION.
Battle, Ellen F. Energy efficiency in Canada's pulp & paper industry /. Calgary, Alta. [1986] xviii, 131, 4 p. : ISBN 0-920522-38-6 (pbk.) : LC Card 87-124507 DDC 333.79 19
HD9834.C22 B37 1986

PAPER INDUSTRY - GERMANY (WEST)
Grefermann, Klaus. Papier- und Pappeverarbeitung . Berlin , c1986. 209 p. : ISBN 3-428-06050-4 LC Card 86-233133
HD9833.5 .G73 1986

PAPER INDUSTRY - HISTORY.
Entwurff und Beschreibung von der Papiermacherey, worinnen der Ursprung des Papiermachens, der Fortgang, wie heutiges Tages das Papier gemachet wird, wie solches viele Mühe und Arbeit hat, benebst denen bey den Papiermachern befindlichen Wörtern, denen Kayserlichen Verordnungen und andern dahin einschlagenden Dingen /. [Mainz , 1962] (Darmstadt : E. Roether) 1 v. (various pagings) : LC Card 87-107659
HD9820.5 .E57 1962

PAPER INDUSTRY - UNITED STATES - FORECASTING.
Special analysis and outlook for E.I. Du Pont De Nemours & Company (Inc.), Chemicals and Pigments Department. Boston, Mass. (7 Liberty Sq., Boston 02109) [1986] 17, [6] p. : LC Card 86-205857 DDC 338.4/766/00973 19
HD9660.P253 U672 1986

PAPER INDUSTRY WORKERS - QUÉBEC (PROVINCE) - HISTORY.
Vanasse, Gilbert, 1948- Histoire de la Fédération des travailleurs du papier et de la forêt /. Montréal, Québec , 1986- v. <1 > : ISBN 2-89035-122-X (t. 1) LC Card 86-231295
HD6528.P332 F438 1986

Paper (Krannert Graduate School of Management. Institute for Research in the Bahavioral, Economic, and Management Sciences) .
(no. 877) Balakrishnan, Anantaram. A composite algorithm for the concave-cost LTL consolidation problem /. West Lafayette, Ind. [1985] 43, 14 p. : LC Card 86-139493
HD6483 .P8 no. 877 T57.85

Paper (Krannert Graduate School of Management. Institute for Research in the Behavioral, Economic, and Management Sciences) .
(no. 859) Carlson, John A., 1933- Stocks, shocks, and price-output dynamics /. West Lafayette, Ind. [1984] 30, 13 p. ; LC Card 84-623131 DDC 658/.001/9 s 332.63/222/0973 19
HD6483 .P8 no. 859 HF5416.5

(no. 893) Smith, Clayton G. Established companies diversifying into young industries . West Lafayette, Ind. [1986] 27, 15 p. ; LC Card 86-621740 DDC 658/.001/9 s 338.8/3 19
HD6483 .P8 no. 893 HD2755.8

(no. 898) Tsai, Hsien-Tang. A 3-interval polynomial approximation for continuous univariate distribution functions /. West Lafayette, Ind. [1986] 7, 14 p. : LC Card 86-622753 DDC 658/.001/9 s 519/.2 19
HD6483 .P8 no. 898 QA273.6

(no. 900) Hu, Sheng C. A game-theoretic approach to the design of an optimal sales policy /. West Lafayette, Ind. [1986] 30, 14 p. : LC Card 86-622755 DDC 658/.001/9 s 658.8/101 19
HD6483 .P8 no. 900 HF5438.25

Paper, Lewis J. Empire : William S. Paley and the making of CBS / Lewis J. Paper.1st ed. New York : St. Martin's Press, 1987. x, 384 p., [16] p. of plates : ill. ; 24 cm. Bibliography: p. 373-374. Includes index. ISBN 0-312-00591-1 : LC Card 87-4368 DDC 384.54/092/4 B 19
1. Paley, William S. (William Samuel), 1901-. 2. Broadcasters - United States - Biography. 3. CBS Inc. - Biography. 4. Broadcasting - United States - History. I. Title.
HE8689.8.P34 P36 1987

Paper (Mekhon Horovits le-ḥeḳer aratsot mitpatḥot) .
(no. 84/3) Eckstein, Zvi. Cotton and wheat production in the Egyptian agriculture . [Tel Aviv] [1984] 40 leaves : LC Card 84-186315 DDC 338.1/711/0962 19
HD9087.E42 E35 1984

(no. 85/2) Lucas, Robert E. B. Motivations to remit . [Tel Aviv] [1985] 27 leaves ; LC Card 86-177234
HG3984.9 .L83 1985

PAPER MONEY - ARGENTINA - HISTORY.
Historia del papel moneda argentino /. Buenos Aires, Argentina , c1984. 47, [1] p. : LC Card 86-180304
HG817 .H57 1984

PAPER MONEY - BRAZIL - HISTORY.
Cédulas brasileiras da República . Rio de Janeiro , 1965. 111 p. : LC Card 85-119119
HG837 .C43 1965

PAPER MONEY - CATALOGS.
Pick, Albert. Standard catalog of world paper money /. Iola, Wis. , München , c1986. 2 v. : ISBN 0-87341-087-4 (v. 1) LC Card 86-222186 DDC 769.5/5/075 19
HG353 .P543 1986

PAPER MONEY - FRANCE - HISTORY - 18TH CENTURY.
Muszynski, Maurice. Les assignats de la Révolution française /. Bruyères-le-Châtel , c1981. 163 p. : LC Card 87-672912
HG978 .M87x 1981

PAPER MONEY - GERMANY (WEST)
Runge, Harry. Haushaltsfinanzierung durch Notendruck /. Berlin , c1986. 69 p. ; ISBN 3-428-05984-0 LC Card 86-165742
HG1004 .R75 1986

PAPER MONEY - PORTUGAL - HISTORY.
O Papel-moeda em Portugal. [Lisbon] [1985?]

502 p. : LC Card 86-226586
HG1147 .P36 1985

PAPER MONEY - UNITED STATES - CATALOGS.
Krause, Chester L. Standard catalog of U. S. paper money /. Iola, WI , c1985. 192 p. : ISBN 0-87341-078-5 (pbk.) LC Card 86-223149 DDC 769.5/5973/0750973 19
HG591 .K7 1985

Paper (New South Wales. Traffic Accident Research Unit) .
(77/3) Fairfield on-scene study of collisions . [Sydney?] [1977] 120 p. : LC Card 85-170609
HE5614.5.A8 F37 1977

Paper (Pastoral Development Network (Overseas Development Institute)) .
(20f) Behnke, Roy H., 1947- Open-range management and property rights in pastoral Africa . London [1985] 29 p. : LC Card 86-209817 DDC 333.2 19
HD977.Z63 B44 1985

The paper trail . Frascona, Oliver E., 1947- Boulder, Colo. , c1987. ix, 185 p. ; ISBN 0-941937-00-3 (pbk.) LC Card 87-8904 DDC 333.33/068 19
HD1386.5 .F7 1987

PAPERMAKING - HISTORY.
Entwurff und Beschreibung von der Papiermacherey, worinnen der Ursprung des Papiermachens, der Fortgang, wie heutiges Tages das Papier gemachet wird, wie solches viele Mühe und Arbeit hat, benebst denen bey den Papiermachern befindlichen Wörtern, denen Kayserlichen Verordnungen und andern dahin einschlagenden Dingen /. [Mainz , 1962] (Darmstadt : E. Roether) 1 v. (various pagings) : LC Card 87-107659
HD9820.5 .E57 1962

Papers from the International Institute for Environment and Society of the Science Center Berlin.
Leipert, Christian. Folgekosten des Wachstums als Wachstumsstimulans . Berlin [1985?] 35 p. : LC Card 86-116361
HD75.6 .L45 1985

Papers of the East-West Population Institute .
(no. 106) Mason, Andrew, 1947- HOMES . Honolulu, Hawaii [1987] x, 114 p. : ISBN 0-86638-102-3 (pbk.) : LC Card 87-22288 DDC 304.6/028/55329 19
HB849.49 .M38 1987

(103) Luther, Norman Y., 1936- Consistent correction of census and vital registration data for Thailand, 1960-80 /. Honolulu, Hawaii [1986] vii, 39 p. ; ISBN 0-86638-089-2 (pbk.) : LC Card 86-32807 DDC 304.6/0723 19
HA39.T4 L87 1986

Papers of the East-West Population Institute, 0732-0531 .
(no. 104) Coale, Ansley J. Basic data on fertility in the provinces of China, 1940-82 /. Honolulu, HI [1987] xvii, 366 p. : ISBN 0-86638-088-4 (pbk.) : LC Card 86-32765 DDC 304.6/32/0951 19
HB1064.A3 C63 1987

(no. 105) Recent trends in fertility and mortality in Indonesia /. Honolulu, Hawaii , 1987. xvi, 96 p. : ISBN 0-86638-092-2 (pbk.) : LC Card 87-11178 DDC 304.6/32/09598 19
HB1057 .R43 1987

(no. 106 (Aug. 1987)) Mason, Andrew, 1947- HOMES . Honolulu, Hawaii [1987] x, 114 p. : ISBN 0-86638-102-3 (pbk.) : LC Card 87-22288 DDC 304.6/028/55329 19
HB849.49 .M38 1987

(no. 107) Hogan, Dennis P. Cultural and economic factors in the fertility of Thai women /. Honolulu, HI [1987] p. cm. ISBN 0-86638-103-1 : LC Card 87-21459 DDC 304.6/32/09593 19
HB1054.55.A3 H64 1987

Papers on monetary economics / edited by the Economics Dept., Monetary Authority of Singapore. [Singapore] : Published by Singapore University Press for the Monetary Authority of Singapore, c1981. xii, 200 p. ; 23 cm. Spine title: MAS papers on monetary economics. Bibliography: p. 197-200. CONTENTS. - The evolution of money in Singapore since 1819 / P.J. Drake -- The development of asset ratios as a monetary policy instrument / C.A.E. Goodhart -- The dynamics of money demand and monetary policy in Singapore / Mohsin S. Khan -- Monetary policy and lagged responses / Wong Kum Poh -- Exchange rate flexibility and monetary policy / Basant K. Kapur -- Monetary stability and exchange rate objectives in Singapore / William H. Branson -- Monetary versus fiscal policy / Lee Soo Ann -- Offshore markets in foreign currencies and monetary control / Ronald I. McKinnon -- Monetary policy and the Asian Dollar Market / John R. Hewson. ISBN 997-16-9044-6 LC Card 82-940575
1. Monetary policy - Singapore. 2. Monetary policy. I. Monetary Authority of Singapore. Economics Dept. II. Monetary Authority of Singapore. III. Title: MAS papers on monetary economics.
HG1250.67 .P37 1981

Papers on planning and design .
(no. 30) Cubukgil, Adil. Urbanization in developing countries . [Toronto] , 1981. ii, 77 p. ; ***NYPL [JLF 87-277]***

Papier- und Pappeverarbeitung . Grefermann, Klaus. Berlin , c1986. 209 p. : ISBN 3-428-06050-4 LC Card 86-233133
HD9833.5 .G73 1986

Papp, Daniel S., 1947- The Political economy of international technology transfer /. Westport, Conn. , c1986. viii, 267 p. : ISBN 0-89930-128-2 (lib. bdg. : alk. paper) LC Card 85-28128 DDC 338.9/26 19
HD45 .P574 1986 ***NYPL [JLE 86-3313]***

Papp, Sándor. A mezőgazdasági ipar, ellenfél vagy partner? / Papp Sándor. [Budapest] : Kossuth, 1985. 154 p. : ill. ; 20 cm. (Gazdaságpolitikai füzetek, 0230-3833) Includes bibliographical references. ISBN 963-09-2547-8 : LC Card 85-230966
1. Agricultural industries - Hungary. I. Title. II. Series.
HD9015.H82 P36 1985

Papp, Zsolt, Dr. Harza, Lajos. Az EGK szőlő- és borgazdaságának szabályozórendszere /. Budapest , 1985. 70 p. : ISBN 963-491-210-9 LC Card 86-196818
HD9259.G7 E864 1985

Pappa, Hellē. Hoi archaioi Hellēnes syngrapheis sto "Kephalaio" tou Marx / Hellēs Pappa. Athēna : Ekdoseis "Synchronē Epochē", 1983. 112 p. ; 21 cm. Includes bibliographical references. LC Card 84-128852
1. Marx, Karl, 1818-1883. Kapital. 2. Capital. 3. Economics. 4. Aristotle - Influence. 5. Plato - Influence. 6. Diodorus, Siculus - Influence. I. Title.
HB501 .P24 1983

Il Pappagallo giallo : la pelle nella moda, nelle arti minori, nell'industrial design, 1900-1940 / a cura di Vanni Bertini e Franco Foggi. [Pisa] : Cassa di risparmio ; Firenze : Alinea, c1986. 194 p., [1] leaf of plates : ill. (some col.) ; 23 cm. (Immagini di memoria . 1) At head of title: Comune di Santa Croce sull'Arno, Museo della zona del cuoio. Associazione conciatori. Bibliography: p. 131-136. LC Card 86-212573
1. Leather industry and trade - Italy - History. 2. Advertising - Italy - History. I. Bertini, Vanni. II. Foggi, Franco. III. Santa Croce sull'Arno (Italy). IV. Museo della zona del cuoio. V. Associazione conciatori.
HD9780.I82 P37 1986

PAPRIKA INDUSTRY - NETHERLANDS.
Goudswaard, A. De ontwikkeling van de paprikateelt . Den Haag [1986] 60 p. : LC Card 86-233094
HD9211.P353 N424 1986

PAPUA NEW GUINEA - ECONOMIC CONDITIONS.
Philp, Norman E. The cash incentive . Canberra , 1986. xii, 135 p. : ISBN 0-86784-984-3 (pbk.) LC Card 87-150813
HD2346.P37 P46 1986

Paqué, Karl-Heinz. Philanthropie und Steuerpolitik : eine ökonomische Analyse der Förderung privater Wohltätigkeit / Karl-Heinz Paqué. Tübingen : J.C.B. Mohr, c1986. xv, 417 p. : 7 ill. ; 24 cm. (Kieler Studien, 0340-6989 . 203) Bibliography: p. 397-417. ISBN 3-16-345154-3 (pbk. : Deut. Bibl.) : LC Card 87-408202 DDC 343.4305/232 344.3035232 19
1. Income tax - Germany (West) - Deductions - Charitable contributions. 2. Income tax - Law and legislation - Germany, West. I. Title. II. Series.
HJ4720.A45 P36 1986

Paquet, Charlotte.
Dumont, René, 1904- Pour l'Afrique, j'accuse . [Paris] , c1986. 457 p., [48] p. of plates : ISBN 2-259-01455-0 LC Card 86-220056
HC1002 .D85 1986

Dumont, René, 1904- Les raisons de la colère, ou, L'utopie et les Verts /. Paris , c1986. 137 p. ; ISBN 2-7266-0075-1 LC Card 86-158407
HC59.72.E5 D85 1986

Par cable. Pigeat, Henri, 1939- La télévision par cable commence demain /. Paris , c1983. 239 p. ; ISBN 2-259-01062-8 : LC Card 83-237808
HE8700.72.F8 P54 1983

Para entender Centroamérica .
(4) Aguilera Peralta, Gabriel Edgardo. Raíces y perspectivas de la crisis económica /. San José, Costa Rica , 1986. 297 p. ; ISBN 997-7990-33-6 LC Card 87-404300 DDC 330.9728/053 19
HC141 .A63 1986

PARADIGMS (SOCIAL SCIENCES)
Alvesson, Mats, 1956- Consensus, control, and critique . Aldershot, Hants, England , Brookfield, Vt., USA , c1987. viii, 162 p. : ISBN 0-566-05285-7 : LC Card 87-8427 DDC 306/.36 19
HD6955 .A442 1987

PARADIGMS (SOCIAL SCIENCES) - CONGRESSES.
Organizational theory and inquiry . Beverly Hills , c1985. 231 p. ; ISBN 0-8039-2494-1 LC Card 85-8137 DDC 302/.072 19
HM131 .O683 1985 ***NYPL [JLD 86-3567]***

Paradis, Adrian A.
Opportunities in vocational & technical careers / Adrian A. Paradis ; foreword by Philip A. Clement. Lincolnwood, Ill., U. S.A. : VGM Career Horizons, c1987. xi, 147 p. : ill. ; 20 cm. (VGM career books) Bibliography: p. 139-147. ISBN 0-8442-6018-5 LC Card 87-60104 DDC 371.4/25/02373 19
1. Vocational guidance - United States. 2. United States - Occupations. 3. Technicians in industry - United States - Vocational guidance. 4. Occupational training - United States. I. Title. II. Title: Opportunities in vocational and technical careers. III. Title: Vocational & technical careers. IV. Title: Vocational and technical careers. V. Series.
HF5382.5.U5 P28 1987

The small business information source book / Adrian A. Paradis. White Hall, Va. : Betterway Publications, c1987. 136 p. ; 28 cm. Includes bibliographies and index. ISBN 0-932620-81-7 (pbk.) LC Card 87-15925 DDC 658/.022/07073 19
1. Small business - Information services - United States. 2. Home-based businesses - Information services - United States. I. Title.
HD2346.U5 P37 1987

Paradise in the Palouse . Prevost, Nancy M., 1953- Fairfield, Wash. , c1985. 35 p. : ISBN 0-87770-365-5 (pbk.) LC Card 85-17842 DDC 338.1/09797/39 19
HD1775.W2 P74 1985 ***NYPL [JFF 86-559]***

The paradox of mass politics . Neuman, W. Russell. Cambridge, Mass. , 1986. 241 p. : ISBN 0-674-65455-2 (alk. paper) LC Card 86-288 DDC 324.973 19
JK1967 .N48 1986 ***NYPL [JLE 86-4140]***

The paradox of poverty . Steidlmeier, Paul, 1942- Cambridge, Mass. , c1987. xx, 318 p. : ISBN 0-88730-184-3 LC Card 86-26589 DDC 338.9 19
HD75 .S75 1987

The paradox of the silicon savior . Venerable, Grant, 1942- San Francisco , c1987. xxx, 190 p. ; ISBN 0-943425-00-X (pbk.) : LC Card 87-17232 DDC 303.4/83 19
HC79.H53 V45 1987

PARAGUAY - CENSUS, 1960.
Chackiel, Juan. La fuerza de trabajo en los países de la Cuenca del Plata según los censos de 1960 /. San José, Costa Rica , 1976. iv, 81 p. : LC Card 83-169596
HD5746.A6 C42 1976

PARAGUAY - COMMERCE - BRAZIL.
Alternativa rodo-hidro-ferroviária para o transporte de parte da safra de soja paraguaia destinada à exportação. [Rio de Janeiro] [19]84. 65 leaves : LC Card 85-187436
HE199.5.S66 A47 1984

PARAGUAY - COMMERCIAL POLICY.
Palacios, Eulalio R. Reflexiones sobre economia nacional e internacional /. [S.l.] 1986

(Asunción, Paraguay : Tall. Gráf. de la Impr. Nacional) 333 p. ; LC Card 86-226634
HC222 .P36 1986

PARAGUAY - ECONOMIC CONDITIONS.
Herken Krauer, Juan Carlos, 1953- El Paraguay rural entre 1869 y 1913 . Asunción, Paraguay , 1984. 224 p., [10] p. of plates : LC Card 84-237050
HC222 .H47 1984

PARAGUAY - ECONOMIC CONDITIONS - 1918-1954.
Seiferheld, Alfredo M., 1950- Economía y petróleo durante la Guerra del Chaco . Asunción , 1983. 535 p. : LC Card 84-121699 DDC 330.9892/071 19
HC222 .S36 1983 ***NYPL [JLD 85-1032]***

PARAGUAY - ECONOMIC CONDITIONS - 1954-
Economía paraguaya, 1985. Asunción, Paraguay , 1986. 285 p. : LC Card 86-182987
HC222 .E27 1986

Flecha, Agustín Oscar. La economía nacional y el costo de vida /. Asunción, Paraguay , 1986. 49 p. ; LC Card 87-122881 DDC 330.9892/073 19
HD7018 .F57 1986

Herken Krauer, Pablo Alfredo. Vía crucis económico, 1982-86 /. Asunción , 1986. 523 p. ; LC Card 86-226871
HC222 .H48 1986

Menezes, Alfredo da Mota, 1944- A herança de Stroessner . Campinas, SP [1987] 186 p. ; LC Card 87-404011 DDC 337.810892 19
HF1524.5.B7 M46 1987

Palacios, Eulalio R. Reflexiones sobre economia nacional e internacional /. [S.l.] 1986 (Asunción, Paraguay : Tall. Gráf. de la Impr. Nacional) 333 p. ; LC Card 86-226634
HC222 .P36 1986

PARAGUAY - ECONOMIC CONDITIONS - 1954- - CONGRESSES.
Flecha, Agustín Oscar. Crisis económica . [Asunción] [1987] 65 p. ; LC Card 87-404003 DDC 331.2/3/09892 19
HD4920.P2 F57 1987

PARAGUAY - ECONOMIC POLICY.
Andrada, René. Reforma estructural de nuestra economía /. [Asunción , 1986] (Asunción, Paraguay : Ediciones y Arte) 150 p. : LC Card 86-227031
HG885 .A85 1986

Martínez Díaz, Nicasio. Economía y política . [Asunción] 1986 ([Asunción] : El Gráfico) 54 p. ; LC Card 87-400204 DDC 338.9892 19
HC222 .M38 1986

Palacios, Eulalio R. Reflexiones sobre economia nacional e internacional /. [S.l.] 1986 (Asunción, Paraguay : Tall. Gráf. de la Impr. Nacional) 333 p. ; LC Card 86-226634
HC222 .P36 1986

PARAGUAY - EMIGRATION AND IMMIGRATION.
El Fenómeno migratorio en el Paraguay /. Asunción, Paraguay [1985] 258 p. : LC Card 86-100044
HB2033 .F45 1985

PARAGUAY - FOREIGN ECONOMIC RELATIONS - BRAZIL.
Menezes, Alfredo da Mota, 1944- A herança de Stroessner . Campinas, SP [1987] 186 p. ; LC Card 87-404011 DDC 337.810892 19
HF1524.5.B7 M46 1987

PARAGUAY - FOREIGN ECONOMIC RELATIONS - CONGRESSES.
Política internacional, economía e integración /. Asunción del Paraguay [1985] 178 p. ; LC Card 86-122468
HF1523 .P65 1985

Paraguay. Itaipu (Power plant) see Itaipu (Power plant)

PARAGUAY - RURAL CONDITIONS.
Herken Krauer, Juan Carlos, 1953- El Paraguay rural entre 1869 y 1913 . Asunción, Paraguay , 1984. 224 p., [10] p. of plates : LC Card 84-237050
HC222 .H47 1984

El Paraguay rural entre 1869 y 1913 . Herken Krauer, Juan Carlos, 1953- Asunción, Paraguay , 1984. 224 p., [10] p. of plates : LC Card 84-237050
HC222 .H47 1984

PARAÍBA (BRAZIL : STATE) - SOCIAL CONDITIONS.
Leite, José Alfredo A. A sócio-economia do semi-árido /. João Pessoa , 1985. 47 p. : LC Card 87-141315 DDC 330.981/33/063 19
HD1875.P34 L45 1985

Santos, Madalena Herculano dos. Condições de vida nos municípios paraibanos /. João Pessoa (PB) : Brasília, DF : 103 p. : LC Card 87-403990 DDC 330.981/33063 19
HC188.P343 S26 1986

PARAÍBA, BRAZIL (STATE) - COMMERCE.
Setor exportador paraibano . João Pessoa , 1976. 72 leaves : LC Card 84-239455
HF3409.P32 S47 1976

PARAÍBA, BRAZIL (STATE) - ECONOMIC CONDITIONS.
Leite, José Alfredo A. A sócio-economia do semi-árido /. João Pessoa , 1985. 47 p. : LC Card 87-141315 DDC 330.981/33/063 19
HD1875.P34 L45 1985

Santos, Madalena Herculano dos. Condições de vida nos municípios paraibanos /. João Pessoa (PB) : Brasília, DF : 103 p. : LC Card 87-403990 DDC 330.981/33063 19
HC188.P343 S26 1986

Parakh, B. S. Population education : inception to institutionalisation / B.S. Parakh. New Delhi : National Council of Educational Research and Training, 1985. xxviii, 355 p. ; 23 cm. Includes some articles in Hindi. With special reference to India. Bibliography: p. [331]-347. Includes index. LC Card 86-903303 DDC 304.6/07/1054 19
1. Population - Study and teaching - India. I. National Council of Educational Research and Training (India). II. Title.
HB850.5.I4 P37 1985

Paralelo .
(2) Gómez Serrano, Jesús. El mayorazgo Rincón Gallardo . [Aguascalientes] [1984] 156 p., [24] p. of plates : LC Card 84-175622
HD329.Z3 G65 1984 ***NYPL [JLD 87-138]***

(5) Gómez Serrano, Jesús. Hacendados y campesinos en Aguascalientes /. [Aguascalientes] , 1985. 221 p., [20] p. of plates : LC Card 86-217321
HD1471.M62 A384 1985

Paralysis of multiple debilitating crises. Adedeji, Adebayo. The African development problematique . Addis Ababa [1985] 33 p. ; LC Card 87-980487 DDC 338.96 19
HC800 .A543 1985

PARAMARIBO (SURINAM) - ECONOMIC CONDITIONS.
Onderzoek naar werkgelegenheid, inkomen en de structuur van de stedelijke economie van Paramaribo . Paramaribo, Suriname [1978] 69 leaves : LC Card 87-115836
HD5759.5.P37 O53 1978

Paramonov, P. F. (Petr Filippovich) Syrovatko, V. G. (Vitaliĭ Grigor′evich) Industrializatsii͡a i kadry sel′skogo khozi͡aĭstva /. Moskva , 1986. 191 p. ; LC Card 86-229171
HD1536.S65 S97 1986

Paraná . Costa, Iraci del Nero da. São Paulo , 1985. 185 p. : LC Card 86-158196
HA984 .C67 1985

Paraná (Brazil : State). Conselho Estadual de Ciência e Tecnologia. Emprego urgente /. Curitiba , 1984. vii, 75 p. ; LC Card 86-177208
HD5713 .E47 1984

Paraná (Brazil : State). Coordenadoria de Desenvolvimento Industrial.
Estudo sobre a adequação floresta-indústria no Estado do Paraná /. [Curitiba] [1982] vi, 106, [4] leaves ; LC Card 86-197076
HD9764.B73 P32 1982

Estudo sobre a soja /. Curitiba , 1980. 61 leaves : LC Card 86-197070
HD9235.S62 B744 1980

Estudo sobre o setor de laticínios no Estado do Paraná /. Curitiba , 1980. iii, 47 leaves : LC Card 86-201233
HD9275.B73 P34 1980

PARANA (BRAZIL : STATE) - POPULATION - STATISTICS - HISTORY - 19TH CENTURY.
Costa, Iraci del Nero da. Paraná . São Paulo , 1985. 185 p. : LC Card 86-158196
HA984 .C67 1985

PARANÁ, BRAZIL (STATE) - INDUSTRIES.
Avila, Luiz Gonçalves. Desenvolvimento industrial e rendimento da terra . Rio de Janeiro, RJ , 1985. 111 p. : LC Card 86-233493
HD1875.S26 A95 1985

Paraná, formação de capital : sociedade anônima e de economia mista / CODESUL. [Pôrto Alegre] : CODESUL, 1965. 185 p. : ill. ; 27 cm. LC Card 85-131098
1. Capital - Brazil - Paraná (State). 2. Saving and investment - Brazil - Paraná (State). I. Codesul.
HC188.P35 P388 1965

PARANÃ RIVER VALLEY (GOIÁS, BRAZIL) - ECONOMIC POLICY.
Projeto de Desenvolvimento Integrado da Bacia do Araguaia-Tocantins. Plano de desenvolvimento da área-programa do Vale do Paranã /. Brasília , 1985. 128 p., [8] folded leaves of plates : LC Card 86-199833
HC188.P36 P76 1985

PARANÃ RIVER VALLEY (GOIÁS, BRAZIL) - SOCIAL POLICY.
Projeto de Desenvolvimento Integrado da Bacia do Araguaia-Tocantins. Plano de desenvolvimento da área-programa do Vale do Paranã /. Brasília , 1985. 128 p., [8] folded leaves of plates : LC Card 86-199833
HC188.P36 P76 1985

Parasochka, V. T. (Valentin Timofeevich) Artemov, ÎU. M. (ÎUriĭ Mikhaĭlovich) Finansovye metody material′nogo stimulirovanii͡a proizvodstva /. Moskva , 1983. 126 p. ; LC Card 84-118738
HF5549.5.I5 A69 1983

PARATRANSIT SERVICES - ECONOMETRIC MODELS.
Weber, Rolf. Vehicle Routing- und Scheduling-Probleme unter besonderer Berücksichtigung von Dial-a-Ride-Problemen /. München , c1985. iii, 158 p. : ISBN 3-88259-349-0 LC Card 86-123392
HE305 .W4 1985

PARATRANSIT SERVICES - UNITED STATES - DIRECTORIES.
A Directory of rural and specialized transit operators /. Washington, D.C. , 1986- v. <1-3 > : LC Card 86-603414 DDC 388.3/22/0973 19
HE203 .D57 1986

Os parceiros do mar . Loureiro, Violeta Refkalefsky. [Brasília] [Belém] , 1985. 227 p. : LC Card 85-211634
HD9464.A4 L68 1985

Pardo V., Lucía. La historia laboral de las mujeres y su efecto en la tasa de salario : una interpretacíon de la evidencia / Lucía Pardo V. Santiago : Departamento de Economía, Universidad de Chile, 1986. 44, 5 p. : ill. ; 27 cm. (Documento Serie investigación . no. 76) Bibliography: p. 43-44. LC Card 86-217486
1. Women - Employment - Chile. 2. Wages - Chile. I. Title. II. Series.
HD6126 .P37 1986

Paredes, Edgar. (joint author) Búfalo, Enzo del. El pensamiento crítico latinoamericano /. [México?] , 1979. 236 p. ; LC Card 79-120323
HC59.7 .B84 ***NYPL [JLC 80-383]***

Parejo Gamir, Alberto. Cuervo García, Alvaro. Manual de sistema financiero . Barcelona , 1987. 427 p. : ISBN 84-344-2013-9 LC Card 87-135198
HG186.S6 C84 1987

PARENT AND CHILD - GERMANY, WEST.
Schneewind, Klaus A., 1939- Eltern und Kinder . Stuttgart , c1983. 229 p. : ISBN 3-17-007744-9 LC Card 83-150745 DDC 303.3/23/0943 19
HQ739 .S29 1983 ***NYPL [JLE 87-1168]***

Parent, Leonard V., 1927- Williams, Anna Fay, 1935- New opportunities to purchase natural gas /. Lilburn, Ga. , c1988. xiv, 372 p. : ISBN 0-88173-034-3 : LC Card 86-46134 DDC 665.7/44/068 19
HD9581.U5 W54 1988

The Parental leave crisis : toward a national policy / edited by Edward F. Zigler and Meryl Frank. New Haven : Yale University Press, c1988. p. cm. Includes index. ISBN 0-300-03984-0

(alk. paper) LC Card 87-10729 DDC 331.25/76 19
1. Parental leave - Government policy - United States. 2. Parental leave - Government policy. I. Zigler, Edward, 1930-. II. Frank, Meryl.
HD6065 .P37 1988

PARENTAL LEAVE - GOVERNMENT POLICY.
The Parental leave crisis . New Haven , c1988. p. cm. ISBN 0-300-03984-0 (alk. paper) LC Card 87-10729 DDC 331.25/76 19
HD6065 .P37 1988

PARENTAL LEAVE - GOVERNMENT POLICY - UNITED STATES.
The Parental leave crisis . New Haven , c1988. p. cm. ISBN 0-300-03984-0 (alk. paper) LC Card 87-10729 DDC 331.25/76 19
HD6065 .P37 1988

PARENTAL LEAVE - UNITED STATES.
The Corporate guide to parental leaves, including Catalyst's Report on a national study of parental leaves /. New York, NY (250 Park Ave. South, New York 10003) , c1986. 145 p. : LC Card 87-161920 DDC 658.3/122 19
HD6065.5.U6 C67 1986

PARENTING.
Hughes, Theodore E. The parents' financial survival guide /. Tucson, Ariz. , c1987. 227 p. ; ISBN 0-89586-644-7 : LC Card 87-10233 DDC 332.024/0431 19
HG179 .H84 1987

PARENTS, AGED - CARE - UNITED STATES.
Carlin, Vivian F., 1919- Where can mom live? . Lexington, Mass. , c1987. viii, 206 p. : ISBN 0-669-13665-4 (alk. paper) LC Card 86-45526 DDC 363.5/9 19
HD7287.92.U54 C37 1987

PARENTS - FINANCE, PERSONAL.
Hughes, Theodore E. The parents' financial survival guide /. Tucson, Ariz. , c1987. 227 p. ; ISBN 0-89586-644-7 : LC Card 87-10233 DDC 332.024/0431 19
HG179 .H84 1987

The parents' financial survival guide /. Hughes, Theodore E. Tucson, Ariz. , c1987. 227 p. ; ISBN 0-89586-644-7 : LC Card 87-10233 DDC 332.024/0431 19
HG179 .H84 1987

Parfënov, I. D. (Igor´ Danilovich) Monopolii͡a i imperii͡a : angliĭskie privilegirovannye kompanii i kolonial´nai͡a ėkspansii͡a 80-90-kh godov XIX veka / I.D. Parfënov ; pod redaktsieĭ A.F. Ostal´tsevoĭ. Saratov : Izd-vo Saratovskogo universiteta, 1980. 191, [1] p. ; 20 cm. Bibliography: p. 183-[192] LC Card 81-142784
1. Corporations, British - Africa - History - 19th century. 2. Investments, British - Africa - History - 19th century. I. Ostal´tseva, Alevtina Fedorovna. II. Title.
HD2845 .P36 1980

Parfenova, V. I. (Valentina Ivanovna) Busurin, K. A. Nauchnai͡a organizatsii͡a truda v dorozhnom khozi͡aĭstve /. Moskva , 1981. 159 p. ; LC Card 87-461013
HD9717.5.R63 S653 1981

Parichno-kreditni i finansovi otnoshenii͡a v sistemata na sŭvremennii͡a dŭrzhavno-monopolisticheski kapitalizŭm / [redaktsionna kolegii͡a S. Kodinov (otgovoren redaktor) ... et al. ; avtorski kolektiv V. Bakhar ... et al.]. Sofii͡a : Izd-vo na Bŭlgarskata akademii͡a na naukite, 1985. 245 p. : ill. ; 25 cm. Titles on added t.p.: Denezhno-kreditnye i finansovye otnoshenii͡a v sisteme sovremennogo gosudarstvenno-monopolisticheskogo kapitalizma; Monetary and financial relations within the system of contemporary state monopoly capitalism. At head of title: Bŭlgarska akademii͡a na naukite. Ikonomicheski institut. Summary in English and Russian. Includes bibliographical references. LC Card 86-153156
1. International finance. I. Kodinov, Stoil. II. Bakhar, V. III. Ikonomicheski institut (Bŭlgarska akademii͡a na naukite). IV. Title: Denezhno-kreditnye i finansovye otnoshenii͡a v sisteme sovremennogo gosudarstvenno-monopolisticheskogo kapitalizma. V. Title: Monetary and financial relations within the system of contemporary state monopoly capitalism.
HG3881 .P2936 1985

Parikh, Girish, 1934- The one minute organizing secret : finding electronic files, papers, books, and almost everything fast! / Girish Parikh.1st ed. Chicago, IL : Shetal Enterprises, c1986. 60, 2 p. ; 28 cm. Bibliography: p. 59-60. ISBN 0-932888-37-2 (pbk.) : LC Card 85-62926 DDC 650.1 19
1. Filing systems. 2. Electronic filing systems. 3. Microcomputers. I. Title.
HF5736 .P34 1986

Parikh, Rajeev N. Orsini, Larry L. World accounting /. New York, NY (11 Penn Plaza, New York 10001) , 1987- c1986- 2 v. (loose-leaf) ; LC Card 86-73012 DDC 657 19
HF5611 .O75 1987

Parikh, S. S. Coal after nationalisation /. Calcutta , 1977. 676, [122] p. : LC Card 77-905030
HD9556.I42 C57 ***NYPL [JLF 78-1568]***

Paris audiovisuel (Firm) Atget, Géniaux, Vert . Paris [1984] 63, [1] p. : ISBN 2-901414-09-5 : LC Card 86-137985
HF5459.F8 A87 1984 ***NYPL [MFW 87-159]***

PARIS CLUB.
Renegociación de la deuda externa, 1985 /. Santo Domingo, República Dominicana , 1985. iv, 168 p. ; LC Card 86-186407
HJ8548 .R46 1985

Civilisations et sociétés. see **Civilisations et sociétés.**

París Eguilaz, Higinio. España en el socialismo actual / por Higinio París Eguilaz. Madrid : [s.n., 1984?] 234 p. ; 24 cm. ISBN 84-398-2401-7 LC Card 87-120643
1. Spain - Economic conditions - 1975-. 2. Spain - Economic policy. 3. Socialism - Spain. I. Title.
HC385 .P313 1984

Paris - Government. see **Paris - Politics and government.**

París, Higinio. see **París Eguilaz, Higinio.**

PARIS - POLITICS AND GOVERNMENT.
Nord, Philip, 1950- Paris shopkeepers and the politics of resentment /. Princeton, N.J. , c1986. xvii, 539 p. : ISBN 0-691-05454-1 : LC Card 85-42695 DDC 322/.3/0944361 19
HF5429.6.F7 N67 1986 ***NYPL [JLD 86-2305]***

Paris. Régie autonome des transports parisiens. see **Régie autonome des transports parisiens.**

Paris shopkeepers and the politics of resentment /. Nord, Philip, 1950- Princeton, N.J. , c1986. xvii, 539 p. : ISBN 0-691-05454-1 : LC Card 85-42695 DDC 322/.3/0944361 19
HF5429.6.F7 N67 1986 ***NYPL [JLD 86-2305]***

PARISH ADMINISTRATION. see **CHURCH MANAGEMENT.**

PARISH MANAGEMENT. see **CHURCH MANAGEMENT.**

Park, Rolla Edward.
Optimal peak-load pricing for local telephone calls / Rolla Edward Park, Bridger M. Mitchell. Santa Monica, CA : Rand, 1986. xiii, 37 p. : ill. ; 23 cm. Bibliography: p. 35-37. "R-3404-RC." ISBN 0-8330-0741-6 (pbk.) LC Card 86-204468 DDC 384.6/3 19
1. Telephone - United States - Rates - Peak-load pricing - Mathematical models. I. Mitchell, Bridger M. II. Title.
HE8825 .P369 1986

Optimal peak-load pricing for local telephone calls : technical appendixes / Rolla Edward Park, Bridger M. Mitchell. Santa Monica, CA : Rand, c1986. x, 72 p. : ill. ; 23 cm. "R-3404/1-RC." "June 1986." Bibliography: p. 70-72. ISBN 0-8330-0747-5 (pbk.) LC Card 86-203146 DDC 384.6/3 19
1. Telephone - United States - Rates - Peak-load pricing - Mathematical models. I. Mitchell, Bridger M. II. Title.
HE8825 .P369 1986 Suppl.

Optimal peak-load pricing for local telephone calls / Rolla Edward Park, Bridger M. Mitchell. Santa Monica, CA : Rand Corp., c1987. xiii, 41 p. : ill. ; 23 cm. "March 1987." Bibliography: p. 39-41. "R-3404-1-RC." ISBN 0-8330-0856-X (pbk.) LC Card 87-410013 DDC 384.6/3 19
1. Telephone - United States - Rates - Peak-load pricing - Mathematical models. I. Mitchell, Bridger M. II. Rand Corporation. III. Title.
HE8825 .P369 1987

Optimal peak-load pricing for local telephone calls : technical appendixes / Rolla Edward Park, Bridger M. Mitchell. Santa Monica, CA : Rand Corp., c1987. x, 75 p. : ill. ; 23 cm. "R-3404/1-1-RC." "March 1987." "Companion volume to Optimal peak-load pricing for local telephone calls, R-3404-1-RC"--P. iii. Bibliography: p. 73-75. ISBN 0-8330-0857-9 (pbk.) LC Card 87-154411 DDC 384.6/3 19
1. Telephone - United States - Rates - Peak-load pricing - Mathematical models. I. Mitchell, Bridger M. II. Title.
HE8825 .P37 1987

Park, Sung-Jo. U. S. labor policy in postwar Japan / Sung-Jo Park. [Berlin] : Express Edition, [c1985] 157 p. : ill. ; 22 cm. (Reihe Horizonte Asiens) Bibliography: p. 152-157. ISBN 3-88548-424-2 LC Card 86-200166 DDC 331.11/0952 19
1. Labor policy - Japan - History. 2. Management - Japan - Employee participation - History. 3. Japan - History - Allied occupation, 1945-1952. I. Title. II. Title: United States labor policy in postwar Japan.
HD5827.A6 P37 1985

Park, Yung Chul. A system for evaluating the performance of government-invested enterprises in Korea / Young C. Park. Washington, D.C. : World Bank, [1986] vi, 49 p. : ill. ; 28 cm. (World Bank discussion papers, 0259-210X . 3) Bibliography: p. 49. ISBN 0-8213-0859-9 (pbk.) LC Card 86-28907 DDC 338.7/4/0723 19
1. Government business enterprises - Korea (South) - Evaluation. I. Title. II. Series.
HD4315.5 .P37 1986

Parker, Cordell. Hamilton, Cheryl. Communicating for results . Belmont, Calif. , c1987. xiii, 418 p. : ISBN 0-534-07956-3 (pbk.) LC Card 86-28108 DDC 658.4/5 19
HD30.3 .H35 1987

Parker, Dennis J.
Penning-Rowsell, Edmund. Floods and drainage . London , Boston , 1986. xx, 199 p. : ISBN 0-04-627001-9 (alk. paper) : LC Card 85-13383 DDC 363.3/4936/0941 19
HD1676.G7 P46 1985 ***NYPL [JLE 86-3996]***

Urban flood protection benefits : a project appraisal guide / Dennis J. Parker, Colin H. Green, and Paul M. Thompson ; with contributions from Edmund C. Penning-Rowsell, John B. Chatterton, and Roger C. Witts. Aldershot, Hants, England ; Brookfield, Vt., U. S. A. : Gower Technical Press, c1987. xvii, 284 p. : ill. ; 31 cm. Bibliography: p. 269-276. Includes index. ISBN 0-291-39707-7 LC Card 87-147842 DDC 363.3/49372 19
1. Flood damage prevention - Great Britain - Cost effectiveness. 2. Flood damage - Economic aspects - Great Britain. 3. City planning - Great Britain. I. Green, Colin H. II. Thompson, Paul M. III. Title.
HD1676.G7 P37 1987

Parker, Frederick. Management techniques for top executives / Frederick Parker. 1st ed. Pompano Beach, Fla. : Exposition Press of Florida, c1985. x, 194 p. : ill. ; 23 cm. ISBN 0-682-40194-3 : LC Card 84-91085 DDC 658.4/09 19
1. Executive ability. 2. Industrial management. I. Title.
HD38.2 .P37 1985

Parker, Martin F. The practical guide to voice mail / Martin F. Parker. Berkeley, Calif. : Osborne McGraw-Hill, c1987. xiv, 306 p. : ill. ; 23 cm. Includes index. ISBN 0-07-881243-7 (pbk.) LC Card 86-210772 DDC 621.385 19
1. Telephone in business. 2. Voice mail systems. I. Title.
HF5541.T4 P37 1987

Parker, R. H. (Robert Henry) The development of the accountancy profession in Britain to the early twentieth century / R.H. Parker. [University, Ala.] : Academy of Accounting Historians, 1986. ix, 74 p. ; 23 cm. (Monograph / the Academy of Accounting Historians . 5) Bibliography: p. 72-74. LC Card 86-226162 DDC 657/.09 19
1. Accounting - Great Britain - History - 20th century. I. Series: Monograph (Academy of Accounting Historians) , 5. II. Title.
HF5616.G7 P36 1986

Parker, Robert Henry. Lee, Thomas Alexander. The evolution of corporate financial reporting /. New York , 1984. x, 307 p. ; ISBN 0-8240-6332-5 (alk. paper) : LC Card 83-49431

DDC 657/.3 19
HF5686.C7 L43 1984 ***NYPL [JLD 86-2835]***

Parker, William Nelson. Economic history and the modern economist /. Oxford, UK , New York, NY, USA , 1986. xi, 105 p. ; ISBN 0-631-14799-3 : LC Card 85-28584 DDC 330/.09 19
HC26 .E26 1986 ***NYPL [JLD 86-2947]***

Parker, Yana. The resume catalog : 200 damm good examples / by Yana Parker. Berkeley, Calif. : Ten Speed Press, 1987. p. cm. Includes index. ISBN 0-89815-219-4 LC Card 87-7057 DDC 650.1/4 19
1. Résumés (Employment). I. Title.
HF5383 .P354 1987

Parkeringsbehov i ældre tætte bydele . Larsen, Flemming. København , 1985. 250 p. : LC Card 86-165642
HE336.P37 L37 1985

Parkin, Michael. Inflation in the world economy /. Manchester [Eng.] , 1976. xvii, 334 p. : ISBN 0-7190-0630-9 LC Card 76-356701
HG229 .I453 1976 ***NYPL [JLD 78-401]***

Parkin, William. Kaplan, Howard J. Scouts on stamps of the world /. [Hicksville, N.Y.] , c1986. 1 v. (loose-leaf) : LC Card 86-224816 DDC 769.56/3 19
HE6183.B63 K36 1986

PARKING, AUTOMOBILE. see **AUTOMOBILE PARKING.**

Parking boys in the city of Kenya "Nairobi" /. Nakhisa, Sellah A. [Nairobi , 1981?] ii, 27 leaves ; LC Card 82-980697 DDC 331.3/1 19
HE367.K43 P376 1981

PARKING LOTS - KENYA - NAIROBI - EMPLOYEES - SOCIAL CONDITIONS.
Nakhisa, Sellah A. Parking boys in the city of Kenya "Nairobi" /. [Nairobi , 1981?] ii, 27 leaves ; LC Card 82-980697 DDC 331.3/1 19
HE367.K43 P376 1981

Parkinson, Lynn K. Using the microcomputer in marketing / Lynn K. Parkinson and Stephen T. Parkinson. London ; New York : McGraw-Hill, c1987. ix, 158 p. : ill. ; 25 cm. (The McGraw-Hill marketing series) Includes bibliographical references and index. ISBN 0-07-084163-2 (pbk.) : LC Card 86-27364 DDC 658.8/0028/5416 19
1. Marketing - Data processing. 2. Microcomputers. I. Parkinson, Stephen T. (Stephen Trent), 1951-. II. Title. III. Series.
HF5415.125 .P36 1987

Parkinson, Stephen T. (Stephen Trent), 1951- Parkinson, Lynn K. Using the microcomputer in marketing /. London , New York , c1987. ix, 158 p. : ISBN 0-07-084163-2 (pbk.) : LC Card 86-27364 DDC 658.8/0028/5416 19
HF5415.125 .P36 1987

Parlamento europeo. see **European Parliament.**

Parlement européen. see **European Parliament.**

The Parliament of labour . Cody, Seamus. Dublin, Ireland , 1986. 253 p. : LC Card 87-102467 DDC 331.88/09418/35 19
HD8400.3.A5 D833 1986

Parliamentary control over public enterprises in India /. Surya Prakash. Allahabad, India , 1985. 293 p. ; LC Card 85-903454 DDC 354.5409/2 19
HD4293 .S87 1985 ***NYPL [JLD 87-325]***

Parliamentary Forum on Public Sector (India) Government media and the public sector . New Delhi , 1983. 270 p. ; LC Card 83-907479 DDC 302.3/24/0954 19
HD59 .G62 1983 ***NYPL [JLD 86-3767]***

PARLIAMENTARY GOVERNMENT. see **REPRESENTATIVE GOVERNMENT AND REPRESENTATION.**

PARMA (ITALY : PROVINCE) - ECONOMIC CONDITIONS - CONGRESSES.
Economia e società della montagna parmense . [Italy , 1984?] (Parma : Officina grafica artigiana) 115 p. ; LC Card 85-156635
HC307.P33 E27 1984

PARMA (ITALY : PROVINCE) - RURAL CONDITIONS - CONGRESSES.
Economia e società della montagna parmense . [Italy , 1984?] (Parma : Officina grafica artigiana) 115 p. ; LC Card 85-156635
HC307.P33 E27 1984

Parnell, Anna, 1852-1911. The tale of a great sham / Anna Parnell ; edited with an introduction by Dana Hearne. Dublin : Arlen House ; Wick, Littlehampton, West Sussex : Distributed in Britain by George Philip Services, 1986. 205 p. ; 22 cm. Bibliography: p. 188-189. ISBN 0-905223-93-4 LC Card 86-234070 DDC 333.33/5/09415 19
1. Ladies' Land League - History. 2. Land tenure - Ireland - History. 3. Eviction - Ireland - History. 4. Land reform - Ireland - History. 5. Home rule (Ireland) - History. 6. Women in politics - Ireland - History. I. Hearne, Dana, 1943-. II. Title.
HD625 .P37 1986

Parnes, Steven. Productivity and the quality of working life / [researched and written by Steven Parnes under the supervision of Michael Rosow]. 1st ed. Scarsdale, N.Y. : Work in America Institute, c1978. 43 p. ; 29 cm. (Work in America Institute studies in productivity . 2) Bibliography: p. 39-43. LC Card 78-51009 DDC 658.31/4
1. Labor productivity - Abstracts. 2. Job satisfaction - Abstracts. 3. Quality of work life. I. Title. II. Title: Quality of working life. III. Series.
HD57 .P33 ***NYPL [JLM 83-380 no.2]***

Parodi Solari, Jorge. Ser obrero es algo relativo-- : obreros, clasismo y política / Jorge Parodi. Lima : Instituto de Estudios Peruanos, [1986] 184 p. ; 21 cm. (Serie Urbanización, migraciones y cambios en la sociedad peruana . 7) Includes bibliographical references. LC Card 87-405297 DDC 331.7/671/0985 19
1. Metal-workers - Peru. 2. Labor and laboring classes - Peru. 3. Trade-unions - Peru. I. Series: Urbanización, migraciones y cambios en la sociedad peruana, 7. II. Title.
HD8039.M52 P46 1986

La parola pubblicitaria . Medici Mario, 1924- Pomezia , Venezia , 1986. 178 p., 40 p. of plates : ISBN 88-317-4902-1 : LC Card 86-219876
HF5813.I8 M43 1986

Los paros nacionales en Chile, 1919-1973 /. Gonzales Torres, Rodrigo. Santiago [Chile] , 1984. 234 p. ; LC Card 86-200794
HD5356.A6 G66 1984

Parquet, Reinerio. Las empresas transnacionales en la economía del Paraguay. 1a ed. Santiago de Chile : Comisión Económica para América Latina y el Caribe, Naciones Unidas, 1987. 115 p. ; 23 cm. (Estudios e informes de la CEPAL, 0256-9795 . 61) Bibliography: p. 79-81. "LC/G.1434, marzo de 1987"--T.p. verso. "Publicación de las Naciones Unidas; número de venta: S.87.II.G.5"--T.p. verso. ISBN 92-1-321223-2 LC Card 87-404657 DDC 338.8/88892 19
1. Investments, Foreign - Paraguay. 2. International business enterprises - Paraguay. I. Title. II. Series.
HG5382 .P37 1987

Parra, Isidro. see **Parra Peña, Isidro, 1936-**

Parra Peña, Isidro, 1936- El subdesarrollo y la crisis en la economía y en la teoría económica / Isidro Parra-Peña ; prólogo de Jorge Méndez Munévar. 1a ed. Bogotá : Plaza & Janés, 1986. 134 p. ; 18 cm. (Selección Cultura colombiana . 40.) Bibliography: p. [133]-134. ISBN 958-1-40133-4 LC Card 87-115003 DDC 338.9 19
1. Economic development. 2. Economics. I. Series: Selección Cultura colombiana , 40. II. Title.
HD85.S7 P36 1986

Parris, Henry. Public enterprise in Western Europe / Henry Parris, Pierre Pestieau, and Peter Saynor. London ; Wolfeboro, N.H. : Croom Helm, c1987. viii, 197 p. : ill. ; 23 cm. Includes index. At head of title on book jacket : The Acton Society. Bibliography: p. [191]-192. ISBN 0-7099-0548-3 : LC Card 86-24133 DDC 338.7/4/094 19
1. Government business enterprises - Europe. I. Pestieau, Pierre, 1943-. II. Saynor, Peter. III. Action Society Trust. IV. Title.
HD4138 .P37 1987 ***NYPL [JLD 87-757]***

Parris, W. H. For survival, development, and prosperity : address at the national launching of Agriculture Month 1985 / by W.H. Parris. Georgetown, Guyana : Publications Division, Ministry of Information, [1985] 28 p. : ill., port. ; 22 cm. LC Card 87-400751 DDC 338.1/8881 19
1. Agriculture and state - Guyana. I. Title.
HD1895.3.Z8 P37 1985

Parrish, Vernon. Great American video retailing : earning megabucks the video way / by Vernon Parrish. Arlington, Va. : V. Parrish Pub., [1983?] viii, 448 p. : ill. ; 24 cm. Cover title: Earning megabucks the video way. Includes bibliographies. ISBN 0-9615774-0-1 LC Card 85-90437 DDC 621.388/332/0688 19
1. Video tape industry - United States - Management. 2. Video disc industry - United States - Management. 3. Retail trade - United States - Management. I. Title. II. Title: Earning megabucks the video way.
HD9697.V543 U544 1983

Parry, J. T. (John T.) Remote sensing and tropical land management /. [New York] , c1986. xii, 365 p., [16] p. of plates : ISBN 0-471-90889-4 : LC Card 85-17932 DDC 333.73/13/028 19
HD108.8 .R45 1986 ***NYPL [JLE 87-943]***

Parsche, Rüdiger.
Die Belastung der Einkünfte aus nichtselbständiger Arbeit mit Einkommensteuern und Sozialabgaben in den EG-Ländern und in Schweden / Rüdiger Parsche. München : Ifo-Institut für Wirtschaftsforschung, 1981. 2 v. ; 21 cm. (Ifo-Studien zur Finanzpolitik . 27) Vol. 2 by Rüdiger Parsche with the collaboration of Heinz Ludwig. Bibliography: v. 1, p. xii-xxii. LC Card 83-115269
1. Income tax - Germany, West. 2. Income tax - Sweden. 3. Income tax - European Economic Community countries. I. Ludwig, Heinz. II. Title. III. Series.
HJ4719 .P37 1981

Hummel, Marlies. Die steuerliche Behandlung des eigengenutzten Wohneigentums in den Ländern Bundesrepublik Deutschland, Österreich, Schweiz, Frankreich, Grossbritannien und den USA /. München , 1986. ii, 73 p. ; ISBN 3-88512-021-6 : LC Card 86-215255
HJ4719 .H85 1986

PARSEES - BIOGRAPHY.
Marker, Kekobad Ardeshir, 1896-1984. A petal from the rose /. [Karachi] 1985 (Karachi : Rosette) 2 v. : LC Card 85-932155
HC440.5.M35 A3 1985

Parson, Mary Jean. Managing the one-person business / Mary Jean Parson. 1st ed. New York : Dodd, Mead, 1987. xii, 274 p. ; 24 cm. Bibliography: p. 255-261. Includes index. ISBN 0-396-09149-0 (pbk.) : LC Card 87-20069 DDC 658/.022 19
1. Self-employed. I. Title.
HD8036 .P37 1987

Parsons, Ben. Contacts . San Rafael, CA (1724 Lincoln Ave., San Rafael 94901) [c1986] 252 p. ; LC Card 86-217208 DDC 332.1/028 19
HG1710 .C66 1986

Parsons, Leonard J. Using microcomputers in marketing / Leonard J. Parsons. [Boston, Mass.?] : American Management Association, Extension Institute, c1986. xi, 141 p. : ill. ; 30 cm. Includes bibliographical references. LC Card 86-216432 DDC 658.8/0028/5416 19
1. Marketing - Data processing. 2. Microcomputers. I. Title.
HF5415.125 .P37 1986

Parsons, W. J. (Will J.) Improving marketing performance / W.J. Parsons. Aldershot, Hants, England ; Brookfield, Vt., USA : Gower, c1987. xiii, 164 p. : ill. ; 23 cm. Includes index. ISBN 0-566-02595-7 : LC Card 86-25681 DDC 658.8 19
1. Marketing. I. Title.
HF5415 .P2496 1987

Part of my soul /. Mandela, Winnie. Harmondsworth , 1985. 163 p., [8] p. of plates :
NYPL [Sc C 86-121]

Part of my soul went with him /. Mandela, Winnie. New York , 1985, c1984. 163 p., [8] p. of plates : ISBN 0-393-02215-3 : LC Card 85-21632 DDC 968/.00496 19
DT779.955.M36 A35 1985
NYPL [JFD 86-7717]

PART-TIME EMPLOYMENT - AUSTRIA.
Was ist bei der Teilzeitbeschäftigung zu beachten? /. Wien , 1985. 64 p. ; LC Card 86-210129
HD5110.2.A9 W37 1985

PART-TIME EMPLOYMENT - DENMARK.
Markussen, Randi. Det fleksible køn .

[Copenhagen] , c1984. 163 p. ; ISBN 87-7445-159-6 : LC Card 84-187146
HD6169 .M37 1984

PART-TIME EMPLOYMENT - ENGLAND - COVENTRY (WEST MIDLANDS)
Beechey, Veronica. A matter of hours . Minneapolis, MN , c1987. 212 p. ; ISBN 0-8166-1641-8 : LC Card 87-12459 DDC 331.4/12/0942498 19
HD6136.Z6 C683 1987

PART-TIME EMPLOYMENT - FRANCE.
Legay, Marie-Agnès. Réduction de la durée du travail et changement des modes de vie . Aix-en-Provence [1984] ix, 366 p. : LC Card 86-185902
HD6066.F8 L44 1984

PART-TIME EMPLOYMENT - GERMANY, WEST.
Burian, Klaus. Betriebliche Erfahrungen mit neuen Arbeitszeitformen . Berlin [1984] iv, 162 p. ; LC Card 84-182592
HD5110.2.G3 B87 1984

Grenzen der Frauenlohnarbeit . Frankfurt/Main , New York , c1986. 250 p. : ISBN 3-593-33628-6 LC Card 86-228323
HD6072.2.G4 G74 1986

PART-TIME EMPLOYMENT - ITALY - CONGRESSES.
Disoccupazione e nuove forme di accesso al lavoro nel mondo bancario /. Milano, Italy , c1986. 186 p. ; LC Card 87-150276
HD5718.B262 I83 1986

PART-TIME EMPLOYMENT - LAW AND LEGISLATION - AUSTRIA.
Was ist bei der Teilzeitbeschäftigung zu beachten? /. Wien , 1985. 64 p. ; LC Card 86-210129
HD5110.2.A9 W37 1985

PART-TIME EMPLOYMENT - QUÉBEC (PROVINCE)
Lewis, Normande. Le travail à temps partiel, le partage du travail comme mesure de sécurité d'emploi et la sous-traitance . [Quebec] , c1985. 90 p. ; ISBN 2-551-08998-0 LC Card 85-213545
HD5110.2.C22 Q45 1985

Part-time employment study . Washington (State). Dept. of Personnel. Olympia, Wash. (600 S. Franklin, FE-11, Olympia 98504) [1984] xi, 82 p. : LC Card 85-621558 DDC 331.25/72 19
HD5110.2.U52 W29 1984
NYPL [JLF 86-517]

PART-TIME EMPLOYMENT - UNITED STATES.
The Changing workplace . Washington, D.C. [Rockville, Md.] , c1986. iv, 140 p. : ISBN 0-87179-910-3 (pbk.) LC Card 86-221689 DDC 331.25/72 19
HD5124 .C46 1986

Kahne, Hilda. Reconceiving part-time work . Totowa, N.J. , 1985. xv, 180 p. : ISBN 0-8476-7376-6 : LC Card 85-2386 DDC 331.3/94 19
HD5110.2.U5 K33 1985
NYPL [JLE 86-1174]

MacDorman, Littleton C. Use of part-time operators /. Washington, D.C. [1986] 33 p. : ISBN 0-309-04403-0 (pbk.) LC Card 86-51175 DDC 331.25/72 19
HD8039.S82 U65 1986

PART-TIME EMPLOYMENT - UNITED STATES - ADDRESSES, ESSAYS, LECTURES.
Rothberg, Diane S., 1930- Part-time professional /. Washington, D.C. , c1985. 158 p. ; ISBN 0-87491-786-7 (pbk.) : LC Card 85-19964 DDC 650.1/4 19
HD5110.2.U5 R67 1985
NYPL [JLE 86-2582]

PART-TIME EMPLOYMENT - WASHINGTON METROPOLITAN AREA - DIRECTORIES.
APTP employer directory. McLean, Va. (7655 Old Springhouse Road, McLean 22102) , c1986. iii, 47 p. ; LC Card 86-213174 DDC 338.7/61/00025753 19
HD8038.U52 W323 1986

PART-TIME EMPLOYMENT - WASHINGTON (STATE)
Washington (State). Dept. of Personnel. Part-time employment study . Olympia, Wash. (600 S. Franklin, FE-11, Olympia 98504) [1984] xi, 82 p. : LC Card 85-621558 DDC 331.25/72 19
HD5110.2.U52 W29 1984
NYPL [JLF 86-517]

PART-TIME FARMING - AUSTRIA.
Aistleitner, Josef. Formen und Auswirkungen des bäuerlichen Nebenerwerbs . [Innsbruck] , 1986. 174 p. : LC Card 87-408342 DDC 338.1/6 19
HD1935 .A66 1986

PART-TIME FARMING - GERMANY (WEST) - NORTH RHINE-WESTPHALIA.
Kreiten, Kurt. Gestalt und Wandel der nebenberuflichen Landwirtschaft in Nordrhein-Westfalen /. Bonn , 1985. xi, 225 p. : ISBN 3-88488-272-4 LC Card 86-205281
HD1960.N67 K74 1985

PART-TIME FARMING - ITALY.
Pieroni, Osvaldo. Agricolture a tempo parziale /. Bologna , c1983. 220 p. : ISBN 88-15-00024-0 LC Card 85-233534
HD1970 .P54 1983

Part-time professional /. Rothberg, Diane S., 1930- Washington, D.C. , c1985. 158 p. ; ISBN 0-87491-786-7 (pbk.) : LC Card 85-19964 DDC 650.1/4 19
HD5110.2.U5 R67 1985
NYPL [JLE 86-2582]

PART-TIME WORK. see **PART-TIME EMPLOYMENT.**

Partap Singh, 1948- Co-operative agricultural finance : utilization and overdues : a study with reference to Patiala District / Partap Singh.1st ed. New Delhi : National Book Organisation : Sole distributor, Sehgal Publishers Service, 1986. xiii, 188 p. : map ; 23 cm. Revision of the author's thesis (Ph. D.--Punjabi University) under the title: Agricultural co-operative finance : utilisation and overdues : a case study of Patiala District. Bibliography: p. [176]-188. LC Card 86-903067
1. Agricultural cooperative credit associations - India - Patiāla District - Case studies. 2. Agricultural cooperative credit associations - India - Case studies. 3. Agriculture - India - Patiāla District - Finance - Case studies. 4. Agriculture - India - Finance - Case studies. I. Title.
HG2051.I5 P376 1986

Parteihochschule "Karl Marx" (Berlin, Germany)
Auf sicherem Kurs . [Berlin] [1976] 80 leaves (some folded) : LC Card 85-190579
HC290.78 .A84 1976

Im Blickpunkt der Leistungsvergleich /. Berlin , 1985. 126 p. ; LC Card 85-155570
HC270.28 .I56 1985

Parti communiste. see **Parti communiste français.**

Parti communiste (bolchevik) de l'U. R. S. S. see **Kommunisticheskai͡a partii͡a Sovetskogo Soi͡uza.**

Parti communiste bulare. see **Bŭlgarska komunisticheska partii͡a.**

PARTI COMMUNISTE FRANÇAIS - PLATFORMS.
Un Chemin pour sortir de la crise /. Paris , c1985. 249 p. ; ISBN 2-209-05753-1 LC Card 86-154397
HC276.2 .C517 1985

Parti communiste français. Section économique.
Un Chemin pour sortir de la crise /. Paris , c1985. 249 p. ; ISBN 2-209-05753-1 LC Card 86-154397
HC276.2 .C517 1985

Parti communiste italien. see **Partito comunista italiano.**

Parti comuniste d'Espagne. see **Partido Comunista de España.**

Le parti des patrons . Weber, Henri. Paris , c1986. 437 p. ; ISBN 2-02-009352-9 : LC Card 87-106644
HD6948.F8 W43 1986

Parti ouvrier bulgare (communistes) see **Bŭlgarska komunisticheska partii͡a.**

PARTIAL EQUILIBRIUM (ECONOMICS) see **EQUILIBRIUM (ECONOMICS)**

PARTIAL MONOPOLIES. see **OLIGOPOLIES.**

A participação da alimentação na inflação brasileira nos anos 70 . Pereira, José Maria Dias. Porto Alegre, RS , 1984. 139 p. : LC Card 85-128694 DDC 338.4/36413/00981 19
HD9014.B82 P47 1984
NYPL [JLE 86-2264]

Participação ou manipulação . Carrion, Rosinha Machado. Porto Alegre, RS , 1984. 111 p. : LC Card 84-209842 DDC 658 19
HD37.P63 C29 1984 *NYPL [JLE 86-2263]*

Participación campesina. ACLO (Organization) "Estudio de participación campesina en la estructura y acción de ACLO" . [Sucre, Bolivia] , 1980. 94 leaves ; LC Card 83-203590
HD1531.B6 A24 1980

Participación, cogestión y autogestión en América Latina / Francisco Iturraspe, ed. 1a ed. Caracas : Editorial Nueva Sociedad, 1986. 2 v. : ill. ; 20 cm. Bibliography: v. 2, p. 309-333. CONTENTS. - 1. América Latina, Argentina, Bolivia, Caribe y Centro América -- 2. Chile, Perú, Venezuela, glosario, bibliografía. ISBN 980-265-396-9 (set) LC Card 87-111263
1. Management - Latin America - Employee participation. 2. Management - Employee participation - Dictionaries - Spanish. 3. Management - Employee participation - Bibliography. I. Iturraspe, Francisco.
HD5660.L29 P37 1986

La participación de los trabajadores en la gestión empresarial en la República del Perú, 1968-1980 /. Neffa, Julio César. Ginebra, Suiza , 1986. vi, 112, x p. : ISBN 92-9014-410-6 LC Card 87-400930 DDC 658.3/152/0985 19
HD5660.P4 N44 1986

Participatie, toegang tot ontwikkeling : verslag van een onderzoek naar de mogelijkheden van participatie in ontwikkelingsprojekten / Benno Galjart ... [et al.].2e druk. Leiden : Instituut voor Culturele Antropologie en Sociologie der Niet-Westerse Volken, Rijksuniversiteit Leiden, 1982, c1983. 313 p. ; 23 cm. (Leiden development studies . no. 1) Bibliography: p. 266-304. ISBN 90-6624-043-1 LC Card 87-158868
1. Economic development projects - Developing countries - Citizen participation. 2. Economic development projects - Developing countries. I. Galjart, B. F. (Benno Franciscus). II. Series.
HC59.72.E44 P37 1983

PARTICIPATION, POLITICAL. see **POLITICAL PARTICIPATION.**

Participatory democracy . Zimmerman, Joseph Francis, 1928- New York , 1986. xi, 229 p. ; ISBN 0-275-92132-8 (alk. paper) : LC Card 86-8129 DDC 323/.042/0973 19
JF493.U6 Z56 1986 *NYPL [JLE 86-3632]*

Partido Comunista de Cuba. Instituto de Historia del Movimiento Comunista y de la Revolución Socialista de Cuba. see **Instituto de Historia del Movimiento Comunista y de la Revolución Socialista de Cuba.**

Partido Comunista de España. Introducción a la historia del movimiento obrero en Montijo . [Montijo?] [1982?] 103 p., 48 p. of plates : ISBN 84-300-6966-6 LC Card 85-177027
HD8590.M65 I57 1982

Partido Comunista Francés. see **Parti communiste français.**

Partido Comunista Ruso. see **Kommunisticheskai͡a partii͡a Sovetskogo Soi͡uza.**

PARTIDO DO MOVIMENTO DEMOCRÁTICO BRASILEIRO.
Esperança e mundança. [Brasília] , 1981. 95 p. ; LC Card 86-202933
HC187 .E83 1981

PARTIDO REPUBLICANO PAULISTA - HISTORY - 19TH CENTURY.
Salles, Iraci Galvão. Trabalho, progresso e a sociedade civilizada . São Paulo [Brasília] , 1986. 145 p. ; LC Card 86-224281
HD8289.S282 S24 1986

Partidul Comunist Italian. see **Partito comunista italiano.**

Parties and pressure groups /. Coxall, W. N. London , New York , 1986. iv, 196 p. ; ISBN 0-582-35189-8 *NYPL [JLD 86-2729]*

PARTIES, POLITICAL. see **POLITICAL PARTIES.**

Partiĭno rŭkovodstvo na ikonomikata /.
Velichkov, Ivan. Sofii͡a , 1985. 40 p. ; LC Card

86-173901
HC403 .V45 1985

Partiĭnoe rukovodstvo sovershenstvovaniem upravleniīa promyshlennost'īu v period stroitel'stva sotsializma, 1926-1937 . Krasnykh, L. M. (Leonid Mikhaĭlovich) Krasnoīarsk , 1986. 150, [2] p. ; LC Card 86-226013
HD70.S63 K73 1986

Partiĭnye gruppy v kolkhozakh i sovkhozakh /. Luukas, Ants. [Majandi parteigrupid. Russian.] Tallin , 1984. 77 p., [8] p. of plates : LC Card 87-115056
HD1492.S652 E85517 1984

Partiĭnye organizatsii Nechernozem'īa v bor'be za povyshenie proizvodstvennoĭ i politicheskoĭ aktivnosti rabochego klassa v period postroeniīa i razvitiīa sotsializma / [redaktsionnaīa kollegiīa ĪU.N. Klimov (otvetstv. redaktor) ... et al.]. Kalinin : Kalininskiĭ gos. universitet, 1985. 152 p. ; 20 cm. At head of title: Ministerstvo vysshego i srednego spetsial'nogo obrazovaniīa RSFSR. Kalininskiĭ gosudarstvennyĭ universitet. Includes bibliographical references. LC Card 86-196840
1. Industrial productivity - Russian S.F.S.R. - Non-Chernozem Region. 2. Labor productivity - Russian S.F.S.R. - Non-Chernozem Region. I. Klimov, ĪU. N. (ĪUriĭ Nikolaevich). II. Kalininskiĭ gosudarstvennyĭ universitet.
HC337.R85 P36 1985

Partito comunista francese. see **Parti communiste français.**

Partito comunista italiano. Dipartimento economico e problemi sociali. Convegno nazionale del PCI (1982 : Milan, Italy) Le nuove frontiere dello sviluppo . Milano, Italy , c1983. 368 p. ; LC Card 85-174697
HD9696.A3 I727 1982

Partito comunista spagnolo. see **Partido Comunista de España.**

Partito della democrazia cristiana. La Politica comunitaria della casa. Roma, 1971. 227 p. LC Card 74-883223 ***NYPL [JLD 72-3595]***

Partito democratico cristiano. see **Partito della democrazia cristiana.**

PARTITO DEMOCRATICO DEL LAVORO - HISTORY.
D'Angelo, Lucio. Ceti medi e ricostruzione . [Milano] , 1981. vi, 287 p. ; LC Card 81-213297
JN5657.D45 D36 1981
NYPL [JLE 86-3459]

Partito di unità proletaria per il comunismo. Sardegna, crisi, dipendenza, alternativa . [Cagliari] [1984?] 223 p. ; LC Card 84-251167
HC307.S3 S29 1984

Partners for Livable Places. McNulty, Robert H., 1940- The economics of amenity . Washington, D.C. , c1985. xvi, 157 p. : ISBN 0-941182-15-0 (pbk.) LC Card 85-6545 DDC 307.7/6/0973 19
HT321 .M36 1985 ***NYPL [JLE 86-4519]***

Partnerschaft in der sozialen Marktwirtschaft : Kooperation statt Konfrontation / Reinhold Biskup (Herausgeber). Bern : P. Haupt, c1986. 367 p. ; 23 cm. (Beiträge zur Wirtschaftspolitik. Bd. 45) Includes bibliographical references and index. ISBN 3-258-03604-7 LC Card 86-226613 DDC 330.943/087 19
1. Germany, West - Economic conditions - 1974-. 2. Switzerland - Economic conditions - 1945-. 3. Economic development. I. Biskup, Reinhold.
HC286.7 .P37 1986

Partnerschaftliche Entwicklungspolitik im Widerstreit der Interessen : neue Formen der Kooperation mit der Dritten Welt : Jahrestagung 1985 / herausgegeben für den Interdisziplinären Arbeitskreis für Entwicklungsländerforschung e.V. vom Institut für Entwicklungsforschung und Entwicklungspolitik der Ruhr-Universität Bochum ; Redaktion, E.-A. v. Renesse. Bochum-Querenburg : Das Institut, 1985. i, 184 leaves ; 30 cm. (IAFEF Texte . 1/85) Includes bibliographical references. CONTENTS. - Partnerschaftliche Entwicklungspolitik im Widerstreit der Interessen / Köhler, Volkmar -- Der Politikdialog / Benecke, Dieter -- Internationale Produktionskooperation / Uhlig, Christian -- Analyse und Schlussfolgerungen von neueren Untersuchungen über den Technologietransfer von deutschen Unternehmen in Entwicklungsländern / Menck, Karl Wolfgang -- Die Genossenschaften als Ausbildungsinstrument / Trappe, Paul -- Formen der Kooperation mit der Dritten Welt auf dem Gebiet der Agrarforschung und der Ausbildung / Basler, Alois -- Erfahrungen in der Vorbereitung von Führungskräften für den Einsatz in der Dritten Welt / Löber, Hanns-Georg -- Qualifizierung von Fach- und Führungskräften in Grossfirmen über den Einsatz in der Dritten Welt / Braun, Wilhelm. LC Card 87-409475 DDC 332.6/7343/01724 19
1. Investments, West German - Developing countries. 2. Technology transfer - Developing countries. I. Renesse, Ernst Albrecht von. II. Interdisziplinärer Arbeitskreis für Entwicklungsländerforschung (Germany). III. Ruhr-Universität Bochum. Institut für Entwicklungsforschung und Entwicklungspolitik. IV. Title: Jahrestagung 1985. V. Series: IAFEF Texte , 85/1.
HG5993 .P37 1985

The Partnership. New York City Partnership. New York, N.Y. , c1986. 44 p. : LC Card 86-223138 DDC 380.1/06/07471 19
HF296.N4 N48 1986

PARTNERSHIP - AUSTRIA - FINANCE.
Pernsteiner, August W. Gestaltkonforme partnerschaftliche "Beteiligungs-" und "Kreditfinanzierung" von "Klein-" und "Mittelbetrieben" /. Wien , 1983. 355, xxx p. : ISBN 3-85369-536-1 LC Card 83-206156
HG4027.7 .P47 1983

PARTNERSHIP - GERMANY, WEST.
Stauf, Wolfgang. Der wichtige Grund bei der personengesellschaftlichen Auflösungs- und Ausschliessungsklage . Göttingen , 1980. xiv, 80 p. ; ISBN 3-88415-549-0 : LC Card 80-150978 DDC 346.73/07 347.3067 19
KK2435.7 .S7 1980 ***NYPL [JLD 86-1591]***

Partsch, Manfred. Prinzipien und Formen sozialer Sicherung in nicht-industriellen Gesellschaften / von Manfred Partsch. Berlin : Duncker & Humblot, c1983. 168 p. ; 24 cm. (Sozialpolitische Schriften. Heft 48) Originally presented as the author's thesis (doctoral--Universität Augsburg) Bibliography: p. [159]-168. ISBN 3-428-05484-9 LC Card 84-148527 DDC 368.4/009172/4 19
1. Social security - Developing countries. 2. Industrialization. 3. Kinship - Developing countries. 4. Old age pensions - Developing countries. I. Title.
HD7252 .P37 1983 ***NYPL [JLE 85-1238]***

PARTY AFFILIATION - GERMANY (WEST) - BAVARIA.
Gesellschaftliches Selbstverständnis und politische Orientierung der Freien Berufe . Nürnberg , 1978. 144 p. : LC Card 86-170378
HD8038.G32 B384 1978

PARTY AFFILIATION - ITALY - VENETO.
Operai e scelte politiche . Milano, Italy , c1986. 267 p., 45 p. of plates : LC Card 86-169148
HD8439.V462 O64 1986

The party and agricultural crisis management in the USSR /. Kaplan, Cynthia Sue. Ithaca , 1987. xvi, 203 p ; ISBN 0-8014-2021-0 (alk. paper) LC Card 86-32223 DDC 338.1/847 19
HD1993 .K36 1987

PARTY COMMITTEES - ESTONIA.
Luukas, Ants. [Majandi parteigrupid. Russian.] Partiĭnye gruppy v kolkhozakh i sovkhozakh /. Tallin , 1984. 77 p., [8] p. of plates : LC Card 87-115056
HD1492.S652 E85517 1984

Parvathamma, C., 1928-
Housing, rural poor, and their living conditions / C. Parvathamma, Satyanarayana. Delhi, India : Gian Pub. House, [1987] vi, 135 p. ; 22 cm. Study of Karnataka. Bibliography: p. [126]-131. Includes index. ISBN 81-212-0088-1 : LC Card 87-900831 DDC 363.5/8 19
1. Housing - India - Karnataka. 2. Rural poor - India - Karnataka. 3. Homelessness - India - Karnataka. I. Satyanarayana. II. Title.
HD7361.K27 P37 1987

Scheduled castes and tribes : a socio-economic survey / C. Parvathamma ; foreword, V.K.R.V. Rao. New Delhi : Ashish, 1984. xiii, 310 p. ; 23 cm. Includes index. Bibliography: p. 297-307.
1. Caste - India - Karnataka. 2. Untouchables - Social conditions. 3. Untouchables - Economic conditions. 4. India - Scheduled tribes - Social conditions. 5. India - Scheduled tribes - Economic conditions. I. Title.
NYPL [JLD 87-707]

Pasang surut pengusaha pejuang . Ning, Hasjim, 1916- Jakarta , 1986. x, 392 p., [1] leaf of plates : LC Card 86-944750
HC446.5.N56 A3 1986

Pasay, Janice L. The effect of the western accord and recent provincial royalty changes on petroleum industry capital expenditures / prepared by Janice L. Pasay. Calgary, Alta. : Canadian Energy Research Institute, 1986. iv, 27, 4 leaves ; 29 cm. (Research report . 86-1) Includes bibliographies. LC Card 86-203742 DDC 338.2/3 19
1. Petroleum industry and trade - Canada - Capital investments. 2. Oil and gas leases - Canada - Provinces. 3. Petroleum industry and trade - Government policy - Canada, Western. I. Series: Research report (Canadian Energy Research Institute) , 86-1. II. Title.
HD9574.C22 P37 1986

Pascha, Werner. Strukturanpassung in schrumpfenden Branchen : Japans Textilindustrie vor dem Hintergrund veränderter Wettbewersbsvorteile / von Werner Pascha. Berlin : Duncker & Humblot, c1986. xx, 364 p. : ill. ; 24 cm. (Schriften zu Regional- und Verkehrsproblemen in Industrie- und Entwicklungsländern. Bd. 42) Bibliography: p. 349-364. ISBN 3-428-05983-2 LC Card 86-151590
1. Textile industry - Japan. . 2. Competition, International. I. Title. II. Series.
HB41 .S3 Bd. 42 HD9866.J32

Paschoal Rossetti, José. see **Rossetti, José Paschoal, 1941-**

Pascoe, George. Weiss, Leonard W. The extent and permanence of market dominance /. Berlin [1984] 30, 7 p. ; LC Card 85-183107 DDC 338.8/2 19
HD2757.3 .W45 1984

Pascon, Paul.
[Haouz de Marrakech. English]
Capitalism and agriculture in the Haouz of Marrakesh / Paul Pascon ; translated by C. Edwin Vaughan and Veronique Ingman ; edited with an introduction to the English edition by John R. Hall. London ; New York : KPI ; 248 p. : ill. ; 23 cm. Translation of: Le Haouz de Marrakech. Bibliography: p. [233]-242. Includes index. ISBN 0-7103-0189-8 LC Card 87-100309 DDC 338.1/0964/6 19
1. Agriculture - Economic aspects - Morocco - Marrakesh Region - History. 2. Agriculture - Morocco - Marrakesh Region - History. 3. Capitalism - Morocco - Marrakesh Region - History. 4. Marrakesh Region (Morocco) - Economic conditions. I. Hall, John R. II. Title.
HD2121.Z9 M37613 1986

Pascual, Julio, 1944- En defensa de la empresa : alegato en crónica, 1976-1984 / Julio Pascual. Madrid : Unión Editorial, c1984. 242 p. ; 22 cm. Includes bibliographical references. ISBN 84-7209-175-9 LC Card 85-215607
1. Industry and state - Spain. 2. Trade and professional associations - Spain. I. Title.
HD3616.S49 P34 1984
NYPL [JLD 87-1507]

Pasewark, William Robert. Willis, Jerry, 1942- Working with SuperCalc 4 /. Blue Ridge Summit, PA , c1987. x, 320 p. : ISBN 0-8306-0214-3 : LC Card 86-30124 DDC 005.36/9 19
HF5548.4.S87 W54 1987

Pasework, William Robert. Willis, Jerry. SuperCalc 3 . Blue Ridge Summit, Pa. , 1986. vi, 248 p. : ISBN 0-8306-0494-4 : LC Card 86-5743 DDC 005.36/9 19
HF5548.4.S86 W55 1986
NYPL [JSE 87-265]

Pashko, A. A. Vklad severnogo krest'īanstva v material'nuīu i dukhovnuīu kul'turu i ego znachenie v reshenii problem agropromyshlennogo kompleksa nechernozemnoĭ zony RSFSR . Vologda , 1984. 93 p. ; LC Card 85-156518
HD9015.S652 V54 1984

Pasinetti, Luigi L. La ricchezza della nazioni / Luigi Pasinetti. Napoli : Guida, c1985. 35 p. ; 21 cm. (Interventi. 27) ISBN 88-7042-841-9 : LC Card 86-196264
1. Economics - History. 2. Economic history. I. Series: Interventi (Guida editori) , 27. II. Title.
HB75 .P27 1985

Paskaleva-Zakharieva, Virzhinii͡a. Sredna Evropa i zemite po Dolnii͡a Dunav prez XVIII-XIX v. : sotsialno-ikonomicheski aspekti / Virzhinii͡a Paskaleva. Sofii͡a : Izd-vo na Bŭlgarskata akademii͡a na naukite, 1986. 317 p. : ill. ; 25 cm. Titles on added t.p.: T͡Sentral'nai͡a Evropa i zemli vdol' Nizhnego Dunai͡a v XVIII i XIX vekakh; Mitteleuropa und die Landen [sic] am unteren Donaulauf im 18. und 19. Jahrhundert. At head of title: Bŭlgarska akademii͡a na naukite. Institut za istorii͡a. Summary in German and Russian. Bibliography: p. 284-293. LC Card 86-219994
1. Central Europe - Economic conditions. 2. Danube River Valley - Economic conditions. 3. Central Europe - Social conditions. 4. Danube River Valley - Social conditions. I. Title. II. Title: T͡Sentral'nai͡a Evropa i zemli vdol' Nizhnego Dunai͡a v XVIII i XIX vekakh. III. Title: Mitteleuropa und die Länder am unteren Donaulauf im 18. und 19. Jahrhundert.
HC244 .P29 1986

Pasko, P. F. Spravochnik rukovoditeli͡a srednego zvena kolkhoza, sovkhoza /. Minsk , 1981. 518 p. ; LC Card 82-147885
HD1492.S65 S67 1981

Pasquet, Sylvie. L'évolution du système postal : la province chinoise du Yunnan à l'époque Qing, 1644-1911 / Sylvie Pasquet. Paris : Collège de France, Institut des hautes études chinoises, c1986. 290 p. : ill., maps ; 25 cm. (Mémoires de l'Institut des hautes études chinoises . v. 28) Revision of thesis (doctoral)--Ecole des hautes études en sciences sociales, 1983. Bibliography: p. [259]-268. Includes index. ISBN 2-85757-038-4 LC Card 87-164960
1. Postal service - China - Yunnan Province - History. I. Title. II. Series.
HE7286.Y8 P37 1986

Passell, Peter. Where to put your money, 1987 / Peter Passell. New York, NY : Warner Books, c1987. 82 p. ; 21 cm. ISBN 0-446-38497-6 (pbk.) : LC Card 86-28917 DDC 332.6/78 19
1. Finance, Personal - United States. 2. Investments - United States. 3. Bank accounts - United States. I. Title.
HG179 .P27 1987

Passi, Michael M. Poverty in the State of Nevada : its extent and distribution / principal authors, Michael M. Passi and John B. Walker. Carson City, Nev. (1100 E. William St., Suite 117, Carson City 89710) : State of Nevada, Office of Community Services, [1986] [11] leaves, 69, 16 p., [1] leaf of plates : ill. ; 28 cm. "March, 1986." LC Card 86-622269 DDC 330.9793/033/08806942 19
1. Poor - Nevada. 2. Nevada - Population. 3. Nevada - Economic conditions. I. Nevada. Office of Community Services. II. Title.
HC107.N33 P623 1986

Passing the baton . Vancil, Richard F. Boston, Mass. , c1987. xxii, 318 p. : ISBN 0-87584-182-1 LC Card 87-11962 DDC 658.4 19
HD38.25.U6 V36 1987

Passing the buck . Wellons, Philip A. Boston, Mass. , c1987. xiv, 342 p. : ISBN 0-87584-146-5 (alk. paper) LC Card 86-19508 DDC 332.1/53 19
HG3891.5 .W46 1987 ***NYPL [JLE 87-1072]***

The passionate investors . Talley, Madelon DeVoe. New York , c1987. 260 p. : ISBN 0-517-56563-3 : LC Card 86-24281 DDC 332.63/22 19
HG4521 .T29 1987

Past masters.
Winch, Donald. Malthus /. Oxford , New York , 1987. 117 p. ; ISBN 0-19-287653-8 : LC Card 87-11179 DDC 330.15/3 19
HB863 .W56 1987

Pasta, David. Shorter, Frederic Claiborne. Computational methods for population projections . New York , 1987, c1974. vii, 192 p. : ISBN 0-87834-056-4 (pbk.) LC Card 87-9303 DDC 304.6/2/0285 19
HB849.53 .S54 1987

PASTIMES. see **GAMES.**

Pastor Antolín, Luis J., 1958- La red de transporte en Castilla y León / Luis J. Pastor Antolín. Valladolid : Ambito, [1986?] 161 p. : ill., maps ; 18 cm. (Colección Ambito Castilla y León . 35) Bibliography: p. 155-161. ISBN 84-86047-71-4 LC Card 86-231524
1. Roads - Spain - Castilla y León. 2. Railroads - Spain - Castilla y León. I. Title. II. Series.
HE363.S64 C376 1986

Pastor, Manuel. The International Monetary Fund and Latin America : economic stabilization and class conflict / Manuel Pastor, Jr. Boulder, Colo. : Westview Press, 1987. xvi, 228 p. : ill. ; 23 cm. (Series in political economy and economic development in Latin America) Bibliography: p. 209-219. Includes index. ISBN 0-8133-7373-5 (pbk. : alk. paper) : LC Card 86-32575 DDC 332.4/98 19
1. Monetary policy - Latin America. 2. Economic stabilization - Latin America. 3. International Monetary Fund - Latin America. 4. Debts, External - Latin America. I. Title. II. Series.
HG660.5 .P33 1987

Pastor, Robert A. Latin America's debt crisis . Boulder, Colo. , 1987. xiii, 176 p. ; ISBN 1-555-87053-8 (lib. bdg. : alk. paper) : LC Card 87-4956 DDC 336.3/435/098 19
HJ8514.5 .L395 1987

Pastoral economics in the Kingdom of Naples /. Marino, John A. Baltimore , c1988. xii, 381 p. : ISBN 0-8018-3437-6 (alk. paper) LC Card 87-9196 DDC 338.1/763145/09457 19
HD9905.I73 N366 1988

PASTORS. see **CLERGY.**

Pastré, Olivier.
L'informatisation et l'emploi / Olivier Pastré. Paris : La Découverte/Maspero, 1983. 127 p. : ill. ; 18 cm. (Collection Repères . 1.) Bibliography: p. 121-124. ISBN 2-7071-1387-5 LC Card 83-161919 DDC 331.12/0944 19
1. Labor supply - France - Effect of automation on. 2. Automation - Economic aspects - France. 3. Automation - Social aspects - France. 4. Unemployment, Technological - France. I. Series: Collection Repères , 1. II. Title.
HD6331.2.F8 P37 1983

La modernisation des banques françaises : rapport remis à Daniel Lebègue, directeur du Trésor / par Olivier Pastré. Paris : Documentation française, [1985] 234 p. : ill. ; 24 cm. (Collection des rapports officiels) At head of title: Ministère de l'économie, des finances et du budget. "Novembre 1985." ISBN 2-11-001537-3 : LC Card 86-179536
1. Banks and banking - France. I. France. Direction du trésor. II. France. Ministère de l'économie, des finances et du budget. III. Title. IV. Series.
HG3026 .P37 1985

PASTURE, RIGHT OF - UNITED STATES - HISTORY.
West, Patrick C. Natural resource bureaucracy and rural poverty . Ann Arbor, MI , c1982. xiii, 168 p. : LC Card 83-102928 DDC 333.7/16/0973 19
HD1761 .W423 1982 ***NYPL [JLE 86-4095]***

PASTURES - AUSTRALIA - WESTERN AUSTRALIA.
Western Australia. Pastoral Tenure Study Group. Final report on pastoral land tenure. Perth, W.A. [1986] [28], 63, 4 p. ; LC Card 87-120095 DDC 333.3/09941 19
HD1641.A9 W47 1986

Pastuszek, Rainer. Leading und Lagging kurzfristig variierbarer gruppeninterner Geldflüsse im Währungsrisikomanagement einer internationalen Unternehmung / Rainer Pastuszek. Pfaffenweiler : Centaurus-Verlagsgesellschaft, 1986. xvi, 275 p. : ill. ; 21 cm. (Reihe Wirtschaftswissenschaften, 0177-283X . Bd. 26) Cover title: Kurzfristiges Leading und Lagging gruppeninterner Geldflüsse. Bibliography: p. 267-275. ISBN 3-89085-122-3 LC Card 87-128258 DDC 658.1/55 19
1. Foreign exchange problem. 2. Risk. 3. Capital market. 4. International business enterprises - Finance. I. Title. II. Title: Kurzfristiges Leading und Lagging gruppeninterner Geldflüsse. III. Series: Reihe Wirtschaftswissenschaften (Pfaffenweiler, Breisgau-Hochschwarzwald, Germany) , Bd. 26.
HG3851 .P295 1986

Pataki, Judit. Közvéleménykutatás népesedési kérdésekről / irták, Pataki Judit, S. Molnár Edit. Budapest : Központi Statisztikai Hivatal, Népességtudományi Kutató Intézet, c1985. 75 p. ; 29 cm. (A Központi Statisztikai Hivatal Népességtudományi Kutató Intézetének és a Magyar Tudományos Akadémia Demográfiai Bizottságának közleményei, 0134-0093 . 60) Includes bibliographical references. LC Card 86-166976
1. Hungary - Population - Public opinion. 2. Family size - Hungary - Public opinion. 3. Public opinion - Hungary. I. Molnár, Edit S. II. Title. III. Series.
HA1201 .A64 no. 60 HB3592.5.A3

Patankar, P. G. Road passenger transport in India / P.G. Patankar. Pune : Central Institute of Road Transport (Training and Research), [1985?] xi, 226 p., [4] p. of plates : ill. ; 25 cm. LC Card 85-905215 DDC 388/.042/0954 19
1. Transportation - India - Passenger traffic. 2. Bus lines - India. I. Title.
HE365.I43 B86 1985 ***NYPL [JLE 86-4230]***

Patel, I. G. (Indraprasad Gordhanbhai), 1924- Essays in economic policy and economic growth / I.G. Patel. Basingstoke, Hampshire : Macmillan, 1986. xii, 261 p. ; 23 cm. Includes bibliographical references and index. ISBN 0-333-39213-2
1. Economic policy - Addresses, essays, lectures. 2. Economic development - Addresses, essays, lectures. 3. India - Economic policy - 1947- - Addresses, essays, lectures. I. Title. ***NYPL [JLD 86-4061]***

Patera, Alan H. Ramsey, Guy Reed. Postmarked Washington . Lake Grove, OR (Box 2093, Lake Grove 97035) , c1987. 148 p. : LC Card 86-72305 DDC 383/.4979791 19
HE6376.A1 W265 1987

Patera, Mario, 1946- Perspektiven der Genossenschaftsrevision . Wien , 1986. x, 322 p. : ISBN 3-85368-775-X LC Card 87-138767 DDC 334/.09436 19
HD3490 .P47 1986

PATERNALISM - UNITED STATES - HISTORY - CASE STUDIES.
Zahavi, Gerald, 1951- Workers, managers, and welfare capitalism . Urbana , c1988. xiii, 261 p., [14] p. of plates : ISBN 0-252-01444-8 (alk. paper) LC Card 87-6035 DDC 331.2/0475/0973 19
HD9787.U6 E654 1988

Paterson, Martin, 1927- Pensions : agenda for change : planning and implementing pension choices after 1988 / Martin Paterson. Cambridge, England ; Wolfeboro, N.H., USA, : Woodhead-Faulkner, 1988. p. cm. ISBN 0-85941-380-2 : LC Card 87-8324 DDC 331.25/2/0941 19
1. Old age pensions - Great Britain. 2. Old age pensions - Law and legislation - Great Britain. I. Title.
HD7105.35.G7 P38 1988

PATERSON (N.J.) - ECONOMIC CONDITIONS.
Tripp, Anne Huber, 1934- The I.W.W. and the Paterson silk strike of 1913 /. Urbana , c1987. xiv, 317 p., [6] p. of plates : ISBN 0-252-01382-4 LC Card 86-24989 DDC 331.89/287739/0974924 19
HD5325.T42 1913 .P387 1987

Paterson, William. Bulmer, Simon. The Federal Republic of Germany and The European community /. London , Boston , 1987. p. cm. ISBN 0-04-382045-X (alk. paper) LC Card 86-25909 DDC 341.24/22 19
HC241.25.G3 B86 1987

Patersoune, Williame. see **Paterson, William.**

Pāṭhaka, Śekhara, 1951- Uttarākhaṇḍa meṃ kulī begāra prathā : eka śoshaka prathā aura usake viruddha hue jana-āndolana kā adhyayana / Śekhara Pāṭhaka.1. saṃskaraṇa. Nayī Dillī : Rādhākṛshṇa, 1987, c1986. 339 p., [16] p. of plates : ill., [2] maps (some folded), ports. ; 23 cm. In Hindi. Originally presented as the author's thesis (Ph. D.--Kumāūṁ Viśvavidyālaya, 1980) Peonage, forced labor, and the popular movements in Uttarākhaṇḍa (northern hill region of Uttar Pradesh) during the British period; a historical study. Bibliography: p. [311]-336. Includes index. LC Card 87-902810
1. Peasantry - India - Uttarkhand Region - History. 2. Forced labor - India - Uttarkhand Region - History. 3. Peonage - India - Uttarkhand Region - History. I. Title.
HD1537.I4 P38 1987

Paths to paradise . Gorz, André. [Chemins du paradis. English.] London , 1985. vii, 120 p. ; ISBN 0-86104-762-1 (pbk.) :
NYPL [JLD 86-3006]

Paths to profits /. Grover, Subhash C. (Shubash Chander), 1938- Dallas , 1985. v, 142 p. ; ISBN 0-930383-04-4 (pbk.) : LC Card 84-25548 DDC 650.1 19
HD62.7 .G75 1985 ***NYPL [JLD 86-1907]***

Paths to progress . McCord, William Maxwell, 1930- New York , c1986. 352 p. ; ISBN 0-393-02307-9 : LC Card 85-29809 DDC 330.9172/4 19
HC59.7 .M358 1986 ***NYPL [JLD 86-3487]***

Pathways through data processing, small business systems. 2nd ed., rev. Cherry Hill, N.J. (140 Barclay Center, Cherry Hill 08034) : Management Information Corp., c1980. 182 p. : ill. ; 28 cm. LC Card 81-118723 DDC 001.64/04/029473 19
1. Small business - Data processing. 2. Minicomputers - Purchasing. 3. Computers - Purchasing. 4. Computer industry - United States - Directories. I. Management Information Corporation.
HF5548.2 P295 1980 ***NYPL [JLF 86-351]***

Pathy, Jaganath, 1948- Tribal peasantry dynamics of development / Jaganath Pathy. New Delhi : Inter-India Publications, 1984, c1983. xiii, 233 p. : map ; 22 cm. Includes index. Bibliography: p. [215]-229. LC Card 84-900095 DDC 330.954/75052 19
1. Peasantry - India - Gujarat - Case studies. 2. Economic assistance, Domestic - India - Gujarat - Case studies. 3. Gujarat (India) - Scheduled tribes - Case studies. I. Title.
HD879.G8 P37 1984 ***NYPL [JLD 87-724]***

Patient monitoring disposables. Patient monitoring disposables and equipment for critical care. Tustin, CA (17722 Irvine Blvd., Tustin 92680) , c1986. 1 v. (various foliations) : LC Card 86-203049 DDC 381/.45681761 19
HD9995.M653 U657 1986

PATIENT MONITORING EQUIPMENT INDUSTRY - UNITED STATES.
Patient monitoring disposables and equipment for critical care. Tustin, CA (17722 Irvine Blvd., Tustin 92680) , c1986. 1 v. (various foliations) : LC Card 86-203049 DDC 381/.45681761 19
HD9995.M653 U657 1986

Pāṭila, Narendra. Āvhāna āṇi āvāhana / Narendra Pāṭila ; sampādana, Sureśa Nagarsekara. Prathamāvṛttī. Mumbaī : Vidyānanda Prakāśana, 1986. 110 p., [13] p. of plates : ill., ports. ; 23 cm. In Marathi. Articles on post-independence economic situation in Maharashtra. LC Card 87-900853
1. Maharashtra (India) - Economic conditions. I. Nagarsekara, Sureśa. II. Title.
HC437.M32 P38 1986

Patiño, Víctor Manuel. Los recursos naturales de Colombia : aproximación y retrospectiva / Víctor Manuel Patiño.1a ed. Bogotá : C. Valencia Editores, 1980. 149 p. : ill. ; 21 cm. Includes bibliographies. ISBN 84-8277-057-8 LC Card 86-208425 DDC 333.7/09861 19
1. Natural resources - Colombia. I. Title.
HC197.5 .P3 1980

Patkoló, Károly. Budapesti pedagógusok közlekedési oktatási és nevelési konferenciája . [Budapest , 1978] ([Budapest] :fKészült az MTI Sokszorosító Üzemében) 100 p. ; LC Card 82-204792
HE5614 .B78 1978

Patmut'yan Institut (Haykakan SSR Gitut'yunneri Akademia). Gyughatntesut'yan ev Gyughats'iut'yan Patmut'yan Handznazhoghov. Nyut'er Hayastani gyughatntesut'yan ev gyughats'iut'yan patmut'yan /. Erevan , 1964- v. <1 > : LC Card 86-225528
HD1995.A7 N98 1964

Patnaik, Utsa. The agrarian question and the development of capitalism in India / Utsa Patnaik. Delhi ; New York : Oxford University Press, 1986. 45 p. ; 23 cm. "The first Daniel Thorner memorial lecture, 1985, under the auspices of the Indian Statistical Institute, New Delhi." Bibliography: p. 38-45. ISBN 0-19-561954-4 : LC Card 86-900017 DDC 338.1/0954 19
1. Agriculture - Economic aspects - India. 2. Capitalism - India. I. Title. II. Title: Daniel Thorner memorial lecture.
HD2072 .P33 1986

Pătrăşcanu, Lucreţiu, 1900-1954. Scrieri, articole, cuvîntări : 1944-1947 / Lucreţiu Pătrăşcanu. Bucureşti : Editura Politică, 1983. 415 p. ; 21 cm. At head of title: Institutul de Studii Istorice şi Social-Politice de pe lîngă C.C. al P.C.R. Includes bibliographical references. LC Card 84-144088
1. Romania - Economic conditions - 1945- - Collected works. 2. Romania - Politics and government - 1944- - Collected works. 3. Marxian economics - Collected works. I. Institutul de Studii Istorice şi Social-Politice de pe lîngă C.C. al P.C.R. II. Title.
HC405 .P345 1983

Patriarchy and accumulation on a world scale . Mies, Maria. London , Atlantic Highlands, NJ , 1986. 251 p. ; ISBN 0-86232-341-X LC Card 86-18916 DDC 305.4 19
HD6060.6 .M54 1986 ***NYPL [JLD 86-3206]***

Patriarchy at work . Walby, Sylvia. Cambridge [Cambrigeshire] , c1986. vii, 292 p. ; ISBN 0-7456-0157-X ***NYPL [JLD 87-941]***

Patriarchy at work . Walby, Sylvia. Minneapolis , c1986. vii, 292 p. ; ISBN 0-8166-1588-8 : LC Card 86-24912 DDC 331.4/133/0941 19
HD6060.65.G7 W35 1986

PATRIARCHY - DENMARK.
Borchorst, Anette. Arbejdsmarkedets kønsopdeling . Aalborg , 1984. 162 p. : ISBN 87-7307-252-4 LC Card 85-106008
HD6060.65.D4 B67 1984
NYPL [JFK 82-214 nr.15]

PATRIARCHY - EUROPE, NORTHERN - HISTORY.
Howell, Martha C. Women, production, and patriarchy in late medieval cities /. Chicago , 1986. xv, 285 p. ; ISBN 0-226-35503-9 : LC Card 85-31816 DDC 331.4/094 19
HD6134 .H69 1986 ***NYPL [JLE 86-4284]***

PATRIARCHY - GREAT BRITAIN.
Walby, Sylvia. Patriarchy at work . Cambridge [Cambrigeshire] , c1986. vii, 292 p. ; ISBN 0-7456-0157-X ***NYPL [JLD 87-941]***

Walby, Sylvia. Patriarchy at work . Minneapolis , c1986. vii, 292 p. ; ISBN 0-8166-1588-8 : LC Card 86-24912 DDC 331.4/133/0941 19
HD6060.65.G7 W35 1986

Patrick, Hugh T.
Japan and the United States today . New York , 1986, c1987. vii, 234 p. : ISBN 0-231-06575-2 LC Card 86-32640 DDC 332/.042/0952 19
HG3903 .J35 1987

The Political economy of Japan. Stanford, Calif. , 1987- v. <1 > : ISBN 0-8047-1380-4 (v. 1 : alk. paper) : LC Card 86-30037 DDC 338.952 19
HC462.9 .P57 1987

PATRIOTISM - MEXICO.
Serrano Illescas, Alfonso. Pobre patria! /. México, D.F. , 1982. 132 p. ; ISBN 968-409-161-3 LC Card 85-122377
HC135 .S368 1982

Pătroiu, Ion. La cumpăna a două epoci, 1849-1877 / Ion Pătroiu. Craiova : Scrisul Românesc, 1983. 316 p. ; 21 cm. Summary in English, French, German, Russian, and Spanish. Table of contents in English, French, German, Romanian, Russian, and Spanish. Includes bibliographical references and index. LC Card 84-234959
1. Land reform - Romania - Oltenia - History - 19th century. 2. Agriculture - Economic aspects - Romania - Oltenia - History - 19th century. 3. Peasantry - Romania - Oltenia - History - 19th century. I. Title.
HD1333.R62 O475 1983

La patronal agraria . González Rodríguez, Juan Jesús. Madrid [1986?] 46 p. ; ISBN 84-7075-335-3 LC Card 87-111477
HD6976.A292 S74 1986

Patroni Griffi, Filena. Il banco di pegni di Cava dei Tirreni del 1495 / Filena Patroni Griffi. Cava dei Tirreni : Avagliano, c1985. 149 p., [8] p. of plates : ill. ; 24 cm. Bibliography: p. 123-147. LC Card 86-195753
1. Pawnbroking - Italy - Cava de' Tirreni - History. 2. Banks and banking - Italy - Cava de' Terreni - History. I. Title.
HG2106.I83 C386 1985

Les patrons et le patronat /. Chotard, Yvon, 1921- [Paris] , c1986. 231 p. ; ISBN 2-7021-1538-1 : LC Card 87-167099
HD6948.F8 C46 1986

The Pattern & problems of population in north-east India / editor, B. Datta Ray. New Delhi : Uppal Pub. House, 1986. xv, 433 p. ; 23 cm. Papers of the Seminar on Pattern and Problems of Population in North-East India: a Multidimensional Study, organized by the North-East India Council for Social Science Research, Shillong, 7-8 December 1984. Includes bibliographies. ISBN 81-85024-03-0 : LC Card 86-902123 DDC 304.6/0954/1 19
1. India, Northeastern - Population - Congresses. 2. Manpower planning - India, Northeastern - Congresses. I. Datta-Ray, B., 1925-. II. North-East India Council for Social Science Research. III. Title: Pattern and problems of population in north-east India.
HA4587.I44 P37 1986

Pattern and problems of population in north-east India. The Pattern & problems of population in north-east India /. New Delhi , 1986. xv, 433 p. ; ISBN 81-85024-03-0 : LC Card 86-902123 DDC 304.6/0954/1 19
HA4587.I44 P37 1986

Pattern for industrial peace /. Whyte, William Foote, 1914- New York , 1987, c1951. ix, 245 p. : ISBN 0-8240-8227-3 (alk. paper) : LC Card 86-25790 DDC 331.89/0469142/0977/311 19
HD6515.I52 C48 1987

Pattern of land ownership and backwardness . Shankar, Kripa. New Delhi , 1986. x, 119 p. ; ISBN 81-7024-021-2 : LC Card 87-900130 DDC 333.3/23/09542 19
HD879.J37 S5 1986

Pattern of land utilization in Assam /. Bora, Ajit Kumar, 1942- Delhi , 1986. x, 203 p. ; ISBN 81-7049-012-X : LC Card 86-902810 DDC 333.73/13/0954162 19
HD873 .B67 1986

Patterns of development in Latin America . Sheahan, John, 1923- Princeton, N.J. , c1987. x, 399 p. : ISBN 0-691-07735-5 (alk. paper) : LC Card 87-2853 DDC 338.98 19
HC125 .S498 1987

Patterns of energy consumption in Florida, 1970-1983 . Llewellyn, Ralph A. Tallahassee, Fla. [1985] xiv, 147 p. : LC Card 86-622312 DDC 333.79/13/09759 19
HD9502.U53 F5846 1985

Patterns of migration and settlement in rural South Africa /. Cilliers, S. P. [Stellenbosch] , 1986. 19, 13 leaves, 5 folded leaves of plates : ISBN 0-908422-81-4 (pbk.) : LC Card 87-126315 DDC 304.8/0968 19
HB2123.4.A3 C56 1986

Patterns of property tax administration in the United States /. Clatanoff, Robert M. Chicago, Ill. , 1986. x, 178 p. : ISBN 0-88329-145-2 (pbk.) LC Card 86-7240 DDC 353.9/37242 19
HJ4120 .C528 1986 ***NYPL [JLF 87-464]***

Patterns of worker's behavior and the enterprise /. Héthy, Lajos. New Brunswick, U. S.A. , c1987. p. cm. ISBN 0-88738-177-4 LC Card 87-13958 DDC 331/.0471/09439 19
HD6956.M5 H47 1987

Patterson, Marc. Wickham, Alexandre. Les carriéristes . Paris , c1983. 358 p. ; ISBN 2-85956-348-2 : LC Card 84-122542 DDC 650.1/4 19
HF5386 .W494 1983 ***NYPL [JLE 86-4124]***

Patti, Charles H. Advertising : a decision-making approach / Charles H. Patti, Charles F. Frazer. Chicago : Dryden Press, c1988. xxxi, 590 p. : ill. (some col.) ; 26 cm. (The Dryden Press series in marketing) Includes bibliographies and indexes. ISBN 0-03-071687-X LC Card 87-6898 DDC 659.1/11 19
1. Advertising. 2. Advertising - Decision making. I. Frazer, Charles F. II. Title.
HF5821 .P27 1988

Patton, Carl V. Spontaneous shelter . Philadelphia , 1988. p. cm. ISBN 0-87722-507-9 (alk. paper) LC Card 87-10002 DDC 363.5/8/091724 19
HD7287.96.D44 S66 1988

Patton, Phil. Open road : a celebration of the American highway / Phil Patton. New York : Simon and Schuster, c1986. 304 p. : ill. ; 25 cm. Includes index. Bibliography: p. [283]-293. ISBN 0-671-53021-6 : LC Card 86-1832 DDC 388.1/0973 19
1. Roads - United States - History. 2. Roads - Social aspects - United States. I. Title.
HE355 .P38 1986 ***NYPL [JLE 86-2812]***

Patwardhan, M. S., 1927- Oil and other multinationals in India / M.S. Patwardhan. Bombay : Popular Prakashan, 1986. xvi, 171 p. : ill. ; 23 cm. Includes bibliographical references and index. LC Card 87-900107 DDC 338.8/87 19

1. Petroleum industry and trade - India. 2. International business enterprises - India. I. Title.
HD9576.I42 P37 1986

Patzig, Werner. Die Haushalte der Flächenländer unter Konsolidierungszwang /. Bonn , 1986. 159 p. ; LC Card 87-409459 DDC 332 s 336.43 19
HJ1120 .B65 Nr. 262

Pau, L.-F. (Louis-François), 1948- Artificial intelligence in economics and management /. Amsterdam ; New York : xv, 292 p. : ISBN 0-444-87961-7 LC Card 85-31139 DDC 330/.028/563 19
HB143.5 .A78 1986 ***NYPL [JLE 86-3612]***

Pauck, Reinhard. Mikroökonomische Modelle des städtischen Verkehrs : theoretische und empirische Grundlagen zur Analyse und Projektion der Verkehrsvorgänge in Städten / Reinhard Pauck.1. Aufl. Baden-Baden : Nomos Verlagsgesellschaft, 1983. 295 p. : ill. ; 23 cm. (Schriften zur öffentlichen Verwaltung und öffentlichen Wirtschaft. Bd. 69) Includes indexes. Bibliography: p. 279-288. ISBN 3-7890-0779-X LC Card 83-157997 DDC 388.4/0724 19
1. Urban transportation - Mathematical models. 2. City traffic - Mathematical models. I. Title.
HE305 .P39 1983 ***NYPL [JLD 87-977]***

Pauken, Joe. Re-tailing ain't easy / by Joe Pauken. Palm Bay, Fla. (2576 First Ave., Post Office Box 990, Palm Bay 32905) : Palm Press, c1985. 160 p., [1] p. of plates : ill. ; 22 cm. LC Card 86-232016 DDC 381/.1/0207 19
1. Retail trade - Caricatures and cartoons. I. Title.
HF5429 .P368 1985

Paukert, Liba. Garnsey, Elizabeth. Industrial change and women's employment . Geneva , 1987. ix, 100, x p. : ISBN 92-9014-411-4 (pbk.) : LC Card 87-163195 DDC 331.4/09172/4 19
HD6223 .G37 1987

Paul, D. Babu (Daniel Babu), 1941- A queen's story : five centuries of Cochin Port / D. Babu Paul. New Delhi : Vikas Pub. House, c1987. xix, 132 p. : ill. (some col.), [8] p. of plates ; 28 cm. Bibliography: p. 127-128. Includes index. ISBN 0-7069-3376-1 : LC Card 86-903827 DDC 387.1/0954/83 19
1. Cochin Port - History. 2. Kerala (India) - Social conditions. I. Title.
HE560.C56 P38 1987

Paul, E. C. (Erik Charles), 1937- Fisheries development and the food needs of Mauritius / by E.C. Paul. Rotterdam ; Boston : A.A. Balkema, 1987. vi, 216 p. : ill. ; 26 cm. Bibliography: p. 205-216. ISBN 90-6191-627-5 LC Card 87-170375 DDC 338.3/7270969/82 19
1. Fish trade - Mauritius. 2. Fishery policy - Mauritius. 3. Food supply - Government policy - Mauritius. I. Title.
HD9468.M452 P38 1987

Paul, Gordon W. Guiltinan, Joseph P. Marketing management . New York , c1988. xvi, 427 p. : ISBN 0-07-048929-7 : LC Card 87-23186 DDC 658.8 19
HF5415.13 .G84 1988

Paul, Jan-Peter. Ekonomiska sanktioner : fällstudie Rhodesia / Jan-Peter Paul. Helsingfors : Institutionen för ekonomisk geografi och ekonomisk politologi, [1985] 46 p. ; 30 cm. (Meddelanden från Svenska handelshögskolan, 0357-4598 = Swedish School of Economics and Business Administration working papers . 132 (1985)) "Februari 1985." Includes bibliographical references. ISBN 951-555-224-9 LC Card 85-212001
1. Economic sanctions - Zimbabwe. 2. Zimbabwe - Foreign economic relations. I. Series: Meddelanden fran Svenska handelshögskolan , 132. II. Title.
HF1613.5 .P38 1985

Paul, Joachim, 1956- Zur politischen Durchsetzungsfähigkeit einer ökologisch orientierten Marktwirtschaft : eine Analyse aus ökonomischer Sicht, dargestellt am Beispiel der Bundesrepublik Deutschland / Joachim Paul. Frankfurt am Main ; New York : P. Lang, c1986. xvii, 569 p. ; 21 cm. (Europäische Hochschulschriften. Reihe V, Volks- und Betriebswirtschaft, 0531-7339 . Bd. 757 = vol. 757 = vol. 757) Bibliography: p. 513-568. ISBN 3-8204-9810-9 LC Card 87-407614 DDC 363.7/056/0943 19
1. Environmental policy - Germany, West. 2. Germany (West) - Industries - Environmental aspects - Government policy. 3. Conservation of natural resources - Government policy - Germany (West). 4. Factory and trade waste - Environmental aspects - Government policy - Germany (West). I. Series: Europäische Hochschulschriften. Reihe V, Volks- und Betriebswirtschaft , Bd. 757. II. Title.
HC290.5.E5 P38 1986

Paul, Karen, 1944- Business environment and business ethics . Cambridge, Mass. , c1987. xi, 151 p. ; ISBN 0-88730-204-1 LC Card 87-3573 DDC 174/.4 19
HF5387 .B867 1987

Paul, Ronald N. The 101 best performing companies in America / Ronald N. Paul, James W. Taylor. Chicago, Ill. : Probus Pub. Co., c1986. vii, 382 p. ; 25 cm. Includes index. ISBN 0-917253-39-6 : LC Card 86-4947 DDC 338.7/4/0973 19
1. Corporations - United States - Case studies. 2. Efficiency, Industrial - United States - Case studies. 3. Success in business - United States - Case studies. 4. Organizational effectiveness - Case studies. I. Taylor, James Walter, 1933-. II. Title. III. Title: One hundred one best performing companies in America.
HD2785 .P38 1986 ***NYPL [JLE 86-3151]***

Paul, Samuel, 1930- Community participation in development projects : the World Bank experience / Samuel Paul. Washington, D.C. : World Bank, [1987]. v, 37 p. : ill. ; 28 cm. (World Bank discussion papers, 0259-210X . 6) Bibliography: p. 32-34. ISBN 0-8213-0886-6 (pbk.) LC Card 87-2183 DDC 338.9/009172/4 19
1. Economic development projects - Developing countries - Citizen participation - Case studies. 2. World Bank - Case studies. I. International Bank for Reconstruction and Development. II. Title. III. Series.
HD75.8 .P38 1987

Paula, Aldo de. Bellardi, Marta. Villas miseria . Buenos Aires , c1986. 157 p. : ISBN 950-25-1423-8 : LC Card 87-125510 DDC 307.3/36 19
HD7321.B9 B45 1986

Paulauskas, T͡S. T͡Sifrovye metody i algoritmy obrabotki signalov . Vil′ni͡us , 1986. 120 p. : LC Card 86-232937
HD38 .S715 vyp. 73 TK5102.5

Paulson, S. Lawrence. Reagan on energy : a special report / by S. Lawrence Paulson ; researched by Cheryl Hoffman. New York, NY (850 3rd Ave., New York 10022) : Oil Daily, 1981. 248 p. in various pagings ; 28 cm. (An Oil daily report) LC Card 82-111477 DDC 333.79/0973 19
1. Energy policy - United States. 2. Petroleum industry and trade - Government policy - United States. I. Hoffman, Cheryl. II. Title. III. Series.
HD9502.U52 P38 ***NYPL [JLF 87-368]***

Pauly, Louis W. Regulatory politics in Japan : the case of foreign banking / Louis W. Pauly. Ithaca, N.Y. : China-Japan Program, Cornell University, c1987. vi, 82 p. ; 22 cm. (Cornell University East Asia papers, 8756-5293 . no. 45) Bibliography: p. 73-82. ISBN 0-939657-45-7 (pbk.) LC Card 87-403245 DDC 332.1/5/0952 19
1. Banks and banking, Foreign - Japan. 2. Banks and banking, Foreign - Law and legislation - Japan. I. Title. II. Series.
HG3324 .P38 1987

Pauly, Mark V., 1941- The Economics of insurance regulation . Houndmills, Basingstoke, Hampshire , 1986. xi, 300 p. : ISBN 0-333-39684-7 ***NYPL [JLD 87-1100]***

PAUPERISM. see **POOR.**

Pautas para la confección de una política económica . Fontaine Talavera, Arturo. Santiago, Chile , 1984. 92 leaves : LC Card 86-177872
HC192 .F58 1984

La pauvreté intolérable . Nicolas, Jean-Pierre, 1941- Toulouse [1984] 208 p. : ISBN 2-86586-026-4 : LC Card 85-118841
HC280.P6 N53 1984

Pavanello, Mariano, 1944- Antropologia ed economia dell'artigianato artistico : il caso di Torre del Greco / Mariano Pavanello, Daniela Borgogni, Alessandra Romano ; a cura di Mariano Pavanello. Milano, Italy : F. Angeli, c1984. 183 p. : ill. ; 22 cm. (Collana di antropologia culturale e sociale) Serie "Studi e ricerche" ; 20 Includes bibliographies. LC Card 84-147193
1. Artisans - Italy - Torre del Greco. 2. Artists - Italy - Torre del Greco. 3. Torre del Greco (Italy) - Economic conditions. I. Borgogni, Daniela, 1949-. II. Romano, Alessandra, 1958-. III. Title.
HD2346.I82 T676 1984

PAVEMENT MARKINGS. see **ROAD MARKINGS.**

PAVEMENTS, ASPHALT CONCRETE - TESTING.
Benson, Fred C. Hot-mix pavement stability performance versus laboratory test results /. College Station, Tex. [1985] xi, 225 p. : LC Card 86-620969 DDC 380.5 s 625.8/5 19
HE203 .T43 no. 285-1 TE200

Roberts, Freddy L. Establishing material properties for thin asphalt concrete surfaces on granular bases /. College Station, Tex. [1985] xvi, 141 p. : LC Card 86-620971 DDC 380.5 s 625.8/5 19
HE203 .T43 no. 345-1 TE270

PAVEMENTS, FLEXIBLE - LIVE LOADS.
The Effect of tire pressures on flexible pavements /. College Station, Tex. , Springfield, Va. , 1985. viii, 235 p. : LC Card 86-622241 DDC 380.5 s 625.8 19
HE203 .T43 no. 372-1F TE270

PAVEMENTS - LIVE LOADS.
Roberts, Freddy L. Establishing material properties for thin asphalt concrete surfaces on granular bases /. College Station, Tex. [1985] xvi, 141 p. : LC Card 86-620971 DDC 380.5 s 625.8/5 19
HE203 .T43 no. 345-1 TE270

Pavia. Università. Dipartimento di ricerche aziendali.
Fruscio, Dario. Il sistema distributivo italiano . [Milano] , 1983. vii, 184 p. ; LC Card 83-233439 DDC 380.1/0945 19
HF5415.6 .F78 1983 ***NYPL [JLE 86-3650]***

Sviluppo della finanza internazionale e interdipendenza dei sistemi finanziari . [Italy] [1984] iv, 204 p. : ISBN 88-14-00203-7 : LC Card 84-238589 DDC 332/.042 19
HG205.S85 S85 1984 ***NYPL [JLE 86-482]***

Pavia. Università. Istituto di finanza. Collana.
(14) Ghessi, Giuseppe. La finanza pubblica in cifre, 1965-1983 /. Milano, Italy , c1985. 186 p. : LC Card 85-180958 DDC 336.45 19
HJ1185 .G43 1985 ***NYPL [JLF 87-249]***

(8) La Crisi delle partecipazioni statali, motivi e prospettive /. Milano , c1981. 240 p. ; ISBN 88-20-42148-8 : LC Card 81-200055
HC310.I53 C74 1981 ***NYPL [JLD 86-3503]***

PAVING. see **PAVEMENTS.**

Pavitt, Keith. Hanson, Philip. The comparative economics of research development in East and West . Chur, Switzerland , New York , c1987. viii, 101 ; ISBN 3-7186-0419-1 (pbk.) LC Card 87-23623 DDC 338/.06 19
HC79.T4 H355 1987

Pavlov, V. S. (Valentin Sergeevich) Finansovye plany i balansy v sisteme ėkonomicheskogo planirovanii͡a / V.S. Pavlov. Moskva : "Finansy", 1978. 238 p. ; 20 cm. Includes bibliographical references. LC Card 81-160805
1. Finance - Soviet Union. 2. Soviet Union - Economic policy - 1976-1980. I. Title.
HG186.S55 P38 1978

Pavlović, Dragiša, 1943- Ko radnike povezuje lažnim koncima : ekonomska preispitivanja / Dragiša Pavlović, Ivan Stojanović. Beograd : Beogradski izdavačko-grafički zavod, 1984. 414 p. ; 23 cm. (Biblioteka Publicistika) In Serbo-Croatian (Roman) Includes bibliographical references. LC Card 84-178578
1. Labor productivity - Yugoslavia. 2. Industrial productivity - Yugoslavia. 3. Employee motivation - Yugoslavia. I. Stojanović, Ivan, Dr. II. Title. III. Series.
HC407.Z9 L36 1984

Pawlowski, Harald. Arbeit, mehr als Kapital . Wuppertal , c1983. 191 p. ; ISBN 3-87294-224-7 LC Card 84-182379
HD6338 .A69 1983

Pawłowski, Zbigniew. Ekonometria / Zbigniew Pawłowski. Wyd. 5., uzup. Warszawa : Państwowe Wydawn. Nauk., 1978. 495 p. : ill. ; 21 cm. Summary in English and Russian. Bibliography: p. 452-[474] Includes indexes. LC Card 81-211573
1. Econometrics. I. Title.
HB139 .P375 1978

PAWNBROKING - ITALY - CAVA DE' TIRRENI - HISTORY.
Patroni Griffi, Filena. Il banco di pegni di Cava dei Tirreni del 1495 /. Cava dei Tirreni , c1985. 149 p., [8] p. of plates : LC Card 86-195753
HG2106.I83 C386 1985

Pay, Diana de. Hennicke, Martin. Zum Förderungssystem für kleine und mittlere Unternehmen . Stuttgart , c1986. 155 p. ; ISBN 3-7910-5012-5 LC Card 86-181544 DDC 338.6/42/0943 19
HD2346.G3 H44 1986

PAY EQUITY.
Kondratas, S. Anna. Comparable worth . Washington, D.C. [c1986] 16 p. ; LC Card 86-212973 DDC 331.2/1 19
HD6061 .K66 1986

PAY EQUITY - CANADA.
Marcotte, Marilee, 1960- Equal pay for work of equal value /. Kingston, Ont., Canada , 1987. 101 p. : ISBN 0-88886-157-5 (pbk.) LC Card 87-163236 DDC 331.2/1 19
HD6061.2.C2 M37 1987

PAY EQUITY - GOVERNMENT POLICY - UNITED STATES.
Comparable worth, pay equity, and public policy /. New York , 1988. xi, 280 p. ; ISBN 0-313-26014-1 (lib. bdg. : alk. paper) LC Card 87-17735 DDC 331.2/1 19
HD6061.2.U6 C656 1988

PAY EQUITY - UNITED STATES.
Responding to comparable worth in today's environment . [Washington, D.C.] , c1986. xi, 160 leaves ; ISBN 0-916559-07-6 (loose-leaf) : LC Card 86-63777 DDC 658.3/2 19
HD6061.2.U6 R47 1986

Women working . Mountain View, Calif. , c1988. xv, 431 p. : ISBN 0-87484-744-3 (pbk.) LC Card 87-3215 DDC 331.4/0973 19
HD6095 .W6976 1988

Pay no taxes with real estate /. Cook, Wade. Orem, Utah , c1982. xvii, 152, [7] p. : ISBN 0-910019-09-6 (pbk.) LC Card 86-228579 DDC 343.7305/46 347.303546 19
HJ4181 .C66 1982

Paying for growth . Snyder, Thomas (Thomas P.) Washington, D.C. , 1986. x, 133 p. : ISBN 0-87420-663-4 (pbk.) LC Card 86-51156 DDC 338.4/3363/0973 19
HJ9156 .S69 1986

Paying for social security . Chaikind, Stephen. [Washington, D.C.], 1981. xix, 47 p. ; LC Card 81-601225 DDC 353.0082/56 19
HD7125 .C47 ***NYPL [JLF 86-252]***

Paying the price . Repetto, Robert C. Washington, DC , c1985. 33 p. ; ISBN 0-915825-12-0 (pbk.) : LC Card 86-225070 DDC 338.4/366865/091724 19
HC59.72.E5 R46 1985

PAYMENT.
Empel, G. van. Betaling, waardepapier en documentair krediet /. Deventer , 1985. viii, 84 p. ; ISBN 90-268-1565-4 : LC Card 85-214764
HG173.6.D8 E46 1985

Vrsaljko, Krešimir. Teorija i praksa domaćih i medunarodnih plaćanja /. Zagreb , 1982. xiv, 460 p. ; LC Card 84-160248
HG2341.Y82 V77 1982

PAYMENT - GREAT BRITAIN.
Frazer, P. A. T. Plastic and electronic money . Cambridge [Cambridgeshire] , Dover, NH. USA , 1985. x, 294 p. ; ISBN 0-85941-290-3 : LC Card 85-22552 DDC 332.1/028 19
HG1710 .F73 1985 ***NYPL [JLE 86-1401]***

Payment in full . Bendell, Leonard, 1941- Gainesville, Fla. , c1987. 174 p. ; ISBN 0-937404-05-5 : LC Card 87-10769 DDC 658.8/8 19
HG3752.5 .B45 1987

PAYMENT - SWITZERLAND - AUTOMATION.
Revolution des Zahlungsverkehrs durch Automation /. Frauenfeld [1984] 160 p. : ISBN 3-7193-0929-0 : LC Card 84-153299
HG1709 .R48 1984

Payment Systems, Inc.
The Affluent market fact book . Tampa, Fla. , c1986. 83 leaves ; LC Card 86-235264 DDC 332.1/7 19
HG1616.C87 A33 1986

Small business market factbook. Tampa, FL (P.O. Box 30168, Tampa 33630) , c1986. 106 leaves : LC Card 87-100402 DDC 338.6/42/0973 19
HG4027.7 .S64 1986

PAYMENT - UNITED STATES.
Cash management and the payments system . Morristown, N.J. , c1986. viii, 102 p. : ISBN 0-910586-62-4 (pbk.) LC Card 86-82305 DDC 658.1/5244 19
HG4028.C45 C359 1986

PAYMENT - YUGOSLAVIA.
Vrsaljko, Krešimir. Teorija i praksa domaćih i medunarodnih plaćanja /. Zagreb , 1982. xiv, 460 p. ; LC Card 84-160248
HG2341.Y82 V77 1982

PAYMENTS, TRANSFER. see **TRANSFER PAYMENTS.**

Payne, Elizabeth Anne, 1943- Reform, labor, and feminism : Margaret Dreier Robins and the National Women's Trade Union League / Elizabeth Anne Payne. Urbana : University of Illinois Press, c1988. p. cm. (Women in American history) Bibliography: p. Includes index. ISBN 0-252-01445-6 (alk. paper) LC Card 87-10794 DDC 331.88/092/4 B 19
1. Robins, Margaret Dreier. 2. Women in trade-unions - United States - Biography. 3. National Women's Trade Union League of America - History. 4. Feminism - United States - History. I. Title. II. Series.
HD6079.2.U5 P38 1988

Payne, Eric. Ethiopia / by Eric Payne. Hampstead Norreys, Newbury, Berkshire, England : P. Cockrill, 1981-1982. 8 v. in 1 : ill. ; 21 cm. (Cockrill series booklet . no. 13-20) Booklet no. 8 by Norman Cape. LC Card 87-166672
1. Postage-stamps - Ethiopia - History. 2. Cancellations (Philately) - Ethiopia - History. 3. Postmarks - Ethiopia - History. 4. Postal service - Ethiopia - History. I. Cape, Norman. II. Title. III. Series.
HE6185.E8 P39 1981

Payne, Richard A. How to get a better job quicker / Richard A. Payne. 3rd new expanded ed. New York : Taplinger Pub. Co., 1987. x, 242 p. ; 24 cm. ISBN 0-8008-3965-X : LC Card 86-23101 DDC 650.1/4 19
1. Applications for positions. 2. Résumés (Employment). 3. Job hunting. 4. Employment interviewing. I. Title.
HF5383 .P36 1987

Payne, Thomas A. Quantitative techniques for management : a practical approach / Thomas A. Payne. Reston, Va. : Reston Pub. Co., c1982. xii, 452 p. : ill. ; 25 cm. Includes bibliographies and index. ISBN 0-8359-6116-8 : LC Card 81-17818 DDC 658.4/033 19
1. Management - Mathematical models. 2. Management - Statistical methods. I. Title.
HD30.25 .P395 1982 ***NYPL [JLE 82-399]***

Payne, W. J. A. (William John Arthur) A preliminary report on the livestock industry in the Jonglei area / by W.J.A. Payne. 2nd ed. [Khartoum?] : United Nations Development Programme : Economic and Social Research Council, 1977. 1 v. (various foliations) : maps ; 28 cm. At head of title: The Democratic Republic of the Sudan. Includes bibliography. LC Card 81-980100
1. Animal industry - Sudan - Jonglei. I. United Nations. Development Programme. II. Majlis al-Abḥāth al-Iqtiṣādīyah wa-al-Ijtimāʻīyah. III. Title.
HD9427.S83 J6664 1977

Payphone magazine. Payphone magazine (formerly Private payphone news) presents the Payphone magazine reference guide. Houston, Tex. (P.O. Box 42371, Houston 77042) , c1986. 1 v. (loose-leaf) ; LC Card 87-112738 DDC 338.4/7621386 19
HD9697.T453 U557 1986

Payphone magazine (formerly Private payphone news) presents the Payphone magazine reference guide. Houston, Tex. (P.O. Box 42371, Houston 77042) : U. S. PayPhone, c1986. 1 v. (loose-leaf) ; 30 cm. LC Card 87-112738 DDC 338.4/7621386 19
1. Telephone supplies industry - United States. 2. Telephone - United States. I. Payphone magazine. II. Title: Payphone magazine reference guide.
HD9697.T453 U557 1986

Payphone magazine reference guide. Payphone magazine (formerly Private payphone news) presents the Payphone magazine reference guide. Houston, Tex. (P.O. Box 42371, Houston 77042) , c1986. 1 v. (loose-leaf) ; LC Card 87-112738 DDC 338.4/7621386 19
HD9697.T453 U557 1986

PAYROLLS.
Risteau, Delores. The American Payroll Association's basic guide to payroll /. Paramus, N.J. , c1986. iv, 251 p. : ISBN 0-13-028242-1 (pbk.) LC Card 87-153688 DDC 658.3/21 19
HG4028.P5 R57 1986

PAYROLLS - DATA PROCESSING.
Mosich, Donna M. Mastering Dac-Easy . Glenview, Ill. , c1988. p. cm. ISBN 0-673-18735-7 LC Card 87-4847 DDC 657/.028/55369 19
HF5679 .M64 1988

West, Gary, 1947- Dac-Easy accounting and payroll made easy /. Blue Ridge Summit, PA , c1987. ix, 261 p. : ISBN 0-8306-2914-9 (pbk.) : LC Card 87-10056 DDC 657/.028/55369 19
HF5679 .W47 1987

Les pays au régime du FMI . Schmitt, Bernard. Albeuve, Suisse , c1984. 91 p. : ISBN 2-88087-013-5 : LC Card 84-240522 DDC 382.1/7 19
HG3882 .S36 1984

Payton, Philip, 1953- The Cornish miner in Australia : cousin Jack down under / Philip J. Payton. Trewolsta, Trewirgie, Kernow [Cornwall] : Dyllansow Turan, 1984. xi, 242 p. : ill. ; 22 cm. Includes index. Bibliography: p. 217-229. ISBN 0-907566-51-0 : LC Card 85-202456 DDC 305.8/9167094 19
1. Miners - Australia - History. 2. Cornish - Australia - History. I. Title.
HD8039.M62 A87 1984
NYPL [JLD 86-4079]

Paz Cárcamo, Guillermo.
Guatemala : reforma agraria / Guillermo Paz C.1a ed. Ciudad Universitaria Rodrigo Facio [Costa Rica] : Editorial Universitaria Centroamericana, 1986. 278 p. : ill., maps ; 19 cm. (Colección Seis) Bibliography: p. 267-272. ISBN 997-7300-95-X LC Card 87-401521
1. Land reform - Guatemala - History - 20th century. 2. Peasantry - Guatemala - History - 20th century. 3. Land tenure - Guatemala. 4. Guatemala - Rural conditions. I. Title.
HD1333.G9 P385 1986

Política agraria : una propuesta para la coyuntura de Guatemala en 1986 / Guillermo Paz Cárcamo. San José, Costa Rica : Instituto Centroamericano de Documentación e Investigación Social, 1986. 84 p. ; 27 cm. Bibliography: p. 83-84. LC Card 87-106764
1. Land reform - Guatemala. I. Title.
HD1333.G9 P39 1986

El universo del café / Guillermo Paz C. Heredia : Universidad Nacional, Facultad de Ciencias Sociales, Unidad Coordinadora de Investigación y Documentación, [1983] 145 p. ; 21 cm. Cover title. Date on cover: 1982. Includes bibliographical references. LC Card 87-400683 DDC 338.1/7373/097286 19
1. Coffee trade - Costa Rica. I. Universidad Nacional (Costa Rica). Unidad Coordinadora de Investigación y Documentación. II. Title.
HD9195.C82 P39 1983

Pazner, Elisha, 1941-1979. Social goals and social organization . Cambridge [Cambridgeshire] , New York , 1985. xii, 365 p. : ISBN 0-521-26204-6 LC Card 85-6668 DDC 330.15/5 19
HB846 .S65 1985 ***NYPL [JLE 86-3786]***

PAZNER, ELISHA, 1941-1979.
Social goals and social organization . Cambridge [Cambridgeshire] , New York , 1985. xii, 365 p. : ISBN 0-521-26204-6 LC Card 85-6668 DDC 330.15/5 19
HB846 .S65 1985 ***NYPL [JLE 86-3786]***

PBS Video.
Hungary, pushing the limits [videorecording] /. Alexandria, VA , 1987. 1 videocassette (60 min.) : LC Card 87-707589 DDC 943.9 11
HC300.28

Will there always be an England? [videorecording] /. Alexandria, VA , 1986. 1 videocassette (60 min.) : LC Card 86-707796

DDC 942.085 11
HC256.5

Pchelintsev, Oleg Sergeevich. Territorial'no-proizvodstvennyĭ kompleks . Moskva , 1982. 107 p. : LC Card 83-200414
HC337.R852 K3685 1982

PDRI-Serra do Mel : repercussões sócio-econômicas / Estado do Rio Grande do Norte, Secretaria da Agricultura, Fundação Estadual de Planejamento Agrícola--CEPA/RN. Natal : A Fundação, 1981. 52 leaves : ill. ; 29 cm. Summary in English. Includes bibliographical references. LC Card 84-246626
1. Land settlement - Brazil - Mel Mountains Region (Rio Grande do Norte) - Case studies. 2. Mel Mountains Region (Rio Grande do Norte, Brazil) - Rural conditions - Case studies. I. Rio Grande do Norte (Brazil). Fundação Estadual de Planejamento Agrícola.
HD499.M45 P37 1981

PEACE - ADDRESSES, ESSAYS, LECTURES.
Fred och säkerhet . [Stockholm] , c1983. 385 p. : ISBN 91-7410-249-4 : LC Card 83-229846
JX1963 .F817 1983 ***NYPL [JLD 84-2639]***

PEACE - CONGRESSES.
Club of Rome Conference (1984 : Helsinki, Finland) Managing global issues . [Lahti] [1985] 216 p. : ISBN 951-45-3807-2 (pbk.) LC Card 87-140928 DDC 909.82/8 19
HC13 .C56 1984

Frieden und Friedenssicherung in Vergangenheit und Gegenwart . München , 1984. 115 p. ; ISBN 3-7705-2147-1 (pbk.) :
NYPL [JFL 76-295 Bd. 7]

Stimme und Aktion der Völker gegen das Wettrüsten . Berlin , 1985. 421 p. ;
NYPL [JLD 86-4257]

World peace and the developing countries . Basingstoke, Hampshire , 1986. xix, 272 p. ; ISBN 0-333-43636-9 ***NYPL [JLD 87-1192]***

Peace Corps in the 80's /. Rice, Gerard T. Washington, D.C. , 1986. v, 89 p. : LC Card 87-601040 DDC 361.2/6/06073 19
HC60.5 .R5 1986

Peace Corps (U. S.) Rice, Gerard T. Peace Corps in the 80's /. Washington, D.C. , 1986. v, 89 p. : LC Card 87-601040 DDC 361.2/6/06073 19
HC60.5 .R5 1986

PEACE CORPS (U. S.)
Landrum, Roger L. The role of the Peace Corps in education in developing countries . Washington, D.C. [1984] iv, 258 p. ; LC Card 86-601664 DDC 371.2/07 19
HC60.5 .L27 1984

Rice, Gerard T. Peace Corps in the 80's /. Washington, D.C. , 1986. v, 89 p. : LC Card 87-601040 DDC 361.2/6/06073 19
HC60.5 .R5 1986

Peace, defence, and economic analysis : proceedings of a conference held in Stockholm jointly by the International Economic Association and the Stockholm International Peace Research Institute / edited by Christian Schmidt and Frank Blackaby. New York : St. Martin's Press, 1987. xxxiii, 450 p. : ill. ; 22 cm. Includes bibliographies and index. ISBN 0-312-01321-3 : LC Card 87-19708 DDC 338.4/7355 19
1. Munitions - Economic aspects - Congresses. 2. Armaments - Economic aspects - Congresses. I. Schmidt, Christian. II. Blackaby, Frank. III. International Economic Association. IV. Stockholm International Peace Research Institute.
HC79.D4 P43 1987

PEACE - RELIGIOUS ASPECTS.
Vance, A. Last chance for peace . Boulder, Colo. , c1985. xviii, 256 p. : ISBN 0-930705-01-7 (pbk.) : LC Card 84-18831 DDC 172/.24 19
BL65.P4 V36 1985 ***NYPL [JLD 86-2214]***

PEACE - RELIGIOUS ASPECTS - CATHOLIC CHURCH.
The Best of This world /. Lanham, MD , c1986. x, 405 p. ; ISBN 0-8191-5605-1 (alk. paper) : LC Card 86-22411 DDC 261.8 19
HB72 .B5 1987 ***NYPL [JFE 86-5571]***

Weigel, George. Tranquillitas ordinis . Oxford , New York , 1987. xiii, 489 p. ; ISBN 0-19-504193-3 (alk. paper) : LC Card 86-12742 DDC 261.8/73/08822 19
BX1795.P43 W45 1987
NYPL [JFE 87-1638]

Peach, Richard Wilson, 1951- Gramley, Lyle E. Real estate finance and housing . Washington, D.C. (1125 15th St., N.W., Washington 20005) , c1987. vii, 132 p. : LC Card 87-124264 DDC 332.7/2/0973021 19
HG2040.5.U5 G73 1987

Peaker, Christine. Making cars . London , Boston , c1985. ix, 131 p. : ISBN 0-7102-0272-5 : LC Card 84-13398 DDC 338.4/76292/0942574 19
HD8039.A82 G75 1984
NYPL [JLE 86-2303]

Peale, Norman Vincent, 1898- Blanchard, Kenneth H. The power of ethical management /. New York , 1988. 139 p. ; ISBN 0-688-07062-0 LC Card 87-24210 DDC 174/.4 19
HF5387 .B56 1988

PEANUT INDUSTRY - SUDAN.
Gibriel, Mohamed Farah. Groundnuts production and marketing in Sudan /. Khartoum, Sudan , 1984. 24 leaves : LC Card 85-981430 DDC 338.1/73368/09624 19
HD9235.P32 S734 1984

PEANUTS - SUDAN - MARKETING.
Gibriel, Mohamed Farah. Groundnuts production and marketing in Sudan /. Khartoum, Sudan , 1984. 24 leaves : LC Card 85-981430 DDC 338.1/73368/09624 19
HD9235.P32 S734 1984

Pearce, Alan. Telecommunications opportunities for colleges and universities /. McLean, Va. (1355 Beverly Rd., Suite 100, McLean 22101) , c1986. 208 p. ; LC Card 86-231086 DDC 384.6/3 19
HD9696.T443 U572 1986

Pearce, David W. (David William) Economics, growth, and sustainable environments . New York , 1988. viii, 205 p. : ISBN 0-312-01240-3 : LC Card 87-12520 DDC 363.7 19
HC79.E5 E2774 1988

Pearce, I. F. (Ivor F.) Demand, equilibrium, and trade . London , 1984. xx, 256 p. : ISBN 0-333-33184-2 LC Card 87-673439
HB34 .D45x 1984b

PEARCE, I. F. (IVOR F.)
Demand, equilibrium, and trade . London , 1984. xx, 256 p. : ISBN 0-333-33184-2 LC Card 87-673439
HB34 .D45x 1984b

Pearce, Jenny. Promised land : peasant rebellion in Chalatenango, El Salvador / Jenny Pearce. London : Latin America Bureau ; [S.l.] : Distribution in the USA by Monthly Review Foundation, 1986. viii, 324 p. : ill. ; 24 cm. Includes index. Bibliography: p. 314-320. ISBN 0-906156-21-1 (pbk.) LC Card 86-141737 DDC 322.4/4/097284 19
1. Peasantry - El Salvador - Chalatenango (Dept.) - Political activity - History. 2. Agricultural laborers - El Salvador - Chalatenango (Dept.) - Political activity - History. 3. Peasant uprisings - El Salvador - Chalatenango (Dept.) - History. I. Title.
HD1531.S2 P4 1986 ***NYPL [JLE 87-471]***

Pearce, John A. Company and industry cases in strategy and policy / John A. Pearce II, Richard B. Robinson Jr., Larry D. Alexander. Homewood, IL : Irwin, 1986. xiv, 711 p. : ill., maps ; 24 cm. (Irwin series in management and the behavioral sciences) "Guide to information sources for use in strategy and policy analysis": p. 671-711. ISBN 0-256-03558-X : LC Card 85-82002
1. Corporate planning - Case studies. 2. Strategic planning - Case studies. I. Robinson, Richard B. (Richard Braden), 1947-. II. Alexander, Larry D. III. Title. ***NYPL [JLE 87-993]***

Pearson, Charles, 1794-1862. Central city terminus : letters / from Charles Pearson, Esq. to W.H. Ashurst, Esq. ... and from Mr. Ashurst to the members of the Corporation of London, and others connected with trade in the city of London, on the importance of a central city terminus to the citizens and to the wholesale and retail trade of the city. [S.l. : s.n.], 1845 (London : Richard and John E. Taylor) 20 p. ; 20 cm. LC Card 85-666155
1. Railroad terminals - Great Britain - London - Economic aspects. I. Ashurst, W. H. (William Henry), 1792-1855. II. Title.
HE3019.L8 P42x 1845

Pearson, Charles S. Down to business : multinational corporations, the environment, and development / Charles S. Pearson. Washington, DC (1735 New York Ave., NW, Washington, DC 20006) : World Resources Institute, c1985. vii, 107 p. ; 23 cm. (Study / World Resources Institute . 2) Reports the principal findings, conclusions, and recommendations of the Institute's Private Sector Initiatives Project. Cf. p. iii. "January 1985." Includes bibliographical references. ISBN 0-915825-04-X (pbk.) : LC Card 84-52795
1. Environmental protection - Developing countries. 2. Pollution - Developing countries. 3. International business enterprises - Developing countries - Management. 4. xnvironmental policy - Developing countries. I. World Resources Institute. II. Private Sector Initiatives Project. III. Title. IV. Title: Multinational corporations, the environment and development. V. Series: Study / World Resources Institute , 2.
HD69.P6 P42 1985 ***NYPL [JLE 86-3186]***

Pearson, Patrick. Kallaway, Peter. Johannesburg . Braamfontein, South Africa , c1986. v, 124 p. : ISBN 0-86975-303-7 (pbk.) LC Card 87-100567 DDC 305.5/62/0968221 19
HD8801.Z8 J6424 1986

Pearson, Richard. UK occupation and employment trends to 1990 . London , Boston , 1986. xxiv, 249 p. : ISBN 0-408-02980-3 : LC Card 86-13617 DDC 331.12/0941 19
HD5765.A6 U38 1986 ***NYPL [JLE 86-4156]***

Pearson, Scott R. Portuguese agriculture in transition /. Ithaca , 1987. 283 p. : ISBN 0-8014-1954-9 (alk. paper) LC Card 86-29198 DDC 338.1/09469 19
HD2027 .P67 1987

Peasant economics . Ellis, Frank. Cambridge [Cambridgeshire] , New York , 1988. p. cm. ISBN 0-521-32446-7 LC Card 87-14815 DDC 338.1/09172/4 19
HD1542 .E43 1988

Peasant organizations in India /. Seth, A. N., 1914- Delhi , New Delhi, India , 1984. xxxxiv, 174 p. ; LC Card 84-902298 DDC 305.5/63 19
HD1339.I4 S48 1984 ***NYPL [JLD 87-644]***

Peasant protest in Japan, 1590-1884 /. Bix, Herbert P. New Haven [Conn.] , c1986. xxxix, 296 p. : ISBN 0-300-03485-7 (alk. paper) LC Card 85-17889 DDC 322.4/4/0952 19
HD1339.J3 B59 1986 ***NYPL [JLE 86-2541]***

PEASANT UPRISING - PERU - ANDAHUAYLAS.
Méndez S., José Fernando. La derrota de Andahuaylas (1974) /. Lima , 1981. 126 p. :
NYPL [JLB 86-27]

PEASANT UPRISINGS - ASIA - CONGRESSES.
Peasants and politics . Melbourne , c1978. 218 p. : ISBN 0-7267-2027-5
NYPL [JLE 81-1456]

PEASANT UPRISINGS - CENTRAL AMERICA.
Barry, Tom, 1950- Roots of rebellion . Boston , c1987. xii, 220 p. : ISBN 0-89608-288-1 : LC Card 87-4519 DDC 338.1/9/728 19
HD9014.C462 B37 1987

PEASANT UPRISINGS - EL SALVADOR - CHALATENANGO (DEPT.) - HISTORY.
Pearce, Jenny. Promised land . London [S.l.] , 1986. viii, 324 p. : ISBN 0-906156-21-1 (pbk.) LC Card 86-141737 DDC 322.4/4/097284 19
HD1531.S2 P4 1986 ***NYPL [JLE 87-471]***

PEASANT UPRISINGS - GERMANY - HISTORY - ADDRESSES, ESSAYS, LECTURES.
Peasants and lords in modern Germany . Boston , 1986. 267 p. ; ISBN 0-04-943037-8 (alk. paper) LC Card 85-6113 DDC 305.5/63 19
HD655 .P34 1986 ***NYPL [JLE 86-1702]***

PEASANT UPRISINGS - GREECE - HISTORY - 20TH CENTURY.
Vrachniarēs, Chrēstos. Anamesa se dyo exegerseis . Athēna , 1985. 139, [5] p. ; LC Card 86-206897
HD1536.G7 V73 1985

PEASANT UPRISINGS - INDIA.
Ghosha, Madana. Bhūmibyabasthā, Kaṃgresa, o Kṛshakasabhā /. Bardhamāna [1986?] 100 p. ; LC Card 87-900325
HD875 .G56 1986

Krishnan-Kutty, G. Peasantry in India /. New Delhi , 1986. 129 p. ; ISBN 81-7017-215-2 : LC Card 86-903053 DDC 305.5/63 19
HD1537.I4 K75 1986

Seshadri, K. Rural unrest in India /. New Delhi , 1983. xiii, 192 p. ; LC Card 83-905323 DDC 303.6/23/0954 19
HC440.P6 S47 1983 NYPL [JLD 86-3704]

PEASANT UPRISINGS - INDIA - 20TH CENTURY.
Agrarian struggles in India after independence /. Delhi , 1986. xxvi, 666 p. :
NYPL [JLD 86-3896]

PEASANT UPRISINGS - ITALY - PUGLIA - HISTORY - 20TH CENTURY.
Snowden, Frank M. (Frank Martin), 1946- Violence and great estates in the south of Italy . Cambridge [Cambridgeshire] , New York , 1986. x, 245 p. : ISBN 0-521-30731-7 LC Card 85-11675 DDC 322.4/4/094575 19
HD679.P83 S66 1986 NYPL [JLD 86-1627]

PEASANT UPRISINGS - JAPAN - HISTORY.
Bix, Herbert P. Peasant protest in Japan, 1590-1884 /. New Haven [Conn.] , c1986. xxxix, 296 p. : ISBN 0-300-03485-7 (alk. paper) LC Card 85-17889 DDC 322.4/4/0952 19
HD1339.J3 B59 1986 NYPL [JLE 86-2541]

PEASANT UPRISINGS - POLAND - HISTORY.
Wycech, Czesław. Z przeszłości ruchów chłopskich, 1768-1861 /. Warszawa , 1952. 221, [3] p. ; LC Card 81-212267
HD1536.P7 W93 1952

PEASANTRY.
Harrod, Jeffrey. Power, production, and the unprotected worker /. New York , 1987. xviii, 347 p. ; ISBN 0-231-05844-6 (alk. paper) LC Card 86-26374 DDC 306/.36 19
HD6971 .H287 1987

Peasants and peasant societies . Oxford [Oxfordshire] , New York, NY, USA , 1987. viii, 497 p. ; ISBN 0-631-15212-1 : LC Card 87-775 DDC 305.5/63 19
HD1521 .P42 1987

PEASANTRY - AFRICA.
Bates, Robert H. Essays on the political economy of rural Africa /. Berkeley , 1987, c1983. p. cm. ISBN 0-520-06014-8 (pbk. : alk. paper) LC Card 86-25120 DDC 330.96/0328/091734 19
HD2117 .B37 1987

Nafziger, E. Wayne. Inequality in Africa . Cambridge [Cambridgeshire] , New York , c1988. p. cm. ISBN 0-521-26881-8 LC Card 87-24263 DDC 339.2/096 19
HC800.Z9 I5136 1988

PEASANTRY - AFRICA, SUB-SAHARAN - MISCELLANEA.
Albagli, Claude. Le rôle économique et social du paysan africain et l'autosuffisance alimentaire /. Abidjan , c1984. 70 p. : ISBN 2-7236-0648-1 LC Card 85-179020
HD9017.S82 A43 1984

The peasantry and nationalism . Mehta, Shirin. New Delhi , 1984. x, 215 p. : LC Card 84-901701 DDC 322.4/4/095475 19
HD1339.I4 M44 1984 NYPL [JLD 86-4424]

PEASANTRY - ANDES REGION.
Sánchez Enríquez, Rodrigo. Organización andina, drama y posibilidad /. Huancayo, Perú [1987] xxii, 219 p. : LC Card 87-404025 DDC 330.98/0038 19
HC167.A5 S26 1987

PEASANTRY - ANDES REGION - CONGRESSES.
Investigación agraria y crisis . Quito , 1986. 498 p. : LC Card 87-400125 DDC 338.1/098 19
HD1860.A53 I58 1986

PEASANTRY - ARGENTINA.
Ringuelet, Andrés. El hombre de la tierra /. [S.l. , 1984] (La Plata, Rep. Argentina : Impr. Ferrograf) 111 p. ; LC Card 85-104745
HD1531.L3 R55 1984

PEASANTRY - ARMENIAN S.S.R. - HISTORY - CONGRESSES.
Nyut'er Hayastani gyughatntesut'yan ev gyughats'iut'yan patmut'yan /. Erevan , 1964- v. <1 > : LC Card 86-225528
HD1995.A7 N98 1964

PEASANTRY - ASIA - CONGRESSES.
Peasants and politics . Melbourne , c1978. 218 p. : ISBN 0-7267-2027-5
NYPL [JLE 81-1456]

PEASANTRY - AUSTRIA - TOTZENBACH REGION - HISTORY.
Landskron, Ferdinand. Von der Bauernfaust zur Bauernkammer /. Totzenbach [1983] 194 p. ; LC Card 84-168829
HD1536.A9 L36 1983

PEASANTRY - BANGLADESH.
Rahamāna, Āsahābura, 1949- Bāṅālādeśera kṛshikāṭhāmo, kṛshaka samāja, o unnaẏan /. Ḍhākā , 1986. 39, 158 p. ; LC Card 86-903304
HD2075.6 .R33 1986

Rahman, Atiur, 1951- Peasants and classes . Dhaka , 1986. xlvi, 295 p. ; LC Card 87-900478 DDC 305.5/63 19
HD1537.B3 R32 1986

PEASANTRY - BOLIVIA.
Segunda reforma agraria . La Paz, Bolivia [1987] 287 p. : LC Card 87-403057 DDC 333.3/1/84 19
HD1333.B5 S44 1987

PEASANTRY - BOLIVIA - CAQUIAVIRI.
Birbuet D., Gustavo. Tierra y ganado en Pacajes . La Paz, Bolivia , 1986. 86 p. : LC Card 87-403087 DDC 333.3/0984/12 19
HD490.C34 B57 1986

PEASANTRY - BOLIVIA - COMANCHE.
Birbuet D., Gustavo. Tierra y ganado en Pacajes . La Paz, Bolivia , 1986. 86 p. : LC Card 87-403087 DDC 333.3/0984/12 19
HD490.C34 B57 1986

PEASANTRY - BOLIVIA - HISTORY.
Bolivia, hoy /. México, D.F. , 1983. 240 p. ; LC Card 84-148626 DDC 330.984/05 19
HC182 .B565 1983 NYPL [JLD 86-2825]

PEASANTRY - BOLIVIA - LA CANCHA (COCHABAMBA)
Calderón G., Fernando. La Cancha . [Cochabamba, Bolivia] , 1984. 208 p. : LC Card 85-238895
HF5473.B62 C363 1984

PEASANTRY - BOLIVIA - POLITICAL ACTIVITY - CONGRESSES.
ACLO (Organization) "Estudio de participación campesina en la estructura y acción de ACLO" . [Sucre, Bolivia] , 1980. 94 leaves ; LC Card 83-203590
HD1531.B6 A24 1980

PEASANTRY - BOLIVIA - SANTA CRUZ (DEPT.)
Gill, Lesley. Peasants, entrepreneurs, and social change . Boulder , 1987. xiv, 246 p. : ISBN 0-8133-7339-5 (pbk. : alk. paper) : LC Card 86-28207 DDC 303.4/0984/3 19
HD1870.S25 G54 1987

PEASANTRY - BRAZIL - CONCEIÇÃO DO ARAGUAIA - CRIMES AGAINST.
Figueira, Ricardo Rezende, 1952- A justiça do lobo . Petrópolis , 1986. 115 p. ; LC Card 87-137552 DDC 305.5/63 19
HD500.C74 F54 1986

PEASANTRY - BRAZIL - CONCEIÇÃO DO ARAGUAIA - POLITICAL ACTIVITY.
Figueira, Ricardo Rezende, 1952- A justiça do lobo . Petrópolis , 1986. 115 p. ; LC Card 87-137552 DDC 305.5/63 19
HD500.C74 F54 1986

PEASANTRY - BRAZIL - GOIÁS (STATE)
Brandão, Carlos Rodrigues. Campesinato goiano . Goiânia , 1986. 156 p. ; ISBN 85-85003-42-1 : LC Card 87-403866 DDC 305.5/63 19
HD1531.B7 B713 1986

PEASANTRY - BRAZIL - GOIÁS (STATE) - POLITICAL ACTIVITY.
Catholic Church. Comissão Pastoral da Terra (Brazil) CPT . Petrópolis , 1983. 105 p. ; LC Card 86-209008
HD499.G65 C38 1983

PEASANTRY - BRAZIL - HISTORY.
Barreiro, José Carlos. Campesinato e capitalismo /. Campinas-SP [1986] 128 p. ; LC Card 86-229683
HD1531.B7 B37 1986

Moura, Margarida Maria. Camponeses /. São Paulo , 1986. 78 p. ; ISBN 85-08-01089-3 LC Card 86-230194
HD1531.B7 M68 1986

PEASANTRY - BRAZIL - PINDARÉ RIVER VALLEY.
Luna, Regina Celi Miranda Reis. A terra era liberta . São Luís, MA , 1985. xxvii, 146 p. : LC Card 87-135907 DDC 333.3/0981/21 19
HD499.P46 L86 1985

PEASANTRY - BRAZIL - SAO PAULO (STATE)
Brandão, Carlos Rodrigues. Os caipiras de São Paulo /. São Paulo-Brasil , 1983. 92, [4] p. : LC Card 84-179661
HD1531.B7 B72 1983

Política agrária /. Porto Alegre-RS , 1985. 79 p. : LC Card 86-198513
HD1531.B7 P65 1985

PEASANTRY - BRAZIL - UBATUBA (SÃO PAULO)
Marcilio, Maria Luiza. Caiçara . São Paulo-SP (Brasil) , c1986. 244 p. : ISBN 85-05-00523-6 LC Card 87-404833 DDC 304.6/0981/61 19
HD1531.B7 M34 1986

PEASANTRY - CHILE - POLITICAL ACTIVITY.
Cruz, María Elena. Chile--opciones y desafíos del sindicalismo rural, 1973-1985 /. Santiago, Chile , 1985. 57 p. ; LC Card 87-100897
HD6619.A29 C78 1985

Tapia Soko, Gonzalo. El problema de la recomposición de los actores campesinos en una perspectiva de democratización /. Santiago [Chile] [1985] ii, 49, 5 leaves ; LC Card 86-159337
HD1531.C5 T36 1985

PEASANTRY - CHINA - CONGRESSES.
The Re-emergence of the Chinese peasantry . London , New York , c1987. ix, 277 p. : LC Card 87-5373 DDC 305.5/63 19
HD1537.C5 R4 1987

PEASANTRY - CHINA - HUNAN PROVINCE - HISTORY.
Perdue, Peter C., 1949- Exhausting the earth . Cambridge, Mass. , 1987. xvii, 331 p. : ISBN 0-674-27504-7 LC Card 87-5067 DDC 338.1/0951/215 19
HD2100.H86 P47 1987

PEASANTRY - COLOMBIA - ADDRESSES, ESSAYS, LECTURES.
Campesinado y capitalismo en Colombia /. Bogotá, Colombia , 1981. 233 p. ; LC Card 82-141108 DDC 338.1/09861 19
HD516 .C35 1981 NYPL [JLD 86-1342]

PEASANTRY - COLOMBIA - BARBOSA (ANTIOQUIA)
Informe general y proyecto de parcelación, Antioquia # 2 (Barbosa y Santo Domingo) /. Bogotá, D.E. , 1964. 2, 73, 16 leaves, [1] leaf of plates : LC Card 85-107102
HD1476.C72 B375 1964

PEASANTRY - COLOMBIA - POLITICAL ACTIVITY.
Problemas agrarios colombianos /. [Bogotá, Colombia] , México, D.F. , 1986. 467 p. : ISBN 958-606-005-5 LC Card 86-221632
HD1882 .P75 1986

Rivera Cusicanqui, Silvia. Política e ideología en el movimiento campesino colombiano . [Bogotá] [s.l.] , 1982. 188 p. ; LC Card 84-155496
HD511.5.A87 R58 1982
NYPL [JLD 86-1208]

PEASANTRY - COLOMBIA - SANTO DOMINGO (ANTIOQUIA)
Informe general y proyecto de parcelación, Antioquia # 2 (Barbosa y Santo Domingo) /. Bogotá, D.E. , 1964. 2, 73, 16 leaves, [1] leaf of plates : LC Card 85-107102
HD1476.C72 B375 1964

PEASANTRY - CONGO (BRAZZAVILLE)
N'Kaloulou, Bernard, 1952- Dynamique paysanne et développement rural au Congo /. Paris , c1984. 260 p. : ISBN 2-85802-416-X LC Card 84-246506 DDC 305.5/63 19
HD1006 .N57 1984 NYPL [JLD 87-304]

PEASANTRY - DEVELOPING COUNTRIES.
Mortimer, Rex, 1926-1979. Stubborn survivors . [Clayton, Vic.] , 1984. xvii, 180 p. : ISBN 0-86746-299-X (pbk.) LC Card 87-672646
HC59.7 .M593x 1984

PEASANTRY - DEVELOPING COUNTRIES - CASE STUDIES.
Critchfield, Richard. The golden bowl be broken . Bloomington , 1988. p. cm. ISBN 0-253-32554-4 LC Card 87-3690 DDC 305.5/63 19
HD1542 .C75 1988

PEASANTRY - DEVELOPING COUNTRIES - ECONOMIC CONDITIONS.
Ellis, Frank. Peasant economics . Cambridge [Cambridgeshire] , New York , 1988. p. cm. ISBN 0-521-32446-7 LC Card 87-14815 DDC 338.1/09172/4 19
HD1542 .E43 1988

PEASANTRY - DEVELOPING COUNTRIES - SOCIAL CONDITIONS.
Ellis, Frank. Peasant economics . Cambridge [Cambridgeshire] , New York , 1988. p. cm. ISBN 0-521-32446-7 LC Card 87-14815 DDC 338.1/09172/4 19
HD1542 .E43 1988

PEASANTRY - DOMINICA - HISTORY.
Trouillot, Michel-Rolph. Peasants and capital . Baltimore , c1988. xiv, 344 p. : ISBN 0-8018-3481-3 (alk. paper) LC Card 87-20018 DDC 305.5/63 19
HD1531.D58 T76 1988

PEASANTRY - ECUADOR - CHIMBORAZO - POLITICAL ACTIVITY - HISTORY.
Sylva Charvet, Paola. Gamonalismo y lucha campesina . [Quito] , 1986. 250 p., [3] leaves of plates : LC Card 87-101122
HD529.C47 S95 1986

PEASANTRY - ECUADOR - COTOPAXI - POLITICAL ACTIVITY.
Farrell, Gilda. Tenencia de la tierra y movimiento campesino en el Ecuador /. Quito, Ecuador , 1981. 158 p., [2] leaves of plates : LC Card 86-174088
HD529.C67 F37 1981

PEASANTRY - ECUADOR - ESMERALDAS (PROVINCE) - CASE STUDIES.
Campesinado y organización en Esmeraldas /. [Quito, Ecuador?] [1986] 213 p. : LC Card 86-171561
HD1531.E2 C36 1986

PEASANTRY - ECUADOR - FLORES (CHIMBORAZO) - CASE STUDIES.
Mariano, Alfonso, José, Lorenzo, Manuel . Quito, Ecuador , 1985. 128 p., [8] leaves of plates : LC Card 86-136793
HD1531.E2 M37 1985

PEASANTRY - ECUADOR - LICTO - CASE STUDIES.
Mariano, Alfonso, José, Lorenzo, Manuel . Quito, Ecuador , 1985. 128 p., [8] leaves of plates : LC Card 86-136793
HD1531.E2 M37 1985

PEASANTRY - ECUADOR - PICHINCHA (PROVINCE) - POLITICAL ACTIVITY.
Farrell, Gilda. Tenencia de la tierra y movimiento campesino en el Ecuador /. Quito, Ecuador , 1981. 158 p., [2] leaves of plates : LC Card 86-174088
HD529.C67 F37 1981

PEASANTRY - ECUADOR - POLITICAL ACTIVITY.
Dubly, Alain. La organización campesina . Quito, Ecuador , 1985. 37 p. : LC Card 87-404544 DDC 322/.2/09866 19
HD1531.E2 D83 1985

PEASANTRY - ECUADOR - TUNGURAHUA - POLITICAL ACTIVITY.
Farrell, Gilda. Tenencia de la tierra y movimiento campesino en el Ecuador /. Quito, Ecuador , 1981. 158 p., [2] leaves of plates : LC Card 86-174088
HD529.C67 F37 1981

PEASANTRY - EGYPT.
Adams, Richard H. Development and social change in rural Egypt /. Syracuse, N.Y. , 1986. xii, 231 p. : ISBN 0-8156-2362-3 (alk. paper) LC Card 85-30251 DDC 307.1/4/0962 19
HN786.Z9 C63 1986 ***NYPL [JLE 86-1999]***

PEASANTRY - EL SALVADOR - CHALATENANGO (DEPT.) - POLITICAL ACTIVITY - HISTORY.
Pearce, Jenny. Promised land . London [S.l.] , 1986. viii, 324 p. : ISBN 0-906156-21-1 (pbk.) LC Card 86-141737 DDC 322.4/4/097284 19
HD1531.S2 P4 1986 ***NYPL [JLE 87-471]***

PEASANTRY - ENGLAND - HISTORY - ADDRESSES, ESSAYS, LECTURES.
Hilton, R. H. (Rodney Howard), 1916- Class conflict and the crisis of feudalism . London , Ronceverte, W. Va. , 1985. 349 p. ; ISBN 0-907628-36-2 : LC Card 85-21855 DDC 305.5/0942 19
HD604 .H48 1985 ***NYPL [JFE 87-391]***

PEASANTRY - ETHIOPIA.
Alemneh Dejene. Peasants, agrarian socialism, and rural development in Ethiopia /. Boulder , 1987. xiii, 162 p. : ISBN 0-8133-7247-X (pbk. : alk. paper) LC Card 86-51527 DDC 338.1/0963 19
HD2124.5 .A79 1987

Tegegne Teke. Cooperatives and national development . Addis Ababa, Ethiopia [1984] iii, 57 leaves ; LC Card 85-980411 DDC 334/.683/0963 19
HD1491.E83 T44 1984 ***NYPL [JLG 86-173]***

PEASANTRY - ETHIOPIA - ATTITUDES.
Habtamu Wondimu. Some factors which affect peasant motivation to work in the Ethiopian agricultural producers cooperatives /. [Addis Ababa] [1983] 60 leaves : LC Card 84-980911 DDC 334/.683/0963 19
HD1491.E83 H3 1983b ***NYPL [JLG 86-163]***

PEASANTRY - EUROPE - HISTORY.
Istoriia krest'ianstva v Evrope, Ėpokha feodalizma . Moskva , 1985- v. :
NYPL [*QGS 86-1566]

PEASANTRY - FRANCE.
Jégouzo, Guenhaël. Petite paysannerie en France /. Paris , c1984. 227 p. : ISBN 2-85340-610-5 LC Card 85-181759 DDC 338.1/6 19
HD1339.F8 J44 1984

PEASANTRY - FRANCE - DÔMES MOUNTAINS.
Système agraire et pratiques paysannes dans les monts Dômes /. Paris , 1983. xi, 318 p., [8] p. of plates : ISBN 2-85340-478-1 LC Card 84-216594
HD1950.D65 S97 1983

PEASANTRY - FRANCE - HISTORY.
Luxardo, Hervé. Rase campagne . Paris , c1984. 253 p. : ISBN 2-7007-0376-6 : LC Card 85-101431
HD1536.F8 L893 1984

PEASANTRY - GERMANY - HISTORY - ADDRESSES, ESSAYS, LECTURES.
Peasants and lords in modern Germany . Boston , 1986. 267 p. ; ISBN 0-04-943037-8 (alk. paper) LC Card 85-6113 DDC 305.5/63 19
HD655 .P34 1986 ***NYPL [JLE 86-1702]***

PEASANTRY - GERMANY (WEST) - LOWER SAXONY.
Landwirtschaftliche Übergangsbetriebe in Niedersachsen . Göttingen , 1985. xiii, 105 p. ; LC Card 86-185987
HD9013.7.L68 L36 1985

PEASANTRY - GERMANY (WEST) - OSTHOLSTEIN - POLITICAL ACTIVITY - HISTORY.
Rüdel, Holger. Landarbeiter und Sozialdemokratie in Ostholstein, 1872 bis 1878 . Neumünster , 1986. 581 p. ; ISBN 3-529-02909-2 LC Card 87-119718 DDC 331.88/13/0943512 19
HD6699.O88 R83 1986

PEASANTRY - GOVERNMENT POLICY - BENIN.
Elwert, Georg. Bauern und Staat in Westafrika . Frankfurt , New York , c1983. 383 p. : ISBN 3-593-33206-X : LC Card 84-152007
HD1538.B46 E49 1983

PEASANTRY - GOVERNMENT POLICY - ETHIOPIA - ADDRESSES, ESSAYS, LECTURES.
Fassil G. Kiros. Mobilizing the peasantry for rural development [microform] . [Addis Ababa , 1982] 20 leaves ; LC Card 82-980723 DDC 334/.683/0963 19
HD1538.E7 F37 1982
NYPL [*Z-3952 no.39]

PEASANTRY - GOVERNMENT POLICY - KENYA.
Wegner, Gerhard, 1953- Bauern, Kapital und Staat in Kenia . Berlin , c1983. 94 p. : ISBN 3-88619-038-2 : LC Card 85-171380
HD1538.K4 W44 1983

PEASANTRY - GOVERNMENT POLICY - PANAMA.
Andrión Alabarca, Aurelio, 1924- Sobre el surco reviven las esperanzas /. Panamá, R. de P. [1978] 84 p. : LC Card 82-100242
HD1531.P2 A53 1978

PEASANTRY - GREAT BRITAIN - HISTORY.
Harrison, J. F. C. (John Fletcher Clews) The common people of Great Britain . Bloomington , 1985. 445 p. : ISBN 0-253-20357-0 (pbk.) LC Card 84-48820 DDC 305.5/62/0942 19
HD8388 .H36 1985 ***NYPL [JLD 86-3656]***

PEASANTRY - GREECE - HISTORY - 20TH CENTURY.
Vrachniarēs, Chrēstos. Anamesa se dyo exegerseis . Athēna , 1985. 139, [5] p. ; LC Card 86-206897
HD1536.G7 V73 1985

PEASANTRY - GUATEMALA.
Hintermeister, Alberto. Modernización de la agricultura y pobreza rural en Guatemala /. [Santiago, Chile] , 1982. 59 leaves : LC Card 87-403247 DDC 338.1/6/097281 19
HC144.Z9 P624 1982

PEASANTRY - GUATEMALA - HISTORY - 20TH CENTURY.
Paz Cárcamo, Guillermo. Guatemala . Ciudad Universitaria Rodrigo Facio [Costa Rica] , 1986. 278 p. : ISBN 997-7300-95-X LC Card 87-401521
HD1333.G9 P385 1986

PEASANTRY - GUATEMALA - POLITICAL ACTIVITY.
Cambranes, J. C. Agrarismo en Guatemala /. Guatemala , 1986. 255 p. : LC Card 87-401042 DDC 322/.2/097281 19
HD1531.G9 C36 1986

PEASANTRY - HISTORY.
Moura, Margarida Maria. Camponeses /. São Paulo , 1986. 78 p. ; ISBN 85-08-01089-3 LC Card 86-230194
HD1531.B7 M68 1986

PEASANTRY - HISTORY - CONGRESSES.
Der Bauer im Wandel der Zeit /. Bonn , 1986. x, 340 p., [1] leaf of plates : ISBN 3-416-04010-4 LC Card 86-228506
HD1521 .B37 1986

PEASANTRY - HUNGARY.
Szelényi, Iván. Socialist entrepreneurs . Madison, Wis. , 1988. p. cm. ISBN 0-299-11360-4 : LC Card 87-16085 DDC 338.1/09439 19
HD1940.5 .S94 1988

PEASANTRY - HUNGARY - HISTORY.
Simon, Péter, 1926- A magyar parasztság sorsfordulója, 1946-1949 /. [Budapest] , 1984. 212 p. : ISBN 963-09-2475-7 :
HD1333.H9 S57 1984 ***NYPL [JLD 86-3163]***

Szabó, László. Munkaszervezet és termelékenység a magyar parasztságnál a XIX-XX. században /. Szolnok , 1968 (Debrecen : Szabadság Lapnyomda) 167 p. : LC Card 86-188720
HD1536.H9 S89 1968

Peasantry in India /. Krishnan-Kutty, G. New Delhi , 1986. 129 p. ; ISBN 81-7017-215-2 : LC Card 86-903053 DDC 305.5/63 19
HD1537.I4 K75 1986

The peasantry in political economy . Deere, Carmen Diana. [Amherst, MA] , 1987. 76 p. ; LC Card 87-404080 DDC 305.5/63 19
HD1531.L3 D44 1987

PEASANTRY - INDIA.
Agrarian struggles in India after independence /. Delhi , 1986. xxvi, 666 p. :
NYPL [JLD 86-3896]

Krishnan-Kutty, G. Peasantry in India /. New Delhi , 1986. 129 p. ; ISBN 81-7017-215-2 : LC Card 86-903053 DDC 305.5/63 19
HD1537.I4 K75 1986

PEASANTRY - INDIA - BARDOLI TALUKA - POLITICAL ACTIVITY - HISTORY.
Mehta, Shirin. The peasantry and nationalism . New Delhi , 1984. x, 215 p. : LC Card 84-901701 DDC 322.4/4/095475 19
HD1339.I4 M44 1984 ***NYPL [JLD 86-4424]***

PEASANTRY - INDIA - BENGAL - HISTORY.
Nag Chowdhury-Zilly, Aditee. The vagrant peasant . Wiesbaden , 1982. xv, 196 p. : ISBN 3-515-03855-8 (pbk.) LC Card 86-214350
HD1537.I4 N327 1982

PEASANTRY - INDIA - BENGAL - POLITICAL ACTIVITY.
Datta, Śekhara. Tebhāgā āndolana /. Ḍhākā , 1985. 103, [1] p. ; LC Card 86-902072
HD1537.I4 D34 1985

PEASANTRY - INDIA - GUJARAT - CASE STUDIES.
Pathy, Jaganath, 1948- Tribal peasantry dynamics of development /. New Delhi , 1984, c1983. xiii, 233 p. : LC Card 84-900095 DDC 330.954/75052 19
HD879.G8 P37 1984 ***NYPL [JLD 87-724]***

PEASANTRY - INDIA - PUNJAB - POLITICAL ACTIVITY - HISTORY.
Hari Singh, Master, 1902- Agrarian scene in British Punjab /. New Delhi , 1983-c1984. 2 v. : LC Card 83-905514 DDC 338.1/0954/5 19
HD2075.P8 H37 1983 ***NYPL [JLK 86-113]***

PEASANTRY - INDIA - SOCIETIES, ETC.
Seth, A. N., 1914- Peasant organizations in India /. Delhi , New Delhi, India , 1984. xxxxiv, 174 p. ; LC Card 84-902298 DDC 305.5/63 19
HD1339.I4 S48 1984 ***NYPL [JLD 87-644]***

PEASANTRY - INDIA - UTTARKHAND REGION - HISTORY.
Pāṭhaka, Śekhara, 1951- Uttarākhaṇḍa meṃ kulī begāra prathā . Nayī Dillī , 1987, c1986. 339 p., [16] p. of plates : LC Card 87-902810
HD1537.I4 P38 1987

PEASANTRY - INDONESIA - BANTUL (KABUPATEN) - CASE STUDIES.
Maurer, Jean-Luc. Modernisation agricole, développement économique et changement social . Paris , c1986. 323 p. : ISBN 2-13-039622-4 : LC Card 86-175394
HD2085.B37 M38 1986

PEASANTRY - INDONESIA - SUMATRA - HISTORY.
Dobbin, Christine E., 1941- Islamic revivalism in a changing peasant economy . London , 1983. xii, 300 p. : ISBN 0-7007-0155-9 (pbk.) : LC Card 83-127619 DDC 303.4/84 19
HD1537.I56 D63 1983
NYPL [JLD 87-1053]

PEASANTRY - ITALY - SAN FELICE SUL PANARO - HISTORY.
Cattini, Marco. I contadini di San Felice . Torino , c1984. xvii, 364 p., [2] leaves of plates : ISBN 88-06-05682-4 : LC Card 84-189545
HD1536.I8 C34 1984

PEASANTRY - ITALY - STATISTICS.
Barberis, Corrado. Agricoltura e strati sociali /. Milano, Italy , c1986. 269 p. ; LC Card 86-214233
HD1536.I8 B328 1986

PEASANTRY - JAPAN - POLITICAL ACTIVITY - HISTORY.
Bix, Herbert P. Peasant protest in Japan, 1590-1884 /. New Haven [Conn.] , c1986. xxxix, 296 p. : ISBN 0-300-03485-7 (alk. paper) LC Card 85-17889 DDC 322.4/4/0952 19
HD1339.J3 B59 1986 ***NYPL [JLE 86-2541]***

PEASANTRY - KARST (YUGOSLAVIA AND ITALY)
Davis, James C. (James Cushman) Rise from want . Philadelphia , 1986. xv, 165 p. : ISBN 0-8122-8034-2 : LC Card 86-19228 DDC 305.5/63 19
HD1536.Y8 D38 1986 ***NYPL [JLE 87-710]***

PEASANTRY - KOREA - HISTORY.
Vanin, IUriĭ Vasil'evich. Agrarnyĭ stroĭ feodal'noĭ Korei XV-XVI vv. /. Moskva , 1981. 309 p. ; LC Card 83-462393
HD1331.K6 V36 1981 ***NYPL [*QI 86-3898]***

PEASANTRY - LATIN AMERICA.
Astori, Danilo. La agricultura campesina en América Latina . Montevideo, Uruguay [1985?] 35 p. ; LC Card 86-204310 DDC 338.1/098 19
HD1790.5 .A85 1985

Deere, Carmen Diana. The peasantry in political economy . [Amherst, MA] , 1987. 76 p. ; LC Card 87-404080 DDC 305.5/63 19
HD1531.L3 D44 1987

Ringuelet, Andrés. El hombre de la tierra /. [S.l. , 1984] (La Plata, Rep. Argentina : Impr. Ferrograf) 111 p. ; LC Card 85-104745
HD1531.L3 R55 1984

PEASANTRY - LATIN AMERICA - CONGRESSES.
Reforma agraria como proceso social . Piura, Perú [1984] 163 p. : LC Card 84-232526 DDC 333.3/1/85 19
HD1333.P4 R44 1984 ***NYPL [JLD 86-2537]***

Taller "Perspectivas y Alternativas de la Agricultura Familiar" (1983 : Montevideo, Uruguay) Taller "Perspectivas y Alternativas de la Agricultura Familiar". Montevideo, Uruguay [1984] 1 v. (various pagings) : LC Card 85-203149 DDC 338.1/6 19
HD1476.L29 T35 1983 ***NYPL [JLF 86-884]***

PEASANTRY - LATIN AMERICA - POLITICAL ACTIVITY - CASE STUDIES.
Luchando por nuestros derechos . Quito , 1984. 50 p. : LC Card 86-174980
HD1531.L3 L79 1984

PEASANTRY - MEXICO.
Bennholdt-Thomsen, Veronika. Bauern in Mexiko . Frankfurt [am Main] , New York , c1982. 214 p. ; ISBN 3-593-33167-5 LC Card 83-139124 DDC 305.5/63 19
HD1531.M6 B46 1982

Trabajo familiar, conducta reproductiva y estratificación social . México, D.F. , 1986. 226 p. ; ISBN 968-8241-06-7 LC Card 87-400355 DDC 304.6/32/0972 19
HB941 .T7 1986

PEASANTRY - MEXICO - AGUASCALIENTES (STATE) - HISTORY - CASE STUDIES.
Gómez Serrano, Jesús. Hacendados y campesinos en Aguascalientes /. [Aguascalientes] , 1985. 221 p., [20] p. of plates : LC Card 86-217321
HD1471.M62 A384 1985

PEASANTRY - MEXICO - JALISCO - POLITICAL ACTIVITY.
Cooperativas agrarias y conflictos políticos en el sur de Jalisco /. México, D.F. , 1985 [i.e. 1986] 201 p. ; ISBN 968-8401-93-5 LC Card 87-405021 DDC 334/.683/097235 19
HD1491.M42 J353 1986

PEASANTRY - MEXICO - POLITICAL ACTIVITY - CONGRESSES.
Movimientos sociales en el noroeste de México /. México , 1985. 282 p. ; ISBN 968-590-072-8 LC Card 87-102068
HD1531.M6 M684 1985

PEASANTRY - MEXICO - YUCATAN.
Villanueva, Eric. Crisis henequenera y movimientos campesinos en Yucatán, 1966-1983 /. México, D.F. , 1985. 220 p., [10] p. of plates : ISBN 968-603-803-5 LC Card 86-118134 DDC 304.8/0972/65 19
HD9156.H463 M67 1985
NYPL [JLD 87-342]

PEASANTRY - MOZAMBIQUE.
Wuyts, Marc. Camponeses e economia rural em Moçambique [microform] /. Maputo , 1978. 31, A1-A6 p. ; LC Card 80-980386 DDC 338.1/0967/9 19
HD2129 .W89 1978
NYPL [*ZT-1564 no.14]

PEASANTRY - NICARAGUA.
Hintermeister, Alberto. El empleo agrícola en una estructra en transformación . [Santiago, Chile] , 1982. 27 p. ; LC Card 87-403249 DDC 331.7/63/097285 19
HD1531.N5 H56 1982

PEASANTRY - NIGERIA - ADDRESSES, ESSAYS, LECTURES.
Nigerian small farmers . Benin-City, Bendel State, Nigeria , 1980. xv, 315 p. ; LC Card 82-206979 DDC 338.1/6 19
HD1339.N5 N54 1980 ***NYPL [Sc D 86-883]***

PEASANTRY - PANAMA.
Andrión Alabarca, Aurelio, 1924- Sobre el surco reviven las esperanzas /. Panamá, R. de P. [1978] 84 p. : LC Card 82-100242
HD1531.P2 A53 1978

Gandásegui, Marco A. La fuerza de trabajo en el agro . Panamá, R.P. , c1985. 404 p. : ISBN 84-8385-002-X LC Card 86-111074 DDC 331.7/63/097287 19
HD1822 .G36 1985 ***NYPL [JLF 86-1350]***

PEASANTRY - PARAGUAY.
Fogel, Ramón B. Movimientos campesinos en el Paraguay /. Asunción, Paraguay , 1986. 230 p., [1] leaf of plates : LC Card 86-189517
HD1531.P3 F64 1986

PEASANTRY - PARAGUAY - CAAZAPÁ (DEPT.)
Campos, Luis A. (Luis Alberto), 1949- Pequeños campesinos y su incertidumbre . Asunción, Paraguay [1986] 224 p. : LC Card 87-400281 DDC 305.5/63 19
HD1531.P3 C36 1986

PEASANTRY - PARAGUAY - CASE STUDIES.
Campos, Luis A. (Luis Alberto), 1949- Pequeños campesinos y su incertidumbre . Asunción, Paraguay [1986] 224 p. : LC Card 87-400281 DDC 305.5/63 19
HD1531.P3 C36 1986

PEASANTRY - PARAGUAY - GUAIRÁ.
Campos, Luis A. (Luis Alberto), 1949- Pequeños campesinos y su incertidumbre . Asunción, Paraguay [1986] 224 p. : LC Card 87-400281 DDC 305.5/63 19
HD1531.P3 C36 1986

PEASANTRY - PARAGUAY - ITAPÚA - CASE STUDIES.
Campos, Luis A. (Luis Alberto), 1949- Pequeños campesinos y su incertidumbre . Asunción, Paraguay [1986] 224 p. : LC Card 87-400281 DDC 305.5/63 19
HD1531.P3 C36 1986

PEASANTRY - PARAGUAY - MISIONES.
Fogel, Ramón B. Movimientos campesinos en el Paraguay /. Asunción, Paraguay , 1986. 230 p., [1] leaf of plates : LC Card 86-189517
HD1531.P3 F64 1986

PEASANTRY - PERU.
Sotomayor, Octavio. Racionalidad campesina y cambio técnico /. Cusco , 1985. 23 p. ; LC Card 86-200944
HD1531.P4 S67 1985

PEASANTRY - PERU - AYACUCHO (DEPT.)
Gianotten, Vera. Organización campesina . Amsterdam , Cinnaminson, N.J. , c1985. ix, 531 p., [4] p. of plates : ISBN 90-6765-162-1 LC Card 85-200688
HD1531.P4 G5 1985

PEASANTRY - PERU - CUZCO (DEPT.)
Barrenechea Lercari, Carlos. Cusco . Cusco [Peru] 1986. 77 p. ; LC Card 87-400243 DDC 338.1/88537 19
HD1905.C87 B37 1986

Cori Castro, Wilfredo. Mercados y precios en la economía campesina . [Cuzco, Peru] , 1986. 29 p. : LC Card 86-200941
HC228.C8 C59 1986

Díaz Gómez, Jorge. Deterioro de los términos de intercambio, migración eventual y pobreza campesina en el departamento del Cusco /. [Cuzco, Peru] , 1986. 17, 3 leaves, 2 leaves of plates : LC Card 86-200938
HD1531.P4 D52 1986

PEASANTRY - PHILIPPINES - POLITICAL ACTIVITY.
Hanisch, Rolf, 1942- Der Staat, ländliche Armutsgruppen und legale Bauernbewegung in den Philippinen /. Baden-Baden , 1983. xii, 432 p. ; ISBN 3-7890-0980-6 LC Card 84-143058
HD1537.P5 H35 1983

PEASANTRY - POLAND - HISTORY.
Wycech, Czesław. Z przeszłości ruchów chłopskich, 1768-1861 /. Warszawa , 1952. 221, [3] p. ; LC Card 81-212267
HD1536.P7 W93 1952

PEASANTRY - PORTUGAL.
Almeida, João Ferreira de. Classes sociais nos campos . Lisboa [1986] 544 p. : LC Card 87-400121 DDC 305.5/63 19
HD1536.P77 A44 1986

Rau, Virginia. Sesmarias medievais portuguesas /. Lisboa [1982] 288 p. : LC Card 87-673341
HD784 .R3x 1982

PEASANTRY - ROMANIA - OLTENIA - HISTORY - 19TH CENTURY.
Pătroiu, Ion. La cumpăna a două epoci, 1849-1877 /. Craiova , 1983. 316 p. ; LC Card 84-234959
HD1333.R62 O475 1983

PEASANTRY - RUSSIAN S.F.S.R. - BASHKIRSKAIA A.S.S.R. - HISTORY - 19TH CENTURY.
Usmanov, Kh. F. Razvitie kapitalizma v sel'skom khoziaistve Bashkirii v poreformennyĭ period, 60-90-e gody XIX v. /. Moskva , 1981. 368 p. ; LC Card 82-118144
HD1995.B38 U86 1981

PEASANTRY - RUSSIAN S.F.S.R. - HISTORY.
Osnovnye kategorii krest'ian v period pozdnego feodalizma, XVII--pervaia polovina XIX vv. . Smolensk , 1985. 134 p., [1] leaf of plates : LC Card 86-120158
HD1536.S65 O86 1985

PEASANTRY - RUSSIAN S.F.S.R. - HISTORY - 17TH CENTURY.
Kopanev, A. I. (Aleksandr Il'ich) Krest'iane Russkogo Severa v XVII v. /. Leningrad , 1984. 242 p. ; LC Card 84-170666
*HD719.R88 K67 1984 NYPL [*QG 86-3646]*

PEASANTRY - RUSSIAN S.F.S.R. - KALININ REGION - HISTORY - 20TH CENTURY.
Altrichter, Helmut, 1945- Die Bauern von Tver . München , 1984. 373 p. : ISBN 3-486-52071-7 LC Card 84-162284
HD1536.S65 A47 1984

PEASANTRY - RUSSIAN S.F.S.R. - SIBERIA - HISTORY.
Voprosy istorii dorevoliutsionnoĭ Sibiri /. Tomsk , 1983. 177 p. ; *NYPL [*QI 87-171]*

PEASANTRY - RUSSIAN S.F.S.R. - SIBERIA, WESTERN - HISTORY.
Vlasova, I. V. (Irina Vladimirovna) Traditsii krest'ianskogo zemlepol'zovaniia v Pomor'e i Zapadnoĭ Sibiri v XVII-XVIII vv. /. Moskva , 1984. 230 p. : LC Card 85-174592
HD719.W45 V55 1984

PEASANTRY - RUSSIAN S.F.S.R. - WHITE SEA REGION - HISTORY.
Vlasova, I. V. (Irina Vladimirovna) Traditsii krest'ianskogo zemlepol'zovaniia v Pomor'e i Zapadnoĭ Sibiri v XVII-XVIII vv. /. Moskva , 1984. 230 p. : LC Card 85-174592
HD719.W45 V55 1984

PEASANTRY - SENEGAL - SINE-SALOUM.
Benoit-Cattin, Michel. L'exploitation agricole familiale en Afrique soudano-sahélienne /. Paris , c1982. 94 p. : ISBN 2-85319-106-0 LC Card 86-116718
HD1476.S382 S563 1982

PEASANTRY - SOVIET UNION - HISTORIOGRAPHY.
Cox, Terry. Peasants, class, and capitalism . Oxford [Oxfordshire] ; New York : xii, 271 p. ; ISBN 0-19-878014-1 : LC Card 86-2362 DDC 305.5/63 19
HD1536.S65 C69 1986
NYPL [JLD 86-3986]

PEASANTRY - SOVIET UNION - HISTORY - 19TH CENTURY.
Macey, David, A. J., 1942- Government and peasant in Russia, 1861-1906 . Dekalb, Ill. , 1987. xviii, 380 p. ; ISBN 0-87580-122-6 LC Card 87-7684 DDC 338.1/847 19
HD1992 .M19 1987

PEASANTRY - SOVIET UNION - HISTORY - 20TH CENTURY.
Istoriia sovetskogo krest'ianstva . Moskva , 1986- v. : *NYPL [*QG 87-3228]*

PEASANTRY - SOVIET UNION - HISTORY - MATHEMATICAL MODELS - ADDRESSES, ESSAYS, LECTURES.
Soviet quantitative history /. Beverly Hills , c1984. 216 p. : ISBN 0-8039-2082-2 LC Card 83-19196 DDC 306/.072047 19
HD715 .S5956 1984 NYPL [JLD 87-841]

PEASANTRY - SOVIET UNION - SOCIAL CONDITIONS.
Istoriia sovetskogo krest'ianstva /. Moskva , 1986-<1987. v. <1-3 > : LC Card 86-230318
HD1492.S65 I88 1986

PEASANTRY - SPAIN - CATALONIA - HISTORY.
Terra, treball i propietat . Barcelona , c1986. 346 p. ; ISBN 84-7423-287-2 LC Card 86-216973
HD2025.C35 T47 1986

PEASANTRY - SRI LANKA.
Capital and peasant production . Colombo, Sri Lanka , 1985. xiv, 230 p. ; LC Card 86-900809 DDC 338.1/3/095493 19
HD2065.8 .C36 1985 NYPL [JLE 87-1667]

PEASANTRY - SWEDEN - ÖSTERGOTLANDS LÄN - HISTORY - 18TH CENTURY.
Bäck, Kalle, 1949- Bondeopposition och bondeinflytande under frihetstiden . Stockholm , c1984. 326 p. : ISBN 91-36-02263-2 : LC Card 84-252422
HD1536.S8 B33 1984

PEASANTRY - TANZANIA.
Collier, Paul. Labour and poverty in rural Tanzania . Oxford [Oxfordhire] , New York , 1986. vii, 143 p. : ISBN 0-19-828531-0 : LC Card 86-5303 DDC 307.1/4/09678 19
HN797.Z9 C625 1986 NYPL [JLD 87-511]

PEASANTRY - UGANDA - BUGISU (DISTRICT) - POLITICAL ACTIVITY.
Bunker, Stephen G., 1944- Double dependency and constraints on class formation in Bugisu, Uganda /. Urbana, Ill. , 1983. v, 88 p. : LC Card 86-229748 DDC 303.3/09676/1 19
HD1538.U43 B86 1983

PEASANTRY - YUGOSLAVIA - SLOVENIA - CASE STUDIES.
Davis, James C. (James Cushman) Rise from want . Philadelphia , 1986. xv, 165 p. : ISBN 0-8122-8034-2 : LC Card 86-19228 DDC 305.5/63 19
HD1536.Y8 D38 1986 NYPL [JLE 87-710]

PEASANTS. see PEASANTRY.

Peasants, agrarian socialism, and rural development in Ethiopia /. Alemneh Dejene. Boulder , 1987. xiii, 162 p. : ISBN 0-8133-7247-X (pbk. : alk. paper) LC Card 86-51527 DDC 338.1/0963 19
HD2124.5 .A79 1987

Peasants and capital . Trouillot, Michel-Rolph. Baltimore , c1988. xiv, 344 p. : ISBN 0-8018-3481-3 (alk. paper) LC Card 87-20018 DDC 305.5/63 19
HD1531.D58 T76 1988

Peasants and classes . Rahman, Atiur, 1951- Dhaka , 1986. xlvi, 295 p. ; LC Card 87-900478 DDC 305.5/63 19
HD1537.B3 R32 1986

Peasants and lords in modern Germany : recent studies in agricultural history / edited by Robert G. Moeller. Boston : Allen & Unwin, 1986. 267 p. ; 24 cm. Includes bibliographical references and index. ISBN 0-04-943037-8 (alk. paper) LC Card 85-6113 DDC 305.5/63 19
1. Peasantry - Germany - History - Addresses, essays, lectures. 2. Peasant uprisings - Germany - History - Addresses, essays, lectures. 3. Farm tenancy - Germany - History - Addresses, essays, lectures. 4. Agriculture and state - Germany - History - Addresses, essays, lectures. I. Moeller, Robert G.
HD655 .P34 1986 NYPL [JLE 86-1702]

Peasants and peasant societies : selected readings / edited by Teodor Shanin.2nd ed. Oxford [Oxfordshire] ; New York, NY, USA : Blackwell, 1987. viii, 497 p. ; 24 cm. Bibliography: p. [476]-489. Includes index. ISBN 0-631-15212-1 : LC Card 87-775 DDC 305.5/63 19
1. Peasantry. 2. Rural conditions. I. Shanin, Teodor.
HD1521 .P42 1987

Peasants and politics : grass roots reaction to change in Asia / editor, D.B. Miller. Melbourne : E. Arnold, c1978. 218 p. : maps ; 24 cm. Rewritten and expanded papers originally presented at a session of the 1st annual conference of the Asian Studies Association of Australia. Includes indexes. Bibliography: p. 203-211. ISBN 0-7267-2027-5
1. Peasant uprisings - Asia - Congresses. 2. Peasantry - Asia - Congresses. 3. Social change - Congresses. 4. Asia - Social conditions - Congresses. I. Miller, D. B.
NYPL [JLE 81-1456]

Peasants become miners . DeWind, Josh. New York , 1987. vii, 421 p. : ISBN 0-8240-1358-1 (alk. paper) LC Card 87-8361 DDC 338.2/0985/23 19
HD8039.M61 P44 1987

Peasants, class, and capitalism . Cox, Terry. Oxford [Oxfordshire] ; New York : xii, 271 p. ; ISBN 0-19-878014-1 : LC Card 86-2362 DDC 305.5/63 19
HD1536.S65 C69 1986
NYPL [JLD 86-3986]

Peasants, entrepreneurs, and social change . Gill, Lesley. Boulder , 1987. xiv, 246 p. : ISBN 0-8133-7339-5 (pbk. : alk. paper) : LC Card 86-28207 DDC 303.4/0984/3 19
HD1870.S25 G54 1987

Pease, Allen.
Appendix for the feasibility report of implementing the International Registration Plan in the State of Maine : a study / prepared by the Motor Vehicle Division, Secretary of State, State of Maine. [Augusta, Me.] : The Division, [1985] 39 leaves : forms, map ; 28 cm. Cover title. Appendix to: Report on the feasibility of implementing the International Registration Plan in the State of Maine. 1985. "June 1985." LC Card 85-622841 DDC 388.3/24 19
1. Trucks - Licenses - Maine. 2. Trucks - Registration and transfer - Maine. 3. American Association of Motor Vehicle Administrators. International Registration Plan. I. Pease, Allen. Report on the feasibility of implementing the International Registration Plan in the State of Maine. II. Maine. Division of Motor Vehicles. III. Title.
HE5633.M2 P39 1985

Report on the feasibility of implementing the International Registration Plan in the State of Maine : a study / prepared by the Division of Motor Vehicles, Secretary of State, State of Maine in conjunction with the American Association of Motor Vehicle Administrators and the northeastern directors of motor vehicles. [Augusta, Me.] : The Division, [1985] ii, 24 leaves ; 28 cm. Cover title. "June 1985." LC Card 85-622840 DDC 388.3/24 19
1. Trucks - Licenses - Maine. 2. Trucks - Registration and transfer - Maine. 3. American Association of Motor Vehicle Administrators. International Registration Plan. I. Maine. Division of Motor Vehicles. II. American Association of Motor Vehicle Administrators. III. Title.
HE5633.M2 P4 1985

Report on the feasibility of implementing the International Registration Plan in the State of Maine. Pease, Allen. Appendix for the feasibility report of implementing the International Registration Plan in the State of Maine : a study / prepared by the Motor Vehicle Division, Secretary of State, State of Maine. [Augusta, Me.] [1985] 39 leaves : LC Card 85-622841 DDC 388.3/24 19
HE5633.M2 P39 1985

Peat, Marwick, Mitchell & Co.
A Guide for selecting ALM microcomputer models . Washington, D.C. (1120 Connecticut Ave., N.W., Washington 20036) , c1987. iv, 147 p. : LC Card 87-159971 DDC 332.1/028/5416 19
HG1615.25 .G85 1987

Haley, Stephen W. Effective credit management in the equipment leasing and finance industry /. Arlington, VA , c1986. ix, 121 p. : ISBN 0-912413-01-8 (pbk.) LC Card 87-105306 DDC 658.1/5242 19
HD39.4 .H35 1986

Peat, Marwick, Mitchell and Company.
Banking in the United Kingdom. London , c1984. 215 p. ; ISBN 1-85061-020-7
NYPL [JLD 86-2506]

International reinsurance . [New York, N.Y.?] , c1985. vii, 164 p. ; LC Card 85-214554 DDC 368/.012 19
HG8083 .I57 1985 NYPL [JLD 86-2530]

Peauger, Claire. 150 meilleures entreprises françaises /. Paris , c1986. 313 p. ; ISBN 2-234-01894-3 : LC Card 87-107207
HF5382.75.F8 A13 1986

Peavy, John W. Block, Stanley B. Personal financial management /. New York , c1988. xvii, 603 p. : ISBN 0-06-040789-1 LC Card 87-19088 DDC 332.024 19
HG179 .B555 1988

Pébereau, Michel. La politique économique de la France. Les instruments / Michel Pébereau. Paris : A. Colin, c1985. 319 p. : ill. ; 23 cm. (Collection U) Includes bibliographies. ISBN 2-200-31217-2 LC Card 86-179163 DDC 338.944 19
1. France - Economic policy - 1945-. 2. France - Economic conditions - 1945-. 3. France - Politics and

government - 1981-. I. Title.
HC276.2 .P42 1985

Pechalbata pri razshirenoto sotsialistichesko vŭzproizvodstvoto . Khadzhiev, Stoian. Sofiia , 1985. 147 p. ; LC Card 85-209903
HC403.Z9 P737 1985

Pechman, Joseph A., 1918-
Comparative tax systems . Arlington, Va. , 1987. xiv, 447 p. : ISBN 0-918255-05-8 (pbk.) : LC Card 87-50143 DDC 336.2 19
HJ2599.5 .C65 1987

Federal tax policy / Joseph A. Pechman. 5th ed. Washington, D.C. : Brookings Institution, c1987. xix, 430 p. : ill. ; 24 cm. (Studies of government finance : Second series) Bibliography: p. 400-420. Includes index. ISBN 0-8157-6962-8 : LC Card 87-13159 DDC 336.2/00973 19
1. Fiscal policy - United States. 2. Taxation - United States. I. Title.
HJ257.2 .P4 1987

Gender in the workplace /. Washington, D.C. , c1987. xiv, 316 p. ; ISBN 0-8157-1170-0 : LC Card 87-668 DDC 331.13/3 19
HD6060.5.U5 G46 1987

Tax reform and the U. S. economy . Washington, D.C. , c1987. ix, 107 p. : ISBN 0-8157-6959-8 (pbk.) LC Card 87-70178 DDC 330.973/0927 19
HJ2381 .T387 1987

Peck, Anne E. Futures markets . Washington, D.C. , c1985. xiii, 325 p. : ISBN 0-8447-3592-2 LC Card 85-26705 DDC 332.64/4 19
HG6049 .F86 1985 *NYPL [JLE 86-1532]*

Peckham, Herbert D.
Luehrmann, Arthur. AppleWorks data bases . Gilroy, Calif. , c1987. viii, 159 p. : ISBN 0-941681-03-3 (pbk.) : LC Card 87-11734 DDC 005.36/9 19
HF5548.4.A68 L838 1987

Luehrmann, Arthur. AppleWorks spreadsheets . Gilroy, Calif. , c1987. viii, 152 p. ; ISBN 0-941681-05-X (pbk.) : LC Card 87-11745 DDC 005.36/9 19
HF5548.4.A68 L847 1987

Pecora, Peter J. Managing human services personnel / Peter J. Pecora, Michael J. Austin. Newbury Park, Calif. : Sage Publications, c1987. 176 p. : forms ; 22 cm. (Sage human services guides. v. 48) Includes bibliographies. ISBN 0-8039-2685-5 (pbk.) LC Card 86-27995 DDC 658.3 19
1. Personnel management. 2. Organizational effectiveness. I. Austin, Michael J. II. Title.
HF5549 .P36 1987

Pécs a szocialista fejlődés útján : megjelent a város felszabadulásának 40. évfordulójára / [a szerkesztő bizottság, Rákos János ... et al.]. Pécs : MSZMP Pécs Városi Bizottsága, [1984] 127 p. : ill. ; 20 cm. "Belső használatra." ISBN 963-00-0782-7 (Magy. nemz. bibl.) LC Card 85-178275
1. Pécs (Hungary) - Economic conditions. 2. Pécs (Hungary) - Social conditions. 3. Education - Hungary - Pécs. I. Rákos, János.
HC300.292.P4 P43 1984

PÉCS (HUNGARY) - ECONOMIC CONDITIONS.
Pécs a szocialista fejlődés útján . Pécs [1984] 127 p. : ISBN 963-00-0782-7 (Magy. nemz. bibl.) LC Card 85-178275
HC300.292.P4 P43 1984

PÉCS (HUNGARY) - SOCIAL CONDITIONS.
Pécs a szocialista fejlődés útján . Pécs [1984] 127 p. : ISBN 963-00-0782-7 (Magy. nemz. bibl.) LC Card 85-178275
HC300.292.P4 P43 1984

Pécsi, Anna. Mit kell tudni a világ szakszervezeteiről? / írta Pécsi Anna. [Budapest] : Kossuth, 1972. 237 p. ; 19 cm. (Mit kell tudni) Bibliography: p. [227] LC Card 85-178719
1. Trade-unions. I. Title.
HD6476 .P29 1972

Pécsi Janus Pannonius Tudományegyetem. Közgazdaságtudományi Kar. A Vállalati magatartást motiváló gazdasági és társadalmi tényezők című konferencia előadásai . Pécs , 1985. 2 v. : LC Card 87-408547
HD70.H8 V334 1985

Pecunia nervus rerum . Stolleis, Michael, 1941- Frankfurt am Main , c1983. 184 p. ; ISBN 3-465-01590-8 (Deut Bibl.) LC Card 83-183704
HJ1000 .S76 1983

PEDAGOGY. see EDUCATION.

Pedani, Diletta P. I Conti finanziari dell'Emilia-Romagna /. [Bologna] , c1984. 157 p. : ISBN 88-15-00522-6 : LC Card 84-235593 DDC 332.1/0945/4 19
HG3089.E45 C66 1984
NYPL [JLE 86-3198]

PEDDLERS AND PEDDLING - BOLIVIA - COCHABAMBA (DEPT.)
Calderón G., Fernando. Jatun Llajta . La Paz, Bolivia , 1982. v, 448 p., [8] leaves of plates : LC Card 83-111937 DDC 381/.1 19
HF5473.B62 C623 1982
NYPL [JLF 86-1794]

PEDDLERS AND PEDDLING - BRAZIL - DISTRITO FEDERAL.
Sobrevivência, aspectos das condições de vida de menores trabalhadores de rua do Distrito Federal /. [Brasília] , 1983. 117 p. ; LC Card 86-197113
HD6276.B73 D577 1983

PEDDLERS AND PEDDLING - BRAZIL - HISTORY.
O Comércio e suas profissões . Rio de Janeiro , 1983. 127, [5] p. : LC Card 84-161651
HF5459.B7 C65 1983 *NYPL [JLF 86-1408]*

PEDDLERS AND PEDDLING - COLOMBIA - MEDELLÍN.
López Castaño, Hugo. El comercio callejero en la ciudad de Medellín . Medellín , 1983. xv, 194 leaves : LC Card 85-131765
HF5459.C7 L67 1983

PEDDLERS AND PEDDLING - FRANCE.
Marchands ambulants et commerçants étrangers en France et en Allemagne fédérale /. Poitiers , 1984. 148 p. : LC Card 87-147724
HF5459.F8 M37 1984

PEDDLERS AND PEDDLING - FRANCE - BIOGRAPHY.
Espagne, Jean-Pierre. Quand les Pyrénéens parcouraient le monde . Saint-Gaudens [France] , c1985. 224 p., [12] leaves of plates : ISBN 2-904458-07-7 : LC Card 86-139944 DDC 381/.18 B 19
HF5459.F8 E844 1985

PEDDLERS AND PEDDLING - FRANCE - PARIS - EXHIBITIONS.
Atget, Géniaux, Vert . Paris [1984] 63, [1] p. : ISBN 2-901414-09-5 : LC Card 86-137985
HF5459.F8 A87 1984 *NYPL [MFW 87-159]*

PEDDLERS AND PEDDLING - GERMANY, WEST.
Marchands ambulants et commerçants étrangers en France et en Allemagne fédérale /. Poitiers , 1984. 148 p. : LC Card 87-147724
HF5459.F8 M37 1984

PEDDLERS AND PEDDLING - HONG KONG - KOWLOON - HISTORY.
Šimko, Dušan. Strassenverkäufer und die Versorgung der Arbeiterfamilien von Kowloon (Hong Kong) im Umfeld der staatlichen Planungspolitik /. Basel , 1983. 196 p., [9] p. of plates : ISBN 3-85977-129-9 : LC Card 83-238672
HF5459.H6 S56 1983

PEDDLERS AND PEDDLING - INDIA, SOUTH - HISTORY.
Bohle, Hans-Georg. Südindische Wochenmarktsysteme . Stuttgart , 1986. 290 p. : ISBN 3-515-04601-1 LC Card 87-136147 DDC 381/.18/09548 19
HF5475.I42 S682 1986

PEDDLERS AND PEDDLING - PERU - LIMA.
Bunster, Ximena. Sellers & servants . New York , 1985. x, 258 p. : ISBN 0-03-060543-1 (alk. paper) : LC Card 85-6259 DDC 331.4/0985/25 19
HD6072.2.P42 L563 1985
NYPL [JLE 86-910]

Grompone, Romeo. Talleristas y vendedores ambulantes en Lima /. Lima , 1985. 319 p. : LC Card 85-243089
HD2346.P42 L564 1985

Peden, D. G. The use of resource survey data in decision-making with special reference to Kitui District in Kenya / D.G. Peden, H. Epp. Nairobi, Kenya : Kenya Rangeland Ecological Monitoring Unit, 1982. 12 leaves ; 30 cm. (KREMU technical report series . no. 93) "December 1982." Bibliography: leaf 12. LC Card 85-980593 DDC 333.74/09676/24 19
1. Rangelands - Kenya - Kitui (District) - Management. 2. Range management - Kenya - Kitui (District) - Decision making. I. Epp, H. II. Series: Technical report (Kenya Rangeland Ecological Monitoring Unit) , no. 93. III. Title.
HD983.Z8 K587 1982

Pedersen, Peder J.
Dynamiska processer på arbejdsmarkedet / af Peder J. Pedersen. Aarhus : Økonomisk institut, Aarhus universitet ; [Copenhagen] : Økonomisk institut, Københavns universitet, [1982] 33 p. : ill. ; 21 cm. (Studies in labor market dynamics, 0108-2469 ; arbejdspapir. 82-7) "November 1982." Cover title. Bibliography: p. 32-33. LC Card 84-125613
1. Labor supply - Mathematical models. 2. Unemployment - Mathematical models. I. Title. II. Series.
HD5701.6 .P43 1982

Unemployment . Berlin , New York , 1987. xx, 353 p. : ISBN 0-89925-277-X : LC Card 87-24369 DDC 331.13/7 19
HD5701.3 .U53 1987

Pedersen, Wesley. Cost-effective management for today's public affairs, or, How to succeed as a PAO in an era of constraints /. Washington, D.C. (1255 Twenty-third St., N.W., Suite 750, Washington 20037) [c1987] xiii, 109 p. : LC Card 87-135276 DDC 659.2 19
HD59 .C645 1987

Pederson, Carlton A. Selling : principles and methods / Carlton A. Pederson, Milburn D. Wright, Barton A. Weitz.9th ed. Homewood, Ill. : Irwin, 1988. xvii, 644 p. : ill. (some col.) ; 25 cm. (The Irwin series in marketing) Includes bibliographies and indexes. ISBN 0-256-03644-6 LC Card 87-81434 DDC 658.8/5 19
1. Selling. I. Wright, Milburn D. II. Weitz, Barton A. III. Title. IV. Series.
HF5438.25 .P42 1988

PEDESTRIAN AREAS - CONGRESSES.
Dix années d'espaces-piétons . Paris [1984] 191 p. : ISBN 2-85723-124-5 LC Card 85-104132
HE336.P43 D59 1984

PEDESTRIAN AREAS - FRANCE.
Les Rues mixtes . [Bagneux] [1982] 40 p. : ISBN 2-11-083325-4 : LC Card 84-104398
HE363.F72 P437 1982

PEDESTRIAN AREAS - GERMANY (WEST) - CASE STUDIES.
Hall, Peter, 1931- Can rail save the city? . Aldershot, Hants , Brookfield, Vt., U. S.A. , c1985. xii, 241 p. : ISBN 0-566-00947-1 : LC Card 85-17659 DDC 388.4/2/0943 19
HE4774 .H35 1985 *NYPL [JLD 86-2622]*

PEDESTRIAN AREAS - GREAT BRITAIN - CASE STUDIES.
Hall, Peter, 1931- Can rail save the city? . Aldershot, Hants , Brookfield, Vt., U. S.A. , c1985. xii, 241 p. : ISBN 0-566-00947-1 : LC Card 85-17659 DDC 388.4/2/0943 19
HE4774 .H35 1985 *NYPL [JLD 86-2622]*

PEDESTRIANS - GERMANY (WEST) - PREVENTION - CONGRESSES.
Die Sicherung des Fussgängerverkehrs. Köln , 1976. ii, 169 p. : LC Card 86-185084
HE5614.5.G3 A7 Bd. 29

PEDICABS - INDIA.
Darbéra, Richard. Le planificateur et le cyclopousse . Caen , 1986. xiii, 190 p. : ISBN 2-86878-015-6 : LC Card 86-192929
HE311.I4 D36 1986

PEDOLOGY (CHILD STUDY) see CHILDREN.

Pedoman pembinaan kewiraswastaan bagi siswa. Jakarta : Departemen Pendidikan dan Kebudayaan, Direktorat Jenderal Pendidikan Dasar dan Menengah, Direktorat Pembinaan Kesiswaan, 1985. 1 v. (various pagings) : forms ; 21 cm. Includes a bibliography. LC Card 86-942929
1. Business education - Indonesia. 2. Entrepreneur - Study and teaching - Indonesia. I. Indonesia. Direktorat Pembinaan Kesiswaan.
HF1171.I5 P43 1985

Pedone, Antonio. Politiche tributarie e struttura industriale in Italia /. Bologna , c1986. 118 p. ;

ISBN 88-15-01224-9 : LC Card 86-224989
HD2753.I7 P65 1986

Pedraja Tomán, René de la. Los Llanos : colonización y economía / por René de la Pedraja Tomán. Bogotá, Colombia : Centro de Estudios Sobre Desarrollo Económico, Facultad de Economía, Universidad de los Andes, 1984. 101 p. : ill. ; 28 cm. (Documento. 072) Bibliography: p. [86]-92. LC Card 84-221343
1. Colombia - Economic conditions - 1970-. 2. Llanos Orientales (Colombia and Venezuela) - Economic conditions. 3. Land settlement - Llanos Orientales (Colombia and Venezuela). 4. Cattle trade - Llanos Orientales (Colombia and Venezuela). I. Series: Documento (Universidad de los Andes (Bogotá, Colombia). Centro de Estudios sobre Desarrollo Económico) , 072. II. Title.
HC198.L56 P4 1984

Pedrero, Mercedes. Indicadores para el estudio de la población económicamente activa basados en la información censal de 1970 / Mercedes Pedrero. México, D.F. : Centro Nacional de Información y Estadísticas del Trabajo, [1977] 495 p. ; 23 cm. (Serie Estudios. 4) Chiefly tables. Includes bibliographical references. LC Card 85-202779
1. Mexico - Population - Economic aspects - Statistics. 2. Mexico - Census, 1970. 3. Labor supply - Mexico - Statistics. 4. Mexico - Occupations - Statistics. I. Centro Nacional de Información y Estadísticas del Trabajo (Mexico). II. Series: Serie Estudios (Centro Nacional de Información y Estadísticas del Trabajo (Mexico)) , 4. III. Title.
HA765 .P43 1977

Peek, Peter.
Peek, Stephen, 1947- Gameplan : the game inventor's handbook / Stephen Peek. White Hall, Va. : Betterway Publications, c1987. 135 p. ; 29 cm. Includes index. ISBN 0-932620-85-X (pbk.) : LC Card 87-15921 DDC 794/.068 19
1. Games - Marketing. I. Title. II. Title: Game plan.
HD9993.G352 P44 1987

Peer review manual /. American Institute of Certified Public Accountants. Private Companies Practice Section. New York, N.Y. (1121 Ave. of the Americas, New York 10036-8775) , 1986. 2 v. in 1 : LC Card 86-217293 DDC 657/.833 19
HF5616.U5 A585 1986a

Peer review manual . American Institute of Certified Public Accountants. SEC Practice Section. New York, NY (1211 Ave. of the Americas, New York 10036-8775) , 1986- 1 v. (loose-leaf) : LC Card 87-108519 DDC 657/.833 19
HF5616.U5 A585 1986b

PEER REVIEW - UNITED STATES.
American Institute of Certified Public Accountants. Private Companies Practice Section. Peer review manual /. New York, N.Y. (1121 Ave. of the Americas, New York 10036-8775) , 1986. 2 v. in 1 : LC Card 86-217293 DDC 657/.833 19
HF5616.U5 A585 1986a

American Institute of Certified Public Accountants. SEC Practice Section. Peer review manual . New York, NY (1211 Ave. of the Americas, New York 10036-8775) , 1986- 1 v. (loose-leaf) : LC Card 87-108519 DDC 657/.833 19
HF5616.U5 A585 1986b

Peet, Richard. International capitalism and industrial restructuring . Boston , 1987. p. cm. ISBN 0-04-338132-4 (alk. paper) LC Card 86-28870 DDC 338.7 19
HD2321 .I58 1987

Peeters, Theo.
International trade and exchange rates in the late eighties /. Amsterdam ; New York : xii, 418 p. : ISBN 2-8004-0892-8
NYPL [JLE 87-120]

International trade and exchange rates in the late eighties /. Amsterdam ; New York : xii, 418 p. : ISBN 0-444-87941-2 LC Card 86-223111 DDC 382.4/5 19
HG203 .I58 1985

Peffer, Michel, 1948- L'Etat anthropophage / Michel Peffer. Bruxelles : Vie ouvrière, c1982. 279 p. ; 19 cm. (Collection Dossiers) Includes bibliographical references. ISBN 2-87005-164-5 LC Card 84-139080
1. Finance, Public - Belgium. 2. Government spending policy - Belgium. 3. Belgium - Economic policy. I. Title.
HJ1197 .P44 1982

Pegels, C. Carl. Management and industry in China / C. Carl Pegels with contributions by J.A. Alutto ... [et al.]. New York : Praeger, 1987. xii, 282 p. ; 25 cm. Includes bibliographical references and index. ISBN 0-275-92553-6 (alk. paper) : LC Card 86-25260 DDC 658/.00951 19
1. Management - China. 2. Industrial management - China. I. Title.
HD70.C5 P44 1987 ***NYPL [JLE 87-1042]***

Pēges oikonomikēs historias .
(3) Pizanias, Petros. Misthoi kai eisodēmata stēn Hellada, 1842-1923 . Athēna , 1985. 324 p., [20] p. of plates : LC Card 87-111106
HG3250.5.A7 P59 1985

PEGMATITES - BRAZIL.
Metais de Minas Gerais, S.A. Programa pegmatitos. Belo Horizonte , 1981. 95 p. : LC Card 83-220720
HD9506.B72 M48 1981

PEINER MASCHINEN- UND SCHRAUBENWERKE - CASE STUDIES.
Fricke, Werner. Beteiligung im Industriebetrieb . Frankfurt/Main , New York , c1985. 291 p. ; ISBN 3-593-32735-X LC Card 85-202742
HD5660.G4 F73 1985

Peiraias, 1835-1870 . Tsokopoulos, Vasias. Athēna , 1984. 280 p., [8] p. of plates : LC Card 86-128354
HC298.P57 T77 1984 ***NYPL [JLD 86-171]***

Peirano Morán, Jorge. Pequeña industria, reactivación y desarrollo industrial /. [Miraflores, Lima] [1986] 127 p. : LC Card 87-127800 DDC 338.6/42/0985 19
HD2346.P4 P47 1986

Peirano, Ricardo. El rol del empresario privado en el desarrollo económico y social en democracia / por Ricardo Peirano, Edgardo Favaro. Montevideo, Uruguay : Asociación Cristiana de Dirigentes de Empresa, 1986. 79 leaves ; 28 cm. Includes bibliographical references. LC Card 87-404359 DDC 338.9895 19
1. Uruguay - Economic policy. 2. Uruguay - Social Policy. 3. Capitalism - Uruguay. 4. Business enterprises - Uruguay. I. Favaro, Edgardo. II. Title.
HC232 .P45 1986

Peiró Arroyo, Antonio. Normante y Carcavilla, Lorenzo. Discurso sobre la utilidad de los conocimientos económico-políticos y la necesidad de su estudio metódico ; Proposiciones de economía civil y comercio ; Espíritu del señor Melón en su ensayo político sobre el comercio /. [Aragón] [1984?] 1 v. (various pagings) ; ISBN 84-505-0473-2 LC Card 87-104302
HC385 .N57 1984

Peláez, Carlos Manuel. O cruzado e o austral : análise das reformas monetárias do Brasil e da Argentina / Carlos Manuel Peláez ; prefácio do Prof. Theóphilo de Azeredo Santos.1a. ed. São Paulo : Editora Atlas, 1986. 174 p. : ill. ; 22 cm. ISBN 85-22-40173-X LC Card 87-102770 DDC 332.4/981 19
1. Monetary policy - Brazil. 2. Monetary policy - Argentina. 3. Brazil - Economic policy. 4. Argentina - Economic policy. I. Title.
HG835 .P43 1986

PELAGIUS, ALVARUS, 1280?-1353 - VIEWS ON ECONOMICS.
Amzalak, Moses Bensabat, 1892- D. Alvaro Pais e o pensamento económico em Portugal na Idade Média /. Lisboa , 1954. 71 p. : LC Card 84-213332
HB79.P45 A49 1954

Pelaksanaan program keterkaitan antar sektor industri dan antara sektor industri dengan sektor ekonomi lainnya . Indonesia. Departemen Perindustrian. [Jakarta] [1985] i, 59 p. ; LC Card 85-941789
HD3616.I53 I49 1985

Pelin, Eli Roberto, 1946- Moldau, Juan Hersztajn. Custo dos recursos domésticos /. Rio de Janeiro , 1985. 94, 4 p. ; LC Card 86-200395
HC190.C7 M64 1985

PELION MOUNTAINS REGION (GREECE) - HISTORY.
Tzamtzēs, A. I. Hē nautilia tou Pēliou stēn Tourkokratia . [Athēnai] [198-] 103 p., [20] p. of plates : LC Card 87-111965
HE872.5.Z6 T98 1980z

Pelkmans, Jacques.
Can the CAP be reformed? /. Maastricht, The Netherlands , c1985. xii, 127 p. ; ISBN 90-6779-013-3 (pbk.) LC Card 86-214732 DDC 338.1/84 19
HD1920.5 .C36 1985

Coming to grips with the internal market /. Maastricht, The Netherlands , c1986. viii, 136 p. ; ISBN 90-6779-019-2 (pbk.) LC Card 86-222624 DDC 337.1/42 19
HC241.2 .C5548 1986

Pell, Arthur R.
Making the most of Medicare / Arthur R. Pell. 1st ed. New York : Prentice Hall Press, c1987. ix, 123 p. : forms ; 28 cm. Includes bibliographical references and index. ISBN 0-13-547696-8 (pbk.) : LC Card 86-25160 DDC 344.73/0226 347.304226 19
1. Medicare - Handbooks, manuals, etc. I. Title.
HD7102.U4 P45 1987

Managing through people /. Garden City, NY (1475 Franklin Ave., Garden City 11530) , c1987. 345 p. ; LC Card 87-167705 DDC 658.4 19
HD31 .M29427 1987

Pellicer Valero, Jesús-Agustín. Sociología del trabajo en Canet de Berenguer / Jesús-Agustín Pellicer Valero. Valencia : [Escuela Universitaria de Estudios Empresariales de la Universidad de Valencia], 1984. 80 p. : ill. ; 24 cm. (Publicaciones de la Escuela Universitaria de Estudios Empresariales de la Universidad de Valencia. Sociología) Bibliography: p. 79-80. ISBN 84-600-3540-9 LC Card 86-216439
1. Labor supply - Spain - Canet de Berenguer. 2. Women - Employment - Spain - Canet de Berenguer. 3. Unemployed - Spain - Canet de Berenguer. 4. Canet de Berenguer (Spain) - Population. 5. Industrial sociology - Spain - Canet de Berenguer. I. Title. II. Series.
HD5808.C33 P45 1984

PELOPONNESUS (GREECE) - POPULATION - HISTORY.
Panagiōtopoulos, Vasilēs, 1932- Plēthysmos kai oikismoi tēs Peloponnēsou . Athēna , 1985. 414 p. : LC Card 86-207132
HB3632.5.P45 P36 1985

Peltason, J. W. (Jack Walter), 1923- Burns, James MacGregor. State and local politics . Englewood Cliffs, N.J. , c1984. xi, 266 p. : ISBN 0-13-843524-3 (pbk.) LC Card 83-21259 DDC 320.973 19
JK2408 .B87 1984 ***NYPL [JLE 87-142]***

Peluso, Nancy Lee. Survival strategies of rural women traders, or, A woman's place is in the market : four case studies from northwestern Sleman in the special region of Yogyakarta / by Nancy Lee Peluso. Geneva : International Labour Office, [1981], c1980. viii, 124 p. ; 30 cm. (World Employment Programme research working paper) "Original paper presented to ILO Jakarta for use by the Department of Manpower, Government of Indonesia, 23 May 1980." "Rural Employment Policy Research Programme." "January 1981." "WEP 10/WP 17." Includes bibliographical references. ISBN 92-2-102633-7 LC Card 83-105710 DDC 331.4/81381/095982 19
1. Women sales personnel - Indonesia - Sleman (Kabupaten) - Case studies. 2. Rural women - Indonesia - Sleman (Kabupaten) - Case studies. I. Title. II. Series.
HD6194.Z6 S566 1981

Pelz, Karl.
Arbeitsplatzpolitik für die Landwirtschaft. 1984. Arbeitsmarktpolitik für die Landwirtschaft und den ländlichen Raum / mit Beiträgen von Otto Lackinger, Karl Pelz, Manfred Sinz ; [Herausgeber, Hans Bach]. Graz , c1984. 138 p. : ISBN 3-900307-15-6 LC Card 85-186643
HD1536.A9 A73 1984

Pelzman, Joseph. Barth, James R. International debt . Fairfax, Va. , 1984. 36 p. ;
NYPL [*ZT-1554 no.21]

Pembangunan ekonomi dan perkembangan bisnis di Indonesia /. Rudianto, Doddy. Jakarta , 1985. 53 p. ; LC Card 86-944718
HC447 .R73 1985

Pemberton, P. A. Pure merinos and others : the "shipping lists" of the Australian Agricultural Company / P.A. Pemberton. Canberra : Australian National University, Archives of Business and Labour : Distributed by Anutech, c1986. 125 p. : maps ; 25 cm. Bibliography: p. 124-125. ISBN 0-86784-796-4 (pbk.) LC Card 87-164515 DDC 382/.41636/0994 19
1. Ship registers - Great Britain. 2. Australian Agricultural Company - History. 3. Australian Agricultural Company - History - Sources. 4. Wool trade and industry - Great Britain - History - Sources. 5. Wool trade and industry - Australia - History - Sources. 6. Sheep industry - Great Britain - History - Sources. 7. Sheep industry - Australia - History - Sources. 8. Coal trade - Great Britain - History - Sources. 9. Coal trade - Australia - History - Sources. I. Australian Agricultural Company. II. Title.
HE565.G7 P46 1986

Pemex. see **Petróleos mexicanos.**

Pempel, T. J., 1942- Ilgen, Thomas L. Trading technology . New York , 1987. x, 203 p. ; ISBN 0-275-92483-1 (alk. paper) : LC Card 86-21197 DDC 338.94/06 19
HC415.15 .I45 1986 ***NYPL [JLE 87-832]***

PEN CANCELLATIONS (PHILATELY) - NEW YORK (STATE) - HISTORY.
Manuscript post offices of New York State /. [Richford, N.Y.?] , 1984. xii, 54 p., [12] p. of plates : LC Card 86-213682 DDC 383/.49747 19
HE6376.A1 N729 1984

Peña, Guillermo de la. Cambio regional, mercado de trabajo y vida obrera en Jalisco /. Guadalajara, Jalisco, México , 1986. 363 p. ; ISBN 968-614-201-0 LC Card 86-218238
HD5731.J35 C36 1986

Peña, Isidro Parra. see **Parra Peña, Isidro, 1936-**

Pena, Maria Valéria Junho. Mulheres e trabalhadoras : presença feminina na constituição do sistema fabril / Maria Valéria Junho Pena. Rio de Janeiro, RJ : Paz e Terra, 1981. iii, 227 p. ; 21 cm. (Coleção O Mundo hoje. vol. 40) Originally presented as the author's thesis (doctoral)--Universidade de São Paulo. Bibliography: p. 223-227. LC Card 81-216820 DDC 331.4/0981 19
1. Women - Employment - Brazil - History. 2. Women - Brazil - Economic conditions. 3. Women - Brazil - Social conditions. 4. Brazil - Industries - History. I. Title.
HD6124 .P46 1981 ***NYPL [JLD 86-1557]***

Peña, Rodolfo F. Aún tiembla . México , c1986. 332 p., [8] p. of plates : ISBN 968-419-620-2 LC Card 87-403523 DDC 363.3/495/097253 19
HC138.M43 A95 1986

Peñalava, Susana. Habitat popular . Buenos Aires , 1986. 162 p. : LC Card 87-404028 DDC 363.5/8 19
HD7305.5 .H32 1986

Penati, Luigi. Strategie di marketing / Luigi Penati. Milano, Italy : F. Angeli, c1986. 332 p. : ill. ; 22 cm. (Azienda moderna. 191) Bibliography: p. [331]-332. LC Card 86-217663
1. Marketing - Italy. I. Title.
HF5415.12.I8 P47 1986

Pendidikan kependudukan untuk perwira. [Jakarta] : Lembaga Keluarga Berencana ABRI bekerja sama dengan BKKBN Pusat dan UNFPA, [1981] vi, 120 p. : ill., ports. ; 28 cm. Includes bibliographies. LC Card 85-940192
1. Population - Study and teaching - Indonesia. I. Lembaga Keluarga Berencana ABRI. II. Indonesia. Badan Koordinasi Keluarga Berencana Nasional. III. United Nations Fund for Population Activities.
HB850.5 .P46 1981

Pendidikan kependudukan untuk peserta diklat Departemen P.U. Bahan instruksional pendidikan kependudukan untuk peserta diklat Departemen P.U. Jakarta , 1982. v, 90 p. ; LC Card 83-941464
HB850.5.I5 B34 1982

Penetrating the international market . Mares, David R. New York , 1987. xvi, 294 p. : ISBN 0-231-06346-6 (alk. paper) LC Card 87-6358 DDC 382/.415/097232 19
HD9014.M62 M38 1987

Penguin business library.
Brown, J. A. C. (James Alexander Campbell), 1911-1964. The social psychology of industry . Harmondsworth, Middlesex, England , New York, N.Y., U. S.A. , c1986. xviii, 335 p. ; ISBN 0-14-009109-2 (pbk.) : LC Card 87-132408 DDC 158.7 19
HF5548.8 .B7 1986

Penkov, Petŭr.
Aktualni ikonomicheski problemi . Sofiia , 1985. 227 p. ; LC Card 86-205815
HC403 .A67 1985

Osnovi na sotsialnoto osiguriavane / Petŭr Penkov. Sofiia : [s.n.], 1984. 191 p. : ill. ; 23 cm. At head of title: Nauchnoizsledovatelski institut po profsŭiuzni problemi "G. Dimitrov." Vissha shkola za sleddiplomna kvalifikatsiia po profsŭiuzni problemi. Bibliography: p. 186-189. LC Card 86-104011
1. Social security. 2. Social security - Bulgaria. I. Title.
HD7091 .P335 1984

Penna, João Camilo de Oliveira.
As empresas estatais na economia brasileira / João Camilo Penna. [Brasília] : Ministério da Indústria e do Comércio, Coordenadoria de Comunicação Social, 1983. 43 p. ; 22 cm. "Palestra proferida pelo Ministro João Camilo Penna no Tribunal de Contas da União." LC Card 86-229392
1. Government business enterprises - Brazil. 2. Economic indicators - Brazil. 3. Brazil - Economic conditions - 1964-1985. I. Title.
HD4093 .P46 1983

O Proálcool vale? /. [São Paulo-SP (Brasil)] , 1985. 52 p. : LC Card 86-220396
HD9502.5.A433 B645 1985

Pennant-Rea, Rupert.
The Economist economics / Rupert Pennant-Rea and Clive Crook. Rev. ed. Harmondsworth, Middlesex, England ; New York, U. S.A. : Penguin Books, 1986. 197 p. : ill. ; 20 cm. (Pelican books) Bibliography: p. 173-189. Includes index. ISBN 0-14-022703-2 (pbk.) : LC Card 86-219602 DDC 330 19
1. Economics. I. Crook, Clive. II. Title.
HB171 .P458 1986

The pocket economist / Rupert Pennant-Rea and Bill Emmott. Oxford, UK ; New York, NY : B. Blackwell and The Economist, 1987, c1983. p. cm. Reprint. Previously published: Cambridge [Cambridgeshire] ; New York : Cambridge University Press, 1983. Bibliography: p. ISBN 0-631-14586-9 : LC Card 87-10361 DDC 330/.03/21 19
1. Economics - Dictionaries. I. Emmott, Bill. II. Title.
HB61 .P435 1987

Penne, R. Leo. Barnes, William R. Employment problems and America's cities /. [Washington, D.C.] , 1984. xiii, 66, 33 p. ;
NYPL [JLF 86-1]

Penne, R. Leo, 1941- McNulty, Robert H., 1940- The economics of amenity . Washington, D.C. , c1985. xvi, 157 p. : ISBN 0-941182-15-0 (pbk.) LC Card 85-6545 DDC 307.7/6/0973 19
HT321 .M36 1985 ***NYPL [JLE 86-4519]***

Pennella, Giuseppe. Le politiche monetarie e di bilancio nei principali paesi industrializzati : aspetti istituzionali e quantitativi / Giuseppe Pennella. Milano, Italy : F. Angeli, c1985. 293 p. : ill. ; 22 cm. Includes bibliographical references. LC Card 86-129450
1. Monetary policy. 2. Balance of payments. 3. International economic relations. I. Title.
HG230.3 .P45 1985

Penner, Hellmut, 1942- Airbus International / Hellmut Penner, Dietmar Plath. 1. Aufl. Stuttgart : Motorbuch Verlag, 1986. 206 p. : ill. (some col.) ; 28 cm. ISBN 3-613-01093-3 LC Card 86-211620
1. Aircraft industry - Europe. 2. Airbus (Jet transport). I. Plath, Dietmar, 1954-. II. Title.
HD9711.E882 P46 1986

Penner, Maria Eunice Soares. A dialética da atividade pesqueira no nordeste amazônico / Maria Eunice Soares Penner. Belém : Universidade Federal do Pará, 1984. 158 p. : ill. ; 23 cm. Presented as the author's thesis (mestre em geografia)--Universidade Federal de Pernambuco. Bibliography: p. 153-158. ISBN 85-24-70006-8 LC Card 86-158128
1. Fish trade - Brazil, Northeast. 2. Fish trade - Amazon River Region. 3. Brazil, Northeast - Economic conditions. 4. Amazon River Region - Economic conditions. I. Title.
HD9464.B73 N676 1984

Penning-Rowsell, Edmund. Floods and drainage : British policies for hazard reduction, agricultural improvement, and wetland conservation / E.C. Penning-Rowsell, D.J. Parker, D.M. Harding. London ; Boston : Allen and Unwin, 1986. xx, 199 p. : ill. ; 23 cm. (Risks & hazards series, 0261-0507 . 2) Includes index. Bibliography: p. 178-192. ISBN 0-04-627001-9 (alk. paper) : LC Card 85-13383 DDC 363.3/4936/0941 19
1. Flood control - Government policy - Great Britain. 2. Drainage - Government policy - Great Britain. 3. Wetland conservation - Government policy - Great Britain. 4. Agriculture and state - Great Britain. I. Parker, Dennis J. II. Harding, Donald M. III. Title.
HD1676.G7 P46 1985 ***NYPL [JLE 86-3996]***

Pennings, Johannes M. New technology as organizational innovation . Cambridge, Mass. , c1987. xvi, 308 p. : ISBN 0-88730-186-X LC Card 86-32110 DDC 658.5/14 19
HD45 .N43 1987

Pennisi, Giuseppe. Development, manpower and migration in the Red Sea region : the case for cooperation / Giuseppe Pennisi. Hamburg : Deutsches Orient-Institut, c1981. xi, 264 p. : ill. ; 30 cm. (Mitteilungen des Deutschen Orient-Institut . Nr. 15) Bibliography: p. 241-264. LC Card 82-109615 DDC 331.6/2/091824 19
1. Alien labor - Red Sea Region. 2. Labor supply - Red Sea Region. 3. Labor policy - Red Sea Region. 4. Red Sea Region - Economic conditions. I. Series: Hamburg. Deutsches Orient-Institut. Mitteilungen, Nr. 15. II. Title.
HD8656 .P46 1981 ***NYPL [JLF 86-1602]***

Pennsylvania. Dept. of Aging. Blank, Thomas O., 1947- Older persons and their homes, today and tomorrow . [Harrisburg] [1986] 60 leaves : LC Card 86-623023 DDC 363.5/9 19
HD7287.92.U54 B55 1986

Pennsylvania. Dept. of Labor and Industry. Office of Employment Security. see **Pennsylvania. Office of Employment Security.**

PENNSYLVANIA - ECONOMIC POLICY.
Allen, David N. Nurturing advanced technology enterprises . New York , c1986. xvi, 268 p. ; ISBN 0-275-92136-0 (alk. paper) : LC Card 86-9411 DDC 338.4/762/0009748 19
HC107.P43 H533 1986
NYPL [JLE 86-3609]

Schweitzer, Mary M. Custom and contract . New York , 1987. xii, 271 p. : ISBN 0-231-06288-5 LC Card 87-8003 DDC 338.9748 19
HC107.P4 S417 1987

Pennsylvania. Employment Security, Office of. see **Pennsylvania. Office of Employment Security.**

Pennsylvania. General Assembly. Legislative Budget and Finance Committee.
A report on mass transit funding needs in Pennsylvania / Legislative Budget and Finance Committee. Rev. Harrisburg, Pa. (Rm. 400, Finance Bldg., Harrisburg 17120) : The Committee, [1986] ii, 151 p. ; 29 cm. "June 11, 1986." LC Card 86-622848 DDC 388.4/042 19
1. Local transit - Pennsylvania - Finance. I. Title.
HE4487.P4 P44 1986

A Sunset performance audit of the Pennsylvania Housing Finance Agency pursuant to Act 1981-142 /. Harrisburg, Pa. (Rm. 400, Finance Bldg., Harrisburg 17120) [1985] ii, 75 p. ; LC Card 85-623018 DDC 353.97480086/5045 19
HD7303.P4 P425 1985
NYPL [JLF 86-1807]

Pennsylvania - Government. see **Pennsylvania - Politics and government.**

Pennsylvania. Health Data Center. Vital statistics for Pennsylvania, 1980 to 1984. Harrisburg, Pa. [1986] x, 103 p. : LC Card 86-622850 DDC 304.6/09748/021 19
HA605 .V58 1986

Pennsylvania. Historical and Museum Commission. Hard coal, hard times . Scranton , 1984, c1983. xv, 193 p. ; ISBN 0-917445-00-7 LC Card 85-156422 DDC 331.7/622335/0974837
HD8039.M62 U633 1984
NYPL [JLE 87-1218]

Pennsylvania history studies .
(no. 4) Miller, Ernest C. (Ernest Conrad), 1912- Pennsylvania's oil industry /. Gettysburg, PA. , 1974, c1954. iii, 69 p. : LC Card

87-100839
HD9567.P4 M5 1974

PENNSYLVANIA HOUSING FINANCE AGENCY - AUDITING.
A Sunset performance audit of the Pennsylvania Housing Finance Agency pursuant to Act 1981-142 /. Harrisburg, Pa. (Rm. 400, Finance Bldg., Harrisburg 17120) [1985] ii, 75 p. ; LC Card 85-623018 DDC 353.97480086/5045 19
HD7303.P4 P425 1985 *NYPL [JLF 86-1807]*

Pennsylvania. Legislature. see **Pennsylvania. General Assembly.**

Pennsylvania occupational trends and outlook for total civilian employment, 1980 and projected 1990 / [developed on a cooperative basis between the Pennsylvania Office of Employment Security and the U. S. Bureau of Labor Statistics]. Harrisburg, Pa. : Department of Labor and Industry, Office of Employment Security, Research and Statistics Division, Occupational Employment Statistics, 1984. ii, 98 p. : ill., map ; 22 x 28 cm. Cover title. Bibliography: p. 96.
1. Employment forecasting - Pennsylvania. 2. Labor supply - Pennsylvania - Statistics. 3. Job vacancies - Pennsylvania - Statistics. 4. Pennsylvania - Occupations - Statistics. I. Pennsylvania. Office of Employment Security. *NYPL [JLF 87-706]*

PENNSYLVANIA - OCCUPATIONS - STATISTICS.
Pennsylvania occupational trends and outlook for total civilian employment, 1980 and projected 1990 /. Harrisburg, Pa. , 1984. ii, 98 p. : *NYPL [JLF 87-706]*

Pennsylvania. Office of Employment Security.
Pennsylvania occupational trends and outlook for total civilian employment, 1980 and projected 1990 /. Harrisburg, Pa. , 1984. ii, 98 p. : *NYPL [JLF 87-706]*

PENNSYLVANIA - POLITICS AND GOVERNMENT - COLONIAL PERIOD, CA. 1600-1775.
Schweitzer, Mary M. Custom and contract . New York , 1987. xii, 271 p. : ISBN 0-231-06288-5 LC Card 87-8003 DDC 338.9748 19
HC107.P4 S417 1987

Pennsylvania Rural Electric Association. Romeo, Mary Ellen. Darkness to daylight . Harrisburg, Pa. , c1986. 152 p. : LC Card 86-216619 DDC 621.319/09748 19
HD9688.U53 P46 1986

PENNSYLVANIA - SOCIAL CONDITIONS.
Schweitzer, Mary M. Custom and contract . New York , 1987. xii, 271 p. : ISBN 0-231-06288-5 LC Card 87-8003 DDC 338.9748 19
HC107.P4 S417 1987

Pennsylvania State University. Dept. of Labor Studies. Forging a union of steel . Ithaca, N.Y. , c1987. vii, 153 p. : ISBN 0-87546-135-2 (pbk.) LC Card 87-21508 DDC 331.88/169142/0973 19
HD6515.I5 F58 1987

PENNSYLVANIA - STATISTICS, VITAL.
Vital statistics for Pennsylvania, 1980 to 1984. Harrisburg, Pa. [1986] x, 103 p. : LC Card 86-622850 DDC 304.6/09748/021 19
HA605 .V58 1986

Pennsylvania. University. Wharton School of Finance and Commerce. Industrial Research Unit.
Industrial Research Unit study. For additional listing of contents, see Old Catalog. For later file
(no. 62) Northrup, Herbert Roof, 1918- Open shop construction revisited /. Philadelphia, Pa., U. S.A. , c1984. xxxv, 674 p. : ISBN 0-89546-047-5 : LC Card 84-48502 DDC 331.88/92 19
HD9715.U52 N67 1984 *NYPL [TB (Pennsylvania. University. Wharton School of Finance and Commerce. Industrial Research Unit. Industrial Research Unit Study. no. 62)]*

Pennsylvania's oil industry /. Miller, Ernest C. (Ernest Conrad), 1912- Gettysburg, PA. , 1974, c1954. iii, 69 p. : LC Card 87-100839
HD9567.P4 M5 1974

Pennsylvania's street railways in early postcard views . Berner, Allan H. [S.l.] , c1986. 106 p. : LC Card 86-221349 DDC 388.4/4/09748 19
HE4487.P4 B47 1986

PennWell Publishing Company. Glossary of the petroleum industry . Tulsa, Okla. , c1982. vi, 378 p. ; ISBN 0-87814-194-4 (pbk.) : LC Card 82-7622 DDC 665.5/03/61 19
TN865 .G63 1982 *NYPL [JSD 86-496]*

PENNZOIL COMPANY.
Petzinger, Thomas. Oil & honor . New York , c1987. 495 p., [8] p. of plates : ISBN 0-399-13276-7 LC Card 87-2255 DDC 338.8/3622338/0973 19
HD9569.T4 P48 1987

Penoyar, William F. Fedspeak : U. S. contracting and grantsmanship made easier / by William F. Penoyar. Arnold, Md. : For additional copies contact G.T.M. Co., c1985. v, 178 p. : ill. ; 22 cm. Bibliography: p. 173-176. ISBN 0-9615112-2-2 (pbk.) : LC Card 85-90360 DDC 353.0071/2 19
1. Government purchasing - United States. 2. Public contracts - United States. I. Title.
JK1673 .P46 1985 *NYPL [JLD 87-568]*

Penrose, John M. Huseman, Richard C. Business communication . Chicago , c1988. xxxi, 702 p., [8] p. of plates : ISBN 0-03-012294-5 LC Card 87-438 DDC 658.4/5 19
HF5718 .H84 1988

Pensamiento agrario ecuatoriano / estudio introductorio y selección, Carlos Marchán Romero. Quito, Ecuador : Banco Central del Ecuador : Corporación Editora Nacional, 1986. 741 p. : ill. ; 22 cm. (Biblioteca básica del pensamiento ecuatoriano . 23) Contains excerpts from publications published between 1904 and 1980. Bibliography: p. 65-71. LC Card 87-403503 DDC 333.3/1/866 19
1. Land reform - Ecuador - History. 2. Land reform - Law and legislation - Ecuador - History. 3. Slavery - Ecuador - History. 4. Slavery - Law and legislation - Ecuador - History. I. Marchán R., Carlos (Marchán Romero). II. Series.
HD1333.E2 P46 1986

Pensamiento de la empresa privada boliviana . Confederación de Empresarios Privados de Bolivia. La Paz, Bolivia [1981] 274 p. : LC Card 82-138113 DDC 322/.3/0984 19
HC181 .C6426 1981 *NYPL [JLF 86-1617]*

Pensamiento monetario y financiero / estudio introductorio y selección, Eduardo Larrea Stacey. Quito, Ecuador : Banco Central del Ecuador : Corporación Editora Nacional, 1986. 2 v. : ill. ; 22 cm. (Biblioteca básica del pensamiento ecuatoriano . 20-21) Contains excerpts from publications published between 1893 and 1979. Bibliography: v. 1, p. [71]-73. LC Card 87-150740 DDC 332.4/9866 19
1. Money - Ecuador. 2. Money - Law and legislation - Ecuador. 3. Finance - Ecuador. 4. Banks and banking - Ecuador. I. Larrea Stacey, Eduardo, 1911-. II. Series.
HG862 .P46 1986

Il pensiero economico italiano /. Nuccio, Oscar. [Sassari] , 1984-<1985. <v. 1, t. 1-2; in 2 > ; LC Card 87-110173
HB109.A2 N833 1984

Pension asset management : an international perspective / edited by Leslie Hannah. Homewood, Ill. : Published for the Pension Research Council, Wharton School, University of Pennsylvania by R.D. Irwin, 1988. xiii, 178 p. : ill. ; 24 cm. Includes bibliographies. ISBN 0-256-06123-8 LC Card 87-81575 DDC 332.6/7254 19
1. Pension trusts - Investments. 2. Portfolio management. 3. Wharton School. Pension Research Council. I. Hannah, Leslie.
HD7105.4 .P45 1988

PENSION BENEFIT GUARANTY CORPORATION.
Overview of current issues relating to single-employer defined benefit pension plans and Pension Benefit Guaranty Corporation (PBGC) premiums . Washington , 1987. iii, 49 p. ; LC Card 87-601357 DDC 331.25/2/0973 19
HD7125 .O88 1987

Pension fund investment / edited by A.G. Shepherd. Cambridge [Cambridgeshire] ; Wolfeboro, NH, U. S.A. : Woodhead-Faulkner, 1988. c. pm. Includes index. ISBN 0-85941-400-0 : LC Card 87-17894 DDC 332.6/7254 19
1. Pension trusts - Great Britain - Investments. 2. Pension trusts - Investments - Law and legislation - Great Britain. I. Shepherd, A. G.
HD7105.45.G7 P45 1988

Pension integration : how large defined benefit plans coordinate benefits with Social Security : briefing report to congressional requesters / United States General Accounting Office. Washington, D.C. : The Office, [1986] 28 p. : ill. ; 28 cm. Cover title. "July 1986." Bibliography: p. 20-21. "GAO/HRD-86-118BR." LC Card 86-603093 DDC 331.25/2/0973 19
1. Old age pensions - United States. 2. Social security - United States. I. United States. General Accounting Office.
HD7125 .P392 1986

Pension plan partial terminations /. Harker, Carlton. Brookfield, Wis. , c1982. 92 p. ; ISBN 0-89154-163-2 (pbk.) : LC Card 82-147078 DDC 344.73/01252 347.3041252 19
KF3512.Z9 H37 1982 *NYPL [JLF 85-605]*

PENSION TRUST INVESTMENTS. see **PENSION TRUSTS - INVESTMENTS.**

PENSION TRUSTS.
Slimmon, Robert F. Successful pension design for small-to medium-sized businesses /. Englewood Cliffs, N.J. , c1987. xix, 440 p. ; ISBN 0-13-860255-7 LC Card 87-2489 DDC 658.3/253
HD7105.4 .S56 1987

Soler Bordetas, Francisco Javier. Fondos de pensiones /. Bilbao [1985?] 152 p. : ISBN 84-234-0575-3 LC Card 86-166028
HD7105.45.S7 S57 1985

PENSION TRUSTS - GERMANY, WEST.
Bethge, Hans, 1951- Die betriebliche Altersversorgung als Möglichkeit zur Deckung von Versorgungslücken in der gesetzlichen Rentenversicherung unter besonderer Berücksichtigung unternehmerischer Entscheidungsgrössen /. Köln , c1986. 269 p. ; ISBN 3-924361-16-9 LC Card 86-222067
HD7105.45.G3 B47 1986

Infratest Sozialforschung. Datenlage zur Alterssicherung . Bonn , 1984. 330 p. : LC Card 86-132439 DDC 331.25/2/0943 19
HD7105.35.G3 I54 1984

Kapitalbildung und Altersvorsorge . Köln , Bergisch Gladbach [1983?] 95 p. : LC Card 84-180205
HD7105.45.G3 K37 1983

Sicherung der Altersvorsorge durch Aufgabenteilung zwischen Individualversicherung und gesetzlicher Rentenversicherung . München , 1986. xi, 242 p. : ISBN 3-88512-017-8 : LC Card 86-163171
HD7105.35.G3 S53 1986

PENSION TRUSTS - GOVERNMENT POLICY - UNITED STATES.
Wendling, Wayne. The regulatory impact on pensions /. Brookfield, Wis. , 1986. xiii, 91 p. : ISBN 0-89154-314-7 (pbk.) : LC Card 87-129712 DDC 331.25/2/0973 19
HD7105.35.U6 W46 1986

PENSION TRUSTS - GREAT BRITAIN - INVESTMENTS.
Pension fund investment /. Cambridge [Cambridgeshire] , Wolfeboro, NH, U. S.A. , 1988. c. pm. ISBN 0-85941-400-0 : LC Card 87-17894 DDC 332.6/7254 19
HD7105.45.G7 P45 1988

Pensions . London , Boston , 1987. xvi, 249 p. : ISBN 0-04-332127-5 (alk. paper) LC Card 86-32086 DDC 331.25/2/0941 19
HD7165 .P46 1987

PENSION TRUSTS - INVESTMENT.
Schuller, Tom. Age, capital, and democracy . Aldershot, Hants., England , Brookfield, Vt., U. S.A. , c1986. ix, 172 p. ; ISBN 0-566-00928-5 : LC Card 85-24950 DDC 332.6/7254 19
HD7105.4 .S38 1986 *NYPL [JLD 86-2477]*

PENSION TRUSTS - INVESTMENTS - LAW AND LEGISLATION - GREAT BRITAIN.
Pension fund investment /. Cambridge [Cambridgeshire] , Wolfeboro, NH, U. S.A. , 1988. c. pm. ISBN 0-85941-400-0 : LC Card 87-17894 DDC 332.6/7254 19
HD7105.45.G7 P45 1988

PENSION TRUSTS - LAW AND LEGISLATION - GERMANY (WEST)
Bethge, Hans, 1951- Die betriebliche Altersversorgung als Möglichkeit zur Deckung von Versorgungslücken in der gesetzlichen Rentenversicherung unter besonderer Berücksichtigung unternehmerischer Entscheidungsgrössen /. Köln , c1986. 269 p. ; ISBN 3-924361-16-9 LC Card 86-222067
HD7105.45.G3 B47 1986

PENSION TRUSTS - LAW AND LEGISLATION - UNITED STATES.
Harker, Carlton. Pension plan partial terminations /. Brookfield, Wis. , c1982. 92 p. ; ISBN 0-89154-163-2 (pbk.) : LC Card 82-147078 DDC 344.73/01252 347.3041252 19
KF3512.Z9 H37 1982 NYPL [JLF 85-605]

PENSION TRUSTS - MANAGEMENT.
Schuller, Tom. Age, capital, and democracy . Aldershot, Hants., England , Brookfield, Vt., U. S.A. , c1986. ix, 172 p. ; ISBN 0-566-00928-5 : LC Card 85-24950 DDC 332.6/7254 19
HD7105.4 .S38 1986 NYPL [JLD 86-2477]

PENSION TRUSTS - SPAIN.
Soler Bordetas, Francisco Javier. Fondos de pensiones /. Bilbao [1985?] 152 p. : ISBN 84-234-0575-3 LC Card 86-166028
HD7105.45.S7 S57 1985

PENSION TRUSTS - TAXATION - UNITED STATES.
Curatola, Anthony P. State income tax consequences of retirement plan distributions /. Brookfield, Wis. , c1986. 20 p. ; ISBN 0-89154-324-4 (pbk.) LC Card 87-158902 DDC 336.24/16 19
HJ4653.P5 C87 1986

PENSION TRUSTS - UNITED STATES.
Andrews, Emily S. The changing profile of pensions in America /. Washington, DC , c1985. xxvii, 234 p. ; ISBN 0-86643-038-5 (pbk.) LC Card 85-25296 DDC 332.6/7254 19
HD7105.45.U6 A53 1985
NYPL [JLE 87-62]

Bernstein, Merton C. Social Security . New York , c1988. xiii, 321 p. : ISBN 0-465-07916-4 : LC Card 86-47762 DDC 368.4/3/00973 19
HD7125 .B48 1988

Harker, Carlton. Pension plan partial terminations /. Brookfield, Wis. , c1982. 92 p. ; ISBN 0-89154-163-2 (pbk.) : LC Card 82-147078 DDC 344.73/01252 347.3041252 19
KF3512.Z9 H37 1982 NYPL [JLF 85-605]

Joanette, Francois P. Funding and asset allocation decisions in corporate pension plans /. Brookfield, Wis. , c1986. 17 p. : ISBN 0-89154-304-X (pbk.) : LC Card 87-118785 DDC 658.2/253/0973 19
HD7105.45.U6 J6 1986

PENSION TRUSTS - UNITED STATES - ACCOUNTING.
Clark, Hal G. Illustrations of accounting for pensions and for settlements and curtailments of defined benefit pension plans . New York, N.Y. (1211 Ave. of the Americas, New York 10036-8775) , c1987. 34 p. ; LC Card 87-401762 DDC 657/.75 19
HF5686.O5 C56 1987

PENSION TRUSTS - UNITED STATES - ADDRESSES, ESSAYS, LECTURES.
Broader perspectives on the interest of pension plan participants /. Charlottesville, Va. (P.O. Box 3665, Charlottesville 22903) , c1985. vii, 43 p. : LC Card 85-196669 DDC 332.6/7254 19
HD7105.45.U6 B76 1985
NYPL [JLL 81-133 no. 22]

PENSION TRUSTS - UNITED STATES - CONGRESSES.
Pensions in the U. S. economy /. Chicago , 1988. ix, 200 p. : ISBN 0-226-06285-6 LC Card 87-19987 DDC 331.25/2/0973 19
HD7105.45.U6 P46 1988

PENSION TRUSTS - UNITED STATES - INVESTMENTS.
Berkowitz, Stephen A. The investment performance of corporate pension plans . New York , 1988. xi, 132 p. ; ISBN 0-89930-224-6 (lib. bdg. : alk. paper) LC Card 87-19030 DDC 332.6/7154 19
HD7105.45.U6 B475 1988

PENSION TRUSTS - UNITED STATES - MANAGEMENT - ADDRESSES, ESSAYS, LECTURES.
Broader perspectives on the interest of pension plan participants /. Charlottesville, Va. (P.O. Box 3665, Charlottesville 22903) , c1985. vii, 43 p. : LC Card 85-196669 DDC 332.6/7254 19
HD7105.45.U6 B76 1985
NYPL [JLL 81-133 no. 22]

PENSION TRUSTS - UNITED STATES - MANAGEMENT - CONGRESSES.
Corporate Benefits Management Conferences (1986 : Phoenix, Ariz., etc.) Managing corporate benefit plans, 1986 /. Brookfield, Wis. , 1986. x, 129 p. : ISBN 0-89154-318-X (pbk.) : LC Card 87-403111 DDC 332.6/7254 19
HD7105.45.U6 C67 1986

Pensions : the problems of today and tomorrow / Bernard Benjamin ... [et al]. London ; Boston : Allen & Unwin, 1987. xvi, 249 p. : ill. ; 23 cm. (Studies in financial institutions and markets . [4]) Includes bibliographies and index. ISBN 0-04-332127-5 (alk. paper) LC Card 86-32086 DDC 331.25/2/0941 19
1. Old age pensions - Great Britain. 2. Pensions - Great Britain. 3. Pension trusts - Great Britain - Investments. I. Benjamin, Bernard, 1910-. II. Series.
HD7165 .P46 1987

Pensions . Paterson, Martin, 1927- Cambridge, England , Wolfeboro, N.H., USA, , 1988. p. cm. ISBN 0-85941-380-2 : LC Card 87-8324 DDC 331.25/2/0941 19
HD7105.35.G7 P38 1988

Pensions & profit sharing. 4th ed. [Chicago, Ill.] : R&R Newkirk, c1987- xiii, 351 p. ; 28 cm. + Multiple choice examination. Third ed. published as: Pensions and profit sharing. 1964. Loose-leaf for updating. ISBN 0-88462-650-4 (pbk.) LC Card 87-1608 DDC 658/.3/25 19
1. Old age pensions - United States. 2. Profit-sharing - United States. I. Pensions and profit sharing.
HD7105.35.U6 P45 1987

Pensions and profit sharing. Pensions & profit sharing. [Chicago, Ill.] , c1987- xiii, 351 p. ; ISBN 0-88462-650-4 (pbk.) LC Card 87-1608 DDC 658/.3/25 19
HD7105.35.U6 P45 1987

PENSIONS - EUROPE - FINANCE - CONGRESSES.
Costi e relativi finanziamenti dei sistemi pensionistici nei paesi europei . Roma , 1985. xi, 486 p. : LC Card 86-206925
HD7164 .C67 1985

PENSIONS - GERMANY, WEST.
Schmähl, Winfried. Änderung der Beitragsfinanzierung in der Rentenversicherung? . Baden-Baden , 1984. 388 p. : ISBN 3-7890-1018-9 LC Card 84-206647
HD7179 .S324 1984

Sicherung der Altersvorsorge durch Aufgabenteilung zwischen Individualversicherung und gesetzlicher Rentenversicherung . München , 1986. xi, 242 p. : ISBN 3-88512-017-8 : LC Card 86-163171
HD7105.35.G3 S53 1986

PENSIONS - GERMANY (WEST) - EFFECT OF INFLATION ON.
Schulz, Erika, 1953- Potentielle Beschäftigungseffekte der Maschinensteuer . Frankfurt am Main , New York , c1986. xiii, 303 p. : ISBN 3-8204-8483-3 LC Card 86-195650
HD7179 .S349 1986

PENSIONS - GREAT BRITAIN.
Pensions . London , Boston , 1987. xvi, 249 p. : ISBN 0-04-332127-5 (alk. paper) LC Card 86-32086 DDC 331.25/2/0941 19
HD7165 .P46 1987

Pensions in the U. S. economy / edited by Zvi Bodie, John B. Shoven, and David A. Wise. Chicago : University of Chicago Press, 1988. ix, 200 p. : ill. ; 24 cm (A National Bureau of Economic Research project report) "Papers presented at a conference held on 21-22 March 1985"--P. ix. Includes bibliographies and indexes. ISBN 0-226-06285-6 LC Card 87-19987 DDC 331.25/2/0973 19
1. Pension trusts - United States - Congresses. 2. Individual retirement accounts - United States - Congresses. I. Bodie, Zvi. II. Shoven, John B. III. Wise, David A. IV. National Bureau of Economic Research. V. Title: Pensions in the US economy. VI. Series.
HD7105.45.U6 P46 1988

Pensions in the US economy. Pensions in the U. S. economy /. Chicago , 1988. ix, 200 p. : ISBN 0-226-06285-6 LC Card 87-19987 DDC 331.25/2/0973 19
HD7105.45.U6 P46 1988

PENSIONS - MANITOBA - CONGRESSES.
An Inquiry into the future of public and private pension plans . Winnipeg [1976] xiii, 54 p. ; LC Card 85-103269
HD7130.M36 I56 1976

PENSIONS - MATHEMATICAL MODELS.
Sahin, Izzet. Job mobility and private pensions /. Brookfield, Wis. , c1986. xv, 49 p. ; ISBN 0-89154-305-8 (pbk.) LC Card 87-129468 DDC 331.25/2/0724 19
HD7105 .S229 1986

PENSIONS - SWITZERLAND - STATISTICS.
Lüthi, Ambros, 1938- Die wirtschaftliche Ungleichheit im Rentenalter in der Schweiz /. Freiburg/Schweiz , 1983. 229 p. : ISBN 3-7278-0282-0 : LC Card 83-163287
HD7105.35.S9 L87 1983

PENSIONS - UNITED STATES.
McFadden, John J. Retirement plans for employees /. Homewood, Ill. , 1988. xviii, 326 p. : ISBN 0-256-05588-2 LC Card 87-81436 DDC 658.3/253 19
HD7105.35.U6 M33 1988

Overview of current issues relating to single-employer defined benefit pension plans and Pension Benefit Guaranty Corporation (PBGC) premiums . Washington , 1987. iii, 49 p. ; LC Card 87-601357 DDC 331.25/2/0973 19
HD7125 .O88 1987

Penteado, Jacob. Memórias de um postalista / Jacob Penteado. São Paulo : Martins, [1963] 199 p., [8] p. of plates : ill. ; 22 cm. Bibliography: p. [187] Includes index. LC Card 85-134575
1. Penteado, Jacob. 2. Postal service - Brazil - Employees - Biography. 3. Postal service - Brazil - History. I. Title.
HE6834.P46 A3 1963

PENTEADO, JACOB.
Penteado, Jacob. Memórias de um postalista /. São Paulo [1963] 199 p., [8] p. of plates : LC Card 85-134575
HE6834.P46 A3 1963

Penteado Neto, Alfredo Camargo, 1939-
Organizações de trabalhadores : comissões de fábrica, greve, autogestão / Alfredo Camargo Penteado Neto. São Paulo : LTr, 1986. 112 p. : ill. ; 21 cm. Bibliography: p. 111-112. LC Card 87-403488 DDC 338.6 19
1. Management - Employee participation. 2. Works councils. 3. Strikes and lockouts. 4. Labor and laboring classes - Brazil - History. I. Title.
HD5650 .P37 1986

Penvenne, Jeanne. Making our own way : women working in Lourenço Marques, 1900-1933 / by Jeanne Penvenne. Boston, MA (270 Bay State Rd., Boston 02215) : African Studies Center, Boston University, 1986. 20 leaves ; 28 cm. (Working papers / African Studies Center, Boston University . no. 114) Bibliography: leaves 17-20. LC Card 87-155233 DDC 331.4/0967/91 19
1. Women - Employment - Mozambique - Maputo - History - 20th century. I. Series: Working papers (Boston University. African Studies Center) , no. 114. II. Title.
HD6211.5 .P46 1986

Penz, G. Peter. Consumer sovereignty and human interests / G. Peter Penz. Cambridge [Cambridgeshire] ; New York : Cambridge University Press, 1986. xiv, 242 p. ; 24 cm. "Developed out of a doctoral dissertation for the University of Oxford"--Acknowledgements. Includes index. Bibliography: p. 226-235. ISBN 0-521-26571-1 LC Card 85-22407 DDC 330.15/5 19
1. Welfare economics. 2. Consumers' preferences. 3. Basic needs. 4. Utilitarianism. 5. Political sociology. I. Title.
HB846 .P46 1986 NYPL [JLE 86-3311]

Penz, Hugo. Das Trentino : Entwicklung und räumliche Differenzierung der Bevölkerung und Wirtschaft Welschtirols / Hugo Penz. Innsbruck : Universitätsverlag Wagner, 1984. 379 p. : ill. ; 25 cm. (Tiroler Wirtschaftsstudien. 37. Folge) Bibliography: p. [347]-365. Includes indexes. ISBN 3-7030-0142-9 : LC Card 86-138251

1. Trentino-Alto Adige (Italy) - Economic conditions - Regional disparities. 2. Trentino-Alto Adige, Italy - Population. 3. Social structure - Italy - Trentino-Alto Adige. I. Title. II. Series.
HC307.T7 P45 1984

PENZBERG (GERMANY) - HISTORY. Tenfelde, Klaus. Proletarische Provinz . München , 1982. xvii, 409 p. : ISBN 3-486-50701-X : LC Card 83-124119
HD8460.P452 T46 1982

Pénzügykutatási Intézet tanulmányai . (1987. 2. sz) World monetary system in a time of change . Budapest [1987] 283 p. ; ISBN 963-01-7937-7 (pbk.) LC Card 87-169001 DDC 332.4/5 19
HG230.3 .W68 1987

PEONAGE - INDIA - MAHARASHTRA. Tāvare, Rāmacandra. Thāpaṭanā /. Mumbaī , 1986. 179 p. ; LC Card 87-900532
HD5820.M29 T38 1986

PEONAGE - INDIA - UTTARKHAND REGION - HISTORY. Pāṭhaka, Śekhara, 1951- Uttarākhaṇḍa meṃ kulī begāra prathā . Nayī Dillī , 1987, c1986. 339 p., [16] p. of plates : LC Card 87-902810
HD1537.I4 P38 1987

People and organisations : the practitioner's view / edited by Andrew Kakabadse. Aldershot, Hants. : Gower, c1982. ix, 143 p. : ill. ; 23 cm. Includes bibliographies. CONTENTS. - Concerns for management in corporate banks / David Robinson -- Organisation development in BL cars / Ray Charlton and Fred Herlihy -- Organisation, culture and work practice / Andrew Kakabadse -- Alienation, participation, and the worker director / John Bank -- Stress among blue-collar workers / Michael J. Kelly -- The stresses and strains of work life / Cary L. Cooper -- Client/consultant relations / Chelvin Hibbert -- Mapping career transitions / Charles Margerison -- L>C / Alan Lawlor. ISBN 0-566-00373-2 LC Card 82-189914 DDC 658.3/124 19
1. Organization - Addresses, essays, lectures. 2. Organizational change - Addresses, essays, lectures. I. Kakabadse, Andrew.
HD31 .P375 1982 NYPL [JLD 86-2775]

People and the organization series. Henry, Lauchland. The professional's guide to working smarter /. Tenafly, N.J. , 1988. xv, 208 p. : ISBN 0-935310-03-7 LC Card 87-23868 DDC 650.1 19
HD8038.A1 H47 1988

People, building neighborhoods . United States. National Commission on Neighborhoods. [Washington?] , Washington [1979] xi, 358 p. : LC Card 79-602955 DDC 307.7/6/0973
HN90.C6 U66 1979 NYPL [JLM 81-194]

People, communication, organization. Organization--communication . Norwood, N.J. , c1986- v. : ISBN 0-89391-274-3 (v. 1) LC Card 85-6159 DDC 302.3/5 19
HD31 .O727 1986 NYPL [JLL 86-382]

A People in focus book. Haddock, Patricia. Standing up for America . Minneapolis, Minn. , c1987. 111 p. : ISBN 0-87518-362-X : LC Card 86-32965 DDC 338.7/6292/0924 B 92 19
HD9710.U52 I246 1987

People skills in action, for loan officers and processors. Module 3, Dealing with objections and irate customers [videorecording] / Chicago, Ill. : Encyclopaedia Britannica Educational Corp., 1986. 1 videocassette (20 min.) : sd., col. + 1 leader's guide. Title from data sheet. Issued as U-matic 3/4 in. or Beta II 1/2 in. or VHS 1/2 in. In this segment of a training course William L. Hopkins teaches how to respond in a natural and instantaneous way with empathy whenever a loan applicant or customer has a problem. He shows the processor or loan officer how to follow the empathy cushion immediately with Stonewell, explain, admit, or ask objective questions. LC Card 86-707349 DDC 658.8 11
1. Loan officers - Training of. 2. Interpersonal communication. I. Hopkins, William L. II. William L. Hopkins, Inc. III. Video Lab (Hudson, N.H.). IV. Encyclopaedia Britannica Educational Corporation. V. Title: Dealing with objections and irate customers.
HG1641

People's Bank (Sri Lanka) In retrospect . Colombo , 1986. 149 p. ; LC Card 86-903248 DDC 334/.2/095493
HG2039.S65 I5 1986

PEOPLE'S BANK (SRI LANKA) In retrospect . Colombo , 1986. 149 p. ; LC Card 86-903248 DDC 334/.2/095493
HG2039.S65 I5 1986

People's banker . Ross, Walter Sanford, 1916- New Canaan, Conn. , c1987. viii, 288 p. ; ISBN 0-87983-429-3 LC Card 87-4066 DDC 332.1/223/0924 B 19
HG2463.R68 R67 1987

PEOPLE'S BANKS. see **BANKS AND BANKING, COOPERATIVE.**

Peoples, David A., 1930- Presentations plus : David Peoples' proven techniques / David A. Peoples. New York : Wiley, c1988. xi, 239 p. : ill. ; 24 cm. Includes index. ISBN 0-471-63391-7 LC Card 87-21691 DDC 658.4/5 19
1. Business communication. 2. Public speaking. 3. Business report writing. I. Title.
HF5718 .P44 1988

People's Media Collective of San Francisco. The Farmer is the man [sound recording]. Los Angeles, Calif. , p1983. 1 sound cassette (58 min.) : LC Card 87-751678
HD8039.F3

People's Republic of Albania. see **Albania.**

People's Republic of Benin. see **Benin.**

The People's Republic of Bulgaria . T͡Sarevski, Nesho Vŭlev. Sofia , 1986. 102 p. ; LC Card 87-123346 DDC 337.1/4977 19
HC403 .T748 1986

People's Union for Democratic Rights (India) Anonymous struggles . New Delhi , 1983. 24 p. ; LC Card 83-904576 DDC 344.54/01 345.4041 19
LAW NYPL [JLD 86-3877]

People's Youth of Bulgaria. see **Dimitrovski komunisticheski mladezhki sŭi͡uz.**

Peopleware . DeMarco, Tom. New York, NY , c1987. x, 188 p. : ISBN 0-932633-05-6 (pbk.) : LC Card 87-22293 DDC 658.3/14 19
HD31 .D42185 1987

Pepper, David. Nuclear power in crisis . New York , 1987. 327 p. : ISBN 0-89397-267-3 : LC Card 86-23710 DDC 333.79/24/0941 19
HD9698.G72 N85 1987

Pepper, Martin. Solomon, Stephen S. Canadian mortgage payments /. New York , c1987. 302 p. ; ISBN 0-8120-3939-4 (pbk.) LC Card 87-13073 DDC 332.8/0212 19
HG1634 .S654 1987

Peppers, Larry C. Managerial economics : theory and applications for decision making / Larry C. Peppers, Dale G. Bails. Englewood Cliffs, N.J. : Prentice-Hall, c1987. xxii, 679 p. : ill. ; 25 cm. Includes bibliographies and index. ISBN 0-13-550055-9 LC Card 86-25278 DDC 338.5/024658 19
1. Managerial economics. I. Bails, Dale. II. Title.
HD30.22 .P43 1987

Pequena empresa : o comportamento empresarial na acumulação e na luta pela sobrevivência / Henrique Rattner (org.) ; José Carlos G. Durand ... [et al.]. São Paulo-Brasil : Brasiliense ; [Brasília] : em co-edição com o CNPq, 1985. 2 v. : ill. ; 21 cm. Includes bibliographies. LC Card 85-180776 DDC 338.6/42/0981 19
1. Automobile supplies industry - Brazil - Addresses, essays, lectures. 2. Textile industry - Brazil - Addresses, essays, lectures. 3. Small business - Brazil - Addresses, essays, lectures. I. Rattner, Henrique. II. Durand, José Carlos Garcia.
HD9710.3.B72 P46 1985
NYPL [JLD 86-1588]

Pequena história dos transportes públicos de São Paulo. Lopes, Miriam B. P. Oelsner (Miriam Bettina Paulina Oelsner) São Paulo [1985] 91 p. : LC Card 86-158179
HE5653.Z7 C675 1985

Pequeña industria, reactivación y desarrollo industrial / Jorge Peirano Morán ... [et al.]. [Miraflores, Lima] : Fundación Friedrich Ebert, [1986] 127 p. : maps ; 21 cm. (Taller de investigación . 6) Includes bibliographies. LC Card 87-127800 DDC 338.6/42/0985 19
1. Small business - Peru. 2. Peru - Industries. I. Peirano Morán, Jorge. II. Friedrich-Ebert-Stiftung. III. Series.
HD2346.P4 P47 1986

Pequeña y mediana empresa. [Mexico City, Mexico] : SHCP, [1983] 220 p. ; 22 cm. Cover title. Includes bibliographical references. ISBN 968-8060-29-01 LC Card 86-144218
1. Small business - Mexico. 2. Small business - Mexico - Taxation. I. Mexico. Secretaría de Hacienda y Crédito Público.
HD2346.M4 P47 1983

As pequenas e médias empresas na expansão industrial brasileira . Ferreira, Assuéro. Fortaleza-Ceará , 1985. 68 p. ; LC Card 87-102632 DDC 338.6/42/098131 19
HD2346.B72 C445 1985

Pequeños campesinos y su incertidumbre . Campos, Luis A. (Luis Alberto), 1949- Asunción, Paraguay [1986] 224 p. : LC Card 87-400281 DDC 305.5/63 19
HD1531.P3 C36 1986

Per una ristrutturazione e riconversione dell'industria italiana / a cura di Romano Prodi e Fabio Gobbo. Bologna : Il mulino, 1980. 244 p. ; 22 cm. (Quaderni de "L'Industria" . 5) Includes bibliographical references. LC Card 82-102594 DDC 338.945 19
1. Industry and state - Italy - Addresses, essays, lectures. 2. Investments - Italy - Addresses, essays, lectures. 3. Credit - Italy - Addresses, essays, lectures. 4. Taxation - Italy - Addresses, essays, lectures. 5. Italy - Commercial policy - Addresses, essays, lectures. 6. Italy - Full employment policies - Addresses, essays, lectures. I. Prodi, Romano. II. Gobbo, Fabio, 1947-.
HD3616.I83 P43 NYPL [JLD 86-599]

Pera, Giuseppe, 1928- Disoccupazione e nuove forme di accesso al lavoro nel mondo bancario /. Milano, Italy , c1986. 186 p. ; LC Card 87-150276
HD5718.B262 I83 1986

Perales, Cesar A., 1940- Utilization of medicaid paid health services by Medicaid recipients in New York City, Nassau, Monroe, and western central counties, 1980-1981 /. Albany, N.Y. (1 Commerce Plaza, Albany 12210) [1985] ii, 31, 17 p. : LC Card 86-622554 DDC 362.1/04252/09747 19
HD7102.U5 N684 1985

Peralta, Gabriel Edgardo Aguilera. see **Aguilera Peralta, Gabriel Edgardo.**

Peralta Ruiz, Víctor. Burga, Manuel. La historia agraria /. Chiclayo, Perú , 1986. 196 p. ;
NYPL [JLD 87-1524]

Percy, Larry. Rossiter, John R. Advertising and promotion management /. New York , 1987. xix, 647 p. : ISBN 0-07-053907-3 : LC Card 86-27381 DDC 659.1 19
HF5821 .R65 1987

Perdía, Roberto Cirilo. Existe otra Argentina posible / Roberto Cirilo Perdía, Fernando Vaca Narvaja. 1a ed. Buenos Aires : E. González Olguin, 1986. 276 p. : ill. ; 20 cm. Bibliography: p. 179-208. ISBN 950-97640-0-0 LC Card 87-139879 DDC 336.3/4/0982 19
1. International Monetary Fund - Argentina. 2. Debts, External - Argentina. 3. Argentina - Economic policy. 4. Argentina - Dependency on foreign countries. 5. Argentina - Politics and government - 1983-. I. Vaca Narvaja, Fernando. II. Title.
HG3881.5.I58 P47 1986

Pérdidas como consecuencia de terremotos . Grases G., José. Caracas , 1986. 71 p. : ISBN 980-265-358-6 LC Card 87-403100 DDC 338.4/33633495 19
HC79.D45 G7 1986

Perdue, Peter C., 1949- Exhausting the earth : state and peasant in Hunan, 1500-1850 / Peter C. Perdue. Cambridge, Mass. : Council on East Asian Studies, Harvard University : Distributed by Harvard University Press, 1987. xvii, 331 p. : maps ; 26 cm. (Harvard East Asian monographs. 130) Bibliography: p. 293-319. Includes index. ISBN 0-674-27504-7 LC Card 87-5067 DDC 338.1/0951/215 19
1. Agriculture and state - China - Hunan Province - History. 2. Land use, Rural - China - Hunan Province - History. 3. Hunan Province (China) - Population - History. 4. Agricultural productivity - China - Hunan Province - History. 5. Peasantry - China - Hunan Province - History. I. Title. II. Series.
HD2100.H86 P47 1987

Peredovye kollektivy ("Legkaia i pishchevaia promyshlennost'" (Firm))
Agarkova, G. D. (Galina Dmitrievna) Leningradskie farforisty /. Moskva , 1984. 61 p. : LC Card 85-111565
HD9616.S653 L463 1984

Peredovye kollektivy (Stroĭizdat (Firm))
Piskunov, F. F. (Fedor Fedorovich) Zabota o stroitel'nykh kadrakh /. Moskva , 1986. 71 p. : LC Card 86-220202
HD8039.B92 S686 1986

Pereira, A. (Armand)
Ethanol, employment, and development : lessons from Brazil / A. Pereira. Geneva : International Labour Office, 1986. xiv, 195 p. : ill. ; 24 cm. Bibliography: p. 181-195. ISBN 92-2-105380-6 (pbk.) : LC Card 87-107819 DDC 338.4/7662669 19
1. Alcohol fuel industry - Brazil. 2. Alcohol fuel industry - Brazil - Employees. I. Title.
HD9502.5.A433 B646 1986

Socio-economic and policy implications of energy price increases / Armand Pereira, Alistair Ulph, and Wouter Tims. Aldershot, Hants, England ; Brookfield, Vt., USA : Gower, c1987. xxiv, 317 p. ; 23 cm. "A study prepared for the International Labour Office within the framework of the World Employment Programme, with financial support from the Government of the Netherlands." Bibliography: p. 297-308. Includes index. ISBN 0-566-05520-1 : LC Card 87-11955 DDC 338.2/3 19
1. Petroleum products - Prices. 2. Energy policy. 3. Economic policy. 4. Social policy. I. Ulph, Alistair. II. Tims, Wouter. III. International Labour Office. IV. World Employment Programme. V. Title.
HD9560.4 .P37 1987

Socioeconomic aspects of renewable energy technologies . New York , 1988. p. cm. ISBN 0-275-92851-9 (alk. paper) : LC Card 87-22890 DDC 333.7/09172/4 19
HD9502.D442 S63 1988

Pereira, D. F. (Dennyson F.) Recent experiences in human resources development /. New Delhi , c1986. xvi, 448 p. ; ISBN 81-204-0120-4 : LC Card 86-902270 DDC 331.11/0954 19
HF5549.5.M3 R38 1985

Pereira, Eduardo Novo da Costa. Bolsa de commodities : mercado futuro / Eduardo Novo da Costa Pereira.1a. ed. Rio de Janeiro, RJ : FGV-Instituto de Documentação, Editora da Fundação Getúlio Vargas, 1985. ix, 69 p. ; 21 cm. (Série Teses EPGE . 08) Originally presented as the author's thesis (doctoral)--Escola de Pós-Graduação em Economia da Fundação Getúlio Vargas. Bibliography: p. 63-65. Includes index. "001-800-016-9"--P. [i] LC Card 86-129753
1. Commodity exchanges. 2. Commodity exchanges - Brazil. I. Series: Série Teses (Escola de Pós-Graduação em Economia) , no. 8. II. Title.
HG6024.B7 P47 1985

Pereira, Fernando Jasmins. Livros de contas da ilha da Madeira, 1504-1537 /. Coimbra , 1985- v. <1 > ; LC Card 86-232733
HJ9930.3.M33 L58 1985

Pereira, Francisco José Piteira. A cultura da vinha na região do Redondo / Francisco José Piteira Pereira e Victor Manuel Pina Dias e Pedro Peixoto e Bourbon. [Lisbon] : Instituto de Gestão e Estruturação Fundiária, 1983. 11, 4, 30, 21 leaves, [2] leaves of plates : ill. ; 30 cm. (Alguns elementos para um banco de dados económicos do ordenamento rural do Alentejo . no. 8) Summary in English, French, German, Portuguese, and Spanish. Cover title: A vinha na região de Redondo. LC Card 84-238378
1. Grape industry - Portugal - Redondo (Evora). 2. Wine industry - Portugal - Redondo (Evora). I. Dias, Victor Manuel Pina. II. Bourbon, Pedro Peixoto e. III. Title. IV. Title: Vinha na região de Redondo. V. Series.
HD9259.G7 P47 1983

Pereira, José Maria Dias. A participação da alimentação na inflação brasileira nos anos 70 : uma contribuição ao debate / José Maria Dias Pereira. Porto Alegre, RS : Fundação de Economia e Estatística, 1984. 139 p. : ill. ; 23 cm. (Teses. n. 7) Summary in English. Originally presented as the author's thesis (mestre em economia rural)--Universidade Federal do Rio Grande do Sul. Bibliography: p. [137]-139. LC Card 85-128694 DDC 338.4/36413/00981 19
1. Food prices - Brazil. 2. Inflation (Finance) - Brazil. I. Series: Teses (Rio Grande do Sul (Brazil). Fundação de Economica e Estatística) , n. 7. II. Title.
HD9014.B82 P47 1984 ***NYPL [JLE 86-2264]***

Pereira, Luiz Carlos Bresser.
[Inflação e recessão. English]
The theory of inertial inflation : the foundation of economic reform in Brazil & Argentina / Luiz Bresser Pereira, Yoshiaki Nakano ; foreword by Rudiger Dornbusch ; [translated from the Portuguese by Colleen Reeks]. Boulder, Colo. : L. Rienner Publishers, 1987. xiii, 206 p. : ill. ; 24 cm. Translation of: Inflação e recessão. Bibliography: p. 187-195. Includes index. ISBN 1-555-87007-4 (alk. paper) : LC Card 86-29832 DDC 332.4/1/0981 19
1. Inflation (Finance) - Brazil. 2. Monetary policy - Brazil. 3. Monetary policy - Argentina. I. Nakano, Yoshiaki, 1944-. II. Title. III. Title: Inertial inflation.
HG835 .P4413 1987

Pereira, Mário.
Alguns elementos para a caracterização da assimetria regional agrária portuguesa / Mário Pereira. Oeiras [Portugal] : Fundação Calouste Gulbenkian, Instituto Gulbenkian de Ciência, Centro de Estudos de Economia Agrária, 1974. 59 p. : maps ; 25 cm. (Estudos / Instituto Gulbenkian de Ciência, Centro de Estudos de Economia Agraria) Summaries in English and French. "Publicações editadas pelo Centro de Estudos de Economia Agraria": p. 55-59. LC Card 85-133550
1. Agricultural productivity - Portugal - Statistics. I. Series: Estudos (Instituto Gulbenkian de Ciência. Centro e Estudos e Economia Agrária). II. Title.
HD2027 .P388 1974

O método dos modelos e a análise económica da exploração agrícola / Mário Pereira. Lisboa : Fundação Calouste Gulbenkian, Centro de Estudos de Economia Agrária, 1962. 233 p. : ill. ; 22 cm. Summary in English and French. Bibliography: p. [231]-233. LC Card 85-221042
1. Agricultural productivity - Portugal - Econometric models. I. Title.
HD2027 .M415 1962

Pereira, Nilda. Economía, organización y planificación de la producción industrial / [edición y corrección, Norma Castillo Falcato ; realización, Nilda Pereira]. La Habana : Editora Política, 1984. 2 v. : ill. ; 23 cm. Date on v. 1, t.p.: 1983. Includes bibliographical references. LC Card 87-401248
1. Industry. 2. Industry and state. 3. Industrial organization. I. Castillo Falcato, Norma. II. Title.
HD2328 .P47 1984

Perelman, Michael. Marx's crises theory : scarcity, labor, and finance / Michael Perelman. New York : Praeger, 1987. v, 250 p. ; 24 cm. Bibliography: p. 221-243. Includes index. ISBN 0-275-92372-X (alk. paper) : LC Card 87-6936 DDC 330.12/2 19
1. Marxian economics. 2. Depressions. 3. Scarcity. 4. Marx, Karl, 1818-1883. I. Title.
HB97.5 .P349 1987

Perepis' naseleniia i zhilishch 1971. Savezni zavod za statistiku (Yugoslavia) [Popis stanovništva i stanova 1971. English.] Population and housing census 1971 . Beograd , 1974. 12 v. ; LC Card 83-122836
HA1631.5 1971 .S38 1974

Perestroĭka i rukovoditel' / [sostavitel' S.N. Krasavchenko ; Evgeniĭ Ivanovich Komarov ... et al.]. Moskva : "Ekonomika", 1987. 143 p. ; 20 cm. Includes bibliographical references. LC Card 87-164793
1. Executives - Soviet Union. 2. Industrial management - Soviet Union. I. Krasavchenko, S. N. II. Komarov, E. I. (Evgeniĭ Ivanovich).
HD38.25.S65 P47 1987

Perevozchikov, V. I. (Viktor Ivanovich)
Stanovlenie i periody razvitiia gosudarstvenno-monopolisticheskogo kapitalizma v Anglii / V.I. Perevozchikov. Kiev : Nauk. dumka, 1982. 153 p. ; 20 cm. At head of title: Akademiia nauk Ukrainskoĭ SSR. Institut sotsial'nykh i ėkonomicheskikh problem zarubezhnykh stran. Includes bibliographical references. LC Card 83-102577
1. Great Britain - Economic conditions - 20th century. I. Title.
HC256 .P47 1982

Pérez Aguirre, Luis. Predicaciones en la plaza / Luis Pérez Aguirre. Montevideo : Ediciones Paulinas, 1985. 228 p. ; 23 cm. LC Card 85-225854 DDC 282/.8 19
1. Catholic Church - Latin America. 2. Church and social problems - Latin America. 3. Latin America - Social conditions - 1945-. I. Title.
BX1426.2 .P46 1985 ***NYPL [JLE 87-456]***

Pérez, Albert. see **Pérez Baró, Albert.**

Pérez Arrarte, Carlos.
Barbato de Silva, Celia. La ganadería vacuna uruguaya . Montevideo, Uruguay [1980] 77 leaves ; ***NYPL [JLF 86-1101]***

Martorelli, Horacio. Nuevo estilo de desarrollo para Uruguay . Montevideo, Uruguay , 1982. 2 v. : LC Card 85-167867 DDC 338.1/09895 19
HD1907 .M376 1982 ***NYPL [JLF 86-935]***

Pérez Baró, Albert. Trenta mesos de col·lectivisme a Catalunya, cinquanta anys després / Albert Pérez Baró ; presentació de Josep Tarradellas. 1a ed. dins "Llibres a l'abast" (corr. i augm.). Barcelona : Edicions 62, 1986. 283 p. : ill. ; 18 cm. (Llibres a l'abast. 212) Includes bibliographical references. ISBN 84-297-2412-5 LC Card 86-186185
1. Collectivism. 2. Government ownership - Spain - Catalonia. I. Title.
HD4245.C3 P45 1986

Pérez Bermúdez, Carlos. El movimiento obrero en Nicaragua : apuntes para el conocimiento de su historia / Carlos Pérez Bermúdez, Onofre Guevara. [S.l. : s.n., 1985] ([Managua, Nicaragua?] : Editorial "El Amanecer") 2 v. in 1 : ill. ; 23 cm. Cover title. LC Card 86-174663
1. Trade-unions - Nicaragua - History. I. Guevara López, Onofre. II. Title.
HD6557 .P473 1985

Pérez de Guinea, María del Carmen. Estudio sobre la sociedad soriana en el siglo XVIII : los censos y distribución de la población / María del Carmen Pérez de Guinea. [Spain] : Consejo General de Castilla y León, [1982?] 296 p. ; 22 cm. Title on spine: La Sociedad soriana en el siglo XVIII. Originally presented as the author's thesis (tesis de licenciatura--Universidad de Zaragoza, 1973) "Apéndice documental": p. [145]-296. Bibliography: p. 141-143. LC Card 85-136714
1. Soria (Spain) - Census, 1752. 2. Soria (Spain) - Census, 1787. 3. Soria (Spain) - Census, 1797. 4. Soria (Spain) - Population - History - 18th century. 5. Spain - Nobility - Statistics - History - 18th century. 6. Clergy - Spain - Statistics - History - 18th century. I. Title. II. Title: Sociedad soriana en el siglo XVIII.
HA1559.S65 P47 1982

Pérez, José. Mauleón, Ignacio. Interest rates determinants and consequences for macroeconomic performance in Spain /. [Madrid] [1984?] 65 p. : ISBN 84-505-0648-7 (pbk.) LC Card 86-215058 DDC 332.8/2/0724 19
HG1623.S7 M38 1984

Pérez, José Cazorla. see **Cazorla Pérez, José.**

Pérez-López, Jorge F. Measuring Cuban economic performance / by Jorge F. Pérez-López. 1st ed. Austin : University of Texas Press, 1987. xii, 202 p. : ill. ; 24 cm. (Special publication / Institute of Latin American Studies) Bibliography: p. [193]-197. Includes index. ISBN 0-292-75092-7 LC Card 86-24907 DDC 339.37291 19
1. Cuba - Economic conditions - 1959-. 2. National income - Cuba - Accounting. 3. Gross national product - Cuba. I. Series: Special publication (University of Texas at Austin. Institute of Latin American Studies). II. Title.
HC152.5 .P47 1987

Pérez, Lourdes. Mántey de Anguiano, M. G. Análisis microeconómico de los factores que determinan el valor de mercado de las empresas industriales mexicanas y su tasa de expansión /. [Mexico City] [1986] iv, 63 leaves : LC Card 87-400949 DDC 658.1/5/0972 19
HG4092 .M36 1986

Pérez, Luis. see **Pérez Aguirre, Luis.**

Pérez Mackenna, Francisco. Fontaine Talavera, Arturo. Pautas para la confección de una política económica . Santiago, Chile , 1984. 92 leaves : LC Card 86-177872
HC192 .F58 1984

Pérez Menayo, Vicente. La protección del desempleo en España y en los países de las Comunidades Europeas / por Vicente Pérez Menayo. [Madrid] : Servicio de Publicaciones, Ministerio de Trabajo : Instituto de Estudios Sociales, [1980?] 303 p. : ill. ; 24 cm. (Cuadernos laborales. Serie Relaciones del trabajo) Bibliography: p. 271-273. ISBN 84-500-3715-8 LC Card 83-240633 DDC 368.4/4/00946 19
1. Insurance, Unemployment - Spain. 2. Insurance, Unemployment - European Economic Community countries. I. Title. II. Series.
HD7096.S7 P47 1980 NYPL [JLE 87-705]

Pérez P., María Dolores. Pérez P., María José. La oferta y la demanda de empleos . Bogotá, Colombia , c1984. 64 p. ; ISBN 84-8276-322-9 LC Card 84-241503
HD5757.A6 P47 1984

Pérez P., María José. La oferta y la demanda de empleos : a su alcance / María José Pérez P., María Dolores Pérez P. Bogotá, Colombia : Editorial Norma, c1984. 64 p. ; 20 cm. Bibliography: p. 64. ISBN 84-8276-322-9 LC Card 84-241503
1. Labor supply - Colombia. I. Pérez P., María Dolores. II. Title.
HD5757.A6 P47 1984

Pérez Planelles, Francisco, fl. 1774-1807. Plan estatístico de la villa de Alcoy / [por Francisco Pérez Planelles] ; introducció a càrrec, d'Ismael Vallès. [València] : Secció de Geografia de la Universitat de València ; [Alcoi] : Ajuntament d'Alcoi, 1983. xiii, 31 p. ; 34 cm. Manuscript facsimile. Text in Spanish; introd. in Catalan. Bibliography: p. xiii. LC Card 86-150151
1. Alcoy (Spain) - Economic conditions. 2. Alcoy (Spain) - Population - History - 18th century. 3. Alcoy (Spain) - Population - History - 19th century. I. Vallès i Sanchis, Ismael. II. Title.
HC388.A44 P47 1983

Perez, Rita. Statistica e pubblica amministrazione . Milano , 1983-1985. 2 v. ; ISBN 88-14-00703-9 (v. 2) : LC Card 86-215546
HA37.I9 S7 1983

Pérez Sáinz, Juan Pablo. Entre la fábrica y la ciudad / Juan Pablo Pérez Sáinz. 1a ed. Quito, Ecuador : Editorial El Conejo, 1986, c1985. 87, [6] p. ; 21 x 10 cm. (Colección Ecuador/hoy) Bibliography: p. [89]-[90]. LC Card 87-403298 DDC 331.7/677/00986613 19
1. Textile workers - Ecuador - Quito Region. I. Title. II. Series.
HD8039.T42 E26 1986

Pérez, Santiago. see **Pérez Triana, Santiago, 1858-1916.**

Pérez Triana, Santiago, 1858-1916. Unificación de deudas : asuntos colombianos / Santiago Pérez Triana. Londres : Impr. de Wertheimer, 1912. 81 p. ; 21 cm. LC Card 85-111033
1. Debts, External - Colombia. I. Title.
HJ8589 .P47 1912

Perfil de empresas. Fortaleza-CE : Ministério do Interior, Fundo de Investimentos do Nordeste, Superintendência do Desenvolvimento do Nordeste, Banco do Nordeste do Brasil, [1984] 248 p. ; 31 cm. Cover title. Spine title: XLVII Leilão do FINOR, Bolsa de Valores Regional (BVRG), Fortaleza (CE), 25 de outubro de 1984. At head of title: XLVII Leilão do FINOR, Bolsa de Valores Regional (BVRG), Fortaleza (CE), 25 de outubro de 1984. Tables. LC Card 85-191373
1. Corporations - Brazil, Northeast - Finance - Directories. 2. Fundo de Investimentos do Nordeste. 3. Securities - Brazil, Northeast. I. Fundo de Investimentos do Nordeste (Brazil). II. Banco do Nordeste do Brasil. III. Title: XLVII Leilão do FINOR, Bolsa de Valores Regional (BVRG), Fortaleza (CE), 25 de outubro de 1984.
HG4111.5.N67 P47 1984

O Perfil do economista. [São Paulo, Brazil] : Ordem dos Economistas de S. Paulo : Sindicato dos Economistas do Estado de São Paulo, [1984?] 60 p. : ill. ; 22 cm. (Série Estudos e pesquisas) LC Card 87-402012 DDC 330/.092/2 19
1. Economists - Brazil. I. Ordem dos Economistas de São Paulo. II. Sindicato dos Economistas do Estado de São Paulo. III. Series: Série Estudos e pesquisas (Ordem dos Economistas de São Paulo).
HB123.B8 P47 1984

Perfiles económicos del Valle del Cauca, Colombia. Cali, Colombia : Fundación para el Desarrollo Industrial : Cámara de Comercio de Cali, [1981?] 40 p. : ill. (some col.) ; 28 cm. Cover title. Includes bibliographical references. LC Card 86-120381 DDC 330.9861/520632 19
1. Valle del Cauca, Colombia - Economic conditions. 2. Investments, Foreign - Colombia. 3. Foreign trade promotion - Colombia. I. Fundación para el Desarrollo Industrial (Cali, Colombia). II. Cámara de Comercio de Cali.
HC198.V3 P47 1981

Perfis indicativos para a industrialização do arroz, milho e soja. Brasília : Projeto de Desenvolvimento Integrado da Bacia do Araguaia-Tocantins, 1985. 189 p. : ill. ; 22 cm. (Série Estudos e pesquisas. no. 13) At head of title: Ministério do Interior; Organização dos Estados Americanos; Governo do Estado de Goiás; Governo do Estado do Maranhão; Governo do Estado do Pará; Governo do Estado de Mato Grosso; PRODIAT, Projeto de Desenvolvimento Integrado da Bacia do Araguaia-Tocantins. LC Card 86-195651
1. Rice trade - Brazil - Araguaia River Watershed. 2. Rice trade - Brazil - Tocantins River Watershed. 3. Corn industry - Brazil - Araguaia River Watershed. 4. Corn industry - Brazil - Tocantins River Watershed. 5. Soybean industry - Brazil - Araguaia River Watershed. 6. Soybean industry - Brazil - Tocantins River Watershed. I. Projeto de Desenvolvimento Integrado da Bacia do Araguaia-Tocantins. II. Series: Série Estudos e pesquisas (Projeto de Desenvolvimento Integrado da Bacia do Araguaia-Tocantins) , no. 13.
HD9066.B83 A737 1985

Performance and credibility : developing excellence in public and nonprofit organizations / edited by Joseph S. Wholey, Mark A. Abramson, Christopher Bellavita. Lexington, Mass. : Lexington Books, c1986. x, 307 p. : ill. ; 24 cm. Includes bibliographies and index. ISBN 0-669-11037-X (alk. paper) LC Card 85-50707 DDC 658/.048 19
1. Corporations, Nonprofit - Management - Evaluation - Addresses, essays, lectures. 2. Public administration - Evaluation - Addresses, essays, lectures. 3. Evaluation research (Social action programs) - Addresses, essays, lectures. I. Wholey, Joseph S. II. Abramson, Mark A., 1947-. III. Bellavita, Christopher.
HD62.6 .P47 1986 NYPL [JLE 86-1159]

Performance appraisals in the public sector . Morrisey, George L. Reading, Mass. , 1983. xiii, 172 p. ; ISBN 0-201-04847-7 (pbk.) : LC Card 83-6049 DDC 353.001/42 19
JK766.6 .M67 1983 NYPL [JLE 83-3164]

PERFORMANCE BUDGET. see **PROGRAM BUDGETING.**

The performance evaluation of Korean public enterprises . Song, Dae-Hee. Seoul, Korea [1986] 109 p. : LC Card 87-404432 DDC 354.519/5092 19
HD4315.5 .S65 1986

The performance management process . Grant, Philip C. Dubuque, Iowa , c1986. xvi, 333 p. : ISBN 0-8403-4086-9 (pbk.) LC Card 86-81844 DDC 658.3 19
HF5549 .G6755 1986

The Performance management sourcebook / edited by Craig Eric Schneier, Richard W. Beatty, Lloyd S. Baird. Amherst, Mass. : Human Resource Development Press, [1987] 393 p. : ill. ; 28 cm. Includes bibliographies. ISBN 0-87425-074-9 (pbk.) LC Card 87-153991 DDC 658.3/125 19
1. Employees, Rating of. I. Schneier, Craig Eric. II. Beatty, Richard W. III. Baird, Lloyd.
HF5549.5.R3 P4755 1987

The performance of Japanese-owned firms in America, 1982-1985 /. Starr, Martin Kenneth, 1927- [New York, NY] , c1987. ii, 41 leaves : LC Card 87-145262 DDC 338.8/8952/073 19
HD2785 .S66 1987

The Performance of small firms : profits, jobs, and failures / David Storey ... [et al.]. London ; Wolfeboro, N.H. : Croom Helm, c1987. 342 p. : ill. ; 22 cm. Bibliography: p. 327-334. Includes index. ISBN 0-7099-4411-X : LC Card 86-29052 DDC 658/.022 19
1. Small business. 2. Business failures. 3. Small business - Government policy. I. Storey, D. J.
HD2341 .P399 1987

PERFORMANCE RATING (OF EMPLOYEES) see **EMPLOYEES, RATING OF.**

Performance review in local government : a handbook for auditors and local authorities. [London : Published by H.M.S.O. for the Audit Commission for Local Authorities in England and Wales, 1986] 1 v. (various pagings) : ill. ; 31 cm. Cover title. Includes bibliographies. CONTENTS. - Introduction -- Education -- Environmental services -- Housing -- Law and order -- Leisure and libraries -- Planning and transportation -- Social services. ISBN 0-11-701302-1 (loose-leaf : set) : LC Card 87-144582 DDC 352.1/72/0942 19
1. Local finance - England - Accounting. 2. Local finance - Wales - Accounting. I. Audit Commission for LocalAuthorities in England and Wales.
HJ9779.G7 P47 1986

PERFUMES INDUSTRY - EUROPE.
Flavors and fragrances market in Europe. New York, N.Y. , c1983. 5, 17, 8, 279 p. ; LC Card 87-141830 DDC 380.1/456645 19
HD9212.E852 F53 1983

PERFUMES INDUSTRY - FRANCE - HISTORY.
Demornex, Jacqueline. Lancôme /. Paris , c1985. 189 p. : ISBN 2-903370-23-0 LC Card 86-201508
HD9999.P3934 L363 1985 NYPL [JSG 87-24]

Pergamon Infotech. Technology-based training. Oxford , New York , c1986. ix, 357 p. : ISBN 0-08-034097-0 LC Card 87-160178 DDC 658.3/12404 19
HF5549.5.T7 T39 1986

Perilaku fertilitas di beberapa daerah di Jawa /. Ananta, Aris. Jakarta , 1986. vi, 56, 26 p. ; LC Card 86-946460
HB1058.J38 A52 1986

PERINATAL MORTALITY - ENGLAND - STATISTICS.
Mortality statistics . London , 1986. viii, 49 p. ; ISBN 0-11-691069-0 (pbk.) : LC Card 87-147154 DDC 614.5/992 19
HB1323.I42 G764 1984

PERINATAL MORTALITY - WALES - STATISTICS.
Mortality statistics . London , 1986. viii, 49 p. ; ISBN 0-11-691069-0 (pbk.) : LC Card 87-147154 DDC 614.5/992 19
HB1323.I42 G764 1984

PERIODICAL ADVERTISING. see **ADVERTISING, MAGAZINE.**

Peripherals for the ISDN D-channel. Norwalk, Conn., U. S.A. (6 Prowitt St., Norwalk 06855) : International Resource Development, c1986. iv, 153 leaves : ill. ; 28 cm. (Report / International Resource Development Inc. . #713) "October 1986." LC Card 87-129535 DDC 380.1/45621385 19
1. Data transmission equipment industry. 2. Market surveys. I. International Resource Development, inc. II. Series: Report / International Resource Development Inc. , #713.
HD9696.D382 P46 1986

Periphere Räume : Strukturen und Entwicklungen in europäischen Problemgebieten / Peter Weber (Hrsg.). Paderborn : Schöningh, 1979. 183 p. : ill. ; 30 cm. (Münstersche geographische Arbeiten . Heft 4) Papers presented at the occasion of the Deutscher Geographentag, held 1979 in Göttingen. Includes bibliographies. CONTENTS. - Nordfinnland / Bernhard Butzin -- Die Förderung von Regionalzentren / Hans Elsasser -- Aspekte eines Vergleichs von regionalen Disparitäten in zwei Ländern unterschiedlicher sozial-ökonomischer Ordnung / Wilfried Heller -- Rückwanderung griechischer Gastarbeiter und Entwicklung ländlicher Räume in Griechenland / Hartmut Hermanns, Cay Lienau -- Regional unterschiedliche Bevölkerungsentwicklungen und der Wandel landwirtschaftlicher Betriebsformen / Rolf Lindemann -- Ursachen und Folgen junger Agrarkolonisationsvorgänge auf Korsika / Hartmut Lücke -- Innere Disparitäten und äussere Steuerungsmechanismen in französischen Wirtschaftsregionen / Frank Robert Nagel -- Erscheinungsformen und Ursachen sozioökonomischer Disparitäten am Beispiel von Jütland / Wolfgang Taubmann. ISBN 3-506-73204-8 LC Card 85-209554
1. Europe - Economic conditions - 1945- - Regional disparities - Congresses. 2. Regional planning - Europe - Congresses. 3. Social structure - Europe - Congresses. I. Weber, Peter, 1935-. II. Deutscher Geographentag (42nd : 1979 : Göttingen, Germany). III. Series.
HC240 .P38 1979

Périphéries urbaines. Colloque Les Périphéries urbaines (1984 : Angers, France) Actes du

Colloque Les Périphéries urbaines . Caen , c1985. 270 p. : ISBN 2-905461-03-9 : LC Card 86-173712
HB2263 .C65 1984

PERKIN-ELMER CORPORATION - HISTORY.
Fahy, Thomas P. Richard Scott Perkin and the Perkin-Elmer Corporation /. [United States] c1987. xv, 271 p. : ISBN 0-9618075-0-4 LC Card 86-63869 DDC 338.7/666156/0973 19
HD9707.U62 P474 1987

PERKIN, RICHARD SCOTT, 1906-1969.
Fahy, Thomas P. Richard Scott Perkin and the Perkin-Elmer Corporation /. [United States] c1987. xv, 271 p. : ISBN 0-9618075-0-4 LC Card 86-63869 DDC 338.7/666156/0973 19
HD9707.U62 P474 1987

PERKINS, FRANCES, 1882-1965.
You may call her madam secretary [motion picture] /. West Tisbury, MA , 1987. 1 film reel (57 min., 40 sec.) : LC Card 87-706816 DDC 973.917 11
HD8073.P38

You may call her madam secretary [videorecording] /. West Tisbury, MA , 1987. 1 videocassette (57 min., 40 sec.) : LC Card 87-706817 DDC 973.917 11
HD8073.P38

Perkins, J. O. N. (James Oliver Newton), 1924- National income and economic progress . New York , 1988. p. cm. ISBN 0-312-01566-6 : LC Card 87-24063 DDC 339.3 19
HB141.5 .N375 1988

Perkins, Tessa. Beechey, Veronica. A matter of hours . Minneapolis, MN , c1987. 212 p. ; ISBN 0-8166-1641-8 : LC Card 87-12459 DDC 331.4/12/0942498 19
HD6136.Z6 C683 1987

Perkins, William, 1558-1602.
TREATISE OF THE VOCATIONS.
Miegge, Mario. Vocazione e lavoro . [Bologna] , c1985. 97 p. : LC Card 87-131793
HF5382.5.G7 M52 1985

Perkinson, Richard C. Data analysis : the key to data base design / Richard C. Perkinson. Wellesley, Mass. : QED Information Sciences, c1984. xvii, 285 p. : ill. ; 25 cm. Bibliography: p. 283-285. ISBN 0-89435-105-2 LC Card 83-63212 DDC 001.64 19
1. Data base management. 2. System design. I. Q.E.D. Information Sciences. II. Title.
QA76.9.D3 P46 1984 ***NYPL [JSE 85-1742]***

Perles, Benjamin M., 1922- Freund, John E. Elementary business statistics . Englewood Cliffs, N.J. , c1988. xiii, 738 p. : ISBN 0-13-253196-8 LC Card 87-20586 DDC 519.5/024658 19
HF1017 .F73 1988

Perlman, Leonard G. Feingold, S. Norman, 1914- Making it on your own /. Washington, D.C. , c1985. 300 p. ; ISBN 0-87491-779-4 (pbk.) : LC Card 85-7560 DDC 658/.022 19
HD62.7 .F44 1985
NYPL [*R-Econ. 85-4850]

Perlmutter, Arnold, 1928- International Scientific Forum on Changes in Energy (1981 : Mexico City, Mexico) Global energy assessment and outlook . Chur, Switzerland , New York, N.Y. , c1984. xxix, 580 p. : ISBN 3-7186-0224-5 LC Card 84-12959 DDC 333.79 19
TJ163.15 .I5678 1981 ***NYPL [JSE 86-509]***

Permanent disability benefits in workers' compensation /. Berkowitz, Monroe, 1919- Kalamazoo, Mich. , 1987. xviii, 459 p. ; ISBN 0-88099-051-1 LC Card 87-22874 DDC 368.4/1/00973 19
HD7105.25.U6 B47 1987

PERMANENT EDUCATION. see **CONTINUING EDUCATION.**

Permanent International Association of Road Congresses. International Seminar on "Road Safety" (1986 : Srinagar, India) International Seminar on "Road Safety", Srinagar, September 17-18, 1986 /. New Delhi [1986] 1 v. (various pagings) : LC Card 87-901986 DDC 363.1/25 19
HE5614 .I5717 1986

Permanent Inter-State Committee for Drought Control in the Sahel. L'Aide publique au développement dans les pays membres du CILSS en 1983 =. Paris , Burkina Faso [1984], c1985. v, 347 p. : LC Card 86-180117
HC1000 .A64 1985

PERMANENT INTER-STATE COMMITTEE FOR DROUGHT CONTROL IN THE SAHEL.
Sall, Alioune. Ressources humaines pour le développement . [Dakar, Sénégal , 1984] 51 p. : LC Card 85-129264 DDC 338.91/09624 19
HC1002 .S25 1984

Permanent Inter-State Commmittee for Drought Control in the Sahel. Berg, Elliot. Absorptive capacity in the Sahel countries. [Paris] [Ouagadougou, Burkina Faso] [1983] xi, 133 p. ; LC Card 87-402541 DDC 338.91/0966 19
HC1002 .B47 1983

Permisos y concesiones, 1890-1912 /. Nuevo León (Mexico : State). Archivo General del Estado. [Monterrey, Mexico] [1981] 43 leaves ; LC Card 81-216459
HD3616.M44 N866 1981

Permskiĭ gosudarstvennyĭ universitet imeni A.M. Gor'kogo. Deiatel'nost' partiĭnykh organizatsiĭ po razvitiiu promyshlennosti Urala v period razvitogo sotsializma . Perm' , 1984. 96 p. ; LC Card 86-181271
HC337.R852 U734 1984

PERNAMBUCO (BRAZIL) - ECONOMIC CONDITIONS.
Bezerra, Agostinho Fernandes. As tarifas internas na 1a. República /. Brasília, DF , 1986. xv, 140 p. : LC Card 87-404990 DDC 381/.5/098134 19
HJ5101.P47 B49 1986

Pôrto, Josè da Costa, 1909- O açúcar num documento colonial /. Recife , 1984. 116 p. ; LC Card 87-102690
HD9114.B7 P448 1984

PERNAMBUCO (BRAZIL) - HISTORY.
Pôrto, Josè da Costa, 1909- O açúcar num documento colonial /. Recife , 1984. 116 p. ; LC Card 87-102690
HD9114.B7 P448 1984

Pernambuco. Secretaria de Habitação. Seminário Permanente de Habitação Popular (1981 : Recife, Brazil) Anais--1981 /. Recife [19]82. 178 p. ; LC Card 84-256147
HD7323.P37 S46 1981

Pernoud, Régine, 1909- Le Moyen Age pour quoi faire? / Régine Pernoud, Raymond Delatouche, Jean Gimpel. [Paris] : Stock, c1986. 315 p. : ill. ; 24 cm. Includes bibliographical references. ISBN 2-234-01940-0 : LC Card 86-189820
1. Economic history - Medieval, 500-1500. 2. Developing countries - Economic conditions. 3. Technology - Social aspects - History. 4. Comparative civilization. 5. Appropriate technology - Developing countries. I. Delatouche, Raymond. II. Gimpel, Jean. III. Title.
HC41 .P46 1986

Pernsteiner, August W. Gestaltkonforme partnerschaftliche "Beteiligungs-" und "Kreditfinanzierung" von "Klein-" und "Mittelbetrieben" / August W. Pernsteiner. Wien : VWGÖ, 1983. 355, xxx p. : ill. ; 21 cm. (Dissertationen der Johannes Kepler-Universität Linz . 42) Bibliography: p. xiii-xxx. ISBN 3-85369-536-1 LC Card 83-206156
1. Small business - Austria - Finance. 2. Small business investment companies - Austria. 3. Credit - Austria. 4. Partnership - Austria - Finance. I. Title. II. Series.
HG4027.7 .P47 1983

Péroche, Marcel, 1907- Les mémoires de Marcel Péroche, "sénateur" du rail / avec la collaboration de Didier Sénécal. Paris : Berger-Levrault, c1984. 256 p., [8] p. of plates : ill. ; 23 cm. ISBN 2-7013-0556-X : LC Card 84-206923
1. Péroche, Marcel, 1907-. 2. Railroads - France - Employees - Biography. 3. Locomotive engineers - France - Biography. I. Sénécal, Didier. II. Title.
HD8039.R322 F87 1984

PÉROCHE, MARCEL, 1907-
Péroche, Marcel, 1907- Les mémoires de Marcel Péroche, "sénateur" du rail /. Paris , c1984. 256 p., [8] p. of plates : ISBN 2-7013-0556-X : LC Card 84-206923
HD8039.R322 F87 1984

PERONISM - HISTORY.
Fernández, Arturo. Ideologías de los grupos dirigentes sindicales /. Buenos Aires , c1986. 2 v. ; ISBN 950-25-1403-3 (v. 1) LC Card 86-205687
HD6603.5 .F47 1986

Perrakēs, Charalambos I. Kazēs, D. A. (Dēmētrēs A.) [Licensing kai viomēchanikē anaptyxē. English.] Licensing and industrial development . Athens , 1986. 208 p. : LC Card 87-170691 DDC 338.09495 19
HF1429 .K3813 1986

Perri, Colleen, 1936-
Entrepreneurial women / by Colleen Perri. Kenosha, WI : Possibilities Pub., c1987. 140 p. : ill. ; 22 cm. (1st in Kenosha-my home town series) Bibliography: p. 137-140. ISBN 0-941579-00-X (pbk.) LC Card 87-154216 DDC 338/.04/088042 19
1. Women-owned business enterprises - Wisconsin - Kenosha - Case studies. 2. New business enterprises - Wisconsin - Kenosha - Case studies. 3. Women in business - Wisconsin - Kenosha - Case studies. I. Series: Perri, Colleen, 1936- Kenosha-my home town series , 1st. II. Title.
HD2346.U52 K376 1987b

Entrepreneurial women ./ by Colleen Perri. 2nd ed. Kenosha, WI : Possibilities Pub., c1988. p. cm. Bibliography: p. ISBN 0-941579-28-X LC Card 87-7380 DDC 338/.04/088042 19
1. Women-owned business enterprises - Wisconsin - Kenosha - Case studies. 2. New business enterprises - Wisconsin - Kenosha - Case studies. 3. Women in business - Wisconsin - Kenosha - Case studies. I. Title.
HD2346.U52 K376 1988

Entrepreneurial women. Book II / by Colleen Perri. Kenosha, WI : Possibilities Pub., c1988. p. cm. Bibliography: p. Includes index. ISBN 0-941579-02-6 LC Card 87-7370 DDC 338/.04/088042 19
1. Women-owned business enterprises - United States - Case studies. 2. New business enterprises - United States - Case studies. 3. Women in business - United States - Case studies. I. Title.
HD2346.U5 P43 1988

Kenosha-my home town series .
(1st) Perri, Colleen, 1936- Entrepreneurial women /. Kenosha, WI , c1987. 140 p. : ISBN 0-941579-00-X (pbk.) LC Card 87-154216 DDC 338/.04/088042 19
HD2346.U52 K376 1987b

Perridon, Louis, 1918- Aktuelle Probleme der Marktwirtschaft in gesamt- und einzelwirtschaftlicher Sicht . Berlin , c1984. 458 p., [1] leaf of plates : ISBN 3-428-05653-1 LC Card 85-128275
HB501 .A514 1984

PERRIDON, LOUIS, 1918-
Aktuelle Probleme der Marktwirtschaft in gesamt- und einzelwirtschaftlicher Sicht . Berlin , c1984. 458 p., [1] leaf of plates : ISBN 3-428-05653-1 LC Card 85-128275
HB501 .A514 1984

Perrin, J. Chaponnière, R. Les fonctions des agents économiques exportant des biens d'équipement, dans le cadre des relations est-ouest et nord-sud, depuis 1970 /. [Paris] [1981] 159 leaves : LC Card 82-180468 DDC 382/.456817 19
HD9705.A2 C55 1981 ***NYPL [JLG 86-212]***

Perrin, Jacqueline. L'enquête de 1848 sur le travail en Isère / Jacqueline Perrin. Grenoble : Université des sciences sociales de Grenoble, Centre de recherche d'histoire économique, sociale et institutionnelle, 1985. 251 p., [1] leaf of plates : ill. ; 21 cm. (Publications du Centre de recherche d'histoire économique, sociale et institutionnelle de Grenoble. Série Histoire économique et sociale . v. 5) Bibliography: p. [246]-248. ISBN 2-904661-03-4 : LC Card 86-227898
1. Isère (France) - Economic conditions. 2. Isère (France) - Industries - History. 3. Agriculture - Economic aspects - France - Isère. I. Title. II. Series.
HC277.I8 P47 1985

Perrings, Charles. Economy and environment : a theoretical essay on the interdependence of economic and environmental systems / Charles Perrings. Cambridge [Cambridgeshire] ; New York : Cambridge University Press, 1987. xv, 179 p. ; 24 cm. Bibliography: p. 168-174. Includes index. ISBN 0-521-34081-0 LC Card 87-18329 DDC 333.7 19
1. Economic development - Environmental aspects. I. Title.
HD75.6 .P47 1987

Perris, Arnold. Music as propaganda : art to persuade, art to control / Arnold Perris. Westport, Conn. : Greenwood Press, c1985. x, 247 p. ; 21 cm. (Contributions to the study of music and dance, 0193-9041 . no. 8) Includes index. Bibliography: p. [227]-242. ISBN 0-313-24505-3 (lib. bdg.) LC Card 84-27969 DDC 781/.15 19
1. Music - Psychology. 2. Propaganda. 3. Persuasion (Psychology). 4. Control (Psychology). 5. Music and state. I. Title. II. Series.
ML3838 .P43 1985 ***NYPL [JMD 86-149]***

Perritt, Gerald W. Expand your investment horizons and increase your stock market profits / Gerald W. Perritt. Chicago, IL : Investment Information Services Press, c1987. viii, 288 p. : ill. ; 23 cm. Includes index. ISBN 0-930369-03-3 (pbk.) LC Card 87-401495 DDC 332.63/2 19
1. Investments - Handbooks, manuals, etc. 2. Stocks - Handbooks, manuals, etc. I. Title.
HG4527 .P39 1987

Perrot, Michelle.
[Jeunesse de la grève. English]
Workers on strike : France, 1871-1890 / Michelle Perrot ; translated from the French by Chris Turner, with the assistance of Erica Carter and Claire Laudet. New Haven : Yale University Press, 1987. 321 p. : ill. ; 23 cm. Translation of: Jeunesse de la grève. Bibliography: p. 320-321. ISBN 0-300-03849-6 LC Card 86-26753 DDC 331.89/2944 19
1. Strikes and lockouts - France - History - 19th century. I. Title.
HD5374 .P4613 1987

Perroux, François, 1903- Regional economic development . Boston , 1987. p. cm. ISBN 0-04-338155-3 (alk. paper) LC Card 87-16749 DDC 338.9 19
HD75 .R44 1987

PERROUX, FRANÇOIS, 1903-
Regional economic development . Boston , 1987. p. cm. ISBN 0-04-338155-3 (alk. paper) LC Card 87-16749 DDC 338.9 19
HD75 .R44 1987

Perry, Charles M. Selling the rope to hang capitalism? . Washington , 1987. viii, 246 p. ; ISBN 0-08-034959-5 : LC Card 86-30401 DDC 382/.091713/01717 19
HF1412 .S45 1987

Perry, Charles R. Union corporate campaigns / by Charles R. Perry. Philadelphia, Pa. : Industrial Research Unit, Wharton School, University of Pennsylvania, c1987. viii, 211 p. : ill. ; 24 cm. (Major Industrial Research Unit studies, 0083-9094 . no. 66) Includes bibliographical references and index. ISBN 0-89546-065-3 : LC Card 86-82727 DDC 331.89/12 19
1. Trade-unions - United States - Organizing. 2. Trade-unions - United States - Organizing - Case studies. 3. Industrial relations - United States. I. Title. II. Series.
HD6490.O72 U665 1987

Perry, Guillermo. Gómez Buendía, Hernando. Sindicalismo y política económica /. Bogotá, Colombia , 1986. 324 p. : ISBN 958-9061-16-8 LC Card 87-401441 DDC 331.88/09861 19
HD6622 .G64 1986

Perry, Jos. Roomsche kinine tegen roode koorts : arbeidersbeweging en katholieke kerk in Maastricht, 1880-1920 / Jos Perry. Amsterdam : Van Gennep, 1983. 334 p. : ill. ; 22 cm. (De Nederlandse arbeidersbeweging . 14) Summary in French. Includes index. Bibliography: p. 315-326. ISBN 90-6012-571-1 : LC Card 83-240733
1. Trade-unions, Catholic - Netherlands - Maastricht - History. 2. Church and labor - Netherlands - Maastricht - History. I. Title.
HD6481.2.N4 P47 1983
NYPL [JLD 86-3418]

Perry, Larry L.
Compilation and review manual / Larry L. Perry. Englewood Cliffs, N.J. : Prentice Hall, c1987- 1 v. (loose-leaf) : forms ; 30 cm. "Guide to quality and efficiency for Prentice Hall's Compilation and review manual" (vii, 52 p.) issued separately. ISBN 0-13-162934-4 (loose-leaf) LC Card 86-63240 DDC 657/.3 19
1. Financial statements, Unaudited - Handbooks, manuals, etc. 2. Financial statements, Unaudited - Forms. I. Title.
HF5681.B2 P42185 1987

Small business audit manual / Larry L. Perry. Englewood Cliffs, N.J. : Prentice Hall, c1987- 1 v. (loose-leaf) : ill. ; 30 cm. Accompanied by a package of blank documentation forms with title: Small business audit manual documentation. "Guide to quality and efficiency for Prentice Hall's Small business audit manual" (vi, 110 p.) issued separately. ISBN 0-13-813155-4 (loose-leaf) LC Card 86-63242 DDC 657/.45 19
1. Small business - Auditing - Handbooks, manuals, etc. 2. Auditing - Handbooks, manuals, etc. I. Perry, Larry L. Small business audit manual documentation. II. Title.
HF5667 .P416 1987

Small business audit manual documentation.
Perry, Larry L. Small business audit manual / Larry L. Perry. Englewood Cliffs, N.J. , c1987- 1 v. (loose-leaf) : ISBN 0-13-813155-4 (loose-leaf) LC Card 86-63242 DDC 657/.45 19
HF5667 .P416 1987

Perry, Martin, 1956-
Fothergill, Steve. Property and industrial development /. London , Wolfeboro, N.H. , 1987. 187 p. : ISBN 0-09-170741-2 (pbk.) : LC Card 87-2627 DDC 333.3/8/0941 19
HD598 .F68 1987

Small factories and economic development / Martin Perry. Aldershot, Hants., England ; Brookfield, VT, USA : Gower, c1986. xvi, 229 p. ; 23 cm. Bibliography: p. 220-229. ISBN 0-566-05208-3 : LC Card 86-9904 DDC 338.6/42/0941 19
1. Industry and state - Great Britain. 2. Small business - Great Britain. 3. Great Britain - Industries - Location. I. Title.
HC260.D5 P47 1986 ***NYPL [JLD 86-3993]***

Perry, Richard D. Money problems / Richard D. Perry. Elgin, Ill. : D.C. Cook Pub. Co., c1987. 111 p. ; 21 cm. (Helping others in crisis) Bibliography: p. 107-111. ISBN 1-555-13797-0 (pbk.) LC Card 86-73209 DDC 332.024 19
1. Finance, Personal. 2. Christian giving. I. Title. II. Series.
HG179 .P367 1987

Perry, Susan. Nightmare : women and the Dalkon Shield / Susan Perry and Jim Dawson. New York : Macmillan, c1985. xvii, 261 p. ; 24 cm. Bibliography included in "Notes" : p. 250-251. ISBN 0-02-595930-1 : LC Card 85-13710 DDC 338.7/616139435 19
1. A.H. Robins Company. 2. Dalkon Shield (Intrauterine contraceptive). 3. Intrauterine contraceptives - Complications and sequelae. 4. Intrauterine contraceptives industry - United States. I. Dawson, Jim (James L.). II. Title.
HD9995.C64 A236 1985
NYPL [JLE 85-3950]

Perry, William E.
The information center / William E. Perry. Englewood Cliffs, N.J. : Prentice-Hall, c1987. xi, 284 p. : ill. ; 25 cm. Includes index. ISBN 0-13-464371-2 LC Card 86-25212 DDC 658.4/038 19
1. Business - Data processing - Information services - United States. 2. Information storage and retrieval systems - Business. I. Title.
HF5548.2 .P47284 1987

Management workstations : strategies for office productivity / William E. Perry.1st ed. Blue Ridge Summit, PA : TAB Professional and Reference Books, c1987. vi, 186 p. : ill. ; 24 cm. Includes index. ISBN 0-8306-2833-9 : LC Card 87-1903 DDC 658/.05 19
1. Management - Data processing. 2. Business - Data processing. I. Title.
HD30.2 .P47 1987

Porter, W. Thomas. EDP, controls and auditing /. Boston, Mass. , c1987. xviii, 617 p. : ISBN 0-534-07092-2 : LC Card 86-27564 DDC 657/.45/0285 19
HF5548.35 .P67 1987

Persaud, B. (Bishnodat) Developing with foreign investment /. London , New York , c1987. viii, 327 p. ; ISBN 0-7099-4825-5 LC Card 87-3603 DDC 332.6/73/091724 19
HG5993 .D47 1987

Persia. see Iran.

PERSIAN GULF REGION - ECONOMIC CONDITIONS.
The Gulf in the early 20th century . [Durham] , c1986. 215 p., [1] leaf of plates : LC Card 87-100795 DDC 330.953/6 19
HC415.3 .G85 1986

PERSIAN GULF REGION - ECONOMIC POLICY.
The Gulf in the early 20th century . [Durham] , c1986. 215 p., [1] leaf of plates : LC Card 87-100795 DDC 330.953/6 19
HC415.3 .G85 1986

PERSIAN GULF REGION - EMIGRATION AND IMMIGRATION.
Feiler, Gil. The number of Egyptian workers in the Arab oil countries, 1974-1983 . Tel Aviv , c1986. i, 30 leaves ; LC Card 87-404430 DDC 331.6/2/620536 19
HD8662 .F45 1986

PERSIAN GULF STATES - ECONOMIC CONDITIONS.
Bazarian, Carl J. The Gulf States =. New York, N.Y. , c1980. 577 p. : ISBN 0-916006-07-7 LC Card 80-65496
HC415.3 .B39 1980

PERSIAN GULF STATES - ECONOMIC POLICY.
Bazarian, Carl J. The Gulf States =. New York, N.Y. , c1980. 577 p. : ISBN 0-916006-07-7 LC Card 80-65496
HC415.3 .B39 1980

PERSIAN GULF STATES - ECONOMIC POLICY - CONGRESSES.
Focus on the Gulf Co-operation Council (GCC) . London , c1984. 48 p. : LC Card 85-211534 DDC 337.53/6/041 19
HF1584.5 .F63 1984

PERSIAN GULF STATES - FOREIGN ECONOMIC RELATIONS - GREAT BRITAIN - CONGRESSES.
Focus on the Gulf Co-operation Council (GCC) . London , c1984. 48 p. : LC Card 85-211534 DDC 337.53/6/041 19
HF1584.5 .F63 1984

The persistence of profits . Geroski, Paul. Berlin [1985] 35, 6 p. : LC Card 86-212315 DDC 338.5/16/0724 19
HG4028.P7 G47 1985

Persistent poverty . Beckford, George L. London , Totowa, N.J. , c1983. xxv, 244 p. : ISBN 0-86232-207-3 (pbk.) LC Card 85-149825 DDC 338.1/09172/4 19
HC59.72.P6 B43 1983 ***NYPL [JLD 87-628]***

Persönlich, an den Manager . Kryka, Milan, 1926- Zürich , c1983. 143 p. : ISBN 3-85505-050-3 LC Card 83-152577
HF5549 .K765 1983

Die persönliche materielle Interessiertheit an der Material- und Energieökonomie /. Kaufmann, Manfred. Jena , 1984. 112 p. : LC Card 85-224317
HF1054.G42 K38 1984

Persoglia, Johann. Projectcontrolling als Subsystem des Rechnungswesens / Johann Persoglia. 1. Aufl. Graz : DBV-Verlag, c1986. 238 p. ; 24 cm. Bibliography: p. 217-235. ISBN 3-7041-0149-4 LC Card 87-407965 DDC 657/.42 19
1. Cost accounting. 2. Industrial project management. I. Title.
HF5686.C8 P475 1986

Person, Ron, 1948-
[1-2-3 business formula handbook. Spanish]
1-2-3 en el mundo de las finanzas : manual de fórmulas y de aplicaciones prácticas / por Ron Person ; [traducido del inglés y adaptado al español por Jorge Tamayo].1a ed. en lengua española. Miami, Fla., E.U.A. : Macrobit Corp., 1988. p. cm. Translation of: 1-2-3 business formula handbook. Includes index. ISBN 0-939573-02-4 LC Card 87-20916 DDC 005.36/9 19
1. Lotus 1-2-3 (Computer program). 2. Business - Data processing. I. Title. II. Title: Uno-dos-tres en el mundo de las finanzas.
HF5548.4.L67 P4718 1988

Person, Samuel. Barron's how to prepare for the certified public accountant examination, CPA / by Person/Wolinsky CPA Review Courses, Samuel Person, Robert Beekman. 3rd ed. New York : Barron's Educational Series, c1987. vi, 537 p. ; 28 cm. Bibliography: p. 48-49. ISBN 0-8120-3880-0 (pbk.) : LC Card 87-17914 DDC 657/.076 19
1. Accounting - Examinations, questions, etc. I. Beekman, Robert. II. Person/Wolinsky CPA Review Courses (Firm). III. Title. IV. Title: How to prepare for

the certified public accountant examination, CPA.
HF5661 .P48 1987

Person to person : helping customers make financial decisions. 1st ed. Chicago, Ill. : Institute of Financial Education, c1986. 310 p. : ill. ; 23 cm. Includes index. ISBN 0-912857-33-1 (pbk.) LC Card 85-81996 DDC 332.1/068/8 19
1. Financial planners. 2. Interpersonal communication.
HG179 .P368 1986 NYPL [JLE 86-3903]

Persona e società .
(2) Understanding poverty /. Milano, Italy , c1984. 355 p. : LC Card 84-249441 DDC 339.4/6/094 19
HC240.9.P6 U53 1984 NYPL [JLD 86-1196]

Personagens da crise /. Formiga, Marcone. Brasília , 1984. 160 p. : LC Card 86-157831
HC187 .F636 1984

PERSONAL ACTIONS. see **ACTIONS AND DEFENSES.**

The Personal computer hardware add-on device market. New York, N.Y. : Frost & Sullivan, c1983. viii, 2, 228 p. : ill. ; 29 cm. "May 1983." "#A1220." LC Card 87-143524
1. Computer industry - United States. 2. Minicomputers - United States. 3. Microcomputers - United States. 4. Market surveys - United States. I. Frost & Sullivan.
HD9696.C63 U52783 1983

The personal consequences of redundancy . Wooden, Mark. [Bedford Park, South Australia] [1987] 102 p. : LC Card 87-155519 DDC 331.13/7 19
HD5707.5 .W66 1987

PERSONAL CONSTRUCT THEORY.
Boose, John H. Expertise transfer for expert system design /. Amsterdam , New York , 1986. viii, 312 p. : ISBN 0-444-42634-5 LC Card 86-9044 DDC 006.3/3 19
QA76.76.E95 B66 1986
NYPL [JSE 86-1840]

PERSONAL DEVELOPMENT. see **SUCCESS.**

Personal economics . Kennedy, Robert A. Tucson, AZ , c1987. xi, 315 p. : ISBN 0-89586-517-3 (pbk.) : LC Card 86-82240 DDC 332.024 19
HG179 .K46 1987

PERSONAL EFFICIENCY. see **SUCCESS.**

Personal finance. Trading gold and silver with futures and options /. Alexandria, VA (1101 King St., Suite 400, Alexandria 22314) , c1986. 149, 10 p. : LC Card 87-110004 DDC 332.64/52 19
HG293 .T73 1986

Personal finance for consumers /. Lee, Stewart Munro. Columbus, Ohio , c1987. xiii, 518 p. : ISBN 0-942280-33-4 : LC Card 86-30503 DDC 381/.3/0973 19
HB301 .L256 1987

Personal financial management /. Block, Stanley B. New York , c1988. xvii, 603 p. : ISBN 0-06-040789-1 LC Card 87-19088 DDC 332.024 19
HG179 .B555 1988

Personal financial markets : an examination of the evolving markets for personal savings and financing in the United Kingdom and the United States / edited by R.L. Carter and B. Chiplin and M.K. Lewis. Deddington, Oxford : P. Allan ; Atlantic Highlands, N.J. : Distributed in the U. S.A. and Canada by Humanities Press, 1986. viii, 279 p. : ill. ; 23 cm. Distributor from label on t.p. Includes bibliographies and indexes. ISBN 0-86003-540-9 LC Card 86-235455 DDC 332.1/7 19
1. Finance - Great Britain. 2. Finance - United States. 3. Finance, Personal - Great Britain. 4. Finance, Personal - United States. I. Carter, R. L. II. Chiplin, Brian. III. Lewis, Mervyn.
HG186.G7 P38 1986

Personal financial planning : the team approach. New York, N.Y. (1211 Ave. of the Americas, New York 10036-8775) : American Institute of Certified Public Accountants, c1987. viii, 131 p. ; 23 cm. (Management advisory services practice aids. Small business consulting practice aid . 7) Bibliography: p. 131. LC Card 87-142958 DDC 332.024 19
1. Finance, Personal - Handbooks, manuals, etc. 2. Small business - Finance - Handbooks, manuals, etc. 3. Business - Forms. I. American Institute of Certified Public Accountants. II. Series.
HG179 .P387 1987

Personal financial planning /. Hallman, G. Victor. New York , c1987. xix, 475 p. : ISBN 0-07-025650-0 : LC Card 87-2584 DDC 332.024 19
HG179 .H24 1987

Personal financial planning /. Woodman, Byron E. Andover, Mass. , c1987. 151 p. ; ISBN 0-931790-77-8 : LC Card 87-13229 DDC 332.024 19
HG179 .W578 1987

Personal financial planning for local government employees / edited by Bruce K. Blaylock, Kenneth F. Kennedy. Washington, D.C. : ICMA, c1987. 203 p. : ill. ; 23 cm. "Published by the International City Management Association in cooperation with the ICMA Retirement Corporation." Bibliography: p. [199]-203. ISBN 0-87326-051-1 (pbk.) LC Card 87-2948 DDC 332.024/354 19
1. Local officials and employees - United States - Finance, Personal. 2. Finance, Personal - United States. I. Blaylock, Bruce K., 1949-. II. Kennedy, Kenneth F., 1945-.
HG179 .P386 1987

Personal financial planning in banks . Seglin, Jeffrey L., 1956- Boston , c1986. xvii, 205 p. ; ISBN 0-87267-059-7 LC Card 85-28738 DDC 332.1/7 19
HG1616.C87 S44 1986 NYPL [JLE 87-820]

Personal financial planning manual : nonauthoritative explanations and illustrations / Personal Financial Planning Division. New York, NY : American Institute of Certified Public Accountants, c1987. 1 v. (loose-leaf) : ill., forms ; 30 cm. LC Card 87-404512 DDC 332.024 19
1. Finance, Personal - Handbooks, manuals, etc. I. American Institute of Certified Public Accountants. Personal Financial Planning Division.
HG179 .P3865 1987

PERSONAL IDENTIFICATION PRODUCTS INDUSTRY.
O'Reilly, Francis J. The "smart card" . Stamford, Conn., U. S.A. [1986] xii, 106 leaves ; ISBN 0-89336-470-3 (soft) : LC Card 87-163972 DDC 380.1/4568 19
HD9696.O672 O74 1986

Personal income taxation in India /. Krishna Rao, Ch. A. (Chitrothu Atchuta), 1940- Allahabad, India , 1987. xii, 284 p. ; ISBN 81-85076-19-7 : LC Card 86-903664 DDC 336.24/2/0954 19
HJ4766 .K75 1987

Personal investing . Senchack, A. J. (Andrew J.) [Texas?] , c1986. 1 v. (various pagings) : LC Card 87-104863 DDC 332.6/78 19
HG4921 .S44 1986

PERSONAL LIBERTY. see **LIBERTY.**

Personal money management with AppleWorks /. Witkin, Ruth K. Hasbrouck Heights, N.J. [New York] , c1986. 418 p. : ISBN 0-471-62575-2 (Wiley : pbk.) : LC Card 87-110545 DDC 332.024/0028/55369 19
HG179 .W554 1986

Personal money mangement with AppleWorks /. Witkin, Ruth K. New York , c1987. p. cm. ISBN 0-471-62575-2 : LC Card 87-6294 DDC 332.024/0028/55369 19
HG179 .W554 1987

Personal narratives of the West series.
Lynch, Gerald, 1908- Roughnecks, drillers, and tool pushers . Austin , 1987. xiv, 262 p. : ISBN 0-292-71553-6 LC Card 87-13857 DDC 331.7/6223382/0924 B 19
HD8039.P42 L95 1987

Personal performance contracts . Fritz, Roger. Los Altos, Calif. , c1987. vi, 71 p. : ISBN 0-931961-12-2 (pbk.) : LC Card 85-73466 DDC 658.3/142 19
HF5549.5.G6 F75 1987

Personal productivity with Lotus 1-2-3 /. Gorham, Kenneth D. Dubuque, Iowa , c1987. x, 164 p. : ISBN 0-697-05227-3 (pbk.) LC Card 87-70158 DDC 005.36/9 19
HF5548.4 L67 G67 1987

PERSONAL PROPERTY - INDIA - CASE STUDIES.
Ghadoliya, M. K. (Mahendra Kumar) Structure of employment, earnings, and assets in India . Delhi , 1986. xi, 248 p. : LC Card 86-903221 DDC 331.12/5/09544 19
HD5820.U33 G47 1986

PERSONAL PROPERTY - INDIA - UDAIPUR (DISTRICT) - CASE STUDIES.
Ghadoliya, M. K. (Mahendra Kumar) Structure of employment, earnings, and assets in India . Delhi , 1986. xi, 248 p. : LC Card 86-903221 DDC 331.12/5/09544 19
HD5820.U33 G47 1986

Personal selling . Marks, Ronald B., 1944- Boston , c1988. xvi, 607 p. : ISBN 0-205-11087-8 LC Card 87-16098 DDC 658.8/5 19
HF5438.25 .M37 1988

Personal selling power. Gschwandtner, Gerhard. Supersellers . New York, N.Y. , c1986. xi, 169 p. : ISBN 0-8144-5883-1 LC Card 86-47586 DDC 658.8/5 19
HF5438.25 .G785 1986
NYPL [JLE 87-1489]

Personal travel in the U. S. . Klinger, Dieter. Washington, D.C. , Springfield, Va. [1986] 2 v. : LC Card 86-603072 DDC 380.5/22/0973021 19
HE199.9 .K535 1986

Personal travel in the United States. Klinger, Dieter. Personal travel in the U. S. . Washington, D.C. , Springfield, Va. [1986] 2 v. : LC Card 86-603072 DDC 380.5/22/0973021 19
HE199.9 .K535 1986

Die Personalberatung bei der Stellenbesetzung /. Franz, Michael. Frankfurt am Main , c1984. viii, 214 p. ; ISBN 3-88129-789-8 LC Card 85-186519
HF5549.5.C8 F7 1984

Personaleadministration /. Andersen, René, 1936- Köbenhavn , 1983. 476 p. : ISBN 87-7040-278-7 : LC Card 84-104119
HF5549.2.D45 A53 1983

PERSONALITY AND INTELLIGENCE.
Peters, Roger. Practical intelligence . New York, N.Y. , c1987. x, 341 p. ; ISBN 0-06-015681-3 : LC Card 86-46096 DDC 650.1 19
HD38.2 .P47 1987

PERSONALITY AND OCCUPATION.
Catálogo de ocupações pesquisadas em Fortaleza. [Fortaleza] . 111, [1] p. ; LC Card 83-222529
HF5382.5.B7 C38 1972

Gardenswartz, Lee. What it takes . New York , 1987. ix, 205 p. ; ISBN 0-385-23820-7 : LC Card 87-13657 DDC 650.1/024042 19
HF5386 .G214 1987

PERSONALITY AND OCCUPATION - MICHIGAN - LONGITUDINAL STUDIES.
Mortimer, Jeylan T., 1943- Work, family, and personality . Norwood, N.J. , c1986. viii, 267 p. : ISBN 0-89391-293-X LC Card 85-20951 DDC 306/.36/09774 19
HD4904.25 .M67 1986 NYPL [JLE 87-869]

Personality and organization . Argyris, Chris, 1923- New York , 1987, c1957. xiii, 291 p. ; ISBN 0-8240-8200-1 (alk. paper) : LC Card 86-27054 DDC 658.4 19
HD58.7 .A75 1987

PERSONALITY AND SITUATION.
Vroom, Victor Harold, 1932- Some personality determinants of the effects of participation /. New York , 1987, c1960. x, 91 p. ; ISBN 0-8240-8225-7 (alk. paper) : LC Card 86-27081 DDC 158.7 19
HF5548.8 .V695 1987

Der Personalmanager im Vorstand . Spie, Ulrich. Stuttgart , 1985. ix, 354 p. : ISBN 3-8202-0313-3 LC Card 86-131051
HF5549.2.G3 S67 1985

Personelle Einkommensverteilung in der Landwirtschaft und Agrarpreise /. Witzke, Harald von. Berlin , 1979. 180 p. : ISBN 3-428-04303-0 LC Card 79-389988
HC290.5.I5 W57 NYPL [JLE 80-439]

Personligt präglat. [Stockholm] : Svenska kraftverksföreningen, [1985] 107 p. : ill. ; 21 cm. "Utgiven till Svenska kraftverksföreningens

75-årsjubileum." LC Card 85-191053
1. Svenska Kraftverksföreningen. 2. Electric utilities - Sweden. I. Svenska Kraftverksföreningen.
HD9685.S854 S945 1985

PERSONNEL ADMINISTRATION. see **PERSONNEL MANAGEMENT.**

Personnel and human resource management. Readings in personnel and human resource management /. St. Paul, MN , c1988. xix, 600 p. : ISBN 0-314-33750-4 (pbk.) LC Card 86-28244 DDC 658.3 19
HF5549 .R38167 1988

Personnel and human resource management in Canada /. Dolan, Shimon. St. Paul, MN , c1987. xvii, 620 p. : ISBN 0-314-32486-0 LC Card 87-2207 DDC 658.3/00971 19
HF5549.2.C3 D65 1987

Personnel and organizational psychology /. Siegel, Laurence. Homewood, Ill. , 1987. xviii, 617 p. : ISBN 0-256-03369-2 LC Card 86-82591 DDC 158.7 19
HF5548.8 .S512 1987

PERSONNEL DIRECTORS - GERMANY, WEST.
Spie, Ulrich. Der Personalmanager im Vorstand . Stuttgart , 1985. ix, 354 p. : ISBN 3-8202-0313-3 LC Card 86-131051
HF5549.2.G3 S67 1985

PERSONNEL DIRECTORS - UNITED STATES - BIOGRAPHY.
Wren, Daniel A. White collar hobo . Ames , 1987. xii, 165 p. : ISBN 0-8138-1922-9 LC Card 87-4048 DDC 331/.092/4 B 19
HD8073.W47 W74 1987

Personnel/human resource management. DeCenzo, David A. Englewood Cliffs, N.J. , c1988. xvii, 637 p. : ISBN 0-13-657198-0 LC Card 87-6983 DDC 658.3 19
HF5549 .D396 1988

Personnel/human resource management . Scarpello, Vida Gulbinas, 1940- Boston, Mass. , c1988. xxii, 794 p. : ISBN 0-534-08346-3 LC Card 87-13678 DDC 658.3 19
HF5549 .S186 1988

Personnel management /. Dessler, Gary, 1942- Englewood Cliffs, N.J. , c1988. viii, 727 p. : ISBN 0-13-658543-4 : LC Card 87-21000 DDC 658.3 19
HF5549 .D4379 1988

PERSONNEL MANAGEMENT - ADDRESSES, ESSAYS, LECTURES.
The Leader-manager /. New York , c1986. xi, 511 p. : ISBN 0-471-83693-1 : LC Card 86-1316 DDC 658.4/092 19
HD38.2 .L42 1986 ***NYPL [JLE 86-2930]***

PERSONNEL MANAGEMENT - ASIA - CASE STUDIES.
In quest of human dynamism . Tokyo, Japan , 1986. viii, 552 p. : ISBN 92-833-1088-2 LC Card 86-210648 DDC 658.3/0095 19
HF5549.2.A75 Q84 1986

PERSONNEL MANAGEMENT - BULGARIA.
Lekov, Kostadin. Nasoki za usŭvŭrshenstvuvane na sistemata za upravlenie na truda /. Sofiia , 1985. 103 p. ; LC Card 86-230344
HF5549.2.B9 L46 1985

PERSONNEL MANAGEMENT - CALIFORNIA - ALAMEDA COUNTY.
McGuire, Nan. Survey of private sector work and family policy . San Francisco , c1986. 41 leaves ; LC Card 87-113810 DDC 331.25/72/0979461 19
HD5126.S4 M38 1986

PERSONNEL MANAGEMENT - CALIFORNIA - SAN FRANCISCO.
McGuire, Nan. Survey of private sector work and family policy . San Francisco , c1986. 41 leaves ; LC Card 87-113810 DDC 331.25/72/0979461 19
HD5126.S4 M38 1986

PERSONNEL MANAGEMENT - CANADA.
Canadian readings in personnel and human resource management /. St. Paul, MN , c1987. xi, 467 p. ; ISBN 0-314-32487-9 (pbk.) LC Card 87-2211 DDC 658.3/00971 19
HF5549.2.C3 C36 1987

Dolan, Shimon. Personnel and human resource management in Canada /. St. Paul, MN , c1987. xvii, 620 p. : ISBN 0-314-32486-0 LC Card 87-2207 DDC 658.3/00971 19
HF5549.2.C3 D65 1987

PERSONNEL MANAGEMENT - CANADA - CASE STUDIES.
Crocker, Olga L. Incidents and cases in Canadian personnel administration /. Toronto , New York , c1986. 216 p. : ISBN 0-458-98690-9 (pbk.) : LC Card 86-218837 DDC 658.3/00971 19
HF5549.2.C3 C76 1986

PERSONNEL MANAGEMENT - CONGRESSES.
Man and work in society . New York , c1975. xiv, 313 p. : ISBN 0-442-29359-3 LC Card 75-26866 DDC 658.3
HF5549 .M299 ***NYPL [JLE 76-2406]***

Occupational stress and organizational effectiveness /. New York , c1987. xii, 285 p. : ISBN 0-275-92281-2 (alk. paper) : LC Card 86-25250 DDC 158.7 19
HF5548.85 .O24 1987

PERSONNEL MANAGEMENT - DATA PROCESSING.
Mülder, Wilhelm. Organisatorische Implementierung von computergestützten Personalinformationssystemen . Berlin , New York , 1984. xix, 257 p. : ISBN 0-387-13360-7 (U. S.) LC Card 84-238144
HF5549.5.D37 M85 1984

PERSONNEL MANAGEMENT - DENMARK.
Andersen, René, 1936- Personaleadministration /. Köbenhavn , 1983. 476 p. : ISBN 87-7040-278-7 : LC Card 84-104119
HF5549.2.D45 A53 1983

PERSONNEL MANAGEMENT - DICTIONARIES.
Shafritz, Jay M. The Facts on File dictionary of personnel management and labor relations /. New York, N.Y. , c1985. 534 p. : ISBN 0-8160-1234-2 LC Card 85-20823 DDC 658.3/003/21 19
HF5549.A23 S52 1985 ***NYPL [JLE 86-4748]***

PERSONNEL MANAGEMENT - EUROPE, EASTERN.
Stimulierung in Industriebetrieben und Kombinaten /. Berlin , c1982. 290 p. : LC Card 83-164671
HF5549.5.M63 S75 1982

PERSONNEL MANAGEMENT - FILM CATALOGS.
National industrial relations film catalogue. [Ottawa, Ont.] , c1986. 31, 21 p. ; ISBN 0-662-54352-1 (pbk.) LC Card 86-203066 DDC 016.331 19
HD6971 .N24 1986

PERSONNEL MANAGEMENT - FORMS, BLANKS, ETC. see **PERSONNEL RECORDS.**

PERSONNEL MANAGEMENT - GERMANY, WEST.
Albach, Horst. Kosten der Arbeit . Stuttgart , c1985. xi, 179 p. : ISBN 3-7910-5003-6 : LC Card 86-162885 DDC 658.3/00943 19
HD5029 .A43 1985 ***NYPL [JLL 73-505 Nr.2]***

Arbeitsgestaltung in der Serienfertigung . Frankfurt [am Main] , New York , c1984. 315 p. : ISBN 3-593-32733-3 LC Card 84-230390
HD58.8 .A73 1984

Huellen, Karl Konrad. Die Motivation von Arbeitnehmern im Innen- und Aussendienst des Vertriebs . Münster [1986] iv, 245 p. : ISBN 3-88660-356-3 (Deut. Bibl.) LC Card 87-114821 DDC 658.3/14 19
HF5549.5.M63 H84 1986

Spie, Ulrich. Der Personalmanager im Vorstand . Stuttgart , 1985. ix, 354 p. : ISBN 3-8202-0313-3 LC Card 86-131051
HF5549.2.G3 S67 1985

Wührer, Gerhard. Strategien des Personalmanagements . Krefeld , 1985. 264 p. : ISBN 3-88358-054-5 LC Card 86-160291
HF5549.2.G3 W84 1985

PERSONNEL MANAGEMENT - GERMANY, WEST - CONGRESSES.
Neue Entwicklungen bei Arbeit, Entgelt und Führung /. Freiburg im Breisgau , c1984. 169 p. : ISBN 3-448-01480-X : LC Card 84-249237
HF5549.2.G3 N48 1984

PERSONNEL MANAGEMENT - HANDBOOKS, MANUALS, ETC.
The IFM guide to the preparation of a company policy manual. Greenvale, N.Y. , c1987. xv, 412 p. ; ISBN 0-916592-71-5 (loose-leaf) LC Card 87-22258 DDC 658.3/01 19
HF5549 .I5643 1987

Sredl, Henry J., 1935- The ASTD reference guide to professional training roles & competencies /. New York , c1987. 2 v. : ISBN 0-394-55915-0 (v. 1) LC Card 86-26006 DDC 658.3/124 19
HF5549.5.T7 S657 1987

PERSONNEL MANAGEMENT - HUNGARY.
Illisz, László. Személyzeti munka, társadalmi környezet /. [Budapest] , 1986. 159 p. : ISBN 963-09-2778-0 : LC Card 87-408532
HF5549.2.H85 I44 1986

Makó, Csaba. A társadalmi viszonyok erőtere, a munkafolyamat /. Budapest , 1985. 192 p. ; ISBN 963-221-528-1 : LC Card 86-187344
HF5549 .M2953 1985

Munkaügy a belkereskedelemben /. [Budapest] , 1986. 272 p. ; ISBN 963-01-7513-4 : LC Card 87-148137
HF5549.2.H85 M86 1986

Personnel management in action . Kelley, Nelson Lane, 1937- St. Paul , c1987. xiv, 338 p. : ISBN 0-314-32168-3 (pbk.) LC Card 86-32445 DDC 658.3 19
HF5549 .K344 1987

PERSONNEL MANAGEMENT - INDIA.
Gangadhara Rao, M. Human resources management in Indian railways /. Delhi , 1986. xvi, 245 p. ; ISBN 81-7049-004-9 : LC Card 86-900747 DDC 385/.068/3 19
HD8039.R12 I437 1986 ***NYPL [JLE 86-4104]***

PERSONNEL MANAGEMENT - INDIA - CONGRESSES.
Recent experiences in human resources development /. New Delhi , c1986. xvi, 448 p. ; ISBN 81-204-0120-4 : LC Card 86-902270 DDC 331.11/0954 19
HF5549.5.M3 R38 1985

PERSONNEL MANAGEMENT - JAPAN.
Iida, Tsuneo, 1932- What is really unique about the Japanese economy? /. Nagoya, Japan , 1985. 13 leaves ; LC Card 87-109242 DDC 331.25 19
HF5549.5.S4 I35 1985

Nötzli, Irene M. A view of Japanese management, especially management development in large business enterprises /. Zürich , c1982. ix, 281 p. : ISBN 3-7255-2191-3 (pbk.) LC Card 82-237094 DDC 658.4/07124 19
HF5549.5.T7 N638 1982 ***NYPL [TB (Zürich. Universität. Handelwissenschafticles Seminar. Mitteilungen. Heft 156)]***

PERSONNEL MANAGEMENT - KENYA.
Wa'Weru, Murathi. Management of human resources in Kenya /. Nairobi , 1984. xv, 174 p. ; LC Card 85-980435 DDC 658.3/009676/2 19
HF5549.2.K4 W39 1984b

PERSONNEL MANAGEMENT - MATHEMATICAL MODELS.
Meiritz, Wolfram. Eignungsorientierte Personaleinsatzplanung . Frankfurt am Main , New York , c1984. xv, 304 p. : ISBN 3-8204-5164-1 LC Card 85-198624
HF5549 .M343 1984

PERSONNEL MANAGEMENT - NETHERLANDS.
Werk en organisatie /. Lisse , 1986- v. <1 > ; ISBN 90-265-0755-0 (deel 1) : LC Card 86-221124
HF5549.2.N4 W47 1986

PERSONNEL MANAGEMENT - PLANNING.
Staffelbach, Bruno. Strategisches Personalmanagement /. Bern [1986] x, 285 p. : ISBN 3-258-03626-8 : LC Card 86-211191
HF5549 .S842416 1986

PERSONNEL MANAGEMENT - POLAND.
Determinanty polityki kadrowej w przedsiębiorstwie . Poznań , 1984. 142 p. : LC Card 86-194984
HB54 .P6 nr. 129 HF5549.2.P6

PERSONNEL MANAGEMENT - PROBLEMS, EXERCISES, ETC.
Kelley, Nelson Lane, 1937- Personnel management in action . St. Paul , c1987. xiv, 338 p. : ISBN 0-314-32168-3 (pbk.) LC Card 86-32445 DDC 658.3 19
HF5549 .K344 1987

The personnel management process . French, Wendell L., 1923- Boston , c1987. xxiv, 685 p. : ISBN 0-395-35661-X LC Card 86-81308 DDC 658.3 19
HF5549 .F73 1987

PERSONNEL MANAGEMENT - PSYCHOLOGICAL ASPECTS.
Lenssen, Adolf K. Konformität und Nichtkonformität im Betrieb . Konstanz , 1986. 400 p. : ISBN 3-89191-064-9 (p. 4. of cover); 3-89191-064-7 LC Card 87-109576 DDC 658.3/001/9 19
HF5549 .L4619 1986

PERSONNEL MANAGEMENT - SOUTH AFRICA.
Botha, Henk. How to manage strikes through strategy . Moreletapark , c1986. vi, 101 p. : ISBN 0-620-10384-1 LC Card 87-148504 DDC 658.3/154 19
HD5442.A6 B68 1986

PERSONNEL MANAGEMENT - SOVIET UNION.
Bakhrakh, D. N. (Dem'ian Nikolaevich) Osnovnye poniatiia teorii sotsial'nogo upravleniia . Perm' , 1978. 100 p. ; LC Card 81-154363
HD70.S63 B35 1978

Nauchnaia organizatsiia truda v promyshlennosti /. Moskva , 1986. 414 p. : LC Card 86-218434
HD36 .N323 1986

Nekotorye problemy internatsional'nogo vospitaniia v mnogonatsional'nom trudovom kollektive /. Moskva , 1985. 135 p. ; LC Card 86-233779
HD8526.5 .N45 1985

Nemtsev, F. L. (Fedor Logvinovich) Upravlenie trudom v usloviiakh nauchno-tekhnicheskogo progressa /. Minsk , 1985. 125 p. ; LC Card 85-231066
HF5549.2.S65 N45 1985

Sotsial'noe upravlenie trudovym kollektivom . Moskva , 1987. 181 p. ; LC Card 87-103391
HF5549.2.S65 S675 1987

Upravlenie sotsial'nymi protsessami v trudovykh kollektivakh /. Kishinev , 1983. 141 p. : LC Card 84-133794
HD6957.S65 U67 1983

PERSONNEL MANAGEMENT - SOVIET UNION - MATHEMATICAL MODELS.
Sulitskii, V. N. (Vladimir Nikolaevich) Organizatsionno-ėkonomicheskie problemy upravleniia kadrami v otrasli /. Moskva , 1986. 164, [3] p. : LC Card 86-233362
HF5549.2.S65 S85 1986

PERSONNEL MANAGEMENT - STUDY AND TEACHING - AFRICA.
Rwegasira, Kami S. P. Administering management development institutions in Africa /. Aldershot, England , Brookfield, Vt. , 1988. p. cm. ISBN 0-566-05501-5 : LC Card 87-17688 DDC 658.4/07124/096 19
HF5549.5.A78 R94 1988

PERSONNEL MANAGEMENT - SWEDEN.
Egemo, Jerry, 1931- Kreativ personalplanering . Malmö , c1984. 99 p. ; ISBN 91-38-61248-8 : LC Card 84-188831
HF5549 .E425 1984

PERSONNEL MANAGEMENT - UNITED STATES.
Connolly, Paul M. Promotional practices and policies . New York , c1985. 52 p. ; ISBN 0-08-029515-0 (pbk.) : LC Card 85-3421 DDC 658.3/142 19
HF5549.2.U5 C66 1985 ***NYPL [JLM 83-380 no.41]***

Derr, C. Brooklyn (Clyde Brooklyn) Managing the new careerists /. San Francisco , 1986. xxii, 288 p. ; ISBN 0-87589-677-4 LC Card 85-45901 DDC 658.3/02 19
HF5549.2.U5 D47 1986 ***NYPL [JLE 86-2427]***

Holoviak, Stephen J. Managing human productivity . New York , 1987. xiii, 216 p. : ISBN 0-275-92481-5 (alk. paper) : LC Card 86-25247 DDC 658.3/14 19
HF5549.2.U5 H65 1987

New York (State). Legislature. Assembly. Standing Committee on Labor. A report on the plight of the collective bargaining system /. [Albany] [1984] 64 p. ; LC Card 86-622572 DDC 331.89/0973 19
HD6508 .N49 1984

United States. Dept. of the Interior. Division of Medical and Health Services. Help for the troubled employee. Washington [1975?] 57 p. ;
NYPL [JLF 86-1309]

PERSONNEL MANAGEMENT - UNITED STATES - CASE STUDIES.
Harrison, Clifford E., 1931- Managing staff reductions in corporations /. Ann Arbor, Mich. , c1986. vi, 138 p. : ISBN 0-8357-1758-5 (alk. paper) LC Card 86-11223 DDC 658.3/134 19
HF5549.5.D55 H37 1986 ***NYPL [JLE 86-3391]***

Jacobson, Beverly. Young programs for older workers . New York , 1980. xvii, 123 p. ; ISBN 0-442-25405-9 LC Card 80-12621 DDC 658.3/042
HD6280 .J3 ***NYPL [JLE 81-438]***

PERSONNEL PROCEDURE MANUALS.
Eimicke, Victor W. Managing human resources . Oxford [Oxfordshire] , New York , 1987. x, 211 p. : ISBN 0-08-034768-1 (U. S.) : LC Card 86-25273 DDC 658.3 19
HF5549 .E44 1987

PERSONNEL RECORDS.
Eimicke, Victor W. Managing human resources . Oxford [Oxfordshire] , New York , 1987. x, 211 p. : ISBN 0-08-034768-1 (U. S.) : LC Card 86-25273 DDC 658.3 19
HF5549 .E44 1987

PERSONNEL RECORDS IN INDUSTRY. see **PERSONNEL RECORDS.**

PERSONNEL RESEARCH - METHODOLOGY.
Manuale di ricerca sul lavoro e sulle organizzazioni /. Roma , 1985. 384 p. : LC Card 86-118313 DDC 306/.36/072 19
HD4824 .M32 1985 ***NYPL [JLD 87-1160]***

Personnel selection and productivity /. Cook, Mark. Chichester [West Sussex] , New York , c1988. p. cm. ISBN 0-471-91148-8 : LC Card 87-21070 DDC 658.3/112 19
HF5549.5.S38 C66 1988

Persons, Robert H., 1922- The investor's encyclopedia of gold, silver, and other precious metals; how to invest successfully in all forms of precious metals [by] Robert H. Persons, Jr.[1st ed. New York, Random House, 1974] x, 316 p. illus. 28 cm. ISBN 0-394-49597-7 LC Card 74-14860 DDC 332.6/328
1. Investments - United States. 2. Metals as an investment. I. Title.
HG5073 .P38 ***NYPL [JLF 86-388]***

Persontrafik i 1975 og 1981 : en sammenlignende undersøgelse. [Copenhagen] : DSB, [1983] 94 p. : ill. ; 30 cm. ISBN 87-88453-06-5 LC Card 84-169450
1. Transportation - Denmark - Passenger traffic.
HE257 .P47 1983

Person/Wolinsky CPA Review Courses (Firm)
Person, Samuel. Barron's how to prepare for the certified public accountant examination, CPA /. New York , c1987. vi, 537 p. ; ISBN 0-8120-3880-0 (pbk.) : LC Card 87-17914 DDC 657/.076 19
HF5661 .P48 1987

Perspectivas de la economía mundial y colombiana / Carlos Medellín ... [et al.]. Bogotá, Colombia : Universidad Externado de Colombia, 1986. 106 p. ; 24 cm. "Ciclo de conferencias para el primer centenario de la universidad." Papers presented at the Seminario de Análisis de la Coyuntura y las Perspectivas de la Economía en Colombia, held in April 1985, organized by the Universidad Externado de Colombia with the collaboration of the Instituto de Altos Estudios de Francia. ISBN 958-616-044-0 LC Card 87-115573 DDC 330.9861/0632 19
1. Colombia - Economic conditions - 1970- - Congresses. 2. Economic history - 1971- - Congresses. I. Medellín, Carlos. II. Seminario de Análisis de la Coyuntura y las Perspectivas de la Economía en Colombia (1985 : Bogotá, Colombia?). III. Universidad Externado de Colombia. IV. Ecole pratique des hautes études (France).
HC197 .P35 1986

Perspectivas de longo prazo da economia brasileira / IPEA, Instituto de Planejamento Econômico e Social, INPES-- Instituto de Pesquisas do IPEA. [Rio de Janeiro, RJ] : IPEA/INPES, 1985. 363 p. : ill. ; 21 cm. Includes bibliographies. LC Card 86-164342
1. Brazil - Economic policy. 2. Economic forecasting - Brazil. I. Instituto de Planejamento Econômico e Social. Instituto de Pesquisas.
HC187 .P415 1985

Perspectivas para a ação do BDMG no período 1983-85. Banco de Desenvolvimento de Minas Gerais. Belo Horizonte, MG, Brasil [1983] 67 p. : LC Card 83-207712
HG2889.M55 B37 1983

Perspectivas sobre o norte de Portugal. Porto : Secretaria de Estado da Cultura, Centro de Estudos Humanísticos, 1981. 242 p. : ill. ; 21 cm. (Studium generale. Estudos contemporâneos . no. 2/3) Cover title. Prepared by the Secção de Estudos Contemporâneos, Centro de Estudos Humanísticos. Includes bibliographical references. LC Card 83-163948
1. Minho (Portugal) - Economic conditions. 2. Minho (Portugal) - Social conditions. 3. Porto Region (Portugal) - Economic conditions. 4. Porto Region (Portugal) - Social conditions. I. Centro de Estudos Humanísticos (Porto, Portugal). II. Series: Studium generale (Centro de Estudos Humanísticos (Porto, Portugal)). Estudos contemporâneos , no. 2/3.
HC393.M55 P47 1981

Perspectivas y Alternativas de la Agricultura Familiar. Taller "Perspectivas y Alternativas de la Agricultura Familiar" (1983 : Montevideo, Uruguay) Taller "Perspectivas y Alternativas de la Agricultura Familiar". Montevideo, Uruguay [1984] 1 v. (various pagings) : LC Card 85-203149 DDC 338.1/6 19
HD1476.L29 T35 1983 ***NYPL [JLF 86-884]***

A perspective on U. S. farm problems and agricultural policy /. McKinzie, Lance. Boulder , 1987. xvii, 189 p. : ISBN 0-8133-7376-X (pbk. : alk. paper) LC Card 86-51501 DDC 338.1/873 19
HD1470.5.U6 M35 1987

Perspective on world energy : the short term 1985-1990 : the medium term 1990-2005 : the long term 2005-2025. Arlington, Va. (1911 Fort Myer Dr., Suite 403, Arlington 22209) : Gulf Futures, c1987. 3, iii, 27, [19] p. : ill. ; 28 cm. "January, 1987." LC Card 87-142737 DDC 333.79 19
1. Petroleum industry and trade - Forecasting. 2. Gas industry - Forecasting. 3. Energy industries - Forecasting. I. Gulf Futures, Inc.
HD9560.5 .P3847 1987

Perspectives and risks of an international division of labour. Albuquerque, Marcos Cintra Cavalcanti de. Riscos e perspectivas da divisão internacional do trabalho =. Brasília, DF [1986] 19, 17, [2] p. ; LC Card 87-403241 DDC 331/.01 19
HF1411 .A3984 1986

Perspectives d'emploi pour les Québécoises dans la décennie 1980 . Messier, Suzanne. Québec [1983] vi, 73 p. ; ISBN 2-550-10439-0 LC Card 84-221697
HD6100.Q4 M47 1983

Perspectives internationales, 0243-2331.
La Serre, Françoise de. La Grande-Bretagne et la Communauté européenne /. Paris , c1987. 223, [1] p. : ISBN 2-13-040114-7 : LC Card 87-165122
HC241.25.G7 L118 1987

Perspectives on Canadian economic history / edited by Douglas McCalla. Toronto : Copp Clark Pitman, c1987. 287 p. : ill. ; 23 cm. (New Canadian readings) Includes bibliographies. ISBN 0-7730-4679-8 LC Card 87-168012 DDC 330.971 19
1. Canada - Economic conditions. I. McCalla, Douglas, 1942-. II. Series.
HC113 .P47 1987

Perspectives on employment /. Freedman, Audrey. New York, N.Y. (845 3rd Ave., New

York 10022) , c1986. 15 p. : LC Card 86-212384 DDC 331.12 19
HD5701.3 .F74 1986

Perspectives on industrial readjustment, the EEC and the developing countries / [research team: Ben Evers, Gerard de Groot, Willy Wagenmans]. Tilburg, Netherlands : Development Research Institute, 1978. ii, 98 p. ; 30 cm. (Research project, industrial readjustment and the internationnal division of labour . report no. 10) Cover title. Includes bibliographies.
1. European Economic Community countries - Commerce - Developing countries. 2. Developing countries - Commerce - European Economic Community countries. 3. Developing countries - Industries. I. Evers, Ben. II. Series.
NYPL [JLF 86-1708]

Perspectives on methodology in consumer research / edited by David Brinberg and Richard J. Lutz. New York : Springer-Verlag, c1986. xi, 301 p. : ill. ; 25 cm. Includes bibliographies and indexes. ISBN 0-387-96238-7 : LC Card 85-26047 DDC 658.8/34 19
1. Consumers - Research - Addresses, essays, lectures. 2. Marketing research - Addresses, essays, lectures. 3. Motivation research (Marketing) - Addresses, essays, lectures. I. Brinberg, David. II. Lutz, Richard John, 1947-.
HF5415.3 .P464 1986 ***NYPL [JLE 86-4371]***

Perspectives on organization theory /. Grandori, Anna. [Teorie dell'organizzazione. English.] Cambridge, Mass. , c1987. xxvi, 199 p. : ISBN 0-88730-214-9 LC Card 87-11359 DDC 302.3/5 19
HD37.I8 G7313 1987

Perspectives on organizational communication /. Daniels, Tom D. Dubuque, Iowa , c1987. xiv, 288 p. : ISBN 0-697-00444-9 LC Card 86-72711 DDC 658.4/5 19
HD30.3 .D33 1987

Perspectives on population : an introduction to concepts and issues / [compiled by] Scott W. Menard and Elizabeth W. Moen. New York : Oxford University Press, 1987. xix, 487 p. : ill. ; 25 cm. Includes bibliographies and indexes. ISBN 0-19-504092-9 (alk. paper) : LC Card 86-23652 DDC 304.6 19
1. Population. I. Menard, Scott W. II. Moen, Elizabeth.
HB871 .P48 1987

Perspectives on safe & sound banking : past, present, and future / by George J. Benston ... [et al.].1st MIT Press ed. Cambridge, Mass. : MIT Press, 1986. xxi, 358 p. ; 24 cm. (MIT Press series on the regulation of economic activity . 12) "A study commissioned by the American Bankers Association." Includes index. Bibliography: p. 327-345. ISBN 0-262-02246-X LC Card 85-23882 DDC 332.1/0973 19
1. Banks and banking - United States. 2. Bank failures - United States. 3. Banks and banking - United States - State supervision. 4. Risk - United States. I. Benston, George J. II. Title: Perspectives on safe and sound banking. III. Series.
HG2481 .P47 1986 ***NYPL [JLE 86-2960]***

Perspectives on safe and sound banking. Perspectives on safe & sound banking . Cambridge, Mass. , 1986. xxi, 358 p. ; ISBN 0-262-02246-X LC Card 85-23882 DDC 332.1/0973 19
HG2481 .P47 1986 ***NYPL [JLE 86-2960]***

Perspectives on social welfare in India /. Bulsara, Jal F. (Jal Feerose), 1899- New Delhi , 1984. xvi, 226 p. ; LC Card 84-900869 DDC 361/.954 19
HV40 .B886 1984 ***NYPL [JLD 86-4376]***

Perspectives on the American Revolution. The Economy of early America . Charlottesville , 1988. xvi, 334 p. : ISBN 0-8139-1139-7 LC Card 87-6169 DDC 330.973/02 19
HC104 .E26 1988

Perspectives on the future of Natal/KwaZulu /. Spies, P. H. Pietermaritzburg , 1986. 149 p. : ISBN 0-909232-59-8 (pbk.) : LC Card 87-166530 DDC 361.2/5/09684 s 361.6/1/09684 19
HC517.N3 A44 vol. 69 JQ2224

Perspektiv på fördelningspolitiken /. Söderström, Lars, 1940- [Stockholm] [1984] 83 p. : ISBN 91-7566-068-7 LC Card 85-108552
HC380.I5 S62 1984

Perspektiven. Issues of the eighties . Wien , 1983. 119 p. : LC Card 83-201354 DDC 338.9 19
HD73 .I86 1983

Perspektiven der Genossenschaftsrevision : Festschrift für Wilhelm Weber zum 70. Geburtstag / herausgegeben von Mario Patera. Wien : A. Orac, 1986. x, 322 p. : port. ; 24 cm. (Wiener Studien des Forschungsinstitutes für Genossenschaftswesen . n.F., Bd. 5) Errata slip laid in. "Univ. Prof. Dr. h.c. mult. Dr. Wilhelm Weber, Schriftenverzeichnis seiner genossenschaftswissenschaftlichen Veröffentlichungen": p. 314-316. Includes bibliographies. ISBN 3-85368-775-X LC Card 87-138767 DDC 334/.09436 19
1. Cooperative societies - Austria. 2. Cooperative societies - Law and legislation - Austria. 3. Weber, Wilhelm, 1916-. I. Weber, Wilhelm, 1916-. II. Patera, Mario, 1946-. III. Series.
HD3490 .P47 1986

Perspektiven der Vollbeschäftigung : ökonomische und gesellschaftliche Rahmenbedingungen : Arbeitstagung zum 40jährigen Bestehen des WSI 1986. Köln : Bund-Verlag, c1987. vi, 263 p. : ill. ; 21 cm. (WSI-Studie zur Wirtschafts- und Sozialforschung . Nr. 58) Papers presented at a meeting in 1986. Includes bibliographies. ISBN 3-7663-3033-0 LC Card 87-135012 DDC 339.5 19
1. Full employment policies - Congresses. I. Deutscher Gewerkschaftsbund. Wirtschafts- und Sozialwissenschaftliches Institut. II. Series.
HD5701.3 .P47 1987

Perspektiven einer ökologischen Ökonomie / Werner Onken (Hrsg.) ; [Ernst Winkler et al.]. Hann. [i.e. Hannoversch] Münden : Fachverlag für Sozialökonomie, c1983. 91 p. ; 21 cm. Includes bibliographical references. ISBN 3-87998-402-6 : LC Card 83-180506
1. Environmental policy - Germany, West. I. Onken, Werner, 1953-.
HC290.5.E5 P47 1983

Perspektiven und Modelle einer Neuorientierung der staatlichen Wohneigentumsforderung /. Kaufmann-Scheuer, Brigitte. Freiburg [i. Br.] , 1983. 235 p. : ISBN 3-8107-2185-9 LC Card 84-108468
HD7339.A3 K34 1983

Perspektiven verkehrswissenschaftlicher Forschung : Festschrift für Fritz Voigt zum 75. Geburtstag / herausgegeben von Sigurd Klatt. Berlin : Duncker & Humblot, c1985. 606 p., [1] leaf of plates : ill. ; 24 cm. Three contributions in English. "Verzeichnis der verkehrs- und regionalwissenschaftlichen Arbeiten von Fritz Voigt": p. [597]-606. Includes bibliographies. ISBN 3-428-05738-4 LC Card 85-155542
1. Transportation and state. 2. Transportation. 3. Voigt, Fritz. I. Voigt, Fritz. II. Klatt, Sigurd.
HE151 .P44 1985

Perspektiven (Vienna, Austria) Issues of the eighties . Wien , 1983. 119 p. : LC Card 83-201354 DDC 338.9 19
HD73 .I86 1983

Perspektivnoe finansovoe planirovanie . Evstigneeva, Li͡udmila Petrovna. Moskva , 1982. 182 p. ; LC Card 83-124268
HG186.S55 E97 1982

Perspektivnoe planirovanie razvitii͡a agrarno-promyshlennogo kompleksa / pod redaktsieĭ A.I. Panchenko. Novosibirsk : Akademii͡a nauk SSSR, Sibirskoe otd-nie, In-t ėkonomiki i organizatsii promyshlennogo proizvodstva, 1979. 159 p. : ill. ; 20 cm. (Sbornik nauchnykh trudov) Includes bibliographies. LC Card 81-143730
1. Agricultural industries - Soviet Union - Mathematical models. 2. Agriculture - Economic aspects - Soviet Union. I. Panchenko, A. I. II. Series: Sbornik nauchnykh trudov (Institut ėkonomiki i organizat͡sii promyshlennogo proizvodstva (Akademii͡a nauk SSSR)).
HD9015.S652 P47 1979

Perspektivy hospodářského a sociálního rozvoje ČSSR /. Závada, Josef. Praha , 1986. 134 p. ; LC Card 87-161408
HC270.28 .Z38 1986

Perspektivy reshenii͡a prodovol'stvennoĭ problemy v razvivai͡ushchikhsi͡a stranakh : sbornik obzorov / [redkollegii͡a Levkovskiĭ A.I. ... et al. ; otvetstvennyĭ redaktor Makarova S.M. ; redaktor-sostavitel' I͡U.V. Chaĭnikov]. Moskva : Akademii͡a nauk SSSR, In-t nauch. informat͡sii po obshchestvennym naukam, 1985. 142 p. ; 20 cm. (Serii͡a Ėkonomika razvivai͡ushchikhsi͡a stran Azii i Afriki) Includes bibliographies. LC Card 85-188217
1. Food supply - Developing countries. 2. Nutrition policy - Developing countries. I. Levkovskiĭ, Alekseĭ Ivanovich. II. Makarova, S. M. III. Chaĭnikov, I͡U. V. IV. Series.
HD9018.D44 P47 1985

PERSUASION (PSYCHOLOGY)
Perris, Arnold. Music as propaganda . Westport, Conn. , c1985. x, 247 p. ; ISBN 0-313-24505-3 (lib. bdg.) LC Card 84-27969 DDC 781/.15 19
ML3838 .P43 1985 ***NYPL [JMD 86-149]***

Persuasive business writing . Cross, Mary. New York, NY , c1987. x, 179 p. : ISBN 0-8144-5898-X LC Card 86-47808 DDC 808/.066651 19
HF5718.3 .C76 1987

Pertempi, Silvia. Montemassi : terra e miniera in una comunità della Maremma / Silvia Pertempi.1a ed. italiana. Torino : Rosenberg & Sellier, 1986. 238 p. ; 21 cm. On spine: 43. Bibliography: p. 233-238. ISBN 88-7011-250-0 : LC Card 87-134525
1. Mineral industries - Italy - Montemassi - History. 2. Agriculture - Economic aspects - Italy - Montemassi - History. 3. Montemassi (Italy) - Economic conditions. 4. Montemassi (Italy) - Social conditions. I. Title.
HD9506.I83 M656 1986

PERTH REGION (W.A.) - POPULATION - STATISTICS.
Projected population of Western Australia and the Perth Statistical Division, 1985-2025. [Perth] [1986] 82 p. : LC Card 87-114601 DDC 304.6/2/09941021 19
HA3007.W47 P76 1986

Perú : estimaciones y proyecciones de la población por años calendarios y edades simples del período, 1970-2000. Lima, Perú : República Peruana, Instituto Nacional de Estadística, Dirección General de Demografía, 1984. 54 p. ; 30 cm. (Boletín especial . no. 7) Chiefly tables. "Edición de 500 ejemplares." Includes bibliographical references. LC Card 86-111841 DDC 304.6/2/0985021 19
1. Population forecasting - Peru - Statistics. 2. Age distribution (Demography) - Peru - Statistics. 3. Peru - Population - Statistics. I. Instituto Nacional de Estadística (Peru). Dirección General de Demografía. II. Series: Boletín especial (Instituto Nacional de Estadística (Peru). Dirección General de Demografía) , no. 7.
HA1055 .P46 1984 ***NYPL [JLG 86-190]***

Perú . Barrón Coral, Marcial. [Lima?] 1983 ([Lima] : General S.R.L.) 191 p. ; LC Card 84-253120
HC227 .B3365 1983

Peru.
LEY DE PROMOCIÓN Y DESARROLLO AGRARIO.
Promoción agraria, para quién? . Lima, Perú , 1980. 162 p. ; ***NYPL [JLD 86-3547]***

Peru and the International Monetary Fund /. Scheetz, Thomas Edward. Pittsburgh, PA , c1986. xi, 257 p. : ISBN 0-8229-3816-2 LC Card 85-40855 DDC 332.1/52 19
HG3881.5.I58 S34 1986
NYPL [JLD 86-2893]

PERU - APPROPRIATIONS AND EXPENDITURES.
Malpica Silva Santisteban, Carlos. La alternativa de la izquierda . [Lima, Peru] [1985] 91 p. : LC Card 87-403544 DDC 338.985 19
HJ2090 .M35 1985

PERU - CENSUS.
Migraciones laborales en el Perú . [Monterrico] [c1984] 47 p. : LC Card 84-235623 DDC 331.12/7985 19
HD5761 .M53 1984 ***NYPL [JLF 86-799]***

PERU - COMMERCE.
Abusada-Salah, Roberto. La crisis del empresariado nacional /. [Lima] [1983] 41 p. ; LC Card 84-236119
HC227 .A57 1983

Iguíñiz, Javier. Crisis y fluctuaciones en la economía peruana, 1950-1983 . Jesús María [Peru] [1985] 245 p. : LC Card 86-116792 DDC 338.5/42/0985 19
HB3779 .I35 1985 ***NYPL [JLC 86-268]***

PERU - COMMERCE - HISTORY - 17TH CENTURY.
Escobari de Querejazu, Laura. Producción y comercio en el espacio sur andino en el siglo XVII . La Paz , 1985. 218 p., [12] p. of plates : LC Card 86-174929
HC167.A5 E83 1985

PERU - COMMERCIAL POLICY.
Herrera, César. Inflación, política devaluatoria y apertura externa en el Perú, 1978-1984 /. Lima, Perú , 1985. 55 p. : LC Card 87-104441
HG895 .H47 1985

Peru. Cooperación Popular. Datos distritales para fines de desarrollo. [Lima] [1964] 92 p. : LC Card 85-134068 DDC 318.5 19
HA1064 .D37 1964

PERU - DEPENDENCY ON FOREIGN COUNTRIES.
Peru, Kolonisation und Abhängigkeit . Saarbrücken , Fort Lauderdale , 1981. 192 p. : ISBN 3-88156-165-X : LC Card 82-104103
HD1905.O75 P47 1981

PERU - DEPENDENCY ON FOREIGN COUNTRIES - HISTORY - 20TH CENTURY.
Dore, Elizabeth. Acumulación y crisis en la minería peruana, 1900-1977 /. [Lima] [1986] 168 p. : LC Card 86-235232
HD9506.P42 D66 1986

Perú, economía no-neoclásica, modelo de acumulación, crisis y alternativa de desarrollo no-monetarista /. Jiménez, Félix. Lima, Perú , 1986. 107 p. : LC Card 87-404229 DDC 338.985 19
HC227 .J53 1986

PERU - ECONOMIC CONDITIONS.
Barrón Coral, Marcial. Perú . [Lima?] 1983 ([Lima] : General S.R.L.) 191 p. ; LC Card 84-253120
HC227 .B3365 1983

Las Crisis económicas en la historia del Perú /. [Lima, Perú] [s.l.] , 1986. 376 p. : LC Card 87-400306 DDC 330.985 19
HC227 .C744 1986

Humala Tasso, Ulises. Subdesarrollo o camino al colapso . [S.l. , 1987?] (Lima, Perú : Graphos 100 Editores) 175 p. ; LC Card 87-403093 DDC 330.985/0633 19
HC227 .H86 1987

Ríos Burga, Jaime R. Ciclos productivos en el espacio peruano colonial, siglos XVI-XIX . Lima, Perú , 1986. 70 p. : LC Card 87-401070 DDC 338.5/42/0983 19
HC227 .R456 1986

PERU - ECONOMIC CONDITIONS - 1918-1968.
Iguíñiz, Javier. Crisis y fluctuaciones en la economía peruana, 1950-1983 . Jesús María [Peru] [1985] 245 p. : LC Card 86-116792 DDC 338.5/42/0985 19
HB3779 .I35 1985 ***NYPL [JLC 86-268]***

PERU - ECONOMIC CONDITIONS - 1968-
Abusada-Salah, Roberto. La crisis del empresariado nacional /. [Lima] [1983] 41 p. ; LC Card 84-236119
HC227 .A57 1983

Basurco Valverde, Gerardo Félix. Herrschaftsformen und Industrialisierungsprozess in Peru . Freiburg [Breisgau] , c1985. xi, 420 p. : ISBN 3-8107-2210-3 LC Card 86-179243
HC227 .B339 1985

Casas Grieve, Luis Felipe de las. Economía y frustración social . Lima, Perú [1982?] 128 p. : LC Card 83-104684
HC227 .C27 1982

Estrategias para el desarrollo de la Sierra /. Cusco , c1986. 418 p. : LC Card 86-199393
HC228.A54 E87 1986

Gall, Norman. Brazil and Peru . Geneva , 1987. x, 123 p., [1] leaf of plates : ISBN 92-2-105506-X (pbk.) : LC Card 87-166425 DDC 338.2/7282/0981 19
HD9574.B82 G34 1987

Iguíñiz, Javier. Crisis y fluctuaciones en la economía peruana, 1950-1983 . Jesús María [Peru] [1985] 245 p. : LC Card 86-116792 DDC 338.5/42/0985 19
HB3779 .I35 1985 ***NYPL [JLC 86-268]***

Lizárraga Bobbio, Raúl. Estrategias para la descentralización y el desarrollo regional /. Lima, Perú , c1985. 356 p. : LC Card 86-146658
HT395.P4 L59 1985 ***NYPL [JLD 87-1315]***

Panorama del Departamento ... /. [Lima?] , 1984-<1987. v. <1-8 > : LC Card 86-202585
HC227 .P354 1984

Sistema de planes de desarrollo de mediano plazo. [Lima] [1987- v. <1-2 > : LC Card 87-404041 DDC 338.985 19
HC227 .S496 1987

Struktur- und Entwicklungsprobleme der Industrie Perus /. Heidelberg , c1985. 338 p. : ISBN 3-88326-165-3 LC Card 86-108518 DDC 338.0985 19
HC227 .S77 1985

PERU - ECONOMIC CONDITIONS - CONGRESSES.
Region and class in modern Peruvian history /. [Liverpool] , 1987. 207 p. : ISBN 0-902806-20-3 LC Card 87-148309 DDC 330.985/0633 19
HC227 .R386 1987

PERU - ECONOMIC POLICY.
Alva Castro, Luis. Deuda o desarrollo . Lima, Perú , 1987. 127 p. : LC Card 87-403115 DDC 336.3/4/0985 19
HJ8604 .A75 1987

Basurco Valverde, Gerardo Félix. Herrschaftsformen und Industrialisierungsprozess in Peru . Freiburg [Breisgau] , c1985. xi, 420 p. : ISBN 3-8107-2210-3 LC Card 86-179243
HC227 .B339 1985

Casas Grieve, Luis Felipe de las. Economía y frustración social . Lima, Perú [1982?] 128 p. : LC Card 83-104684
HC227 .C27 1982

Estrategias para el desarrollo de la Sierra /. Cusco , c1986. 418 p. : LC Card 86-199393
HC228.A54 E87 1986

Iguíñiz, Javier. Política económica 1985-1986 . Lima , 1986. 153 p. : LC Card 87-120200
HC227 .I368 1986

Instituto Nacional de Planificación (Peru) Sistema de planes de desarrollo de corto plazo, 1986. [Lima] [1986- v. <1-35 > : LC Card 86-216851
HC227 .I529 1986

Jiménez, Félix. Perú, economía no-neoclásica, modelo de acumulación, crisis y alternativa de desarrollo no-monetarista /. Lima, Perú , 1986. 107 p. : LC Card 87-404229 DDC 338.985 19
HC227 .J53 1986

Malpica Silva Santisteban, Carlos. La alternativa de la izquierda . [Lima, Peru] [1985] 91 p. : LC Card 87-403544 DDC 338.985 19
HJ2090 .M35 1985

El Mercado de capitales como instrumento de la política económica /. [Miraflores, Lima] [1987] 111 p. ; LC Card 87-169408 DDC 332.6/0985 19
HG5392 .M43 1987

Ortiz, Rolando. CORDES . Lima, Perú , 1987. 96 p. ; LC Card 87-405059 DDC 338.985 19
HC227 .O73 1987

Perú siglo XXI. [Lima] [1986 or 1987] 63 p. : LC Card 87-403080 DDC 338.985 19
HC227 .P416 1986

Planificación por la revolución y la justicia. [Lima, Peru] [1986] 43 p. : LC Card 87-402212 DDC 338.985 19
HC227 .P536 1986

Rosales Díaz, Ramón. Programas de reactivación económica y sistemas financieros . [Lima] , 1986. 68 p. : LC Card 87-400247 DDC 332.4/982 19
HG815 .R67 1986

Sistema de planes de desarrollo de mediano plazo. [Lima] [1987- v. <1-2 > : LC Card 87-404041 DDC 338.985 19
HC227 .S496 1987

Peru - Government. see **Peru - Politics and government.**

PERU - HISTORY - TO 1820.
Ríos Burga, Jaime R. Ciclos productivos en el espacio peruano colonial, siglos XVI-XIX . Lima, Perú , 1986. 70 p. : LC Card 87-401070 DDC 338.5/42/0983 19
HC227 .R456 1986

PERU - HISTORY - CONGRESSES.
Region and class in modern Peruvian history /. [Liverpool] , 1987. 207 p. : ISBN 0-902806-20-3 LC Card 87-148309 DDC 330.985/0633 19
HC227 .R386 1987

PERU - INDUSTRIES.
Basurco Valverde, Gerardo Félix. Herrschaftsformen und Industrialisierungsprozess in Peru . Freiburg [Breisgau] , c1985. xi, 420 p. : ISBN 3-8107-2210-3 LC Card 86-179243
HC227 .B339 1985

Pequeña industria, reactivación y desarrollo industrial /. [Miraflores, Lima] [1986] 127 p. : LC Card 87-127800 DDC 338.6/42/0985 19
HD2346.P4 P47 1986

Struktur- und Entwicklungsprobleme der Industrie Perus /. Heidelberg , c1985. 338 p. : ISBN 3-88326-165-3 LC Card 86-108518 DDC 338.0985 19
HC227 .S77 1985

Peru. Instituto Nacional de Estadística. see **Instituto Nacional de Estadística (Peru)**

Peru, Kolonisation und Abhängigkeit : Untersuchungen zur neuen Strategie ausländischer Interessen im peruanischen Agrarsektor / Wolfgang Heuer und Wolfgang Oberreit (Herausgeber). Saarbrücken ; Fort Lauderdale : Breitenbach, 1981. 192 p. : ill. ; 21 cm. (Sozialwissenschaftliche Studien zu internationalen Problemen, 0584-603X . Heft 58) Includes bibliographical references. ISBN 3-88156-165-X : LC Card 82-104103
1. Agriculture - Economic aspects - Peru - Oriente. 2. Oriente (Peru) - Economic conditions. 3. Peru - Dependency on foreign countries. 4. Land settlement - Peru - Oriente. 5. Education - Peru - Oriente. 6. Public health - Peru - Oriente. I. Heuer, Wolfgang. II. Oberreit, Wolfgang. III. Series.
HD1905.O75 P47 1981

PERU - POLITICS AND GOVERNMENT - 1968-
Basurco Valverde, Gerardo Félix. Herrschaftsformen und Industrialisierungsprozess in Peru . Freiburg [Breisgau] , c1985. xi, 420 p. : ISBN 3-8107-2210-3 LC Card 86-179243
HC227 .B339 1985

PERU - POLITICS AND GOVERNMENT - CONGRESSES.
Region and class in modern Peruvian history /. [Liverpool] , 1987. 207 p. : ISBN 0-902806-20-3 LC Card 87-148309 DDC 330.985/0633 19
HC227 .R386 1987

PERU - POPULATION - CONGRESSES.
Problemas poblacionales peruanos II /. Lima , c1986. 402 p. : LC Card 86-228816
HB3575 .P763 1986

PERU - POPULATION - STATISTICS.
Perú . Lima, Perú , 1984. 54 p. ; LC Card 86-111841 DDC 304.6/2/0985021 19
HA1055 .P46 1984 ***NYPL [JLG 86-190]***

Perú, proyecciones de población por años calendarios, según departamentos, provincias y distritos . Lima , 1985. 84 p. ; LC Card 86-173351
HA1064 .P49 1985

Perú, proyecciones de población por años calendarios, según departamentos, provincias y distritos : período, 1980-1990 / [elaborado por Dirección General de Demografía]. Lima : Instituto Nacional de Estadística, Dirección General de Demografía, Dirección de Proyecciones e Indicadores de Población, 1985. 84 p. ; 30 cm. (Boletín especial . no. 9) Chiefly tables. Limited edition of 500 copies. LC Card 86-173351
1. Population forecasting - Peru - Statistics. 2. Peru - Population - Statistics. I. Instituto Nacional de Estadística (Peru). Dirección General de Demografía. II. Series: Boletín especial (Instituto Nacional de Estadística (Peru). Dirección General de Demografía) , no. 9.
HA1064 .P49 1985

Perú siglo XXI. [Lima] : Presidencia de la República, Instituto Nacional de Planificación, [1986 or 1987] 63 p. : ill. ; 21 cm. LC Card 87-403080 DDC 338.985 19

1. Peru - Economic policy. 2. Peru - Social policy. 3. Political planning - Peru. I. Instituto Nacional de Planificación (Peru).
HC227 .P416 1986

PERU - SOCIAL POLICY.
Perú siglo XXI. [Lima] [1986 or 1987] 63 p. : LC Card 87-403080 DDC 338.985 19
HC227 .P416 1986

PERU - STATISTICS.
Datos distritales para fines de desarrollo. [Lima] [1964] 92 p. : LC Card 85-134068 DDC 318.5 19
HA1064 .D37 1964

Peru. Universidad Nacional Agraria. see **Universidad Nacional Agraria.**

Peruzzo, Dilvo, 1941- Habitação : controle e espoliação / Dilvo Peruzzo. São Paulo-SP : Cortez Editora, [1984] 133 p. ; 21 cm. Bibliography: p. 127-133. LC Card 84-242125 DDC 363.5/0981 19
1. Apartment houses - Brazil. 2. Housing - Brazil. 3. Housing policy - Brazil. 4. Apartment houses - Brazil - Vitória (Espírito Santo). I. Title.
HD7287.6.B7 P47 1984
NYPL [JLD 86-2535]

Pervichnoe opisanie signalov rechi : materialy k seminaru pri Institute matematiki i kibernetiki AN Litovskoĭ SSR "Statisticheskie problemy upravleniia" / pod redaktsieĭ I. Gikis. Vil'nius : In-t matematiki i kibernetiki AN Litovskoĭ SSR, 1980. 67 p. : ill. ; 20 cm. (Statisticheskie problemy upravleniia . vyp. 42) Titles on added t.p.: Pirminis kalbos signalų aprašymas; Primary description of speech signals. At head of title: Institut fizikotekhnicheskikh problem ėnergetiki AN Lit. SSR .... Summaries in English and Lithuanian; table of contents also in English and Lithuanian. Includes bibliographies. LC Card 82-107723
1. Speech processing systems - Congresses. 2. Automatic speech recognition - Congresses. I. Gikis, I. II. Lietuvos TSR Mokslų akademija. Matematikos ir kibernetikos institutas. III. Title: Pirminis kalbos signalų aprašymas. IV. Title: Primary description of speech signals. V. Series.
HD38 .S715 vyp. 42 TK7882.S65

Pervozvanskaia, T. N. (Tat'iana Nikolaevna)
Ėlementy teorii upravleniia zapasami : uchebnoe posobie / T.N. Pervozvanskaia, A.A. Pervozvanskiĭ. Leningrad : Leningradskiĭ universitet, 1983. 108 p. : ill. ; 19 cm. At head of title: Ministerstvo vysshego i srednego spetsial'nogo obrazovaniia RSFSR. Leningradskiĭ ordena Lenina i ordena Trudovogo Krasnogo Znameni gosudarstvennyĭ universitet imeni A.A. Zhdanova. Bibliography: p. 106-108. LC Card 84-217972
1. Inventory control - Mathematical models. I. Pervozvanskiĭ, A. A. (Anatoliĭ Arkad'evich). II. Title.
HD40 .P47 1983

Pervozvanskiĭ, A. A. (Anatoliĭ Arkad'evich)
Pervozvanskaia, T. N. (Tat'iana Nikolaevna) Ėlementy teorii upravleniia zapasami . Leningrad , 1983. 108 p. : LC Card 84-217972
HD40 .P47 1983

Pervushin, S. P. (Serafim Pavlovich) SĖV -- osnovnye napravleniia sotrudnichestva . Moskva , 1984. 203 p. ; LC Card 85-177814
HC243.5 .S48 1984

Pesante, Maria Luisa. Economia e politica / Maria Luisa Pesante. Milano, Italy : F. Angeli, c1986. 94 p. ; 22 cm. (Il Pensiero politico contemporaneo . 11) Bibliography: p. [91]-94. LC Card 86-196256
1. Economics - History. 2. Economic policy - History. I. Title. II. Series.
HB75 .P465 1986

Pesaran, M. Hashem, 1946- The limits to rational expectations / M. Hashem Pesaran. Oxford, UK ; New York, NY, USA : B. Blackwell, 1988, c1987. x, 325 p. : ill. ; 24 cm. Bibliography: p. [305]-316. Includes indexes. ISBN 0-631-14036-0 : LC Card 87-20877 DDC 339 19
1. Rational expectations (Economic theory). I. Title.
HB172.5 .P445 1988

PESARO REGION (ITALY) - INDUSTRIES.
Favaretto, Ilario, 1945- L'impresa artigiana tra economia e territorio . Milano, Italy , c1986. 212 p. : LC Card 86-193238
HD2346.I82 P464 1986

Los pescadores de Tecolutla . Alcalá, Graciela. México, D.F. , 1985. 215 p. : ISBN 968-496-070-0 LC Card 86-191825
HD8039.F652 M62 1985

Peschke, Hans-Peter von, 1951- Elektroindustrie und Staatsverwaltung am Beispiel Siemens, 1847-1914 / Hans-Peter von Peschke. Frankfurt am Main ; Bern : P. Lang, c1981. 393 p. : ill. ; 22 cm. (Europäische Hochschulschriften. Reihe III, Geschichte und ihre Hilfswissenschaften . Bd. 154 = v. 154 = v. 154) Originally presented as the author's thesis (doctoral)--Universität Erlangen-Nürnberg, Erlangen, 1980. Bibliography: p. 361-393. ISBN 3-8204-5902-2 LC Card 81-141438
1. Siemens & Halske - History. 2. Electric industries - Germany - History. 3. Electric machinery industry - Germany - History. 4. Germany - Public works - History. 5. Public contracts - Germany - History. I. Series: Europäische Hochschulschriften. Reihe III, Geschichte und ihre Hilfswissenschaften , Bd. 154. II. Title.
HD9697.A3 G35 1981

Pesotta, Rose, 1896- Bread upon the waters / Rose Pesotta ; with a new introduction by Ann Schofield ; edited by John Nicholas Beffel. Ithaca, N.Y. : ILR Press, c1987. xxiv, 435 p., [10] p. of plates : ill. ; 21 cm. Reprint. Originally published: New York : Dodd, Mead, 1944. Bibliography: p. 417-418. Includes index. ISBN 0-87546-127-1 (pbk. : alk. paper) LC Card 87-2953 DDC 331.88/0973 19
1. Labor and laboring classes - United States - 1914-. 2. Trade-unions - United States - History - 20th century. I. Beffel, John Nicholas. II. Title.
HD8072 .P375 1987

Pesquisa de orçamentos familiares no município de São Paulo /. Endo, Seiti Kaneko. São Paulo [Rio de Janeiro] , 1984. 131 p. : LC Card 85-136517
HB235.B8 E53 1984

Pesquisa--situação de saúde e lazer do comerciário de Fortaleza. Situação de saúde e lazer do comerciário de Fortaleza /. Fortaleza-CE , 1977/1978 [i.e. 1978] 66 leaves ; LC Card 83-116799
HD5755.F6 S58 1978

Pesquisas sobre o problema fundiário urbano. [São Paulo] : Governo do Estado de São Paulo, Secretaria do Interior, Fundação Prefeito Faria Lima, Superintendência de Desenvolvimento Urbano e Rural ; [Brasília?] : Financiadora de Estudos e Projetos, 1983. 6 v. in 8 ; 33 cm. CONTENTS. - v. 1. Instrumentos para aplicação de uma política fundiária urbana. t. 1. I parte-Conclusões e proposicões. t. 2. II parte-Análise dos instrumentos. t. 3. III parte-Análise da documentação existente -- v. 2. A aquisição e cessão da terra urbana pelo estado -- v. 3. Anexo 1, Experiência estrangeira -- v. 4. Anexo 2, Fichas-resumo -- v. 5. Anexo 3, Bibliografia -- v. 6. Anexo 4, Seminários. LC Card 87-404400 DDC 333.77/13/0981 19
1. Land use, Urban - Brazil - Collected works. 2. Land use, Urban - Government policy - Brazil - Collected works. I. Fundação Prefeito Faria Lima. Superintendência de Desenvolvimento Urbano e Rural. II. Financiadora de Estudos e Projetos (Brazil).
HD496 .P47 1983

Pessin, Allan H.
More words of Wall Street : 2,000 investment terms defined / Allan H. Pessin, Joseph A. Ross. Homewood, Ill. : Dow Jones-Irwin, 1986. v, 269 p. ; 23 cm. Sequel to: Words of Wall Street. ISBN 0-87094-701-X LC Card 86-70777
1. Investments - Dictionaries. 2. Finance - Dictionaries. 3. Securities - Dictionaries. I. Ross, Joseph A. II. Pessin, Allan H. Words of Wall Street. III. Title.
NYPL [JLE 86-4060]

Words of Wall Street. Pessin, Allan H. More words of Wall Street : 2,000 investment terms defined / Allan H. Pessin, Joseph A. Ross. Homewood, Ill. , 1986. v, 269 p. ; ISBN 0-87094-701-X LC Card 86-70777
NYPL [JLE 86-4060]

Pessoa, Dirceu Murilo. Espace rural et pauvreté au nord-est du Brésil / par Dirceu Murilo Pessoa. Paris : Ecole des hautes études en sciences sociales, 1981. xvii, 288 leaves : ill. ; 30 cm. Thesis (doctoral)--Ecole des hautes études en sciences sociales, 1981. Bibliography: leaves 281-288. LC Card 86-208627
1. Brazil, Northeast - Economic conditions - 1964-. 2. Rural poor - Brazil, Northeast. 3. Brazil, Northeast - Rural conditions. 4. Brazil, Northeast - Social conditions - 1964-. I. Title.
HC188.N6 P47 1981

PEST CONTROL INDUSTRY - UNITED STATES.
Pinto, Lawrence J. The structural pest control industry . Vienna, Va. (8150 Leesburg Pike, Suite 1100, Vienna 22180) , 1981. 26, [10] p. : LC Card 86-214768 DDC 338.4/762896/0973 19
HD9718.5.P473 U663 1981

Pest Megye (Hungary)
Mezőgazdasági szövetkezetek Pest megyében, 1985 . Budapest , 1985. 442 p. : ISBN 963-02-4206-0 LC Card 87-137365
HD1492.H82 P475 1985

PEST MEGYE (HUNGARY) - POPULATION - STATISTICS.
Szukicsné Serfőző, Klára. Budapest és Pest megye népességfejlődése, az ezredfordulóig várható tendenciák /. Budapest , 1984. 88 p. : LC Card 86-157549
HA1208.B96 S98 1984

Pestana, M. Inácio. Movimento demográfico da matriz de Vila Viçosa nos séculos XVI e XVII / Manuel Inácio Pestana. [Vila Viçosa, Portugal : Câmara Municipal de Vila Viçosa, 1985] 32 p. : ill. ; 21 cm. (II Série dos Cadernos culturais da Câmara Municipal de Vila Viçosa . no. 5) Caption title. Includes bibliographical references. LC Card 86-199468
1. Vila Viçosa (Portugal) - Population - History - 16th century. 2. Vila Viçosa (Portugal) - Population - History - 17th century. 3. Vila Viçosa (Portugal) - History. I. Series: Cadernos culturais da Câmara Municipal de Vila Viçosa , 2a. sér., no. 5. II. Title.
HB3622.V55 P47 1985

PESTICIDE RESIDUES IN FOOD - INTERNATIONAL COOPERATION.
Boardman, Robert. Pesticides in world agriculture . Houndsmills, Basingstoke, Hampshire , c1986. x, 221 p. ; ISBN 0-333-37417-7 *NYPL [JLD 86-2934]*

PESTICIDES - ENVIRONMENTAL ASPECTS.
Boardman, Robert. Pesticides in world agriculture . Houndsmills, Basingstoke, Hampshire , c1986. x, 221 p. ; ISBN 0-333-37417-7 *NYPL [JLD 86-2934]*

PESTICIDES - ENVIRONMENTAL ASPECTS - DEVELOPING COUNTRIES.
Repetto, Robert C. Paying the price . Washington, DC , c1985. 33 p. ; ISBN 0-915825-12-0 (pbk.) : LC Card 86-225070 DDC 338.4/366865/091724 19
HC59.72.E5 R46 1985

PESTICIDES - ENVIRONMENTAL ASPECTS - GOVERNMENT POLICY - UNITED STATES - CONGRESSES.
Agriculture and the environment /. Washington, D.C. , c1986. xvii, 298 p. : ISBN 0-915707-33-0 (pbk.) : LC Card 87-43010 DDC 363.7/31 19
HD1755 .P47 1986

Pesticides in world agriculture . Boardman, Robert. Houndsmills, Basingstoke, Hampshire , c1986. x, 221 p. ; ISBN 0-333-37417-7
NYPL [JLD 86-2934]

PESTICIDES INDUSTRY - ACCOUNTING.
Dubrulle, Louis. Comptabilité analytique de gestion . [Paris] , c1985-c1987. 2 v. : ISBN 2-04-015766-2 (v. 2) : LC Card 86-149033 DDC 668/.65/0681 19
HF5642 .D74 1985

PESTICIDES INDUSTRY - GERMANY (WEST)
Weber, Norbert. Markttransparenz bei Pflanzenschutz- und Düngemitteln . Münster-Hiltrup , 1983. xi, 247 p. : ISBN 3-7843-0277-7 : LC Card 83-234135
HD9660.P33 G328 1983

PESTICIDES INDUSTRY - INDIA - BHOPAL - ACCIDENTS.
Chishti, Anees, 1941- Dateline Bhopal . New Delhi , 1986. 160 p. ; LC Card 86-901993 DDC 363.1/79
HD7269.C452 I5225 1986
NYPL [JLD 87-1050]

Everest, Larry. Behind the poison cloud . Chicago , 1986. 192 p. : ISBN 0-916650-26-X : LC Card 85-26863 DDC 363.1/79 19
HD7269.C452 I524 1986
NYPL [JSD 86-425]

Kurzman, Dan. A killing wind . New York , c1987. xvi, 297 p., [16] p. of plates : ISBN 0-07-035687-4 LC Card 87-3398 DDC

363.1/79 19
HD7269.C452 I525 1987

Shrivastava, Paul. Bhopal . Cambridge, Mass. , c1987. xvi, 184 p. : ISBN 0-88730-084-7 LC Card 86-26575 DDC 363.1/79 19
HD7269.C452 I5268 1987

Shrivastava, Paul. Managing industrial crises . New Delhi, India , 1987. 196 p. : ISBN 81-7094-000-1 : LC Card 87-902160 DDC 363.1/79 19
HD7269.C452 I5269 1987

PESTICIDES POLICY - DEVELOPING COUNTRIES.
Repetto, Robert C. Paying the price . Washington, DC , c1985. 33 p. ; ISBN 0-915825-12-0 (pbk.) : LC Card 86-225070 DDC 338.4/366865/091724 19
HC59.72.E5 R46 1985

Pestieau, Pierre, 1943- Parris, Henry. Public enterprise in Western Europe /. London , Wolfeboro, N.H. , c1987. viii, 197 p. : ISBN 0-7099-0548-3 : LC Card 86-24133 DDC 338.7/4/094 19
HD4138 .P37 1987 *NYPL [JLD 87-757]*

PET FOOD INDUSTRY - ILLINOIS - ROCKFORD - HISTORY.
Rockford . [Rockford, Ill.] , c1987. 98 p. : LC Card 87-61147 DDC 338.7/66466/0977331 19
HD9340.U53 R637 1987

PET FOOD INDUSTRY - UNITED STATES.
The Pet industry . Stamford, Conn., U. S.A. , c1985. xi, 140 leaves : ISBN 0-89336-439-8 (pbk.) LC Card 87-403914 DDC 381/.4568 19
HD9340.U52 P48 1985

The Pet industry : new developments in food & health products / Philip Rothein [i.e. Rotheim], project analyst. Stamford, Conn., U. S.A. : Business Communications Co., c1985. xi, 140 leaves : ill. ; 29 cm. (Business opportunity report . GA-034N) "September 1985"--T.p. verso. ISBN 0-89336-439-8 (pbk.) LC Card 87-403914 DDC 381/.4568 19
1. Pet food industry - United States. 2. Pet supplies industry - United States. I. Rotheim, Philip. II. Business Communications Co. III. Series.
HD9340.U52 P48 1985

PET SUPPLIES INDUSTRY - UNITED STATES.
The Pet industry . Stamford, Conn., U. S.A. , c1985. xi, 140 leaves : ISBN 0-89336-439-8 (pbk.) LC Card 87-403914 DDC 381/.4568 19
HD9340.U52 P48 1985

A petal from the rose /. Marker, Kekobad Ardeshir, 1896-1984. [Karachi] 1985 (Karachi : Rosette) 2 v. : LC Card 85-932155
HC440.5.M35 A3 1985

Peter Barnard Associates. An evaluation of the Ontario Home Renewal Program : a report / prepared for Community Renewal Branch, Ministry of Housing, by Peter Barnard Associates. [Toronto] : The Ministry, 1976. x, 43, [28] p. : ill. ; 28 cm. Includes bibliographical references. LC Card 85-192287
1. Housing authorities - Ontario. 2. Housing rehabilitation - Government policy - Ontario. I. Ontario. Community Renewal Branch. II. Title.
HD7305.O6 P47 1976

Peter, Gerd, 1941- Der Arbeitsschutzbeauftragte : Interessenvertretung und Arbeitspolitik im Steinkohlenbergbau / Gerd Peter, Wolfgang Thon, Hans Vollmer. Frankfurt ; New York : Campus, c1986. 344 p. : ill. ; 21 cm. (Forschungsberichte aus dem Landesinstitut Sozialforschungsstelle Dortmund) Bibliography: p. 329-344. ISBN 3-593-33633-2 LC Card 86-160932
1. Shop stewards - Germany, West. 2. Coal-miners - Germany, West. I. Thon, Wolfgang, 1956-. II. Vollmer, Hans, 1942-. III. Title.
HD6490.S52 G365 1986

Peter, J. Paul.
Certo, Samuel C. Strategic management . New York , c1988. p. cm. ISBN 0-394-35920-8 : LC Card 87-23565 DDC 658.4/012 19
HD30.28 .C43 1988.

Consumer behavior : marketing strategy perspectives / J. Paul Peter, Jerry C. Olson. Homewood, Ill. : Irwin, 1987. xvii, 698 p., [16] p. of plates : ill. (some col.) ; 25 cm. (The Irwin series in marketing) Includes bibliographies and indexes. ISBN 0-256-03177-0 LC Card 86-81801 DDC 658.8/342 19
1. Consumers. 2. Marketing. I. Olson, Jerry C. (Jerry Corrie), 1944-. II. Title. III. Series.
HF5415.3 .P468 1987

A preface to marketing management / J. Paul Peter, James H. Donnelly, Jr. 4th ed. Plano, Tex. : Business Publications, 1988. xii, 320 p. : ill. ; 24 cm. Bibliography: p. 297-307. Includes indexes. ISBN 0-256-06078-9 (pbk.) LC Card 87-71348 DDC 658.8 19
1. Marketing management. I. Donnelly, James H. II. Title.
HF5415.13 .P388 1988

Peter, Johann, Dr. Die Rolle der Rüstung in der Wirtschaft des heutigen Kapitalismus /. Berlin [1984] 127 p. ; LC Card 85-135711
HC281 .B39 1984 Heft 4 HC79.D4

Pētera Stučkas Latvijas Valsts universitāte.
Pravovye voprosy RASU . Riga , 1979. 109, [3] p. ; LC Card 82-100548
HC337.L3 P722 1979

Pētera Stučkas Latvijas Valsts universitāte. Ekonomiskās kibernētikas katedra.
Modelirovanie razvitii͡a mezhotraslevyh kompleksov Latviĭskoĭ SSR . Riga , 1985. 106 p. : LC Card 86-177817
HD9015.S653 L376 1985

Pētera Stučkas Latvijas Valsts universitāte. Kafedra ėkonomiki torgovli. Ėkonomika i upravlenie torgovleĭ v razvitom sotsialisticheskom obshchestve . Riga , 1980. 123 p. : LC Card 82-102627
HF3629.L37 E38 1980

Pētera Stučkas Latvijas valsts universitāte. Kafedra organizatsii mekhanizirovannoĭ obrabotki ėkonomicheskoĭ informatsii.
Sozdanie avtomatizirovannoĭ sistemy upravlenii͡a ėkonomikoĭ administrativnogo raĭona . Riga , 1980. 151 p. ; LC Card 81-215521
HF5679 .S717 1980

Pētera Stučkas Latvijas Valsts universitāte. Kafedra upravlenii͡a narodnym khozi͡aĭstvom.
Khozi͡aĭstvennyĭ mekhanizm proizvodstva i obrashchenii͡a tovarov narodnogo potreblenii͡a /. Riga , 1985. 115 p. ; LC Card 86-177827
HF1040.9.L38 K47 1985

Pētera Stučkas Latvijas Valsts universitāte. Republikas augstskolu politiskās ekonomijas bāzes katedra. Ėkonomicheskie svi͡azi proizvodstva i potreblenii͡a pri sotsializme . Riga , 1978. 152 p. ; LC Card 81-168062
HF1040.9.S65 E36 1978

Pētera Stučkas Latvijas Valsts universitāte. Seno un viduslaiku vēstures katedra. Feodālisms Baltijas regionā . Rīga , 1985. 147 p. : LC Card 86-177836
HC243 .F46 1985

Pētera Stučkas Latvijas Valsts universitāte. Statistikas un demografijas katedra.
Problemy urovni͡a zhizni i demografii . Riga , 1979. 175 p. ; LC Card 82-106660
HD7035.Z8 L376 1979

Peters, A. R. Haigh, R. H. Soviet foreign policy, the League of Nations and Europe, 1917-39 /. Aldershot, Hants , 1986. x, 138 p. ;
NYPL [JFD 86-5778]

Peters, A. R. (Anthony R.) The Guardian book of the General Strike /. Aldershot, Hants, England , Brookfield, Vt. , 1987. p. cm. ISBN 0-7045-3081-3 : LC Card 87-25287 DDC 331.89/25/0941 19
HD5365.A6 G8 1987

Peters, Kathrin. Binnenwirtschaftlich orientierte Hypothesen zur Aussenwirtschaftsentwicklung und ihre Gültigkeit für die Bundesrepublik Deutschland 1969-1982 / Kathrin Peters. Hamburg : Kovač, c1986. vii, 311 p. : 3 ill. ; 21 cm. Originally presented as the author's thesis (doctoral--Universität Hamburg, 1985) Bibliography: p. 302-310. ISBN 3-925630-02-3 : LC Card 86-226488
1. Foreign trade and employment - Germany (West). 2. Export marketing - Germany (West). 3. Foreign trade promotion - Germany (West). I. Title.
HD5710.75.G3 P48 1986

Peters, Nikolaus A. Arbeits- und Organisationsgestaltung in einer post-industriellen Gesellschaft / Nikolaus A. Peters. Bern : P. Haupt, c1981. xi, 351 p. : ill. ; 23 cm. (Veröffentlichungen der Hochschule St. Gallen für Wirtschafts- und Sozialwissenschaften. Schriftenreihe Betriebswirtschaft . Bd. 7) Bibliography: p. 321-350. ISBN 3-258-03066-9 LC Card 87-672718
1. Industrial organization (Economic theory). 2. Industrial sociology. I. Title. II. Series.
HD2326 .P47x 1981

Peters, R. Kyle, 1954- Fiji, a transition to manufacturing. Washington, D.C., U. S.A. , c1987. xvi, 107 p., [1] folded leaf of plates : ISBN 0-8213-0962-5 LC Card 87-23067 DDC 338.4/767/099611 19
HD9738.F55 F55 1987

Peters, Roger. Practical intelligence : working smarter in business and everyday life / Roger Peters.1st ed. New York, N.Y. : Harper & Row, c1987. x, 341 p. ; 25 cm. Bibliography: p. 306-336. Includes index. ISBN 0-06-015681-3 : LC Card 86-46096 DDC 650.1 19
1. Executive ability. 2. Personality and intelligence. 3. Practical judgment. 4. Success in business. I. Title.
HD38.2 .P47 1987

Peters, Thomas J.
The Skunk Camp promises / Tom Peters. New York : Knopf, 1987. p. cm. ISBN 0-394-75314-3 (pbk.) : LC Card 86-46226 DDC 658.4/09 19
1. Leadership. 2. Executive ability. 3. Management. I. Title.
HD57.7 .P47 1987

Thriving on chaos : handbook for a management revolution / Tom Peters.1st ed. New York : Knopf : Distributed by Random House, 1987. xii, 561 p. : ill. ; 24 cm. Bibliography: p. 527-537. Includes index. ISBN 0-394-56784-6 LC Card 87-45575 DDC 658 19
1. Industrial management - United States. I. Title.
HD70.U5 P426 1987

Peters, Ursula, 1950- Hallensleben, Ruth. Frauenarbeit in der Industrie . Berlin-Kreuzberg , c1985. 157 p. : ISBN 3-88940-602-5 : LC Card 86-201457
HD6149 .H27 1985

Petersen, Hans-Georg. Staat, Steuern und Finanzausgleich . Berlin , c1984. 452 p., [1] leaf of plates : ISBN 3-428-05513-6 LC Card 84-166906
HJ1120 .S73 1984

Petersen, Harry C. Mason, John M. (John Michael), 1950- Operational and geometric evaluation of exclusive truck lanes /. College Station, Tex. , Springfield, Va. [1986] vii, 156 p. : LC Card 86-622239 DDC 380.5 s 388.3/14 19
HE203 .T43 no. 331-3F HE356.T4

Petersen, Ib Damgaard. The political economy of long waves : a discussion of definitions, methods, and underlying structures / Ib Damgaard Petersen. København, Denmark : Institute of Political Studies, [1986] 10, [1] p. : ill. ; 21 cm. (Arbejdspapier, 0901-022X . 1986/1) "The ECPR joint sessions in Gothenburg, April 1-6, 1986. Paper presented to the workshop on Cycles in politics." Bibliography: p. [11] ISBN 87-7393-042-3 (pbk.) LC Card 86-214084 DDC 338.9 19
1. Long waves (Economics). I. European Consortium for Political Research. II. Series: Arbejdspapir (Københavns universitet. Institut for samfundsfag og forvaltning) , 1986/1. III. Title.
HB3729 .P47 1986

Petersen, Jógvan, 1947- Thorsen, Thorkil. Alkoholforbrug og trafikulykker . København , 1986. 69 p. : ISBN 87-88225-38-3 LC Card 86-209934
HE5620.D7 T49 1986

Petersen, John E. Innovative capital financing / John E. Petersen and Ronald Forbes. Chicago, IL (1313 E. 60th St., Chicago 60637) : American Planning Association, 1985. ii, 38 p. : ill. ; 28 cm. (Planning Advisory Service report . no. 392) Cover title. Bibliography: p. 35. LC Card 86-175368 DDC 336.73 19
1. Bonds - United States. 2. Debts, Public - United States. 3. United States - Public works - Finance. I. Forbes, Ronald W. II. Series: Report / American Planning Association, Planning Advisory Service , no. 392. III. Title.
HG4936 .P424 1985

Petersen, Keith. Company town : Potlatch, Idaho, and the Potlatch Lumber Company / Keith C. Petersen. Pullman, Wash. : Washington State University Press ; Moscow, Idaho : Latah County Historical Society, 1987. xix, 284 p., [32] p. of plates : ill. ; 24 cm. Bibliography: p.

[270]-276. Includes index. ISBN 0-87422-036-X (alk. paper) : LC Card 87-14980 DDC 307.7/67/0979686 19
1. Potlatch Corporation - History. 2. Lumber trade - Idaho - History. 3. Company towns - Idaho - History. 4. Potlatch (Idaho) - Economic conditions. I. Latah County Historical Society. II. Title.
HD9759.P63 P47 1987

Petersen, Paul. Wohngemeinschaft oder Grossfamilie; Versuch einer neuen Lebenform. Hrsg. von Paul Petersen. [Mit Beiträgen von Halina Holldorf et al. Wuppertal] Jugenddienst-Verlag [c1972] 224 p. illus. 21 cm. LC Card 72-375103
1. Housing - Germany, West. 2. Housing, Cooperative - Germany (West). 3. Community life. I. Title.
NYPL [JLD 77-3003]

Petersen, Sybil. Transportation : danger on the road / [contributors, Sybil Petersen, Brian Lippsett, Will Collette]. Arlington, Va. (P.O. Box 926, Arlington 22216) : Citizen's Clearinghouse for Hazardous Wastes, [1986] [8], 40 p. : ill. ; 28 cm. Cover title. Bibliography: 3rd prelim. p. LC Card 87-401670 DDC 363.1/7 19
1. Hazardous substances - United States - Transportation. I. Lippsett, Brian. II. Collette, Will. III. Citizen's Clearinghouse for Hazardous Wastes (Arlington, Va.). IV. Title.
HE199.5.D3 P48 1986

Peterson, Christine. Why were infant and child mortality rates highest in the poorest states of Peninsular Malaysia, 1941-75? /. Santa Monica, CA (P.O. Box 2138, Santa Monica 90406-2138) [1986] xi, 45 p. ; LC Card 86-210106 DDC 304.6/4/088054 19
HB1323.I42 M49 1986

Peterson, Joyce Shaw, 1939- American automobile workers, 1900-1933 / Joyce Shaw Peterson. Albany : State University of New York Press, c1987. xiv, 231 p. ; 24 cm. (SUNY series in American labor history) Bibliography: p. 201-223. Includes index. ISBN 0-88706-573-2 LC Card 87-1942 DDC 331.7/6292/0973 19
1. Automobile workers - United States - History. I. Title. II. Series.
HD8039.A82 U66 1987

Peterson, Robert A. The Role of affect in consumer behavior . Lexington, Mass. , c1986. ix, 196 p. : ISBN 0-669-12874-0 (alk. paper) LC Card 85-46042 DDC 658.8/342 19
HF5415.3 .R65 1986 ***NYPL [JLE 86-3376]***

Peterson, Robin. Gross, Charles W. Marketing . St. Paul , c1987. xxviii, 700 p. : ISBN 0-314-85242-5 : LC Card 86-26676 DDC 658.8/02 19
HF5415.135 .G76 1987

Peterson, Wallace C. Income, employment, and economic growth / Wallace C. Peterson. 6th ed. New York : Norton, [c1988] xxiii, 750 p. : ill. ; 24 cm. Includes bibliographical references and index. ISBN 0-393-95628-8 LC Card 87-17933 DDC 339 19
1. Macroeconomics. I. Title.
HB172.5 .P453 1988

Peterson, William A. The Cambridge multisectoral dynamic model of the British economy /. Cambridge [Cambridgeshire] , New York , 1988. p. cm. ISBN 0-521-33004-1 LC Card 86-33375 DDC 330.941/00724 19
HC256.6 .C29 1988

Pethick, Donald R. Population and employment forecasts and distribution for the central Puget Sound region, 1975-1990 / by Donald R. Pethick. Seattle, Wash. : Puget Sound Governmental Conference, [1969] 26 p., [2] leaves of plates : ill., maps ; 28 cm. (Special report series / Puget Sound Governmental Conference . no. 1) "May 1969." "Snohomish County population and employment by zone and industry" ([5] p. : map ; 28 cm.) inserted. Includes bibliographical references. LC Card 87-400702 DDC 304.6/2/097977021 19
1. Puget Sound Region (Wash.) - Population - Statistics. 2. Population forecasting - Washington (State) - Puget Sound Region - Statistics. 3. Labor supply - Washington (State) - Puget Sound Region - Statistics. 4. Employment forecasting - Washington (State) - Puget Sound Region - Statistics. I. Series: Special report series / Puget Sound Governmental Conference , no. 1. II. Title.
HA697.P84 P47 1969

Petino, Antonio, 1911- Le Radici intellettuali del progresso economico moderno /. Milano, Italy , c1986. 327 p. ; LC Card 86-197444
HB75 .R13 1986

PETIT-CANAL (GUADELOUPE) - POPULATION - HISTORY.
Boutin, Raymond. Petit-Canal, une commune de la Guadeloupe au XIXe siècle /. Paris , c1983. 221 p. : ISBN 2-85802-251-8 LC Card 84-164720
HB3557.7.P47 B68 1983

Petit-Canal, une commune de la Guadeloupe au XIXe siècle /. Boutin, Raymond. Paris , c1983. 221 p. : ISBN 2-85802-251-8 LC Card 84-164720
HB3557.7.P47 B68 1983

Petit train va loin. Lemieux-Pépin, Madeleine. P'tit train va loin . Ottawa , 1985. vii, 191 p. ; LC Card 86-177382
HE2808.1 .L45 1985

Petite paysannerie en France /. Jégouzo, Guenhaël. Paris , c1984. 227 p. : ISBN 2-85340-610-5 LC Card 85-181759 DDC 338.1/6 19
HD1339.F8 J44 1984

Les Petites Antilles . Chemin Dupontès, P. [Fort-de-France] [Paris] [1979] x, 318 p., [10] p. of plates : ISBN 2-85275-105-4 LC Card 84-164674
HC151 .C49 1979

Petits métiers. Atget, Géniaux, Vert . Paris [1984] 63, [1] p. : ISBN 2-901414-09-5 : LC Card 86-137985
HF5459.F8 A87 1984 ***NYPL [MFW 87-159]***

Petits métiers et types parisiens vers 1900. Atget, Géniaux, Vert . Paris [1984] 63, [1] p. : ISBN 2-901414-09-5 : LC Card 86-137985
HF5459.F8 A87 1984 ***NYPL [MFW 87-159]***

Petits pavés, grands bonheurs : l'univers fabuleux des petites annonces / [choisies par] Fernand Marzelle. [Paris] : Editions Vitamine, c1984. 140 p. : chiefly ill. ; 31 cm. ISBN 2-229-01400-1 : LC Card 85-104866
1. Small-space advertising - France - History. 2. Small-space advertising - France - History - Pictorial works. I. Marzelle, Fernand.
HF6105.F7 P48 1984

Petkov, Krŭst´o.
Sotsiologii͡a na truda / Krŭst´o Petkov. Sofii͡a : Profizdat, 1985- v. <1 > : ill. ; 21 cm. Includes bibliographical references. LC Card 86-232374
1. Industrial sociology. I. Title.
HD6955 .P485 1985

Sot͡siologii͡a na trudovii͡a kolektiv : vŭprosi na teorii͡ata i praktikata / Krŭst´o Petkov, Blagoĭ Kolev. Sofii͡a : Profizdat, 1982. 184 p. ; 21 cm. Errata slip inserted. Includes bibliographical references. LC Card 83-124278
1. Industrial sociology - Bulgaria. 2. Work groups - Bulgaria. I. Kolev, Blagoĭ. II. Title.
HD6957.B85 P47 1982
NYPL [*QK 86-4733]

Petkov, Todor (Todor Iliev) Stopanska samostoi͡atelnost i stopanska otgovornost / Todor Petkov. Sofii͡a : Nauka i izkustvo, 1985. 237 p. ; 22 cm. Includes bibliographical references. LC Card 85-134177
1. Labor and laboring classes - Bulgaria. 2. Labor laws and legislation - Bulgaria. 3. Bulgaria - Economic policy - 1944-. I. Title.
HD8626.5 .P48 1985

Pető, Iván. A hazai gazdaság négy évtizedének története, 1945-1985 / Pető Iván, Szakács Sándor. Budapest : Közgazdasági és Jogi Könyvkiadó, 1985- v. <1 > ; 25 cm. Bibliography: v. 1, p. [719]-735. Includes index. CONTENTS. - 1. Az újjáépítés és a tervutasításos irányítás időszaka, 1945-1968. ISBN 963-221-553-2 (set) LC Card 87-105744
1. Hungary - Economic conditions - 1945-. 2. Hungary - Economic policy - 1945-. I. Szakács, Sándor. II. Title. III. Title: Hazai gazdaság 4 évtizedének története, 1945-1985.
HC300.28 .P47 1985

Petrakov, Nikolaĭ I͡Akovlevich.
Ėkonomicheskoe izmerenie i ot͡senka ėffektivnosti nauchno-tekhnicheskogo progressa /. Moskva , 1982. 172 p. ; LC Card 84-209110
HC79.T4 E55 1982

Khozi͡aĭstvennyĭ mekhanizm funkt͡sionirovanii͡a sotsialisticheskoĭ ėkonomiki /. Moskva , 1982. 358 p. ; LC Card 83-134242
HC243.5 .K47 1982

Khozi͡aĭstvennyĭ mekhanizm v sisteme optimal´nogo funktsionirovanii͡a sotsialisticheskoĭ ėkonomiki /. Moskva , 1985. 346 p. ; LC Card 86-114802
HC336.25 .K474 1985

Modelirovanie ėkonomicheskogo povedenii͡a sot͡sialisticheskogo predprii͡atii͡a /. Moskva , 1984. 131 p. : LC Card 86-144437
HD30.25 .M623 1984

Modin, Anatoliĭ Andreevich. Dinamika proizvodstvennykh ob״edineniĭ i modeli planirovanii͡a ikh dei͡atel´nosti /. Moskva , 1984. 231 p. : LC Card 84-195690
HD9705.S595 M62 1984

Petras, Elizabeth McLean. Jamaican labor migration : white capital and Black labor, 1850-1930 / Elizabeth McLean Petras. Boulder : Westview Press, 1988. x, 297 p. : ill. ; 23 cm. (Westview special studies on Latin America and the Caribbean) Bibliography: p. 267-283. Includes index. ISBN 0-8133-7456-1 (pbk. : alk. paper) LC Card 87-20139 DDC 331.6/2/7292072875 19
1. Alien labor, Jamaican - Panama - Canal Zone - History. 2. Alien labor, Jamaican - Cuba - History. 3. Alien labor, Jamaican - History. 4. Jamaica - Emigration and immigration - History. 5. Labor and laboring classes - Jamaica - History. I. Title.
HD8178 .P47 1988

Petras, James F., 1937- Latin America : bankers, generals, and the struggle for social justice / James F. Petras [with] Howard Brill ... [et al.]. Totowa, N.J. : Rowman & Littlefield, 1986. xi, 187 p. ; 24 cm. Includes bibliographical references and index. ISBN 0-8476-7505-X : LC Card 86-1885 DDC 337.8 19
1. Debts, External - Latin America - Addresses, essays, lectures. 2. Military government - Latin America - Addresses, essays, lectures. 3. Social justice - Addresses, essays, lectures. 4. Latin America - Economic conditions - 1945- - Addresses, essays, lectures. 5. Latin America - Relations - United States - Addresses, essays, lectures. 6. United States - Relations - Latin America - Addresses, essays, lectures. I. Brill, Howard. II. Title.
HC125 .P4643 1986 ***NYPL [JLE 86-4366]***

Petras, Kathryn. Petras, Ross. Inside track . New York , c1986. xv, 508 p. ; ISBN 0-394-74339-3 : LC Card 85-40868 DDC 650.1/4/0973 19
HF5382.U5 P44 1986
NYPL [*R-Econ. 86-3454]

Petras, Ross. Inside track : how to get into and succeed in America's prestige companies / Ross and Kathryn Petras. New York : Vintage Books, c1986. xv, 508 p. ; 21 cm. ISBN 0-394-74339-3 : LC Card 85-40868 DDC 650.1/4/0973 19
1. Vocational guidance - United States. 2. Business enterprises - United States - Case studies. 3. Young adults - Employment - United States. 4. Success in business - United States. I. Petras, Kathryn. II. Title.
HF5382.U5 P44 1986
NYPL [*R-Econ. 86-3454]

Petrecolla, Alberto. Diéguez, Héctor L. Mercados de trabajo y distribución de ingresos en cuatro centros urbanos de Argentina, 1974-1981 /. Buenos Aires, Argentina , 1984. 49 p. ; ISBN 950-621-013-6 LC Card 87-401771 DDC 331.12/982 19
HD5749 .D54 1984

Petrich, K. Germany (West). Bundesministerium für Ernährung, Landwirtschaft und Forsten. Wissenschaftlicher Beirat. Gutachten des Wissenschaftlichen Beirats beim Bundesministerium für Ernährung, Landwirtschaft und Forsten /. Hiltrup bei Münster (Westf.) [1960?] 98 p. ; LC Card 86-185959
HD1957 .G47 1960

Petrillo, Giovanna, 1952- Produttività e improduttività del lavoro domestico : contributo all'analisi della soggettività della donna / Giovanna Petrillo, Marina Bucciero.1a ed. Bologna : Pàtron, 1985. 139 p. ; 22 cm. (Collana di psicologia del lavoro. Sezione Ricerche e studi . 3) Bibliography: p. [131]-134. LC Card 86-132212
1. Housewives - Italy. 2. Sexual division of labor - Italy. 3. Women domestics - Italy. 4. Women - Italy - Social conditions. I. Bucciero, Marina. II. Title. III. Series.
HD8039.H842 I87 1985

Petro chemical industry : energy aspects of structural change. Paris, France : Organisation for Economic Co-operation and Development ; [Washington, D.C. : OECD Publication and

Information Center, distributor], 1985. 161 p. : ill. ; 23 cm. This study was prepared for the OECD by Jean Guinet. Includes bibliographies. ISBN 92-64-12683-X (pbk.) : LC Card 85-177511 DDC 338.4/7661804 19
1. Petroleum chemicals industry. 2. Petroleum industry and trade. 3. Petroleum chemicals - Prices. I. Guinet, Jean. II. Organisation for Economic Co-operation and Development.
HD9579.C32 P48 1985

PETROBRAS. see **Petróleo Brasileiro, S. A.**

Petrochemia a rozwój Płocka /. Chojnacki, Jakub. Płock , 1977. [4], 290, [1] p., [76] p. of plates : LC Card 81-200767
HC340.3.Z7 P573 1977

PETROCHEMICAL INDUSTRY. see **PETROLEUM CHEMICALS INDUSTRY.**

The Petrochemical industry in developing countries : prospects and strategies. [Vienna] : Sectoral Studies Branch, Division for Industrial Studies, United Nations Industrial Development Organization, [1985] xiv, 155 p. : ill. ; 30 cm. (Sectoral studies series . no. 20, v. 1) Cover title. Includes bibliographical references. LC Card 86-204881 DDC 338.4/7661804/091724 19
1. Petroleum chemicals industry - Developing countries. I. United Nations Industrial Development Organization. Sectoral Studies Branch. II. Series.
HD9579.C33 D446 1985

Petrochemical technology . List, H. L. (Harvey L.), 1924- Englewood Cliffs, N.J. , c1986. xxxi, 271 p. : ISBN 0-13-661992-4 : LC Card 85-19225 DDC 661/.804 19
HD9579.C32 L44 1986 *NYPL [JSE 86-1624]*

Petrochemicals . Spitz, Peter H. New York , c1988. xxvii, 588 p. : ISBN 0-471-85985-0 : LC Card 87-23019 DDC 338.4/7661804 19
HD9579.C32 S65 1988

PETROCHEMICALS. see **PETROLEUM PRODUCTS.**

Petrolchemisches Kombinat Schwedt, VEB. Betriebsparteiorganisation der SED. Ein Werk des Sozialismus, der Freundschaft und der Jugend . Berlin , c1985. 296 p. : LC Card 87-112875
HD9579.C34 P4848 1985

PETROLCHEMISCHES KOMBINAT SCHWEDT, VEB. - HISTORY.
Ein Werk des Sozialismus, der Freundschaft und der Jugend . Berlin , c1985. 296 p. : LC Card 87-112875
HD9579.C34 P4848 1985

El Petróleo : la más grande riqueza nacional. 2a ed. México, D.F. : Cámara de Senadores, Sección de Estadística y Anales de Jurisprudencia, 1923. vi, 352 p. ; 24 cm. Includes bibliographical references. LC Card 85-220440
1. Petroleum industry and trade - Mexico. 2. Petroleum law and legislation - Mexico. I. Mexico. Congreso. Cámara e Senadores. Sección de Estadística y Anales de Jurisprudencia.
HD9574.M6 P4475 1923

PETRÓLEO BRASILEIRO, S. A.
Gall, Norman. Brazil and Peru . Geneva , 1987. x, 123 p., [1] leaf of plates : ISBN 92-2-105506-X (pbk.) : LC Card 87-166425 DDC 338.2/7282/0981 19
HD9574.B82 G34 1987

PETRÓLEO BRASILEIRO, S.A. - HISTORY.
Moura, Gerson. A campanha do petróleo /. São Paulo-SP , 1986. 92 p. : LC Card 86-190721
HD9574.B84 P445 1986

Petróleo internacional. Glossary of the petroleum industry . Tulsa, Okla. , c1982. vi, 378 p. ; ISBN 0-87814-194-4 (pbk.) : LC Card 82-7622 DDC 665.5/03/61 19
TN865 .G63 1982 *NYPL [JSD 86-496]*

Petróleo y opinión pública /. Calderón Berti, Humberto. [Caracas?] [1983?] 455 p. : LC Card 85-119987 DDC 338.2/72/0987 19
HD9574.V42 C364 1983 *NYPL [JLE 86-535]*

PETRÓLEOS DE VENEZUELA, S.A.
Randall, Laura. The political economy of Venezuelan oil /. New York , 1987. xiii, 247 p. ; ISBN 0-275-92823-3 (alk. paper) : LC Card 87-15848 DDC 338.2/7282/0987 19
HD9574.V42 R35 1987

Petróleos de Venezuela, S.A. Coordinación de Información y Relaciones. 1976-1985, diez años de la industria petrolera nacional. [Caracas] [1986- v. <1-2 > : ISBN 980-259-069-X (set) LC Card 87-403692 DDC 338.2/7282/0987 19
HD9574.V42 A56 1986

PETRÓLEOS MEXICANOS.
Leduc, Renato. Los diablos del petróleo /. [Mexico City, Mexico] [1986] 131 p. ; LC Card 86-219535 DDC 338.2/7282/0972 19
HD9574.M62 P3745 1986

Los petroleros /. Buendía, Manuel, d. 1984. México, D.F. , c1985. 312 p. ; ISBN 968-493-065-8 LC Card 86-218751
HD9574.M6 B77 1985

PETROLEUM AS FUEL - PRICES - ARGENTINA.
Yornet, Mario E. Combustibles . Buenos Aires [1980] 105, viii leaves : LC Card 84-134419
HD9574.A72 Y67 1980

PETROLEUM CHEMICALS.
List, H. L. (Harvey L.), 1924- Petrochemical technology . Englewood Cliffs, N.J. , c1986. xxxi, 271 p. : ISBN 0-13-661992-4 : LC Card 85-19225 DDC 661/.804 19
HD9579.C32 L44 1986 *NYPL [JSE 86-1624]*

PETROLEUM CHEMICALS - HISTORY.
Spitz, Peter H. Petrochemicals . New York , c1988. xxvii, 588 p. : ISBN 0-471-85985-0 : LC Card 87-23019 DDC 338.4/7661804 19
HD9579.C32 S65 1988

PETROLEUM CHEMICALS INDUSTRY - BRAZIL.
Industria petrolchimica /. [São Paulo] , 1973. 1 v. (various pagings), [22] leaves of plates : LC Card 86-146014
HD9579.C33 B7417 1973

PETROLEUM CHEMICALS INDUSTRY - BRAZIL - RIO GRANDE DO SUL.
Proposta de consolidação do Pólo Petroquímico do Sul . [Porto Alegre] [19]86. 17, [5], 9 p. : LC Card 87-404792 DDC 338.7/661804/098165 19
HD9579.C33 B785 1986

PETROLEUM CHEMICALS INDUSTRY - CHINA - CONGRESSES.
China Energy Workshop I: Petroleum Processing (1985 : Honolulu, Hawaii) China's petroleum industry in the international context . Boulder [Colo.] , 1986. xvii, 166 p. : ISBN 0-86638-072-8 (pbk.) LC Card 86-50695 DDC 338.2/7282/0951 19
HD9576.C52 C524 1985 *NYPL [JLD 86-3885]*

PETROLEUM CHEMICALS INDUSTRY - CONGRESSES.
World petrochemicals . [Staten Island, N.Y. (139 Chestnut Ave., Staten Island 10305)] , c1985. 279 p. : LC Card 85-71088 DDC 338.4/7661804 19
HD9579.C32 W68 1985 *NYPL [JLD 86-2185]*

PETROLEUM CHEMICALS INDUSTRY - DEVELOPING COUNTRIES.
The Petrochemical industry in developing countries . [Vienna] [1985] xiv, 155 p. : LC Card 86-204881 DDC 338.4/7661804/091724 19
HD9579.C33 D446 1985

PETROLEUM CHEMICALS INDUSTRY - DICTIONARIES - RUSSIAN.
Kuznetsov, I͡U. I. (I͡Uriĭ Igorevich) Russko-angliĭskiĭ razgovornik dli͡a neftekhimikov i khimikov-neorganikov /. Moskva , 1985. 359 p. ; LC Card 86-138945 DDC 660/.03/9171 19
HD9579.C32 K88 1985 *NYPL [*QAD 86-3599]*

PETROLEUM CHEMICALS INDUSTRY - GERMANY (EAST) - SCHWEDT - HISTORY.
Ein Werk des Sozialismus, der Freundschaft und der Jugend . Berlin , c1985. 296 p. : LC Card 87-112875
HD9579.C34 P4848 1985

PETROLEUM CHEMICALS INDUSTRY - HISTORY.
Spitz, Peter H. Petrochemicals . New York , c1988. xxvii, 588 p. : ISBN 0-471-85985-0 : LC Card 87-23019 DDC 338.4/7661804 19
HD9579.C32 S65 1988

PETROLEUM CHEMICALS INDUSTRY - SOVIET UNION.
Avrekh, G. L. (Gennadiĭ Lipanovich) Ėkonomika na urovne molekul /. Moskva , 1986. 141 p. : LC Card 86-179247
HD9656.S55 A95 1986

PETROLEUM CHEMICALS INDUSTRY - SOVIET UNION - FORECASTING.
Optimizatsii͡a planirovanii͡a polimerno-neftekhimicheskogo kompleksa /. Moskva , 1984. 141 p. : LC Card 86-143987
HD9579.C33 S655 1984

PETROLEUM CHEMICALS INDUSTRY - TECHNOLOGICAL INNOVATIONS.
List, H. L. (Harvey L.), 1924- Petrochemical technology . Englewood Cliffs, N.J. , c1986. xxxi, 271 p. : ISBN 0-13-661992-4 : LC Card 85-19225 DDC 661/.804 19
HD9579.C32 L44 1986 *NYPL [JSE 86-1624]*

PETROLEUM CHEMICALS - PRICES.
Petro chemical industry . Paris, France [Washington, D.C.] 1985. 161 p. : ISBN 92-64-12683-X (pbk.) : LC Card 85-177511 DDC 338.4/7661804 19
HD9579.C32 P48 1985

PETROLEUM CONSERVATION - SWEDEN.
Internationella förutsättningar för den svenska oljeförsörjningen under 1980-talet. Stockholm , 1981. 172 p. in various pagings : ISBN 91-38-06244-5 LC Card 82-241303
HD9575.S82 I57 1981

Oljeersättningsprogrammet i ett samhällsekonomiskt perspektiv. Stockholm , 1983. 39, 67, 54, 71 p. : ISBN 91-38-07618-7 LC Card 83-232276
HD9502.S82 O55 1983

Sweden. Oljeersättningsdelegationen. Redovisning och analys av kommunernas oljereduktionsplaner /. Stockholm [1983] 59, [91] p. : ISBN 91-38-07458-3 LC Card 83-239703
HD9502.S82 S96 1983a

Sweden. Oljeersättningsdelegationen. Statligt stöd till oljeersättning . [Stockholm] [1983] 1 v. (various pagings) : ISBN 91-38-07657-8 LC Card 84-218524
HD9502.S82 S96 1983

PETROLEUM - DEVELOPING COUNTRIES - RESERVES - STATISTICS.
Fee, Derek. Oil & gas databook for developing countries . London , 1985. 215 p. : ISBN 0-86010-617-9 : LC Card 85-208594 DDC 333.8/23/091724 19
HD9578.D44 F44 1985 *NYPL [JLE 86-3684]*

PETROLEUM - DICTIONARIES.
(1981) Arnould, Michel. Les termes pétroliers . Paris , c1981. xii, 267 p. ; ISBN 2-04-011414-9 LC Card 82-167169 DDC 665.5/03/21 19
TN865 .A66 1981 *NYPL [JSE 84-171]*

PETROLEUM ENGINEERING - DICTIONARIES.
Glossary of the petroleum industry . Tulsa, Okla. , c1982. vi, 378 p. ; ISBN 0-87814-194-4 (pbk.) : LC Card 82-7622 DDC 665.5/03/61 19
TN865 .G63 1982 *NYPL [JSD 86-496]*

PETROLEUM ENGINEERING - DICTIONARIES - SPANISH.
Glossary of the petroleum industry . Tulsa, Okla. , c1982. vi, 378 p. ; ISBN 0-87814-194-4 (pbk.) : LC Card 82-7622 DDC 665.5/03/61 19
TN865 .G63 1982 *NYPL [JSD 86-496]*

PETROLEUM ENGINEERS - MEXICO - POLITICAL ACTIVITY.
Cleaves, Peter S. Professions and the state . Tucson , c1987. xv, 147 p. : ISBN 0-8165-1016-4 (alk. paper) LC Card 87-5911 DDC 331.7/12/0972 19
HD8038.M6 C55 1987

PETROLEUM GEOLOGISTS' WIVES - UNITED STATES - BIOGRAPHY.
Rocks in her head /. Lake Dallas, Tex. (221 Wild Oak, Lake Dallas 75065) , c1987. vii, 97 p. : LC Card 87-151452
HD8039.P42 U676 1987

PETROLEUM - GEOLOGY - UNITED STATES.
Meurer, Heinrich W., 1950- Wirtschaftsgeologische Aspekte bei der privaten Investition in Öl- und Gasbohrvorhaben in den USA /. [Cologne? , 1982] (Aachen : Fotodruck J. Mainz) vi, 163 p., [3] folded leaves of plates : LC Card 84-200100
HD9565 .M48 1982

Petroleum in the Arab Republic of Egypt. Cairo : Arab Republic of Egypt, Ministry of Information, State Information Service, 1983. 19 p. ; 21 cm. LC Card 84-960509 DDC 338.2/7282/0962 19
1. Petroleum industry and trade - Egypt. I. Egypt. Hay'ah al-'Ammah lil-Isti'lāmāt.
HD9577.E32 P48 1983

PETROLEUM INDUSTRY AND TRADE - ACCOUNTING.
Audits of entities with oil and gas producing activities . New York, NY (1211 Ave. of the Americas, New York 10036-8775) , c1986. x, 133 p. ; LC Card 86-209769 DDC 657/.862 19
HF5686.P3 A93 1986

PETROLEUM INDUSTRY AND TRADE - ADDRESSES, ESSAYS, LECTURES.
Calderón Berti, Humberto. Petróleo y opinión pública /. [Caracas?] [1983?] 455 p. : LC Card 85-119987 DDC 338.2/72/0987 19
HD9574.V42 C364 1983 *NYPL [JLE 86-535]*

PETROLEUM INDUSTRY AND TRADE - ALASKA.
Historical and projected oil and gas consumption . [Juneau] [1986] 1 v. (in various pagings) : LC Card 86-622301 DDC 333.8/2313/09798 19
HD9502.U53 A4574 1986

PETROLEUM INDUSTRY AND TRADE - ALASKA - FINANCE.
Livey, Jay. The effect of state income tax policy on the development of marginal oil fields . [Juneau] [1986] vii leaves, 52 p., [17] leaves : LC Card 86-622190 DDC 333.8/232/09798 19
HD9560.8.U53 A445 1986

PETROLEUM INDUSTRY AND TRADE - ALGERIA.
Kukushkin, Vladimir I͡Ur′evich. Neft′ i razvitie, Livii͡a, Alzhir /. Moskva , 1985. 227 p. ; LC Card 85-180876
HD9577.L52 K85 1985 *NYPL [*QIP 87-3410]*

PETROLEUM INDUSTRY AND TRADE - ARAB COUNTRIES.
"Problema neftedollarov" . Moskva , 1984. 231 p. ; LC Card 85-189000
HC498 .P75 1984

Rudnicki, Bohdan. Liga dwudziestu i arabska nafta /. Warszawa , 1979. 469, [3] p. : LC Card 81-109444
HD9578.A55 R83 1979

PETROLEUM INDUSTRY AND TRADE - ARABIAN PENINSULA.
Susani͡an, K. G. (Karen Gevorkovich) Araviĭskie gosudarstva i vneshneėkonomicheskai͡a strategii͡a SShA /. Moskva , 1986. 229, [3] p. : LC Card 86-231698 DDC 337.73053 19
HF1456.5.A625 S87 1986

PETROLEUM INDUSTRY AND TRADE - ARGENTINA.
Energía y petróleo . Capital Federal [1985 or 1986] 60 p. : LC Card 87-403778 DDC 338.2/7282 19
HD9560.5 .E525 1985

PETROLEUM INDUSTRY AND TRADE - ASIA.
Energy conservation in the Asian region . Tokyo, Japan [Honolulu, Hawaii] , 1986. vi, 173 p. : ISBN 92-833-2038-1 LC Card 87-122915 DDC 333.79/16/095 19
HD9502.A782 E53 1986

PETROLEUM INDUSTRY AND TRADE - BOLIVIA.
Granado Cosio, Hugo del. Transnacionales y nación . [La Paz, Bolivia] , 1986. 24 p. ; LC Card 87-115866 DDC 338.8/87 19
HD9574.B82 G73 1986

PETROLEUM INDUSTRY AND TRADE - BRAZIL.
Gall, Norman. Brazil and Peru . Geneva , 1987. x, 123 p., [1] leaf of plates : ISBN 92-2-105506-X (pbk.) : LC Card 87-166425 DDC 338.2/7282/0981 19
HD9574.B82 G34 1987

PETROLEUM INDUSTRY AND TRADE - BRAZIL - HISTORY.
Moura, Gerson. A campanha do petróleo /. São Paulo-SP , 1986. 92 p. : LC Card 86-190721
HD9574.B84 P445 1986

PETROLEUM INDUSTRY AND TRADE - CALIFORNIA - STATISTICS.
California crude oil production, 1960-1985. Los Angeles, Calif. (417 S. Hill St., Suite 930, Los Angeles 90013) , c1986. 149 p., [1] folded leaf of plates : LC Card 87-150171 DDC 338.2/7282/09794021 19
HD9567.C2 C385 1986

PETROLEUM INDUSTRY AND TRADE - CANADA.
Douglas, Gordon W. Energy and regional investment in Canada /. Calgary, Alta. [1983] x, 114 p. : ISBN 0-920522-28-9 (pbk.) : LC Card 83-160268 DDC 332.6/722 19
HD9502.C32 D68 1983 *NYPL [JLD 87-996]*

Oil and natural gas industries in Canada, 1978. [Ottawa] , c1978. viii, 104 p. : LC Card 85-187299
HD9574.C22 O39 1978

PETROLEUM INDUSTRY AND TRADE - CANADA - ACCOUNTING.
Butterworth, John E. Financial reporting . Hamilton, Ont. , 1986. viii, 250 p. : ISBN 0-920212-52-2 (pbk.) LC Card 87-101758 DDC 657/.86203 19
HF5686.P3 B87 1986

PETROLEUM INDUSTRY AND TRADE - CANADA - CAPITAL INVESTMENTS.
Pasay, Janice L. The effect of the western accord and recent provincial royalty changes on petroleum industry capital expenditures /. Calgary, Alta. , 1986. iv, 27, 4 leaves ; LC Card 86-203742 DDC 338.2/3 19
HD9574.C22 P37 1986

PETROLEUM INDUSTRY AND TRADE - CANADA, EASTERN.
Esso Petroleum Canada (Firm) Mémoire présenté à la Commission élue permanente de l'énergie et des ressources de l'Assemblée nationale du Québec /. Québec [1983] 44 leaves : LC Card 85-143347 DDC 338.2/7282/09714 19
HD9574.C23 Q43 1983

PETROLEUM INDUSTRY AND TRADE - CARIBBEAN AREA.
The Caribbean Basin and the changing world economic structure /. Groningen , c1986. 194 p. ; ISBN 90-01-18630-0 (pbk.) : LC Card 87-117415 DDC 330.9729/052 19
HC151 .C26 1986

PETROLEUM INDUSTRY AND TRADE - CHINA - CONGRESSES.
China Energy Workshop I: Petroleum Processing (1985 : Honolulu, Hawaii) China's petroleum industry in the international context . Boulder [Colo.] , 1986. xvii, 166 p. : ISBN 0-86638-072-8 (pbk.) LC Card 86-50695 DDC 338.2/7282/0951 19
HD9576.C52 C524 1985 *NYPL [JLD 86-3885]*

PETROLEUM INDUSTRY AND TRADE - CONGO (BRAZZAVILLE) - ECONOMIC ASPECTS.
Congo . Paris [1983] 19 p. : LC Card 85-118609
HD9577.C62 C65 1983

PETROLEUM INDUSTRY AND TRADE - CONGRESSES.
Global energy interactions /. Ahmedabad , 1987. xxxi, 1290 p. : LC Card 87-902497 DDC 333.79 19
HD9502.A2 G545 1987b

Mercados mundiales de hidrocarburos . México, D.F. , 1983. 377 p. : ISBN 968-12-0231-7 LC Card 84-222729
HD9560.5 .M39 1983

Symposium on the Energy Economy (1984 : Durham, Durham) Prospects for the world oil industry . London , Dover, N.H. , c1985. 131 p. : ISBN 0-7099-4104-8 : LC Card 85-4186 DDC 338.2/7282 19
HD9560.5 .S96 1985 *NYPL [JLD 85-2430]*

PETROLEUM INDUSTRY AND TRADE - COSTS.
Hall, John, 1946- Reducing industrial oil costs /. Aldershot, Hants England , Brookfield, Vt., U. S.A. , c1987. xvii, 118 p. : ISBN 0-291-39740-9 (U. S.) : LC Card 86-29511 DDC 338.2/3 19
HD9560.4 .H35 1987

PETROLEUM INDUSTRY AND TRADE - DEVELOPING COUNTRIES.
McLin, Jon B. Social and economic effects of petroleum development in non-OPEC developing countries . Geneva , 1986. xiii, 104 p., [4] folded leaves of plates : ISBN 92-2-105505-1 (pbk.) : LC Card 87-123328 DDC 338.2/782/091724 19
HD9578.D44 M396 1986

PETROLEUM INDUSTRY AND TRADE - DEVELOPING COUNTRIES - STATISTICS.
Fee, Derek. Oil & gas databook for developing countries . London , 1985. 215 p. : ISBN 0-86010-617-9 : LC Card 85-208594 DDC 333.8/23/091724 19
HD9578.D44 F44 1985 *NYPL [JLE 86-3684]*

PETROLEUM INDUSTRY AND TRADE - DICTIONARIES - RUSSIAN.
Kuznetsov, I͡U. I. (I͡Uriĭ Igorevich) Russko-angliĭskiĭ razgovornik dli͡a neftekhimikov i khimikov-neorganikov /. Moskva , 1985. 359 p. ; LC Card 86-138945 DDC 660/.03/9171 19
HD9579.C32 K88 1985 *NYPL [*QAD 86-3599]*

PETROLEUM INDUSTRY AND TRADE - ECONOMETRIC MODELS.
Farzin, Yeganeh Hossein, 1950- Competition and substitutes in the market for an exhaustible resource /. Greenwich, Conn. , c1985. xvi, 209 : ISBN 0-89232-604-2 : LC Card 85-23765 DDC 338.2/7282/0724 19
HD9560.5 .F385 1985 *NYPL [JLE 86-1585]*

Fertig, Klaus. Ölangebotsmodelle . Hamburg , 1986. 236 p. : ISBN 3-87895-302-X LC Card 86-225350
HD9502.A2 F46 1986

PETROLEUM INDUSTRY AND TRADE - ECONOMIC ASPECTS.
Vidal, Máximo Luis. El fin de la era del petróleo y su impacto sobre la economía mundial . San Pedro de Macorís, R.D. , 1981. 103 p. : LC Card 82-202556
HD9502.5.A433 D658 1981

PETROLEUM INDUSTRY AND TRADE - ECONOMIC ASPECTS - CONGRESSES.
Natural resources and the macroeconomy /. Oxford, UK , 1986. xvi, 352 p. : ISBN 0-631-15087-0 LC Card 86-673943
HC59 .N3194x 1986b

PETROLEUM INDUSTRY AND TRADE - EGYPT.
Petroleum in the Arab Republic of Egypt. Cairo , 1983. 19 p. ; LC Card 84-960509 DDC 338.2/7282/0962 19
HD9577.E32 P48 1983

PETROLEUM INDUSTRY AND TRADE - FINANCE.
Mattione, Richard P. OPEC's investments and the international financial system /. Washington, D.C. , c1985. xi, 201 p. ; ISBN 0-8157-5510-4 : LC Card 84-23242 DDC 332.6/7314 19
HG4538 .M38 1985 *NYPL [JLE 86-3698]*

Orban, John. Money in the ground . Oklahoma City , 1985. xv, 216 p. : ISBN 0-9615776-0-6 (pbk.) : LC Card 86-120440 DDC 332.63 19
HG6047.P47 O73 1985

PETROLEUM INDUSTRY AND TRADE - FINANCE - MATHEMATICAL MODELS.
Tuovila, Olavi. Optimal financing policy of the firm . Vaasa , 1983. 127 p. : ISBN 951-683-199-0 (pbk.) LC Card 84-204398
HG4012 .T86 1983

PETROLEUM INDUSTRY AND TRADE - FORECASTING.
Energy markets after the collapse . Cambridge, MA (56 John F. Kennedy St., Suite 5, Cambridge 02138) , c1987. 164 p. : LC Card

87-142725 DDC 338.2/728 19
HD9560.5 .E54 1987

The Next oil shock . Bala Cynwyd, PA (150 Monument Rd., Bala Cynwyd 19004) , 1986. 2 v. : LC Card 87-109243 DDC 333.82/32 19
HD9560.5 .N47 1986

Perspective on world energy . Arlington, Va. (1911 Fort Myer Dr., Suite 403, Arlington 22209) , c1987. 3, iii, 27, [19] p. : LC Card 87-142737 DDC 333.79 19
HD9560.5 .P3847 1987

PETROLEUM INDUSTRY AND TRADE - GALICIA (POLAND AND UKRAINE) - HISTORY.
Wieleżyński, Leszek. Wspólna praca--wspólny plon . London, England [1986], c1985. 295 p., [24] p. of plates : LC Card 87-111287
HD9575.P62 W549 1986

PETROLEUM INDUSTRY AND TRADE - GOVERNMENT OWNERSHIP - BOLIVIA - HISTORY.
Castrillo M., Hugo. Reseña histórica del petróleo en Bolivia /. La Paz, Bolivia , 1986. 82 p., [1] leaf of plates : LC Card 87-403504 DDC 338.2/7282/0984 19
HD9574.B64 Y294 1986

PETROLEUM INDUSTRY AND TRADE - GOVERNMENT OWNERSHIP - LATIN AMERICA - CASE STUDIES.
Latin American oil companies and the politics of energy /. Lincoln , c1985. xxxix, 282 p. : ISBN 0-8032-4728-1 (alk. paper) LC Card 84-29457 DDC 338.7/6223382/098 19
HD9574.L3 L38 1985 ***NYPL [JLD 86-1289]***

PETROLEUM INDUSTRY AND TRADE - GOVERNMENT OWNERSHIP - MEXICO.
Leduc, Renato. Los diablos del petróleo /. [Mexico City, Mexico] [1986] 131 p. ; LC Card 86-219535 DDC 338.2/7282/0972 19
HD9574.M62 P3745 1986

PETROLEUM INDUSTRY AND TRADE - GOVERNMENT OWNERSHIP - NORWAY.
Organiseringen av statens deltagelse i petroleumsvirksomheten /. Oslo [1983] 44 p. : ISBN 82-00-70798-9 LC Card 83-244370
HD9575.N62 O74 1983

PETROLEUM INDUSTRY AND TRADE - GOVERNMENT OWNERSHIP - VENEZUELA.
Randall, Laura. The political economy of Venezuelan oil /. New York , 1987. xiii, 247 p. ; ISBN 0-275-92823-3 (alk. paper) : LC Card 87-15848 DDC 338.2/7282/0987 19
HD9574.V42 R35 1987

PETROLEUM INDUSTRY AND TRADE - GOVERNMENT OWNERSHIP - VENEZUELA - HISTORY - 20TH CENTURY.
1976-1985, diez años de la industria petrolera nacional. [Caracas] [1986- v. <1-2 > : ISBN 980-259-069-X (set) LC Card 87-403692 DDC 338.2/7282/0987 19
HD9574.V42 A56 1986

PETROLEUM INDUSTRY AND TRADE - GOVERNMENT POLICY - ARGENTINA.
Aspectos económicos de la industria petrolera. Capital Federal [1985 or 1986] 28 p. : LC Card 87-120726
HD9574.A72 A84 1985

PETROLEUM INDUSTRY AND TRADE - GOVERNMENT POLICY - CANADA, WESTERN.
Pasay, Janice L. The effect of the western accord and recent provincial royalty changes on petroleum industry capital expenditures /. Calgary, Alta. , 1986. iv, 27, 4 leaves ; LC Card 86-203742 DDC 338.2/3 19
HD9574.C22 P37 1986

PETROLEUM INDUSTRY AND TRADE - GOVERNMENT POLICY - COLOMBIA.
Eastman, Jorge Mario. Hacia un populismo petrolero? y otros temas /. Bogotá, Colombia , 1986. viii, 145 p., [8] p. of plates : LC Card 86-227075
HD9574.C52 E18 1986

PETROLEUM INDUSTRY AND TRADE - GOVERNMENT POLICY - CUBA - HISTORY.
Dumpierre, Erasmo. La Esso en Cuba . La Habana , 1984. xiii, 148 p., [7] p. of plates : LC Card 86-177066
HD9574.C84 E774 1984

PETROLEUM INDUSTRY AND TRADE - GOVERNMENT POLICY - GREAT BRITAIN.
Hann, Danny. Government and North Sea oil /. Basingstoke, Hampshire , c1986. ix, 175 p. : ISBN 0-333-39436-4 ***NYPL [JLD 86-2581]***

PETROLEUM INDUSTRY AND TRADE - GOVERNMENT POLICY - INDONESIA.
Khong, Cho Oon. The politics of oil in Indonesia . Cambridge [Cambridgeshire] , New York , 1986. x, 253 p. : ISBN 0-521-30901-8 LC Card 85-22416 DDC 338.2/7282/09598 19
HD9567.I52 K48 1986
NYPL [JLD 86-3386]

PETROLEUM INDUSTRY AND TRADE - GOVERNMENT POLICY - ITALY.
Mattei, Enrico. Enrico Mattei, 1945-1953 . [Matelica] [1982] 199 p. : LC Card 84-190191
HD9575.I84 E585 1982

PETROLEUM INDUSTRY AND TRADE - GOVERNMENT POLICY - JAPAN.
Suzuki, Shigeru, 1949- Nihon no enerugī kaihatsu seisaku /. Kyōto-shi , 1985. vii, 274 p. : ISBN 4-623-01582-3 : LC Card 85-221878
HD9502.J32 S89 1985 <Orien Japan>
NYPL [*OSM 86-3954]

PETROLEUM INDUSTRY AND TRADE - GOVERNMENT POLICY - MEXICO.
Teichman, Judith A., 1947- Policymaking in Mexico . Boston , c1988. p. cm. ISBN 0-04-445033-8 : LC Card 87-18704 DDC 338.2/7282/0972 19
HD9574.M6 T45 1988

PETROLEUM INDUSTRY AND TRADE - GOVERNMENT POLICY - MEXICO - CHIAPAS.
Thompson G., Roberto. Problemática agraria y política petrolera en Chiapas /. Tuxtla Gutiérrez, Chiapas , 1983. 37 p., [1] leaf of plates : LC Card 84-243074
HD9574.M63 C457 1983

PETROLEUM INDUSTRY AND TRADE - GOVERNMENT POLICY - NIGERIA.
Establishment of oil refinery in Nigeria. Lagos , 1960. 6 p. ; LC Card 87-401860
HD9577.N52 E84 1960

PETROLEUM INDUSTRY AND TRADE - GOVERNMENT POLICY - NORWAY.
Norway. "Tempo-utvalget." Petroleumsvirksomhetens framtid . Oslo [1983] 167 p. : ISBN 82-00-70810-1 LC Card 83-235609
HD9575.N62 N6855 1983

Organiseringen av statens deltagelse i petroleumsvirksomheten /. Oslo [1983] 44 p. : ISBN 82-00-70798-9 LC Card 83-244370
HD9575.N62 O74 1983

PETROLEUM INDUSTRY AND TRADE - GOVERNMENT POLICY - PERU.
Malpica Silva Santisteban, Carlos. El anti imperialismo del APRA y los contratos petroleros /. [Lima, Peru] [1986 or 1987] 398 p. : LC Card 87-402097 DDC 338.2/7282/0985 19
HD9574.P52 M37 1986

PETROLEUM INDUSTRY AND TRADE - GOVERNMENT POLICY - SAUDI ARABIA.
McHale, Thomas R. Saudi oil policy and the changing world energy balance /. Boulder, Colo., U. S.A. , c1986. 17 p. ; ISBN 0-918714-09-5 (pbk.) : LC Card 87-119219 DDC 338.2/7282/09538 19
HD9502.A1 O28 no. 1 HD9576.S33

PETROLEUM INDUSTRY AND TRADE - GOVERNMENT POLICY - UNITED STATES.
Bull-Berg, Hans Jacob. American international oil policy . New York , 1987. xvi, 209 p. : ISBN 0-312-00465-6 : LC Card 86-31583 DDC 333.8/232/0973 19
HD9566 .B87 1987

Energy conservation . Washington, D.C. , c1986. xii, 270 p. : ISBN 0-8157-7716-7 : LC Card 85-26894 DDC 333.79/16/0973 19
HD9502.U62 E478 1986
NYPL [JLE 86-4084]

Paulson, S. Lawrence. Reagan on energy . New York, NY (850 3rd Ave., New York 10022) , 1981. 248 p. in various pagings ; LC Card 82-111477 DDC 333.79/0973 19
HD9502.U52 P38 ***NYPL [JLF 87-368]***

PETROLEUM INDUSTRY AND TRADE - GOVERNMENT POLICY - UNITED STATES - HISTORY - 20TH CENTURY.
Painter, David S. [Oil and the American century.] Private power and public policy . London , c1986. xii, 302 p. : ISBN 1-85043-021-7 LC Card 87-673320
HD9566 .P24x 1986b

PETROLEUM INDUSTRY AND TRADE - GOVERNMENT POLICY - VENEZUELA - ADDRESSES, ESSAYS, LECTURES.
Calderón Berti, Humberto. Petróleo y opinión pública /. [Caracas?] [1983?] 455 p. : LC Card 85-119987 DDC 338.2/72/0987 19
HD9574.V42 C364 1983
NYPL [JLE 86-535]

PETROLEUM INDUSTRY AND TRADE - GREAT BRITAIN.
Britain's energy resources /. London , 1981. 27 p. : ISBN 0-11-701010-3 (pbk.) LC Card 81-165936 DDC 333.79/0941 19
HD9502.G72 B74 1981

PETROLEUM INDUSTRY AND TRADE - GREAT BRITAIN - CONGRESSES.
Economics of the retail petroleum market . London , c1986. i, 79 p. : LC Card 87-134547 DDC 381/.4566553827/0941 19
HD9579.G5 G63 1986

PETROLEUM INDUSTRY AND TRADE - HISTORY.
Hamilton, Adrian, 1944- Oil . London , 1986. 191 p., [16] p. of plates : ISBN 0-7181-2783-8 : LC Card 87-106290 DDC 338.2/7282/09 19
HD9560.5 .H25 1986

PETROLEUM INDUSTRY AND TRADE - INDIA.
Patwardhan, M. S., 1927- Oil and other multinationals in India /. Bombay , 1986. xvi, 171 p. : LC Card 87-900107 DDC 338.8/87 19
HD9576.I42 P37 1986

PETROLEUM INDUSTRY AND TRADE - JAPAN - CONGRESSES.
Joint Symposium on the Energy Industries: Prospects of Co-operation Between Arab Gulf States and Japan (1984 : Tokyo, Japan) The Arab Gulf States and Japan . London , Dover, N.H. , c1986. xiv, 216 p. : ISBN 0-7099-3393-2 : LC Card 85-12819 DDC 338.2/728/0952 19
HD9576.P52 J65 1984
NYPL [JLD 86-1669]

PETROLEUM INDUSTRY AND TRADE - LATIN AMERICA.
Hernández, Rafael. Estados Unidos y América Latina . La Habana , 1982. 209 p. : LC Card 87-403785 DDC 333.8/232/0973 19
HD9574.L3 H47 1982

Latinskaia Amerika--problemy razvitiia neftianoĭ promyshlennosti /. Moskva , 1984. 192 p. : LC Card 86-181028
HD9574.L3 L4 1984

PETROLEUM INDUSTRY AND TRADE - LATIN AMERICA - CASE STUDIES.
Latin American oil companies and the politics of energy /. Lincoln , c1985. xxxix, 282 p. : ISBN 0-8032-4728-1 (alk. paper) LC Card 84-29457 DDC 338.7/6223382/098 19
HD9574.L3 L38 1985 ***NYPL [JLD 86-1289]***

PETROLEUM INDUSTRY AND TRADE - LIBYA.
Kukushkin, Vladimir IUr'evich. Neft' i razvitie, Liviia, Alzhir /. Moskva , 1985. 227 p. ; LC Card 85-180876
HD9577.L52 K85 1985
NYPL [*QIP 87-3410]

Shamleh, Omar. Erdölinduzierte sozioökonomische Entwicklung in den OAPEC-Staaten . Frankfurt am Main , New York , c1986. 410 p. ; ISBN 3-8204-9097-3 LC Card 86-157642
HC825 .S55 1986

PETROLEUM INDUSTRY AND TRADE - MEXICO.
Buendía, Manuel, d. 1984. Los petroleros /. México, D.F. , c1985. 312 p. ; ISBN 968-493-065-8 LC Card 86-218751
HD9574.M6 B77 1985

El Petróleo . México, D.F. , 1923. vi, 352 p. ; LC Card 85-220440
HD9574.M6 P4475 1923

PETROLEUM INDUSTRY AND TRADE - MEXICO - HISTORY - 20TH CENTURY.
Baldridge, Donald C. (Donald Carl) Mexican petroleum and United States-Mexican relations, 1919-1923 /. New York , 1987. 255 p. ; ISBN 0-8240-8070-X (alk. paper) LC Card 87-23817 DDC 338.2/7282/0972 19
HD9574.M6 B324 1987

PETROLEUM INDUSTRY AND TRADE - MIDDLE EAST - HISTORY - 20TH CENTURY.
Painter, David S. [Oil and the American century.] Private power and public policy . London , c1986. xii, 302 p. : ISBN 1-85043-021-7 LC Card 87-673320
HD9566 .P24x 1986b

PETROLEUM INDUSTRY AND TRADE - NETHERLANDS - SCHOONEBEEK - HISTORY.
Jong, H. J. de (Herman J.) Schoonebeek, olierijk in Zuidoost-Drenthe /. [Zuidwolde] , 1986. 232 p. : ISBN 90-6509-902-6 : LC Card 86-175279
HD9575.N43 N435 1986

PETROLEUM INDUSTRY AND TRADE - NIGERIA.
Nigeria and the international capitalist system /. Boulder, Colo. , 1988. v, 154 p. ; ISBN 1-555-87087-2 (alk. paper) : LC Card 87-23183 DDC 337.669 19
HF1616.7 .N54 1988

State, oil, and agriculture in Nigeria /. Berkeley , c1987. xiv, 327 p. : ISBN 0-87725-166-5 (pbk.) : LC Card 87-2941 DDC 338.1/8669 19
HD2145.5 .S73 1987

PETROLEUM INDUSTRY AND TRADE - NORWAY.
Aarrestad, Jostein. Oljen og norsk økonomi /. [Oslo] , c1984. 118 p. : ISBN 82-508-0285-3 LC Card 86-207964
HD9575.N62 A5 1984

Austvik, Ole Gunnar. Søkelys på mekanismene i oljemarkedet /. Oslo [1986?] 66 p. : LC Card 86-197742
HD9560.5 .A75 1986

Norway. "Tempo-utvalget." Petroleumsvirksomhetens framtid . Oslo [1983] 167 p. : ISBN 82-00-70810-1 LC Card 83-235609
HD9575.N62 N6855 1983

Schreiner, Alette. Virkninger av oljevirksomhet i Nord-Norge /. Oslo , 1984. 43 p. : ISBN 82-537-2118-8 : LC Card 85-146089
HD9575.N62 S37 1984

PETROLEUM INDUSTRY AND TRADE - NORWAY - FINANCE.
Selvig, Erling. Prosjektfinansiering i petroleumsvirksomheten /. Oslo [1983] 30, 5 p. ; LC Card 84-131887
HD9575.N62 S44 1983

PETROLEUM INDUSTRY AND TRADE - NORWAY - MATHEMATICAL MODELS.
Bergan, Roar. Behandlingen av oljevirksomheten i byråets makroøkonomiske årsmodeller /. Oslo , 1983. 30 p. ; ISBN 82-537-1918-3 : LC Card 83-225651
HD9575.N62 B46 1983

PETROLEUM INDUSTRY AND TRADE - OKLAHOMA - FINANCE.
McGuire, Paul F., 1907- Genesis of Oklahoma oil banking /. Muskogee, Okla. , c1986. 160 p. : ISBN 0-86546-068-X (pbk.) LC Card 87-118559 DDC 332.1/223/0924 B 19
HG2463.M36 A3 1986

PETROLEUM INDUSTRY AND TRADE - PANAMA.
Correa V., Virgilio (Correa Vásquez) Centelleo de la industria en Panamá /. [Panama?] 1986 ([Panama, Panama] : Tall. Gráf. del Centro de Impresión Educativa) 279 p., [6] p. of plates : LC Card 87-404562 DDC 338.097287 19
HC147 .C67 1986

PETROLEUM INDUSTRY AND TRADE - PENNSYLVANIA - CORRUPT PRACTICES - HISTORY - 19TH CENTURY.
Tennent, James C. The oil scouts . [Pennsylvania? , 1986] 85 p. : LC Card 87-404148 DDC 338.2/7282/09748 19
HD9567.P4 T46 1986

PETROLEUM INDUSTRY AND TRADE - PENNSYLVANIA - HISTORY.
Miller, Ernest C. (Ernest Conrad), 1912- Pennsylvania's oil industry /. Gettysburg, PA. , 1974, c1954. iii, 69 p. : LC Card 87-100839
HD9567.P4 M5 1974

Wood, Quentin E. Quaker State roots go deep into the world's first oilfield /. New York , 1986 [i.e. 1987] 24 p. : LC Card 86-63307 DDC 338.7/6653/0973 19
HD9569.Q82 W66 1987

PETROLEUM INDUSTRY AND TRADE - PENNSYLVANIA - HISTORY - 19TH CENTURY.
Tennent, James C. The oil scouts . [Pennsylvania? , 1986] 85 p. : LC Card 87-404148 DDC 338.2/7282/09748 19
HD9567.P4 T46 1986

PETROLEUM INDUSTRY AND TRADE - PERSIAN GULF REGION.
The Gulf in the early 20th century . [Durham] , c1986. 215 p., [1] leaf of plates : LC Card 87-100795 DDC 330.953/6 19
HC415.3 .G85 1986

PETROLEUM INDUSTRY AND TRADE - PERSIAN GULF REGION - CONGRESSES.
Joint Symposium on the Energy Industries: Prospects of Co-operation Between Arab Gulf States and Japan (1984 : Tokyo, Japan) The Arab Gulf States and Japan . London , Dover, N.H. , c1986. xiv, 216 p. : ISBN 0-7099-3393-2 : LC Card 85-12819 DDC 338.2/728/0952 19
HD9576.P52 J65 1984 *NYPL [JLD 86-1669]*

PETROLEUM INDUSTRY AND TRADE - PERU.
Gall, Norman. Brazil and Peru . Geneva , 1987. x, 123 p., [1] leaf of plates : ISBN 92-2-105506-X (pbk.) : LC Card 87-166425 DDC 338.2/7282/0981 19
HD9574.B82 G34 1987

Situación petrolera peruana . [Lima, Perú] [1985] iii, 102 leaves : LC Card 86-193466
HD9574.P52 S58 1985

PETROLEUM INDUSTRY AND TRADE - POLAND - EMPLOYEE - BIOGRAPHY.
Wieleżyński, Leszek. Wspólna praca--wspólny plon . London, England [1986], c1985. 295 p., [24] p. of plates : LC Card 87-111287
HD9575.P62 W549 1986

PETROLEUM INDUSTRY AND TRADE - POLAND - PLOCK - HISTORY.
Chojnacki, Jakub. Petrochemia a rozwój Płocka /. Płock , 1977. [4], 290, [1] p., [76] p. of plates : LC Card 81-200767
HC340.3.Z7 P573 1977

PETROLEUM INDUSTRY AND TRADE - POLITICAL ASPECTS - ARAB COUNTRIES.
Rudnicki, Bohdan. Liga dwudziestu i arabska nafta /. Warszawa , 1979. 469, [3] p. : LC Card 81-109444
HD9578.A55 R83 1979

PETROLEUM INDUSTRY AND TRADE - POLITICAL ASPECTS - BOLIVIA - HISTORY.
Seiferheld, Alfredo M., 1950- Economía y petróleo durante la Guerra del Chaco . Asunción , 1983. 535 p. : LC Card 84-121699 DDC 330.9892/071 19
HC222 .S36 1983 *NYPL [JLD 85-1032]*

PETROLEUM INDUSTRY AND TRADE - POLITICAL ASPECTS - HISTORY - 20TH CENTURY.
Venn, Fiona. Oil diplomacy in the twentieth century /. Basingstoke, Hampshire , c1986. xii, 228 p. : ISBN 0-333-35781-7
NYPL [JLD 86-3415]

PETROLEUM INDUSTRY AND TRADE - POLITICAL ASPECTS - NAMIBIA.
Shell out of Namibia and South Africa . London [1986] 19 . : LC Card 87-138719 DDC 338.8/87 19
HD9571.9.S45 S54 1986

PETROLEUM INDUSTRY AND TRADE - POLITICAL ASPECTS - PARAGUAY - HISTORY.
Seiferheld, Alfredo M., 1950- Economía y petróleo durante la Guerra del Chaco . Asunción , 1983. 535 p. : LC Card 84-121699 DDC 330.9892/071 19
HC222 .S36 1983 *NYPL [JLD 85-1032]*

PETROLEUM INDUSTRY AND TRADE - POLITICAL ASPECTS - SOUTH AFRICA.
Shell out of Namibia and South Africa . London [1986] 19 . : LC Card 87-138719 DDC 338.8/87 19
HD9571.9.S45 S54 1986

PETROLEUM INDUSTRY AND TRADE - POLITICAL ASPECTS - SOVIET UNION.
Stern, Jonathan P. Soviet oil and gas exports to the West . Aldershot, Hants, England , Brookfield, Vt., USA , c1987. xi, 123 p. : ISBN 0-566-05124-9 : LC Card 86-32772 DDC 382/.4228/0947 19
HD9575.S652 S74 1987

PETROLEUM INDUSTRY AND TRADE - PRICES. see **PETROLEUM PRODUCTS - PRICES.**

PETROLEUM INDUSTRY AND TRADE - QATAR.
El Mallakh, Ragaei, 1925- Qatar, energy & development /. London , Dover, N.H. , c1985. 184 p. ; ISBN 0-7099-0955-1 : LC Card 84-29317 DDC 330.953/63 19
HC415.37 .E4 1985 *NYPL [JLD 85-1980]*

PETROLEUM INDUSTRY AND TRADE - QUEBEC (PROVINCE)
Esso Petroleum Canada (Firm) Mémoire présenté à la Commission élue permanente de l'énergie et des ressources de l'Assemblée nationale du Québec /. Québec [1983] 44 leaves : LC Card 85-143347 DDC 338.2/7282/09714 19
HD9574.C23 Q43 1983

PETROLEUM INDUSTRY AND TRADE - RUSSIAN S.F.S.R. - BASHKIRSKAIA A.S.S.R.
Puti razvitiia infrastruktury regiona /. Ufa , 1984. 117 p. : LC Card 85-199949
HE255.Z7 B377 1984

PETROLEUM INDUSTRY AND TRADE - RUSSIAN S.F.S.R. - SIBERIA, WESTERN.
Khaĭtun, A. D. (Alekseĭ Davydovich) Ekspeditsionno-vakhtovoe stroitel'stvo v Zapadnoĭ Sibiri /. Leningrad , 1982. 175, [1] p. : LC Card 83-165812
HD9715.S73 S565 1982

PETROLEUM INDUSTRY AND TRADE - RUSSIAN S.F.S.R. - SIBERIA, WESTERN - MANAGEMENT.
Sovershenstvovanie planirovaniia i upravleniia neftegazovym kompleksom /. Novosibirsk , 1986. 208 p. : LC Card 87-124383
HD9575.S653 S577 1986

PETROLEUM INDUSTRY AND TRADE - RUSSIAN S.F.S.R. - SIBERIA, WESTERN - PLANNING.
Sovershenstvovanie planirovaniia i upravleniia neftegazovym kompleksom /. Novosibirsk , 1986. 208 p. : LC Card 87-124383
HD9575.S653 S577 1986

PETROLEUM INDUSTRY AND TRADE - SAUDI ARABIA - HISTORY.
Casillas, Rex J. Oil and diplomacy . New York , 1987. p. cm. ISBN 0-8240-8078-5 : LC Card 87-23769 DDC 337.730538 19
HF1456.5.S33 C37 1987

PETROLEUM INDUSTRY AND TRADE - SOUTH AFRICA.
Mobil in South Africa . [Cape Town] [1986] 64 p. : ISBN 0-620-09921-6 (pbk.) LC Card 87-126457 DDC 338.7/6223382/0968 19
HD9577.S64 M636 1986

PETROLEUM INDUSTRY AND TRADE - SOUTH CAROLINA - HISTORY.
DeMontmollin, Richard Hall. The SCOJA story . [Columbia, S.C.] , c1986. xi, 191 p. : ISBN 0-9617613-0-X LC Card 86-62676 DDC 381/.456655/060757 19
HD9569.S663 D46 1986

PETROLEUM INDUSTRY AND TRADE - SOVIET UNION.
Kozlov, P. T. (Petr Tikhonovich) Sovershenstvovanie khoziaistvennogo

mekhanizma v neftîanoĭ i gazovoĭ promyshlennosti /. Alma-Ata , 1983. 134 p. : LC Card 83-194289
HD9575.S652 K69 1983

Sagers, Matthew J. Refinery throughput in the U. S.S.R. /. Washington, D.C. [1984] v, 81, 2 p. : LC Card 87-601276 DDC 338.4/766553/0947 19
HD9575.S652 S25 1984

Sagers, Matthew J. Restructuring the Soviet petroleum refining industry /. Washington, D.C. [1985] v, 57 p. ; LC Card 87-601278 DDC 338.4/766553/0947 19
HD9575.S652 S254 1985

PETROLEUM INDUSTRY AND TRADE - SOVIET UNION - HISTORY.
Nikitin, V. V. (Vasiliĭ Vasil′evich) Gorîuchee--frontu, 1941-1945 /. Moskva , 1984. 203 p. : LC Card 85-152473
HD9575.S652 N55 1984

PETROLEUM INDUSTRY AND TRADE - STATISTICS.
Champness, Michael. Oil tanker databook, 1985 /. London ; New York : vii, 347 p. ; ISBN 0-85334-311-X LC Card 86-217414 DDC 387.5/448 19
HE566.T3 C42 1985

Facts and figures . Vienna , 1984? 45 p. :
NYPL [JLD 86-2319]

PETROLEUM INDUSTRY AND TRADE - SURINAM.
Jharap, S. E. The production of heavy crude oil reduces fuel oil imports in Suriname /. Paramaribo, Suriname , 1985. [25] p. : LC Card 87-103716 DDC 338.4/76655/09883 19
HD9574.S752 J47 1985

PETROLEUM INDUSTRY AND TRADE - SWEDEN.
Energy and economic adjustment /. Stockholm , 1983. 247 p. : ISBN 91-7204-186-2
NYPL [JLE 86-1351]

Internationella förutsättningar för den svenska oljeförsörjningen under 1980-talet. Stockholm , 1981. 172 p. in various pagings : ISBN 91-38-06244-5 LC Card 82-241303
HD9575.S82 I57 1981

PETROLEUM INDUSTRY AND TRADE - UKRAINE, WESTERN - HISTORY.
Wieleżyński, Leszek. Wspólna praca--wspólny plon . London, England [1986], c1985. 295 p., [24] p. of plates : LC Card 87-111287
HD9575.P62 W549 1986

PETROLEUM INDUSTRY AND TRADE - UNITED STATES.
A Documentary history of the Petroleum Reserves Corporation, 1943-1944 . Washington , 1974. v, 119 p. : LC Card 74-602382
HD9566 .D6 ***NYPL [JLE 78-1181]***

The Domestic U. S. oil industry and low oil prices . [Cambridge, Mass.] , c1987. v, 61 leaves : LC Card 87-402219 DDC 338.2/7282/0973 19
HD9574.U62 D66 1987

The Enhanced oil recovery market, 1980-1990. New York, N.Y. , c1983. vi, 203 leaves : LC Card 87-142370 DDC 381/.45617665/0973 19
HD9565 .E53 1983

Halberstam, David. The reckoning /. New York , c1986. 752 p. ; ISBN 0-688-04838-2 LC Card 86-16427 DDC 338.4/76292/0973 19
HD9710.U52 H28 1986
NYPL [JLE 86-4151]

Hernández, Rafael. Estados Unidos y América Latina . La Habana , 1982. 209 p. : LC Card 87-403785 DDC 333.8/232/0973 19
HD9574.L3 H47 1982

Welker, Anthony J. The oil and gas Publishing /. Tulsa , c1985. xii, 258 p. : ISBN 0-87814-279-7 (pbk.) : LC Card 85-2096 DDC 338.2/728/0973 19
HD9565 .W46 1985 ***NYPL [JLD 86-4010]***

PETROLEUM INDUSTRY AND TRADE - UNITED STATES - CONSOLIDATION.
Petzinger, Thomas. Oil & honor . New York , c1987. 495 p., [8] p. of plates : ISBN 0-399-13276-7 LC Card 87-2255 DDC 338.8/3622338/0973 19
HD9569.T4 P48 1987

PETROLEUM INDUSTRY AND TRADE - UNITED STATES - FINANCE.
Meurer, Heinrich W., 1950- Wirtschaftsgeologische Aspekte bei der privaten Investition in Öl- und Gasbohrvorhaben in den USA /. [Cologne? , 1982] (Aachen : Fotodruck J. Mainz) vi, 163 p., [3] folded leaves of plates : LC Card 84-200100
HD9565 .M48 1982

PETROLEUM INDUSTRY AND TRADE - UNITED STATES - HISTORY.
Coll, Steve. The taking of Getty Oil . New York , 1987. xiii, 528 p. ; ISBN 0-689-11860-0 LC Card 87-11467 DDC 338.8/3622338/0973 19
HD9569.G48 C65 1987

Francis, Devon. Power to fly . [Fallbrook, CA] , 1986. 97 p. : ISBN 0-8168-7632-0 : LC Card 85-20045 DDC 338.4/76655825/0973 19
TL521 .F63 1986 ***NYPL [JSG 86-235]***

Harris, Kenneth, 1919- The wildcatter . New York , c1987. x, 180 p., [8] p. of plates : ISBN 1-555-84048-5 LC Card 87-8183 DDC 338.7/622338/0924 B 19
HD9570.A53 H37 1987

Miller, Russell. The house of Getty /. London , 19. 361 p., [32] p. of plates : ISBN 0-7181-2601-7 : LC Card 86-222703 DDC 332/.092/4 B 19
HD9570.G4 M55 1986b

Miller, Russell. The house of Getty /. South Yarmouth, Ma. [1987], c1985. 669 p. [16] p. of plates : ISBN 1-555-04230-9 LC Card 86-24259 DDC 332/.092/4 B 19
HD9570.G4 M55 1987

Pickens, T. Boone (Thomas Boone) Boone /. Boston , 1987. xii, 304 p., [8] p. of plates : ISBN 0-395-41433-4 : LC Card 86-27648 DDC 338.7/6223382/0924 B 19
HD9570.P53 A3 1987

PETROLEUM INDUSTRY AND TRADE - UNITED STATES - HISTORY - 20TH CENTURY.
Baldridge, Donald C. (Donald Carl) Mexican petroleum and United States-Mexican relations, 1919-1923 /. New York , 1987. 255 p. ; ISBN 0-8240-8070-X (alk. paper) LC Card 87-23817 DDC 338.2/7282/0972 19
HD9574.M6 B324 1987

PETROLEUM INDUSTRY AND TRADE - UNITED STATES - HISTORY - SOURCES.
Lynch, Gerald, 1908- Roughnecks, drillers, and tool pushers . Austin , 1987. xiv, 262 p. : ISBN 0-292-71553-6 LC Card 87-13857 DDC 331.7/6223382/0924 B 19
HD8039.P42 L95 1987

PETROLEUM INDUSTRY AND TRADE - URUGUAY.
Uruguay. Asemblea General. Cámara de Representantes. Investigación en la Administración, Nacional de Combustibles, Alcohol y Portland /. [Montevideo] , 1935. 352 p. ; LC Card 85-105071
HD9574.U72 U78 1935

PETROLEUM INDUSTRY AND TRADE - VENEZUELA.
Gilbert, Alan, 1944- The political economy of land . Aldershot, Hants , Brookfield, Vt., U. S.A. , c1985. xv, 163 p. : ISBN 0-566-05007-2 : LC Card 85-17535 DDC 333.77/13/0987 19
HD576 .G54 1985 ***NYPL [JLD 86-3632]***

Marchand, Bernard. Vénézuela. Paris, 1971. ix, 218 p. LC Card 74-856272
HD9574.V42 M276 ***NYPL [JLE 71-452]***

Randall, Laura. The political economy of Venezuelan oil /. New York , 1987. xiii, 247 p. ; ISBN 0-275-92823-3 (alk. paper) : LC Card 87-15848 DDC 338.2/7282/0987 19
HD9574.V42 R35 1987

PETROLEUM INDUSTRY AND TRADE - VENEZUELA - HISTORY.
Estaba, Rosa M. Geografía de los paisajes urbanos e industriales de Venezuela /. Caracas , c1985. 291 p., [4] folded leaves : ISBN 980-271-006-7 LC Card 86-148810 DDC 307.7/6/0987 19
HC237 .E766 1985 ***NYPL [JLD 86-2340]***

PETROLEUM INDUSTRY AND TRADE - VENEZUELA - HISTORY - 20TH CENTURY.
González G., Godofredo (González González) La revolución de Los Barrosos /. Caracas, Venezuela [19]87. xii, 276 p. ; ISBN 980-263-047-0 LC Card 87-400058 DDC 338.2/7282/0987 19
HD9574.V42 G59 1987

PETROLEUM INDUSTRY AND TRADE - VENEZUELA - ORINOCO RIVER REGION.
Esquema de ordenamiento territorial de la faja petrolífera del Orinoco . Caracas , 1982. 46 p. : LC Card 86-162734
HC238.O75 E87 1982

PETROLEUM INDUSTRY AND TRADE - WYOMING - STATISTICS.
Wyoming oil and gas production by county /. Casper, Wyo. (P.O. Box 2640, Casper 82602) [1986] [40] p. : LC Card 86-622904 DDC 338.2/728/09787021 19
HD9567.W8 W94 1986

Wyoming oil and gas, 1985 /. Casper, Wyo. (P.O. Box 2640, Casper 82602) [1986?] 50 p. ; LC Card 86-622903 DDC 338.2/728/09787021 19
HD9567.W8 W96 1986

Petroleum Information Committee of the Arab Gulf States.
Joint Symposium on the Energy Industries: Prospects of Co-operation Between Arab Gulf States and Japan (1984 : Tokyo, Japan) The Arab Gulf States and Japan . London , Dover, N.H. , c1986. xiv, 216 p. : ISBN 0-7099-3393-2 : LC Card 85-12819 DDC 338.2/728/0952 19
HD9576.P52 J65 1984
NYPL [JLD 86-1669]

Symposium on the Energy Economy (1984 : Durham, Durham) Prospects for the world oil industry . London , Dover, N.H. , c1985. 131 p. : ISBN 0-7099-4104-8 : LC Card 85-4186 DDC 338.2/7282 19
HD9560.5 .S96 1985 ***NYPL [JLD 85-2430]***

Petroleum Information Corporation. Oklahoma casinghead gas production report. [Denver, Colo.] (P.O. Box 2612, Denver 80201) , <[c1986-. v. <1-2 > ; LC Card 86-219814 DDC 338.2/7285/09766021 19
HD9581.U52 O56 1986

PETROLEUM LAW AND LEGISLATION - MEXICO.
El Petróleo . México, D.F. , 1923. vi, 352 p. ; LC Card 85-220440
HD9574.M6 P4475 1923

PETROLEUM LAW AND LEGISLATION - NORWAY.
Selvig, Erling. Prosjektfinansiering i petroleumsvirksomheten /. Oslo [1983] 30, 5 p. ; LC Card 84-131887
HD9575.N62 S44 1983

PETROLEUM LAW AND LEGISLATION - UNITED STATES.
Lowe, John S., 1941- Oil and gas in a nutshell /. St. Paul, Minn. , 1983. xlvii, 443 p. ; ISBN 0-314-73469-4 LC Card 83-6811 DDC 346.7304/6823 347.30646823 19
KF1850 .L68 1983 ***NYPL [JLC 86-226]***

PETROLEUM PIPELINE INDUSTRY - UNITED STATES.
Untiet, Charles J. Competition in the oil pipeline industry . [Washington, D.C.] [1984] iii leaves, 73, [332] p., [10] p. of plates : LC Card 84-602723 DDC 388.5 19
HD9580.U5 U58 1984 ***NYPL [JLF 85-864]***

PETROLEUM PRODUCTS - BRAZIL - MATTO GROSSO DO SUL - TRANSPORTATION.
Alternativa ferro-hidro-rodoviária para o transporte de derivados claros de petróleo para o abastecimento das regiões oeste do Estado do Paraná e sul do Estado de Mato Grosso do Sul /. [Rio de Janeiro] , 1984. 41 leaves : LC Card 87-403934 DDC 380.5/24 19
HE199.5.P4 A48 1984

PETROLEUM PRODUCTS - BRAZIL - PARANÁ (STATE) - TRANSPORTATION.
Alternativa ferro-hidro-rodoviária para o transporte de derivados claros de petróleo para o abastecimento das regiões oeste do Estado do Paraná e sul do Estado de Mato Grosso do Sul /. [Rio de Janeiro] , 1984. 41 leaves : LC Card

87-403934 DDC 380.5/24 19
HE199.5.P4 A48 1984

PETROLEUM PRODUCTS DISTRIBUTION EQUIPMENT INDUSTRY - UNITED STATES.
Petroleum products storage & distribution & information processing. New York, N.Y. , c1983. viii, 249 p. : LC Card 87-143725 DDC 381/.4566554/0973 19
HD9565 .P363 1983

PETROLEUM PRODUCTS - GREAT BRITAIN - PURCHASING.
Hall, John, 1946- Reducing industrial oil costs /. Aldershot, Hants England , Brookfield, Vt., U. S.A. , c1987. xvii, 118 p. : ISBN 0-291-39740-9 (U. S.) : LC Card 86-29511 DDC 338.2/3 19
HD9560.4 .H35 1987

PETROLEUM PRODUCTS - INDIA - MARKETING.
Jayashankar, R., 1954- Distribution of refinery products in India /. New Delhi , 1986, c1985. 152 p. ; LC Card 86-902972 DDC 381/.4566553/0954 19
HD9576.I42 J39 1986

PETROLEUM PRODUCTS - PRICES - BRAZIL.
O'Keefe, Hsu Yuet Heung. A crise do petróleo e a economia brasileira /. São Paulo , 1984. 137 p. : LC Card 85-143617 DDC 338.2/3 19
HD9574.B82 O43 1984
NYPL [JLD 86-2712]

PETROLEUM PRODUCTS - PRICES - BRAZIL - ECONOMETRIC MODELS.
O'Keefe, Hsu Yuet Heung. A crise do petróleo e a economia brasileira /. São Paulo , 1984. 137 p. : LC Card 85-143617 DDC 338.2/3 19
HD9574.B82 O43 1984
NYPL [JLD 86-2712]

PETROLEUM PRODUCTS - PRICES - GERMANY (WEST) - ECONOMETRIC MODELS.
Borrmann, Axel. Die Wettbewerbsposition natürlicher Rohstoffe . Hamburg , 1984. 226 p. : ISBN 3-87895-250-3 LC Card 84-222130
HF1054.G4 B67 1984

PETROLEUM PRODUCTS - PRICES - GOVERNMENT POLICY - ARGENTINA.
Aspectos económicos de la industria petrolera. Capital Federal [1985 or 1986] 28 p. : LC Card 87-120726
HD9574.A72 A84 1985

PETROLEUM PRODUCTS - PRICES - LOUISIANA.
Lam, Manuel. Louisiana crude oil and natural gas report and severance and royalty sensitivity to price, second half 1985 /. Baton Rouge, La (P.O. Box 44156, Baton Rouge 70804-4156) [1986] iii, 31 p. : LC Card 86-621907 DDC 338.2/728/09763 19
HD9560.8.U53 L65 1986

PETROLEUM PRODUCTS - PRICES - MATHEMATICAL MODELS.
Macroeconomics [i.e. Macroeconomic] impacts of energy shocks /. Amsterdam ; New York : xvi, 331 p. : ISBN 0-444-70247-4 (U. S.) LC Card 87-9035 DDC 338.4/36655/0724 19
HG229 .M315 1987

PETROLEUM PRODUCTS - PRICES - QUÉBEC (PROVINCE) - STATISTICS.
Québec (Province). Groupe de travail sur le prix des carburants au Québec. Rapport du Groupe de travail sur le prix des carburants au Québec. [Québec , 1985] xiv, 169, [153] p. : ISBN 2-550-11913-4 LC Card 86-185758
HD9574.C23 Q47 1985

PETROLEUM PRODUCTS - PRICES - SWEDEN.
Energy and economic adjustment /. Stockholm , 1983. 247 p. : ISBN 91-7204-186-2
NYPL [JLE 86-1351]

PETROLEUM PRODUCTS - PRICES - SWITZERLAND.
Schmassmann, Norbert. Verteilungswirkungen von Erdölpreissteigerungen . Diessenhofen , c1983. viii, 326 p. : ISBN 3-7253-0203-0 LC Card 83-219477
HD9575.S92 S27 1983

PETROLEUM PRODUCTS - PRICES - UNITED STATES.
The Domestic U. S. oil industry and low oil prices . [Cambridge, Mass.] , c1987. v, 61 leaves : LC Card 87-402219 DDC 338.2/7282/0973 19
HD9574.U62 D66 1987

PETROLEUM PRODUCTS - SOVIET UNION - FORECASTING.
Optimizatsii͡a planirovanii͡a polimerno-neftekhimicheskogo kompleksa /. Moskva , 1984. 141 p. : LC Card 86-143987
HD9579.C33 S655 1984

Petroleum products storage & distribution & information processing. New York, N.Y. : Frost & Sullivan, c1983. viii, 249 p. : ill. ; 29 cm. "January 1983." "A1101." LC Card 87-143725 DDC 381/.4566554/0973 19
1. Petroleum products distribution equipment industry - United States. 2. Market surveys - United States. I. Frost & Sullivan. II. Title: Petroleum products storage and distribution and information processing.
HD9565 .P363 1983

Petroleum products storage and distribution and information processing. Petroleum products storage & distribution & information processing. New York, N.Y. , c1983. viii, 249 p. : LC Card 87-143725 DDC 381/.4566554/0973 19
HD9565 .P363 1983

PETROLEUM REFINERIES - GOVERNMENT POLICY - NIGERIA.
Establishment of oil refinery in Nigeria. Lagos , 1960. 6 p. ; LC Card 87-401860
HD9577.N52 E84 1960

PETROLEUM REFINERIES - SOVIET UNION.
Sagers, Matthew J. Refinery throughput in the U. S.S.R. /. Washington, D.C. [1984] v, 81, 2 p. : LC Card 87-601276 DDC 338.4/766553/0947 19
HD9575.S652 S25 1984

Sagers, Matthew J. Restructuring the Soviet petroleum refining industry /. Washington, D.C. [1985] v, 57 p. ; LC Card 87-601278 DDC 338.4/766553/0947 19
HD9575.S652 S254 1985

Petroleum refining, June 1985. Williams, Harry B. Industry wage survey . Washington, D.C. [1986] iv, 34 p. ; LC Card 86-602194 DDC 331.2/86553/0973021 19
HD4966.P52 U5556 1986

Petroleum Reserves Croporation. see **War Assets Corporation.**

PETROLEUM - SECONDARY RECOVERY. see **SECONDARY RECOVERY OF OIL.**

PETROLEUM - SOUTH AFRICA - TRANSPORTATION.
Oil tankers to South Africa, 1980-1981. Amsterdam , c1982. vi, 99 p. : ISBN 90-70331-05-5 (pbk.) LC Card 86-213340 DDC 387.5/448 19
HE595.P4 O37 1982

PETROLEUM - TAXATION - ALASKA.
Livey, Jay. The effect of state income tax policy on the development of marginal oil fields . [Juneau] [1986] vii leaves, 52 p., [17] leaves : LC Card 86-622190 DDC 333.8/232/09798 19
HD9560.8.U53 A445 1986

PETROLEUM - TAXATION - LAW AND LEGISLATION - ALASKA.
Livey, Jay. The effect of state income tax policy on the development of marginal oil fields . [Juneau] [1986] vii leaves, 52 p., [17] leaves : LC Card 86-622190 DDC 333.8/232/09798 19
HD9560.8.U53 A445 1986

PETROLEUM - TAXATION - LOUISIANA.
Lam, Manuel. Louisiana crude oil and natural gas report and severance and royalty sensitivity to price, second half 1985 /. Baton Rouge, La (P.O. Box 44156, Baton Rouge 70804-4156) [1986] iii, 31 p. : LC Card 86-621907 DDC 338.2/728/09763 19
HD9560.8.U53 L65 1986

PETROLEUM - TAXATION - UNITED STATES.
Webre, Philip. The budgetary and economic effects of oil taxes. Washington, DC , 19. xvi, 55 p. ; *NYPL [JLF 86-1354]*

PETROLEUM - TRADE AND STATISTICS. see **PETROLEUM INDUSTRY AND TRADE.**

PETROLEUM - TRANSPORTATION.
Gunner, T. J. Gunner and Edwards on the carriage of crude oil by sea /. London , New York , 1986. xii, 137 p. : ISBN 1-85044-073-5 (pbk.) : LC Card 86-224898 DDC 387.5/448 19
HE595.P4 G86 1986

Kapetanakē-Sēphakē, Katerina. Hē diethnopoiēsē tou kephalaiou stēn Hellada, hē periptōsē tōn diylistēriōn . Athēna , 1985. 234 p. : LC Card 86-206498
HE595.P4 K36 1985

PETROLEUM - WELL-BORING. see **OIL WELL DRILLING.**

PETROLEUM - WELLS. see **OIL WELLS.**

PETROLEUM WORKERS - COLOMBIA.
La Ocupación y su remuneración en las empresas petroleras en Colombia, 1977-1984. Bogotá, D.E. [1986] 37 p. : LC Card 87-402964 DDC 331.12/5223382/09861 19
HD8039.P42 V446 1986

PETROLEUM WORKERS - COLOMBIA - BARRANCABERMEJA.
Yunis, José. Barrancabermeja . Bogotá , 1986. 102 p. : ISBN 958-9096-03-4 LC Card 87-400984 DDC 331.7/6223382/0986125 19
HD8310.B372 Y86 1986

PETROLEUM WORKERS - RUSSIAN S.F.S.R. - BIOGRAPHY.
I͡Urasova, M. Neftīanik . Moskva , 1981. 254 p. : LC Card 82-111110
HD8039.P42 S654 1981

PETROLEUM WORKERS - UNITED STATES - BIOGRAPHY.
Lynch, Gerald, 1908- Roughnecks, drillers, and tool pushers . Austin , 1987. xiv, 262 p. : ISBN 0-292-71553-6 LC Card 87-13857 DDC 331.7/6223382/0924 B 19
HD8039.P42 L95 1987

PETROLEUM WORKERS - VENEZUELA.
Marchand, Bernard. Vénézuela. Paris, 1971. ix, 218 p. LC Card 74-856272
HD9574.V42 M276 *NYPL [JLE 71-452]*

PETROLEUM WORKERS - WYOMING - STATISTICS.
Wessel, Louis. Wyoming oil and natural gas extraction industry . Cheyenne, Wyo. (Herschler Bldg., Cheyenne 82002) , 1986. 35 p. : LC Card 86-622902 DDC 331.12/522338/09787021 19
HD4966.P52 U5553 1986

Petroleumsvirksomhetens framtid . Norway. "Tempo-utvalget." Oslo [1983] 167 p. : ISBN 82-00-70810-1 LC Card 83-235609
HD9575.N62 N6855 1983

Petrosi͡an, K. T͡S. (Karmlen T͡Saturovich)
Moiseev, Anatoliĭ Vasil′evich. Ėkonomicheskiĭ slovar'-spravochnik . Moskva , 1978. 239 p. ; LC Card 81-165938
HB61 .M56 1978

Moiseev, Anatoliĭ Vasil′evich. Osnovy ėkonomiki vazhneĭshikh otrasleĭ narodnogo khozi͡aĭsva SSSR . Moskva , 1984. 191 p. : LC Card 85-113764
HC336.25 .M654 1984

Petrov, A. M. Zarubezhnyĭ Vostok . Moskva , 1986. 126 p. ; LC Card 87-126378
HC412 .Z38 1986

Petrov, Milan, k.i.n. Mezhdunarodnite pŭtnicheski prevozi i tekhnite valutno-finansovi problemi / Milan Petrov. Sofii͡a : Bŭlgarska tŭrgovsko-promyshlena palata, 1984. 95, [1] p. ; 21 cm. Bibliography: p. 85-[96] LC Card 85-167160
1. Transit, International - Bulgaria. 2. Foreign exchange problem - Bulgaria. I. Title.
HE265.A2 P48 1984

Petrov, N. A. Razvitie ėnergetiki I͡Akutskoĭ ASSR v svi͡azi s sooruzheniem BAM . I͡Akutsk , 1985. 99, 3 p. : LC Card 86-233736
HD9502.S653 I237 1985

Petrov, N. P. Finansovoe polozhenie russkoĭ zheli͡eznodorozhnoĭ si͡eti i glavni͡eĭshii͡a prichiny ukhudshenii͡a ego v posli͡ednie gody. N. Petrov. S.-Peterburg, Gos. tip., 1909. 185, ii, 17 p. 25 cm. (Vysochaĭshe uchrezhdennai͡a Osobai͡a vysshai͡a komissii͡a dli͡a vsestoronnii͡ago izsli͡edovanii͡a zheli͡eznodorozhnago di͡ela v Rossii. [Trudy] vyp. 5) LC Card 75-564261

1. Railroads - Soviet Union - Finance. I. Series: Vysochaĭshe uchrezhdennaia Osobaia vysshaia komissiia dlia vsestoronniago izsliedovaniia zhelieznodorozhnago diela v Rossii (Series) , vyp. 5. II. Title.
HE3131 .A33 vyp. 5 HE3136

Petrov, Nikolaĭ Ivanovich. Dolzhnost'--direktor /. Moskva , 1985. 333 p. : LC Card 85-145325
HC332.5.A2 D64 1985

Petrov, Tson'o. Revoliutsionnoto profsiiuzno dvizhenie v Gabrovski okrŭg /. Sofiia , 1986. 305 p., [16] p. of plates : LC Card 86-232088
HD6785.G32 R48 1986

Petrov, V. A. (Valeriĭ Arkad'evich)
Sotsial'no-demograficheskaia struktura gorodskogo naseleniia i ego zaniatost' / V.A. Petrov ; pod redaktsieĭ B.D. Breeva. Moskva : "Finansy i statistika," 1981. 151 p. ; 19 cm. Includes bibliographical references. LC Card 82-145197
1. Soviet Union - Population. 2. Soviet Union - Occupations. I. Breev, B. D. (Boris Dmitrievich). II. Title.
HB2277 .P48 1981

Petrov, Vladimir. Izpolzuvaneto na reka Dunav za prevoz na tovari za i ot Sredna i Zapadna Evropa / Vladimir Petrov. Sofiia : Bŭlgarska tŭrgovsko-promishlena palata, 1985. 71 p. ; 21 cm. (Biblioteka / Bŭlgarska tŭrgovsko-promishlena palata . no. 210) Bibliography: p. 71. LC Card 86-105301
1. Shipping - Danube River. 2. Danube River Region - Commerce. I. Series: Biblioteka / Bŭlgarska tŭrgovsko-promishlena palata , kn. 210. II. Title.
HE387.D2 P36 1985

Petrovich, Ė. I. OĖkonomicheskie problemy razvitiia narodnogo khoziaĭstva i povyshenie ėffektivnosti obshchestvennogo proizvodstva /. Minsk , 1984. 148 p. : LC Card 85-147020
HC337.B93 E45 1984

Petry, Almiro. Schneider, José Odelso. Realidade brasileira . Porto Alegre-RS , c1986. 438 p. : LC Card 87-119174
HC187 .S393 1986

Pettavino, Paula J.
Hilton, Robert, 1927- U. S. maritime industries--down for the third time? /. Washington, D.C. , c1987. vi, 60 p. : ISBN 0-89206-099-9 (pbk.) LC Card 86-31768 DDC 387.5/0973 19
HE745 .H66 1987

Ullman, Harlan. Forecasts for U. S. maritime industries in 1989 . Washington, D.C. , c1984. ix, 42 p. : ISBN 0-89206-069-7 (pbk.) LC Card 84-27501 DDC 338.4/76238/0973 19
VM299.6 .U45 1984 ***NYPL [JLD 87-155]***

Pettigrew, Andrew M. The Management of strategic change /. Oxford [Oxfordshire] , New York, NY , 1988, c1987. p. cm. ISBN 0-631-15695-X : LC Card 87-15634 DDC 658.4/012 19
HD30.28 .M344 1988

Petty capitalism in Spanish America . Kinsbruner, Jay. Boulder, Colo. , 1987. xxii, 159 p. : ISBN 0-8133-7272-0 (pbk.) LC Card 86-51526 DDC 381/.456413/0098 19
HD9325.L29 K56 1987

PETTY, WILLIAM, SIR, 1623-1687.
Anikin, Andreĭ Vladimirovich. Uil'iam Petti /. Moskva , 1986. 92, [3] p. ; LC Card 86-206468 DDC 330.15/3 19
HB103.P5 A83 1986

Petunjuk pelaksanaan Program Peningkatan Produktivitas Kerja Tenaga Kerja Wanita Melalui Pendekatan Kesejahteraan Terpadu Tahun 1984/1986. Indonesia. Kantor Menteri Negara Urusan Peranan Wanita. Pokok-pokok petunjuk pelaksanaan Program Peningkatan Produktivitas Kerja Tenaga Kerja Wanita Melalui Pendekatan Kesejahteraan Terpadu, tahun 1984/1986 (Juklak Nakerwan). Jakarta [1984] iii, xii, 47 p. ; LC Card 86-940168
HD6194 .I5 1984

PÉTUR JÓNSSON Á HALLGILSSTÖÐUM, 1911-
Indriði G. Þorsteinsson, 1926- Fimmtán gírar áfram . Reykjavík , 1981. 178 p., [16] p. of plates : LC Card 83-185502
HD8039.M7952 I25 1981

Petzina, Dietmar, 1938- Wirtschaftspolitik im britischen Besatzungsgebiet 1945-1949 /. Düsseldorf , 1984. 338 p. : ISBN 3-590-18124-9 LC Card 84-188669
HC286.5 .W5655 1984

Petzinger, Renate, 1943- Forum wohnen /. Freiburg i. Br. , Giessen , 1986. 158 p. : ISBN 3-89125-009-6 LC Card 86-169106
HD7339.A3 F68 1986

Petzinger, Thomas. Oil & honor : the Texaco-Pennzoil wars / Thomas Petzinger, Jr. New York : Putnam, c1987. 495 p., [8] p. of plates : ports. ; 25 cm. Bibliography: p. 485-486. Includes index. ISBN 0-399-13276-7 LC Card 87-2255 DDC 338.8/3622338/0973 19
1. Texaco, inc. 2. Pennzoil Company. 3. Getty Oil Company. 4. Petroleum industry and trade - United States - Consolidation. 5. Consolidation and merger of corporations - United States. I. Title. II. Title: Oil and honor.
HD9569.T4 P48 1987

Peukert, Detlev.
Arbeit und Arbeitserfahrung in der Geschichte /. Göttingen , c1986. 128 p. ; ISBN 3-525-33516-4 LC Card 86-226588
HD4904 .A6644 1986

Arbeit und Arbeitserfahrung in der Geschichte /. Göttingen , 1986. 128 p. ; ISBN 3-525-33516-4 ***NYPL [JLC 87-12]***

PEWS. see American Sociological Association. Section on Political Economy of the World System.

Pezet, P. (Pierre) Les opérateurs français du commerce international agro-alimentaire / Centre français du commerce extérieur, Direction des produits agro-alimentaires, D.P.A. Paris : La Direction, c1984. 85 p. : ill. ; 30 cm. "Document ... réalisé par M.P. Pezet"--P. 7. "Mai 1984." ISBN 2-279-52812-6 LC Card 85-136648 DDC 382/.456413/00944 19
1. Food industry and trade - France. 2. Food industry and trade. 3. Export marketing - France. I. Centre français du commerce extérieur. Direction des produits agro-alimentaires. II. Title.
HD9012.5 .P43 1984

Pezeu, Fabienne. Gruère, Jean-Pierre. Optimiser les ressources humaines dans l'entreprise . Paris , c1984. 69, 42 p. : ISBN 2-7101-0462-8 : LC Card 84-217427
HF5549.5.A78 G78 1984

Pfaff, Martin.
Finanzsysteme, Ideal- und Realtypen . Berlin , c1983. 278 p. : ISBN 3-428-05419-9 LC Card 83-240120
HJ161 .F575 1983

Gestaltungsspielräume der Arbeitsmarktpolitik auf regionalen Arbeitsmärkten . Berlin , c1984. 180 p. : ISBN 3-428-05614-0 LC Card 84-218530
HD8444 .G47 1984

Methoden und Kriterien zur Überprüfung des Erfolgs von Aufklärungskampagnen . Köln , 1982. 99, [93] p. : LC Card 83-178796
HE5614.5.G3 M37 1982

Pfaltzgraff, Robert L. Selling the rope to hang capitalism? . Washington , 1987. viii, 246 p. ; ISBN 0-08-034959-5 : LC Card 86-30401 DDC 382/.091713/01717 19
HF1412 .S45 1987

Pfankuch, Paula J. 1986 membership profile /. Chicago, Ill. , c1986. ix, 44 p. : ISBN 0-911780-85-8 (pbk.) LC Card 87-144205 DDC 333.33/2/0973 19
HD251 .A17 1986

Pfeffermann, Guy Pierre. Public expenditure in Latin America : effects on poverty / Guy P. Pfeffermann. Washington, D.C. : World Bank, 1987. 38 p. ; 28 cm. (World Bank discussion papers, 0259-210X . 5) Includes bibliographical references. ISBN 0-8213-0906-4 (pbk.) LC Card 87-10650 DDC 336.3/9/098 19
1. Latin America - Appropriations and expenditures. 2. Public investments - Latin America. 3. Poor - Latin America. I. Title. II. Series.
HJ7664.5 .P44 1987

Pfeif, G. H. Boulware, Lemuel Richetts, 1895- What to do about communism in unions . [Schenectady, N.Y.?] [1952?] 62 p. ; ***NYPL [JLD 86-247]***

Pfeiffer, Gabrielle. Mountains of butter, lakes of milk : the International Dairy Arrangement and the international market for dairy products / par Gabrielle Pfeiffer. Genève : Institut universitaire de hautes études internationales, 1986. 78, [4] p. : ill. ; 30 cm. "Mémoire présenté en vue de l'obtention du diplôme." Bibliography: p. [79]-[82] LC Card 87-109400 DDC 382/.417 19
1. Dairy products industry - Government policy. 2. Dairy products industry. 3. Commercial treaties. I. Graduate Institute of International Studies (Geneva, Switzerland). II. Title.
HD9275.A2 P48 1986

Pfeiffer, Paul L. Counter merchandising : for the counter sales person / written and coordinated by Paul L. Pfeiffer. Chicago, Ill. (Suite 2260, 20 N. Wacker Dr., Chicago 60606) : American Supply Association Education Foundation, c1986. 84 p., [1] leaf of plates : ill. ; 28 cm. LC Card 87-404047 DDC 658.8/5 19
1. Selling. 2. Sales personnel. I. ASA Education Foundation. II. Title.
HF5438.25 .P49 1986

Pfeiler, Christine. Die Sozialistische Gemeinschaft . Berlin , 1985. 238 p. ; LC Card 86-120025 DDC 337.1/1717 19
HC243.5 .S685 1985

Pferd, William, 1922- Market report on scanning products & systems /. Falls Church, VA (6609 Rosecroft Pl., Falls Church 22043) [1986]- 1 v. (loose-leaf) ; LC Card 87-151419 DDC 338.7/61006424 19
HD9696.O672 M37 1986

Pfingsten, Andreas. The measurement of tax progression / Andreas Pfingsten. Berlin ; New York : Springer-Verlag, c1986. vi, 131 p. : ill. ; 25 cm. (Studies in contemporary economics . vol. 20) Bibliography: p. [125]-131. ISBN 0-387-16072-8 (U. S. : pbk.) LC Card 86-219663 DDC 336.2/93 19
1. Taxation, Progressive - Mathematical models. 2. Taxation, Progressive - Germany (West) - Mathematical models. I. Series. II. Series: Studies in contemporary economics , v. 20. III. Title.
HJ2326 .P47 1986

Pfister-Langanay, Christian. Ports, navires et négociants à Dunkerque, 1662-1792 / Christian Pfister-Langanay ; préface de Pierre Deyon. Dunkerque : C. Pfister-Langanay : Diffuseur, Société dunkerquoise, 1985. 677 p. : ill., plans ; 23 cm. Bibliography: p. 641-652. Includes indexes. LC Card 87-115474
1. Harbors - France - Dunkerque - History - 17th century. 2. Harbors - France - Dunkerque - History - 18th century. 3. Dunkerque (France) - Commerce - History - 17th century. 4. Dunkerque (France) - Commerce - History - 18th century. 5. Merchants - France - Dunkerque - History - 17th century. 6. Merchants - France - Dunkerque - History - 18th century. I. Title.
HD558.D85 P45 1985

Pflaumer, Peter, 1947- Bevölkerung, Haushalte, Konsum : statistische Analyse und Prognose / Peter Pflaumer. Frankfurt ; New York : Campus, c1986. iv, 218 p. : ill. ; 21 cm. (Campus Forschung. Bd. 507) Bibliography: p. 204-218. ISBN 3-593-33674-X LC Card 87-408990 DDC 339.4/7 19
1. Population forecasting. 2. Households. 3. Consumption (Economics). I. Title.
HB849.53 .P49 1986

Pfohl, Hans-Christian. Unternehmensführung und Logistik /. Wiesbaden , c1984. 151 p. : ISBN 3-409-13038-1 LC Card 85-126091
HD28 .Z46 nr. 84/2 HD30.28

Pfriem, Reinhard.
Betriebswirtschaftslehre in sozialer und ökologischer Dimension / Reinhard Pfriem. Frankfurt [am Main] ; New York : Campus Verlag, c1983. 210 p. ; 21 cm. (Campus Forschung. Bd. 342) Bibliography: p. 194-210. ISBN 3-593-33223-X LC Card 83-190294
1. Industrial management. 2. Industry - Social aspects. I. Title.
HD35 .P45 1983

Ökologische Unternehmenspolitik /. Frankfurt , New York , c1986. 280 p. ; ISBN 3-593-33580-8 LC Card 87-407999 DDC 363.7 19
HD75.6 .O347 1986

Die Phalanx . Schnitzler, Bert, 1933- Herford , c1986. 279 p. ; ISBN 3-512-00752-X LC Card 86-199408
HE8689.9.G4 S36 1986

Phanariōtēs, P. Epicheirēsiakē psychologia : provlēmata anthrōpinōn scheseōn sto ergasiako

plaisio / P. Phanariōtē.3. ekdosē. Athēna : Ekdoseis Papazēsē, 1983. ix, 359, [3] p. : ill. ; 25 cm. Bibliography: p. [360]-[362] LC Card 84-134693
1. Psychology, Industrial. I. Title.
HF5548.8 .P45 1983

PHANGNGA (THAILAND : PROVINCE) - STATISTICS.
Sathiti thī samkhan, 2512. [Bangkok] [19]71. [11], 34 p., [1] leaf of plates : LC Card 83-921120 DDC 315.93 19
HA4600.55.Z9 P428 1971

Phannī Sunth Songsan Ninkamhæng. Čhotmāihēt kānsāng Phraphuttharūp phra prathān Phutthamonthon /. Krung Thēp , 2525 [1982] 172 p. : ISBN 974-7921-05-7 LC Card 83-916060
HB1912.G38 S66 1982

Phares, Donald. Who pays New York taxes? . [Albany, N.Y.] [1985] 2, 101 p. : LC Card 86-621353 DDC 336.2/94/09747 19
HJ2322.N7 W48 1985

Pharmaceutical competitor analysis .
EPHMRA/ESOMAR Seminar (1985 : Lisbon, Portugal) Brooklands, Sale, Cheshire, U.K. [1985] iv, 390 p. : ISBN 92-831-1103-6 (pbk.) : LC Card 86-202276 DDC 338.4/76151 19
HD9665.5 .E64 1985

PHARMACEUTICAL INDUSTRY.
Generic drugs . Stamford, Conn., U. S.A. , c1986. xiii, 311 leaves : ISBN 0-89336-434-7 (soft) LC Card 87-167077 DDC 380.1/456151 19
HD9665.5 .G46 1986

PHARMACEUTICAL INDUSTRY - CANADA.
Maule, Christopher J., 1934- A survey of the economics of the retail pharmacy sector in Canada /. [Toronto, Ont.] , c1986. 42 p. ; ISBN 0-662-14496-1 (pbk.) LC Card 86-206188 DDC 338.4/76151/0971 19
HD9670.C22 M38 1986

PHARMACEUTICAL INDUSTRY - CONGRESSES.
EPHMRA/ESOMAR Seminar (1985 : Lisbon, Portugal) Pharmaceutical competitor analysis . Brooklands, Sale, Cheshire, U.K. [1985] iv, 390 p. : ISBN 92-831-1103-6 (pbk.) : LC Card 86-202276 DDC 338.4/76151 19
HD9665.5 .E64 1985

PHARMACEUTICAL INDUSTRY - DEVELOPING COUNTRIES.
Bühler, Marcel. Geschäfte mit der Armut . Frankfurt/M. , c1982. 200 p. : ISBN 3-923363-02-8 (pbk.) LC Card 86-674004
HD9673.D44 B83x 1982

Wenzel, Gilbert, 1956- Marktstrategien multinationaler Pharmaunternehmen und die Arzneimittelmärkte der Dritten Welt . Frankfurt am Main , New York , c1986. 398 p. : ISBN 3-8204-9721-8 LC Card 87-407426 DDC 381/.456151/091724 19
HD9674.D44 W46 1986

PHARMACEUTICAL INDUSTRY - DEVELOPING COUNTRIES - MORAL AND ETHICAL ASPECTS.
Bühler, Marcel. Geschäfte mit der Armut . Frankfurt/M. , c1982. 200 p. : ISBN 3-923363-02-8 (pbk.) LC Card 86-674004
HD9673.D44 B83x 1982

PHARMACEUTICAL INDUSTRY - FRANCE - STATISTICS.
L'Industrie pharmaceutique, ses réalités. Paris , 1982. 54 p. : LC Card 85-124408
HD9668.4 .I53 1982

PHARMACEUTICAL INDUSTRY - GERMANY (WEST) - HISTORY.
100 Jahre im Dienst der Gesundheit, 1886-1986 /. Ludwigshafen am Rhein , c1986. 159 p. : LC Card 87-408744 DDC 338.7/616151/0943 19
HD9669.9.K56 A15 1986

PHARMACEUTICAL INDUSTRY - STATISTICS.
L'Industrie pharmaceutique, ses réalités. Paris , 1982. 54 p. : LC Card 85-124408
HD9668.4 .I53 1982

PHARMACEUTICAL INDUSTRY - TEXAS - SAN ANTONIO - CONGRESSES.
A Transcription of key addresses at San Antonio's Bio-Medical Seminar /. San Antonio, TX (8961 Tesoro Dr., Suite 308, San Antonio 78217) , c1985. v, 104, [4] leaves of plates : LC Card 87-144092 DDC 338.4/7681761/09764351 19
HD9999.B443 U667 1985

PHARMACEUTICAL INDUSTRY - UNITED STATES - DIRECTORIES.
Top emerging private companies. Tustin, CA, U. S.A. (17722 Irvine Blvd., Tustin 92680) , c1987. iv, 8, 144, [112] leaves : LC Card 87-402028 DDC 681/.761/029473 19
HD9994.U52 T66 1987

PHARMACEUTICAL INDUSTRY - UNITED STATES - FINANCE - DIRECTORIES.
Pharmaceutical manufacturers of the United States /. Park Ridge, N.J., U. S.A. , 1987. vi, 300 p. ; ISBN 0-8155-1109-4 : LC Card 86-33276 DDC 338.7/616151/02573 19
HD9666.3 .P47 1987

PHARMACEUTICAL INDUSTRY - UNITED STATES - HISTORY.
Foster, Lawrence G., 1925- A company that cares . New Brunswick, N.J. , c1986. 175 p. : ISBN 0-9617676-1-8 LC Card 86-27478 DDC 338.7/616151/0973 19
HD9666.9.J6 F67 1986

Liebenau, Jonathan. Medical science and medical industry . Baltimore , 1987. ix, 207 p. ; ISBN 0-8018-3356-6 LC Card 86-27346 DDC 338.4/76151/0973 19
HD9666.5 .L54 1987

Pharmaceutical manufacturers of the United States / edited by D.J. De Renzo. 4th ed. Park Ridge, N.J., U. S.A. : Noyes Data Corp., 1987. vi, 300 p. ; 25 cm. Includes index. ISBN 0-8155-1109-4 : LC Card 86-33276 DDC 338.7/616151/02573 19
1. Pharmaceutical industry - United States - Finance - Directories. 2. Medical supplies industry - United States - Finance - Directories. I. De Renzo, D. J. II. Noyes Data Corporation.
HD9666.3 .P47 1987

Pharmaceutical packaging products market in Europe. Medical products packaging market in Europe. New York, N.Y. , c1983. vi, x, xi, 220 p. : LC Card 87-141779 DDC 380.1/456151 19
HD9671.A2 M43 1983

Pharmaceutical packaging products mkt. in Europe. Medical products packaging market in Europe. New York, N.Y. , c1983. vi, x, xi, 220 p. : LC Card 87-141779 DDC 380.1/456151 19
HD9671.A2 M43 1983

PHARMACEUTICAL POLICY - INDIA - CONGRESSES.
"All India Seminar on National Drug Policy" (1986 : New Delhi, India) Drug industry and the Indian people . New Delhi , Patna , 1986. 333 p. : LC Card 87-900874 DDC 338.4/76151/0954 19
HD9611.I52 A44 1986

PHARMACEUTICAL POLICY - UNITED STATES - HISTORY.
Liebenau, Jonathan. Medical science and medical industry . Baltimore , 1987. ix, 207 p. ; ISBN 0-8018-3356-6 LC Card 86-27346 DDC 338.4/76151/0973 19
HD9666.5 .L54 1987

PHARMACISTS - MANITOBA - WINNIPEG - HISTORY - 20TH CENTURY.
Wilder, Joseph E., 1896- Lotions, potions, and liniments pure . Winnipeg, Man. , c1982. 100 p. : ISBN 0-919576-34-6 (pbk.) : LC Card 83-121333 DDC 381/.456151/0971274 19
HD9670.C23 W568 1982
NYPL [JLE 87-1213]

Phases of economic growth, 1850-1973 .
Solomou, Solomos. Cambridge [Cambridgeshire] , New York , 1987. p. cm. ISBN 0-521-33457-8 LC Card 86-34324 DDC 338.9 19
HB3729 .S65 1987

Phatak, Arvind V.
Boseman, F. Glenn. Cases in strategic management /. New York , c1988. ix, 476 p. : ISBN 0-471-85463-8 (pbk.) LC Card 87-24261 DDC 658.4/012 19
HD30.28 .B67 1988

Schellenberger, Robert Earl. Strategic management . New York , c1986. xiii, 808 p. : ISBN 0-471-88059-0 : LC Card 85-9553 DDC 658.4/012 19
HD30.28 .S34 1986 ***NYPL [JLE 86-1559]***

Phelps, John J. Sheets, Robert G. The impact of service industries on underemployment in metropolitan economies /. Lexington, Mass. , c1987. xii, 185 p. ; ISBN 0-669-14575-0 (alk. paper) LC Card 86-45884 DDC 331.13 19
HD5709.2.U6 S54 1987

Le phénomène Leclerc . Chavane, Laurence. Paris , c1986. 253 p., [16] p. of plates : ISBN 2-259-01481-X : LC Card 86-186372
HF5469.23.F72 L422 1986

Les Phénomènes de "frontière" dans les pays tropicaux : table ronde organisée en l'honneur de Pierre Monbeig, Paris / IHEAL, 12-15 décembre 1979. Paris : Institut des hautes études de l'Amérique latine, 1981. vii, 456 p. : ill. ; 24 cm. (Travaux & mémoires de l'Institut des hautes études de l'Amérique latine . 34) At head of title: Centre de recherche et documentation sur l'Amérique latine, CREDAL (L.A. 111 du CNRS) English, French, Portuguese, and Spanish. Errata slip inserted. Includes bibliographical references. LC Card 83-122397
1. Land settlement - Tropics. 2. Colonization - Tropics. 3. Agriculture - Tropics. 4. Monbeig, Pierre. 5. Frontier and pioneer life - Tropics. I. Monbeig, Pierre. II. Université de Paris III. Institut des hautes études de l'Amérique latine. III. Centre national de la recherche scientifique (France). Laboratoire associé 111. IV. Series.
HD1131 .P47 1981

Philadelphia bus & rail directory : a guide to Philadelphia via the SEPTA system. [Phila., Pa.] (437 Chestnut St., Suite 209, Philadelphia 19106) : Independence Advertising & Marketing, [c1986] 88 p. : ill. ; 20 cm. Cover title. Includes index. LC Card 87-110517 DDC 388.4/09748/11 19
1. Local transit - Pennsylvania - Philadelphia Metropolitan Area - Handbooks, manuals, etc. I. Title: Philadelphia bus and rail directory.
HE4491.P52 P48 1986

Philadelphia bus and rail directory. Philadelphia bus & rail directory . [Phila., Pa.] (437 Chestnut St., Suite 209, Philadelphia 19106) [c1986] 88 p. : LC Card 87-110517 DDC 388.4/09748/11 19
HE4491.P52 P48 1986

Philadelphia. Intercollegiate Studies Institute. see **Intercollegiate Studies Institute.**

PHILADELPHIA METROPOLITAN AREA (PA.) - ECONOMIC CONDITIONS.
Summers, Anita A. Economic development within the Philadelphia metropolitan area /. Philadelphia , c1987. xiv, 268 p. : ISBN 0-8122-1231-2 (pbk.) LC Card 86-25091 DDC 338.9748/11 19
HC108.P5 S85 1987

PHILADELPHIA METROPOLITAN AREA (PA.) - ECONOMIC POLICY.
Summers, Anita A. Economic development within the Philadelphia metropolitan area /. Philadelphia , c1987. xiv, 268 p. : ISBN 0-8122-1231-2 (pbk.) LC Card 86-25091 DDC 338.9748/11 19
HC108.P5 S85 1987

PHILADELPHIA (PA.) - INDUSTRIES - HISTORY.
Scranton, Philip. Work sights . Philadelphia , 1986. 279 p. : ISBN 0-87722-341-6 : LC Card 85-26132 DDC 305.9/009748/11 19
HC108.P5 S37 1986 ***NYPL [JLF 86-1959]***

PHILADELPHIA (PA.) - INDUSTRIES - PICTORIAL WORKS.
Scranton, Philip. Work sights . Philadelphia , 1986. 279 p. : ISBN 0-87722-341-6 : LC Card 85-26132 DDC 305.9/009748/11 19
HC108.P5 S37 1986 ***NYPL [JLF 86-1959]***

Philanthropie und Steuerpolitik . Paqué, Karl-Heinz. Tübingen , c1986. xv, 417 p. : ISBN 3-16-345154-3 (pbk. : Deut. Bibl.) : LC Card 87-408202 DDC 343.4305/232 344.3035232 19
HJ4720.A45 P36 1986

PHILANTHROPISTS - ILLINOIS - CHICAGO - BIOGRAPHY.
Chavers-Wright, Madrue, 1916- The guarantee . New York , 1985. xix, 425 p. : ISBN 0-931505-02-X (pbk.) : LC Card 84-51854

DDC 338/.04/0924 B 19
HG2463.C48 C48 1985
NYPL [Sc D 86-412]

Chavers-Wright, Madrue, 1916- The guarantee . New York , 1987, c1985. xix, 427 p. : ISBN 0-931505-05-4 : LC Card 86-51447 DDC 338/.04/0924 B 19
HG2463.C48 C48 1987

PHILANTHROPISTS - UNITED STATES - BIOGRAPHY.
Matz, Mary Jane. The many lives of Otto Kahn /. New York [1984] x, 299 p., [8] p. of plates : ISBN 0-918728-36-3 : LC Card 83-26326 DDC 361.7/4/0924 B 19
HV28.K32 M37 1984 ***NYPL [JFD 86-2699]***

Wells, Della Wager. George Waldo Woodruff . [Macon, Ga.] c1987. x, 167 p. : ISBN 0-86554-298-8 LC Card 87-24700 DDC 338/.04/0924 B 19
HC102.5.W66 W45 1987

PHILANTHROPY. see **SOCIAL SERVICE; CHARITIES.**

PHILATELY AND PHILATELISTS. see **POSTAGE STAMPS - COLLECTORS AND COLLECTING.**

PHILIP, DUKE OF BURGUNDY, 1342-1404.
Nieuwenhuysen, A. van (Andrée) Les finances du duc de Bourgogne, Philippe le Hardi (1384-1404) . Bruxelles, Belgique , 1984. 556 p. ; ISBN 2-8004-0838-3 : LC Card 85-160639
HJ1099.B85 N54 1984

Philip Lief Group. Jones, Constance. The 220 best franchises to buy . Toronto , New York , 1987. xi, 459 p. ; ISBN 0-553-34385-8 (pbk.) : LC Card 86-47887 DDC 658.8/708 19
HF5429.235.U5 J66 1987

Philip Rosenberg & Associates. Financial administration . Madison, WI , c1986. vi, 97 p. : LC Card 87-620662 DDC 352.1/09775 19
HJ9338 .F56 1986

Philipp, Hans-Jürgen. Die landwirtschaftliche Modernisierung Saudi-Arabiens im 20. Jahrhundert / Hans-Jürgen Philipp. Hamburg : Deutsches Orient-Institut, im Verbund der Stiftung Deutsches Übersee-Institut, c1984. 132 p. : ill., map ; 30 cm. (Mitteilungen des Deutschen Orient-Instituts . Nr. 25) Bibliography p. 116-132. LC Card 85-166668
1. Agricultural innovations - Government policy - Saudi Arabia. 2. Agriculture and state - Saudi Arabia. 3. Agricultural innovations - Saudi Arabia. I. Title. II. Series.
HD2060.Z8 P48 1984

Philippine budget. Philippines. Office of Budget and Management. 1984 Philippine budget . Malacañang, Manila [1984?] viii, 461 p. : LC Card 87-105421 DDC 354.5990072/2 19
HJ2167 .P46 1984

Philippine Council for Agriculture and Resources Research and Development. International Seminar on Recent Improvements in Goat Production in Asia (1984 : Los Baños, Laguna, Philippines) Goat production in Asia . Los Baños, Laguna, Philippines , Taipei, Taiwan, Republic of China , 1985. viii, 186 p. : LC Card 86-200478
HD9438.G632 A785 1984

Philippine Institute for Development Studies. Economic recovery and long-run growth . Makati, Metro Manila [1986- v. <1 > ; LC Card 86-232161 DDC 338.9599 19
HC453 .E27 1986

Philippine postage stamp handbook, 1854-1982 /. Harradine, Peter W. A. Jefferson, N.C. , c1987. xv, 387 p., [71] p. of plates : ISBN 0-89950-178-8 LC Card 84-43212 DDC 769.569599 19
HE6185.P52 H373 1987

The Philippine State and the Marcos regime . Hawes, Gary, 1950- Ithaca , 1987. 196 p. ; ISBN 0-8014-2012-1 (alk. paper) LC Card 86-29237 DDC 382/.41/09599 19
HD9016.P52 H38 1987

The Philippine sugar trading monopoly . Sa-onoy, Modesto P., 1938- Bacolod City, Philippines , c1984. [31] p. ; LC Card 85-165946
HD9116.P61 S2 1984

Philippines : a framework for economic recovery. Washington, D.C., U. S.A. : World Bank, [1987] xiv, 156 p., [1] leaf of plates : col. map ; 27 cm. (A World Bank country study, 0253-2123) Includes bibliographical references. ISBN 0-8213-0942-0 (pbk.) LC Card 87-19697 DDC 330.599/046 19
1. Philippines - Economic conditions - 1946-. 2. Philippines - Economic policy. I. International Bank for Reconstruction and Development. II. Series.
HC455 .P523 1987

Philippines.
International Labour Organisation. National programme for development and training of manpower for employment, Philippines . Geneva , 1979. ii, 54 p. ; LC Card 81-140367 DDC 331.25/92/09599 19
HD5825.A6 I57 1979

Philippines. Agricultural Estimates and Statistics Branch. Selected statistics on rice & corn . Diliman, Quezon City [1969] xxix, 306 p. : LC Card 87-400545 DDC 338.1/7315/09599021 19
HD9066.P62 S45 1969

Philippines. Bureau of Fisheries and Aquatic Resources. Socio-economic and marketing study of municipal fishing households, Bayawan, Negros Oriental, Philippines. Manila, Philippines [1983] vii, 94, 7 p. : LC Card 86-225887
HD8039.F652 P67 1983

PHILIPPINES - COMMERCE - STATISTICS.
Alburo, Florian A. Trade liberalization experience in the Philippines, 1960-84 /. Makati, Metro Manila [1985] 159 p. : LC Card 87-167251 DDC 382/.09599/0021 19
HF1599 .A43 1985

PHILIPPINES - COMMERCIAL POLICY.
Alburo, Florian A. Trade liberalization experience in the Philippines, 1960-84 /. Makati, Metro Manila [1985] 159 p. : LC Card 87-167251 DDC 382/.09599/0021 19
HF1599 .A43 1985

Bautista, Romeo M., 1941- Production incentives in Philippine agriculture . Washington, D.C., USA , c1987. 78 p. : ISBN 0-89629-061-1 (pbk.) LC Card 87-3233 DDC 338.1/8 19
HD2087 .B38 1987

Snow, Robert T. The bourgeois opposition to export-oriented industrialization in the Philippines /. Diliman, Quezon City, Philippines [1983] 45 p. ; LC Card 85-196519 DDC 382/.3/09599 19
HC453 .S66 1983

PHILIPPINES - ECONOMIC CONDITIONS - 1946-
Economic recovery and long-run growth . Makati, Metro Manila [1986- v. <1 > ; LC Card 86-232161 DDC 338.9599 19
HC453 .E27 1986

Philippines . Washington, D.C., U. S.A. [1987] xiv, 156 p., [1] leaf of plates : ISBN 0-8213-0942-0 (pbk.) LC Card 87-19697 DDC 330.599/046 19
HC455 .P523 1987

Stauffer, Robert B. The Philippines under Marcos . Sydney [1986] 207 p. ; ISBN 0-908470-69-X (pbk.) LC Card 87-123266 DDC 338.9599 19
HD3616.P62 S7 1986

Synthesis, before and beyond February 1986 . [Philippines] , 1986. xiv, 114 p. : ISBN 971-91058-0-1 (pbk.) LC Card 87-112023 DDC 338.9599 19
HC452 .S96 1986

PHILIPPINES - ECONOMIC POLICY.
Broad, Robin. Unequal alliance . Berkeley , c1988. p. cm. ISBN 0-520-05905-0 LC Card 87-10745 DDC 332.1/52 19
HG3881.5.W57 B76 1988

Economic recovery and long-run growth . Makati, Metro Manila [1986- v. <1 > ; LC Card 86-232161 DDC 338.9599 19
HC453 .E27 1986

Giesecke, Leonard F. (Leonard Frederick) History of American economic policy in the Philippines during the American colonial period, 1900-1935 /. New York , 1987. 279 p. ; ISBN 0-8240-8082-3 (alk. paper) : LC Card 87-23786 DDC 337.730599 19
HF1456.5.P6 G53 1987

Philippines . Washington, D.C., U. S.A. [1987] xiv, 156 p., [1] leaf of plates : ISBN 0-8213-0942-0 (pbk.) LC Card 87-19697 DDC 330.599/046 19
HC455 .P523 1987

Snow, Robert T. The bourgeois opposition to export-oriented industrialization in the Philippines /. Diliman, Quezon City, Philippines [1983] 45 p. ; LC Card 85-196519 DDC 382/.3/09599 19
HC453 .S66 1983

Synthesis, before and beyond February 1986 . [Philippines] , 1986. xiv, 114 p. : ISBN 971-91058-0-1 (pbk.) LC Card 87-112023 DDC 338.9599 19
HC452 .S96 1986

Towards recovery and sustainable growth /. [Quezon] [1985] 71 leaves ; LC Card 86-147888 DDC 338.9599 19
HC453 .T68 1985

PHILIPPINES - FOREIGN ECONOMIC RELATIONS - JAPAN.
RP-Japan relations and ADB . Metro Manila, Philippines , 1986. x, 137 p. : ISBN 971-08-3156-9 (pbk.) LC Card 86-211088 DDC 337.520599 19
HF1600.15.J3 R68 1986

PHILIPPINES - FOREIGN ECONOMIC RELATIONS - PACIFIC AREA.
The Pacific lake . Manila, Philippines , c1986. xvi, 248 p. : LC Card 87-111641 DDC 337.1/9 19
HF1600.15.P16 P33 1986

PHILIPPINES - FOREIGN ECONOMIC RELATIONS - UNITED STATES.
Giesecke, Leonard F. (Leonard Frederick) History of American economic policy in the Philippines during the American colonial period, 1900-1935 /. New York , 1987. 279 p. ; ISBN 0-8240-8082-3 (alk. paper) : LC Card 87-23786 DDC 337.730599 19
HF1456.5.P6 G53 1987

Stauffer, Robert B. The Philippines under Marcos . Sydney [1986] 207 p. ; ISBN 0-908470-69-X (pbk.) LC Card 87-123266 DDC 338.9599 19
HD3616.P62 S7 1986

The Philippines in the Third World papers . (ser. no. 39) Snow, Robert T. The bourgeois opposition to export-oriented industrialization in the Philippines /. Diliman, Quezon City, Philippines [1983] 45 p. ; LC Card 85-196519 DDC 382/.3/09599 19
HC453 .S66 1983

PHILIPPINES - INDUSTRIES.
Snow, Robert T. The bourgeois opposition to export-oriented industrialization in the Philippines /. Diliman, Quezon City, Philippines [1983] 45 p. ; LC Card 85-196519 DDC 382/.3/09599 19
HC453 .S66 1983

PHILIPPINES - MANUFACTURES.
Hooley, Richard W., 1925- Productivity growth in Philippine manufacturing . [Manila?] , c1985. ix, 128 p. : LC Card 87-112014 DDC 338.4/769/09599 19
HC460.I52 H66 1985

PHILIPPINES. MINISTRY OF ENERGY.
National energy program, 1986-1990. Metro Manila, Philippines [1986] 64 p. : LC Card 86-207642 DDC 333.79/09599 19
HD9502.P62 N373 1986

Philippines. Office of Budget and Management. 1984 Philippine budget : selected staff papers. Malacañang, Manila : Office of Budget and Management, Office of the President, [1984?] viii, 461 p. : ill. ; 23 cm. Includes bibliographical references. LC Card 87-105421 DDC 354.5990072/2 19
1. Budget - Philippines. 2. Program budgeting - Philippines. I. Title. II. Title: Philippine budget.
HJ2167 .P46 1984

PHILIPPINES - POLITICS AND GOVERNMENT - 1898-1935.
Giesecke, Leonard F. (Leonard Frederick) History of American economic policy in the Philippines during the American colonial period, 1900-1935 /. New York , 1987. 279 p. ; ISBN 0-8240-8082-3 (alk. paper) : LC Card 87-23786 DDC 337.730599 19
HF1456.5.P6 G53 1987

PHILIPPINES - POLITICS AND GOVERNMENT - 1946-
Stauffer, Robert B. The Philippines under Marcos . Sydney [1986] 207 p. ; ISBN 0-908470-69-X (pbk.) LC Card 87-123266 DDC 338.9599 19
HD3616.P62 S7 1986

PHILIPPINES - POLITICS AND GOVERNMENT - 1973-
Hanisch, Rolf, 1942- Der Staat, ländliche Armutsgruppen und legale Bauernbewegung in den Philippinen /. Baden-Baden , 1983. xii, 432 p. ; ISBN 3-7890-0980-6 LC Card 84-143058
HD1537.P5 H35 1983

PHILIPPINES - RURAL CONDITIONS.
Hanisch, Rolf, 1942- Der Staat, ländliche Armutsgruppen und legale Bauernbewegung in den Philippinen /. Baden-Baden , 1983. xii, 432 p. ; ISBN 3-7890-0980-6 LC Card 84-143058
HD1537.P5 H35 1983

The Philippines under Marcos . Stauffer, Robert B. Sydney [1986] 207 p. ; ISBN 0-908470-69-X (pbk.) LC Card 87-123266 DDC 338.9599 19
HD3616.P62 S7 1986

Philipps-Universität Marburg.
Politik gegen die Krise . Marburg , 1985. 157 p. : ISBN 3-924800-01-4 : LC Card 86-119259 DDC 338.9 19
HC59 .P584 1985

Wirtschaftsentwicklung und soziale Sicherheit . Köln , 1983. viii, 146 p. : ISBN 3-452-19567-8 LC Card 84-106615
HG9399.G32 W57 1983

Phillip, George J.
A-Z of industrial relations practices at the workplace / George J. Phillip. 1st ed. Kingston, Jamaica : Kingston Publishers, 1987. xiii, 122 p. : ill. ; 22 cm. Bibliography: p. 122. ISBN 976-625-009-X (pbk.) LC Card 87-403438 DDC 331/.097292 19
1. Industrial relations. 2. Industrial relations - Jamaica. I. Title. II. Title: A to Z of industrial relations practices at the workplace.
HD6971 .P46 1987

Alexander, Carlton. Nation building . Kingston, Jamaica , c1983. 100 p. : LC Card 84-172595 DDC 338.97293 19
HC154 .A79 1983

Phillips, Anne. Durkacz, Victor Edward. Financial planning for new businesses /. Chichester [West Sussex] , New York , c1985. 257 p. : ISBN 0-471-90843-6 (pbk.) : LC Card 85-17927 DDC 658.1/5 19
HG4027.6 .D87 1985 ***NYPL [JLE 86-929]***

PHILLIPS CURVE.
Beaumont, Paul (Paul M.) Regional wage rates [microform] . Iowa City , 1982. 22 p. :
NYPL [*ZT-1564 no.29]

The Determinants of negotiated wage settlements in Canada (1966-1975) . [Ottawa] , Hull, Quebec , c1979. x, 256 p. : ISBN 0-660-10162-9 : LC Card 79-313202 DDC 331.2/971
HD4979 .D44 ***NYPL [JLE 80-447]***

Gröschel, Ulrich. Inflation und Beschäftigung in Volkswirtschaften mit Güter- und Arbeitsmarktkontrakten /. Berlin , c1986. 252 p. ; ISBN 3-428-06149-7 LC Card 87-120985 DDC 331.13/72 19
HD5710.2 .G76 1986

Willke, Gerhard. Globalsteuerung und gespaltene Konjunktur . Leyden ; Boston : xiii, 243 p. : ISBN 3-12-915020-X LC Card 84-181249
HD5779 .W55 1978

PHILLIPS CURVE - CASE STUDIES.
Ibler, Josef. Nominallohnentwicklung in der Bundesrepublik Deutschland . Regensburg , c1986. 256 p. : ISBN 3-924956-18-9 LC Card 87-118941 DDC 331.2/943 19
HD5029 .I2 1986

Phillips, David. Restrepo, Iván. La basura . México, D.F. , 1985. 193 p. : LC Card 86-209151
HD9014.M63 M47 1985

Phillips, David R. Rural housing and the public sector / David R. Phillips and Allan M. Williams. Aldershot, Hampshire, England : Gower ; [Brookfield, Vt. : Distributed by Renouf USA], c1982. viii, 174 p. : ill., maps ; 23 cm. Distributor statement from label on fly leaf. Includes index. Bibliography: p. 163-172. Library's copy wanting distributor statement label. ISBN 0-566-00456-9 : LC Card 82-134413 DDC 352.7/5/0941 19
1. Housing, Rural - England - South Hams (Devon). 2. Housing authorities - England - South Hams (Devon). 3. Housing, Rural - Great Britain. I. Williams, Allan M. II. Title.
HD7289.G82 S687 1982
NYPL [JLD 83-2605]

Phillips, David T. Profiting from the insurance revolution / David T. Phillips. 1st ed. Alexandria, VA (1101 King St., Suite 400, Alexandria 22314) : KCI Communications, c1987. vii, 120, 18 p. : forms ; 28 cm. LC Card 87-401086 DDC 368.3/2/00973 19
1. Insurance, Life - United States. I. Title.
HG8951 .P47 1987

Phillips, Jack J., 1945- Recruiting, training, and retaining new employees : managing the transition from college to work / Jack J. Phillips, with the assistance of Sharon L. Oswald.1st ed. San Francisco : Jossey-Bass Publishers, 1987. xxii, 324 p. ; 24 cm. (The Jossey-Bass management series) Bibliography: p. 301-311. Includes index. ISBN 1-555-42042-7 (alk. paper) LC Card 86-46332 DDC 658.3/14 19
1. Recruiting of employees - United States. 2. Employees, Training of - United States. 3. College graduates - Employment - United States. I. Oswald, Sharon L. II. Title. III. Series.
HF5549.5.R44 P49 1987

Phillips, John A. S. Deutsch-englische Komödie der Irrungen um Südwestafrika : eine Studie zu Bismarcks Kolonialpolitik und deren Folgen / John A.S. Phillips. Pfaffenhofen, West Germany : Afrika Verlag, 1986. 184 p., [12] p. of plates : ill. ; 21 cm. Summary in German and English. Bibliography: p. 157-169. Includes index. ISBN 3-87010-105-9 LC Card 87-146587 DDC 338.4/76686366/09688 19
1. Guano industry - Namibia - History - 19th century. 2. Germans - Namibia - History - 19th century. 3. British - Namibia - History - 19th century. 4. Namibia - History - 1884-1915. 5. Lüderitz Region (Namibia) - History. I. Title.
HD9484.G9 N366 1986

Phillips, John L., 1923-
How to think about statistics / John L. Phillips, Jr. [3rd ed.]. New York : W.H. Freeman, c1988. xiv, 198 p. : ill. ; 24 cm. Rev. ed. of: Statistical thinking. 2nd ed. c1982. Bibliography: p. [191]. Includes index. ISBN 0-7167-1923-1 (pbk.) LC Card 87-15056 DDC 519.5 19
1. Social sciences - Statistical methods. 2. Psychometrics. 3. Statistics. I. Phillips, John L., 1923- Statistical thinking. II. Title.
HA29 .P517 1988

Statistical thinking. Phillips, John L., 1923- How to think about statistics / John L. Phillips, Jr. [3rd ed.]. New York , c1988. xiv, 198 p. : ISBN 0-7167-1923-1 (pbk.) LC Card 87-15056 DDC 519.5 19
HA29 .P517 1988

Phillips, Judith A. Ludwick, David E. The competitive position of U. S. and European Community pork and the United States and third-country markets . Washington, DC [1985] xxiii, 341 p. : LC Card 86-601366 DDC 380.1/4566492/0973 19
HD9435.U52 L83 1985

Phillips, Patrick. Inside the new gilt-edged market / Patrick Phillips. 2nd ed. Cambridge, England ; Wolfeboro, N.H. : Woodhead-Faulkner, 1987. p. cm. Includes index. ISBN 0-85941-346-2 : LC Card 86-24692 DDC 332.63/232/0941 19
1. Securities - Great Britain. I. Title.
HG5432 .P48 1987

Phillips Publishing. The Videotex marketplace. Bethesda, Md. , c1984. 203 p. : ISBN 0-934960-17-8 (pbk.) : LC Card 84-201507 DDC 384 19
HD9696.D383 U638 1984
NYPL [JSF 86-430]

Phillips, Steven R. Solutions : a guide to better problem solving / Steven R. Phillips, William H. Bergquist. San Diego, Calif. : University Associates, c1987. xi, 127 p. ; 28 cm. ISBN 0-88390-205-2 (pbk.) : LC Card 87-5894 DDC 658.4/03 19
1. Problem solving. I. Bergquist, William H. II. Title.
HD30.29 .P48 1987

Le philosophe plébéien /. Gauny, Gabriel, 1806-1889. [Selections. 1983.] Paris , Saint-Denis , c1983. 205 p. ; ISBN 2-7071-1420-0 : LC Card 84-105473
HD4853 .G382 1983

Philosophical and radical thought in marketing / [edited by] A. Fuat Firat, Nikhilesh Dholakia, Richard P. Bagozzi. Lexington, Mass. : Lexington Books, c1987. xxi, 392 p. : ill. ; 24 cm. Includes bibliographies. ISBN 0-669-14301-4 (alk. paper) LC Card 86-45791 DDC 658.8 19
1. Marketing. 2. Consumers. I. Firat, A. Fuat. II. Dholakia, Nikhilesh, 1947-. III. Bagozzi, Richard P.
HF5415 .P485 1987

"Philosophical and social aspects of science and technology" series .
(1) Moving towards the year 2000 . Moscow , 1987. 204 p. ; LC Card 87-163642 DDC 333.7 19
HC79.E5 M69 1987

Philosophie und Ökonomie, oder, Das Exempel Bernstein /. Tetzel, Manfred. Berlin , 1984. 187 p. : LC Card 84-166815
HB107.B52 T48 1984

PHILOSOPHY - CONGRESSES.
Economics and philosophy /. Tübingen , 1985. ix, 284 p. : ISBN 3-16-244944-8 LC Card 85-236925 DDC 330 19
HB72 .E27 1985 ***NYPL [JFE 86-2159]***

Philosophy, ideology, and social science . Mészáros, István, 1930- Brighton, Sussex , 1986. xix, 284 p. ; ISBN 0-85527-717-3
NYPL [JLD 87-1334]

PHILOSOPHY, MARXIST.
Haug, Wolfgang Fritz. Pluraler Marxismus . Berlin , 1985- v. ; ISBN 3-88619-303-9 (Bd. 1) LC Card 86-119293 DDC 355.43/09/04 19
HX40 .H27 1985 ***NYPL [JLK 86-57]***

PHILOSOPHY, MORAL. see **ETHICS.**

PHILOTHEOS, BISHOP OF SALONA.
Dokos, Kōnstantinos. Hē Sterea Hellas kata ton Henetotourkikon polemon, 1684-1699 kai ho Salōnōn Philotheos /. Athēnai , 1985. 255 p. ; LC Card 86-211599
HB2092.5.A3 D64 1985

Philp, Norman E. The cash incentive : the economic response of semi-subsistent craftworkers in Papua New Guinea / Norman E. Philp. Canberra : National Centre for Development Studies, Australian National University, 1986. xii, 135 p. : ill. ; 25 cm. (Pacific research monograph. 13) Bibliography: p. 131-135. ISBN 0-86784-984-3 (pbk.) LC Card 87-150813
1. Cottage industries - Papua New Guinea. 2. Hand weaving - Economic aspects - Papua New Guinea. 3. Subsistence economy - Papua New Guinea. 4. Papua New Guinea - Economic conditions. 5. Artisans - Papua New Guinea. I. Title. II. Series.
HD2346.P37 P46 1986

Phimister, I. R. (Ian R.) An economic and social history of Zimbabwe, 1890-1948 : capital accumulation and class struggle / Ian Phimister. London ; New York : Longman, 1987. p. cm. Includes index. ISBN 0-582-64423-2 LC Card 87-12471 DDC 330.96891/02 19
1. Saving and investment - Zimbabwe - History. 2. Social conflict - Zimbabwe - History. 3. Zimbabwe - Economic conditions - To 1965. 4. Zimbabwe - Social conditions - 1890-1965. I. Title.
HC910.Z9 S36 1987

Phipps, Tim. Agriculture and the environment /. Washington, D.C. , c1986. xvii, 298 p. : ISBN 0-915707-33-0 (pbk.) : LC Card 87-43010 DDC 363.7/31 19
HD1755 .P47 1986

Phlips, Louis. Oligopoly, competition, and welfare /. Oxford, OX, UK , New York, NY, USA , 1985. 191 p. : ISBN 0-631-14479-X (pbk.) LC Card 85-11200 DDC 338.8/2 19
HD2757.3 .O44 1985 ***NYPL [JLE 86-1961]***

Phoenix and the lame lion . Liu, Alan P. L., 1937- Stanford, Calif. , c1987. x, 182 p. ; ISBN 0-8179-8581-6 LC Card 87-13555 DDC 338.951 19
HC430.5 .L568 1987

Phon kānphatthanā nai raya khrng Phæn Phatthanā-- Chabap thī 5, Ph Thailand. Samnakngān Khana Kammakān Phatthanākān

Sētthakit læ Sangkhom hæ̆ng Chāt. [Bangkok] [2529 i.e. 1986] 2, 215, 25 p. ; LC Card 86-915872
HC445 .T448 1986

The phone book . Klein, Jean H., 1938- Norfolk , c1987. p. cm. ISBN 0-89865-542-0 (pbk.) : LC Card 87-20897 DDC 651.7/3 19
HF5541.T4 K56 1987

Phone power . Gross, LeRoy. New York, N.Y. , c1987. xiii, 208 p. : ISBN 0-13-664350-7 LC Card 87-7740 DDC 332.6/068/8 19
HG4621 .G776 1987

Phonewriting . Simon, Sam, 1945- [Washington, D.C.] , c1986. iv, 92 p., [4] p. of plates : ISBN 0-943444-03-9 (pbk.) LC Card 86-214171 DDC 004.6 19
HE6239.E54 S56 1986

Photocopies des vignettes françaises de Croix-Rouge. Granger, Louis. Catalogue des vignettes françaises de Croix-Rouge /. [Aurillac] [1964] 117 p. ; LC Card 68-39071
HE6184.S42 G7 1964

PHOTOGRAPHY - AESTHETICS. see **PHOTOGRAPHY, ARTISTIC.**

PHOTOGRAPHY, ARTISTIC - EXHIBITIONS.
Atget, Géniaux, Vert . Paris [1984] 63, [1] p. : ISBN 2-901414-09-5 : LC Card 86-137985
HF5459.F8 A87 1984 ***NYPL [MFW 87-159]***

PHOTOGRAPHY, CRIME. see **PHOTOGRAPHY, LEGAL.**

PHOTOGRAPHY, FORENSIC. see **PHOTOGRAPHY, LEGAL.**

PHOTOGRAPHY, LEGAL - CASE STUDIES.
Kizorek, Bill. Disability or deception /. [Naperville, Ill., USA] (Suite 12, 6 S 235 Steeple Run Dr., Naperville 60540) [c1986] 140 p. : LC Card 86-206432 DDC 363.2/5 19
HD7105.25.U6 K59 1986

PHOTOGRAPHY, LENSLESS. see **HOLOGRAPHY.**

PHOTOGRAPHY, PICTORIAL. see **PHOTOGRAPHY, ARTISTIC.**

PHOTOGRAPHY, POLICE. see **PHOTOGRAPHY, LEGAL.**

Phrankos, Dionysios M., 1926- Hoi makrochronies exelixeis tou oikonomika mē energou plēthysmou tēs Hellados / tou Dionysiou M. Phrankou. Athēna : Ethniko Kentro Koinōnikōn Ereunōn, 1983. 148 p. : ill. ; 24 cm. Bibliography: p. [124]-125. LC Card 85-152730
1. Unemployment - Greece. 2. Unemployed - Greece. I. Ethniko Kentro Koinōnikōn Ereunōn (Greece). II. Title.
HD5811.83.A6 P47 1983

Phūmisāt sētthakit kh Barton, Thomas Frank, 1905- [Bangkok] 2500 [1957] 2, 5, 392 p. : LC Card 83-921251
HC445 .B36 1957

Phylaktis, Kate. Finance. Oxford [Oxfordshire] , New York , 1987. xiii, 495 p. ; ISBN 0-08-034780-0 : LC Card 87-7247 DDC 332/.0941 19
HG186.G7 F53 1987

Physica-Schriften zur Betriebswirtschaft .
(Bd. 15) Wondrak, Bernhard. Management von Zinsänderungschancen und -risiken /. Heidelberg , c1986. xv, 254 p. : ISBN 3-7908-0341-3 LC Card 86-213976
HG6024.5 .W66 1986

(10) Wahl, Jack. Informationsbewertung und -effizienz auf dem Kapitalmarkt /. Würzburg , 1983. 211 p. : ISBN 3-7908-0308-1 LC Card 84-154688
HG4515 .W34 1983

(17) Rothacker, Hartmut. Zeitstetige Bewertungsmodelle für Tilgungsanleihen . Heidelberg , c1986. xxiv, 350 p. : ISBN 3-7908-0343-X LC Card 86-222052
HG4523 .R68 1986

(19) Jäger, Hubert. Die Bewertung von konzerninternen Lieferungen und Leistungen in der operativen Planung /. Heidelberg , c1987. xii, 345 p. ; ISBN 3-7908-0367-7 LC Card 87-145912 DDC 658.1/5/0943 19
HG4156 .J336 1987

PHYSICAL DISTRIBUTION OF GOODS - DIRECTORIES.
The Standard handbook of industrial distributors. Fairfield, CT, USA , c1987- v. <1-2 > ; ISBN 0-917408-02-0 (pbk. : v. 1) LC Card 86-73258 DDC 380.1/456218/025 19
HD9680.A2 S72 1987

PHYSICAL DISTRIBUTION OF GOODS - GOVERNMENT POLICY - INDIA.
Ojha, Ghanshyam Das, 1947- Organisation & management of public distribution system /. Delhi, India , 1987. x, 235 p. ; LC Card 87-900491 DDC 381/.1/0954 19
HF5415.12.I5 O44 1987

PHYSICAL DISTRIBUTION OF GOODS - ITALY.
Fruscio, Dario. Il sistema distributivo italiano . [Milano] , 1983. vii, 184 p. ; LC Card 83-233439 DDC 380.1/0945 19
HF5415.6 .F78 1983 ***NYPL [JLE 86-3650]***

Industria e commercio . Milano, Italy , c1985. 194 p. : LC Card 86-112174 DDC 658.7/88/0945 19
HF5415.12.I8 I53 1985 ***NYPL [JLD 87-432]***

L'Affiliazione commerciale . Milano , 1986. 100 p. : ***NYPL [JLD 87-531]***

PHYSICAL DISTRIBUTION OF GOODS - MANAGEMENT.
Ballou, Ronald H., 1937- Basic business logistics . Englewood Cliffs, N.J. , c1987. x, 438 p. : ISBN 0-13-057464-3 LC Card 86-22691 DDC 658.7/88 19
HF5415.7 .B338 1987

PHYSICAL DISTRIBUTION OF GOODS - MANAGEMENT - DATA PROCESSING.
Barrett, Colin. The practical handbook of computerization for distribution managers /. Washington , c1987. xvi, 317 p. ; ISBN 0-87408-040-1 LC Card 86-51299 DDC 658.7/8/0285 19
HF5415.7 .B36 1987

PHYSICAL DISTRIBUTION OF GOODS - NEPAL - BIRENDRANAGAR.
Basic needs delivery system in Birendranagar, Surkhet /. Kathmandu , 1985. 143, [23], iii p. (some folded) ; LC Card 86-903561 DDC 338.9549/6 19
HF5415.12.N35 B36 1985

PHYSICAL DISTRIBUTION OF GOODS - RUSSIAN S.F.S.R. - SIBERIA.
Bernval'd, A. R. (Arngol'd Reĭngol'dovich) Regional'nye problemy tovarnogo obrashchenii͡a . Novosibirsk , 1984. 207 p. ; LC Card 85-104041
HF5415.6 .B46 1984 ***NYPL [*QIP 87-2770]***

PHYSICAL DISTRIBUTION OF GOODS - RUSSIAN S.F.S.R. - SOVIET FAR EAST.
Bernval'd, A. R. (Arngol'd Reĭngol'dovich) Regional'nye problemy tovarnogo obrashchenii͡a . Novosibirsk , 1984. 207 p. ; LC Card 85-104041
HF5415.6 .B46 1984 ***NYPL [*QIP 87-2770]***

PHYSICAL DISTRIBUTION OF GOODS - SOVIET UNION.
Tret'i͡ak, V. P. (Vladimir Petrovich) Pri͡amye khozi͡aĭstvennye svi͡azi v sot͡sialisticheskoĭ ėkonomike /. Leningrad , 1986. 141 p. : LC Card 87-146709
HF5415.6 .T74 1986

PHYSICAL DISTRIBUTION OF GOODS - UNITED STATES.
An evaluation of industrial purchasing and distribution trends . Cleveland, Ohio (1230 Keith Bldg., Cleveland 44115) , c1985. 173 p. : LC Card 86-219582 DDC 658.7 19
HD39.5 .E93 1985

PHYSICAL GEOGRAPHY - ARGENTINA - COMAHUE REGION.
Reboratti, Carlos E. Condicionantes físicos del asentamiento humano en el norte de la Patagonia /. Buenos Aires , 1982. 47 p. : LC Card 83-185201
HD479.C57 R43 1982

PHYSICAL GEOGRAPHY - BRAZIL - RIO GRANDE DO SUL.
Silva, J. Resende. A fronteira do sul . Rio de Janeiro , 1922. 723 p., [1] leaf of plates : LC Card 85-223002
HF3409.R56 S55 1922

PHYSICAL GEOGRAPHY - BRITISH COLUMBIA - SLOCAN RIVER VALLEY.
Biophysical resources of the Slocan Valley /. Victoria, B.C. , 1982. ix, 102 p. : ISBN 0-7718-8310-2 (pbk.) LC Card 84-117204 DDC 333.7/09711/43 19
HC117.B8 B46 1982

PHYSICAL GEOGRAPHY - ICELAND.
Glässer, Ewald. Island /. Darmstadt , 1986. xii, 315 p., [20] p. of plates (4 folded) : ISBN 3-534-01225-9 LC Card 87-101040
HC360.5 .G57 1986

PHYSICAL GEOGRAPHY - MEXICO - QUINTANA ROO (STATE)
Quintana Roo . Puerto Morelos, Q.R. , 1980. iv, 203 p., [32] leaves of plates : LC Card 84-222175
HC137.Q5 Q55 1980

PHYSICAL GEOGRAPHY - MEXICO - STATES.
Méndez Morales, José Silvestre. México por entidades federativas /. México, D.F. , c1986. 318 p., [32] p. of plates : ISBN 968-493-098-4 LC Card 87-400185 DDC 330.972/083 19
HC135 .M52524 1986

PHYSICAL GEOGRAPHY - SOUTH AFRICA - NATAL.
Natal (South Africa). South Coast Regional Planning Committee. Draft regional plan for the South Coast. Pietermaritzburg, Natal, South Africa , 1974. 144 p., [2] folded leaves of plates : ISBN 0-909232-03-2 (pbk.) LC Card 84-246771
HC517.N3 A44 vol. 29 HC905.Z7N37

PHYSICAL GEOGRAPHY - SPAIN - ESTREMADURA.
Gurría Gascón, José Luis. El paisaje de montaña en Extremadura . Cáceres [1985?] 273 p. : ISBN 84-600-3949-8 LC Card 87-111451
HC387.E7 G87 1985

PHYSICAL GEOGRAPHY - SPAIN - SEGURA MOUNTAINS REGION.
Ruiz Avilés, Pedro. Estudio integral de la Sierra de Segura . [Jaén] [1985] 130 leaves : ISBN 84-505-1249-2 LC Card 86-187282
HC387.S438 R85 1985

Physical models and equilibrium methods in programming and economics /. Razumikhin, Boris Sergeevich. [Fizicheskie modeli i metody teorii ravnovesii͡a v programmirovanii i ėkonomike. English.] Dordrecht ; Boston : xv, 351 p. : ISBN 90-277-1644-7 LC Card 83-17791 DDC 330/.0724 19
HB135 .R3913 1984 ***NYPL [JSD 86-491]***

Physical planning inputs in national and state development plans : workshop, 9-14 July 1984. Ibadan : Urban and Regional Planning Programme, Dept. of Geography, University of Ibadan : Physical Planning Division, Nigerian Institute of Social and Economic Research, [1984?] v, 312 p. : ill. ; 29 cm. Lectures delivered at the Workshop on Physical Development Planning. Includes bibliographies. LC Card 87-400745 DDC 338.9669 19
1. Nigeria - Economic policy - Congresses. 2. Nigeria - Social policy - Congresses. I. University of Ibadan. Urban and Regional Planning Programme. II. Nigerian Institute of Social and Economic Research. Physical Planning Division. III. Workshop on Physical Development Planning (1984 : Ibadan, Nigeria).
HC1055 .P488 1984

Physical security : readings from Security management magazine / edited by Shari Mendelson Gallery. Boston : Butterworths, c1986. xii, 409 p. : ill. ; 24 cm. Includes bibliographical references. ISBN 0-409-95105-6 (pbk.) LC Card 85-29083 DDC 658.4/73 19
1. Private security services - Management. 2. Security systems. I. Gallery, Shari Mendelson. II. Security management.
HD38 .P49 1986 ***NYPL [JLE 86-3699]***

PHYSICALLY HANDICAPPED - EMPLOYMENT - UNITED STATES.
The Role of the sheltered workshops in the rehabilitation of the severely handicapped. New York , 1976. xxiv, 467 p. ;
NYPL [JLF 86-1287]

PHYSICIANS - CANADA - ATTITUDES.
Taylor, Malcolm G. (Malcolm Gordon) Medical perspectives on Canadian Medicare . Downsview, Ont. , 1984. vii, 201 p. : ISBN

0-919762-57-3 (pbk.) LC Card 87-673411
HD7102.C2 T34x 1984

PHYSICIANS, FOREIGN - ETHIOPIA - BIOGRAPHY.
Harris, Myles F. Breakfast in hell . New York , c1987. 271 p. ; ISBN 0-671-63272-8 : LC Card 86-25504 DDC 363.8/83/0963 19
HC845.Z9 F345 1987

PHYSICIANS - MEXICO - POLITICAL ACTIVITY.
Cleaves, Peter S. Professions and the state . Tucson , c1987. xv, 147 p. : ISBN 0-8165-1016-4 (alk. paper) LC Card 87-5911 DDC 331.7/12/0972 19
HD8038.M6 C55 1987

The physiocrats . Higgs, Henry, 1864-1940. New York, N.Y. , 1988. p. cm. ISBN 0-678-00398-X LC Card 87-17066 DDC 330.15/2 19
HB93 .H6 1988

PHYSIOGRAPHY. see **GEOLOGY; PHYSICAL GEOGRAPHY.**

The physiology of industry . Mummery, A. F. (Albert Frederick), 1855-1895. Fairfield, NJ , 1988. p. cm. ISBN 0-678-00673-3 LC Card 87-17943 DDC 330.1 19
HB171 .M95 1988

Physische und psychische Erkrankungen bei Arbeitsmigranten in der BRD . Görtz, Vera. Gelsenkirchen [1986?] 250 p. : ISBN 3-89049-007-7 LC Card 87-141880 DDC 331.6/2/0943 19
HD8458.A2 G67 1986

Pi.Ā'ī.Ae. ṭayyāre kā ighvā, dahshat gardī kī intihā, 'amle aur musāfiroṇ ke ta'assurāt, Pishāvar, 18 Mārc, 1981. Islāmābād : Maṭbū'āt-i Pākistān, [1981] 27 p. ; 27 cm. In Urdu. LC Card 82-930104
1. Hijacking of aircraft - Pakistan. I. Pakistan International Airlines.
HE9871.5.Z7 H56 1981

Piac és pénz a modern gazdaságban /. Bokros, Lajos. Budapest , 1985. 340, [1] p. ; ISBN 963-221-551-6 : LC Card 86-185991
HB95 .B65 1985

Piacentini, Paolo, 1948- Palazzi, Paolo. Domanda di lavoro e produttività nell'industria italiana /. Bologna , c1980. 177 p. ; LC Card 82-156294 DDC 331.13/7945 19
HD5784 .P28 1980 ***NYPL [JLD 86-2811]***

Il piano del lavoro /. De Michelis, G. (Gianni) Roma , 1986. xii, 267 p. : ISBN 88-420-2753-7 : LC Card 86-219772
HD8481 .D42 1986

PIANO TRADE. see **MUSIC TRADE.**

Pi͡atibratova, V. N. (Vera Nikolaevna)
I͡Usufovich, B. E. (Boris Efimovich) Sovershenstvovanie operativnogo upravlenii͡a osnovnym proizvodstvom mashinostroitel'nogo predprii͡atii͡a /. Moskva , 1982. 91 p. : LC Card 82-204954
HD9705.S595 I94 1982

Pi͡atiletka, god vtoroĭ : oni otvechai͡ut delom : [ocherki / redaktory V.I. Chernetsova, I͡U.V. Sli͡usareva]. Petrozavodsk : Izd-vo "Karelii͡a", 1977. 101 p. ; 16 cm. LC Card 81-161405
1. Karel'skai͡a A.S.S.R. (R.S.F.S.R.) - Economic conditions. 2. Labor and laboring classes - Russian S.F.S.R. - Karel'skai͡a A.S.S.R. I. Chernetsova, V. I. II. Sli͡usareva, I͡U. V.
HC337.K265 P52 1977

PIAUÍ (BRAZIL) - ECONOMIC CONDITIONS.
Mott, Luiz R. B. (Luiz Roberto de Barros) Piauí colonial . [Teresina] [1985] 142 p. : LC Card 86-131892
HC188.P5 M67 1985

PIAUÍ, BRAZIL - HISTORY.
Mott, Luiz R. B. (Luiz Roberto de Barros) Piauí colonial . [Teresina] [1985] 142 p. : LC Card 86-131892
HC188.P5 M67 1985

PIAUÍ (BRAZIL) - POPULATION - HISTORY.
Mott, Luiz R. B. (Luiz Roberto de Barros) Piauí colonial . [Teresina] [1985] 142 p. : LC Card 86-131892
HC188.P5 M67 1985

PIAUÍ (BRAZIL) - SOCIAL CONDITIONS.
Mott, Luiz R. B. (Luiz Roberto de Barros) Piauí colonial . [Teresina] [1985] 142 p. : LC Card 86-131892
HC188.P5 M67 1985

Piauí colonial . Mott, Luiz R. B. (Luiz Roberto de Barros) [Teresina] [1985] 142 p. : LC Card 86-131892
HC188.P5 M67 1985

Piazzo, Pietrenzo, 1935- Una valutazione intersettoriale costi benefici estesa al territorio : note metodologiche e sintesi delle elaborazioni di Cassa per il Mezzogiorno e OTE per il progetto speciale n. 12 / Pietrenzo Piazzo. Roma : Edizioni dell'Ateneo, c1984. viii, 224 p., 6 folded leaves of plates : maps ; 24 cm. Bibliography: p. 223-224. LC Card 84-250428
1. Infrastructure (Economics) - Italy - Abruzzi. 2. Regional planning - Italy - Abruzzi. 3. Land use - Italy - Abruzzi. I. Title.
HC307.A2 P53 1984

Picado Hidalgo, Roberto. La inflación y la política económica, el caso de Costa Rica : ponencia / presentada por Roberto Picado Hidalgo, a nombre del presidente ejecutivo del Banco Central de Costa Rica, en la XL Reunión de Gobernadores de Bancos Centrales Latinoamericanos y de España, celebrada en Guadalajara, México, entre el 11 y 12 de abril de 1985. [San José] : Banco Central de Costa Rica, 1985. 16, 20 p. ; 28 cm. (Serie "Comentarios sobre asuntos económicos" . no. 55) Cover title. At head of title: Licda. Rosa Roig de González, Lic. Carlos Vega. LC Card 86-219388
1. Costa Rica - Economic Policy. 2. Costa Rica - Economic conditions - 1948-. 3. Inflation (Finance) - Costa Rica. I. Roig de González, Rosa. II. Vega, Carlos, Lic. III. Title. IV. Series.
HC143 .P52 1985

Picaper, Jean-Paul, 1938- Le pont invisible : ces radios et télévisions que l'Est veut réduire au silence / Jean-Paul Picaper. Paris : Plon, c1986. 345 p. ; 24 cm. ISBN 2-259-01619-7; 0-225-91619-7 : LC Card 87-147835
1. International broadcasting - Europe. 2. International broadcasting - Europe, Eastern. I. Title.
HE8697.45.E87 P52 1986

Picard, Pierre. Théorie du déséquilibre et politique économique / Pierre Picard. Paris : Economica, 1985. 253 p. : ill. ; 24 cm. (Collection Approfondissement de la connaissance économique) Bibliography: p. [243]-250. ISBN 2-7178-0877-9 : LC Card 86-109716 DDC 339.5 19
1. Equilibrium (Economics). 2. Economic policy - Mathematical models. I. Series: Collection Approfondissement de la connaissance économique. II. Title.
HB145 .P53 1985

Picchi, Fernando. Economics and business : Dizionario enciclopedico economico e commerciale inglese italiano, italiano inglese / di Fernando Picchi.1a ed. Bologna : Zanichelli, 1986. 1333 p. ; 25 cm. ISBN 88-08-04550-1 LC Card 86-201141 DDC 330/.03/51 19
1. Economics - Dictionaries. 2. Economics - Dictionaries - Italian. 3. Commerce - Dictionaries. 4. Commerce - Dictionaries - Italian. 5. Business - Dictionaries. 6. Business - Dictionaries - Italian. 7. English language - Dictionaries - Italian. 8. Italian language - Dictionaries - English. I. Title. II. Title: Dizionario enciclopedico economico e commerciale inglese italiano, italiano inglese.
HB61 .P49 1986

Piccioni, Alessandro. La Cgil nei suoi congressi / Alessandro Piccioni ; prefazione di Sergio Turone. Roma : Ediesse, c1986. 168 p. ; 21 cm. (Primopiano) LC Card 87-103188
1. Confederazione generale italiana del lavoro - History - 20th century. 2. Trade-unions - Italy - History - 20th century. I. Title.
HD8473 .P53 1986

Pick, Albert. Standard catalog of world paper money / by Albert Pick ; Colin R. Bruce II, Neil Shafer, cataloging editor & market analyst. 5th ed. Iola, Wis. : Krause Publications ; München : Battenberg Verlag, c1986. 2 v. : chiefly ill. ; 29 cm. Bibliography: v. 2, p. 34-35. Includes indexes. CONTENTS. - v. 1. Specialized issues -- v. 2. General issues. ISBN 0-87341-087-4 (v. 1) LC Card 86-222186 DDC 769.5/5/075 19
1. Paper money - Catalogs. I. Bruce, Colin R. II. Shafer, Neil. III. Title. IV. Title: World paper money.
HG353 .P543 1986

Pick, Franz.
The U. S. dollar : an advance obituary / by Dr. Franz Pick.3rd ed. Bethel, CT : Silver & Gold Report, c1986. xvi, 103 p., [1] folded leaf of plates : ill. (1 col.) ; 28 cm. Rev. ed. of: The United States dollar, 1940-1980. ISBN 0-916373-04-5 (pbk.): LC Card 86-210094 DDC 332.4/973 19
1. Money - United States - History. 2. Inflation (Finance) - United States - History. 3. Devaluation of currency - United States - History. I. Pick, Franz. United States dollar, 1940-1980. II. Title. III. Title: US dollar.
HG539 .P5 1986

United States dollar, 1940-1980. Pick, Franz. The U. S. dollar : an advance obituary / by Dr. Franz Pick.3rd ed. Bethel, CT , c1986. xvi, 103 p., [1] folded leaf of plates : ISBN 0-916373-04-5 (pbk.): LC Card 86-210094 DDC 332.4/973 19
HG539 .P5 1986

Pick, Hartmut.
Entwicklungspolitik im Spannungsfeld von Solidarität und Eigeninteresse . Stuttgart , New York , 1986. 155 p. ; ISBN 3-437-50306-5 LC Card 87-408212 DDC 338.91/43/01724 19
HC60 .E527 1986

Kontinuität und Wandel in vier Jahrzehnten deutscher Wirtschaftspolitik /. Stuttgart , New York , 1986. 111 p. ; ISBN 3-437-50310-3 LC Card 87-116017 DDC 338.943 19
HC286.5 .K618 1986

Steuerpolitik für die soziale Marktwirtschaft . Stuttgart , New York , 1986. 85 p. ; ISBN 3-437-50311-1 LC Card 87-122642 DDC 336.2/00943 19
HJ2687 .S73 1986

Pickens, T. Boone (Thomas Boone) Boone / T. Boone Pickens, Jr. Boston : Houghton Mifflin, 1987. xii, 304 p., [8] p. of plates : ill. ; 24 cm. "A Richard Todd book." Includes index. ISBN 0-395-41433-4 : LC Card 86-27648 DDC 338.7/6223382/0924 B 19
1. Pickens, T. Boone (Thomas Boone). 2. Mesa Petroleum Co. - History. 3. Industrialists - Texas - Biography. 4. Petroleum industry and trade - United States - History. I. Title.
HD9570.P53 A3 1987

PICKENS, T. BOONE (THOMAS BOONE)
Pickens, T. Boone (Thomas Boone) Boone /. Boston , 1987. xii, 304 p., [8] p. of plates : ISBN 0-395-41433-4 : LC Card 86-27648 DDC 338.7/6223382/0924 B 19
HD9570.P53 A3 1987

PICKLING. see **CANNING AND PRESERVING.**

Pickman, James. Producing lower income housing . Washington, D.C. , c1986. xiv, 373 p. ; ISBN 0-87179-533-7 (pbk.) LC Card 86-26424 DDC 363.5/ 19
HD7288.78.U5 P76 1986

Picot, W. Garnett. The changing labour market for postsecondary graduates, 1975-1984 / W. Garnett Picot and Ted Wannell, Doug Lynd. Ottawa : Statistics Canada, c1987. 86, 94 p. : ill. ; 23 cm. Added t.p. in French: L'évolution du marché du travail pour les diplômés du postsecondaire. English and French. "Catalogue 89-518"--Cover. ISBN 0-660-52896-7 (pbk.) : LC Card 87-169612 DDC 331.11/423 19
1. College graduates - Employment - Canada. I. Wannell, Ted. II. Lynd, D. III. Title. IV. Title: Evolution du marché du travail pour les diplômés du postsecondaire.
HD6278.C3 P52 1987

PICTORIAL PHOTOGRAPHY. see **PHOTOGRAPHY, ARTISTIC.**

PICTURE POST-CARDS. see **POSTAL CARDS.**

PIDS monograph series, 0115-9194 .
(no. 9) Hooley, Richard W., 1925- Productivity growth in Philippine manufacturing . [Manila?] , c1985. ix, 128 p. : LC Card 87-112014 DDC 338.4/769/09599 19
HC460.I52 H66 1985

PIECE-WORK - BRAZIL - RIO DE JANEIRO.
Abreu, Alice R. de Paiva. O avesso da moda . São Paulo , 1986. 302 p. ; LC Card 87-129109 DDC 331.4/887/098153 19
HD6073.C62 B62 1986

Piedmont. see **Piemonte, Italy.**

Piedmont Carolinas, where wealth awaits you. Charlotte, N.C. : Industrial Dept. of the Duke Power Co., [1930?] 47 p. : ill ; 22 cm. LC Card 85-666462
1. North Carolina - Economic conditions. 2. South Carolina - Economic conditions. I. Duke Power Company. Industrial Dept.
HC107.N8 P53x 1930

Piedmont, Italy (Region) see **Piemonte, Italy.**

Piel, Manfred, 1945-
[Staatsverschuldung, Schicksalsfrage der Nation]
Staatsverschuldung, Hintergründe und Probleme / von Manfred Piel und Diethard B. Simmert. Stuttgart : Deutscher Sparkassenverlag, [1982] 128 p. ; 22 cm. (Informationsdienst der Sparkassen und Landesbanken/Girozentralen) Previously published as: Staatsverschuldung, Schicksalsfrage der Nation? 1981. Bibliography: p. 126-128. LC Card 83-118137
1. Debts, Public - Germany, West. 2. Germany, West - Economic conditions - 1974-. I. Simmert, Diethard B., 1944-. II. Title.
HJ8654 .P52 1982

PIEMONTE (ITALY) - INDUSTRIES - HISTORY.
Rapetti, Vittorio, 1955- Uomini, collina e vigneto in Piemonte, da metà Ottocento agli anni trenta /. Alessandria , 1984. 342 p., [16] p. of plates : LC Card 86-151345
HD9385.I82 P547 1984

Piepenbrock, Hartwig.
Ladenschluss kontrovers . Stuttgart [1984] 232 p. : ISBN 3-512-00712-0 LC Card 85-138606
HD5178 .L33 1984

Verbraucherpolitik in der sozialen Marktwirtschaft . Bonn , c1984. 146 p. ; ISBN 3-922335-04-7 LC Card 85-228004
HC240.9.C63 V47 1984

Pieper, Antje, 1943-
Pieper, Beate. Vom Lehrermangel zur Lehrerarbeitslosigkeit : Bildungspolitik als geschichtliches Dilemma / Beate Pieper.1. Aufl. Münster : Wurf Verlag, 1984. ix, 265 p. : 6 ill. ; 21 cm. (Wissenschaftliche Texte. Bd. 4) Bibliography: p. 243-251. ISBN 3-923881-11-8 : LC Card 85-195712 DDC 331.12 19
1. Teachers - Germany (West) - Supply and demand. 2. Unemployment - Germany (West). 3. Education and state - Germany, West. I. Title.
LB2833.4.G4 P54 1984
NYPL [JLD 87-1161]

Pierce, Brad. The timber industry in interior Alaska : prices, products, markets, and the economics of production / Brad Pierce. [Juneau] : House Research Agency, Alaska State Legislature, [1986] 65 p. ; 28 cm. (House Research Agency report . 86-B) "January 1986." Bibliography: p. 61-65. LC Card 86-621755 DDC 338.1/7498/09798 19
1. Lumber trade - Alaska. 2. Forest products industry - Alaska. I. Alaska. Legislature. House of Representatives. Research Agency. II. Title. III. Series.
HD9757.A7 P54 1986

Pierce, Deborah L. Feigenbaum, Todd R. New York's highway system . Albany, N.Y. (150 State St., Albany 12207) [1986] 2, iv, 130 p. : LC Card 87-620939 DDC 388.1/09747 19
HE356.N7 F45 1986

Piero Sraffa . Ahijado, Manuel. Madrid , 1985. 90 p. ; ISBN 84-85942-31-0 LC Card 87-104173
HB109.S73 A35 1985

Pieroni, Osvaldo. Agricolture a tempo parziale / Osvaldo Pieroni. Bologna : Società editrice il Mulino, c1983. 220 p. : ill. ; 22 cm. (Studi e ricerche / Instituto nazionale di economia agraria . 3) ISBN 88-15-00024-0 LC Card 85-233534
1. Part-time farming - Italy. 2. Farmers, Part-time - Italy. I. Series: Studi e ricerche (Istituto nazionale di economia agraria) , 3. II. Title.
HD1970 .P54 1983

Pieroni, W. (Walter) Le 150 ore e la formazione professionale in azienda . Milano, Italy , c1985. 178 p. : LC Card 86-141990
HD5716.T242 I82 1985
NYPL [JFD 87-3739]

Pierre, Andrew J.
A High technology gap? . New York, N.Y. , c1987. xii, 114 p. : ISBN 0-87609-021-8 (pbk.) : LC Card 87-6713 DDC 338/.06 19
HC240.9.T4 H54 1987

Unemployment and growth in the Western economies /. New York, N.Y. , c1984. x, 142 p. ; ISBN 0-87609-001-3 (pbk.) : LC Card 84-9415 DDC 331.13/791812 19
HD5707.5 .U54 1984 *NYPL [JLE 86-1564]*

Pierwsza pięciolatka w Związku Radzieckim . Wilk, Marian. Wrocław , 1986. 314 p., [21] p. of plates : ISBN 83-04-02190-0 : LC Card 87-110627
HC335.4 .W55 1986

Pigeat, Henri, 1939- La télévision par cable commence demain / Henri Pigeat. Paris : Plon, c1983. 239 p. ; 20 cm. Bibliography: p. [235]-236. ISBN 2-259-01062-8 : LC Card 83-237808
1. Cable television - France. 2. Cable television. I. Title. II. Title: Par cable.
HE8700.72.F8 P54 1983

Piggybacking--the federal-state collection act of 1972 /. Ware, Ray M. Lexington, Ky. , 1980. ix leaves, 35 p. ;
NYPL [JLM 79-1230 no.10]

Pigott, William, 1927- Henning, Charles N. Financial markets and the economy /. Englewood Cliffs, N.J. , c1988. xvi, 638 p. : ISBN 0-13-316894-8 LC Card 87-24413 DDC 332/.0973 19
HG181 .H37 1988

Pihkala, Erkki. Toisen maailmansodan aikaisesta huoltotasosta Suomessa ja analogioista 1980-luvun alun tilanteeseen / Erkki Pihkala. [Helsinki] : Puolustustalouden suunnittelukeskus, 1986. 49 leaves ; 30 cm. (Selvityksiä ja raportteja, 0782-5277 . n:o 5) Cover title. Bibliography: leaves 48-49. ISBN 951-46-9497-X LC Card 86-221750
1. Finland - Economic conditions - 1918-. 2. Finland - Economic conditions - 1945-. I. Title. II. Series.
HC340.2 .P54 1986

Pike, Clarence Edward, 1917- Chronicles of hunger / Clarence Edward Pike. Millwood, N.Y. : Associated Faculty Press, 1988. p. cm. Bibliography: p. Includes index. ISBN 0-8046-9410-9 LC Card 87-12332 DDC 363.8 19
1. Food supply. 2. Famines. I. Title.
HD9000.5 .P55 1988

PIKE PLACE MARKET (SEATTLE, WASH.) - PICTORIAL WORKS.
Stamets, John, 1949- Portrait of a market . Seattle , 1987. 95 p. : ISBN 0-941104-17-6 (pbk.) : LC Card 87-4746 DDC 381/.18/0979777 19
HF5472.U7 S48 1987

PILAS (SEVILLE, SPAIN) - POPULATION - HISTORY.
Camacho Rueda, Eduardo. Propiedad y explotación agrarias en el aljarafe sevillano . Sevilla , 1984. 199 p. : ISBN 84-500-9772-X LC Card 85-135028
HD773 .C18 1984

Pilder, Christhard. Die empirische Erhebung von Unternehmenserwartungen als Beitrag zur Konjunkturprognose / Christhard Pilder. Frankfurt am Main : Haag + Herchen, c1984. vii, 185 p. : ill. ; 21 cm. Originally presented as the author's thesis (doctoral--Gesamthochschule Wuppertal, 1983) Bibliography: p. 171-185. ISBN 3-88129-769-3 LC Card 84-173409
1. Economic forecasting. 2. Rational expectations (Economic theory). I. Title.
HB3730 .P53 1984

Pilgrim Trust (Great Britain) Men without work . New York , 1985. xii, 447 p. ; ISBN 0-8240-7619-2 (alk. paper) : LC Card 85-13069 DDC 331.13/7941 19
HD5765.A6 M46 1985
NYPL [JLD 87-1031]

Pilipenko, Nikolaĭ Nikolaevich. Moiseev, Anatoliĭ Vasil'evich. Ėkonomicheskiĭ slovar'-spravochnik . Moskva , 1978. 239 p. ; LC Card 81-165938
HB61 .M56 1978

Piller, L. Beleggen in effecten / L. Piller. 1e druk. Utrecht : Spectrum, 1984. 195 p. ; 19 cm. (Marka) Includes index. ISBN 90-274-6126-0 : LC Card 85-134084
1. Stock-exchange - Netherlands. 2. Stock-exchange. I. Title.
HG5562 .P55 1984

Pilling, András. Az önelszámoló rendszer alkalmazásának, a kistermelők integrálásának és a kihelyezett részlegeknek a hatása a mezőgazdasági vállalatok szervezeti felépitésére, s annak müködésére / Pilling András, Horváth János. Budapest : Agrárgazdasági Kutató Intézet, 1985. 89 p. ; 28 cm. (Agrárgazdasági Kutató Intézet, 0209-5696 . 1985/5) Bibliography: p. 88-89. ISBN 963-491-206-0 LC Card 86-196755
1. Collective farms - Hungary - Finance. 2. Private plot agriculture - Hungary - Finance. 3. Agriculture - Hungary - Finance. I. Horváth, János. II. Series: Agrárgazdasági Kutató Intézet (Series) , 1985/5. III. Title.
HD1492.H8 P55 1985

Pillsbury, Hobart B. Armed forces guide to personal financial planning : strategies for managing your budget, savings, insurance, taxes, and investments / Hobart B. Pillsbury, Jr. and Robert H. Baldwin, Jr. Harrisburg, PA : Stackpole Books, c1987. p. cm. Includes bibliographies and index. ISBN 0-8117-2123-X LC Card 86-30201 DDC 332.024/355 19
1. United States - Armed Forces - Finance, Personal. I. Baldwin, Robert H. II. Title.
HG179 .P55 1987

Pilot evaluation report on Mahalapye Development Trust /. Gobotswang, Z. Gaborone, Botswana [1982] v leaves, 61, 3 p. ; LC Card 87-122810
HD5710.85.B59 G63 1982

Piloty, Robert, 1863-1926. Müller, Fr. (Friedrich), Dr. Ferdinand von Steinbeis . Tübingen , 1907. vi, 215 p. : LC Card 85-666358
HC282.5.S67 M85x 1907

Piltz, Detlev Jürgen. Vorschlag zur Verbesserung der Behandlung nichtabziehbarer Ausgaben im KStG 1977 / [Bearbeiter, Detlev Jürgen Piltz]. Bonn : Institut "Finanzen und Steuern", 1987. 42 leaves ; 29 cm. (Brief / Institut "Finanzen und Steuern" . Nr. 263) Cover title. Includes bibliographical references. LC Card 87-401366 DDC 332 s 343.4305/267 332 s 344.3035267 19
1. Corporations - Taxation - Law and legislation - Germany (West). 2. Income tax - Germany, West - Deductions - Expenses. I. Series: Brief (Institut "Finanz und Steuern" (Germany)) , Nr. 263. II. Title.
HJ1120 .B65 Nr. 263 KK7226

Pimenta, Haydn Coutinho. Plano Cruzado . Rio de Janeiro , 1987. xii, 203 p. : LC Card 87-127770 DDC 338.981 19
HC187 .P59 1987

Pimentão, Luís Nuno de Matos. Anwendungen der Variationsrechnung auf makroökonomische Modelle / Luís Nuno de Matos Pimentão. Berlin ; New York : Springer-Verlag, c1986. xii, 220 p. : ill. ; 24 cm. (Studies in contemporary economics) Bibliography: p. [215]-220. ISBN 0-387-16484-7 (U. S.) LC Card 86-209488
1. Macroeconomics - Econometric models. I. Title. II. Series.
HB141 .P55 1986

Pimentel, José Graciliano Alves, 1903- Memórias doces e amargas de um fabricante de açúcar / José Graciliano Alves Pimentel. Recife : [s.n.], 1980 (Recife, Pernambuco : Editora Universitária da Univ. Fed. de Pernambuco) 172 p. ; 23 cm. LC Card 86-158546
1. Pimentel, José Graciliano Alves, 1903-. 2. Sugar workers - Brazil - Pernambuco - Biography. 3. Sugar trade - Brazil - Pernambuco - History. I. Title.
HD8039.S86 B755 1980

PIMENTEL, JOSÉ GRACILIANO ALVES, 1903-
Pimentel, José Graciliano Alves, 1903- Memórias doces e amargas de um fabricante de açúcar /. Recife , 1980 (Recife, Pernambuco : Editora Universitária da Univ. Fed. de Pernambuco) 172 p. ; LC Card 86-158546
HD8039.S86 B755 1980

Pimentel, Richard. Job placement for the industrially injured worker / written by Richard Pimentel, Denise Bissonnette, Anita Lee Wright. Northridge, Calif. (17624 Romar St., Northridge 91325) : M. Wright, c1987. v, 93, [1] leaves : ill., forms ; 28 cm. Bibliography: leaf [94]. LC Card 87-401986 DDC 650.1/4/0240816 19
1. Handicapped - Employment. 2. Vocational guidance for the handicapped. I. Bissonette, Denise. II. Wright, Anita Lee. III. Title.
HD7255 .P54 1987

PIMES (Program) A Questão Nordeste . Rio de Janeiro-RJ , 1984. 137 p. ; LC Card 84-191031
HC188.N6 Q47 1984

The PIMS principles . Buzzell, Robert D. (Robert Dow), 1933- New York , London , c1987. xiii, 322 p. : ISBN 0-02-904430-8 LC Card 87-416 DDC 658.8/02 19
HF5415.13 .B893 1987

Pina, Amílcar. Análise de empresas em inflação : projectos de investimento, projectos de saneamento financeiro. [Porto] : Banco Português do Atlântico, Direcção de Estudos Económicos e de Marketing, 1985. 142 p. : ill. ; 29 cm. (BPA cadernos) LC Card 86-174401
1. Accounting - Portugal - Effect of inflation on. 2. Investments - Portugal - Effect of inflation on. I. Banco Português do Atlântico. Direcção de Estudos Económicos e de Marketing. II. Title. III. Series.
HF5658.5 .P56 1985

Pinal Verges, Jorge. México es mágico : reflexiones de un patriota / Jorge Pinal Verges. México : EDAMEX, c1986. 92 p. ; 20 cm. Subtitle on cover: sencillas fórmulas para salir de la crisis. ISBN 968-409-352-7 LC Card 87-401447 DDC 338.972 19
1. Mexico - Economic policy 1970-. 2. Mexico - Economic conditions - 1970-. I. Title.
HC135 .P54 1986

PINANG ISLAND (PINANG) - COMMERCE. Majlis Perbandaran Pulau Pinang. Report of survey . [Georgetown] [1984?] xv, 193 p. : LC Card 86-945200 DDC 307/.09595/1 19
HC445.Z7 P526 1984

PINANG ISLAND (PINANG) - ECONOMIC CONDITIONS. Majlis Perbandaran Pulau Pinang. Report of survey . [Georgetown] [1984?] xv, 193 p. : LC Card 86-945200 DDC 307/.09595/1 19
HC445.Z7 P526 1984

PINANG ISLAND (PINANG) - INDUSTRIES. Majlis Perbandaran Pulau Pinang. Report of survey . [Georgetown] [1984?] xv, 193 p. : LC Card 86-945200 DDC 307/.09595/1 19
HC445.Z7 P526 1984

PINANG ISLAND (PINANG) - SOCIAL CONDITIONS. Majlis Perbandaran Pulau Pinang. Report of survey . [Georgetown] [1984?] xv, 193 p. : LC Card 86-945200 DDC 307/.09595/1 19
HC445.Z7 P526 1984

Piñango, Ramón. Mejías, Tulio. La coordinación como consecuencia de razones y pasiones . Caracas, Venezuela , c1983. 37, [2] p. : ISBN 980-217-002-X LC Card 86-193647
HD37.S66 M37 1983

Piṇḍāṃ dī ḍāiraikaṭarī, 1983-84. Caṇḍīgaṛha : Ārathika Salāhakāra, Pañjāba Sarakāra, [1985- v. <1- > ; 30 cm. (Prakāshana . no. 480-) In Panjabi. Directory of villages in Punjab. CONTENTS. - [1] Ziḷā Saṅgarūra. LC Card 86-902359
1. Punjab (India) - Statistics. 2. Villages - India - Punjab - Statistics. I. Punjab (India). Economic and Statistical Organization. II. Series: Publication (Punjab (India). Economic and Statistical Organisation) , no. 480.
HA4587.P86 P56 1985

Pineda Siriany, Lorena. Fabián, Miguel Angel. Monografía del café /. [San Salvador] , 1984. 39 leaves : LC Card 86-177543
HD9199.S142 F33 1984

Pinedo Brigé, Lucía. Estadísticas sociales . Caracas, Venezuela , 1983. 2 v. ; LC Card 84-183391 DDC 312/.0987 19
HA1095 .E88 1983 ***NYPL [JLM 85-550]***

Pinhas Sapir Conference on Development (4th : 1986 : Tel-Aviv University) Economic effects of the government budget /. Cambridge, Mass. , c1988. p. cm. ISBN 0-262-08172-5 LC Card 87-26187 DDC 338.9 19
HJ2005 .E25 1988

Pinheiro, Saramago. Reforma agrária : discuros e projetos de lei / apresentados pelo Deputado Saramago Pinheiro. Brasília : Câmara dos Deputados, Centro de Documentação e Informação, Coordenação de Publicações, 1986. 46 p. ; 23 cm. (Separatas de discursos, pareceres e projetos / Câmara dos Deputados, 47a. Legislatura, 3a. Sessão Legislativa . no. 174) LC Card 86-228887
1. Land reform - Brazil. 2. Brazil - Politics and government - 1964-1985. I. Series: Separatas de discursos, pareceres e projetos , 47a. Legislatura--3a. Sessão Legislativa, no. 174. II. Title.
HD1333.B6 P56 1986

Pinho, Diva Benevides. Economia informal, tecnologia apropriada e associativismo /. São Paulo , 1986. 176 p. : LC Card 86-233370
HC190.P6 E34 1986

Pinkas, Klara. Vŭznikvane, razvitie i zalez na oporti͡unizma v bŭlgarskoto rabotnichesko dvizhenie, 1891/1948 /. Sofii͡a , 1986. 696 p. ; LC Card 86-200229
HD8628 .V89 1986

Pinnarò, Gabriella. Ricerca sociale e movimento operaio . Milano , c1982. 294 p. ; LC Card 82-246648 DDC 331/.0945 19
HD8481 .R53 1982 ***NYPL [JLD 86-3380]***

Pinney, William E., 1941- Management science : an introduction to quantitative analysis for management / William E. Pinney, Donald B. McWilliams.2nd ed. New York : Harper & Row, c1987. xvii, 620 p. : ill. ; 25 cm. Bibliography: p. 599-604. Includes index. ISBN 0-06-045229-3 LC Card 86-22933 DDC 658.4/033 19
1. Management - Mathematical models. 2. Decision-making - Mathematical models. 3. Management science. I. McWilliams, Donald B., 1936-. II. Title.
HD30.25 .P56 1987

Pinoy management /. Franco, Ernesto A. Metro Manila, Philippines , 1986. 230 p. : ISBN 971-08-2961-0 (pbk.) LC Card 86-217631 DDC 658/.009599 19
HD70.P5 F73 1986

Pinoy overseas handbook : mga dapat malaman ng isang manggagawang mangingibang-bansa. [Manila, Philippines] : Kaibigan, 1982. 88 p. : ill. ; 22 cm. Tagalog, Arabic, and English. LC Card 83-207976
1. Alien labor, Philippine - Near East - Handbooks, manuals, etc. 2. Alien labor, Philippine - Korea (South) - Handbooks, manuals, etc. I. Friends of Filipino Migrant Workers.
HD8656 .P56 1982

Pintel, Gerald. Retailing / Gerald Pintel, Jay Diamond. 4th ed. Englewood Cliffs, N.J. : Prentice-Hall, c1987. iv, 488 p. : ill. ; 25 cm. Includes index. ISBN 0-13-778549-6 LC Card 86-25397 DDC 658.8/7 19
1. Retail trade - Management. 2. Retail trade - Vocational guidance. I. Diamond, Jay. II. Title.
HF5429 .P57 1987

Pintér, György, 1921- Közgazdasági bizottságok kézikönyve /. Budapest , 1984. 324 p. ; ISBN 963-322-017-3 : LC Card 85-126303
HC300.28 .K68 1984

Pinto, Antônio Carlos Figueiredo. Investidores institucionais : efeitos da regulamentação econômica / Antônio Carlos Figueiredo Pinto. Rio de Janeiro : Instituto Brasileiro de Mercado de Capitais, 1985. 74 p. : ill. ; 21 cm. Bibliography: p. 73-74. LC Card 86-140523
1. Institutional investments - Brazil. I. Instituto Brasileiro de Mercado de Capitais. II. Title.
HG5332 .P56 1985

Pinto, Armando Sevinate. A Agricultura portuguesa no período 1950-1980 . Lisboa [1984] 74 p. : LC Card 85-207313
HD2027 .A635 1984

Pinto, Claudio. Fecundabilidad y edad de la mujer en las áreas rurales y semi-urbanas de cuatro países latinoamericanos / Claudio Pinto, Shea O. Rutstein. Santiago de Chile : Centro Latinoamericano de Demografía, [1978] 21, [2] p. : ill. ; 27 cm. (Serie A . no. 151) Summary also in English. Bibliography: p. [23] LC Card 83-175823
1. Fertility, Human - Latin America - Case studies. I. Rutstein, Shea Oscar. II. Series: Serie A (CELADE (Organization)) , no. 151. III. Title.
HA755 .U5 no. 151 HB940.5

Pinto Cohén, Gustavo. Foro . San Felipe, Venezuela , 1984. ii, 92 p. ; LC Card 85-132901 DDC 338.1/0987 19
HD1912 .F67 1984 ***NYPL [JLD 86-424]***

Pinto, Isaac de, 1715-1787. [Selections. 1960]
O economista Isaac de Pinto, o seu "Tratado da circulação e do crédito," e outros escritos económicos / Moses Bensabat Amzalak. Lisboa : Editorial Império, 1960. 247 p. : ill. ; 25 cm. French and Portuguese. Includes bibliographical references. LC Card 85-125396
1. Finance, Public. 2. Debt, Public. 3. Credit. 4. Luxury. 5. Commerce - Early works to 1800. 6. Pinto, Isaac de, 1715-1787. I. Amzalak, Moses Bensabat, 1892-. II. Pinto, Isaac de, 1715-1787. Traité de la circulation et du crédit. 1960. III. Title.
HJ150 .P552 1960

Traité de la circulation et du crédit. 1960. Pinto, Isaac de, 1715-1787. [Selections. 1960.] O economista Isaac de Pinto, o seu "Tratado da circulação e do crédito," e outros escritos económicos / Moses Bensabat Amzalak. Lisboa , 1960. 247 p. : LC Card 85-125396
HJ150 .P552 1960

PINTO, ISAAC DE, 1715-1787. Pinto, Isaac de, 1715-1787. [Selections. 1960.] O economista Isaac de Pinto, o seu "Tratado da circulação e do crédito," e outros escritos económicos /. Lisboa , 1960. 247 p. : LC Card 85-125396
HJ150 .P552 1960

Pinto, L. M. Teixeira (Luis Maria Teixeira) Cooperação e coexistência / L.M. Teixeira Pinto. [Lisboa] : Atica, 1965. 205 p., [1] folded leaf of plates : ill. ; 20 cm. CONTENTS. - Desenvolvimento económico e comércio internacional -- Aspectos fundamentais da cooperação económica internacional após a Segunda Guerra Mundial -- Cooperação económica internacional -- Desenvolvimento económico e comércio internacional -- Coexistência entre sistemas e estruturas. LC Card 85-205639
1. International economic relations. 2. International finance. 3. International cooperation. I. Title.
HF1411 .P52 1965

Pinto, Lawrence J. The structural pest control industry : description and impact on the nation / prepared by Lawrence J. Pinto. Vienna, Va. (8150 Leesburg Pike, Suite 1100, Vienna 22180) : National Pest Control Association, 1981. 26, [10] p. : ill. ; 28 cm. Bibliography: p. [27]-[30] LC Card 86-214768 DDC 338.4/762896/0973 19
1. Pest control industry - United States. I. National Pest Control Association. II. Title.
HD9718.5.P473 U663 1981

Pinto, Maurício Barata de Paula. O potencial das exportações brasileiras de manufaturados / Maurício Barata de Paula Pinto. Rio de Janeiro : Programa Nacional de Pesquisa Econômica, 1983. 46 p. ; 30 cm. (Série Fac-símile . no. 12) "Versão apresentada ao PNPE em março/83." Bibliography: p. 28. LC Card 87-403022 DDC 382/.4567/0981 19
1. Brazil - Manufactures. 2. Brazil - Commerce. 3. Export marketing - Brazil. I. Title. II. Series.
HD9734.B72 P56 1983

Pinzolits, Herbert. Gergely, Stefan M. Wirtschaftswissenschaften /. Wien , 1985. 170 p. ; ISBN 3-205-06108-X LC Card 85-229521
HB74.9.A9 G47 1985

Pinzón Santos, Rómulo Enrique. Cortés de Pinzón, Magdalena. Bases de contabilidad nacional /. [Bogotá, Colombia] [1982] 96 p. : LC Card 82-216044
HC79.I5 C675 1982

Pioneer American businessman in Korea . Cook, Harold F., 1929- Seoul, Korea , 1981. ix, 104 p. : LC Card 83-140523 DDC 382/.09519/0730924 B 19
HF3023.T68 C66 1981
NYPL [JFE 86-4650]

Pioneering economic theory, 1630-1980 . Brems, Hans. Baltimore , c1986. xv, 411 p. : ISBN 0-8018-2667-5 (alk. paper) LC Card 85-19819 DDC 330.1 19
HB75 .B7845 1986 ***NYPL [JLE 86-2408]***

Pioneers in development. Second series / Theodore W. Schultz ... [et al.] ; Gerald M. Meier, editor. New York : Published for the World Bank [by] Oxford University Press, c1987. viii, 244 p. ; 24 cm. Includes bibliographical references and index. ISBN 0-19-520542-1 LC Card 86-23511 DDC 338.9 19
1. Economic development. I. Schultz, Theodore William, 1902-. II. Meier, Gerald M. III. International Bank for Reconstruction and Development.
HD74 .P56 1987

Pioneers of a profession . Stewart, James C.

(James Cathcart) New York , 1986, c1977. xii, 181 p., [2] leaves of plates : ISBN 0-8240-7888-8 : LC Card 86-25636 DDC 657/.092/2 B 19
HF5604 .S73 1986

Pioneros de la selva . Salazar, Ernesto, 1946- Quito, Ecuador , 1986. 228 p., [11] leaves of plates : LC Card 87-400290 DDC 338.1/09866/43 19
HD1516.E25 S25 1986

Pionniers suisses de l'économie et de la technique .
(9) Jéquier, François. Charles Veillon . Zürich , 1985. 142 p. : LC Card 85-139330 DDC 338.092/4 B 19
HC395.5.V45 J45 1985

Piotet, F. (Françoise) Neue Arbeits- und Tätigkeitsformen . Dublin, Ireland [Washington, D.C.] c1986. xvi, 339 p. ; ISBN 92-825-6418-5 LC Card 87-408469 DDC 306/.36/094 19
HD6957.E86 N48 1986

PIPE INDUSTRY - SOVIET UNION - SAFETY MEASURES.
Okhrana truda v trubnom proizvodstve /. Moskva , 1986. 151, [1] p. : LC Card 85-163240
HD9529.P53 S686 1986

PIPE LINES, GAS, NATURAL. see **GAS, NATURAL - PIPE LINES.**

Piping Industry Progress & Education. A Practical guide to investigating public works violations /. Oakland, CA (520 3rd St., Suite 204, Oakland 94607) , 1986. 73 p., [3] leaves of plates : LC Card 86-209657 DDC 363.2/5 19
HD3890.C2 P7 1986

PIRAEUS (GREECE) - ECONOMIC CONDITIONS.
Tsokopoulos, Vasias. Peiraias, 1835-1870 . Athēna , 1984. 280 p., [8] p. of plates : LC Card 86-128354
HC298.P57 T77 1984 ***NYPL [JLD 86-171]***

PIRAEUS (GREECE) - HISTORY.
Tsokopoulos, Vasias. Peiraias, 1835-1870 . Athēna , 1984. 280 p., [8] p. of plates : LC Card 86-128354
HC298.P57 T77 1984 ***NYPL [JLD 86-171]***

PIRAEUS (GREECE) - SOCIAL CONDITIONS.
Tsokopoulos, Vasias. Peiraias, 1835-1870 . Athēna , 1984. 280 p., [8] p. of plates : LC Card 86-128354
HC298.P57 T77 1984 ***NYPL [JLD 86-171]***

PIRAJUÍ (BRAZIL) - POPULATION.
Rocha, José Carlos Rodrigues. O êxodo rural no município de Pirajuí /. Bauru-SP , 1984. iv, 66 p. : LC Card 86-158771
HB2024.P57 R62 1984

PIRAN (SLOVENIA) - ECONOMIC CONDITIONS.
Mihelič, Darja. Neagrarno gospodarstvo Pirana od 1280 do 1340 =. Ljubljana , 1985. 244 p., [12] p. on folded leaves : LC Card 86-202646
HC407.Z7 P576 1985

PIRATE RADIO BROADCASTING.
Machado, Arlindo. Rádios livres . São Paulo-SP , 1986. 181 p. : LC Card 86-157835
HE8697.P57 M33 1986

PIRATE RADIO BROADCASTING - BRAZIL.
Machado, Arlindo. Rádios livres . São Paulo-SP , 1986. 181 p. : LC Card 86-157835
HE8697.P57 M33 1986

PIRATE RADIO BROADCASTING - FRANCE.
Benhaïm, J.-P. (Jean-Pierre) Les radios locales privées /. Paris , c1985. 153 p. : ISBN 2-7101-0528-4 : LC Card 85-205602
HE8697.P57 B45 1985

Pirec, Dušan. Iskušenja marksizma : azijski način proizvodnje i vanevropska društva / Dušan Pirec, Miomir Jakšić. Beograd : Ekonomika, 1985. 461 p. : ill. ; 24 cm. (Biblioteka Izazov) In Serbo-Croatian (roman) Summary in English and Russian. Bibliography: p. 446-455. Includes index. LC Card 86-128661
1. Asiatic mode of production. 2. Economic history. I. Jakšić, Miomir. II. Title.
HB97.5 .P498 1985

Pires, Maria Eugénia. La Conjoncture économique en Europe . Lisboa, Portugal [1982] 78 p. : LC Card 83-181663
HC240 .C588 1982

A pirita humana . Volpato, Terezinha Gascho. Florianópolis , 1984. 159 p. : LC Card 85-150574
HD8039.M62 B78 1984

Pirityi, Ottó. Életszínvonal és közhangulat /. Budapest , 1984. 69 p. ; LC Card 86-147705
HD7027.5 .E44 1984

Pirkl, Fritz, 1925- Dritte-Welt-Kongress (1985 : Hof (Hof, Germany)) Entwicklungspolitik im Wandel . Stuttgart , 1986. 256 p. ; ISBN 3-87959-271-3 LC Card 86-193768
HD73 .D75 1985

Pirminis kalbos signalų aprašymas. Pervichnoe opisanie signalov rechi . Vil'nīūs , 1980. 67 p. : LC Card 82-107723
HD38 .S715 vyp. 42 TK7882.S65

Pirog, Robert L. Energy economics . Englewood Cliffs, N.J. , c1987. viii, 328 p. : ISBN 0-13-277245-0 : LC Card 86-25254 DDC 333.79/0973 19
HD9502.U52 E4874 1987

Pirogova, S. V. Ėkonomicheskie funktsii upravleniīa proizvoditel'nym trudom /. Kiev , 1986. 167 p. ; LC Card 87-152432
HD9705.S595 E37 1986

Pirsume mifkad ha-ukhlusin yeha-diyur, 1983 .
(mis. 7) Tekhunot demografiyot shel ha-ukhlusiyah . Yerushalayim , 1985. 31, 175, xxxiv p. : LC Card 86-204169
HA4560 .A4 1983

Pirsumim mekhuyane mediniyut .
(7) Laufer, Leopold Yehuda. U. S. aid to Israel . [Jerusalem] [1983] 55 p. : LC Card 87-400279 DDC 338.91/73/05694 19
HC415.25 .L38 1983

Pirzio Ammassari, Gloria. I sindacalisti : inchiesta sui dirigenti delle confederazioni italiane / Gloria Pirzio Ammassari, Francesco Mattioli. Bari : De Donato, c1982. 155 p. ; 21 cm. (Movimento operaio. 69) Includes bibliographical references. LC Card 82-131644 DDC 331.87/33/0945 19
1. Trade-unions - Officials and employees - Italy. 2. Industrial relations - Italy. 3. Trade-unions - Italy. I. Mattioli, Francesco, 1947-. II. Title.
HD6709 .P57 1982 ***NYPL [JLD 86-2840]***

Pisa (Italy) Conferenza economica dell'area pisana (1984 : Pisa, Italy) Atti /. Pisa [1985-1986], c1985. 2 v. : LC Card 86-223161
HC308.P58 C66 1984

PISA REGION (ITALY) - ECONOMIC CONDITIONS - CONGRESSES.
Conferenza economica dell'area pisana (1984 : Pisa, Italy) Atti /. Pisa [1985-1986], c1985. 2 v. : LC Card 86-223161
HC308.P58 C66 1984

PISA REGION (ITALY) - ECONOMIC POLICY - CONGRESSES.
Conferenza economica dell'area pisana (1984 : Pisa, Italy) Atti /. Pisa [1985-1986], c1985. 2 v. : LC Card 86-223161
HC308.P58 C66 1984

Pisani-Ferry, Jean. Problèmes de macroéconomie / Jean Pisani-Ferry, Henri Sterdyniak, Pierre Villa. Paris : Economica, 1984. 452 p. : ill. ; 24 cm. (Collection "Economie et statistiques avancées." Série Ecole nationale de la statistique et de l'administration économique et Centre d'études des programmes économiques) Includes bibliographies. ISBN 2-7178-0801-9 : LC Card 85-100663 DDC 339 19
1. Macroeconomics. I. Sterdyniak, Henri. II. Villa, Pierre. III. Title. IV. Series.
HB173 .P534 1984

Pisarski, Alan.
Briggs, Dwight. Journey-to-work trends . Washington, D.C. , Springfield, VA [1986] 1 v. (various pagings) : LC Card 86-602387 DDC 388.4/1314/0973 19
HE371.A3 B75 1986

Commuting in America : a national report on commuting patterns and trends / prepared by Alan E. Pisarski ; under direction of the Steering Committee for the National Commuting Study. Westport, Conn. (P.O. Box 2055, Westport 06880-2055) : Eno Foundation for Transportation, c1987. 78 p. : ill. (some col.) ; 28 cm. Includes index. LC Card 86-82787 DDC 388.3/14/0973 19
1. Commuting - United States. I. Steering Committee for the National Commuting Study. II. Title.
HD5717.5.U6 P57 1987

Pisatel' i vremīa. Pis'ma iz derevni.
Vasil'ev, Ivan Afanas'evich. Korennye i priezzhie /. Moskva , 1980. 86 p. ; LC Card 81-178115
HD1536.S65 V375 1980

Pisatel' i vremīa. Pis'ma s zavodov i stroek.
Kaplinskaīa, Elena. Puteshestvie v Rīazan' /. Moskva , 1978. 84 p. ; LC Card 81-155441
HD8039.M22 S654 1978

Pisciotta, John L. (John Lee) Development policy, inflation, and politics in Chile, 1938-1958 : an essay in political economy / John Lee Pisciotta. New York : Garland Pub., 1987. v, 188 p. ; 24 cm. (South American and Latin American economic history) Thesis (Ph. D.)--University of Texas at Austin, 1971. Bibliography: p. 178-188. ISBN 0-8240-1367-0 (alk. paper) : LC Card 87-7617 DDC 338.983 19
1. Chile - Economic policy. 2. Inflation (Finance) - Chile - History - 20th century. 3. Chile - Politics and government - 1920-1970. 4. Chile - Economic conditions - 1918-1970. I. Title. II. Series.
HC192 .P625 1987

Pishchulin, N. P. Chelovek, svobodnoe vremīa i profsoīūzy /. Moskva , 1980. 256 p., [32] p. of plates : LC Card 81-137052
HD7395.R4 C42 1980

Piskunov, F. F. (Fedor Fedorovich) Zabota o stroitel'nykh kadrakh / F.F. Piskunov. 2-e izd., dop. Moskva : Stroĭizdat, 1986. 71 p. : ill. ; 20 cm. (Peredovye kollektivy) LC Card 86-220202
1. Construction workers - Services for - Soviet Union. 2. Construction industry - Soviet Union - Employees. I. Series: Peredovye kollektivy (Stroĭizdat (Firm)). II. Title.
HD8039.B92 S686 1986

Pisma o rzeczypospolitej morskiej /.
Kwiatkowski, Eugeniusz. Szczecin , 1985. 277 p., [24] p. of plates : ISBN 83-7007-012-4 :
NYPL [*QO 86-2539]

PISTOIA (ITALY) - ECONOMIC CONDITIONS.
Reti terziarie ed economie locali . Milano, Italy , c1983. 174 p. ; LC Card 85-215649
HD9986.I83 P577 1983

PISTOIA (ITALY) - INDUSTRIES.
Reti terziarie ed economie locali . Milano, Italy , c1983. 174 p. ; LC Card 85-215649
HD9986.I83 P577 1983

Pitelis, Christos. Corporate capital : control, ownership, saving, and crisis / Christos Pitelis. Cambridge [Cambridgeshire] ; New York : Cambridge University Press, 1987. viii, 136 p. ; 24 cm. Bibliography: p. 111-127. Includes index. ISBN 0-521-32848-9 LC Card 86-26807 DDC 658.1/5 19
1. Corporations - Finance. 2. Capital investments. 3. Saving and investment. I. Title.
HG4026 .P575 1987

The pitmen of the northern coalfield . Colls, Robert. Manchester, UK , Wolfeboro, NH, USA , c1987. xv, 386 p., [2] p. of plates : ISBN 0-7190-2202-9 (U. S.) : LC Card 87-11029 DDC 305/.9622/09427 19
HD8039.M62 G737 1987

Pitsela, Angelika. Straffälligkeit und Viktimisierung ausländischer Minderheiten in der Bundesrepublik Deutschland : dargestellt am Beispiel der griechischen Bevölkerungsgruppe / von Angelika Pitsela. Freiburg [i.B.] : Max-Planck-Institut für Ausländisches und Internationales Strafrecht, 1986. xxvii, 479 p. ; 21 cm. (Kriminologische Forschungsberichte aus dem Max-Planck-Institut für Ausländisches und Internationales Strafrecht, Freiburg i. Br. . Bd. 15) Originally presented as the author's thesis (doctoral)--Universität Freiburg i.Br. Bibliography: p. 448-479. ISBN 3-922498-16-7 LC Card 87-131111 DDC 331.6/2/495043 19
1. Alien labor, Greek - Germany (West) - Social conditions. 2. Alien labor criminals - Germany (West). 3. Victims of crimes - Germany, West. 4. Greeks - Germany (West) - Crimes against. I. Series: Kriminologische Forschungsberichte aus dem Max-Planck-Institut für Ausländisches und Internationales Strafrecht, Freiburg , Bd. 15. II. Title.
HD8458.G7 P57 1986

Pitt, David C. New ideas in environmental education /. London , New York , c1988. xiv, 219 p. ; ISBN 0-7099-5042-X LC Card 87-15696 DDC 363.7/007/1 19
HC79.E5 N45 1988

Pitt series in policy and institutional studies. Reed, Steven R., 1947- Japanese prefectures and policy making /. Pittsburgh, Pa. , 1986. ix, 197 p. ; ISBN 0-8229-3527-9 LC Card 85-22528 DDC 352/.00047 19
JS7373.A3 R44 1986 ***NYPL [JLE 86-3757]***

West, Darrell M., 1954- Congress and economic policymaking /. Pittsburgh, Pa. , c1987. xiv, 203 p. ; ISBN 0-8229-5396-X (pbk.) LC Card 87-40160 DDC 338.973 19
HC106.8 .W45 1987

Pitts, Mary Anne, 1927- Economic development in Chile under two growth strategies, 1925-1968 / Mary A. Pitts. New York : Garland Pub., 1987. vii, 246 p. ; 24 cm. (South American and Latin American economic history) Originally presented as the author's thesis (doctoral--Syracuse University, 1975) Bibliography: p. 237-246. ISBN 0-8240-1368-9 (alk. paper) : LC Card 87-7618 DDC 338.983 19
1. Chile - Economic policy. 2. Import substitution - Chile - History - 20th century. 3. Industry and state - Chile - History - 20th century. 4. Foreign trade promotion - Chile - History - 20th century. I. Title. II. Series.
HC192 .P627 1987

Pittsburgh. Carnegie-Mellon University. see **Carnegie-Mellon University.**

Pittsburgh series in social and labor history. Hoerr, John P., 1930- And the wolf finally came . Pittsburgh, PA , 1988. p. cm. ISBN 0-8229-3572-4 LC Card 87-24932 DDC 338.4/7669142/097488 19
HD9517.M85 H64 1988

Jones, Mother, 1843?-1930. [Selections. 1988.] The speeches and writings of Mother Jones /. Pittsburgh, Pa. , 1988. p. cm. ISBN 0-8229-3575-9 LC Card 87-25192 DDC 331.88/0973 19
HD8072 .J7832 1988

Pivato, Giorgio. Sviluppo della finanza internazionale e interdipendenza dei sistemi finanziari . [Italy] [1984] iv, 204 p. : ISBN 88-14-00203-7 : LC Card 84-238589 DDC 332/.042 19
HG205.S85 S85 1984 ***NYPL [JLE 86-482]***

Pivert, Marceau, 1895- Los problemas del socialismo en nuestra tiempo [microform]. México, 1944. 119 p. DDC 335.082
HX40 .P73 ***NYPL [*ZT-1711 no.21]***

Pizanias, Petros. Misthoi kai eisodēmata stēn Hellada, 1842-1923 : to paradeigma tōn hypallēlōn tēs Ethnikēs Trapezas / Petrou Pizania. Athēna : Morphōtiko Hidryma Ethnikēs Trapezēs, 1985. 324 p., [20] p. of plates : ill., facsims., ports. ; 22 cm. (Pēges oikonomikēs historias . 3) Bibliography: p. 309-317. Includes index. LC Card 87-111106
1. Ethnikē Trapeza tēs Hellados - Officials and employees - Salaries, allowances, etc. - History. I. Title. II. Series.
HG3250.5.A7 P59 1985

Pizarro, Crisóstomo. La huelga obrera en Chile, 1890-1970 / Crisóstomo Pizarro. Santiago, Chile : Ediciones SUR, [1986] 227 p. : ill. ; 25 cm. (Colección Estudios históricos) Bibliography: p. 215-222. LC Card 87-115190 DDC 331.89/2983 19
1. Strikes and lockouts - Chile - History. 2. Trade-unions - Chile - History. I. Series: Colección Estudios históricos (Santiago, Chile). II. Title.
HD5356.A6 P59 1986

Pizarro, Eduardo. McGranahan, Donald V. Measurement and analysis of socioeconomic development . Geneva , 1985. xx, 504 p. :
NYPL [JLK 74-447 no.85.5]

Pizzanelli, Giuliano. Economia tra teoria e politica /. Milano , c1984. 295 p. ; LC Card 84-171327 DDC 330/.09 19
HB75 .E28 1984 ***NYPL [JLD 87-819]***

Pla d'organització social agrària de Catalunya /. Rendé, Josep M. Barcelona , 1924. 138 p., [1] folded leaf of plates : LC Card 86-202164 DDC 334/.683/09467 19
HD1491.S82 C317 1924

Plachno, Larry, 1943. Used intercity bus pricing, 1978-1986 / Larry Plachno. Polo, Ill. : Transportation Trails, c1987. 40 p. : ill. ; 28 cm. ISBN 0-933449-03-8 (pbk.) LC Card 87-19189 DDC 629.2/2233/029473 19
1. Used buses - United States - Prices. I. Title.
HD9710.33.U52 P42 1987

Placier, Anne. Les métiers de la publicité / Anne et Bertrand Placier. Paris : Editions Génération : Diffusion, Bordas, c1984. 247 p., [15] p. of plates : ill. (some col.) ; 22 cm. (Collection L'Etudiant pratique, 0759-9064 . 19) Bibliography: p. 247. Includes indexes. ISBN 2-86745-019-5 LC Card 85-118630
1. Advertising - Vocational guidance. I. Placier, Bertrand. II. Title. III. Series.
HF5828.4 .P58 1984

Placier, Bertrand. Placier, Anne. Les métiers de la publicité /. Paris , c1984. 247 p., [15] p. of plates : ISBN 2-86745-019-5 LC Card 85-118630
HF5828.4 .P58 1984

Plaksin, V. I. (Viktor Ivanovich) Sovershenstvovanie sistem upravleniia trudom na predpriiatiiakh mashinostroeniia / V.I. Plaksin. Kiev : Gol. izd-vo izdatel'skogo ob"edineniia "Vyshcha shkola", 1986. 137, [3] p. : ill. ; 20 cm. Bibliography: p. 132-[138] LC Card 85-241056
1. Machine-tool industry - Soviet Union - Management. I. Title.
HD9703.S652 P42 1986

Plan "Afrique," Libreville 1983. Plan général de développement du réseau régional en Afrique =. Genève , 1983. 134 p. : ISBN 92-71-02066-9 LC Card 85-146412
HE8465 .P54 1983

Le plan dans l'économie française /. Bauchet, Pierre. Paris , c1986. 246 p. : ISBN 2-7246-0532-2 : LC Card 86-223474
HC276.2 .B292 1986

Plan de desarrollo regional /. Universidad de los Andes (Mérida, Venezuela). Instituto de Investigaciones Económicas. Mérida , 1973- v. <1-5 > : LC Card 86-202604
HC238.A683 U55 1973

Plan de red de transportes frigoríficos en España /. Instituto Nacional de Industria (Spain). Departamento de Industrias de la Alimentación. Madrid , 1965. 188 p., [1] folded leaf of plates : LC Card 85-107661
HE199.5.R43 I57 1965

Plan d'entreprise 1983/1987. Régie autonome des transports parisiens. RATP plan d'entreprise 1983/1987. Paris [1982] 164 p. : LC Card 83-203335
HE4769.P33 R47 1982

Plan económico de Andalucía, 1984-1986 /. Junta de Andalucía. Grupo de Trabajo 14, Planificación Económica de las Corporaciones Locales y Comarcalización. [Andalucía] , 1983. 133 p. ; ISBN 84-505-1243-3 LC Card 86-223752
HJ1249.A4 J86 1983

Plan económico para Andalucía, 1984-1986 / documento elaborado en el Grupo de Trabajo no. 3 sobre Industria, Energía y Minería. Andalucía : Consejería de Economía, Planificación, Industria y Energía, Junta de Andalucía, [1985?] 164 p. ; 24 cm. ISBN 84-505-0611-5 LC Card 86-205786
1. Industry and state - Spain - Andalusia. 2. Energy policy - Spain - Andalusia. 3. Mineral industries - Government policy - Spain - Andalusia. I. Grupo de Trabajo no. 3 sobre Industria, Energía y Minería (Andalusia, Spain).
HD3616.S495 A536 1985

Plan económico para Andalucía, 1984-1986. Junta de Andalucía. Grupo de Trabajo 14, Planificación Económica de las Corporaciones Locales y Comarcalización. Plan económico de Andalucía, 1984-1986 /. [Andalucía] , 1983. 133 p. ; ISBN 84-505-1243-3 LC Card 86-223752
HJ1249.A4 J86 1983

Plan estatístico de la villa de Alcoy /. Pérez Planelles, Francisco, fl. 1774-1807. [València] [Alcoi] , 1983. xiii, 31 p. ; LC Card 86-150151
HC388.A44 P47 1983

A Plan for an industrial survey for Kalamazoo, August 1, 1926. New York : Technical Advisory Corporation, 1926. 30 p. ; 21 cm. LC Card 85-666471
1. Kalamazoo (Mich.) - Industries. 2. Kalamazoo, Mich. - Economic conditions. I. Technical Advisory Corporation (New York, N.Y.).
HC108.K34 P52x 1926

Plan for information society-a national goal toward year 2000. Italian. Verso una società dell'informazione : il caso giapponese / Japan Computer Usage Development Institute ; introduzione di Roberto Olivetti. Milano : Edizioni di Comunità, 1974. 157 p. : ill ; 23 cm. (Studi e ricerche di scienze sociali. 60) Translation of: "The plan for information society - a national goal toward year 2000." Cover title.
1. Computer industry - Japan - Addresses, essays, lectures. 2. Japan - Industries - Information Services - Addresses, essays, lectures. 3. Business forecasting - Addresses, essays, lectures. I. Japan Computer Usage Development Institute. II. Title. III. Series.
NYPL [TB (Studi e ricerche di scienze sociali. v.60)]

Plan (France. Commissariat général du plan) (10) Le Renouvellement du tissu industriel . Paris [1986] 130 p. ; ISBN 2-11-001568-3 : LC Card 86-191910
HD3616.F83 R46 1986

(11) Pour un rôle actif de la Communauté économique européenne sur la scène agricole internationale . Paris , c1986. 184 p. ; ISBN 2-11-001582-9 : LC Card 86-174918
HD1431 .P68 1986

(8) France. Groupe de stratégie industrielle no 8. Sous-groupe Travaux publics. La branche des travaux publics en France et sur les marchés extérieurs /. Paris , c1985. 202 p. : ISBN 2-11-001524-1 : LC Card 86-183130
HD4168 .F69 1985

(9) Evaluation de la planification décentralisée /. Paris , c1986. 97 p. : ISBN 2-11-001562-4 : LC Card 86-193163
HC276.2 .E89 1986

Les Industries agro-alimentaires . Paris [1986], c1987. 164 p. : ISBN 2-11-001722-8 : LC Card 87-167615
HD9012.5 .I53 1987

Der Plan Freycinet und die Provinzen . Beck, Robert, 1953- Frankfurt am Main , New York , c1986. 354 p. : ISBN 3-8204-9791-9 LC Card 87-408148 DDC 385/.068 19
HE3067 .B43 1986

Plan général de développement du réseau régional en Afrique = General plan for the development of the regional network in Africa : 1982-1986-1990. Genève : Union internationale des télécommunications, 1983. 134 p. : ill. (1 col.) ; 30 cm. Chiefly tables. Parallel English, French, and Spanish texts. On spine: Plan "Afrique," Libreville 1983. At head of title: CCITT-CCIR, Commission régionale du plan pour le développement des réseaux des télécommunications en Afrique. ISBN 92-71-02066-9 LC Card 85-146412
1. Telecommunication policy - Africa. I. Commission régionale du plan pour le développement des réseaux des télécommunications en Afrique. II. International Telecommunication Union. III. Title: General plan for the development of the regional network in Africa. IV. Title: Plan "Afrique," Libreville 1983.
HE8465 .P54 1983

Plan integral de desarrollo del predio Putumayo. Proyecto La Chorrera. Bogotá : Caja Agraria, [1986] 29 p. : ill. (some col.), maps ; 23 cm. Cover title. LC Card 87-401011 DDC 338.9861/7 19
1. Proyecto La Chorrera. 2. Economic development projects - Colombia - La Chorrera Region (Amazonas). I. Caja de Crédito Agrario, Industrial y Minero (Colombia).
HC198.C49 P55 1986

Plan laboral de Izquierda Unida. Izquierda Unida (Political party) [Lima?] , 1986. 67 p. ; LC Card 87-107365
HD8346.5 .I97 1986

Plan Nacional de Desarrollo, 1985-1988 /. Consejo Nacional de Desarrollo (Ecuador). Secretaría General de Planificación. [Quito, Ecuador] [1985] 3 leaves, iv, 218 p. : LC Card 86-146646 DDC 338.9866 19
HC202 .C675 1985b

Plan nacional de rehabilitación : plan social para la paz / Presidencia de la República, Departamento Nacional de Planeación, Ministerio de Gobierno. [Bogotá, Colombia] :

La Presidencia, 1985. 86 leaves : ill. ; 27 cm. LC Card 87-103481 DDC 338.9861 19
1. Colombia - Economic policy. 2. Colombia - Social policy. 3. Colombia - Politics and government - 1974-. I. Colombia. Presidencia de la República. II. Colombia. Departamento Nacional de Planeación. III. Colombia. Ministerio de Gobierno.
HC197 .P59 1985

Plan quinquennal de développement économique et social, 1979-1983 /. Niger. Ministère du plan. [Niamey] [1980] 666 p. : LC Card 86-138814
HC1020 .N535 1980

Plan régional de développement . Martinique. [Fort-de-France] [1984?] 96 p. : LC Card 87-101613
HC158.6 .M36 1984

Plan to restructure professional standards. New York, N.Y. (1211 Ave. of the Americas, New York 10036-8775) : American Institute of Certified Public Accountants, c1987. xii, 68 p. ; 23 cm. LC Card 87-160205 DDC 657/.0218 19
1. Accounting - Standards - United States. 2. Accountants - Professional ethics - United States. 3. Accounting - Study and teaching (Continuing education) - United States. I. American Institute of Certified Public Accountants.
HF5616.U5 P53 1987

Plan your work with plans of action /. Wall, William C. Huntsville, Ala. , c1987. p. cm. ISBN 0-938745-03-4 : LC Card 87-3629 DDC 658.4/012 19
HD30.28 .W336 1987

Plandecor, Plan de desarrollo de Córdoba . Córdoba (Argentina : Province) Córdoba , 1981-<1982. v. <1-3 > : LC Card 87-401182 DDC 330.982/54064 19
HC177.C7 C66 1981

Planeación familiar y cambio demográfico. 1a ed. México, D.F. : Instituto Mexicano del Seguro Social, Secretaría General, Subdirección General Médica, Jefatura de Servicios del Secretariado Técnico, Centro de Documentación [y] Jefatura de Servicios de Planificación Familiar, [1983], c1982. 554 p. : ill. ; 24 cm. (Lecturas en materia de seguridad social) Includes bibliographical references. ISBN 968-8241-63-6 LC Card 84-227488 DDC 304.6/0972 19
1. Birth control - Mexico. 2. Fertility, Human - Mexico. 3. Mortality - Mexico. 4. Mexico - Population. I. Instituto Mexicano del Seguro Social. Centro de Documentación. II. Instituto Mexicano del Seguro Social. Jefatura de Servicios de Planificación Familiar. III. Series.
HB3531 .P57 1983 ***NYPL [JLE 86-3248]***

Planejamento, ciência e tecnologia . Bahia, Brazil (State) Secretaria do Planejamento, Ciência e Tecnologia. [Salvador , 1983?] 93 p. : LC Card 85-136375
HC188.B3 B334 1983

O planejamento e os pré-investimentos /. Banco Regional de Desenvolvimento do Extremo sul. [Porto Alegre?] [19]85. 71, [6], p. 21 leaves ; LC Card 86-201808
HC188.S68 B35 1985

Planejamento e os pré-investimentos na Região Sul. Banco Regional de Desenvolvimento do Extremo sul. O planejamento e os pré-investimentos /. [Porto Alegre?] [19]85. 71, [6], p. 21 leaves ; LC Card 86-201808
HC188.S68 B35 1985

Los planes del capitalismo para la década de los 80 /. Larrazábal, Radamés. [Caracas, Venezuela? , 1982] (Caracas, Venezuela : Cooperative Mixta de Trabajadores Gráficos) 81 p. ; LC Card 83-201901
HC237 .L325 1982

Planificación por la revolución y la justicia. [Lima, Peru] : Presidencia de la República, Instituto Nacional de Planificación, [1986] 43 p. : ill. ; 29 cm. "Agosto 85/Julio 86." LC Card 87-402212 DDC 338.985 19
1. Peru - Economic policy. I. Instituto Nacional de Planificación (Peru).
HC227 .P536 1986

Le planificateur et le cyclopousse . Darbéra, Richard. Caen , 1986. xiii, 190 p. : ISBN 2-86878-015-6 : LC Card 86-192929
HE311.I4 D36 1986

La planification économique du développement . Martens, André. Montréal [1982] 2 v. : LC Card 83-178486
HC59.7 .M323 1982

Planification et aménagement des communes, des départements et des régions /. Lefebvre, André, docteur en droit. Paris , c1985. 335 p. : ISBN 2-7013-0620-5 : LC Card 86-113657 DDC 338.944 19
HT395.F7 L43 1985 ***NYPL [JLD 87-1577]***

Planirovanie ėkonomicheskogo rosta v razvivai͡ushchikhsi͡a stranakh . I͡Ashkin, V. A. (Vladimir Andreevich) Moskva , 1986. 120 p. ; LC Card 86-220878
HC59.7 .I13 1986

Planirovanie ėkonomiki Moldavskoĭ SSR / [redkollegii͡a P.S. Soltan (otvetstvennyĭ redaktor) ... et al.]. Kishinev : "Shtiint͡sa", 1986. 161 p. ; 22 cm. At head of title: Gosplan Moldavskoĭ SSR. Nauchno-issledovatel′skiĭ institut planirovanii͡a. Includes bibliographies. LC Card 86-203680
1. Agricultural industries - Moldavian S.S.R. - Management. 2. Industrial management - Moldavian S.S.R. I. Soltan, Petr Semenovich. II. Nauchno-issledovatel′skiĭ institut planirovanii͡a (Moldavian S.S.R.).
HD9015.S653 M6457 1986

Planirovanie narodnogo khozi͡aĭstva SSSR /. Terekhov, I͡U. I. (I͡Uriĭ Ivanovich) Khar′kov , 1985. 176 p. ; LC Card 86-102455
HC336.25 .T465 1985

Planirovanie otdelochnogo proizvodstva s primeneniem matematicheskikh metodov i ĖVM . Denisova, N. F. (Nina Fedorovna) Moskva , 1984. 59, [5] p. : LC Card 85-131509
HD9865.S652 D46 1984

Planirovanie potrebnosti v material′nykh resursakh na predprii͡atii /. Baskin, A. I. (Arkadiĭ Isaakovich) Kiev , 1983. 48 p. ; LC Card 83-243488
HD39.5 .B37 1983

Planirovanie pribyli i rentabel′nosti na promyshlennom predprii͡atii . Vasil′eva, E. S. (Elena Stepanovna) Moskva , 1985. 40 p. : LC Card 86-204680
HG4028.P7 V39 1985

Plänitz, Günther. Das bisschen Fahren-- : Arbeits- und Lebensbedingungen von Fernfahrern / Günther Plänitz. Hamburg : VSA-Verlag, 1983. 317 p. : ill. ; 21 cm. Bibliography: p. 316-317. ISBN 3-87975-248-6 LC Card 84-187043
1. Truck drivers - Germany (West). 2. Job stress - Germany (West). 3. Trucking - Germany (West) - Safety measures. I. Title.
HD8039.M7952 G37 1983

Planned development in Turkey and the State Planning Organization. [Ankara] : Dept. of Publication and Press, [1986] 47 p. : ill. ; 24 cm. "July 1986." "Periodicals": p. 47. LC Card 87-151757 DDC 338.9561 19
1. Devlet Planlama Teşkilatı (Turkey). 2. Turkey - Economic policy. 3. Turkey - Social policy. 4. Central planning - Turkey. I. Devlet Planlama Teşkilatı (Turkey). Yayin ve Temsil Dairesi Başkanliği.
HC492 .P63 1986

Planned unit developments . Tomioka, Seishiro. New York , c1984. xviii, 192 p. : ISBN 0-471-08595-2 : LC Card 82-13419 DDC 307/.12/0973 19
HD257 .T65 1984 ***NYPL [JLF 86-1316]***

PLANNED UNIT DEVELOPMENTS.
Schwanke, Dean. Mixed-use development handbook /. Washington, D.C. , 1987. xv, 364 p. : ISBN 0-08-742665-0 LC Card 86-51443 DDC 333.3/8 19
HD1390 .S38 1987

PLANNED UNIT DEVELOPMENTS - UNITED STATES.
Tomioka, Seishiro. Planned unit developments . New York , c1984. xviii, 192 p. : ISBN 0-471-08595-2 : LC Card 82-13419 DDC 307/.12/0973 19
HD257 .T65 1984 ***NYPL [JLF 86-1316]***

PLANNING.
Brooks, Julie K. How to write a successful business plan /. New York, NY , c1987. vii, 231 p. : ISBN 0-8144-5873-4 LC Card 86-22355 DDC 658.4/012 19
HD30.28 .B775 1987

Planning in turbulence /. Jerusalem , 1986. xii, 158 p. : ISBN 965-223-657-8 (pbk.) LC Card 87-163701 DDC 658.4/012 19
HD87.5 .P5 1986

Reigado, Felisberto Marques. Introdução ao planeamento . Lisboa , 1983. 370 p. : LC Card 84-164510 DDC 361.2 19
HD85.P65 R45 1983 ***NYPL [JLD 86-3065]***

Schlesinger, James R. Organizational structures and planning /. [Santa Monica, Calif. , 1966] iii, 45 p. : LC Card 87-404140 DDC 353.6 19
HD58.9 .S35 1966

Sullivan, George, 1927- Work smart, not hard /. New York, N.Y. , c1987. xii, 196 p. ; ISBN 0-8160-1393-4 : LC Card 86-24320 DDC 658.3/14 19
HF5549.5.P35 S85 1987

Willis, Raymond E. (Raymond Edson), 1930- A guide to forecasting for planners and managers /. Englewood Cliffs, N.J. , c1987. xii, 404 p. : ISBN 0-13-369539-5 : LC Card 86-25532 DDC 658.4/0355 19
HD30.27 .W55 1987

Planning a project and building your project team. Project management. Chicago, Ill. , 1987, c1985. 1 videocassette (30 min.) : LC Card 87-705140 DDC 658.4 11
HD69.P75

Planning and employment trends in India /. Chaudhary, S. K. New Delhi , c1987. 300 p. ; LC Card 86-903543 DDC 331.11/0954/12 19
HD5819 .C47 1987

Planning and financial evaluation of housing strategies / edited by Errol Haarhoff. Durban : Economic Research Unit/School of Architecture and Allied Disciplines, University of Natal, 1983. viii, 233 p. : ill. ; 30 cm. (Low-income housing in the Durban metropolitan region . project report no. 4) Cover title: Planning & financial evaluation of housing strategies. Bibliography: p. 231-233. ISBN 0-86980-360-3 (pbk.) LC Card 86-205849 DDC 363.5/8 19
1. Poor - Housing - South Africa - Durban Metropolitan Area. 2. Housing policy - South Africa - Durban Metropolitan Area. I. Haarhoff, E. J. (Errol J.). II. Title: Planning & financial evaluation of housing strategies. III. Series.
HD7287.96.S682 D876 1983

Planning & financial evaluation of housing strategies. Planning and financial evaluation of housing strategies /. Durban , 1983. viii, 233 p. : ISBN 0-86980-360-3 (pbk.) LC Card 86-205849 DDC 363.5/8 19
HD7287.96.S682 D876 1983

Planning & implementing an apparel sourcing strategy : 1986 report of the Technical Advisory Committee, American Apparel Manufacturers Association. Arlington, Va. (2500 Wilson Blvd., Suite 301, Arlington 22209) : The Association, c1986. 41 p. : ill. ; 28 cm. LC Card 87-107327 DDC 687/.068/7 19
1. Clothing trade - United States. 2. Clothing trade - International cooperation. 3. Textile fabrics - Purchasing. 4. Textile industry. 5. International division of labor. I. American Apparel Manufacturers Association. Technical Advisory Committee. II. Title: Planning and implementing an apparel sourcing strategy.
HD9940.U4 P52 1986

Planning and implementing an apparel sourcing strategy. Planning & implementing an apparel sourcing strategy . Arlington, Va. (2500 Wilson Blvd., Suite 301, Arlington 22209) , c1986. 41 p. : LC Card 87-107327 DDC 687/.068/7 19
HD9940.U4 P52 1986

Planning and implementing information resource centers for end-user computing /. Head, Robert V. Wellesley, MA , c1985. viii, 186 p. : ISBN 0-89435-123-0 : LC Card 84-61536
NYPL [JLE 86-2117]

Planning and zoning for farmland protection : a community based approach / prepared by American Farmland Trust. East Lansing, MI : The Trust, c1987. 58 p. : ill. ; 28 cm. Bibliography: p. 58. LC Card 87-119320 DDC 333.76/17/0973 19
1. Land use, Rural - United States - Planning. 2. Farms - United States. 3. Zoning - United States. I. American Farmland Trust.
HD256 .P57 1987

PLANNING - BRAZIL.
A Renda da terra . [São Paulo, Brazil] , Petrópolis , c1980. 152 p. : LC Card 81-214665
HC186 .C36a no. 27 HB401

PLANNING - CITIZEN PARTICIPATION.
Garbe, Detlef, 1949- Die Planungszelle und ihre Umwelt . Frankfurt a.M. ; Bern ; xiv, 339 p. ; ISBN 3-8204-6017-9 LC Card 81-464829
HC79.E5 G33 1980 ***NYPL [JLD 81-2376]***

PLANNING, CITY. see **CITY PLANNING.**

Planning control : philosophies, prospects and practice / edited by M.L. Harrison and R. Mordey. London : Wolfeboro, N.H. : Croom Helm, c1987. 234 p. ; 23 cm. (Croom Helm series in geography and environment) Includes index. Bibliography: p. 227-232. ISBN 0-7099-3790-3 : LC Card 86-24079 DDC 333.73/17/0941 19
1. Land use - Government policy - Great Britain. 2. Real estate development - Government policy - Great Britain. 3. Regional planning - Government policy - Great Britain. 4. Land use - Law and legislation - Great Britain. I. Harrison, M. L. (Malcolm L.). II. Mordey, R. (Richard).
HD596 .P53 1987 ***NYPL [JLD 87-803]***

PLANNING, CORPORATA. see **CORPORATE PLANNING.**

Planning Division special studies .
(no. 20) Safilios-Rothschild, Constantina, 1934- The policy implications of the roles of women in agriculture in Zambia /. [Lusaka] [1985] 49, [25] p. ; LC Card 87-980047 DDC 331.4/83/096894 19
HD6073.A292 Z337 1985

(no. 9) A Report on the resources, activities, and constraints in tobacco schemes . Lusaka , 1985. iii, 37 p. ; LC Card 85-981599 DDC 338.1/7371/096894 19
HD9147.Z34 R46 1985

PLANNING, ECONOMIC. see **ECONOMIC POLICY.**

Planning for adult career counseling /. Bhaerman, Robert D. Columbus, Ohio (1960 Kenny Rd., Columbus 43210-1090) , 1985. ix, 64 p. ; LC Card 87-108253 DDC 331.12/8 19
HF5381 .B4225 1985

Planning for changing energy conditions / edited by John Byrne and Daniel Rich. New Brunswick, N.J., U. S.A. : Transaction Books, c1988. xiii, 300 p. : ill. ; 23 cm. (Energy policy studies, 0882-3537 . v. 4) Includes bibliographies. ISBN 0-88738-713-6 (pbk.) : LC Card 87-13977 DDC 333.79 19
1. Energy policy. 2. Energy industries - Planning. I. Byrne, John, 1949-. II. Rich, Daniel. III. Series.
HD9502.A2 P59 1988

PLANNING - HISTORY.
Friedmann, John. Planning in the public domain . Princeton, N.J. , c1987. xii, 501 p. : ISBN 0-691-07743-6 (alk. paper) : LC Card 87-3194 DDC 361.6 19
HD87.5 .F745 1987

Planning, implementing, and evaluating targeted communication programs . Selnow, Gary W. New York , 1987. vi, 291 p. : ISBN 0-89930-208-4 (lib. bdg. : alk. paper) LC Card 86-30418 DDC 659.1 19
HD30.3 .S46 1987

Planning in decentralized firms . Meijboom, Bert R., 1957- Berlin , New York , c1987. x, 168 p. : ISBN 0-387-17795-7 (U. S. : pbk.) : LC Card 87-9824 DDC 658.4/012 19
HD30.28 .M43 1987

Planning in India . Sinha, R. K. (Raj Kishore), 1946- New Delhi , c1987. ix, 247 p. ; ISBN 81-7003-079-X : LC Card 87-901786 DDC 338.954 19
HC435.2 .S565 1987

PLANNING IN POLITICS. see **POLITICAL PLANNING.**

Planning in the public domain . Friedmann, John. Princeton, N.J. , c1987. xii, 501 p. : ISBN 0-691-07743-6 (alk. paper) : LC Card 87-3194 DDC 361.6 19
HD87.5 .F745 1987

Planning in turbulence / edited by David Morley and Arie Shachar. Jerusalem : Magnes Press, Hebrew University, 1986. xii, 158 p. : ill., maps ; 23 cm. At head of title: The Programme of Canadian Studies at the Hebrew University of Jerusalem. Includes bibliographies and index. ISBN 965-223-657-8 (pbk.) LC Card 87-163701 DDC 658.4/012 19
1. Planning. 2. Risk. 3. Uncertainty. 4. Planning - Israel. I. Morley, C. D. II. Shachar, A., 1935-. III. Universitah ha-'Ivrit bi-Yerushalayim. Programme of Canadian Studies.
HD87.5 .P5 1986

Planning income generating projects . Else, John F. Harare, Zimbabwe [1986?] 46 p. : LC Card 87-400416 DDC 338.96891/0068 19
HC910 .E43 1986

PLANNING - ISRAEL.
Planning in turbulence /. Jerusalem , 1986. xii, 158 p. : ISBN 965-223-657-8 (pbk.) LC Card 87-163701 DDC 658.4/012 19
HD87.5 .P5 1986

PLANNING, NATIONAL. see **ECONOMIC POLICY; SOCIAL POLICY.**

PLANNING - PORTUGAL.
Reigado, Felisberto Marques. Introdução ao planeamento . Lisboa , 1983. 370 p. : LC Card 84-164510 DDC 361.2 19
HD85.P65 R45 1983 ***NYPL [JLD 86-3065]***

PLANNING-PROGRAMMING-BUDGETING. see **PROGRAM BUDGETING.**

PLANNING, STATE. see **ECONOMIC POLICY; SOCIAL POLICY.**

Planning strategies that work / edited by Arnoldo C. Hax. New York : Oxford University Press, 1987. xii, 287 p. : ill. ; 24 cm. (The Executive bookshelf) A selection of articles from the Sloan management review. Bibliography: p. 252-275. Includes index. ISBN 0-19-504883-0 (alk. paper) LC Card 86-31117 DDC 658.4/012 19
1. Strategic planning. I. Hax, Arnoldo C. II. Sloan management review. III. Series.
HD30.28 .P555 1987

Planning under indeterminacy /. Zauberman, Alfred. Bielefeld, Federal Republic of Germany [1976] 153, 5 p. ; LC Card 85-127554
HC336.25 .Z38 1976

Planning under pressure . Friend, John. Oxford [Oxfordshire] , New York , 1987. xix, 338 p. : ISBN 0-08-018766-8 : LC Card 86-25219 DDC 658.4/012 19
HD30.28 .F75 1987

O Plano Beveridge criticado /. Costa, F. Ramos da. Lisboa , 1943. 75 p. ; LC Card 85-211958
HD7165.A72 C66 1943

Plano Cruzado : ataque e defesa / coordenação editorial de Haydn Coutinho Pimenta.1a. ed. Rio de Janeiro : Forense-Universitária, 1987. xii, 203 p. : ill. ; 22 cm. At head of title: CEDEPLAR/UFMG. Includes bibliographical references. LC Card 87-127770 DDC 338.981 19
1. Brazil - Economic policy. 2. Brazil - Economic conditions - 1985-. I. Pimenta, Haydn Coutinho. II. Universidade Federal de Minas Gerais. Centro de Desenvolvimento e Planejamento Regional.
HC187 .P59 1987

Plano de desenvolvimento da área-programa do Vale do Paraná /. Projeto de Desenvolvimento Integrado da Bacia do Araguaia-Tocantins. Brasília , 1985. 128 p., [8] folded leaves of plates : LC Card 86-199833
HC188.P36 P76 1985

Plano de desenvolvimento das áreas-programa de Araguaína e Tocantinópolis /. Projeto de Desenvolvimento Integrado da Bacia do Araguaia-Tocantins. Brasília , 1985. 95 p., [8] leaves of plates : LC Card 86-200369
HC189.A67 P76 1985

Plano de desenvolvimento regional do Centro-Oeste . Brazil. Superintendência do Desenvolvimento da Região Centro-Oeste. Brasília , 1985. 101 p. : LC Card 86-146677
HC188.C46 B7 1985

Plano Diretor do Distrito Agropecuário /. Brazil. Superintendência da Zona Franca de Manaus. Manaus , 1984. 86 p. : LC Card 85-209805
HD1875.M325 B73 1984

Plano nacional de armazenagem, 1985 /. Companhia Brasileira de Armazenamento. Brasília, DF [1985 or 1986] 1 v. (various foliations) : LC Card 87-403918 DDC 381 19
HF5489.B73 C66 1985

Plano Operativo 1983, Governo Divaldo Suruagy. Alagoas (Brazil) [Maceió] [1983?] 196 p. ; LC Card 85-200834
HC188.A46 A44 1983a

Planomernoe razreshenie protivorechiĭ razvitiia sotsializma kak pervoĭ fazy kommunizma /. Popov, Mikhail V. Leningrad , 1986. 156 p. ; LC Card 87-146874
HB97.5 .P7994 1986

Planomernoe razvitie sotsialisticheskoĭ ėkonomiki / [kniga podgotovlena kollektivom sovetskikh i chekhoslovatskikh avtorov pod redaktsieĭ S.V. Rogacheva i Zdenko IAury]. Sovmestnoe izd. Moskva : Izd-vo "Ėkonomika" ; Bratislava : Izd-vo "Pravda", 1977. 262 p. ; 23 cm. Includes bibliographical references. LC Card 87-100683
1. Central planning - Soviet Union. 2. Soviet Union - Economic policy - 1976-1980. 3. Central planning - Czechoslovakia. 4. Czechoslovakia - Economic policy - 1965-. I. Rogachev, S. V. (Sergeĭ Vladimirovich). II. Jaura, Zdeno.
HC336.25 .P448 1977

Planomernost′ i ėffektivnost′ sotsialisticheskogo obshchestvennogo proizvodstva /. Martyniuk, S. M. (Stanislav Mikhaĭlovich) Kiev , 1982. 141 p. ; LC Card 83-219823
HC335 .M3675 1982

Planovoe regulirovanie vozmeshcheniia orudiĭ truda v promyshlennosti /. Liakh, L. V. (Lidiia Vasil′evna) Kiev , 1983. 122, [1] p. : LC Card 84-105177
HD39.3 .L53 1983

Planovoe upravlenie ėkonomikoĭ razvitogo sotsializma .
(t. 1) Narodno-khoziaĭstvennye proportsii, ikh planirovanie i prognozirovanie /. Kiev , 1985. 318 p. : LC Card 86-210651
HC337.U5 P5 1985 t. 1

(t. 2) Resursy narodnogo khoziaĭstva . Kiev , 1985. 308 p. : LC Card 86-226867
HC337.U5 P5 1985 t. 2 HC337.U53I52

PLANT AND EQUIPMENT INVESTMENTS. see **CAPITAL INVESTMENTS.**

PLANT AND OFFICE LAYOUT. see **OFFICE LAYOUT.**

Plant closing : advance notice and rapid response : special report. Washington, D.C. : Congress of the U. S., Office of Technology Assessment : For sale by the Supt. of Docs., U. S. G.P.O., 1986. viii, 60 p. ; 26 cm. "September 1986"--P. [4] of cover. "OTA-ITE-321"--P. [4] of cover. Includes bibliographical references. LC Card 86-600573 DDC 338.6/042 19
1. Plant shutdowns - United States. I. United States. Congress. Office of Technology Assessment.
HD5708.55.U6 P519 1986

Plant closings . Rothstein, Lawrence E. Dover, Mass. , c1986. xv, 201 p. ; ISBN 0-86569-121-5 : LC Card 85-23025 DDC 338.6/042 19
HD5708.55.U6 R68 1986
NYPL [JLE 86-1884]

PLANT MAINTENANCE - ACCOUNTING - ADDRESSES, ESSAYS, LECTURES.
Depreciation and capital maintenance /. New York , 1984. xi, 137 p. : ISBN 0-8240-6304-X (alk. paper) : LC Card 83-49437 DDC 657/.73 19
HF5681.D5 D45 1984 ***NYPL [JLE 86-1715]***

Plant, Roger. Sugar and modern slavery : a tale of two countries / Roger Plant. London ; Atlantic Highlands, N.J. : Zed Books, 1987. xiv, 177 p. : map ; 23 cm. Bibliography: p. [168]-172. Includes index. ISBN 0-86232-572-2 : LC Card 87-13315 DDC 331.7/6361/097293 19
1. Sugar workers - Dominican Republic. 2. Sugarcane industry - Dominican Republic. 3. Alien labor, Haitian - Dominican Republic. 4. Haitians - Employment - Dominican Republic. 5. Forced labor - Dominican Republic. I. Title.
HD8039.S86 D652 1987

PLANT SHUTDOWNS - AUSTRALIA - CASE STUDIES.
Wooden, Mark. The effects of redundancy . [Bedford Park, S. Aust.] [1987] 52 p. : LC Card 87-170621 DDC 331.13/7994 19
HD5708.55.A8 W66 1987

PLANT SHUTDOWNS - ENGLAND - CORBY (NORTHAMPTONSHIRE)
Maunders, A. R. A process of struggle . Aldershot, Hampshire, England , Brookfield, Vt., USA , c1987. xi, 283 p. : ISBN 0-566-05227-X : LC Card 86-25640 DDC

338.6/042 19
HD9521.8.C85 M38 1987
NYPL [JLD 87-1533]

PLANT SHUTDOWNS - FRANCE.
Rothstein, Lawrence E. Plant closings . Dover, Mass. , c1986. xv, 201 p. ; ISBN 0-86569-121-5 : LC Card 85-23025 DDC 338.6/042 19
HD5708.55.U6 R68 1986
NYPL [JLE 86-1884]

PLANT SHUTDOWNS - GERMANY (WEST) - SPEYER.
Kirchen kämpfen mit . Mainz , 1981. 106 p. : ISBN 3-7867-0873-8 LC Card 81-188986 DDC 261.8/34562/094343 19
HD6338.2.G32 S634 1981
NYPL [JLD 86-2786]

PLANT SHUTDOWNS - GOVERNMENT POLICY - NEW YORK (STATE)
New York (State). Lieutenant Governor's Task Force on Plant Closings. Final report /. [Albany] [1985] 1 v. (various foliations) ; LC Card 86-622454 DDC 338.6/042 19
HD5708.55.U62 N76 1985

PLANT SHUTDOWNS - GREAT BRITAIN - CASE STUDIES.
Love, Cohn, 1938- Conflicts over closure . Aldershot, Hants, England , Brookfield, Vt., U. S.A. [1987] p. cm. ISBN 0-566-05367-5 : LC Card 86-29496 DDC 338.6/042 19
HD5708.55.G7 L68 1987

PLANT SHUTDOWNS - NEW YORK (STATE)
New York (State). Lieutenant Governor's Task Force on Plant Closings. Final report /. [Albany] [1985] 1 v. (various foliations) ; LC Card 86-622454 DDC 338.6/042 19
HD5708.55.U62 N76 1985

PLANT SHUTDOWNS - OHIO.
Logue, John, 1947- Buyout! . [Kent, Ohio] [1986] vi, 98 p. : ISBN 0-933522-15-0 (pbk.) LC Card 86-623028 DDC 658.1/6 19
HD2746.5 .L64 1986

PLANT SHUTDOWNS - SWEDEN - CASE STUDIES.
Samhällsekonomiska kalkyler vid industrinedläggningar . Stockholm [1982] 213 p. : ISBN 91-38-07164-9 LC Card 83-219569
HD5708.55.S8 S25 1982

PLANT SHUTDOWNS - UNITED STATES.
Plant closing . Washington, D.C. , 1986. viii, 60 p. ; LC Card 86-600573 DDC 338.6/042 19
HD5708.55.U6 P519 1986

Rothstein, Lawrence E. Plant closings . Dover, Mass. , c1986. xv, 201 p. ; ISBN 0-86569-121-5 : LC Card 85-23025 DDC 338.6/042 19
HD5708.55.U6 R68 1986
NYPL [JLE 86-1884]

United States. Secretary of Labor's Task Force on Economic Adjustment and Worker Dislocation. Economic adjustment and worker dislocation in a competitive society . Washington, D.C. [1986] 189 p. in various pagings : LC Card 87-601034 DDC 331.13/7973 19
HC106.8 .U545 1986

PLANT SHUTDOWNS - UNITED STATES - CASE STUDIES.
Berenbeim, Ronald. Company programs to ease the impact of shutdowns /. New York, N.Y. , c1986. ix, 57 p. : ISBN 0-8237-0320-7 (pbk.) LC Card 86-207794 DDC 331.25 19
HF5549.5.D55 B47 1986

PLANTATION LIFE - MISSISSIPPI - HISTORY.
Moore, John Hebron. The emergence of the Cotton Kingdom in the Old Southwest . Baton Rouge , c1988. xii, 323 p. : ISBN 0-8071-1404-9 (pbk.) LC Card 87-2803 DDC 330.9762 19
HC107.M7 M66 1988

PLANTATION LIFE - SRI LANKA.
Dawood, Nawaz. Tea and poverty . Kowloon, Hong Kong , 1980. xii, 166 p. ; LC Card 80-154803 DDC 338.1/7372/095493 19
HC424 .D36 1980

PLANTATIONS - BRAZIL - BAHIA (STATE) - HISTORY.
Schwartz, Stuart B. Sugar plantations in the formation of Brazilian society . Cambridge [Cambridgeshire] , New York , 1985. xxiii, 616 p. : ISBN 0-521-30934-4 LC Card 85-6716 DDC 306/.0981/42 19
HD9114.B7 B347 1985
NYPL [JLE 86-2276]

PLANTATIONS - BRAZIL - PIAUÍ - HISTORY.
Mott, Luiz R. B. (Luiz Roberto de Barros) Piauí colonial . [Teresina] [1985] 142 p. : LC Card 86-131892
HC188.P5 M67 1985

PLANTATIONS - DEVELOPING COUNTRIES.
Beckford, George L. Persistent poverty . London , Totowa, N.J. , c1983. xxv, 244 p. : ISBN 0-86232-207-3 (pbk.) LC Card 85-149825 DDC 338.1/09172/4 19
HC59.72.P6 B43 1983 *NYPL [JLD 87-628]*

PLANTATIONS - INDIA - JALPAIGURI (DISTRICT)
Bhowmik, Sharit, 1948- Class formation in the plantation system /. New Delhi , 1981. xix, 263 p. : LC Card 81-903777 DDC 305/.93633 19
HD1470.5.I42 J342 1981
NYPL [JLD 86-2612]

PLANTATIONS - SRI LANKA.
Capital and peasant production . Colombo, Sri Lanka , 1985. xiv, 230 p. ; LC Card 86-900809 DDC 338.1/3/095493 19
HD2065.8 .C36 1985 *NYPL [JLE 87-1667]*

PLANTING. see **AGRICULTURE.**

Planung des Personalbedarfs in indirekten Bereichen /. Hemmers, K. (Karlheinz) Berlin , New York , 1986. viii, 141 p. : ISBN 0-387-16702-1 (U. S.) : LC Card 86-200805
HF5549.5.M3 H46 1986

Die Planung langfristiger Kosten . Winkelmann, Jürgen. Thun , c1982. 281 p. : ISBN 3-87144-702-1 LC Card 83-129316
HD47 .W54 1982

Planung und Erwartungsbildung in der Investitionsentscheidung . Mors, Matthias. Frankfurt am Main , c1983. 190 p. : ISBN 3-88129-619-0 LC Card 83-174677
HG4028.C4 M65 1983

Planung und Nutzung des technischen Fortschritts /. Schmidt-Tiedemann, K. J. [Dortmund?] , 1976. 37 p. : LC Card 86-123518
HD30 .A7 Heft 173 T177.G4

Planung und Partizipation . Rucht, Dieter. München , c1982. 321 p. ; ISBN 3-88073-105-5 LC Card 83-672501
JN3971.A91 R82x 1982
NYPL [JLD 86-2900]

Die Planung von Distributionssystemen der Konsumgüterindustrie unter besonderer Berücksichtigung der Tourenauslieferung . Kipshagen, Lothar. Thun , c1983. v, 336 p. : ISBN 3-87144-748-X LC Card 83-185464
HF5415.6 .K56 1983

Die Planung von Liquidationsstrategien . Wöbbeking, Karlheinz. Münster [1986] vii, 273 p. : ISBN 3-88660-328-8 LC Card 86-213801
HD2747 .W6 1986

Planung von Marketing-Strategien . Müller, Wolfgang, 1955- Frankfurt am Main , New York , c1986. xxvi, 514 p. : ISBN 3-8204-8992-4 LC Card 86-205571
HF5415.13 .M833 1986

Planungsbeispiele für Knotenpunkte des Strassenverkehrs /. Feuchtinger, Max Erich. Bad Godesberg [1960] 93 p., [2] folded leaves of plates : LC Card 86-191612
HE363.G3 F48 1960

Planungshefte Ruhrgebiet.
Radverkehrskonzept Sprockhövel /. Essen , c1985. 55 p., [3] folded col. leaves of plates : ISBN 3-923494-51-3 LC Card 86-113993
HE5739.G3 R33 1985

Planwirtschaft im Zerrspiegel des Linksradikalismus /. Nörenberg, Günther. Berlin , 1984. 108 p. ; LC Card 84-196372
HC59 .N652 1984

Plas, W. Inventaris van het archief van Regeringscommissariaat voor de Buitenlandse Agrarische Aangelegenheden (RECOBAA), 1946-1950 / W. Plas. [Hague] : Ministerie van Landbouw en Visserij, Directie Materiële Zaken, Centrale Afdeling Algemene Secretarie, [1985] 111 p. ; 30 cm. "December 1985." Includes index. LC Card 87-101964

1. Produce trade - Netherlands. 2. Food industry and trade - Netherlands. 3. Netherlands. Regeringscommissariaat voor de Buitenlandse Agrarische Aangelegenheden - Archives. I. Title.
HD9015.N42 P55 1985

Plaschka, Gerhard. Unternehmenserfolg : eine vergleichende empirische Untersuchung von erfolgreichen und nicht erfolgreichen Unternehmensgründern / Gerhard Plaschka. Wien : Service, c1986. viii, 228 p. ; 21 cm. (Schriftenreihe der Abteilung für Gewerbe, Klein- und Mittelbetriebe an der Wirtschaftsuniversität Wien . Bd. 7) Bibliography: p. 207-228. LC Card 87-103428 DDC 658.4/09 19

1. Executive ability. 2. Success in business. 3. Leadership. I. Title.
HD38.2 .P55 1986

Plaschka, Martina. Gründungsfinanzierung : eine empirische Analyse potentieller Unternehmer / Martina Plaschka. Wien : Service, c1986. vii, 159 p. : 17 ill. ; 21 cm. (Schriftenreihe der Abteilung für Gewerbe, Klein- und Mittelbetriebe an der Wirtschaftsuniversität Wien . Bd. 4) Bibliography: p. 154-159. ISBN 3-85428-067-X LC Card 86-225844

1. Business enterprises - Austria - Finance. 2. Businessmen - Austria - Attitudes. 3. Entrepreneur. I. Series: Schriftenreihe der Abteilung für Gewerbe, Klein- und Mittelbetriebe an der Wirtschaftsuniversität Wien , Bd. 4. II. Title.
HG4146 .P57 1986

Plastic and electronic money . Frazer, P. A. T. Cambridge [Cambridgeshire] , Dover, NH. USA , 1985. x, 294 p. ; ISBN 0-85941-290-3 : LC Card 85-22552 DDC 332.1/028 19
HG1710 .F73 1985 *NYPL [JLE 86-1401]*

PLASTIC INDUSTRIES. see **PLASTICS INDUSTRY AND TRADE.**

PLASTIC SCRAP - RECYCLING - CONGRESSES.
Technology Exchange Program (1986 : Washington, D.C.) Plastics recycling as a future business opportunity, Friday, June 20, 1986 at the Sheraton-Carlton Hotel, Washington, D.C. . Lancaster, Pa., U. S.A. , c1986. iii, 139 p. : ISBN 0-87762-510-7 (pbk.) LC Card 86-51296 DDC 668.4/192 19
HD9661.U62 T39 1986

PLASTIC SCRAP - UNITED STATES - RECYCLING - CONGRESSES.
Technology Exchange Program (1986 : Washington, D.C.) Plastics recycling as a future business opportunity, Friday, June 20, 1986 at the Sheraton-Carlton Hotel, Washington, D.C. . Lancaster, Pa., U. S.A. , c1986. iii, 139 p. : ISBN 0-87762-510-7 (pbk.) LC Card 86-51296 DDC 668.4/192 19
HD9661.U62 T39 1986

Plastics EMI shielding . Mooney, Peter. Stamford, Conn., U. S.A. , c1985. xxii, 297 leaves : ISBN 0-89336-409-6 (soft) LC Card 87-168832 DDC 338.4/76684 19
HD9661.U62 M654 1985

PLASTICS IN AUTOMOBILES.
The Changing passenger car markets . Stamford, Conn., U. S.A. , c1985. viii, 227 leaves : ISBN 0-89336-479-7 (pbk.) LC Card 87-404429 DDC 381/.4566849 19
HD9710.U52 C385 1985

Plastics in business machines : domestic and international developments / Peter J. Mooney, project analyst. Stamford, Conn. : Business Communications, c1986. vii, 215 leaves : ill. ; 29 cm. (Business opportunity report . P-064R) ISBN 0-89336-433-6 (soft) : LC Card 87-165036 DDC 380.1/456684 19

1. Electronic office machine industry. 2. Plastics industry and trade. 3. Electronic office machines - Materials. 4. Substitute products. I. Mooney, Peter. II. Business Communications Co. III. Series.
HD9801.A2 P56 1986

PLASTICS IN ELECTRIC ENGINEERING - UNITED STATES.
Mooney, Peter. Plastics EMI shielding . Stamford, Conn., U. S.A. , c1985. xxii, 297 leaves : ISBN 0-89336-409-6 (soft) LC Card 87-168832 DDC 338.4/76684 19
HD9661.U62 M654 1985

PLASTICS INDUSTRY AND TRADE.
(1986) Plastics in business machines . Stamford, Conn. , c1986. vii, 215 leaves : ISBN

0-89336-433-6 (soft) : LC Card 87-165036 DDC 380.1/456684 19
HD9801.A2 P56 1986

PLASTICS INDUSTRY AND TRADE - CONGRESSES.
Technology Exchange Program (1986 : Washington, D.C.) Plastics recycling as a future business opportunity, Friday, June 20, 1986 at the Sheraton-Carlton Hotel, Washington, D.C. . Lancaster, Pa., U. S.A. , c1986. iii, 139 p. : ISBN 0-87762-510-7 (pbk.) LC Card 86-51296 DDC 668.4/192 19
HD9661.U62 T39 1986

PLASTICS INDUSTRY AND TRADE - EUROPE.
Vinyl and acrylic latices markets in Europe. New York, N.Y. , c1983. 2 v. (xxxv, 328 leaves) : LC Card 87-143984 DDC 380.1/456684232/094 19
HD9661.E82 V55 1983

PLASTICS INDUSTRY AND TRADE - HEALTH ASPECTS - QUÉBEC (PROVINCE)
Caoutchouc et produits en matières plastiques au Québec . [Québec] , 1984. 249 p. : ISBN 2-550-10690-3 LC Card 85-155214 DDC 363.1/196684/09714 19
HD7269.R92 C23 1984

PLASTICS INDUSTRY AND TRADE - SWITZERLAND - MANAGEMENT - CASE STUDIES.
Kurmann, Bernadette, 1950- Firmenkultur am Beispiel der Sarna /. Bern [1985] 119 p. ; ISBN 3-258-03560-1 : LC Card 86-123837 DDC 338.7/6684/09494 19
HD9661.S94 S275 1985 ***NYPL [JLD 86-4028]***

PLASTICS INDUSTRY AND TRADE - UNITED STATES.
Plastics industry research manual /. [S.l.] [1985] 69 leaves ; LC Card 86-219855 DDC 338.4/7668497/0973 19
HD9661.U62 P489 1985

Shea, Moira M. The United States engineering plastics industry . Washington, D.C. , 1987. 51 p. : LC Card 87-601518 DDC 338.4/76684/0973 19
HD9661.U62 S54 1987

PLASTICS INDUSTRY AND TRADE - UNITED STATES - CONGRESSES.
Technology Exchange Program (1986 : Washington, D.C.) Plastics recycling as a future business opportunity, Friday, June 20, 1986 at the Sheraton-Carlton Hotel, Washington, D.C. . Lancaster, Pa., U. S.A. , c1986. iii, 139 p. : ISBN 0-87762-510-7 (pbk.) LC Card 86-51296 DDC 668.4/192 19
HD9661.U62 T39 1986

PLASTICS INDUSTRY AND TRADE - UNITED STATES - ELECTRIC EQUIPMENT.
Mooney, Peter. Plastics EMI shielding . Stamford, Conn., U. S.A. , c1985. xxii, 297 leaves : ISBN 0-89336-409-6 (soft) LC Card 87-168832 DDC 338.4/76684 19
HD9661.U62 M654 1985

Plastics industry research manual / prepared by the Food and Allied Service Trades Department, AFL-CIO. [S.l.] : FAST, [1985] 69 leaves ; 28 cm. "October 1985." LC Card 86-219855 DDC 338.4/7668497/0973 19
1. Plastics industry and trade - United States. I. AFL-CIO. Food and Allied Service Trades Dept.
HD9661.U62 P489 1985

Plastics Institute of America. Technology Exchange Program (1986 : Washington, D.C.) Plastics recycling as a future business opportunity, Friday, June 20, 1986 at the Sheraton-Carlton Hotel, Washington, D.C. . Lancaster, Pa., U. S.A. , c1986. iii, 139 p. : ISBN 0-87762-510-7 (pbk.) LC Card 86-51296 DDC 668.4/192 19
HD9661.U62 T39 1986

Plastics recycling as a future business opportunity, Friday, June 20, 1986 at the Sheraton-Carlton Hotel, Washington, D.C. . Technology Exchange Program (1986 : Washington, D.C.) Lancaster, Pa., U. S.A. , c1986. iii, 139 p. : ISBN 0-87762-510-7 (pbk.) LC Card 86-51296 DDC 668.4/192 19
HD9661.U62 T39 1986

Platão. see **Plato.**

Plateau State (Nigeria) Government views and decisions on the Report of the Panel on the Allocation of Stalls in the Three Temporary Markets in Jos : 18th October 1976. Jos [Nigeria] : Plateau State of Nigeria, [1976?] 9 p. ; 25 cm. LC Card 87-401792 DDC 381/.18/096695 19
1. Markets - Government policy - Nigeria - Jos. I. Report of the Panel on the Allocation of Stalls in the Three Temporary Markets in Jos. II. Title.
HF5475.N52 J66 1976

Plath, Dietmar, 1954- Penner, Hellmut, 1942- Airbus International /. Stuttgart , 1986. 206 p. : ISBN 3-613-01093-3 LC Card 86-211620
HD9711.E882 P46 1986

PLATO - INFLUENCE.
Pappa, Hellē. Hoi archaioi Hellēnes syngrapheis sto "Kephalaio" tou Marx /. Athēna , 1983. 112 p. ; LC Card 84-128852
HB501 .P24 1983

Platon. see **Plato.**

Platon, Clarck. Amapá, fundamento de minha luta : atividades parlamentares desenvolvidas pelo Deputado Clarck Platon durante o ano de 1983. Brasília : Câmara dos Deputados, Centro de Documentação e Informação, Coordenação de Publicações, 1983. 155 p. : ill. ; 23 cm. (Separatas de discursos, pareceres e projetos . 47a. Legislatura--1a. Sessão Legislativa, no. 212) LC Card 86-127813
1. Amapá (Brazil : Territory) - Economic policy. 2. Amapá (Brazil : Territory) - Politics and government. I. Title. II. Series.
HC188.A48 P53 1983

Platt, Barbara. Residential real estate : how to find, buy, manage, and sell for a profit! / Barbara Platt, as told to Carl Platt ; [editor, Linda Bowman]. Austin, Tex. : Roscher House, c1987. 206 p. : ill., forms ; 24 cm. "Key 1986 tax revisions used in real-life examples"--Cover. Includes index. ISBN 0-941089-17-7 (lib. bdg.) LC Card 87-60697 DDC 332.63/243 19
1. House buying. 2. House selling. 3. Real estate business. I. Platt, Carl. II. Bowman, Linda. III. Title.
HD1379 .P57 1987

Platt, Brenda. Morris, David J. Garbage disposal economics . Washington, DC [1987] v, 101 p. : ISBN 0-917582-44-6 (pbk.) : LC Card 87-4182 DDC 338.4/3363728/0973 19
HD4483 .G37 1987

Platt, Carl. Platt, Barbara. Residential real estate . Austin, Tex. , c1987. 206 p. : ISBN 0-941089-17-7 (lib. bdg.) LC Card 87-60697 DDC 332.63/243 19
HD1379 .P57 1987

Platt, LaVonne. Hope for the family farm . Newton, Kan. , c1987. viii, 231 p. : ISBN 0-87303-126-1 (pbk.) LC Card 87-81635 DDC 338.1/6 19
HD1476.U5 H67 1987

Platt, Robert B., 1936- Controlling interest rate risk . New York , c1986. xv, 414 p. : ISBN 0-471-82354-6 : LC Card 85-22504 DDC 332.8/2 19
HG1621 .C6 1986 ***NYPL [JLE 86-2850]***

Platt, Tristan. Estado tributario y librecambio en Potosí (siglo XIX) : mercado indígena, proyecto proteccionista y lucha de ideologías monetarias / Tristán Platt. [La Paz?] : Instituto de Historia Social Boliviana, c1986. 73 p. ; 19 cm. Binder's title: Potosí, siglo XIX. Bibliography: p. 59-73. LC Card 87-401159 DDC 330.984/1404 19
1. Potosí Region (Bolivia) - Economic conditions. I. Title. II. Title: Potosí, siglo XIX. III. Title: Potosí, siglo diecinueve. IV. Title: Potosí, siglo 19.
HC183.P67 P55 1986

Platzer, Hans-Wolfgang. Unternehmensverbände in der EG, ihre nationale und transnationale Organisation und Politik : dargestellt am Beispiel des Bundesverbandes der Deutschen Industrie, der Bundesvereinigung der Deutschen Arbeitgeberverbände, [und] der deutschen industriellen Branchenverbände und deren EG-Verbandszusammenschlüsse / Hans-Wolfgang Platzer.1. Aufl. Kehl am Rhein : Engel, 1984. xi, 283 p. ; 23 cm. (Schriftenreihe Europa-Forschung . Bd. 9) Revision of the author's thesis (doctoral)--Universität Tübingen, 1983. Bibliography: p. 276-280. ISBN 3-88357-024-9 LC Card 85-131940
1. Employers associations - Germany, West. 2. Employers' associations - European Economic Community countries. 3. Bundesverband der Deutschen Industrie. 4. Bundesvereinigung der Deutschen Arbeitgeberverbände. I. Title. II. Series.
HD6948.G3 P58 1984

Plaxico, James Sam, 1924- Financial status of Oklahoma farmers and ranchers, 1985 : a survey / by James S. Plaxico, Marcia L. Tilley, and John Cochrane. [Stillwater] : Agricultural Experiment Station, Division of Agriculture, Oklahoma State University, [1986] 42 p. ; 28 cm. (Research report / Agricultural Experiment Station, Division of Agriculture, Oklahoma State University . P-879) "May 1986"--Cover. LC Card 86-622478 DDC 338.1/3/09766021 19
1. Agriculture - Oklahoma - Finance. 2. Farm income - Oklahoma. 3. Farmers - Oklahoma - Economic conditions. 4. Ranchers - Oklahoma - Economic conditions. I. Tilley, Marcia L. II. Cochrane, John. III. Title. IV. Title: Oklahoma farmers and ranchers. V. Series: Research report (Oklahoma Agricultural Experiment Station) , P-879.
HD1775.O5 P57 1986

Playing to win . Tarkenton, Francis A. New York , c1984. viii, 116 p. ; ISBN 0-06-015242-7 : LC Card 83-48390 DDC 650.1 19
HF5386 .T22 1984 ***NYPL [JLD 86-3515]***

Pleck, Joseph H. Working wives, working husbands / Joseph H. Pleck. Beverly Hills, Calif. : Sage Publications, c1985. 167 p. ; 23 cm. (New perspectives on family) "Published in cooperation with the National Council on Family Relations." Bibliography: p. 160-167. ISBN 0-8039-2489-5 LC Card 85-11974 DDC 306.8/7 19
1. Married people - Employment - Social aspects - United States. 2. Sexual division of labor - United States. 3. Sex role - United States. 4. Time management - United States. 5. Family life surveys - United States. I. National Council on Family Relations. II. Title.
HQ536 .P59 1985 ***NYPL [JLD 86-1130]***

Die Pleite . Martin, Paul C. (Paul Christoph), 1939- München , c1984. 416 p. : ISBN 3-7844-7145-5 : LC Card 85-188703
HJ8011 .M36 1984

Plenum studies in work and industry.
Kalleberg, Arne L. Work and industry . New York , c1987. xviii, 244 p. ; ISBN 0-306-42344-8 LC Card 87-2333 DDC 306/.36 19
HD4904 .K294 1987

Workers, managers, and technological change . New York , c1987. xxii, 362 p. : ISBN 0-306-42450-9 LC Card 87-2327 DDC 331/.0973 19
HD6331.2.U5 W67 1987

Plessy, Bernard, 1939- La vie quotidienne des mineurs au temps de Germinal / Bernard Plessy, Louis Challet. [Paris] : Hachette littérature, c1984. 339 p. : map ; 20 cm. Bibliography: p. [329]-336. ISBN 2-01-009272-4 : LC Card 85-160775
1. Coal miners - France - History - 19th century. I. Challet, Louis. II. Title.
HD8039.M6152 F86 1984

Plēthysmos kai oikismoi tēs Peloponnēsou . Panagiōtopoulos, Vasilēs, 1932- Athēna , 1985. 414 p. : LC Card 86-207132
HB3632.5.P45 P36 1985

Pletnev, V. Lena : ocherk istorii lenskikh sobytiĭ : s prilozheniiami / V. Pletnev. Moskva : Vseros. proletkul't, 1925. 103 p., [4] leaves of plates : ill. ; 26 cm. CONTENTS. - Ocherk istorii lenskikh sobytiĭ ; "Lena"--p'esa. LC Card 85-217266
1. Gold mines and mining - Russian S.F.S.R. - Siberia, Eastern - History. 2. Strikes and lockouts - Gold mining - Russian S.F.S.R. - Siberia, Eastern - History. I. Title.
HD9536.S653 S536 1925

Pliūshch, M. R. Vklad robitnychoho klasu Ukraïns'koï RSR u pryskorenniā naukovo-tekhnichnoho prohresu v promyslovosti, 50-70-i roky / M.R. Pliūshch. Kyïv : "Nauk. dumka," 1981. 244 p. ; 23 cm. At head of title: Akademiiā nauk Ukraïns'koï RSR. Instytut istoriï. Includes bibliographical references. LC Card 82-200854
1. Technological innovations - Ukraine. 2. Industrial productivity - Ukraine. 3. Labor and laboring classes - Ukraine. I. Title. II. Title: Vklad robitnychoho klasu Ukraïns'koï R.S.R. u pryskorenniā

naukovo-tekhnichnoho prohresu v promyslovosti, 50-70-i roky.
HC337.U53 T465 1981

PLOCK, POLAND - ECONOMIC CONDITIONS.
Chojnacki, Jakub. Petrochemia a rozwój Płocka /. Płock , 1977. [4], 290, [1] p., [76] p. of plates : LC Card 81-200767
HC340.3.Z7 P573 1977

Plogstedt, Sibylle. Übergriffe : sexuelle Belästigung in Büros und Betrieben : eine Dokumentation der Grünen Frauen im Bundestag / Sibylle Plogstedt, Kathleen Bode.Originalausg. Reinbek bei Hamburg : Rowohlt, 1984. 157 p. ; 19 cm. (Frauen aktuell) Rororo aktuell Bibliography: p. 156-157. ISBN 3-499-15353-X (pbk.) LC Card 87-672604
1. Sexual harassment of women - Germany (West). 2. Sex role in the work environment. I. Bode, Kathleen, 1947-. II. Title. III. Series.
HD6060.3 .P56x 1984

Plotkin, Sidney. Keep out : the struggle for land use control / Sidney Plotkin. Berkeley : University of California Press, c1987. xiii, 360 p. ; 24 cm. Bibliography: p. 323-344. Includes index. ISBN 0-520-05806-2 LC Card 86-30807 DDC 333.3/0973 19
1. Land use - Government policy - United States. 2. Right of property - United States. 3. Capitalism - United States. I. Title.
HD205 .P56 1987

Plotnikov, Viktor Petrovich. Vernulsi͡a soldat k poli͡u, 1945-1985 /. Moskva , 1985. 429, [16] p. : LC Card 85-228297
HD1536.S65 V47 1985

Hai ploutoparagōgikai dynameis tēs nēsou Androu /. Moustakas, Dion. E. En Athēnais , 1924. 25 p. : LC Card 87-100195
HC297.A53 M68 1924

Plumez, Jacqueline Hornor. Divorcing a corporation : how to know when - and if - a job change is right for you / Jacqueline Hornor Plumez with Karla Dougherty. New York, N.Y. : Villard Books, 1985. xxiii, 198 p. : ill. ; 25 cm. Includes index. Bibliography: p. 185-192. ISBN 0-394-54457-9 : LC Card 85-40183 DDC 650.1/4 19
1. Career changes. 2. Job hunting. I. Dougherty, Karla. II. Title.
HF5384 .P58 1986 *NYPL [JLE 86-2346]*

Plunkett, Jack W. The almanac of American employers : a guide to America's 500 most successful, large corporations / Jack W. Plunkett. Chicago : Contemporary Books, 1985. 340 p. ; 28 cm. Includes index. ISBN 0-8092-5407-7 LC Card 85-14908 DDC 331.2/0973 19
1. Compensation management - United States - Handbooks, manuals, etc. 2. Corporations - United States - Handbooks, manuals, etc. 3. Job satisfaction - United States - Handbooks, manuals, etc. I. Title.
HF5549.5.C67 P58 1985
*NYPL [*R-Econ. 85-3166]*

Pluraler Marxismus . Haug, Wolfgang Fritz. Berlin , 1985- v. ; ISBN 3-88619-303-9 (Bd. 1) LC Card 86-119293 DDC 355.43/09/04 19
HX40 .H27 1985 *NYPL [JLK 86-57]*

PLURALISM (SOCIAL SCIENCES) - GERMANY (WEST)
Wersebe, Hilmar von, 1943- Struktureller und funktionaler Pluralismus in der öffentlichen Verwaltung /. Frankfurt am Main , New York , c1986. 100 p. : ISBN 3-8204-9136-8 LC Card 86-229888
HD58.7 .W36 1986

Pluto Press workers' handbooks.
Eaton, Jack. The trade union directory . London , 1981. xii, 323 p. ; ISBN 0-86104-350-2 (pbk.) LC Card 86-673635
HD6663 .E27x 1981

PLYWOOD INDUSTRY - NORTHWEST, PACIFIC - MANAGEMENT - EMPLOYEE PARTICIPATION - CASE STUDIES.
Greenberg, Edward S., 1942- Workplace democracy . Ithaca , 1986. 257 p. ; ISBN 0-8014-1921-2 (alk. paper) LC Card 86-47641 DDC 674/.834/068 19
HD5658.P622 U554 1986
NYPL [JLE 86-4586]

PLYWOOD INDUSTRY - UNITED STATES - STATISTICS.
Fuller, Bernard. Treated wood update . Lexington, Mass., USA (24 Hartwell Ave., Lexington 02173) , c1985. iii, 121 p. : LC Card 86-201219 DDC 381/.45674/0973 19
HD9754 .F85 1985

PME, ayudas, estímulos e instituciones especializadas en la C.E.E. P.M.E., ayudas, estímulos e instituciones especializadas en la C.E.E. . [Madrid] [1983?] 141 p. ; ISBN 84-500-8571-3 LC Card 85-135456
HD2346.E93 P16 1983

PNEU MICHELIN (FIRM)
Barrière, Antoine. Michelin . Nonette , 1983. 289 p. ; ISBN 2-902894-20-1
NYPL [JLD 86-4467]

Po visochinite na sŭrtseto : ochert͡si za pŭrvent͡si ot zavod "Vida" / [sŭstavitel Velko Atanasov]. Sofii͡a : Profizdat, 1986. 75 p., [16] p. of plates : ill. ; 21 cm. LC Card 87-101682
1. Clothing workers - Bulgaria - Vidin. 2. "Vida" (Factory). I. Atanasov, Velko.
HD8039.C62 B97 1986

Pobeda kolkhoznogo stroi͡a v Uzbekistane . Aminova, R. Kh. Tashkent , 1981. 289 p. ; LC Card 82-161362
HD1492.S652 U9226 1981

La población de la ciudad de Corrientes a mediados del siglo XIX /. Sonzogni, Cristina María. Corrientes , 1980. 50, [4] leaves, [14] leaves of plates : LC Card 85-209374
HB3560.C67 S65 1980

La población de Mérida en el siglo XVII /. Rodríguez Grajera, Alfonso. [Badajoz] , 1985. xv, 162 p. : ISBN 84-505-1500-9 LC Card 86-232003
HB3620.M47 R63 1985

La población de Tepic bajo la organización regional, 1530-1821 /. López González, Pedro. Tepic, Nay. , 1984. 80 p. : LC Card 86-119610
HB3532.T47 L66 1984

Población, fecundidad y desarrollo en Costa Rica, 1950-1970 /. Denton L., Carlos F. [Heredia, Costa Rica] , 1984. iv, 150 p. : LC Card 86-117583 DDC 304.6/097286 19
HB3531 .D44 1984 *NYPL [JLF 87-144]*

Población y energía en la República Dominicana, 1990-2000. Gómez, Carmen. Santo Domingo, República Dominicana [1985] vi, 86 p. : LC Card 86-176044
HD9502.D652 G65 1985

Población y familia rural en Colombia /. Ordóñez G., Myriam. Bogotá , 1986. 179 p. : LC Card 86-208940
HB2447 .O73 1986

Población y recursos . Puyol Antolín, Rafael. Madrid , c1984. 157 p. : ISBN 84-368-0258-6 LC Card 87-105824
HB871 .P89 1984

Población y vivienda en la República Dominicana . Gómez, Carmen. Santo Domingo, República Dominicana , 1984. 116 p. : LC Card 85-154466
HD7316.5.A3 G65 1984
NYPL [JLF 86-1146]

Poblete, Martiniano O. Una jornada ferroviaria : recuerdos de 38 años de vida carrilana / por Martiniano O. Poblete. Santiago de Chile : Impr. y Estampería Claret, 1930. 2 v. : ill. ; 21 cm. Vol. 2: 2a ed. LC Card 87-162075 DDC 385/.0983 19
1. Empresa de los Ferrocarriles del Estado (Chile) - History. 2. Railroads - Chile - History. 3. Poblete, Martiniano O. I. Title.
HE2940.F47 P63 1930

POBLETE, MARTINIANO O.
Poblete, Martiniano O. Una jornada ferroviaria . Santiago de Chile , 1930. 2 v. : LC Card 87-162075 DDC 385/.0983 19
HE2940.F47 P63 1930

Pobre patria! /. Serrano Illescas, Alfonso. México, D.F. , 1982. 132 p. ; ISBN 968-409-161-3 LC Card 85-122377
HC135 .S368 1982

La Pobreza en España y sus causas / obra dirigida por Jesús García Valcárcel. 2a ed. Madrid : Fundación AGAPE, 1985. xx, 759 p. : maps ; 24 cm. Includes bibliographical references. ISBN 84-398-3252-4 : LC Card 86-230170
1. Poor - Spain. 2. Spain - Economic conditions - 1975-. 3. Spain - Social conditions - 1975-. 4. Poverty. I. García Valcárcel, Jesús. II. Fundación AGAPE (Madrid, Spain).
HC390.P6 P63 1985

Pobreza, participación y desarrollo regional / Margarita Jaramillo de Botero, Francisco Uribe-Echevarría, editores. 1a ed. [Bogotá, D.E., Colombia] : Centro Interdisciplinario de Estudios Regionales de la Universidad de los Andes : Banco Central Hipotecario, 1986. 536 p. : ill. ; 21 cm. Papers from the Seminario Internacional sobre Pobreza y Desarrollo Regional, held in March 1984 in Bogotá, sponsored by CIDER and the Institute of Social Studies, Netherlands. Includes bibliographies. LC Card 87-103266
1. Latin America - Economic policy. 2. Rural poor - Latin America - Political activity. 3. Regional development - Latin America - Case studies. I. Jaramillo de Botero, Margarita. II. Uribe-Echevarría, Francisco. III. Seminario Internacional sobre Pobreza y Desarrollo Regional (1984 : Bogotá, Colombia). IV. Universidad de los Andes (Bogotá, Colombia). Centro Interdisciplinario de Estudios Regionales. V. Institute of Social Studies (Netherlands).
HC125 .P6 1986

Pobreza y riqueza en 378 municipios de México /. Acevedo Conde, María Luisa. México, D.F. , 1984. 281 p. : LC Card 86-219445
HC140.P6 A25 1984

Pochtovye marki : Respubliki Kuba, 1978-1982 / [sostavitel′ Morgunov I͡Uriĭ Grigor′evich] : Chekhoslovatskoĭ Sotsialisticheskoĭ Respubliki, 1973-1983 : katalog / [sostavitel′ Nemchinov Sergeĭ Valentinovich]. Moskva : T͡Sentr. filatelisticheskoe agentstvo "Soi͡uzpechat′" Ministerstva svi͡azi SSSR, 1984. 223 p. : ill. ; 21 cm. Includes bibliographies and index. LC Card 85-185295
1. Postage-stamps - Cuba - Catalogs. 2. Postage-stamps - Czechoslovakia - Catalogs. I. Morgunov, I͡U. G. (I͡Uriĭ Grigor′evich). II. Nemchinov, Sergeĭ Valentinovich. III. T͡Sentral′noe filatelisticheskoe agentstvo "Soi͡uzpechat′.".
HE6185.C92 P63 1984

Pochun, Malati J. Determinants of import prices in Mauritius / Malati J. Pochun. Réduit, Mauritius : University of Mauritius, School of Administration, 1981. 15 p. ; 33 cm. Cover title. "May 1981." Bibliography: p. 11. LC Card 82-980680
1. Prices - Mauritius. 2. Mauritius - Commerce. I. University of Mauritius. School of Administration. II. Title.
HB235.M38 P63 1981

The pocket economist /. Pennant-Rea, Rupert. Oxford, UK , New York, NY , 1987, c1983. p. cm. ISBN 0-631-14586-9 : LC Card 87-10361 DDC 330/.03/21 19
HB61 .P435 1987

The Pocket guide to business numeracy /. Targett, David. Oxford, OX ; New York, NY, USA : x, 184 p. : ISBN 0-631-15124-9 : LC Card 86-31032 DDC 513/.93/0321 19
HF5695 .T34 1987

Pocket negotiator /. Kennedy, Gavin. Oxford, OX, UK ; New York, NY, USA : xi, 264 p. : ISBN 0-631-15451-5 : LC Card 87-6302 DDC 658 19
HD58.6 .K47 1987

Poddar, B. N. Development of irrigation and Indian agriculture / B.N. Poddar. New Delhi : Deep & Deep Publications, c1987. 331 p. ; 22 cm. Study, with reference to Bihar. Bibliography: p. [323]-328. Includes index. LC Card 87-901300 DDC 338.1/62 19
1. Agriculture - Economic aspects - India - Bihar. 2. Irrigation - Economic aspects - India - Bihar. I. Title.
HD2075.B5 P63 1967

Poddubnyĭ, Vladimir Andreevich. Suĭmenko, I͡E. I. Kerivnyk-orhanizator i vykhovatel′ /. Kyïv , 1985. 189 p. ; LC Card 87-109649
HD38.2 .S85 1985

Podēmata, Anny. Hellēniko syndikalistiko kinēma . Athēna , 1984. 215 p. ; LC Card 86-193159
HD6795.5 .H44 1984

El poder norteamericano y la renegociación de la deuda externa brasileña, 1982-1983 /. Alcalde Cardoza, Xavier. Lima, Perú , 1985. 62 p. ; LC Card 86-223475
HJ8579 .A44 1985

Podestá, Ricardo Augusto. Argentina, país productor de capitales / Ricardo Augusto Podestá. Mendoza : [s.n.], 1976. 11 p. ; 26 cm. "Separata de Idearium, revista de la Facultad de Ciencias Jurídicas y Sociales de la Universidad de Mendoza, no. 2." Includes bibliographical references. LC Card 84-196569
1. Capital - Argentina. I. Title.
HC180.C3 P62 1976

Podgotovka upravlencheskikh kadrov--opyt, problemy, perspektivy (po zarubezhnym materialam) : referativnyĭ sbornik / [otvetstvennye redaktory S.N. Krasavchenko i I.G. Minervin]. Moskva : INION AN SSSR, 1984. 188 p. ; 20 cm. (Serii͡a Problemy upravlenii͡a ėkonomikoĭ) At head of title: Akademii͡a nauk SSSR. Institut nauchnoĭ informat͡sii po obshchestvennym naukam. Akademii͡a narodnogo khozi͡aĭstva pri Sovete Ministrov SSSR. Includes bibliographies. LC Card 85-188986
1. Executives, Training of. 2. Executives - Training of - Soviet Union. I. Krasavchenko, S. N. II. Minervin, I. G. III. Institut nauchnoĭ informat͡sii po obshchestvennym naukam (Akademii͡a nauk SSSR). IV. Akademii͡a narodnogo khozi͡aĭstva SSSR. V. Series.
HD30.4 .P6 1984

Podoplelov, V. P. Malʹt͡sev, V. I. (Valerʹi͡an Ivanovich) Ėkonomicheskie osnovy industrializat͡sii selʹskogo khozi͡aĭstva Severa /. Moskva , 1985. 142 p. ; LC Card 86-165352
HD1995.N55 M34 1985

Podryv vekovykh ustoev . Rymalov, V. V. (Viktor Vladimirovich) Moskva , 1984. 268, [3] p. : LC Card 85-112238
HC59 .R839 1984

Podsolonko, Vladimir Andreevich. Upravlenie ėffektivnostʹi͡u proizvodstva /. Kiev , 1985. 125 p. : LC Card 85-181580
HD30.23 .U67 1985

Podstatzky, Aloisius, Graf. Prokopp, Ludwig Ferdinand. Europäische Commerzreisen um die Mitte des 18. Jahrhunderts /. Linz , c1982. xiii, 446 p., [1] folded leaf of plates : ISBN 3-85320-296-1 LC Card 83-150921
HF3548.C36 P76 1982

Podstawowe problemy polityki rolnej w PRL /. Mazurkiewicz, Eugeniusz. Warszawa , 1979. 306 p. ; LC Card 81-172693
HD1995.7.Z8 M39 1979

Podvig na pochtovoĭ marke : katalog-spravochnik : geroi Velikoĭ Otechestvennoĭ voĭny na pochtovykh markakh SSSR / [sostaviteli Lurʹe I͡Uliĭ Solomonovich, Busel Anatoliĭ Fedorovich]. Moskva : T͡Sentr. filatelisticheskoe agentstvo "Soi͡uzpechatʹ" Ministerstva svi͡azi SSSR, 1985. 135 p. : ill. ; 20 cm. "40-letii͡u pobedy posvi͡ashchaetsi͡a." Includes index. Bibliography: p. 133. LC Card 86-113767
1. Postage-stamps - Topics - Geroĭ Sovetskogo Soi͡uza - Catalogs. 2. Postage-stamps - Topics - World War, 1939-1945 - Catalogs. 3. Postage-stamps - Soviet Union - Catalogs. I. Lurʹe, I͡Uliĭ Solomonovich. II. Busel, Anatoliĭ Fedorovich. III. T͡Sentralʹnoe filatelisticheskoe agenstvo "Soi͡uzpechatʹ.".
HE6183.G47 P63 1985

Podvoĭskiĭ, G. L. (Gleb Lʹvovich) Gosplan RSFSR. Metodicheskie ukazanii͡a k razrabotke planov ėkonomicheskogo i sot͡sialʹnogo razvitii͡a RSFSR /. Moskva , 1985. 462 p. ; LC Card 85-232541
HC337.R85 G67 1985

Pöhl, Karl Otto, 1929- DIHT-Kongress (1983 : Frankfurt am Main, Germany) Kapital, Zins, Währung . Bonn , 1984. 68 p. : LC Card 84-212399
HC290.5.C3 D53 1983

Poel, J. H. R. van de. Groot, T. L. C. M. Financieël management van non-profit organisaties /. Groningen , c1985. 200 p. : ISBN 90-01-30316-1 : LC Card 85-214807
HG4027.65 .G76 1985

Pogorelova, O. A. (Oksana Afanasʹevna) Ėkologicheskiĭ krizis v uslovii͡akh sovremennogo kapitalizma : politiko-ėkonomicheskiĭ aspekt / O.A. Pogorelova. Kiev : Nauk. dumka, 1986. 110, [2] p. ; 20 cm. At head of title: Akademii͡a nauk Ukrainskoĭ SSR. Institut ėkonomiki. Bibliography: p. 103-[111]. LC Card 86-233475
1. Economic development - Environmental aspects. 2. Environmental policy. I. Title.
HD75.6 .P64 1986

Pohier, Jacques. Unemployment and the right to work /. Edinburgh , New York , c1982. x, 98 p. ; ISBN 0-8164-2391-1 (Seabury Press : pbk.) LC Card 87-150638
HD5707.5 .U544 1982

Pohier, Jacques Marie. Christian ethics and economics . Edinburgh , New York , c1980. xii, 114 p. ; ISBN 0-8164-2282-6 (Seabury Press : pbk.) LC Card 80-50892
HF1411 .C422 1980

Pohjois-Suomen Maantieteellinin Seura. Policies of population redistribution /. Oulu , 1981. 199 p. : ISBN 951-675-071-0 (pbk.) LC Card 83-148782 DDC 304.8 19
HB1952 .P65 1981

Pohl, Hans. Goetzeler, Herbert. Wilhelm und Carl Friedrich von Siemens . Stuttgart , 1986. 131 p. : ISBN 3-515-04558-9 LC Card 86-141456
HD9695.G43 S514 1986

Pohl, Harald.
Finke, B. (Barbara) Studien zur kommunalen Industrieförderung im 20. Jahrhundert . Regensburg , c1986. 125, [45], xxv p. : ISBN 3-924956-19-7 : LC Card 87-129091 DDC 338.943/34 19
HC289.R36 F56 1986

Kommunale Wirtschafts- und Finanzpolitik in Bayern zur Zeit der Weimarer Republik : dargestellt am Beispiel der Wirtschaftsregion Inglostadt / Harald Pohl. Regensburg : Transfer Verlag, c1985. xiv, 312 p. : ill. ; 24 cm. Originally presented as the author's thesis (doctoral)--Universität Regensburg, 1984. Bibliography: p. 284-312. ISBN 3-924956-01-4 LC Card 86-230648
1. Finance, Public - Germany (West) - Ingolstadt Metropolitan Area - History - 20th century. 2. Finance, Public - Germany (West) - Bavaria - History - 20th century. I. Title.
HJ9494.I53 P63 1985

Pohl, Manfred, 1944- Hamburger Bankengeschichte / Manfred Pohl. Mainz : V. Hase & Koehler, c1986. 264 p., [20] p. of plates : ill. (1 col.) ; 25 cm. "Quellen- und Literaturverzeichnis": p. 243-255. Includes index. ISBN 3-7758-1136-2 LC Card 87-104548
1. Banks and banking - Germany (West) - Hamburg - History. I. Title.
HG3060.H22 P64 1986

Pohl, Sigrid, 1954- Entwicklung und Ursachen der Frauenlohndiskriminierung : ein feministisch-marxistischer Erklärungsansatz / Sigrid Pohl. Frankfurt am Main ; New York : P. Lang, c1984. x, 387 p. : ill. ; 21 cm. (Europäische Hochschulschriften. Reihe V, Volks- und Betriebswirtschaft, 0361-7339 . Bd. 496 = vol. 496 = vol. 496) Bibliography: p. 357-387. ISBN 3-8204-8017-X LC Card 85-189325 DDC 331.13/3/0943 19
1. Sex discrimination in employment - Germany (West) - History. 2. Wages - Women - Germany (West) - History. 3. Sexual division of labor - Germany (West) - History. I. Series: Europäische Hochschulschriften. Reihe V, Volks- und Betriebswirtschaft , Bd. 496. II. Title.
HD6060.5.G3 P64 1984

Pohle, Ernst. Die Leistungsbewertung in der Industrie . Jena , 1983. 241 p. ; LC Card 84-176546
HD56.25 .L45 1983

Pohle, Michael. Industriebrachen und extensiv genutzte Flächen in innenstadtnahen Gewerbegebieten : räumliche Nutzungsreserven und Strategien zu ihrer Reaktivierung dargestellt am Beispiel des Industriegebietes Hamburg-Eidelstedt / Michael Pohle. Paderborn : F. Schöningh, 1985. viii, 121 p. : ill. ; 30 cm. (Arbeitsberichte und Ergebnisse zur wirtschafts- und sozialgeographischen Regionalforschung . Heft 12) Bibliography: p. 98-106. ISBN 3-506-73577-2 : LC Card 86-183775
1. Hamburg (Germany) - Industries - Location. 2. Eidelstedt (Hamburg, Germany) - Industries - Location. 3. Enterprise zones - Germany (West) - Hamburg. 4. Eidelstedt (Hamburg, Germany). I. Title. II. Series.
HC289.H2 P64 1985

Pohlig, Rolf. Probleme der Aufbauorganisation des Finanz- und Rechnungswesens / Rolf Pohlig. Bochum : Studienverlag N. Brockmeyer, 1984. xi, 465 p. : ill. ; 21 cm. (Bochumer wirtschaftswissenschaftliche Studien. Nr. 99) Bibliography: p. 394-465. ISBN 3-88339-354-1 LC Card 84-162112
1. Accounting. I. Title.
HF5645 .P64 1984

Pöhlmann, Helmut. Jahresabschlussprüfung auf Stichprobenbasis : die Anwendung von Verfahren der statistischen Qualitätskontrolle auf die Jahresabschlussprüfung / Helmut Pöhlmann. Pfaffenweiler : Centaurus, 1987. xii, 187 p. ; 21 cm. (Reihe Wirtschaftswissenschaften, 0177-283X . Bd. 31) Bibliography: p. 158-187. ISBN 3-89085-142-8 LC Card 87-133413 DDC 657/.458 19
1. Auditing, Internal - Statistical methods. 2. Sampling (Statistics). 3. Quality control - Statistical methods. I. Series: Reihe Wirtschaftswissenschaften (Pfaffenweiler, Breisgau-Hochschwarzwald, Germany) , Bd. 31. II. Title.
HF5668.25 .P64 1987

Pohmer, Karlheinz. Mikroökonomische Theorie der personellen Einkommens- und Vermögensverteilung : Allokation und Distribution als Ergebnis intertemporaler Wahlhandlungen / Karlheinz Pohmer. Berlin ; New York : Springer-Verlag, c1985. ix, 214 p. : ill. ; 25 cm. (Studies in contemporary economics . vol. 16) Bibliography: p. [202]-214. ISBN 0-387-15174-5 (U. S.) LC Card 85-164096
1. Income distribution - Mathematical models. 2. Microeconomics - Mathematical models. I. Title. II. Series.
HB523 .P64 1985

Le poids de l'Etat /. Meyer, Jean, 1924- Paris , c1983. 304 p. : ISBN 2-13-037770-X : LC Card 83-175028
HC280.D4 M49 1983

POINCARÉ, HENRI, 1854-1912 - PHILOSOPHY.
Siemianowski, Andrzej. Fakty, prawa, decyzje . [Wrocław] , 1983. 103 p. ; LC Card 85-113022
HB9 .B7522 nr. 245 Q175

Point de mire . De Vos, Wouter. Antwerpen, Belgiëlai 147 a , 1977. 125 p. : ISBN 90-02-01132-6 : LC Card 78-370280 DDC 309.1
HC59 .D464 ***NYPL [JLD 80-3135]***

POINT FOUR PROGRAM. see **TECHNICAL ASSISTANCE, AMERICAN.**

POINT-OF-SALE SYSTEMS - UNITED STATES.
American Bankers Association. Retail Payments Task Force. Ad Hoc Committee. Implementation guidelines for online debit card systems at the point of sale /. [Washington, D.C.] , c1986. 1 v. (various pagings) : LC Card 86-224882 DDC 332.1/028 19
HG1710.5 .A47 1986

Points, a guide to frequent flyer bonus programs /. Michaels, Susan. New York , c1987. 161 p. : ISBN 0-87052-375-9 (pbk.) : LC Card 87-8681 DDC 387.7/1 19
HF6161.A38 M53 1987

POISONS, ECONOMIC. see **PESTICIDES.**

POISONS, INDUSTRIAL. see **INDUSTRIAL TOXICOLOGY.**

POITIERS (FRANCE) - ECONOMIC CONDITIONS - CONGRESSES.
Colloque "Poitiers 1981" (1981 : Université de Poitiers) Actes du Colloque "Poitiers 1981" . Poitiers [France] [1983] 472 p. : LC Card 84-119227
HB3594.P65 C65 1981

POITIERS (FRANCE) - POPULATION - CONGRESSES.
Colloque "Poitiers 1981" (1981 : Université de Poitiers) Actes du Colloque "Poitiers 1981" . Poitiers [France] [1983] 472 p. : LC Card 84-119227
HB3594.P65 C65 1981

"Poitiers 1981." Colloque "Poitiers 1981" (1981 : Université de Poitiers) Actes du Colloque "Poitiers 1981" . Poitiers [France] [1983] 472 p. : LC Card 84-119227
HB3594.P65 C65 1981

Pojatina, Stipe. Društvena reprodukcija u djelu Vladimira Bakarića /. Zagreb , 1985 printing. 204 p. ; LC Card 86-233326
HD5650 .D68 1985

Pokataeva, T. S. Problemy khozi͡aĭstvennogo razvitii͡a osvobodivshikhsi͡a stran . Moskva ,

1987. 2 v. (306 p.) ; LC Card 87-157281
HC59.7 .P7354 1987

Poklad, B. I. (Boris Iosifovich) Real'nosti sovremennogo mira i politika konfrontatsii / B.I. Poklad. Moskva : "Mezhdunarodnye otnosheniia", 1985. 157 p. ; 20 cm. Includes bibliographical references. LC Card 85-170137
1. Nuclear disarmament. 2. Arms control. 3. United States - Military policy. I. Title.
JX1974.7 .P585 1985 ***NYPL [*QIK 87-1550]***

Pokok-pokok petunjuk pelaksanaan Program Peningkatan Produktivitas Kerja Tenaga Kerja Wanita Melalui Pendekatan Kesejahteraan Terpadu, tahun 1984/1986 (Juklak Nakerwan). Indonesia. Kantor Menteri Negara Urusan Peranan Wanita. Jakarta [1984] iii, xii, 47 p. ; LC Card 86-940168
HD6194 .I5 1984

Pokorny, Michael. An introduction to econometrics / Michael Pokorny. Oxford, [Oxfordshire], UK ; New York, NY, USA : B. Blackwell, 1987. p. cm. Includes bibliographies and index. ISBN 0-631-15002-1 : LC Card 86-32707 DDC 330/.028 19
1. Econometrics. I. Title.
HB139 .P635 1987

Pokrytan, A. K. (Anatoliĭ Karpovich) Leninskie raboty 90-kh godov i sovremennost' / A.K. Pokrytan. Kiev : Gol. izd-vo izdatel'skogo ob"edineniia "Vyshcha shkola", 1985. 159 p. ; 20 cm. Bibliography: p. 157-158. LC Card 87-113578
1. Marxian economics - History - 19th century. 2. Lenin, Vladimir Il'ich, 1870-1924. I. Title.
HB97.5 .P538 1985

Pol, Louis G. Business demography : a guide and reference for business planners and marketers / Louis G. Pol. New York : Quorum Books, c1987. p. cm. Bibliography: p. Includes index. ISBN 0-89930-218-1 (lib. bdg. : alk. paper) LC Card 87-2494 DDC 304.6 19
1. Demography. 2. United States - Population. 3. Marketing research. I. Title.
HB849.41 .P63 1987

Pola dasar pembangunan daerah Propinsi Daerah Tingkat I Maluku. Maluku (Indonesia) [Ambon] , 1984. vii, 69 p. ; LC Card 86-943211
HC448.M34 M33 1984a

POLAND - COMMERCIAL POLICY.
Basiuk, Jerzy. Eksport warunkiem importu /. Warszawa , 1978. 57 p. ; LC Card 81-192725
HF1558.7 .B32 1978

Dmowski, Zygmunt. Organizacja i technika handlu zagranicznego . Gdańsk , 1979. 201 p. ; LC Card 81-181043
HF1558.7 .D59 1979

POLAND - ECONOMIC CONDITIONS.
Kostrowicka, Irena. Historia gospodarcza Polski XIX i XX wieku /. Warszawa , 1984. 583 p., [3] folded leaves of plates : ISBN 83-05-11411-2 : LC Card 85-218322
HC340.3 .K67 1984

Landau, Zbigniew. Wirtschaftsgeschichte Polens im 19. und 20. Jahrhundert /. Berlin , 1986. vi, 300 p. : LC Card 86-223591
HC340.3 .L367 1986

POLAND - ECONOMIC CONDITIONS - 1918-
Landau, Zbigniew. The Polish economy in the twentieth century /. London , c1985. vi, 346 p. ; ISBN 0-7099-1607-8 LC Card 86-673496
HC340.3 .L36x 1985b

POLAND - ECONOMIC CONDITIONS - 1918-1945.
Gołębiowski, Jerzy. Sektor państwowy w gospodarce Polski międzywojennej /. Warszawa , 1985. 366 p. ; ISBN 83-01-06292-4 : LC Card 86-108406
HD4215.7 .G65 1985

POLAND - ECONOMIC CONDITIONS - 1945-
Gabrisch, Hubert. Polen im RGW . Hamburg , 1986. 308 p. ; ISBN 3-87895-316-X LC Card 87-407406 DDC 330.9438/056 19
HC340.3 .G34 1986

Poland's renewal and U. S. options . Washington , 1987. xv, 41 p. : LC Card 87-601374 DDC 337.438073 19
HC340.3 .P646 1987

Prace z zakresu planowania i ekonomiki regionu /. Kraków , 1980. 220 p. : LC Card 80-131017
HB9 .K53 nr. 116 HC340.3

Probleme monetärer und finanzwirtschaftlicher Steuerung im Systemvergleich /. Duisburg , c1986. 175 p. : ISBN 3-921473-43-8 LC Card 86-211745
HC286.6 .P754 1986

POLAND - ECONOMIC CONDITIONS - 1945- - REGIONAL DISPARITIES.
Regionale Aspekte der Wirtschaftsplanung in den Mitteleuropäischen RGW-Staaten. Marburg/Lahn , 1983. 95 p. : ISBN 3-87969-178-9 LC Card 84-249235
HC270.28 .R42 1983

POLAND - ECONOMIC CONDITIONS - 1980- - REGIONAL DISPARITIES - CONGRESSES.
Przestrzenne aspekty gospodarki żywnościowej do 2000 r. . Warszawa , 1986. 166 p. : ISBN 83-208-0497-3 : LC Card 86-223691
HD9015.P72 P72 1986

POLAND - ECONOMIC CONDITIONS - 1981-
Rozwój sytuacji i polityki gospodarczej w Polsce w latach 1981-1984 /. Warszawa , 1985. 161 p. ; ISBN 83-03-00866-8 : LC Card 85-229473
HC340.3 .R69 1985

POLAND - ECONOMIC POLICY.
Landau, Zbigniew. The Polish economy in the twentieth century /. London , c1985. vi, 346 p. ; ISBN 0-7099-1607-8 LC Card 86-673496
HC340.3 .L36x 1985b

Landau, Zbigniew. Wirtschaftsgeschichte Polens im 19. und 20. Jahrhundert /. Berlin , 1986. vi, 300 p. : LC Card 86-223591
HC340.3 .L367 1986

POLAND - ECONOMIC POLICY - 1945-
Magierska, Anna. Przywrócić Polsce . Warszawa , 1986. 467 p. ; ISBN 83-01-06606-7 : LC Card 86-228089
HC340.3.Z7 W4765 1986

Polish People's Republic national report to the habitat . [S.l.] 1976 (Warszawa : Dom Słowa Polskiego) 48 p. : LC Card 83-226226
HC340.3 .P656 1976

Probleme monetärer und finanzwirtschaftlicher Steuerung im Systemvergleich /. Duisburg , c1986. 175 p. : ISBN 3-921473-43-8 LC Card 86-211745
HC286.6 .P754 1986

Regionale Aspekte der Wirtschaftsplanung in den Mitteleuropäischen RGW-Staaten. Marburg/Lahn , 1983. 95 p. : ISBN 3-87969-178-9 LC Card 84-249235
HC270.28 .R42 1983

POLAND - ECONOMIC POLICY - 1966-1980.
Elementy polityki ekonomicznej . Kraków , 1977. 306 p. ; LC Card 81-173152
HC340.3 .E515 1977

Strategy of socio-economic development . Warsaw , 1980. 122 p. : LC Card 81-107307
HD75 .S8 1980

POLAND - ECONOMIC POLICY - 1981-
Böhm, Edward. Wechselkurspolitik in der Planwirtschaft . Hamburg , 1986. 139 p. : ISBN 3-87895-301-1 LC Card 86-210978
HG3947.5 .B64 1986

Gospodarka w procesie reformowania /. Warszawa , 1986. 423 p. : ISBN 83-208-0514-7 : LC Card 87-102275
HC340.3 .G68 1986

Kapustka, Aleksander. Gospodarka inwestycyjna i remontowa w latach 1984-1985 /. Zielona Góra , 1984. 294 p. ; LC Card 86-670001
HC340.3.Z9 C35 1984

Kapustka, Aleksander. Inwestycje w reformie . Zielona Góra , 1985. 282 p. ; LC Card 86-125896
HJ2132 .K37 1985

Rozwój sytuacji i polityki gospodarczej w Polsce w latach 1981-1984 /. Warszawa , 1985. 161 p. ; ISBN 83-03-00866-8 : LC Card 85-229473
HC340.3 .R69 1985

Samecki, Wiesław. Czego można oczekiwać od ekonomii /. Warszawa , 1981. 35 p. ; ISBN 83-202-0150-0 LC Card 86-150577
HC340.3 .S24 1981

POLAND - FOREIGN ECONOMIC RELATIONS.
Basiuk, Jerzy. Eksport warunkiem importu /. Warszawa , 1978. 57 p. ; LC Card 81-192725
HF1558.7 .B32 1978

Dmowski, Zygmunt. Organizacja i technika handlu zagranicznego . Gdańsk , 1979. 201 p. ; LC Card 81-181043
HF1558.7 .D59 1979

POLAND - FOREIGN ECONOMIC RELATIONS - UNITED STATES.
Poland's renewal and U. S. options . Washington , 1987. xv, 41 p. : LC Card 87-601374 DDC 337.438073 19
HC340.3 .P646 1987

POLAND - FOREIGN RELATIONS - UNITED STATES.
Poland's renewal and U. S. options . Washington , 1987. xv, 41 p. : LC Card 87-601374 DDC 337.438073 19
HC340.3 .P646 1987

Poland. Główny Urząd Statystyczny.
Ceny detaliczne 1971-1985 /. Warszawa , 1985. 160 p. ; LC Card 86-196060
HB235.P6 C45 1985

Definicje z zakresu inwestycji . Warszawa , 1977. 42 p. ; LC Card 81-172624
HG4528 .D44 1977

Nomenklatura artykułów i usług do badania spożycia (NAS). Warszawa , 1980. 87 p. ; LC Card 81-109132
HF1044.P6 N66 1980

Polska 1973 . Warszawa , 1973. 199 p., [8] p. of plates : LC Card 82-102013
HA1455 .P66 1973

Spis ludności i mieszkań metodą reprezentacyjną z dnia 6 XII 1984 r. . Warszawa , 1985. xx, 93 p., [2] p. of plates : LC Card 86-176185
HD7345.7.A3 S65 1985

Warunki życia ludności w 1984 r. /. Warszawa , 1985. 108 p. ; LC Card 86-225456
HD7035.7 .W35 1985

Zasady metodyczne statystyki przemysłu. Warszawa , 1979. 224 p. ; LC Card 81-115708
HC340.3 .Z373 1979

Poland - Government. see **Poland - Politics and government.**

POLAND - INDUSTRIES - CLASSIFICATION.
Nomenklatura artykułów i usług do badania spożycia (NAS). Warszawa , 1980. 87 p. ; LC Card 81-109132
HF1044.P6 N66 1980

POLAND - INDUSTRIES - ENVIRONMENTAL ASPECTS.
Bonenberg, Wojciech. Przemysł w mieście . Gliwice , 1985. 181 p., [8] folded leaves of plates : LC Card 86-219523
HC340.3.Z9 D52 1985

POLAND - INDUSTRIES - STATISTICAL METHODS.
Zasady metodyczne statystyki przemysłu. Warszawa , 1979. 224 p. ; LC Card 81-115708
HC340.3 .Z373 1979

POLAND - INDUSTRY - LOCATION.
Bonenberg, Wojciech. Przemysł w mieście . Gliwice , 1985. 181 p., [8] folded leaves of plates : LC Card 86-219523
HC340.3.Z9 D52 1985

Poland. Konsultacyjna Rada Gospodarcza.
Rozwój sytuacji i polityki gospodarczej w Polsce w latach 1981-1984 /. Warszawa , 1985. 161 p. ; ISBN 83-03-00866-8 : LC Card 85-229473
HC340.3 .R69 1985

Poland. Ministerstwo Administracji, Gospodarki Terenowej i Ochrony Środowiska. Polish People's Republic national report to the habitat . [S.l.] 1976 (Warszawa : Dom Słowa Polskiego) 48 p. : LC Card 83-226226
HC340.3 .P656 1976

Poland - Politics. see **Poland - Politics and government.**

POLAND - POLITICS AND GOVERNMENT - 1945-1980.
Wałęsa, Lech, 1943- [Chemin d'espoir. English.] A way of hope /. New York , c1987. 325 p., [17] p. of plates : ISBN 0-8050-0668-0 LC Card

87-21194 DDC 322/.2/0924 B 19
HD6735.7.Z55 W34813 1987

POLAND - POLITICS AND GOVERNMENT - 1980-
A Lengyel földindulás /. Malakoff , New York , 1980. 150 p. ; LC Card 81-177379
HD8537.N783 L45 1980 NYPL [JLB 86-24]

Poland's renewal and U. S. options . Washington , 1987. xv, 41 p. : LC Card 87-601374 DDC 337.438073 19
HC340.3 .P646 1987

Stelmach, Waldemar. Drugie oblicze "Solidarności" /. Warszawa , 1985. 222 p. : ISBN 83-202-0391-0 : LC Card 86-208212
HD8537.N783 S74 1985

Wałęsa, Lech, 1943- [Chemin d'espoir. English.] A way of hope /. New York , c1987. 325 p., [17] p. of plates : ISBN 0-8050-0668-0 LC Card 87-21194 DDC 322/.2/0924 B 19
HD6735.7.Z55 W34813 1987

POLAND - POLITICS AND GOVERNMENT - 1980- - PUBLIC OPINION.
A Lengyel földindulás /. Malakoff , New York , 1980. 150 p. ; LC Card 81-177379
HD8537.N783 L45 1980 NYPL [JLB 86-24]

POLAND - POPULATION.
Rozwój ludności krajów socjalistycznych . Warszawa , Moskva , 1978. 381 p. ; LC Card 81-206832
HB3608.7.A3 R69 1978

POLAND - POPULATION, RURAL.
Rudnicki, Leszek. Zróżnicowania wzorców konsumpcji ludności rolniczej dwuzawodowej /. Kraków , 1985. 313 p. : LC Card 86-174377
HC340.3.Z9 C6177 1985

POLAND - POPULATION - STATISTICS.
Migracje wewnętrzne ludności . Warszawa , 1980. xvi, 389 p. ; LC Card 86-215694
HB2068.7.A3 M54 1980

Spis ludności i mieszkań metodą reprezentacyjną z dnia 6 XII 1984 r. . Warszawa , 1985. xx, 93 p., [2] p. of plates : LC Card 86-176185
HD7345.7.A3 S65 1985

POLAND - RURAL CONDITIONS.
Inglot, Stefan. Z dziejów wsi polskiej i rolnictwa /. Warszawa , 1986. 448 p. : ISBN 83-205-3734-7 : LC Card 85-126716
HD1995.7 .I54 1986

POLAND - SOCIAL CONDITIONS - 1945-
Strategy of socio-economic development . Warsaw , 1980. 122 p. : LC Card 81-107307
HD75 .S8 1980

Wałęsa, Lech, 1943- [Chemin d'espoir. English.] A way of hope /. New York , c1987. 325 p., [17] p. of plates : ISBN 0-8050-0668-0 LC Card 87-21194 DDC 322/.2/0924 B 19
HD6735.7.Z55 W34813 1987

POLAND - SOCIAL CONDITIONS - ADDRESSES, ESSAYS, LECTURES.
Karpiński, Wojciech. Szkice o wolności /. Chicago, Ill. (2886 Milwaukee Ave., Chicago, Ill. 60618) , 1980. 95 p. ; LC Card 81-201974
*JC585 .K32 1980 NYPL [*QR 86-4376]*

POLAND - STATISTICS.
Polska 1973 . Warszawa , 1973. 199 p., [8] p. of plates : LC Card 82-102013
HA1455 .P66 1973

Poland's renewal and U. S. options : a policy reconnaissance : report / prepared for the Subcommittee on Europe and the Middle East of the Committee on Foreign Affairs, U. S. House of Representatives, by the Congressional Research Service, Library of Congress. Washington : U. S. G.P.O. : For sale by the Supt. of Docs., Congressional Sales Office, U. S. G.P.O., 1987. xv, 41 p. : 1 map ; 24 cm. At head of title: 100th Congress, 1st session. Committee print. Distributed to some depository libraries in microfiche. Shipping list no.: 87-175-P. "March 5, 1987." Includes bibliographical references. Item 1017-A, 1017-B (microfiche) LC Card 87-601374 DDC 337.438073 19
1. Poland - Economic conditions - 1945-. 2. Poland - Politics and government - 1980-. 3. United States - Foreign relations - Poland. 4. Poland - Foreign relations - United States. 5. United States - Foreign economic relations - Poland. 6. Poland - Foreign economic relations - United States. I. United States. Congress. House. Committee on Foreign Affairs. Subcommittee on Europe and the Middle East. II. Library of Congress. Congressional Research Service. III. Title: Poland's renewal and US options.
HC340.3 .P646 1987

Poland's renewal and US options. Poland's renewal and U. S. options . Washington , 1987. xv, 41 p. : LC Card 87-601374 DDC 337.438073 19
HC340.3 .P646 1987

Polanyi, Karl, 1886-1964.
[Livelihood of man. Hungarian. Selections] Kereskedelem, piacok és pénz az ókori Görögországban / Polányi Károly. Budapest : Gondolat, 1984. 327 p. ; 19 cm. Selected translation of: The livelihood of man. Includes bibliographical references. ISBN 963-281-335-9 : LC Card 85-189578
1. Greece - Economic conditions - To 146 B.C. I. Title.
HC37 .P65155 1984

POLANYI, KARL, 1886-1964.
Stanfield, J. Ron, 1945- The economic thought of Karl Polanyi . Basingstoke, Hampshire , 1986. x, 162 p. ; ISBN 0-333-39629-4 LC Card 87-673390
HB102.P64 S73x 1986b

POLAR EXPEDITIONS. see **ANTARCTIC REGIONS.**

Polary, José Henrique Braga. Reflexões sobre o quadro global e setorial da economia maranhense / José Henrique Braga Polary. São Luís [Brazil] : Estado do Maranhão, Instituto de Pequisas Econômicas e Sociais, 1981. 60 p. ; 29 cm. (Série Estudos monográficos . 1) Bibliography: p. 60. LC Card 87-404934 DDC 330.981/21063 19
1. Maranhão (Brazil) - Economic conditions. I. Title. II. Series.
HC188.M29 P65 1981

Poleman, Thomas T. Ewell, Peter T., 1947- Uxpanapa . Ithaca, N.Y. [1982] xiv, 218 p., [35] leaves of plates : LC Card 84-621492 DDC 338.1/0972/6 19
HD1795.P3 E94 1982

Polen im RGW . Gabrisch, Hubert. Hamburg , 1986. 308 p. ; ISBN 3-87895-316-X LC Card 87-407406 DDC 330.9438/056 19
HC340.3 .G34 1986

POLES - GERMANY (WEST) - WILHELMSBURG (HAMBURG) - SOCIAL LIFE AND CUSTOMS.
Hauschildt, Elke. Polnische Arbeitsmigranten in Wilhelmsburg bei Hamburg während des Kaiserreichs und der Weimarer Republik /. Dortmund , c1986. xv, 330 p. : ISBN 3-923293-17-8 LC Card 87-127027 DDC 331.6/2/438043515 19
HD8458.P65 H38 1986

POLES - GERMANY (WEST) - WILHEMSBURG (HAMBURG) - HISTORY - 20TH CENTURY.
Hauschildt, Elke. Polnische Arbeitsmigranten in Wilhelmsburg bei Hamburg während des Kaiserreichs und der Weimarer Republik /. Dortmund , c1986. xv, 330 p. : ISBN 3-923293-17-8 LC Card 87-127027 DDC 331.6/2/438043515 19
HD8458.P65 H38 1986

Poletaev, Vladimir Evgen′evich. Iz istorii razvitii͡a metallurgicheskoĭ promyshlennosti Moskvy, 1883-1932 gg. . Moskva , 1981. 219 p. ; LC Card 84-163581
HD9525.S653 M64 1981
*NYPL [*QIP 87-3316]*

Poletti, Ronaldo. Estado, economia e liberdade / Ronaldo Poletti. Brasília, DF : Instituto Tancredo Neves de Estudos Políticos e Sociais, [1986] 11 p. ; 30 cm. (Cadernos liberais . 18/86) LC Card 87-403230 DDC 330 19
1. Economics. 2. Capitalism. 3. Socialism. 4. Liberty. I. Series: Cadernos liberais , 86/18. II. Title.
HB179.P75 P65 1986

Polgár, Tibor, Dr. Illisz, László. Személyzeti munka, társadalmi környezet /. [Budapest] , 1986. 159 p. : ISBN 963-09-2778-0 : LC Card 87-408532
HF5549.2.H85 I44 1986

Polii͡anskiĭ, F. I͡A. (Fedor I͡Akovlevich) Ėkonomicheskai͡a mysl′ Drevnego Rima : kurs lektsiĭ / F.I͡A. Polii͡anskiĭ. Moskva : Izd-vo Moskovskogo universiteta, 1978. 355 p. ; 22 cm. At head of title: Moskovskiĭ gosudarstvennyĭ universitet imeni M.V. Lomonosova. Ėkonomicheskiĭ fakul′tet. Includes bibliographical references. LC Card 81-167944
1. Rome - Economic conditions. 2. Economics - Rome - History. I. Title.
HC39 .P65 1978

POLICE - ENGLAND - HISTORY - 20TH CENTURY.
Morgan, Jane. Conflict and order . Oxford [Oxfordshire] , New York , c1987. p. cm. ISBN 0-19-820128-1 : LC Card 87-11027 DDC 331.89/2942 19
HD5366.A6 M67 1987

POLICE - JAPAN - HISTORY.
Westney, D. Eleanor. Imitation and innovation . Cambridge, Mass. , 1987. viii, 252 p. : ISBN 0-674-44437-X (alk. paper) LC Card 87-273 DDC 338.6/0952 19
HD70.J3 W47 1987

POLICE PHOTOGRAPHY. see **PHOTOGRAPHY, LEGAL.**

POLICE - SALARIES, ETC. - WASHINGTON METROPOLITAN AREA.

POLICE - WALES - HISTORY - 20TH CENTURY.
Morgan, Jane. Conflict and order . Oxford [Oxfordshire] , New York , c1987. p. cm. ISBN 0-19-820128-1 : LC Card 87-11027 DDC 331.89/2942 19
HD5366.A6 M67 1987

Polich, Cynthia Longseth. Oberg, Charles N. Medicaid, entering the third decade . Excelsior, Minn. (P.O. Box 458, Excelsior 55331-0458) , c1986. vii, 70 p. : LC Card 86-233259 DDC 362.1/0425/0973 19
HD7102.U4 O58 1986

Policies and measures to promote industrial co-operatives in Africa / prepared by the Regional and Country Studies Branch, Division for Industrial Studies for the Regional Expert Consultation on the Role of Rural Co-operatives in the Productive Sectors in Africa, Addis Ababa, 7-11 October 1985. [New York] : United Nations Industrial Development Organization, [1985] 23 p. ; 30 cm. Cover title. "UNIDO/IS.561." "17 September 1985." Bibliography: p. 23. LC Card 87-104469 DDC 334/.6/096 19
1. Producer cooperatives - Africa. 2. Africa - Industries. 3. Small business - Africa. 4. Industry and state - Africa. 5. Rural development - Africa. I. United Nations Industrial Development Organization. Regional and Country Studies Branch. II. United Nations Industrial Development Organization. Regional Expert Consultation on the Role of Rural Co-operatives in the Productive Sectors in Africa.
HD3247 .P65 1985

Policies for maintaining social development through collective bargaining, legislation, and adequate social security protection to cope with structural change in the iron and steel industry /. International Labour Organisation. Iron and Steel Committee. Geneva , 1986. 45 p. ; ISBN 92-2-105497-7 (pbk.) : LC Card 86-222047 DDC 331.89/0469142 19
HD8039.I5 I6 1986

Policies for prosperity . Tobin, James, 1918- Cambridge, Mass. , 1987. xiv, 508 p. : ISBN 0-262-20066-X LC Card 87-2967 DDC 330.15/6 19
HB99.7 .T63 1987

Policies of population redistribution / edited by John W. Webb, Arvo Naukkarinen, Leszek A. Kosiński. Oulu : Geographical Society of Northern Finland for the IGU Commission on Population Geography, 1981. 199 p. : ill. ; 25 cm. (Nordia, 0356-1437 . 1981, vol. 15, no. 2, p. 1-201) Revised and amended papers originally presented at a symposium organized by the IGU Commission on Population Geography, held in Oulu, Finland, in 1978. Includes bibliographies and index. ISBN 951-675-071-0 (pbk.) LC Card 83-148782 DDC 304.8 19
1. Migration, Internal - Congresses. 2. Population policy - Congresses. 3. Population density - Congresses. I. Webb, John Winter. II. Naukkarinen, Arvo. III. Kosiński, Leszek A. IV. International Geographical Union. Commission of Population Geography. V. Pohjois-Suomen Maantieteellinin Seura. VI. Series: Nordia , v. 15, no. 2.
HB1952 .P65 1981

Policies with regard to grants to local authorities : report / prepared by the

Committee of Experts on Local and Regional Finance of the Steering Committee for Regional and Municipal Matters and drafted by J. Lotz. Strasbourg : Council of Europe, 1986. 35 p. : ill. ; 30 cm. (Study series, Local and regional authorities in Europe . 36) LC Card 86-218329 DDC 336.1/85 19
1. Grants-in-aid - Europe. I. Lotz, J. II. Council of Europe. Committee of Experts on Local and Regional Finances. III. Series: Study series, Local and regional authorities in Europe , study no. 36.
HJ1000 .P65 1986

Policy analyses in international economics .
(13) Bergsten, C. Fred, 1941- The United States-Japan economic problem /. Washington, D.C. , c1985. x, 164 p. : ISBN 0-262-52108-3 LC Card 85-18106 DDC 382/.0973/052 19
HF3127 .B47 1985 NYPL [JLE 87-19]

(16) Wonnacott, Paul. The United States and Canada . Washington, DC , 1987. xii, 173 p. : ISBN 0-88132-056-0 (pbk.) : LC Card 87-2660 DDC 382.71073 19
HF1456.5.C2 W65 1987

(17) Balassa, Bela A. Adjusting to success . Washington, DC , 1987. x, 121 p. : ISBN 0-88132-061-7 (pbk.) LC Card 87-3309 DDC 382.1/7/0951 19
HG3883.H66 B34 1987

(18) Cline, William R. Mobilizing bank lending to debtor countries /. Washington, DC , 1987. viii, 92 p. : ISBN 0-88132-062-5 (pbk.) LC Card 87-16857 DDC 332.1/5 19
HG3891.5 .C58 1987

(19) Auction quotas and United States trade policy /. Washington, DC , c1987. xiii, 241 p. : ISBN 0-88132-050-1 (pbk.) LC Card 87-12948 DDC 382/.52/0973 19
HF1455 .A83 1987

(20) Hathaway, Dale E. Agriculture and the GATT . Washington, DC , c1987. xii, 157 p. : ISBN 0-88132-052-8 LC Card 87-21430 DDC 382/.41/0973 19
HD9006 .H28 1987

(21) Destler, I. M. Anti-protection . Washington, DC , c1987. xii, 204 p. ; ISBN 0-88132-065-X (pbk.) LC Card 87-22545 DDC 382/.3/0973 19
HF1455 .D482 1987

(22) Williamson, John, 1937- Targets and indicators . Washington, DC , 1987. xii, 108 p. : ISBN 0-88132-064-1 LC Card 87-22724 DDC 332.4/5 19
HG3881 .W4936 1987

(23) Lessard, Donald R. Capital flight . Washington, DC , 1987. x, 64 p. ; ISBN 0-88132-059-5 LC Card 87-17279 DDC 332/.042 19
HG3891 .C367 1987

Policy and methods in German and American antitrust law . Maxeiner, James. New York , 1986. xiii, 174 p. ; ISBN 0-275-92113-1 (alk. paper) : LC Card 86-8108 DDC 343/.072 342.372 19
K3856 .M38 1986 NYPL [JLE 86-4413]

Policy implementation in the Federal system . Van Horn, Carl E. Lexington, Mass. , c1979. xiv, 177 p. ; ISBN 0-669-02435-X LC Card 78-19929 DDC 353.007/25
HJ275 .V35 NYPL [JLE 80-794]

The policy implications of the roles of women in agriculture in Zambia /. Safilios-Rothschild, Constantina, 1934- [Lusaka] [1985] 49, [25] p. ; LC Card 87-980047 DDC 331.4/83/096894 19
HD6073.A292 Z337 1985

Policy monograph .
(no. 2) Agricultural policies in the European Community . Canberra , 1985. xii, 373 p. : ISBN 0-644-04293-1 (pbk.) LC Card 86-673733
HD1920.5.Z8 A37x 1985

The policy of protection in regard to textiles and clothing . South Africa. Committee of Inquiry into the Textile and Clothing Industries. Pretoria , 1982?] ix, 110, [28] p. ; ISBN 0-621-08170-1 (pbk.) : LC Card 86-207580 DDC 382/.45677/00968 19
HF2651.C635 S627 1982

Policy paper (Australian Institute for Public Policy) .
(no. 5) Albon, Robert, 1951- The Telecom monopoly . Perth, W.A. , 1986. 56 p. : ISBN 0-949186-10-4 (pbk.) : LC Card 86-213521 DDC 384/.0994 19
HE8540.T44 A42 1986

(no. 6) Hussey, Denis D. Australian grain marketing . Perth, W.A. , 1986. 72 p. : ISBN 0-949186-11-2 (pbk.) : LC Card 86-213695 DDC 338.1/731/0994 19
HD9048.A82 H87 1986

Policy papers in ethnic relations, 0268-3970 .
(no. 5) Wrench, John. Unequal comrades . Coventry , 1986. 30 p. ; ISBN 0-948303-65-4 (pbk.) : LC Card 87-146518 DDC 331.6 19
HD6490.R22 G78 1986

Policy prescriptions for solving the infrastructure problem in Nebraska /. Stauss, Connie. [Lincoln , 1986] xi, 101 leaves : LC Card 87-102492 DDC 363/.09782 s 363/.09782 19
HC107.N23 C37 1986 pt. 1

Policy relevance of findings of the world fertility survey for developing countries /. Acsádi, György. New York , 1986. vi, 160 p. ; LC Card 85-37681 DDC 304.6/32/091724 19
HB1108 .A28 1986

Policy research series (Dublin, Dublin) .
(no. 7) FitzGerald, John D. The national debt and economic policy in the medium term /. Dublin , c1986. 62 p. : ISBN 0-7070-0089-0 (pbk.) : LC Card 87-110464 DDC 336.3/4/09417 19
HJ8630.A2 F58 1986

Policy responses to the changing international environment : (proceedings of the First Hungarian-Swiss roundtable, 8-12 April 1980) / edited by István Dobozi and Harriet Matejka. Budapest : Hungarian Scientific Council for World Economy, 1981. 170 p. ; 24 cm. (Trends in world economy, 0133-7769 . no. 33) Papers from a roundtable held in Budapest, April 8-April 12, 1980, sponsored by the Institute for World Economy of the Hungarian Academy of Sciences and the Graduate Institute of International Studies, Geneva. Includes bibliographical references. CONTENTS. - Changes of the international economic environment / by Mihály Simai -- Policy responses to the energy crisis / by István Dobozi -- The external relations of the European Economic Community / by Marlis Steinert -- The commodity pattern of east-west trade / by Béla Kádár -- The scope for structural adaptation in east-west trade and co-operation / by Norman Scott -- A note on free trade areas between market and centrally planned economies / by Harriet Matejka -- Towards an integrated international division of labour / by Károly Nyiri -- The Hungarian economic reform / by Tamás Nagy -- A comparative discussion of the reform of the economic mechanism and of enterprise management / by Hans Peter Graf. ISBN 963-301-077-2 (pbk.) LC Card 81-179118 DDC 337/.09/048 19
1. Economic history - 1971- - Congresses. 2. Economic policy - Congresses. I. Dobozi, István. II. Matejka, Harriet. III. Magyar Tudományos Akadémia, Budapest. Világgazdasági Kutató Intézet. IV. Geneva. Graduate Institute of International Studies.
HC59 .P573 1981 NYPL [JLL 79-189 no.33]

POLICY SCIENCES - ADDRESSES, ESSAYS, LECTURES.
Organizational theory and public policy /. Beverly Hills, Calif. , c1983. 304 p. : ISBN 0-8039-2006-7 LC Card 83-9704 DDC 302.3/5 19
HD38 .O75 1983 NYPL [JLD 87-1123]

The Private exercise of public functions /. Port Washington, N.Y. , 1985. 251 p. ; ISBN 0-8046-9368-4 LC Card 84-9254 DDC 361.6/1 19
H97 .P76 1985 NYPL [JLE 86-2611]

Policy Studies Institute.
Daniel, W. W. (William Wentworth), 1938- Workplace industrial relations and technical change /. London , c1987. 312 p. : ISBN 0-86187-917-1 LC Card 87-154801 DDC 331/.0941 19
HD8391 .D3535 1987

Streeck, Wolfgang, 1946- Industrial relations in West Germany . London , 1984. 178 p. ; ISBN 0-435-83839-3 LC Card 87-673421
HD6698.A8 S77x 1984b

Policy studies (Makhon li-yeḥasim benle'umiyim 'al-shem Le'onard Deiyis) .
(12) Laufer, Leopold Yehuda. U. S. aid to the West Bank and Gaza . [Jerusalem] [1985] 54 p. ; LC Card 87-400340 DDC 338.91/73/056951 19
HC415.25.Z7 W4735 1985

Policy Studies Organization.
Citizen participation in public decision making /. Westport, Conn. , 1987. xii, 237 p. ; ISBN 0-313-25478-8 (lib. bdg. : alk. paper) : LC Card 86-7571 DDC 323/.042/0973 19
JK1764 .C525 1987 NYPL [JLD 87-932]

Intergovernmental relations and public policy /. New York , 1986. viii, 224 p. : ISBN 0-313-25443-5 (lib. bdg. : alk. paper) LC Card 86-3155 DDC 353.9/29 19
JK325 .I575 1986 NYPL [JLE 87-749]

Market-based public policy /. New York , 1988. xiv, 265 p. : ISBN 0-312-00747-7 : LC Card 87-19703 DDC 361.6 19
HD3612 .M36 1988

Urban policy problems . New York , 1986. vi, 261 p. : ISBN 0-03-004218-6 (alk. paper) : LC Card 86-596 DDC 307.7/6/0973 19
HT123 .U7466 1986 NYPL [JLE 86-3613]

Policy Studies Organization series (New York, N. Y.)
The Distributional impacts of public policies /. New York , 1988. xvii, 257 p. ; ISBN 0-312-00749-3 : LC Card 87-11877 DDC 339.2/0973 19
HC110.I5 D535 1988

Market-based public policy /. New York , 1988. xiv, 265 p. : ISBN 0-312-00747-7 : LC Card 87-19703 DDC 361.6 19
HD3612 .M36 1988

A Policy Studies Organization series publication.
The Private exercise of public functions /. Port Washington, N.Y. , 1985. 251 p. ; ISBN 0-8046-9368-4 LC Card 84-9254 DDC 361.6/1 19
H97 .P76 1985 NYPL [JLE 86-2611]

Policy study (C.D. Howe Institute) .
(no. 1) Howitt, Peter, 1946- Monetary policy in transition . Toronto , Scarborough, Ont. [1986] viii, 140 p. : ISBN 0-88806-136-6 (pbk.) LC Card 86-229489 DDC 332.1/12/0971 19
HG655 .H69 1986

Policy vs. paper clips . Fram, Eugene H. Milwaukee, Wis. , 1988. p. cm. ISBN 0-87304-227-1 LC Card 87-24377 DDC 658/.048 19
HD62.6 .F73 1988

A Policy working paper of the National League of Cities.
Pagano, Michael A. How the public works . Washington, D.C. , c1986. ix, 68, 6 p. : ISBN 0-933729-13-8 (pbk.) : LC Card 87-129719 DDC 338.4/3363/0973 19
HJ9145 .P343 1986

Policymaking in Mexico . Teichman, Judith A., 1947- Boston , c1988. p. cm. ISBN 0-04-445033-8 : LC Card 87-18704 DDC 338.2/7282/0972 19
HD9574.M6 T45 1988

Polikarov, Azarii͡a Prizenti. Globalni problemi . Sofii͡a , 1986. 268 p. : LC Card 86-231293
HD75 .G555 1986

Polish Academy of Sciences. see **Polska Akademia Nauk.**

The Polish economy in the twentieth century /. Landau, Zbigniew. London , c1985. vi, 346 p. ; ISBN 0-7099-1607-8 LC Card 86-673496
HC340.3 .L36x 1985b

Polish economy in the 20th century. Landau, Zbigniew. The Polish economy in the twentieth century /. London , c1985. vi, 346 p. ; ISBN 0-7099-1607-8 LC Card 86-673496
HC340.3 .L36x 1985b

Polish People's Republic national report to the habitat : the United Nations Conference on Human Settlements, Vancouver, Canada, 31 May-11 June, 1976. [S.l. : s.n.], 1976 (Warszawa : Dom Słowa Polskiego) 48 p. : ill. ; 23 cm. + 1 portfolio. "April 1976." LC Card 83-226226
1. Poland - Economic policy - 1945-. 2. Regional planning - Poland. 3. Housing policy - Poland. I. Instytut Kształtowania Środowiska (Poland). II. Poland. Ministerstwo Administracji, Gospodarki Terenowej i Ochrony Środowiska.
HC340.3 .P656 1976

Politechnika Poznańska. Ekonomia polityczna kapitalizmu . Poznań , 1978. 240 p. : LC Card 81-172481
HB179.P7 E37 1978

Política agrária / Amilton Sinatora ... [et al.]. Porto Alegre-RS : Mercado Aberto : Fundação Wilson Pinheiro, 1985. 79 p. : ill. ; 19 cm. (Série Tempo de pensar) LC Card 86-198513
1. Agricultural laborers - Brazil - São Paulo (State). 2. Peasantry - Brazil - Sao Paulo (State). 3. Land reform - Brazil - São Paulo (State). 4. Agriculture and State - Brazil - São Paulo (State). I. Sinatora, Amilton. II. Series.
HD1531.B7 P65 1985

Política agraria . Paz Cárcamo, Guillermo. San José, Costa Rica , 1986. 84 p. ; LC Card 87-106764
HD1333.G9 P39 1986

La política agraria actual . Guadamuz López, Ernesto. San José, Costa Rica , 1986. 33 p. ; LC Card 87-402782 DDC 338.1/87286 19
HD1803 .G83 1986

La política agraria de la Comunidad Económica Europea . Reig Martínez, Ernest. [Valencia] [1986?] 129 p. ; ISBN 84-00-06370-8 LC Card 87-125600
HD1920.5.Z8 R45 1986

La Politica agraria della CEE / a cura di Alberto Mattei. Torino : G. Giappichelli, [1986] 330 p. : ill. ; 25 cm. Includes bibliographical references. LC Card 86-212028
1. Agriculture and state - European Economic Community countries. I. Mattei, Alberto.
HD1920.5.Z8 P625 1986

Política agrícola, eficiência e concentração na agricultura brasileira . Manoel, Alvaro. São Paulo , 1986. 180 p. : LC Card 86-234338
HD1873 .M35 1986

Política ambiental y desarrollo : un debate para América Latina / edición, Martha Cárdenas.1a ed. [Bogotá, Colombia] : Fundación Friedrich Ebert de Colombia : Instituto Nacional de Recursos Naturales Renovables y del Ambiente, 1986. 221 p. : ill. ; 21 cm. Includes bibliographies. LC Card 86-207035
1. Environmental policy - Latin America. 2. Environmental policy. I. Cárdenas, Martha. II. Fundación Friedrich Ebert de Colombia. III. Instituto Nacional de los Recursos Naturales Renovables y del Ambiente (Colombia).
HC130.E5 P65 1986

Política ambiental y sociedad /. Gabaldón, Arnoldo. Caracas, Venezuela , 1986. 225 p. : ISBN 980-01-0034-2 LC Card 87-115207 DDC 363.7/056/0987 19
HC239.5.E5 G32 1986

La politica commerciale italiana, 1945-1952 . Cavalcanti, Maria Luisa, 1943- Napoli , c1984. 288 p. ; LC Card 86-121609 DDC 380.1/3/0945 19
HF1549 .C38 1984

La política cultural del estado mexicano y el desarrollo de la T.V. /. Esparza Oteo T., Luis. México, D.F. , 1984. 116 p. ; LC Card 87-404017 DDC 384.55/4/0972 19
HE8700.9.M6 E84 1984

Política de endeudamiento público interno en el Perú . Ycaza Clerc, Mónica de. Lima, Perú , 1985. ii, 23, [39] p. : LC Card 86-223472
HJ8604 .Y33 1985

La política de protección en el desarrollo económico de México /. Kate, Adriaan ten. México , 1979. 376 p. ; ISBN 968-16-0352-4 LC Card 87-672671
HF1775 .K37x 1979

Política de rentas . Cuadrado Roura, Juan R. [Madrid] [1980?] 471 p. : ISBN 84-7196-297-7 LC Card 85-131138
HC390.I5 C8 1980

Política de transportes. Conferência do Ministro dos Transportes na Escola Superior de Guerra . [Brasília] [198-] [61] p. : LC Card 86-193198
HE233 .C59 1980z

A política de transportes marítimos no Brasil . Sanson, João Rogério. Rio de Janeiro , 1986. vii, 178, 5 p. : LC Card 87-403931 DDC 387.5/44/0981 19
HE597.B7 S26 1986

La politica degli investimenti in titoli nelle banche di deposito /. Fabrizi, Pier Luigi. [Milano] , 1982. xii, 138 p. ; LC Card 82-165568
HG1616.I5 F33 1982

La politica del debito pubblico in Italia, 1919-1943 /. Confalonieri, Antonio. Milano , Roma , c1986. 2 v. (536 p.) ; ISBN 88-420-2794-4 : LC Card 87-125992
HJ8678 .C64 1986

La política del Ministerio de Desarrollo. Agudelo Villa, Hernando. (comp) Bogotá, 1972-73. 3 v. LC Card 73-208936
HC197 .A63

La politica del pane . Grab, Alexander I., 1946- Milano, Italy , c1986. 180 p. ; LC Card 86-168239
HD9015.I85 L664 1986

Política demográfica / [Manoel A. Costa ... et al.]. Salvador : Fundação Bahiana para Estudos Econômicos e Sociais, [1983] 82 p. : ports. ; 23 cm. Report of debates held in Salvador, July 22, 1983. Includes bibliographical references. LC Card 87-138903 DDC 304.6/0981 19
1. Brazil - Population - Congresses. 2. Brazil - Population policy - Congresses. 3. Birth control - Brazil - Congresses. I. Costa, Manoel Augusto. II. Fundação Bahiana para Estudos Econômicos e Sociais.
HB3563 .P65 1983

La Politica di bilancio in condizioni di stress fiscale : profili istituzionali / E. Buglione ... [et al.] ; a cura di Franco Fichera. Milano, Italy : F. Angeli, c1986. 377 p. ; 22 cm. (Ricerche / Centro studi e iniziative per la riforma dello Stato . 2.2) Includes bibliographies. LC Card 87-134343
1. Budget - Italy - Congresses. 2. Government spending policy - Italy - Congresses. 3. Fiscal policy - Italy - Congresses. 4. Intergovernmental fiscal relations - Italy - Congresses. 5. Administrative agencies - Italy - Congresses. I. Buglione, Enrico, 1948-. II. Fichera, Franco. III. Series: Ricerche (Centro studi e iniziative per la riforma dello Stato (Italy)) , 2.2.
HJ2119 .P65 1986

A política dos transportes no Brasil, 1979/85 /. Severo, Cloraldino. [Brasília] , 1983. 91 p. : LC Card 86-153346
HE233 .S44 1983

Política e ideología en el movimiento campesino colombiano . Rivera Cusicanqui, Silvia. [Bogotá] [s.l.] , 1982. 188 p. ; LC Card 84-155496
HD511.5.A87 R58 1982
NYPL [JLD 86-1208]

Politica, economia, corporativismo . (v. 3) De Franchis, Carlo. Giammaria Ortes . Napoli , 1930. 165 p. ; LC Card 87-139766
HB109.O68 D4 1930

Política econômica da Nova República / Ricardo Carneiro ... [et al.] ; prefácio de Maria da Conceição Tavares ; organização de Ricardo Carneiro. Rio de Janeiro, RJ : Paz e Terra, [1986] 275 p. : ill. ; 21 cm. (Coleção Economia. vol. 15) LC Card 87-102398
1. Brazil - Economic policy. 2. Brazil - Economic conditions - 1985-. 3. Economic stabilization - Brazil. I. Carneiro, Ricardo.
HC187 .P67 1986

La Política económica del gobierno de Febres Cordero. Quito, Ecuador : Centro de Estudios y Difusión Social, [1986] 84 p. : ill. ; 22 cm. (Serie La Economía ecuatoriana de los últimos años . no. 3) Bibliography: p. 81. LC Card 87-403470
1. Ecuador - Economic policy. 2. Ecuador - Economic conditions - 1972-. I. CEDIS (Organization). II. Series.
HC202 .P65 1986

La política económica en el Ecuador . Pacheco, Lucas. Quito, Ecuador , 1985. 219 p. ; LC Card 87-400294 DDC 338.9866 19
HC202 .P26 1985

Política económica y movimiento laboral . Vega F., Humberto (Vega Fernández) Santiago, Chile , 1986. 52 p. : LC Card 87-101128
HC192 .V355 1986

Política económica 1985-1986 . Iguíñiz, Javier. Lima , 1986. 153 p. : LC Card 87-120200
HC227 .I368 1986

Politica ed economia . Convegno "La scienza politica in Italia, bilancio e prospettive" (1984 : Milan, Italy) Milano, Italy , c1987. 159 p. ; LC Card 87-139661
HC305 .C6767 1984

Política española. Gómez Fuentes, Angel, 1950- Así cambiará España . Esplugues de Llobregat, Barcelona , 1986. 333 p. ; ISBN 84-01-33317-2 LC Card 87-100798
HC241.25.S6 G65 1986

Política habitacional /. Matta, Nelson da. [Salvador] [1984] 59 p. : LC Card 87-138899 DDC 363.5/8 19
HD7323.A3 M37 1984

Política industrial da Bahia. Seminário sobre Política Industrial da Bahia (1986 : Salvador, Brazil) Síntese das exposições e dos debates /. [Salvador] [1986] 89 p. ; LC Card 87-403843 DDC 338.981/42 19
HD3616.B84 B37 1986

A política industrial da nova república. Brazil. Ministério da Indústria e do Comércio. [Brasília, Brazil] [1985] 44 p. ; LC Card 87-404994 DDC 338.981 19
HD3616.B83 B66 1985

Uma política industrial para o Brasil /. Magalhães, João Paulo de Almeida. [Rio de Janeiro] [between 1985 and 1987] 161 p. ; LC Card 87-403992 DDC 338.981 19
HD3616.B83 M34 1985

Política industrial y adquisición de tecnología en la actividad química en Costa Rica /. Morales C., Pedro A. [San José, Costa Rica] [1984] ii, 55 p. ; LC Card 86-199221
HD9655.C82 M67 1984

Política internacional, economía e integración / Antonio Salum Flecha ... [et al.] ; prólogo de Julia Velilla de Arréllaga. 1a ed. Asunción del Paraguay : Editorial Araverá, [1985] 178 p. ; 19 cm. (Serie Relaciones internacionales . no. 1) Proceedings of the V Jornadas sobre Relaciones Internacionales, Economía e Integración, organized by the Instituto Paraguayo de Estudios Geopolíticos e Internacionales and held at the Colegio de Graduados en Ciencias Económicas del Paraguay, with the collaboration of the Fundación Friedrich Naumann, Sept. 25-27, 1985. Limited edition of 500 copies. LC Card 86-122468
1. Paraguay - Foreign economic relations - Congresses. 2. Latin America - Economic integration - Congresses. 3. Debts, External - Paraguay - Congresses. 4. Debts, External - Latin America - Congresses. I. Salum-Flecha, Antonio, 1927-. II. Jornadas sobre Relaciones Internacionales, Economía e Integración (5th : 1985 : Colegio de Graduados en Ciencias Económicas del Paraguay). III. Instituto Paraguayo de Estudios Geopolíticos e Internacionales. IV. Colegio de Graduados en Ciencias Económicas del Paraguay. V. Friedrich Naumann Stiftung. VI. Series.
HF1523 .P65 1985

Política macroeconômica no Brasil, 1964/66 e 1980/84 /. Cysne, Rubens Penha. Rio de Janeiro, RJ [1986?] 125 p. : LC Card 86-229936
HC187 .C983 1986

Politica monetaria e debito pubblico : l'esperienza italiana dell'ultimo decennio / a cura di Riccardo Azzolini e Ugo Marani. Milano, Italy : F. Angeli, c1984. 209 p. : ill. ; 22 cm. At head of title: Cespe-Centro studi di politica economica. Includes bibliographical references. LC Card 85-111306 DDC 332.4/945 19
1. Debts, Public - Italy - Congresses. 2. Monetary policy - Italy - Congresses. I. Azzolini, Riccardo. II. Marani, Ugo. III. CESPE (Organization).
HJ8678 .P65 1984 ***NYPL [JLD 86-1207]***

Politica monetaria e politica dell'occupazione in Italia, in un contesto di innovazione finanziaria / L. Frey ... [et al.]. Milano : F. Angeli, c1984. 166 p. ; 22 cm. (Quaderni di economia del lavoro. 20 [i.e. 24]) Includes bibliographical references. LC Card 84-245111 DDC 332/.0945 19
1. Monetary policy - Italy. 2. Italy - Economic policy. 3. Italy - Full employment policies. 4. Finance - Italy. I. Frey, Luigi. II. Series: Quaderni di economia del lavoro (Franco Angeli editore) , 24.
HG1029.5 .P63 1984

Política monetaria y desarrollo industrial en el Ecuador, 1970-1983 /. Abril-Ojeda, Galo. Quito , 1985. 118 p. : ISBN 91-85894-10-9 LC Card 86-103812
HG865 .A27 1985

Política salarial. [Rio de Janeiro] : Instituto Euvaldo Lodi, [19]85. 31 leaves ; 30 cm. LC Card 86-152437
1. Wages - Government policy - Brazil. 2. Wages -

Brazil - Effect of inflation on. 3. Indexation (Economics) - Brazil. I. Instituto Euvaldo Lodi.
HD5004 .P65 1985

La Política tributaria en Latinoamérica : seminario, San José, Costa Rica, 1984 : (documentos y conclusiones) / Centro Interamericano de Estudios Tributarios (CIET) con la colaboración del Instituto Centroamericano de Administración Pública (ICAP). Washington, D.C. : Secretaría General, Organización de los Estados Americanos, 1986. ix, 180 p. ; 23 cm. Papers presented at the Seminario Interamericano sobre Política Tributaria sponsored by the General Secretariat of the OEA and ICAP, held in San José, Costa Rica, Oct. 29-Nov. 2, 1984. Includes bibliographies. ISBN 0-8270-2496-7 (pbk.) LC Card 87-403563 DDC 336.2/0098 19
1. Taxation - Latin America - Congresses. I. Centro Interamericano de Estudios Tributarios. II. Instituto Centroamericano de Administración Pública. III. Organization of American States. General Secretariat. IV. Seminario Interamericano sobre Política Tributaria (1984 : San José, Costa Rica).
HJ3374.5 .P65 1986

Política versus técnica no planejamento. Política x técnica no planejamento . São Paulo [Brasília] , 1982. 251 p. ; LC Card 86-150182
HD85.P65 P65 1982

Política x técnica no planejamento : perspectivas críticas / Ray Bromley, Eduardo S. Bustelo (org.). São Paulo : Brasiliense ; [Brasília] : UNICEF, 1982. 251 p. ; 22 cm. Includes bibliographies. CONTENTS. - O planejamento numa era de revolução social / Bertram M. Gross -- Aspectos políticos do planejamento na América Latina / Marcos Kaplan -- O processo de planejamento / Ray Bromley -- Planejamento e política social / Eduardo S. Bustelo -- Participacão é conquista / Pedro Demo -- A economia política de eficiência ; Salvando a análise de políticas do método de orçamento-programa / Aaron Wildavsky -- Técnicas de sistemas para gerir a sociedade / Ida R. Hoos -- Avaliação dos programas de objectivo amplo / Robert S. Weiss e Martin Rein. LC Card 86-150182
1. Economic policy. 2. Social policy. 3. Policy sciences. I. Bromley, R. J. II. Bustelo, Eduardo S. III. UNICEF. IV. Title: Política versus técnica no planejamento.
HD85.P65 P65 1982

POLITICAL ACTION COMMITTEES - UNITED STATES.
Matasar, Ann B. Corporate PACs and federal campaign financing laws . New York , 1986. x, 161 p. ; ISBN 0-89930-086-3 (lib. bdg. : alk. paper)
NYPL [JLE 86-2492]

Political broadcast catechism. 10th ed. Washington : National Association of Broadcasters, c1984. 61 p. : form. ; 28 cm. "Prepared for the members of the National Association of Broadcasters." On cover: You've got what it takes. Includes index.
1. Television in politics - United States. 2. Radio in politics - United States. 3. Fairness doctrine (Broadcasting) - United States.
NYPL [MWGH 85-3267]

Political economy : public policies in the United States and Britain / edited by Jerold L. Waltman and Donley T. Studlar. Jackson : University Press of Mississippi, c1987. vii, 276 p. ; 23 cm. Includes index. ISBN 0-87805-313-1 (alk. paper) LC Card 87-10425 DDC 361.6/1/0941 19
1. United States - Economic policy. 2. United States - Economic conditions - 1945-. 3. Great Britain - Economic policy - 1945-. 4. Great Britain - Economic conditions - 1945-. I. Waltman, Jerold L., 1945-. II. Studlar, Donley T.
HC106 .P68 1987

Political economy . Reynolds, Peter J. Brighton, Sussex , New York , 1987. viii, 279 p. : ISBN 0-312-01328-0 (St. Martin's Press) : LC Card 87-23307 DDC 330 19
HB171 .R42 1987

Political economy /. Sismondi, J.-C.-L. Simonde de (Jean-Charles-Léonard Simonde), 1773-1842. Fairfield, N.J. , 1988. p. cm. ISBN 0-678-00120-0 LC Card 87-17084 DDC 330 19
HB163 .S5853 1988

POLITICAL ECONOMY. see **ECONOMICS.**

Political economy and international money . Williamson, John, 1937- New York , 1987. xii, 292 p. ; ISBN 0-8147-5434-1 : LC Card 86-23484 DDC 332.4/5 19
HG3881 .W4934 1987

Political economy and monetary management . Ambirajan, S. Madras , c1984. viii, 203 p. ; LC Card 87-900241 DDC 332.4/954 19
HC433 .A42 1984

The political economy in perspective [microform] . Wanniski, Jude, 1936- Morristown, N.J. (66 Macculloch Ave., Morristown 07960) [1983] 5 p. ; LC Card 83-239685 DDC 332.4/973 19
HG540 .W36 1983 ***NYPL [*ZT-1708 no.21]***

The Political economy of Argentina, 1946-83 / Guido di Tella and Rudiger Dornbusch, editors. Pittsburgh, Pa. : University of Pittsburgh Press, 1988. p. cm. (Pitt Latin American series) Includes bibliographies and index. ISBN 0-8229-1148-5 LC Card 87-24412 DDC 338.982 19
1. Argentina - Economic policy. 2. Argentina - Economic conditions - 1945-1983. I. Di Tella, Guido, 1931-. II. Dornbusch, Rudiger.
HC175 .P623 1988

The political economy of Central America since 1920 /. Bulmer-Thomas, V. Cambridge , New York , 1987. xxiii, 416 p. : ISBN 0-521-34284-8 LC Card 87-11779 DDC 338.9728 19
HC141 .B78 1987

The Political economy of development and underdevelopment / edited by Charles K. Wilber. 4th ed. New York : Random House, Business Division, c1988. xi, 611 p. ; 24 cm. Bibliography: p. 589-594. Includes indexes. ISBN 0-394-37499-1 (pbk.) LC Card 87-9668 DDC 330.9172/4 19
1. Economic development. 2. Developing countries - Economic conditions. I. Wilber, Charles K.
HD82 .P546 1988

The political economy of food in Nigeria 1960-1982 . Sano, Hans-Otto. Uppsala , 1983. 108 p. : ISBN 91-7106-210-6
NYPL [JLD 84-860]

The political economy of global energy /. Pachauri, R. K. Delhi , New York , 1985. xiii, 191 p. : LC Card 85-900034 DDC 333.79 19
HD9502.A2 P32 1985

The political economy of industrial democracies /. Hibbs, Douglas A., 1943- Cambridge, Mass. , 1987. viii, 327 p. : ISBN 0-674-68580-6 LC Card 86-9799 DDC 339.5/09171/3 19
HB3743 .H53 1987 ***NYPL [JLE 87-1430]***

The Political economy of international change.
Conybeare, John A. C. Trade wars . New York , 1987. xv, 319 p. ; ISBN 0-231-06234-6 LC Card 87-8097 DDC 382 19
HF1414 .C665 1987

McNeil, William C. American money and the Weimar Republic . New York , 1986. x, 352 p. : ISBN 0-231-06236-2 LC Card 85-29962 DDC 336.3/4/0943 19
HG3949 .M38 1986 ***NYPL [JLE 86-3268]***

Mares, David R. Penetrating the international market . New York , 1987. xvi, 294 p. : ISBN 0-231-06346-6 (alk. paper) LC Card 87-6358 DDC 382/.415/097232 19
HD9014.M62 M38 1987

Rodman, Kenneth Aaron. Sanctity versus sovereignty . New York , 1988. p. cm. ISBN 0-231-06448-9 LC Card 87-24970 DDC 332.6/7373/01724 19
HG5993 .R63 1988

Political economy of international change series.
McNeil, William C. American money and the Weimar Republic . New York , 1986. x, 352 p. : ISBN 0-231-06236-2 LC Card 85-29962 DDC 336.3/4/0943 19
HG3949 .M38 1986 ***NYPL [JLE 86-3268]***

The political economy of international debt . Bouchet, Michel Henri. New York , 1987. xix, 219 p. : ISBN 0-89930-185-1 (lib. bdg. : alk. paper) LC Card 87-2474 DDC 336.3/435 19
HJ8015 .B68 1987

The political economy of international relations /. Gilpin, Robert. Princeton, N.J. , 1987. xvi, 449 p. ; ISBN 0-691-07732-0 (alk. paper) : LC Card 86-25562 DDC 337 19
HF1411 .G55 1987

The Political economy of international technology transfer / edited by John R. McIntyre and Daniel S. Papp. Westport, Conn. : Quorum Books, c1986. viii, 267 p. : tables ; 24 cm. Includes index. Bibliography: p.253-255. ISBN 0-89930-128-2 (lib. bdg. : alk. paper) LC Card 85-28128 DDC 338.9/26 19
1. Technology transfer - Addresses, essays, lectures. 2. Economic development - Addresses, essays, lectures. I. McIntyre, John R. II. Papp, Daniel S., 1947-.
HD45 .P574 1986 ***NYPL [JLE 86-3313]***

The political economy of Israel /. Sharkansky, Ira. New Brunswick, N.J., U. S.A. , c1987. xi, 157 p. ; ISBN 0-88738-117-0 : LC Card 86-25090 DDC 338.95694/054 19
HC415.25 .S49 1987

The Political economy of Japan. Stanford, Calif. : Stanford University Press, 1987- v. <1 > : ill. ; 24 cm. "Under the general editorship of Yasuske Murakami and Hugh T. Patrick." Bibliography: v. 1, p. [595]-650. Includes indexes. CONTENTS. - v. 1. The Domestic transformation / edited by Kōzō Yamamura and Yasukichi Yasuba. ISBN 0-8047-1380-4 (v. 1 : alk. paper) : LC Card 86-30037 DDC 338.952 19
1. Japan - Economic conditions - 1945-. 2. Japan - Economic policy - 1945-. I. Murakami, Yasusuke, 1931-. II. Patrick, Hugh T. III. Yamamura, Kōzō.
HC462.9 .P57 1987

The Political economy of Kenya / edited by Michael G. Schatzberg. New York : Praeger, 1987. viii, 245 p. ; 25 cm. (A SAIS study on Africa) Papers from a conference held in Apr. 1986 at the Johns Hopkins University School of Advanced International Studies. Bibliography: p. [203]-236. Includes index. ISBN 0-275-92672-9 (alk. paper) : LC Card 87-22889 DDC 330.9676/204 19
1. Kenya - Economic conditions - 1963- - Congresses. 2. Kenya - Social conditions - 1963- - Congresses. I. Schatzberg, Michael G. II. Series.
HC865 .P65 1987

The political economy of land . Gilbert, Alan, 1944- Aldershot, Hants , Brookfield, Vt., U. S.A. , c1985. xv, 163 p. : ISBN 0-566-05007-2 : LC Card 85-17535 DDC 333.77/13/0987 19
HD576 .G54 1985 ***NYPL [JLD 86-3632]***

The political economy of land reforms /. Thimmaiah, G. New Delhi [1983?] xiii, 94 p. ; LC Card 84-900237 DDC 333.3/1/5487 19
HD1333.I42 K3778 1983
NYPL [JLD 87-752]

The political economy of Latin American development . Hirschman, Albert O. La Jolla, Calif. [1986] 57 p. ; LC Card 87-621614 DDC 338.98 19
HC125 .H544 1986

The political economy of long waves . Petersen, Ib Damgaard. København, Denmark [1986] 10, [1] p. : ISBN 87-7393-042-3 (pbk.) LC Card 86-214084 DDC 338.9 19
HB3729 .P47 1986

The political economy of Mexico under de la Madrid . Cornelius, Wayne A., 1945- La Jolla, Calif. , 1986. 50 p. ; LC Card 87-621352 DDC 330.972/0834 19
HC135 .C7185 1986

The political economy of national defense /. Weida, William J. Boulder , 1987. xvii, 230 p. ; ISBN 0-8133-0432-6 (alk. paper) : LC Card 86-19015 DDC 355.6/22/0973 19
UA23 .W3694 1987 ***NYPL [JLE 87-1043]***

The political economy of natural gas /. Banks, Ferdinand E. London , New York , c1987. 200 p. ; ISBN 0-7099-3940-X : LC Card 87-14098 DDC 338.2/7285 19
HD9581.A2 B36 1987

Political economy of neocolonialism in Third World countries /. Ghosh, B. N. New Delhi , c1985. vii, 174 p. ; LC Card 85-903172 DDC 338.9/009172/4 19
HC59.7 .G485 1985 ***NYPL [JLD 87-1141]***

The Political economy of rent-seeking / edited and with contributions by Charles K. Rowley, Robert D. Tollison, Gordon Tullock. Boston : Kluwer Academic Publishers, c1988. xvi, 492 p. : ill. ; 24 cm. (Topics in regulatory economics and policy . 1) Includes bibliographies and index. ISBN 0-89838-241-6 LC Card 87-16887 DDC 333/.012 19
1. Rent (Economic theory). 2. Social choice. I. Rowley, Charles Kershaw. II. Tollison, Robert D. III. Tullock, Gordon. IV. Series.
HB401 .P64 1988

The Political economy of risk and choice in Senegal / edited by Mark Gersovitz and John Waterbury. London, England ; Totowa, N.J. : F. Cass, 1987. xv, 363 p. : ill. ; 24 cm. Bibliography: p. 327-343. Includes index. ISBN 0-7146-3297-X : LC Card 86-26859 DDC 338.966/3 19
1. Senegal - Economic conditions. 2. Senegal - Economic policy. I. Gersovitz, Mark. II. Waterbury, John.
HC1045 .P65 1987

Political economy of tax and expenditure determination . Govinda Rao, M. New Delhi , 1981. vii, 212 p. ; LC Card 81-905062 DDC 336.54 19
HJ1337 .G68 1981 ***NYPL [JLD 86-2603]***

The political economy of the Brazilian State, 1889-1930 /. Topik, Steven. Austin , 1987. xii, 241 p. : ISBN 0-292-76500-2 LC Card 87-5835 DDC 338.981 19
HC187 .T558 1987

The Political economy of the new Asian industrialism / edited by Frederic C. Deyo. Ithaca, N.Y. : Cornell University Press, 1987. 252 p. ; 24 cm. (Cornell studies in political economy) Includes bibliographies and index. CONTENTS. - Export-oriented industrializing states in the capitalist world system / Richard E. Barrett and Soomi Chin -- The origins and development of the Northeast Asian political economy / Bruce Cumings -- State and foreign capital in the East Asian NICs / Stephan Haggard and Tun-jen Cheng -- Political institutions and economic performance / Chalmers Johnson -- The interplay of state, social class, and world system in East Asian development / Hagen Koo -- State and labor / Frederic C. Deyo -- Class, state, and dependence in East Asia / Peter Evans -- Coalitions, institutions, and linkage sequencing toward a strategic capacity model of East Asian development / Frederic C. Deyo. ISBN 0-8014-1948-4 (alk. paper) LC Card 86-29103 DDC 338.95 19
1. East Asia - Economic policy. 2. Korea (South) - Economic policy. 3. Taiwan - Economic policy. 4. Singapore - Economic policy. 5. Hong Kong - Economic policy. I. Deyo, Frederic C. II. Series.
HC460.5 .P65 1987

Political Economy of the World-System Conference (10th : 1986 : San Francisco State University) Rethinking the nineteenth century . New York , c1988. p. cm. ISBN 0-313-25997-6 (lib. bdg. : alk. paper) LC Card 87-17791 DDC 330.9/034 19
HC53 .R48 1988

Political Economy of the World System Section. see **American Sociological Association. Section on Political Economy of the World System.**

The political economy of trade and development /. Evans, H. David (Henry David) New York , 1988- p. cm. ISBN 0-312-00955-0 (v. 1) : LC Card 87-16370 DDC 382 19
HF1008 .E83 1988

The political economy of underdevelopment in Northern Rhodesia, 1918-1960 . Kanduza, Ackson M. Lanham, MD , c1986. x, 336 p. : ISBN 0-8191-5189-0 (alk. paper) : LC Card 85-29835 DDC 338.96894 19
HC915 .K36 1986 ***NYPL [JLD 86-2962]***

The political economy of Venezuelan oil /. Randall, Laura. New York , 1987. xiii, 247 p. ; ISBN 0-275-92823-3 (alk. paper) : LC Card 87-15848 DDC 338.2/7282/0987 19
HD9574.V42 R35 1987

The political economy of West Germany, 1945-85 . Leaman, Jeremy, 1947- New York , 1988. xii, 287 p. : ISBN 0-312-00541-5 : LC Card 87-9458 DDC 338.943 19
HC286.5 .L4 1988

Political economy of world poverty .
(3) Leo, Christopher. Land and class in Kenya /. Toronto , Buffalo [N.Y.] , c1984. xii, 244 p. : ISBN 0-8020-2532-3 ***NYPL [JLE 86-1242]***

Political education in the Southern Farmers' Alliance, 1887-1900 /. Mitchell, Theodore R. Madison, Wis. , 1987. xiv, 242 p. : ISBN 0-299-11470-8 : LC Card 87-40141 DDC 338.1/06/075 19
HD1485.N35 M58 1987

Political mobilization and industry in Libya /. Naur, Maja. [Uppsala] , c1986. 268 p. : ISBN 87-500-2648-8 (pbk.) : LC Card 87-141231 DDC 338.961/2 19
HD3616.L752 N38 1986

POLITICAL PARTICIPATION - BOLIVIA.
Sandoval, Godofredo. Las mil caras del movimiento social boliviano /. La Paz, Bolivia [1986] 132 p. : LC Card 86-227792
HD6608.5 .S25 1986

POLITICAL PARTICIPATION - CHILE.
Campero, Guillermo. El sindicalismo internacional y la redemocratización de Chile /. Santiago, Chile , 1984. 77 p. ; LC Card 86-139122 DDC 331.88/0983 19
HD6617 .C357 1984

POLITICAL PARTICIPATION - FRANCE.
Séguin, Philippe, 1943- Réussir l'alternance . Paris , c1985. 220 p. ; ISBN 2-221-04633-1 : LC Card 85-187945 DDC 944.083/8 19
JN2594.2 .S37 1985 ***NYPL [JLC 87-46]***

POLITICAL PARTICIPATION - GERMANY, WEST.
Roth, Rainer A., 1942- Zur Problematik der politischen Kultur der Jungwähler in der Bundesrepublik Deutschland /. Passau , c1984. 516 p. : ISBN 3-922016-46-4 ***NYPL [JLE 87-703]***

Rucht, Dieter. Planung und Partizipation . München , c1982. 321 p. ; ISBN 3-88073-105-5 LC Card 83-672501
JN3971.A91 R82x 1982 ***NYPL [JLD 86-2900]***

POLITICAL PARTICIPATION - MEXICO.
Salinas de Gortari, Carlos. Producción y participación política en el campo /. México , 1980. 320 p. : ISBN 968-582-934-9 LC Card 82-199421 DDC 338.1/0972 19
HD1792 .S287 1980 ***NYPL [JLD 86-2602]***

POLITICAL PARTICIPATION - UNITED STATES.
Citizen participation in public decision making /. Westport, Conn. , 1987. xii, 237 p. ; ISBN 0-313-25478-8 (lib. bdg. : alk. paper) : LC Card 86-7571 DDC 323/.042/0973 19
JK1764 .C525 1987 ***NYPL [JLD 87-932]***

Delli Carpini, Michael X., 1953- Stability and change in American politics . New York , 1986. xxv, 374 p. ; ISBN 0-8147-1780-2 (alk. paper) : LC Card 85-15348 DDC 323/.042/0973 19
JK1764 .D45 1986 ***NYPL [JLE 86-2183]***

Hollander, Richard S. Video democracy . Mt. Airy, Md. , c1985. ix, 161 p. : ISBN 0-912338-51-2 LC Card 85-81818 DDC 384.55/5 19
HE8700.76.U6 H65 1985 ***NYPL [MWGT 86-1503]***

LeMay, Michael C., 1941- The struggle for influence . Lanham , c1985. xv, 452 p. : ISBN 0-8191-4653-6 (alk. paper) : LC Card 85-6105 DDC 323.1/73 19
E184.A1 L44 1985 ***NYPL [IE 85-3562]***

McCann, Michael W., 1952- Taking reform seriously . Ithaca , 1986. 345 p. ; ISBN 0-8014-1952-2 LC Card 86-47647 DDC 322.4/3/0973 19
JK1118 .M37 1986 ***NYPL [JLE 87-1009]***

Oettinger, Craig Milton, 1945- The politics of excluded groups . 1978. xvi, 454 leaves : ***NYPL [Sc Micro R-4615]***

Stone, Clarence N. (Clarence Nathan), 1935- Urban policy and politics in a bureaucratic age /. Englewood Cliffs, N.J. , c1986. xv, 397 p. ; ISBN 0-13-939562-8 LC Card 85-6481 DDC 320.8/0973 19
JS331 .S76 1986 ***NYPL [JLE 86-3158]***

Zimmerman, Joseph Francis, 1928- Participatory democracy . New York , 1986. xi, 229 p. ; ISBN 0-275-92132-8 (alk. paper) : LC Card 86-8129 DDC 323/.042/0973 19
JF493.U6 Z56 1986 ***NYPL [JLE 86-3632]***

POLITICAL PARTIES - BRAZIL.
State and society in Brazil . Boulder , 1987. x, 349 p. ; ISBN 0-8133-7401-4 (pbk. : alk. paper) : LC Card 87-2160 DDC 981/.063 19
HC187 .S78 1987

POLITICAL PARTIES - FRANCE.
Mouriaux, René. Syndicalisme et politique /. Paris , c1985. 212 p. : LC Card 86-159539
HD6687 .M68 1985

Séguin, Philippe, 1943- Réussir l'alternance . Paris , c1985. 220 p. ; ISBN 2-221-04633-1 : LC Card 85-187945 DDC 944.083/8 19
JN2594.2 .S37 1985 ***NYPL [JLC 87-46]***

POLITICAL PARTIES - GERMANY, WEST.
Das Politische System der BRD . Berlin , 1985. 479 p. ; LC Card 86-123928 DDC 320.943 19
JN3971.A2 P59 1985 ***NYPL [JLD 86-3144]***

POLITICAL PARTIES - GREAT BRITAIN.
Coxall, W. N. Parties and pressure groups /. London , New York , 1986. iv, 196 p. ; ISBN 0-582-35189-8 ***NYPL [JLD 86-2729]***

POLITICAL PARTIES - INDIA - STATES - CASE STUDIES.
Kohli, Atul. The state and poverty in India . Cambridge [Cambridgeshire] , New York , 1987. x, 262 p. : ISBN 0-521-32008-9 LC Card 85-25554 DDC 333.3/1/54 19
HD1333.I4 K65 1986 ***NYPL [JLD 87-1517]***

POLITICAL PARTIES - ITALY.
Keszthelyi, Csaba. Az autonómia kérdése az olasz szakszervezeti egységért folytatott küzdelemben /. [Budapest] , 1985. 75 p. ; ISBN 963-673-322-8 LC Card 86-185901
HD6680.5.Z65 K47 1985

POLITICAL PARTIES - ROMANIA - HISTORY - 19TH CENTURY.
Condițiile istorice ale apariției și dezvoltării clasei muncitoare din România . București , 1984. 652 p. ; LC Card 84-234192
HD8648 .C65 1984

POLITICAL PARTIES - SOUTH AFRICA.
Hauck, David. U. S. corporate withdrawal from South Africa . Washington, D.C. (Suite 600, 1755 Massachusetts Ave., N.W., Washington 20036) [1986] 22 p. ; LC Card 86-209299 DDC 332.6/7373/068 19
HG5851.A3 H39 1986

POLITICAL PLANNING - FRANCE.
Herzog, Philippe. La France peut se ressaisir /. Paris , c1987. 416 p. : ISBN 2-209-05941-0 : LC Card 87-169995
HC276.3 .H47 1987

POLITICAL PLANNING - GERMANY, WEST.
Rucht, Dieter. Planung und Partizipation . München , c1982. 321 p. ; ISBN 3-88073-105-5 LC Card 83-672501
JN3971.A91 R82x 1982 ***NYPL [JLD 86-2900]***

POLITICAL PLANNING - GERMANY, WEST - ADDRESSES, ESSAYS, LECTURES.
Verwaltung und Planung im Wandel /. Köln , 1979. 112 p. ; ISBN 3-7745-6438-8 : LC Card 81-473982
HT395.G4 V48 ***NYPL [JLE 86-2107]***

POLITICAL PLANNING - HISTORY.
Friedmann, John. Planning in the public domain . Princeton, N.J. , c1987. xii, 501 p. : ISBN 0-691-07743-6 (alk. paper) : LC Card 87-3194 DDC 361.6 19
HD87.5 .F745 1987

POLITICAL PLANNING - PERU.
Perú siglo XXI. [Lima] [1986 or 1987] 63 p. : LC Card 87-403080 DDC 338.985 19
HC227 .P416 1986

POLITICAL PLANNING - SOUTH AFRICA - KWAZULU.
Spies, P. H. Perspectives on the future of Natal/KwaZulu /. Pietermaritzburg , 1986. 149 p. : ISBN 0-909232-59-8 (pbk.) : LC Card 87-166530 DDC 361.2/5/09684 s 361.6/1/09684 19
HC517.N3 A44 vol. 69 JQ2224

POLITICAL PLANNING - SOUTH AFRICA - NATAL.
Spies, P. H. Perspectives on the future of Natal/KwaZulu /. Pietermaritzburg , 1986. 149 p. : ISBN 0-909232-59-8 (pbk.) : LC Card 87-166530 DDC 361.2/5/09684 s 361.6/1/09684 19
HC517.N3 A44 vol. 69 JQ2224

POLITICAL PLANNING - UNITED STATES - CONGRESSES.
Carson, Carol S. The use of national income and product accounts for public policy . Washington, D.C. , 1986. 26 p. : LC Card 86-601338 DDC 339.5/0973 19
HC110.I5 C37 1986

POLITICAL PLATFORMS. see **POLITICAL PARTIES.**

The political realities of African management /.

Leonard, David K. Binghamton, NY, USA (P.O. Box 818, Binghamton 13902) [1984] 39 p. ; LC Card 87-153761 DDC 338.1/86 19
HD2118 .L46 1984

POLITICAL REFUGEES. see **REFUGEES, POLITICAL.**

POLITICAL RIGHTS - DEVELOPING COUNTRIES - CONGRESSES.
Les Libéraux et le dialogue Nord-Sud . Bonn , c1982. 220 p. ; ISBN 3-920590-36-8 LC Card 84-204748
HC59.7 .L4177 1982

POLITICAL RIGHTS - LATIN AMERICA.
Sheahan, John, 1923- Patterns of development in Latin America . Princeton, N.J. , c1987. x, 399 p. : ISBN 0-691-07735-5 (alk. paper) : LC Card 87-2853 DDC 338.98 19
HC125 .S498 1987

Political risk management . Kennedy, Charles R. New York , 1987. xiv, 163 p. : ISBN 0-89930-157-6 (lib. bdg. : alk. paper) LC Card 86-25588 DDC 332.6/7373 19
HG4538 .K44 1987

POLITICAL SCIENCE. Here and with local subdivision are entered works on the discipline of political science. Works on the politics of particular countries, regions, cities, etc., are entered under the name of the place subdivided by Politics and government.

POLITICAL SCIENCE - ADDRESSES, ESSAYS, LECTURES.
Gonella, Guido, 1905- Contestazioni /. Roma , 1983. 3 v. ; LC Card 84-237282 DDC 945.092 19
JN5451 .G57 1983 ***NYPL [JFE 86-1367]***

POLITICAL SCIENCE - DICTIONARIES.
Andrlić, Vlasta. Rječnik terminologije jugoslavenskog političko-ekonomskog sistema . Zagreb , 1985. viii, 135 p. ; LC Card 86-182784
HB61 .A55 1985 ***NYPL [*QKK 87-1803]***

Erdsiek, Gerhard. Wörterbuch für Recht, Wirtschaft und Politik. Bleckede bei Hamburg [1964-1968] 2 v. LC Card 65-42077
NYPL [JLE 85-408]

Raghu Vira. A comprehensive English-Hindi dictionary of governmental & educational words & phrases ... /. New Delhi , 1962. 189, 1572 p. ; ***NYPL [JLF 87-203]***

POLITICAL SCIENCE - DICTIONARIES - SERBO-CROATIAN.
Andrlić, Vlasta. Rječnik terminologije jugoslavenskog političko-ekonomskog sistema . Zagreb , 1985. viii, 135 p. ; LC Card 86-182784
HB61 .A55 1985 ***NYPL [*QKK 87-1803]***

POLITICAL SCIENCE - EUROPE - HISTORY.
Kloppenberg, James T. Uncertain victory . New York , 1986. x, 546 p. ; ISBN 0-19-503749-9 : LC Card 85-21636 DDC 320.5/315/094 19
JA84.E9 K57 1986 ***NYPL [JLE 86-2574]***

POLITICAL SCIENCE - HISTORY - ADDRESSES, ESSAYS, LECTURES.
The Rise of the modern state /. Brighton, Sussex , 1986. viii, 255 p. ; ISBN 0-7450-0059-2
NYPL [JLD 86-2353]

POLITICAL SCIENCE - METHODOLOGY.
Sylvan, David J., 1953- A rationalist methodology for the social sciences /. Oxford [Oxfordshire] , 1985. 188 p. : ISBN 0-631-13443-3 : LC Card 84-14480 DDC 300/.1/8 19
HM24 .S95 1985 ***NYPL [JLE 86-1125]***

POLITICAL SCIENCE - PHILOSOPHY.
Hamlin, Alan P., 1951- Ethics, economics, and the state /. Brighton, Sussex , 1986. x, 198 p. ;
NYPL [JLD 86-3648]

POLITICAL SCIENCE - UNITED STATES - HISTORY.
Kloppenberg, James T. Uncertain victory . New York , 1986. x, 546 p. ; ISBN 0-19-503749-9 : LC Card 85-21636 DDC 320.5/315/094 19
JA84.E9 K57 1986 ***NYPL [JLE 86-2574]***

Osiatyński, Wiktor, 1945- Współczesny konserwatyzm i liberalizm amerykański /. Warszawa , 1984. 552 p. ; ISBN 83-01-04929-4 (pbk.) : ***NYPL [*QO 86-3450]***

The Political self-assessment of Bulgarian respondents in terms of a left-right continuum. [Munich?] : Radio Free Europe/Radio Liberty, [1986] 16 p. ; 30 cm. (East European area audience and opinion research) Cover title. "August 1986." "727." Includes bibliographical references. LC Card 87-142360 DDC 384.55/43 19
1. Radio Free Europe - Public opinion. 2. Public opinion - Bulgaria. 3. Radio audiences - Bulgaria. I. RFL/RL, inc. II. Series.
HE8697.A8 P67 1986

POLITICAL SOCIALIZATION - SOVIET UNION.
Akopov, Mykhaĭlo Arutiūnovych. Dukhovnyĭ mir sovetskogo cheloveka /. Kiev , 1985. 124, [3] p. ; LC Card 86-139846
JN6581 .A64 1985 ***NYPL [*QIK 87-3448]***

POLITICAL SOCIOLOGY.
Badaloni, Nicola. Forme della politica e teorie del cambiamento . Pisa , c1983. xxii, 264 p. ; LC Card 85-163265 DDC 306/.2 19
JA76 .B23 1983 ***NYPL [JLD 86-3306]***

Mészáros, István, 1930- Philosophy, ideology, and social science . Brighton, Sussex , 1986. xix, 284 p. ; ISBN 0-85527-717-3
NYPL [JLD 87-1334]

Penz, G. Peter. Consumer sovereignty and human interests /. Cambridge [Cambridgeshire] , New York , 1986. xiv, 242 p. ; ISBN 0-521-26571-1 LC Card 85-22407 DDC 330.15/5 19
HB846 .P46 1986 ***NYPL [JLE 86-3311]***

Vance, A. Last chance for peace . Boulder, Colo. , c1985. xviii, 256 p. : ISBN 0-930705-01-7 (pbk.) : LC Card 84-18831 DDC 172/.24 19
BL65.P4 V36 1985 ***NYPL [JLD 86-2214]***

POLITICAL SOCIOLOGY - ADDRESSES, ESSAYS, LECTURES.
White collar workers, trade unions, and class /. London , Dover, N.H. , c1986. 215 p. : ISBN 0-7099-0571-8 : LC Card 85-28806 DDC 331.88/041 19
HD8039.M39 W45 1986
NYPL [JLD 86-1602]

Political stability and neo-corporatism : corporatist integration and societal cleavages in Western Europe / edited by Ilja Scholten. London ; Beverly Hills : Sage Publications, 1987. x, 276 p. ; 23 cm. (Sage series in neo-corporatism) Includes bibliographies and index. ISBN 0-8039-8028-0 LC Card 86-63492 DDC 321.9 19
1. Corporate state - Europe. 2. Europe - Politics and government - 1945-. I. Scholten, Ilja. II. Series.
HD3616.E8 P64 1987

POLITICAL STABILITY - EVALUATION.
Ting, Wenlee. Multinational risk assessment and management . New York , c1987. p. cm. ISBN 0-89930-175-4 (lib. bdg. : alk. paper) LC Card 87-5970 DDC 658 19
HD61 .T56 1987

Political strikes . Hain, Peter, 1950- Harmondsworth, Middlesex, England , New York, N.Y., U. S.A. , 1986. 357 p. ; ISBN 0-670-80601-3 : LC Card 86-216642 DDC 331.89/2941 19
HD5365.A6 H35 1986

Political strikes . Hain, Peter, 1950- Harmondsworth, Middlesex, England , New York , 1986. 357 p. ; ISBN 0-670-80601-3
NYPL [JLD 87-532]

POLITICAL STRIKES - GREAT BRITAIN.
Hain, Peter, 1950- Political strikes . Harmondsworth, Middlesex, England , New York, N.Y., U. S.A. , 1986. 357 p. ; ISBN 0-670-80601-3 : LC Card 86-216642 DDC 331.89/2941 19
HD5365.A6 H35 1986

Políticas de ajuste y grupos más vulnerables en América Latina : hacia un enfoque alternativo / compilador, Eduardo S. Bustelo.1a ed. [Bogotá, Colombia] : Fondo de las Naciones Unidas para la Infancia : Fondo de Cultura Económica, 1987. 278 p. : ill. ; 21 cm. (Sección de obras de economía) Serie de economía Errata slip inserted. Papers presented at the Seminario sobre Políticas de Ajuste y Grupos más Vulnerables en América Latina, held in Bogotá, Colombia on Feb. 20-21, 1986, organized by the Departamento Nacional de Planeación de la República de Colombia and the Fondo de las Naciones Unidas para la Infancia-UNICEF. Includes bibliographical references. ISBN 958-9093-01-9 LC Card 87-404285 DDC 338.98 19
1. Latin America - Economic policy - Congresses. 2. Economic stabilization - Latin America - Congresses. 3. Latin America - Economic conditions - 1945- - Congresses. I. Bustelo, Eduardo S. II. Seminario sobre Políticas de Ajuste y Grupos Más Vulnerables en América Latina (1986 : Bogotá, Colombia). III. Colombia. Departamento Nacional de Planeación. IV. UNICEF. V. Series: Sección de obras de economía (Bogotá, Colombia).
HC125 .P647 1987

Las políticas de distribución y redistribución del ingreso en Costa Rica en la década de los años setenta /. Trejos S., Juan Diego. Ciudad Universitaria Rodrigo Facio , 1983. 117 p. ; LC Card 85-242016
HC143.Z9 I527 1983

Políticas de incentivos a la exportación de manufacturas en América Latina . Lejavitzer, Moisés. México, D.F. , 1985. iv, 155 leaves ; LC Card 87-122013 DDC 382/.4567/098 19
HF1480.5 .L44 1985

Políticas macro-económicas : una perspectiva latinoamericana / René Cortázar, editor ; José Pablo Arellano ... [et al.]. Santiago de Chile : Corporación de Investigaciones Económicas para Latinoamérica, [1986] 409 p. : ill. ; 23 cm. Includes bibliographies. CONTENTS. - Políticas de estabilización / Joseph Ramos -- La literatura económica y los costos de equilibrar la balanza de pagos en América Latina / José Pablo Arellano -- La política fiscal macroeconómica / Manuel Marfán -- Política monetaria y financiera / Roberto Zahler -- Aspectos conceptuales sobre política cambiaria relevantes para América Latina / Andrés Solimano -- Empleo y remuneraciones / René Cortázar -- Keynesianismo y monetarismo / Patricio Meller -- Modelos y políticas de crecimiento / Jorge Marshall -- Modelos macroeconómicos aplicados en América Latina / Juan Foxley y Joaquín Vial. LC Card 87-403669 DDC 338.98 19
1. Latin America - Economic policy. 2. Debts, External - Latin America. 3. Economic stabilization - Latin America. 4. Fiscal policy - Latin America. 5. Monetary policy - Latin America. 6. Chicago school of economics. I. Cortázar, René. II. Arellano, José Pablo. III. Corporación de Investigaciones Económicas para Latinoamérica.
HC125 .P657 1986

Políticas oleícolas nacionales / Consejo Oleícola Internacional. [S.l.] : El Consejo, [1985] 130 p. in various pagings ; 28 cm. "E.108/Doc. no. 4, actualización no. 17, 15 de abril de 1985." LC Card 86-131977 DDC 338.4/7664362 19
1. Olive-oil industry. 2. Olive-oil industry - Government policy. I. International Olive Oil Council.
HD9490.5.O462 P65 1985

Politiche dell'impresa e sistema tributario /. Leccisotti, Mario. Napoli , 1984. 174 p. : ISBN 88-20-70883-3 : ***NYPL [JLD 86-3651]***

Politiche di mercato dei beni industriali /. Brondoni, Silvio M. [Milano] [1983] ix, 279 p. : LC Card 83-234353
HD9680.A2 B76 1983

Le politiche monetarie e di bilancio nei principali paesi industrializzati . Pennella, Giuseppe. Milano, Italy , c1985. 293 p. : LC Card 86-129450
HG230.3 .P45 1985

Le politiche regionali del lavoro . Runggaldier, Ulrich. Milano, Italy , c1986. 160 p. ; LC Card 86-169484
HD8376.5 .R93 1986

Politiche tributarie e struttura industriale in Italia / a cura di Antonio Pedone. Bologna : Il Mulino, c1986. 118 p. ; 22 cm. (Quaderni de "L'Industria" . 36) Bibliography: p. 79-81. ISBN 88-15-01224-9 : LC Card 86-224989
1. Corporations - Taxation - Italy. 2. Investments - Taxation - Italy. 3. Tax incentives - Italy. 4. Industry and state - Italy. I. Pedone, Antonio. II. Series: Quaderni de L'Industria (Società editrice Il Mulino) , 36.
HD2753.I7 P65 1986

Politicheskaia͡ bor'ba v Chekhoslovakii v 1944-1948 gg. i natsionalizatsii͡a sredstv proizvodstva /. Murashko, G. P. (Galina Pavlovna) Moskva , 1986. 326, [2] p. ; LC Card 86-202951
HC270.28 .M87 1986

Politicheskata ikonomii͡a kato teorii͡a i metodologii͡a / Nikola Popov ... [et al.]. 1. izd. Sofii͡a : "Nauka i izkustvo", 1986. 397 p. ; 21 cm. (Metodologicheski vŭprosi na politicheskata

ikonomiia v pet toma . t. 1) Summary in English and Russian. Includes bibliographical references. LC Card 86-210685
1. Marxian economics - Methodology. I. Popov, Nikola Grigorov. II. Series.
HB71 .M59 1986 t. 1 HB97.5

POLITICIANS - GREAT BRITAIN - BIOGRAPHY.
Brown, J. Gordon. Maxton /. Edinburgh , 1986. 336 p., [8] p. of plates : ISBN 1-85158-042-5 *NYPL [JFE 87-30]*

POLITICIANS - INDIA.
Singh, V. B., 1941- Profiles of political elites in India /. Delhi , 1984. xii, 178 p. : LC Card 84-900272 DDC 305.5/24/0954 19
JQ281 .S565 1984 NYPL [JLD 86-4319]

POLITICIANS - UNITED STATES - PUBLIC OPINION.
Lipset, Seymour Martin. The confidence gap . Baltimore , 1987. xxiv, 460 p. : ISBN 0-8018-3044-3 (pbk.) LC Card 86-27416 DDC 303.3/8/0973 19
HD2785 .L53 1987

POLITICS AND BUSINESS. see **BUSINESS AND POLITICS.**

Politics and economic policy . Withers, William, 1905-1987. New York, N.Y. , c1986. 240 p. : ISBN 0-8062-2722-2 : LC Card 86-201185 DDC 338.973 19
HC106 .W82 1986

Politics and land system in Bangladesh /. Shawkat Ali, A. M. M. Dhaka , 1986. x, 354 p. ; LC Card 86-900954 DDC 333.3/1/5492 19
HD880.6 .S53 1986 NYPL [JLD 86-4018]

Politics and nuclear power . Hatch, Michael T., 1945- Lexington, KY , 1986. xi, 219 p. ; ISBN 0-8131-1583-3 : LC Card 85-29545 DDC 333.79/24/094 19
HD9698.E82 H38 1986 NYPL [JLD 86-2137]

POLITICS AND RELIGION. see **RELIGION AND POLITICS.**

Politics and the budget . Shuman, Howard E. Englewood Cliffs, N.J. , c1988. p. cm. ISBN 0-13-684416-2 (pbk.) : LC Card 87-14521 DDC 353.0072/231 19
HJ2051 .S49 1988

Politics and the Ethiopian famine, 1984-1985 /. Clay, Jason W. Cambridge, MA (11 Divinity Ave., Cambridge 02138) , 1985. xi, 250 p. : LC Card 86-153948 DDC 363.8/56/0963 19
HC845.Z9 F33 1985 NYPL [JLF 87-364]

POLITICS AND THE PRESS. see **PRESS AND POLITICS.**

Politics and tyranny . Friedman, Milton, 1912- San Francisco, Calif. , c1984. 68 p. ; ISBN 0-936488-00-X (pbk.) : LC Card 84-61364 DDC 330 19
HB98.3 .F75 1984 NYPL [JLE 87-857]

Politics, economics, and welfare reform . Lenkowsky, Leslie, 1946- Lanham, MD [Washington, D.C.] , c1986. vii, 207 p. ; ISBN 0-8191-5215-3 (alk. paper) : LC Card 85-29456 DDC 362.5/82 19
HC260.I5 L46 1986 NYPL [JLE 86-2801]

The politics of a guaranteed income. Moynihan, Daniel P. (Daniel Patrick), 1927- New York [1973] xiii, 579 p. ISBN 0-394-46354-4 LC Card 77-37069 DDC 362.5
HC110.I5 M65 NYPL [JLE 74-384]

The politics of airline deregulation /. Brown, Anthony E. Knoxville , c1987. xiii, 224 p. ; ISBN 0-87049-532-1 (alk. paper) : LC Card 86-30888 DDC 387.7/1 19
HE9803.A4 B68 1987

The Politics of American economic policy making / edited by Paul Peretz. Armonk, N.Y. : M.E. Sharpe, c1987. 455 p. : ill. ; 24 cm. Includes bibliographies. ISBN 0-87332-406-4 : LC Card 87-12827 DDC 338.973 19
1. Finance, Public - United States. 2. Industry and state - United States. 3. Fiscal policy - United States. 4. United States - Economic policy. 5. United States - Politics and government.
HJ257 .P59 1987

The politics of baby foods . Chetley, Andrew. London , 1986. xv, 189 p. ; ISBN 0-86187-293-2 *NYPL [JLE 86-2969]*

The Politics of broadcasting / edited by Raymond Kuhn. New York : St. Martin's Press, 1985. 305 p. ; 23 cm. Includes bibliographies and index. ISBN 0-312-62660-6 : LC Card 84-15996 DDC 384.54 19
1. Broadcasting - Addresses, essays, lectures. 2. Broadcasting - Political aspects - Addresses, essays, lectures. 3. Broadcasting policy - Addresses, essays, lectures. I. Kuhn, Raymond.
HE8689.4 .P65 1985 NYPL [MWGT 86-5102]

The politics of development . Seitz, John L., 1931- New York, NY, USA , 1988. xiii, 194 p. : ISBN 0-631-15801-4 (pbk.) LC Card 87-20825 DDC 338.9 19
HD82 .S399 1988

The politics of economic interdependence /. Dell, Edmund. New York , 1987. x, 268 p. ; ISBN 0-312-00526-1 : LC Card 86-31345 DDC 337 19
HF1411 .D332 1987

The politics of economic power in southern Africa /. Libby, Ronald T. Princeton, N.J. , c1987. xxii, 361 p. : ISBN 0-691-07723-1 (alk. paper) : LC Card 87-2406 DDC 337.68 19
HF1613.3.Z4 S65 1987

The politics of energy conservation /. Nivola, Pietro S. Washington, D.C. , c1986. x, 294 p. ; ISBN 0-8157-6088-4 : LC Card 85-48265 DDC 333.79/16/0973 19
TJ163.4.U6 N58 1986 NYPL [JLE 86-2515]

The Politics of energy forecasting : a comparative study of energy forecasting in Western Europe and North America / edited by Thomas Baumgartner and Atle Midttun. Oxford [Oxfordshire] : Clarendon Press ; New York : Oxford University Press, 1987. xiii, 314 p. : ill. ; 24 cm. Includes bibliographies and indexes. ISBN 0-19-828547-7 : LC Card 86-23885 DDC 333.79 19
1. Energy industries - Forecasting - Case studies. 2. Power resources - Forecasting - Case studies. 3. Energy policy - Case studies. I. Baumgartner, Thomas (Thomas Martin). II. Midttun, Atle, 1952-.
HD9502.A2 P66 1987

The Politics of energy research and development / edited by John Byrne and Daniel Rich. New Brunswick, U. S.A. : Transaction Books, c1986. 181 p. : ill. ; 23 cm. (Energy policy studies, 0882-3537 . v. 3) Includes bibliographies. ISBN 0-88738-653-9 (pbk.) LC Card 86-1307 DDC 333.79/0973 19
1. Energy policy - United States - Addresses, essays, lectures. 2. Power resources - Research - United States - Addresses, essays, lectures. 3. Energy development - United States - Addresses, essays, lectures. I. Byrne, John, 1949-. II. Rich, Daniel. III. Series. IV. Series: Energy policy studies (Newark, Del.).
HD9502.U52 P63 1986 NYPL [JLE 86-3577]

The politics of hunger . Warnock, John W., 1933- Toronto , New York , c1987. xv, 334 p. ; ISBN 0-458-80630-7 (pbk.) : LC Card 87-1659 DDC 363.8/09172/4 19
HD9018.D44 W37 1987

The Politics of international debt / edited by Miles Kahler. Ithaca : Cornell University Press, 1986. 272 p. ; 25 cm. (Cornell studies in political economy) Includes bibliographical references. ISBN 0-8014-1911-5 (alk. paper) LC Card 85-48243 DDC 327.1/11 19
1. Debts, External - Political aspects - Addresses, essays, lectures. 2. Loans, Foreign - Political aspects - Addresses, essays, lectures. I. Kahler, Miles, 1949-. II. Series.
HJ8083 .P65 1986 NYPL [JLE 86-2405]

The politics of manpower, 1914-1918 /. Grieves, Keith. New York, NY , 1988. vii, 241 p. ; ISBN 0-312-01320-5 LC Card 87-20511 DDC 331.12/042/0941 19
HD5765.A6 G77 1988

The politics of neglect . Frieden, Bernard J. Cambridge, Mass. [1975] x, 281 p. ; ISBN 0-262-06061-2 LC Card 75-6792 DDC 309.2/62/0973
HT167 .F74 NYPL [JLE 80-1135]

The politics of nuclear defence . Rumble, Greville. Cambridge [Cambridgeshire] , 1985. xi, 285 p. ; ISBN 0-7456-0194-4 : LC Card 85-18643 DDC 355/.0217 19
U263 .R86 1985 NYPL [JLD 86-1092]

The politics of oil in Indonesia . Khong, Cho Oon. Cambridge [Cambridgeshire] , New York , 1986. x, 253 p. : ISBN 0-521-30901-8 LC Card 85-22416 DDC 338.2/7282/09598 19
HD9567.I52 K48 1986 NYPL [JLD 86-3386]

The politics of penury . Tenenbaum, Barbara, 1946- Albuquerque , c1986. xviii, 250 p. ; ISBN 0-8263-0890-2 : LC Card 86-16027 DDC 336.72 19
HJ802 .T46 1986 NYPL [JLE 87-482]

The Politics of professionalism, opportunity, employment, and gender / Sarah Slavin, editor. New York : Haworth Press, c1987. xx, 110 p. ; 23 cm. "Also been published as Women & politics, volume 6, number 3, fall 1986."--T.p. verso. Includes bibliographies. CONTENTS. - Professionalism, occupational segregation by gender and control of nursing / David G. Allen -- Comparable worth, skill groups, and market interactions / Frederick G. Floss -- Dual career academic couples / Elizabeth Monk-Turner, Charlie G. Turner -- Political marriages : when the wife is the politician / Joan Bartczak Cannon, Mary Ann Marusich-Smith -- Support for academic women in political science, 1890-1945 / Beverly B. Cook. ISBN 0-86656-626-0 LC Card 86-29491 DDC 331.4/81/000973 19
1. Women in the professions - United States. 2. Dual career families - United States. I. Slavin, Sarah.
HD6054.2.U6 P64 1987

The politics of public expenditure /. Mullard, Maurice, 1946- London , New York , c1987. 220 p. : ISBN 0-7099-4674-0 : LC Card 87-6777 DDC 336.3/9/0941 19
HJ7764 .M85 1987

The politics of sentiment . Sincere, Richard E. Washington, D.C. : Lanham, MD ; xiv, 164 p. : ISBN 0-89633-116-4 (alk. paper) : LC Card 87-13441 DDC 332.6/73/0968 19
HG5851.A3 S56 1987

The politics of state and city administration /. Abney, Glenn. Albany, N.Y. , c1986. xvi, 260 p. ; ISBN 0-88706-255-5 LC Card 85-14873 DDC 353.9 19
JK2408 .A26 1986 NYPL [JLE 86-3711]

The politics of the nuclear freeze /. Garfinkle, Adam M., 1951- Philadelphia, Pa. , 1984. xviii, 258 p. ; ISBN 0-910191-08-5 : LC Card 84-6030 DDC 327.1/74 19
JX1974.7 .G34 1984 NYPL [JLE 86-710]

The politics of the South Africa run . Berridge, Geoff. Oxford [Oxfordshire] , New York , 1987. x, 254 p. ; ISBN 0-19-827484-X : LC Card 87-1600 DDC 387.5/094 19
HE903.4 .B47 1987

The politics of the UCS work-in . Foster, John. London , Atlantic Highlands, N.J. , 1986. 446 p. : ISBN 0-85315-663-8 (pbk.) : LC Card 86-235159 DDC 331.89/282383/094141 19
HD5365.S512 1971 .C584 1986

The politics of United States foreign aid /. Guess, George M. New York , 1987. 297 p. ; ISBN 0-312-00448-6 : LC Card 86-26301 DDC 338.91/09172/4 19
HC60 .G7383 1987

The Politics of urban fiscal policy / editors, Terrence J. McDonald and Sally K. Ward. Beverly Hills : Sage Publications, c1984. 176 p. : ill. ; 23 cm. (New approaches to social science history . v. 5) Principally versions of papers presented at the 1982 Meeting of the Social Science History Association. Includes bibliographical references. ISBN 0-8039-2373-2 LC Card 84-13431 DDC 336/.014/73 19
1. Municipal finance - United States - History - Addresses, essays, lectures. 2. Municipal government - United States - History - Addresses, essays, lectures. I. McDonald, Terrence J. II. Ward, Sally K. III. Social Science History Association. IV. Series.
HJ9144 .P64 1984 NYPL [JLD 87-126]

POLITICS, PRACTICAL - UNITED STATES.
Abney, Glenn. The politics of state and city administration /. Albany, N.Y. , c1986. xvi, 260 p. ; ISBN 0-88706-255-5 LC Card 85-14873 DDC 353.9 19
JK2408 .A26 1986 NYPL [JLE 86-3711]

Politieke bibliotheek.
Florizoone, Patrick, 1958- De groenen . [Deurne] , c1985. x, 194 p. : ISBN 90-6716-272-8 LC Card 86-148321
HC329.5.E5 F56 1985

Politik als Investitionsmotor? . Wolffsohn, Michael. Frankfurt am Main , New York , c1985. 141 p. : ISBN 3-8204-7487-0 (pbk.) LC Card 87-672289
HD2810.5 W64x 1985

Politik der Armut. Politik der Armut und die Spaltung des Sozialstaats /. Frankfurt am Main , 1985. 474 p. : ISBN 3-518-11233-3 : LC Card 85-183026
HC290.5.P6 P65 1985

Politik der Armut und die Spaltung des Sozialstaats / herausgegeben von Stephan Leibfried und Florian Tennstedt. 1. Aufl. Frankfurt am Main : Suhrkamp, 1985. 474 p. : ill. ; 18 cm. (Edition Suhrkamp. 1233 = n.F., Bd. 233) Bibliography: p. 429-[468] ISBN 3-518-11233-3 : LC Card 85-183026
1. Poor - Germany, West. 2. Unemployment - Germany (West). 3. Germany, West - Social policy. I. Leibfried, Stephan, 1944-. II. Tennstedt, Florian. III. Title: Politik der Armut.
HC290.5.P6 P65 1985

Politik gegen die Krise : Beiträge zu einer alternativen Wirtschaftspolitik / Hartmut Elsenhans ... [et al.] ; Herausgeber, Michael Birk, Harald Eggerstedt, Andre P. Tegtmeier. Marburg : SP-Verlag, 1985. 157 p. : 1 ill. ; 20 cm. (Texte zur politischen Theorie und Praxis) Contains the most important reports, some rev. and some previously published, given as part of a series of lectures at Philipps-Universität Marburg during the summer semester of 1984. Includes bibliographies. CONTENTS. - Die Krise des "Keynesianischen Staates" : Ursachen des Scheiterns der sozialdemokratischen Politik in der Bundesrepublik Deutschland / Jürgen Hoffmann -- Wirtschaftspolitik in der Krise / Hajo Riese -- Monetaristische Politik in den Industrieländern, oder, Der beste Weg zur Zerstörung einer liberalen Weltwirtschaft / Hartmut Elsenhans -- Die ostasiatischen Schwellenländer--Modell für die Dritte Welt? / Ulrich Menzel -- Wirtschaftsdemokratie und betriebliche Mitbestimmung / Hans G. Nutzinger -- Godesberger Erneuerung / Heinz Rapp. ISBN 3-924800-01-4 : LC Card 86-119259 DDC 338.9 19
1. Economic history - 1945-. 2. Economic policy. I. Elsenhans, Hartmut, 1941-. II. Birk, Michael. III. Eggerstedt, Harald. IV. Tegtmeier, Andre P. V. Philipps-Universität Marburg.
HC59 .P584 1985

Politik, Recht, Gesellschaft .
(Bd. 6) Energie und Gerechtigkeit /. München , c1984. xii, 254 p. : ISBN 3-597-10259-X LC Card 84-175053
HD9502.A2 E5192 1984

Politik som rationellt handlande .
(10) Nordfors, Lennart. Makten hälsan och vinsten . Lund, Sweden , c1985. 195 p. : ISBN 91-44-23331-0 : LC Card 85-204849
HD7732 .N66 1985

Politik und Ökonomie als Kultur /. Stehl, Jan. Würzburg , 1982. viii, 449 p. ; ISBN 3-88479-093-5 LC Card 83-183293
HB175 .S88 1982

Politikai gazdaságtan füzetek, 0324-6396 .
(43) Halmai, Péter. Integráció és tulajdon az iparosodó mezőgazdaságban /. [Budapest] , 1984. 124 p. ; ISBN 963-673-278-7 LC Card 85-126691
HD1940.5 .H35 1984

(46) Dévai, Katalin. A nagyvállalatok helyzetéről /. [Budapest] , 1984. 68 p. ; ISBN 963-673-293-0 LC Card 85-175237
HD2852.5 .D48 1984

(47) Vigvári, András. A gazdaságirányítási rendszer egyes kérdései, elmélettörténeti megközelítésben /. [Budapest] , 1985. 87 p. ; ISBN 963-673-302-3 LC Card 85-231820
HC300.28 .V53 1985

(48) Tanulmányok az anyagi érdekeltség, jövedelemszabályozás témaköréből /. [Budapest] , 1985. 126 p. : ISBN 963-673-308-2 LC Card 86-147619
HD5022.5 .T37 1985

(50) Bató, Sándor. Az áru mint történelmi kategória /. [Budapest] , 1985. 104 p. ; ISBN 963-673-332-5 LC Card 86-228016
HB97.5 .B3245 1985

Politikai gazdaságtan (Szeged, Hungary)
A Gazdaság és társadalom viszonya a szocializmus építésének jelenlegi időszakában . Szeged , 1985. 181 p. ; LC Card 86-207975
HC300.28 .G27 1985

Politikē oikonomia gia holous . Liverēs, Anastasēs I. Athēna , 1985. 424 p. ; LC Card 86-178760
HB97.5 .L555 1985

Hoi politikes pleures tēs entaxēs tēs Helladas stēn EOK . Sarlēs, Dēmētrēs. Athēna , 1981. 212 p. ; LC Card 83-170595
HC241.25.G8 S27 1981

Politikwissenschaftliche Paperbacks .
(Bd. 4) Kress, Roland, 1961- Die politischen Stiftungen in der Entwicklungspolitik . Bochum , 1985. iv, 224 p. ; ISBN 3-88339-426-2 : LC Card 85-175519
HC60 .K727 1985

(Bd. 6) Ungleiche Entwicklung und Regionalpolitik in Südeuropa . Bochum , 1985. 282 p. : ISBN 3-88339-441-6 : LC Card 85-205651
HC244.5 .U48 1985

La Politique agraire en Chine : structure et évolution / Centre tricontinental. Ottignies, Louvain-la-Neuve, Belgique : CETRI, [1981] 84 leaves ; 30 cm. Bibliography: leaves 83-84. LC Card 86-203953
1. Land reform - China - History - 20th century. 2. China - Rural conditions. 3. Agriculture, Cooperative - China - History - 20th century. I. Centre tricontinental (Louvain-la-Neuve, Belgium).
HD926 .P65 1981

Politique agricole commune : revenus et fiscalité des agriculteurs en Belgique / G. Bublot ... [et al.] ; textes rassemblés par Max Frank. Bruxelles, Belgique : Université de Bruxelles, c1982. 126 p. ; 24 cm. "Les articles de G. Bublot, J.F. Breuer, M. Frank, J. Herinckx, B. Lange, et R. Praet sont extraits des 'Cahiers économiques de Bruxelles' no 91/3e trimestre 1981"--P. [4]. ISBN 1-8004-0773-5 LC Card 87-672469
1. Farm income - Belgium. 2. Farm income - Taxation - Belgium. 3. Agriculture and state - European Economic Community countries. I. Bublot, Georges. II. Frank, Max, 1913-. III. Title: Revenus et fiscalité des agriculteurs en Belgique.
HD1803 .P64x 1982

Politique communautaire de développement. The European Community's development policy . Bruges , 19. 285 p. : LC Card 87-135534 DDC 338.94 19
HC60 .E7626 1986

Politique d'aujourd'hui.
Harouel, Jean Louis. Essai sur l'inégalité /. Paris , c1984. 287, [1] p. ; ISBN 2-13-038354-8 : LC Card 84-150958
HC280.I5 H35 1984

Kolm, Serge Christophe. La bonne économie . Paris , 1984. 472 p. : ISBN 2-13-038695-4 : LC Card 84-254896 DDC 330 19
HB173 .K64 1984

La Politique de l'emploi-formation au Maghreb, 1970-1980 / Chantal Bernard ; avec la participation de R. Abdelkrim ... [et al.]. Paris : Editions du Centre national de la recherche scientifique, 1982. 472 p. : ill. ; 24 cm. (Collection "Etudes de l'Annuaire de l'Afrique du Nord") "Extrait de l'Annuaire de l'Afrique du Nord 1980." Includes bibliographical references. ISBN 2-222-03122-2 LC Card 84-222103 DDC 331.11/0961 19
1. Labor supply - Africa, North. 2. Manpower policy - Africa, North. 3. Occupational training - Africa, North. I. Bernard, Chantal. II. Series.
HD5838 .P65 1982

Politique des transports. France. Groupe de politique des transports. Rapport du Groupe de politique des transports. Paris , c1984. 246 p. : ISBN 2-11-001216-1 : LC Card 84-163968
HE248 .F716 1984

Politique d'organisation du territoire.
Raumordnungspolitik im Vollzug . Grüsch , c1985. 507 p. : ISBN 3-7253-0258-8 : LC Card 86-149201
HC397 .R36 1985

La politique économique de la France. Pébereau, Michel. Paris , c1985. 319 p. : ISBN 2-200-31217-2 LC Card 86-179163 DDC 338.944 19
HC276.2 .P42 1985

Politiques d'aménagement hydro-agricole /. Funel, Jean Marie. Paris , c1980. 212 p. : ISBN 2-85319-083-8 LC Card 86-112826
HD1699.S37 F86 1980

Politiques de population .
(no 3-4) Loriaux, M. Economie, population et politique démographique /. Louvain-la-Neuve [c1984] 169 p. : ISBN 2-87085-041-7 : LC Card 86-144677
HB883.5 .L67 1984

Politiques vivrières, dépendances alimentaires et développement / fruit du travail collectif mené au sein du Réseau "Stratégies alimentaires, Stratégies paysannes" à la suite des ateliers "Technologies et développement" de septembre 1983 ; rédaction finale ... Jean-Christophe Bureau, avec le concours de Vincent Minier et Jean-Marc Pradelle. [Paris] : Groupe de recherches et d'échanges technologiques : Editions L'Harmattan, diffusion, c1984. iv, 129 p. : ill. ; 22 cm. (Collection des ateliers Technologie et développement . no 1) "Janvier 1984." Bibliography: p. 127-128. ISBN 2-86844-000-2 : LC Card 84-248912
1. Food supply - Sahel - Congresses. 2. Food relief - Sahel - Congresses. I. Bureau, Jean-Christophe. II. Minier, Vincent. III. Pradelle, Jean-Marc. IV. Réseau Stratégies alimentaires, stratégies paysannes (France). V. Series.
HD9017.S152 P65 1984

Politische Ökonomie und Persönlichkeitstheorie . Kurthen, Hermann. Köln , 1985. 245 p. ; ISBN 3-7609-5181-3 LC Card 85-155083
HB74.P8 K87 1985

Politische System der B.R.D. Das Politische System der BRD . Berlin , 1985. 479 p. ; LC Card 86-123928 DDC 320.943 19
JN3971.A2 P59 1985 ***NYPL [JLD 86-3144]***

Die politischen Stiftungen in der Entwicklungspolitik . Kress, Roland, 1961- Bochum , 1985. iv, 224 p. ; ISBN 3-88339-426-2 : LC Card 85-175519
HC60 .K727 1985

Politökonomische Probleme des Gebrauchswerts, der Nützlichkeit und der Bewertung von Gebrauchswerten / Autorenkollektiv der Forschungsgruppe "Politökonomische Probleme des Wissenschaftlich-Technischen Fortschritts" ; Leitung, Ulrich Hoffmann ; Technische Hochschule Karl-Marx-Stadt, Sektion Marxismus-Leninismus. Karl-Marx-Stadt : Rektor der Technischen Hochschule Karl-Marx-Stadt, Sektion Marxismus-Leninismus, [1983] 92 p. ; 21 cm. (Wissenschaftliche Schriftenreihe der Technischen Hochschule Karl-Marx-Stadt, 0323-6374 . 13/1983) Includes bibliographies. LC Card 84-167577
1. Value. 2. Utility theory. 3. Technological innovations. 4. Communism and technology. I. Hoffmann, Ulrich, Prof. Dr. sc. oec. II. Technische Hochschule Karl-Marx-Stadt. Forschungsgruppe "Politökonomische Probleme des Wissenschaftlich-Technischen Fortschritts.". III. Series: Wissenschaftliche Schriftenreihe der Technischen Hochschule Karl-Marx-Stadt, 1983/13.
HB201 .P63 1983

Politologische Studien .
(Bd. 27) Sonnewald, Bernd, 1947- Die "Berliner Linie" und die Hausbesetzer-Szene /. Berlin , c1983. 149 p. ; ISBN 3-87061-170-7 LC Card 83-190228
HD7287.96.G32 B477 1983

Polityka finansowa PRL . Tegler, Eugeniusz. Szczecin , 1984. 128 p. ; LC Card 86-100923
HJ1213.Z6 T44 1984

Polityka ochrony środowiska w krajach socjalistycznych : wybór opracowań / pod redakcją nauk. Barbary Prandeckiej.Wyd. 1. Warszawa : Państwowe Wydawn. Ekonomiczne, 1980. 318 p. ; 20 cm. Partly translated from Bulgarian, Czech, German, Hungarian, and Russian. Includes bibliographical references. ISBN 83-208-0067-6 LC Card 81-101337
1. Environmental policy - Europe, Eastern. 2. Environmental policy - Soviet Union. 3. Environmental protection - Europe, Eastern. 4. Environmental protection - Soviet Union. I. Prandecka, Barbara Karolina.
HC244.Z9 E56 1980

Polityka rolna PRL : wybrane problemy : praca zbiorowa / pod redakcją Augustyna Wosia ; [napisali Jerzy Wojtecki ... et al.].Wyd. 2., popr. Warszawa : Książka i Wiedza, 1977. 246, [2] p., [24] p. of plates : col. ill. ; 21 cm. Includes

bibliographies. LC Card 81-201110
1. Agriculture and state - Poland. I. Woś, Augustyn.
HD1995.7.Z8 P65 1977

Pollack, Irving M., 1918- The Handbook of fixed income securities /. Homewood, Ill. , 1987. xxx, 1376 p. : ISBN 0-87094-745-1 LC Card 86-50815 *NYPL [JLE 87-939]*

Pollard, J. H.
Methodologies for the collection and analysis of mortality data . Liège, Belgium , 1984. vi, 510 p. : ISBN 2-87040-032-2 (pbk.) LC Card 86-205582 DDC 304.6/4/072 19
HB1321 .M48 1984

Mortality, expectation of life, and the Hungarian experience / J.H. Pollard. [North Ryde, N.S.W.] : Macquarie University, School of Economic and Financial Studies, [1986] 59 p. ; 30 cm. (Research paper / Macquarie University, School of Economic and Financial Studies . no. 304) Cover title. "January 1986." Bibliography: p. 29. ISBN 0-85837-578-8 (pbk.) LC Card 87-110257 DDC 304.6/4/09439 19
1. Mortality - Hungary - Mathematical models. 2. Hungary - Statistics, Vital - Mathematical models. 3. Life expectancy - Hungary - Mathematical models. I. Series: Research paper / Macquarie University, School of Economic and Financial Studies , no. 304. II. Title.
HB1422.5.A3 P65 1986

Pollard, Sidney.
Region und Industrialisierung im Vergleich, Minden-Ravensberg und die englischen Industriegebiete. 1983. Henning, Friedrich-Wilhelm. Vorindustrielles Gewerbe und wirtschaftlicher Wandel im Paderborner Land im 19. Jahrhundert / von Friedrich-Wilhelm Henning. Region und Industrialisierung im Vergleich, Minden-Ravensberg und die englischen Industriegebiete / Sidney Pollard. Dortmund , 1983. 67 p. ; LC Card 83-198581
HC288.P27 H46 1983

Studies in capital formation in Great Britain . Oxford [Oxfordshire] , New York , c1988. p. cm. ISBN 0-19-828408-X : LC Card 87-15196 DDC 332/.0415/0941 19
HC260.S3 S78 1988

Pollard, Walker A. Ludwick, David E. The competitive position of U. S. and European Community pork and the United States and third-country markets . Washington, DC [1985] xxiii, 341 p. : LC Card 86-601366 DDC 380.1/4566492/0973 19
HD9435.U52 L83 1985

Pollert, Anna. Girls, wives, factory lives / Anna Pollert. London, England : Macmillan, 1981. 251 p. ; 23 cm. Bibliography: p. [244]-251. ISBN 0-333-29177-8
1. Women - Employment - Great Britain. 2. Labor and laboring classes - Great Britain. I. Title.
NYPL [JLD 83-884]

POLLS. see **ELECTIONS; VOTING.**

Pollution and the struggle for the world product . Leonard, H. Jeffrey. Cambridge [Cambridgeshire] , New York , 1988. p. cm. ISBN 0-521-34042-X LC Card 87-17766 DDC 338.6/042 19
HD75.6 .L46 1988

POLLUTION - COSTA RICA.
Bonilla, Alexander. Situación ambiental de Costa Rica /. [San José] [1985] 271 p. : ISBN 997-7590-57-5 LC Card 86-156609
HC143.Z9 E52 1985

POLLUTION - COSTS.
Schäkermann, Thomas, 1957- Umweltschutz, Umweltverschmutzung und Wirtschaftswachstum . München , c1986. v, 249 p. ; ISBN 3-88259-404-7 LC Card 86-226458 DDC 363.7/32 19
HC79.P55 S355 1986

POLLUTION - DEVELOPING COUNTRIES.
Knödgen, Gabriele, 1949- Umweltschutz und industrielle Standortentscheidung /. Frankfurt/Main , New York , c1982. 219 p. : ISBN 3-593-33158-6 LC Card 83-110653
HC59.72.P55 K58 1982

Pearson, Charles S. Down to business . Washington, DC (1735 New York Ave., NW, Washington, DC 20006) , c1985. vii, 107 p. ; ISBN 0-915825-04-X (pbk.) : LC Card 84-52795
HD69.P6 P42 1985 *NYPL [JLE 86-3186]*

POLLUTION - ECONOMIC ASPECTS.
Employers and the environmental challenge /. Geneva , 1986. vii, 101 p. ; ISBN 92-2-105647-3 (pbk.) : LC Card 87-123427 DDC 363.7/056 19
HD69.P6 E46 1986

Kneese, Allen V. [Economics and the environment. Russian.] Ėkonomika i okruzhaiushchaia sreda /. Moskva , 1981. 189 p. : LC Card 82-187223
HC79.E5 K57517 1981

Møllmann Boye, Erik. Miljøstatistik og lidt forureningsøkonomi . [Århus] , 1978. 53 leaves : LC Card 86-460199
HC79.P55 M65 1978

Schäkermann, Thomas, 1957- Umweltschutz, Umweltverschmutzung und Wirtschaftswachstum . München , c1986. v, 249 p. ; ISBN 3-88259-404-7 LC Card 86-226458 DDC 363.7/32 19
HC79.P55 S355 1986

POLLUTION - ECONOMIC ASPECTS - ADDRESSES, ESSAYS, LECTURES.
United States. Library of Congress. Environment and Natural Resources Policy Division. Pollution taxes, effluent charges, and other alternatives for pollution control . Washington , 19. iv, 869 p. : LC Card 78-602626
HC110.E5 U58 1977a *NYPL [JLE 79-2372]*

POLLUTION - ECONOMIC ASPECTS - BELGIUM.
Kock, Suzan de, 1949- Milieuvervuiling en milieubeleid economisch bekeken /. Antwerpen [1977] 140 p. ; ISBN 90-289-0313-1 : LC Card 78-384758
HC320.E5 K6 *NYPL [JLD 80-3195]*

POLLUTION - ECONOMIC ASPECTS - KOREA (SOUTH)
Lee, Mu-Choon. Entwicklungen in der Umweltpolitik Südkoreas im Widerspruch zwischen Industrialisierung und Umweltschutz /. Offenbach/Main, West Germany [1984] 21 p. : LC Card 86-172511
HC79.P55 L44 1984

POLLUTION - ECONOMIC ASPECTS - NETHERLANDS.
Kock, Suzan de, 1949- Milieuvervuiling en milieubeleid economisch bekeken /. Antwerpen [1977] 140 p. ; ISBN 90-289-0313-1 : LC Card 78-384758
HC320.E5 K6 *NYPL [JLD 80-3195]*

POLLUTION - ENVIRONMENTAL ASPECTS.
Bellini, James. High tech holocaust /. Newton Abbot , c1986. 255 p. ; ISBN 0-7153-8812-6
NYPL [JLE 87-827]

Førsund, Finn R. Environmental economics and management . London , New York , c1988. 307 p. : ISBN 0-85664-900-7 LC Card 87-9179 DDC 363.7/0525 19
HC79.E5 F64 1988

POLLUTION - GERMANY (EAST)
Wensierski, Peter. Von oben nach unten wächts gar nichts . Frankfurt am Main , 1986. 206 p. : ISBN 3-596-24274-6 LC Card 87-115154 DDC 363.7/058/09431 19
HC290.795.E5 W46 1986

POLLUTION - JAPAN.
Environmental protection in the industrial sector in Japan . Tokyo, Japan , c1983. 168 p. : LC Card 87-672736
HC465.P55 E58x 1983

Huddle, Norie, 1944- Island of dreams . Cambridge, Mass. , c1987. xxiii, 355 p. : ISBN 0-87047-027-2 : LC Card 86-33842 DDC 363.7/00952 19
HC465.E5 H82 1987

POLLUTION - KOREA (SOUTH)
Lee, Mu-Choon. Entwicklungen in der Umweltpolitik Südkoreas im Widerspruch zwischen Industrialisierung und Umweltschutz /. Offenbach/Main, West Germany [1984] 21 p. : LC Card 86-172511
HC79.P55 L44 1984

POLLUTION - LAW AND LEGISLATION - ECONOMIC ASPECTS - UNITED STATES - ADDRESSES, ESSAYS, LECTURES.
United States. Library of Congress. Environment and Natural Resources Policy Division. Pollution taxes, effluent charges, and other alternatives for pollution control . Washington , 19. iv, 869 p. : LC Card 78-602626
HC110.E5 U58 1977a *NYPL [JLE 79-2372]*

POLLUTION OF WATER. see **WATER - POLLUTION.**

POLLUTION - SPAIN - CATALONIA.
Vilanova, Santiago, 1947- L'econacionalisme . Barcelona , 1981. 142 p. ; ISBN 84-7031-281-2 LC Card 81-212886
HC387.C25 V527 1981

Pollution taxes, effluent charges, and other alternatives for pollution control . United States. Library of Congress. Environment and Natural Resources Policy Division. Washington , 19. iv, 869 p. : LC Card 78-602626
HC110.E5 U58 1977a *NYPL [JLE 79-2372]*

Polnische Akademie der Wissenschaften. see **Polska Akademia Nauk.**

Polnische Arbeitsmigranten in Wilhelmsburg bei Hamburg während des Kaiserreichs und der Weimarer Republik /. Hauschildt, Elke. Dortmund , c1986. xv, 330 p. : ISBN 3-923293-17-8 LC Card 87-127027 DDC 331.6/2/438043515 19
HD8458.P65 H38 1986

PÓLO PETROQUÍMICO DO RIO GRANDE DO SUL.
Proposta de consolidação do Pólo Petroquímico do Sul . [Porto Alegre] [19]86. 17, [5], 9 p. : LC Card 87-404792 DDC 338.7/661804/098165 19
HD9579.C33 B785 1986

Pólo Petroquímico do Sul. Proposta de consolidação do Pólo Petroquímico do Sul . [Porto Alegre] [19]86. 17, [5], 9 p. : LC Card 87-404792 DDC 338.7/661804/098165 19
HD9579.C33 B785 1986

Polozov, Vladimir Romanovich. Kupriianov, L. A. (Leonid Aleksandrovich) Sotsial'noe planirovanie na predpriiatiiakh NRB, GDR i ChSSR /. Leningrad , 1984. 111 p. ; LC Card 85-116781
HD7741.5 .K86 1984

Polska Akademia Nauk. (Old Catalog form: Polska Akademia Nauk, Warsaw)

Polska Akademia Nauk. Komitet Przestrzennego Zagospodarowania Kraju. Przestrzenne aspekty gospodarki żywnościowej do 2000 r. . Warszawa , 1986. 166 p. : ISBN 83-208-0497-3 : LC Card 86-223691
HD9015.P72 P72 1986

Polska Akademia Nauk. Komitet Statystyki i Ekonometrii. Macromodels and forecasts of national economy . Warszawa , 1986. 284 p. : ISBN 83-01-06464-1 (pbk.) : LC Card 86-226942 DDC 338.947 19
HC244 .M227 1986

Polska polityka morska /. Sójka, Zygmunt. Gdańsk , 1986. 237, [1] : ISBN 83-215-1646-7(pbk.) :
*NYPL [*QO 87-1818]*

Polska Reczpospolita Ludowa. see **Poland.**

Polska 1973 : rozwój społeczno-gospodarczy / [komitet redakcyjny Głównego Urzędu Statystycznego Eugenia Krzeczkowska (przewodniczący)]. Warszawa : Główny Urząd Statystyczny, 1973. 199 p., [8] p. of plates : col. ill. ; 17 cm. Errata slip inserted. LC Card 82-102013
1. Poland - Statistics. I. Krzeczkowska, Eugenia. II. Poland. Główny Urząd Statystyczny.
HA1455 .P66 1973

Biblioteka "Spraw międzynarodowych". see **Biblioteka "Spraw międzynarodowych".**

Polunina, G. V. Rol' bankov v usilenii gospodstva finansovogo kapitala /. Moskva , 1985. 206 p. ; LC Card 86-102078
HG3881 .R615 1985

Polyethnikes hetairies dēmētriakōn kai hē diamorphōsē timōn /. Gkekos, Giōrgos. Athēna , 1985. 292 p. : LC Card 86-212325
HD9030.5 .G58 1985

POLYNOMIALS.
Tsai, Hsien-Tang. A 3-interval polynomial approximation for continuous univariate distribution functions /. West Lafayette, Ind. [1986] 7, 14 p. : LC Card 86-622753 DDC

658/.001/9 s 519/.2 19
HD6483 .P8 no. 898 QA273.6

Polytechnic Institute of New York. Transportation Training and Research Center. Bloch, Arnold J. Interstate highway trade-in process. Vol. 1. Assessment /. New York , 1982. [45] p. : *NYPL [*XME-11,324]*

Pomareda, Carlos. Crop insurance for agricultural development . Baltimore , c1986. xviii, 322 p. ISBN 0-8018-2673-X (alk. paper) LC Card 85-9810 DDC 368.1/22 19
HG9968 .C76 1985 NYPL [JLE 86-1082]

Pombo, José Ignacio de, 1761-1815. Comercio y contrabando en Cartagena de Indias, 2 de junio de 1800 / José Ignacio de Pombo. 1a ed. Bogotá, Colombia : Procultura, 1986. 124 p. ; 19 cm. (Nueva biblioteca colombiana de cultura. Serie breve. Historia) Bibliography: p. 123-124. LC Card 87-107126
1. Smuggling - Colombia - Cartegena. 2. Cartagena (Colombia) - Commerce. I. Title. II. Series.
HJ6864 .P66 1986

POMERELIA (POLAND) - ECONOMIC CONDITIONS.
Kwiatkowski, Eugeniusz. Pisma o rzeczypospolitej morskiej /. Szczecin , 1985. 277 p., [24] p. of plates : ISBN 83-7007-012-4 : *NYPL [*QO 86-2539]*

Pommerehne, Werner W.
Präferenzen für öffentliche Güter : Ansätze zu ihrer Erfassung / von Werner W. Pommerehne ; mit einem Geleitwort von Alan T. Peacock. Tübingen : J.C.B. Mohr, 1987. xv, 290 p. : ill. ; 24 cm. (Die Einheit der Gesellschaftswissenschaften, 0424-6985 . Bd. 50) Bibliography: p. [254]-285. Includes index. ISBN 3-16-945040-9 LC Card 87-138780 DDC 363 19
1. Public goods. 2. Economic policy. I. Title. II. Series.
HB846.5 .P66 1987

Weck-Hannemann, Hannelore. Die heimliche Wirtschaft . Bern , c1986. 112 p. : ISBN 3-258-03541-5 LC Card 86-159961
HD2346.S9 W43 1986

Pomorski, Jerzy Mikułowski- see Mikułowski-Pomorski, Jerzy.

Ponce, Antonio García. see García Ponce, Antonio, 1929-

Ponce Dávila, Vicente O. Presupuestos : aplicación práctica a la planeación / Vicente O. Ponce Dávila.[1a ed.]. [Armenia, Colombia : s.n., 1986] (Armenia : SERVICOPIAR) v, 149 p. : ill. ; 25 cm. Bibliography: p. 148-149. LC Card 87-400649
1. Budget in business. 2. Corporate planning. I. Title.
HG4028.B8 P66 1986

Ponce Vega, Luis. El propietario ausente : ineficiencia interna y sistema institucional : el caso de SIDERPERU / Luis Ponce Vega. Lima : Fundación Friedrich Ebert, 1986. 80 p. ; 21 cm. (Diagnóstico y debate . 20) Bibliography: p. 75-80. LC Card 86-221571
1. SiderPerú (Organization) - Management - Evaluation. 2. Government business enterprises - Peru - Management - Evaluation. I. Title. II. Series.
HD9524.P44 S565 1986

Poncins, Michel de. Tous capitalistes, ou, La réponse au socialisme / Michel de Poncins. Vouillé [France] : Editions de Chiré, c1983. 164 p. ; 21 cm. LC Card 83-244442 DDC 338.944 19
1. Socialism - France. 2. Capitalism - France. 3. France - Economic policy - 1945-. 4. France - Social policy. 5. France - Politics and government - 1981-. I. Title. II. Title: Tous capitalistes.
HC276.2 .P63 1983 NYPL [JLD 86-427]

PONCITLÁN (MEXICO) - ECONOMIC CONDITIONS - STATISTICS.
Municipio de Poncitlán. Guadalajara, Jal., México [1979] 71 p. : LC Card 86-188934
HC138.P63 M85 1979

PONDICHERRY (INDIA) - CENSUS, 1981.
Census of India, 1981. New Delhi , <1982-[1985]. v. in : LC Card 87-915039 DDC 304.6/0954/86021 19
HA4587.P647 C46 1982

Pongrácz, Antal. Gazdaságpolitika, elméletben és gyakorlatban : a magyar gazdaság 1970-1990 közötti fejlődésének főbb vonásai / Pongrácz Antal. [Budapest] : Ifjúsági Lap- és Könyvkiadó, 1985. 73 p. ; 20 cm. (Gazdaságpolitika, szociálpolitika, 0231-0279) ISBN 963-422-739-2 : LC Card 87-105897
1. Hungary - Economic policy - 1968-. 2. Hungary - Economic conditions - 1968-. I. Title. II. Series.
HC300.28 .P66 1985

Pongrácz, Tiborné. A terhességmegszakításon átesett 18 éven aluli hajadonok társadalmi-demográfiai jellemzői / írták, Pongrácz Tiborné, S. Molnár Edit. Budapest : Központi Statisztikai Hivatal Népességtudományi Kutató Intézet, c1986. 115 p. ; 29 cm. (Központi Statisztikai Hivatal Népességtudományi Kutató Intézetének és a Magyar Tudományos Akadémia Demográfiai Bizottságának közleményei, 0134-0093 . 62) LC Card 87-409645
1. Abortion - Hungary - Statistics. 2. Pregnancy, Adolescent - Hungary - Statistics. I. Molnár, Edit S. II. Title. III. Series.
HA1201 .A64 no. 62 HQ767.5.H8

Poniachek, Harvey A. Direct foreign investment in the United States / Harvey A. Poniachek. Lexington, Mass. : Lexington Books, c1986. xiii, 256 p. : ill. ; 24 cm. Includes index. Bibliography: p. [251]-252. ISBN 0-669-11076-0 (alk. paper) LC Card 85-40457 DDC 332.6/73/0973 19
1. Investments, Foreign - United States. 2. International business enterprises - United States. 3. United States - Economic conditions - 1981-. I. Title.
HG4910 .P66 1986 NYPL [JLE 86-4295]

Poniatowski, Michel. Les technologies nouvelles : la chance de l'homme / Michel Poniatowski ; préface de Pierre Pflimlin. Paris : Plon, c1986. 334 p. ; 23 cm. Includes bibliographical references. ISBN 2-259-01439-9 : LC Card 86-182131
1. Technological innovations - Economic aspects - Europe. 2. High technology industries - Europe. I. Title.
HC240.9.T4 P65 1986

Ponomarev, Alekseĭ Mikhaĭlovich. Rozvytok kapitalistychnykh vidnosyn u promyslovosti Ukraïny XVIII st. / O.M. Ponomar′ ov. L′viv : Vyd-vo L′vivs′koho universytetu, 1971. 181 p. ; 21 cm. Title in colophon: Razvitie kapitalisticheskikh otnosheniĭ v promyshlennosti Ukrainy XVIII v. Includes bibliographical References. LC Card 82-105634
1. Ukraine - Industries - History - 18th century. 2. Capitalism - Ukraine - History - 18th century. 3. Ukraine - Manufactures - History - 18th century. I. Title. II. Title: Razvitie kapitalisticheskikh otnosheniĭ v promyshlennosti Ukrainy XVIII v.
HC337.U5 P58 1971

Pons Deutsch-Englisch Globalwörterbuch. Collins English-German dictionary =. London , Stuttgart , 1986, c1983. 2 v. (xviii, 1390, xxiii, 1380 p.) ; ISBN 3-12-517131-8 (v. 1) *NYPL [JFC 86-2613]*

Pons Englisch-Deutsch Globalwörterbuch. Collins English-German dictionary =. London , Stuttgart , 1986, c1983. 2 v. (xviii, 1390, xxiii, 1380 p.) ; ISBN 3-12-517131-8 (v. 1) *NYPL [JFC 86-2613]*

Le pont invisible . Picaper, Jean-Paul, 1938- Paris , c1986. 345 p. ; ISBN 2-259-01619-7; 0-225-91619-7 : LC Card 87-147835
HE8697.45.E87 P52 1986

Pontificia Universidad Católica del Perú, Lima. see Lima. Pontificia Universidad Católica del Perú.

Pontones S., Jaime. Condicionantes estructurales del desarrollo tecnológico / Jaime Pontones S., Pilar Charles C. [Mexico City, Mexico] : Universidad Iberoamericana, [1982] 27, [2] leaves ; 28 cm. (Cuadernos del Centro de Servicio y Promoción Social. Serie Investigación . no. 3) Bibliography: leaves [28]-[29] LC Card 85-203882
1. Technological innovations - Economic aspects. 2. Saving and investment. I. Charles Creel, Pilar. II. Title. III. Series.
HC79.T4 P66 1982

Pontos básicos para uma política de eletrificação rural . Brazil. Departamento Nacional de Aguas e Energia Elétrica. Brasília, D.F. , 1984. 190 p. : LC Card 86-158852
HD9688.B72 B73 1984

PONY EXPRESS - HISTORY.
Forster, Dale E. Oregon express companies /. Eugene, Ore. , c1985. vi, 231 p. : LC Card 87-121202 DDC 383/.143/09795 19
HE6376.A1 O735 1985

PONY EXPRESS - HISTORY - JUVENILE LITERATURE.
Brandt, Betty. Special delivery /. Minneapolis, Minn. , c1988. 40 p. : ISBN 0-87614-312-5 (lib. bdg.) LC Card 87-15647 DDC 383/.4973 19
HE6371 .B77 1988

Pool, John Charles. The ABCs of international finance : understanding the trade and debt crisis / John Charles Pool, Steve Stamos. Lexington, Mass. : Lexington Books, c1987. xii, 138 p. ; 25 cm. Bibliography: p. [131]-132. Includes index. ISBN 0-669-15605-1 (alk. paper) LC Card 86-45933 DDC 332/.042 19
1. International finance. 2. Balance of payments. 3. Debts, External - Developing countries. 4. International economic relations. I. Stamos, Steve, 1947-. II. Title.
HG3851 .P66 1987

Poole, Keith T. Women, public opinion, and politics : the changing political attitudes of American women / Keith T. Poole, L. Harmon Zeigler. New York : Longman, c1985. xii, 196 p. : ill. ; 23 cm. Includes bibliographies and index. ISBN 0-582-28274-8 LC Card 84-7155 DDC 305.4/0973 19
1. Women - United States - Attitudes. 2. Women in politics - United States. 3. Women - United States - Social conditions. 4. Public opinion - United States. 5. Women - United States - Public opinion. 6. United States - Politics and government - 1981- - Public opinion. I. Zeigler, Luther Harmon, 1936-. II. Title.
HQ1410 .P66 1985 NYPL [JLE 85-1580]

Poon, Raymond S. Biotechnology instrumentation : creating a product niche in a dynamic industry / Raymond S. Poon, Pepi Ross, Walter C. Ogier. Menlo Park, Calif. (333 Ravenswood Ave., Menlo Park 94025-3476) : Business Intelligence Program, SRI International, c1985. 32 p. : col. ill. ; 28 cm. (Report / Business Intelligence Program, SRI International . no. 722 (Summer 1985)) Cover title. LC Card 87-160671 DDC 338.4/766063 19
1. Biological laboratory equipment industry. 2. Biotechnology - Equipment and supplies. 3. Market surveys. I. Ross, Pepi. II. Ogier, Walter C. III. Series: Research report (Business Intelligence Program (SRI International)) , no. 722. IV. Title.
HD9706.65.B552 P66 1985

Poonia, M. S. (Mohan Singh), 1955-
Development banking in India / M.S. Poonia. Jaipur : Prateeksha Publications : Sole distributors, Shri Ram Book Co., 1987. 140, iii, [i] p. ; 22 cm. Bibliography: p. i-[iv] LC Card 87-901804 DDC 332.2 19
1. Industrial Finance Corporation of India. 2. Development banks - India. 3. Banks and banking - India. I. Title.
HG3284 .P66 1987

POOR.
Grasnick, Georg, 1927- Alter Kapitalismus, "neue Armut" /. Berlin , 1985. 78 p. : LC Card 86-132510 DDC 330.12/2 19
HB501 .G64 1985

Hakemulder, Roel. Subcultuur en stigma van de armoede . Leiden , 1985. 96 p. ; ISBN 90-6624-058-X LC Card 86-172398
HC79.P6 H34 1985

Poverty amidst plenty . Boulder, Colo. , 1989. p. cm. ISBN 0-8133-0523-3 LC Card 87-12829 DDC 330.9/048 19
HC59 .P639 1989

Rigdon, Susan M., 1943- The culture facade . Urbana , c1988. p. cm. ISBN 0-252-01495-2 (alk. paper) LC Card 87-19063 DDC 305.5/69 19
HC79.P6 R57 1988

POOR - ADDRESSES, ESSAYS, LECTURES.
Armut und Reichtum . Hamburg , Göttingen , 1981. 80 p. : ISBN 3-921620-14-7 LC Card 81-159683 DDC 305.5/6 19
HC79.P6 A75 NYPL [JLG 85-309]

POOR - AFRICA.
Nafziger, E. Wayne. Inequality in Africa . Cambridge [Cambridgeshire] , New York , c1988. p. cm. ISBN 0-521-26881-8 LC Card 87-24263 DDC 339.2/096 19
HC800.Z9 I5136 1988

POOR - AFRICA - HISTORY.
Iliffe, John. The African poor . Cambridge [Cambridgeshire] , New York , 1987. ix, 387 p. ; ISBN 0-521-34415-8 LC Card 87-14622 DDC 305.5/62/096 19
HC800.Z9 P625 1987

POOR - AMERICA.
Mauro, Frédéric. [Des origines de l'inégalité

entre les peuples d'Amérique. Portuguese.] Origens da desigualdade entre os povos da América /. São Paulo, SP , 1986. 113 p. : LC Card 87-120229 DDC 339.2/097 19
HC94.Z9 I56317 1986

POOR AND THE CHURCH. see **CHURCH AND THE POOR.**

POOR AS CONSUMERS - UNITED STATES.
Hammond, Claire Holton, 1951- The benefits of subsidized housing programs . Cambridge [Cambridgeshire] , New York , 1987. ix, 140 p. ; ISBN 0-521-32752-0 LC Card 86-32638 DDC 363.5/8 19
HD7288.83 .H36 1987

POOR - AUSTRALIA.
Hollingworth, Peter John, 1935- Australians in poverty /. Melbourne, Vic. , 1985. x, 166 p. : ISBN 0-17-006741-6 (pbk.) : LC Card 87-108662 DDC 305.5/69/0994 19
HC610.P6 H62 1985

POOR - AUSTRIA.
Armut in Österreich . Graz , c1977. 168 p. : ISBN 3-7011-7080-0 LC Card 86-176543
HC270.P6 A75 1977

POOR - BRAZIL.
Calsing, Elizeu F. Extensão e características da pobreza no Brasil /. Brasília , 1983. 44, [1] p. : LC Card 86-178277
HC190.P6 C29 1983

Economia informal, tecnologia apropriada e associativismo /. São Paulo , 1986. 176 p. : LC Card 86-233370
HC190.P6 E34 1986

Singer, Paul Israel, 1932- Repartição da renda . Rio de Janeiro , 1986. 95 p. ; ISBN 85-85061-40-5 : LC Card 86-157852
HC190.I5 S56 1986

A Transição incompleta . Rio de Janeiro-RJ , 1986. 2 v. ; LC Card 86-224684
HC187 .T72 1986

POOR - BRAZIL - RIO GRANDE DE NORTE.
Agripino, Jose. Compromisso com o povo . [Natal, Brazil] [1983?] 19 p. ; LC Card 86-215313
HC188.R38 A54 1983

POOR - BRAZIL - UBATUBA (SÃO PAULO)
Marcilio, Maria Luiza. Caiçara . São Paulo-SP (Brasil) , c1986. 244 p. : ISBN 85-05-00523-6 LC Card 87-404833 DDC 304.6/0981/61 19
HD1531.B7 M34 1986

POOR - CENTRAL AMERICA.
Brockett, Charles D., 1946- Land, power, and poverty . Boston , c1988. p. cm. ISBN 0-04-497027-7 LC Card 87-22746 DDC 338.1/09728 19
HD1797 .B76 1988

POOR - CHILE - SANTIAGO.
Schkolnik, Mariana. Sobrevivir en la población José M. Caro y en Lo Hermida /. [Santiago, Chile] [1986] 150 p., [20] p. of plates : LC Card 87-400080 DDC 362.5/8/098331 19
HC193.S2 S35 1986

POOR - COLOMBIA.
Barco, Virgilio. La lucha contra la pobreza /. [Bogotá] , 1985. 193 p. ; ISBN 958-9044-11-5 LC Card 85-239429
HC197 .B2765 1985

POOR - COMMUNIST COUNTRIES.
Eberstadt, Nick, 1955- The poverty of communism /. New Brunswick, N.J., U. S.A. , c1987. p. cm. ISBN 0-88738-188-X : LC Card 87-19097 DDC 362.5/09171/7 19
HC710.P6 E24 1987

POOR - CONNECTICUT.
Hadden, Kenneth. Poverty in Connecticut, 1979 /. Storrs, CT [1986] 24 p. : LC Card 86-623148 DDC 362.5/09746 19
HC107.C8 H33 1986

POOR - DEVELOPING COUNTRIES.
Beckford, George L. Persistent poverty . London , Totowa, N.J. , c1983. xxv, 244 p. : ISBN 0-86232-207-3 (pbk.) LC Card 85-149825 DDC 338.1/09172/4 19
HC59.72.P6 B43 1983 ***NYPL [JLD 87-628]***

The Economic demography of mass poverty. [Williamsburg, Va., U. S.A. , c1986] xiv, 142 p. : LC Card 85-73339 DDC 339.4/6/091724 19
HB884 .E36 1986

Haq, Mahbub ul, 1934- The poverty curtain . Lahore , 1983. li, 247 p. ; LC Card 83-931275 DDC 338.9/009172/4 19
HC59.7 .H35 1983 ***NYPL [JLD 87-439]***

Kruijer, G. J. (Gerardus Johannes), 1919- Development through liberation . Atlantic Highlands, NJ , 1987. x, 257 p. ; ISBN 0-391-03538-X LC Card 87-3710 DDC 338.9/009172/4 19
HC59.72.P6 K78 1987

POOR - DEVELOPING COUNTRIES - ADDRESSES, ESSAYS, LECTURES.
Armut und Reichtum . Hamburg , Göttingen , 1981. 80 p. : ISBN 3-921620-14-7 LC Card 81-159683 DDC 305.5/6 19
HC79.P6 A75 ***NYPL [JLG 85-309]***

POOR - EGYPT.
Radwān, Samīr Muhammad. Agrarian change in Egypt . London , Dover, N.H. , c1986. xii, 167 p. : ISBN 0-7099-4214-1 : LC Card 85-11356 DDC 305.5/69/0962 19
HN786.A8 R33 1985 ***NYPL [JLD 86-1045]***

POOR - EMPLOYMENT - UNITED STATES.
Levitan, Sar A. Working but poor . Baltimore , c1987. ix, 142 p. : ISBN 0-8018-3583-6 (alk. paper) LC Card 87-16973 DDC 362.5/0973 19
HC110.I5 L468 1987

POOR - ENGLAND - YORK (NORTH YORKSHIRE)
Rowntree, B. Seebohm (Benjamin Seebohm), 1871-1954. Poverty . New York , 1980. xxi, 426 p. : ISBN 0-8240-0120-6 (alk. paper) : LC Card 79-56969 DDC 305.5/6 19
HC258.Y6 R64 1980 ***NYPL [JLD 86-3436]***

POOR - EUROPE.
Schmitz, Heinz. Vermeidung von Armut im Alter . München , c1983. 267 p. : ISBN 3-89019-099-5 LC Card 84-197886
HD7164 .S29 1983

POOR - EUROPE - HISTORY.
La Storia dei poveri . Roma , c1985. xii, 300 p. ; ISBN 88-382-3530-9 : LC Card 86-198943
HC240.9.P6 S76 1985

POOR - EUROPEAN ECONOMIC COMMUNITY COUNTRIES - ADDRESSES, ESSAYS, LECTURES.
Understanding poverty /. Milano, Italy , c1984. 355 p. : LC Card 84-249441 DDC 339.4/6/094 19
HC240.9.P6 U53 1984 ***NYPL [JLD 86-1196]***

POOR - FRANCE.
Godinot, Xavier, 1951- Les travailleurs sous-prolétaires face aux mutations de l'emploi /. Paris [1985] 155 p. ; ISBN 2-904972-04-08 LC Card 86-166442
HD5775 .G63 1985

POOR - FRANCE - CASE STUDIES.
Nicolas, Jean-Pierre, 1941- La pauvreté intolérable . Toulouse [1984] 208 p. : ISBN 2-86586-026-4 : LC Card 85-118841
HC280.P6 N53 1984

POOR - FRANCE - PARIS - HISTORY.
Shapiro, Ann-Louise, 1944- Housing the poor of Paris, 1850-1902 /. Madison, Wis. , 1985. xx, 224 p. : ISBN 0-299-09880-X : LC Card 84-40159 DDC 363.5/8 19
HD7288.78.F82 P357 1985
NYPL [JLE 85-1534]

POOR - GERMANY, WEST.
Kovacic, Anton. Suppe genug, aber Seele kaputt . München , c1986. 185 p. ; ISBN 3-453-43075-1 : LC Card 86-230927
HC290.5.P6 K68 1986

Politik der Armut und die Spaltung des Sozialstaats /. Frankfurt am Main , 1985. 474 p. : ISBN 3-518-11233-3 : LC Card 85-183026
HC290.5.P6 P65 1985

POOR - GERMANY (WEST) - DÜSSELDORF.
Arbeitslosigkeit und Neue Armut in Düsseldorf . Bochum , c1986. 65 p. : ISBN 3-925222-03-0 LC Card 87-409036 DDC 331.13/794355 19
HD5780.D85 A73 1986

POOR - GOVERNMENT POLICY - LATIN AMERICA - CONGRESSES.
La Opción preferencial por los pobres . [Santiago] [1987] 360 p. : LC Card 87-403060 DDC 362.5/098 19
HC130.P6 O63 1987

POOR - GREAT BRITAIN.
Fattigdom i England . København [1986] 24 columns : ISBN 87-7296-008-6 : LC Card 87-168467
HC260.P6 F37 1986

Will there always be an England? [videorecording] /. Alexandria, VA , 1986. 1 videocassette (60 min.) : LC Card 86-707796 DDC 942.085 11
HC256.5

POOR - GREAT BRITAIN - HISTORY.
Pound, John. Poverty and vagrancy in Tudor England /. London , New York , 1986. xii, 116 p. ; ISBN 0-582-35508-7 : LC Card 85-19747 DDC 305.5/69/0942 19
HC260.P6 P68 1986 ***NYPL [JLD 86-2366]***

Slack, Paul. Poverty and policy in Tudor and Stuart England /. London , New York , 1988. p. cm. ISBN 0-582-48965-2 (alk. paper) LC Card 87-2657 DDC 362.5/561/0942 19
HC254.4 .S42 1988

POOR - GREAT BRITAIN - HISTORY - 20TH CENTURY.
The Worst of times . London , 1985. 201 p., [8] p. of plates : ISBN 0-7045-0513-4
NYPL [JLD 86-1799]

POOR - HAITI.
Anglade, Georges. Eloge de la pauvreté /. Montréal, Québec, Canada , c1983. 63 p. ; ISBN 2-920418-04-1 LC Card 84-140110
HC153.Z9 P612 1983

POOR - HONDURAS - SAN PEDRO SULA.
Estudio de diagnóstico de la población de los barrios--Chamelecón, Suyapa, Fe y Esperanza, San Antonio, San José y San Miguel /. Tegucigalpa, D.C. [1984] 1 v. (various foliations) : LC Card 85-205996
HC145.Z7 T434 1984

POOR - HONDURAS - TEGUCIGALPA.
Estudio de diagnóstico de la población de los barrios--Chamelecón, Suyapa, Fe y Esperanza, San Antonio, San José y San Miguel /. Tegucigalpa, D.C. [1984] 1 v. (various foliations) : LC Card 85-205996
HC145.Z7 T434 1984

POOR - HOUSING - AFRICA.
Die Verplante Wohnmisere . Saarbrücken , Fort Lauderdale , 1986. 334 p. : ISBN 3-88156-329-6 LC Card 87-408292 DDC 363.5/1/096 19
HD7287.96.A4 V47 1986

POOR - HOUSING - DEVELOPING COUNTRIES.
Spontaneous shelter . Philadelphia , 1988. p. cm. ISBN 0-87722-507-9 (alk. paper) LC Card 87-10002 DDC 363.5/8/091724 19
HD7287.96.D44 S66 1988

POOR - HOUSING - ECUADOR.
Landivar, Jorge F. The role of housing in development models . Swansea, U.K. , 1986. 60 p. ; ISBN 0-906250-12-9 (pbk.) LC Card 87-166136 DDC 363.5/8 19
HD7287.96.E2 L36 1986

POOR - HOUSING - ECUADOR - FINANCE.
Landivar, Jorge F. The role of housing in development models . Swansea, U.K. , 1986. 60 p. ; ISBN 0-906250-12-9 (pbk.) LC Card 87-166136 DDC 363.5/8 19
HD7287.96.E2 L36 1986

POOR - HOUSING - EL SALVADOR - SAN SALVADOR.
Lungo, Mario. El terremoto de octubre de 1986 en San Salvador y la situación habitacional de los sectores populares /. Ciudad Universitaria Rodrigo Facio [Costa Rica] , 1987. 26 leaves ; LC Card 87-125001 DDC 363.3/495 19
HD7287.96.S22 S265 1987

POOR - HOUSING - FINANCE.
The Promotion of non-conventional approaches to housing finance for low-income groups. Nairobi , 1984. ii, 54 p. ; LC Card 86-980642 DDC 363.5/8 19
HD7287.95 .P76 1984

POOR - HOUSING - GOVERNMENT POLICY - DEVELOPING COUNTRIES.
Cheema, G. Shabbir. Urban shelter and services . New York , 1987. x, 220 p. ; ISBN 0-275-92653-2 (alk. paper) : LC Card 87-6982 DDC 363.5/8 19
HD7287.96.D44 C47 1987

Spontaneous shelter . Philadelphia , 1988. p.

cm. ISBN 0-87722-507-9 (alk. paper) LC Card 87-10002 DDC 363.5/8/091724 19
HD7287.96.D44 S66 1988

POOR - HOUSING - GOVERNMENT POLICY - ECUADOR.
Landivar, Jorge F. The role of housing in development models . Swansea, U.K. , 1986. 60 p. ; ISBN 0-906250-12-9 (pbk.) LC Card 87-166136 DDC 363.5/8 19
HD7287.96.E2 L36 1986

POOR - HOUSING - GOVERNMENT POLICY - PANAMA.
Pacheco D., Rubén. Industria de la construcción . [Panamá] , 1974. 17, [1] leaves, [4] leaves of plates : LC Card 87-400643
HD9715.P223 P367 1974

POOR - HOUSING - LATIN AMERICA.
Die Verplante Wohnmisere . Saarbrücken , Fort Lauderdale , 1986. 334 p. : ISBN 3-88156-329-6 LC Card 87-408292 DDC 363.5/1/096 19
HD7287.96.A4 V47 1986

POOR - HOUSING - LATIN AMERICA - CONGRESSES.
Habitat popular . Buenos Aires , 1986. 162 p. : LC Card 87-404028 DDC 363.5/8 19
HD7305.5 .H32 1986

POOR - HOUSING - SOUTH AFRICA - DURBAN METROPOLITAN AREA.
Planning and financial evaluation of housing strategies /. Durban , 1983. viii, 233 p. : ISBN 0-86980-360-3 (pbk.) LC Card 86-205849 DDC 363.5/8 19
HD7287.96.S682 D876 1983

POOR - HOUSING - UNITED STATES.
Housing America's poor /. Chapel Hill , c1987. ix, 203 p. ; ISBN 0-8078-1738-4 LC Card 86-40449 DDC 363.5/8 19
HD7287.96.U5 H68 1987

POOR - HOUSING - URUGUAY - MONTEVIDEO.
Vicario, Luis B. Lineamientos básicos del Programa Habitacional de Emergencia, 1985-86 /. [Montevideo] , 1985. 25 p. : LC Card 87-122422 DDC 363.5/8 19
HD7287.96.U82 M668 1985

The Poor in Asia : productivity raising programmes and strategies / edited by Swapna Mukhopadhyay. Kuala Lumpur, Malaysia : Asian and Pacific Development Centre, 1985- v. <1 > ; 23 cm. (Human Resource Mobilization Programme publications) Includes bibliographies. ISBN 967-99954-0-2 (v. 1) LC Card 86-944764 DDC 362.5/8/095 19
1. Rural poor - Government policy - Asia - Case studies. 2. Economic assistance, Domestic - Asia - Case studies. 3. Agricultural productivity - Government policy - Asia - Case studies. 4. Land reform - Asia - Case studies. I. Sukhopadhyay, Swapna. II. Series.
HC415.P6 P66 1985

POOR - INDIA.
Arya, Dwarika Prasas, 1922- Swastika removes India's poverty and problems within 100 days . Calcutta, West Bengal , 1982. vi, 153 p. ; LC Card 82-904556 DDC 338.954 19
HC435.2 .A887 1982

Gupta, S. P. (Shiv Prakash), 1957- Structural dimensions of poverty in India /. Delhi, India , 1987. xii, 427 p. : LC Card 87-901423 DDC 362.5/0954 19
HC440.P6 G86 1987

Mina Swaminathan, 1933- Who cares? . New Delhi , 1985. xi, 159 p. : LC Card 86-900126
HV861.I4 M56 1985 ***NYPL [JLD 86-3265]***

POOR - INDIA - EAST GODAVĀRI.
Subrahmanyam, S. Poverty, unemployment, and perspective of development /. Allahabad, India , 1987. xi, 311 p. : ISBN 81-85076-22-7 : LC Card 87-900803 DDC 330.954/84 19
HC440.P6 S9 1987

POOR - INDIA - JHĀBUA (DISTRICT)
Pais, H. Poverty alleviation programmes . New Delhi , 1986. xii, 48, [3] p. (some folded) : LC Card 86-903597 DDC 362.5/8/09543 19
HC437.J43 P35 1986

POOR - INDIA - KARNATAKA.
Prabhakara, N. R. Population growth and unemployment in India /. New Delhi , 1986. ix, 102 p. ; ISBN 81-7024-041-7 : LC Card 86-902156 DDC 331.13/795487 19
HD5820.K37 P7 1986

Thimmaiah, G. Inequality and poverty . Bombay , 1983. xiv, 106 p. ; LC Card 83-903408 DDC 339.4/6/095487 19
HC437.K27 T47 1983 ***NYPL [JLD 86-3792]***

POOR - INDIA - PSYCHOLOGICAL ASPECTS - ADDRESSES, ESSAYS, LECTURES.
Psycho-ecological dimensions of poverty /. New Delhi , 1983. x, 115 p. : LC Card 83-906411 DDC 305.5/69/0954 19
HC440.P6 P78 1983 ***NYPL [JLD 87-491]***

POOR - ITALY - LOMBARDY - HISTORY.
Bressan, E. (Edoardo) Povertà e assistenza in Lombardia nell'età napoleonica /. [Milano] , Bari , c1985. viii, 339 p. : ISBN 88-420-2653-0 : LC Card 86-162978
HC307.L8 B74 1985

POOR - KENYA.
Collier, Paul. Labour and poverty in Kenya, 1900-1980 /. Oxford , New York , 1986. xi, 296 p. : ISBN 0-19-828505-1 : LC Card 86-1352 DDC 331.12/09676/2 19
HD5840.5.A6 C65 1986
NYPL [JLE 86-3282]

POOR - LATIN AMERICA.
Pfeffermann, Guy Pierre. Public expenditure in Latin America . Washington, D.C. , 1987. 38 p. ; ISBN 0-8213-0906-4 (pbk.) LC Card 87-10650 DDC 336.3/9/098 19
HJ7664.5 .P44 1987

Poverty in Latin America . Washington, D.C., U. S.A. [1986] 25 p. ; ISBN 0-8213-0836-X (pbk.) LC Card 86-225244 DDC 330.98/0038 19
HC130.I5 P68 1986

Sheahan, John, 1923- Patterns of development in Latin America . Princeton, N.J. , c1987. x, 399 p. : ISBN 0-691-07735-5 (alk. paper) : LC Card 87-2853 DDC 338.98 19
HC125 .S498 1987

POOR - LATIN AMERICA - CONGRESSES.
La Opción preferencial por los pobres . [Santiago] [1987] 360 p. : LC Card 87-403060 DDC 362.5/098 19
HC130.P6 O63 1987

POOR LAWS - ENGLAND - HISTORY.
Pound, John. Poverty and vagrancy in Tudor England /. London , New York , 1986. xii, 116 p. ; ISBN 0-582-35508-7 : LC Card 85-19747 DDC 305.5/69/0942 19
HC260.P6 P68 1986 ***NYPL [JLD 86-2366]***

POOR - MADAGASCAR - ANTANANARIVO.
Camacho, Martine. Les poubelles de la survie . Paris , c1986. 207 p. : ISBN 2-85802-590-5 LC Card 86-180208
HC895.Z7 A443 1986

POOR - MALAYSIA - MORTALITY.
Why were infant and child mortality rates highest in the poorest states of Peninsular Malaysia, 1941-75? /. Santa Monica, CA (P.O. Box 2138, Santa Monica 90406-2138) [1986] xi, 45 p. ; LC Card 86-210106 DDC 304.6/4/088054 19
HB1323.I42 M49 1986

POOR - MARYLAND - BALTIMORE METROPOLITAN AREA - STATISTICS.
Census '80 . Baltimore, Md. (2225 N. Charles St., Baltimore 21218) [1983] xv, 106 leaves : LC Card 83-622347 DDC 339.2/2/097526 19
HC108.B2 C46 1983 ***NYPL [JLF 86-1594]***

POOR - MEDICAL CARE - UNITED STATES.
Oberg, Charles N. Medicaid, entering the third decade . Excelsior, Minn. (P.O. Box 458, Excelsior 55331-0458) , c1986. vii, 70 p. : LC Card 86-233259 DDC 362.1/0425/0973 19
HD7102.U4 O58 1986

POOR - MEXICO - HOUSING.
Ziss, Roland. Baumaterialien und Selbsthilfe . Saarbrücken , Fort Lauderdale, Fl. , 1986. 319 p. : ISBN 3-88156-333-4 LC Card 86-197177
HD7287.96.M6 Z57 1986

POOR - NEPAL.

POOR - NEVADA.
Passi, Michael M. Poverty in the State of Nevada . Carson City, Nev. (1100 E. William St., Suite 117, Carson City 89710) [1986] [11] leaves, 69, 16 p., [1] leaf of plates : LC Card 86-622269 DDC 330.9793/033/08806942 19
HC107.N33 P623 1986

POOR - NEW JERSEY - STATISTICS.
Crowley, Charles. Income and poverty in New Jersey [microform] . Trenton, N.J. [1982] 32 p. ; LC Card 83-620831 DDC 339.2/2/09749 19
HC107.N53 I5113 1982
NYPL [*ZT-1712 no.31]

POOR - OHIO - STATISTICS.
Ohio poverty indicators. Cleveland, Ohio (668 Euclid Ave, Suite 700, Cleveland 44114) , c1986-<c1987. v. <1-2 > : LC Card 87-107608 DDC 362.5/2/09771 19
HC107.O323 P6355 1986

POOR - PERU - AREQUIPA - NUTRITION.
Pacheco S., Janette. Situación y posibilidades alimentarias de la población urbano marginal de Arequipa /. Arequipa, Perú [1986] 38 p., 8 folded leaves of plates : LC Card 86-232480
HD9014.P53 A746 1986

POOR - PERU - AYACUCHO (DEPT.)
Díaz Martínez, Antonio, 1933- Ayacucho . Lima , 1985. xvi, 224 p. ; LC Card 86-134530
HC228.A9 D5 1985

POOR - PERU - LIMA.
Bunster, Ximena. Sellers & servants . New York , 1985. x, 258 p. : ISBN 0-03-060543-1 (alk. paper) : LC Card 85-6259 DDC 331.4/0985/25 19
HD6072.2.P42 L563 1985
NYPL [JLE 86-910]

Grompone, Romeo. Talleristas y vendedores ambulantes en Lima /. Lima , 1985. 319 p. : LC Card 85-243089
HD2346.P42 L564 1985

POOR - PSYCHOLOGY. see **POVERTY - PSYCHOLOGICAL ASPECTS.**

POOR RELIEF. see **PUBLIC WELFARE; CHARITIES.**

POOR - SAINT VINCENT AND THE GRENADINES - CASE STUDIES.
Rubenstein, Hymie. Coping with poverty . Boulder, Colo. , 1987. xx, 389 p. : ISBN 0-8133-7387-5 (pbk. : alk. paper) : LC Card 86-32530 DDC 972.98/4400496 19
HC156.5.Z7 S296 1987

POOR - SOVIET UNION.
Matthews, Mervyn. Poverty in the Soviet Union . Cambridge [Cambridgeshire] , New York , 1986. xv, 227 p. ; ISBN 0-521-32544-7 LC Card 86-993 DDC 305.5/69/0947 19
HC340.P6 M38 1986 ***NYPL [JLD 87-262]***

POOR - SPAIN.
La Pobreza en España y sus causas /. Madrid , 1985. xx, 759 p. : ISBN 84-398-3252-4 : LC Card 86-230170
HC390.P6 P63 1985

POOR - SPAIN - CASTILE - HISTORY.
López Alonso, Carmen. Los rostros y la realidad de la pobreza en la sociedad castellana medieval (siglos XIII-XV) /. Madrid [1983?] 54 p. ; ISBN 84-7075-284-7 LC Card 87-110606
HC387.C244 L66 1983

POOR - TANZANIA.
Collier, Paul. Labour and poverty in rural Tanzania . Oxford [Oxfordhire] , New York , 1986. vii, 143 p. : ISBN 0-19-828531-0 : LC Card 86-5303 DDC 307.1/4/09678 19
HN797.Z9 C625 1986 ***NYPL [JLD 87-511]***

POOR - UNITED STATES.
Bernstein, Blanche, 1912- Saving a generation /. New York , 1986. vi, 63 p. ; ISBN 0-87078-206-1 (pbk.) : LC Card 87-102738 DDC 362.5/8/0973 19
HC110.P6 B47 1986

Dumas, Lloyd J. The overburdened economy . Berkeley , c1986. xiv, 297 p. ; ISBN 0-520-05686-8 (alk. paper) LC Card 85-20856 DDC 331.13/7973 19
HD5724 .D775 1986 ***NYPL [JLD 86-2582]***

Estimates of poverty, including the value of noncash benefits, 1985. Washington, D.C. [1986] v, 86 p. ; LC Card 86-603442 DDC 362.5/8/0973 19
HC110.P63 E783 1986

Morris, Michael, 1949- Poverty and public policy . Westport, Conn. , 1986. xii, 236 p. ; ISBN 0-313-24942-3 (lib. bdg. : alk. paper) LC Card 86-398 DDC 361.6/1/0973 19
HV95 .M67 1986 ***NYPL [JLD 87-510]***

United States. President's Commission on

Income Maintenance Programs. Poverty amid plenty, the American paradox. [Washington] 1969. ix, 155 p. LC Card 71-605334 DDC 362.5/0973
HC110.P63 A59 ***NYPL [JLF 86-478]***

Williams, Terry (Terry M.) Growing up poor /. Lexington, MA , c1985. xvi, 136 p. ; ISBN 0-669-09687-3 (alk. paper) LC Card 84-48564 DDC 362.7/044 19
HV1431 .W55 1985 ***NYPL [JLE 85-2236]***

POOR - UNITED STATES - CONGRESSES.
Fighting poverty . Cambridge, Mass. , 1986. viii, 418 p. : ISBN 0-674-30085-8 (alk. paper) LC Card 85-24848 DDC 362.5/8/0973 19
HC110.P63 F54 1986 ***NYPL [JLE 86-4089]***

POOR - UNITED STATES - ENERGY ASSISTANCE.
Sweet, David C. Public utilities and the poor . New York , 1987. xxiii, 174 p. : ISBN 0-275-92572-2 (alk. paper) : LC Card 87-6979 DDC 362.5/82 19
HC110.P6 S894 1987

POOR - UNITED STATES - INTERVIEWS.
Richards, Eugene. Below the line . Mount Vernon, N.Y. , c1987. 218 p. : ISBN 0-89043-062-4 LC Card 86-70834 DDC 305.5/69/0973 19
HC110.P6 R52 1987

POOR - UNITED STATES - PICTORIAL WORKS.
Richards, Eugene. Below the line . Mount Vernon, N.Y. , c1987. 218 p. : ISBN 0-89043-062-4 LC Card 86-70834 DDC 305.5/69/0973 19
HC110.P6 R52 1987

POOR - WEST VIRGINIA - STATISTICS.
State of West Virginia Job Training Partnership Act planning statistics /. Charleston, W. Va. (112 California Ave., Charleston 25305-0112) [1985] v, 122 p. ; LC Card 85-623225 DDC 331.1/09754/021 19
HD5725.W4 S7 1985

Poor women, poor families . Rodgers, Harrell R. Armonk, N.Y. , 1986. viii, 167 p. ; ISBN 0-87332-372-6 : LC Card 86-6449 DDC 362.8/3/0973 19
HV1445 .R64 1986 ***NYPL [JLE 86-4042]***

Poors Corporate Register, 1974* (hq. New York, N. Y.) see Texaco, inc.

Pope, W. H. (William Henry), 1923- Bingham, Robert C. Economic concepts . New York , c1987. xv, 444 p. ; ISBN 0-07-044963-5 (pbk.) LC Card 87-3351 DDC 330/.07/7 19
HB171.5 .B52 1987

Popham, Estelle L. Tilton, Rita Sloan. Secretarial procedures and administration /. Cincinnati , c1987. vi, 874 p. : ISBN 0-538-11790-7 LC Card 86-63074 DDC 651.3/74 19
HF5547.5 .S4 1987

Popivanov, Ivan, prof. Biografii͡a ot mnogo imena . Sofii͡a , 1983. 232 p. : LC Card 84-163061
HD8627.A1 B56 1983

La Popolazione italiana nell'Ottocento : continuità e mutamenti : relazioni e comunicazioni presentate al convegno tenuto ad Assisi nei giorni 26-28 aprile 1983 / [saggi di L. Del Panta ... et al.]. Bologna : CLUEB, [1985] xxv, 534 p. : ill., maps ; 24 cm. Italian and Spanish. At head of title: Società italiana di demografia storica. Summaries in English and French. Includes bibliographical references. LC Card 86-157672
1. Italy - Population - History - 19th century - Congresses. I. Società italiana di demografia storica.
HB3599 .P663 1985

Popov, I͡U. N. (I͡Uriĭ Nikolaevich), 1931- Essays in political economy / Yuri Popov ; [translated from the Russian by Yuri Sdobnikov]. Moscow : Progress Publishers, c1984- v. ; 21 cm. (Progress guides to the social sciences) Includes bibliographical references. CONTENTS. - [pt. 1] Imperialism and the developing countries. LC Card 84-202086 DDC 335.43 19
1. Economics - Collected works. 2. Marxian economics - Collected works. I. Title.
HB53 .P64 1984 ***NYPL [JLK 86-18]***

Popov, Mikhail V. Planomernoe razreshenie protivorechiĭ razvitii͡a sotsializma kak pervoĭ fazy kommunizma / M.V. Popov. Leningrad : Izd-vo Leningradskogo universiteta, 1986. 156 p. ; 22 cm. At head of title: Leningradskiĭ ordena Lenina i ordena Trudovogo Krasnogo Znameni gosudarstvennyĭ universitet imeni A.A. Zhdanova. Institut povysheni͡ia kvalifikat͡sii prepodavateleĭ obshchestvennykh nauk. Includes bibliographical references. LC Card 87-146874
1. Marxian economics. 2. Soviet Union - Economic policy. 3. Socialism - Soviet Union. I. Title.
HB97.5 .P7994 1986

Popov, Nikola Grigorov.
Politicheskata ikonomii͡a kato teorii͡a i metodologii͡a /. Sofii͡a , 1986. 397 p. ; LC Card 86-210685
HB71 .M59 1986 t. 1 HB97.5

Sŭshtnost, formi i nasoki na izzhivi͡avane na chastnata stopanska deĭnost pri sot͡sializma / Nikola Popov. Sofii͡a : "Nauka i izkustvo", 1985. 363 p. ; 21 cm. Summary in English and Russian. Includes bibliographical references. LC Card 85-169713
1. Capitalism - Communist countries. 2. Small business - Communist countries. I. Title.
HC704 .P66 1985 ***NYPL [*QK 87-1471]***

Popov, Todor. Rol′mezhdunarodnykh monopoliĭ v prodovol′stvennoĭ sisteme /. Sofii͡a , 1985. 113 p. ; LC Card 86-109190
HD9000.5 .R62 1985

Popov, V. D. (Vladimir Dmitrievich) Ėkonomika pli͡us pedagogika : ocherki ob ėkonomicheskom vospitanii molodezhi / V.D. Popov. Moskva : "Molodai͡a gvardii͡a", 1986. 288 p. ; 20 cm. (Molodezh′--problemy i perspektivy) Includes bibliographical references. LC Card 86-103180
1. Economics - Study and teaching (Secondary) - Soviet Union. I. Title. II. Series.
HB74.9.S65 P66 1986

Popov, V. Ė. (Vitaliĭ Ėrastovich) KATĖK i razvitie otrasleĭ khozi͡aĭstva Sibiri /. Novosibirsk , 1984. 164 p. ; LC Card 84-167870
HC337.R852 S5246 1984

Popov, V. (Vladimir) Razvitie promyshlennosti Urala na zavershai͡ushchem ėtape sozdanii͡a razvitogo sotsializma, 1951-1961 gg. : uchebnoe posobie po spet͡skursu / V.F. Popov. Perm′ : Permskiĭ gos. universitet, 1984. 70 p. ; 22 cm. At head of title: Ministerstvo vysshego i srednego spet͡sial′nogo obrazovanii͡a RSFSR. Permskiĭ ordena Trudovogo Krasnogo Znameni gosudarstvennyĭ universitet imeni A.M. Gor′kogo. Includies bibliographical references. LC Card 87-151346
1. Ural Mountains Region (R.S.F.S.R.) - Industries - Histories - 20th century. 2. Ural Mountains Region (R.S.F.S.R.) - Economic conditions. 3. Socialist competition - Russian S.F.S.R. - Ural Mountains Region - History - 20th century. I. Title.
HC337.R852 U73577 1984

Popova, E. I. (Elena Ivanovna) Problemy sovershenstvovanii͡a material′no-tekhnicheskoĭ bazy otrasleĭ obshchestvennogo proizvodstva . Moskva , 1983. 167 p. : LC Card 84-211670
HD70.S63 P753 1983

Popović, Dejan. Ekonomski efekti posrednih poreza / Dejan Popović. Beograd : Centar za publikacije Pravnog fakulteta Univerziteta u Beogradu, 1983. 286 p. : ill. ; 20 cm. In Serbo-Croatian (roman) Originally presented as the author's thesis (doctoral--Pravni fakultet Univerziteta u Beogradu, 1980) Bibliography: p. 275-286. LC Card 86-173775
1. Excise tax - Yugoslavia - Econometric models. 2. Yugoslavia - Economic conditions - 1945- - Econometric models. I. Title.
HJ5156.5 P67 1983

Popović, Strašimir, 1916- Ogled o privrednom sistemu Jugoslavije / Strašimir Popović. Beograd : NIO Poslovna politika, [1983?] 165 p. ; 20 cm. In Serbo-Croatian (roman) Bibliography: p. 161-163. LC Card 86-197560
1. Yugoslavia - Economic conditions - 1945-. I. Title.
HC407 .P65 1983

Popovich, Charles J. Business and economics databases online : environmental scanning with a personal computer / Charles J. Popovich. Littleton, Colo. : Libraries Unlimited, 1987. xviii, 276 p. : ill. ; 28 cm. (Advanced online searching series) Includes bibliographies and index. ISBN 0-87287-454-0 (pbk. : alk. paper) : LC Card 87-2672 DDC 300/.28/5 19
1. Business - Data bases. 2. Economics - Data bases. I. Title. II. Series.
HF5548.2 .P612 1987

Popovych, I. F. V i͡edynomu narodnohospodars′komu kompleksi /. Uzhhorod , 1982. 179 p. : LC Card 83-180335
HC337.U52 W485 1982

Popp, Judy. Financial planners and planning organizations directory . Detroit, Mich. , c1987. viii, 605 p. ; ISBN 0-8103-4397-5 : LC Card 87-21259 DDC 332.6/2 19
HG179.5 .F56 1987

Popp, Wolfgang. Schertler, Walter. Attraktivitätsanalyse von Dienstleistungen . München , c1983. 183 p. : ISBN 3-597-10420-7 LC Card 83-140207
HD9984.5 .S25 1983

Poppe, Fred C. 50 rules to keep a client happy / Fred C. Poppe. 1st ed. New York : Harper & Row, c1987. 90 p. : ill. ; 22 cm. Bibliography: p. 88. Includes index. ISBN 0-06-015779-8 : LC Card 87-45139 DDC 659.1/125 19
1. Advertising agencies. 2. Customer relations. I. Title. II. Title: Fifty rules to keep a client happy.
HF6178 .P66 1987

Poppe, Johann Heinrich Moritz von, 1776-1854. Ausführliche Volks-Gewerbslehre, oder, Allgemeine und besondere Technologie zur Belehrung und zum Nutzen für alle Stände / nach dem neuesten Zustande der technischen Gewerbe und deren Hilfswissenschaften bearbeitet von J.H.M. Poppe. Stuttgart : C. Hoffmann ; Wien : C. Gerold'sche Buchh., 1833- v. <1 > : ill. ; 21 cm. Includes bibliographical references. CONTENTS. - 1. Bd. Allgemeine Technologie. LC Card 87-409525 DDC 331.7/02/024042 19
1. Vocational guidance - Europe. 2. Job descriptions. 3. Europe - Occupations. 4. Technical education - Europe. I. Title. II. Title: Ausführliche Volks-Gewerbslehre. III. Title: Allgemeine und besondere Technologie zur Belehrung und zum Nutzen für alle Stände. IV. Title: Ausführliche Volksgewerbslehre.
HF5382.5.E84 P66 1833

Poppe, Jürgen. Mikroelektronik, Jobkiller oder Jobknüller? : Versuch einer Einschätzung für die Bundesrepublik Deutschland / Jürgen Poppe. Pfaffenweiler : Centaurus-Verlagsgesellschaft, 1984. 93 p. : ill. ; 21 cm. (Reihe Wirtschaftswissenschaften . Bd. 6) Revision of a Diplomarbeit (Universität Bremen, 1983) jointly presented by the author and B. Heyden under the title: Technischer Wandel und der Arbeitsmarkt in der Bundesrepublik Deutschland, dargestellt am Beispiel der Mikroelektronik. Bibliography: p. 89-93. ISBN 3-89085-027-8 : LC Card 85-129494
1. Unemployment, Technological - Germany, West. 2. Microelectronics - Social aspects - Germany (West). I. Series. II. Series: Reihe Wirtschaftswissenschaften (Pfaffenweiler, Breisgau-Hochschwarzwald, Germany) , Bd. 6. III. Title.
HD6331.2.G28 P66 1984

Poppe, René. Interior mina : testimonio / René Poppe.[1a ed.]. La Paz, Bolivia : [Empresa Editora Khana Cruz], 1986. 236 p. ; 20 cm. (Biblioteca popular boliviana de "Ultimo Hora") Includes bibliographies. LC Card 87-400962 DDC 331.7/622/0984 19
1. Miners - Bolivia. I. Title. II. Series.
HD8039.M61 B634 1986

Poppel, Harvey L. Information technology : the trillion-dollar opportunity / Harvey L. Poppel, Bernard Goldstein ; with foreword by John Sculley. New York : McGraw-Hill, c1987. xx, 207 p. : ill. ; 24 cm. Includes bibliographical references and index. ISBN 0-07-050511-X : LC Card 86-27782 DDC 338.4/7004/0973 19
1. Computer industry. 2. Telecommunication equipment industry. 3. Market surveys. I. Goldstein, Bernard. II. Title.
HD9696.C62 P623 1987

A População de Portugal / Portugal, Centro e Estudos Demográficos, Instituto Nacional de Estatística. [Lisbon] : O Centro, 1976. 116 p., [1] folded leaf of plates : ill. ; 24 cm. (Caderno . no. 2) Includes bibliographical references. LC Card 85-204353
1. Portugal - Population. 2. Migration, Internal - Portugal. 3. Labor supply - Portugal. I. Centro de Estudios Demográficos (Portugal). II. Series: Caderno (Centro de Estudos Demográficos (Portugal)) , no. 2.
HB3621 .P67 1976

População, migração e desenvolvimento econômico . Milone, Paulo Cesar. São Paulo , 1986. 150 p. : LC Card 87-118486 DDC

304.6/0981 19
HB3563 .M45 1986

Popular Front, France. see **Front populaire.**

POPULAR FRONTS - MEXICO.
The Mexican Left, the popular movements, and the politics of austerity /. La Jolla, Calif. , 1986. vi, 96 p. ; LC Card 87-621353 DDC 322/.2/0972 19
HC135 .M525535 1986

POPULAR PARTICIPATION - LATIN AMERICA.
Buscando la equidad. English. In search for equity . Aldershot, Hants, England , Brookfield, USA , c1987. xvi, 249 p. ; ISBN 0-566-05537-6 : LC Card 87-21225 DDC 338.98 19
HC130.B38 B8713 1987

Popular radicalism . Wright, D. G. London , New York , 1988. p. cm. ISBN 0-582-49440-0 LC Card 87-4093 DDC 322/.2/0942 19
HD8395 .W75 1988

Population abstract, 1970-1981. Trinidad and Tobago : Ministry of Finance and Planning, Central Statistical Office, c1986. ix, 48 p. : ill. ; 28 cm. Cover title. LC Card 87-125348 DDC 304.6/097298/3021 19
1. Trinidad and Tobago - Population - Statistics. I. Trinidad and Tobago. Central Statistical Office.
HA867 .P66 1986

POPULATION - ADDRESSES, ESSAYS, LECTURES.
Population structures and models . London , Boston , 1986. xxii, 417 p. : ISBN 0-04-301200-0 (alk. paper) LC Card 85-30642 DDC 304.6 19
HB1951 .P67 1986 ***NYPL [JLE 86-4134]***

The State of population theory . Oxford, OX , New York, NY, USA , 1986. 311 p. : ISBN 0-631-13975-3 : LC Card 85-26668 DDC 304.6/01 19
HB849.4 .S73 1986 ***NYPL [JLE 86-2411]***

Population and agriculture in the developing countries /. Cairncross, John. Rome , 1980. ii, 52 p. ; ISBN 92-5-100885-X (pbk.) LC Card 81-198370 DDC 338.1/09172/4 19
HD1417 .C34 1980 ***NYPL [JLF 86-1573]***

Population and development . Population and Development Symposium (1985 : Cairo, Egypt) Cairo , 1986. 616 p. : LC Card 86-969481 DDC 304.6 19
HB849 .P575 1986

Population and development in the Third World /. Findlay, Allan M. London , New York , 1987. xii, 84 p. : ISBN 0-416-91950-2 (pbk.) : LC Card 86-31094 DDC 304.6/09172/4 19
HB884 .F56 1987

Population and development projects in Africa / edited by John I. Clarke, Mustafa Khogali, Leszek A. Kosiński for International Geographical Union, Commission on Population Geography. Cambridge [Cambridgeshire] ; New York : Cambridge University Press, 1985. xvi, 329 p. : ill. ; 26 cm. Includes bibliographies and index. ISBN 0-521-30527-6 LC Card 84-29323 DDC 304.6/096 19
1. Migration, Internal - Africa - Addresses, essays, lectures. 2. Economic development projects - Africa - Addresses, essays, lectures. 3. Rural development projects - Africa - Addresses, essays, lectures. 4. Africa - Population - Addresses, essays, lectures. I. Clarke, John Innes. II. Khogali, M. (Mustafa). III. Kosiński, Leszek A. IV. International Geographical Union. Commission on Population Geography.
HB2121.A3 P67 1985 ***NYPL [JLF 86-186]***

Population and development review. Vol. 12 (Supplement)
Below-replacement fertility in industrial societies . Cambridge [Cambridgeshire] , New York , c1987. x, 360 p. : ISBN 0-521-34324-0 LC Card 87-6371 DDC 304.6/32 19
HB901 .B45 1987b

Below-replacement fertility in industrial societies . New York, N.Y., USA , c1987. x, 360 p. : LC Card 87-2458 DDC 304.6/32 19
HB901 .B45 1987

Population and Development Symposium, 1985.
Population and Development Symposium (1985 : Cairo, Egypt) Population and development . Cairo , 1986. 616 p. : LC Card 86-969481 DDC 304.6 19
HB849 .P575 1986

Population and Development Symposium (1985 : Cairo, Egypt) Population and development : proceedings of the symposium held at Cairo Demographic Centre, 3-7 November 1985. Cairo : The Centre, 1986. 616 p. : ill. ; 24 cm. (Research monograph series / Cairo Demographic Centre . no. 14) Cover title: Population and Development Symposium, 1985. "Special issue." Includes bibliographies. LC Card 86-969481 DDC 304.6 19
1. Population - Congresses. 2. Economic development - Congresses. 3. Population policy - Congresses. I. Cairo Demographic Centre. II. Title. III. Title: Population and Development Symposium, 1985. IV. Series: Research monograph series / Cairo Demographic Centre , no. 14.
HB849 .P575 1986

Population and economic projections for the State of Hawaii, 1980-2005 [microform]. [Honolulu, Hawaii] : Research and Economic Analysis Division, Dept. of Planning and Economic Development, State of Hawaii, [1984] 22 p. ; 28 cm. "July 1984." Microfilm. New York : New York Public Library, 1986. 1 microfilm reel ; 35 mm. (MN *ZZ-26,873) LC Card 84-622934 DDC 304.6/2/09969021 19
1. Population forecasting - Hawaii - Statistics. 2. Economic forecasting - Hawaii - Statistics. 3. Hawaii - Economic conditions - 1959- - Statistics. I. Hawaii. Dept. of Planning and Economic Development. Research and Economic Analysis Division.
HB3525.H3 P67 1984
NYPL [*ZT-1745 no.28]

Population and employment forecasts and distribution for the central Puget Sound region, 1975-1990 /. Pethick, Donald R. Seattle, Wash. [1969] 26 p., [2] leaves of plates : LC Card 87-400702 DDC 304.6/2/097977021 19
HA697.P84 P47 1969

Population and housing census 1971 . Savezni zavod za statistiku (Yugoslavia) [Popis stanovništva i stanova 1971. English.] Beograd , 1974. 12 v. ; LC Card 83-122836
HA1631.5 1971 .S38 1974

Population and settlement in U.P. . Singh, Alok Kumar, 1958- New Delhi, India , 1985. xx, 231 p., [10] p. of plates : LC Card 86-900123 DDC 304.6/0954/2 19
HB2100.U88 S55 1985
NYPL [JLD 86-3156]

Population and socioeconomic development / [translated from the Russian by Sergeĭ Sosinsky ; authors D. Horlacher ... et al.]. Moscow : Progress Publishers, 1986. 186 p. ; 21 cm. Title on verso of t.p.: Narodonaselenie i sotsial′ no-ėkonomicheskoe razvitie. LC Card 86-226273 DDC 304.6/09172/4 19
1. Developing countries - Population policy. 2. Developing countries - Economic policy. I. Horlacher, D. II. Title: Narodonaselenie i sotsial′ no-ėkonomicheskoe razvitie.
HB849.41 .P644 1986

Population and the world economy in the 21st century / edited by Just Faaland. Oxford : B. Blackwell, 1982. viii, 264 p. : ill. ; 24 cm. Background papers, summaries of discussions, and an overview of the Nobel Symposium on "Population Growth and World Development: a Fifty-year Perspective," held at Noresund, Norway, Sept. 7-11, 1981. Includes bibliographies and index. ISBN 0-631-12964-2 LC Card 86-673281
1. Economic history - 1971- - Congresses. 2. Population - Congresses. 3. Population - Economic aspects - Congresses. 4. Economic forecasting - Congresses. 5. Population forecasting - Congresses. I. Faaland, Just. II. Nobel Symposium on "Population Growth and World Development: a Fifty-year Perspective" (1981 : Noresund, Norway).
HC59 .P638x 1982b

Population, birth, death, and marriage statistics of the Cayman Islands : 1986 with some comparative statistics for earlier years. [George Town] : Govt. Statistics Unit, Dept. of Finance & Development, Cayman Islands, [1987] 10 leaves ; 28 cm. "March 1987"--Leaf 2. Chiefly tables. LC Card 87-403402 DDC 304.6/097292/1021 19
1. Cayman Islands - Statistics, Vital. I. Cayman Islands. Dept. of Finance and Development. Statistics Unit.
HA916.Z9 C2968 1987

Population census 1980, selected statistical region Port Elizabeth/Uitenhage/Kirkwood. Bevolkingsensus 1980, uitgesoekte statistiese streek Port Elizabeth/Uitenhage/Kirkwood =. [Pretoria] [1985] xix, 317 p. : ISBN 0-621-09480-3 : LC Card 85-241531
HA4701.Z9 P673 1985

Population census 1980, selected statistical region, Pretoria/Wonderboom. Bevolkingsensus 1980, uitgesoekte statistiese streek, Pretoria/Wonderboom =. [Pretoria] [1985?] xx, 476 p. : ISBN 0-621-09483-8 : LC Card 85-238587
HA4701.Z9 P743 1985

Population census 1980, selected statistical region Vereeniging/Vanderbijlpark/Sasolburg. Bevolkingsensus 1980 uitgesoekte statistiese streek Vereeniging/Vanderbijlpark/Sasolburg =. Pretoria [1985] xx, 301 p. : ISBN 0-621-09484-6 : LC Card 85-235498
HA4701.Z9 V474 1985

Population census, 1981--Nepal. Kathmandu, Nepal : His Majesty's Govt., National Planning Commission Secretariat, Central Bureau of Statistics, 1984- <v. 1, pt. 1-4, 5-7; v. 2; v. 3 in 9 > ; 23 x 29 cm. Cover title. CONTENTS. - v. 1, pt. 1. General characteristics tables. pt. 2-4. Social characteristics tables (2 v.) pt. 5-7. Economic characteristics tables (3 v.) -- v. 2. Geographic region tables -- v. 3. Urban areas tables. LC Card 85-904528
1. Nepal - Population - Statistics. 2. Nepal - Census, 1981. I. Nepal. Kendrīya Tathyāṅka Vibhāga.
HA4570.9 .A4 1981c

Population change, natural resources, and regionalism / edited by Ann Christine Reid. Milford, Pa. : Grey Towers Press, c1986. viii, 104 p. : ill. ; 23 cm. (Breaking new ground . no. 1) Proceedings of a symposium held Sept. 18-19, 1985. ISBN 0-938549-00-6 (pbk.) LC Card 86-25682 DDC 304.6/0973 19
1. United States - Population - Congresses. 2. United States - Population density - Congresses. 3. United States - Population policy - Congresses. 4. Conservation of natural resources - United States - Congresses. 5. Environmental policy - United States - Congresses. 6. Regional planning - United States - Congresses. I. Reid, Ann Christine. II. Series.
HB3505 .P62 1986

POPULATION - CONGRESSES.
Bevölkerungswissenschaft . Frankfurt , New York , c1985. 227 p. ; ISBN 3-593-33461-5 LC Card 85-178756
HB849 .B48 1985

International Population Conference (1985 : Florence, Italy) International Population Conference, Florence 1985, 5-12 June =. Liège, Belgium , c1985- v. : ISBN 2-87108-004-6 (set) LC Card 86-113476 DDC 304.6 19
HB849 .I616 1985 ***NYPL [JLL 86-265]***

Journalist Workshop on Population and Development Reporting (1981 : Islāmābād, Pakistan) Journalist Workshop on Population and Development Reporting, Oct. 31-Nov. 5, 1981, Islamabad /. [Pakistan , 1982? (Lahore : Directorate of Production and Publication) 63, 12 p. ; LC Card 83-930293 DDC 304.6 19
HB849 .J67 1981

Population and Development Symposium (1985 : Cairo, Egypt) Population and development . Cairo , 1986. 616 p. : LC Card 86-969481 DDC 304.6 19
HB849 .P575 1986

Population and the world economy in the 21st century /. Oxford , 1982. viii, 264 p. : ISBN 0-631-12964-2 LC Card 86-673281
HC59 .P638x 1982b

Population Council, New York.
Jackson, Cecile, 1953- The Kano River Irrigation Project /. West Hartford, Conn. , 1985. xviii, 66 p. ; ISBN 0-931816-19-X LC Card 85-5242 DDC 331.4/83/09669 19
HD6073.F32 N64 1985
NYPL [JLF 86-1634]

Palmer, Ingrid. The impact of agrarian reform on women /. West Hartford, Conn. , c1985. xiv, 55 p. ; ISBN 0-931816-21-1 (pbk.) LC Card 85-5250 DDC 331.4/83/091724 19
HD6073.A292 D447 1985
NYPL [JLF 86-1633]

Palmer, Ingrid. The impact of male out-migration on women in farming /. West Hartford, Conn. , c1985. xviii, 78 p. ; ISBN 0-931816-22-X (pbk.) LC Card 85-5240 DDC

331.4/83/091724 19
HD6073.A292 D4472 1985
NYPL [JLF 86-1626]

Spiro, Heather M. The Ilora farm settlement in Nigeria /. West Hartford, Conn. , 1985. xvii, 50 p. : ISBN 0-931816-20-3 LC Card 85-5230 DDC 331.4/83/089963 19
HD6073.F3 N667 1985
NYPL [JLF 86-1629]

POPULATION - DATA PROCESSING.
Mode, Charles J., 1927- Stochastic processes in demography and their computer implementation /. Berlin , New York , c1985. xvii, 389 p. : ISBN 0-387-13622-3 (U. S.) LC Card 84-26707 DDC 304.6/028/54 19
HB849.51 .M635 1985 NYPL [JSE 86-1952]

Population de la Côte d'Ivoire . Ahonzo, Etienne. Abidjan , 1984. ix, 324 p. : LC Card 86-110796 DDC 304.6/09666/8 19
HB3666.A3 A46 1984 NYPL [JLF 86-1466]

La population de la Wallonie dans la dualité démographique de la Belgique /. André, Robert, 1925- Bruxelles , Charleroi , 1983. 192 p. : LC Card 85-175936
HB3604.W34 A53 1983

Population de Madagascar . Andrianarivelo Rafrezy, Vincent. [Antananarivo] [1985] 154 p. : LC Card 86-981367
HA4699 .A84 1985

POPULATION DENSITY.
Miyao, Takahiro. Urban dynamics and urban externalities /. Chur, Switzerland , New York , c1987. viii, 107 p. : ISBN 3-7186-0333-0 (pbk.) LC Card 86-25629 DDC 330.9173/2 19
HB2161 .M595 1987

POPULATION DENSITY - CONGRESSES.
Policies of population redistribution /. Oulu , 1981. 199 p. : ISBN 951-675-071-0 (pbk.) LC Card 83-148782 DDC 304.8 19
HB1952 .P65 1981

Population distribution and urbanization : a review of policy options. Nairobi, Kenya : United Nations Centre for Human Settlements (Habitat), 1985. 95 p. ; 30 cm. "HS/73/85/E"--T.p. verso. Bibliography: p. 89-90. LC Card 85-980971 DDC 304.6/1 19
1. Developing countries - Population. 2. Developing countries - Population density. 3. Urbanization - Government policy - Developing countries. 4. Developing countries - Population policy. I. United Nations Centre for Human Settlements.
HB2160 .P67 1985

Population distribution and urbanization [in] ECA member states. [Addis Ababa?] : United Nations, Economic Commission for Africa, 1983. ix, 81 p. : map ; 28 cm. (African population studies series. no. 7) Includes bibliographical references. "E/ECA/SER.A/5" LC Card 86-980945 DDC 304.6/1 19
1. Africa - Population. 2. Urbanization - Africa. 3. Africa - Population, Rural. I. United Nations. Economic Commission for Africa. II. Series.
HB2121 .P66 1983

POPULATION - DOCUMENTATION - HANDBOOKS, MANUALS, ETC.
Unesco. Regional Office for Education in Asia and the Pacific. Manual for repackaging of information on population education. Bangkok , 1986. 94 p. : LC Card 86-915865 DDC 304.6/07/1 19
HB850 .U57 1986

Population dynamics . Expert Group Meeting on Fertility and Mortality Levels and Trends in Africa and Their Policy Implications (1979 : Monrovia, Liberia) [Addis Ababa] [1981] ix, 581 p. : LC Card 82-980086 DDC 304.6/3/096 19
HB3661.A3 E9 1979 NYPL [JLF 83-591]

POPULATION - ECONOMIC ASPECTS.
Makalová, Eva. Ekonomické aspekty globálních problémů lidstva /. Praha , 1984. 97 p. ; LC Card 86-207353
HB9 .P72a 1984, 4/20 HD75

POPULATION - ECONOMIC ASPECTS - CONGRESSES.
Population and the world economy in the 21st century /. Oxford , 1982. viii, 264 p. : ISBN 0-631-12964-2 LC Card 86-673281
HC59 .P638x 1982b

Population, economics, and unemployment : an economic demographic analysis / prepared by the Population Studies and Research Institute, University of Nairobi, for the Presidential Committee on Unemployment. [Nairobi] : The Institute, [1982] 55 leaves ; 30 cm. "July 1982." Includes bibliographical references. LC Card 85-980190
1. Unemployment, Structural - Kenya. 2. Kenya - Population. I. University of Nairobi. Population Studies and Research Institute. II. Kenya. Presidential Committee on Unemployment.
HD5708.47.K4 P67 1982

Population education . Parakh, B. S. New Delhi , 1985. xxviii, 355 p. ; LC Card 86-903303 DDC 304.6/07/1054 19
HB850.5.I4 P37 1985

Population education programme service. Unesco. Regional Office for Education in Asia and the Pacific. Manual for repackaging of information on population education. Bangkok , 1986. 94 p. : LC Card 86-915865 DDC 304.6/07/1 19
HB850 .U57 1986

Population, environment, and agricultural change . Abdel-Rahman, Awad Ibrahim. [Khartoum] [1984] iii, 37 leaves : LC Card 84-980808 DDC 338.1/8624 19
HD2123.5 .A64 1984

Population estimation methods, Canada. Statistics Canada. Demography Division. Ottawa , c1987. 117 p. : ISBN 0-660-12028-3 (pbk.) : LC Card 87-168812 DDC 304.6/0724 19
HB3529 .S73 1987

Population et progrès socio-économique au Togo /. Gù-Konu, E. Y. Lome , 1980. 291 p. : LC Card 87-148380
HB3665.8.A3 G8 1980

POPULATION FORECASTING - AFRICA - CASE STUDIES.
Uses of census data for demographic research and development planning in Africa . New York , 1986. iv, 24 p. ; LC Card 87-118612 DDC 304.6/096 19
HB3661 .U94 1986

POPULATION FORECASTING - AUSTRALIA.
Hugo, Graeme. Australia's changing population . Melbourne , New York , 1986. x, 354 p. : ISBN 0-19-554680-6 LC Card 87-107294 DDC 304.6/0994 19
HB3675 .H84 1986

POPULATION FORECASTING - AUSTRALIA - PERTH REGION (W.A.) - STATISTICS.
Projected population of Western Australia and the Perth Statistical Division, 1985-2025. [Perth] [1986] 82 p. : LC Card 87-114601 DDC 304.6/2/09941021 19
HA3007.W47 P76 1986

POPULATION FORECASTING - AUSTRALIA - WESTERN AUSTRALIA - STATISTICS.
Projected population of Western Australia and the Perth Statistical Division, 1985-2025. [Perth] [1986] 82 p. : LC Card 87-114601 DDC 304.6/2/09941021 19
HA3007.W47 P76 1986

POPULATION FORECASTING - BERMUDA ISLANDS.
Roberts, G. W. (George W.) Provisional estimates of population movements in Bermuda to 1990 /. Hamilton, Bermuda [198-?] 12, [8] p. : LC Card 86-173218
HB3668.A3 R63 1980z

POPULATION FORECASTING - BOLIVIA - STATISTICS.
Bolivia . [La Paz, Bolivia] [Santiago, Chile] [1985] 107 p. : LC Card 86-160849
HA954 .B64 1985

POPULATION FORECASTING - BRAZIL - AMAZONAS - STATISTICS.
Projeção da população do Estado do Amazonas e seus municípios /. Manaus, Amazonas , 1984. 37 leaves ; LC Card 87-402133 DDC 304.6/0981/13021 19
HA988.A5 P76 1984

POPULATION FORECASTING - CALIFORNIA.
California. Legislature. Senate. Select Committee on Long Range Policy Planning. California and the 21st century . Sacramento, CA [1986] 3 v. : LC Card 86-622352 DDC 338.5/443/09794 19
HC107.C2 C227 1986

POPULATION FORECASTING - CANADA - METHODOLOGY.
Statistics Canada. Demography Division. Population estimation methods, Canada. Ottawa , c1987. 117 p. : ISBN 0-660-12028-3 (pbk.) : LC Card 87-168812 DDC 304.6/0724 19
HB3529 .S73 1987

POPULATION FORECASTING - CANADA - STATISTICS.
Household and population projections for Canadian provinces and territories, 1981-2046. Edmonton, Alta., Canada , c1984. 53 p. ; LC Card 84-670146 DDC 312/.8/0971 19
HA745 .H69 1984 NYPL [JLF 86-642]

Interim household and family projections for Canada, provinces, and territories to 2006 =. [Ottawa] [1987] 67 p. ; LC Card 87-162270 DDC 304.6/2/0971021 19
HA745 .I62 1987

POPULATION FORECASTING - CONGRESSES.
Population and the world economy in the 21st century /. Oxford , 1982. viii, 264 p. : ISBN 0-631-12964-2 LC Card 86-673281
HC59 .P638x 1982b

Projecting migration for integrated rural and urban development planning. Liege, Belgium , c1980. 46 p. ; LC Card 84-221919 DDC 304.8 19
HB1952 .P76 1980
NYPL [JLL 77-289 no. 16]

POPULATION FORECASTING - DATA PROCESSING.
Mason, Andrew, 1947- HOMES . Honolulu, Hawaii [1987] x, 114 p. : ISBN 0-86638-102-3 (pbk.) : LC Card 87-22288 DDC 304.6/028/55329 19
HB849.49 .M38 1987

Shorter, Frederic Claiborne. Computational methods for population projections . New York , 1987, c1974. vii, 192 p. : ISBN 0-87834-056-4 (pbk.) LC Card 87-9303 DDC 304.6/2/0285 19
HB849.53 .S54 1987

POPULATION FORECASTING - DEVELOPING COUNTRIES.
Kitay, Michael G. Land acquisition in developing countries . Boston , c1985. xx, 199 p. ; ISBN 0-89946-192-1 LC Card 85-7225 DDC 333.1/3/091724 19
HD1131 .K58 1985 NYPL [JLE 86-3827]

POPULATION FORECASTING - ETHIOPIA - STATISTICS.
Population of weredas and towns, by sex and average household size, based on the preliminary census results, and population projections by age, sex groups, and rural-urban, for total country and regions, 1984-1995 /. Addis Ababa [1985] 370 p. ; LC Card 86-980450 DDC 304.6/0963/021 19
HA4689 .P67 1985

POPULATION FORECASTING - EUROPE.
Wattenberg, Ben J. The birth dearth /. New York, NY , 1987. viii, 182 p. : ISBN 0-88687-304-5 : LC Card 83-63759 DDC 304.6/32 19
HB915 .W29 1987

POPULATION FORECASTING - GERMANY, WEST.
Leben im Jahr 2000 und danach . Berlin , c1984. 213 p. : ISBN 3-7605-8571-X LC Card 85-128359
HB3595 .L43 1984

Merklein, Renate. Die Rentenkrise /. Reinbek bei Hamburg , 1986. 190 p. : ISBN 3-499-33072-5 : LC Card 87-100842
HD7105.35.G3 M47 1986

Raumordnungsprognose 1990 . Bonn-Bad-Godesberg , 1977. 95 p. : LC Card 86-100310
HB3595 .R38 1977

POPULATION FORECASTING - GERMANY (WEST) - NORTH RHINE-WESTPHALIA - STATISTICS.
Vorausberechnung der Bevölkerung in den kreisfreien Städten und Kreisen Nordrhein-Westfalens . Düsseldorf [1983] 103

p. : LC Card 86-202728
HA1320.N6 A32 Heft 500

POPULATION FORECASTING - GREAT BRITAIN.
Variant population projections . London , 1986. 17 p. : ISBN 0-11-690777-0 (pbk.) : LC Card 86-234516 DDC 304.6/2/0941021 19
HB3583 .V368 1986

POPULATION FORECASTING - GREAT BRITAIN - STATISTICS.
Variant population projections . London , 1986. 17 p. : ISBN 0-11-690777-0 (pbk.) : LC Card 86-234516 DDC 304.6/2/0941021 19
HB3583 .V368 1986

POPULATION FORECASTING - HAWAII - STATISTICS.
Population and economic projections for the State of Hawaii, 1980-2005 [microform]. [Honolulu, Hawaii] [1984] 22 p. ; LC Card 84-622934 DDC 304.6/2/09969021 19
HB3525.H3 P67 1984
NYPL [*ZT-1745 no.28]

POPULATION FORECASTING - HUNGARY - BUDAPEST - STATISTICS.
Szukicsné Serfőző, Klára. Budapest és Pest megye népességfejlődése, az ezredfordulóig várható tendenciák /. Budapest , 1984. 88 p. : LC Card 86-157549
HA1208.B96 S98 1984

POPULATION FORECASTING - HUNGARY - PEST MEGYE - FORECASTING - STATISTICS.
Szukicsné Serfőző, Klára. Budapest és Pest megye népességfejlődése, az ezredfordulóig várható tendenciák /. Budapest , 1984. 88 p. : LC Card 86-157549
HA1208.B96 S98 1984

POPULATION FORECASTING - HUNGARY - STATISTICS.
Csernák, Józsefné. A családok és háztartások előreszámítása, 1981-2001 /. Budapest , 1985. 125 p. : LC Card 86-166603
HA1201 .A64 no. 59 HA1205

POPULATION FORECASTING - INDIA - STATISTICS.
Hobbs, Frank. Demographic estimates, projections, and selected social characteristics of the population of India /. Washington, D.C. [1986] vii, 148 p. : LC Card 87-601294 DDC 304.6/0954/021 19
HA4585 .H63 1986

POPULATION FORECASTING - LATIN AMERICA.
Wiarda, Howard J., 1939- Population, internal unrest, and U. S. security in Latin America /. [Amherst] , 1986. 50 p. ; LC Card 87-621399 DDC 304.6/098 19
HB3530.5.A3 W5 1986

POPULATION FORECASTING - MADAGASCAR - STATISTICS.
Andrianarivelo Rafrezy, Vincent. Population de Madagascar . [Antananarivo] [1985] 154 p. : LC Card 86-981367
HA4699 .A84 1985

POPULATION FORECASTING - MARYLAND - MONTGOMERY COUNTY - STATISTICS.
Montgomery County census update survey . [Silver Spring, Md.] (8787 Georgia Ave., Silver Spring 20907) [1985] 59 p. : LC Card 86-622600 DDC 304.6/09752/84 19
HA427.M65 M66 1985

POPULATION FORECASTING - MATHEMATICAL MODELS.
Foot, David H.S. A comparison of some land-use allocation/interaction models [microform] /. Reading [Berkshire] , 1974. 36 p. : ISBN 0-7049-0338-5
NYPL [*ZT-1712 no.13]

POPULATION FORECASTING - METHODOLOGY.
Kayani, Ashraf K. Preparing subnational population projections . Santiago de Chile [1980] ii, 68 p. ; LC Card 84-256007 DDC 304.6/2/072 19
HB849.53 .K39 1980

POPULATION FORECASTING - MEXICO - STATES - STATISTICS.
Proyecciones de la población de México y de las entidades federativas, 1980-2010. México, D.F. , c1985. xiii, 134 p. ; ISBN 968-8097-66-7 LC Card 86-223751
HB3531 .P78 1985

POPULATION FORECASTING - NEW JERSEY - STATISTICS.
Population projections for New Jersey and counties . Trenton, N.J. , 1985. 2 v. ; LC Card 86-622231 DDC 304.6/2/09749021 19
HA525 .P66 1985

POPULATION FORECASTING - OREGON - LINN COUNTY - STATISTICS.
Population trends, Linn County, Oregon . [Eugene] [1964] 20 leaves : LC Card 85-209473
HA597.L56 P66 1964

POPULATION FORECASTING - PERU - STATISTICS.
Perú . Lima, Perú , 1984. 54 p. ; LC Card 86-111841 DDC 304.6/2/0985021 19
HA1055 .P46 1984 ***NYPL [JLG 86-190]***

Perú, proyecciones de población por años calendarios, según departamentos, provincias y distritos . Lima , 1985. 84 p. ; LC Card 86-173351
HA1064 .P49 1985

POPULATION FORECASTING - SOUTH DAKOTA - STATISTICS.
Goss, De Vee E. South Dakota county and subcounty population estimates (1980, 1982, 1984) /. Vermillion, S.D. [1985] 42 p. ; LC Card 87-620701 DDC 304.6/2/09783021 19
HA635 .G67 1985

South Dakota county population estimates, 1984 (age by race by sex). Vermillion, S.D. [1986] [25] leaves ; LC Card 87-620702 DDC 304.6/09783/021 19
HA635 .S68 1986

POPULATION FORECASTING - STATISTICAL METHODS.
London, Dick, 1943- Survival models and their estimation /. Winsted, Conn. , c1986 (1987 printing) xii, 282 p. : ISBN 0-936031-01-8 (pbk.) LC Card 87-402847 DDC 304.6/4/015195 19
HG8782 .L57 1987

POPULATION FORECASTING - STATISTICS.
Vu, My T., 1939- World population projections, 1985 . Baltimore , 1985. xxvi, 451 p. ; ISBN 0-8018-3322-1 LC Card 85-23083 DDC 304.6 19
HA155 .V83 1985
NYPL [*R-Econ. 86-3764]

POPULATION FORECASTING - SWEDEN.
Trender och prognoser inför 90-talet. Stockholm , Örebro , 1985. 147 p. : ISBN 91-618-0001-5 LC Card 86-115921
LB2833 .S9 1985:2 HC375
NYPL [JLG 86-230]

POPULATION FORECASTING - UNITED STATES.
Forecasting interstate migration with limited data . Iowa City , 1982. 37 p. :
NYPL [*ZT-1564 no.33]

Wattenberg, Ben J. The birth dearth /. New York, NY , 1987. viii, 182 p. : ISBN 0-88687-304-5 : LC Card 83-63759 DDC 304.6/32 19
HB915 .W29 1987

POPULATION FORECASTING - VENEZUELA - STATISTICS.
Estimaciones y proyecciones de población, 1950-2025 /. [Caracas] , 1985-[1987] 2 v. : ISBN 980-280-006-6 (set) LC Card 87-123959 DDC 304.6/2/0987021 19
HA1095 .E885 1985

POPULATION FORECASTING - VIRGINIA - STATISTICS.
Lillywhite, Donald P. Virginia population projections 2000 /. Richmond, VA (P.O. Box 1422, Ninth St. Office Building, Richmond 23219) [1986] 96 p. : LC Card 87-621004 DDC 304.6/2/09755021 19
HA685 .L542 1986

POPULATION FORECASTING - WASHINGTON (D.C.)
Grier, George W. Greater Washington at mid decade . Washington, DC (1717 Massachusetts Ave., N.W., Washington 20036-2076) , c1985- v. <1> : LC Card 86-200647 DDC 338.5/443/09753 19
HC108.W3 G73 1985

POPULATION FORECASTING - WASHINGTON METROPOLITAN AREA - STATISTICS.
Growth trends to the year 2010. Washington, D.C. , c1986. i, 32 p. : LC Card 87-129483 DDC 304.6/2/09753021 19
HA305 .G76 1986

Growth trends to the year 2010. Washington, D.C. , c1986. i, 9 p. : LC Card 87-153125 DDC 304.6/2/09753021 19
HA305 .G77 1986

POPULATION FORECASTING - WASHINGTON (STATE) - PUGET SOUND REGION - STATISTICS.
Pethick, Donald R. Population and employment forecasts and distribution for the central Puget Sound region, 1975-1990 /. Seattle, Wash. [1969] 26 p., [2] leaves of plates : LC Card 87-400702 DDC 304.6/2/097977021 19
HA697.P84 P47 1969

POPULATION FORECASTING - ZAMBIA - PROVINCES - STATISTICS.
Fahmy, H. A. African population projection according to eight models, sex & age groups (1970-2000) /. [Lusaka] [198-?] 34, 9, 62 leaves, [3] leaves of plates : LC Card 85-980559 DDC 304.6/2/096894021 19
HA4703 .F34 1980z

POPULATION, FOREIGN. see **EMIGRATION AND IMMIGRATION.**

Population geography : progress & prospect / edited by Michael Pacione. London ; Dover, N.H. : Croom Helm, c1986. 322 p. : ill., maps ; 23 cm. (Croom Helm progress in geography series) Includes bibliographies and index. ISBN 0-7099-4045-9 : LC Card 86-6210 DDC 304.6 19
1. Census. 2. Fertility, Human. 3. Population policy. I. Pacione, Michael. II. Series.
HB1951 .P653 1986 ***NYPL [JLD 86-3692]***

POPULATION GEOGRAPHY - ADDRESSES, ESSAYS, LECTURES.
Multiregional demography . Laxenburg, Austria , c1984. v, 81 p. : LC Card 84-218929 DDC 304.6 19
HB1951 .M85 1983 ***NYPL [JLE 86-583]***

Population structures and models . London , Boston , 1986. xxii, 417 p. : ISBN 0-04-301200-0 (alk. paper) LC Card 85-30642 DDC 304.6 19
HB1951 .P67 1986 ***NYPL [JLE 86-4134]***

POPULATION, GEOGRAPHY OF. see **POPULATION GEOGRAPHY.**

POPULATION GEOGRAPHY - SPAIN - ANDALUSIA.
Jordá Borrell, Rosa Ma. (Rosa Maria) Dinámica y distribución recientes de la población andaluza /. [Sevilla] [1985?] 80 p. : ISBN 84-600-3827-0 LC Card 87-124031
HB3620.A5 J67 1985

POPULATION - GREAT BRITAIN - STATISTICS.
ISBA area information, 1978 /. London , 1978. 147 p. : ISBN 0-906241-00-6 (pbk.) LC Card 83-225656 DDC 381/.1/0941021 19
HA1134 .I83 1978

Population growth /. McGraw, Eric. Vero Bleach, FL , 1987. 46 p. : ISBN 0-86592-276-4 LC Card 87-12729 DDC 304.6/2 19
HB871 .M325 1987

Population growth and economic development : policy questions / Working Group on Population Growth and Economic Development, Committee on Population, Commission on Behavioral and Social Sciences and Education, National Research Council. Washington, D.C. : National Academy Press, 1986. ix, 108 p. ; 23 cm. Includes index. Bibliography: p. 94-104. ISBN 0-309-03641-0 (pbk.) LC Card 86-862 DDC 304.6/09172/4 19
1. Developing countries - Population. 2. Developing countries - Economic conditions. I. National Research Council. Working Group on Population Growth and Economic Development.
HB884 .P6655 1986 ***NYPL [JLE 86-3533]***

Population growth and economic development : issues and evidence / edited by D. Gale Johnson and Ronald D. Lee. Madison, Wis. : University of Wisconsin Press, 1987. xiii, 702 p. ; 24 cm. (Social demography) "Working Group on Population Growth and Economic Development;

Committee on Population, Commission on Behavioral and Social Sciences and Education, National Research Council." Includes bibliographies and index. ISBN 0-299-11130-X : LC Card 86-40447 DDC 338.9/009172/4 19
1. Developing countries - Population. 2. Food supply - Developing countries. 3. Labor supply - Developing countries. 4. Natural resources - Developing countries. 5. Developing countries - Economic policy. I. Johnson, D. Gale (David Gale), 1916-. II. Lee, Ronald Demos, 1941-. III. National Research Council (U. S.). Working Group on Population Growth and Economic Development. IV. National Research Council (U. S.). Committee on Population. V. Series.
HB884 .P66547 1987

Population growth and unemployment in India /. Prabhakara, N. R. New Delhi , 1986. ix, 102 p. ; ISBN 81-7024-041-7 : LC Card 86-902156 DDC 331.13/795487 19
HD5820.K37 P7 1986

POPULATION - HISTORY.
Russell, Josiah Cox, 1900- The control of late ancient and medieval population /. Philadelphia , 1985. xv, 272 p. ; ISBN 0-87169-160-4 LC Card 83-71298
NYPL [JLF 85-844]

Population, human and national resources in Pakistan / edited by Jahangir Khan. [Karachi : Dept. of Sociology, University of Karachi, 198-?] 19 p. ; 25 cm. Cover title. "Proceedings of the special symposium sponsored jointly by the Pakistan Population Planning Council, Islamabad and Pakistan Sociological Association on the occasion of 8th annual conference held at the University of Karachi, Karachi." Bibliography: p. 19. CONTENTS. - An anaylsis of the first release from the third Population census of Pakistan, 1972 / Anwarul Haq -- Effect of Population pressure on human and national resources in Pakistan / Talat Khan -- Population and health services in Karachi city / S. Kamil. LC Card 85-931341
1. Pakistan - Population - Congresses. 2. Pakistan - Population policy - Congresses. 3. Human capital - Pakistan - Congresses. 4. Pakistan - Economic conditions - Congresses. I. Khan, Jahangir. II. Pakistan Population Planning Council. III. Pakistan Sociological Association.
HA4590.5 .P66 1980z

POPULATION - INFORMATIONAL SERVICES - HANDBOOKS, MANUALS, ETC.
Unesco. Regional Office for Education in Asia and the Pacific. Manual for repackaging of information on population education. Bangkok , 1986. 94 p. : LC Card 86-915865 DDC 304.6/07/1 19
HB850 .U57 1986

Population, internal unrest, and U. S. security in Latin America /. Wiarda, Howard J., 1939- [Amherst] , 1986. 50 p. ; LC Card 87-621399 DDC 304.6/098 19
HB3530.5.A3 W5 1986

Population, labour, and migration in 19th- and 20th-century Germany / edited by Klaus J. Bade. Leamington Spa [UK] ; New York : Berg ; xii, 200 p. : ill. ; 23 cm. (German historical perspectives . 1) Bibliography: p. 189-196. ISBN 0-85496-503-3 : LC Card 86-24470 DDC 331.6/2/0943 19
1. Migrant labor - Germany - History. 2. Migration, Internal - Germany - History. 3. Alien labor - Germany - History. 4. Germany - Population - History. 5. Labor and laboring classes - Germany - History. I. Bade, Klaus J. II. Series.
HD5856.G3 P66 1987

POPULATION - MAPS.
Census mapping survey /. New Delhi , 1984. xxiii, 299 p. : LC Card 84-902653 DDC 304.6 19
HA31.25 .C46 1984 ***NYPL [JLE 85-3881]***

POPULATION - MATHEMATICAL MODELS.
Iskakov, B. I. (Boris Ivanovich) Demograficheskoe modelirovanie . Moskva , 1982. 75 p. ; LC Card 83-179019
HB849.51 .I85 1982

Mode, Charles J., 1927- Stochastic processes in demography and their computer implementation /. Berlin , New York , c1985. xvii, 389 p. : ISBN 0-387-13622-3 (U. S.) LC Card 84-26707 DDC 304.6/028/54 19
HB849.51 .M635 1985 ***NYPL [JSE 86-1952]***

Müller, Karl-Wilhelm, 1953- Die Theorie erschöpfbarer natürlicher Ressourcen bei wachsender Bevölkerung /. Frankfurt am Main , New York , c1984. 191 p. : ISBN 3-8204-5315-6 LC Card 85-197540
HD75.6 .M85 1984

Simon, Julian Lincoln, 1932- Theory of population and economic growth /. Oxford , 1986. xi, 232 p. : ISBN 0-631-14427-7 : LC Card 85-28574 DDC 338.9/00724 19
HB849.41 .S55 1986 ***NYPL [JLE 86-3702]***

Population mobility and multilocality in Ilorin, Kwara State, Nigeria /. Watts, Susan J. [Liverpool , 1981-] v. <1 > : LC Card 86-226489 DDC 304.8/09669/5 19
HB2126.7.I46 W37 1981

Population of Ghana, 1850-1960 /. Engmann, E. V. T. Accra, Ghana , 1986. xvii, 300 p. : ISBN 996-430-088-3 (pbk.) LC Card 87-127395 DDC 304.6/09669 19
HB3666.8.A3 E535 1986

The Population of Hawaii, 1980-1985.
[Honolulu] : Research and Economic Analysis Division, Dept. of Planning and Economic Development, State of Hawaii, [1986] 12 p. ; 28 cm. (Statistical report . 190) "July 2, 1986." Includes bibliographical references. LC Card 86-622982 DDC 319.69 s 304.6/09969 19
1. Hawaii - Population - Statistics. I. Series: Statistical report (Hawaii. Dept. of Planning and Economic Development) , 190.
HA329.1 .A25 no. 190 HA329.5

Population of Japan / [edited and published by Statistics Bureau, Management and Coordination Agency]. Tokyo : The Bureau, c1986. 124 p. : ill. ; 21 cm. LC Card 86-230476 DDC 304.6/0952 19
1. Japan - Population. I. Japan. Sōrifu. Tōkeikyoku. II. Japan. Sōmuchō.
HB3651 .P67 1986

Population of the Sudan and its regions : a joint project on mapping and analysing the 1983 population census data. [Wad Medani, Sudan?] : Population Studies Centre, Faculty of Economics and Rural Development, University of Gezira, [1984?- <1 > v. : ill. ; 32 cm. Cover title. At head of title: Democratic Republic of the Sudan, Department of Statistics, Census Office. "Third population census, 1983." CONTENTS. - Project documentation no. 1. Total populations by region, province & district. LC Card 86-980678 DDC 304.6/09624/021 19
1. Sudan - Census, 1983. 2. Sudan - Population - Statistics. I. Sudan. Census Office.
HA4687 .A4 1983

The Population of the United States in the 1980s.
Adams, John S., 1938- Housing America in the 1980s /. New York , c1987. p. cm. ISBN 0-87154-003-7 : LC Card 86-42950 DDC 363.5/0973 19
HD7293 .A625 1987

Levy, Frank, 1941- Dollars and dreams . New York , 1987. p. cm. ISBN 0-87154-523-3 : LC Card 86-42952 DDC 339.2/0973 19
HC110.I5 L47 1987

Population of weredas and towns, by sex and average household size, based on the preliminary census results, and population projections by age, sex groups, and rural-urban, for total country and regions, 1984-1995 / the Provisional Military Government of Socialist Ethiopia, Office of the National Committee for Central Planning, Central Statistical Office. Addis Ababa : Central Statistical Office, [1985] 370 p. ; 30 cm. (Census supplement . 1) "December 1985." LC Card 86-980450 DDC 304.6/0963/021 19
1. Ethiopia - Population - Statistics. 2. Population forecasting - Ethiopia - Statistics. I. Ethiopia. Central Statistical Office. II. Series: Census supplement (Ethiopia. Central Statistical Office) , 1.
HA4689 .P67 1985

POPULATION - PHILIPPINES - MINDANAO ISLAND.
Socio economic factbook of Mindanao. Davao City, Philippines [1985] 568 p. ; LC Card 85-234433
HA4617.M56 S63 1985

POPULATION POLICY.
Demograficheskaia͡ politika sot͡sialisticheskogo obshchestva /. Moskva , 1986. 190 p. ;
NYPL [*QIP 87-2842]

Johnson, Stanley, 1940- World population and the United Nations . Cambridge [Cambridgeshire] , New York , 1987. xxxviii, 357 p. ; ISBN 0-521-32207-3 LC Card 87-5126 DDC 363.9 19
HB884.5 .J64 1987

Loriaux, M. Economie, population et politique démographique /. Louvain-la-Neuve [c1984] 169 p. : ISBN 2-87085-041-7 : LC Card 86-144677
HB883.5 .L67 1984

Nerlove, Marc, 1933- Household and economy . Boston , 1987. xiii, 155 p. : ISBN 0-12-515752-5 LC Card 86-10764 DDC 304.6/32 19
HB901 .N47 1987 ***NYPL [JLE 87-1715]***

Population geography . London , Dover, N.H. , c1986. 322 p. : ISBN 0-7099-4045-9 : LC Card 86-6210 DDC 304.6 19
HB1951 .P653 1986 ***NYPL [JLD 86-3692]***

Repetto, Robert C. World enough and time . New Haven , c1986. xiv, 147 p. ; ISBN 0-300-03648-5 LC Card 85-20180 DDC 333.7 19
HC59 .R43 1986 ***NYPL [JLD 86-1434]***

Stevens, Charles J. Confronting the world food crisis /. Muscatine, Iowa [1981] 24 p. : LC Card 82-127279 DDC 338.1/9 19
HD9000.6 .S73 ***NYPL [JLK 75-198 no. 27]***

Teorii͡a i praktika ėkonomiki demoprot͡sessa . Kiev , 1982. 181 p., [2] folded leaves of plates : LC Card 83-145373
HB883.5 .T46 1982

United Nations. Dept. of International Economic and Social Affairs. Review and appraisal of the World Population Plan of Action . New York , 1986. vi, 169 p. : ISBN 92-1-151158-5 (pbk.) LC Card 87-105369 DDC 304.6 19
HB883.5 .U55 1986

Wereldbevolking groeiend ontwikkelingsprobleem. Den Haag [1975] 66 p. : LC Card 87-118557
HB883.5 .W47 1975

World food, population, and development /. Totowa, N.J. , 1985. xvi, 346 p. : ISBN 0-8476-7455-X : LC Card 85-14398 DDC 338.1/9 19
HD9000.5 .W59 1985 ***NYPL [JLE 86-1741]***

Population policy and individual choice . Nerlove, Marc, 1933- Washington, D.C., U. S.A. , 1987. 52 p. : ISBN 0-89629-062-X (pbk.) LC Card 87-16802 DDC 363.9 19
HB901 .N474 1987

Population policy briefs : the current situation in developing countries, 1985. New York : United Nations, 1986. viii, 49 p. ; 28 cm. (Population policy paper / Department of International Economic and Social Affairs . no. 2) "Prepared by the Population Division of the Department of International Economic and Social Affairs of the United Nations Secretariat"--Pref. "ST/ESA/SER.R/62." LC Card 87-117649 DDC 304.6/09172/4 19
1. Developing countries - Population policy. I. United Nations. Dept. of International Economic and Social Affairs. Population Division. II. Series: Population policy paper , no. 2.
HB884 .P66557 1986

POPULATION POLICY - CONGRESSES.
International Congress on New Dimensions in Population Planning and Development (1978 : Colombo, Sri Lanka) The International Congress on New Dimensions in Population Planning and Development, Bandaranaike Memorial International Conference Hall, Colombo, 26-28 March 1978 /. Colombo, Sri Lanka , 1978. 114 p., [5] leaves of plates : LC Card 84-902651 DDC 304.6/6/095493 19
HB883.5 .I57 1978 ***NYPL [JLF 86-1970]***

Policies of population redistribution /. Oulu , 1981. 199 p. : ISBN 951-675-071-0 (pbk.) LC Card 83-148782 DDC 304.8 19
HB1952 .P65 1981

Population and Development Symposium (1985 : Cairo, Egypt) Population and development . Cairo , 1986. 616 p. : LC Card 86-969481 DDC 304.6 19
HB849 .P575 1986

POPULATION POLICY - MATHEMATICAL MODELS.
Nerlove, Marc, 1933- Population policy and individual choice . Washington, D.C., U. S.A. ,

1987. 52 p. : ISBN 0-89629-062-X (pbk.) LC Card 87-16802 DDC 363.9 19
HB901 .N474 1987

Population policy paper .
(no. 2) Population policy briefs . New York , 1986. viii, 49 p. ; LC Card 87-117649 DDC 304.6/09172/4 19
HB884 .P66557 1986

Population, poverty, and basic needs in southern Sudan . House, William J. [Juba, Sudan , 1985] vi, 94 leaves ; LC Card 86-981127 DDC 338.9629 19
HC835.Z7 S684 1985

Population profile, Nuwara Eliya District.
[Colombo] : Population Division, Ministry of Plan Implementation, [1985?] viii, 35 p. : ill., map ; 26 cm. Cover title: The population profile of the Nuwara Eliya District. LC Card 86-902529 DDC 304.6/09549/3 19
1. Nuwara Eliya (Sri Lanka : District) - Population - Statistics. I. Sri Lanka. Sālasum Kriyātmaka Kirīmē Amātyāṃśaya. Janagahana Aṃśaya. II. Title: Population profile of the Nuwara Eliya District.
HA4570.8.Z9 N886 1985

Population profile of the Nuwara Eliya District.
Population profile, Nuwara Eliya District. [Colombo] [1985?] viii, 35 p. : LC Card 86-902529 DDC 304.6/09549/3 19
HA4570.8.Z9 N886 1985

POPULATION PROJECTIONS. see **POPULATION FORECASTING.**

Population projections for New Jersey and counties : 1990 to 2020. Trenton, N.J. : State of New Jersey, Dept. of Labor, Office of Demographic and Economic Analysis, Division of Planning and Research, 1985. 2 v. ; 28 cm. "November 1985." LC Card 86-622231 DDC 304.6/2/09749021 19
1. New Jersey - Population - Statistics. 2. Population forecasting - New Jersey - Statistics. I. New Jersey. Office of Demographic and Economic Analysis.
HA525 .P66 1985

Population redistribution and development in South Asia / edited by Leszek A. Kosiński and K. Maudood Elahi. Dordrecht ; Boston : D. Reidel, 1985. 243 p. : ill. ; 24 cm. Bibliography: p. 235-236. Includes index. ISBN 90-277-1938-1 : LC Card 84-26260 DDC 304.8/0959 19
1. Migration, Internal - South Asia - Addresses, essays, lectures. 2. Refugees - South Asia - Addresses, essays, lectures. 3. South Asia - Population - Addresses, essays, lectures. I. Kosiński, Leszek A. II. Elahi, K. Maudood.
HB2096.5 .P66 1985 ***NYPL [JLE 86-3852]***

POPULATION - STATISTICS.
Vu, My T., 1939- World population projections, 1985 . Baltimore , 1985. xxvi, 451 p. ; ISBN 0-8018-3322-1 LC Card 85-23083 DDC 304.6 19
HA155 .V83 1985
NYPL [*R-Econ. 86-3764]

World population prospects . New York , 1986. x, 330 p. : ISBN 92-1-151159-3 (pbk.) LC Card 87-104085 DDC 304.6/2/021 19
HA155 .W693 1986

The population structure and living circumstances of Irish travellers . Rottman, David B. Dublin , 1986. 134 p. : ISBN 0-7070-0084-X (pbk.) : LC Card 86-215759 DDC 330.9417 s 305.5/68 19
HC257.I6 E3 no. 131 DX217

Population structures and models : developments in spatial demography / edited by Robert Woods and Philip Rees. London ; Boston : G. Allen and Unwin, 1986. xxii, 417 p. : ill. ; 24 cm. Includes index. Bibliography: p. 390-409. ISBN 0-04-301200-0 (alk. paper) LC Card 85-30642 DDC 304.6 19
1. Population geography - Addresses, essays, lectures. 2. Population - Addresses, essays, lectures. I. Woods, Robert. II. Rees, P. H. (Philip H.), 1944-. III. Title: Spatial demography.
HB1951 .P67 1986 ***NYPL [JLE 86-4134]***

Population studies (New York, N.Y.) .
(no. 98) World population prospects . New York , 1986. x, 330 p. : ISBN 92-1-151159-3 (pbk.) LC Card 87-104085 DDC 304.6/2/021 19
HA155 .W693 1986

(no. 99) United Nations. Dept. of International Economic and Social Affairs. Review and appraisal of the World Population Plan of Action . New York , 1986. vi, 169 p. : ISBN 92-1-151158-5 (pbk.) LC Card 87-105369 DDC 304.6 19
HB883.5 .U55 1986

Population studies translation series .
(no. 3) Henry, Louis, writer on demography. [Fécondité des marriages. English.] Fertility of marriage . New York , 1980. iv, 136 p. : LC Card 81-133059
HB901 .H4613 1980

POPULATION - STUDY AND TEACHING - INDIA.
Parakh, B. S. Population education . New Delhi , 1985. xxviii, 355 p. ; LC Card 86-903303 DDC 304.6/07/1054 19
HB850.5.I4 P37 1985

POPULATION - STUDY AND TEACHING - INDONESIA.
Bahan instruksional pendidikan kependudukan untuk peserta diklat Departemen P.U. Jakarta , 1982. v, 90 p. ; LC Card 83-941464
HB850.5.I5 B34 1982

Pendidikan kependudukan untuk perwira. [Jakarta] [1981] vi, 120 p. : LC Card 85-940192
HB850.5 .P46 1981

POPULATION - STUDY AND TEACHING - NEPAL.
Nepālamā janasaṅkhyā śikshā. Kāṭhamāḍauṃ, Nepāla , 2042 [1985] 195 p. ; LC Card 87-902146
HB850.5.N35 N46 1985

POPULATION - STUDYING AND TEACHING - HANDBOOKS, MANUALS, ETC.
Unesco. Regional Office for Education in Asia and the Pacific. Manual for repackaging of information on population education. Bangkok , 1986. 94 p. : LC Card 86-915865 DDC 304.6/07/1 19
HB850 .U57 1986

POPULATION SURVEYS - GREAT BRITAIN.
Todd, Jean Elizabeth. Changing the definition of a household . London , 1986. viii, 43 p. : ISBN 0-11-691071-2 (pbk.) : LC Card 87-132272
HB849.49 .T63 1986

Population trends and public policy .
(no. 10) Diaz-Briquets, Sergio. Conflict in Central America . Washington, D.C. (777 14th St. NW, Washington 20005) , 1986. 16 p. : LC Card 87-401095 DDC 304.6/09728 19
HB3533 .D5 1986

Population trends, Linn County, Oregon : a planning study / prepared for Linn County and the cities of Albany, Brownsville, Lebanon, and Sweet Home by the Bureau of Municipal Research and Service, University of Oregon. [Eugene] : The Bureau, [1964] 20 leaves : col. ill. ; 28 cm. "The preparation of this report was financially aided through a federal grant from the Urban Renewal Administration of the Housing Finance Agency, under the Urban Planning Assistance Program ... Oregon Project no. P-41." LC Card 85-209473
1. Population forecasting - Oregon - Linn County - Statistics. 2. Linn County (Or.) - Population - Statistics. I. University of Oregon. Bureau of Municipal Research and Service.
HA597.L56 P66 1964

Popul͡iarnai͡a politėkonomii͡a /. Nechaev, I͡U. V. (I͡Uriĭ Vasilʹevich) Kiev , 1986. 246 p. : LC Card 87-169729
HC336.25 .N43 1986

POPULISM - CHILE.
Vega Tapia, Héctor. L'économie du populisme et le projet de passage au socialisme proposé par l'Unité populaire au Chili /. [Brussels] , 1984. 511 p. ; LC Card 85-146534 DDC 338.983 19
HC192 .V37 1984 ***NYPL [JLE 86-3663]***

POPULISM - LATIN AMERICA - HISTORY.
Godio, Julio. Sindicalismo y política en América Latina /. Caracas, Venezuela [1983] 315 p. ; LC Card 83-157510 DDC 322/.2/098 19
HD8110.5 .G64 1983 ***NYPL [JLD 86-1758]***

POPULISM - POLAND - HISTORY.
Wycech, Czesław. Z przeszłości ruchów chłopskich, 1768-1861 /. Warszawa , 1952. 221, [3] p. ; LC Card 81-212267
HD1536.P7 W93 1952

POPULISM - SOUTH ASIA.
Bhairav, Kalki Kaal. Populist manifesto /. Grand Forks, ND, USA (830 S. 48th St., Grand Forks 58201) [c1986] vii, 85 p. ; LC Card 86-201038 DDC 338.954 19
HC430.6 .B46 1986

POPULISM - SOUTHERN STATES - HISTORY - 19TH CENTURY.
Mitchell, Theodore R. Political education in the Southern Farmers' Alliance, 1887-1900 /. Madison, Wis. , 1987. xiv, 242 p. : ISBN 0-299-11470-8 : LC Card 87-40141 DDC 338.1/06/075 19
HD1485.N35 M58 1987

POPULISM - UNITED STATES.
Zimmerman, Joseph Francis, 1928- Participatory democracy . New York , 1986. xi, 229 p. ; ISBN 0-275-92132-8 (alk. paper) : LC Card 86-8129 DDC 323/.042/0973 19
JF493.U6 Z56 1986 ***NYPL [JLE 86-3632]***

POPULISM - URUGUAY - HISTORY - 20TH CENTURY - ADDRESSES, ESSAYS, LECTURES.
El Primer batllismo . Montevideo [1985] 159 p. : LC Card 85-233561 DDC 338.9895 19
HC232 .P75 1985 ***NYPL [JLC 86-259]***

Populist manifesto /. Bhairav, Kalki Kaal. Grand Forks, ND, USA (830 S. 48th St., Grand Forks 58201) [c1986] vii, 85 p. ; LC Card 86-201038 DDC 338.954 19
HC430.6 .B46 1986

Popyk, Marilyn K., 1945-
Up and running! : microcomputer applications / Marilyn K. Popyk. Reading, Mass. : Addison-Wesley, c1987. xxv, 647, [28] p. : ill. (some col.) ; 23 cm. Includes index. ISBN 0-201-06274-7 (pbk.) : LC Card 86-26620 DDC 650/.028/5536 19
1. Business - Computer programs. 2. Business - Data processing. 3. Microcomputers. I. Title.
HF5548.2 .P614 1987

Word processing and information systems : a practical approach to concepts / Marilyn K. Popyk.2nd ed. New York : Gregg Division/McGraw-Hill, c1986. xx, 345 p., [15] p. of plates : ill. (some col.) ; 24 cm. Includes index. ISBN 0-07-050594-2 (pbk.) : LC Card 85-23813 DDC 652/.5 19
1. Word processing. 2. Office practice - Automation. I. Title.
HF5548.115 .P66 1986 ***NYPL [JSE 87-273]***

Por qué cayó Jaime Michelsen? /. Donadío, Alberto, 1953- Bogotá , c1984. 142 p. : ISBN 84-89209-42-1 LC Card 85-122262
HG2908.C65 D66 1984

Por qué nos confunden-- el comunismo, el capitalismo, los economistas, las elites? /. Guiba (Writer) Montevideo , 1981. 211 p. ; LC Card 82-125535 DDC 330.9/04 19
HC54 .G79 1981 ***NYPL [JLC 86-320]***

Por una causa agraria . Hurtado Miller, Juan Carlos. Lima, Perú , 1986. 348 p. : LC Card 87-400122 DDC 338.1/885 19
HD1903 .H87 1986

Por una nueva política alimentaria / compilación, David Barkin y Ayari Prieto ; coordinación, Gustavo Esteva. 1a ed. [México, D.F.] : Sociedad Mexicana de Planificación : Comité Promotor de Investigaciones para el Desarrollo Rural, 1984. 114 p. ; 18 cm. LC Card 85-131176 DDC 338.1/9/72 19
1. Food supply - Government policy - Mexico - Addresses, essays, lectures. 2. Nutrition policy - Mexico - Addresses, essays, lectures. 3. Food industry and trade - Government policy - Mexico - Addresses, essays, lectures. 4. Food consumption - Mexico - Addresses, essays, lectures. I. Barkin, David. II. Prieto, Ayari. III. Esteva, Gustavo. IV. Sociedad Mexicana de Planificación. V. Comité Promotor de Investigaciones para el Desarrollo Rural (Mexico).
HD9014.M62 P67 1984 ***NYPL [JLC 86-348]***

Por una visión del desarrollo latinoamericano con autodeterminación, democracia y paz / Francisco Javier Alejo ... [et al.]. San Isidro, Lima, Perú : Departamento de Comunicaciones e Información, Junta del Acuerdo de Cartagena, [1984] 191 p. ; 21 cm. Spine title: 1969-1984, XV aniversario del Acuerdo de Cartagena. Papers from a meeting held May 24-25, 1984 in Lima, Peru. Includes bibliographical references. LC Card 86-226515
1. Andes region - Economic integration - Congresses. 2.

Latin America - Economic integration - Congresses. I. Alejo, Francisco Javier. II. Board of the Cartagena Agreement. Departamento de Comunicaciones e Información. III. Title: 1969-1984, XV aniversario del Acuerdo de Cartagena. IV. Title: 1969-1984, 5o aniversario del Acuerdo de Cartagena.
HC167.A5 P67 1984

P'oraže mtkic'eni. Zakariadze, M. Krepche stali /. Tbilisi , 1986. 51 p., [16] p. of plates : LC Card 85-172385
HD9525.S653 G469 1986

Porcaro, Mimmo, 1953- I difficili inizi di Karl Marx : contro chi e per che cosa leggere "Il capitale" oggi / Mimmo Porcaro. Bari : Dedalo, c1986. 112 p. ; 18 cm. (Piccola biblioteca Dedalo . 15) Includes bibliographical references. ISBN 88-22-03815-0 : LC Card 86-195836
1. Marx, Karl, 1818-1883. Kapital. I. Title.
HB501.M37 P63 1986

Porcaro, Rosa Maria. Oliveira, Lúcia Elena Garcia de. O lugar do negro na força de trabalho /. Rio de Janeiro , 1983. 86 p. ; ISBN 85-24-00024-4 LC Card 86-129924
HD8288.5.B55 O45 1983

PORCELAIN INDUSTRY - RUSSIAN S.F.S.R. - LENINGRAD.
Agarkova, G. D. (Galina Dmitrievna) Leningradskie farforisty /. Moskva , 1984. 61 p. : LC Card 85-111565
HD9616.S653 L463 1984

Poreditsa "Ikonomicheski znaniia" .
(1982, 1) Pamukchiev, Minko Stoĭchev. Intelektualizatsiia na truda i proizvodstvoto /. Sofiia , 1982. 48 p. ; LC Card 82-183037
HF5548.8 .P255 1982

Poreditsa Kategorii na politicheskata ikonomiia.
Khadzhiev, Stoian. Pechalbata pri razshirenoto sotsialistichesko vŭzproizvodstvoto . Sofiia , 1985. 147 p. ; LC Card 85-209903
HC403.Z9 P737 1985

Kostov, Ivan Dimitrov. Obshtestvenata sobstvenost pri sotsializma /. Sofiia , 1985. 111 p. ; LC Card 86-122395
HD4263 .K67 1985

PORK INDUSTRY AND TRADE - AUSTRALIA - VICTORIA - LOCATION.
Victoria. Saleyard Working Party. Distribution of saleyards in Victoria . [Melbourne] , 1986. 69, 7, 7 p. : LC Card 87-159450 DDC 338.1/760831 19
HD9428.A83 V538 1986

PORK INDUSTRY AND TRADE - DEVELOPING COUNTRIES.
Ludwick, David E. The competitive position of U. S. and European Community pork and the United States and third-country markets . Washington, DC [1985] xxiii, 341 p. : LC Card 86-601366 DDC 380.1/4566492/0973 19
HD9435.U52 L83 1985

PORK INDUSTRY AND TRADE - EUROPEAN ECONOMIC COMMUNITY COUNTRIES.
Ludwick, David E. The competitive position of U. S. and European Community pork and the United States and third-country markets . Washington, DC [1985] xxiii, 341 p. : LC Card 86-601366 DDC 380.1/4566492/0973 19
HD9435.U52 L83 1985

PORK INDUSTRY AND TRADE - UNITED STATES.
Ludwick, David E. The competitive position of U. S. and European Community pork and the United States and third-country markets . Washington, DC [1985] xxiii, 341 p. : LC Card 86-601366 DDC 380.1/4566492/0973 19
HD9435.U52 L83 1985

PORK INDUSTRY AND TRADE - URUGUAY.
Producción y comercialización porcina en Uruguay . Montevideo , 1986. 91 p. : LC Card 87-401290 DDC 338.1/764/009895 19
HD9435.U82 P76 1986

Pormale, V. M. Ėkonomicheskie sviazi proizvodstva i potrebleniia pri sotsializme . Riga , 1978. 152 p. ; LC Card 81-168062
HF1040.9.S65 E36 1978

Porras, J. Conte. see Conte Porras, J.

Port development policy : proceedings of a seminar-cum-study tour, Japan, October 1984. Bangkok, Thailand : Economic and Social Commission for Asia and the Pacific, United Nations, 1985. ix, 83 p. : ill. (some col.) ; 28 cm. (ESCAP port development series, 0252-3396 . no. 7) Proceedings and papers of the Seminar-cum-Study Tour on Port Development Policy, organized by the Economic and Social Commission for Asia and the Pacific, and held in Yokohama, Japan, Oct. 1-8, 1984. LC Card 87-106926 DDC 387.1/0952 19
1. Harbors - Government policy - Japan - Congresses. 2. Harbors - Government policy - Japan - Case studies - Congresses. 3. Harbors - Government policy - Congresses. 4. Harbors - Government policy - Case studies - Congresses. I. United Nations. Economic and Social Commission for Asia and the Pacific. II. Seminar-cum-Study Tour on Port Development Policy (1984 : Yokohama-shi, Japan). III. Series.
HE559.J3 P653 1985

PORT ELIZABETH (SOUTH AFRICA) - CENSUS, 1980.
Bevolkingsensus 1980, uitgesoekte statistiese streek Port Elizabeth/Uitenhage/Kirkwood =. [Pretoria] [1985] xix, 317 p. : ISBN 0-621-09480-3 : LC Card 85-241531
HA4701.Z9 P673 1985

Port guide on African major ports. [Addis Ababa, Ethiopia] : United Nations, [1986?] ii, 256 p. ; 28 cm. Cover title. At head of title: United Nations transport and communications decade in Africa, 1978-1988. "E/ECA/TCD/30." LC Card 86-980946 DDC 387.1/096 19
1. Harbors - Africa. I. United Nations. II. Title: United Nations transport and communications decade in Africa, 1978-1988.
HE559.5 .P68 1986

The Port of Mobile, Alabama / prepared by the Water Resources Support Center. Rev. 1986. Washington : U. S. G.P.O ; Fort Belvoir, Va. : For sale by The Center, 1986. vi, 99 p. : ill. ; 26 cm. (Port series / U. S. Army, Corps of Engineers . no. 18) "Supersedes a similar report revised in 1978"--P. v. Rev. ed. of: The port of Mobile, Alabama / prepared by the Board of Engineers for Rivers and Harbors. 1978. Folded map in pocket. LC Card 86-603154 DDC 387.1/09761/22 19
1. Harbors - Alabama - Mobile. I. Water Resources Support Center (U. S.). II. United States. Board of Engineers for Rivers and Harbors. Port of Mobile, Alabama. III. Series: Port series (United States. Army. Corps of Engineers) , no. 18.
HE554.M7 P67 1986

Port of Québec (Canada) Economic impact of the Port of Québec. [Québec, Québec] [1974] [16], [18] leaves ; LC Card 85-183731 DDC 386/.8/09714471 19
HE554.Q4 E27 1974

Port planning and development /. Frankel, Ernst G. New York , c1987. xxiv, 795 p. : ISBN 0-471-83708-3 LC Card 86-24747 DDC 387.1/068 19
HE551 .F7 1987

Port series (United States. Army. Corps of Engineers) .
(no. 18) The Port of Mobile, Alabama /. Washington , Fort Belvoir, Va. , 1986. vi, 99 p. : LC Card 86-603154 DDC 387.1/09761/22 19
HE554.M7 P67 1986

(no. 49) The Ports of Duluth, MN, and Superior, WI, Taconite Harbor, Silver Bay, and Two Harbors, Mdd, and Ashland, WI /. Washington , Fort Belvoir, Va. , 1987. vi, 62 p. : LC Card 87-601753 DDC 386/.8/0977512 19
HE554.A5 P66 1987

Porta, Pier Luigi. Scuola classica e teoria economica / Pier Luigi Porta. Milano : Giuffrè, 1984. xi, 145 p. ; 25 cm. (Studi economici e aziendali . 2) At head of title: Università degli studi di Milano, Facoltà di scienze politiche. Includes bibliographical references and index. ISBN 88-14-00004-2 : LC Card 84-177305 DDC 330.15/3 19
1. Classical school of economics. 2. Economics - History. I. Title. II. Series.
HB167 .P67 1984 ***NYPL [JLE 86-4055]***

The Portable compressor market. New York, N.Y. (106 Fulton St., New York 10038) : Frost & Sullivan, c1983. xi, 254 p. : ill. ; 29 cm. "September 1983." "#A1238." LC Card 87-142051
1. Compressor industry - United States. 2. Market surveys - United States. I. Frost & Sullivan.
HD9705.5.C643 U66 1983

Portable computer market. The Markets and competitive environment for portable computers. New York, N.Y. , c1983. xii, 356 p. : LC Card 87-143515 DDC 380.1/4500416 19
HD9696.C62 M369 1983

Portable kitchen appliance market. New York, N.Y. : Frost & Sullivan, c1983. 2 v. (x, 405 p.) : ill. ; 29 cm. Spine title: Portable kitchen appliances in the U. S. "September 1983." "(#A1184)." LC Card 87-143951 DDC 381/.4568383/0973 19
1. Kitchen utensils industry - United States. 2. Electric household appliances industry - United States. 3. Market surveys - United States. I. Frost & Sullivan. II. Title: Portable kitchen appliances in the U. S.
HD9971.5.K583 U656 1983

Portable kitchen appliances in the U. S. Portable kitchen appliance market. New York, N.Y. , c1983. 2 v. (x, 405 p.) : LC Card 87-143951 DDC 381/.4568383/0973 19
HD9971.5.K583 U656 1983

The portable office . Bates, Jefferson D., 1920- Washington, D.C. , c1987. 262 p. : ISBN 0-87491-491-3 :; 0-87491-841-3 (jacket) LC Card 87-1773 DDC 658.4/093 19
HD38 .B325 1987

Portela, José, 1950- Trabalho cooperativo em duas aldeias de Trás-os-Montes / José Portela. Porto : Edições Afrontamento, 1986. 79 p., [4] p. of plates : ill. ; 21 cm. (Colecção Biblioteca das ciências do homem. Antropologia . 2) "Edição subsidiada pela Universidade de Trás-os-Montes e Alto Douro." Bibliography: p. 69-71. LC Card 87-400109 DDC 334/.683/094692 19
1. Agriculture, Cooperative - Portugal - Trás-os-Montes - Case studies. I. Title. II. Series.
HD1491.P82 T736 1986

Porter, Douglas R. Growth management . Washington, D.C. , c1986. iv, 218 p. : ISBN 0-87420-655-3 (pbk.) LC Card 86-50332 DDC 307.1/4/0973 19
HD205 .G76 1986 ***NYPL [JLE 87-558]***

Porter, Gary A., 1950- Wolk, Harry I. Management accounting . Boston, Mass. , c1988. xiii, 754 p. : ISBN 0-534-07050-7 : LC Card 87-7348 DDC 658.1/511 19
HF5657.4 .W64 1988

Porter, James. Integrating the computer with your business : accounting for computer charges / by James Porter & Jonathan Chapple ; edited by R. B. Yearsley. London : H.F.L. Publishers, 1980. 308 p. ; 22 cm. Includes index. ISBN 0-372-30032-4
1. Electronic data processing departments - Costs. 2. Electronic data processing departments - Accounting. I. Chapple, Jonathan. II. Yearsley, Ronald. III. Title.
NYPL [JLD 86-2442]

Porter, Lyman W. Motivation and work behavior /. New York , c1987. xii, 595 p. : ISBN 0-07-060948-9 : LC Card 86-27865 DDC 658.3/14 19
HF5549.5.M63 M667 1987

Porter, Marilyn, 1942- Women, work, and family in the British, Canadian, and Norwegian oilfields /. New York , 1987. p. cm. ISBN 0-312-00528-8 : LC Card 86-31393 DDC 305.4/3665 19
HD9560.5 .W66 1987

Porter, Mattie C. Francia, Arthur J. Managerial accounting /. Houston, Tex. , 1984. xiv, 651 p. : ISBN 0-931920-70-1 LC Card 83-72203 DDC 658.1/511 19
HF5657.4 .F72 1984

Porter, Steven L., 1952- Save your home : avoid foreclosure and make a fat profit / by Steven L. Porter.1st ed. Bellaire, Tex. : Java Pub. Co., c1987. 167 p. : ill. ; 28 cm. Includes index. ISBN 0-941599-02-7 (pbk.) : LC Card 87-3916 DDC 332.7/22 19
1. Mortgage loans. 2. Foreclosure. I. Title.
HG2040.15 .P67 1987

Porter, W. Thomas. EDP, controls and auditing / W. Thomas Porter, William E. Perry. 5th ed. Boston, Mass. : Kent Pub. Co., c1987. xviii, 617 p. : ill. ; 25 cm. Bibliography: p. 587-589. Includes index. ISBN 0-534-07092-2 : LC Card 86-27564 DDC 657/.45/0285 19
1. Electronic data processing departments - Auditing. I. Perry, William E. II. Title.
HF5548.35 .P67 1987

PORTERS - BOLIVIA - COCHABAMBA - ALCOHOL USE.

Moscoso Pacheco, Arturo C. Con la vida a cuestas . Oruro, Bolivia , 1987. 122 p. : LC Card 87-403838 DDC 362.2/922/088388 19
HD8039.P66 B56 1987

Portes, Richard. Threats to international financial stability /. Cambridge , New York , 1987. xviii, 307 p. : ISBN 0-521-34556-1 LC Card 87-10310 DDC 332/.042 19
HG3881 .T495 1987

Portfolio analysis /. Alexander, Gordon J., 1947- Englewood Cliffs, N.J. , c1986. xiv, 306 p. : ISBN 0-13-686825-8 : LC Card 85-28317 DDC 332.6 19
HG4521 .A42 1986 ***NYPL [JLE 86-4286]***

PORTFOLIO MANAGEMENT.

Coulson, Robert D. The intelligent investor's guide to profiting from stock market inefficiencies /. Chicago, Ill. , c1987. xii, 261 p. : ISBN 0-917253-46-9 : LC Card 86-25341 DDC 332.6 19
HG4529.5 .C68 1987

Fischer, Donald E. Security analysis and portfolio management /. Englewood Cliffs, N.J. , c1987. xii, 708 p. : ISBN 0-13-798901-6 LC Card 86-25484 DDC 332.6 19
HG4529 .F57 1987

Harrington, Diana R., 1940- Modern portfolio theory, the capital asset pricing model, and arbitrage pricing theory . Englewood Cliffs, N.J. , c1987. x, 229 p. : ISBN 0-13-597261-2 (pbk.) LC Card 86-22693 DDC 332.6 19
HG4637 .H37 1987

Haugen, Robert A. Introductory investment theory /. Englewood Cliffs, N.J. , c1987. xv, 524 p. : ISBN 0-13-501933-8 LC Card 86-25373 DDC 332.6 19
HG4529 .H378 1987

Hirsch, Michael D. Multifund investing . Homewood, Ill. , c1987. xx, 237 p. : ISBN 0-87094-912-8 LC Card 86-71215 DDC 332.63/27 19
HG4530 .H57 1987

Huang, Stanley S. C. Investment analysis and management /. Boston , c1987. xiv, 605 p. : ISBN 0-205-10501-7 LC Card 87-986 DDC 332.6 19
HG4529 .H8 1987

Ibbotson, Roger G. Investment markets . New York , c1987. ix, 294 p. : ISBN 0-07-031673-2 : LC Card 86-33740 DDC 332.6 19
HG4523 .I23 1987

Pension asset management . Homewood, Ill. , 1988. xiii, 178 p. : ISBN 0-256-06123-8 LC Card 87-81575 DDC 332.6/7254 19
HD7105.4 .P45 1988

Solberg, Ronald L., 1953- Sovereign rescheduling . London , Boston , 1988. p. cm. ISBN 0-04-332122-4 (alk. paper) LC Card 87-18805 DDC 336.3/435 19
HG3891.5 .S65 1988

Wahl, Jack. Informationsbewertung und -effizienz auf dem Kapitalmarkt /. Würzburg , 1983. 211 p. : ISBN 3-7908-0308-1 LC Card 84-154688
HG4515 .W34 1983

Williams, Alex O., 1934- Managing risk in mortgage portfolios /. New York , c1987. xx, 161 p. : ISBN 0-89930-058-8 (lib. bdg. : alk. paper) LC Card 87-2497 DDC 332.63/244 19
HG4655 .W55 1987

PORTFOLIO MANAGEMENT - ADDRESSES, ESSAYS, LECTURES.

CFA readings in fixed income securities analysis /. Charlottesville, VA (P.O. Box 3668, Charlottesville, VA 22903) , c1985. v, 255 p. :
NYPL [JLF 86-1994]

PORTFOLIO MANAGEMENT - ECONOMETRIC MODELS.

Alexander, Gordon J., 1947- Portfolio analysis /. Englewood Cliffs, N.J. , c1986. xiv, 306 p. : ISBN 0-13-686825-8 : LC Card 85-28317 DDC 332.6 19
HG4521 .A42 1986 ***NYPL [JLE 86-4286]***

PORTFOLIO MANAGEMENT - GERMANY (WEST)

Skutlartz, Ekkehard. Branchenportfolioanalyse und Wirtschaftsförderungsstrategien . [Karlsruhe] [1986] a-m, 205, vi p. : LC Card 87-103969
HG4529.5 .S58 1986

PORTFOLIO MANAGEMENT - GERMANY (WEST) - BADEN-WÜRTTEMBERG.

Skutlartz, Ekkehard. Branchenportfolioanalyse und Wirtschaftsförderungsstrategien . [Karlsruhe] [1986] a-m, 205, vi p. : LC Card 87-103969
HG4529.5 .S58 1986

PORTFOLIO MANAGEMENT - MATHEMATICAL MODELS.

Firchau, Volker. Information evaluation in capital markets /. Berlin , New York , c1986. iv, 103 p. : ISBN 0-387-16462-6 (U. S.) : LC Card 86-6655 DDC 332.6/0724 19
HG4523 .F57 1986
NYPL [JLM 72-289 v.268]

Markowitz, H. (Harry), 1927- Mean-variance analysis in portfolio choice and capital markets /. Oxford, OX, UK , New York, NY, USA , 1987. xi, 387 p. : ISBN 0-631-15381-0 : LC Card 87-2975 DDC 332.6 19
HG4529.5 .M37 1987

Wondrak, Bernhard. Management von Zinsänderungschancen und -risiken /. Heidelberg , c1986. xv, 254 p. : ISBN 3-7908-0341-3 LC Card 86-213976
HG6024.5 .W66 1986

PORTFOLIO MANAGEMENT - UNITED STATES.

Mortgage-backed securities . Chicago, Ill. , c1987. xi, 474 p. : ISBN 0-917253-47-7 : LC Card 86-15087 DDC 332.63/232 19
HG4655 .M65 1987 ***NYPL [JLE 87-783]***

Seligman, Barnard. Choosing an investment company /. Cambridge, Mass. , c1987. xvii, 174 p. : ISBN 0-88730-094-4 LC Card 87-1437 DDC 332.6 19
HG4930 .S45 1987

Supply-side portfolio strategies /. Westport, Conn. , 1988. xii, 180 p. : ISBN 0-89930-286-6 (lib. bdg. : alk. paper) LC Card 87-13091 DDC 332.6/0973 19
HG4910 .S775 1988

Portilla, Belfor. Alimentos : dependencia o desarrollo nacional / Belfor Portilla, Rebeca Salazar, Silvia del Valle.1a ed. México : Centro de Estudios Económicos y Sociales del Tercer Mundo : Editorial Nueva Imagen, 1983. 149, [53] p. : ill., maps ; 20 cm. (Serie CEESTEM-Nueva Imagen) Bibliography: p. 133-149. ISBN 968-429-384-4 LC Card 84-172348 DDC 338.1/9/1724 19
1. Food supply - Political aspects - Developing countries. 2. Food industry and trade - United States. 3. International business enterprises - Developing countries. 4. Developing countries - Foreign economic relations - United States. 5. United States - Foreign economic relations - Developing countries. I. Salazar, Rebeca. II. Valle, Silvia del. III. Title.
HD9018.D44 P67 1983
NYPL [JLD 86-1520]

PORTNEUF (QUÉBEC : COUNTY) - ECONOMIC CONDITIONS.

Le Projet Delaney . [St-Raymond, Québec] [1983] 76 leaves in various foliations : LC Card 84-224364
HD9685.C3 Q456 1983

Portney, Kent E. The Distributional impacts of public policies /. New York , 1988. xvii, 257 p. ; ISBN 0-312-00749-3 : LC Card 87-11877 DDC 339.2/0973 19
HC110.I5 D535 1988

PORTO ALEGRE (BRAZIL) - COMMERCE - STATISTICS.

Porto Alegre (Brazil). Mayor. Mensagem apresentada á Camara Municipal /. Pôrto Alegre , 1936. 686 p., [7] folded leaves of plates : LC Card 85-135614
HD4635.P6 P67 1936

Porto Alegre (Brazil). Mayor. Mensagem apresentada á Camara Municipal / pelo prefeito Alberto Bins em 3 de outubro de 1936. Pôrto Alegre : Livraria do Globo, 1936. 686 p., [7] folded leaves of plates : ill. (some col.) ; 27 cm. LC Card 85-135614
1. Porto Alegre (Brazil) - Public works. 2. Municipal services - Brazil - Porto Alegre. 3. Public utilities - Brazil - Porto Alegre. 4. Finance, Public - Brazil - Porto Alegre. 5. Porto Alegre (Brazil) - Commerce - Statistics. I. Bins, Alberto, 1869-1957. II. Title.
HD4635.P6 P67 1936

PORTO ALEGRE (BRAZIL) - PUBLIC WORKS.

Porto Alegre (Brazil). Mayor. Mensagem apresentada á Camara Municipal /. Pôrto Alegre , 1936. 686 p., [7] folded leaves of plates : LC Card 85-135614
HD4635.P6 P67 1936

PORTO ALEGRE METROPOLITAN AREA (BRAZIL) - ECONOMIC POLICY - CONGRESSES.

Seminário para Compatibilização da Ação Pública na Região Metropolitana de Porto Alegre (1983) Seminário para Compatibilização da Ação Pública na Região Metropolitana de Porto Alegre . Porto Alegre, RS [1983] 83 p. : LC Card 84-216956
HC189.P64 S45 1983

PORTO ALEGRE METROPOLITAN AREA (BRAZIL) - SOCIAL POLICY - CONGRESSES.

Seminário para Compatibilização da Ação Pública na Região Metropolitana de Porto Alegre (1983) Seminário para Compatibilização da Ação Pública na Região Metropolitana de Porto Alegre . Porto Alegre, RS [1983] 83 p. : LC Card 84-216956
HC189.P64 S45 1983

Pôrto, Josè da Costa, 1909- O açúcar num documento colonial / Costa Porto. Recife : Centro de Estudos de História Municipal, Fundação de Desenvolvimento Municipal do Interior de Pernambuco, 1984. 116 p. ; 23 cm. (Coleção Tempo municipal . 4) LC Card 87-102690
1. Sugar trade - Brazil - Pernambuco - History - 16th century. 2. Sugar trade - Brazil - Pernambuco - History - 17th century. 3. Pernambuco (Brazil) - History. 4. Pernambuco (Brazil) - Economic conditions. I. Title. II. Series.
HD9114.B7 P448 1984

PORTO REGION (PORTUGAL) - ECONOMIC CONDITIONS.

Perspectivas sobre o norte de Portugal. Porto , 1981. 242 p. : LC Card 83-163948
HC393.M55 P47 1981

PORTO REGION (PORTUGAL) - SOCIAL CONDITIONS.

Perspectivas sobre o norte de Portugal. Porto , 1981. 242 p. : LC Card 83-163948
HC393.M55 P47 1981

Portocarrero de Guzmán, Blancanieve. El capitalismo dependiente y su incidencia en el problema agrario venezolano / Blancanieve Portocarrero de Guzmán. Valencia, Venezuela : Vadell Hnos. Editores, c1985. 189 p. : ill. ; 22 cm. Bibliography: p. 183-189. LC Card 86-226697
1. Land reform - Venezuela. 2. Social conflict - Venezuela. 3. Agriculture and state - Venezuela. I. Title.
HD1333.V4 P67 1985

Portocarrero Lasso de la Vega, Melchor, conde de la Monclova, 1636-1705. Numeracion general de todas las personas de ambos sexos, edades y calidades q[ue] se hà hecho en esta ciudad de Lima, año de 1700 /. Lima , 1985. xv, 358 p. : LC Card 87-400680
HA1069.L7 N86 1985

Portocarrero Maisch, Javier. Promoción de las exportaciones no tradicionales . [Lima, Peru] . 145 p. ; LC Card 86-146920
HF1569 .P76 1985 ***NYPL [JLD 87-1165]***

Portrait of a market . Stamets, John, 1949- Seattle , 1987. 95 p. : ISBN 0-941104-17-6 (pbk.) : LC Card 87-4746 DDC 381/.18/0979777 19
HF5472.U7 S48 1987

PORTRAIT PAINTINGS - 18TH CENTURY - MEXICO - MEXICO CITY.

Cortina Portilla, Manuel. Algo sobre la plata en México en el siglo XVIII /. México , 1986. 48 p., [1] folded leaf of plates : LC Card 87-404604 DDC 332.4/042/097253 19
HG661 .C67 1986

Portraits of success . Caddes, Carolyn, 1935- Palo Alto, Calif. , 1986. viii, 138 p. : ISBN 0-935382-56-9 : LC Card 86-40032 DDC 338.4/7621/0979473 19
HD9696.A3 U53173 1986
NYPL [MFX (Caddes) 87-542]

PORTS. see **HARBORS.**

Les ports maritimes . France. Conseil économique et social. Paris [1983] 1 v. (various pagings) : LC Card 83-186600
HE557.F8 F67 1983

Ports, navires et négociants à Dunkerque, 1662-1792 /. Pfister-Langanay, Christian. Dunkerque , 1985. 677 p. : LC Card 87-115474
HD558.D85 P45 1985

Ports of California. Davis, Charlotte. Los Angeles [1970] 80 p. LC Card 79-114863 DDC 387.1/09794
HE554.C16 D3

The Ports of Duluth, MN, and Superior, WI, Taconite Harbor, Silver Bay, and Two Harbors, Mdd, and Ashland, WI / prepared by the Water Resources Support Center ; U. S. Army Corps of Engineers. Rev. 1987. Washington : U. S. G.P.O. ; Fort Belvoir, Va. : For sale by Water Resources Support Center, 1987. vi, 62 p. : ill., col. maps ; 26 cm. (Port series . no. 49) Shipping list no.: 87-347-P. Two folded maps in pocket. Item 340 LC Card 87-601753 DDC 386/.8/0977512 19
1. Harbors - Minnesota. 2. Harbors - Wisconsin. I. Water Resources Support Center (U. S.). II. United States. Army. Corps of Engineers. III. Series: Port series (United States. Army. Corps of Engineers) , no. 49.
HE554.A5 P66 1987

The Ports of Tacoma, Grays Harbor, and Olympia, Washington / prepared by the Water Resources Support Center. Rev. 1983. Washington, D.C. : U. S. G.P.O. ; Fort Belvoir, Va. : For sale by the Center, Casey Bldg., 1983. vi, 98 p. : ill., maps ; 26 cm. (Port series / U. S. Army, Corps of Engineers . no. 35) "This report supersedes a similar report revised in 1975." Two folded maps in pocket. Includes index. LC Card 83-603527 DDC 387.1/09797/7 19
1. Harbors - Washington (State) - Tacoma. 2. Harbors - Washington (State) - Olympia. 3. Harbors - Washington (State). 4. Grays Harbor, Wash. - Harbor. I. Water Resources Support Center (U. S.). II. Series: Water Resources Support Center (U. S.). Port series, no. 35.
HE554.T2 P67 1983 ***NYPL [JLF 85-2000]***

PORTUGAL - CIVILIZATION.
Portugal, 1386-1986 . London [c1987] 156 p. : ISBN 0-947991-01-8 (pbk.) LC Card 87-404164 DDC 382/.09469/04 19
HF3698.E8 P67 1987

PORTUGAL - COLONIES - ECONOMIC CONDITIONS.
Martinez, José Fernando Trindade. Recursos económicos do Ultramar Português, sua valorização e perspectivas futuras . Lisboa , 1960. 113 p. ; LC Card 86-169892
HC890 .M37 1960

PORTUGAL - COMMERCE.

PORTUGAL - COMMERCE - AFRICA, WEST - HISTORY.
Carreira, António. Os portuguêses nos rios de Guiné, 1500-1900 /. Lisboa , 1984. 205 p. : LC Card 85-149851
HF3698.A358 C37 1984

PORTUGAL - COMMERCE - EUROPE - HISTORY.
Portugal, 1386-1986 . London [c1987] 156 p. : ISBN 0-947991-01-8 (pbk.) LC Card 87-404164 DDC 382/.09469/04 19
HF3698.E8 P67 1987

PORTUGAL - COMMERCE - HISTORY.
Ferreira, António Fonseca. A acumulação capitalista em Portugal . Porto , 1977. 156 p. ; LC Card 85-194898
HF3696 .F47 1977

PORTUGAL - COMMERCE - INDIA - HISTORY - 16TH CENTURY.
Solis, Duarte Gomes. Armadas da carreira da India de 1560 a 1590 . Lisboa , 1938. xvi, 20 p. : LC Card 86-140347
HF3698.I4 S65 1938

PORTUGAL - COMMERCIAL POLICY.
Evolução da situação económica em 1983 /. Lisboa , 1984. ix, 149 p. : LC Card 85-208352
HC392 .E963 1984

PORTUGAL - DESCRIPTION AND TRAVEL.
Coelho, Antonio Borges. Quadros para uma viagem a Portugal no Sec. XVI /. Lisboa , c1986. 403 p., [2] folded leaves of plates : LC Card 87-401474
HC392 .C573 1986

PORTUGAL - ECONOMIC CONDITIONS.
Coelho, Antonio Borges. Quadros para uma viagem a Portugal no Sec. XVI /. Lisboa , c1986. 403 p., [2] folded leaves of plates : LC Card 87-401474
HC392 .C573 1986

Reflexões sobre história e cultura portuguesa . Lisboa , 1985. 286 p. ; LC Card 86-135021 DDC 946.9 19
HC392 .R34 1985

PORTUGAL - ECONOMIC CONDITIONS - 1918-1974.
A Agricultura portuguesa no período 1950-1980 . Lisboa [1984] 74 p. : LC Card 85-207313
HD2027 .A635 1984

PORTUGAL - ECONOMIC CONDITIONS - 1974-
A Agricultura portuguesa no período 1950-1980 . Lisboa [1984] 74 p. : LC Card 85-207313
HD2027 .A635 1984

Evolução da situação económica em 1983 /. Lisboa , 1984. ix, 149 p. : LC Card 85-208352
HC392 .E963 1984

Melo, M. Teixeira de. A economia portuguesa após o 25 de abril /. Queluz [Portugal] [1978] 149 p. ; LC Card 79-104785
HC392 .M45 1978

PORTUGAL - ECONOMIC CONDITIONS - 1974- - MATHEMATICAL MODELS.
Barbosa, Manuel P. (Manuel Pinto), 1944- Growth, migration, and the balance of payments in a small open economy, Portugal /. New York , 1984. xv, 212 p. : ISBN 0-8240-4169-0 : LC Card 79-53646 DDC 382.1/7/0724 19
HD5809.A6 B37 1984 ***NYPL [JLE 86-4171]***

PORTUGAL - ECONOMIC POLICY.
Almeida, João António R. Simões de. Financiamento do desenvolvimento económico . Lisboa , 1961. 60 p. ; LC Card 85-220891
HC392 .A466 1961

Evolução da situação económica em 1983 /. Lisboa , 1984. ix, 149 p. : LC Card 85-208352
HC392 .E963 1984

Rosa, Eugénio. O fracasso dos governos de direita em Portugal (1978 a 1981) . [Lisbon?] [1982] 351 p. ; LC Card 85-228499
HC392 .R592 1982

PORTUGAL - EMIGRATION AND IMMIGRATION.
Barbosa, Manuel P. (Manuel Pinto), 1944- Growth, migration, and the balance of payments in a small open economy, Portugal /. New York , 1984. xv, 212 p. : ISBN 0-8240-4169-0 : LC Card 79-53646 DDC 382.1/7/0724 19
HD5809.A6 B37 1984 ***NYPL [JLE 86-4171]***

Emigración y retorno . [Madrid] , 1981. 325 p., [2] folded leaves of plates : ISBN 84-500-5097-9 LC Card 82-145134 DDC 325.46 19
JV8251 .E49 1981 ***NYPL [JLE 86-3179]***

PORTUGAL - EMIGRATION AND IMMIGRATION - GOVERNMENT POLICY.
Ferreira, Eduardo de Sousa, 1936- Reintegração dos emigrantes portugueses . [Lisbon] , 1984. xiv, 137 p. ; LC Card 86-132652
HD8380.5 .F47 1984

PORTUGAL - EMIGRATION AND IMMIGRATION - HISTORY - CASE STUDIES.
Brettell, Caroline. Men who migrate, women who wait . Princeton , c1986. xv, 329 p., [8] p. of plates : ISBN 0-691-09424-1 (alk. paper) : LC Card 86-11270 DDC 304.6/09469/12 19
HB2082.L36 B74 1986 ***NYPL [JLE 87-1417]***

Portugal, Europa face ao Mercado Comum . Azevedo, J. Cândido de. Amadora , c1978. 300 p. ; LC Card 80-121153
HC241.25.P6 A94 1978

Portugal. Finanças, Ministerio das. see **Portugal. Ministerio das Finanças.**

PORTUGAL - FOREIGN ECONOMIC RELATIONS - SPAIN.
Dauderstädt, Michael. Las relaciones hispano-portuguesas y la integración europea /. Madrid [1987?] 36 p. ; ISBN 84-398-8593-8 LC Card 87-161277
HF1570.15.P8 D38 1987

Portugal - Government. see **Portugal - Politics and government.**

PORTUGAL. GUARDA FISCAL - HISTORY.
Santos, Pedro Ribeiro dos. Génese e estrutura da Guarda Fiscal . [Lisbon] [1985] 193 p., [9] leaves of plates : LC Card 87-400399 DDC 354.4690072/46 19
HJ6996 .A25 1985

PORTUGAL - INDUSTRIES.

PORTUGAL - INDUSTRIES - CONGRESSES.
Milhano, Vicente. Problemas sociais e económicos . Covilhã , 1958. 185 p. ; LC Card 86-126181 DDC 338.09469 19
HC392 .M58 1958

PORTUGAL - INDUSTRIES - LOCATION - CONGRESSES.
Milhano, Vicente. Problemas sociais e económicos . Covilhã , 1958. 185 p. ; LC Card 86-126181 DDC 338.09469 19
HC392 .M58 1958

Portugal. Ministerio das Finanças. Arquivo Histórico. Diário da navegação de Macau, 1759-1761 . Lisboa , 1970. 274 p. ; LC Card 86-201114
HF1009.7.M25 D53 1970

Portugal. Ministério do Trabalho e Segurança Social. Ribeiro, Maria Eduarda. Aspectos analíticos da distribuição da massa salarial no período de 1972 a 1983 /. Lisboa , 1985. 58 p. : LC Card 86-132683
HC394.5.I5 R52 1985

Portugal na Associação Europeia de Comércio Livre /. André, J. L. da Costa. Lisboa , 1960. 98 p. ; LC Card 85-216282
HC241.4 .A56 1960

Portugal na CEE . Álvares, Pedro. [Lisbon] , 1986. 543 p. ; LC Card 87-403268 DDC 341.24/22 19
HC241.25.P6 A48 1986

PORTUGAL - POLITICS AND GOVERNMENT - 1974-
Rosa, Eugénio. O fracasso dos governos de direita em Portugal (1978 a 1981) . [Lisbon?] [1982] 351 p. ; LC Card 85-228499
HC392 .R592 1982

PORTUGAL - POPULATION.
Arroteia, Jorge Carvalho, 1947- A evolução demográfica portuguesa . Lisboa , Amadora, Portugal , 1984 [i.e. 1985] 119 p. : LC Card 86-125507 DDC 304.6/09469 19
HB3621 .A77 1985

A População de Portugal /. [Lisbon] , 1976. 116 p., [1] folded leaf of plates : LC Card 85-204353
HB3621 .P67 1976

PORTUGAL - POPULATION DENSITY.
Arroteia, Jorge Carvalho, 1947- A evolução demográfica portuguesa . Lisboa , Amadora, Portugal , 1984 [i.e. 1985] 119 p. : LC Card 86-125507 DDC 304.6/09469 19
HB3621 .A77 1985

PORTUGAL - POPULATION - HISTORY - 16TH CENTURY.
Coelho, Antonio Borges. Quadros para uma viagem a Portugal no Sec. XVI /. Lisboa , c1986. 403 p., [2] folded leaves of plates : LC Card 87-401474
HC392 .C573 1986

PORTUGAL - RURAL CONDITIONS.
Almeida, João Ferreira de. Classes sociais nos campos . Lisboa [1986] 544 p. : LC Card 87-400121 DDC 305.5/63 19
HD1536.P77 A44 1986

Portugal. Secretaria de Estado da Integração Europeia. Álvares, Pedro. Portugal na CEE . [Lisbon] , 1986. 543 p. ; LC Card 87-403268 DDC 341.24/22 19
HC241.25.P6 A48 1986

Portugal. Serviços de Informação para o Planeamento. Evolução da situação económica em 1983 /. Lisboa , 1984. ix, 149 p. : LC Card 85-208352
HC392 .E963 1984

PORTUGAL - SOCIAL CONDITIONS.
Coelho, Antonio Borges. Quadros para uma

viagem a Portugal no Sec. XVI /. Lisboa , c1986. 403 p., [2] folded leaves of plates : LC Card 87-401474
HC392 .C573 1986

Ferreira, António Fonseca. A acumulação capitalista em Portugal . Porto , 1977. 156 p. ; LC Card 85-194898
HF3696 .F47 1977

Reflexões sobre história e cultura portuguesa . Lisboa , 1985. 286 p. ; LC Card 86-135021 DDC 946.9 19
HC392 .R34 1985

Portugal, 1386-1986 : business partners in Europe / edited by Martim Cabral ; commissioned by the Anglo-Portuguese Foundation. London : De Montfort Pub., [c1987] 156 p. : ill. (some col.) ; 30 cm. Cover title: 1386-1986--Portugal, business partners in Europe. ISBN 0-947991-01-8 (pbk.) LC Card 87-404164 DDC 382/.09469/04 19
1. Portugal - Commerce - Europe - History. 2. Europe - Commerce - Portugal - History. 3. Portugal - Civilization. I. Cabral, Martim. II. Anglo-Portuguese Foundation. III. Title: 1386-1986--Portugal, business partners in Europe.
HF3698.E8 P67 1987

Portugal--desafios e soluções .
(4) A Reforma do mercado de capitais. [Lisbon] [1985] 143 p. : LC Card 87-127037 DDC 332.63 19
HG4523 .R44 1985

(5) A Televisão em Portugal. [Lisbon] [1985] 95 p. : LC Card 87-102704 DDC 384.55/4/09469 19
HE8700.9.P8 T45 1985

Portuguese agriculture in transition / Scott R. Pearson ... [et al.]. Ithaca : Cornell University Press, 1987. 283 p. : ill., 2 maps ; 24 cm. Includes bibliographies and index. ISBN 0-8014-1954-9 (alk. paper) LC Card 86-29198 DDC 338.1/09469 19
1. Agriculture - Economic aspects - Portugal. 2. Agriculture and state - Portugal. 3. Agriculture - Portugal. I. Pearson, Scott R.
HD2027 .P67 1987

Portuguese West Africa. see **Angola.**

Os portuguêses nos rios de Guiné, 1500-1900 /. Carreira, António. Lisboa , 1984. 205 p. : LC Card 85-149851
HF3698.A358 C37 1984

POSADAS (ARGENTINA) - POPULATION.
Baranger, Dionisio. Migración y marginalidad en Posadas . Posadas , 1982. 53 p. : LC Card 86-205276 DDC 304.8/0982/23 19
HB2020.P67 B37 1982

Pöschl, Josef. Die Preisbildung in der industrialisierten Marktwirtschaft : Studien anhand der Theorie Michal Kaleckis / Josef Pöschl. Hamburg : Verlag Dr. Kovač, c1987. v, 149 p. : ill. ; 21 cm. Summary in English and German. Bibliography: p. 147-149. ISBN 3-925630-12-0 LC Card 87-146592 DDC 338.5/2 19
1. Prices. 2. Distribution (Economic theory). 3. Kalecki, Michał. I. Title.
HB221 .P65 1987

Posibilidades de intercambio compensado entre Argentina y Chile y exportaciones graníferas al area del Pacífico, ambos por el paso de San Francisco /. Argerich, Federico Raúl. Córdoba , 1985. 35 p. ; LC Card 87-402749 DDC 382/.0983/082 19
HF3418.A7 A8 1985

Posibilidades y limitaciones del funcionamiento de los mercados en los países menos desarrollados . Naím, Moisés. Caracas , c1985. 88 p. : ISBN 980-217-006-2 LC Card 86-193990
HB501 .N255 1985

Posição : a grandeza da empresa catarinense. [Florianópolis] : Secretaria da Indústria e do Comércio, 1982. 135 p. ; 21 cm. Cover title. LC Card 86-200246
1. Santa Catarina, Brazil (State) - Industries. 2. Santa Catarina (Brazil : State) - Economic conditions. I. Santa Catarina (Brazil : State). Secretaria da Indústria e do Comércio.
HC188.S26 P67 1982

Posición de los países en desarrollo frente a la crisis económica mundial /. García Bocanegra, Angela Victoria. Bogotá, D.E. , 1984. 146 p. ; LC Card 85-205412
HF1413 .G312 1984

Posicionamento das finanças de Alagoas na atual crise /. Alagoas (Brazil). Secretaria da Fazenda. [Maceió] , 1983. 97 p. : LC Card 86-201070
HJ929.A52 A42 1983

Position and policy statement on enhancing the Alberta capital market. Alberta. [Edmonton, Alta.] [1985] iii, 43 p. ; LC Card 86-137218 DDC 332.63/23 19
HG5150 .A42 1985

Position paper (Development Bank of Southern Africa) .
(no. 1) La Grange, A. B. DBSA in the southern African development framework /. Sandton, Republic of South Africa [1985] 36 p. : LC Card 87-150256 DDC 332.2 19
HC900 .L3 1985

(no. 2) Coetzee, S. F. Regional economic development in the Southern African development area /. Sandton, Republic of South Africa , 1985. xvi, 105 p. : LC Card 87-150264 DDC 338.968 19
HC905 .C64 1985

(no. 4) An Introduction to economic development in Southern Africa and the role of DBSA /. Sandton, Republic of South Africa [1985] 78 p. ; LC Card 87-127414 DDC 338.968 19
HG3401.A8 D485 1985

Posluns, Ronald J. Negotiate your way to financial success / Ronald J. Posluns. New York : Putnam, c1987. 176 p. ; 24 cm. ISBN 0-399-13239-2 LC Card 87-2408 DDC 658.1/5 19
1. Negotiation in business. I. Title.
HD58.6 .P67 1987

Posner, Barry Z.
Kouzes, James M., 1945- The leadership challenge . San Francisco , 1987. xxx, 362 p. : ISBN 1-555-42061-3 (alk. paper) LC Card 87-45428 DDC 658.4/092 19
HD57.7 .K68 1987

Randolph, W. Alan. Effective project planning and management . Englewood Cliffs, N.J. [1987], c1988. x, 163 p. : ISBN 0-13-244815-7 LC Card 87-11399 DDC 658.4/04 19
HD69.P75 R36 1988

Pospelov, E. M. (Evgeniĭ Mikhaĭlovich)
Geograficheskie problemy razvitii͡a narodnogo khozi͡aĭstva Moskovskogo regiona /. Moskva , 1986. 104 p. : LC Card 87-135959
HC338.M6 G46 1986

Pospelov, Germogen Sergeevich. Prot͡sedury i algoritmy formirovanii͡a kompleksnykh programm / G.S. Pospelov, V.A. Irikov, A.E. Kurilov ; pod redaktsieĭ G.S. Pospelova. Moskva : "Nauka," Glav. red. fiziko-matematicheskoĭ lit-ry, 1985. 422, [2] p. : ill. ; 23 cm. (Ėkonomiko-matematicheskai͡a biblioteka) Includes bibliographical references. Bibliography: p. 413-[423] LC Card 86-203758
1. Soviet Union - Economic policy - 1981- - Mathematical models. 2. Energy policy - Soviet Union - Mathematical models. I. Irikov, V. A. (Valeriĭ Alekseevich). II. Kurilov, A. E. (Alekseĭ Evgrafovich). III. Title. IV. Series.
HC336.25 .P567 1985

Possas, Cristina de Albuquerque. Saúde e trabalho : a crise da previdência social / Cristina de Albuquerque Possas. Rio de Janeiro, RJ : Graal, 1981. xxxix, 324 p. : ill. ; 21 cm. (Biblioteca de saúde e sociedade . vol. no. 8) Bibliography: p. 313-322. LC Card 82-132979 DDC 362.1/0981 19
1. Social medicine - Brazil. 2. Industrial hygiene - Brazil. 3. Public welfare - Brazil. 4. Public health - Brazil. I. Title.
RA418.3.B6 P68 1981 ***NYPL [JLD 86-1896]***

Posse, Achim Ulrich, 1960- Föderative Politikverflechtung in der Umweltpolitik / Achim Ulrich Posse. München : Minerva Publikation, c1986. xiv, 181 p. : ill. ; 21 cm. (Innenpolitik in Theorie und Praxis . 16) Originally presented as the author's Diplomarbeit--Universität Konstanz, 1985. Bibliography: p. 166-176. ISBN 3-597-10526-2 LC Card 86-222201
1. Environmental policy - Germany, West. 2. Federal government - Germany, West. I. Title. II. Series.
HC290.5.E5 P67 1986

Posselt, Siegfried G. Budgetkontrolle als Instrument zur Unternehmungssteuerung / Siegfried G. Posselt. Darmstadt : Toeche-Mittler, c1986. 272 p. : ill. ; 23 cm. (Controlling-Praxis . CP 12) Bibliography: p. [225]-251. Includes index. ISBN 3-87820-068-4 LC Card 87-113335 DDC 658.1/54 19
1. Budget in business. 2. Industrial management. I. Title. II. Series.
HG4028.B8 P67 1986

The possibility of politics . Ringen, Stein. Oxford [Oxfordshire] : Oxford [Oxfordshire] ; x, 303 p. ; ISBN 0-19-828574-4 :$42.00 (U. S.) LC Card 86-28472 DDC 361.6/5 19
HB846.8 .R56 1987

POST-CARDS. see **POSTAL CARDS.**

Post, James E. Frederick, William Crittenden, 1925- Business and society . New York , c1988. xxvii, 626 p. : ISBN 0-07-015561-5 : LC Card 87-21436 DDC 658.4/08 19
HD60 .F72 1988

Post Keynesian economic theory : a challenge to neo classical economics / edited by Philip Arestis, Thanos Skouras. Sussex : Wheatsheaf Books ; Armonk, N.Y. : M.E. Sharpe, 1985. xii, 235 p. ; 23 cm. Includes index. Bibliography: p. 213-229. ISBN 0-87332-318-1 LC Card 84-23615 DDC 330/.09/04 19
1. Economics - History - 20th century - Addresses, essays, lectures. 2. Keynesian economics - Addresses, essays, lectures. 3. Neoclassical school of economics - Addresses, essays, lectures. I. Arestis, Philip, 1941-. II. Skouras, Thanos, 1943-.
HB87 .P62 1985 ***NYPL [JLD 87-1155]***

Post Keynesian monetary economics /. Rousseas, Stephen William. Armonk, N.Y. , c1986. x, 126 p.; ISBN 0-87332-355-6 LC Card 85-14181 DDC 332.4/6 19
HG230.3 .R68 1986 ***NYPL [JLE 86-4326]***

Post offices in the United States, 1876 / [reprinted by Don Simmons]. Melber, Ky. : Simmons Historical Publications, [1986] 125 p. ; 28 cm. Caption title: List of post offices in the United States, March 1, 1876. LC Card 87-400310 DDC 383/.42/0973 19
1. Postal service - United States - States - Registers. I. Simmons, Don, 1934-. II. Title: List of post offices in the United States, March 1, 1876.
HE6366 .P67 1986

POSTAGE-STAMP DESIGN - HISTORY - 19TH CENTURY.
Mueses, Danilo A. Seebeck . [S.l.] , República Dominicana [1986?] 170, [5] p. : LC Card 86-177691
HE6185.L29 M84 1986

POSTAGE-STAMP PRINTING - HISTORY - 19TH CENTURY.
Mueses, Danilo A. Seebeck . [S.l.] , República Dominicana [1986?] 170, [5] p. : LC Card 86-177691
HE6185.L29 M84 1986

POSTAGE-STAMPS - ASIA - HISTORY.
Vladinets, N. I. (Nikolaĭ Ivanovich) Filatelisticheskai͡a geografii͡a . Moskva , 1984. 175 p. : LC Card 85-153635
HE6185.A7 V53 1984

POSTAGE-STAMPS - BULGARIA - CATALOGS.
Georgiev, Petŭr Borisov. Katalog na bŭlgarskite poshtenski marki 1979-1984 /. Sofii͡a , 1985. 119 p. : LC Card 86-112123
HE6185.B82 G47 1985

POSTAGE STAMPS - COLLECTORS AND COLLECTING.
Buchan, Bryan, 1945- Discovering stamps /. Richmond Hill, Ont. , New York [1977], c1973. 91 p. : LC Card 85-148831
HE6213 .B83 1977

Tripcovici, Nicolae. Filatelia . București , 1985. 213 p., [16] p. of plates : LC Card 87-164874
HE6213 .T75 1985

POSTAGE-STAMPS - COLLECTORS AND COLLECTING - CHINA.
Yang, Jan-Syau. English-Chinese philatelic dictionary and identification key =. Winter Park, Fla. (340 Park Ave., N., Winter Park 32789) , c1986. [55] p. : LC Card 87-169624 DDC 769.56/014 19
HE6204.C6 Y36 1986

POSTAGE-STAMPS - COLLECTORS AND COLLECTING - FRANCE - PERIODICALS - BIBLIOGRAPHY.
Rabier, Pascal. Regard sur la presse philatélique française . [Paris] , 1986. 2 v. (586 p.) : ISBN 2-9501543-0-1 (set) LC Card 87-166808
HE6185.F8 R32 1986

POSTAGE-STAMPS - COLLECTORS AND COLLECTING - HISTORY.
Brühl, Carlrichard, 1925- Geschichte der Philatelie /. Hildesheim , New York , 1985-1986. 2 v. : ISBN 3-487-07619-5 (v. 1) LC Card 86-118167 DDC 769.569 19
HE6203 .B78 1985 ***NYPL [JFM 86-350]***

Haefeli-Meylan, Traugott. Die Entstehung der Briefmarke und ihre weltweite Verbreitung /. Lausanne , c1985. 167 p. : LC Card 86-202635
HE6203 .H25 1985

POSTAGE-STAMPS - COLLECTORS AND COLLECTING - JUVENILE LITERATURE.
Vigilev, A. N. (Aleksandr Nikolaevich) Imi͡a tvoe--kollektsioner /. Moskva , 1981. 93 p. : LC Card 82-103288
HE6213 .V54 1981

POSTAGE-STAMPS - COLLECTORS AND COLLECTING - MISCELLANEA.
Levitas, I. I͡A. (Iosif I͡Akovlevich) I ser′ëzno, i kur′ëzno . Moskva , 1985. 232 p. : LC Card 85-184912
HE6182 .L48 1985

POSTAGE STAMPS, COMMEMORATIVE. see **COMMEMORATIVE POSTAGE STAMPS.**

POSTAGE-STAMPS - CONFEDERATE STATES OF AMERICA - CATALOGS.
Skinner, Hubert C. The new Dietz Confederate States catalog and handbook /. Miami, Fla. (1007 Kane Concourse, Bay Harbor Islands 33154) , 1986. viii, 270 p. : LC Card 86-206685 DDC 769.56975/075/0973 19
HE6500 .S58 1986

POSTAGE-STAMPS - CUBA - CATALOGS.
Pochtovye marki . Moskva , 1984. 223 p. : LC Card 85-185295
HE6185.C92 P63 1984

POSTAGE-STAMPS - CZECHOSLOVAKIA - CATALOGS.
Pochtovye marki . Moskva , 1984. 223 p. : LC Card 85-185295
HE6185.C92 P63 1984

POSTAGE-STAMPS - DEALERS - HISTORY.
Brühl, Carlrichard, 1925- Geschichte der Philatelie /. Hildesheim , New York , 1985-1986. 2 v. : ISBN 3-487-07619-5 (v. 1) LC Card 86-118167 DDC 769.569 19
HE6203 .B78 1985 ***NYPL [JFM 86-350]***

POSTAGE-STAMPS - ENGLAND - LONDON - HISTORY.
London's postal history /. [London] , c1978. 16 p. : LC Card 84-172225
HE6946.L6 L65 1978

POSTAGE-STAMPS - ETHIOPIA - HISTORY.
Payne, Eric. Ethiopia /. Hampstead Norreys, Newbury, Berkshire, England , 1981-1982. 8 v. in 1 : LC Card 87-166672
HE6185.E8 P39 1981

POSTAGE-STAMPS - EUROPE - HISTORY.
Vladinets, N. I. (Nikolaĭ Ivanovich) Filatelisticheskai͡a geografii͡a . Moskva , 1981. 159 p. : LC Card 82-110957
HE6185.E84 V54 1981

POSTAGE-STAMPS - FINLAND - CATALOGS.
Grosfils-Berger, P. Finlande . Southfield, MI (15565 Northland Dr., Suite 605 W, Southfield 48075-5308) , 1947, i.e. [1986?] 320 p. : LC Card 86-206197 DDC 769.5694897 19
HE6185.F52 G76 1986

POSTAGE-STAMPS - FINLAND - HISTORY - 19TH CENTURY.
Grosfils-Berger, P. Finlande . Southfield, MI (15565 Northland Dr., Suite 605 W, Southfield 48075-5308) , 1947, i.e. [1986?] 320 p. : LC Card 86-206197 DDC 769.5694897 19
HE6185.F52 G76 1986

POSTAGE-STAMPS - FRANCE - COLLECTORS AND COLLECTING - FRANCE - PERIODICALS - BIBLIOGRAPHY.
Rabier, Pascal. Regard sur la presse philatélique française . [Paris] , 1986. 2 v. (586 p.) : ISBN 2-9501543-0-1 (set) LC Card 87-166808
HE6185.F8 R32 1986

POSTAGE-STAMPS - FRANCE - COLONIES - CATALOGS.
Catalogue des timbres-poste de la France et des colonies françaises. Southfield, MI (15565 Northland Dr., Suite 605 West, Southfield 48075-5308) , <[1985]-. v. <2 > : LC Card 86-210422
HE6185.F82 C37 1985

POSTAGE-STAMPS - FRANCE - TERRITORIES AND POSSESSIONS - CATALOGS.
Catalogue des timbres-poste de la France et des colonies françaises. Southfield, MI (15565 Northland Dr., Suite 605 West, Southfield 48075-5308) , <[1985]-. v. <2 > : LC Card 86-210422
HE6185.F82 C37 1985

POSTAGE-STAMPS - GEORGIAN S.S.R. - CATALOGS.
Barefoot, John. Georgia /. York, England , c1983. 66 p. : ISBN 0-906845-19-X (pbk.) LC Card 87-100272 DDC 769.5694795 19
HE6185.S653 G463 1983

POSTAGE-STAMPS - GERMANY - CATALOGS.
Michel Privatpostkarten-Katalog Deutschland (Ganzsachen auf Privatbestellung) . München , c1984. 368 p. : ISBN 3-87858-418-0 LC Card 86-167804
HE6185.G62 M48 1984

POSTAGE-STAMPS - GREECE - CRETE - HISTORY.
Marinakēs, Markos, 1945- Tachydromikē historia Krētikēs Politeias, 1900-1913 /. Athēna , 1983. 127 p. : LC Card 85-151773
HE7180.5.Z7 C746 1983
NYPL [JFD 86-10347]

POSTAGE-STAMPS - HISTORY - MISCELLANEA.
Levitas, I. I͡A. (Iosif I͡Akovlevich) I ser′ëzno, i kur′ëzno . Moskva , 1985. 232 p. : LC Card 85-184912
HE6182 .L48 1985

Postage stamps honoring animals [slide] / Educational Images Ltd. ; author/photographer, Derrick Ditchburn. Elmira, NY : Educational Images, 1984. 20 slides : col. + 1 script. Title from data sheet. General. Presents postage stamps from Canada, the United States, New Guinea, Great Britain, and New Zealand, featuring rare and spectacular birds, mammals, and reptiles. LC Card 83-720055 DDC 769.56 11
1. Postage-stamps - Topics - Animals. I. Ditchburn, Derrick. II. Educational Images (Firm).
HE6183.A5

POSTAGE-STAMPS - HUNGARY - HISTORY - 19TH CENTURY.
A Magyar bélyegek kézikönyve /. Budapest , 1986. 551 p., viii p. of plates : ISBN 963-281-692-7 : LC Card 87-151573 DDC 769.569439 19
HE6185.H8 M32 1986

POSTAGE-STAMPS - HUNGARY - HISTORY - 20TH CENTURY.
A Magyar bélyegek kézikönyve /. Budapest , 1986. 551 p., viii p. of plates : ISBN 963-281-692-7 : LC Card 87-151573 DDC 769.569439 19
HE6185.H8 M32 1986

POSTAGE-STAMPS - INDIA.
Jain, Manik, 1938- The silver key to the golden treasure of Indian philately /. Calcutta , 1986. xvi, 326, [1] p. : LC Card 86-903670 DDC 769.56954 19
HE6185.I5 J35 1986

POSTAGE-STAMPS - INDIA - HISTORY.
Jain, Manik, 1938- The silver key to the golden treasure of Indian philately /. Calcutta , 1986. xvi, 326, [1] p. : LC Card 86-903670 DDC 769.56954 19
HE6185.I5 J35 1986

POSTAGE-STAMPS - INDIA - JAMMU AND KASHMIR - HISTORY - 19TH CENTURY.
Staal, Frits. The stamps of Jammu & Kashmir /. New York , 1983. xvii, 286 p., 16 p. of plates : ISBN 0-912574-37-X LC Card 87-402877 DDC 769.56954/6 19
HE6185.I53 J357 1983

POSTAGE-STAMPS - LATIN AMERICA - HISTORY - 19TH CENTURY.
Mueses, Danilo A. Seebeck . [S.l.] , República Dominicana [1986?] 170, [5] p. : LC Card 86-177691
HE6185.L29 M84 1986

POSTAGE STAMPS - LIBERIA - HISTORY.
Cockrill, Philip. Liberia /. Newbury, Berkshire, England [198-?] 15 v. in 2 : LC Card 86-217641
HE6185.L49 C63 1980z

POSTAGE-STAMPS, LOCAL - GERMANY - CATALOGS.
Michel Privatpostkarten-Katalog Deutschland (Ganzsachen auf Privatbestellung) . München , c1984. 368 p. : ISBN 3-87858-418-0 LC Card 86-167804
HE6185.G62 M48 1984

POSTAGE-STAMPS - NORWAY - TOPICS - KINGS AND RULERS.
Tuffs, V. Norway number one . York, England , c1983. 52 p. : ISBN 0-906845-26-2 (pbk.) LC Card 87-100273 DDC 769.569481 19
HE6183.K56 T83 1983

POSTAGE-STAMPS - NORWAY - TOPICS - REGALIA (INSIGNIA)
Tuffs, V. Norway number one . York, England , c1983. 52 p. : ISBN 0-906845-26-2 (pbk.) LC Card 87-100273 DDC 769.569481 19
HE6183.K56 T83 1983

POSTAGE-STAMPS - PALESTINE - CATALOGS.
Filasṭīn fī ṭawābiʻ al-barīd (1865-1981). English. Palestine stamps (1865-1981) [Abdel-Wahab Elmessiri, Jean O'Hanlon, translation]. Beirut , Cairo , 1981. [80] p. : LC Card 84-960260
HE6185.P14 F5513 1981

POSTAGE-STAMPS - PALESTINE - HISTORY - 20TH CENTURY.
Collins, Norman J. Palestine Mandate issues, 1921-1948 . [New York] , c1987. 52 p. : LC Card 87-400470 DDC 383/.495694 19
HE7186 .C65 1987

POSTAGE-STAMPS - PHILIPPINES - CATALOGS.
Harradine, Peter W. A. Philippine postage stamp handbook, 1854-1982 /. Jefferson, N.C. , c1987. xv, 387 p., [71] p. of plates : ISBN 0-89950-178-8 LC Card 84-43212 DDC 769.569599 19
HE6185.P52 H373 1987

POSTAGE-STAMPS - POLAND - CATALOGS.
Katalog specjalizowany znaków pocztowych ziem polskich 1985 /. Warszawa , 1984-1985. 4 v. : ISBN 83-03-00691-6 (cz. 1-2) : LC Card 87-120964
HE6185.P62 K28 1984

POSTAGE-STAMPS - SOVIET UNION - CATALOGS.
Arakelov, S. N. (Suren Nersesovich) Armenii͡a v filatelii /. Erevan , 1980. 175 p., [24] p. of plates : LC Card 82-105026
HE6183.A69 A72 1980

Podvig na pochtovoĭ marke . Moskva , 1985. 135 p. : LC Card 86-113767
HE6183.G47 P63 1985

POSTAGE STAMPS - SWITZERLAND - CATALOGS.
Zumstein, Ernst. Handbook of the postage stamps of Switzerland from the German of Ernst Zumstein. [Germany , Southfield, MI [1986?] 61 p., 4 p. of plates : LC Card 86-202597 DDC 769.569494 19
HE6185.S92 Z78 1986

POSTAGE-STAMPS - SWITZERLAND - HISTORY - 19TH CENTURY.
Zumstein, Ernst. Handbook of the postage stamps of Switzerland from the German of Ernst Zumstein. [Germany , Southfield, MI [1986?] 61 p., 4 p. of plates : LC Card 86-202597 DDC 769.569494 19
HE6185.S92 Z78 1986

POSTAGE-STAMPS - TERRES AUSTRALES ET ANTARCTIQUES FRANÇAISES - CATALOGS.
Terres australes et antarctiques françaises . [France] , 1982. 216 p. : LC Card 82-171424
HE6185.F83 T477 1982

POSTAGE-STAMPS - TOPICS - HITLER, ADOLF, 1889-1945 - HISTORY.
Thomas, Earl. A history of Adolf Hitler and the Third Reich in postage stamps and postal stationery /. Silver Spring, Md. , c1987. p. cm. ISBN 0-918184-06-1 LC Card 87-755 DDC 769.56/3 19
HE6183.H53 T46 1987

POSTAGE-STAMPS - TOPICS - ANIMALS.
Postage stamps honoring animals [slide] /. Elmira, NY , 1984. 20 slides : LC Card 83-720055 DDC 769.56 11
HE6183.A5

POSTAGE-STAMPS - TOPICS - ARMED FORCES.
Maier, Lotte. Militärmarken /. Dortmund , 1981. 158 p. : ISBN 3-88379-253-5 (kart.) : LC Card 81-180793
HE6184.S42 M35 1981

POSTAGE-STAMPS - TOPICS - ARMENIA - CATALOGS.
Arakelov, S. N. (Suren Nersesovich) Armeniia v filatelii /. Erevan , 1980. 175 p., [24] p. of plates : LC Card 82-105026
HE6183.A69 A72 1980

POSTAGE-STAMPS - TOPICS - BIRDS.
Ridgely, Beverly S. Supplement to Birds of the world in philately /. Johnstown, PA , c1986. 62 p., [3] p. of plates : ISBN 0-935991-00-X (pbk.): LC Card 86-217462 DDC 769.56/4/075 769.56/432 19
HE6187 .A635 no. 106-1 HE6183.B53

POSTAGE-STAMPS - TOPICS - BOY SCOUTS.
Kaplan, Howard J. Scouts on stamps of the world /. [Hicksville, N.Y.] , c1986. 1 v. (loose-leaf) : LC Card 86-224816 DDC 769.56/3 19
HE6183.B63 K36 1986

POSTAGE-STAMPS - TOPICS - CHESS - CATALOGS.
Voĭshko, V. B. (Vladimir Boleslavovich) Shakhmatnaia filateliia . Moskva , 1984. 192 p. : LC Card 84-174397
HE6183.C415 V65 1984

POSTAGE-STAMPS - TOPICS - CHRISTIANITY - CATALOGS.
Schönen, Hans G. Christliche Motive auf Briefmarken . Rommerskirchen-Oekoven , 1984, c1983. xv, 830 p. ; ISBN 3-9800824-0-7 : LC Card 84-208011
HE6183.C47 S36 1984

POSTAGE-STAMPS - TOPICS - COMMEMORATIVES. see **COMMEMORATIVE POSTAGE STAMPS.**

POSTAGE-STAMPS - TOPICS - GEROĬ SOVETSKOGO SOIUZA - CATALOGS.
Podvig na pochtovoĭ marke . Moskva , 1985. 135 p. : LC Card 86-113767
HE6183.G47 P63 1985

POSTAGE-STAMPS - TOPICS - GIRL SCOUTS.
Kaplan, Howard J. Scouts on stamps of the world /. [Hicksville, N.Y.] , c1986. 1 v. (loose-leaf) : LC Card 86-224816 DDC 769.56/3 19
HE6183.B63 K36 1986

POSTAGE-STAMPS - TOPICS - GLIDING AND SOARING.
Short, Simine, 1944- Glider mail . Cinnaminson, NJ , 1987. 261 p. : ISBN 0-939429-00-4 : LC Card 86-72751 DDC 383/.144 19
HE6239.G54 S56 1987

POSTAGE-STAMPS - TOPICS - GRAF ZEPPELIN (AIRSHIP) - CATALOGS.
Sieger. Zeppelinpost Spezial-Katalog /. Lorch/Württemberg , c1981. 384 p. : LC Card 83-214233
HE6183.G735 S54 1981

POSTAGE-STAMPS - TOPICS - OUTER SPACE.
Hubl, Peter. Interplanetare Raumsonden /. Lorch/Württemberg [1983?] 98 p. : LC Card 83-218116
HE6183.O95 H83 1983

POSTAGE-STAMPS - TOPICS - PUSHKIN, ALEKSANDR SERGEEVICH, 1799-1837.
Gdalin, A. D. (Aleksandr Davidovich) Filatelisticheskaia Pushkiniana /. Moskva , 1981. 124 p. : LC Card 86-174858
HE6183.P86 G43 1981

POSTAGE-STAMPS - TOPICS - ROCKET MAIL.
Kronstein, Max. Rocket mail flights of the world to 1986 /. Cinnaminson, N.J. , 1986. 191 p. : LC Card 87-400297 DDC 383/.144 19
HE6239.R6 K76 1986

POSTAGE-STAMPS - TOPICS - SCIENCE.
Science/earth science on stamps and banknotes [slide] /. Lincoln, Neb. , 1984. 30 slides : LC Card 85-702119 DDC 551 11
HE6183.S36

POSTAGE-STAMPS - TOPICS - SOVIET UNION.
Sovetskiĭ Soiuz na inostrannykh markakh /] Moskva , 1979. 286 p. : LC Card 81-136372
HE6183.S56 S68 1979

POSTAGE-STAMPS - TOPICS - SPACE FLIGHT.
Hubl, Peter. Interplanetare Raumsonden /. Lorch/Württemberg [1983?] 98 p. : LC Card 83-218116
HE6183.O95 H83 1983

POSTAGE-STAMPS - TOPICS - VOLLEYBALL.
Gilardi, Mauro. Volley e bolli . Milano , c1985. 107 p. : LC Card 86-128270
HE6183.V64 G55 1985

POSTAGE-STAMPS - TOPICS - WISCONSIN.
Wisconsin on stamps. [Wisconsin?] , c1986 (Green Bay, Wis. : insty-prints) i, 53 leaves : LC Card 86-206933 DDC 769.56/49775 19
HE6185.U7 W578 1986

POSTAGE-STAMPS - TOPICS - WORLD WAR, 1939-1945 - CATALOGS.
Podvig na pochtovoĭ marke . Moskva , 1985. 135 p. : LC Card 86-113767
HE6183.G47 P63 1985

POSTAGE-STAMPS - UNITED STATES - COLLECTORS AND COLLECTING - WISCONSIN.
Wisconsin on stamps. [Wisconsin?] , c1986 (Green Bay, Wis. : insty-prints) i, 53 leaves : LC Card 86-206933 DDC 769.56/49775 19
HE6185.U7 W578 1986

POSTAGE-STAMPS - UNITED STATES - FLAWS.
Datz, Stephen R. Errors . Loveland, Colo. (P.O. Box 402, Loveland 80537) , 1986. vi, 100 p. : LC Card 87-128178 DDC 769.56973 19
HE6184.E7 D38 1986

Postai szakkifejezések ötnyelvű szótára : (francia, német, angol, orosz, magyar) / [készitette, Almásy György]. Budapest : Közlekedési Dokumentációs Vállalat, 1978. 349 p. ; 15 x 21 cm. (Közlekedés- és Postaügyi Minisztérium Postafőosztályának kiadványa) "Az Egyetemes Postaegyesület ... 1972. évben Bernben kiadott hétnyelvű postai szakkifejezés-szótára alapján"--T.p verso. LC Card 84-248004
1. Postal service - Dictionaries - Polyglot. 2. Dictionaries, Polyglot. I. Almásy, György. II. Series.
HE6035 .P67 1978

POSTAL CARDS - PENNSYLVANIA - HISTORY.
Berner, Allan H. Pennsylvania's street railways in early postcard views . [S.l.] , c1986. 106 p. : LC Card 86-221349 DDC 388.4/4/09748 19
HE4487.P4 B47 1986

Postal history journal. Migliavacca, Giorgio. The postal history of Lombardy under Austrian rule, 1707-1796 . [S.l.] , 1985. [40] p. : ISBN 0-934139-03-2 (pbk.) LC Card 87-149625 DDC 383/.49452 19
HE7016.L66 M54 1985

The postal history of Coles County, Illinois . Redlich, Paul R. Des Plaines, Ill. (P.O. Box 1513, Des Plaines 60018) , c1986. v, 175 p. : LC Card 87-400110 DDC 383/.4977372 19
HE6376.A1 I58 1986

Postal History of Cretan Administration, 1900-1913. Marinakēs, Markos, 1945- Tachydromikē historia Krētikēs Politeias, 1900-1913 /. Athēna , 1983. 127 p. : LC Card 85-151773
HE7180.5.Z7 C746 1983 ***NYPL [JFD 86-10347]***

The postal history of Lombardy under Austrian rule, 1707-1796 . Migliavacca, Giorgio. [S.l.] , 1985. [40] p. : ISBN 0-934139-03-2 (pbk.) LC Card 87-149625 DDC 383/.49452 19
HE7016.L66 M54 1985

The postal history of the Australian Imperial Forces during World War One, 1914-1918 /. Emery, R. C. Worthing, West Sussex, England [1984] viii, 343 p. : LC Card 85-123155 DDC 355.3/41 19
HE7395 .E47 1984 ***NYPL [JLF 86-1054]***

POSTAL LIFE INSURANCE. see **INSURANCE, LIFE.**

Postal rate history of China and Hong Kong . Scamp, Lee C. Houston, Tex., U. S.A. , c1986. xx, 284 p. : LC Card 87-145274 DDC 383/.23/0951 19
HE7305.Z8 S33 1986

POSTAL SERVICE - AFRICA.
United Nations transport and communications decade in Africa (1978-1988) . [S.l.] [1983?] iii, 32 p. ; LC Card 87-115721 DDC 380.3/096 19
HE8465 .U55 1983

POSTAL SERVICE - AUSTRALIA - HISTORY.
Maddock, John, 1917- Mail for the back of beyond /. Kenthurst , 1986. 160 p. : ISBN 0-86417-063-7 LC Card 86-207558 DDC 383/.143/0994 19
HE5709.A6 M33 1986

POSTAL SERVICE - AUSTRALIA - HISTORY - 20TH CENTURY.
Emery, R. C. The postal history of the Australian Imperial Forces during World War One, 1914-1918 /. Worthing, West Sussex, England [1984] viii, 343 p. : LC Card 85-123155 DDC 355.3/41 19
HE7395 .E47 1984 ***NYPL [JLF 86-1054]***

POSTAL SERVICE - AUSTRIA - HISTORY - 18TH CENTURY.
Migliavacca, Giorgio. The postal history of Lombardy under Austrian rule, 1707-1796 . [S.l.] , 1985. [40] p. : ISBN 0-934139-03-2 (pbk.) LC Card 87-149625 DDC 383/.49452 19
HE7016.L66 M54 1985

POSTAL SERVICE - AUSTRIA - TYROL - HISTORY.
Bianco, Christian. Postgeschichte Südtirols /. [S.l. , 1981?] 207 p. : LC Card 86-168698
HE7016.T74 B53 1981

POSTAL SERVICE - BOTSWANA - HISTORY.
Putzel, Ralph F. Encyclopaedia of South African post offices and postal agencies (including their forerunners in the Cape, Natal, Orange Free State, and Transvaal, Basutoland, Bechuanaland, and Swaziland, etc.) /. Cape Town , 1986- v. <1 > : ISBN 0-620-09781-7 LC Card 87-143880 DDC 383/.4968 19
HE7351 .P88 1986

POSTAL SERVICE - BRAZIL - EMPLOYEES - BIOGRAPHY.
Penteado, Jacob. Memórias de um postalista /. São Paulo [1963] 199 p., [8] p. of plates : LC Card 85-134575
HE6834.P46 A3 1963

POSTAL SERVICE - BRAZIL - HISTORY.
Penteado, Jacob. Memórias de um postalista /. São Paulo [1963] 199 p., [8] p. of plates : LC Card 85-134575
HE6834.P46 A3 1963

POSTAL SERVICE - CENTRAL AMERICA - HISTORY.
Central America postal history and a listing of prephilatelic postmarks =. New York [Yonkers, N.Y.?] , 1986. xiv, 142 p. : ISBN 0-912574-41-0 (pbk.) LC Card 87-402819 DDC 383/.49728 19
HE6674 .C46 1986

POSTAL SERVICE - CHINA - HISTORY - 19TH CENTURY.
Scamp, Lee C. Postal rate history of China and Hong Kong . Houston, Tex., U. S.A. , c1986. xx, 284 p. : LC Card 87-145274 DDC 383/.23/0951 19
HE7305.Z8 S33 1986

POSTAL SERVICE - CHINA - YUNNAN PROVINCE - HISTORY.
Pasquet, Sylvie. L'évolution du système postal . Paris , c1986. 290 p. : ISBN 2-85757-038-4 LC Card 87-164960
HE7286.Y8 P37 1986

POSTAL SERVICE - CONFEDERATE STATES OF AMERICA - HANDBOOKS, MANUALS, ETC.
Skinner, Hubert C. The new Dietz Confederate States catalog and handbook /. Miami, Fla. (1007 Kane Concourse, Bay Harbor Islands 33154) , 1986. viii, 270 p. : LC Card 86-206685 DDC 769.56975/075/0973 19
HE6500 .S58 1986

POSTAL SERVICE - DICTIONARIES - POLYGLOT.
Postai szakkifejezések ötnyelvű szótára . Budapest , 1978. 349 p. ; LC Card 84-248004
HE6035 .P67 1978

POSTAL SERVICE - EMPLOYEES - SALARIES, ETC. - CONGRESSES.
Matthew, J. Purchasing power of PTT personnel, 1965 /. Brussels [1966] 1 v. (various pagings) ; LC Card 87-165119
HE6241 .M37 1966

POSTAL SERVICE - ENGLAND - LONDON - HISTORY.
London's postal history /. [London] , c1978. 16 p. : LC Card 84-172225
HE6946.L6 L65 1978

POSTAL SERVICE - EQUIPMENT AND SUPPLIES - HISTORY.
Newman, Geoffrey R. (Geoffrey Richard), 1933- The Bickerdike machine papers /. Toronto , c1986. 144 p. : ISBN 0-919801-51-X (pbk.) : LC Card 87-167878 DDC 681/.7676 19
HE6237 .N48 1986

POSTAL SERVICE - ETHIOPIA - HISTORY.
Payne, Eric. Ethiopia /. Hampstead Norreys, Newbury, Berkshire, England , 1981-1982. 8 v. in 1 : LC Card 87-166672
HE6185.E8 P39 1981

POSTAL SERVICE - EUROPE - HISTORY.
Vladinets, N. I. (Nikolaĭ Ivanovich) Filatelisticheskaīa geografīīa . Moskva , 1981. 159 p. : LC Card 82-110957
HE6185.E84 V54 1981

POSTAL SERVICE - FINLAND - BIOGRAPHY - DICTIONARIES.
Ranta, Niilo, 1914- Suomen postimestarit 1809-1984 . Helsinki [1986] 144 p. : LC Card 87-101716
HE7064 .R35 1986

POSTAL SERVICE - FINLAND - HISTORY - 19TH CENTURY.
Ranta, Niilo, 1914- Suomen postimestarit 1809-1984 . Helsinki [1986] 144 p. : LC Card 87-101716
HE7064 .R35 1986

POSTAL SERVICE - FINLAND - POSTMASTERS - BIOGRAPHY - DICTIONARIES.
Ranta, Niilo, 1914- Suomen postimestarit 1809-1984 . Helsinki [1986] 144 p. : LC Card 87-101716
HE7064 .R35 1986

POSTAL SERVICE - FRANCE - COLONIES.
Catalogue des timbres-poste de la France et des colonies françaises. Southfield, MI (15565 Northland Dr., Suite 605 West, Southfield 48075-5308) , <[1985]-. v. <2 > : LC Card 86-210422
HE6185.F82 C37 1985

POSTAL SERVICE - FRANCE - HISTORY.
Charbon, Paul. Le facteur et ses métamorphoses /. Barembach , c1984. 266 p., [24] p. of plates : ISBN 2-902912-40-4 LC Card 85-118656 DDC 383/.4944 19
HE6989.P4 C48 1984 ***NYPL [JLG 86-165]***

POSTAL SERVICE - FRANCE - LETTER CARRIERS - HISTORY.
Charbon, Paul. Le facteur et ses métamorphoses /. Barembach , c1984. 266 p., [24] p. of plates : ISBN 2-902912-40-4 LC Card 85-118656 DDC 383/.4944 19
HE6989.P4 C48 1984 ***NYPL [JLG 86-165]***

POSTAL SERVICE - FRANCE - NORD-PAS-DE-CALAIS - HISTORY - CONGRESSES.
Histoire de la poste et des télécommunications dans la région Nord-Pas-de-Calais . [Lille] , c1983. 156 p. : LC Card 86-115052
HE6986.N67 H57 1983

POSTAL SERVICE - FRANCE - TERRITORIES AND POSSESSIONS.
Catalogue des timbres-poste de la France et des colonies françaises. Southfield, MI (15565 Northland Dr., Suite 605 West, Southfield 48075-5308) , <[1985]-. v. <2 > : LC Card 86-210422
HE6185.F82 C37 1985

POSTAL SERVICE - GERMANY - HISTORY.
Beyrer, Klaus. Die Postkutschenreise /. Tübingen , 1985. 284 p. : ISBN 3-925340-35-1 LC Card 86-198761
HE6995 .B49 1985

POSTAL SERVICE - GERMANY, WEST.
Herrmann, Ernst. Die Deutsche Bundespost . Baden-Baden , 1986. 261 p. ; ISBN 3-7890-1323-4 LC Card 87-116897 DDC 383/.4943 19
HE6995 .H44 1986

POSTAL SERVICE - GERMANY (WEST) - BAVARIA - CATALOGS.
Winkler, Karl. Handbuch der bayerischen Poststempel /. Southfield, MI [198-?] 383 p., [18] p. of plates : LC Card 86-155089
HE6185.G32 B389 1980z

POSTAL SERVICE - GERMANY (WEST) - HEILBRONN - HISTORY.
Sinzinger, Friedrich, 1911- Heilbronner Postgeschichte bis zur Einführung der Briefmarke 1851 /. Heilbronn , c1984. 133 p. : LC Card 87-409273 DDC 383/.494346 19
HE6185.G32 H457 1984

POSTAL SERVICE - GERMANY (WEST) - MANAGEMENT.
Detjen, Günther, 1930- Betriebswirtschaftslehre des Post- und Fernmeldewesens /. Gelsenkirchen-Buer , c1984-c1985. 2 v. : ISBN 3-87333-070-9 (Bd. 1) LC Card 87-104294 DDC 383/.4943 19
HE6995 .D37 1984

POSTAL SERVICE - GERMANY (WEST) - RATES.
Die Gebührenpolitik der Deutschen Bundespost im Kleingut- und Fernmeldebereich . [Mainz] [1984?] xi, 300 p. ; LC Card 87-407592 DDC 383/.23/0943 19
HE6998 .G42 1984

Hammer, Karl-Heinrich. Posttips . Bonn , 1982. 108 p. : LC Card 83-193275
HE6998 .H35 1982

POSTAL SERVICE - GREAT BRITAIN - SECURITY MEASURES - HISTORY.
Dear cats . London , 1986. 128 p. : LC Card 87-126969 DDC 628.9/693 19
HE6939.S42 D42 1986

POSTAL SERVICE - GREECE - CRETE - HISTORY.
Marinakēs, Markos, 1945- Tachydromikē historia Krētikēs Politeias, 1900-1913 /. Athēna , 1983. 127 p. : LC Card 85-151773
HE7180.5.Z7 C746 1983 ***NYPL [JFD 86-10347]***

POSTAL SERVICE - HONG KONG - HISTORY - 19TH CENTURY.
Scamp, Lee C. Postal rate history of China and Hong Kong . Houston, Tex., U. S.A. , c1986. xx, 284 p. : LC Card 87-145274 DDC 383/.23/0951 19
HE7305.Z8 S33 1986

POSTAL SERVICE - HUNGARY - HISTORY.
Kamody, Miklós. Észak-Magyarország hírközlésének története /. Miskolc , 1985. 153 p., [3] leaves of plates : ISBN 963-01-6902-9 : LC Card 87-408020
HE6980.5 .K36 1985

POSTAL SERVICE - HUNGARY - HISTORY - 19TH CENTURY.
Zlatev, István. A magyar postahivatalok, 1867-1871. években használt hely-keletbélyegzései . Budapest , 1983. 255 p. : ISBN 963-01-4848-X LC Card 86-148361
HE6980.5 .Z55 1983

POSTAL SERVICE - ILLINOIS - COLES COUNTY - HISTORY.
Redlich, Paul R. The postal history of Coles County, Illinois . Des Plaines, Ill. (P.O. Box 1513, Des Plaines 60018) , c1986. v, 175 p. : LC Card 87-400110 DDC 383/.4977372 19
HE6376.A1 I58 1986

POSTAL SERVICE - INDIA - JAMMA AND KASHMIR - HISTORY - 19TH CENTURY.
Staal, Frits. The stamps of Jammu & Kashmir /. New York , 1983. xvii, 286 p., 16 p. of plates : ISBN 0-912574-37-X LC Card 87-402877 DDC 769.56954/6 19
HE6185.I53 J357 1983

POSTAL SERVICE - ITALY - LOMBARDY - HISTORY - 18TH CENTURY.
Migliavacca, Giorgio. The postal history of Lombardy under Austrian rule, 1707-1796 . [S.l.] , 1985. [40] p. : ISBN 0-934139-03-2 (pbk.) LC Card 87-149625 DDC 383/.49452 19
HE7016.L66 M54 1985

POSTAL SERVICE - ITALY - TRENTINO-ALTO ADIGE - HISTORY.
Bianco, Christian. Postgeschichte Südtirols /. [S.l. , 1981?] 207 p. : LC Card 86-168698
HE7016.T74 B53 1981

POSTAL SERVICE - JAPAN - HISTORY.
Westney, D. Eleanor. Imitation and innovation . Cambridge, Mass. , 1987. viii, 252 p. : ISBN 0-674-44437-X (alk. paper) LC Card 87-273 DDC 338.6/0952 19
HD70.J3 W47 1987

POSTAL SERVICE - LIBERIA - HISTORY.
Cockrill, Philip. Liberia /. Newbury, Berkshire, England [198-?] 15 v. in 2 : LC Card 86-217641
HE6185.L49 C63 1980z

POSTAL SERVICE - MACAO - HISTORY - 19TH CENTURY.
Scamp, Lee C. Postal rate history of China and Hong Kong . Houston, Tex., U. S.A. , c1986. xx, 284 p. : LC Card 87-145274 DDC 383/.23/0951 19
HE7305.Z8 S33 1986

POSTAL SERVICE - NEW YORK (STATE) - HISTORY.
Manuscript post offices of New York State /. [Richford, N.Y.?] , 1984. xii, 54 p., [12] p. of plates : LC Card 86-213682 DDC 383/.49747 19
HE6376.A1 N729 1984

POSTAL SERVICE - OHIO - CHILLICOTHE - HISTORY.
Grabb, John R., 1915- A history of the Chillicothe and other Ross County, Ohio, post offices, 1799-1987 /. Chillicothe, Ohio (206 Caldwell St., Chillicothe 45601) , c1987. iv, 76 p. : LC Card 87-80919 DDC 383/.4977182 19
HE6376.C45 G73 1987

POSTAL SERVICE - OHIO - ROSS COUNTY - HISTORY.
Grabb, John R., 1915- A history of the Chillicothe and other Ross County, Ohio, post offices, 1799-1987 /. Chillicothe, Ohio (206 Caldwell St., Chillicothe 45601) , c1987. iv, 76 p. : LC Card 87-80919 DDC 383/.4977182 19
HE6376.C45 G73 1987

POSTAL SERVICE - OREGON - HISTORY.
Forster, Dale E. Oregon express companies /. Eugene, Ore. , c1985. vi, 231 p. : LC Card 87-121202 DDC 383/.143/09795 19
HE6376.A1 O735 1985

POSTAL SERVICE - OREGON - UNION COUNTY - HISTORY.
Barklow, Irene. From trails to rails . Enterprise, Or. , c1987. ix, 300 p. : ISBN 0-9618185-2-2 : LC Card 87-15709 DDC 383/.4979571 19
HE6376.A1 O727 1987

POSTAL SERVICE - PALESTINE - HISTORY - 20TH CENTURY.
Collins, Norman J. Palestine Mandate issues, 1921-1948 . [New York] , c1987. 52 p. : LC Card 87-400470 DDC 383/.495694 19
HE7186 .C65 1987

POSTAL SERVICE - RÍO DE LA PLATA REGION (ARGENTINA AND URUGUAY) - HISTORY.
Marcó del Pont, José. El correo marítimo en el Río de la Plata /. Buenos Aires , 1913. 161 p. : LC Card 85-125707
HE6819.M3 M37 1913

POSTAL SERVICE - SOUTH AFRICA - HISTORY.
Putzel, Ralph F. Encyclopaedia of South African post offices and postal agencies (including their forerunners in the Cape, Natal, Orange Free State, and Transvaal, Basutoland, Bechuanaland, and Swaziland, etc.) /. Cape Town , 1986- v. <1 > : ISBN 0-620-09781-7 LC Card 87-143880 DDC 383/.4968 19
HE7351 .P88 1986

POSTAL SERVICE - SPAIN - RATES.
Catálogo de tarifas postales y telegráficas. Madrid [1964?] 256, [42] p. : LC Card 85-106223
HE8277 .C37 1964

POSTAL SERVICE - SWAZILAND - HISTORY.
Putzel, Ralph F. Encyclopaedia of South African post offices and postal agencies (including their forerunners in the Cape, Natal, Orange Free State, and Transvaal, Basutoland, Bechuanaland, and Swaziland, etc.) /. Cape Town , 1986- v. <1 > : ISBN 0-620-09781-7 LC Card 87-143880 DDC 383/.4968 19
HE7351 .P88 1986

POSTAL SERVICE - SWITZERLAND - HISTORY.
75 Jahre Postauto . Bern [1981] 104 p. : LC Card 86-221362 DDC 388.3/22/09494 19
HE5683.A6 A14 1981

POSTAL SERVICE - TEXAS - HISTORY - 19TH CENTURY.
Austerman, Wayne R. (Wayne Randolph), 1948- Sharps rifles and Spanish mules . College Station , c1985. x, 367 p., [8] p. of plates : ISBN 0-89096-220-0 : LC Card 84-40557 DDC 383/.49764 19
HE6376.A1 T417 1985
NYPL [JLE 85-3346]

POSTAL SERVICE - UNITED STATES - AIR MAIL. see **AIR MAIL SERVICE - UNITED STATES.**

POSTAL SERVICE - UNITED STATES - EXAMINATIONS, QUESTIONS, ETC.
Barkus, Philip. How to prepare for the U. S. Postal Service mailhandler/mail processor examination /. New York , c1987. viii, 295 p. : ISBN 0-8120-2995-X (pbk.) : LC Card 87-14435 DDC 383/.1/076 19
HE6499 .B296 1987

POSTAL SERVICE - UNITED STATES - HISTORY - JUVENILE LITERATURE.
Brandt, Betty. Special delivery /. Minneapolis, Minn. , c1988. 40 p. : ISBN 0-87614-312-5 (lib. bdg.) LC Card 87-15647 DDC 383/.4973 19
HE6371 .B77 1988

POSTAL SERVICE - UNITED STATES - STATES - REGISTERS.
Post offices in the United States, 1876 /. Melber, Ky. [1986] 125 p. ; LC Card 87-400310 DDC 383/.42/0973 19
HE6366 .P67 1986

POSTAL SERVICE - WASHINGTON (STATE) - PACIFIC COUNTY - HISTORY.
Ramsey, Guy Reed. Postmarked Washington . Lake Grove, OR (Box 2093, Lake Grove 97035) , c1987. 148 p. : LC Card 86-72305 DDC 383/.4979791 19
HE6376.A1 W265 1987

POSTAL SERVICE - WASHINGTON (STATE) - WAHKIAKUM COUNTY - HISTORY.
Ramsey, Guy Reed. Postmarked Washington . Lake Grove, OR (Box 2093, Lake Grove 97035) , c1987. 148 p. : LC Card 86-72305 DDC 383/.4979791 19
HE6376.A1 W265 1987

POSTAL SERVICE - WISCONSIN - HISTORY - SOURCES.
1902 Wisconsin alphabetical postal scheme. [Madison, Wis.] (5401 Raymond Rd., Madison 53711) [1984] 19 p. : LC Card 86-175627 DDC 383/.49775 19
HE6376.A1 W645 1984

POSTAL STATIONERY - GERMANY - HISTORY - 20TH CENTURY.
Thomas, Earl. A history of Adolf Hitler and the Third Reich in postage stamps and postal stationery /. Silver Spring, Md. , c1987. p. cm. ISBN 0-918184-06-1 LC Card 87-755 DDC 769.56/3 19
HE6183.H53 T46 1987

POSTAL TELEGRAPH. see **TELEGRAPH.**

Postanovlenie Verkhovnogo Soveta SSSR ob utverzhdenii otcheta ob ispolnenii Gosudarstvennogo bi͡udzheta SSSR za 1984 god. Dementsev, V. V. (Viktor Vladimirovich) O Gosudarstvennom bi͡udzhete SSSR na 1986 god i ob ispolnenii Gosudarstvennogo bi͡udzheta SSSR za 1984 god . Moskva , 1985. 28 p. ; LC Card 86-203425
HJ2129 .D46 1985

Post-capitalist industrialization . Luttrell, William L. New York , 1986. xv, 189 p. : ISBN 0-275-92310-X : LC Card 86-9452 DDC 338.9678 19
HD3616.T343 L88 1986
NYPL [JLE 87-351]

Postcard deck media. Lynch, Christine M. (Christine Marie), 1962- The national directory of postcard deck media /. Westbury, N.Y. , c1987. ix, 238 p. ; ISBN 0-87280-156-X (pbk.) LC Card 87-1071 DDC 659.13/3 19
HF5861 .L96 1987

POSTCARDS - FRANCE - HISTORY - 19TH CENTURY.
Cabaud, Michel. 1900, la Française au quotidien /. Paris , c1985. 204 p. : ISBN 2-200-37097-0 LC Card 86-137649
HD6059.F8 C33 1985

POSTCARDS - FRANCE - HISTORY - 19TH CENTURY - PICTORIAL WORKS.
Cabaud, Michel. 1900, la Française au quotidien /. Paris , c1985. 204 p. : ISBN 2-200-37097-0 LC Card 86-137649
HD6059.F8 C33 1985

Poste Des Cantons, lignes Nicolet-Des Cantons et Des Cantons-Nouvelle-Angleterre / Bureau d'audiences publiques sur l'environnement. [Sainte-Foy, Qc] : Le Bureau, [1983] 1 v. (various pagings) ; 29 cm. (Rapport d'enquête et d'audience publique . 14) ISBN 2-550-10466-8 LC Card 85-121505
1. Electric utilities - Environmental aspects - Québec (Province). 2. Hydro-Québec. I. Québec (Province). Bureau d'audiences publiques sur l'environnement. II. Series.
HD9685.C3 Q455 1983

Postel, Rainer. Stadt und Hafen . Hamburg , 1986. 209 p. : ISBN 3-7672-0951-9 LC Card 87-130912 DDC 387.1/0943/515 19
HE558.H3 S7 1986

POSTEMPLOYMENT BENEFITS - ACCOUNTING.
Public record . Stamford, Conn. (P.O. Box 3821, Stamford 06905-0821) [1986] 424 p. ; LC Card 86-81700 DDC 657/.75 19
HF5686.O5 P83 1986

POSTEMPLOYMENT BENEFITS - UNITED STATES - ACCOUNTING.
Measuring and funding corporate liabilities for retiree health benefits. Washington, D.C. , c1987. xxxviii, 226 p. : ISBN 0-86643-054-7 (pbk.) LC Card 87-24534 DDC 657/.75 19
HG9396 .M4 1987

POSTERS, AMERICAN - CATALOGS.
Strauss, Bob. American sporting advertising /. Jefferson, Me. (Box 1060, Jefferson 04348) , 1987- v. <1 > : LC Card 87-155421 DDC 741.67/0973/074013 19
HF6161.S65 S77 1987

Les postes de traite de fourrure sur la Côte-Nord et dans l'Outaouais /. Caron, Diane. [Québec] [1984] xvi, 150 p. : ISBN 2-551-06277-2 LC Card 84-220957
HD9944.C22 C34 1984

Postgeschichte Südtirols /. Bianco, Christian. [S.l. , 1981?] 207 p. : LC Card 86-168698
HE7016.T74 B53 1981

Postgraduate Institute of International Studies, Geneva. see **Geneva. Graduate Institute of International Studies.**

POST-GRADUATE WORK. see **UNIVERSITIES AND COLLEGES - GRADUATE WORK.**

Postharvest losses, technology, and employment . Greeley, Martin. Boulder, Colo. , 1987. xvii, 345 p. : ISBN 0-8133-7371-9 (pbk. : alk. paper) : LC Card 87-10648 DDC 338.1/7318/095492 19
HD9066.B32 G73 1987

Post-harvest losses, technology, and employment. Greeley, Martin. Postharvest losses, technology, and employment . Boulder, Colo. , 1987. xvii, 345 p. : ISBN 0-8133-7371-9 (pbk. : alk. paper) : LC Card 87-10648 DDC 338.1/7318/095492 19
HD9066.B32 G73 1987

Postilion publications.
Catalogue des timbres-poste de la France et des colonies françaises. Southfield, MI (15565 Northland Dr., Suite 605 West, Southfield 48075-5308) , <[1985]-. v. <2 > : LC Card 86-210422
HE6185.F82 C37 1985

Grosfils-Berger, P. Finlande . Southfield, MI (15565 Northland Dr., Suite 605 W, Southfield 48075-5308) , 1947, i.e. [1986?] 320 p. : LC Card 86-206197 DDC 769.5694897 19
HE6185.F52 G76 1986

Winkler, Karl. Handbuch der bayerischen Poststempel /. Southfield, MI [198-?] 383 p., [18] p. of plates : LC Card 86-155089
HE6185.G32 B389 1980z

Zumstein, Ernst. Handbook of the postage stamps of Switzerland from the German of Ernst Zumstein. [Germany , Southfield, MI [1986?] 61 p., 4 p. of plates : LC Card 86-202597 DDC 769.569494 19
HE6185.S92 Z78 1986

Postimperialism : international capitalism and development in the late twentieth century / David G. Becker ... [et al.]. Boulder : L. Rienner Publishers, 1987. x, 252 p. : ill. ; 24 cm. Bibliography: p. 227-244. Includes index. CONTENTS. - Why postimperialism? / David G. Becker and Richard L. Sklar -- Postimperialism, a class analysis of multinational corporate expansion / Richard L. Sklar -- Development, democracy, and dependency in Latin America ; "Bonanza development" and the "new bourgeoisie" / David G. Becker -- Assertive pragmatism and the multinational enterprise / Sayre P. Schatz -- Third World indebted industrialization / Jeff Frieden -- Socializing adaptation / Sayre P. Schatz -- International capital and national development / Jeff Frieden -- Postimperialism and the great competition / Sayre P. Schatz -- Postimperialism, a first quarterly report / David G. Becker. ISBN 1-555-87046-5 (lib. bdg. : alk. paper) : LC Card 87-4455 DDC 338.8/881724 19
1. International business enterprises - Developing countries. 2. Industry and state - Developing countries. 3. Elite (Social sciences) - Developing countries. I. Becker, David G., 1938-. II. Title: Post-imperialism.
HD2932 .P67 1987

Post-imperialism. Postimperialism . Boulder , 1987. x, 252 p. : ISBN 1-555-87046-5 (lib. bdg. : alk. paper) : LC Card 87-4455 DDC 338.8/881724 19
HD2932 .P67 1987

Die Postkutschenreise /. Beyrer, Klaus. Tübingen , 1985. 284 p. : ISBN 3-925340-35-1 LC Card 86-198761
HE6995 .B49 1985

Postman, Andrew. Using HAL : a guide to achieving greater productivity with Lotus 1-2-3's companion product / by Andrew Postman ; foreword by Bill Gross and Larry Gross. Berkeley, Calif. : Osborne McGraw-Hill, c1987. xvi, 557 p. : ill. ; 24 cm. On t.p. the registered trademark symbol "TM" is superscript following "HAL" in title. Includes index. ISBN 0-07-881268-2 (pbk.) : LC Card 87-403738 DDC 005.36/9 19
1. Lotus HAL (Computer program). 2. Business - Data processing. I. Title.
HF5548.4.L68 P67 1987

Postmarked . Whitford, Craig A. Lansing, Mich. (P.O. Box 14225, Lansing 48901) , c1987. 27 p., [2] p. of plates : LC Card 87-402869 DDC 769.56/7/0977427 19
HE6185.U7 M59 1987

Postmarked Washington . Ramsey, Guy Reed. Lake Grove, OR (Box 2093, Lake Grove 97035) , c1987. 148 p. : LC Card 86-72305 DDC 383/.4979791 19
HE6376.A1 W265 1987

POSTMARKS - BELGIUM.
Silverberg, René. Le courrier des militaires belges internés aux Pays-Bas et en Suisse 1914-1919, et essai de classement des marques néerlandaises de censure et autres /. Bruxelles , 1978. 154 p. : LC Card 80-452392 DDC 769.56/7
HE6184.C3 S55 ***NYPL [JFD 81-1659]***

POSTMARKS - CENTRAL AMERICA - HISTORY.
Central America postal history and a listing of prephilatelic postmarks =. New York [Yonkers, N.Y.?] , 1986. xiv, 142 p. : ISBN 0-912574-41-0 (pbk.) LC Card 87-402819

DDC 383/.49728 19
HE6674 .C46 1986

POSTMARKS - ENGLAND - LONDON - HISTORY.
London's postal history /. [London] , c1978. 16 p. : LC Card 84-172225
HE6946.L6 L65 1978

POSTMARKS - ETHIOPIA - HISTORY.
Payne, Eric. Ethiopia /. Hampstead Norreys, Newbury, Berkshire, England , 1981-1982. 8 v. in 1 : LC Card 87-166672
HE6185.E8 P39 1981

POSTMARKS - FINLAND.
Gummesson, Rolf. Finnland . [Sweden , 1964] ([Kristianstad] : Kristianstads Länstryckeri) 96 p. : LC Card 86-209484
HE6185.F5 G85 1964

POSTMARKS - FINLAND - HISTORY - 19TH CENTURY.
Grosfils-Berger, P. Finlande . Southfield, MI (15565 Northland Dr., Suite 605 W, Southfield 48075-5308) , 1947, i.e. [1986?] 320 p. : LC Card 86-206197 DDC 769.5694897 19
HE6185.F52 G76 1986

POSTMARKS - FRANCE - COLONIES - CATALOGS.
Catalogue des timbres-poste de la France et des colonies françaises. Southfield, MI (15565 Northland Dr., Suite 605 West, Southfield 48075-5308) , <[1985]-. v. <2 > : LC Card 86-210422
HE6185.F82 C37 1985

POSTMARKS - FRANCE - COLONIES - HISTORY.
Bergier, J. (Joseph) Marques d'entrée maritime du XVIIIème et du XIXème siècle et études diverses s'y rapportant, dont taxes et mouvements portuaires de provenance ou à destination des principaux ports d'outremer au XVIIIe s. /. Nantes [1981] 131, x p. : LC Card 82-228434
HE6986 .B47 1981

POSTMARKS - FRANCE - TERRITORIES AND POSSESSIONS - CATALOGS.
Catalogue des timbres-poste de la France et des colonies françaises. Southfield, MI (15565 Northland Dr., Suite 605 West, Southfield 48075-5308) , <[1985]-. v. <2 > : LC Card 86-210422
HE6185.F82 C37 1985

POSTMARKS - GERMANY (WEST) - BADEN (GRAND DUCHY)
Die Abstempelungen des Grossherzogtums Baden ab 1851 . [Soest] , c1980. 393 p. : LC Card 86-152444
HE6185.G32 B333 1980

POSTMARKS - GERMANY (WEST) - BAVARIA - CATALOGS.
Winkler, Karl. Handbuch der bayerischen Poststempel /. Southfield, MI [198-?] 383 p., [18] p. of plates : LC Card 86-155089
HE6185.G32 B389 1980z

POSTMARKS - GERMANY (WEST) - HESSE-KASSEL (ELECTORATE) - CATALOGS.
Köhler, H. (Heinz) Thurn und Taxis, Kurhessen 1816-1867 . Kassel [1970?]- v. <1 > : LC Card 86-235280
HE6185.G32 H474 1970

POSTMARKS - GREECE - CRETE - HISTORY.
Marinakēs, Markos, 1945- Tachydromikē historia Krētikēs Politeias, 1900-1913 /. Athēna , 1983. 127 p. : LC Card 85-151773
HE7180.5.Z7 C746 1983
NYPL [JFD 86-10347]

POSTMARKS - HUNGARY - HISTORY - 19TH CENTURY.
Zlatev, István. A magyar postahivatalok, 1867-1871. években használt hely-keletbélyegzései . Budapest , 1983. 255 p. : ISBN 963-01-4848-X LC Card 86-148361
HE6980.5 .Z55 1983

POSTMARKS - INDIA - JAMMU AND KASHMIR - HISTORY - 19TH CENTURY.
Staal, Frits. The stamps of Jammu & Kashmir /. New York , 1983. xvii, 286 p., 16 p. of plates : ISBN 0-912574-37-X LC Card 87-402877 DDC 769.56954/6 19
HE6185.I53 J357 1983

POSTMARKS - ITALY - TRENTINO-ALTO ADIGE - HISTORY.
Bianco, Christian. Postgeschichte Südtirols /. [S.l. , 1981?] 207 p. : LC Card 86-168698
HE7016.T74 B53 1981

POSTMARKS - LIBERIA - HISTORY.
Cockrill, Philip. Liberia /. Newbury, Berkshire, England [198-?] 15 v. in 2 : LC Card 86-217641
HE6185.L49 C63 1980z

POSTMARKS - MICHIGAN - LANSING - HISTORY - 19TH CENTURY.
Whitford, Craig A. Postmarked . Lansing, Mich. (P.O. Box 14225, Lansing 48901) , c1987. 27 p., [2] p. of plates : LC Card 87-402869 DDC 769.56/7/0977427 19
HE6185.U7 M59 1987

POSTMARKS - NETHERLANDS.
Silverberg, René. Le courrier des militaires belges internés aux Pays-Bas et en Suisse 1914-1919, et essai de classement des marques néerlandaises de censure et autres /. Bruxelles , 1978. 154 p. : LC Card 80-452392 DDC 769.56/7
HE6184.C3 S55 *NYPL [JFD 81-1659]*

POSTMARKS - PALESTINE - HISTORY.
Buzzetti, Luciano. Il distaccamento italiano di Palestina, 1917-1921 /. Milano , c1976. 55 p. : LC Card 86-179004
HE6185.P13 B89 1976

POSTMARKS - POLAND - CATALOGS.
Katalog specjalizowany znaków pocztowych ziem polskich 1985 /. Warszawa , 1984-1985. 4 v. : ISBN 83-03-00691-6 (cz. 1-2) : LC Card 87-120964
HE6185.P62 K28 1984

POSTMARKS - SWITZERLAND.
Müller, Alfred. Die schweizerischen Bahnpoststempel . Bern , 1977. 28 p. : LC Card 85-138287
HE7139.R2 M85 1977

Silverberg, René. Le courrier des militaires belges internés aux Pays-Bas et en Suisse 1914-1919, et essai de classement des marques néerlandaises de censure et autres /. Bruxelles , 1978. 154 p. : LC Card 80-452392 DDC 769.56/7
HE6184.C3 S55 *NYPL [JFD 81-1659]*

POSTMARKS - TOPICS - AMERICAN REVOLUTIION BICENNTENIAL, 1776-1976.
Rothenberg, Bertram. U. S. Postal Service bicentennial postmarks, 1972-1984 /. Johnstown, PA, USA , c1986. 42 p. : ISBN 0-935991-01-8 (pbk.): LC Card 86-224991 DDC 769.56/7/0973 19
HE6187 .A635 no. 110 HE6183.A45

POSTMARKS - TOPICS - GLIDING AND SOARING.
Short, Simine, 1944- Glider mail . Cinnaminson, NJ , 1987. 261 p. : ISBN 0-939429-00-4 : LC Card 86-72751 DDC 383/.144 19
HE6239.G54 S56 1987

POSTMARKS - UNITED STATES.
Rothenberg, Bertram. U. S. Postal Service bicentennial postmarks, 1972-1984 /. Johnstown, PA, USA , c1986. 42 p. : ISBN 0-935991-01-8 (pbk.): LC Card 86-224991 DDC 769.56/7/0973 19
HE6187 .A635 no. 110 HE6183.A45

POSTMARKS - WISCONSIN - HISTORY - 19TH CENTURY.
Bournique, Raymond A. County & postmaster postmarks of Wisconsin. Madison, WI (5401 Raymond Rd., Madison 53711) , 1985. 12 p. : LC Card 86-174748 DDC 769.56/7/09775 19
HE6185.U7 W573 1985

Post-revolutionary Nicaragua . Colburn, Forrest D. Berkeley , c1986. xi, 145 p. : ISBN 0-520-05524-1 LC Card 85-5798 DDC 338.1/097285 19
HD1817 .C63 1986 *NYPL [JLD 86-2414]*

Posttips . Hammer, Karl-Heinrich. Bonn , 1982. 108 p. : LC Card 83-193275
HE6998 .H35 1982

Potapov, V. V. (Viktor Vladimirovich)
Modifikatsii teorii "poleznosti" / V.V. Potapov. Moskva : "Mysl′", 1984. 132 p. ; 20 cm. (Sovremennye burzhuaznye ėkonomicheskie teorii: kriticheskiĭ analiz) Includes bibliographical references. LC Card 84-247447
1. Utility theory. 2. Capitalism. I. Series: Sovremennye burzhuaznye ėkonomicheskie teorii. II. Title.
HB201 .P65 1984

POTASH INDUSTRY AND TRADE - EARLY WORKS TO 1800.
Lavoisier, Antoine Laurent, 1743-1794. L'art de fabriquer le salin, et la potasse ... /. A Paris , 1779. [2], viij, 84 p., IV, [1] folded leaves of plates : LC Card 85-666435
HD9660.A42 L38x 1779

POTATO. see **POTATOES.**

POTATOES - BOLIVIA - CHUQUISACA - STORAGE.
Estudio de factibilidad para una cadena de silos intercomunales de papa . [Sucre, Bolivia] 1982. 178 p., [2] leaves of plates : LC Card 83-202593 DDC 338.1/6 19
HD9235.P82 B525 1982
NYPL [JLF 87-711]

POTATOES - BOLIVIA - POTOSÍ (DEPT.) - STORAGE.
Estudio de factibilidad para una cadena de silos intercomunales de papa . [Sucre, Bolivia] 1982. 178 p., [2] leaves of plates : LC Card 83-202593 DDC 338.1/6 19
HD9235.P82 B525 1982
NYPL [JLF 87-711]

POTATOES - BOLIVIA - TARIJA (DEPT.) - STORAGE.
Estudio de factibilidad para una cadena de silos intercomunales de papa . [Sucre, Bolivia] 1982. 178 p., [2] leaves of plates : LC Card 83-202593 DDC 338.1/6 19
HD9235.P82 B525 1982
NYPL [JLF 87-711]

O potencial das exportações brasileiras de manufaturados /. Pinto, Maurício Barata de Paula. Rio de Janeiro , 1983. 46 p. ; LC Card 87-403022 DDC 382/.4567/0981 19
HD9734.B72 P56 1983

Potential effects of section 3 of the Federal Coal Leasing Amendments Act of 1976. Washington, D.C. : Congress of the U. S., Office of Technology Assessment : For sale by the Supt. of Docs., U. S. G.P.O., 1986. vii, 186 p. : ill. ; 26 cm. At head of title: OTA special report. Shipping list no.: 86-237-P. "March 1986"--P. [4] of cover. "OTA-ITE-300"--P. [4] of cover. S/N 052-003-01029-1 Item 1070-M Includes bibliographical references. LC Card 86-600512 DDC 333.33/9 19
1. Coal leases - United States. 2. Coal trade - United States.
HD242.3 .P68 1986 *NYPL [JLF 86-1368]*

Potential for foreign investment in rubber products manufacture with information on special projects and a selection of local collaborators /. Karunaratne, S. W. [Colombo] , 1985. vii, 100 p. ; LC Card 86-902791 DDC 332.6/73/095493 19
HD9161.S752 K37 1985

Potentielle Beschäftigungseffekte der Maschinensteuer . Schulz, Erika, 1953- Frankfurt am Main , New York , c1986. xiii, 303 p. : ISBN 3-8204-8483-3 LC Card 86-195650
HD7179 .S349 1986

Potent͡sial ėffektivnosti / [redaktor-sostavitel′ V.E. Kukushkin]. I͡Uzhno-Sakhalinsk : Dal′nevostochnoe knizhnoe izd-vo, Sakhalinskoe otd-nie, 1985. 67 p. ; 20 cm. LC Card 87-100690
1. Farmers - Russian S.F.S.R. - Sakhalinskai͡a oblast′. 2. Agricultural productivity - Russian S.F.S.R. - Sakhalinskai͡a oblast′. 3. State farms - Russian S.F.S.R. - Sakhalinskai͡a oblast′. I. Kukushkin, V. E.
HD8039.F32 S656 1985

Potgieter, J. F. Kruger, Gudrun. Development region D . Port Elizabeth [1985] iv, 89 p. : ISBN 0-86988-274-0 (pbk.) LC Card 86-233113 DDC 304.6/09687/5 19
HA4701.Z9 C354 1985

POTLATCH CORPORATION - HISTORY.
Petersen, Keith. Company town . Pullman, Wash. , Moscow, Idaho , 1987. xix, 284 p., [32] p. of plates : ISBN 0-87422-036-X (alk. paper) : LC Card 87-14980 DDC 307.7/67/0979686 19
HD9759.P63 P47 1987

POTLATCH (IDAHO) - ECONOMIC CONDITIONS.
Petersen, Keith. Company town . Pullman,

Wash. , Moscow, Idaho , 1987. xix, 284 p., [32] p. of plates : ISBN 0-87422-036-X (alk. paper) : LC Card 87-14980 DDC 307.7/67/0979686 19
HD9759.P63 P47 1987

POTOSÍ REGION (BOLIVIA) - ECONOMIC CONDITIONS.
Platt, Tristan. Estado tributario y librecambio en Potosí (siglo XIX) . [La Paz?] , c1986. 73 p. ; LC Card 87-401159 DDC 330.984/1404 19
HC183.P67 P55 1986

Potosí, siglo diecinueve. Platt, Tristan. Estado tributario y librecambio en Potosí (siglo XIX) . [La Paz?] , c1986. 73 p. ; LC Card 87-401159 DDC 330.984/1404 19
HC183.P67 P55 1986

Potosí, siglo XIX. Platt, Tristan. Estado tributario y librecambio en Potosí (siglo XIX) . [La Paz?] , c1986. 73 p. ; LC Card 87-401159 DDC 330.984/1404 19
HC183.P67 P55 1986

Potosí, siglo 19. Platt, Tristan. Estado tributario y librecambio en Potosí (siglo XIX) . [La Paz?] , c1986. 73 p. ; LC Card 87-401159 DDC 330.984/1404 19
HC183.P67 P55 1986

Potrebitel´naia stoimost´ pri sotsializme /. Krotov, M. I. (Mikhail Iosifovich) Moskva , 1983. 151 p. ; LC Card 83-166303
HB201 .K965 1983

Potrebitel´skaia kooperatsiia v odinnadtsatoĭ piatiletke /. Smirnov, A. A. (Alekseĭ Alekseevich) Moskva , 1981. 88 p. : LC Card 82-106193
HD3355 .S65 1981

Potrebitel´skaia kooperatsiia v 11-ĭ piatiletke. Smirnov, A. A. (Alekseĭ Alekseevich) Potrebitel´skaia kooperatsiia v odinnadtsatoĭ piatiletke /. Moskva , 1981. 88 p. : LC Card 82-106193
HD3355 .S65 1981

Potsdam. Akademie für Staats- und Rechtswissenschaft der DDR. see **Akademie für Staats- und Rechtswissenschaft der DDR.**

Pott, Philipp. Marktpolitik von Privatbankiers : die Preis-, Leistungs- und Zweigstellenpolitik, die Werbung und Öffentlichkeitsarbeit von Privatbankiers / Philipp Pott. Frankfurt : R.G. Fischer, c1983. 66 p. ; 21 cm. Bibliography: p. 52-65. ISBN 3-88323-443-5 LC Card 84-154560
1. Banks and banking - Germany, West. 2. Bank marketing - Germany (West). I. Title.
HG2021.G4 P67 1983

Potter, Gregory C. Pritchard, Robert E., 1941- Be your own financial advisor /. Englewood Cliffs, N.J. , c1988. xiv, 187 p. ; ISBN 0-13-071242-6 LC Card 87-14366 DDC 332.024 19
HG179 .P737 1988

POTTERY INDUSTRY - KOREA (SOUTH) - HISTORY.
Sayers, Robert. The Korean onggi potter /. Washington, D.C. , 1987. 288 p. : LC Card 86-600366 DDC 338.4/77382/095195 19
HD9617.K82 S29 1987

POTTERY INDUSTRY - NORTHEASTERN STATES - HISTORY.
Domestic pottery of the northeastern United States, 1625-1850 /. Orlando , 1985. xxi, 319 p. : ISBN 0-12-703870-1 (alk. paper) LC Card 85-9038 DDC 338.4/76663974 19
HD9611.7.A115 D66 1985 ***NYPL [3-MPH 86-2845]***

POTTERY - IVORY COAST - KATIOLA (CENTRE)
Traoré, Aminata. La mine d'argile est notre champ /. [Abidjan?] [1985] (Abidjan : Société d'impr. ivoirienne) [36] p. : LC Card 86-200373
HD6073.P82 1967 1985

POTTERY, KOREAN.
Sayers, Robert. The Korean onggi potter /. Washington, D.C. , 1987. 288 p. : LC Card 86-600366 DDC 338.4/77382/095195 19
HD9617.K82 S29 1987

POTTERY - NORTHEASTERN STATES - HISTORY.
Domestic pottery of the northeastern United States, 1625-1850 /. Orlando , 1985. xxi, 319 p. : ISBN 0-12-703870-1 (alk. paper) LC Card 85-9038 DDC 338.4/76663974 19
HD9611.7.A115 D66 1985 ***NYPL [3-MPH 86-2845]***

Potthoff, Erich. Eugen Schmalenbach . Stuttgart , 1984. xvii, 478 p. : ISBN 3-8202-0295-1 LC Card 84-215889
HF5616.G3 E93 1984

Potts, Mark. The leading edge : CEOs who turned their companies around : what they did and how they did it / Mark Potts, Peter Behr. New York : McGraw-Hill, c1987. iv, 220 p. ; 24 cm. Includes index. ISBN 0-07-050599-3 LC Card 86-10567 DDC 658.4/06 19
1. Organizational change - Case studies. 2. Success in business - Case studies. I. Behr, Peter. II. Title.
HD58.8 .P68 1987 ***NYPL [JLE 87-33]***

Pou, Francis. Duarte, Isis. Trabajadores urbanos . Santo Domingo, República Dominicana , c1986. 314 p. ; LC Card 87-402153 DDC 331/.097293 19
HD8218.5 .D83 1986

Les poubelles de la survie . Camacho, Martine. Paris , c1986. 207 p. : ISBN 2-85802-590-5 LC Card 86-180208
HC895.Z7 A443 1986

Poulat, Émile. Debès, Joseph. L'appel de la J.O.C., 1926-1928 /. Paris , 1986. 292 p. : ISBN 2-204-02529-1 : LC Card 86-189508
HD8430 .D37 1986

Poulsen, Per Thygesen. Dansk ledelse '90 i et internationalt perspektiv . [Copenhagen] , 1983. 226 p. : ISBN 87-7553-128-3 : LC Card 83-185958
HD57.7 .D38 1983

POULTRY INDUSTRY - DENMARK.
Landsudvalget for fjerkræ (Denmark) Den danske fjerkræsektor 1985, en beskrivelse . [Denmark? , 1986] 152 p. ; LC Card 86-224129
HD9437.D42 L35 1986

POULTRY INDUSTRY - SAUDI ARABIA.
Analytical study for the market of white meat and eggs /. Jeddah [1985?] 159 p. : LC Card 85-964046 DDC 381/.4566493/09538 19
HD9437.S332 A53 1985

POULTRY TRADE. see **POULTRY INDUSTRY.**

POULTRY - TRADE AND STATISTICS. see **POULTRY INDUSTRY.**

Pound, John. Poverty and vagrancy in Tudor England / John Pound. 2nd ed. London ; New York : Longman, 1986. xii, 116 p. ; 20 cm. (Seminar studies in history) Includes index. Bibliography: p. 104-113. ISBN 0-582-35508-7 : LC Card 85-19747 DDC 305.5/69/0942 19
1. Poor - Great Britain - History. 2. Poor laws - England - History. 3. Tramps - England - History. I. Title.
HC260.P6 P68 1986 ***NYPL [JLD 86-2366]***

Pour assurer le renouveau économique. The Agenda for economic renewal . [Ottawa] [1987] 25, 26 p. : LC Card 87-140803 DDC 338.971 19
HC115 .A624 1987

Pour assurer le renouveau économique. Securing economic renewal . [Ottawa] [1987] 147, 161 p. : LC Card 87-144360 DDC 336.71 19
HJ793 .S43 1987

Pour en sortir-- /. Véron, Emile. Paris , c1984. 185 p. : ISBN 2-226-02060-8 : LC Card 84-197071
HC276.2 .V465 1984

Pour l'Afrique, j'accuse . Dumont, René, 1904- [Paris] , c1986. 457 p., [48] p. of plates : ISBN 2-259-01455-0 LC Card 86-220056
HC1002 .D85 1986

Pour un rôle actif de la Communauté économique européenne sur la scène agricole internationale : rapport du Groupe de travail sur la prospective des échanges mondiaux agricoles / présidé par B. Auberger ; coprésidé par Ph. Neeser ; animé par A. Azouvi. Paris : La Documentation française, c1986. 184 p. ; 24 cm. (Plan / Commissariat général du plan. 11) At head of title: Ministère du plan et de l'aménagement du territoire, Commissariat général du plan. "Décembre 1985." Bibliography: p. 180-184. ISBN 2-11-001582-9 : LC Card 86-174918
1. Agricultural assistance, European - Developing countries. 2. Agriculture - Economic aspects - European Economic Community countries. I. Auberger, Bernard. II. Neeser, Ph. III. Azouvi, A. IV. France. Groupe de travail sur la prospective des échanges mondiaux agricoles. V. Series: Plan (France. Commissariat général du plan) 11.
HD1431 .P68 1986

Pour une histoire économique vraie /. Morineau, Michel. [Lille] , c1985. 512 p. : ISBN 2-85939-234-3 : LC Card 86-142388 DDC 330.9 19
HC51 .M64 1985

Pour une mesure indirecte de la mortalité. Locoh, Thérèse. La fécondité en Afrique noire /. Lomé [1985] 36, 22 leaves : LC Card 87-126644
HB1071 .L63 1985

Pour une nouvelle culture d'entreprise /. Mothé-Gautrat, Daniel, 1924- Paris , 1986. 173 p. ; ISBN 2-7071-1596-7 : LC Card 86-185142
HD8431 .M63 1986

A Pournelle users guide.
Grieb, William E. The small business computer today and tomorrow /. New York, N.Y. , c1984. 287 p. : ISBN 0-671-55907-9 (pbk.) : LC Card 86-207213 DDC 658/.05416 19
HF5548.2 .G733 1984

Pourquoi la pauvreté-- quand les produits abondent? . Puel, Gaston. [France] [1986] 255 p. ; LC Card 86-189201
HC79.W4 P84 1986

Pourquoi, où et comment investir / Banque marocaine pour le commerce et l'industrie. Ed. 1985/86. Casablanca, Maroc : La Banque, [1985] 126 p. ; 20 cm. Cover title: Investir au Maroc. LC Card 86-198948
1. Investments, Foreign - Morocco. 2. Morocco - Foreign economic relations. 3. Morocco - Economic policy. 4. Morocco - Economic conditions. I. Banque marocaine pour le commerce et l'industrie. II. Title: Investir au Maroc.
HG5832.A3 P68 1985

Pousset, Henri, 1914- Mögliche globale Wirtschaftsstrategie im 3. Jahrtausend / Henri Pousset. Frankfurt am Main : Haag + Herchen, c1986. 190 p. : ill. ; 21 cm. Bibliography: p. 189. ISBN 3-88129-956-4 LC Card 86-160350
1. Economic policy. 2. International cooperation. 3. International economic relations. 4. Twenty-first century - Forecasts. I. Title. II. Title: Mögliche globale Wirtschaftsstrategie im dritten Jahrtausend.
HD84 .P65 1986

Poveda Blanco, Francisco. La valoración de bases imponibles en los impuestos sobre la renta y el patrimonio / Francisco Poveda Blanco. [Alicante] : Secretariado de Publicaciones, Universidad de Alicante, E.U. de Estudios Empresariales, Facultad de Ciencias Económicas y Empresariales, [1984?] 395 p. ; 24 cm. Includes bibliographical references. LC Card 84-216651 DDC 333.33/2/0946 19
1. Valuation - Spain. 2. Property tax - Spain. 3. Income tax - Spain. 4. Property tax - Law and legislation - Spain. 5. Income tax - Law and legislation - Spain. I. Title.
HJ4125.S8 P68 1984 ***NYPL [JLE 86-1461]***

Poveda, Gabriel. see **Poveda Ramos, Gabriel.**

Poveda Ramos, Gabriel. Nueva alternativa para el desarrollo : realidad, potencial y futuro del sector rural / preparado por DINPROA, Grupo de Consulta Industrial y Asesoría Jurídica y Económica ; Gabriel Poveda Ramos, Jaime Jiménez, Edgar Gutiérrez Castro. Bogotá : Sociedad de Agricultores de Colombia, 1974. 249 p. : ill. ; 24 cm. Includes bibliographical references. LC Card 78-345029
1. Agriculture and state - Colombia. 2. Agriculture - Economic aspects - Colombia. 3. Agricultural industries - Colombia. I. Jiménez, Jaime, joint author. II. Dinproa, Grupo de Consulta Industrial y Asesoría Jurídica y Económica. III. Title.
HD1883 1974 .P68 ***NYPL [JLE 80-482]***

O poveiro /. Santos Graça, A. (António), 1882-1956. Póvoa de Varzim , 1982. 238, xvi p., [29] p. of plates : LC Card 83-215678
HD8039.F66 P67 1982

Povertà e assistenza in Lombardia nell'età napoleonica /. Bressan, E. (Edoardo) [Milano] , Bari , c1985. viii, 339 p. : ISBN 88-420-2653-0 : LC Card 86-162978
HC307.L8 B74 1985

Poverty . Rowntree, B. Seebohm (Benjamin Seebohm), 1871-1954. New York , 1980. xxi, 426 p. : ISBN 0-8240-0120-6 (alk. paper) : LC Card 79-56969 DDC 305.5/6 19
HC258.Y6 R64 1980 ***NYPL [JLD 86-3436]***

POVERTY - ADDRESSES, ESSAYS, LECTURES.
Armut und Reichtum . Hamburg , Göttingen , 1981. 80 p. : ISBN 3-921620-14-7 LC Card 81-159683 DDC 305.5/6 19
HC79.P6 A75 ***NYPL [JLG 85-309]***

George, Susan. Ill fares the land . Washington, D.C. , c1984. xviii, 102 p. ; ISBN 0-89758-039-7 (pbk.) : LC Card 84-25124 DDC 363.8 19
HD9000.5 .G385 1984
NYPL [JLD 86-3899]

Understanding poverty /. Milano, Italy , c1984. 355 p. : LC Card 84-249441 DDC 339.4/6/094 19
HC240.9.P6 U53 1984 ***NYPL [JLD 86-1196]***

Poverty alleviation programmes . Pais, H. New Delhi , 1986. xii, 48, [3] p. (some folded) : LC Card 86-903597 DDC 362.5/8/09543 19
HC437.J43 P35 1986

Poverty amid plenty, the American paradox. United States. President's Commission on Income Maintenance Programs. [Washington] 1969. ix, 155 p. LC Card 71-605334 DDC 362.5/0973
HC110.P63 A59 ***NYPL [JLF 86-478]***

Poverty amidst plenty : world political economy and distributive justice / edited by Edward Weisband. Boulder, Colo. : Westview Press, 1989. p. cm. Includes index. ISBN 0-8133-0523-3 LC Card 87-12829 DDC 330.9/048 19
1. Economic history - 1945-. 2. Distributive justice. 3. Poor. I. Weisband, Edward, 1939-.
HC59 .P639 1989

Poverty among black families in the nonmetro South /. Ghelfi, Linda M. Washington, D.C. , Supt. of Docs., U. S. G.P.O. [distributor, 1986] vii, 27 p. : LC Card 86-602435 DDC 330.975/043/0899607301734 19
HC107.A13 G48 1986

Poverty and policy in Tudor and Stuart England /. Slack, Paul. London , New York , 1988. p. cm. ISBN 0-582-48965-2 (alk. paper) LC Card 87-2657 DDC 362.5/561/0942 19
HC254.4 .S42 1988

Poverty and politics . Hahner, June Edith, 1940- Albuquerque , 1986. xvi, 415 p. : ISBN 0-8263-0878-3 : LC Card 86-1258 DDC 305.5/69/0981 19
HC190.P6 H34 1986 ***NYPL [JLE 86-4407]***

Poverty and public policy . Morris, Michael, 1949- Westport, Conn. , 1986. xii, 236 p. ; ISBN 0-313-24942-3 (lib. bdg. : alk. paper) LC Card 86-398 DDC 361.6/1/0973 19
HV95 .M67 1986 ***NYPL [JLD 87-510]***

Poverty and state support /. Alcock, Peter, 1951- London , New York , 1987. xi, 215 p. : ISBN 0-582-29652-8 (pbk.) LC Card 86-27857 DDC 368.4/00941 19
HD7165 .A77 1987

Poverty and vagrancy in Tudor England /. Pound, John. London , New York , 1986. xii, 116 p. ; ISBN 0-582-35508-7 : LC Card 85-19747 DDC 305.5/69/0942 19
HC260.P6 P68 1986 ***NYPL [JLD 86-2366]***

POVERTY - ASIA - CONGRESSES.
Movement for a no poverty society . Calcutta , 1980. 78 p. ; LC Card 81-902107
HC415.P6 M68 1980

The poverty curtain . Haq, Mahbub ul, 1934- Lahore , 1983. li, 247 p. ; LC Card 83-931275 DDC 338.9/009172/4 19
HC59.7 .H35 1983 ***NYPL [JLD 87-439]***

Poverty, development, and exchange relations . Majumder, Arun. New Delhi , 1987. xiii, 141 p. : ISBN 81-7027-108-8 : LC Card 87-900910
HC438.B24 M35 1987

POVERTY - ENVIRONMENTAL ASPECTS - INDIA - ADDRESSES, ESSAYS, LECTURES.
Psycho-ecological dimensions of poverty /. New Delhi , 1983. x, 115 p. : LC Card 83-906411 DDC 305.5/69/0954 19
HC440.P6 P78 1983 ***NYPL [JLD 87-491]***

POVERTY - GOVERNMENT POLICY - INDIA - GHAZIPUR (DISTRICT)
Ghate, Prabhu, 1941- Direct attacks on rural poverty . New Delhi , 1984. xvi, 597 p. : LC Card 84-902455 DDC 338.954/2 19
HC437.G48 G46 1984 ***NYPL [JLD 87-651]***

Poverty in Connecticut, 1979 /. Hadden, Kenneth. Storrs, CT [1986] 24 p. : LC Card 86-623148 DDC 362.5/09746 19
HC107.C8 H33 1986

Poverty in Latin America : the impact of depression. Washington, D.C., U. S.A. : World Bank, [1986] 25 p. ; 23 cm. Includes bibliographical references. ISBN 0-8213-0836-X (pbk.) LC Card 86-225244 DDC 330.98/0038 19
1. Income distribution - Latin America. 2. Poor - Latin America. 3. Labor supply - Latin America. 4. Public welfare - Latin America. I. International Bank for Reconstruction and Development.
HC130.I5 P68 1986

Poverty in rural Asia / edited by Azizur Rahman Khan and Eddy Lee. Bangkok : International Labour Organisation, Asia Employment Programme (ARTEP), 1984, c1983. xii, 276 p. ; 23 cm. Includes bibliographical references and index. ISBN 92-2-103286-8 (pbk.)
1. Rural poor - East Asia. 2. Rural poor - Indonesia. 3. Rural poor - Thailand. I. Lee, Eddy. II. Khan, Azizur Rahman. ***NYPL [JLE 86-1050]***

Poverty in the Soviet Union . Matthews, Mervyn. Cambridge [Cambridgeshire] , New York , 1986. xv, 227 p. ; ISBN 0-521-32544-7 LC Card 86-993 DDC 305.5/69/0947 19
HC340.P6 M38 1986 ***NYPL [JLD 87-262]***

Poverty in the State of Nevada . Passi, Michael M. Carson City, Nev. (1100 E. William St., Suite 117, Carson City 89710) [1986] [11] leaves, 69, 16 p., [1] leaf of plates : LC Card 86-622269 DDC 330.9793/033/08806942 19
HC107.N33 P623 1986

Poverty, income distribution, the family, and public policy : a study / prepared for the use of the Subcommittee on Trade, Productivity, and Economic Growth of the Joint Economic Committee, Congress of the United States. Washington : U. S. G.P.O. : For sale by the Supt. of Docs., Congressional Sales Office, U. S. G.P.O., 1986. viii, 125 p. : ill. ; 24 cm. (S. prt. . 99-199) At head of title: 99th Congress, 2d session. Joint committee print. Distributed to some depository libraries in microfiche. Shipping list no.: 86-1007-P. "December 19, 1986." Includes bibliographical references. Item 1000-B, 1000-C (microfiche) LC Card 87-601355 DDC 339.2/2/0973 19
1. Income distribution - United States. 2. United States - Economic policy - 1981-. 3. United States - Economic conditions - 1981-. 4. Poverty. I. United States. Congress. Joint Economic Committee. Subcommittee on Trade, Productivity, and Economic Growth. II. Series.
HC110.I5 P68 1986

POVERTY - MATHEMATICAL MODELS.
Greer, Joel William, 1948- Food poverty and consumption patterns in Kenya /. Geneva , 1986. xii, 170 p. : ISBN 92-2-105374-1 (pbk.) : LC Card 87-115091 DDC 338.1/9/6762 19
HD9017.K42 G74 1986

The poverty of Coloured labour preference . Goldin, Ian. Cape Town [1984] ii, 97 p. : ISBN 0-7992-0570-2 (pbk.) LC Card 84-195453
HD8801.Z8 C324 1984

The poverty of communism /. Eberstadt, Nick, 1955- New Brunswick, N.J., U. S.A. , c1987. p. cm. ISBN 0-88738-188-X : LC Card 87-19097 DDC 362.5/09171/7 19
HC710.P6 E24 1987

POVERTY - PACIFIC AREA - CONGRESSES.
Movement for a no poverty society . Calcutta , 1980. 78 p. ; LC Card 81-902107
HC415.P6 M68 1980

Poverty policy and poverty research . Haveman, Robert H. Madison, Wis. , 1987. xi, 307 p. : ISBN 0-299-11150-4 : LC Card 86-40453 DDC 362.5/8/0973 19
HC110.P6 H38 1987

POVERTY - PSYCHOLOGICAL ASPECTS.
Alarcón, Reynaldo. Psicología, pobreza y subdesarrollo /. Lima, Perú , 1986. 153 p. ; LC Card 87-126266 DDC 155.9/2 19
HC79.P6 A55 1986

Hakemulder, Roel. Subcultuur en stigma van de armoede . Leiden , 1985. 96 p. ; ISBN 90-6624-058-X LC Card 86-172398
HC79.P6 H34 1985

Rigdon, Susan M., 1943- The culture facade . Urbana , c1988. p. cm. ISBN 0-252-01495-2 (alk. paper) LC Card 87-19063 DDC 305.5/69 19
HC79.P6 R57 1988

POVERTY RESEARCH - UNITED STATES.
Haveman, Robert H. Poverty policy and poverty research . Madison, Wis. , 1987. xi, 307 p. : ISBN 0-299-11150-4 : LC Card 86-40453 DDC 362.5/8/0973 19
HC110.P6 H38 1987

Morrissey, Elizabeth S. Characteristics of poverty in nonmetro counties /. Washington, D.C. , 1985. iv, 10 p. : LC Card 86-602555 DDC 362.5/0973 19
HC110.P6 M67 1985

Poverty, unemployment, and perspective of development /. Subrahmanyam, S. Allahabad, India , 1987. xi, 311 p. : ISBN 81-85076-22-7 : LC Card 87-900803 DDC 330.954/84 19
HC440.P6 S9 1987

Povesti o delakh i li͡udi͡akh partii.
Rotov, Viktor. Li͡ubimoe pole /. Moskva , 1980. 149 p. ; LC Card 81-143989
HD1492.S652 K76 1980

PÓVOA DE VARZIM (PORTUGAL) - SOCIAL LIFE AND CUSTOMS.
Santos Graça, A. (António), 1882-1956. O poveiro /. Póvoa de Varzim , 1982. 238, xvi p., [29] p. of plates : LC Card 83-215678
HD8039.F66 P67 1982

Povolot͡skai͡a, S. I. (Sarra Isaakovna)
I͡Ukhimenko, V. V. (Vladimir Vasil'evich) Izuchenie i prognozirovanie sprosa na bytovye uslugi /. Kiev , 1983. 103 p. ; LC Card 83-218585
HD9986.S683 U385 1983

Povyshat' ėffektivnost' partiĭnoĭ raboty /. Turkin, V. G. (Vladimir Gavrilovich) Moskva , 1978. 63 p. ; LC Card 81-170148
HF5549.5.M63 T87 1978

Povyshenie ėffektivnosti ASUP : kont͡sept͡sii͡a i opyt / [avtory N.I. Ivanov ... et al. ; otvetstvennyĭ redaktor L.Sh. Gaft]. Kiev : Nauk. dumka, 1985. 303 p. : ill. ; 21 cm. At head of title: Akademii͡a nauk SSSR. Institut ėkonomiki promyshlennosti. Bibliography: p. 294-[302] LC Card 85-210269
1. Industrial management - Data processing. 2. Industrial management - Ukraine. I. Ivanov, N. I. (Nikolaĭ Ivanovich). II. Gaft, L. Sh. (Leonid Shevelevich). III. Institut ekonomiky promyslovosti (Akademii͡a nauk Ukraïns'koï RSR).
HD30.2 .P68 1985 ***NYPL [*QIP 87-2760]***

Povyshenie ėffektivnosti proizvodstva v uslovii͡akh sovershenstvovanii͡a khozi͡aĭstvennogo mekhanizma : sbornik nauchnykh trudov / [redakt͡sionnai͡a kollegii͡a A.N. Zolotarev (otvetstvennyĭ redaktor) ... et al.]. Kiev : IĖ AN USSR, 1982. 106 p. ; 20 cm. At head of title: Akademii͡a nauk Ukrainskoĭ SSR. Institut ėkonomiki. Includes bibliographical references. LC Card 83-145049
1. Technological innovations - Ukraine. I. Zolotarev, Anatoliĭ Nikolaevich. II. Instytut ekonomiky (Akademii͡a nauk Ukraïns'koï RSR).
HC337.U5 T46 1982

Povyshenie ėffektivnosti raboty morskogo transporta /. Mikhin, A. A. (Al'bert Afanas'evich) Moskva , 1985. 110, [2] p. ; LC Card 86-115398
HE848 .M55 1985

Povyshenie nadezhnosti i kachestva snabzhenii͡a /. Ini͡utina, K. V. (Klara Vasil'evna) Leningrad , 1983. 239 p. ; LC Card 84-196942
HD39.5 .I55 1983

Povyshenie proizvoditel'nosti truda--kli͡uchevai͡a zadacha sovetskoĭ ėkonomiki . Bukhval'd, E. M. Moskva , 1984. 63 p. ; LC Card 85-188977
HC340.L3 B85 1984

Povyshenie trudovoĭ i obshchestvenno-politicheskoĭ aktivnosti mass kak reshai͡ushchiĭ faktor uskorenii͡a sot͡sial'no-ėkonomicheskogo progressa sotsialisticheskogo obshchestva : materialy Vsesoi͡uznoĭ nauchnoĭ konferent͡sii, Kaliningrad, 4-6 senti͡abri͡a 1985 g. / [chleny redkollegii E.A. Anufriev ... et al.]. Kaliningrad : Kaliningradskiĭ gos. universitet, 1986. 382 p. ; 23 cm. At head of title: Ministerstvo vysshego i srednego spet͡sial'nogo obrazovanii͡a SSSR ... Includes bibliographical references. LC Card 87-136621
1. Labor and laboring classes - Soviet Union -

Congresses. 2. Labor and laboring classes - Soviet Union - Political activity - Congresses. 3. Labor productivity - Soviet Union - Congresses. 4. Management - Soviet Union - Employee participation - Congresses. 5. Soviet Union - Economic policy - 1981- - Congresses. 6. Soviet Union - Social policy - Congresses. I. Anufriev, Evgeniĭ Aleksandrovich. II. Kaliningradskiĭ gosudarstvennyĭ universitet.
HD8526.5 .P62 1986

Powell, James B. The Dow Jones-Irwin guide to high tech investing : picking tomorrow's winners today / James B. Powell. Homewood, Ill. : Dow Jones-Irwin, c1986. xix, 356 p. : ill. ; 24 cm. ISBN 0-87094-596-3 : LC Card 85-72178 DDC 332.6/7253 19
1. Investments. 2. High technology industries. 3. Energy industries. 4. Computer industry. I. Dow Jones-Irwin. II. Title. III. Title: High tech investing.
HG4521 .P63 1986 ***NYPL [JLE 86-2261]***

Powell, Marvin A. Labor in the ancient Near East /. New Haven, Conn. , 1987. xiv, 289 p. : ISBN 0-940490-68-4 LC Card 86-32227 DDC 305.5/62/09394 19
HD8656 .L33 1987 ***NYPL [*OAC (American Oriental series)]***

Powell, Victor. Improving public enterprise performance : concepts and techniques / Victor Powell. Geneva : International Labour Office, 1987. x, 226 p. : ill. ; 24 cm. (Management development series, 0074-6703 . no. 22) "Prepared within the INTERMAN project with the financial support of the UNDP Inter-regional Programme." Includes bibliographies. ISBN 92-2-105563-9 (pbk.) : LC Card 87-166309 DDC 350/.0092/091724 19
1. Government business enterprises - Developing countries - Management. 2. Government executives - Training of - Developing countries. I. Title. II. Series.
HD4420.8 .P68 1987

Powelson, John P., 1920- Facing social revolution : the personal journey of a Quaker economist / by Jack Powelson ; with a foreword by Jim Corbett and an afterword by Kenneth Boulding. Boulder, Colo. : Horizon Society Publications in cooperation with the Social Order Series of the Pacific Yearly Meeting of the Religious Society of Friends, c1987. v, 146 p. ; 22 cm. Bibliography: p. 137-140. Includes index. ISBN 0-934449-03-1 : LC Card 86-32186 DDC 330/.092/4 B 19
1. Powelson, John P., 1920-. 2. Economists - United States - Biography. 3. Quakers - United States - Biography. I. Title.
HB119.P68 A3 1987

POWELSON, JOHN P., 1920-
Powelson, John P., 1920- Facing social revolution . Boulder, Colo. , c1987. v, 146 p. ; ISBN 0-934449-03-1 : LC Card 86-32186 DDC 330/.092/4 B 19
HB119.P68 A3 1987

Power & culture . Gutman, Herbert George, 1928- New York, N.Y. , c1987. xi, 452 p. ; ISBN 0-394-56171-6 LC Card 87-43018 DDC 305.5/62/0973 19
HD8072 .G97 1987

Power and culture. Gutman, Herbert George, 1928- Power & culture . New York, N.Y. , c1987. xi, 452 p. ; ISBN 0-394-56171-6 LC Card 87-43018 DDC 305.5/62/0973 19
HD8072 .G97 1987

Power and economic change . McLewin, Philip J., 1939- New York , 1987. ii, 271 p. : ISBN 0-8240-1366-2 (alk. paper) : LC Card 87-8344 DDC 330.97292/04 19
HC154 .M36 1987

Power and poverty : development and development projects in the Third World / edited by Donald W. Attwood, Thomas C. Bruneau, and John G. Galaty. Boulder : Westview Press, 1988. v, 186 p. ; 23 cm. (Westview special studies in social, political and economic development) Results from a series of seminars held at the Centre for Developing-Area Studies of McGill University"--T.p. verso. Includes bibliographies and index. ISBN 0-8133-7351-4 (pbk. : alk. paper) : LC Card 86-32578 DDC 338.9/009172/4 19
1. Economic development projects - Developing countries. 2. Economic development projects - Developing countries - Case studies. 3. Developing countries - Economic conditions. I. Attwood, Donald W. II. Bruneau, Thomas C. III. Galaty, John G. IV. McGill University. Centre for Developing-Area Studies.
HC59.72.E44 P68 1988

Power and powerlessness in industry . Harris, Rosemary. London , New York , 1987. viii, 245 p. : ISBN 0-422-60920-X LC Card 86-14420 DDC 338.4/766134/0941 19
HD6956.A497 H37 1986 ***NYPL [JLD 87-825]***

Power, Anne. Property before people : the management of twentieth-century council housing / Anne Power. London ; Boston : Allen & Unwin, c1987. xvi, 268 p. : ill. ; 23 cm. Bibliography: p. 249-259. Includes index. ISBN 0-04-350069-2 (alk. paper) LC Card 86-28751 DDC 363.5/8 19
1. Public housing - Great Britain - Management. I. Title.
HD7288.78.G7 P69 1987

POWER DISTRIBUTION, ELECTRIC. see **ELECTRIC POWER DISTRIBUTION.**

Power, Eileen Edna, 1889-1940. The wool trade in English medieval history / by Eileen Power. New York : Greenwood Press, [1987], c1941. viii, 128 p. ; 23 cm. Reprint. Originally published: London ; New York : Oxford University Press, 1941. (The Ford lectures ; 1939) Includes index. ISBN 0-313-25656-X (lib. bdg. : alk. paper) LC Card 86-29442 DDC 338.4/767731/0942 19
1. Wool trade and industry - England - History. 2. England - Economic conditions. 3. Great Britain - History - Medieval period, 1066-1485. I. Series: Ford lectures, 1939. II. Title.
HD9901.7.E54 P68 1987

Power in numbers . Forst, Brian. New York , c1987. xiv, 257 p. ; ISBN 0-471-62809-3 LC Card 87-21555 DDC 658.1/51 19
HG4028.B2 F58 1987

Power investing : generating profits from utility stocks / by the editors of KCI Communications, Inc. Alexandria, VA (P.O. Box 1467, Alexandria 22313) : KCI Communications, Inc., c1987. vi, 42 leaves : ill. ; 23 cm. LC Card 87-403629 DDC 332.63/22 19
1. Stocks - Prices - United States. 2. Electric utilities - United States - Finance. I. KCI Communications, Inc.
HG4915 .P65 1987

Power, Jane. Hunter, Jane, 1943- Undercutting sanctions . Washington, DC (918 16th St. NW, Suite 501, Washington 20006) , c1987. iv, 71 p. ; LC Card 87-403525 DDC 337.68 19
HF1613.4 .H86 1987

Power, labor, and livelihood . Hart, Gillian Patricia. Berkeley , c1986. xvi, 228 p. : ISBN 0-520-05499-7 (alk. paper) LC Card 85-8435 DDC 330.9598/2 19
HD1537.I56 H37 1986 ***NYPL [JLE 86-3039]***

Power management in India /. Sah, A. K. (Anirudh Kumar) New Delhi [1986] x, 142, [14] p., [4] p. of plates : LC Card 87-902432 DDC 621.4/068 19
HD9697.A3 I48 1986

The power of consultative selling /. Webster, Bryce. Englewood Cliffs, N.J. , c1987. xvi, 200 p. ; ISBN 0-13-685918-6 LC Card 87-2251 DDC 658.8/1 19
HF5438.25 .W287 1987

The power of ethical management /. Blanchard, Kenneth H. New York , 1988. 139 p. ; ISBN 0-688-07062-0 LC Card 87-24210 DDC 174/.4 19
HF5387 .B56 1988

POWER (PHILOSOPHY)
Janicaud, Dominique, 1937- La puissance du rationnel /. [Paris] , c1985. 386 p. ; ISBN 2-07-070343-6 : ***NYPL [JFD 86-638]***

POWER-PLANTS, ELECTRIC. see **ELECTRIC POWER-PLANTS.**

POWER PLANTS, HYDROELECTRIC. see **HYDROELECTRIC POWER PLANTS.**

POWER-PLANTS - INDIA - MANAGEMENT.
Sah, A. K. (Anirudh Kumar) Power management in India /. New Delhi [1986] x, 142, [14] p., [4] p. of plates : LC Card 87-902432 DDC 621.4/068 19
HD9697.A3 I48 1986

Power production . Fremlin, J. H. Bristol , Boston , c1985. x, 318 p. : ISBN 0-85274-479-X : LC Card 85-115642 DDC 363.1/19621042/0941 19
HD7269.E472 G744 1985 ***NYPL [JLE 86-3055]***

Power production . Fremlin, J. H. Oxford [Oxfordshire] , New York , 1987. p. cm. ISBN 0-19-286078-X (pbk.) : LC Card 87-1564 DDC 363.1/9621042/0941 19
HD7269.E472 G744 1987

Power, production, and the unprotected worker /. Harrod, Jeffrey. New York , 1987. xviii, 347 p. ; ISBN 0-231-05844-6 (alk. paper) LC Card 86-26374 DDC 306/.36 19
HD6971 .H287 1987

POWER PRODUCTION, ELECTRIC. see **ELECTRIC POWER PRODUCTION.**

POWER RESOURCES - AFRICA, SUB-SAHARAN.
Diop, Cheikh Anta. [Fondements économiques et culturels d'un état fédéral d'Afrique noire. English.] Black Africa . Westport, Conn. , Trenton, N.J. , 1987. 125 p. ; ISBN 0-88208-223-X (pbk.) : LC Card 87-17704 DDC 330.967 19
HC800 .D5413 1987

POWER RESOURCES - ALASKA.
Rainery, Richard. Alaska's public energy resources . [Juneau?] [1985] 8, 124, 3, 7 p. : LC Card 86-622191 DDC 333.79/09798 19
HD9502.U53 A473 1985

POWER RESOURCES - ASIA - STATISTICS.
Asian energy problems . New York, N.Y., U. S.A. , Singapore , 1982. xxxviii, 363 p. : ISBN 0-03-061566-6 (pbk.) LC Card 81-84610
HD9502.A782 A84x 1982

POWER RESOURCES - AUSTRALIA - WESTERN AUSTRALIA.
Taylor, Neil. The security of energy supplies in Western Australia /. Murdoch, W.A. , 1986. 35 p. : ISBN 0-86905-099-0 (pbk.) : LC Card 87-118009 DDC 333.79/09941 19
HD9502.A873 W45673 1986

POWER RESOURCES - BRAZIL - CONGRESSES.
Opções energéticas . Belo Horizonte, MG , 1983. 328 p., [30] leaves of plates : LC Card 83-205480
HD9502.B72 O63 1983

POWER RESOURCES - BRAZIL - MINAS GERAIS.
Fluxo energético estadual, 1983 /. [Belo Horizonte, Brazil] , 1985. 105 p. : LC Card 87-404947 DDC 333.79/0981/51 19
HD9502.B73 M5646 1985

POWER RESOURCES - BRAZIL, NORTHEAST - CONGRESSES.
Lopes, Marcos José. Atendimento ao mercado de energia elétrica do Nordeste /. Recife, PE [1984] 2 v. in 4 : LC Card 86-166126
HD9685.B83 N675 1984

POWER RESOURCES - CANADA.
Connections . [Ottawa] , Ottawa, Canada , 1985. x, 207 p. : ISBN 0-660-11743-6 (pbk.) : LC Card 85-136746 DDC 333.79/0971 19
TJ163.25.C2 C66 1985 ***NYPL [JLF 87-326]***

POWER RESOURCES - CHINA.
Smil, Vaclav. Energy in China's modernization . Armonk, N.Y. , c1988. xiv, 250 p. : ISBN 0-87332-423-4 LC Card 87-12922 DDC 333.79/0951 19
HD9502.C62 S644 1988

POWER RESOURCES - CONGRESSES.
International Scientific Forum on Changes in Energy (1981 : Mexico City, Mexico) Global energy assessment and outlook . Chur, Switzerland , New York, N.Y. , c1984. xxix, 580 p. : ISBN 3-7186-0224-5 LC Card 84-12959 DDC 333.79 19
TJ163.15 .I5678 1981 ***NYPL [JSE 86-509]***

POWER RESOURCES - DEVELOPING COUNTRIES - CONGRESSES.
Management Training Seminar (1982 : Joint Research Centre, Ispra, Italy) National energy planning and management in developing countries . Dordrecht, Holland , Hingham, MA , c1983. xiii, 442 p. ; ISBN 90-277-1589-0 LC Card 83-4407 DDC 333.79/09172/4 19
HD9502.A2 M343 1982 ***NYPL [JLE 87-302]***

POWER RESOURCES DEVELOPMENT. see **ENERGY DEVELOPMENT.**

POWER RESOURCES - ECONOMIC ASPECTS - CONGRESSES.
IASTED Symposia on Modelling, Policy and Economics of Energy and Power Systems, and Alternative Energy Sources and Technology (1981 : San Francisco, Calif.) Proceedings of the IASTED Energy Symposia : Modelling, Policy and Economics of Energy and Power Systems [and] Alternative Energy Sources and Technology, May 20-22, 1981, San Francisco, U. S.A. /. Anaheim, Calif. [1981?] 209 p. : ISBN 0-88986-027-0 ***NYPL [JSF 86-1103]***

POWER RESOURCES - ECONOMIC ASPECTS - SOVIET UNION.
Mineral'noe syr'e i ėkonomiia material'nykh i ėnergeticheskikh resursov /. Moskva , 1986. 333, [3] p. : LC Card 87-119481
HD9502.S652 M56 1986

POWER RESOURCES - ECUADOR.
Kublank, Peter. Balances energéticos del Ecuador . Quito, Ecuador , 1983. 1 v. (various foliations) : LC Card 86-153116
HD9502.E22 K82 1983

POWER RESOURCES - EUROPE.
Braathu, Jan. Diversification strategies and security-of-supply . Oslo [1984?] 74 p. ; LC Card 85-129223 DDC 382/.42285/094 19
HD9581.E8552 B7 1984
NYPL [JLM 78-136 no.88]

Weyman-Jones, Thomas G., 1947- Energy in Europe . London , New York , 1986. xii, 176 p. : ISBN 0-416-36590-6 LC Card 86-18169 DDC 333.79/094 19
TJ163.25.E85 W48 1986
NYPL [JLD 87-1305]

POWER RESOURCES - FORECASTING.
Energy after the eighties . Amsterdam , New York , 1984. xxii, 298 p. : ISBN 0-444-42404-0 : LC Card 84-13742 DDC 333.79 19
HD9502.A2 E537 1984
NYPL [JLE 86-1572]

POWER RESOURCES - FORECASTING - CASE STUDIES.
The Politics of energy forecasting . Oxford [Oxfordshire] , New York , 1987. xiii, 314 p. : ISBN 0-19-828547-7 : LC Card 86-23885 DDC 333.79 19
HD9502.A2 P66 1987

POWER RESOURCES - GERMANY, WEST.
Gesamtkonzeption nachwachsende Rohstoffe des Bundesministeriums für Ernährung, Landwirtschaft und Forsten . Münster-Hiltrup , 1983. vi, 196 p. : ISBN 3-7843-0202-5 : LC Card 84-126491
HD9502.G42 G47 1983

POWER RESOURCES - GREAT BRITAIN.
Britain's energy resources /. London , 1981. 27 p. : ISBN 0-11-701010-3 (pbk.) LC Card 81-165936 DDC 333.79/0941 19
HD9502.G72 B74 1981

POWER RESOURCES - HUNGARY.
Márton, Géza. A hazai energiaszerkezet-változás fontosabb regionális kérdései /. Budapest , 1974. 271 p. : ISBN 963-05-0062-0 LC Card 86-187425
HD9502.H92 M37 1974

POWER RESOURCES - HUNGARY - STATISTICS.
Az Energiatermelés és az energiafelhasználás szerkezete . Budapest , 1970. 44 p. ; LC Card 86-189699
HD9502.H92 E54 1970

POWER RESOURCES - INDIA.
Energy problem and world economic development . New Delhi , c1983. vi, 192 p. ; LC Card 83-906441 DDC 333.79/0954 19
HD9502.I42 E54 1983 ***NYPL [JLD 87-629]***

Guru, D. D. Energy and economic development /. Delhi , c1987. xi, 257 p. : ISBN 81-85061-53-6 : LC Card 87-901433 DDC 333.79/0954 19
HD9502.I4 G87 1987

POWER RESOURCES - INDIA - CONGRESSES.
Energy alternatives for rural development /. Jaipur , 1985. vi, 303 p. : LC Card 86-902191 DDC 333.79/0954 19
HD9556.I42 E54 1985

POWER RESOURCES - INDIA - GUJARAT.
Energy use in rural Gujarat /. New Delhi , c1987. iv, 186 p. : ISBN 81-204-0216-2 : LC Card 87-901949 DDC 333.79/13/095475 19
HD9502.I43 G844 1987

POWER RESOURCES - INDIA - MANAGEMENT.
Sah, A. K. (Anirudh Kumar) Power management in India /. New Delhi [1986] x, 142, [14] p., [4] p. of plates : LC Card 87-902432 DDC 621.4/068 19
HD9697.A3 I48 1986

POWER RESOURCES - INFORMATION SERVICES - DEVELOPING COUNTRIES - CONGRESSES.
National energy data systems . New Delhi , 1984, c1983. xxvi, 511 p. ; LC Card 84-901310 DDC 333.79/09172/4 19
HD9502.D442 N37 1984
NYPL [JLD 86-4320]

POWER RESOURCES - JUVENILE LITERATURE.
Gibson, Michael, 1942- The energy crisis /. Vero Beach, FL , 1987. 46 p. : ISBN 0-86592-277-2 LC Card 87-12768 DDC 333.79 19
HD9502.A2 G525 1987

POWER RESOURCES - KENYA.
Hosier, Richard. Energy use in rural Kenya . Stockholm , Uppsala , c1985. xi, 177 p. : ISBN 91-7106-241-6 ***NYPL [JLD 86-2653]***

POWER RESOURCES - MATHEMATICAL MODELS.
Ströbele, Wolfgang. Wirtschaftswachstum bei begrenzten Energieressourcen /. Berlin , c1984. 173 p. : ISBN 3-428-05541-1 LC Card 84-176734
HD84 .S747 1984

POWER RESOURCES - MATHEMATICAL MODELS - CONGRESSES.
IASTED Symposia on Modelling, Policy and Economics of Energy and Power Systems, and Alternative Energy Sources and Technology (1981 : San Francisco, Calif.) Proceedings of the IASTED Energy Symposia : Modelling, Policy and Economics of Energy and Power Systems [and] Alternative Energy Sources and Technology, May 20-22, 1981, San Francisco, U. S.A. /. Anaheim, Calif. [1981?] 209 p. : ISBN 0-88986-027-0 ***NYPL [JSF 86-1103]***

POWER RESOURCES - PACIFIC AREA.
The Pacific rim . Vancouver , 1987, c1986. ix, 319 p. : ISBN 0-7748-0266-9 (pbk.) LC Card 87-140238 DDC 330.99 19
HF4030.7 .P33 1987

POWER RESOURCES - PRICES.
Rente et structures des industries de l'énergie /. [Saint-Martin-d'Hères] , 1983. 268 p. : ISBN 2-7061-0217-9 : LC Card 84-173320
HD9502.A2 R45 1983 ***NYPL [JLE 87-1263]***

POWER RESOURCES - RESEARCH - SWEDEN.
Wittrock, Björn. De stora programmens tid . Stockholm , 1984. 186 p. ; ISBN 91-7410-200-1 : LC Card 84-189613
HD9502.S82 W58 1984

POWER RESOURCES - RESEARCH - UNITED STATES - ADDRESSES, ESSAYS, LECTURES.
The Politics of energy research and development /. New Brunswick, U. S.A. , c1986. 181 p. : ISBN 0-88738-653-9 (pbk.) LC Card 86-1307 DDC 333.79/0973 19
HD9502.U52 P63 1986
NYPL [JLE 86-3577]

POWER RESOURCES - RWANDA.
Joint UNDP/World Bank Energy Sector Assessment Program. Rwanda . [Washington, D.C.?] [1982] ii, 68 p., [1] folded leaf : LC Card 87-136863 DDC 333.79/0967/571 19
HD9502.R932 J65 1982

POWER RESOURCES - SOVIET UNION - TRANSPORTATION.
Sagers, Matthew J. The transportation of Soviet energy resources /. Totowa, N.J. , 1986. xvi, 177 p. : ISBN 0-8476-7504-1 : LC Card 86-15508 DDC 380.5/24 19
HD9502.S652 S24 1986 ***NYPL [JLE 87-38]***

POWER RESOURCES - SPAIN.
Comisión Energía y Recursos de AEPDEN-Amigos de la Tierra. Modelo energético de tránsito /. Madrid [1979?] 136 p. ; ISBN 84-85639-02-2 LC Card 79-126051
HD9502.S662 C66 1979 ***NYPL [JLC 87-71]***

POWER RESOURCES - SWEDEN.
Försörjningstryggheten för olja, kol och uran . Stockholm [1982] 175 p. : ISBN 91-38-07030-8 LC Card 82-240448
HD9502.S82 F68 1983

Sweden. Oljeersättningsdelegationen. Uppföljning av oljeersättningsprogrammet . [Stockholm] [1982] 83, [74] p. : ISBN 91-38-07111-8 LC Card 83-217864
HD9502.S82 S96 1982

POWER RESOURCES - UNITED STATES.
Bloch, Carolyn. Federal energy information sources and data bases /. Park Ridge, N.J. , 1979. x, 115 p. ; ISBN 0-8155-0764-X : LC Card 79-15543 DDC 016.33379/0973 19
HD9502.U52 B58 ***NYPL [JLE 86-4259]***

Handbook of alternative energy technology development and policy /. [Washington, D.C.] , 1983. xiv, 341 p. : ***NYPL [JLF 86-1486]***

Rosenbaum, Walter A. Energy, politics, and public policy /. Washington, D.C. , c1987. viii, 221 p. : ISBN 0-87187-412-1 (pbk.) : LC Card 87-5301 DDC 333.79/0973 19
HD9502.U52 R64 1987

POWER RESOURCES - UNITED STATES - FORECASTING.
United States. Dept. of Energy. Office of Policy, Planning, and Analysis. National energy policy plan projections to 2010 . Washington, D.C. [1985] 1 v. (various pagings) : LC Card 86-601637 DDC 333.79/0973 19
HD9502.U52 U5125 1985

The power sector in India /. Hans, Asha. New Delhi , c1986. vi, 149 p. ; LC Card 86-901959 DDC 333.79/32/0954 19
HD9502.I42 H36 1986

POWER (SOCIAL SCIENCES) - HISTORY.
Cox, Robert W., 1926- Production, power, and world order . New York , 1987. xii, 500 p. ; ISBN 0-231-05808-X LC Card 86-26387
HD6971 .C78 1987

POWER SUPPLY. see **POWER RESOURCES.**

Power, Thomas M. The economic pursuit of quality / by Thomas M. Power. Armonk, N.Y. : M.E. Sharpe, c1987. p. cm. ISBN 0-87332-436-6 LC Card 87-12128 DDC 330 19
1. Economics. I. Title.
HB171 .P697 1987

Power to fly . Francis, Devon. [Fallbrook, CA] , 1986. 97 p. : ISBN 0-8168-7632-0 : LC Card 85-20045 DDC 338.4/76655825/0973 19
TL521 .F63 1986 ***NYPL [JSG 86-235]***

Power user's guide to one-two-three. Lunsford, E. Michael. Power user's guide to 1-2-3 /. San Francisco , c1988. xx, 367 p. : ISBN 0-89588-421-6 (pbk.) LC Card 87-61528 DDC 005.36/9 19
HF5548.4.L67 L87 1988

Power user's guide to 1-2-3 /. Lunsford, E. Michael. San Francisco , c1988. xx, 367 p. : ISBN 0-89588-421-6 (pbk.) LC Card 87-61528 DDC 005.36/9 19
HF5548.4.L67 L87 1988

POWERS, SEPARATION OF. see **SEPARATION OF POWERS.**

Poyo, Jeffrey. Los bancos agropecuarios y la captación de depósitos / Jeffrey Poyo. 1a ed. Santo Domingo, República Dominicana : Centro de Estudios Monetarios y Bancarios, 1986. 39 p. : ill. ; 21 cm. (Biblioteca Mercados financieros . 2) Serie Estudios Bibliography: p. 39. LC Card 87-400523 DDC 332.7/1/097293 19
1. Agricultural credit - Dominican Republic. 2. Bank deposits - Dominican Republic. 3. Banks and banking - Dominican Republic. I. Series. II. Series: Serie Estudios (Centro de Estudios Monetarios y Bancarios (Santo Domingo, Dominican Republic)). III. Title.
HG2051.D6 P69 1986

Poznań, Poland. Akademia Ekonomiczna. see **Akademia Ekonomiczna w Poznaniu.**

Poznań, Poland. Politechnika. see **Politechnika Poznańska.**

Poznański, Kazimierz. Technology, competition, & the Soviet bloc in the world

market / Kazimierz Z. Poznański. Berkeley : Institute of International Studies, University of California, Berkeley, c1987. ix, 226 p. ; 24 cm. (Research studies, 0068-6093 . no. 70) Bibliography: p. 211-221. Includes index. ISBN 0-87725-170-3 (pbk.) : LC Card 87-3505 DDC 338/.06 19
1. Technological innovations - Europe, Eastern. 2. Export marketing - Europe, Eastern. 3. Quality of products - Europe, Eastern. 4. Europe, Eastern - Manufactures. I. Title. II. Title: Technology, competition, and the Soviet bloc in the world market. III. Series: Research series (University of California, Berkeley. Institute of International Studies) , no. 70.
HC244.Z9 T4716 1987

Poznavate li svoeto predpriiatie?
Kadiev, Ivan. Khronika za "Proletarii" /. [Sofia] , 1985. 140, [3] p., [32] p. of plates : LC Card 86-195264
HD9969.K7 B855 1985

Pozsonyi, Pál. A Nemzeti vagyon és az állóeszközállomány 1970-1978 /. [Budapest] [1979] 140 p. ; LC Card 82-193609
HC300.295.W4 N454 1979

PPC self-study CPE.
Clay, John R. Advanced compilation and review . Fort Worth, Tex. , c1987. 1 v. (various pagings) : LC Card 87-160681 DDC 657/.3 19
HF5667.65 .M42 1986 Suppl.

PPC self-study library.
Clay, John R. Accounting for S corporations and noncorporate entities . Fort Worth, Tex. , c1987. 1 v. (various pagings) ; LC Card 87-163295 DDC 657/.95/076 19
HF5686.C7 C58 1987

PR . Blyskal, Jeff. New York , c1985. 241 p. ; ISBN 0-688-04788-2 : LC Card 85-80602
NYPL [JLE 86-268]

Prabhakara, N. R.
Internal migration and population redistribution in India : some reflections / N.R. Prabhakara. New Delhi : Concept Pub. Co., 1986, c1985. xi, 117 p. ; 23 cm. Bibliography: p. [110]-113. Includes index. LC Card 86-902406 DDC 304.8/0954/87 19
1. Migration, Internal - India - Karnataka. 2. Karnataka (India) - Population. I. Title.
HB2100.K37 P73 1985

Population growth and unemployment in India / N.R. Prabhakara, M.N. Usha. New Delhi : Ashish Pub. House, 1986. ix, 102 p. ; 23 cm. Bibliography: p. 97-99. Includes index. ISBN 81-7024-041-7 : LC Card 86-902156 DDC 331.13/795487 19
1. Unemployment - India - Karnataka. 2. Poor - India - Karnataka. 3. Labor supply - India - Karnataka. I. Usha, M. N. II. Title.
HD5820.K37 P7 1986

Prabhakara Rao, D. (Devisetti), 1954- Human resource accounting / D. Prabhakara Rao. New Delhi, India : Inter-India Publications, 1986. xviii, 247 p. : ill. ; 23 cm. Empirical study based on data from the Hindustan Shipyard Limited. Bibliography: p. [228]-244. Includes index. ISBN 81-210-0169-2 : LC Card 86-902848
1. Human capital - Accounting. 2. Hindustan Shipyard Limited. I. Title.
HF5681.H8 P73 1986

Praca zawodowa a życie rodzinne kobiet / [redaktor Stefania Dzięcielska-Machnikowska]. Wyd. 1. [Łódź] : Uniwersytet Łódzki, 1979. 120 p. ; 24 cm. (Acta Universitatis Lodziensis = Zeszyty naukowe Uniwersytetu Łódzkiego. Nauki ekonomiczne i socjologiczne. Seria 3 . nr 44) Summaries in English. Includes bibliographical references. LC Card 81-109965
1. Women - Employment - Poland - Łódź. 2. Mothers - Employment - Poland - Łódź. I. Dzięcielska-Machnikowska, Stefania.
HD6054.2.P72 L636 1979

Prace habilitacyjne (Wrocław, Poland)
Dąbrowski, Marek. Ekonomiczne konsekwencje samorządności pracowniczej /. Wrocław , 1986. 140 p. ; ISBN 83-04-02213-3 : LC Card 86-199502
HD5660.P6 D33 1986

Prace naukowe Akademii Ekonomicznej imienia Oskara Langego we Wrocławiu .
(nr. 122) Studencki ruch naukowy /. Wrocław , 1978. 98 p. : LC Card 81-206830
HB9 .B7522 nr. 122 HD36

(nr. 188) Systemy organizacyjne /. [Wrocław] , 1981. 75 p. : LC Card 83-161920
HB9 .B7522 nr. 188 HM131

(nr. 191) Technologia /. [Wrocław] , 1982. 188 p. : LC Card 83-176194
HB9 .B7522 nr. 191 TP185

(nr. 216) Lichtarski, Jan. Kryteria i metody oceny efektywności przedsięwzięć organizatorskich w przedsiębiorstwie /. [Wrocław] , 1982. 197 p. : LC Card 83-153426
HB9 .B7522 nr. 216 HD58.9

(nr. 218) Rymarczyk, Jan. Migracja siły roboczej do krajów EWG i jej konsekwencje społeczno-gospodarcze /. [Wrocław] , 1982. 239 p., [4] folded leaves ; LC Card 83-153742
HB9 .B7522 nr. 218 HD8378.5.A2

(nr. 218) Rymarczyk, Jan. Migracja siły roboczej do krajów EWG i jej konsekwencje społeczno-gospodarcze /. [Wrocław] , 1982. 239 p., [4] folded leaves ; LC Card 83-153742
HB9 .B7522 nr. 218 HD8378.5.A2

(nr. 245) Siemianowski, Andrzej. Fakty, prawa, decyzje . [Wrocław] , 1983. 103 p. ; LC Card 85-113022
HB9 .B7522 nr. 245 Q175

(nr. 301) Problems of decision making based on experimental data /. Wrocław , 1985. 186 p. : LC Card 86-207027
HB9 .B7522 nr. 301 QA279.4

(nr. 304) Wybrane problemy ekonomiki przemysłu /. Wrocław , 1985. 110 p. ; LC Card 86-155957
HB9 .B7522 nr. 304 HD70.P6

(nr. 355) Funkcjonowanie rynku usług w Polsce /. Wrocław , 1986. 176 p. ; ISBN 83-7011-034-7 : LC Card 87-169457
HB9 .B7522 nr. 355 HD9986.P7

(nr. 8) Rymarczyk, Jan. Migracja siły roboczej do krajów EWG i jej konsekwencje społeczno-gospodarcze /. [Wrocław] , 1982. 239 p., [4] folded leaves ; LC Card 83-153742
HB9 .B7522 nr. 218 HD8378.5.A2

(zesz. 122 (144)) Studencki ruch naukowy /. Wrocław , 1978. 98 p. : LC Card 81-206830
HB9 .B7522 nr. 122 HD36

(zesz. 141) Statystyka i ekonometria /. Wrocław , 1978. 193 p. : LC Card 81-206821
HB9 .B7522 zesz. 141 HB135

Prace naukowe Instytutu Organizacji i Ekonomiki Politechniki Wrocławskiej. Studia i materiały .
(1) Organizacja produkcji w przemyśle /. Wrocław , 1970. 64 p. : LC Card 87-137344
HD70.P6 O745 1970

Prace z zakresu ekonomiki i organizacji przedsiębiorstw handlowych / [redaktor naukowy zeszytu Zbigniew Misiaszek]. Kraków : Akademia Ekonomiczna w Krakowie, 1978. 176 p. ; 24 cm. (Zeszyty naukowe / Akademia Ekonomiczna w Krakowie . nr. 101) Summaries in English and Russian. Includes bibliographical references. LC Card 81-200309
1. Retail trade - Poland. I. Misiaszek, Zbigniew. II. Series: Zeszyty naukowe / Akademia Ekonomiczna w Krakowie , nr. 101.
HB9 .K53 nr. 101 HF5429.6.P6

Prace z zakresu ekonomiki produkcji / [redaktor naukowy Edmund Kurtys]. Wyd. 1. Poznań : Wydawn. Akademii Ekonomicznej w Poznaniu, 1984. 219 p. : ill. ; 24 cm. (Zeszyty naukowe / Akademia Ekonomiczna w Poznaniu. Seria I . zesz. nr. 122) Summaries also in English and Russian. Includes bibliographical references. LC Card 86-127229
1. Industrial management - Poland. I. Kurtys, Edmund. II. Series: Zeszyty naukowe / Akademia Ekonomiczna w Poznaniu. Seria I , zesz. nr. 122.
HB54 .P6 nr. 122 HD70.P6

Prace z zakresu planowania i ekonomiki regionu / [redaktor naukowy zeszytu Jan Steczkowski]. Kraków : Akademia Ekonomiczna w Krakowie, 1980. 220 p. : ill. ; 24 cm. (Zeszyty naukowe / Akademia Ekonomiczna w Krakowie . nr. 116) Summaries in English and Russian. Includes bibliographical references. LC Card 80-131017
1. Poland - Economic conditions - 1945-. 2. Regional planning - Poland. 3. Europe, Eastern - Economic conditions - 1945-. 4. Regional planning - Europe, Eastern. I. Steczkowski, Jan. II. Series: Zeszyty naukowe / Akademia Ekonomiczna w Krakowie , nr. 116.
HB9 .K53 nr. 116 HC340.3

Prace z zakresu socjologii / [redaktor naukowy zeszytu Jerzy Mikułowski-Pomorski]. Kraków : Akademia Ekonomiczna w Krakowie, 1979. 137 p. ; 24 cm. (Zeszyty naukowe / Akademia Ekonomiczna w Krakowie . nr. 117) Summaries in English and Russian. Includes bibliographical references. LC Card 80-129964
1. Kraków (Poland) - Economic conditions. 2. Consumption (Economics) - Poland - Kraków. I. Mikułowski-Pomorski, Jerzy. II. Series: Zeszyty naukowe / Akademia Ekonomiczna w Krakowie , nr. 117.
HB9 .K53 nr. 117 HC340.3.Z7K7

Pracher, Christian. Schauer, Reinbert. Die Verwaltung als betriebliches Teilsystem . Wien , 1984. v, 258 p. : ISBN 3-85436-014-2 LC Card 84-173337
HD35 .S2655 1984

Prācīna Bhārata meṃ vyāvasāyika samudāya, 600 Ī. Pū. se 200 Ī. taka =. Rāya, Śaśikānta, 1957- Naī Dillī , 1986. 176 p. ; LC Card 87-902475
HB3639 .R39 1986

A practical and simple guide to a home mortgage /. Bass, Gary J. Irving, Tex. , c1987. v, 66 p. : ISBN 0-944319-00-9 (pbk.) LC Card 87-82025 DDC 332.7/22/0973 19
HG2040.5.U5 B367 1987

Practical business math procedures /. Slater, Jeffrey, 1947- Homewood, Ill. , 1987. xiv, 440 p. : ISBN 0-256-03654-3 (pbk.) LC Card 85-82557 DDC 513/.93 19
HF5694 .S57 1987

Practical business planning /. Chandler, John. London , New York , c1987. 210 p. ; ISBN 0-07-084172-1 (pbk.) : LC Card 87-3240 DDC 658.4/012 19
HD30.28 .C45 1987

A Practical guide to investigating public works violations / developed by California State Building and Construction Trades Council [and] Painting and Drywall Work Preservation Fund, Inc. [and] Piping Industry Progress and Education. Oakland, CA (520 3rd St., Suite 204, Oakland 94607) : Painting and Drywall Work Preservation Fund, 1986. 73 p., [3] leaves of plates : ill. ; 28 cm. Cover title. Bibliography: p. 71-73. LC Card 86-209657 DDC 363.2/5 19
1. California - Public works - Corrupt practices. 2. Public contracts - California - Criminal provisions. 3. Corruption investigation - California. I. California State Building and Construction Trades Council. II. Painting and Drywall Work Preservation Fund. III. Piping Industry Progress & Education.
HD3890.C2 P7 1986

The practical guide to voice mail /. Parker, Martin F. Berkeley, Calif. , c1987. xiv, 306 p. : ISBN 0-07-881243-7 (pbk.) LC Card 86-210772 DDC 621.385 19
HF5541.T4 P37 1987

The practical handbook and guide to focus group research /. Greenbaum, Thomas L. Lexington, Mass. , c1988. xii, 191 p. ; ISBN 0-669-14775-3 (alk. paper) LC Card 86-45946 DDC 658.8/3 19
HF5415.2 .G695 1988

The practical handbook of computerization for distribution managers /. Barrett, Colin. Washington , c1987. xvi, 317 p. ; ISBN 0-87408-040-1 LC Card 86-51299 DDC 658.7/8/0285 19
HF5415.7 .B36 1987

Practical handbook of industrial traffic management /. Morse, Leon William. Washington , 1987. xiii, 642 p. : ISBN 0-87408-039-8 LC Card 86-51249 DDC 658.7/882 19
HF5761 .M74 1987

Practical handbook of transportation contracting and rate negotiations /. Barrett, Colin. Washington , c1987. ix, 269 p. ; ISBN 0-87408-037-1 LC Card 86-50988 DDC 380.5/24/068 19
HE199.U5 B37 1987

Practical intelligence . Peters, Roger. New York, N.Y. , c1987. x, 341 p. ; ISBN 0-06-015681-3 : LC Card 86-46096 DDC 650.1 19
HD38.2 .P47 1987

PRACTICAL JUDGMENT.
Peters, Roger. Practical intelligence . New York, N.Y. , c1987. x, 341 p. ; ISBN 0-06-015681-3 : LC Card 86-46096 DDC

650.1 19
HD38.2 .P47 1987

Practical management series.
Long-term financial planning . Washington, D.C. , 1987. 188 p. ; ISBN 0-87326-076-7 (pbk.) : LC Card 87-2613 DDC 352.1/0973 19
HJ275 .L66 1987

PRACTICAL POLITICS. see **POLITICS, PRACTICAL.**

Practical steps in raising business finance from banks /. Akwaeze, G. C. Enugu, Nigeria , 1985. 290 p. : ISBN 978-15-6214-5 (pbk.) LC Card 87-118106 DDC 658.1/5224 19
HG3754.5.N6 A38 1985

Prácticas y orientaciones del movimiento sindical en la lucha por la democracia /. Frías F., Patricio. Santiago, Chile , 1986. 57 p. ; LC Card 87-101389
HD6618.5 .F75 1986

The practice of collective bargaining /. Beal, Edwin Fletcher. Homewood, Ill. , 1985. xvi, 560 p. : ISBN 0-256-03214-9 LC Card 84-82023 DDC 331.89 19
HD6508 .B375 1985 ***NYPL [*R-Econ. 86-3458]***

The practice of marketing management . Cohen, William A., 1937- New York , London , c1988. xix, 695 p. : ISBN 0-02-323150-5 LC Card 87-11281 DDC 658.8 19
HF5415.13 .C635 1988

The practice of modern internal auditing /. Sawyer, Lawrence B. Altamonte Springs, Fla. , 1981. xiv, 882 p. : ISBN 0-89413-092-7 LC Card 87-462054 DDC 657/.458 19
HF5668.25 .S28 1981

The practice of supervision . DuBrin, Andrew J. Plano, Tex. , 1987. xvi, 571 p. : ISBN 0-256-03685-3 (pbk.) LC Card 86-71880 DDC 658.3/02 19
HF5549 .D82 1987

Practicing management /. Griffin, Ricky W. Boston , c1987. xii, 368 p. : ISBN 0-395-42584-0 (pbk.) LC Card 87-163492 DDC 658 19
HD31 .G7635 1987

Practicing management. Griffin, Ricky W. Instructor's manual, Practicing management, second edition /. Boston , c1987. xiii, 167 p. ; ISBN 0-395-42585-9 (pbk.) LC Card 87-400618 DDC 658 19
HD31 .G7627 1987

Practising Law Institute. Tax, SEC, and accounting aspects of corporate acquisitions, 1984 /. New York, N.Y. (810 Seventh Ave., New York 10019) , c1984. 584 p. : LC Card 84-231882 DDC 343.7306/7 347.30367 19
KF6499.M4 T39 1984 ***NYPL [JLD 87-57]***

Pradeep Kumar. see **Kumar, Pradeep.**

Pradelle, Jean-Marc. Politiques vivrières, dépendances alimentaires et développement /. [Paris] , c1984. iv, 129 p. : ISBN 2-86844-000-2 : LC Card 84-248912
HD9017.S152 P65 1984

Pradhan, Radhe S. Public corporations of Nepal : a study of financial ratios / Radhe S. Pradhan.1st ed. New Delhi, India : National Book Organisation, 1986. xiii, 173 p. ; 23 cm. Based on a study of ten corporations in the manufacturing sector and ten in the non-manufacturing sector over a period of twelve years. Bibliography: p. [158]-161. Includes index. LC Card 86-903436 DDC 338.7/4/095496 19
1. Ratio analysis. 2. Corporations - Nepal - Finance. I. Title.
HF5681.R25 P73 1986

Prado Moura, Angel de. El movimiento obrero en Valladolid durante la II República, 1931-1936 / Angel de Prado Moura. [Castilla y León] : Junta de Castilla y León, Consejería de Educación y Cultura, 1985. 234 p. : ill. ; 25 cm. Bibliography: p. 231-232. ISBN 84-505-2341-9 LC Card 86-214605
1. Labor and laboring classes - Spain - Valladolid (Province) - Political activity - History. 2. Trade-unions - Spain - Valladolid (Province) - History. 3. Valladolid (Spain : Province) - Economic conditions. I. Title.
HD8119.V34 P72 1985

Präferenzen für öffentliche Güter . Pommerehne, Werner W. Tübingen , 1987. xv, 290 p. : ISBN 3-16-945040-9 LC Card 87-138780 DDC 363 19
HB846.5 .P66 1987

Präferenzregelung der Forschungs- und Entwicklungsförderung in Berlin /. Hornschild, Kurt. Berlin , 1985. v, 55 p. ; ISBN 3-428-05800-3 LC Card 86-156799
HD30.42.G39 H67 1985

Prael, Charles E. Tymes, Elna. Lotus 1-2-3 financial models /. Indianapolis, Ind. , c1988. vi, 307 p. ; ISBN 0-672-48410-2 (pbk.) LC Card 87-72205 DDC 005.36/9 19
HF5548.4.L67 T95 1988

Praet, Peter.
International trade and exchange rates in the late eighties /. Amsterdam ; New York : xii, 418 p. : ISBN 0-444-87941-2 LC Card 86-223111 DDC 382.4/5 19
HG203 .I58 1985

International trade and exchange rates in the late eighties /. Amsterdam ; New York : xii, 418 p. : ISBN 2-8004-0892-8
NYPL [JLE 87-120]

Prager, Jonas. Fundamentals of money, banking, and financial institutions / Jonas Prager. 2nd ed. New York : Harper & Row, c1987. xix, 783, 11 p. : ill. ; 24 cm. Includes bibliographies and index. ISBN 0-06-045253-6 LC Card 86-27023 DDC 332.1 19
1. Money. 2. Banks and banking. 3. Financial institutions. I. Title.
HG221 .P9195 1987

Práger, László. Gazdaságon innen és túl : a szocialista vállalat parttalan funkciói / Práger László. Budapest : Akadémiai Kiadó, 1986. 194 p. : ill. ; 21 cm. Bibliography: p. 185-190. ISBN 963-05-4355-9 : LC Card 87-407707
I. Title.
HD70.H8 P7 1986

Prague, Cary N. Programming with dBase III / Cary N. Prague and James E. Hammitt. 1st ed. Blue Ridge Summit, Pa. : Tab Books, 1985. ix, 292 p. ; 24 cm. Includes index. ISBN 0-8306-0976-8 : LC Card 84-23979 DDC 001.64/2 19
1. Data base management. 2. dBase III (Computer program). 3. Microcomputers - Programming. I. Hammitt, James E. II. Title.
QA76.9.D3 P728 1985 ***NYPL [JSE 87-75]***

PRAGUE (CZECHOSLOVAKIA) - POPULATION - STATISTICS.
Sčítání lidu, domů a bytů 1970. Praha [1970?] 132, [64] p. ; LC Card 82-143437
HA1198.P7 S38 1970

Prague, N. Cary. Programming with dBASE III PLUS / by Cary N. Prague and James E. Hammitt. 1st ed. Blue Ridge Summit, PA : Tab Books, c1986. vi, 375 p. : ill. ; 24 cm. On t.p. the registered trademark symbol "®" is superscript following "dBASE III" in the title. Includes index. "No. 2726." ISBN 0-8306-0326-3 : LC Card 86-5736 DDC 005.74 19
1. Data base management. 2. dBASE III PLUS (Computer program). 3. Microcomputers - Programming. I. Hammitt, James E. II. Title.
QA76.9.D3 P729 1986 ***NYPL [JSE 87-539]***

Prahalad, C. K. The multinational mission : balancing local demands and global vision / C.K. Prahalad, Yves L. Doz. New York : Free Press ; London : Collier Macmillan, c1987. ix, 290 p. : ill. ; 25 cm. Bibliography: p. 273-281. Includes index. ISBN 0-02-925050-1 LC Card 87-11970 DDC 658/.049 19
1. International business enterprises - Management. I. Doz, Yves L. II. Title.
HD62.4 .P69 1987

Praiphol Koomsup. The Minerals industries of ASEAN and Australia . Sydney , Boston , 1988. p. cm. ISBN 0-04-301284-1 LC Card 87-18339 DDC 338.2/0959 19
HD9506.A6592 M56 1988

The prairies and the pampas . Solberg, Carl E. Stanford, Calif. , 1987. xii, 297 p. : ISBN 0-8047-1346-4 (alk. paper) : LC Card 86-27854 DDC 338.1/8 19
HD9049.W5 C297 1987

Prakasam, C. P. Student research abstracts in population studies /. Bombay , 1986, c1985. xi, 434 p. ; LC Card 86-902278 DDC 304.6/095 19
HA4553 .S78 1986

Prakash, Arun J. Financial, commercial, and mortgage mathematics and their applications / Arun J. Prakash, Gordon V. Karels, Ray Fernandez. New York : Praeger, 1987. x, 245 p. ; 24 cm. Rev. ed. of Financial, commercial, and mortgage mathematics and their applications / Gordon V. Karels. Includes bibliographies and index. ISBN 0-275-92119-0 (alk. paper) : LC Card 86-30579 DDC 513/.93 19
1. Business mathematics. 2. Business mathematics - Real estate business. I. Karels, Gordon V. II. Fernandez, Ray. III. Title.
HF5691 .P69 1987

Prakash, Ishwar. Mann, H. S. (Haracharan Singh), 1922- Halting the march . [New Delhi] [1983] 35, [1] p., [4] p. of plates : LC Card 86-204352 DDC 338.1/0954/4 19
HC437.T47 M36 1983

Prakash, Om, 1927- Guided incomes policy / Om Prakash. 1st ed. New Delhi : Sterling, 1983. vi, 214 p. ; 22 cm. Includes bibliographical references and index. LC Card 83-902415 DDC 339.5/0954 19
1. Income - Government policy - India. 2. Social justice. 3. India - Economic policy. I. Title.
HC440.I5 P72 1983 ***NYPL [JLD 86-3834]***

De praktijk van de inkomensverdeling /. Hoek, M. P. van der. Groningen , c1987. 183 p. : ISBN 90-01-39430-2 : LC Card 87-157808
HC329.5.I5 H634 1987

Praktikum po demografii /. Boi͡arskiĭ, Aron I͡Akovlevich, 1906- Moskva , 1985. 141, [3] p. : LC Card 86-170070
HB3607 .B64 1985

Praktikum po organizat͡sii i planirovanii͡u proizvodstva na promyshlennykh predprii͡atii͡akh / [nauchnyĭ redaktor I.V. Zaikin]. Izd. 3-e, perer. i dop. Voronezh : Izd-vo Voronezhskogo universiteta, 1985. 209, [3] p. ; 20 cm. Bibliography: p. 208-[210] LC Card 84-172797
1. Industrial management - Soviet Union - Problems, exercises, etc. I. Zaikin, I. V.
HD70.S63 P69 1985

Praktikum po statistike promyshlennosti / [V.N. Sivt͡sov ... et al.]. Moskva : Finansy i statistika, 1985. 239 p. ; 21 cm. Authorized for instructional purposes. LC Card 85-153243
1. Industrial organization (Economic theory) - Statistical methods - Problems, exercises, etc. I. Sivt͡sov, V. N.
HD30.413 .P72 1985

Prandecka, Barbara Karolina. Polityka ochrony środowiska w krajach socjalistycznych . Warszawa , 1980. 318 p. ; ISBN 83-208-0067-6 LC Card 81-101337
HC244.Z9 E56 1980

Prasad, Anubhuti Ranjan. Coal industry of India / Anubhuti Ranjan Prasad. New Delhi : Ashish Pub. House, 1986. xxvi, 516 p. : ill., map ; 23 cm. Revision of the author's thesis (Ph. D.--Banaras Hindu University, 1982) Bibliography: p. [506]-511. Includes index. ISBN 81-7024-055-7 : LC Card 86-902669 DDC 338.2/724/0954 19
1. Coal trade - India. I. Title.
HD9556.I42 P72 1986

Prasad, Maheshwari, 1944- Social aspects of mining towns of the tribal region / by Maheshwari Prasad. New Delhi : Today & Tomorrow's Printers and Publishers, 1986- v. <1- > ; 22 cm. Revision of the author's thesis (D. Litt.--Ranchi University, 1976) under the title: Mining towns of Chotanagpur : a study in social geography. Study, with reference to the Chotanagpur Region in Bihar. Includes bibliographical references and index. CONTENTS. - v. 1. Text. LC Card 86-902979 DDC 307.7/66/095412 19
1. Mineral industries - Social aspects - India - Chota Nāgpur. 2. Miners - India - Chota Nāgpur. 3. Tribes - India - Chota Nāgpur. 4. Anthropo-geography - India - Chota Nagpur. I. Title.
HD9506.I43 C486 1986

Prasad, R. R., 1955- Change and continuity among the scheduled caste leather workers / R.R. Prasad. Hyderabad : National Institute of Rural Development, 1986. 132 p., [4] leaves of plates : ill. ; 25 cm. Study relates to the workers in Uttar Pradesh. Includes bibliographies. LC Card 87-902216
1. Leather workers - India - Uttar Pradesh. 2. Leather industry and trade - India - Uttar Pradesh. 3. Untouchables - India - Pradesh. I. Title.
HD8039.L42 I575 1986

Prasad, Ranga N., 1957- Levitsky, Jacob, 1924- Credit guarantee schemes for small and medium enterprises /. Washington, D.C. , 1987. vi, 91 p. ; ISBN 0-8213-0866-1 (pbk.) LC Card 86-32571 DDC 658.8/7 19
HG9977 .L48 1987

Prasifka, David W., 1951- Current trends in water-supply planning : issues, concepts, and risks / David W. Prasifka. New York : Van Nostrand Reinhold Co., c1988. xi, 266 p. : ill. ; 24 cm. Bibliography: p. 255-256. Includes index. ISBN 0-442-27511-0 : LC Card 87-12157 DDC 333.91/212 19
1. Water-supply - Planning. I. Title. II. Title: Water-supply planning.
HD1691 .P7 1988

Prather, Dewitt G. United States national bank notes and their seals / by Dewitt G. Prather ; edited by J.S. Prather & Angela Prather. Charlotte, NC : D.G. Prather, c1986. xvi, 200 p., 16 p. of plates : ill. (some col.) ; 29 cm. ISBN 0-9616836-0-0 LC Card 86-90441 DDC 769.5/5973 19
1. National bank notes - United States - Catalogs. 2. Seals (Numismatics) - United States - Catalogs. I. Title.
HG607 .P73 1986

La pratique bancaire française en matière de financement sur le marché intérieur /. Bizot, Alain. Paris , c1985. 238 p. : ISBN 2-86325-033-7 : LC Card 86-159009
HG1642.F8 B59 1985

La pratique de l'audit financier dans les entreprises au Sénégal, à travers le cabinet Helios . Sougue, Matthieu Kounabé. [Dakar] [1983?] 194, [18] leaves : LC Card 85-121418
HF5686.C7 S67 1984

Prätsch, Joachim, 1951- Langfristige Finanzplanung und Simulationsmodelle : methodische Grundlegung sowie Beurteilung der Eignung der Simulation für die langfristige Finanzplanungspraxis / Joachim Prätsch. Frankfurt am Main ; New York : P. Lang, c1986. xii, 481 p. : ill. ; 21 cm. (Europäische Hochschulschriften. Reihe V, Volks- und Betriebswirtschaft, 0531-7339 . Bd. 740 = vol. 740 = vol. 740) Originally presented as the author's thesis (doctoral)--Universität Hamburg, 1985. Bibliography: p. 405-481. ISBN 3-8204-9403-0 LC Card 86-219850
1. Business enterprises - Germany (West) - Finance - Mathematical models. 2. Industrial management - Germany, West - Mathematical models. I. Series: Europäische Hochschulschriften. Reihe V, Volks- und Betriebswirtschaft , Bd. 740. II. Title.
HG4157 .P73 1986

Pratt, George J. Korn, Errol R. Hyper-performance . New York , c1987. xi, 195 p. : ISBN 0-471-85344-5 LC Card 86-33984 DDC 650.1 19
HF5386 .K775 1987

Pratt, Jane. Marks, Georgette A. Harrap's slang dictionary English-French/French-English /. London , 1984. 476 p. ; ISBN 0-245-54047-4
NYPL [JFC 86-640]

Pratt, Shannon P. Valuing small businesses and professional practices / Shannon P. Pratt. Homewood, Ill. : Dow Jones-Irwin, c1986. xxvii, 483 p. : ill. ; 29 cm. Includes index. Bibliography: p. 462-478. ISBN 0-87094-598-X LC Card 85-72255
1. Small business - Valuation. 2. Professions - Valuation. I. Title. ***NYPL [*R-Econ. 86-1421]***

Praude, V. R. (Valeriĭ Robertovich)
Ėkonomicheskie svi͡azi proizvodstva i potreblenii͡a pri sotsializme . Riga , 1978. 152 p. ; LC Card 81-168062
HF1040.9.S65 E36 1978

Khozi͡aĭstvennyĭ mekhanizm proizvodstva i obrashchenii͡a tovarov narodnogo potreblenii͡a /. Riga , 1985. 115 p. ; LC Card 86-177827
HF1040.9.L38 K47 1985

Pravovye problemy RASU / [avtory O.F. Andriĭko ... et al. ; otvetstvennye redaktory V.V. T͡Svetkov, V.F. Sirenko]. Kiev : Nauk. dumka, 1985. 303 p. : ill. ; 20 cm. At head of title: Akademii͡a nauk Ukrainskoĭ SSR. Institut gosudarstva i prava. Includes bibliographical references. LC Card 86-139849
1. Ukraine - Economic policy - Data processing. 2. Data protection - Ukraine. I. Andriĭko, O. F. (Ol'ga Fedorovna). II. T͡Svetkov, V. V. III. Sirenko, Vasiliĭ Fedorovich. IV. Instytut derz͡havy i prava (Akademii͡a nauk Ukraïns'koï RSR).
HC337.U5 P65 1985

Pravovye voprosy RASU : na materiale Latviĭskoĭ SSR / [otvetstvennyĭ redaktor G.I͡A. Kli͡ava]. Riga : "Zinatne", 1979. 109, [3] p. ; 20 cm. At head of title: Latviĭskiĭ ordena Trudovogo Krasnogo Znameni gosudarstvennyĭ universitet im. Petra Stuchki. "Spisok publikat͡sii latviĭskikh avtorov po pravovym voprosam ASU": p. 108-[110] Includes bibliographical references. LC Card 82-100548
1. Latvia - Economic policy - Data processing. 2. Data protection - Latvia. I. Kli͡ava, G. I͡A., 1906-. II. Pētera Stučkas Latvijas Valsts universitāte.
HC337.L3 P722 1979

Praxisbezug im wirtschaftswissenschaftlichen Studium . Bachmann, Gerhard, 1935- Frankfurt am Main , New York , c1986. 277 p. : ISBN 3-8204-9052-3 LC Card 86-147278
HB74.9.G3 B33 1986

Praxisleitfaden Privatisierung / Deutscher Industrie- und Handelstag. Bonn : Der Handelstag, 1984. 202 p. : ill. ; 21 cm. (DIHT . 213) LC Card 84-194479
1. Privatization - Germany (West). 2. Germany, West - Economic policy - 1974-. I. Deutscher Industrie- und Handelstag. II. Series: DIHT (Series) , 213.
HD4175 .P73 1984

Praxisratgeber.
Ferk, Hans S., 1945- Gemeinkosten abbauen durch Wertanalyse . Zürich , c1983. 128 p. : ISBN 3-478-36120-6 : LC Card 84-108512
HD47.3 .F47 1983

PREACHERS. see **CLERGY.**

Prebisch, Raúl.
La crisis del desarrollo argentino : de la frustración al crecimiento vigoroso / Raúl Prebisch. Buenos Aires : Librería "El Ateneo" Editorial, c1986. 195 p. ; 20 cm. Includes bibliographical references. ISBN 950-0-26293-2 LC Card 86-229773
1. Saving and investment - Argentina. 2. Argentina - Economic policy. 3. Argentina - Foreign economic relations. 4. Economic development. I. Title.
HC180.S3 P74 1986

Problemas económicos del Tercer Mundo /. Buenos Aires, República Argentina , c1983. 210 p. : ISBN 950-577-070-7 LC Card 84-120737 DDC 337/.09172/4 19
HF1413 .P75 1983 ***NYPL [JLC 86-394]***

Los precios sociales en la evaluación de proyectos en Costa Rica /. Pucci, Carlos. San José, Costa Rica , 1979. [108] leaves ; LC Card 83-238167
HC143.Z9 L36 1979

Precious, Mark. Rational expectations, non-market clearing, and investment theory / Mark Precious. Oxford : Clarendon Press ; New York : Oxford University Press, 1987. vi, 167 p. : ill. ; 23 cm. Bibliography: p. [161]-163. Includes index. ISBN 0-19-877256-4 : LC Card 87-1552 DDC 332.6 19
1. Investment analysis. 2. Rational expectations (Economic theory). 3. Equilibrium (Economics). I. Title.
HG4529 .P74 1987

PRECIOUS METALS - AMERICA - HISTORY.
Attman, Artur, 1910- American bullion in the European world trade, 1600-1800 /. Göteborg , 1986. 115 p. ; ISBN 91-85252-38-7 (pbk.) LC Card 87-147250 DDC 382/.4242/0973 19
HG285.A45 A88 1986

Morineau, Michel. Incroyables gazettes et fabuleux métaux . London ; New York : 687 p. : ISBN 0-521-25384-5 : LC Card 83-7177 DDC 330.94/022 19
HC240 .M73 1985 ***NYPL [JLE 85-1587]***

PRECIOUS METALS - EUROPE - HISTORY.
Attman, Artur, 1910- American bullion in the European world trade, 1600-1800 /. Göteborg , 1986. 115 p. ; ISBN 91-85252-38-7 (pbk.) LC Card 87-147250 DDC 382/.4242/0973 19
HG285.A45 A88 1986

Morineau, Michel. Incroyables gazettes et fabuleux métaux . London ; New York : 687 p. : ISBN 0-521-25384-5 : LC Card 83-7177 DDC 330.94/022 19
HC240 .M73 1985 ***NYPL [JLE 85-1587]***

PRECIOUS METALS - HANDBOOKS, MANUALS, ETC.
Cavelti, Peter C., 1947- New profits in gold, silver, strategic metals . New York , 1984, c1985. 221 p. : ISBN 0-07-010288-0 LC Card 84-12268 DDC 332.63 19
HG261 .C38 1985 ***NYPL [JLE 84-2956]***

PRECIOUS METALS - PORTUGAL - HISTORY.
Morineau, Michel. Incroyables gazettes et fabuleux métaux . London ; New York : 687 p. : ISBN 0-521-25384-5 : LC Card 83-7177 DDC 330.94/022 19
HC240 .M73 1985 ***NYPL [JLE 85-1587]***

PRECIOUS METALS - SPAIN - HISTORY.
Morineau, Michel. Incroyables gazettes et fabuleux métaux . London ; New York : 687 p. : ISBN 0-521-25384-5 : LC Card 83-7177 DDC 330.94/022 19
HC240 .M73 1985 ***NYPL [JLE 85-1587]***

Precision guided munitions : worldwide market study & forecast / Leland S. Ness, project director. Greenwich, CT., U. S.A. (P.O. Box 4585, Greenwich 06830) : Defense Marketing Services, c1986. 606, 4 p. ; 29 cm. LC Card 86-207047 DDC 380.1/456234 19
1. Precision guided munitions industry. 2. Market surveys. I. Ness, Leland S. II. Defense Marketing Services, inc.
HD9744.P732 P74 1986

PRECISION GUIDED MUNITIONS INDUSTRY.
Military electro-optics markets. Norwalk, Conn., U. S.A. (6 Prowitt St., Norwalk 06855) , c1986. vi, 238 leaves : LC Card 86-226982 DDC 380.1/456234 19
HD9744.P732 M55 1986

Precision guided munitions . Greenwich, CT., U. S.A. (P.O. Box 4585, Greenwich 06830) , c1986. 606, 4 p. ; LC Card 86-207047 DDC 380.1/456234 19
HD9744.P732 P74 1986

Precondiciones para la implementación de la economía social de mercado en América Latina . Cartas, José María. Buenos Aires, República Argentina , c1985. 80 p. ; LC Card 87-101628
HC125 .C374 1985

Preda, Michele. Sury, Paul de. Milano, centro finanziario internazionale /. [Milano] [1984] viii, 138 p. : ISBN 88-14-00312-2 : LC Card 86-114645
HG3090.M52 S87 1984

Predicaciones en la plaza /. Pérez Aguirre, Luis. Montevideo , 1985. 228 p. ; LC Card 85-225854 DDC 282/.8 19
BX1426.2 .P46 1985 ***NYPL [JLE 87-456]***

Predicasts, inc.
New Product Announcements (NPA) user's guide. Cleveland, Ohio (11001 Cedar Ave., Cleveland 44106) , 1986- 1 v. (loose-leaf) ; LC Card 86-220025 DDC 025/.0633802 19
HF5415.153 .N46 1986

Predicasts terminal system users manual. Cleveland, OH (11001 Cedar Ave., Cleveland 44106) , c1986- 1 v. (loose-leaf) ; LC Card 86-219849 DDC 025/.0633 19
HF5548.4.P74 P74 1986

Regional Business News (RBN) user's guide. Cleveland, Ohio (11001 Cedar Ave., Cleveland 44106) , 1986- 1 v. (loose-leaf) ; LC Card 86-220007 DDC 025/.0633 19
HF5548.4.P74 R44 1986

PREDICASTS TERMINAL SYSTEM (INFORMATION RETRIEVAL SYSTEM)
Predicasts terminal system users manual. Cleveland, OH (11001 Cedar Ave., Cleveland 44106) , c1986- 1 v. (loose-leaf) ; LC Card 86-219849 DDC 025/.0633 19
HF5548.4.P74 P74 1986

Predicasts terminal system users manual. Cleveland, OH (11001 Cedar Ave., Cleveland 44106) : Predicasts, c1986- 1 v. (loose-leaf) ; 30 cm. Cover title: PTS user's manual. LC Card 86-219849 DDC 025/.0633 19
1. Predicasts Terminal System (Information retrieval system). I. Predicasts, inc. II. Title: PTS user's manual.
HF5548.4.P74 P74 1986

Predicting which disabled employees will return to work . Hester, Edward J. Topeka, Kan. (700 Jackson, 9th floor, Topeka 66603) , c1986. x, 86 p. : LC Card 86-231920 DDC 331.5/9 19
HD7256.U5 H43 1986

PREDICTION, EARTHQUAKES. see **EARTHQUAKE PREDICTION.**

PREDICTION, SOCIAL. see **SOCIAL PREDICTION.**

Predpriiatie--samostoiatel'nost' i otvetstvennost'. Akhrameev, V. N. (Vasiliĭ Nikiforovich) "IUzhdizel'mash"--podgotovka k ėkonomicheskomu ėksperimentu /. Moskva , 1984. 96 p. : LC Card 85-144706
HD9705.S595 A36 1984

Astaf'ev, Vladimir Egorovich. Ėkonomicheskiĭ ėksperiment v ėlektrotekhnicheskoĭ promyshlennosti /. Moskva , 1984. 108, [3] p. ; LC Card 85-125403
HD9697.A3 A77 1984

Moskovskiĭ, I. D. (Igor' Dmitrievich) Finansy i khoziaĭstvennyĭ raschet v usloviiakh ėkonomicheskogo ėksperimenta /. Moskva , 1984. 60 p. ; LC Card 87-100142
HD9697.A3 S656 1984

Muzhitskikh, V. V. (Viktor Vasil'evich) Finansirovanie i kreditovanie kapital'nogo stroitel'stva v usloviiakh ėkonomicheskogo ėksperimenta /. Moskva , 1985. 157 p. ; LC Card 86-169842
HD9715.S72 M894 1985

Predpriiatie--samostoiatel'nost' i otvetstvennost' ("Finansy i statistika" (Firm))
Moskovskiĭ, I. D. (Igor' Dmitrievich) Finansy i khoziaĭstvennyĭ raschet v usloviiakh ėkonomicheskogo ėksperimenta /. Moskva , 1984. 60 p. ; LC Card 87-100142
HD9697.A3 S656 1984

Muzhitskikh, V. V. (Viktor Vasil'evich) Finansirovanie i kreditovanie kapital'nogo stroitel'stva v usloviiakh ėkonomicheskogo ėksperimenta /. Moskva , 1985. 157 p. ; LC Card 86-169842
HD9715.S72 M894 1985

Preeg, Ernest H. New dimensions in foreign economic policy . Washington, DC , 1986. xiii, 118 p. ; LC Card 86-600514 DDC 337.73 19
HF1410.5 .N488 1986

PRE-EMPTION - INDIA - KARNATAKA - HISTORY.
Pani, Narendar, 1954- Reforms to pre-empt change . New Delhi , 1983. ix, 122 p. ; LC Card 83-902691 DDC 333.3/1/5487 19
HD1333.I42 K376 1983 *NYPL [JLD 86-3841]*

Preemstvennost' stakhanovskikh traditsiĭ : stat'i i ocherki / [sostavitel' L.P. Kravchenko]. Moskva : Profizdat, 1985. 222 p. ; 17 cm. LC Card 85-234107
1. Socialist competition - Soviet Union. 2. Stakhanov movement. I. Kravchenko, L. P. (Leonid Petrovich).
HC340.S6 P68 1985

PREFABRICATED BUILDINGS. see **BUILDINGS, PREFABRICATED.**

PREFABRICATED HOUSES - AFRICA, EASTERN - MARKETING.
Export promotion of furniture/joinery products from east/southern Africa. Addis Ababa [1983] 34 p. in various pagings : LC Card 86-981008
HD9773.A472 E96 1983

PREFABRICATED HOUSES - QUÉBEC (PROVINCE)
Duchaine, Paul. Bâtiments préfabriqués résidentiels et industriels à ossature de bois . [Québec] , c1985. 36 p. : ISBN 2-550-12116-3 LC Card 86-133426
HD9715.5.C23 Q43 1985

PREFABRICATED HOUSES - SWEDEN.
Sweden. Exportstödsutredningen. Ökad trähusexport . [Stockholm] [1984] 51 p. ; ISBN 91-38-08165-2 LC Card 84-219457
HD9715.5.S82 S94 1984

A preface to marketing management /. Peter, J. Paul. Plano, Tex. , 1988. xii, 320 p. : ISBN 0-256-06078-9 (pbk.) LC Card 87-71348 DDC 658.8 19
HF5415.13 .P388 1988

Preface to quantitative economics & econometrics. Brennan, Michael Joseph, 1928- Cincinnati , c1987. x, 580 p. : ISBN 0-538-08230-5 (pbk.) LC Card 86-60209 DDC 330/.028 19
HB139 .B74 1987

Preface to the international frequency list and the weekly IFRB circular /. International Frequency Registration Board. Geneva , 1985. 1 v. (loose-leaf) : ISBN 92-71-04001-5 LC Card 86-207597 DDC 384.54/52 19
HE8675 .I5525 1985

Pre-feasibility study of the integrated Ras Hafun project in north east Somalia . Hinzen, Eckhard. Kronberg [West Germany] [1981] xii, 186 leaves : LC Card 85-980733
HC850.Z9 E444 1981

PREFERENTIAL DUTY. see **TARIFF PREFERENCES.**

PREFERENTIAL TARIFF. see **TARIFF PREFERENCES.**

PREFERRED STOCKS - HANDBOOKS, MANUALS, ETC.
The Handbook of fixed income securities /. Homewood, Ill. , 1987. xxx, 1376 p. : ISBN 0-87094-745-1 LC Card 86-50815
NYPL [JLE 87-939]

PREFERRED STOCKS - UNITED STATES.
Wilson, Richard S. Corporate senior securities . Chicago, Ill. , c1987. xiv, 459 p. : ISBN 0-917253-79-5 : LC Card 87-6980 DDC 332.63/2 19
HG4963 .W56 1987

PREGNANCY, ADOLESCENT - HUNGARY - STATISTICS.
Pongrácz, Tiborné. A terhességmegszakításon átesett 18 éven aluli hajadonok társadalmi-demográfiai jellemzői /. Budapest , c1986. 115 p. ; LC Card 87-409645
HA1201 .A64 no. 62 HQ767.5.H8

PREGNANCY IN ADOLESCENCE. see **PREGNANCY, ADOLESCENT.**

PREGNANCY, TEEN-AGE. see **PREGNANCY, ADOLESCENT.**

Prehn, Edward C. Alexander, Albert. The economic world of 1787 and the Constitution /. New York (150 Nassau St., Rm. 1625, New York 10038) [1987] 18 p. ; LC Card 87-403433 DDC 330.973/0318 19
HC105.6 .A44 1987

Preĭger, D. K. (Davyd Kasparovich) Alymov, Aleksandr Nikolaevich. Sbalansirovannost' narodnokhoziaĭstvennogo razvitiia . Kiev , 1986. 221, [3] p. ; LC Card 86-214583
HC337.U5 A793 1986

Preis- und Lohndirigismen im Dienste der Stabilisierungspolitik . Dobrovolny, Jiri, 1943- Bern , New York , c1985. xi, 433 p. : ISBN 3-261-03517-X LC Card 86-105626 DDC 338.5/2/0945 19
HB236.G7 D63 1985

Preisbildung bei Rüstungsgütern /. Bontrup, Heinz-J. Köln , c1986. 247 p. ; ISBN 3-8046-8677-X LC Card 87-122749 DDC 338.4/36234 19
HD9743.A2 B59 1986

Die Preisbildung in der industrialisierten Marktwirtschaft . Pöschl, Josef. Hamburg , c1987. v, 149 p. : ISBN 3-925630-12-0 LC Card 87-146592 DDC 338.5/2 19
HB221 .P65 1987

Preispolitik und Akkumulation . Welzmüller, Rudolf. Köln , c1982. 283 p. : ISBN 3-7663-0522-0 : LC Card 82-140922 DDC 338.8/266/00943 19
HD9654.5 .W44 1982 *NYPL [JLD 86-2908]*

Die Preistypdebatte, ihre Grundlagen und ihr Einfluss auf die praktische Ausgestaltung des Preissystems der DDR /. Bardmann, Manfred. Berlin , c1986. 99 p. : ISBN 3-87061-300-9 LC Card 86-148984
HB235.G32 B37 1986

Prékopa, András. System modelling and optimization . Berlin , New York , c1986. xii, 1046 p. : ISBN 0-387-16854-0 (U. S.) LC Card 86-15637 DDC 003 19
QA402 .S95822 1986 *NYPL [JSE 86-1775]*

A preliminary report on the livestock industry in the Jonglei area /. Payne, W. J. A. (William John Arthur) [Khartoum?] , 1977. 1 v. (various foliations) : LC Card 81-980100
HD9427.S83 J6664 1977

Preliminary study report on promotion of small-medium scale industries in the Republic of Venezuela. [Tokyo] : Japan International Cooperation Agency, [1978] ii, 27 p. : ill. ; 30 cm. Cover title. "November 1978." LC Card 84-249328
1. Metal-work - Venezuela. 2. Machinery industry - Venezuela. 3. Small business - Venezuela. 4. Industrial promotion - Venezuela. I. Kokusai Kyōryoku Jigyōdan.
HD9506.V42 P74 1978

PREMEN. Gerência do Ceará. Catálogo de ocupações pesquisadas em Fortaleza. [Fortaleza] . 111, [1] p. ; LC Card 83-222529
HF5382.5.B7 C38 1972

Premier plan quinquennal de développement populaire, 1986-1990. Burkina Faso. [Burkina Faso , 1986?] 2 v. : LC Card 87-159604
HC1040 .B87 1986

Premières mesures de mise en application du programme du CMRN. Guinea. Comité militaire de redressement national. [Conakry, R.G. , 1984] 84 p. ; LC Card 85-143345
HD2143.Z8 G85 1984

Premium Audit Advisory Service.
Classification guide for commercial building construction. [New York, N.Y.?] , c1986. 72 p. : LC Card 87-119406 DDC 368.4/1 19
HD7116.R3152 U63 1986

Classification guide for street and road construction /. New York, NY , c1986. 44 p. : LC Card 86-232165 DDC 368.4/1 19
HD7116.R62 U63 1986

Guidelines for auditing governmental subdivisions /. [New York, NY] [c1987] ii, 50 p. ; LC Card 87-121255 DDC 350.72/32 19
HJ9733 .G85 1987

Premssler, Manfred. Dötsch, Jochen. EG und Arbeiterrechte . Berlin , 1981. 143 p. ; LC Card 81-145834 DDC 331.11/094 19
HD8380.5 .D67 1981 *NYPL [JLD 86-2739]*

PRENATAL CARE - MICHIGAN - STATISTICS.
Southeastern Michigan minor civil divisions . Detroit, Mich. (1200 Book Bldg., Detroit 48226) , c1986. i, 285 p. : LC Card 87-105776 DDC 304.6/3/09774021 19
HB935.M5 S68 1986

The Prentice Hall business tax deduction master guide /. Bradford, W. Murray. New York , c1987. 368 p. : ISBN 0-13-108234-5 (pbk.) : LC Card 87-2252 DDC 343.7305/23 347.303523 19
HJ4653.D4 B68 1987

The Prentice-Hall directory of executive search firms /. Lewis, William, 1946- New York , c1986. v, 328 p. ; ISBN 0-671-55518-9 (pbk.) LC Card 85-30190 DDC 658.4/07111/02573 19
HD38.25.U6 L49 1986
*NYPL [*R-Econ. 87-1586]*

Prentice-Hall, inc.
Bradford, W. Murray. The Prentice Hall business tax deduction master guide /. New York , c1987. 368 p. : ISBN 0-13-108234-5 (pbk.) : LC Card 87-2252 DDC 343.7305/23 347.303523 19
HJ4653.D4 B68 1987

Prentice-Hall, inc. Information Services Division.
Modern job safety and health /. Paramus, N.J. , c1987- 1 v. (loose-leaf) : LC Card 87-403957 DDC 363.1/1/068 19
HD6067.2.U6 M63 1987

Prentice-Hall series in accounting.
Arens, Alvin A. Auditing, an integrated approach /. Englewood Cliffs, N.J. , c1988. p. cm. ISBN 0-13-051814-X LC Card 87-26359 DDC 657/.45 19
HF5667 .A69 1988

Horngren, Charles T., 1926- Introduction to financial accounting /. Englewood Cliffs, N.J. , c1987. xx, 795 p. ; ISBN 0-13-483264-7 LC Card 86-25310 DDC 657 19
HF5635 .H813 1987

Horngren, Charles T., 1926- Introduction to management accounting /. Englewood Cliffs, N.J. , c1987. xxi, 762 p. : ISBN 0-13-487885-X LC Card 86-25138 DDC 658.1/511 19
HF5635 .H814 1987

Prentice-Hall series in industrial relations and personnel.
Belcher, David W. Compensation administration

/. Englewood Cliffs, N.J. , c1987. xv, 464 p. : ISBN 0-13-154790-9 : LC Card 86-25494 DDC 658.3/2 19
HF5549.5.C67 B45 1987

The Prentice-Hall series in marketing.
Kleppner, Otto, 1899- [Advertising procedure.] Kleppner's advertising procedure. Englewood Cliffs, N.J. , 1987, c1988. p. cm. ISBN 0-13-516451-6 LC Card 87-19346 DDC 659.1 19
HF5823 .K45 1988

Kotler, Philip. Strategic marketing for nonprofit organizations /. Englewood Cliffs, N.J. , c1987. xvi, 670 p. : LC Card 86-25538 DDC 658.8 19
HF5415 .K6312 1987

Stern, Louis W., 1935- Marketing channels /. Englewood Cliffs, N.J. , c1988. xiv, 609 p. : ISBN 0-13-557158-8 : LC Card 87-17396 DDC 658.8/4 19
HF5415.129 .S75 1988

The Prentice-Hall series in security and insurance.
Black, Kenneth. Life insurance. Englewood Cliffs, N.J. , c1987. xiii, 608 p. : ISBN 0-13-535881-7 LC Card 86-25375 DDC 368.3/2 19
HG8771 .B55 1987

Dorfman, Mark S., 1945- Introduction to insurance /. Englewood Cliffs, NJ , c1987. xix, 501 p. : ISBN 0-13-484809-8 LC Card 86-30319 DDC 368 19
HG8051 .D65 1987

Preobrazovanie chastnoĭ promyshlennosti i torgovli vo V′etname /. Glazunov, E. P. Moskva , 1981. 213, [1] p. ; LC Card 82-112489
HC444 .G58 1981

Prepackaged kits & trays markets in the U. S. New York, N.Y. : Frost & Sullivan, c1983. xxiii, 188 p. : charts ; 29 cm. Spine title: Prepackaged trays & kits market in the U. S. "October 1983." "#A1139." LC Card 87-142284 DDC 381/.45681761 19
1. Disposable medical supplies industry - United States. 2. Market surveys - United States. I. Frost & Sullivan. II. Title: Prepackaged kits and trays markets in the U. S. III. Title: Prepackaged trays & kits market in the U. S.
HD9995.D563 U665 1983

Prepackaged kits and trays markets in the U. S. Prepackaged kits & trays markets in the U. S. New York, N.Y. , c1983. xxiii, 188 p. : LC Card 87-142284 DDC 381/.45681761 19
HD9995.D563 U665 1983

Prepackaged trays & kits market in the U. S. Prepackaged kits & trays markets in the U. S. New York, N.Y. , c1983. xxiii, 188 p. : LC Card 87-142284 DDC 381/.45681761 19
HD9995.D563 U665 1983

PREPAID GROUP MEDICAL PRACTICE. see **HEALTH MAINTENANCE ORGANIZATIONS.**

PREPAID MEDICAL CARE. see **INSURANCE, HEALTH.**

Preparación y presentación de proyectos de inversión / República de Chile, Presidencia de la República, Oficina de Planificación Nacional, ODEPLAN. [Santiago] : ODEPLAN, 1985. v, 138 p. : ill. ; 26 cm. Includes bibliographical references. LC Card 87-116769
1. Capital investments - Evaluation. 2. Economic development projects - Evaluation. I. Chile. Oficina de Planificación Nacional.
HD39 .P72 1985

Préparation du IXe plan, 1984-1988.
France. Groupe de politique des transports. Rapport du Groupe de politique des transports. Paris , c1984. 246 p. : ISBN 2-11-001216-1 : LC Card 84-163968
HE248 .F716 1984

France. Groupe de travail "Calcul économique." Calcul économique et résorption des déséquilibres . Paris , c1984. 149 p. ; ISBN 2-11-001233-1 : LC Card 84-227039
HB135 .F72 1984

L'Impasse Nord-Sud . Paris , c1984. 103 p. : ISBN 2-11-001207-2 : LC Card 84-163951
HC59 .I44 1984

Preparation report, rural development programme, 1980-85 /. Gambia. Banjul [1979- v. <1 > : LC Card 86-203596
HD2147 .G35 1980a

Prepare power-packed reports /. Wall, William C. Huntsville, Ala. , c1987. p. cm. ISBN 0-938745-04-2 LC Card 87-13581 DDC 658.4/53 19
HF5719 .W35 1987

Preparing documents with U.N.I.X. Brown, Constance C., 1952- Preparing documents with UNIX /. Englewood Cliffs, N.J. , c1986. xv, 206 p. : ISBN 0-13-699976-X LC Card 85-17016 DDC 652/.5 19
Z52.5.U54 B76 1986 ***NYPL [JSE 86-1215]***

Preparing documents with UNIX /. Brown, Constance C., 1952- Englewood Cliffs, N.J. , c1986. xv, 206 p. : ISBN 0-13-699976-X LC Card 85-17016 DDC 652/.5 19
Z52.5.U54 B76 1986 ***NYPL [JSE 86-1215]***

Preparing subnational population projections . Kayani, Ashraf K. Santiago de Chile [1980] ii, 68 p. ; LC Card 84-256007 DDC 304.6/2/072 19
HB849.53 .K39 1980

Prepress graphic arts equipment and supplies market in Europe. New York, N.Y. : Frost & Sullivan, c1983. xxiii, 268 p. ; 28 cm. Spine title: Prepress graphic arts market in Europe. "February 1983." "E588." LC Card 87-141770 DDC 380.1/456816 19
1. Graphic arts equipment industry - Europe. 2. Market surveys - Europe. I. Frost & Sullivan. II. Title: Prepress graphic arts market in Europe.
HD9790.E85 P74 1983

Prepress graphic arts market in Europe. Prepress graphic arts equipment and supplies market in Europe. New York, N.Y. , c1983. xxiii, 268 p. ; LC Card 87-141770 DDC 380.1/456816 19
HD9790.E85 P74 1983

Prescott, Edward C. Contractual arrangements for intertemporal trade /. Minneapolis, MN , c1987. p. cm. ISBN 0-8166-1533-0 : LC Card 86-24888 DDC 332.64/4/0724 19
HB801 .C629 1987

Presença de Angola na IX Feira Internacional de Lisboa, 1968. Representação do produtos alimentares de Angola na IX Feira Internacional de Lisboa . Luanda [1968] 248 p. : LC Card 87-400609 DDC 338.7/6413/0025673 19
HD9017.A532 R46 1968

La Presencia del tercer mundo / edición a cargo de Carlos Roberto López Leal. 1a ed. San José, Costa Rica : Universidad de Costa Rica, 1982. 239 p., [1] leaf of plates : ill. ; 21 cm. (Introducción a la cultura contemporánea . v. 3) "Selección de textos y documentos para el programa regular de historia de la cultura de la Escuela de Estudios Generales de la Universidad de Costa Rica; XXV aniversario de los estudios generales." Includes bibliographical references. LC Card 83-161829
1. Developing countries - Economic policy. 2. Developing countries - Social policy. 3. International cooperation. I. López Leal, Carlos Roberto. II. Series.
HC59.7 .P718 1982

The present state of consumer theory /. Roth, Timothy P. Lanham, MD , c1987. vi, 168 p. ; ISBN 0-8191-5708-2 (alk. paper) : LC Card 86-24619 DDC 339.4/7/01 19
HB801 .R687 1987

PRESENT-VALUE TABLES. see **INSURANCE, LIFE - RATES AND TABLES.**

Presentations. Wall, William C. Create and deliver dynamite presentations /. Huntsville, Ala. , c1987. p. cm. ISBN 0-938745-02-6 : LC Card 87-14130 DDC 658.8/5 19
HF5438.25 .W275 1987

Presentations plus . Peoples, David A., 1930- New York , c1988. xi, 239 p. : ISBN 0-471-63391-7 LC Card 87-21691 DDC 658.4/5 19
HF5718 .P44 1988

PRESERVATION OF FORESTS. see **NATURAL RESOURCES.**

PRESERVATION OF FRUIT. see **CANNING AND PRESERVING.**

PRESERVATION OF HISTORICAL RECORDS. see **ARCHIVES.**

PRESERVATION OF VEGETABLES. see **CANNING AND PRESERVING.**

PRESERVATION OF WILDLIFE. see **WILDLIFE CONSERVATION.**

Preservation programs of the Federal government in the area of housing ... United States. Congress. House. Committee on Banking, Currency and Housing. Subcommittee on Historic Preservation and Coinage. Preservation programs of the Federal government in the area of housing and community development /. Washington , 1976. vi, 86 p. ; LC Card 77-601749
HT175 .U583 1976 ***NYPL [JLE 78-1181]***

PRESERVATIVES. see **CANNING AND PRESERVING.**

PRESERVING. see **CANNING AND PRESERVING.**

Presidency College, Calcutta. Statistical laboratory. Indian Statistical Institute. see **Indian Statistical Institute.**

The Presidential documents series.
The War on poverty, 1964-1968 [microform] . Frederick, MD , c1986- microfilm reel ISBN 0-89093-495-9 (microfilm : set) : LC Card 87-10510 DDC 338.973 19
HC110 .P63

President's Private Sector Survey on Cost Control (U. S.) President's private sector survey on cost control : report on financial asset management. Washington, D.C. : The Survey : For sale by the Supt. of Docs., U. S. G.P.O., 1983. viii, 320 p. ; 28 cm. "Approved by the Subcommittee for the Full Executive Committee, Spring-Fall 1983."
1. Government lending - United States. 2. Collecting of accounts - United States. I. Title: Report on financial asset management. ***NYPL [JLF 86-727]***

The President's tax reform proposal : the impact on New York State. [Albany, N.Y.] : New York State Dept. of Taxation and Finance, New York State Division of the Budget, [1985] 48 leaves : ill. ; 28 cm. "October, 1985"--Cover. Includes bibliographical references. LC Card 86-622434 DDC 336.2/009747 19
1. Taxation - New York (State). 2. Income tax - New York (State). 3. Taxation - United States. 4. Income tax - United States. 5. Intergovernmental tax relations - New York (State). I. New York (State). Dept. of Taxation and Finance. II. New York (State). Division of the Budget.
HJ2424 .P84 1985

PRESIDENTS - UNITED STATES - ELECTION - 1984.
Broh, C. Anthony. A horse of a different color . Washington, D.C. , 1987. xiv, 93 p. : ISBN 0-941410-54-4 (pbk.) : LC Card 87-2869 DDC 324.973/0927 19
HE8700.76.U6 B76 1987

PRESS AND POLITICS - CONGRESES.
Famine in Ukraine, 1932-1933 /. Edmonton , Downsview, Ont., Canada , 1986. 192 p. ; ISBN 0-09-286243-8 LC Card 87-148658 DDC 363.8/0947/71 19
HC337.U53 F314 1986

Press Foundation of Asia. Journalist Workshop on Population and Development Reporting (1981 : Islāmābād, Pakistan) Journalist Workshop on Population and Development Reporting, Oct. 31-Nov. 5, 1981, Islamabad /. [Pakistan , 1982? (Lahore : Directorate of Production and Publication) 63, 12 p. ; LC Card 83-930293 DDC 304.6 19
HB849 .J67 1981

Press, Frank. A High technology gap? . New York, N.Y. , c1987. xii, 114 p. : ISBN 0-87609-021-8 (pbk.) : LC Card 87-6713 DDC 338/.06 19
HC240.9.T4 H54 1987

PRESS, LABOR - GERMANY - HISTORY - 19TH CENTURY.
Simon, Dan, 1937- Das Frankreichbild der deutschen Arbeiterbewegung 1859-1865 /. [Gerlingen] , 1984. 334 p. ; ISBN 3-88350-451-3 LC Card 84-173175
HD8450 .S56 1984 ***NYPL [JLD 86-2711]***

PRESS RELEASES.
Evans, Fred J. Managing the media . New York , 1987. xvii, 172 p. : ISBN 0-89930-156-8 (lib. bdg. : alk. paper) : LC Card 86-25736 DDC 659.2 19
HD59 .E93 1987

Lima, Gerson Moreira, 1952- Releasemania, uma contribuição para o estudo do press-release no Brasil /. São Paulo, SP , c1985. 114 p. : LC Card 85-184576 DDC 659.2 19
HM263 .L478 1985 ***NYPL [JFD 86-2728]***

Press, Volker. Städtewesen und Merkantilismus in Mitteleuropa /. Köln , 1983. xii, 333 p. : ISBN 3-412-00382-4 LC Card 83-155285
HF1531 .S688 1983

Pressekomitee für Fiskalfragen (Switzerland) Die Kalte Progression . Bern , 1982. 107 p. : LC Card 83-128720
HJ4747 .K35 1982

Pressen, reklamen och konkurrensen, 1935-1978 /. Jonsson, Sverker, 1941- Göteborg , 1982. 406 p. : ISBN 91-85196-24-X : LC Card 84-157282
HF6105.S8 J66 1982

Pressler, Larry, 1942- Trip report, a visit to Eastern Europe in the wake of the 27th Soviet Party Congress and the Chernobyl nuclear accident (Czechoslovakia, Hungary, Yugoslavia, and Romania) on June 28, 1986 : a report to the Committee on Foreign Relations, United States Senate / by Larry Pressler. Washington : U. S. G.P.O. : For sale by the Supt. of Docs., Congressional Sales Office, U. S. G.P.O., 1987. vi, 58 p. ; 24 cm. (S. prt. . 100-13) At head of title: 100th Congress, 1st session. Committee print. Distributed to some depository libraries in microfiche. Shipping list no.: 87-150-P. "February 1987." Item 1039-A, 1039-B (microfiche) LC Card 87-601360 DDC 337.47 19
1. Europe, Eastern - Economic conditions - 1945-. 2. Europe, Eastern - Foreign relations - 1945-. 3. Human rights - Europe, Eastern. 4. Europe, Eastern - Religion. I. United States. Congress. Senate. Committee on Foreign Relations. II. Title. III. Series.
HC244 .P744 1987

Pressure at work . Arroba, Tanya. London , New York , c1987. xvi, 192 p. : ISBN 0-07-084931-5 (pbk.) : LC Card 87-3925 DDC 658.4/095 19
HF5548.85 .A77 1987

Pressure for the poor . Whiteley, Paul. London , New York , 1987. 174 p. ; ISBN 0-416-36370-9 LC Card 87-11205 DDC 362.5/8/0941 19
HC260.P63 W47 1987

PRESSURE GROUPS - GERMANY - HISTORY.
Abraham, David, 1946- The collapse of the Weimar Republic . New York , 1986. liii, 352 p. ; ISBN 0-8419-1083-9 LC Card 86-27033 DDC 338.0943 19
HD3616.G35 A27 1986

PRESSURE GROUPS - GERMANY, WEST.
Leonhard, Martin. Umweltverbände . Opladen , c1986. xiii, 352 p. ; ISBN 3-531-11820-X LC Card 86-192568
HC290.5.E5 L46 1986

PRESSURE GROUPS - GREAT BRITAIN.
Coxall, W. N. Parties and pressure groups /. London , New York , 1986. iv, 196 p. ; ISBN 0-582-35189-8 ***NYPL [JLD 86-2729]***

Whiteley, Paul. Pressure for the poor . London , New York , 1987. 174 p. ; ISBN 0-416-36370-9 LC Card 87-11205 DDC 362.5/8/0941 19
HC260.P63 W47 1987

PRESSURE GROUPS - SWEDEN.
Micheletti, Michele. Organizing interest and organized protest . [Stockholm] , 1985. vii, 253 p. ; ISBN 91-7146-451-4 (pbk.) LC Card 86-145828 DDC 322/.2/09481 19
HD8572.T5 M53 1985
NYPL [JLL 74-316 no.29]

PRESSURE GROUPS - SWITZERLAND.
Aeberhardt, Werner. Die Umweltpolitik im Spannungsfeld politischer und wirtschaftlicher Interessen /. Köln , 1985. 134, [9] p. : ISBN 3-921471-55-9 : LC Card 86-145456
HC400.E5 A33 1985

Farago, Peter. Verbände als Träger öffentlicher Politik . Grüsch , c1987. xi, 185 p. : ISBN 3-7253-0290-1 LC Card 87-140606 DDC 322/.3/09494 19
HD2429.S92 F37 1987

Wirtschaftsverbände in der Schweiz . Grüsch , c1986. xv, 294 p. : ISBN 3-7253-0260-X : LC Card 86-136455 DDC 322/.3/09494 19
HD2429.S92 W57 1986
NYPL [JLD 86-2919]

PRESSURE GROUPS - UNITED STATES.
Browne, William Paul, 1945- Private interests, public policy, and American agriculture /. Lawrence, Kan. , c1988. p. cm. ISBN 0-7006-0334-4 : LC Card 87-23131 DDC 338.1/873 19
HD1761 .B73 1988

McCann, Michael W., 1952- Taking reform seriously . Ithaca , 1986. 345 p. ; ISBN 0-8014-1952-2 LC Card 86-47647 DDC 322.4/3/0973 19
JK1118 .M37 1986 ***NYPL [JLE 87-1009]***

Préstamo del BID al sector pesquero . Pacheco O., Amparo. [San José] , 1984. 50 p. : LC Card 86-185463
HD9464.A2 P33 1984

Prestes Motta, Fernando C. see **Motta, Fernando C. Prestes.**

Preston, A. Scott. Martin, Dale R. Lotus 1-2-3 applications with disk /. Englewood Cliffs, N.J. , c1986. viii, 120 p. : ISBN 0-13-540717-6 (pbk.) LC Card 86-200542 DDC 657/.044/02855369 19
HF5679 .M37 1986

Preston, Edmund, 1941- Troubled passage : the Federal Aviation Administration during the Nixon-Ford term, 1973-1977 / by Edmund Preston. Washington, D.C. : U. S. Dept. of Transportation, Federal Aviation Administration : For sale by the Superintendent of Documents, U. S. G.P.O., 1987 vii, 340 p. ; 21 cm. "The fifth in FAA's narrative history serie"--P. iv. Bibliography: p. 267-320. Includes index. LC Card 87-25500 DDC 353.0087/77 19
1. United States. Federal Aviation Administration. 2. Aeronautics, Commercial - Government policy - United States - History. I. Title.
HE9803.A35 P74 1987

Preston, Jill. Barnes, Ian. The European Community /. London , New York , 1988. p. cm. ISBN 0-582-29716-8 LC Card 87-16765 DDC 337.1/42 19
HC241.2 .B293 1988

PRESTON (LANCASHIRE) - POLITICS AND GOVERNMENT.
Savage, Michael. The dynamics of working-class politics . Cambridge [Cambridgeshire] , New York , 1987. xii, 280 p. : LC Card 87-14636 DDC 322/.2/0941 19
HD8397.P74 S28 1987

Preston, P. W. (Peter Wallace), 1949- Rethinking development : essays on development and Southeast Asia / P.W. Preston. London ; New York : Routledge & Kegan Paul, 1987. xv, 261 p. ; 24 cm. Bibliography: p. [252]-258. Includes index. ISBN 0-7102-1263-1 LC Card 87-4905 DDC 338.959 19
1. Asia, Southeastern - Economic policy. 2. Asia, Southeastern - Social policy. I. Title.
HC441 .P75 1987

Presupuesto de la administración nacional, 1961-1979. Argentina. Dirección Nacional de Programación Presupuestaria. [Buenos Aires] [1982] 79 leaves : LC Card 82-199149
HJ2076 .A74 1982

Presupuestos . Ponce Dávila, Vicente O. [Armenia, Colombia , 1986] (Armenia : SERVICOPIAR) v, 149 p. : LC Card 87-400649
HG4028.B8 P66 1986

Pretiale Lenkung bei sicheren und unsicheren Erwartungen /. Winter, Richard, 1946- Frankfurt am Main , New York , c1986. 243 p. ; ISBN 3-8204-9816-8 LC Card 87-407541 DDC 658.8/16 19
HD62.45 .W56 1986

PRETORIA (SOUTH AFRICA) - CENSUS, 1980.
Bevolkingsensus 1980, uitgesoekte statistiese streek, Pretoria/Wonderboom =. [Pretoria] [1985?] xx, 476 p. : ISBN 0-621-09483-8 : LC Card 85-238587
HA4701.Z9 P743 1985

Preusch, Deb. Barry, Tom, 1950- The soft war . New York , 1988. xv, 304 p. ; ISBN 0-8021-0003-1 LC Card 87-13238 DDC 338.91/73/0728 19
HC141 .B375 1988

Preventing dishonest behavior in the electronics industry . Oren, Ditza L. [United States , 1985] vii, 115 leaves : LC Card 86-224386 DDC 621.381/068/3 19
HD8039.E38 U65 1985

PREVENTION OF ACCIDENTS. see **ACCIDENTS - PREVENTION.**

Previews & premises /. Toffler, Alvin. Montréal, Québec , 1984, c1983. 230 p. ; ISBN 0-920057-37-3 (pbk.) ***NYPL [JFD 86-3191]***

Previews and premises. Toffler, Alvin. Previews & premises /. Montréal, Québec , 1984, c1983. 230 p. ; ISBN 0-920057-37-3 (pbk.)
NYPL [JFD 86-3191]

La prévision des ventes /. Maricourt, Renaud de. Paris , c1985. 159 p. : ISBN 2-13-039013-7 : LC Card 86-138110 DDC 658.8/18 19
HF5415 .M2794 1985

Previts, Gary John.
John Raymond Wildman : first president, American Accounting Association, 1917, professor and professional accountant / Gary John Previts and Richard F. Taylor. University, Ala. : Academy of Accounting Historians, 1978. viii, 84 p. ; 22 cm. (Monograph / the Academy of Accounting Historians . 2) "A Chronological bibliography of the known writings of John R. Wildman": p. 75-80. LC Card 86-224716
1. Wildman, John Raymond, 1878-. 2. Accountants - United States - Biography. 3. Accounting - United States - History. 4. Wildman, John Raymond, 1878- - Bibliography. I. Taylor, Richard F. II. Series: Monograph (Academy of Accounting Historians) , 2. III. Title.
HF5604.5.W55 P74 1978

The scope of CPA services : a study of the development of the concept of independence and the profession's role in society / Gary John Previts. New York : Wiley, c1985. xv, 187 p. ; 24 cm. (Modern accounting perspectives and practice) "A Ronald Press publication." Includes index. Bibliography: p. 177-180. ISBN 0-471-01149-5 : LC Card 85-22455 DDC 657/.09 19
1. Accounting - History. 2. Accountants - Professional ethics - History. I. Title. II. Title: Scope of C P A services.
HF5611 .P73 1985 ***NYPL [JLE 86-2961]***

Prevost, Nancy M., 1953- Paradise in the Palouse : the development of a farming empire in eastern Washington, 1870-1900 / by Nancy M. Prevost. Fairfield, Wash. : Ye Galleon Press, c1985. 35 p. : ill. ; 26 cm. Includes index. Bibliography: p. 29-31. ISBN 0-87770-365-5 (pbk.) LC Card 85-17842 DDC 338.1/09797/39 19
1. Agriculture - Economic aspects - Washington (State) - History - 19th century. 2. Agriculture - Economic aspects - Palouse River Valley (Idaho and Wash.) - History - 19th century. 3. Palouse River Valley (Idaho and Wash.) - History, Local. 4. Palouse River Valley (Idaho and Wash.) - Social life and customs. 5. Whitman County (Wash.) - History. 6. Spokane County, Wash. - History. I. Title.
HD1775.W2 P74 1985 ***NYPL [JFF 86-559]***

Prevrashchenie sel´skokhoziaistvennogo truda v raznovidnost´ industrial´nogo v usloviiakh razvitogo sotsializma. . Toshpŭlatov, Mirzapŭlat. Tashkent , 1980. 68 p. ; LC Card 81-149078
HD1536.S65 T67 1980

Priamye khoziaistvennye sviazi v sotsialisticheskoĭ ėkonomike /. Tret´iak, V. P. (Vladimir Petrovich) Leningrad , 1986. 141 p. : LC Card 87-146709
HF5415.6 .T74 1986

Price, Courtney H. The entrepreneur's resource handbook / Courtney Price, Richard H. Buskirk, R. Mack Davis. Denver, Colo. : Creative Management Unlimited, 1987. 178 p. : ill., forms ; 28 cm. Includes indexes. ISBN 0-944303-00-5 (pbk.) LC Card 87-62190
1. Entrepreneurship - Dictionaries. 2. New business enterprises - Information services - United States. 3. Business - Forms. I. Buskirk, Richard Hobart, 1927-. II. Davis, R. Mack. III. Title.
HD62.5 .P65 1987

Price elasticity of export demand . Gardiner, Walter H. Washington, D.C. [1986] iv, 43 p. ; LC Card 86-602820 DDC 382/.41/0973 19
HD9004 .G37 1986

PRICE FLUCTUATIONS AND ACCOUNTING. see **ACCOUNTING AND**

PRICE FLUCTUATIONS.

PRICE INDEXES.
Industrial product price indexes, 1981=100 . Ottawa , c1986. 216 p. : ISBN 0-660-52876-2 (pbk.) : LC Card 87-168891
HB235.C2 I53 1986

Landeswirtschaftlicher Paritätsspiegel . Wien [1982] 11 leaves ; LC Card 86-181563
HD1935 .L325 1982

Meinlschmidt, Gerhard. Statistische Methoden zur Berechnung von Preisniveauindizes integrierter Wirtschaftsräume /. Göttingen , c1985. 142 p. : ISBN 3-525-11262-9 LC Card 85-213565
HB225 .M45 1985

Methodologie der EG-Agrarpreisindizes (Output und Input) =. Luxembourg , Washington, DC , 1985. 228 p. ; ISBN 92-825-5463-5 : LC Card 87-107275 DDC 338.1/3/094021 19
HD1920.5 .M47 1985

Nikitin, Sergeĭ Mikhaĭlovich. Indeksy t͡sen i produkt͡sii v kapitalisticheskikh stranakh /. Moskva , 1981. 255 p. ; LC Card 86-460234
HB225 .N52 1981

PRICE INDICES. see **PRICE INDEXES.**

Price, Kent A. Agriculture and the environment /. Washington, D.C. , c1986. xvii, 298 p. : ISBN 0-915707-33-0 (pbk.) : LC Card 87-43010 DDC 363.7/31 19
HD1755 .P47 1986

PRICE LABELS. see **LABELS.**

The price of power . Lowe, D. A. (Douglas Ackley), 1942- South Melbourne , 1984. viii, 184 p., [12] p. of plates : ISBN 0-333-38088-6 LC Card 84-254286 DDC 333.91/62/099466 19
HD9685.A83 T385 1984
NYPL [JLD 87-795]

Price policy and economic development in India /. Lal, Shyam, 1942- Delhi , 1987. xiii, 272 p. : LC Card 87-900801 DDC 338.5/26/0954552 19
HB236.I4 L35 1987

PRICE POLICY - CASE STUDIES.
Welzmüller, Rudolf. Preispolitik und Akkumulation . Köln , c1982. 283 p. : ISBN 3-7663-0522-0 : LC Card 82-140922 DDC 338.8/266/00943 19
HD9654.5 .W44 1982 *NYPL [JLD 86-2908]*

PRICE POLICY - COLOMBIA - ADDRESSES, ESSAYS, LECTURES.
Thomas, Vinod, 1949- Linking macroeconomic and agricultural policies for adjustment with growth . Baltimore , c1985. xv, 252 p. ; ISBN 0-8018-3121-0 : LC Card 85-45105 DDC 338.9861 19
HC197 .T38 1985 *NYPL [JLE 86-1438]*

PRICE POLICY - FINLAND.
Neilimo, Kari, 1944- Hinnanasetanta, toiminta-analyyttinen tutkimus pienyrityksistä /. Tampere , 19. 90, [8] leaves : ISBN 951-44-1729-1 LC Card 86-140431
HF5416.5 .N45 1985

PRICE POLICY - INDIA - PUNJAB.
Lal, Shyam, 1942- Price policy and economic development in India /. Delhi , 1987. xiii, 272 p. : LC Card 87-900801 DDC 338.5/26/0954552 19
HB236.I4 L35 1987

PRICE POLICY, INDUSTRIAL. see **PRICE POLICY.**

PRICE POLICY - MATHEMATICAL MODELS.
Angebotsentwicklung und Preisbildung natürlicher Ressourcen /. München , 1986. vii, 148, 10 p. : ISBN 3-486-26171-1 LC Card 86-182074
HC59 .A794 1986

Bruse, Helmut. Der Absatzbereich von Unternehmen . Bonn , 1980. xiv, 323 p. : LC Card 85-164955
HF5415 .B7713 1980

Frenkel, Roberto. Decisiones de precio en alta inflación /. Buenos Aires, Argentina , 1979. 58 p. ; LC Card 80-125798 DDC 332.4/15 19
HF5416.5 .F73 *NYPL [JLD 86-2701]*

Schoch, Hans. Size and price in oligopoly /. Königstein, Ts. , Cambridge, Mass. , 1981. viii, 151 p. : ISBN 3-445-12157-5 LC Card 80-84489 DDC 338.8/2/0724 19
HD2757.3 .S36 1981

PRICE POLICY - UNITED STATES.
Pricing consumer credit . Washington, D.C. (1120 Connecticut Ave., N.W., Washington 20036) , c1986. 136 p. : LC Card 86-209981 DDC 332.1/753 19
HG1642.U5 P75 1986

PRICE POLICY - UNITED STATES - ECONOMETRIC MODELS.
Carlson, John A., 1933- Stocks, shocks, and price-output dynamics /. West Lafayette, Ind. [1984] 30, 13 p. ; LC Card 84-623131 DDC 658/.001/9 s 332.63/222/0973 19
HD6483 .P8 no. 859 HF5416.5

PRICE REGULATION - AUSTRALIA.
Hall, Richard, 1937- The Prices Surveillance Authority /. Melbourne [1987] 24 p. ; ISBN 0-85801-167-0 (pbk.) LC Card 87-156317 DDC 338.5/26/0994 19
HB236.A8 H35 1987

PRICE REGULATION - DEVELOPING COUNTRIES.
Saksena, K. D. Pricing policy and price controls in developing countries /. London , Boulder, Colo. , c1986. x, 240 p. ; ISBN 0-931477-85-9 (U. S.) : LC Card 86-3287 DDC 338.5/26/091724 19
HB236.D44 S25 1986 *NYPL [JLD 86-4069]*

PRICE REGULATION - FINLAND.
Wahlroos, Björn. A comment on the goals and potential implications of Finnish average cost price regulation /. Helsingfors , 1978. 12, [1] leaves : ISBN 951-555-053-X LC Card 85-192907
HB236.F55 W328 1978

PRICE REGULATION - GERMANY, WEST.
Mestmäcker, Ernst Joachim. Vereinbarkeit von Preisregelungen auf dem Arzneimittelmarkt mit dem Recht der Europäischen Wirtschaftsgemeinschaft /. Baden-Baden , 1979. 83 p. ; ISBN 3-7890-0444-8 : LC Card 80-515375
KK6444.D78 M47 *NYPL [JLD 81-684]*

PRICE REGULATION - INDIA.
Saksena, K. D. Pricing policy and price controls in developing countries /. London , Boulder, Colo. , c1986. x, 240 p. ; ISBN 0-931477-85-9 (U. S.) : LC Card 86-3287 DDC 338.5/26/091724 19
HB236.D44 S25 1986 *NYPL [JLD 86-4069]*

PRICE REGULATION - INDIA - CONGRESSES.
Workshop on Impact of Regulatory Mechanism on Corporate Sector (1984 : Bangalore, India) Workshop on Impact of Regulatory Mechanism on Corporate Sector . New Delhi [1985] 104 p. : LC Card 87-902536 DDC 338.954 19
HC435.2 .W67 1984

PRICE REGULATION - SPAIN - HISTORY - 17TH CENTURY - SOURCES.
Ebersole, Alva Vernon. Dos documentos de 1627 sobre la economía de España /. Valencia [1986?] 49 p. ; ISBN 84-7274-144-3 LC Card 87-107711
HG1133 .E24 1986

PRICE REGULATION - SWEDEN.
Sweden. 1983 års livsmedelskommitté. Expertgruppen för prisregleringsfrågor. Prisstöd och jordbruksprisreglering . Stockholm [1984] xvi, 260 p. ; ISBN 91-38-08461-9 LC Card 86-109988
HD9015.S86 S883 1984

Underbilaga till rapport från 1983 års livsmedelskommittés expertgrupp för prisregleringsfrågor . [Sweden , 1983] (Jönköping . 1 v. (various pagings) : LC Card 85-191640
HD9015.S86 U47 1983

Price responses of Malawi smallholder farmers--fast, slow or none? [microform] /. Mills, J. C. (Joseph C.) [Zomba] [1975] 42, [2] p. ; LC Card 80-980238 DDC 338.1/3/096897 19
HD1476.M33 M54 1975
*NYPL [*ZT-1646 no.53]*

The price system and resource allocation. Eckert, Ross D. Chicago , c1988. xviii, 648 p. : ISBN 0-03-012533-2 LC Card 87-5068 DDC 338.5/2 19
HB172 .L45 1988

PRICE THEORY. see **MICROECONOMICS.**

PRICE-WAGE POLICY. see **WAGE-PRICE POLICY.**

The Price Waterhouse book of personal financial planning /. Breitbard, Stanley H. New York , 1988. xi, 447 p. ; ISBN 0-8050-0387-8 LC Card 87-8493 DDC 332.024 19
HG179 .B727 1988

Price Waterhouse (Firm)
Breitbard, Stanley H. The Price Waterhouse book of personal financial planning /. New York , 1988. xi, 447 p. ; ISBN 0-8050-0387-8 LC Card 87-8493 DDC 332.024 19
HG179 .B727 1988

Doing business in Texas. [Austin, Tex.] [1986], c1985. 52, [64] p. : LC Card 87-621557 DDC 332.6/7322764 19
HC107.T4 D65 1986

Financing foreign development of non-fuel mineral resources . [Washington, D.C.] [1986] 308 p. : LC Card 86-602175 DDC 332.1/5 19
HD9506.D452 F56 1986

Making the right turn . [Salem? Or.] [1986] iv, 39 p. : LC Card 87-621891 DDC 388.1/14/09795 19
HE356.O7 M35 1986

El Manejo de los riesgos de la informática . Bogotá, D.E. [1984?] 61 p. : LC Card 85-183870
HF5548.2 .M2985 1984

PRICEFORBES FEDERALE VOLKSKAS (FIRM) - HISTORY.
Uberrima fides . [Johannesburg , 1985?] 69 p. : ISBN 0-620-08481-2 LC Card 87-146303 DDC 368/.006 19
HG8724.3.Z9 P758 1985

Prices and choices . Hemenway, David. Cambridge, Mass. , c1988. xii, 315 p. : ISBN 0-88730-242-4 (pbk.) LC Card 87-17437 DDC 338.5 19
HB172 .H47 1988

PRICES AND WAGES. see **WAGE-PRICE POLICY.**

PRICES - ARGENTINA.
Salarios e inflación, Argentina, 1970-1983 /. [Santiago, Chile] [c1984] iv, 116 p. : LC Card 85-156959
HC180.W24 S25 1984

PRICES - BRAZIL - ECONOMETRIC MODELS.
Modiano, Eduardo Marco. Salários, preços e câmbio . Rio de Janeiro, RJ , 1984. 55, [5] leaves ; LC Card 84-234066
HD5004 .M56 1984

PRICES - BRAZIL - SÃO PAULO.
Endo, Seiti Kaneko. Pesquisa de orçamentos familiares no município de São Paulo /. São Paulo [Rio de Janeiro] , 1984. 131 p. : LC Card 85-136517
HB235.B8 E53 1984

PRICES - BULGARIA - STATISTICS.
Statistika na t͡senite na stokite v tŭrgoviiata na edro i drebno. Statistika na t͡senitie na stokitie v tŭrgoviiata na edro i drebno =. Sofiia , 1937. 117 p. ; LC Card 86-222130
HB235.B85 S7 1937

PRICES - CANADA.
Industrial product price indexes, 1981=100 . Ottawa , c1986. 216 p. : ISBN 0-660-52876-2 (pbk.) : LC Card 87-168891
HB235.C2 I53 1986

PRICES - CAYMAN ISLANDS - STATISTICS.
A Guide to the new consumer price index. [George Town, Grand Caymon, B.W.I.] [1985] 26 leaves ; LC Card 86-221984 DDC 338.5/28/0972921 19
HB235.C29 G85 1985

PRICES - CHILE.
Desormeaux J., Jorge. Determinación de precios del sector exportador chileno, 1978-1982 /. Santiago, Chile , 1983. 88 p. : LC Card 87-403699 DDC 338.5/2/0983 19
HB235.C57 D47 1983

PRICES - COLOMBIA - MATHEMATICAL MODELS.
Mayer, Thomas, 1927- Instabile Exportmärkte und wirtschaftliche Entwicklung . Tübingen , c1983. vii, 181 p. : ISBN 3-16-344673-6 LC Card 83-218666
HF3426.5 .M39 1983

PRICES - COMMUNIST COUNTRIES.

Prices, costs, and margins in the production and distribution of compound feeding stuff for cattle, pigs, and poultry . Great Britain. Price Commission. London [1978] v, 35 p. ; ISBN 0-10-233878-7 (pbk.) LC Card 85-146987
HD9056.G72 G76 1978

PRICES - DENMARK.
Discountbutikker i dagligvarehandelen . København , 1983. 175 p. : ISBN 87-88149-11-0 : LC Card 83-237411
HF5429.215.D4 D57 1983

PRICES - DEVELOPING COUNTRIES.
World prices and development /. Aldershot, Hants, England , Brookfield, Vt., U. S.A. , c1985. xi, 377 p. : ISBN 0-566-00890-4 LC Card 86-134604 DDC 338.5/2/0971724 19
HC59.7 .W684 1985 ***NYPL [JLD 86-4068]***

PRICES - EUROPE, EASTERN.
Brabant, Jozef M. van. Regional price formation in Eastern Europe . Boston ; Dordrecht : xiv, 290 p. ; ISBN 90-247-3540-8 LC Card 87-12238 DDC 338.5/26/0947 19
HB235.E8 B73 1987

PRICES - EUROPEAN ECONOMIC COMMUNITY COUNTRIES.
Almedia, Maria Henriqueta de. O ganho médio do operário na indústria transformadora em Portugal e noutros países da OCDE de 1972 a 1982 /. Lisboa , 1985. 88 p. : LC Card 86-189354
HD5059 .A65 1985

PRICES - FORECASTING - STATISTICAL METHODS.
Sipos, Béla. Vállalati árelőrejelzések . Budapest , 1985. 290, [1] p. : ISBN 963-221-515-X : LC Card 86-190915
HB3730 .S495 1985

PRICES - FRANCE - HISTORY.
Douët-d'Arcq, L. (Louis), 1808-1882. (ed) Comptes de l'hôtel des rois de France aux XIVe et XVe siècles. Paris, 1865. 3 p.l., xlii p., 1 l., 437 p., 1 l. LC Card 05-5875
HJ1077 .D6

PRICES - GERMANY, EAST.
Bardmann, Manfred. Die Preistypdebatte, ihre Grundlagen und ihr Einfluss auf die praktische Ausgestaltung des Preissystems der DDR /. Berlin , c1986. 99 p. : ISBN 3-87061-300-9 LC Card 86-148984
HB235.G32 B37 1986

PRICES - GERMANY, WEST.
Gerster, Hans Joachim, 1946- Flexibilität und Rigidität in der Preisbewegung . Frankfurt am Main , New York , c1984. xii, 298, 69 p. : ISBN 3-8204-5109-9 LC Card 85-195018
HB235.G3 G48 1984

Vormbaum, Herbert. Differenzierte Preise . Köln , 1960. xi, 291 p. : LC Card 86-191408
HB235.G3 V67 1960

Wechselwirkungen von Geldpolitik, Inflation und Strukturwandel . Hamburg , 1984. 179 p. : ISBN 3-87895-243-0 LC Card 84-221405
HB235.G3 W42 1984

PRICES - GERMANY (WEST) - STATISTICS.
Döhrn, Roland. Privater Verbrauch und Einzelhandel in der Bundesrepublik Deutschland . Essen , 1981. 280 p. ; LC Card 87-408859 DDC 338.5/28/0943 19
HB235.G3 D57 1981

PRICES - GREAT BRITAIN.
Dobrovolny, Jiri, 1943- Preis- und Lohndirigismen im Dienste der Stabilisierungspolitik . Bern , New York , c1985. xi, 433 p. : ISBN 3-261-03517-X LC Card 86-105626 DDC 338.5/2/0945 19
HB236.G7 D63 1985

PRICES - HAWAII.
The Honolulu consumer price index, 1940-1986. [Honolulu] [1986] 19 p. ; LC Card 86-622085 DDC 319.69 s 338.5/28/09969 19
HA329.1 .A25 no. 187 HB235.U6

PRICES - HUNGARY.
A Folyamatos árszinvonal-emelkedés társadalmi hatásai . Budapest [1985] 176 p. ; ISBN 963-608-087-9 LC Card 87-407751
HG970.5 .F65 1985

A Hazai áralakulásról /. [Budapest] , 1986. 342 p. ; ISBN 963-09-2758-6 : LC Card 87-407741
HG970.5 .H39 1986

PRICES - HUNGARY - FORECASTING - STATISTICAL METHODS.
Sipos, Béla. Vállalati árelőrejelzések . Budapest , 1985. 290, [1] p. : ISBN 963-221-515-X : LC Card 86-190915
HB3730 .S495 1985

PRICES - HUNGARY - STATISTICS.
Beruházási árindexek, 1968-1971 /. [Budapest] [1972] 56 p. ; LC Card 86-189972
HB235.H8 B48 1972

Kiskereskedelmi áralakulás, 1981-1985 /. Budapest , 1986. 81 p. ; LC Card 86-202239
HB235.H8 K56 1986

Külkereskedelmi árstatisztikai adatok, 1950-1985 /. Budapest , 1986. 114 p. ; LC Card 87-409625
HB235.H8 K84 1986

Külkereskedelmi árstatisztikai adatok, 1957-1977 /. Budapest [1978] 125 p. ; LC Card 86-196922
HB235.H8 K85 1978

PRICES - INDEX NUMBERS. see **PRICE INDEXES.**

PRICES - INDEXES. see **PRICE INDEXES.**

PRICES - MARTINIQUE.
Guglielmetti, Francis. L'indice des prix de la Martinique, base 100 en 1979 . [Fort de France?] [1985] 130, xxiii p. : ISBN 2-11-062943-6 : LC Card 86-176702
HB235.M37 G83 1985

PRICES - MATHEMATICAL MODELS.
Blang, Hans-Georg, 1953- Die Variabilität relativer Preisänderungen und die Varianz monetärer Aggregate /. Frankfurt am Main , New York , c1986. xxvii, 338 p. : ISBN 3-8204-9074-4 LC Card 86-156110
HG229 .B555 1986

Borgmeier, Bernd, 1955- Der Einfluss verschiedener Preisbildungsmechanismen auf die gesamtwirtschfliche Beschäftigung /. Frankfurt am Main , New York , c1984. 362 p. : ISBN 3-8204-5601-5 : LC Card 85-198888
HB221 .B592 1984

Kucher, Eckhard. Scannerdaten und Preissensitivität bei Konsumgütern /. Wiesbaden , c1985. 282 p. : ISBN 3-409-13608-8 LC Card 86-128961
HB801 .K789 1985

Le Vaillant de Folleville, Patrice, 1954- Nicht-sequentielle Suche, Preiswerbung und Marktgleichgewicht /. Frankfurt am Main , New York , c1986. 198 p. : ISBN 3-8204-9058-2 LC Card 86-153194
HB221 .L42 1986

Silva, Adroaldo Moura da. Emprego e preços no curto prazo /. São Paulo, SP (C.P. 11474, 01000 São Paulo, SP) , 1983. 94 p. ;
NYPL [JLD 86-3819]

Thomée, Friedrich, 1920- Dynamische Preisbildungsprozesse in Monopol /. Wiesbaden , c1983. 247 p. : ISBN 3-409-13035-7 : LC Card 84-116637
HB221 .T465 1983

Vollmer, Friedrich Uwe, 1958- Informations- und Veränderungskosten in makroökonomischen Transmissionsmodellen /. Frankfurt am Main , New York , c1986. 169 p. : ISBN 3-8204-9142-2 LC Card 86-194476
HB221 .V64 1986

Wied-Nebbeling, Susanne. Sektorale Preisbildung und gesamtwirtschaftliche Preisstabilität /. Tübingen , 1986. xiii, 368 p. : ISBN 3-16-345102-0 LC Card 87-132436 DDC 338.5/2/0724 19
HB221 .W484 1986

Wittmann, Uli. Das Konzept rationaler Preiserwartungen /. Berlin , New York , c1985. xi, 310 p. : ISBN 0-387-15221-0 LC Card 86-194342
HB221 .W56 1985

PRICES - MAURITIUS.
Pochun, Malati J. Determinants of import prices in Mauritius /. Réduit, Mauritius , 1981. 15 p. ; LC Card 82-980680
HB235.M38 P63 1981

PRICES - MEXICO - HISTORY.
Bortz, Jeff. El salario en México /. México, D.F. , 1986. 198 p. : ISBN 968-612-519-1 LC Card 87-404064 DDC 331.2/972 19
HD4981 .B677 1986

PRICES - NORWAY.
Engrosprisstatistikk . Oslo , 1982. 120 p. ; ISBN 82-537-1833-0 : LC Card 83-139816
HB235.N6 E54 1982

Holm, Yngvar. Engrosomsetningsindeks /. Oslo , 1984. 18 leaves ; ISBN 82-537-2141-2 : LC Card 85-178075
HB235.N6 H65 1984

PRICES - PAKISTAN.
Consumer price index numbers of Pakistan, 1980-81 =. Karachi [1985] 118 p. ; LC Card 86-930250 DDC 338.5/28/095491 19
HB235.P25 C65 1985

PRICES - PERU.
Herrera, César. Inflación, política devaluatoria y apertura externa en el Perú, 1978-1984 /. Lima, Perú , 1985. 55 p. : LC Card 87-104441
HG895 .H47 1985

PRICES - POLAND - STATISTICS.
Ceny detaliczne 1971-1985 /. Warszawa , 1985. 160 p. ; LC Card 86-196060
HB235.P6 C45 1985

PRICES - PORTUGAL.
Almedia, Maria Henriqueta de. O ganho médio do operário na indústria transformadora em Portugal e noutros países da OCDE de 1972 a 1982 /. Lisboa , 1985. 88 p. : LC Card 86-189354
HD5059 .A65 1985

Prices, quantities, and expectations : Keynes and macroeconomics in the fifty years since the publication of the General theory / edited by P.J.N. Sinclair. Oxford [Oxfordshire] : Clarendon Press ; New York : Oxford University Press, 1987. xxiv, 487 p. : ill. ; 24 cm. Includes bibliographies and index. ISBN 0-19-828589-2 (pbk.) : LC Card 87-7770 DDC 330.15/6 19
1. Keynesian economics. 2. Macroeconomics. 3. Keynes, John Maynard, 1883-1946. I. Sinclair, P. J. N.
HB99.7 .P74 1987

PRICES, SECURITIES. see **STOCKS - PRICES.**

PRICES - SOVIET UNION.
Kirillov, S. R. (Sergeĭ Rufovich) Soizmerenie zatrat i rezul'tatov v teorii planovogo tsenoobrazovaniia /. Moskva , 1987. 188 p. ; LC Card 87-157208
HB235.S73 K57 1987

TSena i khozraschet /. Moskva , 1986. 144 p. ; LC Card 87-163568
HB235.S73 T72 1986

TSeny i tarify /. Moskva , 1983. 150 p. : LC Card 84-117348
HB235.S73 T735 1983

PRICES - SOVIET UNION - MATHEMATICAL MODELS.
Khoziaistvennyĭ mekhanizm i tsenoobrazovanie /. Moskva , 1983. 77 p. ; LC Card 85-180519
HB235.S73 K47 1983

PRICES - SRI LANKA - MATHEMATICAL MODELS.
Athukoralge, Premachandra. Export instability and growth . London , Wolfeboro, N.H. , c1987. 244 p. : ISBN 0-7099-3739-3 : LC Card 86-32833 DDC 382/.6/095493 19
HF3770.8.Z5 A84 1987

The Prices Surveillance Authority /. Hall, Richard, 1937- Melbourne [1987] 24 p. ; ISBN 0-85801-167-0 (pbk.) LC Card 87-156317 DDC 338.5/26/0994 19
HB236.A8 H35 1987

PRICES - SWEDEN.
Isacsson, Göthe. Index för prisregleringar. Stockholm [1985?] 80 p. : ISBN 91-618-0082-1 LC Card 85-206079
HB235.S8 I83 1985

PRICES - UNITED STATES.
Gerster, Hans Joachim, 1946- Flexibilität und Rigidität in der Preisbewegung . Frankfurt am Main , New York , c1984. xii, 298, 69 p. : ISBN 3-8204-5109-9 LC Card 85-195018
HB235.G3 G48 1984

PRICING.
Montgomery, Stephen L. Profitable pricing strategies /. New York , c1988. xiii, 174 p. : ISBN 0-07-042860-3 : LC Card 87-4089 DDC

658.8/16 19
HF5416.5 .M67 1988

Pricing consumer credit : PC2 sourcebook. Washington, D.C. (1120 Connecticut Ave., N.W., Washington 20036) : American Bankers Association, c1986. 136 p. : ill. ; 23 cm. LC Card 86-209981 DDC 332.1/753 19
1. Bank loans - United States. 2. Consumer credit - United States. 3. Price policy - United States. 4. Bank management - United States. I. American Bankers Association.
HG1642.U5 P75 1986

PRICING - DICTIONARIES.
Woelfel, Charles J. Budgeting, pricing, and cost controls . Chicago, Ill. , c1987. p. cm. ISBN 0-917253-91-4 : LC Card 87-17921 DDC 658.1/5/0321 19
HG151 .W63 1987

Pricing financial services /. Moebs, G. Michael. Homewood, Ill. , c1986. xviii, 246 p. : ISBN 0-87094-594-7 LC Card 85-73688
NYPL [JLE 86-2817]

PRICING - MATHEMATICAL MODELS.
Hwang, Hae-Shin. Dominant firm price leadership . Toronto, Ont. [1986] 40 p. : ISBN 0-7729-2122-9 : LC Card 87-161006 DDC 338.2/3 19
HD9539.N5 H93 1986

Wied-Nebbeling, Susanne. Sektorale Preisbildung und gesamtwirtschaftliche Preisstabilität /. Tübingen , 1986. xiii, 368 p. : ISBN 3-16-345102-0 LC Card 87-132436 DDC 338.5/2/0724 19
HB221 .W484 1986

Pricing of water services /. Herrington, Paul. Paris , Washington, D.C. , 1987. 145 p. : ISBN 92-64-12921-9 (pbk.) : LC Card 87-167536 DDC 338.4/336361 19
HD4456 .H47 1987

Pricing policies and price controls in developing countries. Saksena, K. D. Pricing policy and price controls in developing countries /. London , Boulder, Colo. , c1986. x, 240 p. ; ISBN 0-931477-85-9 (U. S.) : LC Card 86-3287 DDC 338.5/26/091724 19
HB236.D44 S25 1986 NYPL [JLD 86-4069]

Pricing policy and investment criteria in public enterprises : proceedings of two international workshops / organized by ICPE in collaboration with the United Nations Development Administration Division ; edited by Zia U. Ahmed. Ljubljana, Yugoslavia : International Center for Public Enterprises in Developing Countries, 1982. 297 p. : ill. ; 24 cm. Includes bibliographical references. ISBN 92-9038-024-1 (pbk.) LC Card 85-242542 DDC 338.7/4 19
1. Government business enterprises - Price policy - Congresses. 2. Government business enterprises - Finance - Congresses. I. Ahmed, Zia U. (Zia Uddin). II. International Center for Public Enterprises in Developing Countries. III. United Nations. Dept. of Technical Cooperation for Development. Development Administration Division.
HD3842 .P75 1985 NYPL [JLE 87-547]

Pricing policy and price controls in developing countries /. Saksena, K. D. London , Boulder, Colo. , c1986. x, 240 p. ; ISBN 0-931477-85-9 (U. S.) : LC Card 86-3287 DDC 338.5/26/091724 19
HB236.D44 S25 1986 NYPL [JLD 86-4069]

Pricing policy in the social sectors . Jimenez, Emmanuel, 1952- Baltimore , 1987. v, 170 p. ; ISBN 0-8018-3501-1 : LC Card 86-27590 DDC 338.4/33621/091724 19
HJ7469 .J56 1987

The pride and the fall . Barnett, Correlli. New York , 1987, c1986. xii, 359 p. ; ISBN 0-02-901851-X LC Card 86-25701 DDC 330.941/0854 19
HC256.4 .B28 1987

Priebe, Hermann, 1907- Agrarpolitik in der EG : Probleme und Perspektiven / Hermann Priebe, Wilhelm Scheper, Winfried von Urff, unter Mitarbeit von Heino von Meyer ... [et al.].1. Aufl. Baden-Baden : Nomos Verlagsgesellschaft, 1984. 269 p. ; 23 cm. Includes bibliographical references. ISBN 3-7890-1060-X LC Card 85-138555 DDC 338.1/84 19
1. Agriculture and state - European Economic Community countries. I. Scheper, Wilhelm. II. Urff, Winfried von. III. Title.
HD1920.5.Z8 P74 1984

Priemus, Hugo. Nederlandse woontheorieën / Hugo Priemus. Delft : Delftse Universitaire Pers, 1984. vi, 92 p. : ill. ; 24 cm. (Volkshuisvesting in theorie en praktijk . 6) Bibliography: p. 76-92. ISBN 90-6275-126-1 : LC Card 84-226472
1. Housing - Netherlands. 2. Housing policy - Netherlands. I. Title. II. Series.
HD7344.A3 P67 1984 NYPL [JLE 86-2510]

Prieto, Ayari. Por una nueva política alimentaria /. [México, D.F.] , 1984. 114 p. ; LC Card 85-131176 DDC 338.1/9/72 19
HD9014.M62 P67 1984 NYPL [JLC 86-348]

Priewe, Jan, 1949- Zur Kritik konkurrierender Arbeitsmarkt- und Beschäftigungstheorien und ihrer politischen Implikationen : Ansatzpunkte für eine Neuorientierung einer Theorie der Arbeitslosigkeit / Jan Priewe. Frankfurt am Main ; New York : P. Lang, c1984. 385 p. ; 21 cm. (Europäische Hochschulschriften. Reihe V, Volks- und Betriebswirtschaft, 0531-7339 . Bd. 501 = vol. 501 = vol. 501) Bibliography: p. 351-385. ISBN 3-8204-8033-1 LC Card 85-198523
1. Unemployment. 2. Labor supply. I. Series: Europäische Hochschulschriften. Reihe V, Volks- und Betriebswirtschaft , Bd. 501. II. Title.
HD5707.5 .P75 1984

Prigarin, V. S. (Valentin Stepanovich) Usloviia truda pri sotsializme : politiko-ėkonomicheskiĭ analiz / V.S. Prigarin. Leningrad : Izd-vo Leningradskogo universiteta, 1985. 125 p. ; 22 cm. At head of title: Leningradskiĭ ordena Lenina i ordena Trudovogo Krasnogo Znameni gosudarstvennyĭ universitet imeni A.A. Zhdanova. LC Card 86-124818
1. Work environment - Soviet Union. 2. Industrial hygiene - Soviet Union. I. Title.
HD7725 .P83 1985

Prigorodnye passazhirskie perevozki /. Artynov, Aleksandr Petrovich. Moskva , 1985. 160 p. : LC Card 86-208093
HE4834 .A78 1985

Primary commodities : market developments and outlook / by the Commodities Division of the Research Department. Washington, D.C. : International Monetary Fund, 1987. p. cm. (World economic and financial surveys, 0258-7440) ISBN 0-939934-87-6 LC Card 87-17225 DDC 382/.4 19
1. Commercial products. 2. Raw materials. I. International Monetary Fund. Commodities Division. II. Series.
HF1040.7 .P718 1987

Primary commodities . Mukerjee, Dilip. Kuala Lumpur, Malaysia , c1985. 39 p. ; ISBN 967-99974-7-2 (pbk.) : LC Card 87-105669 DDC 338/.02 19
HF1040.7 .M85 1985

Primary commodities, security of supply. Probleme der Rohstoffsicherung =. Bonn [1981] 215 p. : LC Card 85-206699
HF1051 .P76 1980

Primary description of speech signals. Pervichnoe opisanie signalov rechi . Vil'nius , 1980. 67 p. : LC Card 82-107723
HD38 .S715 vyp. 42 TK7882.S65

Prime cut . Skaggs, Jimmy M. College Station , c1986. xiii, 263 p., [8] p. of plates : ISBN 0-89096-249-9 : LC Card 85-40742 DDC 338.1/76213/0973 19
HD9415 .S58 1986 NYPL [JLE 86-3913]

Primeaux, Walter J. Direct electric utility competition : the natural monopoly myth / by Walter J. Primeaux, Jr. New York, NY, USA : Praeger, 1986. xiii, 297 p. ; 25 cm. Includes bibliographical references and index. ISBN 0-03-004858-3 (alk. paper) : LC Card 85-20487 DDC 338.8/26136362/0973 19
1. Electric utilities - United States. 2. Monopolies - United States. 3. Competition - United States. I. Title.
HD9685.U5 P74 1985 NYPL [JLE 86-4075]

Primeiro de maio. Roio, José Luiz del. 1o. de maio /. São Paulo , 1986. 152, [16] p. : LC Card 86-197367
HD7791 .R59 1986

Primeiro de maio. 1o. de maio . [São Paulo] , 1985. 80 p. : LC Card 86-200658
HD8286 .A13 1985

Primeiro plano nacional de reforma agrária da Nova República. Instituto Nacional de Colonização e Reforma Agraria. 1o. plano nacional de reforma agrária da Nova República . Brasília, DF , 1985. 73 leaves : LC Card 86-225850
HD1333.B6 I54 1985

Primenenie ėkonomiko-matematicheskikh metodov v sovershenstvovanii upravleniia narodnym khoziaistvom / [otvetstvennyĭ redaktor V.K. Gorbunov]. Frunze : Izd-vo "Ilim", 1982. 225 p. : ill. ; 20 cm. At head of title: Akademiia nauk Kirgizskoĭ SSR. Institut fiziki i matematiki. Includes bibliographies. LC Card 83-193778
1. Sugar beet industry - Soviet Union - Planning - Mathematical models. 2. Sugar beet industry - Kirghiz S.S.R. - Planning - Mathematical models. I. Gorbunov, V. K. (Vladimir Konstantinovich). II. Institut fiziki i matematiki (Kyrgyz SSR Ilimder Akademiiasy).
HD9115.S652 P75 1982

Primer censo artesanal, 1978. Directorio artesanal, 1978 /. Guatemala , 1981. 6 v. ; LC Card 87-403025
HD2346.G8 D57 1981

Primer censo artesanal 1978. Principales indicadores económicos . Guatemala , 1982. 487 p. ; LC Card 87-403026 DDC 331.7/94 19
HD2346.G8 P75 1982

A primer for buying and selling small manufacturing companies /. Kellogg, Douglas E. New York , c1987. xiv, 225 p. : ISBN 0-471-85235-X LC Card 87-19017 DDC 658.1/6 19
HD2341 .K44 1987

Prince Edward Island. Human Resource Development Division. Research and Planning Division. Prince Edward Island's migration patterns . [Charlottetown, P.E.I.] [1986] 40 leaves : LC Card 87-165892 DDC 304.8/09717 19
HB1990.P74 P75 1986

Prince Edward Island Labour-management Relations Council. Twentieth joint conference . [Charlottetown, P.E.I. , 1986] 94 p. ; LC Card 87-147512 DDC 338/.06 19
HC120.T4 T84 1986

Prince Edward Island's migration patterns : past, present, and future / prepared by Research & Analytical Services, Human Resource Development Division, PEI Department of Industry. [Charlottetown, P.E.I.] : The Dept., [1986] 40 leaves : ill. ; 28 cm. "January, 1986." Bibliography: leaf 40. LC Card 87-165892 DDC 304.8/09717 19
1. Migration, Internal - Prince Edward Island. I. Prince Edward Island. Human Resource Development Division. Research and Planning Division.
HB1990.P74 P75 1986

Princeton studies in international finance. For other vols. in this series, see Old Catalog.
(no. 58) Cuddington, John T. Capital flight . Princeton, N.J. , c1986. 44 p. ; ISBN 0-88165-230-X (pbk.) : LC Card 86-21386 DDC 332/.041 19
HG3891 .C83 1986

(no. 59) Crawford, Vincent P., 1950- International lending, long-term credit relationships, and dynamic contract theory /. Princeton, N.J. [1987] c1986. 34 p. ; ISBN 0-88165-231-8 (pbk.) : LC Card 86-33743 DDC 336.3/435 19
HG3891.5 .C7 1987

(no. 60) Gylfason, Thorvaldur. Credit policy and economic activity in developing countries with IMF stabilization programs /. Princeton, N.J. , c1987. 44 p. ; ISBN 0-88165-232-6 (pbk.) : LC Card 87-3389 DDC 332.7/09172/4 19
HG3711.D48 G94 1987

Principales indicadores económicos : I censo artesanal / Dirección General de Estadística, Ministerio de Economía, República de Guatemala. Guatemala : El Ministerio, 1982. 487 p. ; 20 x 27 cm. Cover title: I censo artesanal 1978. Spine title: Indicadores económicos, I censo artesanal 1978. LC Card 87-403026 DDC 331.7/94 19
1. Artisans - Guatemala - Statistics. 2. Cottage industries - Guatemala - Statistics. 3. Guatemala - Census, 1978. I. Guatemala. Dirección General de Estadística. II. Title: I censo artesanal 1978. III. Title:

lo censo artesanal 1978. IV. Title: Primer censo artesanal 1978. V. Title: Indicadores económicos, I censo artesanal 1978.
HD2346.G8 P75 1982

Principales productos del comercio exterior mexicano del siglo XIX /. Alvarado Gómez, Armando. México, D.F. , 1985. v. <1 > ; LC Card 87-401206 DDC 382/.0972 19
HF3236 .A5 1985

Principles of accounting /. Emery, Mary Ann. San Diego , <c1987-. v. <2- > : ISBN 0-15-600029-6 (pbk.) : LC Card 86-27103 DDC 657 19
HF5635 .E537 1987

Principles of accounting /. Flamholtz, Eric. New York , London , c1987. xli, 1159, [90] p. : ISBN 0-02-338210-4 LC Card 86-31086 DDC 657 19
HF5635 .F5645 1987

Principles of accounting /. Needles, Belverd E. Boston, MA , c1987. xx, 1100, [38] p. : ISBN 0-395-35702-0 LC Card 86-80401 DDC 657 19
HF5635 .N35 1987

Principles of auditing / Walter B. Meigs ... [et al.]. 3rd Canadian ed. Homewood, Ill. : Irwin, 1987. xv, 724 p. : ill. ; 25 cm. Includes bibliographical references and index. ISBN 0-256-03580-6 LC Card 86-82588 DDC 657/.45 19
1. Auditing. I. Meigs, Walter B.
HF5667 .P73 1987

Principles of dynamical classification of stochastic processes and systems. Shpilevskiĭ, Ė. Printsipy dinamicheskoĭ klassifikatsii stokhasticheskikh protsessov i sistem . Vil′nius , 1978. 138 p. ; LC Card 81-173567
HD38 .S715 vyp. 28 QA274

Principles of economics /. Ruffin, Roy, 1938- Glenview, Ill. , c1988. xxxi, 918, [42] p. : ISBN 0-673-18871-X : LC Card 87-23369 DDC 330 19
HB171.5 .R82 1988

Principles of financial management /. Gup, Benton E. New York , c1987. xii, 672, 16 p. : ISBN 0-471-81203-X LC Card 86-28937 DDC 658.1/5 19
HG4026 .G88 1987

Principles of health & disability insurance selling. 3rd ed. Chicago : Longman/R&R Newkirk, c1987. 179 p. ; 28 cm. ISBN 0-88462-700-4 (pbk.) LC Card 87-16281 DDC 368.3/8/00688 19
1. Insurance, Health - United States. 2. Insurance, Disability - United States. 3. Insurance, Health - Agents. I. R & R Newkirk. II. Title: Principles of health and disability insurance selling.
HG9396 .P75 1987

Principles of health and disability insurance selling. Principles of health & disability insurance selling. Chicago , c1987. 179 p. ; ISBN 0-88462-700-4 (pbk.) LC Card 87-16281 DDC 368.3/8/00688 19
HG9396 .P75 1987

Principles of international finance /. Kane, Daniel R., 1949- London , New York , c1988. xiv, 301 p. : ISBN 0-7099-3134-4 (pbk.) LC Card 87-24388 DDC 332.042 19
HG3881 .K263 1988

Principles of macroeconomics /. Fleisher, Belton M. Dubuque, Iowa , c1987. xix, 427 p. : ISBN 0-697-01035-X (pbk.) LC Card 86-72959 DDC 339 19
HB172.5 .F545 1987

Principles of marketing /. Evans, Joel R. New York , London , c1988. xxiii, 528, 44, 22 p. : ISBN 0-02-334340-0 LC Card 87-15223 DDC 658.8 19
HF5415 .E865 1988

Principles of microeconomics /. Fleisher, Belton M. Dubuque, Iowa , c1987. xxi, 458 p. : ISBN 0-697-01038-4 (pbk.) LC Card 86-72958 DDC 338.5 19
HB172 .F54 1987

Principles of political economy . Malthus, T. R. (Thomas Robert, 1766-1834. London , 1986. 2 v. (18, x, 439 p.) : ISBN 1-85196-105-4 (v. 1) LC Card 87-672115
HB861 .A2x 1986 vol. 5-6

Principles of political economy /. Malthus, T. R. (Thomas Robert, 1766-1834. Cambridge , New York , 1987. p. cm. ISBN 0-521-32363-0 (set) LC Card 86-32742 DDC 330.15/3 19
HB161 .M25 1987

Principles of political economy . Mill, John Stuart, 1806-1873. Fairfield, NJ , 1987. liii, 1013 p. ; ISBN 0-678-00073-5 LC Card 86-21290 DDC 330 19
HB161 .M6 1987

Pringle, John J. Essentials of managerial finance / John J. Pringle, Robert S. Harris. 2nd ed. Glenview, Ill. : Scott, Foresman, c1987. xxxi, 811, [98] p. : col. ill. ; 24 cm. Includes bibliographies and indexes. ISBN 0-673-18331-9 : LC Card 86-31333 DDC 658.1/5 19
1. Business enterprises - Finance. 2. Corporations - Finance. I. Harris, Robert S., 1949-. II. Title.
HG4026 .P73 1987

Prini͡atie reshenii͡ v upravlenii khozi͡aĭstvennymi svi͡azi͡ami / [otvetstvennyĭ redaktor E.A. Khrutskiĭ]. Moskva : Akademii͡a nauk SSSR, T͡Sentr. ėkonomiko-matematicheskiĭ in-t, 1982. 80 p. : ill. ; 21 cm. Includes bibliographies. LC Card 85-180526
1. Industrial management - Soviet Union - Decision making - Mathematical models. I. Khrutskiĭ, E. A. II. T͡Sentral′nyĭ ėkonomiko-matematicheskiĭ institut (Akademii͡a nauk SSSR).
HD30.23 .P745 1982

Prinosŭt na dr. Todor Zhivkov za razvitieto na sotsialno-ikonomicheskata politika na BKP v etapa na izgrazhdane na razvitoto sotsialistichesko obshtestvo : nauchno-prakticheska konferentsii͡a / [ezikov redaktor Vasilka Ivanova]. Sofii͡a : [s.n.], 1983. 398 p. ; 22 cm. At head of title: Kolarovski raĭonen komitet na BKP--Sofii͡a. Vissh ikonomicheski institut "Karl Marks"--Sofii͡a. Includes bibliographical references. LC Card 84-103348
1. Bulgaria - Economic policy - 1944- - Congresses. 2. Bulgaria - Economic conditions - 1944- - Congresses. 3. Zhivkov, Todor - Congresses. I. Ivanova, Vasilka. II. Kolarovski raĭonen komitet na BKP--Sofii͡a. III. Vissh ikonomicheski institut "Karl Marks"--Sofii͡a.
HC403 .P72 1983

Print Project.
The Wholesale-by-mail catalog. New York , 1986. iv, 364 p. ; ISBN 0-312-90379-0 (pbk.) : LC Card 87-139567 DDC 381/.2/02573 19
HF5861 .W54 1986

The Wholesale-by-mail catalog, 1987 /. New York [1987] p. cm. ISBN 0-312-00205-X (pbk.) : LC Card 86-27890 DDC 381/.2/02573 19
HF5861 .W527 1987

The printed circuit board industry /. Castrovilla, Joseph A. Stamford, Conn., U. S.A. , c1985. ix, 116 leaves : ISBN 0-89336-451-7 (soft) LC Card 87-403911 DDC 381/.4562138174/0973 19
HD9696.P743 U634 1985

Printed circuit board market opportunities. Norwalk, Conn., U. S.A. (6 Prowitt St., Norwalk 06855) : International Resource Development Inc., [1986] v, 153 leaves : ill. ; 28 cm. (Report / International Resource Development Inc. . #694) "May 1986." LC Card 86-224533 DDC 381/.4562/38174/0973 19
1. Printed circuits industry - United States. 2. Market surveys - United States. I. International Resource Development, inc. II. Series: Report / International Resource Development Inc. , #649.
HD9696.P743 U66 1986

PRINTED CIRCUITS - DICTIONARIES.
Böhss, Günther. Dictionary of printed circuit technology . Amsterdam , New York , 1985. 187 p. ; ISBN 0-444-99555-2 (U. S.) : LC Card 85-12955 DDC 621.381/74/0331 19
TK7868.P7 B65 1985 ***NYPL [JSD 86-621]***

PRINTED CIRCUITS - DICTIONARIES - GERMAN.
Böhss, Günther. Dictionary of printed circuit technology . Amsterdam , New York , 1985. 187 p. ; ISBN 0-444-99555-2 (U. S.) : LC Card 85-12955 DDC 621.381/74/0331 19
TK7868.P7 B65 1985 ***NYPL [JSD 86-621]***

PRINTED CIRCUITS INDUSTRY - MANAGEMENT - DATA PROCESSING - CONGRESSES.
Symposium on Management Data Processing for PCB Manufacturing (1982 : Luxembourg, Luxembourg) Symposium on Management Data Processing for PCB Manufacturing . Lugano [1982?] 1 v. (various pagings) : LC Card 84-211066 DDC 621.381/74/0685 19
HD9696.P742 S96 1982
NYPL [JSG 86-145]

PRINTED CIRCUITS INDUSTRY - QUALITY CONTROL - CONGRESSES.
Symposium on Management Data Processing for PCB Manufacturing (1982 : Luxembourg, Luxembourg) Symposium on Management Data Processing for PCB Manufacturing . Lugano [1982?] 1 v. (various pagings) : LC Card 84-211066 DDC 621.381/74/0685 19
HD9696.P742 S96 1982
NYPL [JSG 86-145]

PRINTED CIRCUITS INDUSTRY - UNITED STATES.
Castrovilla, Joseph A. The printed circuit board industry /. Stamford, Conn., U. S.A. , c1985. ix, 116 leaves : ISBN 0-89336-451-7 (soft) LC Card 87-403911 DDC 381/.4562138174/0973 19
HD9696.P743 U634 1985

Printed circuit board market opportunities. Norwalk, Conn., U. S.A. (6 Prowitt St., Norwalk 06855) [1986] v, 153 leaves : LC Card 86-224533 DDC 381/.4562/38174/0973 19
HD9696.P743 U66 1986

Printsipy dinamicheskoĭ klassifikatsii stokhasticheskikh protsessov i sistem . Shpilevskiĭ, Ė. Vil′nius , 1978. 138 p. ; LC Card 81-173567
HD38 .S715 vyp. 28 QA274

Printsipy ėkonomicheskogo upravlenii͡a nauchno-tekhnicheskim progressom : sbornik nauchnykh trudov / [redaktsionnai͡a kollegii͡a N.P. Goncharova ... et al.]. Kiev : IĖ AN USSR, 1982. 122 p. ; 20 cm. At head of title: Akademii͡a nauk Ukrainskoĭ SSR. Institut ėkonomiki. Includes bibliographical references. LC Card 83-143870
1. Technological innovations - Soviet Union. I. Goncharova, N. P. II. Instytut ekonomiky (Akademii͡a nauk Ukraïns′koï RSR).
HC340.T4 P67 1982

Prinz, Michael, 1952- Novy, Klaus. Illustrierte Geschichte der Gemeinwirtschaft . Berlin , c1985. 239 p. : ISBN 3-8012-0111-2 LC Card 86-122604
HD3498 .N68 1985

Prinzipien und Formen sozialer Sicherung in nicht-industriellen Gesellschaften /. Partsch, Manfred. Berlin , c1983. 168 p. ; ISBN 3-428-05484-9 LC Card 84-148527 DDC 368.4/009172/4 19
HD7252 .P37 1983 ***NYPL [JLE 85-1238]***

PRIO report .
(85/15) Vargas, Ines. The right to work and the situation of workers /. Oslo [1985] 47 p. ; ISBN 82-7288-122-5 (pbk.) LC Card 86-204949 DDC 331.88/92 19
HD4903 .V34 1985

(85/6) Buvollen, H. P. (Hans Petter) The situation of workers in the industrialised countries with special reference to Scandinavia /. Oslo [1985] 24 p. ; LC Card 86-205580 DDC 331.13/7948 19
HD8540 .B86 1985

(85/8) Vargas, Ines. The NIEO and the situatuon of workers . Oslo [1985] xiv, 290 p. ; ISBN 82-7288-121-7 (pbk.) LC Card 86-205407 DDC 331/.098 19
HD6530.5 .V36 1985

(85/9) Vargas, Ines. The situation of workers in Latin America /. Oslo , 1985. 92 p. ; ISBN 82-7288-123-3 (pbk.) LC Card 86-205392 DDC 331/.098 19
HD6530.5 .V37 1985

(86/14) Vargas, Ines. Conclusions from "The NIEO and the situation of workers" . Oslo :International Peace Research Institute, [1986] 21 p. ; LC Card 87-128390 DDC 337.8 19
HF1480.5 .V37 1986

(86/21) Gleditsch, Nils Petter, 1942- Economic incentives to arm? . Oslo [1986] 72 p. : ISBN 82-7288-134-9 LC Card 87-163647 DDC 338.4/36234 19
HC79.D4 G54 1986

(87/2) Haugstveit, Nils. The Nicaraguan

development process, 1979-85 . Oslo [1987] 148 p. : ISBN 82-7288-136-5 (pbk.) LC Card 87-164230 DDC 338.97285 19
HC146 .H38 1987

Prioridade agrícola . Homem de Melo, Fernando Bento, 1942- São Paulo , 1985. xiii, 200 p. : LC Card 86-126447 DDC 338.1/881 19
HD1872 .H66 1985 ***NYPL [JLD 86-3809]***

Prioritások gazdaságunk fejlesztésében /. Nyitrai, Ferencné. [Budapest] , 1986. 270 p. ; ISBN 963-09-2782-9 : LC Card 87-408568
HC300.28 .N954 1986

PRISON SENTENCES - UNITED STATES.
The Drunk driver and jail /. [Washington, D.C.?] , 1987- v. : LC Card 87-600837 DDC 363.1/255 19
HE5620.D7 D77 1987

PRISONERS OF WAR - GERMANY - HISTORY.
Herrenmensch und Arbeitsvölker . Berlin , c1986. 189 p. : ISBN 3-88022-952-X (cover); 3-88022-925-X : LC Card 87-119712 DDC 331.11/732/0943 19
HD4875.G4 H47 1986

PRISONERS OF WAR - GERMANY - HISTORY - 20TH CENTURY.
Siegfried, Klaus-Jörg, 1940- Rüstungsproduktion und Zwangsarbeit im Volkswagenwerk, 1939-1945 . Frankfurt , New York , c1986. 239 p. : ISBN 3-593-33765-7 LC Card 87-133375 DDC 338.4/76234/0943 19
HD9743.G48 S56 1986

PRISONERS OF WAR - GERMANY (WEST) - MÜNSTER IN WESTFALEN - HISTORY.
Weidner, Marcus, 1964- Nur Gräber als Spuren . Münster , c1984. 134 p. : ISBN 3-924550-02-6 LC Card 86-116688 DDC 331.11/732/094355 19
HD4875.G4 W45 1984

Prisstöd och jordbruksprisreglering . Sweden. 1983 års livsmedelskommitté. Expertgruppen för prisregleringsfrågor. Stockholm [1984] xvi, 260 p. ; ISBN 91-38-08461-9 LC Card 86-109988
HD9015.S86 S883 1984

Pristupko, Viktor Aleksandrovich. Molodost´, trud, romantika . Moskva , 1985. 183 p., [8] p. of plates : LC Card 86-113851
HD4870.S65 M65 1985

Pritchard, Robert E., 1941- Be your own financial advisor / Robert E. Pritchard, Gregory C. Potter, Larry E. Howe. Englewood Cliffs, N.J. : Prentice-Hall, c1988. xiv, 187 p. ; 24 cm. Bibliography: p. 171-181. Includes index. ISBN 0-13-071242-6 LC Card 87-14366 DDC 332.024 19
1. Finance, Personal - United States. 2. Investments - United States. I. Potter, Gregory C. II. Howe, Larry E. III. Title.
HG179 .P737 1988

Pritchett, Janie. Fencl, George. The central Florida career guide /. Altamonte Springs, FL. , c1987. 56, 48 p. : ISBN 0-942827-00-7 (pbk.) : LC Card 87-402073 DDC 650.1/4/09759 19
HF5382.75.U62 F64 1987

Pritchett, Price. Making mergers work : a guide to managing mergers and acquisitions / Price Pritchett. Homewood, Ill. : Dow Jones-Irwin, c1987. xii, 108 p. ; 24 cm. Includes bibliographical references and index. ISBN 0-87094-980-2 LC Card 86-73001 DDC 658.1/6 19
1. Consolidation and merger of corporations. I. Title.
HD2746.5 .P743 1987

Prittwitz, Volker. Umweltaussenpolitik : grenzüberschreitende Luftverschmutzung in Europa / Volker Prittwitz. Frankfurt ; New York : Campus Verlag, c1984. vii, 211 p. : ill. ; 21 cm. (Arbeitsberichte des Wissenschaftszentrums Berlin, Internationales Institut für Umwelt und Gesellschaft) Bibliography: p. 207-211. ISBN 3-593-33369-4 LC Card 84-202897
1. Air quality management - Europe - International cooperation. 2. Air - Pollution - Europe. I. Title. II. Series.
HC240.9.A4 P75 1984

Private Auslandsinvestitionen in Lateinamerika. (10) Issel, Catarina Irene. Die Geldwertberichtigung in Brasilien im Rechnungswesen der Unternehmung /. Hamburg , 1983. iii, 181 p. : LC Card 84-112596 DDC 332.6/73/098 s 657/.48 19
HG5160.5.A3 P7 Nr. 10 HF5658.5 ***NYPL [JLK 73-84 Nr.10]***

PRIVATE BRANCH EXCHANGE TELEPHONE EQUIPMENT INDUSTRY - UNITED STATES.
Customer premises telecom equipment & the regional Bell companies. Norwalk, Conn., U. S.A. (6 Prowitt St., Norwalk 06855) , c1987. ix, 193 leaves ; LC Card 87-403216 DDC 381/.45621385 19
HD9697.T453 U5245 1987

PRIVATE COMPANIES - FINANCE - LAW AND LEGISLATION - INDIA.
Kulshreshtha, V. D. (Visheshwar Dayal), 1922- Government regulation of financial management of private corporate sector in India /. Bombay , 1986. xxiv, 306 p. ; LC Card 87-902600
HG4241 .K85 1986

PRIVATE COMPANIES - INDIA - FINANCE.
Kulshreshtha, V. D. (Visheshwar Dayal), 1922- Government regulation of financial management of private corporate sector in India /. Bombay , 1986. xxiv, 306 p. ; LC Card 87-902600
HG4241 .K85 1986

PRIVATE COMPANIES - INFORMATION SERVICES - UNITED STATES - HANDBOOKS, MANUALS, ETC.
How to find information about private companies /. Washington, DC , c1987. iii, 149 p. ; ISBN 0-934940-47-9 (pbk.) : LC Card 86-51566 DDC 016.3387/4/0973 19
HG4013.5 .H69 1987

Private enterprise in Africa . Marsden, Keith. Washington, D.C. [1987] xiii, 66 p. ; ISBN 0-8213-0945-5 (pbk.) LC Card 87-18419 DDC 330.96/032 19
HC800 .M353 1987

The Private exercise of public functions / edited by Dennis L. Thompson. Port Washington, N.Y. : Associated Faculty Press, 1985. 251 p. ; 24 cm. (A Policy Studies Organization series publication) Includes bibliographies and index. ISBN 0-8046-9368-4 LC Card 84-9254 DDC 361.6/1 19
1. Policy sciences - Addresses, essays, lectures. 2. Government ownership - Addresses, essays, lectures. 3. Associations, institutions, etc. - Addresses, essays, lectures. I. Thompson, Dennis L. II. Series.
H97 .P76 1985 ***NYPL [JLE 86-2611]***

Private health insurance in the United States . Farley, Pamela J. Rockville, MD , Springfield, VA [1986] 106 p. : LC Card 86-23618 DDC 368.3/82/00973 19
HG9396 .F3 1986

A private health plan option strategy for Medicare /. Ginsburg, Paul B. Santa Monica, CA [1987] xvi, 116 p. ; ISBN 0-8330-0863-3 (pbk.) LC Card 87-17593 DDC 368.4/26/00973 19
HD7102.U4 G56 1987

Private interests, public policy, and American agriculture /. Browne, William Paul, 1945- Lawrence, Kan. , c1988. p. cm. ISBN 0-7006-0334-4 : LC Card 87-23131 DDC 338.1/873 19
HD1761 .B73 1988

Private investment /. International Industrial Conference, 1st, San Francisco, 1957. New York , 1980, c1958. xi, 282 p. ; ISBN 0-405-13355-3 LC Card 80-606 DDC 332.6/7314
HG4538 .I537 1957d ***NYPL [JLD 81-249]***

Private means--public ends : private business in social service delivery / edited by Barry J. Carroll, Ralph W. Conant, Thomas A. Easton. New York : Praeger, 1987. xiii, 187 p. ; 25 cm. Includes bibliographies and index. ISBN 0-275-92429-7 (alk. paper) : LC Card 86-25251 DDC 361.6/1/0973 19
1. Social service - United States. 2. Privatization - United States. 3. Industry and education - United States. 4. Public welfare - United States. 5. United States - Social policy. I. Carroll, Barry J. II. Conant, Ralph Wendell, 1926-. III. Easton, Thomas A.
HN65 .P69 1987 ***NYPL [JLE 87-1390]***

PRIVATE PLOT AGRICULTURE - HUNGARY.
Halász, Péter. Nemzedéki vonások a mezőgazdasági kistermelésben /. Budapest , 1984. 72 p. ; ISBN 963-491-192-7 LC Card 86-198744
HD1476.H8 H252 1984

Vasary, Ildiko. Beyond the plan . Boulder , 1987. xvii, 308 p. : ISBN 0-8133-7412-X (soft : alk. paper) : LC Card 87-8219 DDC 307.7/2/09439 19
HD1492.H8 V35 1987

PRIVATE PLOT AGRICULTURE - HUNGARY - FINANCE.
Pilling, András. Az önelszámoló rendszer alkalmazásának, a kistermelők integrálásának és a kihelyezett részlegeknek a hatása a mezőgazdasági vállalatok szervezeti felépitésére, s annak müködésére /. Budapest , 1985. 89 p. ; ISBN 963-491-206-0 LC Card 86-196755
HD1492.H8 P55 1985

PRIVATE PLOT AGRICULTURE - HUNGARY - STATISTICS.
A Háztáji és kisegitő gazdaság szerepe az életmód alakulásában . Budapest , 1983. 263 p. ; ISBN 963-02-2948-X (Magy. nemz. bibl.) LC Card 84-216989
HD1476.H8 H28 1983

PRIVATE PLOT AGRICULTURE - SOVIET UNION.
Shinn, William T., 1936- The decline of the Russian peasant household /. New York , 1987. xvii, 122 p. ; ISBN 0-275-92767-9 (alk. paper) LC Card 87-2554 DDC 338.1/0947 19
HD1992 .S4735 1987

PRIVATE PLOT AGRICULTURE - UKRAINE.
Savenko, V. N. (Valentina Nikolaevna) Prodovol´stvennyĭ kompleks goroda . Kiev , 1986. 173, [3] p. : LC Card 87-161654
HD9015.S653 U473 1986

Private power and public policy . Painter, David S. [Oil and the American century.] London , c1986. xii, 302 p. : ISBN 1-85043-021-7 LC Card 87-673320
HD9566 .P24x 1986b

PRIVATE PROPERTY, RIGHT OF. see **RIGHT OF PROPERTY.**

The private provision of public services in developing countries /. Roth, Gabriel Joseph, 1926- New York , c1987. xv, 278 p. : ISBN 0-19-520544-8 : LC Card 86-23880 DDC 338.91/09172/4 19
HD4420.8 .R68 1987

The Private residential landlord and tenant in Christchurch : a profile of the private residential landlord and tenant in the Christchurch urban area / Synergy Applied Research Ltd, planning and research consultants, Wellington, for the National Housing Commission. Wellington, N.Z. : The Commission, [1986] viii, 105 p. : ill. ; 30 cm. (Research paper / National Housing Commission, 0110-1609 . 86/4) Bibliography: p. 74-75. "November 1986." ISBN 0-477-03810-7 (pbk.) LC Card 87-147647 DDC 333.33/8 19
1. Rental housing - New Zealand - Christchurch. 2. Landlord and tenant - New Zealand - Christchurch. I. Synergy Applied Research Limited. II. New Zealand. National Housing Commission. III. Series: Research paper (New Zealand. National Housing Commission) , 86/4.
HD7288.85.N452 C576 1986

Private Sector Initiatives Project. Pearson, Charles S. Down to business . Washington, DC (1735 New York Ave., NW, Washington, DC 20006) , c1985. vii, 107 p. ; ISBN 0-915825-04-X (pbk.) : LC Card 84-52795
HD69.P6 P42 1985 ***NYPL [JLE 86-3186]***

PRIVATE SECURITY SERVICES - MANAGEMENT.
Physical security . Boston , c1986. xii, 409 p. : ISBN 0-409-95105-6 (pbk.) LC Card 85-29083 DDC 658.4/73 19
HD38 .P49 1986 ***NYPL [JLE 86-3699]***

Private wants, public means . Tullock, Gordon. Lanham , c1987. viii, 262 p. : ISBN 0-8191-6370-8 (pbk. : alk. paper) : LC Card 87-8273 DDC 330.15/5 19
HB99.3 .T8 1987

Privateigentum, Patriarchat, Geldwirtschaft . Heinsohn, Gunnar. Frankfurt am Main , 1984. 218 p. ; ISBN 3-518-28055-4 : LC Card 84-150578
HC31 .H45 1984

Privater Verbrauch und Einzelhandel in der Bundesrepublik Deutschland . Döhrn, Roland.

Essen , 1981. 280 p. ; LC Card 87-408859 DDC 338.5/28/0943 19
HB235.G3 D57 1981

Privatisation : l'art et les manières / sous la direction d'Edouard Cointreau. Paris : L'Harmattan : Centre d'observation et de prospective sociales, c1986. 188 p. ; 22 cm. (Collection du COPS) "Ce livre décrit dix cas concrets de privatisations et les programmes de 19 pays"--P. 4 of cover. ISBN 2-85802-651-3 : LC Card 86-161183
1. Privatization - Cast studies. I. Cointreau, Edouard. II. Series.
HD3854 .P75 1986

Privatisation de sociétés d'Etat. English. Privatization of Crown corporations : orientation and prospects. [Québec] : Ministère des finances, Minister Responsible for Privatization, [1986] 71 p. : ill. ; 28 cm. Translation of: Privatisation de sociétés d'Etat. "February 1986." LC Card 86-220606 DDC 338.9714 19
1. Corporations, Government - Québec (Province). 2. Privatization - Québec (Province). I. Québec (Province). Ministre délégué à la privatisation. II. Title.
HD4010.Q4 P7513 1986

Privatisierung kommunaler Aufgaben? . Linzer Kommunalwissenschaftliche Tagung (1978) Linz , c1978. 62 p. ; ISBN 3-7141-7871-6 LC Card 85-185084
HD4651 .L56 1978

PRIVATIZATION.

Briançon, Pierre. A droite en sortant de la gauche? /. Paris , c1986. 270 p. ; ISBN 2-246-34901-X : LC Card 86-159681
HC276.2 .B66 1986

Competition policy and deregulation . Paris , 1986. 35 p. ; LC Card 86-217040 DDC 338.6/048 19
HD3612 .C65 1986

Entrepreneurship and the privatizing of government /. New York , 1987. x, 216 p. ; ISBN 0-89930-196-7 (lib. bdg. : alk. paper) LC Card 86-25555 DDC 338.9 19
HD3850 .E57 1987

Market-based public policy /. New York , 1988. xiv, 265 p. : ISBN 0-312-00747-7 : LC Card 87-19703 DDC 361.6 19
HD3612 .M36 1988

Paillet, Marc. Le grand inventaire . Paris , c1985. 176 p. ; ISBN 2-207-23172-0 : LC Card 86-127029 DDC 338.944 19
HD4168 .P35 1985 ***NYPL [JLE 87-1232]***

Prospects for privatization /. New York , 1987. x, 214 p. ; LC Card 87-70470 DDC 338.973 19
HD3885 .P76 1987

PRIVATIZATION - AUSTRIA - CONGRESSES.

Linzer Kommunalwissenschaftliche Tagung (1978) Privatisierung kommunaler Aufgaben? . Linz , c1978. 62 p. ; ISBN 3-7141-7871-6 LC Card 85-185084
HD4651 .L56 1978

PRIVATIZATION - BERLIN (GERMANY) - CASE STUDIES.

Huter, Otto, 1952- Die Berliner Eigenbetriebe als Instrumente kommunaler Politik /. Berlin , c1984. 275 p. : ISBN 3-87061-910-4 LC Card 84-231849
HD4180.B47 H87 1984

PRIVATIZATION - BRAZIL.

Setor público, reordenamento e privatização /. [Rio de Janeiro, RJ , 1986] 47 p. : LC Card 87-403308 DDC 338.981 19
HC187 .S436 1986

PRIVATIZATION - CAST STUDIES.

Privatisation . Paris , c1986. 188 p. ; ISBN 2-85802-651-3 : LC Card 86-161183
HD3854 .P75 1986

PRIVATIZATION - CONGRESSES.

Innovation and entrepreneurship in organizations . Amsterdam ; New York : vii, 207 p. : ISBN 0-444-42716-3 (U. S.) : LC Card 86-24207 DDC 658.4/012 19
HD41 .I56 1986

PRIVATIZATION - DENMARK.

Denmark. Privatiseringsudvalget. Rapport afgivet af Privatiseringsudvalget. [Copenhagen] [1983] 2, 243, [65] p. ; LC Card 85-134270
HD4224 .D45 1983

PRIVATIZATION - DEVELOPING COUNTRIES.

Berg, Elliot. Divestiture in developing countries /. Washington, D.C. , 1987. vii, 30 p. : ISBN 0-8213-0917-X (pbk.) LC Card 87-14235 DDC 338.9/009172/4 19
HD4420.8 .B45 1987

Roth, Gabriel Joseph, 1926- The private provision of public services in developing countries /. New York , c1987. xv, 278 p. : ISBN 0-19-520544-8 : LC Card 86-23880 DDC 338.91/09172/4 19
HD4420.8 .R68 1987

PRIVATIZATION - FLORIDA.

The Role of privatization in Florida's growth /. [Tallahassee?] , c1987. iv, 474 p. ; LC Card 87-403210 DDC 338.9 19
HD3865.F6 R65 1987

PRIVATIZATION - FRANCE.

Chalandon, Albin. Quitte ou double /. Paris , c1986. 317 p. ; ISBN 2-246-37401-4 : LC Card 86-170477
HD4165 .C47 1986

Paillet, Marc. Le grand inventaire . Paris , c1985. 176 p. ; ISBN 2-207-23172-0 : LC Card 86-127029 DDC 338.944 19
HD4168 .P35 1985 ***NYPL [JLE 87-1232]***

Tuppen, John N. France under recession, 1981-1986 /. Albany , c1988. p. cm. ISBN 0-88706-580-5 LC Card 87-1980 DDC 338.944 19
HC276.3 .T86 1988

Vedie, Henri-Louis, 1943- L'Etat-pieuvre /. Paris , c1986. 172 p. : LC Card 86-219134
HD4165 .V38 1986

PRIVATIZATION - GERMANY (WEST)

Knieps, Günter. Entstaatlichung im Telekommunikationsbereich . Tübingen , 1985. xi, 205 p. : ISBN 3-16-344955-7 LC Card 86-156485
HE8154 .K55 1985

Praxisleitfaden Privatisierung /. Bonn , 1984. 202 p. : LC Card 84-194479
HD4175 .P73 1984

Wolfgart, Ludger. Die technische Entwicklung als Element des sozialen Wandels und ihre Auswirkungen auf den öffentlichen Sektor in der Bundesrepublik Deutschland /. Münster [1986] ii, 213 p. ; ISBN 3-88660-230-3 (cover); 3-88600-230-3 (Deut. Bibl.) LC Card 87-106473 DDC 338.943 19
HD4175 .W65 1986

Ziele und Möglichkeiten der Privatisierung in volkswirtschaftlicher Sicht . Bonn , 1985. 83 leaves ; LC Card 86-185728
HJ1120 .B65 Nr. 244 HD4178

PRIVATIZATION - GREAT BRITAIN.

Curwen, Peter J. Public enterprise . Brighton, Sussex , 1986. xvii, 318 p. : ISBN 0-312-65435-9 : LC Card 85-26234 DDC 354.4109/2 19
HD4145 .C87 1986 ***NYPL [JLD 86-1636]***

PRIVATIZATION - GREAT BRITAIN - CASE STUDIES.

Newman, Karin. The selling of British Telecom /. London , New York , c1986. viii, 176 p. : ISBN 0-03-910639-X ***NYPL [JLF 86-853]***

PRIVATIZATION - LAW AND LEGISLATION - FLORIDA.

The Role of privatization in Florida's growth /. [Tallahassee?] , c1987. iv, 474 p. ; LC Card 87-403210 DDC 338.9 19
HD3865.F6 R65 1987

PRIVATIZATION - NORWAY.

Grund, Jan. Velferdsstat i motvind /. Oslo , 1986, c1985. 139 p. : ISBN 82-00-07590-7 : LC Card 86-132818
HC365 .G78 1985 ***NYPL [JLD 86-4433]***

PRIVATIZATION - OCEANIA.

Feinstein, Charles, 1954- Privatization possibilities among Pacific island countries /. Honolulu, Hawaii, USA , 1986. iv, 48 p. ; ISBN 0-86638-084-1 LC Card 86-24012 DDC 338.99 19
HD4415.6 .F45 1986

Privatization of Crown corporations . Privatisation de sociétés d'Etat. English. [Québec] [1986] 71 p. : LC Card 86-220606 DDC 338.9714 19
HD4010.Q4 P7513 1986

Privatization possibilities among Pacific island countries /. Feinstein, Charles, 1954- Honolulu, Hawaii, USA , 1986. iv, 48 p. ; ISBN 0-86638-084-1 LC Card 86-24012 DDC 338.99 19
HD4415.6 .F45 1986

PRIVATIZATION - QUÉBEC (PROVINCE)

Privatisation de sociétés d'Etat. English. Privatization of Crown corporations . [Québec] [1986] 71 p. : LC Card 86-220606 DDC 338.9714 19
HD4010.Q4 P7513 1986

Québec (Province). Groupe de travail sur la déréglementation. Réglementer moins et mieux . [Quebec] [1986] 2 v. ; ISBN 2-551-08729-5 (v. 1) LC Card 86-206349
HD3616.C24 Q47 1986

PRIVATIZATION - UNITED STATES.

Financing a common wealth . Washington, DC , 1985. xx, 304 p. : ISBN 0-89125-090-5 LC Card 84-81918
HD3888 .F5 1985 ***NYPL [JLE 86-2519]***

Knieps, Günter. Entstaatlichung im Telekommunikationsbereich . Tübingen , 1985. xi, 205 p. : ISBN 3-16-344955-7 LC Card 86-156485
HE8154 .K55 1985

Private means--public ends . New York , 1987. xiii, 187 p. ; ISBN 0-275-92429-7 (alk. paper) : LC Card 86-25251 DDC 361.6/1/0973 19
HN65 .P69 1987 ***NYPL [JLE 87-1390]***

Prospects for privatization /. New York , 1987. x, 214 p. ; LC Card 87-70470 DDC 338.973 19
HD3885 .P76 1987

PRIVATIZATION - WASHINGTON (STATE)

Joint development financing for public works . Olympia, Wash. (9th & Columbia Bldg., MS/GH-51, Olympia 98504) [1986] 1 v. (various pagings) : LC Card 86-622101 DDC 338.4/3363/09797 19
HD3890.W2 J65 1986

PRIVILEGED DEBTS. see **BANKRUPTCY.**

Privilegierung und Regulierung im Bankwesen . Seifert, Ekkehard. Baden-Baden , 1984. 332 p. ; ISBN 3-7890-0861-3 LC Card 84-186059
HG3054 .S42 1984

Privilegios y capital transnacional . Alarcón Aliaga, Carlos. [Peru?] [1985 or 1986] 168 p. : LC Card 87-127159 DDC 338.8/87 19
HD2841.Z75 S683 1985

PRIVITIZATION - CHILE.

Análisis de la previsión en Chile /. Santiago, Chile [1986] 309 p. : LC Card 87-115194
HD7156 .A78 1986

O Proálcool vale? / [Camilo Penna ... et al.]. 2a. ed. [São Paulo-SP (Brasil)] : Sopral, 1985. 52 p. : ill., ports. ; 22 cm. (Coleção Sopral . 5) LC Card 86-220396
1. Programa Nacional do Alcool (Brazil). 2. Alcohol fuel industry - Brazil. I. Penna, João Camilo de Oliveira. II. Series.
HD9502.5.A433 B645 1985

Probáld, Ferenc, 1941- Az európai tőkés országok gazdaságföldrajza : egyetemi tankönyv / Probáld Ferenc, Sárfalvi Béla, Szegedi Nándor. Budapest : Tankönyvkiadó, 1984. 361 p. : ill., maps ; 25 cm. Bibliography: p. 355-356. ISBN 963-17-7607-7 : LC Card 85-154701
1. Europe - Economic conditions. I. Sárfalvi, Béla. II. Szegedi, Nándor. III. Title.
HC240 .P738 1984

Problación y desarrollo socioeconómico en Honduras /. Suazo, Margarita. Chicago, Ill., USA (1313 E. 60th St., Chicago 60637) , c1984. 90 p., [2] leaves of plates : LC Card 85-203746
HB3540.A3 S82 1984

PROBLEM EMPLOYEES.

Sherman, V. Clayton. From losers to winners . New York, NY , c1987. xi, 188 p. : ISBN 0-8144-5918-8 LC Card 87-47710 DDC 658.3/045 19
HF5549.5.E42 S54 1987b

Sherman, V. Clayton. From losers to winners . New York, NY , c1987. 1 v. (various pagings) : ISBN 0-8144-1146-0 (loose-leaf) LC Card

86-47823 DDC 658.3/045 19
HF5549.5.E42 S54 1987

A problem-finding approach to effective corporate planning /. Thierauf, Robert J. New York , c1987. p. cm. ISBN 0-89930-262-9 (lib. bdg. : alk. paper) LC Card 87-5971 DDC 658.4/012 19
HD30.28 .T45 1987

The Problem isn't age : work and older Americans / edited by Steven H. Sandell. New York : Praeger, 1987. xiii, 265 p. : ill. ; 25 cm. Bibliography: p. 247-257. Includes index. ISBN 0-275-92371-1 (alk. paper) : LC Card 86-30642 DDC 331.3/94/0973 19
1. Aged - Employment - United States. I. Sandell, Steven H.
HD6280 .P75 1987

Problem of economic order. Röpke, Wilhelm, 1899-1966. [Problem of economic order.] 2 essays /. Lanham, MD , c1987. x, 103 p. ; ISBN 0-8191-6125-X (alk. paper) : LC Card 86-33982 DDC 338.9 19
HD82 .R682 1987

The problem of the distressed areas /. Hannington, Wal, 1895- New York , 1985. 286 p. : ISBN 0-8240-7613-3 : LC Card 85-14663 DDC 338.941 19
HC256.3 .H265 1985 ***NYPL [JLD 86-3420]***

Problem solving . Kahney, Hank. Milton Keynes , Philadelphia , 1986. 155 p. : ISBN 0-335-15327-5 (pbk.) LC Card 85-21651 DDC 153.4/3 19
BF441 .K24 1986 ***NYPL [JFE 86-1837]***

PROBLEM SOLVING.
Adams, James L. The care and feeding of ideas . Reading, Mass. , 1986. xv, 223 p. : ISBN 0-201-10160-2 : LC Card 86-10895 DDC 153.3/5 19
BF408 .A3 1986 ***NYPL [JFE 87-1553]***

Adams, James L. Conceptual blockbusting . Reading, Mass. , c1986. xi, 161 p. : ISBN 0-201-10149-1 LC Card 85-28722 DDC 153.4 19
BF441 .A28 1986 ***NYPL [JFE 86-4947]***

Bennett, Steven J. Executive chess /. New York , c1987. xv, 256 p. ; ISBN 0-453-00550-0 LC Card 87-1723 DDC 658.4/03 19
HD30.29 .B46 1987

Burton, John W. (John Wear), 1915- Resolving deep-rooted conflict . Lanham, MD , c1987. vii, 74 p. ; ISBN 0-8191-6284-1 (alk. paper) : LC Card 87-6144 DDC 658.4 19
HD42 .B87 1987

Conflict management and problem solving . New York , 1987. x, 321 p. : ISBN 0-8147-7866-6 : LC Card 87-11072 DDC 658.4 19
HD42 .C65 1987

Elbracht-Hülseweh, Bettina. Problemlösungsverhalten und Problemlösungsmethoden bei schlecht-strukturierten Problemen /. Bochum , 1985. vi, 220 p. : ISBN 3-88339-425-4 LC Card 85-170755
HD30.29 .E42 1985

Ellis, R. Jeffery. Managing strategy in the real world . Lexington, Mass. , c1988. xviii, 340 p. : ISBN 0-669-15898-4 (alk. paper) LC Card 87-4259 DDC 658.4/012 19
HD30.28 .E45 1988

How to solve problems [videorecording] /. Del Mar, CA , 1986. 1 videocassette (22 min.) : ISBN 0-07-109096-7 (3/4 in.) LC Card 86-700129 DDC 658.4 11
HD30.29

Kahney, Hank. Problem solving . Milton Keynes , Philadelphia , 1986. 155 p. : ISBN 0-335-15327-5 (pbk.) LC Card 85-21651 DDC 153.4/3 19
BF441 .K24 1986 ***NYPL [JFE 86-1837]***

Lupton, Tom. Achieving change . Aldershots, Hants, England , Brookfield, Vt., U. S.A. , c1987. xv, 86 p. : ISBN 0-566-02526-4 : LC Card 87-17665 DDC 658.4/06 19
HD58.9 .L86 1987

Phillips, Steven R. Solutions . San Diego, Calif. , c1987. xi, 127 p. ; ISBN 0-88390-205-2 (pbk.) : LC Card 87-5894 DDC 658.4/03 19
HD30.29 .P48 1987

Quick, Thomas L. Quick solutions . New York , c1987. xi, 377 p. ; ISBN 0-471-85229-5 LC Card 87-10540 DDC 658.4/03 19
HD30.29 .Q53 1987

Thierauf, Robert J. A problem-finding approach to effective corporate planning /. New York , c1987. p. cm. ISBN 0-89930-262-9 (lib. bdg. : alk. paper) LC Card 87-5971 DDC 658.4/012 19
HD30.28 .T45 1987

VanGundy, Arthur B. Techniques of structured problem solving /. New York , c1988. xiv, 386 p. : ISBN 0-442-28847-6 LC Card 87-6168 DDC 658.4/03 19
HD30.29 .V36 1988

PROBLEM SOLVING - CROSS-CULTURAL STUDIES.
Elbracht-Hülseweh, Bettina. Problemlösungsverhalten und Problemlösungsmethoden bei schlecht-strukturierten Problemen /. Bochum , 1985. vi, 220 p. : ISBN 3-88339-425-4 LC Card 85-170755
HD30.29 .E42 1985

PROBLEM SOLVING, GROUP.
Brightman, Harvey J. Group problem solving . Atlanta, Ga. , 1987. p. cm. ISBN 0-88406-201-5 : LC Card 87-21876 DDC 658.4/036 19
HD30.29 .B735 1987

Fox, William M. Effective group problem solving . San Francisco , 1987. xvii, 204 p. : ISBN 1-555-42033-8 (alk. paper) LC Card 86-33742 DDC 658.4/036 19
HD30.29 .F69 1987

Problem solving in industrial marketing. Seminar on Problem Solving in Industrial Marketing (1986 : Lucerne, Switzerland) Seminar on Problem Solving in Idustrial Marketing, Lucerne (Switzerland) 26th-28th February 1986. Amsterdam, Netherlands [1986] iv, 179 p. : ISBN 92-831-1111-7 (pbk.) : LC Card 86-213119 DDC 658.8 19
HF5415 .S3687 1986

El problema de la recomposición de los actores campesinos en una perspectiva de democratización /. Tapia Soko, Gonzalo. Santiago [Chile] [1985] ii, 49, 5 leaves ; LC Card 86-159337
HD1531.C5 T36 1985

El problema de la tierra urbana . Lungo, Mario. Ciudad Universitaria Rodrigo Facio [Costa Rica] , 1986. 42 p. ; LC Card 87-127789 DDC 333.77/13 19
HD1391 .L86 1986

"Problema neftedollarov" : referativnyĭ sbornik / [redakt͡sionnai͡a kollegii͡a sbornika Makarova S.M., otvetstvennyĭ redaktor, Smyslov D.V., Chernı͡akhovskai͡a N.I. ; otvetstvennai͡a za vypusk Bodanskai͡a K.M.]. Moskva : Akademii͡a nauk SSSR, In-t nauch. informatsii po obshchestvennym naukam, 1984. 231 p. ; 20 cm. (Serii͡a Ėkonomika razvivai͡ushchikhsi͡a stran Azii i Afriki) Includes bibliographies. LC Card 85-189000
1. Arab countries - Economic policy. 2. Arab countries - Economic conditions. 3. Finance - Arab countries. 4. Petroleum industry and trade - Arab countries. 5. Organization of Petroleum Exporting Countries. 6. Investments, Arab. I. Makarova, S. M. II. Smyslov, D. V. (Dmitriĭ Vasil'evich). III. Cherni͡akhovskai͡a, N. I. IV. Bodanskai͡a, K. M. V. Institut nauchnoĭ informat͡sii po obshchestvennym naukam (Akademii͡a nauk SSSR). VI. Series.
HC498 .P75 1984

Problema tempov ėkonomicheskogo rosta v sovremennom mire / otvetstvennyĭ redaktor K.I. Mikul'skiĭ. Moskva : "Nauka", 1986. 383 p. : ill. ; 23 cm. At head of title: Akademii͡a nauk SSSR. Nauchnyĭ sovet "Ėkonomicheskie zakonomernosti razvitii͡a sot͡sializma i sorevnovanie dvukh sistem." Nauchnyĭ sovet "Mirovai͡a sot͡sialisticheskai͡a sistema." Includes bibliographical references. LC Card 87-124359
1. Europe, Eastern - Economic conditions - 1945-. 2. Developing countries - Economic conditions. 3. Economic history - 1971-. I. Mikul'skiĭ, Konstantin Ivanovich. II. Nauchnyĭ sovet AN SSSR "Ėkonomicheskie zakonomernosti razvitii͡a sot͡sializma i sorevnovanie dvukh sistem.". III. Nauchnyĭ sovet "Mirovai͡a sot͡sialisticheskai͡a sistema." (Akademii͡a nauk SSSR).
HC244 .P747 1986

Problema tovarnogo proizvodstva . Illarionov, Sergeĭ Ivanovich. Moskva , 1984. 109 p. ; LC Card 85-111933
HF3626 .I64 1984

Problemas agrarios colombianos / Absalón Machado C. ... [et al.] ; Absalón Machado C., coordinador. 1a ed. [Bogotá, Colombia] : CEGA ; México, D.F. : Siglo Veintiuno Editores, 1986. 467 p. : ill. ; 23 cm. (Economía y demografía) Includes bibliographies. ISBN 958-606-005-5 LC Card 86-221632
1. Agriculture - Economic aspects - Colombia. 2. Produce trade - Colombia. 3. Agriculture and state - Colombia. 4. Peasantry - Colombia - Political activity. 5. Food industry and trade - Colombia. 6. Malnutrition - Colombia. I. Machado C., Absalón. II. Corporación de Estudios Ganaderos y Agrícolas (Bogotá, Colombia). III. Series: Economía y demografía (Mexico City, Mexico).
HD1882 .P75 1986

Los problemas ambientales del sistema de transporte urbano /. Matas, Jaime. Santiago de Chile , 1981. 30 leaves : LC Card 82-201768
HE234.Z7 S355 1981

Problemas contemporâneos (Editora Hucitec)
Abreu, Alice R. de Paiva. O avesso da moda . São Paulo , 1986. 302 p. ; LC Card 87-129109 DDC 331.4/887/098153 19
HD6073.C62 B62 1986

Los Problemas de la inflación en la República Dominicana / [editor, Frank Moya Pons]. Santo Domingo, República Dominicana : FORUM, 1986. 111 p. : ill. ; 22 cm. (Forum. 20) Spine title: Inflación. "Este libro recoge las exposiciones que fueron presentadas en el encuentro sobre los problemas de la inflación en la República Dominicana, celebrado por FORUM en el Hotel Santo Domingo Sur, el viernes 12 de abril de 1985"--P. 9. LC Card 86-208576
1. Inflation (Finance) - Dominican Republic - Congresses. I. Moya Pons, Frank, 1944-. II. FORUM (Debating society). III. Title: Inflación. IV. Series: FORUM (Series : Santo Domingo, Dominican Republic) , 20.
HG767 .P76 1986

Los Problemas del conocimiento y la perspectiva ambiental del desarrollo / José María Montes ... [et al.] ; coordinado por Enrique Leff. 1a ed. México, D.F. : Siglo Veintiuno Editores, 1986. 476 p., [1] folded leaf of plates : ill. ; 23 cm. Includes bibliographies. ISBN 968-231-372-4 LC Card 87-119336 DDC 363.7/0098 19
1. Economic development - Environmental aspects. 2. Environmental policy. 3. Environmental policy - Latin America. I. Montes, José María. II. Leff, Enrique.
HD75.6 .P76 1986

Problemas e política de emprego no continente /. Moura, João. Lisboa , 1977. 56 p. ; LC Card 85-214189
HD5809.A6 M68 1977

Problemas económicos del Tercer Mundo / Raúl Prebisch ... [et al.] ; prólogo de Luciano Tomassini. Buenos Aires, República Argentina : Editorial de Belgrano, c1983. 210 p. : ill. ; 20 cm. (Colección Temas de política internacional) Bibliography: p. 171-172. CONTENTS. - La crisis del capitalismo y la periferia / por Raúl Prebisch -- Análisis del carácter de la crisis internacional actual / por Johan Galtung -- La crisis económica internacional y las perspectivas de América Latina / por Enrique V. Iglesias -- El comercio Norte-Sur y la autonomía socioeconómica / por Wolfgang Hager -- Hacia una nueva apreciación del sistema de comercio internacional / por Reynaldo Figueredo -- El deterioro de la relación de intercambio / por John Spraos -- Deuda Externa y balanza de pagos de América Latina / por Ricardo Ffrench-Davis -- América Latina : aspectos principales del financiamiento externo / por Carlos Massad -- La deuda externa y las políticas nacionales / por Aldo Ferrer -- La interdependencia económica global y el cambio social / por Víctor L. Urquidi. ISBN 950-577-070-7 LC Card 84-120737 DDC 337/.09172/4 19
1. Developing countries - Foreign economic relations - Addresses, essays, lectures. 2. International economic relations - Addresses, essays, lectures. 3. Latin America - Foreign economic relations - Addresses, essays, lectures. I. Prebisch, Raúl. II. Series.
HF1413 .P75 1983 ***NYPL [JLC 86-394]***

Los Problemas financieros en el Estado regionalizado / Aubert ... [et al.] ; prefacio de Pierre Ansiaux ; traducción, J. Zamit. Madrid : Ministerio de Economía y Hacienda, Instituto de Estudios Fiscales, 1983. 207 leaves ; 29 cm. (Monografia. no. 23) Cover title. Includes bibliographical references. CONTENTS. - La relaciones financieras en el sistema federal Aleman / de Dieter Grimm -- Relaciones fiscales en un estado federal: el ejempio de los Estados Unidos / de Patrick L. Kelley -- Las relaciones financieras entre la federación y los Länder en Austria / Theo Öhlinger -- Las relaciones financieras entre la confederación Suiza y los cantones / de Jean-François Aubert -- Las relaciones financieras entre el estado central, las regiones y las comunidades de Belgica / de Philippe Quertaonmont. LC Card 85-177739

1. Intergovernmental fiscal relations - Germany, West. 2. Intergovernmental fiscal relations - United States. 3. Intergovernmental fiscal relations - Austria. 4. Intergovernmental fiscal relations - Switzerland. 5. Intergovernmental fiscal relations - Belgium. I. Series: Monografías (Instituto de Estudios Financieros (Spain)) , no. 23.

HJ1120 .P75 1983

Problemas internacionales .
(11) Manifiesto contra el hambre en el mundo. Madrid , c1985. 95 p. ; ISBN 84-85436-23-7 (IEPALA) LC Card 86-165078
HD9018.D44 M35 1985
NYPL [JLD 87-1535]

Problemas metodológicos de una encuesta rural en Chile y estructura del empleo / Organización Internacional del Trabajo, Programa Mundial del Empleo, Programa Regional del Empleo para América Latina y el Caribe. [Santiago, Chile] : PREALC, [c1983] ii, 27 leaves ; 28 cm. (Documento de trabajo / PREALC . 227) Includes bibliographical references. LC Card 84-225128

1. Agricultural laborers - Chile - Supply and demand. 2. Household surveys - Chile. 3. Chile - Rural conditions. I. Regional Employment Program for Latin America and the Caribbean. II. Series: Documento de trabajo (Regional Employment Program for Latin America and the Caribbean) , 227.

HD1531.C5 P76 1983

Problemas poblacionales peruanos II / [J. Wicht et al.] ; Roger Guerra-García, editor. Lima : Asociación Multidisciplinaria de Investigación y Docencia en Población, c1986. 402 p. : ill. ; 21 cm. Papers presented at the Segunda Reunión Nacional sobre Población, held in Tarma, Junín, Peru during July, 1985 and sponsored by the Asociación. Includes bibliographies. CONTENTS. - Realidad demográfica y crisis de la sociedad peruana / Juan J. Wicht -- Expansión demográfica, migración y desarrollo en el Perú / Héctor Martínez -- Aspectos sociales y económicos de la educación en el Perú / Hernán Fernández -- El estado de salud / Federico Ugarte -- Alimentación en el Perú / Luis Paz Silva -- Evolución y perspectivas del empleo / Edgar Flores Bevavente -- La familia y el niño en el Perú / Hilda Mercado Avalos -- Mujer, población y desarrollo / Marfil Francke B. -- Política de población / Luis Sobrevilla Alcázar -- Conclusiones y recomendaciones. LC Card 86-228816

1. Peru - Population - Congresses. I. Wicht, Juan J. II. Guerra García, R. (Roger). III. Asociación Multidisciplinaria de Investigación y Docencia en Población (Peru). IV. Reunión Nacional sobre Población (2nd : 1985 : Tarma, Junín, Peru).

HB3575 .P763 1986

Problemas sociais e económicos . Milhano, Vicente. Covilhã , 1958. 185 p. ; LC Card 86-126181 DDC 338.09469 19
HC392 .M58 1958

Problemática agraria y política petrolera en Chiapas /. Thompson G., Roberto. Tuxtla Gutiérrez, Chiapas , 1983. 37 p., [1] leaf of plates : LC Card 84-243074
HD9574.M63 C457 1983

La problemática de los almacenes generales de depósito como instituciones financieras no bancarias en el Perú (1970-1983) /. Hinojosa Tapia, Juan. Lima, Perú , 1985. iii, 29, [43] p. : LC Card 86-218257
HG3751.9.P4 H56 1985

A Problemática e a política da terra e água do Nordeste. Recife : Superintendência do Desenvolvimento do Nordeste, Coordenação do Planejamento Regional, 1985. 296 p. : ill., maps ; 23 cm. (Série Projeto Nordeste . v. 7) At head of title: Secretaria de Planejamento da Presidência da República, Instituto de Planejamento Econômico e Social, Ministério do Interior, Superintendência do Desenvolvimento do Nordeste, Banco do Nordeste do Brasil. Bibliography: p. 287-289. LC Card 87-124121 DDC 333.91/00981/3 19

1. Water resources development - Brazil, Northeast. 2. Water-supply - Brazil, Northeast. 3. Irrigation - Brazil, Northeast. 4. Land reform - Brazil, Northeast. 5. Land tenure - Brazil, Northeast. I. Brazil. Superintendência do Desenvolvimento do Nordeste. Coordenação de Planejamento Regional.

HD1696.B84 N675 1985

Problemática energética .
(1) Energía y petróleo . Capital Federal [1985 or 1986] 60 p. : LC Card 87-403778 DDC 338.2/7282 19
HD9560.5 .E525 1985

(4) Aspectos económicos de la industria petrolera. Capital Federal [1985 or 1986] 28 p. : LC Card 87-120726
HD9574.A72 A84 1985

Die Problematik der Informationsgewinnung und -verarbeitung bei der Bewertung von Sand- und Kiesabbaugelände /. Kohrs-Barrmeyer, Andrea. Münster [1986] xviii, 379 p. : ISBN 3-88660-330-X LC Card 86-223939 DDC 622/.3622/068 19
HD9585.S162 K64 1986

Probleme der Aufbauorganisation des Finanz- und Rechnungswesens /. Pohlig, Rolf. Bochum , 1984. xi, 465 p. : ISBN 3-88339-354-1 LC Card 84-162112
HF5645 .P64 1984

Probleme der modernen Welt .
(55) Die Wirtschaftliche Expansion der USA . Moskau , 1986. 175 p. ; LC Card 87-408806 DDC 337.7305 19
HF1456.5.A64 W57 1986

Probleme der Ordnungs- und Strukturpolitik : Hellmuth Stefan Seidenfus zur Vollendung des 60. Lebensjahres gewidmet / herausgegeben von Hans-Jürgen Ewers und Helmut Schuster. Göttingen : Vandenhoeck & Ruprecht, c1984. viii, 311 p., [1] leaf of plates : ill., maps ; 24 cm. One article in English. List of H.S. Seidenfus' works: p. [304]-309. Includes bibliographies. ISBN 3-525-85925-2 LC Card 84-203472

1. Transportation. 2. Government business enterprises. 3. Economic policy. 4. Regional planning. 5. Energy policy. 6. Seidenfus, Hellmuth Stefan. I. Seidenfus, Hellmuth Stefan. II. Ewers, Hans-Jürgen. III. Schuster, Helmut.

HE152.6 .P76 1984

Die Probleme der Prognose des Kapitalbedarfs im Rahmen der strategischen Plannung /. Stomberg, Peter. Göttingen , c1984. x, 212 p. ; ISBN 0-352-51266-3 LC Card 84-240131
HD30.28 .S729 1984

Probleme der Rohstoffsicherung = primary commodities, security of supply : Expertengespräche der Friedrich-Ebert-Stiftung, Bonn, 26. und 27. Juni 1980 : Washington, 11. und 12. Dezember 1980. Bonn : Forschungsinstitut der Friedrich-Ebert-Stiftung, [1981] 215 p. : ill. ; 21 cm. (Analysen aus der Abteilung Entwicklungsländerforschung . Nr. 92/93) German and English; summaries in English. Papers of conferences sponsored by the Forschungsinstitut of the Friedrich-Ebert-Stiftung. Bibliography: p. 213-215. LC Card 85-206699

1. Raw materials - Congresses. I. Friedrich-Ebert-Stiftung. Forschungsinstitut. II. Title: Primary commodities, security of supply. III. Series.

HF1051 .P76 1980

Probleme der Sanierung der Deutschen Bundesbahn durch die Änderung institutioneller Rahmenbedingungen /. Michelbach, Roger. Thun , c1984. xi, 450 p. : ISBN 3-87144-865-6 LC Card 85-137676
HE3080.D4 M53 1984

Probleme der staatsmonopolistischen Wirtschaftsregulierung : Laudatio und Beiträge des Ehrenkolloquiums vom 2. Oktober 1980 anlässlich des 65. Geburtstages von Prof. Dr. sc. oec. Alfred Klein / [Redaktion, Abt. Wissenschaftspublizistik der Wilhelm-Pieck-Universität Rostock]. Rostock : Die Universität, Sektion Sozialistische Betriebswirtschaft, 1981. 35 p. ; 21 cm. CONTENTS. - Wertgesetz und staatsmonopolistische Wirtschaftsregulierung / Lemmnita, A. -- Methodologische Probleme der Auseinandersetzung mit bürgerlichen politischen Ideologien / Meissner, h. -- Zur staatsmonopolistischen Regulierung der Seeschifffahrt in den kapitalistischen Ländern / Breitzmann, K.-H., Pawelzig, K., Schaumburg, J. LC Card 86-211250

1. Capitalism - Congresses. 2. Economic policy - Congresses. 3. Industry and state - Congresses. 4. Monopolies - Congresses. 5. Klein, Alfred, 1915-. I. Klein, Alfred, 1915-. II. Wilhelm-Pieck-Universität Rostock. Abteilung Wissenschaftspublizistik.

HB501 .P694 1981

Probleme des Kapitalmarkts. Kolloquien-Beiträge.
(27) Die Internationale Finanzierungskrise /. Frankfurt am Main , c1985. 153 p. ; ISBN 3-7819-2536-6 LC Card 87-146671 DDC 336.3/435 19
HG3891.5 .I587 1985

Probleme des Kapitalmarkts. Monographien.
(10) Hess, Stephan M. Liquiditätswirkungen alternativer Geldvermögensanlagen /. Frankfurt am Main , c1983. 193 p. ; ISBN 3-7819-2533-1 LC Card 84-109572
HG173.5 .H47 1983

Le problème du mur d'argent . Néré, Jacques. Paris , c1985. 159 p. ; ISBN 2-214-06264-5 : LC Card 86-149791
HG979 .N47 1985

Probleme einer Privatgeldordnung . Honeck, Gerhard. Frankfurt am Main , c1985. 93 p. ; ISBN 3-88129-964-5 LC Card 86-153829
HG230.3 .H56 1985

Probleme monetärer und finanzwirtschaftlicher Steuerung im Systemvergleich / herausgegeben von E. Ulrich Cichy, Günther Neumann. Duisburg : Verlag der Sozialwissenschaftlichen Kooperative, c1986. 175 p. : ill. ; 21 cm. (Sozialwissenschaftliche Schriften . 32) Includes bibliographical references. ISBN 3-921473-43-8 LC Card 86-211745

1. Germany, West - Economic policy. 2. Germany, West - Economic conditions. 3. Monetary policy - Germany, West. 4. Fiscal policy - Germany, West. 5. Poland - Economic policy - 1945-. 6. Poland - Economic conditions - 1945-. 7. Monetary policy - Poland. 8. Fiscal policy - Poland. I. Cichy, E. Ulrich. II. Neumann, Günther, 1945-.

HC286.6 .P754 1986

Problèmes d'adaptation des structures au développement socialiste /. Senegal. Présidence du Conseil du gouvernement. Direction de l'animation. Bureau d'études. [Dakar?] [1962] 50 leaves ; LC Card 83-113563
HC1045 .S465 1962a

Problèmes de macroéconomie /. Pisani-Ferry, Jean. Paris , 1984. 452 p. : ISBN 2-7178-0801-9 : LC Card 85-100663 DDC 339 19
HB173 .P534 1984

Problèmes économiques généraux /. Salles, Pierre, 1913- Paris , 1984-19. 2 v. : ISBN 2-04-016910-5 (v. 1) LC Card 87-116907
HB173 .S355 1986

Problemi e prospettive. Serie di economia.
Le Crisi finanziarie /. Bologna , c1985. 348 p. : ISBN 88-15-00807-1 : LC Card 85-201934 DDC 332.1 19
HG1591 .C75 1985

Problemi na dŭrzhavnoto i obshtestvenoto osiguri͡avane na rabotnitsite i sluzhitelite. Stara Zagora : Okrŭzhen sŭvet na Bŭlgarskite profesionalni sŭi͡uzi, 1984. 17 p. ; 21 cm. (Init͡siativi, dela, chelen opit) LC Card 86-204115

1. Social security - Bulgaria. I. Bŭlgarski profesionalni sŭi͡uzi. Okrŭzhen sŭvet (Starozagorski okrŭg). II. Series.

HD7211.5 .P75 1984

Problemi na sot͡sialisticheskata organizat͡sii͡a na truda / [sŭstavitel Isak Mashiakh]. Sofii͡a : Profizdat, 1986. 146 p. : ill. ; 20 cm. Includes bibliographical references. LC Card 87-128832

1. Labor supply - Bulgaria. 2. Industrial management - Bulgaria. I. Mashiakh, Isak.

HD5811.5.A6 P76 1986

Problemi na stopanskata smetka / [redakt͡sionna kolegii͡a Kiril Kiri͡akov (otg. redaktor) ... et al.]. Sofii͡a : Izd-vo na Bŭlgarskata akademii͡a na naukite, 1981. 207 p. ; 21 cm. At head of title: Bŭlgarska akademii͡a na naukite. Ikonomicheski institut. Includes bibliographical references. LC Card 82-133037

1. Bulgaria - Industries - Auditing. 2. Industrial productivity - Bulgaria. I. Kiri͡akov, Kiril Todorov. II. Ikonomicheski institut (Bŭlgarska akademii͡a na naukite).

HC403.Z9 A865 1981

Problemi na valutnii͡a sŭi͡uz na stranite-chlenki na EIO i razvitie na mezhdunarodnata valutna sistema n kapitalizma. Problemy vali͡utnogo soi͡uza stran-chlenov Evropeĭskogo ėkonomicheskogo soobshchestva i razvitie mezhdunarodnoĭ vali͡utnoĭ sistemy kapitalizma . Sofii͡a , 1984. 151 p. ; LC Card 85-224144
HG3942.8 .P76 1984

Problemi samoupravne organizacije / M. Novak ... [et al.] ; redakcija Mijo Novak. Zagreb : Informator, 1981. xi, 237 p. ; 24 cm. (Organizacija i ekonomika) In Serbo-Croatian (Roman) Includes bibliographical references. LC Card 83-110609
1. Management - Yugoslavia - Employee participation. 2. Yugoslavia - Economic policy - 1945-. 3. Yugoslavia - Politics and government - 1945-. I. Novak, Mijo.
HD5660.Y8 P675 1981

Problemlösungsverhalten und Problemlösungsmethoden bei schlecht-strukturierten Problemen /. Elbracht-Hülseweh, Bettina. Bochum , 1985. vi, 220 p. : ISBN 3-88339-425-4 LC Card 85-170755
HD30.29 .E42 1985

Problemnai͡a komissii͡a mnogostoronnego nauchnogo sotrudnichestva akademiĭ nauk sotsialisticheskikh stran "Voprosy sovershenstvovanii͡a planirovanii͡a i upravlenii͡a narodnym khozi͡aĭstvom stran--chlenov SĖV." Khozi͡aĭstvennyĭ mekhanizm funktsionirovanii͡a sotsialisticheskoĭ ėkonomiki /. Moskva , 1982. 358 p. ; LC Card 83-134242
HC243.5 .K47 1982

Problems in macroeconomic theory . Whiteman, Charles H. Boston , c1987. ix, 266 p. ; ISBN 0-12-619752-0 (pbk.) LC Card 87-17398 DDC 339 19
HB172.5 .S27 1987 Suppl. 2

Problems of decision making based on experimental data / [redaktorzy Zdzisław Hellwig, Lech Warężak]. Wrocław : Wydawn. Uczelniane Akademii Ekonomicznej we Wrocławiu, 1985. 186 p. : ill. ; 24 cm. (Prace naukowe Akademii Ekonomicznej imienia Oskara Langego we Wrocławiu, 0324-8445 . nr. 301/1985) English and German. Includes bibliographies. LC Card 86-207027
1. Decision-making. 2. Mathematical statistics. I. Hellwig, Zdzisław. II. Warężak, Lech. III. Series: Prace naukowe Akademii Ekonomicznej imienia Oskara Langego we Wrocławiu , nr. 301.
HB9 .B7522 nr. 301 QA279.4

Problems of Indian fiscal structure /. Agarwal, A. K. (Ashok Kumar), 1949- Delhi, India , 1987. xii, 157 p. ; LC Card 86-903836 DDC 336.54 19
HJ1334. A38 1987

Problems of the aged in unorganised sector /. Mahajan, Amarjit. Delhi, India , 1987. viii, 106 p. ; LC Card 87-901315 DDC 362.6/042 19
HD7105.35.I5 M34 1987

Problems of trade in fishery products. Paris, France : Organisation for Economic Co-operation and Development ; Washington, D.C. : OECD Publications and Information Center [distributor], c1985. 384 p. : ill. ; 27 cm. "This study has been prepared by the Committee for Fisheries in response to a mandate given by the OECD Council meeting at Ministerial level of May 1982"--P. 3. Includes bibliographies. ISBN 92-64-12775-5 (pbk.) : LC Card 86-203595 DDC 382/.437 19
1. Fish trade. 2. Fisheries. 3. Fishery law and legislation. I. Organisation for Economic Co-operation and Development. Committee for Fisheries.
HD9450.5 .P76 1985

Problems of urban circulation in the 90's. Afghani, Abdus Sattar. Traffic growth in Karachi . [Karachi] [1985] [25] leaves : LC Card 85-931413 DDC 388.4/13142/09549183 19
HE373.P183 K372 1985

Problems of urban unemployment. Calcutta : Dept. of Economics, Rabindra Bharati University, 1981. ix, 114 p. ; 26 cm. (Occasional papers . 1981) "Papers/notes presented by various participants at the U.G.C. sponsored Seminar on Problems of Urban Unemployment held at the Department of Economics, Rabindra Bharati University, during March 19 to 21, 1979"--Pref. Includes bibliographical references. LC Card 83-907262 DDC 331.13/77/0954 19
1. Unemployed - Government policy - India - Congresses. 2. Urban policy - India - Congresses. I. Rabindra Bharati University. Dept. of Economics. II. Seminar on Problems of Urban Unemployment (1979 : Rabindra Bharati University). III. Series: Occasional papers (Rabindra Bharati University. Dept. of Economics) , 1981.
HD5819 .P76 1981 ***NYPL [JLF 86-1766]***

Problems of workers in the meat, dairy, edible oils, and fats industries : working papers of the Trade Committe meeting, Berlin, 1985. Sofia : Trade Unions International of Food, Tobacco, Hotel and Allied Industries' Workers (WFTU), 1986. 43 p. ; 23 cm. LC Card 86-222996 DDC 338.4/7664 19
1. Food industry and trade - Employees. I. Trade Unions International of Food, Tobacco, Hotel and Allied Industries' Workers.
HD8039.F7 P76 1986

Problemy agropromyshlennoĭ integrat͡sii v I͡Aponii /. Markar'i͡an, S. B. (Seda Bagdasarovna) Moskva , 1982. 286 p. ; LC Card 83-143582
HD9017.J32 M37 1982

Problemy amerikanistiki (Unnumbered) Rogulev, I͡U. N. (I͡Uriĭ Nikolaevich) Krakh rabocheĭ politiki administratsii Trumėna . Moskva , 1981. 135 p. ; LC Card 82-155486
HD8072.5 .R64 1981

Problemy ėffektivnosti ispolʹzovanii͡a trudovykh resursov / pod redaktsieĭ V.G. Kostakova. Moskva : Nauchno-issl. ėkon. in-t pri Gosplane SSSR, 1981. 147 p. ; 21 cm. (Nauchnye trudy) Includes bibliographical references. LC Card 82-150334
1. Labor productivity - Soviet Union. 2. Labor supply - Soviet Union. I. Kostakov, V. G. (Vladimir Georgievich). II. Series: Nauchnye trudy (Nauchno-issledovatelʹskiĭ ėkonomicheskiĭ institut (Soviet Union)).
HC340.L3 P64 1981

Problemy ėkonomicheskogo rosta na sovremennom ėtape. Moskva : Akademii͡a nauk SSSR, In-t ėkonomiki, 1984. 137 p. : ill. ; 20 cm. Cover title. Includes bibliographical references. LC Card 85-240336
1. Soviet Union - Economic conditions - 1976-. I. Institut ėkonomiki (Akademii͡a nauk SSSR).
HC336.25 .P624 1984

Problemy formirovanii͡a i upravlenii͡a agrarno-promyshlennym kompleksom : sbornik nauchnykh trudov / redaktor A.I. Panchenko. Novosibirsk : Akademii͡a nauk SSSR, Sibirskoe otd-nie, In-t ėkonomiki i organizat͡sii promyshl. proizvodstva, 1979. 157 p. : ill. ; 20 cm. Includes bibliographies. LC Card 81-143766
1. Agricultural industries - Soviet Union - Mathematical models. 2. Agricultural industries - Russian S.F.S.R. - Siberia, Western - Mathematical models. I. Panchenko, A. I. II. Institut ėkonomiki i organizat͡sii promyshlennosti proizvodstva (Akademii͡a nauk SSSR).
HD9015.S652 P73 1979

Problemy khozi͡aĭstvennogo razvitii͡a osvobodivshikhsi͡a stran : sbornik nauchnykh trudov / [otvetstvennyĭ redaktor Pokataeva T.S.]. Moskva : Akademii͡a nauk SSSR, In-t mirovoĭ ėkonomiki i mezhdunar. otnosheniĭ, 1987. 2 v. (306 p.) ; 21 cm. Includes bibliographies. LC Card 87-157281
1. Developing countries - Economic conditions. I. Pokataeva, T. S. II. Institut mirovoĭ ėkonomiki i mezhdunarodnykh otnosheniĭ (Akademii͡a nauk SSSR).
HC59.7 .P7354 1987

Problemy modelirovanii͡a makroėkonomicheskikh sistem : sbornik nauchnykh trudov / [redaktsionnai͡a kollegii͡a A.A. Bakaev, I͡U.A. Chizhov (otvetstv. redaktory ... et al.]. Kiev : Akademii͡a nauk Ukrainskoĭ SSR, In-t kibernetiki im. V.M. Glushkova, 1982. 100 p. ; 20 cm. At head of title: Akademii͡a nauk Ukrainskoĭ SSR. Nauchnyĭ sovet po probleme "Kibernetika." Ordena Lenina Institut kibernetiki im. V.M. Glushkova. Includes bibliographies. LC Card 83-144893
1. Econometrics. I. Bakaev, Aleksandr Aleksandrovich. II. Chizhov, I͡U. A. (I͡Uriĭ Alekseevich). III. Naukova rada z kibernetyky (Akademii͡a nauk Ukraïnsʹkoï RSR). IV. Institut kibernetiki im. V.M. Glushkova.
HB139 .P755 1982

Problemy narodno-khozi͡aĭstvennogo optimuma. Valʹtukh, Konstantin Kurtovich. T͡Selevai͡a funktsii͡a potreblenii͡a . Novosibirsk , 1980. 381, [3] p. ; LC Card 81-134031
HB801 .V265 1980

Problemy nauchno-tekhnicheskogo progressa v bratskikh sotsialisticheskikh stranakh : referativnyĭ sbornik / [redaktsionnai͡a kollegii͡a sbornika Aleksandrov V.A. ... Shanshieva L.N. (otvetstvennyĭ redaktor) ... et al.]. Moskva : Akademii͡a nauk SSSR, In-t nauch. informatsii po obshchestvennym naukam, 1985. 234 p. ; 20 cm. (Serii͡a Problemy razvitii͡a sotsialisticheskikh stran) Includes bibliographies. LC Card 86-179196
1. Technological innovations - Europe, Eastern. I. Aleksandrov, V. A. II. Shanshieva, L. N. III. Series.
HC244.Z9 T472 1985

Problemy obosnovanii͡a gosudarstvennogo plana /. Efimov, A. N. (Anatoliĭ Nikolaevich) Moskva , 1980. 197, [3] p. ; LC Card 81-135658
HC336.25 .E346 1980

Problemy optimizat͡sii mezhotraslevykh svi͡azeĭ : tematicheskiĭ sbornik / [redaktsionnai͡a A.V. Zharinov, V.K. Dobrovolʹskiĭ, V.A. Tochilin]. Kiev : In-t ėkonomiki AN USSR, 1976. 135 p. : ill. ; 20 cm. At head of title: Institut ėkonomiki AN USSR. Includes bibliographical references. LC Card 87-100694
1. Agricultural industries - Ukraine - Mathematical models. 2. Mathematical optimization. I. Zharinov, Artem Viktorovich. II. Dobrovolʹskiĭ, V. K. (Vladimir Konstantinovich). III. Tochilin, Viktor Aleksandrovich. IV. Instytut ekonomiky (Akademii͡a nauk Ukraïnsʹkoï RSR).
HD9015.S653 U4547 1976

Problemy osvoenii͡a prirodnykh resursov Uralʹskogo Severa / [otvetstvennyĭ redaktor V.P. Pakhomov]. Sverdlovsk : Akademii͡a nauk SSSR, Uralʹskiĭ nauch. t͡sentr, 1985. 70 p. : ill. ; 22 cm. Includes bibliographical references. LC Card 86-195834
1. Natural resources - Russian S.F.S.R. - Ural Mountains Region. 2. Natural resources - Soviet Union, Northern. I. Pakhomov, V. P. (Vi͡acheslav Petrovich). II. Akademii͡a nauk SSSR. Uralʹskiĭ nauchnyĭ t͡sentr.
HC337.R852 U7359 1985

Problemy povyshenii͡a ėkonomicheskoĭ ėffektivnosti kapitalʹnykh vlozheniĭ v territorialʹnye promyshlennye kompleksy. Moskva : Akademii͡a nauk SSSR, Institut ėkonomiki, 1983. 170 p. : ill. ; 21 cm. At head of title: Nauchnyĭ sovet po probleme "Ėkonomicheskai͡a ėffektivnostʹ osnovnykh fondov, kapitalʹnykh vlozheniĭ i novoĭ tekhniki." Includes bibliographical references. LC Card 84-202808
1. Territorial production complexes - Soviet Union - Capital productivity. 2. Capital productivity - Soviet Union. I. Institut ėkonomiki (Akademii͡a nauk SSSR). II. Nauchnyĭ sovet po probleme "Ėkonomicheskai͡a ėffektivnostʹ osnovnykh fondov, kapitalʹnykh vlozheniĭ i novoĭ tekhniki" (Akademii͡a nauk SSSR).
HC340.C3 P747 1983

Problemy rasselenii͡a v SSSR : Sotsialʹno-demograficheskiĭ analiz seti poseleniĭ i zadachi upravlenii͡a / [B.S. Khorev, D.G. Khodzhaev, I͡U.A. Avdeev ... et al.] ; Pod redaktsieĭ B.S. Khoreva. Moskva : "Statistika", 1980. 254 p. : ill. ; 20 cm. Includes bibliographical references. LC Card 81-135093
1. Russian S.F.S.R. - Population density. 2. Cities and towns - Russian S.F.S.R. 3. Soviet Union - Population density. 4. Cities and towns - Soviet Union. I. Khorev, Boris Sergeevich.
HB2068.S65 P76 1980

Problemy razvitii͡a i sovershenstvovanii͡a materialʹno-tekhnicheskoĭ bazy torgovli i obshchestvennogo pitanii͡a v dvenadtsatoĭ pi͡atiletke : sokrashchennye doklady nauchnoĭ konferentsii, Vilʹni͡us, 3-4 okti͡abri͡a 1985 g. / [redaktsionnai͡a kollegii͡a A. Ventskus ... A. Pai͡uodis (otvetstvennyĭ redaktor) ... et al.]. Vilʹni͡us : Vilʹni͡usskiĭ gosuniversitet im. V. Kapsukasa, 1985. 169 p. ; 20 cm. At head of title: Ministerstvo torgovli Litovskoĭ SSR ... LC Card 86-102743
1. Lithuania - Commerce - Congresses. 2. Food service - Lithuania - Congresses. I. Ventskus, A. II. Pai͡uodis, A. III. Vilniaus Valstybinis V. Kapsuko vardo universitetas.
HF3629.L5 P76 1985

Problemy razvitii͡a narodnogo khozi͡aĭstva Severo-Zapada SSSR . Kulibanov, V. S. (Vadim Sergeevich) Leningrad , 1980. 33, [3] p. ; LC Card 82-115046
HC336.9.N65 K85 1980

Problemy razvitiia sotsialisticheskikh finansov /. Shirshov, V. O. (Viacheslav Osipovich) Moskva , 1984. 87 p. ; LC Card 85-131694
HG4186 .S47 1984

Problemy razvitiia transporta Kazakhstana . Bekkulov, A. B. (Ablkaĭ Bekkulovich) Alma-Ata , 1984. 229 p. ; LC Card 84-226651
HE255.Z7 K393 1984

Problemy rynku i handlu w Łodzi i regionie łódzkim / [redaktor zeszytu Jerzy Dietl]. Wyd. 1. [Łódź] : Uniwersytet Łódzki, 1978. 193 p. : ill. ; 24 cm. (Acta Universitatis Lodziensis. Seria 3, Nauki ekonomiczne i socjologiczne . nr. 31) Summaries in English. Includes bibliographical references. LC Card 80-129744
1. Service industries - Poland - Łódź Region. 2. Consumption (Economics) - Poland - Łódź Region. I. Dietl, Jerzy.
HD9986.P72 L636 1978

Problemy sovershenstvovaniia material'no-tekhnicheskoĭ bazy otrasleĭ obshchestvennogo proizvodstva : sbornik stateĭ / pod redaktsieĭ S.A. Kheĭnmana, E.I. Popovoĭ. Moskva : Akademiia nauk SSSR, In-t ėkonomiki, 1983. 167 p. : ill. ; 21 cm. Includes bibliographical references. LC Card 84-211670
1. Industrial organization - Soviet Union. 2. Technological innovations - Soviet Union. I. Kheĭnman, S. A. (Solomon Aronovich). II. Popova, E. I. (Elena Ivanovna). III. Institut ėkonomiki (Akademiia nauk SSSR).
HD70.S63 P753 1983

Problemy tselevoĭ orientatsii razvitiia resursnogo potentsiala / [otvetstvennye redaktory E.Z. Maĭminas, V.V. Ivanov]. Moskva : Akademiia nauk SSSR, TSentr. ėkonomiko-matematicheskiĭ in-t, 1984. 205 p. : ill. ; 21 cm. Includes bibliographies. LC Card 86-143993
1. Natural resources - Soviet Union - Forecasting. 2. Soviet Union - Economic policy - 1981- - Mathematical models. I. Maĭminas, E. Z. (Efrem Zalmanovich), 1932-. II. Ivanov, V. V., k.ė.n. III. TSentral'nyĭ ėkonomiko-matematicheskiĭ institut (Akademiia nauk SSSR).
HC333.5 .P77 1984

Problemy ukrepleniia trudovoĭ distsipliny i predotvrashcheniia tekuchesti kadrov na predpriiatiiakh TSentral'nogo Kazakhstana : sbornik nauchnykh trudov, mezhduvedomstvennyĭ / [redaktsionnaia kollegiia E.N. Nurgalieva (otv. redaktor) ... et al.]. Karaganda : Karagandinskiĭ gos. universitet, 1982. 126 p. ; 20 cm. At head of title: Ministerstvo vysshego i srednego spetsial'nogo obrazovaniia Kazakhskoĭ SSR. Karagandinskiĭ gosudarstvennyĭ universitet. Includes bibliographies. LC Card 84-226131
1. Labor discipline - Kazakh S.S.R. 2. Labor turnover - Kazakh S.S.R. 3. Labor discipline - Law and legislation - Kazakh S.S.R. I. Nurgalieva, E. N. II. Karagandinskiĭ gosudarstvennyĭ universitet.
HF5549.5.L3 P76 1982

Problemy urovnia zhizni i demografii : mezhvedomstvennyĭ sbornik nauchnykh trudov / [Redkollegiia Kh.A. Zile (otv. redaktor), P.P. Zvidrin'sh, A.N. Lapin'sh ... et al.]. Riga : Latviĭskiĭ gos. universitet im. P. Stuchki, 1979. 175 p. ; 20 cm. At head of title: Ministerstvo vysshego i srednego spetsial'nogo obrazovaniia Latviĭskoĭ SSR. Latviĭskiĭ ordena Trudovogo Krasnogo Znameni gosudarstvennyĭ universitet imeni Petra Stuchki. Kafedra statistiki i demografii. Includes bibliographical references. LC Card 82-106660
1. Cost and standard of living - Latvia. 2. Latvia - Population. I. Zile, Kh. II. Pētera Stučkas Latvijas Valsts universitāte. Statistikas un demografijas katedra.
HD7035.Z8 L376 1979

Problemy valiutnogo soiuza stran-chlenov Evropeĭskogo ėkonomicheskogo soobshchestva i razvitie mezhdunarodnoĭ valiutnoĭ sistemy kapitalizma : materialy mezhdunarodnogo simpoziuma, noiabr', 1980, Sofiia / [redaktsionnaia kollegiia Khr. Nokov (otvetstvennyĭ redaktor), T. Vylchev, T. Khubenova]. Sofiia : Izd-vo Bolgarskoĭ akademii nauk, 1984. 151 p. ; 20 cm. Title on added t.p.: Problemi na valutniia sŭiuz na stranite-chlenki na EIO i razvitie na mezhdunarodnata valutna sistema na kapitalizma. At head of title: Bolgarskaia akademiia nauk. Institut ėkonomiki. Includes bibliographical references. LC Card 85-224144
1. Foreign exchange problem - European Economic Community countries - Congresses. 2. Currency question - European Economic Community countries - Congresses. 3. Monetary policy - European Economic Community countries - Congresses. 4. Monetary unions - Congresses. I. Nokov, Khristo. II. Vŭlchev, Todor Iordanov. III. Khubenova-Delisivkova, Tatiana. IV. Ikonomicheski institut (Bŭlgarska akademiia na naukite). V. Title: Problemi na valutniia sŭiuz na stranite-chlenki na EIO i razvitie na mezhdunarodnata valutna sistema n kapitalizma.
HG3942.8 .P76 1984

Problemy valiutnoĭ integratsii v Evropeĭskom soobshchestve . Murtazina, E. N. Moskva , 1985. 75 p. ; LC Card 85-224384
HG3942.8 .M87 1985

Proceedings /. AWWA Seminar on the Rate Making Process: Going Beyond the Cost of Service (1986 : Denver, Colo.) Denver, CO , c1986. vi, 58 p. ; ISBN 0-89867-368-2 (pbk.) LC Card 87-107641 DDC 338.4/336361/0973 19
HD4461 .A915 1986

Proceedings /. Conference on Cable Television (1981 : Brooklyn College Student Union) [Albany, N.Y.] (P.O. Box 167, Albany 12248) [1982] 77 p. ; LC Card 86-622177 DDC 384.55/47/09747 19
HE8700.72 'J6 C66 1981

Proceedings from The Future is Now, A Home Equity (›nversion Conference. The Future is Now: A Home Equity Conversion Conference (1985 : Washington, D.C.) Washington, D.C. [1985?] ix, 76 p. ; LC Card 86-601425 DDC 332.7/22 19
HG2040.45 .F87 1985

Proceedings of a National Conference on Rural Development. National Conference on Rural Development, Des Moines, 1973. Proceedings. Washington, 1974. iii, 108 p. LC Card 74-600918 DDC 309.2/63/0973
HN65 .N35 1973 ***NYPL [JLE 81-564 no.2]***

Proceedings of a symposium on competitiveness of U. S. grains in international markets / edited by William W. Wilson. Fargo, N.D. : Dept. of Agricultural Economics, Agricultural Experiment Station, North Dakota State University, [1986] ii leaves, 67 p. : ill. ; 28 cm. (Agricultural economics miscellaneous report . no. 97) Cover title. Papers presented at a symposium held during the annual meeting of the American Agricultural Economics Association in Ames, Iowa, Aug. 1985. "May 1986." Includes bibliographies. LC Card 86-622839 DDC 382/.4131/0973 19
1. Grain trade - United States - Congresses. 2. United States - Commerce - Congresses. 3. Competition, International - Congresses. I. Wilson, William W. II. American Agricultural Economics Association.
HD9035 .P76 1986

Proceedings of an international conference on genetic algorithms and their applications : July 24-26, 1985 at Carnegie-Mellon University, Pittsburgh, Pa./ sponsored by Texas Instruments, Inc., U. S. Navy Center for Applied Research in Artificial Intelligence (NCARAI) ; John J. Grefenstette, editor. [S.l. : s.n., 1985] 225 p. : ill. ; 28 cm. Includes bibliographies.
1. Artificial intelligence - Congresses. 2. Algorithms - Congresses. 3. Adaptation (Biology) - Congresses. 4. Mathematical optimization - Congresses. 5. Self-organizing systems - Congresses. I. Grefenstette, John J. II. Texas Instruments Incorporated. III. United States. Navy Center for Applied Research in Artificial Intelligence. IV. Title: Genetic algorithms and their applications. ***NYPL [JSF 87-413]***

Proceedings of second (special) general conference : Africa Hall, Addis Ababa, Ethiopia, 30th October to 1st November, 1985. Accra, Ghana : Executive Director, African Development Experts, [1985?] 73 p. ; 24 cm. LC Card 86-220781 DDC 338.96 19
1. African cooperation. 2. Economic assistance - Africa. 3. Technical assistance - Africa. I. African Development Experts (Organization). II. Title: Proceedings of 2nd (special) general conference.
HC800 .P77 1985

Proceedings of the Academy of Political Science in the city of New York .
(v. 36, no. 3) Prospects for privatization /. New York , 1987. x, 214 p. ; LC Card 87-70470 DDC 338.973 19
HD3885 .P76 1987

[Proceedings of the annual conference of First Ministers, held in Halifax, N.S., November 28-29, 1985]. First Ministers' Conference (1985 : Halifax, N.S.) [Canada , 1986-] portfolios <1-4 > : LC Card 86-201687 DDC 338.971 19
HC115 .F485 1985

Proceedings of the IASTED Energy Symposia : Modelling, Policy and Economics of Energy and Power Systems [and] Alternative Energy Sources and Technology, May 20-22, 1981, San Francisco, U. S.A. /. IASTED Symposia on Modelling, Policy and Economics of Energy and Power Systems, and Alternative Energy Sources and Technology (1981 : San Francisco, Calif.) Anaheim, Calif. [1981?] 209 p. : ISBN 0-88986-027-0 ***NYPL [JSF 86-1103]***

Proceedings of the International Symposium on the Role of the Asia-Pacific Region in World Economic Development . International Symposium on the Role of the Asia-Pacific Region in World Economic Development (1984 : Tokyo, Japan) Tokyo , c1985. iv, 325 p. : LC Card 87-108109 DDC 337.9 19
HC681 .I58 1984

Proceedings of the Lupande Development Workshop . Lupande Development Workshop (1983 : Nyamaluma Wildlife Conservation Camp) Chipata, Zambia , 1984. x, 121 p. : LC Card 84-980605 DDC 333.73/17/096894 19
HD993.Z8 L835 1983 ***NYPL [JLG 87-67]***

Proceedings of the Regional Workshop on Wood Energy in East Africa . Regional Workshop on Wood Energy in East Africa (1982 : Nairobi, Kenya) Ottawa, Canada [1983] 241 p. : LC Card 86-185703 DDC 333.75 19
HD9769.F843 A367 1982

Proceedings of the Specialty Conference on Engineering and Construction Projects . Specialty Conference on Engineering and Construction Projects (1982 : New Orleans, La.) New York, N.Y. , c1982. vi, 329 p. : ISBN 0-87262-299-1 (pbk.) LC Card 82-70492 DDC 658.5 19
TA190 .S67 1982 ***NYPL [JLD 86-1905]***

Proceedings of the Tokyo Forum: Ethics of Human Survival . Tokyo Forum: Ethics of Human Survival (1985) Tokyo, Japan , c1986. v, 88 p. : ISBN 4-7955-1024-5 LC Card 87-142747
HD73 .T65 1985

Proceedings of the Workshop on Exact Matching Methodologies. Workshop on Exact Matching Methodologies (May 9-10, 1985 : Arlington, Va.) Record linkage techniques--1985 . [Washington, D.C.] , 1985. vii, 397 p. : ***NYPL [JLF 86-1723]***

Proceedings of the workshop on the "Interrelationship between agricultural settlement, agricultural development, and population change" in selected Eastern Africa Countries, Ethiopia, Kenya, Sudan, and Tanzania, held at the Population Studies and Research Institute, University of Nairobi, April 13-16, 1981. Nairobi : The Institute, [1981] 304 p. : maps ; 30 cm. "Prepared by the Population Studies and Research Institute, University of Nairobi"--Cover. "July 1981." Includes bibliographies. LC Card 85-980248 DDC 338.1/09676 19
1. Land settlement - Africa, Eastern - Congresses. 2. Agriculture and state - Africa, Eastern - Congresses. 3. Migration, Internal - Africa, Eastern - Congresses. I. University of Nairobi. Population Studies and Research Institute.
HD982.Z63 P76 1981

Proceedings of 2nd (special) general conference. Proceedings of second (special) general conference . Accra, Ghana [1985?] 73 p. ; LC Card 86-220781 DDC 338.96 19
HC800 .P77 1985

Proceedings, Symposium on Logic in Computer Science, Cambridge, Massachusetts, June 16-18, 1986 /. Symposium on Logic in Computer Science (1986 : Cambridge, Mass.) Washington, D.C. , Los Angeles, CA , 1986. xi, 383 p. : ISBN 0-8186-0720-3 (pbk.) LC Card 86-81090 DDC 004 19
QA75.5 .S9813 1986 ***NYPL [JSF 86-1041]***

Proces odlučivanja u organizacijama udruženog rada /. Zver, Boris. Zagreb , 1983. ix, 169 p. ; LC Card 85-171946
HD30.23 .Z87 1983

Proces samoupravne integracije . Mirić, Rade. Bačka Topola , 1984. 147 p. ; LC Card 85-194104
HD5660.Y8 M57 1984

Procès-verbaux de la Conférence européenne des horaires des trains de voyageurs pour les années 1985/87 . Conférence européenne des horaires des trains de voyageurs (1984 : Paris, France) Paris , 1984. 619 p. ; LC Card 85-152699
HE3004 .C64 1984

El proceso de colonización en el impenetrable chaqueño /. Borrini, Héctor R. Corrientes , 1981. 60 leaves : LC Card 86-204205 DDC 333.3/1/8234 19
HD479.C47 B67 1981

El proceso de implantación del IVA . Sevilla Segura, Jorge. [Madrid] [1982?] iii, 182 p. ; LC Card 85-201954
HJ5715.G7 S4 1982

El proceso de industrialización en la región aragonesa en el período 1900-1920 /. Biescas, José Antonio, 1946- Zaragoza , 1985. 335 p. : ISBN 84-00-06130-6 LC Card 87-111810
HC387.A68 B536 1985

El Proceso de integración en América Latina en 1985 / INTAL. Buenos Aires, República Argentina : Instituto para la Integración de América Latina, Banco Interamericano de Desarrollo, 1986. 271 p. : ill. ; 23 cm. Includes bibliographical references. LC Card 87-169476 DDC 337.1/8 19
1. Latin America - Economic integration. I. Institute for Latin American Integration.
HC125 .P768 1986

El Proceso de trabajo en México / M. de la Luz Arriaga ... [et al.]. [Iztapalapa, Mexico] : Universidad Autónoma Metropolitana, Unidad Iztapalapa, División Ciencias Sociales y Humanidades, Carrera de Sociología, [1983 or 1984] 227 p. : ill. ; 18 cm. (Cuadernos Teoría y sociedad . 4) Includes bibliographical references. LC Card 87-401038 DDC 331/.0972 19
1. Labor and laboring classes - Mexico. I. Arriaga, M. de la Luz (María de la Luz). II. Series.
HD8116.5 .P76 1983

Proceso y significado del cooperativismo uruguayo /. Terra, Juan Pablo, 1924. Montevideo [1986] 171 p. ; LC Card 87-403179 DDC 334/.09885 19
HD3482.A4 T47 1986

PROCESS CONTROL EQUIPMENT INDUSTRY - LATIN AMERICA.
Process control instrumentation in Latin America. New York, N.Y. , c1983. vi, 404 p. ; LC Card 87-141802 DDC 380.1/456817 19
HD9696.P763 L296 1983

PROCESS CONTROL EQUIPMENT INDUSTRY - UNITED STATES.
The Distributed digital process control systems market in the U. S. New York, N.Y. , c1983. 229 p. ; LC Card 87-141853
HD9696.P763 U527 1983

The Process control equipment market (1982-1992). New York, N.Y. : Frost & Sullivan, c1983. vii, 241 leaves : ill. ; 29 cm. "September 1983." "(#1242)" LC Card 87-142195 DDC 380.1/456817 19
1. Automatic control equipment industry - United States. 2. Market surveys - United States. I. Frost & Sullivan.
HD9696.A963 U66 1983

Process control instrumentation in Latin America. New York, N.Y. : Frost & Sullivan, c1983. vi, 404 p. ; 29 cm. "January, 1983." "W 591." LC Card 87-141802 DDC 380.1/456817 19
1. Process control equipment industry - Latin America. 2. Market surveys - Latin America. I. Frost & Sullivan.
HD9696.P763 L296 1983

PROCESS ENGINEERING. see **PRODUCTION ENGINEERING.**

PROCESS ENGINEERING (MANUFACTURES) see **MANUFACTURING PROCESSES.**

The process of economic development in Costa Rica, 1948-1970 . Jacobstein, Helen L., 1925- New York , 1987. 338 p. : ISBN 0-8240-1363-8 (alk. paper) : LC Card 87-8519 DDC 338.97286 19
HC143 .J28 1987

The process of occupational sex-typing . Cohn, Samuel, 1954- Philadelphia , 1985. viii, 279 p. ; ISBN 0-87722-402-1 : LC Card 85-14864 DDC 331.4/8165137/0941 19
HD6060.65.G7 C64 1985 ***NYPL [JLE 86-917]***

The process of presentational speaking /. Howell, William Smiley. New York , c19. p. cm. ISBN 0-06-042929-1 LC Card 87-8673 DDC 658.4/52 19
HF5718 .H7 1988

A process of struggle . Maunders, A. R. Aldershot, Hampshire, England , Brookfield, Vt., USA , c1987. xi, 283 p. : ISBN 0-566-05227-X : LC Card 86-25640 DDC 338.6/042 19
HD9521.8.C85 M38 1987 ***NYPL [JLD 87-1533]***

The process of technological change : new technology and social choice in the workplace / Jon Clark ... [et al.]. Cambridge [Cambridgeshire] ; New York : Cambridge University Press, 1988. p. cm. (Cambridge studies in management . 11) Bibliography: p. Includes index. ISBN 0-521-32303-7 LC Card 87-6641 DDC 658.5/14 19
1. Technological innovations - Management. 2. Industrial relations - Effect of technological innovations on. I. Clark, Jon, Ph.D. II. Series.
HD45 .P757 1988

PROCESSES, MANUFACTURING. see **MANUFACTURING PROCESSES.**

Processi formativi e coscienza operaia : un'esperienza italo-tedesca / a cura di Enrico Taliani e Edgar Weick. Pisa : ETS, c1983. 509 p. ; 24 cm. At head of title: Istituto di sociologia, Pisa; Institut für sozialforschung, Francoforte sul Meno; Hessische Erwachsendibildungsstätte [i.e. Erwachsenenbildungsstätte], Falkenstein. Includes bibliographical references. LC Card 86-136656 DDC 658.3/124/0945 19
1. Employees, Training of - Germany, West. 2. Employees, Training of - Italy. 3. Employee motivation - Germany (West) - Congresses. 4. Employee motivation - Italy - Congresses. I. Taliani, Enrico. II. Weick, Edgar. III. Università di Pisa. Istituto di sociologia. IV. Institut für Sozialforschung (Frankfurt am Main, Germany). V. Hessische Erwachsenenbildungsstätte Falkenstein (Königstein im Taunus, Germany).
HF5549.5.T7 P69 1983 ***NYPL [JLE 87-1466]***

PROCESSING, INDUSTRIAL. see **MANUFACTURING PROCESSES.**

O processo de relações públicas /. Wey, Hebe. São Paulo, SP , c1983. 166 p. ; LC Card 86-152248
HD59 .W44 1983

Procesų dinaminės klasifikacijos algoritmų sudarymas ir tyrimas. Razrabotka i issledovanie algoritmov dinamicheskoĭ klassifikatsii protsessov . Vil'nius , 1979. 93 p. : LC Card 82-150323
HD38 .S715 vyp. 37 T57.83

Procesul investițional /. Cistelecan, Lazăr M. București , 1983. 264 p. : LC Card 84-135967
HG5692 .C57 1983

PROCUREMENT, INDUSTRIAL. see **INDUSTRIAL PROCUREMENT.**

Procurement under IBRD loans and IDA credits : guidelines. 3rd ed., rev. and expanded. Washington, D.C. : World Bank, c1985. 38 p. ; 23 cm. ISBN 0-8213-0562-X (pbk.) LC Card 86-211637 DDC 332.1/532 19
1. World Bank. 2. International Development Association. 3. Industrial procurement. 4. Loans, Foreign. I. International Bank for Reconstruction and Development.
HG3881.5.W57 P76 1985

Prodavets i Pokupatel', ili rasskaz o tom, kakimi mogli by stat' ikh otnosheniia, bud' riadom Psikholog /. Bel'chikov, IA. M. Riga , 1986. 157, [3] p. : LC Card 87-129915
HF5438.8.P75 B45 1986

Prodemocracia (Organization) Deuda externa y reforma del sistema monetario internacional . Bogotá, D.E., Colombia , 1986. 235 p. ; ISBN 958-608-037-4 LC Card 87-400468 DDC 336.3/435/098 19
HJ8514.5 .D487 1986

Prodhan, B. Multinational accounting : segment disclosure and risk / Bimal Prodhan. London ; Dover, N.H. : Croom Helm, c1986. xi, 399 p. : ill. ; 23 cm. Includes index. Bibliography: p. 271-294. ISBN 0-7099-4010-6 : LC Card 86-4521 DDC 657/.95 19
1. International business enterprises - Accounting. 2. Disclosure in accounting. I. Title.
HF5686.I56 P76 1986 ***NYPL [JLD 86-2595]***

Prodi, Romano. Per una ristrutturazione e riconversione dell'industria italiana /. Bologna , 1980. 244 p. ; LC Card 82-102594 DDC 338.945 19
HD3616.I83 P43 ***NYPL [JLD 86-599]***

Prodolzhenie podviga : o "TSeline" i tselinnikakh / [sostavitel' V.V. Vladimirov]. Moskva : Izd-vo polit. lit-ry, 1979. 165 p., [16] p. of plates : ill., ports. ; 20 cm. LC Card 81-150822
1. Brezhnev, Leonid Il'ich, 1906- TSelina. 2. Agriculture and state - Kazakh S.S.R. - History. 3. Agricultural colonies - Kazakh S.S.R. - History. 4. Agricultural development projects - Kazakh S.S.R. - History. I. Vladimirov, Vladislav Vasil'evich.
HD1995.K36 B7337 1979

Prodovol'stvennaia problema i perspektivy ee resheniia v arabskikh stranakh . Shestopalova, Zoia Vladimirovna. Moskva , 1985. 151, [4] p. : LC Card 86-130508
HD9016.S92 S44 1985 ***NYPL [*QIP 87-3413]***

Prodovol'stvennaia problema i sel'skoe khoziaistvo stran Latinskoĭ Ameriki / [avtorskiĭ kollektiv IU.G. Onufriev ... et al. ; otvetstvennyĭ redaktor IU.G. Onufriev]. Moskva : Izd-vo "Nauka", 1981. 311 p. ; 21 cm. At head of title: Akademiia nauk SSSR. Institut Latinskoĭ Ameriki. Includes bibliographies. LC Card 82-108167
1. Food supply - Latin America. 2. Agricultural industries - Latin America. I. Onufriev, IU. G. II. Institut Latinskoĭ Ameriki (Akademiia nauk SSSR).
HD9014.L32 P76 1981

Prodovol'stvennaia programma SSSR : voprosy i otvety / [kollektiv avtorov Gorlanov I.A. ... et al. ; pod obshcheĭ redaktsieĭ Florent'eva L.IA. ; sostaviteli Kopanev N.G., Seleznev F.IA.]. Moskva : Izd-vo polit. lit-ry, 1986. 285 p. ; 17 cm. LC Card 87-110478 DDC 338.1/9/47 19
1. Food industry and trade - Soviet Union - Miscellanea. 2. Agriculture and state - Soviet Union - Miscellanea. I. Gorlanov, I. A. II. Florent'ev, L. IA. (Leonid IAkovlevich). III. Kopanev, N. G. IV. Seleznev, F. (Fedor).
HD9015.S652 P743 1986

Prodovol'stvennyĭ kompleks goroda . Savenko, V. N. (Valentina Nikolaevna) Kiev , 1986. 173, [3] p. : LC Card 87-161654
HD9015.S653 U473 1986

Produção agrícola brasileira : municípios mais importantes. [Rio de Janeiro] : Fundação Getúlio Vargas, 1986. 188 p. : ill ; 31 cm. "Este trabalho foi realizado ... sob a direção do ... Sylvio Wanick Ribeiro ... Boris Gheventer e Martha Macedo de Lima Barata"--P. 1. LC Card 87-403944 DDC 338.1/0981/021 19
1. Farm produce - Brazil - Statistics. I. Ribeiro, Sylvio Wanick. II. Gheventer, Boris. III. Barata, Martha Macedo de Lima. IV. Fundação Getúlio Vargas.
HD9014.B82 P765 1986

A Produção capitalista da casa (e da cidade) no Brasil industrial / Ermínia Maricato, organizadora ; pref., Francisco de Oliveira ; [capa, Vera Altemberg]. Ed. ilustrada. São Paulo : Editora Alfa-Omega, 1979. 166 p. : ill. ; 21 cm. (Biblioteca Alfa-Omega de ciências sociais ; Série 1a, Urbanismo ; v. 1) Includes bibliographical references. CONTENTS. - Singer, P. O uso do solo urbano na economía capitalista.--Bolaffi, G. Habitação e urbanismo.--Maricato, E. Autoconstrução, a arquitetura possível.--Lefévre, R. Notas sobre o papel dos preços de terrenos em negócios imobiliários de apartamentos e escritórios na cidade de São Paulo.--Bonduki, R., Bonduki, N. Periferia da Grande São Paulo, reprodução do espaço como expediente de reprodução da força de trabalho.--Ferracini, G. Fotos: o processo de expansão horizontal das áreas metropolitanas. LC Card 80-100793
1. Housing - Brazil - Addresses, essays, lectures. 2. Housing policy - Brazil - Addresses, essays, lectures. 3. City planning - Brazil - Addresses, essays, lectures. I. Maricato, Ermínia.
HD7323.A3 P76 1979 ***NYPL [JLD 80-3858]***

Producción corredores de seguros 1985. [Chile] : Superintendencia de Valores y Seguros, 1986. 390 p. ; 26 cm. Errata slips inserted. LC Card 87-403786 DDC 368/.0025/83 19
1. Insurance - Chile - Directories. 2. Insurance - Chile - Statistics. I. Chile. Superintendencia de Valores y Seguros.
HG8576 .P76 1986

Producción versus consumo de alimentos : desafío y oportunidades de la presente década / asesoría, Gentil Rojas L. [Santo Domingo, Dominican Republic] : Secretaría de Estado de Agricultura, Subsecretaría Técnica de Planificación Sectorial Agropecuaria, Departamento Planes, Programas y Proyectos, 1981. 74 p. ; 21 cm. Bibliography: p. 43-44. LC Card 82-207744
1. Food supply - Dominican Republic. 2. Food consumption - Dominican Republic. I. Rojas L., Gentil. II. Dominican Republic. Subsecretaría Técnica de Planificación Sectorial Agropecuaria. Departamento Planes, Programas y Proyectos.
HD9014.D62 P76 1981

Producción y comercialización de la coca : informe preliminar / Universidad Boliviana Mayor de San Simón, Instituto de Estudios Sociales y Económicos, IESE, Facultad de Ciencias Económicas. Cochabamba, Bolivia : La Facultad, 1972. 92 leaves in various foliations, [3] folded leaves of plates : maps ; 33 cm. Cover title. LC Card 85-138614
1. Coca industry - Bolivia - Chaparé. 2. Coca industry - Bolivia - Yungas. I. Universidad Boliviana Mayor de San Simón. Facultad de Ciencias Económicas.
HD9019.C632 B646 1972

Producción y comercialización porcina en Uruguay : un análisis de coyuntura / por Alvaro Azzarini ... [et al.]. Montevideo : Instituto de Promoción Económico-Social del Uruguay, 1986. 91 p. : ill. ; 26 cm. (Publicaciones técnicas . 8) Bibliography: p. 87-88. LC Card 87-401290 DDC 338.1/764/009895 19
1. Pork industry and trade - Uruguay. I. Azzarini, Alvaro. II. Instituto de Promoción Económico-Social del Uruguay. III. Series: Publicaciones técnicas (Instituto de Promoción Económico-Social del Uruguay) , 8.
HD9435.U82 P76 1986

Producción y comercio en el espacio sur andino en el siglo XVII . Escobari de Querejazu, Laura. La Paz , 1985. 218 p., [12] p. of plates : LC Card 86-174929
HC167.A5 E83 1985

Producción y exportación de lácteos / Ministerio de Economía y Finanzas, Dirección General de Comercio Exterior. Montevideo, Uruguay : La Dirección, 1977. 21 p. ; 22 cm. LC Card 85-205438
1. Dairy products industry - Uruguay. 2. Dairy plants - Uruguay. I. Uruguay. Dirección General de Comercio Exterior.
HD9275.U92 P76 1977

Producción y participación política en el campo /. Salinas de Gortari, Carlos. México , 1980. 320 p. : ISBN 968-582-934-9 LC Card 82-199421 DDC 338.1/0972 19
HD1792 .S287 1980 ***NYPL [JLD 86-2602]***

PRODUCE EXCHANGES. see **COMMODITY EXCHANGES.**

Produce Marketing Association. Retail produce operations, 1986 /. Washington, D.C. (1750 K. St., N.W. Washington 20006) , Newark, Del. [1986] viii, 20 p. ; LC Card 87-101803 DDC 381/.456648/00973 19
HD9321.4 .R47 1986

PRODUCE TRADE - BOLIVIA - COCHABAMBA (DEPT.)
Calderón G., Fernando. Jatun Llajta . La Paz, Bolivia , 1982. v, 448 p., [8] leaves of plates : LC Card 83-111937 DDC 381/.1 19
HF5473.B62 C623 1982
NYPL [JLF 86-1794]

PRODUCE TRADE - BRAZIL - ALAGOAS - STATISTICS.
Distribuição da produção dos principais produtos agropecuários do Estado de Alagoas. [S.l.] [198-] [29] p. : LC Card 86-179132
HD9014.B83 A653 1980z

PRODUCE TRADE - BRAZIL - SÃO PAULO (STATE)
Disponibilidade de alimentos a nível regional no Estado de São Paulo, 1974-83 /. São Paulo , 1985. 75 p. ; LC Card 86-196482
HD9014.B83 S433 1985

PRODUCE TRADE - BRAZIL - STATISTICS.
Balanço e disponibilidade interna de gêneros alimentícios de origem vegetal 1975 a 1980 /. Rio de Janeiro, RJ, Brasil , 1983. 72 p. ;
NYPL [JLG 85-94]

Balanço e disponibilidade interna de gêneros alimentícios de origem vegetal, 1979 a 1983 /. Rio de Janeiro, Brasil , 1985. 67 p. ; LC Card 87-404963 DDC 339.4/86413/00981021 19
HD9014.B82 B345 1985

PRODUCE TRADE - BRAZIL - STATISTICS - HISTORY.
Lima, José Luiz. Estatísticas básicas do setor agrícola no Brasil /. São Paulo , 1983- v. : LC Card 83-219032 DDC 338.1/0981 19
HD9014.B82 L55 1983 ***NYPL [JLL 86-432]***

PRODUCE TRADE - BULGARIA.
Atanasov, Mikhail, k.i.n. Vŭshnotŭrgovski aspekti na selskostopanskite i khranitelno-vkusovite stoki i problemi pred bŭlgarskiia iznos /. Sofiia , 1984. 118 p. ; LC Card 85-163481
HD9015.B82 A86 1984

PRODUCE TRADE - CARIBBEAN AREA.
Agricultural marketing handbook for Caribbean Basin products. Spanish. Manual--mercadeo de productos agrícolas de la Cuenca del Caribe /. San José, Costa Rica . x, 434 p. : ISBN 92-9039-101-4 LC Card 86-204686
HD9014.C442 A4718 1986

PRODUCE TRADE - CENTRAL AMERICA.
Agricultural marketing handbook for Caribbean Basin products. Spanish. Manual--mercadeo de productos agrícolas de la Cuenca del Caribe /. San José, Costa Rica . x, 434 p. : ISBN 92-9039-101-4 LC Card 86-204686
HD9014.C442 A4718 1986

PRODUCE TRADE - COLOMBIA.
Isaza Tobón, Gabriela. El IDEMA, hacia una pérdida de los objetivos sociales. [Colombia? , between 1984 and 1987] ([Colombia?] : Litoarte) 126 p., [1] leaf of plates : LC Card 87-404223 DDC 381/.41/09861 19
HD9014.C72 I8 1984

Problemas agrarios colombianos /. [Bogotá, Colombia] , México, D.F. , 1986. 467 p. : ISBN 958-606-005-5 LC Card 86-221632
HD1882 .P75 1986

PRODUCE TRADE - DEVELOPING COUNTRIES.
Abbott, John Cave, 1919- Agricultural marketing enterprises for the developing world . Cambridge [Cambridgeshire] , New York , 1987. xi, 217 p. : ISBN 0-521-32597-8 LC Card 86-24462 DDC 381/.41/091724 19
HD9018.D44 A228 1987

Agricultural trade with developing countries. Paris [Washington, D.C.] 1984. 113 p. ; ISBN 92-64-12579-5 (pbk.) LC Card 84-221780 DDC 382/.41/091724 19
HD9018.D44 A37 1984
NYPL [JLE 86-3906]

Junginger-Dittel, K.-O. Marketing Boards für Agrarexportgüter in Entwicklungsländern /. [Kiel] , 1980. iii, 48 leaves ; LC Card 85-160428
HD9018.D44 J86 1980

PRODUCE TRADE - DEVELOPING COUNTRIES - CASE STUDIES.
Abbott, John Cave, 1919- Agricultural marketing enterprises for the developing world . Cambridge [Cambridgeshire] , New York , 1987. xi, 217 p. : ISBN 0-521-32597-8 LC Card 86-24462 DDC 381/.41/091724 19
HD9018.D44 A228 1987

PRODUCE TRADE - DEVELOPING COUNTRIES - CONGRESSES.
The Common agricultural policy and the Third World . London , 1986. 97 p. : ISBN 0-946848-79-3 (pbk.) : LC Card 87-150069 DDC 338.1/81/094 19
HD9015.E82 C665 1986

U. S. agriculture and Third World economic development . Washington, D.C. , c1987. xv, 103 p. : ISBN 0-89068-086-8 (pbk.): LC Card 86-62757 DDC 338.9/009172/4 19
HD1755 .U173 1987

PRODUCE TRADE - DOMINICAN REPUBLIC.
Ross, Jaime. Instrumentos tributarios de financiamientos coadyuvantes a la producción agraria de alimentos /. Santo Domingo, R.D. [1983] i, 229 p. ; LC Card 84-159753
HJ4308 .R67 1983

PRODUCE TRADE - EUROPE, EASTERN.
Deutsch, Robert. The food revolution in the Soviet Union and Eastern Europe /. Boulder , 1986. xxii, 256 p. : ISBN 0-8133-7161-9 (pbk.) : LC Card 85-26625 DDC 338.1/9/47 19
HD9015.S652 D47 1986
NYPL [JLE 86-1588]

PRODUCE TRADE - EUROPEAN ECONOMIC COMMUNITY COUNTRIES.
Ahn, Lothar. Ökonomische und ökologische Perspektiven der Agrarpolitik . Köln , 1983. 98 p. : ISBN 3-7609-5124-4 LC Card 83-155478
HD1920.5 .A627 1983

Japanese import barriers to U. S. agricultural exports and the Common agricultural policy of the European Community and implications for U. S. agricultural trade . Washington , 1986. vii, 65 p. : LC Card 87-601384 DDC 382/.5/0952 19
HF1601 .J363 1986

Qarouach, Mostafa. L'agriculture marocaine face au deuxième élargissement de la CEE /. [S.l.] 1983 (Casablanca : Editions maghrébines) 117 p. ; LC Card 83-192279 DDC 382/.41/0964 19
HD9017.M82 Q37 1983
NYPL [JLD 86-4326]

PRODUCE TRADE - GAMBIA - HISTORY.
Barrett, Hazel R., 1955- The marketing of foodstuffs in the Gambia, 1400-1980 . Aldershot, Hants., England , Brookfield, Vt., U. S.A. , 1988, c1987. p. cm. ISBN 0-566-05487-6 LC Card 87-23063 DDC 381/.41/096651 19
HD9017.G262 B37 1988

PRODUCE TRADE - GERMANY, WEST.
Kühl, Rainer. Wettbewerbstheoretische Analyse des Landwarenmarktes in der Bundesrepublik Deutschland . Kiel , 1986. 77 p. : ISBN 3-922553-79-6 LC Card 86-172903
HD9013.5 .K84 1986

PRODUCE TRADE - GOVERNMENT POLICY.
Agricultural trade with developing countries. Paris [Washington, D.C.] 1984. 113 p. ; ISBN 92-64-12579-5 (pbk.) LC Card 84-221780 DDC 382/.41/091724 19
HD9018.D44 A37 1984
NYPL [JLE 86-3906]

Hathaway, Dale E. Agriculture and the GATT . Washington, DC , c1987. xii, 157 p. : ISBN 0-88132-052-8 LC Card 87-21430 DDC 382/.41/0973 19
HD9006 .H28 1987

PRODUCE TRADE - GOVERNMENT POLICY - DEVELOPING COUNTRIES.
Agricultural trade with developing countries. Paris [Washington, D.C.] 1984. 113 p. ; ISBN 92-64-12579-5 (pbk.) LC Card 84-221780 DDC 382/.41/091724 19
HD9018.D44 A37 1984
NYPL [JLE 86-3906]

PRODUCE TRADE - GOVERNMENT POLICY - EUROPEAN ECONOMIC COMMUNITY COUNTRIES - CONGRESSES.
The Common agricultural policy and the Third World . London , 1986. 97 p. : ISBN 0-946848-79-3 (pbk.) : LC Card 87-150069 DDC 338.1/81/094 19
HD9015.E82 C665 1986

Confrontation or negotiation . Millwood, N.Y. , 1985. xvi, 303 p. : ISBN 0-8046-9397-8 : LC Card 85-18667 DDC 382/.41/094 19
HD9015.E82 C67 1985
NYPL [JLE 86-4594]

PRODUCE TRADE - GOVERNMENT POLICY - ITALY - CONGRESSES.
L'Imprenditore coltivatore nella società che cambia . [Italy] [1983] (Roma : Arti grafiche Jasillo) 364 p. : LC Card 86-185731
HD1972 .I44 1983

PRODUCE TRADE - GOVERNMENT POLICY - JAPAN.
Hillman, Jimmye S., 1923- Agricultural trade

and protection in Japan /. Aldershot, Hants, England , Brookfield, Vt. , 1988. p. cm. ISBN 0-566-05339-X : LC Card 87-15043 DDC 382.7/3/0952 19
HD9016.J42 H55 1988

PRODUCE TRADE - GOVERNMENT POLICY - MIDDLE WEST - CONGRESSES.
Ninth Federal Reserve District Farm Forum (1965 : Minneapolis, Minn.) Farm Forum of the Ninth Federal Reserve District . Hopkins, Minn. [1965] 99 p. : LC Card 87-110732
HD9007.A14 N56 1965

PRODUCE TRADE - GOVERNMENT POLICY - PHILIPPINES.
Bautista, Romeo M., 1941- Production incentives in Philippine agriculture . Washington, D.C., USA , c1987. 78 p. : ISBN 0-89629-061-1 (pbk.) LC Card 87-3233 DDC 338.1/8 19
HD2087 .B38 1987

PRODUCE TRADE - GOVERNMENT POLICY - UNITED STATES.
Agriculture in the GATT . Washington , 1986. v, 47 p. ; LC Card 86-603393 DDC 382/.41/0973 19
HD9006 .A77 1986

Gold, Kenneth A. (Kenneth Alan) United States foreign economic policy-making . New York , 1987. 349 p. ; ISBN 0-8240-8083-1 : LC Card 87-23785 DDC 382/.456413/00973 19
HD9006 .G64 1987

Hathaway, Dale E. Agriculture and the GATT . Washington, DC , c1987. xii, 157 p. : ISBN 0-88132-052-8 LC Card 87-21430 DDC 382/.41/0973 19
HD9006 .H28 1987

Paarlberg, Robert L. Fixing farm trade . Cambridge, Mass. , c1988. xiv, 159 p. ; ISBN 0-88730-196-7 LC Card 87-24118 DDC 382/.41/0973 19
HD9006 .P27 1988

PRODUCE TRADE - GOVERNMENT POLICY - UNITED STATES - CONGRESSES.
Confrontation or negotiation . Millwood, N.Y. , 1985. xvi, 303 p. : ISBN 0-8046-9397-8 : LC Card 85-18667 DDC 382/.41/094 19
HD9015.E82 C67 1985
NYPL [JLE 86-4594]

Ninth Federal Reserve District Farm Forum (1965 : Minneapolis, Minn.) Farm Forum of the Ninth Federal Reserve District . Hopkins, Minn. [1965] 99 p. : LC Card 87-110732
HD9007.A14 N56 1965

PRODUCE TRADE - GREECE.
Delēs, Dēmētrēs I. Hē anaptyxē tēs hellēnikēs geōrgias . Athēna , 1985. 3 v. in 2 : LC Card 86-203175
HD2055.5 .D44 1985

PRODUCE TRADE - GREECE - DIRECTORIES.
Hodēgos geōrgikōn viomēchaniōn. Athēna , 1985. 510 p. : LC Card 86-193419
HD9015.G82 H58 1985

PRODUCE TRADE - GREECE - FINANCE.
Baltas, Nik. K. Chrēmatodotēsē ependyseōn tou agrotikou tomea . Athēna , 1984. 142 p. ; LC Card 86-201892
HD2055.5 .B35 1984

PRODUCE TRADE - HUNGARY.
Éliás, András. Mezőgazdasági és élelmiszeripari termékeink a külpiaci versenyben /. Budapest , 1985. 197 p. ; ISBN 963-232-064-6 : LC Card 86-185883
HD9015.H82 E59 1985

Forgács, Katalin. A zöldség-gyümölcs szindróma . Budapest , 1986. 134, [1] p. ; ISBN 963-221-901-5 : LC Card 87-148760
HD9220.H82 F67 1986

PRODUCE TRADE - ILLINOIS - FINANCE.
Seger, Daniel J. Financing Illinois agricultural exports /. [Urbana?] [1985] 74 p. : LC Card 86-621070 DDC 382/.63 19
HD9007.I3 S44 1985

PRODUCE TRADE - INDIA, SOUTH - HISTORY.
Bohle, Hans-Georg. Südindische Wochenmarktsysteme . Stuttgart , 1986. 290 p. : ISBN 3-515-04601-1 LC Card 87-136147 DDC 381/.18/09548 19
HF5475.I42 S682 1986

PRODUCE TRADE - ISLAMIC COUNTRIES - STATISTICS.
Quazi, Mohammed Hanif. Food insecurity in the Muslim world /. Jeddah, Saudi Arabia (P.O. Box 9833, Jeddah) , 1985. 21, [26] p. : LC Card 87-133798 DDC 338.1/9/17671 19
HD9018.I84 Q39 1985

PRODUCE TRADE - IVORY COAST.
Trueblood, Michael A. The Ivory Coast . Washington, DC , 1986. iv, 32 p. : LC Card 86-602806 DDC 338.1 s 382/.41/096668 19
HD1411 .F59 no. 223 HD9017.I912

PRODUCE TRADE - LATIN AMERICA.
Arroyo, Gonzalo. Agricultura y alimentos en América Latina . México, D.F. , 1985. 267 p. ; ISBN 968-8373-33-8 LC Card 86-208283
HD9014.L32 A77 1985

Basco, Carlos A. El comercio intrarregional de alimentos básicos. [S.l.] , 1986. xi, 558 p. : LC Card 87-404784 DDC 382/.41/098 19
HD9014.L32 B37 1986

PRODUCE TRADE - MALAYSIA.
Profile of the primary commodity sector in Malaysia. [Kuala Lumpur] [1984] 77 p. : LC Card 86-945653 DDC 338.09595 19
HD9016.M32 P76 1984

PRODUCE TRADE - MATHEMATICAL MODELS.
Sapounas, Giōrgos S. Epharmosmenē analysē tēs zētēsēs . Athēna , 1985. 483 p. : LC Card 86-212306
HD9000.5 .S29 1985

Thompson, Robert L. A survey of recent U. S. developments in international agricultural trade models /. Washington, D.C. , 1981. v, 74 p. ; LC Card 81-603138 DDC 382/.41/0973 19
HD1433 .T48 ***NYPL [JLF 84-568]***

PRODUCE TRADE - MEXICO.
Mares, David R. Penetrating the international market . New York , 1987. xvi, 294 p. : ISBN 0-231-06346-6 (alk. paper) LC Card 87-6358 DDC 382/.415/097232 19
HD9014.M62 M38 1987

Rama, Ruth. Las relaciones económicas México-Estados Unidos . Miami, FL (Tamiami Trail, Miami 33199) [1984] 55 p. ; LC Card 85-226824
HD9014.M62 R36 1984

PRODUCE TRADE - MOROCCO.
Qarouach, Mostafa. L'agriculture marocaine face au deuxième élargissement de la CEE /. [S.l.] 1983 (Casablanca : Editions maghrébines) 117 p. ; LC Card 83-192279 DDC 382/.41/0964 19
HD9017.M82 Q37 1983
NYPL [JLD 86-4326]

PRODUCE TRADE - MOZAMBIQUE.
Caballero, Lorenzo. Mozambique, food and agriculture sector /. Uppsala , 1984. 223, [30] p. : ISBN 91-576-2129-2 (pbk.) LC Card 86-218958 DDC 338.1/0967/9 19
HD9017.M86 C33 1984

PRODUCE TRADE - NETHERLANDS.
Plas, W. Inventaris van het archief van Regeringscommissariaat voor de Buitenlandse Agrarische Aangelegenheden (RECOBAA), 1946-1950 /. [Hague] [1985] 111 p. ; LC Card 87-101964
HD9015.N42 P55 1985

PRODUCE TRADE - NIGERIA.
Mabbs-Zeno, Carl. Nigeria . Washington, D.C. [1986] vi, 54 p. : LC Card 86-601597 DDC 382/.41/09669 19
HD9017.N52 M3 1986

PRODUCE TRADE - PERU - CONGRESSES.
Agricultura y alimentación . [Lima] , 1982. 536 p. : LC Card 83-174688 DDC 338.1/9/85 19
HD9014.P52 A57 1982 ***NYPL [JLD 86-268]***

PRODUCE TRADE - PHILIPPINES.
Hawes, Gary, 1950- The Philippine State and the Marcos regime . Ithaca , 1987. 196 p. ; ISBN 0-8014-2012-1 (alk. paper) LC Card 86-29237 DDC 382/.41/09599 19
HD9016.P52 H38 1987

PRODUCE TRADE - PHILIPPINES - HISTORY - STATISTICS.
Selected statistics on rice & corn . Diliman, Quezon City [1969] xxix, 306 p. : LC Card 87-400545 DDC 338.1/7315/09599021 19
HD9066.P62 S45 1969

PRODUCE TRADE - RUSSIA.
Deutsch, Robert. The food revolution in the Soviet Union and Eastern Europe /. Boulder , 1986. xxii, 256 p. : ISBN 0-8133-7161-9 (pbk.) : LC Card 85-26625 DDC 338.1/9/47 19
HD9015.S652 D47 1986
NYPL [JLE 86-1588]

PRODUCE TRADE - SIERRA LEONE - BO (DISTRICT)
Yearwood, John. Storage facilities in the chiefdoms of Bo and Pujehun District /. Bo [1983] vi, 31 leaves : LC Card 87-110214 DDC 338.1/6 19
HD9017.S53 B599 1983

PRODUCE TRADE - SIERRA LEONE - PUJEHUN (DISTRICT)
Yearwood, John. Storage facilities in the chiefdoms of Bo and Pujehun District /. Bo [1983] vi, 31 leaves : LC Card 87-110214 DDC 338.1/6 19
HD9017.S53 B599 1983

PRODUCE TRADE - SOUTH AFRICA - CONGRESSES.
1985-bedryfskongresse =. [South Africa] [1985?] 1 v. (various pagings) ; LC Card 85-206777
HD9017.S72 A14 1985

PRODUCE TRADE - TURKEY.
Hale, William M. Turkish agriculture and Community enlargement /. [Ankara] , 1984. 37 p. ; LC Card 87-113782 DDC 338.9561 s 338.1/09561 19
HC401 .A356 no. 1949 HD9016.T82

PRODUCE TRADE - UNITED STATES.
Agricultural marketing handbook for Caribbean Basin products. Spanish. Manual--mercadeo de productos agrícolas de la Cuenca del Caribe /. San José, Costa Rica . x, 434 p. : ISBN 92-9039-101-4 LC Card 86-204686
HD9014.C442 A4718 1986

Coyle, Barry. Economic gains from agricultural trade . Washington, D.C. [Springfield, VA , 1986] iii, 41 p. : LC Card 86-602417 DDC 382/.41/0973 19
HD9005 .C86 1986

Federal marketing programs in agriculture . Danville, Ill. , c1983. x, 326 p. ; ISBN 0-8134-2292-2 : LC Card 83-80130
NYPL [JLE 86-4572]

Japanese import barriers to U. S. agricultural exports and the Common agricultural policy of the European Community and implications for U. S. agricultural trade . Washington , 1986. vii, 65 p. : LC Card 87-601384 DDC 382/.5/0952 19
HF1601 .J363 1986

Kohls, Richard L. Marketing of agricultural products /. New York , London , c1985. xi, 624 p. : ISBN 0-02-365670-0 LC Card 84-817 DDC 381/.41 19
HD9000.5 .K57 1985 ***NYPL [JLE 86-4145]***

Mares, David R. Penetrating the international market . New York , 1987. xvi, 294 p. : ISBN 0-231-06346-6 (alk. paper) LC Card 87-6358 DDC 382/.415/097232 19
HD9014.M62 M38 1987

Rama, Ruth. Las relaciones económicas México-Estados Unidos . Miami, FL (Tamiami Trail, Miami 33199) [1984] 55 p. ; LC Card 85-226824
HD9014.M62 R36 1984

Trueblood, Michael A. The Ivory Coast . Washington, DC , 1986. iv, 32 p. : LC Card 86-602806 DDC 338.1 s 382/.41/096668 19
HD1411 .F59 no. 223 HD9017.I912

U. S. agriculture & Third World development . Boulder , 1987. xi, 258 p. ; ISBN 1-555-87011-2 (lib. bdg.) : LC Card 86-29860 DDC 338.1/09172/4 19
HD1765 .U15 1987

PRODUCE TRADE - UNITED STATES - CONGRESSES.
Economic efficiency in agricultural and food marketing /. Ames , 1987. xii, 315 p. ; ISBN 0-8138-0533-3 LC Card 87-2821 DDC 381/.41/0973 19
HD9000.5 .E26 1987

U. S. agriculture and Third World economic development . Washington, D.C. , c1987. xv, 103 p. : ISBN 0-89068-086-8 (pbk.): LC Card 86-62757 DDC 338.9/009172/4 19
HD1755 .U173 1987

PRODUCE TRADE - UNITED STATES - STATISTICS.
Retail produce operations, 1986 /. Washington, D.C. (1750 K. St., N.W. Washington 20006) , Newark, Del. [1986] viii, 20 p. ; LC Card 87-101803 DDC 381/.456648/00973 19
HD9321.4 .R47 1986

PRODUCE TRADE - URUGUAY - STATISTICS.
Estadísticas agropecuarias. Montevideo, República Oriental del Uruguay , 1979. [79] p. ; LC Card 82-209370
HD9014.U82 E78 1979

Producer consumer dialogue : opinion / Economic and Social Committee of the European Communities. Brussels : The Committee, [1984] ii, 55 p. ; 21 cm. "October 1984." LC Card 85-178866 DDC 381/.34/094 19
1. Consumer protection - European Economic Community countries. 2. Environmental policy - European Economic Community countries. I. Economic and Social Committee of the European Communities.
HC240.9.C63 P77 1984 ***NYPL [JLD 86-2369]***

PRODUCER COOPERATIVES - AFRICA.
Policies and measures to promote industrial co-operatives in Africa /. [New York] [1985] 23 p. ; LC Card 87-104469 DDC 334/.6/096 19
HD3247 .P65 1985

PRODUCER COOPERATIVES - BRAZIL - STATISTICS.
As Cooperativas na balança comercial brasileira . [Brasília] [1986] 98 p. : LC Card 87-403826 DDC 334/.63/0981021 19
HF3401.5 .C66 1986

PRODUCER COOPERATIVES - DENMARK.
Nørrung, Per. The producing commune /. Aalborg Ø., Denmark , 1985. 39 p. ; ISBN 87-88353-11-7 (pbk.) LC Card 87-100060 DDC 334/.6/09489 19
HD3209.A4 N67 1985

PRODUCER COOPERATIVES - ETHIOPIA.
Habtamu Wondimu. Some factors which affect peasant motivation to work in the Ethiopian agricultural producers cooperatives /. [Addis Ababa] [1983] 60 leaves : LC Card 84-980911 DDC 334/.683/0963 19
HD1491.E83 H3 1983b ***NYPL [JLG 86-163]***

Tegegne Teke. Cooperatives and national development . Addis Ababa, Ethiopia [1984] iii, 57 leaves ; LC Card 85-980411 DDC 334/.683/0963 19
HD1491.E83 T44 1984 ***NYPL [JLG 86-173]***

PRODUCER COOPERATIVES - EUROPEAN ECONOMIC COMMUNITY COUNTRIES.
Buiren, S. van. The quantitative and qualitative significance of the emergence of local initiatives for employment creation . Luxembourg , Washington, D.C. , 1986. iii, 141, 14, [12] p. : ISBN 92-825-6048-1 (pbk.) : LC Card 86-222030 DDC 331.12/042/094 19
HD5764.5.A6 B85 1986

PRODUCER COOPERATIVES - FRANCE.
Programme of research and actions on the development of the labour market . Luxembourg , Washington, DC , 1986. 1 v. (various pagings) : ISBN 92-825-6077-5 (pbk.) : LC Card 86-216010 DDC 334/.6/094 19
HD3184 .P76 1986

PRODUCER COOPERATIVES - GERMANY (WEST)
Janetzki, Annemarie. Das Verbundwinzersystem . Münster , 1982. xxiv, 406 p., [3] folded leaves of plates : ISBN 3-7923-0486-4 LC Card 83-157892
HD9383.5 .J35 1982

PRODUCER COOPERATIVES - GERMANY (WEST) - BREMEN REGION - HISTORY.
Selbsthilfe zum Beispiel . Hannover , 1984. 264 p. : ISBN 3-921951-18-6 LC Card 85-233577
HD3190.A3 L687 1984

PRODUCER COOPERATIVES - GERMANY (WEST) - LOWER SAXONY - HISTORY.
Selbsthilfe zum Beispiel . Hannover , 1984. 264 p. : ISBN 3-921951-18-6 LC Card 85-233577
HD3190.A3 L687 1984

PRODUCER COOPERATIVES - GHANA.
Dadson, J. A. Production co-operatives and rural development in Ghana /. [Addis Ababa] [1985] 53 p. ; LC Card 87-105501 DDC 334/.6/09667 19
HD3258.3.A4 D34 1985

PRODUCER COOPERATIVES - GREAT BRITAIN.
Programme of research and actions on the development of the labour market . Luxembourg , Washington, DC , 1986. 1 v. (various pagings) : ISBN 92-825-6077-5 (pbk.) : LC Card 86-216010 DDC 334/.6/094 19
HD3184 .P76 1986

PRODUCER COOPERATIVES - HUNGARY.
Bennó, Pál. A bedolgozás helye és szerepe, perspektívája a szövetkezeti iparban . Budapest , 1985. 153 p. ; LC Card 85-226119
HD2336.H9 B46 1985

Kőhegyi, Kálmán. Az ipari szövetkezetek összevonásai a 70-es években /. [Budapest] [1983] 119 p. ; LC Card 86-145163
HD3182.5.A4 K64 1983

PRODUCER COOPERATIVES - ITALY.
Programme of research and actions on the development of the labour market . Luxembourg , Washington, DC , 1986. 1 v. (various pagings) : ISBN 92-825-6077-5 (pbk.) : LC Card 86-216010 DDC 334/.6/094 19
HD3184 .P76 1986

PRODUCER COOPERATIVES - NORTHWEST, PACIFIC - MANAGEMENT - EMPLOYEE PARTICIPATION - CASE STUDIES.
Greenberg, Edward S., 1942- Workplace democracy . Ithaca , 1986. 257 p. ; ISBN 0-8014-1921-2 (alk. paper) LC Card 86-47641 DDC 674/.834/068 19
HD5658.P622 U554 1986
NYPL [JLE 86-4586]

PRODUCER COOPERATIVES - SPAIN - MADRID.
Vara Miranda, Ma. Jesús (María Jesús) Análisis de las cooperativas de trabajo asociado en Madrid /. [Madrid] , c1985. 463 p. : ISBN 84-7434-332-1 LC Card 87-109103 DDC 334/.6/094643 19
HD3218.M38 V37 1985

The producing commune /. Nørrung, Per. Aalborg Ø., Denmark , 1985. 39 p. ; ISBN 87-88353-11-7 (pbk.) LC Card 87-100060 DDC 334/.6/09489 19
HD3209.A4 N67 1985

Producing lower income housing : local initiatives / James Pickman ... [et al.]. Washington, D.C. : Bureau of National Affairs, c1986. xiv, 373 p. ; 23 cm. Includes index. ISBN 0-87179-533-7 (pbk.) LC Card 86-26424 DDC 363.5/ 19
1. Public housing - United States. 2. Public housing - United States - Finance. 3. Housing, Cooperative - United States. I. Pickman, James. II. Bureau of National Affairs, Washington, D. C.
HD7288.78.U5 P76 1986

PRODUCT CODING EQUIPMENT INDUSTRY.
Delson, Erwin B. The bar coding systems industry. New York, N.Y. , c1986. 1 v. (various pagings) : ISBN 0-931634-64-4 (pbk.) LC Card 87-156445 DDC 380.1/45621399 19
HD9801.6.P762 D45 1986

PRODUCT CODING VERIFICATION EQUIPMENT INDUSTRY - UNITED STATES.
Bar code markets . Norwalk, Conn., U. S.A. (6 Prowitt St., Norwalk 06855) , c1987. iv, 221 leaves : LC Card 87-401927 DDC 381/.45621399 19
HD9801.6.P763 U624 1987

PRODUCT COUNTERFEITING.
Freemantle, Brian. The steal . London , 1986. xi, 244 p. ; ISBN 0-7181-2584-3 : LC Card 87-105381 DDC 364.1/63 19
HD38.7 .F74 1986

Product differentiation and non-price competition /. Ireland, Norman J. Oxford, UK , New York, NY, USA , 1987. 192 p. : ISBN 0-631-13846-3 : LC Card 86-24504 DDC 658.8/16 19
HF5415.15 .I74 1987

Product differentiation & non-price competition. Ireland, Norman J. Product differentiation and non-price competition /. Oxford, UK , New York, NY, USA , 1987. 192 p. : ISBN 0-631-13846-3 : LC Card 86-24504 DDC 658.8/16 19
HF5415.15 .I74 1987

PRODUCT DIVERSIFICATION. see **DIVERSIFICATION IN INDUSTRY.**

PRODUCT LIFE CYCLE - CONGRESSES.
Carpenter, Gregory. Business strategy and the life cycle concept . Cambridge, Mass. (1000 Massachusetts Ave., Cambridge 02138) [1985] [19] leaves ; LC Card 87-108925 DDC 658.5/038 19
HF5415.155 .C37 1985

PRODUCT MANAGEMENT - DECISION MAKING.
Kilhey, Ulrike. Die Beurteilung des Erfolgs von Bankprodukten als Grundlage produktpolitischer Entscheidungen /. Frankfurt am Main , c1987. xiv, 289 p. : ISBN 3-7819-0374-5 LC Card 87-136157 DDC 332.1/068/5 19
HF5415.15 .K55 1987

PRODUCT MANAGEMENT - ENVIRONMENTAL ASPECTS.
Thomé, Gotthardt, 1949- Produktgestaltung und Ökologie /. München , c1981. xii, 212 p. : ISBN 3-88259-086-6 : LC Card 81-146058
HD69.N4 T54 1981 ***NYPL [JLD 86-2800]***

Product publicity sources. The National directory of product publicity sources /. Westbury, N.Y. , 1987. p. cm. ISBN 0-87280-157-8 : LC Card 87-17542 DDC 338.7/616592/025 19
HD59 .N245 1987

PRODUCT QUALITY. see **QUALITY OF PRODUCTS.**

Product standardization and competitive strategy / edited by H. Landis Gabel. Amsterdam ; New York : North-Holland ; xii, 316 p. : ill. ; 23 cm. (Advanced series in management . v. 11) Includes bibliographies. ISBN 0-444-70232-6(U. S.) LC Card 87-8849 DDC 338/.02 19
1. Standardization. 2. Competition. I. Gabel, H. Landis. II. Series.
HD62 .P75 1987

PRODUCTION. see **INDUSTRY.**

Production and decision theory under uncertainty /. Aiginger, Karl. Oxford [Oxfordshire] , New York, NY, USA , 1987. p. cm. ISBN 0-631-14792-6 : LC Card 87-23854 DDC 338.5 19
HB241 .A52 1987

Production by the masses . Dāśagupta, Pānnālāla, 1909- Calcutta , 1983. vi, 54 p. ; LC Card 83-906787 DDC 331.11/8/0954 19
HC440.I52 D37 1983 ***NYPL [JLD 87-708]***

PRODUCTION CONTROL - DATA PROCESSING.
Computer models for production and inventory control /. La Jolla, Calif. , c1984. ix, 148 p. : LC Card 84-189641 DDC 658.5/0028/54 19
TS157 .C63 1984 ***NYPL [JSF 86-930]***

PRODUCTION CONTROL - MATHEMATICAL MODELS.
Computer models for production and inventory control /. La Jolla, Calif. , c1984. ix, 148 p. : LC Card 84-189641 DDC 658.5/0028/54 19
TS157 .C63 1984 ***NYPL [JSF 86-930]***

PRODUCTION, COOPERATIVE. see **COOPERATION; PRODUCER COOPERATIVES.**

Production co-operatives and rural development in Ghana /. Dadson, J. A. [Addis Ababa] [1985] 53 p. ; LC Card 87-105501 DDC 334/.6/09667 19
HD3258.3.A4 D34 1985

Production costs for cereals in the European community . Stanton, B. F. (Bernard Freeland), 1925- Ithaca, N.Y. [1986] 178 p., 2 p. of plates : LC Card 86-622607 DDC 338.1/331/094 19
HD9045.E82 S73 1986

PRODUCTION (ECONOMIC THEORY)
Bató, Sándor. Az áru mint történelmi kategória /. [Budapest] , 1985. 104 p. ; ISBN 963-673-332-5 LC Card 86-228016
HB97.5 .B3245 1985

Chambers, Robert G. Applied production

analysis /. Cambridge [Cambridgeshire] , New York , 1988. p. cm. ISBN 0-521-30699-X LC Card 87-12511 DDC 338.5 19
HB241 .C452 1988

Chiang, Hsüeh-mo. She hui chu i so yu chih yen chiu /. Hang-chou , 1985. [3], 211 p. ;
*NYPL [*OVL 86-3601]*

Christoffersen, Mads. Fysisk planlægning og samfundsmæssige reproduktionsproblemer . København , 1980, c1979. 317 p. ; ISBN 87-500-1922-8 *NYPL [JLD 86-2303]*

Costa, Beatriz B. O trabalhador e a produção hoje . Petrópolis , Rio de Janeiro, RJ, Brasil , 1985. 78 p. ; LC Card 86-150042 DDC 331.11/8 19
HC79.L3 C67 1985

Folom'ev, A. N. (Aleksandr Nikolaevich) Orudiia truda . Moskva , 1984. 107, [4] p. ; LC Card 85-138858
HC336.25 .F64 1984

Haupt, Reinhard. Produktionstheorie und Ablaufmanagement . Stuttgart , c1987. xiv, 217 p. : ISBN 3-7910-0398-4 LC Card 87-134161 DDC 338.6 19
HB241 .H37 1987

Liu, Shih-pai. She hui chu i so yu chih yen chiu /. Shang-hai , 1985. 2, 6, 223 p. ;
*NYPL [*OVY 86-3647]*

Mummery, A. F. (Albert Frederick), 1855-1895. The physiology of industry . Fairfield, NJ , 1988. p. cm. ISBN 0-678-00673-3 LC Card 87-17943 DDC 330.1 19
HB171 .M95 1988

Ricketts, Martin J. The economics of business enterprise . Brighton, Sussex , 1987. xii, 306 p. : ISBN 0-7108-0221-8 : LC Card 87-104594 DDC 338.5 19
HD2731 .R53 1987

Romitelli, Valerio. Critica dell'economia politica e teoria delle forze produttive /. Milano , c1982. 241 p. ; LC Card 82-200332 DDC 338.5 19
HB241 .R66 1982 *NYPL [JLD 87-812]*

Roski, Reinhold. Einsatz von Aggregaten, Modellierung und Planung /. Berlin , c1986. xi, 321 p. : ISBN 3-428-06038-5 LC Card 86-188767
HB241 .R67 1986

Tani, Piero. Analisi microeconomica della produzione /. Roma , 1986. viii, 351 p. : LC Card 86-169971
HB241 .T36 1986

PRODUCTION (ECONOMIC THEORY) - CONGRESSES.
Sheng ch'an li kuei lü yen chiu /. Pei-ching , 1985. 5, 3, 466 p. : LC Card 85-242399 DDC 335.4/12 19
HB241 .S519 1985 <Orien China>
*NYPL [*OVL 87-507]*

Uchenie K. Marksa ob ėtapakh razvitiia sposoba proizvodstva i problemy zrelogo sotsializma . Leningrad , 1985. 150 p. ; LC Card 86-140577
HB97.5 .U24 1985

PRODUCTION (ECONOMIC THEORY) - MATHEMATICAL MODELS. see **PRODUCTION FUNCTIONS (ECONOMIC THEORY)**

PRODUCTION ENGINEERING - DATA PROCESSING.
Computerized manufacturing automation [microform] . Washington, D.C. , 1984. 35 p. :
*NYPL [*ZV-326 no.31]*

PRODUCTION FUNCTIONS (ECONOMIC THEORY) - ECONOMETRIC MODELS.
Santos, José Carlos de Souza. Demanda de fatores, energia e substituição na indústria brasileira, 1970/79 /. São Paulo , 1986. 183 p. : LC Card 86-234783
HB241 .S26 1986

PRODUCTION FUNCTIONS (ECONOMIC THEORY) - MATHEMATICAL MODELS.
Ghosh, A., 1921- Income distribution and the structure of production /. New Delhi , c1984. ix, 186 p. ; LC Card 83-907762 DDC 339.2/0724 19
HB523 .G46 1984 *NYPL [JLD 86-4234]*

Püschel, Manfred, 1953- Die Wahl der optimalen Wärmeversorgungskonfiguration als betriebswirtschaftliches Produktions- und Investitionsproblem /. Frankfurt am Main , New York , c1984. iv, 298 p. : ISBN 3-8204-7432-3 LC Card 86-108875
HD30.25 .P87 1984

Production incentives in Philippine agriculture . Bautista, Romeo M., 1941- Washington, D.C., USA , c1987. 78 p. : ISBN 0-89629-061-1 (pbk.) LC Card 87-3233 DDC 338.1/8 19
HD2087 .B38 1987

PRODUCTION-LINE METHODS. see **ASSEMBLY-LINE METHODS.**

Production links in the agro-industrial sphere. Vŭlchev, Nikola. Proizvodstvenite vrŭzki v agrarno-promishlenata oblast /. Sofiia , 1986. 183 p. ; LC Card 86-195329
HD9015.B82 V84 1986

PRODUCTION MANAGEMENT - CASE STUDIES.
Schonberger, Richard. World class manufacturing casebook . New York , London , c1987. xxvi, 253 p. : ISBN 0-02-929340-5 LC Card 86-25822 DDC 658 19
HD31 .S3386 1987

PRODUCTION MANAGEMENT - JAPAN - CASE STUDIES.
Kyanon no seisan kakushin. English. Canon production system . Stamford, Conn. , c1987. xxi, 230 p. : ISBN 0-915299-06-2 : LC Card 85-63498 DDC 681/.418/0683 19
HD9708.5.C354 K92513 1987

PRODUCTION MANAGEMENT - MATHEMATICAL MODELS.
Ballot, Michael. Decision-making models in production & operations management /. Malabar, Fla. , 1986. xi, 295 p. : ISBN 0-89874-825-9 LC Card 84-29740 DDC 658.5/036 19
TS155 .B2435 1984 *NYPL [JLF 86-1851]*

The production of heavy crude oil reduces fuel oil imports in Suriname /. Jharap, S. E. Paramaribo, Suriname , 1985. [25] p. : LC Card 87-103716 DDC 338.4/76655/09883 19
HD9574.S752 J47 1985

PRODUCTION PLANNING - DECISION-MAKING.
Döring, Ulrich. Kostensteuern, der Einfluss von Steuern auf kurzfristige Produktions- und Absatzentscheidungen /. Stuttgart , c1984. x, 228 p. ; ISBN 3-7910-0369-0 LC Card 86-134925
HD2753.G3 D73 1984

PRODUCTION PLANNING - MATHEMATICAL MODELS.
Haupt, Reinhard. Produktionstheorie und Ablaufmanagement . Stuttgart , c1987. xiv, 217 p. : ISBN 3-7910-0398-4 LC Card 87-134161 DDC 338.6 19
HB241 .H37 1987

Production, power, and world order . Cox, Robert W., 1926- New York , 1987. xii, 500 p. ; ISBN 0-231-05808-X LC Card 86-26387
HD6971 .C78 1987

Production prices and dynamical processes of the gravitation of market prices /. Franke, Reiner. Frankfurt am Main , New York , c1987. 231 p. : ISBN 3-8204-9435-9 (pbk.) LC Card 87-170397 DDC 338/.01 19
HB171.S7253 F73 1987

PRODUCTION PROCESSES. see **MANUFACTURING PROCESSES.**

The Production, promotion, and marketing of Western Australian table grapes : proceedings, September 25 & 26, 1985, held at Mulberry Farm, Hamersley Road, Caversham. Perth, WA : Rural and Allied Industries Council, [1985] viii, 180 p. : ill. ; 30 cm. LC Card 87-120107 DDC 338.1/748/09941 19
1. Grape industry - Australia - Western Australia - Congresses. I. Rural and Allied Industries Council (W.A.).
HD9259.G7 A827 1985

La production sociale des femmes /. Coomans, Géry, 1949- Bruxelles , c1983. 223 p. : ISBN 2-8004-0820-0 : LC Card 84-199167
HD6158 .C66 1983

Production, work, territory : the geographical anatomy of industrial capitalism / edited by Allen J. Scott and Michael Storper. Boston : Allen & Unwin, 1986. xix, 344 p. : ill. ; 24 cm. Includes index. ISBN 0-04-338126-X (alk. paper) LC Card 85-20006 DDC 330 19
1. Economic history - 1971- - Addresses, essays, lectures. 2. Capitalism - Addresses, essays, lectures. 3. Regional economic disparities - Addresses, essays, lectures. I. Scott, Allen, John. II. Storper, Michael.
HC59 .P682 1986 *NYPL [JLE 86-1745]*

Productive workplaces . Weisbord, Marvin Ross. San Francisco , 1987. xxv, 405 p. : ISBN 1-555-42054-0 (alk. paper) LC Card 87-45425 DDC 658.3/14 19
HD31 .W424 1987

Productividad y participación : la experiencia de los círculos de participación en empresas colombianas / [editado por] Camilo Gaitán García, Carlos Dávila L. de Guevara, Luis Armando Zarruk Zarruk. [Bucaramanga, Colombia] : Talleres de la Cámara de Comercio de Bucaramanga, c1985. 165 p. : ill. ; 21 cm. Papers presented at the Primer Foro Nacional sobre Círculos de Participación organized by Hilanderías del Fonce, held in Bucaramanga, Colombia, June, 1983. Includes bibliographical references. ISBN 958-9302-15-6 LC Card 86-166141
1. Industrial management - Colombia - Employee participation - Congresses. 2. Work groups - Colombia - Congresses. I. Gaitán García, Camilo. II. Dávila L. de Guevara, Carlos. III. Zarruk Zarruk, Luis Armando. IV. Foro Nacional sobre Círculos de Participación (1st : 1983 : Bucaramanga, Colombia). V. Hilanderías del Fonce (Bucaramanga, Colombia).
HD5660.C7 P76 1985

Productivité dans l'industrie. Productivity in industry . Paris , 1986. 108 p. ; ISBN 92-64-12816-6 (pbk.) : LC Card 86-213264 DDC 338/.06 19
HC79.I52 P78 1986

PRODUCTIVITY ACCOUNTING.
Gerhardt, Jürgen. Dienstleistungsproduktion . Bergisch Gladbach , c1987. 251 p. ; ISBN 3-89012-075-X LC Card 87-141416 DDC 338.4/6 19
HD9980.5 .G46 1987

Pucci, Carlos. Los precios sociales en la evaluación de proyectos en Costa Rica /. San José, Costa Rica , 1979. [108] leaves ; LC Card 83-238167
HC143.Z9 L36 1979

PRODUCTIVITY, AGRICULTURAL. see **AGRICULTURAL PRODUCTIVITY.**

Productivity and human factors in construction / edited by Peter R. Lansley and Peter A. Harlow. London ; New York : E. & F.N. Spon, 1987. p. cm. (Managing construction worldwide . v. 2) Bibliography: p. Includes index. ISBN 0-419-14010-7 LC Card 87-20547 DDC 624/.068 s 624/.068/3 19
1. Construction industry - Labor productivity - Congresses. 2. Construction industry - Labor productivity - Case studies - Congresses. I. Lansley, Peter R. II. Harlow, P. A. (Peter Alan). III. Series.
HD9715.A2 M296 vol. 2

Productivity and role of top management. Tokyo : Asian Productivity Organization, 1986. x, 94 p. : ill. ; 26 cm. Papers presented at a forum held in March 1985 in Tokyo. ISBN 92-833-2041-1 (pbk.) LC Card 87-146526 DDC 658.3/14/0952 19
1. Industrial productivity - Japan - Congresses. 2. Industrial management - Japan - Congresses. I. Asian Productivity Organization.
HC465.I52 P76 1986

Productivity and the quality of working life /. Parnes, Steven. Scarsdale, N.Y. , c1978. 43 p. ; LC Card 78-51009 DDC 658.31/4
HD57 .P33 *NYPL [JLM 83-380 no.2]*

Productivity and the self-fulfilling prophecy [motion picture] : the Pygmalion effect / McGraw-Hill Training Systems ; [produced by] CRM Productions, Inc. ; writers, Kirby Timmons, Joan Owens.2nd ed. Del Mar, CA : McGraw-Hill Training Systems, 1987. 1 film reel (27 min.) : sd., col. ; 16 mm. + 1 leader's guide. Title from data sheet. Management training classes and senior high school through college students. Issued also as videorecording. Explores the Pygmalion effect: the notion that the prediction or expectation of an event can actually cause it to happen. Explains the evolution of this self-fulfilling prophecy, and shows how a leader's expectations alone can influence another person's performance. The four-factor theory of how expectations are transmitted is also discussed. LC Card 87-700078 DDC 658.4 11
1. Incentives in industry. 2. Employee motivation. 3.

Supervision of employees. 4. Interpersonal relations. I. McGraw-Hill Training Systems (Firm). II. CRM Productions.
HF5549.5.I5

Productivity and the self-fulfilling prophecy [videorecording] : the Pygmalion effect / McGraw-Hill Training Systems ; [produced by] CRM Productions, Inc. ; writers, Kirby Timmons, Joan Owens.2nd ed. Del Mar, CA : McGraw-Hill Training Systems, 1987. 1 videocassette (27 min.) : sd., col. + 1 leader's guide. Title from data sheet. Management training classes and senior high school through college students. Issued as U-matic 3/4 in. or VHS 1/2 in. Issued also as motion picture. Explores the Pygmalion effect: the notion that the prediction or expectation of an event can actually cause it to happen. Explains the evolution of this self-fulfilling prophecy, and shows how a leader's expectations alone can influence another person's performance. The four-factor theory of how expectations are transmitted is also discussed. LC Card 87-700079 DDC 658.4 11
1. Incentives in industry. 2. Employee motivation. 3. Supervision of employees. 4. Interpersonal relations. I. CRM Productions.
HF5549.5.I5

Productivity and U. S. economic growth /. Jorgenson, Dale Weldeau, 1933- Cambridge, Mass. , 1987. 567 p. : ISBN 0-674-71175-0 (alk. paper) LC Card 87-12098 DDC 338/.06/0973 19
HC110.I52 J67 1987

Productivity and US economic growth. Jorgenson, Dale Weldeau, 1933- Productivity and U. S. economic growth /. Cambridge, Mass. , 1987. 567 p. : ISBN 0-674-71175-0 (alk. paper) LC Card 87-12098 DDC 338/.06/0973 19
HC110.I52 J67 1987

Productivity and value . Dovring, Folke. New York , 1987. vii, 194 p. ; ISBN 0-275-92668-0 (alk. paper) : LC Card 87-2347 DDC 338/.06 19
HC79.I52 D68 1987

PRODUCTIVITY BARGAINING - GREAT BRITAIN.
The Future of pay determination . London [1977] 56 p. ; LC Card 84-255776 DDC 331.2/15 19
HD5015 .F88 1977

Productivity centers . Limp, Wolfgang. Frankfurt am Main , 1975. 64 p. ; LC Card 82-219310
HD30.4 .L55 1975

PRODUCTIVITY CENTERS. see **INDUSTRIAL PRODUCTIVITY CENTERS.**

Productivity growth in Indian industry /. Goldar, B. N. New Delhi , 1986, c1985. xvi, 206 p. ; ISBN 81-7023-062-4 : LC Card 86-902812 DDC 338/.06/0954 19
HC440.I52 G65 1986

Productivity growth in Philippine manufacturing . Hooley, Richard W., 1925- [Manila?] , c1985. ix, 128 p. : LC Card 87-112014 DDC 338.4/769/09599 19
HC460.I52 H66 1985

Productivity improvement and its effects on the level of employment and working conditions in the iron and steel industry /. International Labour Organisation. Iron and Steel Committee. Geneva , 1986. ii, 66 p. : ISBN 92-2-105498-5 (pbk.) : LC Card 86-222063 DDC 338.4/56691 19
HD9510.5 .I525 1986

Productivity improvement management . Bialek, Jacques, 1919- San Francisco [c1986] 339 p. ; ISBN 0-941883-01-9 (pbk.) : LC Card 87-6557 DDC 658.5 19
HD56 .B49 1986

Productivity in industry : prospects and policies. Paris : Organisation for Economic Co-operation and Development, 1986. 108 p. ; 23 cm. Title on verso t.p.: La productivité dans l'industrie. Bibliography: p. 70-78. ISBN 92-64-12816-6 (pbk.) : LC Card 86-213264 DDC 338/.06 19
1. Industrial productivity. 2. Labor productivity. 3. Efficiency, Industrial. I. Organisation for Economic Co-operation and Development. II. Title: Productivité dans l'industrie.
HC79.I52 P78 1986

PRODUCTIVITY, INDUSTRIAL. see **INDUSTRIAL PRODUCTIVITY.**

PRODUCTIVITY OF CAPITAL. see **CAPITAL PRODUCTIVITY.**

PRODUCTIVITY OF LABOR. see **LABOR PRODUCTIVITY.**

Productivity plus /. Belcher, John G. Houston , 1987. p. cm. ISBN 0-87201-451-7 LC Card 87-9222 DDC 658.3/14 19
HD56 .B45 1987

The Productivity sourcebook / edited by Richard W. Beatty, H. John Bernardin, James E. Nickel. Amherst, Mass. : Human Resource Development Press, [1987] x, 467 p. : ill. ; 28 cm. Includes bibliographies. ISBN 0-87425-075-7 (pbk.) LC Card 87-404037 DDC 658.3/14 19
1. Labor productivity - United States. 2. Incentives in industry - United States. 3. Industrial management - United States. I. Beatty, Richard W. II. Bernardin, H. John. III. Nickel, James E.
HD57 .P7114 1987

Productivity, supervision, and morale in an office situation, part I /. Katz, Daniel, 1903- New York , 1987, c1950. vii, 84 p. ; ISBN 0-8240-8211-7 (alk. paper) : LC Card 86-25804 DDC 658.3 19
HF5549 .K282 1987

Productivity, technology, and industrial development . Pack, Howard. New York , c1987. x, 193 p. : ISBN 0-19-520543-X : LC Card 86-33271 DDC 331.11/8 19
HD9870.5 .P25 1987

Productivity versus OSHA and EPA regulations /. Gray, Wayne B. (Wayne Burger), 1955- Ann Arbor, Mich. , c1986. xii, p. : ISBN 0-8357-1721-6 (alk. paper) LC Card 85-28873 DDC 338/.06/0973 19
HC110.I52 G73 1986 ***NYPL [JLE 86-2375]***

Producto bruto geográfico : Provincia de Río Negro, 1970-1975. [Viedma, Argentina] : Secretaría de Planeamiento, Dirección de Estadística y Censos, 1977. 153 p. ; 22 cm. Bibliography: p. 39. LC Card 79-107106
1. Gross national product - Argentina - Río Negro - Statistics. I. Río Negro (Argentina). Dirección de Estadística y Censos.
HC177.R5 P76 1977

Producto interno bruto y gasto, cuaderno 1970-1979. [Mexico City] : Banco de México, Subdirección de Investigación Económica, [1980] 123 p. ; 21 x 28 cm. (Información económica) Cover title. Chiefly tables. "IPI/BG. 003-00-10-80." LC Card 82-197714
1. Gross national product - Mexico - Statistics. 2. Input-output tables - Mexico. I. Banco de México (1925-). Subdirección de Investigación Económica. II. Series.
HC140.I5 P76 1980

PRODUCTS, COMMERCIAL. see **COMMERCIAL PRODUCTS.**

PRODUCTS, MANUFACTURED. see **MANUFACTURES.**

PRODUCTS, NEW. see **NEW PRODUCTS.**

Produits alimentaires et des boissons de la Suisse. Lebensmittel und Getränke aus der Schweiz =. Zürich , 1984. 113 p. : ISBN 0-390-92140-3 ***NYPL [JFE 86-3409]***

Produktbeurteilung der Konsumenten . Bleicker, Ulrike. Würzburg , c1983. 245 p. : ISBN 3-7908-0292-1 LC Card 83-191583
HF5415.3 .B52 1983

Produkteigenschaften und das Nachfrageverhalten von Konsumenten . Riepe, Claudia. Thun , c1984. 341 p. : ISBN 3-87144-841-9 LC Card 85-113523
HB801 .R45 1984

Produktgestaltung und Ökologie /. Thomé, Gotthardt, 1949- München , c1981. xii, 212 p. : ISBN 3-88259-086-6 : LC Card 81-146058
HD69.N4 T54 1981 ***NYPL [JLD 86-2800]***

Produktion, Intensivierung, Effektivität / herausgegeben von der Sektion Wirtschaftswissenschaften, Wissenschaftsbereich Sozialistische Betriebswirtschaft der Friedrich-Schiller-Universität Jena. Jena : Die Universität, 1978. 180 p. : ill. ; 21 cm. (Wissenschaftliche Beiträge der Friedrich-Schiller-Univeritát Jena) Includes bibliographical references. LC Card 85-183724
1. Industrial productivity - Germany, East. 2. Central planning - Germany (East). 3. Germany, East - Economic policy. I. Friedrich-Schiller-Universität Jena. Sektion Wirtschaftswissenschaften. II. Series.
HC290.795.I52 P75 1978

Die Produktion von Dienstleistungen . Corsten, Hans. Berlin , c1985. xii, 439 p. : ISBN 3-503-02523-5 LC Card 86-113978 DDC 658 19
HD9980.5 .C67 1985

Produktionstheorie und Ablaufmanagement . Haupt, Reinhard. Stuttgart , c1987. xiv, 217 p. : ISBN 3-7910-0398-4 LC Card 87-134161 DDC 338.6 19
HB241 .H37 1987

Die Produktionsverhältnisse /. Friedrich, Horst, 1935- Berlin , 1981. 228 p. ; LC Card 81-175348
HC79.I52 F75 1981

Produktivitätslücken nach Wirtschaftszweigen im internationalen Vergleich . Conrad, Klaus, 1940- Berlin , New York , c1985. 165 p. ; ISBN 0-387-15571-6 (U. S.) LC Card 85-233665
HC110.I52 C67 1985

Produktivitätswachstum und Umweltschutz /. Seyfried, Manfred, 1957- Frankfurt am Main , New York , c1986. x, 198 p. : ISBN 3-8204-8985-1 LC Card 86-195597
HC79.I52 S49 1986

Der Produktivitätszuwachs als Massstab für eine beschäftigungsorientierte Lohnpolitik . Wansleben, Martin. Baden-Baden , 1986. 153 p. : ISBN 3-7890-1312-9 LC Card 87-128291 DDC 331.1/18 19
HD4945 .W36 1986

Produktwettbewerb und Dienstleistungsfreiheit auf Versicherungsmärkten /. Eggerstedt, Harald. Berlin , c1987. 320 p. : ISBN 3-428-06167-5 LC Card 87-143175 DDC 368/.94 19
HG8593.5.Z75 E34 1987

Produto interno bruto do Paraná, 1970-84 / Fundação Edison Vieira, Instituto Paranaense de Desenvolvimento Econômico e Social. Curitiba : IPARDES, 1985. vi, 63 leaves : ill. ; 30 cm. Bibliography: leaves [62]-63. LC Card 87-403687 DDC 339.381/62 19
1. Gross national product - Brazil - Paraná (State). I. Fundação Edison Vieira.
HC188.P35 P76 1985

Produttività e improduttività del lavoro domestico . Petrillo, Giovanna, 1952- Bologna , 1985. 139 p. ; LC Card 86-132212
HD8039.H842 I87 1985

Produttività potenziale e classificazione dei terreni. Roma : Regione Lazio, Assessorato agricoltura, foreste, caccia e pesca, 1985- v. <1 > in <5 > : ill. (some col.), maps ; 24 cm. Errata slip inserted. "Supplemento Annali [dell'] Istituto sperimentale per la nutrizione delle piante." Includes bibliographies. CONTENTS. - nota 1. Valle del fiume Sacco. Allegato n. 1-4 (5 v.) LC Card 87-105342
1. Land use - Italy - Lazio - Classification - Collected works. 2. Soil productivity - Italy - Lazio - Collected works. 3. Land capability for agriculture - Italy - Lazio - Collected works. 4. Land use - Italy - Sacco River Valley - Classification. 5. Soil productivity - Italy - Sacco River Valley. 6. Land capability for agriculture - Italy - Sacco River Valley. I. Annali dell'Istituto sperimentale per la nutrizione delle piante. Supplement. II. Lazio (Italy). Assessorato agricoltura, foreste, caccia e pesca.
HD679.L39 P76 1985

Produzione non rurale di Pirano dal 1280 al 1340. Mihelič, Darja. Neagrarno gospodarstvo Pirana od 1280 do 1340 =. Ljubljana , 1985. 244 p., [12] p. on folded leaves : LC Card 86-202646
HC407.Z7 P576 1985

Proektirovanie ėkonomicheskikh informatsionnykh sistem /. Zherebin, V. M. Moskva , 1983. 182, [2] p., [2] folded p. of plates : LC Card 83-224346
HD30.25 .Z52 1983

Proektirovanie mashinnoĭ obrabotki ėkonomicheskoĭ informatsii / [avt. kollektiv G.A. Titorenko ... et al.]. Izd. 3-e, perer. i dop. Moskva : "Statistika", 1979. 287 p. : ill. ; 22 cm. Authorized for instructional purposes. Bibliography: p. 283-[285] LC Card 81-159368
1. Business - Data processing. I. Titorenko, G. A.

(Galina Anton′evna).
HF5548.2 .P79 1979

Proektno-tekhnicheskiĭ institut Ministerstva bytovogo obsluzhivaniia ESSR. Voprosy razvitiia obsluzhivaniia naseleniia . Tallin , 1985. 140 p. : LC Card 85-158428
HD9986.S683 E888 1985

Los profesionales . Ferrer Roselló, Clemente, 1938- Madrid [1984?] 643 p. : ISBN 84-256-0424-9 LC Card 86-213550
HF5813.S8 F47 1984

Professional accounting in foreign countries series. The Accounting profession in [name of country] . New York, N.Y. , c1987- v. <1-5 > ; LC Card 87-150526 DDC 657 19
HF5611 .A34 1987

Professional certification & licensing examination series.
Lindsell, Sheryl L. CPS®--Certified Professional Secretary® examination /. New York, N.Y. , c1987. xxx, 286 p. : ISBN 0-13-122805-6 (pbk.) : LC Card 87-11381 DDC 651.3/741/076 19
HF5547.5 .L554 1987

The professional decision-thinker . Heirs, Ben J. New York , c1987. xiv, 294 ; ISBN 0-396-09203-9 : LC Card 87-15575 DDC 658.4/03 19
HD30.23 .H445 1987

PROFESSIONAL EDUCATION.
National CPE curriculum . New York, N.Y. , c1987- 1 v. (loose-leaf) : ISBN 0-87051-001-0 (loose-leaf : CIP data sheet) : LC Card 87-18832 DDC 657/.07/15 19
HF5635 .N25 1987

PROFESSIONAL EDUCATION - MEXICO.
Cleaves, Peter S. Professions and the state . Tucson , c1987. xv, 147 p. : ISBN 0-8165-1016-4 (alk. paper) LC Card 87-5911 DDC 331.7/12/0972 19
HD8038.M6 C55 1987

PROFESSIONAL EDUCATION OF WOMEN - GERMANY (WEST)
Hegelheimer, Armin. Gleichwertigkeit von allgemeiner und beruflicher Bildung /. Bonn , Bad Honnef , 1986. v, 74 p. ; ISBN 3-87066-628-5 : LC Card 87-409371 DDC 331.4/2592/0943 19
HD6059.6.G4 H42 1986

PROFESSIONAL EMPLOYEES - ESTONIA.
Osobennosti popolneniia osnovnykh otriadov intelligentsii /. Tallin , 1981. 131 p. : LC Card 82-125732
HD8038.S652 E775 1981

PROFESSIONAL EMPLOYEES - FRANCE.
Le Guen, René. Oxygène pour tous les cerveaux /. Paris , c1985. 204 p. : ISBN 2-209-05743-4 : LC Card 86-117864 DDC 331.7/12/0944 19
HD8038.F7 L4 1985

PROFESSIONAL EMPLOYEES - FRANCE - ANECDOTES, FACETIAE, SATIRE, ETC.
Bondt, Frank de. Délivrez-nous des cadres /. [Paris] , c1984. 248 p. ; LC Card 85-103087 DDC 331.7/12/0944 19
HD8038.F7 B65 1984

PROFESSIONAL EMPLOYEES - GERMANY (WEST) - BAVARIA.
Gesellschaftliches Selbstverständnis und politische Orientierung der Freien Berufe . Nürnberg , 1978. 144 p. : LC Card 86-170378
HD8038.G32 B384 1978

PROFESSIONAL EMPLOYEES - GOVERNMENT POLICY - MEXICO.
Cleaves, Peter S. Professions and the state . Tucson , c1987. xv, 147 p. : ISBN 0-8165-1016-4 (alk. paper) LC Card 87-5911 DDC 331.7/12/0972 19
HD8038.M6 C55 1987

PROFESSIONAL EMPLOYEES - ITALY - CONGRESSES.
Tecnici, ricercatori, quadri e sindacato /. Roma , 1985. 126 p. : LC Card 86-169979
HD8038.I8 T43 1985

PROFESSIONAL EMPLOYEES - SOVIET UNION.
Main, V. N. (Valentin Nikolaevich) Sel′skaia intelligentsiia v gody Velikoĭ Otechestvennoĭ voĭny . Voronezh , 1985. 158 p. ; LC Card 84-172657
HC340.D4 M35 1985

PROFESSIONAL EMPLOYEES - UNITED STATES - ATTITUDES - LONGITUDINAL STUDIES.
Hopkins, David M. Changing career values . Bethlehem, PA , 1986. x, 126 p. : ISBN 0-914885-10-3 (pbk.) LC Card 87-112752 DDC 331.25 19
HD8038.U5 H66 1986

PROFESSIONAL EMPLOYEES - WASHINGTON METROPOLITAN AREA - DIRECTORIES.
APTP employer directory. McLean, Va. (7655 Old Springhouse Road, McLean 22102) , c1986. iii, 47 p. ; LC Card 86-213174 DDC 338.7/61/00025753 19
HD8038.U52 W323 1986

PROFESSIONAL ETHICS.
Behrman, Jack N. Essays on ethics in business and the professions /. Englewood Cliffs, N.J. , c1988. x, 358 p. ; ISBN 0-13-283623-8 (pbk.) LC Card 87-13697 DDC 174/.4 19
HF5387 .B44 1988

Professional/executive workstations. The U. S. professional/executive workstations market. New York, N.Y. , c1983. vi, 284 p. : LC Card 87-142071 DDC 381/.4500416/0973 19
HD9801.U542 U18 1983

The professional option trader's manual /. Caplan, David L. Malibu, Calif. (P.O. Box 2126, Malibu 90265) , c1987. 2 v. in 1 (viii, 177 p.) : LC Card 87-116716 DDC 332.64/52 19
HG6042 .C36 1987

Professional project management . Adams, John R. Dayton, OH (1616 Mardon Dr., Dayton 45432-2634) , c1987. viii, 154 p. : LC Card 86-51558 DDC 658.4/04 19
HD69.P75 A33 1987

Professional Secretaries International. Certified professional secretary examination review series. [Kansas City, Mo.?] , New York , c1986- v. <1, 6 > : ISBN 0-471-84353-9 (pbk. : v. 1) LC Card 87-100577 DDC 651.3/74/076 19
HF5547.5 .C44 1986

PROFESSIONAL SOCIALIZATION.
Henry, Lauchland. The professional's guide to working smarter /. Tenafly, N.J. , 1988. xv, 208 p. : ISBN 0-935310-03-7 LC Card 87-23868 DDC 650.1 19
HD8038.A1 H47 1988

Professional training roles and competencies. Sredl, Henry J., 1935- The ASTD reference guide to professional training roles & competencies /. New York , c1987. 2 v. : ISBN 0-394-55915-0 (v. 1) LC Card 86-26006 DDC 658.3/124 19
HF5549.5.T7 S657 1987

Professional training roles & competencies. Sredl, Henry J., 1935- The ASTD reference guide to professional training roles & competencies /. New York , c1987. 2 v. : ISBN 0-394-55915-0 (v. 1) LC Card 86-26006 DDC 658.3/124 19
HF5549.5.T7 S657 1987

Professionalità e formazione nel settore delle costruzioni . Franciosi, Franco B. Venezia , 1985. 178 p. ; ISBN 88-317-4781-9 : LC Card 86-234138
HD5716.B92 I724 1985

The professional's desktop guide to real estate finance /. G-Yohannes, Arefaine. Chicago, Ill. , c1988. p. cm. ISBN 0-917253-93-0 : LC Card 87-17918 DDC 332.7/2 19
HG2040.5.U5 G125 1988

The professional's guide to working smarter /. Henry, Lauchland. Tenafly, N.J. , 1988. xv, 208 p. : ISBN 0-935310-03-7 LC Card 87-23868 DDC 650.1 19
HD8038.A1 H47 1988

Professions and the state . Cleaves, Peter S. Tucson , c1987. xv, 147 p. : ISBN 0-8165-1016-4 (alk. paper) LC Card 87-5911 DDC 331.7/12/0972 19
HD8038.M6 C55 1987

PROFESSIONS - CHOICE. see **VOCATIONAL GUIDANCE.**

Les Professions de l'informatique : [dossier / réalisé conjointement par l'Agence de l'informatique et al.]. Paris : Documentation française, [1986-1987] 2 v. : ill. ; 24 cm. (Dossier professionnel) Includes bibliographies. ISBN 2-11-001675-2 (v. 1) : LC Card 87-156366
1. Electronic data processing. 2. Electronic data processing - Vocational guidance. I. France. Agence de l'informatique. II. Series.
HF5548.2 .P7925 1986

Les professions del futur /. Triadú, Joaquim, 1959- Barcelona , 1986. 186 p. : ISBN 84-86421-20-9 LC Card 86-214981
HF5382.5.S7 T75 1986

PROFESSIONS - FLORIDA.
Fencl, George. The central Florida career guide /. Altamonte Springs, FL. , c1987. 56, 48 p. : ISBN 0-942827-00-7 (pbk.) : LC Card 87-402073 DDC 650.1/4/09759 19
HF5382.75.U62 F64 1987

PROFESSIONS - FORECASTING.
Jobs for the '90s [videorecording] /. Pleasantville, NY , 1987. 1 videocassette (48 min.) : LC Card 87-705264 DDC 331.7 11
HF5382

PROFESSIONS - GERMANY (WEST) - CASE STUDIES.
Gesinnungs überprüft! . Berlin [1978] 263 p. : LC Card 84-198533
HD4903.5.G4 G47 1978

PROFESSIONS - GOVERNMENT POLICY - MEXICO.
Cleaves, Peter S. Professions and the state . Tucson , c1987. xv, 147 p. : ISBN 0-8165-1016-4 (alk. paper) LC Card 87-5911 DDC 331.7/12/0972 19
HD8038.M6 C55 1987

PROFESSIONS - MARKETING.
Connor, Richard A. Getting new clients /. New York , c1987. xxiii, 305 p. : ISBN 0-471-62778-X LC Card 87-21657 DDC 658.8 19
HD8038.A1 C665 1987

Davidson, Jeffrey P. Blow your own horn . New York, NY , c1987. xv, 271 p. : ISBN 0-8144-5908-0 LC Card 86-47809 DDC 650.1/4 19
HF5549.5.C35 D375 1987

PROFESSIONS - POLAND.
U nas dole i niedole /. Warszawa , 1978. 283 p. ; LC Card 81-208722
HD8038.P6 U25 1978

PROFESSIONS - UNITED STATES - ADDRESSES, ESSAYS, LECTURES.
Rothberg, Diane S., 1930- Part-time professional /. Washington, D.C. , c1985. 158 p. ; ISBN 0-87491-786-7 (pbk.) : LC Card 85-19964 DDC 650.1/4 19
HD5110.2.U5 R67 1985
NYPL [JLE 86-2582]

PROFESSIONS - VALUATION.
Pratt, Shannon P. Valuing small businesses and professional practices /. Homewood, Ill. , c1986. xxvii, 483 p. : ISBN 0-87094-598-X LC Card 85-72255 ***NYPL [*R-Econ. 86-1421]***

Professor Dr. F. de Vries lectures in economics . (v. 8) Nelson, Richard R. Understanding technical change as an evolutionary process /. Amsterdam ; New York : viii, 125 p. ; ISBN 0-444-70207-5 (pbk.) LC Card 87-9109 DDC 338/.06 19
HC79.T4 N45 1987

Professor Monimohan Sen memorial lectures. Datta, Bhabatosh, 1911- Social justice in a mixed economy /. Calcutta , 1982. ii, 64 p. ; LC Card 82-905698 DDC 338.954 19
HC435.2 .D353 1982 ***NYPL [JLD 86-3172]***

Profil de l'industrie canadienne de la chaussure / [preparé par la Direction des études sectorielles, Direction générale de la recherche et de la planification]. [Québec] : Gouvernement du Québec, Ministère de l'industrie et du commerce, Direction des communications, [1985] xv, 65 p. : ill. ; 28 cm. Includes bibliographical references. ISBN 2-550-12407-3 LC Card 86-177298
1. Shoe industry - Québec (Province). 2. Shoe industry - Canada. I. Québec (Province). Direction des études sectorielles. II. Québec (Province). Direction générale de la recherche et de la planification.
HD9787.C23 Q436 1985

Profil de l'industrie québécoise des éléments d'architecture et de structure préfabriqués en béton /. Ristic, Veselin. [Québec] , c1983. 168 p. : LC Card 85-100163
HD9622.C23 Q437 1983

Profile of social welfare and development in India /. Chowdhry, D. Paul. New Delhi , 1985. viii, 340 p. ; LC Card 85-901093 DDC 362/.954 19
HV393 .C515 1985 ***NYPL [JLD 86-2575]***

A Profile of the baking industry. [Washington, D.C.] : Food and Allied Service Trades Department, AFL-CIO, [1985] 49 leaves ; 28 cm. Cover title: Baking industry profile. "October, 1985." Bibliography: p. 47-49. LC Card 86-211982 DDC 338.4/7664752/0973 19
1. Bakers and bakeries - United States. 2. Baked products. 3. Baking. I. AFL-CIO. Food and Allied Service Trades Dept. II. Title: Baking industry profile.
HD9057.U59 P76 1985

Profile of the primary commodity sector in Malaysia. [Kuala Lumpur] : Ministry of Primary Industries, Malaysia, [1984] 77 p. : ill. (some col.), maps, col. ports. ; 27 cm. "March 1984." LC Card 86-945653 DDC 338.09595 19
1. Produce trade - Malaysia. 2. Forest products industry - Indonesia. 3. Tin industry - Indonesia. I. Malaysia. Kementerian Perusahaan Utama.
HD9016.M32 P76 1984

Profile of the '80's / U. S. Department of Transportation, Assistant Secretary for Policy and International Affairs. [Washington, D.C.?] : U. S. Dept. of Transportation, [Office of the] Assistant Secretary for Policy and International Affairs : For sale by the Supt. of Docs., U. S. G.P.O., 1980. v, 77 p. : ill., maps ; 28 cm. "Prepared by SG Associates, Inc. [and] the Urban Institute"--P. 3 of cover. "February 1980." Includes bibliographical references. LC Card 81-600725 DDC 380.5/0973 19
1. Transportation and state - United States. 2. Economic forecasting - United States. 3. United States - Economic conditions - 1971-1981. I. United States. Dept. of Transportation. Office of the Assistant Secretary for Policy and International Affairs. II. SG Associates. III. Urban Institute.
HE206.2 .P765 ***NYPL [JLF 86-1445]***

A profile of 1984 Texas homebuyers /. Albrecht, Don E. College Station, Tex. [1986] 70 p. : LC Card 86-622194 DDC 333.33/8 19
HD7287.82.U62 T434 1986

Profile, State of Wyoming. Cheyenne, Wyo. : Economic Development and Stabilization Board, [1986] 30 leaves ; 28 cm. LC Card 86-622611 DDC 330.9787/033 19
1. Wyoming - Economic conditions. 2. Wyoming - Economic conditions - Statistics. I. Wyoming Economic Development and Stabilization Board.
HC107.W9 P76 1986

Profiles of political elites in India /. Singh, V. B., 1941- Delhi , 1984. xii, 178 p. : LC Card 84-900272 DDC 305.5/24/0954 19
JQ281 .S565 1984 ***NYPL [JLD 86-4319]***

Profili funzionali e operativi delle casse rurali e artigiane /. Santoro, Vittorio. Milano [1984] 181 p. ; ISBN 88-14-00380-7 : LC Card 85-147834
HG2039.I8 S26 1984 ***NYPL [JLE 86-3669]***

PROFIT.
Hanan, Mack. If you don't have a plan, stay in the car /. New York, NY , c1987. x, 277 p. ; ISBN 0-8144-5936-6 LC Card 87-47706 DDC 658.8/1 19
HF5438.25 .H347 1987

Maennig, Wolfgang. Die Effekte der Preisstabilisierung auf internationalen Rohstoffmärkten auf Erlöshöhe und -stabilität /. Berlin , 1985. 168 p. : ISBN 3-428-05947-6
NYPL [JLE 86-1670]

Mehrwert heute . Berlin , c1981. 285 p. ; LC Card 82-189316 DDC 338.5/21 19
HB206 .M44 1981 ***NYPL [JLD 86-2837]***

Sloma, Richard S. Getting it to the bottom line . New York , London , c1987. ix, 196 p. : ISBN 0-02-929540-8 LC Card 87-411 DDC 658.4/063 19
HD58.9 .S56 1987

Tammer, Hans. Monopole, Profite, Ausbeutung /. Berlin , 1983. 237 p. : LC Card 84-142912
HD2757.2 .T35 1983

Utton, Michael A. Profits and stability of monopoly /. Cambridge [Cambridgeshire] , New York , 1986. vii, 96 p. ; ISBN 0-521-32550-1 LC Card 86-4226 DDC 338.8/2/0941 19
HD2757.3 .U88 1986 ***NYPL [TB (National Institute of Economic and Social Research. Occasional papers. v.38)]***

Weingarten, Richard. Eine kapitaltheoretische Untersuchung zum Gesetz vom tendenziellen Fall der Profitrate einschliesslich der Bestimmung seiner empirischen Relevanz /. München , c1982. ix, 342 p. ; ISBN 3-597-10136-4 LC Card 83-134240
HB601 .W37 1982

Woelfel, Charles J. The operating executive's guide to profit planning tools and techniques /. Chicago, Ill. , c1986. ix, 199 p. : ISBN 0-917253-24-8 : LC Card 86-3222 DDC 658.1/55 19
HF5635 .W848 1986 ***NYPL [JLE 86-3007]***

PROFIT AND LOSS STATEMENTS. see **FINANCIAL STATEMENTS.**

PROFIT - BULGARIA.
Khadzhiev, Stoîan. Pechalbata pri razshirenoto sotsialisticheskо vŭzproizvodstvoto . Sofiîa , 1985. 147 p. ; LC Card 85-209903
HC403.Z9 P737 1985

PROFIT - GERMANY, EAST.
Brandt, Horst. Kostensenkung und Gewinn /. Berlin , 1985. 100 p. ; LC Card 87-144350 DDC 338.5/1/09431 19
HC290.795.C7 B7 1985

PROFIT - GREAT BRITAIN.
Utton, Michael A. Profits and stability of monopoly /. Cambridge [Cambridgeshire] , New York , 1986. vii, 96 p. ; ISBN 0-521-32550-1 LC Card 86-4226 DDC 338.8/2/0941 19
HD2757.3 .U88 1986 ***NYPL [TB (National Institute of Economic and Social Research. Occasional papers. v.38)]***

PROFIT - HANSA TOWNS - HISTORY.
Stark, Walter. Untersuchungen zum Profit beim hansischen Handelskapital in der ersten Hälfte des 15. Jahrhunderts /. Weimar , 1985. 147 p. ; LC Card 86-148303
HF458 .S73 1985

Profit in small firms . Andersson, Tommy D., 1947- Aldershot, Hants, England , Brookfield, Vt., USA , c1987. 407 p. : ISBN 0-566-05468-X : LC Card 87-21321 DDC 338.6/42/091724 19
HD2346.5 .A53 1987

PROFIT - INDIA.
Chopra, Kiran. Managing profits, profitability & productivity in public sector banking /. Jalandhar , 1987. 320 p. : ISBN 81-7072-012-5 : LC Card 87-901014 DDC 332.1/0954 19
HG3284 .C56 1987

PROFIT - INDIA - ECONOMETRIC MODELS.
Shrivastava, S. C., 1939- Wages, profits, and productivity in selected industries of India since 1950 . Bombay , 1984. xii, 254 p. : LC Card 84-900745 DDC 338/.06/0954 19
HD5069 .S46 1984 ***NYPL [JLD 86-4260]***

PROFIT - MATHEMATICAL MODELS.
Helmedag, Fritz, 1953- Die Technikwahl bei linearer Einzelproduktion, oder, Die dritte Krise der Profitrate /. Frankfurt am Main , New York , c1986. viii, 301 p. : ISBN 3-8204-9645-9 LC Card 86-219002
HB601 .H44 1986

PROFIT-SHARING.
Slimmon, Robert F. Successful pension design for small-to medium-sized businesses /. Englewood Cliffs, N.J. , c1987. xix, 440 p. ; ISBN 0-13-860255-7 LC Card 87-2489 DDC 658.3/253
HD7105.4 .S56 1987

PROFIT-SHARING - GERMANY, WEST.
Schultz, Reinhard. Gewinn- und Kapitalbeteiligung der Arbeitnehmer (Vermögensbildung) /. München , c1987. 256 p. ; ISBN 3-597-10525-4 LC Card 87-127356 DDC 331.2/164 19
HD3038 .S365 1987

Profit sharing in 38 large companies . Metzger, Bertram L. Evanston, Ill. , 1975-78. 2 v. : ISBN 0-911192-25-5 : LC Card 75-39379 DDC 658.32/25
HD2984 .M47 ***NYPL [JLF 86-389]***

PROFIT-SHARING - INDIA.
Singh, Nar, 1952- Sharing of productivity gains in Indian industry /. Delhi , 1984. x, 180 p. ;
NYPL [JLD 86-4253]

Profit-Sharing Research Foundation. Metzger, Bertram L. Profit sharing in 38 large companies . Evanston, Ill. , 1975-78. 2 v. : ISBN 0-911192-25-5 : LC Card 75-39379 DDC 658.32/25
HD2984 .M47 ***NYPL [JLF 86-389]***

PROFIT-SHARING TRUSTS. see **INVESTMENT TRUSTS.**

PROFIT-SHARING - UNITED STATES.
Metzger, Bertram L. Profit sharing in 38 large companies . Evanston, Ill. , 1975-78. 2 v. : ISBN 0-911192-25-5 : LC Card 75-39379 DDC 658.32/25
HD2984 .M47 ***NYPL [JLF 86-389]***

Pensions & profit sharing. [Chicago, Ill.] , c1987- xiii, 351 p. ; ISBN 0-88462-650-4 (pbk.) LC Card 87-1608 DDC 658/.3/25 19
HD7105.35.U6 P45 1987

PROFIT - SOVIET UNION.
TSena i khozraschet /. Moskva , 1986. 144 p. ; LC Card 87-163568
HB235.S73 T72 1986

Vasil'eva, E. S. (Elena Stepanovna) Planirovanie pribyli i rentabel'nosti na promyshlennom predpriîatii . Moskva , 1985. 40 p. : LC Card 86-204680
HG4028.P7 V39 1985

Profitable careers in nonprofit /. Lewis, William, 1946- New York , c1987. vi, 202 p. ; ISBN 0-471-83699-0 (pbk.) : LC Card 87-6102 DDC 331.7/02 19
HF5382.5.U5 L44 1987

Profitable equipment leasing . Winders, Terry J., 1942- Boston , c1987. xii, 252 p. ; ISBN 0-87267-101-1 : LC Card 86-26601 DDC 332.1/068/7 19
HD39.4 .W56 1987 ***NYPL [JLE 87-1512]***

Profitable inventory management strategies /. Kleutghen, Paul P. New York, NY, U. S.A. , c1986. viii, 208 p. : ISBN 0-86604-233-4 (pbk.) LC Card 86-205426 DDC 658.7/87 19
HD40 .K54 1986

Profitable no-load mutual fund trading techniques for the individual investor /. Mallory, Norman. Brightwaters, N.Y. , c1987. 153 p. : ISBN 0-930233-11-5 (pbk.) LC Card 87-400302 DDC 332.63/27 19
HG4530 .M25 1987

Profitable pricing strategies /. Montgomery, Stephen L. New York , c1988. xiii, 174 p. : ISBN 0-07-042860-3 : LC Card 87-4089 DDC 658.8/16 19
HF5416.5 .M67 1988

Profitable ratio analysis techniques /. Moore, Carl L. New York, N.Y., U. S.A. , c1986. ix leaves, 201 p. : ISBN 0-86604-206-7 (pbk.) LC Card 86-208178 DDC 658.4/033 19
HF5681.R25 M58 1986

Profitable service marketing /. Johnson, Eugene M. Homewood, Ill. , c1986. xiv, 303 p. : ISBN 0-87094-613-7 LC Card 86-70516 DDC 658.8 19
HF5415.122 .J64 1986 ***NYPL [JLE 87-666]***

Profiting from the insurance revolution /. Phillips, David T. Alexandria, VA (1101 King St., Suite 400, Alexandria 22314) , c1987. vii, 120, 18 p. : LC Card 87-401086 DDC 368.3/2/00973 19
HG8951 .P47 1987

Profits and stability of monopoly /. Utton, Michael A. Cambridge [Cambridgeshire] , New York , 1986. vii, 96 p. ; ISBN 0-521-32550-1 LC Card 86-4226 DDC 338.8/2/0941 19
HD2757.3 .U88 1986 ***NYPL [TB (National Institute of Economic and Social Research. Occasional papers. v.38)]***

Profits without production /. Melman, Seymour. Philadelphia , 1987, c1983. p. cm. ISBN 0-8122-1258-4 (pbk.) LC Card 87-13796 DDC 338.0973 19
HD70.U5 M425 1987

Profmex monograph series.
Cleaves, Peter S. Professions and the state . Tucson , c1987. xv, 147 p. : ISBN 0-8165-1016-4 (alk. paper) LC Card 87-5911 DDC

331.7/12/0972 19
HD8038.M6 C55 1987

Profsoiūzy sovetskoĭ Moldavii v sotsialisticheskom stroitel'stve. Burlaku, I. N. Sindikatele Moldoveĭ sovetiche yn konstruktsiīa sochialistė /. Kishinėu , 1980. 148 p. ; LC Card 81-135331
HD6735.M56 B87 1980

Profsoiūzy Ukrainy na zavershaiūshchem ėtape stroitel'stva sotsializma /. Kondratiūk, K. K. (Konstantin Konstantinovich) L'vov , 1985. 173 p. ; LC Card 87-165263
HD6735.U5 K65 1985

PROFSŬIŪZ NA MIN'ORITE, METALURZITE, ENERGETITSITE E GEOLOZITE (BULGARIA) - ANNIVERSARIES, ETC.
75 godini borba i sŭzidanie . Sofiīa , 1985. 144 p. ; LC Card 86-195265
HD6784.M62 P762 1985

Profsŭiūz na min'orite, metalurzite, energetitsite i geolozite. TSentralen komitet. 75 godini borba i sŭzidanie . Sofiīa , 1985. 144 p. ; LC Card 86-195265
HD6784.M62 P762 1985

Profsŭiūzno stroitelstvo : uchebnik za bŭlgarskite kursove / [napisan ot avtorski kolektiv pod nauchnoto rŭkovodstvo i sŭstavitelstvo na Stoīan Andreev].2., prer. i dop. izd. Sofiīa : Nauchnoizsledovatelski in-t po profsŭiūzni problemi "G. Dimitrov" pri TSS na BPS, 1985. 310 p. : ill. ; 22 cm. Includes bibliographical references. LC Card 86-209854
1. Trade-unions - Bulgaria. I. Andreev, Stoīan. II. Nauchnoizsledovatelski institut po profsŭiūzni problemi Georgi Dimitrov.
HD6782 .P78 1985

Prognose van het budget van de Provincie op middellange termijn (zgn. meerjarenramingen) behorende bij de Ontwerp-Provinciale Begroting 1982. ['s-Hertogenbosch] : Provincie Noord-Brabant, [1982?] 7, [52] p. ; 30 cm. "Nummer 76/81." LC Card 86-232148
1. North Brabant (Netherlands) - Appropriations and expenditures - Forecasting. 2. Budget - Netherlands - North Brabant - Forecasting. I. North Brabant (Netherlands).
HJ2128.5.N6 P76 1982

Prognosepublizität . Mennenöh, Hartwig. Bochum , 1984. ii, 329 p. : ISBN 3-88339-366-5 : LC Card 84-181938
HB3730 .M396 1984

Prognozirovanie i ėffektivnost' raboty flota : sbornik nauchnykh trudov / [otvetstvennyĭ redaktor IŪ.I. Panin ; nauchnyĭ redaktor A.G. Shchelkanov]. Leningrad : "Transport," Leningradskoe otd-nie, 1985. 104 p. : ill. ; 22 cm. At head of title: Ministerstvo Morskogo flota SSSR. Vsesoiūznoe ob"edinenie "Mortekhinformreklama." TSentral'nyĭ ordena Trudovogo Krasnogo Znameni nauchno-issledovatel'skiĭ institut morskogo flota. Includes bibliographies. LC Card 86-170274
1. Merchant marine - Soviet Union - Management - Data processing. I. Panin, IŪ. I. II. Shchelkanov, A. G. III. Vsesoiūznoe ob"edinenie "Mortekhinformreklama" (Soviet Union). IV. TSentral'nyĭ nauchno-issledovatel'skiĭ institut morskogo flota (Leningrad, R.S.F.S.R.).
HE847 .P77 1985

Prognozirovanie razvitiīa regional'nogo gorno-promyshlennogo kompleksa /. Nikitin, V. S. (Vadim Semenovich) Moskva , 1982. 141, [3] p. : LC Card 83-154711
HD9506.S7473 S656 1982

Program analysis and design . Eliason, Alan L. Chicago , c1987. ix, 134 p. : ISBN 0-574-18660-3 (pbk.) LC Card 87-4521 DDC 658/.055265 19
HF5548.2 .E4275 1987

Program analysis and utilization review report . (2) Utilization of medicaid paid health services by Medicaid recipients in New York City, Nassau, Monroe, and western central counties, 1980-1981 /. Albany, N.Y. (1 Commerce Plaza, Albany 12210) [1985] ii, 31, 17 p. : LC Card 86-622554 DDC 362.1/04252/09747 19
HD7102.U5 N684 1985

Program and background materials for Tanzania/USAID bilateral talks, November 30 and December 1, 1983. USAID/Tanzania. [Dar es Salaam, Tanzania] [1983?] 1 v. (various pagings) ; LC Card 86-980179 DDC 338.91/73/0678 19
HC885 .U8 1983

Program and fiscal review . Washington (State). Legislature. Legislative Budget Committee. Olympia (506 E. 16th Ave., Olympia 98504) [1985] v, 69 p. ; LC Card 86-621785 DDC 353.97970072/32 s 353.97970082/43 19
HJ11 .W2453 no. 85-13 KFN329.A25

PROGRAM BUDGETING - MEXICO - ZACATECAS (STATE) - STATISTICS.
Zacatecas (Mexico : State). Governor (1980- : Cervantes Corona) Tercer informe de gobierno. Zacatecas , 1983. 350 p. : LC Card 86-202257
HJ15.Z3 Z33 1980

PROGRAM BUDGETING - PHILIPPINES.
Philippines. Office of Budget and Management. 1984 Philippine budget . Malacañang, Manila [1984?] viii, 461 p. : LC Card 87-105421 DDC 354.5990072/2 19
HJ2167 .P46 1984

Program development and evaluation resource book for trainers /. Caffarella, Rosemary S. (Rosemary Shelly), 1946- New York , c1988. xxi, 266 p. : ISBN 0-471-84235-4 LC Card 87-15990 DDC 658.3/12404 19
HF5549.5.T7 C23 1988

Programa Centroamericano de Ciencias Sociales. see **Programa Centroamericano de Desarrollo de las Ciencias Sociales.**

Programa Centroamericano de Desarrollo de las Ciencias Sociales. Costa Rica colonial . [San José, Costa Rica , 1984] 83 p. ; LC Card 86-173945
HC389 .C67 1984

Programa de aproveitamento de recursos hídricos do Nordeste . Brazil. Ministério do Interior. Subsecretaria de Programas Regionais. Brasília [1980] [73] leaves ; LC Card 87-403686 DDC 333.91/00981/3 19
HD1696.B84 N649 1980

Programa de Asesoramiento Minero (Bolivia) Desabastecimiento de alimentos y alternativas de solución en las minas . La Paz [Bolivia] , 1986. 128 : LC Card 87-401454 DDC 331.7/6223453/098413 19
HD8039.M72 B624 1986

El programa de braceros ferroviarios /. Driscoll, Bárbara A. Tijuana, Baja California , 1985. 45 p. ; ISBN 968-607-501-1 LC Card 86-188661
HD8039.R432 U62 1985

Programa de Contribuições ao Estudo de Problemas Mineiros (Minas Gerais, Brazil) Opções energéticas . Belo Horizonte, MG , 1983. 328 p., [30] leaves of plates : LC Card 83-205480
HD9502.B72 O63 1983

Programa de cooperación técnica Perú-Venezuela-OEA . Buroz Castillo, Eduardo. Caracas , 1976. [11], 62 p. ; LC Card 84-136478
HD1696.P5 B87 1976

Programa de dispêndios globais para 1986 . Alagoas (Brazil). Comissão de Controle das Entidades Estatais. [Maceió, Brazil] , 1985. 76 p. : LC Card 87-404783 DDC 354.81/35092 19
HD4095.A4 A4 1985

Programa de Economía del Trabajo (Academia de Humanismo Cristiano)
Bustamante G., Jaime. Algunos antecedentes estadísticos sobre las organizaciones económicas populares /. Santiago, Chile , 1986. 23 p. ; LC Card 87-101323
HD2346.C53 B87 1986

Errázuriz, Enrique. Industria eléctrica, 1960-1985 . [Santiago, Chile] [1986] 243 p. : LC Card 87-403870 DDC 338.4/762131/0983 19
HD9685.C52 E77 1986

Schkolnik, Mariana. Sobrevivir en la población José M. Caro y en Lo Hermida /. [Santiago, Chile] [1986] 150 p., [20] p. of plates : LC Card 87-400080 DDC 362.5/8/098331 19
HC193.S2 S35 1986

Vega F., Humberto (Vega Fernández) Política económica y movimiento laboral . Santiago, Chile , 1986. 52 p. : LC Card 87-101128
HC192 .V355 1986

PROGRAMA DE EMPLEO MÍNIMO.
Ruiz-Tagle P., Jaime. Los trabajadores del Programa del Empleo Mínimo . Santiago , 1984. 179 p. : LC Card 84-234738
HD5756.A6 R86 1984

PROGRAMA DE INVERSIONES PARA EL DESARROLLO RURAL (MEXICO)
Cernea, Michael M. Measuring project impact . Washington, D.C., U. S.A. , c1979. vi, 93 p. ; LC Card 81-170764
HD1792 .C43 1979

Programa de investigación y servicio sobre propiedad social en Costa Rica, con énfasis en cooperativismo. Propuesta para el desarrollo de un programa de investigación sobre propiedad social con énfasis en cooperativismo /. San José, Costa Rica , 1986. ii, 70 p. : LC Card 87-125056 DDC 334/.097286 19
HD3454.A4 P76 1986

Programa de Investigaciones Sociales sobre Problemas de Población Relevantes para Políticas de Población en América Latina. Estructura política y políticas de población /. [Santiago, Chile] [1977] 442 p. ; LC Card 83-168971
HB3530.5 .E88 1977

Programa de Irrigação do Nordeste--PROINE . Brazil. Ministerio do Interior. Brasília , 1986. 30 p. ; LC Card 87-400672 DDC 333.91/3/09813 19
HD1741.B82 N623 1986

El programa de la CONAPRO y las perspectivas económicas inmediatas /. Cancela Vilanova, Walter, 1948- [Montevideo, Uruguay] [1985] 39 p. ; LC Card 85-235957 DDC 338.9895 19
HC232 .C283 1985

Programa de modernização e expansão da indústria de cal em Minas Gerais. Belo Horizonte : Banco de Desenvolvimento de Minas Gerais, Assessoria de Comunicação Social, 1977. 57 leaves, [8] leaves of plates : forms ; 30 cm. Bibliography: leaves 54-55. LC Card 79-123546
1. Lime industry - Brazil - Minas Gerais. I. Banco de Desenvolvimento de Minas Gerais. Assessoria de Comunicação Social.
HD9585.L52 B77 1977

Programa Interdisciplinario de Investigaciones en Educación (Academia de Humanismo Cristiano) Tapia Soko, Gonzalo. El problema de la recomposición de los actores campesinos en una perspectiva de democratización /. Santiago [Chile] [1985] ii, 49, 5 leaves ; LC Card 86-159337
HD1531.C5 T36 1985

Programa nacional de apoio às migrações internas /. Brazil. Ministério do Interior. Secretaria de Planejamento. Brasília , 1980. 42 p. ; LC Card 86-203543 DDC 362.8/5 19
HB2023 .B73 1980

Programa Nacional de Desburocratização (Brazil) Cidadão, estado e políticas no Brasil contemporâneo /. Brasília-Distrito Federal , c1986. 290 p. : ISBN 85-23-00214-6 LC Card 87-405054 DDC 338.981 19
HD1873 .C53 1986

Programa Nacional de Pesquisa Econômica (Brazil) Saboia, João, 1944- Evolução histórica do salário mínimo no Brasil . Rio de Janeiro , 1984. 106 p. ; LC Card 87-403844 DDC 331.2/3 19
HD4920.B8 S265 1984

PROGRAMA NACIONAL DO ALCOOL (BRAZIL)
O Proálcool vale? /. [São Paulo-SP (Brasil)] , 1985. 52 p. : LC Card 86-220396
HD9502.5.A433 B645 1985

Programa pegmatitos. Metais de Minas Gerais, S.A. Belo Horizonte , 1981. 95 p. : LC Card 83-220720
HD9506.B72 M48 1981

Programa Regional para el Desarrollo del Sur (Ecuador) Informe cuatrianual, 1980-1983 /. Cuenca, Ecuador [1983] 222 p. : LC Card 86-206868
HC203.O76 I53 1983

Programa subregional de apoyo a la pequeña y mediana industria /. Board of the Cartagena Agreement. [S.l.] [between 1983 and 1986] (Lima, Perú : Europrint) 29 p. ; LC Card

87-400442 DDC 338.6/42/098 19
HD2346.A64 B63 1983

Programas de estabilización y condicionalidad en Costa Rica /. Delgado Q., Félix. San José, Costa Rica , 1986. 30, [6] leaves ; LC Card 87-404196 DDC 338.97286 19
HC143 .D45 1986

Programas de reactivación económica y sistemas financieros . Rosales Díaz, Ramón. [Lima] , 1986. 68 p. : LC Card 87-400247 DDC 332.4/982 19
HG815 .R67 1986

Programas especiais . Brazil. Ministério do Interior. Subsecretaria de Programas Regionais. [Brasília] [1981] 1 v. (various foliations) ; LC Card 87-403680 DDC 338.981/1 19
HD1875.A347 B7 1981

Programas especiais do governo, 1983-1987. Rio Grande do Norte (Brazil) Natal , 1984. [83] leaves ; LC Card 87-403924 DDC 331.12/0981/32 19
HC188.R38 P76 1984

Programma ependyseōn se geōrgikes viomēchanies to 1986 / Agrotikē Trapeza tēs Hellados, Dieuthynsē Geōrgikōn Viomēchaniōn. Athēna : Hē Trapeza, 1986. 32, 91 leaves, [1] folded leaf of plates : ill. ; 30 cm. LC Card 86-193452
1. Agricultural credit - Greece. 2. Agricultural industries - Greece - Finance. I. Agrotikē Trapeza tēs Hellados. Dieuthynsē Geōrgikōn Viomēchaniōn.
HG2051.G9 P76 1986

Il programma INEA per la progettazione e le analisi statistiche di un campione rappresentativo /. Istituto nazionale di economia agraria. Roma , 1986. 122 p. : LC Card 86-213865
HD1970 .I773 1986

Programmazione e sviluppo in Unione Sovietica /. Marrama, Vittorio. Torino , c1983. 146 p. : LC Card 85-175586
HC336.25 .M358 1983

Programmazione lineare e teoria dell'impresa /. Moro, Beniamino, 1945- Milano [1980] 182 p. : ISBN 88-20-41708-1 : LC Card 80-489699
T57.74 .M67 ***NYPL [JLD 87-792]***

Programmazione regionale. Sezione 2 . ([2]) Il Consolidamento regionale della finanza locale /. Milano [1980] 332 p. : ISBN 88-20-41859-2 : LC Card 80-143023
HJ9497 .C63 ***NYPL [JLD 87-1397]***

Programme, Analysen, Tatbestände . (Bd. 6) Verwaltung und Planung im Wandel /. Köln , 1979. 112 p. ; ISBN 3-7745-6438-8 : LC Card 81-473982
HT395.G4 V48 ***NYPL [JLE 86-2107]***

Programme d'aide aux médias communautaires, 1979-80 : rapport du jury / Denise Dufour ... [et al.]. [Québec] : Editeur officiel du Québec, Service des impressions en régie, [1979] 97 leaves ; 35 cm. Report prepared for the Ministry of Communications. "Québec, le 7 novembre 1979." LC Card 83-200428
1. Public broadcasting - Québec (Province). 2. Local mass media - Québec (Province). I. Dufour, Denise. II. Québec (Province). Ministère des communications.
HE8689.9.C3 P755 1979

Programme de coopération. Agenda for co-operation . [Ottawa?] [1977?] 63, 66 p. ; LC Card 84-246582
HC120.W24 A64 1977

Programme de renouveau économique. The Agenda for economic renewal . [Ottawa] [1987] 25, 26 p. : LC Card 87-140803 DDC 338.971 19
HC115 .A624 1987

Programme for research and actions on the development of the labour market. Buiren, S. van. The quantitative and qualitative significance of the emergence of local initiatives for employment creation . Luxembourg , Washington, D.C. , 1986. iii, 141, 14, [12] p. : ISBN 92-825-6048-1 (pbk.) : LC Card 86-222030 DDC 331.12/042/094 19
HD5764.5.A6 B85 1986

Programme of research and actions on the development of the labour market : forms of organisation, type of employment, working conditions and industrial relations in co-operatives, any collectiveness or other self-managing structures of the EEC. Luxembourg : Office for Official Publications of the European Communities ; Washington, DC : European Community Information Service [distributor], 1986. 1 v. (various pagings) : ill. ; 30 cm. English, French, and Italian. At head of title: Commission of the European Communities. "Catalogue number: CB-46-86-395-EN-C"--P. 2 of cover. Includes bibliographies. ISBN 92-825-6077-5 (pbk.) : LC Card 86-216010 DDC 334/.6/094 19
1. Producer cooperatives - France. 2. Producer cooperatives - Great Britain. 3. Producer cooperatives - Italy. I. Commission of the European Communities.
HD3184 .P76 1986

Programme of research and actions on the development of the labour market . Junankar, P. N. Luxembourg [Washington, DC] 1986. vi, 76, 35 p. : ISBN 92-825-6084-8 (pbk.) : LC Card 86-220947
HD5764.5.A6 J85 1986

Programme populaire de développement, octobre 1984 décembre 1985 /. Conseil national de la révolution (Burkina Faso) [Ouagadougou, Burkina Faso] [1985?] 1 v. (various pagings) : LC Card 87-160992
HC1040 .C66 1985

Programme populaire de développement, octobre 1984-décembre 1985 . Conseil national de la révolution (Burkina Faso) [Ouagadougou] [1986] 2 v. : LC Card 87-158925
HC1040 .C66 1986

Programmes d'encouragement et d'expansion à l'intention de l'industrie canadienne. Incentive and development programs for Canadian industry. Ottawa, Canada , 1973, c1975. 14, 14 p. ; LC Card 85-158119
HC120.I53 I48 1975

Les Programmes spéciaux d'emploi et de formation de la jeunesse ... Addis Abéba : Organisation internationale du travail, Bureau international du travail, Programme des emplois et des compétences techniques pour l'Afrique, 1985- v. <1-6 > : ill. ; 29 cm. Comparative studies prepared by PECTA. Includes bibliographies. CONTENTS. - [1] Bénin -- [2] Burkina Faso -- [3] Côte d'Ivoire -- [4] Mali -- [5] Mauritanie -- [6] Rapport de synthèse. LC Card 86-981200
1. Youth - Employment - Government policy - Africa - Collected works. 2. Manpower policy - Africa - Collected works. I. Jobs and Skills Programme for Africa.
HD6276.A3 P76 1985

Programming in C with a bit of UNIX /. Moore, F. Richard. Englewood Cliffs, NJ , 1985. vii, 193 p. : ISBN 0-13-730102-2 : LC Card 84-26642 DDC 001.64/24 19
QA76.73.C15 M66 1985
NYPL [JSE 86-1377]

PROGRAMMING (MATHEMATICS)
(1984) Razumikhin, Boris Sergeevich. [Fizicheskie modeli i metody teorii ravnovesiia v programmirovanii i ėkonomike. English.] Physical models and equilibrium methods in programming and economics /. Dordrecht ; Boston : xv, 351 p. : ISBN 90-277-1644-7 LC Card 83-17791 DDC 330/.0724 19
HB135 .R3913 1984 ***NYPL [JSD 86-491]***

PROGRAMMING (MATHEMATICS) - CONGRESSES.
IIASA (International Institute for Applied Systems Analysis) Workshop on Nondifferentiable Optimization (1984 : Sopron, Hungary) Nondifferentiable optimization . Berlin , New York , 1985. vi, 349 p. : ISBN 0-387-15979-7 (U. S.) LC Card 85-25029 DDC 658.4/03/4 19
T57.6 .I46 1984
NYPL [JLM 72-289 no.255]

Programming the IBM PC user interface /. Simpson, Henry. New York , c1985. vii, 228 p. : ISBN 0-07-057297-6 (pbk.) : LC Card 85-7924 DDC 005.265 19
QA76.8.I2594 S575 1985
NYPL [JSE 86-1154]

Programming with A.P.S.E. software tools. Freedman, Roy S. Programming with APSE software tools /. Princeton, N.J. , c1984. viii, 253 p. : ISBN 0-89433-220-1 LC Card 84-20739 DDC 001.64/24 19
QA76.73.A35 F74 1984
NYPL [JSE 86-1512]

Programming with APSE software tools /. Freedman, Roy S. Princeton, N.J. , c1984. viii, 253 p. : ISBN 0-89433-220-1 LC Card 84-20739 DDC 001.64/24 19
QA76.73.A35 F74 1984
NYPL [JSE 86-1512]

Programming with dBase III /. Prague, Cary N. Blue Ridge Summit, Pa. , 1985. ix, 292 p. ; ISBN 0-8306-0976-8 : LC Card 84-23979 DDC 001.64/2 19
QA76.9.D3 P728 1985 ***NYPL [JSE 87-75]***

Programming with dBASE III PLUS /. Prague, N. Cary. Blue Ridge Summit, PA , c1986. vi, 375 p. : ISBN 0-8306-0326-3 : LC Card 86-5736 DDC 005.74 19
QA76.9.D3 P729 1986 ***NYPL [JSE 87-539]***

Programmno-tselevoĭ metod v planirovanii / [otvetstvennyĭ redaktor N.P. Fedorenko ; monografiia podgotovlena avtorskim kollektivom, A.G. Fonotov ... et al.]. Moskva : Izd-vo "Nauka," 1982. 150 p. : ill. ; 20 cm. (Problemy sovetskoĭ ėkonomiki) At head of title: Akademiia nauk SSSR. TSentral'nyĭ ėkonomiko-matematicheskiĭ institut. Nauchnyĭ sovet po kompleksnoĭ probleme "Optimal'noe planirovanie i upravlenie narodnym khoziaĭstvom." Bibliography: p. 147-[149] LC Card 83-162853
1. Soviet Union - Economic policy - 1981-. I. Fedorenko, Nikolaĭ Prokof'evich. II. Fonotov, A. G. III. TSentral'nyĭ ėkonomiko-matematicheskiĭ institut (Akademiia nauk SSSR). IV. Nauchnyĭ sovet po kompleksnoĭ probleme "Optimal'noe planirovanie i upravlenie narodnym khoziaĭstvom" (Akademiia nauk SSSR).
HC336.25 .P6577 1982

Programmnoe obespechenie ėkonomiko-matematicheskikh issledovaniĭ / [sostaviteli Aĭvazian S.A. ... et al. ; otvetstvennyĭ redaktor Ershov Ė.B.]. Moskva : Akademiia nauk SSSR, TSentr. ėkonomiko-matematicheskiĭ in-t, 1982. 142 p. : ill. ; 21 cm. (Programmy i algoritmy . vyp. 100) Includes bibliographies. LC Card 84-209065
1. Industrial management - Linear programming. 2. Economics - Linear programming. I. Aĭvazian, Sergeĭ Artem'evich. II. Ershov, Ė. B. III. TSentral'nyĭ ėkonomiko-matematicheskiĭ institut (Akademiia nauk SSSR). IV. Series.
HD30.25 .P76 1982

Programmpaket zur Verbesserung der Rahmenbedingungen für die Wirtschaft im Ruhrgebiet : Vorschlagspapier / [Herausgeber], Siedlungsverband Ruhrkohlenbezirk. Essen : Der Siedlungsverband, [197-?] 42 p. : ill. ; 21 cm. LC Card 85-153643
1. Ruhr (Germany : Region) - Economic policy. I. Siedlungsverband Ruhrkohlenbezirk.
HC288.R8 P76 1970z

Programmy i algoritmy .
(vyp. 100) Programmnoe obespechenie ėkonomiko-matematicheskikh issledovaniĭ /. Moskva , 1982. 142 p. : LC Card 84-209065
HD30.25 .P76 1982

Programno-tselevi kolektiv "Prebroiavane na naselenieto i zhilishtniia fond" (Bulgaria)
Nauchno-prakticheska konferentsiia "Prebroiavane na naselenieto i zhilishtniia fond--teoriia i praktika" (1986 : Slŭnchev briag, Bulgaria) Nauchno-prakticheska konferentsiia "Prebroiavane na naselenieto i zhilishtniia fond--teoriia i praktika," 9-11 oktomvri 1986 g., Slŭnchev briag /. Sofiia , 1986- v. <1 > : LC Card 87-156528
HA1621.5 1985

PROGRAMS, COMPUTER. see **COMPUTER PROGRAMS.**

Programs for productivity and quality of work life /. Guzzo, Richard A. New York , c1983. 38 p. ; ISBN 0-08-030964-X (pbk.) : LC Card 83-22029 DDC 658.3/14 19
HC110.L3 G89 1983
NYPL [JLM 83-380 no.32]

PROGRAMS, TELEVISION. see **TELEVISION PROGRAMS.**

Programs to improve coverage in the 1980 census. Census of population and housing (1980). Evaluation and research reports. Programs to improve coverage in the 1980 census. 1980 census of population and housing. Washington, D.C. [1987] 83 p. : LC Card

87-601259
HA201 1980aa

Progreso y miseria /. George, Henry, 1839-1897. [Progress and poverty. Spanish.] [Madrid , 1985?] cxv, 384 p. : ISBN 84-7479-375-0 : LC Card 87-112201
HB171 .G276 1985

Progresos de la administración del trabajo en las últimas décadas . Difrieri, Jorge A. (Jorge Alberto) Lima, Perú , 1985. 19 p. ; LC Card 86-152814
HD8110.5 .D54 1985

Progress of development banking in India /. Lakshmana Rao, V., 1940- Allahabad, India , 1986. xvi, 139 p. ; ISBN 81-85076-07-3 : LC Card 86-902782 DDC 332.2 19
HG3284 .L35 1986

Progress of the working class, 1832-1867 /. Ludlow, John Malcolm Forbes, 1821-1911. New York , 1984. xv, 304 p. ; ISBN 0-8240-5717-1 (alk. paper) : LC Card 83-48490 DDC 305.5/62/0942 19
HD8390 .L93 1984 ***NYPL [JLC 86-387]***

Progression à froid. Die Kalte Progression . Bern , 1982. 107 p. : LC Card 83-128720
HJ4747 .K35 1982

PROGRESSIVISM (UNITED STATES POLITICS)
Sklar, Martin J., 1935- The corporate reconstruction of American capitalism, 1890-1916 . Cambridge [Cambridgeshire] , New York , 1987. p. cm. ISBN 0-521-30921-2 LC Card 87-9408 DDC 338.8/0973 19
HC110.C3 S58 1987

Progresso técnico e evolução estratégica na indústria de máquinas-ferramentas . Rendeiro, João Oliveira. Lisboa , 1985. 111 p. : LC Card 86-189891
HD9703.E92 R45 1985

Proizvoditel´nost´ i oplata truda v APK /. Vorontsov, A. P. (Alekseĭ Pavlovich) Moskva , 1985. 191 p. ; LC Card 86-130051
HD9015.S652 V67 1985

Proizvoditel´nost´ truda--glavnoe zveno ėffektivnosti /. Vinogradov, I. P. (Igor´ Petrovich) Moskva , 1980. 192 p. ; LC Card 81-134882
HC340.L3 V459 1980

Proizvoditel´nost´ truda i zarabotnai͡a plata v stroitel´stve sooruzhenii͡ svi͡azi /. Ivanov, V. R. (Vladimir Romanovich) Moskva , 1985. 159 p. : LC Card 85-224803
HD9715.S72 I9 1985

Proizvoditel´nost´ truda v razvitom sotsialisticheskom obshchestve / pod redakt͡sieĭ M.G. Nazarova, I.D. Kostova. Moskva : "Ėkonomika", 1982. 214 p. ; 22 cm. Includes bibliographical references. LC Card 83-166417
1. Labor productivity - Soviet Union. 2. Labor productivity - Bulgaria. I. Nazarov, Mikhail Georgievich. II. Kostov, Ivan Dimitrov.
HC340.L3 P687 1982

Proizvoditel´nost´ truda v stroitel´stve . Serov, V. M. (Viktor Mikhaĭlovich) Moskva , 1986. 253 p. : LC Card 85-179119
HD9715.S72 S47 1986

Proizvoditel´nost´ truda--vazhneĭshiĭ faktor povyshenii͡a ėffektivnosti proizvodstva / pod redakt͡sieĭ P.A. Khromova ; [rabota napisana kollektivom avtorov P.A. Khromov ... et al.]. Moskva : Izd-vo "Nauka", 1982. 358 p. ; 21 cm. At head of title: Akademii͡a nauk SSSR. Institut ėkonomiki. Includes bibliographical references. LC Card 83-140430
1. Labor productivity - Soviet Union. 2. Industrial productivity - Soviet Union. I. Khromov, P. A. (Pavel Alekseevich). II. Institut ėkonomiki (Akademii͡a nauk SSSR).
HC340.L3 P693 1982

Proizvoditel´nost´ truda--samoe vazhnoe, samoe glavnoe (Stroĭizdat (Firm))
Borisov, I͡U. D. (I͡Uriĭ Dmitrievich) Ėkonomicheskie problemy povyshenii͡a proizvoditel´nosti truda v stroitel´stve /. Moskva , 1985. 183 p. ; LC Card 86-208622
HD9715.S72 B67 1985

Serov, V. M. (Viktor Mikhaĭlovich) Proizvoditel´nost´ truda v stroitel´stve . Moskva , 1986. 253 p. : LC Card 85-179119
HD9715.S72 S47 1986

Proizvoditel´nye sily i monopolisticheskiĭ kapital v Rossii i Germanii v kontse XIX-nachale XX vv. / [otvetstvennye redaktory V.I. Bovykin, Kh. Nussbaum]. Moskva : In-t istorii SSSR AN SSSR, 1986. 223 p. ; 20 cm. At head of title: Akademii͡a nauk SSSR. Institut istorii SSSR. Akademii͡a nauk GDR. Institut ėkonomicheskoĭ istorii. Includes bibliographies. LC Card 87-159751
1. Industrial concentration - Germany - History. 2. Monopolies - Germany - History. 3. Industry and state - Germany - History. 4. Industrial concentration - Soviet Union - History. 5. Monopolies - Soviet Union - History. 6. Industry and state - Soviet Union - History. I. Bovykin, Valeriĭ Ivanovich. II. Nussbaum, Helga. III. Institut istorii SSSR (Akademii͡a nauk SSSR). IV. Akademie der Wissenschaften der DDR. Institut für Wirtschaftsgeschichte.
HD2859 .P76 1986

Proizvodstvenite vrŭzki v agrarno-promishlenata oblast /. Vŭlchev, Nikola. Sofii͡a , 1986. 183 p. ; LC Card 86-195329
HD9015.B82 V84 1986

Proizvodstvennai͡a sfera sovremennogo sela /. Kuznetsova, T. E. Moskva , 1986. 199 p. ; LC Card 86-164902
HD9015.S652 K89 1986

Proizvodstvennoe nakoplenie . Puzanov, V. D. (Valeriĭ Dmitrievich) Moskva , 1983. 109 p. ; LC Card 83-194433
HC340.S3 P89 1983

Proizvodstvennye fondy kak ėkonomicheskai͡a kategorii͡a /. Lenskai͡a, S. A. (Svetlana Alekseevna) Moskva , 1982. 126 p. ; LC Card 83-134249
HC340.C3 L396 1982

Proizvodstvennye ob˝edinenii͡a : organizat͡sii͡a, ėffektivnost´, perspektivy razvitii͡a / [I͡U.A. Lavrikov ... et al.]. Moskva : "Ėkonomika", 1982. 173 p. ; 20 cm. Includes bibliographical references. LC Card 83-123241
1. Industrial organization - Soviet Union. I. Lavrikov, I͡Uriĭ Aleksandrovich.
HD70.S63 P764 1982

Proizvodstvennye resursy predprii͡atii͡a . Lebedev, I. P. (Igor´ Pavlovich) Moskva , 1984. 198 p. : LC Card 85-138003
HC340.I52 L42 1984

Proizvodstvennye svi͡azi v agrarno-promyshlennoĭ oblasti. Vŭlchev, Nikola. Proizvodstvenite vrŭzki v agrarno-promishlenata oblast /. Sofii͡a , 1986. 183 p. ; LC Card 86-195329
HD9015.B82 V84 1986

Proizvodstvo i potreblenie v regione /. Lipko, A. G. (Alekseĭ Gennad´evich) Moskva , 1986. 142 p. : LC Card 86-211374
HC336.25 .L56 1986

Proizvodstvo tovarov narodnogo potreblenii͡a . Kostin, Leonid Alekseevich. Moskva , 1980. 212 p. ; LC Card 87-107901
HF1040.9.S65 K67 1980

Projeção da população do Estado do Amazonas e seus municípios / Governo do Estado do Amazonas, Secretaria de Estado de Planejamento e Cooordenação [sic] Geral--SEPLAN, Centro de Desenvolvimento, Pesquisa e Tecnologia do Estado do Amazonas--CODEAMA. Manaus, Amazonas : Coordenadoria de Estudos e Pesquisas, 1984. 37 leaves ; 34 cm. Chiefly tables. LC Card 87-402133 DDC 304.6/0981/13021 19
1. Amazonas (Brazil) - Population - Statistics. 2. Population forecasting - Brazil - Amazonas - Statistics. I. Centro de Desenvolvimento, Pesquisa e Tecnologia do Estado do Amazonas. Coordenadoria de Estudos e Pesquisas.
HA988.A5 P76 1984

Project evaluation . Sang, Heng-Kang. New York, N.Y. , c1987. p. cm. ISBN 0-9617304-0-4 : LC Card 87-6074 DDC 338.9/0068 19
HD75.9 .S26 1987

Project Financing . Frank, Hermann. Wien , c1986. xii, 313 p. : ISBN 3-85428-066-1 LC Card 86-225790
HG4028.C4 F76 1986

Project identification . Mogridge, M. C. Nairobi [1971] 81 leaves in various pagings : LC Card 87-118674
HE283.5.Z7 N456 1971

Project management. 2, Planning a project and building your project team [videorecording] / Chicago, Ill. : Encyclopaedia Britannica Educational Corp., 1987, c1985. 1 videocassette (30 min.) : sd., col. + 1 teacher's guide. Title from data sheet. Issued as U-matic 3/4 in. or Beta II 1/2 in. or VHS 1/2 in. Project management authority A. Richard De Luca covers the process of project management including the elements of the planning process, making a project definition statement, project phases, selection of a project team, communication formats, and initial team meeting. LC Card 87-705140 DDC 658.4 11
1. Industrial project management. I. De Luca, A. Richard. II. Instrument Society of America. III. Encyclopaedia Britannica Educational Corporation. IV. Title: Planning a project and building your project team.
HD69.P75

Project management . Ahmed, Mumtaz. Hamilton, Ont. [1986] xv, 254 p. : ISBN 0-920212-56-5 (pbk.) LC Card 87-158681 DDC 658.4/04 19
HF5635 .A26 1986

Project management . Goel, Brij Bhushan. New Delhi , c1987. 352 p. : LC Card 87-900676 DDC 338.954/0068 19
HD69.P75 G635 1987

PROJECT MANAGEMENT - DEVELOPING COUNTRIES - DECISION MAKING.
Hellinger, Steve. Aid for just development . Washington, D.C. (1010 Vermont Ave., N.W., Suite 521, Washington 20005) , c1987. vii, 191 p. ; LC Card 87-404422 DDC 338.91/09172/4 19
HC60 .H38516 1987

Project management handbook / edited by David I. Cleland, William R. King. 2nd ed. New York : Van Nostrand Reinhold, 1988. p. cm. Includes index. ISBN 0-442-22114-2 LC Card 87-23151 DDC 658.4/04 19
1. Industrial project management. I. Cleland, David I. II. King, William Richard, 1938-.
HD69.P75 P75 1988

PROJECT MANAGEMENT, INDUSTRIAL.
see **INDUSTRIAL PROJECT MANAGEMENT.**

Project manpower management . Anderson, S. D. (Stuart D.) New York , c1987. ix, 509 p. : ISBN 0-471-86189-8 LC Card 86-26728 DDC 624/.068 19
HD9715.A2 A515 1987

Project monitoring and evaluation in agriculture /. Casley, D. J. Baltimore , c1987. xiii, 159 p. : ISBN 0-8018-3616-6 (pbk.) LC Card 87-22632 DDC 351.82/33 19
HD1415 .C335 1987

Project on the Federal Social Role (U. S.). Committee on Federalism and National Purpose. To form a more perfect union / the report of the Committee on Federalism and National Purpose, Daniel J. Evans and Charles S. Robb, Chairmen. Washington, D.C. (1730 M St., Suite 911, Washington 20036) : National Conference on Social Welfare, c1985. xi, 52 p. ; 25 cm. "The Committee on Federalism and National Purpose was convened in the summer of 1984 under the auspices of the National Conference on Social Welfare's Project on the Federal Social Role"--P. vii. Includes bibliographical references.
1. Public welfare - United States - Finance. 2. Federal government - United States. 3. Intergovernmental fiscal relations - United States. ***NYPL [JLE 86-1879]***

Project on United States-Mexico Relations. U. S.-Mexico relations . Stanford, Calif. , c1987. xii, 401 p. ; ISBN 0-8047-1319-7 (alk. paper) LC Card 86-23103 DDC 338.1/872 19
HD1792 .U19 1987

Project planning and management . Goodman, Louis J. New York , 1988. ix, 302 p. : ISBN 0-442-22762-0 LC Card 87-6192 DDC 658.4/04 19
HD69.P75 G65 1988

Project 1.04 . Clifton-Brown, E. Salisbury, Zimbabwe [1977] 46 leaves ; LC Card 84-256608
HD3562.3.A4 C55 1977

Project 1.07 . Whitsun Foundation. Harare, Zimbabwe [1983?] 2 v. ; ISBN 0-7974-0597-6 LC Card 84-981092 DDC 380.1/096891 19
HF3902 .W48 1983 ***NYPL [JLM 87-272]***

Project 1.09 . Whitsun Foundation. Harare, Zimbabwe [1983?] ix, 260 p. : ISBN 0-7974-0607-7 (pbk.) LC Card 87-402552

DDC 332.1/096891 19
HG1352 .W48 1983

Project 3,04(a), Peasant sector credit plan (revised) . Whitsun Foundation. Salisbury, Rhodesia [1978] ii, 18 leaves ; LC Card 86-981359
HG2051.Z55 W45 1978

Project 3.05, rural workshop and machinery centre . Kirk, T. Salisbury, Zimbabwe , 1977. 1 v. (various pagings) : LC Card 85-104610
HD2131.Z9 S265 1977

Projectcontrolling als Subsystem des Rechnungswesens /. Persoglia, Johann. Graz , c1986. 238 p. ; ISBN 3-7041-0149-4 LC Card 87-407965 DDC 657/.42 19
HF5686.C8 P475 1986

Projected population of Western Australia and the Perth Statistical Division, 1985-2025. [Perth] : Western Australian Treasury, [1986] 82 p. : ill. ; 30 cm. "March 1986." LC Card 87-114601 DDC 304.6/2/09941021 19
1. Western Australia - Population - Statistics. 2. Population forecasting - Australia - Western Australia - Statistics. 3. Perth Region (W.A.) - Population - Statistics. 4. Population forecasting - Australia - Perth Region (W.A.) - Statistics. I. Western Australia. Treasury. II. Title.
HA3007.W47 P76 1986

Projecting migration for integrated rural and urban development planning. Liege, Belgium : I.U. S.S.P., c1980. 46 p. ; 24 cm. (IUSSP papers . no. 16) "Committee on Demographic Aspects of Family Planning Programs." Summaries of major issues addressed and abstracts of papers presented at the Seminar on Innovative Approaches to Projecting Migration for Integrated Rural and Urban Development Planning that was held in Oulu, Finland, 8/22-26/78, under the auspices of the IUSSP Committee on Urbanization and Population Redistribution. Includes bibliographical references. LC Card 84-221919 DDC 304.8 19
1. Migration, Internal - Congresses. 2. Population forecasting - Congresses. I. International Union for the Scientific Study of Population. Committee on Demographic Aspects of Family Planning Programs. II. International Union for the Scientific Study of Population. Committee on Urbanization and Population Redistribution. III. Seminar on Innovative Approaches to Projecting Migration for Integrated Rural and Urban Development Planning (1978 : Oulu, Finland). IV. Series: International Union for the Scientific Study of Population. IUSSP papers, no. 16.
HB1952 .P76 1980
NYPL [JLL 77-289 no. 16]

Projection series.
Employment and labor force in Maryland . Baltimore, Md. (301 W. Preston St., Baltimore) [1986] xliv, 164, [51] p. : LC Card 86-622107 DDC 331.12/5/09752 19
HD5725.M35 E43 1986

Projections provisoires des ménages et des familles pour le Canada, les provinces et territoires jusqu'à 2006. Interim household and family projections for Canada, provinces, and territories to 2006 =. [Ottawa] [1987] 67 p. ; LC Card 87-162270 DDC 304.6/2/0971021 19
HA745 .I62 1987

Projekt-Controlling bei der Entwicklung neuer Produkte /. Offermann, Andreas. Thun , c1985. 524 p. : ISBN 3-87144-885-0 LC Card 85-208022
HD69.N4 O36 1985

Projektgruppe Arbeitslosigkeit und Neue Armut (Germany) Arbeitslosigkeit und Neue Armut in Düsseldorf . Bochum , c1986. 65 p. : ISBN 3-925222-03-0 LC Card 87-409036 DDC 331.13/794355 19
HD5780.D85 A73 1986

Projektgruppe Automation und Qualifikation (Freie Universität Berlin. Psychologisches Institut) Widersprüche der Automationsarbeit . West-Berlin , c1987. 228 p. ; ISBN 3-88619-362-4 LC Card 87-145099 DDC 331.12/0943 19
HD6331.2.G28 W55 1987

Projektmanagement, INTERNATIONAL / herausgegeben von Eberhard Dülfer ; Ko[m]mission Internationales Management im Verband der Hochschullehrer für Betriebswirtschaft e.V. Stuttgart : C.E. Poeschel, c1982. x, 244 p. : ill. ; 24 cm. Includes bibliographies and index. CONTENTS. - Projekte und Projektmanagement im internationalen Kontext / Eberhard Dülfer -- Projektmanagement von Anlagengeschäften insbesondere in Entwicklungsländern / Heiner Schmitz -- Projektmanagement in der technischen Zusammenarbeit am Beispiel der GTZ / Hans-Peter Merz -- Management von Industrieförderungsprojekten in Entwicklungsländern / Norbert Fromm -- Management von Forschungsprojekten über multinationale Unternehmen beim Internationalen Arbeitsamt (IAA) / Paul J. Bailey -- Stochastische Methoden der Planung betriebswirtschaftlicher Projekte in Entwicklungsländern / Hans-Jürgen Wurl -- Aspekte der Angemessenheit von Techniken für industrielle Projekte in Entwicklungsländern / Bernd Schiemenz -- Internationale Projektfinanzierungen / Frank Heintzeler -- Probleme des internationalen Projektmanagements aus sozialorganisatorischer Sicht / Friedrich Fürstenberg -- Zum Problem des Auslandseinsatzes von Stammhaus-Mitarbeiten in Rahmen des internationalen Projektmanagements / Brij Kumar und Horst Steinmann -- INTERCO / Lothar G. Winter. ISBN 3-7910-0339-9 LC Card 83-183718
1. Industrial project management. I. Dülfer, Eberhard. II. Verband der Hochschullehrer für Betriebswirtschaft. Kommission Internationales Management. III. Title: INTERNATIONAL.
HD69.P75 P764 1982

Projektplanung in der kleinbäuerlichen Produktion /. Brandt, Hartmut. Berlin , 1982. xv, 208 p. : LC Card 83-193407
HD1476.G3 B73 1982 ***NYPL [JLE 87-2903]***

Projektübergabe bei der technischen Zusammenarbeit mit Entwicklungsländer /. Neun, Hansjörg, 1953- Augsburg [1985] viii, 315 p. : ISBN 3-87512-135-X : LC Card 86-228570
HD84 .N43 1985

Le Projet Delaney : instrument essentiel pour bâtir le Québec : considérations socio-économiques sur le projet d'une centrale hydro-électrique à réserve-pompée dans Portneuf. [St-Raymond, Québec] : Le Comité Delaney, [1983] 76 leaves in various foliations : ill. ; 28 cm. "Mars 1983." On cover: Mémoire sur le projet de la centrale Delaney. Bibliography: leaf [31] LC Card 84-224364
1. Electric utilities - Québec (Province) - Portneuf (County). 2. Hydroelectric power plants - Québec (Province) - Portneuf (County). 3. Pumped storage power plants - Québec (Province) - Portneuf (County). 4. Portneuf (Québec : County) - Economic conditions. I. Comité Delaney. II. Title: Mémoire sur le projet de la centrale Delaney.
HD9685.C3 Q456 1983

Projet pour la France : construire nos communautés / Le Cercle de la cité, Le Club de l'astrolabe. Paris : Livre-Essor, c1983. 196 p. ; 23 cm. Includes bibliographical references. ISBN 2-7340-0032-6 : LC Card 83-196098
1. France - Economic policy - 1945-. 2. France - Social policy - 1945-. 3. Community development - France. I. Cercle de la cité (Paris, France). II. Club de l'astrolabe (Lyon, France).
HC276.2 .P767 1983

Projeto "Alternativas de Atendimento aos Meninos de Rua" (Brazil) Eu preciso trabalhar . Rio de Janeiro [between 1983 and 1986] 85 p. ; LC Card 86-150189
HD6276.B72 E9 1983

Projeto de Desenvolvimento Integrado da Bacia do Araguaia-Tocantins.
Descrição da área e caracterização do projeto / PRODIAT, Projeto de Desenvolvimento Integrado da Bacia do Araguaia-Tocantins. Brasília : PRODIAT, 1983. 129 p. : ill., maps ; 22 cm. "Ministério do Interior, Organização dos Estados Americanos; Governo do Estado de Goiás, Governo do Estado do Pará, Governo do Estado do Maranhão, Governo do Estado do Mato Grosso." LC Card 87-130908 DDC 338.981/73 19
1. Economic development projects - Brazil - Araguaia River Watershed. 2. Economic development projects - Brazil - Tocantins River Watershed. I. Title.
HC188.A73 P76 1983

Estudo do mercado de carne bovina /. Brasília , 1985. 89 p. : LC Card 86-197081
HD9433.B82 A74 1985

Finanças públicas dos Estados de Goiás, Maranhão, Mato Grosso e Pará /. Brasília , 1985. 114, [34] p. ; LC Card 87-404251 DDC 336.81 19
HJ929.G65 F56 1985

Finanças públicas municipais da região do PRODIAT /. Brasília , 1985. 420 p. ; LC Card 86-195656
HJ9388.A2 A734 1985

Fontes de financiamento para projetos de desenvolvimento / Projeto de Desenvolvimento Integrado da Bacia do Araguaia-Tocantins. Brasília : PRODIAT, 1985. 450 p. : ill. ; 22 cm. (Série Estudos e pesquisas. no. 9) At head of title: Ministério do Interior, Organização dos Estados Americanos, Governo do Estado de Goiás, Governo do Estado do Maranhão, Governo do Estado do Pará, Governo do Estado de Mato Grosso. Bibliography: p. 449. LC Card 86-195649
1. Economic development projects - Brazil - Araguaia River Region - Finance. 2. Economic development projects - Brazil - Tocantins River Region - Finance. I. Series: Série Estudos e pesquisas (Projeto de Desenvolvimento Integrado da Bacia do Araguaia-Tocantins) , no. 9. II. Title.
HC188.A7 P76 1985

Perfis indicativos para a industrialização do arroz, milho e soja. Brasília , 1985. 189 p. : LC Card 86-195651
HD9066.B83 A737 1985

Plano de desenvolvimento da área-programa do Vale do Paraná / PRODIAT, Projeto de Desenvolvimento Integrado da Bacia do Araguaia-Tocantins. Brasília : PRODIAT, 1985. 128 p., [8] folded leaves of plates : maps ; 26 cm. (Série Planejamento e programação . no. 4) At head of title: Ministério do Interior, Organização dos Estados Americanos, Governo do Estado de Goiás, Governo do Estado do Pará, Governo do Estado do Maranhão, Governo do Estado de Mato Grosso. Includes bibliographical references. LC Card 86-199833
1. Paranã River Valley (Goiás, Brazil) - Economic policy. 2. Paranã River Valley (Goiás, Brazil) - Social policy. 3. Natural resources - Brazil - Paranã River Valley (Goiás). I. Title. II. Series.
HC188.P36 P76 1985

Plano de desenvolvimento das áreas-programa de Araguaína e Tocantinópolis / PRODIAT, Projeto de Desenvolvimento Integrado da Bacia do Araguaia-Tocantins. Brasília : PRODIAT, 1985. 95 p., [8] leaves of plates : maps ; 26 cm. (Série Planejamento e programação . no. 3) At head of title: Ministério do Interior, Organização dos Estados Americanos, Governo do Estado de Goiás, Governo do Estado do Pará, Governo do Estado do Maranhão, Governo do Estado de Mato Grosso. Includes bibliographical references. LC Card 86-200369
1. Araguaína Region (Brazil) - Economic policy. 2. Tocantinópolis Region (Brazil) - Economic policy. 3. Araguaína Region (Brazil) - Social policy. 4. Tocantinópolis Region (Brazil) - Social policy. 5. Regional planning - Brazil - Araguaína Region. 6. Regional planning - Brazil - Tocantinópolis Region. I. Title. II. Series.
HC189.A67 P76 1985

Projeto de pesquisa--política de preços para a agricultura .
(v. especial 5) Análise das distorções dos preços domésticos em relação aos preços de fronteira . Brasília , 1983. 125 p. : LC Card 86-200859
HD9014.B82 A66 1983

Projeto perfil empresarial. Análise econômico-financeira da indústria de mineração, 1978-1982 /. Brasília , 1984. viii, 105 p. : LC Card 86-146667
HD9506.B72 A65 1984

Projeto Pesca Industrial à Vela. Paiva, Francisco Ismar Martins. [Natal, Brazil] [1982 or 1983] 91 p. : LC Card 85-102872
HD9464.B73 R487 1982

Projeto sertanejo : região Nordeste e estado do Piauí : realizações 1982. [Brasília] : Ministério do Interior, Secretaria Geral, Secretaria de Planejamento : Secretaria de Programas Regionais, [1982?] 20 leaves, [1] leaf of plates : map ; 30 cm. (Série Programas especiais . 61) LC Card 87-405007
1. Agriculture and state - Brazil, Northeast. 2. Agriculture and state - Brazil - Piauí. 3. Water resources development - Brazil, Northeast. 4. Water resources development - Brazil - Piauí. I. Brazil. Ministério do Interior. Secretaria de Planejamento. II. Brazil. Ministério do Interior. Secretaria de Programas Regionais. III. Series.
HD1875.N6 P76 1982

Projeto Tabuleiros Norte de Sergipe /

CONDESE, Conselho do Desenvolvimento de Sergipe, CEPA/SE, Comissão Estadual de Planejamento Agrícola de Sergipe. Aracaju : A Comissão, 1977. 521 p. : maps ; 29 cm. "Convênio: MA/SUDENE/CONDESE/SUDAP/EMATER-SE." Bibliography: p. 515-521. LC Card 86-131158
1. Agriculture - Economic aspects - Brazil - Sergipe. 2. Agriculture - Brazil - Sergipe. 3. Rural development - Brazil - Sergipe. I. Comissão Estadual de Planejamento Agrícola de Sergipe.
HD1875.S4 P76 1977

Prokhorova, Galina Nikolaevna. Mezhdunarodnye organizatsii vo vneshneėkonomicheskoĭ politike imperializma / G.N. Prokhorova ; otvetstvennyĭ redaktor P.I. Khvoĭnik. Moskva : "Nauka", 1986. 183 p. ; 22 cm. At head of title: Akademiia nauk SSSR. Ordena Trudovogo Krasnogo Znameni Institut mirovoĭ ėkonomiki i mezhdunarodnykh otnosheniĭ. Includes bibliographical references. LC Card 86-232949
1. Commercial policy. I. Khvoĭnik, Pavel Ignat'evich. II. Title.
HF1411 .P692 1986

Prokhorova, V. A. Voprosy istorii sotsialisticheskogo preobrazovaniia i razvitiia sel'skogo khoziaĭstva Chuvashskoĭ ASSR /. Cheboksary , 1985. 176 p. ; LC Card 86-100164
HD1492.5.S65 C488 1985

Prokof'ev, A. P. (Aleksandr Pavlovich) Ėkonomika, organizatsiia i planirovanie proizvodstva v khimicheskoĭ promyshlennosti /. Moskva , 1986. 254 p. : LC Card 86-227240
HD9656.S55 E38 1986

Prokopp, Ludwig Ferdinand. Europäische Commerzreisen um die Mitte des 18. Jahrhunderts / von Ludwig Ferdinand Prokopp, Aloisius Graf Podstatzky und Karl Graf Haugwitz ; [Herausgeber], Gustav Otruba. Linz : R. Trauner, c1982. xiii, 446 p., [1] folded leaf of plates : ill. ; 25 cm. (Linzer Schriften zur Sozial- u. Wirtschaftsgeschichte . Bd. 5) Bibliography: p. 414-423. Includes indexes. ISBN 3-85320-296-1 LC Card 83-150921
1. Austria - Commerce - Central Europe - History - 18th century - Sources. 2. Central Europe - Commerce - Austria - History - 18th century - Sources. 3. Central Europe - Description and travel - Sources. I. Podstatzky, Aloisius, Graf. II. Haugwitz, Karl, Graf. III. Otruba, Gustav. IV. Title. V. Series.
HF3548.C36 P76 1982

Proletariat : Kultur und Lebensweise im 19. Jahrhundert / [herausgegeben von] Dietrich Mühlberg. Wien : H. Böhlau, 1986. 275 p. : ill. (some col.) ; 28 cm. (Kulturstudien. Sonderband . 2) Bibliography: p. [268]-271. Includes index. ISBN 3-205-00561-9 LC Card 86-673962
1. Labor and laboring classes - History - 19th century. 2. Labor and laboring classes - Social conditions. I. Mühlberg, Dietrich. II. Series.
HD4853 .P76x 1986

PROLETARIAT - ADDRESSES, ESSAYS, LECTURES.
Confrontation, class consciousness, and the labor process . Westport, Conn. , 1986. viii, 261 p. ; ISBN 0-313-25140-1 (lib. bdg. : alk. paper) LC Card 85-17734 DDC 305.5/62 19
HD4851 .C63 1986 ***NYPL [JLE 86-3558]***

Les Sauvages dans la cité . Seyssel , c1985. 229 p. ; ISBN 2-903528-53-5
NYPL [JLD 86-1133]

PROLETARIAT - COLLECTED WORKS.
Gauny, Gabriel, 1806-1889. [Selections. 1983.] Le philosophe plébéien /. Paris , Saint-Denis , c1983. 205 p. ; ISBN 2-7071-1420-0 : LC Card 84-105473
HD4853 .G382 1983

PROLETARIAT - HISTORY.
The German worker . Berkeley , c1987. p. cm. ISBN 0-520-05972-7 (alk. paper) LC Card 87-5076 DDC 305.5/62/0922 B 19
HD8453.A1 G47 1987

PROLETARIAT - SPAIN - ANDALUSIA - HISTORY - 19TH CENTURY.
Seis estudios sobre el proletariado andaluz (1868-1939). [Córdoba] , 1984. 247 p. ; ISBN 84-500-9584-0 LC Card 86-142680 DDC 305.5/62/09468 19
HD8589.A52 S45 1984
NYPL [JLD 87-1550]

PROLETARIAT - SPAIN - ANDALUSIA - HISTORY - 20TH CENTURY.
Seis estudios sobre el proletariado andaluz (1868-1939). [Córdoba] , 1984. 247 p. ; ISBN 84-500-9584-0 LC Card 86-142680 DDC 305.5/62/09468 19
HD8589.A52 S45 1984
NYPL [JLD 87-1550]

Proletarische Provinz . Tenfelde, Klaus. München , 1982. xvii, 409 p. : ISBN 3-486-50701-X : LC Card 83-124119
HD8460.P452 T46 1982

PROLIFERATION, NUCLEAR. see **NUCLEAR NONPROLIFERATION.**

Promemorior från SCB .

Promised land . Pearce, Jenny. London [S.l.] , 1986. viii, 324 p. : ISBN 0-906156-21-1 (pbk.) LC Card 86-141737 DDC 322.4/4/097284 19
HD1531.S2 P4 1986 ***NYPL [JLE 87-471]***

PROMISSORY NOTES - UNITED STATES.
Story, Joseph, 1779-1845. Commentaries on the law of promissory notes [microform]. Boston, 1868. xliv, 739 p. LC Card 12-34848
NYPL [*ZT-1734]

Promoción agraria, para quién? : análisis de la Ley de promoción y desarrollo agrario / José Manuel Mejía, compilador ; [ensayos de] Bruno Revesz Long ... [et al.].1a ed. Lima, Perú : Tiempo Presente, 1980. 162 p. ; 21 cm. CONTENTS. - De la reforma agraria a la promoción agropecuaria. Un análisis crítico de la nueva política agraria / José Manuel Mejía -- La ley : promoción y desarrollo agrario? / Bruno Revesz Long -- La nueva conquista de la Amazonía / Francisco Ballón Aguirre -- La reestructuración de la tenencia de la tierra y de las empresas asociativas / Hernán Castillo Ardiles -- La crisis de la alimentación y el papel de la agroindustria / Manuel Lajo Lazo -- Comentarios finales / José Manuel Mejía -- Apéndice 1 : Bases para una política agraria alternativa -- Apéndice 2 : El campesinado y los productores ante la ley.
1. Peru. Ley de promoción y desarrollo agrario. 2. Peru. Ley orgánica del sector agrario. 3. Land reform - Peru. 4. Land tenure - Peru. I. Mejía, José Manuel. II. Revesz Long, Bruno. ***NYPL [JLD 86-3547]***

Promoción de las exportaciones no tradicionales : intercambio de experiencias entre España y el Perú / editor, Javier Portocarrero Maisch. [Lima, Peru] : Instituto de Investigaciones Cambio y Desarrollo : Instituto de Cooperación Iberoamericana : 145 p. ; 21 cm. Includes bibliographical references. LC Card 86-146920
1. Foreign trade promotion - Spain. 2. Foreign trade promotion - Peru. I. Portocarrero Maisch, Javier. II. Instituto de Investigaciones Cambio y Desarrollo (Peru). III. Instituto de Cooperación Iberoamericana (Madrid, Spain).
HF1569 .P76 1985 ***NYPL [JLD 87-1165]***

La promoción industrial en Argentina /. Ferrucci, Ricardo Jorge. [Buenos Aires] , c1986. 274 p. : ISBN 950-23-0307-5 LC Card 87-124151 DDC 338.982 19
HD3616.A73 F47 1986

Promoting energy conservation . Katzev, Richard D. Boulder , 1987. xvi, 218 p. : ISBN 0-8133-7337-9 (pbk.) : LC Card 86-32587 DDC 333.79/16 19
HD9502.A2 K38 1987

Promoting high-technology industry : initiatives and policies for state governments / edited by Jurgen Schmandt and Robert Wilson. Boulder : Westview Press, 1987. 283 p. ; 23 cm. (Westview special studies in science, technology and public policy) A project of the Lyndon B. Johnson School of Public Affairs. "Published in cooperation with the Houston Area Research Center." Includes bibliographies and index. ISBN 0-8133-7427-8 (pbk. : alk. paper) LC Card 87-61327 DDC 338.4/762/000973 19
1. High technology industries - United States - States. 2. Industrial promotion - United States - States. 3. Technology and state - United States - States. 4. United States - Population. 5. United States - Economic conditions - 1981-. I. Schmandt, Jurgen. II. Wilson, Robert Hines. III. Lyndon B. Johnson School of Public Affairs. IV. Houston Area Research Center.
HC110.H53 P76 1987

Promoting issues & ideas : a guide to public relations for nonprofit organizations / by Public Interest Public Relations. New York, N.Y. : Foundation Center, 1987. 183 p. : ill. ; 24 cm. Bibliography: p. [177]-178. Includes index. ISBN 0-87954-192-X (pbk.) : LC Card 87-7600 DDC 659.2/88 19
1. Corporations, Nonprofit - Management. 2. Public relations. I. Public Interest Public Relations, inc. II. Title: Promoting issues and ideas.
HD62.6 .P76 1987

Promoting issues and ideas. Promoting issues & ideas . New York, N.Y. , 1987. 183 p. : ISBN 0-87954-192-X (pbk.) : LC Card 87-7600 DDC 659.2/88 19
HD62.6 .P76 1987

Promotion de la petite industrie dans les pays en développement / ... compte-rendu ... rédigé par Stanislas Hutin. Paris : Centre d'information et de formation des agents en coopération et à l'étranger : Groupe de recherche et d'échanges technologiques, c1985. 103 p. : ill. ; 21 cm. (Collection des ateliers du développement . no 5) "Ce texte fait suite au séminaire conçu et animé en septembre 1984." "Ce séminaire ... s'inscrit dans la continuité de la réflexion engagée depuis deux ans par la Cellule industrie du GRET"--P. iii. Bibliography: p. 93-95. ISBN 2-86844-008-8 LC Card 85-242526 DDC 338.6/42/0943 19
1. Small business - Government policy - Developing countries - Congresses. 2. Industrial promotion - Developing countries - Congresses. I. Hutin, Stanislas. II. France. Groupe de recherche et d'échanges technologiques. Cellule Industrie. III. Series.
HD2346.5 .P76 1985 ***NYPL [JLD 86-3171]***

Promotion of cooperation amongst research and development organizations in the field of vocational training : working meeting papers-20/21 May 1985 / CEDEFOP.1st ed. Berlin : CEDEFOP, European Centre for the Development of Vocational Training ; Washington, DC : European Community Information Service [distributor], 1986. 111 p. ; 30 cm. (CEDEFOP document) ISBN 92-825-6570-X (pbk.) : LC Card 87-133749 DDC 331.25/92/094
1. Occupational training - Government policy - Europe. I. European Centre for the Development of Vocational Training. II. Series.
HD5715.5.E78 P77 1986

Promotion of employment and incomes for the rural poor, including rural women, through non-farm activities : second item on the agenda / Advisory Committee on Rural Development. Geneva : International Labour Office, 1983. 131 p. ; 24 cm. "Table of Contents": v. p. inserted. Errata slip inserted. Includes bibliographical references. ISBN 92-2-103506-9 (pbk.) : LC Card 86-221308 DDC 331.12/042/091734 19
1. Rural poor - Employment - Congresses. 2. Rural development - Congresses. I. International Labour Organisation. Advisory Committee on Rural Development.
HD5710.8 .P76 1983

The Promotion of non-conventional approaches to housing finance for low-income groups. Nairobi : United Nations Centre for Human Settlements (Habitat), 1984. ii, 54 p. ; 30 cm. "HS/62/84/E"--T.p. verso. Bibliography: p. 54. LC Card 86-980642 DDC 363.5/8 19
1. Poor - Housing - Finance. I. United Nations Centre for Human Settlements.
HD7287.95 .P76 1984

Promotion strategies for household cleaning products. New York, N.Y. : Frost & Sullivan, c1983. 2 v. (xx, 635 p.) ; 29 cm. "March 1983." "#A989." LC Card 87-142358 DDC 381/.456671/0973 19
1. Cleaning compounds industry - United States. 2. Synthetic detergents industry - United States. 3. Soap trade - United States. 4. Cleaning compounds - Marketing. 5. Detergents, Synthetic - Marketing. 6. Soap - Marketing. 7. Market surveys - United States. I. Frost & Sullivan.
HD9999.C4863 U56 1983

Promotional management : issues and perspectives / [compiled by] Norman Govoni, Robert Eng, Morton Galper. Englewood Cliffs, N.J. : Prentice-Hall, c1988. xi, 305 p. : ill. ; 24 cm. Includes bibliographies. ISBN 0-13-731035-8 (pbk.) LC Card 87-12041 DDC 658.8 19
1. Marketing. 2. Sales promotion. 3. Advertising. I. Govoni, Norman A. P. II. Eng, Robert J. III. Galper, Morton.
HF5415 .P727 1988

Promotional practices and policies . Connolly, Paul M. New York , c1985. 52 p. ; ISBN 0-08-029515-0 (pbk.) : LC Card 85-3421 DDC

658.3/142 19
HF5549.2.U5 C66 1985
NYPL [JLM 83-380 no.41]

PROMOTIONS.
Chapman, Jack, 1945- How to make $1,000 a minute . Berkeley, Calif. , c1987. xii, 90 p. : ISBN 0-89815-191-0 (pbk.) : LC Card 86-23099 DDC 650.1/4 19
HF5549.5.P7 C48 1987

Lewis, Diane, 1936- Why women fail in business /. Nashville , c1987. p. cm. ISBN 0-8407-4219-3 : LC Card 87-15370 DDC 658.4/09088042 19
HD6054.3 .L48 1987

Mrkvicka, Edward F. Moving up . New York , 1985. 193 p. ; ISBN 0-688-02427-0 : LC Card 84-27272 DDC 650.1/4 19
HF5382.7 .M75 1985 ***NYPL [JLD 86-4148]***

Your job [filmstrip] . Pleasantville, NY , 1986. 2 filmstrips (ca. 74 fr. each) : LC Card 86-700184 DDC 650.1 11
HF5549.5.C35

Your job [videorecording] . Pleasantville, NY , 1986. 1 videocassette (30 min.) : LC Card 87-705039 DDC 650.1 11
HF5549.5.C35

PROMOTIONS - ITALY.
Organizzazione del lavoro, mobilità e aspetti formativi nella contrattazione . Milano, Italy , c1982. 172 p. ; LC Card 83-106874
HD6709 .O73 1982

Promyshlennost'. Guber, A. A. (Aleksandr Andreevich) Industry /. Moscow , 1985. 46 p., [16] p. of plates : LC Card 86-208070 DDC 338.947 19
HC336.25 .G8 1985

Promyshlennost' GDR . Volchenko, M. ÎA. (Maîa ÎAkovlevna) Moskva , 1981. 179 p. ; LC Card 82-115880
HC290.74 .V63 1981

Promyshlennost' i rabochiĭ klass Moldavskoĭ SSR v gody Velikoĭ Otechestvennoĭ voĭny /. Shornikov, P. M. (Petr Mikhaĭlovich) Kishinev , 1986. 148, [4] p. ; LC Card 86-141169
HC337.M553 D47 1986

Promyshlennost' Sotsialisticheskoĭ Respubliki Rumynii /. Samorukova, A. N. (Angara Nikolaevna) Moskva , 1986. 143 p. ; LC Card 86-202797
HC405 .S253 1986

Promyshlennost' Urala v gody Velikoĭ Otechestvennoĭ voĭny 1941-1945 /. Vasil'ev, A. F. (Aleksandr Filippovich) Moskva , 1982. 279 p., [1] folded leaf of plates : LC Card 83-165021
HC337.R852 U7387 1982

Promysly sibirskogo krest'îanstva v poreformennyĭ period /. Solov'eva, E. I., d-r ist. nauk. Novosibirsk , 1981. 327 p. : LC Card 82-111175
HD2346.S652 S527 1981

PRONAL.

PROPAGANDA.
Huxley, Aldous, 1894-1963. [Brave new world.] Brave new world ; and, Brave new world revisited /. London , 1984. xxii, 387 p. ; ISBN 0-7011-2769-4 : LC Card 84-134715 DDC 823/.912 19
PR6015.U9 B65 1984 ***NYPL [JFE 86-4706]***

Perris, Arnold. Music as propaganda . Westport, Conn. , c1985. x, 247 p. ; ISBN 0-313-24505-3 (lib. bdg.) LC Card 84-27969 DDC 781/.15 19
ML3838 .P43 1985 ***NYPL [JMD 86-149]***

PROPAGANDA AND RADIO. see **RADIO IN PROPAGANDA.**

PROPAGANDA, COMMUNIST - HUNGARY.
A Munkavédelem agitációs és propaganda rendszere /. Budapest , 1983. 51 p. : ISBN 963-7006-04-4 LC Card 85-110318
HD7702.5 .M85 1983

PROPAGANDA, GERMAN - HISTORY.
Surmann, Rolf. Die Münzenberg-Legende . Köln , c1983. 307 p. : ISBN 3-922009-53-0 LC Card 83-155325
HD8450 .S87 1983

PROPAGANDA IN RADIO. see **RADIO IN PROPAGANDA.**

Property and industrial development /. Fothergill, Steve. London , Wolfeboro, N.H. , 1987. 187 p. : ISBN 0-09-170741-2 (pbk.) : LC Card 87-2627 DDC 333.3/8/0941 19
HD598 .F68 1987

Property and kinship . Ditz, Toby L., 1951- Princeton, N.J. , c1986. xvi, 213 p. : ISBN 0-691-04735-9 (alk. paper) : LC Card 86-5051 DDC 333.33 19
HB715 .D58 1986 ***NYPL [JLE 86-4624]***

Property before people . Power, Anne. London , Boston , c1987. xvi, 268 p. : ISBN 0-04-350069-2 (alk. paper) LC Card 86-28751 DDC 363.5/8 19
HD7288.78.G7 P69 1987

PROPERTY - BRAZIL - SÃO PAULO (STATE) - HISTORY - 19TH CENTURY.
Mello, Zélia Maria Cardoso de. Metamorfoses da riqueza, São Paulo, 1845-1895 . São Paulo , 1985. 188 p. : LC Card 85-207635
HC188.S3 M49 1985

PROPERTY - CONNECTICUT - HISTORY.
Ditz, Toby L., 1951- Property and kinship . Princeton, N.J. , c1986. xvi, 213 p. : ISBN 0-691-04735-9 (alk. paper) : LC Card 86-5051 DDC 333.33 19
HB715 .D58 1986 ***NYPL [JLE 86-4624]***

PROPERTY INSURANCE. see **INSURANCE, PROPERTY.**

Property-liability insurance accounting / written and prepared by twenty authors, thirty-one reviewers, fourteen IASA textbook committeemen ; editor, Robert W. Strain. 3rd ed. Durham, N.C. : Insurance Accounting and Systems Association ; Wingdale, N.Y. : Available from Strain Pub., c1986. 1 v. (loose-leaf) : ill. ; 27 cm. Includes bibliographical references and index. LC Card 86-207635 DDC 657/.836 19
1. Insurance - Accounting. I. Strain, Robert W. II. Insurance Accounting and Systems Association.
HG8077 .P7 1986

Property management /. Kyle, Robert C. Chicago, IL , c1988. x, 422 p. : ISBN 0-88462-669-5 (pbk.) LC Card 87-17906 DDC 332.63/24/068 19
HD1394 .K94 1988

Property management reinvented . Shear, Mel A. Englewood-Cliffs, N.J. , c1988. xiii, 306 p. : ISBN 0-13-731191-5 LC Card 87-18852 DDC 333.3/068 19
HD1394 .S52 1988

Property, power, and public choice . Schmid, A. Allan (Alfred Allan), 1935- New York , 1987. xv, 332 p. : ISBN 0-275-92797-0 (alk. paper) : LC Card 87-22893 DDC 330.1 19
HB73 .S35 1987

PROPERTY, REAL. see **REAL PROPERTY.**

PROPERTY, RIGHT OF. see **RIGHT OF PROPERTY.**

Property rights, Freiheit und Wettbewerbspolitik /. Schmidtchen, Dieter. Tübingen , 1983. 71 p. ; ISBN 3-16-344630-2 (Deut. Bibl.) LC Card 84-100421
HF1410.5 .S36 1983

PROPERTY, SOCIALIST. see **SOCIALIST PROPERTY.**

PROPERTY TAX CREDIT - UNITED STATES.
Guggenheim, Joseph. Tax credits for low income housing . Washington, D.C. , c1986. vii, 117 p. : ISBN 0-941239-00-4 (pbk.) LC Card 87-112304 DDC 363.5/8 19
HJ4653.C73 G85 1986

Property tax delinquency in Minnesota : taxes payable in 1982 and 1983, delinquent in 1983 and 1984 / Department of Revenue. St. Paul, Minn. : The Department, Local Government Aids and Analysis Division, [1984?] iv, 84 p. : ill., maps ; 28 cm. Cover title. LC Card 86-622652 DDC 336.22 19
1. Real property tax - Minnesota. 2. Tax collection - Minnesota. I. Minnesota. Local Government Aids & Analysis Division.
HJ4232.A25 P76 1984

PROPERTY TAX - LAW AND LEGISLATION - SPAIN.
Poveda Blanco, Francisco. La valoración de bases imponibles en los impuestos sobre la renta y el patrimonio /. [Alicante] [1984?] 395 p. ; LC Card 84-216651 DDC 333.33/2/0946 19
HJ4125.S8 P68 1984 ***NYPL [JLE 86-1461]***

PROPERTY TAX - LAW AND LEGISLATION - UNITED STATES.
Property taxation /. Washington, D.C. , c1987. 1 v. (various pagings) ; LC Card 87-3326 DDC 336.22/0973 19
HJ4120 .P6717 1987

PROPERTY TAX - MISSOURI - RATES AND TABLES.
Kelly, Margaret. Review of 1985 property tax rates /. Jefferson City [1986] i, 6 leaves, 109, 2 p. ; LC Card 87-620606 DDC 336.22/2 19
HJ4121.M82 K45 1986

PROPERTY TAX - NEW JERSEY.
New Jersey. Bureau of Urban Strategies. Proposed solutions to local fiscal resource disparities in the state of New Jersey . Trenton, N.J. [1980] vi, 353 p. ; LC Card 81-622089 DDC 336.02/749 19
HJ585 .N38 1980 ***NYPL [JLF 86-1372]***

PROPERTY TAX - SPAIN.
Poveda Blanco, Francisco. La valoración de bases imponibles en los impuestos sobre la renta y el patrimonio /. [Alicante] [1984?] 395 p. ; LC Card 84-216651 DDC 333.33/2/0946 19
HJ4125.S8 P68 1984 ***NYPL [JLE 86-1461]***

PROPERTY TAX - UNITED STATES.
Property taxation /. Washington, D.C. , c1987. 1 v. (various pagings) ; LC Card 87-3326 DDC 336.22/0973 19
HJ4120 .P6717 1987

PROPERTY TAX - UNITED STATES - STATES.
Clatanoff, Robert M. Patterns of property tax administration in the United States /. Chicago, Ill. , 1986. x, 178 p. : ISBN 0-88329-145-2 (pbk.) LC Card 86-7240 DDC 353.9/37242 19
HJ4120 .C528 1986 ***NYPL [JLF 87-464]***

Property taxation / edited by Jerrold F. Janata. Washington, D.C. : Institute of Property Taxation, c1987. 1 v. (various pagings) ; 24 cm. Bibliography: p. rr1-rr4. Includes index. LC Card 87-3326 DDC 336.22/0973 19
1. Property tax - United States. 2. Property tax - Law and legislation - United States. I. Janata, Jerrold F., 1936-. II. Institute of Property Taxation (Washington, D.C.).
HJ4120 .P6717 1987

Propiedad y explotación agrarias del aljarafe sevillano. Camacho Rueda, Eduardo. Propiedad y explotación agrarias en el aljarafe sevillano . Sevilla , 1984. 199 p. : ISBN 84-500-9772-X LC Card 85-135028
HD773 .C18 1984

Propiedad y explotación agrarias en el aljarafe sevillano . Camacho Rueda, Eduardo. Sevilla , 1984. 199 p. : ISBN 84-500-9772-X LC Card 85-135028
HD773 .C18 1984

Propiedad y explotación agrarias en Puente Genil /. Jurado Carmona, María Isabel. Córdoba , 1984. 229 p. : ISBN 84-505-0063-X LC Card 85-139166 DDC 338.1/0946/84 19
HD2025.P84 J87 1984
NYPL [JLD 86-2522]

Propiedad y usos de la tierra en el Marquesado del Cenete /. Arias Abellán, Jesús. [Granada] , 1984. iv, 439 p. : ISBN 84-338-0229-1 LC Card 86-214060
HD779.C4 A75 1984

El propietario ausente . Ponce Vega, Luis. Lima , 1986. 80 p. ; LC Card 86-221571
HD9524.P44 S565 1986

Proposal to review the minimum age at which children may drive or ride on agricultural machinery /. Great Britain. Health and Safety Commission. London [1982] 12 p. ; ISBN 0-11-883635-8 (pbk.) LC Card 82-214120 DDC 363.1/89 19
HD6247.A4 G74 1982

Proposals for a cattle marketing strategy for Transkei /. Tapson, D. R. [Fort Hare] [1982] ii, 45 leaves, 4 leaves of plates : ISBN 0-949974-68-4 LC Card 86-209520 DDC 381/.4162/00968791 19
HD9433.S643 T77 1982

Proposals for an industrial and science strategy for Albertans, 1985-1990. Alberta. Position and policy statement on enhancing the Alberta

capital market. [Edmonton, Alta.] [1985] iii, 43 p. ; LC Card 86-137218 DDC 332.63/23 19
HG5150 .A42 1985

Proposals for the establishment of an African Institute of Chartered Accountants. Monday, H. R. [New York?] [1984] 10 p. ; LC Card 86-122510 DDC 657/.06/06 19
HF5616.A35 M65 1984

Proposed computer acquisition by the Australian Audit Office /. Australia. Parliament. Joint Committee of Public Accounts. Canberra , 1986. xiii, 256 p. : ISBN 0-644-05079-9 (pbk.) LC Card 86-234536 DDC 354.940072/32 19
HJ9931 .A875 1986

Proposed national strategies for the prevention of leading work-related diseases and injuries. [Washington, D.C.] : Association of Schools of Public Health, 1986- v. <1 > ; 28 cm. Reports from the National Symposium on the Prevention of Leading Work-related Diseases and Injuries, held May 1-3, 1985 in Atlanta, Ga. "Published ... under a cooperative agreement with the National Institute for Occupational Safety and Health." Includes bibliographical references. LC Card 87-111984 DDC 363.1/17/0973 19
1. Industrial hygiene - United States - Congresses. 2. Industrial accidents - United States - Congresses. I. Association of Schools of Public Health. II. National Symposium on the Prevention of Leading Work-related Diseases and Injuries (1985 : Atlanta, Ga.). III. National Institute for Occupational Safety and Health.
HD7262.5.U6 P75 1986

Proposed solutions to local fiscal resource disparities in the state of New Jersey . New Jersey. Bureau of Urban Strategies. Trenton, N.J. [1980] vi, 353 p. ; LC Card 81-622089 DDC 336.02/749 19
HJ585 .N38 1980 ***NYPL [JLF 86-1372]***

Proposiciones de economía civil y comercio. Normante y Carcavilla, Lorenzo. Discurso sobre la utilidad de los conocimientos económico-políticos y la necesidad de su estudio metódico ; Proposiciones de economía civil y comercio ; Espíritu del señor Melón en su ensayo político sobre el comercio /. [Aragón] [1984?] 1 v. (various pagings) ; ISBN 84-505-0473-2 LC Card 87-104302
HC385 .N57 1984

Proposta de consolidação do Pólo Petroquímico do Sul : horizonte 1995. [Porto Alegre] : Banco Regional de Desenvolvimento do Extremo Sul, [19]86. 17, [5], 9 p. : ill. ; 23 cm. Cover title: Pólo Petroquímico do Sul. "Este documento foi elaborado no âmbito da Gerência de Planejamento da Agência de Porto Alegre do BRDE." LC Card 87-404792 DDC 338.7/661804/098165 19
1. Pólo Petroquímico do Rio Grande do Sul. 2. Petroleum chemicals industry - Brazil - Rio Grande do Sul. I. Banco Regional de Desenvolvimento do Extremo Sul. Agência de Porto Alegre. Gerência de Planejamento. II. Title: Pólo Petroquímico do Sul.
HD9579.C33 B785 1986

Propostas cooperativistas / [Organização das Cooperativas do Estado do Paraná-OCEPAR] ; colaboração, Fundação Friedrich Naumann e OCB. Curitiba : OCEPAR, 1986. 56 p. : ill. ; 22 cm. (Série Cooperativismo . 1) Includes bibliographies. CONTENTS. - Integração cooperativista no setor agropecuário / Guntolf Vank [sic] Kaick -- Capitalização das cooperativas ; Autofiscalização em execução no Paraná / João Paulo Koslovski -- Comunicação, quale é o nosso ideal / Eloy Olindo Setti. LC Card 87-403655 DDC 334 19
1. Cooperative societies - Congresses. 2. Cooperative societies - Brazil - Paraná - Congresses. I. Koslovski, João Paulo. II. Kaick, Guntolf van. Integração cooperativista no setor agropecuário. 1986. III. Setti, Eloy Olindo. Comunicação, quale é o nosso ideal. 1986. IV. Organização das Cooperativas do Estado do Paraná. V. Friedrich Naumann Stiftung. VI. Organização das Cooperativas Brasileiras. VII. Series: Série Cooperativismo (Curitiba, Brazil) , 1.
HD2953 .P76 1986

A propriedade privada e a livre iniciativa no tufão agro-reformista /. Oliveira, Plinio Corrêa de, 1908- [São Paulo] [1985] xvi, 174 p., [16] p. of plates : LC Card 87-104428
HD1333.B6 O385 1985

Proprietary capitalism . Scranton, Philip. Philadelphia , 1987. p. cm. ISBN 0-87722-461-7 (pbk.) : LC Card 87-488 DDC 338.4/7677/00974811 19
HD9858.P5 S35 1987

La Propriété foncière / préface de Jean-Louis Guigou ; avec des contributions de D. Barthélémy ... [et al.]. Paris : Economica, c1984. vii, 252 p. : ill. ; 24 cm. At head of title: ADEF. "Cet ouvrage a été élaboré à partir des contributions présentées aux journées de rencontre de l'ADEF (avril 1983) et des débats qu'elles ont provoqués." Bibliography: p. [245]-250. ISBN 2-7178-0783-7 LC Card 84-249621
1. Real property - France. 2. Land tenure - France. I. Barthélemy, Denis. II. ADEF (Association : France).
HD643 .N49 1984

Propst, Robert. The office, a facility based on change / by Robert Propst. Rev. Zeeland, MI : H. Miller, 1986 printing, c1968. 71 p. : ill. (some col.) ; 29 cm. ISBN 0-936658-01-0 (pbk.) : LC Card 86-23653 DDC 651.3 19
1. Office management. I. Title.
HF5547 .P76 1986

Propuesta para el desarrollo de un programa de investigación sobre propiedad social con énfasis en cooperativismo / [Luis Fernando Mayorga Acuña, coordinador ... et al.]. San José, Costa Rica : Universidad de Costa Rica, Facultad de Ciencias Sociales, Instituto de Investigaciones Sociales, 1986. ii, 70 p. : ill. ; 27 cm. (Avances de investigación . anõ 1986, no. 56) "Programa de investigación y servicio sobre propiedad social en Costa Rica, con énfasis en cooperativismo." Includes bibliographical references. LC Card 87-125056 DDC 334/.097286 19
1. Cooperative societies - Research - Costa Rica. 2. Cooperation - Research - Costa Rica. I. Mayorga Acuña, Luis Fernando. II. Universidad de Costa Rica. Instituto de Investigaciones Sociales. III. Title: Programa de investigación y servicio sobre propiedad social en Costa Rica, con énfasis en cooperativismo. IV. Series: Avance de investigación , no. 56.
HD3454.A4 P76 1986

Prosjektevaluering i u-land . Sandanger, Runar. Oslo [1983] viii, 97 p. : LC Card 83-144428
HC60 .S156 1983

Prosjektfinansiering i petroleumsvirksomheten /. Selvig, Erling. Oslo [1983] 30, 5 p. ; LC Card 84-131887
HD9575.N62 S44 1983

The prospect for gold . Green, Timothy, 1936- New York, N.Y. , 1987. xi, 204 p. : ISBN 0-8027-1002-6 LC Card 87-16046 DDC 338.2/741 19
HG289 .G7395 1987

PROSPECTING - CANADA - COSTS.
Whillans, Robert T. Mineral exploration expenditures in Canada, 1969-1975 /. [Ottawa] , c1978. vi, 13 p. : LC Card 85-182002 DDC 338.2/3 19
HD9506.C2 W45 1978

PROSPECTING - ECONOMIC ASPECTS - UNITED STATES.
Meurer, Heinrich W., 1950- Wirtschaftsgeologische Aspekte bei der privaten Investition in Öl- und Gasbohrvorhaben in den USA /. [Cologne?] , 1982] (Aachen : Fotodruck J. Mainz) vi, 163 p., [3] folded leaves of plates : LC Card 84-200100
HD9565 .M48 1982

Prospective changes for handling of commodities in Canadian ports. Brouillette, Benoît, 1904-1979. [Perspectives de changements dans la manutention des marchandises aux ports canadiens. English.] Montréal, Québec, Canada [1974] iv, 93, [3] p. ; LC Card 82-219246
HE553 .B7613 1974

Prospective evolution of EEC common agricultural policy : its relevance for Mediterranean members / [edited by Fernando Brito Soares]. Lisboa : Fundação Calouste Gulbenkian ; Oeiras : Instituto Gulbenkian de Ciência, Centro de Estudos de Economia Agrária, 1985. 122 p. : ill. ; 24 cm. English and Portuguese. Papers presented at an international workshop organized by the Agricultural Economics Research Center of the Calouste Gulbenkian Foundation, took place at Oeiras from 9-11 May 1984. Includes bibliographies. LC Card 86-221785
1. Agriculture and state - Europe, Southern - Congresses. 2. Agriculture and state - European Economic Community countries - Congresses. 3. European Economic Community - Europe, Southern - Congresses. I. Soares, Fernando Brito. II. Instituto Gulbendian de Ciência. Centro de Estudos de Economia Agrária.
HD1920.5.Z8 P77 1985

The Prospects for economic recovery. Washington, D.C. : Congress of the United States, Congressional Budget Office : For sale by the Supt. of Docs., U. S. G.P.O., 1982. xx, 120 p. : ill. ; 26 cm. "A report to the Senate and House Committees on the Budget--part I as required by Public Law 93-344"--Cover. "February 1982"--Cover. Includes bibliographical references.
1. Interest and usury - United States. 2. Monetary policy - United States. 3. United States - Economic policy - 1971-. ***NYPL [JLF 86-1215]***

Prospects for privatization / edited by Steve H. Hanke. New York : Academy of Political Science, 1987. x, 214 p. ; 23 cm. (Proceedings of the Academy of Political Science, 0065-0684 . v. 36, no. 3) Includes bibliographies and index. LC Card 87-70470 DDC 338.973 19
1. Privatization - United States. 2. Privatization. I. Hanke, Steve H. II. Series: Proceedings of the Academy of Political Science in the city of New York , v. 36, no. 3.
HD3885 .P76 1987

Prospects for sustainable development in Sub-Saharan Africa . United States. Congress. House. Committee on Science and Technology. Washington , 1986. vii, 88 p. ; LC Card 86-603140 DDC 338.967 19
HD2117 .U48 1986

Prospects for the world oil industry . Symposium on the Energy Economy (1984 : Durham, Durham) London , Dover, N.H. , c1985. 131 p. : ISBN 0-7099-4104-8 : LC Card 85-4186 DDC 338.2/7282 19
HD9560.5 .S96 1985 ***NYPL [JLD 85-2430]***

Prospects of industrial estates in under-developed countries /. Agrawal, Deepak, 1955- Allahabad, India , 1987. 279 p. ; ISBN 81-85076-13-8 : LC Card 86-903605 DDC 338.6/042/09542 19
HC440.D5 A37 1987

Prospects, programmes, and policies for economic development-III (PPPED-III) /. Sudan. Wizārat al-Mālīyah wa-al-Takhṭīṭ al-Iqtiṣādī. Planning. Khartoum [1984] 232 p. ; LC Card 86-980066 DDC 338.9624 19
HC835 .S8335 1984

Der Prospekt über steuerbegünstigte Kapitalanlagen . Hergarten, Lothar, 1953- Köln , c1986. v, 209 p. ; ISBN 3-924361-18-5 : LC Card 87-103997 DDC 332.63 19
HG4028.C4 H456 1986

Prospektive Erfolgsanalyse und Unternehmensbonität /. Mühlbayer, Michael, 1955- Frankfurt am Main , New York , c1986. vii, 388 p. : ISBN 3-8204-9462-6 LC Card 86-190036
HG4156 .M84 1986

Prosperity and public spending . Nell, Edward J. Boston , 1987. p. cm. ISBN 0-04-339044-7 (alk. paper) LC Card 87-1383 DDC 339.5/22 19
HJ7451 .N44 1987

Prosser, Larry. For rent by owner / Larry Prosser. New York : F. Watts, 1987. xii, 217 p. : ill. ; 24 cm. Includes index. ISBN 0-531-15526-9 LC Card 87-16206 DDC 333.33/8 19
1. Rental housing. 2. Rental housing - Management. I. Title.
HD1394 .P77 1987

Prosterman, Roy L.
Egyptian development and U. S. aid : a 6-year report / Roy L. Prosterman and Jeffrey M. Riedinger. [Seattle, Wash.?] : Rural Development Institute, c1985. i, 32, A1-A10 p. ; 22 cm. (RDI monographs on foreign aid and development, 0748-0644 . #2) "November 1985." LC Card 87-104139 DDC 338.91/73/062 19
1. Economic development projects - Egypt. 2. Economic assistance, American - Egypt. 3. Egypt - Economic conditions - 1952-. I. Riedinger, Jeffrey M. II. Rural Development Institute (U. S.). III. Title. IV. Series.
HC830.Z9 E446 1985

Land reform and democratic development / Roy L. Prosterman and Jeffrey M. Riedinger. Baltimore : Johns Hopkins University Press, c1987. xii, 313 p. ; 24 cm. (The Johns Hopkins studies in development) Bibliography: p. [253]-303. Includes index. ISBN 0-8018-3482-1 (alk. paper) LC

Card 87-4188 DDC 333.3/1/1724 19
1. Land reform - Developing countries. 2. Revolutions - Developing countries. 3. Developing countries - Economic conditions. 4. Developing countries - Social conditions. 5. Developing countries - Politics and government. 6. Democracy. I. Riedinger, Jeffrey M. II. Title. III. Series.
HD1333.5 .P76 1987

PROSTHESIS - EQUIPMENT AND SUPPLIES - MARKETING.
Strategic marketing of surgical products. Tustin, CA, U. S.A. (17722 Irvine Blvd., Tustin 92680) , c1987. 1 v. (various foliations) : LC Card 87-168617 DDC 380.1/45681761 19
HD9995.S92 S77 1987

PROSTHETICS. see **PROSTHESIS.**

PROSTITUTION, JUVENILE - THAILAND.
Föste, Wolfgang. Verkaufte Träume . München , c1982. 53 p. : ISBN 3-88676-011-1 (pbk.) LC Card 87-672593
HD6250.T52 F67x 1982

Prostranstvennye sistemy proizvodstva . Baklanov, Petr ÎAkovlevich. Moskva , 1986. 149 p. : LC Card 86-202803
HC340.D5 B35 1986

Protasi, Juan Carlos. La flotación cambiaría : la experiencia uruguaya reciente / Juan Carlos Protasi. Montevideo, Uruguay : Dirección General de Extensión Universitaria, División Publicaciones y Ediciones, [1985] 33 leaves : ill. ; 28 cm. Cover title. At head of title: Universidad de la República, Facultad de Ciencias Económicas y de Administración, Instituto de Estadísticas. Includes bibliographical references. LC Card 86-160085
1. Foreign exchange administration - Uruguay. I. Universidad de la República (Uruguay). Instituto de Estadísticas. II. Title.
HG3940 .P76 1985

Protección efectiva en Chile, 1974-1979 /. Aedo, Cristián. Santiago [1984] 56 leaves ; LC Card 85-152465
HF1956 .A35 1984

Protecting environmental & nuclear whistleblowers . Kohn, Stephen M. (Stephen Martin) Washington, D.C. , c1985. xiii, 346 p. : ISBN 0-9615323-0-0 (pbk.) LC Card 85-61844 DDC 342.73/0684 347.302684 19
KF5342 .K64 1985 ***NYPL [JLE 86-1787]***

Protecting environmental and nuclear whistleblowers. Kohn, Stephen M. (Stephen Martin) Protecting environmental & nuclear whistleblowers . Washington, D.C. , c1985. xiii, 346 p. : ISBN 0-9615323-0-0 (pbk.) LC Card 85-61844 DDC 342.73/0684 347.302684 19
KF5342 .K64 1985 ***NYPL [JLE 86-1787]***

Protecting the environment : a free market strategy / edited by Doug Bandow. Washington, D.C. : Heritage Foundation, c1986. iii, 88 p. ; 23 cm. (Critical issues) Includes bibliographical references. ISBN 0-89195-040-0 (pbk.) : LC Card 86-82962 DDC 363.7/056/0973 19
1. Environmental policy - United States. 2. Environmental protection - Government policy - United States. 3. United States - Economic policy - 1981-. I. Bandow, Doug. II. Heritage Foundation (Washington, D.C.).
HC110.E5 P77 1986

PROTECTION AGAINST BURGLARY. see **BURGLARY PROTECTION.**

Protection and competition in international trade : essays in honor of W.M. Corden / edited by Henryk Kierzkowski. Oxford [Oxfordshire] ; New York, NY, USA : Blackwell, 1987. vi, 242 p. : ill. ; 24 cm. Includes bibliographies and index. ISBN 0-631-15004-8 : LC Card 86-29915 DDC 382/.3 19
1. Commercial policy. 2. Free trade and protection. 3. Competition, International. 4. Corden, W. M. (Warner Max). I. Corden, W. M. (Warner Max). II. Kierzkowski, Henryk.
HF1411 .P697 1987

Protection and liberalization . Corden, W. M. (Warner Max) Washington, D.C. , c1987. v, 28 p. ; ISBN 0-939934-95-7 (pbk.) : LC Card 87-16932 DDC 382.7 19
HF1411 .C5954 1987

PROTECTION OF CHILDREN. see **CHILD WELFARE.**

PROTECTION OF ENVIRONMENT. see **ENVIRONMENTAL PROTECTION.**

PROTECTION OF WILDLIFE. see **WILDLIFE CONSERVATION.**

Protectionism and the future of international shipping . Ademuni-Odeke, Dr. Dordrecht ; Boston : xxviii, 446 p. ; ISBN 90-247-2918-1 LC Card 83-25055 DDC 387.5/068 19
HE736 .A34 1984 ***NYPL [JLE 85-1539]***

Protectionism in the European community against Brazilian exports : IPEA/ECLAC agreement / Institute for Economic and Social Planning (IPEA) [and] Economic Commission for Latin America and the Caribbean (ECLAC). Brasília : IPEA : ECLAC, 1985. 125 p. ; 23 cm. Bibliography: p. 123-125. LC Card 86-119107 DDC 382.7/3/094 19
1. European Economic Community countries - Commerce - Brazil. 2. Brazil - Commerce - European Economic Community countries. 3. European Economic Community countries - Commercial policy. 4. Brazil - Commercial policy. 5. Free trade and protection - Protection. I. Instituto de Planejamento Econômico e Social. II. United Nations. Economic Commission for Latin America and the Caribbean.
HF3499.5.Z7 B76 1985

The Protectionist threat : fair for all or free for all? : alternative global scenarios. Philadelphia, PA (3624 Science Center, Philadelphia 19104) : Wharton Econometric Forecasting Associates, c1985. 85 p. : ill. ; 28 cm. "October 1985." LC Card 87-106782 DDC 382.7/3/0973 19
1. Tariff - United States - Econometric models. 2. Free trade and protection - Protection - Econometric models. I. Wharton Econometric Forecasting Associates.
HF1716 .P76 1985

PROTEIN PRODUCTS INDUSTRY - FRANCE.
Les Protéines françaises, un enjeu économique . Paris [1984] 6, xiii, 258 p. : LC Card 86-187038
HD9019.P753 F76 1984

Les Protéines françaises, un enjeu économique : [colloque], Paris, 27 au 29 novembre 1984 / APRIA, Association pour la promotion industrie agriculture. Paris : APRIA, [1984] 6, xiii, 258 p. : ill. ; 30 cm. Cover title. "Président du colloque ... C. Calet." LC Card 86-187038
1. Protein products industry - France. I. Calet, C. II. Association pour la promotion industrie-agriculture.
HD9019.P753 F76 1984

Protektionismus . Nestone, Alberto. München , c1984. 76 p. : ISBN 3-89019-108-8 LC Card 85-127389
HF1713 .N38 1984

Protektionismus in der Weltwirtschaft : Verstösse gegen die Spielregeln der Marktwirtschaft und das Freihandelsprinzip / herausgegeben von Bodo B. Gemper. Hamburg : Verlag Weltarchiv, 1984. viii, 147 p. ; 24 cm. (Veröffentlichung des HWWA-Institut für Wirtschaftsforschung-Hamburg und des Unabhängigen Instituts für Rechts-, Sozial- und Wirtschaftswissenschaften e.V) Chiefly papers read at the 10th Walberberger System-Symposium. Includes bibliographical references and indexes. ISBN 3-87895-253-8 LC Card 84-233895
1. Free trade and protection - Protection - Congresses. 2. Free trade and protection - European Economic Community countries - Congresses. I. Gemper, Bodo B. II. Walberberger System-Symposium (10th : 1983?). III. Series.
HF1703 .P77 1984

Protest and perish . Towle, Philip, 1945- London , 1982. 121 p. ; ISBN 0-907967-02-7 (pbk.) : LC Card 83-198296 DDC 355/.0217/0941 19
UA647 .T69 1982 ***NYPL [JLD 86-1904]***

Die Protestantische Ethik und der Verfall des Kapitalismus : zur Verleihung der Goldenen Doktorurkunde an Werner Stark : Ansprachen bei der Feierstunde des Fachbereichs Wirtschaftswissenschaften der Universität Hamburg am 23. Mai 1984. [Hamburg] : Pressestelle der Universität Hamburg, 1985. 31 p. : 1 port. ; 21 cm. (Hamburger Universitätsreden, 0438-4822 . 44) Includes bibliographical references. LC Card 86-112068
1. Capitalism. 2. Religion and sociology. 3. Capitalism - Religious aspects - Protestant churches. 4. Stark, Werner, 1909-. I. Stark, Werner, 1909-. II. Universität Hamburg. Fachbereich Wirtschaftswissenschaften. III. Series.
HB501 .P76 1985

Protestkultur und Jugend . Hein, Peter Ulrich. Münster , 1984. iii, 151 p. ; ISBN 3-88660-109-9
NYPL [JLD 86-2444]

Prothero, R. Mansell. Watts, Susan J. Population mobility and multilocality in Ilorin, Kwara State, Nigeria /. [Liverpool , 1981-] v. <1 > : LC Card 86-226489 DDC 304.8/09669/5 19
HB2126.7.I46 W37 1981

Protivorechiiа i perspektivy formirovaniia "Tikhookeanskogo soobshchestva" /. Kovrigin, E. B. (Evgeniĭ Borisovich) Moskva , 1986. 173, [3] p. ; LC Card 86-200677
HC681 .K68 1986

Proto-industrialisation in Scandinavia . Isacson, Maths, 1948- Leamington Spa, UK ; New York : p. cm. ISBN 0-85496-514-9 : LC Card 86-32062 DDC 338.09485 19
HC375 .I8 1987

Protokoll über das Kolloquium zur Gewerkschaftlichen Interessenvertretung beim Umfassenden Aufbau des Sozialismus in der Deutschen Demokratischen Republik am 31. Januar 1964. Kolloquium zur Gewerkschaftlichen Interessenvertretung beim Umfassenden Aufbau des Sozialismus in der Deutschen Demokratischen Republik (1964) [Bernau] [1964] iv, 246 p. ; LC Card 85-125499
HD6700.5 .K65 1964

Protsedury i algoritmy formirovaniia kompleksnykh programm /. Pospelov, Germogen Sergeevich. Moskva , 1985. 422, [2] p. : LC Card 86-203758
HC336.25 .P567 1985

Protsent sverkh plana /. Babakov, V. M. (Viktor Mikhaĭlovich) Volgograd , 1986. 45 p. : LC Card 86-220320
HC340.S6 B23 1986

Protz, Michael. Administrative Zusammenarbeit in der Entwicklungspolitik : Länderberichte, USA, Grossbritannien, Frankreich, Bundesrepublik Deutschland / Michael Protz. Speyer : Forschungsinstitut für Öffentliche Verwaltung bei der Hochschule für Verwaltungswissenschaften Speyer, 1982. ix, 382, 2 p. ; 29 cm. (Speyerer Forschungsberichte . 25) Bibliography: p. 358-382. LC Card 86-218043
1. Economic assistance, American - Developing countries. 2. Economic assistance, British - Developing countries. 3. Economic assistance, French - Developing countries. 4. Economic assistance, West German - Developing countries. 5. Decolonization - Developing countries. I. Title. II. Series.
HC60 .P77 1982

Proudhon, P.-J. (Pierre Joseph), 1809-1865. Des réformes à opérer dans l'exploitation des chemins de fer, et des conséquences qui peuvent en résulter, soit pour l'augmentation du revenu des compagnies, soit pour l'abaissement des prix de transport, l'organisation de l'industrie voiturière, et la constitution économique de la société ... Paris, Garnier frères, 1855. 2 p.l., 392 p. 18 cm. LC Card 05-35562
1. Railroads. I. Title.
HE1031 .P92

PROUDHON, P.-J. (PIERRE-JOSEPH), 1809-1865 - CONTRIBUTIONS IN BUREAUCRACY.
Motta, Fernando C. Prestes. Burocracia e autogestão . São Paulo, Brasil , 1981. 170 p. ; LC Card 82-106136
HD2961 .M658 1981

PROUDHON, P.-J. (PIERRE-JOSEPH), 1809-1865 - CONTRIBUTIONS IN MUTUALISM.
Motta, Fernando C. Prestes. Burocracia e autogestão . São Paulo, Brasil , 1981. 170 p. ; LC Card 82-106136
HD2961 .M658 1981

Proutat, Jacques. Barbier, André. Guide pratique de l'analyse financière à l'usage des banquiers /. Paris , c1985. viii, 313 p. : ISBN 2-86325-038-8 : LC Card 86-165653
HF5686.C7 B32 1985

PROVIDENT LOAN ASSOCIATIONS. see **BUILDING AND LOAN ASSOCIATIONS.**

Providing personal financial planning services in your CPA practice /. Clark-James, Suzanne. New York, NY (11 Penn Plaza, New York 10001) , 1987. 1 v. (various pagings) : LC Card

87-61984 DDC 657/.068/5 19
HG179 .C59 1987

Provincia de Buenos Aires . Buenos Aires (Argentina : Province). Dirección Provincial de Estadística. [Buenos Aires] , 1985. 107 p. : LC Card 86-107759
HA958.B8 B85 1985

Provincia de Coquimbo. Chouteau, Eujenio. Informe sobre la provincia de Coquimbo /. Santiago de Chile , 1887. 262 p. ; LC Card 85-165581
HC193.C64 C46 1887

Provincie Friesland financieel meerjarenplan, 1986-1989. Financieel meerjarenplan, 1986-1989 /. [Leeuwarden] [1985?] vii, 169 p. ; LC Card 87-111957
HJ2128.5.F75 F563 1985

Provisional estimates of population movements in Bermuda to 1990 /. Roberts, G. W. (George W.) Hamilton, Bermuda [198-?] 12, [8] p. : LC Card 86-173218
HB3668.A3 R63 1980z

PROXY - UNITED STATES.
Heard, James E. Conflicts of interest in the proxy voting system /. Washington, D.C. , c1987. 100 p. : ISBN 0-931035-18-X (pbk.) LC Card 87-404270 DDC 338.8/3/0973 19
HD2743 .H43 1987

Proyecciones de la población de México y de las entidades federativas, 1980-2010. México, D.F. : Instituto Nacional de Estadística, Geografía e Informática : CONAPO, c1985. xiii, 134 p. ; 28 cm. Chiefly tables. Bibliography: p. xiii. ISBN 968-8097-66-7 LC Card 86-223751
1. Population forecasting - Mexico - States - Statistics. 2. Mexico - Population - Statistics. I. Instituto Nacional de Estadística, Geografía e Informática (Mexico). II. Consejo Nacional de Población (Mexico).
HB3531 .P78 1985

Proyecciones de población, 1980-2000.
Estimaciones y proyecciones de población, 1950-2025 /. [Caracas] , 1985-[1987] 2 v. : ISBN 980-280-006-6 (set) LC Card 87-123959 DDC 304.6/2/0987021 19
HA1095 .E885 1985

Proyecto crisis y alternativas en Centroamérica-- documentos de trabajo.
López, Roberto. Los orígenes económicos de la crisis en Centroamérica /. San José, Costa Rica [1986] 134 p. : LC Card 87-106423
HC141 .L67 1986

Rovira Mas, Jorge, 1950- La crisis de Costa Rica /. San José, Costa Rica , 1986. 175 p. ; LC Card 87-125520 DDC 338.97286 19
HC143 .R667 1986

Proyecto de desarrollo local de La Paz, Intibucá /. Consejo Superior de Planificación Económica (Honduras). Secretaría Técnica. [Tegucigalpa, Honduras] [1984- v. <1 > : LC Card 86-213886
HC145.Z9 E443 1984

Proyecto de parcelación, Antioquia no. 2. Informe general y proyecto de parcelación, Antioquia # 2 (Barbosa y Santo Domingo) /. Bogotá, D.E. , 1964. 2, 73, 16 leaves, [1] leaf of plates : LC Card 85-107102
HD1476.C72 B375 1964

Proyecto E.I.-5-3. Proyecto EI-5-3 . México, D.F. [1977] ca. 150 p. : LC Card 82-119251
HC137.Q5 P76 1977

Proyecto EI-5-3 : estudio de gran visión para la colonización de la zona de Ucum, Estado de Quintana Roo / Secretaría de la Presidencia, Comisión de Estudios del Territorio Nacional, Subdirección Técnica, Departamento de Estudios Interdisciplinarios. México, D.F. : El Departamento, [1977] ca. 150 p. : ill. ; 21 cm. "Septiembre de 1975." LC Card 82-119251
1. Quintana Roo (Mexico : State) - Economic conditions. 2. Land settlement - Mexico - Quintana Roo (State). I. Mexico. Comisión de Estudios del Territorio Nacional. Departamento de Estudios Interdisciplinarios. II. Title: Proyecto E.I.-5-3.
HC137.Q5 P76 1977

Proyecto estratificación social .
(no. 1) Algunos aspectos sociográficos del área metropolitana de San José, Costa Rica /. [Ciudad Universitaria "Rodrigo Facio"] , 1970. 105 p. : LC Card 82-196053
HC143.Z7 S3515 1970

Proyecto harinas compuestas : informe final / Ministerio de Industria, Comercio y Turismo, Dirección General de Normas y Tecnología, Misión USAID Bolivia, Western Regional Research Center. La Paz, Bolivia : El Ministerio, 1982. 272, [2], 3 p., [9] p. of plates : ill. ; 34 cm. Bibliography: p. [273]-[274] LC Card 83-195592
1. Grain trade - Bolivia. 2. Wheat trade - Bolivia. 3. Bread industry - Bolivia. 4. Food supply - Bolivia. 5. Nutrition policy - Bolivia. I. Bolivia. Dirección General de Normas y Tecnología. II. USAID-Bolivia (Mission). III. United States. Agricultural Research Service. Western Regional Research Center. IV. Title: Harinas compuestas.
HD9044.B52 P76 1982

PROYECTO LA CHORRERA.
Plan integral de desarrollo del predio Putumayo. Bogotá [1986] 29 p. : LC Card 87-401011 DDC 338.9861/7 19
HC198.C49 P55 1986

Proyecto Paraná Medio : conclusiones y recomendaciones finales en el área de antropología cultural : provincias de Entre Ríos y Corrientes / Amaya, Luis Esteban ... [et al.]. Buenos Aires : Asociación Amigos del Instituto Nacional de Antropología, 1985. 44 leaves : ill. ; 28 cm. Cover title. Bibliography: leaf 44. LC Card 86-218225
1. Fishers - Argentina - Entre Ríos - Case studies. 2. Fishers - Argentina - Corrientes - Case studies. 3. Fishers - Paraná River Valley (Brazil-Argentina) - Case studies. 4. Hunters - Argentina - Entre Ríos - Case studies. 5. Hunters - Argentina - Corrientes - Case studies. 6. Hunters - Paraná River Valley (Brazil-Argentina) - Case studies. 7. Ethnology - Argentina - Entre Ríos - Case studies. 8. Ethnology - Argentina - Corrientes - Case studies. 9. Ethnology - Paraná River Valley (Brazil-Argentina) - Case studies. I. Amaya, Luis Esteban. II. Instituto Nacional de Antropología (Argentina). Asociación Amigos.
HD8039.F66 A746 1985

Proyectos políticos y estrategias de planificación en los planes nacionales de desarrollo de Costa Rica: 1974-1982. Gamboa Conejo, Rita Ma. (Rita María) Resultados preliminares del análisis metodológico de los planes nacionales de desarrollo, 1974-1982 /. Heredia , 1985. 1 v. (various pagings) : LC Card 87-402159 DDC 338.97286 19
HC143 .G36 1985

Proyek Pengaturan Pengupahan Daerah Sumatera Selatan (Indonesia) Analysa hasil survey pengupahan dan draft pedoman kebijaksanaan penetapan upah minimum, tahun 1977/1978 / Proyek Pengaturan Pengupahan [Daerah Sumatera Selatan]. [S.l.] : Kantor Wilayah Direktorat Jenderal Perlindungan dan Per[a]watan Tenaga Kerja Prop. Sumatera Selatan & Bengkulu, [1978?] 21, [2], 3 leaves ; 30 cm. LC Card 80-941072
1. Wages - Minimum wage - Indonesia - Sumatera Selatan. 2. Wages - Minimum wage - Indonesia - Bengkulu (Province). I. Title.
HD4922.I5 P75 1978

Proyek Sumber Daya Ekonomi (Indonesia)
Monografi sumber daya ekonomi di bidang kehutanan Kalimantan Timur . Bogor , 1975. ix, 67 leaves : LC Card 80-941771
HD9766.I73 K356 1975

Prud'homme, Rémy. Le Financement des équipements publics de demain /. Paris , c1986. 432 p. : ISBN 2-7178-1186-9 : LC Card 87-117264
HC280.C3 F56 1986

Prudinskiĭ, G. A. (Grigoriĭ Aronovich) Shvart͡s, M. A. (Mikhail Aleksandrovich) Ėkonomicheskiĭ analiz deiatelʹnosti proizvodstvennogo obʺedineni͡ia po dobyche ugl͡ia /. Moskva , 1986. 222 p. ; LC Card 85-236907
HF5686.M6 S48 1986

Die Prüfung der Geschäftsführung . Kofler, Herbert. Wien , 1985. 196 p. ; ISBN 3-85122-183-4 : LC Card 86-203497
HF5668.25 .K68 1985

PRUSSIA (GERMANY) - ECONOMIC CONDITIONS.
Wolffsohn, Seew, 1916- Wirtschaftliche und soziale Entwicklungen in Brandenburg, Preussen, Schlesien und Oberschlesien in den Jahren 1640-1853, Frühindustrialisierung in Oberschlesien /. Frankfurt am Main , New York , c1985. 182 p., [2] p. of folded plates : ISBN 3-8204-8197-4 LC Card 85-219539
HC288.B68 W65 1985

PRUSSIA (GERMANY) - ECONOMIC POLICY.
Schmoller, Gustav von, 1838-1917. The mercantile system and its historical significance . Fairfield, NJ , 1988. p. cm. ISBN 0-678-00252-5 LC Card 87-17247 DDC 330.15/13/0943 19
HB91 .S3 1988

PRUSSIA (GERMANY) - SOCIAL CONDITIONS.
Wolffsohn, Seew, 1916- Wirtschaftliche und soziale Entwicklungen in Brandenburg, Preussen, Schlesien und Oberschlesien in den Jahren 1640-1853, Frühindustrialisierung in Oberschlesien /. Frankfurt am Main , New York , c1985. 182 p., [2] p. of folded plates : ISBN 3-8204-8197-4 LC Card 85-219539
HC288.B68 W65 1985

Pruzner, S. L. (Saul Lʹvovich) Ėkonomika, organizatsii͡a i planirovanie ėnergeticheskogo proizvodstva / S.L. Pruzner. Izd. 5-e, perer. Moskva : Ėnergoatomizdat, 1984. 334 p. : ill., map ; 21 cm. Authorized for instructional purposes. Bibliography: p. 330-331. Includes index. LC Card 84-214102
1. Electric utilities - Soviet Union. I. Title.
HD9685.S762 P78 1984

Pryde, J. G. Survey of New Zealand farmer intentions and opinions, November 1985-January 1986 / by J.G. Pryde, P.J. McCartin. Canterbury, N.Z. : Agricultural Economics Research Unit, Lincoln College, [1986] 133 p. ; 30 cm. (Research report, 0069-3790 . no. 181) "June 1986." LC Card 87-107903 DDC 338.1/09931 19
1. Farmers - New Zealand - Attitudes. I. McCartin, P. J. II. Series: Research report (Lincoln College (University of Canterbury). Agricultural Economics Research Unit) , no. 181. III. Title.
HD8039.F32 N486 1986

Pryke, Richard. Competition among international airlines / by Richard Pryke. Aldershot ; Brookfield, USA : Gower for the Trade Policy Research Centre, London, 1987. xi, 113 p. : ill. ; 22 cm. (Thames essay, 0306-6991 . no. 46) Bibliography: p. [106]-109. ISBN 0-566-05333-0 : LC Card 86-31877 DDC 387.7/1 19
1. Aeronautics, Commercial. 2. Competition, International. 3. Aeronautics, Commercial - Deregulation. 4. Air lines - Rates. I. Trade Policy Research Centre. II. Title. III. Series.
HE9780 .P79 1987

Pryor, Frederic L. Revolutionary Grenada : a study in political economy / Frederic L. Pryor. New York : Praeger, 1986. xx, 395 p. : ill. ; 24 cm. Includes index. Bibliography: p. 375-382. ISBN 0-275-92155-7 (alk. paper) : LC Card 86-8109 DDC 338.97298/45 19
1. Economic assistance, Communist - Grenada - History. 2. Socialism - Grenada - History. 3. Grenada - Economic policy. 4. Grenada - Economic conditions. 5. Grenada - Politics and government - 1974-. I. Title.
HC156.5.Z7 G747 1986
NYPL [JLE 86-3969]

Przed kolejną reformą. Samecki, Wiesław. Czego można oczekiwać od ekonomii /. Warszawa , 1981. 35 p. ; ISBN 83-202-0150-0 LC Card 86-150577
HC340.3 .S24 1981

Przemiany we współczesnej gospodarce światowej : praca zbiorowa / pod red. A. Makacia.Wyd. 1. Gdańsk : Wydawn. Uniwersytetu Gdańskiego, 1978. 360 p. ; 24 cm. (Skrypty uczelniane / Uniwersytet Gdański) Bibliography: p. 355-360. LC Card 81-200306
1. Economic history - 1945-. 2. Commercial policy. I. Makać, Antoni. II. Series: Skrypty uczelniane / Uniwersytet Gdański.
HC59 .P78 1978

Przemysł w mieście . Bonenberg, Wojciech. Gliwice , 1985. 181 p., [8] folded leaves of plates : LC Card 86-219523
HC340.3.Z9 D52 1985

Przestrzenne aspekty gospodarki żywnościowej do 2000 r. : materiały z seminarium w Jadwisinie 18-20 października 1981 r. / pod redakcją Andrzeja Stasiaka i Przemysława Dąbrowskiego.Wyd. 1. Warszawa : Państwowe Wydawn. Ekonomiczne, 1986. 166 p. : ill. ; 24

cm. (Studia / Polska Akademia Nauk, Komitet Przestrzennego Zagospodarowania Kraju . t. 90) Includes bibliographical references. ISBN 83-208-0497-3 : LC Card 86-223691
1. Food industry and trade - Poland - Congresses. 2. Food supply - Poland - Congresses. 3. Poland - Economic conditions - 1980- - Regional disparities - Congresses. 4. Dąbrowski, Przemysław. I. Stasiak, Andrzej. II. Polska Akademia Nauk. Komitet Przestrzennego Zagospodarowania Kraju. III. Series: Studia / Polska Akademia Nauk, Komitet Przestrzennego Zagospodarowania Kraju , t. 90.
HD9015.P72 P72 1986

Przestrzenne zróżnicowanie gospodarki rolnej w Polsce /. Wiatrak, Andrzej Piotr. Warszawa , 1986. 207 p. : ISBN 83-01-05118-3 : LC Card 86-212769
HD1995.7 .W45 1986

Przestrzenne zróżnicowanie państwowej gospodarki rolnej w Polsce /. Dramowicz, Elżbieta. Warszawa , 1986. 125 p. ; ISBN 83-01-05021-7 : LC Card 86-212594
HD1995.7 .D73 1986

Przewodnik metodyczny do ekonomii politycznej dla doktorantów nieekonomistów /. Borcz, Leszek. Gliwice , 1979. 79 p. ; LC Card 81-182800
HB74.5 .B67 1979

Przywrócić Polsce . Magierska, Anna. Warszawa , 1986. 467 p. ; ISBN 83-01-06606-7 : LC Card 86-228089
HC340.3.Z7 W4765 1986

Psacharopoulos, George. Education for development : an analysis of investment choices / George Psacharopoulos, Maureen Woodhall. New York : Oxford University Press, 1985. ix, 337 p. : ill. ; 25 cm. "A World Bank publication."--half t.p. Includes bibliographies and indexes. ISBN 0-19-520477-8 LC Card 85-13782 DDC 338.9 19
1. Economic development - Effect of education on. 2. Education - Developing countries - Finance. I. Woodhall, Maureen. II. Title.
HD75.7 .P77 1985 NYPL [JLE 86-1073]

Pshennikov, S. New international economic order /. Moscow , 1984. 196 p. ; LC Card 85-151148 DDC 337/.09/047 19
HF1411 .N398 1984 NYPL [JLD 86-2664]

Psicología, pobreza y subdesarrollo /. Alarcón, Reynaldo. Lima, Perú , 1986. 153 p. ; LC Card 87-126266 DDC 155.9/2 19
HC79.P6 A55 1986

Psicosociología de la organización . Uriarte, Pedro. Bilbao , 1985. 284 p. : ISBN 84-7485-049-5 LC Card 86-151352
HD6955 .U75 1985

P.S.O.E. (POLITICAL PARTY) - HISTORY.
Biglino Campos, Paloma. El socialismo español y la cuestión agraria (1890-1936) /. Madrid [1986?] 564 p. ; ISBN 84-7434-368-2 LC Card 87-136300
HD6764.A29 B54 1986

Psychische Belastungen in der Arbeitswelt . Marstedt, Gerd. Opladen , c1986. vii, 366 p. : ISBN 3-531-11757-2 LC Card 87-135624
HF5548.8 .M373 1986

Psycho-ecological dimensions of poverty / edited by M.G. Husain. New Delhi : Manohar, 1983. x, 115 p. : ill. ; 23 cm. Includes bibliographies and index. LC Card 83-906411 DDC 305.5/69/0954 19
1. Poor - India - Psychological aspects - Addresses, essays, lectures. 2. Poverty - Environmental aspects - India - Addresses, essays, lectures. I. Husain, M. G., 1949-.
HC440.P6 P78 1983 NYPL [JLD 87-491]

PSYCHOANALYSIS.
Lichtenstein, Heinz, 1904- The dilemma of human identity /. New York , c1983. xiv, 399 p. ; ISBN 0-87668-677-3 : LC Card 84-45086 DDC 155.2 19
BF697 .L52 1983 NYPL [JFE 86-2218]

The Psychology of men . New York , c1986. x, 310 p. ; ISBN 0-465-06718-2 LC Card 85-48022 DDC 155.3/32 19
BF692.5 .P78 1986 NYPL [JFE 86-2975]

Sanford, John A. The invisible partners . New York , c1980. 139 p. ; ISBN 0-8091-2277-4 : LC Card 79-56604 DDC 150.19/54
BF175 .S24 NYPL [JFE 86-5093]

Psychological economics : development, tensions, prospects / edited by Peter E. Earl. Boston : Kluwer Academic Publishers, c1987. p. cm. Bibliography: p. Includes index. ISBN 0-89838-234-3 LC Card 87-3050 DDC 330/.01/9 19
1. Economics - Psychological aspects. I. Earl, Peter E.
HB74.P8 P697 1987

Psychological testing in personnel selection /. Venne, Rosemary Amelia, 1956- Kingston, Ont., Canada , 1987. 65 p. ; ISBN 0-88886-152-4 (pbk.) LC Card 87-163203 DDC 658.3/1125 19
HF5549.5.E5 V46 1987

PSYCHOLOGICAL TESTS.
Venne, Rosemary Amelia, 1956- Psychological testing in personnel selection /. Kingston, Ont., Canada , 1987. 65 p. ; ISBN 0-88886-152-4 (pbk.) LC Card 87-163203 DDC 658.3/1125 19
HF5549.5.E5 V46 1987

Psychologie des Entscheidungsverhaltens und des Konfliktes .
(Bd. 3) Experimental social dilemmas /. Frankfurt am Main , New York , c1986. vi, 234 p. : ISBN 3-8204-8574-0 (pbk.) : LC Card 86-10307 DDC 302 19
HM132 .E96 1986 NYPL [JLD 87-1177]

Psychologische Forschungsgruppe Schönhals. Zur Problematik der Abbrecher der beruflichen Rehabilitation /. Bonn [1985?] 118, [29] p. ; LC Card 86-190824
HD7256.G3 Z87 1985

Psychology applied to work . Muchinsky, Paul M. Chicago, Ill. , c1987. xxvi, 712, xix p. : ISBN 0-256-03671-3 LC Card 86-81818 DDC 158.7 19
HF5548.8 .M756 1987

PSYCHOLOGY, CRIMINAL. see **CRIMINAL PSYCHOLOGY.**

PSYCHOLOGY, EXISTENTIAL. see **EXISTENTIAL PSYCHOLOGY.**

Psychology in administration . Costello, Timothy W. New York , 1987. xii, 500 p. : ISBN 0-8240-8202-8 (alk. paper) : LC Card 86-25805 DDC 658/.001/9 19
HF5548.8 .C6 1987

PSYCHOLOGY, INDUSTRIAL - ADDRESSES, ESSAYS, LECTURES.
Handbook of industrial and organizational psychology /. New York , c1983. xxvii, 1740 p. : ISBN 0-471-88642-4 LC Card 83-42702 DDC 158.7 19
HF5548.8 .H265 1983 NYPL [JLE 86-1120]

Herzberg, Frederick. The managerial choice . Salt Lake City, Utah , c1982. xviii, 360 p. : ISBN 0-913420-97-2 LC Card 81-85925 DDC 658.3/14 19
HF5549.5.I5 H47 1982 NYPL [JLE 86-2591]

Industrial relations . Chichester , New York , c1979. xii, 412 p. ; ISBN 0-471-99701-3 LC Card 78-18452 DDC 301.5/5
HD6971 .I547 NYPL [JLE 80-1770]

Qualitative Arbeitsanalyse . Frankfurt , New York , c1983. 352 p. ; ISBN 3-593-32721-X LC Card 83-161600 DDC 158.7 19
HD6955 .Q35 1983 NYPL [JLD 87-1014]

PSYCHOLOGY, INDUSTRIAL - CONGRESSES.
Man and work in society . New York , c1975. xiv, 313 p. : ISBN 0-442-29359-3 LC Card 75-26866 DDC 658.3
HF5549 .M299 NYPL [JLE 76-2406]

PSYCHOLOGY, INDUSTRIAL - EUROPE - CONGRESSES.
West European Conference on the Psychology of Work and Organization (1985 : Aachen, Germany) The psychology of work and organization . Amsterdam ; New York : xi, 407 p. : ISBN 0-444-70029-3 (U. S.) LC Card 86-8947 DDC 158.7 19
HF5548.8 .W475 1985 NYPL [JLE 86-4341]

PSYCHOLOGY, INDUSTRIAL - GERMANY (WEST)
Ansprüche an die Arbeit . Frankfurt [am Main] , New York , c1984. 298 p. : ISBN 3-593-33390-2 LC Card 85-103333
HF5548.8 .A683 1984

PSYCHOLOGY, INDUSTRIAL - NETHERLANDS.
Modern organiseren en menselijker werken /. 's-Gravenhage , 1985. 198 p. : ISBN 90-6095-314-2 : LC Card 85-214437
HF5548.8 .M55 1985

PSYCHOLOGY, INDUSTRIAL - SOUTH AFRICA.
Behaviour in organisations . Johannesburg , New York , 1986, c1983. 924 p. : ISBN 0-07-450690-0 (pbk.) : LC Card 87-113321 DDC 158.7/0968 19
HD58.7 .B426 1986

The psychology of consumer behavior /. Mullen, Brian. Hillsdale, N.J. , 1988. p. cm. ISBN 0-89859-857-5 LC Card 87-15601 DDC 658.8/342 19
HF5415.3 .M85 1988

The Psychology of gender : advances through meta-analysis / edited by Janet Shibley Hyde and Marcia C. Linn. Baltimore : Johns Hopkins University Press, c1986. vii, 293 p. : ill. ; 24 cm. Includes bibliographies and index. ISBN 0-8018-2974-7 (alk. paper) LC Card 85-19822 DDC 155.3/3 19
1. Sex differences (Psychology). 2. Sex role - Psychological aspects. 3. Meta-analysis. I. Hyde, Janet Shibley. II. Linn, Marcia C.
BF692.2 .P76 1986 NYPL [JFE 86-2969]

Psychology of industrial conflict /. Stagner, Ross, 1909- New York , 1987, c1956. ix, 550 p. : ISBN 0-8240-8218-4 (alk. paper) : LC Card 86-27080 DDC 158.7 19
HF5548.8 .S713 1987

The Psychology of men : new psychoanalytic perspectives / edited by Gerald I. Fogel, Frederick M. Lane, and Robert S. Liebert. New York : Basic Books, c1986. x, 310 p. ; 24 cm. Includes bibliographical references and index. ISBN 0-465-06718-2 LC Card 85-48022 DDC 155.3/32 19
1. Men - Psychology. 2. Psychoanalysis. I. Fogel, Gerald I. II. Lane, Frederick M. III. Liebert, Robert, 1930-.
BF692.5 .P78 1986 NYPL [JFE 86-2975]

The psychology of work and organization . West European Conference on the Psychology of Work and Organization (1985 : Aachen, Germany) Amsterdam ; New York : xi, 407 p. : ISBN 0-444-70029-3 (U. S.) LC Card 86-8947 DDC 158.7 19
HF5548.8 .W475 1985 NYPL [JLE 86-4341]

PSYCHOLOGY - PHILOSOPHY.
Nuttin, Jozef, 1909- [Théorie de la motivation humaine. English.] Motivation, planning, and action . Leuven, Belgium , Hillsdale, N.J. , c1984. viii, 251 p. ; ISBN 0-89859-332-8 (L. Erlbaum) LC Card 83-16416 DDC 153.8 19
BF503 .N8713 1984 NYPL [JFE 86-2315]

PSYCHOLOGY, SOCIAL. see **SOCIAL PSYCHOLOGY.**

PSYCHOLOGY, VOCATIONAL. see **PSYCHOLOGY, INDUSTRIAL.**

PSYCHOTECHNICS. see **PSYCHOLOGY, INDUSTRIAL.**

P'tit train va loin . Lemieux-Pépin, Madeleine. Ottawa , 1985. vii, 191 p. ; LC Card 86-177382
HE2808.1 .L45 1985

PTS user's manual. Predicasts terminal system users manual. Cleveland, OH (11001 Cedar Ave., Cleveland 44106) , c1986- 1 v. (loose-leaf) ; LC Card 86-219849 DDC 025/.0633 19
HF5548.4.P74 P74 1986

Pubblicazioni dell'Istituto di studi politico-economici .
(4) Targetti Lenti, Renata. Struttura produttiva e distribuzione personale del reddito . Milano [1984] 263 p. : ISBN 88-14-00277-0 : LC Card 84-251227 DDC 339.2/2/0945 19
HC310.I5 T346 1984 NYPL [JLF 86-1305]

Pubblicazioni dell'Università degli studi di Salerno. Sezione Atti, convegni, miscellanee .
(12) I Fondi comuni di investimento . Napoli , c1985. 183 p. ; LC Card 86-193326
HG5526 .F66 1985

Publ. (Institute for Latin American Integration) .
(no. 232) Kaplan, Marcos. El sistema de las relaciones políticas y económicas entre los países latinoamericanos . [Buenos Aires] [1985] 62 leaves ; LC Card 86-200041
HC125 .K32 1985

(no. 237) Obras hidroeléctricas binacionales en América Latina. [Buenos Aires, Argentina] , 1985. vii leaves, 385 p., 3 leaves of plates : LC Card 86-180644
HD1696.A7 O27 1985

(no. 238) Reunión Técnica sobre el Financiamiento de la Integración Subregional en América Latina (1985 : Buenos Aires, Argentina) Reunión Técnica sobre el Financiamiento de la Integración Subregional en América Latina . [Buenos Aires, Argentina] . 335 p. : LC Card 86-217551
HC125 .R479 1985

(no. 247) Interconexión de cuencas sudamericanas. [Buenos Aires] , 1986. 159 leaves, [5] leaves of plates : LC Card 86-225024
HE650 .I58 1986

(no. 267) Zorn, Stephen. Minería y elaboración de minerales . Buenos Aires , 1986. ii, 84 p. ; LC Card 87-402781 DDC 338.2/098 19
HD9506.L252 Z67 1986

PUBLIC ACCOUNTANTS. see **ACCOUNTANTS.**

PUBLIC ACCOUNTING. see **FINANCE, PUBLIC - ACCOUNTING; MUNICIPAL FINANCE - ACCOUNTING.**

PUBLIC ADMINISTRATION - DICTIONARIES.
Glossary of terms . [Ottawa] [1981]-1984. 3 v. ; ISBN 0-662-52389-X (v. 2) LC Card 81-180363 DDC 350/.0003/41 19
JA61 .G55 ***NYPL [JLF 87-379]***

PUBLIC ADMINISTRATION - DICTIONARIES - FRENCH.
Glossary of terms . [Ottawa] [1981]-1984. 3 v. ; ISBN 0-662-52389-X (v. 2) LC Card 81-180363 DDC 350/.0003/41 19
JA61 .G55 ***NYPL [JLF 87-379]***

PUBLIC ADMINISTRATION - EVALUATION - ADDRESSES, ESSAYS, LECTURES.
Performance and credibility . Lexington, Mass. , c1986. x, 307 p. : ISBN 0-669-11037-X (alk. paper) LC Card 85-50707 DDC 658/.048 19
HD62.6 .P47 1986 ***NYPL [JLE 86-1159]***

PUBLIC ADMINISTRATION - GERMANY (WEST)
Rucht, Dieter. Planung und Partizipation . München , c1982. 321 p. ; ISBN 3-88073-105-5 LC Card 83-672501
JN3971.A91 R82x 1982 ***NYPL [JLD 86-2900]***

PUBLIC ADMINISTRATION - GREECE - HISTORY.
Lowry, S. Todd. The archaeology of economic ideas . Durham , 1987. xviii, 366 p. ; ISBN 0-8223-0774-X LC Card 87-15507 DDC 330/.0938 19
HB108.A2 L68 1987

Public administration in India : emerging trends / editors, S.L. Kaushik, Pardeep Sahni.1st ed. Allahabad : Kitab Mahal, 1983. xii, 308 p. ; 25 cm. Includes bibliographical references. LC Card 83-907416 DDC 354.54 19
1. Rural development - India. 2. Municipal government - India. 3. Government business enterprises - India. 4. India - Politics and government - 1947-. I. Kaushik, S. L., 1946-. II. Sahni, Pardeep, 1955-.
JQ224 .P75 1983 ***NYPL [JLE 86-4197]***

PUBLIC ADMINISTRATION - ITALY - DATA PROCESSING - CONGRESSES.
Statistica e pubblica amministrazione . Milano , 1983-1985. 2 v. ; ISBN 88-14-00703-9 (v. 2) : LC Card 86-215546
HA37.I9 S7 1983

Public Administration, National Academy of. see **National Academy of Public Administration.**

PUBLIC ADMINISTRATION - STATISTICAL METHODS.
Meier, Kenneth J., 1950- Applied statistics for public administration /. Monterey, Calif. , c1987. xix, 460 p. ; LC Card 87-10342 DDC 350/.0001/5195 19
HA29 .M46 1987

PUBLIC ADMINISTRATION - TURKEY.
Heper, Metin. Development administration in Turkey . Bebek, Istanbul [1980] vi, 116 p. ; LC Card 87-400032 DDC 338.9561 19
HC492 .H47 1980

A Public Affairs Council handbook. Cost-effective management for today's public affairs, or, How to succeed as a PAO in an era of constraints /. Washington, D.C. (1255 Twenty-third St., N.W., Suite 750, Washington 20037) [c1987] xiii, 109 p. : LC Card 87-135276 DDC 659.2 19
HD59 .C645 1987

Public affairs pamphlet (Public Affairs Committee) .
(no. 644) Irwin, Michael H. K. Risks to health and safety on the job /. New York, NY , c1986. 28 p. : ISBN 0-88291-096-5 (pbk.) : LC Card 87-402515 DDC 363.1/1/0973 19
HD7654 .I79 1986

Public Agenda Foundation. The Trade gap . Dayton, Ohio (100 Commons Rd., Dayton 45459-2777) , c1987. 35 p. : LC Card 87-71294 DDC 382.1/7/0973 19
HF3031 .T7 1987

PUBLIC ASSISTANCE. see **PUBLIC WELFARE.**

PUBLIC AUTHORITIES. see **CORPORATIONS, GOVERNMENT.**

PUBLIC BROADCASTING - AUSTRALIA.
Etzioni-Halevy, Eva. National broadcasting under siege . New York , 1987. xii, 228 p. ; ISBN 0-312-00772-8 : LC Card 87-4702 DDC 384.54 19
HE8689.6 .E89 1987

PUBLIC BROADCASTING - GERMANY (WEST)
Etzioni-Halevy, Eva. National broadcasting under siege . New York , 1987. xii, 228 p. ; ISBN 0-312-00772-8 : LC Card 87-4702 DDC 384.54 19
HE8689.6 .E89 1987

PUBLIC BROADCASTING - GREAT BRITAIN.
The BBC and public service broadcasting /. Manchester , c1986. viii, 116 p. ; ISBN 0-7190-1964-8 : LC Card 86-209725 DDC 384.54/4/0941 19
HE8689.9.G7 B34 1986

Etzioni-Halevy, Eva. National broadcasting under siege . New York , 1987. xii, 228 p. ; ISBN 0-312-00772-8 : LC Card 87-4702 DDC 384.54 19
HE8689.6 .E89 1987

PUBLIC BROADCASTING - ISRAEL.
Etzioni-Halevy, Eva. National broadcasting under siege . New York , 1987. xii, 228 p. ; ISBN 0-312-00772-8 : LC Card 87-4702 DDC 384.54 19
HE8689.6 .E89 1987

PUBLIC BROADCASTING - QUÉBEC (PROVINCE)
Programme d'aide aux médias communautaires, 1979-80 . [Québec] [1979] 97 leaves ; LC Card 83-200428
HE8689.9.C3 P755 1979

PUBLIC BROADCASTING - UNITED STATES.
Statement of principles of editorial integrity in public broadcasting /. Columbia, S.C. (P.O. Box 5966, Columbia 29250) [1985] 21 p. : LC Card 87-126452 DDC 384.54/53 19
HE8689.8 .S72 1986

Public budgeting with Lotus 1-2-3 /. Baker, Keith, 1938- Portland, Or. , 1988. p. cm. ISBN 0-943518-46-6 : LC Card 87-24020 DDC 350.72/2/02855369 19
HJ2009 .B34 1988

PUBLIC CHARITIES. see **PUBLIC WELFARE.**

Public choice . Ross, Murray N. [Washington, D.C.] [c1987] 8 p. ; LC Card 87-403005 DDC 338.9 19
HB846.8 .R66 1987

PUBLIC CHOICE. see **SOCIAL CHOICE.**

Public choice and regulation : a view from inside the Federal Trade Commission / edited by Robert J. Mackay, James C. Miller III & Bruce Yandle. Stanford, Calif. : Hoover Institution Press, 1987. xiii, 363 p. ; 23 cm. Bibliography: p. [345]-363. ISBN 0-8179-8562-X (pbk.) : LC Card 87-3984 DDC 353.0082/6 19
1. United States. Federal Trade Commission. I. Mackay, Robert J. II. Miller, James Clifford. III. Yandle, Bruce. IV. United States. Federal Trade Commission.
HD3616.U47 P796 1987

PUBLIC CONTRACTS - CALIFORNIA - CRIMINAL PROVISIONS.
A Practical guide to investigating public works violations /. Oakland, CA (520 3rd St., Suite 204, Oakland 94607) , 1986. 73 p., [3] leaves of plates : LC Card 86-209657 DDC 363.2/5 19
HD3890.C2 P7 1986

PUBLIC CONTRACTS - ESTIMATES - UNITED STATES.
Cost estimating for government contracts . [Washington, D.C.] (1120 20th St., NW, Washington 20036) , c1986. 1 v. (various pagings) : LC Card 87-100120 DDC 658.1/552 19
HD3860 .C67 1986

PUBLIC CONTRACTS - GERMANY - HISTORY.
Peschke, Hans-Peter von, 1951- Elektroindustrie und Staatsverwaltung am Beispiel Siemens, 1847-1914 /. Frankfurt am Main , Bern , c1981. 393 p. : ISBN 3-8204-5902-2 LC Card 81-141438
HD9697.A3 G35 1981

PUBLIC CONTRACTS - NEW YORK (N.Y.)
New York (State). Office of the Special Deputy Comptroller for the City of New York. Reforming the contract process in New York City /. [Albany] [1986] 13 leaves ; LC Card 86-623049
HD3861.U6 N48 1986

PUBLIC CONTRACTS - NEW YORK (N.Y.) - MANAGEMENT.
New York (State). Office of the Special Deputy Comptroller for the City of New York. Reforming the contract process in New York City /. [Albany] [1986] 13 leaves ; LC Card 86-623049
HD3861.U6 N48 1986

PUBLIC CONTRACTS - UNITED STATES.
Cohen, Leah. A summary of the American experience with the Federal Contract Compliance Program . [Ottawa] , 1979. 72 leaves ; ***NYPL [JLF 86-1657]***

Kettl, Donald F. Government by proxy . Washington, D.C. , c1988. x, 170 p. ; ISBN 0-87187-429-6 (pbk.) : LC Card 87-13645 DDC 353.009 19
HD3861.U6 K47 1988

Penoyar, William F. Fedspeak . Arnold, Md. , c1985. v, 178 p. : ISBN 0-9615112-2-2 (pbk.) : LC Card 85-90360 DDC 353.0071/2 19
JK1673 .P46 1985 ***NYPL [JLD 87-568]***

United States. Dept. of Transportation. Office of the Secretary. Contracting with the United States Department of Transportation [microform]. Washington, D.C. , 1984. iii, 40 p. : ***NYPL [*ZT-1711 no.25]***

PUBLIC CORPORATIONS. see **CORPORATIONS; MUNICIPAL CORPORATIONS.**

Public corporations of Nepal . Pradhan, Radhe S. New Delhi, India , 1986. xiii, 173 p. ; LC Card 86-903436 DDC 338.7/4/095496 19
HF5681.R25 P73 1986

Public debt in a medium-term context and its implications for fiscal policy /. Chouraqui, Jean Claude. [Paris, France] , c1986. 67 p. : LC Card 86-218210 DDC 339.5 19
HJ8030 .C48 1986

PUBLIC DEBTS. see **DEBTS, PUBLIC.**

Public development finance corporations . Mitsotaki, Alexandra Gourdain. Paris , 1986. 40 p. ; LC Card 86-221546 DDC 332.6/734/01724 19
HG5993 .M57 1986

Public enterprise : developments in social ownership and control in Great Britain / [edited by] William Robson. New York : Garland, 1985. 416 p. ; 21 cm. (English workers and the coming of the welfare state, 1918-1945) Includes bibliographical references and index. Reprint. Originally published: London : Allen & Unwin, 1937. CONTENTS. - The Port of London Authority / by Lincoln Gordon -- The Forestry Commission / by John Parker -- The British Broadcasting Corporation / by William A. Robson -- The Central Electricity Board and other electricity authorities / by Graeme Haldane -- The London Passenger Transport Board / by Ernest Davies -- The Coal Mines Reorganization Commission / by Ivor Thomas -- The agricultural marketing boards

/ by W.H. Jones -- The Post Office / by John Dugdale -- The organization of the co-operative movement / by G. Walworth -- The Public Service Board / by William A. Robson. ISBN 0-8240-7626-5 (alk. paper) : LC Card 85-13105 DDC 354.4109/1 19
1. Government business enterprises - Great Britain - Case studies. 2. Public service commissions - Great Britain - Case studies. 3. Public utilities - Great Britain - Case studies. I. Robson, William Alexander, 1895-. II. Series.
HD4147 .P83 1985 ***NYPL [JLD 86-3467]***

Public enterprise . Curwen, Peter J. Brighton, Sussex , 1986. xvii, 318 p. : ISBN 0-312-65435-9 : LC Card 85-26234 DDC 354.4109/2 19
HD4145 .C87 1986 ***NYPL [JLD 86-1636]***

Public enterprise economics /. Rees, Ray, 1943- London , 1984. xiii, 238 p. : ISBN 0-297-78336-X LC Card 87-672956
HD3840 .R43x 1984b

Public enterprise in Western Europe /. Parris, Henry. London , Wolfeboro, N.H. , c1987. viii, 197 p. : ISBN 0-7099-0548-3 : LC Card 86-24133 DDC 338.7/4/094 19
HD4138 .P37 1987 ***NYPL [JLD 87-757]***

Public enterprise policy in India and U.K. in 1980s / editors, T.L. Sankar ... [et al.]. 1st ed. Bombay : Himalaya Pub. House, 1987. xx, 286 p. ; 23 cm. Proceedings and selected papers presented at the International Seminar on Public Enterprise Policy in the Eighties, held at Hyderabad, February 11-14, 1985, organised jointly by the London Business School, U.K. and Institute of Public Enterprise, Hyderabad, India. Includes bibliographies. LC Card 86-903771 DDC 338.6/2/0941 19
1. Government business enterprises - India - Congresses. 2. Government business enterprises - Great Britain - Congresses. 3. India - Economic policy - 1980- - Congresses. 4. Great Britain - Economic policy - 1945- - Congresses. I. Sankar, T. L. (T. Lakshmana), 1934-. II. London Graduate School of Business Studies. III. Institute of Public Enterprise, Hyderabad, India. IV. International Seminar on Public Enterprise Policy in the Eighties (1985 : Hyderabad, India).
HD4293 .P775 1987

PUBLIC ENTERPRISES. see **GOVERNMENT BUSINESS ENTERPRISES.**

Public enterprises, a state level perspective / [editor], Y. Saraswathy Rao. Delhi : B.R. Pub. Corp. ; New Delhi : Distributed by D.K. Publishers' Distributors, 1986. xix, 287 p. ; 23 cm. Study of Andhra Pradesh. Bibliography: p. [279]-287. ISBN 81-7018-370-7 : LC Card 86-902715 DDC 338.6/2/095484 19
1. Government business enterprises - India - Andhra Pradesh. I. Saraswathy Rao, Y.
HD4295.A5 P8 1986

Public enterprises in economic development . Hassan, Shabir. Delhi , 1987. xiii, 230 p. ; LC Card 86-903835
HD2900.12.J35 H37 1987

Public enterprises in India : the focus on researches / T.L. Sankar, editor-in-chief, R.K. Mishra, S. Ravishankar, managing editors.1st ed. Bombay : Himalaya Pub. House, 1983. xxii, 524 p. ; 23 cm. Papers presented at National Seminar of Senior Research Workers on Public Enterprise, 1982, conducted by the Institute of Public Enterprise, Hyderabad. Includes bibliographical references. LC Card 83-905617 DDC 354.5409/2 19
1. Government business enterprises - India - Congresses. 2. Government business enterprises - Research - India - Congresses. I. Sankar, T. L. (T. Lakshman), 1934-. II. Mishra, R. K., 1948-. III. Ravishankar, S., 1956-. IV. National Seminar of Senior Research Workers on Public Enterprise (1982 : Hyderabad, India).
HD4293 .P793 1983 ***NYPL [JLD 87-723]***

Public enterprises in Sub-Saharan Africa /. Nellis, John R. Washington, D.C., U. S.A. [1986] vii, 66 p. : ISBN 0-8213-0845-9 (pbk.) LC Card 86-24756 DDC 338.7/4/0967 19
HD4338 .N45 1986

Public expenditure : the key issues / edited by John Bristow and Declan McDonagh. Dublin, Ireland : Institute of Public Administration, 1986. 138 p. ; 22 cm. Proceedings of National Conference on Public Expenditure: the Key Issues, held Nov. 1985 in Dublin, organized by the Institute. Includes bibliographies. CONTENTS. - Public expenditure and public debt / Vito Tanzi -- The political economy of public expenditure / Alan Peacock -- Public employment and public expenditure / Richard Rose -- Public expenditure and the bureaucracy / Peter Jackson -- An Irish overview / Alan Dukes. ISBN 0-906980-56-9 (pbk.) : LC Card 86-143826 DDC 336.3/9 19
1. Expenditures, Public - Congresses. 2. Debts, Public - Congresses. 3. Civil service - Congresses. 4. Bureaucracy - Congresses. 5. Ireland - Appropriations and expenditures - Congresses. I. Bristow, J. A. (John A.). II. McDonagh, Declan. III. Institute of Public Administration (Dublin, Dublin). IV. National Conference on Public Expenditure: the Kay Issues (1985 : Dublin, Dublin).
HJ7461 .P83 1986 ***NYPL [JLD 87-553]***

Public expenditure in Latin America . Pfeffermann, Guy Pierre. Washington, D.C. , 1987. 38 p. ; ISBN 0-8213-0906-4 (pbk.) LC Card 87-10650 DDC 336.3/9/098 19
HJ7664.5 .P44 1987

PUBLIC EXPENDITURES. see **EXPENDITURES, PUBLIC.**

PUBLIC FINANCE. see **FINANCE, PUBLIC.**

Public finance and monetary policy in open economies . Jones-Hendrickson, S. B. (Simon B.) [Kingston, Jamaica] , 19. 172 p. ;
NYPL [Sc D 86-830]

Public finance in Hungary, 0230-9718 .
(24) Turnover tax-system in Hungary /. Budapest , 1985. 21 p. ; ISBN 963-621-208-2 (pbk.) : LC Card 86-202548 DDC 336.2/7 19
HJ5715.H9 T87 1985

(31) Management of public budgetary institutions /. Budapest , 1986. 37 p. ; ISBN 963-03-2343-5 (pbk.) : LC Card 86-230773 DDC 336.439 19
HJ2103 .M33 1986

PUBLIC GOODS - COST EFFECTIVENESS.
Rondorf, Dieter, 1955- Die Bewertung öffentlicher Leistungen durch die Bürger . Frankfurt am Main , New York , c1985. 231 p. : ISBN 3-8204-5652-X LC Card 85-229645
HB846.5 .R65 1985

PUBLIC GOODS - MATHEMATICAL MODELS.
Altenburg, Lutz, 1943- Zur Einbeziehung öffentlicher Zwischenprodukte in Mehrsektorenmodelle /. Frankfurt am Main , New York , c1985. 315 p. : ISBN 3-8204-9046-9 LC Card 85-231430 DDC 338.4/3363/0724 19
HB846.5 .A47 1985

Bonus, Holger. Öffentliche Güter und der Öffentlichkeitsgrad von Gütern /. Konstanz [1979] 39, 3 p. ; LC Card 85-171986
HB846.5 .B66 1979

PUBLIC HEALTH - ARGENTINA.
Funciones y servicios de competencia municipal /. Córdoba, República Argentina , 1984. 94 leaves ; LC Card 87-121632 DDC 352.082 19
HD4629 .F86 1984

PUBLIC HEALTH - BRAZIL.
Possas, Cristina de Albuquerque. Saúde e trabalho . Rio de Janeiro, RJ , 1981. xxxix, 324 p. : LC Card 82-132979 DDC 362.1/0981 19
RA418.3.B6 P68 1981 ***NYPL [JLD 86-1896]***

A Transição incompleta . Rio de Janeiro-RJ , 1986. 2 v. ; LC Card 86-224684
HC187 .T72 1986

PUBLIC HEALTH - BRAZIL - GOIÁS (STATE)
O Estado de Goiás . Goiânia-GO , 1983. 406 p. : LC Card 86-224747
HC188.G6 E85 1983

PUBLIC HEALTH - BRAZIL - RIO GRANDE DO SUL.
Rio Grande do Sul (Brazil) Relatorios provinciaes. [1850-1859] 19 pamphlets in 1 v. ; LC Card 84-217966
HD4635.R54 R56 1850

PUBLIC HEALTH - COSTA RICA.
Avance de resultados, encuesta de fecundidad y salud /. [San José] Costa Rica , 1986. [32] leaves : LC Card 87-400666 DDC 304.6/32/097286 19
HB947 .A96 1986

PUBLIC HEALTH - CUBA.
Cuba's socialist economy toward the 1990s /. Boulder, Colo. , 1987. ix, 188 p. : ISBN 1-555-87080-5 (lib. bdg. : alk. paper) : LC Card 87-12867 DDC 338.97291 19
HC152.5 .C824 1987

PUBLIC HEALTH - DEVELOPING COUNTRIES.
Nath, Uma Ram. Smoking, Third World alert /. Oxford [Oxfordshire] , New York , 1986. x, 291 p. : ISBN 0-19-261402-9 : LC Card 86-5201 DDC 363.1/9 19
HD9148.D44 N37 1986
NYPL [JLD 87-992]

PUBLIC HEALTH - ECONOMIC ASPECTS - DEVELOPING COUNTRIES.
Jimenez, Emmanuel, 1952- Pricing policy in the social sectors . Baltimore , 1987. v, 170 p. ; ISBN 0-8018-3501-1 : LC Card 86-27590 DDC 338.4/33621/091724 19
HJ7469 .J56 1987

PUBLIC HEALTH - FINANCE.
Finanzsysteme, Ideal- und Realtypen . Berlin , c1983. 278 p. : ISBN 3-428-05419-9 LC Card 83-240120
HJ161 .F575 1983

PUBLIC HEALTH - FRANCE - PARIS - HISTORY.
Shapiro, Ann-Louise, 1944- Housing the poor of Paris, 1850-1902 /. Madison, Wis. , 1985. xx, 224 p. : ISBN 0-299-09880-X : LC Card 84-40159 DDC 363.5/8 19
HD7288.78.F82 P357 1985
NYPL [JLE 85-1534]

PUBLIC HEALTH - GREAT BRITAIN - HISTORY - 20TH CENTURY.
Winter, J. M. The great war and the British people /. Basingstoke, Hampshire , 1986, c1985. xiv, 360 p. : ISBN 0-333-26582-3
NYPL [JLD 86-1426]

PUBLIC HEALTH - PERU - ORIENTE.
Peru, Kolonisation und Abhängigkeit . Saarbrücken , Fort Lauderdale , 1981. 192 p. : ISBN 3-88156-165-X : LC Card 82-104103
HD1905.O75 P47 1981

PUBLIC HEALTH SERVICES. see **PUBLIC HEALTH.**

Public health statistics bulletin.
Changing fertility patterns in Vermont. Burlington, Vt. (Box 70, 60 Main St., Burlington 05402) [1986] 18 p. : LC Card 86-622900 DDC 304.6/32/09743 19
HB935.V4 C46 1986

Cooley, Walter L. Vermont's urban population, 1950 to 1985 /. Burlington, Vt. (Box 70, 60 Main St., Burlington 05402) [1986] 9 leaves : LC Card 86-622184 DDC 304.6/09743 19
HA675 .C66 1986

PUBLIC HEALTH - SWITZERLAND - LUCERNE - HISTORY.
Schüpbach, Werner. Die Bevölkerung der Stadt Luzern 1850-1914 . Luzern , 1983. 323 p., [17] p. of plates : ISBN 3-7252-0432-2 LC Card 83-201416
HB3624.L8 S38 1983

PUBLIC HEALTH - VENEZUELA - GUAYANA REGION - ADDRESSES, ESSAYS, LECTURES.
Exploración de la Guayana /. [Caracas] [1983] 158 p., [20] p. of plates : LC Card 85-178221 DDC 333.7/0988/1 19
HC238.G8 E98 1983 ***NYPL [JSF 86-461]***

PUBLIC HEALTH - VENEZUELA - STATISTICS.
Estadísticas sociales . Caracas, Venezuela , 1983. 2 v. ; LC Card 84-183391 DDC 312/.0987 19
HA1095 .E88 1983 ***NYPL [JLM 85-550]***

Public hearing before Emergency Response System Study Commission on implementation of a statewide enhanced 911 service . New Jersey. Legislature. Emergency Response System Study Commission. [Trenton, N.J.] [1986] 49 p. ; LC Card 87-621252 DDC 384.6/42 19
HE8840.N5 N48 1986

PUBLIC HOUSES. see **HOTELS, TAVERNS, ETC.**

Public housing / editors, M.A. Muttalib, Mohd. Akbar Ali Khan. Hyderabad, A.P. : Regional Centre for Urban & Environmental Studies, c1983. xx, 345 p. ; 26 cm. LC Card 85-903848 DDC 363.5/8 19

1. Public housing - India - Congresses. 2. Housing policy - India - Congresses. I. Muttalib, M. A. II. Khan, Mohd. Akbar Ali. III. Regional Centre for Urban Environmental Studies (Hyderabad, India).
HD7288.78.I4 P83 1983
NYPL [JLF 86-1782]

Public housing : current trends and future developments / edited by David Clapham and John English. London ; Wolfeboro, N.H. : Croom Helm, c1987. 174 p. : ill. ; 23 cm.
Bibliography: p. 165-170. ISBN 0-7099-4826-3 : LC Card 86-24056 DDC 363.5/8 19
1. Public housing - Great Britain. 2. Rental housing - Great Britain. I. Clapham, David. II. English, John, 1944-.
HD7288.78.G7 P83 1987

PUBLIC HOUSING - ENGLAND - LONDON METROPOLITAN AREA - MANAGEMENT.
The Relationship between the GLC Housing Department, its tenants, and the public /. London , c1977. iv, 107 p. ; ISBN 0-7168-0895-1 (pbk.) LC Card 87-107202
HD7288.78.G72 L68 1977

PUBLIC HOUSING - FINANCE - LAW AND LEGISLATION - UNITED STATES.
Guggenheim, Joseph. Tax credits for low income housing . Washington, D.C. , c1986. vii, 117 p. : ISBN 0-941239-00-4 (pbk.) LC Card 87-112304 DDC 363.5/8 19
HJ4653.C73 G85 1986

PUBLIC HOUSING - FRANCE - PARIS - HISTORY.
Shapiro, Ann-Louise, 1944- Housing the poor of Paris, 1850-1902 /. Madison, Wis. , 1985. xx, 224 p. : ISBN 0-299-09880-X : LC Card 84-40159 DDC 363.5/8 19
HD7288.78.F82 P357 1985
NYPL [JLE 85-1534]

PUBLIC HOUSING - GERMANY, WEST.
Echter, Claus-Peter. Konzepte städtischer Wohnungspolitik . Berlin , 1985. 97 p. : ISBN 3-88118-123-7 LC Card 86-145702
HD7288.78.G3 E265 1985

Fuhrich, Manfred, 1950- Sicherung des Sozialmietwohnungsbestandes /. Frankfurt am Main , c1986. xxiii, 180, 16 p. : ISBN 3-88129-996-3 LC Card 86-223886
HD7288.78.G3 F84 1986

PUBLIC HOUSING - GERMANY (WEST) - FINANCE.
Fuhrich, Manfred, 1950- Sicherung des Sozialmietwohnungsbestandes /. Frankfurt am Main , c1986. xxiii, 180, 16 p. : ISBN 3-88129-996-3 LC Card 86-223886
HD7288.78.G3 F84 1986

PUBLIC HOUSING - GERMANY (WEST) - MANNHEIM - FINANCE - CASE STUDIES.
Ipsen, Detlev. Markt und Raum . Frankfurt , New York , c1986. 250 p. : ISBN 3-593-33685-5 LC Card 87-127593 DDC 363.5/8 19
HD7339.M35 I67 1986

PUBLIC HOUSING - GERMANY (WEST) - MANNHEIM - HISTORY.
Hahn, Barbara. Der geförderte Wohnungsbau in Mannheim 1850-1985 /. Mannheim , 1986. 236 p. : ISBN 3-87804-185-3 LC Card 87-121543 DDC 363.5/8/0943/46 19
HD7339.M35 H34 1986

PUBLIC HOUSING - GOVERNMENT POLICY - NEW YORK (STATE)
New York (State). Division of Housing and Community Renewal. Special needs housing demonstration program report. New York, N.Y. (2 World Trade Center, New York 10047) [1984] 1 v. (various foliations) : LC Card 86-622827 DDC 363.5/8 19
HD7288.85.U62 N754 1984

PUBLIC HOUSING - GREAT BRITAIN.
Navarro, Hugo. La vivienda de interés social en Panamá . Panamá , 1975. 288 p. : LC Card 84-100873
HD7312.A3 N38 1975

Public housing . London , Wolfeboro, N.H. , c1987. 174 p. : ISBN 0-7099-4826-3 : LC Card 86-24056 DDC 363.5/8 19
HD7288.78.G7 P83 1987

PUBLIC HOUSING - GREAT BRITAIN - ADDRESSES, ESSAYS, LECTURES.
The Housing crisis /. London , Dover, N.H. , c1986. 243 p.: ISBN 0-7099-4605-8 : LC Card 85-31113 DDC 363.5/0941 19
HD7333.A3 H684 1986
NYPL [JLD 86-2181]

PUBLIC HOUSING - GREAT BRITAIN - MANAGEMENT.
Power, Anne. Property before people . London , Boston , c1987. xvi, 268 p. : ISBN 0-04-350069-2 (alk. paper) LC Card 86-28751 DDC 363.5/8 19
HD7288.78.G7 P69 1987

PUBLIC HOUSING - INDIA - CONGRESSES.
Public housing /. Hyderabad, A.P. , c1983. xx, 345 p. ; LC Card 85-903848 DDC 363.5/8 19
HD7288.78.I4 P83 1983
NYPL [JLF 86-1782]

PUBLIC HOUSING - MASSACHUSETTS - LOWELL - HISTORY.
Leney, Julie M. Lowell as a laboratory . [Lowell, Mass.?] , 1987. 92 p. : LC Card 87-158220 DDC 363.5/8 19
HD7288.78.U52 M44 1987

PUBLIC HOUSING - NETHERLANDS.
Toekomstverkenning volkshuisvesting . Delft , 1985. 100 p. : ISBN 90-6275-193-8 : LC Card 86-157352
HD7288.78.N4 T64 1985

PUBLIC HOUSING - UNITED STATES.
Housing America's poor /. Chapel Hill , c1987. ix, 203 p. ; ISBN 0-8078-1738-4 LC Card 86-40449 DDC 363.5/8 19
HD7287.96.U5 H68 1987

Producing lower income housing . Washington, D.C. , c1986. xiv, 373 p. ; ISBN 0-87179-533-7 (pbk.) LC Card 86-26424 DDC 363.5/ 19
HD7288.78.U5 P76 1986

PUBLIC HOUSING - UNITED STATES - ADDRESSES, ESSAYS, LECTURES.
Critical perspectives on housing /. Philadelphia , 1986. xxi, 686 p. : ISBN 0-87722-395-5 LC Card 85-17274 DDC 363.5/0973 19
HD7293 .C738 1986 ***NYPL [JLE 86-3639]***

PUBLIC HOUSING - UNITED STATES - FINANCE.
Guggenheim, Joseph. Tax credits for low income housing . Washington, D.C. , c1986. vii, 117 p. : ISBN 0-941239-00-4 (pbk.) LC Card 87-112304 DDC 363.5/8 19
HJ4653.C73 G85 1986

Producing lower income housing . Washington, D.C. , c1986. xiv, 373 p. ; ISBN 0-87179-533-7 (pbk.) LC Card 86-26424 DDC 363.5/ 19
HD7288.78.U5 P76 1986

PUBLIC HYGIENE. see PUBLIC HEALTH.

PUBLIC INSTITUTIONS - BRAZIL - BAHIA (STATE)
Bahia, Brazil (State) Secretaria do Planejamento, Ciência e Tecnologia. Planejamento, ciência e tecnologia . [Salvador , 1983?] 93 p. : LC Card 85-136375
HC188.B3 B334 1983

Public Interest Public Relations, inc. Promoting issues & ideas . New York, N.Y. , 1987. 183 p. : ISBN 0-87954-192-X (pbk.) : LC Card 87-7600 DDC 659.2/88 19
HD62.6 .P76 1987

PUBLIC INTEREST - UNITED STATES.
McCann, Michael W., 1952- Taking reform seriously . Ithaca , 1986. 345 p. ; ISBN 0-8014-1952-2 LC Card 86-47647 DDC 322.4/3/0973 19
JK1118 .M37 1986 ***NYPL [JLE 87-1009]***

Public investment and agrarian transformation in northern Nigeria /. Beckman, Björn, 1938- [Zaria , 1983] 33 p. ; LC Card 87-402849 DDC 338.1/8669 19
HD2145.5 .B43 1983

Public investment, 1983-1987. Colombo : National Planning Division, Ministry of Finance and Planning, 1983. 232 p. ; 26 cm. LC Card 83-905444 DDC 332.6/7252/095493 19
1. Infrastructure (Economics) - Sri Lanka. 2. Economic forecasting - Sri Lanka. 3. Sri Lanka - Economic policy. I. Sri Lanka. Jātika Krama Sampādana Aṃśaya.
HC424 .P82 1983 ***NYPL [JLF 87-290]***

PUBLIC INVESTMENTS - BRAZIL - SÃO PAULO (STATE)
Fontes de financiamento aos municípios. São Paulo , 1984. 175 p. ; LC Card 85-221901
HJ925 .F66 1984

PUBLIC INVESTMENTS - CANADA - QUÉBEC (PROVINCE)
Raynauld, André. L'impact économique et financier de la Caisse de dépôt et placement du Québec /. Montréal [1983?] 23 p. ; LC Card 85-164461
HG5160.Q4 C357 1983

PUBLIC INVESTMENTS - EVALUATION.
Quirk, James P. The choice of discount rate applicable to government resource use . Santa Monica, CA [1987] xviii, 52 p. : ISBN 0-8330-0849-8 (pbk.) LC Card 87-9867 DDC 336.3/9 19
HJ7451 .Q57 1987

PUBLIC INVESTMENTS - GERMANY (WEST)
Gornas, Jürgen. Zur Berücksichtigung der finanziellen Leistungsfähigkeit in kommunalen Investitions- und Finanzplanungsmodellen /. Hamburg , 1984. 40 p. ; LC Card 85-166310
HJ9473 .G67 1984

PUBLIC INVESTMENTS - HAITI.
Haiti . Washington, D.C., U. S.A. [1987] xix, 254 p. ; ISBN 0-8213-0872-6 (pbk.) LC Card 86-32599 DDC 339.5/22/097294 19
HC153.Z9 P834 1987

PUBLIC INVESTMENTS - LATIN AMERICA.
Pfeffermann, Guy Pierre. Public expenditure in Latin America . Washington, D.C. , 1987. 38 p. ; ISBN 0-8213-0906-4 (pbk.) LC Card 87-10650 DDC 336.3/9/098 19
HJ7664.5 .P44 1987

PUBLIC INVESTMENTS - LIBERIA.
Economic recovery program, 1986/87-1988/89. Monrovia, Liberia [1986] 76, a-n p. ; LC Card 87-104460 DDC 338.9666/2 19
HC1075 .E25 1986

PUBLIC INVESTMENTS - NIGERIA.
Beckman, Björn, 1938- Public investment and agrarian transformation in northern Nigeria /. [Zaria , 1983] 33 p. ; LC Card 87-402849 DDC 338.1/8669 19
HD2145.5 .B43 1983

PUBLIC INVESTMENTS - SPAIN - BARCELONA.
Barcelona (Spain). Ayuntamiento. Departament d'Estudis i Programació. Estat d'execució dels programes d'actuació i pressupostos d'inversió de l'Ajuntament de Barcelona durant 1982. [Barcelona] [1983] 126 leaves ; LC Card 84-249883
HC388.B3 B36 1983

PUBLIC INVESTMENTS - SUDAN.
Sudan. Wizārat al-Mālīyah wa-al-Takhṭīṭ al-Iqtiṣādī. Planning. Prospects, programmes, and policies for economic development-III (PPPED-III) /. Khartoum [1984] 232 p. ; LC Card 86-980066 DDC 338.9624 19
HC835 .S8335 1984

PUBLIC INVESTMENTS - UNITED STATES.
Local infrastructure investment in rural America /. Boulder , 1988. xxi, 291 p. ; ISBN 0-8133-7460-X (soft : alk. paper) LC Card 87-21606 DDC 332.6/7252 19
HC110.P83 L63 1988

PUBLIC INVESTMENTS - UNITED STATES - HISTORY - 20TH CENTURY.
Economics U$A. Chicago, IL , 1986. 1 videocassette (28 min.) : LC Card 86-708020 DDC 330.15 11
HB99.7

PUBLIC INVESTMENTS - ZIMBABWE.
Whitsun Foundation. Project 1.07 . Harare, Zimbabwe [1983?] 2 v. ; ISBN 0-7974-0597-6 LC Card 84-981092 DDC 380.1/096891 19
HF3902 .W48 1983 ***NYPL [JLM 87-272]***

PUBLIC LABOR POLICY. see LABOR POLICY.

Public land distribution in Saudi Arabia /. Hajrah, Hassan Hamza. London , New York , 1982. xxi, 280 p. : ISBN 0-582-78301-1 LC Card 83-232929 DDC 333.1/6/09538 19
HD853.Z7 H34 1982 ***NYPL [JLE 87-1566]***

PUBLIC LAND SALES - ITALY - NAPLES (KINGDOM) - HISTORY - 18TH

CENTURY.
Rao, Anna Maria, 1949- L'"Amaro della feudalità" . Napoli , c1984. 382 p. ; ISBN 88-7042-265-8 : LC Card 85-200705
HD1333.I82 N367 1984

PUBLIC LANDS - WEST (U. S.) - HISTORY.
Layton, Stanford J., 1941- To no privileged class . Provo, Utah , Salt Lake City, Utah , c1987. p. cm. ISBN 0-941214-59-1 : LC Card 87-14299 DDC 333.1/6/0978 19
HD1339.U5 L39 1987

PUBLIC LIBRARIES - NETHERLANDS.
Boon, Irene. Mannen in een vrouwenberoep . Den Haag , 1984. 139 p. : ISBN 90-6252-426-5 : LC Card 84-243593
Z682.4.W65 B66 1984 ***NYPL [JLG 87-4]***

Public limited companies in India, 1980-82 : a profile. Bombay : Reserve Bank of India, Dept. of Statistical Analysis and Computer Services, 1986. xvi, 359 p. ; 25 cm. LC Card 87-902505 DDC 338.7/4/0954021 19
1. Corporations - India - Finance. I. Reserve Bank of India. Dept. of Statistical Analysis and Computer Services.
HG4242 .P83 1986

Public Management Institute. Capital campaign resource guide. San Francisco, Calif. , c1984. x, 1229 p. : LC Card 87-122608 DDC 658.1/5224 19
HG177.5.U6 C36 1984

PUBLIC OPINION - AUSTRIA.
Jäggle, Martin. Öffentlichkeitsarbeit 3. Welt in Österreich /. Wien , 1975- v. <1 > ; LC Card 86-234031
HC60 .J344 1975

PUBLIC OPINION - BRAZIL.
Formiga, Marcone. Personagens da crise /. Brasília , 1984. 160 p. : LC Card 86-157831
HC187 .F636 1984

PUBLIC OPINION - BULGARIA.
The Political self-assessment of Bulgarian respondents in terms of a left-right continuum. [Munich?] [1986] 16 p. ; LC Card 87-142360 DDC 384.55/43 19
HE8697.A8 P67 1986

PUBLIC OPINION - DENMARK.
Henriksen, Ingrid. Holdninger til den økonomiske fordeling =. København , 1985. 349 p. : ISBN 87-7487-265-6 : LC Card 85-186400
HC360.I5 S25 1985 vol. 1
NYPL [JLD 86-2002]

PUBLIC OPINION - GERMANY - HISTORY - 19TH CENTURY.
Simon, Dan, 1937- Das Frankreichbild der deutschen Arbeiterbewegung 1859-1865 /. [Gerlingen] , 1984. 334 p. ; ISBN 3-88350-451-3 LC Card 84-173175
HD8450 .S56 1984 ***NYPL [JLD 86-2711]***

PUBLIC OPINION - GERMANY, WEST.
Gewandelte Werte, erstarrte Strukturen . Bonn , c1985. ix, 329 p. : ISBN 3-87831-423-X LC Card 86-117688 DDC 330/.0943 19
HD8451 .G54 1985

Krämer, Georg. Pädagogische Aspekte entwicklungspolitischer Öffentlichkeitsarbeit /. Frankfurt/Main , 1980. 233 p. : ISBN 3-88129-332-9 LC Card 81-466304
HC59.7 .K687 ***NYPL [JLD 87-528]***

PUBLIC OPINION - HONDURAS.
Análisis de la encuesta a líderes nacionales /. Tegucigalpa, D.C. , 1983. 49, [12] leaves ; LC Card 85-203745
HB3540.A3 A52 1983

PUBLIC OPINION - HUNGARY.
A Lengyel földindulás /. Malakoff , New York , 1980. 150 p. ; LC Card 81-177379
HD8537.N783 L45 1980 ***NYPL [JLB 86-24]***

Pataki, Judit. Közvéleménykutatás népesedési kérdésekről /. Budapest , c1985. 75 p. ; LC Card 86-166976
HA1201 .A64 no. 60 HB3592.5.A3

Salamin, Pálné. Vélemények az életszínvonalról /. Budapest , 1986. 88 p. : LC Card 86-218875
HD7027.5 .S25 1986

PUBLIC OPINION - JAPAN.
A Comparative study on accounting policy between Japanese and the U. S. companies /. Tokyo, Japan , c1986. iv, 56 p. : LC Card 87-169003 DDC 657/.0952 19
HF5686.C7 C635 1986

PUBLIC OPINION - NETHERLANDS.
Szirmai, Adam, 1946- Inequality observed . Aldershot, Hants, England , Brookfield, Vt., USA , c1988. p. cm. ISBN 0-566-05549-X : LC Card 87-23071 DDC 339.2/09492 19
HC329.5.I5 S96 1988

PUBLIC OPINION - NORWAY.
Attidues to Norwegian development assistance, 1974. Oslo , 1975. 57 p. ; LC Card 86-460167
HA1503 .A18 nr. 34 HC60

Colbjørnsen, Tom. Så samles vi på valen--? . [Oslo?] [1985] 88 p. : ISBN 82-991187-5-1 LC Card 85-220350
HD6752 .C644 1985

PUBLIC OPINION - QUEBEC (PROVINCE)
Comportement électoral au Québec /. Chicoutimi, Québec, Canada , c1984. xv, 447 p. : ISBN 2-89105-063-0 LC Card 85-177886 DDC 324.9714 19
JL258 .C65 1984 ***NYPL [JLD 87-1351]***

PUBLIC OPINION - SOUTH AFRICA.
Orkin, Mark. Disinvestment, the struggle, and the future . Johannesburg , 1986. xii, 78 p. : ISBN 0-86975-305-3 (pbk.) LC Card 87-100474 DDC 332.6/73/0968 19
HG5851.A3 O47 1986

Voorhes, Meg. Black South African views on disinvestment /. Washington, D.C. (Suite 600, 1755 Massachusetts Ave., N.W., Washington 20036) [1986] 36 p. ; LC Card 86-209279 DDC 332.6/73/0968 19
HG5851.A3 V66 1986

PUBLIC OPINION - SOVIET UNION.
Akopov, Mykhaĭlo Arutiunovych. Dukhovnyĭ mir sovetskogo cheloveka /. Kiev , 1985. 124, [3] p. ; LC Card 86-139846
JN6581 .A64 1985 ***NYPL [*QIK 87-3448]***

PUBLIC OPINION - SPAIN - ASTURIAS.
Argüelles, Alfonso. Los Oscos y la Cuenca del Eo . [Asturias] [1984?] ix, 317 p. : ISBN 84-505-0237-3 LC Card 86-174593
HC387.A7 A74 1984

PUBLIC OPINION - SWEDEN.
Sannerstedt, Anders, 1945- Attityder till kommunal service /. [Stockholm] [1981] vi, 166 p. : ISBN 91-38-06586-X LC Card 82-244101
HD4485.S8 S26 1981

PUBLIC OPINION - UNITED STATES.
The American dream . [New York] , c1987. 103 p. : LC Card 87-404096 DDC 330.973/0927 19
HC106.8 .A437 1987

The American farmer book . [Smithshire, Ill.] (Box 181, Smithshire 61478) [c1986] 192 p. : LC Card 86-203314 DDC 338.1/0973 19
HD8039.F32 U614 1986

Blyskal, Jeff. PR . New York , c1985. 241 p. ; ISBN 0-688-04788-2 : LC Card 85-80602
NYPL [JLE 86-268]

A Comparative study on accounting policy between Japanese and the U. S. companies /. Tokyo, Japan , c1986. iv, 56 p. : LC Card 87-169003 DDC 657/.0952 19
HF5686.C7 C635 1986

How consumers view credit unions . New York, NY (1 Penn Plaza, Suite 1631, New York 10119) , c1986. 37, 7 leaves, [166] p. ; LC Card 87-111937 DDC 334/.22/0973 19
HG2037 .H68 1986

Lipset, Seymour Martin. The confidence gap . Baltimore , 1987. xxiv, 460 p. : ISBN 0-8018-3044-3 (pbk.) LC Card 86-27416 DDC 303.3/8/0973 19
HD2785 .L53 1987

Margin accounts. Chicago, IL , c1987. iii leaves, 59 p. : LC Card 87-403672 DDC 332.64/5 19
HG4963 .M34 1987

Neuman, W. Russell. The paradox of mass politics . Cambridge, Mass. , 1986. 241 p. : ISBN 0-674-65455-2 (alk. paper) LC Card 86-288 DDC 324.973 19
JK1967 .N48 1986 ***NYPL [JLE 86-4140]***

Poole, Keith T. Women, public opinion, and politics . New York , c1985. xii, 196 p. : ISBN 0-582-28274-8 LC Card 84-7155 DDC 305.4/0973 19
HQ1410 .P66 1985 ***NYPL [JLE 85-1580]***

Reinarman, Craig. American states of mind . New Haven , c1987. x, 262 p. ; ISBN 0-300-03817-8 (alk. paper) LC Card 86-26752 DDC 330.12/2/0973 19
HD3616.U47 R1464 1987

A Study of the attitudes toward and an assessment of the Financial Accounting Standards Board /. Stamford, CT , 1985. x, 141 p. : LC Card 86-230871 DDC 657/.0218 19
HF5616.U5 S78 1985

United States. Congress. House. Committee on Foreign Affairs. Subcommittee on International Organizations and Movements. Modern communications and foreign policy. Washington, 1967. vii, 13R, iv, 216 p. LC Card 67-61749
E744 .U45 1967 ***NYPL [JLE 73-233]***

A View of unions /. [Washington? D.C.] [1985] 25 p. ; LC Card 86-211350 DDC 331.88/0973 19
HD6508 .V39 1985

PUBLIC OWNERSHIP. see **GOVERNMENT OWNERSHIP.**

Public policies and private actions : a multinational study of local energy conservation schemes / [edited by] George Gaskell and Bernward Joerges. Aldershot, Hants, England ; Brookfield, Vt., U. S.A. : Gower Pub. Co., c1987. p. cm. Includes bibliographies. ISBN 0-566-05436-1 : LC Card 87-14909 DDC 333.79/16 19
1. Energy conservation - Case studies. I. Gaskell, George. II. Joerges, Bernward.
HD9502.A2 P82 1987

Public policy and industrial development . Bennett, Mark. Boulder, Colo. , 1986. xii, 134 p. : ISBN 0-86531-821-2 : LC Card 83-23456 DDC 338.4/76292/0972 19
HD9710.3.M42 B46 1986
NYPL [JLE 86-2581]

PUBLIC POLICY MANAGEMENT. see **POLICY SCIENCES.**

The public policy roots of recent thrift crises /. Ford, William F. (William Frank), 1934- Washington, D.C. , c1986. 14 p. ; ISBN 0-8447-1376-7 (pbk.) LC Card 87-164463 DDC 332.3/2/0973 19
HG2152 .F67 1986

Public policy toward corporate takeovers / edited by Murray L. Weidenbaum and Kenneth W. Chilton. New Brunswick (USA) : Transaction Books, c1988. xvi, 176 p. ; 24 cm. Papers resulting from a research project conducted in the winter and spring of 1986 by the Center for the Study of American Business at Washington University in St. Louis, Mo. Includes bibliographies and index. ISBN 0-88738-166-9 : LC Card 87-10750 DDC 338.8/3/0973 19
1. Consolidation and merger of corporations - Government policy - United States. I. Weidenbaum, Murray L. II. Chilton, Kenneth. III. Washington University (Saint Louis, Mo.). Center for the Study of American Business.
HD2795 .P825 1988

Public policy toward corporations / edited by Arnold A. Heggestad. Gainesville : University of Florida Press, 1987. p. cm. ISBN 0-8130-0880-8 LC Card 87-21324 DDC 338.973 19
1. Industry and state - United States. I. Heggestad, Arnold A., 1943-.
HD3616.U47 P82 1987

Public record : employer's accounting for settlements and curtailments of defined benefit pension plans and for termination benefits : position papers submitted in respect of Exposure draft. Stamford, Conn. (P.O. Box 3821, Stamford 06905-0821) : Financial Accounting Standards Board, [1986] 424 p. ; 28 cm. (Statement of financial accounting standards . no. 88) "PB 188." LC Card 86-81700 DDC 657/.75 19
1. Old age pensions - Accounting. 2. Postemployment benefits - Accounting. I. Financial Accounting Standards Board. II. Exposure draft. III. Series.
HF5686.O5 P83 1986

Public record, FASB technical bulletin no. 86-1, Accounting for certain effects of the Tax Reform Act of 1986. Stamford, Conn. (P.O. Box 3821, Stamford 06905-0821) : Financial Accounting Standards Board, [1987] 172 p. ; 28 cm. Consists of proposed bulletin no. 86-a and

comments on it received by the Board. Includes index. LC Card 87-80349 DDC 657/.46 19
1. Tax accounting - United States. I. Financial Accounting Standards Board. II. Title: FASB technical bulletin no. 86-1. III. Title: Accounting for certain effects of the Tax Reform Act of 1986.
HF5681.T3 P83 1987

PUBLIC RECORDS - PRESERVATION. see **ARCHIVES.**

PUBLIC RECORDS - UNITED STATES.
Workshop on Exact Matching Methodologies (May 9-10, 1985 : Arlington, Va.) Record linkage techniques--1985 . [Washington, D.C.] , 1985. vii, 397 p. : ***NYPL [JLF 86-1723]***

Public regulation : new perspectives on institutions and policies / edited by Elizabeth E. Bailey. Cambridge, Mass. : MIT Press, c1987. xiv, 404 p. ; 24 cm. (MIT Press series on the regulation of economic activity . 14) "Essays ... presented at a conference on public regulation sponsored by Carnegie Mellon University" -- Pref. Includes bibliographies and index. ISBN 0-262-02258-3 LC Card 86-21302 DDC 338.973 19
1. Trade regulation - United States - Congresses. 2. Trade regulation - Congresses. I. Bailey, Elizabeth E. II. Carnegie-Mellon University. III. Series.
HD3616.U47 P83 1987

Public relations : the Malaysian experience / [edited by Benedict Morais, Hamdan Adnan]. Kuala Lumpur : Institute of Public Relations Malaysia, 1986. 259 p. : ill. ; 22 cm. Includes bibliographies. LC Card 86-944684 DDC 659.2/09595 19
1. Public relations - Malaysia. I. Morais, Benedict. II. Mohd. Hamdan Adnan. III. Institut Perhubungan Raya Malaysia.
HD59.6.M4 P83 1986

PUBLIC RELATIONS - BANKS AND BANKING.
Burns, Thomas J., 1942- Effective communications and advertising for financial institutions /. Englewood Cliffs, N.J. , c1986. xvi, 299 p. : ISBN 0-8359-1556-5 LC Card 85-25641 DDC 659.1/93321 19
HG1616.M3 B87 1986 ***NYPL [JLE 86-1689]***

PUBLIC RELATIONS - BRAZIL.
Wey, Hebe. O processo de relações públicas /. São Paulo, SP , c1983. 166 p. ; LC Card 86-152248
HD59 .W44 1983

PUBLIC RELATIONS - BUSINESS. see **PUBLIC RELATIONS.**

PUBLIC RELATIONS - CORPORATIONS.
Effective corporate relations . London , New York , c1987. xii, 207 p. : ISBN 0-07-084940-4 (pbk.) : LC Card 87-21520 DDC 659.2/85 19
HD59 .E33 1987

PUBLIC RELATIONS - DATA PROCESSING.
New technology and public relations . New York, NY (310 Madison Ave., New York 10017) , c1986. xviii, 170 p. : LC Card 87-105313 DDC 659.2/028/5 19
HD59 .N44 1986

PUBLIC RELATIONS - DIRECTORIES.
The National directory of product publicity sources /. Westbury, N.Y. , 1987. p. cm. ISBN 0-87280-157-8 : LC Card 87-17542 DDC 338.7/616592/025 19
HD59 .N245 1987

PUBLIC RELATIONS - GERMANY (WEST) - BANKS AND BANKING.
Metz, Matthias. Kundenfreundliches Verhalten . Frankfurt am Main , c1985. xxi, 349 p. : ISBN 3-7819-0326-5 LC Card 85-202352
HG1616.P8 M47 1985

PUBLIC RELATIONS - INDUSTRY. see **PUBLIC RELATIONS.**

PUBLIC RELATIONS - MALAYSIA.
Public relations . Kuala Lumpur , 1986. 259 p. : LC Card 86-944684 DDC 659.2/09595 19
HD59.6.M4 P83 1986

PUBLIC RELATIONS - SOCIAL SERVICE - CASE STUDIES.
Egan, Gerard. Change agent skills in helping and human service settings /. Monterey, Calif. , c1985. xi, 306 p. : ISBN 0-534-03624-4 : LC Card 84-7804 DDC 361.3/07 19
HV11 .E43 1985 ***NYPL [JLE 86-1963]***

PUBLIC RELATIONS - SPAIN.
Televisió, federalisme. Barcelona [1986] 209 p. ; LC Card 86-210066
HE8700.9.S63 T44 1986

PUBLIC RELATIONS - TRADE-UNIONS.
Kolozsvári, Ernő. Szemelvények a szakszervezetek agitációs, propaganda- és kulturális tevékenységéből, 1948-1980 /. Budapest , 1982. 43 p. : ISBN 963-321-957-4 LC Card 83-229170
HD6680.5.Z6 K64 1982

A Szakszervezetek kulturális, agitációs és propagandamunkájának kézikönyve /. [Budapest] , 1986. 246 p. : ISBN 963-322-335-0 : LC Card 87-409655
HD6680.5 .S874 1986

PUBLIC RELATIONS - UNITED STATES.
Blyskal, Jeff. PR . New York , c1985. 241 p. ; ISBN 0-688-04788-2 : LC Card 85-80602 ***NYPL [JLE 86-268]***

Chamber of Commerce of the United States of America. Contact . Washington, D.C. , c1980. v, 129 p. : ISBN 0-89834-024-1 (pbk.) LC Card 80-80440 DDC 650/.07/073 19
HF5351 .C46 1980 ***NYPL [JLF 86-1414]***

PUBLIC RELATIONS - UNITED STATES - EVALUATION.
The velvet ghetto . San Francisco , 1986. 147 leaves in various foliations : LC Card 86-161157 DDC 331.4/816592/0973 19
HD6054.2.U6 V45 1986

PUBLIC RELATIONS - UNITED STATES - HISTORY.
Olasky, Marvin N. Corporate public relations and American private enterprise . Hillsdale, NJ , 1987. p. cm. ISBN 0-8058-0052-2 LC Card 87-3551 DDC 659.2/0973 19
HD59.6.U6 O4 1987

PUBLIC RELIEF. see **PUBLIC WELFARE.**

PUBLIC SCHOOLS - ARGENTINA.
Funciones y servicios de competencia municipal /. Córdoba, República Argentina , 1984. 94 leaves ; LC Card 87-121632 DDC 352.082 19
HD4629 .F86 1984

PUBLIC SCHOOLS - FINANCE. see **EDUCATION - FINANCE.**

Public sector deficits in OECD countries : causes, consequences, and remedies / edited by Henry Cavanna. New York : St. Martin's Press, 1987. p. cm. Bibliography: p. Includes index. ISBN 0-312-00533-4 : LC Card 87-11876 DDC 339.5/23/091724 19
1. Budget deficits. 2. Organisation for Economic Co-operation and Development. I. Cavanna, Henry.
HJ2043 .P8 1987

Public sector economics /. Holcombe, Randall G. Belmont, Calif. [1987], c1988. xxxii, 414 p. : ISBN 0-534-08190-8 LC Card 87-13344 DDC 338.9 19
HJ141 .H58 1988

Public sector financial control and accounting /. Glynn, John J. Oxford [Oxfordshire] , New York, N.Y., USA , 1987. x, 278 p. : ISBN 0-631-14686-5 : LC Card 86-31725 DDC 657/.835 19
HJ9733 .G58 1987

Public sector labor relations : analysis and readings / [edited by] David Lewin ... [et al.].[3rd ed.]. Lexington, Mass. : Lexington Books, c1988. xi, 648 p. ; 24 cm. Rev. ed. of: Public sector labor relations / David Lewin. 1977. Includes bibliographies and index. ISBN 0-669-12893-7 (alk. paper) LC Card 82-64038 DDC 331.89/041353 19
1. Collective bargaining - Government employees - United States. 2. Trade-unions - Government employees - United States. 3. Employee-management relations in government - United States. I. Lewin, David, 1943-. II. Lewin, David, 1943- Public sector labor relations.
HD8005.6.U5 P83 1988

PUBLIC SECURITIES. see **SECURITIES.**

PUBLIC SERVICE COMMISSIONS - GREAT BRITAIN - CASE STUDIES.
Public enterprise . New York , 1985. 416 p. ; ISBN 0-8240-7626-5 (alk. paper) : LC Card 85-13105 DDC 354.4109/1 19
HD4147 .P83 1985 ***NYPL [JLD 86-3467]***

Public service employment . Cook, Robert F., 1943- Kalamazoo, Mich. , 1985. xiii, 131 p. ; ISBN 0-88099-031-7 (pbk.) LC Card 85-22495 DDC 331.13/77/0973 19
HD5713.6.U54 C66 1985 ***NYPL [JLE 86-3877]***

PUBLIC SERVICE EMPLOYMENT - CALIFORNIA - SAN DIEGO COUNTY.
Goldman, Barbara. Final report on the San Diego job search and work experience demonstration /. New York, N.Y. (3 Park Ave., New York 10016) , c1986. xliv, 269 p. : LC Card 87-118376 DDC 331.12/042/0979498 19
HD5713.6.U542 S395 1986

PUBLIC SERVICE EMPLOYMENT - CONGRESSES.
Le Iniziative locali per l'occupazione . Milano, Italy , c1985. 244 p. : LC Card 85-221711 DDC 331 s 331.12/042 19
HD85.I7 I68 no. 75 HD5713.5 ***NYPL [JLD 87-446]***

PUBLIC SERVICE EMPLOYMENT - EUROPE.
Rein, Martin. Women in the social welfare labor market /. Berlin [1985] 180 p. ; LC Card 86-213535 DDC 331.4/129136294 19
HD6134 .R45 1985

PUBLIC SERVICE EMPLOYMENT - INDIA.
Varma, S. C. Millions in poverty grip . New Delhi , 1984. xv, 172 p. ; LC Card 84-900600 DDC 331.12/042/0954 19
HD5710.85.I4 V37 1984 ***NYPL [JLD 86-4236]***

PUBLIC SERVICE EMPLOYMENT - UNITED STATES.
Cook, Robert F., 1943- Public service employment . Kalamazoo, Mich. , 1985. xiii, 131 p. ; ISBN 0-88099-031-7 (pbk.) LC Card 85-22495 DDC 331.13/77/0973 19
HD5713.6.U54 C66 1985 ***NYPL [JLE 86-3877]***

Rein, Martin. Women in the social welfare labor market /. Berlin [1985] 180 p. ; LC Card 86-213535 DDC 331.4/129136294 19
HD6134 .R45 1985

PUBLIC SERVICES. see **MUNICIPAL SERVICES.**

PUBLIC SPENDING POLICY. see **GOVERNMENT SPENDING POLICY.**

Public Strategies (Firm) Federal tax reform and the states . Washington, D.C. (1616 H St., N.W., Suite 600, Washington 20006) , c1987. 84 p. ; LC Card 87-404532 DDC 336.2/05/0973 19
HJ2381 .F37 1987

PUBLIC TELEVISION - SPAIN.
La Televisión en España mañana . Madrid , 1986. 331 p. ; ISBN 84-323-0563-X LC Card 86-199326
HE8700.9.S63 T45 1986 ***NYPL [MWGV (Spain) 87-2054]***

Public utilities and the poor . Sweet, David C. New York , 1987. xxiii, 174 p. : ISBN 0-275-92572-2 (alk. paper) : LC Card 87-6979 DDC 362.5/82 19
HC110.P6 S894 1987

PUBLIC UTILITIES - BRAZIL - PORTO ALEGRE.
Porto Alegre (Brazil). Mayor. Mensagem apresentada á Camara Municipal /. Pôrto Alegre , 1936. 686 p., [7] folded leaves of plates : LC Card 85-135614
HD4635.P6 P67 1936

PUBLIC UTILITIES - BRAZIL - STATISTICS.
Inquéritos especiais /. Rio de Janeiro, Brasil , 1984. 4 v. in 5. ; ***NYPL [JLF 86-202]***

PUBLIC UTILITIES - CALIFORNIA.
Shapiro, Michael E. Utility diversification . Sacramento, CA [1986] 50 p. ; LC Card 86-621960 DDC 338.8/3613636/0973 19
HD2766 .S47 1986

PUBLIC UTILITIES - FINANCE.
Bozem, Karlheinz. Controlling in Versorgungsunternehmen /. München , 1986. xiv, 468, 10 p. : ISBN 3-486-26236-X LC Card 87-135246 DDC 363.6/2/0681 19
HD2763 .B66 1986

PUBLIC UTILITIES - GERMANY (EAST)
Bartsch, Heinz. Örtliche Versorgungswirtschaft . Potsdam-Babelsberg , 1985. 79 p. : LC Card 86-121253
HD2768.G4 B27 1985

PUBLIC UTILITIES - GERMANY, WEST.
Erklärungen zur kommunalen Versorgungswirtschaft. Köln , 1985. 146 p. ; ISBN 3-87750-141-9
NYPL [K-10 8934 Heft 63]

Schröter, Klaus, 1953- Die wettbewerbspolitische Behandlung der leitungsgebundenen Energiewirtschaft . Frankfurt am Main , New York , c1986. viii, 300 p. ; ISBN 3-8204-9551-7 LC Card 87-407422 DDC 363.6/2/0943 19
HD9685.G3 S375 1986

PUBLIC UTILITIES - GERMANY (WEST) - MANAGEMENT - EMPLOYEE PARTICIPATION.
Ehinger, Jürgen. Erfahrungen mit der Mitbestimmung in kommunalen Unternehmen . Baden-Baden , 1986. 147 p. ; ISBN 3-7890-1289-0 LC Card 87-118963 DDC 350.87/00943 19
HD2768.G44 E38 1986

PUBLIC UTILITIES - GOVERNMENT POLICY.
Regulating utilities in an era of deregulation /. New York , 1987. xii, 201 p. : ISBN 0-312-00527-X : LC Card 86-29639 DDC 363.6/0973 19
HD2763 .R43 1987

PUBLIC UTILITIES - GOVERNMENT POLICY - UNITED STATES.
Regulatory reform . Washington, D.C. , c1984. ii, 267 p. : ISBN 0-913097-02-0 (pbk.) LC Card 84-80846 DDC 363.6/0973 19
HD2766 .R357 1984

PUBLIC UTILITIES - GOVERNMENT POLICY - WASHINGTON (STATE)
Washington (State). Governor's Citizens Utility and Telecommunication Advisory Committee. Utilities in transition . [Olympia, Wash.] [1984] 61, 18, [20] p. ; LC Card 85-622797 DDC 363.6/09797 19
HE7791.W2 W37 1984
NYPL [JLF 86-1773]

PUBLIC UTILITIES - GREAT BRITAIN - CASE STUDIES.
Public enterprise . New York , 1985. 416 p. ; ISBN 0-8240-7626-5 (alk. paper) : LC Card 85-13105 DDC 354.4109/1 19
HD4147 .P83 1985 *NYPL [JLD 86-3467]*

Public Utilities Reports, Inc. Purview. [Arlington, Va.] , c1985. 1 v. (various pagings) : LC Card 86-222822 DDC 363.6/0973 19
HD2766 .P87 1985

PUBLIC UTILITIES - SPAIN - ASTURIAS.
Argüelles, Alfonso. Los Oscos y la Cuenca del Eo . [Asturias] [1984?] ix, 317 p. : ISBN 84-505-0237-3 LC Card 86-174593
HC387.A7 A74 1984

PUBLIC UTILITIES - UNITED STATES.
Purview. [Arlington, Va.] , c1985. 1 v. (various pagings) : LC Card 86-222822 DDC 363.6/0973 19
HD2766 .P87 1985

Shapiro, Michael E. Utility diversification . Sacramento, CA [1986] 50 p. ; LC Card 86-621960 DDC 338.8/3613636/0973 19
HD2766 .S47 1986

PUBLIC UTILITIES - UNITED STATES - COSTS.
Regulatory reform . Washington, D.C. , c1984. ii, 267 p. : ISBN 0-913097-02-0 (pbk.) LC Card 84-80846 DDC 363.6/0973 19
HD2766 .R357 1984

PUBLIC UTILITIES - UNITED STATES - ENERGY CONSERVATION.
Energy conservation . Washington, D.C. , c1986. xii, 270 p. : ISBN 0-8157-7716-7 : LC Card 85-26894 DDC 333.79/16/0973 19
HD9502.U62 E478 1986
NYPL [JLE 86-4084]

PUBLIC UTILITIES - UNITED STATES - RATES.
Regulatory reform . Washington, D.C. , c1984. ii, 267 p. : ISBN 0-913097-02-0 (pbk.) LC Card 84-80846 DDC 363.6/0973 19
HD2766 .R357 1984

PUBLIC UTILITIES - URUGUAY - MONTEVIDEO.
Vicario, Luis B. Algunas características del inventario de vivienda . [Montevideo] , 1985. 42 p. : LC Card 86-152477
HD7330.M64 V53 1985

PUBLIC WELFARE - ADDRESSES, ESSAYS, LECTURES.
Sozialreform und Rhetorik =. Wiesbaden , 1984. 174 p. ; ISBN 3-515-02857-9
NYPL [L-11 3778 Bd. 4]

PUBLIC WELFARE - BRAZIL.
Possas, Cristina de Albuquerque. Saúde e trabalho . Rio de Janeiro, RJ , 1981. xxxix, 324 p. : LC Card 82-132979 DDC 362.1/0981 19
RA418.3.B6 P68 1981 *NYPL [JLD 86-1896]*

PUBLIC WELFARE - COST EFFECTIVENESS.
Tasgian, Astrig. La valutazione economica della vita umana . Torino , 1980. 117 p. : LC Card 81-124532 DDC 331/.01/1 19
HD4904.7 .T34 1980 *NYPL [JLE 86-1600]*

PUBLIC WELFARE - ENGLAND - BRIGHTON (EAST SUSSEX)
Brighton on the rocks . Brighton [1983?] 192 p. : ISBN 0-904733-00-4 (pbk.) : LC Card 84-173777 DDC 336.3/9/0942256 19
HJ9438.B75 B75 1983 *NYPL [JLD 87-104]*

PUBLIC WELFARE - EUROPE - HISTORY.
La Storia dei poveri . Roma , c1985. xii, 300 p. ; ISBN 88-382-3530-9 : LC Card 86-198943
HC240.9.P6 S76 1985

PUBLIC WELFARE - GERMANY, WEST.
Böpple, Arthur. "Sozialstaat" im Abbruch . Frankfurt/Main , c1986. 277 p. : ISBN 3-88367-062-6 LC Card 87-104497
HD7179 .B624 1986

PUBLIC WELFARE - INDIA.
Bulsara, Jal F. (Jal Feerose), 1899- Perspectives on social welfare in India /. New Delhi , 1984. xvi, 226 p. ; LC Card 84-900869 DDC 361/.954 19
HV40 .B886 1984 *NYPL [JLD 86-4376]*

Chowdhry, D. Paul. Profile of social welfare and development in India /. New Delhi , 1985. viii, 340 p. ; LC Card 85-901093 DDC 362/.954 19
HV393 .C515 1985 *NYPL [JLD 86-2575]*

PUBLIC WELFARE - INDIA - KARNATAKA.
Hanumantha Rayappa, P. (Pullikunta), 1938- Backwardness and welfare of scheduled castes and scheduled tribes in India /. New Delhi , 1986. xi, 121 p. ; ISBN 81-7024-059-X : LC Card 86-902970
HC437.K27 H36 1986

PUBLIC WELFARE - INDIA - RAJASTHAN - HISTORY.
Maloo, Kamala, 1948- The history of famines in Rajputana, 1858-1900 A.D. /. Udaipur , 1987. xii, 296 p. : ISBN 81-85167-00-1 : LC Card 87-901599 DDC 363.8/0954/4 19
HC437.R3 M28 1987

PUBLIC WELFARE - ITALY - LOMBARDY - HISTORY.
Bressan, E. (Edoardo) Povertà e assistenza in Lombardia nell'età napoleonica /. [Milano] , Bari , c1985. viii, 339 p. : ISBN 88-420-2653-0 : LC Card 86-162978
HC307.L8 B74 1985

PUBLIC WELFARE - ITALY - STATISTICAL SERVICES - CONGRESSES.
Statistica e pubblica amministrazione . Milano , 1983-1985. 2 v. ; ISBN 88-14-00703-9 (v. 2) : LC Card 86-215546
HA37.I9 S7 1983

PUBLIC WELFARE - LATIN AMERICA.
Poverty in Latin America . Washington, D.C., U. S.A. [1986] 25 p. ; ISBN 0-8213-0836-X (pbk.) LC Card 86-225244 DDC 330.98/0038 19
HC130.I5 P68 1986

PUBLIC WELFARE - LAW AND LEGISLATION - NETHERLANDS.
Braakman, T. C. Sociale zekerheid in Nederland /. Utrecht , 1984. 199 p. : ISBN 90-274-5513-9 : LC Card 85-110890
HD7192 .B73 1984 *NYPL [JLC 86-295]*

PUBLIC WELFARE - NETHERLANDS.
Braakman, T. C. Sociale zekerheid in Nederland /. Utrecht , 1984. 199 p. : ISBN 90-274-5513-9 : LC Card 85-110890
HD7192 .B73 1984 *NYPL [JLC 86-295]*

PUBLIC WELFARE - UNITED STATES.
Bernstein, Blanche, 1912- Saving a generation /. New York , 1986. vi, 63 p. ; ISBN 0-87078-206-1 (pbk.) : LC Card 87-102738 DDC 362.5/8/0973 19
HC110.P6 B47 1986

For crying out loud . New York , c1986. ix, 397 p. ; ISBN 0-8298-0581-8 (pbk.) : LC Card 86-9302 DDC 305.4/2/0973 19
HQ1426 .F757 1986 *NYPL [JLD 86-3989]*

Malone, Margaret Sahlin, 1933- Work and welfare /. Washington , 1986. ix, 162 p. ; LC Card 86-603383 DDC 362.5/84/0973 19
HD5715.2 .M34 1986

The Mean season . New York, c1987. xvi, 205 p. ; ISBN 0-394-55338-1 : LC Card 86-43126 DDC 361/.973 19
HC110.P63 M42 1987

Morris, Michael, 1949- Poverty and public policy . Westport, Conn. , 1986. xii, 236 p. ; ISBN 0-313-24942-3 (lib. bdg. : alk. paper) LC Card 86-398 DDC 361.6/1/0973 19
HV95 .M67 1986 *NYPL [JLD 87-510]*

Moynihan, Daniel P. (Daniel Patrick), 1927- The politics of a guaranteed income. New York [1973] xiii, 579 p. ISBN 0-394-46354-4 LC Card 77-37069 DDC 362.5
HC110.I5 M65 *NYPL [JLE 74-384]*

Private means--public ends . New York , 1987. xiii, 187 p. ; ISBN 0-275-92429-7 (alk. paper) : LC Card 86-25251 DDC 361.6/1/0973 19
HN65 .P69 1987 *NYPL [JLE 87-1390]*

Rodgers, Harrell R. Poor women, poor families . Armonk, N.Y. , 1986. viii, 167 p. ; ISBN 0-87332-372-6 : LC Card 86-6449 DDC 362.8/3/0973 19
HV1445 .R64 1986 *NYPL [JLE 86-4042]*

PUBLIC WELFARE - UNITED STATES - CONGRESSES.
Fighting poverty . Cambridge, Mass. , 1986. viii, 418 p. : ISBN 0-674-30085-8 (alk. paper) LC Card 85-24848 DDC 362.5/8/0973 19
HC110.P63 F54 1986 *NYPL [JLE 86-4089]*

PUBLIC WELFARE - UNITED STATES - FINANCE.
Project on the Federal Social Role (U. S.). Committee on Federalism and National Purpose. To form a more perfect union /. Washington, D.C. (1730 M St., Suite 911, Washington 20036) , c1985. xi, 52 p. ;
NYPL [JLE 86-1879]

PUBLIC WORKS - COSTS.
López Nieto, Antonio. Los costes de las obras a cargo del sector público . Madrid , 1962. xiv, 214 p. : LC Card 85-107655
HD3856.S7 L66 1962

PUBLIC WORKS - MANAGEMENT - ADDRESSES, ESSAYS, LECTURES.
Management of local public works /. Washington, D.C. , c1986. xvii, 402 p. : ISBN 0-87326-048-1 : LC Card 86-125 DDC 363/.068 19
HD4431 .M35 1986 *NYPL [JLF 86-1543]*

Publicação (Biblioteca do Exército (Brazil)) .
(231) Carvalho, Osvaldo Ferraro de. Ensaio sôbre a problemática dos transportes /. Rio de Janeiro , 1957. 324 p., [5] folded leaves of plates : LC Card 85-197985
HE233 .C345 1957

Publicação (Brazil. Inspectoria Federal de Obras contra as Seccas) .
(n. 70, sér. 2, M) Brazil. Inspectoria Federal de Obras contra as Seccas. Relatorio dos trabalhos executados durante o anno de 1925 . Rio de Janeiro , 1926. xiv, 75 p. ; LC Card 85-186786
HD1696.B8 B73 1926

Publicação (Brazil. Ministério do Interior. Coordenadoria de Comunicação Social) .
(86/01) Brazil. Ministerio do Interior. Programa de Irrigação do Nordeste--PROINE . Brasília , 1986. 30 p. ; LC Card 87-400672 DDC 333.91/3/09813 19
HD1741.B82 N623 1986

Publicação (Brazil. Secretaria de Planejamento. Coordenadoria de Comunicação Social) .
(82/07) Delfim Netto, Antônio. Brasil 82, a grande luta para manter o espaço para crescer . Brasília , 1982. 37 p. : LC Card 84-249919
HC187 .D552 1982

Publicação (Universidade Federal de Goiás) .
(no. 115) Brandão, Carlos Rodrigues. Campesinato goiano . Goiânia , 1986. 156 p. ; ISBN 85-85003-42-1 : LC Card 87-403866 DDC 305.5/63 19
HD1531.B7 B713 1986

Publicación ... del Centro de Estudios Darocenses .

Publicación divulgativa .
(no. 22) Buroz Castillo, Eduardo. Programa de cooperación técnica Perú-Venezuela-OEA . Caracas , 1976. [11], 62 p. ; LC Card 84-136478
HD1696.P5 B87 1976

Publicación Emilio Obregón.
Mueses, Danilo A. Seebeck . [S.l.] , República Dominicana [1986?] 170, [5] p. : LC Card 86-177691
HE6185.L29 M84 1986

Publicaciones de la Comisión Preparatoria de la IV Asamblea General del Instituto Panamericano de Geografía e Historia.
Hacienda colonial venezolana /. Caracas , 1946. 170 p. ; LC Card 85-105445
HJ991 .H323 1946

Publicaciones de la Escuela Universitaria de Estudios Empresariales de la Universidad de Valencia. Sociología.
Pellicer Valero, Jesús-Agustín. Sociología del trabajo en Canet de Berenguer /. Valencia , 1984. 80 p. : ISBN 84-600-3540-9 LC Card 86-216439
HD5808.C33 P45 1984

Publicaciones de la Excma. Diputación Provincial de Sevilla. Sección Historia .
(ser. 1a, no. 17) Herrera García, Antonio. El Aljarafe sevillano durante el antiguo régimen . [Sevilla] , 1980. 517 p., [9] leaves of plates : ISBN 84-500-4373-5 LC Card 81-173649 DDC 946/.86 19
HD779.A39 H475 1980 ***NYPL [JLF 86-928]***

(ser. 1a, no. 27) Camacho Rueda, Eduardo. Propiedad y explotación agrarias en el aljarafe sevillano . Sevilla , 1984. 199 p. : ISBN 84-500-9772-X LC Card 85-135028
HD773 .C18 1984

(ser. 1a, no. 29) Morell Peguero, Blanca. Mercaderes y artesanos en la Sevilla del descubrimiento /. Sevilla , 1986. 222 p. ; ISBN 84-505-2883-6 LC Card 86-199625
HD2346.S72 S465 1986

Publicaciones de la Facultad de Derecho. Cuaderno .
(no. 15) Conferencias sobre desarrollo económico, presupuesto, estabilización y nacionalización de empresas económicas. La Paz, Bolivia , 1955. 180 p. : LC Card 86-167406
HC182 .C54 1955

Publicaciones de la Universidad Autónoma de Santo Domingo. Colección Estudios sociales .
(no. 1) Duarte, Isis. Trabajadores urbanos . Santo Domingo, República Dominicana , c1986. 314 p. ; LC Card 87-402153 DDC 331/.097293 19
HD8218.5 .D83 1986

Publicaciones de la Universidad Autónoma de Santo Domingo. Colección Historia y sociedad .
(no. 43) Domínguez, Jaime de Jesús, 1947- Feudalismo, capitalismo mercantil y capitalismo industrial /. Santo Domingo, República Dominicana , 1981. 229 p. ; ISBN 84-89527-00-8 LC Card 82-200900
HC21 .D66 1981

Publicaciones de la Universidad de Deusto. Sociología .
(v. 5) Uriarte, Pedro. Psicosociología de la organización . Bilbao , 1985. 284 p. : ISBN 84-7485-049-5 LC Card 86-151352
HD6955 .U75 1985

Publicaciones de la Universidad de Murcia.
Chacón Jiménez, Francisco. Murcia, un modelo económico en el mundo mediterráneo durante el siglo XVI /. [Murcia] , 1978. 29 p., [7] folded leaves of plates : ISBN 84-600-1243-3 LC Card 86-133743
HC387.M8 C48 1978

Publicaciones técnicas (Instituto de Promoción Económico-Social del Uruguay) .
(8) Producción y comercialización porcina en Uruguay . Montevideo , 1986. 91 p. : LC Card 87-401290 DDC 338.1/764/009895 19
HD9435.U82 P76 1986

Publicacions de la Caixa d'Estalvis i Socors de Sagunt.
Estructura social de la comarca "El Camp de Morvedre" /. Sagunt, València [Madrid] , 1982. 2 v. (1133 p.) : ISBN 84-7231-763-3 (set) LC Card 85-188040
HB3620.S24 E87 1982

Publicatie ... van de Stichting Comité Oud-Muiderberg .
(nr. 26) Handel en wandel in de dertiende eeuw /. Amsterdam , c1986. 139 p. : ISBN 90-6707-112-9 LC Card 86-199144
HC324 .H36 1986

Publication (Canada. Agriculture Canada. Marketing and Economics Branch) .
(no. 83/3) Hassan, Zuhair A. Handbook of food expenditures, prices, and consumption /. Ottawa , c1983. 270 p., [2] p. of plates : LC Card 86-228246 DDC 339.4/8664/00971 19
HD9014.C3 H29 1983

Publication (Mahatma Phule Krishi Vidyapeeth. Dept. of Agricultural Economics) .
(9) Dhongade, M. P. Farmers' attitude survey in the Mula Command Area, Maharashtra /. Rahuri, Maharashtra, India , 1986. vi, 69 p. ; LC Card 86-903408 DDC 338.1/0954/792 19
HD8039.F32 I44 1986

Publication of HWWA-Institut für Wirtschaftsforschung-Hamburg.
Indebtedness and growth in developing countries /. Hamburg , 1986. 344 p. ; ISBN 3-87895-300-3 (pbk.) LC Card 86-213057 DDC 336.3/435/091724 19
HJ8899 .I53 1986

Publication (Punjab (India). Economic and Statistical Organisation) .
(no. 296) Punjab (India). Economic and Statistical Organisation. Report on the evaluation study of working of the Punjab Scheduled Castes Land Development and Finance Corporation. Chandigarh [pref. 1978] viii, 98 p. ; LC Card 79-903307
HC437.P8 P85 1978a

(no. 480) Piṇḍāṃ dī ḍairaikaṭarī, 1983-84. Caṇḍīgaṛha [1985- v. <1- > ; LC Card 86-902359
HA4587.P86 P56 1985

Publications de l'Institut universitaire de hautes études internationales, Genève.
Maurer, Jean-Luc. Modernisation agricole, développement économique et changement social . Paris , c1986. 323 p. : ISBN 2-13-039622-4 : LC Card 86-175394
HD2085.B37 M38 1986

Publications de l'Université de Tunis, Faculté des lettres et sciences humaines de Tunis. Deuxième série, Géographie .
(v. 20) Jedidi, Mohammed. Croissance économique et espace urbain dans le Sahel tunisien depuis l'indépendance /. [Tunis] , 1986. 2 v. : LC Card 87-123401
HC820 .J43 1986

Publications du Centre de recherche d'histoire économique, sociale et institutionnelle de Grenoble. Série Histoire économique et sociale .
(v. 5) Perrin, Jacqueline. L'enquête de 1848 sur le travail en Isère /. Grenoble , 1985. 251 p., [1] leaf of plates : ISBN 2-904661-03-4 : LC Card 86-227898
HC277.I8 P47 1985

Publications in octavo (Société de l'histoire de France) .
(130) Douët-d'Arcq, L. (Louis), 1808-1882. (ed) Comptes de l'hôtel des rois de France aux XIVe et XVe siècles. Paris, 1865. 3 p.l., xlii p., 1 l., 437 p., 1 l. LC Card 05-5875
HJ1077 .D6

Publications of the European University Institute .
(2) Willke, Gerhard. Globalsteuerung und gespaltene Konjunktur . Leyden ; Boston : xiii, 243 p. : ISBN 3-12-915020-X LC Card 84-181249
HD5779 .W55 1978

Publications of the Institute of Social Studies.
Somasekhara, N. Rural energy . New Delhi , 1985. xii, 113 p. ; ISBN 81-207-0121-6 : LC Card 86-900467 DDC 333.79/0954 19
HD9502.I42 S66 1985 ***NYPL [JLD 86-3315]***

Publications of the Institute of World Economics, University of Kiel.
Free trade in the world economy . Boulder , 1987. p. cm. ISBN 0-8133-0596-9 LC Card 87-20148 DDC 382.7/1 19
HF1703 .F74 1987

The International debt problem . Boulder , 1987. p. cm. ISBN 0-8133-0595-0 LC Card 87-20149 DDC 336.3/435 19
HG3891.5 .I557 1987

New opportunities for entrepreneurship /. Boulder , 1987. p. cm. ISBN 0-8133-0597-7 LC Card 87-20143 DDC 338/.04 19
HD62.5 .N48 1987

Reassessing the role of government in the mixed economy /. Boulder , 1987. p. cm. ISBN 0-8133-0598-5 : LC Card 87-20142 DDC 338.9 19
HD73 .R43 1987

Publicité dans un pays plurilingue. Werbung in einem mehrsprachigen Land /. Freiburg, Schweiz , c1986. 152 p. : ISBN 3-7278-0382-7 LC Card 87-409238 DDC 659.1/09494 19
HF5808.S9 W47 1986

PUBLICITY.
Krämer, Georg. Pädagogische Aspekte entwicklungspolitischer Öffentlichkeitsarbeit /. Frankfurt/Main , 1980. 233 p. : ISBN 3-88129-332-9 LC Card 81-466304
HC59.7 .K687 ***NYPL [JLD 87-528]***

Lima, Gerson Moreira, 1952- Releasemania, uma contribuição para o estudo do press-release no Brasil /. São Paulo, SP , c1985. 114 p. : LC Card 85-184576 DDC 659.2 19
HM263 .L478 1985 ***NYPL [JFD 86-2728]***

PUBLICITY, INDUSTRIAL. see INDUSTRIAL PUBLICITY.

Publikatie (Sociaal-Economische Raad) .
(86/10) Sociaal-Economische Raad. Advies inzake het sociaal-economisch beleid op middellange termijn 1986-1990 /. Den Haag [1986] 142, 150 p. ; ISBN 90-6587-248-5 LC Card 86-234847
HC321 .S63 1986, nr. 10 HC325

(86/11) Advies wijziging Winkelsluitingswet . Den Haag [1986] 78 p. ; ISBN 90-6587-250-7 LC Card 86-234857
HC321 .S63 1986, nr. 11 KKM3419

(86/14) Sociaal-Economische Raad. Commissie Ondernemingsraden. Advies vereenvoudiging Wet OR . Den Haag [1986] 61 p. ; ISBN 90-6587-254-X LC Card 87-165080
HC321 .S63 1986, nr. 14 KKM1350

(86/6) Advies samenloop Wet OR en ARBO-wet . Den Haag [1986] 37 p. ; ISBN 90-6587-243-4 LC Card 87-104667
HC321 .S63 1986, nr. 6 KKM1430

Publikatiereeks milieubeheer .
(85/24) Meijenfeldt, C. F. W. M. von. Gebruik van en alternatieven voor tropisch hout. 's-Gravenhage , c1985. 207, [14] p. : ISBN 90-346-0647-3 : LC Card 86-231435
HD9750.8.T73 M45 1985

Publikaties van de Nationale Advies Raad voor Ontwikkelingssamenwerking .
(84) Netherlands. Nationale Advies Raad voor Ontwikkelingssamenwerking. Advies minimum internationale arbeidsnormen /. 's-Gravenhage [1984] 97 p. ; ISBN 90-12-04950-4 LC Card 86-193168
HC60 .N465 no. 84a K1705.4

(85) Netherlands. Nationale Advies Raad voor Ontwikkelingssamenwerking. Advies vrouwen en ontwikkeling /. [The Hague , 1985] 53 p. ; ISBN 90-12-04985-7 LC Card 86-198854
HC60 .N465 no. 85 HQ1240

Publikationen des Beirates für Wirtschafts- und Sozialfragen .
(53) Budgetvorschau 1986-1990. Wien , 1986. 45 p. : LC Card 86-227246
HJ2101 .B83 1986

Publikationen des Schweizerischen Nationalfonds aus den nationalen Forschungsprogrammen .
(Bd. 34, 2) Flückiger, Hans. Siedlungsstruktur . Bern , c1985. 118 p. : ISBN 3-258-03529-6 : LC Card 86-134805
HN603.5 .F58 1985 NYPL [JLE 86-3789]

(Bd. 38) Finsinger, Jörg. Der Submissionswettbewerb . Bern , c1986. 104 p. : ISBN 3-258-03617-9 : LC Card 86-224617
HD9715.S92 F56 1986

Publikationer fra Boligministeriet, Boligstyrelsen og Byggestyrelsen .
(41) Denmark. Udvalget vedrørende byfornyelse og støtte til ejerboliger. Redegørelse om støtte til ejerboliger i forbindelse med byfornyelse . København [1981] 128 p. : ISBN 87-503-3873-0 LC Card 82-194685
HD7347.A4 D455 1981

Publikationer fra Institut for geografi, samfundsanalyse og datalogi, Roskilde universitetscenter. Arbejdspapir, 0106-5920 .

Publikationer fra Institut for geografi, samfundsanalyse og datalogi, Roskilde universitetscenter. Arbejdspapir .
(nr. 25) Vedel, Gitte. Om kvindearbejdets igangværende udvikling og perspektiver, i relation til den teknologiske udvikling /. Roskilde , 1982. 103 leaves : LC Card 83-172895
HD6060.65.D4 V42 1982

(nr. 36) Kongstad, Per. Industri, fagbevægelse og lønarbejde i Kenya . Roskilde [1983] 76 p. ; LC Card 85-238103
HC865 .K66 1983

Pucci, Carlos. Los precios sociales en la evaluación de proyectos en Costa Rica / por Carlos Pucci. San José, Costa Rica : Oficina e Planificación Nacional y Política Económica, División de Inversiones, 1979. [108] leaves ; 27 cm. Cover title. LC Card 83-238167
1. Labor productivity - Costa Rica. 2. Productivity accounting. 3. Capital - Costa Rica. I. Title.
HC143.Z9 L36 1979

Puchert, Berthold. Landau, Zbigniew. Wirtschaftsgeschichte Polens im 19. und 20. Jahrhundert /. Berlin , 1986. vi, 300 p. : LC Card 86-223591
HC340.3 .L367 1986

Puchinskas, K. K. (Kazis Kazio) Vasil'ev, A. F. (Alekseĭ Fedorovich) Avtomatizirovannaia obrabotka uchetnoĭ informatsii v sel'skokhoziaĭstvennykh predpriiatiiakh /. Moskva , 1984. 198 p. ; LC Card 85-113739
HF5686.A36 V37 1984

PUEBLO INDIANS - LAND TENURE - HISTORY.
Land, water, and culture . Albuquerque , c1987. ix, 422 p. : ISBN 0-8263-0989-5 (pbk.) LC Card 87-10957 DDC 333.1/6/09788 19
HD243.N5 L36 1987

Puel, Gaston. Pourquoi la pauvreté-- quand les produits abondent? : ce que l'on ne vous dit pas-- / Gaston Puel. [France] : Editions Tiers-Monde, [1986] 255 p. ; 21 cm. LC Card 86-189201
1. Wealth. 2. Income distribution. 3. Poverty. 4. Prices. I. Title.
HC79.W4 P84 1986

Pümpin, Cuno Beat. The essence of corporate strategy / Cuno Pümpin. Aldershot, Hants, England ; Brookfield, Vt., U. S.A. : Gower, c1987. xi, 183 p. : ill. ; 26 cm. Bibliography: p. 177-179. Includes index. ISBN 0-566-02565-5 : LC Card 87-14907 DDC 658.4/012 19
1. Strategic planning. I. Title.
HD30.28 .P85 1987

Puerto Rico . Curet, Eliezer. Rio Piedras, P.R. (Calle Roble No. 51, Rio Piedras 00925) , 1986. xiii, 257 p. : LC Card 87-100359 DDC 338.97295 19
HC154.5 .C87 1986

PUERTO RICO - COMMERCE - HISTORY.
Dietz, James L., 1947- Economic history of Puerto Rico . Princeton , c1986. xxiii, 337 p., [11] p. of plates : ISBN 0-691-07716-9 (alk. paper) : LC Card 86-12313 DDC 330.97295 19
HC154.5 .D54 1986 NYPL [JLE 87-1592]

PUERTO RICO - ECONOMIC CONDITIONS.
Dietz, James L., 1947- Economic history of Puerto Rico . Princeton , c1986. xxiii, 337 p., [11] p. of plates : ISBN 0-691-07716-9 (alk. paper) : LC Card 86-12313 DDC 330.97295 19
HC154.5 .D54 1986 NYPL [JLE 87-1592]

PUERTO RICO - ECONOMIC CONDITIONS - 1952-
Curet, Eliezer. Puerto Rico . Rio Piedras, P.R. (Calle Roble No. 51, Rio Piedras 00925) , 1986. xiii, 257 p. : LC Card 87-100359 DDC 338.97295 19
HC154.5 .C87 1986

PUERTO RICO - ECONOMIC POLICY.
Curet, Eliezer. Puerto Rico . Rio Piedras, P.R. (Calle Roble No. 51, Rio Piedras 00925) , 1986. xiii, 257 p. : LC Card 87-100359 DDC 338.97295 19
HC154.5 .C87 1986

PUERTO RICO - HISTORY.
Dietz, James L., 1947- Economic history of Puerto Rico . Princeton , c1986. xxiii, 337 p., [11] p. of plates : ISBN 0-691-07716-9 (alk. paper) : LC Card 86-12313 DDC 330.97295 19
HC154.5 .D54 1986 NYPL [JLE 87-1592]

Los puertos del Perú /. Flórez Nohesell, Miguel. Lima, Perú , 1986. 947 p. : LC Card 86-210075
HE555.P5 F58 1986

Los puertos marítimos del País Vasco /. Ciriquiain-Gaiztarro, M. San Sebastián [1986?] 270 p. : ISBN 84-7148-180-4 LC Card 87-105513
HE558.P15 C57 1986

Püschel, Herbert. Die Rentenversorgung der Arbeiter und Angestellten in der DDR / Herbert Püschel, Rudolf Hoppe. 6. Aufl. Berlin : Tribüne, c1986. 206 p. ; 21 cm. Includes legislation. ISBN 3-7303-0068-7 LC Card 87-408895 DDC 331.25/2/09431 19
1. Old age pensions - Germany, East. 2. Old age pensions - Law and legislation - Germany (East). I. Hoppe, Rudolf. II. Title.
HD7180.5 .P87 1986

Puette, William. Stern, Bernard W., 1912- Rutledge unionism . Honolulu , 1986. x, 147 p. ; LC Card 86-51020 DDC 331/.04138841322/0996931 19
HD6515.T72 H37 1986

Püttner, Günter. Gesellschaft für Öffentliche Wirtschaft und Gemeinwirtschaft. Wissenschaftlicher Beirat. Zum Problem der Aufgabenverlagerung auf öffentliche Unternehmen . Baden-Baden , 1984. 73 p. ; ISBN 3-7890-1048-0 LC Card 85-143795
HD4177 .G47 1984

Pugel, Thomas A. Gray, H. Peter. International trade, employment, and structural adjustment . Geneva , 1986. x, 108 p. ; ISBN 92-2-105325-3 (pbk.) : LC Card 87-119470 DDC 331.12/0973 19
HD5710.75.U6 G73 1986

PUGET SOUND POWER AND LIGHT COMPANY - HISTORY.
A Century of service . Bellevue, Wash. , c1987. 178 p. : ISBN 0-9619061-0-3 (pbk.) : LC Card 87-16582 DDC 338.7/6136362/097977 19
HD9685.U7 P923 1987

Kramer, Arthur, 1908- Among the livewires . [Edmonds, Wash. , c1986] 141 p. : ISBN 0-939116-14-6 (pbk.) LC Card 86-91152 DDC 338.7/6136362/09797 19
HD9685.U7 P925 1986

PUGET SOUND REGION (WASH.) - POPULATION - STATISTICS.
Pethick, Donald R. Population and employment forecasts and distribution for the central Puget Sound region, 1975-1990 /. Seattle, Wash. [1969] 26 p., [2] leaves of plates : LC Card 87-400702 DDC 304.6/2/097977021 19
HA697.P84 P47 1969

PUGLIA (ITALY) - ECONOMIC CONDITIONS.
Snowden, Frank M. (Frank Martin), 1946- Violence and great estates in the south of Italy . Cambridge [Cambridgeshire] , New York , 1986. x, 245 p. : ISBN 0-521-30731-7 LC Card 85-11675 DDC 322.4/4/094575 19
HD679.P83 S66 1986 NYPL [JLD 86-1627]

PUGLIA (ITALY) - SOCIAL CONDITIONS.
Snowden, Frank M. (Frank Martin), 1946- Violence and great estates in the south of Italy . Cambridge [Cambridgeshire] , New York , 1986. x, 245 p. : ISBN 0-521-30731-7 LC Card 85-11675 DDC 322.4/4/094575 19
HD679.P83 S66 1986 NYPL [JLD 86-1627]

Pugwash (Organization) World peace and the developing countries . Basingstoke, Hampshire , 1986. xix, 272 p. ; ISBN 0-333-43636-9
NYPL [JLD 87-1192]

Puig Vilazar, Carlos. Sacrificio de un pueblo, 15 de noviembre de 1922 / Carlos Puig Vilazar. [2a ed.]. [Guayaquil, Ecuador] : Litografía e Impr. de la Universidad de Guayaquil, 1983. 88 p. ; 22 cm. (Colección Movimiento obrero ecuatoriano . no. 2) Cover title. LC Card 86-115462
1. General Strike, Ecuador, 1922. 2. Socialism - Ecuador - History - 20th century. 3. Ecuador - Industries - History - 20th century. I. Title. II. Series.
HD5358.A6 P85 1983

Pulai, Miklós. Gazdaságirányítás, 1985 /. Budapest , 1984. 175 p. ; ISBN 963-221-540-0 : LC Card 85-229856
HC300.28 .G338 1984

Pulatov, Kh. Toshpŭlatov, Mirzapŭlat. Prevrashchenie sel'skokhoziaĭstvennogo truda v raznovidnost' industrial'nogo v usloviiakh razvitogo sotsializma. . Tashkent , 1980. 68 p. ; LC Card 81-149078
HD1536.S65 T67 1980

Pullan, Robert. Ansett, Bob, 1933- Bob Ansett, an autobiography /. Hartwell, Vic. , 1986. 221 p., [16] p. of plates : ISBN 0-9588161-0-7 LC Card 86-228002 DDC 338.7/4/0924 B 19
HC602.5.A57 A33 1986

Pullat, Raimo. Osobennosti popolneniia osnovnykh otriadov intelligentsii /. Tallin , 1981. 131 p. : LC Card 82-125732
HD8038.S652 E775 1981

Pullen, J. M. Lord Grenville's manuscript notes on Malthus / by J.M. Pullen. [Newcastle] : University of Newcastle, N.S.W., Australia, Dept. of Economics, [1986] 94 p. ; 30 cm. (Research report or occasional paper, 0812-1664 . no. 130) "September 1986." Bibliography: p. 81-94. ISBN 0-7259-0557-3 (pbk.) LC Card 87-150102 DDC 330.15/3 19
1. Malthus, T. R. (Thomas Robert), 1766-1834. Principles of political economy. 2. Economics. 3. Classical school of economics. 4. Grenville, William Wyndham Grenville, Baron, 1759-1834 - Views on economics. I. Grenville, William Wyndham Grenville, Baron, 1759-1834. II. Title. III. Series.
HB161.M28 P85 1986

Pullen, John, 1933- Malthus, T. R. (Thomas Robert, 1766-1834. Principles of political economy /. Cambridge , New York , 1987. p. cm. ISBN 0-521-32363-0 (set) LC Card 86-32742 DDC 330.15/3 19
HB161 .M25 1987

Pullen, William George. World War debts and United States foreign policy, 1919-1929 / William George Pullen. New York : Garland, 1987. 157 p. ; 23 cm. (Foreign economic policy of the United States) Originally presented as the author's thesis (Ph. D.--University of Georgia, 1972). Bibliography: p. 151-157. ISBN 0-8240-8088-2 : LC Card 87-23789 DDC 337.7304 19
1. United States - Foreign economic relations - Europe. 2. Europe - Foreign economic relations - United States. 3. World War, 1914-1918 - Finance - United States. 4. World War, 1914-1918 - Finance - Europe. 5. Loans, American - Europe - History - 20th century. I. Title. II. Series.
HF1456.5.E8 P84 1987

Puls, Heinz. Finanzkraft der Gemeinden und kommunaler Ausgleichsstock in NW / [Heinz Puls] ; herausgegeben vom Institut für Landes- und Stadtentwicklungsforschung des Landes Nordrheine-Westfalen (ILS). Dortmund : Das Institut, [1977] [15] p. : 1 col. map ; 30 cm. (Kurzberichte zur Landes- und Stadtentwicklungsforschung) Cover title. Includes bibliographical references. LC Card 86-211554
1. Local finance - Germany, West - North Rhine-Westphalia. I. Institut für Landes- und Stadtentwicklungsforschung des Landes Nordrhein-Westfalen. II. Title. III. Series.
HJ9493.5.N6 P85 1977

Pulvino, Charles J. Communicating with clients : a guide for financial professionals / Charles J. Pulvino, James L. Lee, and Cynthia E. Forman. Paramus, NJ : Prentice Hall Information Services, c1987. ix, 194 p. : ill. ; 24 cm.

Bibliography: p. 185-187. Includes index. ISBN 0-13-153578-1 (pbk.) LC Card 87-153498 DDC 332.1/068/8 19
1. Financial planners. 2. Interpersonal communication. I. Lee, James L. II. Forman, Cynthia E. III. Title.
HG179.5 .P86 1987

PUMPED STORAGE POWER PLANTS - QUÉBEC (PROVINCE) - PORTNEUF (COUNTY)
Le Projet Delaney . [St-Raymond, Québec] [1983] 76 leaves in various foliations : LC Card 84-224364
HD9685.C3 Q456 1983

PUMPING MACHINERY - FUEL CONSUMPTION - HISTORY - STATISTICS.
Sloggett, Gordon. Energy and U. S. agriculture . Washington, D.C. , 1985] iii, 43 p. : LC Card 86-600880 DDC 338.1 s 338.1/3 19
HD1751 .A91854 no. 545 S619.E53

PUMPING MACHINERY INDUSTRY - UNITED STATES.
The U. S. market for hazardous duty liquid pumps and valves. New York, N.Y. , c1983. 2 v. (viii, 343 leaves) : LC Card 87-401677 DDC 381/.456216 19
HD9651.5 .U16 1983

Punchiwilaththawa, household study of a dry zone village /. Fernando, Vijita. Colombo, Sri Lanka , 1986. 36 p. : LC Card 86-902299 DDC 330.9549/3 19
HC424.Z7 P864 1986

PUNCHIWILATHTHAWA (SRI LANKA) - ECONOMIC CONDITIONS.
Fernando, Vijita. Punchiwilaththawa, household study of a dry zone village /. Colombo, Sri Lanka , 1986. 36 p. : LC Card 86-902299 DDC 330.9549/3 19
HC424.Z7 P864 1986

PUNCHIWILATHTHAWA (SRI LANKA) - SOCIAL CONDITIONS.
Fernando, Vijita. Punchiwilaththawa, household study of a dry zone village /. Colombo, Sri Lanka , 1986. 36 p. : LC Card 86-902299 DDC 330.9549/3 19
HC424.Z7 P864 1986

PUNJAB (INDIA) - CENSUS, 1981.
Census of India, 1981. Delhi , <[1982]-[1983?]. v. in : LC Card 87-915023 DDC 304.6/0954/552021 19
HA4587.P86 C46 1982

Punjab (India). Economic and Statistical Organisation. Report on the evaluation study of working of the Punjab Scheduled Castes Land Development and Finance Corporation. Chandigarh : Economic Adviser to Govt., Punjab, [pref. 1978] viii, 98 p. ; 26 cm. (Publication / Economic and Statistical Organisation, Government of Punjab . no. 296) LC Card 79-903307
1. Punjab Scheduled Castes Land Development and Finance Corporation. 2. Economic assistance, Domestic - India - Punjab. 3. Punjab (India) - Scheduled tribes - Economic conditions. 4. Untouchables - Economic conditions. I. Series: Publication (Punjab (India). Economic and Statistical Organisation) , no. 296. II. Title.
HC437.P8 P85 1978a

Punjab (India). Economic and Statistical Organization. Piṇḍāṃ dī ḍāiraikaṭarī, 1983-84. Caṇḍīgaṛha [1985- v. <1- > ; LC Card 86-902359
HA4587.P86 P56 1985

PUNJAB (INDIA) - ECONOMIC POLICY.
Lal, Shyam, 1942- Price policy and economic development in India /. Delhi , 1987. xiii, 272 p. : LC Card 87-900801 DDC 338.5/26/0954552 19
HB236.I4 L35 1987

PUNJAB (INDIA) - SCHEDULED TRIBES - ECONOMIC CONDITIONS.
Punjab (India). Economic and Statistical Organisation. Report on the evaluation study of working of the Punjab Scheduled Castes Land Development and Finance Corporation. Chandigarh [pref. 1978] viii, 98 p. ; LC Card 79-903307
HC437.P8 P85 1978a

PUNJAB (INDIA) - STATISTICS.
Piṇḍāṃ dī ḍāiraikaṭarī, 1983-84. Caṇḍīgaṛha [1985- v. <1- > ; LC Card 86-902359
HA4587.P86 P56 1985

Punjab peasant freedom struggle. Hari Singh, Master, 1902- Agrarian scene in British Punjab /. New Delhi , 1983-c1984. 2 v. : LC Card 83-905514 DDC 338.1/0954/5 19
HD2075.P8 H37 1983 ***NYPL [JLK 86-113]***

PUNJAB SCHEDULED CASTES LAND DEVELOPMENT AND FINANCE CORPORATION.
Punjab (India). Economic and Statistical Organisation. Report on the evaluation study of working of the Punjab Scheduled Castes Land Development and Finance Corporation. Chandigarh [pref. 1978] viii, 98 p. ; LC Card 79-903307
HC437.P8 P85 1978a

Punset, Eduard, 1936- La España impertinente / Eduardo Punset. Madrid : Espasa Calpe, c1986. 188 p. ; 24 cm. (Espasa mañana) Includes bibliographical references. ISBN 84-239-2420-3 LC Card 87-136770
1. Spain - Foreign economic relations. 2. International economic relations. 3. Spain - Politics and government - 1939-1975. 4. Spain - Politics and government - 1975-. I. Title.
HF1569 .P86 1986

Punzo, Lionello F. Goodwin, Richard M. (Richard Murphey), 1913- The dynamics of a capitalist economy /. Boulder , 1987. p. cm. ISBN 0-8133-0482-2 : LC Card 86-33965 DDC 330.12/2 19
HB501 .G622 1987

Purcell, Kate. The Changing experience of employment . Houndmills, Basingstoke, Hampshire , 1986. x, 230 p. ; ISBN 0-333-39695-2 ***NYPL [JLD 87-933]***

Purcell, Randall B. U. S. agriculture & Third World development . Boulder , 1987. xi, 258 p. ; ISBN 1-555-87011-2 (lib. bdg.) : LC Card 86-29860 DDC 338.1/09172/4 19
HD1765 .U15 1987

PURCHASERS. see **VENDORS AND PURCHASERS.**

Purchasing and supply management /. Baily, Peter J. H. London , New York , 1987. viii, 296 p. : ISBN 0-412-28940-7 (pbk.) LC Card 87-11760 DDC 658.7 19
HD39.5 .B335 1987

Purchasing and the management of materials /. Zenz, Gary Joseph. New York , c1981. xiii, 514 p. : ISBN 0-471-06091-7 LC Card 80-21649 DDC 658.7/2 19
HD39.5 .W47 1981 ***NYPL [JLE 86-3384]***

Purchasing and the management of materials /. Zenz, Gary Joseph. New York , c1987. xvi, 542 p. : ISBN 0-471-81802-X LC Card 86-32589 DDC 658.7/2 19
HD39.5 .W47 1987

PURCHASING - DATA PROCESSING.
Sinkel, Dimitri. Computers in purchasing [microform] /. New York , c1984. 48 p. : ISBN 0-8144-2305-1 : LC Card 84-9034 DDC 658.7/2/02854 19
HF5437 .S52 1984 ***NYPL [*ZT-1565 no.12]***

PURCHASING, INDUSTRIAL. see **INDUSTRIAL PROCUREMENT.**

PURCHASING - MANAGEMENT.
Baily, Peter J. H. Purchasing principles and management /. London , Marshfield, Mass. , 1985. 324 p. : ISBN 0-273-02242-3 LC Card 85-16704 DDC 658.7/2 19
HF5437 .B3415 1985 ***NYPL [JLE 86-3321]***

PURCHASING POWER.
Beck, Horst. Auswirkungen von nicht kostenniveauneutralen Lohnänderungen auf Beschäftigung und Preisniveau . Krefeld , 1983. iii, 227 p. : ISBN 3-88358-033-3 LC Card 83-202725
HD4911 .B4 1983

World comparisons of purchasing power and real product for 1980 . New York , 1986- v. <1 > ; LC Card 86-225798 DDC 339.3 19
HC79.I5 W675 1986

PURCHASING POWER - GERMANY, WEST.
Beck, Horst. Auswirkungen von nicht kostenniveauneutralen Lohnänderungen auf Beschäftigung und Preisniveau . Krefeld , 1983. iii, 227 p. : ISBN 3-88358-033-3 LC Card 83-202725
HD4911 .B4 1983

Vajna, Thomas. Das Kaufkraftargument /. Köln , c1982. 52 p. ; ISBN 3-602-24710-4 : LC Card 83-193844
HD5029 .V35 1982

Purchasing power of PTT personnel, 1965 /. Matthew, J. Brussels [1966] 1 v. (various pagings) ; LC Card 87-165119
HE6241 .M37 1966

Purchasing power parities for international comparisons /. Voeller, Joachim, 1946- Königstein/Ts. , Cambridge, Mass. , c1981. 104 p. ; ISBN 3-445-02225-9 (pbk.) LC Card 81-84382
HG3821 .V63x 1981

PURCHASING POWER PARITY - MATHEMATICAL MODELS.
Meinlschmidt, Gerhard. Statistische Methoden zur Berechnung von Preisniveauindizes integrierter Wirtschaftsräume /. Göttingen , c1985. 142 p. : ISBN 3-525-11262-9 LC Card 85-213565
HB225 .M45 1985

PURCHASING POWER PARITY - STATISTICAL METHODS.
Voeller, Joachim, 1946- Purchasing power parities for international comparisons /. Königstein/Ts. , Cambridge, Mass. , c1981. 104 p. ; ISBN 3-445-02225-9 (pbk.) LC Card 81-84382
HG3821 .V63x 1981

Purchasing principles and management /. Baily, Peter J. H. London , Marshfield, Mass. , 1985. 324 p. : ISBN 0-273-02242-3 LC Card 85-16704 DDC 658.7/2 19
HF5437 .B3415 1985 ***NYPL [JLE 86-3321]***

PURCHASING - STATISTICS.
Zur Neuberechnung der Indizes des Auftragseingangs und des Auftragsbestands für das Verarbeitende Gewerbe und das Bauhauptgewerbe auf Basis 1976. English. Indices of orders received and unfilled orders /. Wiesbaden , Stuttgart , 1986. 16 p. ; LC Card 86-215307
HF5437 .Z8713 1976

PURCHASING - UNITED STATES - DIRECTORIES.
Davidson, Jeffrey P. Marketing to the Fortune 500 and other corporations /. Homewood, Ill. , c1987. xv, 291 p. : ISBN 0-87094-984-5 LC Card 86-51669 DDC 658.8 19
HF5415.1 .D28 1987

Purdah to profession . Chauhan, Indira, 1949- Delhi , New Delhi , 1986. vi, 295 p. ; ISBN 81-7018-375-8 : LC Card 86-902846 DDC 331.4/0954/3 19
HD6190.B48 C47 1986

PURE FOOD. see **FOOD ADULTERATION AND INSPECTION.**

Pure merinos and others . Pemberton, P. A. Canberra , c1986. 125 p. : ISBN 0-86784-796-4 (pbk.) LC Card 87-164515 DDC 382/.41636/0994 19
HE565.G7 P46 1986

Puri, Vijay Kumar. Nabhi's manual for Indian residents abroad, 1985 / by V.K. Puri, S.C. Malhotra. 4th rev. ed. New Delhi : Nabhi Publications, 1985. xv, 352 p., [1] leaf of plate : col. port. ; 23 cm. LC Card 86-901951 DDC 346.54/07 345.4067 19
1. Investments, Foreign - India. 2. East Indians - Foreign countries. 3. Foreign exchange - India. 4. Banks and banking - India. I. Malhotra, S. C. II. Title. III. Title: Manual for Indian residents abroad, 1985.
HG5732 .P83 1985

Purono dinera kathā /. Sen, P. K. (Prabhat Kumar), 1905- Kalakātā , 1985. 49 p. ; LC Card 85-904772
HD6812.5.S46 A3 1985

Pursuing food security : strategies and obstacles in Africa, Asia, Latin America, and the Middle East / edited by W. Ladd Hollist & F. LaMond Tullis. Boulder : L. Rienner Publishers, 1987. xv, 357 p. : ill. ; 24 cm. (International political economy yearbook, 8755-8335 . v. 3) Bibliography: p. 312-333. Includes indexes. ISBN 1-555-87032-5 (lib. bdg. : alk. paper) : LC Card 87-4524 DDC 337/.05 s 338.1/9/1724 19
1. Food supply - Developing countries - Congresses. 2. Agriculture - Economic aspects - Developing countries - Congresses. I. Hollist, W. Ladd, 1947-. II. Tullis, F. LaMond, 1935-. III. Series.
HF1410 .I579 vol. 3 HD9018.D44

The pursuit of growth . Funkhouser, G. Ray. Redmond, Wash. , c1987. 261 p. ; ISBN 1-556-15043-1 : LC Card 87-20230 DDC 658/.00973 19
HD70.U5 F86 1987

Purview. [Arlington, Va.] : Public Utilities Reports, c1985. 1 v. (various pagings) : col. ill. ; 28 cm. Caption title. LC Card 86-222822 DDC 363.6/0973 19
1. Public utilities - United States. I. Public Utilities Reports, Inc.
HD2766 .P87 1985

Purvis, Douglas D. Lipsey, Richard G., 1928- Economics /. New York , c1987. xxvii, 942 p. : ISBN 0-06-043917-3 LC Card 86-29422 DDC 330 19
HB171.5 .L733 1987

Purwanto, Bambang. Kepemimpinan dan masalah pertanahan di pedesaan Jawa : kasus desa Nampu dan desa Ngandagan / oleh Bambang Purwanto. [Yogyakarta] : Departemen Pendidikan dan Kebudayaan, Direktorat Jenderal Kebudayaan, Proyek Penelitian dan Pengkajian Kebudayaan Nusantara, 1985. ix, 58 p. : maps ; 23 cm. Bibliography: p. 52-54. LC Card 86-943756
1. Land tenure - Indonesia - Nampu. 2. Land tenure - Indonesia - Ngandagan. 3. Community leadership - Indonesia - Nampu. 4. Community leadership - Indonesia - Ngandagan. I. Title.
HD900.N36 P87 1985

Pusat Pembinaan dan Pengembangan Bahasa. Kamus istilah ekonomi /. Jakarta , 1984. v, 216 p. ; LC Card 85-941380
HB61 .K26 1984

Pusat Pendidikan dan Latihan Tenaga Kerja (Indonesia) Bahan instruksional pendidikan kependudukan untuk peserta diklat Departemen P.U. Jakarta , 1982. v, 90 p. ; LC Card 83-941464
HB850.5.I5 B34 1982

Püschel, Manfred, 1953- Die Wahl der optimalen Wärmeversorgungskonfiguration als betriebswirtschaftliches Produktions- und Investitionsproblem / Manfred Püschel. Frankfurt am Main ; New York : P. Lang, c1984. iv, 298 p. : ill. ; 21 cm. (Betriebswirtschaftliche Beiträge zu Energie-, Rohstoff- und Umweltfragen, 0721-2933 . Bd. 3) Bibliography: p. 289-298. ISBN 3-8204-7432-3 LC Card 86-108875
1. Industrial management - Mathematical models. 2. Production functions (Economic theory) - Mathematical models. 3. Capital investments - Mathematical models. I. Title. II. Series.
HD30.25 .P87 1984

"Push down" accounting. Goodman, Hortense. Illustrations of "push down" accounting /. New York, N.Y. (1211 Ave., of the Americas, New York 10036) , c1985. 52 p. ; LC Card 87-100703 DDC 657/.3 19
HF5681.B2 G663 1985

Pushkin, Ann B. Auditing . Houston, TX , 1986. xvii, 919 p. : ISBN 0-87393-016-9 LC Card 86-127902 DDC 657/.45 19
HF5667 .A832 1986

Pusse, Leo. Arbeitsproduktivität und Beschäftigung : eine wirtschaftstheoretische und ökonometrische Analyse mit empirischen Ergebnissen für deutsche Industriesektoren / Leo Pusse. Freiburg im Breisgau : R. Haufe, c1984. viii, 311 p. : ill. ; 21 cm. (Band 24 der Schriftenreihe des Instituts für Allgemeine Wirtschaftsforschung der Albert-Ludwigs-Universität Freiburg i. Br) Bibliography: p. 260-308. Includes index. ISBN 3-448-01512-1 LC Card 85-138794
1. Labor productivity - Germany, West. 2. Labor supply - Germany, West. I. Series: Schriftenreihe des Instituts für Allgemeine Wirtschaftsforschung der Albert-Ludwigs-Universität Freiburg i. Br. , Bd. 24. II. Title.
HC290.5.L3 P87 1984

PUT AND CALL TRANSACTIONS - ACCOUNTING - STANDARDS - UNITED STATES.
Accounting for options /. New York, NY (1211 Ave. of the Americas, New York 10036-8775) [1986] 182 p., [4] p. of plates (some folded) : LC Card 86-221314 DDC 657/.76 19
HF5686.I6 A28 1986

PUT AND CALL TRANSACTIONS - BRAZIL.
Você e as opções de compra. [São Paulo, Brazil] [19]82. [24] p. ; LC Card 86-217458
HG6042 .V63 1982

Você e as opções de venda. [São Paulo, Brazil] [19]82. [28] p. ; LC Card 86-217459
HG6042 .V64 1982

PUT AND CALL TRANSACTIONS - FRANCE.
Augros, Jean-Claude. Finance . Paris , c1985. 320 p. : ISBN 2-7178-0911-2 : LC Card 85-219227 DDC 332.64/52/0944 19
HG6042 .A94 1985 ***NYPL [JLE 87-295]***

PUT AND CALL TRANSACTIONS - HANDBOOKS, MANUALS, ETC.
Handbook of financial markets . Homewood, Ill. , c1986. xix, 785 p. : ISBN 0-87094-600-5 LC Card 85-71920 DDC 332.6/78 19
HG4527 .H25 1986
NYPL [*R-Econ 86-3815]

Handbook of financial markets--securities, options, futures /. Homewood, Ill. , c1981. xxiii, 794 p. : ISBN 0-87094-216-6 LC Card 80-70448 DDC 332.6/78 19
HG4527 .H25 ***NYPL [JLE 86-1500]***

PUT AND CALL TRANSACTIONS - MATHEMATICAL MODELS.
Ritchken, Peter. Options . Glenview, Ill. , c1987. xiii, 414 p. : ISBN 0-673-18307-6 (pbk.) LC Card 86-29721 DDC 332.64/52 19
HG6042 .R57 1987

PUT AND CALL TRANSACTIONS - UNITED STATES.
Angell, George. Agricultural options . New York, NY , c1986. ix, 230 p. : ISBN 0-8144-5822-X LC Card 85-48215 DDC 332.64/25 19
HG6047.G8 A54 1986 ***NYPL [JLE 86-2854]***

Gross, LeRoy. The stockbroker's guide to put and call option strategies. [New York, 1974] viii, 116 p. ISBN 0-13-846741-9 LC Card 74-166476 DDC 332.6/45
HG6041 .G75 ***NYPL [JLE 87-573]***

Hadady, R. Earl (Robert Earl), 1920- Winning with the insiders /. West Palm Beach, Fla. , c1987. vi, 115 p. : ISBN 0-9613048-8-X : LC Card 87-40003 DDC 332.64/4 19
HG4910 .H18 1987

Put′ mongol′skogo aratstva k sot͡sializmu /. Ulymzhiev, D. B. (Dashi Batuevich) Novosibirsk , 1987. 283, [5] p. ; LC Card 87-159668
HD1491.M55 U49 1987

Puteshestvie v Ri͡azan′ /. Kaplinskai͡a, Elena. Moskva , 1978. 84 p. ; LC Card 81-155441
HD8039.M22 S654 1978

Puth, Robert Christian, 1936- American economic history / Robert C. Puth. 2nd ed. Chicago : Dryden Press, c1988. xv, 640 p. : ill. ; 24 cm. (Dryden Press series in economics) Includes bibliographies and index. ISBN 0-03-011892-1 LC Card 87-6782 DDC 330.973 19
1. United States - Economic conditions. I. Title. II. Series.
HC103 .P9 1988

Puti razvitii͡a infrastruktury regiona / [redaktsionnai͡a kollegii͡a, L.V. Mitrofanova (otv. redaktor), G.V. Surovtseva, V.P. I͡Urina]. Ufa : BFAN SSSR, 1984. 117 p. : ill. ; 22 cm. At head of title: Akademii͡a nauk SSSR. Bashkirskiĭ filial. Otdel ėkonomicheskikh issledovaniĭ. Includes bibliographies. LC Card 85-199949
1. Transportation - Russian S.F.S.R. - Bashkirskai͡a A.S.S.R. 2. Petroleum industry and trade - Russian S.F.S.R. - Bashkirskai͡a A.S.S.R. I. Mitrofanova, L. V. II. Surovtseva, G. V. III. I͡Urina, V. P. IV. Akademii͡a nauk SSSR. Bashkirskiĭ filial. Otdel ėkonomicheskikh issledovaniĭ.
HE255.Z7 B377 1984

Pŭtishta za podobri͡avane na kachestvoto /. Tomov, Mitko. Pleven , 1984. 68, [4] p. ; LC Card 85-179053
HC403.Z9 L38 1984

Putnam, Bluford H. The Blackwell guide to Wall Street / Bluford H. Putnam and Sandra C. Zimmer. Oxford, UK ; New York, NY, USA : Blackwell, 1987. viii, 222 p. : ill. ; 24 cm. Includes index. ISBN 0-631-14183-9 : LC Card 87-10299 DDC 332.63/2 19
1. Securities - United States. 2. Investments - United States. I. Zimmer, Sandra G. II. Title.
HG4910 .P87 1987

Putnam, Robert D. Hanging together : cooperation and conflict in the seven-power summits / Robert D. Putnam and Nicholas Bayne.Rev. and enl. ed. Cambridge, Mass. : Harvard University Press, 1987. x, 293 p. ; 22 cm. Includes bibliographies and index. ISBN 0-674-37226-3 (pbk.) LC Card 87-23593 DDC 337 19
1. International economic relations - Congresses. I. Bayne, Nicholas, 1937-. II. Title.
HF1410.5 .P87 1987

PUTNOK REGION (HUNGARY) - SOCIAL CONDITIONS.
Dobrossy, István. Termelés és életmód . Debrecen , 1983. 282 p. : ISBN 963-471-276-2 LC Card 86-100359
HD1492.H82 P873 1983

PUTS (COMMERCE) see PUT AND CALL TRANSACTIONS.

Putting America first : [a conservative trade alternative / edited by Anthony H. Harrigan]. Washington, D.C. : USIC Educational Foundation, c1987. 87 p. ; 25 cm. Bibliography: p. 68-70. Includes index. ISBN 0-944468-00-4 (pbk.) : LC Card 87-50998 DDC 382/.3/0973 19
1. United States - Commercial policy. 2. Free trade and protection - Protection. I. Harrigan, Anthony H.
HF1455 .P87 1987

Putting democracy to work . Adams, Frank T. Eugene, OR , 1987. p. cm. ISBN 0-938493-03-5 : LC Card 87-4246 DDC 658.1/147 19
HD5650 .A3 1987

Putting on appearances . Barthel, Diane L., 1949- Philadelphia , 1988. p. cm. ISBN 0-87722-528-1 (alk. paper) : LC Card 87-20010 DDC 659.1/042 19
HF5827 .B37 1988

Putzel, Ralph F. Encyclopaedia of South African post offices and postal agencies (including their forerunners in the Cape, Natal, Orange Free State, and Transvaal, Basutoland, Bechuanaland, and Swaziland, etc.) / by Ralph F. Putzel. 1st ed. Cape Town : Hale & Putzel, 1986- v. <1 > : ill. ; 31 cm. CONTENTS. - v. 1. A-E ISBN 0-620-09781-7 LC Card 87-143880 DDC 383/.4968 19
1. Postal service - South Africa - History. 2. Postal service - Swaziland - History. 3. Postal service - Botswana - History. I. Title.
HE7351 .P88 1986

Puumanen, Kari. Three essays on money, wealth, and the exchange rate / Kari Puumanen. Helsinki : Bank of Finland, 1986. 143 p. : ill. ; 25 cm. (Bank of Finland publications. Series B . 41) Bibliography: p. [139]-143. ISBN 951-686-119-9 (pbk.) LC Card 86-235460 DDC 332.4/0724 19
1. Money - Mathematical models. 2. Wealth - Mathematical models. 3. Foreign exchange - Mathematical models. I. Title.
HG221 .P97 1986

Puutteellisen asumisen parantaminen kunnissa vuosina 1985-1989 /. Harju, Hely. [Helsinki , 1986] 69, [16] p. : ISBN 951-46-9022-2 LC Card 86-215457
HD7345.3.A3 H367 1986

Puxty, Anthony G. Organization and management : an accountant's perspective / Anthony G. Puxty. London : Pitman, 1986. viii, 280 p. ; 23 cm. Bibliography: p. [268]-273. Includes index. ISBN 0-273-02138-9 (pbk.) : LC Card 87-122002 DDC 658 19
1. Management. 2. Organization. I. Title.
HD31 .P88 1986

Puyenbroek, R. (Rien)
Exportgids Japan / R. Puyenbroek, J.G. Schouten. Amsterdam : Elsevier, 1985. 149 p. : ill. ; 21 cm. (Innovatiereeks) Bibliography: p. [134]-149. ISBN 90-10-05277-X LC Card 85-236503
1. Netherlands - Commerce - Japan. 2. Export marketing - Netherlands. I. Schouten, J. G. (Jan Gijs). II. Title.
HF3618.J33 P89 1985

Exportgids Verenigde Staten / R. Puyenbroek, J.G. Schouten. Amsterdam : Elsevier, 1985. 140 p. : ill. ; 21 cm. (Innovatiereeks) Bibliography: p. [131]-140. ISBN 90-10-05276-1 LC Card 85-236520
1. Netherlands - Commerce - United States. 2. Export marketing - Netherlands. I. Schouten, J. G. (Jan Gijs). II. Title.
HF3618.U6 P89 1985

Puyol Antolín, Rafael. Población y recursos : el incierto futuro / Rafael Puyol. Madrid : Ediciones Pirámide, c1984. 157 p. : maps ; 21 cm. (Escuela de Salamanca) Bibliography: p. [155]-157. ISBN 84-368-0258-6 LC Card 87-105824
1. Population. 2. Natural resources. I. Title.
HB871 .P89 1984

Puzanov, V. D. (Valeriĭ Dmitrievich) Proizvodstvennoe nakoplenie : sushchnost′, ėffektivnost′ ispol′zovaniia / V.D. Puzanov. Moskva : "Mysl′", 1983. 109 p. ; 20 cm. Bibliography: p. 102-[108] LC Card 83-194433
1. Saving and investment - Soviet Union. 2. Capital productivity - Soviet Union. 3. Soviet Union - Economic policy - 1981-. I. Title.
HC340.S3 P89 1983

Puzynin, R. G. (Roman Gavrilovich) IUkhimenko, V. V. (Vladimir Vasil′evich) Izuchenie i prognozirovanie sprosa na bytovye uslugi /. Kiev , 1983. 103 p. ; LC Card 83-218585
HD9986.S683 U385 1983

Pyburn, Phillip J. Gremillion, Lee L. (Lee Louis) Computers and information systems in business . New York , c1988. xxi, 359 p., [16] p. of plates : ISBN 0-07-051007-5 (pbk.) LC Card 87-20300 DDC 650/.028/5 19
HF5548.2 .G7196 1988

Pychlau, Matthias. Temporale Entwicklungstheorie / Matthias Pychlau. Pfaffenweiler : Centaurus-Verlagsgesellschaft, 1986. viii, 79 p. ; 21 cm. (Reihe Wirtschaftswissenschaften, 0177-283X . Bd. 24) Bibliography: p. 72-79. ISBN 3-89085-110-X LC Card 87-409006 DDC 338.9 19
1. Economic development. I. Series: Reihe Wirtschaftswissenschaften (Pfaffenweiler, Breisgau-Hochschwarzwald, Germany) , Bd. 24. II. Title.
HD84 .P9 1986

Pyle, William W.
Fundamental accounting principles.
Fundamental accounting principles / Kermit D. Larson ... [et al.]. 5th Canadian ed. Homewood, Ill. , 1987. xvii, 1230 p. : ISBN 0-256-03601-2 LC Card 86-83105 DDC 657 19
HF5635 .P975 1987b

Larson, Kermit D. Fundamental accounting principles /. Homewood, Ill. , 1987. xxxi, 1076 p. : ISBN 0-256-03574-1 LC Card 86-81958 DDC 657 19
HF5635 .P975 1987

Pynoos, Jon. Housing the aged . New York , c1987. xvii, 500 p. : ISBN 0-444-01012-2 LC Card 87-5253 DDC 363.5/9
HD7287.9 .H7 1987

Qāmūs al-iqtiṣād wa-al-tijārah. A Dictionary of economics & commerce . Beirut , 1983. 383 p. ; LC Card 83-961782 DDC 330/.03/21 19
HB61 .D4896 1983 ***NYPL [*OEO 87-1397]***

Qāmūs Inkilīzī-'Arabī khāṣṣ bi-muṣṭalaḥāt idārat al-a'māl. The English-Arabic dictionary of professional business terms /. London , Boulder, Colo. , c1987. 210 p. ; ISBN 0-946510-33-4 : LC Card 87-163985 DDC 650/.03/21 19
HF1002 .E583 1987

QANTAS AIRWAYS.
Findlay, Christopher C. (Christopher Charles) The flying kangaroo, an endangered species? . Sydney , Boston , 1985. xii, 121 p. : ISBN 0-86861-406-8 (pbk.) LC Card 85-71362 DDC 387.7/065/94 19
HE9889.A4 F56 1985

Qarouach, Mostafa. L'agriculture marocaine face au deuxième élargissement de la CEE / Mostafa Qarouach. 1ère éd. [S.l. : s.n.], 1983 (Casablanca : Editions maghrébines) 117 p. ; 22 cm. Bibliography: p. 115-117. LC Card 83-192279 DDC 382/.41/0964 19
1. Produce trade - Morocco. 2. Produce trade - European Economic Community countries. 3. Morocco - Commerce - European Economic Community countries. 4. European Economic Community countries - Commerce - Morocco. I. Title.
HD9017.M82 Q37 1983
NYPL [JLD 86-4326]

Qāsim, Ṣubḥī, 1934-
Mulakhkhaṣ kitāb Naẓrah taḥlīlīyah fī mushkilat al-ghidhā' fī al-buldān al-'Arabīyah / Ṣubḥī al-Qāsim. al-Ṭab'ah 1. [Jordan?] : Mu'assasat 'Abd al-Ḥamīd Shūmān, 1982. 103 p. ; 24 cm. LC Card 86-203782
1. Food supply - Arab countries. I. Qāsim, Ṣubḥī, 1934- Naẓrah taḥlīlīyah fī mushkilat al-ghidhā' fī al-buldān al-'Arabīyah. II. Title.
HD9018.A55 Q269 1982

Naẓrah taḥlīlīyah fī mushkilat al-ghidhā' fī al-buldān al-'Arabīyah. Qāsim, Ṣubḥī, 1934- Mulakhkhaṣ kitāb Naẓrah taḥlīlīyah fī mushkilat al-ghidhā' fī al-buldān al-'Arabīyah / Ṣubḥī al-Qāsim. al-Ṭab'ah 1. [Jordan?] , 1982. 103 p. ; LC Card 86-203782
HD9018.A55 Q269 1982

QATAR - ECONOMIC CONDITIONS.
El Mallakh, Ragaei, 1925- Qatar, energy & development /. London , Dover, N.H. , c1985. 184 p. ; ISBN 0-7099-0955-1 : LC Card 84-29317 DDC 330.953/63 19
HC415.37 .E4 1985 ***NYPL [JLD 85-1980]***

Ritter, Wigand. Qatar, ein arabisches Erdölemirat /. Nürnberg , 1985. 201 p. : LC Card 86-205396
HC415.37 .R58 1985

Qatar, ein arabisches Erdölemirat /. Ritter, Wigand. Nürnberg , 1985. 201 p. : LC Card 86-205396
HC415.37 .R58 1985

Qatar, energy & development /. El Mallakh, Ragaei, 1925- London , Dover, N.H. , c1985. 184 p. ; ISBN 0-7099-0955-1 : LC Card 84-29317 DDC 330.953/63 19
HC415.37 .E4 1985 ***NYPL [JLD 85-1980]***

Qatar, energy and development. El Mallakh, Ragaei, 1925- Qatar, energy & development /. London , Dover, N.H. , c1985. 184 p. ; ISBN 0-7099-0955-1 : LC Card 84-29317 DDC 330.953/63 19
HC415.37 .E4 1985 ***NYPL [JLD 85-1980]***

Q.E.D. Information Sciences. Perkinson, Richard C. Data analysis . Wellesley, Mass. , c1984. xvii, 285 p. : ISBN 0-89435-105-2 LC Card 83-63212 DDC 001.64 19
QA76.9.D3 P46 1984 ***NYPL [JSE 85-1742]***

Quadagno, Jill S. The transformation of old age security : class and politics in the American welfare state / Jill Quadagno. Chicago : University of Chicago Press, 1988. p. cm. Bibliography: p. Includes index. ISBN 0-226-69923-4 : LC Card 87-18754 DDC 368.4/00973 19
1. Social security - United States. 2. Social security - Europe. 3. Old age pensions - United States. 4. Old age pensions - Europe. I. Title.
HD7125 .Q46 1988

Quaderni (Cisem) .
(10) Le 150 ore e la formazione professionale in azienda . Milano, Italy , c1985. 178 p. : LC Card 86-141990
HD5716.T242 I82 1985
NYPL [JFD 87-3739]

(2) L'Insegnamento dell'economia politica nella scuola secondaria superiore . Milano, Italy , c1982. 261 p. ; LC Card 87-673404
HB74.9.I8 I57x 1982

Quaderni de L'Industria (Società editrice Il Mulino) .
(25) Bertelè, Umberto. Un modello interpretativo dell'import-export italiano, 1970-1983 /. Bologna , c1985. 172 p. : ISBN 88-15-00919-1 : LC Card 86-176592
HF3586.5 .B47 1985

(30) Quintano, Claudio. Il sistema industriale del Molise /. Bologna , c1986. 106 p. : ISBN 88-15-01163-3 : LC Card 86-214879
HC307.M64 Q56 1986

(34) Struttura industriale e politiche macroeconomiche in Italia /. Bologna , c1986. 152 p. : ISBN 88-15-01193-5 : LC Card 87-100465
HC305 .S845 1986

(36) Politiche tributarie e struttura industriale in Italia /. Bologna , c1986. 118 p. ; ISBN 88-15-01224-9 : LC Card 86-224989
HD2753.I7 P65 1986

Quaderni della Fondazione Giacomo Brodolini.
Franciosi, Franco B. Professionalità e formazione nel settore delle costruzioni . Venezia , 1985. 178 p. ; ISBN 88-317-4781-9 : LC Card 86-234138
HD5716.B92 I724 1985

Quaderni di AREA .
(3) Mancini, Andrea, 1954- La contabilità analitica dei costi . [Torino] , 1986. 53 p. : ISBN 88-85851-00-2 : LC Card 87-114718
HF5686.C8 M265 1986

Quaderni di banca, borsa e titoli di credito .
(5) La Riforma della legge bancaria . Milano [1984] 283 p. ; ISBN 88-14-00126-X : LC Card 84-190853 DDC 346.45/082 344.50682 19
LAW ***NYPL [JLE 86-3654]***

(7) Allegri, Vincenzo. Credito di scopo e finanziamento bancario delle imprese /. Milano [1984] 166 p. ; ISBN 88-14-00299-1 : LC Card 85-187365 DDC 332.7/0945 19
HG1642.I8 A44 1984 ***NYPL [JLE 86-3661]***

(8) Santoro, Vittorio. Profili funzionali e operativi delle casse rurali e artigiane /. Milano [1984] 181 p. ; ISBN 88-14-00380-7 : LC Card 85-147834
HG2039.I8 S26 1984 ***NYPL [JLE 86-3669]***

Quaderni di banca, impresa, società .
(2) I Conti finanziari dell'Emilia-Romagna /. [Bologna] , c1984. 157 p. : ISBN 88-15-00522-6 : LC Card 84-235593 DDC 332.1/0945/4 19
HG3089.E45 C66 1984
NYPL [JLE 86-3198]

Quaderni di documentazione (Italy. Parlamento. Camera dei deputati. Servizio relazioni comunitarie e internazionali) .
(5) La Politica industriale della CEE . Roma , 1983. 371 p. ; LC Card 86-104849 DDC 338.94 19
HD3616.E83 P65 1983
NYPL [JLD 87-1225]

Quaderni di economia del lavoro (Franco Angeli editore) .
(23) Albertini, Sergio. Il consolidamento strutturale dell'occupazione in specifiche aree con particolare riguardo alla provincia di Gorizia /. Milano , c1984. 184 p. ; LC Card 84-234951 DDC 331.12/0945/392 19
HD5785.G67 A42 1984

(24) Politica monetaria e politica dell'occupazione in Italia, in un contesto di innovazione finanziaria /. Milano , c1984. 166 p. ; LC Card 84-245111 DDC 332/.0945 19
HG1029.5 .P63 1984

Quaderni di formazione ISFOL .
(n. 84/6) Società di terziario avanzato e professionalità . Roma [1984] 159 p. : LC Card 85-232870
HD69.C6 S66 1984

(n. 85/1) Gatti, M. (Mario) Servizi innovativi e professionalità . Roma [1985] 231 p. : LC Card 85-237680
HD5716.S452 T84 1985

(n. 85/3) Relazioni industriali nell'impresa degli anni '80 . Roma , 1985. 308 p. ; LC Card 86-192682
HD8481 .R45 1985

(n. 85/4) Automazione d'ufficio . Roma [1985] 248 p. : LC Card 86-213829
HF1152.P28 A95 1985

Quaderni di storia urbana e rurale .
(7) Epstein, Stephan R., 1960- Alle origini della fattoria toscana . Firenze , c1986. 315 p. : LC Card 87-104355
HD1470.5.I82 S544 1986

Quaderno (Italy. Servizi delle informazioni e della proprietà letteraria, artistica e scientifica) .
(n. 21) La Tutela del lavoro in Italia. [Roma] [1976] 144 p. ; LC Card 86-233354
HD8481 .T85 1976

Quaderns de l'I. E. I. .
(2) Materials per a l'estudi geogràfic dels pobles de l'àrea econòmica de Bellpuig /. [Lleida , 1985. 253 p. : LC Card 87-131722
HA1559.B45 M38 1985

Quaderns d'història d'Algaida . Sastre de Sá Torreta, Antoni. Algaida , 1983. 139 p., [8] p. of plates : LC Card 86-181627
HD780.R36 S27 1983

Quadri Castillo, Mario. La Argentina descentralizada / Mario Quadri Castillo. [Buenos Aires] : Editorial Universitaria de Buenos Aires, c1986. 236 p. : ill., maps ; 23 cm. (Colección Temas) Bibliography: p. 227-233. ISBN 950-23-0322-9 LC Card 87-402244 DDC 330.982/064 19
1. Argentina - Economic conditions - Regional

disparities - History. 2. Decentralization in government - Argentina - History. 3. Infrastructure (Economics) - Argentina - History. 4. Geopolitics - Argentina - History. I. Series: Colección Temas (Editorial Universitaria de Buenos Aires). II. Title.
HC175 .Q33 1986

Quadros para uma viagem a Portugal no Sec. XVI /. Coelho, Antonio Borges. Lisboa , c1986. 403 p., [2] folded leaves of plates : LC Card 87-401474
HC392 .C573 1986

Quaisser, Wolfgang, 1955- Crisis and reform in socialist economies /. Boulder , 1987. xi, 196 p. ; ISBN 0-8133-7332-8 (pbk. : alk. paper) : LC Card 86-32602 DDC 338.9/009171/7 19
HC704 .C75 1987

Quaker Oats Company. Rockford Pet Foods Division.
Rockford . [Rockford, Ill.] , c1987. 98 p. : LC Card 87-61147 DDC 338.7/66466/0977331 19
HD9340.U53 R637 1987

QUAKER OATS COMPANY ROCKFORD PET FOODS DIVISION - HISTORY.
Rockford . [Rockford, Ill.] , c1987. 98 p. : LC Card 87-61147 DDC 338.7/66466/0977331 19
HD9340.U53 R637 1987

QUAKER STATE OIL REFINING CORPORATION - HISTORY.
Wood, Quentin E. Quaker State roots go deep into the world's first oilfield /. New York , 1986 [i.e. 1987] 24 p. : LC Card 86-63307 DDC 338.7/6653/0973 19
HD9569.Q82 W66 1987

Quaker State roots go deep into the world's first oilfield /. Wood, Quentin E. New York , 1986 [i.e. 1987] 24 p. : LC Card 86-63307 DDC 338.7/6653/0973 19
HD9569.Q82 W66 1987

QUAKERS - UNITED STATES - BIOGRAPHY.
Powelson, John P., 1920- Facing social revolution . Boulder, Colo. , c1987. v, 146 p. ; ISBN 0-934449-03-1 : LC Card 86-32186 DDC 330/.092/4 B 19
HB119.P68 A3 1987

Yates, W. Ross (Willard Ross) Joseph Wharton . Bethlehem , London , c1987. 413 p. : ISBN 0-934223-00-9 (alk. paper) LC Card 86-81983 DDC 338.7/6691/0924 B 19
HC102.5.W47 Y38 1987

Quale strategia per l'industria? : primo rapporto sull'industria e la politica industriale italiana / a cura del Centro Europa ricerche e dell'Istituto per la ricerca sociale. Bologna : Il Mulino, c1986. 221 p. : ill. ; 22 cm. (Studi e ricerche. 205) Includes bibliographical references. ISBN 88-15-00975-2 : LC Card 86-182300
1. Industrial promotion - Italy. 2. Italy - Industries. 3. Industry and state - Italy. 4. Commercial policy - Italy. I. Centro Europa ricerche (Rome, Italy). II. Istituto per la ricerca sociale (Milan, Italy).
HC310.I53 Q35 1986

Qualificação, divisão do trabalho e mercado do trabalho /. Oliveira, José Gonçalves Grosso de. Lisboa , 1985. 60 p. ; LC Card 86-132680
HF5549.5.J62 O44 1985

Qualitäts- und Werbestrategien bei Qualitätsunsicherheit der Konsumenten /.
Ringbeck, Jürgen. Wiesbaden , c1986. 256 p. ; ISBN 3-409-13612-6 LC Card 87-111545 DDC 658.8/02 19
HF5415.135 .R56 1986

Qualitätspolitik in der industriellen Beschaffung . Boeker, Heiner, 1955- Bochum , 1986. ix, 296 p. ; ISBN 3-88339-525-0 LC Card 87-127490 DDC 687/.068/5 19
HD9940.A2 B64 1986

Qualitätszirkel als Instrument zeitgemässer Betriebsführung / Walter Bungard, Gerd Wiendieck (Hrsg.). Landsberg/Lech : Moderne Industrie, c1986. 328 p. : ill. ; 23 cm. Includes bibliographies. ISBN 3-478-32520-X LC Card 86-200304
1. Quality circles - Germany (West). 2. Quality circles - Japan. 3. Quality circles - Germany (West) - Case studies. I. Bungard, Walter. II. Wiendieck, Gerd.
HD66 .Q33 1986

Qualitätszirkel und Kleingruppenarbeit als praktische Organisationsentwicklung / Manfred E. Strombach (Hrsg) ; mit Beiträgen von Walter Bungard ... [et al.]. Frankfurt am Main : Kommentator Verlag, 1984. vii, 149 p. : ill. ; 21 cm. (Schriften zur Personalwirtschaft) Bibliography: p. [143]-145. Includes index. CONTENTS. - Qualitätszirkel und Kleingruppenarbeit in der Bundesrepublik Deutschland / Manfred E. Strombach -- Das Training von Qualitätszirkel-Moderatoren / Walter Bungard -- Qualitätszirkel nach japanischem Muster / Siegfried Rehm -- Lernstatt in der Hannen-Brauerei / Helmut Morjan -- Gruppenarbeit in der 1B-Montage / Friedjung Elter. ISBN 3-7824-0348-7 LC Card 85-131916
1. Quality circles - Germany (West). 2. Quality circles - Germany (West) - Case studies. I. Strombach, Manfred E., 1950-. II. Bungard, Walter. III. Series.
HD66 .Q332 1984

Qualitative Arbeitsanalyse : neue Verfahren zur Beurteilung von Tätigkeiten / Eva Dürholt ... [et al.] ; Institut für Psychologie der Universität München. Frankfurt ; New York : Campus, c1983. 352 p. ; 22 cm. (Schriftenreihe "Humanisierung des Arbeitslebens" . Bd. 36) Includes indexes. Bibliography: p. 321-335. ISBN 3-593-32721-X LC Card 83-161600 DDC 158.7 19
1. Quality of work life - Addresses, essays, lectures. 2. Psychology, Industrial - Addresses, essays, lectures. I. Dürholt, Eva. II. Universität München. Institut für Psychologie. III. Series.
HD6955 .Q35 1983 ***NYPL [JLD 87-1014]***

Qualitative research . Advertising Research Foundation Qualitative Research Workshop (1985 : New York, N.Y.) New York, NY (3 E. 54th St., New York 10022-3180) , c1985. 121 p. : LC Card 86-212738 DDC 659.1/072 19
HF5802.5 .A383 1985

Qualitative research methods .
(v. 4) Fielding, Nigel. Linking data /. Beverly Hills , c1986. 96 p. ; ISBN 0-8039-2518-2 (pbk.) LC Card 85-62290 DDC 300/.72 19
H62 .F425 1986 ***NYPL [JLD 86-3863]***

Quality and reliability .
(12) Human resources management /. New York , Milwaukee, Wis. , c1987. xiv, 276 p. : ISBN 0-8247-7716-6 LC Card 86-29321 DDC 658.3 19
HF5549 .H8727 1987

QUALITY ASSURANCE.
Townsend, Patrick L. Commit to quality /. New York , c1986. xvii, 189 p. : ISBN 0-471-83953-1 LC Card 85-29639 DDC 658.5/62 19
HD66 .T65 1986 ***NYPL [JLE 86-3004]***

Quality assurance in service organizations /. DiPrimio, Anthony. Radnor, Pa. , c1987. xiv, 210 p. : ISBN 0-8019-7730-4 : LC Card 86-47961 DDC 658.5/62 19
HD9980.5 .D52 1987

QUALITY ASSURANCE - JAPAN - MANAGEMENT.
Garvin, David A. Managing quality . New York , London , c1988. xiv, 319 p. ; ISBN 0-02-911380-6 LC Card 87-15145 DDC 658.5/62 19
HF5415.157 .G37 1988

QUALITY ASSURANCE - JAPAN - MANAGEMENT - CASE STUDIES.
Garvin, David A. Managing quality . New York , London , c1988. xiv, 319 p. ; ISBN 0-02-911380-6 LC Card 87-15145 DDC 658.5/62 19
HF5415.157 .G37 1988

QUALITY ASSURANCE - MANAGEMENT.
Edosomwan, Johnson Aimie, 1953- Integrating productivity and quality management /. New York , c1987. xvii, 360 p. : ISBN 0-8247-7657-7 LC Card 86-32780 DDC 658.5 19
HD56 .E28 1987

QUALITY ASSURANCE - UNITED STATES - MANAGEMENT.
Garvin, David A. Managing quality . New York , London , c1988. xiv, 319 p. ; ISBN 0-02-911380-6 LC Card 87-15145 DDC 658.5/62 19
HF5415.157 .G37 1988

QUALITY ASSURANCE - UNITED STATES - MANAGEMENT - CASE STUDIES.
Garvin, David A. Managing quality . New York , London , c1988. xiv, 319 p. ; ISBN 0-02-911380-6 LC Card 87-15145 DDC 658.5/62 19
HF5415.157 .G37 1988

QUALITY CIRCLES.
Katzan, Harry. A manager's guide to productivity, quality circles, and industrial robots /. New York , c1985. vii, 136 p. : ISBN 0-442-24823-7 LC Card 84-25739 DDC 658.5 19
HD56 .K377 1985 ***NYPL [JLE 86-4510]***

Nemoto, Masao. [TQC to toppu bu-kachō no yakuwari. English.] Total quality control for management . Englewood Cliffs, N.J. , c1987. xix, 238 p. : ISBN 0-13-925637-7 : LC Card 87-2329 DDC 658.4/036 19
HD66 .N4613 1987

Nicoletti, Bernardo. I circoli di qualità . Milano, Italy , c1986. 249 p. ; LC Card 86-207976
HD66 .N53 1986

Townsend, Patrick L. Commit to quality /. New York , c1986. xvii, 189 p. : ISBN 0-471-83953-1 LC Card 85-29639 DDC 658.5/62 19
HD66 .T65 1986 ***NYPL [JLE 86-3004]***

QUALITY CIRCLES - ASIA, SOUTHEASTERN - CONGRESSES.
Quality control circle . Tokyo , 1986. x, 170 p. : ISBN 92-833-2040-3 LC Card 87-133710 DDC 658.5/62 19
HD9987.A7852 Q35 1986

QUALITY CIRCLES - GERMANY (WEST)
Qualitätszirkel als Instrument zeitgemässer Betriebsführung /. Landsberg/Lech , c1986. 328 p. : ISBN 3-478-32520-X LC Card 86-200304
HD66 .Q33 1986

Qualitätszirkel und Kleingruppenarbeit als praktische Organisationsentwicklung /. Frankfurt am Main , 1984. vii, 149 p. : ISBN 3-7824-0348-7 LC Card 85-131916
HD66 .Q332 1984

QUALITY CIRCLES - GERMANY (WEST) - CASE STUDIES.
Qualitätszirkel als Instrument zeitgemässer Betriebsführung /. Landsberg/Lech , c1986. 328 p. : ISBN 3-478-32520-X LC Card 86-200304
HD66 .Q33 1986

Qualitätszirkel und Kleingruppenarbeit als praktische Organisationsentwicklung /. Frankfurt am Main , 1984. vii, 149 p. : ISBN 3-7824-0348-7 LC Card 85-131916
HD66 .Q332 1984

QUALITY CIRCLES - ITALY - CASE STUDIES.
Nicoletti, Bernardo. I circoli di qualità . Milano, Italy , c1986. 249 p. ; LC Card 86-207976
HD66 .N53 1986

QUALITY CIRCLES - JAPAN.
Qualitätszirkel als Instrument zeitgemässer Betriebsführung /. Landsberg/Lech , c1986. 328 p. : ISBN 3-478-32520-X LC Card 86-200304
HD66 .Q33 1986

Quality control circles at work . Tokyo , 1984. v, 232 p. : ISBN 92-833-1074-9 LC Card 85-133901 DDC 658.5/62/0952 19
HD66 .Q36 1984 ***NYPL [JLD 87-806]***

QUALITY CIRCLES - UNITED STATES - CASE STUDIES.
Grenier, Guillermo J. Inhuman relations . Philadelphia , 1988. xx, 232 p. ; ISBN 0-87722-502-8 (alk. paper) : LC Card 87-10116 DDC 331.25 19
HD6490.O72 U645 1988

Quality control circle : activities in the service sector : a symposium report. Tokyo : Asian Productivity Organization, 1986. x, 170 p. : ill. ; 26 cm. ISBN 92-833-2040-3 LC Card 87-133710 DDC 658.5/62 19
1. Service industries - Asia, Southeastern - Quality control - Congresses. 2. Quality circles - Asia, Southeastern - Congresses. I. Asian Productivity Organization.
HD9987.A7852 Q35 1986

Quality control circles at work : cases from Japan's manufacturing and service sectors / with special contribution by Kaoru Ishikawa. Tokyo : Asian Productivity Organization, 1984. v, 232 p. : ill. ; 22 cm. Includes index. ISBN 92-833-1074-9 LC Card 85-133901 DDC 658.5/62/0952 19
1. Quality circles - Japan. 2. Quality control - Japan. 3. Industrial management - Japan - Employee

participation. I. Ishikawa, Kaoru, 1915-.
HD66 .Q36 1984 ***NYPL [JLD 87-806]***

QUALITY CONTROL - JAPAN.
Quality control circles at work . Tokyo , 1984. v, 232 p. : ISBN 92-833-1074-9 LC Card 85-133901 DDC 658.5/62/0952 19
HD66 .Q36 1984 ***NYPL [JLD 87-806]***

QUALITY CONTROL - STATISTICAL METHODS.
Pöhlmann, Helmut. Jahresabschlussprüfung auf Stichprobenbasis . Pfaffenweiler , 1987. xii, 187 p. ; ISBN 3-89085-142-8 LC Card 87-133413 DDC 657/.458 19
HF5668.25 .P64 1987

Quality of earnings . O'glove, Thornton L. New York , c1987. xviii, 204 p. : ISBN 0-02-922630-9 LC Card 86-25631 DDC 657/.33 19
HG4028.B2 O35 1987

QUALITY OF LIFE.
Baumol, William J. The theory of environmental policy /. Cambridge [Cambridgeshire] , New York , 1988. x, 299 p. : ISBN 0-521-32224-3 LC Card 87-24975 DDC 363.7/001 19
HC79.E5 B375 1988

Gasparini, Giovanni, 1940- Il tempo e il lavoro /. Milano, Italy , c1986. 178 p. ; LC Card 86-180970
HD5106 .G37 1986

Labour market flexibility . Paris , Washington, D.C. , 1986. 23 p. ; LC Card 86-215799 DDC 331.12 19
HD5707 .L28 1986

Ravaioli, Carla. Tempo da vendere, tempo da usare . Milano, Italy , c1986. 142 p. ; LC Card 86-182560
HD5106 .R357 1986

Repetto, Robert C. World enough and time . New Haven , c1986. xiv, 147 p. ; ISBN 0-300-03648-5 LC Card 85-20180 DDC 333.7 19
HC59 .R43 1986 ***NYPL [JLD 86-1434]***

Research on the quality of life /. Ann Arbor, Mich. , 1986. xiv, 365 p. ; ISBN 0-87944-308-1 : LC Card 86-15179 DDC 305/.0973 19
HN60 .R47 1986 ***NYPL [JLE 86-3621]***

A quality of life and basic needs measurement system with application to Elsies River /. Ellis, George Francis Rayner. Cape Town [1983] 101, [84] p. : ISBN 0-7992-0551-6 LC Card 84-146635 DDC 338.968/00723 19
HC905.Z7 E473 1983 ***NYPL [JLF 86-1126]***

QUALITY OF LIFE - ARMENIAN S.S.R.
Karapetian, S. A. Regional'nye osobennosti sotsial'no-demograficheskogo razvitiia Armianskoĭ SSR /. Erevan , 1986. 215 p. ; LC Card 87-118556
HB3608.A75 K37 1986

QUALITY OF LIFE - CONGRESSES.
Individuelle und gesellschaftliche Kosten der Massenarbeitslosigkeit . Weinheim , 1985. xxvi, 506 p. : ISBN 3-407-54689-0 LC Card 86-118545 DDC 331.13/7/019 19
HD5708 .I53 1985 ***NYPL [JLD 87-387]***

QUALITY OF LIFE - DEVELOPING COUNTRIES.
Ellis, Frank. Peasant economics . Cambridge [Cambridgeshire] , New York , 1988. p. cm. ISBN 0-521-32446-7 LC Card 87-14815 DDC 338.1/09172/4 19
HD1542 .E43 1988

QUALITY OF LIFE - HUNGARY - STATISTICS.
A Háztáji és kisegitő gazdaság szerepe az életmód alakulásában . Budapest , 1983. 263 p. ; ISBN 963-02-2948-X (Magy. nemz. bibl.) LC Card 84-216989
HD1476.H8 H28 1983

QUALITY OF LIFE - MEXICO - TECOLUTLA.
Alcalá, Graciela. Los pescadores de Tecolutla . México, D.F. , 1985. 215 p. : ISBN 968-496-070-0 LC Card 86-191825
HD8039.F652 M62 1985

QUALITY OF LIFE - NETHERLANDS - STATISTICS.
Beek, P. van. De leefsituatie van Surinamers en Antillianen in Nederland, 1985 /. 's-Gravenhage , 1986- v. <1 > : ISBN 90-357-0558-0 : LC Card 87-120083
HD8518.5.S87 B44 1986

De Leefsituatie van Turken en Marokkanen in Nederland 1984 /. 's-Gravenhage , 1985-<1987. v. <1-3 > : ISBN 90-357-0457-6 : LC Card 86-234067
HD8518.5.T87 L44 1985

Quality of life of Turks and Moroccans in the Netherlands 1984. De Leefsituatie van Turken en Marokkanen in Nederland 1984 /. 's-Gravenhage , 1985-<1987. v. <1-3 > : ISBN 90-357-0457-6 : LC Card 86-234067
HD8518.5.T87 L44 1985

QUALITY OF LIFE - PARAGUAY - CONGRESSES.
Flecha, Agustín Oscar. Crisis económica . [Asunción] [1987] 65 p. ; LC Card 87-404003 DDC 331.2/3/09892 19
HD4920.P2 F57 1987

QUALITY OF LIFE - SOUTH AFRICA - ELSIES RIVER.
Ellis, George Francis Rayner. A quality of life and basic needs measurement system with application to Elsies River /. Cape Town [1983] 101, [84] p. : ISBN 0-7992-0551-6 LC Card 84-146635 DDC 338.968/00723 19
HC905.Z7 E473 1983 ***NYPL [JLF 86-1126]***

QUALITY OF LIFE - SOVIET UNION - STATISTICAL METHODS.
Statisticheskie metody v issledovaniiakh truda, dokhodov i potrebleniia /. Moskva , 1981. 382 p. : LC Card 82-155399
HA1.A38 A15 t. 42 HD7035

QUALITY OF LIFE - SPAIN.
Nuevas tecnologías, economía y sociedad en España /. Madrid , c1986. 2 v. (xvi, 1056 p.) : ISBN 84-206-9495-9 (set) LC Card 86-205429
HC390.T4 N84 1986

QUALITY OF LIFE - SPAIN - BADAJOZ (PROVINCE) - HISTORY.
Bohoyo Velázquez, Isidoro Francisco. Situación socio-económica y condiciones de vida en la Provincia de Badajoz, 1880-1902 /. Badajoz [1984?] 149 p., [3] p. of plates : ISBN 84-309-1055-7 LC Card 86-151914
HC387.B14 B64 1984

QUALITY OF LIFE - SPAIN - CASTILLA-LA MANCHA.
Sánchez Sánchez, Isidro. Castilla-La Mancha en la época contemporánea, 1808-1939 /. [Castilla-La Mancha] [1986] iii, 204 p. : ISBN 84-505-3538-7 LC Card 87-122049
HC387.C245 S36 1986

QUALITY OF LIFE - THAILAND - BANGKOK METROPOLITAN AREA.
Charoon Vitiprod. Rapid population growth, living conditions, and fertility reduction implication (Bangkok metropolis) /. [Singapore] 1979. ii, 41 leaves : LC Card 82-940038
HB3644.55.B36 C48 1979

QUALITY OF LIFE - UNITED STATES.
Bowman, Thomas F. Finding your best place to live in America /. New York , c1981. xiii, 337 p. : ISBN 0-940162-00-8 (pbk.) : LC Card 81-51506 DDC 973.927 19
HT123 .B665 ***NYPL [Pub. Cat. 86-574]***

Cutter, Susan L. Rating places . Washington, D.C. , c1985. viii, 76 p. : ISBN 0-89291-191-3 (pbk.) : LC Card 85-13469 DDC 307/.0973 19
GF503 .C87 1985 ***NYPL [JLD 86-2715]***

McNulty, Robert H., 1940- The economics of amenity . Washington, D.C. , c1985. xvi, 157 p. : ISBN 0-941182-15-0 (pbk.) LC Card 85-6545 DDC 307.7/6/0973 19
HT321 .M36 1985 ***NYPL [JLE 86-4519]***

Research on the quality of life /. Ann Arbor, Mich. , 1986. xiv, 365 p. ; ISBN 0-87944-308-1 : LC Card 86-15179 DDC 305/.0973 19
HN60 .R47 1986 ***NYPL [JLE 86-3621]***

QUALITY OF PRODUCTS - BULGARIA.
Ikonomika i upravlenie na kachestvoto. Svishtov , 1985. 201 p. : LC Card 86-155955
HC403.Z9 I5239 1985

Narŭchnik na profsŭiuzniia aktivist . [[Sofia?] , 1985. 264 p. ; LC Card 85-216969
HC403.Z9 L366 1985

Tomov, Mitko. Pŭtishta za podobriavane na kachestvoto /. Pleven , 1984. 68, [4] p. ; LC Card 85-179053
HC403.Z9 L38 1984

QUALITY OF PRODUCTS - CONGRESSES.
Empirical approaches to consumer protection economics . Washington, D.C. [1986] ii, 484 p. : ***NYPL [JLE 86-3552]***

QUALITY OF PRODUCTS - EUROPE, EASTERN.
Poznański, Kazimierz. Technology, competition, & the Soviet bloc in the world market /. Berkeley , c1987. ix, 226 p. ; ISBN 0-87725-170-3 (pbk.) : LC Card 87-3505 DDC 338/.06 19
HC244.Z9 T4716 1987

QUALITY OF PRODUCTS - JAPAN - MANAGEMENT.
Garvin, David A. Managing quality . New York , London , c1988. xiv, 319 p. ; ISBN 0-02-911380-6 LC Card 87-15145 DDC 658.5/62 19
HF5415.157 .G37 1988

QUALITY OF PRODUCTS - JAPAN - MANAGEMENT - CASE STUDIES.
Garvin, David A. Managing quality . New York , London , c1988. xiv, 319 p. ; ISBN 0-02-911380-6 LC Card 87-15145 DDC 658.5/62 19
HF5415.157 .G37 1988

QUALITY OF PRODUCTS - MANAGEMENT.
Edosomwan, Johnson Aimie, 1953- Integrating productivity and quality management /. New York , c1987. xvii, 360 p. : ISBN 0-8247-7657-7 LC Card 86-32780 DDC 658.5 19
HD56 .E28 1987

QUALITY OF PRODUCTS - UNITED STATES - CONGRESSES.
Empirical approaches to consumer protection economics . Washington, D.C. [1986] ii, 484 p. : LC Card 86-602207 DDC 381/.34/0973 19
HC110.C63 E46 1986

QUALITY OF PRODUCTS - UNITED STATES - MANAGEMENT.
Garvin, David A. Managing quality . New York , London , c1988. xiv, 319 p. ; ISBN 0-02-911380-6 LC Card 87-15145 DDC 658.5/62 19
HF5415.157 .G37 1988

QUALITY OF PRODUCTS - UNITED STATES - MANAGEMENT - CASE STUDIES.
Garvin, David A. Managing quality . New York , London , c1988. xiv, 319 p. ; ISBN 0-02-911380-6 LC Card 87-15145 DDC 658.5/62 19
HF5415.157 .G37 1988

QUALITY OF WORK LIFE.
Befreiung der Arbeit . Bonn , c1986. 197 p. : ISBN 3-87831-429-9 LC Card 86-194157
HD6955 .B389 1986

Enke, Harald. Konsumtive Arbeit . Freiburg im Breisgau , c1983. 354 p. : ISBN 3-448-01239-4 LC Card 83-224110
HF5549.5.J63 E54 1983

Flexibility in the labour market . Paris [Washington, D.C.] 1986. 146 p. ; ISBN 92-64-12892-1 (pbk.) LC Card 87-123763 DDC 331.12 19
HD5707 .F59 1986

Francis, Arthur. New technology at work /. Oxford [Oxfordshire] , New York , 1986. vi, 216 p. ; ISBN 0-19-878016-8 : LC Card 86-12705 DDC 338/.06 19
HD6331 .F66 1987 ***NYPL [JLD 87-912]***

Lawler, Edward E. High-involvement management /. San Francisco, Calif. , 1986. xvii, 252 p. : ISBN 0-87589-686-3 (alk. paper) LC Card 85-45909 DDC 658.3/152 19
HD5650 .L35 1986 ***NYPL [JLE 86-3096]***

Magyar, Lajosné. A munkaviszonyok humanizálása . Budapest [1985] 210 p. ; ISBN 963-608-075-5 LC Card 85-154632
HD6955 .M27 1985

Parnes, Steven. Productivity and the quality of working life /. Scarsdale, N.Y. , c1978. 43 p. ; LC Card 78-51009 DDC 658.31/4
HD57 .P33 ***NYPL [JLM 83-380 no.2]***

Schmied, Volker. Alternativen der Arbeitsgestaltung und ihre Bewertung . Wiesbaden , c1982. 423 p. : ISBN 3-409-38642-4

LC Card 83-187066
HD6955 .S345 1982

Stoîanov, Khristo. Khumanizatsiîa na truda . Sofiîa , 1985. 191 p. ; LC Card 85-243365
HD6955 .S85 1985

Sul "movimento" della qualità della vita di lavoro /. Milano , c1982. 117 p. ; LC Card 82-246606
HD6955 .S94 1982 ***NYPL [JLD 87-1159]***

Szathmári, Gábor. Kinek lehet igaza? . Budapest , 1985. 118 p. ; ISBN 963-322-273-7 : LC Card 86-156416
HD6955 .S975 1985

Weisbord, Marvin Ross. Productive workplaces . San Francisco , 1987. xxv, 405 p. : ISBN 1-555-42054-0 (alk. paper) LC Card 87-45425 DDC 658.3/14 19
HD31 .W424 1987

Wells, Don, 1946- Empty promises . New York , c1987. xviii, 167 p. ; ISBN 0-85345-710-7 : LC Card 87-24687 DDC 331.25 19
HD6957.U6 W34 1987

QUALITY OF WORK LIFE - ADDRESSES, ESSAYS, LECTURES.
Qualitative Arbeitsanalyse . Frankfurt , New York , c1983. 352 p. ; ISBN 3-593-32721-X LC Card 83-161600 DDC 158.7 19
HD6955 .Q35 1983 ***NYPL [JLD 87-1014]***

QUALITY OF WORK LIFE - BRAZIL.
De que adoecem e morrem os trabalhadores /. São Paulo , 1985. 236 p. ; LC Card 85-231487
HD7683 .D4 1985

QUALITY OF WORK LIFE - CONGRESSES.
Mehr Technik, weniger Arbeit? . Karlsruhe , c1984. 228 p. : ISBN 3-7880-9697-7 LC Card 85-108996
HD6331 .M384 1984

QUALITY OF WORK LIFE - EUROPEAN ECONOMIC COMMUNITY COUNTRIES.
Sul "movimento" della qualità della vita di lavoro /. Milano , c1982. 117 p. ; LC Card 82-246606
HD6955 .S94 1982 ***NYPL [JLD 87-1159]***

QUALITY OF WORK LIFE - FRANCE.
Drancourt, Michel. La fin du travail /. Paris , c1984. 329 p. : ISBN 2-01-009476-X LC Card 84-222228 DDC 306/.36 19
HD6957.F8 D7 1984 ***NYPL [JLC 86-444]***

QUALITY OF WORK LIFE - GERMANY (WEST)
Elsenau, Detlef von. Arbeitnehmerorientierte Sozialforschung . Münster [1986] ii, 233 p. ; ISBN 3-88660-246-X LC Card 86-200305
HD6957.G3 E59 1986

QUALITY OF WORK LIFE - INDIA - PUNE.
Lambert, Richard D. The transformation of an Indian labor market . Amsterdam , Philadelphia , 1986. ix, 249 p. ; ISBN 0-915027-63-1 (alk. paper) : LC Card 86-26900 DDC 331.11/0954/792 19
HD5820.P78 L36 1986

QUALITY OF WORK LIFE - ITALY.
Sul "movimento" della qualità della vita di lavoro /. Milano , c1982. 117 p. ; LC Card 82-246606
HD6955 .S94 1982 ***NYPL [JLD 87-1159]***

QUALITY OF WORK LIFE - LATIN AMERICA.
Galin, Pedro. Condiciones de trabajo y coordinación de las inspecciones /. Lima, Perú , 1986. 19 p. ; LC Card 87-401748 DDC 331.25 19
HD6957.L29 G35 1986

QUALITY OF WORK LIFE - MEXICO - BARROTERÁN.
Arenal, Sandra. Barroterán! . [Mexico City?] , c1984. 116 p. ; ISBN 968-495-016-0 LC Card 85-195552
HD8039.M62 M63 1984

QUALITY OF WORK LIFE - SOCIETIES, ETC. - DIRECTORIES.
Conditions of work and quality of working life . Geneva , 1986. xxi, 306 p. ; ISBN 92-2-105328-8 (pbk.) : LC Card 86-215659 DDC 306/.36/025 19
HD7260 .C64 1986

QUALITY OF WORK LIFE - SOVIET UNION.
Aktivnaîa sotsial'naîa politika . Moskva , 1986. 156 p., [16] p. of plates : LC Card 86-216405 DDC 354.47001/6 19
HD60.5.S77 A38 1986

QUALITY OF WORK LIFE - UNITED STATES.
EAPs and the information revolution . New York , c1987. 106 p. ; ISBN 0-86656-606-6 LC Card 86-33519 DDC 331.25 19
HF5549.5.E42 E37 1987

Fernandez, John P., 1941- Survival in the corporate fishbowl . Lexington, Mass. , c1987. xiii, 314 p. : ISBN 0-669-10336-5 (alk. paper) LC Card 85-40021 DDC 302.3/5 19
HD6957.U6 F47 1987

Moral rights in the workplace /. Albany , c1987. xii, 312 p. ; ISBN 0-88706-362-4 LC Card 86-6949 DDC 331.25 19
HD6957.U6 M67 1987
NYPL [JLE 87-1197]

Wells, Don, 1946- Empty promises . New York , c1987. xviii, 167 p. ; ISBN 0-85345-710-7 : LC Card 87-24687 DDC 331.25 19
HD6957.U6 W34 1987

QUALITY OF WORK LIFE - UNITED STATES - ABSTRACTS.
Guzzo, Richard A. Programs for productivity and quality of work life /. New York , c1983. 38 p. ; ISBN 0-08-030964-X (pbk.) : LC Card 83-22029 DDC 658.3/14 19
HC110.L3 G89 1983
NYPL [JLM 83-380 no.32]

Weinberg, Edgar. Labor-management cooperation for productivity /. New York , c1983. 61 p. ; ISBN 0-08-029511-8 (pbk.) LC Card 83-2361 DDC 016.33111/8/0973 19
HD56 .W44 1983
NYPL [JLM 83-380 no.30]

QUALITY OF WORK LIFE - UNITED STATES - ADDRESSES, ESSAYS, LECTURES.
Labor-management cooperation . [Washington, D.C.?] , 1984. v, 77 p. ; LC Card 85-602044 DDC 331.01/12/0973 19
HD6490.L332 U55 1984
NYPL [JLF 86-559]

QUALITY OF WORK LIFE - UNITED STATES - CASE STUDIES.
Grenier, Guillermo J. Inhuman relations . Philadelphia , 1988. xx, 232 p. ; ISBN 0-87722-502-8 (alk. paper) : LC Card 87-10116 DDC 331.25 19
HD6490.O72 U645 1988

QUALITY OF WORK LIFE - UNITED STATES - HISTORY.
Katz, Harry Charles, 1951- Shifting gears . Cambridge, Mass. , c1985. xii, 230 p. : ISBN 0-262-11098-9 LC Card 84-26105 DDC 331/.04292/0973 19
HD6976.A82 U528 1985
NYPL [JLE 85-2260]

Quality of working life. Mikheev, S. Glossary of economic and social terminology in Eastern European socialist countries /. Geneva , 1986. 52, x p. ; ISBN 92-9014-413-0 : LC Card 86-214600 DDC 335.4/03/21 19
HB61 .M487 1986

Quality of working life. Mikheev, S. Remuneration in Eastern European countries /. Geneva , 1985. vi, 45, ix p. ; ISBN 92-9014-408-4 (pbk.) : LC Card 86-216036 DDC 331.2/947 19
HD5014 .M55 1985

Quality of working life. Parnes, Steven. Productivity and the quality of working life /. Scarsdale, N.Y. , c1978. 43 p. ; LC Card 78-51009 DDC 658.31/4
HD57 .P33 ***NYPL [JLM 83-380 no.2]***

Quality, productivity, and innovation : strategies for gaining competitive advantage / edited by Y.K. Shetty, Vernon M. Buehler ; foreword by Roger Smith. New York : Elsevier, c1987. xx, 427 p. : ill. ; 24 cm Bibliography: p. [399]-416. Includes index. ISBN 0-444-01194-3 LC Card 87-6815 DDC 658.5 19
1. Organizational effectiveness. 2. Personnel management. 3. Quality of products. 4. Industrial productivity. 5. Technological innovations - Management. 6. Competition, International. I. Shetty, Y. Krishna. II. Buehler, Vernon M.
HD58.9 .Q35 1987

Qualls, P. David. Bain, Joe Staten, 1912- Industrial organization . Greenwich, Conn. , c1987. 2 v. ; ISBN 0-89232-702-2 (set) LC Card 87-2618 DDC 338.6 19
HD2326 .B34 1987

Quamina, Odida T. Mineworkers of Guyana : the making of a working class / Odida T. Quamina. London ; Atlantic Highlands, N.J., USA : Zed Books, 1987. xv, 118 p., [7] p. of plates : ill. ; 23 cm. Bibliography: p. 111-116. Includes index. ISBN 0-86232-308-8 : LC Card 87-14719 DDC 305/.9622/098814 19
1. Aluminum industry and trade - Guyana - Mackenzie - Employees. 2. Aluminum mines and mining - Guyana - Mackenzie. 3. Mackenzie (Guyana) - Social conditions. I. Title.
HD8039.A492 G9558 1987

Quand les Pyrénéens parcouraient le monde . Espagne, Jean-Pierre. Saint-Gaudens [France] , c1985. 224 p., [12] leaves of plates : ISBN 2-904458-07-7 : LC Card 86-139944 DDC 381/.18 B 19
HF5459.F8 E844 1985

Die Quantifizierung der Steuerbelastung im internationalen Bereich . Widdau, Peter, 1952- Frankfurt am Main , New York , c1984. xx, 413 p. : ISBN 3-8204-8044-7 : LC Card 85-191946
HJ2321 .W46 1984

Quantifizierung des systematischen Fehlers in wirtschafts- und sozialstatistischen Daten . Krug, Walter, Prof. Dr. Berlin , 1976. 109 p. : ISBN 3-428-03710-3 LC Card 76-487801
HD5711 .K78 ***NYPL [JLE 80-187]***

Quantifying the impact of the Tax Reform Act of 1986 on effective corporate tax rates /. Starcher, Mark L. [Arlington, Va.] , c1986. 45, 3 leaves, 12 leaves of plates : LC Card 87-402048 DDC 336.24/3/0973021 19
HJ4653.C7 S675 1986

The quantitative and qualitative significance of the emergence of local initiatives for employment creation . Buiren, S. van. Luxembourg , Washington, D.C. , 1986. iii, 141, 14, [12] p. : ISBN 92-825-6048-1 (pbk.) : LC Card 86-222030 DDC 331.12/042/094 19
HD5764.5.A6 B85 1986

Quantitative applications in the social sciences. (no. 57) Schroeder, Larry D. Understanding regression analysis . Beverly Hills , c1986. 95 p. : ISBN 0-8039-2758-4 LC Card 85-63790
NYPL [JLK 77-39 no.57]

(no. 59) Wolf, Fredric M. (Fredric Marc) Meta-analysis . Beverly Hills , c1986. 65 p. : ISBN 0-8039-2756-8 LC Card 85-52372
NYPL [JLK 77-39 no.59]

Quantitative economics & econometrics. Brennan, Michael Joseph, 1928- Preface to quantitative economics & econometrics. Cincinnati , c1987. x, 580 p. : ISBN 0-538-08230-5 (pbk.) LC Card 86-60209 DDC 330/.028 19
HB139 .B74 1987

Quantitative Entwicklungsplanung für ländliche Regionen . Bauer, Jürgen. Bochum , 1979. 382 p. in various pagings : ISBN 3-88339-087-9 : LC Card 80-470152
HT395.G4 B39 1979 ***NYPL [JLD 86-1628]***

Quantitative Latin American studies : methods and findings / edited by James W. Wilkie, Kenneth Ruddle. Los Angeles : UCLA Latin American Center Publications, University of California, 1977. xiv, 91 p. : graphs ; 28 cm. (Statistical abstract of Latin America. Supplement series . v. 6) Includes bibliographies. ISBN 0-87903-227-8 LC Card 77-620011 DDC 330.9/8/003
1. Labor supply - Mexico - Addresses, essays, lectures. 2. Elections - Mexico - Addresses, essays, lectures. 3. Industrial productivity - Cuba - Addresses, essays, lectures. 4. Latin America - Social conditions - Addresses, essays, lectures. 5. Latin America - Politics and government - Addresses, essays, lectures. I. Wilkie, James Wallace. II. Ruddle, Kenneth. III. Series. IV. Series: Statistical abstract of Latin America. Supplement series , suppl. 6.
HD5731.A6 Q36 ***NYPL [JLF 80-242]***

Quantitative methods for business decisions /. Curwin, Jon. New York , 1985. xii, 343 p. : ISBN 0-442-30640-7 (pbk.) LC Card 85-3267

DDC 519.5/024658 19
HF5691 .C87 1985

Quantitative methods for financial analysis / edited by Stephen J. Brown, Mark P. Kritzman ; sponsored by the Institute of Chartered Financial Analysts. Homewood, Ill. : Dow Jones-Irwin, c1987. xv, 229 p. : ill. ; 25 cm. Includes bibliographies and index. ISBN 0-87094-978-0 LC Card 86-72275 DDC 332.6/01/51 19
1. Investments - Decision making - Mathematics. 2. Investments - Decision making - Statistical methods. I. Brown, Stephen J. II. Kritzman, Mark P. III. Institute of Chartered Financial Analysts.
HG4515.3 .Q36 1987

Quantitative techniques for management . Payne, Thomas A. Reston, Va. , c1982. xii, 452 p. : ISBN 0-8359-6116-8 : LC Card 81-17818 DDC 658.4/033 19
HD30.25 .P395 1982 NYPL [JLE 82-399]

Quantitative und qualitative Konsolidierung /. Fuest, Winfried, 1946- Köln , c1986. 44 p. : ISBN 3-602-24741-4 LC Card 86-214118
HJ2110 .F84 1986

Quantity and quality in economic research / edited by Roy Chamberlain Brown. Lanham, MD : University Press of America, c1985- v. : ill. ; 24 cm. "Outgrowth of the First International Conference on Quantity and Quality in Economic Research which met in Princeton, New Jersey, U. S.A., June 17-19, 1984. Sponsored by the International Society of Statistical Science in Economics."--V. 1, p. iii. "Co-published by arrangement with the International Society of Statistical Science in Economics"--V. 1, t.p. verso. Includes bibliographies. ISBN 0-8191-5112-2 (v. 1 : alk. paper) : LC Card 85-26360 DDC 330/.072 19
1. Economics, Mathematical - Research - Congresses. 2. Economics - Statistical methods - Congresses. I. Brown, Roy Chamberlain, 1927-. II. International Society of Statistical Science in Economics. III. International Conference on Quantity and Quality in Economic Research (1st : 1984 : Princeton, N.J.).
HB135 .Q38 1985 NYPL [JLL 86-232]

QUANTITY OF MONEY. see MONEY SUPPLY.

QUANTITY THEORY OF MONEY.
Cencini, Alvaro. Money, income, and time . London , New York , 1988. p. cm. ISBN 0-86187-943-0 : LC Card 87-7279 DDC 332.4 19
HG221 .C39 1988

García, Valeriano F. A critical inquiry into Argentine economic history, 1946-1970 /. New York , 1987. vi, 127 p. : ISBN 0-8240-1361-1 (alk. paper) : LC Card 87-7620 DDC 330.982/062 19
HG815 .G27 1987

El quantum de exportaciones del Ecuador (1970-1983) /. León, I. Josefina. [Guayaquil] , 1985. 93 p. : LC Card 87-123381 DDC 382/.6/09866 19
HF3431.5 .L46 1985

Quarré, Dominique. Les agents de l'Etat au 31 décembre 1980 / Dominique Quarré, et Direction de la Fonction publique. Paris : INSEE, [1985] 305 p. ; 30 cm. (Archives & documents . no 127) "Avril 1985." ISBN 2-11-064767-1 : LC Card 86-162558
1. France - Officials and employees - Statistics. I. France. Direction générale de l'administration et de la fonction publique. II. Series: Archives & documents (Institut national de la statistique et des études économiques (France)) , no 127. III. Title.
HD8013.F6 Q373 1985

Quarrey, Michael. Taking stock : employee ownership at work / Michael Quarrey, Joseph Blasi, and Corey Rosen. Cambridge, Mass. : Ballinger Pub. Co., c1986. xii, 176 p. ; 24 cm. Includes index. Bibliography: p. 165-170. ISBN 0-88730-131-2 LC Card 86-14045 DDC 338.7/4 19
1. Employee ownership - United States. 2. Employee stock options - United States. 3. Job satisfaction - United States. I. Blasi, Joseph R. II. Rosen, Corey M. III. Title.
HD5660.U5 Q37 1986 NYPL [JLE 87-49]

QUARTERLY LABOUR FORCE STATISTICS.
Standardised unemployment rates . Paris, France [Washington, D.C.] 1985. 93 p. ; LC Card 86-143095 DDC 331.13/7/072 19
HD5711 .S77 1985 NYPL [JLF 86-1743]

Quarterly national accounts, 1978-1983. Kvartalsvis nasjonalregnskap 1978-1983 =. Oslo , 1984. 99 p. ; ISBN 82-537-2143-9 : LC Card 85-223735
HA1501 B, nr. 510 HC370.I5

Quatrième plan quinquennal de développement économique et social du Burundi, 1983-1987. Burundi. Ministère à la présidence chargé du plan. IVème plan quinquennal de développement économique et social du Burundi, 1983-1987 /. [Bujumbura] [1983?-] <v. 1, pt. 1; v. 2, 4, 7 > : LC Card 86-980056
HC880 .B88 1983

Quatro plano mineiro de desenvolvimento econômico e social. Minas Gerais, Brazil. IV plano mineiro de desenvolvimento econômico e social . [Belo Horizonte] [1983] 347 p. : LC Card 86-201630
HC188.M6 M48 1983

Quazi, Mohammed Hanif. Food insecurity in the Muslim world / by Mohammed Hanif Quazi. Jeddah, Saudi Arabia (P.O. Box 9833, Jeddah) : Islamic Foundation for Science, Technology, and Development, 1985. 21, [26] p. : ill. ; 21 cm. (IFSTAD studies series . no. 1) Bibliography: p. 19-20 (1st group) LC Card 87-133798 DDC 338.1/9/17671 19
1. Food supply - Islamic countries. 2. Food supply - Islamic countries - Statistics. 3. Agricultural productivity - Islamic countries - Statistics. 4. Produce trade - Islamic countries - Statistics. I. Title. II. Series.
HD9018.I84 Q39 1985

Quddus, Syed Abdul. Rail transport in Pakistan / by Syed Abdul Quddus. Lahore : Directorate of Research & Training, Pakistan Railways, [1984?] 277 p. ; 25 cm. Bibliography: p. 274-277. LC Card 85-932263 DDC 385/.09549/1 19
1. Railroads and state - Pakistan. 2. Railroads - Pakistan. 3. Urban transportation - Pakistan. I. Title.
HE3300.5 .Q33 1984

Que Corporation. Using 1-2-3 /. Carmel, Ind. , c1987. xxviii, 905 p. : ISBN 0-88022-332-4 (pbk.) LC Card 87-61897 DDC 005.36/9 19
HF5548.4.L67 U85 1987

Que nous a appris la crise de l'endettement international? /. Leroux, François, 1945- Montréal, Québec, Canada [1985] 41 leaves ; LC Card 86-144447 DDC 336.3/4/091724 19
HJ8899 .L47 1985

O que todo cidadão precisa saber sobre comissões de fábrica /. Ibrahim, José. São Paulo, SP [1986] 96 p. : ISBN 85-26-00095-0 LC Card 87-402908 DDC 338.6 19
HD5660.B7 I27 1986

Que todo cidadão precisa saber sobre comissões de fábrica. Ibrahim, José. O que todo cidadão precisa saber sobre comissões de fábrica /. São Paulo, SP [1986] 96 p. : ISBN 85-26-00095-0 LC Card 87-402908 DDC 338.6 19
HD5660.B7 I27 1986

Quebec Federation of Labor (Founded 1957) see **Fédération des travailleurs du Québec.**

Québec (Province). Assemblée nationale. The Legislature of Quebec Province was, until 1968, composed of two chambers: the Legislative Council and the Legislative Assembly. In that year the Council was abolished and the Legislative Assembly was renamed National Assembly.) // Works published 1975- are entered under form as above.

Québec (Province). Assemblée nationale. Commission permanente de l'énergie et des ressources.
"L'Energie, levier de développement économique" . [Ottawa?] [1983] 30 leaves ; LC Card 85-128816
HD9685.C3 Q4425 1983

Esso Petroleum Canada (Firm) Mémoire présenté à la Commission élue permanente de l'énergie et des ressources de l'Assemblée nationale du Québec /. Québec [1983] 44 leaves : LC Card 85-143347 DDC 338.2/7282/09714 19
HD9574.C23 Q43 1983

Québec (Province). Bureau d'audiences publiques sur l'environnement. Poste Des Cantons, lignes Nicolet-Des Cantons et Des Cantons-Nouvelle-Angleterre /. [Sainte-Foy, Qc] [1983] 1 v. (various pagings) ; ISBN 2-550-10466-8 LC Card 85-121505
HD9685.C3 Q455 1983

Québec (Province). Bureau du vérificateur général. Vérification spéciale : (mandat confié par l'arrêté en conseil 1796-78 du 7 juin 1978). [Québec] : Bureau du vérificateur général, [1978-<1987? >] v. <1-3 > ; 30 cm. At head of title: Office de la construction du Québec. CONTENTS. - [1] Rapport relatif aux traitements, honoraires et autres bénéfices des membres de l'Office de la construction du Québec, du 27 juin 1975 au 31 mai 1978 -- [2] Rapport d'étape au 6 octobre 1978 -- [3] Rapport relatif à l'administration des régimes d'avantages sociaux des salaries de la construction. LC Card 82-212701
1. Office de la construction du Québec - Auditing. I. Title. II. Title: Rapport relatif aux traitements, honoraires et autres bénéfices des membres de l'Office de la construction du Québec.
HD9715.C33 Q45 1978

Québec (Province). Centre de recherche et de statistiques sur le marché du travail. Lewis, Normande. Le travail à temps partiel, le partage du travail comme mesure de sécurité d'emploi et la sous-traitance . [Quebec] , c1985. 90 p. ; ISBN 2-551-08998-0 LC Card 85-213545
HD5110.2.C22 Q45 1985

Québec (Province). Comité sur les questions économiques. Messier, Suzanne. Perspectives d'emploi pour les Québécoises dans la décennie 1980 . Québec [1983] vi, 73 p. ; ISBN 2-550-10439-0 LC Card 84-221697
HD6100.Q4 M47 1983

QUEBEC (PROVINCE) - COMMERCE.
Le Secteur manufacturier, le commerce et le tourisme au Québec en 1983. [Québec] [1984] 34 leaves : LC Card 85-127334
HD9734.C3 Q485 1984

QUÉBEC (PROVINCE) - COMMERCE - STATISTICS.
Destination des expéditions des manufacturiers exportateurs du Québec, 1976-1980 /. Québec, Québec [1983] ix, 249 p. : LC Card 85-115007
HF3229.Q4 D47 1983

Québec (Province). Communications, Ministère des. see **Québec (Province). Ministère des communications.**

Québec (Province). Conseil du statut de la femme. Messier, Suzanne. Perspectives d'emploi pour les Québécoises dans la décennie 1980 . Québec [1983] vi, 73 p. ; ISBN 2-550-10439-0 LC Card 84-221697
HD6100.Q4 M47 1983

Québec (Province). Conseil du trésor. Bureau de la recherche sur la rémunération.
Morin, André, analyste en rémunération. Analyse de l'évolution des principaux indicateurs économiques au Québec, en Ontario, au Canada et aux Etats-Unis . [Québec] [1982] 209 p. ; ISBN 2-551-04641-6 LC Card 83-103355
HC117.Q4 M66 1982

Nadeau, Jean. Les indicateurs globaux de la productivité . Québec [1982] 41 p. : ISBN 2-551-05072-3 LC Card 83-221751
HC120.I52 N33 1982

Québec (Province). Direction des études industrielles. L'Industrie québécoise du matériel médical jetable . Québec [1983] xv, 235 p. : LC Card 84-235956
HD9995.D563 C35 1983

Québec (Province). Direction des études sectorielles. Profil de l'industrie canadienne de la chaussure /. [Québec] [1985] xv, 65 p. : ISBN 2-550-12407-3 LC Card 86-177298
HD9787.C23 Q436 1985

Québec (Province). Direction des politiques de santé. Charron, Marie-France, 1952- Le suicide au Québec . [Quebec] , 1983. 221 p. : ISBN 2-551-05209-2 LC Card 83-168606
HB1323.S82 C352 1983

Québec (Province). Direction générale de la recherche et de la planification. Profil de l'industrie canadienne de la chaussure /. [Québec] [1985] xv, 65 p. : ISBN 2-550-12407-3 LC Card 86-177298
HD9787.C23 Q436 1985

Québec (Province). Direction générale de l'industrie. Ristic, Veselin. Profil de l'industrie québécoise des éléments d'architecture et de structure préfabriqués en béton /. [Québec] , c1983. 168 p. : LC Card 85-100163
HD9622.C23 Q437 1983

QUEBEC (PROVINCE) - ECONOMIC CONDITIONS.
Aperçu de la situation économique au Québec en 1980 /. Québec [1980] 42 leaves : LC Card 83-150001
HC117.Q4 A794 1980

Brunelle, Dorval. L'Etat solide . Montréal, Québec , 1982. 174 p. : ISBN 2-89132-677-6 (pbk.) LC Card 87-672120
HC115 .B773x 1982

Fortin, Pierre. [Unemployment, inflation, and economic stabilization in Quebec. French.] Chômage, inflation et régulation de la conjoncture au Québec /. Montréal, Québec [1980] viii, 144 p. : ISBN 0-88806-063-7 (pbk.) LC Card 87-673448
HC117.Q4 F63x 1980

QUÉBEC (PROVINCE) - ECONOMIC CONDITIONS - REGIONAL DISPARITIES.
Gagnon, Alain. Le modèle centre-périphérique appliqué à l'est du Québec . Rimouski , c19. ix, 154 p. ; LC Card 80-143484
HC117.G37 G33 1980

QUÉBEC (PROVINCE) - ECONOMIC CONDITIONS - STATISTICS.
Morin, André, analyste en rémunération. Analyse de l'évolution des principaux indicateurs économiques au Québec, en Ontario, au Canada et aux Etats-Unis . [Québec] [1982] 209 p. ; ISBN 2-551-04641-6 LC Card 83-103355
HC117.Q4 M66 1982

QUEBEC (PROVINCE) - ECONOMIC POLICY - CONGRESSES.
Le Bilan des conférences socio-économiques . [Quebec] [1983] xi, 124 p. : ISBN 2-551-05784-1 LC Card 84-134997
HC117.Q4 B535 1983

Québec (Province). Groupe de travail sur la déréglementation. Réglementer moins et mieux : rapport final / du Groupe de travail sur la déréglementation. [Quebec] : Gouvernement du Québec, Conseil exécutif, [1986] 2 v. ; 28 cm. (Les Publications du Québec) Bibliography: v. [1], p. 257-270. CONTENTS. - [1] Le processus de réglementation, la réglementation sociale, la réglementation économique -- [2] Inventaire sectoriel de la réglementation économique au Québec. ISBN 2-551-08729-5 (v. 1) LC Card 86-206349
1. Deregulation - Québec (Province). 2. Industry and state - Québec (Province). 3. Privatization - Québec (Province). I. Title.
HD3616.C24 Q47 1986

Québec (Province). Groupe de travail sur le prix des carburants au Québec. Rapport du Groupe de travail sur le prix des carburants au Québec. [Québec : Ministère des finances, 1985] xiv, 169, [153] p. : ill. ; 28 cm. Report presented to the Ministre des finances, Gouvernement du Québec. Includes bibliographical references. ISBN 2-550-11913-4 LC Card 86-185758
1. Petroleum products - Prices - Québec (Province) - Statistics. I. Québec (Province). Ministère des finances. II. Title.
HD9574.C23 Q47 1985

QUEBEC (PROVINCE) - MANUFACTURES.
Le Secteur manufacturier, le commerce et le tourisme au Québec en 1983. [Québec] [1984] 34 leaves : LC Card 85-127334
HD9734.C3 Q485 1984

Québec (Province). Ministère de l'agriculture et de l'alimentation. Conseil de planification et de développement du Québec. Le réseau décisionnel en agro-alimentation au Québec . [Québec] [1979] 29 p. ; LC Card 85-102587
HD9014.C4 Q425 1979

Québec (Province). Ministère de l'Énergie et des ressources.
Répertoire administratif du Ministère de l'énergie et des ressources. Québec : Le Ministère, [1984?] 111 p. ; 28 cm. Cover title. Errata slip inserted. LC Card 84-222485
1. Québec (Province). Ministère de l'énergie et des ressources - Officials and employees - Directories. I. Title.
HD9502.C33 Q444 1984

QUÉBEC (PROVINCE). MINISTÈRE DE L'ÉNERGIE ET DES RESSOURCES - OFFICIALS AND EMPLOYEES - DIRECTORIES.
Québec (Province). Ministère de l'Énergie et des ressources. Répertoire administratif du Ministère de l'énergie et des ressources. Québec [1984?] 111 p. ; LC Card 84-222485
HD9502.C33 Q444 1984

Québec (Province). Ministère de l'industrie, du commerce et du tourisme.
Le Secteur manufacturier, le commerce et le tourisme au Québec en 1983. [Québec] [1984] 34 leaves : LC Card 85-127334
HD9734.C3 Q485 1984

Québec (Province). Ministère de l'industrie, du commerce et du tourisme. Direction de l'analyse et de la prévision économiques.
Aperçu de la situation économique au Québec en 1980 /. Québec [1980] 42 leaves : LC Card 83-150001
HC117.Q4 A794 1980

Québec (Province). Ministère des communications.
Programme d'aide aux médias communautaires, 1979-80 . [Québec] [1979] 97 leaves ; LC Card 83-200428
HE8689.9.C3 P755 1979

Se lancer en affaires . [Quebec] , c1986. 450 p. : ISBN 2-551-09144-6 LC Card 86-138587 DDC 658.1/1 19
HD62.5 .S4 1986

Québec (Province). Ministère des finances.
Québec (Province). Groupe de travail sur le prix des carburants au Québec. Rapport du Groupe de travail sur le prix des carburants au Québec. [Québec , 1985] xiv, 169, [153] p. : ISBN 2-550-11913-4 LC Card 86-185758
HD9574.C23 Q47 1985

Québec (Province). Ministère du travail. Lewis, Normande. Le travail à temps partiel, le partage du travail comme mesure de sécurité d'emploi et la sous-traitance . [Quebec] , c1985. 90 p. ; ISBN 2-551-08998-0 LC Card 85-213545
HD5110.2.C22 Q45 1985

Québec (Province). Ministre délégué à la privatisation. Privatisation de sociétés d'Etat. English. Privatization of Crown corporations . [Québec] [1986] 71 p. : LC Card 86-220606 DDC 338.9714 19
HD4010.Q4 P7513 1986

Québec (Province). Premier ministre. Conseil de planification et de développement du Québec. Le réseau décisionnel en agro-alimentation au Québec . [Québec] [1979] 29 p. ; LC Card 85-102587
HD9014.C4 Q425 1979

Québec (Province). Secrétariat des conférences socio-économiques.
Le Bilan des conférences socio-économiques . [Quebec] [1983] xi, 124 p. : ISBN 2-551-05784-1 LC Card 84-134997
HC117.Q4 B535 1983

Le Meuble . [Québec] [1983] xiii, 109 p. : ISBN 2-550-10196-0 LC Card 85-124226
HD9773.C23 Q425 1983

Québec (Province). Service des produits du bâtiment. Duchaine, Paul. Bâtiments préfabriqués résidentiels et industriels à ossature de bois . [Québec] , c1985. 36 p. : ISBN 2-550-12116-3 LC Card 86-133426
HD9715.5.C23 Q43 1985

QUÉBEC (PROVINCE) - SOCIAL POLICY - CONGRESSES.
Le Bilan des conférences socio-économiques . [Quebec] [1983] xi, 124 p. : ISBN 2-551-05784-1 LC Card 84-134997
HC117.Q4 B535 1983

Québec (Province). Statut de la femme, Conseil du. see **Québec (Province). Conseil du statut de la femme.**

QUEBRACHO.
Dargoltz, Raúl E. (Raúl Eduardo) La alianza anglo argentina . Buenos Aires [1983] 168 p. : LC Card 84-117468
HD9764.A73 S353 1983

Queen's papers in industrial relations .
(1987-1) Kumar, Pradeep. Recent wage deceleration . Kingston, Ont., Canada , 1987. 21, [12] p. ; ISBN 0-88886-158-3 (pbk.) LC Card 87-163251 DDC 331.2/971 19
HD4979 .K816 1987

(1987-4) Abbott, Michael G. Alternative estimates of union-nonunion and public-private wage differentials in Ontario, 1981 /. Kingston, Ont., Canada , 1987. ii, 47 p. ; ISBN 0-88886-166-4 (pbk.) LC Card 87-170767 DDC 331.2/2/09713 19
HD4980.O5 A64 1987

A queen's story . Paul, D. Babu (Daniel Babu), 1941- New Delhi , c1987. xix, 132 p. : ISBN 0-7069-3376-1 : LC Card 86-903827 DDC 387.1/0954/83 19
HE560.C56 P38 1987

Queen's University, Kingston, Ont. Industrial Relations Centre. (Old Catalog form: Queen's University, Kingston, Ont. Industrial Relations Dept.)
Stocks, Alex M. Union raiding . Kingston, Ont., Canada , 1985. 61 p. ; ISBN 0-88886-125-7 (pbk.) LC Card 86-145321 DDC 331.87/09711 19
HD6528.B9 S86 1985 ***NYPL [JLF 87-422]***

QUEENSLAND - PUBLIC LANDS - HISTORY - 19TH CENTURY.
Walker, Jan, 1954- Jondaryan station . St. Lucia , New York , 1988. p. cm. ISBN 0-7022-2093-0 (pbk.) LC Card 87-13816 DDC 333.3/09943 19
HD1039.Q43 W34 1988

QUEENSLAND. STATE GOVERNMENT INSURANCE OFFICE - HISTORY.
Thomis, Malcolm I. From SGIO to Suncorp /. [Brisbane?] , 1986. xii, 272 p., [32] p. of plates : ISBN 0-7242-1698-7 LC Card 87-158138 DDC 368.4/009943 19
HG8220.A9 T56 1986

QueenSpark new series .
(1) Brighton on the rocks . Brighton [1983?] 192 p. : ISBN 0-904733-00-4 (pbk.) : LC Card 84-173777 DDC 336.3/9/0942256 19
HJ9438.B75 B75 1983 ***NYPL [JLD 87-104]***

QueenSpark Rates Book Group. Brighton on the rocks . Brighton [1983?] 192 p. : ISBN 0-904733-00-4 (pbk.) : LC Card 84-173777 DDC 336.3/9/0942256 19
HJ9438.B75 B75 1983 ***NYPL [JLD 87-104]***

Quéinnec, Y. (Yvon) Copsey, S. M. Shiftwork review . Luxembourg , Washington, DC , 1986. xi, 122 p. : ISBN 92-825-6419-3 (pbk.) : LC Card 87-137298 DDC 331.25/72 19
HD5111.6.E86 C66 1986

Quelch, John A.
Cases in advertising and promotion management / John A. Quelch, Paul W. Farris. 2nd ed. Plano, Tex. : Business Publications, 1987. xv, 759 p. : ill. ; 25 cm. Includes bibliographical references and index. ISBN 0-256-03713-2 LC Card 86-72244 DDC 659.1 19
1. Advertising - Case studies. 2. Sales promotion - Case studies. I. Farris, Paul. II. Title.
HF5823 .Q44 1987

Farris, Paul. Advertising & promotion management . Malabar, Fla. , 1987, c1983. x, 301 p. : ISBN 0-89464-261-8 (pbk.) LC Card 87-15902 DDC 659.1 19
HF5821 .F36 1987

Multinational marketing management . Reading, Mass. , c1988. x, 500 p. : ISBN 0-201-07996-8 (pbk.) : LC Card 87-12599 DDC 658.8/48 19
HF1009.5 .M85 1988

Quellen. Reininghaus, Wilfried. Quellen zur Geschichte des Deutschen Industrie- und Handelstages in Kammerarchiven, 1861 bis 1918 /. Bonn , 1986. 158 p. : ISBN 3-925925-01-5 LC Card 87-408272 DDC 354.430082/09 19
HF308 .R343 1986

Quellen und Darstellungen zur Geschichte Niedersachsens .
(Bd. 50) Schatz- und Zinsverzeichnisse des 15. Jahrhunderts aus dem Fürstentum Lüneburg . Hildesheim , 1942. 153 p. ; LC Card 87-409521 DDC 336.2/00943/59 19
HJ2110.5.L86 S3 1942

Quellen und Darstellungen zur Hansischen Geschichte. For additional listing of contents, see Old Catalog.
(n.F., Bd. 29) Gilde und Korporation in den nordeuropäischen Städten des späten Mittelalters /. Köln , 1984. 114 p. ; ISBN 3-412-06883-3 LC Card 84-194645
HD6473.E853 G55 1984

Quellen und Studien zur baltischen Geschichte. (Bd. 5) Engelhardt, Hans Dieter von. Die Livländische Gemeinnützige und Ökonomische Sozietät (1792-1939) . Köln , 1983. ix, 215 p., [3] leaves of plates : ISBN 3-412-04282-X LC Card 84-117318
HD1486.S65 E54 1983

Quellen zur deutschen Wirtschafts- und Sozialgeschichte im 19. Jahrhundert bis zur Reichsgründung. Quellen zur deutschen Wirtschafts- und Sozialgeschichte von der Reichsgründung bis zum ersten Weltkrieg /. Darmstadt , 1985. xviii, 553 p. : ISBN 3-534-07561-7 LC Card 85-229315
HC285 .Q45 1985

Quellen zur deutschen Wirtschafts- und Sozialgeschichte von der Reichsgründung bis zum ersten Weltkrieg / herausgegeben von Walter Steitz. Darmstadt : Wissenschaftliche Buchgesellschaft, 1985. xviii, 553 p. : ill. ; 23 cm. (Ausgewählte Quellen zur deutschen Geschichte der Neuzeit, 0571-9178 . Bd. 37) Continues: Quellen zur deutschen Wirtschafts- und Sozialgeschichte im 19. Jahrhundert bis zur Reichsgründung. Bibliography: p. [535]-549. Includes index. ISBN 3-534-07561-7 LC Card 85-229315
1. Germany - Economic conditions - Sources. 2. Germany - Social conditions - Sources. 3. Germany - Industries - History - Sources. I. Steitz, Walter. II. Title: Quellen zur deutschen Wirtschafts- und Sozialgeschichte im 19. Jahrhundert bis zur Reichsgründung. III. Series.
HC285 .Q45 1985

Quellen zur Geschichte der deutschen Gewerkschaftsbewegung im 20. Jahrhundert . (Bd. 3) Die Gewerkschaften von der Stabilisierung bis zur Weltwirtschaftskrise, 1924-1930 /. Köln , c1986. 2 v. (1586 p.) ; ISBN 3-7663-0902-1 (Bd. 1) LC Card 87-123987
HD6694 .Q44 1985 Bd. 3

Quellen zur Geschichte des Deutschen Industrie- und Handelstages in Kammerarchiven, 1861 bis 1918 /. Reininghaus, Wilfried. Bonn , 1986. 158 p. : ISBN 3-925925-01-5 LC Card 87-408272 DDC 354.430082/09 19
HF308 .R343 1986

Quellen zur Geschichte Unnas und der Grafschaft Mark .
(Bd. 1) Mark (Grafschaft) Schatzbuch der Grafschaft Mark, 1486 /. Unna , 1986. 176 p. ; ISBN 3-87298-042-4 LC Card 87-116701 DDC 336.2/00943/55 19
HJ2110.5.M36 M37 1986

Queremos hechos /. Flores Domínguez, David. México, D.F. , c1982. 154 p. ; ISBN 968-7163-01-1 LC Card 83-142817
HC135 .F54 1982

Querol Bellido, Vicente. Herrero Suazo, Santiago. Técnicas presupuestarias en la administración pública /. Alcalá de Henares-Madrid, España [1984?] 382 p. : ISBN 84-7351-173-5 LC Card 85-185202
HJ1248 .H47 1984

Quesada Pérez, Felino. El Sistema de dirección y planificación de la economía en las empresas. La Habana , 1981. xi, 203 p. : LC Card 83-212653
HC152.5 .S57 1981

Quesnay, François, 1694-1774.
MAXIMES GÉNÉRALES DU GOUVERNEMENT ÉCONOMIQUE D'UN ROYAUME AGRICOLE.
Lluch, Ernest, 1937- Acaecimientos de Manuel Belgrano, fisiócrata, y su traducción de las "Máximas generales del gobierno económico de un reyno agricultor" de François Quesnay /. Madrid , 1984. 107 p. ; ISBN 84-7232-332-3 LC Card 85-179398
HB159 .L58 1984

QUESNAY, FRANÇOIS, 1694-1774.
Vaggi, Gianni. The economics of François Quesnay /. Durham , 1987. xv, 247 p. : ISBN 0-8223-0757-X LC Card 87-3549 DDC 330.15/2 19
HB105.Q5 V34 1987

Quest for gold /. Wattone, Mike, 1939- Scarborough, W.A. , 1985. 103 p. : ISBN 0-949731-03-X (pbk.) LC Card 86-142484 DDC 338.2/741/09941 19
HD9536.A83 C669 1985
NYPL [JLE 87-662]

Questão agrária e agroindústria /. Amaro, Antonio Ambrosio. Brasília, DF [1986] 13 p. ; LC Card 87-403237 DDC 338.1/881 19
HD1873 .A49 1986

A questão do bóia-fria /. Incao, Maria da Conceição d'. São Paulo-Brasil , 1984. 93 p. : LC Card 85-187274
HD5856.B6 I53 1984

A questão energética /. Castanho Filho, Eduardo Pires. São Paulo , 1984. 15 p. ; LC Card 86-159794
HD9502.A2 C385 1984

A questão fundiária /. Ferreira, Benedito, 1932- Brasília , 1986. 171 p. ; LC Card 86-229678
HD496 .F42 1986

Questão fundiária (ocupação das terras brasileiras) Ferreira, Benedito, 1932- A questão fundiária /. Brasília , 1986. 171 p. ; LC Card 86-229678
HD496 .F42 1986

A Questão Nordeste : estudos sobre formação histórica, desenvolvimento e processos políticos e ideológicos / Sílvio Maranhão, organizador ; Sílvio Maranhão ... [et al.]. Rio de Janeiro-RJ : Paz e Terra, 1984. 137 p. ; 21 cm. (Coleção Estudos sobre o Nordeste . vol. 16) Includes papers presented at the Seminário "Nordeste--Estrutura Econômica e Social, Desenvolvimento e Processos Políticos" organized by the Curso de mestrado em sociologia, Programa Integrado de Mestrado em Economia e Sociologia, Universidade Federal de Pernambuco, and held in Recife, 1982. Includes bibliographical references. LC Card 84-191031
1. Brazil, Northeast - Economic conditions - Congresses. 2. Brazil, Northeast - Social conditions - Congresses. 3. Brazil, Northeast - Politics and government - Congresses. 4. Regional development - Brazil, Northeast - Congresses. I. Maranhão, Sílvio. II. Seminário "Nordeste--Estrutura Econômica e Social, Desenvolvimento e Processos Políticos" (1982 : Recife, Brazil). III. PIMES (Program). IV. Series: Coleção Estudos sobre o Nordeste , v. 16.
HC188.N6 Q47 1984

Questers . Kanchier, Carole. Saratoga, Calif. , c1987. xi, 225 p. ; ISBN 0-88247-767-6 (pbk.) : LC Card 87-60351 DDC 658.4/09 19
HF5384 .K36 1987

La Questione demaniale in Terra d'Otranto nel XIX secolo : catalogo della mostra, Lecce, Museo provinciale Sigismondo Castromediano, 15 dicembre 1984-30 gennaio 1985. [Roma] : Ministero per i beni culturali e ambientali ; [Lecce] : Archivio di stato di Lecce, [1985?] 183 p., [6] leaves of plates : ill. (some col.) ; 21 x 22 cm. Bibliography: p. 178. LC Card 86-180857
1. Land tenure - Italy - Otranto Region - History - 19th century - Sources - Exhibitions. I. Italy. Ministero per i beni culturali e ambientali. II. Archivio di Stato di Lecce. III. Museo provinciale Sigismondo Castromediano.
HD680.O87 Q47 1985

La Questione meridionale oggi / Alatri ... [et al.] ; a cura di Vincenzo Guarrasi. Caltanissetta : S. Sciascia, 1985. 186 p. ; 20 cm. (Studi dell'Istituto Gramsci siciliano, 0518-4053 . 4) LC Card 86-214162
1. Italy, Southern - Economic conditions - Congresses. 2. Italy, Southern - Social conditions - Congresses. I. Alatri, Paolo. II. Guarrasi, Vincenzo. III. Series.
HC307.S69 Q47 1985

QUESTIONING.
Leeds, Dorothy. Smart questions . New York , c1987. x, 309 p. ; ISBN 0-07-036996-8 LC Card 86-27469 DDC 658.4/52 19
HD38 .L3867 1987

QUESTIONNAIRES.
Grootaert, Christiaan, 1950- Measuring and analyzing levels of living in developing countries . Washington, D.C., U. S.A. , c1986. x, 139 p. : ISBN 0-8213-0758-4 (pbk.) LC Card 86-5611 DDC 339.4/7/091724 19
HD7067 .G76 1986b

Questions and recommendations on the telephone [videorecording] / McGraw-Hill Training Systems ; [produced by] CRM Productions, Inc. ; script, Murray Krow. Del Mar, CA : McGraw-Hill Training Systems, 1987. 1 videocassette (13 min.) : sd., col. + 1 leader's guide. Title from data sheet. Telemarketing/sales classes and senior high school through college students. Issued as U-matic 3/4 in. or VHS 1/2 in. Teaches specific steps that lead to a successful sale over the telephone. By following a specific line of questioning, development of strategy, and understanding of information gathered, the telemarketing representative learns how to make a good recommendation to the customer. LC Card 87-700084 DDC 658.8 11
1. Telemarketing. 2. Telephone selling. 3. Telephone etiquette. I. McGraw-Hill Training Systems (Firm). II. CRM Productions.
HF5415.1265

Quibrera Matienzo, Enrique. La informática nacional : primeras aproximaciones / Enrique Quibrera Matienzo. [Xochimilco, Mexico] : Universidad Autónoma Metropolitana-Xochimilco, División de Ciencias Sociales y Humanidades, Departamento de Educación y Comunicación, Taller de Investigación para la Comunicación Masiva, 1984. 133 p. ; 27 cm. (Cuadernos del TICOM . no. 32) Includes bibliographical references. LC Card 86-124964 DDC 338.4/7004/0972 19
1. Computer industry - Mexico. 2. Electronic industries - Mexico. I. Title. II. Series.
HD9696.C63 M617 1984

Quick and easy guide to learning Lotus 1-2-3. Wolf, Douglas, 1948- Compute!'s quick & easy guide to learning Lotus 1-2-3 /. Greensboro, N.C. , c1987. vi, 139 p. : ISBN 0-87455-106-4 (pbk.) : LC Card 87-163385 DDC 005.36/9 19
HF5548.4.L67 W65 1987

Quick & easy guide to learning Lotus 1-2-3. Wolf, Douglas, 1948- Compute!'s quick & easy guide to learning Lotus 1-2-3 /. Greensboro, N.C. , c1987. vi, 139 p. : ISBN 0-87455-106-4 (pbk.) : LC Card 87-163385 DDC 005.36/9 19
HF5548.4.L67 W65 1987

Quick, James C. Work stress . New York , 1987. xvii, 329 p. : ISBN 0-275-92329-0 (alk. paper) : LC Card 86-30636 DDC 616.85/2 19
HF5548.85 .W67 1987

Quick, Rolf H. Informationsprozesse auf spekulativen Märkten : eine Analyse des Terminkontrakthandels / Rolf H. Quick. Thun : H. Deutsch, c1984. vii, 291 p. : ill. ; 21 cm. (Reihe Wirtschaftswissenschaften, 0253-1488 . Bd. 300) Bibliography: p. 282-291. ISBN 3-87144-790-0 : LC Card 84-159793
1. Forward exchange. 2. Commodity exchanges. 3. Uncertainty. I. Title. II. Series.
HG3853 .Q53 1984

Quick solutions . Quick, Thomas L. New York , c1987. xi, 377 p. ; ISBN 0-471-85229-5 LC Card 87-10540 DDC 658.4/03 19
HD30.29 .Q53 1987

Quick, Thomas L. Quick solutions : 500 people problems managers face and how to solve them / Thomas L. Quick. New York : Wiley, c1987. xi, 377 p. ; 24 cm. Includes index. ISBN 0-471-85229-5 LC Card 87-10540 DDC 658.4/03 19
1. Problem solving. 2. Management. I. Title. II. Title: 500 people problems managers face and how to solve them. III. Title: Five hundred people problems managers face and how to solve them.
HD30.29 .Q53 1987

Quien es quien en la empresa mexicana. 1a ed. México : Quien es Quien en la Empresa Mexicana, 1985. 381 p. ; 29 cm. On cover: Who is who in Mexican business. LC Card 86-190341
1. Businessmen - Mexico - Biography. I. Title: Who is who in Mexican business.
HF3234.5 .Q54 1985

Quijano, José Manuel. Finanzas, desarrollo económico y penetración extranjera / José Manuel Quijano, Hilda Sánchez, Fernando Antía. 1a ed. Puebla, Pue. : Universidad Autónoma de Puebla, 1985. 395 p. : ill. ; 21 cm. (Colección Pensamiento económico . 2) "Problemas financieros de México y América Latina"--Cover. Includes bibliographical references. LC Card 86-112589 DDC 332/.0972 19
1. Finance - Mexico - History. 2. Banks and banking - Mexico - History. 3. Debts, External - Mexico -

History. 4. Finance - Latin America. 5. Banks and banking, Foreign - Latin America. I. Sánchez Martínez, Hilda. II. Antía, Fernando. III. Title. IV. Series.
HG185.M6 Q55 1985 ***NYPL [JLD 86-2195]***

Quilitzsch, Siegmar.
Die DDR in der Welt des Sozialismus /. Berlin , 1985. 237 p. ; LC Card 85-188821 DDC 335.43/09431 19
HX280.5.A6 D38 1985 ***NYPL [JLD 87-1167]***

Die sozialistische Gemeinschaft zu Beginn der 80er Jahre : Haupttendenzen ihrer Entwicklung und Politik / Siegmar Quilitzsch, Erhard Crome.1. Aufl. Berlin : Staatsverlag der Deutschen Demokratischen Republik, 1984. 141 p. : ill. ; 22 cm. (Blickpunkt Weltpolitik) Includes bibliographical references. LC Card 84-180106
1. Council for Mutual Economic Assistance. I. Crome, Erhard. II. Title.
HC243.5 .Q55 1984

Quilligan, James B. Logue, John, 1947- Buyout! . [Kent, Ohio] [1986] vi, 98 p. : ISBN 0-933522-15-0 (pbk.) LC Card 86-623028 DDC 658.1/6 19
HD2746.5 .L64 1986

Quin, Claude. France. Conseil économique et social. L'évolution des transports urbains de voyageurs face aux nouvelles technologies . [Paris] [1986] 184 p. in various pagings : LC Card 86-179126
HE4764 .F73 1986

Quinke, Hermann. Microanalytic simulation models to support social and financial policy /. Amsterdam ; New York : xvii, 553 p. : ISBN 0-444-87876-9 (U. S.) LC Card 85-25231 DDC 361.6/0724 19
HD87 .M52 1986 ***NYPL [JLD 86-3485]***

Quinn, Daniel J. Skov, Paul B. Strategy, analysis, and decisions . Menlo Park, Calif. (333 Ravenswood Ave., Menlo Park 94025-3476) , c1985. 40 p. : LC Card 87-119164 DDC 658.4/012
HD30.28 .S49 1985

Quinn, Dennis Patrick, 1955- Restructuring the automobile industry : a study of firms and states in modern capitalism / Dennis Patrick Quinn. New York : Columbia University Press, 1988. p. cm. (Columbia studies in business, government, and society) Bibliography: p. Includes index. ISBN 0-231-06524-8 LC Card 87-15919 DDC 338.4/76292/0941 19
1. Automobile industry and trade - United States. 2. Automobile industry and trade - Great Britain. 3. Industry and state - United States. 4. Industry and state - Great Britain. I. Title. II. Series.
HD9710.U52 Q56 1988

Quinn, James Brian, 1928- The strategy process : concepts, contexts, and cases / James Brian Quinn, Henry Mintzberg, Robert M. James. Englewood Cliffs, N.J. : Prentice-Hall, c1988. p. cm. Bibliography: p. Includes index. ISBN 0-13-850892-5 LC Card 87-1160 DDC 658.4/012 19
1. Strategic planning. 2. Strategic planning - Case studies. I. Mintzberg, Henry. II. James, Robert M., 1922-. III. Title.
HD30.28 .Q53 1988

Quinn, Robert E. Organizational theory and public policy /. Beverly Hills, Calif. , c1983. 304 p. : ISBN 0-8039-2006-7 LC Card 83-9704 DDC 302.3/5 19
HD38 .O75 1983 ***NYPL [JLD 87-1123]***

Quiñones Rodríguez, Federico, 1940- Sindicalismo y política en Puerto Rico : (ideas y opiniones) / Federico Quiñones Rodríguez. [Río Piedras, P.R.] : Editorial Edil, [c1977] 147 p., [4] p. of plates : ill. ; 20 cm. Articles previously published in La Hora, 1973-1974. ISBN 84-399-6989-9 LC Card 82-159544
1. Trade-unions - Puerto Rico. 2. Trade-unions - Puerto Rico - Political activity. 3. Strikes and lockouts - Puerto Rico. I. Title.
HD6592 .Q56 1977

Quintana Roo : organización espacial : trabajo / realizado por el Departamento de Geografía Económica del Instituto de Geografía de la Universidad Nacional Autónoma de México, a solicitud del Centro de Investigaciones de Quintana Roo, A.C. Puerto Morelos, Q.R. : CIQRO, 1980. iv, 203 p., [32] leaves of plates : ill., maps ; 28 cm. Bibliography: p. 193-197. LC Card 84-222175
1. Quintana Roo (Mexico : State) - Economic conditions. 2. Land use - Mexico - Quintana Roo (State). 3. Physical geography - Mexico - Quintana Roo (State). I. Universidad Nacional Autónoma de México. Departamento de Geografía Económica. II. CIQRO (Organization).
HC137.Q5 Q55 1980

QUINTANA ROO (MEXICO : STATE) - ECONOMIC CONDITIONS.
Proyecto EI-5-3 . México, D.F. [1977] ca. 150 p. : LC Card 82-119251
HC137.Q5 P76 1977

Quintana Roo . Puerto Morelos, Q.R. , 1980. iv, 203 p., [32] leaves of plates : LC Card 84-222175
HC137.Q5 Q55 1980

Quintano, Claudio. Il sistema industriale del Molise / di Claudio Quintano. Bologna : Il Mulino, c1986. 106 p. : ill., maps ; 22 cm. (Quaderni de "L'Industria" . 30) Bibliography: p. 99-106. ISBN 88-15-01163-3 : LC Card 86-214879
1. Molise (Italy) - Industries. 2. Molise (Italy) - Economic conditions. I. Series: Quaderni de L'Industria (Società editrice Il Mulino) , 30. II. Title.
HC307.M64 Q56 1986

Quintas reuniones técnicas de información, evaluación y perspectivas de las empresas / coordinadas por Corpalmar, San Mateo, Edo. Aragua, Venezuela, 29 al 30 de junio de 1984. [Caracas, Venezuela] : Central El Palmar, [1984?] 245 p. : ill. ; 22 cm. Spine title: Memoria. LC Card 87-404408 DDC 338.8/6/09877 19
1. Central El Palmar (Caracas, Venezuela) - Management. 2. Holding companies - Venezuela - Management. I. Central El Palmar (Caracas, Venezuela). II. Title: Memoria.
HD2843.Z75 C467 1984

Quirk, James P. The choice of discount rate applicable to government resource use : theory and limitations / James P. Quirk, Katsuaki L. Terasawa ; prepared for the Director, Program Analysis and Evaluation. Santa Monica, CA : Rand, [1987] xviii, 52 p. : 1 ill. ; 23 cm. "December 1987." "R-3464-PA&E" Bibliography: p. 47-52. ISBN 0-8330-0849-8 (pbk.) LC Card 87-9867 DDC 336.3/9 19
1. Expenditures, Public. 2. Public investments - Evaluation. I. Terasawa, Katsuaki. II. United States. Office of the Assistant Secretary of Defense (Program Analysis and Evaluation). III. Title.
HJ7451 .Q57 1987

Quirk, Peter J. Floating exchange rates in developing countries . Washington, D.C. , 1987. v, 43 p. : ISBN 0-939934-89-2 (pbk.) : LC Card 87-3025 DDC 332.4/56/091724 19
HG3877 .F58 1987

Quit your job! . Levinson, Jay Conrad. New York , c1987. 216 p. ; ISBN 0-396-08882-1 LC Card 87-15545 DDC 650.1 19
HF5384 .L48 1987

Quito. Casa de la Cultura Ecuatoriana. see **Casa de la Cultura Ecuatoriana.**

QUOTAS, IMPORT. see **IMPORT QUOTAS.**

Qureahi, Sarfraz Khan. Some aspects of agricultural price and taxation policies in Pakistan /. Islamabad, Pakistan [1985] x, 223 p. ; LC Card 86-930932 DDC 338.1/8 19
HD2075.5 .S66 1985

Qureshi, S. M. Moin. Social security scheme / by S.M. Moin Qureshi. Karachi : Public Relations Wing-cum-Training & Research Institute, Sind Employees' Social Security Institution, 1984. 146 p. : ill. ; 22 cm. Bibliography: p. 145-146. LC Card 85-932136 DDC 368.4/009549/1 19
1. Social security - Pakistan. I. Title.
HD7220.5 .Q73 1984

R & D management systems in Japanese industry / edited by Hajime Eto and Konomu Matsui. Amsterdam ; New York : North Holland : ix, 331 p. : ill. ; 24 cm. Includes bibliographies. ISBN 0-444-86808-9 (U. S.) LC Card 83-20489 DDC 658.5/7/0952 19
1. Technological innovations - Japan - Addresses, essays, lectures. 2. Research, Industrial - Japan - Addresses, essays, lectures. I. Etō, Hajime, 1935-. II. Matsui, Konomu, 1931-. III. Title: R and D management systems in Japanese industry.
HD45 .R2 1984 ***NYPL [JLD 87-107]***

R. A. T. P. see **Régie autonome des transports parisiens.**

R.A.T.P. plan d'entreprise 1983/1987. Régie autonome des transports parisiens. RATP plan d'entreprise 1983/1987. Paris [1982] 164 p. : LC Card 83-203335
HE4769.P33 R47 1982

R and D management systems in Japanese industry. R & D management systems in Japanese industry /. Amsterdam ; New York : ix, 331 p. : ISBN 0-444-86808-9 (U. S.) LC Card 83-20489 DDC 658.5/7/0952 19
HD45 .R2 1984 ***NYPL [JLD 87-107]***

R & R Newkirk.
Investment planning. Chicago, IL , c1987. p. cm. ISBN 0-88462-694-6 LC Card 87-15222 DDC 332.6/78 19
HG179 .I488 1987

Michigan study manual for life and accident and health insurance. Chicago , c1987. v, 56 p. ; ISBN 0-88462-729-2 (unb.) LC Card 87-18552 DDC 368.3/009774 19
HG8101.M5 M53 1987

New Jersey study manual for life and accident and health insurance. Chicago , c1987. p. cm. ISBN 0-88462-726-8 LC Card 87-13103 DDC 368.3/009749 19
HG8101.N48 N47 1987

New York study manual for life and accident and health insurance. Chicago , c1987. p. cm. ISBN 0-88462-725-X LC Card 87-13102 DDC 368.3/009747 19
HG8101.N49 N47 1987

Principles of health & disability insurance selling. Chicago , c1987. 179 p. ; ISBN 0-88462-700-4 (pbk.) LC Card 87-16281 DDC 368.3/8/00688 19
HG9396 .P75 1987

Survey of advanced sales. Chicago , c1987. v, 214 p. : ISBN 0-88462-703-9 (pbk.) LC Card 87-13112 DDC 368/.0068/8 19
HG8091 .S87 1987

Total needs selling. Chicago , c1986. viii, 174 p. : ISBN 0-88462-564-8 (pbk.) LC Card 86-23542 DDC 368.3/2/00688 19
HG8877 .T68 1986

R C A. see **Radio Corporation of America.**

R. C. Fuller Associates. Strategic real estate submarkets . Denver, Colo. (1009 Grant St., Suite 304, Denver 80203) , c1986. 195 p. : LC Card 86-228061 DDC 333.33/22/0973 19
HD255 .S77 1986

R.D., frente a su propia realidad . Castro, Aníbal de. [Santo Domingo, Dominican Republic? , 1986] 450, [2] p. ; LC Card 87-115306 DDC 330.97293/054 19
HC153.5 .C383 1986

R. E. A. see **United States. Rural Electrification Administration.**

R. F. E. see **Radio Free Europe.**

R. g. W. see **Sovet ėkonomicheskoĭ vzaimopomoshchi.**

R. K. W. see **Rationalisierungs-Kuratorium der Deutschen Wirtschaft.**

R. MEES & ZOONEN, FA. (ROTTERDAM, NETHERLANDS) - HISTORY.
Mees en Chabot, twee kassiers te Rotterdam . Delft , c1986. 87 p. : ISBN 90-70879-40-9 : LC Card 86-205783
HG3120.R62 M44 1986

Rǣngngān Thai. Krung Thēp : Samākhom Sangkhomsāt hǣng Prathēt Thai, 2528 [1985] 53 p. ; 31 cm. (Čhunlasān wichākān = Monograph . chabap thī 1, pi thi 1 (Phrtsačhikāyon 2528) In Thai. On Thai labor force; contributed articles. Includes bibliographies. CONTENTS. - Botwikhrǫ b LC Card 86-915944
1. Labor supply - Thailand. I. Samret Siphongkun. Botwikhrǫ b
HD5822.55.A6 R35 1985

R.P.M. realize your power to motivate /. Sanders, Mary. Farmington Hills, Mich. , c1986. 153 p., [2] p. of plates : ISBN 0-9616833-0-9 (pbk.) LC Card 87-111586

DDC 658.3/14 19
HF5549.5.M63 S26 1986

R.S. Wallace Station, East Peoria, Illinois . Urban Land Institute. Washington, D.C. (1090 Vermont Ave., N.W., Washington 20005) , c1986. 36 p. : LC Card 86-216045 DDC 333.77/17/0977352 19
HD268.E26 U73 1986

R. V. H. P. [i. e. Rada vzájemné hospodářské pomici] see **Sovet ėkonomicheskoĭ vzaimopomoshchi.**

Raab, Steven S., 1949- The blueprint for franchising a business / Steven S. Raab with Gregory Matusky. New York : Wiley, c1987. ix, 244 p. : ill. ; 25 cm. Includes index. ISBN 0-471-85617-7 LC Card 87-15932 DDC 658.8/7 19
1. Franchises (Retail trade) - United States. 2. Franchises (Retail trade) - Law and legislation - United States. I. Matusky, Gregory. II. Title.
HF5429.235.U5 R32 1987

Raabe, John. Lenchek, Tom. Superinsulated design and construction . New York , c1987. ix, 172 p. : ISBN 0-442-26051-2 : LC Card 86-7089 DDC 693.8/32 19
TJ163.5.D86 L46 1987 *NYPL [JSF 87-235]*

Raabe-Zimmermann, Jürgen, 1950- Sonnewald, Bernd, 1947- Die "Berliner Linie" und die Hausbesetzer-Szene /. Berlin , c1983. 149 p. ; ISBN 3-87061-170-7 LC Card 83-190228
HD7287.96.G32 B477 1983

Raad van Advies voor het Wetenschappelijk Onderzoek in het kader van Ontwikkelingssamenwerking (Netherlands) International dimension of development problems . Amsterdam , New York , 1984. 103 p. ; ISBN 0-444-85621-8 (pbk.) LC Card 85-209291 DDC 338.9 19
HD75 .I59 1984 *NYPL [JLE 86-1391]*

RABBIT MEAT INDUSTRY - HUNGARY. Szajkó, Pál. A nyúlhústermelés és export gazdasági problémái /. Budapest , 1985. 57 p. : ISBN 963-491-207-9 LC Card 86-196798
HD9438.R4 H97 1985

Rabelo, Genival. Brasil, país das oportunidades perdidas / Genival Rabelo. [Brazil : s.n.], 1977. 112 p. ; 21 cm. LC Card 85-210978
1. Brazil - Economic policy. 2. Brazil - Dependency on foreign countries. I. Title.
HC187 .R27 1977

Räber, Josef. Subventionen als volkswirtschaftliche und finanzwirtschaftliche Erscheinung, mit besonderer Berücksichtigung der schweizerischen Verhältnisse in den Nachkriegsjahren / Josef Räber. Winterthur : H. Schellenberg, 1965. xxvii, 191 p. : ill. ; 23 cm. Originally presented as the author's thesis (doctoral)--Hochschule St. Gallen für Wirtschafts- und Sozialwissenschaften. Bibliography: p. xvi-xxiv. LC Card 85-162566
1. Subsidies - Switzerland. 2. Subsidies. I. Title.
HD3646.S9 R33 1965

Rabier, Pascal. Regard sur la presse philatélique française : mémoire / présenté par Rabier Pascal. [Paris] : P. Rabier, 1986. 2 v. (586 p.) : ill. ; 30 cm. At head of title: Université de Paris II, Institut national de gestion des P.T.T. d'Evry. Bibliography: p. 216-219. Includes indexes. CONTENTS. - t. 1. Organisation, fonction, audience -- t. 2. Les publications commerciales depuis 1864. ISBN 2-9501543-0-1 (set) LC Card 87-166808
1. Postage-stamps - Collectors and collecting - France - Periodicals - Bibliography. 2. Postage-stamps - France - Collectors and collecting - France - Periodicals - Bibliography. I. Title.
HE6185.F8 R32 1986

Rabindra Bharati University. Dept. of Economics. Problems of urban unemployment. Calcutta , 1981. ix, 114 p. ; LC Card 83-907262 DDC 331.13/77/0954 19
HD5819 .P76 1981 *NYPL [JLF 86-1766]*

Rabino, Giovanni A. L'Analisi degli insediamenti umani e produttivi /. Milano, Italy , c1984. 295 p. : LC Card 84-179265 DDC 330.945/0928 19
HC305 .A6618 1984 *NYPL [JLD 86-3298]*

Rabinovich Woloshin, Catalina. El Mercado de capitales como instrumento de la política económica /. [Miraflores, Lima] [1987] 111 p. ; LC Card 87-169408 DDC 332.6/0985 19
HG5392 .M43 1987

Rabochaia molodezh' SSSR v period razvitogo sotsializma . Davidovich, IA. A. Moskva , 1985. 37 p. ; LC Card 86-187709
HD6276.S59 D38 1985

Rabochee dvizhenie v Belorussii v 1861-1904 gg. /. Bich, M. O. Minsk , 1983. 278 p. ; LC Card 83-182369
HD8529.B952 B52 1983
*NYPL [*QM 87-2378]*

Rabochee dvizhenie v Moldavii, 1895-fevral' 1917 g. : sbornik dokumentov / [redaktsionnaia kollegiia, Zhukov V.I., Ivanov IU.G. (otv. redaktor) ... et al.]. Kishinev : "Shtiintsa", 1985. 322 p. ; 23 cm. At head of title: Akademiia nauk Moldavskoĭ SSR. Institut istorii imeni IA.S. Grosula. Glavnoe arkhivnoe upravlenie pri Sovete Ministrov MSSR. TSentral'nyĭ gosudarstvennyĭ arkhiv MSSR. Summary in English and French. Includes bibliographical references and index. LC Card 86-100092
1. Labor and laboring classes - Moldavian S.S.R. - History - Sources. 2. Socialism - Moldavian S.S.R. - History - Sources. I. Zhukov, V. I. II. Ivanov, IUriĭ Grigor'evich. III. Institut istorii imeni akademika AN MSSR IA.S. Grosula. IV. Arkhiva Chentrale de Stat a RSS Moldoveneshti'.
HD8529.M57 R32 1985

Rabochee dvizhenie v razvitykh kapitalisticheskikh stranakh : problemy bor'by za demokratiiu v kontse 70-kh--nachale 80-kh godov / otvetstvennyĭ redaktor R.IA. Evzerov. Moskva : "Nauka", 1987. 268 p. ; 23 cm. At head of title: Akademiia nauk SSSR. Institut mezhdunarodnogo rabochego dvizheniia. Includes bibliographical references. LC Card 87-164460
1. Labor and laboring classes - Europe - Political activity. 2. Europe - Politics and government - 1945-. 3. Labor and laboring classes - United States - Political activity. 4. United States - Politics and government - 1977-. I. Evzerov, R. IA. II. Institut mezhdunarodnogo rabochego dvizheniia (Akademiia nauk SSSR).
HD8378 .R29 1987

Rabochee dvizhenie v Rossii v period imperializma : sbornik stateĭ / [redaktsionnaia kollegiia, Ivanova N.A., Kir'ianov IU.I., Tiutiukin S.V. (otv. red.)]. Moskva : Akademiia nauk SSSR, In-t istorii SSSR, 1982. 144 p. ; 20 cm. Includes bibliographies. LC Card 83-174879
1. Labor and laboring classes - Soviet Union - History. I. Tiutiukin, S. V. (Stanislav Vasil'evich). II. Institut istorii SSSR (Akademiia nauk SSSR).
HD8526 .R3112 1982

Rabochee i svobodnoe vremia v usloviiakh razvitogo sotsializma /. Maksimov, A. L. (Alekseĭ L'vovich) Moskva , 1981. 95 p. ; LC Card 82-104233
HD5195 .M34 1981

Rabochie dinastii Urala / I. Davydov ... [et al.]. Sverdlovsk : Sredne-Ural'skoe knizhnoe izd-vo, 1977. 340 p. : ill. ; 15 cm. CONTENTS. - V polnuiu meru / I. Davydov -- Iz shchedrykh ruk / B. Batarchuk -- Gorshchiki Kitaevy / A. Fomenko -- Dobytchiki gornogo l'na / V. Pankratov -- Ural'skiĭ kharakter / A. Vorob'ev. LC Card 81-170557
1. Labor and laboring classes - Russian S.F.S.R. - Ural Mountains Region - Biography. I. Davydov, I. (Iosif).
HD8527.A1 R33 1977

Rabochie-moriaki Kaspiia . Guseĭnova, D. S. Baku , 1981. 113 p. ; LC Card 82-166385
HD8039.S42 C424 1981

Rabochie Sibiri v bor'be za sotsialisticheskuiu revoliutsiiu i postroenie sotsializma : sbornik nauchnykh trudov / [redaktsionnaia kollegiia Gushchina V.V. ... Zol'nikov D.M. (otvetstvennyĭ redaktor)]. Novosibirsk : Novosibirskiĭ gos. universitet, 1975. 119 p. ; 21 cm. At head of title: Ministerstvo vysshego i srednego spetsial'nogo obrazovaniia RSFSR. Novosibirskiĭ gosudarstvennyĭ universitet. Includes bibliographies. LC Card 85-187793
1. Labor and laboring classes - Russian S.F.S.R. - Siberia - History. I. Gushchina, V. V. II. Zol'nikov, D. M. III. Novosibirskiĭ gosudarstvennyĭ universitet.
HD8529.S652 R283 1975

Rabochie zolotodobyvaiushcheĭ promyshlennosti Vostochnoĭ Sibiri 1921--1937 gg. /. Khatylaev, M. M. (Mikhail Mikhaĭlovich) Novosibirsk , 1986. 171, [4] p. ; LC Card 86-231511
HD8039.M74 S545 1986

Rabochiĭ klass i profsoiuzy Frantsii v bor'ybe protiv monopoliĭ, 1968-1981 gody /. Kolomiĭtsev, Valentin Fedorovich. Moskva , 1981. 173 p. ; LC Card 82-134380
HD8435 .K65 1981

Rabochiĭ klass i stroitel'stvo sotsializma v stranakh TSentral'noĭ i IUgo-Vostochnoĭ Evropy / [redkollegiia, A.I. Nedorezov (otvetstvennyĭ redaktor), M.G. Sazina, N.S. Dolgikh]. Moskva : Izd-vo "Nauka", 1977. 382 p. ; 22 cm. On page preceding t.p.: Akademiia nauk SSSR. Institut slavianovedeniia i balkanistiki. Includes bibliographical references. LC Card 81-174150
1. Labor and laboring classes - Europe, Eastern. 2. Socialism - Europe, Eastern. 3. Europe, Eastern - Economic conditions - 1945-. I. Nedorezov, A. I. (Aleksandr Ivanovich). II. Sazina, M. G. III. Dolgikh, N. S. IV. Institut slavianovedeniia i balkanistiki (Akademiia nauk SSSR).
HD8376.5 .R33 1977

Rabochiĭ klass Ispanii boretsia . Baranova, T. N. (Tat'iana Nikolaevna) Moskva , 1978. 151 p. ; LC Card 81-147187
HD8586.5 .B37 1978

Rabochiĭ klass Narodnoĭ Vengrii . Shman'ko, G. I. Kiev , 1982. 165 p. ; LC Card 83-143426
HD8420.5 .S55 1982

Rabochiĭ klass Shri Lanki . Voronin, S. V. Moskva , 1979. 278, [2] p. ; LC Card 81-147848
HD8670.8 .V67 1979

Rabochiĭ klass Sibiri : 1961-1980 gg. / [redkollegiia toma E.V. Vasil'evskaia ... I.I. Komogortsev (otv. redaktor) ... et al.]. Novosibirsk : Izd-vo "Nauka," Sibirskoe otd-nie, 1986. 355 p., [16] p. of plates : ill., ports. ; 25 cm. (Istoriia rabochego klassa Sibiri) On p. preceding t.p.: Akademiia nauk SSSR. Sibirskoe otdelenie. Institut istorii, filologii i filosofii. Includes bibliographical references and index. LC Card 86-211294
1. Labor supply - Russian S.F.S.R. - Siberia. 2. Siberia (R.S.F.S.R.) - Industries. 3. Siberia (R.S.F.S.R.) - Social conditions. I. Vasil'evskaia, E. V. (Emiliia Viktorovna). II. Komogortsev, I. I. (Ivan Ivanovich). III. Institut istorii, filologii i filosofii (Akademiia nauk SSSR). IV. Series.
HD5797.S5 R33 1986

Rabochiĭ klass Ukrainskoĭ SSR : traditsii i sovremennost' / [avtory IU.IU Kondufor ... et al. ; otvetstvennyĭ redaktor IU.IU. Kondufor]. Kiev : Nauk. dumka, 1986. 238 p. ; 25 cm. On p. preceding t.p.: Akademiia nauk Ukrainskoĭ SSR. Institut istorii. Bibliography: p. 230-[237] LC Card 86-155918
1. Labor and laboring classes - Ukraine - History - 20th century. 2. Ukraine - Economic conditions - 1918-. I. Kondufor, IUriĭ IUr'evich. II. Instytut istoriï (Akademiia nauk Ukraïns'koï RSR).
HD8529.U42 R33 1986

Rabochiĭ klass Uzbekistana v usloviiakh nauchno-tekhnicheskoĭ revoliutsii /. Akhunova, M. A. Tashkent , 1984. 181 p. ; LC Card 85-232015
HD6331.2.S652 U93 1984

Rabochiĭ klass v proshlom i nastoiashchem : problemy istorii i istoriografii / [redaktsionnaia kollegiia T.T. Timofeev (otvetstvennyĭ redaktor) ... et al.]. Moskva : Izd-vo "Nauka", 1984, c1983. 255 p. ; 21 cm. At head of title: Akademiia nauk SSSR. Institut mezhdunarodnogo rabochego dvizheniia. Includes bibliographical references. LC Card 84-169518
1. Labor and laboring classes - History - 20th century. 2. Economic history - 20th century. 3. Labor and laboring classes - France - History - 20th century. 4. France - Economic conditions - 1918-. I. Timofeev, Timur Timofeevich. II. Institut mezhdunarodnogo rabochego dvizheniia (Akademiia nauk SSSR).
HD4854 .R273 1984

Rabotnicheskoto profsŭiuzno dvizhenie vŭv Varnenski okrŭg / [redaktor, Ivanka Bogdanova]. Sofiia : Profizdat, 1985. 348 p., [16] p. of plates : ill., facsims., ports. ; 21 cm. Includes bibliographical references. LC Card 86-111781
1. Labor and laboring classes - Bulgaria - Varnenski okrŭg - History. 2. Trade-unions - Bulgaria - Varnenski okrŭg - History. 3. Socialism - Bulgaria - Varnenski okrŭg - History. 4. Varnenski okrŭg (Bulgaria) - Economic conditions. I. Bogdanova, Ivanka.
HD8629.V372 R37 1985

Rabotniki khoroshie i plokhie /. Aitov, Nariman Abdrakhmanovich. Moskva , 1983. 134 p. ; LC Card 84-178331
HD6957.S65 A37 1983

Rabushka, Alvin. The new China : comparative economic development in Mainland China, Taiwan, and Hong Kong / Alvin Rabushka. San Francisco : Pacific Research Institute for Public Policy ; Boulder, Colo. : Westview Press, 1987. xii, 254 p. ; 23 cm. "Ching chi fa chan"--Cover. Bibliography: p. 233-242. Includes index. ISBN 0-936488-15-8 (pbk. : alk. paper) LC Card 87-10574 DDC 338.951 19
1. China - Economic policy - 1976-. 2. Taiwan - Economic policy - 1975-. 3. Hong Kong - Economic policy. I. Pacific Research Institute for Public Policy. II. Title.
HC427.92 .R33 1987

Race, class, and state housing . Henderson, J. W. (Jeffrey William), 1947- Aldershot, Hants, England ;Brookfield, Vt. , c1987. xxiii, 331 p. : ISBN 0-566-00785-1 :
NYPL [JLD 87-1476]

RACE DISCRIMINATION - GREAT BRITAIN.
Jenkins, Richard, 1952- Racism and recruitment . Cambridge [Cambridgeshire] , New York , 1986. xi, 281 p. ; ISBN 0-521-32028-3 LC Card 85-17483 DDC 331.13/3/0941 19
HG4903.5.G7 J46 1986
NYPL [JLE 86-3305]

Little, Alan. Loading the law . London , 1982. 67 p. ; ISBN 0-902355-98-8 (pbk.)
NYPL [JLD 87-1941]

Race, ethnicity, and minority housing in the United States / edited by Jamshid A. Momeni ; foreword by Joe T. Darden. New York : Greenwood Press, 1986. xxv, 224 p. ; 24 cm. (Contributions in ethnic studies, 0196-7088 . no. 16) Includes index. Bibliography: p.[217]-220. ISBN 0-313-24848-6 (lib. bdg. : alk. paper) LC Card 86-9971 DDC 363.5/9 19
1. Minorities - Housing - United States. 2. Discrimination in housing - United States. 3. Minorities - Housing - Government policy - United States. I. Momeni, Jamshid A., 1938-. II. Series.
HD7288.72.U5 R33 1986
NYPL [JLE 87-946]

RACE PREJUDICE. see **RACE DISCRIMINATION; RACISM.**

RACE PROBLEMS. see **RACE RELATIONS.**

RACE QUESTION. see **RACE RELATIONS.**

RACE RELATIONS - RELIGIOUS ASPECTS - CATHOLIC CHURCH.
United States Catholic Conference. Administrative Board. Divestment, disinvestment, and South Africa . Washington, D.C. , c1986. 36 p. ; ISBN 1-555-86137-7 (pbk.) LC Card 87-136857 DDC 332.6/7373/068 19
HG5851.A3 U55 1986

RACE RELATIONS - RELIGIOUS ASPECTS - CHRISTIANITY.
Williams, Oliver F. The apartheid crisis . San Francisco , 1986. xiv, 124 p. : ISBN 0-06-250951-9 (pbk.) : LC Card 85-45726 DDC 332.6/7373/068 19
HG5851.A3 W55 1986
NYPL [JLD 86-4023]

The race to the year 2000, our future. Baade, Fritz, 1893- [Wettlauf zum Jahre 2000. English.] Garden City, N.Y., 1962. xix, 246 p. LC Card 62-7600 DDC 330.9/04 19
HC59 .B2513 1962

Race, training, and employment /. Verma, Gajendra K. London , New York , 1987. vi, 134 p. : ISBN 1-85000-243-6 : LC Card 87-15470 DDC 331.3/46/0941 19
HD5715.5.G7 V47 1987

RACES OF MAN. see **ETHNOLOGY.**

RACETRACKS (AUTOMOBILE RACING)
Sport und Werbung, Präsenz und Erinnerungswirkung ausgewählter Werbeträger an Rennstrecken . München [1986] 70, lii, [iii] p. : LC Card 87-409557 DDC 659.13/42 19
HF5843 .S69 1986

Rachhpal Singh, 1944- Farm production in rainfed sub-mountainous Punjab / Rachhpal Singh. Delhi : B.R. Pub. Corp. ; New Delhi : Distributed by D.K. Publishers' Distributors, 1987. vi, 349 p. ; 23 cm. Revision of the author's thesis (Ph. D.--Punjab Agricultural University, Ludhiana) under the title: Farm production strategy under rainfed conditions for the sub-mountainous areas of the Punjab. Bibliography: p. [341]-345. Includes index. ISBN 81-7018-450-9 : LC Card 87-902161 DDC 338.1/0954/552 19
1. Agricultural productivity - India - Punjab. 2. Farm management - India - Punjab. 3. Crops and climate - India - Punjab. I. Title.
HD2075.P8 R33 1987

Rachidzadeh, Esfandiar. Le secteur rural et le développement économique : le cas de l'Iran / par Esfandiar Rachidzadeh. Genève : Service Rapide, 1978. ix, 389 p. : maps ; 23 cm. Thesis--Geneva. Bibliography: p. 354-389. LC Card 79-376015 DDC 338.1/0955
1. Agriculture - Economic aspects - Iran. 2. Agriculture, Cooperative - Iran. I. Title.
HD2065.2 .R3 *NYPL [JLE 80-2370]*

Rachlin, Robert, 1937- Return on investment strategies for decision-making / Robert Rachlin. New York : F. Watts, 1987. x, 306 p. : ill. ; 24 cm. (Advanced management skills) Spine title: ROI. Includes index. ISBN 0-531-15528-5 LC Card 87-10633 DDC 658.1/52 19
1. Capital investments - Evaluation. 2. Corporations - Finance. I. Title. II. Title: ROI. III. Series.
HG4028.C4 R255 1987

Rachman, Budhy Munawar. Indonesia dan masalah-masalah pembangunan /. [Jakarta] , 1986. viii, 277 p. : LC Card 87-940526
HC447 .I555936 1986

Rachman, David J.
Business today / David J. Rachman, Michael H. Mescon. 5th ed. New York : Random House, c1987. xxiii, 643 p. : ill. (some col.) ; 27 cm. Bibliography: p. 594-600. Includes indexes. ISBN 0-394-35114-2 LC Card 86-24784 DDC 658 19
1. Business. 2. Management - United States. I. Mescon, Michael H. II. Title.
HF5351 .R26 1987

Marketing today / David J. Rachman ; with cases by W. Wayne Talarzyk. 2nd ed. Chicago : Dryden Press, c1988. xxvii, 654 p. : col. ill. ; 26 cm. (The Dryden Press series in marketing) Bibliography: p. [615]-628. Includes indexes. ISBN 0-03-013573-7 (pbk.) LC Card 87-22239 DDC 658.8 19
1. Marketing. I. Title.
HF5415 .R2354 1988

Racines du présent, 0757-6366.
Godin, Francine. Bénin, 1972-1982 . Paris , c1986. 325 p. ; ISBN 2-85802-609-X LC Card 87-112975
HC1010 .G63 1986

Racionalidad campesina y cambio técnico /. Sotomayor, Octavio. Cusco , 1985. 23 p. ; LC Card 86-200944
HD1531.P4 S67 1985

Racism and recruitment . Jenkins, Richard, 1952- Cambridge [Cambridgeshire] , New York , 1986. xi, 281 p. ; ISBN 0-521-32028-3 LC Card 85-17483 DDC 331.13/3/0941 19
HG4903.5.G7 J46 1986
NYPL [JLE 86-3305]

RACISM - UNITED STATES.
Morse, Roberta. The Black female professional /. Washington, D.C. [1983] i, 48 p. ; LC Card 83-80187 DDC 305.4/8896073 19
HQ1426 .M88 1983 *NYPL [Sc F 86-230]*

RACISM - UNITED STATES - HISTORY.
Andolsen, Barbara Hilkert. "Daughters of Jefferson, daughters of bootblacks" . Macon, GA , c1986. xiv, 130 p. ; ISBN 0-86554-204-X : LC Card 86-816 DDC 305.4/2/0973 19
HQ1426 .A6827 1986 *NYPL [JLE 86-3359]*

Racjonalny podział przewozów ładunków między gałęzie transportu /. Blotko, Kazimierz. Warszawa , 1978. 126 p. ; LC Card 81-206824
HF5780.P7 B57 1978

RACKETEERING - UNITED STATES.
United States. President's Commission on Organized Crime. The edge . Washington, D.C. , 1985. 356 p. ; *NYPL [JLE 87-41]*

United States. President's Commission on Organized Crime. The edge . Washington, D.C. , 1986. xxii, 393 p. ;
NYPL [JLE 86-2671]

Rada, Juan F. La microelectrónica, la tecnología de la información y sus efectos en los países en vía de desarrollo / Juan F. Rada. 1a ed. México, D.F. : Programa de Ciencia y Tecnología para el Desarrollo, Colegio de México, c1983. 158 p. ; 17 cm. (Jornadas. 97) Includes bibliographical references. ISBN 968-12-0214-7 LC Card 85-243097
1. Electronic industries - Developing countries. 2. Electronic data processing - Developing countries. I. Title. II. Series.
HD9696.A3 D447 1983

Rada po vyvchenniu produktyvnykh syl URSR.
Kompleksnoe ispol'zovanie prirodnykh resursov . Kiev , 1985. 174 p. ; LC Card 86-175133
HC337.U5 K6372 1985

Territorial'naia organizatsiia prodovol'stvennogo kompleksa . Kiev , 1985. 163 p. ; LC Card 86-175134
HD9015.S653 U4755 1985

Territorial'nye osobennosti razmeshcheniia pishchevoĭ promyshlennosti USSR /. Kiev , 1982. 282 p. ; LC Card 83-197067
HD9015.S653 U476 1982

Vosproizvodstvo trudovykh resursov /. Kiev , 1984. 177, [3] p. ; LC Card 86-189052
HD5797.U37 V67 1984

Rada Wzajemnej Pomocy Gospodarczej. see **Sovet ėkonomicheskoĭ vzaimopomoshchi.**

Radaev, Valeriĭ Viktorovich.
Intensifikatsiia sotsialisticheskogo proizvodstva i khoziaĭstvennyĭ mekhanizm /. Moskva , 1984. 228 p. ; LC Card 84-247548
HC340.I52 I58 1984

Obshchestvennyĭ kharakter proizvodstva i sotsialisticheskaia sobstvennost' /. Moskva , 1985. 286 p. ; LC Card 85-173513
HC340.I52 O27 1985

Radar 33 : spring 1986 : based on surveys conducted in-- fall 1985, May 1, 1985 to October 22, 1985 (excluding July 3-9), spring 1986, October 30, 1985 to April 22, 1986 (excluding Dec. 25-31). Westfield, N.J. (111 Prospect St., Westfield 07090) : Statistical Research, <c1986- > <v. 2, pt. 1-2; v. 3, pt. 2 > ; 22 x 28 cm. Chiefly tables. CONTENTS. - -- v. 2. Network audiences to all commercials (including commercials within and outside of programs) projections and ratings for dayparts -- v. 3. Network audiences to commercials within programs (excluding commercials outside of programs), projections and ratings for dayparts. LC Card 86-218886 DDC 384.54/3 19
1. Radio audiences - United States - Statistics. I. Statistical Research, Inc.
HE8697.A8 R243 1986

Radchenko, V. V. (Viktor Vladimirovich) Modeli i metody resheniia zadach vzaimodeĭstviia ėkonomicheskikh sistem /. Novosibirsk , 1982. 160 p. ; LC Card 83-164468
HB137 .M6 1982

Radding, Cynthia.
[Acumulación originaria de capital agrario en Sonora]
La acumulación originaria de capital agrario en Sonora ; Registro de los archivos del Estado de Sonora / Cynthia Radding. [Hermosillo, Sonora] : Centro Regional del Noroeste, INAH, SEP, 1981. 90 p. : maps ; 28 cm. (Noroeste de México . no. 5) Cover title. Bibliography: p. 83. LC Card 82-118209
1. Land tenure - Mexico - Sonora (State) - History. 2. Sonora (Mexico : State) - History. 3. Archives - Mexico - Sonora (State) - Catalogs. I. Radding, Cynthia. Registro de los archivos del Estado de Sonora. 1981. II. Title. III. Series.
HD329.S6 R33 1981

Registro de los archivos del Estado de Sonora. 1981. Radding, Cynthia. [Acumulación originaria de capital agrario en Sonora.] La acumulación originaria de capital agrario en Sonora ; Registro de los archivos del Estado de Sonora / Cynthia Radding. [Hermosillo, Sonora] , 1981. 90 p. : LC Card 82-118209
HD329.S6 R33 1981

Raddock, David M. Assessing corporate political risk . Totowa, NJ , 1986. xvii, 212 p. ; ISBN 0-86598-114-0 LC Card 85-19618 DDC 658 19
HD61 .A87 1986 *NYPL [JLE 86-3102]*

RÅDET FOR TRAFIKSIKKERHEDSFORSKNING.
Virksomheden i årene 1981-1983 . Gentofte ,

København , 1984. 80 p. : ISBN 87-7327-022-9 LC Card 86-100414
HE5614.5.D4 V57 1984

Rådet for trafiksikkerhedsforskning (Denmark) Virksomheden i årene 1981-1983 . Gentofte , København , 1984. 80 p. : ISBN 87-7327-022-9 LC Card 86-100414
HE5614.5.D4 V57 1984

Radev, Georgi. Vŭznikvane, razvitie i zalez na oportiūnizma v bŭlgarskoto rabotnichesko dvizhenie, 1891/1948 /. Sofiia , 1986. 696 p. ; LC Card 86-200229
HD8628 .V89 1986

Radev, Ivan. 75 godini borba i sŭzidanie . Sofiia , 1985. 144 p. ; LC Card 86-195265
HD6784.M62 P762 1985

Radev, Simeon. Sotsialnata programa na partiiata-delo na trudoviia kolektiv / Simeon Radev, Dimitŭr Kamenov. 1. izd. Sofiia : Partizdat, 1984. 173 p. ; 16 cm. Includes bibliographical references. LC Card 84-172433
1. Labor policy - Bulgaria. 2. Bulgaria - Social policy. I. Kamenov, Dimitŭr. II. Title.
HD8626.5 .R32 1984

Radians'ka Ukraïna : sotsial'no-ekonomichnyĭ dovidnyk / [avtors'kyĭ kolektyv, V.I. Senchenko (kerivnyk) ... et al.]. Kyïv : Vyd-vo polit. lit-ry Ukraïny, 1985. 205 p., [2] p. of plates : ill. (some col.) ; 21 cm. Title in colophon: Sovetskaia Ukraina. LC Card 87-151437
1. Ukraine - Economic conditions - 1945-. 2. Ukraine - Social conditions - 1945-. I. Senchenko, Volodymyr Ivanovych. II. Title: Sovetskaia Ukraina.
HC337.U5 R215 1985

Radical aristocrats . Fuller, Ken. London , Atlantic Highlands, N.J. , 1985. 256 p. : ISBN 0-85315-649-2 (pbk.) : LC Card 86-214586 DDC 331.88/1138841322/09421 19
HD8039.M82 G74 1985

Radical economics.
Bhaduri, Amit. Macroeconomics . Houndmills, Basingstoke, Hampshire , 1986. xii, 278 p. : ISBN 0-333-29194-8 LC Card 86-673605
HB172.5 .B48x 1986b

Radical science essays / edited by Les Levidow. London : Free Association Books ; Atlantic Highlands, N.J. : Humanities Press International, 1986. 230 p. : ill. ; 22 cm. Includes bibliographies and indexes. CONTENTS. - Introduction / Bob Young -- Technology and the construction of social reality / David Dickson -- The "Relevance" of anthropology to colonialism and imperialism / Jack Stauder -- Management science and the "Second industrial revolution" / Mike Hales -- The politics of abortion as "family planning" / Sheila Ernst -- Science as alienated consciousness / Alfred Sohn-Rethel -- "Life" in a biology lab / Simon Pickvance -- Death in the plastic industry / Charlie Clutterbuck -- Mathematics as ideology and politics / Luke Hodgkin -- IQ as ideological reality / Les Levidow -- Why socialism? / Albert Einstein. LC Card 86-7425 DDC 303.4/83 19
1. Science - Social aspects. 2. Technology - Social aspects. I. Levidow, Les.
Q175.55 .R33 1986 ***NYPL [JLD 87-615]***

RADICALISM - EUROPE.
Glotz, Peter, 1939- Manifest für eine Neue Europäische Linke /. Berlin , c1985. 112, [1] p. ; ISBN 3-88680-162-4 LC Card 86-100474 DDC 320.5/31/094 19
HX238.5 .G56 1985 ***NYPL [JLD 87-1162]***

RADICALISM - FRANCE.
Lash, Scott. The militant worker . London , 1984. vii, 264 p. ; ISBN 0-435-82516-X LC Card 87-673366
HD8076 .L37x 1984b

RADICALISM - UNITED STATES.
Lash, Scott. The militant worker . London , 1984. vii, 264 p. ; ISBN 0-435-82516-X LC Card 87-673366
HD8076 .L37x 1984b

RADICALS - UNITED STATES - BIOGRAPHY.
O'Connor, Jessie Lloyd, 1904- Harvey and Jessie . Philadelphia , 1988. p. cm. ISBN 0-87722-519-2 (alk. paper) LC Card 87-21737 DDC 322/.2/0922 B 19
HD8073.A1 O25 1988

Le Radici intellettuali del progresso economico moderno / a cura di Antonio Petino ; scritti di C. Fohlen ... [et al.]. Milano, Italy : F. Angeli, c1986. 327 p. ; 22 cm. Includes bibliographical references and index. LC Card 86-197444
1. Economics - History. 2. Economic history. I. Petino, Antonio, 1911-. II. Fohlen, Claude.
HB75 .R13 1986

La Radio : storia di sessant'anni, 1924-1984 / [curatori della mostra e del catalogo, Franco Monteleone e Peppino Ortoleva]. Torino : ERI, c1984. 126 p., [41] p. of plates : ill. (some col.), facsims., ports. ; 24 cm. Includes bibliographical references. LC Card 86-201755
1. Radiotelevisione italiana - Anniversaries, etc. - Exhibitions. 2. Radio broadcasting - Italy - History - Exhibitions. I. Monteleone, Franco, 1938-. II. Ortoleva, Peppino. III. Radiotelevisione italiana.
HE8699.I8 R335 1984

RADIO AND PROPAGANDA. see **RADIO IN PROPAGANDA.**

RADIO AS AN AID TO NAVIGATION. see **RADIO IN NAVIGATION.**

RADIO AUDIENCES - BULGARIA.
The Political self-assessment of Bulgarian respondents in terms of a left-right continuum. [Munich?] [1986] 16 p. ; LC Card 87-142360 DDC 384.55/43 19
HE8697.A8 P67 1986

RADIO AUDIENCES - GREAT BRITAIN.
Taylor, Laurie, 1935- Uninvited guests . London , 1986. 218 p. : ISBN 0-7011-2973-5 : LC Card 86-183414 DDC 791.44/75/0941 19
HE8689.7.A8 T39 1986

RADIO AUDIENCES - KENYA.
Trends in Kenyan short wave listening . Nairobi, Kenya , c1979. vii, 87 [26] leaves : LC Card 85-980967 DDC 384.54/3 19
HE8697.A8 T74 1979

RADIO AUDIENCES - SOVIET UNION.
Ostrogorskiĭ, V. M. (Vladimir Mikhaĭlovich) Ostorozhno--"Nemetskaia volna" . Moskva , 1985. 254 p. ; LC Card 85-197423
HE8699.G3 O86 1985

RADIO AUDIENCES - UNITED STATES - STATISTICS.
Radar 33 . Westfield, N.J. (111 Prospect St., Westfield 07090) , <c1986-. <v. 2, pt. 1-2; v. 3, pt. 2 > ; LC Card 86-218886 DDC 384.54/3 19
HE8697.A8 R243 1986

RADIO BROADCASTING - ARGENTINA - HISTORY.
Horvath, Ricardo. La trama secreta de la radiodifusión argentina . Cap. Fed. [i.e. Buenos Aires, Argentina] [1986] 153 p. ; ISBN 950-9458-13-9 LC Card 86-226636
HE8699.A7 H67 1986

RADIO BROADCASTING - BELGIUM.
La Guerre des ondes . Paris , Lausanne , c1985. 382 p. : ISBN 2-601-00475-4 (Payot)
NYPL [MWGK (France) 87-550]

RADIO BROADCASTING - CANADA - QUÉBEC.
La Guerre des ondes . Paris , Lausanne , c1985. 382 p. : ISBN 2-601-00475-4 (Payot)
NYPL [MWGK (France) 87-550]

RADIO BROADCASTING - FRANCE.
La Guerre des ondes . Paris , Lausanne , c1985. 382 p. : ISBN 2-601-00475-4 (Payot)
NYPL [MWGK (France) 87-550]

RADIO BROADCASTING - GERMANY - HISTORY.
Bierbach, Wolf. Rundfunk zwischen Kommerz und Politik . Frankfurt am Main , New York , c1986. 2 v. (595 p.) : ISBN 3-8204-9692-0 LC Card 86-233794
HE8699.G3 B54 1986

RADIO BROADCASTING - GERMANY, WEST.
Nach fünfundzwanzig Jahren . Köln , 1980. 399 p. : ISBN 3-7745-6465-5
NYPL [MWGK (Germany) 74-75 Bd.4]

Ostrogorskiĭ, V. M. (Vladimir Mikhaĭlovich) Ostorozhno--"Nemetskaia volna" . Moskva , 1985. 254 p. ; LC Card 85-197423
HE8699.G3 O86 1985

RADIO BROADCASTING - GHANA.
Golden jubilee, July 1935-1985 /. Accra [Ghana] [1985] 64 p. : LC Card 86-155961 DDC 384.54/06/0667 19
HE8689.9.G45 G65 1985

RADIO BROADCASTING - GOVERNMENT POLICY - CANADA.
Canada. Task Force on Broadcasting Policy. Report of the Task Force on Broadcasting Policy. [Toronto] , c1986. 730 p. : ISBN 0-660-12164-6 (pbk.) : LC Card 86-231885 DDC 384.54/0971 19
HE8689.9.C3 C37 1986

RADIO BROADCASTING - GREAT BRITAIN - FEES.
Two studies concerning the British Broadcasting Corporation /. London , 1979. 48 p. : ISBN 0-11-340763-7 (pbk.) LC Card 83-221765
HE8689.9.G7 T85 1979

RADIO BROADCASTING - GREAT BRITAIN - PLANNING.
Two studies concerning the British Broadcasting Corporation /. London , 1979. 48 p. : ISBN 0-11-340763-7 (pbk.) LC Card 83-221765
HE8689.9.G7 T85 1979

RADIO BROADCASTING - ITALY.
Il Gigante nano . Torino , c1985. 382 p. : LC Card 86-128171 DDC 384.54/0945 19
HE8689.9.I8 G54 1985
NYPL [MWGK (Italy) 86-2853]

RADIO BROADCASTING - ITALY - HISTORY - EXHIBITIONS.
La Radio . Torino , c1984. 126 p., [41] p. of plates : LC Card 86-201755
HE8699.I8 R335 1984

RADIO BROADCASTING - MEXICAN-AMERICAN BORDER REGION.
Fowler, Gene, 1950- Border radio . Austin, Tex. , c1987. p. cm. ISBN 0-87719-066-6 : LC Card 87-17975 DDC 384.54/53/09721 19
HE8699.M4 F68 1987

RADIO BROADCASTING - MEXICO.
Arredondo Ramírez, Pablo. Comunicación social, poder y democracia en México /. Guadalajara, Jalisco, México , c1986. 214 p. : LC Card 86-227944
HE8689.9.M6 A77 1986

RADIO BROADCASTING - NEWS. see **RADIO JOURNALISM.**

RADIO BROADCASTING - PROPAGANDA. see **RADIO IN PROPAGANDA.**

RADIO BROADCASTING - SOCIAL ASPECTS - GREAT BRITAIN.
Taylor, Laurie, 1935- Uninvited guests . London , 1986. 218 p. : ISBN 0-7011-2973-5 : LC Card 86-183414 DDC 791.44/75/0941 19
HE8689.7.A8 T39 1986

RADIO BROADCASTING - SOMALIA.
Somalia. Commission on National Broadcasting. Report of the Commission on National Broadcasting. Mogadishu [1966] ii, 108 leaves (2 folded) : LC Card 85-981107
HE8699.S65 S64 1966

RADIO BROADCASTING - SWITZERLAND, FRENCH-SPEAKING.
La Guerre des ondes . Paris , Lausanne , c1985. 382 p. : ISBN 2-601-00475-4 (Payot)
NYPL [MWGK (France) 87-550]

Radio Broadcasting to Cuba (Organization). Advisory Board.
Report / by the Advisory Board for Radio Broadcasting to Cuba. Washington, D.C. (400 6th St., S.W., Washington 20547) : The Board, 1986. [16] p. ; 27 cm. Cover title. LC Card 87-110428 DDC 384.54/46 19
1. Radio Marti (Radio program). 2. International broadcasting - Cuba. 3. International broadcasting - United States. I. Title.
HE8697.45.C9 R33 1986

Report by the Advisory Board for Radio Broadcasting to Cuba. Washington, D.C. (400 6th St., S.W., Rm. 3850, Washington 20547) : The Board, 1986. [20] p. : map, ports. ; 28 cm. Cover title. LC Card 87-402533 DDC 384.54/4 19
1. Radio Marti (Radio program). 2. International broadcasting - United States. 3. International broadcasting - Cuba. I. Title.
HE8698 .R27 1986

RADIO BROADCASTING - UNITED STATES - HISTORY.
Douglas, George H., 1934- The early days of radio broadcasting /. Jefferson, N.C. , c1987. viii, 248 p. : ISBN 0-89950-285-7 (lib. bdg. : alk.

paper) : LC Card 86-43090 DDC 384.54/0973 19
HE8698 .D68 1987

Douglas, Susan J. (Susan Jeanne), 1950- Inventing American broadcasting, 1899-1922 /. Baltimore , c1987. xxix, 363 p. : ISBN 0-8018-3387-6 (alk. paper) LC Card 87-3717 DDC 384.54/0973 19
HE8698 .D685 1987

Radio call-ins and covert politics . Verwey, Norma Ellen. Aldershot, Hants, England , Brookfield, Vt., U. S.A. , 1987. p. cm. ISBN 0-566-05349-7 : LC Card 86-33490 DDC 324.7/3 19
HE8697.P6 V47 1987

Radio Cologne. see **Westdeutscher Rundfunk.**

RADIO CORPORATION OF AMERICA - HISTORY.
Bilby, Kenneth. The general . New York , c1986. 326 p. ; ISBN 0-06-015568-X : LC Card 85-45621 DDC 384.54/092/4 B 19
HE8689.8 B55 1985
NYPL [MWES (Sarnoff, D.) 86-4682]

RADIO FEBA SEYCHELLES (MAHÉ ISLAND)
Trends in Kenyan short wave listening . Nairobi, Kenya , c1979. vii, 87 [26] leaves : LC Card 85-980967 DDC 384.54/3 19
HE8697.A8 T74 1979

Radio-France internationale. Africascope . Paris [1985] 426 p. : LC Card 86-192167
HC945 .A65 1985

RADIO FREE EUROPE - PUBLIC OPINION.
The Political self-assessment of Bulgarian respondents in terms of a left-right continuum. [Munich?] [1986] 16 p. ; LC Card 87-142360 DDC 384.55/43 19
HE8697.A8 P67 1986

RADIO FREQUENCY ALLOCATION.
International Frequency Registration Board. Preface to the international frequency list and the weekly IFRB circular /. Geneva , 1985. 1 v. (loose-leaf) : ISBN 92-71-04001-5 LC Card 86-207597 DDC 384.54/52 19
HE8675 .I5525 1985

RADIO FREQUENCY ALLOCATION - GREAT BRITAIN.
CSP International (Firm) Deregulation of the radio spectrum in the UK /. London , 1987. vi, 182, [30] p. : ISBN 0-11-513979-6 (pbk.) : LC Card 87-170465 DDC 384.54/52 19
HE8689.9.G7 C76 1987

RADIO IN NAVIGATION - AUSTRALIA - HISTORY.
Durrant, Lawrence L. The seawatchers . North Ryde, NSW, Australia , 1986. xii, 248 p. : ISBN 0-207-15198-9 LC Card 86-228332 DDC 384.5/3 19
HE8683.A8 D87 1986

RADIO IN POLITICS.
Soley, Lawrence C. Clandestine radio broadcasting . New York , 1987. xiv, 384 p. ; ISBN 0-275-92259-6 (alk. paper) : LC Card 86-21169 DDC 384.54 19
HE8697.P6 S59 1986
NYPL [MWGH 87-1678]

RADIO IN POLITICS - CANADA.
Verwey, Norma Ellen. Radio call-ins and covert politics . Aldershot, Hants, England , Brookfield, Vt., U. S.A. , 1987. p. cm. ISBN 0-566-05349-7 : LC Card 86-33490 DDC 324.7/3 19
HE8697.P6 V47 1987

RADIO IN POLITICS - GREAT BRITAIN.
Verwey, Norma Ellen. Radio call-ins and covert politics . Aldershot, Hants, England , Brookfield, Vt., U. S.A. , 1987. p. cm. ISBN 0-566-05349-7 : LC Card 86-33490 DDC 324.7/3 19
HE8697.P6 V47 1987

RADIO IN POLITICS - UNITED STATES.
News and views from National Public Radio /. Memphis, Tenn. , 1989. p. cm. LC Card 87-23331 DDC 384.54/06/073 19
HE8697.P6 N48 1989

Political broadcast catechism. Washington , c1984. 61 p. : ***NYPL [MWGH 85-3267]***

RADIO IN PROPAGANDA.
La Guerre des ondes . Paris , Lausanne , c1985. 382 p. : ISBN 2-601-00475-4 (Payot)
NYPL [MWGK (France) 87-550]

Soley, Lawrence C. Clandestine radio broadcasting . New York , 1987. xiv, 384 p. ; ISBN 0-275-92259-6 (alk. paper) : LC Card 86-21169 DDC 384.54 19
HE8697.P6 S59 1986
NYPL [MWGH 87-1678]

RADIO JOURNALISM - UNITED STATES.
News and views from National Public Radio /. Memphis, Tenn. , 1989. p. cm. LC Card 87-23331 DDC 384.54/06/073 19
HE8697.P6 N48 1989

RADIO - LAW AND LEGISLATION - FRANCE.
Benhaïm, J.-P. (Jean-Pierre) Les radios locales privées /. Paris , c1985. 153 p. : ISBN 2-7101-0528-4 : LC Card 85-205602
HE8697.P57 B45 1985

RADIO MARTI (RADIO PROGRAM)
Radio Broadcasting to Cuba (Organization). Advisory Board. Report /. Washington, D.C. (400 6th St., S.W., Washington 20547) , 1986. [16] p. ; LC Card 87-110428 DDC 384.54/46 19
HE8697.45.C9 R33 1986

Radio Broadcasting to Cuba (Organization). Advisory Board. Report by the Advisory Board for Radio Broadcasting to Cuba. Washington, D.C. (400 6th St., S.W., Rm. 3850, Washington 20547) , 1986. [20] p. : LC Card 87-402533 DDC 384.54/4 19
HE8698 .R27 1986

RADIO NEWS. see **RADIO JOURNALISM.**

RADIO PROGRAMS - GERMANY (WEST) - HAMBURG.
Renckstorf, Karsten. Landesprogramme von Hörfunk und Fernsehen in Hamburg . Hamburg , c1985. xlvii, vi, 388 p. : ISBN 3-87296-067-9 (pbk.) LC Card 86-109817 DDC 384.54/43/0943515 19
HE8700.9.G4 R45 1985 ***NYPL [MWGK (Germany, West) 86-4239]***

RADIO PROGRAMS - RATINGS.
Beville, Hugh Malcolm. Audience ratings . Hillsdale, N.J. , 1987. p. cm. ISBN 0-8058-0175-8 LC Card 87-21001 DDC 384.54/3 19
HE8697.A8 B46 1987

RADIO PROGRAMS - UNITED STATES - HISTORY.
Douglas, George H., 1934- The early days of radio broadcasting /. Jefferson, N.C. , c1987. viii, 248 p. : ISBN 0-89950-285-7 (lib. bdg. : alk. paper) : LC Card 86-43090 DDC 384.54/0973 19
HE8698 .D68 1987

RADIO PROGRAMS - UNITED STATES - REVIEWS.
Selected radio and television criticism /. Metuchen, N.J. , c1987. ix, 203 p. ; ISBN 0-8108-1942-2 LC Card 86-27891 DDC 791.44/75/0973 19
PN1990.6.U5 S4 1987
NYPL [MWGI 87-1890]

RADIO, SHORTWAVE - KENYA.
Trends in Kenyan short wave listening . Nairobi, Kenya , c1979. vii, 87 [26] leaves : LC Card 85-980967 DDC 384.54/3 19
HE8697.A8 T74 1979

RADIO STATIONS - MEXICAN-AMERICAN BORDER REGION.
Fowler, Gene, 1950- Border radio . Austin, Tex. , c1987. p. cm. ISBN 0-87719-066-6 : LC Card 87-17975 DDC 384.54/53/09721 19
HE8699.M4 F68 1987

RADIO STATIONS - UNITED STATES - MANAGEMENT.
Marcus, Norman, 1934- Broadcast and cable management /. Englewood Cliffs, N.J. , c1986. xii, 308 p. : ISBN 0-13-083577-3 LC Card 85-3565 DDC 384.54/068 19
HE8700.8 .M37 1986 ***NYPL [JLE 86-3127]***

RADIO SUPPLIES INDUSTRY - EUROPE.
The Mobile radio market in Western Europe. New York, N.Y. , c1982. x, 283 p. : LC Card 87-141850 DDC 380.1/45621384165/094 19
HD9696.R363 E855 1982

RADIO SUPPLIES INDUSTRY - UNITED STATES.
The U. S. mobile radio communications equipment market. New York, N.Y. , c1983. viii, 253 p. : LC Card 87-142226 DDC 384.5/3 19
HD9696.R363 U684 1983

RADIO SUPPLIES INDUSTRY - UNITED STATES - HISTORY.
Douglas, George H., 1934- The early days of radio broadcasting /. Jefferson, N.C. , c1987. viii, 248 p. : ISBN 0-89950-285-7 (lib. bdg. : alk. paper) : LC Card 86-43090 DDC 384.54/0973 19
HE8698 .D68 1987

Radio Telefís Éireann.
Ireland in transition /. Cork , 1986. 178 p. ; ISBN 0-85342-786-0 (pbk.) : LC Card 87-111629 DDC 306/.09417 19
HC260.5 .I735 1986

O'Connor, Nuala. Jobsuss . Cork , c1985. 96 p. ; ISBN 0-85342-748-8 (pbk.) : LC Card 86-220513 DDC 658/.022/09417 19
HD62.7 .O36 1985

Rádió-televízió anno-- /. Lévai, Béla. Budapest , 1985. 94 p. : ISBN 963-223-331-X : LC Card 86-128497
HE8689.9.H8 L49 1985

Radio Tirana. Marxismus-Leninismus, eine immer junge und wissenschaftliche Lehre (Radio Program). Selections. Neue Phänomene der kapitalistischen Gesellschaft ändern nichts an ihrem Wesen . Wien , 1976. 35 p. : LC Card 85-144894
HB501 .M338 1976

RADIO - UNITED STATES - HISTORY.
Douglas, Susan J. (Susan Jeanne), 1950- Inventing American broadcasting, 1899-1922 /. Baltimore , c1987. xxix, 363 p. : ISBN 0-8018-3387-6 (alk. paper) LC Card 87-3717 DDC 384.54/0973 19
HE8698 .D685 1987

RADIO VISION. see **TELEVISION.**

RADIOACTIVE POLLUTION - IRELAND.
Closing the door on a nuclear future . [Harbour View, Bantry, Co. Cork , 1986] [7] leaves : LC Card 87-111333 DDC 333.79/27/0941 19
HD9698.G72 C56 1986

RADIOACTIVE WASTE DISPOSAL - ENVIRONMENTAL ASPECTS - UNITED STATES.

RADIOACTIVE WASTE DISPOSAL - GOVERNMENT POLICY - CASE STUDIES.
Carter, Luther J. Nuclear imperatives and public trust . Washington, D.C. [Baltimore, Md.] , c1987. xii, 473 p. ; ISBN 0-915707-29-2 : LC Card 87-4706 DDC 363.7/28 19
HC110.E5 C358 1987

RADIOACTIVE WASTE DISPOSAL - GOVERNMENT POLICY - UNITED STATES.
Carter, Luther J. Nuclear imperatives and public trust . Washington, D.C. [Baltimore, Md.] , c1987. xii, 473 p. ; ISBN 0-915707-29-2 : LC Card 87-4706 DDC 363.7/28 19
HC110.E5 C358 1987

RADIOACTIVE WASTE DISPOSAL - SAFETY MEASURES - GOVERNMENT POLICY - INTERNATIONAL COOPERATION.
IAEA safeguards, 1980-1985 . Vienna , 1986. 15 p. ; LC Card 87-114776 DDC 363.1/79 19
HD9698.5 .I24 1986

RADIOACTIVE WASTE SITES - LOCATION - GOVERNMENT POLICY - UNITED STATES.

RADIOACTIVE WASTE SITES - UNITED STATES - LOCATION - PLANNING - CONGRESSES.
Facility location and land use . New York, N.Y. , c1986. vii, 40 p. : ISBN 0-87262-574-5 (pbk.) LC Card 86-25926 DDC 338.6/042 19
HD171.A15 F33 1986

Rádios livres . Machado, Arlindo. São Paulo-SP , 1986. 181 p. : LC Card 86-157835
HE8697.P57 M33 1986

Les radios locales privées /. Benhaïm, J.-P. (Jean-Pierre) Paris , c1985. 153 p. : ISBN 2-7101-0528-4 : LC Card 85-205602
HE8697.P57 B45 1985

RADIOSCOPIC DIAGNOSTIC EQUIPMENT INDUSTRY - UNITED STATES.
The Diagnostic radiology market in the U. S. New York, N.Y. , c1983. xxxix, 261 p. : LC Card 87-143803 DDC 381/.45681761 19
HD9995.R333 U53 1983

Radiotelevisione italiana.
La Radio . Torino , c1984. 126 p., [41] p. of plates : LC Card 86-201755
HE8699.I8 R335 1984

RADIOTELEVISIONE ITALIANA - ANNIVERSARIES, ETC. - EXHIBITIONS.
La Radio . Torino , c1984. 126 p., [41] p. of plates : LC Card 86-201755
HE8699.I8 R335 1984

Radke, Detlef. Auflagenpolitik und Politik-Dialog in der entwicklungspolitischen Zusammenarbeit / Detlef Radke. Berlin : Deutsches Institut für Entwicklungspolitik, 1985. xiii, 91 p. : ill. ; 24 cm. (Schriften des Deutschen Instituts für Entwicklungspolitik, DIE . Bd. 81) Includes bibliographical references. ISBN 3-88985-036-7 LC Card 85-134788
1. Economic assistance - Developing countries. 2. Developing countries - Economic conditions. 3. Economic development. I. Series. II. Series: Schriften des Deutschen Instituts für Entwicklungspolitik, DIE , Bd. 81. III. Title.
HC60 .R183 1985

Radna snaga u samoupravnom društvu .
Čelenković, Teodosije. Beograd , 1980. 241 p. ; LC Card 82-166188
HD5811.6.A6 C45 1980

Radnóti, Éva. Életszínvonal és közhangulat /. Budapest , 1984. 69 p. ; LC Card 86-147705
HD7027.5 .E44 1984

Radó, Lászlóné. Hatékony vezetői időgazdálkodás . Budapest , 1984. 62 p. ; ISBN 963-7902-09-0 (Magy. nemz. bibl.) LC Card 85-177403
HD69.T54 H38 1984

Radogna, Lamberto. Ogliari, Francesco. Trasporti marittimi di linea /. Milano , 1975- v. : LC Card 76-507610
HE839 .O35 ***NYPL [JSK 86-35]***

RADOM (POLAND : VOIVODESHIP) - ECONOMIC CONDITIONS.
Zdrojkowski, Józef. Rola partii robotniczych w życiu społeczno-politycznym Ziemi Radomskiej w latach 1930-1939 /. Radom , 1983. 168 p. : LC Card 86-100120
HD8539.R332 Z38 1983

RADOM (POLAND : VOIVODESHIP) - POLITICS AND GOVERNMENT.
Zdrojkowski, Józef. Rola partii robotniczych w życiu społeczno-politycznym Ziemi Radomskiej w latach 1930-1939 /. Radom , 1983. 168 p. : LC Card 86-100120
HD8539.R332 Z38 1983

Rados, David L., 1933- Gilmour, Peter, 1942- Australian marketing casebook /. St. Lucia , c1988. p. cm. ISBN 0-7022-2091-4 (pbk.) LC Card 87-16220 DDC 658.8/00994 19
HF5415.12.A9 G54 1988

Radosevich, George. Regional Symposium on Water Resoures Policy in Agro-Socio-Economic Development (1985 : Dhaka, Bangladesh) Water resources policy for Asia . Rotterdam , Boston , 1987. xii, 627 p. : ISBN 90-6191-684-4 LC Card 87-170039 DDC 333.91/0095 19
HD1698.A1 R45 1985

Radukin, V. P. (Viktor Pavlovich) Nauchnaia organizatsiia truda na mashinostroitel'nykh predpriiatiiakh /. Moskva , 1986. 240 p. : LC Card 86-214776
HD9703.S652 N38 1986

Radverkehrskonzept Sprockhövel / Kommunalverband Ruhrgebiet, Abteilung Planung ; Leiter, Stephan Reiss-Schmidt ; Bearbeiter, Reinhold Budde (Projektleiter), Uwe Trillitzsch, in Zusammenarbeit mit Arbeitsgemeinschaft Stadtplanung, Struktur- und Sozialforschung, Bochum, Dieter Holdorf u. Ulrich Krause. Essen : Der Kommunalverband, c1985. 55 p., [3] folded col. leaves of plates : ill. (some col.) ; 30 cm. (Planungshefte Ruhrgebiet) Bibliography: p. 42. ISBN 3-923494-51-3 LC Card 86-113993
1. Bicycle commuting - Germany (West) - Sprockhövel. 2. Sprockhövel (Germany) - Social conditions. I. Reiss-Schmidt, Stephan. II. Budde, Reinhold. III. Trillitzsch, Uwe. IV. Kommunalverband Ruhrgebiet. Abteilung Planung. V. Series.
HE5739.G3 R33 1985

Radwān, Samīr Muḥammad.
Agrarian change in Egypt : an anatomy of rural poverty / by Samir Radwan and Eddy Lee. London ; Dover, N.H. : Croom Helm, c1986. xii, 167 p. : ill. ; 23 cm. "A study prepared for the International Labour Office within the framework of the World Employment Programme." Includes bibliographical references and index. ISBN 0-7099-4214-1 : LC Card 85-11356 DDC 305.5/69/0962 19
1. Poor - Egypt. 2. Agriculture - Economic aspects - Egypt. 3. Egypt - Rural conditions. I. Lee, Eddy. II. International Labor Organization. World Employment Programme. III. Title.
HN786.A8 R33 1985 ***NYPL [JLD 86-1045]***

Collier, Paul. Labour and poverty in rural Tanzania . Oxford [Oxfordhire] , New York , 1986. vii, 143 p. : ISBN 0-19-828531-0 : LC Card 86-5303 DDC 307.1/4/09678 19
HN797.Z9 C625 1986 ***NYPL [JLD 87-511]***

Rae, Leslie. The skills of interviewing / Leslie Rae. New York, N.Y. : Nichols Pub. Co., 1988. p. cm. Bibliography: p. Includes index. ISBN 0-89397-293-2 : LC Card 87-25066 DDC 658.3/1124 19
1. Employment interviewing. I. Title.
HF5549.5.I6 R34 1988

Räumliche Einkommens-, Preis- und Verbrauchsunterschiede in der Bundesrepublik Deutschland /. Struff, Richard. Bonn , 1983. xi, 258 p. : ISBN 3-88488-262-7 LC Card 84-196141
HC286.7 .S836 1983

Raffaele Mattioli Foundation. The Debate over stabilization policy /. Cambridge [Cambridgeshire] , New York , 1986. xiv, 270 p. : ISBN 0-521-26790-0 LC Card 84-21366 DDC 338.9 19
HB3732 .D43 1986 ***NYPL [JLF 86-1945]***

Raffaele Mattioli lectures.
The Debate over stabilization policy /. Cambridge [Cambridgeshire] , New York , 1986. xiv, 270 p. : ISBN 0-521-26790-0 LC Card 84-21366 DDC 338.9 19
HB3732 .D43 1986 ***NYPL [JLF 86-1945]***

Raffée, Hans. Warentest und Konsument . Frankfurt/Main , New York , c1984. 268 p. : ISBN 3-593-33295-7 LC Card 84-150919
HF1040.9.G3 W37 1984

Raffegeau, Jean. Les comptes consolidés : étude méthodologique et analyse comparée des normes françaises, communautaires, internationales et étrangères / [Jean Raffegeau, Pierre Dufils, Jean Corre]. Paris : F. Lefebvre, c1984. 971 p. : ill. ; 25 cm. Includes index. ISBN 2-85115-064-2 : LC Card 84-245353 DDC 657/.3 19
1. Financial statements, Consolidated. I. Dufils, Pierre. II. Corre, Jean. III. Title.
HF5681.B2 R25 1984

Raffer, Kunibert, 1951- Unequal exchange and the evolution of the world system : reconsidering the impact of trade on North-South relations / Kunibert Raffer. New York : St. Martin's Press, 1987. ix, 301 p. ; 24 cm. Bibliography: p. 277-294. Includes index. ISBN 0-312-00440-0 : LC Card 86-31306 DDC 337 19
1. International economic relations. 2. Free trade and protection. 3. Balance of trade. I. Title.
HF1411 .R26 1987

Raghu Vira. A comprehensive English-Hindi dictionary of governmental & educational words & phrases ... / by Raghu Vira with the collaboration of numerous scientists and scholars. 3d ed. New Delhi : International Academy of Indian Culture, 1962. 189, 1572 p. ; 26 cm. (Sarasvati vihara series. v. 35)
1. Political science - Dictionaries. 2. English language - Dictionaries - Hindi. I. Title. II. Series.
NYPL [JLF 87-203]

Raghunadha Reddy, C. (Chinnathimmanna), 1950- Changing status of educated working women : a case study / C. Raghunadha Reddy. Delhi : B.R. Pub. Corp. ; New Delhi : Distributed by D.K. Publishers' Distributors, 1986. 210 p. ; 23 cm. Revision of the author's thesis ((Ph. D.--Sri Venkateswara University) Bibliography: p. [196]-205. Includes index. ISBN 81-7018-379-0 : LC Card 86-902900 DDC 305.4/3/0095484 19
1. Women - Employment - India - Andhra Pradesh - Case studies. 2. Women - Employment - India - Case studies. 3. Women - India - Andhra Pradesh - Social conditions - Case studies. 4. Women - India - Social conditions - Case studies. I. Title.
HD6190.A5 R34 1986

Rāġib, Yūsuf. Marchands d'étoffes du Fayyoum au IIIe/IXe siècle d'après leurs archives (actes et lettres) / par Yūsuf Rāġib. Le Caire : Institut français d'archéologie orientale, 1982- v. : ill. ; 28 cm. (Supplément aux Annales islamologiques, 0254-282X . cahier no 2, 5) Includes bibliographical references. CONTENTS. - 1. Les actes des ban u 'Abd al-Mj'min. LC Card 83-156837 DDC 380.1/0962/2 19
1. Merchants - Egypt - Fayyum - Correspondence. 2. Merchants - Egypt - Fayyum - History - Sources. 3. Manuscripts, Arabic - Egypt - Fayyum. 4. al-Fayyum, Egypt - Commerce - History - Sources. I. Title. II. Series.
HF366 .R34 1982 ***NYPL [*OFP 86-3324]***

RAHAD AGRICULTURAL PROJECT.
Abdel-Rahman, Awad Ibrahim. Population, environment, and agricultural change . [Khartoum] [1984] iii, 37 leaves : LC Card 84-980808 DDC 338.1/8624 19
HD2123.5 .A64 1984

Rahamāna, Āsahābura, 1949- Bāṅalādeśera kṛshikāṭhāmo, kṛshaka samāja, o unnaẏan / Āsahābura Rahamāna. Ḍhākā : Iunibhārsiṭi Presa, 1986. 39, 158 p. ; 22 cm. In Bengali. On Bangladesh agricultural system, peasant society, and development. Bibliography: p. 138-151. Includes index. LC Card 86-903304
1. Agriculture - Economic aspects - Bangladesh. 2. Peasantry - Bangladesh. 3. Rural development - Bangladesh. I. Title.
HD2075.6 .R33 1986

Rahamāna, Matiura, 1946- Dhanikagoshṭhīra luṭapāṭera kāhinī / Matiura Rahamāna, Saiẏada Ājijula Haka. Ḍhākā : Sūcanā, 1987. 136 p. : ill. ; 22 cm. In Bengali. On banks and banking of Bangladesh; includes cases of economic exploitation by the privileged people. LC Card 87-902373
1. Banks and banking - Bangladesh. 2. Banks and banking - Bangladesh - Corrupt practices. I. Haka, Saiẏada Ājijula. II. Title.
HG3290.6.A6 R35 1987

Rahfeldt, Dan. Hadady, R. Earl (Robert Earl), 1920- Winning with the insiders /. West Palm Beach, Fla. , c1987. vi, 115 p. : ISBN 0-9613048-8-X : LC Card 87-40003 DDC 332.64/4 19
HG4910 .H18 1987

Rahman, Alimur. Capacity utilisation in the large-scale manufacturing industry in Bangladesh / Alimur Rahman. [Dhaka] : Institute of Business Administration, University of Dhaka, [1983] 123 p. ; 24 cm. Revised version of author's thesis (Ph. D.)--University of Sussex, 1978) Includes index. Bibliography: p. [107]-120. LC Card 83-903801 DDC 338.6/44/095492 19
1. Industrial capacity - Bangladesh. 2. Big business - Bangladesh. 3. Bangladesh - Manufactures. I. Title.
HD69.C3 R34 1983 ***NYPL [JLE 86-4622]***

Rahman, Anisur, 1950- Oteiza, Enrique. Technical co-operation among Third World countries and the international order /. Mexico, D.F. , 1978. 72 p. ; LC Card 86-223022 DDC 338.9/26 19
HC60 .O838 1978

Rahman, Atiur, 1951- Peasants and classes : a study in differentiation in Bangladesh / Atiur Rahman. Dhaka : University Press, 1986. xlvi, 295 p. ; 22 cm. Based on the author's thesis (Ph. D.--University of London, 1983) Bibliography: p. [282]-291. Includes index. LC Card 87-900478 DDC 305.5/63 19
1. Peasantry - Bangladesh. 2. Social classes - Bangladesh. I. Title.
HD1537.B3 R32 1986

Rahman, Habibur. Elahi, Mahboob. Rural labour market, with special reference to hired labour in Pakistan's Punjab /. Lahore, Pakistan [1983] ii, ix, 186 leaves ; LC Card 86-930467
HD1537.P2 E4 1983

Rahman Khan, Azizur. see **Khan, Azizur Rahman.**

Rahman, M. L. (Mohammad Lutfur), 1933- SAARC facts and economic development / M.L. Rahman. Dhaka : SARC Association, Bangladesh, 1986. xvi, 200 p. : map, ports. ; 29 cm. History of South Asian Association for Regional Cooperation (SAARC), comprising Bangladesh, Bhutan, India, Maldives, Nepal, Pakistan, and Sri Lanka. Bibliography: p. 200. LC Card 87-901419 DDC 338.954 19
1. South Asia - Economic conditions. 2. South Asian Association for Regional Cooperation. I. SARC Association, Bangladesh. II. Title.
HC430.6 .R37 1986

Rahman, Mahfoozur. Sami Uddin. Cooperative sector in India after independence /. New Delhi , 1983. vi, 597 p. ; LC Card 83-903263 DDC 334/.0954 19
HD3538 .S25 1983 *NYPL [JLD 86-3874]*

Rahman, Mushtaqur. Muslim world . Lanham, MD , c1987. viii, 190 p. : ISBN 0-8191-6558-1 (alk. paper) : LC Card 87-14087 DDC 330.917/671 19
HC499 .M875 1987

Rahman, Rushidan Islam. The wage employment market for rural women in Bangladesh / Rushidan Islam Rahman. Dhaka, Bangladesh : Bangladesh Institute of Development Studies, 1986. xi, 97 p. ; 23 cm. (Research monograph . no. 6) LC Card 86-903129 DDC 331.4/295492 19
1. Wages - Women - Bangladesh. 2. Rural women - Employment - Bangladesh. I. Bangladesh Institute of Development Studies. II. Series: Research monograph (Bangladesh Institute of Development Studies) , no. 6. III. Title.
HD6061.2.B3 R34 1986

Rahman Saghayroun, Atif A. see Saghayroun, Atif A. Rahman.

Rahmann, Bernd. Staat und Beschäftigung . Nürnberg , 1985. 471 p. : LC Card 86-674027
HD5713 .S72x 1985

Rahmentarifverträge, Gehaltstarifverträge, Vermögensbildungstarifverträge, Tabelle der Kündigungsfristen, Auslösungssätze für die technischen und kaufmännischen Angestellten und für die Poliere und Schachtmeister des Baugewerbes im Gebiet der Bundesrepublik Deutschland / herausgegeben von Udo Knitter. Stand, 1. Mai 1977. Düsseldorf : Werner, 1977. 102 p. ; 17 cm. (Bau-Tarifverträge) Includes index. ISBN 3-8041-1158-0 LC Card 85-166026
1. Collective labor agreements - Construction industry - Germany (West). 2. Collective bargaining - Construction industry - Germany (West). 3. Wages - Construction workers - Germany (West). I. Knitter, Udo, 1931-. II. Series.
HD6698.R315 R34 1977

Rahmeyer, Fritz. Gahlen, Bernhard. Zur internationalen Wettbewerbsfähigkeit der deutschen Wirtschaft /. [Berlin] [1985] 41, 4 p. ; LC Card 86-204589
HC286.7 .G29 1985

Rahn, Horst-J. Formen der Aufbauorganisation des betrieblichen Bildungswesens in industriellen Grossbetrieben : eine empirische Untersuchung / von Horst-J. Rahn. Berlin : Duncker & Humblot, c1984. 99 p. : ill. ; 24 cm. (Betriebswirtschaftliche Schriften. Heft 115) Includes bibliographical references. ISBN 3-428-05503-9 LC Card 84-147527
1. Employees, Training of. 2. Corporations. I. Title.
HF5549.5.T7 R254 1984

Rai, Ravi Prakash. Mishra, G. P. Village industries and agriculture in changing agrarian situation /. New Delhi , c1985. 120 p. ; ISBN 81-7024-010-7 LC Card 85-904926 DDC 338.6/34/0954 19
HD2346.I5 M49 1985 *NYPL [JLD 86-3746]*

Raiatskas, R. L. (Raimundas Leonovich), 1937- Okruzhaiushchaia sreda i problemy planirovaniia / R.L. Raiatskas, V.P. Sutkaitis. Moskva : Izd-vo "Nauka," 1981. 272 p. ; 20 cm. (Problemy sovetskoĭ ėkonomiki) At head of title: Akademiia nauk SSSR. Tsentral'nyĭ ėkonomiko-matematicheskiĭ institut. Nauchnyĭ sovet po kompleksnoĭ probleme "Optimal noe planirovanie i upravlenie narodnym khoziaistvom." Includes bibliographies. LC Card 87-462039
1. Economic development - Environmental aspects. I. Sutkaitis, V. P. (Virgilis Povilovich). II. Title.
HD75.6 .R35 1981

Raíces y perspectivas de la crisis económica /. Aguilera Peralta, Gabriel Edgardo. San José, Costa Rica , 1986. 297 p. ; ISBN 997-7990-33-6 LC Card 87-404300 DDC 330.9728/053 19
HC141 .A63 1986

Raiffeisen, F. W. (Friedrich Wilhelm), 1818-1888. [Correspondence]
Briefe : 1875-1883 / F.W. Raiffeisen ; bearbeitet von Walter Koch. Wien : Österreichischer Agrarverlag, 1986. 207 p. : facsims. ; 22 cm. Bibliography: p. 206-207. ISBN 0-370-40867-2 LC Card 87-139235 DDC 332.1/092/4 B 19
1. Raiffeisen, F. W. (Friedrich Wilhelm), 1818-1888. Correspondence. 2. Bankers - Germany - Correspondence. I. Koch, Walter, 1942-. II. Title.
HG1552.R35 A4 1986

CORRESPONDENCE
Raiffeisen, F. W. (Friedrich Wilhelm), 1818-1888. [Correspondence.] Briefe . Wien , 1986. 207 p. : ISBN 0-370-40867-2 LC Card 87-139235 DDC 332.1/092/4 B 19
HG1552.R35 A4 1986

Raikom i nauchno-tekhnicheskaia intelligentsiia / [sostavitel' S.V. Sharenkov]. Leningrad : Lenizdat, 1981. 117 p. ; 20 cm. LC Card 82-177893
1. Technological innovations - Soviet Union. 2. Technological innovations - Russian S.F.S.R. - Leningrad. 3. Science and industry - Soviet Union. I. Sharenkov, S. V. (Stanislav Vasil'evich).
HC340.T4 R35 1981

Le rail franco-éthiopien en détresse /. Rosso, Max. Paris , c1983. 311 p. : ISBN 2-214-04961-4 : LC Card 83-173267
HE3416.Z8 F737 1983

Rail passenger development plan . California. Division of Mass Transportation. Sacramento, CA (1120 N St., Sacramento 95814) [1985] x, 98 p. : LC Card 86-622128 DDC 385/.22/09794 19
HE2583 .C25 1985

Rail transport in Pakistan /. Quddus, Syed Abdul. Lahore [1984?] 277 p. ; LC Card 85-932263 DDC 385/.09549/1 19
HE3300.5 .Q33 1984

Rail transport pricing in India /. Saxena, R. N. (Rajendra Narain), 1937- New Delhi , 1985. 549 p. : LC Card 86-903024 DDC 385/.12/0954 19
HE1911 .S29 1985

Railpax. see **Amtrak.**

RAILROAD COMPANIES - GREAT BRITAIN - HISTORY - 19TH CENTURY.
Joby, R. S. The railway builders . Newton Abbot [Devon] , North Pomfret, Vt. , c1983. 200 p. : ISBN 0-7153-7959-3 : LC Card 84-147746 DDC 338.7/6251/00941 19
HE3018 .J63 1983 *NYPL [JLD 86-918]*

RAILROAD ENGINEERS - TRAINING OF - PAKISTAN.
Ghias-ud-Din, Mian. Role of management, training & research in railroad operations /. [Pakistan , 1983?] (Lahore : Caxton Printing Press) 98 p., A-C folded leaves of plates : LC Card 86-903113 DDC 385/.068 19
HE3300.5 .G48 1983

RAILROAD EQUIPMENT INDUSTRY - GERMANY (WEST)
Mayer, Ralph-Dieter. Stahl- und Leichtmetallbau, Schienenfahrzeugbau . Berlin , c1985. 352 p. : ISBN 3-428-05771-6 LC Card 85-161158
HD9523.5 .M3 1985

Railroad ferries of the Hudson . Baxter, Raymond J., 1928- Woodcliff Lake, NJ , 1987. viii, 254 p. : ISBN 0-910389-01-2 : LC Card 87-22782 DDC 386/.2234/097473 19
HE5774. B39 1987

RAILROAD LAW - MEXICO - HISTORY - SOURCES.
Diversos documentos y datos relativos al proyectado ferrocarril de Chamela a Aguascalientes /. Guadalajara, México , 1982. 24, iii, 98 p. : LC Card 86-115748 DDC 385/.0972 19
HE2818 .D58 1982

RAILROAD LAW - SCOTLAND.
Scotchman. Letter to Joseph Locke, Esq. ... in reference to his bill "to regulate Sunday travelling on railways" /. Glasgow , 1849. 16 p. ; LC Card 85-666156
HE3037. S36x 1849

RAILROAD TERMINALS - GREAT BRITAIN - LONDON - ECONOMIC ASPECTS.
Pearson, Charles, 1794-1862. Central city terminus . [S.l.] 1845 (London : Richard and John E. Taylor) 20 p. ; LC Card 85-666155
HE3019.L8 P42x 1845

RAILROAD TRAVEL - SPAIN.
Demanche, Georges, b. 1855. En Espagne . Paris , 1883. 40 p. ; LC Card 85-665876
HE3195 .D45x 1883

RAILROADS.
Proudhon, P.-J. (Pierre Joseph), 1809-1865. Des réformes à opérer dans l'exploitation des chemins de fer. Paris, 1855. 2 p.l., 392 p. LC Card 05-35562
HE1031 .P92

RAILROADS - AFRICA.
United Nations transport and communications decade in Africa . [Addis Ababa?] [1985?- v. <1 > : LC Card 86-981012 DDC 385/.096 19
HE3395 .U65 1985

RAILROADS AND STATE - CALIFORNIA.
California. Division of Mass Transportation. Rail passenger development plan . Sacramento, CA (1120 N St., Sacramento 95814) [1985] x, 98 p. : LC Card 86-622128 DDC 385/.22/09794 19
HE2583 .C25 1985

RAILROADS AND STATE - CANADA.
Canadian Railway Labour Association. CRLA submission to the government of Canada /. Ottawa [1977] 28, 31 p. ; LC Card 84-256714
HE2807 .C33 1977

RAILROADS AND STATE - FRANCE - PROVINCES - HISTORY - 19TH CENTURY.
Beck, Robert, 1953- Der Plan Freycinet und die Provinzen . Frankfurt am Main , New York , c1986. 354 p. : ISBN 3-8204-9791-9 LC Card 87-408148 DDC 385/.068 19
HE3067 .B43 1986

RAILROADS AND STATE - GERMANY, WEST.
Vom Gleis abgekommen . Bonn , 1977. 60 p. ; LC Card 86-176591
HE2445 .V65 1977

RAILROADS AND STATE - OHIO - HISTORY - 19TH CENTURY.
Scheiber, Harry N. Ohio canal era . Athens , 1987. xxvi, 430 p. ; ISBN 0-8214-0048-7 LC Card 86-23800 DDC 386/.48/09771 19
HE395.O34 S34 1987

RAILROADS AND STATE - PAKISTAN.
Quddus, Syed Abdul. Rail transport in Pakistan /. Lahore [1984?] 277 p. ; LC Card 85-932263 DDC 385/.09549/1 19
HE3300.5 .Q33 1984

RAILROADS AND STATE - RHODE ISLAND.
Rhode Island. Dept. of Transportation. Division of Planning. Rhode Island state rail plan, 1985. Providence, R.I. [1985] 1 v. (various pagings) : LC Card 87-621867 DDC 385/.068 19
HE2771.R4 R48 1985

RAILROADS AND STATE - UNITED STATES.
Black, William Richard, 1942- Railroads for rent . Bloomington , c1986. x, 341 p. ; ISBN 0-253-34774-2 LC Card 84-48546 DDC 385/.1 19
HE1061 .B57 1986 *NYPL [JLE 86-3354]*

Hines, Walker Downer, 1870-1934. War history of American railroads /. [S.l.] , 1974. xviii, 327 p. : LC Card 74-75240 *NYPL [JLD 87-638]*

RAILROADS - ARGENTINA - HISTORY.
Fleming, William J. Regional development and transportation in Argentina . New York , 1987. ii, 218 p. : ISBN 0-8240-1360-3 (alk. paper) : LC Card 87-8401 DDC 385/.065/82 19
HE2910.G64 F54 1987

RAILROADS - ARGENTINA - MENDOZA (PROVINCE) - HISTORY.
Fleming, William J. Regional development and transportation in Argentina . New York , 1987. ii, 218 p. : ISBN 0-8240-1360-3 (alk. paper) : LC Card 87-8401 DDC 385/.065/82 19
HE2910.G64 F54 1987

RAILROADS - ARGENTINA - SANTIAGO DEL ESTERO (PROVINCE) - HISTORY.
Dargoltz, Raúl E. (Raúl Eduardo) La alianza anglo argentina . Buenos Aires [1983] 168 p. : LC Card 84-117468
HD9764.A73 S353 1983

RAILROADS - AUSTRIA - HISTORY - 19TH CENTURY.
Kupka, P. F. (Peter Friedrich), 1846- Die Eisenbahnen Österreich-Ungarns, 1822-1867 /. Leipzig , 1888. x, 386 p. : LC Card 83-217358
HE3058 .K86 1888

RAILROADS - AUSTRIA - TYROL - HISTORY.
Zwanowetz, Georg. Das Strassenwesen Tirols seit der Eröffnung der Eisenbahn Innsbruck-Kufstein (1858) . Innsbruck , 1986. 163 p., 32 leaves of plates : ISBN 3-7030-0165-8 LC Card 87-142160 DDC 388.1/09436/42 19
HE247.Z7 T99 1986

RAILROADS - BRAZIL - HISTORY.
Topik, Steven. The political economy of the Brazilian State, 1889-1930 /. Austin , 1987. xii, 241 p. : ISBN 0-292-76500-2 LC Card 87-5835 DDC 338.981 19
HC187 .T558 1987

RAILROADS - BRAZIL - PARANA (STATE) - HISTORY.
Trevisan, Edilberto. Ao apito do trem . [Curitiba] , 1985-1986 [i.e. 1986] 123 p. : LC Card 87-121016 DDC 385/.0981/62 19
HE2930.P34 T74 1986

RAILROADS - CALIFORNIA - PASSENGER TRAFFIC.
California. Division of Mass Transportation. Rail passenger development plan . Sacramento, CA (1120 N St., Sacramento 95814) [1985] x, 98 p. : LC Card 86-622128 DDC 385/.22/09794 19
HE2583 .C25 1985

RAILROADS - CHILE - HISTORY.
Poblete, Martiniano O. Una jornada ferroviaria . Santiago de Chile , 1930. 2 v. : LC Card 87-162075 DDC 385/.0983 19
HE2940.F47 P63 1930

RAILROADS - CONGRESSES.
Leber, Maximilien, Edler von. Die Beschlüsse des internationalen Eisenbahn-Congresses zu St. Petersburg nach dem am 20.-31. August 1892 angenommenen französischen Texte in getreuer deutscher Uebersetzung /. Wien , 1893. 25 p. ; LC Card 85-666030
HE1005.I553 L4x 1893

RAILROADS - DJIBOUTI - HISTORY.
Rosso, Max. Le rail franco-éthiopien en détresse /. Paris , c1983. 311 p. : ISBN 2-214-04961-4 : LC Card 83-173267
HE3416.Z8 F737 1983

RAILROADS - ETHIOPIA - HISTORY.
Rosso, Max. Le rail franco-éthiopien en détresse /. Paris , c1983. 311 p. : ISBN 2-214-04961-4 : LC Card 83-173267
HE3416.Z8 F737 1983

RAILROADS - EUROPE - CONGRESSES.
Report of the international seminar held in Paris on 15th-16th-17th January 1986 on the following topic, European dimension and future prospects of the railways /. Paris, France [Washington, D.C.] c1986. 289 p. : ISBN 92-821-1109-1 (pbk.) : LC Card 86-215627 DDC 385/.094 19
HE3005 .R47 1986

RAILROADS - EUROPE - TIME-TABLES - CONGRESSES.
Conférence européenne des horaires des trains de voyageurs (1984 : Paris, France) Procès-verbaux de la Conférence européenne des horaires des trains de voyageurs pour les années 1985/87 . Paris , 1984. 619 p. ; LC Card 85-152699
HE3004 .C64 1984

Railroads for rent . Black, William Richard, 1942- Bloomington , c1986. x, 341 p. ; ISBN 0-253-34774-2 LC Card 84-48546 DDC 385/.1 19
HE1061 .B57 1986 ***NYPL [JLE 86-3354]***

RAILROADS - FRANCE.
Berthelin, E. (Egmont), 1807-1860. Chemin de fer de Paris à Lyon par Troyes et Dijon . Troyes , 1843. 54, [2] p. ; LC Card 85-665948
HE3068 .B47x 1843

RAILROADS - FRANCE - EMPLOYEES - BIOGRAPHY.
Péroche, Marcel, 1907- Les mémoires de Marcel Péroche, "sénateur" du rail /. Paris , c1984. 256 p., [8] p. of plates : ISBN 2-7013-0556-X : LC Card 84-206923
HD8039.R322 F87 1984

RAILROADS - FRANCE - EMPLOYEES - HISTORY - 19TH CENTURY.
Stein, Margot B. (Margot Ballou), 1945- The social origins of a labor elite . New York , 1987. xxiv, 515 p. : ISBN 0-8240-8043-2 (alk. paper) : LC Card 87-6913 DDC 305/.9385 19
HD8039.R322 F88 1987

RAILROADS - FRANCE - HISTORY.
Reverdy, Georges. Histoire des grandes liaisons françaises /. Paris, France , c1981-c1982. 2 v. : LC Card 83-129286
HE363.F7 R48 1981

RAILROADS - FRANCE - PROVINCES - HISTORY - 19TH CENTURY.
Beck, Robert, 1953- Der Plan Freycinet und die Provinzen . Frankfurt am Main , New York , c1986. 354 p. : ISBN 3-8204-9791-9 LC Card 87-408148 DDC 385/.068 19
HE3067 .B43 1986

RAILROADS - GERMANY - HISTORY.
Offizieller Jubiläumsband der Deutschen Bundesbahn . München , 1985. 239 p. : ISBN 3-923967-03-9 LC Card 86-168073
HE3078 .O44 1985b

RAILROADS - GERMANY, WEST.
Hoffmann, Klaus G. Raumbedeutsamkeit von Schnellfahrstrecken im Schienenverkehr /. Berlin , c1985. xxviii, 547, [1] p. : ISBN 3-428-05770-8 LC Card 85-155640
HE3078 .H64 1985

RAILROADS - GERMANY (WEST) - BAVARIA - PASSENGER TRAFFIC - CASE STUDIES.
Marcinowski, Bernhard. Auswirkungen von Streckenstillegungen, dargestellt am Beispiel von Nebenbahnen in Bayern /. Nürnberg , 1983. xviii, 260 p. : LC Card 84-162065
HE3079.B5 M28 1983

RAILROADS - GERMANY, WEST - FREIGHT.
Vom Gleis abgekommen . Bonn , 1977. 60 p. ; LC Card 86-176591
HE2445 .V65 1977

RAILROADS - GERMANY (WEST) - HANNOVER - PERSONNEL MANAGEMENT - HISTORY - 19TH CENTURY.
Voigt, Wolfgang. Der Eisenbahnkönig, oder, Rumänien lag in Linden . München , 1982. 142 p. : ISBN 3-923126-15-8 (pbk.) LC Card 87-672921
HD7289.5.R1 V64x 1982

RAILROADS - GERMANY (WEST) - NORTH RHINE-WESTPHALIA - FREIGHT - CASE STUDIES.
Dick, Walter, 1949- Die ökonomische Bedeutung der Qualität des Schienengüterverkehrs . Berlin , c1980. xi, 331 p. : ISBN 3-428-04731-1 LC Card 84-130833
HE2446.N67 D52 1980

RAILROADS - GREAT BRITAIN.
Sandars, Joseph. A letter on the subject of the projected rail road between Liverpool & Manchester . Liverpool , 1825. 46 p. ; LC Card 85-666157
HE3018 .S36x 1825

RAILROADS - GREAT BRITAIN - ACCIDENTS.
Railway accident . London , 1922-<1985. <74 > v. LC Card 47-22771
HE1783.G7 A52

RAILROADS - GREAT BRITAIN - HISTORY - 19TH CENTURY.
Joby, R. S. The railway builders . Newton Abbot [Devon] , North Pomfret, Vt. , c1983. 200 p. : ISBN 0-7153-7959-3 : LC Card 84-147746 DDC 338.7/6251/00941 19
HE3018 .J63 1983 ***NYPL [JLD 86-918]***

RAILROADS - GREAT BRITAIN - ROLLING STOCK - HISTORY.
Johnson, Peter, 1949- The British travelling post office /. London , 1985. 104 p. : ISBN 0-7110-1459-0 : LC Card 86-164160 DDC 383/.143 19
HE6939.R2 J64 1985

RAILROADS - GREAT BRITAIN - TIME-TABLES.
Richardson's railway guide and time and fare tables : shewing the departure and arrival of the trains of every railway in England . London , 1841. 64 p., 1 folded leaf of plates : LC Card 85-666126
HE3014 .R5x 1841

RAILROADS - HISTORY.
Wolf, Winfried. Eisenbahn und Autowahn . Hamburg , c1987. 565 p. : ISBN 3-89136-105-X LC Card 87-167400 DDC 388/.09 19
HE151 .W58 1987

RAILROADS - HONDURAS - FINANCE - HISTORY - 19TH CENTURY.
Relación histórica de los contratiempos que ha sufrido la construcción de un ferro-carril á través de la República de Honduras, fracasos de los empréstitos pedidos al público para llevar á cabo esa empresa y principales dificultades que han sobrevenido á cada nueva combinación intentada para terminar la línea. Lóndres , 1875. vii, 94 p. ; LC Card 85-127957
HE2843 .R45 1875

RAILROADS - HUNGARY - EMPLOYEES - HISTORY.
Gadanecz, Béla. A vasutas munkásmozgalom története . Budapest , 1985. 351 p. ; ISBN 963-322-262-1 LC Card 86-227921
HD8039.R12 H93 1985

RAILROADS - HUNGARY - HISTORY - 19TH CENTURY.
Kupka, P. F. (Peter Friedrich), 1846- Die Eisenbahnen Österreich-Ungarns, 1822-1867 /. Leipzig , 1888. x, 386 p. : LC Card 83-217358
HE3058 .K86 1888

RAILROADS - INDIA - EMPLOYEES.
Gangadhara Rao, M. Human resources management in Indian railways /. Delhi , 1986. xvi, 245 p. ; ISBN 81-7049-004-9 : LC Card 86-900747 DDC 385/.068/3 19
HD8039.R12 I437 1986
NYPL [JLE 86-4104]

RAILROADS - INDIA - FREIGHT.
Raza, Moonis. Transport geography of India . New Delhi , 1986. xii, 299 p. : LC Card 86-903251 DDC 380.5/0954 19
HE3298 .R39 1986

RAILROADS - INDIA - FREIGHT - HISTORY.
Sthanunathan, V. K. Railway economics /. Madras , 1986. 319 p. : LC Card 87-900868 DDC 385/.1 19
HE1911 .S74 1986

RAILROADS - INDIA - RATES.
Saxena, R. N. (Rajendra Narain), 1937- Rail transport pricing in India /. New Delhi , 1985. 549 p. : LC Card 86-903024 DDC 385/.12/0954 19
HE1911 .S29 1985

RAILROADS - INDIA - RATES - HISTORY.
Sthanunathan, V. K. Railway economics /. Madras , 1986. 319 p. : LC Card 87-900868 DDC 385/.1 19
HE1911 .S74 1986

RAILROADS - IRELAND.
Irish railways . London , 1839. 8 p. ; LC Card 85-665175
HE3047 .I74x 1839

Monsell, William, 1812-1894. On some of the impediments to Irish manufacturing industry /. Dublin , 1865. 48 p. ; LC Card 85-666368
HC260.5 .M66x 1865

RAILROADS - ITALY.
Blasi, Benedetto. Della strada ferrata Pia-Cassia da citta della Pieve a Civitavecchia e del ristauro del Porto Neroniano in Anzio . Roma , 1846. 56 p., [3] folded leaves of plates : LC Card 85-665949
HE3098 .B51x 1846

Blasi, Benedetto. Sulle strade ferrate nello stato pontificio . Roma , 1847. 32 p. ; LC Card 85-665950
HE3098 .B52x 1847

RAILROADS - ITALY - EMPLOYEES - CASE STUDIES.
Carmignani, Fabrizo. Assenteismo e

presenteismo . Milano, Italy , c1984. 211 p. ; LC Card 84-175594 DDC 658.3/14 19
HD5115 .C37 1984 ***NYPL [JLD 86-3383]***

RAILROADS - MALAWI - FREIGHT.
Transportation of imports and exports . Lilongwe , 1984. i, 23 leaves ; LC Card 86-980329 DDC 385/.24/096897 19
HE3432 .T7 1984

Railroads--methods of valuing operating property and the amounts of tax payments : a report to the 1986 Minnesota Legislature / prepared by the Minnesota Department of Revenue. [Minneapolis] : The Department, [1986] 18 leaves : ill. ; 28 cm. "February 1986." LC Card 87-620974 DDC 336.22/5 19
1. Railroads - Valuation - Minnesota. 2. Railroads - Taxation - Minnesota. I. Minnesota. Legislature. II. Minnesota. Dept. of Revenue.
HE1075.M6 R35 1986

RAILROADS - MEXICO - FUERTE RIVER VALLEY - HISTORY.
Gill, Mario. La conquista del Valle del Fuerte /. Culiacán, Rosales, Sinaloa, México , c1983. 273 p., [4] folded leaves of plates : LC Card 86-121747
HC137.F84 G54 1983

RAILROADS - MEXICO - HISTORY - SOURCES.
Diversos documentos y datos relativos al proyectado ferrocarril de Chamela a Aguascalientes /. Guadalajara, México , 1982. 24, iii, 98 p. : LC Card 86-115748 DDC 385/.0972 19
HE2818 .D58 1982

RAILROADS - MEXICO - PUEBLA (STATE) - HISTORY.
Schmidt, Arthur, 1943- The social and economic effect of the railroad in Puebla and Veracruz, Mexico, 1867-1911 /. New York , 1987. 297 p. : ISBN 0-8240-1370-0 (alk. paper) : LC Card 87-8628 DDC 385/.0972/48 19
HE2819.P84 S35 1987

RAILROADS - MEXICO - VERACRUZ (STATE) - HISTORY.
Schmidt, Arthur, 1943- The social and economic effect of the railroad in Puebla and Veracruz, Mexico, 1867-1911 /. New York , 1987. 297 p. : ISBN 0-8240-1370-0 (alk. paper) : LC Card 87-8628 DDC 385/.0972/48 19
HE2819.P84 S35 1987

RAILROADS - MIDDLE EAST - HISTORY.
Fiedler, Ulrich. Der Bedeutungswandel der Hedschasbahn . Berlin , 1984. ix, 338 p. : ISBN 3-922968-37-6 LC Card 86-135345
HE3380.5.M53 F54 1984

RAILROADS - NEW YORK (STATE)
New York (State). Legislature. Legislative Commission on Critical Transportation Choices. Conrail . [Albany] [1986] i, 134 p. ; LC Card 87-620569 DDC 385/.065/73 19
HE2791.C899 N48 1986

RAILROADS - OHIO - HISTORY - 19TH CENTURY.
Scheiber, Harry N. Ohio canal era . Athens , 1987. xxvi, 430 p. ; ISBN 0-8214-0048-7 LC Card 86-23800 DDC 386/.48/09771 19
HE395.O34 S34 1987

RAILROADS - PAKISTAN.
Quddus, Syed Abdul. Rail transport in Pakistan /. Lahore [1984?] 277 p. ; LC Card 85-932263 DDC 385/.09549/1 19
HE3300.5 .Q33 1984

RAILROADS - PAKISTAN - MANAGEMENT.
Ghias-ud-Din, Mian. Role of management, training & research in railroad operations /. [Pakistan , 1983?] (Lahore : Caxton Printing Press) 98 p., A-C folded leaves of plates : LC Card 86-903113 DDC 385/.068 19
HE3300.5 .G48 1983

RAILROADS - QUÉBEC (PROVINCE) - EMPLOYEES - INTERVIEWS.
Lemieux-Pépin, Madeleine. P'tit train va loin . Ottawa , 1985. vii, 191 p. ; LC Card 86-177382
HE2808.1 .L45 1985

RAILROADS - RESEARCH - PAKISTAN.
Ghias-ud-Din, Mian. Role of management, training & research in railroad operations /. [Pakistan , 1983?] (Lahore : Caxton Printing Press) 98 p., A-C folded leaves of plates : LC Card 86-903113 DDC 385/.068 19
HE3300.5 .G48 1983

RAILROADS - RHODE ISLAND.
Rhode Island. Dept. of Transportation. Division of Planning. Rhode Island state rail plan, 1985. Providence, R.I. [1985] 1 v. (various pagings) : LC Card 87-621867 DDC 385/.068 19
HE2771.R4 R48 1985

RAILROADS - RHODE ISLAND - FREIGHT.
Rhode Island. Dept. of Transportation. Division of Planning. Rhode Island state rail plan, 1985. Providence, R.I. [1985] 1 v. (various pagings) : LC Card 87-621867 DDC 385/.068 19
HE2771.R4 R48 1985

RAILROADS - RHODE ISLAND - PLANNING.
Rhode Island. Dept. of Transportation. Division of Planning. Rhode Island state rail plan, 1985. Providence, R.I. [1985] 1 v. (various pagings) : LC Card 87-621867 DDC 385/.068 19
HE2771.R4 R48 1985

RAILROADS - RUSSIAN S.F.S.R. - KOLA PENINSULA - HISTORY.
Kharitonov, S. F. (Sergeĭ Fedorovich) Rasskaz o velikom severnom puti /. Petrozavodsk , 1984. 143 p. : LC Card 84-247171
HE3140.M87 K46 1984

RAILROADS - SAUDI ARABIA - HISTORY.
Fiedler, Ulrich. Der Bedeutungswandel der Hedschasbahn . Berlin , 1984. ix, 338 p. : ISBN 3-922968-37-6 LC Card 86-135345
HE3380.5.M53 F54 1984

RAILROADS - SOUTHWEST, NEW - EMPLOYEES - HISTORY - 20TH CENTURY.
Driscoll, Bárbara A. El programa de braceros ferroviarios /. Tijuana, Baja California , 1985. 45 p. ; ISBN 968-607-501-1 LC Card 86-188661
HD8039.R432 U62 1985

RAILROADS - SOVIET UNION.
Lomonosov, I͡U. (I͡Uriĭ), 1876-1952. Tekhnicheskie perspektivy zheleznodorozhnogo transporta v blizhaĭshee vremi͡a. Moskva, 1924. 67 p. LC Card 60-59178
HE3135 .L6

RAILROADS - SOVIET UNION - FINANCE.
Petrov, N. P. Finansovoe polozhenie russkoĭ zheli͡eznodorozhnoĭ si͡eti i glavni͡eĭshii͡a prichiny ukhudshenii͡a ego v posli͡ednie gody. S.-Peterburg, 1909. 185, ii, 17 p. LC Card 75-564261
HE3131 .A33 vyp. 5 HE3136

RAILROADS - SOVIET UNION - FREIGHT.
Ėkonomika promyshlennogo zheleznodorozhnogo transporta /. Moskva , 1981. 295 p. ; LC Card 82-124231
HE2457 .E38 1981

Galaburda, V. G. Optimal′noe planirovanie gruzopotokov /. Moskva , 1985. 255 p. : LC Card 85-243810
HE2457 .G35 1985

RAILROADS - SOVIET UNION - RATES.
Sagers, Matthew J. The freight rate structure on Soviet railroads /. Washington, D.C. [1985] vii, 28 p. : LC Card 87-601285 DDC 385/.12/0947 19
HE1895 .S25 1985

RAILROADS - SPAIN.
Demanche, Georges, b. 1855. En Espagne . Paris , 1883. 40 p. ; LC Card 85-665876
HE3195 .D45x 1883

Ubach i Soler, Tomàs M., 1955- El ferrocarril . Barcelona , 1984. 232 p. : ISBN 84-85256-39-5 LC Card 84-254098
HE3199.C38 U23 1984 ***NYPL [JSD 86-434]***

RAILROADS - SPAIN - CASTILLA Y LEÓN.
Pastor Antolín, Luis J., 1958- La red de transporte en Castilla y León /. Valladolid [1986?] 161 p. : ISBN 84-86047-71-4 LC Card 86-231524
HE363.S64 C376 1986

RAILROADS - SPAIN - CATALONIA.
Ubach i Soler, Tomàs M., 1955- El ferrocarril . Barcelona , 1984. 232 p. : ISBN 84-85256-39-5 LC Card 84-254098
HE3199.C38 U23 1984 ***NYPL [JSD 86-434]***

RAILROADS - SPAIN - FREIGHT - HISTORY.
Gómez Mendoza, Antonio. Ferrocarril y mercado interior en España, 1874-1913 /. Madrid , 1984- v. : ISBN 84-500-9728-2 (v. 1) LC Card 85-215275 DDC 385/.24/0946 19
HE2469 .G66 1984 ***NYPL [JLL 86-176]***

RAILROADS - SPAIN - TRAFFIC - HISTORY.
Gómez Mendoza, Antonio. Ferrocarril y mercado interior en España, 1874-1913 /. Madrid , 1984- v. : ISBN 84-500-9728-2 (v. 1) LC Card 85-215275 DDC 385/.24/0946 19
HE2469 .G66 1984 ***NYPL [JLL 86-176]***

RAILROADS - STATISTICS.
Bermingham, Thomas. A statistical account of foreign and English railways . London , 1839. 24 p. ; LC Card 85-665741
HE2271 .B47x 1839

RAILROADS, STREET. see **STREET-RAILROADS.**

RAILROADS - SUMATRA - HISTORY.
Meijer, H., 1904- De Deli Spoorweg Maatschappij . Zutphen , c1987. 152 p. : ISBN 90-6011-540-6 : LC Card 87-157915
HE3340.D45 M45 1987

RAILROADS - SWITZERLAND - AAR RIVER VALLEY - HISTORY.
Aebi, Ernst. SBB im Aaretal . Luzern , c1984. 111 p. : LC Card 84-234665
HE3898.A37 A42 1984

RAILROADS - TAXATION - MINNESOTA.
Railroads--methods of valuing operating property and the amounts of tax payments . [Minneapolis] [1986] 18 leaves : LC Card 87-620974 DDC 336.22/5 19
HE1075.M6 R35 1986

RAILROADS - TURKEY - HISTORY - 20TH CENTURY.
Hiller, Marlene P., 1948- Krisenregion Nahost . Frankfurt am Main , New York , c1985. 335 p. : ISBN 3-8204-8249-0 LC Card 85-191941
HF1558.15.T8 H55 1985

RAILROADS - UKRAINE - EMPLOYEES.
Saltovskiĭ, I. A. (Ivan Aleksandrovich) Sotsialisticheskai͡a distsiplina truda i sotsial′nye faktory ee ukreplenii͡a v trudovykh kollektivakh /. Kiev , 1985. 118, [2] p. ; LC Card 86-220755
HF5549.5.L3 S27 1985

RAILROADS, UNDERGROUND. see **SUBWAYS.**

RAILROADS - UNITED STATES.
Hines, Walker Downer, 1870-1934. War history of American railroads /. [S.l.] , 1974. xviii, 327 p. : LC Card 74-75240 ***NYPL [JLD 87-638]***

RAILROADS - UNITED STATES - BRANCH LINES.
Black, William Richard, 1942- Railroads for rent . Bloomington , c1986. x, 341 p. ; ISBN 0-253-34774-2 LC Card 84-48546 DDC 385/.1 19
HE1061 .B57 1986 ***NYPL [JLE 86-3354]***

RAILROADS - UNITED STATES - EMPLOYEES - HISTORY - 20TH CENTURY.
Driscoll, Bárbara A. El programa de braceros ferroviarios /. Tijuana, Baja California , 1985. 45 p. ; ISBN 968-607-501-1 LC Card 86-188661
HD8039.R432 U62 1985

RAILROADS - UNITED STATES - FINANCE.
Black, William Richard, 1942- Railroads for rent . Bloomington , c1986. x, 341 p. ; ISBN 0-253-34774-2 LC Card 84-48546 DDC 385/.1 19
HE1061 .B57 1986 ***NYPL [JLE 86-3354]***

RAILROADS - UNITED STATES - FREIGHT.
Black, William Richard, 1942- Railroads for rent . Bloomington , c1986. x, 341 p. ; ISBN 0-253-34774-2 LC Card 84-48546 DDC 385/.1 19
HE1061 .B57 1986 ***NYPL [JLE 86-3354]***

RAILROADS - UNITED STATES - HISTORY.
Klein, Maury, 1939- The life and legend of Jay Gould /. Baltimore , c1986. xvi, 595 p., [24] p. of plates : ISBN 0-8018-2880-5 (alk. paper) LC Card 85-24107 DDC 332/.092/4 B 19
HC102.5.G68 K55 1986
NYPL [JFE 86-2364]

RAILROADS - UNITED STATES - HISTORY - 19TH CENTURY.
Lewty, Peter J., 1934- To the Columbia gateway . Pullman, Wash. , 1987. p. cm. ISBN

0-87422-030-0 (alk. paper) : LC Card 87-21041 DDC 385/.09795 19
HE2791.N855 L48 1987

RAILROADS - UNITED STATES - PASSENGER TRAFFIC.
Ferris, Sally A. Federal subsidies to rail passenger service . Washington, D.C. , Congress of the United States, Congressional Budget Office [1982] xxiii, 85, [1] p. : LC Card 82-602556 DDC 385/.1 19
HE1061 .F47 1982 ***NYPL [JLF 86-1384]***

RAILROADS - VALUATION - MINNESOTA.
Railroads--methods of valuing operating property and the amounts of tax payments . [Minneapolis] [1986] 18 leaves : LC Card 87-620974 DDC 336.22/5 19
HE1075.M6 R35 1986

RAILROADS - ZAMBIA - RATES - HISTORY.
Kanduza, Ackson M. The political economy of underdevelopment in Northern Rhodesia, 1918-1960 . Lanham, MD , c1986. x, 336 p. : ISBN 0-8191-5189-0 (alk. paper) : LC Card 85-29835 DDC 338.96894 19
HC915 .K36 1986 ***NYPL [JLD 86-2962]***

Railway accident : report on .... London : H.M.S.O., 1922-<1985 > <74 > v. illus. 25-34 cm. At head of title: Department of Transport. Some issues have title: Railway accidents. Collection of reports on railway accidents in Great Britain. Some reports issued by Department of the Environment. LC Card 47-22771
1. Railroads - Great Britain - Accidents. I. Great Britain. Ministry of Transport. II. Great Britain. Dept. of the Environment. III. Title: Railway accidents.
HE1783.G7 A52

Railway accidents. Railway accident . London , 1922-<1985. <74 > v. LC Card 47-22771
HE1783.G7 A52

The railway builders . Joby, R. S. Newton Abbot [Devon] , North Pomfret, Vt. , c1983. 200 p. : ISBN 0-7153-7959-3 : LC Card 84-147746 DDC 338.7/6251/00941 19
HE3018 .J63 1983 ***NYPL [JLD 86-918]***

Railway economics /. Sthanunathan, V. K. Madras , 1986. 319 p. : LC Card 87-900868 DDC 385/.1 19
HE1911 .S74 1986

RAILWAY MAIL SERVICE - GREAT BRITAIN - HISTORY.
Johnson, Peter, 1949- The British travelling post office /. London , 1985. 104 p. : ISBN 0-7110-1459-0 : LC Card 86-164160 DDC 383/.143 19
HE6939.R2 J64 1985

RAILWAY MAIL SERVICE - OREGON - UNION COUNTY - HISTORY.
Barklow, Irene. From trails to rails . Enterprise, Or. , c1987. ix, 300 p. : ISBN 0-9618185-2-2 : LC Card 87-15709 DDC 383/.4979571 19
HE6376.A1 O727 1987

RAILWAY MAIL SERVICE - SWITZERLAND.
Müller, Alfred. Die schweizerischen Bahnpoststempel . Bern , 1977. 28 p. : LC Card 85-138287
HE7139.R2 M85 1977

RAILWAY MAIL SERVICE - WISCONSIN - HISTORY - SOURCES.
1902 Wisconsin alphabetical postal scheme. [Madison, Wis.] (5401 Raymond Rd., Madison 53711) [1984] 19 p. : LC Card 86-175627 DDC 383/.49775 19
HE6376.A1 W645 1984

RAILWAYS - SWITZERLAND - SEELAND - HISTORY.
Waldburger, Hans. Die Seetalbahn . Luzern , c1983. 143 p. : LC Card 84-190252
HE4918.S44 W35 1983

Raimbault, René. France. Conseil économique et social. Les surplus agricoles et la pénurie alimentaire . [Paris] [1986] 1 v. (various pagings) : LC Card 86-179100
HD1431 .F7 1986

Raimond, Jean-Marie. Vocational training of young migrants in France / this study was drawn up by Jean-Marie Raimond. 1st ed. Berlin : CEDEFOP, 1986. x, 101 p. : ill. ; 30 cm. (CEDEFOP document) "Catalogue no.: HX-45-85-034-EN-C"--T.p. verso. Bibliography: p. 96-100. ISBN 92-825-6118-6
1. Vocational education - France. 2. Children of alien laborers - Vocational education - France. 3. Alien labor - France. I. European Centre for the Development of Vocational Training. II. Title. III. Series.
NYPL [JLG 87-134]

Raimundi, Virginia M. Mach mich nicht an . Berlin , c1986. [48] p. : ISBN 3-88114-313-0 : LC Card 87-118837 DDC 331.4/133/0943 19
HD6060.5.G3 M33 1986

RAIN FOREST ECOLOGY - AMAZON RIVER REGION.
Fearnside, Philip M. (Philip Martin) Human carrying capacity of the Brazilian rain-forest /. New York , 1986. xii, 293 p. : ISBN 0-231-06104-8 (alk. paper) LC Card 85-6643 DDC 330.981/1063 19
HC188.A5 F42 1986 ***NYPL [JLE 86-4554]***

Rainer, Norbert.
Anwendung der Arbeitsmarktorientierten Input-Output-Analyse am beispiel der Gastarbeiterbeschäftigung / Nobert Rainer. Wien : Verband der Assistenten der Wirtschaftsuniversität Wien, 1977. 47 leaves ; 31 cm. (Arbeitshefte / Wirtschaftsuniversität Wien . Nr. 10 =) Bibliography: leaves 37-38. LC Card 86-194737
1. Input-output tables - Austria. 2. Alien labor - Austria. I. Series: Arbeitshefte / Wirtschaftsuniversität Wien , Nr. 10. II. Title.
HC270.I57 R35 1977

Clement, Werner. Einkommensverteilung und Qualifikation . Wien , 1984. vi, 201 p. : ISBN 3-85436-020-7 LC Card 84-191161
HC270.I5 C56 1984

Rainery, Richard. Alaska's public energy resources : distribution of benefits of thermal energy and electric power energy resource consumption / by Richard Rainery, Allison Fargnoli, Jennifer Klein. [Juneau?] : Rural Research Agency, Alaska State Senate, [1985] 8, 124, 3, 7 p. : ill. ; 28 cm. "July 1985." Bibliography: p. 1-7 (last group) LC Card 86-622191 DDC 333.79/09798 19
1. Energy industries - Alaska. 2. Power resources - Alaska. 3. Energy consumption - Alaska. I. Fargnoli, Allison. II. Klein, Jennifer. III. Alaska. Rural Research Agency. IV. Alaska. Legislature. Senate. V. Title.
HD9502.U53 A473 1985

Raines, John C. Modern work and human meaning / by John C. Raines and Donna C. Day-Lower. 1st ed. Philadelphia : Westminster Press, c1986. 150 p. ; 23 cm. Includes index. Bibliography: p. [141]-148. ISBN 0-664-24703-2 (pbk.) LC Card 85-26370 DDC 241/.64 19
1. Economics - Religious aspects - Christianity. 2. Social classes - United States. 3. Distributive justice - Religious aspects - Christianity. I. Day-Lower, Donna C., 1951-. II. Title.
BJ1498 .R335 1986 ***NYPL [JLD 86-2382]***

Rāingān phon kānsksā wičhai . Thailand. Krom Sētthakit Kānphānit. [Krung Thēp Mahā Nakh 2521 [1978] 24, [7] folded p., [7] p. of plates : LC Card 81-183926
HD9766.T52 T47 1978

Raising business finance from banks. Akwaeze, G. C. Practical steps in raising business finance from banks /. Enugu, Nigeria , 1985. 290 p. : ISBN 978-15-6214-5 (pbk.) LC Card 87-118106 DDC 658.1/5224 19
HG3754.5.N6 A38 1985

Les raisons de la colère, ou, L'utopie et les Verts /. Dumont, René, 1904- Paris , c1986. 137 p. ; ISBN 2-7266-0075-1 LC Card 86-158407
HC59.72.E5 D85 1986

Rajagopal Rao, Narayanamurthy, 1925-
Municipal finance in India : theory and practice / N.R. Rao. New Delhi, India : Inter-India Publications, 1986. xix, 411 p. ; 23 cm. Bibliography: p. [404]-406. Includes index. ISBN 81-210-0067-X : LC Card 86-901947 DDC 336/.014/54 19
1. Municipal finance - India. I. Title.
HJ9565 .R35 1986

Rajan, Amin, 1942-
Services--the second industrial revolution? : business and jobs outlook for UK growth industries / Amin Rajan. London ; Boston : Butterworths, 1987. xviii, 257 p. : ill. ; 24 cm. "An employer-based study by the Institute of Manpower Studies for the Occupations Study Group." Bibliography: p. 240-244. ISBN 0-408-02003-2 LC Card 86-32739 DDC 331.12/9042 19
1. Service industries - Great Britain - Forecasting. 2. Service industries workers - Great Britain - Supply and demand - Forecasting. I. Institute of Manpower Studies (Great Britain). II. Occupations Study Group (Great Britain). III. Title.
HD9982.5 .R34 1987

UK occupation and employment trends to 1990 . London , Boston , 1986. xxiv, 249 p. : ISBN 0-408-02980-3 : LC Card 86-13617 DDC 331.12/0941 19
HD5765.A6 U38 1986 ***NYPL [JLE 86-4156]***

Rajan, M. A. S. (Mandyam Anandampullai Srirangarajan), 1921- Land reforms in Karnataka : an account by a participant observer / M.A.S. Rajan. Delhi : Hindustan Pub. Corp., 1986. viii, 178 p. : folded map ; 24 cm. Bibliography: p. [173]-174. Includes index. LC Card 86-902976 DDC 333.3/1/5487 19
1. Land reform - India - Karnataka. I. Title.
HD1333.I42 K377 1986

Rajapatirana, Sarath. Lal, Deepak. Trade liberalization in Sri Lanka /. Aldershop, Hants, England , Brookfield, Vt. , 1988. p. cm. ISBN 0-566-05340-3 : LC Card 87-15044 DDC 382/.3/095493 19
HF1586.8 .L35 1988

RAJASTHAN (INDIA) - COMMERCE - HISTORY - 18TH CENTURY.
Gupta, B. L. (Babu Lal), 1949- Trade and commerce in Rajasthan during the 18th century /. Jaipur , 1987. iv, 274 p. : LC Card 87-902534 DDC 380.1/0954/4 19
HF3789.R33 G86 1987

RAJASTHAN (INDIA) - ECONOMIC CONDITIONS - REGIONAL DISPARITIES.
Singh, H. P. Regional disparity in industrial growth /. New Delhi, India , 1987. xvi, 304 p. : ISBN 81-7041-029-0 : LC Card 87-902685 DDC 338.0954/4 19
HC437.R3 S37 1987

RAJASTHAN, INDIA - INDUSTRIES.
Singh, H. P. Regional disparity in industrial growth /. New Delhi, India , 1987. xvi, 304 p. : ISBN 81-7041-029-0 : LC Card 87-902685 DDC 338.0954/4 19
HC437.R3 S37 1987

RAJASTHAN, INDIA - RURAL CONDITIONS.
Gupta, Satya Prakash, 1940- The agrarian system of eastern Rajasthan, c. 1650-c. 1750 /. Delhi , 1986. xvi, 352 p. : ISBN 81-85054-11-8 : LC Card 87-900814 DDC 338.1/0954/4 19
HD2075.R27 G86 1986

Rajeswaran, K. A feasibility study on the ox-driven scotch cart project : possible extension of ox-cart technology in the Eastern Province : benefits and obstacles / prepared by K. Rajeswaran. Lusaka, Zambia : Institute for African Studies, University of Zambia, [1985] vii leaves, 66 p., [3] leaves of plates : ill., map ; 30 cm. (IAS commissioned studies reports . no. 5, 1985) Includes bibliographical references. LC Card 87-980373 DDC 388.3/41/096894 19
1. Carriages and carts - Zambia - Eastern Province. 2. Ox driving - Zambia - Eastern Province. 3. Ox industry - Zambia - Eastern Province. 4. Rural development - Zambia - Eastern Province. I. Series: IAS commissioned studies reports , 1985, no. 5. II. Title.
HE153 .R35 1985

Raju, B. Yerram, 1941- Khemani, C. L., 1934- How and why of rural banking /. New Delhi , 1987. 255, [41] p. : LC Card 87-901033 DDC 332.1/0954 19
HG3288 .K44 1987

Rajyagor, S. B. Gujarātanāṃ bandaro : eka paricaya / Śivaprasāda Rājagora.1. āvṛtti. Amadāvāda : Bī. Esa. Rājagora, 1986. 6, 167 p. : ill., maps ; 23 cm. In Gujarati. Introduction to harbors in Gujarat. Bibliography: p. [165]-167. LC Card 87-900295
1. Harbors - India - Gujarat. I. Title.
HE559.I4 R34 1986

Rakesh Hooja. see **Hooja, Rakesh.**

Rakhahari Chatterji. see **Chatterji, Rakhahari, 1943-**

Rakhovetskiĭ, A. N. (Anatoliĭ Nikolaevich) Operativnaia frakhtovaia deiatel'nost' na morskom transporte / A.N. Rakhovetskiĭ. Moskva : "Transport", 1986. 159 p. : ill. ; 22 cm. Bibliography: p. 157-159. LC Card 86-115637
1. Freight and freightage - Soviet Union. 2. Cargo ships - Soviet Union. I. Title.
HE597.S615 R36 1986

Rakin, Aleksandr Petrovich. Myt' i vichnist' rekordu . Kyïv , 1985. 124 p., [24] p. of plates : LC Card 86-178641
HC340.S6 M97 1985

Rakorong, K. Gobotswang, Z. Pilot evaluation report on Mahalapye Development Trust /. Gaborone, Botswana [1982] v leaves, 61, 3 p. ; LC Card 87-122810
HD5710.85.B59 G63 1982

Rákos, János. Pécs a szocialista fejlődés útján . Pécs [1984] 127 p. : ISBN 963-00-0782-7 (Magy. nemz. bibl.) LC Card 85-178275
HC300.292.P4 P43 1984

Rákosi, Miklós. Lukács, Lajos. Szövetkezeti gazdálkodás elemzése /. Budapest , 1983. 155 p. : ISBN 963-03-2028-2 (Magy. nemz. bibl.) LC Card 85-184472
HF5686.C67 L84 1983

Rakovskiĭ, S. N. (Sergeĭ Nikolaevich) Migratsii naseleniia v zarubezhnykh sotsialisticheskikh stranakh Evropy : uchebnoe posobie k spetsial'nomu kursu (po spetsial'nosti "Ekonomicheskaia i sotsial'naia geografiia zarubezhnykh stran") / S.N. Rakovskiĭ. Moskva : Moskovskiĭ gos. pedagog. in-t im. V.I. Lenina, 1983. 152 p. ; 21 cm. At head of title: Ministerstvo prosveshcheniia RSFSR. Moskovskiĭ ordena Lenina i ordena Trudovogo Krasnogo Znameni gosudarstvennyĭ pedagogicheskiĭ institut imeni V.I. Lenina. Includes bibliographical references. LC Card 85-181642
1. Migration, Internal - Europe, Eastern. 2. Europe, Eastern - Population. I. Title.
HB2041 .R35 1983

Rakshit, Gangadhar, 1929- Steel industry in the public sector / G. Rakshit. Calcutta : World Press, 1985. xii, 72 p. ; 22 cm. Includes index. Bibliography: p. 65-70. LC Card 85-904175 DDC 338.4/7669142/0954 19
1. Steel industry and trade - India. 2. Steel industry and trade - Government policy - India. I. Title.
HD9526.I62 R28 1985
NYPL [JLD 86-2180]

Rallis, Tom. City transport in developed and developing countries / Tom Rallis. New York : St. Martin's Press, 1988. xiv, 202 p. : ill. ; 22 cm. Bibliography: p. 191-197. Includes index. ISBN 0-312-00450-8 : LC Card 86-29789 DDC 388.4 19
1. Urban transportation. 2. Local transit. I. Title.
HE305 .R35 1988

Ram K. Vepa. see **Vepa, Ram K.**

Ram, S. (Sundaresan), 1957- Sheth, Jagdish N. Bringing innovation to market . New York , c1987. xii, 247 p. : ISBN 0-471-84977-4 LC Card 87-17611 DDC 658.5/78 19
HD69.N4 S494 1987

Ram Singh, Sita. see **Singh, Sita Ram.**

Rama, Germán W. Escenarios políticos y sociales del desarrollo latinoamericano /. [S.l.] [Buenos Aires] , c1986. 231 p. ; ISBN 950-23-0274-5 LC Card 87-400175 DDC 338.98 19
HC125 .E82 1986

Rama, Ruth.
Arroyo, Gonzalo. Agricultura y alimentos en América Latina . México, D.F. , 1985. 267 p. ; ISBN 968-8373-33-8 LC Card 86-208283
HD9014.L32 A77 1985

Las relaciones económicas México-Estados Unidos : el comercio alimentario, 1950-1982 / Ruth Rama. Miami, FL (Tamiami Trail, Miami 33199) : Latin American and Caribbean Center, Florida International University, [1984] 55 p. ; 28 cm. (Occasional papers series / Latin American and Caribbean Center, Florida International University . #8 (Spring 1984)) Bibliography: p. 53-55. LC Card 85-226824
1. Produce trade - Mexico. 2. Produce trade - United States. I. Series: Occasional papers series (Florida International University. Latin American and Caribbean Center) , #8. II. Title.
HD9014.M62 R36 1984

Ramachandra Rao, B. All about priority sector advances / B. Ramachandra Rao. 1st ed. New Delhi : Suneja, 1984. 350 p. : forms ; 22 cm. LC Card 84-901313 DDC 332.7/0954 19
1. Credit - India. 2. Rural development - India - Finance. I. Title.
HG3729.I42 R36 1984 *NYPL [JLD 87-574]*

Ramakrishna Sarma, K. Financial institutions and regional development in India / K. Ramakrishna Sarma ; foreword by J. Satyanarayana. 1st ed. Allahabad, India : Chugh Publications, 1986. xvii, 211 p. ; 22 cm. Bibliography: p. [206]-207. Includes index. ISBN 81-85076-04-9 : LC Card 86-902692 DDC 332.2 19
1. Government financial institutions - India. 2. Development banks - India. 3. Rural development - India. I. Title.
HG3288 .R32 1986

Ramalho, José Ricardo Garcia Pereira. Brandão, Carlos Rodrigues. Campesinato goiano . Goiânia , 1986. 156 p. ; ISBN 85-85003-42-1 : LC Card 87-403866 DDC 305.5/63 19
HD1531.B7 B713 1986

Ramalho, Luiz.
Lateinamerikanische Gewerkschaften zwischen staatlicher Gängelung und Autonomie . Saarbrücken , Fort Lauderdale , 1985. 306 p. ; ISBN 3-88156-315-6 LC Card 87-135045 DDC 331.88/098 19
HD6571 .L38 1985

Die Verplante Wohnmisere . Saarbrücken , Fort Lauderdale , 1986. 334 p. : ISBN 3-88156-329-6 LC Card 87-408292 DDC 363.5/1/096 19
HD7287.96.A4 V47 1986

Ramamurti, Ravi. State-owned enterprises in high technology industries : studies in India and Brazil / Ravi Ramamurti. New York : Praeger, 1987. xii, 306 p. ; 25 cm. Includes index. Bibliography: p. 289-294. ISBN 0-03-068767-5 (alk. paper) : LC Card 85-30751 DDC 338.4/762/00954 19
1. High technology industries - Government ownership - India. 2. High technology industries - Government ownership - Brazil. I. Title.
HC440.H53 R36 1986 *NYPL [JLE 87-1514]*

Ramana, D. V. A monograph on access planning as an essay on explorations in alternatives / by D.V. Ramana. Kuala Lumpur : APDC, [1982] 86 p. : ill. ; 23 cm. At head of title: United Nations, Asian and Pacific Development Centre. "30 June 1982." Includes bibliographical references. LC Card 84-940306 DDC 338.954 19
1. Economic development. 2. Economic development projects - India - Citizen participation. I. Asian and Pacific Development Centre. II. Title. III. Title: Access planning as an essay on explorations in alternatives.
HD75 .R36 1982

Ramanadham, Venkata Vemuri, 1920- The Nature of public enterprise / edited by V.V. Ramanadham. New York : St. Martin's Press, 1984. 302 p. : ill. ; 23 cm. Includes bibliographical references and index. ISBN 0-312-86778-6 : LC Card 83-40570
1. Government business enterprises - Developing countries. 2. Government business enterprises - Management. I. Title. *NYPL [JLD 86-1037]*

Ramanamma, A., 1936- Women in Indian industry / A. Ramanamma, Usha Bambawale. Delhi, India : Mittal Publications, 1987. 232 p. ; 23 cm. Bibliography: p. [223]-227. Includes index. LC Card 87-901258 DDC 331.4/821381/0954 19
1. Women - Employment - India. 2. Women electronic industry workers - India. I. Bambawale, Usha. II. Title.
HD6189 .R347 1987

Ramanantoanison, R. Willaert, Y. Ressources humaines et développement régional en Côte d'Ivoire . [Addis Ababa] [1977] 3, 108, [6] leaves (1 folded) ; LC Card 82-980560
HD5846.9.A6 W55 1977

Ramanlal Desai, Akshayakumar. see **Desai, Akshayakumar Ramanlal.**

Ramdin, Ron. The making of the Black working class in Britain / Ron Ramdin. Aldershot, Hants, England ; Brookfield, Vt., USA : Gower, c1987. x, 626 p. ; 23 cm. Includes index. Bibliography: p. [523]-605. ISBN 0-566-00943-9 LC Card 87-127153 DDC 305.5/62 19
1. Labor and laboring classes - Great Britain. 2. Blacks - Great Britain - Economic conditions. 3. Blacks - Great Britain - Social conditions. I. Title.
HD8398.B55 R36 1987

Ramírez Bautista, Elia.
Estadísticas bancarias : promedios anuales de los balances mensuales de los bancos mexicanos, 1882-1910 / Elia Ramírez Bautista.1a ed. México, D.F. : Dirección de Estudios Históricos, Instituto Nacional de Antropología e Historia, 1985. 10, ca. 200 p. ; 27 cm. (Recopilación de estadísticas económicas del siglo XIX en México . v. 3) Cuaderno de trabajo / Instituto Nacional de Antropología e Historia ; 47 Chiefly tables. ISBN 968-603-813-2 LC Card 87-401719 DDC 332.1/0972/021 19
1. Banks and banking - Mexico - History - 19th century - Statistics. 2. Banks and banking - Mexico - History - 20th century - Statistics. I. Series. II. Series: Cuaderno de trabajo (Instituto Nacional de Antropología e Historia (Mexico). Dirección de Estudios Históricos) , 47. III. Title.
HG2714 .R36 1985

Flores Clair, Eduardo. Estadísticas mineras de México en el siglo XIX /. México, D.F. , 1985. 181 p. ; LC Card 87-401718 DDC 338.2/0972 19
HD9506.M62 F57 1985

Ramírez C., Luis Alfonso. Chilchota, un pueblo al pie de la sierra : integración regional y cambio económico en el noroeste de Michoacán / Luis Alfonso Ramírez C. Zamora, Mich. [i.e. Michoacán] : Colegio de Michoacán ; [Morelia, Mexico] : Gobierno del Estado de Michoacán, 1986. 306 p. : ill. ; 21 cm. Bibliography: p. 299-306. ISBN 968-7230-23-1 LC Card 87-401034 DDC 330.972/37 19
1. Chilchota Region (Mexico) - Economic conditions. 2. Artisans - Mexico - Chilchota Region. 3. Agriculture - Economic aspects - Mexico - Chilchota Region. I. Title.
HC138.C45 R36 1986

Ramírez C., Valeria (Ramírez Ceballos) Desarrollo socio-económico de la Octava Región de Chile / Valeria Ramírez C. Santiago, Chile : Centro de Estudios del Desarrollo, 1985. i, 45 leaves ; 28 cm. (Materiales para discusión . no. 95) Includes bibliographical references. LC Card 86-115542
1. Biobío (Chile) - Economic conditions. 2. Regional planning - Chile - Biobío. I. Title. II. Series.
HC193.B5 R35 1985

Ramirez, Francisco O. Rethinking the nineteenth century . New York , c1988. p. cm. ISBN 0-313-25997-6 (lib. bdg. : alk. paper) LC Card 87-17791 DDC 330.9/034 19
HC53 .R48 1988

Ramírez L., Fernando (Ramírez López) Estado y crisis del desarrollo nacional : planeación de la administración pública / Fernando Ramírez L., Raúl Díaz Ontiveros.1a ed. México, D.F. : Ediciones Contables y Administrativas, 1983. 242 p. ; 22 cm. Bibliography: p. 225-242. LC Card 86-220975
1. Mexico - Economic policy. 2. Mexico - Economic conditions - 1918-. I. Díaz Ontiveros, Raúl. II. Title.
HC135 .R234 1983

Ramírez, Ligia. Abitazione e periferie urbane nei paesi in via di sviluppo . Milano, Italy , c1985. 450 p. : LC Card 86-132019
HD7287.96.L29 A25 1985
NYPL [JLD 87-1173]

Ramírez, Mirta Beatriz. Sonzogni, Cristina María. La población de la ciudad de Corrientes a mediados del siglo XIX /. Corrientes , 1980. 50, [4] leaves, [14] leaves of plates : LC Card 85-209374
HB3560.C67 S65 1980

Ramírez, Nelson. Gómez, Carmen. Población y vivienda en la República Dominicana . Santo Domingo, República Dominicana , 1984. 116 p. : LC Card 85-154466
HD7316.5.A3 G65 1984
NYPL [JLF 86-1146]

Ramona y el robot . Cárdenas, Isabel Laura. Buenos Aires, Argentina , 1986. 155 p. : ISBN 950-560-032-1 LC Card 87-100727
HD6072.2.A72 B843 1986

Ramos Allup, Henry. Veinte temas, una posición / Henry Ramos Allup. Caracas, Venezuela : Ediciones Centauro, [19]85. 153 p. ; 16 cm. ISBN 980-263-018-7 LC Card 87-401543 DDC 330.987/0633 19
1. Venezuela - Economic conditions - 1958-. 2.

Venezuela - Politics and government - 1958-. I. Title.
HC237 .R315 1985

Ramos, Gabriel Poveda. see **Poveda Ramos, Gabriel.**

Ramos, Segundo, d. 1960.
Rasgos salientes de la tragedia histórica de noviembre de 1922. 1983. Capelo C., J. Alejo (J. Alejo Capelo Cabello), d. 1973. El crimen del 15 de noviembre de 1922 / por J. Alejo Capelo C. Rasgos salientes de la tragedia histórica de noviembre de 1922 / por Segundo Ramos. La hora trágica : (15 de noviembre de 1922) y otros apuntes sobre el movimiento obrero / por José I. Guzmán S. [Guayaquil] , 1983. 10, 14, 19 p. : LC Card 86-114097
HD5358.A6 C36 1983

Ramphal, S. S. The trampling of the grass : the inaugural silver jubilee lecture of the Economic Commission for Africa / given by Shridath S. Ramphal, Addis Ababa, 29 April 1985. [Addis Ababa?] : The Commission, [1985] 41 p. : port. ; 24 cm. "No. 1." LC Card 85-981035 DDC 338.96 19
1. Africa - Economic policy. 2. Africa - Economic integration. 3. United Nations. Economic Commission for Africa. I. United Nations. Economic Commission for Africa. II. Title.
HC800 .R36 1985

Ramsa, Georges. Binst, Olivier. Banques, le grand secret /. Paris , c1987. 166 p. ; ISBN 2-234-02032-8 : LC Card 87-156884
HG3026 .B48 1987

Ramsey, Douglas K. The corporate warriors / Douglas K. Ramsey. Boston : Houghton Mifflin, 1987. xxi, 261 p. ; 24 cm. Bibliography: p. 261. ISBN 0-395-35487-0 : LC Card 86-20954 DDC 338.8/3/0973 19
1. Competition - United States - Case studies. 2. Competition, International - Case studies. 3. Strategic planning - Case studies. I. Title.
HD41 .R27 1987 ***NYPL [JLE 87-1347]***

Ramsey, Gerald D. The Impact of zero base budgeting on managerial behavior /. Hempstead, N.Y. , 1986. vii, 288 p. ; LC Card 86-80005 DDC 658.1/54 19
HG4028.B8 I55 1986

Ramsey, Guy Reed. Postmarked Washington : Pacific and Wahkiakum counties / by Guy Reed Ramsey ; editor, Alan H. Patera. Lake Grove, OR (Box 2093, Lake Grove 97035) : Depot, c1987. 148 p. : ill. ; 22 cm. Includes index. LC Card 86-72305 DDC 383/.4979791 19
1. Postal service - Washington (State) - Pacific County - History. 2. Postal service - Washington (State) - Wahkiakum County - History. I. Patera, Alan H. II. Title.
HE6376.A1 W265 1987

Rana, Pradumna Bickram, 1947- The impact of the current exchange rate system on trade and inflation of selected developing member countries / by Pradumna B. Rana. Manila, Philippines : Asian Development Bank, c1983. iv, 78 p. : ill. ; 28 cm. (Asian Development Bank economic staff paper . no. 18) "September 1983"--Cover. Bibliography: p. 77-78. LC Card 87-105105 DDC 332.4/56 19
1. Foreign exchange problem - Developing countries. 2. Developing countries - Commerce. 3. Inflation (Finance) - Developing countries. I. Title. II. Series.
HG3877 .R36 1983

Ranade, Sudhanshu, 1952- Rural banking adrift / Sudhanshu Ranade. Bombay : Jaico, c1984. x, 126 p. ; 23 cm. Includes bibliographical references. LC Card 84-903073 DDC 332.1/0954 19
1. Banks and banking - India. 2. Rural development - India. I. Title.
HG3284 .R325 1984 ***NYPL [JLD 87-561]***

Ranadive, K. R. Accumulation, employment, and labour aristocracy : towards understanding working class reality in India / by K.R. Ranadive. Bombay : Tata Institute of Social Sciences, [1982] 55 p. ; 25 cm. (T.I.S.S. series . 53) Dr. S.D. Punekar memorial lectures ; 2 Includes bibliographical references. LC Card 83-903051 DDC 305.5/62/0954 19
1. Labor and laboring classes - India - Addresses, essays, lectures. 2. Labor policy - India - Addresses, essays, lectures. 3. Wages - India - Addresses, essays, lectures. 4. Industry and state - India - Addresses, essays, lectures. I. Title. II. Title: Dr. S.D. Punekar memorial lecture. III. Series.
HD8686.5 .R325 1982 ***NYPL [JLF 87-500]***

RANCHERS - OKLAHOMA - ECONOMIC CONDITIONS.
Plaxico, James Sam, 1924- Financial status of Oklahoma farmers and ranchers, 1985 . [Stillwater] [1986] 42 p. ; LC Card 86-622478 DDC 338.1/3/09766021 19
HD1775.O5 P57 1986

RANCHERS - OREGON - HARNEY COUNTY - HISTORY.
Simpson, Peter K., 1930- The community of cattlemen . Moscow, Idaho , c1987. xiv, 228 p. ; ISBN 0-89301-117-7 (pbk.) LC Card 87-5855 DDC 338.1/762/00979595 19
HD9433.U5 H277 1987

RANCHERS - PRAIRIE PROVINCES - POLITICAL ACTIVITY - HISTORY.
Breen, David. The Canadian prairie west and the ranching frontier, 1874-1924 /. Toronto , Buffalo , c1983. xiii, 302 p., [4] p. of plates : ISBN 0-8020-5548-6 LC Card 83-143575 DDC 338.1/762/009712 19
HD9433.C22 P733 1983 ***NYPL [HY 87-755]***

RANCHES - ARGENTINA - CÓRDOBA (PROVINCE) - HISTORY.
Tagle Frías de Cuenca, Matilde. Historia de la Estancia "Pozo de Correa" /. [Córdoba, Argentina] , 1984. 88 p. : LC Card 86-157022
HD1471.A72 C677 1984

RANCHES - OREGON - HARNEY COUNTY - HISTORY.
Simpson, Peter K., 1930- The community of cattlemen . Moscow, Idaho , c1987. xiv, 228 p. ; ISBN 0-89301-117-7 (pbk.) LC Card 87-5855 DDC 338.1/762/00979595 19
HD9433.U5 H277 1987

Rancière, Jacques. Gauny, Gabriel, 1806-1889. [Selections. 1983.] Le philosophe plébéien /. Paris , Saint-Denis , c1983. 205 p. ; ISBN 2-7071-1420-0 : LC Card 84-105473
HD4853 .G382 1983

Rand Corporation.
Ginsburg, Paul B. A private health plan option strategy for Medicare /. Santa Monica, CA [1987] xvi, 116 p. ; ISBN 0-8330-0863-3 (pbk.) LC Card 87-17593 DDC 368.4/26/00973 19
HD7102.U4 G56 1987

Health insurance and the demand for medical care . Santa Monica, CA , 1987. p. cm. ISBN 0-8330-0864-1 LC Card 87-17587 DDC 368.3/82/00973 19
HD7102.U4 H413 1987

Neu, C. R. (Carl Richard), 1949- Toward a profile of Soviet behavior in international financial markets /. Santa Monica, CA [1987] xv, 58 p. : ISBN 0-8330-0865-X (pbk.) LC Card 87-13084 DDC 332/.042/0947 19
HG3955 .N48 1987

Park, Rolla Edward. Optimal peak-load pricing for local telephone calls /. Santa Monica, CA , c1987. xiii, 41 p. : ISBN 0-8330-0856-X (pbk.) LC Card 87-410013 DDC 384.6/3 19
HE8825 .P369 1987

Schlesinger, James R. Organizational structures and planning /. [Santa Monica, Calif. , 1966] iii, 45 p. : LC Card 87-404140 DDC 353.6 19
HD58.9 .S35 1966

Rand Health Insurance Study. Health insurance and the demand for medical care . Santa Monica, CA , 1987. p. cm. ISBN 0-8330-0864-1 LC Card 87-17587 DDC 368.3/82/00973 19
HD7102.U4 H413 1987

A Rand note .
(N-2329-FF/RF/WFHF) Why were infant and child mortality rates highest in the poorest states of Peninsular Malaysia, 1941-75? /. Santa Monica, CA (P.O. Box 2138, Santa Monica 90406-2138) [1986] xi, 45 p. ; LC Card 86-210106 DDC 304.6/4/088054 19
HB1323.I42 M49 1986

(N-2516-HHS) Marquis, M. Susan. Choice under uncertainty and the demand for health insurance /. Santa Monica, CA (P.O. Box 2138, Santa Monica 90406-2138) [1986] ix, 50 p. ; LC Card 87-118503 DDC 368.3/8/00973 19
HG9396 .M268 1986

Randak, Harald, 1942- Die soziale Marktwirtschaft / Harald Randak. 1. Aufl. München : Bayerische Landeszentrale für Politische Bildungsarbeit, 1985. 143 p. : ill. (some col.) ; 17 x 24 cm. (Elementar . E 6) Bibliography: p. 137-138. Includes index. LC Card 85-216985
1. Germany, West - Economic conditions. 2. Germany, West - Economic policy. I. Bayerische Landeszentrale für Politische Bildungsarbeit. II. Title. III. Series.
HC286.5 .R36 1985

Randall, Alan, 1944- Resource economics : an economic approach to natural resource and environmental policy / Alan Randall.2nd ed. New York : Wiley, c1987. xiii, 434 p. ; 24 cm. Includes bibliographies and indexes. ISBN 0-471-87468-X LC Card 87-4988 DDC 333.7 19
1. Nonrenewable natural resources. 2. Environmental policy. 3. Economics. I. Title.
HC59 .R256 1987

Randall, Laura. The political economy of Venezuelan oil / Laura Randall. New York : Praeger, 1987. xiii, 247 p. ; 25 cm. Bibliography: p. 231-239. Includes index. ISBN 0-275-92823-3 (alk. paper) : LC Card 87-15848 DDC 338.2/7282/0987 19
1. Petroleum industry and trade - Venezuela. 2. Petroleum industry and trade - Government ownership - Venezuela. 3. Petróleos de Venezuela, S.A. 4. Venezuela - Economic policy. I. Title.
HD9574.V42 R35 1987

Randall, Maury R. Huang, Stanley S. C. Investment analysis and management /. Boston , c1987. xiv, 605 p. : ISBN 0-205-10501-7 LC Card 87-986 DDC 332.6 19
HG4529 .H8 1987

Randle, Yvonne. Flamholtz, Eric. The inner game of management . New York, NY , c1987. xiv, 225 p. ; ISBN 0-8144-5867-X LC Card 87-47705 DDC 658.4/09 19
HD31 .F538 1987

The Randlords /. Wheatcroft, Geoffrey. New York , 1987, c1985. xix, 314 p. : ISBN 0-671-63993-5 (pbk.) : LC Card 87-4513 DDC 338.2/0968 19
HD9536.S62 W44 1985

Randolph, W. Alan. Effective project planning and management : getting the job done / W. Alan Randolph, Barry Z. Posner. Englewood Cliffs, N.J. : Prentice-Hall, [1987], c1988. x, 163 p. : ill. ; 24 cm. Bibliography: p. 141-143. Includes index. ISBN 0-13-244815-7 LC Card 87-11399 DDC 658.4/04 19
1. Industrial project management. I. Posner, Barry Z. II. Title.
HD69.P75 R36 1988

Random House (Firm) Chilnick, Lawrence D. The complete guide to drug testing . New York, N.Y. , c1987. p. cm. ISBN 0-394-56058-2 : LC Card 87-9631 DDC 658.3/82 19
HF5549.5.D7 C46 1987

RANDOM PROCESSES. see **STOCHASTIC PROCESSES.**

Randretsa, Iarivony. Andrianarivelo Rafrezy, Vincent. Population de Madagascar . [Antananarivo] [1985] 154 p. : LC Card 86-981367
HA4699 .A84 1985

Randse Afrikaanse Universiteit. Departement Vervoerekonomie. Inligtingsimposium, 23 Oktober 1981 /. [Pretoria] [1981] 115 p. : LC Card 86-213181 DDC 380.5/0968 19
HE284.4.A2 I55 1981

Range economics /. Workman, John P. New York , London , c1986. xvi, 217 p. : ISBN 0-02-948810-9 LC Card 85-18882 DDC 333.74 19
HD1635 .W67 1986 ***NYPL [JLE 86-2382]***

RANGE MANAGEMENT.
Workman, John P. Range economics /. New York , London , c1986. xvi, 217 p. : ISBN 0-02-948810-9 LC Card 85-18882 DDC 333.74 19
HD1635 .W67 1986 ***NYPL [JLE 86-2382]***

RANGE MANAGEMENT - KENYA - KITUI (DISTRICT) - DECISION MAKING.
Peden, D. G. The use of resource survey data in decision-making with special reference to Kitui District in Kenya /. Nairobi, Kenya , 1982. 12 leaves ; LC Card 85-980593 DDC 333.74/09676/24 19
HD983.Z8 K587 1982

RANGE MANAGEMENT - SUDAN.
Behnke, Roy H., 1947- Open-range management and property rights in pastoral Africa . London [1985] 29 p. : LC Card 86-209817 DDC 333.2 19
HD977.Z63 B44 1985

Rangel Belis, Gonzalo. Sector económico externo, industrialización y conflictos laborales en Venezuela / Gonzalo Rangel Belis. Valencia : Vadell Hnos. Editores, 1985. 141 p. : ill. ; 21 cm. Bibliography: p. 137-141. ISBN 980-212-007-3 LC Card 86-226708
1. Venezuela - Foreign economic relations. 2. Industry and state - Venezuela. 3. Venezuela - Commercial policy. 4. Venezuela - Economic conditions - 1958-. I. Title.
HF1529 .R36 1985

Rangel, Domingo Alberto. Fin de fiesta / Domingo Alberto Rangel. 1a ed. Valencia, Venezuela : Vadell, 1982. 181 p. ; 19 cm. LC Card 83-200321
1. Latin America - Economic conditions - 1945-. 2. Latin America - Politics and government - 1948-. I. Title.
HC125 .R29 1982

Rangel Guevara, Carlos.
[Tercermundismo. English]
Third world ideology and Western reality : manufacturing of political myth / Carlos Rangel ; foreword by Jean-François Revel ; with the assistance of Vladimir Tismaneanu. New Brunswick : Transaction Books, c1986. xiii, 180 p. ; 24 cm. Translation of: El tercermundismo. Includes index. ISBN 0-88738-601-6 (pbk.) LC Card 85-24486 DDC 330.9172/4 19
1. Socialism - Developing countries. 2. Capitalism - Developing countries. 3. Developing countries. I. Title.
HC59.7 .R26513 1985 NYPL [JLE 86-3009]

RANGELANDS - ECONOMIC ASPECTS.
Workman, John P. Range economics /. New York , London , c1986. xvi, 217 p. : ISBN 0-02-948810-9 LC Card 85-18882 DDC 333.74 19
HD1635 .W67 1986 NYPL [JLE 86-2382]

RANGELANDS - KENYA.
Agatsiva, J. L. Land use mapping of Kenya using remote sensing techniques /. [Nairobi] , 1982. iv, 39 p. : LC Card 84-980919 DDC 333.73/13/028 19
HD983.Z7 A38 1982

RANGELANDS - KENYA - KITUI (DISTRICT) - MANAGEMENT.
Peden, D. G. The use of resource survey data in decision-making with special reference to Kitui District in Kenya /. Nairobi, Kenya , 1982. 12 leaves ; LC Card 85-980593 DDC 333.74/09676/24 19
HD983.Z8 K587 1982

Ranis, Gustav.
Li, Kuo-ting. The evolution of policy behind Taiwan's development success /. New Haven , c1988. p. cm. ISBN 0-300-04080-6 LC Card 87-23035 DDC 338.951/249 19
HC430.5 .L4725 1988

Otsuka, Keijiro. Comparative technology choice in development . New York , 1988. viii, 247 p. : ISBN 0-312-00516-4 : LC Card 86-29666 DDC 338.4/567721/0952 19
HD9886.I42 O87 1988

RANK. see **SOCIAL CLASSES.**

Ránki, György, 1930- Berend, T. Iván (Tibor Iván), 1930- The Hungarian economy in the twentieth century /. London , c1985. 316 p. ; ISBN 0-7099-2209-4 LC Card 86-673483
HC300.24 .B44 1985b

Rankin, H. C. D. Corporation tax for students / H.C.D. Rankin and D.M. Catterall. 2nd ed. Wokingham, Berkshire, England : Van Nostrand Reinhold, 1985. x, 230 p. : ill. ; 22 cm. Includes indexes. ISBN 0-85258-242-0 (pbk.) LC Card 85-3272 DDC 657/.46/0941 19
1. Corporations - Taxation - Great Britain. 2. Tax accounting - Great Britain. I. Catterall, D. M. II. Title.
HD2753.G7 R36 1985

RANKING AND SELECTION (STATISTICS)
Meddis, Ray. Statistics using ranks . Oxford, OX, UK , New York, NY, USA , 1984. vi, 449 p. : ISBN 0-631-13788-2 (pbk.) : LC Card 84-11087 DDC 519.5 19
HA29 .M43885 1984 NYPL [JLE 86-4708]

Ranky, Paul G., 1951- Computer integrated manufacturing : an introduction with case studies / Paul G. Ranky. Englewood Cliffs, N.J. : Prentice-Hall International, c1986. xiii, 513 p. : ill. ; 24 cm. Includes bibliographies and index. ISBN 0-13-165655-4 : LC Card 85-19199 DDC 670.42/7 19
1. Computer integrated manufacturing systems. 2. CAD/CAM systems. 3. Flexible manufacturing systems. I. Title.
TS155.6 .R36 1985 NYPL [JSE 87-587]

Ranta, Niilo, 1914- Suomen postimestarit 1809-1984 : virkoihin nimitetyt postimestarit, postinhoitajat, posti- sekä posti- ja lennätinkonttorien konttorinhoitajat, kuin myös postikonttorien päälliköt / Niilo Ranta. Helsinki : Postikonttorien päälliköt, [1986] 144 p. : ill., 1 facsim., 4 maps, ports. ; 26 cm. Maps on lining papers. "Liite: Postijärjestys v. 1881": p. 114-144. Includes index. LC Card 87-101716
1. Postal service - Finland - Postmasters - Biography - Dictionaries. 2. Postal service - Finland - Biography - Dictionaries. 3. Postal service - Finland - History - 19th century. I. Title.
HE7064 .R35 1986

Rantala, Olavi, 1949- A study of housing investment and housing market behaviour / Olavi Rantala. Helsinki : Bank of Finland, 1986. 117 p. : ill. ; 25 cm. (Bank of Finland publications. Series B, 0357-4776 . 40) Bibliography: p. [113]-117. ISBN 951-686-116-4 (pbk.) LC Card 86-204998 DDC 338.4/369083/0724 19
1. Housing - Econometric models. I. Title.
HD7287.5 .R33 1986

Rao, Anna Maria, 1949- L'"Amaro della feudalità" : la devoluzione di Arnone e la questione feudale a Napoli alla fine del '700 / Anna Maria Rao. Napoli : Guida, c1984. 382 p. ; 23 cm. (Esperienze. 119) Includes bibliographical references and index. ISBN 88-7042-265-8 : LC Card 85-200705
1. Land reform - Italy - Naples (Kingdom) - History - 18th century. 2. Feudalism - Italy - Naples (Kingdom) - History - 18th century. 3. Inheritance and succession - Italy - Naples (Kingdom) - History - 18th century. 4. Land tenure - Law and legislation - Italy - Naples (Kingdom) - History - 18th century. 5. Public land sales - Italy - Naples (Kingdom) - History - 18th century. 6. Social conflict - Italy - Naples (Kingdom) - History - 18th century. 7. Naples (Kingdom) - Social conditions. I. Title.
HD1333.I82 N367 1984

Rao, B. Ramachandra. see **Ramachandra Rao, B.**

Rao, Dileep.
National emerging industries resourceguide /. Minneapolis, MN , c1986. 368, 124 p. ; ISBN 0-8144-5851-3 LC Card 85-82163 DDC 338.7/61/0002573 19
HD62.5 .N38 1986 NYPL [JLF 86-1717]

National emerging industries site selection guide /. Minneapolis, MN , c1986. 124 p. ; LC Card 86-231272 DDC 338.6/042/02573 19
HC110.D5 N38 1986

Rao, M. Gangadhara. see **Gangadhara Rao, M.**

Rao, M. S. A. Studies in migration . Delhi , 1986. x, 400 p. : ISBN 81-85054-08-8 : LC Card 86-902753 DDC 304.8/0954 19
HB2099 .S78 1986

Rao, P. S. Fishery economics and management in India / P.S. Rao. 1st ed. Bombay, India : Pioneer Publishers, 1983. 356, [1] p. : ill. ; 24 cm. Errata slip mounted on p. [357] Includes bibliographical references and index. LC Card 83-906523 DDC 338.3/714/0954 19
1. Fish trade - India. 2. Fisheries - Economic aspects - India. 3. Fishery management - India. I. Title.
HD9466.I52 R36 1983 NYPL [JLE 86-290]

Rao, Ramesh K. S. Financial management : concepts and applications / Ramesh K.S. Rao. New York : Macmillan ; London : Collier Macmillan, c1987. xvii, 798 p. : ill. ; 24 cm. Tables: [4] p. inserted. Includes bibliographies and index. ISBN 0-02-398210-1 LC Card 86-26406 DDC 658.1/5 19
1. Corporations - Finance. I. Title.
HG4026 .R36 1987

Rao, T. Venkateswara. see **Venkateswara, Rao T.**

Rao, Y. Saraswathy. see **Saraswathy Rao, Y.**

Rao, Y. V. Krishna. see **Krishna Rao, Y. V.**

Rapajić, Nikola. Kongres privrednih stručnjaka Hrvatske (1943-1944 : Otočac and Čazma, Croatia) Kongres privrednih stručnjaka Hrvatske . Zagreb , 1985. 252 p., [16] p. of plates : ISBN 86-80359-01-7 LC Card 86-176200
HC407.Z7 C7637 1943

Rapawy, Stephen. Civilian employment in the U. S.S.R., 1950 to 1983 / by Stephen Rapawy. Washington, D.C. : Soviet Social Studies Branch, Center for International Research, Bureau of the Census, U. S. Dept. of Commerce, [1985] 35 leaves ; 22 x 36 cm. (CIR staff paper . no. 10) Bibliography: leave 35. LC Card 87-601284 DDC 331.12/5/0947021 19
1. Labor supply - Soviet Union - Statistics. I. Title. II. Series.
HD5796 .R358 1985

Rapetti, Vittorio, 1955- Uomini, collina e vigneto in Piemonte, da metà Ottocento agli anni trenta / Vittorio Rapetti ; prefazione di Piero Bolchini. 1a ed. Alessandria : Edizioni dell'orso, 1984. 342 p., [16] p. of plates : ill. ; 24 cm. (ISRA . 4) At head of title: Istituto per la storia della resistenza in provincia di Alessandria, Istituto per la storia della resistenza in provincia di Asti. Bibliography: p. 302-333. LC Card 86-151345
1. Wine industry - Italy - Piemonte - History. 2. Viticulture - Italy - Piemonte - History. 3. Agriculture - Economic aspects - Italy - Piemonte - History. 4. Piemonte (Italy) - Industries - History. I. Istituto per la storia della resistenza in provincia di Alessandria. II. Istituto per la storia della resistenza in provincia di Asti. III. Title. IV. Series.
HD9385.I82 P547 1984

Raphaelson, Joel. Ogilvy, David, 1911- The unpublished David Ogilvy /. New York , c1986. 178 p., [6] p. of plates : ISBN 0-517-56609-5 : LC Card 87-13583 DDC 659.1/092/4 B 19
HF5810.O34 A3 1986

Raphel, Murray, 1928- The do-it-yourself direct mail handbook / by Murray Raphel & Ken Erdman. Philadelphia, PA (402 Bethlehem Pike, Philadelphia 19118) : Marketers Bookshelf, c1986. xix, 218 p. : ill. ; 24 cm. LC Card 86-203353
1. Advertising, Direct-mail. 2. Mail-order business. I. Erdman, Ken. II. Title.
HF5861 .R35 1986

Rapid population growth, living conditions, and fertility reduction implication (Bangkok metropolis) /. Charoon Vitiprod. [Singapore] 1979. ii, 41 leaves : LC Card 82-940038
HB3644.55.B36 C48 1979

RAPID READING.
Saperstein, Rose, 1956- Read your way to the top with the guide /. Seattle, Wash. , c1987. 83 p. : ISBN 0-930251-00-8 (pbk.) : LC Card 87-310 DDC 428.4/3 19
HF5351 .S34 1987

RAPID TRANSIT. see **LOCAL TRANSIT.**

RAPO . Shiriaev, A. V. (Andreĭ Vasil'evich) Moskva , 1985. 155 p. ; LC Card 86-142380
HD9015.S653 R8775 1985

Rapone, Anita. The Guardian Life Insurance Company, 1860-1920 : a history of a German-American enterprise / Anita Rapone. New York : New York University Press, c1987. xiv, 209 p., [10] p. of plates : ill. ; 24 cm. Bibliography: p. [201]-204. Includes index. ISBN 0-8147-7401-6 : LC Card 87-7913 DDC 368.3/2/0068 19
1. Guardian Life Insurance Company - History. 2. German Americans - History. I. Title.
HG8963.G942 R36 1987

Rapoport, IU. M. (IUriĭ Mikhaĭlovich)
Osushchestvlenie ėkonomicheskoĭ politiki Kommunisticheskoĭ partii v usloviiakh Evropeĭskogo Severa RSFSR, 1917-1925 gg. / IU.M. Rapoport ; pod redaktsieĭ V.A. Selezneva. Leningrad : Izd-vo Leningradskogo universiteta, 1984. 216 p. ; 22 cm. At head of title: Ministerstvo vysshego i srednego spetsial'nogo obrazovaniia RSFSR. Includes bibliographical references. LC Card 84-217989
1. Soviet Union, Northern - Economic conditions. 2. Soviet Union - Economic policy - 1917-1928. 3. Russian S.F.S.R. - Economic conditions. I. Seleznev, V. A. (Valeriĭ Aleksandrovich). II. Title.
HC336.9.N65 R36 1984

Rapoport, Vladimir Samuilovich. Mil'ner, Bentsion Zakharovich. Sistemnyĭ podkhod k organizatsii upravleniia /. Moskva , 1983. 223 p. : LC Card 83-229946
HD70.S63 M54 1983

Rappaport, Stephen P. Lamb, Robert. Municipal bonds /. New York , c1987. xx, 327 p. ; ISBN 0-07-036084-7 : LC Card 86-27539 DDC 336.3/1 19
HJ9145 .L35 1987

Rapport afgivet af Privatiseringsudvalget. Denmark. Privatiseringsudvalget. [Copenhagen] [1983] 2, 243, [65] p. ; LC Card 85-134270
HD4224 .D45 1983

Rapport (ATA-projektet (Aalborg universitetscenter)) . (nr. 4, etc) Jørgensen, Henning, 1949- Arbejdsmarkedsnævn i arbejdsmarkedspolitikken /. [Aalborg] [1985?]-<[1986]. v. <1-2 > : ISBN 87-88706-12-5 LC Card 87-104729
HD5799.A6 J64 1985

Rapport aux assemblées régionales . Guadeloupe. Conseil régional. [Basse-Terre] [1982] 62 p. ; LC Card 85-136896 DDC 338.97297/6 19
HC158.5 .G83 1982a

Rapport de la Mission sur le programme de développement des industries métallurgiques de base et mécaniques en République du Sénégal. ECA/UNIDO Basic Metals and Engineering Industries Development Programme Mission. [S.l.] [1979] 41, 3 p. (2 fold.) ; LC Card 80-981173
HD9506.S42 E33 1979

Rapport de la Table de concertation sur l'industrie du vêtement . Table de concertation sur l'industrie du vêtement (1985 : Montréal, Québec) [Québec] [1985] v, 174, 12 p. ; LC Card 87-103889
HD9940.C22 Q847 1985

Rapport (Denmark. Direktoratet for toldvæsenet) . (2) Denmark. Direktoratet for toldvæsenet. Information og kontrol . [Copenhagen] [1985] 125, [49] p. : LC Card 86-209910
HJ6971 .D46 1985

Rapport d'enquête et d'audience publique . (14) Poste Des Cantons, lignes Nicolet-Des Cantons et Des Cantons-Nouvelle-Angleterre /. [Sainte-Foy, Qc] [1983] 1 v. (various pagings) ; ISBN 2-550-10466-8 LC Card 85-121505
HD9685.C3 Q455 1983

Rapport d'exécution du plan intérimaire, 1982-1983 / Secrétariat d'Etat auprès du Premier Ministre, Commissariat général du plan. Paris : La Documentation française, c1984. 146 p. : ill. ; 24 cm. "23 novembre 1983." ISBN 2-11-001229-3 : LC Card 85-121410
1. France - Economic policy - 1945-. 2. Industry and state - France. 3. France - Social policy. I. France. Commissariat général du plan.
HC276.2 .R32 1984

Rapport du Groupe de politique des transports. France. Groupe de politique des transports. Paris , c1984. 246 p. : ISBN 2-11-001216-1 : LC Card 84-163968
HE248 .F716 1984

Rapport du Groupe de travail sur le prix des carburants au Québec. Québec (Province). Groupe de travail sur le prix des carburants au Québec. [Québec , 1985] xiv, 169, [153] p. : ISBN 2-550-11913-4 LC Card 86-185758
HD9574.C23 Q47 1985

Rapport fra Underavdeligen for intervjuundersøkelser . (nr. 34) Attidues to Norwegian development assistance, 1974. Oslo , 1975. 57 p. ; LC Card 86-460167
HA1503 .A18 nr. 34 HC60

Rapport från Kommunaldemokratiska forskningsgruppen . (9) Sannerstedt, Anders, 1945- Attityder till kommunal service /. [Stockholm] [1981] vi, 166 p. : ISBN 91-38-06586-X LC Card 82-244101
HD4485.S8 S26 1981

Rapport intérimaire sur la promotion des exportations de produits de bois. Export promotion of furniture/joinery products from east/southern Africa. Addis Ababa [1983] 34 p. in various pagings : LC Card 86-981008
HD9773.A472 E96 1983

Rapport intérimaire sur l'étude de marketing sur le potentiel d'exportation de mobilier et de produits de ménuiserie des pays du MULPOC de Lusaka vers les états du Golfe, l'Algérie et la Jamahiriya arabe libyenne. 1983. Export promotion of furniture/joinery products from east/southern Africa. Addis Ababa [1983] 34 p. in various pagings : LC Card 86-981008
HD9773.A472 E96 1983

Rapport om administrationsbudgettering. [Copenhagen] : Fællesudgiftsudvalget, Administrationsudvalget, [1984] 85, 33 p. ; 21 cm. "Marts 1984." LC Card 85-129140
1. Budget - Denmark. I. Denmark. Fællesudgiftsudvalget.
HJ2133 .R36 1984

Rapport om betalingskort : en undersøgelse af købe- og kreditkortsystemer og elektronisk betalingsformidling ved forbrugerkøb / Industriministeriet. [Copenhagen] : Direktoratet for statens indkøb, [1982] 302, 4, 17 p. ; 24 cm. "December 1982." "Betænkning nr. 965." Bibliography: p. 101-103. ISBN 87-503-4413-7 LC Card 83-243151
1. Credit cards - Denmark. I. Denmark. Industriministeriet.
HG3756.D4 R36 1982

Rapport relatif aux traitements, honoraires et autres bénéfices des membres de l'Office de la construction du Québec. Québec (Province). Bureau du vérificateur général. Vérification spéciale . [Québec] [1978-<1987? >] v. <1-3 > ; LC Card 82-212701
HD9715.C33 Q45 1978

Rapport sur la situation économique et sociale, stratégie de développement et besoins d'assistance, 1986-1990 . Laos. Genève [1986- v. <1 > : LC Card 86-204475
HC443 .L36 1986

Rapport (Sweden. Konsumentverket) . (1984:4-O3) Kombinationserbjudanden. Vällingby [1984] 269, [45] p. : ISBN 91-7398-243-1 LC Card 85-115578
HF5438.5 .K66 1984

Rapporter /. Lauritzen, Niels, 1947- København [1983] 59 p. : ISBN 87-503-4574-5 LC Card 84-169893
HD4465.D4 L38 1983

Rapporter fra Statistisk sentralbyrå, 0332-8422 . (82/17) Ressursregnskap for fisk. Oslo , 1982. 53 p. : ISBN 82-537-1765-2 : LC Card 82-229877
HD9465.N62 R47 1982

(82/29) Engrosprisstatistikk . Oslo , 1982. 120 p. ; ISBN 82-537-1833-0 : LC Card 83-139816
HB235.N6 E54 1982

(83/1) Naturressurser 1982 . Oslo , 1983. 62 p. : ISBN 82-537-1837-3 : LC Card 83-174054
HC363.5 .N372 1983

(83/29) Stølen, Nils Martin. Etterspørsel etter arbeidskraft i norske industrinæringer /. Oslo , 1983. 66 p. : ISBN 82-537-2001-7 : LC Card 84-191739
HD5800.A6 S76 1983

(83/30) Siring, Erling. To notater om sammenlikning av data fra fruktbarhetsundersøkelsen 1977 med data fra registre /. Oslo , 1983. 43 p. : ISBN 82-537-2006-8 : LC Card 84-161768
HB1025 .S57 1983

(83/32) Skoglund, Tor. Regionale strukturendringer belyst ved sysselsettingstall /. Oslo , 1983. 52 p. ; ISBN 82-537-2003-3 : LC Card 84-161751
HD5800.A6 S58 1983

(83/7) Bergan, Roar. Behandlingen av oljevirksomheten i byråets makroøkonomiske årsmodeller /. Oslo , 1983. 30 p. ; ISBN 82-537-1918-3 : LC Card 83-225651
HD9575.N62 B46 1983

(84/1) Naturressurser og miljø 1983 . Oslo , 1984. 100 p. : ISBN 82-537-1993-0 : LC Card 84-161695
HC363.5 .N38 1984

(84/13) Knudsen, Jon Paschen. Boligstandard . Oslo , 1984. 66 p. : ISBN 82-537-2088-2 : LC Card 85-125379
HD7349.A3 K58 1984

(84/17) Schreiner, Alette. Virkninger av oljevirksomhet i Nord-Norge /. Oslo , 1984. 43 p. : ISBN 82-537-2118-8 : LC Card 85-146089
HD9575.N62 S37 1984

(84/23) Bergan, Roar. MINK . Oslo , 1984. 71 p. : ISBN 82-537-2138-2 : LC Card 85-178061
HC365 .B388 1984

(84/24) Holm, Yngvar. Engrosomsetningsindeks /. Oslo , 1984. 18 leaves ; ISBN 82-537-2141-2 : LC Card 85-178075
HB235.N6 H65 1984

Rapporter udarbejdet af Forvaltningshøjskolen og Miljøstyrelsens økonomifunktion. København : Miljøministeriet, [1983] 59 p. : ill. ; 24 cm. At head of title: Rapportbilag II til Vandprisudvalgets betænkning. "Oktober 1983." ISBN 87-503-4574-5 LC Card 85-150558
1. Municipal water supply - Denmark - Rates. 2. Water consumption - Denmark. I. Danmarks forvaltningshøjskole. II. Denmark. Miljøstyrelsen. III. Denmark. Udvalget til undersøgelse af vandforsyningernes økonomiske baggrund. Vandpriser.
HD4465.D4 R36 1983

Rapporteur's report : second conference of ambassadors/high commissioners of Sierra Leone, Freetown, 15th-21st Dec. 1978 : policy statements. [Freetown : Ministry of Foreign Affairs, Sierra Leone, 1978?] 70 leaves ; 29 cm. Cover title. LC Card 87-401796 DDC 338.966/4 19
1. Sierra Leone - Economic policy - Congresses. 2. Sierra Leone - Social policy - Congresses. 3. Sierra Leone - Politics and government - 1961- - Congresses. I. Sierra Leone. Ministry of Foreign Affairs. II. Title: Second conference of ambassadors/high commissioners of Sierra Leone, Freetown, 15th-21st Dec. 1978.
HC1065 .R36 1978

Rapporto CNEL su risparmio e borsa . Consiglio nazionale dell'economia e del lavoro (Italy) Roma , 1984. 308 p. : LC Card 85-242331 DDC 332/.0415/0945021 19
HC310.S3 C66 1984

Rapporto ISFOL 1985 : formazione, nuove tecnologie, professionalità. Milano, Italy : F. Angeli, c1985. 533 p. : ill. ; 22 cm. (Strumenti e ricerche . 11) Bibliography: p. [509]-522. LC Card 86-156267
1. Occupational training - Italy. 2. Occupational retraining - Italy. 3. Vocational education - Italy. 4. Labor supply - Italy - Effect of technological innovations on. I. Istituto per lo sviluppo della formazione professionale dei lavoratori. II. Series.
HD5715.5.I8 R393 1985

Rapporto sulle partecipazioni statali / [di] G. De Michelis ... [et al.]. Milano : F. Angeli, [1981] 1 v. (in various pagings) ; 22 cm. (Collana di economia e politica industriale. 14) Includes bibliographical references. ISBN 88-20-42161-5 : LC Card 81-199972 DDC 338.945 19
1. Industrial promotion - Italy. 2. Industry and state - Italy. 3. Economic development projects - Italy. 4. Italy - Economic policy. I. De Michelis, G. (Gianni).
HC310.I53 R35 ***NYPL [JLD 83-2970]***

Rasche, Robert H. Controlling the growth of monetary aggregates / Robert H. Rasche, James M. Johannes ; with a foreword by Karl Brunner. Boston : Kluwer Academic Publishers, c1987. xviii, 212 p. : ill. ; 24 cm. (Rochester studies in economics and policy issues) "Published in cooperation with the Center for Research in Government Policy & Business, William E. Simon Graduate School of Business, University of Rochester, Rochester, New York"--Verso t.p. Bibliography: p. 189-193. Includes indexes. ISBN 0-89838-226-2 : LC Card 87-3737 DDC 332.4/6 19
1. Monetary policy - Econometric models. 2. Money supply - Econometric models. I. Johannes, James M. II. University of Rochester. Center for Research in Government Policy and Business. III. Title.
HG230.3 .R37 1987

Raschet zatrat i opredelenie ėkonomicheskoĭ ėffektivnosti avtomatizirovannykh sistem operativno-proizvodstvennogo planirovaniia na avtoremontnykh predpriiatiiakh . Dergachev, A. F. Moskva , 1978. 35 p. ; LC Card 81-173259
HD9710.A2 D47 1978

Raschke, Freddy, 1950- Bevölkerungsstruktur, Mobilität und Lohn : eine ungleichgewichtstheoretische Analyse des Zusammenhangs zwischen der Mobilitäts- und Lohnentwicklung unter besonderer Berücksichtigung der Bevölkerungsstruktur / Freddy Raschke. Frankfurt am Main ; New York : Lang, c1985. vi, 194 p. : ill. ; 22 cm.

(Europäische Hochschulschriften. Reihe V, Volks- und Betriebswirtschaft, 0531-7339 . Bd. 629 = vol. 629 = vol. 629) Bibliography: p. 190-194. ISBN 3-8204-5697-X LC Card 85-221450
1. Wages - Effect of labor mobility on - Mathematical models. 2. Migration, Internal - Mathematical models. I. Series: Europäische Hochschulschriften. Reihe V, Volks- und Betriebswirtschaft , Bd. 629. II. Title.
HD4911 .R37 1985

Rase campagne . Luxardo, Hervé. Paris , c1984. 253 p. : ISBN 2-7007-0376-6 : LC Card 85-101431
HD1536.F8 L893 1984

Rasgos salientes de la tragedia histórica de noviembre de 1922. Capelo C., J. Alejo (J. Alejo Capelo Cabello), d. 1973. El crimen del 15 de noviembre de 1922 /. [Guayaquil] , 1983. 10, 14, 19 p. : LC Card 86-114097
HD5358.A6 C36 1983

Rashed, Saeed Ahmed. Pakistan's energy policy : towards a new strategy / Saeed Ahmed Rashed. Islamabad, Pakistan : Institute of Policy Studies, 1983. iv, 102 p. : ill. ; 23 cm. Bibliography: p. 101-102. LC Card 83-930777 DDC 333.79/09549/1 19
1. Energy policy - Pakistan. 2. Energy consumption - Pakistan. I. Title. II. Title: Energy policy.
HD9502.P272 R373 1983
NYPL [JLD 86-3857]

Rashid, A. Characteristics of high income families, 1980 / by A. Rashid = Caractéristiques des familles à revenu élevé, 1980 / par A. Rashid. Ottawa : Statistics Canada, Labour and Household Surveys Analysis Division, [1986] 97 p. : ill. ; 28 cm. "June 1986." "Catalogue 13-584." Bibliography: p. 95. ISBN 0-660-52875-4 (pbk.) : LC Card 86-210700
1. Income - Canada - Statistics. 2. Income distribution - Canada - Statistics. 3. Wealth - Canada - Statistics. I. Statistics Canada. Labour and Household Surveys Analysis Division. II. Title. III. Title: Caractéristiques des familles à revenu élevé, 1980.
HC120.I5 R36 1986

Raskin, Patricia M., 1943- Vocational counseling : a guide for the practitioner / Patricia M. Raskin. New York, NY : Teachers College Press, c1987. xiii, 160 p. ; 23 cm. (Guidance and counseling series) Bibliography: p. 149-154. Includes index. ISBN 0-8077-2860-8 (pbk.) LC Card 87-1972 DDC 371.4/25 19
1. Vocational guidance. I. Title. II. Series.
HF5381 .R325 1987

Rasmussen, Jørgen, 1948- Virksomheden, lønarbejderen og samfundet : et oplæg til erhvervsøkonomisk debat / Jørgen Rasmussen. [Aalborg] : Aalborg universitetscenter, Institut for produktion, 1978. 264 p. ; 21 cm. Bibliography: p. 260-264. LC Card 86-460208
1. Industry - Social aspects - Denmark. I. Title.
HD60.5.D4 R37 1978

Raspoznavanie sluchaĭnykh prot͡sessov s peremennoĭ strukturoĭ veroi͡atnostnykh raspredeleniĭ . Kligene, Nerute. Vil′ni͡us , 1986. 136 p. : LC Card 87-146330
HD38 .S715 vyp.76 QA274

Rassegna congiunturale. N. 2 (Supplement) L'Economia in cifre, 1971-1985 /. Roma [1986] viii, 154 p. ; LC Card 86-233222
HC305 .E246 1986

Rasshirenie samostoi͡atel′nosti predprii͡atiĭ i nauchno-tekhnicheskoe razvitie proizvodstva / otvetstvennyĭ redaktor sbornika G.A. T͡Saritsina. Moskva : Akademii͡a nauk SSSR, In-t ėkonomiki, 1986. 205 p. ; 20 cm. Includes bibliographical references. LC Card 87-162795
1. Business enterprises - Soviet Union - Finance. 2. Technological innovations - Economic aspects - Soviet Union. I. T͡Saritsina, G. A. II. Institut ėkonomiki (Akademii͡a nauk SSSR).
HG4186 .R37 1986

Rasskaz o velikom severnom puti /. Kharitonov, S. F. (Sergeĭ Fedorovich) Petrozavodsk , 1984. 143 p. : LC Card 84-247171
HE3140.M87 K46 1984

Rasskazy o kalinint͡sakh. Moskva : Moskovskiĭ rabochiĭ, 1978. 172 p. : ill., ports. ; 20 cm. (Geroi nashikh dneĭ) LC Card 81-147895
1. Labor and laboring classes - Russian S.F.S.R. - Kaliningradskai͡a oblast′ - Biography. I. Series.
HD8529.K3162 R37 1978

Rasti͡annikov, V. G. (Viktor Georgievich) Gosudarstvo i agrarnai͡a ėvoli͡utsii͡a v razvivai͡ushchikhsi͡a stranakh Azii i Afriki /. Moskva , 1980. 227 p. ; LC Card 81-143353
HD2056 .G67 1980

Rastoin, Pierre. Marseille, quai d'avenir / Pierre Rastoin. [Paris] : J.C. Lattès, c1985. 184 p. ; 22 cm. LC Card 86-151556
1. Marseille (France) - Economic conditions. I. Title.
HC278.M3 R37 1985 *NYPL [JLD 87-253]*

Rastro de Cobra /. Silvia Helena. [Brazil , 1984] (Rio de Janeiro, RJ : Alphaset Gráfica e Editora) 124 p., [4] p. of plates : LC Card 87-130372 DDC 338.4/7004/0981 19
HD9696.C63 B77 1984

Rat des Kreises Burg. Die Sozialistische Gemeinschaftsarbeit im Territorium . Potsdam-Babelsberg , 1986. 175 p. ; LC Card 86-212526
HD3616.G48 S68 1986

Rat für Gegenseitige Wirtschaftshilfe. see **Sovet ėkonomicheskoĭ vzaimopomoshchi.**

Rat für Wissenschaftlichen Kommunismus (Germany) Die Sozialistische Gemeinschaft . Berlin , 1985. 238 p. ; LC Card 86-120025 DDC 337.1/1717 19
HC243.5 .S685 1985

RATAIONAL EXPECTATIONS (ECONOMIC THEORY)
Wittmann, Uli. Das Konzept rationaler Preiserwartungen /. Berlin , New York , c1985. xi, 310 p. : ISBN 0-387-15221-0 LC Card 86-194342
HB221 .W56 1985

Rate making process : going beyond the cost of service. AWWA Seminar on the Rate Making Process: Going Beyond the Cost of Service (1986 : Denver, Colo.) Proceedings /. Denver, CO , c1986. vi, 58 p. ; ISBN 0-89867-368-2 (pbk.) LC Card 87-107641 DDC 338.4/336361/0973 19
HD4461 .A915 1986

RATE OF RETURN.
Anderson, Dennis, 1937- Economic growth and the returns to investment /. Washington, D.C. [1987] 93 p. : ISBN 0-8213-0918-8 (pbk.) LC Card 87-14178 DDC 338.9 19
HD75 .A53 1987

Bierwag, Gerald O. Duration analysis . Cambridge, Mass. , c1987. xvi, 341 p. : ISBN 0-88730-116-9 LC Card 86-28745 DDC 332.8/2 19
HG4515.3 .B54 1987

Brownlie, William D. Life insurance . Cincinnati, Ohio , 1983. xii, 201 p. : ISBN 0-87218-033-6 (pbk.) LC Card 83-61584 DDC 368.3/2015 19
HG8853 .B87 1983
*NYPL [*R-Econ. 86-3488]*

Gheysens, Lieven. International diversification through the government bond market . [Leuven] , 1977. 188 leaves ; LC Card 85-186317 DDC 332.63/232 19
HG4715 .G44 1977
NYPL [JLM 86-1310 nr.24]

Stockton, Richard B. ROI, planning for profitable growth /. New York, N.Y., U. S.A. , c1984. x, 141 leaves : ISBN 0-86604-150-8 (pbk.) LC Card 86-232254 DDC 332.63 19
HG4028.C4 S72 1984b

Rate your executive potential /. Fritz, Roger. New York , c1988. xv, 239 p. : ISBN 0-471-62598-1 (pbk.) : LC Card 87-13705 DDC 658.4/09 19
HD38.2 .F74 1988

Ratemaking . Ishmael, Cheryl. [Albany, N.Y.] [1984] xi, 152 p. : *NYPL [JLF 86-598]*

RATERPILLAR TRACTOR COMPANY - HISTORY.
Zinman, Michael. The history of the decline and fall of the Raterpillar Tractor Company . Ardsley, N.Y. , c1986. 231 p. : ISBN 0-937704-03-2 (pbk.) : LC Card 86-82887 DDC 338.7/629225 19
HD9710.4.U64 R388 1986

Rates reform . Midwinter, Arthur F. Edinburgh , 1987. 182 p. ; ISBN 1-85158-062-X : LC Card 87-167866 DDC 336/.014/41 19
HJ9421 .M53 1987

Rating America's corporate conscience . Lydenberg, Steven D. Reading, Mass. , c1986. x, 499 p. : ISBN 0-201-15886-8 : LC Card 86-8064 DDC 338.7/4/0973 19
HD60.5.U5 L93 1986
*NYPL [*R-Econ. 87-1830]*

RATING, JOB. see **JOB EVALUATION.**

RATING OF EMPLOYEES. see **EMPLOYEES, RATING OF.**

RATING OF EXECUTIVES. see **EXECUTIVES, RATING OF.**

Rating places . Cutter, Susan L. Washington, D.C. , c1985. viii, 76 p. : ISBN 0-89291-191-3 (pbk.) : LC Card 85-13469 DDC 307/.0973 19
GF503 .C87 1985 *NYPL [JLD 86-2715]*

RATIO ANALYSIS.
Barbier, André. Guide pratique de l'analyse financière à l'usage des banquiers /. Paris , c1985. viii, 313 p. : ISBN 2-86325-038-8 : LC Card 86-165653
HF5686.C7 B32 1985

Helfert, Erich A. Techniques of financial analysis /. Homewood, Ill. , 1987. xiii, 458 p. : ISBN 0-256-03625-X (pbk.) LC Card 86-82589 DDC 658.1/51 19
HG4026 .H44 1987

Moore, Carl L. Profitable ratio analysis techniques /. New York, N.Y., U. S.A. , c1986. ix leaves, 201 p. : ISBN 0-86604-206-7 (pbk.) LC Card 86-208178 DDC 658.4/033 19
HF5681.R25 M58 1986

Pradhan, Radhe S. Public corporations of Nepal . New Delhi, India , 1986. xiii, 173 p. ; LC Card 86-903436 DDC 338.7/4/095496 19
HF5681.R25 P73 1986

Westwick, C. A. How to use management ratios /. Aldershot, Hants, England , 1987. xviii, 421 p. : ISBN 0-566-02425-X LC Card 87-126440 DDC 658.4/001/512924 19
HF5681.R25 W47 1987

Yadav, R. A. (Ram Avtar), 1949- Financial ratios and the prediction of corporate failure /. New Delhi , 1986. xvi, 196 p. ; LC Card 86-903341 DDC 338.7/4/0954 19
HF5681.R25 Y33 1986

Rational association /. Frohock, Fred M. Syracuse, N.Y. , 1987. xi, 201 p. ; ISBN 0-8156-2390-9 (alk. paper) LC Card 86-23026 DDC 302/.13 19
HB846.8 .F76 1987 *NYPL [JLE 87-1126]*

Rational choice . Behavioral foundations of economic theory. Chicago , 1987. ix, 332 p. : ISBN 0-226-34857-1 (alk. paper) LC Card 86-27241 DDC 330/.01/9 19
HB74.P8 B44 1987

Rational ecology . Dryzek, John S., 1953- Oxford, OX, UK , New York, NY, USA , 1987. ix, 270 p. : ISBN 0-631-15574-0 : LC Card 87-6587 DDC 363.7/0561 19
HC79.E5 D79 1987

Rational economics /. Jackson, Robin. New York , c1987. v, 145 p. ; ISBN 0-8022-2529-2 : LC Card 86-30260 DDC 330.1 19
HB501 .J27 1987

RATIONAL EXPECTATIONS (ECONOMIC THEORY)
Adolph, Brigitte. Rationale Erwartungen, Arbeitsverträge und Wirtschaftspolitik /. München , c1986. ii, 127 p. : ISBN 3-88259-346-6 LC Card 87-104701 DDC 330/.01/9 19
HB175 .A26 1986

Apostolopoulos, Athanase, 1955- Aktienkurse und rationale Erwartungen . Frankfurt am Main , New York , c1986. 364 p. : ISBN 3-8204-9157-0 LC Card 86-220281
HG5494 .A66 1986

Bökenkamp, Joachim. Methodologische Betrachtungen der Annahmen zum menschlichen Verhalten aus der Sicht der Volkswirtschaftslehre . Göttingen , c1985. v, 446 p. ; ISBN 3-925391-01-0 LC Card 87-121278 DDC 330/.01/9 19
HB74.P8 B59 1985

Hankel, Wilhelm, 1929- Gegenkurs . Berlin , c1984. 261 p. : ISBN 3-88680-114-4 LC Card 84-174753
HB3723 .H26 1984

Helmer, Hans-Josef. Merkantilismus und Kapitalismus im modernen

Rationalisierungsprozess /. Frankfurt , c1986. iii, 223 p. ; ISBN 3-88323-647-0 LC Card 87-113030 DDC 330.15/13 19
HB91 .H436 1986

Pesaran, M. Hashem, 1946- The limits to rational expectations /. Oxford, UK , New York, NY, USA , 1988, c1987. x, 325 p. : ISBN 0-631-14036-0 : LC Card 87-20877 DDC 339 19
HB172.5 .P445 1988

Pilder, Christhard. Die empirische Erhebung von Unternehmenserwartungen als Beitrag zur Konjunkturprognose /. Frankfurt am Main , c1984. vii, 185 p. : ISBN 3-88129-769-3 LC Card 84-173409
HB3730 .P53 1984

Precious, Mark. Rational expectations, non-market clearing, and investment theory /. Oxford , New York , 1987. vi, 167 p. : ISBN 0-19-877256-4 : LC Card 87-1552 DDC 332.6 19
HG4529 .P74 1987

Strong, Norman, 1954- Information and capital markets /. Oxford, UK , New York, NY, USA , 1987. x, 222 p. : ISBN 0-631-13834-X : LC Card 86-31721 DDC 332/.041 19
HG4523 .S77 1987

RATIONAL EXPECTATIONS (ECONOMIC THEORY) - CONGRESSES.
Behavioral foundations of economic theory. Rational choice . Chicago , 1987. ix, 332 p. : ISBN 0-226-34857-1 (alk. paper) LC Card 86-27241 DDC 330/.01/9 19
HB74.P8 B44 1987

Monetary policy and uncertainty . Baden-Baden , 1986. 262 p. : ISBN 3-7890-1257-2 (pbk.) LC Card 86-225786 DDC 332.4/0724 19
HG230.3 .M655 1986

Rational expectations, non-market clearing, and investment theory /. Precious, Mark. Oxford , New York , 1987. vi, 167 p. : ISBN 0-19-877256-4 : LC Card 87-1552 DDC 332.6 19
HG4529 .P74 1987

Rationale Erwartungen, Arbeitsverträge und Wirtschaftspolitik /. Adolph, Brigitte. München , c1986. ii, 127 p. : ISBN 3-88259-346-6 LC Card 87-104701 DDC 330/.01/9 19
HB175 .A26 1986

Rationalisierung im Energiebereich . Böttges, Norbert. Essen , Bielefeld , 1984. 159 p. : ISBN 3-7736-0106-9 LC Card 85-130852
HD9502.A2 B68 1984

Rationalisierung im Konjunkturverlauf /. Buchholz, Günter, 1946- Spardorf , c1983. 207 p. ; ISBN 3-922919-18-9 LC Card 84-135309
HD35 .B77 1983

Rationalisierungs-Kuratorium der Deutschen Wirtschaft. Limp, Wolfgang. Productivity centers . Frankfurt am Main , 1975. 64 p. ; LC Card 82-219310
HD30.4 .L55 1975

Rationalisierungsmassnahmen der Nachinflationszeit im Urteil der deutschen freien Gewerkschaften. Schalldach, Elisabeth, 1904- Jena, 1930. ix, [1], 186 p. LC Card AC34-383
HD70.G2 S26 1930

RATIONALISM.
Janicaud, Dominique, 1937- La puissance du rationnel /. [Paris] , c1985. 386 p. ; ISBN 2-07-070343-6 : ***NYPL [JFD 86-638]***

Sylvan, David J., 1953- A rationalist methodology for the social sciences /. Oxford [Oxfordshire] , 1985. 188 p. : ISBN 0-631-13443-3 : LC Card 84-14480 DDC 300/.1/8 19
HM24 .S95 1985 ***NYPL [JLE 86-1125]***

RATIONALISM - ADDRESSES, ESSAYS, LECTURES.
Rationalism, humanism, and democracy . Meerut , 1985. xcii, 514 p., [2] p. of plates : LC Card 85-901252 DDC 144 19
B833 .R29 1985 ***NYPL [JFD 86-3589]***

Rationalism, humanism, and democracy : a commemoration vol. in honour of Professor R.S. Yadava / by V.M. Tarkunde ... [et al.] ; K. Gopal, editor, B.S. Saxena, associate editor. Meerut : Professor R.S. Yadava Commemoration Volume Committee, 1985. xcii, 514 p., [2] p. of plates : ports. ; 22 cm. Includes bibliographical references. LC Card 85-901252 DDC 144 19
1. Yadava, R. S., 1922- - Addresses, essays, lectures. 2. Rationalism - Addresses, essays, lectures. 3. Humanism - Addresses, essays, lectures. 4. Democracy - Addresses, essays, lectures. 5. India - Politics and government - 1977- - Addresses, essays, lectures. 6. India - Civilization - 1947- - Addresses, essays, lectures. I. Yadave, R. S., 1922-. II. Tarkunda, V. M. III. Gopal, Krishna, 1937-.
B833 .R29 1985 ***NYPL [JFD 86-3589]***

A rationalist methodology for the social sciences /. Sylvan, David J., 1953- Oxford [Oxfordshire] , 1985. 188 p. : ISBN 0-631-13443-3 : LC Card 84-14480 DDC 300/.1/8 19
HM24 .S95 1985 ***NYPL [JLE 86-1125]***

RATIONALIZATION OF INDUSTRY. see **INDUSTRIAL MANAGEMENT.**

Rationelle Energieverwendung im Industriebetrieb . Nosko, Herbert. Berlin , c1986. xiii, 289 p. : ISBN 3-503-02547-2 LC Card 86-192206
HD9502.A2 N67 1986

RATIONING, CONSUMER - ECONOMETRIC MODELS.
Lambert, Jean-Paul, 1952- Disequilibrium macroeconomic models . Cambridge [Cambridgeshire] , New York , 1988. p. cm. ISBN 0-521-32209-X LC Card 86-24966 DDC 339.5/0724 19
HB145 .L36 1988

Tobin, James, 1918- Essays in economics. Cambridge, Mass. , 1987. vii, 492 p. : ISBN 0-262-20064-3 LC Card 87-3913 DDC 330/.028 19
HB801 .T6 1987

Ratiu, Ion. Moscow challenges the world / Ion Ratiu ; with an introduction by Brian Crozier. London : Sherwood Press, 1986. 410 p. ; 24 cm. Includes index. Bibliography: p. 381-388. ISBN 0-907671-23-5
1. Communism - Soviet Union. 2. World politics - 20th century. 3. Soviet Union - Foreign relations. 4. Soviet Union - History - 20th century. I. Crozier, Brian. II. Title. ***NYPL [JLE 87-1665]***

Ratjen, Wolfgang. Die bayerischen Bauernkammern von 1920 bis 1933 / Wolfgang Ratjen. München : Kommissionsbuchhandlung R. Wölfle, 1981. vi, 204 p. ; 21 cm. (Miscellanea Bavarica Monacensia . Heft 94) Neue Schriftenreihe des Stadtarchivs München ; Bd. 115 Bibliography: p. 198-204. ISBN 3-87913-108-2 : LC Card 83-194708 DDC 338.1/06/0433 19
1. Agriculture - Germany (West) - Bavaria - Societies, etc. - History. I. Title.
HD1486.G3 R34 1981

Ratnam, C. Dairy development : demand and supply aspects / C. Ratnam. Allahabad, India : Chugh Publications, 1986. xii, 168 p., [2] p. of plates : ill., map ; 23 cm. Revision of the author's thesis (Ph. D.--Andhra University, 1980) Study conducted in the Vishakhapatnam District, Andhra Pradesh. Includes bibliographies and index. ISBN 81-85076-06-5 : LC Card 86-903085 DDC 338.1/77/095484 19
1. Dairy products - India - Vishākhapatnam (District) - Marketing. 2. Dairy products industry - India - Vishākhapatnam (District). 3. Dairying - India - Vishākhapatnam (District). I. Title.
HD9275.I53 V587 1986

RATP plan d'entreprise 1983/1987. Régie autonome des transports parisiens. Paris [1982] 164 p. : LC Card 83-203335
HE4769.P33 R47 1982

Rattigan, G. A. (Godfrey Alfred), 1911- Industry assistance : the inside story / Alf Rattigan. Carlton, Vic. : Melbourne University Press ; Beaverton, Or. : International Specialized Book Services, 1986. viii, 289 p., [4] p. of plates : ill. ; 23 cm. Includes index. ISBN 0-522-84313-1 LC Card 86-202866 DDC 338.994 19
1. Tariff - Australia. 2. Australia - Commercial policy. 3. Industry and state - Australia. 4. Australia. Tariff Board. 5. Australia. Industries Assistance Commission. I. Title.
HF2483 .R38 1986

Rattinger, Hans. Wirtschaftlicher Wandel, religiöser Wandel und Wertwandel . Berlin , c1985. 411 p. : ISBN 3-428-05784-8 LC Card 85-218417
HC286.7 .W58 1985

Rattner, Henrique.
Informática e sociedade / Henrique Rattner. São Paulo-SP : Brasiliense, 1985. 219 p. : ill. ; 21 cm. (Série Comunicação e informática) Includes bibliographies. LC Card 85-221850
1. Technological innovations - Economic aspects. 2. Tecnological innovations - Social aspects. 3. Computer industry. 4. Economic history - 1971-. I. Series: Série Comunicação & informática. II. Title.
HC79.T4 R387 1985

Pequena empresa . São Paulo-Brasil [Brasília] , 1985. 2 v. : LC Card 85-180776 DDC 338.6/42/0981 19
HD9710.3.B72 P46 1985 ***NYPL [JLD 86-1588]***

Ratto, Luciano. Dizionario di management, matematica, statistica, R.O., logistica, produzione, personale, psicologia e sociologia del lavoro e delle organizzazioni /. Milano, Italy , c1986. 779 p. : LC Card 86-225959
HD30 .E5 vol. 30 HD30.15

Rau, Heinrich. Vergleichende Statistik des Handels der deutschen Staaten / von Heinrich Rau. Wien : W. Braumüller, 1863. vii, 183 p. ; 24 cm. LC Card 85-217948
1. Germany - Commerce - Statistics. 2. Austria - Commerce - Statistics. 3. Zollverein. I. Title.
HF3561.5 .R38 1863

Rau, Karl Heinrich.
Grundsätze der Volkswirthschaftslehre.
Menger, Carl, 1840-1921. Carl Mengers erster Entwurf zu seinem Hauptwerk "Grundsätze" geschrieben als Anmerkungen zu den "Grundsätzen der Volkswirthschaftslehre" von Karl Heinrich Rau. Tokio , 1963. xxviii, 236 p., [3] leaves of plates : LC Card 85-210245
HB175 .M47 1963

Rau, Thomas. Bodenallokation und Bodenpolitik im Ruhrgebiet : eine allokationstheoretische Untersuchung des "Grundstücksfonds Ruhr" / von Thomas Rau. Bochum : Studienverlag Brockmeyer, 1982. viii, 323 p. : ill. ; 21 cm. (Beiträge zur Struktur- und Konjunkturforschung . Bd. 19) Bibliography: p. 301-323. ISBN 3-88339-269-3 LC Card 83-130477 DDC 333.73/13/094355 19
1. Land use - Government policy - Germany (West) - Ruhr (Region). 2. Land use - Germany (West) - Ruhr (Region) - Planning. 3. Regional planning - Germany (West) - Ruhr (Region). I. Title. II. Series.
HD659.R8 R38 1982 ***NYPL [JLD 86-1715]***

Rau, Virginia. Sesmarias medievais portuguesas / Virgínia Rau ; prólogo e adenda documental por José Manuel Garcia. Lisboa : Editorial Presença, [1982] 288 p. : facsims. ; 22 cm. (Biblioteca de textos universitários . 53) Originally presented as the author's thesis (doctoral--Universidade de Lisboa). Includes bibliographical references. LC Card 87-673341
1. Land tenure - Portugal. 2. Land tenure - Law and legislation - Portugal. 3. Peasantry - Portugal. 4. Agriculture - Economic aspects - Portugal. I. Garcia, José Manuel. II. Title.
HD784 .R3x 1982

Raubenheimer, L. P. Cilliers, S. P. Patterns of migration and settlement in rural South Africa /. [Stellenbosch] , 1986. 19, 13 leaves, 5 folded leaves of plates : ISBN 0-908422-81-4 (pbk.) : LC Card 87-126315 DDC 304.8/0968 19
HB2123.4.A3 C56 1986

Rauch, Nizan. Kunert-Schroth, Heidrun. Jugendarbeitslosigkeit, lokale Ausprägungen und kommunale Strategien . Berlin , 1987. 172 p. ; ISBN 3-88118-135-0 LC Card 87-409103 DDC 331.3/412/0943 19
HD6276.G4 K86 1987

Rauf, Mohammad A. (Mohammad Abdur)
Rural-urban migration and rural emigration in Pakistan : a socio-economic impact study / Mohammad A. Rauf. Islamabad, Pakistan : Dept. of Anthropology, Quaid-i-Azam University, [1984?] 201 p. ; 24 cm. Bibliography: p. 198-201. LC Card 86-931437 DDC 307.2 19
1. Rural-urban migration - Pakistan. I. Title.
HB1955 .R38 1984

Raumbedeutsamkeit von Schnellfahrstrecken im Schienenverkehr /. Hoffmann, Klaus G. Berlin , c1985. xxviii, 547, [1] p. : ISBN 3-428-05770-8 LC Card 85-155640
HE3078 .H64 1985

Raumordnung und Industrialisierung /. Timmer, Reinhard. Hannover , 1977. 103 p. : LC Card 84-150907
HC286.5 .T55 1977

Raumordnungspolitik im Vollzug : Anspruch und Wirklichkeit / Herausgeber, Heinz D. Hänni = Politique d'organisation du territoire : impératifs et réalités / Editeur, Heinz D. Hänni. Grüsch : Rüegger, c1985. 507 p. : ill. ; 21 cm. (Thema = Thème) German and French. "Dieser Themaband enthält die überarbeiteten Vorträge eines Seminars, das im Rahmen des Nationalen Forschungsprogrammes 'Regionalprobleme' vom Januar 1984 in Bern durchgeführt wurde"--P. [5] Includes bibliographies. ISBN 3-7253-0258-8 : LC Card 86-149201
1. Switzerland - Economic conditions - 1918- - Regional disparities. 2. Regional planning - Switzerland. 3. Switzerland - Politics and government - 1945-. I. Hänni, Heinz D. II. Schweizerischer Nationalfonds zur Förderung der Wissenschaftlichen Forschung. NFP "Regionalprobleme.". III. Title: Politique d'organisation du territoire. IV. Series: Thème.
HC397 .R36 1985

Raumordnungsprognose 1990 : aktualisierte Prognose der Bevölkerung und der Arbeitsplatzzahl in den 38 Gebietseinheiten der Raumordnung für die Jahre 1980, 1985 und 1990. Bonn-Bad-Godesberg : Der Bundesminister für Raumordnung, Bauwesen und Städtebau, 1977. 95 p. : ill. col. maps ; 30 cm. (Schriftenreihe "Raumordnung" des Bundesministers für Raumordnung, Bauwesen und Städtebau . 06.012) Includes bibliographical references. LC Card 86-100310
1. Population forecasting - Germany, West. 2. Employment forecasting - Germany, West. I. Germany (West). Bundesministerium für Raumordnung, Bauwesen und Städtebau. II. Series.
HB3595 .R38 1977

Raumplanung und Flächennutzung. Rumley, Pierre-Alain. Aménagement du territoire et utilisation du sol . Zürich , c1984. x, 176 p. : LC Card 85-104773
HD796 .R86 1984

Raumwirkungen des Budgets der gesetzlichen Rentenversicherung . Blum, Ulrich. Karlsruhe , c1986. xii, 184, 35 p. : ISBN 3-88652-029-3 LC Card 87-124826 DDC 368.4/00943 19
HD7179 .B57 1986

Raunikar, Robert. Food demand analysis . Ames , 1987. xvi, 285 p. : ISBN 0-8138-1841-9 LC Card 86-30534 DDC 338.4/76413 19
HD9000.5 .F5947 1987

Rausch, Helmar. Grundsätze ordnungsmässiger EDV-Dokumentation : Möglichkeiten ihrer maschinellen Erfüllung und Konsequenzen für die Prüfungsdurchführung / vorgelegt von Helmar Rausch. Schwarzenbek : R. Martienss, 1985. vii, 323 p. : ill. ; 21 cm. Imprint on t.p.: Hamburg, 1983. Originally presented as the author's thesis (doctoral--Universität Hamburg, 1983) Bibliography: p. 302-323. ISBN 3-921757-21-5 LC Card 86-227042
1. Auditing - Germany (West) - Data processing. I. Title.
HF5667 .R335 1985

Rauscher, Anton.
Alternative Ökonomie? /. Köln , 1982. 244 p. ; ISBN 3-7616-0671-0 (pbk.) LC Card 84-109717 DDC 338.9 19
HD88 .A48 1982 ***NYPL [JLC 86-230]***

Soziallehre der Kirche und katholische Verbände /. Köln , 1980. 244 p. ; ISBN 3-7616-0568-4 (pbk.) : LC Card 81-122896 DDC 306/.6/0943 19
HN39.G3 S693 ***NYPL [JLC 86-231]***

Rauziński, Robert. Ludność Nadodrza, 1945-2000 / Robert Rauziński. Opole : Instytut Śląski w Opolu, 1985. 44 p. ; 24 cm. (Odra i Nadodrze) Bibliography: p. 36. LC Card 86-207214
1. Oder River Region - Population. 2. Western and Northern Territories (Poland) - Population. I. Title. II. Series.
HB3608.7.O34 R38 1985

Ravages du dogmatisme. Walbert, F. Non aux économistes, ou, Les ravages du dogmatisme /. Paris , c1984. 170 p. ; LC Card 87-152097
HB173 .W15 1984

Ravaioli, Carla. Tempo da vendere, tempo da usare : lavoro produttivo e lavoro riproduttivo nella società microelettronica / Carla Ravaioli. Milano, Italy : F. Angeli, c1986. 142 p. ; 22 cm. (La Società. 114) Includes bibliographical references. LC Card 86-182560
1. Hours of labor. 2. Work sharing. 3. Full employment policies. 4. Automation. 5. Leisure. 6. Quality of life. I. Title.
HD5106 .R357 1986

Ravallion, Martin. Markets and famines / Martin Ravallion. Oxford [Oxfordshire] : Clarendon Press ; New York : Oxford University Press, 1987. viii, 203 p. : ill. ; 23 cm. Bibliography: p. [181]-198. Includes index. ISBN 0-19-828514-0 : LC Card 86-23724 DDC 381/.456413/0095492 19
1. Famines. 2. Famines - Bangladesh. I. Title.
HC79.F3 R38 1987

Ravazzi, Giancarlo. L'Affiliazione commerciale . Milano , 1986. 100 p. : ***NYPL [JLD 87-531]***

Ravell, James J. Konings, Piet. The state and rural class formation in Ghana . London ; Boston : xvi, 391 p. : ISBN 0-7103-0117-0 LC Card 85-28109 DDC 305.5/09667 19
HN832.Z9 S65 1986 ***NYPL [Sc D 86-574]***

The raven of Zürich . Somary, Felix, 1881-1956. [Erinnerungen aus meinem Leben. English.] London , New York , c1986. xii, 310 p. : ISBN 0-312-66407-9 LC Card 86-6662 DDC 330/.092/4 B 19
HB101.S6 A313 1986 ***NYPL [JFE 87-54]***

RAVENSBURG REGION (GERMANY) - ECONOMIC CONDITIONS.
Henning, Friedrich-Wilhelm. Vorindustrielles Gewerbe und wirtschaftlicher Wandel im Paderborner Land im 19. Jahrhundert /. Dortmund , 1983. 67 p. ; LC Card 83-198581
HC288.P27 H46 1983

Ravenscraft, David J., 1952- Mergers, sell-offs, and economic efficiency / David J. Ravenscraft, F.M. Scherer. Washington, D.C. : Brookings Institution, c1987. xiii, 290 p. : ill. ; 24 cm. Cover title: Mergers, sell-offs & economic efficiency. Includes bibliographical references and index. ISBN 0-8157-7348-X : LC Card 87-14018 DDC 338.8/3/0973 19
1. Consolidation and merger of corporations - United States. 2. Corporate divestiture - United States. I. Scherer, F. M. (Frederic M.). II. Title. III. Title: Mergers, sell-offs & economic efficiency.
HD2746.5 .R38 1987

Raventós R., José María, 1940- 1880-1980, un siglo de publicidad gráfica en Colombia /. [Bogotá?] [1984] 286 p. : LC Card 84-202348 DDC 659.1/09861 19
HF5813.C63 A16 1984
NYPL [3-MDW+ 86-17]

Raventos Vorst, Ciska. El café en Costa Rica : desarrollo capitalista y diferenciación social de los productores, 1950-1980 / Ciska Raventos Vorst. San José, Costa Rica : Programa Centroamericano de Ciencias Sociales del CSUCA, 1985. iii, 145 p. : ill. ; 21 cm. (Cuadernos centroamericanos de ciencias sociales . 12) "Esta edición consta de 500 ejemplares"--Colophon. Bibliography: p. [101]-104. LC Card 86-174756
1. Coffee trade - Costa Rica - History. I. Title. II. Series.
HD9199.C82 R39 1985

Ravishankar, S., 1956-
Management of human resources in public enterprises /. New Delhi, India , 1985. vi, 304 p. ; LC Card 87-402995 DDC 354.5409/2/0683 19
HD4293 .M355 1985

Public enterprises in India . Bombay , 1983. xxii, 524 p. ; LC Card 83-905617 DDC 354.5409/2 19
HD4293 .P793 1983 ***NYPL [JLD 87-723]***

Ravitie ėkonomiki nezavisimoĭ Angoly /. Fituni, L. L. (Leonid Leonidovich) Moskva , 1981. 171, [3] p. ; LC Card 82-115411
HC950 .F57 1981

RAW MATERIALS.
Chalmin, Philippe. Négociants et chargeurs . Paris , 1985. 299 p. : ISBN 2-7178-0851-5 : LC Card 85-149921 DDC 333.7 19
HF1051 .C42 1985

Domdey, Karl Heinz. Weltenergie- und Weltrohstoffwirtschaft /. Berlin , 1981. 198 p. ; LC Card 85-132039
HD9502.A2 D65 1981

Kompleksnye problemy obespecheniia ėkonomiki mineral'nym syr'em /. Moskva , 1984. 115 p. : LC Card 85-192528
HF1051 .K64 1984

Maennig, Wolfgang. Die Effekte der Preisstabilisierung auf internationalen Rohstoffmärkten auf Erlöshöhe und -stabilität /. Berlin , 1985. 168 p. : ISBN 3-428-05947-6
NYPL [JLE 86-1670]

Mukerjee, Dilip. Primary commodities . Kuala Lumpur, Malaysia , c1985. 39 p. ; ISBN 967-99974-7-2 (pbk.) : LC Card 87-105669 DDC 338/.02 19
HF1040.7 .M85 1985

Primary commodities . Washington, D.C. , 1987. p. cm. ISBN 0-939934-87-6 LC Card 87-17225 DDC 382/.4 19
HF1040.7 .P718 1987

RAW MATERIALS - ASIA.
Gantskiĭ, Vladimir Alekseevich. Razvivaiushchiesia strany Azii v mirovom kapitalisticheskom syr'evom khoziaĭstve /. Moskva , 1985. 204 p. ; LC Card 86-154165
HF1054.A8 G36 1985

RAW MATERIALS - CONGRESSES.
Probleme der Rohstoffsicherung =. Bonn [1981] 215 p. : LC Card 85-206699
HF1051 .P76 1980

RAW MATERIALS - DEVELOPING COUNTRIES.
Gantskiĭ, Vladimir Alekseevich. Razvivaiushchiesia strany Azii v mirovom kapitalisticheskom syr'evom khoziaĭstve /. Moskva , 1985. 204 p. ; LC Card 86-154165
HF1054.A8 G36 1985

Habermayer, Wolfgang, 1959- Internationale Rohstoffabkommen als Beispiel des Nord-Süd Dialoges /. Frankfurt am Main , New York , c1985. xxxiii, 264 p. : ISBN 3-8204-8896-0 LC Card 86-111744
HF1054.D44 H33 1985

Hagemann, Hermann. Die Formierung der rohstoffpolitischen Forderungen der Entwicklungsländer auf der Ebene der Vereinten Nationen bis zur ersten Konferenz für Handel und Entwicklung (UNCTAD 1) 1946 /. Münster , 1983. xix, 384, [14], 42 p. : ISBN 3-923676-11-5 LC Card 84-172079
HC59.7 .H27 1983

Rodman, Kenneth Aaron. Sanctity versus sovereignty . New York , 1988. p. cm. ISBN 0-231-06448-9 LC Card 87-24970 DDC 332.6/7373/01724 19
HG5993 .R63 1988

RAW MATERIALS - GERMANY, EAST.
Kaufmann, Manfred. Die persönliche materielle Interessiertheit an der Material- und Energieökonomie /. Jena , 1984. 112 p. : LC Card 85-224317
HF1054.G42 K38 1984

RAW MATERIALS - GERMANY, WEST.
Eschenbaum, Gerhard. Krisenbevorratung von Rohstoffen unter spezieller Berücksichtigung einer Finanzierung aus Währungsreserven der Deutschen Bundesbank /. Bochum , 1983. xix, 464 p. : ISBN 3-88339-314-2 : LC Card 83-218426
HF1054.G4 E83 1983

Köhler, Axel, 1938- Konturen bundesdeutscher Rohstoffpolitik /. Köln , c1983. 56 p. : ISBN 3-602-24713-9 LC Card 83-215016
HF1054.G4 K64 1983

RAW MATERIALS - GOVERNMENT POLICY.
Tietenberg, Thomas H. Environmental and natural resource economics /. Glenview, Ill. , c1988. 559 p. : ISBN 0-673-18945-7 LC Card 87-23250 DDC 333.7 19
HC79.E5 T525 1988

RAW MATERIALS - INDIA.
Raza, Moonis. Transport geography of India . New Delhi , 1986. xii, 299 p. : LC Card 86-903251 DDC 380.5/0954 19
HE3298 .R39 1986

RAW MATERIALS - INDIA - DICTIONARIES.
The Wealth of India . New Delhi , c1985- v.

<1- > : ISBN 81-85038-00-7 (set) LC Card 87-900740 DDC 333.7/0954 19
HF1054.I5 W4 1985

RAW MATERIALS - KAZAKH S.S.R.
Ėkonomicheskaia otsenka i prognozirovanie ispol'zovaniia prirodnykh resursov Kazakhstana /. Alma-Ata , 1980. 161 p. ; LC Card 82-106708
HC337.K3 E34 1980

RAW MATERIALS - PRICES.
Behnke, Hartmut, 1941- Verletzbarkeitsmanagement bei parallelen Rohstoffpreis- und Devisenkursrisiken /. Frankfurt am Main , New York , c1986. vi, 288 p. : ISBN 3-8204-9365-4 LC Card 86-190114
HG3853 .B44 1986

Delmas, Philippe. La stabilisation des prix des matières premières . Paris , 1983. vii, 359 p. : ISBN 2-7178-0657-1 : LC Card 84-116258
HF1051 .D38 1983

RAW MATERIALS - PRICES - GERMANY (WEST) - ECONOMETRIC MODELS.
Borrmann, Axel. Die Wettbewerbsposition natürlicher Rohstoffe . Hamburg , 1984. 226 p. : ISBN 3-87895-250-3 LC Card 84-222130
HF1054.G4 B67 1984

RAW MATERIALS - SOVIET UNION.
Kompleksnye problemy obespecheniia ėkonomiki mineral'nym syr'em /. Moskva , 1984. 115 p. : LC Card 85-192528
HF1051 .K64 1984

Rawlins, V. Lane. Cook, Robert F., 1943- Public service employment . Kalamazoo, Mich. , 1985. xiii, 131 p. ; ISBN 0-88099-031-7 (pbk.) LC Card 85-22495 DDC 331.13/77/0973 19
HD5713.6.U54 C66 1985 NYPL [JLE 86-3877]

Rawson, Donald William.
Australian unions, 1984 / D.W. Rawson and Sue Wrightson Sydney : Croom Helm Australia, c1985. 123 p. ; 23 cm. Rev. ed. of: A handbook of Australian trade unions and employees' associations. 4th ed. 1980. ISBN 0-949614-13-0 LC Card 85-169297 DDC 331.88/025/94 19
1. Trade-unions - Australia - Directories. 2. Trade-unions - Australia - Statistics. I. Wrightson, Suzanne Nancy. II. Rawson, Donald William. Handbook of Australian trade unions and employees' associations. III. Title.
HD6891 .R35 1985 NYPL [JLD 86-1566]

Handbook of Australian trade unions and employees' associations. Rawson, Donald William. Australian unions, 1984 / D.W. Rawson and Sue Wrightson Sydney , c1985. 123 p. ; ISBN 0-949614-13-0 LC Card 85-169297 DDC 331.88/025/94 19
HD6891 .R35 1985 NYPL [JLD 86-1566]

Ray, B. Datta- see **Datta-Ray, B., 1925-**

Ray, D. Michael (David Michael), 1935- Berry, Brian Joe Lobley, 1934- Economic geography . Englewood Cliffs, N.J. , c1987. xi, 447 p. : ISBN 0-13-231440-1 : LC Card 87-2250 DDC 330.9 19
HC59 .B52 1987

Ray, Edward J. (Edward John), 1944-
Fleisher, Belton M. Principles of macroeconomics /. Dubuque, Iowa , c1987. xix, 427 p. : ISBN 0-697-01035-X (pbk.) LC Card 86-72959 DDC 339 19
HB172.5 .F545 1987

Fleisher, Belton M. Principles of microeconomics /. Dubuque, Iowa , c1987. xxi, 458 p. : ISBN 0-697-01038-4 (pbk.) LC Card 86-72958 DDC 338.5 19
HB172 .F54 1987

Ray, R.
Mikheev, S. Glossary of economic and social terminology in Eastern European socialist countries /. Geneva , 1986. 52, x p. ; ISBN 92-9014-413-0 : LC Card 86-214600 DDC 335.4/03/21 19
HB61 .M487 1986

Mikheev, S. Remuneration in Eastern European countries /. Geneva , 1985. vi, 45, ix p. ; ISBN 92-9014-408-4 (pbk.) : LC Card 86-216036 DDC 331.2/947 19
HD5014 .M55 1985

Ray, Renuka Mukerji, 1903- My reminiscences : social development during Gandhian era and after / Renuka Ray. New Delhi : Allied, 1982. ix, 294 p., [5] p. of plates : ill., ports. ; 22 cm. Autobiographical. Includes index. Bibliography: p. [279]-282. LC Card 82-905707 DDC 954.03/5 19
1. Ray, Renuka Mukerji, 1903-. 2. Women - India - Social conditions. 3. Legislators - India - Biography. 4. Social reformers - India - Biography. 5. India - Politics and government - 20th century. 6. India - Social conditions. I. Title.
DS481.R33 A38 1982 NYPL [JFD 85-9372]

RAY, RENUKA MUKERJI, 1903-
Ray, Renuka Mukerji, 1903- My reminiscences . New Delhi , 1982. ix, 294 p., [5] p. of plates : LC Card 82-905707 DDC 954.03/5 19
DS481.R33 A38 1982 NYPL [JFD 85-9372]

Ray, S. N., M.A. Migrant women workers : a study / by S.N. Ray. Ranchi : Bihar Tribal Welfare Research Institute, [1982] iii, 92 p., [3] leaves of plates : ill. ; 23 cm. Bibliography: p. 92. LC Card 85-903727 DDC 331.4/0954 19
1. Women - Employment - India. 2. Migrant labor - India. I. Title.
HD6189 .R39 1982 NYPL [JLD 86-3370]

Rāya, Manorañjana. Śramika āndolane aikya prasaṅge / Manorañjana Rāya. Kalikātā : Niśāna Prakāśanī, 1986. 226 p. ; 22 cm. In Bengali. Labor and trade union movements in West Bengal, covers the period, 1945-46 to 1955. LC Card 87-900228
1. Trade-unions - India - West Bengal - History. I. Title.
HD6815.W47 R39 1986

Rāya, Śaśikānta, 1957- Prācīna Bhārata meṃ vyāvasāyika samudāya, 600 Ī. Pū. se 200 Ī. taka = Occupational groups in ancient India / Śaśikānta Rāya.1. saṃskaraṇa. Naī Dillī : Rāmānanda Vidyā Bhavana, 1986. 176 p. ; 23 cm. In Hindi. Bibliography: p. [160]-[167] Includes index. LC Card 87-902475
1. India - Occupations - History. 2. India - Civilization - To 1200. I. Title. II. Title: Occupational groups in ancient India.
HB3639 .R39 1986

Raymond, Alex. Evaluation de la planification décentralisée /. Paris , c1986. 97 p. : ISBN 2-11-001562-4 : LC Card 86-193163
HC276.2 .E89 1986

Raynaud, Hervé. Arrow, Kenneth Joseph, 1921- Social choice and multicriterion decision-making /. Cambridge, Mass. , c1986. vii, 127 p. : ISBN 0-262-01087-9 LC Card 85-19913 DDC 302/.13 19
HM271 .A73 1986 NYPL [JLD 86-3628]

Raynauld, André. L'impact économique et financier de la Caisse de dépôt et placement du Québec / par André Raynauld. Montréal : Université de Montréal, [1983?] 23 p. ; 28 cm. (Cahier, 0709-9231 . 8336) "Communication présentée à l'Institut C.D. Howe le 10 novembre 1983 (texte révisé)" Summary in English. Includes bibliographical references. LC Card 85-164461
1. Caisse de dépôt et placement du Québec. 2. Public investments - Canada - Québec (Province). I. Series: Cahier (Université de Montréal. Département de sciences économiques) , 8336. II. Title.
HG5160.Q4 C357 1983

Raza, Moonis. Transport geography of India : commodity flows and the regional structure of the Indian economy / Moonis Raza, Yash Aggarwal. New Delhi : Concept Pub. Co., 1986. xii, 299 p. : ill., maps ; 25 cm. Bibliography: p. [287]-295. Includes index. LC Card 86-903251 DDC 380.5/0954 19
1. Transportation - India. 2. Railroads - India - Freight. 3. Commercial products - India. 4. Raw materials - India. 5. Geography, Economic. 6. India - Economic conditions - 1947-. I. Aggarwal, Yash, 1948-. II. Title.
HE3298 .R39 1986

Razeto, Luis. see **Razeto M., Luis, 1945-**

Razeto M., Luis, 1945- Las organizaciones económicas populares en la nueva coyuntura económica / Luis Razeto M. Santiago, Chile : Programa de Economía del Trabajo, Academia de Humanismo Cristiano, 1984. 23 p. ; 21 cm. "Preparado para el Seminario 'El Movimiento Laboral Frente a la Nueva Política Económica,' organizado por el P.E.T. en Santiago, el 19 de mayo de 1984." LC Card 84-227565
1. Cottage industries - Chile. 2. Self-help housing - Chile. 3. Consumer cooperatives - Chile. I. Title.
HD2346.C53 R39 1984

Razeto Migliaro, Luis. see **Razeto M., Luis, 1945-**

Razin, Assaf.
Economic effects of the government budget /. Cambridge, Mass. , c1988. p. cm. ISBN 0-262-08172-5 LC Card 87-26187 DDC 338.9 19
HJ2005 .E25 1988

Frenkel, Jacob A. Fiscal policies and the world economy . Cambridge, Mass. , c1987. xix, 484 p. : ISBN 0-262-06109-0 LC Card 87-3276 DDC 339.5/2 19
HJ141 .F74 1987

Nerlove, Marc, 1933- Household and economy . Boston , 1987. xiii, 155 p. : ISBN 0-12-515752-5 LC Card 86-10764 DDC 304.6/32 19
HB901 .N47 1987 NYPL [JLE 87-1715]

Nerlove, Marc, 1933- Population policy and individual choice . Washington, D.C., U. S.A. , 1987. 52 p. : ISBN 0-89629-062-X (pbk.) LC Card 87-16802 DDC 363.9 19
HB901 .N474 1987

La razionalità contrattata . Nacamulli, Raoul C. D. Bologna , c1986. 166 p. : ISBN 88-15-01189-7 : LC Card 87-122104
HD6709 .N296 1986

Razmeshchenie proizvoditel'nykh sil v Narynskoĭ oblasti /. Israilov, A. (Asangazy) Frunze , 1978. 56 p. ; LC Card 81-147534
HC337.K5452 N375 1978

Razrabotka i issledovanie algoritmov dinamicheskoĭ klassifikatsii protsessov : materialy k seminaru pri Institute matematiki i kibernetiki AN Litovskoĭ SSR "Statisticheskie problemy upravleniia" ; pod redaktsieĭ Ė. Shpilevskogo. Vil'nius : In-t matematiki i kibernetiki Akademii nauk Litovskoĭ SSR, 1979. 93 p. : ill. ; 20 cm. (Statisticheskie problemy upravleniia . vyp. 37) Titles on added t.p.: Procesų dinaminės klasifikacijos algoritmų sudarymas ir tyrimas; Elaboration and investigation of algorithms for dynamic classification of processes. At head of title: Institut matematiki i kibernetiki AN Litovskoĭ SSR. Institut fiziko-tekhnicheskikh problem ėnergetiki AN Lit. SSR. Litovskaia territorial'naia gruppa NKAU SSSR Mezhdunarodnoĭ federatsii po avtomaticheskokmu upravleniiu. Summaries in English and Lithuanian; table of contents also in English and Lithuanian. Includes bibliographies. LC Card 82-150323
1. Dynamic programming - Congresses. I. Shpilevskiĭ, Ė. II. Lietuvos TSR Mokslų akademija. Matematikos ir kibernetikos institutas. III. Fizikinių-techninių energetikos problemų institutas (Lietuvos TSR Mokslų akademija). IV. Natsional'nyĭ komitet SSSR po avtomaticheskomu upravleniiu. Litovskaia territorial'naia gruppa. V. Title: Procesų dinaminės klasifikacijos algoritmų sudarymas ir tyrimas. VI. Title: Elaboration and investigation of algorithms for dynamic classification of processes. VII. Series.
HD38 .S715 vyp. 37 T57.83

Razumikhin, Boris Sergeevich.
[Fizicheskie modeli i metody teorii ravnovesiia v programmirovanii i ėkonomike. English] Physical models and equilibrium methods in programming and economics / B.S. Razumikhin ; [translated from the Russian by M. Hazewinkel]. Dordrecht ; Boston : D. Reidel Pub. Co. ; xv, 351 p. : ill. ; 23 cm. (Mathematics and its applications) Translation of: Fizicheskie modeli i metody teorii ravnovesiia v programmirovanii i ėkonomike. "Revised and augmented compared to the original Russian edition and the French translation." Includes index. Bibliography: p. 344-348. ISBN 90-277-1644-7 LC Card 83-17791 DDC 330/.0724 19
1. Economics - Mathematical models. 2. Programming (Mathematics). 3. Equilibrium. I. Series: Mathematics and its applications (Dordrecht, Holland). II. Title.
HB135 .R3913 1984 NYPL [JSD 86-491]

Razumovskiĭ, A. V. (Al'bert Vadimovich)
Ėkonomika promyshlennosti stroitel'nykh materialov / A.V. Razumovskiĭ, S.G. Gusev. Izd. 2-e, perer. i dop. Moskva : Stroĭizdat, 1986. 350 p. : ill. ; 21 cm. Authorized for instructional purposes. Bibliography: p. [346]. LC Card 86-204591
1. Building materials industry - Soviet Union. I. Gusev, S. G. (Sergeĭ Georgievich). II. Title.
HD9715.8.S652 R39 1986

Razvitie agropromyshlennogo kompleksa Turkmenskoĭ SSR /. Stanchin, I. M. (Ivan

Mikhaĭlovich) Ashkhabad , 1985. 181, [3] p. : LC Card 85-185696
HD9015.S653 T878 1985

Razvitie ėnergetiki ÎAkutskoĭ ASSR v svîazi s sooruzheniem BAM : sbornik nauchnykh trudov / [redaktsionnaîa kollegiîa A.D. Alekseev ... N.A. Petrov (otv. redaktor) ... et al.]. ÎAkutsk : ÎAkutskiĭ filial SO AN SSSR, 1985. 99, 3 p. : ill. ; 20 cm. At head of title: Akademiîa nauk SSSR. Ordena Lenina Sibirskoe otdelenie. ÎAkutskiĭ filial. Institut fiziko-tekhnicheskikh problem Severa. Includes bibliographies. LC Card 86-233736
1. Energy industries - Russian S.F.S.R. - ÎAkutskaîa A.S.S.R. 2. ÎAkutskaîa A.S.S.R. (R.S.F.S.R.) - Economic conditions. I. Alekseev, A. D. II. Petrov, N. A. III. Institut fiziko-tekhnicheskikh problem Severa (Akademiîa nauk SSSR).
HD9502.S653 I237 1985

Razvitie i razmeshchenie mashinostroeniîa v investitsionnom komplekse / otvetstvennyĭ redaktor A.P. Levin. Moskva : "Nauka", 1986. 128 p. : ill. ; 20 cm. (Problemy sovetskoĭ ėkonomiki) At head of title: Akademiîa nauk SSSR. Gosplan SSSR. Sovet po izucheniîu proizvoditel'nykh sil. Includes bibliographical references. LC Card 86-232328
1. Machinery industry - Soviet Union - Capital investments. I. Levin, A. P. II. Sovet po izucheniîu proizvoditel'nykh sil (Soviet Union).
HD9705.S595 R39 1986

Razvitie kapitalisticheskikh otnosheniĭ v promyshlennosti Ukrainy XVIII v. Ponomarev, Alekseĭ Mikhaĭlovich. Rozvytok kapitalistychnykh vidnosyn u promyslovosti Ukraïny XVIII st. /. L'viv , 1971. 181 p. ; LC Card 82-105634
HC337.U5 P58 1971

Razvitie kapitalisticheskoĭ manufaktury v Anglii i Germanii XVI-XVII vv. : mezhvuzovskiĭ sbornik nauchnykh trudov / pod redaktsieĭ A.A. Kirillovoĭ. Moskva : Moskovskiĭ gos. pedagog. in-t im. V.I. Lenina, 1981. 132 p. : ill. ; 22 cm. At head of title: Ministerstvo prosveshcheniîa RSFSR. Moskovskiĭ ordena Lenina i ordena Trudovogo Krasnogo Znameni gosudarstvennyĭ pedagogicheskiĭ institut imeni V.I. Lenina. Includes bibliographical references. LC Card 83-111684
1. Manufactures - Germany - History. 2. Manufactures - Great Britain - History. 3. Capitalism - Germany - History. 4. Capitalism - Great Britain - History. I. Kirillova, A. A. II. Moskovskiĭ gosudarstvennyĭ pedagogicheskiĭ institut imeni V.I. Lenina.
HD9735.G32 R39 1981

Razvitie kapitalizma v sel'skom khoziaĭstve Bashkirii v poreformennyĭ period, 60-90-e gody XIX v. /. Usmanov, Kh. F. Moskva , 1981. 368 p. ; LC Card 82-118144
HD1995.B38 U86 1981

Razvitie khimicheskoĭ promyshlennosti Sibiri . Vsesoîuznaîa konferentsiîa "Razvitie proizvoditel'nykh sil Sibiri i zadachi uskoreniîa nauchno-tekhnicheskogo progressa" (1985 : Tomsk, R.S.F.S.R.). Sektsiîa "Khimicheskaîa promyshlennost'." Tomsk , 1985. 177 p. : LC Card 86-176713
HD9656.S56 S538 1985

Razvitie obshchestvennykh fondov potrebleniîa na sovremennom ėtape / otv. redaktory V.F. Maĭer, I.K. Zolotova. Moskva : In-t ėkonomiki AN SSSR, 1984. 140 p. ; 20 cm. Includes bibliographical references. LC Card 85-240059
1. Social security - Soviet Union. I. Maĭer, V. F. II. Zolotova, I. K. III. Institut ėkonomiki (Akademiîa nauk SSSR).
HD7196 .R39 1984

Razvitie prodovol'stvennogo kompleksa Kazakhstana /. Abdil'din, S. A. (Serikbolsyn Abdil'daevich) Alma-Ata , 1985. 158 p. ; LC Card 85-226938
HD9015.S653 K393 1985

Razvitie promyshlennosti Urala na zavershaîushchem ėtape sozdaniîa razvitogo sotsializma, 1951-1961 gg. . Popov, V. (Vladimir) Perm' , 1984. 70 p. ; LC Card 87-151346
HC337.R852 U73577 1984

Razvivaîushchiesîa strany : ėkonomika i politika / [glavnyĭ redaktor A.I. Chekhutov ; otvetstvennye redaktory T. Fel'vintsi ... et al.]. Moskva : In-t mirovoĭ ėkonomiki i mezhdunarodnykh otnosheniĭ AN SSSR : In-t nauch. informatsii po obshchestvennym naukam AN SSSR, 1982. 307 p. ; 20 cm. (Informatsionnyĭ biîulleten' . 8) At head of title: Problemnaîa komissiîa mnogostoronnego sotrudnichestva akademiĭ nauk sotsialisticheskikh stran "Ėkonomika i politika razvivaîushchikhsîa stran." Includes bibliographies. LC Card 85-115259
1. Developing countries - Economic conditions. 2. Developing countries - Foreign economic relations. I. Chekhutov, A. I. II. Fel'vintsi, T. III. Series: Informatsionnyĭ biîulleten' (Problemnaîa komissiîa mnogostoronnego sotrudnichestva akademiĭ nauk sotsialisticheskikh stran "Ėkonomika i politika razvivaîushchikhsîa stran") , 8.
HC59.7 .R33858 1982

Razvivaîushchiesîa strany . Ivanov, S. F. (Sergeĭ Feliksovich) Moskva , 1984. 63 p. : LC Card 85-125223
HB884 .I93 1984

Razvivaîushchiesîa strany Azii v mirovom kapitalisticheskom syr'evom khoziaĭstve /. Gantskiĭ, Vladimir Alekseevich. Moskva , 1985. 204 p. ; LC Card 86-154165
HF1054.A8 G36 1985

Razvivaîushchiesîa strany i mezhdunarodnoe sotrudnichestvo . Kupriîanov, A. B. (Alekseĭ Borisovich) Moskva , 1980. 262 p. ; LC Card 81-131557
HC59.7 .K863 1980

Razvivashti se strani : spravochnik / [sŭstaviteli i redaktsionna kolegiîa Ivan Ganev ... et al.].1. izd. Sofiîa : Partizdat, 1986. 423 p. ; 21 cm. Includes bibliographical references. LC Card 86-231951
1. Developing countries - Economic conditions - Dictionaries. I. Ganev, Ivan.
HC59.7 .R3395 1986

RBN user's guide. Regional Business News (RBN) user's guide. Cleveland, Ohio (11001 Cedar Ave., Cleveland 44106) , 1986- 1 v. (loose-leaf) ; LC Card 86-220007 DDC 025/.0633 19
HF5548.4.P74 R44 1986

RD, frente a su propia realidad. Castro, Aníbal de. R.D., frente a su propia realidad . [Santo Domingo, Dominican Republic? , 1986] 450, [2] p. ; LC Card 87-115306 DDC 330.97293/054 19
HC153.5 .C383 1986

Rdesiński, Maciej. Rummel, Julian. Narodziny żeglugi /. Gdańsk , 1980. 333 p., [32] leaves of plates : ISBN 83-215-3235-7 LC Card 80-147019
HE848.7 .R86 1980

RDI monographs on foreign aid and development, 0748-0644 .
(#2) Prosterman, Roy L. Egyptian development and U. S. aid . [Seattle, Wash.?] , c1985. i, 32, A1-A10 p. ; LC Card 87-104139 DDC 338.91/73/062 19
HC830.Z9 E446 1985

Rea, Kathryn P. Lientz, Bennet P. Data communications for business /. St. Louis , 1987. xx, 326 p. : ISBN 0-8016-3013-4 LC Card 86-23012 DDC 650/.028/546 19
HF5548.2 .L535 1987

Rea, Rupert Pennant- see Pennant-Rea, Rupert.

Reactivación con transformación : el efecto empleo. [Santiago, Chile] : Oficina Internacional del Trabajo, Programa Mundial del Empleo, Programa Regional del Empleo para América Latina y el Caribe, [c1984] 29 leaves ; 28 cm. (Documento de trabajo / PREALC . 238) "Abril 1984. Original: español." Bibliography: leaves [28]-29. LC Card 85-156967
1. Unemployment, Structural - Chile. 2. Chile - Economic policy. I. Regional Employment Program for Latin America and the Caribbean. II. Series: Documento de trabajo (Regional Employment Program for Latin America and the Caribbean) , 238.
HD5708.47.C5 R43 1984

Read your way to the top with the guide /. Saperstein, Rose, 1956- Seattle, Wash. , c1987. 83 p. : ISBN 0-930251-00-8 (pbk.) : LC Card 87-310 DDC 428.4/3 19
HF5351 .S34 1987

Reader, W. J. (William Joseph), 1920- Grand Metropolitan : a history, 1962-1987 / W.J. Reader. Oxford [Oxfordshire] ; New York : Oxford University Press, 1988. p. cm. Includes index. ISBN 0-19-822976-3 : LC Card 87-21942 DDC 338.8/8941 19
1. Grand Metropolitan (Firm) - History. 2. Conglomerate corporations - Great Britain - History. I. Title.
HD2845.Z75 G77 1988

Reader zum Kongress "Ausländerpolitik und Menschenrechte" /. Kongress "Ausländerpolitik und Menschenrechte" (1983 : Frankfurt am Main, Germany) Frankfurt , 1984. 60 p. ; LC Card 87-133583 DDC 331.6/2/0943 19
HD8458.A2 K594 1983

READING (ADULT EDUCATION) - UNITED STATES.
Workplace literacy /. New York , c1986. 74 p. : ISBN 0-8144-2325-6 LC Card 86-14013 DDC 331.25/92 19
HF5549.5.T7 W66 1986 ***NYPL [JLE 86-3510]***

READING COMPREHENSION.
Saperstein, Rose, 1956- Read your way to the top with the guide /. Seattle, Wash. , c1987. 83 p. : ISBN 0-930251-00-8 (pbk.) : LC Card 87-310 DDC 428.4/3 19
HF5351 .S34 1987

Geographical papers. see **Geographical papers. [Reading, Eng.]**

READING INTERESTS - ITALY - STATISTICS.
Indagine sulla lettura e su altri aspetti dell'impiego del tempo libero . [Roma] , 1986. 140 p., [5] p. of plates : LC Card 87-165864
HA1363 .A27 no. 3 Z1003.5.I8

Readings and cases in basic marketing / edited by E. Jerome McCarthy, John F. Grashof, Andrew A. Brogowicz. 5th ed. Homewood, Ill. : Irwin, 1987. ix, 365 p. : ill. ; 25 cm. (The Irwin series in marketing) Designed to accompany Basic marketing, ninth ed. by E. Jerome McCarthy and William K. Perreault, Jr. Includes bibliographies. ISBN 0-256-05795-8 (pbk.) LC Card 86-83136 DDC 658.8 19
1. Marketing. 2. Marketing - Case studies. I. McCarthy, E. Jerome (Edmund Jerome). II. Grashof, John F. III. Brogowicz, Andrew A. IV. McCarthy, E. Jerome (Edmund Jerome). Basic marketing. V. Series.
HF5415 .R334 1987

Readings and cases in macroeconomics / [edited by] Ben Bernanke. New York : McGraw-Hill, c1987. x, 485 p. : ill. ; 24 cm. Supplement to: Macroeconomics / Rudiger Dornbusch, Stanley Fischer. 4th ed. Includes bibliographies. ISBN 0-07-017779-1 (pbk.) : LC Card 86-27423 DDC 339 19
1. Macroeconomics. I. Bernanke, Ben. II. Dornbusch, Rudiger. Macroeconomics. 4th ed.
HB172.5 .D67 1987 Suppl.

Readings and cases in marketing management / edited by Alvin C. Burns, David W. Cravens. Homewood, Ill. : Irwin, 1987. xv, 443 p. : ill. ; 24 cm. (The Irwin series in marketing) Includes bibliographies and indexes. ISBN 0-256-03161-4 (pbk.) LC Card 86-82585 DDC 658.8 19
1. Marketing management. 2. Marketing management - Case studies. I. Burns, Alvin C. II. Cravens, David W. III. Series.
HF5415.13 .R362 1987

Readings and cases in Nigerian corporate policy and strategy /. Osaze, Bob. Es. [Benin City, Nigeria] [between 1982 and 1984] vi, 185, 17, 23 p. : LC Card 84-237026 DDC 658.4/012/09669 19
HD70.N43 O83 1982

Readings in contemporary transportation / [edited by] Donald F. Wood, James C. Johnson. 2nd ed. Tulsa, OK : PennWell Pub. Co., c1983. x, 325 p. : ill. ; 28 cm. Includes index. ISBN 0-87814-215-0 (pbk.) LC Card 82-22379 DDC 380.5 19
1. Transportation - Addresses, essays, lectures. 2. Transportation - United States - Addresses, essays, lectures. I. Wood, Donald F. II. Johnson, James C., 1944-.
HE151 .R37 1983 ***NYPL [JLF 86-2000]***

Readings in management / Phillip B. DuBose, editor. Englewood Cliffs, NJ : Prentice-Hall, c1988. viii, 343 p. : ill. ; 24 cm. Designed to be used in conjunction with Management, principles, and practices by David H. Holt. Includes bibliographies. ISBN 0-13-755166-5 (pbk.) : LC Card 87-2301 DDC 658.4 19
1. Management. 2. Industrial management. I. DuBose, Philip B., 1949-. II. Holt, David H. Management.

principles, and practices.
HD31 .R4175 1988

Readings in personnel and human resource management / [selected by] Randall S. Schuler, Stuart A. Youngblood, Vandra L. Huber. 3rd ed. St. Paul, MN : West Pub. Co., c1988. xix, 600 p. : ill. ; 25 cm. Bibliography: p. 555-600. ISBN 0-314-33750-4 (pbk.) LC Card 86-28244 DDC 658.3 19
1. Personnel management. I. Schuler, Randall S. II. Youngblood, Stuart A. III. Huber, Vandra L. (Vandra Lee), 1949-. IV. Title: Personnel and human resource management.
HF5549 .R38167 1988

Readings in strategic marketing : analysis, planning, and implementation / [compiled by] Barton A. Weitz, Robin Wensley. Chicago : Dryden Press, c1988. x, 534 p. : ill. ; 24 cm. (The Dryden Press series in marketing) Includes bibliographies and index. ISBN 0-03-020864-5 (pbk.) LC Card 87-22274 DDC 658.8/02 19
1. Marketing - Decision making. 2. Marketing management. I. Weitz, Barton A. II. Wensley, Robin, 1944-.
HF5415.135 .R42 1988

Reagan and the economy . Boskin, Michael J. San Francisco, Calif. , New York , c1987. xvi, 301 p. : ISBN 0-917616-80-4 : LC Card 87-22544 DDC 338.973 19
HC106.8 .B656 1987

Reagan and the States /. Nathan, Richard P. Princeton, N.J. , c1987. xv, 375 p. : ISBN 0-691-07748-7 (alk. paper) : LC Card 87-45529 DDC 353.0072/5 19
HJ2051 .N167 1987

Reagan, James, 1931- Gerstein, Arnold, 1940- Win-win approaches to conflict avoidance /. Salt Lake City, Utah , 1986. xvii, 110 p. : ISBN 0-87905-215-5 LC Card 85-26261 DDC 303.6 19
HM136 .G46 1986 ***NYPL [JLD 86-2104]***

Reagan on energy . Paulson, S. Lawrence. New York, NY (850 3rd Ave., New York 10022) , 1981. 248 p. in various pagings ; LC Card 82-111477 DDC 333.79/0973 19
HD9502.U52 P38 ***NYPL [JLF 87-368]***

REAGAN, RONALD.
Boskin, Michael J. Reagan and the economy . San Francisco, Calif. , New York , c1987. xvi, 301 p. : ISBN 0-917616-80-4 : LC Card 87-22544 DDC 338.973 19
HC106.8 .B656 1987

Reagan und die Entwicklungsländer . May, Bernhard. München , 1987. xiv, 271 p. ; ISBN 3-486-53981-7 LC Card 87-139481 DDC 337.730172/4 19
HF1456.5.D44 M39 1987

Reagans gesammelte Alpträume. Arbeit, Entropie, Apokalypse . Zürich , 1982. 134 p. : LC Card 83-128724
HC106.8 .A73 1982

REAL ACTIONS. see **ACTIONS AND DEFENSES.**

Réal, Bernard. Chaponnière, R. Les fonctions des agents économiques exportant des biens d'équipement, dans le cadre des relations est-ouest et nord-sud, depuis 1970 /. [Paris] [1981] 159 leaves : LC Card 82-180468 DDC 382/.456817 19
HD9705.A2 C55 1981 ***NYPL [JLG 86-212]***

The real Coke, the real story /. Oliver, Thomas, 1950- New York , 1986. 195 p. ; ISBN 0-394-55273-3 : LC Card 86-10151 DDC 338.7/66362/0973 19
HD9349.S634 C67 1986
NYPL [JLE 86-4489]

The real Coke, the real story /. Oliver, Thomas, 1950- New York , 1987, c1986. 234 p., [9] p. of plates : ISBN 0-14-010408-9 (pbk.) LC Card 87-11836 DDC 338.7/66362/0973 19
HD9349.S634 C67 1987

REAL EATATE INVESTMENT.
Cook, Wade. Real estate . Orem, Utah , c1983. 142 p. : ISBN 0-910019-10-X (pbk.) LC Card 86-220658 DDC 332.63/24 19
HD1382.5 .C6697 1983

Real estate . Chinloy, Peter, 1950- Boston, Mass. , c1987. p. cm. ISBN 0-89838-237-8 LC Card 87-3249 DDC 332.63/24 19
HD1382.5 .C475 1987

Real estate . Cook, Wade. Orem, Utah , c1983. 142 p. : ISBN 0-910019-10-X (pbk.) LC Card 86-220658 DDC 332.63/24 19
HD1382.5 .C6697 1983

Real estate . Eldred, Gary W. New York , c1987. xxii, 567 p. : ISBN 0-06-041893-1 LC Card 86-22936 DDC 333.33 19
HD1375 .E354 1987

REAL ESTATE. see **REAL PROPERTY.**

Real estate after tax reform . Shenkman, Martin. New York , c1987. xii, 307 p. ; ISBN 0-471-85984-2 LC Card 87-2196 DDC 343.7305/46 347.303546 19
HJ4181 .S45 1987

REAL ESTATE AGENTS - LICENSES - CALIFORNIA.
Lush, Minnie. California real estate exam guide /. Chicago , c1987. p. cm. ISBN 0-88462-591-5 LC Card 87-3290 DDC 333.33/09794 19
HD266.C2 L87 1987

REAL ESTATE AGENTS - LICENSES - UNITED STATES.
French, William B. Guide to real estate licensing examinations for salespersons and brokers /. New York , c1986. ix, 367 p. : ISBN 0-471-87754-9 : LC Card 83-23484 DDC 333.33/0973 19
HD1375 .F74 1984
NYPL [*R-Econ. 86-3475]

Martin, Joseph H. Real estate license examinations . New York, N.Y. , 1987. p. cm. ISBN 0-668-06616-4 (pbk.) : LC Card 86-25376 DDC 333.33/076 19
HD1381.5.U5 M37 1987

REAL ESTATE AGENTS - MALPRACTICE.
Frascona, Oliver E., 1947- The paper trail . Boulder, Colo. , c1987. ix, 185 p. ; ISBN 0-941937-00-3 (pbk.) LC Card 87-8904 DDC 333.33/068 19
HD1386.5 .F7 1987

REAL ESTATE AGENTS - TEXAS - HISTORY.
Matlock, Cora Biesele. Sixty-five years the realtor in Texas . Austin, Texas , c1986. xii, 207 p. : LC Card 86-220747 DDC 333.33/06/0764 19
HD266.T4 M38 1986

REAL ESTATE AGENTS - UNITED STATES.
Cyr, John E. Real estate brokerage . Chicago , c1988. xiii, 367 p. : ISBN 0-88462-674-1 (pbk.) LC Card 87-16650 DDC 333.33/068 19
HD278 .C95 1988

Doeleman, David. Real estate financial management /. Chicago, Ill. [1987], c1986. 152 p. : ISBN 0-913652-61-X (pbk.) LC Card 86-62851 DDC 333.33/068/1 19
HD278 .D64 1987

Thompson, Pauline J. Up and running in real estate sales /. Santa Barbara, Calif. , c1987. vi, 202 p. : ISBN 0-918785-02-2 (pbk.) : LC Card 87-16916 DDC 333.33 19
HD255 .T49 1987

REAL ESTATE AGENTS - UNITED STATES - RECRUITING.
Reyhons, Ken. Recruiting sales associates /. [Chicago, Ill.] , c1986. 151 p. : ISBN 0-931652-62-8 (pbk.) LC Card 86-63281 DDC 333.33/068/3 19
HD278 .R49 1986

Real estate and mortgage banking software. Guide to real estate and mortgage banking software /. Washington, D.C. , 1986. 3 v. ; ISBN 0-917935-14-4 (pbk. : set) LC Card 86-63061 DDC 333.3/028/553 19
HD1380 .G85 1986a

Real estate appraisal /. Smith, Halbert C., 1934- Dayton, Ohio , Columbus, OH [c1987] xii, 341 p. ; ISBN 0-939787-01-6 (pbk.) : LC Card 86-24520 DDC 333.33/2 19
HD1387 .S5152 1987

Real estate appraisal, finance, investment, and business management : a text / sponsored and approved by the Florida Real Estate Commission for FREC course II ; by the Real Estate Research Center, University of Florida and the Division of Real Estate, Department of Professional Regulation.5th ed. [Tallahassee] : The Commission, c1986. ix, 441, iv, 86 p. : ill. ; 28 cm. Cover title: Brokers course textbook. Spine title: FREC brokers course. Bibliography: p. 413-415. Includes index. LC Card 87-159867 DDC 333.33 19
1. Real estate business. I. Florida. Real Estate Commission. II. University of Florida. Real Estate Research Center. III. Florida. Division of Real Estate. IV. Title: Brokers course textbook. V. Title: FREC brokers course.
HD1375 .R375 1986

REAL ESTATE APPRAISERS - UNITED STATES - STATISTICS.
1986 membership profile /. Chicago, Ill. , c1986. ix, 44 p. : ISBN 0-911780-85-8 (pbk.) LC Card 87-144205 DDC 333.33/2/0973 19
HD251 .A17 1986

Real estate brokerage . Cyr, John E. Chicago , c1988. xiii, 367 p. : ISBN 0-88462-674-1 (pbk.) LC Card 87-16650 DDC 333.33/068 19
HD278 .C95 1988

REAL ESTATE BROKERS. see **REAL ESTATE AGENTS.**

REAL ESTATE BUSINESS.
Bloch, H. I. Sonny. Inside real estate . New York , c1987. xx, 375 p. ; ISBN 1-555-84030-2 LC Card 86-28303 DDC 333.33/8 19
HD1379 .B515 1987

Bresnan, Bill, 1940- WABC Talkradio 77 AM financial expert Bill Bresnan speaks on real estate-- in words of one syllable /. Englewood Cliffs, NJ , c1987. xx, 172 p. ; ISBN 0-13-949629-7 LC Card 87-60220 DDC 332.63/24 19
HD1379 .B744 1987

Commercial real estate . Dallas, Tex. , c1986. 219 p. : ISBN 0-87833-459-9 : LC Card 85-27108 DDC 332.63/243 19
HD1393.25 .C65 1986 ***NYPL [JLE 86-4267]***

Danks, Lawrence J. Contemporary real estate principles /. Medford, N.J. , c1987. x, 439 p. : ISBN 0-9610624-1-X (pbk.) LC Card 86-63861 DDC 333.33 19
HD1375 .D25 1987

Earle, Gary. How to sell apartment buildings . [Chicago] [1987], c1988. xiv, 183 p. : ISBN 0-88462-716-0 LC Card 87-13964 DDC 333.33/8 19
HD1394 .E24 1988

Eldred, Gary W. Real estate . New York , c1987. xxii, 567 p. : ISBN 0-06-041893-1 LC Card 86-22936 DDC 333.33 19
HD1375 .E354 1987

Johnson, Ross H. Real estate finance /. Columbus, Ohio , c1985. ix, 445 p. : ISBN 0-675-20195-0 LC Card 84-61298 DDC 332.7/2 19
HG2040 .J6 1985 ***NYPL [JLE 86-3033]***

Ochsner, Neal. Common sense real estate /. New York , c1987. xi, 239 p. : ISBN 0-8050-0509-9 LC Card 87-8420 DDC 332.63/24 19
HD1382.5 .O36 1987

Platt, Barbara. Residential real estate . Austin, Tex. , c1987. 206 p. : ISBN 0-941089-17-7 (lib. bdg.) LC Card 87-60697 DDC 332.63/243 19
HD1379 .P57 1987

Real estate appraisal, finance, investment, and business management . [Tallahassee] , c1986. ix, 441, iv, 86 p. : LC Card 87-159867 DDC 333.33 19
HD1375 .R375 1986

Real estate market analysis . New York , 1988. xvii, 350 p. : ISBN 0-275-92414-9 (alk. paper) : LC Card 87-15832 DDC 333.33/22 19
HD1382.5 .R396 1988

Rosenauer, Johnnie L. Effective real estate sales and marketing /. Chicago, Ill. , c1988. xiv, 258 p. : ISBN 0-88462-599-0 (pbk.) LC Card 87-9544 DDC 333.33/068/8 19
HD1375 .R597 1988

Unger, Maurice Albert, 1917- Real estate, principles, and practices /. Cincinnati , c1987. ix, 650 p. : ISBN 0-538-19761-7 LC Card 86-61595 DDC 333.33 19
HD1375 .U6 1987

Wickman, Floyd. Successful strategies for real estate agents . Dubuque, Iowa , c1987. xii, 226 p. ; ISBN 0-8403-4185-7 (pbk.) : LC Card 86-82782 DDC 333.33/068/8 19
HD1382 .W53 1987

Wurtzebach, Charles H. Modern real estate /.

New York , c1987. xii, 772 p. : ISBN 0-471-84890-5 LC Card 86-23412 DDC 333.33/0973 19
HD1375 .W873 1987

REAL ESTATE BUSINESS - ACCOUNTING.
Liegenschaftenbuchhaltung /. Zürich , c1977. 128 p. : ISBN 3-85567-073-1 LC Card 85-141656
HF5686.R3 L54 1977

REAL ESTATE BUSINESS - BRAZIL - PORT ALEGRE.
Clichevsky, Nora. O mercado de terra na região metropolitana de Porto Alegre /. Porto Alegre , 1982. 60 p. : LC Card 84-256219
HD500.P67 C57 1982

REAL ESTATE BUSINESS - CALIFORNIA.
Bowman, Arthur G. California real estate principles. Glenview, Ill. , c1987. xiv, 368 p. : ISBN 0-673-16667-8 : LC Card 86-25985 DDC 333.33/09794 19
HD266.C2 B68 1987

California real estate principles /. New York , c1987. ix, 364 p. : ISBN 0-471-63274-0 LC Card 87-404650 DDC 333.33/09794 19
HD266.C2 C25 1987

Stapleton, Charles O. California real estate principles /. Chicago , c1987. xvi, 428, 8 p. : ISBN 0-88462-569-9 (pbk.) LC Card 86-24870 DDC 333.33/09794 19
HD266.C2 S73 1987

REAL ESTATE BUSINESS - CALIFORNIA - EXAMINATIONS, QUESTIONS, ETC.
Lush, Minnie. California real estate exam guide /. Chicago , c1987. p. cm. ISBN 0-88462-591-5 LC Card 87-3290 DDC 333.33/09794 19
HD266.C2 L87 1987

REAL ESTATE BUSINESS - COMPUTER PROGRAMS - CATALOGS.
Guide to real estate and mortgage banking software /. Washington, D.C. , 1986. 3 v. ; ISBN 0-917935-14-4 (pbk. : set) LC Card 86-63061 DDC 333.3/028/553 19
HD1380 .G85 1986a

REAL ESTATE BUSINESS - DICTIONARIES.
The Dictionary of real estate appraisal. Chicago, Ill. , c1984. ix, 368 p. ; ISBN 0-911780-74-2 LC Card 84-16834 DDC 333.33/2/0321 19
HD1387 .D435 1984 ***NYPL [JLE 86-2371]***

Friedman, Jack P. Dictionary of real estate terms /. New York , c1987. v, 329 p. : ISBN 0-8120-3898-3 (pbk.) : LC Card 87-19869 DDC 333.33/03/21 19
HD1365 .F75 1987

Gross, Jerome S. Webster's new world illustrated encyclopedic dictionary of real estate /. New York , c1987. 418 p. : ISBN 0-13-947318-1 (pbk.) : LC Card 87-2360 DDC 333.33/03/21 19
HD1365 .G76 1987

West, Bill W. Street talk in real estate /. Alameda, Calif. [1987] vi, 216 p. : ISBN 0-934189-04-8 (pbk. : trade) : LC Card 86-50605 DDC 333.33/03/21 19
HD1365 .W47 1987

REAL ESTATE BUSINESS - ENGLAND - LONDON - FORECASTING.
The London property market in AD 2000 /. London , New York , 1986. xi, 155 p. : ISBN 0-419-14100-6 : LC Card 86-217227 DDC 333.33/22/09421 19
HD610.L6 L66 1986

REAL ESTATE BUSINESS - GERMANY (WEST) - HANDBOOKS, MANUALS, ETC.
Falk, Bernd R. Immobilien-Handbuch . Stuttgart , c1985. xlii, 972 p. : ISBN 3-17-008062-8 LC Card 86-129985
HD656 .F35 1985

REAL ESTATE BUSINESS - HANDBOOKS, MANUALS, ETC.
Falk, Bernd R. Immobilien-Handbuch . Stuttgart , c1985. xlii, 972 p. : ISBN 3-17-008062-8 LC Card 86-129985
HD656 .F35 1985

REAL ESTATE BUSINESS - JURISPRUDENCE. see REAL ESTATE BUSINESS - LAW AND LEGISLATION.

REAL ESTATE BUSINESS - KENTUCKY - EMPLOYEES - SUPPLY AND DEMAND - STATISTICS.
Kentucky occupational profiles, finance, insurance, and real estate /. [Frankfort, Ky.] [1985] v, 33 p. : LC Card 85-622996 DDC 331.12/51/0009769 19
HD5718.B262 U66 1985

REAL ESTATE BUSINESS - LAW AND LEGISLATION.
Frascona, Oliver E., 1947- The paper trail . Boulder, Colo. , c1987. ix, 185 p. ; ISBN 0-941937-00-3 (pbk.) LC Card 87-8904 DDC 333.33/068 19
HD1386.5 .F7 1987

REAL ESTATE BUSINESS - LAW AND LEGISLATION - GERMANY (WEST) - HANDBOOKS, MANUALS, ETC.
Falk, Bernd R. Immobilien-Handbuch . Stuttgart , c1985. xlii, 972 p. : ISBN 3-17-008062-8 LC Card 86-129985
HD656 .F35 1985

REAL ESTATE BUSINESS - LAW AND LEGISLATION - HANDBOOKS, MANUALS, ETC.
Falk, Bernd R. Immobilien-Handbuch . Stuttgart , c1985. xlii, 972 p. : ISBN 3-17-008062-8 LC Card 86-129985
HD656 .F35 1985

REAL ESTATE BUSINESS - LAW AND LEGISLATION - UNITED STATES.
Ficek, Edmund F. Real estate principles and practices /. Columbus , c1983. viii, 550 p. : ISBN 0-675-20016-4 LC Card 82-73775 DDC 346.7304/37 347.306437 19
KF2042.R4 F46 1983 ***NYPL [JLE 86-2010]***

REAL ESTATE BUSINESS - LICENSES - CALIFORNIA - EXAMINATIONS, QUESTIONS, ETC.
Calhoun, David E. A step-by-step guide to real estate principles in California . Los Angeles, Calif. , c1987. 351 p. : LC Card 87-403596 DDC 333.33/09794 19
HD266.C2 C22 1987

REAL ESTATE BUSINESS - LICENSES - CALIFORNIA - OUTLINES, SYLLABI, ETC.
Calhoun, David E. A step-by-step guide to real estate principles in California . Los Angeles, Calif. , c1987. 351 p. : LC Card 87-403596 DDC 333.33/09794 19
HD266.C2 C22 1987

REAL ESTATE BUSINESS - MARYLAND - STATISTICS.
Owen, Gail T. Residential property sales in Maryland . Baltimore, Md. (2225 N. Charles St., Baltimore 21218-5767) [1985] iv, 79 leaves : LC Card 86-622370 DDC 333.33/8 19
HD266.M3 O9 1985

REAL ESTATE BUSINESS - MATHEMATICS. see BUSINESS MATHEMATICS - REAL ESTATE BUSINESS.

REAL ESTATE BUSINESS - NEW YORK (STATE) - ADIRONDACK MOUNTAINS REGION - STATISTICS.
Kay, David L. The Adirondack land market . Ithaca, N.Y. [1985] 53 p. : LC Card 86-621939 DDC 333.33/22/0974753 19
HD266.N72 A265 1985

REAL ESTATE BUSINESS - NORTH DAKOTA - EMPLOYEES - STATISTICS.
Finance, insurance, and real estate . Bismarck, N.D. (1000 E. Divide, Bismarck 58502) [1986] 55 p. : LC Card 86-623003 DDC 332.12/51/0009784 19
HD5718.B262 U64 1986

REAL ESTATE BUSINESS - RECORDS AND CORRESPONDENCE.
Frascona, Oliver E., 1947- The paper trail . Boulder, Colo. , c1987. ix, 185 p. ; ISBN 0-941937-00-3 (pbk.) LC Card 87-8904 DDC 333.33/068 19
HD1386.5 .F7 1987

REAL ESTATE BUSINESS - TEXAS.
Harris, Jack C., 1945- 1985-86 real estate review and outlook /. College Station, Tex. [1985?] 22 p. ; LC Card 86-621364 DDC 333.33/09764 19
HD266.T4 H37 1985

REAL ESTATE BUSINESS - TEXAS - FINANCE.
Texas real estate finance /. New York , c1987. xviii, 365 p. : ISBN 0-471-82300-7 (pbk.) LC Card 86-29004 DDC 332.7/2/09764 19
HD266.T4 T5 1987

REAL ESTATE BUSINESS - TEXAS - FORECASTING.
Harris, Jack C., 1945- 1985-86 real estate review and outlook /. College Station, Tex. [1985?] 22 p. ; LC Card 86-621364 DDC 333.33/09764 19
HD266.T4 H37 1985

REAL ESTATE BUSINESS - TEXAS - HISTORY.
Matlock, Cora Biesele. Sixty-five years the realtor in Texas . Austin, Texas , c1986. xii, 207 p. : LC Card 86-220747 DDC 333.33/06/0764 19
HD266.T4 M38 1986

REAL ESTATE BUSINESS - UNITED STATES.
Cyr, John E. Real estate brokerage . Chicago , c1988. xiii, 367 p. : ISBN 0-88462-674-1 (pbk.) LC Card 87-16650 DDC 333.33/068 19
HD278 .C95 1988

Ficek, Edmund F. Real estate principles and practices /. Columbus , c1983. viii, 550 p. : ISBN 0-675-20016-4 LC Card 82-73775 DDC 346.7304/37 347.306437 19
KF2042.R4 F46 1983 ***NYPL [JLE 86-2010]***

Floyd, Charles F. Real estate principles /. Chicago , c1987. xxix, 511 p. : ISBN 0-88462-672-5 LC Card 87-3391 DDC 333.33/0973 19
HD255 .F57 1987

French, William B. Guide to real estate licensing examinations for salespersons and brokers /. New York , c1986. ix, 367 p. : ISBN 0-471-87754-9 : LC Card 83-23484 DDC 333.33/0973 19
HD1375 .F74 1984
NYPL [*R-Econ. 86-3475]

The Kiplinger/Changing times guide to buying and selling a home /. Washington, DC , New York, NY , c1987. iii, 311 p. : ISBN 0-938721-02-X (pbk.) : LC Card 87-167806 DDC 643/.12 19
HD1379 .K52 1987

Olin, Harold Bennett. Realty brokerage operations by savings institutions /. Chicago, IL (111 E. Wacker Dr., Chicago 60601) , c1986. 38, [96] p. : LC Card 86-212493 DDC 332.3/2 19
HD255 .O45 1986

Thompson, Pauline J. Up and running in real estate sales /. Santa Barbara, Calif. , c1987. vi, 202 p. : ISBN 0-918785-02-2 (pbk.) : LC Card 87-16916 DDC 333.33 19
HD255 .T49 1987

Wurtzebach, Charles H. Modern real estate /. New York , c1987. xii, 772 p. : ISBN 0-471-84890-5 LC Card 86-23412 DDC 333.33/0973 19
HD1375 .W873 1987

REAL ESTATE BUSINESS - UNITED STATES - EXAMINATIONS, QUESTIONS, ETC.
French, William B. Guide to real estate licensing examinations for salespersons and brokers /. New York , c1986. ix, 367 p. : ISBN 0-471-87754-9 : LC Card 83-23484 DDC 333.33/0973 19
HD1375 .F74 1984
NYPL [*R-Econ. 86-3475]

Martin, Joseph H. Real estate license examinations . New York, N.Y. , 1987. p. cm. ISBN 0-668-06616-4 (pbk.) : LC Card 86-25376 DDC 333.33/076 19
HD1381.5.U5 M37 1987

REAL ESTATE BUSINESS - UNITED STATES - FINANCE.
Doeleman, David. Real estate financial management /. Chicago, Ill. [1987], c1986. 152 p. : ISBN 0-913652-61-X (pbk.) LC Card 86-62851 DDC 333.33/068/1 19
HD278 .D64 1987

REAL ESTATE BUSINESS - VOCATIONAL GUIDANCE.
Edwards, Kenneth W., 1928- Your successful real estate career /. New York, NY , c1987. vii, 184 p. ; ISBN 0-8144-7675-9 (pbk.) : LC Card 86-47810 DDC 333.33/023/73 19
HD1375 .E33 1987

Real estate debt financing /. Hines, Mary Alice. New York , c1987. xviii, 405 p. ; ISBN 0-471-85493-X LC Card 87-6200 DDC 332.7/2/0973 19
HG2040.5.U5 H55 1987

REAL ESTATE DEVELOPERS - UNITED STATES - BIOGRAPHY.
Trump, Donald, 1946- Trump . New York , 1988. p. cm. ISBN 0-394-55528-7 LC Card 87-42663 DDC 333.33/092/4 B 19
HC102.5.T78 A3 1988

REAL ESTATE DEVELOPMENT - GOVERNMENT POLICY - GERMANY (WEST)
Schlüsselgewalt . Dortmund , c1981. 190 p. : ISBN 3-88142-261-7 : LC Card 81-206444
HD7339.A3 S25 1981

REAL ESTATE DEVELOPMENT - GOVERNMENT POLICY - GREAT BRITAIN.
Ambrose, Peter J. Whatever happened to planning? /. London , New York , 1986. xiv, 288 p. : ISBN 0-416-37100-0 LC Card 86-12415 DDC 333.73/17/0941 19
HD596 .A43 1986 ***NYPL [JLD 87-1402]***

Planning control . London , Wolfeboro, N.H. , c1987. 234 p. ; ISBN 0-7099-3790-3 : LC Card 86-24079 DDC 333.73/17/0941 19
HD596 .P53 1987 ***NYPL [JLD 87-803]***

REAL ESTATE DEVELOPMENT - GOVERNMENT POLICY - HAWAII.
Cooper, George. Land and power in Hawaii . Honolulu, Hawaii , c1985. x, 518 p. ; ISBN 0-9615052-0-6 : LC Card 85-72037 DDC 333.73/13/09969 19
HD266.H3 C66 1985 ***NYPL [JLE 87-361]***

REAL ESTATE DEVELOPMENT - GREAT BRITAIN.
Fothergill, Steve. Property and industrial development /. London , Wolfeboro, N.H. , 1987. 187 p. : ISBN 0-09-170741-2 (pbk.) : LC Card 87-2627 DDC 333.3/8/0941 19
HD598 .F68 1987

REAL ESTATE DEVELOPMENT - ILLINOIS - EAST PEORIA.
Urban Land Institute. R.S. Wallace Station, East Peoria, Illinois . Washington, D.C. (1090 Vermont Ave., N.W., Washington 20005) , c1986. 36 p. : LC Card 86-216045 DDC 333.77/17/0977352 19
HD268.E26 U73 1986

REAL ESTATE DEVELOPMENT - JAPAN - TOKYO METROPOLITAN AREA.
Hanayama, Yuzuru, 1939- Land markets and land policy in a metropolitan area . Boston, MA , 1986. xiv, 162 p. : ISBN 0-89946-197-2 LC Card 85-13867 DDC 333.77/13/0952135 19
HD920.T62 H36 1986 ***NYPL [JLE 86-4398]***

REAL ESTATE DEVELOPMENT - KANSAS - LENEXA.
Bedford Properties, Lenexa, Kansas . Washington, D.C. (1090 Vermont Ave., N.W., Washington 20005) [1986?] 37 p. : LC Card 87-141440 DDC 333.3/8/09781675 19
HD268.L46 B43 1986

REAL ESTATE DEVELOPMENT - MANAGEMENT - CASE STUDIES.
Suchman, Diane R. Managing a development company . Washington, D.C. [1987] v, 179 p. ; ISBN 0-87420-672-3 (pbk.) LC Card 87-82097 DDC 333.3/8/068 19
HD1390 .S93 1987

REAL ESTATE DEVELOPMENT - SOUTHERN STATES.
Healy, Robert G. Competition for land in the American South . Washington, D.C. , c1985. xxxii, 333 p. : ISBN 0-89164-094-0 (pbk.) LC Card 85-25459 DDC 333.76/13/0975 19
HD266.A13 H43 1985 ***NYPL [JLE 86-2724]***

REAL ESTATE DEVELOPMENT - TURKEY - MATHEMATICAL MODELS.
Boratav, Korkut. Housing yearbook /. Ankara, Turkey , 1985. 32, [2] p. ; LC Card 87-403323 DDC 363.5/09561 19
HD7358.25.A3 B67 1985

REAL ESTATE DEVELOPMENT - UNITED STATES.
The Development trends, 1986 /. Washington, D.C. , c1986. 48 p. : ISBN 0-87420-657-X (pbk.) LC Card 86-227316 DDC 333.3/8/0973 19
HD1390 .D485 1986

Hines, Mary Alice. Shopping center development and investment /. New York , c1987. p. cm. ISBN 0-471-62427-6 LC Card 87-26342 DDC 332.63/24 19
HF5430 .H56 1987

Weiss, Marc A. (Marc Allan) The rise of the community builders . New York , 1987. xii, 228 p. : ISBN 0-231-06504-3 LC Card 87-5115 DDC 333.77/17/0973 19
HD257 .W46 1987

REAL ESTATE DEVELOPMENT - UNITED STATES - CONGRESSES.
ULI/UMTA Policy Forum on Joint Development of Rail Transit Facilities (1986 : Washington, D.C.) ULI-UMTA Policy Forum on Joint Development of Rail Transit Facilities . [Washington, D.C.] [1987] iv, 107 p. : ISBN 0-87420-671-5 (pbk.) LC Card 87-82098 DDC 333.3/8 19
HD257 .U43 1986

REAL ESTATE DEVELOPMENT - UNITED STATES - FINANCE.
Economic development and real estate financing /. N[ew] Y[ork], N.Y. (41 E. 42nd St., N[ew] Y[ork] 10017) [c1985] iii, 203 p. : LC Card 86-221586 DDC 332.7/2/0973 19
HD255 .E26 1985

Financing land acquisition and development /. Washington, D.C. , c1987. 134 p. : ISBN 0-86718-281-4 (pbk.) LC Card 87-61069 DDC 332.7/2/0973 19
HD1390 .F56 1987

G-Yohannes, Arefaine. The professional's desktop guide to real estate finance /. Chicago, Ill. , c1988. p. cm. ISBN 0-917253-93-0 : LC Card 87-17918 DDC 332.7/2 19
HG2040.5.U5 G125 1988

Hines, Mary Alice. Real estate debt financing /. New York , c1987. xviii, 405 p. ; ISBN 0-471-85493-X LC Card 87-6200 DDC 332.7/2/0973 19
HG2040.5.U5 H55 1987

Real estate finance /. Johnson, Ross H. Columbus, Ohio , c1985. ix, 445 p. : ISBN 0-675-20195-0 LC Card 84-61298 DDC 332.7/2 19
HG2040 .J6 1985 ***NYPL [JLE 86-3033]***

Real estate finance /. Unger, Maurice Albert, 1917- Cincinnati , c1984. vi, 426 p. : ISBN 0-538-19630-0 LC Card 83-61343 DDC 332.7/2 19
HG2040 .U53 1984 ***NYPL [JLE 86-4718]***

Real estate finance /. Wiedemer, John P., 1918- Englewood Cliffs, N.J. , c1987. xvi, 396 p. : ISBN 0-13-762774-2 LC Card 86-30471 DDC 332.7/2/0973 19
HG2040.5.U5 W54 1987

Real estate finance and housing . Gramley, Lyle E. Washington, D.C. (1125 15th St., N.W., Washington 20005) , c1987. vii, 132 p. : LC Card 87-124264 DDC 332.7/2/0973021 19
HG2040.5.U5 G73 1987

Real estate financial management /. Doeleman, David. Chicago, Ill. [1987], c1986. 152 p. : ISBN 0-913652-61-X (pbk.) LC Card 86-62851 DDC 333.33/068/1 19
HD278 .D64 1987

REAL ESTATE INVESTMENT - FINANCE - MATHEMATICAL MODELS.
Hamilton, S. W. (Stanley William), 1939- Foundations of real estate financing . Vancouver , c1982. xv, 319 p. : ISBN 0-409-98843-X LC Card 87-143264
HF5695.5.R3 H36 1982

REAL ESTATE INVESTMENT - JAPAN.
Hines, Mary Alice. Investing in Japanese real estate /. New York , 1987. xiv, 287 p. : ISBN 0-89930-184-3 (lib. bdg. : alk. paper) LC Card 86-30582 DDC 332.63/24/0952 19
HD918 .H55 1987

REAL ESTATE INVESTMENT - JUVENILE LITERATURE.
Epstein, Rachel S. Alternative investments /. New York , c1988. 47 p. : ISBN 1-555-46633-8 LC Card 87-21766 DDC 332.6/78 19
HG4521 .E685 1988

REAL ESTATE INVESTMENT - LAW AND LEGISLATION - UNITED STATES.
Arnold, Alvin L. Real estate investor's deskbook /. Boston , c1982. 1 v. (various pagings) : ISBN 0-88262-732-5 LC Card 82-70717 DDC 346.7304/3 347.30643 19
KF665 .A8 1982 ***NYPL [JLF 86-907]***

REAL ESTATE INVESTMENT - SYNDICATION.
Stanger, Robert A. How to evaluate real estate partnerships /. Shrewsbury, N.J. , c1986. xvi, 256 p. ; ISBN 0-943570-10-7 LC Card 85-90539 DDC 332.63/247 19
HD1382.55 .S73 1986

REAL ESTATE INVESTMENT - TAXATION - LAW AND LEGISLATION - UNITED STATES.
Arnold, Alvin L. Real estate investor's deskbook /. Boston , c1982. 1 v. (various pagings) : ISBN 0-88262-732-5 LC Card 82-70717 DDC 346.7304/3 347.30643 19
KF665 .A8 1982 ***NYPL [JLF 86-907]***

Reed, John T. Aggressive tax avoidance for real estate investors . Danville, CA , 1986. 267 p. : ISBN 0-939224-13-5 (pbk.) :
NYPL [JLF 86-1562]

REAL ESTATE INVESTMENT TRUSTS - GERMANY, WEST.
Bölter, Hendrick H., 1957- Der geschlossene Immobilienfonds . Frankfurt am Main , New York , c1986. xv, 290 p. : ISBN 3-8204-9460-X LC Card 86-195280
HG5502 .B65 1986

REAL ESTATE INVESTMENT TRUSTS - UNITED STATES.
Haight, G. Timothy. REITs . Chicago, Ill. , c1987. x, 227 p. : ISBN 0-917253-71-X : LC Card 87-2558 DDC 346.7304/37 347.306437 19
HG5095 .H33 1987

REAL ESTATE INVESTMENT - UNITED STATES.
Economic development and real estate financing /. N[ew] Y[ork], N.Y. (41 E. 42nd St., N[ew] Y[ork] 10017) [c1985] iii, 203 p. : LC Card 86-221586 DDC 332.7/2/0973 19
HD255 .E26 1985

Guggenheim, Joseph. Tax credits for low income housing . Washington, D.C. , c1986. vii, 117 p. : ISBN 0-941239-00-4 (pbk.) LC Card 87-112304 DDC 363.5/8 19
HJ4653.C73 G85 1986

Hines, Mary Alice. Shopping center development and investment /. New York , c1987. p. cm. ISBN 0-471-62427-6 LC Card 87-26342 DDC 332.63/24 19
HF5430 .H56 1987

Strategic real estate submarkets . Denver, Colo. (1009 Grant St., Suite 304, Denver 80203) , c1986. 195 p. : LC Card 86-228061 DDC 333.33/22/0973 19
HD255 .S77 1986

REAL ESTATE INVESTMENTS - ENGLAND - LONDON - FORECASTING.
The London property market in AD 2000 /. London , New York , 1986. xi, 155 p. : ISBN 0-419-14100-6 : LC Card 86-217227 DDC 333.33/22/09421 19
HD610.L6 L66 1986

Real estate investor's deskbook /. Arnold, Alvin L. Boston , c1982. 1 v. (various pagings) : ISBN 0-88262-732-5 LC Card 82-70717 DDC 346.7304/3 347.30643 19
KF665 .A8 1982 ***NYPL [JLF 86-907]***

Real estate license examinations . Martin, Joseph H. New York, N.Y. , 1987. p. cm. ISBN 0-668-06616-4 (pbk.) : LC Card 86-25376 DDC 333.33/076 19
HD1381.5.U5 M37 1987

REAL ESTATE LOANS. see **MORTGAGE LOANS.**

Real estate management. Sirota, David. Essentials of real estate investment /. Chicago , 1988. xiii, 254 p. ; ISBN 0-88462-667-9 (p. 4 of cover) LC Card 87-23222 DDC 332.63/24 19
HD1382.5 .S52 1988

REAL ESTATE MANAGEMENT.
Holland, Barbara Kamanitz. Managing single-family homes /. Chicago, Ill. , c1987. xiv, 155 p. ; ISBN 0-912104-92-9 (pbk.) LC Card

87-81672 DDC 333.33/8 19
HD1394 .H63 1987

Kyle, Robert C. Property management /. Chicago, IL , c1988. x, 422 p. : ISBN 0-88462-669-5 (pbk.) LC Card 87-17906 DDC 332.63/24/068 19
HD1394 .K94 1988

Shear, Mel A. Property management reinvented . Englewood-Cliffs, N.J. , c1988. xiii, 306 p. : ISBN 0-13-731191-5 LC Card 87-18852 DDC 333.3/068 19
HD1394 .S52 1988

REAL ESTATE MANAGEMENT - CASE STUDIES.
Suchman, Diane R. Managing a development company . Washington, D.C. [1987] v, 179 p. ; ISBN 0-87420-672-3 (pbk.) LC Card 87-82097 DDC 333.3/8/068 19
HD1390 .S93 1987

Real estate market analysis : methods and applications / edited by John M. Clapp, Stephen D. Messner. New York : Praeger, 1988. xvii, 350 p. : ill. ; 25 cm. Bibliography: p. 323-338. Includes index. ISBN 0-275-92414-9 (alk. paper) : LC Card 87-15832 DDC 333.33/22 19
1. Real estate investment. 2. Real estate development. 3. Real estate business. I. Clapp, John M. II. Messner, Stephen D.
HD1382.5 .R396 1988

Real estate mortgage lending for bankers. Construction lending for income-producing properties . Washington, D.C. (1120 Connecticut Ave., N.W. Washington 20036) , c1986. xiv, 163 p. : LC Card 86-209027 DDC 332.1/753 19
HG2040.5.U5 M49 1986

Real estate principles /. Floyd, Charles F. Chicago , c1987. xxix, 511 p. : ISBN 0-88462-672-5 LC Card 87-3391 DDC 333.33/0973 19
HD255 .F57 1987

Real estate principles and practices /. Ficek, Edmund F. Columbus , c1983. viii, 550 p. : ISBN 0-675-20016-4 LC Card 82-73775 DDC 346.7304/37 347.306437 19
KF2042.R4 F46 1983 ***NYPL [JLE 86-2010]***

Real estate, principles, and practices /. Unger, Maurice Albert, 1917- Cincinnati , c1987. ix, 650 p. : ISBN 0-538-19761-7 LC Card 86-61595 DDC 333.33 19
HD1375 .U6 1987

Real estate principles in California. Calhoun, David E. A step-by-step guide to real estate principles in California . Los Angeles, Calif. , c1987. 351 p. : LC Card 87-403596 DDC 333.33/09794 19
HD266.C2 C22 1987

REAL ESTATE SALESMEN. see **REAL ESTATE AGENTS.**

Real Estate Solutions, Inc. Guide to real estate and mortgage banking software /. Washington, D.C. , 1986. 3 v. ; ISBN 0-917935-14-4 (pbk. : set) LC Card 86-63061 DDC 333.3/028/553 19
HD1380 .G85 1986a

REAL ESTATE TAX. see **REAL PROPERTY TAX.**

Real-financial linkages among open economies / edited by Sven W. Arndt, J. David Richardson. Cambridge, Mass. : MIT Press, c1987. x, 215 p. : ill. ; 24 cm. Includes bibliographies and index. ISBN 0-262-01096-8 LC Card 87-15153 DDC 337 19
1. International economic relations. 2. International finance. I. Arndt, Sven W. II. Richardson, J. David.
HF1411 .R4135 1987

Real inside [motion picture] / National Film Board of Canada. Deerfield, IL : MTI Film & Video, 1985. 1 film reel (12 min.) : sd., col. ; 16 mm. Title from data sheet. Adults. Issued also as videorecording. An amusing film about a weary personnel director who interviews a prospective applicant for an executive assistant position. The candidate is dynamic, charming, and creative. However, he is also a cartoon character looking for a change from the animated life. LC Card 87-705522 DDC 791.43 11
1. Employment interviewing - Anecdotes, facetiae, satire, etc. I. National Film Board of Canada. II. MTI Film & Video.
HF5549.5.I6

Real inside [videorecording] / National Film Board of Canada. Deerfield, IL: MTI Film & Video, 1985. 1 videocassette (12 min.) : sd., col. Title from data sheet. Adults. Issued as U-matic 3/4 in. or Beta 1/2 in. or VHS 1/2 in. Issued also as motion picture. An amusing film about a weary personnel director who interviews a prospective applicant for an executive assistant position. The candidate is dynamic, charming, and creative. However, he is also a cartoon character looking for a change from the animated life. LC Card 87-705515 DDC 791.43 11
1. Employment interviewing - Anecdotes, facetiae, satire, etc. I. National Film Board of Canada. II. MTI Film & Video.
HF5549.5.I6

Real law books series.
Frascona, Oliver E., 1947- The paper trail . Boulder, Colo. , c1987. ix, 185 p. ; ISBN 0-941937-00-3 (pbk.) LC Card 87-8904 DDC 333.33/068 19
HD1386.5 .F7 1987

Real life, real answers . Shilling, Dana. New York , c1988. xiv, 309 p. ; ISBN 1-557-10004-7 LC Card 87-19538 DDC 332.024 19
HG179 .S465 1988

Real life, real answers . Shilling, Dana. New York , c1988. p. cm. ISBN 0-87795-942-0 : LC Card 87-24380 DDC 332.024 19
HG179 .S465 1988b

Real managers /. Luthans, Fred. Cambridge, Mass. , c1988. xvi, 192 p. : ISBN 0-88730-103-7 LC Card 87-19080 DDC 658.4 19
HD31 .L865 1988

REAL PROPERTY AND TAXATION.
Bush, Vanessa A. How to buy a house when you're cash poor . Chicago , c1986. 92 p. ; ISBN 0-8092-4834-4 (pbk.) : LC Card 86-24053 DDC 332.7/22 19
HG2040.15 .B87 1986

Calder, Eugene B. Advising clients on real estate investments /. New York, NY (11 Penn Plaza, New York 10001) , 1987. 95 p. in various pagings : LC Card 87-61983 DDC 332.63/24 19
HD1382.5 .C34 1987

REAL PROPERTY AND TAXATION - UNITED STATES.
Buying or selling a home . Chicago, Ill. (4025 W. Peterson Ave., Chicago 60646) , c1986. 31 p. : LC Card 86-209128 DDC 343.7305/46 347.303546 19
HJ4182.A5 B89 1986

Ferguson, Jerry T., 1938- Managing real estate taxes /. Westport, Conn. , 1986. x, 185 p. ; ISBN 0-89930-106-1 (lib. bdg. : alk. paper) LC Card 85-6360 DDC 343.7305/46 347.303546 19
HJ4181 .F47 1986 ***NYPL [JLE 86-2439]***

Guggenheim, Joseph. Tax credits for low income housing . Washington, D.C. , c1986. vii, 117 p. : ISBN 0-941239-00-4 (pbk.) LC Card 87-112304 DDC 363.5/8 19
HJ4653.C73 G85 1986

Norton, Hollis. The new real estate game . Chicago , c1987. 233 p. : ISBN 0-8092-4794-1 : LC Card 86-32902 DDC 346.7304/37 347.306437 19
HD1382.5 .N675 1987

Robinson, Gerald J. Federal income taxation of real estate . Boston, Mass. , c1984. ca. 750 p. in various pagings ; ISBN 0-88712-081-4 LC Card 83-50925 DDC 343.7305/2 347.30352 19
KF6535 .R6 1984 ***NYPL [JLL 87-136]***

Robinson, Gerald J. Federal income taxation of real estate . Boston, Mass. , c1987. ca. 480 p. in various pagings ; ISBN 0-88712-743-6 LC Card 83-50925
NYPL [JLL 87-136 Suppl. 1987/1]

Robinson, Gerald J. Federal income taxation of real estate : text, forms, and tax planning ideas : 4th ed. Cumulative supplement /. Boston, Mass. , c1985- v. ISBN 0-88712-305-8 (pbk.) LC Card 83-50925
NYPL [*R-Econ. 85-1660 Suppl.]

Shenkman, Martin. Real estate after tax reform . New York , c1987. xii, 307 p. ; ISBN 0-471-85984-2 LC Card 87-2196 DDC 343.7305/46 347.303546 19
HJ4181 .S45 1987

REAL PROPERTY - BERLIN.
Breitkopf, Stephan. Die Behandlung von Immobilienrechten Deutscher mit Wohnsitz in der Bundesrepublik Deutschland und Berlin (West), in der DDR und Berlin (Ost) /. Berlin , 1983. xii, 203 p. ; ISBN 3-921374-25-1 LC Card 84-167165 DDC 330 s 346.431/55043 19
HC244.A1 B4 Heft 129 KK1315
NYPL [STN+ (Berlin. Freie Universität. Osteuropa-Institut. Berichte. Heft 129)]

REAL PROPERTY - CALIFORNIA.
Stapleton, Charles O. California real estate principles /. Chicago , c1987. xvi, 428, 8 p. : ISBN 0-88462-569-9 (pbk.) LC Card 86-24870 DDC 333.33/09794 19
HD266.C2 S73 1987

REAL PROPERTY - CALIFORNIA - EXAMINATIONS, QUESTIONS, ETC.
Calhoun, David E. A step-by-step guide to real estate principles in California . Los Angeles, Calif. , c1987. 351 p. : LC Card 87-403596 DDC 333.33/09794 19
HD266.C2 C22 1987

Lush, Minnie. California real estate exam guide /. Chicago , c1987. p. cm. ISBN 0-88462-591-5 LC Card 87-3290 DDC 333.33/09794 19
HD266.C2 L87 1987

REAL PROPERTY - CALIFORNIA - OUTLINES, SYLLABI, ETC.
Calhoun, David E. A step-by-step guide to real estate principles in California . Los Angeles, Calif. , c1987. 351 p. : LC Card 87-403596 DDC 333.33/09794 19
HD266.C2 C22 1987

REAL PROPERTY - DENMARK - STATISTICS.
Danmarks areal. København , 1968. 228 p., [1] folded leaf of plates : LC Card 83-223613
HD736 .D36 1968

REAL PROPERTY - DICTIONARIES.
The Dictionary of real estate appraisal. Chicago, Ill. , c1984. ix, 368 p. ; ISBN 0-911780-74-2 LC Card 84-16834 DDC 333.33/2/0321 19
HD1387 .D435 1984 ***NYPL [JLE 86-2371]***

Friedman, Jack P. Dictionary of real estate terms /. New York , c1987. v, 329 p. : ISBN 0-8120-3898-3 (pbk.) : LC Card 87-19869 DDC 333.33/03/21 19
HD1365 .F75 1987

West, Bill W. Street talk in real estate /. Alameda, Calif. [1987] vi, 216 p. : ISBN 0-934189-04-8 (pbk. : trade) : LC Card 86-50605 DDC 333.33/03/21 19
HD1365 .W47 1987

REAL PROPERTY - FINANCE.
Johnson, Ross H. Real estate finance /. Columbus, Ohio , c1985. ix, 445 p. : ISBN 0-675-20195-0 LC Card 84-61298 DDC 332.7/2 19
HG2040 .J6 1985 ***NYPL [JLE 86-3033]***

REAL PROPERTY - FOREIGN OWNERSHIP.
Hines, Mary Alice. Marketing real estate internationally /. New York , c1988. p. cm. ISBN 0-89930-205-X (lib. bdg. : alk. paper) LC Card 87-24935 DDC 333.33/0688 19
HD1382.5 .H557 1988

REAL PROPERTY - FRANCE.
Guichard-Ayoub, Éliane. Les associations syndicales de propriétaires /. Paris , 1984. 127 p. ; ISBN 2-13-038290-8 ***NYPL [JLC 87-57]***

La Propriété foncière /. Paris , c1984. vii, 252 p. : ISBN 2-7178-0783-7 LC Card 84-249621
HD643 .N49 1984

REAL PROPERTY - GERMANY (EAST)
Breitkopf, Stephan. Die Behandlung von Immobilienrechten Deutscher mit Wohnsitz in der Bundesrepublik Deutschland und Berlin (West), in der DDR und Berlin (Ost) /. Berlin , 1983. xii, 203 p. ; ISBN 3-921374-25-1 LC Card 84-167165 DDC 330 s 346.431/55043 19
HC244.A1 B4 Heft 129 KK1315
NYPL [STN+ (Berlin. Freie Universität. Osteuropa-Institut. Berichte. Heft 129)]

REAL PROPERTY - GERMANY, WEST.
Breitkopf, Stephan. Die Behandlung von Immobilienrechten Deutscher mit Wohnsitz in der Bundesrepublik Deutschland und Berlin (West), in der DDR und Berlin (Ost) /. Berlin , 1983. xii, 203 p. ; ISBN 3-921374-25-1 LC Card

84-167165 DDC 330 s 346.431/55043 19
HC244.A1 B4 Heft 129 KK1315
NYPL [STN+ (Berlin. Freie Universität. Osteuropa-Institut. Berichte. Heft 129)]

REAL PROPERTY - GREAT BRITAIN.
Dart, Joseph Henry, 1817-1887. A compendium of the law and practice of vendors and purchasers of real estate [microform]. New York, Albany, 1851. civ, 665 (i.e. 856) p. LC Card 17-19132 *NYPL [*ZT-1719]*

Fothergill, Steve. Property and industrial development /. London , Wolfeboro, N.H. , 1987. 187 p. : ISBN 0-09-170741-2 (pbk.) : LC Card 87-2627 DDC 333.3/8/0941 19
HD598 .F68 1987

REAL PROPERTY - GREECE - ATHENS - HISTORY.
Finley, M. I. (Moses I.), 1912- Studies in land and credit in ancient Athens, 500-200 B.C. . New Brunswick, U. S.A. , c1985. xli, 332 p. ; ISBN 0-88738-066-2 : LC Card 85-14091 DDC 333.3/0938/5 19
HD134 .F5 1985 *NYPL [JLE 86-4293]*

REAL PROPERTY INVESTMENT. see **REAL ESTATE INVESTMENT.**

REAL PROPERTY - PRICES - ALBERTA - FORECASTING - MATHEMATICAL MODELS.
Weideman, Donald James. A model to predict urban influenced land prices /. [Edmonton, Alta.] [1986] xi, 294 p. : ISBN 0-88654-148-4 (pbk.) LC Card 86-231786 DDC 333.33/7 19
HD319.A4 W45 1986

REAL PROPERTY - PRICES - JAPAN - TOKYO METROPOLITAN AREA.
Hanayama, Yuzuru, 1939- Land markets and land policy in a metropolitan area . Boston, MA , 1986. xiv, 162 p. : ISBN 0-89946-197-2 LC Card 85-13867 DDC 333.77/13/0952135 19
HD920.T62 H36 1986 *NYPL [JLE 86-4398]*

REAL PROPERTY - PRICES - SWITZERLAND - ZURICH (CANTON) - STATISTICS.
Der Grundeigentumswechsel im Kanton Zürich 1973-1980 . [Zürich] [1982] 74 p. : LC Card 85-161363
HA1608.Z6 A3 Heft 107, Folge 3 HD799.Z8

REAL PROPERTY - PRICES - ZAMBIA - LUSAKA REGION.
Van den Berg, L. M. Anticipating urban growth in Africa . Lusaka, Zambia , 1984. viii, 167 p., [4] p. of plates : LC Card 86-980297 DDC 307.7/6/096894 19
HD993.Z9 L88 1984

REAL PROPERTY - SPAIN - CATALONIA - FINANCE.
Trilla i Bellart, Carme. Finançament del l'accés a l'habitatge a Catalunya en els darrers anys /. [Barcelona] [1984] 58 p. : LC Card 86-160332
HD7351.C37 T75 1984

REAL PROPERTY - SWITZERLAND.
Usteri, Martin. Bodenrecht in Bewegung . Zürich [1985] 27 p. ; LC Card 86-195037
HC395 .Z43 Nr. 126 KKW683

REAL PROPERTY TAX - CALIFORNIA.
Assessment practices survey. [Sacramento, Calif.] , 1987- v. ; LC Card 87-167612 DDC 332.22/2 19
HJ4191 .A74 1987

Barbaria, Janet. The growth revolt . Sacramento, Calif. [1980] 66 p. : LC Card 81-620644 DDC 336.794 19
HJ4191 .B37 1980 *NYPL [JLF 86-369]*

California. Legislature. Assembly. Committee on Local Government. The impact of Proposition 13 (the Jarvis-Gann property tax initiative) on local government programs and services /. [Sacramento, CA.] 1978. iv, 367, 108 p. : LC Card 79-621409 DDC 352/.0794
HJ4191 .C34 1978 *NYPL [JLF 86-1607]*

Reis, Karl Eugen. Fesseln für den Leviathan . Pfaffenweiler , 1987. xi, 338 p. ; ISBN 3-89085-159-2 LC Card 87-134876 DDC 336.973 19
HJ2381 .R356 1987

REAL PROPERTY TAX - DOMINICAN REPUBLIC.
Ross, Jaime. Instrumentos tributarios de financiamientos coadyuvantes a la producción agraria de alimentos /. Santo Domingo, R.D. [1983] i, 229 p. ; LC Card 84-159753
HJ4308 .R67 1983

REAL PROPERTY TAX - FLORIDA.
Florida. Legislature. Senate. Finance, Tax & Claims Committee. The homestead exemption . [Tallahassee, Fla.] [1986] ii leaves, 104 p. ; LC Card 86-623229 DDC 336.22 19
HJ4204.A27 F57 1986

REAL PROPERTY TAX - FRANCE - STATISTICS.
France. Service de la législation fiscale. Taxe d'habitation . [Paris] [1984] 192 p. in various pagings ; LC Card 85-103723
HJ4346 .F73 1984

REAL PROPERTY TAX - GERMANY, WEST.
Jasper, Lothar Th. Entwicklung der Realsteuerhebesätze der Gemeinden mit mehr als 50.000 Einwohnern 1984 gegenüber 1983 /. Bonn , 1984. 29 leaves ; LC Card 86-186306
HJ1120 .B65 nr. 238 HJ4125.G35

REAL PROPERTY TAX - MINNESOTA.
Property tax delinquency in Minnesota . St. Paul, Minn. [1984?] iv, 84 p. : LC Card 86-622652 DDC 336.22 19
HJ4232.A25 P76 1984

REAL PROPERTY TAX - NEW YORK (STATE)
Murphy, Barbara (Barbara Anne) New York State property valuation trends by class . Albany, N.Y. [1986] viii, 47 p. : LC Card 86-623052 DDC 336.22/2 19
HJ4249 .M87 1986

REAL PROPERTY TAX - NEW YORK (STATE) - RATES AND TABLES.
Understanding the equalization rate /. Albany, N.Y. (Governor Nelson A. Rockefeller Empire State Plaza, Albany 12223) [1986] 28 p. : LC Card 87-620729 DDC 336.22/2 19
HJ4249 .U53 1986

REAL PROPERTY TAX - UNITED STATES.
Buying or selling a home . Chicago, Ill. (4025 W. Peterson Ave., Chicago 60646) , c1986. 31 p. : LC Card 86-209128 DDC 343.7305/46 347.303546 19
HJ4182.A5 B89 1986

Cook, Wade. Pay no taxes with real estate /. Orem, Utah , c1982. xvii, 152, [7] p. : ISBN 0-910019-09-6 (pbk.) LC Card 86-228579 DDC 343.7305/46 347.303546 19
HJ4181 .C66 1982

Reis, Karl Eugen. Fesseln für den Leviathan . Pfaffenweiler , 1987. xi, 338 p. ; ISBN 3-89085-159-2 LC Card 87-134876 DDC 336.973 19
HJ2381 .R356 1987

Shenkman, Martin. Real estate after tax reform . New York , c1987. xii, 307 p. ; ISBN 0-471-85984-2 LC Card 87-2196 DDC 343.7305/46 347.303546 19
HJ4181 .S45 1987

REAL PROPERTY TAX - WISCONSIN.
Wise, Gregory J. The effect of tax exempt forestland on town property tax revenues . Madison [1986] 40 leaves : LC Card 86-623093 DDC 336.22/09775 19
HJ4284.A3 W59 1986

REAL PROPERTY - TAXATION. see **REAL PROPERTY TAX.**

REAL PROPERTY - UNITED STATES.
Arnold, Alvin L. Real estate investor's deskbook /. Boston , c1982. 1 v. (various pagings) : ISBN 0-88262-732-5 LC Card 82-70717 DDC 346.7304/3 347.30643 19
KF665 .A8 1982 *NYPL [JLF 86-907]*

Ausländische Investitionen in U. S.-Grundvermögen /. Herne , 1984, c1983. 86 p. ; ISBN 3-482-69041-3 LC Card 84-203818 DDC 346.43/07 344.3067 19
K3830.4 .A97 1984 *NYPL [JLD 86-2326]*

Dart, Joseph Henry, 1817-1887. A compendium of the law and practice of vendors and purchasers of real estate [microform]. New York, Albany, 1851. civ, 665 (i.e. 856) p. LC Card 17-19132 *NYPL [*ZT-1719]*

Ficek, Edmund F. Real estate principles and practices /. Columbus , c1983. viii, 550 p. : ISBN 0-675-20016-4 LC Card 82-73775 DDC 346.7304/37 347.306437 19
KF2042.R4 F46 1983 *NYPL [JLE 86-2010]*

REAL PROPERTY - UNITED STATES - FINANCE.
Wiedemer, John P., 1918- Real estate finance /. Englewood Cliffs, N.J. , c1987. xvi, 396 p. : ISBN 0-13-762774-2 LC Card 86-30471 DDC 332.7/2/0973 19
HG2040.5.U5 W54 1987

REAL PROPERTY - VALUATION - CALIFORNIA.
Miller, George H. California real estate appraisal . Englewood Cliffs, N.J. , c1987. xiv, 348 p. : ISBN 0-13-112558-3 : LC Card 87-6956 DDC 333.33/2/09794 19
HD1387 .M545 1987

REAL PROPERTY - VALUATION - DENMARK.
Vurderingen af landets faste ejendomme pr. 1 april 1981 . København [1982] 225 p. ; ISBN 87-503-4048-4 LC Card 82-232266
HD736 .V87 1982

REAL PROPERTY - VALUATION - DICTIONARIES.
The Dictionary of real estate appraisal. Chicago, Ill. , c1984. ix, 368 p. ; ISBN 0-911780-74-2 LC Card 84-16834 DDC 333.33/2/0321 19
HD1387 .D435 1984 *NYPL [JLE 86-2371]*

REAL PROPERTY - VALUATION - HUNGARY.
Fórizs, Józsefné. Földértékelés, termőhelyi értékelés problémái . Budapest , 1985. 211 p., [4] folded leaves of plates : ISBN 963-491-204-4 LC Card 86-196842
HD1387 .F596 1985

REAL PROPERTY - VALUATION - INDIA.
Dange, Manohar N. Theory and practice of urban land values in India /. Bombay , 1983. xii, 132 p. ; LC Card 83-903969 DDC 333.33/2/0954 19
HD878 .D36 1983 *NYPL [JLD 87-729]*

REAL PROPERTY - VALUATION - PROBLEMS, EXERCISES, ETC.
Akerson, Charles B. The appraiser's workbook /. Chicago, Ill. , c1985. xv, 263 p. in various pagings : ISBN 0-911780-75-0 (pbk.) LC Card 84-3008 DDC 333.33/2/076 19
HD1387 .A518 1985 *NYPL [JLF 86-1025]*

REAL PROPERTY - VIRGINIA - FAIRFAX COUNTY - DIRECTORIES.
Lusk's Fairfax County, Virginia assessment directory . Washington, D.C. (1824 Jefferson Pl., NW, Washington 20036) , 1986. 1251, [81] p. ; LC Card 87-144674 DDC 333.33/2/09755291 19
HD266.V82 F24 1986

Real-world intelligence . Meyer, Herbert E., 1945- New York , c1987. 102 p. ; ISBN 1-555-84147-3 LC Card 87-20787 DDC 658.4/7 19
HD38.7 .M47 1987

The real world of the small business owner /. Scase, Richard. London , New York , c1987. 170 p. ; ISBN 0-7099-5416-6 (pbk.) LC Card 87-6756 DDC 338.6/42/0941 19
HD2346.G7 S28 1987

Realengo y municipio . Romeo Mateo, María Cruz, 1960- Alicante , 1986. 171 p. : ISBN 84-505-3131-4 LC Card 87-137181
HD780.A435 R66 1986

Realidad nacional (Culiacán, Mexico) . (19) Movimientos sociales en el noroeste de México /. México , 1985. 282 p. ; ISBN 968-590-072-8 LC Card 87-102068
HD1531.M6 M684 1985

Realidade brasileira . Schneider, José Odelso. Porto Alegre-RS , c1986. 438 p. : LC Card 87-119174
HC187 .S393 1986

Realidade social portuguesa .
(1) Rosa, Eugénio. O fracasso dos governos de direita em Portugal (1978 a 1981) . [Lisbon?] [1982] 351 p. ; LC Card 85-228499
HC392 .R592 1982

Realistic economics /. Light, John J. Indianapolis, IN (P.O. Box 1606, Indianapolis 46206) , c1984. 111 p. ; ISBN 0-933021-00-3 : LC Card 84-249506 DDC 331.12/0973 19
HD5724 .L4236 1984 *NYPL [JLE 86-4650]*

The realities of nuclear power . Thomas, S. D. (Steve D.) Cambridge , New York , 1988. p. cm. ISBN 0-521-32750-4 LC Card 87-22488

DDC 338.4/7621483 19
HD9698.A2 T53 1988

Realizatsiia na Ė.V.M. uchetno-planovykh rabot material'no-tekhnicheskogo snabzheniia. Realizatsiia na ĖVM uchetno-planovykh rabot material'no-tekhnicheskogo snabzheniia /. Moskva , 1983. 63 p. : LC Card 84-210458
HD39.5 .R43 1983

Realizatsiia na ĖVM uchetno-planovykh rabot material'no-tekhnicheskogo snabzheniia / [otvetstvennyĭ redaktor M.D. Il'menskiĭ]. Moskva : TSentr. ėkonomiko-matematicheskiĭ institut AN SSSR, 1983. 63 p. : ill. ; 21 cm. At head of title: Akademiia nauk SSSR. TSentral'nyĭ ėkonomiko-matematicheskiĭ institut. Includes bibliographies. LC Card 84-210458
1. Industrial procurement - Soviet Union - Data processing. I. Il'menskiĭ, M. D. II. TSentral'nyĭ ėkonomiko-matematicheskiĭ institut (Akademiia nauk SSSR). III. Title: Realizatsiia na Ė.V.M. uchetno-planovykh rabot material'no-tekhnicheskogo snabzheniia.
HD39.5 .R43 1983

Realkredit . Goedecke, Wolfgang. Frankfurt am Main , c1982. 120 p. ; ISBN 3-7819-0275-7 LC Card 83-139826
HG2040.5.G4 G64 1982

Realniiat sotsializŭm--teoriia i praktika. Shopov, Dimitŭr. Kachestvoto na truda . Sofiia , 1984. 202 p. : LC Card 85-117683
HC403.Z9 L375 1984

Real'nosti sovremennogo mira i politika konfrontatsii /. Poklad, B. I. (Boris Iosifovich) Moskva , 1985. 157 p. ; LC Card 85-170137
*JX1974.7 .P585 1985 NYPL [*QIK 87-1550]*

REALTORS. see **REAL ESTATE AGENTS.**

REALTY. see **REAL PROPERTY.**

Realty brokerage operations by savings institutions /. Olin, Harold Bennett. Chicago, IL (111 E. Wacker Dr., Chicago 60601) , c1986. 38, [96] p. : LC Card 86-212493 DDC 332.3/2 19
HD255 .O45 1986

Reason Foundation. Local Government Center. The Role of privatization in Florida's growth /. [Tallahassee?] , c1987. iv, 474 p. ; LC Card 87-403210 DDC 338.9 19
HD3865.F6 R65 1987

Reason in the air : towards a balance of international aviation needs. [S.l.] : International Air Transport Association, [1977] 31 p. : ill. (some col.) ; 20 cm. LC Card 85-149832 DDC 387.7/068 19
1. Aeronautics, Commercial - Government policy. 2. Air lines - Government policy. I. International Air Transport Association.
HE9777.7 .R43 1977

The Reasoning criminal : rational choice perspectives on offending / edited by Derek B. Cornish, Ronald V. Clarke. New York : Springer-Verlag, c1986. xiv, 246 p. : ill. ; 25 cm. (Research in criminology) "The chapters in this volume are the outcome of a conference sponsored by the Home Office at Christ's College, Cambridge, England, in July 1985."--Introd. Includes bibliographies and indexes. ISBN 0-387-96272-7 : LC Card 86-1275 DDC 364.3 19
1. Criminal psychology - Congresses. 2. Crime and criminals - Congresses. 3. Decision-making - Congresses. 4. Choice (Psychology) - Congresses. I. Cornish, Derek B. (Derek Blaikie), 1939-. II. Clarke, R. V. G. III. Series.
HV6080 .R38 1986 NYPL [JLE 86-3522]

Reassessing the role of government in the mixed economy / edited by Herbert Giersch. Boulder : Westview Press, 1987. p. cm. (Publications of the Institute of World Economics, University of Kiel) Based on a symposium held by the Kiel Institute of World Economics, June 23-25, 1982. Includes bibliographies. ISBN 0-8133-0598-5 : LC Card 87-20142 DDC 338.9 19
1. Economic policy - Congresses. 2. Economic development - Political aspects - Congresses. 3. Mixed economy - Congresses. I. Giersch, Herbert. II. Universität Kiel. Institut für Weltwirtschaft. III. Series.
HD73 .R43 1987

Reavis, Marshall W. Florida life and health study manual . [Chicago] , c1987. x, 358 p. : ISBN 0-88462-727-6 (pbk.) LC Card 87-17254 DDC 368.3/009759 19
HG8961.F6 F56 1987

Reay, D. A. (David Anthony) Innovation for energy efficiency . Oxford [Oxfordshire] , 1988. p. cm. ISBN 0-08-034798-3 : LC Card 87-19016 DDC 333.79/094 19
HD9502.E8 I55 1988

REBATES - UNITED STATES.
Samtur, Susan J. Cashing in at the checkout /. New York , c1979. 152 p. : ISBN 0-448-15704-7 : LC Card 79-51120 DDC 381/.1 19
HF6127 .S25 NYPL [JLD 81-566]

Rebel pen . Vorse, Mary Heaton, 1874-1966. New York , c1985. 345 p. : ISBN 0-85345-669-0 : LC Card 85-7130 DDC 331.4/0973 19
HD8072 .V755 1985 NYPL [JLD 86-2459]

REBELLIONS. see **REVOLUTIONS.**

Rebels and reformers of the airways /. Davies, R. E. G. (Ronald Edward George) Washington, D.C. , c1987. xvi, 440 p. : ISBN 0-87474-354-0 (alk. paper) LC Card 86-26243 DDC 387.7/092/2 19
HE9775 .D38 1987

Rebolledo Soberón, Luis. Deuda externa : en búsqueda de salidas viables para la crisis / [Luis Rebolledo Soberón, Enrique Cornejo Ramírez]. [Lima] : Universidad de Lima, Facultad de Economía, Centro de Investigaciones Económicas y Sociales, c1985. 58 p. : ill. ; 21 cm. (Serie Documentos. no. 2) LC Card 86-120059
1. Debts, External - Latin America. 2. Debt relief - Latin America. I. Cornejo Ramírez, Enrique. II. Universidad de Lima. Centro de Investigaciones Económicas y Sociales. III. Series: Serie Documentos (Universidad de Lima. Centro de Investigaciones Económicas y Sociales) , no. 2. IV. Title.
HJ8514.5 .R43 1985

Reboratti, Carlos E. Condicionantes físicos del asentamiento humano en el norte de la Patagonia / Carlos E. Reboratti. Buenos Aires : Centro de Estudios Urbanos y Regionales, 1982. 47 p. : maps ; 28 cm. (Cuadernos del CEUR, 0326-1417 . no. 5) Bibliography: p. 47. LC Card 83-185201
1. Land settlement - Argentina - Comahue Region. 2. Physical geography - Argentina - Comahue Region. I. Title. II. Series.
HD479.C57 R43 1982

Rebovich, Donald. Understanding hazardous waste crime : a multistate examination of offense and offender characteristics in the northeast / by Donald Rebovich ; project participants, Philip Ahrens ... [et al.]. [Trenton?] : Northeast Hazardous Waste Project, New Jersey Division of Criminal Justice, [1986] viii, 70 p. : ill. ; 28 cm. "June 1986"--Cover. Bibliography: p. 58. LC Card 86-622805 DDC 364.1/42 19
1. Hazardous waste management industry - Northeastern States - Corrupt practices. 2. Organized crime - Northeastern States. I. Ahrens, Philip. II. Northeast Hazardous Waste Project (U. S.). III. New Jersey. Division of Criminal Justice. IV. Title.
HD9975.U53 A1157 1986

Rebuilding America's cities . Meyers, Edward M. Cambridge, Mass. , c1986. xxi, 290 p. : ISBN 0-88730-051-0 LC Card 85-30780 DDC 307.3/4/0973 19
HT175 .U59 1986 NYPL [JLE 86-2874]

Rebuilding New York--the next phase, from recovery to resurgence . Tese, Vincent. [New York, NY (1515 Broadway, New York 10036) , 1985] 74 leaves ; LC Card 86-622413 DDC 338.9747 19
HC107.N7 T47 1985

Re-building Zimbabwe at 5 years of independence. Zimbabwe at 5 years of independence. [Harare?] [1984?] ix, 265 p. : LC Card 87-103323 DDC 338.96891 19
HC910 .Z3173 1984

Rebuttal and commentaries to the third report on the progress of land reform in Cuba as rendered by the United Nations in 1962. Barro y Segura, Antonio. Miami, Fla. , 1963. 17 p. ; LC Card 86-181697
HD1333.C9 B37 1963

RECALL - UNITED STATES.
Zimmerman, Joseph Francis, 1928- Participatory democracy . New York , 1986. xi, 229 p. ; ISBN 0-275-92132-8 (alk. paper) : LC Card 86-8129 DDC 323/.042/0973 19
JF493.U6 Z56 1986 NYPL [JLE 86-3632]

Recensement de la population et de l'habitation de 1971. Savezni zavod za statistiku (Yugoslavia) [Popis stanovništva i stanova 1971. English.] Population and housing census 1971 . Beograd , 1974. 12 v. ; LC Card 83-122836
HA1631.5 1971 .S38 1974

Recensement des marchés et commandes des entreprises publiques et sociétés d'économie mixte : art. 35, 36, 37 du Code des marchés publics : instruction et nomenclature. Paris : Ministère de l'économie, des finances et du budget, Secrétariat général de la Commission centrale des marchés, [1984] 71 p. : ill. ; 30 cm. "Janvier 1984." "Cette instruction abroge et remplace l'instruction prédédente émise en 1980." LC Card 85-133146
1. Government business enterprises - France. 2. France - Statistical services. I. France. Commission centrale des marchés. Secrétariat général.
HD4163 .R43 1984

Recensement fédéral des entreprises 1985. Eidgenössische Betriebszählung 1985. Bern , 1986. 108 p. ; ISBN 3-303-07007-5 LC Card 87-407623 DDC 338.1/7498/09494021 19
HD9765.S92 E37 1986

Recensement général de la population de 1982, France métropolitaine, sondage au 1/20. Kerromes, Armelle. Tableaux normalisés simplifiés par région et département . Paris [1984] 273 p. ; ISBN 2-11-064692-6 : LC Card 86-176720
HA1214 1982p

Recensement général de la population 1977 : résultats définitifs. Niamey : République du Niger, Ministère du Plan, Direction de la statistique et de l'informatique, 1985-<1986 > v. <1-3 > : ill. ; 30 cm. Vol. 2 lacks other title info. CONTENTS. - [1] Rapport d'analyse -- [2] Rapport méthodologique -- [3] Données brutes, ensemble du Niger. LC Card 87-157638
1. Niger - Census, 1977. 2. Niger - Population - Statistics. I. Niger. Direction de la statistique et de l'informatique.
HA4724 .A4 1977

Recensement général 1982, population et logement. Résultats préliminaires du recensement général (septembre 1982) /. [Port-au-Prince] [1982 or 1983] vii, 60 p., [1] leaf of plates : LC Card 84-138275 DDC 304.6/097294/021 19
HD7316.A3 R47 1982 NYPL [JLF 86-1280]

Recent advances in labour economics / edited by Gillian Hutchinson & John Treble. London : Croom Helm ; New York : St. Martin's Press, c1984. 258 p. : ill. ; 22 cm. Papers presented at a conference of the S.S.R.C. Labour Economics Study Group, held July 1983 at Hull University. Bibliography: p. 247-258. ISBN 0-312-66575-X (St. Martin's) : LC Card 83-40628 DDC 331 19
1. Labor economics - Congresses. 2. Trade-unions - Congresses. I. Hutchinson, Gillian. II. Treble, John. III. S.S.R.C. Labour Economics Study Group.
HD4813 .R28 1984 NYPL [JLD 86-2455]

Recent advances in system modelling and optimization . IFIP Working Conference on System Modelling and Optimization (1984 : Santiago, Chile) Berlin , New York , c1986. 199 p. : ISBN 0-387-17083-9 (U. S.) LC Card 86-29770 DDC 003 19
QA402 .I43 1984 NYPL [JSE 87-639]

Recent advances in the techniques for demographic analysis / edited by P.C. Saxena, P.P. Talwar. 1st ed. Bombay : Himalaya Pub. House, 1987. xiv, 456 p. ; 23 cm. Papers presented at a workshop held in Bombay, 1982, organized by the Indian Association for the Study of Population. Includes bibliographies. LC Card 87-900498
1. Demography - Congresses. 2. Cohort analysis - Congresses. 3. India - Population - Congresses. I. Saxena, P. C. (Prem Chandra), 1939-. II. Talwar, Prem P., 1936-. III. Indian Association for the Study of Population.
HB849 .R42 1987

Recent developments in monetary policy . Holmes, Frank Wakefield, Sir, 1924- [Wellington] [1976] 5 p. ; LC Card 82-216052
HG1480.5 .H65 1976

Recent economic thought.
Classical political economy . Boston , c1988. viii, 275 p. : ISBN 0-89838-229-7 : LC Card 87-3394 DDC 330.15/3 19
HB94 .C42 1988

International economics /. Boston , c1987. x, 274 p. : ISBN 0-89838-196-7 LC Card 86-33776 DDC 337 19
HF1411 .I51725 1987

Recent economic thought series.
International economics /. Boston , c1987. x, 274 p. : ISBN 0-89838-196-7 LC Card 86-33776 DDC 337 19
HF1411 .I51725 1987

Natural resource economics . Boston , c1986. xiv, 234 p. : ISBN 0-89838-203-3 LC Card 85-24215 DDC 333.7 19
HC59 .N318 1986 ***NYPL [JLE 86-3471]***

Theories of income distribution /. Boston , c1988. x, 255 p. : ISBN 0-89838-232-7 LC Card 87-3248 DDC 339.2 19
HB523 .T44 1988

Recent experience with multilateral official debt rescheduling /. Dillon, K. Burke. Washington, D.C. , c1987. v, 22 p. : LC Card 87-2633 DDC 336.3/435 19
HG3891.5 .D55 1987

Recent experiences in human resources development / editors, T.V. Rao and D.F. Pereira. New Delhi : Oxford & IBH Pub. Co., c1986. xvi, 448 p. ; 23 cm. "A work of the Centre for Human Resources Development, XLRI, Jamshedpur." Papers presented at a national seminar, Bombay, 1985. Includes bibliographies and indexes. ISBN 81-204-0120-4 : LC Card 86-902270 DDC 331.11/0954 19
1. Manpower planning - India - Congresses. 2. Personnel management - India - Congresses. I. Venkateswara, Rao T. II. Pereira, D. F. (Dennyson F.). III. Xavier Labour Relations Institute. Centre for Human Resources Development.
HF5549.5.M3 R38 1985

Recent findings on the determinants of urban-rural income transfers in Kenya /. Mukras, M. S. [Nairobi?] , 1985. ii, 33 leaves : LC Card 85-980600
HC865.Z9 I516 1985

Recent industrial research unit studies. see **Pennsylvania. University. Wharton School of Finance and Commerce. Industrial Research Unit. Industrial Research Unit study.**

Recent trends in fertility and mortality in Indonesia / Panel on Indonesia, Committee on Population and Demography, Commission on Behavioral and Social Sciences and Education, National Research Council. Honolulu, Hawaii : East-West Center, 1987. xvi, 96 p. : ill. ; 23 cm. (Papers of the East-West Population Institute, 0732-0531 . no. 105) Report / Committee on Population and Demography ; no. 29 "May 1987." Bibliography: p. 85-88. ISBN 0-86638-092-2 (pbk.) : LC Card 87-11178 DDC 304.6/32/09598 19
1. Fertility, Human - Indonesia. 2. Mortality - Indonesia. 3. Indonesia - Statistics, Vital. I. National Research Council (U. S.). Committee on Population and Demography. Panel on Indonesia. II. Series. III. Series: Report (National Research Council (U. S.). Committee on Population and Demography) , no. 29.
HB1057 .R43 1987

Recent wage deceleration . Kumar, Pradeep. Kingston, Ont., Canada , 1987. 21, [12] p. ; ISBN 0-88886-158-3 (pbk.) LC Card 87-163251 DDC 331.2/971 19
HD4979 .K816 1987

Récession et relance /. Colloque d'étude des politiques économiques Récession et relance (1984 : Paris, France) Paris , 1984. 218 p. : ISBN 2-7178-0690-3 : LC Card 85-158199 DDC 338.5/42 19
HB3711 .C59 1984

Recession survival handbook. Helping handbook /. Lansing, MI (300 N. Washington Square, Suite 401, Lansing 48933) , 1986. v, 101 p. ; LC Card 87-110874 DDC 361.6/025/774 19
HC107.M53 P633 1986

RECESSIONS - GREAT BRITAIN.
Redundancy and recession . Norwich, England , c1986. xii, 174 p. : ISBN 0-86094-201-5 : LC Card 86-218942 DDC 330.941/0858 19
HC256.6 .R44 1986

Recettes, dépenses et revenus des exploitations agricoles en 1983 / République française, Ministère de l'agriculture, Service central des enquêtes et études statistiques. Paris : SCEES, [1986] 138 p. : ill. ; 30 cm. (SSCR, 0244-5271 . no 68) Chiefly tables. Cover title. "Décembre 1985." LC Card 86-187878
1. Agriculture - Economic aspects - France - Statistics. I. France. Service central des enquêtes et études statistiques. II. Series: Synthèses statistiques, comptes et revenus , no 68.
HD1945 .R374 1986

Recherche et coopération avec le Tiers Monde . France. Mission "Recherche, technologie et progrès en coopération." Paris , c1983. 120 p. ; ISBN 2-11-001071-1 : LC Card 83-196852
HC60 .F727 1983

Recherches démographiques .
(cahier no 4) Sala-Diakanda, Mpembele. Approche ethnique des phénomènes démographiques . Louvain-la-Neuve , 1980. 433 p. : LC Card 84-118066
HB3664.5.A3 S23 1980

Recherches économiques et sociales, 0396-3683 .
(nouv. sér., no 3) Economie monétaire internationale. Paris [1982] 156 p. : LC Card 85-131349 DDC 332/.042 19
HG3881 .E27 1982

Recherches Panthéon-Sorbonne, Université de Paris I. Série Sciences économiques, 0338-8719.
Formation et rôle des taux d'intérêt /. Paris , c1982. 204 p. : ISBN 2-7178-0562-1 : LC Card 83-103493
HB539 .F63 1982

Recherches politiques.
Vérin, Hélène, 1940- Entrepreneurs, entreprise . Paris , c1982. 262 p. ; ISBN 2-13-037449-2 (pbk.) : LC Card 82-153537 DDC 338/.04/09 19
HB615 .V44 1982 ***NYPL [JLD 86-3019]***

Rechin, V. D. Upravlenie nauchno-tekhnicheskim progressom na predpriiatii /. Novosibirsk , 1986. 222 p. ; LC Card 87-124400
HD45 .U52 1986

Rechmann, Bernhard. Noll, Wulf. Lokales Informationssystem Arbeitsmarkt (LISA) /. Essen , 1986. 262 p. ; ISBN 3-923494-64-5 LC Card 87-409105 DDC 331.12/5/094355 19
HD5780.R82 N65 1986

Rechnungslegung für Beteiligungen nach der Anschaffungskostenmethode und nach der Equity-Methode /. Fricke, Gabriele. Bochum , 1983. xv, 374 p. : ISBN 3-88339-310-X : LC Card 83-218419
HF5686.I6 F75 1983

Rechnungslegung, Gläubigerschutz und Agency-Probleme /. Ewert, Ralf. Wiesbaden , c1986. 429 p. ; ISBN 3-409-13710-6 LC Card 87-134169 DDC 657/.3 19
HG4028.B2 E92 1986

Recht auf Arbeit und Beruf? . Baruzzi, Arno, 1935- Freiburg , c1983. 88 p. ; ISBN 3-495-47518-4 LC Card 83-152808
HD4903 .B37 1983

Recht, Wirtschaft, Aussenhandel .
(Bd. 6) Löschner, Ernst. Souveräne Risken und internationale Verschuldung /. Wien , 1983. 187 p. : ISBN 3-214-06553-X : LC Card 84-152762 DDC 336.3/435/091724 19
HJ8899 .L67 1983 ***NYPL [JLE 86-1553]***

Recht, Wirtschaft, Gesellschaft. Wirtschaft .
(2) Steingräber, Carola, 1956- Geld- und Fiskalpolitik in Portfolio-orientierten Modellen kleiner offener Volkswirtschaften . Rheinfelden , c1986. ix, 219 p. : ISBN 3-87718-532-0 LC Card 86-182509
HG230.3 .S74 1986

Rechtsdogmatik und Wirtschaft . Bürge, Alfons. Berlin , c1987. 280 p. ; ISBN 3-428-06124-1 LC Card 87-134998 DDC 332.8/3/094 19
HB551 .B87 1987

Rechtspolitische Schriften .
(7) Demontage des Sozialstaats . Köln , 1986. 177 p. ; ISBN 3-8161-0107-0 LC Card 87-104505 DDC 338.943 19
HC286.7 .D455 1986

Rechtsprobleme der Innovation . Gaul, Dieter. München , 1984. xiv, 126 p. ; ISBN 3-88709-084-5 ***NYPL [JLD 85-2917]***

Recker, Marie-Luise. Von der Konkurrenz zur Rivalität . Stuttgart , 1986. 186 p. ; ISBN 3-515-04760-3 LC Card 87-134320 DDC 337/.09/04 19
HF1411 .V665 1986

The reckoning /. Halberstam, David. New York , c1986. 752 p. ; ISBN 0-688-04838-2 LC Card 86-16427 DDC 338.4/76292/0973 19
HD9710.U52 H28 1986
NYPL [JLE 86-4151]

Recktenwald, Horst Claus. Smith, Adam, 1723-1790. [Inquiry into the nature and causes of the wealth of nations. German.] Der Wohlstand der Nationen . München , c1974. lxxix, 859 p., [14] p. of plates : ISBN 3-406-05393-9 LC Card 87-672505
HB161 .S654x 1974

Recktenwald, Werner.
Wie errechne ich meinen Nettolohn? : mit der Monatslohnsteuertabelle für rentenversicherungspflichtige Arbeitnehmer 1985 : Auszug / [Bearbeitung, Werner Recktenwald].8. Aufl. Saarbrücken : Arbeitskammer des Saarlandes, [1985?] 112 p. ; 21 cm. ISBN 3-88968-029-1 LC Card 85-171297 DDC 343.4305/242 344.3035242 19
1. Wages - Taxation - Germany (West) - Tables. I. Arbeitskammer des Saarlandes. II. Title. III. Title: Nettolohn?.
HJ4720.A7 R42 1985

Wie errechne ich meinen Nettolohn? Mit der Monatslohnsteuertabelle für rentenversicherungspflichtige Arbeitnehmer, 1986 und 1987, Auszug / [Bearbeitung, Werner Recktenwald, Barbara Scheidhauer]. 10. Aufl. Saarbrücken : Arbeitskammer des Saarlandes, [1987]. 128 p. ; 21 cm. LC Card 87-408789 DDC 343.4305/242 344.3035242 19
1. Wages - Taxation - Germany (West) - Tables. I. Scheidhauer, Barbara. II. Title.
HJ4720.A7 R42 1987

RECLAMATION OF LAND - HUNGARY.
Ács, Rudolf. A komplex meliorációs beruházások történeti áttekintése és gazdasági hatásának vizsgálata különböző agroökológiai tipusu gazdaságokban /. Budapest , 1986. 118 p. ; ISBN 963-491-237-0 LC Card 87-137972
HD1940.5 .A65 1986

RECLAMATION OF LAND - INDIA.
Wastelands . New Delhi , 1987. xii, 249 p. : LC Card 86-903086 DDC 333.73 19
HD1671.I5W37 1987

RECLAMATION OF LAND - ITALY - HISTORY - ADDRESSES, ESSAYS, LECTURES.
Le Bonifiche in Italia dal '700 a oggi /. Roma , 1984. viii, 437 p. : ISBN 88-420-2429-5 : LC Card 85-173148
HD1683.I8 B66 1984 ***NYPL [JSD 87-50]***

RECLAMATION OF LAND - ITALY, SOUTHERN.
Barone, Giuseppe, 1947- Mezzogiorno e modernizzazione . Torino , c1986. xii, 408 p. ; ISBN 88-06-59238-6 : LC Card 86-219130
HC307.S69 B37 1986

RECLAMATION OF LAND - UZBEK S.S.R.
Ergashev, N. (Nazirzhon) Rukovodstvo Kompartii Uzbekistana osvoeniem tselinnykh zemel′ /. Tashkent , 1985. 159 p. ; LC Card 86-231568
HD1741.S782 U84 1985

Recognition of stochastic processes with the changing structure of probabilities distributions. Kligene, Nerute. Raspoznavanie sluchaĭnykh protsessov s peremennoĭ strukturoĭ veroiatnostnykh raspredeleniĭ . Vil′nius , 1986. 136 p. : LC Card 87-146330
HD38 .S715 vyp.76 QA274

Recollections of an "old China hand" /. Holzberger, Peter. [Hongkong , c1984] 233 p. : LC Card 86-135690 DDC 338.092/2 B 19
HC282.5.H64 A3 1984

Les récoltants vendeurs au kilo champenois face au contrat interprofessionnel /. Berger, Alain. Paris , Epernay [1984] 45, 63 p. : ISBN 2-85340-534-6 LC Card 85-111856
HD9382.7.C5 B47 1984

RECOM, residential computing. The Home terminal II . [Boston, Ma.] (89 Broad St., Boston 02110) [1986] 63 leaves : LC Card

86-211108 DDC 381/.45621396/0973 19
HD9696.C63 U518327 1986

Reconceiving part-time work . Kahne, Hilda. Totowa, N.J. , 1985. xv, 180 p. : ISBN 0-8476-7376-6 : LC Card 85-2386 DDC 331.3/94 19
HD5110.2.U5 K33 1985
NYPL [JLE 86-1174]

RECONSTRUCTION FINANCE CORPORATION - HISTORY.
Olson, James Stuart, 1946- Saving capitalism . Princeton, N.J. , c1988. p. cm. ISBN 0-691-04749-9 (alk. paper) : LC Card 87-7275 DDC 353.0082/5/09 19
HG3729.U5 O47 1988

The reconstruction of economics . Gruchy, Allan Garfield, 1906- New York , 1987. xx, 173 p. ; ISBN 0-313-25679-9 (lib. bdg. : alk. paper) LC Card 86-25721 DDC 330 19
HB99.5 .G79 1987

RECONSTRUCTION (1914-1939) - FRANCE.
Fourcaut, Annie, 1950- Femmes à l'usine . Paris , 1982. 268 p. : ISBN 2-7071-1258-5 : LC Card 82-151587
HD6145 .F65 1982

RECONSTRUCTION (1914-1939) - GREAT BRITAIN.
Britain's industrial future . New York , 1985. xxiv, 503 p. ; ISBN 0-8240-7605-2 (alk. paper) : LC Card 85-13042 DDC 338.941 19
HC256.3 .B728 1985 ***NYPL [JLD 86-3461]***

RECONSTRUCTION (1914-1939) - ITALY.
Caroleo, Anna, 1948- Il movimento cooperativo in Italia nel primo dopoguerra (1918-1925) /. Milano, Italy , c1986. 376 p. ; LC Card 86-192160
HD3503 .C36 1986

RECONSTRUCTION (1939-1951) - GERMANY.
Wirtschaftspolitik im britischen Besatzungsgebiet 1945-1949 /. Düsseldorf , 1984. 338 p. : ISBN 3-590-18124-9 LC Card 84-188669
HC286.5 .W5655 1984

RECONSTRUCTION (1939-1951) - GERMANY (WEST)
Abelshauser, Werner. Wirtschaftsgeschichte der Bundesrepublik Deutschland (1945-1980) /. Frankfurt am Main , 1983. 186 p. : ISBN 3-518-11241-4 : LC Card 83-180531
HC286.7 .A26 1983

Engelmann, Bernt, 1921- Wir hab'n ja den Kopf noch fest auf dem Hals . Köln , c1987. 257 p. : ISBN 3-462-01688-1 LC Card 87-146658
HC286.5 .E594 1987

RECONSTRUCTION (1939-1951) - GREAT BRITAIN.
Robertson, Alex. The bleak midwinter, 1947 /. Manchester, U.K. , Wolfeboro, N.H., U. S.A. , 1987. x, 207 p. : ISBN 0-7190-1902-8 : LC Card 87-11085 DDC 333.8/22/0941 19
HD9551.5 .R56 1987

RECONSTRUCTION (1939-1951) - ITALY.
D'Angelo, Lucio. Ceti medi e ricostruzione . [Milano] , 1981. vi, 287 p. ; LC Card 81-213297
JN5657.D45 D36 1981
NYPL [JLE 86-3459]

Harper, John Lamberton. America and the reconstruction of Italy, 1945-1948 /. Cambridge [Cambridgeshire] , New York , 1986. x, 213 p. ; ISBN 0-521-32518-8 LC Card 85-30915 DDC 338.91/73/045 19
HC305 .H36 1986 ***NYPL [JLE 86-3600]***

Maione, Giuseppe, 1942- Tecnocrati e mercanti . Milano, Italia , c1986. 354 p. ; LC Card 86-194293
HC305 .M274 1986

Ortona, Egidio. Anni d'America /. Bologna , c1984- v. ; ISBN 88-15-00531-5 (v. 1) : LC Card 84-240652 DDC 338.91/73/045 19
HC305 .O78 1984 ***NYPL [JLL 86-503]***

RECONSTRUCTION (1939-1951) - ITALY, NORTHERN.
Soldini, Bruno, 1939- Uomini da soma . [Lugano] , c1985. 289 p. : LC Card 86-136358
HJ6947 .S65 1985

RECONSTRUCTION (1939-1951) - ITALY - TRIESTE REGION.
--Anche l'uomo doveva essere di ferro . Milano, Italy , c1986. 441 p. : LC Card 86-213675
HD8490.T742 A53 1986

RECONSTRUCTION (1939-1951) - POLAND.
Mazurkiewicz, Eugeniusz. Podstawowe problemy polityki rolnej w PRL /. Warszawa , 1979. 306 p. ; LC Card 81-172693
HD1995.7.Z8 M39 1979

RECONSTRUCTION (1939-1951) - POLAND - OPOLE (VOIVODESHIP)
Lis, Michał. Odbudowa podstaw gospodarki Śląska Opolskiego na przykładzie przemysłu, 1945-1949 /. [Opole] , 1978. 254 p. : LC Card 81-201084
HC340.Z7 O665 1978

RECONSTRUCTION (1939-1951) - SOVIET UNION, WESTERN - CONGRESSES.
Vozrozhdenie prifrontovykh i osvobozhdennykh raĭonov SSSR v gody Velikoĭ Otechestvennoĭ voĭny 1941-1945 /. Moskva , 1986. 214 p., [24] p. of plates : LC Card 86-232256
HC336.9.W47 V69 1986

RECONSTRUCTION (1939-1951) - UKRAINE.
V bitvakh za sovetskuiu Ukrainu . Kiev , 1985. 172 p. ; LC Card 85-170194
HC337.U53 D48 1985

La Reconversión industrial, la crisis y reforma agraria. [Madrid] : Fundación Friedrich Ebert, [1984] 148 p. : ill. ; 23 cm. (Documentos y estudios . 37) "Estudio realizado por el Equipo de Investigación Sociológica"--P. [5] Includes bibliographical references. ISBN 84-398-1197-7 LC Card 86-216324
1. Spain - Economic conditions - 1975-. 2. Industry and state - Spain. 3. Manpower policy - Spain. 4. Land reform - Spain. I. Cáritas Española. Departamento de Investigación Sociológica. II. Series.
HC385 .R375 1984

Recopilación de estadísticas económicas del siglo XIX en México .
(v. 2) Flores Clair, Eduardo. Estadísticas mineras de México en el siglo XIX /. México, D.F. , 1985. 181 p. ; LC Card 87-401718 DDC 338.2/0972 19
HD9506.M62 F57 1985

(v. 3) Ramírez Bautista, Elia. Estadísticas bancarias . México, D.F. , 1985. 10, ca. 200 p. ; ISBN 968-603-813-2 LC Card 87-401719 DDC 332.1/0972/021 19
HG2714 .R36 1985

Recopilaciones INDEC .
(2) Evolución de la industria manufacturera, 1982-1984. Buenos Aires, República Argentina [1986] 115 p. : LC Card 86-226786
HD4999 .E95 1986

(3) Edificación, 1972-1984. Buenos Aires , 1986. 36 p. : LC Card 87-404780 DDC 338.4/7624/0982021 19
HD9715.A72 E35 1986

Record linkage techniques--1985 . Workshop on Exact Matching Methodologies (May 9-10, 1985 : Arlington, Va.) [Washington, D.C.] , 1985. vii, 397 p. : ***NYPL [JLF 86-1723]***

Record of hearing I, federal perspective. United States. President's Commission on Organized Crime. Organized crime . Washington, D.C. , 1983. vi, 159 p. : ***NYPL [JLE 86-1587]***

Record of hearing II, money laundering. United States. President's Commission on Organized Crime. Organized crime and money laundering . Washington, D.C. [1985]. vi, 189 p. : ***NYPL [JLE 86-1282]***

RECORDS, BUSINESS. see **BUSINESS RECORDS.**

RECORDS - MANAGEMENT.
Knepp, Jay. Tax[s]aver. Menlo Park, Calif. , c1987. 143 p. : ISBN 0-376-07015-3 (pbk.) : LC Card 86-80874 DDC 343.7305/23 347.303523 19
HJ4653.D4 K56 1987

Smith, Milburn D. Information and records management . New York , c1986. xiv, 285 p. : ISBN 0-89930-111-8 (lib. bdg. : alk. paper) LC Card 86-638 DDC 651.5 19
HF5736 .S58 1986 ***NYPL [JLE 87-1454]***

Taylor, Mary Sue, 1938- Clear & simple filing and records management /. New York, NY , c1987. 171 p. : ISBN 0-671-62397-4 (pbk.) : LC Card 86-28534 DDC 651.5 19
HF5736 .T388 1987

Workshop on Exact Matching Methodologies (May 9-10, 1985 : Arlington, Va.) Record linkage techniques--1985 . [Washington, D.C.] , 1985. vii, 397 p. : ***NYPL [JLF 86-1723]***

Records of the U. S. Department of State relating to commercial relations between the United States and Russia/the Soviet Union, 1910-1949 [microform]. Wilmington, DE : Scholarly Resources, c1987. microfilm reel. Accompanied by printed reel guides. Department of State Decimal File 611.61 and Decimal File 611.11. CONTENTS. - pt. 1. U. S. Commercial relations with Russia/the Soviet Union, 611.61 -- pt. 2. Russian/Soviet commercial relations with the United States, 661.11. ISBN 0-8420-3053-0 (microfilm : set) : LC Card 87-23223 DDC 337.73047 19
1. United States - Commerce - Soviet Union - History - 20th century - Sources. 2. Soviet Union - Commerce - United States - History - 20th century - Sources. 3. United States - Commercial policy - History - 20th century - Sources. 4. Soviet Union - Commercial policy - History - 20th century - Sources. 5. United States. Dept. of State - Archives. I. United States. Dept. of State. II. Scholarly Resources, inc. III. Title: Records of the US Department of State relating to commercial relations between the United States and Russia/the Soviet Union, 1910-1949.
HF3105

Records of the U. S. Department of State relating to commercial relations between the United States and Japan, 1910-1949 [microform]. Wilmington, Del. : Scholarly Resources, c1987. microfilm reel "Department of State Decimal Files 611.94 and 694.11"--CIP galley. Includes index. CONTENTS. - pt. 1. U. S. commercial relations with Japan, 611.94 -- pt. 2. Japanese commercial relations with the United States, 694.11. ISBN 0-8420-3061-1 (microfilm : set) : LC Card 87-23376 DDC 337.73052 19
1. United States - Commerce - Japan - History - 20th century - Sources. 2. Japan - Commerce - United States - History - 20th century - Sources. 3. United States - Commercial policy - History - 20th century - Sources. 4. Japan - Commercial policy - History - 20th century - Sources. 5. United States. Dept. of State - Archives. I. United States. Dept. of State. II. Scholarly Resources, inc. III. Records of the US Department of State relating to commercial relations between the United States and Japan, 1910-1949.
HF3127

Records of the US Department of State relating to commercial relations between the United States and Russia/the Soviet Union, 1910-1949. Records of the U. S. Department of State relating to commercial relations between the United States and Russia/the Soviet Union, 1910-1949 [microform]. Wilmington, DE , c1987. microfilm reel. ISBN 0-8420-3053-0 (microfilm : set) : LC Card 87-23223 DDC 337.73047 19
HF3105

Records of the US Department of State relating to commercial relations between the United States and Japan, 1910-1949. Records of the U. S. Department of State relating to commercial relations between the United States and Japan, 1910-1949 [microform]. Wilmington, Del. , c1987. microfilm reel ISBN 0-8420-3061-1 (microfilm : set) : LC Card 87-23376 DDC 337.73052 19
HF3127

Records of the Women's Bureau of the Department of Labor, 1918-1965 [microform] /. United States. Women's Bureau. Frederick, MD , 1987- microfilm reel ISBN 0-89093-870-9 (microfilm : pt. 1) : LC Card 87-6239 DDC 331.4/0973 19
HD6095

RECOVERY OF NATURAL RESOURCES. see **RECYCLING (WASTE, ETC.)**

RECOVERY OF WASTE MATERIALS. see **RECYCLING (WASTE, ETC.)**

RECREATION AREAS - ALBERTA.
Swinnerton, Guy S. Recreation on agricultural land in Alberta /. Edmonton, Alta. [1982] x, 211 p. : LC Card 83-149875 DDC 333.76/17/097123 19
HD319.A4 S94 1982 ***NYPL [JLF 86-851]***

RECREATION AREAS - UNITED STATES - LOCATION - PLANNING - CONGRESSES.
Facility location and land use . New York,

N.Y. , c1986. vii, 40 p. : ISBN 0-87262-574-5 (pbk.) LC Card 86-25926 DDC 338.6/042 19
HD171.A15 F33 1986

RECREATION, INDUSTRIAL. see **INDUSTRIAL RECREATION.**

Recreation on agricultural land in Alberta /. Swinnerton, Guy S. Edmonton, Alta. [1982] x, 211 p. : LC Card 83-149875 DDC 333.76/17/097123 19
HD319.A4 S94 1982 *NYPL [JLF 86-851]*

Recreation Vehicle Industry Association (U. S.) Understanding first-time recreation vehicle buyers . Reston, VA (P.O. Box 2999, Prepared for Recreation Vehicle Industry Association, c1986. xxvi, 80 p. ; LC Card 87-108982 DDC 381/45629226/0973 19
HD9710.37.U62 U53 1986

RECREATIONAL VEHICLE INDUSTRY - UNITED STATES.
Understanding first-time recreation vehicle buyers . Reston, VA (P.O. Box 2999, Prepared for Recreation Vehicle Industry Association, c1986. xxvi, 80 p. ; LC Card 87-108982 DDC 381/45629226/0973 19
HD9710.37.U62 U53 1986

RECREATIONS. see **GAMES.**

RECRUITING OF EMPLOYEES - GERMANY (WEST)
Windolf, Paul. Recruitment and selection in the labour market . Aldershot, Hants, England , Brookfield, Vt. , c1988. p. cm. ISBN 0-566-00937-4 : LC Card 87-19763 DDC 658.3/11/0941 19
HF5549.5.R44 W494 1988

RECRUITING OF EMPLOYEES - GREAT BRITAIN.
Jenkins, Richard, 1952- Racism and recruitment . Cambridge [Cambridgeshire] , New York , 1986. xi, 281 p. ; ISBN 0-521-32028-3 LC Card 85-17483 DDC 331.13/3/0941 19
HG4903.5.G7 J46 1986 *NYPL [JLE 86-3305]*

Windolf, Paul. Recruitment and selection in the labour market . Aldershot, Hants, England , Brookfield, Vt. , c1988. p. cm. ISBN 0-566-00937-4 : LC Card 87-19763 DDC 658.3/11/0941 19
HF5549.5.R44 W494 1988

RECRUITING OF EMPLOYEES - SOUTH AFRICA.
Jeeves, Alan. Migrant labour in South Africa's mining economy . Kingston, Canada , 1985. xiv, 323 p. ; ISBN 0-7735-0420-6 DDC 331.7'6223422 *NYPL [JLE 85-3148]*

RECRUITING OF EMPLOYEES - UNITED STATES.
Hiring costs and strategies . New York , c1986. v, 82 p. : ISBN 0-8144-3153-4 *NYPL [JLF 86-960]*

Phillips, Jack J., 1945- Recruiting, training, and retaining new employees . San Francisco , 1987. xxii, 324 p. ; ISBN 1-555-42042-7 (alk. paper) LC Card 86-46332 DDC 658.3/14 19
HF5549.5.R44 P49 1987

Recruiting sales associates /. Reyhons, Ken. [Chicago, Ill.] , c1986. 151 p. : ISBN 0-931652-62-8 (pbk.) LC Card 86-63281 DDC 333.33/068/3 19
HD278 .R49 1986

Recruiting, training, and retaining new employees . Phillips, Jack J., 1945- San Francisco , 1987. xxii, 324 p. ; ISBN 1-555-42042-7 (alk. paper) LC Card 86-46332 DDC 658.3/14 19
HF5549.5.R44 P49 1987

Recruitment and selection in the labour market . Windolf, Paul. Aldershot, Hants, England , Brookfield, Vt. , c1988. p. cm. ISBN 0-566-00937-4 : LC Card 87-19763 DDC 658.3/11/0941 19
HF5549.5.R44 W494 1988

RECTORS. see **CLERGY.**

Recueil du Centre d'études européennes de Waterloo .
(no 3) L'Information financière . Bruxelles , 1983. 220 p. ; ISBN 2-8027-0298-X LC Card 84-104169
HG151.5 .I56 1983

Recuentos preliminares : VI censo general de población y IV de viviendas, 1985. [Montevideo] : República Oriental del Uruguay, Dirección General de Estadística y Censos, [1986] 188 p. : ill., maps (some col.) ; 26 cm. Chiefly tables. Cover title. LC Card 87-122427 DDC 304.6/09895/021 19
1. Uruguay - Census, 1985. 2. Uruguay - Population - Statistics. 3. Housing - Uruguay - Statistics. I. Uruguay. Dirección General de Estadística y Censos. II. Title: VI censo general de población y IV de viviendas, 1985. III. Title: Sexto censo general de población y cuarto de viviendas, 1985.
HA1074 1985

Recuerdos de un diplomático /. Bernstein Carabantes, Enrique. Santiago de Chile [1984- v. : LC Card 84-172336 DDC 327.83 19
F3099 .B43 1984 *NYPL [JFL 84-297]*

RECURRENT EDUCATION. see **CONTINUING EDUCATION.**

Recursos e desempenhos dos programas de formação de mão-de-obra /. Campino, Antonio Carlos Coelho. São Paulo, SP , Brasília, DF , 1985. 78 p. ; ISBN 85-21-30276-2 LC Card 85-187505
HD5754 .C34 1985

Recursos económicos do Ultramar Português, sua valorização e perspectivas futuras . Martinez, José Fernando Trindade. Lisboa , 1960. 113 p. ; LC Card 86-169892
HC890 .M37 1960

Los recursos naturales de Colombia . Patiño, Víctor Manuel. Bogotá , 1980. 149 p. : ISBN 84-8277-057-8 LC Card 86-208425 DDC 333.7/09861 19
HC197.5 .P3 1980

RECYCLING INDUSTRY - GERMANY (WEST) - HAMBURG.
Meyer, Rolf. Die Entsorgungswirtschaft einer Wirtschaftsregion . Schwarzenbek , 1983. 400 p. : ISBN 3-921757-20-7 LC Card 84-103993
HD9975.G43 H355 1983

RECYCLING (WASTE, ETC.) - ECONOMIC ASPECTS - FINLAND.
Wallin, Markku. Jätteiden hyötykäyttö kansantaloudessa /. [Helsinki] [1986] 87 p. : ISBN 951-46-9505-4 LC Card 86-216953
HD9975.F52 W35 1986

RECYCLING (WASTE, ETC.) - ECONOMIC ASPECTS - UNITED STATES - CASE STUDIES.
Morris, David J. Garbage disposal economics . Washington, DC [1987] v, 101 p. : ISBN 0-917582-44-6 (pbk.) : LC Card 87-4182 DDC 338.4/3363728/0973 19
HD4483 .G37 1987

La red de transporte en Castilla y León /. Pastor Antolín, Luis J., 1958- Valladolid [1986?] 161 p. : ISBN 84-86047-71-4 LC Card 86-231524
HE363.S64 C376 1986

Red Dog project analysis /. Alaska. Office of Mineral Development. [Juneau?] [1984] 300 p. in various pagings : LC Card 84-622211 DDC 333.8/5/097986 19
HD9506.U63 R422 1984

Red multinationals or red herrings? : the activities of enterprises from socialist countries in the West / edited by Geoffrey Hamilton. London : Frances Pinter, 1986. xi, 202 p. ; 23 cm. Includes bibliographical references and index. ISBN 0-86187-583-4
1. International business enterprises - Europe, Eastern. 2. International business enterprises - Europe, Eastern - Case studies. 3. Industrial management - Europe, Eastern. I. Hamilton, Geoffrey.
NYPL [JLD 86-2751]

RED RIVER REGION (TEX.-LA.) - ECONOMIC CONDITIONS.
Secondary benefits associated with the Red River Waterway, Mississippi River to Shreveport, Louisiana . Baton Rouge, La. (P.O. Box 14787, Baton Rouge 70898) [1986] 2 v. : LC Card 87-620750 DDC 330.9766/6053 19
HC107.A15 S43 1986

RED RIVER REGION (TEX.-LA.) - INDUSTRIES.
Secondary benefits associated with the Red River Waterway, Mississippi River to Shreveport, Louisiana . Baton Rouge, La. (P.O. Box 14787, Baton Rouge 70898) [1986] 2 v. : LC Card 87-620750 DDC 330.9766/6053 19
HC107.A15 S43 1986

Red River Waterway Commission. Secondary benefits associated with the Red River Waterway, Mississippi River to Shreveport, Louisiana . Baton Rouge, La. (P.O. Box 14787, Baton Rouge 70898) [1986] 2 v. : LC Card 87-620750 DDC 330.9766/6053 19
HC107.A15 S43 1986

RED SEA REGION - ECONOMIC CONDITIONS.
Pennisi, Giuseppe. Development, manpower and migration in the Red Sea region . Hamburg , c1981. xi, 264 p. : LC Card 82-109615 DDC 331.6/2/091824 19
HD8656 .P46 1981 *NYPL [JLF 86-1602]*

Redaktion Deutschland Archiv (Germany) Umweltprobleme und Umweltbewusstsein in der DDR /. Köln , c1985. 252 p. : ISBN 3-8046-8649-4 LC Card 86-119841
HC290.795.E5 U585 1985

Redaktionsgruppe Info 35 (Frankfurt am Main, Germany) Aktive Kolleginnen und Kollegen ziehen Bilanz . Frankfurt/M. , 1984. 100 p. : ISBN 3-88332-092-7 : LC Card 85-233569 DDC 331.89/2 19
HD5378 .A64 1984

Redclift, M. R. Sustainable development : exploring the contradictions / Michael Redclift. London ; New York : Methuen, 1987. 221 p. : ill. ; 23 cm. Bibliography: p. [205]-217. Includes index. ISBN 0-416-90240-5 LC Card 87-5710 DDC 363.7 19
1. Economic development - Environmental aspects. 2. Environmental policy. I. Title.
HD75.6 .R43 1987

Redding, J. W. (John W.) Uberrima fides . [Johannesburg , 1985?] 69 p. : ISBN 0-620-08481-2 LC Card 87-146303 DDC 368/.006 19
HG8724.3.Z9 P758 1985

Redding, Rodney J. Miller, Paul B. W. The FASB . Homewood, Ill. , 1986. xvi, 145 p. : ISBN 0-256-03520-2 LC Card 85-82340 *NYPL [JLE 87-872]*

Reddy, C. R. Cooperative long term finance : a regional study / C.R. Reddy. Delhi, India : Mittal Publications, 1987. ix, 128 p. : ill. ; 22 cm. Study of the Andhra Pradesh Cooperative Agricultural Development Bank. Bibliography: p. [119]-124. Includes index. LC Card 87-900729 DDC 334/.2/095484 19
1. Agricultural cooperative credit associations - India - Andhra Pradesh. 2. Banks and banking, Cooperative - India - Andhra Pradesh. 3. Development banks - India - Andhra Pradesh. I. Title.
HG2051.I5 A652 1987

Reddy, K. N. (Kaipa Narayana), 1936- Central government expenditure : growth, structure, and impact, 1950-51 to 1977-78 / K.N. Reddy, J.V.M. Sarma, Narain Sinha. New Delhi : National Institute of Public Finance and Policy, 1984. xvi, 175 p. ; 22 cm. Includes index. Includes statistical tables. Bibliography: p. [166]-172. LC Card 84-901866 DDC 336.3/9/0954 19
1. Government purchasing - India - Gujarat - History. 2. Finance, Public - India - History. 3. India - Appropriations and expenditures - History. 4. Gujarat (India) - Appropriations and expenditures - History. I. Sharma, J. V. M. II. Sinha, Narain. III. Title.
HJ2157 .R43 1984 *NYPL [JLD 87-66]*

Reddy, P. J. Fertility and mortality . New Delhi , Beverly Hills , 1986. 351 p. ; ISBN 0-8039-9497-4 LC Card 85-22287 DDC 304.6/3 19
HB901 .F468 1986 *NYPL [JLE 86-4122]*

Reddy, William M. Money and liberty in modern Europe : a critique of historical understanding / William M. Reddy. Cambridge [Cambridgeshire] ; New York : Cambridge University Press, 1987. xii, 264 p. ; 24 cm. Includes index. Bibliography: p. 224-256. ISBN 0-521-30445-8 LC Card 86-11709 DDC 332.4/94 19
1. Money - Europe - History. 2. Social structure - Europe - History. I. Title.
HG922 .R43 1987 *NYPL [JLE 87-1346]*

Rede Ferroviária Federal (Brazil) Trevisan, Edilberto. Ao apito do trem . [Curitiba] , 1985-1986 [i.e. 1986] 123 p. : LC Card

87-121016 DDC 385/.0981/62 19
HE2930.P34 T74 1986

Rede zur Einbringung des Bundeshaushalts 1982 . Germany (West). Bundesministerium der Finanzen. Bonn , 1982. 56 p. : LC Card 82-221425
HJ2109 .G45 1982

Redegørelse fra Monopoltilsynet.
Discountbutikker i dagligvarehandelen . København , 1983. 175 p. : ISBN 87-88149-11-0 : LC Card 83-237411
HF5429.215.D4 D57 1983

Rugbrødsbranchen . København , 1985. 112 p. : ISBN 87-88149-23-4 : LC Card 86-161889
HD9058.B743 D47 1985

Redegørelse om støtte til ejerboliger i forbindelse med byfornyelse . Denmark. Udvalget vedrørende byfornyelse og støtte til ejerboliger. København [1981] 128 p. : ISBN 87-503-3873-0 LC Card 82-194685
HD7347.A4 D455 1981

REDENCIÓN PAMPA (BOLIVIA) - ECONOMIC CONDITIONS.
Estudio cultural y socio económico de Mojocoya--Redención Pampa. Estudio cultural socio económico, Mojocoya y Redención Pampa. Sucre, Bolivia , 1979. 266 p. : LC Card 83-204567
HC183.M65 E77 1979

Réder, Gyula. Helyzetkép az élelmiszeripari müvezetőkről / Réder Gyula. Budapest : Agrárgazdasági Kutató Intézet, 1985. 81 p. ; 28 cm. (Agrárgazdasági Kutató Intézet, 0209-5696 . 1985/4) Bibliography: p. 79-81. ISBN 963-491-205-2 LC Card 86-196825
1. Food industry and trade - Hungary. 2. Supervisors, Industrial - Hungary. I. Series: Agrárgazdasági Kutató Intézet (Series) , 1985/4. II. Title.
HD9015.H82 R43 1985

Reder, Melvin Warren, 1919- Behavioral foundations of economic theory. Rational choice . Chicago , 1987. ix, 332 p. : ISBN 0-226-34857-1 (alk. paper) LC Card 86-27241 DDC 330/.01/9 19
HB74.P8 B44 1987

Redeterminación de usos del suelo en Ancón y redelimitación del sitio de defensa de Albrook /. Panama. Ministerio de Vivienda. [Panama, Panama] [between 1981 and 1987] [15] leaves : LC Card 87-403861 DDC 333.73/17/097287 19
HD385.A4 P36 1981

REDEVELOPMENT, URBAN. see **CITY PLANNING.**

Reding, Paul.
International trade and exchange rates in the late eighties /. Amsterdam ; New York : xii, 418 p. : ISBN 2-8004-0892-8
NYPL [JLE 87-120]

International trade and exchange rates in the late eighties /. Amsterdam ; New York : xii, 418 p. : ISBN 0-444-87941-2 LC Card 86-223111 DDC 382.4/5 19
HG203 .I58 1985

Redlich, Paul R. The postal history of Coles County, Illinois : the first hundred years, 1830-1930 / Paul R. Redlich. Des Plaines, Ill. (P.O. Box 1513, Des Plaines 60018) : Illinois Postal History Society, c1986. v, 175 p. : ill. ; 28 cm. Bibliography: p. 170-175. LC Card 87-400110 DDC 383/.4977372 19
1. Postal service - Illinois - Coles County - History. 2. Coles County (Ill.) - History. I. Illinois Postal History Society. II. Title.
HE6376.A1 I58 1986

Redovisning och analys av kommunernas oljereduktionsplaner /. Sweden. Oljeersättningsdelegationen. Stockholm [1983] 59, [91] p. : ISBN 91-38-07458-3 LC Card 83-239703
HD9502.S82 S96 1983a

Redressement national (Society : Switzerland)
Allenspach, Heinz. Bevorzugter Beamtenstatus, Möglichkeiten und Grenzen einer Reform . Zürich [1986] 32 p. ; LC Card 87-407830 DDC 330.9494 s 331.7/61354494 19
HC395 .Z43 Nr. 130 JN8831

Usteri, Martin. Bodenrecht in Bewegung . Zürich [1985] 27 p. ; LC Card 86-195037
HC395 .Z43 Nr. 126 KKW683

Reducing highway crashes through administrative license revocation. [Washington, D.C.?] : U. S. Dept. of Transportation, National Highway Traffic Safety Administration, 1986. 89 p. : ill. ; 28 cm. Cover title. Shipping list no.: 86-413-P. "April 1986"--P. [4] of cover. "DOT HS 806 921"--P. [4] of cover. Includes bibliographical references.
1. Drunk driving - United States. 2. Automobile drivers' licenses - United States. 3. Traffic violations - United States. ***NYPL [JLF 86-1382]***

Reducing industrial oil costs /. Hall, John, 1946- Aldershot, Hants England , Brookfield, Vt., U. S.A. , c1987. xvii, 118 p. : ISBN 0-291-39740-9 (U. S.) : LC Card 86-29511 DDC 338.2/3 19
HD9560.4 .H35 1987

Reducing New York State's deficit /. Green, Cynthia B. New York, N.Y. (110 E. 42nd St., New York 10017) [1986] ii leaves, 33 p. ; LC Card 87-108691 DDC 336.747 19
HJ2053.N7 G74 1986

Reducing soil erosion . Ribaudo, Marc. Washington, D.C. , 1986. v, 24 p. : LC Card 86-603068 DDC 338.1 s 333.73 19
HD1751 .A91854 no. 561 S624.A1

Reducing the federal deficit : strategies and options. Washington, D.C. : Congress of the United States, Congressional Budget Office : For sale by the Supt. of Docs., U. S. G.P.O., 1982. 1 v. (various pagings) : ill. ; 27 cm. "A report to the Senate and House Committees on the Budget--part III, as required by Public Law 93-344"--Cover. "February 1982"--Cover. Includes bibliographical references.
1. Budget - United States. 2. Deficit financing - United States. 3. Government spending policy - United States.
NYPL [JLF 86-1219]

Reducing workweeks to prevent layoffs . Best, Fred. Philadelphia , 1988. p. cm. ISBN 0-87722-506-0 LC Card 87-10097 DDC 331.25/72 19
HD5110.5 .B467 1988

Réduction de la durée du travail et changement des modes de vie . Legay, Marie-Agnès. Aix-en-Provence [1984] ix, 366 p. : LC Card 86-185902
HD6066.F8 L44 1984

Redundancy and recession : restructuring the regions? / edited by Mike Danson. Norwich, England : Geo Books, c1986. xii, 174 p. : ill. ; 22 cm. Includes bibliographies. ISBN 0-86094-201-5 : LC Card 86-218942 DDC 330.941/0858 19
1. Great Britain - Economic conditions - 1945- - Regional disparities. 2. Recessions - Great Britain. 3. Economic assistance, Domestic - Great Britain. I. Danson, Mike.
HC256.6 .R44 1986

Redundancy and recession in South Wales /. Harris, C. C. (Christopher Charles) Oxford, OX, UK , New York, NY, USA , 1987. p. cm. ISBN 0-631-15106-0 : LC Card 87-6301 DDC 331.13/794294 19
HD5766.A6 H37 1987

Redundant women /. Coyle, Angela. London , 1984. 154 p. : ISBN 0-7043-3923-4 (pbk.) : LC Card 84-100906 DDC 331.4/137941 19
HD5708.55.G7 C68 1984
NYPL [JLD 86-3916]

Reed, David A. (David Albert), 1947- Johnston, William B., 1945- Michigan beyond 2000 /. Lanham , Indianapolis, IN , c1987. xxv, 161 p. : ISBN 0-8191-6462-3 (alk. paper) LC Card 87-10725 DDC 338.9774 19
HC107.M5 J64 1987

Reed, John T.
Aggressive tax avoidance for real estate investors : how to make sure you aren't paying one more cent in taxes than the law requires / by John T. Reed.6th ed. Danville, CA : Reed Pub., 1986. 267 p. : ill. ; 28 cm. Includes index. ISBN 0-939224-13-5 (pbk.) :
1. Real estate investment - Taxation - Law and legislation - United States. 2. Tax planning - United States. I. Title. ***NYPL [JLF 86-1562]***

How to use leverage to maximize your real estate investment return : sensible finance techniques for real estate investors / by John T. Reed. Danville, Calif. : Reed Pub. ; Cambridge, MA : Order c/o Publishers Business Services, c1986. iii, 301 p. : ill. ; 28 cm. Includes index. ISBN 0-939224-12-7 (pbk.) LC Card 85-90486 DDC 332.63/24 19
1. Real estate investment. 2. Mortgage loans. I. Title.
HD1382.5 .R426 1986

Reed, Steven R., 1947- Japanese prefectures and policy making / Steven R. Reed. Pittsburgh, Pa. : University of Pittsburgh Press, 1986. ix, 197 p. ; 24 cm. (Pitt series in policy and institutional studies) Includes index. Bibliography: p. 181-193. ISBN 0-8229-3527-9 LC Card 85-22528 DDC 352/.00047 19
1. Local government - Japan. 2. Environmental policy - Japan. 3. Housing policy - Japan. 4. Education and state - Japan. I. Title. II. Series.
JS7373.A3 R44 1986 ***NYPL [JLE 86-3757]***

Reeder, Betty H., 1936- Reeder, Robert R., 1935- Industrial marketing . Englewood Cliffs, N.J. , c1987. xviii, 654 p. : ISBN 0-13-461526-3 LC Card 86-25195 DDC 658.8 19
HF5415 .R355 1987

Reeder, Robert R., 1935- Industrial marketing : analysis, planning, and control / Robert R. Reeder, Edward G. Brierty, Betty H. Reeder. Englewood Cliffs, N.J. : Prentice-Hall, c1987. xviii, 654 p. : ill. ; 25 cm. Includes bibliographies and index. ISBN 0-13-461526-3 LC Card 86-25195 DDC 658.8 19
1. Industrial marketing. I. Brierty, Edward G., 1925-. II. Reeder, Betty H., 1936-. III. Title.
HF5415 .R355 1987

Reekie, W. Duncan. Managerial economics / W. Duncan Reekie, Jonathan N. Crook. 3rd ed. Oxford [Oxfordshire] ; Atlantic Highlands, N.J. : P. Allan, 1987. xi, 522 p. : ill. ; 24 cm. Includes bibliographies and index. ISBN 0-86003-070-9 LC Card 87-12627 DDC 338.5/024/658 19
1. Managerial economics. I. Crook, Jonathan N. II. Title.
HD30.22 .R39 1987

Reekmans, T. Inleiding tot de antieke economie / T. Reekmans. 1e uitg. Leuven : Acco, 1984. 129 leaves in various foliations ; 29 cm. + 1 suppl. Polyglot. Includes bibliographical references. ISBN 90-334-0834-1 : LC Card 86-203767
1. Economics - Greece - History. 2. Economics - Rome - History. 3. Greece - Economic conditions - To 146 B.C. 4. Rome - Economic conditions. I. Title.
HB77 .R44 1984

Reeks C (University of Port Elizabeth. Institute for Planning Research) .
(verslag nr. 3) Kruger, Gudrun. Development region D . Port Elizabeth [1985] iv, 89 p. : ISBN 0-86988-274-0 (pbk.) LC Card 86-233113 DDC 304.6/09687/5 19
HA4701.Z9 C354 1985

The Re-emergence of the Chinese peasantry : aspects of rural decollectivisation / edited by Ashwani Saith. London ; New York : Croom Helm, c1987. ix, 277 p. : ill. ; 23 cm. Papers presented at a workshop held at the Institute of Social Studies, The Hague. Includes bibliographies and index. CONTENTS. - Collectivisation and decollectivisation in Guanzhong, Central Shaanxi, 1934-1984 / Eduard Vermeer -- The people's commune, responsibility systems, and rural development in China, 1965-1984 / Ajit Kunar Ghose -- Towards an appraisal of the impact of rural reform in China, 1978-85 / Peter Nolan and Suzanne Paine -- Some implications of the rural economic reforms for the Chinese peasant household / Elisabeth Croll --The disintegration and reconstruction of the rural science and technology system / Richard Conroy -- Changes in the system of basic social security in the countryside since 1979 / Stephan Feuchtwang -- China's new population policies / Ashwani Saith -- Riding the tiger / Gordon White. LC Card 87-5373 DDC 305.5/63 19
1. Peasantry - China - Congresses. I. Saith, Ashwani. II. Institute of Social Studies (Netherlands).
HD1537.C5 R4 1987

Rees, Albert, 1921- Hamermesh, Daniel S. The economics of work and pay /. New York , c1988. xii, 452 p. : ISBN 0-06-045356-7 LC Card 87-18355 DDC 331 19
HD4901 .H18 1988

Rees, Gwilym.
Thody, Philip Malcolm Waller, 1928- Faux amis & key words . London , 1985. 224 p. ; ISBN 0-485-11243-4 : LC Card 84-108125 DDC 443/.21 19
PC2593 .T45 1985 ***NYPL [JFD 86-5704]***

Thody, Philip Malcolm Waller, 1928- Mistakable French . New York , 1985. 224 p. ;

ISBN 0-684-18324-2 : LC Card 84-51853 DDC 443/.21 19
PC2593 .T46 1985 ***NYPL [JFD 86-5781]***

Rees, John, 1948- Technology, regions, and policy /. Totowa, N.J. , 1986. xiv, 322 p. : ISBN 0-8476-7409-6 LC Card 85-24970 DDC 338.4/76213817/0973 19
HC110.H53 T43 1986 ***NYPL [JLE 86-3327]***

Rees-Mogg, William, 1928- Davidson, James Dale. Blood in the streets . New York , c1987. 386 p. ; ISBN 0-671-62735-X : LC Card 87-9935 DDC 332.6 19
HG4516 .D38 1987

Rees, P. H. (Philip H.), 1944- Population structures and models . London , Boston , 1986. xxii, 417 p. : ISBN 0-04-301200-0 (alk. paper) LC Card 85-30642 DDC 304.6 19
HB1951 .P67 1986 ***NYPL [JLE 86-4134]***

Rees, Ray, 1943- Public enterprise economics / Ray Rees. 2nd ed. London : Weidenfeld and Nicolson, 1984. xiii, 238 p. : ill. ; 23 cm. (London School of Economics Handbooks in economic analysis) Bibliography: p. [231]-235. Includes index. ISBN 0-297-78336-X LC Card 87-672956
1. Government business enterprises. 2. Microeconomics. I. Title.
HD3840 .R43x 1984b

Reese, Hartmut. Arbeiterbewegung in der Zusammenbruchsgesellschaft : ein methodischer Versuch zur Rekonstruktionsproblematik der Arbeiterbewegung in Westdeutschland 1945-1947 / Hartmut Reese. Münster : Lit, [1984?] 209 p. ; 22 cm. ([Arbeiterkultur . Bd. 13]) Series taken from CIP statement and p. [210] Bibliography: p. 195-209. ISBN 3-88660-133-1 LC Card 85-128699
1. Trade-unions - Germany (West) - History - 20th century. 2. Labor and laboring classes - Germany (West) - History - 20th century. 3. Germany, West - Economic conditions. I. Title. II. Series.
HD6694 .R35 1984

Reessing, Ludwig. Analyse der Wettbewerbsfähigkeit von Extensivblattfrüchten in Niedersachsen unter ökonomischen und ökologischen Gesichtspunkten / von Ludwig Reessing. Kiel : Wissenschaftsverlag Vauk, 1986. xiv, 251 p. : ill. ; 21 cm. (Empirische Studien zur Agrarökonomie, 0177-0675 . Bd. 5) "Arbeit aus dem Institut für Agrarökonomie der Georg-August-Universität Göttingen." Originally presented as the author's thesis (doctoral)--Georg-August-Universität zu Göttingen. Bibliography: p. 241-251. ISBN 3-922553-81-8 LC Card 86-163003
1. Agriculture - Economic aspects - Germany (West) - Lower Saxony. 2. Field crops - Germany (West) - Lower Saxony. 3. Agricultural ecology - Germany (West) - Lower Saxony. I. Title. II. Series.
HD1960.L69 R44 1986

Reestudo da parte de cereais e estivas relacionado com a viabilidade técnico-econômico-financeira da Central de Abastecimento de Gêneros Alimentícios da Região Metropolitana de Fortaleza. [Fortaleza] : Superintendência do Desenvolvimento do Estado do Ceará, 1973. 72 leaves : ill. ; 31 cm. LC Card 82-147387
1. Food industry and trade - Brazil - Fortaleza. 2. Central de Abastecimento de Gêneros Alimentícios da Região Metropolitana de Fortaleza. I. Superintendência do Desenvolvimento do Estado do Ceará.
HD9014.B83 F587 1973

Reetz, Norbert. Konjunktur und Wachstum : eine Einführung an Hand der vier grundlegenden Modelle von Harrod, Samuelson und Hicks, Domar und Solow : Vorlesung / von Norbert Reetz. St. Gallen : W. Surbir, 1983. viii, 121 p. : ill. ; 21 cm. "Vorlesung an der Hochschule St. Gallen für Wirtschafts- und Sozialwissenschaften, Wintersemester 1981/82 und 1982/83"--Verso t.p. Bibliography: p. iv. LC Card 83-141234
1. Economic development - Mathematical models. 2. Business cycles - Mathematical models. I. Title.
HD75.5 .R44 1983

REFA-Verband (Hamburg, Germany) Neue Entwicklungen bei Arbeit, Entgelt und Führung /. Freiburg im Breisgau , c1984. 169 p. : ISBN 3-448-01480-X : LC Card 84-249237
HF5549.2.G3 N48 1984

Referate zum Deutsch-Französischen Arbeitstreffen auf dem Gebiet der Demographie vom 30. September bis 3. Oktober 1985 in Dijon. Deutsch-Französisches Arbeitstreffen auf dem Gebiet der Demographie (1985 : Dijon, France) Wiesbaden , 1986. 134 p. : LC Card 87-409287 DDC 304.6/0943 19
HB3595 .D45 1985

REFERENCE BOOKS - BUSINESS - BIBLIOGRAPHY.
Encyclopedia of geographic information sources, international volume . Detroit, Mich. , c1988. 479 p. ; ISBN 0-8103-0410-4 : LC Card 87-23777 DDC 016.33 19
HF5341 .E53 1988

Johnson, H. Herbert Webster, 1906- How to use the business library . Cincinnati , c1984. iv, 267 p. : ISBN 0-538-05750-5 (pbk.) LC Card 83-60484 DDC 027.6/9 19
Z675.B8 J6 1984 ***NYPL [JLE 86-3971]***

Lavin, Michael R. Business information . Phoenix, Ariz. , 1987. x, 299 p. : ISBN 0-89774-157-9 (alk. paper) : LC Card 86-42787 DDC 650/.072 19
HF5356 .L36 1987

Reference (Canada. Tariff Board) .
(161.1) Canada. Tariff Board. Relating to the reinstatement of the general preferential tariff on imports of rubber footwear . Ottawa, Canada , c1985. vi, 88 p. ; ISBN 0-660-11961-7 (pbk.) : LC Card 87-109471 DDC 382/.0971 s 382/.4568531/00971 19
HF1762 .A3 no. 161, pt. 1 HF2651.F757C22

Reference guide of permits and licenses. Baton Rouge, La. (P.O. Box 94185, Baton Rouge 71808-9185) : State of Louisiana, Dept. of Commerce, Office of Commerce and Industry, [1986?] ix, 222 p. ; 28 cm. LC Card 86-621904 DDC 353.97630082/4046 19
1. Licenses - Louisiana - Handbooks, manuals, etc. I. Louisiana. Office of Commerce & Industry.
HD3630.U7 R44 1986

Reference guide to management techniques and activities /. Bloor, Ian G. Oxford, England , New York , 1987. xi, 80 p. ; ISBN 0-08-034268-X : LC Card 86-30266 DDC 658/.003/21 19
HD30.15 .B46 1987

Références (Presses de la Fondation nationale des sciences politiques) .
(15) Balandier, Georges. Sociologie des Brazzavilles noires /. Paris , c1985. xviii, 306 p., [2] leaves of plates : ISBN 2-7246-0524-1 : LC Card 86-138199
HB2125.B73 B34 1985

REFERENDUM - QUÉBEC (PROVINCE)
Comportement électoral au Québec /. Chicoutimi, Québec, Canada , c1984. xv, 447 p. : ISBN 2-89105-063-0 LC Card 85-177886 DDC 324.9714 19
JL258 .C65 1984 ***NYPL [JLD 87-1351]***

REFERENDUM - UNITED STATES.
Zimmerman, Joseph Francis, 1928- Participatory democracy . New York , 1986. xi, 229 p. ; ISBN 0-275-92132-8 (alk. paper) : LC Card 86-8129 DDC 323/.042/0973 19
JF493.U6 Z56 1986 ***NYPL [JLE 86-3632]***

Referent USSR economic and demographic statistics for normalization of Berkeley-Duke emigre questionnaire data /. Treml, Vladimir G. [Durham, N.C. [1986] 1 v. (various pagings) ; LC Card 86-70618 DDC 304.6/0947/021 19
HB3607 .T74 1986

Das Referenzbüro der Gemeinschaften /. Lauer, Karl Friedrich. [Dortmund?] , 1976. 76 p. ; LC Card 85-241026
HD30 .A7 Heft 171 T59.A1

Refinery throughput in the U. S.S.R. /. Sagers, Matthew J. Washington, D.C. [1984] v, 81, 2 p. : LC Card 87-601276 DDC 338.4/766553/0947 19
HD9575.S652 S25 1984

Reflections on the Indian economy / edited by B.P.S. Bhadouria ; foreword by S.P. Nagendra. 1st ed. Delhi, India : Commonwealth Publishers : Distributed by Anupama Publishers Distributors, 1987. xxxi, 439 p. : ill. ; 22 cm. "Published in the Chambal Valley Development Foundation (CVDF) series"--P. [xv] Research papers and articles. Includes bibliographies and index. ISBN 81-900026-0-0 : LC Card 87-901043 DDC 338.9 19
1. India - Economic policy - 1980-. I. Bhadouria, B. P. S.
HC435.2 .R425 1987

Reflective raised pavement markers. Noel, James S. Retention of reflective raised pavement markers /. College Station, Tex. , Springfield, Va. [1986] xiii, 170 p. : LC Card 87-620642 DDC 380.5 s 625.7/042 19
HE203 .T43 no. 322-3 TE203

REFLECTORS (SAFETY DEVICES)
McNees, Roger W. State-of-the-art and objectives of reflective raised pavement markers /. College Station, Tex. , Springfield, Va. [1986] vii, 162 p. : LC Card 87-620643 DDC 380.5 s 625.7/97 19
HE203 .T43 no. 322-1 TE203

Noel, James S. Retention of reflective raised pavement markers /. College Station, Tex. , Springfield, Va. [1986] xiii, 170 p. : LC Card 87-620642 DDC 380.5 s 625.7/042 19
HE203 .T43 no. 322-3 TE203

Reflexiones en torno al proceso de coordinación latinoamericano sobre la deuda externa /. Kisic Wagner, Drago. [Lima, Perú] [1985] 29 p. ; LC Card 87-403187 DDC 336.3/435/098 19
HJ8514.5 .K57 1985

Reflexiones para la acción /. Sánchez Meleán, Jorge. [Venezuela?] , 1986. xv, 322 p. : ISBN 980-232-049-8 LC Card 87-134702 DDC 338.987 19
HC237 .S275 1986

Reflexiones sobre apertura financiera . Gutiérrez Urrutia, Mario. Santiago , 1982. 36 p. : LC Card 82-203323
HG845 .G87 1982

Reflexiones sobre economia nacional e internacional /. Palacios, Eulalio R. [S.l.] 1986 (Asunción, Paraguay : Tall. Gráf. de la Impr. Nacional) 333 p. ; LC Card 86-226634
HC222 .P36 1986

Les Réflexions sur l'état présent du commerce, fabriques et manufactures des Païs-Bas autrichiens (1765) du négociant bruxellois, Nicolas Bacon (1710-1779), conseiller député aux affaires du commerce /. Hasquin, Hervé, 1942- Bruxelles , 1978. vi, 190 p. ; LC Card 87-672234
HF3595 .H37x 1978

Reflexões sobre história e cultura portuguesa : ciclo de conferências para professores de história do ensino secundário realizadas no Museu de Etnologia no ano lectivo de 1981/1982 / coordenação, Maria Emília Cordeiro Ferreira. Lisboa : Centro de Estudos de História e Cultura Portuguesa, Instituto Português de Ensino a Distância, 1985. 286 p. ; 22 cm. (Colecção Temas de cultura portuguesa . no. 9) Bibliography: p. 248. LC Card 86-135021 DDC 946.9 19
1. Portugal - Economic conditions. 2. Portugal - Social conditions. 3. Portugal - Politics and government. I. Ferreira, Maria Emília Cordeiro. II. Instituto Português de Ensino a Distância. Centro de Estudos de História e Cultura Portuguesa. III. Series.
HC392 .R34 1985

Reflexões sobre o quadro global e setorial da economia maranhense /. Polary, José Henrique Braga. São Luís [Brazil] , 1981. 60 p. ; LC Card 87-404934 DDC 330.981/21063 19
HC188.M29 P65 1981

Reform der Entwicklungsfinanzierung durch "Automatisierung"? . Hauser, Heinz-Michael. Baden-Baden , 1986. vi, 531 p. ; ISBN 3-7890-1235-1 LC Card 87-407969 DDC 338.91/09172/4 19
HC60 .H329 1986

Reform in China . Kai ko. English. Armonk, N.Y., USA , c1987. p. cm. ISBN 0-87332-458-7 : LC Card 87-23537 DDC 338.951 19
HC427.92 .K32 1987

Reform, labor, and feminism . Payne, Elizabeth Anne, 1943- Urbana , c1988. p. cm. ISBN 0-252-01445-6 (alk. paper) LC Card 87-10794 DDC 331.88/092/4 B 19
HD6079.2.U5 P38 1988

Reform oder Revolution? : Diskussion um die Änderung der Struktur in der gesetzlichen

Rentenversicherung 1990 : Materialauswahl. Bonn : Hauptabteilung Wissenschaftliche Dienste der Verwaltung des Deutschen Bundestages, 1987. vi, 241, A 140 p. : ill. ; 30 cm. (Materialie[n] / Deutscher Bundestag, Wissenschaftliche Dienste, 0344-9130 . Nr. 98) "Die Materialauswahl ... wurde in der Abteilung Wissenschaftliche Dokumentation von Frau Regierungsdirektorin Traute Hoffmann erstellt"--P. iii. Bibliography: p. 225-232. Includes index. LC Card 87-409091 DDC 368.4/00943 19
1. Social security - Germany, West. 2. Social security - Law and legislation - Germany, West. I. Hoffmann, Traute. II. Germany (West). Bundestag. Hauptabteilung Wissenschaftliche Dienste. III. Series: Materialien (Germany (West). Bundestag. Hauptabteilung Wissenschaftliche Dienste) , Nr. 98.
HD7179 .R384 1987

REFORM OF CRIMINALS. see **CRIME AND CRIMINALS.**

REFORM, SOCIAL. see **SOCIAL PROBLEMS.**

Reforma agrária . Pinheiro, Saramago. Brasília , 1986. 46 p. ; LC Card 86-228887
HD1333.B6 P56 1986

Reforma agraria como proceso social : análisis y perspectiva nacional / Christian Deverre ... [et al.]. Piura, Perú : Centro de Investigación y Promoción del Campesinado, [1984] 163 p. : ill. ; 21 cm. Proceedings of the "Seminario sobre Reforma Agraria, Cooperativismo y Autogestión en el Proceso del Agro Nacional," organized by CIPCA in 1982. LC Card 84-232526 DDC 333.3/1/85 19
1. Land reform - Peru - Congresses. 2. Land reform - Latin America - Congresses. 3. Land reform - Congresses. 4. Peasantry - Latin America - Congresses. 5. Agricultural laborers - Latin America - Congresses. 6. Agriculture, Cooperative - Latin America - Congresses. 7. Employee ownership - Latin America - Congresses. I. Deverre, Christian. II. Centro de Investigación y Promoción del Campesinado. III. "Seminario sobre Reforma Agraria, Cooperativismo y Autogestión en el Proceso del Agro Nacional" (1982).
HD1333.P4 R44 1984 ***NYPL [JLD 86-2537]***

Reforma agraria en Bolivia /. Espinoza C., Jorge. Cochabamba, Bolivia , 1984. 78 p. ; LC Card 86-166584
HD1333.B5 E87 1984

Reforma agrária socialista e confiscatória. Oliveira, Plinio Corrêa de, 1908- A propriedade privada e a livre iniciativa no tufão agro-reformista /. [São Paulo] [1985] xvi, 174 p., [16] p. of plates : LC Card 87-104428
HD1333.B6 O385 1985

A Reforma do mercado de capitais. [Lisbon] : Instituto Progresso Social e Democracia Francisco Sá Carneiro : Editorial Progresso Social e Democracia, [1985] 143 p. : ill. ; 23 cm. (Portugal--desafios e soluções . 4) Papers presented at an international seminar sponsored by the Instituto Progresso Social e Democracia Francisco Sá Carneiro. Bibliography: p. 54-55. LC Card 87-127037 DDC 332.63 19
1. Capital market - Portugal - Congresses. 2. Capital market - Congresses. I. Instituto Progresso Social e Democracia Francisco Sá Carneiro. II. Series.
HG4523 .R44 1985

Reforma estructural de nuestra economía /. Andrada, René. [Asunción , 1986] (Asunción, Paraguay : Ediciones y Arte) 150 p. : LC Card 86-227031
HG885 .A85 1986

Reforma financiera en pequeñas economías abiertas /. Dauhajre, Andrés. Santo Domingo, República Dominicana , 1986. 97 p. : LC Card 87-402920 DDC 332.4/56097293 19
HG3926.5 .D38 1986

Reforma tributária . Nunes, Helvídio. Brasília , 1982. 108 p. ; LC Card 86-128083
HJ2527 .N85 1982

Reforma tributária, federalismo e desenvolvimento nacional /. Baptista, Lourival. Brasília , 1983. 255 p. : LC Card 86-210783
HJ2525 .B36 1983

Reformen für Wirtschaft und Gesellschaft . Kleinewefers, Henner. Frankfurt , New York , c1985. 532 p. : ISBN 3-593-33466-6 LC Card 85-143393
HD84 .K543 1985

Reforming capital income taxation in Canada . Davies, James B., 1951- [Ottawa] , c1987. ix, 153 p. : ISBN 0-660-12454-8 (pbk.) : LC Card 87-168079 DDC 336.24/24/0971 19
HJ4133.C2 .D38 1987

Reforming the contract process in New York City /. New York (State). Office of the Special Deputy Comptroller for the City of New York. [Albany] [1986] 13 leaves ; LC Card 86-623049
HD3861.U6 N48 1986

Réformisme et révisionnisme dans les socialismes allemand, autrichien et français / publié sous la direction de François-Georges Dreyfus. Paris : Editions de la Maison des sciences de l'homme, c1984. 195 p. ; 23 cm. (Collection Les Publications de la Maison des sciences de l'homme de Strasbourg) "Actes du colloque organisé par la Maison des sciences de l'homme de Strasbourg ... en novembre 1981"--Verso t.p. French and German. Includes bibliographies. ISBN 2-7351-0053-7 : LC Card 85-105830
1. Socialism - Germany - History - 20th century. 2. Socialism - Austria - History - 20th century. 3. Socialism - France - History - 20th century. I. Dreyfus, François G. II. Maison des sciences de l'homme de Strasbourg. III. Series.
HX273 .R39 1984 ***NYPL [JLE 86-4752]***

Reforms to pre-empt change . Pani, Narendar, 1954- New Delhi , 1983. ix, 122 p. ; LC Card 83-902691 DDC 333.3/1/5487 19
HD1333.I42 K376 1983 ***NYPL [JLD 86-3841]***

Reformulação . Brazil. Grupo de Trabalho para Reformulação do Sistema Financeiro da Habitação. [Brasília] , 1986. 94 leaves ; LC Card 87-144710 DDC 363.5/8 19
HD7323.A3 B7 1986

REFRIGERATED TRANSPORT - GOVERNMENT POLICY - SPAIN.
Instituto Nacional de Industria (Spain). Departamento de Industrias de la Alimentación. Plan de red de transportes frigoríficos en España /. Madrid , 1965. 188 p., [1] folded leaf of plates : LC Card 85-107661
HE199.5.R43 I57 1965

REFRIGERATOR INDUSTRY - EUROPE.
Frozen foods market in Europe. New York, N.Y. , c1983. 2 v. (vii, 438 p.) ; LC Card 87-142593 DDC 380.1/4566402853/094 19
HD9326.A2 F76 1983

REFUGEES - CALIFORNIA.
Strand, Paul J., 1949- Indochinese refugees in America . Durham, N.C. , 1985. x, 182 p. ; ISBN 0-8223-0629-8 LC Card 84-25888 DDC 362.8/49592 19
HV640.5.I5 S77 1985 ***NYPL [JLE 86-4772]***

REFUGEES - CHAGOS ISLANDS.
Mauritius. Legislative Assembly. Public Accounts Committee. Special report of the Public Accounts Committee for the 1980 session . Port Louis, Mauritius , 1981. 13 p. ; LC Card 82-980151 DDC 333.1/6/09697 19
HD1030.3.Z63 M38 1981

REFUGEES - ETHIOPIA.
Clay, Jason W. Politics and the Ethiopian famine, 1984-1985 /. Cambridge, MA (11 Divinity Ave., Cambridge 02138) , 1985. xi, 250 p. : LC Card 86-153948 DDC 363.8/56/0963 19
HC845.Z9 F33 1985 ***NYPL [JLF 87-364]***

Ethiopia's bitter medicine, settling for disaster . London , 1986. 55 p. : ISBN 0-946592-01-2 (pbk.) LC Card 86-232852 DDC 333.3/1/63
HD979.Z63 E74 1986

REFUGEES - ETHIOPIA - INTERVIEWS.
Niggli, Peter, 1950- [Äthiopien, Deportationen und Zwangsarbeitslager. English.] Ethiopia, deportations and forced-labour camps . [Berlin , 1986] 86 p., [1] leaf of plates : LC Card 87-131977 DDC 333.3/1/63 19
HD979 .N3413 1986

REFUGEES - INDOCHINA.
Strand, Paul J., 1949- Indochinese refugees in America . Durham, N.C. , 1985. x, 182 p. ; ISBN 0-8223-0629-8 LC Card 84-25888 DDC 362.8/49592 19
HV640.5.I5 S77 1985 ***NYPL [JLE 86-4772]***

REFUGEES - MAURITIUS.
Mauritius. Legislative Assembly. Public Accounts Committee. Special report of the Public Accounts Committee for the 1980 session . Port Louis, Mauritius , 1981. 13 p. ; LC Card 82-980151 DDC 333.1/6/09697 19
HD1030.3.Z63 M38 1981

REFUGEES, POLITICAL - AFGHANISTAN.
Shinwari, Ahmad Nawaz. Small scale industry in North West Frontier Province . Peshawar , 1983. 103 p., [3] leaves of plates : LC Card 84-931673 DDC 338.6/422/0899159 19
HD2346.P32 N677 1983

REFUGEES, POLITICAL - PSYCHOLOGY.
Liu, William Thomas, 1930- Transition to nowhere . Nashville , c1979. 214 p., [2] leaves of plates : ISBN 0-8202-0189-8 : LC Card 78-21129 DDC 361.5/3/09597
HV640.5.V5 L58 ***NYPL [JLD 87-670]***

REFUGEES - SOUTH ASIA - ADDRESSES, ESSAYS, LECTURES.
Population redistribution and development in South Asia /. Dordrecht , Boston , 1985. 243 p. : ISBN 90-277-1938-1 : LC Card 84-26260 DDC 304.8/0959 19
HB2096.5 .P66 1985 ***NYPL [JLE 86-3852]***

REFUGEES - UNITED STATES.
Liu, William Thomas, 1930- Transition to nowhere . Nashville , c1979. 214 p., [2] leaves of plates : ISBN 0-8202-0189-8 : LC Card 78-21129 DDC 361.5/3/09597
HV640.5.V5 L58 ***NYPL [JLD 87-670]***

Mason, Sarah R. Training Southeast Asian refugee women for employment . Minneapolis, Minn. , 1986. viii, 142 p. : LC Card 86-72303 DDC 331.4/2592/08995073 19
HD5715.2 .M37 1986

Mason, Sarah R. Training Southeast Asian refugee women for employment . Minneapolis, Minn. , 1986. viii, 142 p. : LC Card 86-72303 DDC 331.4/2592/08995073 19
HD5715.2 .M37 1986

Strand, Paul J., 1949- Indochinese refugees in America . Durham, N.C. , 1985. x, 182 p. ; ISBN 0-8223-0629-8 LC Card 84-25888 DDC 362.8/49592 19
HV640.5.I5 S77 1985 ***NYPL [JLE 86-4772]***

REFUGEES - VIETNAM.
Liu, William Thomas, 1930- Transition to nowhere . Nashville , c1979. 214 p., [2] leaves of plates : ISBN 0-8202-0189-8 : LC Card 78-21129 DDC 361.5/3/09597
HV640.5.V5 L58 ***NYPL [JLD 87-670]***

REFUSE AND REFUSE DISPOSAL - ECONOMIC ASPECTS - UNITED STATES - CASE STUDIES.
Morris, David J. Garbage disposal economics . Washington, DC [1987] v, 101 p. : ISBN 0-917582-44-6 (pbk.) : LC Card 87-4182 DDC 338.4/3363728/0973 19
HD4483 .G37 1987

REFUSE AND REFUSE DISPOSAL - GOVERNMENT POLICY - GERMANY (WEST) - BADEN-WÜRTTEMBERG.
Koch, Thilo. Müllverwertung und -Beseitigung in Baden-Württemberg . Stuttgart , 1984. ii, 177 p. : LC Card 84-158868
HD4485.G32 B335 1984

REFUSE AND REFUSE DISPOSAL - MEXICO - DISTRITO FEDERAL.
Restrepo, Iván. La basura . México, D.F. , 1985. 193 p. : LC Card 86-209151
HD9014.M63 M47 1985

Regaining the lead . Striner, Herbert E. Millwood, N.Y. , c1987. xvii, 205 p. ; ISBN 0-8046-9408-7 (pbk. : alk. paper) : LC Card 86-32218 DDC 338.973 19
HC106.8 .S77 1987

Regalia, Ida, 1946- Eletti e abbandonati : modelli e stili di rappresentanza in fabbrica : una ricerca promossa dal CESOS, Centro di studi sociali e sindacali / Ida Regalia. Bologna : Mulino, c1984. 355 p. : ill. ; 22 cm. (Studi e ricerche. 188) Includes bibliographical references. ISBN 88-15-00592-7 : LC Card 84-250543 DDC 331.87/33/0945 19
1. Trade-unions - Italy - Officials and employees. 2. Works councils - Italy. 3. Shop stewards - Italy. I. Centro di studi sociali e sindacali (Rome, Italy). II. Title.
HD6490.O42 I87 1984 ***NYPL [JLD 86-211]***

Regalsky, Andrés Martín. Las inversiones extranjeras en la Argentina, 1860-1914 / Andrés Martín Regalsky. Buenos Aires : Centro Editor de América Latina, c1986. 129 p. ; 18

cm. (Biblioteca Política argentina . 151) Bibliography: p. 52-57. ISBN 950-25-1412-2 : LC Card 87-100719
1. Investments, Foreign - Argentina - History. I. Title. II. Series.
HG5312 .R44 1986

Regard sur la presse philatélique française . Rabier, Pascal. [Paris] , 1986. 2 v. (586 p.) : ISBN 2-9501543-0-1 (set) LC Card 87-166808
HE6185.F8 R32 1986

Regards sur Kinshasa . Sakombi Inongo. [Zaire] [1981?] 94 p. ; LC Card 82-226585
HC955.Z7 K497 1981

Die Regeneration der Stadt . Kujath, Hans Joachim. Hamburg , c1986. 282 p. ; ISBN 3-7672-0943-8 LC Card 87-113493 DDC 363.5/8 19
HD7339.A3 K85 1986

Regensburger Diskussionsbeiträge zur Wirtschaftswissenschaft .
(Nr. 124) Drukarczyk, Jochen. Zum Problem der Auslösung insolvenzrechtlicher Verfahren /. [Regensburg] [198-?] 30, iv leaves : LC Card 84-181525
HG3761 .D79 1980z

(Nr. 168) Drukarczyk, Jochen. Credit contracts, collateral-based security agreements, and bankruptcy /. Regensburg [1983?] 25 leaves ; LC Card 84-181506 DDC 332.7/5/0943 19
HG3769.G34 D78 1983

(Nr. 172) Niemeyer, Gerhard. Eine automatentheoretische Baumkonstruktion zur Simulation hierarchischer Management-Strukturen /. [Regensburg] [1984] 64 p. : LC Card 84-181485
HD38 .N513 1984

Regeringens berättelse om utvecklingssamarbetet till riksdagen. Helsingfors : Statens tryckericentral, 1986. 30 p. : ill. ; 25 cm. "1986 rd. nr 1." LC Card 86-224775
1. Economic assistance, Finnish - Developing countries.
HC60 .R33 1986

Regessa Kebede. The effect of leader behavior on worker job satisfaction and job performance in Ethiopian textile factories : an empirical investigation / Regassa Kebede. [Turku] : Turku School of Economics, c1987. 138 p. : ill. ; 21 cm. (Publications of the Turku School of Economics. Series D, 0782-8330 . 4:1987 = 4:1987) "Summary." Bibliography: p. 116-122. LC Card 87-170154 DDC 677/.0068 19
1. Textile industry - Ethiopia - Management - Employee participation. 2. Job satisfaction - Ethiopia. 3. Textile workers - Ethiopia. I. Title.
HD5658.T42 E87 1987

Regesti marittimi croati / [a cura di] Nikola Colak. Padova : Centro di studi storici croati--Venezia, 1985- v. <v. 1, pt. 1 > : 1 map ; 25 cm. (Fonti . vol. 1. vol. 1 = svez. 1. svez. 1) Italian with Serbo-Croatian translations. Title on added t.p.: Hrvatski pomorski regesti. Map on lining papers. Includes bibliographical references and indexes. CONTENTS. - 1. Settecento. la pt. Navigazione nell'adriatico. LC Card 86-215640
1. Ship registers - Yugoslavia - Croatia. 2. Shipping - Yugoslavia - Croatia - History - Sources. I. Čolak, Nikola. II. Title: Hrvatski pomorski regesti. III. Series: Fonti (Padova, Italy) , vol. 1.
HE565.Y8 R42 1985

Região geo-econômica de Brasília . Distrito Federal (Brazil). Coordenação do Sistema de Planejamento. [Brasília] [1980?] [28] leaves : LC Card 86-204066
HC189.B7 D57 1980

Região geoeconômica de Brasília . Franz, Paulo Renato Ferreira. Planaltina-DF [Brazil] , 1985. 70 p. : LC Card 87-143606 DDC 338.1/3/098174 19
HD1875.B7 F7 1985

Região metropolitana do Rio de Janeiro : informações básicas, 1984. [Rio de Janeiro, Brazil] : Governadoria do Estado do Rio de Janeiro, Secretaria de Estado para o Desenvolvimento da Região Metropolitana, Fundação para o Desenvolvimento da Região Metropolitana do Rio de Janeiro, [1984?] 242 p. : maps ; 30 cm. Chiefly tables. Bibliography: p. 241-242. LC Card 87-404930 DDC 330.981/53 19
1. Rio de Janeiro Metropolitian Area (Brazil) - Economic conditions - Statistics. 2. Rio de Janeiro Metropolitian Area (Brazil) - Social conditions - Statistics. I. Fundação para o Desenvolvimento da Região Metropolitana do Rio de Janeiro.
HC189.R45 R44 1984

Régie autonome des transports parisiens. RATP plan d'entreprise 1983/1987. Paris : Régie autonome des transports parisiens, [1982] 164 p. : (col.) ill. ; 28 cm. Includes index. LC Card 83-203335
1. Régie autonome des transports parisiens. 2. Local transit - France - Paris Metropolitan Area. I. Title. II. Title: R.A.T.P. plan d'entreprise 1983/1987. III. Title: Plan d'entreprise 1983/1987.
HE4769.P33 R47 1982

RÉGIE AUTONOME DES TRANSPORTS PARISIENS.
Régie autonome des transports parisiens. RATP plan d'entreprise 1983/1987. Paris [1982] 164 p. : LC Card 83-203335
HE4769.P33 R47 1982

Régie des rentes du Québec.
La Compensation des charges familiales au Québec /. [Quebec] [1986] xxi, 197 p. ; ISBN 2-551-08707-4 LC Card 86-179318
HD4925.5.C2 C65 1986

Régime de rentes du Québec : rapport actuariel / Régie des rentes du Québec. Québec : La Régie, [1983] 45 leaves : ill. ; 28 cm. "Mai 83." LC Card 85-131814
1. Old age pensions - Québec (Province). 2. Old age pensions - Law and legislation - Economic aspects - Québec (Province). I. Title.
HD7130.Z8 Q47 1983

Régime de rentes du Québec . Régie des rentes du Québec. Québec [1983] 45 leaves : LC Card 85-131814
HD7130.Z8 Q47 1983

Régimen de zonas francas en Colombia. Bogotá : Cámara de Comercio de Bogotá, Vicepresidencia Comercial, 1984. 157 leaves ; 29 cm. Papers of a seminar held in Bogotá, May 23-24, 1984, organized by the Cámara de Comercio de Bogotá. CONTENTS. - Las zonas francas y la promoción del sector externo colombiano / Germán Jaramillo Rojas -- Zonas francas colombianas / Jaime Ardila Gómez -- Que hacer con las zonas francas en Colombia / Martín Gustavo Ibarra -- Ventajas de instalar una empresa en una zona franca colombiana / Ramón Olave Cortés -- Papel de las zonas francas en las exportaciones colombianas / Héctor Trujillo Vélez -- Conclusiones de la Mesa Redonda sobre el Futuro de las Zonas Francas en Colombia. LC Card 86-185156
1. Free ports and zones - Colombia - Congresses. 2. Free ports and zones - Law and legislation - Colombia. I. Cámara de Comercio de Bogotá.
HF1418 .R44 1984

Regiões de governo : indicadores da evolução sócio-econômica / Governo do Estado de São Paulo, Secretaria de Economia e Planejamento, Coordenadoria de Ação Regional. São Paulo : A Coordenaria, 1985. [255] p. : ill. ; 33 cm. LC Card 86-164322
1. São Paulo, Brazil (State) - Economic conditions - Statistics. 2. São Paulo (Brazil : State) - Social conditions - Statistics. I. São Paulo, Brazil (State). Secretaria de Economia e Planejamento. Coordenadoria de Ação Regional.
HC188.S3 R44 1985

Region and class in modern Peruvian history / edited by Rory Miller. [Liverpool] : University of Liverpool, Institute of Latin American Studies, 1987. 207 p. : ill. ; 21 cm. (Monograph series / University of Liverpool, Institute of Latin American Studies . no. 14) "Most of these papers were initially given at a seminar of Peruvianists working in Great Britain which was held at the Institute of Latin American Studies in the University of Liverpool in December of 1984"--P. 5. Includes bibliographies. CONTENTS. - Introduction, some reflections on foreign research and Peruvian history / Rory Miller -- Imperialism, centralism, and regionalism in Peru, 1776-1845 / John Fisher -- The Socavónof Quiulacocha and the Steam Engine Company / José Deustua -- Patterns of urban and regional development in Peru on the eve of the Pacific War / Clifford T. Smith -- Earning a living in Hualgayoc, 1870-1900 / Lewis Taylor -- The conflict between indigenous and immigrant commerical systems in the Peruvian Central Sierrra, 1900-1940 / Fiona Wilson -- Reordering disorder / Nigel Haworth -- The rise of Sendero Luminoso / Colin Harding. ISBN 0-902806-20-3 LC Card 87-148309 DDC 330.985/0633 19
1. Peru - Economic conditions - Congresses. 2. Peru - Politics and government - Congresses. 3. Peru - History - Congresses. I. Miller, Rory. II. Series: Monograph series / University of Liverpool, Institute of Latin American Studies , no. 14.
HC227 .R386 1987

Región sur, problemática y perspectivas / Janette Pacheco Santos, Patricia Salas O'Brien, editores ; Amauta, Asociación Cultural ... [et al., participantes]. Arequipa : CECYCAP : CIED, [1986?] 164 p. ; 21 cm. Papers presented at the Seminario Taller "Problemática del Desarrollo Regional y los Procesos de Regionalización y Microregionalización," held in Jan. 1986 and at the Seminario Taller "El Problema Regional y la Regionalización en Arequipa," held in May 1986. LC Card 87-404224 DDC 330.984/052 19
1. Bolivia - Economic conditions - 1982- - Congresses. 2. Bolivia - Social conditions - 1982- - Congresses. I. Pacheco S., Janette. II. Salas O'Brien, Patricia. III. Asoción Amauta (Cuzco, Peru). IV. Seminario Taller "Problemática del Desarrollo Regional y los Procesos de Regionalización y Microregionalización" (1986). V. Seminario Taller "El Problema Regional y la Regionalización en Arequipa" (1986 : Arequipa, Peru?).
HC182 .R39 1986

Region und Industrialisierung im Vergleich, Minden-Ravensberg und die englischen Industriegebiete. Henning, Friedrich-Wilhelm. Vorindustrielles Gewerbe und wirtschaftlicher Wandel im Paderborner Land im 19. Jahrhundert /. Dortmund , 1983. 67 p. ; LC Card 83-198581
HC288.P27 H46 1983

Region versus nation. Fleming, William J. Region vs nation . Tempe , c1986. 82 p. ; ISBN 0-87918-066-8 LC Card 86-29919 DDC 330.982/64 19
HC177.M4 F55 1986

Region vs nation . Fleming, William J. Tempe , c1986. 82 p. ; ISBN 0-87918-066-8 LC Card 86-29919 DDC 330.982/64 19
HC177.M4 F55 1986

REGIONAL BUSINESS NEWS (DATA BASE)
Regional Business News (RBN) user's guide. Cleveland, Ohio (11001 Cedar Ave., Cleveland 44106) , 1986- 1 v. (loose-leaf) ; LC Card 86-220007 DDC 025/.0633 19
HF5548.4.P74 R44 1986

Regional Business News (RBN) user's guide. Cleveland, Ohio (11001 Cedar Ave., Cleveland 44106) : Predicasts, 1986- 1 v. (loose-leaf) ; 30 cm. Spine title: RBN user's guide. On t.p. the registered trademark symbol "TM" is superscript following "Regional Business News" in the title. Includes index. LC Card 86-220007 DDC 025/.0633 19
1. Regional Business News (Data base). I. Predicasts, inc. II. Title: RBN user's guide.
HF5548.4.P74 R44 1986

Regional Centre for Urban Environmental Studies (Hyderabad, India) Public housing /. Hyderabad, A.P. , c1983. xx, 345 p. ; LC Card 85-903848 DDC 363.5/8 19
HD7288.78.I4 P83 1983
NYPL [JLF 86-1782]

Regional Conference for Asia on Women and the Household (1985 : New Delhi, India) Invisible hands . New Delhi , Newbury Park, Calif. , 1987. 273 p. ; ISBN 0-8039-9524-5 (U. S.) LC Card 87-4337 DDC 331.4/0954 19
HD6181.85 .A85 1987

Regional development and transportation in Argentina . Fleming, William J. New York , 1987. ii, 218 p. : ISBN 0-8240-1360-3 (alk. paper) : LC Card 87-8401 DDC 385/.065/82 19
HE2910.G64 F54 1987

Regional development and vocational training analysis and discussion of the relationship development . Gizard, Xavier. Berlin , Washington, DC , 1986. 49 p. ; ISBN 92-825-5911-4 (pbk.) : LC Card 87-137374 DDC 331.25/92/094 19
HD5715.5.E8 G58 1986

REGIONAL DEVELOPMENT - BRAZIL, NORTHEAST - CONGRESSES.
A Questão Nordeste . Rio de Janeiro-RJ , 1984. 137 p. ; LC Card 84-191031
HC188.N6 Q47 1984

REGIONAL DEVELOPMENT - LATIN AMERICA - CASE STUDIES.
Pobreza, participación y desarrollo regional /. [Bogotá, D.E., Colombia] , 1986. 536 p. : LC

Card 87-103266
HC125 .P6 1986

Regional disparities and imbalances in India's planned economic development /. Mandal, S. K. (Sushil Kumar), 1954- New Delhi [1986], c1987. 380 p. ; LC Card 87-900589 DDC 338.954 19
HC435.2 .M335 1987

Regional disparity in industrial growth /. Singh, H. P. New Delhi, India , 1987. xvi, 304 p. : ISBN 81-7041-029-0 : LC Card 87-902685 DDC 338.0954/4 19
HC437.R3 S37 1987

Regional economic development : essays in honour of François Perroux / edited by Ben Higgins and Donald J. Savoie. Boston : Allen & Unwin, 1987. p. cm. Papers presented at a conference held during the summer of 1985 at Grand Pré, Nova Scotia, Canada, sponsored by the Canadian Institute for Research on Regional Development. Includes bibliographies and index. ISBN 0-04-338155-3 (alk. paper) LC Card 87-16749 DDC 338.9 19
1. Economic development. 2. Regional economics. 3. Perroux, François, 1903-. I. Perroux, François, 1903-. II. Higgins, Benjamin Howard, 1912-. III. Savoie, Donald J. IV. Université de Moncton. Canadian Institute for Research on Regional Development.
HD75 .R44 1987

Regional economic development in the Southern African development area /. Coetzee, S. F. Sandton, Republic of South Africa , 1985. xvi, 105 p. : LC Card 87-150264 DDC 338.968 19
HC905 .C64 1985

REGIONAL ECONOMIC DISPARITIES.
Booth, Douglas E. Regional long waves, uneven growth, and the cooperative alternative /. New York , 1987. 121 p. ; ISBN 0-275-92567-6 (alk. paper) : LC Card 87-2348 DDC 338.973 19
HB3729 .B66 1987

REGIONAL ECONOMIC DISPARITIES - ADDRESSES, ESSAYS, LECTURES.
Production, work, territory . Boston , 1986. xix, 344 p. : ISBN 0-04-338126-X (alk. paper) LC Card 85-20006 DDC 330 19
HC59 .P682 1986 ***NYPL [JLE 86-1745]***

REGIONAL ECONOMICS.
Agnew, John A. The United States in the world-economy . Cambridge , New York , 1987. xvii, 264 p. : ISBN 0-521-30410-5 LC Card 86-32743 DDC 337.73 19
HC103 .A37 1987

Economic and regional development agreements . [Ottawa?] [1985] 11, 12, [8] p. : LC Card 86-214896 DDC 338.971 19
HC113 .E26 1985

Odén, Bertil, 1939- Sydafrika i södra Afrika /. Uppsala , 1985. 181 p. : ISBN 91-7106-236-X LC Card 85-221741
HC905 .O34 1985 ***NYPL [Sc E 86-483]***

Regional economic development . Boston , 1987. p. cm. ISBN 0-04-338155-3 (alk. paper) LC Card 87-16749 DDC 338.9 19
HD75 .R44 1987

Reunión Técnica sobre el Financiamiento de la Integración Subregional en América Latina (1985 : Buenos Aires, Argentina) Reunión Técnica sobre el Financiamiento de la Integración Subregional en América Latina . [Buenos Aires, Argentina] . 335 p. : LC Card 86-217551
HC125 .R479 1985

Sadolin, Pia. Regional udvikling i Danmark /. [Aarhus] , 1983. 92 p. : LC Card 84-164625
HC355 .S26 1983

REGIONAL ECONOMICS - ADDRESSES, ESSAYS, LECTURES.
Human behaviour in geographical space . Aldershot, Hants, England , Brookfield, Vt., U. S.A. , c1986. x, 328 p. : ISBN 0-566-00807-6 : LC Card 85-5528 DDC 338.9 19
HT391 .H785 1986 ***NYPL [JLD 86-1630]***

REGIONAL ECONOMICS - CONGRESSES.
International Symposium on Technological Change and Employment: Urban and Regional Dimensions (1985 : Zandvoort, Netherlands) Technological change, employment, and spatial dynamics . Berlin , New York , c1986. vii, 466 p. : ISBN 0-387-16478-2 (U. S. : pbk.) LC Card 86-10081 DDC 331.12 19
HD6331 .I6 1985
NYPL [JLM 72-289 v.270]

REGIONAL ECONOMICS - MATHEMATICAL MODELS.
Kuiper, J. H. Distribution of distances in pregeographical space /. Brookfield, Vt. , 1986. viii, 296 p. : ISBN 0-566-05214-8 : LC Card 86-7673 DDC 910 19
HT391.3 .K85 1986 ***NYPL [JSD 86-605]***

Regional Employment Program for Latin America and the Caribbean.
Buscando la equidad. English. In search for equity . Aldershot, Hants, England , Brookfield, USA , c1987. xvi, 249 p. ; ISBN 0-566-05537-6 : LC Card 87-21225 DDC 338.98 19
HC130.B38 B8713 1987

Cambio y polarización ocupacional en Centroamérica. [San José, Costa Rica?] , 1986. 202 p. : ISBN 92-2-305432-X LC Card 86-231773
HD5733.A6 C36 1986

García, Norberto E. Absorción creciente con subempleo persistente (América Latina, 1950-80) /. [Santiago, Chile] , 1982. 35 p. ; LC Card 87-403250 DDC 331.12/098 19
HD5730.5.A6 G355 1982

Honduras . [Santiago, Chile] , 1983. vii, 99 p. ; LC Card 84-225233
HD5736.A6 H66 1983

Problemas metodológicos de una encuesta rural en Chile y estructura del empleo /. [Santiago, Chile] [c1983] ii, 27 leaves ; LC Card 84-225128
HD1531.C5 P76 1983

Reactivación con transformación . [Santiago, Chile] [c1984] 29 leaves ; LC Card 85-156967
HD5708.47.C5 R43 1984

Salarios e inflación, Argentina, 1970-1983 /. [Santiago, Chile] [c1984] iv, 116 p. : LC Card 85-156959
HC180.W24 S25 1984

Regional Energy Development Programme (United Nations) Energy Pricing Policy Workshop (1984 : Bangkok, Thailand) Criteria for energy pricing policy . London , Gaithersburg, MD, USA , 1985. 247 p. : ISBN 0-86010-618-1 : LC Card 86-147259 DDC 333.79/17 19
HD9502.D442 E56 1984

Regional environmental policy : the economic issues / edited by Horst Siebert, Ingo Walter, and Klaus Zimmermann. New York : New York University Press, c1979. xii, 290 p. : ill. ; 24 cm. Proceedings of a conference held in Berlin, Nov. 13-14, 1978. Includes bibliographies and index. ISBN 0-8147-7805-4 : LC Card 79-2058 DDC 301.31
1. Environmental policy - Congresses. 2. Regional planning - Congresses. I. Siebert, Horst, 1938-. II. Walter, Ingo. III. Zimmermann, Klaus, 1944-.
HC79.E5 R44 ***NYPL [JLE 80-1854]***

Regional industrial co-operation . Wong, John, 1939- Vienna , 1986. xi, 102 p. : ISBN 92-1-106204-7 (pbk.) LC Card 86-214910 DDC 337.1/5 19
HC441 .W66 1986

Regional integrations in the new world economic environment /. Inotai, András. [Regionális integrációk az új világgazdasági helyzetben. English.] Budapest , 1986. vii, 286 p. ; ISBN 963-05-4353-2 LC Card 87-111425 DDC 337.1 19
HF1418.5 .I5513 1986

Regional labour markets : analytical contributions and cross-national comparisons / edited by Manfred M. Fischer and Peter Nijkamp. Amsterdam ; New York : North-Holland ; xvii, 500 p. : ill. ; 23 cm (Contributions to economic analysis. 168) Includes bibliographies and indexes. ISBN 0-444-70323-3 LC Card 87-22200 DDC 331.12 19
1. Labor supply - Regional disparities. I. Fischer, Manfred M. II. Nijkamp, Peter. III. Series.
HD5707 .R37 1987

Regional long waves, uneven growth, and the cooperative alternative /. Booth, Douglas E. New York , 1987. 121 p. ; ISBN 0-275-92567-6 (alk. paper) : LC Card 87-2348 DDC 338.973 19
HB3729 .B66 1987

Regional Meeting on Socio-economic and Policy Aspects of Water Resources Management in Africa, 2-7 June 1986, Addis Ababa, Ethiopia /. Regional Meeting on Socio-economic and Policy Aspects of Water Resources Management in Africa (1986 : Addis Ababa, Ethiopia) [Addis Ababa?] [1986] 19 v. : LC Card 86-981006 DDC 333.91/0096 19
HD1699.A1 R44 1986

Regional Meeting on Socio-economic and Policy Aspects of Water Resources Management in Africa (1986 : Addis Ababa, Ethiopia)
Regional Meeting on Socio-economic and Policy Aspects of Water Resources Management in Africa, 2-7 June 1986, Addis Ababa, Ethiopia / organized by United Nations Economic Commission for Africa, United Nations Educational, Scientific, and Cultural Organization ; co-sponsored by United Nations International Research and Training Institute for the Advancement of Women ... [et al.]. [Addis Ababa?] : Unesco, [1986] 19 v. : ill. ; 33 cm. Cover title. English and French. [United Nations publications list]: 4 pages (p. 180-183) inserted. Includes bibliographies. CONTENTS. - [1] Country paper, Ethiopia -- [2] Country report, Sierra Leone / by I.S. Kabia -- [3] Development and management of water resources in Nigeria -- [4] Education, training, and research in water resources development in Nigeria / by A.U. Oteri -- [5] Environmental and health aspects / John Pickford -- [6] First draft of recommendations on environmental and health aspects -- [7] Planning and management of water resources and their assessment / by Nii Boi Ayibotele -- [8] Problems of water resources development in Africa -- [9] The role of the Economic Commission for Africa in water resources management -- [10] Some constraints to Africa's water resources development / by Kwame Amoako Tuffuor -- [11] Statement by the Economic Commission for Africa on the status of water resources development in Africa -- [12] Statement by the representative of UNCHS (Habitat) -- [13] Summary of Unesco's activities of water resources in Africa / by K.A. Tuffuor -- [14] Training and research for water supply development in Africa / Eustace Gondwe -- [15] Water, women and Health / Shafika Nasser -- [16] Women and water resources management for socio-economic development in Africa / by Ralphina Phillott-Almeida -- [17] Zambia country report on planning and management of water resources and their assessment in Zambia / prepared by L.L. Mbumwae, E.M. Siamachoka -- [18] Provisional list of participants / Liste provisoire des participants -- [19] [without special title]. LC Card 86-981006 DDC 333.91/0096 19
1. Water resources development - Africa - Congresses. I. Unesco. II. International Research and Training Institute for the Advancement of Women. III. Title.
HD1699.A1 R44 1986

Regional modelling of social reproduction.
Regional'noe modelirovanie obshchestvennogo vosproizvodstva . Vil'nius , 1980. 280 p. : LC Card 81-191307
HC337.L5 R44 1980

REGIONAL PLANNING - AMAZON RIVER REGION.
Miranda Neto, Manoel José de. O dilema da Amazônia /. Belém, Pará [1986] 154 p. ; LC Card 87-119394 DDC 330.981/1063 19
HC188.A5 M57 1986

REGIONAL PLANNING - ARGENTINA.
Boneo, Horacio. Desarrollo regional, incentivos fiscales y localización industrial /. Buenos Aires, Argentina [1985] 160 p. : ISBN 950-95720-8-X ***NYPL [JLD 86-4218]***

REGIONAL PLANNING - AUSTRALIA - WESTERN AUSTRALIA.
Goldfields-Esperance regional profile. Kalgoorlie, W.A. , Perth, W.A. [1986] 58 p. : LC Card 87-169717 DDC 330.9941/7 19
HC607.W47 G65 1986

Western Australia's North . [Perth, W.A.] [1985?] [32] p. : LC Card 86-232759 DDC 338.9941 19
HC607.W47 W485 1985

REGIONAL PLANNING - BRAZIL.
Estudos e propostas para a organização territorial e desenvolvimento urbano do Brasil. Brasilia , 1981. 126 leaves, [7] folded leaves of plates : ***NYPL [JLG 86-151]***

Harber, Richard P. Tax policy, economic development, and regional inequality [microform] . Austin , 1984. 33 p. ; LC Card

84-623077 DDC 339.5/2/09813 19
HJ2527 .H37 1984 ***NYPL [*ZT-1646 no.22]***

REGIONAL PLANNING - BRAZIL - ARAGUAÍNA REGION.
Projeto de Desenvolvimento Integrado da Bacia do Araguaia-Tocantins. Plano de desenvolvimento das áreas-programa de Araguaína e Tocantinópolis /. Brasília , 1985. 95 p., [8] leaves of plates : LC Card 86-200369
HC189.A67 P76 1985

REGIONAL PLANNING - BRAZIL - BRASÍLIA REGION.
Distrito Federal (Brazil). Coordenação do Sistema de Planejamento. Região geo-econômica de Brasília . [Brasília] [1980?] [28] leaves : LC Card 86-204066
HC189.B7 D57 1980

REGIONAL PLANNING - BRAZIL, NORTHEAST.
Guerra, Paulo de Brito, 1914- A civilização da seca . Fortaleza , 1981. 324 p. : LC Card 82-231215 DDC 361.6/0981/3 19
HT395.B72 N63 1981 ***NYPL [JLD 86-2873]***

Magalhães, Antonio Rocha. Industrialização e desenvolvimento regional . Brasília , 1983. 315 p. : LC Card 84-160221 DDC 338.981/3 19
HD3616.B84 N676 1983
NYPL [JLD 86-3120]

REGIONAL PLANNING - BRAZIL, NORTHEAST - CONGRESSES.
Dinâmica da economia e absorção de mão-de-obra . Recife , 1984. 79 p. ; ISBN 85-7019-063-8 LC Card 85-156612 DDC 338.981/3 19
HD5755.N63 D56 1984
NYPL [JLE 86-3545]

REGIONAL PLANNING - BRAZIL - SÃO PAULO (STATE)
Identificação e caracterização de agrupamentos industriais como subsídio à política de desenvolvimento regional. São Paulo , 1981. 134, 17, 60 p. : LC Card 86-146114
HC188.S3 I34 1981

REGIONAL PLANNING - BRAZIL, SOUTH.
Banco Regional de Desenvolvimento do Extremo sul. O planejamento e os pré-investimentos /. [Porto Alegre?] [19]85. 71, [6], p. 21 leaves ; LC Card 86-201808
HC188.S68 B35 1985

REGIONAL PLANNING - BRAZIL - TOCANTINÓPOLIS REGION.
Projeto de Desenvolvimento Integrado da Bacia do Araguaia-Tocantins. Plano de desenvolvimento das áreas-programa de Araguaína e Tocantinópolis /. Brasília , 1985. 95 p., [8] leaves of plates : LC Card 86-200369
HC189.A67 P76 1985

REGIONAL PLANNING - BYELORUSSIAN S.S.R.
Regional'nye problemy razvitiia infrastruktury i mezhotraslevykh proizvodstv /. Minsk , 1985. 243, [4] p. ; LC Card 86-161744
HC337.B933 C37 1985
NYPL [*QM 87-2108]

REGIONAL PLANNING - CANADA.
The Canadian economy . Toronto , New York , c1986. 291 p. : ISBN 0-458-99950-4 (pbk.) : LC Card 86-218828 DDC 338.971 19
HC113 .C37 1986

Economic and regional development agreements . [Ottawa?] [1985] 11, 12, [8] p. : LC Card 86-214896 DDC 338.971 19
HC113 .E26 1985

REGIONAL PLANNING - CHILE - BIOBÍO.
Ramírez C., Valeria (Ramírez Ceballos) Desarrollo socio-económico de la Octava Región de Chile /. Santiago, Chile , 1985. i, 45 leaves ; LC Card 86-115542
HC193.B5 R35 1985

REGIONAL PLANNING - COLOMBIA.
Jiménez, Margarita. Historia del desarrollo regional en Colombia /. Bogotá, Colombia , 1985. 338 p. ; ISBN 958-9061-04-4 LC Card 85-242811
HC197 .J57 1985

Latorre, Emilio. Transporte y crecimiento regional en Colombia /. Bogotá, Colombia , 1986. 137 p. : ISBN 958-9061-14-1 LC Card 87-115019 DDC 380.5/09861 19
HE235 .L37 1986

REGIONAL PLANNING - COLOMBIA - ANTIOQUIA (DEPT.)
Vellinga, Menno. Industrialization and regional development in Colombia /. Amsterdam, The Netherlands , 1983. 183 p. : ISBN 90-70280-80-9 LC Card 83-209247 DDC 338.09861/26 19
HC198.C296 V45 1983

REGIONAL PLANNING - COLOMBIA - CAUCA RIVER REGION.
Vellinga, Menno. Industrialization and regional development in Colombia /. Amsterdam, The Netherlands , 1983. 183 p. : ISBN 90-70280-80-9 LC Card 83-209247 DDC 338.09861/26 19
HC198.C296 V45 1983

REGIONAL PLANNING - CONGRESSES.
Regional environmental policy . New York , c1979. xii, 290 p. : ISBN 0-8147-7805-4 : LC Card 79-2058 DDC 301.31
HC79.E5 R44 ***NYPL [JLE 80-1854]***

Regional Planning Council (Md.) Owen, Gail T. Residential property sales in Maryland . Baltimore, Md. (2225 N. Charles St., Baltimore 21218-5767) [1985] iv, 79 leaves : LC Card 86-622370 DDC 333.33/8 19
HD266.M3 O9 1985

REGIONAL PLANNING - DENMARK.
Christoffersen, Mads. Fysisk planlægning og samfundsmæssige reproduktionsproblemer . København , 1980, c1979. 317 p. ; ISBN 87-500-1922-8 ***NYPL [JLD 86-2303]***

REGIONAL PLANNING - DEVELOPING COUNTRIES.
Cubukgil, Adil. Urbanization in developing countries . [Toronto] , 1981. ii, 77 p. ;
NYPL [JLF 87-277]

The Socialist Third World . Oxford, UK , New York, NY , 1987. vii, 333 p. : ISBN 0-631-13442-5 : LC Card 87-5165 DDC 338.9/009172/4 19
HC59.7 .S5857 1987

REGIONAL PLANNING - DICTIONARIES - POLYGLOT.
Logie, Gordon. Glossary of planning and development . Amsterdam , New York , 1986. xxv, 254 p. ; ISBN 0-444-42608-6 (U. S.) : LC Card 86-521 DDC 338.9/003 19
HT391 .L64 1987 ***NYPL [JLE 86-4010]***

REGIONAL PLANNING - EUROPE - CONGRESSES.
Periphere Räume . Paderborn , 1979. 183 p. : ISBN 3-506-73204-8 LC Card 85-209554
HC240 .P38 1979

The Regionalisation of transport and regional planning in practice . Paris, France [Washington, D.C.] c1984. 199 p. : ISBN 92-821-1091-5 (pbk.) : LC Card 85-180250 DDC 380.5/068 19
HE242 .R44 1984 ***NYPL [JLG 86-138]***

REGIONAL PLANNING - EUROPE, EASTERN.
Prace z zakresu planowania i ekonomiki regionu /. Kraków , 1980. 220 p. : LC Card 80-131017
HB9 .K53 nr. 116 HC340.3

REGIONAL PLANNING - EUROPE, SOUTHERN - CONGRESSES.
Ungleiche Entwicklung und Regionalpolitik in Südeuropa . Bochum , 1985. 282 p. : ISBN 3-88339-441-6 : LC Card 85-205651
HC244.5 .U48 1985

REGIONAL PLANNING - EUROPEAN ECONOMIC COMMUNITY COUNTRIES.
Hackenbroch, Inge. Zur Theorie und Politik eines supranationalen Finanzausgleichs . München , c1983. xvi, 350 p. ; ISBN 3-8039-0259-2 LC Card 83-167962
HJ1000.5 .H33 1983

Sweeney, G. P. (Gerald Patrick), 1928- Innovation, entrepreneurs, and regional development /. London , 1987. xvi, 271 p. : ISBN 0-86187-647-4 ***NYPL [JLD 87-1403]***

Sweeney, G. P. (Gerald Patrick), 1928- Innovation, entrepreneurs, and regional development /. New York , c1987. xvi, 271 p. : ISBN 0-312-00489-3 : LC Card 86-27999 DDC 338/.06/094 19
HC240.9.T4 S94 1987

REGIONAL PLANNING - FLORIDA.
The Saddlebrook papers . [Fort Lauderdale] [Tallahassee] [1985] v leaves, 177 p. : LC Card 86-621089 DDC 338.9759 19
HC107.F63 E547 1985

REGIONAL PLANNING - FRANCE.
Laborie, Jean Paul. La politique française d'amenagement du territoire de 1950 à 1985 /. Paris , 1985. 176 p., [8] p. of plates : ISBN 2-11-001488-1(pbk.) : ***NYPL [JLG 87-38]***

Lefebvre, André, docteur en droit. Planification et aménagement des communes, des départements et des régions /. Paris , c1985. 335 p. : ISBN 2-7013-0620-5 : LC Card 86-113657 DDC 338.944 19
HT395.F7 L43 1985 ***NYPL [JLD 87-1577]***

REGIONAL PLANNING - GERMANY, WEST.
Arnold-Palussiére, Martine. Die grenzüberschreitende regionale Zusammenarbeit auf dem Gebiet der Raumordnung . Hannover , 1983. xvii, 393 p. ; ISBN 3-87870-869-6 : LC Card 83-239646 DDC 361.6/1/0943 19
HT395.G4 A76 1983
NYPL [JLL 72-326 Bd. 71]

Gewerbeentwicklung und Gewerbepolitik in der Grossstadtregion /. Gerlingen , c1987. 390 p., [3] leaves of plates : ISBN 3-88350-596-X LC Card 87-146643 DDC 332.6/732243 19
HC290.5.I53 G4797 1987

Klemmer, Paul. Abgrenzung von Fördergebieten /. Bochum , 1983. 206 p. : ISBN 3-88339-298-7 LC Card 83-183564
HC286.7 .K59 1983

Timmer, Reinhard. Raumordnung und Industrialisierung /. Hannover , 1977. 103 p. : LC Card 84-150907
HC286.5 .T55 1977

Wagner, Gerhard. Abbau regionaler Strompreisdisparitäten durch raumwirksame Massnahmen und Planungen /. Bonn , 1985. xv, 356 p. : ISBN 3-87994-415-6 LC Card 87-408008 DDC 338.4/336362/0943 19
HD9685.G3 W34 1985

REGIONAL PLANNING - GERMANY, WEST - ADDRESSES, ESSAYS, LECTURES.
Verwaltung und Planung im Wandel /. Köln , 1979. 112 p. ; ISBN 3-7745-6438-8 : LC Card 81-473982
HT395.G4 V48 ***NYPL [JLE 86-2107]***

REGIONAL PLANNING - GERMANY, WEST - BADEN-WÜRTTEMBERG.
Friedrich, R. (Rainer) Energie und Umwelt . Stuttgart [1985] 115 p. : LC Card 87-409534 DDC 333.79/0943/46 19
HD9502.G43 B324 1985

Friedrich, R. (Rainer) Energie und Umwelt . Stuttgart [1985] 124 p. : LC Card 87-409533 DDC 333.79/0943/46 19
HD9502.G43 B3238 1985

REGIONAL PLANNING - GERMANY, WEST - CASE STUDIES.
Funktionsräumliche Arbeitsteilung. Hannover , <1986-. v. <3 > : ISBN 3-87870-770-3 (T. III) : LC Card 87-409060 DDC 361.6/0943 19
HD51 .F86 1986

REGIONAL PLANNING - GERMANY, WEST - CONGRESSES.
Beiträge zur empirischen Bürostandortforschung /. Kallmünz , 1983. 167 p. : ISBN 3-7847-6050-3 : LC Card 84-176770
HF5547.25 .B45 1983

Stand der grenzüberschreitenden Raumordnung am Oberrhein /. [Heidelberg] , 1981. 105 p. : ISBN 3-88570-071-9 LC Card 81-197772 DDC 361.6/0943/4 19
HT395.G4 S735 1981
NYPL [L-10 4979 Heft 71]

REGIONAL PLANNING - GERMANY, WEST - GRAFSCHAFT DIEPHOLZ (LANDKREIS) - CA E STUDIES.
Bauer, Jürgen. Quantitative Entwicklungsplanung für ländliche Regionen . Bochum , 1979. 382 p. in various pagings : ISBN 3-88339-087-9 : LC Card 80-470152
HT395.G4 B39 1979 ***NYPL [JLD 86-1628]***

REGIONAL PLANNING - GERMANY (WEST) - HESSE - ECONOMETRIC MODELS.
Krietemeyer, Hartmut, 1955- Der Erklärungsgehalt der Exportbasistheorie /. Hamburg , 1983. 224 p. : ISBN 3-87895-240-6 : LC Card 84-147595
HC287.H4 K75 1983

REGIONAL PLANNING - GERMANY, WEST - MATHEMATICAL MODELS.
Bauer, Jürgen. Quantitative Entwicklungsplanung für ländliche Regionen . Bochum , 1979. 382 p. in various pagings : ISBN 3-88339-087-9 : LC Card 80-470152
HT395.G4 B39 1979 ***NYPL [JLD 86-1628]***

REGIONAL PLANNING - GERMANY (WEST) - REMOTE SENSING.
Angewandte Fernerkundung . Hannover , 1984. x, 285 p. : ISBN 3-87870-904-8 LC Card 85-147235
HD108.8 .A54 1984

REGIONAL PLANNING - GERMANY (WEST) - RHINELAND.
Ebel, Friedhelm. Landwirtschaft am Niederrhein . Bonn , 1976. 223 p. : LC Card 87-408419
HD1407 .L3 Heft 33 HD1960.R48

REGIONAL PLANNING - GERMANY (WEST) - RUHR (REGION)
Rau, Thomas. Bodenallokation und Bodenpolitik im Ruhrgebiet . Bochum , 1982. viii, 323 p. : ISBN 3-88339-269-3 LC Card 83-130477 DDC 333.73/13/094355 19
HD659.R8 R38 1982 ***NYPL [JLD 86-1715]***

REGIONAL PLANNING - GERMANY (WEST) - SCHLESWIG-HOLSTEIN - CONGRESSES.
Gestaltung künftiger Raumstrukturen durch veränderte Verkehrskonzepte . Hannover , 1986. xii, 173 p. : ISBN 3-87870-767-3 LC Card 87-401351 DDC 380.5/0943/512 19
HE249.Z7 S343 1986

REGIONAL PLANNING - GOVERNMENT POLICY - GREAT BRITAIN.
Planning control . London , Wolfeboro, N.H. , c1987. 234 p. ; ISBN 0-7099-3790-3 : LC Card 86-24079 DDC 333.73/17/0941 19
HD596 .P53 1987 ***NYPL [JLD 87-803]***

REGIONAL PLANNING - GREAT BRITAIN.
Ambrose, Peter J. Whatever happened to planning? /. London , New York , 1986. xiv, 288 p. : ISBN 0-416-37100-0 LC Card 86-12415 DDC 333.73/17/0941 19
HD596 .A43 1986 ***NYPL [JLD 87-1402]***

Bruton, Michael J. Local planning in practice /. London , 1987. 452 p. : ISBN 0-09-165381-9
NYPL [JLE 87-1201]

Loebl, Herbert. Government factories and the origins of British regional policy, 1934-1948 . Aldershot, Hants, England , Brookfield, Vt., USA , c1987. p. cm. ISBN 0-566-05343-8 LC Card 87-23075 DDC 338.6/2/0941 19
HD4145 .L64 1987

REGIONAL PLANNING - GREAT BRITAIN - CONGRESSES.
Developing local economic strategies . Milton Keynes [England] , Philadelphia , 1987. p. cm. ISBN 0-335-15522-7 LC Card 87-22681 DDC 338.941 19
HC256.6 .D48 1987

REGIONAL PLANNING - HUNGARY - STATISTICS.
Nagyné Szauter, Edit. A gazdaságilag elmaradott térségek társadalmi-gazdasági jellemzői /. Budapest , 1986. 41 p. : LC Card 86-215345
HC300.28 .N26 1986

REGIONAL PLANNING - INDIA.
Kundu, Amitabh, 1948- Location of public enterprises and regional development /. New Delhi , 1986. xv, 178 p. ; LC Card 86-903373 DDC 338.954 19
HD9697.A3 I45 1986

Nanjundappa, D. M., 1930- Area planning and rural development /. New Delhi , c1981. viii, 52 p. ; LC Card 81-903723 DDC 307/.12/0954 19
HN690.Z9 C6649 1981
NYPL [JLD 86-2687]

Vyasulu, Vinod. Development of backward areas . New Delhi, India , 1987. xi, 188 p. : ISBN 81-85030-05-7 : LC Card 87-902689 DDC 332.6/42/0954 19
HD2346.I5 V93 1987

REGIONAL PLANNING - INDIA - KORAPUT (DISTRICT)
Mahapatro, Prafulla Ch. Economic development of tribal India /. New Delhi , 1987. xvi, 408 p. : ISBN 81-7024-077-8 : LC Card 87-900212 DDC 338.954/13 19
HC437.K63 M34 1987

REGIONAL PLANNING - IRAN.
Contribution to national and regional planning problems /. Calcutta , 1983. vii, 174 p., [2] leaves of plates (some folded) : LC Card 83-907550 DDC 338.954 19
HC435.2 .C63 1983 ***NYPL [JLD 86-3868]***

Nattagh, Nima. Agriculture & regional development in Iran /. Wisbech, Cambridgeshire, England , 1986. 105 p. : ISBN 0-906559-26-X (pbk.) : LC Card 86-230845 DDC 338.1/0955 19
HD1565.2 .N37 1986

REGIONAL PLANNING - ITALY - ABRUZZI.
Piazzo, Pietrenzo, 1935- Una valutazione intersettoriale costi benefici estesa al territorio . Roma , c1984. viii, 224 p., 6 folded leaves of plates : LC Card 84-250428
HC307.A2 P53 1984

REGIONAL PLANNING - ITALY - BOLOGNA (PROVINCE)
Modello padano, localismo e modernizzazione . Bologna , c1986. 470 p. : ISBN 88-15-01220-6 : LC Card 87-103653
HC307.B57 M63 1986

REGIONAL PLANNING - ITALY - MILAN REGION.
Metropoli e agricoltura /. Milano , c1982. 319 p. : LC Card 82-246692 DDC 333.76/13/094521 19
HD680.M54 M47 1982
NYPL [JLD 86-3678]

REGIONAL PLANNING - IVORY COAST.
Willaert, Y. Ressources humaines et développement régional en Côte d'Ivoire . [Addis Ababa] [1977] 3, 108, [6] leaves (1 folded) ; LC Card 82-980560
HD5846.9.A6 W55 1977

REGIONAL PLANNING - LIBYA.
Khalaf Allāh, Ramaḍān 'Uraybī. Ḥarakat al-quwá al-'āmilah wa-al-tanmiyah al-iqlīmīyah fī Lībiyā /. Ṭarābulus, al-Jamāhīrīyah al-'Arabīyah al-Lībīyah al-Sha'bīyah al-Ishtirākīyah , 1984. 279 p. : LC Card 86-965535
HB2121.6.A3 K47 1984

REGIONAL PLANNING - MASSACHUSETTS - WORCESTER COUNTY.
Doeringer, Peter B. Invisible factors in local economic development /. New York , 1987. vii, 144 p. : ISBN 0-19-504965-9 (alk. paper) LC Card 87-13550 DDC 338.9744/3 19
HC107.M42 W674 1987

REGIONAL PLANNING - MATHEMATICAL MODELS.
Foot, David H.S. A comparison of some land-use allocation/interaction models [microform] /. Reading [Berkshire] , 1974. 36 p. : ISBN 0-7049-0338-5
NYPL [*ZT-1712 no.13]

REGIONAL PLANNING - NORWAY.
Næringslivets utviklingsmuligheter i innlandet /. Oslo [1983] 291 p. : ISBN 82-00-70803-9 LC Card 83-237323
HC365 .N32 1983

REGIONAL PLANNING - PERU.
Instituto Nacional de Planificación (Peru) Sistema de planes de desarrollo de corto plazo, 1986. [Lima] [1986- v. <1-35 > : LC Card 86-216851
HC227 .I529 1986

Lizárraga Bobbio, Raúl. Estrategias para la descentralización y el desarrollo regional /. Lima, Perú , c1985. 356 p. : LC Card 86-146658
HT395.P4 L59 1985 ***NYPL [JLD 87-1315]***

Ortiz, Rolando. CORDES . Lima, Perú , 1987. 96 p. ; LC Card 87-405059 DDC 338.985 19
HC227 .O73 1987

REGIONAL PLANNING - POLAND.
Polish People's Republic national report to the habitat . [S.l.] 1976 (Warszawa : Dom Słowa Polskiego) 48 p. : LC Card 83-226226
HC340.3 .P656 1976

Prace z zakresu planowania i ekonomiki regionu /. Kraków , 1980. 220 p. : LC Card 80-131017
HB9 .K53 nr. 116 HC340.3

REGIONAL PLANNING - REMOTE SENSING.
Angewandte Fernerkundung . Hannover , 1984. x, 285 p. : ISBN 3-87870-904-8 LC Card 85-147235
HD108.8 .A54 1984

REGIONAL PLANNING - RHINE VALLEY.
Arnold-Palussiére, Martine. Die grenzüberschreitende regionale Zusammenarbeit auf dem Gebiet der Raumordnung . Hannover , 1983. xvii, 393 p. ; ISBN 3-87870-869-6 : LC Card 83-239646 DDC 361.6/1/0943 19
HT395.G4 A76 1983
NYPL [JLL 72-326 Bd. 71]

REGIONAL PLANNING - RHINE VALLEY - CONGRESSES.
Stand der grenzüberschreitenden Raumordnung am Oberrhein /. [Heidelberg] , 1981. 105 p. : ISBN 3-88570-071-9 LC Card 81-197772 DDC 361.6/0943/4 19
HT395.G4 S735 1981
NYPL [L-10 4979 Heft 71]

REGIONAL PLANNING - RUSSIAN S.F.S.R. - SIBERIA.
Khozi͡aĭstvennoe osvoenie novykh raĭonov i ėkonomicheskiĭ rost Sibiri . Novosibirsk , 1980. 173 p. : LC Card 83-182452
HC337.R852 S5247 1980

REGIONAL PLANNING - SIBERIA (R.S.F.S. R.)
Dienes, Leslie. Soviet Asia . Boulder , 1987. xx, 289 p. ; ISBN 0-8133-7437-5 (pbk.) LC Card 87-8331 DDC 338.957 19
HC336.9.S53 D53 1987

REGIONAL PLANNING - SOUTH AFRICA.
Coetzee, S. F. Regional economic development in the Southern African development area /. Sandton, Republic of South Africa , 1985. xvi, 105 p. : LC Card 87-150264 DDC 338.968 19
HC905 .C64 1985

An Introduction to economic development in Southern Africa and the role of DBSA /. Sandton, Republic of South Africa [1985] 78 p. ; LC Card 87-127414 DDC 338.968 19
HG3401.A8 D485 1985

REGIONAL PLANNING - SOUTH AFRICA - KWAZULU.
Spies, P. H. Perspectives on the future of Natal/KwaZulu /. Pietermaritzburg , 1986. 149 p. : ISBN 0-909232-59-8 (pbk.) : LC Card 87-166530 DDC 361.2/5/09684 s 361.6/1/09684 19
HC517.N3 A44 vol. 69 JQ2224

REGIONAL PLANNING - SOUTH AFRICA - NATAL.
Spies, P. H. Perspectives on the future of Natal/KwaZulu /. Pietermaritzburg , 1986. 149 p. : ISBN 0-909232-59-8 (pbk.) : LC Card 87-166530 DDC 361.2/5/09684 s 361.6/1/09684 19
HC517.N3 A44 vol. 69 JQ2224

REGIONAL PLANNING - SOVIET CENTRAL ASIA.
Dienes, Leslie. Soviet Asia . Boulder , 1987. xx, 289 p. ; ISBN 0-8133-7437-5 (pbk.) LC Card 87-8331 DDC 338.957 19
HC336.9.S53 D53 1987

REGIONAL PLANNING - SOVIET UNION.
Bugaev, V. K. (Vladimir Konstantinovich) Territorial'nai͡a struktura ėkonomicheskogo raĭona . Leningrad , 1986. 164, [3] p. : LC Card 87-120624
HC336.25 .B84 1986

Chisti͡akov, E. G. (Evgeniĭ Gavrilovich) Metody sochetanii͡a otraslevogo i territorial'nogo planirovanii͡a /. Moskva , 1982. 147, [3] p. : LC Card 82-189489
HC336.25 .C516 1982

Novit͡skiĭ, N. A. (Nikolaĭ Aleksandrovich) Faktornyĭ analiz ėffektivnosti razmeshchenii͡a proizvodstva /. Moskva , 1982. 126 p. : LC Card 83-193429
HC340.D5 N68 1982

Teoreticheskie i metodologicheskie problemy regional'noĭ ėkonomiki . Moskva , 1983. 158 p. : LC Card 87-100005
HC340.D5 T437 1983

REGIONAL PLANNING - SPAIN - CATALONIA.
Conte, Jesús. La Catalunya a mig fer /.

Barcelona , c1985. 259 p. ; ISBN 84-86006-64-5X LC Card 86-164880
HC387.C25 C57 1985

REGIONAL PLANNING - SWEDEN.
Andersson, Göran, 1944- Industrihotell och industribyar . Stockholm [1984] 150 p. : ISBN 91-38-08268-3 LC Card 85-106828
HC375 .A72 1984

Hur planeras Sverige? /. Stockholm , c1986. 179 p. : ISBN 91-38-90679-1 : LC Card 87-151788
HC375 .H85 1986

Omfattning och erfarenheter . Stockholm [1984] 127 p. : ISBN 91-38-08319-1 LC Card 85-106802
HC375 .O39 1984

Regionala effekter av en kärnkraftsavveckling . [Stockholm] [1979] 254 p. : ISBN 91-38-05243-1 LC Card 82-219566
HD9698.S82 O42 1979b Suppl.

De Regionala utvecklingsfonderna . Stockholm , 1981. 260 p. ; ISBN 91-38-06693-9 LC Card 82-234113
HC380.I53 R44 1981

REGIONAL PLANNING - SWITZERLAND.
Arnold-Palussiére, Martine. Die grenzüberschreitende regionale Zusammenarbeit auf dem Gebiet der Raumordnung . Hannover , 1983. xvii, 393 p. ; ISBN 3-87870-869-6 : LC Card 83-239646 DDC 361.6/1/0943 19
HT395.G4 A76 1983
NYPL [JLL 72-326 Bd. 71]

Flückiger, Hans. Siedlungsstruktur . Bern , c1985. 118 p. : ISBN 3-258-03529-6 : LC Card 86-134805
HN603.5 .F58 1985 ***NYPL [JLE 86-3789]***

Hanser, Christian. Erfolgskontrolle der Industrieansiedlungspolitik . Bern , New York , c1986. 375 p. ; ISBN 3-261-03610-9 LC Card 87-407957 DDC 338.6/042/09494 19
HD58 .H36 1986

Held, Daniel. Marché de l'emploi . Lausanne , 1984. 205 p. : ISBN 2-88074-028-2
NYPL [JLE 86-679]

Raumordnungspolitik im Vollzug . Grüsch , c1985. 507 p. : ISBN 3-7253-0258-8 : LC Card 86-149201
HC397 .R36 1985

Rumley, Pierre-Alain. Aménagement du territoire et utilisation du sol . Zürich , c1984. x, 176 p. : LC Card 85-104773
HD796 .R86 1984

REGIONAL PLANNING - SWITZERLAND - CONGRESSES.
Stand der grenzüberschreitenden Raumordnung am Oberrhein /. [Heidelberg] , 1981. 105 p. : ISBN 3-88570-071-9 LC Card 81-197772 DDC 361.6/0943/4 19
HT395.G4 S735 1981
NYPL [L-10 4979 Heft 71]

REGIONAL PLANNING - TURKMEN S.S.R.
Egengel'dyev, Ė. (Ėsengel'dy) Teoreticheskie issledovaniīa regional'nykh faktorov razmeshcheniīa khoziaīstva /. Ashkabad , 1985. 227 p. : LC Card 86-172008
HC337.T853 D53 1985

REGIONAL PLANNING - UNITED STATES.
Committee on Science, Technology, and Regional Economic Development. The impact of science and technology on regional economic development. Washington, 1969. xi, 111 p. LC Card 72-604009 DDC 338.973
HC110.R4 C65 1969b ***NYPL [JLE 87-898]***

Financing a common wealth . Washington, DC , 1985. xx, 304 p. : ISBN 0-89125-090-5 LC Card 84-81918
HD3888 .F5 1985 ***NYPL [JLE 86-2519]***

Tomioka, Seishiro. Planned unit developments . New York , c1984. xviii, 192 p. : ISBN 0-471-08595-2 : LC Card 82-13419 DDC 307/.12/0973 19
HD257 .T65 1984 ***NYPL [JLF 86-1316]***

REGIONAL PLANNING - UNITED STATES - CONGRESSES.
Population change, natural resources, and regionalism /. Milford, Pa. , c1986. viii, 104 p. : ISBN 0-938549-00-6 (pbk.) LC Card 86-25682 DDC 304.6/0973 19
HB3505 .P62 1986

Regional price formation in Eastern Europe . Brabant, Jozef M. van. Boston ; Dordrecht : xiv, 290 p. ; ISBN 90-247-3540-8 LC Card 87-12238 DDC 338.5/26/0947 19
HB235.E8 B73 1987

Regional Seminar on an Integrated Approach to Population, Food, and Nutrition Policies and Programmes for National Development (1979 : Bangkok, Thailand) An Integrated approach to population, food, and nutrition policies and programmes for national development . Bangkok, Thailand [1979 or 1980] 39 p. ; LC Card 82-169080
HA4553 .I58 1979

Regional statistical abstract, 1972-1980 / by Division of Statistics, Regional Ministry of Finance and Economic Affairs, Juba, Equatoria Region. Juba [Sudan] : The Division, 1986. xiii, 113 leaves ; 33 cm. Cover title. Chiefly tables. LC Card 86-981387 DDC 316.24 19
1. Sudan - Statistics. I. Equatoria Region (Sudan). Ministry of Finance and Economic Affairs. Division of Statistics.
HA4687 .R45 1986

Regional Symposium on Water Resoures Policy in Agro-Socio-Economic Development (1985 : Dhaka, Bangladesh) Water resources policy for Asia : proceedings of the Regional Symposium on Water Resources Policy in Agro-Socio-Economic Development, Dhaka, Bangladesh, 4-8 August 1985 / edited by Mohammed Ali, George E. Radosevich, Akbar Ali Khan. Rotterdam ; Boston : Balkema, 1987. xii, 627 p. : ill. ; 24 cm. Includes bibliographies. ISBN 90-6191-684-4 LC Card 87-170039 DDC 333.91/0095 19
1. Water resources development - Government policy - Asia - Congresses. I. Ali, Mohammed. II. Radosevich, George. III. Khan, Akbar Ali, 1944-. IV. Title.
HD1698.A1 R45 1985

Regional udvikling i Danmark /. Sadolin, Pia. [Aarhus] , 1983. 92 p. : LC Card 84-164625
HC355 .S26 1983

Regional wage rates [microform] . Beaumont, Paul (Paul M.) Iowa City , 1982. 22 p. :
NYPL [*ZT-1564 no.29]

Regional Workshop on the Role and Prospects of Copper and Aluminium in African Development (1985 : Lusaka, Zambia) Final report / Regional Workshop on the Role and Prospects of Copper and Aluminium in African Development, 27 February-2 March 1985, Lusaka, Zambia. [Addis Ababa] : Economic Commission for Africa, 1985. 9 p. ; 28 cm. Cover title: Final report of the Regional Workshop on the Role and Prospects of Copper and Aluminium in African Development. "2 March 1985." "ECA/NRD/WCA/5." LC Card 86-980966 DDC 338.2/743/096 19
1. Copper industry and trade - Africa - Congresses. 2. Aluminum industry and trade - Africa - Congresses. I. United Nations. Economic Commission for Africa. II. Title. III. Title: Final report of the Regional Workshop on the Role and Prospects of Copper and Aluminium in African Development.
HD9539.C7 A427 1985

Regional Workshop on Wood Energy in East Africa (1982 : Nairobi, Kenya) Proceedings of the Regional Workshop on Wood Energy in East Africa : Nairobi, Kenya, 5-8 October 1982 / organized by the International Development Research Centre, in collaboration with the African Energy Programme/Commonwealth Science Council. Ottawa, Canada : The Centre, [1983] 241 p. : ill. ; 28 cm. (Manuscript reports / International Development Research Centre) IDRC ; MR73e Cover title: Wood energy in East Africa. "April 1983"--Cover. Includes bibliographies. LC Card 86-185703 DDC 333.75 19
1. Fuelwood industry - Africa, Eastern - Congresses. 2. Fuelwood consumption - Africa, Eastern - Congresses. I. International Development Research Centre (Canada). II. African Energy Programme (Commonwealth Science Council). III. Title. IV. Title: Wood energy in East Africa. V. Series: Manuscript reports (International Development Research Centre (Canada)).
HD9769.F843 A367 1982

Regionala effekter av en kärnkraftsavveckling : rapport / från Konsekvensutredningens D-grupp. [Stockholm] : Industridepartementet : LiberFörlag, [1979] 254 p. : ill. ; 24 cm. "Ds I 1979:13." Includes bibliographical references. "Bilaga 4." Supplement to: Om vi avvecklar kärnkraften / Konsekvensutredningen, 1979. ISBN 91-38-05243-1 LC Card 82-219566
1. Nuclear industry - Sweden. 2. Regional planning - Sweden. 3. Energy policy - Sweden. I. Sweden. Konsekvensutredningen. D-gruppen. II. Sweden. Konsekvensutredningen. Om vi avvecklar kärnkraften.
HD9698.S82 O42 1979b Suppl.

De regionala utvecklingsbolagen . Olofsson, Christer. Stockholm [1983] 118 p. ; ISBN 91-38-07479-6 LC Card 83-234309
HC380.I53 O46 1983

De Regionala utvecklingsfonderna : erfarenheter av verksamheten 1978-1981 : utredning från Statens industriverk. Stockholm : LiberFörlag, 1981. 260 p. ; 25 cm. (SIND, 0346-5748 . 1981:7) Bibliography: p. 255-256. ISBN 91-38-06693-9 LC Card 82-234113
1. Industrial promotion - Sweden. 2. Sweden - Economic conditions - 1945-. 3. Regional planning - Sweden. I. Sweden. Statens industriverk. II. Series.
HC380.I53 R44 1981

Regionalbericht Region Oberfranken-West / Herausgeber, Bayerisches Staatsministerium für Landesentwicklung und Umweltfragen, Regionaler Planungsverband Oberfranken-West ; Bearbeiter, Bezirksplanungsstelle bei der Regierung von Oberfranken. [München] : Das Staats ministerium, 1976. 83 p. : ill. ; 30 cm. + portfolio (30 leaves of plates : 30 folded col. maps ; 30 cm.) LC Card 86-231827
1. Oberfranken (Germany) - Economic conditions. 2. Oberfranken (Germany) - Population. 3. Oberfranken (Germany) - Social conditions. I. Bavaria (Germany). Bayerisches Staatsministerium für Landesentwicklung und Umweltfragen. II. Regionaler Planungsverband Oberfranken-West (Germany). III. Oberfranken (Germany). Bezirksplanungsstelle.
HC288.O16 R44 1976

Regionale Aspekte der Wirtschaftsplanung in den Mitteleuropäischen RGW-Staaten. Marburg/Lahn : J.G. Herder-Institut, 1983. 95 p. : ill., maps ; 24 cm. (Wirtschafts- und sozialwissenschaftliche Ostmitteleuropa-Studien . 6) Includes bibliographies. CONTENTS. - Vorwort / Ekkehard Buchhofer -- Wirtschaftsräumliche Strukturen der Tschechoslowakei / Horst Förster -- Wirtschaftsräumliche Struckturen der Volksrepublik Polen / Ekkehard Buchhofer -- Territorialplanung in sozialistischen Ländern / Hans E. Gramatzki -- Territoriale Autonomie in der polnischen Reformdiskussion der 80er Jahre / Karl von Delhaes. ISBN 3-87969-178-9 LC Card 84-249235
1. Czechoslovakia - Economic conditions - 1945- - Regional disparities. 2. Czechoslovakia - Economic policy - 1945-. 3. Poland - Economic conditions - 1945- - Regional disparities. 4. Poland - Economic policy - 1945-. 5. Communist countries - Economic conditions - Regional disparities. 6. Communist countries - Economic policy. I. Series.
HC270.28 .R42 1983

Die regionale Ausstrahlung der Universität Basel /. Frey, René Leo. Basel , c1984. 73 p. : LC Card 84-166545 DDC 378/.103 19
HC395 .A75 no. 8 LC238.4.S92B37

Regionale Besonderheiten der Preisbildung und Ansätze zur Förderung des Wettbewerbs auf dem Berliner Baustoffmarkt /. Ring, Peter. Berlin , 1986. 187 p. : ISBN 3-428-06112-8 LC Card 87-114036 DDC 330 s 338.4/3691/09431554 19
HC281 .B33 Heft 91 HD9715.G33B52

Regionale dødelighedsforskelle i Danmark 1971-79. København : Danmarks statistik, 1983. 136 p. : ill. ; 30 cm. (Statistiske undersøgelser, 0039-0682 . nr. 39) ISBN 87-501-0582-5 : LC Card 84-169325
1. Mortality - Denmark - Statistics. 2. Denmark - statistics, Vital. I. Danmarks statistik. II. Series: Statistiske undersøgelser (Danmarks statistik) , nr. 39.
HA1473 .A35 nr. 39 HB1441

Regionale Entwicklungspolitik und Massenarmut im ländlichen Raum Nordost-Brasiliens . Rönick, Volker. Paderborn , 1986. 136 p. : ISBN 3-506-73225-0 LC Card 87-407836 DDC 338.981/3 19
HC188.N6 R66 1986

Regionale Struktur des Personenverkehrs in der Bundesrepublik Deutschland im Jahre 1980 / von Jutta Kloas ... [et al.]. Berlin : Duncker & Humblot, 1985. ix, 320 p. : ill. ; 30 cm. (Beiträge zur Strukturforschung . Heft 88) At head of title:

Deutsches Institut für Wirtschaftsforschung. Includes numerous tables. Bibliography: p. 150-155. ISBN 3-428-05961-1 LC Card 86-165242
1. Transportation - Germany, West - Passenger traffic. I. Kloas, Jutta. II. Deutsches Institut für Wirtschaftsforschung.
HC281 .B33 Heft 88 HE249

Regionale strukturendringer belyst ved sysselsettingstall /. Skoglund, Tor. Oslo , 1983. 52 p. ; ISBN 82-537-2003-3 : LC Card 84-161751
HD5800.A6 S58 1983

Die regionalen Verteilungswirkungen des kommunalen Finanzausgleichs . Kops, Manfred. Thun , c1983. xvii, 537, 259 p. : ISBN 3-87144-728-5 : LC Card 83-159176
HJ9493.5.N6 K66 1983

Regionaler Planungsverband Oberfranken-West (Germany) Regionalbericht Region Oberfranken-West /. [München] , 1976. 83 p. : LC Card 86-231827
HC288.O16 R44 1976

The Regionalisation of transport and regional planning in practice : an examination based on case studies : seminar, Strasbourg, 5-6 December 1983 : introductory reports and summary of the discussion. Paris, France : ECMT ; [Washington, D.C. : OECD Publications and Information Center, distributor], c1984. 199 p. : ill. ; 30 cm. Organized by the European Conference of Ministers of Transport, the European Conference of Ministers Responsible for Regional Planning, and the Steering Committee for Regional Planning of the Council of Europe. Includes bibliographical references. ISBN 92-821-1091-5 (pbk.) : LC Card 85-180250 DDC 380.5/068 19
1. Transportation - Europe - Congresses. 2. Transportation and state - Europe - Congresses. 3. Regional planning - Europe - Congresses. I. European Conference of Ministers Responsible for Regional Planning. II. Council of Europe. Steering Committee for Regional Planning.
HE242 .R44 1984 ***NYPL [JLG 86-138]***

Regionalisierte Arbeitsmarkt- und Beschäftigungspolitik / Dietrich Garlichs, Friederike Maier, Klaus Semlinger (Hg.) ; mit Beiträgen von G. Schmid ... [et al.]. Frankfurt/Main ; New York : Campus, c1983. 322 p. : ill. ; 21 cm. (Arbeitsberichte des Wissenschaftszentrums Berlin, Internationales Institut für Management und Verwaltung/Arbeitsmarktpolitik) Papers of a conference held Sept. 23-24, 1982, at the Internationales Institut für Management und Verwaltung (IIMV) of the Wissenschaftszentrum Berlin. Includes bibliographies. ISBN 3-593-33241-8 LC Card 84-106151
1. Germany (West) - Economic conditions - 1974- - Regional disparities - Congresses. 2. Labor supply - Germany (West) - Congresses. 3. Germany (West) - Full employment policies - Congresses. I. Garlichs, Dietrich. II. Maier, Friederike. III. Semlinger, Klaus. IV. Schmid, Gunther, 1942-. V. International Institute of Management. VI. Series.
HC286.7 .R44 1983

REGIONALISM - FRANCE.
Evaluation de la planification décentralisée /. Paris , c1986. 97 p. : ISBN 2-11-001562-4 : LC Card 86-193163
HC276.2 .E89 1986

Lefebvre, André, docteur en droit. Planification et aménagement des communes, des départements et des régions /. Paris , c1985. 335 p. : ISBN 2-7013-0620-5 : LC Card 86-113657 DDC 338.944 19
HT395.F7 L43 1985 ***NYPL [JLD 87-1577]***

REGIONALISM - FRANCE - HISTORY - 19TH CENTURY.
Beck, Thomas D. French notables . New York , c1987. 254 p. : ISBN 0-8204-0393-8 : LC Card 87-12156 DDC 338.0944 19
HC275 .B37 1987

REGIONALISM - UNITED STATES.
Burleson, Clyde W., 1934- Interstate commerce . New York , 1987. viii, 230 p. ; ISBN 0-531-15519-6 LC Card 86-29019 DDC 381/.5/0973 19
HF5387 .B856 1987

REGIONALISM - VENEZUELA - TÁCHIRA - HISTORY - 19TH CENTURY.
Muñoz, Arturo Guillermo. El Táchira fronterizo . Caracas , 1985. 315 p. ; ISBN 980-265-178-8 LC Card 87-402928 DDC 330.987/120633 19
HC238.T3 M86 1985

Regional'naia effektivnost' obshchestvennogo proizvodstva . Shimov, V. N. (Vladimir Nikolaevich) Minsk , 1986. 167 p. ; LC Card 86-204677
HC337.B93 S55 1986

Regional'noe modelirovanie obshchestvennogo vosproizvodstva : sbornik stateĭ / otv. red. A.I. Burachas. Vil'nius : Akademiia nauk Litovskoĭ SSR, In-t ėkonomiki, 1980. 280 p. : ill. ; 21 cm. Title on verso t.p.: Regional modelling of social reproduction. Includes bibliographies. LC Card 81-191307
1. Lithuania - Economic conditions - 1945- - Econometric models. 2. Economic forecasting - Lithuania. I. Buračas, A. (Antanas). II. Ekonomikos institutas (Lietuvos TSR Mokslų akademija). III. Title: Regional modelling of social reproduction.
HC337.L5 R44 1980

Regional'nye osobennosti ratsionalizatsii prirodopol'zovaniia i okhrany sredy / [otvetstvennyĭ redaktor B.M. Ishmuratov]. Irkutsk : Akademiia nauk SSSR, Sibirskoe otd-nie, In-t geografii Sibiri i Dal'nego Vostoka, 1980. 177 p. ; 20 cm. Includes bibliographies. LC Card 82-111826
1. Natural resources - Russian S.F.S.R. - Siberia. 2. Siberia (R.S.F.S.R.) - Environmental policy. 3. Natural resources - Russian S.F.S.R. - Soviet Far East. 4. Soviet Far East (R.S.F.S.R.) - Environmental policy. I. Ishmuratov, Baĭron Mustafovich. II. Institut geografii Sibiri i Dal'nego Vostoka (Akademiia nauk SSSR).
HC337.R852 S5266 1980

Regional'nye osobennosti sotsial'no-demograficheskogo razvitiia Armianskoĭ SSR /. Karapetian, S. A. Erevan , 1986. 215 p. ; LC Card 87-118556
HB3608.A75 K37 1986

Regional'nye problemy razvitiia infrastruktury i mezhotraslevykh proizvodstv / pod redaktsieĭ L.V. Kozlovskoĭ. Minsk : "Nauka i tekhnika", 1985. 243, [4] p. ; 20 cm. At head of title: Akademiia nauk Belorusskoĭ SSR. Institut ėkonomiki. Bibliography: p. 241-[244] LC Card 86-161744
1. Infrastructure (Economics) - Byelorussian S.S.R. 2. Regional planning - Byelorussian S.S.R. I. Kozlovskaia, L. V. II. Instytut ėkanomiki (Akademiia navuk Belaruskaĭ SSR).
HC337.B933 C37 1985
NYPL [*QM 87-2108]

Regional'nye problemy tovarnogo obrashcheniia . Bernval'd, A. R. (Arngol'd Reĭngol'dovich) Novosibirsk , 1984. 207 p. ; LC Card 85-104041
HF5415.6 .B46 1984 ***NYPL [*QIP 87-2770]***

Regional'nyĭ aspekt mezhotraslevykh proizvodstv . Atarov, N. Z. Moskva , 1980. 173 p. : LC Card 81-132091
HD9705.S595 A73 1980

Regionalverband Neckar-Alb. Heinzmann, Ute. Umzugsverhalten der Bevölkerung in ausgewählten ländlichen Teilräumen am Beispiel der Region Neckar-Alb . Tübingen , 1985. 69, [4] p. : LC Card 86-195573
HB2056.N43 H45 1985

Regione Piemonte. see **Piemonte, Italy.**

Register. Organisation for Economic Co-operation and Development. Development Centre. Répertoire . Paris , Washington, D.C. , 1986. xxiv, 523 p. ; ISBN 92-64-02872-2 : LC Card 87-146730
HD77.5.A34 O75 1986

Register, Charles A. Sharp, Ansel Miree, 1924- Economics of social issues /. Plano, Tex. , 1988. xiii, 431 p. : ISBN 0-256-06173-4 (pbk.) LC Card 87-71674 DDC 330 19
HB171.5 .S5498 1988

Register, David L., 1925-1983. Jones, Robert C., 1934- Two feet to tidewater . Boulder, Colo. , c1987. xvi, 269 p., [1] leaf of plates : ISBN 0-87108-729-4 LC Card 87-2428 DDC 385/.065/741 19
HE2791.W76647 J66 1987

REGISTERS OF BIRTHS, ETC. - CANADA - DIRECTORIES.
Burgess, Michael, 1948- The state and province vital records guide /. San Bernardino, Calif. , 1988. p. cm. ISBN 0-89370-815-1 : LC Card 87-6312 DDC 929/.1/02573 19
HA38 .B87 1988

REGISTERS OF BIRTHS, ETC. - COSTA RICA - HISTORY.
Daremblum, Jaime. El auge del café y la apertura de la economía costarricense /. San José, Costa Rica , 1980. 62 p. ; LC Card 84-247131
HF3255 .D37 1980

REGISTERS OF BIRTHS, ETC. - FRANCE.
France. Direction générale des collectivités locales. Instruction aux maires relative aux bulletins statistiques de l'état civil . [Paris] [1983] 50 p. : LC Card 84-112361
HA37.F8 F73 1983

REGISTERS OF BIRTHS, ETC. - HUNGARY - HISTORY.
A Népmozgalmi statisztika fejlődése Magyarországon. Budapest , 1985- v. <1 > ; LC Card 86-190535
HA37.H92 N46 1985

REGISTERS OF BIRTHS, ETC. - THAILAND.
Luther, Norman Y., 1936- Consistent correction of census and vital registration data for Thailand, 1960-80 /. Honolulu, Hawaii [1986] vii, 39 p. ; ISBN 0-86638-089-2 (pbk.) : LC Card 86-32807 DDC 304.6/0723 19
HA39.T4 L87 1986

REGISTERS OF BIRTHS, ETC. - UNITED STATES - DIRECTORIES.
Burgess, Michael, 1948- The state and province vital records guide /. San Bernardino, Calif. , 1988. p. cm. ISBN 0-89370-815-1 : LC Card 87-6312 DDC 929/.1/02573 19
HA38 .B87 1988

Registration list /. International Beverage Industry Exhibition & Congress (1986 : Dallas, Tex.) Washington, D.C. (1101-16th St., N.W., Washington 20036) , c1986. ca. 400 p. ; LC Card 87-107458 DDC 338.4/7663/025 19
HD9348.A2 I57 1986

REGISTRATION OF TITLE. see **LAND TITLES - REGISTRATION AND TRANSFER.**

Registro civil y el processo electoral en Costa Rica. Daremblum, Jaime. El auge del café y la apertura de la economía costarricense /. San José, Costa Rica , 1980. 62 p. ; LC Card 84-247131
HF3255 .D37 1980

El registro contable en moneda constante . Badillo, Juan A. Capital Federal, Argentina , 1985. 249 p. ; LC Card 85-203677
HF5658.5 .B34 1985

Réglementer moins et mieux . Québec (Province). Groupe de travail sur la déréglementation. [Quebec] [1986] 2 v. ; ISBN 2-551-08729-5 (v. 1) LC Card 86-206349
HD3616.C24 Q47 1986

Regnier, Victor, 1947- Housing the aged . New York , c1987. xvii, 500 p. : ISBN 0-444-01012-2 LC Card 87-5253 DDC 363.5/9
HD7287.9 .H7 1987

Regnskaber og statistikker for den offentlige sektor 1970-1981 = Konten und Statistiken des Staates, 1970-1981 = General government accounts and statistics, 1970-1981. Luxembourg : Europæiske fællesskabers statistiske kontor ; Washington, DC : Sales and subscriptions, European Community Information Service, 1983. clxxii, 279 p. ; 30 cm. "Manuscript completed in October 1983." Danish, Dutch, English, French, German, and Italian. ISBN 92-825-4066-9 LC Card 84-174459
1. National income - European Economic Community countries - Accounting - Statistics. I. Statistical Office of the European Communities. II. Title: Konten und Statistiken des Staates, 1970-1981. III. Title: General government accounts and statistics, 1970-1981.
HC240.9.I5 R45 1983

Regourd, Florence. La Vendée ouvrière : grèves et ouvriers vendéens, 1840-1940 / Florence Regourd. Les Sables-d'Olonne : Cercle d'or, [1981] 353 p., [16] p. of plates : ill. ; 25 cm. Revision of the author's thesis (doctoral--U.E.R. de Nantes 1980) under the title: Grèves et ouvriers vendéens de 1840 à 1940. Includes indexes. Bibliography: p. 331-344. ISBN 2-7188-0098-4 : LC Card 82-161939 DDC 331.89/294461 19
1. Strikes and lockouts - France - Vendée - History. 2. Labor and laboring classes - France - Vendée - History.

I. Title.
HD5376.V46 R43 1981
NYPL [JLF 85-1433]

REGRESSION ANALYSIS.
Dworschak, Franz. Struktur von Arbeitseinkommen . Idstein , 1986. ix, 408 p. : ISBN 3-925196-16-1 LC Card 86-225347
HB523 .D86 1986

Schroeder, Larry D. Understanding regression analysis . Beverly Hills , c1986. 95 p. : ISBN 0-8039-2758-4 LC Card 85-63790
NYPL [JLK 77-39 no.57]

Studenmund, A. H. Using econometrics . Boston , c1987. xii, 440 p. : ISBN 0-316-82010-5 LC Card 86-21382 DDC 330/.028 19
HB139 .S795 1987

West, Bruce J. An essay on the importance of being nonlinear /. Berlin , New York , c1985. viii, 204 p. : ISBN 0-387-16038-8 (U. S.)
NYPL [JSK 75-186 v.62]

Regulated markets in Orissa : a case study / Dept. of Rural Economics, Sociology, and Applied Economics. Bhubaneswar, Orissa : Utkal University, [1973] 56 p. ; 25 cm. LC Card 82-903827
1. Markets - India - Sākhi Gopāl - Case studies. 2. Markets - India - Kendupatna - Case studies. 3. Markets - India - Orissa - Case studies. I. Utkal University. Dept. of Rural Economics, Sociology, and Applied Economics.
HF5415.12.I5 R44 1973

Regulating the automobile / Robert W. Crandall ... [et al.]. Washington, D.C. : Brookings Institution, c1986. xiii, 202 p. ; 24 cm. (Studies in the regulation of economic activity) Includes bibliographical references and index. ISBN 0-8157-1594-3 : LC Card 85-48171 DDC 343.73/078629222 347.30378629222 19
1. Automobiles - Safety regulations - United States - Cost effectiveness. 2. Automobiles - Motors - Exhaust gas - Law and legislation - Cost effectiveness. 3. Automobiles - Fuel consumption - Law and legislation - United States - Cost effetiveness. I. Crandall, Robert W.
HD9710.U52 R39 1986
NYPL [JLE 86-3240]

Regulating the city . Clarke, Michael, 1945- Milton Keynes, Eng. , Philadelphia, Pa. , 1986. 194 p. ; ISBN 0-335-15381-X LC Card 85-29715 DDC 332.1/09421/2 19
HG186.G7 C53 1985 ***NYPL [JLE 86-3357]***

Regulating utilities in an era of deregulation / edited by Michael A. Crew. New York : St. Martin's Press, 1987. xii, 201 p. : ill. ; 23 cm. "A result of two seminars held at Rutgers-The State University of New Jersey on 1 November 1985 and 2 May 1986"--P. ix. Includes bibliographies and index. ISBN 0-312-00527-X : LC Card 86-29639 DDC 363.6/0973 19
1. Public utilities - Government policy. I. Crew, Michael A.
HD2763 .R43 1987

Regulation of insurance . Alliance of American Insurers. Chicago, Ill. , 1977. 68 p. ;
NYPL [JLE 86-1584]

Regulation of the firm and natural monopoly /. Waterson, Michael, 1950- Oxford [Oxfordshire] , New York, NY, USA , 1988. p. cm. ISBN 0-631-14007-7 : LC Card 87-20925 DDC 338.8 19
HD3611 .W35 1988

REGULATION OF TRADE. see **TRADE REGULATION.**

Regulations in vain? . Martinussen, John. Roskilde, Denmark , 1986. 239 p. : LC Card 87-100775 DDC 338.8/8854 19
HD2900 .M37 1986

The Regulatory framework of accounting / general editors, Emile Woolf, Suresh Tanna, Karam Singh. Estover, Plymouth : Macdonald and Evans, 1985. [12], 391 p. : ill. ; 25 cm. (M & E professional studies) Includes index. ISBN 0-7121-0491-7
1. Corporations - Great Britain - Accounting. 2. Accounting - Great Britain. I. Woolf, Emile. II. Tanna, Suresh. III. Singh, Karam, M.B.A. IV. Series.
NYPL [JLF 87-84]

The regulatory impact on pensions /. Wendling, Wayne. Brookfield, Wis. , 1986. xiii, 91 p. : ISBN 0-89154-314-7 (pbk.) : LC Card 87-129712 DDC 331.25/2/0973 19
HD7105.35.U6 W46 1986

Regulatory politics in Japan . Pauly, Louis W. Ithaca, N.Y. , c1987. vi, 82 p. ; ISBN 0-939657-45-7 (pbk.) LC Card 87-403245 DDC 332.1/5/0952 19
HG3324 .P38 1987

Regulatory reform : the state of the regulatory art : emerging concepts and procedures / editors, J. Rhoads Foster ... [et al.]. Washington, D.C. : Institute for Study of Regulation, c1984. ii, 267 p. : ill. ; 23 cm. Bibliography: p. 259-260. ISBN 0-913097-02-0 (pbk.) LC Card 84-80846 DDC 363.6/0973 19
1. Public utilities - Government policy - United States. 2. Public utilities - United States - Rates. 3. Public utilities - United States - Costs. I. Foster, J. Rhoads. II. Institute for Study of Regulation.
HD2766 .R357 1984

REHABILITATION - ARGENTINA.
Argentina. Comisión Nacional de Rehabilitación del Lisiado. Comisión Nacional de Rehabilitación del Lisiado. [Buenos Aires] , 1965. [24] leaves ; LC Card 85-110867
HD7256.A7 A74 1965

REHABILITATION CENTERS - DIRECTORIES.
Social and vocational rehabilitation resources . Geneve , 1984- v. ; ISBN 92-2-003776-9 (pbk. : v. 1) LC Card 86-126143 DDC 362/.0425 19
HD7255 .S62 1984 ***NYPL [JLL 85-184]***

REHABILITATION CENTERS - PERSONNEL MANAGEMENT.
Human resources management . Springfield, Ill., U. S.A. , c1987. xiv, 170 p. : ISBN 0-398-05296-4 LC Card 86-23016 DDC 362/.0425 19
HD7255 .H86 1987

REHABILITATION CENTERS - UNITED STATES - COST CONTROL.
Thomas, Dale F. Fees for services . Menomonie, WI [1986] v, 90 p. : LC Card 86-622897 DDC 338.4/33620425 19
HD7256.U5 T47 1986

REHABILITATION CENTERS - UNITED STATES - FEES.
Thomas, Dale F. Fees for services . Menomonie, WI [1986] v, 90 p. : LC Card 86-622897 DDC 338.4/33620425 19
HD7256.U5 T47 1986

REHABILITATION COUNSELING.
Rubin, Stanford E. Foundations of the vocational rehabilitation process /. Austin, Tex. , c1987. xiii, 400 p. : ISBN 0-89079-147-3 (pbk.) LC Card 86-30600 DDC 362/.0425 19
HD7255.5 .R823 1987

Tews, Hans Peter. Abbrüche beruflicher Rehabilitationsmassnahmen . Hamburg , 1986. 277 p. ; ISBN 3-925408-04-5 LC Card 87-127427 DDC 362/.0425 19
HD7256.G3 T48 1986

REHABILITATION - DIRECTORIES.
Social and vocational rehabilitation resources . Geneve , 1984- v. ; ISBN 92-2-003776-9 (pbk. : v. 1) LC Card 86-126143 DDC 362/.0425 19
HD7255 .S62 1984 ***NYPL [JLL 85-184]***

REHABILITATION - GERMANY (EAST)
Rehabilitationspädagogik für Körperbehinderte /. Berlin , 1986. 132 p. ; LC Card 86-193835
HD7256.G32 R44 1986

REHABILITATION - GERMANY, WEST.
Tews, Hans Peter. Abbrüche beruflicher Rehabilitationsmassnahmen . Hamburg , 1986. 277 p. ; ISBN 3-925408-04-5 LC Card 87-127427 DDC 362/.0425 19
HD7256.G3 T48 1986

REHABILITATION, RURAL. see **RURAL DEVELOPMENT.**

REHABILITATION, VOCATIONAL. see **VOCATIONAL REHABILITATION.**

Rehabilitationspädagogik für Körperbehinderte / Helmut Berndt und Autorenkollektiv. 1. Aufl. Berlin : Verlag Volk und Gesundheit, 1986. 132 p. ; 24 cm. (Beiträge zum Sonderschulwesen und zur Rehabilitationspädagogik, 0138-1725 . Bd. 44) Bibliography: p. 123-128. Includes index. LC Card 86-193835
1. Rehabilitation - Germany (East). I. Berndt, Helmut, ao. Prof. Dr. paed. habil. II. Series.
HD7256.G32 R44 1986

Reheis, Fritz. Konkurrenz und Gleichgewicht als Fundamente von Gesellschaft : interdisziplinäre Untersuchung zu einem sozialwissenschaftlichen Paradigma / von Fritz Reheis. Berlin : Duncker & Humblot, c1986. xi, 401 p. : ill. ; 24 cm. (Sozialwissenschaftliche Schriften . Heft 13) Originally presented as the author's thesis (doctoral)--Universität Regensburg, 1985. Bibliography: p. 380-401. ISBN 3-428-06102-0 LC Card 87-131057 DDC 339.5 19
1. Competition. 2. Equilibrium (Economics). I. Series: Sozialwissenschaftliche Schriften (Duncker & Humblot) , Heft 13. II. Title.
HB238 .R44 1986

Rehfeld, Dieter, 1951- Bestimmungsfaktoren der Energiepolitik in der Bundesrepublik Deutschland : zugleich ein Beitrag zur aktuellen Diskussion staatlicher Willensbildungs-, Entscheidungs- und Funktionsmuster / Dieter Rehfeld. Frankfurt am Main ; New York : Lang, c1986. vii, 287 p. ; 21 cm. (Beiträge zur Politikwissenschaft, 0170-8384 . Bd. 33) Bibliography: p. 256-287. ISBN 3-8204-9354-9 LC Card 86-194761
1. Energy policy - Germany, West. I. Title. II. Series.
HD9502.G42 R44 1986

Rehsche, Guntram. Brain Drain : Fachleute aus Entwicklungsländern in der Schweiz : eine Analyse von Ursachen, Ausmass, Wirkungen und Gegenstrategien zur Abwanderung hochqualifizierter Arbeitskräfte aus der Dritten Welt / Guntram Rehsche.1. Aufl. Adliswil : Institut für Sozialethik SEK, Entwicklungsstudien, 1981. 71 p. ; 21 cm. (Entwicklungspolitische Diskussionsbeiträge . 20) Bibliography: p. 69-71. ISBN 3-7229-4019-2 LC Card 81-206028 DDC 331.12/79 19
1. Brain drain - Switzerland. 2. Brain drain - Developing countries. I. Title. II. Series.
HD8038.S85 R44 1981

Reich, Michael, 1950- Huddle, Norie, 1944- Island of dreams . Cambridge, Mass. , c1987. xxiii, 355 p. : ISBN 0-87047-027-2 : LC Card 86-33842 DDC 363.7/00952 19
HC465.E5 H82 1987

Reich, Utz-Peter. Darstellungskonzepte der Input-Output-Rechnung / Utz Peter Reich, Carsten Stahmer u.a. ; Herausgeber, Statistisches Bundesamt, Wiesbaden. Stuttgart : Kohlhammer, 1984. 185 p. : ill. ; 25 cm. (Schriftenreihe Forum der Bundesstatistik . Bd. 2) Includes bibliographies. ISBN 3-17-003301-8
1. Input-output tables. 2. Input-output analysis. I. Stahmer, Carsten, 1942-. II. Germany (Federal Republic, 1949-). Statistisches Bundesamt. III. Series. IV. Series: Forum der Bundesstatistik , Bd. 2. V. Title.
NYPL [JLE 86-1264]

Reichelt, Matthias. Mein Vaterland ist international . Oberhausen , 1986. 331 p. : ISBN 3-921541-62-X LC Card 86-224091
HD7791 .M45 1986

Reichert, Thomas. Andorra, eine Landeskunde : Möglichkeiten und Grenzen endogener Regionalentwicklung / Thomas Reichert. Nürnberg : Im Selbstverlag des Wirtschafts- und Sozialgeographischen Instituts der Friedrich-Alexander-Universität, 1986. xviii, 320 p. : ill. ; 21 cm. (Nürnberger wirtschafts- und sozialgeographische Arbeiten, 0546-9112 . Bd. 39) Summary in English, German, and Spanish. Bibliography: p. 296-320. LC Card 87-131037 DDC 330.946/79083 19
1. Andorra - Economic conditions. I. Title. II. Series.
HC390.5 .R45 1986

Reichman, Shalom, 1935- Les transports, servitude ou liberté? / Shalom Reichman. 1re éd. Paris : Presses universitaires de France, c1983. 197 p. ; 22 cm. (Espace et liberté, 0222-3376) Includes bibliographical references and indexes. ISBN 2-13-037934-6 : LC Card 83-230014
1. Transportation and state. 2. Transportation - Social aspects. I. Title. II. Title: Transports. III. Series.
HE151 .R44 1983

REICHSBANK (GERMANY) - HISTORY.
Flaskamp, Jürgen, 1958- Aufgaben und Wirkungen der Reichsbank in der Zeit des Dawes-Planes /. Bergisch Gladbach , c1986. 210 p. : ISBN 3-89012-060-1 LC Card 87-108166 DDC 332.1/1/0943 19
HG3054 .F58 1986

REICHSWERKE AKTIENGESELLSCHAFT FÜR ERZBERGBAU UND

EISENHÜTTEN "HERMANN GÖRING" - HISTORY.
Meyer, August. Das Syndikat . Braunschweig , c1986. 348 p. ; ISBN 3-925151-18-4 LC Card 87-129940 DDC 338.2/73/0943 19
HD9523.9.R45 M49 1986

Reid, Ann Christine. Population change, natural resources, and regionalism /. Milford, Pa. , c1986. viii, 104 p. : ISBN 0-938549-00-6 (pbk.) LC Card 86-25682 DDC 304.6/0973 19
HB3505 .P62 1986

Reid, Frank. Meltz, Noah M. Sharing the work . Toronto , Buffalo , 1981. viii, 90 p. : ISBN 0-8020-2383-5 *NYPL [JLD 82-233]*

Reid, Gavin C. Theories of industrial organization / Gavin C. Reid. Oxford, UK ; New York, NY, USA : B. Blackwell, 1987. 234 p. : ill. ; 24 cm. Bibliography: p. [215]-229. Includes index. ISBN 0-631-15172-9 : LC Card 86-31007 DDC 338.7 19
1. Industrial organization (Economic theory). I. Title.
HD2326 .R45 1987

Reid, Ian. Maney, Tracy. A management guide to artificial intelligence /. Aldershot, Hants, England , c1986. viii, 188 p. ; *NYPL [JLD 87-862]*

Reid, Stanley D. Managing export entry and expansion . New York , 1987. xx, 439 p. : ISBN 0-275-92361-4 (alk. paper) : LC Card 86-30330 DDC 658.8/48 19
HF1009.5 .M345 1987

Reid, Stuart. Working with statistics : an introduction to quantitative methods for social scientists / Stuart Reid. Totowa, N.J. : Rowman & Littlefield, 1987. xiv, 183 p. ; 23 cm. Bibliography: p. [176]-177. Includes index. ISBN 0-8476-7590-4 (pbk.) : LC Card 87-20508 DDC 300/.72 19
1. Social sciences - Statistical methods. I. Title.
HA29 .R43 1987

Reidegeld, Eckart. Die Sozialversicherung zwischen Neuordnung und Restauration : soziale Kräfte, Reformen und Reformpläne unter besonderer Berücksichtigung der Versicherungsanstalt Berlin (VAB) / Eckart Reidegeld. Frankfurt am Main : Haag + Herchen, c1982. 481 p. ; 20 cm. Originally presented as the author's thesis (doctoral)--Freie Universität Berlin. Bibliography: p. 464-477. ISBN 3-88129-519-4 : LC Card 83-155896
1. Social security - Berlin (Germany) - History. 2. Social security - Germany, West - History. I. Title.
HD7180.B4 R45 1982

Reidenbach, Michael. Verfällt die öffentliche Infrastruktur? : eine Bestandsaufnahme unter Einbeziehung britischer und amerikanischer Erfahrungen / Michael Reidenbach ; [Organisation und Schreibarbeiten, Claudia Eichenhöfer ... et al.]. Berlin : Deutsches Institut für Urbanistik, 1986. 212 p. : ill. ; 30 cm. Bibliography: p. 202-212. ISBN 3-88118-125-3 LC Card 86-233141
1. Infrastructure (Economics) - Germany (West). I. Eichenhöfer, Claudia. II. Deutsches Institut für Urbanistik. III. Title.
HC290.5.C3 R45 1986

Reidenbach, R. Eric. Developing new banking products : a manager's guide / R. Eric Reidenbach, M. Ray Grubbs. Englewood Cliffs, N.J. : Prentice-Hall, c1987. xii, 206 p. : ill. ; 24 cm. Includes bibliographical references and index. ISBN 0-13-204603-2 LC Card 86-22708 DDC 332.1/7/0685 19
1. Banks and banking - Customer services. I. Grubbs, M. Ray. II. Title.
HG1616.C87 R45 1987
NYPL [JLE 87-1141]

Reifenhäuser, Irene. Koch, Thilo. Müllverwertung und -Beseitigung in Baden-Württemberg . Stuttgart , 1984. ii, 177 p. : LC Card 84-158868
HD4485.G32 B335 1984

Reig Martínez, Ernest. La política agraria de la Comunidad Económica Europea : repercusiones internacionales / Ernest Reig. [Valencia] : Edicions "Alfons el Magnànim," Institució Valenciana d'Estudis i Investigació, [1986?] 129 p. ; 19 cm. (Libros de bolsillo. 5) Bibliography: p. 127-129. ISBN 84-00-06370-8 LC Card 87-125600
1. Agriculture and state - European Economic Community countries. I. Series: Libros de bolsillo (Valencia, Spain) , 5. II. Title.
HD1920.5.Z8 R45 1986

Reigado, Felisberto Marques. Introdução ao planeamento : teorias e técnicas / F. Marques Reigado.1a ed. Lisboa : Publicações Dom Quixote, 1983. 370 p. : ill. ; 21 cm. (Universidade moderna . 76.) LC Card 84-164510 DDC 361.2 19
1. Planning - Portugal. 2. Planning. I. Title.
HD85.P65 R45 1983 *NYPL [JLD 86-3065]*

REIGN OF TERROR. see **FRANCE - HISTORY - REVOLUTION, 1789-1799.**

Reihe Arbeit. Sonderheft .
(6) Befreiung der Arbeit . Bonn , c1986. 197 p. : ISBN 3-87831-429-9 LC Card 86-194157
HD6955 .B389 1986

Reihe Arbeiterbewegung und Kirche .
(Nr. 1) Aussperrung und Streik . Mainz , 1981, c1980. 173 p. ; ISBN 3-7867-0854-1 LC Card 81-101514 DDC 331.89/2943 19
HD5378 .A97 1981 *NYPL [JLD 86-2787]*

(Nr. 3) Kirchen kämpfen mit . Mainz , 1981. 106 p. : ISBN 3-7867-0873-8 LC Card 81-188986 DDC 261.8/34562/094343 19
HD6338.2.G32 S634 1981
NYPL [JLD 86-2786]

(Nr. 3) Kirchen kämpfen mit . Mainz , 1981. 106 p. : ISBN 3-7867-0873-8 LC Card 81-188986 DDC 261.8/34562/094343 19
HD6338.2.G32 S634 1981
NYPL [JLD 86-2786]

(Nr. 7) Schwarz, Heino, 1936- Katholisch, proletarisch und in der Einheitsgewerkschaft /. Mainz , c1983. 141 p. : ISBN 3-7867-1046-5 LC Card 83-193395 DDC 331.88/0943 19
HD6694 .S34 1983 *NYPL [JLD 86-2783]*

Reihe Berichte und Dokumentationen (Bonn, Germany)
Arbeitssicherheit '86 . Bonn [1986] 47, 46, 22 p. : LC Card 87-409083 DDC 363.1/12/0943 19
HD7708 .A7 1986

Germany (West). Bundesministerium der Finanzen. Rede zur Einbringung des Bundeshaushalts 1982 . Bonn , 1982. 56 p. : LC Card 82-221425
HJ2109 .G45 1982

Reihe Finanzierung, Steuern, Wirtschaftsprüfung .
(Bd. 1) Hergarten, Lothar, 1953- Der Prospekt über steuerbegünstigte Kapitalanlagen . Köln , c1986. v, 209 p. ; ISBN 3-924361-18-5 : LC Card 87-103997 DDC 332.63 19
HG4028.C4 H456 1986

Reihe Geschichtswissenschaft, 0177-2767 .
(Bd. 7) Bartels, Christoph. Schieferdörfer . Pfaffenweiler , 1986. xiv, 370 p. : ISBN 3-89085-124-X LC Card 87-134379 DDC 338.943/43 19
HD9621.G33 R463 1986

Reihe Japanwirtschaft .
(Heft 3) Frese, Dirk. Japan, Markt für deutsche Konsumgüter /. Düsseldorf [1978?] 32 p. : LC Card 85-242493
HF3568.J3 F74 1978

Reihe Oikos .
(Bd. 14) Hopf, Michael. Informationen für Märkte und Märkte für Informationen /. Frankfurt am Main , 1983. iv, 237 p. : ISBN 3-922182-14-3 : LC Card 84-180866
HB133 .H66 1983

(Bd. 17) Christians, Volker C. Neue Zahlungsverkehrsinstrumente . Frankfurt am Main , 1985. 216 p. ; ISBN 3-922182-17-8 : LC Card 86-100407
HG1710 .C48 1985

Reihe Personalwesen, Organisation, Unternehmungsführung .
(Bd. 1) Müller, Christoph, 1957- Organisatorische Gestaltung des Job Sharing in der Unternehmung . Köln , c1986. xiii, 404 p. ; ISBN 3-924361-12-6 LC Card 87-114139 DDC 331.25/72 19
HD5110.2.G3 M85 1986

(Bd. 2) Bethge, Hans, 1951- Die betriebliche Altersversorgung als Möglichkeit zur Deckung von Versorgungslücken in der gesetzlichen Rentenversicherung unter besonderer Berücksichtigung unternehmerischer Entscheidungsgrössen /. Köln , c1986. 269 p. ; ISBN 3-924361-16-9 LC Card 86-222067
HD7105.45.G3 B47 1986

Reihe Planung, Information und Unternehmungsführung .
(Bd. 1) Mayntz, Renate. Dokumentation und Organisation . Bergisch Gladbach , 1984. 132 p. : ISBN 3-89012-008-3 : LC Card 85-131112
HD30.3 .M394 1984

(Bd. 10) Walbrück, Hans-Jürgen, 1956- Entwicklung von branchen-spezifischen integrierten Bürokommunikationssystemen . Bergisch Gladbach , c1986. 368 p. : ISBN 3-89012-044-X : LC Card 86-174155
HF5547.5 .W345 1986

(Bd. 13) Schmidt-Prestin, Barbara, 1953- Bildschirmtext in Unternehmen . Bergisch Gladbach , c1986. xvi, 308 p. : ISBN 3-89012-064-4 LC Card 87-129114 DDC 651.8/0943 19
HD9696.T463 G365 1986

(Bd. 14) Fronhoff, Bernd, 1956- Die Gestaltung von Marketingstrategien . Bergisch Gladbach , 1986. ix, 369 p. : ISBN 3-89012-067-9 LC Card 87-122913 DDC 658.8/02 19
HF5415.135 .F76 1986

Reihe Planung, Organisation, Unternehmensführung .
(Bd. 1) Meyer, Petra. Die Entwicklung der Organisationswissenschaft im deutschsprachigen Raum . München , c1985. 309 p. : ISBN 3-924361-10-X LC Card 87-114143
HD70.E8 M48 1985

Reihe Politik-Informationen, 0173-0525.
Zwei Jahre Politik der Erneuerung . Bonn [1984] 110 p. : LC Card 85-180111
HC286.7 .Z865 1984

Reihe Sozialwissenschaften, 0177-2813 .
(Bd. 8) Heipel, Gerd. Nichtkapitalistische Produktionsverhältnisse und Konkurrenz . Pfaffenweiler , 1986. vii, 459 p. ; ISBN 3-89085-116-9 LC Card 86-171832
HD9199.B8 S22 1986

Reihe Steuer, Wirtschaft und Recht .
(Bd. 28) Schulte, Karl-Werner. Bilanzpolitik und Publizitätsverhalten deutscher Aktiengesellschaften . Bergisch Gladbach , c1986. xx, 553 p. : ISBN 3-89012-070-9 LC Card 87-122912 DDC 658.1/5/0943 19
HF5686.C7 S357 1986

(Bd. 4) Binz, Hans-Bert, 1954- Kritik an deutschen Wirtschaftsprüfern, ein Glaubwürdigkeitsproblem? . Bergisch Gladbach , 1984. ix, 325 p. : ISBN 3-89012-004-0 : LC Card 84-174776
HF5627 .B55 1984

(Bd. 9) Russ, Wolfgang, 1955- Der Anhang als dritter Teil des Jahresabschlusses . Bergisch Gladbach , 1984. xi, 332 p. : ISBN 3-89012-013-X : LC Card 85-195717
HF5681.B2 R817 1984

Reihe Unterhaltungsliteratur.
Loeliger, Walter. Sind Sie frei? . Basel , 1982. 99 p. : ISBN 3-85816-043-1 : LC Card 83-100470
HD8039.T162 L64 1982

Reihe Weltwirtschaft (Bonn, Germany)
Der Neue Protektionismus . Bonn , c1983. 195 p. : ISBN 3-87831-370-5 LC Card 83-198686
HF1756 .N58 1983

Wirtschaftskrieg oder Entspannung? . Bonn , c1984. 328 p. ; ISBN 3-87831-392-6 LC Card 84-251713
HF4050 .W57 1984

Reihe Wirtschaft und Beschäftigung .
(Bd. 3) Gewandelte Werte, erstarrte Strukturen . Bonn , c1985. ix, 329 p. : ISBN 3-87831-423-X LC Card 86-117688 DDC 330/.0943 19
HD8451 .G54 1985

Reihe Wirtschafts- und Rechtsgeschichte .
(Bd. 4) Gilles, Martina, 1956- Die Standortfrage in der Versicherungswirtschaft . Köln , c1987. xv, 309 p., [4] folded leaves of plates : ISBN 3-924361-26-6 LC Card 87-144415 DDC 368/.006 19
HG8618 .G55 1987

Reihe Wirtschaftswissenschaften .
(Bd. 6) Poppe, Jürgen. Mikroelektronik, Jobkiller oder Jobknüller? . Pfaffenweiler , 1984.

93 p. : ISBN 3-89085-027-8 : LC Card 85-129494
HD6331.2.G28 P66 1984

Reihe Wirtschaftswissenschaften (Pfaffenweiler, Breisgau-Hochschwarzwald, Germany) .
(Bd. 12) Lutz, Stefan. Die Körperschaftsteuer in der Europäischen Gemeinschaft . Pfaffenweiler , 1984. xii, 346 p. : ISBN 3-89085-037-5 : LC Card 85-142851
HD2753.E8 L87 1984

(Bd. 22) Faller, Eberhard. Zur Problematik der Zulässigkeit des Abweichens vom Grundsatz der Einzelerfassung und Einzelbewertung im aktienrechtlichen Jahresabschluss . Pfaffenweiler , 1985. xiv, 386 p. : ISBN 3-89085-078-2 : LC Card 86-140803
HF5681.S8 F34 1985

(Bd. 24) Pychlau, Matthias. Temporale Entwicklungstheorie /. Pfaffenweiler , 1986. viii, 79 p. ; ISBN 3-89085-110-X LC Card 87-409006 DDC 338.9 19
HD84 .P9 1986

(Bd. 26) Pastuszek, Rainer. Leading und Lagging kurzfristig variierbarer gruppeninterner Geldflüsse im Währungsrisikomanagement einer internationalen Unternehmung /. Pfaffenweiler , 1986. xvi, 275 p. : ISBN 3-89085-122-3 LC Card 87-128258 DDC 658.1/55 19
HG3851 .P295 1986

(Bd. 28) Friderichs, Hans. Lohndispersionen auf strukturierten Arbeitsmärkten . Pfaffenweiler , 1986. xvi, 404 p. : ISBN 3-89085-133-9 LC Card 87-134875 DDC 331.2/943 19
HD5029 .F75 1986

(Bd. 31) Pöhlmann, Helmut. Jahresabschlussprüfung auf Stichprobenbasis . Pfaffenweiler , 1987. xii, 187 p. ; ISBN 3-89085-142-8 LC Card 87-133413 DDC 657/.458 19
HF5668.25 .P64 1987

(Bd. 32) Reis, Karl Eugen. Fesseln für den Leviathan . Pfaffenweiler , 1987. xi, 338 p. ; ISBN 3-89085-159-2 LC Card 87-134876 DDC 336.973 19
HJ2381 .R356 1987

(Bd. 6) Poppe, Jürgen. Mikroelektronik, Jobkiller oder Jobknüller? . Pfaffenweiler , 1984. 93 p. : ISBN 3-89085-027-8 : LC Card 85-129494
HD6331.2.G28 P66 1984

Reihe Wirtschaftswissenschaften, 0253-1488 .
(Bd. 276) Kops, Manfred. Die regionalen Verteilungswirkungen des kommunalen Finanzausgleichs . Thun , c1983. xvii, 537, 259 p. : ISBN 3-87144-728-5 : LC Card 83-159176
HJ9493.5.N6 K66 1983

(Bd. 280) Walter, Herbert. Standortpolitik multinationaler Banken /. Thun , c1983. viii, 255 p. : ISBN 3-87144-737-4 : LC Card 83-159195
HG3881 .W273 1983

(Bd. 281) Weis, Hans Christian. Marketingkommunikation in der Investitionsgüterindustrie . Thun , c1983. v, 319, xxxix p. : ISBN 3-87144-741-2 : LC Card 83-159201
HF5415.123 .W45 1983

(Bd. 285) Kipshagen, Lothar. Die Planung von Distributionssystemen der Konsumgüterindustrie unter besonderer Berücksichtigung der Tourenauslieferung . Thun , c1983. v, 336 p. : ISBN 3-87144-748-X LC Card 83-185464
HF5415.6 .K56 1983

(Bd. 293) Kupitz, Rolf. Die Kreditwirtschaft als wettbewerbspolitischer Ausnahmebereich . Thun , c1983. 300 p. ; ISBN 3-87144-773-0 : LC Card 84-129435
HG3754.5.G3 K86 1983

(Bd. 300) Quick, Rolf H. Informationsprozesse auf spekulativen Märkten . Thun , c1984. vii, 291 p. : ISBN 3-87144-790-0 : LC Card 84-159793
HG3853 .Q53 1984

(Bd. 319) Riepe, Claudia. Produkteigenschaften und das Nachfrageverhalten von Konsumenten . Thun , c1984. 341 p. : ISBN 3-87144-841-9 LC Card 85-113523
HB801 .R45 1984

(Bd. 320) Langkamp, Peter. Die Erfassung von Carryover-Effekten im Marketing . Thun , c1984. 335 p. : ISBN 3-87144-844-3 : LC Card 85-113501
HF5415.3 .L36 1984

(Bd. 323) Michelbach, Roger. Probleme der Sanierung der Deutschen Bundesbahn durch die Änderung institutioneller Rahmenbedingungen /. Thun , c1984. xi, 450 p. : ISBN 3-87144-865-6 LC Card 85-137676
HE3080.D4 M53 1984

(Bd. 329) Offermann, Andreas. Projekt-Controlling bei der Entwicklung neuer Produkte /. Thun , c1985. 524 p. : ISBN 3-87144-885-0 LC Card 85-208022
HD69.N4 O36 1985

(Bd. 334) Schöll, Wolfgang. Konsumentenverhalten in der Bundesrepublik Deutschland 1958-1982 . Thun , c1985. 226, 70, [9] p. : ISBN 3-87144-900-8 (Deut. Bibl.) : LC Card 85-232693
HC290.5.C6 S35 1985

(Bd. 338) Stahl, Herbert. Clusteranalyse grosser Objektmengen mit problemorientierten Distanzmassen /. Thun , c1985. ii, vi, 323 p. : ISBN 3-87144-908-3 LC Card 86-112498
HA29.5.G4 S68 1985

(Bd. 344) Sandler, Christian Heinrich. Innovative Technologien im Vertrieb . Thun , c1986. xvii, 313 p. : ISBN 3-87144-926-1 LC Card 86-171131
HD9850.5 .S25 1986

Reihe Wirtschaftswissenschaften, 0253-1488 .
(Bd. 265) Winkelmann, Jürgen. Die Planung langfristiger Kosten . Thun , c1982. 281 p. : ISBN 3-87144-702-1 LC Card 83-129316
HD47 .W54 1982

(Bd. 272) Schäfer, Harald. Bilanzierung von Beteiligungen an assoziierten Unternehmen nach der Equity-Methode . Thun , c1982. xxiii, 428 p. ; ISBN 3-87144-714-5 LC Card 83-129280
HF5686.I6 S33 1982

(Bd. 302) Massat, Dieter. Die ökonomische Problematik von Zuweisungen an Kommunen /. Thun , c1984. vii, 321 p. : ISBN 3-87144-792-7 LC Card 84-183709
HJ1121 .M37 1984

Reihe Wissenschaft (Augsburg, Germany)
Schlager, Errol, 1950- Konjunkturzyklen . Augsburg , 1986. ii, 99 p. : ISBN 3-925274-08-1 LC Card 87-127445 DDC 338.5/42 19
HB3716 .S35 1986

Reihe Wissenschaft (Munich, Germany)
Nestone, Alberto. Protektionismus . München , c1984. 76 p. : ISBN 3-89019-108-8 LC Card 85-127389
HF1713 .N38 1984

Schmitz, Heinz. Vermeidung von Armut im Alter . München , c1983. 267 p. : ISBN 3-89019-099-5 LC Card 84-197886
HD7164 .S29 1983

Reihe "Zeitgeschehen"
Stange, Sabine. Kriegsvorbereitung im Hunsrück . Essen , 1985. 157, [35] p., [4] folded leaves of plates : ISBN 3-88474-409-7 : LC Card 86-148061
HC290.5.D4 S84 1985

Die Reihenfolge der Informationssuche von Konsumenten . Hertrich, Roland, 1954- Frankfurt am Main , New York , c1985. iv, 272 p. ; ISBN 3-8204-8594-5 LC Card 85-230707
HB801 .H43 1985

Reihlen, Helmut. Lauer, Karl Friedrich. Das Referenzbüro der Gemeinschaften /. [Dortmund?] , 1976. 76 p. ; LC Card 85-241026
HD30 .A7 Heft 171 T59.A1

Reilly, John W. Lush, Minnie. California real estate exam guide /. Chicago , c1987. p. cm. ISBN 0-88462-591-5 LC Card 87-3290 DDC 333.33/09794 19
HD266.C2 L87 1987

Reilly, Michael E., 1947- Law, Gordon T., 1945- A guide to information on closely held corporations /. Buffalo, N.Y. , c1986. p. cm. ISBN 0-9615917-1-4 : LC Card 86-32812 DDC 338.7/4/072073 19
HD2785 .L38 1986

Rein, Martin. Women in the social welfare labor market / Martin Rein. Berlin : Wissenschaftszentrum Berlin, [1985] 180 p. ; 30 cm. (Discussion papers / International Institute of Management, IIM, Labour Market Policy, 0722-673X . IIM/LMP 85-18) "December 1985." Includes bibliographical references. LC Card 86-213535 DDC 331.4/129136294 19
1. Women - Employment - Europe. 2. Women - Employment - United States. 3. Public service employment - Europe. 4. Public service employment - United States. 5. Manpower policy - Europe. 6. Manpower policy - United States. I. Series: Discussion papers (International Institute of Management. Labour Market Policy) , IIM/LMP 85-18. II. Title.
HD6134 .R45 1985

Reinarman, Craig. American states of mind : political beliefs and behavior among private and public workers / Craig Reinarman. New Haven : Yale University Press, c1987. x, 262 p. ; 25 cm. Bibliography: p. 243-254. Includes index. ISBN 0-300-03817-8 (alk. paper) LC Card 86-26752 DDC 330.12/2/0973 19
1. Trade regulation - United States - Public opinion. 2. Capitalism - United States - Public opinion. 3. Public opinion - United States. 4. Truck drivers - United States - Attitudes. 5. Social workers - United States - Attitudes. I. Title.
HD3616.U47 R1464 1987

Reinders, Judy A. Ross, Steven C. Understanding and using SuperCalc 3 /. St. Paul , c1987. xiii, 184, [27] p. : ISBN 0-314-30123-2 (pbk.) LC Card 86-32548 DDC 005.36/9 19
HF5548.4.S86 R67 1987

Reinecke, Heike. Schlieper, Andreas. 150 Jahre Ruhrgebiet . Düsseldorf , 1986. 224 p. : ISBN 3-590-18150-8 LC Card 86-231681
HC288.R8 S34 1986

Reinecke, Rainer. Bonk, Heinz. Rüstungspolitik und Arbeiterklasse . Berlin , 1986. 299 p. ; LC Card 86-174039
HC79.D4 B65 1986

Reineke, Ulrich, 1955- Segmentationstheorien des Arbeitsmarktes und Beschäftigungsniveau : eine Auseinandersetzung mit der theoretischen und empirischen Relevanz der Entkopplungshypothese / Ulrich Reineke. Frankfurt am Main ; New York : P. Lang, c1986. iv, 333 p. : ill. ; 21 cm. (Europäische Hochschulschriften. Reihe V, Volks- und Betriebswirtschaft, 0531-7339 . Bd. 743 = vol. 743 = vol. 743) Originally presented as the author's thesis (doctoral)--Universität-GH-Paderborn, 1984. Bibliography: p. 298-321. ISBN 3-8204-9671-8 LC Card 87-407583 DDC 331.12/0943 19
1. Labor supply. 2. Full employment policies. 3. Market segmentation. I. Series: Europäische Hochschulschriften. Reihe V, Volks- und Betriebswirtschaft , Bd. 743. II. Title.
HD5706 .R43 1986

Reiners, H. (Hartmut) Meifort, J. (Joachim) Arbeitsbedingungen von Linienbus- und Strassenbahnfahrern der Dortmunder Stadtwerke Aktiengesellschaft /. Dortmund , 1983. 137 p. : ISBN 3-88314-249-2 LC Card 83-204902
HD8039.T72 G36 1983

REINFORCED CONCRETE, FIBER.
Button, Joe W. Synthetic fibers in asphalt paving mixtures /. College Station, Tex. [1984] vi, 153 p. : LC Card 86-620835 DDC 380.5 s 625.8/5 19
HE203 .T43 no. 319-1F TA443.A7

Reinforced plastics : the next five years / Joseph Mongiello, project analyst. Stamford, Conn., U. S.A. : Business Communications Co., c1986. v, 136 leaves : ill. ; 29 cm. (Business opportunity report . P-055R) "March 1986"--T.p. verso. ISBN 0-89336-478-9 (pbk.) LC Card 87-167989 DDC 381/.45668494/0973 19
1. Fiber reinforced plastics industry - United States. 2. Market surveys - United States. I. Mongiello, Joseph. II. Series.
HD9662.F523 U57 1986

Reingold, Edwin M. Morita, Akio, 1921- Made in Japan . New York , c1986. viii, 309 p., [8] p. of plates : ISBN 0-525-24465-4 : LC Card 86-11479 DDC 338.7/6213/0924 B 19
HD9696.A3 J3658 1986
NYPL [JFE 86-5112]

Reinhold, Otto. Mehr, besser, billiger, aber wie? / Otto Reinhold. Berlin : Dietz, 1985. 80 p. : ill. (some col.) ; 23 cm. (Ökonomie aktuell) Bibliography: p. 80. LC Card 86-179312
1. Industrial management - Germany, East. 2. Germany, East - Economic policy. 3. Germany, East - Industries. I. Title. II. Series.
HD70.G22 R45 1985

Reininghaus, Wilfried. Quellen zur Geschichte des Deutschen Industrie- und Handelstages in Kammerarchiven, 1861 bis 1918 / Wilfried Reininghaus, Klara van Eyll ; Anne Hermann, Angela Toussaint, Jürgen Weise. Bonn : DIHT, 1986. 158 p. : 11 facsims. ; 24 cm. (DIHT-Materialien zur Geschichte) Cover title: Quellen. "DIHT-Arbeitskreis Kammerarchive/Dokumentation"--T.p. verso. Bibliography: p. 18-19. Includes indexes. ISBN 3-925925-01-5 LC Card 87-408272 DDC 354.430082/09 19
1. Deutscher Industrie- und Handelstag - History - Sources. 2. Boards of trade - Germany - History - Sources. I. Eyll, Klara van. II. Deutscher Industrie- und Handelstag. III. DIHT-Arbeitskreis Kammerarchive/Dokumentation. IV. Title. V. Title: Quellen. VI. Series.
HF308 .R343 1986

Reinsch, Anthony Ernest. Industrial cogeneration in Canada : prospects and perspectives / Anthony E. Reinsch and Ellen F. Battle. Calgary, Alta. : Canadian Energy Research Institute, [1987] xviii, 137 p. : ill. ; 22 cm. (Study / Canadian Energy Research Institute . no. 24) "March 1987." Bibliography: p.135-137. ISBN 0-920522-41-6 (pbk.) : LC Card 87-163062 DDC 333.79/3 19
1. Cogeneration of electric power and heat - Economic aspects - Canada. 2. Energy conservation - Canada. 3. Canadian Energy Research Institute. I. Battle, Ellen F. II. Series: Study / Canadian Energy Research Institute , no. 24. III. Title.
HD9685.C2 R45 1987

REINSURANCE.
International reinsurance . [New York, N.Y.?] , c1985. vii, 164 p. ; LC Card 85-214554 DDC 368/.012 19
HG8083 .I57 1985 ***NYPL [JLD 86-2530]***

REINSURANCE - LAW AND LEGISLATION.
International reinsurance . [New York, N.Y.?] , c1985. vii, 164 p. ; LC Card 85-214554 DDC 368/.012 19
HG8083 .I57 1985 ***NYPL [JLD 86-2530]***

REINSURANCE - UNITED STATES.
Catastrophic losses . Oak Brook, Ill. (1200 Harger Rd., Suite 222, Oak Brook 60521) , c1986. vi, 73 p. : LC Card 87-106114 DDC 368.1/22014/0973 19
HG9979.3 .C38 1986

Reintegração dos emigrantes portugueses . Ferreira, Eduardo de Sousa, 1936- [Lisbon] , 1984. xiv, 137 p. ; LC Card 86-132652
HD8380.5 .F47 1984

Reis, Karl Eugen. Fesseln für den Leviathan : die Steuerrevolte in den Vereinigten Staaten und die Problematik budgetärer Schranken / Karl Eugen Reis. Pfaffenweiler : Centaurus-Verlagsgesellschaft, 1987. xi, 338 p. ; 21 cm. (Reihe Wirtschaftswissenschaften, 0177-283X . Bd. 32) Includes English summary. Originally presented as the author's thesis (doctoral)--Johannes Gutenberg-Universität Mainz, 1986. Bibliography: p. 309-335. ISBN 3-89085-159-2 LC Card 87-134876 DDC 336.973 19
1. Tax and expenditure limitations - United States. 2. Real property tax - United States. 3. Tax and expenditure limitations - California. 4. Real property tax - California. I. Series: Reihe Wirtschaftswissenschaften (Pfaffenweiler, Breisgau-Hochschwarzwald, Germany) , Bd. 32. II. Title.
HJ2381 .R356 1987

Reis, Ulysses A. (Ulysses Alves) Educação & produtividade / Ulysses A. Reis, Aroldo Rodrigues, Elio Vieira. Salvador-BA : Fundação Emílio Odebrecht ; [Rio de Janeiro] : Forense Universitária, 1984. 184 p. : ill. ; 21 cm. Bibliography: p. 169-172. ISBN 85-85023-05-8 LC Card 87-130042 DDC 331.11/8/0981 19
1. Labor productivity - Brazil. 2. Education - Economic aspects - Brazil. I. Title. II. Title: Educação e produtividade.
HC190.L3 R45 1984

Reischl, Dennis K. Managing for Uncle Sam : the supervisor's handbook on labor relations in the Federal Government / by Dennis K. Reischl and Ralph R. Smith. Huntsville, Ala. : WordSmith, c1986. ix, 271 p. : ill. ; 21 cm. Includes index. ISBN 0-936295-01-5 (pbk.) : LC Card 87-115055 DDC 353.001/7 19
1. Trade-unions - Government employees - United States. 2. Employee-management relations in government - United States. I. Smith, Ralph R. (Ralph Russell), 1947-. II. Title.
HD8005.2.U5 R45 1986

Reisman, David A.
Alfred Marshall, progress and politics / David Reisman. New York : St. Martin's Press, 1987. vii, 499 p. ; 22 cm. Bibliography: p. 365-488. Includes index. ISBN 0-312-00773-6 : LC Card 87-4811 DDC 330.15/5 19
1. Neoclassical school of economics. 2. Marshall, Alfred, 1842-1924. I. Title.
HB98.2 .R44 1987

The economics of Alfred Marshall / David Reisman ; foreword by G.L.S. Shackle. New York : St. Martin's Press, 1986. ix, 433 p. ; 23 cm. Bibliography: p. 322-425. Includes index. ISBN 0-312-23430-9 : LC Card 85-22321 DDC 330.15/5 19
1. Neoclassical school of economics. 2. Marshall, Alfred, 1842-1924. I. Title.
HB98.2 .R45 1986

Reisner, Marc. Cadillac desert : the American West and its disappearing water / Marc Reisner. New York, N.Y., U. S.A. : Penguin Books, 1987, c1986. 582 p., [18] p. of plates : ill. ; 20 cm. Reprint. Originally published: New York, N.Y., U. S.A. : Viking, 1986. Bibliography: p. [419]-564. Includes index. ISBN 0-14-010432-1 (pbk.) : LC Card 87-7602 DDC 333.91/00978 19
1. Irrigation - Government policy - West (U. S.) - History. 2. Water resources development - Government policy - West (U. S.) - History. 3. Corruption (in politics) - West (U. S.) - History. I. Title.
HD1739.A17 R45 1987

Reiss-Schmidt, Stephan. Radverkehrskonzept Sprockhövel /. Essen , c1985. 55 p., [3] folded col. leaves of plates : ISBN 3-923494-51-3 LC Card 86-113993
HE5739.G3 R33 1985

Reiss, Winfried, 1941- Umwegproduktion und Positivität des Zinses : eine neo-österreichische Analyse / von Winfried Reiss. Berlin : Duncker & Humblot, c1981. 152 p. : ill. ; 24 cm. (Volkswirtschaftliche Schriften. Heft 312) The author's Habilitationsschrift, Universität Heidelberg. Bibliography: p. 150-152. ISBN 3-428-05009-6 LC Card 82-146836 DDC 332.8/2/0724 19
1. Interest and usury - Mathematical models. 2. Capital - Mathematical models. 3. Austrian school of economists. I. Title. II. Series.
HB539 .R423 1981 ***NYPL [JLE 86-2623]***

Reissig, Rolf. Die Sozialistische Gemeinschaft . Berlin , 1985. 238 p. ; LC Card 86-120025 DDC 337.1/1717 19
HC243.5 .S685 1985

Reisz, Terézia W. Érettségizettek a munkaerőpiacon /. Budapest , 1985. 124 p. ; ISBN 963-404-026-8 LC Card 87-409614
HD6276.H82 E73 1985

Reĭtman, L. I. (Leonid Il'ich) Rol' finansovo-kreditnogo mekhanizma v povyshenii ėffektivnosti obshchestvennykh zatrat . Moskva , 1984. 153 p. ; LC Card 86-113408
HG186.S55 R64 1984

REITs . Haight, G. Timothy. Chicago, Ill. , c1987. x, 227 p. : ISBN 0-917253-71-X : LC Card 87-2558 DDC 346.7304/37 347.306437 19
HG5095 .H33 1987

Reitsma, Feike. Denis, Pierre. L'ASEAN (Association des pays de l'Asie et du Sud-Est) . Ottignies, Louvain-la-Neuve [1981] 61 p., [3] leaves of plates : LC Card 86-204495
HC441 .D45 1981

Reizinho, Eduardo J. Costa (Eduardo José Costa) A adesão portuguesa à CEE : manual prático / Eduardo J. Costa Reizinho. Mem Martins, Portugal : Publicações Europa-América, c1985. 396 p. ; 18 cm. (Colecção Saber . 184) Bibliography: p. [395]-396. LC Card 86-205515
1. European Economic Community - Portugal. I. Title.
HC241.25.P6 R45 1985

Reke, Barnabás. Forgóeszköz-gazdálkodás a mezőgazdaságban / Reke Barnabás. Budapest : Mezőgazdasági Kiadó, 1986. 175 p. ; 20 cm. Bibliography: p. 170-[174]. ISBN 963-232-219-3 : LC Card 87-408500
1. Agricultural credit - Hungary. 2. Agriculture - Hungary - Finance. I. Title.
HD1440.H9 R45 1986

Reklam i satellit-tv . Holmlöv, Per Gunnar, 1951- Stockholm [1984] 147 p. ; ISBN 91-7258-183-2 : LC Card 84-229824
HF6146.T42 H64 1984

Reklama knig segodni͡a /. Bekleshov, Dmitriĭ. Moskva , 1986. 201 p. : LC Card 87-132362 DDC 659.1/90705 19
HF6161.B37 B44 1986

Rekomendat͡sii po ukreplenii͡u trudovoĭ i proizvodstvennoĭ distsipliny / [nauchnyĭ redaktor N.S. Gerasimchuk]. Kiev : [s.n.], 1984. 41 p. ; 21 cm. At head of title: Gosudarstvennyĭ komitet po trudu Ukrainskoĭ SSR. Ukrainskiĭ respublikanskiĭ sovet professional'nykh soi͡uzov. Institut ėkonomiki AN USSR. LC Card 86-181301
1. Labor discipline - Ukraine. I. Gerasimchuk, Nikolaĭ Semenovich. II. Gosudarstvennyĭ komitet po trudu Ukrainskoĭ SSR. III. Ukraïns'ka respublikans'ka rada profesiĭnykh spilok. IV. Instytut ekonomiky (Akademii͡a nauk Ukraïns'koï RSR).
HF5549.5.L3 R45 1984

Rekonstrukt͡sii͡a predprii͡atiĭ i ėffektivnost' proizvodstva /. Palamarchuk, Aleksandr Semenovich. Moskva , 1981. 62, [2] p. ; LC Card 81-179552
HD39.3 .P34 1981

Relación histórica de los contratiempos que ha sufrido la construcción de un ferro-carril á través de la República de Honduras, fracasos de los empréstitos pedidos al público para llevar á cabo esa empresa y principales dificultades que han sobrevenido á cada nueva combinación intentada para terminar la línea. Lóndres : Impr. de Clayton y Ca., 1875. vii, 94 p. ; 25 cm. LC Card 85-127957
1. Railroads - Honduras - Finance - History - 19th century.
HE2843 .R45 1875

Relaciones agrarias en el socialismo. Moscú : Redacción "Ciencias Sociales Contemporáneas", 1986. 223 p. ; 21 cm. (Serie "La Ciencia económica soviética" . 2) Title in colophon: Agrarnye otnoshenii͡a pri sot͡sializme. At head of title: Academia de Ciencias de la URSS, Consejo Científico de la AC de la URSS para Problemas Económicos, Sociales y Jurídicos del Complejo Agroindustrial. Bibliography: p. 209-[211] LC Card 87-126164
1. Agricultural industries - Soviet Union. 2. Agriculture and state - Soviet Union. I. Nauchnyĭ sovet po ėkonomicheskim, sot͡sial'nym i pravovym problemam APK (Akademii͡a nauk SSSR). II. Title: Agrarnye otnoshenii͡a pri sot͡sializme. III. Series.
HD9015.S652 R45 1986

Relaciones colectivas del trabajo en América Latina. Portuguese. As relações coletivas de trabalho na América Latina : um estudo de seus atores, suas diversas manifestações e seus conflitos, com especial referência ao setor privado / publicado sob a direção de Efrén Córdova ; [tradução de Maria Luiza Jacobson].Versão corr., aum. e atualizada. São Paulo : Editora LTr : OIT : 327 p. ; 23 cm. Translation of: Las Relaciones colectivas del trabajo en América Latina. Includes bibliographies. LC Card 87-151930 DDC 331/.098 19
1. Industrial relations - Latin America. I. Córdova, Efrén. II. Jacobson, Maria Luiza. III. International Labour Office. IV. Instituto Brasileiro de Relações do Trabalho. V. Title.
HD8110.5 .R3817 1985

Las relaciones de trabajos de las mujeres en zonas rurales . Martorelli, Horacio. Montevideo, Uruguay , 1981. 264 p. : LC Card 86-202374 DDC 331.4/83/09895 19
HD6132 .M375 1981

Las relaciones económicas México-Estados Unidos . Rama, Ruth. Miami, FL (Tamiami Trail, Miami 33199) [1984] 55 p. ; LC Card 85-226824
HD9014.M62 R36 1984

Las relaciones hispano-portuguesas y la integración europea /. Dauderstädt, Michael. Madrid [1987?] 36 p. ; ISBN 84-398-8593-8 LC Card 87-161277
HF1570.15.P8 D38 1987

As relações coletivas de trabalho na América Latina . Relaciones colectivas del trabajo en América Latina. Portuguese. São Paulo . 327 p. ; LC Card 87-151930 DDC 331/.098 19
HD8110.5 .R3817 1985

As relações dos Estados Unidos com as potências médias na América Latina, México e Brasil /. Hirst, Mônica. [Rio de Janeiro] , 1985. 48 leaves ; LC Card 87-143873 DDC 337.73072 19
HF1456.5.M6 H57 1985

Relações externas da economia do Rio Grande do Sul, 1949/79 /. Leite, Manoel Marques. [Porto Alegre] , 1985. 114 p. : ISBN 85-7025-097-5 : LC Card 87-104433 DDC 382/.098165 19
HF3409.R5 L45 1985

Relaţiile comerciale româno-engleze în contextul politicii orientale a Marii Britanii . Cernovodeanu, Paul. Cluj-Napoca , 1986. 404 p. ; LC Card 87-143711
HF3508.R6 C47 1986

Relating to the reinstatement of the general preferential tariff on imports of rubber footwear . Canada. Tariff Board. Ottawa, Canada , c1985. vi, 88 p. ; ISBN 0-660-11961-7 (pbk.) : LC Card 87-109471 DDC 382/.0971 s 382/.4568531/00971 19
HF1762 .A3 no. 161, pt. 1 HF2651.F757C22

Relation between education, employment, and productivity and their impact on education and labour market policies . Wagner, Karin. Berlin , Washington, DC , 1986. ix, 80 p. ; ISBN 92-825-6371-5 : LC Card 87-136255 DDC 331.12/042/0941 19
HD5715.5.G4 W35 1986

Relations between the European Community and the member states of the Association of South-East Asian Nations / rapporteur, Herbert Nierhaus ; co-rapporteur, Alma Williams. Brussels : European Community, Economic and Social Committee, [1986] 55 p. : ill. ; 30 cm. LC Card 87-135576 DDC 337.4059 19
1. European Economic Community countries - Foreign economic relations - Asia, Southeastern. 2. Asia, Southeastern - Foreign economic relations - European Economic Community countries. I. Nierhaus, Herbert. II. Williams, Alma. III. Economic and Social Committee of the European Community.
HF1532.5 .R46 1986

Les relations du Liban avec la Communauté économique européenne /. Mesropian, André. Beyrouth, Liban [between 1972 and 1984] 65 p. ; LC Card 84-196415
HF1583.9.Z4 E865 1972

RELATIONS, RACE. see **RACE RELATIONS.**

The Relationship between the GLC Housing Department, its tenants, and the public / by the Behavioural Science Unit and an interdepartmental working party. London : Greater London Council, c1977. iv, 107 p. ; 30 cm. (Research memorandum / Greater London Council, 0306-7203 . RM 503) ISBN 0-7168-0895-1 (pbk.) LC Card 87-107202
1. Public housing - England - London Metropolitan Area - Management. I. GLC Housing Dept. II. Greater London Council. Behavioural Science Unit. III. Series: Research memorandum (Greater London Council) , RM503.
HD7288.78.G72 L68 1977

Relationships between losses and vehicle density, 1982-84 models. Washington, D.C. (Watergate 600, Washington 20037) : Highway Loss Data Institute, c1985. 24 p. : ill. ; 28 cm. (Research report HLDI . A-25 (Oct. 1985)) Insurance special report / Highway Loss Data Institute LC Card 87-107842 DDC 368.5/72/00973 19
1. Insurance, Automobile - United States. 2. Traffic accidents - United States. I. Highway Loss Data Institute. II. Series: Research report HLDI , A-25.
HG9970.3 .R45 1985

Relative mobility in Texas cities, 1975 to 1984 /. Lomax, Timothy J. College Station, Tex. [1986] xiii, 30, 9 p. : LC Card 87-620994 DDC 380.5 s 388.4/1314/09764 19
HE203 .T43 no. 339-8 HE356.T4

Relatório da Comissão Especial de Automação Bancária. Brasília : Secretaria Especial de Informática, 1985. 304 p. : ill. ; 23 cm. LC Card 86-230558
1. Banks and banking - Brazil - Automation. 2. Banks and banking - Brazil - Data processing. I. Conselho Nacional de Informática e Automação (Brazil). Comissão Especial de Automação Bancária.
HG1709 .R35 1985

Relatório da Comissão Instaladora do Instituto de Gestão Financeira das Empresas Públicas . Instituto de Gestão Financeira das Empresas Públicas (Portugal). Comissão Instaladora. Lisboa , 1984. 81 p. ; LC Card 84-240299
HD4248 .I57 1984

Relatório de pesquisa (São Paulo (Brazil : State). Instituto de Economia Agrícola) .
(no. 84/14) Castanho Filho, Eduardo Pires. A questão energética /. São Paulo , 1984. 15 p. ; LC Card 86-159794
HD9502.A2 C385 1984

(no. 85/7) Disponibilidade de alimentos a nível regional no Estado de São Paulo, 1974-83 /. São Paulo , 1985. 75 p. ; LC Card 86-196482
HD9014.B83 S433 1985

(no. 85/9) Desgualdo Netto, Domingos. Aspectos agroeconômicos da soja /. São Paulo , 1985. 139 p. ; LC Card 86-158570
HD9235.S62 B74 1985

(no. 86/18) Tsunechiro, Alfredo. O desempenho dos mercados a termo . São Paulo , 1986. xi, 123 p. : LC Card 87-404554 DDC 332.64/4 19
HG6046 .T75 1986

(no. 86/9) Camargo, Ana Maria M. Pires de. Comportamento dos preços de olerícolas nos mercados atacadistas e fluxo de produção regional no Brasil, 1977-83 /. São Paulo , 1986. 79 p. : LC Card 87-403840 DDC 338.1/35/0981/61021 19
HD9220.B73 S263 1986

Relatorio dos trabalhos executados durante o anno de 1925 . Brazil. Inspectoria Federal de Obras contra as Seccas. Rio de Janeiro , 1926. xiv, 75 p. ; LC Card 85-186786
HD1696.B8 B73 1926

Relatório final /. Encontro de Trabalho sobre Descentralização dos Serviços Municipais (1983 : Rio de Janeiro, Brazil) [Rio de Janeiro] [1983] 60 leaves ; LC Card 84-160735
HD4634 .E53 1983

Relatório final da Subcomissão de Pesca da Comissão de Agricultura e Política Rural, durante a sessão legislativa de 1984. Brazil. Congresso Nacional. Câmara dos Deputados. Comissão de Agricultura e Política Rural. Subcomissão de Pesca. Brasília , 1985. 66 p. ; LC Card 86-203945
HD9464.B72 B64 1985

Relatório final do GTR/SFH. Brazil. Grupo de Trabalho para Reformulação do Sistema Financeiro da Habitação. Reformulação . [Brasília] , 1986. 94 leaves ; LC Card 87-144710 DDC 363.5/8 19
HD7323.A3 B7 1986

Relatório preliminar dos municípios de Mato Grosso / Estado de Mato Grosso, Gabinete de Planejamento e Coordenação do Governo do Estado, Assessoria de Informações Técnicas-AIT. [Cuiabá] : AIT, 1984. 404 p. ; 33 cm. Cover title. LC Card 85-202292
1. Mato Grosso, Brazil (State) - Economic conditions. 2. Mato Grosso (Brazil : State) - Social conditions. 3. Mato Grosso (Brazil : State) - Administrative and political divisions. I. Mato Grosso (Brazil : State). Gabinete de Planejamento e Coordenação. Assessoria de Informações Técnicas.
HC188.M3 R45 1984

Relatorios provinciaes. Rio Grande do Sul (Brazil) [1850-1859] 19 pamphlets in 1 v. ; LC Card 84-217966
HD4635.R54 R56 1850

Relazione programmatica delle partecipazioni statali per il 1984 : allegata, ai sensi dell'articolo 15 della legge 5 agosto 1978, n. 468, alla relazione previsionale e programmatica per l'anno 1984. Roma : Instituto poligrafico e Zecca dello Stato, 1985. 563 p. ; 29 cm. At head of title: Ministero delle partecipazioni statali. LC Card 86-176014
1. Industrial promotion - Italy. 2. Industry and state - Italy. 3. Italy - Economic policy. 4. Italy - Commercial policy. 5. Economic assistance, Domestic - Italy. 6. Subsidies - Italy. I. Italy. Ministero delle partecipazioni statali.
HC310.I53 R45 1985

Le relazioni industriali di tipo sovietico . Grancelli, Bruno, 1943- Milano, Italy , c1986. 337 p. ; LC Card 86-222589
HD8526.5 .G73 1986

Relazioni industriali nell'impresa degli anni '80 : analisi di alcuni casi aziendali sull'interazione tra cambiamento economico, tecnologico, organizzativo e sistemi di relazioni industriali. Roma : Istituto per lo sviluppo della formazione professionale dei lavoratori, 1985. 308 p. ; 24 cm. (Quaderni di formazione ISFOL, 0390-3532 . n. 3/85 (maggio giugno 1985)) Cover title. Bibliography: p. 287. LC Card 86-192682
1. Industrial relations - Italy. I. Istituto per lo sviluppo della formazione professionale dei lavoratori. II. Series: Quaderni di formazione ISFOL , n. 85/3.
HD8481 .R45 1985

Releasemania, uma contribuição para o estudo do press-release no Brasil /. Lima, Gerson Moreira, 1952- São Paulo, SP , c1985. 114 p. : LC Card 85-184576 DDC 659.2 19
HM263 .L478 1985 ***NYPL [JFD 86-2728]***

Relevance . Sperber, Dan. Oxford [Oxfordshire] , 1986. viii, 279 p. : ISBN 0-631-13756-4
NYPL [JFE 86-1728]

RELEVANCE.
Sperber, Dan. Relevance . Oxford [Oxfordshire] , 1986. viii, 279 p. : ISBN 0-631-13756-4 ***NYPL [JFE 86-1728]***

Relevance lost . Johnson, H. Thomas, 1938- Boston, Mass. , c1987. xiii, 269 p. ; ISBN 0-87584-138-4 LC Card 86-29474 DDC 658.1/511/09 19
HF5605 .J64 1987

Die Relevanz nicht-tarifärer Handelshemmnisse im internationalen Handel und ihre Wirkungen auf die Integration der Entwicklungsländer in die Weltwirtschaft /. Ohlinger, Hans A., 1954- Frankfurt am Main , New York , c1986. iii, 400 p. : ISBN 3-8204-8344-6 LC Card 87-407585 DDC 382/.5/091724 19
HF1430 .O38 1986

RELIEF (AID) see **PUBLIC WELFARE; CHARITIES.**

RELIGION AND POLITICS - CONGRESSES.
Morality of the market . Vancouver, B.C., Canada , c1985. xxv, 601 p. ; ISBN 0-88975-074-2 (pbk.) : LC Card 86-158049 DDC 174/.4 19
HB72 .M56 1985

RELIGION AND POLITICS - GERMANY (WEST) - MATHEMATICAL MODELS.
Wirtschaftlicher Wandel, religiöser Wandel und Wertwandel . Berlin , c1985. 411 p. : ISBN 3-428-05784-8 LC Card 85-218417
HC286.7 .W58 1985

RELIGION AND SOCIAL PROBLEMS. see **CHURCH AND SOCIAL PROBLEMS; RELIGION AND SOCIOLOGY.**

RELIGION AND SOCIETY. see **RELIGION AND SOCIOLOGY.**

RELIGION AND SOCIOLOGY - CONGRESSES.
Morality of the market . Vancouver, B.C., Canada , c1985. xxv, 601 p. ; ISBN 0-88975-074-2 (pbk.) : LC Card 86-158049 DDC 174/.4 19
HB72 .M56 1985

RELIGION - ECONOMIC ASPECTS - INDIA - CONGRESSES.
Indien, Probleme eines Schwellenlandes . Tübingen , c1984. 75 p. ; ISBN 3-922362-02-8 LC Card 85-157722
HC435.2 .I6235 1984

RELIGION - PHILOSOPHY.
Vance, A. Last chance for peace . Boulder, Colo. , c1985. xviii, 256 p. : ISBN 0-930705-01-7 (pbk.) : LC Card 84-18831 DDC 172/.24 19
BL65.P4 V36 1985 ***NYPL [JLD 86-2214]***

RELIGIOUS SOCIOLOGY. see **RELIGION AND SOCIOLOGY.**

Rello, Fernando.
Arroyo, Gonzalo. Agricultura y alimentos en América Latina . México, D.F. , 1985. 267 p. ; ISBN 968-8373-33-8 LC Card 86-208283
HD9014.L32 A77 1985

Estado y ejidos en México : el caso del crédito rural en La Laguna / Fernando Rello ; introducción de Cynthia Hewitt de Alcántara.1a ed. Ginebra : Instituto de Investigaciones de las Naciones Unidas para el Desarrollo Social, 1986. xxvi, 122 p. : 1 map ; 21 cm. (Informe . no. 85.2) Includes bibliographical references. LC Card 86-210274
1. Agricultural credit - Mexico - Laguna Region. 2. Ejidos - Mexico - Laguna Region. 3. Agriculture and

state - Mexico - Laguna Region. I. United Nations. Research Institute for Social Development. II. Series: Report / United Nations Research Institute for Social Development , no. 85.2. III. Title.
HG2051.M62 L37 1986

The relocating spouse's guide to employment . Bastress, Frances. Chevy Chase, Md. , c1987. xviii, 258 p. : ISBN 0-937623-01-6 (pbk.) : LC Card 87-16045 DDC 650.1/4 19
HF5382.7 .B375 1987

Relocation Resources (Firm) Selling your home for the best price in the shortest time . [Norwell, Mass.] , c1986. 48 leaves : LC Card 87-150628 DDC 333.33/8 19
HD1379 .S36 1986

Remaking the World Bank /. De Vries, Barend A. Washington, DC , Lanham, Md. , c1987. xvi, 184 p. ; ISBN 0-932020-49-6 (pbk.) LC Card 87-23406 DDC 332.1/532 19
HG3881.5.W57 D4 1987

The Remarkables and Hector mountains, Otago, New Zealand : a management study. Dunedin, N.Z. : Published for the Land Settlement Board by the Dept. of Lands & Survey, 1977. 215 p., [9] leaves of plates (some folded) : ill. (some col.), maps (some col.) ; 30 cm. Cover title: Remarkables and Hector mountains, Otago, N.Z. "March 1977." Two folded maps inserted. LC Card 85-115616
1. Land use surveys - New Zealand - Remarkables, The, Region. 2. Land use surveys - New Zealand - Hector Mountains Region. 3. Land use - New Zealand - Remarkables, The, Region - Planning. 4. Land use - New Zealand - Hector Mountains Region - Planning. I. New Zealand. Land Settlement Board. II. New Zealand. Dept. of Lands and Survey.
HD1120.5.Z8 R457 1977

Remmele, Werner. Arbeitsplätze morgen /. Stuttgart , c1986. 431 p. : ISBN 3-519-02446-2 LC Card 86-171663
HD6331 .A695 1986

Remmes Lenicov, Jorge. La industria curtidora en Argentina : cueros vacunos. [Buenos Aires] : Ministerio de Economía, Secretaría de Estado de Programación y Coordinación Económica, Instituto Nacional de Planificación Económica, Dirección Nacional de Planeamiento de los Sectores Productores de Bienes, Departamento Industria, 1976. 46 leaves ; 30 cm. Cover title. LC Card 86-157645
1. Leather industry and trade - Argentina. I. Instituto Nacional de Planificación Económica. Departamento Industria. II. Title.
HD9780.A52 R45 1976

REMODELING OF BUILDINGS. see **BUILDINGS - REPAIR AND RECONSTRUCTION.**

REMODELING OF BUILDINGS FOR OTHER USE. see **BUILDINGS - REMODELING FOR OTHER USE.**

Rémond, Bruno. Soisson, Jean Pierre, 1934- L'enjeu de la formation professionnelle /. [Paris] , c1986. iv, 315 p. : ISBN 2-213-01752-2 : LC Card 86-194690
HD5715.5.F8 S65 1986

REMOTE FACSIMILE DUPLICATOR. see **FACSIMILE TRANSMISSION.**

Remote sensing and tropical land management / edited by M.J. Eden and J.T. Parry. [New York] : J. Wiley, c1986. xii, 365 p., [16] p. of plates : ill. (some col.) ; 24 cm. Based on papers presented at a workshop of the Commonwealth Geographical Bureau hosted by McGill University, Montreal, Aug. 20-27, 1983. Includes bibliographical references and index. ISBN 0-471-90889-4 : LC Card 85-17932 DDC 333.73/13/028 19
1. Land use - Remote sensing - Congresses. 2. Land use - Tropics - Congresses. I. Eden, M. J. (Michael John). II. Parry, J. T. (John T.). III. Commonwealth Geographical Bureau.
HD108.8 .R45 1986 ***NYPL [JLE 87-943]***

REMOTE SENSING - GOVERNMENT POLICY - UNITED STATES.
Commercial newsgathering from space. Washington, DC [1987] ix, 51 p. : LC Card 87-619818 DDC 070.4/3 19
HE9721.U5 C65 1987

REMOTE TERRAIN SENSING. see **REMOTE SENSING.**

Removal of price supports and supply controls for U. S. tobacco . Sumner, Daniel A. (Daniel Alan), 1950- Demoines, Iowa , Washington, D.C. , c1985. viii, 64 p. ; ISBN 0-89068-084-1 LC Card 85-63194 ***NYPL [JLF 86-1014]***

REMSCHEID (GERMANY) - ECONOMIC CONDITIONS.
Lindmüller, Peter. Remscheid und Solingen im industriegeographischen Entwicklungsvergleich /. Bochum , 1986. 423 p. : ISBN 3-88339-544-7 LC Card 87-146590 DDC 330.943/55 19
HC289.R38 L56 1986

REMSCHEID (GERMANY) - INDUSTRIES - HISTORY.
Lindmüller, Peter. Remscheid und Solingen im industriegeographischen Entwicklungsvergleich /. Bochum , 1986. 423 p. : ISBN 3-88339-544-7 LC Card 87-146590 DDC 330.943/55 19
HC289.R38 L56 1986

Remscheid und Solingen im industriegeographischen Entwicklungsvergleich /. Lindmüller, Peter. Bochum , 1986. 423 p. : ISBN 3-88339-544-7 LC Card 87-146590 DDC 330.943/55 19
HC289.R38 L56 1986

Remuneration in Eastern European countries /. Mikheev, S. Geneva , 1985. vi, 45, ix p. ; ISBN 92-9014-408-4 (pbk.) : LC Card 86-216036 DDC 331.2/947 19
HD5014 .M55 1985

R'emy, Ernst. La diplomatie : vers la coexistence dans la paix Ernest R'emy. Port-au-Prince : Impr. H. Deschamps, 1983. 299 p. ; 21 cm. Bibliography: p. [294]-299.
1. Diplomacy. 2. World politics. I. Title.
NYPL [Sc D 85-315]

Remyga, V. N. (Vladimir Nikolaevich) Sistema upravleniia promyshlennost'iu KNR, 1949-1980 / V.N. Remyga. Moskva : Izd-vo "Nauka," Glav. red. vostochnoĭ lit-ry, 1982. 189, [3] p. ; 20 cm. At head of title: Akademiia nauk SSSR. Institut Dal'nego Vostoka. Bibliography: p. 181-[190] LC Card 82-180587
1. Industrial management - China - History. I. Title.
HD70.C5 R45 1982

Remz, Carol L. Remz it! : a simple method for developing inexpensive & effective training / Carol L. Remz. Seattle, Wash. : Human Resource Connections, c1987. 1 v. (various pagings) ; 30 cm. ISBN 0-941999-01-7 (loose-leaf) LC Card 87-80592 DDC 658.3/12404 19
1. Employees, Training of. I. Title. II. Title: Simple method for developing inexpensive & effective training.
HF5549.5.T7 R374 1987

Remz it! . Remz, Carol L. Seattle, Wash. , c1987. 1 v. (various pagings) ; ISBN 0-941999-01-7 (loose-leaf) LC Card 87-80592 DDC 658.3/12404 19
HF5549.5.T7 R374 1987

Renault, Susan Stetson. Faaborg, Barbara Laue. Job resources for Colorado women . Colorado Springs, CO , c1986. 128 p. : ISBN 0-939411-00-8 (pbk.) : LC Card 87-103489 DDC 650.1/4/024042 19
HF5382.65 .F33 1986

Renberg, Werner. Making money with mutual funds : investment strategies to beat the market / Werner Renberg, Jeremiah Blitzer. New York : Wiley, c1988. xviii, 217 p. : ill. ; 24 cm. Includes bibliographical references and index. ISBN 0-471-85555-3 LC Card 87-26366 DDC 332.63/27 19
1. Mutual funds. I. Blitzer, Jeremiah. II. Title.
HG4530 .R46 1988

Renckstorf, Karsten. Landesprogramme von Hörfunk und Fernsehen in Hamburg : eine empirische Studie zur Weiterentwicklung regionaler Programmangebote / Karsten Renckstorf, Alex Ehmcke. Hamburg : Verlag Hans-Bredow-Institut, c1985. xlvii, vi, 388 p. : ill. ; 21 cm. (Forschungsberichte und Materialien . Bd. 7) Bibliography: p. 265-268. ISBN 3-87296-067-9 (pbk.) LC Card 86-109817 DDC 384.54/43/0943515 19
1. Television programs - Germany (West) - Hamburg. 2. Radio programs - Germany (West) - Hamburg. I. Ehmcke, Alex. II. Title. III. Series.
HE8700.9.G4 R45 1985 ***NYPL [MWGK (Germany, West) 86-4239]***

A Renda da terra : acumulação, uso do solo, progresso técnico e poder político : universidade, economia e poder : planejamento, estado e grande empresa / L.C.B. Pereira ... [et al.]. [São Paulo, Brazil] : CEBRAP ; Petrópolis : Distribuição, Editora Vozes, c1980. 152 p. : ill. ; 21 cm. (Estudos CEBRAP . no. 27) Cover title. Includes bibliographical references. CONTENTS. - Notas intempestivas sobre a questão da universidade, I / José Arthur Giannotti -- Notas intempestivas sobre a questão da universidade, II / Francisco de Oliveira e Wanderley J. Borges -- Notas críticas sobre a relação entre rendas fundiárias e uso do solo urbano / Paulo Vieira da Cunha e Martim O. Smolka -- Renda diferencial, renda absoluta e progresso técnico na agricultura ricardiana / Antônio C. Sechaczewski e José Serra -- Estrutura agrária e democracia na América Latina / Vinícius Caldeira Brant -- Estado e planejamento no Brasil, 1974/1976 / Sebastião C. Velasco e Cruz -- Licões do aprendiz de feiticeiro ou tecnoburocracia e empresa monopolista / Luiz C. Bresser Pereira. LC Card 81-214665
1. Rent (Economic theory). 2. Universities and colleges - Brazil. 3. Agriculture - Latin America. 4. Planning - Brazil. 5. Bureaucracy. 6. Business enterprises. I. Pereira, Luiz Carlos Bresser. II. Centro Brasileiro de Análise e Planejamento. III. Series.
HC186 .C36a no. 27 HB401

Rendé, Josep M. Pla d'organització social agrària de Catalunya / per Josep M. Rendé. Barcelona : Mancomunitat de Catalunya, 1924. 138 p., [1] folded leaf of plates : col. map ; 22 cm. (Arxius dels serveis tècnics d'agricultura . fasc. 3) LC Card 86-202164 DDC 334/.683/09467 19
1. Agriculture, Cooperative - Spain - Catalonia. 2. Cooperative societies - Spain - Catalonia. 3. Agriculture - Spain - Catalonia - Societies, etc. I. Title. II. Series.
HD1491.S82 C317 1924

Rendeiro, João Oliveira. Progresso técnico e evolução estratégica na indústria de máquinas-ferramentas : implicações para Portugal / João Oliveira Rendeiro. Lisboa : Banco de Fomento Nacional, 1985. 111 p. : ill. ; 24 cm. (Estudos (Banco de Fomento Nacional) . 24) Bibliography: p. [107]-111. LC Card 86-189891
1. Machine-tool industry - Europe. 2. Machine-tool industry - Japan. 3. Machine-tool industry - Portugal. I. Series. II. Series: Estudos (Banco de Fomento Nacional) , 24. III. Title.
HD9703.E92 R45 1985

Rendell, John. An economic survey of intensive bush cider orchards, 1972-1981 : results of a survey carried out in the South West Midlands and South-Western England over the period 1972 to 1981 / J. Rendell. [Reading, Berks.] : University of Reading, Dept. of Agricultural Economics & Management, [1984] 24 p. : ill. ; 30 cm. (Miscellaneous study / University of Reading, Dept. of Agricultural Economics & Management . no. 72) "March 1984." Includes bibliographical references. ISBN 0-7049-0814-X (pbk.) : LC Card 85-111963 DDC 338.1/74117 19
1. Cider industry - England. 2. Orchards - England. I. Series: Miscellaneous study / University of Reading, Dept. of Agricultural Economics & Management , no. 72. II. Title.
HD9398.G83 E57 1984

RENDENCIÓN PAMPA (BOLIVIA) - SOCIAL CONDITIONS.
Estudio cultural y socio económico de Mojocoya--Redención Pampa. Estudio cultural socio económico, Mojocoya y Redención Pampa. Sucre, Bolivia , 1979. 266 p. : LC Card 83-204567
HC183.M65 E77 1979

Rendimientos de beneficiado de café . Cléves S., Rodrigo. San José, Costa Rica , 1986. 35 leaves : LC Card 87-403521 DDC 338.1/6 19
HD9199.C82 C57 1986

Rendszerkutatási tanulmányok, 0139-2352 . (3) Kockázat és társadalom /. Budapest , 1987. 309 p. : ISBN 963-05-4450-4 : LC Card 87-425562
HD61 .K6 1987

Renegociación de la deuda externa, 1985 / Banco Central de la República Dominicana. Santo Domingo, República Dominicana : El Banco, 1985. iv, 168 p. ; 28 cm. Prefatory material in Spanish and English; text in English. LC Card 86-186407
1. Debts, External - Dominican Republic. 2. Loans, Foreign - Dominican Republic. 3. Paris Club. 4. Debt relief - Dominican Republic. I. Banco Central de la República Dominicana.
HJ8548 .R46 1985

Renesse, Ernst Albrecht von. Partnerschaftliche Entwicklungspolitik im Widerstreit der Interessen . Bochum-Querenburg , 1985. i, 184 leaves ; LC Card 87-409475 DDC 332.6/7343/01724 19
HG5993 .P37 1985

Renewable Energy Institute. Fenn, Scott. Institutional investment in renewable energy technologies /. Washington, D.C. , c1987. iii, 50 p. : ISBN 0-930135-17-1 (pbk.) LC Card 87-401940 DDC 332.6/722 19
HD9502.U52 F46 1987

RENEWABLE ENERGY SOURCES.
Kristoferson, Lars A. Renewable energy technologies . Oxford [Oxfordshire] , New York , 1986. xviii, 319 p. : ISBN 0-08-034061-X : LC Card 86-766 DDC 621.042 19
TJ808 .K75 1986 ***NYPL [JSG 87-45]***

Worldwide remote power sites. New York, N.Y. , c1983. 2 v. (xx, xxvii, 500 p.) : LC Card 87-141748
HD9695.A2 W67 1983

RENEWABLE ENERGY SOURCES - AFRICA, WEST.
Busacker, Dietrich. Energies à la mesure des villages . Bielefeld, Federal Republic of Germany , 1985. 21 leaves ; LC Card 85-160345
HD9502.A4993 B87 1985

RENEWABLE ENERGY SOURCES - BRAZIL - CONGRESSES.
Opções energéticas . Belo Horizonte, MG , 1983. 328 p., [30] leaves of plates : LC Card 83-205480
HD9502.B72 O63 1983

RENEWABLE ENERGY SOURCES - BRAZIL - ECONOMETRIC MODELS.
Santos, José Carlos de Souza. Demanda de fatores, energia e substituição na indústria brasileira, 1970/79 /. São Paulo , 1986. 183 p. : LC Card 86-234783
HB241 .S26 1986

RENEWABLE ENERGY SOURCES - CONGRESSES.
All India Seminar on Renewable Sources of Energy (1982 : Allahabad, India) All India Seminar on Renewable Sources of Energy, Allahabad, 20th and 21st October '82 . Allahabad [1982] 1 v. (various pagings) : LC Card 84-911087 ***NYPL [JSF 86-685]***

ENERGEX '84 (1984 : Regina, Sask.) Energy developments . Toronto , New York , 1984. xxiv, 1026 p. : ISBN 0-08-025407-1 LC Card 85-122124 DDC 333.79 19
TJ163.15 .E46 1984 ***NYPL [JSF 86-799]***

IASTED Symposia on Modelling, Policy and Economics of Energy and Power Systems, and Alternative Energy Sources and Technology (1981 : San Francisco, Calif.) Proceedings of the IASTED Energy Symposia : Modelling, Policy and Economics of Energy and Power Systems [and] Alternative Energy Sources and Technology, May 20-22, 1981, San Francisco, U. S.A. /. Anaheim, Calif. [1981?] 209 p. : ISBN 0-88986-027-0 ***NYPL [JSF 86-1103]***

RENEWABLE ENERGY SOURCES - DEVELOPING COUNTRIES.
Kristoferson, Lars A. Renewable energy technologies . Oxford [Oxfordshire] , New York , 1986. xviii, 319 p. : ISBN 0-08-034061-X : LC Card 86-766 DDC 621.042 19
TJ808 .K75 1986 ***NYPL [JSG 87-45]***

RENEWABLE ENERGY SOURCES - DEVELOPING COUNTRIES - CASE STUDIES.
Socioeconomic aspects of renewable energy technologies . New York , 1988. p. cm. ISBN 0-275-92851-9 (alk. paper) : LC Card 87-22890 DDC 333.7/09172/4 19
HD9502.D442 S63 1988

RENEWABLE ENERGY SOURCES - DOMINICAN REPUBLIC.
Vidal, Máximo Luis. El fin de la era del petróleo y su impacto sobre la economía mundial . San Pedro de Macorís, R.D. , 1981. 103 p. : LC Card 82-202556
HD9502.5.A433 D658 1981

RENEWABLE ENERGY SOURCES - GREAT BRITAIN.
Britain's energy resources /. London , 1981. 27 p. : ISBN 0-11-701010-3 (pbk.) LC Card 81-165936 DDC 333.79/0941 19
HD9502.G72 B74 1981

RENEWABLE ENERGY SOURCES - INDIA - CONGRESSES.
All India Seminar on Renewable Sources of Energy (1982 : Allahabad, India) All India Seminar on Renewable Sources of Energy, Allahabad, 20th and 21st October '82 . Allahabad [1982] 1 v. (various pagings) : LC Card 84-911087 ***NYPL [JSF 86-685]***

RENEWABLE ENERGY SOURCES - JUVENILE LITERATURE.
Gibson, Michael, 1942- The energy crisis /. Vero Beach, FL , 1987. 46 p. : ISBN 0-86592-277-2 LC Card 87-12768 DDC 333.79 19
HD9502.A2 G525 1987

RENEWABLE ENERGY SOURCES - RESEARCH - UNITED STATES - FINANCE.
Fenn, Scott. Institutional investment in renewable energy technologies /. Washington, D.C. , c1987. iii, 50 p. : ISBN 0-930135-17-1 (pbk.) LC Card 87-401940 DDC 332.6/722 19
HD9502.U52 F46 1987

RENEWABLE ENERGY SOURCES - SWEDEN.
Sweden. Oljeersättningsdelegationen. Statligt stöd till oljeersättning . [Stockholm] [1983] 1 v. (various pagings) : ISBN 91-38-07657-8 LC Card 84-218524
HD9502.S82 S96 1983

RENEWABLE ENERGY SOURCES - UNITED STATES.
Cogan, Douglas. Generating energy alternatives . Washington, D.C. , c1987. xi, 358 p. : ISBN 0-931035-16-3 (pbk.) LC Card 87-403993 DDC 333.79 19
HD9685.U5 C588 1987

Energy economics . Englewood Cliffs, N.J. , c1987. viii, 328 p. : ISBN 0-13-277245-0 : LC Card 86-25254 DDC 333.79/0973 19
HD9502.U52 E4874 1987

Van der Ryn, Sim. Sustainable communities . San Francisco [1986] xvii, 238 p. : ISBN 0-87156-800-4 LC Card 83-4676 DDC 307/.14 19
HN90.C6 V36 1986 ***NYPL [JLF 86-1241]***

RENEWABLE ENERGY SOURCES - UNITED STATES - FINANCE.
Fenn, Scott. Institutional investment in renewable energy technologies /. Washington, D.C. , c1987. iii, 50 p. : ISBN 0-930135-17-1 (pbk.) LC Card 87-401940 DDC 332.6/722 19
HD9502.U52 F46 1987

Renewable energy technologies . Kristoferson, Lars A. Oxford [Oxfordshire] , New York , 1986. xviii, 319 p. : ISBN 0-08-034061-X : LC Card 86-766 DDC 621.042 19
TJ808 .K75 1986 ***NYPL [JSG 87-45]***

RENEWABLE NATURAL RESOURCES.
Krelle, Wilhelm. Wachstum bei Erschöpfbaren Ressourcen, gibt es das? . Münster , c1982. 59 p. : ISBN 3-402-04434-X LC Card 83-215135
HC55 .K74 1982

RENEWABLE NATURAL RESOURCES - PACIFIC ISLANDS (TRUST TERRITORY) - MANAGEMENT.
Integrated renewable resource management for U. S. insular areas. Washington, DC [1987] vi, 443 p. : LC Card 86-600595 DDC 333.7 19
HC154.5 .I58 1987

RENEWABLE NATURAL RESOURCES - PUERTO RICO - MANAGEMENT.
Integrated renewable resource management for U. S. insular areas. Washington, DC [1987] vi, 443 p. : LC Card 86-600595 DDC 333.7 19
HC154.5 .I58 1987

RENEWABLE NATURAL RESOURCES - UNITED STATES.
Morandi, Larry B. Renewing resources . Denver, Colo. , 1984. vii, 133 p. ;
NYPL [JSF 86-712]

RENEWABLE NATURAL RESOURCES - VIRGIN ISLANDS OF THE UNITED STATES - MANAGEMENT.
Integrated renewable resource management for U. S. insular areas. Washington, DC [1987] vi, 443 p. : LC Card 86-600595 DDC 333.7 19
HC154.5 .I58 1987

The renewal factor . Waterman, Robert H. Toronto , New York , 1987. xiv, 338 p. ; ISBN 0-553-05226-8 LC Card 87-18662 DDC 658.4/06 19
HD58.8 .W387 1987

Renewing resources . Morandi, Larry B. Denver, Colo. , 1984. vii, 133 p. ;
NYPL [JSF 86-712]

Renn, Ortwin. Technik auf dem Prüfstand . Essen , Gräfelfing [1982] 183 p. : ISBN 3-7736-0340-1 LC Card 83-187518
HD9698.G42 T43 1982

RENNELL ISLAND (SOLOMON ISLANDS) - ECONOMIC CONDITIONS.
Infrastructural survey report for the development of the alumina resources in Rennell Island, Solomon Islands. [S.l.] [1976] xv, 321 p. : LC Card 84-230135
HC684.Z7 R455 1976

Rennhoff, Harley A. Get that business loan : convince your banker to say "yes" / Harley A. Rennhoff. Gretna, La. : Pelican Pub. Co., 1987. viii, 163 p. ; 22 cm. ISBN 0-88289-602-4 LC Card 87-2245 DDC 658.1/5224 19
1. Small business - Finance. 2. Loans. I. Title.
HG4027.7 .R46 1987

Le Renouvellement du tissu industriel : rapport du Groupe de stratégie industrielle no 11 / président du groupe, Philippe Demaegdt ; vice-présidents, François Reingold et François Cantegreil [et] Daniel Houri ; rapporteurs, Francis Merrien, Bernard Roy, avec la collaboration de Sylvie Cauet. Paris : Documentation française, [1986] 130 p. ; 30 cm. (Plan . 10) At head of title: Plan, Commissariat général du plan [et] Ministère d'Etat chargé du plan et de l'aménagement du territoire [et] Ministère du redéploiement industriel et du commerce extérieur. "Janvier 1986." ISBN 2-11-001568-3 : LC Card 86-191910
1. Industry and state - France. 2. Industrial promotion - France. 3. Technological innovations - France. I. Demaegdt, Philippe. II. Merrien, Francis. III. Roy, Bernard. IV. Cauet, Sylvie. V. France. Groupe de stratégie industrielle no 11. VI. France. Commissariat général du plan. VII. Series: Plan (France. Commissariat général du plan) 10.
HD3616.F83 R46 1986

Renovación .
(11) López Díaz, Pedro. Crítica de la economía y la política /. México , 1985. 255 p. ; ISBN 968-590-060-4 LC Card 86-156378
HB501 .L856 1985

RENOVATION OF BUILDINGS FOR OTHER USE. see **BUILDINGS - REMODELING FOR OTHER USE.**

Renshaw, Geoffrey. Adjustment and economic performance in industrialised countries : a synthesis / Geoffrey Renshaw. Geneva : International Labour Office, 1986. xiv, 180 p. ; 24 cm. (Employment, adjustment, and industrialisation, 0257-3415 . 8) Includes bibliographies. ISBN 92-2-105510-8 (pbk.) : LC Card 87-123435 DDC 338.9/009172/2 19
1. Germany, West - Economic policy - 1974-. 2. Japan - Economic policy - 1945-. 3. Great Britain - Economic policy - 1945-. 4. Netherlands - Economic policy. 5. Germany, West - Industries. 6. Japan - Industries. 7. Great Britain - Industries. 8. Netherlands - Industries. I. Title. II. Series.
HC286.7 .R46 1986

Rent. Renta . Moskva , 1984. 95 p. : LC Card 85-192538
HB401 .R48 1984

RENT AND EVICTION CONTROL. see **RENT CONTROL.**

RENT CHARGES - GERMANY (WEST)
Fuhrich, Manfred, 1950- Sicherung des Sozialmietwohnungsbestandes /. Frankfurt am Main , c1986. xxiii, 180, 16 p. : ISBN 3-88129-996-3 LC Card 86-223886
HD7288.78.G3 F84 1986

Rent control /. Albon, Robert, 1951- London ; New York : xi, 128 p. : ISBN 0-7099-5411-5 LC Card 87-15899 DDC 363.5/6/0941 19
HD7288.85.G7 A4 1987

RENT CONTROL - GERMANY (WEST)
Eucker-Herresthal, Waltraud. Staatliche

Eingriffe in den Mietwohnungsmarkt, Erfolgskontrolle und Reformvorschläge /. [Mainz] [1985?] v, 242 p. ; LC Card 87-407601 DDC 363.5/8 19
HD7288.85.G3 E92 1985

RENT CONTROL - GREAT BRITAIN.
Albon, Robert, 1951- Rent control /. London ; New York : xi, 128 p. : ISBN 0-7099-5411-5 LC Card 87-15899 DDC 363.5/6/0941 19
HD7288.85.G7 A4 1987

RENT (ECONOMIC THEORY)
Dämpfling, Björn, 1949- Die Marxsche Theorie der Grundrente . Hamburg , 1985. 161 p. ; ISBN 3-87975-302-4 LC Card 86-172913
HB401 .D35 1985

The Political economy of rent-seeking /. Boston , c1988. xvi, 492 p. : ISBN 0-89838-241-6 LC Card 87-16887 DDC 333/.012 19
HB401 .P64 1988

A Renda da terra . [São Paulo, Brazil] , Petrópolis , c1980. 152 p. : LC Card 81-214665
HC186 .C36a no. 27 HB401

Rudolph, Günther. Karl Rodbertus (1805-1875) und die Grundrententheorie . Berlin , 1984. 332 p. ; LC Card 84-158301
HB401 .R83 1984

Solé, Miguel José. Las condiciones de vida y de trabajo de los tamberos de la pampa húmeda . Stockholm , 1983. 33 p. ; LC Card 84-107283
HD1865.P35 S65 1983

Vieira, Cláudio Afonso. Urbanização e custo de reprodução da força de trabalho /. São Paulo , 1984. 175 p., [5] folded leaves ; LC Card 85-136502
HD5755.S3 V54 1984

RENT (ECONOMIC THEORY) - MATHEMATICAL MODELS.
Renta . Moskva , 1984. 95 p. : LC Card 85-192538
HB401 .R48 1984

RENT - JURISPRUDENCE. see **RENT CONTROL.**

RENT REGULATION. see **RENT CONTROL.**

RENT RESTRICTIONS. see **RENT CONTROL.**

RENT SUBSIDIES - CALIFORNIA - LOS ANGELES.
Aroni, Samuel. How successful was Section 8 in Los Angeles? . Berkeley , 1986. 18 p. ; ISBN 0-87772-311-7 (pbk.) LC Card 86-27180 DDC 363.5/8 19
HD7288.85.U62 L73 1986

RENT SUBSIDIES - GERMANY (WEST)
Eucker-Herresthal, Waltraud. Staatliche Eingriffe in den Mietwohnungsmarkt, Erfolgskontrolle und Reformvorschläge /. [Mainz] [1985?] v, 242 p. ; LC Card 87-407601 DDC 363.5/8 19
HD7288.85.G3 E92 1985

RENT SUBSIDIES - UNITED STATES.
Guggenheim, Joseph. HUD's rental rehabilitation program, HUD's housing development grant program /. Washington, D.C. [c1984] 13 p. ; LC Card 87-100358 DDC 363.5/8 19
HD7288.85.U6 G84 1984

Hammond, Claire Holton, 1951- The benefits of subsidized housing programs . Cambridge [Cambridgeshire] , New York , 1987. ix, 140 p. ; ISBN 0-521-32752-0 LC Card 86-32638 DDC 363.5/8 19
HD7288.83 .H36 1987

Renta : problemy teorii, izmereniīa i funktsionirovaniīa v khoziaĭstvennom mekhanizme sotsialisticheskoĭ ėkonomiki / [otvetstvennye redaktory S.S. Shatalin, V.G. Grebennikov]. Moskva : Vses. nauchno-issl. in-t sistemnykh issledovaniĭ, 1984. 95 p. : ill. ; 27 cm. (Sbornik trudov . vyp. 10) Title on verso t.p.: Rent. Includes bibliographies. LC Card 85-192538
1. Rent (Economic theory) - Mathematical models. 2. Marxian economics. I. Shatalin, S. S. (Stanislav Sergeevich). II. Grebennikov, Valeriĭ Grigor'evich. III. Title: Rent. IV. Series: Sbornik trudov (Vsesoiūznyĭ nauchno-issledovatel'skiĭ institut sistemnykh issledovaniĭ) , 1984, vyp. 10.
HB401 .R48 1984

La renta de la tierra en Castilla la Vieja y León (1836-1913) /. Robledo Hernández, Ricardo. [Madrid] [1984?] 245 p. : ISBN 84-505-0885-1 LC Card 87-104999
HJ4375.C27 R63 1984

Rentabilität, Produktivität, Liquidität der Unternehmung . Weber, Helmut Kurt, 1933- Stuttgart , c1983. x, 161 p. ; ISBN 3-7910-0346-1 LC Card 83-167883
HG4026 .W4 1983

Rentabilität und Risiko im Kreditgeschäft der Banken . Wiegel, Klaus Dieter. Köln , c1985. 342 p. : ISBN 3-87951-125-X LC Card 87-140074 DDC 332.1/753 19
HG1641 .W54 1985

Rentabilitätsrisiken aus dem Hypothekargeschäft von Kreditinstituten in Zeiten der Geldentwertung /. Dieckhöner, Bruno. Wiesbaden , c1984. xi, 395 p. : ISBN 3-409-14002-6 : LC Card 85-119494
HG2040.5.G4 D53 1984

RENTAL HOUSING.
Prosser, Larry. For rent by owner /. New York , 1987. xii, 217 p. : ISBN 0-531-15526-9 LC Card 87-16206 DDC 333.33/8 19
HD1394 .P77 1987

RENTAL HOUSING - AUSTRIA - VIENNA - COSTS.
Czasny, Karl. Erfassung des Wohnungsangebotes /. Wien , 1985. 284 p. ; ISBN 3-900551-04-9 LC Card 87-103427 DDC 333.33/8 19
HD7337.V3 C93 1985

RENTAL HOUSING - GERMANY (WEST) - MANNHEIM - FINANCE - CASE STUDIES.
Ipsen, Detlev. Markt und Raum . Frankfurt , New York , c1986. 250 p. : ISBN 3-593-33685-5 LC Card 87-127593 DDC 363.5/8 19
HD7339.M35 I67 1986

RENTAL HOUSING - GOVERNMENT POLICY - GERMANY (WEST)
Eucker-Herresthal, Waltraud. Staatliche Eingriffe in den Mietwohnungsmarkt, Erfolgskontrolle und Reformvorschläge /. [Mainz] [1985?] v, 242 p. ; LC Card 87-407601 DDC 363.5/8 19
HD7288.85.G3 E92 1985

RENTAL HOUSING - GOVERNMENT POLICY - NEW YORK (STATE)
New York (State). Division of Housing and Community Renewal. Special needs housing demonstration program report. New York, N.Y. (2 World Trade Center, New York 10047) [1984] 1 v. (various foliations) : LC Card 86-622827 DDC 363.5/8 19
HD7288.85.U62 N754 1984

RENTAL HOUSING - GOVERNMENT POLICY - UNITED STATES.
Gilderbloom, John Ingram. Rethinking rental housing /. Philadelphia , 1987. p. cm. ISBN 0-87722-498-6 (alk. paper) LC Card 87-1958 DDC 363.5/8 19
HD7288.85.U6 G55 1987

RENTAL HOUSING - GREAT BRITAIN.
Public housing . London , Wolfeboro, N.H. , c1987. 174 p. : ISBN 0-7099-4826-3 : LC Card 86-24056 DDC 363.5/8 19
HD7288.78.G7 P83 1987

RENTAL HOUSING - MANAGEMENT.
Prosser, Larry. For rent by owner /. New York , 1987. xii, 217 p. : ISBN 0-531-15526-9 LC Card 87-16206 DDC 333.33/8 19
HD1394 .P77 1987

RENTAL HOUSING - NEW YORK (N.Y.) - HISTORY - 20TH CENTURY.
The Tenant movement in New York City, 1904-1984 /. New Brunswick, N.J. , c1986. xiv, 289 p. : ISBN 0-8135-1203-4 (pbk.) : LC Card 85-27894 DDC 333.33/8 19
HD7288.85.U62 N58 1986 ***NYPL [JLE 86-4565]***

RENTAL HOUSING - NEW ZEALAND - CHRISTCHURCH.
The Private residential landlord and tenant in Christchurch . Wellington, N.Z. [1986] viii, 105 p. : ISBN 0-477-03810-7 (pbk.) LC Card 87-147647 DDC 333.33/8 19
HD7288.85.N452 C576 1986

RENTAL HOUSING - NEW ZEALAND - COSTS.
Brooks, R. Inflation, tax rules, and housing in New Zealand /. Wellington, N.Z. [1986] 22, [22] p. : LC Card 87-132461 DDC 363.5/8 19
HD7387.5.A3 B76 1986

RENTAL HOUSING - PORTUGAL - EVORA.
Inquérito às rendas e a outras características das habitações arrendadas na cidade de Evora em 1955-56 /. Lisboa [1958] 26 p. : LC Card 85-185037
HA1571 .A32 no. 33 HD7288.85.P82E93

RENTAL HOUSING - UNITED STATES.
United States. Dept. of Housing and Urban Development. Office of Policy Development and Research. Division of Policy Studies. The conversion of rental housing to condominiums and cooperatives . [Washington, D.C.] , 1982. 95 p. : ***NYPL [JLF 86-442]***

RENTAL HOUSING - UNITED STATES - FINANCE.
Guggenheim, Joseph. HUD's rental rehabilitation program, HUD's housing development grant program /. Washington, D.C. [c1984] 13 p. ; LC Card 87-100358 DDC 363.5/8 19
HD7288.85.U6 G84 1984

RENTAL INDUSTRIES. see **LEASE AND RENTAL SERVICES.**

RENTAL SERVICES. see **LEASE AND RENTAL SERVICES.**

Rente et structures des industries de l'énergie / Jean-Pierre Angelier ... [et al.]. [Saint-Martin-d'Hères] : Presses universitaires de Grenoble, 1983. 268 p. : ill. ; 25 cm. ("Energie et société", 0338-6120) Includes bibliographies. CONTENTS. - Rente minière, prix et marchés des ressources naturelles non renouvelables / Gérard Gaudet -- Réexamen de la théorie marxiste de la rente gazière / Laurent Benzoni -- La théorie de la rente dans un cadre néo-ricardien / Francis Bidault -- Rente gazière et économie internationale du gaz naturel / Christian Christeller -- Histoire de la concurrence entre énergies fossiles et construction de la rente pétrolière / Jean-Claude Werrebrouck -- "Juste prix" du pétrole, concurrence et complémentarité entre énergies / Jean-Pierre Angelier -- Structure de l'industrie pétrolière et répartition de la rente / Francis Bidault. ISBN 2-7061-0217-9 : LC Card 84-173320
1. Power resources - Prices. I. Angelier, Jean Pierre. II. Series. III. Series: Énergie et societé.
HD9502.A2 R45 1983 ***NYPL [JLE 87-1263]***

Renten zweitausend. Renten 2000 . München , c1985. 124 p. : ISBN 3-7892-7267-1 LC Card 87-118239 DDC 331.25/2/0943 19
HD7105.35.G3 R46 1985

Renten 2000 : längerfristige Finanzierungsprobleme der Alterssicherung und Lösungsansätze / Beiträge von Willi Albers ... [et al.] ; herausgegeben im Auftrag der Akademien von Peter Hampe. München : G. Olzog, c1985. 124 p. : ill. ; 24 cm. (Akademiebeiträge zur politischen Bildung . Bd. 14) Papers presented at a conference held in 1985 and sponsored by Evangelische Akademie Tutzing and Akademie für Politische Bildung Tutzing. CONTENTS. - Langfristprobleme der gesetzlichen Rentenversicherung / Helmut Meinhold -- Demographische Entwicklung und Finanzierung der Alterssicherung / Heinz Grohmann -- Die gesetzliche Rentenversicherung / Rudolf Kolb -- Gesamtwirtschaftliche Gründe für eine Reform der Rentenversicherung / Ernst-Moritz Lipp -- Grundversorgung und private Alterssicherung / Meinhard Miegel -- Zum Vorschlag "Grundversorgung und private Alterssicherung" / Walter Wellner -- Harmonisierung von Sozialleistungen / Willi Albers -- Exkurs, Betriebliche Altersversorgung in der Bundesrepublik Deutschland. ISBN 3-7892-7267-1 LC Card 87-118239 DDC 331.25/2/0943 19
1. Old age pensions - Germany (West) - Congresses. I. Albers, Willi. II. Hampe, Peter. III. Evangelische Akademie (Tutzing, Germany). IV. Akademie für Politische Bildung (Tutzing, Germany). V. Title: Renten zweitausend. VI. Series.
HD7105.35.G3 R46 1985

Rentenfinanzierung und Rentenbesteuerung . Weise, Herbert. Kiel , 1978. iii, 64 leaves ; LC Card 85-188549
HJ4720.A7 W45 1978

Die Rentenkrise /. Merklein, Renate. Reinbek bei Hamburg , 1986. 190 p. : ISBN 3-499-33072-5 : LC Card 87-100842
HD7105.35.G3 M47 1986

Die Rentenversorgung der Arbeiter und Angestellten in der DDR /. Püschel, Herbert. Berlin , c1986. 206 p. ; ISBN 3-7303-0068-7 LC Card 87-408895 DDC 331.25/2/09431 19
HD7180.5 .P87 1986

Renuka Mukerji Ray. see **Ray, Renuka Mukerji, 1903-**

Renzo, D. J. de. see **De Renzo, D. J.**

REORGANIZATION OF CORPORATIONS. see **CORPORATE REORGANIZATIONS.**

Reorientação da assistência à saúde no âmbito da previdência social . Fonseca, Aloysio de Salles. [Brasília] , 1983. 67 p. ; LC Card 86-171863
HD7102.B7 F66 1983

Re-orientation of industrial policies : studies undertaken for ad-hoc group of ministers of industry. [Bangkok] : Economic and Social Commission for Asia and the Pacific, [1979. iii, 196 p. ; 24 cm. Includes bibliographical references. LC Card 83-187259
1. Industry and state - Asia. 2. Industry and state - Oceania. 3. Industry and state - Bangladesh. 4. Industry and state - Papua New Guinea. 5. Industry and state - Philippines. 6. Industry and state - Thailand. I. United Nations. Economic and Social Commission for Asia and the Pacific.
HD3616.A772 R46 1979

REPAIRING TRADES - NEW YORK (STATE) - CASE STUDIES.
Harper, Douglas A. Working knowledge . Chicago , 1987. x, 214 p. : ISBN 0-226-31688-2 LC Card 86-30708 DDC 302.3/4 19
HD4904 .H335 1987

Repartição da renda . Singer, Paul Israel, 1932- Rio de Janeiro , 1986. 95 p. ; ISBN 85-85061-40-5 : LC Card 86-157852
HC190.I5 S56 1986

Reparto Guía Postal y Telegráfica (Spain)
Catálogo de tarifas postales y telegráficas. Madrid [1964?] 256, [42] p. : LC Card 85-106223
HE8277 .C37 1964

Repères pour négocier. Quéinnec, Y. (Yvon) Le travail posté . [Toulouse-Le Mirail] , 1985. 261 p. : ISBN 2-85816-030-9 LC Card 87-133427
HD5111.5 .Q45 1985

Répertoire . Organisation for Economic Co-operation and Development. Development Centre. Paris , Washington, D.C. , 1986. xxiv, 523 p. ; ISBN 92-64-02872-2 : LC Card 87-146730
HD77.5.A34 O75 1986

Répertoire administratif du Ministère de l'énergie et des ressources. Québec (Province). Ministère de l'Énergie et des ressources. Québec [1984?] 111 p. ; LC Card 84-222485
HD9502.C33 Q444 1984

Répertoire des organismes de commerce d'etat des pays en développement. Handbook of state trading organizations of developing countries =. New York , 1985. clxxxix, 542 p. : ISBN 92-1-012014-0 (pbk.) LC Card 86-233995
HF1009.7.D44 H35 1985

Répertoire financier et fiscal du Cameroun : 1986-1987. Le Vésinet, France : EDITM, [1987?] 147 p. ; 30 cm. Includes related legislation. LC Card 87-124445
1. Finance, Public - Cameroon. 2. Economic assistance - Cameroon. 3. Taxation - Cameroon. 4. Finance, Public - Law and legislation - Cameroon. 5. Taxation - Law and legislation - Cameroon. I. EDITM (Firm).
HJ1489 .R46 1987

Répertoire financier et monétaire du Sénégal, 1985. Le Vésinet, France : EDITM, [1985?] ii, 98 leaves ; 30 cm. Bibliography: leaf [1] LC Card 86-202435
1. Budget - Senegal. 2. Money - Senegal. 3. Senegal - Economic conditions. 4. Senegal - Economic policy. 5. Finance, Public - Senegal. I. EDITM (Firm).
HJ2184.5 .R46 1985

Répertoire "Les entreprises du Brabant Flamand." Adresboek "Bedrijven in Vlaams-Brabant" =. Vilvoorde , 1985. lxi, 186, 62, 63 p. : LC Card 87-111619
HC317.B7 A37 1985

Repertorio de las organizaciones comerciales estatales de países en desarrollo. Handbook of state trading organizations of developing countries =. New York , 1985. clxxxix, 542 p. : ISBN 92-1-012014-0 (pbk.) LC Card 86-233995
HF1009.7.D44 H35 1985

Repetto, Robert C.
Paying the price : pesticide subsidies in developing countries / Robert Repetto. Washington, DC : World Resources Institute, c1985. 33 p. ; 28 cm. (Research report, 0880-2582 . 2) "December 1985." Bibliography: p. 18. ISBN 0-915825-12-0 (pbk.) : LC Card 86-225070 DDC 338.4/366865/091724 19
1. Pesticides policy - Developing countries. 2. Pesticides - Environmental aspects - Developing countries. 3. Agricultural subsidies - Developing countries. 4. Agriculture and state - Developing countries. I. Series: Research report (World Resources Institute) , #2. II. Title.
HC59.72.E5 R46 1985

World enough and time : successful strategies for resource management Robert Repetto. New Haven : Yale University Press, c1986. xiv, 147 p. ; 22 cm. Includes bibliographical references and index. ISBN 0-300-03648-5 LC Card 85-20180 DDC 333.7 19
1. Natural resources - Management. 2. Population policy. 3. Quality of life. I. Title.
HC59 .R43 1986 ***NYPL [JLD 86-1434]***

Repida, A. V. (Afanasiĭ Vasil'evich) Burlaku, I. N. Sindikatele Moldoveĭ sovetiche yn konstruktsii͡a sochialistė /. Kishinėu , 1980. 148 p. ; LC Card 81-135331
HD6735.M56 B87 1980

REPLACEMENT OF INDUSTRIAL EQUIPMENT.
Ėkonomicheskai͡a ėffektivnost' rekonstruktsii deĭstvui͡ushchikh predprii͡atiĭ /. Sverdlovsk , 1981. 171 p. ; LC Card 83-192125
HD39.3 .E37 1981

Li͡akh, L. V. (Lidii͡a Vasil'evna) Planovoe regulirovanie vozmeshchenii͡a orudiĭ truda v promyshlennosti /. Kiev , 1983. 122, [1] p. : LC Card 84-105177
HD39.3 .L53 1983

Report /. Barbados. Duffus Commission of Enquiry. [Bridgetown, Barbados] [1978] vi, 118, 270 p. : LC Card 82-243628 DDC 354.7298/10072 19
HJ2073.B37 B37 1978 ***NYPL [JLG 86-221]***

Report /. Radio Broadcasting to Cuba (Organization). Advisory Board. Washington, D.C. (400 6th St., S.W., Washington 20547) , 1986. [16] p. ; LC Card 87-110428 DDC 384.54/46 19
HE8697.45.C9 R33 1986

Report / United Nations Research Institute for Social Development .
(no. 84.1) Barrera, Manuel. Trade unions and the state in the present day Chile . Geneva, Switzerland , Santiago, Chile , 1986. xx, 154 p. : LC Card 87-128364 DDC 331.89/0983 19
HD6617 .B273 1986

(no. 84.1) Barrera, Manuel. Sindicatos y estado en el Chile actual . Geneva, Switzerland , Santiago, Chile , c1985. v, 196 p. : LC Card 87-118607
HD6617 .B27 1985

(no. 84.1) Barrera, Manuel. Trade unions and the state in the present day Chile . Geneva, Switzerland , Santiago, Chile , 1986. xx, 154 p. : LC Card 87-128364 DDC 331.89/0983 19
HD6617 .B273 1986

(no. 85.2) Rello, Fernando. Estado y ejidos en México . Ginebra , 1986. xxvi, 122 p. : LC Card 86-210274
HG2051.M62 L37 1986

Report (Australia. Parliament. Joint Committee of Public Accounts) .
(246) Australia. Parliament. Joint Committee of Public Accounts. Income maintenance programs . Canberra , 1986. viii, 49 p. ; ISBN 0-644-04993-6 (pbk.) LC Card 86-234535 DDC 362.5/82 19
HC610.I5 A95 1986

(253) Australia. Parliament. Joint Committee of Public Accounts. Proposed computer acquisition by the Australian Audit Office /. Canberra , 1986. xiii, 256 p. : ISBN 0-644-05079-9 (pbk.) LC Card 86-234536 DDC 354.940072/32 19
HJ9931 .A875 1986

Report (Australian Academy of Science. Science and Industry Forum) .
(no. 20) An Industrial research and development and marketing package for Australia . [Canberra?] [1984] 48, 4 leaves : LC Card 87-153477 DDC 338/.06 19
HC610.T4 I53 1984

Report (Biomedical Business International, Inc.) .
(#3111) Marketing communications effectiveness to the dentist. Tustin, CA (17722 Irvine Blvd., Tustin 92680) , c1986. 130 leaves in various foliations : LC Card 86-231569 DDC 681/.761 19
HD9995.D43 U55 1986

(#3112) Sales representative effectiveness to the dentist. Tustin, CA (17722 Irvine Blvd., Tustin 92680) , c1986. 113 leaves in various foliations : LC Card 86-231841 DDC 681/.761 19
HD9995.D43 U56 1986

(#3251) Strategic marketing of hospital pharmacy products. Tustin, CA, U. S.A. (17722 Irvine Blvd., Tustin 92680) , c1986. iii leaves, 2, 12, 134, 111 p. : LC Card 87-149442 DDC 380.1/456151 19
HD9665.5 .S77 1986

(#3261) Strategic marketing of surgical products. Tustin, CA, U. S.A. (17722 Irvine Blvd., Tustin 92680) , c1987. 1 v. (various foliations) : LC Card 87-168617 DDC 380.1/45681761 19
HD9995.S92 S77 1987

(#3291) Strategic marketing of oncology products /. Tustin, CA, U. S.A. (17722 Irvine Blvd., Tustin 92680) , c1987. 242 p. in various pagings : LC Card 87-402026 DDC 381/.45681761 19
HD9995.C353 U67 1987

(#7013) Patient monitoring disposables and equipment for critical care. Tustin, CA (17722 Irvine Blvd., Tustin 92680) , c1986. 1 v. (various foliations) : LC Card 86-203049 DDC 381/.45681761 19
HD9995.M653 U657 1986

(#7021) Catheter devices for interventional cardiology, angiography, and radiology--U. S. and international. Tustin, CA, U. S.A. (17722 Irvine Blvd., Tustin 92680) , c1987. 1 v. (various foliations) : LC Card 87-168823 DDC 381/.45681761 19
HD9995.C383 U628 1987

(#7026) Nerve, muscle, bone stimulation, and augmentation. Tustin, CA, U. S.A. (17722 Irvine Blvd., Tustin 92680) , c1987. iv, 8, 144, [112] p. : LC Card 87-402023 DDC 338.4/7681761 19
HD9995.E43 U56 1987

(#7027) Cardiovascular therapy market . Tustin, CA, U. S.A. (17722 Irvine Blvd., Tustin 92680) , c1987. 1 v. (various foliations) ; LC Card 87-402037 DDC 380.1/45681761 19
HD9995.C363 U62 1987

(#7040) U. S. clinical testing market /. Tustin, CA, U. S.A. (17722 Irvine Blvd., Tustin 92680) , c1987. 223 leaves in various foliations ; LC Card 87-402039 DDC 381/.45681761 19
HD9995.L33 U5484 1987

(#7042) Sensors and transducers for biomedical applications. Tustin, CA, U. S.A. (17722 Irvine Blvd., Tustin 92680) , c1987. 1 v. (various foliations) : LC Card 87-403749 DDC 381/.45681761 19
HD9995.T733 U675 1987

(#7045) Noninvasive cardiovascular and cardiorespiratory diagnostic devices (U. S. and international). Tustin, CA (17722 Irvine Blvd., Tustin 92680) , c1986. 1 v. (various pagings) : LC Card 87-101739 DDC 380.1/45681761 19
HD9995.C363 U65 1986

(#7062) Urology and incontinence products /. Tustin, CA (17722 Irvine Blvd., Tustin 92680) , c1986. 1 v. (various foliations) : LC Card 86-235104
HD9995.U742 U76 1986a

(#7070) Growth areas in dentistry . Tustin, CA (17722 Irvine Blvd., Tustin 92680) , c1986. 1 v. (various foliations) : LC Card 86-212546 DDC 381/.45681761 19
HD9995.D42 G76 1986

(#7075) Specimen collection and transport market. Tustin, CA, U. S.A. (17722 Irvine

Blvd., Tustin 92680) , c1987. 1 v. (various foliations) : LC Card 87-402105 DDC 380.1/45681761 19
HD9995.L32 S64 1987

(#7079) Top emerging private companies. Tustin, CA, U. S.A. (17722 Irvine Blvd., Tustin 92680) , c1987. iv, 8, 144, [112] leaves : LC Card 87-402028 DDC 681/.761/029473 19
HD9994.U52 T66 1987

(#7088) Alternate site clinical testing. Tustin, CA, U. S.A. (17722 Irvine Blvd., Tustin 92680) , c1987. 167 leaves in various foliations : LC Card 87-402110 DDC 381/.45681761 19
HD9995.L33 U5412 1987

(#7096) Maximizing sales to hospital national accounts /. Tustin, CA, U. S.A. (17722 Irvine Blvd., Tustin 92680) , c1987. 524 p. in various pagings : LC Card 87-401688 DDC 681/.761/0688 19
HD9994.U52 M39 1987

(7050) Anesthesiology products and marketplace. Tustin, CA, U. S.A. (17722 Irvine Blvd., Tustin 92680) , c1987. 1 v. (various foliations) : LC Card 87-142979 DDC 381/.45681761 19
HD9995.A532 A54 1987

Report by the Advisory Board for Radio Broadcasting to Cuba. Radio Broadcasting to Cuba (Organization). Advisory Board. Washington, D.C. (400 6th St., S.W., Rm. 3850, Washington 20547) , 1986. [20] p. : LC Card 87-402533 DDC 384.54/4 19
HE8698 .R27 1986

Report (Calcutta Metropolitan Development Authority) .
(44) An Approach to economic renewal and promotion programme . [Calcutta] , 1977. 55 leaves ; LC Card 83-908562 DDC 338.954/14 19
HC438.C3 A66 1977

Report (California. Dept. of Finance. Program Evaluation Unit) .
(no. D85-2) California. Dept. of Finance. Program Evaluation Unit. The Conservation and Liquidation Division, Department of Insurance /. [Sacramento, Calif.] [1985] xii, 62 p. ; LC Card 85-622857 DDC 353.97940082/55 19
HG8538.C2 C35 1985

Report (Canada. Energy, Mines and Resources Canada) .
(ER78-2) Oil and natural gas industries in Canada, 1978. [Ottawa] , c1978. viii, 104 p. : LC Card 85-187299
HD9574.C22 O39 1978

Report (Canadian Transport Commission. Research Branch) .
(no. 1985/06E) Lin, Leesha. U. S. essential air services study /. Ottawa-Hull , c1986. viii, 118 p. : ISBN 0-662-14800-2 (pbk.) LC Card 87-102545 DDC 387.7/1 19
HE9803.A4 L55 1986

Report (International Resources Development, inc.) .
(#703) Database management systems. Norwalk, Conn., U. S.A. (6 Prowitt St., Norwalk 06855) , c1986. iv, 149 leaves ; LC Card 86-226965 DDC 381/.4500574/0973
HD9696.C63 U515925 1986

Report (Kenya. Ministry of Co-operative Development. Development Planning Division. Research & Evaluation Unit) .
(no. 9) A Base-line study of Farm Input Supply Scheme. Nairobi , 1981. 65 leaves, [1] leaf of plates : LC Card 87-980116
HD1491.K42 K583 1981

Report (Kenya NGO Organising Committee--Forum '85) .
(no. 1) Women and employment in Kenya . [Nairobi] [1985] iii, 46 p. ; LC Card 85-981502 DDC 331.4/09676/2 19
HD6210.5 .W65 1985

(no. 2) Exhibition and income generation for women . [Nairobi?] [1985] 17, 11 p. ; LC Card 85-981503 DDC 331.4/09676/2 19
HD6210.5 .E94 1985

(no. 3) Women and credit . [Nairobi?] [1985] 17, 2 p. ; LC Card 85-981504 DDC 332.7/088042 19
HG3756.K4 W65 1985

(no. 6) Women in co-operatives . [Nairobi?] [1985] 30 p. ; LC Card 85-981507 DDC 334/.088042 19
HA3560.5.A4 W66 1985

Report (Missouri. State Auditor) .
(no. 86-62) Kelly, Margaret. Review of 1985 property tax rates /. Jefferson City [1986] i, 6 leaves, 109, 2 p. ; LC Card 87-620606 DDC 336.22/2 19
HJ4121.M82 K45 1986

Report (National Research Council (U. S.). Committee on Population and Demography) .
(no. 29) Recent trends in fertility and mortality in Indonesia /. Honolulu, Hawaii , 1987. xvi, 96 p. : ISBN 0-86638-092-2 (pbk.) : LC Card 87-11178 DDC 304.6/32/09598 19
HB1057 .R43 1987

Report (New Zealand Energy Research and Development Committee) .
(no. 80) Copeland, M. C. (Michael Campbell) Transport energy in New Zealand's overseas trade . Auckland, N.Z. [1982] iv, 130 p. : LC Card 84-159485 DDC 387.5/1 19
HE597.N4 C63 1982
NYPL [JSK 82-15 no.80]

Report of JASPA Steering Group Meeting on Priority Employment Policies and Projects for Africa. JASPA Steering Group Meeting on Priority Employment Policies and Projects for Africa (1985 : Addis Ababa, Ethiopia) Addis Ababa , 1986. 43 leaves ; LC Card 87-980227 DDC 331.12/042/096 19
HD5837.A6 J37 1985

Report of survey . Majlis Perbandaran Pulau Pinang. [Georgetown] [1984?] xv, 193 p. : LC Card 86-945200 DDC 307/.09595/1 19
HC445.Z7 P526 1984

Report of the Bangladesh household expenditure survey, 1981-82. Bangladesh household expenditure survey, 1981-82. Dhaka, Bangladesh , 1986. 160 p., [13] leaves of plates : LC Card 86-902560 DDC 339.4/1/095492021 19
HD7051.6 .B36 1986

Report of the Central Committee of the Socialist Unity Party of Germany to the 11th Congress of the SED /. Sozialistische Einheitspartei Deutschlands. Zentralkomitee. [Bericht des Zentralkomitees der Sozialistischen Einheitspartei Deutschlands an den XI. Parteitag der SED. English.] Dresden [1986] 109 p. : LC Card 86-220057 DDC 338.9431 19
HC290.78 .S66 1986

Report of the Commission of Enquiry into the Banana Industry of Jamaica. Jamaica. Commission of Enquiry into the Banana Industry of Jamaica. Kingston , 1959- v. <1 > ; LC Card 86-221011
HD9259.B3 J346 1959

Report of the Commission of Inquiry into the Agricultural Industry / under the chairmanship of G.L. Chavunduka. [Harare?] : The Commission, [1982] ix, 205 p. : maps ; 30 cm. LC Card 85-980325 DDC 338.1/096891 19
1. Agriculture - Economic aspects - Zimbabwe. I. Chavunduka, G. L. II. Zimbabwe. Commission of Inquiry into the Agricultural Industry.
HD2131 .R47 1982

Report of the Commission of Inquiry into the Dairy Industry, 1961 /. Rhodesia and Nyasaland. Commission of Inquiry into the Dairy Industry. Salisbury , 1962. 91 p., [1] folded leaf of plates : LC Card 86-105139
HD9275.Z552 R46 1962

Report of the Commission of Inquiry into the Possible Introduction of a Five-Day Working Week in the Mining Industry of the Republic of South Africa. South Africa. Commission of Inquiry into the Possible Introduction of a Five-Day Working Week in the Mining Industry. [Pretoria] , 1977. iii, 194 p. : LC Card 85-148007
HD5119.M5982 S68 1977

Report of the Commission of Inquiry on the Sugar Industry. Mauritius. Commission of Inquiry into the Sugar Industry. Port Louis, Mauritius , 1984. iii, 213 p. ; LC Card 85-980302 DDC 338.1/7361/096982 19
HD9118.M45 M33 1984

Report of the Commission of Inquiry on the Sugar Industry. Mauritius. Commission of Inquiry into the Sugar Industry. The human factor, the sugar industry, and Mauritius . Port Louis, Mauritius [1984] 157 p. ; LC Card 85-980119 DDC 338.1/7361/096982 19
HD9118.M45 M33 1984a

Report of the Commission on National Broadcasting. Somalia. Commission on National Broadcasting. Mogadishu [1966] ii, 108 leaves (2 folded) : LC Card 85-981107
HE8699.S65 S64 1966

Report of the commissioner appointed to inquire into the operation of the land tenure scheme in Ankole. Low, G. C. Entebbe, Uganda [1961?] 30 p. ; LC Card 85-208468
HD994.Z8 A55 1961

Report of the Committee of Review of Aboriginal Employment and Training Programs. Aboriginal employment and training programs . Canberra , 1985. ix, 453 p. ; ISBN 0-644-00712-5 (pbk.) LC Card 87-107756 DDC 331.25/92/089011094 19
HD5850.A6 A26 1985

Report of the Committee to Review the Working of the Monetary System. Reserve Bank of India. Committee to Review the Working of the Monetary System. Bombay [1985] vii, 371 p. ; LC Card 87-902447 DDC 332.4/954 19
HG1235 .R47 1985

Report of the Consultation Panel on Pay Equity. Toronto, Ont., Canada : Ontario Women's Directorate, [1986] 123 p. ; 30 cm. Cover title. "Green paper on pay equity"--P. i. Bibliography: p. 119-122. ISBN 0-7729-1657-8 (pbk.) LC Card 87-117472 DDC 331.2/1 19
1. Equal pay for equal work - Ontario. 2. Women - Employment - Ontario. I. Ontario. Consultation Panel on Pay Equity.
HD6061.2.C22 O577 1986

Report of the Courseware Committee . Ireland. Courseware Committee. Dublin [1986] vii, 79 p. ; LC Card 86-226148 DDC 338.4/70053 19
HD9811.I732 I74 1986

Report of the Governor's Economic Research Council on the Idaho economy, submitted to John V. Evans, governor. Idaho. Governor's Economic Research Council. [Boise] [1984] v, 30 p. : LC Card 86-621917 DDC 330.9796/033 19
HC107.I2 I164 1984

Report of the inquiry into the collapse of the CCB and Northland Bank /. Estey, Willard Z. Ottawa, Canada , c1986. xiii, 641 p. : ISBN 0-660-12171-9 (pbk.) : LC Card 87-134617 DDC 332.1/2/0971 19
HG2708.C36 E89 1986

Report of the Interministerial Task Force on Agricultural Finance. Ontario. Interministerial Task Force on Agricultural Finance. [Toronto, Ont. , 1986] vii, 65, [42] p. : LC Card 87-127476 DDC 332.7/1/09713 19
HD1790.O6 O573 1986

Report of the international seminar held in Paris on 15th-16th-17th January 1986 on the following topic, European dimension and future prospects of the railways / European Conference of Ministers of Transport, Economic Research Centre. Paris, France : ECMT ; [Washington, D.C. : OECD Publications and Information Centre, distributor], c1986. 289 p. : ill. ; 27 cm. Includes bibliographies. CONTENTS. - Actions recommended by international organisations / Messrs. Malaurie ... [et al.] -- Economic changes / A. De Waele -- Innovative areas : high speeds / J. Bouley -- Innovative areas : computer technologies / A.A.I. Holtgrefe -- The German network / R. Heinisch -- The British network / I. Phillips -- The Swedish network / P. Jönsson. ISBN 92-821-1109-1 (pbk.) : LC Card 86-215627 DDC 385/.094 19
1. Railroads - Europe - Congresses. I. European Conference of Ministers of Transport. Economic Research Centre. II. Title: European dimension and future prospects of the railways.
HE3005 .R47 1986

Report of the joint Somali government and World Bank study of agricultural incentives and grain marketing in Somalia / Mohamud Ibrahim Asser ... [et al.]. [Alexandria, Va. : E. Berg Associates, 1984] xviii, 170, 2 p. : ill. ; 28 cm. "10 January 1984." LC Card 87-404086 DDC

338.1/8 19
1. Grain trade - Somalia. 2. Grain - Somalia - Marketing. 3. Grain - Prices - Government policy - Somalia. I. Asser, Mohamud Ibrahim. II. Somalia. III. International Bank for Reconstruction and Development.
HD9047.S582 R47 1984

Report of the National Manpower Commission on an investigation into the small business sector in the Republic of South Africa, with specific reference to the factors that may retard the growth and development thereof. South Africa. National Manpower Commission. Verslag van die Nasionale Mannekragkommissie oor 'n ondersoek na die kleinsakesektor in die Republiek van Suid-Afrika, in die besonder die faktore wat die groei en ontwikkeling daarvan kan belemmer =. [Pretoria] [1983] 58 p. ; ISBN 0-620-07511-2 LC Card 85-116407 DDC 338.6/42/0968 19
HD2346.S63 S64 1983

Report of the National Manpower Commission on in-service training in the Republic of South Africa, 1980/81. Verslag van die Nasionale Mannekragkommissie oor indiensopleiding in die Republiek van Suid-Afrika, 1980/81 =. [Pretoria] [1984] 267 p. ; ISBN 0-621-08502-2 : LC Card 86-109914
HF5549.5.T7 V44 1984

Report of the Panel on the Allocation of Stalls in the Three Temporary Markets in Jos. Plateau State (Nigeria) Government views and decisions on the Report of the Panel on the Allocation of Stalls in the Three Temporary Markets in Jos . Jos [Nigeria] [1976?] 9 p. ; LC Card 87-401792 DDC 381/.18/096695 19
HF5475.N52 J66 1976

Report of the Public Accounts Committee on the Special report of the Controller and Auditor-General on the City Council of Nairobi. Kenya. Public Accounts Committee. Nairobi [1981] i, 23 p. ; LC Card 85-980597
HJ9620.5.Z9 N344 1981

Report of the Registrar General on vital statistics, 1981, Sri Lanka. [Colombo] : Dept. of Census and Statistics, Ministry of Plan Implementation, Sri Lanka, [1986] viii, 178 p. ; 29 cm. LC Card 86-903546 DDC 304.6/09549/3021 19
1. Sri Lanka - Statistics, Vital. I. Sri Lanka. Rejistrār Janarāl Depārtamēntuva.
HA4570.8 .R47 1986

Report of the Royal Commission on the Status of Women in Canada. Canada. Royal Commission on the Status of Women in Canada. [Ottawa, Ont.] , 1970. xii, 488 p. :
NYPL [JLE 73-1102]

Report of the Select Committee on Toll Financing of Roads. South Africa. Parliament. House of Assembly. Select Committee on Toll Financing of Roads. Verslag van die Gekose Komitee oor Tolfinansiering van Paaie =. [Pretoria] [1982] xix, 54 p. ; ISBN 0-621-07457-8 : LC Card 83-215629
HE367.S63 T647 1982

Report of the Special House Committee to Study Consumers Power Company . Michigan. Legislature. House of Representatives. Special House Committee to Study Consumers Power Company. Lansing, Mich. (The Capitol, Lansing 48909) [1985] iv leaves, 57 p. ; LC Card 86-622638 DDC 338.7/6136362/09774 19
HD9685.U7 C785 1985

Report of the Taju-Deen Commission of Inquiry into the status, administration, and activities of the Sierra Leone Labour Congress from 1976 following the amalgamation of the then Sierra Leone Labour Congress and the Sierra Leone Council of Labour, and to inquire into all aspects of industrial relations in Sierra Leone and to make recommendations for any improvements which it may consider necessary. Sierra Leone. Taju-Deen Commission of Inquiry. [Freetown] [198-] vi, 149 leaves ; LC Card 87-118833
HD8833.A5 S57 1980

Report of the Task Force on Broadcasting Policy. Canada. Task Force on Broadcasting Policy. [Toronto] , c1986. 730 p. : ISBN 0-660-12164-6 (pbk.) : LC Card 86-231885 DDC 384.54/0971 19
HE8689.9.C3 C37 1986

Report of the Task Force on Business Training of the Legislative Commission on Economic Development. Kansas. Legislature. Task Force on Business Training. [Topeka, Kansas] [1986] 1 v. (various pagings) ; LC Card 87-621700 DDC 331.25/92/09781 19
HD5715.3.K2 K37 1986

Report of the Task Force on the Quality of Audits of Governmental Units . Task Force on the Quality of Audits of Governmental Units. New York, N.Y. , c1987. viii, 71 p. : LC Card 87-149765 DDC 350.72/32 19
HJ9777.A3 T37 1987

Report of the Union Delegation to the U. S.S.R. : November & December, 1946. London : Amalgamated Engineering Union, [1946?] iii, 40 p. : ill. ; 22 cm. LC Card 87-100506
1. Labor and laboring classes - Soviet Union. 2. Trade-unions - Soviet Union. I. Amalgamated Engineering Union. Delegation to the U. S.S.R.
HD8526.5 .R46 1946

Report on a national study of parental leaves. 1986. The Corporate guide to parental leaves, including Catalyst's Report on a national study of parental leaves /. New York, NY (250 Park Ave. South, New York 10003) , c1986. 145 p. : LC Card 87-161920 DDC 658.3/122 19
HD6065.5.U6 C67 1986

Report on an income tax in Texas /. Greenhut, Melvin L. College Station, Tex. , c1986. 40 p. : ISBN 0-86599-057-3 (pbk.) LC Card 86-622258 DDC 336.24/09764 19
HJ4655.T4 G74 1986

Report on competition in the telephone industry. Huber, Peter W. (Peter William), 1952- The geodesic network . Washington, D.C. , 1987. 1 v. (various pagings) : LC Card 87-601031 DDC 384/.041 19
HE8819 .H76 1987

Report on demographic socio-economic survey : communal lands of Manicaland Province, 1983/84. Harare, Zimbabwe : Permanent Sample Survey Unit, Central Statistical Office, [1984 or 1985] 18 p. : map ; 30 cm. (Report / Zimbabwe National Household Survey Capability Programme (ZNHSCP) . no. 2) Cover title. LC Card 86-980590 DDC 304.6/096891 19
1. Manicaland Province (Zimbabwe) - Population - Statistics. 2. Manicaland Province (Zimbabwe) - Economic conditions - Statistics. 3. Manicaland Province (Zimbabwe) - Social conditions - Statistics. I. Zimbabwe. Central Statistical Office. Permanent Sample Survey Unit. II. Series: Report (Zimbabwe National Household Survey Capability Programme) , no. 2.
HA4702.Z9 M356 1984

Report on development cooperation with Pakistan. Islamabad, Pakistan : United Nations Development Programme, [1985] xxxvi, 267 p. : all forms ; 28 cm. "January 1985." LC Card 85-931852 DDC 338.91/09549/2 19
1. Economic development projects - Pakistan. 2. Economic assistance - Pakistan. I. United Nations. Development Programme.
HC440.5.Z9 E447 1985

Report on development of India's handloom fabrics for export to the United States of America, September 1957 / by Handloom Fabrics Survey Team invited by the Government of India with the cooperation of the Ford Foundation. [S.l. : s.n., 1957] (Delhi : Albion Press) ii, ii, 108 p., [8] p. of plates : ill. ; 24 cm. Cover title. "September 1957." LC Card 81-911063
1. Handloom industry - India. 2. Textile fabrics - India. 3. India - Commerce - United States. 4. United States - Commerce - India. I. Handloom Fabrics Survey Team (U. S.).
HD9866.I62 R46 1957

Report on extraordinary session of the General Assembly, May 1985 : subject, savings and loan associations, state chartered associations insured by Maryland Savings-Share Insurance Corporation / prepared by Department of Fiscal Servies, Department of Legislative Reference. Annapolis, Md. : Dept. of Fiscal Services : Dept. of Legislative Reference, [1985] ii, 26 leaves ; 28 cm. Cover title. LC Card 86-622373 DDC 332.3/2/09752 19
1. Building and loan associations - Maryland. 2. Building and loan associations - Maryland - State supervision. I. Maryland. General Assembly. Dept. of Fiscal Services. II. Maryland. General Assembly. State Dept. of Legislative Reference.
HG2153.M3 R46 1985

Report on financial asset management. President's Private Sector Survey on Cost Control (U. S.) President's private sector survey on cost control . Washington, D.C. , 1983. viii, 320 p. ; ***NYPL [JLF 86-727]***

Report on housing and urban development in Zimbabwe : public and private sector partnership : presented at the 10th Conference on Housing and Urban Development in Sub-Saharan Africa, 24th-28th February, 1986, Harare, Zimbabwe. [Harare, Zimbabwe : Ministry of Public Construction and National Housing, 1986] vi, 46 p., [1] folded leaf of plates : map ; 30 cm. Cover title. At head of title: Zimbabwe. Co-sponsored by the Ministry of Public Construction and National Housing, Zimbabwe, and the United States Agency for International Development. "G.P. & S. 33463-X." Bibliography: p. 46. LC Card 87-980381 DDC 363.5/8 19
1. Housing policy - Zimbabwe. 2. Urban policy - Zimbabwe. 3. Housing - Zimbabwe. 4. Urbanization - Zimbabwe. I. Conference on Housing and Urban Development in Sub-Saharan Africa (10th : 1986 : Harare, Zimbabwe). II. Zimbabwe. Ministry of Public Construction and National Housing. III. United States. Agency for International Development.
HD7374.5.A3 R46 1986

A Report on index numbers of parity between prices received and prices paid by the farmers in the state of Orissa / Government of Orissa, Bureau of Statistics & Economics. Bhubaneswar, Orissa : The Bureau, [1985] 11 p. : ill. (some col.) ; 28 cm. LC Card 87-401032 DDC 338.1/3/095413 19
1. Agricultural prices - India - Orissa. I. Orissa, India. Bureau of Statistics and Economics. II. Title: Index numbers of parity between prices received and prices paid by the farmers in the state of Orissa.
HD2075.O7 R46 1985

A report on mass transit funding needs in Pennsylvania /. Pennsylvania. General Assembly. Legislative Budget and Finance Committee. Harrisburg, Pa. (Rm. 400, Finance Bldg., Harrisburg 17120) [1986] ii, 151 p. ; LC Card 86-622848 DDC 388.4/042 19
HE4487.P4 P44 1986

Report on programme implementation, 1984-85. Geneva : International Labour Office, [1986] 116 p. ; 30 cm. At head of title: International Labour Conference, 72nd session, 1986. "Supplement to the Report of the Director-General: Documents of the 233rd (May-June 1986) Session of the Governing Body." ISBN 92-2-105179-X (pbk.) : LC Card 87-101092 DDC 354.1/83 19
1. International Labour Office. I. International Labour Office. II. International Labour Conference (72nd : 1986 : Geneva, Switzerland).
HD7801 .R462 1986

Report on survey of job evaluation practices in some Nigerian organisations / Nigerian Institute of Management, Management Research Unit. Lagos : The Unit, [1981] 2, 59, [1] leaves ; 30 cm. "November 1981." Bibliography: leaf [60] LC Card 87-110199 DDC 331.25 19
1. Job evaluation - Nigeria. I. Nigerian Institute of Management. Management Research Unit.
HF5549.5.J62 R46 1981

Report on the activities of the Special Investigations Committee of the SEC Practice Section of the AICPA Division for CPA Firms : for the period from inception through December 31, 1985. New York, N.Y. (1211 Ave. of the Americas, New York 10036-8775) : American Institute of Certified Public Accountants, c1986. iii, 6 p. ; 28 cm. LC Card 86-209679 DDC 657/.0218 19
1. American Institute of Certified Public Accountants. SEC Practice Section. Special Investigations Committee. 2. Accounting - Standards - United States. 3. Accounting - United States - Quality control. I. American Institute of Certified Public Accountants. SEC Practice Section. Special Investigations Committee.
HF5657 .R46 1986

Report on the coffee service industry / prepared for the Coffee Development Group by Strategic Information Services, Inc. Columbus, Ohio : Strategic Information Services, [1984] 1 v. (various foliations) : ill. ; 28 cm. Cover title. LC Card 87-100404 DDC 381/.4566393 19
1. Coffee trade - United States. 2. Consumers - United

States - Attitudes. 3. Consumers' preferences - United States. 4. Coffee brewing. 5. Coffee, Instant. 6. Rest periods - United States. 7. White collar workers - United States - Attitudes. 8. Market surveys - United States. I. Strategic Information Services. II. Coffee Development Group (U. S.).
HD9199.U48 R47 1984

Report on the evaluation study of working of the Punjab Scheduled Castes Land Development and Finance Corporation. Punjab (India). Economic and Statistical Organisation. Chandigarh [pref. 1978] viii, 98 p. ; LC Card 79-903307
HC437.P8 P85 1978a

Report on the feasibility of implementing the International Registration Plan in the State of Maine . Pease, Allen. [Augusta, Me.] [1985] ii, 24 leaves ; LC Card 85-622840 DDC 388.3/24 19
HE5633.M2 P4 1985

Report on the marketing of sandalwood in India. Faridabad : Directorate of Marketing and Inspection, Ministry of Rural Development, Govt. of India, 1986. viii, 196 p. : ill. ; 22 cm. (MRPC . 19) "Published by the Controller of Publications, Delhi"--P. [4] of cover. Includes bibliographical references. "PAMA-183/1000-1985 (DSK-II)"--P. [4] of cover. LC Card 86-903266 DDC 381/.41497394/0954 19
1. Sandalwood trade - India. I. India. Directorate of Marketing and Inspection. II. Series: MRPC (Series) , no. 19.
HD9769.S33 I47 1986

Report on the medium term prospects for Latin American countries. Roma : Istituto italo-latino americano, 1986. 109 p. : ill. ; 24 cm. Bibliography: p. 107-109. LC Card 86-223594 DDC 336.3/435/098 19
1. Debts, External - Latin America. 2. Latin America - Economic policy. 3. Latin America - Commercial policy. 4. Debt relief - Latin America. I. Istituto italo-latino americano.
HJ8514.5 .R46 1986

Report on the National Programme on Worker's Participation and Development, 3-14 October, 1983, Mauritius. National Programme on Worker's Participation and Development (1983 : Mauritius) [Mauritius? , between 1983 and 1985] 33 p. ; LC Card 86-980341 DDC 658.3/152/096982 19
HD6890.5 .N37 1983

A report on the plight of the collective bargaining system /. New York (State). Legislature. Assembly. Standing Committee on Labor. [Albany] [1984] 64 p. ; LC Card 86-622572 DDC 331.89/0973 19
HD6508 .N49 1984

A Report on the resources, activities, and constraints in tobacco schemes : appraisal of tobacco schemes in Zambia. Lusaka : Govt. Printer, 1985. iii, 37 p. ; 30 cm. (Planning Division special studies . no. 9) Cover title. At head of title: Republic of Zambia, Ministry of Agriculture and Water Development. "April/May 1984." LC Card 85-981599 DDC 338.1/7371/096894 19
1. Tobacco industry - Zambia. I. Zambia. Ministry of Agriculture and Water Development. II. Title: Appraisal of tobacco schemes in Zambia. III. Series.
HD9147.Z34 R46 1985

Report on the safety of aircraft under charter to the Department of Defense . United States. Congress. House. Committee on Armed Services. Subcommittee on Investigations. Washington , 1986. iii, 17 p. ; LC Card 86-603401 DDC 363.1/24 19
HE9803.Z7 C538 1986

Report on the Victorian Wheat Advisory Committee . Victoria. Parliament. Public Bodies Review Committee. Melbourne [1986] xiii, 34 p. ; LC Card 87-168597 DDC 338.1/7311/09945 19
HD9049.W5 A949 1986

Report on the 1986-87 Budget Act (as amended May 21, 1986) /. California. Legislature. Senate. Committee on Budget and Fiscal Review. [Sacramento, Calif.] [1986] 3 v. (1105 leaves) ; LC Card 86-622935 DDC 336.794 19
HJ2053.C3 C36 1986

Report (South Carolina Council on Vocational and Technical Education) .
(#4) Meeting labor needs in South Carolina . Columbia, S.C. (2221 Devine St., Suite 420, Columbia 29205) [1986] 52 leaves ; LC Card 86-623031 DDC 331.12/3/09757 19
HD5725.S6 M44 1986

Report to Congress on the capital gains tax reductions of 1978. United States. Office of Tax Analysis. [Washington, D.C.] [1985] xix, 199 p. ; LC Card 85-602710 DDC 336.24/3 19
HJ4653.C3 U55 1985

Report to the Administrator on the analysis of the management and administration of the Procurement and Technical Assistance programs /. United States. Small Business Administration. Office of Procurement and Technical Assistance. [Washington, D.C.] , 1984. 1 v. (various pagings) :
NYPL [JLF 86-1066]

Report to the Legislature . California. Public Utilities Commission. [San Francisco] [1984] 40 leaves ; LC Card 86-622236 DDC 384.6/09794 19
HE8840.C2 C35 1984

Report to the World Bank, Amazônia Mineração S.A. : Carajas iron ore project : financial and economic appraisal / report prepared by Hill Samuel & Co. Ltd., London, in conjunction with Amazônia Mineração S.A. and Companhia Vale do Rio Doce. London : Hill Samuel, [1979?] v, 57, [31] leaves : ill. ; 31 cm. LC Card 85-154695
1. Iron industry and trade - Brazil - Carajás Mountains Region. 2. Iron mines and mining - Brazil - Carajás Mountains Region. I. Hill Samuel & Co. II. Amazônia Mineração S.A. III. Companhia Vale do Rio Doce. IV. Title: Carajas iron ore project.
HD9524.B8 R46 1979

Report (University of Fort Hare. Agricultural and Rural Development Research Institute) .
(no. 82/1) Tapson, D. R. Proposals for a cattle marketing strategy for Transkei /. [Fort Hare] [1982] ii, 45 leaves, 4 leaves of plates : ISBN 0-949974-68-4 LC Card 86-209520 DDC 381/.4162/00968791 19
HD9433.S643 T77 1982

Report (University of Winnipeg. Institute of Urban Studies) .
(no. 7) Downtown and regional shopping centre retailing in Winnipeg /. Winnipeg, Man., Canada , 1985. x, 90, [8] p. : ISBN 0-920213-22-7 (pbk.) LC Card 86-137592 DDC 381/.1/0971274 19
HF5429.6.C3 D69 1985
NYPL [JLF 86-1331]

Report (Washington (State). Legislature. Legislative Budget Committee) .
(no. 85-13) Washington (State). Legislature. Legislative Budget Committee. Program and fiscal review . Olympia (506 E. 16th Ave., Olympia 98504) [1985] v, 69 p. ; LC Card 86-621785 DDC 353.97970072/32 s 353.97970082/43 19
HJ11 .W2453 no. 85-13 KFN329.A25

REPORT WRITING.
Blicq, Ron, 1925- Writing reports to get results . New York , c1987. x, 203 p. : ISBN 0-87942-228-9 LC Card 87-16850 DDC 808/.066651 19
HF5719 .B55 1987

Report (Zimbabwe National Household Survey Capability Programme) .
(no. 2) Report on demographic socio-economic survey . Harare, Zimbabwe [1984 or 1985] 18 p. : LC Card 86-980590 DDC 304.6/096891 19
HA4702.Z9 M356 1984

Report 1969-1984 /. Jamaica National Export Corporation. [Kingston, Jamaica] [1984] x, 62, 8 p. : LC Card 87-110047 DDC 354.72920082/76/06 19
HF1009.7.J25 J35 1984

REPORTERS AND REPORTING - UNITED STATES.
Commercial newsgathering from space. Washington, DC [1987] ix, 51 p. : LC Card 87-619818 DDC 070.4/3 19
HE9721.U5 C65 1987

Reporting systems for bank management . Walker, John R. (John Rex), 1922- Boston , c1987. xii, 292 p. : ISBN 0-87267-106-2 LC Card 87-17424 DDC 332.1/068 19
HG1615 .W35 1987

REPORTS, CORPORATION. see **CORPORATION REPORTS.**

Reports on fraud. The Institute of Internal Auditors reports on fraud . Altamonte Springs, Fla. , c1987. xv, 74 p. : ISBN 0-89413-164-8 (pbk.) LC Card 87-401942 DDC 657/.3 19
HF5686.C7 I53 1987

Reports on the Tobacco Leaf Marketing Board, Tobacco Quota Committee, Tobacco Quota Appeals Tribunal . Victoria. Parliament. Public Bodies Review Committee. Melbourne [1986] xix, 107 p. ; LC Card 87-168528 DDC 354.9450082/332 19
HD9148.A8 V53 1986

Reports (University of Winnipeg. Institute of Urban Studies) .
(no. 8) Levin, Earl A. A model for joint public sector/private sector participation in core area housing development and core area revitalization /. [Winnipeg, Man., Canada] , 1985. ix leaves, 93 p. ; LC Card 86-137674 DDC 363.5/8 19
HD7305.M3 L48 1985 NYPL [JLF 86-1313]

Representação do produtos alimentares de Angola na IX Feira Internacional de Lisboa : Lisboa, 9 a 23 de junho de 1968. Luanda : Associação Industrial de Angola, [1968] 248 p. : ill. ; 22 cm. Cover title: Presença de Angola na IX Feira Internacional de Lisboa, 1968. LC Card 87-400609 DDC 338.7/6413/0025673 19
1. Food industry and trade - Angola - Directories. 2. Agricultural industries - Angola - Directories. 3. Business enterprieses - Angola - Directories. I. Feira Internacional de Lisboa (9th : 1968 : Lisbon, Portugal). II. Associação Industrial de Angola. III. Title: Presença de Angola na IX Feira Internacional de Lisboa, 1968.
HD9017.A532 R46 1968

REPRESENTATION. see **REPRESENTATIVE GOVERNMENT AND REPRESENTATION.**

REPRESENTATIVE GOVERNMENT AND REPRESENTATION - ARGENTINA.
Figuerola, Francisco José. Teoría de la democracia social . Buenos Aires , 1986. xxv, 492 p. ; ISBN 950-43-0832-5 LC Card 86-184525
HD2081 .F54 1986

Rubinstein, Juan Carlos, 1928- Estructura social, estado democrático y cambio político /. [Buenos Aires] , c1986. 159 p. : ISBN 950-23-0292-3 LC Card 87-114981 DDC 330.982/064 19
HC175 .R783 1986

REPRESENTATIVE GOVERNMENT AND REPRESENTATION - EUROPE - HISTORY - 20TH CENTURY.
Maier, Charles S. In search of stability . Cambridge [Cambridgeshire] , New York , 1987. x, 291 p. ; ISBN 0-521-23001-2 LC Card 87-6383 DDC 338.94 19
HC240 .M17 1987

REPRESSURING (PETROLEUM ENGINEERING) see **SECONDARY RECOVERY OF OIL.**

Reprint (Budapest, Hungary)
Horváth, Mihály, 1809-1878. Az ipar és kereskedés története Magyarországban a három utolsó század alatt /. [Budapest , 1984] xiv, 390 p. ; ISBN 963-02-2781-9 : LC Card 85-138953
HC300.26 .H67 1984

Reprint series (Peace Corps (U. S.). Information Collection and Exchange) .
(R-49) Landrum, Roger L. The role of the Peace Corps in education in developing countries . Washington, D.C. [1984] iv, 258 p. ; LC Card 86-601664 DDC 371.2/07 19
HC60.5 .L27 1984

Reprint series (Queen's University (Kingston, Ont.). Industrial Relations Centre) .
(no. 5) Duncan, A. R. C. (Alastair Robert Campbell), 1915- The concept of leisure. Kingston, Ont. [1970?] 8 p. LC Card 70-534907 DDC 331/.08 s
HD8102 .K52 no. 5

(no. 54) Carter, D. D. The changing face of Canadian labour relations law /. Kingston, Ont., Canada , 1985. 15 p. ; ISBN 0-88886-126-5 (pbk.) LC Card 86-145328 DDC 331 s 344.71/01 331 s 347.1041 19
HD8102 .K52 no. 54 KE3009

Repro-serie (Københavns universitet. Institut for kultursociologi) .
(1984, nr. 7) Andersen, Kirsten Gøgsig. Det skal stampes halv stamp presses og klædeskæres . København [1984] 179 columns : LC Card 85-242146
HD9999.C483 D43 1984

Reproducción de fuerza de trabajo, educación y migración en el sector rural colombiano / por Alejandro Sanz de Santamaría ... [et al.]. Bogotá, Colombia : Centro de Estudios sobre Desarrollo Económico, Universidad de los Andes : Instituto SER de Investigación, 1985. 98, [52] p. : forms ; 28 cm. (Documento CEDE-SER . 079) Bibliography: p. [50]-[52] (2nd group). LC Card 87-402979 DDC 331.1/09861 19
1. Labor supply - Colombia. 2. Agricultural laborers - Colombia. 3. Education - Colombia. 4. Migration, Internal - Colombia. 5. Colombia - Rural conditions. I. Sanz de Santamaría, Alejandro. II. Series: Documento (Universidad de los Andes (Bogotá, Colombia). Centro de Estudios sobre Desarrollo Económico) , 079.
HD5757.A6 R46 1985

Reproducciones de billetes y cheques de viaje extranjeros / Banco Hispano Americano. [Madrid] : El Banco, [1972?] 140 p. : col. ill. ; 23 x 31 cm. Cover title. LC Card 85-140130
1. Paper money. 2. Traveler's checks. I. Banco Hispano Americano (Madrid, Spain).
HG353 .R44 1972

Reproducing families . Levine, David, 1946- Cambridge [Cambridgeshire] , New York , 1987. ix, 251 p. ; ISBN 0-521-33256-7 LC Card 86-26372 DDC 304.6/0942 19
HB3585 .L48 1987

Reproduktion und Infrastruktur /. Koziolek, Helmut. Berlin , c1986. 224 p. : ISBN 3-349-00017-7 LC Card 87-130782 DDC 363/.09431 19
HC290.795.C3 K675 1986

Le repubbliche cisalpina e italiana . Frumento, Armando. Milano , 1985. xii, 608 p. ; LC Card 86-215881
HD9525.I82 F72 1985

Republic of Biafra. see **East-Central State, Nigeria; South-Eastern State, Nigeria.**

Republic of Indonesia. see **Indonesia.**

Republic of Nigeria. see **Nigeria.**

Republic of South Africa. see **South Africa.**

Republic of the United States of Indonesia. see **Indonesia.**

Republic of Viet Nam. see **Vietnam.**

Republic of Zambia, economic memorandum / prepared by the Bank of Zambia with the kind assistance of Meridien International Bank Limited. [Lusaka?] : Bank of Zambia with the assistance of Meridien International Bank, [1983?] 28 p. : map ; 28 cm. Cover title. LC Card 86-980289 DDC 330.96894/04 19
1. Zambia - Economic conditions - 1964-. I. Bank of Zambia. II. Meridien International Bank.
HC915 .R46 1983

República de Colombia. see **Colombia.**

República de Nueva Granada. see **Colombia.**

La República Dominicana : perfil ambiental del país : un estudio de campo / por Gary Hartshorn ... [et al.]. McLean, Va. : JRB Associates, 1981. xii, 134 p. : ill. ; 28 cm. Bibliography: p. 127-130. "AID contract no. AID/SOD/PDC-C-0247." LC Card 86-218146
1. Natural resources - Dominican Republic. 2. Environmental policy - Dominican Republic. I. Hartshorn, Gary S. II. JRB Associates.
HC153.5 .R45 1981

República Dominicana. Censo nacional de población y vivienda, 1981 . Santo Domingo, Distrito Nacional, República Dominicana , 1985- v. <1 > : LC Card 86-223758
HA886.5 1981c

Republički zavod za društveno planiranje SR Hrvatske. Osnove dugoročnog razvoja SR Hrvatske--svodna studija /. Zagreb , 1984. 437 p. ; LC Card 87-151188
HC407.Z7 C7647 1984

Republički zavod za statistiku SR Srbije.
Babić, Bogdan. Statistički informacioni sistem SR Srbije u društvenom sistemu informisanja republike . Beograd , 1986- v. <1 > ; LC Card 87-168381
HA37.Y83 S43 1986

Industrija SR Srbije, 1981-1982. godina /. Beograd , 1984. 76 p. ; LC Card 86-212264
HA1651 .A334 no. 239 HA1634.S47

Republik Indonesia Serikat. see **Indonesia.**

République autonome du Togo. see **Togo.**

République Centrafricaine. see **Central African Republic.**

République de Guinée. see **Guinea.**

République du Niger. see **Niger.**

République du Togo. see **Togo.**

République fédérale du Cameroun. see **Cameroon.**

République gabonaise. see **Gabon.**

République Populaire du Bénin. see **Benin.**

Requeijo, Jaime. Introducción a la balanza de pagos de España / Jaime Requeijo. Madrid : Tecnos, 1985. 174 p. : ill. ; 24 cm. (Serie de historia) Includes bibliographical references. ISBN 84-309-1221-5 LC Card 86-150983
1. Balance of payments - Spain. 2. Balance of trade - Spain. I. Title.
HG3883.S69 R46 1985

Requerimientos de mano de obra en la agricultura peruana /. Maletta, Héctor. Lima, Perú , 1985. 184 p. ; LC Card 86-156077
HD1531.P4 M34 1985

Res, Zannis, 1941- International debt and central banking in the 1980s /. New York , 1987. viii, 234 p. ; ISBN 0-312-00530-X : LC Card 87-4300 DDC 336.3/435/091724 19
HJ8899 .I574 1987

Research and consulting as a business /. Davis, Nancy Yaw. Washington, D.C. , c1987. v, 41 p. : ISBN 0-913167-21-5 (pbk.) LC Card 87-20254 DDC 658.4/6 19
HD69.C6 D38 1987

Research and current issues series, 0317-2546 .
(no. 44) Coates, Mary Lou. Employment equity . Kingston, Ont., Canada , 1986. 109 p. : ISBN 0-88886-131-1 (pbk.) LC Card 86-182985 DDC 331.13/3/0971 19
HD4903.5.C2 C6 1986

RESEARCH AND DEVELOPMENT CONTRACTS, GOVERNMENT - UNITED STATES.
Johnston, Robert F. Entrepreneurial science . New York , 1987. 157 p. ; ISBN 0-89930-260-2 (lib. bdg. : alk. paper) LC Card 87-2518 DDC 338/.06 19
HC110.H53 J65 1987

Nonprofit organizations, a government management tool /. New York , 1980. xxi, 173 p. ; ISBN 0-03-053966-8 : LC Card 79-23632 DDC 350 19
JK468.R45 N66 ***NYPL [JLE 80-1874]***

United States. Dept. of Transportation. Office of the Secretary. Contracting with the United States Department of Transportation [microform]. Washington, D.C. , 1984. iii, 40 p. : ***NYPL [*ZT-1711 no.25]***

Research and development series .
Research & development series .
(no 253) Warmbrod, Catharine P. Skills for the changing workplace . Columbus, Ohio (1960 Kenny Rd., Columbus 43210-1090) , 1985. ix, 86 p. ; LC Card 86-205842 DDC 658.8/007/15 19
HF5415 .W3155 1985

(no. 254) Warmbrod, Catharine P. Skills for the changing workplace . Columbus, Ohio (1960 Kenny Rd., Columbus 43210-1090) , 1985. ix, 93 p. ; LC Card 86-205907 DDC 651/.07/15 19
HF1106 .W36 1985

Research and information series .
(no. 5) Clatanoff, Robert M. Patterns of property tax administration in the United States /. Chicago, Ill. , 1986. x, 178 p. : ISBN 0-88329-145-2 (pbk.) LC Card 86-7240 DDC 353.9/37242 19
HJ4120 .C528 1986 ***NYPL [JLF 87-464]***

(no. 6) Langhoff, Gary M., 1952- Assessment jurisdictions and agency resources in the United States . Chicago, Ill. , 1987. p. cm. ISBN 0-88329-061-8 : LC Card 87-4101 DDC 336.22/2 19
HJ3241 .L36 1987

Research and Information System for the Non-aligned and Other Developing Countries.
Research and Information System for the Nonaligned and Other Developing Countries.
Low income countries . New Delhi , 1987. x, 106 p. ; ISBN 81-7027-101-0 : LC Card 87-900104 DDC 330.9172/4 19
HF1413 .L68 1987

South-South economic cooperation . New Delhi , 1987. xii, 262 p. ; ISBN 81-7027-102-9 : LC Card 86-903797 DDC 337/.09172/4 19
HF1413 .S617 1987

World economy in the mid-eighties . New Delhi, India , c1986. xii, 222 p. ; LC Card 86-903369 DDC 330.9/048 19
HB171 .W83 1986

Research and other activities of the Development Centre, 1983-1985. Paris, France : Development Centre of the Organisation for Economic Co-operation and Development, 1985. 50 p. ; 23 cm. LC Card 86-213499 DDC 338.9 19
1. Economic development - Research. I. Organisation for Economic Co-operation and Development. Development Centre.
HD77 .R47 1985

Research & Review Service of America.
Individual and family markets. [Chicago] , c1986. ii, 243 p. ; ISBN 0-88462-594-X (loose-leaf) LC Card 86-29692 DDC 368.3/2/0688 19
HG8951 .I44 1986

Research bulletin (Conference Board) .
(no. 183) Lees, Francis A. Financing export sales /. New York, N.Y. (845 3rd Ave., New York 10022) , c1986. 12 p. : LC Card 86-212400 DDC 658.1/5 19
HF3031 .L36 1986

(no. 186) Weber, Nathan. Communicating with security analysts /. New York, N.Y. (845 3rd Ave., New York 10022) , c1985. 22 p. : LC Card 86-212395 DDC 658.4/5 19
HD59 .W36 1985

(no. 190) Schein, Lawrence. Current issues in human-resource management /. New York, N.Y. (845 3rd Ave., New York 10022) , c1986. 17 p. : LC Card 86-212364 DDC 658.3/01 19
HF5549.5.M3 S34 1986

(no. 194) Freedman, Audrey. Perspectives on employment /. New York, N.Y. (845 3rd Ave., New York 10022) , c1986. 15 p. : LC Card 86-212384 DDC 331.12 19
HD5701.3 .F74 1986

(no. 196) Davey, Patrick J. Corporate financing in international markets /. New York, N.Y. (845 3rd Ave., New York 10022) , c1986. 15 p. ; LC Card 86-212373 DDC 658.1/599 19
HG4061 .D384 1986

(no. 199) The 1986-87 outlook . New York, N.Y. (845 3rd Ave., New York 10022) , c1986. 18 p. : LC Card 86-212392 DDC 338.5/443/0973 19
HC106.8 .A14 1986

(no. 200) Basche, James R., 1926- Eliminating barriers to international trade and investment in services /. New York, N.Y. (845 Third Ave., New York 10022) , c1986. 15 p. ; LC Card 87-147770 DDC 382/.45 19
HD9980.6 .B37 1986

Research Bureau Limited. ISBA area information, 1978 /. London , 1978. 147 p. : ISBN 0-906241-00-6 (pbk.) LC Card 83-225656 DDC 381/.1/0941021 19
HA1134 .I83 1978

Research Center for International Agrarian Development.
Publications .
(9) Klempin, Arno. Contribution of state-directed land settlement to agricultural development . Saarbrücken , Fort Launderdale, 1979. viii, 169 p. : ISBN 3-88156-121-8 LC Card 80-464363 DDC 333.3/1/593
HD890.55 .K57 ***NYPL [JLE 80-1270]***

Research Centre for International Agrarian Development.
Publications.
(8) Tschiersch, Joachim E. Appropriate mechanization for small farmers in developing countries /. Saarbrücken , 1978. iii, 106 p. ; ISBN 3-88156-112-9 LC Card 80-472522 DDC

338.1/61/091724
S675 .T72 ***NYPL [JLE 80-1482]***

Research collections in women's studies.
United States. Women's Bureau. Records of the Women's Bureau of the Department of Labor, 1918-1965 [microform] /. Frederick, MD , 1987- microfilm reel ISBN 0-89093-870-9 (microfilm : pt. 1) : LC Card 87-6239 DDC 331.4/0973 19
HD6095

Research colloquium (Harvard University. Graduate School of Business Administration)
The Uneasy alliance . Boston, Mass. , c1985. x, 485 p. : ISBN 0-87584-172-4 LC Card 85-8709 DDC 658.5 19
HD56 .U53 1985 ***NYPL [JLE 86-2361]***

Research Conference on Trends Impacting Tax Administration, November 20-22, 1985.
Research Conference on Trends Impacting Tax Administration (1985 : Washington, D.C.) Washington, D.C. (1111 Constitution Ave., N.W., Washington 20224) [1985] 2 v. ; 28 cm. LC Card 87-601252 DDC 350.72/4/00973 19
HJ3252 .R357 1985

Research Conference on Trends Impacting Tax Administration (1985 : Washington, D.C.)
Research Conference on Trends Impacting Tax Administration, November 20-22, 1985. Washington, D.C. (1111 Constitution Ave., N.W., Washington 20224) : Office of the Assistant Commissioner, Planning, Finance and Research, Internal Revenue Service, [1985] 2 v. ; 28 cm. LC Card 87-601252 DDC 350.72/4/00973 19
1. Tax administration and procedure - United States - Congresses. 2. Tax administration and procedure - United States - Technological innovations - Congresses. 3. United States - Population - Congresses. 4. United States - Economic conditions - 1981- - Congresses. I. Title.
HJ3252 .R357 1985

Research Consultancy Bureau (India) Tractor industry in India. New Delhi [1982?]. 3 v. ; LC Card 83-906487 DDC 338.4/7629225 19
HD9710.4.I42 T73 1982
NYPL [JLM 86-469]

RESEARCH - ECONOMIC ASPECTS - BYELORUSSIAN S.S.R.
Ėkonomicheskie aspekty integratsii nauki i proizvodstva /. Minsk , 1986. 204, [4] p. ; LC Card 87-106384
HC337.B933 R43 1986

RESEARCH - ECONOMIC ASPECTS - PAKISTAN - STATISTICS.
Growth of R & D manpower and expenditure in Pakistan. Islamabad , 1985. 66 p. ; LC Card 85-932022 DDC 331.12/510014/095491021 19
HC440.5.Z9 R44 1985

RESEARCH - ECONOMIC ASPECTS - SOVIET UNION.
Kompleksnaia organizatsiia issledovaniĭ . Moskva , 1981. 191 p. : LC Card 82-130582
HC340.R4 K66 1981

Marek, A. I. (Aleksandr Isaevich) Nauchno-proizvodstvennye kompleksy . Moskva , 1985. 141, [3] p. : LC Card 86-118921
HC340.R4 M37 1985

Rodionenkov, P. A. (Petr Andreevich) Zatraty i rezul'taty proizvodstvennykh issledovaniĭ i razrabotok /. Leningrad , 1986. 143 p. ; LC Card 87-136354
HC340.R4 R63 1986

Sovershenstvovanie metodologii ėkonomicheskogo analiza v nauchnykh uchrezhdeniiakh i nauchno-tekhnicheskikh kompleksakh . Kiev , 1986. 116 p. ; LC Card 87-126466
HC340.R4 S68 1986

RESEARCH - ECONOMIC ASPECTS - UKRAINE.
Ėkonomizatsiia nauki . Kiev , 1986. 221 p. ; LC Card 87-102107
HC337.U53 R44 1986

RESEARCH - ECONOMIC ASPECTS - UNITED STATES.
Committee on Science, Technology, and Regional Economic Development. The impact of science and technology on regional economic development. Washington, 1969. xi, 111 p. LC Card 72-604009 DDC 338.973
HC110.R4 C65 1969b ***NYPL [JLE 87-898]***

Research funding as an investment--can we measure the returns? Washington, D.C. [1986] vi, 72 p. : LC Card 86-600525 DDC 338/.06 19
HC110.R4 R47 1986

RESEARCH - ECONOMIC ASPECTS - YUGOSLAVIA - SLOVENIA.
Vloga znanosti pri oblikovanju strategije razvoja SR Slovenije /. Ljubljana , 1981. 174 p. : LC Card 82-151266
HC407.Z7 S57 1981

RESEARCH - EUROPE.
Research for public transit : new directions : strategic transportation research study : transit. Washington, D.C. : Transportation Research Board, National Research Council, 1987. vi, 146 p. : ill. ; 23 cm. (Special report . 213) Includes bibliographies. ISBN 0-309-04461-8 (pbk.) LC Card 87-22878 DDC 388.4/0973 19
1. Local transit - Research - United States. 2. Transportation - Research - United States. I. Series: Special report (National Research Council (U. S.). Transportation Research Board) , 213.
HE4451 .R47 1987

Research funding as an investment--can we measure the returns? Washington, D.C. : Congress of the U. S., Office of Technology Assessment : For sale by the Supt. of Docs., U. S. G.P.O., [1986] vi, 72 p. : ill. ; 26 cm. (A Technical memorandum / Congress of the United States, Office of Technology Assessment) "April 1986." Includes bibliographical references. "OTA-TM-SET-36"--P. [4] of cover. LC Card 86-600525 DDC 338/.06 19
1. Research - Economic aspects - United States. 2. Research, Industrial - Economic aspects - United States. 3. Industry and state - United States. 4. Technology and state - United States. I. United States. Congress. Office of Technology Assessment. II. Series: Technical memoranda (United States. Congress. Office of Technology Assessment).
HC110.R4 R47 1986

RESEARCH GRANTS - UNITED STATES.
Kalas, John W. The grant system /. Albany , c1987. xii, 168 p. : ISBN 0-88706-583-X LC Card 87-6156 DDC 001.4/4 19
HJ275 .K34 1987

Research in business economics and public policy .
(no. 11) Williams, Donald R., 1956- Labor force participation of black and white youth /. Ann Arbor, Mich. , c1987. 125 p. ; ISBN 0-8357-1804-2 (alk. paper) LC Card 87-5868 DDC 331.3/412/0973 19
HD6273 .W48 1987

(no. 12) Wolff, Nancy, 1955- Income redistribution and the Social Security program /. Ann Arbor , c1987. vi, 181 p. : ISBN 0-8357-1807-7 LC Card 87-10791 DDC 368.4/3/00973 19
HD7105.35.U6 W65 1987

Research in criminology.
The Reasoning criminal . New York , c1986. xiv, 246 p. : ISBN 0-387-96272-7 : LC Card 86-1275 DDC 364.3 19
HV6080 .R38 1986 ***NYPL [JLE 86-3522]***

Research in ethnic relations series.
Cohen, Robin. The new helots . Aldershot, Hants, England , Brookfield, Vt., USA , c1987. xiii, 290 p. : ISBN 0-566-00932-3 : LC Card 87-19807 DDC 331.6/2 19
HD6304 .C64 1987

Research in international marketing / edited by Peter W. Turnbull & Stanley J. Paliwoda. London ; Dover, N.H. : Croom Helm, c1986. 376 p. : ill. ; 23 cm. Includes bibliographies. ISBN 0-7099-4313-X : LC Card 85-29052 DDC 382/.6 19
1. Export marketing - Addresses, essays, lectures. 2. Export marketing - Research - Addresses, essays, lectures. I. Turnbull, Peter W. II. Paliwoda, Stanley J.
HF1009.5 .R46 1986 ***NYPL [JLD 86-2264]***

RESEARCH, INDUSTRIAL - ADDRESSES, ESSAYS, LECTURES.
(1968) Tagiuri, Renato. Organizational climate. Boston, 1968. viii, 246 p. LC Card 68-8418 DDC 301.4
HM131 .T27 ***NYPL [JLD 86-684]***

RESEARCH, INDUSTRIAL - AUSTRALIA - CONGRESSES.
An Industrial research and development and marketing package for Australia . [Canberra?] [1984] 48, 4 leaves : LC Card 87-153477 DDC 338/.06 19
HC610.T4 I53 1984

RESEARCH, INDUSTRIAL - BERLIN (GERMANY)
Hornschild, Kurt. Präferenzregelung der Forschungs- und Entwicklungsförderung in Berlin /. Berlin , 1985. v, 55 p. ; ISBN 3-428-05800-3 LC Card 86-156799
HD30.42.G39 H67 1985

RESEARCH, INDUSTRIAL - BYELORUSSIAN S.S.R.
Ėkonomicheskie aspekty integratsii nauki i proizvodstva /. Minsk , 1986. 204, [4] p. ; LC Card 87-106384
HC337.B933 R43 1986

RESEARCH, INDUSTRIAL - ECONOMIC ASPECTS - JAPAN - ECONOMETRIC MODELS.
Audretsch, David B. Industrial policy, R&D, and U. S.-Japanese trade /. Berlin [1986] 39 p. ; LC Card 87-156721 DDC 382/.0952/073 19
HF3127 .A93 1986

RESEARCH, INDUSTRIAL - ECONOMIC ASPECTS - UNITED STATES.
Research funding as an investment--can we measure the returns? Washington, D.C. [1986] vi, 72 p. : LC Card 86-600525 DDC 338/.06 19
HC110.R4 R47 1986

RESEARCH, INDUSTRIAL - EUROPE.
Nauchno-tekhnicheskiĭ progress i strukturnye sdvigi v ėkonomike sovremennogo kapitalizma . Moskva , 1987. 168 p. ; LC Card 87-165811
HC240.9.T4 N38 1987

RESEARCH, INDUSTRIAL - GERMANY, EAST.
Intensivierung der Forschung . Berlin , 1984. 354 p. ; LC Card 84-195559
HD30.42.G4 I57 1984

RESEARCH, INDUSTRIAL - GERMANY, WEST.
Hornschild, Kurt. Präferenzregelung der Forschungs- und Entwicklungsförderung in Berlin /. Berlin , 1985. v, 55 p. ; ISBN 3-428-05800-3 LC Card 86-156799
HD30.42.G39 H67 1985

RESEARCH, INDUSTRIAL - GERMANY (WEST) - CONGRESSES.
Rembser, Josef. Die Förderung des wirtschaftlichen und sozialen Wandels durch die Forschungs- und Entwicklungspolitik als präventive Strukturpolitik /. Dortmund , 1977. 100 p. : LC Card 84-130876
HD30 .A7 Heft 184 HD6331.2.G28

RESEARCH, INDUSTRIAL - GERMANY (WEST) - MANAGEMENT.
Schmidt-Tiedemann, K. J. Planung und Nutzung des technischen Fortschritts /. [Dortmund?] , 1976. 37 p. : LC Card 86-123518
HD30 .A7 Heft 173 T177.G4

RESEARCH, INDUSTRIAL - ITALY - FINANCE - CONGRESSES.
Il Finanziamento dell'innovazione nelle imprese industriali /. Milano, Italy , c1985. 271 p. : LC Card 86-157239
HC310.T4 F55 1985

RESEARCH, INDUSTRIAL - JAPAN - ADDRESSES, ESSAYS, LECTURES.
R & D management systems in Japanese industry /. Amsterdam ; New York : ix, 331 p. : ISBN 0-444-86808-9 (U. S.) LC Card 83-20489 DDC 658.5/7/0952 19
HD45 .R2 1984 ***NYPL [JLD 87-107]***

RESEARCH, INDUSTRIAL - MANAGEMENT.
Foster, Richard N. Innovation . New York , c1986. 316 p. : ISBN 0-671-62250-1 : LC Card 86-1945 DDC 658.4/062 19
HD45 .F67 1986 ***NYPL [JLE 86-1899]***

RESEARCH, INDUSTRIAL - MANAGEMENT - CONGRESSES.
Technology management '85 . London , c1985. 160 p. : ISBN 0-903748-61-4
NYPL [JLG 87-124]

RESEARCH, INDUSTRIAL - NETHERLANDS.
Kleinknecht, A. Industriële innovatie in Nederland . Assen , 1987. viii, 140 p. ; ISBN

90-232-2261-X : LC Card 87-157579
HC329.5.T4 K58 1987

RESEARCH, INDUSTRIAL - SOVIET UNION.
Kompleksnaia organizatsiia issledovaniĭ . Moskva , 1981. 191 p. : LC Card 82-130582
HC340.R4 K66 1981

Sovershenstvovanie metodologii ėkonomicheskogo analiza v nauchnykh uchrezhdeniiakh i nauchno-tekhnicheskikh kompleksakh . Kiev , 1986. 116 p. ; LC Card 87-126466
HC340.R4 S68 1986

RESEARCH, INDUSTRIAL - SOVIET UNION - REPUBLICS - CONGRESSES.
Upravlenie nauchno-tekhnicheskim progressom v soiuznykh respublikakh /. Tallin , 1986. 158 p. ; LC Card 87-123175
HC340.T4 U77 1986

RESEARCH, INDUSTRIAL - UNITED STATES.
Johnston, Robert F. Entrepreneurial science . New York , 1987. 157 p. ; ISBN 0-89930-260-2 (lib. bdg. : alk. paper) LC Card 87-2518 DDC 338/.06 19
HC110.H53 J65 1987

Nauchno-tekhnicheskiĭ progress i strukturnye sdvigi v ėkonomike sovremennogo kapitalizma . Moskva , 1987. 168 p. ; LC Card 87-165811
HC240.9.T4 N38 1987

Technology and trade . Washington , 1986. x, 80 p. : LC Card 86-603362 DDC 338/.06 19
HC110.T4 T393 1986

RESEARCH, INDUSTRIAL - YUGOSLAVIA.
Čubra, Nikola. Naučnoistraživački i razvojni rad u organizacijama udruženog rada /. Beograd , 1982. 165 p. : LC Card 82-166181
HD30 .C83 1982

Research Institute for Agrucultural Economics. see **Agrárgazdasági Kutató Intézet.**

RESEARCH INSTITUTES - SOVIET UNION.
Sovershenstvovanie metodologii ėkonomicheskogo analiza v nauchnykh uchrezhdeniiakh i nauchno-tekhnicheskikh kompleksakh . Kiev , 1986. 116 p. ; LC Card 87-126466
HC340.R4 S68 1986

Research memorandum (Greater London Council) .
(RM498) Weatheritt, L. Manufacturing industry in Greater London /. London , c1975. ii, 26 p. ; ISBN 0-7168-0853-6 (pbk.) LC Card 82-213745
HD5766.L66 W43 1975

(RM503) The Relationship between the GLC Housing Department, its tenants, and the public /. London , c1977. iv, 107 p. ; ISBN 0-7168-0895-1 (pbk.) LC Card 87-107202
HD7288.78.G72 L68 1977

Research memorandum (Institut für Höhere Studien, Wien) .
(no. 210) Amanshauser, Wilfried. Jugendarbeitsmarktförderung in Österreich /. Wien [1985] ii, 71, 3 p. ; LC Card 86-165982
HD6276.A9 A43 1985

(no. 212, 218) Diekmann, Andreas. Einkommensunterschiede zwischen Frauen und Männern . Wien [1985] 2 v. (244, 4 p.) : LC Card 86-150241
HD6061 .D54 1985

Research methodology for economists . Johnson, Glenn Leroy, 1918- New York , London , c1986. xx, 252 p. ; ISBN 0-02-949840-6 LC Card 85-24240 DDC 300/.72 19
HB74.5 .J65 1986 ***NYPL [JLE 86-4300]***

Research methods /. McNeill, Patrick. London , New York , 1985. 136 p. ; ISBN 0-422-79540-2 (pbk.) LC Card 85-4656 DDC 301/.072 19
HM24 .M37 1985 ***NYPL [JLD 86-4181]***

Research monograph (Australian National University. Health Economics Research Unit) .
(3) Brown, Malcolm C. (Malcolm Clarence), 1941- National health insurance in Canada and Australia . Canberra , 1983. vii, 108 p. ; ISBN 0-86784-281-4 (pbk.) LC Card 86-214526 DDC 368.4/2/00971 19
HD7102.A8 B75 1983

Research monograph (Bangladesh Institute of Development Studies) .
(no. 6) Rahman, Rushidan Islam. The wage employment market for rural women in Bangladesh /. Dhaka, Bangladesh , 1986. xi, 97 p. ; LC Card 86-903129 DDC 331.4/295492 19
HD6061.2.B3 R34 1986

Research monograph (Georgia State University. College of Business Administration) .
(no. 100) Wagner, Nancy A. Eric Louis Kohler in the accounting profession /. Atlanta, Ga. , 1987. vi, 210 p. ; ISBN 0-88406-196-5 (pbk.) : LC Card 86-25633 DDC 657/.092/4 19
HF5604.5.K64 W34 1987

(no. 87) Wacht, Richard F. A new approach to capital budgeting for city and county governments /. Atlanta, Ga. , 1987. ix, 149 p. : ISBN 0-88406-190-6 (pbk.) : LC Card 87-21157 DDC 352.1/2 19
HJ9147 .W33 1987

Research monographs (Egypt. Jihāz Tanẓīm al-Usrah wa-al-Sukkān. Maktab al-Buḥūth) .
(series no. 5) Ibrahim, Saad Eddin. Internal migration in Egypt . Cairo, Egypt [1982] 86, viii p. : LC Card 84-960007 DDC 304.8/0962 19
HB2121.7.A3 I27 1982

Research notes and discussions paper .
(no. 56) Grubel, Herbert G. Multinational banking /. Singapore , 1985. iii, 21 p. ; ISBN 997-19-8817-8 (pbk.) LC Card 86-940563 DDC 332.1/6 19
HG3881 .G747 1985

Research notes (National Institute of Development and Cultural Research (Botswana)) .
(no. 7) Gobotswang, Z. Pilot evaluation report on Mahalapye Development Trust /. Gaborone, Botswana [1982] v leaves, 61, 3 p. ; LC Card 87-122810
HD5710.85.B59 G63 1982

Research on rural-non farm employment in Lesotho . Senaoana, M. P. Roma, Lesotho [1984] 88 leaves : LC Card 86-214032 DDC 331.12/5/096816 19
HD5842.7.A6 S46 1984

Research on the quality of life / edited by Frank M. Andrews. Ann Arbor, Mich. : Survey Research Center, Institute for Social Research, University of Michigan, 1986. xiv, 365 p. ; ill. : 24 cm. Includes bibliographies. ISBN 0-87944-308-1 : LC Card 86-15179 DDC 305/.0973 19
1. Quality of life - United States. 2. Quality of life. 3. Social indicators - United States. I. Andrews, Frank M. II. Michigan. University. Survey Research Center.
HN60 .R47 1986 ***NYPL [JLE 86-3621]***

RESEARCH - PAKISTAN - FINANCE - STATISTICS.
Growth of R & D manpower and expenditure in Pakistan. Islamabad , 1985. 66 p. ; LC Card 85-932022 DDC 331.12/510014/095491021 19
HC440.5.Z9 R44 1985

Research paper (Australia. Dept. of Social Security. Development Division) .
(no. 29) Whiteford, Peter. Issues in assistance for families . Woden, ACT [1986] iii, 56 p. ; ISBN 0-642-51604-9 (pbk.) LC Card 86-231139 DDC 362/.0425 19
HD4925.5.A8 W47 1986

(no. 31) Moore, Jim. Trends in the disposable incomes of Australian families, 1964-65 to 1985-86 /. Woden, ACT [1986] vii, 103 p. ; ISBN 0-642-51700-2 (pbk.) LC Card 87-154435 DDC 339.394 19
HC610.I5 M66 1986

Research paper (Australia. Dept. of Social Security. Research and Statistics Branch) .
(no. 26) Retirement income provisions overseas. [Canberra] [1984] 162 p. ; ISBN 0-642-51580-8 (pbk.) LC Card 84-252861 DDC 331.25/22 19
HD7105.3 .R46 1984

Research paper (Australia-Japan Research Centre) .
(no. 102) Anderson, Kym. Australia's trade growth with developing countries /. Canberra, Australia , 1983. iv, 55 p. ; ISBN 0-86413-001-5 (pbk.) LC Card 86-673748
HF3948.D44 A52x 1983

Research paper (Chuo Kikuu cha Dar es Salaam. Bureau of Resource Assessment and Land Use Planning) .
(no. 38) Joseph, G. An econometric approach to forecasting demand for electricity in Tanzania to the year 2000 A.D. /. [Dar es Salaam] [between 1978 and 1984] 42, [44] p. ; LC Card 84-980076 DDC 333.7/09678 333.79/3213/09678 19
HD107 .D36 no. 38a HD9685.T352

(no. 71) Workshop on the Institutionalization of the Shallow Wells Programme under Tanzanian Administration (1981 : University of Dar es Salaam) Proceedings of the Workshop on the Institutionalization of the Shallow Wells Programme under Tanzanian Administration /. [Dar es Salaam?] , 1981. 3, 16, 12 p. ; LC Card 85-980881 DDC 333.7/09678 s 333.91/22/09678 19
HD107 .D36 no. 71 HD1699.T33

Research paper (Chuo Kikuu cha Dar es Salaam. Institute of Resource Assessment) .
(6) Bantje, Han. Mechanised food production in Tanzania . [Dar es Salaam] [1984] 3 leaves, 73 p. : LC Card 86-980118 DDC 338.1/61/09678 19
HD1471.T34 B36 1984

Research paper (New Zealand. National Housing Commission) .
(86/4) The Private residential landlord and tenant in Christchurch . Wellington, N.Z. [1986] viii, 105 p. : ISBN 0-477-03810-7 (pbk.) LC Card 87-147647 DDC 333.33/8 19
HD7288.85.N452 C576 1986

Research paper (Reserve Bank of New Zealand) .
(no. 40) Clements, R. T. The Reserve Bank econometric model of the New Zealand economy . Wellington [1986] 62 p., [2] leaves of plates : LC Card 87-142103 DDC 330.9931/00724 19
HC665 .C54 1986

Research paper series .
(no. 2) Mukras, M. S. Recent findings on the determinants of urban-rural income transfers in Kenya /. [Nairobi?] , 1985. ii, 33 leaves : LC Card 85-980600
HC865.Z9 I516 1985

(no. 38) Solé, Miguel José. Las condiciones de vida y de trabajo de los tamberos de la pampa húmeda . Stockholm , 1983. 33 p. ; LC Card 84-107283
HD1865.P35 S65 1983

(paper no. 42) Feuer, Björn. Consideraciones aproximativas en torno a la investigación laboral en América Latina /. Stockholm [1985] 18 p. ; LC Card 85-205735
HD4824.5.L29 F48 1985

Research paper series (Latinamerika-institutet i Stockholm) .
(paper no. 42) Feuer, Björn. Consideraciones aproximativas en torno a la investigación laboral en América Latina /. Stockholm [1985] 18 p. ; LC Card 85-205735
HD4824.5.L29 F48 1985

Research paper series (Latinamerikainstitutet i Stockholm) .
(paper no. 38) Solé, Miguel José. Las condiciones de vida y de trabajo de los tamberos de la pampa húmeda . Stockholm , 1983. 33 p. ; LC Card 84-107283
HD1865.P35 S65 1983

Research paper (University of Chicago. Committee on Geographical Studies) .
(no. 223) Astroth, Joseph H., 1955- Understanding peasant agriculture . Chicago, Ill. , 1987. p. cm. ISBN 0-89065-127-2 (pbk.) : LC Card 87-15099 DDC 333.76/13/0724 19
HD879.P8 A77 1987

Research paper (University of Swaziland. Social Science Research Unit) .
(no. 8) Guma, Xolile P. Small farmer credit and small farmer attitudes towards co-operatives /. [Kwaluseni, Swaziland] [1982] 94 p. : LC Card 86-101161 DDC 332.7/1/096813 19
HD1491.S855 G85 1982
NYPL [JLG 86-262]

Research papers in geography .
(no. 30) Camm, J. C. R. (Jack Charles Robert) Hardtimes--a cartographic and graphic representation of selected aspects of the depression years, 1925-1935, in Australia /. [Newcastle, N.S.W.] , 1985. 59, iii p. : ISBN 0-7259-0542-5 (pbk.) : LC Card 86-222404 DDC 330.994/042 19
HC603 .C36 1985

Research project, industrial readjustment and the internationnal division of labour .
(report no. 10) Perspectives on industrial readjustment, the EEC and the developing countries /. Tilburg, Netherlands , 1978. ii, 98 p. ; ***NYPL [JLF 86-1708]***

Research publication (Salt Lake City, Utah) .
(85-10) Katayama, Leslee. Hotel sales, room rents, and transient room taxes in Utah, 1978-1985 /. Salt Lake City, Utah (519 Heber Wells Bldg., Salt Lake City 84134) [1985] i, 49 leaves : LC Card 86-620905 DDC 336.2/7864794 19
HJ5715.U62 U85 1985

Research report / Bureau of Market Research, University of South Africa = Navorsingsverslag / Buro vir Marknavorsing, Universiteit van Suid-Afrika .
(no. 130.4) Van Wyk, H. de J. Income and expenditure patterns of urban Black multiple households in Durban, 1985 /. Pretoria , 1986. xi, 130 p. : ISBN 0-908408-59-5 (pbk.) LC Card 87-151639 DDC 658.8/3968 s 339.4/1/0968455021 19
HC517.S7 S48 no. 130, pt. 4 HD7064.4.Z8D8

(no. 59) Nel, P. A. The BM industrial register and its application in industrial marketing /. Pretoria , 1977. iii, 29, [34] p. ; ISBN 0-949951-74-9 (pbk.) LC Card 85-127469
HC905 .N45 1977

Research report / Ekonomiska forskningsinstitutet vid Handelshögskolan i Stockholm.
Krusell, Per. The demand for money in Sweden, 1970-1983 /. Stockholm, Sweden [1986] 91 p. ; ISBN 0-917258-21-5 (pbk.) LC Card 87-151531 DDC 332.4/14 19
HG1125 .K78 1986

Research report (Addis Ababa University. Institute of Development Research) .
(no. 21) Habtamu Wondimu. Some factors which affect peasant motivation to work in the Ethiopian agricultural producers cooperatives /. [Addis Ababa] [1983] 60 leaves : LC Card 84-980911 DDC 334/.683/0963 19
HD1491.E83 H3 1983b ***NYPL [JLG 86-163]***

Research report (Addis Abeba University. Institute of Development Research) .
(no. 24) Yeraswork Admassie. Food-for-work in Ethiopia . Addis Abeba , 1985. viii, 102, [58] leaves : LC Card 86-980537 DDC 339.5/0963 19
HD5839.7.A6 Y47 1985

Research report (American Institute of Real Estate Appraisers) .
(no. 1) 1986 membership profile /. Chicago, Ill. , c1986. ix, 44 p. : ISBN 0-911780-85-8 (pbk.) LC Card 87-144205 DDC 333.33/2/0973 19
HD251 .A17 1986

Research report (Bangladesh Agricultural University. Bureau of Socio-economic Research and Training) .
(no. 13) Ali, Md. Harun, 1944- An economic study on guava cultivation in some selected areas of Bangladesh /. Mymensingh , 1986. 38 p. ; LC Card 87-902187 DDC 338.1/74421/095492 19
HD9259.G83 B353 1986

Research report (Business Intelligence Program (SRI International)) .
(no. 709) Carlson, Richard C. Managing the changing work force . Menlo Park, Calif. (333 Ravenswood Ave., Menlo Park 94025-3476) , c1984. 44 p. : LC Card 86-212936 DDC 658.3 19
HD5706 .C29 1984

(no. 716) Skov, Paul B. Strategy, analysis, and decisions . Menlo Park, Calif. (333 Ravenswood Ave., Menlo Park 94025-3476) , c1985. 40 p. : LC Card 87-119164 DDC 658.4/012
HD30.28 .S49 1985

(no. 722) Poon, Raymond S. Biotechnology instrumentation . Menlo Park, Calif. (333 Ravenswood Ave., Menlo Park 94025-3476) , c1985. 32 p. : LC Card 87-160671 DDC 338.4/766063 19
HD9706.65.B552 P66 1985

(704) McPherson, Joseph H. Bringing innovations to market . Menlo Park, Calif. (333 Ravenswood Ave., Menlo Park 94025-3476) , c1984. 36 p. : LC Card 87-118382 DDC 658.5/75 19
HF5415.153 .M35 1984

(706) Gollub, James O. Business opportunities among the aging population . Menlo Park, Calif. (333 Ravenswood Ave., Menlo Park 94025-3476) , c1984. 36 p. : LC Card 86-210219 DDC 658.8/348 19
HC110.C6 G62 1984

(710) Business opportunities in China . Menlo Park, Calif. (333 Ravenswood Ave., Menlo Park 94025-3476) , c1984. 32 p. : LC Card 86-210279 DDC 338.8/8851 19
HC427.92 .B85 1984

(713) Kliachko, Valerie A. World diesel engine markets . Menlo Park, Calif. (333 Ravenswood Ave., Menlo Park 94025-3476) , c1985. 36 p. : LC Card 87-145492 DDC 338.4/7621436 19
HD9705.5.M672 K65 1985

(714) George, J. John. Opportunities in computer-assisted medical diagnostics . Menlo Park, Calif. (333 Ravenswood Ave., Menlo Park 94025-3476) , c1985. 32 p. : LC Card 86-232002 DDC 381/.45681761 19
HD9995.D543 U63 1985

(715) Harman, Willis W. Creativity and intuition in business . Menlo Park, Calif. (333 Ravenswood Ave., Menlo Park 94025-3476) , c1985. 28 p. : LC Card 86-232128 DDC 658.4/09 19
HD53 .H37 1985

(718) Morse, Diane McGinty. Managing competitive intelligence . Menlo Park, Calif. , c1985. 36 p. : LC Card 87-404501 DDC 658.4/7 19
HD38.7 .M674 1985

(720, etc) Schmidt, Klaus D. Business customs and protocol in the ASEAN region /. Menlo Park, Calif. [c1985- v. <1 > : LC Card 87-404513 DDC 395/.52 19
HF5387 .S36 1985

Research report (Canadian Energy Research Institute) .
(86-1) Pasay, Janice L. The effect of the western accord and recent provincial royalty changes on petroleum industry capital expenditures /. Calgary, Alta. , 1986. iv, 27, 4 leaves ; LC Card 86-203742 DDC 338.2/3 19
HD9574.C22 P37 1986

Research report (Financial Accounting Foundation. Governmental Accounting Standards Board)
Ingram, Robert W. Financial reporting practices of local governments /. Stamford, Conn. (P.O. Box 3821, Stamford 06905-0821) , c1987. viii, 93 p. : LC Card 87-80564 DDC 657/.835 19
HJ9777.A3 I55 1987

Van Daniker, Relmond P., 1942- Infrastructure assets . Stamford, Conn. (High Ridge Park, P.O. Box 3821, Stamford 06905-0821) , c1986. xii, 155 p. ; LC Card 86-90661 DDC 657/.835 19
HJ9816 .V35 1986

Research report (Handelshögskolan i Stockholm. Ekonomiska forskningsinstitutet)
Krusell, Per. The demand for money in Sweden, 1970-1983 /. Stockholm, Sweden [1986] 91 p. ; ISBN 0-917258-21-5 (pbk.) LC Card 87-151531 DDC 332.4/14 19
HG1125 .K78 1986

Thimrén, Claes. Imperfectly competitive markets for exhaustible resources . Stockholm, Sweden [1986] 94 p. : ISBN 91-7258-212-X (pbk.) LC Card 87-151530 DDC 333.7/0724 19
HB238 .T54 1986

Research report (International Food Policy Research Institute) .
(55) Oyejide, T. Ademola. The effects of trade and exchange rate policies on agriculture in Nigeria /. Washington, D.C., USA , c1986. 61 p. : ISBN 0-89629-056-5 (pbk.) LC Card 86-21309 DDC 338.1/09669 19
HD2145.5 .O94 1986

(56) Tshibaka, Tshikala B., 1949- The effects of trade and exchange rate policies on agriculture in Zaire /. Washington, D.C., USA , 1986. 65 p. : ISBN 0-89629-057-3 LC Card 86-27449 DDC 338.1/09675/1 19
HD2135.5 .T75 1986

(56) Tshibaka, Tshikala B., 1949- The effects of trade and exchange rate policies on agriculture in Zaire /. Washington, D.C., USA , 1986. 65 p. : ISBN 0-89629-057-3 LC Card 86-27449 DDC 338.1/09675/1 19
HD2135.5 .T75 1986

(57) Sarma, J. S. Cereal feed use in the Third World . Washington, D.C. , c1986. 68 p. : ISBN 0-89629-058-1 (pbk.) LC Card 86-27355 DDC 338.1/7325/091724 19
HD9052.D44 S27 1986

(59) Bautista, Romeo M., 1941- Production incentives in Philippine agriculture . Washington, D.C., USA , c1987. 78 p. : ISBN 0-89629-061-1 (pbk.) LC Card 87-3233 DDC 338.1/8 19
HD2087 .B38 1987

(60) Nerlove, Marc, 1933- Population policy and individual choice . Washington, D.C., U. S.A. , 1987. 52 p. : ISBN 0-89629-062-X (pbk.) LC Card 87-16802 DDC 363.9 19
HB901 .N474 1987

(60) Nerlove, Marc, 1933- Population policy and individual choice . Washington, D.C., U. S.A. , 1987. 52 p. : ISBN 0-89629-062-X (pbk.) LC Card 87-16802 DDC 363.9 19
HB901 .N474 1987

Research report (International Foundation of Employee Benefit Plans) .
(rept. 86-1) Joanette, Francois P. Funding and asset allocation decisions in corporate pension plans /. Brookfield, Wis. , c1986. 17 p. : ISBN 0-89154-304-X (pbk.) : LC Card 87-118785 DDC 658.2/253/0973 19
HD7105.45.U6 J6 1986

(rept. 86-2) Sahin, Izzet. Job mobility and private pensions /. Brookfield, Wis. , c1986. xv, 49 p. ; ISBN 0-89154-305-8 (pbk.) LC Card 87-129468 DDC 331.25/2/0724 19
HD7105 .S229 1986

(rept. 86-2) Sahin, Izzet. Job mobility and private pensions /. Brookfield, Wis. , c1986. xv, 49 p. ; ISBN 0-89154-305-8 (pbk.) LC Card 87-129468 DDC 331.25/2/0724 19
HD7105 .S229 1986

(rept. 86-5) Curatola, Anthony P. State income tax consequences of retirement plan distributions /. Brookfield, Wis. , c1986. 20 p. ; ISBN 0-89154-324-4 (pbk.) LC Card 87-158902 DDC 336.24/16 19
HJ4653.P5 C87 1986

(rpt. 86-4) Coudroglou, Aliki. Employee assistance programs within the context of personnel policies /. Brookfield, Wis. , c1986. 26 p. ; ISBN 0-89154-322-8 (pbk.) LC Card 87-158924 DDC 658.3/82 19
HF5549.5.E42 C676 1986

Research report (Kentucky. General Assembly. Legislative Research Commission) .
(no. 221) Kentucky. General Assembly. Tobacco Task Force. Final report of the Kentucky Tobacco Task Force /. Frankfort, Ky. [1986] vii, 91 p. : LC Card 86-622267 DDC 338.1/7371/09769 19
HD9137.K4 K45 1986

Research report (Lincoln College (University of Canterbury). Agricultural Economics Research Unit) .
(no. 180) St. Hill, R. L. Labour mobility between New Zealand and Australia /. Canterbury, N.Z. [1986] ix, 68 p. : LC Card 87-109510 DDC 331.12/791 19
HD8848.5.N45 S7 1986

(no. 181) Pryde, J. G. Survey of New Zealand farmer intentions and opinions, November 1985-January 1986 /. Canterbury, N.Z. [1986] 133 p. ; LC Card 87-107903 DDC 338.1/09931 19
HD8039.F32 N486 1986

Research report (Majlis al-Abḥāth al-Iqtiṣādīyah wa-al-Ijtimāʻīyah) .
(no. 19) Affan, Bodour O. Abu. Traffic and public transport in metropolitan Khartoum . Khartoum [1985] iv, 73 leaves ; LC Card 86-980566 DDC 388.4/1/096262 19
HE311.S742 K472 1985

Research report (National University of Lesotho. Institute of Southern African Studies) .
(no. 13) Swallow, Brent M. Cattle marketing in Lesotho /. Maseru, Lesotho [1986] iv, 75 leaves : LC Card 87-132309 DDC 381/.416213/096816 19
HD9433.L452 S9 1986

(no. 6) Senaoana, M. P. Research on rural-non farm employment in Lesotho . Roma, Lesotho

[1984] 88 leaves : LC Card 86-214032 DDC 331.12/5/096816 19
HD5842.7.A6 S46 1984

Research report (Nordiska Afrikainstitutet) .
(no. 77) Fadahunsi, Akin. The development process and technology . Uppsala , 1986. 41 p. ; ISBN 91-7106-257-2 (pbk.) LC Card 87-119156 DDC 338.9669/07 19
HC1055.Z9 T43 1986

Research report (Oklahoma Agricultural Experiment Station) .
(P-879) Plaxico, James Sam, 1924- Financial status of Oklahoma farmers and ranchers, 1985 . [Stillwater] [1986] 42 p. ; LC Card 86-622478 DDC 338.1/3/09766021 19
HD1775.O5 P57 1986

Research report or occasional paper, 0812-1664 .
(no. 130) Pullen, J. M. Lord Grenville's manuscript notes on Malthus /. [Newcastle] [1986] 94 p. ; ISBN 0-7259-0557-3 (pbk.) LC Card 87-150102 DDC 330.15/3 19
HB161.M28 P85 1986

Research report (Roskilde universitetscenter. Institut for samfundsøkonomi og planlægning) .
(1984/nr. 1) Vesterø Jensen, Carsten. Det tvedelte pensionssystem /. Roskilde [1984] 284 p. ; LC Card 84-181865
HD7105.35.D4 J45 1984

Research report (Sathāban Prachāk
(no. 12) Goldstein, Sidney, 1927- Urban-rural migration differentials in Thailand /. [Bangkok] , 1974. 49 p. ; LC Card 78-301310 DDC 301.36/1
HB2104.55.A3 G64
NYPL [JLM 83-719 no.12]

Research report series (Pacific Islands Development Program (East-West Center)) .
(no. 2) Feinstein, Charles, 1954- Privatization possibilities among Pacific island countries /. Honolulu, Hawaii, USA , 1986. iv, 48 p. ; ISBN 0-86638-084-1 LC Card 86-24012 DDC 338.99 19
HD4415.6 .F45 1986

(no. 4) Edo, Junko, 1947- Japanese aid to the Pacific islands region /. Honolulu, Hawaii, USA , 1986. x, 94 p. ; ISBN 0-86638-090-6 (pbk.) LC Card 87-5293 DDC 338.91/52/09 19
HC681. E36 1986

(no. 5) Hudgins, Linda Lucas, 1946- Development of the Mexican tuna industry, 1976-86 /. Honolulu, Hawaii , 1987. p. cm. ISBN 0-86638-091-4 LC Card 87-505 DDC 338.3/72758 19
HD9469.T83 M64 1987

(no. 8) Doulman, David J., 1950- Options for U. S. fisheries investment in the Pacific Islands region /. Honolulu, Hawaii, U. S.A. , 1987. vi, 30 p. ; ISBN 0-86638-097-3 (pbk.) LC Card 87-9198 DDC 338.3/72758 19
HD9469.T83 I743 1987

Research report series (United States. National Commission for Employment Policy) .
(RR-85-09) Goldstein, Harold. Training for work in the computer age . Washington, D.C. , 1986. iv, 109 p. ; LC Card 86-601422 DDC 331.25/92 19
HD5715.2 .G63 1986

Research report series (University of California, San Diego. Center for U. S.-Mexican Studies) .
(43) Cornelius, Wayne A., 1945- The political economy of Mexico under de la Madrid . La Jolla, Calif. , 1986. 50 p. ; LC Card 87-621352 DDC 330.972/0834 19
HC135 .C7185 1986

(44) De Murguía, Valdemar. Capital flight and economic crisis . La Jolla, Calif. , 1986. 27 p. ; LC Card 87-621351 DDC 332/.042 19
HG3916 .D4 1986

Research report series (University of Michigan. Institute for Social Research)
Burpee, C. Gaye. 1985 household survey of Grenada . Ann Arbor, Mich. , 1986. 168 p. : ISBN 0-87944-317-0 (pbk.) LC Card 86-217405 DDC 339.4/1/0723 19
HD7009.9.Z8 G843 1986

Research report (Stout Vocational Rehabilitation Institute. Research and Training Center)
Thomas, Dale F. Fees for services . Menomonie, WI [1986] v, 90 p. : LC Card 86-622897 DDC 338.4/33620425 19
HD7256.U5 T47 1986

Research report summaries.
Schwartz, Moshe. Non-agricultural employment for moshav youth in the Galilee /. Rehovot, Israel , c1985. 36, [2] p. ; LC Card 86-115596 DDC 331.3/4/0956945 19
HD6276.I66 G347 1985

Research report (Sūn Wichākān Thīyū'āsai lǣ Kāntang Thinthān Manut (Thailand)) .
(no. 7) Chadsri Bunnag. Housing in urban development . [Bangkok] [Rotterdam] Netherlands [1985] 49, [2] leaves : LC Card 86-915989 DDC 363.5/09593 19
HD7363.55.A3 C46 1985

Research report (Texas Transportation Institute) .
(285-1) Benson, Fred C. Hot-mix pavement stability performance versus laboratory test results /. College Station, Tex. [1985] xi, 225 p. : LC Card 86-620969 DDC 380.5 s 625.8/5 19
HE203 .T43 no. 285-1 TE200

(285-1) Benson, Fred C. Hot-mix pavement stability performance versus laboratory test results /. College Station, Tex. [1985] xi, 225 p. : LC Card 86-620969 DDC 380.5 s 625.8/5 19
HE203 .T43 no. 285-1 TE200

(319-1F) Button, Joe W. Synthetic fibers in asphalt paving mixtures /. College Station, Tex. [1984] vi, 153 p. : LC Card 86-620835 DDC 380.5 s 625.8/5 19
HE203 .T43 no. 319-1F TA443.A7

(322-1) McNees, Roger W. State-of-the-art and objectives of reflective raised pavement markers /. College Station, Tex. , Springfield, Va. [1986] vii, 162 p. : LC Card 87-620643 DDC 380.5 s 625.7/97 19
HE203 .T43 no. 322-1 TE203

(322-1) McNees, Roger W. State-of-the-art and objectives of reflective raised pavement markers /. College Station, Tex. , Springfield, Va. [1986] vii, 162 p. : LC Card 87-620643 DDC 380.5 s 625.7/97 19
HE203 .T43 no. 322-1 TE203

(322-3) Noel, James S. Retention of reflective raised pavement markers /. College Station, Tex. , Springfield, Va. [1986] xiii, 170 p. : LC Card 87-620642 DDC 380.5 s 625.7/042 19
HE203 .T43 no. 322-3 TE203

(331-3F) Mason, John M. (John Michael), 1950- Operational and geometric evaluation of exclusive truck lanes /. College Station, Tex. , Springfield, Va. [1986] vii, 156 p. : LC Card 86-622239 DDC 380.5 s 388.3/14 19
HE203 .T43 no. 331-3F HE356.T4

(337-1F) McFarland, William F. New approaches to project ranking . College Station, Tex. , Springfield, Va. [1985] xvii, 116 p. : LC Card 86-622422 DDC 380.5 s 388.1/12/09764 19
HE203 .T43 no. 337-1F HE356.T4

(339-5) Lomax, Timothy J. Guidelines for estimating the cost effectiveness of high-occupancy vehicle lanes /. College Station, Tex. , Springfield, Va. [1985] xiii, 55 p. : LC Card 86-622240 DDC 380.5 s 388.3/142 19
HE203 .T43 no. 339-5 HE356.T4

(339-8) Lomax, Timothy J. Relative mobility in Texas cities, 1975 to 1984 /. College Station, Tex. [1986] xiii, 30, 9 p. : LC Card 87-620994 DDC 380.5 s 388.4/1314/09764 19
HE203 .T43 no. 339-8 HE356.T4

(345-1) Roberts, Freddy L. Establishing material properties for thin asphalt concrete surfaces on granular bases /. College Station, Tex. [1985] xvi, 141 p. : LC Card 86-620971 DDC 380.5 s 625.8/5 19
HE203 .T43 no. 345-1 TE270

(345-1) Roberts, Freddy L. Establishing material properties for thin asphalt concrete surfaces on granular bases /. College Station, Tex. [1985] xvi, 141 p. : LC Card 86-620971 DDC 380.5 s 625.8/5 19
HE203 .T43 no. 345-1 TE270

(346-1F) Sicking, Dean. Roadside concrete barriers . College Station, Tex. , Springfield, Va. [1985] vii, 60, 64, [51] p. : LC Card 86-622864 DDC 380.5 s 625.7/95 19
HE203 .T43 no. 346-1F TE228

(372-1F) The Effect of tire pressures on flexible pavements /. College Station, Tex. , Springfield, Va. , 1985. viii, 235 p. : LC Card 86-622241 DDC 380.5 s 625.8 19
HE203 .T43 no. 372-1F TE270

(425-2F) McCasland, William R. Transitway surveillance, communications, and control /. College Station, Tex. [1986] vi, 76 p. : LC Card 87-620995 DDC 380.5 s 388.3/143 19
HE203 .T43 no. 425-2F HE336.B8

Research report (University of Cape Town. School of Environmental Studies) .
(no. 20) Sinclair, Sharyn. The rural settlement of Verlorenvlei in historical perspective /. Rondebosch, South Africa [1980] 234 leaves : LC Card 86-210654
HD991.Z9 V477 1980

(no. 34) Stauth, Roy. A methodology for determining the socially optimum uses of estuarine resources . Rondebosch, South Africa [1982] v, 119 leaves : LC Card 86-210152
HC905.Z7 G87 1982

Research report (University of Dhaka, Bureau of Economic Research) .
(new ser. no. 3) Muqtada, M. Social and economic formations in Bangladesh agriculture . Dacca, Bangladesh , 1986. 68 p. ; LC Card 86-902421 DDC 338.1/09549/2 19
HD2075.6 .M86 1986

Research report (University of South Africa. Bureau of Market Research) .
(no. 130.1) Martins, J. H. Income and expenditure patterns of urban Indian multiple households in Durban, 1985 /. Pretoria , 1986. xi, 126 p. : ISBN 0-908408-54-4 (pbk.) LC Card 86-208481 DDC 658.8/3968 s 339.4/1/09684 19
HC517.S7 S48 no. 130, pt. 1 HD7064.4.Z8D8

(no. 130.2) Martins, J. H. Income and expenditure patterns of urban black multiple households in Pretoria, 1985 /. Pretoria , 1986. xi, 128 p. : ISBN 0-908408-57-9 (pbk.) LC Card 86-220725 DDC 658.8/3968 s 339.4/1/0968235 19
HC517.S7 S48 no. 130, pt. 2 HD7064.4.Z8P74

(no. 130.4) Van Wyk, H. de J. Income and expenditure patterns of urban Black multiple households in Durban, 1985 /. Pretoria , 1986. xi, 130 p. : ISBN 0-908408-59-5 (pbk.) LC Card 87-151639 DDC 658.8/3968 s 339.4/1/0968455021 19
HC517.S7 S48 no. 130, pt. 4 HD7064.4.Z8D8

(no. 130.5) Martins, J. H. Income and expenditure patterns of urban Indian households in Pietermaritzburg, 1985 /. Pretoria , 1986. xi, 126 p. : ISBN 0-908408-60-9 (pbk.) LC Card 87-140863 DDC 658.8/3968 s 339.4/1/0968475 19
HC517.S7 S48 no. 130, pt. 5 HD7064.4.Z8P54

(no. 59) Nel, P. A. The BM industrial register and its application in industrial marketing /. Pretoria , 1977. iii, 29, [34] p. ; ISBN 0-949951-74-9 (pbk.) LC Card 85-127469
HC905 .N45 1977

Research report (University of South Africa. Bureau of Market Research report) .
(no. 125) Van Zyl, S. J. J. Trends in capital expenditure on fixed assets /. Pretoria , 1985. ix, 100 p. : ISBN 0-908408-49-8 (pbk.) LC Card 86-206341 DDC 658.8/3968 s 332/.0414/0968 19
HC517.S7 S48 no. 125 HG4028.C4

Research report (University of Sydney. Dept. of Agricultural Economics) .
(no. 10) Fisher, Brian S. An economic and technical assessment of the establishment of an Australian fat-tail sheep industry /. [Sydney], N.S.W. , c1986. vi, 52 p. ; LC Card 87-154531 DDC 338.1/76386 19
HD9436.A82 F57 1986

Research report (University of Texas at Austin. Center for Transportation Research) .
(no. 356-1) Massimi, John J. Truck lane needs methodology . Austin , Springfield, Va. [1985] xii, 63 p. : LC Card 86-622425 DDC 388.1/3 19
HE336.T79 M37 1985

Research report (University of Wisconsin--Madison. College of Agricultural and Life Sciences. Research Division) .
(R3331) Saupe, William E. Rural poverty in Wisconsin counties /. Madison, WI [198-] 26

p. : LC Card 86-622097
HC107.W63 P6249 1980z

(R3377) Tienda, Marta. The structural transformation of employment in Wisconsin, 1960-1980 /. Madison, WI (Rm. 245, 30 N. Murray St., Madison 53715) [1986] ii, 47 p. ; LC Card 86-623091 DDC 331.12/09775 19
HD5725.W5 T54 1986

Research report (World Resources Institute) .
(#2) Repetto, Robert C. Paying the price . Washington, DC , c1985. 33 p. ; ISBN 0-915825-12-0 (pbk.) : LC Card 86-225070 DDC 338.4/366865/091724 19
HC59.72.E5 R46 1985

Research reports (Interntional Institute for Applied Systems Analysis) .
(RR84-2) Multiregional demography . Laxenburg, Austria , c1984. v, 81 p. : LC Card 84-218929 DDC 304.6 19
HB1951 .M85 1983 ***NYPL [JLE 86-583]***

Research series (Hawaii Institute of Tropical Agriculture and Human Resources)
Leong, Jerrold K. (Jerrold Kim), 1947- Economic implications of import barriers to protect the U. S. sugar industry with particular reference to Hawaii /. Manoa , 1987. p. cm. LC Card 87-11855 DDC 382/.456641/09969 19
HD9107.H3 L46 1987

Research series (International Institute for Labour Studies) .
(no. 82) Mikheev, S. Remuneration in Eastern European countries /. Geneva , 1985. vi, 45, ix p. ; ISBN 92-9014-408-4 (pbk.) : LC Card 86-216036 DDC 331.2/947 19
HD5014 .M55 1985

(no. 82) Mikheev, S. Remuneration in Eastern European countries /. Geneva , 1985. vi, 45, ix p. ; ISBN 92-9014-408-4 (pbk.) : LC Card 86-216036 DDC 331.2/947 19
HD5014 .M55 1985

(no. 84) Neffa, Julio César. La participación de los trabajadores en la gestión empresarial en la República del Perú, 1968-1980 /. Ginebra, Suiza , 1986. vi, 112, x p. : ISBN 92-9014-410-6 LC Card 87-400930 DDC 658.3/152/0985 19
HD5660.P4 N44 1986

(no. 85) Mikheev, S. Glossary of economic and social terminology in Eastern European socialist countries /. Geneva , 1986. 52, x p. ; ISBN 92-9014-413-0 : LC Card 86-214600 DDC 335.4/03/21 19
HB61 .M487 1986

(no. 86) Garnsey, Elizabeth. Industrial change and women's employment . Geneva , 1987. ix, 100, x p. : ISBN 92-9014-411-4 (pbk.) : LC Card 87-163195 DDC 331.4/09172/4 19
HD6223 .G37 1987

Research series (Statistics Canada. Labour Force Activity Section) .
(45) Self-employment in Canada =. Ottawa , c1985. 33 p. : ISBN 0-660-52868-1 (pbk.) : LC Card 87-101519
HD8037.C2 S45 1985

Research series (University of California, Berkeley. Institute of International Studies) .
(no. 66) State, oil, and agriculture in Nigeria /. Berkeley , c1987. xiv, 327 p. : ISBN 0-87725-166-5 (pbk.) : LC Card 87-2941 DDC 338.1/8669 19
HD2145.5 .S73 1987

(no. 68) Blatherwick, David E. S. The international politics of telecommunications /. [Berkeley, Calif.] , c1987. ix, 107 p. ; ISBN 0-87725-168-1 (pbk.) : LC Card 87-3509 DDC 384/.068 19
HE7645 .B57 1987

(no. 69) Wilensky, Harold L. Democratic corporatism and policy linkages . Berkeley , c1987. ix, 97 p. ; ISBN 0-87725-169-X (pbk.) : LC Card 87-3525 DDC 338.9 19
HD3616.E8 W54 1987

(no. 70) Poznański, Kazimierz. Technology, competition, & the Soviet bloc in the world market /. Berkeley , c1987. ix, 226 p. ; ISBN 0-87725-170-3 (pbk.) : LC Card 87-3505 DDC 338/.06 19
HC244.Z9 T4716 1987

Research studies in accounting.
Bhaskar, Krish N. The impact of microprocessors on the small accounting practice /. Englewood Cliffs, N.J. , c1986. xvi, 167 p. ; ISBN 0-13-453291-0 (pbk.) LC Card 85-25764 DDC 657/.028/5416 19
HF5679 .B45 1986 ***NYPL [JLE 86-4067]***

Macve, Richard, 1940- A survey of Lloyds syndicate accounts . Englewood Cliffs, NJ , 1986. xxv, 263 p. : ISBN 0-13-878273-3 : LC Card 85-12147 DDC 368/.012/094212 19
HG8039 .M33 1986 ***NYPL [JLE 87-864]***

Research study (Committee for Economic Development of Australia) .
(P24) Norman, Neville R. The economics of personal tax escalation in Australia /. [Sydney] : Sydney ; xii, 173 p. : ISBN 0-86861-652-4 (pbk.) LC Card 84-72057 DDC 336.24/2/0994 19
HJ4802 .N67 1985 ***NYPL [JLD 86-1906]***

(P25) Niland, John R. Control, consensus, or chaos? . Sydney , Boston , 1985. xiv, 330 p. : ISBN 0-86861-447-5 (pbk.) LC Card 85-70461 DDC 331.89/0994 19
HD8846.5 .N55 1985 ***NYPL [JLD 87-354]***

(P25) Niland, John R. Control, consensus, or chaos? . Sydney , Boston , 1985. xiv, 330 p. : ISBN 0-86861-447-5 (pbk.) LC Card 85-70461 DDC 331.89/0994 19
HD8846.5 .N55 1985 ***NYPL [JLD 87-354]***

Research Triangle Institute. NACS convenience store customer purchasing patterns research report /. [Falls Church, Va. , 1985?] vi, 76 p. : LC Card 86-157648 DDC 381/.1 19
HF5469.55.U62 N33 1985
NYPL [JLF 87-810]

Researches of the Jeddah Chamber of Commerce and Industry .
(research no. 3) Analytical study for the market of white meat and eggs /. Jeddah [1985?] 159 p. : LC Card 85-964046 DDC 381/.4566493/09538 19
HD9437.S332 A53 1985

Le réseau décisionnel en agro-alimentation au Québec . Conseil de planification et de développement du Québec. [Québec] [1979] 29 p. ; LC Card 85-102587
HD9014.C4 Q425 1979

Réseau Stratégies alimentaires, stratégies paysannes (France) Politiques vivrières, dépendances alimentaires et développement /. [Paris] , c1984. iv, 129 p. : ISBN 2-86844-000-2 : LC Card 84-248912
HD9017.S152 P65 1984

Reseña histórica del petróleo en Bolivia /. Castrillo M., Hugo. La Paz, Bolivia , 1986. 82 p., [1] leaf of plates : LC Card 87-403504 DDC 338.2/7282/0984 19
HD9574.B64 Y294 1986

Reseña histórica del primero de mayo en Mendoza. Vélez, Roberto. Reseña histórica del 1o de mayo en Mendoza . Buenos Aires , 1983. 125 p. : LC Card 87-400123 DDC 394.2/683 19
HD7791 .V4 1983

Reseña histórica del 1o de mayo en Mendoza . Vélez, Roberto. Buenos Aires , 1983. 125 p. : LC Card 87-400123 DDC 394.2/683 19
HD7791 .V4 1983

Reseña histórico-económica de los partidos de la provincia de Buenos Aires. [Buenos Aires] : Banco de la Provincia de Buenos Aires, [1981- v. <1-2 > : ill. (some col.) ; 30 cm. Bibliography: v. 1, p. 315. Includes indexes. CONTENTS. - 1 v. [1]. Eje pampeano -- v. 2. Eje mediterráneo. LC Card 87-114686 DDC 330.982/12/064 19
1. Buenos Aires (Argentina : Province) - Economic conditions - Statistics. 2. Buenos Aires (Argentina : Province) - Social conditions - Statistics. I. Banco de la Provincia de Buenos Aires.
HC177.B8 R47 1981

Resende, Mara Lúcia S. Dal-Rosso, Sadi. As condições de emprego do menor trabalhador . [Brasília] , c1986. 114 p. ; LC Card 86-224647
HD6231 .D35 1986

Resenha SENAI-MG, 10 anos. Belo Horizonte : SENAI, Departamento Regional de Minas Gerais, Assessoria de Comunicação, 1985. 128 p. ; 21 cm. LC Card 86-200862
1. Brazil. Serviço Nacional de Aprendizagem Industrial. Departamento Regional de Minas Gerais. Resenha SENAI-MG - History. I. Brazil. Serviço Nacional de Aprendizagem Industrial. Departamento Regional de Minas Gerais. Assessoria de Comunicação. II. Brazil. Serviço Nacional de Aprendizagem Industrial. Departamento Regional de Minas Gerais. Resenha SENAI-MG.
HD5715 .R46 1985

The Reserve Bank econometric model of the New Zealand economy . Clements, R. T. Wellington [1986] 62 p., [2] leaves of plates : LC Card 87-142103 DDC 330.9931/00724 19
HC665 .C54 1986

Reserve Bank of India.
Explanatory notes on current statistics. Bombay [1978] iii, 74 p. ; LC Card 85-229381
HG187.I4 E98 1978

Reserve Bank of India. Committee to Review the Working of the Monetary System. Report of the Committee to Review the Working of the Monetary System. Bombay : Reserve Bank of India, [1985] vii, 371 p. ; 25 cm. Includes bibliographical references. LC Card 87-902447 DDC 332.4/954 19
1. Monetary policy - India. 2. Money supply - India. I. Title.
HG1235 .R47 1985

Reserve Bank of India. Dept. of Statistical Analysis and Computer Services. Public limited companies in India, 1980-82 . Bombay , 1986. xvi, 359 p. ; LC Card 87-902505 DDC 338.7/4/0954021 19
HG4242 .P83 1986

RESIDENCES. see **ARCHITECTURE, DOMESTIC.**

RESIDENTAL MOBILITY - QUÉBEC (PROVINCE)
Garon-Audy, Muriel. Mobilités professionnelles et géographiques au Québec, 1954-64-74 /. Montréal , 1980. 61 p. ; LC Card 81-105620 DDC 331.12/7971 19
HD5717.5.C22 Q44 1980
NYPL [JLM 79-970 no.22]

RESIDENTIAL CONSTRUCTION. see **HOUSE CONSTRUCTION.**

Residential heating, ventilating & cooling systems market. New York, N.Y. : Frost & Sullivan, c1983. iv, 269 leaves : ill. ; 29 cm. "A 1124." "March, 1983." LC Card 87-138699 DDC 381/.45697/000973 19
1. Heating equipment industry - United States. 2. Air conditioning equipment industry - United States. 3. Market surveys - United States. I. Frost & Sullivan. II. Title: Residential heating, ventilating, and cooling systems market.
HD9683.U52 R47 1983

Residential heating, ventilating, and cooling systems market. Residential heating, ventilating & cooling systems market. New York, N.Y. , c1983. iv, 269 leaves : LC Card 87-138699 DDC 381/.45697/000973 19
HD9683.U52 R47 1983

RESIDENTIAL MOBILITY - GERMANY, WEST - MANNHEIM.
Miodek, Wolfgang. Innerstädtische Umzüge und Stadtentwicklung in Mannheim, 1977-1983 . Mannheim , 1986. 244 p. : ISBN 3-923750-18-8 : LC Card 86-181776
HD7288.92.G32 M355 1986

RESIDENTIAL MOBILITY - HUNGARY - STATISTICS.
Lakásváltoztatási szándékok, lakáskörülmények az 1984. évi mikrocenzus alapján /. Budapest , 1986. 199 p. ; ISBN 963-340-798-2 LC Card 87-110348
HD7337.5.A3 L355 1986

RESIDENTIAL MOBILITY - MATHEMATICAL MODELS.
Lierop, Wal F. J. van. Spatial interaction modelling and residential choice analysis /. Aldershot, Hants, England , Brookfield, Vt., USA , c1986. xii, 286 p. : ISBN 0-566-05036-6
NYPL [JLD 87-695]

RESIDENTIAL MOBILITY - MEXICO - CHIHUAHUA.
Verbeek, Henk. Residentiële mobiliteit in Ciudad Chihuahua, Mexico /. Utrecht [1986] iii, 142 p. : LC Card 86-172646
HD7288.92.M62 C488 1986

RESIDENTIAL MOBILITY - WASHINGTON METROPOLITAN AREA.
Gale, Dennis E. Black and white

urban-to-suburban outmigrants . Washington, D.C. [1986] 46 p. : LC Card 87-404424 DDC 307.2 19
HB1987.W34 G35 1986

Residential property sales in Maryland . Owen, Gail T. Baltimore, Md. (2225 N. Charles St., Baltimore 21218-5767) [1985] iv, 79 leaves : LC Card 86-622370 DDC 333.33/8 19
HD266.M3 O9 1985

Residential real estate . Platt, Barbara. Austin, Tex. , c1987. 206 p. : ISBN 0-941089-17-7 (lib. bdg.) LC Card 87-60697 DDC 332.63/243 19
HD1379 .P57 1987

Residential real estate appraisal . Miller, George H. Englewood Cliffs, N.J. , c1988. xiv, 336 p. : ISBN 0-13-762428-X (pbk.) : LC Card 87-6960 DDC 333.33/2 19
HD1387 .M547 1988

RESIDENTIAL SUBDIVISIONS. see **REAL ESTATE DEVELOPMENT.**

Residentiële mobiliteit in Ciudad Chihuahua, Mexico /. Verbeek, Henk. Utrecht [1986] iii, 142 p. : LC Card 86-172646
HD7288.92.M62 C488 1986

Resin systems in India . Gurdev Singh. Bombay , 1986. xiii, 100 p. ; ISBN 0-86132-128-6 : LC Card 86-903469 DDC 338.4/766837/0954 19
HD9660.R43 I44 1986

RESISTANCE MOVEMENTS (WORLD WAR, 1939-1945) see **ANTI-NAZI MOVEMENT.**

Resizing for organizational effectiveness . Ginzberg, Eli, 1911- New York, N.Y. (316 Uris Hall, New York 10027) , c1985. vii, 43 p. ; LC Card 86-162474 DDC 658.1/6 19
HD58.9 .G56 1985

Reskin, Barbara F. Women's work, men's work . Washington, D.C. , 1986. xii, 173 p. : ISBN 0-309-03429-9 (pbk.) LC Card 85-11541 DDC 331.1/33/0973 19
HD6060.5.U5 W66 1986
NYPL [JLF 86-1430]

Resnick, Stephen A.
Knowledge and class : a Marxian critique of political economy / Stephen A. Resnick and Richard D. Wolff. Chicago : University of Chicago Press, c1987. vii, 352 p. ; 25 cm. Bibliography: p. 283-342. Includes indexes. ISBN 0-226-71021-1 LC Card 86-32631 DDC 335.4 19
1. Marxian economics. 2. Capitalism. 3. Communist state. I. Wolff, Richard D. II. Title.
HB97.5 .R48 1987

Wolff, Richard D. Economics . Baltimore , c1987. xiv, 279 p. : ISBN 0-8018-3479-1 (alk. paper) LC Card 87-4131 DDC 330.1 19
HB90 .W65 1987

Resolving deep-rooted conflict . Burton, John W. (John Wear), 1915- Lanham, MD , c1987. vii, 74 p. ; ISBN 0-8191-6284-1 (alk. paper) : LC Card 87-6144 DDC 658.4 19
HD42 .B87 1987

RESOURCE ALLOCATION - MATHEMATICAL MODELS.
Sinn, Hans-Werner. [Kapitaleinkommensbesteuerung. English.] Capital income taxation and resource allocation /. Amsterdam ; New York : xiv, 411 p. ; ISBN 0-444-70208-3 LC Card 87-9126 DDC 336.24/3 19
HD2753.A3 S47413 1987

Toward a new Iron Age? . Cambridge, Mass. , 1987. vi, 173 p. : ISBN 0-674-89818-4 (alk. paper) LC Card 86-22923 DDC 333.8/5 19
HC59 .T63 1987

Resource analysis for integrated development, Sultanpur District, Uttar Pradesh. New Delhi : Water Technology Centre, Indian Agricultural Research Institute, I.C.A.R., 1986. xii, 436 p. : ill., maps ; 25 cm. Spine title: Sultanpur District, Uttar Pradesh, resource analysis for integrated development. Includes statistical tables. LC Card 87-902515
1. Sultānpur (India) - Economic conditions. 2. Natural resources - India - Sultānpur. I. Water Technology Centre (Indian Agricultural Research Institute). II. Title: Sultanpur District, Uttar Pradesh, resource analysis for integrated development.
HC437.S85 R47 1986

Resource bulletin NE .
(89) Nevel, Robert L. The timber industries of New Hampshire and Vermont . Broomall, Pa. , 1986. 56 p. : LC Card 86-601144 DDC 338.1/7498/09742 19
HD9757.N4 N48 1986

(91) Frieswyk, Thomas S. Biomass statistics for Vermont . [Broomall, Pa.] , 1986. 105 p. : LC Card 86-602390 DDC 333.79/38 19
HD9502.5.B543 U635 1986

Resource economics . Randall, Alan, 1944- New York , c1987. xiii, 434 p. ; ISBN 0-471-87468-X LC Card 87-4988 DDC 333.7 19
HC59 .R256 1987

Resource extraction and market structure /. Schäfer, Martin, 1951- Berlin , New York , c1986. ix, 154 p. : ISBN 0-387-16081-7 (U. S.) LC Card 86-1786 DDC 333.7/0973 19
HC59 .S344 1986
NYPL [JLM 72-289 no.263]

Resource mobilisation, medium and long-term issues : proceedings of Assocham Workshop. New Delhi : Associated Chambers of Commerce & Industry of India, [1986] viii, 98 p. ; 25 cm. In the context of the Seventh Five Year Plan of India. LC Card 87-902180 DDC 338.954 19
1. India - Economic policy - 1980- - Congresses. I. Associated Chambers of Commerce & Industry of India.
HC435.2 .R46 1986

RESOURCE RECOVERY. see **RECYCLING (WASTE, ETC.)**

Resource series (Maine. Bureau of Health Planning and Development. Division of Data and Research) .
(no. 13) Welch, Dale E. Suicides in Maine for the 25 year period, 1958-1982 /. Augusta, Me. [1986] ii, 14, [5] p. : LC Card 86-622276 DDC 362.2 19
HB1323.S8 W45 1986

Resource studies of the Navajo Indian Reservation : administrative report / prepared by U. S. Geological Survey for U. S. Bureau of Indian Affairs. [Denver? Colo.] : The Survey, 1986. 187 p. in various pagings : ill., maps ; 28 cm. Includes bibliographies. LC Card 86-603130 DDC 333.7/09791/3 19
1. Natural resources - Navajo Indian Reservation. I. Geological Survey (U. S.). II. United States. Bureau of Indian Affairs.
HC107.A165 R47 1986

Resources, Inc. Occupations in energy-related industries [microform] . Washington, D.C. , 1981. ca. 300 p. ; ***NYPL [*XME-11,557]***

RESOURCES, MARINE. see **MARINE RESOURCES.**

RESOURCES, NATURAL. see **NATURAL RESOURCES.**

Resources, power and women . African and Asian Inter-regional Workshop on Strategies for Improving the Employment Conditions of Rural Women (1984 : Arusha, Tanzania) Geneva , 1985. ix, 82 p. ; ISBN 92-2-105009-2 (pbk.) : LC Card 86-208830 DDC 331.4/83/095 19
HD6207 .A78 1984

RESOURCES, RENEWABLE NATURAL. see **RENEWABLE NATURAL RESOURCES.**

Responding to comparable worth in today's environment : a basic training course resource manual / edited by G. John Tysse. [Washington, D.C.] : National Foundation for the Study of Equal Employment Policy, c1986. xi, 160 leaves ; 30 cm. Includes bibliography. ISBN 0-916559-07-6 (loose-leaf) : LC Card 86-63777 DDC 658.3/2 19
1. Pay equity - United States. I. Tysse, G. John. II. National Foundation for the Study of Equal Employment Policy (U. S.).
HD6061.2.U6 R47 1986

The response of local authorities to central government incitement to reduce expenditure . Meadows, W. J. Strasbourg , 1986. 33 p. ; LC Card 87-135687 DDC 336.3/9/094 19
HJ9415 .M43 1986

RESPONSIBILITY, ADMINISTRATIVE. see **ADMINISTRATIVE RESPONSIBILITY.**

The responsive workplace . Kamerman, Sheila B. New York , 1987. xi, 329 p. ; ISBN 0-231-06480-2 LC Card 87-6636 DDC 658.3 19
HF5549 .K253 1987

Respubliki Strany Sovetov.
Solomentsev, M. S. (Mikhail Sergeevich) Rossiĭskaia Federatsiia /. Moskva , 1978. 212 p. ; LC Card 81-170399
HC337.R85 S65 1978

La respuesta de Latinoamérica a la crisis internacional /. Silva Ruete, Javier. [Lima, Peru?] [1984] 99 p. ; LC Card 86-154728
HF1480.5 .S55 1984

Ressourcenumverteilung zugunsten von Problemregionen . Meyer, Willm Rolf. Frankfurt/Main , New York , c1982. 262 p. : ISBN 3-593-33036-9 LC Card 82-161064 DDC 336.1/85 19
HJ1121 .M49 1982 ***NYPL [JLD 86-3292]***

Ressources humaines et développement régional en Côte d'Ivoire . Willaert, Y. [Addis Ababa] [1977] 3, 108, [6] leaves (1 folded) ; LC Card 82-980560
HD5846.9.A6 W55 1977

Ressources humaines pour le développement . Sall, Alioune. [Dakar, Sénégal , 1984] 51 p. : LC Card 85-129264 DDC 338.91/09624 19
HC1002 .S25 1984

Ressursregnskap for fisk. Oslo : Statistisk sentralbyrå, 1982. 53 p. : ill. ; 30 cm. (Rapporter fra Statistisk sentralbyrå, 0332-8422 . 82/17) ISBN 82-537-1765-2 : LC Card 82-229877
1. Fish trade - Norway - Statistics. I. Norway. Statistisk sentralbyrå. II. Series.
HD9465.N62 R47 1982

Ressursregnskap og ressursbudsjett / utarbeidet av Miljøverndepartementet. [Oslo] : Miljøverndepartementet, [1984?] 28 p. : ill. ; 28 cm. "Særskilt vedlegg til St. meld. nr. 83 (1984-85) Langtidsprogrammet 1986-1989." LC Card 85-239023
1. Natural resources - Norway. I. Norway. Miljøverndepartementet.
HC363.5 .R46 1984

REST PERIODS.
Neven, Peter, 1953- Arbeits- und Freizeitpädagogik . Düsseldorf [1982?] 424 p. ; ISBN 3-87864-087-0 LC Card 84-119072
HD4901 .N47 1982

REST PERIODS - UNITED STATES.
Report on the coffee service industry /. Columbus, Ohio [1984] 1 v. (various foliations) : LC Card 87-100404 DDC 381/.4566393 19
HD9199.U48 R47 1984

RESTAURANTS, LUNCH ROOMS, ETC. - ACCOUNTING.
Cote, Raymond. Understanding hospitality accounting I /. East Lansing, Mich. , c1987. p. cm. ISBN 0-86612-035-1 : LC Card 87-15724 DDC 657/.837 19
HF5686.H75 C63 1987

RESTAURANTS, LUNCH ROOMS, ETC. - GERMANY (WEST) - RHINELAND-PALATINATE - STATISTICS.
Die Unternehmen des Gastgewerbes in Rheinland-Pfalz 1979 . Bad Ems [1982] 46 p., [2] p. of plates : LC Card 83-207906 DDC 314.3/43 s 338.4/7647/944343021 19
HA1320 .R453 Bd. 294 TX910.G4

RESTAURANTS, LUNCH ROOMS, ETC. - MANAGEMENT.
Food courts . New York , c1987. 70 p. : ISBN 0-913598-66-6 (pbk.) LC Card 87-604 DDC 647/.9573 19
HF5430 .F66 1987

RESTAURANTS, LUNCH ROOMS, ETC. - UNITED STATES - STATISTICS.
Food retailing review . Fair Lawn, NJ , 1985. 178 p. : ***NYPL [JLF 86-868]***

Die restlose Erfassung . Aly, Götz, 1947- Berlin , c1984. 157 p. : ISBN 3-88022-282-7 : LC Card 84-206488
HA37.G3 A49 1984

Restoring growth in the debt-laden Third World : a draft task force report to the Trilateral Commission / authors, Martin Feldstein ... [et al.]. New York : The Commission, 1987. x, 82 p. : ill. ; 23 cm. (Triangle papers . 33) "April 1987." Bibliography: p. 81-82. ISBN 0-930503-02-3 : LC Card 87-23778 DDC 336.3/435/091724 19
1. Debts, External - Developing countries. 2. Developing countries - Economic policy. I. Feldstein,

Martin S. II. Trilateral Commission. III. Series.
HJ8899 .R47 1987

Restraining the economy : social credit, economic policies for B. C. in the eighties / edited by Robert C. Allen & Gideon Rosenbluth. Vancouver : New Star Books, c1986. 320 p. ; 22 cm. Includes bibliographies. ISBN 0-919573-60-6 LC Card 87-107157 DDC 338.9711 19
1. British Columbia - Economic policy. 2. British Columbia - Economic conditions. 3. British Columbia - Politics and government. I. Allen, Robert C., 1947-. II. Rosenbluth, Gideon.
HC117.B8 R475 1986

RESTRAINT OF TRADE - EUROPEAN ECONOMIC COMMUNITY COUNTRIES - CONGRESSES.
Neuorientierung des Wettbewerbsschutzes . Köln , 1986. viii, 231 p. ; ISBN 3-452-20666-1 : LC Card 87-138003
HB41 .F22 Heft 120 KK6456

RESTRAINT OF TRADE - GERMANY, WEST.
Maxeiner, James. Policy and methods in German and American antitrust law . New York , 1986. xiii, 174 p. ; ISBN 0-275-92113-1 (alk. paper) : LC Card 86-8108 DDC 343/.072 342.372 19
K3856 .M38 1986 ***NYPL [JLE 86-4413]***

RESTRAINT OF TRADE - GERMANY (WEST) - CONGRESSES.
Neuorientierung des Wettbewerbsschutzes . Köln , 1986. viii, 231 p. ; ISBN 3-452-20666-1 : LC Card 87-138003
HB41 .F22 Heft 120 KK6456

RESTRAINT OF TRADE - SWITZERLAND.
Weber, Rolf H. Wirtschaftsregulierung in wettbewerbspolitischen Ausnahmebereichen . Baden-Baden , 1986. 710 p. : ISBN 3-7890-1288-2 LC Card 87-128141
HD3616.S93 W425 1986

RESTRAINT OF TRADE - UNITED STATES.
Caves, Richard E. American industry . Englewood Cliffs, N.J. , c1987. x, 124 p. : ISBN 0-13-027665-0 (pbk.) : LC Card 86-22706 DDC 338.0973 19
HC106.5 .C34 1987

Caves, Richard E. American industry: structure, conduct, performance. Englewood Cliffs, N.J. [c1972] vii, 117 p. ISBN 0-13-027573-5 LC Card 72-170034 DDC 338/.0973
HC106.5 .C34 1972

Maxeiner, James. Policy and methods in German and American antitrust law . New York , 1986. xiii, 174 p. ; ISBN 0-275-92113-1 (alk. paper) : LC Card 86-8108 DDC 343/.072 342.372 19
K3856 .M38 1986 ***NYPL [JLE 86-4413]***

Weber, Rolf H. Wirtschaftsregulierung in wettbewerbspolitischen Ausnahmebereichen . Baden-Baden , 1986. 710 p. : ISBN 3-7890-1288-2 LC Card 87-128141
HD3616.S93 W425 1986

Restrepo Correa, Alejandro. Manual de crédito industrial y agropecuario : directorio de instituciones financieras / elaborado por Alejandro Restrepo Correa, Mario Londoño Mejía.[Ed. 1985]. [Bogotá, D.E. : Corporación Editorial Interamericana, 1985] 270, 30, 4 p. : ill. (some col.) ; 25 cm. Cover title. LC Card 86-110073
1. Commercial credit - Colombia. 2. Agricultural credit - Colombia. I. Londoño Mejía, Mario. II. Title. III. Title: Directorio de instituciones financieras.
HG3751.9.C7 R47 1985

Restrepo, Iván. La basura : consumo y desperdicio en el Distrito Federal / Iván Restrepo y David Phillips.2a ed. México, D.F. : Centro de Ecodesarrollo, 1985. 193 p. : ill. ; 20 cm. Bibliography: p. 191-193. LC Card 86-209151
1. Food consumption - Mexico - Distrito Federal. 2. Nutrition surveys - Mexico - Distrito Federal. 3. Refuse and refuse disposal - Mexico - Distrito Federal. I. Phillips, David. II. Title.
HD9014.M63 M47 1985

Restrepo Uribe, Jorge. Foro El Suroeste de Antioquia y el Chocó Norte (1984 : Urrao, Colombia) Foro El Suroeste de Antioquia y el Chocó Norte . [Medellín] [1985] 65 p. : LC Card 87-400457 DDC 338.9861/2 19
HC198.A5 F595 1984

Restructuration et croissance de l'économie libanaise /. Yachoui, Elie. Beyrouth , 1983. 230 p. ; LC Card 86-148239
HC415.24 .Y32 1983

Restructuration industrielle et filières de main-d'œuvre . Tiger, Henri. Paris , 1979. 389 p. : LC Card 85-126419
HD5776.G74 T54 1979

Restructuring, a vital concern of the people . Gorbachev, Mikhail Sergeevich, 1931- [Perestroĭka--krovnoe delo naroda. English.] Moscow , 1987. 28 p. ; LC Card 87-165567 DDC 338.947 19
HC336.26 .G6713 1987

Restructuring professional standards to achieve professional excellence in a changing environment . American Institute of Certified Public Accountants. Special Committee on Standards of Professional Conduct for Certified Public Accountants. New York, N.Y. (1211 Ave. of the Americas, New York 10036-8775) , c1986. vi, 66 p. : LC Card 86-211085 DDC 657/.0218 19
HF5616.U5 A585 1986

Restructuring the automobile industry . Quinn, Dennis Patrick, 1955- New York , 1988. p. cm. ISBN 0-231-06524-8 LC Card 87-15919 DDC 338.4/76292/0941 19
HD9710.U52 Q56 1988

Restructuring the Soviet petroleum refining industry /. Sagers, Matthew J. Washington, D.C. [1985] v, 57 p. ; LC Card 87-601278 DDC 338.4/766553/0947 19
HD9575.S652 S254 1985

Resultados de la encuesta sobre expectativas de producción e inversión de las empresas industriales / Presidencia de la Nación, Consejo Nacional de Desarrollo, Sector Presupuesto Económico Nacional. Buenos Aires : El Sector, 1965. 81 leaves : ill. ; 29 cm. "Encuesta sobre expectativas de producción e inversión de las empresas industriales" (9 leaves) inserted. LC Card 85-114982
1. Industrial productivity - Argentina. 2. Investments - Argentina. 3. Argentina - Industries. I. Consejo Nacional de Desarrollo (Argentina). Sector Presupuesto Económico Nacional.
HC180.I52 R47 1965

Resultados preliminares del análisis metodológico de los planes nacionales de desarrollo, 1974-1982 /. Gamboa Conejo, Rita Ma. (Rita María) Heredia , 1985. 1 v. (various pagings) : LC Card 87-402159 DDC 338.97286 19
HC143 .G36 1985

Resultados y perspectivas de la economía ecuatoriana, 1984-1985. Quito, Ecuador : Corporación de Estudios para el Desarrollo, [1985] 27, 7 p. ; 29 cm. (Serie Apuntes técnicos . no. 1) LC Card 85-215488
1. Ecuador - Economic conditions - 1972-. 2. Ecuador - Economic policy. 3. Economic forecasting - Ecuador. 4. Gross national product - Ecuador. I. Corporación de Estudios para el Desarrollo (Ecuador). II. Series.
HC202 .R47 1985

Résultats des élections aux conseils de prud'hommes par département . Bon, Frédéric, 1943- St. Martin d'Hères [France] [1982] 303 p. ; LC Card 84-152037
HD5555 .B65 1982

Résultats du projet et recommandations en découlant. International Labour Organisation. Côte-d'Ivoire . Genève , 1984. 94 p. : ISBN 92-2-203860-6 LC Card 86-219971
HD5846.9.A6 I57 1984

Résultats du projet et recommandations en découlant. International Labour Organisation. Organisation de l'Institut national de formation et de perfectionnement professionnels de Bangui (INFPP) . Genève , 1980. 14 p. ; ISBN 92-2-202448-6 LC Card 82-214934
HD5716.M342 C335 1980

Résultats préliminaires du recensement de 1960 . Morocco. Maṣlaḥah al-Markazīyah lil-Iḥṣāʾīyāt. [Rabat] [1964?] 43 leaves ; LC Card 82-960641
HD7372.3.A3 M67 1964

Résultats préliminaires du recensement général de la population et du logement (septembre 1982) Résultats préliminaires du recensement général (septembre 1982) /. [Port-au-Prince] [1982 or 1983] vii, 60 p., [1] leaf of plates : LC Card 84-138275 DDC 304.6/097294/021 19
HD7316.A3 R47 1982 ***NYPL [JLF 86-1280]***

Résultats préliminaires du recensement général (septembre 1982) / République d'Haïti, Secrétairerie d'Etat du plan, Institut haïtien de statistique et d'informatique. [Port-au-Prince] : L'Institut, [1982 or 1983] vii, 60 p., [1] leaf of plates : map ; 28 cm. Cover title. Caption title: Résultats préliminaires du recensement général de la population et du logement (septembre 1982). Cover also has title: Recensement général 1982, population et logement. Chiefly tables. LC Card 84-138275 DDC 304.6/097294/021 19
1. Housing - Haiti - Statistics. 2. Households - Haiti - Statistics. 3. Haiti - Population - Statistics. 4. Haiti - Census, 1982. I. Institut haïtien de statistique et d'informantique. II. Title: Résultats préliminaires du recensement général de la population et du logement (septembre 1982). III. Title: Recensement général 1982, population et logement.
HD7316.A3 R47 1982 ***NYPL [JLF 86-1280]***

Results of the maritime transport study for the years 1972-1975. Commodity trade (by sea) statistics . New York , 1980. v, 396 p. ; LC Card 87-112992 DDC 387.5/55/021 19
HE562.8 .C667 1980

Results of the 1983 world programme of industrial statistics, Hungary. Az 1983. évi iparstatisztikai világprogram adatai, Magyarország /. [Budapest , 1986. 289 p. ; LC Card 86-219027
HC300.28 .A14 1986

The resume catalog . Parker, Yana. Berkeley, Calif. , 1987. p. cm. ISBN 0-89815-219-4 LC Card 87-7057 DDC 650.1/4 19
HF5383 .P354 1987

Resumes for better jobs /. Brennan, Lawrence D. (Lawrence David), 1915- New York, NY , c1987. 202 p. ; ISBN 0-13-329152-9 : LC Card 87-2383 DDC 650.1/4 19
HF5383 .B68 1987

Résumés that get interviews, interviews that get jobs [videorecording] / Guidance Associates, Inc. Mt. Kisco, NY : Guidance Associates, 1986, c1987. 1 videocassette (42 min.) : sd., col. + 1 program guide. Title from data sheet. In four parts. Senior high school through college. Issued as U-matic 3/4 in. or Beta 1/2 in. or VHS 1/2 in. Tells how to organize and write effective résumés and cover letters. Gives helpful tips on the job interview, including questions employers are most likely to ask, questions to ask about the job and company, and how to use body language to advantage. LC Card 86-707973 DDC 650.1 11
1. Résumés (Employment). 2. Employment interviewing. I. Guidance Associates.
HF5383

The resurgence of the states /. Bowman, Ann O'M., 1948- Englewood Cliffs, N.J. , c1986. x, 269 p. : ISBN 0-13-774969-4 (pbk.) LC Card 85-19213 DDC 353.9 19
JK2408 .B68 1986 ***NYPL [JLE 86-4496]***

Resurgir (Agency : Colombia). Junta Directiva. Foro de la Esperanza (1985 : Ibagué, Colombia) Foro de la Esperanza . [Bogotá?] [1985] 154 p. ; LC Card 87-401285 DDC 338.9861 19
HC197 .F59 1985

Resursy narodnogo khozi͡aĭstva : planirovanie i ėffektivnostʹ ispolʹzovanii͡a / redaktsionnai͡a kollegii͡a toma I.K. Bondarʹ (otvetstvennyĭ redaktor) ... [et al.]. Kiev : Nauk. dumka, 1985. 308 p. : ill. ; 21 cm. (Planovoe upravlenie ėkonomikoĭ razvitogo sotsializma . t. 2) On p. preceding t.p.: Nauchno-issledovatelʹskiĭ ėkonomicheskiĭ institut Gosplana USSR. Bibliography: p. 303-[307] Includes index. LC Card 86-226867
1. Industrial productivity - Ukraine. 2. Labor supply - Ukraine. 3. Natural resources - Ukraine. I. Bondarʹ, I. K. (Interna Kasʹi͡anovna). II. Naukovo-doslidnyĭ ekonomichnyĭ instytut. III. Series.
HC337.U5 P5 1985 t. 2 HC337.U53I52

RETAIL ADVERTISING. see **ADVERTISING.**

RETAIL FRANCHISES. see **FRANCHISES (RETAIL TRADE)**

Retail produce operations, 1986 / produced by the Food Marketing Institute, the Produce Marketing Association. Washington, D.C. (1750 K. St., N.W. Washington 20006) : FMI ; Newark, Del. : PMA, [1986] viii, 20 p. ; 28 cm. LC Card 87-101803 DDC 381/.456648/00973 19

1. Grocery trade - United States - Statistics. 2. Produce trade - United States - Statistics. 3. Supermarkets - United States - Statistics. 4. Retail trade - United States - Statistics. 5. Retail trade surveys - United States. I. Food Marketing Institute. II. Produce Marketing Association.
HD9321.4 .R47 1986

The retail sales tax in Canada /. Robinson, Albert J., 1926- Toronto, Ont. , c1986. viii, 165 p. ; ISBN 0-88808-025-5 (pbk.) : LC Card 86-210098 DDC 336.2/713/0971 19
HJ5715.C2 R63 1986

RETAIL STORES. see **STORES, RETAIL.**

RETAIL TRADE.
Boeker, Heiner, 1955- Qualitätspolitik in der industriellen Beschaffung . Bochum , 1986. ix, 296 p. ; ISBN 3-88339-525-0 LC Card 87-127490 DDC 687/.068/5 19
HD9940.A2 B64 1986

Laulajainen, Risto. Spatial strategies in retailing /. Dordrecht ; Boston : xiii, 253 p. : ISBN 90-277-2595-0 LC Card 87-20803 DDC 658.8/7 19
HF5429.275 .L38 1987

Mason, Joseph Barry. Modern retailing . Plano, Tex. , 1987. xviii, 834 p. : ISBN 0-256-03706-X LC Card 86-71842 DDC 658.8/7 19
HF5429 .M328 1987

Mwanza Mujila. La gestion planifiée de l'entreprise commerciale de détail . Lubumbashi [Zaire] , 1984. 287 p. : LC Card 85-177323
HF5429 .M88 1984

Rogers, Dorothy S., 1929- Retailing . Hinsdale, IL , 1987, c1988. p. cm. ISBN 0-03-001997-4 LC Card 87-5337 DDC 658.8/7 19
HF5429 .R5793 1988

RETAIL TRADE - ARGENTINA.
Cimillo, Elsa. La terciarización del empleo en la Argentina. [Buenos Aires] [1985] 23, [41], 3 p. ; LC Card 87-123708 DDC 381/.1/0982 19
HF5429.6.A7 C56 1985

RETAIL TRADE - ARGENTINA - BUENOS AIRES METROPOLITAN AREA.
Cimillo, Elsa. La terciarización del empleo en la Argentina. [Buenos Aires] [1985] 23, [41], 3 p. ; LC Card 87-123708 DDC 381/.1/0982 19
HF5429.6.A7 C56 1985

RETAIL TRADE - ARGENTINA - BUENOS AIRES METROPOLITAN AREA - EMPLOYEES.
Cimillo, Elsa. La terciarización del empleo en la Argentina. [Buenos Aires] [1985] 23, [41], 3 p. ; LC Card 87-123708 DDC 381/.1/0982 19
HF5429.6.A7 C56 1985

RETAIL TRADE - ARGENTINA - EMPLOYEES.
Cimillo, Elsa. La terciarización del empleo en la Argentina. [Buenos Aires] [1985] 23, [41], 3 p. ; LC Card 87-123708 DDC 381/.1/0982 19
HF5429.6.A7 C56 1985

RETAIL TRADE - BRAZIL - FORTALEZA - EMPLOYEES.
Situação de saúde e lazer do comerciário de Fortaleza /. Fortaleza-CE , 1977/1978 [i.e. 1978] 66 leaves ; LC Card 83-116799
HD5755.F6 S58 1978

RETAIL TRADE - BRAZIL - HISTORY.
O Comércio e suas profissões . Rio de Janeiro , 1983. 127, [5] p. : LC Card 84-161651
HF5459.B7 C65 1983 ***NYPL [JLF 86-1408]***

RETAIL TRADE - CARICATURES AND CARTOONS.
Pauken, Joe. Re-tailing ain't easy /. Palm Bay, Fla. (2576 First Ave., Post Office Box 990, Palm Bay 32905) , c1985. 160 p., [1] p. of plates : LC Card 86-232016 DDC 381/.1/0207 19
HF5429 .P368 1985

RETAIL TRADE - COSTS. see **MARKETING - COSTS.**

RETAIL TRADE - EMPLOYEES - MATHEMATICAL MODELS.
Kaufhold, Klaus, 1943- Die wirtschaftlichen Wirkungen der Fluktuation in der Einzelwirtschaft . Frankfurt am Main , New York , c1985. 357 p. : ISBN 3-8204-5665-1 LC Card 85-195373
HF5429 .K4156 1985

RETAIL TRADE - EMPLOYEES - TRAINING OF - BRAZIL - PARANÁ (STATE)
Federação do Comércio Varejista do Estado do Paraná. Empresa forte, mais trabalho . [Curitiba] , 1983. 67 leaves : LC Card 83-225279
HF5429.6.B7 F44 1983

RETAIL TRADE - EQUIPMENT AND SUPPLIES.
Mertens, Jürgen. Zur Entwicklung und zum konstellationsadäquaten Einsatz eines Beschaffungsmarketinginstrumentariums im Einzelhandel /. Köln , 1986. 379 p. : ISBN 3-922292-13-7 LC Card 87-143182 DDC 658.8/7 19
HF5429.225 .M47 1986

RETAIL TRADE - EUROPE - CONGRESSES.
Seminar on Retail Strategies for Profit and Growth (1986 : Brussels, Belgium) Seminar on Retail Strategies for Profit and Growth . Amsterdam, Netherlands [1986] vi, 324 p. : ISBN 92-831-1113-3 (pbk.) : LC Card 86-218316 DDC 658.8/7/0094 19
HF5429.6.E9 S45 1986

RETAIL TRADE - FLORIDA - STATISTICS.
Lacrosse, James. Florida index of retail activity /. [Tallahassee] [1983] [22] leaves : LC Card 86-621941 DDC 381/.1/09759021 19
HF5429.4.F6 L33 1983

RETAIL TRADE - FRANCHISES. see **FRANCHISES (RETAIL TRADE)**

RETAIL TRADE - GERMANY (EAST) - HISTORY.
Berekoven, Ludwig. Geschichte des deutschen Einzelhandels /. Frankfurt am Main , c1986. 175 p. : ISBN 3-87150-246-4 LC Card 87-121881
HF5429.6.G42 B46 1986

RETAIL TRADE - GERMANY - HISTORY.
Berekoven, Ludwig. Geschichte des deutschen Einzelhandels /. Frankfurt am Main , c1986. 175 p. : ISBN 3-87150-246-4 LC Card 87-121881
HF5429.6.G42 B46 1986

RETAIL TRADE - GERMANY, WEST.
Die Wirksamkeit staatlicher Mittelstandsförderung im Einzelhandel /. Berlin , c1981. 223 p. : ISBN 3-428-04919-5 LC Card 82-175986 DDC 658.8 s 338.6/42/0943 19
HF5415.A2 S37 Bd. 12 HD2346.G3 ***NYPL [JLE 86-3464]***

Rösch, Willi. Das tägliche Duell zwischen Handel und Verbraucher . [München-Gräfelfing] , c1975. 110 p. : LC Card 84-121903
HF5429.6.G42 R67 1975

Straaten, Martin. Wettbewerb und Kooperation im Landhandel . Berlin , c1985. 82 p. ; ISBN 3-428-05712-0 LC Card 85-167800
HF5429.6.G42 S77 1985

RETAIL TRADE - GERMANY (WEST) - HISTORY.
Berekoven, Ludwig. Geschichte des deutschen Einzelhandels /. Frankfurt am Main , c1986. 175 p. : ISBN 3-87150-246-4 LC Card 87-121881
HF5429.6.G42 B46 1986

RETAIL TRADE - GERMANY (WEST) - NORTH RHINE-WESTPHALIA.
Döhne, Ulrich. Analyse der Ansiedlung von Einkaufszentren und Verbrauchermärkten in Nordrhein-Westfalen /. Dortmund , Essen , 1977. 39 p. : LC Card 86-181973
HF5429.6.G42 D64 1977

RETAIL TRADE - GERMANY (WEST) - STATISTICS.
Döhrn, Roland. Privater Verbrauch und Einzelhandel in der Bundesrepublik Deutschland . Essen , 1981. 280 p. ; LC Card 87-408859 DDC 338.5/28/0943 19
HB235.G3 D57 1981

RETAIL TRADE - GOVERNMENT POLICY - BRAZIL - PARANÁ (STATE)
Federação do Comércio Varejista do Estado do Paraná. Empresa forte, mais trabalho . [Curitiba] , 1983. 67 leaves : LC Card 83-225279
HF5429.6.B7 F44 1983

RETAIL TRADE - GREAT BRITAIN - CASE STUDIES.
Kay, William. Battle for the high street /. London , 1987. 194 p., [16] p. of plates : ISBN 0-86188-621-6 : LC Card 87-143764 DDC 658.8/7 19
HF5429.6.G7 K38 1987

RETAIL TRADE - GREAT BRITAIN - CONGRESSES.
Economics of the retail petroleum market . London , c1986. i, 79 p. : LC Card 87-134547 DDC 381/.4566553827/0941 19
HD9579.G5 G63 1986

RETAIL TRADE - GREAT BRITAIN - STATISTICS.
ISBA area information, 1978 /. London , 1978. 147 p. : ISBN 0-906241-00-6 (pbk.) LC Card 83-225656 DDC 381/.1/0941021 19
HA1134 .I83 1978

RETAIL TRADE - HUNGARY - PERSONNEL MANAGEMENT.
Munkaügy a belkereskedelemben /. [Budapest] , 1986. 272 p. ; ISBN 963-01-7513-4 : LC Card 87-148137
HF5549.2.H85 M86 1986

RETAIL TRADE - MANAGEMENT.
Bolen, William H., 1943- Contemporary retailing /. Englewood Cliffs, N.J. , c1988. xviii, 622 p. : ISBN 0-13-170309-9 LC Card 87-17514 DDC 658.8/7 19
HF5429 .B595 1988

Büttner, Herbert. Die segmentorientierte Marketingplanung im Einzelhandelsbetrieb /. Göttingen , 1986. 413 p. : ISBN 3-509-01424-3 LC Card 87-134581 DDC 658.8/7 19
HF5429 .B87 1986

Davidson, William R. Retailing management /. New York , c1988. xix, 876 p. : ISBN 0-471-85094-2 LC Card 87-10555 DDC 658.8/7 19
HF5429 .D334 1988

Medla, Karsten, 1954- Shop-in-the-shop . München , c1987. xxxi, 207, 6 p. ; ISBN 3-88259-428-4 LC Card 87-141864 DDC 658.8/7 19
HF5429 .M36 1987

Mertens, Jürgen. Zur Entwicklung und zum konstellationsadäquaten Einsatz eines Beschaffungsmarketinginstrumentariums im Einzelhandel /. Köln , 1986. 379 p. : ISBN 3-922292-13-7 LC Card 87-143182 DDC 658.8/7 19
HF5429.225 .M47 1986

Mwanza Mujila. La gestion planifiée de l'entreprise commerciale de détail . Lubumbashi [Zaire] , 1984. 287 p. : LC Card 85-177323
HF5429 .M88 1984

Pintel, Gerald. Retailing /. Englewood Cliffs, N.J. , c1987. iv, 488 p. : ISBN 0-13-778549-6 LC Card 86-25397 DDC 658.8/7 19
HF5429 .P57 1987

Shopping center managers and retailers . New York , c1988. p. cm. ISBN 0-913598-73-9 (pbk.) : LC Card 87-22546 DDC 658.8/7 19
HF5430 .S557 1988

RETAIL TRADE - MANITOBA - WINNIPEG.
Downtown and regional shopping centre retailing in Winnipeg /. Winnipeg, Man., Canada , 1985. x, 90, [8] p. : ISBN 0-920213-22-7 (pbk.) LC Card 86-137592 DDC 381/.1/0971274 19
HF5429.6.C3 D69 1985 ***NYPL [JLF 86-1331]***

RETAIL TRADE - NETHERLANDS.
Jong, K. J. de. Schijnwerper op de detailhandel /. Deventer , 1986. 221 p. : ISBN 90-267-1058-5 : LC Card 86-177114
HF5429.6.N4 J663 1986

RETAIL TRADE - NEW ZEALAND - STATISTICS.
Census of distribution, 1977-78 . Wellington, N.Z. [1980]-<[1981]. v. <11 > : LC Card 86-204705
HF5429.6.N47 C46 1980

RETAIL TRADE - POLAND.
Prace z zakresu ekonomiki i organizacji przedsiębiorstw handlowych /. Kraków , 1978. 176 p. ; LC Card 81-200309
HB9 .K53 nr. 101 HF5429.6.P6

RETAIL TRADE - POLAND - STATISTICS.
Ceny detaliczne 1971-1985 /. Warszawa , 1985. 160 p. ; LC Card 86-196060
HB235.P6 C45 1985

RETAIL TRADE - SEASONAL VARIATIONS - MATHEMATICAL MODELS.
Kaufhold, Klaus, 1943- Die wirtschaftlichen Wirkungen der Fluktuation in der Einzelwirtschaft . Frankfurt am Main , New

York , c1985. 357 p. : ISBN 3-8204-5665-1 LC Card 85-195373
HF5429 .K4156 1985

RETAIL TRADE SURVEYS - UNITED STATES.
NACS convenience store customer purchasing patterns research report /. [Falls Church, Va. , 1985?] vi, 76 p. : LC Card 86-157648 DDC 381/.1 19
HF5469.55.U62 N33 1985
NYPL [JLF 87-810]

Retail produce operations, 1986 /. Washington, D.C. (1750 K. St., N.W. Washington 20006) , Newark, Del. [1986] viii, 20 p. ; LC Card 87-101803 DDC 381/.456648/00973 19
HD9321.4 .R47 1986

RETAIL TRADE - SWEDEN.
Larsson, Folke. Varuhandeln. [Stockholm] [1981] 137 p. : ISBN 91-38-06014-0 LC Card 84-120411
HF5429.6.S9 L368 1981

RETAIL TRADE - SWEDEN - CASE STUDIES.
Wolvén, Lars-Erik. Konsumenter, konsumentpolitik, rationalitet och välfärd . Umeå , 1981. 83 leaves ; LC Card 82-105540 DDC 658.8/342/09485 19
HC380.C63 W64 ***NYPL [JLM 74-106 no.61]***

RETAIL TRADE - SWEDEN - DATA PROCESSING.
Bra affärer med datorer? . [Stockholm] , 1982. 176 p. : ISBN 91-38-06989-X LC Card 83-235564
HF5429.15 .B72 1982

RETAIL TRADE - SWITZERLAND.
Moser, R. (René), 1941- Marketing-Strategie für den Detailhandel /. Münsingen , Zürich , 1981. 159 p. : ISBN 3-85681-059-5 LC Card 83-240590
HF5429.6.S92 M67 1981

RETAIL TRADE - UNITED STATES - MANAGEMENT.
Parrish, Vernon. Great American video retailing . Arlington, Va. [1983?] viii, 448 p. : ISBN 0-9615774-0-1 LC Card 85-90437 DDC 621.388/332/0688 19
HD9697.V543 U544 1983

RETAIL TRADE - UNITED STATES - STATISTICS.
Retail produce operations, 1986 /. Washington, D.C. (1750 K. St., N.W. Washington 20006) , Newark, Del. [1986] viii, 20 p. ; LC Card 87-101803 DDC 381/.456648/00973 19
HD9321.4 .R47 1986

RETAIL TRADE - VOCATIONAL GUIDANCE.
Pintel, Gerald. Retailing /. Englewood Cliffs, N.J. , c1987. iv, 488 p. : ISBN 0-13-778549-6 LC Card 86-25397 DDC 658.8/7 19
HF5429 .P57 1987

RETAIL TRADING AREAS. see **MARKET SURVEYS.**

Retailing /. Pintel, Gerald. Englewood Cliffs, N.J. , c1987. iv, 488 p. : ISBN 0-13-778549-6 LC Card 86-25397 DDC 658.8/7 19
HF5429 .P57 1987

Retailing . Rogers, Dorothy S., 1929- Hinsdale, IL , 1987, c1988. p. cm. ISBN 0-03-001997-4 LC Card 87-5337 DDC 658.8/7 19
HF5429 .R5793 1988

Re-tailing ain't easy /. Pauken, Joe. Palm Bay, Fla. (2576 First Ave., Post Office Box 990, Palm Bay 32905) , c1985. 160 p., [1] p. of plates : LC Card 86-232016 DDC 381/.1/0207 19
HF5429 .P368 1985

Retailing management /. Davidson, William R. New York , c1988. xix, 876 p. : ISBN 0-471-85094-2 LC Card 87-10555 DDC 658.8/7 19
HF5429 .D334 1988

RETALIATION (ECONOMICS) see **TARIFF.**

Reteŭm, Alekseĭ IŪr'evich. Kompleksnye problemy obespechenii͡a ėkonomiki mineral'nym syr'em /. Moskva , 1984. 115 p. : LC Card 85-192528
HF1051 .K64 1984

Retention of land for agriculture . Schnidman, Frank. Boston, MA , 1988. p. cm. ISBN 0-89946-219-7 LC Card 87-5580 DDC 333.76/16/0974 19
HD266.A11 S36 1988

Retention of reflective raised pavement markers /. Noel, James S. College Station, Tex. , Springfield, Va. [1986] xiii, 170 p. : LC Card 87-620642 DDC 380.5 s 625.7/042 19
HE203 .T43 no. 322-3 TE203

Rethinking development . Apter, David Ernest, 1924- Newbury Park, Calif. , c1987. 326 p. : ISBN 0-8039-2971-4 LC Card 86-29642 DDC 338.9 19
HD82 .A657 1987

Rethinking development . Preston, P. W. (Peter Wallace), 1949- London , New York , 1987. xv, 261 p. ; ISBN 0-7102-1263-1 LC Card 87-4905 DDC 338.959 19
HC441 .P75 1987

Rethinking rental housing /. Gilderbloom, John Ingram. Philadelphia , 1987. p. cm. ISBN 0-87722-498-6 (alk. paper) LC Card 87-1958 DDC 363.5/8 19
HD7288.85.U6 G55 1987

Rethinking the company's selling and distribution channels /. Sutton, Howard, 1930- New York, N.Y. , c1986. v, 26 p. : ISBN 0-8237-0328-2 (pbk.) LC Card 87-404502 DDC 658.8/4 19
HF5415.129 .S87 1986

Rethinking the nineteenth century : contradictions and movements / edited by Francisco O. Ramirez. New York : Greenwood Press, c1988. p. cm. (Contributions in economics and economic history, 0084-9235 . no. 76) Studies in the political economy of the world-system Papers presented at the 10th Annual Political Economy of the World-System Conference held at the San Francisco State University, Mar. 1986, sponsored by the School of Behavioral and Social Sciences and the Dept. of Sociology of San Francisco State University and the Political Economy of the World System Section of the American Sociological Association. Includes bibliographies and index. ISBN 0-313-25997-6 (lib. bdg. : alk. paper) LC Card 87-17791 DDC 330.9/034 19
1. Economic history - 1750-1918 - Congresses. 2. Social sciences - History - 19th century - Congresses. I. Ramirez, Francisco O. II. Political Economy of the World-System Conference (10th : 1986 : San Francisco State University). III. San Francisco State University. School of Behavioral and Social Sciences. IV. San Francisco State University. Dept. of Sociology. V. American Sociological Association. Section on Political Economy of the World System. VI. Series.
HC53 .R48 1988

Rethinking young drivers / J. Peter Rothe, editor. [North Vancouver, B.C.] : Insurance Corporation of British Columbia, c1987. ii, 291 p. : ill. ; 22 cm. "Traffic Safety Planning and Research"--Cover. Includes bibliographies. ISBN 0-7726-0588-2 (pbk.) LC Card 87-167603 DDC 363.1/251 19
1. Juvenile automobile drivers - British Columbia. 2. Juvenile automobile drivers - British Columbia - Attitudes. 3. Traffic accidents - British Columbia. I. Rothe, John Peter, 1948-. II. Insurance Corporation of British Columbia. Traffic Safety Planning and Research Department.
HE5620.J8 R47 1987

Reti terziarie ed economie locali : il caso di Pistoia. Milano, Italy : F. Angeli, c1983. 174 p. ; 22 cm. (Materiali di ricerca . 6) At head of title: CENSIS, Centro studi investimenti sociali. Includes bibliographical references. LC Card 85-215649
1. Service industries - Italy - Pistoia. 2. Pistoia (Italy) - Industries. 3. Pistoia (Italy) - Economic conditions. I. Centro studi investimenti sociali. II. Series.
HD9986.I83 P577 1983

RETIRED MILITARY PERSONNEL - EMPLOYMENT - UNITED STATES.
Transitional career counseling from the Air Force to the private sector . Washington, D.C. , c1987. iv, 153 leaves : LC Card 87-401057 DDC 358.4/1154/0973 19
HF5382.75.U6 T7 1987

RETIREMENT AGE - SWEDEN.
Klevmarken, N. Anders. Höj och sänk pensionsåldern /. Göteborg [1985?] 9 leaves : LC Card 86-195492
HD7203 .K57 1985

RETIREMENT - ECONOMIC ASPECTS - UNITED STATES.
Andrews, Emily S. The changing profile of pensions in America /. Washington, DC , c1985. xxvii, 234 p. ; ISBN 0-86643-038-5 (pbk.) LC Card 85-25296 DDC 332.6/7254 19
HD7105.45.U6 A53 1985
NYPL [JLE 87-62]

RETIREMENT - GREAT BRITAIN - CASE STUDIES.
Lyon, Phil, 1948- Nearing retirement . Aldershot, Hants , Brookfield, Vt., USA , c1987. xix, 196 p. : ISBN 0-566-05233-4 : LC Card 86-25680 DDC 331.3/94/0941 19
HD6283.G7 L86 1987

RETIREMENT INCOME.
Retirement income provisions overseas. [Canberra] [1984] 162 p. ; ISBN 0-642-51580-8 (pbk.) LC Card 84-252861 DDC 331.25/22 19
HD7105.3 .R46 1984

RETIREMENT INCOME - AUSTRALIA.
Crompton, Cathy. Too old for a job, too young for a pension? . Canberra , 1986. x, 69 p. ; ISBN 0-644-05599-5 LC Card 87-150775 DDC 368.4/4/00880564 19
HD6283.A8 C76 1986

Retirement income provisions overseas. [Canberra] : Research and Statistics Branch, Development Division, Dept. of Social Security, [1984] 162 p. ; 30 cm. (Research paper / Research and Statistics Branch, Development Division, Department of Social Security . no. 26) "April 1984"--Cover. Bibliography: p. 162. ISBN 0-642-51580-8 (pbk.) LC Card 84-252861 DDC 331.25/22 19
1. Old age pensions. 2. Retirement income. I. Australia. Dept. of Social Security. Research and Statistics Branch. II. Series: Research paper (Australia. Dept. of Social Security. Research and Statistics Branch) , no. 26.
HD7105.3 .R46 1984

RETIREMENT INCOME - UNITED STATES.
Andrews, Emily S. The changing profile of pensions in America /. Washington, DC , c1985. xxvii, 234 p. ; ISBN 0-86643-038-5 (pbk.) LC Card 85-25296 DDC 332.6/7254 19
HD7105.45.U6 A53 1985
NYPL [JLE 87-62]

Cheeks, James E. Keoghs . New York , c1986. xviii, 248 p. ; ISBN 0-531-15505-6 LC Card 85-31753 DDC 332.024/01 19
HG1660.U5 C48 1986 ***NYPL [JLD 86-3669]***

Dunn, Pat. Script for an employee flipchart presentation titled The 401(k) plan . Chicago, Ill. , c1986. [40] p. : ISBN 0-88462-610-5 (pbk.) LC Card 86-201609 DDC 331.25/5 19
HG1660.U5 D86 1986

Earnings sharing options for the social security system. [Washington, D.C.?] [1986] xxv, 137 p. : LC Card 86-601147 DDC 368.4/3015/0973 19
HD7125 .E227 1986 ***NYPL [JLF 86-1058]***

Vicker, Ray. The Dow Jones-Irwin guide to retirement planning /. Homewood, Ill. , c1987. ix, 332 p. : ISBN 1-556-23005-2 LC Card 86-72973 DDC 332.024/01 19
HG179 .V54 1987

Wendling, Wayne. The regulatory impact on pensions /. Brookfield, Wis. , 1986. xiii, 91 p. : ISBN 0-89154-314-7 (pbk.) : LC Card 87-129712 DDC 331.25/2/0973 19
HD7105.35.U6 W46 1986

Wolff, Nancy, 1955- Income redistribution and the Social Security program /. Ann Arbor , c1987. vi, 181 p. : ISBN 0-8357-1807-7 LC Card 87-10791 DDC 368.4/3/00973 19
HD7105.35.U6 W65 1987

RETIREMENT PENSIONS. see **OLD AGE PENSIONS.**

Retirement planning. Vicker, Ray. The Dow Jones-Irwin guide to retirement planning /. Homewood, Ill. , c1987. ix, 332 p. : ISBN 1-556-23005-2 LC Card 86-72973 DDC 332.024/01 19
HG179 .V54 1987

Retirement plans for employees /. McFadden, John J. Homewood, Ill. , 1988. xviii, 326 p. : ISBN 0-256-05588-2 LC Card 87-81436 DDC 658.3/253 19
HD7105.35.U6 M33 1988

RETIREMENT - UNITED STATES.
Morrison, Malcolm H. The transition to retirement . Washington, D.C. (1990 M St., N.W., Washington 20036) , c1985. 85 p. : LC Card 85-169472 DDC 306/.38/0973 19
HQ1062 .M64 1985 ***NYPL [JLE 86-2236]***

RETIREMENT - UNITED STATES - MANAGEMENT.
Leedy, Jack J., 1921- Executive retirement management . New York, N.Y. , c1987. xi, 260 p. ; ISBN 0-8160-1286-5 LC Card 86-24010 DDC 658.4/07132 19
HD7125 .L43 1987

RETIREMENT - UNITED STATES - PLANNING.
Morrison, Malcolm H. The transition to retirement . Washington, D.C. (1990 M St., N.W., Washington 20036) , c1985. 85 p. : LC Card 85-169472 DDC 306/.38/0973 19
HQ1062 .M64 1985 ***NYPL [JLE 86-2236]***

RETRAINING, OCCUPATIONAL. see **OCCUPATIONAL RETRAINING.**

Retribuzioni a confronto . Valvo, Tino, 1948- Milano, Italy , c1986. 247 p. : LC Card 86-170001
HD5035.T87 V34 1986

Rettenbacher, Karl. Die Kraftfahrzeughaftpflichtversicherung in Österreich : (Geschichte und Gegenwart) / Karl Rettenbacher. Linz : R. Trauner, c1984. 183 p. : ill. ; 24 cm. (Linzer Schriften zur Sozial- u. Wirtschaftsgeschichte . Bd. 11) Bibliography: p. 178-183. ISBN 3-85320-328-0 LC Card 85-162917
1. Insurance, Automobile - Austria. 2. Insurance, Automobile - Law and legislation - Austria. I. Title. II. Series.
HG9970.4.A9 R48 1984

Rettig, Rudi. Korthaus, E. Input-Output-Tabellen für die Bundesrepublik Deutschland, 1962 bis 1975 /. Essen , 1979. 279 p. ; LC Card 87-408858 DDC 339.2/3/0943 19
HC290.5.I57 K67 1979

Retuerto, Enrique. Determinación de necesidades de formación profesional : metodología y manual / Enrique Retuerto.1a ed. Montevideo : CINTERFOR/OIT, 1983. 110 p. ; 23 cm. (Estudios y monografías . no. 60) Bibliography: p. 109-110. LC Card 86-149551
1. Occupational training. I. Series: Estudios y monografías (CINTERFOR (Organization)) , no. 60. II. Title.
HD5715 .R47 1983

RETURN MIGRATION - ALGERIA.
Voss, Timm. Die algerisch-französische Arbeitsmigration . Königstein/Ts. , 1981. xiii, 193 p. : ISBN 3-7756-6937-X : LC Card 81-176949 DDC 331.6/2/65044 19
HD8438.A4 V67 1981 ***NYPL [JLD 86-2466]***

RETURN MIGRATION - GOVERNMENT POLICY - ALGERIA.
Voss, Timm. Die algerisch-französische Arbeitsmigration . Königstein/Ts. , 1981. xiii, 193 p. : ISBN 3-7756-6937-X : LC Card 81-176949 DDC 331.6/2/65044 19
HD8438.A4 V67 1981 ***NYPL [JLD 86-2466]***

RETURN MIGRATION - PORTUGAL.
Emigración y retorno . [Madrid] , 1981. 325 p., [2] folded leaves of plates : ISBN 84-500-5097-9 LC Card 82-145134 DDC 325.46 19
JV8251 .E49 1981 ***NYPL [JLE 86-3179]***

Ferreira, Eduardo de Sousa, 1936- Reintegração dos emigrantes portugueses . [Lisbon] , 1984. xiv, 137 p. ; LC Card 86-132652
HD8380.5 .F47 1984

RETURN MIGRATION - SPAIN.
Emigración y retorno . [Madrid] , 1981. 325 p., [2] folded leaves of plates : ISBN 84-500-5097-9 LC Card 82-145134 DDC 325.46 19
JV8251 .E49 1981 ***NYPL [JLE 86-3179]***

RETURN MIGRATION - TURKEY.
Ölçen, Ali Nejat. Türken und Rückkehr . Frankfurt a.M. , 1986. 132 p. ; ISBN 3-924320-51-9 LC Card 87-138316 DDC 331.6/2/56104355 19
HD8458.T9 O43 1986

Return on investment strategies for decision-making /. Rachlin, Robert, 1937- New York , 1987. x, 306 p. : ISBN 0-531-15528-5 LC Card 87-10633 DDC 658.1/52 19
HG4028.C4 R255 1987

Reule, Fred J. Nuclear winter and national security . Maxwell Air Force Base, Ala. , Washington, D.C. , 1986. xiii, 76 p. ; LC Card 86-7967 DDC 355/.0217 19
U263 .N845 1986 ***NYPL [JFE 87-751]***

Reunión coloquio sobre como ven nuestros hombres de empresa la economía de Cantabria para 1984 / presidida por, Fernando Correa Gutiérrez, Enrique Campos Pedraja. [Santander] : Centro Montañés de Investigación y Desarrollo Empresarial : Camara de Comercio, Industria y Navegación de Santander, [1984?] 54 p. ; 22 cm. Cover title: Como ven nuestros hombres de empresa la economía de Cantabria para 1984. ISBN 84-505-0186-5 LC Card 86-187513
1. Cantabria (Spain) - Commerce - Congresses. I. Centro Montañés de Investigación y Desarrollo Empresarial (Santander, Spain). II. Cámara de Comercio, Industria y Navegación de Santander (Spain). III. Title: Como ven nuestros hombres de empresa la economía de Cantabria para 1984.
HF3690.C35 R48 1984

Reunión coloquio sobre como ven nuestros hombres de empresa la economía de Cantabria para 1985 / presidida por Fernando Correa Gutiérrez, Enrique Campos Pedraja. [Santander] : Cámara Oficial de Comercio, Industria y Navegación de Santander, [1985?] 78 p. ; 22 cm. Cover title: Como ven nuestros hombres de empresa la economía de Cantabria para 1985. ISBN 84-505-1440-1 LC Card 86-193783
1. Cantabria (Spain) - Commerce - Congresses. I. Cámara de Comercio, Industria y Navegación de Santander (Spain). II. Title: Como ven nuestros hombres de empresa la economía de Cantabria para 1985.
HF3690.C35 R49 1985

RÉUNION - ECONOMIC CONDITIONS.
Abramovici, G. Comptes économiques de la Réunion, série 1975-1980 . Ste Clotilde, [Réunion] [1983?] 133 p. ; LC Card 86-980541
HC598 .A37 1983

Reunión Nacional de la AMIC (2nd : 1982 : Centro de Estudios Económicos y Sociales del Tercer Mundo) Medios de comunicación, hegemonía y proyectos de desarrollo. [Mexico City] [between 1982 and 1987] 179 p. ; LC Card 87-127821 DDC 338.9/007/1 19
HD77 .M43 1982

Reunión Nacional para el Desarrollo de la Industria, el Comercio, la Distribución y Otros Servicios (1981 : Mexico City, Mexico) Memoria / Reunión Nacional para el Desarrollo de la Industria, el Comercio, la Distribución y Otros Servicios, Ciudad de México, 9, 10 y 11 de marzo de 1981. [Mexico City] : Confederación de Trabajadores de México, 1981. 428 p., [4] folded leaves of plates : ill. ; 22 cm. LC Card 84-228700
1. Industry and state - Mexico - Congresses. 2. Mexico - Commercial policy - Congresses. 3. Transportation and state - Mexico - Congresses. 4. Mexico - Economic policy - Congresses. I. Confederación de Trabajadores de México. II. Title.
HD3616.M42 R46 1981

Reunión Nacional sobre Población (2nd : 1985 : Tarma, Junín, Peru) Problemas poblacionales peruanos II /. Lima , c1986. 402 p. : LC Card 86-228816
HB3575 .P763 1986

RÉUNION - STATISTICS.
Abramovici, G. Comptes économiques de la Réunion, série 1975-1980 . Ste Clotilde, [Réunion] [1983?] 133 p. ; LC Card 86-980541
HC598 .A37 1983

Reunión Técnica sobre el Financiamiento de la Integración Subregional en América Latina . Reunión Técnica sobre el Financiamiento de la Integración Subregional en América Latina (1985 : Buenos Aires, Argentina) [Buenos Aires, Argentina] . 335 p. : LC Card 86-217551
HC125 .R479 1985

Reunión Técnica sobre el Financiamiento de la Integración Subregional en América Latina (1985 : Buenos Aires, Argentina) Reunión Técnica sobre el Financiamiento de la Integración Subregional en América Latina : memoria, Buenos Aires, 16 y 17 de mayo de 1985. [Buenos Aires, Argentina] : Instituto para la Integración de América Latina : Banco Interamericano de Desarrollo : 335 p. : ill. ; 29 cm. (Public. . no. 238) Cover title: El financiamiento de la integración subregional en América Latina. Includes bibliographical references. "Distrib. general, BID.INTAL/DP 335/85." LC Card 86-217551
1. Latin America - Economic integration - Congresses. 2. Regional economics. I. Institute for Latin American Integration. II. FONPLATA (Organization). III. Title. IV. Title: Financiamiento de la integración subregional en América Latina. V. Series: Publ. (Institute for Latin American Integration) , no. 238.
HC125 .R479 1985

Reuniones y seminarios.
Financiamiento agrícola. México, D.F. , 1985. i, 156 p. ; LC Card 86-156375
HG2051.L26 F55 1985

REUS REGION (SPAIN) - ECONOMIC CONDITIONS.
Calleja Xifré, Carlos. El Baix Camp . Barcelona [1986] xv, 367 p. : ISBN 84-505-3567-9 LC Card 86-205881
HC388.R482 C35 1986

REUS REGION (SPAIN) - POLITICS AND GOVERNMENT.
Calleja Xifré, Carlos. El Baix Camp . Barcelona [1986] xv, 367 p. : ISBN 84-505-3567-9 LC Card 86-205881
HC388.R482 C35 1986

REUS REGION (SPAIN) - POPULATION.
Calleja Xifré, Carlos. El Baix Camp . Barcelona [1986] xv, 367 p. : ISBN 84-505-3567-9 LC Card 86-205881
HC388.R482 C35 1986

REUS REGION (SPAIN) - SOCIAL CONDITIONS.
Calleja Xifré, Carlos. El Baix Camp . Barcelona [1986] xv, 367 p. : ISBN 84-505-3567-9 LC Card 86-205881
HC388.R482 C35 1986

Reuschenbach, Ruth. Ziele, Instrumente und Bedingungen der Geschäftsstellenorganisation im filialisierten Universalbankbetrieb / Ruth Reuschenbach. Köln : Wison, c1984. 385 p. ; 21 cm. (Kölner bankwirtschaftliche Studien. Bd. 6) Bibliography: p. 332-385. ISBN 3-87951-122-5 LC Card 85-131689
1. Banks and banking - Germany, West - Branch banks. 2. Bank management - Germany (West). I. Title. II. Series.
HG1616.B7 R48 1984

Reuss, Martin. Interview with Professor Arthur Maass / by Martin Reuss. Fort Belvoir, Va. : Office of History, U. S. Army Corps of Engineers, 1987. p. cm. (Water resources--people and issues) LC Card 86-32033 DDC 333.91/15/0973 19
1. Water resources development - United States - Planning - History. 2. Water resources development - United States - Planning - History - Sources. I. Maass, Arthur. II. Title. III. Series.
HD1694.A5 R46 1987

Réussir l'alternance . Séguin, Philippe, 1943- Paris , c1985. 220 p. ; ISBN 2-221-04633-1 : LC Card 85-187945 DDC 944.083/8 19
JN2594.2 .S37 1985 ***NYPL [JLC 87-46]***

Reuter, Edzard, 1928- Vom Geist der Wirtschaft : Europa zwischen Technokraten und Mythokraten / Edzard Reuter. Stuttgart : Deutsche Verlags-Anstalt, c1986. 288 p. ; 22 cm. Bibliography: p. 285-288. ISBN 3-421-06311-7 LC Card 86-181795
1. Europe - Economic conditions - 1945-. 2. Economic forecasting - Europe. 3. Europe - Industries. I. Title.
HC240 .R44 1986

Reuter, Frank, Dr. Grundzüge der internationalen Unternehmenspolitik des Versicherungsunternehmens / von Frank Reuter. Berlin : Duncker & Humblot, c1983. 178 p. : 48 ill. ; 24 cm. (Schriftenreihe des Instituts für Versicherungswissenschaft an der Universität zu Köln . n.F., Heft 39) Bibliography: p. [166]-178. ISBN 3-428-05308-7 LC Card 83-161541
1. Insurance, Business. 2. International business enterprises. I. Title. II. Series.
HG8018 .C6 n.F., Heft 39 HG8059

Reutersberg, Bernhard. Logistik als Instrument zur Steigerung der Marktleistungsfähigkeit von Stahlhandlungen / Bernhard Reutersberg. Göttingen : Vandenhoeck & Ruprecht, 1985. 301 p. : ill. ; 24 cm. (Beiträge aus dem Institut für Verkehrswissenschaft an der Universität Münster . Heft 107) Bibliography: p. 285-301. ISBN 3-525-85697-0 : LC Card 86-162333
1. Steel - Transportation - Planning. 2. Steel - Marketing. I. Title. II. Series.
HE131 .M8 Heft 107 HE199.5.M4

Los revalúos técnicos de bienes . Troiano, Alberto C. (Alberto Carlos) Buenos Aires [1982] 63,

[2] p. : ISBN 950-0-37018-2 LC Card 84-237340
HF5658.5 .T76 1982

Revéiz, Edgar. Deuda externa latinoamericana y proceso de ajuste . Bogotá, Colombia , 1985. 335 p. : LC Card 86-164491
HJ8514.5 .D484 1985

REVEL, CHASE.
Tepper, Ron, 1937- Secrets of a successful mail order guru . New York , c1988. ix, 230 p. : ISBN 0-471-84857-3 LC Card 87-21658 DDC 658.8/72 19
HF5466 .T36 1988

Revenue and equity effects of the 1983 income tax reform in Malawi /. Kandoole, B. F. [Zomba, Malaŵi?] [1986] 20 p. ; LC Card 86-981440 DDC 336.2/0096897 19
HJ4791 .K36 1986

REVENUE - AUSTRALIA - STATISTICS - HISTORY.
Barnard, A. (Alan) Some government financial data, 1850 to 1982 /. Canberra, Australia [1986] 47, 2 p. ; ISBN 0-86784-850-2 (pbk.) LC Card 86-211320 DDC 336.94 19
HJ2193.Z7 B37 1986

REVENUE - BRAZIL - MINAS GERAIS.
Economia mineira e o financiamento do setor público . Belo Horizonte , 1985. 126 p. : LC Card 85-207952
HJ2529.M5 E26 1985

REVENUE - ILLINOIS.
Tax report . Springfield, Ill. (703 Stratton Office Bldg., Springfield 62706) [1986] iv, 30, 3 leaves ; LC Card 86-622596 DDC 336.2/009773 19
HJ2403 .T39 1986

REVENUE - INDIA - ASSAM - HISTORY.
Goswami, Shrutidev, 1947- Aspects of revenue administration in Assam, 1826-1874 /. Delhi, India , 1987. xii, 184 p. ; LC Card 87-900200 DDC 336.02/54162 19
HJ2939.A87 G67 1987

Goswami, Surendra Kumar, 1929-1985. A history of revenue administration in Assam, 1228-1826 A.D. . Delhi , 1986. xii, 321 p. : LC Card 86-903188 DDC 354.54/16200726/09 19
HJ2939.Z9 A874 1986

REVENUE - ITALY - STATISTICS.
Ghessi, Giuseppe. La finanza pubblica in cifre, 1965-1983 /. Milano, Italy , c1985. 186 p. : LC Card 85-180958 DDC 336.45 19
HJ1185 .G43 1985 ***NYPL [JLF 87-249]***

REVENUE - LOUISIANA.
Lam, Manuel. Louisiana crude oil and natural gas report and severance and royalty sensitivity to price, second half 1985 /. Baton Rouge, La (P.O. Box 44156, Baton Rouge 70804-4156) [1986] iii, 31 p. : LC Card 86-621907 DDC 338.2/728/09763 19
HD9560.8.U53 L65 1986

REVENUE - MAINE - STATISTICS.
Compendium of state fiscal information /. [Augusta?] [1985] 40 leaves : LC Card 86-621730 DDC 336.741/021 19
HJ2410 .C65 1985

REVENUE - MALAWI.
Kandoole, B. F. Revenue and equity effects of the 1983 income tax reform in Malawi /. [Zomba, Malaŵi?] [1986] 20 p. ; LC Card 86-981440 DDC 336.2/0096897 19
HJ4791 .K36 1986

Revenue mobilization and responsiveness of Philippine income taxes . Diokno, Benjamin E. [Quezon City, Philippines] [1986] 26 p. : LC Card 87-120920 DDC 339.5/25/09599 19
HJ4743 .D56 1986

REVENUE - NEBRASKA - STATISTICS.
Nebraska. Legislature. Appropriations and revenues, fiscal year 1985-86 . [Lincoln] [1985] i, 49 leaves ; LC Card 85-623111 DDC 336.782 19
HJ2053.N34 A66 1985

REVENUE - ONTARIO - FORECASTING.
Economic and fiscal review . Toronto, Ont. [1986] i, 89 p. : ISBN 0-7729-1950-X (pbk.) LC Card 87-169450 DDC 330.9713/04 19
HJ2460.O5 E28 1986

REVENUE - PHILIPPINES.
Diokno, Benjamin E. Revenue mobilization and responsiveness of Philippine income taxes . [Quezon City, Philippines] [1986] 26 p. : LC Card 87-120920 DDC 339.5/25/09599 19
HJ4743 .D56 1986

REVENUE SHARING - AUSTRIA - PROVINCES - STATISTICS.
Daten zum Finanzausgleich . Wien [1986] xx, 331 p. : LC Card 86-209464
HJ1066 .D37 1986

REVENUE SHARING - BRAZIL.
Longo, Carlos Alberto. Ajustamentos de impostos na fronteira e a alocação de receitas tributárias . São Paulo , 1979. 208 p. ; LC Card 80-152384
HJ5715.B8 L6617 ***NYPL [JLD 86-3846]***

REVENUE SHARING - FLORIDA.
Sapolsky, Joann. Catalogue of state shared revenue sources distributed between 1973-1986. Tallahassee, Fla. (House Office Bldg., Tallahassee 32301) [1986] v, 76 leaves : LC Card 86-623224 DDC 336.1/85/09759 19
HJ375 .S26 1986

REVENUE SHARING - GERMANY (WEST)
Finanzwirtschaftliche Folgen kommunaler Gebiets- und Funktionalreformen . Baden-Baden , 1986. 209 p. : ISBN 3-7890-1163-0 (Deut. Bibl.) LC Card 86-169111
HJ1121 .F55 1986

REVENUE SHARING - NEW JERSEY.
New Jersey. Bureau of Urban Strategies. Proposed solutions to local fiscal resource disparities in the state of New Jersey . Trenton, N.J. [1980] vi, 353 p. ; LC Card 81-622089 DDC 336.02/749 19
HJ585 .N38 1980 ***NYPL [JLF 86-1372]***

REVENUE SHARING - NIGERIA.
REVENUE SHARING - UNITED STATES.
An Alphabetical guide to Office of Revenue Sharing account numbers /. Washington, D.C. , 1981. iii, 187 p. ; ***NYPL [JLF 87-470]***

Van Horn, Carl E. Policy implementation in the Federal system . Lexington, Mass. , c1979. xiv, 177 p. ; ISBN 0-669-02435-X LC Card 78-19929 DDC 353.007/25
HJ275 .V35 ***NYPL [JLE 80-794]***

REVENUE-STAMPS - BALTIC STATES - CATALOGS.
Hall, Andrew. Baltic states revenues /. York, England , c1983. 40 p. : ISBN 0-906845-14-9 (pbk.) LC Card 87-100278 DDC 769.5/7 19
HJ5429.B34 H34 1983

REVENUE-STAMPS - FRANCE - CATALOGS.
Catalogue des timbres fiscaux et sociaux de France /. Le Havre , 1982. 135 p. : LC Card 86-159729
HJ5412 .C37 1982

REVENUE-STAMPS - HAWAII - HISTORY.
Burt, Randall E. Adhesive revenue stamps of Hawaii . Honolulu, Hawaii (P.O. Box 10115, Honolulu 96816-0115) , c1986. ix, 114 p. : LC Card 87-136622 DDC 769.5/7 19
HJ5346.5 .B87 1986

REVENUE-STAMPS - SWITZERLAND - CATALOGS.
Kelly, Gene. [Catalog of the fiscal stamps of the Kantone and Gemeinden of Switzerland.] Gene Kelly's catalog of the fiscal stamps of the Kantone and Gemeinden of Switzerland. [Diessenhofen, Switzerland] [1986- v. <1 > : LC Card 87-112466 DDC 769.5/7 19
HJ5437.Z7 K45 1986

REVENUE - TEXAS.
Hamilton, Billy. Outlook for state spending and revenues in the late '80s . College Station, Tex. , c1985. 14 p. : ISBN 0-86599-055-7 (pbk.) LC Card 86-622256 DDC 336.764 19
HJ2053.T5 H36 1985

REVENUE - UNITED STATES - STATES.
Federal tax reform and the states . Washington, D.C. (1616 H St., N.W., Suite 600, Washington 20006) , c1987. 84 p. ; LC Card 87-404532 DDC 336.2/05/0973 19
HJ2381 .F37 1987

Revenus et fiscalité des agriculteurs en Belgique. Politique agricole commune . Bruxelles, Belgique , c1982. 126 p. ; ISBN 1-8004-0773-5 LC Card 87-672469
HD1803 .P64x 1982

Reverdy, Georges. Histoire des grandes liaisons françaises / Georges Reverdy. Paris, France : Revue générale des routes et des aérodromes, c1981-c1982. 2 v. : ill. ; 24 cm. Bibliography: v. 2, p. 311-312. Includes index. LC Card 83-129286
1. Roads - France - History. 2. Railroads - France - History. I. Title.
HE363.F7 R48 1981

Reverse marketing . Leenders, Michiel R. New York , London , c1988. ix, 198 p. : ISBN 0-02-918381-2 LC Card 87-15146 DDC 658.7/2 19
HD39.5 .L435 1988

Revesz Long, Bruno. Promoción agraria, para quién? . Lima, Perú , 1980. 162 p. ; ***NYPL [JLD 86-3547]***

Review and appraisal of the World Population Plan of Action . United Nations. Dept. of International Economic and Social Affairs. New York , 1986. vi, 169 p. : ISBN 92-1-151158-5 (pbk.) LC Card 87-105369 DDC 304.6 19
HB883.5 .U55 1986

Review of a mid-year review of the economy, 1984 /. Balakrishnan, C. B. New Delhi , 1984. 132 p. ; LC Card 86-903796 DDC 330.954/052 19
HC435.2 .B323 1984

A review of aerodrome statistics in Tanzania, 1970-1982. Mkwawa, D. A. Y. Dar es Salaam [1984] xix, 143 p. : LC Card 87-403351 DDC 387.7/36/09678021 19
HE9797.5.T34 M58 1984

Review of African Political Economy Conference (1984 : University of Keele) World recession and the food crisis in Africa /. London , 1986. 314 p. ; ISBN 0-85255-309-9 : LC Card 86-235333 DDC 363.8/526/096 19
HD9017.A2 W67 1986b

A review of Bay Area public transportation financing. California. Legislature. Joint Legislative Budget Committee. Legislative Analyst. Sacramento, Calif. (925 L St., Suite 650, Sacramento 95814) [1986] 57 p. : LC Card 86-621890 DDC 388.4/042 19
HE4491.S45 C33 1986

A Review of birth statistics, Bermuda, 1971-1978 / Statistical Office, Ministry of Finance. [Hamilton] : The Office, [1980] 62 p. ; 29 cm. "May, 1980." Chiefly tables. LC Card 85-189032 DDC 304.6/3/097299021 19
1. Childbirth - Bermuda Islands - Statistics. 2. Fertility, Human - Bermuda Islands - Statistics. I. Bermuda Islands. of Finance Ministry. Statistical Office.
HB1078.A3 R48 1980 ***NYPL [JLF 85-3121]***

A review of Essentials of accounting, 4th edition /. Anthony, Robert Newton, 1916- Reading, Mass. , 1988. p. cm. ISBN 0-201-05905-3 : LC Card 87-21949 DDC 657 19
HF5635 .A69143 1988

Review of exporters and importers of Yugoslavia : Zagreb International Fair / editorial board Ljubo Babić ... [et al.] ; translated by Marko Pavičić. Zagreb : The Fair : Grafički zavod Hrvatske, 1965. ca. 650 p. : ill. (some col.) ; 33 cm. LC Card 84-149403
1. Yugoslavia - Commerce. 2. Commercial products - Yugoslavia. 3. Yugoslavia - Industries. I. Babić, Ljubo. II. Zagreb International Fair (10th : 1965). III. Grafički zavod Hrvatske.
HF3732.3 .R46 1965

Review of Federal-Aid Urban System program. United States. Office of Highway Planning. Urban Planning and Transportation Management Division. [Washington, D.C.?] [1985] 55 p. : ***NYPL [JLF 86-340]***

Review of food consumption surveys 1981. Review of food consumption surveys-1985 . Rome , 1986. xxiv, 212 p. ; ISBN 92-5-102375-1 (pbk.) LC Card 86-222995 DDC 339.4/8664 19
HD9000.4 .R483 1986

Review of food consumption surveys-1985 : household food consumption by economic groups. Rome : Food and Agriculture Organization of the United Nations, 1986. xxiv, 212 p. ; 30 cm. (FAO food and nutrition paper . 35) Continues: Review of food consumption surveys 1981. ISBN 92-5-102375-1 (pbk.) LC Card 86-222995 DDC 339.4/8664 19
1. Food consumption - Statistics. 2. Nutrition surveys. I. Food and Agriculture Organization of the United Nations. II. Title: Review of food consumption surveys

1981. III. Series.
HD9000.4 .R483 1986

Review of ILO rural development activities since 1979 : first item on the agenda / Advisory Committee on Rural Development. Geneva : International Labor Office, 1983. ii, 61 p. ; 24 cm. "ACRD X/1983/1." "Tenth session, Geneva, 22 November to 1 December 1983." ISBN 92-2-103505-0 (pbk.) : LC Card 86-221297 DDC 331.11/09173/4 19
1. Manpower policy, Rural. 2. Rural development. I. International Labour Organisation. Advisory Committee on Rural Development.
HD5707 .R44 1983

Review of Shannon Free Airport Development Company Limited . Ireland. Oireachtas. Dáil. Committee on Public Expenditure. Dublin [1983?] 79 p. : LC Card 87-146082 DDC 387.7/36/094193 19
HE9797.5.I72 S54 1983

A Review of technologies for the provision of basic infrastructure in low-income settlements. Nairobi : United Nations Centre for Human Settlements (Habitat), 1984. viii, 82 p. ; 30 cm. Bibliography: p. 75-82. "HS/40/84/E"--T.p. verso. LC Card 86-980643 DDC 363/.09172/4 19
1. Infrastructure (Economics) - Developing countries. I. United Nations Centre for Human Settlements.
HC59.72.C3 R47 1984

Review of the economy. Adiseshiah, Malcolm S. Mid year review of the economy, 1986-87 /. New Delhi , 1987. 193 p. : ISBN 81-7062-016-3 : LC Card 87-900477 DDC 330.954/052 19
HC435.2 .A648 1987

Review of the European Foundation's research into shiftwork, 1981-1984. Copsey, S. M. Shiftwork review . Luxembourg , Washington, DC , 1986. xi, 122 p. : ISBN 92-825-6419-3 (pbk.) : LC Card 87-137298 DDC 331.25/72 19
HD5111.6.E86 C66 1986

Review of the implementation of the Food Security Act of 1985 . United States. Congress. Senate. Committee on Agriculture, Nutrition, and Forestry. Washington , 1987. iv, 180 p. : LC Card 87-601199 DDC 338.1/9/73 19
HD1761 .U515 1987

Review of the ITV and ILR levy structures, 1984-85 : report of a working group of officials of the Home Office, Treasury, and Independent Broadcasting Authority, May 1985. London : Broadcasting Dept., Home Office, c1986. 44 p. ; 30 cm. "February 1986." ISBN 0-86252-236-6 (pbk.) LC Card 86-202703 DDC 384.54/3 19
1. Broadcasting - Taxation - Great Britain. I. Great Britain. Home Office. II. Great Britain. Treasury. III. Independent Broadcasting Authority.
HE8689.9.G7 R48 1986

A Review of U. S. competitiveness in agricultural trade. Washington, D.C. : Congress of the U. S., Office of Technology Assessment : For sale by the Supt. of Docs., U. S. G.P.O., [1986] ix, 101 p. : ill. ; 26 cm. (A technical memorandum) Shipping list no.: 86-830-P. "October 1986." Includes bibliographical references. "OTA-TM-TET-29"--P. [4] of cover. S/N 052-003-01054-2 Item 1070-M LC Card 86-600586 DDC 382/.41/0973 19
1. Agriculture - Economic aspects - United States. 2. Farm produce - United States - Marketing. 3. Agricultural productivity - United States. 4. Agriculture and state - United States. 5. Competition, International. I. United States. Congress. Office of Technology Assessment. II. Title: Review of US competitiveness in agricultural trade. III. Series: Technical memoranda (United States. Congress. Office of Technology Assessment).
HD1761 .R48 1986

Review of US competitiveness in agricultural trade. A Review of U. S. competitiveness in agricultural trade. Washington, D.C. [1986] ix, 101 p. : LC Card 86-600586 DDC 382/.41/0973 19
HD1761 .R48 1986

Review of 1985 property tax rates /. Kelly, Margaret. Jefferson City [1986] i, 6 leaves, 109, 2 p. ; LC Card 87-620606 DDC 336.22/2 19
HJ4121.M82 K45 1986

Review on the development of antibiotics industry in selected countries . Aizawa, Minoru. [Vienna, Austria] , 1985. 92 p. : LC Card 86-151674 DDC 338.4/7615329/0952 19
HD9675.A63 J33 1985

Review report (National Fertilizer Development Centre (Pakistan)) . (2) Suleman, R. M. U. 1983-84 rabi (winter) season fertilizer review . Islamabad [1984] iv, 28 leaves : LC Card 85-930451 DDC 338.4/766862/095491 19
HD9483.P22 S844 1984

Reviews of the Tobacco Leaf Marketing Board, Tobacco Quota Committee, Tobacco Quota Appeals Tribunal. Victoria. Parliament. Public Bodies Review Committee. Reports on the Tobacco Leaf Marketing Board, Tobacco Quota Committee, Tobacco Quota Appeals Tribunal . Melbourne [1986] xix, 107 p. ; LC Card 87-168528 DDC 354.9450082/332 19
HD9148.A8 V53 1986

Reviews of United Kingdom statistical sources . (v. 21) Finance. Oxford [Oxfordshire] , New York , 1987. xiii, 495 p. ; ISBN 0-08-034780-0 : LC Card 87-7247 DDC 332/.0941 19
HG186.G7 F53 1987

Revinskiĭ, I. A. Upravlenie v sisteme proizvodstvennykh otnosheniĭ /. Novosibirsk , 1974. 82 p. ; LC Card 83-120398
HD70.S63 U68 1974

Revised annual estimates of population for census divisions, 1971-1976 / Statistics Canada, Census and Household Surveys Field, Demography Division = Estimations annuelles révisées de la population des divisions de recensement, 1971-1976 / Statistique Canada, Secteur du recensement et des enquêtes ménages, Division de la démographie. Ottawa : Statistics Canada, c1979. 21 p. ; 28 cm. English and French. "July 1979." Includes bibliographical references. "Catalogue 91-521 occasional"--Cover. "Catalogue 91-521." LC Card 82-216681
1. Canada - Population - Statistics. 2. Census districts - Canada - Statistics. I. Statistics Canada. Census and Household Surveys Field. II. Title: Estimations annuelles révisées de la population des divisions de recensement, 1971-1975.
HA745 .R473 1979

Revised life tables by sex and ethnic group for Peninsular Malaysia, 1970 and 1980. Kajian semula jadual-jadual hayat mengikut jantina dan kumpulan etnik bagi Semenanjung Malaysia, 1970 dan 1980 =. Kuala Lumpur [1986] v, 27, v, 38 p. : ISBN 967-99995-2-1 (pbk.) : LC Card 87-941374
HB1474.6.A3 K35 1986

Una revisión de políticas de empleo para América Latina /. Meller, Patricio. Santiago, Chile , 1981. 72 leaves ; LC Card 83-182110
HD5730.5.A6 M44 1981

Revisión del índice del costo de la construcción de vivienda en la Ciudad de Guatemala, años 1975-1979. Guatemala : Dirección General de Estadística, Ministerio de Economía, 1979. 35 p. : ill. ; 28 cm. LC Card 82-182718
1. Dwellings - Guatemala - Guatemala - Costs. 2. Construction industry - Guatemala - Guatemala - Costs. 3. Building materials - Prices - Guatemala - Guatemala. 4. Wages - Construction workers - Guatemala - Guatemala. I. Guatemala. Dirección General de Estadística.
HD9715.G983 G827 1979

A revision of demand theory /. Hicks, John Richard, Sir, 1940- Oxford [Oxfordshire] , New York , 1986, c1956. vii, 196 p. : ISBN 0-19-828110-2 LC Card 86-154241 DDC 338.5/212 19
HB801 .H48 1986 ***NYPL [JLD 86-3663]***

REVISIONISM, COMMUNIST. see **COMMUNIST REVISIONISM.**

Reviving industry in America . Shapiro, H. Jack (Harris Jack) Cambridge, Mass. , c1987. xii, 204 p. : ISBN 0-88730-118-5 LC Card 87-17585 DDC 338.4/767/0973 19
HD9725 .S46 1987

Revoli͡ut͡sionnoto profsi͡uzno dvizhenie v Gabrovski okrŭg / [sŭstavitel T͡Son′o Petrov]. Sofii͡a : Profizdat, 1986. 305 p., [16] p. of plates : ill. ; 21 cm. Bibliography: p. 300-[304] LC Card 86-232088
1. Trade-unions - Bulgaria - Gabrovski okrŭg - History. 2. Trade-unions and communism - Bulgaria - Gabrovski okrŭg - History. I. Petrov, Tson′o.
HD6785.G32 R48 1986

A Revolta dos Parceiros /. Witter, José Sebastião. São Paulo, SP , 1986. 77 p. : LC Card 87-102716
HD4875.B8 W58 1986

La revolución de Los Barrosos /. González G., Godofredo (González González) Caracas, Venezuela [19]87. xii, 276 p. ; ISBN 980-263-047-0 LC Card 87-400058 DDC 338.2/7282/0987 19
HD9574.V42 G59 1987

Una revolución en las comunicaciones . Colombia. Ministerio de Comunicaciones. [Bogotá] 1986. 307 p., [5] leaves of plates : LC Card 87-401464 DDC 384/.09861 19
HE8011 .C65 1986

Revolución y mujeres del campo : el impacto de la Reforma Agraria Sandinista sobre la subordinación de la mujer rural / [autores, Ana Criquillion, et al.]. Managua : Asociación de Trabajadores del Campo, [1985] 46 p. : ill. ; 21 cm. Bibliography: p. [45]-46. LC Card 86-231936
1. Land reform - Nicaragua. 2. Rural women - Nicaragua. 3. Women in agriculture - Nicaragua. 4. Frente Sandinista de Liberación Nacional. I. Criquillion, Ana. II. Asociación de Trabajadores del Campo (Nicaragua).
HD1333.N5 R48 1985

La révolution aux pieds nus . Schneider, Bertrand. Paris , c1985. 344 p. ; ISBN 2-213-01684-4 : LC Card 86-179661
HC60 .S314 1985

Revolution des Zahlungsverkehrs durch Automation / herausgegeben von Leo Schuster. Frauenfeld : Huber, [1984] 160 p. : ill. ; 22 cm. Includes bibliographical references and index. CONTENTS. - Der Zahlungsverkehr als Teil des strategischen Managements einer Bank / Markus Graf -- Entwicklungen im schweizerischen Banken-Zahlungsverkehr / Médard Storz -- Point of Sale-Systeme / Alex W. Widmer -- Strategien von Kreditkartenorganisationen / Hans Jürg Malär -- Cash Management in Unternehmungen / Jürgen Wilhelm Westphal -- Die PTT als Substitutionskonkurrentin der Banken im Zahlungsverkehr / Rolf Stahel -- Auswirkungen des EDV-gestützten Zahlungsverkehrs auf die Zweigstellenpolitik der Banken / Leo Schuster. ISBN 3-7193-0929-0 : LC Card 84-153299
1. Banks and banking - Switzerland - Automation. 2. Payment - Switzerland - Automation. I. Schuster, Leo.
HG1709 .R48 1984

REVOLUTION, FRENCH. see **FRANCE - HISTORY - REVOLUTION, 1789-1799.**

Revolution in financial services /. Gourgues, Harold W. Washington, D.C. , c1987. xiii, 248 p. : ISBN 0-87179-561-2 LC Card 87-18390 DDC 332.1/0973 19
HG2491 .G68 1987

La révolution industrielle /. Verley, Patrick. Paris , c1985. 270 p. : ISBN 2-86676-194-4 LC Card 86-116016 DDC 338.09 19
HD2321 .V47 1985

REVOLUTIONÄRE GEWERKSCHAFTSOPPOSITION (ORGANIZATION) - CONGRESSES.
Der I. Kongress der Revolutionären Gewerkschafts-Opposition (RGO) im Bezirk Mittelrhein (Raum Aachen-Köln-Koblenz) im Jahre 1930 /. Reinbek , c1982. 136 p. : ISBN 3-88756-024-8 : LC Card 84-135308
HD6699.R47 I18 1982

Revolutionary Grenada . Pryor, Frederic L. New York , 1986. xx, 395 p. : ISBN 0-275-92155-7 (alk. paper) : LC Card 86-8109 DDC 338.97298/45 19
HC156.5.Z7 G747 1986
NYPL [JLE 86-3969]

REVOLUTIONS - DEVELOPING COUNTRIES.
Prosterman, Roy L. Land reform and democratic development /. Baltimore , c1987. xii, 313 p. ; ISBN 0-8018-3482-1 (alk. paper) LC Card 87-4188 DDC 333.3/1/1724 19
HD1333.5 .P76 1987

Rex-Kiss, Béla. Vizsgálatok az újszülöttek nemi arányának alakulásáról / Rex-Kiss Béla. Budapest : Medicina, 1986. 124 p. : ill. ; 20 cm. (Aesculap, 0133-7513) Bibliography: p. 121-124. ISBN 963-241-457-8 : LC Card 87-138601
1. Sex. 2. Sex ratio. 3. Hungary - Statistics, Vital. I. Title.
HB1741 .R49 1986

Rey, Heinz, 1943- Usteri, Martin. Bodenrecht in Bewegung . Zürich [1985] 27 p. ; LC Card 86-195037
HC395 .Z43 Nr. 126 KKW683

Rey Romay, Benito. La ofensiva empresarial contra la intervención del estado / por Benito Rey Romay. 1a ed. México : Siglo Veintiuno Editores, 1984. 160 p. ; 21 cm. (Economía y demografía) Includes bibliographical references. ISBN 968-231-283-3 LC Card 86-151140
1. Government business enterprises - Mexico. 2. Industry and state - Mexico. I. Series: Economía y demografía (Mexico City, Mexico). II. Title.
HD4013 .R49 1984

Rey Salgado, Rafael del. La crisis de la deuda en América Latina / por Rafael del Rey Salgado. [Spain] : Instituto de Cuestiones Internacionales, [1985] ii, 88 p. ; 28 cm. (Una Publicación INCI . no. 28) "Marzo 1985." Bibliography: p. 81-88. LC Card 86-131407
1. Debts, External - Latin America. 2. Loans, Foreign - Latin America. 3. Latin America - Economic policy. I. Series: INCI publication , nr. 28. II. Title.
HJ8514.5 .R49 1985

Reyes Osorio, Sergio. Estructura agraria y desarrollo agrícola en México . México , 1974 (1979 printing) xvi, 1174 p. : LC Card 81-126616 DDC 338.1/0972 19
HD1792 .E85 1974 ***NYPL [JLE 81-372]***

Reyes, Sergio. see **Reyes Osorio, Sergio.**

Reyhons, Ken. Recruiting sales associates / Ken Reyhons. [Chicago, Ill.] : Real Estate Brokerage Council, Realtors National Marketing Institute, National Association of Realtors, c1986. 151 p. : forms ; 28 cm. Includes index. ISBN 0-931652-62-8 (pbk.) LC Card 86-63281 DDC 333.33/068/3 19
1. Real estate agents - United States - Recruiting. I. Title.
HD278 .R49 1986

Reynaud, Françoise. Atget, Géniaux, Vert . Paris [1984] 63, [1] p. : ISBN 2-901414-09-5 : LC Card 86-137985
HF5459.F8 A87 1984 ***NYPL [MFW 87-159]***

Reynolds, Barbara, 1914-
[Cambridge Italian dictionary]
Cambridge dizionario italiano-inglese, inglese-italiano, Signorelli : dal "Cambridge Italian dictionary" di Barbara Reynolds. Cambridge [Cambridgeshire] ; New York : Cambridge University Press ; 2276 p. ; 25 cm. Translation of: Cambridge Italian dictionary. ISBN 0-521-32702-4 LC Card 86-1898 DDC 453/.21 19
1. Italian language - Dictionaries - English. 2. English language - Dictionaries - Italian. I. Title.
PC1640 .R4 1986 ***NYPL [*R-REK 86-3799]***

Reynolds, Bruce Lloyd, 1944- Kai ko. English. Reform in China . Armonk, N.Y., USA , c1987. p. cm. ISBN 0-87332-458-7 : LC Card 87-23537 DDC 338.951 19
HC427.92 .K32 1987

Reynolds, Lloyd George, 1910-
Economics of labor / Lloyd G. Reynolds, Stanley H. Masters, Collette H. Moser. Englewood Cliffs, NJ : Prentice-Hall, c1987. x, 518 p. : ill. ; 25 cm. Includes bibliographies and index. ISBN 0-13-225772-6 LC Card 86-25149 DDC 331 19
1. Labor economics. I. Masters, Stanley H., 1940-. II. Moser, Colletta H., 1940-. III. Title.
HD4901 .R469 1987

REYNOLDS, LLOYD GEORGE, 1910- - CONGRESSES.
How labor markets work . Lexington, Mass. , c1988. viii, 256 p. : ISBN 0-669-15126-2 (alk. paper) LC Card 87-22718 DDC 331.12 19
HD5701.3 .H68 1988

Reynolds, Morgan O., 1942- Making America poorer : the cost of labor law / Morgan O. Reynolds. Washington, D.C. : Cato Institute, c1987. ix, 218 p. ; 24 cm. Bibliography: p. 195-209. Includes index. ISBN 0-932790-63-1 LC Card 87-6569 DDC 338.5/1/0973 19
1. Trade-unions - United States. 2. Industrial productivity - United States. 3. Wages - United States. 4. Labor laws and legislation - United States - Compliance costs. I. Title.
HD6508 .R435 1987

Reynolds, Peter J. Political economy : a synthesis of Kaleckian and post Keynesian economics / Peter J. Reynolds. Brighton, Sussex : Wheatsheaf Books ; New York : St. Martin's Press, 1987. viii, 279 p. : ill. ; 23 cm. Bibliography: p. 253-272. Includes index. ISBN 0-312-01328-0 (St. Martin's Press) : LC Card 87-23307 DDC 330 19
1. Economics. I. Title.
HB171 .R42 1987

Rezer, Semen Moiseevich. Vzaimodeĭstvie transportnykh sistem / S.M. Rezer ; otvetstvennyĭ redaktor A.F. Volkov. Moskva : "Nauka", 1985. 243 p. : ill. ; 22 cm. At head of title: Akademii͡a nauk SSSR. Institut problem upravlenii͡a. Vsesoi͡uznyĭ institut nauchnoĭ i tekhnicheskoĭ informat͡sii. Bibliography: p. 239-241. Includes index. LC Card 85-223225
1. Transportation - Soviet Union. I. Volkov, Al'bert Fedorovich. II. Title.
HE255 .R493 1985

Rezervy ėffektivnosti upravlenii͡a proizvodstvom /. Sinavina, V. S. (Valentina Semenovna) Moskva , 1984. 167 p. : LC Card 84-244689
HD70.S63 S575 1984

Rezervy intensifikat͡sii vosproizvodstva osnovnykh fondov i ikh ispol'zovanii͡a / [otvetstvennyĭ redaktor Smyshli͡aeva L.M.]. Moskva : Akademii͡a nauk SSSR, In-t ėkonomiki, 1984. 204 p. ; 21 cm. Includes bibliographical references. LC Card 85-240369
1. Capital productivity - Soviet Union. 2. Capital investments - Soviet Union. I. Smyshli͡aeva, Li͡udmila Matveevna. II. Institut ėkonomiki (Akademii͡a nauk SSSR).
HC340.C3 R48 1984

Rezervy povysheniia ėffektivnosti proizvodstva na magnitogorskom metallurgicheskom kombinate /. Zubets, V. M. (Vasiliĭ Mikhaĭlovich) Cheli͡abinsk , 1975. 183 p. ; LC Card 81-170397
HD9525.S653 M39 1975

Rezervy v ekonomice /. Kazimour, Jan, engineer. Praha , 1981. 227 p. ; LC Card 81-208368
HC270.28 .K38 1981

Reznikov, Iosif Emmanuilovich. Die Organisation der Gewerkschaften der Sowjetunion / I. Resnikow. Moskau : Kommission für Auswärtige Beziehungen des Zentralrats der Gewerkschaften der USSR, 1927. 76 p. ; 18 cm. LC Card 86-231829
1. Trade-unions - Soviet Union - History - 20th century. I. Title.
HD6732 .R398 1927

Le Rézo . Fortin, Andrée. Québec, Québec , 1985. 282 p. : ISBN 2-89224-052-2 LC Card 86-225353
HD3290.A3 Q435 1985

RFL/RL, inc. The Political self-assessment of Bulgarian respondents in terms of a left-right continuum. [Munich?] [1986] 16 p. ; LC Card 87-142360 DDC 384.55/43 19
HE8697.A8 P67 1986

RGK Foundation. Frontiers in creative and innovative management /. Cambridge, Mass. , 1985, c1986. xxv, 391 p. : ISBN 0-88730-057-X LC Card 85-15125 DDC 658.4 19
HD53 .F76 1986 ***NYPL [JLE 86-3614]***

RGN-ondersoek na werkkragvraagstukke. Werkkragstudies .
(nr. 4) Van der Walt, Sunette. Die vrou in die werksituasie in die RSA . Pretoria , 1986. vii, 156 p. : ISBN 0-7969-0373-5 LC Card 87-121977
HD6212 .V363 1986

RGW-Staaten und Dritte Welt . Machowski, Heinrich. Bonn , 1981. iii, 84 p. ; ISBN 3-7713-0167-X LC Card 85-224767
HF1532.15.D44 M33 1981

Rheault, Sylvie. Les femmes et l'emploi / Sylvie Rheault, Francine Lepage, Micheline Boivin. [Québec] : Gouvernement du Québec, Conseil du statut de la femme, [1983] 64 p. ; 28 cm. "1983-10-19." Bibliography: p. [59]-64. ISBN 2-550-10471-4 LC Card 85-108850 DDC 331.4/09714 19
1. Women - Employment - Québec (Province). I. Lepage, Francine. II. Boivin, Micheline, 1950-. III. Title.
HD6100.Q4 R44 1983

Rhein-Main-Donau : Tagungen und Kundgebungen. [Nürnberg : Verein zur Wahrung der Main- und Donau-Schiffahrtsinteressen, 1937?] 195 p. : ill. ; 25 cm. (Schriften des Vereins zur Wahrung der Main- und Donau-Schiffahrtsinteressen e.V. . Heft 4) CONTENTS. - Die Rhein-Main-Donau-Grossschiffahrtsstrasse im Dienste der Rohstofferschliessung -- Die Rhein-Main-Donau-Tagung in Würzburg am 17. November 1935 -- Die Rhein-Main-Donau-Kundgebung in Nürnberg am 12. Januar 1936 -- Die Wasserstrassen-Tagung in Nürnberg am 22. Februar 1937. LC Card 86-216951
1. Rhein-Main-Donau-Kanal (Germany) - Centennial celebrations, etc. 2. Shipping - Germany (West) - Rhein-Main-Donau-Kanal - History. I. Verein zur Wahrung der Main- und Donau-Schiffahrtsinteressen (Germany). II. Series.
HE449.R38 R48 1937

RHEIN-MAIN-DONAU-KANAL (GERMANY) - CENTENNIAL CELEBRATIONS, ETC.
Rhein-Main-Donau . [Nürnberg , 1937?] 195 p. : LC Card 86-216951
HE449.R38 R48 1937

Rheinisch-Westfälische Technische Hochschule Aachen. Büro Technologie-Transfer.
Wirtschaftsreformen und neue Entwicklungsstrategien in der Volksrepublik China /. Frankfurt am Main , New York , c1986. 185 p. ; ISBN 3-8204-9101-5 LC Card 86-220822
HC427.92 .W56 1986

Rheinisch-Westfälische Technische Hochschule Aachen. Institut für Soziologie.
Wirtschaftsreformen und neue Entwicklungsstrategien in der Volksrepublik China /. Frankfurt am Main , New York , c1986. 185 p. ; ISBN 3-8204-9101-5 LC Card 86-220822
HC427.92 .W56 1986

Rheinisch-Westfälisches Institut für Wirtschaftsforschung Essen. Krüger-Hemmer, Christiane. Der Staatssektor in der Input-Output-Rechnung . Essen , 1982. 175 p. ; LC Card 87-408033 DDC 339.2/3/0943 19
HC290.5.I57 K78 1982

Rheinisch-Westfälisches Wirtschaftsarchiv.
Wirtschaftsarchive und Kammern--Aspekte wirtschaftlicher selbstverwaltung gestern und heute . Köln , 1982. 250 p. ; LC Card 86-198576
HC286 .W59 1982

Rheinische Braunkohlenwerke (Cologne, Germany) Kleinebeckel, Arno. Unternehmen Braunkohle . Köln , 1986. 287 p. : ISBN 3-7743-0225-1 LC Card 86-193426
HD9559.L6 G36 1986

Rheinisches Amt für Denkmalpflege.
Arbeitersiedlungen im 19. Jahrhundert . Bochum , c1985. 189 p. : ISBN 3-88339-427-0 LC Card 85-164690
HD7289.5.A3 G42 1985

Rhenman, Eric. Edgren, Jan, 1940- Divisionalisering och därefter . Stockholm , c1983. 157 p. : ISBN 91-7722-013-7 : LC Card 83-186664
HD50 .E34 1983

Rhetoric of welfare. Sozialreform und Rhetorik =. Wiesbaden , 1984. 174 p. ; ISBN 3-515-02857-9 ***NYPL [L-11 3778 Bd. 4]***

RHINELAND (GERMANY) - ECONOMIC CONDITIONS.
Bartels, Christoph. Schieferdörfer . Pfaffenweiler , 1986. xiv, 370 p. : ISBN 3-89085-124-X LC Card 87-134379 DDC 338.943/43 19
HD9621.G33 R463 1986

RHINELAND-PALATINATE (GERMANY) - ECONOMIC CONDITIONS.
Hasenfratz, Eberhard. Gemeindetypen der Pfalz . Mannheim , 1986. 197 p. : ISBN 3-923750-19-6 LC Card 86-185643
HB3596.R46 H37 1986

Die Kreisfreien Städte und Landkreise in Rheinland-Pfalz /. Bad Ems , 1977. 420 p. : LC Card 85-244499
HC287.R7 K74 1977

RHINELAND-PALATINATE (GERMANY). LANDTAG - ELECTIONS - STATISTICS.
Die Wahl zum 9. Landtag in Rheinland-Pfalz am 18. März 1979 /. Bad Ems , 1979. 153, [18], 23 p. : LC Card 86-128836
HA1320 .R453 Bd. 284 JN4945.R4565

RHINELAND-PALATINATE (GERMANY) - MAPS.
Die Kreisfreien Städte und Landkreise in Rheinland-Pfalz /. Bad Ems , 1977. 420 p. : LC Card 85-244499
HC287.R7 K74 1977

RHINELAND-PALATINATE (GERMANY) - POLITICS AND GOVERNMENT.
Die Kreisfreien Städte und Landkreise in Rheinland-Pfalz /. Bad Ems , 1977. 420 p. : LC Card 85-244499
HC287.R7 K74 1977

RHINELAND-PALATINATE (GERMANY) - POPULATION.
Hasenfratz, Eberhard. Gemeindetypen der Pfalz . Mannheim , 1986. 197 p. : ISBN 3-923750-19-6 LC Card 86-185643
HB3596.R46 H37 1986

Die Kreisfreien Städte und Landkreise in Rheinland-Pfalz /. Bad Ems , 1977. 420 p. : LC Card 85-244499
HC287.R7 K74 1977

RHINELAND-PALATINATE (GERMANY) - POPULATION DENSITY - MATHEMATICAL MODELS.
König, Robert. Die Wohnflächenbestände der Gemeinden der Vorderpfalz . Heidelberg , 1980. [14], 226 p. : ISBN 3-88570-068-9 LC Card 81-136631 DDC 333.73/13/0724 19
HD659.P34 K66 1980
NYPL [L-10 4979 Heft 68]

RHINELAND-PALATINATE (GERMANY) - RURAL CONDITIONS.
Migration und Dorfkultur . Stuttgart , 1984. viii, 429 p. : ISBN 3-515-04199-0 LC Card 85-131269
HB2056.R53 M54 1984

RHINELAND-PALATINATE (GERMANY) - SOCIAL CONDITIONS.
Hasenfratz, Eberhard. Gemeindetypen der Pfalz . Mannheim , 1986. 197 p. : ISBN 3-923750-19-6 LC Card 86-185643
HB3596.R46 H37 1986

Rhode Island. Dept. of Transportation. Division of Planning. Rhode Island state rail plan, 1985. Providence, R.I. : Rhode Island Dept. of Transportation, Planning Division, [1985] 1 v. (various pagings) : maps ; 29 cm. "June 1985." LC Card 87-621867 DDC 385/.068 19
1. Railroads - Rhode Island. 2. Railroads - Rhode Island - Freight. 3. Railroads and state - Rhode Island. 4. Railroads - Rhode Island - Planning. I. Title.
HE2771.R4 R48 1985

Rhode Island nonprofit organizations . Salamon, Lester M. Washington, D.C. , Providence, RI , c1987. vii, 40 p. : LC Card 87-148803 DDC 338.7/4/09745 19
HD2769.2.U6 S25 1987

Rhode Island state rail plan, 1985. Rhode Island. Dept. of Transportation. Division of Planning. Providence, R.I. [1985] 1 v. (various pagings) : LC Card 87-621867 DDC 385/.068 19
HE2771.R4 R48 1985

Rhodes, Lucien.
Little, Jeffrey B. Understanding Wall Street /. Blue Ridge Summit, PA , c1987. 219 p. : ISBN 0-8306-3120-8 : LC Card 87-3628 DDC 332.6/78 19
HG4910 .L54 1987

Little, Jeffrey B. [Wall Street library.] Understanding Wall Street /. Blue Ridge Summit, PA , 1986. p. cm. ISBN 0-8306-3010-4 (pbk.) : LC Card 86-27791 DDC 332.6/78 19
HG4921 .L63 1986

Rhodes, R. A. W. The national world of local government / R.A.W. Rhodes. London ; Boston : Allen & Unwin, 1986. xviii, 441 p. ; 23 cm. (The New local government series. no. 26) Includes indexes. Bibliography: p. [417]-428. ISBN 0-04-320170-9 (alk. paper) LC Card 85-15103 DDC 352.041 19
1. Local government - Great Britain. 2. Intergovernmental fiscal relations - Great Britain. I. Title.
JS3137 .R49 1986 ***NYPL [JLD 86-1931]***

Rhodesia and Nyasaland. Commission of Inquiry into the Dairy Industry. Report of the Commission of Inquiry into the Dairy Industry, 1961 / presented to the Federal Assembly. Salisbury : Govt. Printer, 1962. 91 p., [1] folded leaf of plates : ill., map ; 34 cm. At head of title: Rhodesia Nyasaland. Cover title. Includes bibliographical references. LC Card 86-105139
1. Dairy products industry - Zimbabwe. 2. Dairy products industry - Malawi. 3. Dairy products industry - Zambia. I. Title.
HD9275.Z552 R46 1962

RHÔNE-ALPES (FRANCE) - INDUSTRIES - STATISTICS.
Robert, Jacqueline. 1977 à 1982 . [Lyon] [1985] 143 p. ; LC Card 86-187676
HC277.R58 R62 1985

Rhyne, Elisabeth. Bosworth, Barry, 1942- The economics of federal credit programs /. Washington, D.C. , c1987. xii, 214 p. : ISBN 0-8157-1038-0 : LC Card 85-48205 DDC 336.3/44/0973 19
HJ8119 .B67 1987

Ri͡abushkin, T. V. (Timon Vasil'evich)
Demograficheska͡ia politika sotsialisticheskogo obshchestva /. Moskva , 1986. 190 p. : LC Card 87-120466
HB3607 .D425 1986

Demograficheska͡ia politika sot͡sialisticheskogo obshchestva /. Moskva , 1986. 190 p. ;
NYPL [*QIP 87-2842]

Statisticheskie metody v issledovanii͡akh truda, dokhodov i potreblenii͡a /. Moskva , 1981. 382 p. : LC Card 82-155399
HA1.A38 A15 t. 42 HD7035

Statisticheskoe izuchenie proizvoditel'nosti truda /. Moskva , 1981. 407 p. ; LC Card 82-155063 DDC 330/.018 s 331.11/8/0947 19
HA1.A38 A15 t. 41 HC340.L3
NYPL [*QIP 87-1311]

Riad el Ghonemy, Mohamad. see El Ghonemy, Mohamad Riad, 1924-

Ri͡ashchenko, B. R. Dolgosrochnoe sotsial'no-ėkonomicheskoe planirovanie /. Leningrad , 1986. 165 p. : LC Card 87-146872
HC338.T5 D65 1986

Ribas, Armando P. Mercados de capitales bajo inflación /. New York, N.Y. , c1982. xxi, 471 p. : ISBN 0-910365-00-8 : LC Card 82-50965 DDC 332.64 19
HG4523 .M47 1982 ***NYPL [JLE 86-3568]***

Ribaudo, Marc. Reducing soil erosion : offsite benefits / Marc O. Ribaudo. Washington, D.C. : U. S. Dept. of Agriculture, Economic Research Service : [Supt. of Docs., U. S. G.P.O., distributor], 1986. v, 24 p. : 1 map ; 28 cm. (Agricultural economic report . no. 561) Cover title. Distributed to depository libraries in microfiche. "September 1986"--P. iii. Bibliography: p. 23-24. S/N 001-019-00468-1 Item 42-C (microfiche) LC Card 86-603068 DDC 338.1 s 333.73 19
1. Soil conservation - United States. 2. Soil erosion - United States. 3. Soil conservation - Economic aspects - United States. 4. Soil erosion - Economic aspects - United States. I. United States. Dept. of Agriculture. Economic Research Service. II. Title. III. Series.
HD1751 .A91854 no. 561 S624.A1

Ribbers, P. Omgeving, doelstellingen en organisatie . Assen , 1986. viii, 464 p. : ISBN 90-232-2208-3 : LC Card 86-182876
HG4181 .O44 1986

RIBBON INDUSTRY - SWITZERLAND - BASEL - HISTORY.
Fink, Paul. Geschichte der Basler Bandindustrie 1550-1800 /. Basel , 1983. 216 p. : ISBN 3-7190-0836-3 LC Card 83-220231 DDC 338.4/767776 19
HD9929.R6 S94 1983 ***NYPL [JLE 86-2781]***

Ribeiro, Herval Pina. De que adoecem e morrem os trabalhadores /. São Paulo , 1985. 236 p. ; LC Card 85-231487
HD7683 .D4 1985

Ribeiro, Lêda Cristina de O. Santana Cançado. Considerações sobre o mercado das indústrias de confecções brasileiras. Belo Horizonte [Brazil] : Banco de Desenvolvimento de Minas Gerais, Area de Coordenação do Planejamento, 1985. 66 leaves : ill. ; 30 cm. "Técnico responsável pela elaboração deste documento: Lêda Cristina de O. Santana Cançado Ribeiro"--Leaf 66. Bibliography: leaves 43-45. LC Card 87-404932 DDC 338.4/7687/0981 19
1. Clothing trade - Brazil. 2. Dry-goods - Brazil. 3. Clothing trade - Brazil - Minas Gerais. 4. Dry-goods - Brazil - Minas Gerais. I. Banco de Desenvolvimento de Minas Gerais. Area de Coordenação e Planejamento. II. Title.
HD9940.B82 R53 1985

Ribeiro, Sérgio. Situação e perspectivas dos recursos humanos na República da Guiné-Bissau / [Sérgio Ribeiro]. Addis Ababa : Organização Internacional de Trabalho, Programa de Empregos e Competências Técnicas para Africa, [1984 or 1985] 49, 19 p., [8] leaves : ill. ; 30 cm. "Missão PECTA, dezembro 83-janeiro 84; relatório ao govêrno"--Prelim. p. [3] Bibliography: p. 47-48. LC Card 85-981187 DDC 331.11/0966/57 19
1. Manpower policy - Guinea-Bissau. 2. Labor supply - Guinea-Bissau. 3. Guinea-Bissau - Population. I. Jobs and Skills Programme for Africa. II. Title.
HD5849.A6 R53 1984

Ribeiro, Sylvio Wanick. Produção agrícola brasileira . [Rio de Janeiro] , 1986. 188 p. : LC Card 87-403944 DDC 338.1/0981/021 19
HD9014.B82 P765 1986

Ricardo-Campbell, Rita.
Below-replacement fertility in industrial societies . Cambridge [Cambridgeshire] , New York , c1987. x, 360 p. : ISBN 0-521-34324-0 LC Card 87-6371 DDC 304.6/32 19
HB901 .B45 1987b

Below-replacement fertility in industrial societies . New York, N.Y., USA , c1987. x, 360 p. : LC Card 87-2458 DDC 304.6/32 19
HB901 .B45 1987

Ricardo, David, 1772-1823. Scritti monetari / David Ricardo ; introduzione di Bernard Schmitt. Roma : Istituto della Enciclopedia italiana, [1985] 495 p. ; 21 cm. (Bibliotheca biographica. Sezione di scienze sociali) Includes bibliographical references. LC Card 86-207988
1. Currency question - Great Britain. 2. Foreign exchange problem - Great Britain. 3. Banks and banking - Great Britain. 4. Money - Great Britain. 5. Monetary policy - Great Britain. I. Title. II. Series.
HG938 .R63 1985

RICARDO, DAVID, 1772-1823.
Schmidt, Christian, 1950- Essai sur l'économie ricardienne /. Paris , 1984. 168 p. ; ISBN 2-7178-0693-8 : LC Card 84-218068
HB103.R5 S25 1984

Stamatis, Georg. Sraffa und sein Verhältnis zu Ricardo und Marx /. Göttingen , Lollar , c1984. ix, 459 p. : ISBN 3-921701-04-X LC Card 84-213549
HB103.S7 S73 1984

The Value dimension . London , New York , 1986. 239 p. ; ISBN 0-7102-0766-2 (pbk.) : LC Card 87-109334 DDC 338.5/21 19
HB203 .V33 1986

La ricchezza della nazioni /. Pasinetti, Luigi L. Napoli , c1985. 35 p. ; ISBN 88-7042-841-9 : LC Card 86-196264
HB75 .P27 1985

Riccomini, Donald R., 1952- Unexpected Japan : why American business should return to its own traditional values - and not imitate the Japanese / Donald R. Riccomini & Philip M. Rosenzweig. New York : Walker, 1985. iv, 132 p. ; 22 cm. Includes index. Bibliography: p. [129]-130. ISBN 0-8027-0858-7 : LC Card 85-7313 DDC 658/.00952 19
1. Management - Japan - Miscellanea. 2. Management - United States - Miscellanea. 3. Japan - Social life and customs - Miscellanea. I. Rosenzweig, Phil, 1955-. II. Title.
HD70.J3 R53 1985 ***NYPL [JLD 86-1348]***

RICE - ASIA - COOPERATIVE MARKETING.
Gaikwad, V. R., 1933- Managing paddy-rice business of small farmers . Bombay , 1986. xxiii, 239 p. : ISBN 0-86132-129-4 : LC Card 86-903247 DDC 334/.68318/0954 19
HD9066.A7 G35 1986

RICE - BANGLADESH - PROCESSING - COST EFFECTIVENESS.
Greeley, Martin. Postharvest losses, technology, and employment . Boulder, Colo. , 1987. xvii, 345 p. : ISBN 0-8133-7371-9 (pbk. : alk. paper) : LC Card 87-10648 DDC 338.1/7318/095492 19
HD9066.B32 G73 1987

RICE - BRAZIL, SOUTH - MARKETING - HISTORY - 20TH CENTURY.
Smith, Gordon Whitford, 1934- Agricultural marketing and economic development . New York , 1987. iii, 417 p. ; ISBN 0-8240-1371-9

(alk. paper) : LC Card 87-11833 DDC 381/.41318/09816 19
HD9066.B84 S687 1987

RICE - BURUNDI - IRRIGATION.
Bergen, D. Etude socio-économique sur la culture du riz irrigué dans le périmètre de Mugerero (S.R.D. Imbo) /. Bujumbura , 1985. 96 leaves : LC Card 86-980581
HD9066.B952 B47 1985

The rice economies . Bray, Francesca. Oxford [Oxfordshire] , New York , 1986. xvii, 254 p. : ISBN 0-631-14877-9 : LC Card 85-30819 DDC 338.1/7318/095 19
HD9066.A7 B73 1986 NYPL [JLE 87-793]

RICE FARMERS - MALAYSIA - KELANTAN - SUPPLEMENTARY EMPLOYMENT.
Chew, T. A. The off-farm labour supply of padi farmers in Kelantan, Malaysia [microform] /. [Canberra] , c1984. 19 p. ; ISBN 0-86784-513-9 (pbk.) LC Card 85-670027 DDC 331.12/93318/095951 19
HD5854.55.M4 C47 1984
*NYPL [*ZF-1745 no.58]*

Rice, Gerard T. Peace Corps in the 80's / by Gerard T. Rice. Washington, D.C. : Peace Corps, 1986. v, 89 p. : ill. (some col.), col. maps ; 27 cm. Cover title. Shipping list no.: 87-104-P. "June, 1986"--P. iv. Bibliography: p. 78-82. Item 900-D LC Card 87-601040 DDC 361.2/6/06073 19
1. Peace Corps (U. S.). I. Peace Corps (U. S.). II. Title.
HC60.5 .R5 1986

RICE - JAPAN - NAKADA-CHŌ (MIYAGI-KEN)
Moore, Richard H. Japanese agriculture . Boulder , 1987. p. cm. ISBN 0-8133-7406-5 LC Card 87-13553 DDC 338.1/0952/115 19
HD920.N33 M65 1987

Rice, John, 1944- British trade unionism, 1750-1850 . London , New York , 1988. p. cm. ISBN 0-582-49459-1 LC Card 87-22614 DDC 331.88/0941 19
HD6664 .B83 1988

Rice, Jonathan. How to survive and profit from the coming currency recall / Jonathan Rice and Francis Ciabattoni. Chicago : Contemporary Books, c1986. xiii, 258 p. : ill. ; 24 cm. Includes index. ISBN 0-8092-4998-7 : LC Card 86-6215 DDC 332.4/973 19
1. Currency question - United States. 2. Money - History. I. Ciabattoni, Francis. II. Title.
HG540 .R53 1986 NYPL [JLE 86-3508]

Rice-Maximin, Edward Francis, 1941-
Accomodation and resistance : the French left, Indochina, and the Cold War, 1944-1954 / Edward Rice-Maximin. New York : Greenwood Press, 1986. xi, 175 p. ; 25 cm. (Contribution to the study of world history, 0885-9159 . no. 2) Includes index. Bibliography: p. [153]-157. ISBN 0-313-25355-2 (lib. bdg. : alk. paper) LC Card 86-4624 DDC 959.704/1 19
1. Indochina War, 1946-1954 - France. 2. Communism - France - History. 3. Socialism - France - History. 4. World politics - 1945-. 5. France - Politics and government - 1945-1958. I. Title. II. Series.
DS553.1 .R53 1986 NYPL [JFE 87-1024]

Rice, Richard E. Kloepfer, Deanne. The Watt record . Washington, D.C. [1983] ii, 66, 9, 3 p. : LC Card 86-232533 DDC 333.1/0973 19
HD183.L3 K58 1983

Rice, Ronald E. Johnson, Bonnie McDaniel, 1944- Managing organizational innovation . New York , 1987. xiv, 242 p. ; ISBN 0-231-06398-9 LC Card 87-307 DDC 652/.5 19
HF5548.115 .J64 1987

RICE TRADE.
Rice, selected aspects of production, trade, and price policies /. Rome , 1985. ii, 83 p. : ISBN 92-5-102329-8 (pbk.) LC Card 86-213105 DDC 338.1/7318 19
HD9066.D44 R53 1985

RICE - TRADE AND STATISTICS. see **RICE TRADE.**

RICE TRADE - ASIA.
Bray, Francesca. The rice economies . Oxford [Oxfordshire] , New York , 1986. xvii, 254 p. : ISBN 0-631-14877-9 : LC Card 85-30819 DDC 338.1/7318/095 19
HD9066.A7 B73 1986 NYPL [JLE 87-793]

RICE TRADE - BANGLADESH.
Greeley, Martin. Postharvest losses, technology, and employment . Boulder, Colo. , 1987. xvii, 345 p. : ISBN 0-8133-7371-9 (pbk. : alk. paper) : LC Card 87-10648 DDC 338.1/7318/095492 19
HD9066.B32 G73 1987

RICE TRADE - BRAZIL - ARAGUAIA RIVER WATERSHED.
Perfis indicativos para a industrialização do arroz, milho e soja. Brasília , 1985. 189 p. : LC Card 86-195651
HD9066.B83 A737 1985

RICE TRADE - BRAZIL - RIO GRANDE DO SUL - HISTORY.
Beskow, Paulo Roberto. O arrendamento capitalista na agricultura . São Paulo , Brasília , 1986. 219 p. : LC Card 86-229665
HD9066.B83 R463 1986

RICE TRADE - BRAZIL - TOCANTINS RIVER WATERSHED.
Perfis indicativos para a industrialização do arroz, milho e soja. Brasília , 1985. 189 p. : LC Card 86-195651
HD9066.B83 A737 1985

RICE TRADE - BURUNDI.
Bergen, D. Etude socio-économique sur la culture du riz irrigué dans le périmètre de Mugerero (S.R.D. Imbo) /. Bujumbura , 1985. 96 leaves : LC Card 86-980581
HD9066.B952 B47 1985

RICE TRADE - DEVELOPING COUNTRIES.
Rice, selected aspects of production, trade, and price policies /. Rome , 1985. ii, 83 p. : ISBN 92-5-102329-8 (pbk.) LC Card 86-213105 DDC 338.1/7318 19
HD9066.D44 R53 1985

RICE TRADE - GHANA.
Konings, Piet. The state and rural class formation in Ghana . London ; Boston : xvi, 391 p. : ISBN 0-7103-0117-0 LC Card 85-28109 DDC 305.5/09667 19
HN832.Z9 S65 1986 NYPL [Sc D 86-574]

RICE TRADE - GOVERNMENT POLICY - INDIA - ORISSA.
Mishra, Bhagabat, 1940- Economics of public distribution system in food-grains /. New Delhi , 1985. xviii, 306 p. (some folded) ; LC Card 85-902748 DDC 381/.4131/095413 19
HD9066.I63 O756 1982
NYPL [JLD 86-1149]

RICE TRADE - INDONESIA - BANTUL (KABUPATEN) - CASE STUDIES.
Maurer, Jean-Luc. Modernisation agricole, développement économique et changement social . Paris , c1986. 323 p. : ISBN 2-13-039622-4 : LC Card 86-175394
HD2085.B37 M38 1986

RICE TRADE - INDONESIA - JAVA.
Budidaya padi di Jawa /. Jakarta , 1986. x, 339 p. : LC Card 87-941451
HD9066.I63 J3493 1986

RICE TRADE - PHILIPPINES - HISTORY - STATISTICS.
Selected statistics on rice & corn . Diliman, Quezon City [1969] xxix, 306 p. : LC Card 87-400545 DDC 338.1/7315/09599021 19
HD9066.P62 S45 1969

RICE TRADE - SOUTHERN STATES - STATISTICS.
Wharton, Robert B. Analysis of rice export flows from southern states /. [Baton Rouge?] [1986] iii, 44 p. ; LC Card 87-620886 DDC 338.1/09763 s 382/.41318/0975021 19
HD1775.L8 L7 no. 662 HD9066.U46A13

Ricerca sociale e movimento operaio : tre anni di incontro di studio / introduzione e cura di Gabriella Pinnarò. Milano : F. Angeli, c1982. 294 p. ; 22 cm. On cover: Cespe - Centro studi di politica economica, Partito comunista italiano. Includes bibliographical references. LC Card 82-246648 DDC 331/.0945 19
1. Labor and laboring classes - Italy - Addresses, essays, lectures. 2. Industrial sociology - Italy - Addresses, essays, lectures. 3. Industrial relations - Italy - Addresses, essays, lectures. I. Pinnarò, Gabriella. II. CESPE (Organization).
HD8481 .R53 1982 NYPL [JLD 86-3380]

Ricerche (Centro studi e iniziative per la riforma dello Stato (Italy)) .
(2.2) La Politica di bilancio in condizioni di stress fiscale . Milano, Italy , c1986. 377 p. ; LC Card 87-134343
HJ2119 .P65 1986

Ricerche di tecnologia dell'architettura .
(22) Bianchi, Roberto, 1954- Le tecniche esecutive nell'edilizia residenziale degli anni '80 . Milano, Italy , c1986. 144 p. : LC Card 87-126093
HD9715.5.I83 L653 1986

Ricerche e progetti (Firm) Italia multinazionale . Milano , 1986. 2 v. : LC Card 87-158571
HD2864 .I82 1986

RICH AS CONSUMERS - UNITED STATES.
The Affluent market fact book . Tampa, Fla. , c1986. 83 leaves ; LC Card 86-235264 DDC 332.1/7 19
HG1616.C87 A33 1986

Rich countries and poor countries . Rostow, W. W. (Walt Whitman), 1916- Boulder , 1987. xiv, 194 p. : ISBN 0-8133-0497-0 (alk. paper) : LC Card 87-8280 DDC 337 19
HC51 .R665 1987

Rich, D. C. The industrial geography of Australia / David C. Rich. London ; Wolfeboro, N.H. : Croom Helm, c1987. xvi, 384 p. : ill., maps ; 23 cm. (Croom Helm industrial geography series) Bibliography: p. 350-372. Includes index. ISBN 0-7099-2214-0 : LC Card 86-29383 DDC 338.0994 19
1. Australia - Industries - Location. I. Title. II. Series.
HC610.D5 R53 1987

Rich, Daniel.
Energy and cities /. New Brunswick, U. S.A. , c1985. 173 p. : ISBN 0-87855-813-6 (pbk.) LC Card 84-24074 DDC 333.79/13/091732 19
HD108.2 .E525 1985 NYPL [JLE 86-4441]

Planning for changing energy conditions /. New Brunswick, N.J., U. S.A. , c1988. xiii, 300 p. : ISBN 0-88738-713-6 (pbk.) : LC Card 87-13977 DDC 333.79 19
HD9502.A2 P59 1988

The Politics of energy research and development /. New Brunswick, U. S.A. , c1986. 181 p. : ISBN 0-88738-653-9 (pbk.) LC Card 86-1307 DDC 333.79/0973 19
HD9502.U52 P63 1986
NYPL [JLE 86-3577]

Rich man, poor man /. Hilton, John, 1880-1943. New York , 1985. 174 p. ; ISBN 0-8240-7614-1 (alk. paper) : LC Card 85-13078 DDC 339.2/2/0941 19
HC256.4 .H54 1985 NYPL [JLC 86-342]

Richard, Claude. McGranahan, Donald V. Measurement and analysis of socioeconomic development . Geneva , 1985. xx, 504 p. :
NYPL [JLK 74-447 no.85.5]

Richard E. Neustadt lecture, May 13, 1986. Neustadt, Richard E. Seattle, WA [1986] 35 p. : LC Card 87-402984 DDC 339.5/2/0973 19
HJ257.2 .N48 1986

Richard Scott Perkin and the Perkin-Elmer Corporation /. Fahy, Thomas P. [United States] c1987. xv, 271 p. : ISBN 0-9618075-0-4 LC Card 86-63869 DDC 338.7/666156/0973 19
HD9707.U62 P474 1987

Richards, E. G. (Edward Graham) Forestry and the forest industries . Dordrecht ; Boston : xi, 428 p. : ISBN 90-247-3592-0 LC Card 87-20400 DDC 338.1/749 19
HD9765.A2 F64 1987

Richards, Eric. A history of the Highland clearances / Eric Richards. London : Croom Helm, c1982-1985. 2 v. : maps ; 23 cm. Includes bibliographies and indexes. CONTENTS. - [v. 1] Agrarian transformation and the evictions, 1746-1886.--v. 2. Emigration, protest, reasons. ISBN 0-85664-496-X : LC Card 81-208122 DDC 333.33/5 19
1. Crofters - History. 2. Farm tenancy - Scotland - Highlands - History. 3. Eviction - Scotland - Highlands - History. 4. Highlands (Scotland) - Economic conditions. I. Title.
HD1511.G7 R53 1982 NYPL [JLL 82-171]

Richards, Eugene. Below the line : living poor in America / photographs and interviews by Eugene Richards ; text editor, Christiane Bird ; story researcher, Janine Altongy. Mount Vernon, N.Y. : Consumers Union, c1987. 218 p. : ill. ; 29 cm. ISBN 0-89043-062-4 LC Card 86-70834 DDC 305.5/69/0973 19

1. Poor - United States - Interviews. 2. United States - Economic conditions - 1981- - Case studies. 3. United States - Social conditions - 1980- - Case studies. 4. Poor - United States - Pictorial works. 5. United States - Economic conditions - 1981- - Pictorial works. 6. United States - Social conditions - 1980- - Pictorial works. I. Bird, Christiane. II. Altongy, Janine. III. Title.
HC110.P6 R52 1987

Richards, P. J. (Peter J.) Rural roads and poverty alleviation . London , 1984. vii, 191 p. : ISBN 0-946688-05-2 : LC Card 86-673296
HE336.R85 R87x 1984

Richardson, Clinton. The Venture magazine complete guide to venture capital / Clinton Richardson ; with an introduction by Arthur Lipper III. New York : New American Library, c1987. xxiv, 261 p. : ill. ; 23 cm. Includes index. ISBN 0-452-25918-5 (pbk.) : LC Card 87-5721 DDC 332/.0415 19
1. Venture capital. I. Venture (New York, N.Y. : 1979). II. Title. III. Title: Complete guide to venture capital.
HG4751 .R52 1987

Richardson, J. David.
Current U. S. trade policy . Cambridge, Mass. (1050 Massachusetts Ave., Cambridge 02138) , 1986. iii, 128 p. ; LC Card 86-201110 DDC 382/.3/0973 19
HF1455 .C87 1986

Real-financial linkages among open economies /. Cambridge, Mass. , c1987. x, 215 p. : ISBN 0-262-01096-8 LC Card 87-15153 DDC 337 19
HF1411 .R4135 1987

Richardson, William, Sir, 1909- A union of many trades : the history of USDAW / by Sir William Richardson. Manchester : Union of Shop, Distributive, and Allied Workers, [197-?] xv, 388 p., [16] p. of plates : ill. ; 23 cm. Errata: p. 388. Includes index. ISBN 0-906957-01-X : LC Card 83-222175
1. Union of Shop, Distributive and Allied Workers - History. 2. Trade-unions - Great Britain - History. I. Title.
HD8383.U553 R53 1970z

Richardson's railway guide and time and fare tables : shewing the departure and arrival of the trains of every railway in England : with a copious and very interesting description of all the principal towns on the line : with many historical and highly amusing records : illustrated with several views, and a railway map of England, engraved expressly for this work. London : Sherwood, Gilbert, & Piper, 1841. 64 p., 1 folded leaf of plates : ill., map ; 15 cm. LC Card 85-666126
1. Railroads - Great Britain - Time-tables.
HE3014 .R5x 1841

Richelle Giampiccoli, Emma. La langue de l'économie, de la technique à la banalisation / Emma Richelle Giampiccoli. Torino : G. Giappichelli, [1983] 114 p. ; 25 cm. Includes bibliographies and index. LC Card 84-141597
1. Economics - Language. 2. French language - Semantics. I. Title.
HB62 .R53 1983

Richer, Laurette B. Ludger Gravel, 1864-1933 : contre l'oubli / Laurette B. Richer. [Montréal] : L.B. Richer, c1986. 170 p. : ill., geneal. tables ; 23 cm. Includes bibliographical references. ISBN 2-9800028-1-X LC Card 87-115031
1. Gravel, Ludger, 1864-1933. 2. Businessmen - Québec (Province) - Biography. 3. Collectors and collecting - Québec (Province) - Biography. I. Title.
HC112.5.G73 R53 1986

RICHES. see **WEALTH.**

Richet, Xavier. La Voie hongroise . [Paris] , c1986. 319 p. : ISBN 2-7021-1378-8 : LC Card 86-221784
HC300.28 .V65 1986

Richmond Newspapers, Inc. The Climate of persuasion . [Richmond, VA.] , 1959. 58 p. :
NYPL [JLF 86-1150]

Richter, Bernd, 1954- Der mitbestimmte Aktiengesellschaftskonzern : eine ökonomisch-empirische Analyse zum Mitbestimmungsgesetz 1976 / Bernd Richter. Köln : Bund, c1983. ix, 394 p. : ill. ; 21 cm. Originally presented as the author's thesis (doctoral)--Friedrich-Alexander-Universität Erlangen-Nürnberg, 1982. Bibliography: p. 361-394. ISBN 3-7663-0820-3 LC Card 83-215341
1. Industrial management - Germany (West) - Employee participation. 2. Industrial management - Employee participation - Law and legislation - Germany (West). I. Title.
HD5660.G4 R53 1983

Richter, Gerhard, 1920- Effektivität und Reproduktion . Berlin , c1985. 148 p. ; LC Card 86-166628
HC290.78 .E365 1985

Richter, Josef. Energiekosten und Anpassungsverhalten der Wirtschaft / Josef Richter, Werner Teufelsbauer. Wien : Institut für Angewandte Sozial- und Wirtschaftsforschung im Signum-Verlag, 1985. iv, 184 p. : ill. ; 21 cm. Bibliography: p. 169-173. ISBN 3-85436-031-2 LC Card 86-154099
1. Austria - Industries - Energy consumption - Costs. 2. Energy consumption - Austria - Costs. 3. Austria - Economic conditions - 1945-. I. Teufelsbauer, Werner. II. Title.
HD9502.A92 R53 1985

Richter, Lothar. Training needs : assessment and monitoring / L. Richter. Geneva : International Labour Office, 1986. viii, 83 p. : ill. ; 25 cm. Bibliography: p. 76-83. ISBN 92-2-105458-6 (pbk.) : LC Card 86-222104 DDC 331.25/92 19
1. Occupational training. 2. Employment forecasting. 3. Manpower policy. I. International Labour Office. II. Title.
HD5715 .R53 1986

Richter, Rudolf, 1926- Geld- und Währungsordnung /. Berlin , c1983. 249 p. : ISBN 3-428-05530-6 LC Card 84-141547
HG999.5 .G4556 1983

Richter, W. F. Bamberg, Günter, 1940- Decision-theoretic analysis of envisaged income tax reforms for FRG and U. S. /. [Augsburg] [1986] 11 leaves : LC Card 87-101962 DDC 336.24/0724 19
HJ4719 .B35 1986

Richter, Wolfgang, Dipl.-Ing. Schlüsselgewalt . Dortmund , c1981. 190 p. : ISBN 3-88142-261-7 : LC Card 81-206444
HD7339.A3 S25 1981

Rick, Josef. Bewertung und Abgeltungskonditionen bei der Veräusserung mittelständischer Unternehmen / von Josef Rick. Berlin : Duncker & Humblot, c1985. 191 p. : ill. ; 24 cm. (Forschungsergebnisse aus dem Revisionswesen und der betriebswirtschaftlichen Steuerlehre. Bd. 4) Originally presented as the author's thesis (doctoral)--Westfälische Wilhelms-Universität Münster, 1984. Bibliography: p. [172]-191. ISBN 3-428-05785-6 : LC Card 85-186420
1. Business enterprises - Valuation. 2. Small business - Valuation. I. Title.
HG4028.V3 R52 1985

Ricke, Keith G. Credit union membership study, 1986 / conducted by Concepts in Marketing Research. St. Paul, Minn. : CIMR, [c1987] 72 leaves : map ; 28 cm. LC Card 87-154030 DDC 334/.22 19
1. Credit unions - United States. I. Concepts in Marketing Research (Firm). II. Title.
HG2037 .R54 1987

Rickert, Heinrich. Der Sozialvertrag für die Finanzierung kommunaler Einrichtungen und Gemeinschaftsaufgaben : eine Theorie neutraler Kapitalmacht bei fallender Staatsrate / Heinrich Rickert. Stuttgart : Kohlhammer, c1982. 268 p. : ill. ; 24 cm. Bibliography: p. 266-268. ISBN 3-17-007760-0 : LC Card 83-152669
1. Local finance - Germany, West. 2. Local taxation - Germany, West. 3. Social contract. I. Title.
HJ9473 .R53 1982

Ricketts, Martin J.
The economics of business enterprise : new approaches to the firm / Martin Ricketts. Brighton, Sussex : Wheatsheaf Books, 1987. xii, 306 p. : ill. ; 23 cm. Bibliography: p. 282-299. Includes indexes. ISBN 0-7108-0221-8 : LC Card 87-104594 DDC 338.5 19
1. Corporations. 2. Production (Economic theory). 3. Entrepreneur. 4. Competition. I. Title.
HD2731 .R53 1987

The new industrial economics : an introduction to modern theories of the firm / Martin Ricketts. New York : St. Martin's Press, 1987. xii, 306 p. : ill. ; 23 cm. Bibliography: p. 282-299. Includes indexes. ISBN 0-312-00458-3 : LC Card 86-27918 DDC 338.6 19
1. Industrial organization (Economic theory). I. Title.
HD2326 .R53 1987

Ricks, Betty R. Business communication : systems and applications / Betty R. Ricks, Kay F. Gow. New York : Wiley, c1987. xiii, 479 p. : ill. ; 25 cm. Includes index. ISBN 0-471-81824-0 LC Card 86-26747 DDC 651.7 19
1. Communication in management. I. Gow, Kay F. II. Title.
HF5718 .R53 1987

Ricostruire e/o trasformare .
(2) Terremoto e crisi urbana . Napoli , 1981. 207 p. ; ***NYPL [JLE 86-4532]***

Riddell, Roger. Foreign aid reconsidered / Roger C. Riddell. Baltimore : Johns Hopkins University Press, 1987. x, 309 p. ; 25 cm. (The Johns Hopkins studies in development) Bibliography: p. 279-301. Includes index. ISBN 0-8018-3546-1 LC Card 87-2949 DDC 338.91 19
1. Economic assistance. 2. Technical assistance. I. Title. II. Series.
HC60 .R49 1987

Riddell, W. Craig (William Craig), 1946-
Adapting to change . Toronto [Ont.] , Buffalo , c1986. xv, 221 p. ; ISBN 0-8020-7260-7 (pbk.) LC Card 86-673029 DDC 331.12/0971 19
HD5728 .A596 1986 ***NYPL [JLD 87-1967]***

Ridgely, Beverly S.
Birds of the world in philately. Ridgely, Beverly S. Supplement to Birds of the world in philately / Beverly S. Ridgely & Gustavs E. Eglajs. Johnstown, PA , c1986. 62 p., [3] p. of plates : ISBN 0-935991-00-X (pbk.): LC Card 86-217462 DDC 769.56/4/075 769.56/432 19
HE6187 .A635 no. 106-1 HE6183.B53

Supplement to Birds of the world in philately / Beverly S. Ridgely & Gustavs E. Eglajs. Johnstown, PA : American Topical Association, c1986. 62 p., [3] p. of plates : ill. ; 23 cm. (ATA handbook . 106-1) Cover title. Includes index. ISBN 0-935991-00-X (pbk.): LC Card 86-217462 DDC 769.56/4/075 769.56/432 19
1. Postage-stamps - Topics - Birds. I. Eglajs, Gustav. II. Ridgely, Beverly S. Birds of the world in philately. III. Title. IV. Series.
HE6187 .A635 no. 106-1 HE6183.B53

Riechey, Gunter. Möglichkeiten und Grenzen der Beeinflussung der Preissetzungsmöglichkeiten der Unternehmen / Gunter Riechey. München : Minerva Publikation, c1982. 286 p. : ill. ; 21 cm. (Minerva-Fachserie Wirtschafts- und Sozialwissenschaften) Bibliography: p. 273-286. ISBN 3-597-10144-5 LC Card 83-160762
1. Wage-price policy - Germany, West. 2. Wage-price policy - United States. I. Title. II. Series.
HC290.5.W24 R54 1982

Riedel, James. Myths and reality of external constraints on development / by James Riedel. Aldershot, Hampshire, U.K. ; Brookfield, Vt., USA : Gower for the Trade Policy Research Centre, London, 1987. xvi, 111 p. : ill. ; 22 cm. (Thames essay, 0306-6991 . no. 47) Bibliography: p. [104]-107. ISBN 0-566-05336-5 (pbk.) : LC Card 86-31801 DDC 330.9172/4 19
1. Developing countries - Economic conditions. 2. Developing countries - Economic policy. 3. Investments, Foreign - Developing countries. 4. Economic development. 5. International economic relations. I. Trade Policy Research Centre. II. Title. III. Series.
HC59.7 .R494 1987

Riedinger, Jeffrey M.
Prosterman, Roy L. Egyptian development and U. S. aid . [Seattle, Wash.?] , c1985. i, 32, A1-A10 p. ; LC Card 87-104139 DDC 338.91/73/062 19
HC830.Z9 E446 1985

Prosterman, Roy L. Land reform and democratic development /. Baltimore , c1987. xii, 313 p. ; ISBN 0-8018-3482-1 (alk. paper) LC Card 87-4188 DDC 333.3/1/1724 19
HD1333.5 .P76 1987

Riedl-Ehrenberg, Renate. Alfred Kern (1850-1893), Edouard Sandoz (1853-1928) : Gründer der Sandoz AG, Basel / von Renate Riedl-Ehrenberg. Zürich : Verein für Wirtschaftshistorische Studien, c1986. 90 p. : ill. ; 24 cm. (Schweizer Pioniere der Wirtschaft und Technik. 44) Includes bibliographies. LC Card

86-159933 DDC 338/.09494 s 338.7/66/0094943 19
1. Kern, Alfred, 1850-1893. 2. Sandoz, Edouard, 1853-1928. 3. Sandoz AG. - History. 4. Chemists - Switzerland - Biography. 5. Businessmen - Switzerland - Biography. I. Title. II. Series.
HC395.5.A2 S3 no. 44 QD21

Riedmann, Josef. Festschrift für Univ.-Prof. Dr. Georg Zwanowetz anlässlich der Vollendung des 65. Lebensjahres /. [Innsbruck] , c1984. 332 p. : LC Card 84-183487
HC244 .F48 1984

Rieger, Hans Christoph. Grundbedürfnisse als Gegenstand der Entwicklungspolitik . Wiesbaden , 1982. viii, 220 p. : ISBN 3-515-03838-8 (Deut. Bibl.) LC Card 85-134671
HC59.72.B38 G78 1982

Rieger, Sören. Engelhardt, Werner Hans. Der Direktvertrieb im Konsumgüterbereich . Stuttgart , c1984. 158 p. : ISBN 3-17-008550-6 : LC Card 84-234886
HF5415.126 .E54 1984

Riehm, Sarah, 1952- The teenage enterpreneur's guide : fifty money-making ideas / by Sarah Riehm. Chicago, IL : Surrey Books, c1987. viii, 211 p. : ill. ; 22 cm. Includes index. ISBN 0-940625-00-8 (pbk.) : LC Card 87-1904 DDC 658/.041 19
1. Youth - Employment - United States. 2. Self-employed - United States. I. Title.
HD6273 .R53 1987

Riekhof, Hans-Christian. Schanz, Günther, 1943- Mitarbeiter-Kapitalbeteiligung in der Wirtschaft Niedersachsens . Spardorf , c1984. 228 p. : ISBN 3-922919-26-X : LC Card 84-162288
HD5660.G412 L687 1984

Riemann, Friedrich. Theorie und Empirie in Wirtschaftspolitik und Wirtschaftsgeschichte . Göttingen , 1984. 242 p. : ISBN 3-509-01366-2 : LC Card 85-120064
HC240 .T45 1984

Riemer, Martin. Beschwerdemanagement / Martin Riemer. Frankfurt ; New York : Campus, c1986. 295 p. ; 21 cm. (Campus Forschung. Bd. 515.) Bibliography: p. 287-295. ISBN 3-593-33756-8 LC Card 87-129210 DDC 658.8/12 19
1. Consumer complaints. 2. Consumer satisfaction. I. Series: Campus Forschung. Schwerpunktreihe "Marketing und Verbraucherarbeit" , Bd. 3. II. Title.
HF5415.3 .R45 1986

Riepe, Claudia. Produkteigenschaften und das Nachfrageverhalten von Konsumenten : eine vergleichende Analyse von Lancasters "Neuer Nachfragetheorie" und "Multi-Attribute-Attitude"-Modellen / Claudia Riepe. Thun : H. Deutsch, c1984. 341 p. : ill. ; 21 cm. (Reihe Wirtschaftswissenschaften, 0253-1488 . Bd. 319) Bibliography: p. 323-341. ISBN 3-87144-841-9 LC Card 85-113523
1. Consumers - Mathematical models. 2. Lancaster, Kelvin. I. Title. II. Series.
HB801 .R45 1984

Rier, David C. The guide to Lotus HAL : techniques for experienced 1-2-3 users / David C. Rier. Reading, Mass. : Addison-Wesley Pub. Co., [1987], c1988. xv, 266 p. : ill. ; 24 cm. "Lotus books." Includes index. ISBN 0-201-16827-8 (pbk.) : LC Card 87-22885 DDC 005.36/9 19
1. Lotus HAL (Computer program). 2. Lotus 1-2-3 (Computer program). 3. Business - Data processing. I. Title.
HF5548.4.L68 R54 1988

Riese, Martin. Die Messung der Arbeitslosigkeit / von Martin Riese. Berlin : Duncker & Humblot, c1986. 199 p. : 17 ill. ; 24 cm. (Volkswirtschaftliche Schriften. Heft 366) Bibliography: p. [180]-199. ISBN 3-428-06034-2 LC Card 86-215265 DDC 331.12/0724 19
1. Labor supply - Econometric models. 2. Unemployment - Econometric models. I. Title. II. Series.
HD5707.5 .R54 1986

Riesenfellner, Stefan. Der Sozialreporter : Max Winter im alten Österreich / Stefan Riesenfellner. Wien : Verlag für Gesellschaftskritik, c1987. vi, 278 p. ; 22 cm. Bibliography: p. 264-278. ISBN 3-900351-67-8 LC Card 87-137993 DDC 305.5/62/09436 19
1. Labor and laboring classes - Austria - History. 2. Labor and laboring classes - Czechoslovakia - History. 3. Austria - Social conditions. 4. Czechoslovakia - Social conditions. 5. Winter, Max, 1870-1937. I. Title.
HD8410 .R54 1987

Riesgo, Rodolfo. Cuba, el movimiento obrero y su entorno socio-politico, 1865-1983 / Rodolfo Riesgo. Miami : Saeta Ediciones, 1985. 251 p. ; 21 cm. (Colección Realidades) Bibliography: p. 241-242. Includes index. ISBN 0-917049-02-0 (pbk.) LC Card 86-673864
1. Trade-unions - Cuba - Political activity. 2. Trade-unions - Cuba - History. 3. Labor and laboring classes - Cuba - Political activity. I. Title.
HD6578.5 .R53x 1985

Rigdon, Susan M., 1943- The culture facade : art, science, and politics in the work of Oscar Lewis / Susan M. Rigdon. Urbana : University of Illinois Press, c1988. p. cm. "Publications of Oscar Lewis": p. Bibliography: p. Includes index. ISBN 0-252-01495-2 (alk. paper) LC Card 87-19063 DDC 305.5/69 19
1. Poverty - Psychological aspects. 2. Poor. 3. Lewis, Oscar, 1914-1970 - Views on Poverty. I. Lewis, Oscar, 1914-1970. II. Title.
HC79.P6 R57 1988

The right choice . Wells, Richard C. New York, N.Y., U. S.A. , c1985. viii, 178 p. : ISBN 0-86604-198-2 (pbk.) LC Card 86-201105 DDC 658.4/033 19
HD31 .W457 1985

The right move . Zey, Michael G. New York , 1987. ix, 225 p. ; ISBN 0-531-15523-4 LC Card 86-29015 DDC 650.1/4 19
HF5382.7 .Z49 1987

RIGHT OF PRIVATE PROPERTY. see **RIGHT OF PROPERTY.**

RIGHT OF PROPERTY - CONGRESSES.
Schmidtchen, Dieter. Property rights, Freiheit und Wettbewerbspolitik /. Tübingen , 1983. 71 p. ; ISBN 3-16-344630-2 (Deut. Bibl.) LC Card 84-100421
HF1410.5 .S36 1983

Symposion "Marktwirtschaft und Umwelt" (1980 : Walter Eucken Institut) Marktwirtschaft und Umwelt . Tübingen , 1981. ix, 303 p. : ISBN 3-16-343372-3 : LC Card 81-128698 DDC 363.7/0526 19
HC79.E5 S92 1980 ***NYPL [TB (Walter Eucken Institut. Wirtschaftswissenschaftliche und wirtschaftsrechtliche Untersuchungen. Bd. 17)]***

RIGHT OF PROPERTY - HISTORY.
Heinsohn, Gunnar. Privateigentum, Patriarchat, Geldwirtschaft . Frankfurt am Main , 1984. 218 p. ; ISBN 3-518-28055-4 : LC Card 84-150578
HC31 .H45 1984

RIGHT OF PROPERTY - HUNGARY.
Halmai, Péter. Integráció és tulajdon az iparosodó mezőgazdaságban /. [Budapest] , 1984. 124 p. ; ISBN 963-673-278-7 LC Card 85-126691
HD1940.5 .H35 1984

RIGHT OF PROPERTY - UNITED STATES.
Plotkin, Sidney. Keep out . Berkeley , c1987. xiii, 360 p. ; ISBN 0-520-05806-2 LC Card 86-30807 DDC 333.3/0973 19
HD205 .P56 1987

RIGHT TO LABOR.
Arbeit, Arbeit über alles? . Köln , 1985. 160 p. : ISBN 3-8025-2167-6 LC Card 86-148728
HD4854 .A725 1985

Baruzzi, Arno, 1935- Recht auf Arbeit und Beruf? . Freiburg , c1983. 88 p. ; ISBN 3-495-47518-4 LC Card 83-152808
HD4903 .B37 1983

Unemployment and the right to work /. Edinburgh , New York , c1982. x, 98 p. ; ISBN 0-8164-2391-1 (Seabury Press : pbk.) LC Card 87-150638
HD5707.5 .U544 1982

Vargas, Ines. The right to work and the situation of workers /. Oslo [1985] 47 p. ; ISBN 82-7288-122-5 (pbk.) LC Card 86-204949 DDC 331.88/92 19
HD4903 .V34 1985

RIGHT TO LABOR - GERMANY (WEST) - CASE STUDIES.
Gesinnungs überprüft! . Berlin [1978] 263 p. : LC Card 84-198533
HD4903.5.G4 G47 1978

RIGHT TO LABOR - INDIA.
Anonymous struggles . New Delhi , 1983. 24 p. ; LC Card 83-904576 DDC 344.54/01 345.4041 19
LAW ***NYPL [JLD 86-3877]***

RIGHT TO LABOR - ITALY.
La Tutela del lavoro in Italia. [Roma] [1976] 144 p. ; LC Card 86-233354
HD8481 .T85 1976

RIGHT TO LABOR - LATIN AMERICA.
Vargas, Ines. The right to work and the situation of workers /. Oslo [1985] 47 p. ; ISBN 82-7288-122-5 (pbk.) LC Card 86-204949 DDC 331.88/92 19
HD4903 .V34 1985

RIGHT TO LABOR - SCOTLAND - CASE STUDIES.
Foster, John. The politics of the UCS work-in . London , Atlantic Highlands, N.J. , 1986. 446 p. : ISBN 0-85315-663-8 (pbk.) : LC Card 86-235159 DDC 331.89/282383/094141 19
HD5365.S512 1971 .C584 1986

RIGHT TO LABOR - UNITED STATES - ADDRESSES, ESSAYS, LECTURES.
Job equity and other studies in industrial relations . Los Angeles , c1982. 274 p. : LC Card 82-621216 DDC 331/.0973 19
HD5708.45.U6 J6 1982 ***NYPL [JLD 87-273]***

The right to manage . Harris, Howell John, 1951- Madison, Wis. , 1982. ix, 296 p. ; ISBN 0-299-08640-2 : LC Card 81-69820 DDC 331./0973 19
HD8072 .H2874 ***NYPL [JLE 86-4147]***

RIGHT TO PROPERTY. see **RIGHT OF PROPERTY.**

RIGHT TO WORK. see **RIGHT TO LABOR.**

The right to work and the situation of workers /. Vargas, Ines. Oslo [1985] 47 p. ; ISBN 82-7288-122-5 (pbk.) LC Card 86-204949 DDC 331.88/92 19
HD4903 .V34 1985

The right work . Caple, John. New York, N.Y. , 1977. xvi, 269 p. ; ISBN 0-396-09064-8 LC Card 87-15734 DDC 650.1/4 19
HF5381 .C2634 1987

RIGHTS, CIVIL. see **CIVIL RIGHTS.**

RIGHTS OF EMPLOYEES. see **EMPLOYEE RIGHTS.**

RIGHTS OF WOMEN. see **WOMEN'S RIGHTS.**

Rigney, Peter. Cody, Seamus. The Parliament of labour . Dublin, Ireland , 1986. 253 p. : LC Card 87-102467 DDC 331.88/09418/35 19
HD8400.3.A5 D833 1986

Riikonen, Eila. Työnteon turvallisuus : yritystason ja yksilötason tekijöiden yhteys työpaikkatapaturmiin / Eila Riikonen. Tampere : Työsuojeluhallitus : Myy Valtion painatuskeskus, 1985 x, 131, [66] p. : ill., forms ; 25 cm. (Tutkimusraportti / Työsuojeluhallitus, 0357-0029 . 50) Summary in English and Swedish. Bibliography: p. [133]-[142] ISBN 951-860-009-0 LC Card 86-222051
1. Industrial accidents - Finland. 2. Industrial safety - Finland. I. Series: Tutkimusraportti (Finland. Työsuojeluhallitus) , 50. II. Title.
HD7262.5.F5 R55 1986

Rijksuniversiteit Limburg. Faculteit der Economische Wetenschappen. Economische wetenschappen . Maastricht , Assen , 1985. 224 p. ; ISBN 90-232-2148-6 LC Card 86-111599
HB21 .E248 1985

Rijksuniversiteit te Leiden. Werkgroep voor de Geschiedenis van de Europese Expansie. All of one company . Utrecht , 1986. 230 p. : ISBN 90-6194-036-2 (pbk.) : LC Card 86-203885 DDC 382/.06/01 19
HF483.E6 A65 1986

Rikert, Richard. Disclosure checklists for banks . New York, N.Y. , c1986. 64 p. ; LC Card 86-224924 DDC 657/.833 19
HG1708 .D57 1986

Riley, Anne W. Occupational stress and organizational effectiveness /. New York , c1987. xii, 285 p. : ISBN 0-275-92281-2 (alk. paper) : LC Card 86-25250 DDC 158.7 19
HF5548.85 .O24 1987

Riley, Dennis D. Controlling the federal bureaucracy / Dennis D. Riley. Philadelphia : Temple University Press, 1987. xiv, 200 ; 22 cm. Includes index. Bibliography: p. [189]-194. ISBN 0-87722-455-2 (alk. paper) : LC Card 86-14469 DDC 353.07/5 19

1. Administrative agencies - United States. 2. Bureaucracy - United States. I. Title.

JK421 .R52 1987 ***NYPL [JLD 87-1396]***

Riley, James C. The Seven Years War and the old regime in France : the economic and financial toll / James C. Riley. Princeton, N.J. : Princeton University Press, 1986. xxii, 256 p. : ill. ; 25 cm. Includes bibliographical references and index. ISBN 0-691-05488-6 (alk. paper) : LC Card 86-42847 DDC 330.944/034 19

1. Seven Years' War, 1756-1763 - Economic aspects - France. 2. Anglo-French War, 1755-1763 - Economic aspects - France. 3. Finance, Public - France - History - 18th century. 4. France - Economic conditions. I. Title.

HC275 .R54 1986 ***NYPL [JLE 87-932]***

Riley, John J. (John Joseph), 1920- Human resources management /. New York , Milwaukee, Wis. , c1987. xiv, 276 p. : ISBN 0-8247-7716-6 LC Card 86-29321 DDC 658.3 19

HF5549 .H8727 1987

Riley, Jonathan, 1955- Liberal utilitarianism : social choice theory and J.S. Mill's philosophy / Jonathan Riley. Cambridge [Cambridgeshire] ; New York : Cambridge University Press, 1987. p. cm. Originally presented as the author's thesis (D. Phil--Oxford, 1983)under the title: Collective choice and individual liberty. Bibliography: p. Includes index. ISBN 0-521-30692-2 LC Card 87-6598 DDC 302/.13 19

1. Social choice. 2. Utilitarianism. 3. Liberalism. 4. Mill, John Stuart, 1806-1873. I. Title.

HB846.8 .R55 1987

Rimashevskaia͡, Natal'i͡a Mikhaĭlovna. Sistema ėkonomiko-matematicheskikh modeleĭ dli͡a analiza i prognoza urovni͡a zhizni /. Moskva , 1986. 262 p. : LC Card 86-232874

HD6978 .S56 1986

Rimele-Petzold, Ursula. Frauen und Beruf, zwischen Wunsch und Realität . Bonn , Bad Honnef , 1986. 142 p. ; ISBN 3-87066-629-3 : LC Card 87-409372 DDC 331.4/0943 19

HD6149 .F719 1986

Rimmer, Douglas. The economies of West Africa / Douglas Rimmer. London : Weidenfeld and Nicolson, c1984. xii, 308 p. : ill. ; 23 cm. (The International economies series) Bibliography: p. 268-296. Includes index. ISBN 0-297-78095-6 LC Card 87-673367

1. Africa, West - Economic conditions - 1960-. 2. Africa, West - Economic policy. I. Title. II. Series.

HC1000 .R56x 1984b

Rinascimento prossimo venturo /. Vacca, Roberto, 1927- Milano , 1986. 281 p. : LC Card 87-100469

HC59 .V24 1986

RINCÓN GALLARDO, JOSÉ MARÍA, MARQUÉS DE GUADALUPE, B. 1802.
Gómez Serrano, Jesús. El mayorazgo Rincón Gallardo . [Aguascalientes] [1984] 156 p., [24] p. of plates : LC Card 84-175622

HD329.Z3 G65 1984 ***NYPL [JLD 87-138]***

Ring, Peter. Regionale Besonderheiten der Preisbildung und Ansätze zur Förderung des Wettbewerbs auf dem Berliner Baustoffmarkt / Peter Ring. Berlin : Duncker & Humblot, 1986. 187 p. : ill. ; 30 cm. (Beiträge zur Strukturforschung . Heft 91) Originally presented as the author's thesis (doctoral--Freie Universität Berlin). Bibliography: p. 181-187. ISBN 3-428-06112-8 LC Card 87-114036 DDC 330 s 338.4/3691/09431554 19

1. Building materials - Prices - Berlin (Germany). 2. Competition - Berlin (Germany). I. Title.

HC281 .B33 Heft 91 HD9715.G33B52

Ringbeck, Jürgen. Qualitäts- und Werbestrategien bei Qualitätsunsicherheit der Konsumenten / Jürgen Ringbeck. Wiesbaden : Gabler, c1986. 256 p. ; 24 cm. (Beiträge zur betriebswirtschaftlichen Forschung. Bd. 60) Bibliography: p. [252]-256. ISBN 3-409-13612-6 LC Card 87-111545 DDC 658.8/02 19

1. Marketing - Decision making. 2. Quality of products. 3. Consumers. I. Title. II. Series.

HF5415.135 .R56 1986

Ringen, Stein. The possibility of politics : a study in the political economy of the welfare state / Stein Ringen. Oxford [Oxfordshire] : Clarendon Press ; Oxford [Oxfordshire] ; x, 303 p. ; 23 cm. Bibliography: p. [267]-295. Includes index. ISBN 0-19-828574-4 :$42.00 (U. S.) LC Card 86-28472 DDC 361.6/5 19

1. Social choice. 2. Welfare state. 3. Income distribution - Government policy. I. Title.

HB846.8 .R56 1987

Ringier Reihe Kommunikation .
(3. Bd) Kutter, Markus, 1925- Werbung in der Schweiz . [Zürich] , 1983. 271 p., xvi p. of plates : ISBN 3-85859-202-1 : LC Card 84-142450

HF5813.S94 K87 1983

Ringuelet, Andrés. El hombre de la tierra / Andrés Ringuelet. [S.l. : s.n., 1984] (La Plata, Rep. Argentina : Impr. Ferrograf) 111 p. ; 22 cm. Cover title. LC Card 85-104745

1. Peasantry - Latin America. 2. Peasantry - Argentina. I. Title.

HD1531.L3 R55 1984

Rinneberg, Karl-Jürgen. Das betriebliche Ausbildungswesen in der Zeit der industriellen Umgestaltung Deutschlands / Karl-Jürgen Rinneberg. Köln : In Kommission bei Böhlau, 1985. xvi, 481 p. : ill. ; 22 cm. (Studien und Dokumentationen zur deutschen Bildungsgeschichte. Bd. 29) Originally presented as the author's thesis (doctoral)--Freie Universität Berlin, 1984. Bibliography: p. 454-478. ISBN 3-412-02885-1 LC Card 86-121691

1. Employees, Training of - Germany - History - 19th century. 2. Germany - Industries - History - 19th century. I. Title. II. Series.

HF5549.5.T7 R486 1985

Rinzler, Ralph. Sayers, Robert. The Korean onggi potter /. Washington, D.C. , 1987. 288 p. : LC Card 86-600366 DDC 338.4/77382/095195 19

HD9617.K82 S29 1987

Rio de Janeiro. Banco Nacional da Habitação. see **Banco Nacional da Habitação.**

RIO DE JANEIRO (BRAZIL) - COMMERCE - HISTORY.
Os Assinantes da praça 1834-1984. Rio de Janeiro , 1984. 72 p. ; LC Card 85-160423

HF300.B66 A78 1984

Rio de Janeiro. Centro de Estudos Agrícolas. see **Instituto Brasileiro de Economia. Centro de Estudos Agrícolas.**

Rio de Janeiro. Escola Interamericana de Administração Pública. see **Escola Interamericana de Administração Pública.**

RIO DE JANEIRO METROPOLITAN AREA (BRAZIL) - SOCIAL CONDITIONS - STATISTICS.
Região metropolitana do Rio de Janeiro . [Rio de Janeiro, Brazil] [1984?] 242 p. : LC Card 87-404930 DDC 330.981/53 19

HC189.R45 R44 1984

Rio de Janeiro. Museu da Fazenda Federal. see **Museu da Fazenda Federal.**

RIO DE LA PLATA REGION - HISTORY - 18TH CENTURY.
Santos, Corcino Medeiros dos. Economia e sociedade do Rio Grande do Sul . São Paulo, SP, Brasil , 1984. xxi, 216 p. : ISBN 85-04-00203-9 : LC Card 85-199838

HF3409.R56 S25 1984

Rio Grande do Norte (Brazil)
Agregados econômicos estaduais do Rio Grande do Norte, 1970-1982 /. Natal , 1985. 35 leaves : LC Card 86-158766

HC188.R38 A53 1985

Programas especiais do governo, 1983-1987. Natal : Governo do Estado do Rio Grande do Norte, Secretaria do Planejamento, Fundação Instituto de Desenvolvimento do Rio Grande do Norte, 1984. [83] leaves ; 28 cm. LC Card 87-403924 DDC 331.12/0981/32 19

1. Rio Grande do Norte (Brazil) - Economic policy. 2. Rural development - Brazil - Rio Grande do Norte. 3. Manpower policy - Brazil - Rio Grande do Norte. I. Title.

HC188.R38 P76 1984

Rio Grande do Norte (Brazil). Companhia de Desenvolvimento Industrial. Paiva, Francisco Ismar Martins. Projeto Pesca Industrial à Vela. [Natal, Brazil] [1982 or 1983] 91 p. : LC Card 85-102872

HD9464.B73 R487 1982

RIO GRANDE DO NORTE (BRAZIL) - ECONOMIC POLICY.
Rio Grande do Norte (Brazil) Programas especiais do governo, 1983-1987. Natal , 1984. [83] leaves ; LC Card 87-403924 DDC 331.12/0981/32 19

HC188.R38 P76 1984

Rio Grande do Norte (Brazil). Fundação Estadual de Planejamento Agrícola.
PDRI-Serra do Mel . Natal , 1981. 52 leaves : LC Card 84-246626

HD499.M45 P37 1981

Séries históricas da produção agrícola do Estado do Rio Grande do Norte, 1947-1982 . Natal , 1983. 159 leaves : LC Card 84-246432

HD1875.R48 S47 1983

Rio Grande do Norte (Brazil). Secretaria da Indústria e Comércio. Estudos de viabilidade técnica da implantação e plano diretor do distrito industrial de Mossoró . [Natal] , 1979. ca. 250 leaves, 8 folded leaves of plates : LC Card 84-256137

HC189.M6 E86 1979

Rio Grande do Sul (Brazil)
Relatorios provinciaes. [1850-1859] 19 pamphlets in 1 v. ; 28 cm. Reports presented by various provincial officials between 1850 and 1859. Binder's title on spine. LC Card 84-217966

1. Rio Grande do Sul (Brazil) - Public works. 2. Finance, Public - Brazil - Rio Grande do Sul. 3. Municipal services - Brazil - Rio Grande do Sul. 4. Education - Brazil - Rio Grande do Sul. 5. Public health - Brazil - Rio Grande do Sul. 6. Rio Grande do Sul (Brazil) - Armed forces. I. Title.

HD4635.R54 R56 1850

RIO GRANDE DO SUL (BRAZIL) - ARMED FORCES.
Rio Grande do Sul (Brazil) Relatorios provinciaes. [1850-1859] 19 pamphlets in 1 v. ; LC Card 84-217966

HD4635.R54 R56 1850

Rio Grande do Sul (Brazil). Assembléia Legislativa. Comissão Especial dos Agricultores Desalojados do Passo Real.
Afogados, até quando? : relatório da Comissão Especial dos Agricultores Desalojados do Passo Real. [Porto Alegre] : Estado do Rio Grande do Sul, Assembléia Legislativa, [1984] 99 p. : ill. ; 23 cm. Cover title. LC Card 85-150200

1. Land tenure - Brazil - Passo Real. 2. Agricultural laborers - Brazil - Passo Real. 3. Eminent domain - Brazil - Passo Real. 4. Hydoelectric power plants - Brazil - Passo Real. I. Title.

HD500.P39 R56 1984

Rio Grande do Sul (Brazil). Comissão de Estudos Municipais. Os Municípios do Rio Grande do Sul . [Porto Alegre] , 1985. 250, [7] p. : LC Card 87-401216 DDC 318.1/65 19

HA988.R8 M86 1985

Rio Grande do Sul (Brazil). Comissão Estadual de Energia. Energia e assentamentos humanos. Porto Alegre , 1983. 40 p. : LC Card 86-200513

HD9502.A2 E513 1983

RIO GRANDE DO SUL (BRAZIL) - COMMERCE - HISTORY.
Silva, J. Resende. A fronteira do sul . Rio de Janeiro , 1922. 723 p., [1] leaf of plates : LC Card 85-223002

HF3409.R56 S55 1922

RIO GRANDE DO SUL (BRAZIL) - COMMERCE - HISTORY - 18TH CENTURY.
Santos, Corcino Medeiros dos. Economia e sociedade do Rio Grande do Sul . São Paulo, SP, Brasil , 1984. xxi, 216 p. : ISBN 85-04-00203-9 : LC Card 85-199838

HF3409.R56 S25 1984

RIO GRANDE DO SUL (BRAZIL) - COMMERCE - HISTORY - 20TH CENTURY.
Leite, Manoel Marques. Relações externas da economia do Rio Grande do Sul, 1949/79 /. [Porto Alegre] , 1985. 114 p. : ISBN 85-7025-097-5 : LC Card 87-104433 DDC 382/.098165 19

HF3409.R5 L45 1985

RIO GRANDE DO SUL (BRAZIL) - ECONOMIC CONDITIONS.
Carrion Júnior, Francisco M. (Francisco Machado), 1944- O Rio Grande em busca de novos caminhos por um projeto regional /. Porto Alegre, RS , 1986. 78 p. : LC Card 87-129162 DDC 330.981/65063 19
HC188.R4 C35 1986

RIO GRANDE DO SUL (BRAZIL) - ECONOMIC CONDTIONS - STATISTICS.
Areas estatísticamente comparáveis do Rio Grande do Sul, 1940-80 . Porto Alegre, RS , 1986. 186 p. : LC Card 87-403481 DDC 339.381/65 19
HC188.R4 A73 1986

Rio Grande do Sul (Brazil). Fundação de Economia e Estatística.
Areas estatísticamente comparáveis do Rio Grande do Sul, 1940-80 . Porto Alegre, RS , 1986. 186 p. : LC Card 87-403481 DDC 339.381/65 19
HC188.R4 A73 1986

Cunha, Rafael Alves de. Duas décadas da produção e do produto da agropecuária RS, 1964-84 /. Porto Alegre , 1986- v. <1 > : LC Card 87-404979 DDC 338.1/0981/65 19
HD9014.B83 R5416 1986

O Emprego no Rio Grande do Sul . Porto Alegre , 1985. 163 p. : LC Card 85-207909
HD5755.R54 E46 1985

Rio Grande do Sul (Brazil). Fundação Metropolitana de Planejamento. Seminário para Compatibilização da Ação Pública na Região Metropolitana de Porto Alegre (1983) Seminário para Compatibilização da Ação Pública na Região Metropolitana de Porto Alegre . Porto Alegre, RS [1983] 83 p. : LC Card 84-216956
HC189.P64 S45 1983

RIO GRANDE DO SUL (BRAZIL) - HISTORY.
Silva, J. Resende. A fronteira do sul . Rio de Janeiro , 1922. 723 p., [1] leaf of plates : LC Card 85-223002
HF3409.R56 S55 1922

RIO GRANDE DO SUL (BRAZIL) - HISTORY - 18TH CENTURY.
Santos, Corcino Medeiros dos. Economia e sociedade do Rio Grande do Sul . São Paulo, SP, Brasil , 1984. xxi, 216 p. : ISBN 85-04-00203-9 : LC Card 85-199838
HF3409.R56 S25 1984

RIO GRANDE DO SUL (BRAZIL) - POLITICS AND GOVERNMENT.
Silva, J. Resende. A fronteira do sul . Rio de Janeiro , 1922. 723 p., [1] leaf of plates : LC Card 85-223002
HF3409.R56 S55 1922

RIO GRANDE DO SUL (BRAZIL) - PUBLIC WORKS.
Rio Grande do Sul (Brazil) Relatorios provinciaes. [1850-1859] 19 pamphlets in 1 v. ; LC Card 84-217966
HD4635.R54 R56 1850

Rio Grande do Sul (Brazil). Secretaria da Indústria e Comércio. Departamento Técnico. Divisão de Estudos Especiais. Catálogo da indústria têxtil e do vestuário do Rio Grande do Sul /. [Porto Alegre] , 1985. 96 p. ; LC Card 86-209398
HD9864.B83 R593 1985

RIO GRANDE DO SUL (BRAZIL) - STATISTICS.
Os Municípios do Rio Grande do Sul . [Porto Alegre] , 1985. 250, [7] p. : LC Card 87-401216 DDC 318.1/65 19
HA988.R8 M86 1985

O Rio Grande em busca de novos caminhos por um projeto regional /. Carrion Júnior, Francisco M. (Francisco Machado), 1944- Porto Alegre, RS , 1986. 78 p. : LC Card 87-129162 DDC 330.981/65063 19
HC188.R4 C35 1986

Río Negro (Argentina). Dirección de Estadística y Censos. Producto bruto geográfico . [Viedma, Argentina] , 1977. 153 p. ; LC Card 79-107106
HC177.R5 P76 1977

The Rio Tinto Company . Harvey, Charles E. Penzance, Cornwall , 1981. xiv, 390 p. : ISBN 0-906720-03-6 : LC Card 82-127720 DDC 338.8/87 19
HD9506.G74 R564 1981 *NYPL [JLD 86-2605]*

RIO TINTO COMPANY - HISTORY.
Harvey, Charles E. The Rio Tinto Company . Penzance, Cornwall , 1981. xiv, 390 p. : ISBN 0-906720-03-6 : LC Card 82-127720 DDC 338.8/87 19
HD9506.G74 R564 1981 *NYPL [JLD 86-2605]*

Ríos Burga, Jaime R. Ciclos productivos en el espacio peruano colonial, siglos XVI-XIX : una aproximación a una síntesis cuantitativa / Jaime R. Ríos Burga.1a ed. Lima, Perú : Ediciones Trabajo, 1986. 70 p. : ill. ; 21 cm. (Serie Síntesis) "Ponencia al VII Simposio Internacional de Historia Económica, Comisión de Historia Económica del Consejo Latinoamericano de Ciencias Sociales, Lima, 26-29 de junio de 1986"--Verso t.p. Includes bibliographical references. LC Card 87-401070 DDC 338.5/42/0983 19
1. Peru - Economic conditions. 2. Business cycles - Peru - History. 3. Mineral industries - Peru - History. 4. Agriculture - Economic aspects - Peru - History. 5. Peru - History - To 1820. I. Title.
HC227 .R456 1986

Riscophobie et étalement à moyenne constante . Boyer, Marcel. Montréal [1982] 32 p. : LC Card 85-160864
HB615 .B68 1982

Riscos e perspectivas da divisão internacional do trabalho =. Albuquerque, Marcos Cintra Cavalcanti de. Brasília, DF [1986] 19, 17, [2] p. ; LC Card 87-403241 DDC 331/.01 19
HF1411 .A3984 1986

The rise and decline of the Great Atlantic & Pacific Tea Company /. Walsh, William I. Secaucus, N.J. , c1986. 254 p., [24] p. of plates : ISBN 0-8184-0382-9 : LC Card 85-24987 DDC 381/.456413/006073 19
HD9321.9.G7 W35 1986 *NYPL [JLE 86-1952]*

Rise from want . Davis, James C. (James Cushman) Philadelphia , 1986. xv, 165 p. : ISBN 0-8122-8034-2 : LC Card 86-19228 DDC 305.5/63 19
HD1536.Y8 D38 1986 *NYPL [JLE 87-710]*

The Rise in unemployment / edited by C.R. Bean, P.R.G. Layard, and S.J. Nickell. Oxford, UK ; New York, NY, USA : B. Blackwell, 1987, c1986. 382 p. : ill. ; 23 cm. Includes bibliographies and indexes. ISBN 0-631-15419-1 (pbk.) : LC Card 87-699 DDC 331.13/7 19
1. Unemployment. I. Bean, C. R. (Charles R.), 1953-. II. Layard, P. R. G. (P. Richard G.). III. Nickell, S. J.
HD5707.5 .R57 1987

The rise of large American corporations, 1889-1919 /. Bunting, David G. New York , 1986, c1987. 224 p. ; ISBN 0-8240-8353-9 (alk. paper) : LC Card 86-29527 DDC 338.6/44 19
HD2785 .B76 1987

The rise of modern business in Great Britain, the United States, and Japan /. Blackford, Mansel G., 1944- Chapel Hill , c1988. xi, 176 p. : ISBN 0-8078-1760-0 (alk. paper) LC Card 87-10022 DDC 338.09 19
HC255 .B59 1988

The rise of the community builders . Weiss, Marc A. (Marc Allan) New York , 1987. xii, 228 p. : ISBN 0-231-06504-3 LC Card 87-5115 DDC 333.77/17/0973 19
HD257 .W46 1987

The Rise of the modern state / edited by James Anderson. Brighton, Sussex : Wheatsheaf Books : Distributed by Harvester Press, 1986. viii, 255 p. ; 22 cm. Includes index. Bibliography: p. 231-239. ISBN 0-7450-0059-2
1. State, The - Addresses, essays, lectures. 2. Political science - History - Addresses, essays, lectures. 3. Comparative government - Addresses, essays, lectures. I. Anderson, James. *NYPL [JLD 86-2353]*

The rise of the phoenix . Behrman, Jack N. Boulder , 1987. xiii, 104 p. ; ISBN 0-8133-7511-8 (pbk. : alk. paper) : LC Card 87-21689 DDC 338.973 19
HC106.8 .B43 1987

The rise of the trading state . Rosecrance, Richard N. New York , c1986. xiii, 268 p. : ISBN 0-465-07035-3 : LC Card 85-47558 DDC 382/.09/04 19
HF1007 .R549 1985 *NYPL [JLE 86-951]*

Risiken im Auslandsgeschäft . Köpplinger, Herbert, 1954- Nürnberg , 1986. xli, 227 p. : ISBN 3-89078-005-9 LC Card 87-145527 DDC 332.6/73 19
HG4538 .K64 1986

Risiko-Management / [Matthias Haller ... et al.]. Wiesbaden : Gabler, [1986] 145 p. : ill. ; 24 cm. (Schriften zur Unternehmensführung, 0582-0545 . 33) Cover title. Includes bibliographical references. ISBN 3-409-17902-X LC Card 86-161867
1. Risk management. 2. Risk (Insurance). I. Haller, Matthias. II. Series.
HD70.G2 S3 Bd. 33 HD61

Risikokapital über die Börse . Mannheimer Bankenforum (1985) Berlin , New York , c1986. x, 190 p. ; ISBN 0-387-16671-8 (U. S.) LC Card 86-225903
HG5492 .M35 1985

Risikovorsorge : das Rechnungswesen als Informationsinstrument zur Steuerung und Kontrolle bankbetrieblicher Risiken / herausgegeben von Rosemarie Kolbeck ; mit Beiträgen von Erich Dreher ... [et al.]. Frankfurt am Main : F. Knapp, c1985. 130 p. : ill. ; 24 cm. Bibliography: p. 123-124. CONTENTS. - Risikovorsorge im Jahresabschluss der Kreditinstitute / von Klaus Mertin -- Möglichst sicherer Einblick versus true and fair view / von Eberhard Spieth -- Der Konzernabschluss als Spiegel der Konzernbilanzpolitik / von Martin Kohlhaussen -- Probleme der Erfassung und Steuerung des Zinsänderungsrisikos mit Hilfe des bankbetrieblichen Rechnungswesens / von Johann Remmers -- Das interne Rechnungswesen als Planungs- und Steuerungsinstrument / von Erich Dreher -- Die Bankenstatistik der Deutschen Bundesbank / von Helmut Schlesinger. ISBN 3-7819-0323-0 LC Card 85-217569
1. Bank management. 2. Risk management. I. Kolbeck, Rosemarie. II. Dreher, Erich.
HG1615 .R57 1985

RISK.
Brenner, Reuven. Rivalry . Cambridge , New York , 1987. xi, 244 p. ; ISBN 0-521-33187-0 LC Card 86-24415 DDC 338.6/048 19
HD41 .B743 1987

Dieckhöner, Bruno. Rentabilitätsrisiken aus dem Hypothekargeschäft von Kreditinstituten in Zeiten der Geldentwertung /. Wiesbaden , c1984. xi, 395 p. : ISBN 3-409-14002-6 : LC Card 85-119494
HG2040.5.G4 D53 1984

Ford, J. L. Economic choice under uncertainty . New York , c1987. ix, 146 p. ; ISBN 0-312-01244-6 : LC Card 87-18806 DDC 330.1 19
HB615 .F674 1987

Galts, Helmut. Ungewissheit und Planungsmethodik . Münster [1983] vi, 234 p. : ISBN 3-88660-143-9 LC Card 84-178712
HB615 .G35 1983

Heffernan, Shelagh A., 1956- Sovereign risk analysis /. London , Boston , 1986. xvii, 181 p. : ISBN 0-04-332119-4 (alk. paper) LC Card 85-32069 DDC 332.1/5/0685 19
HG3891.5 .H44 1986 *NYPL [JLD 86-2957]*

Jones, Eric T. (Eric Thomas) Hedging foreign exchange . New York , c1987. xiv, 239 p. : ISBN 0-471-84986-3 LC Card 86-26639 DDC 332.4/5 19
HG3853 .J66 1987

Katz, Reinhard. Informationsquellen der Konsumenten . Wiesbaden , c1983. xxix, 297 p. : ISBN 3-409-13602-9 LC Card 84-118615
HF5415.3 .K35 1983

Kockázat és társadalom /. Budapest , 1987. 309 p. : ISBN 963-05-4450-4 : LC Card 87-425562
HD61 .K6 1987

Marchés, capital et incertitude . Paris , c1986. 265 p. : ISBN 2-7178-1002-1 : LC Card 86-160930
HB615 .M37 1986

Möller, Hans Peter. Bilanzkennzahlen und Ertragsrisiken des Kapitalmarktes . Stuttgart , 1986. xii, 240 p. : ISBN 3-7910-0382-8 LC Card 86-149711
HF5681.C25 M64 1986

Pastuszek, Rainer. Leading und Lagging kurzfristig variierbarer gruppeninterner

Geldflüsse im Währungsrisikomanagement einer internationalen Unternehmung /. Pfaffenweiler , 1986. xvi, 275 p. : ISBN 3-89085-122-3 LC Card 87-128258 DDC 658.1/55 19
HG3851 .P295 1986

Planning in turbulence /. Jerusalem , 1986. xii, 158 p. : ISBN 965-223-657-8 (pbk.) LC Card 87-163701 DDC 658.4/012 19
HD87.5 .P5 1986

Schoemaker, Paul J. H. Experiments on decisions under risk . Boston , c1980. xxii, 211 p. : ISBN 0-89838-035-9 LC Card 79-27948 DDC 658.4/03
HB615 .S36 ***NYPL [JLE 81-559]***

Shin, Kilman. Interest rate, risk, and income distribution /. [Taegu, Korea] , c1986. v, 378 p. : LC Card 87-105107 DDC 330/.01/51 19
HG229 .S436 1986

Tietzel, Manfred. Wirtschaftstheorie und Unwissen . Tübingen , 1985. viii, 208 p. ; ISBN 3-16-944919-2 LC Card 86-147807
HB175 .T55 1985

Wiegel, Klaus Dieter. Rentabilität und Risiko im Kreditgeschäft der Banken . Köln , c1985. 342 p. : ISBN 3-87951-125-X LC Card 87-140074 DDC 332.1/753 19
HG1641 .W54 1985

RISK - ADDRESSES, ESSAYS, LECTURES.
Controlling interest rate risk . New York , c1986. xv, 414 p. : ISBN 0-471-82354-6 : LC Card 85-22504 DDC 332.8/2 19
HG1621 .C6 1986 ***NYPL [JLE 86-2850]***

Risk and failure in English business, 1700-1800 /. Hoppit, Julian. Cambridge [Cambridgeshire] , New York , 1987. vii, 228 p. : ISBN 0-521-32624-9 LC Card 87-743 DDC 332.7/5/0942 19
HG3769.G73 E54 1987

Risk and the control of technology . Irwin, Alan. Manchester [Greater Manchester] , Dover, N.H., USA , c1985. vii, 265 p. : ISBN 0-7190-1723-8 : LC Card 84-17153 DDC 363.1/25561/0941 19
HE5614.2 .I79 1985 ***NYPL [JLD 87-929]***

Risk assessment and management / edited by Lester B. Lave. New York : Plenum Press, c1987. xii, 740 p. : ill. ; 26 cm. (Advances in risk analysis . v. 5) "Proceedings of the annual meeting of the Society for Risk Assessment [i.e. Analysis] held November 1985, in Washington, D.C."--T.p. verso. Includes bibliographies and index. ISBN 0-306-42683-8 LC Card 87-21288 DDC 658 19
1. Risk management - Congresses. 2. Risk - Congresses. I. Lave, Lester B. II. Society for Risk Analysis. III. Series.
HD61 .R5684 1987

Risk assessments . Soldati, John M. Washington, D.C. (1120 Connecticut Ave., N.W., Washington 20036) , c1987. 21 p. : LC Card 87-148315 DDC 332.64/52 19
HG6042 .S65 1987

RISK CAPITAL. see **VENTURE CAPITAL.**

RISK - CONGRESSES.
Risk assessment and management /. New York , c1987. xii, 740 p. : ISBN 0-306-42683-8 LC Card 87-21288 DDC 658 19
HD61 .R5684 1987

Society for Risk Analysis International Workshop on Uncertainty in Risk Assessment, Risk Management, and Decision Making (1984 : Knoxville, Tenn.) Uncertainty in risk assessment, risk management, and decision making /. New York , c1987. x, 538 p. : ISBN 0-306-42557-2 LC Card 87-2403 DDC 658 19
HD61 .S625 1984

RISK - DEVELOPING COUNTRIES.
Mugglin, Markus. Exportrisikogarantie, internationale Verschuldung und schweizerische Entwicklungspolitik /. Adliswil , 1985. 56 p. : ISBN 3-7229-4036-X LC Card 85-148130
HF1574.5.D44 M84 1985

RISK - EUROPEAN ECONOMIC COMMUNITY COUNTRIES.
Kirschke, Dieter, 1952- Agrarmarktpolitik bei Unsicherheit . Berlin , c1987. 225 p. : ISBN 3-428-06111-X LC Card 87-131255 DDC 338.1/8 19
HD1920.5 .K57 1987

RISK - GERMANY, WEST.
Seifert, Ekkehard. Privilegierung und Regulierung im Bankwesen . Baden-Baden , 1984. 332 p. ; ISBN 3-7890-0861-3 LC Card 84-186059
HG3054 .S42 1984

RISK - GERMANY (WEST) - CONGRESSES.
Mannheimer Bankenforum (1985) Risikokapital über die Börse . Berlin , New York , c1986. x, 190 p. ; ISBN 0-387-16671-8 (U. S.) LC Card 86-225903
HG5492 .M35 1985

RISK - GERMANY (WEST) - MATHEMATICAL MODELS.
Bamberg, Günter, 1940- Decision-theoretic analysis of envisaged income tax reforms for FRG and U. S. /. [Augsburg] [1986] 11 leaves : LC Card 87-101962 DDC 336.24/0724 19
HJ4719 .B35 1986

RISK (INSURANCE) - ITALY.
Padoa, Fabio. L'assicurazione internazionale . Milano , c1983. 140 p. : ISBN 88-20-31384-7 LC Card 85-189997
HG8059 .P33 1983

RISK (INSURANCE) - MATHEMATICAL MODELS.
Cresta, Jean-Paul. Théorie des marchés d'assurance /. Paris , 1984. vii, 231 p. : ISBN 2-7178-0696-2 : LC Card 84-235141
HG8054.5 .C74 1984

Ruohonen, Matti. On the use of Ventcel-Freidlin estimates in approximating the probability of ruin /. Vaasa , 1979. 27 p. : ISBN 951-683-103-6 (pbk.) LC Card 83-223364
HG8054.5 .R86 1979

Schlesinger, Harris. Extending Arrow-Pratt risk premiums /. Berlin [1985] 13, 4 leaves : LC Card 86-206602 DDC 368 19
HG8054.5 .S35 1985

RISK (INSURANCE) - UNITED STATES.
Abraham, Kenneth S., 1946- Distributing risk . New Haven , c1986. x, 254 p. ; ISBN 0-300-03460-1 (alk. paper) LC Card 85-22459 DDC 346.73/086 347.30686 19
KF1164 .A72 1986 ***NYPL [JLE 86-4347]***

Keenan, Gerald M. Insurance redlining . Chicago, Ill. , c1979. 135 p. :
NYPL [JLF 86-1590]

RISK (INSURANCE) - UNITED STATES - ECONOMETRIC MODELS.
Marquis, M. Susan. Choice under uncertainty and the demand for health insurance /. Santa Monica, CA (P.O. Box 2138, Santa Monica 90406-2138) [1986] ix, 50 p. ; LC Card 87-118503 DDC 368.3/8/00973 19
HG9396 .M268 1986

RISK (INSURANCE) - UNITED STATES - HANDBOOKS, MANUALS, ETC.
Lenz, Matthew. Risk management manual /. Santa Monica, Calif. (P.O. Box 955, Santa Monica 90406) , <1972-. 3 v. (loose-leaf) : LC Card 86-209050
HG8054.5 .L46 1972

RISK (ISLAMIC LAW)
Saleh, Nabil A. Unlawful gain and legitimate profit in Islamic law . Cambridge [Cambridgeshire] , New York , 1986. xii, 130 p. ; ISBN 0-521-32298-7 LC Card 85-25547 DDC 297/.14 19
LAW ***NYPL [JLE 86-2377]***

RISK MANAGEMENT.
Assessing corporate political risk . Totowa, NJ , 1986. xvii, 212 p. ; ISBN 0-86598-114-0 LC Card 85-19618 DDC 658 19
HD61 .A87 1986 ***NYPL [JLE 86-3102]***

Borghesi, Antonio. La gestione dei rischi di azienda . Padova , 1985. 299 p. : LC Card 86-214201
HD61 .B65 1985

Commercial liability risk management and insurance /. Malvern, Pa. , 1986. 2 v. : ISBN 0-89463-049-0 (set) LC Card 86-72708 DDC 368.8/1 19
HG8059 .C64 1986

Essentials of risk control /. Malvern, Pa. , 1986. 2 v. : ISBN 0-89462-033-9 (pbk.) LC Card 86-82833 DDC 368 19
HD61 .E84 1986

Evans, Thomas G. Foreign exchange risk management under statement 52 /. Stamford, Conn. , c1986. ix, 133 p. : ISBN 0-910065-21-7 (pbk.) LC Card 86-91435 DDC 657/.48 19
HG3853.7 .E935 1986

Gardner, Mona J. Managing financial institutions . Chicago , c1988. xii, 795 p. : ISBN 0-03-005479-6 LC Card 86-32805 DDC 332.1/068/1 19
HG1615.25 .G37 1988

Grose, Vernon L., 1928- Managing risk . Englewood Cliffs, N.J. , c1987. xii, 404 p. : ISBN 0-13-551110-0 : LC Card 87-12309 DDC 658 19
HD61 .G76 1987

Kockázat és társadalom /. Budapest , 1987. 309 p. : ISBN 963-05-4450-4 : LC Card 87-425562
HD61 .K6 1987

Oxelheim, Lars. Macroeconomic uncertainty . Chichester [West Sussex] , New York , c1987. xv, 251 p. : ISBN 0-471-91480-0 : LC Card 87-8333 DDC 658.1/55 19
HG3821 .O894 1987

Risiko-Management /. Wiesbaden [1986] 145 p. : ISBN 3-409-17902-X LC Card 86-161867
HD70.G2 S3 Bd. 33 HD61

Risikovorsorge . Frankfurt am Main , c1985. 130 p. : ISBN 3-7819-0323-0 LC Card 85-217569
HG1615 .R57 1985

Risk management and retention . Monterey, Calif. (1 Mission Plaza, Monterey 93940) , c1986. v, 71 p. : LC Card 86-202599 DDC 658 19
HD61 .R569 1986

Schlangen, Gerhard. Die Systematik der unternehmerischen Sicherungsmassnahmen /. Münster [1984?] vii, 179 p. : ISBN 3-88660-063-7 LC Card 84-166733
HD61 .S34 1984

Williams, Alex O., 1934- Managing risk in mortgage portfolios /. New York , c1987. xx, 161 p. : ISBN 0-89930-058-8 (lib. bdg. : alk. paper) LC Card 87-2497 DDC 332.63/244 19
HG4655 .W55 1987

Risk management and retention : minimizing risk and using self-insurance / from the editors of Small business report. Monterey, Calif. (1 Mission Plaza, Monterey 93940) : Business Research & Communications, c1986. v, 71 p. : ill. ; 28 cm. (Management information studies) Management information series LC Card 86-202599 DDC 658 19
1. Risk management. 2. Insurance, Business. 3. Self-insurance. I. Small business report (Monterey, Calif.). II. Series. III. Series: Management information series (Monterey, Calif.).
HD61 .R569 1986

RISK MANAGEMENT - CASE STUDIES.
Assessing corporate political risk . Totowa, NJ , 1986. xvii, 212 p. ; ISBN 0-86598-114-0 LC Card 85-19618 DDC 658 19
HD61 .A87 1986 ***NYPL [JLE 86-3102]***

RISK MANAGEMENT - CONGRESSES.
Insuring and managing hazardous risks--from Seveso to Bhopal and beyond /. Berlin , New York , c1987. ix, 534 p. : ISBN 0-387-17732-9 (U. S.) LC Card 87-4963 DDC 346.03/8 342.638 19
HG9994 .I57 1987

Risk assessment and management /. New York , c1987. xii, 740 p. : ISBN 0-306-42683-8 LC Card 87-21288 DDC 658 19
HD61 .R5684 1987

Society for Risk Analysis International Workshop on Uncertainty in Risk Assessment, Risk Management, and Decision Making (1984 : Knoxville, Tenn.) Uncertainty in risk assessment, risk management, and decision making /. New York , c1987. x, 538 p. : ISBN 0-306-42557-2 LC Card 87-2403 DDC 658 19
HD61 .S625 1984

RISK MANAGEMENT - GERMANY (WEST) - CONGRESSES.
Langfristiges Anlagengeschäft, Risiko-Management und Controlling /. Düsseldorf , c1986. 148 p. : ISBN 3-7754-0016-8 LC Card 86-227044
HG4534 .L36 1986

RISK MANAGEMENT - HANDBOOKS, MANUALS, ETC.

The Business insurance handbook /. Homewood, Ill. , c1981. xvii, 753 p. : ISBN 0-87094-237-9 LC Card 80-70437 DDC 368.8/1/00202 19
HG8059 .B87 ***NYPL [*R-Econ. 86-2502]***

Risk management manual /. Lenz, Matthew. Santa Monica, Calif. (P.O. Box 955, Santa Monica 90406) , <1972-. 3 v. (loose-leaf) : LC Card 86-209050
HG8054.5 .L46 1972

RISK MANAGEMENT - MATHEMATICAL MODELS.
Dimmer, Klaus. Die optimale Versicherungsentscheidung als risikopolitisches Problem . Karlsruhe , c1986. xiv, 320 p. : LC Card 87-114755 DDC 368/.0072 19
HG8054.5 .D555 1986

Vörös, József. A kockázat, haszon és a termelési szerkezet összefüggése /. Pécs , 1983. 77 leaves : LC Card 85-111246
HD61 .V67 1983

RISK MANAGEMENT - POLITICAL ASPECTS.
Ting, Wenlee. Multinational risk assessment and management . New York , c1987. p. cm. ISBN 0-89930-175-4 (lib. bdg. : alk. paper) LC Card 87-5970 DDC 658 19
HD61 .T56 1987

RISK MANAGEMENT - UNITED STATES.
Kennedy, Charles R. Political risk management . New York , 1987. xiv, 163 p. : ISBN 0-89930-157-6 (lib. bdg. : alk. paper) LC Card 86-25588 DDC 332.6/7373 19
HG4538 .K44 1987

RISK MANAGEMENT - UNITED STATES - HANDBOOKS, MANUALS, ETC.
Lenz, Matthew. Risk management manual /. Santa Monica, Calif. (P.O. Box 955, Santa Monica 90406) , <1972-. 3 v. (loose-leaf) : LC Card 86-209050
HG8054.5 .L46 1972

RISK MANAGERS - UNITED STATES.
Dietz, Thomas. The risk professionals /. New York , c1987. p. cm. ISBN 0-87154-214-5 : LC Card 87-19992 DDC 363.7/056/0973 19
HC110.E5 D54 1987

RISK - MATHEMATICAL MODELS.
Boyer, Marcel. Riscophobie et étalement à moyenne constante . Montréal [1982] 32 p. : LC Card 85-160864
HB615 .B68 1982

The risk professionals /. Dietz, Thomas. New York , c1987. p. cm. ISBN 0-87154-214-5 : LC Card 87-19992 DDC 363.7/056/0973 19
HC110.E5 D54 1987

RISK - SWEDEN.
Lindmark, Leif. Företagsstöd och kommunalt risktagande /. Stockholm [1984] iv, 49 p. : ISBN 91-38-08297-7 LC Card 85-106839
HD3646.S8 L55 1984

Risk to riche$: women and entrepreneurship in America : a special report / Edie Fraser, editor. Washington, DC (600 Maryland Ave., S.W., Suite 700, Washington 20024) : Institute for Enterprise Advancement, c1986. vii, 204 p. : ill. ; 27 cm. Bibliography: p. 203-204. LC Card 87-158511 DDC 338/.04/088042 19
1. Women-owned business enterprises - United States - Case studies. 2. Women in business - United States - Case studies. 3. Entrepreneurship - United States - Case studies. 4. Success in business - United States - Case studies. 5. Women executives - United States - Case studies. I. Fraser, Edie. II. Institute for Enterprise Advancement (U. S.).
HD2346.U5 R57 1986

RISK - UNITED STATES.
Perspectives on safe & sound banking . Cambridge, Mass. , 1986. xxi, 358 p. ; ISBN 0-262-02246-X LC Card 85-23882 DDC 332.1/0973 19
HG2481 .P47 1986 ***NYPL [JLE 86-2960]***

RISK - UNITED STATES - MATHEMATICAL MODELS.
Bamberg, Günter, 1940- Decision-theoretic analysis of envisaged income tax reforms for FRG and U. S. /. [Augsburg] [1986] 11 leaves : LC Card 87-101962 DDC 336.24/0724 19
HJ4719 .B35 1986

Riskalla, Rafat Riad. Nakhla, Afaf Fouad. Update the transportation problem /. Cairo [1985- v. <1 > ; LC Card 87-401510 DDC 361.6/0962 s 380.5/24 19
HD82 .C23 no. 1415 HE199.A2

Risks & rewards of entrepreneurship / by M. Catherine Ashmore ... [et al.]. Saint Paul, Minn. : EMC Publishing, c1988. 123 p. : ill. ; 29 cm. "The National Center for Research in Vocational Education, the Ohio State University, Columbus, Ohio." Describes the skills needed to become an entrepreneur, how to start your own business, and how to be your own boss. ISBN 0-8219-0323-3 (pbk.) LC Card 87-21787 DDC 338/.04 19
1. Entrepreneurship - Juvenile literature. 2. New business enterprises - Juvenile literature. I. Ashmore, M. Catherine. II. Changing Times Education Service. III. National Center for Research in Vocational Education (U. S.). IV. Title: Risks and rewards of entrepreneurship.
HB615 .R56 1988

Risks and rewards of entrepreneurship. Risks & rewards of entrepreneurship /. Saint Paul, Minn. , c1988. 123 p. : ISBN 0-8219-0323-3 (pbk.) LC Card 87-21787 DDC 338/.04 19
HB615 .R56 1988

Risks to health and safety on the job /. Irwin, Michael H. K. New York, NY , c1986. 28 p. : ISBN 0-88291-096-5 (pbk.) : LC Card 87-402515 DDC 363.1/1/0973 19
HD7654 .I79 1986

Risorse umane e redditi da lavoro . Antonelli, Gilberto. Milano , c1985. 256 p. : LC Card 85-191554
HC310.I5 A66 1985

Rist, Gilbert, 1938- Towards a new United Nations development strategy : some major United Nations resolutions in perspective / Gilbert Rist. Nyon : International Foundation for Development Alternatives, 1977. 74 p. ; 30 cm. Bibliography: p. 74. LC Card 81-118524
1. United Nations - Economic assistance. I. International Foundation for Development Alternatives. II. Title.
HC60 .R539 1977

Risteau, Delores. The American Payroll Association's basic guide to payroll / by Delores Risteau. Paramus, N.J. : Prentice-Hall Information Services, c1986. iv, 251 p. : forms ; 24 cm. Includes index. ISBN 0-13-028242-1 (pbk.) LC Card 87-153688 DDC 658.3/21 19
1. Payrolls. I. American Payroll Association. II. Title. III. Title: Basic guide to payroll.
HG4028.P5 R57 1986

Ristic, Veselin. Profil de l'industrie québécoise des éléments d'architecture et de structure préfabriqués en béton / [préparé par Veselin Ristic]. [Québec] : Industrie Québec, c1983. 168 p. : ill. ; 28 cm. Bibliography: p. 81-82. LC Card 85-100163
1. Concrete products industry - Québec (Province). 2. Building materials industry - Québec (Province). I. Québec (Province). Direction générale de l'industrie. II. Title.
HD9622.C23 Q437 1983

Ritchken, Peter. Options : theory, strategy, and applications / Peter Ritchken. Glenview, Ill. : Scott, Foresman, c1987. xiii, 414 p. : ill. ; 24 cm. Includes bibliographies and index. ISBN 0-673-18307-6 (pbk.) LC Card 86-29721 DDC 332.64/52 19
1. Put and call transactions - Mathematical models. I. Title.
HG6042 .R57 1987

Rites of passage at $100,000+ . Lucht, John, 1933- New York , c1988. ix, 547 p. ; ISBN 0-942785-07-X : LC Card 87-50459 DDC 658.4/09 19
HD38.25.U6 L83 1988

Ritoók, Pálné. Személyiségfejlesztés és pályaválasztás / Ritoók Pálné. Budapest : Tankönyvkiadó, 1986. 192 p. ; 20 cm. (Korszerű nevelés, 0324-704X) Bibliography: p. 185-192. ISBN 963-17-8713-3 : LC Card 87-408516
1. Vocational guidance. I. Title. II. Series.
HF5381 .R635 1986

Il ritorno del gigante /. Scheggi Merlini, Lorenzo, 1944- Milano, Italy , c1985. 140 p. ; LC Card 86-137491 DDC 331.88/0945 19
HD6709 .S39 1985

Rittaler, Jan B. Schmidt, Ingo. Die Chicago School of Antitrust Analysis . Baden-Baden , 1986. 119 p. : ISBN 3-7890-1285-8 LC Card 87-409043 DDC 330.15/6 19
HB98.3 .S35 1986

Ritter, Wigand.
Arabian gulf studies /. Nürnberg , 1985- v. <1 > : LC Card 86-205380 DDC 330.953/053 19
HC415.3 .A7 1985

Qatar, ein arabisches Erdölemirat / Wigand Ritter. Nürnberg : Im Selbstverlag des Wirtschafts- und Sozialgeographischen Instituts der Friedrich-Alexander-Universität, 1985. 201 p. : ill. ; 21 cm. (Nürnberger wirtschafts- und sozialgeographische Arbeiten, 0546-9112 . Bd. 38) Summary in English. Bibliography: p. 193-197. LC Card 86-205396
1. Qatar - Economic conditions. 2. Economic development projects - Qatar. 3. Urbanization - Qatar. 4. Self-organizing systems. I. Title. II. Series.
HC415.37 .R58 1985

Ritzer, George. Working, conflict and change / George Ritzer, David Walczak. 3rd ed. Englewood Cliffs, N.J. : Prentice-Hall, c1986. xii, 451 p. ; 24 cm. Includes bibliographical references and indexes. ISBN 0-13-967589-2 : LC Card 85-28135 DDC 306/.36/0973 19
1. Industrial sociology - United States. 2. Labor and laboring classes - United States. 3. United States - Occupations. I. Walczak, David, 1950-. II. Title.
HD6957.U6 R5 1986 ***NYPL [JLE 86-3160]***

Riuso e riqualificazione edilizia negli anni '80 / a cura di C. Di Biase ... [et al.] ; [scritti] di L.B. Belgiojoso ... [et al.]. Milano : F. Angeli, [1981] 706 p. :ill. ; 22 cm. (Collana di studi urbani e regionali. 25) Includes bibliographical references. ISBN 88-20-42135-6 (pbk.) : LC Card 81-210070
1. Housing rehabilitation - Italy - Addresses, essays, lectures. 2. Buildings - Italy - Conservation and restoration - Addresses, essays, lectures. 3. Buildings - Italy - Remodeling for other use - Addresses, essays, lectures. I. Di Biase, C. (Carolina). II. Belgiojoso, L. B. (Lodovico Barbiano), 1909-.
HD7341.A3 R58 1981 ***NYPL [JSD 86-493]***

Riv pyramiderna! . Carlzon, Jan. [Stockholm] , c19. 219 p. : ISBN 91-0-046844-4 LC Card 86-139896
HE9860.S28 C375 1986

Riva, Alberto. Scelte strategiche e riorganizzazione aziendale . Milano, Italy , c1985. 312 p. ; LC Card 86-146459
HD2864 .S36 1985 ***NYPL [JLD 87-1549]***

Rivalry . Brenner, Reuven. Cambridge , New York , 1987. xi, 244 p. ; ISBN 0-521-33187-0 LC Card 86-24415 DDC 338.6/048 19
HD41 .B743 1987

River Associates. see **Charles River Associates.**

River (Charles) Associates. see **Charles River Associates.**

RIVER FRONTS. see **WATERFRONTS.**

River Transportation Seminar (1986 : Iquitos, Peru) Tratado de cooperación amazónica : seminario realizado en la ciudad de Iquitos, Peru, del 18 al 21 de marzo de 1986, en el ámbito del Tratado de cooperación amazónica. Washington, D.C. : Secretaría Ejecutiva para Asuntos Económicos y Sociales, Departamento de Desarrollo Regional, 1986. iii, 110 p. ; 23 cm. English, Portuguese and Spanish. Spine title: TCA, Seminario sobre Transporte Fluvial. ISBN 0-8270-2473-8 (pbk.) LC Card 87-115058
1. Shipping - Amazon River Region - Congresses. I. Organization of American States. Dept. of Regional Development. II. Title. III. Title: TCA, Seminario sobre Transporte Fluvial.
HE387.A6 R58 1986

Rivera Castro, José. Los Sindicatos nacionales en el México contemporáneo /. [México, D.F.] , 1986- v. <1 > ; ISBN 968-498-020-5 (set) LC Card 87-401211 DDC 331.88/0972 19
HD6532 .S55 1986

Rivera Cusicanqui, Silvia. Política e ideología en el movimiento campesino colombiano : el caso de la ANUC (Asociación Nacional de Usuarios Campesinos) / Silvia Rivera Cusicanqui. [Bogotá] : CINEP ; [s.l.] : United Nations Research Institute for Social Development, 1982. 188 p. ; 22 cm. (Colección agraria . 7) Bibliography: p. 183-188. LC Card 84-155496
1. Asociación Nacional de Usuarios Campesinos (Colombia). 2. Peasantry - Colombia - Political activity. 3. Agriculture and state - Colombia. 4. Rural

development - Colombia. I. Series: Colombia agraria , 7. II. Title.
HD511.5.A87 R58 1982
NYPL [JLD 86-1208]

Rivera, Eugenio. Centroamérica, política económica y crisis / Eugenio Rivera Urrutia, Ana Sojo, José Roberto López. San José, Costa Rica : ICADIS : DEI, c1986. 201 p. : ill. ; 21 cm. (Colección universitaria) Includes bibliographical references. ISBN 997-7904-37-5 LC Card 87-404079 DDC 338.9728 19
1. Central America - Economic policy. 2. Central America - Economic conditions - 1979-. I. Sojo, Ana, 1954-. II. López, José Roberto. III. Series: Colección universitaria (San José, Costa Rica). IV. Title.
HC141 .R58 1986

Rivera P., Alberto.
Calderón G., Fernando. La Cancha . [Cochabamba, Bolivia] , 1984. 208 p. : LC Card 85-238895
HF5473.B62 C363 1984

Calderón G., Fernando. Jatun Llajta . La Paz, Bolivia , 1982. v, 448 p., [8] leaves of plates : LC Card 83-111937 DDC 381/.1 19
HF5473.B62 C623 1982
NYPL [JLF 86-1794]

Rivera Ríos, Miguel Angel. Crisis y reorganización del capitalismo mexicano, 1960-1985 / Miguel Angel Rivera Ríos. 1a ed. México, D.F. : Ediciones Era, 1986. 227 p. : ill. ; 20 cm. (Colección Problemas de México) Bibliography: p. 198-227. ISBN 968-411-149-5 LC Card 87-401541 DDC 330.972/083 19
1. Mexico - Economic conditions - 1970-. 2. Capitalism - Mexico. 3. Mexico - Economic policy 1970-. I. Series: Colección Problemas de México (Ediciones Era). II. Title.
HC135 .R435 1986

Rivera V., Fredy (Rivera Vélez) Campesinado y organización en Esmeraldas /. [Quito, Ecuador?] [1986] 213 p. : LC Card 86-171561
HD1531.E2 C36 1986

RIVERFRONTS. see **WATERFRONTS.**

Riveros C., Luis. Structural reforms and wage setting across sectors : a test of the Chilean labor market efficiency / Luis Riveros C. Santiago : Departamento de Economía, Universidad de Chile, 1984. 37, [5], 13 p. ; 27 cm. (Documento Serie investigación . no. 66) Bibliography: p. [38]-[39]
1. Labor supply - Chile. 2. Wages - Chile. I. Title. II. Title: Test of the Chilean labor market efficiency. III. Series.
NYPL [JLF 87-136]

RIVERS - ENGLAND.
Atterbury, Paul. English rivers and canals /. London , 1984. 152 p. : ISBN 0-297-78318-1
NYPL [JFF 87-598]

RIVERS - ITALY - REGULATION - CONGRESSES.
Convegno nazionale "Qualche idea sui fiumi" (1983 : Iesi, Italy) Atti del Convegno nazionale "Qualche idea sui fiumi," Jesi, aprile 1983. Ancona , c1983-c1984. 2 v. ; ISBN 88-7663-030-9 (v. 1) : LC Card 84-119835
HD1697.I8 C62 1983 NYPL [JLK 87-40]

RIVERS - POLLUTION. see **WATER - POLLUTION.**

Rivière, Jean, professeur. Les Etats-Unis à l'horizon de la troisième révolution industrielle / Jean Rivière. Nancy : Presses universitaires de Nancy, c1986. 207 p. : ill. ; 24 cm. Bibliography: p. 192-203. ISBN 2-86480-174-4 LC Card 86-202607
1. United States - Economic conditions - 1981-. 2. United States - Industries. I. Title.
HC106.8 .R57 1986

Rivista trimestrale (Turin, Italy : 1985). N. 1-2, 1986 (Supplement) Mancini, Andrea, 1954- La contabilità analitica dei costi . [Torino] , 1986. 53 p. : ISBN 88-85851-00-2 : LC Card 87-114718
HF5686.C8 M265 1986

Rivlin, Alice M. The Swedish economy /. Washington, D.C. , c1987. xvi, 338 p. : ISBN 0-8157-1042-9 : LC Card 86-29920 DDC 330.9485/058 19
HC375 .S977 1987

Rizos, Kōstas. Hodēgos tachydromikōn tomeōn Athēnōn /. Athēnai [1962] 124 p. : LC Card 86-234916
HE7180.5.Z7 A744 1962

Rizzieri, Juarez Alexandre Baldini.
Desenvolvimento econômico e urbanização : produtividade das cidades e custos de serviços públicos por ordem de tamanho urbano / Juarez Alexandre Baldini Rizzieri. São Paulo : Instituto de Pesquisas Econômicas, 1982. 219 p. : ill. ; 21 cm. (Série Ensaios econômicos . no. 18) Originally presented as the author's thesis (doctoral--Universidade de São Paulo, 1980) under the title: Estrutura urbana, produtividade e custos de urbanização. Bibliography: p. [213]-219. LC Card 83-150574 DDC 330.9173/2 19
1. Industries, Location of. 2. Central places. 3. Municipal services - Finance. I. Series: Ensaios econômicos (Universidade de São Paulo. Instituto de Pesquisas Econômicas) , 18. II. Title.
HT321 .R59 1982 NYPL [JLD 86-3817]

Rizzo, Michael R. How to make profits with service contracts / Michael R. Rizzo. New York, NY : American Management Association, c1987. xii, 367 p. ; 26 cm. Includes index. ISBN 0-8144-5807-6 LC Card 86-47590 DDC 658 19
1. Service industries - Management. 2. Contracts for work and labor. I. Title.
HD9980.5 .R59 1987

Rizzo, Sócrates. Opciones de política económica, 1979-1982 / por Sócrates Rizzo y Leopoldo Solís. México, D.F. : Banco de México, Subdirección de Investigación Económica : Edición y distribución, Oficina de Divulgación, [1983] 133 p. : ill. ; 28 cm. (Serie Documentos de investigación . documento no. 12) "Septiembre, 1979." An edition of 400 copies. LC Card 86-205260 DDC 338.972 19
1. Mexico - Economic policy 1970-. I. Solís M., Leopoldo. II. Title. III. Series.
HC135 .R44 1983

Rječnik terminologije jugoslavenskog političko-ekonomskog sistema . Andrlić, Vlasta. Zagreb , 1985. viii, 135 p. ; LC Card 86-182784
HB61 .A55 1985 NYPL [*QKK 87-1803]

Roach, Thomas R. Gillis, R. Peter. Lost initiatives . New York , 1986. 326 p. : ISBN 0-313-25415-X (lib. bdg. : alk. paper) LC Card 86-3122 DDC 333.75/0971 19
HD9764.C3 G55 1986 NYPL [JLE 87-947]

ROAD ACCIDENTS. see **TRAFFIC ACCIDENTS.**

ROAD BUILDING. see **ROAD CONSTRUCTION.**

ROAD CONSTRUCTION - AMAZON RIVER REGION - CONGRESSES.
Tratado de cooperación amazónica . Washington, D.C. , 1986. iii, 101 p. ; ISBN 0-8270-2304-9 (pbk.) LC Card 86-152493
HE359.A5 T73 1986

ROAD CONSTRUCTION - FINANCE.
Ludlow, Nicholas H. The Development Bank highways market, 1987-1991 . Washington, D.C., USA (1735 Eye St., NW, Suite 710, Washington 20006) , c1987. 387, 2 p. : LC Card 87-71066 DDC 388.1/14 19
HG3881 .L737 1987

ROAD CONSTRUCTION - GERMANY (WEST) - CONGRESSES.
Deutscher Strassenkongress (1984 : Mannheim, Germany) Deutscher Strassenkongress, Mannheim, 1984 /. Köln [1985?] 255 p. : LC Card 87-408263 DDC 388.1/0943 19
HE363.G3 D48 1984

ROAD CONSTRUCTION - GERMANY (WEST) - STATISTICS.
Strassenbau und Mineralölindustrie im Spiegel der Statistik . Hamburg , 1976. [48] p. : LC Card 83-126399
HD9582.A7 G37 1976

ROAD CONSTRUCTION INDUSTRY - RUSSIAN S.F.S.R.
Busurin, K. A. Nauchnaia͡ organizatsii͡a truda v dorozhnom khozi͡aĭstve /. Moskva , 1981. 159 p. ; LC Card 87-461013
HD9717.5.R63 S653 1981

ROAD CONSTRUCTION - TEXAS - COST EFFECTIVENESS.
McFarland, William F. New approaches to project ranking . College Station, Tex. , Springfield, Va. [1985] xvii, 116 p. : LC Card 86-622422 DDC 380.5 s 388.1/12/09764 19
HE203 .T43 no. 337-1F HE356.T4

ROAD CONSTRUCTION WORKERS - INDIA - ANDHRA PRADESH.
Andhra Pradesh (India). Finance and Planning (Planning Wing) Dept. Evaluation Wing. Evaluation study on the working of crash scheme for rural employment. Hyderabad , 1983. 89 p. : LC Card 86-144139 DDC 331.12/042/095484 19
HD5710.85.I42 A532 1983

ROAD CONSTRUCTION WORKERS - RUSSIAN S.F.S.R.
Busurin, K. A. Nauchnaia͡ organizatsii͡a truda v dorozhnom khozi͡aĭstve /. Moskva , 1981. 159 p. ; LC Card 87-461013
HD9717.5.R63 S653 1981

ROAD CONSTRUCTION WORKERS - UNITED STATES - CLASSIFICATION - CODE NUMBERS.
Classification guide for street and road construction /. New York, NY , c1986. 44 p. : LC Card 86-232165 DDC 368.4/1 19
HD7116.R62 U63 1986

ROAD MARKINGS.
McNees, Roger W. State-of-the-art and objectives of reflective raised pavement markers /. College Station, Tex. , Springfield, Va. [1986] vii, 162 p. : LC Card 87-620643 DDC 380.5 s 625.7/97 19
HE203 .T43 no. 322-1 TE203

Noel, James S. Retention of reflective raised pavement markers /. College Station, Tex. , Springfield, Va. [1986] xiii, 170 p. : LC Card 87-620642 DDC 380.5 s 625.7/042 19
HE203 .T43 no. 322-3 TE203

Road passenger transport in India /. Patankar, P. G. Pune [1985?] xi, 226 p., [4] p. of plates : LC Card 85-905215 DDC 388/.042/0954 19
HE365.I43 B86 1985 NYPL [JLE 86-4230]

ROAD SIGNS. see **TRAFFIC SIGNS AND SIGNALS.**

The road to revolution in Spain . Shubert, Adrian, 1953- Urbana , c1987. 183 p. : ISBN 0-252-01368-9 (alk. paper) LC Card 86-24998 DDC 331.7/622334/094615 19
HD8039.M62 S68 1987

ROAD TRAFFIC. see **TRAFFIC ENGINEERING.**

Road Traffic Safety Research Council (N.Z.)
Road Traffic Safety Seminar (1984 : Wellington, N.Z.) Road Traffic Safety Seminar, 15-17 August, 1984 . Wellington, N.Z. [1985?] 2 v. : LC Card 87-101217 DDC 363.1/25/09931 19
HE5614.5.N45 R62 1984

Road Traffic Safety Seminar, 15-17 August, 1984 . Road Traffic Safety Seminar (1984 : Wellington, N.Z.) Wellington, N.Z. [1985?] 2 v. : LC Card 87-101217 DDC 363.1/25/09931 19
HE5614.5.N45 R62 1984

Road Traffic Safety Seminar (1984 : Wellington, N.Z.) Road Traffic Safety Seminar, 15-17 August, 1984 : seminar papers. Wellington, N.Z. : Road Traffic Safety Research Council, [1985?] 2 v. : ill. ; 30 cm. Includes bibliographies. LC Card 87-101217 DDC 363.1/25/09931 19
1. Traffic safety - New Zealand - Congresses. 2. Traffic safety - Congresses. I. Road Traffic Safety Research Council (N.Z.). II. Title.
HE5614.5.N45 R62 1984

Road transport passenger policy issues / Office of the President and Cabinet, Economic Planning Division. [Lilongwe, Malawi] : The Division, [1984] i, 22 leaves : 2 ill. ; 30 cm. (Economic policy review paper . 1st issue (1984)) On cover: Malaŵi Government. LC Card 86-980328 DDC 388.3/22/096897 19
1. Bus lines - Government policy - Malawi. I. Malawi. Economic Planning Division. II. Series: Economic policy review paper , 1st issue.
HE5705.A6 R6 1984

Road transport research.
Co-ordinated urban transport pricing . Paris [Washington, D.C.] 1985. 151 p. : ISBN 92-64-12692-9 (pbk.) : LC Card 86-125699 DDC 388.4/042 19
HE305 .C58 1985

Effectiveness of road safety education programmes . Paris [Washington, D.C.] 1986.

134 p. : ISBN 92-64-12881-6 : LC Card 87-119891 DDC 363.1/2575/07 19
HE5613.5 .E33 1986

OECD road safety research . Paris [Washington, D.C.] 1986. 106 p. : ISBN 92-64-12814-X (pbk.) : LC Card 86-212506 DDC 363.1/25 19
HE5614 .O34 1986

Technico-economic analysis of the role of road freight transport . Paris [Washington, D.C.] 1986. 135 p. : ISBN 92-64-12843-3 (pbk.) : LC Card 86-215619 DDC 388.3/24 19
HE5611 .T43 1986

ROAD TRANSPORTATION. see **TRANSPORTATION, AUTOMOTIVE.**

Roadmap for change. Part II, The Deming legacy [motion picture] / Chicago, Ill. : Encyclopaedia Britannica Educational Corp., 1987. 1 film reel (28 min.) : sd., col. ; 16 mm. + 1 teacher's guide. Title from data sheet. Adults. Issued also as videorecording. Shows methods used by W. Edwards Deming to improve quality and productivity at the Pontiac Fiero plant. Explains how his philosophy has been accepted and how the plant's managers and workers have responded to the challenges of innovation and problem solving. LC Card 87-705133 DDC 658 11
1. Deming, W. Edwards (William Edwards), 1900-. 2. General Motors Corporation. Pontiac Motor Division. 3. Automobile industry and trade - United States - Management - Case studies. I. Chuck Olin Associates. II. Encyclopaedia Britannica Educational Corporation. III. Title: Deming legacy.
HD9710

ROADS - ALASKA - RIGHT OF WAY.
Roberts, Malcolm B. Senate Transportation Committee, RS 2477 Task Force report /. [Anchorage, Alaska] [1986] 121 leaves, 27 p. : LC Card 86-622718 DDC 333.78/09798 19
HE356.A4 R63 1986

ROADS - AUSTRIA - TYROL - HISTORY.
Forcher, Michael. Felbertauern . Thaur/Tirol [1982] 152 p. : ISBN 3-85395-044-2 LC Card 86-166479
HE363.A94 F454 1982

Zwanowetz, Georg. Das Strassenwesen Tirols seit der Eröffnung der Eisenbahn Innsbruck-Kufstein (1858) . Innsbruck , 1986. 163 p., 32 leaves of plates : ISBN 3-7030-0165-8 LC Card 87-142160 DDC 388.1/09436/42 19
HE247.Z7 T99 1986

ROADS - BASE COURSES - TESTING.
Roberts, Freddy L. Establishing material properties for thin asphalt concrete surfaces on granular bases /. College Station, Tex. [1985] xvi, 141 p. : LC Card 86-620971 DDC 380.5 s 625.8/5 19
HE203 .T43 no. 345-1 TE270

ROADS - BRAZIL - HISTORY.
Oliveira, Maria Chambarelli de. Achegas à história do rodoviarismo no Brasil /. Rio de Janeiro-RJ , c1986. 137 p., [1] leaf of plates : LC Card 86-232581
HE359.B7 O45 1986

ROADS - BURUNDI - CASE STUDIES.
Groupement Berger-BCEOM. Etude de factibilité routière, Bujumbura-Cibitoke . [[Bujumbura] [1977] 162 p. : LC Card 82-980356
HE367.B872 G76 1977a

ROADS - CONSTRUCTION. see **ROAD CONSTRUCTION.**

ROADS - ECONOMIC ASPECTS - AUSTRALIA.
Abelson, P. W. The economic evaluation of roads in Australia /. Mosman, N.S.W. , 1986. xi, 144 p. : ISBN 0-949416-06-1 (pbk.) : LC Card 87-142110 DDC 388.1/0994 19
HE368.Z55 E33 1986

ROADS - ECONOMIC ASPECTS - KENYA.
Shimeles Asfaw. The economic evaluation of low traffic roads . [Nairobi? , 1980?] ii, 28, 13 leaves, [2] leaves of plates : LC Card 85-981138
HE367.K43 E374 1980

ROADS - ENGLAND - HISTORY.
Hindle, Brian Paul. Medieval roads /. Aylesbury, Bucks, UK , 1982. 62 p. : ISBN 0-85263-600-8 (pbk.) : LC Card 83-228901 DDC 388.1/0942 19
HE363.G72 H56 1982 ***NYPL [JLD 86-1755]***

ROADS - ESTIMATES - SOUTH CAROLINA.
1984 needs vs. funds expected to be available July 1983 through September 1990. [Columbia, S.C.] [1984] [49] leaves ; LC Card 86-622435 DDC 388.1/14/09757 19
HE356 .A57 1984

ROADS - FRANCE - HISTORY.
Reverdy, Georges. Histoire des grandes liaisons françaises /. Paris, France , c1981-c1982. 2 v. : LC Card 83-129286
HE363.F7 R48 1981

ROADS - GERMANY, WEST.
Sack, Manfred, 1928- Lebensraum . Bonn , 1982. 81 p. : ISBN 3-922153-01-1 LC Card 85-128580
HE363.G3 S23 1982

ROADS - GERMANY (WEST) - CONGRESSES.
Deutscher Strassenkongress (1984 : Mannheim, Germany) Deutscher Strassenkongress, Mannheim, 1984 /. Köln [1985?] 255 p. : LC Card 87-408263 DDC 388.1/0943 19
HE363.G3 D48 1984

ROADS - GERMANY (WEST) - INTERCHANGES AND INTERSECTIONS.
Kockelke, Wilhelm. Untersuchung der Vorfahrtregelung "Rechts vor Links" unter dem Aspekt der Verkehrssicherheit /. Bergisch Gladbach [1983] 63, 3 p. : LC Card 84-147884
HE363.G32 U744 1983

ROADS - GERMANY (WEST) - RIGHT OF WAY.
Kockelke, Wilhelm. Untersuchung der Vorfahrtregelung "Rechts vor Links" unter dem Aspekt der Verkehrssicherheit /. Bergisch Gladbach [1983] 63, 3 p. : LC Card 84-147884
HE363.G32 U744 1983

ROADS - GOVERNMENT POLICY - KENYA.
Shimeles Asfaw. The economic evaluation of low traffic roads . [Nairobi? , 1980?] ii, 28, 13 leaves, [2] leaves of plates : LC Card 85-981138
HE367.K43 E374 1980

ROADS - GOVERNMENT POLICY - NEW YORK (STATE)
Feigenbaum, Todd R. New York's highway system . Albany, N.Y. (150 State St., Albany 12207) [1986] 2, iv, 130 p. : LC Card 87-620939 DDC 388.1/09747 19
HE356.N7 F45 1986

New York (State). Legislature. Legislative Commission on Critical Transportation Choices. CHIPS, the Consolidated Local Street and Highway Improvement Program . [Albany, N.Y.] [1986] i, 18 leaves ; LC Card 87-620568 DDC 388.1/12 19
HE356.N7 N37 1986

ROADS - GOVERNMENT POLICY - UNITED STATES - HISTORY - 20TH CENTURY.
St. Clair, David James, 1950- The motorization of American cities /. New York , 1986. xi, 192 p. ; ISBN 0-275-92126-3 (alk. paper) : LC Card 86-523 DDC 388.4/1321/0973 19
HE5623 .S617 1986 ***NYPL [JLE 86-3608]***

ROADS - GUARD FENCES.
(1985) Sicking, Dean. Roadside concrete barriers . College Station, Tex. , Springfield, Va. [1985] vii, 60, 64, [51] p. : LC Card 86-622864 DDC 380.5 s 625.7/95 19
HE203 .T43 no. 346-1F TE228

ROADS - HUNGARY.
Az Ország közuthálózatának müszaki minősitése és nyilvántartása /. [Budapest] , 1983. 2 v. : LC Card 84-253458
HE363.H82 O76 1983

ROADS - HUNGARY - EVALUATION.
Az Ország közuthálózatának müszaki minősitése és nyilvántartása /. [Budapest] , 1983. 2 v. : LC Card 84-253458
HE363.H82 O76 1983

ROADS - INTERCHANGES AND INTERSECTIONS.
Leisch, Jack E. Capacity analysis techniques for signalized intersections /. Washington, D.C., USA (525 School St., S.W., Suite 410, Washington 20024-2729) , c1986. 46 p. : LC Card 86-212242 DDC 388.3/14 19
HE336.H48 L45 1986

ROADS - KENYA - KISII DISTRICT.
Rural access roads programme . Nairobi [1976- v. : LC Card 86-981034
HE367.K43 R8576 1976

ROADS - MAINTENANCE AND REPAIR - BOTSWANA.
Botswana Transport Sector I (Road Maintenance) (633-0073). [Botswana? , 1979?] 1 v. (various pagings) : LC Card 86-148788
HE367.B652 B67 1979

ROADS - MAINTENANCE AND REPAIR - GOVERNMENT POLICY - NEW YORK (STATE)
New York (State). Legislature. Legislative Commission on Critical Transportation Choices. CHIPS, the Consolidated Local Street and Highway Improvement Program . [Albany, N.Y.] [1986] i, 18 leaves ; LC Card 87-620568 DDC 388.1/12 19
HE356.N7 N37 1986

ROADS - MALAWI - STATISTICS.
Inventory of designated roads in Malaŵi, 1983. [Lilongwe, Malawi] , 1984. i, 57 leaves : LC Card 86-980326 DDC 388.1/096897 19
HE367.M32 I58 1984

ROADS - NEVADA.
1985 log, federal-aid urban routes /. Carson City, Nev. [1984] iii leaves, 165 p. ; LC Card 86-622235 DDC 388.4/042 19
HE356.N37 A17 1984

ROADS - NEVADA - FINANCE.
Nevada. Legislature. Legislative Commission. Study of the fees and taxes which produce revenue for the construction and maintenance of the highways. [Carson City, Nev.] [1986] viii, 74 p. ; LC Card 86-623141 DDC 388.1/14/09793 19
HE356.N37 N42 1986

ROADS - NEVADA - STATISTICS.
Log of the federal-aid interstate system comprising the Nevada primary state highway system, 1985 /. Carson City, Nev. [Washington] [1985] 41 leaves ; LC Card 86-622234 DDC 388.1/09793 19
HE356.N37 L632 1985

ROADS - NEW JERSEY.
New Jersey. Legislature. General Assembly. Transportation, Communications & High Technology Committee. Public hearing before the Assembly Transportation, Communications & High Technology Committee on transportation infrastructure . [Trenton, N.J.] [1986]. 95 p. ;
NYPL [JLF 86-1583]

ROADS - NEW YORK (STATE)
Feigenbaum, Todd R. New York's highway system . Albany, N.Y. (150 State St., Albany 12207) [1986] 2, iv, 130 p. : LC Card 87-620939 DDC 388.1/09747 19
HE356.N7 F45 1986

ROADS - NEW YORK (STATE) - FINANCE.
New York's highway system . Albany, N.Y. , 1986. S-2, iv, 130 p. : ***NYPL [JLD 86-2346]***

ROADS - NORTH DAKOTA - FINANCE.
Federal, state, and local highway financing /. Bismarck, N.D. [1986] 33 leaves : LC Card 87-620924 DDC 388.1/14/09784 19
HE356.N9 F42 1986

ROADS - OREGON - FINANCE.
Making the right turn . [Salem? Or.] [1986] iv, 39 p. : LC Card 87-621891 DDC 388.1/14/09795 19
HE356.O7 M35 1986

ROADS, ROMAN - FRANCE.
Roman, Yves. De Narbonne à Bordeaux . Lyon , c1983. 333 p. : ISBN 2-7297-0200-8 : LC Card 84-179554
HF377 .R65 1983

ROADS - SAFETY MEASURES - CONGRESSES.
International Seminar on "Road Safety" (1986 : Srinagar, India) International Seminar on "Road Safety", Srinagar, September 17-18, 1986 /. New Delhi [1986] 1 v. (various pagings) : LC Card 87-901986 DDC 363.1/25 19
HE5614 .I5717 1986

ROADS - SIGNS. see **TRAFFIC SIGNS AND SIGNALS.**

ROADS - SOCIAL ASPECTS - UNITED STATES.
Patton, Phil. Open road . New York , c1986. 304 p. : ISBN 0-671-53021-6 : LC Card 86-1832

DDC 388.1/0973 19
HE355 .P38 1986 ***NYPL [JLE 86-2812]***

ROADS - SOUTH CAROLINA - FINANCE.
1984 needs vs. funds expected to be available July 1983 through September 1990. [Columbia, S.C.] [1984] [49] leaves ; LC Card 86-622435 DDC 388.1/14/09757 19
HE356 .A57 1984

ROADS - SPAIN - CASTILLA Y LEÓN.
Pastor Antolín, Luis J., 1958- La red de transporte en Castilla y León /. Valladolid [1986?] 161 p. : ISBN 84-86047-71-4 LC Card 86-231524
HE363.S64 C376 1986

ROADS - SWITZERLAND.
Studer, Stefan. Nationalstrasse, Nationalstrafe, oder, Die Demokratie bleibt auf der Strecke /. Zürich , 1985. 191 p. : ISBN 3-85869-037-6 : LC Card 86-129406
HE363.S92 S83 1985

ROADS - TEXAS - COST EFFECTIVENESS.
McFarland, William F. New approaches to project ranking . College Station, Tex. , Springfield, Va. [1985] xvii, 116 p. : LC Card 86-622422 DDC 380.5 s 388.1/12/09764 19
HE203 .T43 no. 337-1F HE356.T4

ROADS, TOLL. see **TOLL ROADS.**

ROADS - TOLLS. see **TOLL ROADS.**

ROADS - TRAFFIC SIGNS. see **TRAFFIC SIGNS AND SIGNALS.**

ROADS - UNITED STATES - FINANCE.
Federal, state, and local highway financing /. Bismarck, N.D. [1986] 33 leaves : LC Card 87-620924 DDC 388.1/14/09784 19
HE356.N9 F42 1986

Highway finance . [Washington] [1983] iii, 96 p. ; ***NYPL [JLF 87-431]***

ROADS - UNITED STATES - HISTORY.
Patton, Phil. Open road . New York , c1986. 304 p. : ISBN 0-671-53021-6 : LC Card 86-1832 DDC 388.1/0973 19
HE355 .P38 1986 ***NYPL [JLE 86-2812]***

ROADS - WALES - HISTORY.
Hindle, Brian Paul. Medieval roads /. Aylesbury, Bucks, UK , 1982. 62 p. : ISBN 0-85263-600-8 (pbk.) : LC Card 83-228901 DDC 388.1/0942 19
HE363.G72 H56 1982 ***NYPL [JLD 86-1755]***

Roadside concrete barriers . Sicking, Dean. College Station, Tex. , Springfield, Va. [1985] vii, 60, 64, [51] p. : LC Card 86-622864 DDC 380.5 s 625.7/95 19
HE203 .T43 no. 346-1F TE228

ROADSIDE TRAFFIC SIGNS. see **TRAFFIC SIGNS AND SIGNALS.**

Robbins, Bradley. Economic development in a conscious state : a growth management perspective / by Bradley Robbins. Tallahassee, Fla. : Select Committee on Growth Management, Florida House of Representatives, [1984] viii, 41, [5] p. : ill. ; 28 cm. "September 1984." Bibliography: p. [43]-[46] LC Card 86-621090 DDC 338.9759 19
1. Florida - Economic conditions. 2. Florida - Economic policy. 3. Environmental policy - Florida. I. Florida. Legislature. House of Representatives. Select Committee on Growth Management. II. Title.
HC107.F6 R63 1984

Robbins, Diana. Little, Alan. Loading the law . London , 1982. 67 p. ; ISBN 0-902355-98-8 (pbk.) ***NYPL [JLD 87-1941]***

Robbins, Linda. Hassan, Zuhair A. Handbook of food expenditures, prices, and consumption /. Ottawa , c1983. 270 p., [2] p. of plates : LC Card 86-228246 DDC 339.4/8664/00971 19
HD9014.C3 H29 1983

Robbins, Stephen P., 1943-
DeCenzo, David A. Personnel/human resource management. Englewood Cliffs, N.J. , c1988. xvii, 637 p. : ISBN 0-13-657198-0 LC Card 87-6983 DDC 658.3 19
HF5549 .D396 1988

Essentials of organizational behavior / Stephen P. Robbins. 2nd ed. Englewood Cliffs, N.J. : Prentice-Hall, c1988. p. cm. Includes index. ISBN 0-13-286485-1 LC Card 87-19876 DDC 658.3 19
1. Organizational behavior. I. Title.
HD58.7 .R6 1988

Robbins, Walter A. Ingram, Robert W. Financial reporting practices of local governments /. Stamford, Conn. (P.O. Box 3821, Stamford 06905-0821) , c1987. viii, 93 p. : LC Card 87-80564 DDC 657/.835 19
HJ9777.A3 I55 1987

Robek, Mary F. Information and records management / Mary F. Robek, Gerald F. Brown, Wilmer O. Maedke. 3rd ed. Encino, Calif. : Glencoe Pub. Co., c1987. vi, 580 p. : ill. ; 24 cm. Rev. ed. of: Information and records management / Wilmer O. Maedke. 2nd ed. c1981. ISBN 0-02-820590-1 LC Card 87-135683 DDC 651.5 19
1. Business records - Management. 2. Information storage and retrieval systems - Business. I. Maedke, Wilmer O. Information and records management. II. Brown, Gerald F. III. Title.
HF5736 .R53 1987

Röber, Manfred, 1947- Fleischer, Manfred. Organisationstheoretische Analyse von Marketing-Entscheidungsprozessen . Berlin [1977] 93 p. : LC Card 85-111320
HF5415.135 .F58 1977

ROBERT BOSCH GMBH - HISTORY.
Herdt, Hans Konradin, 1935- Bosch, 1886-1986 . [Stuttgart] [1986] 174 p., [88] p. of plates : ISBN 3-421-06324-9 LC Card 86-229723
HD9710.3.G44 R634 1986

Robert Cassen & Associates. Does aid work? . Oxford [Oxfordshire] , New York , 1986. xv, 381 p. ; ISBN 0-19-877250-5 : LC Card 86-12621 DDC 338.91/09172/4 19
HC60 .D53 1986 ***NYPL [JLE 86-4563]***

Robert Gerberg's job changing system . Gerberg, Robert J. [Job changing system.] Kansas City , c1986. xxii, 265 p. : ISBN 0-8362-7932-8 : LC Card 86-17298 DDC 650.1/4 19
NYPL [JD 87-125]

Robert Half's success guide for accountants /. Half, Robert. [Success guide for accountants.] New York , c1987. x, 167 p. ; ISBN 0-07-172107-X LC Card 87-16430 DDC 657/.023/72 19
HF5657 .H34 1987

Robert, Jacqueline. 1977 à 1982 : données sur l'industrie régionale / Jacqueline Robert. [Lyon] : Institut national de la statistique et des études économiques, Direction régionale de Lyon, [1985] 143 p. ; 21 x 30 cm. (Les Dossiers de l'INSEE Rhône-Alpes . no 24) "Juillet 1985." Chiefly tables. LC Card 86-187676
1. Rhône-Alpes (France) - Industries - Statistics. I. Title. II. Title: Données sur l'industrie régionale. III. Series.
HC277.R58 R62 1985

Robert Ley, Hitler's labor leader /. Smelser, Ronald, 1942- New York , 1988. p. cm. ISBN 0-85496-161-5 : LC Card 87-20960 DDC 331/.092/4 B 19
HD8453.L49 S64 1988

Robert, Michel, 1941- The strategist CEO : how visionary executives build organizations / Michel Robert. New York : Quorum Books, 1988. viii, 140 p. : ill. ; 25 cm. Bibliography: p. [135]-138. Includes index. ISBN 0-89930-268-8 (lib. bdg. : alk. paper) LC Card 87-10945 DDC 658.4/012 19
1. Strategic planning. 2. Organizational effectiveness. 3. Chief executive officers. I. Title.
HD30.28 .R63 1988

Robert Morris Associates.
Credit analysis . Philadelphia, Pa. , c1987. 146 p. : ISBN 0-936742-38-0 (pbk.) : LC Card 86-28628 DDC 332.1/753/0685 19
HG1641 .C66 1987

A Guide to the spreading and analysis of Japanese bank statements. Philadelphia, PA (1616 Philadelphia National Bank Bldg. Philadelphia 19107) , c1986. 60 p. ; LC Card 86-203674 DDC 657/.833 19
HG3324 .G85 1986

Pace, Edmond E. Developing a basic loan training program /. Philadelphia, Pa. , c1987. 108 p. ; ISBN 0-936742-41-0 (pbk.) : LC Card 87-7936 DDC 332.1/753/0683 19
HG1642.U5 P33 1987

Small business financing . Philadelphia, Pa. , c1987. 118 p. ; ISBN 0-936742-40-2 (pbk.) : LC Card 87-5534 DDC 332.1/753/0685 19
HG3754.5.U6 S6 1987

The Robert N. Anthony/Willard J. Graham series in accounting.
Engler, Calvin. Managerial accounting /. Homewood, Ill. , 1987. xvi, 926 p. : ISBN 0-256-03318-8 LC Card 86-81610 DDC 658.1/511 19
HF5657 .E54 1987

Hay, Leon Edwards, 1923- Essentials of accounting for governmental and not-for-profit organizations /. Homewood, Ill. , 1987. x, 310 p. ; ISBN 0-256-03454-0 (pbk.) LC Card 86-82587 DDC 657/.98 19
HJ9801 .H39 1987

Larson, Kermit D. Fundamental accounting principles /. Homewood, Ill. , 1987. xxxi, 1076 p. : ISBN 0-256-03574-1 LC Card 86-81958 DDC 657 19
HF5635 .P975 1987

Miller, Paul B. W. The FASB . Homewood, Ill. , 1986. xvi, 145 p. : ISBN 0-256-03520-2 LC Card 85-82340 ***NYPL [JLE 87-872]***

Welsch, Glenn A. Fundamentals of financial accounting /. Homewood, Ill. , 1987. xviii, 958 p. : ISBN 0-256-03614-4 LC Card 86-82802 DDC 657 19
HF5635 .W458 1987b

Robert Nicolait & Associates. Belize . Belize City, Belize , 1984. xvi, 151 p. : LC Card 86-136310 DDC 333.7/097282 19
HC142 .B447 1984 ***NYPL [JLF 87-170]***

Robert R. Nathan Associates. An Evaluation of ROCAP activities in marketing, 1965-71 /. Washington, D.C. (1200 18th St., N.W., Washington 20036) [1971] xvii, 82, 3 leaves, [1] leaf of plates : LC Card 81-146599
HC141 .E93 1971

Roberts, B. C. (Benjamin Charles), 1917-
Industrial relations in Europe . London , Dover, N.H. , c1985. ix, 277 p. ; ISBN 0-7099-4212-5 : LC Card 85-21321 DDC 331/.094 19
HD8376.5 .I54 1985 ***NYPL [JLD 86-1065]***

Roberts, C. W. (Colin William), 1916- A legacy from Victorian enterprise : the Briton Ferry Ironworks and the daughter companies / C.W. Roberts. [Farnborough, Berkshire?] : C.W. Roberts, 1983. x, 277 p. : ill. ; 22 cm. Includes index. Bibliography: p. 270-271. ISBN 0-9509107-1-6 (pbk.) : LC Card 85-109000 DDC 338.7/6691/0942984 19
1. Briton Ferry Ironworks - History. 2. Iron industry and trade - Wales - Briton Ferry (West Glamorgan) - History. 3. Iron industry and trade - Great Britain - History. I. Title.
HD9521.9.B74 R62 1983
NYPL [JLD 86-2141]

Roberts, Edward Baer. Generating technological innovation /. New York , 1987. xii, 299 p. : ISBN 0-19-505023-1 (alk. paper) LC Card 86-33119 DDC 658.5/14 19
HD45 .G39 1987

Roberts, Freddy L.
The Effect of tire pressures on flexible pavements /. College Station, Tex. , Springfield, Va. , 1985. viii, 235 p. : LC Card 86-622241 DDC 380.5 s 625.8 19
HE203 .T43 no. 372-1F TE270

Establishing material properties for thin asphalt concrete surfaces on granular bases / by Freddy L. Roberts and Barry T. Rosson ; conducted for State Department of Highways and Public Transportation in cooperation with the U. S. Department of Transportation, Federal Highway Administration by the Texas Transportation Institute, Texas A&M University. College Station, Tex. : The Institute, [1985] xvi, 141 p. : ill. ; 28 cm. (Research report (Texas Transportation Institute) . 345-1) "November, 1985." Bibliography: p. 85-86. "TTI-2-9-84-345-1"--Cover. LC Card 86-620971 DDC 380.5 s 625.8/5 19
1. Pavements, Asphalt concrete - Testing. 2. Roads - Base courses - Testing. 3. Pavements - Live loads. I. Rosson, Barry T. II. Texas Transportation Institute. III. Texas. State Dept. of Highways and Public Transportation. IV. United States. Federal Highway Administration. V. Series. VI. Series: Research report (Texas Transportation Institute) , 345-1.
HE203 .T43 no. 345-1 TE270

Roberts, G. W. (George W.) Provisional estimates of population movements in Bermuda to 1990 / by G.W. Roberts. Hamilton, Bermuda : Statistical Dept., Ministry of Finance, [198-?] 12, [8] p. : ill. ; 28 cm. "Prepared for the Statistical Office." LC Card 86-173218
1. Population forecasting - Bermuda Islands. 2. Bermuda Islands - Population. I. Bermuda Islands. Finance Ministry. Statistical Office. II. Title.
HB3668.A3 R63 1980z

Roberts, Ivan. Agricultural policies in the European Community . Canberra , 1985. xii, 373 p. : ISBN 0-644-04293-1 (pbk.) LC Card 86-673733
HD1920.5.Z8 A37x 1985

Roberts, Kenneth, 1940- School-leavers and their prospects : youth in the labour market in the 1980s / Kenneth Roberts. Milton Keynes : Open University Press, 1984. viii, 133 p. ; 23 cm. Bibliography: p. [116]-128. Includes index. ISBN 0-335-10418-5 (pbk.) LC Card 87-672221
1. Youth - Employment - Great Britain. 2. High school graduates - Employment - Great Britain. I. Title.
HD6276.G72 R62x 1984

Roberts, Malcolm B. Senate Transportation Committee, RS 2477 Task Force report / submitted by Malcolm B. Roberts and Valerie Tailman Chavez. [Anchorage, Alaska] : The Task Force, [1986] 121 leaves, 27 p. : ill., maps ; 28 cm. "January 17, 1986." LC Card 86-622718 DDC 333.78/09798 19
1. Trails - Alaska. 2. Roads - Alaska - Right of way. 3. National parks and reserves - Alaska. 4. Wildlife refuges - Alaska. I. Chavez, Valerie Taliman. II. Alaska. Legislature. Senate. Transportation Committee. RS 2477 Task Force. III. Title.
HE356.A4 R63 1986

Roberts, Richard. From Eden to Eros : origins of the put down of women / by Richard Roberts.1st ed. San Anselmo, Ca. : Vernal Equinox Press, 1985. 166 p. : ill. ; 22 cm. Bibliography: p. 162-166. ISBN 0-942380-05-3 (pbk.) LC Card 85-51722
1. Women - Psychology. 2. Women - Religion. 3. Identity (Psychology). I. Title.
NYPL [JLD 87-224]

Roberts, Richard L., 1949- Warriors, merchants, and slaves : the state and the economy in the Middle Niger Valley, 1700-1914 / Richard L. Roberts. Stanford, Calif. : Stanford University Press, 1987. xii, 293 p. : maps ; 23 cm. Originally presented as the author's thesis, University of Toronto, 1978. Bibliography: p. [250]-277. Includes index. ISBN 0-8047-1378-2 (alk. paper) : LC Card 86-23138 DDC 330.966/23 19
1. Mali - Economic conditions. 2. Niger River Valley - Economic conditions. 3. Mali - History. I. Title.
HC1035 .R63 1987

Roberts, William W. Johnson, Ivan C. Money and banking . Chicago , c1988. xix, 604 p. : ISBN 0-03-012518-9 LC Card 87-15002 DDC 332.1 19
HG221 .J667 1988

Robertson, A. F. The dynamics of productive relationships : African share contracts in comparative perspective / A.F. Robertson. Cambridge [Cambridgeshire] ; New York : Cambridge University Press, 1987. xix, 321 p. : ill. ; 24 cm. Includes index. Bibliography: p. [278]-311. ISBN 0-521-32834-9 LC Card 86-11801 DDC 333.33/5 19
1. Métayer system - Ghana. 2. Métayer system - Sudan. 3. Métayer system - Lesotho. 4. Métayer system - Senegal. 5. Métayer system - Gambia. I. Title.
HD1478.A35 R63 1987
NYPL [JLE 87-1299]

Robertson, Alex. The bleak midwinter, 1947 / Alex J. Robertson. Manchester, U.K. ; Wolfeboro, N.H., U. S.A. : Manchester University Press, 1987. x, 207 p. : ill. ; 24 cm. Bibliography: p. 197-199. Includes index. ISBN 0-7190-1902-8 : LC Card 87-11085 DDC 333.8/22/0941 19
1. Coal trade - Great Britain - History - 20th century. 2. Great Britain - Economic conditions - 1945-. 3. Great Britain - Social conditions - 1945-. 4. Reconstruction (1939-1951) - Great Britain. I. Title. II. Title: Bleak mid-winter, 1947.
HD9551.5 .R56 1987

Robertson, Dennis Holme, Sir, 1890-1963. Banking policy and the price level : an essay in the theory of the trade cycle / by D.H. Robertson. New York : A.M. Kelley, 1988. p. cm. (Reprints of economic classics) Reprint. Originally published: New York : A.M. Kelley, 1949. ISBN 0-678-00675-X LC Card 87-7140 DDC 338.5/42 19
1. Business cycles. 2. Prices. 3. Banks and banking. I. Title.
HB3725 .R63 1988

Robertson, James E., 1944- Sales, the whole body approach / James E. Robertson. Portland, Or. : Metamorphous Press, 1988. p. cm. Bibliography: p. ISBN 0-943920-78-7 : LC Card 87-24679 DDC 658.8/5 19
1. Selling - Psychological aspects. I. Title.
HF5438.8.P75 R63 1988

Robey, Daniel. Bjørn-Andersen, Niels. Managing computer impact . Norwood, N.J. , c1986. viii, 248 p. : ISBN 0-89391-358-8 LC Card 85-30754 DDC 658/.05 19
HD30.2 .B55 1986 ***NYPL [JLE 86-2806]***

Robins, David, 1944- We hate humans / David Robins. Harmondsworth, Middlesex, England ; New York, N.Y. : Penguin Books, 1984. 155 p. ; 20 cm. Includes bibliographical references. ISBN 0-14-007062-1
1. Soccer - Social aspects - Great Britain. 2. Labor and laboring classes - Great Britain. 3. Youth - Employment - Great Britain. I. Title.
NYPL [JLD 86-4404]

ROBINS, MARGARET DREIER.
Payne, Elizabeth Anne, 1943- Reform, labor, and feminism . Urbana , c1988. p. cm. ISBN 0-252-01445-6 (alk. paper) LC Card 87-10794 DDC 331.88/092/4 B 19
HD6079.2.U5 P38 1988

Robins, Paul. Advanced accounting practice book 1 : CACA paper 2.9 / Paul Robins. Wokingham, Berkshire, England : Van Nostrand Reinhold (UK) Co. Ltd., 1987. p. cm. (VNR accountancy passbooks) Includes index. ISBN 0-278-00014-2 : LC Card 87-13803 DDC 657/.046 19
1. Accounting. 2. Accounting - Great Britain. I. Title. II. Series.
HF5635 .R66 1987

Robinson, Albert J., 1926- The retail sales tax in Canada / A.J. Robinson. Toronto, Ont. : Canadian Tax Foundation, c1986. viii, 165 p. ; 23 cm. (Canadian tax paper . no. 77) Bibliography: p. 152-161. Includes index. ISBN 0-88808-025-5 (pbk.) : LC Card 86-210098 DDC 336.2/713/0971 19
1. Sales tax - Canada - Provinces. 2. Sales tax - Canada. I. Series: Canadian tax papers , no. 77. II. Title.
HJ5715.C2 R63 1986

Robinson, David Alexander, 1909- Accounts receivable and inventory lending : how to establish and operate an asset-based lending department / David A. Robinson.3rd ed. Boston : Bankers Pub. Co., 1987. xii, 299 p. : ill., forms ; 28 cm. Includes index. ISBN 0-87267-104-6 LC Card 86-32252 DDC 332.1/753/068 19
1. Accounts receivable loans. 2. Inventory loans. I. Title.
HG3752.3 .R63 1987

Robinson, Dean L. Network marketing / prepared for Embassy Consulting by Dean L. Robinson & D. Reid Hilton. Salt Lake City, Utah : Embassy Consulting Corp., c1983. 137 p. : ill. ; 19 cm. LC Card 86-202974 DDC 658.8/4 19
1. Multilevel marketing. 2. Direct marketing. I. Hilton, D. Reid. II. Embassy Consulting (Firm : Salt Lake City, Utah). III. Title.
HF5415.126 .R63 1983

Robinson, Derek, 1932 (Feb. 9)- Introduction to economics : a revision aid / Derek Robinson. Cambridge, Cambridgeshire, England ; Wolfeboro, N.H., USA : ICSA Pub., 1987. p. cm. ISBN 0-902197-53-3 (pbk.) : LC Card 87-3746 DDC 330 19
1. Economics. I. Title.
HB171.5 .R65 1987

Robinson, Gerald J.
Federal income taxation of real estate : text, forms, and tax planning ideas / by Gerald J. Robinson.4th ed. Boston, Mass. : Warren, Gorham & Lamont, c1984. ca. 750 p. in various pagings ; 25 cm. (WG & L tax series) "Special update" ([79] p.) issued 1984 under title: Tax Reform Act of 1984. Includes index. Kept up to date by supplements. Library lacks: "Special update." ISBN 0-88712-081-4 LC Card 83-50925 DDC 343.7305/2 347.30352 19
1. Real property and taxation - United States. 2. Income tax - Law and legislation - United States. 3. Tax planning - United States. I. Robinson, Gerald J. Tax Reform Act of 1984. II. Title.
KF6535 .R6 1984 ***NYPL [JLL 87-136]***

Federal income taxation of real estate : text, forms, and tax planning ideas : 1987 cumulative supplement no. 1, including Tax Reform Act of 1986 : analysis and tax planning strategies / by Gerald J. Robinson.4th ed. Boston, Mass. : Warren, Gorham & Lamont, c1987. ca. 480 p. in various pagings ; 24 cm. (WG & L tax series) Includes indexes. ISBN 0-88712-743-6 LC Card 83-50925
1. Real property and taxation - United States. 2. Income tax - Law and legislation - United States. 3. Tax planning - United States. I. Robinson, Gerald J. Tax Reform Act of 1986. II. Title.
NYPL [JLL 87-136 Suppl. 1987/1]

Federal income taxation of real estate : text, forms, and tax planning ideas : 4th ed. Cumulative supplement / by Gerald J. Robinson. Boston, Mass. : Warren, Gorham & Lamont, c1985- v. 25 cm. Includes indexes. ISBN 0-88712-305-8 (pbk.) LC Card 83-50925
1. Real property and taxation - United States. 2. Income tax - Law and legislation - United States. 3. Tax planning - United States. I. Title.
NYPL [*R-Econ. 85-1660 Suppl.]

Tax Reform Act of 1984. Robinson, Gerald J. Federal income taxation of real estate : text, forms, and tax planning ideas / by Gerald J. Robinson.4th ed. Boston, Mass. , c1984. ca. 750 p. in various pagings ; ISBN 0-88712-081-4 LC Card 83-50925 DDC 343.7305/2 347.30352 19
KF6535 .R6 1984 ***NYPL [JLL 87-136]***

Tax Reform Act of 1986. Robinson, Gerald J. Federal income taxation of real estate : text, forms, and tax planning ideas : 1987 cumulative supplement no. 1, including Tax Reform Act of 1986 : analysis and tax planning strategies / by Gerald J. Robinson.4th ed. Boston, Mass. , c1987. ca. 480 p. in various pagings ; ISBN 0-88712-743-6 LC Card 83-50925
NYPL [JLL 87-136 Suppl. 1987/1]

Robinson, Jancis. Loftus, Simon. Anatomy of the wine trade . New York , c1985. 179 p. ; ISBN 0-06-015785-2 : LC Card 87-45066 DDC 380.1/456632 19
HD9370.5 .L64 1985

Robinson, Joe. You're the boss / Joe Robinson. 1st ed. New York : St. Martin's Press, c1987. x, 342 p. ; 22 cm. Bibliography: p. [330]-333. Includes index. ISBN 0-312-01027-3 : LC Card 87-16149 DDC 658.4/2 19
1. New business enterprises. 2. Success in business. I. Title.
HD62.5 .R59 1987

Robinson, John L. United Nations University Symposium on Energy and Agriculture Futures--Policy Implications of Global Models (1982 : Paris, France) Energy and agriculture . [Chur, Switzerland , New York] , c1984. xii, 370 p. : ISBN 3-7186-0187-7 LC Card 83-18363 DDC 333.79 19
HD1405 .E53 1983 ***NYPL [JLD 86-1837]***

Robinson, Kathryn Mae, 1949- Migrasi /. Ujung Pandang , 1985. xi, 205 p. : LC Card 87-940461
HB2108.S8 M54 1985

Robinson, Kathryn May, 1949- Stepchildren of progress : the political economy of development in an Indonesian mining town / Kathryn May Robinson. Albany, N.Y. : State University of New York Press, c1986. xvi, 315 p. : ill., maps ; 24 cm. (SUNY series in the anthropology of work) Originally presented as the author's thesis (Ph.D.--Australian National University, 1983). Includes index. Bibliography: p. 295-307. ISBN 0-88706-119-2 LC Card 86-5847 DDC 307.7/66/095984 19
1. Nickel industry - Indonesia - Saroako. 2. Economic anthropology - Indonesia - Saroako. 3. Saroako (Indonesia) - Economic conditions. 4. Saroako (Indonesia) - Social conditions. I. Title. II. Series.
HD9539.N52 I547 1986
NYPL [JLE 86-4126]

Robinson, Larry E. Lillywhite, Donald P. Virginia population projections 2000 /. Richmond, VA (P.O. Box 1422, Ninth St. Office Building,

Richmond 23219) [1986] 96 p. : LC Card 87-621004 DDC 304.6/2/09755021 19
HA685 .L542 1986

Robinson, Patricia A. (Patricia Ann) Women's work interruptions : results from the 1984 family history survey / by Patricia Robinson. Ottawa : Statistics Canada, [1987], c1986. 36, 40 p. ; 28 cm. English and French. Title on added t.p.: Interruptions de travail chez les femmes. "January 1987." "Catalogue 99-962." ISBN 0-660-52895-9 (pbk.) : LC Card 87-146334 DDC 331.4/12/0971 19
1. Women - Employment - Canada. 2. Wives - Employment - Canada. I. Title. II. Title: Interruptions de travail chez les femmes.
HD6099 .R63 1987

Robinson, Richard B. (Richard Braden), 1947- Pearce, John A. Company and industry cases in strategy and policy /. Homewood, IL , 1986. xiv, 711 p. : ISBN 0-256-03558-X : LC Card 85-82002 ***NYPL [JLE 87-993]***

Robinson, Richard D., 1921-
Direct foreign investment . New York , 1987. xvii, 227 p. ; ISBN 0-275-92717-2 (alk. paper) : LC Card 87-17750 DDC 332.6732 19
HG4538 .D557 1987

Foreign capital and technology in China /. New York , 1987. xvii, 191 p. : ISBN 0-275-92716-4 (alk. paper) : LC Card 87-2450 DDC 332.6/7314/0951 19
HG5782 .F67 1987

Robison L. J. Models for investment and disinvestment decision making under uncertainty [microform] /. East Lansing , 1982. 173 p. : ***NYPL [*XME-11,286]***

Robison, Maynard T. Ferguson, Gary D. Evaluation of the small cities community development block grant program--the role of the counties [microform] /. Cambridge, Mass. , 1981. vii, vi, 186 p. ; ***NYPL [*XME-11,283]***

Robison, Richard, 1943- Southeast Asia in the 1980s . Sydney , Boston , 1987. p. cm. ISBN 0-04-301289-2 LC Card 87-19550 DDC 338.959 19
HC441 .S69 1987

Robledo Hernández, Ricardo. La renta de la tierra en Castilla la Vieja y León (1836-1913) / Ricardo Robledo Hernández. [Madrid] : Banco de España, Servicio de Estudios, [1984?] 245 p. : ill. ; 24 cm. (Estudios de historia económica . no. 11) Includes bibliographical references. ISBN 84-505-0885-1 LC Card 87-104999
1. Land value taxation - Spain - Castilla y León - History. 2. Farm rents - Spain - Castilla y León - History. 3. Land tenure - Spain - Castilla y León - History. I. Title. II. Series.
HJ4375.C27 R63 1984

Robles, Albert G. Attitudes toward vended coffee /. [Chicago? , 1983] 1 v. (various pagings) : LC Card 86-235525 DDC 381/.4566393 19
HD9199.U48 A88 1983

Robles Bohórquez, Isabel. La agricultura colombiana en la encrucijada : evolución de las políticas financieras, logros y perspectivas / Isabel Robles Bohórquez. Bogotá, Colombia : Ediciones Tercer Mundo, [1982] 165 p. ; 19 cm. Bibliography: p. 163-165. LC Card 83-103208
1. Agriculture and state - Colombia. 2. Agriculture - Colombia - Finance. I. Title.
HD1883 1982 .R62

ROBOT INDUSTRY.
The Robotics industry. Washington, D.C. , 1983. 54 p. : ***NYPL [JLF 86-713]***

ROBOT INDUSTRY - EUROPE.
Industrial robots market in Europe. New York, N.Y. , c1983. vi, 320 p. : LC Card 87-141842 DDC 380.1/45629892 19
HD9696.R623 E854 1983

ROBOT INDUSTRY - HUNGARY - STATISTICS.
Az Ipari robotok termelésének és felhasználásának trendjei /. Budapest , 1985. 63 p. : LC Card 86-199458
HD9696.R623 H852 1985

ROBOT INDUSTRY - ITALY.
Il Robot italiano . Milano , 1984. 194 p. : LC Card 86-129858
HD9696.R623 I837 1984
NYPL [JLD 87-1277]

ROBOT INDUSTRY - STATISTICS.
Az Ipari robotok termelésének és felhasználásának trendjei /. Budapest , 1985. 63 p. : LC Card 86-199458
HD9696.R623 H852 1985

ROBOT INDUSTRY - SWEDEN.
Investering i industrirobotar . [Stockholm] [1983] 263 p. : ISBN 91-38-07833-3 LC Card 84-218538
HD9696.R623 S845 1983

ROBOT INDUSTRY - UNITED STATES.
A Competitive assessment of the U. S. robotics industry /. Washington, D.C. [1987] xiii, 85 p. ; LC Card 87-601316 DDC 338.4/7629892 19
HD9696.R623 U615 1987

Delson, Erwin B. The factory automation industry /. New York, N.Y. , c1985. 1 v. (various pagings) : ISBN 0-931634-16-4 (pbk.) LC Card 86-203033 DDC 338.4/76298/0973 19
HD9696.A963 U635 1985

Industrial robots market. New York, N.Y. , <c1983-. v. <2 > ; LC Card 87-166012 DDC 381/.45629892 19
HD9696.R623 U634 1983

The Robotics industry. Washington, D.C. , 1983. 54 p. : ***NYPL [JLF 86-713]***

ROBOT VISION.
Miller, Richard Kendall, 1946- Color machine vision . Madison, GA [c1986] 174 leaves : ISBN 0-89671-079-3 (pbk.) LC Card 87-116822 DDC 380.1/4500637 19
HD9696.C62 M55 1986

Robotics/artificial intelligence/productivity . Chacko, George Kuttickal, 1930- Princeton, N.J. , c1986. 2 v. in 1 (xvii, 335 p.) : ISBN 0-89433-228-7 LC Card 86-12177 DDC 658.5/14 19
HD9725 .C48 1986 ***NYPL [JLE 87-1001]***

ROBOTICS - GERMANY (WEST) - ADDRESSES, ESSAYS, LECTURES.
Neue Technologien und Arbeitswelt . Köln , c1984. 197 p. : ISBN 3-7663-0893-9 LC Card 85-160745
HD6331.2.G28 N475 1984
NYPL [JLD 86-3861]

The Robotics industry. Washington, D.C. : U. S. Dept. of Commerce, International Trade Administration : For sale by the Supt. of Docs., U. S. G.P.O., 1983. 54 p. : ill. ; 28 cm. (High technology industries, profiles and outlooks)
1. Robot industry - United States. 2. Robot industry. I. United States. International Trade Administration.
NYPL [JLF 86-713]

ROBOTICS - JAPAN.
Chacko, George Kuttickal, 1930- Robotics/artificial intelligence/productivity . Princeton, N.J. , c1986. 2 v. in 1 (xvii, 335 p.) : ISBN 0-89433-228-7 LC Card 86-12177 DDC 658.5/14 19
HD9725 .C48 1986 ***NYPL [JLE 87-1001]***

ROBOTICS - UNITED STATES.
Chacko, George Kuttickal, 1930- Robotics/artificial intelligence/productivity . Princeton, N.J. , c1986. 2 v. in 1 (xvii, 335 p.) : ISBN 0-89433-228-7 LC Card 86-12177 DDC 658.5/14 19
HD9725 .C48 1986 ***NYPL [JLE 87-1001]***

A Competitive assessment of the U. S. robotics industry /. Washington, D.C. [1987] xiii, 85 p. ; LC Card 87-601316 DDC 338.4/7629892 19
HD9696.R623 U615 1987

Robotization, its implications for management / Researched by JMA Research Institute, a division of Japan Management Association. Tokyo, Japan : Fuji Corporation, c1983. vi, 316 p. : ill. ; 29 cm.
1. Robots, Industrial. 2. Industrial management - Japan. I. JMA Research Institute. ***NYPL [JLF 86-1055]***

Robotnicze drogi Śląska i Zagłębia Dąbrowskiego do roku 1939 /. Walczak, Jan. Katowice , 1985. 493 p. ; ISBN 83-7008-096-0 : LC Card 86-101066
HD8539.S52 W35 1985

Robots and automated manufacture / edited by J. Billingsley. London, U.K. : P. Peregrinus on behalf of the Institution of Electrical Engineers, c1985. xii, 233 p. : ill. ; 24 cm. (IEE control engineering series. 28) Includes bibliograhies and index. ISBN 0-86341-053-7
1. Robots, Industrial. 2. Manufacturing processes - Automation. I. Billingsley, J. II. Series.
NYPL [JSK 77-191 v.28]

ROBOTS, INDUSTRIAL.
Computerized manufacturing automation [microform] . Washington, D.C. , 1984. 35 p. : ***NYPL [*ZV-326 no.31]***

Industrial robots market. New York, N.Y. , <c1983-. v. <2 > ; LC Card 87-166012 DDC 381/.45629892 19
HD9696.R623 U634 1983

Katzan, Harry. A manager's guide to productivity, quality circles, and industrial robots /. New York , c1985. vii, 136 p. : ISBN 0-442-24823-7 LC Card 84-25739 DDC 658.5 19
HD56 .K377 1985 ***NYPL [JLE 86-4510]***

Light, John J. Realistic economics /. Indianapolis, IN (P.O. Box 1606, Indianapolis 46206) , c1984. 111 p. ; ISBN 0-933021-00-3 : LC Card 84-249506 DDC 331.12/0973 19
HD5724 .L4236 1984 ***NYPL [JLE 86-4650]***

Robotization, its implications for management /. Tokyo, Japan , c1983. vi, 316 p. : ***NYPL [JLF 86-1055]***

Robots and automated manufacture /. London, U.K. , c1985. xii, 233 p. : ISBN 0-86341-053-7 ***NYPL [JSK 77-191 v.28]***

ROBOTS, INDUSTRIAL - STATISTICS.
Az Ipari robotok termelésének és felhasználásának trendjei /. Budapest , 1985. 63 p. : LC Card 86-199458
HD9696.R623 H852 1985

ROBOTS, INDUSTRIAL - SWEDEN.
Investering i industrirobotar . [Stockholm] [1983] 263 p. : ISBN 91-38-07833-3 LC Card 84-218538
HD9696.R623 S845 1983

Robson, Peter, 1926- The economics of international integration / Peter Robson. 3rd rev. ed. London ; Boston : Allen & Unwin, 1987. 285 p. : ill. ; 22 cm. Bibliography: p. [260]-279. Includes index. ISBN 0-04-445005-2 (pbk. : alk. paper) LC Card 87-11472 DDC 337.1 19
1. International economic integration. I. Title.
HF1418.5 .R63 1987

Robson, William Alexander, 1895- Public enterprise . New York , 1985. 416 p. ; ISBN 0-8240-7626-5 (alk. paper) : LC Card 85-13105 DDC 354.4109/1 19
HD4147 .P83 1985 ***NYPL [JLD 86-3467]***

Roca, José Luis, 1935- Derrotemos al hambre : observaciones sobre la seguridad alimentaria en Bolivia / José Luis Roca. La Paz, Bolivia : UNICEF, 1985. 157, [16] leaves of plates : ill. ; 23 cm. "E/ICEF/BOL/12485"--Verso t.p. Bibliography: p. 153-157. LC Card 85-241330 DDC 363.8/56/0984 19
1. Food supply - Bolivia. 2. Diet - Bolivia. 3. Food supply - Government policy - Bolivia. I. Title.
HD9014.B62 R63 1985 ***NYPL [JLD 87-385]***

Rocard, Michel, 1930- Economie sociale et cycle de vie des institutions /. Paris , 1983. 162 p. : ISBN 2-7178-0631-8 : LC Card 83-174618 DDC 334/.0944 19
HD3494 .E26 1983 ***NYPL [JLE 86-537]***

Rocca, José. Excedentes financieros y sistema bancario, Uruguay, 1974-1982 / José Rocca, Jorge Simón y la colaboración de Carlos Méndez. Montevideo, Uruguay : Centro Interdisciplinario de Estudios sobre el Desarrollo Uruguay, 1985. 39 p. : ill. ; 28 cm. (Serie Investigaciones. no. 20) Includes bibliographies. LC Card 85-213768
1. Saving and investment - Uruguay. 2. Banks and banking - Uruguay. I. Simón, Jorge. II. Méndez, Carlos. III. Series: Serie Investigaciones (Montevideo, Uruguay) . IV. Title.
HC235.S3 R63 1985

Roccella, Massimo. I salari / Massimo Roccella. Bologna : Il Mulino, c1986. 342 p. ; 22 cm. (La Nuova scienza: Serie di diritto) Includes bibliographical references. ISBN 88-15-01204-4 : LC Card 86-216417
1. Wages - Italy. 2. Wages. I. Title.
HD5034 .R63 1986

Rocha C., Julio César de la (Rocha Corzo) Un análisis de la rentabilidad accionaria de la Bolsa de Valores de Lima, 1980-1983 / Julio César de la Rocha C. Lima, Perú : Universidad de

Lima, Facultad de Economía, Centro de Investigaciones Económicas y Sociales, 1984. ii, 56 p. ; 30 cm. (Serie Avances de investigación . no. 5) Includes bibliographical references. LC Card 86-154699
1. Securities - Peru. 2. Bolsa de Valores de Lima. I. Series: Avances de de investigación (Universidad de Lima. Centro de Investigaciones Económicas y Sociales) , 5. II. Title.
HG5392 .R66 1984

Rocha, Everardo P. Guimarães, 1951- Magia e capitalismo : um estudo antropológico da publicidade / Everardo P. Guimarães Rocha. São Paulo, SP : Brasiliense, 1985. 162 p. : ill. ; 21 cm. Originally presented as the author's thesis (master's)--Universidade Federal do Rio de Janeiro. Bibliography: p. [160]-162. LC Card 85-199925
1. Advertising - Social aspects. 2. Symbolism in advertising. 3. Advertising agencies. I. Title.
HF5827 .R58 1985

Rocha, José Carlos Rodrigues. O êxodo rural no município de Pirajuí / José Carlos Rodrigues Rocha. Bauru-SP : Faculdades do Sagrado Coração, 1984. iv, 66 p. : ill. ; 22 cm. (Cadernos de divulgação cultural . 14) Thesis (mestre em ciências humanas)--Faculdade de Filosofia, Ciências e Letras "Sagrado Coração de Jesus.". Summary also in English. Bibliography: p. 65-66. LC Card 86-158771
1. Pirajuí (Brazil) - Population. 2. Rural-urban migration - Brazil - Sao Paulo (State). I. Series: Cadernos de divulgação cultural (Bauru, Brazil) , 14. II. Title.
HB2024.P57 R62 1984

Rocha, Roberto Rezende. Melo, Valdir Ramalho de. Seleção de agregados monetários /. [Brasília] [1981] 136 p. : LC Card 85-161532
HG835 .M45 1981

ROCHDALE (GREATER MANCHESTER) - SOCIAL CONDITIONS.
Higgs, Edward, 1952- Domestic servants and households in Rochdale, 1851-1871 /. New York , 1986. 423 p. ; ISBN 0-8240-6682-0 : LC Card 84-46002 DDC 305.5/6 19
HD8039.D52 G7755 1986
NYPL [JLE 86-4591]

Roche, Daniel.
Ménétra, Jacques-Louis, b. 1738. Journal de ma vie . Paris , c1982. 431 p. : ISBN 2-85870-022-2 : LC Card 82-166496 DDC 666/.1/0924 B 19
HD8039.G52 F73 1982
NYPL [JFD 86-6795]

Ménétra, Jacques-Louis, b. 1738. [Journal de ma vie. English.] Journal of my life /. New York , 1986. xviii, 368 p., [1] leaf of plate : ISBN 0-231-06128-5 LC Card 85-28068 DDC 666/.1/0924 B 19
HD8039.G52 F7313 1986
NYPL [JFE 86-2978]

Rochell, Carlton C. Dreams betrayed : working in the technological age / by Carlton Rochell with Christina Spellman. Lexington, Mass. : Lexington Books, c1987. 138 p. ; 24 cm. Bibliography: p. [121]-132. Includes index. ISBN 0-669-11105-8 (alk. paper) LC Card 85-45019 DDC 331.25 19
1. Automation - Social aspects - United States. 2. Labor supply - United States - Effect of technological innovations on. I. Spellman, Christina. II. Title.
HD6331.2.U5 R63 1987

Rochette, Edward C., 1927- Making money / Edward C. Rochette. Frederick, CO : Renaissance House, c1986. 107 p. : ill. ; 23 cm. Cover subtitle: Rogues & rascals who made their own. Includes index. ISBN 0-939650-25-8 (pbk.) : LC Card 86-22120 DDC 364.1/33/09 19
1. Counterfeits and counterfeiting - History. 2. Money - History. I. Title.
HG335 .R63 1986

Rock, Reinhard. Marketing=Philosophie / Reinhard Rock, Klaus Rosenthal. Frankfurt am Main ; New York : P. Lang, c1986. 220 p. ; 21 cm. Bibliography: p. 219-220. ISBN 3-8204-9700-5 LC Card 87-407971 DDC 658.8/001 19
1. Marketing. I. Rosenthal, Klaus. II. Title. III. Title: Marketing ist Philosophie.
HF5415 .R557 1986

ROCKEFELLER FAMILY.
Scholl, Heinz. Bilderberger & Trilaterale . Euskirchen, Bundesrepublik Deutschland , c1977. 92 p. ; LC Card 85-199172
HD2785 .S396 1977

ROCKEFELLER, JOHN D. (JOHN DAVISON), 1839-1937.
Akin, Edward N. Flagler, Rockefeller partner and Florida baron /. Kent, Ohio , c1988. xiii, 305 p. : ISBN 0-87338-348-6 (alk. paper) LC Card 87-2070 DDC 338/.04/0924 B 19
HC102.5.F55 A75 1988

Rocker, Rudolf, 1873-1958.
Zur Geschichte der parlamentarischen Tätigkeit in der modernen Arbeiterbewegung. 1978. Wozu noch in die Parlamente? / [Zusammenstellung, Trotzdem-Kollektiv]. [1. Aufl.]. [Reutlingen] , 1978. 81 p. : LC Card 82-223081 DDC 322/.2/0943 19
HD6697 .W69 1978 *NYPL [JLD 87-886]*

Rocket mail flights of the world to 1986 /. Kronstein, Max. Cinnaminson, N.J. , 1986. 191 p. : LC Card 87-400297 DDC 383/.144 19
HE6239.R6 K76 1986

ROCKET MAIL - HISTORY.
Kronstein, Max. Rocket mail flights of the world to 1986 /. Cinnaminson, N.J. , 1986. 191 p. : LC Card 87-400297 DDC 383/.144 19
HE6239.R6 K76 1986

Rockford : the pet food story, 1923-1987. 1st ed. [Rockford, Ill.] : Rockford Pet Foods Division, Quaker Oats Co., c1987. 98 p. : ill. ; 30 cm. LC Card 87-61147 DDC 338.7/66466/0977331 19
1. Quaker Oats Company Rockford Pet Foods Division - History. 2. Pet food industry - Illinois - Rockford - History. I. Quaker Oats Company. Rockford Pet Foods Division.
HD9340.U53 R637 1987

Rocks in her head / edited by Dorchen Forman ; landscapes by Andy Alpha. Lake Dallas, Tex. (221 Wild Oak, Lake Dallas 75065) : Siwash Enterprises, c1987. vii, 97 p. : ill. ; 22 cm. LC Card 87-151452
1. Petroleum geologists' wives - United States - Biography. I. Forman, Dorchen.
HD8039.P42 U676 1987

RODBERTUS, KARL, 1805-1875 - VIEWS ON RENT.
Rudolph, Günther. Karl Rodbertus (1805-1875) und die Grundrententheorie . Berlin , 1984. 332 p. ; LC Card 84-158301
HB401 .R83 1984

Rode, Reinhard, 1947-
US-Technologietransferpolitik gegenüber der UdSSR und der VR China : Weltmachtpolitik im Dreieck / Reinhard Rode. Frankfurt am Main : Hessische Stiftung Friedens- und Konfliktforschung, [1986] 39 p. : ill. ; 30 cm. (HSFK-Report. 4/1986) Includes bibliographical references. ISBN 3-926197-01-3 LC Card 87-120584 DDC 338.9/26 19
1. Technology transfer - Economic aspects - Soviet Union. 2. Technology transfer - Economic aspects - China. 3. Technology transfer - Economic aspects - United States. I. Series. II. Series: HSFK-Report, 1986/4. III. Title.
HC340.T4 R63 1986

Wirtschaftskrieg oder Entspannung? . Bonn , c1984. 328 p. ; ISBN 3-87831-392-6 LC Card 84-251713
HF4050 .W57 1984

Rodemer, Horst. Glismann, Hans H. Zur Natur der Wachstumsschwäche in der Bundesrepublik Deutschland . Kiel [1978] 32 p. : LC Card 85-166323
HB44 .K45 no. 55 HB3789

Roden, Peyton Foster. Cooley, Philip L. Business financial management /. Chicago , c1988. xxv, 924, [34] p. : ISBN 0-03-009979-X LC Card 87-20079 DDC 658.1/5 19
HG4026 .C63 1988

RODENTS - CONTROL - GREAT BRITAIN - HISTORY.
Dear cats . London , 1986. 128 p. : LC Card 87-126969 DDC 628.9/693 19
HE6939.S42 D42 1986

Roder, Hartmut, 1951- Der christlich-nationale Deutsche Gewerkschaftsbund (DGB) im politisch-ökonomischen Kräftefeld der Weimarer Republik : ein Beitrag zur Funktion und Praxis der bürgerlichen Arbeitnehmerbewegung vom Kaiserreich bis zur faschistischen Diktatur / Hartmut Roder. Frankfurt am Main ; New York : Lang, c1986. 804 p. : ill. ; 21 cm. (Europäische Hochschulschriften. Reihe III, Geschichte und ihre Hilfswissenschaften, 0531-7320 . Bd. 291 = vol. 291 = vol. 291) Bibliography: p. 726-778. Includes index. ISBN 3-8204-9325-5 LC Card 86-194815
1. Deutscher Gewerkschaftsbund - History. 2. Gesamtverband der Christlichen Gewerkschaften Deutschlands - History. 3. Trade-unions, Catholic - Germany - History. 4. Trade-unions and Christianity - Germany - History. I. Series: Europäische Hochschulschriften. Reihe III, Geschichte und ihre Hilfswissenschaften , Bd. 291. II. Title.
HD8443.D457 R63 1986

Röder, Karl Heinz. Das Politische System der BRD . Berlin , 1985. 479 p. ; LC Card 86-123928 DDC 320.943 19
JN3971.A2 P59 1985 *NYPL [JLD 86-3144]*

Rodgers, F. G. (Francis G.)
Getting the best out of yourself and others / by Buck Rodgers with Irv Levey. 1st ed. New York : Harper & Row, c1987. xi, 227 p. ; 25 cm. ISBN 0-06-015670-8 : LC Card 86-46125 DDC 658.3/4 19
1. Employee motivation. 2. Achievement motivation. 3. Performance. 4. Employee assistance programs. I. Levey, Irv. II. Title.
HF5549.5.M63 R63 1987

The IBM way : insights into the world's most successful marketing organization / F.G. "Buck" Rodgers, with Robert L. Shook.1st ed. New York : Harper & Row, c1986. xiv, 235 p. ; 25 cm. Includes index. ISBN 0-06-015522-1 : LC Card 85-45223 DDC 338.7/61004/0973 19
1. Computers - Marketing - Case studies. 2. Electronic office machines - Marketing - Case studies. 3. Marketing - Case studies. I. Shook, Robert L., 1938-. II. Title. III. Title: I.B.M. way.
HD9696.C64 I4875 1986
NYPL [JLE 86-1374]

Rodgers, Harrell R. Poor women, poor families : the economic plight of America's female-headed households / Harrell R. Rodgers, Jr. Armonk, N.Y. : M.E. Sharpe, 1986. viii, 167 p. ; 24 cm. Bibliography: p. 150-161. ISBN 0-87332-372-6 : LC Card 86-6449 DDC 362.8/3/0973 19
1. Women heads of households - United States. 2. Women, Poor - United States. 3. Women - Employment - United States. 4. Public welfare - United States. I. Title.
HV1445 .R64 1986 *NYPL [JLE 86-4042]*

Rodgers, Mervyn. Kaiser, Martin. The New Zealand software industry . Wellington, N.Z. , c1986. 1 v. (various pagings) : ISBN 0-477-06783-2 (pbk.) LC Card 86-212843 DDC 381/.450053/09931 19
HD9696.C63 N455 1986

Rodionenkov, P. A. (Petr Andreevich) Zatraty i rezul′taty proizvodstvennykh issledovaniĭ i razrabotok / P.A. Rodionenkov. Leningrad : Izd-vo Leningradskogo universiteta, 1986. 143 p. ; 21 cm. At head of title: Leningradskiĭ Ordena Lenina i Ordena Trudovogo Krasnogo Znameni gosudarstvennyĭ universitet imeni A.A. Zhdanova. Includes bibliographical references. LC Card 87-136354
1. Research - Economic aspects - Soviet Union. 2. Technological innovations - Soviet Union. 3. Science and industry - Soviet Union. I. Title.
HC340.R4 R63 1986

Rodman, Kenneth Aaron. Sanctity versus sovereignty : the United States and the nationalization of natural resource investments / Kenneth A. Rodman. New York : Columbia University Press, 1988. p. cm. (The Political economy of international change) Bibliography: p. Includes index. ISBN 0-231-06448-9 LC Card 87-24970 DDC 332.6/7373/01724 19
1. Investments, American - Developing countries. 2. Raw materials - Developing countries. 3. Government ownership - Developing countries. I. Title. II. Series.
HG5993 .R63 1988

Rodman, Margaret, 1947- Masters of tradition : consequences of customary land tenure in Longana, Vanuatu / Margaret Critchlow Rodman. Vancouver : University of British Columbia Press, 1987. 198 p. : ill. ; 24 cm. Bibliography: p. [179]-189. Includes index. ISBN 0-7748-0234-0 LC Card 87-158135 DDC 333.3/0993/4 19
1. Land tenure - Vanuatu - Longana. 2. Farm tenancy - Vanuatu - Longana. 3. Agriculture - Economic aspects - Vanuatu - Longana. I. Title.
HD1125.Z9 L657 1987

Rodney, Walter. How Europe underdeveloped Africa / by Walter Rodney with a postcript by A.M. Babu. Rev. ed. Washington, D.C. : Howard University Press, 1981, c1972. xxiv, 312 p. ; 24 cm. Title page dated 1982. Includes bibliographies and index. ISBN 0-88258-105-8 LC Card 87-142601
1. Africa - Economic conditions. 2. Africa - Colonial influence. 3. Europe - Foreign economic relations - Africa. 4. Africa - Foreign economic relations - Europe. 5. Europe - Colonies - Africa - Economic policy. I. Title.
HC800 .R62 1981b

RODOVIA TRANSAMAZÔNICA, BRAZIL. Fearnside, Philip M. (Philip Martin) Human carrying capacity of the Brazilian rain-forest /. New York , 1986. xii, 293 p. : ISBN 0-231-06104-8 (alk. paper) LC Card 85-6643 DDC 330.981/1063 19
HC188.A5 F42 1986 ***NYPL [JLE 86-4554]***

Rodríguez Cancho, Manuel. Alvarado Corrales, Eduardo J. Extremadura . Cáceres [1984?] 101 p. : ISBN 84-600-3663-4 LC Card 86-165503
HD1333.S712 E783 1984

Rodríguez Daza, Myriam. Santa María de Cárdenas, Cecilia. El seguro agrícola como factor de desarrollo económico /. Bogotá , 1978. 168, 2, [43] p. : LC Card 85-203482
HG9966 .S25 1978

Rodríguez Grajera, Alfonso. La población de Mérida en el siglo XVII / Alfonso Rodríguez Grajera. [Badajoz] : Excma. Diputación Provincial de Badajoz, 1985. xv, 162 p. : ill. ; 24 cm. (Colección Historia. no. 3) Bibliography: p. 161-162. ISBN 84-505-1500-9 LC Card 86-232003
1. Mérida (Spain) - Population - History - 17th century - Statistics. 2. Births - Spain - Mérida - History - 17th century - Statistics. 3. Mortality - Spain - Mérida - History - 17th century - Statistics. 4. Marriage - Spain - Mérida - History - 17th century - Statistics. 5. Mérida (Spain) - Statistics, Vital - History - 17th century. I. Series: Colección Historia (Badajoz, Spain) , 3. II. Title.
HB3620.M47 R63 1985

Rodríguez, Gumersindo, 1933- Era posible la gran Venezuela? / Gumersindo Rodríguez. Caracas : Editorial Ateneo de Caracas, 1986. 215 p. : ill. ; 22 cm. (Colección Ensayo) Cover subtitle: Los 5 años de CAP. ISBN 980-255-004-3 LC Card 87-118414 DDC 338.987 19
1. Venezuela - Economic policy. I. Title.
HC237 .R617 1986

Rodríguez, Héctor, 1918- Lucha y polémica sindical, 1968-1973. [Montevideo?] , 1985. 4 v. ; LC Card 86-107744 DDC 322/.2/09895 19
HD6647 .L83 1985 ***NYPL [JLC 86-368]***

Rodriguez, Jose E., 1958- Lehr, Jay H., 1936- Orbital management . Lanham, MD [Cambridge, MA] , c1987. xvi, 104 p. : ISBN 0-8191-6264-7 (alk. paper) : LC Card 87-143 DDC 658.4/02 19
HD50 .L44 1987

Rodríguez, Luis Hernando. Análisis descriptivo de las exportaciones colombianas, 1950-1980 / por Luis Hernando Rodríguez R. Bogotá, Colombia : Centro de Estudios sobre Desarrollo Económico, Universidad de los Andes, 1985. 3, 169 p. : ill. ; 28 cm. (Documento CEDE . no. 078) Bibliography: p. 165-169. LC Card 87-402978 DDC 382/.6/09861 19
1. Colombia - Commerce - History - 20th century. I. Series: Documento (Universidad de los Andes (Bogotá, Colombia). Centro de Estudios sobre Desarrollo Económico) , 078. II. Title.
HF3426.5 .R63 1985

Rodríguez, Martha de. Fabián, Miguel Angel. Monografía del café /. [San Salvador] , 1984. 39 leaves : LC Card 86-177543
HD9199.S142 F33 1984

Rodríguez Prada, Gonzalo. Fanjul Martín, Enrique. La evolución de la política monetaria española (1940-1978) . [Madrid] , 1979. 164 p. ; LC Card 85-202991
HG1135 .F35 1979

Rodriguez, Rita M., 1944- The Export-Import Bank at fifty . Lexington, Mass. , c1987. xii, 206 p. : ISBN 0-669-14828-8 (alk. paper) LC Card 86-21521 DDC 332.1/54 19
HG3754.U5 E94 1987 ***NYPL [JLE 87-1153]***

Rodríguez Sáiz, L. (Luis) Cuervo García, Alvaro. Manual de sistema financiero . Barcelona , 1987. 427 p. : ISBN 84-344-2013-9 LC Card 87-135198
HG186.S6 C84 1987

Rodríguez Silvero, Ricardo.
Campos, Luis A. (Luis Alberto), 1949- Pequeños campesinos y su incertidumbre . Asunción, Paraguay [1986] 224 p. : LC Card 87-400281 DDC 305.5/63 19
HD1531.P3 C36 1986

Las Transnacionales en el Paraguay /. Asunción, Paraguay [1985] 317 p. : LC Card 86-112866 DDC 338.8/88892 19
HD2840 .T7 1985 ***NYPL [JLD 86-2210]***

Rodríquez, Pedro. Conde de Campomanes. see **Campomanes, Pedro Rodríguez, Conde de, 1723-1803.**

Rødseth, Tor, 1928- Kvinner i arbeid . Oslo , c1984. 290 p. : ISBN 82-00-06835-8 : LC Card 85-102185
HD6170 .K85 1984

Rodwin, Lloyd. Shelter, settlement, and development /. Boston , 1987. xvii, 476 p. : ISBN 0-04-711023-6 (alk. paper) LC Card 87-1038 DDC 363.5/09172/4 19
HD7391 .S54 1987

Roehl, Thomas W. Itami, Hiroyuki, 1945- Mobilizing invisible assets /. Cambridge, Mass. , 1987. xi, 186 p. : ISBN 0-674-57770-1 (alk. paper) LC Card 86-26972 DDC 658.4/012 19
HD30.28 .I85 1987

Röhm, Helmut. Der Förderungsauftrag im Zielsystem der Bankgenossenschaften : Untersuchungen über den Zielbildungsprozess, die Erwartungsstrukturen und die Beurteilung des Förderungsauftrags durch das Management und die Mitglieder von Genossenschaftsbanken / von Helmut Röhm, under Mitarbeit von Martin Doll. Stuttgart : E. Ulmer, c1983. 306 p. ; 22 cm. (Hohenheimer Arbeiten. Heft 127.) Bibliography: p. 298-306. ISBN 3-8001-8187-8 LC Card 84-106807
1. Banks and banking, Cooperative - Germany, West. I. Doll, Martin. II. Series: Hohenheimer Arbeiten, Heft 127. III. Title.
HG2039.G4 R568 1983

Roemer, John E.
Analytical Marxism /. Cambridge, CB ; New York : viii, 313 p. : ISBN 0-521-30025-8 LC Card 85-11697 DDC 335.4 19
HB97.5 .A487 1986 ***NYPL [JLE 86-1742]***

Free to lose : an introduction to Marxist economic philosophy / John E. Roemer. Cambridge, Mass. : Harvard University Press, 1988. p. cm. Bibliography: p. Includes index. ISBN 0-674-31875-7 (alk. paper) LC Card 87-12121 DDC 335.4/12 19
1. Marxian economics - Mathematical models. I. Title.
HB97.5 .R6167 1988

Röper, Burkhardt.
Der Einfluss des Staates auf den Wettbewerb /. Berlin , c1986. 101 p. ; ISBN 3-428-06084-9 LC Card 87-132303 DDC 338.943 19
HD3616.G35 E38 1986

Strukturpolitische Probleme der Automobil-Industrie unter dem Aspekt des Wettbewerbs /. Berlin , c1985. 247 p. : ISBN 3-428-05924-7 LC Card 86-165212 DDC 338.4/76292/094 19
HD9710.E82 S77 1985

Roericht, Reinhard. Wirtschaftsreformen und neue Entwicklungsstrategien in der Volksrepublik China /. Frankfurt am Main , New York , c1986. 185 p. ; ISBN 3-8204-9101-5 LC Card 86-220822
HC427.92 .W56 1986

Roesler, Jörg. Wirtschaftswachstum in der Industrie der DDR, 1945-1970 / Jörg Roesler, Veronika Siedt, Michael Elle. Berlin : Akademie-Verlag, 1986. 280 p. ; 24 cm. (Forschungen zur Wirtschaftsgeschichte, 0138-5100 . Bd. 23) Includes bibliographical references and index. ISBN 3-05-000074-0 LC Card 86-196020
1. Germany (East) - Industries - History. 2. Industrial productivity - Germany (East) - History. 3. Germany, East - Economic policy. I. Siedt, Veronika. II. Elle, Michael. III. Title. IV. Series.
HC290.78 .R64 1986

Roessler, Helmut R. Deutsche Geschäftskorrespondenz : an introduction to the German business world for native speakers of English who study German business procedures and their legal implications / Helmut R. Roessler. Lanham, MD : University Press of America, c1987. xii, 218 p. : ill. ; 24 cm. English and German. Bibliography: p. 165-166. Includes index. ISBN 0-8191-6277-9 (alk. paper) : LC Card 87-6086 DDC 658.4/53 19
1. Commercial correspondence, German - Handbooks, manuals, etc. 2. German language - Business German - Handbooks, manuals, etc. 3. Business law - Germany (West) - Handbooks, manuals, etc. 4. Commercial correspondence - Dictionaries - German. 5. German language - Dictionaries - English. I. Title.
HF5728.G3 R64 1987

Roessler, Richard, 1944- Rubin, Stanford E. Foundations of the vocational rehabilitation process /. Austin, Tex. , c1987. xiii, 400 p. : ISBN 0-89079-147-3 (pbk.) LC Card 86-30600 DDC 362/.0425 19
HD7255.5 .R823 1987

Roessner, J. David. The Impact of office automation on clerical employment, 1985-2000 : forecasting techniques and plausible futures in banking and insurance / J. David Roessner ... [et al.]. Westport, Conn. : Quorum Books, 1985. xii, 297 p. : ill. ; 24 cm. Includes bibliographical references and index. ISBN 0-89930-119-3 (lib. bdg. : alk. paper) LC Card 85-6523 DDC 331.12/9165137 19
1. Bank employees - United States - Supply and demand - Forecasting. 2. Insurance companies - United States - Employees - Supply and demand - Forecasting. 3. Office practice - Automation.
HD8039.B27 U548 1986 ***NYPL [JLE 86-1424]***

Rogach, A. I. (Aleksandr Igorevich) Ėkspansii͡a mezhdunarodnykh monopoliĭ v razvivai͡ushchiesi͡a strany Azii / A.I. Rogach. Nauchno-populi͡arnoe izd. Kiev : Izd-vo polit. lit-ry Ukrainy, 1987. 236, [4] p. ; 17 cm. Bibliography: p. 227-[237]. LC Card 86-234922
1. International business enterprises - Developing countries. 2. International business enterprises - Asia. I. Title.
HD2932 .R65 1987

Rogachev, S. V. (Sergeĭ Vladimirovich)
Aktual′nye problemy planomernogo razvitii͡a narodnogo khozi͡aĭstva /. Moskva , 1980. 247 p. ; LC Card 81-131558
HC336.25 .A455 1980

Planomernoe razvitie sot͡sialisticheskoĭ ėkonomiki /. Moskva , Bratislava , 1977. 262 p. ; LC Card 87-100683
HC336.25 .P448 1977

Rogalla, Dieter. Heute Grenzen-- morgen Europa /. Bonn , c1984. 107 p. : ISBN 3-7713-0227-7 LC Card 85-146220
HE197.E86 H48 1984

Røgeberg, Svein Lasse. Sektorberegninger for fiske og fangst / av Svein Røgeberg. Oslo : Statistisk sentralbyrå, 1979. 34 p. ; 30 cm. (Det Norske nasjonalregnskapet. Dokumentasjonsnotat . nr. 14) Rapporter fra Statistisk sentralbyrå ; 79/8 ISBN 82-537-0977-3 LC Card 86-460230
1. Fish trade - Norway - Finance. I. Title. II. Series.
HD9465.N62 R64 1979

Rogers, Andrei.
Migration and settlement . Dordrecht ; Boston : xix, 496 p. ; ISBN 90-277-2119-X LC Card 85-25626 DDC 304.8 19
HB1952 .M539 1986 ***NYPL [JLE 86-4091]***

Multiregional demography . Laxenburg, Austria , c1984. v, 81 p. : LC Card 84-218929 DDC 304.6 19
HB1951 .M85 1983 ***NYPL [JLE 86-583]***

Rogers, David J. Waging business warfare : lessons from the military masters in achieving corporate superiority / David J. Rogers.1st ed. New York : Scribner, c1987. x, 341 p. ; 25 cm. Bibliography: p. 317-327. Includes index. ISBN 0-684-18596-2 : LC Card 86-31584 DDC 658.4 19
1. Management. 2. Success in business. 3. Military art and science. I. Title.
HD38 .R5776 1987

Rogers, Dorothy S., 1929- Retailing : new perspectives / Dorothy S. Rogers, Mercia Grassi. Hinsdale, IL : Dryden Press, 1987, c1988. p. cm. Includes bibliographical references and index. ISBN 0-03-001997-4 LC Card 87-5337

DDC 658.8/7 19
1. Retail trade. I. Grassi, Mercia. II. Title.
HF5429 .R5793 1988

Rogers, Everett M. Communication technology : the new media in society / Everett M. Rogers. New York : Free Press ; London : Collier Macmillan, c1986. xii, 273 p. : ill. ; 25 cm. (Series in communication technology and society) Includes indexes. Bibliography: p. 247-260. ISBN 0-02-927110-X LC Card 85-27555 DDC 621.38 19
1. Interactive video. 2. Teleconferencing. 3. Videotex systems. I. Title.
TK5102.5 .R55 1986 ***NYPL [JSE 86-1913]***

Rogers, Gerry. Economics of changing age distributions in developed countries /. Oxford [Oxfordshire] , Topsfield, Mass. , 1987. p. cm. ISBN 0-19-829503-0 : LC Card 86-25098 DDC 304.6/2/091722 19
HB1531 .E28 1987

Rogers, James E., 1945- Life insurance for Canadians : how much? what Kind? from whom? / James E. Rogers.New rev. ed. Vancouver, B.C. : International Self-Council Press, [1980] 84 p. : ill. ; 21 cm. (Self-council series) "Second edition"--2nd prelim. p. Bibliography: p. 83-84. ISBN 0-88908-073-9 (pbk.) LC Card 81-131363
1. Insurance, Life. 2. Insurance, Life - Canada. I. Title. II. Series.
HG8773 .R63 1980

Rogers, Michael, 1949- Yang, Jan-Syau. English-Chinese philatelic dictionary and identification key =. Winter Park, Fla. (340 Park Ave., N., Winter Park 32789) , c1986. [55] p. : LC Card 87-169624 DDC 769.56/014 19
HE6204.C6 Y36 1986

Rogers, Ronald C. (Ronald Clifton), 1946- Doeleman, David. Real estate financial management /. Chicago, Ill. [1987], c1986. 152 p. : ISBN 0-913652-61-X (pbk.) LC Card 86-62851 DDC 333.33/068/1 19
HD278 .D64 1987

Rogerson, Peter. Job turnover and interregional migration [microform] / Peter Rogerson. Iowa City : Institute of Urban and Regional Research, University of Iowa, 1981. 25 p. : ill. ; 28 cm. (ASA/census working paper . 5 5) "October 1981." Bibliography: p. 24-25. Microfilm. New York : New York Public Library, 1985. 1 microfilm reel ; 35 mm. (MN *ZZ-25,047)
1. Migration, Internal - United States. 2. Labor turnover - United States. I. Iowa. University. Institute of Urban and Regional Research. II. Title. III. Series.
NYPL [*ZT-1564 no.31]

Rogerson, S. A Casebook for systems development /. London , Baltimore, Md., USA , 1986. iv, 88, [1] p. : ISBN 0-7131-3600-6 LC Card 87-114266 DDC 658 19
HD31 .C3554 1986

Rogge, Werner. Die Arbeit mit dem Prämienfonds / Werner Rogge. 1. Aufl. Berlin : Tribüne, c1984. 70 p. ; 21 cm. Bibliography: p. 69-70. LC Card 86-100311 DDC 331.2/164 19
1. Bonus system - Germany, East. 2. Incentives in industry - Germany, East. I. Title.
HD4928.B62 G357 1984

Rogoff, Rosalind Louise. The training wheel : a simple model for instructional design / Rosalind L. Rogoff. New York : Wiley, c1987. 151 p. : ill. ; 23 cm. (Wiley series in training and development) Includes index. ISBN 0-471-83467-X LC Card 86-32409 DDC 658.3/12404 19
1. Employees, Training of. 2. Instructional systems - Design. I. Title. II. Series.
HF5549.5.T7 R565 1987

Roguenant, Albert. Lyon, l'argent, le commerce et la soie /. Lyon , c1986. 138 p. : ISBN 2-904638-63-6 : LC Card 86-184131
HC278.L9 L96 1986

Rogulev, ÎU. N. (ÎUriĭ Nikolaevich) Krakh rabocheĭ politiki administratsii Trumėna : 1950-nachalo 1953 g. / ÎU.N. Rogulev. Moskva : Izd-vo Moskovskogo universiteta, 1981. 135 p. ; 21 cm. (Problemy amerikanistiki) Bibliography: p. 130-[134] LC Card 82-155486
1. Labor policy - United States - History. 2. United States - Politics and government - 1945-1953. 3. Truman, Harry S., 1884-1972. 4. International relations - United States - History. I. Series: Problemy amerikanistiki (Unnumbered). II. Title.
HD8072.5 .R64 1981

Rohde, Horst. Sterbetafeln für Personenkraftwagen und Kombinationskraftwagen : 1965, 1970, 1975-1980 / von Horst Rohde. Essen : RWI Essen, 1981. 64 p. ; 30 cm. (RWI-Papiere . Nr. 13) Includes bibliographical references. LC Card 87-408032 DDC 363.1/252/0943021 19
1. Traffic accidents - Germany (West) - Statistics. 2. Mortality - Germany (West) - Statistics. 3. Germany - Statistics, Vital. I. Title. II. Series.
HE5614.5.G3 R64 1981

Rohde, Jörg. Die Gebührenpolitik der Deutschen Bundespost im Kleingut- und Fernmeldebereich . [Mainz] [1984?] xi, 300 p. ; LC Card 87-407592 DDC 383/.23/0943 19
HE6998 .G42 1984

Rohlen, Thomas P. Inside the Japanese system . Stanford, Calif. , c1988. xiii, 286 p. : ISBN 0-8047-1425-8 (alk. paper) LC Card 87-18820 DDC 330.952/04 19
HC462.9 .I587 1988

Röhling, Wolfgang.
Einsatz nachfragewirksamer Staatsausgaben als konjunkturelle Steuergrösse. 1982.
Aktuelle Probleme der Wirtschaftspolitik : ökonometrische Untersuchungen anhand des F&T-Modells / von Joachim Fronia ; Wolfgang Röhling. Tübingen , 1982. vi, 69, vii, 62 p. : ISBN 3-16-344473-3 LC Card 84-125468
HJ5715.G3 A67 1982

Ökonometrische Systeme mit variablen Strukturen : die Konstruktion adaptiver lernfähiger Systeme als Möglichkeit zur Weiterentwicklung der ökonometrischen Modellbildung / Wolfgang Röhling. Freiburg im Breisgau : R. Haufe, c1983. x, 263 p. : ill. ; 21 cm. (Bd. 21 der Schriftenreihe des Instituts für Allgemeine Wirtschaftsforschung der Albert-Ludwigs-Universität Freiburg i. Br) Bibliography: p. [249]-258. Includes index. ISBN 3-448-01353-6 LC Card 84-132199
1. Econometrics. 2. Economics - Mathematical models. I. Series: Schriftenreihe des Instituts für Allgemeine Wirtschaftsforschung der Albert-Ludwigs-Universität Freiburg i. Br. , Bd. 21. II. Title.
HB139 .R63 1983

Rohrbeck, Benson W. Berner, Allan H. Pennsylvania's street railways in early postcard views . [S.l.] , c1986. 106 p. : LC Card 86-221349 DDC 388.4/4/09748 19
HE4487.P4 B47 1986

Röhrenbacher, Hans. Die Kosten- und Leistungsrechnung im Handelsbetrieb : unter besonderer Berücksichtigung der industriellen Vertriebskosten- und Absatzsegmenterfolgsrechnung / von Hans Röhrenbacher. Berlin : Duncker & Humblot, c1985. 176 p. : ill. ; 24 cm. (Betriebswirtschaftliche Schriften. Heft 118) Originally presented as the author's thesis (doctoral)--Wirtschaftsuniversität Wien, 1982. Bibliography: p. [168]-176. ISBN 3-428-05808-9 LC Card 86-129151 DDC 657/.42 19
1. Cost accounting. I. Title.
HF5686.C8 R583 1985

Rohrmoser, Günter. Wende wohin? . Köln , c1983. 139 p. ; ISBN 3-921349-34-6 LC Card 84-150290
HC286.7 .W4 1983 ***NYPL [JFC 87-1258]***

Rohstoffwirtschaftliche Länderberichte. (28) Wagner, Hermann, Dr. Italien /. Hannover , Stuttgart , 1982. xv, 190 p., 4 folded leaves of plates : LC Card 83-235644
HD9506.I82 W34 1982

ROI. Rachlin, Robert, 1937- Return on investment strategies for decision-making /. New York , 1987. x, 306 p. : ISBN 0-531-15528-5 LC Card 87-10633 DDC 658.1/52 19
HG4028.C4 R255 1987

ROI, planning for profitable growth /. Stockton, Richard B. New York, N.Y., U. S.A. , c1984. x, 141 leaves : ISBN 0-86604-150-8 (pbk.) LC Card 86-232254 DDC 332.63 19
HG4028.C4 S72 1984b

Roig de González, Rosa. Picado Hidalgo, Roberto. La inflación y la política económica, el caso de Costa Rica . [San José] , 1985. 16, 20 p. ; LC Card 86-219388
HC143 .P52 1985

Roio, José Luiz del. 1o. de maio / José Luiz del Roio. São Paulo : Global Editora, 1986. 152, [16] p. : ill. ; 21 cm. Cover title: 1o. de maio, cem anos de luta, 1886-1986. Title on added t.p.: 1o. de maio, sua origem, seu significado e suas lutas. "Organizado pelo Centro de Memória Sindical"--Cover. Bibliography: p. 151-152. LC Card 86-197367
1. May Day (Labor holiday) - History. 2. Trade-unions - Brazil - Political activity - History. I. Centro de Memória Sindical (São Paulo, Brazil). II. Title. III. Title: Primeiro de maio. IV. Title: 1o. de maio, cem anos de luta, 1886-1986. V. Title: 1o. de maio, sua origem, seu significado e suas lutas.
HD7791 .R59 1986

Roithmayr, Friedrich. Heinrich, Lutz J. (Lutz Jürgen) Wirtschaftsinformatik-Lexikon /. München , c1986. xxi, 539 p. : ISBN 3-486-20045-3 LC Card 87-122992 DDC 330/.03/31 19
HB61 .H365 1986

Rojas, Fernando [i. e. Fernando Rojas H.] see **Rojas H., Fernando.**

Rojas H., Fernando. Alviar Ramírez, Oscar, d. 1984. Elementos de finanzas públicas en Colombia /. Bogotá, Colombia , 1985. xx, 584 p. ; ISBN 958-604-045-3 (pbk.) LC Card 86-129809 DDC 336.861 19
HJ945 .A48 1985

Rojas L., Gentil. Producción versus consumo de alimentos . [Santo Domingo, Dominican Republic] , 1981. 74 p. ; LC Card 82-207744
HD9014.D62 P76 1981

Rojas Ramos, Patricio. Demanda dinámica por trabajo / Patricio Rojas Ramos. Santiago : Banco Central de Chile, 1986. 58 p. : ill. ; 27 cm. (Serie de estudios económicos . no. 27) An edition of 300 copies. Bibliography: p. 53-55. LC Card 87-404328 DDC 331.12/5/0983 19
1. Labor supply - Chile. 2. Unemployment - Chile. I. Series: Serie de estudios económicos (Banco Central de Chile) , no. 27. II. Title.
HD5756.A6 R65 1986

Rojas Rojas, Edgar. Indices de eficiencia económica para la industria beneficiadora de café : convenio, ICAFE-Escuela Economía Agrícola U.C.R. / Edgar Rojas Rojas, Jorge Moya Rodríguez. San José, Costa Rica : Instituto del Café de Costa Rica, Departamento de Estudios Agrícolas y Económicos, 1986. 14 leaves : ill. ; 29 cm. LC Card 87-403520 DDC 338.1/6 19
1. Coffee trade - Costa Rica - Capital productivity. 2. Coffee trade - Costa Rica - Labor productivity. I. Moya Rodríguez, Jorge. II. Instituto del Café de Costa Rica. Departamento de Estudios Agrícolas y Económicos. III. Universidad de Costa Rica. Escuela de Economía Agrícola. IV. Title.
HD9199.C82 R65 1986

Rojas Senisse, Hugo. Azúcar : crisis y alternativa / Hugo Rojas Senisse. Lima : Instituto de Apoyo Agrario ; [Lima?] : Federación de Trabajadores Azucareros del Perú, [1984] 131 p. : ill. ; 21 cm. Bibliography: p. 90. LC Card 84-234204 DDC 338.1/7361/0985 19
1. Sugar trade - Peru. 2. Agriculture, Cooperative - Peru. I. Title.
HD9114.P52 R65 1984 ***NYPL [JLD 85-1982]***

Rol´ bankov v usilenii gospodstva finansovogo kapitala / pod redaktsieĭ V.V. Shcherbakova, G.P. Solīusa, V.V. Motyleva ; [avtorami glav īavlīaīutsīa, G.V. Polunina ... et al.]. Moskva : "Finansy i statistika", 1985. 206 p. ; 21 cm. Includes bibliographies. LC Card 86-102078
1. Banks and banking, International. 2. International finance. 3. Capitalism. I. Shcherbakov, Vladimir Vasil´evich. II. Solīus, G. P. III. Motylev, Veniamin Vol´fovich. IV. Polunina, G. V.
HG3881 .R615 1985

El rol del empresario mediano en el desarrollo argentino . Frediani, Ramón O. Buenos Aires, República Argentina , c1985. 123 p. : LC Card 87-101993
HD2346.A73 F73 1985

El rol del empresario privado en el desarrollo económico y social en democracia /. Peirano, Ricardo. Montevideo, Uruguay , 1986. 79 leaves ; LC Card 87-404359 DDC 338.9895 19
HC232 .P45 1986

Rol′ finansovo-kreditnogo mekhanizma v povyshenii ėffektivnosti obshchestvennykh zatrat : sbornik nauchnykh trudov / [redkollegiia, Atlas M.S., Reĭtman L.I., Lavrushin O.I.]. Moskva : [s.n.], 1984. 153 p. ; 21 cm. At head of title: Ministerstvo vysshego i srednego spetsial′nogo obrazovaniia SSSR. Moskovskiĭ finansovyĭ institut. Includes bibliographical references. "V nastoiashchiĭ sbornik vkliucheny pererabotannye v stat′i doklady i vystupleniia na proiskhodivsheĭ v 1983 g. v Moskovskom finansovym institute nauchnoĭ konferentsii po teme: Zakon povysheniia proizvoditel′nosti truda i rol′ finansov i kredita v ego ispol′zovanii v stroitel′stve kommunizma"--P. 3. LC Card 86-113408
1. Finance - Soviet Union - Congresses. 2. Credit - Soviet Union - Congresses. I. Atlas, M. S. II. Reĭtman, L. I. (Leonid Il′ich). III. Lavrushin, O. I. (Oleg Ivanovich). IV. Moskovskiĭ finansovyĭ institut. V. Nauchnaia konferentsiia po teme "Zakon povysheniia proizvoditel′nosti truda i rol′ finansov i kredita v ego ispol′zovanii v stroitel′stve kommunizma" (1983 : Moskovskiĭ finansovyĭ institut).
HG186.S55 R64 1984

Rol′ gosudarstva v razvitii ėkonomiki Pakistana . Illarionov, Sergeĭ Ivanovich. Moskva , 1981. 196, [3] p. ; LC Card 82-112505
HC440.5 .I39 1981

Rol′ nauchno-tekhnicheskogo progressa v intensifikatsii obshchestvennogo proizvodstva / otv. redaktor Veger L.L. Moskva : Akademiia nauk SSSR, In-t ėkonomiki, 1986. 177 p. : ill. ; 20 cm. Includes bibliographical references. LC Card 87-163537
1. Technological innovations - Economic aspects - Soviet Union. I. Veger, L. L. (Leonid Leonidovich). II. Institut ėkonomiki (Akademiia nauk SSSR).
HC340.T4 R65 1986

De rol van de technologie in de ekonomische theorievorming /. Roobeek, Annemieke J. M., 1958- Amsterdam , c1987. 175 p. : ISBN 90-71302-06-7 : LC Card 87-132353
HC79.T4 R64 1987

Rola, funkcje i zadania mistrza w systemie dokształcania i wychowania robotników /. Kowtun, Józef. Warszawa , 1979. 151, [1] p. ; LC Card 81-180277
HF5549.5.T7 K687 1979

Rola partii robotniczych w życiu społeczno-politycznym Ziemi Radomskiej w latach 1930-1939 /. Zdrojkowski, Józef. Radom , 1983. 168 p. : LC Card 86-100120
HD8539.R332 Z38 1983

Rola pomocy gospodarczej w polityce zagranicznej USA wobec krajów rozwijających się /. Winiecki, Jan. Warszawa , 1979. 310, [1] p. ; LC Card 81-205172
HC60 .W54 1979

Roland, Ferenc.
Szakszervezetek agitációs és propagandamunkájának kézikönyve. 1986.
A Szakszervezetek kulturális, agitációs és propagandamunkájának kézikönyve / [szerkesztette, Roland Ferenc ; szerzők, Balog István ... et al.]. [Budapest] , 1986. 246 p. : ISBN 963-322-335-0 : LC Card 87-409655
HD6680.5 .S874 1986

A Szakszervezetek kulturális, agitációs és propagandamunkájának kézikönyve /. [Budapest] , 1986. 246 p. : ISBN 963-322-335-0 : LC Card 87-409655
HD6680.5 .S874 1986

Roland, Marcos M. O valor de uso em Marx / Marcos M. Roland. [Brasília] : Fundação Universidade de Brasília, [19]81. 52, [2] leaves ; 30 cm. (Texto para discussão . no. 083) Bibliography: leaves [53]-[54] LC Card 85-228336
1. Labor theory of value. I. Series: Texto para discussão (Universidade de Brasília. Departamento de Economia) , no. 83. II. Title.
HB206 .R65 1981

Le rôle du mouvement coopératif dans le développement du Sénégal . Sourang, Abdou. [Dakar] [1981] 44 leaves : LC Card 85-207626
HD3567.7.A4 S67 1981

Le rôle économique et social du paysan africain et l'autosuffisance alimentaire /. Albagli, Claude. Abidjan , c1984. 70 p. : ISBN 2-7236-0648-1 LC Card 85-179020
HD9017.S82 A43 1984

The role fulfilled by the International Trade Centre UNCTAD/GATT within the framework of the United Nations development policy /. Nicanovich, Marta Beatriz. Genève , 1986. xii, 248, 103, xix p. : LC Card 86-225702 DDC 382/.06/01 19
HF1417.5 .N52 1986

The Role of affect in consumer behavior : emerging theories and applications / edited by Robert A. Peterson, Wayne D. Hoyer, William R. Wilson. Lexington, Mass. : Lexington Books, c1986. ix, 196 p. : ill. ; 24 cm. Papers from a symposium held Sept. 21-22, 1984, at the University of Texas at Austin and sponsored by the College of Business Administration and the IC Institute of the University of Texas at Austin. Includes index. Bibliography: p. [161]-184. ISBN 0-669-12874-0 (alk. paper) LC Card 85-46042 DDC 658.8/342 19
1. Consumers - Congresses. 2. Affect (Psychology) - Congresses. I. Peterson, Robert A. II. Hoyer, Wayne D. III. Wilson, William R. (William Raft), 1947-. IV. Texas. University. College of Business Administration. V. IC Institute.
HF5415.3 .R65 1986 ***NYPL [JLE 86-3376]***

The role of demand and supply in the generation and diffusion of technical change /. Thirtle, Colin G., 1944- Chur, Switzerland , New York , c1987. viii, 173 p. : ISBN 3-7186-0384-5 (U. S. : pbk.) LC Card 87-138 DDC 338/.06 19
HC79.T4 T495 1987

The Role of embassies in promoting business : a symposium / edited by Martin F. Herz ; introduction by Erland H. Heginbotham ; overview by Theodore H. Moran. Lanham, MD : University Press of America, 1987, c1981. p. cm. "In which are presented the opinions, experiences, and recommendations of 19 experts--business executives, scholars, and government officials from the Departments of State and Commerce--who discuss what is right and what is wrong, what works and what does not, what must be changed, and what has already changed in order to improve what is being done in this important field of diplomacy." Reprint. Originally published: Washington, D.C. : Institute for the Study of Diplomacy, Edmund A. Walsh School of Foreign Service, Georgetown University, c1981. "Co-published by arrangement with the Institute for the Study of Diplomacy, Georgetown University"--T.p. verso. Bibliography: p. ISBN 0-8191-5053-3 (pbk. : alk. paper) LC Card 87-14027 DDC 382/.3/0973 19
1. Foreign trade promotion - United States - Congresses. 2. Commercial attachés - United States - Congresses. I. Herz, Martin Florian, 1917-. II. Georgetown University. Institute for the Study of Diplomacy.
HF1417.5 .R64 1987

Role of foreign trade in Indian economy / Malcolm S. Adiseshiah. 1st ed. New Delhi : Lancer International in association with India International Centre, 1986. 216 p. ; 23 cm. Spine title: Foreign trade. Includes bibliographies and index. ISBN 81-7062-001-5 : LC Card 86-902110 DDC 382/.0954 19
1. India - Commerce. 2. India - Foreign economic relations. 3. India - Economic conditions - 1947-. I. Adiseshiah, Malcolm S. II. Lancer International. III. India International Centre. IV. Title: Foreign trade.
HF3782 .R65 1986

The role of housing in development models . Landivar, Jorge F. Swansea, U.K. , 1986. 60 p. ; ISBN 0-906250-12-9 (pbk.) LC Card 87-166136 DDC 363.5/8 19
HD7287.96.E2 L36 1986

Role of international monopolies in the food system. Rol′mezhdunarodnykh monopoliĭ v prodovol′stvennoĭ sisteme /. Sofiia , 1985. 113 p. ; LC Card 86-109190
HD9000.5 .R62 1985

The role of large firms in local job creation : local initiatives for employment creation. Paris : Organisation for Economic Co-operation and Development ; [Washington, D.C. : OECD Publications and Information Centre, distributor], c1986. 31 p. ; 23 cm. LC Card 87-130519 DDC 331.12/4 19
1. Job vacancies. 2. Big business. 3. Industrial promotion. 4. Industry and state. I. Organisation for Economic Co-operation and Development.
HD5710.5 .R65 1986

Role of management, training & research in railroad operations /. Ghias-ud-Din, Mian. [Pakistan , 1983?] (Lahore : Caxton Printing Press) 98 p., A-C folded leaves of plates : LC Card 86-903113 DDC 385/.068 19
HE3300.5 .G48 1983

Role of multinationals in India's foreign trade /. Saxena, Usha, 1957- New Delhi , 1987. xx, 237 p. ; ISBN 81-7024-081-6 : LC Card 87-900766 DDC 382/.0954 19
HD2899 .S29 1987

The Role of privatization in Florida's growth / by Law & Economics Center, University of Miami and Local Government Center, Reason Foundation. [Tallahassee?] : Florida Chamber of Commerce Foundation, c1987. iv, 474 p. ; 30 cm. + 3 computer disks (5 1/4 in.) System requirements for computer disks: IBM PC and 100% compatibles. Includes bibliographies. LC Card 87-403210 DDC 338.9 19
1. Privatization - Florida. 2. Contracting out - Florida. 3. Privatization - Law and legislation - Florida. I. University of Miami. Law and Economics Center. II. Reason Foundation. Local Government Center.
HD3865.F6 R65 1987

Role of science in forming the development strategy for SR Slovenia. Vloga znanosti pri oblikovanju strategije razvoja SR Slovenije /. Ljubljana , 1981. 174 p. : LC Card 82-151266
HC407.Z7 S57 1981

Role of the Asia-Pacific Region in World Economic Development. International Symposium on the Role of the Asia-Pacific Region in World Economic Development (1984 : Tokyo, Japan) Proceedings of the International Symposium on the Role of the Asia-Pacific Region in World Economic Development . Tokyo , c1985. iv, 325 p. : LC Card 87-108109 DDC 337.9 19
HC681 .I58 1984

The role of the current account in asset market models of exchange rate determination /. Gross, Alexander, 1953- Berlin , New York , 1987. xiii, 391 p. : ISBN 0-89925-373-3 (U. S.) : LC Card 87-8852 DDC 332.4/56 19
HG3882 .G75 1987

The role of the Peace Corps in education in developing countries . Landrum, Roger L. Washington, D.C. [1984] iv, 258 p. ; LC Card 86-601664 DDC 371.2/07 19
HC60.5 .L27 1984

The Role of the SDR in the international monetary system : studies / by the Research and Treasurer's departments of the International Monetary Fund. Washington, D.C. : The Fund, 1987. vii, 62 p. : ill. (some col.) ; 28 cm. (Occasional paper / International Monetary Fund, 0251-6365 . no. 51) "March 1987." Edited by Juanita Roushdy. Includes bibliographies. ISBN 0-939934-81-7 (pbk.) : LC Card 87-4184 DDC 332.4/5 19
1. Special drawing rights. 2. European currency unit. 3. International finance. I. Roushdy, Juanita. II. International Monetary Fund. Research Dept. III. International Monetary Fund. Treasurer's Dept. IV. Series: Occasional paper (International Monetary Fund) , no. 51.
HG3898 .R65 1987

The Role of the sheltered workshops in the rehabilitation of the severely handicapped. 2nd print. New York : Greenleigh Associates, Inc., 1976. xxiv, 467 p. ; 28 cm. Includes bibliographical references.
1. Sheltered workshops - United States. 2. Vocational Rehabilitation - United States. 3. Physically handicapped - Employment - United States. I. Greenleigh Associates, inc. II. United States. Rehabilitation Services Administration.
NYPL [JLF 86-1287]

Role playing the principles of selling . Sellars, David. Chicago , c1987. xiii, 102 p. ; ISBN 0-03-013048-4 (pbk.) LC Card 86-24073 DDC 658.8/5/071173 19
HF5438.2 .S45 1987

Roliata na mezhdunarodnite monopoli v proizvodstvoto na prodovolstviia. Rol′mezhdunarodnykh monopoliĭ v prodovol′stvennoĭ sisteme /. Sofiia , 1985. 113 p. ; LC Card 86-109190
HD9000.5 .R62 1985

Die Rolle der Rüstung in der Wirtschaft des heutigen Kapitalismus / Autorenkollektiv [Johann Peter ... et al. ; Klaus Engelhardt, Leiter des Autorenkollektivs]. Berlin : Institut

für Internationale Politik und Wirtschaft der DDR, [1984] 127 p. ; 22 cm. (IPW-Forschungshefte, 0323-3901 . 4/1984) Summary in English, French, German, Russian, and Spanish. Bibliography: p. 119-124. LC Card 85-135711
1. Armaments - Economic aspects. 2. Armaments - Economic aspects - United States. 3. Armaments - Economic aspects - Germany (West). 4. Capitalism. 5. Capitalism - United States. 6. Capitalism - Germany (West). 7. Imperialism. I. Peter, Johann, Dr. II. Engelhardt, Klaus. III. Series: IPW-Forschungshefte , 1984ns4.
HC281 .B39 1984 Heft 4 HC79.D4

Die Rolle öffentlicher Industrieunternehmen im Exportsektor Indiens /. Nunnenkamp, Peter. Hamburg , 1985. xiv, 268 p. : ISBN 3-87895-285-6 : LC Card 87-111454
HD4293 .N85 1985

Rollo, Vera A. Foster. Aviation insurance / by Vera Foster Rollo. Lanham, Md. : Maryland Historical Press, 1987. x, 438 p. : ill. ; 24 cm. "SAN #202-6147"--T.p. verso. Bibliography: p. 406. Includes index. ISBN 0-917882-22-9 LC Card 86-62107 DDC 368/.093/0973 19
1. Insurance, Aviation - United States. I. Title.
HG9972.3 .R65 1987

Rol'mezhdunarodnykh monopoliĭ v prodovol'stvennoĭ sisteme / [T. Popov (otvetstvennyĭ redaktor)]. Sofiia : Izd-vo Bolgarskoĭ akademii nauk, 1985. 113 p. ; 20 cm. Title on added t.p.: Role of international monopolies in the food system. Title in colophon: Roliata na mezhdunarodnite monopoli v proizvodstvoto na prodovolstviia. At head of title: Bolgarskaia akademiia nauk. NIL po problemam prodovol'stvennogo kompleksa. Summaries in English. Includes bibliographical references. LC Card 86-109190
1. Food industry and trade. 2. Food supply. 3. International business enterprises. I. Popov, Todor. II. NIL po problemam prodovol'stvennogo kompleksa (Bŭlgarska akademiia na naukite). III. Title: Role of international monopolies in the food system. IV. Title: Roliata na mezhdunarodnite monopoli v proizvodstvoto na prodovolstviia.
HD9000.5 .R62 1985

Roloff, Otto, 1937- Umweltschutz in öffentlichen Budgets / Otto Roloff, Werner Wild. Regensburg : Transfer, c1986. 278 p. : ill. ; 24 cm. Includes bibliographies. ISBN 3-924956-14-6 LC Card 87-129127 DDC 363.7/00943 19
1. Environmental policy - Germany - History. 2. Local government - Germany - History. 3. Environmental policy - Germany (West) - Nordrhein-Westfalen. 4. Local government - Germany (West) - Nordrhein-Westfalen. I. Wild, Werner. II. Title.
HC290.5.E5 R65 1986

Rolova, Aleksandra, 1920- Feodālisms Baltijas reģionā . Rīga , 1985. 147 p. : LC Card 86-177836
HC243 .F46 1985

Roma. see **Rome.**

Romagnoli, Gian Cesare, 1948- Nuove politiche di finanziamento degli enti locali in Italia : confronti con l'esperienza nord-americana / Gian Cesare Romagnoli ; presentazione di Francesco Forte. Milano, Italy : F. Angeli, c1985. 260 p. : ill. ; 22 cm. (Collana di pubblicazioni dell'Istituto di politica economica e finanziaria della Facoltà di economia e commercio della Università di Roma . 9) Bibliography: p. [237]-251. Includes index. LC Card 86-169439
1. Local finance - Italy. 2. Local finance - United States. 3. Intergovernmental fiscal relations - Italy. 4. Intergovernmental fiscal relations - United States. I. Title. II. Series.
HJ9497 .R65 1985

ROMAN ANTIQUITIES. see **ROADS, ROMAN.**

Román, Arquímedes. Belardi C., Arturo. La industria frente a la inflación . Valencia [Venezuela] , 1981. 92 leaves : LC Card 85-187972
HG915 .B44 1981

Roman Catholic Church. see **Catholic Church.**

Roman Catholicism and the right to work /. McLean, Edward B. Lanham , c1985. ix, 175 p. ; ISBN 0-8191-5009-6 (alk. paper) : LC Card 85-20379 DDC 261.8/5 19
HD6338 .M436 1985 NYPL [JLD 86-2803]

Román de Silgado, Manuel. Burocracia y cambio social / Manuel Román de Silgado. [Lima] : Centro de Investigación, Universidad del Pacífico, 1975. 327 p. : ill. ; 20 cm. (Serie Departamentos académicos . no. 2) On cover: Universidad del Pacífico, Departamento de Ciencias Sociales y Políticas. Includes bibliographical references. LC Card 77-553812
1. Bureaucracy. 2. Developing countries - Politics and government. I. Title. II. Series.
JF1355 .R688 NYPL [JLC 77-327]

Román Egea, Antonio. Supuestos y consultas sobre licencia fiscal : actividades comerciales e industriales y de profesionales y artistas / Antonio Román Egea. Madrid : Editoriales de Derecho Reunidas, [1984?] 235 p. ; 22 cm. (Textos fiscales) ISBN 84-7130-439-2 LC Card 86-149143 DDC 343.4606/8 344.60368 19
1. Business tax - Spain - Accounting. I. Title. II. Series.
HJ5627.S7 R66 1984

Román, Manuel [i. e. Manuel Román de Silgado] see **Román de Silgado, Manuel.**

ROMAN ROADS. see **ROADS, ROMAN.**

Roman, Yves. De Narbonne à Bordeaux : un axe économique au Ier siècle avant J.-C. : (125 av. J.-C.-14 ap. J.-C.) / Yves Roman. Lyon : Presses universitaires de Lyon, c1983. 333 p. : ill. ; 24 cm. Bibliography: p. [255]-328. ISBN 2-7297-0200-8 : LC Card 84-179554
1. Rome - Commerce - Gaul - History. 2. Gaul - Commerce - Rome - History. 3. Narbonne Region (France) - Antiquities, Roman. 4. Bordeaux Region (France) - Antiquities, Roman. 5. France - Antiquities, Roman. 6. Rome - Economic policy. 7. Roads, Roman - France. I. Title. II. Title: Axe économique au Ier siècle avant J.-C. III. Title: Axe économique au 1er siècle avant J.-C. IV. Title: Axe économique au premier siècle avant J.-C.
HF377 .R65 1983

Romanes lecture .
(1986-7) St. John-Stevas, Norman. The omnipresence of Walter Bagehot /. Oxford [Oxfordshire] , New York , 1987. p. cm. ISBN 0-19-951554-9 (pbk.) : LC Card 87-13923 DDC 330/.092/4 19
HB103.B2 S29 1987

ROMANIA - COMMERCE - GREAT BRITAIN - HISTORY - 19TH CENTURY.
Cernovodeanu, Paul. Relaţiile comerciale româno-engleze în contextul politicii orientale a Marii Britanii . Cluj-Napoca , 1986. 404 p. ; LC Card 87-143711
HF3508.R6 C47 1986

ROMANIA - DEFENSES - ECONOMIC ASPECTS.
Pagini din gîndirea economică militară românească /. Bucureşti , 1983. 219 p. ; LC Card 84-116220
HC405.Z9 D443 1983

ROMANIA - ECONOMIC CONDITIONS.
Doh, Rainer. Bevölkerungsentwicklung, Wirtschaftsordnung und Industrialisierungsprozess in Südosteuropa . Neuried , c1985. [12], 486, 19 p. : ISBN 3-88893-045-6 LC Card 87-140271 DDC 304.6/09498 19
HB3631 .D64 1985

ROMANIA - ECONOMIC CONDITIONS - 1945-
Eficienţa economico-socială /. Craiova , 1983. 392 p. ; LC Card 84-152996
HC405.Z9 I523 1983

Samorukova, A. N. (Angara Nikolaevna) Promyshlennost' Sotsialisticheskoĭ Respubliki Rumynii /. Moskva , 1986. 143 p. ; LC Card 86-202797
HC405 .S253 1986

ROMANIA - ECONOMIC CONDITIONS - 1945- - COLLECTED WORKS.
Pătrăşcanu, Lucreţiu, 1900-1954. Scrieri, articole, cuvîntări . Bucureşti , 1983. 415 p. ; LC Card 84-144088
HC405 .P345 1983

ROMANIA - ECONOMIC POLICY - 1945-
Ceauşescu, Nicolae. Cuvîntare la Plenara Consiliului Naţional al Oamenilor Muncii, din 19-20 ianuarie 1981 /. Bucureşti , 1981. 31 p. ; LC Card 81-153290
HC405 .C4215 1981

ROMANIA - ECONOMIC POLICY - 1945- - CONGRESSES.
Congress of Working People of Romania (3rd : 1986 : Bucharest, Romania) Third Congress of Working People of Romania. Bucharest [1986?] ii, 56 p. ; LC Card 86-225999 DDC 331/.09498 19
HD8642 .C59 1986

ROMANIA - ECONOMIC POLICY - 1954-
Romania from the perspective opened by the 1986-1990 five-year plan. Bucharest [1986?] iii, 119 p. ; LC Card 87-124268 DDC 338.9498 19
HC405 .R563 1986

ROMANIA - FOREIGN ECONOMIC RELATIONS.
Linden, Ronald Haly. Communist states and international change . Boston , c1987. xviii, 201 p. ; ISBN 0-04-497050-1 : LC Card 87-11389 DDC 337.497 19
HF1581 .L56 1987

Romania from the perspective opened by the 1986-1990 five-year plan. Bucharest : Romanian News Agency, [1986?] iii, 119 p. ; 21 cm. Cover title. CONTENTS. - Nicolae Ceauşescu's speech at the plenary meeting of the CC of the RCP -- Nicolae Ceauşescu's speech at the joint plenary meeting of the National Council for Working People and the Supreme Council of Economic and Social Development -- Session of the Grand National Assembly, memoranda and laws. LC Card 87-124268 DDC 338.9498 19
1. Central planning - Romania. 2. Romania - Economic policy - 1954-. I. Ceauşescu, Nicolae.
HC405 .R563 1986

Romania - Government. see **Romania - Politics and government.**

ROMANIA - INDUSTRIES.
Samorukova, A. N. (Angara Nikolaevna) Promyshlennost' Sotsialisticheskoĭ Respubliki Rumynii /. Moskva , 1986. 143 p. ; LC Card 86-202797
HC405 .S253 1986

ROMANIA - INDUSTRIES - STATISTICS.
Ştefan, C. Statistică industrială . Bucureşti , 1985. 223 p. ; LC Card 86-155097
HB137 .S76 1985

ROMANIA - POLITICS AND GOVERNMENT - 19TH CENTURY.
Condiţiile istorice ale apariţiei şi dezvoltării clasei muncitoare din România . Bucureşti , 1984. 652 p. ; LC Card 84-234192
HD8648 .C65 1984

ROMANIA - POLITICS AND GOVERNMENT - 1944-
Linden, Ronald Haly. Communist states and international change . Boston , c1987. xviii, 201 p. ; ISBN 0-04-497050-1 : LC Card 87-11389 DDC 337.497 19
HF1581 .L56 1987

ROMANIA - POLITICS AND GOVERNMENT - 1944- - COLLECTED WORKS.
Pătrăşcanu, Lucreţiu, 1900-1954. Scrieri, articole, cuvîntări . Bucureşti , 1983. 415 p. ; LC Card 84-144088
HC405 .P345 1983

ROMANIA - POPULATION.
Doh, Rainer. Bevölkerungsentwicklung, Wirtschaftsordnung und Industrialisierungsprozess in Südosteuropa . Neuried , c1985. [12], 486, 19 p. : ISBN 3-88893-045-6 LC Card 87-140271 DDC 304.6/09498 19
HB3631 .D64 1985

Trebici, Vladimir. Demografia teritorială a României /. Bucureşti , 1986. 160 p. : LC Card 87-151036
HB3631 .T72 1986

ROMANIA - RELATIONS (GENERAL) WITH BULGARIA.
Bâldescu, Emil. Din istoria legăturilor revoluţionare româno-bulgare (1909-1916) [microform]. [Bucureşti, 1966] 181 p. LC Card 81-475045
*HD8646 .B34 **NYPL [*ZT-1732 no.1]***

ROMANIA - SOCIAL POLICY - CONGRESSES.
Congress of Working People of Romania (3rd : 1986 : Bucharest, Romania) Third Congress of Working People of Romania. Bucharest [1986?] ii, 56 p. ; LC Card 86-225999 DDC 331/.09498 19
HD8642 .C59 1986

ROMANIES. see **GYPSIES.**

Romanized English-Japanese, Japanese-English dictionary /. Takahashi, M. (Morio), 1892-1959. [Tokyo] , 1958. 457, 1226 p. ; *NYPL [*O-*OSG 87-870]*

Romano, Alessandra, 1958- Pavanello, Mariano, 1944- Antropologia ed economia dell'artigianato artistico . Milano, Italy , c1984. 183 p. : LC Card 84-147193
HD2346.I82 T676 1984

Romanov, A. K. (Arnol'd Konstantinovich) Matematicheskoe modelirovanie dvizheniia kadrov v organizatsiiakh / A.K. Romanov, A.I. Terekhov. Moskva : Otdel vychislitel'noĭ matematiki AN SSSR, 1986. 154 p. : ill. ; 22 cm. Bibliography: p. 136-144. LC Card 87-158073
1. Labor turnover - Mathematical models. I. Terekhov, A. I. II. Title.
HF5549.5.T8 R56 1986

The romantic ethic and the spirit of modern consumerism /. Campbell, Colin, 1940- Oxford, UK , New York, NY, USA , 1987. 301 p. ; ISBN 0-631-15539-2 : LC Card 86-30979 DDC 339.4/7 19
HC79.C6 C36 1987

Rome (City). Istituto italo-latino americano. see **Istituto italo-latino americano.**

Rome (City). Istituto nazionale de economia agraria. see **Istituto nazionale di economia agraria.**

ROME - COMMERCE - GAUL - HISTORY.
Roman, Yves. De Narbonne à Bordeaux . Lyon , c1983. 333 p. : ISBN 2-7297-0200-8 : LC Card 84-179554
HF377 .R65 1983

ROME - ECONOMIC CONDITIONS.
Greene, Kevin. The archaeology of the Roman economy /. London , 1986. 192 p. : ISBN 0-7134-4593-9 : LC Card 86-226151 DDC 330.937/06 19
HC39 .G72 1986

Polianskiĭ, F. IA. (Fedor IAkovlevich) Ėkonomicheskaia mysl' Drevnego Rima . Moskva , 1978. 355 p. ; LC Card 81-167944
HC39 .P65 1978

Reekmans, T. Inleiding tot de antieke economie /. Leuven , 1984. 129 leaves in various foliations ; ISBN 90-334-0834-1 : LC Card 86-203767
HB77 .R44 1984

ROME - ECONOMIC POLICY.
Roman, Yves. De Narbonne à Bordeaux . Lyon , c1983. 333 p. : ISBN 2-7297-0200-8 : LC Card 84-179554
HF377 .R65 1983

ROME - HISTORY - JULIAN, 361-363.
Pack, Edgar. Städte und Steuern in der Politik Julians . Bruxelles , 1986. 420 p. ; ISBN 2-87031-134-6 LC Card 87-105922 DDC 336.2/014/37 19
HJ9497.A3 P33 1986

Romeo, Mary Ellen. Darkness to daylight : an oral history of rural electrification in Pennsylvania and New Jersey / by Mary Ellen Romeo. Harrisburg, Pa. : Pennsylvania Rural Electric Association, c1986. 152 p. : ill. ; 23 cm. Includes index. LC Card 86-216619 DDC 621.319/09748 19
1. Rural electrification - Pennsylvania - History - Sources. 2. Rural electrification - New Jersey - History - Sources. I. Pennsylvania Rural Electric Association. II. Title.
HD9688.U53 P46 1986

Romeo Mateo, María Cruz, 1960- Realengo y municipio : marco de formación de una burguesía (Alcoi en el siglo XVIII) / María Cruz Romeo Mateo. Alicante : Instituto de Estudios Juan Gil-Albert : Excma. Diputación Provincial, 1986. 171 p. : ill. ; 21 cm. (Ensayo e investigación . 6) Originally presented as the author's thesis (licenciatura--Universidad de Valencia, 1984). Bibliography: p. 161-171. ISBN 84-505-3131-4 LC Card 87-137181
1. Land tenure - Spain - Alcoy - History - 18th century. 2. Municipal government - Spain - History - 18th century. 3. Municipal finance - Spain - History - 18th century. 4. Landowners - Spain - History - 18th century. I. Title. II. Series.
HD780.A435 R66 1986

Romero, Carlos, 1946- Introducción a la financiación empresarial y al análisis bursátil / Carlos Romero. Madrid : Alianza, c1984. 238 p. : ill. ; 23 cm. (Alianza universidad. Textos . 80) Bibliography: p. 229-232. Includes indexes. ISBN 84-206-8080-X LC Card 85-135755
1. Business enterprises - Finance. 2. Stocks. I. Title.
HG4011 .R57 1984

Romero, Carmelo, 1950- Historia contemporánea de Soria, 1860-1936 : aspectos demográficos, socioeconómicos, culturales y políticos / Carmelo Romero.2a ed. [Soria] : Macondo, 1982. 510 p. : ill. ; 23 cm. (Colección Soria existe) "Apéndice documental": p. [235]-499. Bibliography: p. 211-234. Includes index. ISBN 84-85792-02-5 LC Card 85-136084
1. Soria (Spain : Province) - Economic conditions. 2. Soria (Spain : Province) - Social conditions. 3. Soria (Spain : Province) - Politics and government. 4. Soria (Spain : Province) - Population - History. 5. Elections - Spain - Soria (Province) - History. 6. Soria (Spain : Province) - Civilization. I. Title. II. Series.
HC387.S67 R66 1982

Romero Rodríguez, José J. Loring, Jaime. Los sectores agrarios de Andalucía ante la integración en la C.E.E. /. Madrid , 1984. 303 p. : ISBN 84-7114-149-3 LC Card 86-152628
HD2025.A5 L67 1984

Romich, Manfred F. Wirtschaftsreformen und neue Entwicklungsstrategien in der Volksrepublik China /. Frankfurt am Main , New York , c1986. 185 p. ; ISBN 3-8204-9101-5 LC Card 86-220822
HC427.92 .W56 1986

Romitelli, Valerio. Critica dell'economia politica e teoria delle forze produttive / Valerio Romitelli. Milano : F. Angeli, c1982. 241 p. ; 22 cm. (Collana Università . 11) Bibliography: p. [237]-241. LC Card 82-200332 DDC 338.5 19
1. Production (Economic theory). 2. Marxian economics. I. Title. II. Series.
HB241 .R66 1982 *NYPL [JLD 87-812]*

Romney, Brad. Romney, Keith B. Condominium development guide . Boston , c1984- v. ; ISBN 0-88712-195-0 LC Card 83-50498
NYPL [JLL 87-76]

Romney, Keith B. Condominium development guide : procedures, analysis, forms : rev. ed. Supplement / by Keith B. Romney and Brad Romney. Boston : Warren, Gorham & Lamont, c1984- v. ; 25 cm. Includes bibliographies and indexes. ISBN 0-88712-195-0 LC Card 83-50498
1. Condominiums - United States - Handbooks, manuals, etc. 2. Condominiums - Handbooks, manuals, etc. I. Romney, Brad. II. Title.
NYPL [JLL 87-76]

Ronald, Dana M. Successfully developing your accounting practice : a practical guide with forms, letters, and checklists / Dana M. Ronald. New York : Wiley, 1987. x, 314 p. ; 24 cm. Includes index. ISBN 0-471-84736-4 LC Card 86-32388 DDC 657/.068/8 19
1. Accounting - Marketing. 2. Advertising - Accountants. I. Title.
HF5657 .R644 1987

Ronceray, Hubert de. Notre projet de société pour Haïti / Hubert de Ronceray. [Port-au-Prince?] : Graphisme & impression Le Natal, [1986?] 52 p. : ill., port. ; 21 cm. LC Card 86-210570
1. Haiti - Economic policy. 2. Haiti - Economic conditions - 1981-. 3. Economic assistance - Haiti. I. Title.
HC153 .R66 1986

Roncolini, Giuliana, 1948- La crisi della legittimità borghese : capitalismo e razionalità nel pensiero di Jürgen Habermas / Giuliana Roncolini ; premessa di Franco Ferrarotti.1. ed. Napoli : Liguori, 1978. 115 p. ; 21 cm. (Contributi di sociologia ; 48) Bibliography: p. [114]-115. ISBN 88-20-70809-4 : LC Card 79-368996
1. Habermas, Jürgen. 2. Economic history - 20th century. 3. Social history - 20th century. 4. Capitalism. I. Title.
HC54 .R64 *NYPL [JLD 81-254]*

Rondinelli, Dennis A. Development administration and U. S. foreign aid policy / by Dennis A. Rondinelli. Boulder : L. Rienner Publishers, 1987. xi, 188 p. ; 25 cm. (Studies in development management) Bibliography: p. 165-176. Includes index. ISBN 0-931477-97-2 (lib. bdg.) : LC Card 87-4555 DDC 338.9/0068 19
1. Economic development projects - Developing countries - Management. 2. Economic assistance, American - Developing countries. I. Title. II. Series.
HC59.72.E44 R66 1987

RONDÔNIA (BRAZIL : STATE) - ECONOMIC POLICY.
Gonçalves, Sérgio Ricardo Vieira, 1940- Rondônia--política, agrária e transformação . Porto Velho , 1982. 40 p. : LC Card 87-401465 DDC 338.981/75 19
HC188.R6 G66 1982

Rondônia (Brazil : State). Núcleo Estadual Responsável por Migrações. 5 anos de migração em Rondônia, 1979/83 /. Porto Velho , 1984. 7, [19] leaves : LC Card 87-151286 DDC 304.8/0981/75 19
HB2024.R65 A12 1984

RONDÔNIA (BRAZIL : STATE) - POPULATION.
5 anos de migração em Rondônia, 1979/83 /. Porto Velho , 1984. 7, [19] leaves : LC Card 87-151286 DDC 304.8/0981/75 19
HB2024.R65 A12 1984

Rondônia--política, agrária e transformação . Gonçalves, Sérgio Ricardo Vieira, 1940- Porto Velho , 1982. 40 p. : LC Card 87-401465 DDC 338.981/75 19
HC188.R6 G66 1982

Rondorf, Dieter, 1955- Die Bewertung öffentlicher Leistungen durch die Bürger : ihre Bedeutung für die Effizienz des staatlichen Sektors und Ansätze zu ihrer Messung / Dieter Rondorf. Frankfurt am Main ; New York : P. Lang, c1985. 231 p. : ill. ; 21 cm. (Europäische Hochschulschriften. Reihe V, Volks- und Betriebswirtschaft, 0531-7339 . Bd. 636 = vol. 636 = vol. 636) A slight revision of the author's thesis (doctoral)--Universität zu Köln, 1984. Bibliography: p. 217-231. ISBN 3-8204-5652-X LC Card 85-229645
1. Public goods - Cost effectiveness. 2. Fiscal policy - Public opinion. I. Series: Europäische Hochschulschriften. Reihe V, Volks- und Betriebswirtschaft , Bd. 636. II. Title.
HB846.5 .R65 1985

Rönick, Volker. Regionale Entwicklungspolitik und Massenarmut im ländlichen Raum Nordost-Brasiliens : Ursachen des Elends und Hindernisse bei der Erfüllung der Grundbedürfnisse / Volker Rönick. Paderborn : Schöningh, 1986. 136 p. : ill., maps ; 30 cm. (Münstersche geographische Arbeiten, 0176-1064 . Heft 25) Summary in German and English. Bibliography: p. 128-136. ISBN 3-506-73225-0 LC Card 87-407836 DDC 338.981/3 19
1. Brazil, Northeast - Economic policy. 2. Brazil, Northeast - Economic conditions. 3. Brazil, Northeast - Social conditions. 4. Basic needs - Brazil, Northeast. I. Title. II. Series.
HC188.N6 R66 1986

Ronka-Chmielowiec, Wanda. Statystyka i ekonometria /. Wrocław , 1978. 193 p. : LC Card 81-206821
HB9 .B7522 zesz. 141 HB135

Ronkainen, Ilkka A. Czinkota, Michael R. International marketing /. Chicago , c1988. xxi, 649 p. : ISBN 0-03-070297-6 LC Card 86-32959 DDC 658.8/48 19
HF1009.5 .C95 1988

Rønne, Henning. Dødelighed og førtidspensionering blandt ansatte på danske kraftværker / Henning Rønne. 1. udg. København : Arbejdsmiljøfondet, 1985. 73 p. : ill. ; 24 cm. (Arbejdsmiljøfondets forskningsrapporter) Bibliography: p. 69-73. ISBN 87-7359-155-6 LC Card 85-228083
1. Industrial accidents - Denmark. 2. Occupational mortality - Denmark. I. Title.
HD7262.5.D4 R66 1985

Roobeek, Annemieke J. M., 1958- De rol van de technologie in de ekonomische theorievorming / Annemieke J.M. Roobeek. Amsterdam : Scheltema Holkema Vermeulen, c1987. 175 p. : ill. ; 21 cm. (Economische monografieën/Universiteit van Amsterdam . 4) Bibliography: p. 163-175. ISBN 90-71302-06-7 : LC Card 87-132353
1. Technological innovations. 2. Economics. I. Title. II. Series.
HC79.T4 R64 1987

Rooduijn, M. J. Beek, P. van. De leefsituatie van Surinamers en Antillianen in Nederland, 1985 /. 's-Gravenhage , 1986- v. <1 > : ISBN

90-357-0558-0 : LC Card 87-120083
HD8518.5.S87 B44 1986

A roof over their heads . Burke, Terry, 1942- Melbourne , 1984. xiv, 178 p. : ISBN 0-642-87172-8 ***NYPL [JLD 86-2639]***

ROOMING HOUSES. see **HOTELS, TAVERNS, ETC.**

Roomsche kinine tegen roode koorts . Perry, Jos. Amsterdam , 1983. 334 p. : ISBN 90-6012-571-1 : LC Card 83-240733
HD6481.2.N4 P47 1983 ***NYPL [JLD 86-3418]***

Roos, Harry. Small and medium-sized enterprises . Tilburg, Netherlands , 1986. xi, 219 p. : ISBN 90-361-9711-2 (pbk.) : LC Card 86-221122 DDC 338.6/42/094 19
HD2346.E9 S58 1986

Roos, Jean-Louis.
IFAC/IFORS/IFIP/IASC/AFCET Conference on Economics and Artificial Intelligence (1986 : Aix-en-Provence, France) Economics and artificial intelligence . Oxford [Oxfordshire] , New York , 1987. xiii, 194 p. : ISBN 0-08-034350-3 (U. S.) : LC Card 87-6943 DDC 330/.028/563 19
HB143.5 .I44 1986

Roosa, Robert V. The United States and Japan in the international monetary system, 1946-1985 / Robert V. Roosa. New York : Group of Thirty, 1986. ii, 76 p. ; 23 cm. (Occasional papers / Group of Thirty . no. 21) LC Card 86-230043 DDC 332.4/560952 19
1. International finance. 2. Foreign exchange problem - United States. 3. Foreign exchange problem - Japan. I. Series: Occasional papers / Group of Thirty , no. 21. II. Title.
HG3881 .R66 1986

Root, Jane. Open the box : about television / by Jane Root. London : Comedia Pub. Group, 1986. 126 p. : ill. ; 21 cm. (Comedia series . no. 34) "A Channel four book"--Cover. Bibliography: p. 122-123. ISBN 0-906890-78-0 (pbk.) : LC Card 86-206072 DDC 302.2/345/0941 19
1. Television broadcasting - Social aspects - Great Britain. I. Title. II. Series.
HE8700.9.G7 R66 1986

The roots of crisis in southern Africa /. Seidman, Ann Willcox, 1926- Trenton, N.J. [1985] xvii, 209 p. : ISBN 0-86543-026-8 (pbk.) : LC Card 85-72995 DDC 968.06/3 19
E183.8.S6 S45 1985 ***NYPL [Sc E 86-368]***

Roots of rebellion . Barry, Tom, 1950- Boston , c1987. xii, 220 p. : ISBN 0-89608-288-1 : LC Card 87-4519 DDC 338.1/9/728 19
HD9014.C462 B37 1987

Roper, Carl A. Kelley, Clarence M. Security for you and your home-- . Blue Ridge Summit, Pa. , c1984. viii, 391 p. : ISBN 0-8306-0680-7 : LC Card 83-18134 DDC 643/.16 19
HV7431 .K44 1984 ***NYPL [JSE 86-649]***

Roper Organization. The American dream . [New York] , c1987. 103 p. : LC Card 87-404096 DDC 330.973/0927 19
HC106.8 .A437 1987

Röpke, Wilhelm, 1899-1966.
[Problem of economic order]
2 essays / by Wilhelm Roepke ; edited with an introduction by Johannes Overbeek. Lanham, MD : University Press of America, c1987. x, 103 p. ; 23 cm. Essays originally published in 1951 and 1957. CONTENTS. - The problem of economic order -- Welfare, freedom, and inflation. ISBN 0-8191-6125-X (alk. paper) : LC Card 86-33982 DDC 338.9 19
1. Economic policy. 2. Inflation (Finance). 3. Welfare economics. I. Overbeek, Johannes. II. Röpke, Wilhelm, 1899-1966. Welfare, freedom, and inflation. 1987. III. Title. IV. Title: Two essays. V. Title: Problem of economic order. VI. Title: Welfare, freedom, and inflation.
HD82 .R682 1987

Welfare, freedom, and inflation. 1987. Röpke, Wilhelm, 1899-1966. [Problem of economic order.] 2 essays / by Wilhelm Roepke ; edited with an introduction by Johannes Overbeek. Lanham, MD , c1987. x, 103 p. ; ISBN 0-8191-6125-X (alk. paper) : LC Card 86-33982 DDC 338.9 19
HD82 .R682 1987

Rosa, Eugénio. O fracasso dos governos de direita em Portugal (1978 a 1981) : do governo PS/CDS ao governo Pinto Balsemão/Freitas do Amaral / Eugénio Rosa. [Lisbon?] : Edições Um de Outubro, [1982] 351 p. ; 21 cm. (Realidade social portuguesa . 1) LC Card 85-228499
1. Portugal - Economic policy. 2. Portugal - Politics and government - 1974-. I. Title. II. Series.
HC392 .R592 1982

Rosales Díaz, Ramón. Programas de reactivación económica y sistemas financieros : los casos de Argentina y Perú / Ramón Rosales Díaz.1era. ed. [Lima] : Fundación Friedrich Ebert, 1986. 68 p. : ill. ; 21 cm. Includes bibliographies. LC Card 87-400247 DDC 332.4/982 19
1. Monetary policy - Argentina. 2. Argentina - Economic policy. 3. Monetary policy - Peru. 4. Peru - Economic policy. I. Title.
HG815 .R67 1986

Rosbrow, James M. Fifty years of unemployment insurance--a legislative history, 1935-1985. Washington, D.C. : U. S. Dept. of Labor, Employment and Training Administration, Unemployment Insurance Service, 1986. vii, 97 p. ; 28 cm. (Unemployment insurance occasional paper . 86-5) Shipping list no.: 87-116-P. Item 780-A-10 LC Card 86-601117 DDC 368.4/4/00973 s 344.73/024/0262 368.4/4/00973 s 347.304240262 19
1. Insurance, Unemployment - Law and legislation - United States - History. I. United States. Unemployment Insurance Service. II. Title.
HD7096.U5 U637 no. 86-5 KF3675

Roşca, Teodor. Creşterea eficienţei mijloacelor circulante, cerinţă actuală / Teodor Roşca. Bucureşti : Editura Academiei Republicii Socialiste România, 1983. 234 p. : ill. ; 21 cm. Title on spine: Creşterea eficienţei mijloacelor circulante. Summary in Russian. Table of contents in Romanian and Russian. Bibliography: p. 227-[228] LC Card 84-152999
1. Working capital. 2. Business enterprises - Romania - Finance. I. Title.
HG4028.W65 R67 1983 ***NYPL [JLD 87-49]***

Rösch, Willi. Das tägliche Duell zwischen Handel und Verbraucher : Erklärungen zum Verständnis der Spannungen an Orten der Bedarfsdeckung / Willi Rösch. [München-Gräfelfing] : Albrechtverlag, c1975. 110 p. : ill. ; 22 cm. (Fachinformationen) LC Card 84-121903
1. Retail trade - Germany, West. 2. Consumers - Germany, West. I. Title. II. Series.
HF5429.6.G42 R67 1975

Roscher, Volker, 1948- Wohnen . Hamburg , c1983. 230 p. : ISBN 3-7672-0808-3 LC Card 83-219819 DDC 363.5/0943 19
HD7339.A3 W616 1983 ***NYPL [JLE 86-3338]***

Rose-Ackerman, Susan. Knights, raiders, and targets . New York , 1987. p. cm. ISBN 0-19-504405-3 (alk. paper) LC Card 86-33293 DDC 338.8/3 19
HD2746.5 .K58 1987

Rose, Adam Zachary. Forecasting natural gas demand in a changing world / by Adam Rose, David Kolk. Greenwich, Conn. : JAI Press, c1987. xix, 152 p. : ill. ; 24 cm. (Contemporary studies in economic and financial analysis. v. 60) Bibliography: p. 139-146. Includes index. ISBN 0-89232-838-X : LC Card 87-21390 DDC 333.8/23312 19
1. Gas industry - Forecasting - Mathematical models. I. Kolk, David. II. Title.
HD9581.A2 R67 1987

Rose, Adam Zachery. Natural resource policy and income distribution / Adam Rose, Brandt Stevens, and Gregg Davis. Baltimore : Johns Hopkins University Press, c1988. xvi, 139 p. : ill. ; 26 cm. Bibliography: p. 125-132. Includes index. ISBN 0-8018-3523-2 (alk. paper) LC Card 87-2788 DDC 333.7/0973 19
1. Natural resources - United States. 2. United States - Economic policy - 1981-. 3. Income distribution - United States. I. Stevens, Brandt. II. Davis, Gregg. III. Title.
HC103.7 .R67 1988

Rose, Michael, 1937- Travail et sa sociologie. English. Industrial sociology . London , Newbury Park, Calif. , 1987. xvi, 184 p. ; ISBN 0-8039-8053-1 LC Card 87-50308 DDC 306/.36/0944 19
HD6957.F8 T7313 1987

Rose, Peter S. Financial institutions and markets in a changing world /. Plano, Tex. , 1987. xiii, 697 p. : ISBN 0-256-03695-0 (pbk.) LC Card 86-61850 DDC 332.1/0973 19
HG181 .F633 1987

Rose, Richard, 1933-
Getting by in three economies : the resources of the official, unofficial, and domestic economies / by Richard Rose. Glasgow : Centre for the Study of Public Policy, University of Strathclyde, 1983. 40 p. ; 20 cm. (Studies in public policy, 0140-8240 . no. 110) Bibliography: p. 35-39. LC Card 83-150133 DDC 330.941/0858 19
1. Great Britain - Economic conditions - 1945-. 2. Informal sector (Economics) - Great Britain. 3. Home economics - Great Britain. I. Title. II. Series.
HC256.6 .R67 1983

Taxation by political inertia : financing the growth of government in Britain / Richard Rose, Terence Karran. London ; Boston : Allen & Unwin, 1987. viii, 264 p. : ill. ; 23 cm. Bibliography: p. 253-261. Includes index. ISBN 0-04-320197-0 (alk. paper) LC Card 87-11478 DDC 336.2/00941 19
1. Taxation - Great Britain. I. Karran, Terence. II. Title.
HJ2619 .R68 1987

Rose, Stephen J., (Stephen Jay), 1947- The American economy poster and fact book / Stephen J. Rose ; poster designed by Dennis Livingston. 1st ed. New York : Pantheon Books, c1987. vi, 56 p. : ill. ; 28 cm. Includes colored pull-out poster. Bibliography: p. 55. ISBN 0-394-74390-3 (pbk.) : LC Card 86-43119 DDC 338.973 19
1. United States - Economic conditions - 1981-. 2. United States - Economic policy - 1981-. 3. United States - Economic conditions - 1981- - Charts, diagrams, etc. 4. United States - Economic policy - 1981- - Charts, diagrams, etc. I. Title.
HC106.8 .R658 1987

Rose, W. D. (William Dennis) Gapes, R. F. (Robert Francis) The heavy engineering industry in New Zealand . [Wellington, N.Z. , 1976] 105 p. : LC Card 84-255451
HD9705.N44 G36 1976

Rosecrance, Richard N. The rise of the trading state : commerce and conquest in the modern world / Richard Rosecrance. New York : Basic Books, c1986. xiii, 268 p. : ill. ; 24 cm. Includes index. Bibliography: p. 240-249. ISBN 0-465-07035-3 : LC Card 85-47558 DDC 382/.09/04 19
1. Commerce - History - 20th century. 2. World politics - 1945-. 3. Munitions - Economic aspects - History - 20th century. I. Title.
HF1007 .R549 1985 ***NYPL [JLE 86-951]***

Rosélie, Roland. L'habitation sucrière au Quartier La Dumaine, Le François / par Roland Rosélie et Elyane Jean-Louis. [Fort-deFrance? ; s.n., 1986] ([Fort-de-France] : Impr. Désormeaux) 59 p. : ill. ; 21 x 30 cm. Bibliography: p. 56. LC Card 86-203128
1. Sugar workers - Martinique - Dumaine. 2. Sugar workers - Martinique - Le François. 3. Dumaine (Martinique) - Social conditions. 4. Le François (Martinique) - Social conditions. I. Jean-Louis, Elyane. II. Title.
HD8039.S86 M327 1986

Rosen, Arnold, 1932- Office automation and information systems / Arnold Rosen. Columbus : Merrill Pub. Co., c1987. xvi, 363 p. : ill. ; 24 cm. (The Merrill series in computer information systems) Includes index. ISBN 0-675-20557-3 (pbk.) LC Card 86-62495 DDC 651.8 19
1. Office practice - Automation. 2. Business - Data processing. I. Title. II. Series.
HF5548 .R67 1987

Rosen, Christine Meisner, 1951- The limits of power : great fires and the process of city growth in America / Christine Meisner Rosen. Cambridge [Cambridgeshire] ; New York : Cambridge University Press, 1986. xii, 395 p. : ill. ; 24 cm. Includes index. Bibliography: p. 339-382. ISBN 0-521-30319-2 LC Card 85-7753 DDC 307.7/6/0973 19
1. Urbanization - United States. 2. Urban renewal - United States. 3. Fires - Social aspects - Case studies. I. Title.
HT371 .R67 1986 ***NYPL [JLE 86-2388]***

Rosen, Corey M. Quarrey, Michael. Taking stock . Cambridge, Mass. , c1986. xxii, 176 p. ; ISBN 0-88730-131-2 LC Card 86-14045 DDC 338.7/4 19
HD5660.U5 Q37 1986 NYPL [JLE 87-49]

Rosen, Ellen Israel. Bitter choices : blue-collar women in and out of work / Ellen Israel Rosen. Chicago : University of Chicago Press, 1987. x, 220 p. : ill. ; 24 cm. (Women in culture and society) Bibliography: p. 197-214. Includes index. ISBN 0-226-72644-4 LC Card 87-5867 DDC 331.4/125/0973 19
1. Women - Employment - United States. 2. Labor and laboring classes - United States. I. Title. II. Series.
HD6095 .R74 1987

Rosen, Howard. Job generation . Salt Lake City, Utah , c1986. xiv, 138 p. ; ISBN 0-913420-89-1 (pbk.) LC Card 86-31285 DDC 331.12/094 19
HD5724 .J63 1986

Rosen, Josef. Verwaltung und Ungeld in Basel, 1360-1535 : zwei Studien zu Stadtfinanzen im Mittelalter / Josef Rosen. Stuttgart : F. Steiner Verlag Wiesbaden, 1986. 231 p. ; 23 cm. (Vierteljahrschrift für Sozial- und Wirtschaftsgeschichte. Beihefte, 0506-9416 . Nr. 77) Bibliography: p. [120]-121. ISBN 3-515-03348-3 : LC Card 86-184510
1. Money - Switzerland - Basel-Stadt - History. 2. Finance, Public - Switzerland - Basel-Stadt - History. 3. Taxation - Switzerland - Basel-Stadt - History. I. Title. II. Series.
HG1160.B37 R67 1986

Rosen, Rita. --Muss kommen, aber nix von Herzen : zur Lebenssituation von Migrantinnen, unter besonderer Berücksichtigung der Biographien türkischer Frauen / Rita Rosen. Opladen : Leske + Budrich, 1986. 262 p. : ill. ; 21 cm. (Forschungstexte Wirtschafts- und Sozialwissenschaften . Bd. 20) Bibliography: p. 253-262. ISBN 3-8100-0572-X LC Card 87-112784
1. Women, Muslim - Employment - Germany (West). 2. Women immigrants - Germany (West). 3. Women, Muslim - Germany (West). 4. Women's rights - Germany, West. 5. Alien labor, Turkish - Germany, West. I. Title. II. Series.
HD6149 .R67 1986

Rosenauer, Johnnie L. Effective real estate sales and marketing / Johnnie Rosenauer. 2nd ed. Chicago, Ill. : Real Estate Education Co., c1988. xiv, 258 p. : ill. ; 24 cm. Includes index. ISBN 0-88462-599-0 (pbk.) LC Card 87-9544 DDC 333.33/068/8 19
1. Real estate business. 2. Real estate agents. I. Title.
HD1375 .R597 1988

Rosenbaum, Virginia.
Mathiasen, Karen. Corporate governance and shareholder rights . Washington, DC (1755 Massachusetts Ave., N.W., Suite 600, Washington 20036) , c1986. 96 p. ; LC Card 86-230362 DDC 346.73/0666 347.306666 19
HD2743 .M34 1986

Takeover defenses : profiles of the Fortune 500 / by Virginia K. Rosenbaum. Washington, D.C. : Investor Responsibility Research Center, c1987. 227 p. ; 23 cm. ISBN 0-931035-13-9 (pbk.) LC Card 87-400095 DDC 338.7/4/02573 19
1. Consolidation and merger of corporations - United States - Prevention - Directories. 2. Tender offers (Securities) - United States - Directories. 3. Big business - United States - Directories. I. Investor Responsibility Research Center. II. Title.
HD2746.5 .R67 1987

Rosenbaum, Virginia K. Antitakeover charter amendments : a directory of major American corporations. 1985 supplement / Virginia K. Rosenbaum. Washington, D.C. : Investor Responsibility Research Center, 1986. 100 p. : ill. ; 28 cm. Main directory compiled by Joseph Kruger. ISBN 0-931035-07-4
1. Corporations - United States - Directories. 2. Consolidation and merger of corporations - United States - Directories. I. Kruger, Joseph. II. Title.
NYPL [JLF 86-1964]

Rosenbaum, Walter A. Energy, politics, and public policy / Walter A. Rosenbaum. 2nd ed. Washington, D.C. : CQ Press, c1987. viii, 221 p. : maps ; 23 cm. Bibliography: p. 211. Includes index. ISBN 0-87187-412-1 (pbk.) : LC Card 87-5301 DDC 333.79/0973 19
1. Energy policy - United States. 2. Power resources - United States. I. Title.
HD9502.U52 R64 1987

Rosenberg, Claude N. Stock market primer : the classic guide to investment success for the novice and the expert / Claude N. Rosenberg, Jr.Rev. and updated ed., Warner Books ed. New York, NY : Warner Books, c1987. xii, 372 p. ; 24 cm. Includes index. ISBN 0-446-51257-5 LC Card 87-40163 DDC 332.63/22 19
1. Investments - United States - Handbooks, manuals, etc. 2. Stocks - United States - Handbooks, manuals, etc. 3. Stock-exchange - United States - Handbooks, manuals, etc. I. Title.
HG4921 .R58 1987

Rosenberg, Daniel, 1953- New Orleans dockworkers : race, labor, and unionism, 1892-1923 / Daniel Rosenberg. Albany : State University of New York Press, c1988. x, 233 p. ; 24 cm. (SUNY series in American labor history) Bibliography: p. 215-228. Includes index. ISBN 0-88706-649-6 LC Card 87-10156 DDC 331.7/61387164/0976335 19
1. Stevedores - Louisiana - New Orleans - History. 2. Trade-unions - Stevedores - Louisiana - New Orleans - History. 3. Strikes and lockouts - Stevedores - Louisiana - New Orleans - History. 4. New Orleans (La.) - Race relations. I. Title. II. Series.
HD8039.L82 U664 1988

Rosenberg, Emily S., 1944- World War I and the growth of United States predominance in Latin America / Emily S. Rosenberg. New York : Garland, 1987. p. cm. (Foreign economic policy of the United States) Bibliography: p. ISBN 0-8240-8089-0 : LC Card 87-23683 DDC 337.7308 19
1. United States - Foreign economic relations - Latin America. 2. Latin America - Foreign economic relations - United States. 3. World War, 1914-1918 - Influence. 4. United States - Foreign relations - 1913-1921. 5. Latin America - Neutrality - History. I. Title. II. Series.
HF1456.5.L3 R67 1987

Rosenberg, Gerald I. How to find information about acquisition candidates / by Washington Researchers Publishing ; contributors, Gerald I. Rosenberg, Teresa M. Flynn. Ed. 1. Washington, D.C. : Washington Researchers, c1987. 79 p. ; 28 cm. (Executive reports series) Includes bibliographies and index. ISBN 0-934940-45-2 LC Card 86-51570 DDC 016.3387/4/0973 19
1. Consolidation and merger of corporations - Information services - United States. 2. Consolidation and merger of corporations - United States - Directories. 3. Corporations - United States - Directories. I. Flynn, Teresa M. II. Washington Researchers Publishing. III. Title. IV. Series.
HD2785 .R58 1987

Rosenberg, Jerry Martin.
Dictionary of banking and finance. Rosenberg, Jerry Martin. Dictionary of banking and financial services / Jerry M. Rosenberg. 2nd ed. New York , c1985. xv, 708 p. ; ISBN 0-471-83088-7 LC Card 85-12461 DDC 332/.03/21 19
HG151 .R67 1985
*NYPL [*R-Econ. 86-3275]*

Dictionary of banking and financial services / Jerry M. Rosenberg. 2nd ed. New York : Wiley, c1985. xv, 708 p. ; 26 cm. Rev. ed. of: Dictionary of banking and finance. c1982. Bibliography: p. 706-708. ISBN 0-471-83088-7 LC Card 85-12461 DDC 332/.03/21 19
1. Finance - Dictionaries. 2. Banks and banking - Dictionaries. I. Rosenberg, Jerry Martin. Dictionary of banking and finance. II. Title.
HG151 .R67 1985
*NYPL [*R-Econ. 86-3275]*

Rosenberg, R. Robert (Reuben Robert), 1900-
Business mathematics. Business mathematics / Lloyd D. Brooks ... [et al.]. 10th ed. New York , c1988. p. cm. ISBN 0-07-008166-2 LC Card 87-4210 DDC 513/.93 19
HF5691 .B9 1988

Rosenblatt, Robert M. Gramley, Lyle E. Real estate finance and housing . Washington, D.C. (1125 15th St., N.W., Washington 20005) , c1987. vii, 132 p. : LC Card 87-124264 DDC 332.7/2/0973021 19
HG2040.5.U5 G73 1987

Rosenblatt, Samuel M. East-West trade in technology : a purpose in search of a policy / by Samuel M. Rosenblatt. Washington, D.C. : International Economic Studies Institute, c1980. viii, 64 p. ; 22 cm. (Contemporary issues . no. 4) Includes bibliographical references. LC Card 80-81923 DDC 382/.4560973 19
1. Export controls - United States. 2. East-West trade (1945-). 3. United States - Commercial policy. 4. United States - Commerce - Russia. 5. Russia - Commerce - United States. I. Title. II. Series.
HF1414.5 .R67 NYPL [JLD 81-233]

Rosenbloom, Jerry S. Hallman, G. Victor. Personal financial planning /. New York , c1987. xix, 475 p. : ISBN 0-07-025650-0 : LC Card 87-2584 DDC 332.024 19
HG179 .H24 1987

Rosenblum, Gerald. Immigrant workers; their impact on American labor radicalism. New York, Basic Books, inc. [1973] vi, 189 p. 24 cm. Includes bibliographical references. ISBN 0-465-03207-9 LC Card 72-89280
1. Alien labor - United States. 2. Labor and laboring classes - United States - Political activity. 3. Trade-unions - United States - Political activity. I. Title.
HD8081.A5 R67 NYPL [JLE 73-3033]

Rosenbluth, Gideon. Restraining the economy . Vancouver , c1986. 320 p. ; ISBN 0-919573-60-6 LC Card 87-107157 DDC 338.9711 19
HC117.B8 R475 1986

Rosende Ramírez, Francisco.
Consideraciones acerca del estado del debate en teoría macroeconómica / Francisco Rosende R. Santiago : Pontificia Universidad Católica de Chile, Instituto de Economía, 1986. 51 leaves ; 27 cm. (Trabajo docente . no. 46) "Trabajo presentado en el Encuentro Anual de Economistas 1985, organizado por la Universidad de Santiago." Bibliography: leaves 47-51. LC Card 87-116226 DDC 339 19
1. Macroeconomics. I. Series: Trabajo docente (Pontificia Universidad Católica de Chile. Instituto de Economía) , no. 46. II. Title.
HB178.5 .R67 1986

Tipo de cambio y salarios reales : consideraciones sobre el caso chileno / Francisco Rosende R. Santiago : Departamento de Informaciones, Estadísticas y Publicaciones del Banco Central de Chile, 1985. 28 p. : ill. ; 27 cm. (Serie de estudios económicos : documentos de investigación . no. 25) "Edición de 300 ejemplares"--Verso t.p. LC Card 86-106380 DDC 332.4/5/0983 19
1. Foreign exchange problem - Chile - Econometric models. 2. Wages - Chile - Econometric models. I. Series: Serie de estudios económicos (Banco Central de Chile) , no. 25. II. Title.
HG3934 .R67 1985

Rosenfeld, Martin. Ausgabeneffekte kommunaler Funktionalreformen : zum Problem der Operationalisierung und empirischen Überprüfung des Popitzschen "Gesetzes von der Anziehungskraft des übergeordneten Etats" / Martin Rosenfeld.1. Aufl. Baden-Baden : Nomos, 1985. 395 p. : ill. ; 23 cm. (Die Kommunale Gebietsreform . Bd. III, 4) Summary in English, French, and German. Includes bibliographical references. ISBN 3-7890-1077-4 LC Card 86-156503
1. Local finance - Germany (West) - Lower Saxony. 2. Local finance. 3. Decentralization of government - Germany (West) - Lower Saxony. 4. Decentralization of government. I. Title. II. Series.
HJ9493.5.L6 R67 1985

Rosenfield, James, 1957- Energy markets after the collapse . Cambridge, MA (56 John F. Kennedy St., Suite 5, Cambridge 02138) , c1987. 164 p. : LC Card 87-142725 DDC 338.2/728 19
HD9560.5 .E54 1987

Rosenkrantz, Stuart A. Luthans, Fred. Real managers /. Cambridge, Mass. , c1988. xvi, 192 p. : ISBN 0-88730-103-7 LC Card 87-19080 DDC 658.4 19
HD31 .L865 1988

Rosenkranz, Otto. (ed) Handbuch des Genossenschaftsbauern. [Berlin] Deutsche Akademie der Landwirtschaftswissenschaften [1954-<1959 > v. <v. 1, pt. 1-2; v. 3; in 3 > illus. (some col.) 25 cm. Includes other editions of some volumes. Includes bibliographical reference and indexes. CONTENTS. - Bd. 1. Organisation und Planung. (2 v.). --Bd. 3. Tierische Produktion, von K. Vieweg und O. Rosenkranz. LC Card 60-21317
1. Collective farms - Germany, East. I. Vieweg, K., ed. II. Title.
HD1491.G33 R6

Rosenlew, Andreas. Intern marknadsföring : en begreppsanalys / Andreas Rosenlew. [Helsinki] : Institutionen för marknadsekonomi, Svenska handelshögskolan, [1985] 51 p. : ill. ; 30 cm. (Meddelanden från Svenska handelshögskolan, 0357-4598 = Working papers / Swedish School of Economics and Business Administration . 135 (1985)) "April 1985." Bibliography: p. 46-51. ISBN 951-555-227-3 LC Card 85-214635
1. Marketing. 2. Marketing - Scandinavia. I. Series: Meddelanden fran Svenska handelshögskolan , 135. II. Title.
HF5415 .R5795 1985

Rosenthal, Daniel M.
The case for South African gold mining stocks : the opportunities and hidden hazards for all gold investors / by Daniel Rosenthal and Ellen Young. Bethel, CT : Institute for the Preservation of Wealth, c1987. vi, 57 p. : ill. ; 28 cm. ISBN 0-938689-05-3 (pbk.) LC Card 87-160603 DDC 332.63/22 19
1. Gold - Prices. 2. Gold - Prices - South Africa. 3. Gold industry - South Africa. 4. South Africa - Politics and government - 1978-. I. Young, Ellen. II. Title.
HG293 .R676 1987

The new case for silver / by Daniel M. Rosenthal & Ellen Young. 2nd ed. Lafayette, CA : D. Rosenthal, c1986. ix, 157 p. : ill. ; 28 cm. ISBN 0-9615814-1-7 (pbk.): LC Card 86-208965 DDC 332.63/28 19
1. Silver. 2. Investments. I. Young, Ellen. II. Title.
HG305 .R67 1986

A short course in gold investing : a guide to financial security / by Daniel Rosenthal and Ellen Young. Bethel, CT : Institute for the Preservation of Wealth, c1986. 91 leaves : ill. ; 28 cm. ISBN 0-938689-00-2 (pbk.) : LC Card 86-207234 DDC 332.63 19
1. Gold - United States - Purchasing. 2. Investments - United States. I. Young, Ellen. II. Title.
HG295.U6 R67 1986

The silver & gold investor's profit guide : where to get the best prices on the best silver & gold investments / by Daniel Rosenthal and Ellen Young. Bethel, CT : Institute for the Preservation of Wealth, c1986. viii, 90 leaves : ill. ; 28 cm. ISBN 0-938689-02-9 (pbk.) : LC Card 86-232188 DDC 332.63 19
1. Silver - United States. 2. Gold - United States. 3. Investments - United States. I. Young, Ellen. II. Title.
HG307.U5 R67 1986

Which 3 silver and gold dealers give you the worst prices? : and which give you the best! / by Daniel Rosenthal and Ellen Young. Lafayette, CA : D. Rosenthal, c1986. 58 leaves : ill. ; 28 cm. ISBN 0-9615814-3-3 (pbk.) : LC Card 86-209287 DDC 332.63 19
1. Silver - United States - Purchasing. 2. Gold - United States - Purchasing. I. Young, Ellen. II. Title. III. Title: Which three silver and gold dealers give you the worst prices?.
HG307.U5 R673 1986

Rosenthal, Klaus. Rock, Reinhard. Marketing=Philosophie /. Frankfurt am Main , New York , c1986. 220 p. ; ISBN 3-8204-9700-5 LC Card 87-407971 DDC 658.8/001 19
HF5415 .R557 1986

Rosenthal, Walter, 1929- The complete portfolio of sales personnel tests with recruiting, screening, and selecting guidelines / Walter Rosenthal. Westbury, N.Y. : Asher-Galant Press, c1987. p. cm. ISBN 0-87280-011-3 LC Card 87-17523 DDC 658.3/1125 19
1. Sales personnel - Recruiting. 2. Sales personnel - Ability testing. I. Title.
HF5439.65 .R67 1987

Rosentraub, Mark S., 1950- Urban policy problems . New York , 1986. vi, 261 p. : ISBN 0-03-004218-6 (alk. paper) : LC Card 86-596 DDC 307.7/6/0973 19
HT123 .U7466 1986 ***NYPL [JLE 86-3613]***

Rosenzweig, Phil, 1955- Riccomini, Donald R., 1952- Unexpected Japan . New York , 1985. iv, 132 p. ; ISBN 0-8027-0858-7 : LC Card 85-7313 DDC 658/.00952 19
HD70.J3 R53 1985 ***NYPL [JLD 86-1348]***

Roser, Thomas. Technik auf dem Prüfstand . Essen , Gräfelfing [1982] 183 p. : ISBN 3-7736-0340-1 LC Card 83-187518
HD9698.G42 T43 1982

Roshchin, S. K. (Stanislav Kuz´mich) Opyt stroitel´stva sotsialisticheskoĭ ėkonomiki v stranakh Azii /. Moskva , 1986. 290 p. ; LC Card 87-126301
HC412 .O675 1986

Rosie the Riveter revisited . Gluck, Sherna Berger. Boston , c1987. xiii, 282 p. : ISBN 0-8057-9022-5 (alk. paper) LC Card 86-31852 DDC 331.4/0973 19
HD6073.A452 U64 1987

Rosin, Mark Bruce. Fogel, Steven Jay, 1942- The yes-I-can guide to mastering real estate . New York , c1987. xviii, 302 p. ; ISBN 0-8129-1637-9 : LC Card 86-28503 DDC 332.63/24 19
HD1382.5 .F64 1987

Roskamp, Karl W. International Institute of Public Finance . Detroit , 1987. vi, 106 p. : ISBN 0-8143-1984-X LC Card 87-10724 DDC 336/.006/01 19
HJ203 .I57 1987

Roski, Reinhold. Einsatz von Aggregaten, Modellierung und Planung / von Rheinhold Roski. Berlin : Duncker & Humblot, c1986. xi, 321 p. : ill. ; 24 cm. (Betriebswirtschaftliche Schriften. Heft 121) Originally presented as the author's thesis (doctoral)--Georg-August-Universität in Göttingen, 1986? Bibliography: p. [273]-321. ISBN 3-428-06038-5 LC Card 86-188767
1. Production functions (Economic theory). 2. Production (Economic theory). I. Title.
HB241 .R67 1986

ROSKILDE AMT (DENMARK) - ECONOMIC CONDITIONS.
Godsejerrøster . København , 1984. 320 p. : ISBN 87-7526-018-2 : LC Card 84-224395
HD1333.D42 R674 1984

Rosner, David, 1947- Slaves of the Depression . Ithaca, N.Y. , 1987. x, 229 p. ; ISBN 0-8014-9464-8 (pbk. : alk. paper) LC Card 87-6671 DDC 331.25/0973 19
HD8072 .S6164 1987

Rosow, Jerome M. Teamwork, joint labor-management programs in America /. New York , 1986. xvi, 199 p. : ISBN 0-08-032799-0 : LC Card 85-28397 DDC 331.01/12/0973 19
HD8072.5 .T43 1986 ***NYPL [JLE 86-3139]***

Ross, David, 1947- Walstad, William B. An annotated catalog of microcomputer software in economics /. New York, NY (2 Park Ave., New York 10016) , c1986. viii, 160 p. ; LC Card 86-210285 DDC 330/.028/5536 19
HB74.8 .W34 1986

Ross, Derek. International treasury management / Derek Ross. New York, N.Y. : New York Institute of Finance, c1988. p. cm. Includes index. ISBN 0-13-473968-X : LC Card 87-16118 DDC 658.1/599 19
1. International business enterprises - Finance. 2. Cash management. 3. Foreign exchange. I. Title.
HG4027.5 .R67 1988

Ross, H. Edward. Free airline tickets--worldwide!! : how to negotiate free flights to overseas vacation and tax havens / by H. Edward Ross for the International Services Guild. St. Paul, Minn., U. S.A. : The Guild, c1986. 154 p. ; 23 cm. ISBN 0-9616129-0-8 (pbk.) LC Card 87-117304 DDC 387.7/1 19
1. Airlines - Rates. 2. Air travel. 3. Business travel. 4. Tax havens. I. International Services Guild. II. Title.
HE9783.5 .R67 1986

Ross, Hayes E. Sicking, Dean. Roadside concrete barriers . College Station, Tex. , Springfield, Va. [1985] vii, 60, 64, [51] p. : LC Card 86-622864 DDC 380.5 s 625.7/95 19
HE203 .T43 no. 346-1F TE228

Ross, Howard D. Handbook for raising capital . Homewood, Ill. , c1987. xxiv, 666 p. : ISBN 0-87094-705-2 LC Card 86-71216
NYPL [*R-Econ. 87-1124]

Ross, Jaime. Instrumentos tributarios de financiamientos coadyuvantes a la producción agraria de alimentos / Jaime Ross. Santo Domingo, R.D. : Instituto de Capacitación Tributaria de la Secretaría de Estado de Finanzas, [1983] i, 229 p. ; 21 cm. (Colección Manuales de finanzas públicas . 17) Cover title. "Enero de 1983." Includes bibliographical references. LC Card 84-159753
1. Real property tax - Dominican Republic. 2. Agriculture - Taxation - Dominican Republic. 3. Produce trade - Dominican Republic. I. Title. II. Series.
HJ4308 .R67 1983

Ross, Joseph A. Pessin, Allan H. More words of Wall Street . Homewood, Ill. , 1986. v, 269 p. ; ISBN 0-87094-701-X LC Card 86-70777
NYPL [JLE 86-4060]

Ross, Kenton E. Swanson, Robert M. Century 21 accounting . Cincinnati , c1988. xi, 653 p. : ISBN 0-538-02470-4 LC Card 87-60958 DDC 657/.046 19
HF5635 .C4228 1988

Ross, Murray N. Public choice : the new political economy / Murray N. Ross. [Washington, D.C.] : American Enterprise Institute for Public Policy Research, [c1987] 8 p. ; 28 cm. (The AEI economist, 0149-9785) Caption title. "June 1987." LC Card 87-403005 DDC 338.9 19
1. Social choice. I. American Enterprise Institute for Public Policy Research. II. Title. III. Series.
HB846.8 .R66 1987

Ross, Novella. National Center for Research in Vocational Education (U. S.) A National entrepreneurship education agenda for action /. Columbus, Ohio , 1984. xiv, 114 p. : LC Card 86-201272 DDC 658.4/2 19
HF1131 .N28 1984

Ross, Pepi. Poon, Raymond S. Biotechnology instrumentation . Menlo Park, Calif. (333 Ravenswood Ave., Menlo Park 94025-3476) , c1985. 32 p. : LC Card 87-160671 DDC 338.4/766063 19
HD9706.65.B552 P66 1985

Ross, Stephen A. Corporate finance / Stephen A. Ross, Randolph W. Westerfield. [International ed.]. St. Louis : Times Mirror/Mosby College Pub., 1988. xxvii, 857 p. : ill. (some col.) ; 24 cm. Includes bibliographies. Includes index. ISBN 0-8016-4211-6 (pbk.) LC Card 87-18076 DDC 658.1/5 19
1. Corporations - Finance. I. Westerfield, Randolph. II. Title.
HG4026 .R675 1988

Ross, Steven C.
Understanding and using Lotus 1-2-3 : release 2 / Steven C. Ross. St. Paul : West Pub. Co., c1987. xv, 232, [34] p. : ill. ; 26 cm. (The Microcomputing series) Includes indexes. ISBN 0-314-34741-0 (pbk.) LC Card 86-33964 DDC 650/.028/55369 19
1. Lotus 1-2-3 (Computer program). 2. Business - Data processing. I. Title. II. Title: Understanding and using Lotus one-two-three. III. Series.
HF5548.4.L67 R673 1987

Understanding and using SuperCalc 3 / Steven C. Ross, Judy A. Reinders. St. Paul : West Pub. Co., c1987. xiii, 184, [27] p. : ill. ; 26 cm. (The Microcomputing series) Includes index. ISBN 0-314-30123-2 (pbk.) LC Card 86-32548 DDC 005.36/9 19
1. SuperCalc3 (Computer program). 2. Business - Data processing. I. Reinders, Judy A. II. Title. III. Series.
HF5548.4.S86 R67 1987

Ross, Steven S.
Goldman, Benjamin A. Hazardous waste management . Washington, D.C. , c1986. xx, 316 p. : ISBN 0-933280-30-0 : LC Card 86-2748 DDC 363.7/28 19
HD9975.U52 G65 1986
NYPL [JLE 87-1159]

SPREADSTAT : how to build statistics into your Lotus 1-2-3 spreadsheets / Steven S. Ross. New York : McGraw-Hill, c1988. p. cm. Accompanying disk available. Includes index. ISBN 0-07-053909-X : LC Card 87-22811 DDC 005.36/9 19
1. Lotus 1-2-3 (Computer program). 2. Electronic spreadsheets. 3. Commercial statistics - Data processing. I. Title.
HF1017 .R67 1988

Ross, Walter Sanford, 1916- People's banker : the story of Arthur T. Roth and the Franklin National Bank / by Walter S. Ross. New Canaan, Conn. : Keats Pub., c1987. viii, 288 p. ; 24 cm. Bibliography: p. 277-280. Includes index. ISBN 0-87983-429-3 LC Card 87-4066 DDC 332.1/223/0924 B 19
1. Roth, Arthur T. 2. Bankers - United States - Biography. 3. Franklin National Bank. 4. Bank failures - United States. I. Title.
HG2463.R68 R67 1987

Rosser, M. J., 1949- Mallier, A. T., 1931- Women and the economy . Houndmills, Basingstoke, Hampshire , 1987. xiv, 221 p. : ISBN 0-333-37938-1 *NYPL [JLD 87-1151]*

Rossett, Allison. Training needs assessment / Allison Rossett. Englewood Cliffs, N.J. : Educational Technology Publications, c1987. xvi, 294 p. : ill. ; 25 cm. (Techniques in training and performance development series) Includes bibliographies and index. ISBN 0-87778-195-8 LC Card 87-9070 DDC 658.3/124 19
1. Training needs. 2. Employees, Training of. I. Title. II. Series.
HF5549.5.T7 R65 1987

Rossetti, José Paschoal, 1941- O Brasil do cruzado : antecedentes e perspectivas / José Paschoal Rossetti. São Paulo-SP : IOB, 1986. 135 p. : ill. ; 22 cm. LC Card 87-129096 DDC 338.981 19
1. Brazil - Economic conditions - 1985-. 2. Brazil - Economic policy. I. Title.
HC187 .R673 1986

Rossi, Aldo, 1931- Tecnici, ricercatori, quadri e sindacato /. Roma , 1985. 126 p. : LC Card 86-169979
HD8038.I8 T43 1985

ROSSI, ALESSANDRO, 1819-1898 - CONGRESSES.
Convegno nazionale di studi storici (1979 : Schio, Italy) Schio e Alessandro Rossi . Roma , 1985-1986. 2 v. (1487 p., [1] folded leaf of plates) : LC Card 87-110167
HC302.5.R6 C66 1979

Rossi, Carlo. Franciosi, Franco B. Professionalità e formazione nel settore delle costruzioni . Venezia , 1985. 178 p. ; ISBN 88-317-4781-9 : LC Card 86-234138
HD5716.B92 I724 1985

Rossi-Doria, Manlio, 1905- Le Bonifiche in Italia dal '700 a oggi /. Roma , 1984. viii, 437 p. : ISBN 88-420-2429-5 : LC Card 85-173148
HD1683.I8 B66 1984 *NYPL [JSD 87-50]*

Rossi, Guido. La scalata del mercato : la borsa e i valori mobiliari / Guido Rossi. Bologna : Il Mulino, c1986. 152 p. ; 22 cm. (Studi e ricerche. 209) Includes bibliographical references. ISBN 88-15-01123-4 : LC Card 86-180921
1. Stocks - Italy. 2. Stock-exchange - Italy. 3. Securities - Italy. 4. Investments - Italy. I. Title.
HG5522 .R66 1986

Rossiĭskaia Federatsiia /. Solomentsev, M. S. (Mikhail Sergeevich) Moskva , 1978. 212 p. ; LC Card 81-170399
HC337.R85 S65 1978

Rossiĭskaia Kommunisticheskaia Partiia (Bol'shevikov) see Kommunisticheskaia partiia Sovetskogo Soiuza.

Rossiter, John R. Advertising and promotion management / John R. Rossiter, Larry Percy. New York : McGraw-Hill, 1987. xix, 647 p. : ill. ; 25 cm. (McGraw-Hill series in marketing) Includes bibliographies and indexes. ISBN 0-07-053907-3 : LC Card 86-27381 DDC 659.1 19
1. Advertising. 2. Sales promotion. I. Percy, Larry. II. Title.
HF5821 .R65 1987

Rosslyn, Va. Inter-American Foundation. see **Inter-American Foundation.**

Rosso, Max. Le rail franco-éthiopien en détresse / Max Rosso. Paris : Pensée universelle, c1983. 311 p. : ill. ; 22 cm. ISBN 2-214-04961-4 : LC Card 83-173267
1. Chemin de fer franco-éthiopien. 2. Railroads - Ethiopia - History. 3. Railroads - Djibouti - History. I. Title.
HE3416.Z8 F737 1983

Rosson, Barry T. Roberts, Freddy L. Establishing material properties for thin asphalt concrete surfaces on granular bases /. College Station, Tex. [1985] xvi, 141 p. : LC Card 86-620971 DDC 380.5 s 625.8/5 19
HE203 .T43 no. 345-1 TE270

Rosson, Philip J. Managing export entry and expansion . New York , 1987. xx, 439 p. : ISBN 0-275-92361-4 (alk. paper) : LC Card 86-30330 DDC 658.8/48 19
HF1009.5 .M345 1987

Rosted, Jørgen. Macroeconomic medium-term models in the Nordic countries /. Amsterdam ; New York : x, 324 p. : ISBN 0-444-70262-8 (U. S.) LC Card 87-13422 DDC 330.948/00724 19
HC345 .M33 1987

Roster of certified public accountants, public accountants, and accounting practitioners registered with the South Carolina Board of Accountancy. South Carolina Board of Accountancy. Columbia, S.C. (P.O. Box 11376, Columbia 29211) [1986] 74 p. ; LC Card 87-620717 DDC 657/.025/757 19
HF5616.U6 S68 1986

Rostow, W. W. (Walt Whitman), 1916- Rich countries and poor countries : reflections on the past, lessons for the future / W.W. Rostow. Boulder : Westview Press, 1987. xiv, 194 p. : ill. ; 24 cm. Includes bibliographies and index. ISBN 0-8133-0497-0 (alk. paper) : LC Card 87-8280 DDC 337 19
1. Economic history. 2. Economic development. 3. International economic relations. I. Title.
HC51 .R665 1987

Los rostros y la realidad de la pobreza en la sociedad castellana medieval (siglos XIII-XV) /. López Alonso, Carmen. Madrid [1983?] 54 p. ; ISBN 84-7075-284-7 LC Card 87-110606
HC387.C244 L66 1983

ROTARY INTERNATIONAL.
Leitão, Renato de Castro. Uma visão de Rotary /. Olinda [Brazil] 1985. 55 p. ; LC Card 86-158781
HF5001 .L47 1985

Rotblat, Joseph, 1908- World peace and the developing countries . Basingstoke, Hampshire , 1986. xix, 272 p. ; ISBN 0-333-43636-9 *NYPL [JLD 87-1192]*

Rotch, William. The executive's guide to management accounting and control systems / William Rotch, Brandt R. Allen, C. Ray Smith. 3rd ed. Houston, Tex. : Dame Publications, 1987. ix, 225 p. : ill. ; 29 cm. Includes index. ISBN 0-87393-044-4 LC Card 87-163287 DDC 658.1/511 19
1. Managerial accounting. 2. Cost accounting. I. Allen, Brandt R. II. Smith, C. Ray (Clyde Ray), 1935-. III. Title.
HF5635 .R829 1987

Das rote Chaos . Broer, Wolfgang, 1944- München , c1982. 237 p. ; ISBN 3-7844-7100-55 LC Card 87-672594
HC244 .B76x 1982

Der rote Faden . Heintzeler, Wolfgang. Stuttgart , c1983. 292 p. ; ISBN 3-512-00664-7 LC Card 83-183709
HD9654.9.B27 H45 1983

Roth, Alvin E., 1951- Laboratory experimentation in economics . Cambridge , New York , 1987. ix, 219 p. : ISBN 0-521-33392-X LC Card 87-10343 DDC 330/.0724 19
HB131 .L32 1987

ROTH, ARTHUR T.
Ross, Walter Sanford, 1916- People's banker . New Canaan, Conn. , c1987. viii, 288 p. ; ISBN 0-87983-429-3 LC Card 87-4066 DDC 332.1/223/0924 B 19
HG2463.R68 R67 1987

Roth, Bernhard. Weltökonomie oder Nationalökonomie? : Tendenzen des Internationalisierungsprozesses seit Mitte des 19. Jahrhunderts / Bernhard Roth. Marburg : Verlag Arbeiterbewegung und Gesellschaftswissenschaft, c1984. xiv, 377 p. : ill. ; 21 cm. (Schriftenreihe der Studiengesellschaft für Sozialgeschichte und Arbeiterbewegung . Bd. 46) Bibliography: p. 360-377. ISBN 3-921630-48-7 : LC Card 84-252964
1. International economic integration. 2. International finance. 3. International division of labor. I. Title. II. Series.
HF1411 .R69 1984

Roth, Gabriel Joseph, 1926- The private provision of public services in developing countries / Gabriel Roth. New York : Oxford University Press, c1987. xv, 278 p. : ill. ; 24 cm. (EDI series in economic development) "Published for the World Bank." Includes bibliographies and index. ISBN 0-19-520544-8 : LC Card 86-23880 DDC 338.91/09172/4 19
1. Privatization - Developing countries. I. International Bank for Reconstruction and Development. II. Title. III. Series.
HD4420.8 .R68 1987

Roth, Karl Heinz.
Aly, Götz, 1947- Die restlose Erfassung . Berlin , c1984. 157 p. : ISBN 3-88022-282-7 : LC Card 84-206488
HA37.G3 A49 1984

Ermittlungen gegen die Dresdner Bank, 1946 /. Nördlingen , 1986. cxxxiv, 353 p., [8] p. of plates : ISBN 3-89190-297-2 : LC Card 87-121689
HG3058.D7 E76 1986

Roth, Rainer A., 1942- Zur Problematik der politischen Kultur der Jungwähler in der Bundesrepublik Deutschland / Rainer A. Roth. Passau : Passavia Universitätsverlag, c1984. 516 p. : ill. ; 24 cm. (Schriften der Universität Passau. Reihe Geisteswissenschaften . Bd. 7) Bibliography: p. 491-516. ISBN 3-922016-46-4
1. Voting - Germany, West. 2. Youth - Germany, West - Political activity. 3. Political participation - Germany, West. 4. Germany, West - Politics and government. I. Title. II. Series.
NYPL [JLE 87-703]

Roth, Stephanie F., 1949- Weidlein, Marianne S., 1944- Visions & business . Boulder, Colo. , 1987, c1986. 261 p. in various pagings : ISBN 0-942097-11-4 (3-ring binder ed.) : LC Card 87-7935 DDC 658/.007/7 19
HD30.4 .W43 1987

Roth, Thomas. Buchholz, Steve. Creating the high performance team /. New York , c1987. xiii, 202 p. : ISBN 0-471-85672-X : LC Card 86-32623 DDC 658.4/02 19
HD66 .B82 1987a

Roth, Timothy P. The present state of consumer theory / Timothy P. Roth. Lanham, MD : University Press of America, c1987. vi, 168 p. ; 24 cm. Bibliography: p. 155-168. ISBN 0-8191-5708-2 (alk. paper) : LC Card 86-24619 DDC 339.4/7/01 19
1. Consumption (Economics). I. Title.
HB801 .R687 1987

Rothacker, Hartmut. Zeitstetige Bewertungsmodelle für Tilgungsanleihen : eine empirische Studie des deutschen Kapitalmarktes / Hartmut Rothacker. Heidelberg : Physica-Verlag, c1986. xxiv, 350 p. : 88 ill. ; 25 cm. (Physica-Schriften zur Betriebswirtschaft . 17) Bibliography: p. 339-350. ISBN 3-7908-0343-X LC Card 86-222052
1. Capital market - Germany (West) - Mathematical models. 2. Stocks - Prices - Germany (West) - Mathematical models. I. Title. II. Series.
HG4523 .R68 1986

Rothberg, Diane S., 1930- Part-time professional / by Diane S. Rothberg & Barbara Ensor Cook. Washington, D.C. : Acropolis Books, c1985. 158 p. ; 23 cm. Includes index. ISBN 0-87491-786-7 (pbk.) : LC Card 85-19964 DDC 650.1/4 19
1. Part-time employment - United States - Addresses, essays, lectures. 2. Professions - United States - Addresses, essays, lectures. I. Cook, Barbara Ensor, 1950-. II. Title.
HD5110.2.U5 R67 1985
NYPL [JLE 86-2582]

Rothberg, Robert R. Funkhouser, G. Ray. The pursuit of growth . Redmond, Wash. , c1987. 261 p. ; ISBN 1-556-15043-1 : LC Card 87-20230 DDC 658/.00973 19
HD70.U5 F86 1987

Rothe, John Peter, 1948-
Rethinking young drivers /. [North Vancouver, B.C.] , c1987. ii, 291 p. : ISBN 0-7726-0588-2 (pbk.) LC Card 87-167603 DDC 363.1/251 19
HE5620.J8 R47 1987

Young drivers involved in injury producing crashes : what do they say about life and the accidents? / by J. Peter Rothe. North Vancouver, B.C. : Insurance Corporation of British Columbia, c1986. ii, 77 p. : ill. ; 22 cm. "Traffic Safety Planning and Research"--Cover. Bibliography: p. 72-73. ISBN 0-7726-0530-0 (pbk.) LC Card 87-167610 DDC 363.1/251 19
1. Juvenile automobile drivers - British Columbia - Attitudes. 2. Juvenile automobile drivers - British Columbia. 3. Traffic accidents - British Columbia. I. Insurance Corporation of British Columbia. Traffic Safety Planning and Research Department. II. Title.
HE5620.J8 R67 1986

Rotheim, Philip.
Biotechnology in agriculture . Stamford, Conn., U. S. A. , c1985. xvii, 192 leaves : ISBN

0-89336-485-1 (pbk.) LC Card 87-403883 DDC 381/.456606 19
HD9999.B443 U615 1985

New biotechnology comes to market /. Stamford, Conn., U. S.A. , c1985. viii, 205 leaves : ISBN 0-89336-436-3 (soft) LC Card 87-167067 DDC 381/.456606 19
HD9999.B442 N48 1985

New materials for new semiconductors /. Stamford, Conn., U. S.A. , c1986. xii, 198 leaves : ISBN 0-89336-475-4 (soft) LC Card 87-404262 DDC 381/.4562138152/0973 19
HD9696.S43 U492 1986

The Pet industry . Stamford, Conn., U. S.A. , c1985. xi, 140 leaves : ISBN 0-89336-439-8 (pbk.) LC Card 87-403914 DDC 381/.4568 19
HD9340.U52 P48 1985

Rötheli, Tobias F. Das Volkseinkommen und die internationalen Kapitalbewegungen / Tobias F. Rötheli. Bern : P. Haupt, c1986. 128 p. ; 23 cm. (Berner Beiträge zur Nationalökonomie. Bd. 50) Bibliography: p. 124-128. ISBN 3-258-03669-1 LC Card 87-110633 DDC 332.4/5/0724 19
1. Capital movements - Econometric models. 2. National income - Econometric models. 3. Monetary policy - Econometric models. 4. Foreign exchange - Econometric models. I. Title. II. Series.
HG3891 .R67 1986

Rothenberg, Bertram. U. S. Postal Service bicentennial postmarks, 1972-1984 / Bertram Rothenberg. Johnstown, PA, USA : American Topical Association, c1986. 42 p. : ill. ; 23 cm. (ATA handbook . no. 110) Cover title. ISBN 0-935991-01-8 (pbk.): LC Card 86-224991 DDC 769.56/7/0973 19
1. Postmarks - Topics - American Revolutiion Bicenntenial, 1776-1976. 2. Postmarks - United States. I. Series. II. Series: ATA handbook , 110. III. Title.
HE6187 .A635 no. 110 HE6183.A45

Rothenberg, Robert A. Hillman, Jimmye S., 1923- Agricultural trade and protection in Japan /. Aldershot, Hants, England , Brookfield, Vt. , 1988. p. cm. ISBN 0-566-05339-X : LC Card 87-15043 DDC 382.7/3/0952 19
HD9016.J42 H55 1988

Rothermund, Dietmar. Die Peripherie in der Weltwirtschaftskrise, Afrika, Asien und Lateinamerika, 1929-1939 /. Paderborn , c1982. 295 p. : ISBN 3-506-77461-1 LC Card 83-167120 DDC 330.9172/4 19
HC59.7 .P457 1982 ***NYPL [JLE 87-1202]***

Rothfelder, Helmut. Zyklisches Wachstum, Struktureffekte und Stabilisierungspolitik / Helmut Rothfelder. Regensburg : Transfer Verlag, c1985. iii, 240 p. : ill. ; 24 cm. Bibliography: p. 229-240. ISBN 3-924956-03-0 LC Card 86-212369
1. Business cycles. 2. Economic stabilization. 3. Saving and investment. 4. Economic policy. 5. Neoclassical school of economics. I. Title.
HB3711 .R77 1985

Röthlin, Niklaus. Die Basler Handelspolitik und deren Träger in der zweiten Hälfte des 17. und im 18. Jahrhundert / von Niklaus Röthlin. Basel : Helbing & Lichtenhahn, 1986. 424 p., [3] folded leaves of plates : ill. ; 24 cm. (Basler Beiträge zur Geschichtswissenschaft. Bd. 152) Bibliography: p. 407-424. ISBN 3-7190-0920-3 LC Card 86-187799
1. Basel (Switzerland) - Commerce - History. 2. Basel (Switzerland) - Economic conditions. I. Title. II. Series.
HF3710.B3 R67 1986

Rothman, David J. The Consumers' League of New York . New York , 1987. 47, 47, 55 p. : ISBN 0-8240-7684-2 (alk. paper) : LC Card 87-19804 DDC 331.4/2/09747 19
HD6096.N6 C66 1987

Rothman, Sheila M. The Consumers' League of New York . New York , 1987. 47, 47, 55 p. : ISBN 0-8240-7684-2 (alk. paper) : LC Card 87-19804 DDC 331.4/2/09747 19
HD6096.N6 C66 1987

Rothschild, Constantina Safilios- see Safilios-Rothschild, Constantina, 1934-

ROTHSCHILD FAMILY - HISTORY.
Martín Martín, Victoriano. Los Rothschild y las minas de Almadén . Madrid , 1980. xiv, 639 p. ; ISBN 84-7196-338-8 LC Card 83-149823
HJ8738 .M37 1980

ROTHSCHILD, JAMES, BARON DE, 1792-1868.
Muhlstein, Anka. James de Rothschild . [Paris] , c1981. 242 p., [16] p. of plates : LC Card 82-149581 DDC 332.1/092/4 B 19
HG1552.R816 M84 1981
NYPL [*PWZ (Rothschild, J.) 86-6471]

Los Rothschild y las minas de Almadén . Martín Martín, Victoriano. Madrid , 1980. xiv, 639 p. ; ISBN 84-7196-338-8 LC Card 83-149823
HJ8738 .M37 1980

Rothstein, Lawrence E. Plant closings : power, politics, and workers / Lawrence E. Rothstein. Dover, Mass. : Auburn House Pub. Co., c1986. xv, 201 p. ; 25 cm. Includes bibliographical references and index. ISBN 0-86569-121-5 : LC Card 85-23025 DDC 338.6/042 19
1. Plant shutdowns - United States. 2. Plant shutdowns - France. I. Title.
HD5708.55.U6 R68 1986
NYPL [JLE 86-1884]

Rothstein, Theodore. From chartism to labourism / Theodore Rothstein. New York : Garland, 1984. vi, 365 p. ; 23 cm. (The World of labour : English workers, 1850-1890) Includes index. Reprint. Originally published: London : M. Lawrence, 1929. ISBN 0-8240-5722-8 (alk. paper) : LC Card 83-48495 DDC 335/.1 19
1. Labour Party (Great Britain) - History - 19th century. 2. Socialism - Great Britain - History - 19th century. 3. Trade-unions - Great Britain - Political activity - History - 19th century. 4. Labor and laboring classes - Great Britain - Political activity - History - 19th century. 5. Chartism - History. I. Series: World of labour. II. Title.
HX249 .R68 1984 ***NYPL [JLD 86-1828]***

Rothwell, William J., 1951- Sredl, Henry J., 1935- The ASTD reference guide to professional training roles & competencies /. New York , c1987. 2 v. : ISBN 0-394-55915-0 (v. 1) LC Card 86-26006 DDC 658.3/124 19
HF5549.5.T7 S657 1987

Rotleĭder, A. IA. (Arkadiĭ IAkovlevich) Organizatsiia i planirovanie kredita i denezhnogo obrashcheniia /. Moskva , 1984. 350 p. ; LC Card 85-108172
HG3729.S632 O74 1984

Rotov, Viktor. Liubimoe pole / Viktor Rotov. Moskva : Izd-vo polit. lit-ry, 1980. 149 p. ; 17 cm. (Povesti o delakh i liudiakh partii) LC Card 81-143989
1. Collective farms - Russian S.F.S.R. - Krasnodarskiĭ kraĭ. I. Title. II. Series.
HD1492.S652 K76 1980

Roubíček, V. (Vladimír) Československá demografická společnost. 20 let Československé demografické společnosti při ČSAV /. Praha , 1985. 198 p. : LC Card 86-208016
HB3592.3.A3 C47 1985

Roughnecks, drillers, and tool pushers . Lynch, Gerald, 1908- Austin , 1987. xiv, 262 p. : ISBN 0-292-71553-6 LC Card 87-13857 DDC 331.7/6223382/0924 B 19
HD8039.P42 L95 1987

Round Table Discussions on Japan in the Global Community. Japan in the global community : its role and contribution on the eve of the 21st century / edited by Yasusuke Murakami, Yutaka Kosai. [Tokyo] : Distributed by University of Tokyo Press, c1986. 129, [38] p. : ill. ; 23 cm. Final report of series of eight international conferences held, the 1st in Sept. 1985 and the last in Apr. 1986, which were organized by Ministry of International Trade and Industry. Cf. Pref. ISBN 4-13-057014-5 : LC Card 87-129161 DDC 337.52 19
1. Japan - Foreign economic relations - Congresses. 2. Economic assistance, Japanese - Congresses. 3. Japan - Relations - Foreign countries - Congresses. I. Murakami, Yasusuke, 1931-. II. Kōsai, Yutaka, 1933-. III. Title.
HF1601 .R68 1986

Rounds, Christopher R., 1945- From hacienda to ejido : land reform and economic development in Yautepec, Morelos, 1920-1970 / Christopher R. Rounds. New York : Garland, 1987. viii, 268 p. ; 24 cm. (South American and Latin American economic history) Thesis (Ph. D.)--State University of New York at Stony Brook, 1977. Bibliography: p. 260-265. Includes index. ISBN 0-8240-1369-7 (alk. paper) : LC Card 87-8526 DDC 333.3/1/7249 19
1. Land reform - Mexico - Yautepec (Morelos) - History. 2. Land tenure - Mexico - Yautepec (Morelos) - History. 3. Ejidos - Mexico - Yautepec (Morelos) - History. 4. Sugar trade - Mexico - Yautepec (Morelos) - History. I. Title. II. Series.
HD1333.M62 Y387 1987

Rouner, Leroy S. Corporations and the common good /. Notre Dame, Ind. [Boston] , c1986. xii, 147 p. ; ISBN 0-268-00754-3 : LC Card 85-40597 DDC 174/.4 19
HB501 .C7614 1986 ***NYPL [JLD 86-2145]***

Roush, Fred William. Kim, Ki Hang. Team theory /. Chichester , New York , 1987. viii, 246 p. ; ISBN 0-7458-0154-4 : LC Card 87-4137 DDC 658.4/036 19
HD30.23 .K396 1987

Roushdy, Juanita. The Role of the SDR in the international monetary system . Washington, D.C. , 1987. vii, 62 p. : ISBN 0-939934-81-7 (pbk.) : LC Card 87-4184 DDC 332.4/5 19
HG3898 .R65 1987

Rousseas, Stephen William. Post Keynesian monetary economics / Stephen Rousseas. Armonk, N.Y. : M.E. Sharpe, c1986. x, 126 p.; 24 cm. Includes index. Bibliography: p.120-121 ISBN 0-87332-355-6 LC Card 85-14181 DDC 332.4/6 19
1. Monetary policy - History. 2. Keynesian economics. 3. Chicago school of economics. I. Title.
HG230.3 .R68 1986 ***NYPL [JLE 86-4326]***

ROUSSILLON (FRANCE : PROVINCE) - POPULATION - HISTORY.
Iglésies, Josep, 1902- El moviment de població de les comarques de la Catalunya de sobirania francesa en el curs dels segles XIX i XX /. Barcelona , 1979. 63 p. ; LC Card 81-120813
HB3620.C3 I325 1979

Roustang, Guy. Legay, Marie-Agnès. Réduction de la durée du travail et changement des modes de vie . Aix-en-Provence [1984] ix, 366 p. : LC Card 86-185902
HD6066.F8 L44 1984

ROUTES OF TRADE. see **TRADE ROUTES.**

ROUTES OF TRAVEL. see **AIR TRAVEL.**

Roux, Dominique. Analyse économique et gestion de l'entreprise / Dominique Roux. Paris : Dunod, c1986- v. <1 > : ill. ; 24 cm. (Economie "module," 0338-6074) Includes bibliographies and indexes. CONTENTS. - Théories, méthodes et pratiques. ISBN 2-04-016455-3 LC Card 87-114498
1. Industrial management. 2. Industrial management - France. I. Title. II. Series.
HD33 .R647 1986

Roux, Marianne Cornelia. The Sullivan principles at Ford--audit a [microform] /. [s.l.] , 1981. 16 p. ; ***NYPL [*ZT-1745 no.32]***

Roux, Pierre, docteur en sciences économiques. Economie agricole / Pierre Roux. Paris : Lavoisier, c1986- v. <1 > : ill. ; 24 cm. (Agriculture d'aujourd'hui) Tec & doc Includes bibliographies. CONTENTS. - v. 1. Les fondements de l'économie. ISBN 2-85206-353-0 (set) LC Card 87-106675
1. Agriculture - Economic aspects. 2. Economics. I. Series. II. Series: Technique & documentation. III. Title.
HD1415 .R62 1986

Rouyn-Noranda . Berthiaume, Nicole, 1952- Rouyn [Québec] , 1981. xiii, 169 p. : ISBN 2-89073-103-0 LC Card 83-132846
HD9524.C23 R683 1981

ROUYN (QUÉBEC) - ECONOMIC CONDITIONS.
Berthiaume, Nicole, 1952- Rouyn-Noranda . Rouyn [Québec] , 1981. xiii, 169 p. : ISBN 2-89073-103-0 LC Card 83-132846
HD9524.C23 R683 1981

Rovira Mas, Jorge, 1950- La crisis de Costa Rica / Jorge Rovira Mas. San José, Costa Rica : Instituto Centroamericano de Documentación e Investigación Social, 1986. 175 p. ; 28 cm. (Proyecto crisis y alternativas en Centroamérica--documentos de trabajo) "Para la elaboración de este trabajo, el autor contó con la colaboración de Mario A. Sánchez Machado." Bibliography: p. 155-175. LC Card 87-125520 DDC 338.97286 19
1. Costa Rica - Economic conditions - 1948-. 2. Costa Rica - Economic Policy. I. Sánchez Machado, Mario. II. Title. III. Series.
HC143 .R667 1986

Rowbottom, Ralph William. Organisational design : the work-levels approach / Ralph Rowbottom and David Billis. Aldershot, Hants, England ; Brookfield, Vt., USA : Gower Pub. Co., 1987. 165 p. : ill. ; 23 cm. Includes bibliographies and index. ISBN 0-566-05408-6 : LC Card 86-31946 DDC 658.4/02 19
1. Delegation of authority. 2. Organization. I. Billis, David. II. Title.
HD50 .R68 1987

Rowe, Alan J. Managing with style : a guide to understanding, assessing, and improving decision making / Alan J. Rowe, Richard O. Mason.1st ed. San Francisco : Jossey-Bass, 1987. xviii, 225 p. : ill. ; 24 cm. (The Jossey-Bass management series) Bibliography: p. 207-218. Includes index. ISBN 1-555-42074-5 (alk. paper) LC Card 87-45570 DDC 658.4/03 19
1. Decision-making. 2. Executive ability. I. Mason, Richard O. II. Title. III. Series.
HD30.28 .R676 1987

Rowe, Anita. Gardenswartz, Lee. What it takes . New York , 1987. ix, 205 p. ; ISBN 0-385-23820-7 : LC Card 87-13657 DDC 650.1/024042 19
HF5386 .G214 1987

Rowe, Stanford H. Business telecommunications / Stanford H. Rowe II. Chicago : Science Research Associates, c1988. xx, 529 p. : ill. ; 25 cm. Bibliography: p. 519-522. Includes index. ISBN 0-574-18690-5 : LC Card 87-14001 DDC 651.7 19
1. Telecommunication. 2. Business - Communication systems. I. Title.
HE7631 .R69 1988

Rowland, Benjamin M. Commercial conflict and foreign policy : a study in Anglo-American relations, 1932-1938 / Benjamin M. Rowland. New York : Garland, 1987. 431 p. ; 23 cm. (Foreign economic policy of the United States) Originally presented as the author's thesis (Ph. D.--Johns Hopkins School of Advanced International Studies, 1975). Bibliography: p. 415-431. ISBN 0-8240-8090-4 (alk. paper) : LC Card 87-23787 DDC 337.73041 19
1. United States - Foreign economic relations - Great Britain. 2. Great Britain - Foreign economic relations - United States. 3. United States - Foreign relations - 1933-1945. 4. Great Britain - Foreign relations - 1910-1936. 5. Great Britain - Foreign relations - 1936-1945. I. Title. II. Series.
HF1456.5.G7 R68 1987

Rowland, Diane. Davis, Karen, 1942- Medicare policy . Baltimore , c1986. xiii, 137 p. ; ISBN 0-8018-2874-0 (alk. paper) LC Card 85-45048 DDC 368.4/26/00973 19
HD7102.U4 D279 1986 ***NYPL [JLE 86-3782]***

Rowland, Ronald. Stevenson, Eric. The secondary market and securitization for income property mortgages /. Washington, D.C. (1125 15th St., N.W., Washington 20005) , c1986. xiii, 129 p. : LC Card 87-153518 DDC 332.1/753 19
HG2040.5.U5 S73 1986

Rowley, Anthony, 1939- Asian stockmarkets : the inside story / Anthony Rowley. Homewood, Ill. : Dow Jones-Irwin, 1987. 290 p. : ill. ; 23 cm. Bibliography: p. [286]-290. Includes index. ISBN 962-7010-29-4; 0-87094-987-X (jacket) LC Card 87-137156 DDC 332.64/25 19
1. Securities - Asia. 2. Stock-exchange - Asia. I. Title.
HG5702 .R69 1987

Rowley, Charles Kershaw.
Democracy and public choice . Oxford [Oxfordshire] , New York, NY, USA , 1987. x, 265 p. : ISBN 0-631-15029-3 : LC Card 87-6402 DDC 302/.13 19
HB846.8 .D46 1987

The Political economy of rent-seeking /. Boston , c1988. xvi, 492 p. : ISBN 0-89838-241-6 LC Card 87-16887 DDC 333/.012 19
HB401 .P64 1988

Rowley, Eric E. The financial system today / Eric E. Rowley. Manchester, UK ; Wolfeboro, NH, USA : Manchester University Press, c1987. p. cm. ISBN 0-7190-1487-5 LC Card 87-7938 DDC 332/.0941 19
1. Finance - Great Britain. I. Title.
HG186.G7 R64 1987

Rowney, Don Karl, 1936- Soviet quantitative history /. Beverly Hills , c1984. 216 p. : ISBN 0-8039-2082-2 LC Card 83-19196 DDC 306/.072047 19
HD715 .S5956 1984 ***NYPL [JLD 87-841]***

Rowntree, B. Seebohm (Benjamin Seebohm), 1871-1954. Poverty : a study of town life / B. Seebohm Rowntree. New York : Garland Pub., 1980. xxi, 426 p. : ill. ; 23 cm. (The English working class) Reprint of the 2nd ed. published by Macmillan, London, 1910. Includes bibliographical references and index. ISBN 0-8240-0120-6 (alk. paper) : LC Card 79-56969 DDC 305.5/6 19
1. Social surveys - England - York (North Yorkshire). 2. Poor - England - York (North Yorkshire). 3. York (North Yorkshire) - Economic conditions. I. Series: English working class. II. Title.
HC258.Y6 R64 1980 ***NYPL [JLD 86-3436]***

Rowsell, Edmund Penning- see **Penning-Rowsell, Edmund.**

Rowthorn, Bob. De-industrialization and foreign trade / R.E. Rowthorn, J.R. Wells. Cambridge [Cambridgeshire] ; New York : Cambridge University Press, 1987. xi, 422 p. : ill. ; 24 cm. Bibliography: p. [411]-416. Includes index. ISBN 0-521-26360-3 LC Card 87-6331 DDC 338.0941 19
1. Great Britain - Industries. 2. Great Britain - Commerce. 3. Great Britain - Economic conditions - 1945-. I. Wells, J. R. (John R.). II. Title.
HC256.5 .R683 1987

Roy, B. (Bernard), 1934- Méthodologie multicritère d'aide à la décision / Bernard Roy. Paris : Economica, c1985. xxii, 423 p. : ill. ; 25 cm. (Collection Gestion. Série Production et techniques quantitatives appliquées à la gestion) Bibliography: p. [407]-412. Includes index. ISBN 2-7178-0901-5 : LC Card 86-166619
1. Decision-making - Mathematical models. 2. Management - Mathematical models. I. Series: Collection Gestion (Economica (Firm)). Série Production et techniques quantitatives appliquées à la gestion. II. Title.
HD30.25 .R68 1985

Roy, Bernard. Le Renouvellement du tissu industriel . Paris [1986] 130 p. ; ISBN 2-11-001568-3 : LC Card 86-191910
HD3616.F83 R46 1986

Roy Burman, B. K. Towards poverty alleviation programmes in Nagaland and Manipur / B.K. Roy Burman ; assistance in data compilation in Manipur, Lava Yamben ; supplementary field study in Nagaland, Lanu Imchen. Delhi : Mittal Publications, 1984. xxxi, 123 p. ; 23 cm. Includes index. Bibliography: p. [93]-95. LC Card 84-902780 DDC 338.954/165 19
1. Economic assistance, Domestic - India - Nāgāland. 2. Economic assistance, Domestic - India - Manipur. I. Lava Yamben. II. Lanu Imchen. III. Title.
HC437.N25 R69 1984 ***NYPL [JLD 87-903]***

Roy, Dietrich. Klatt, Edmund. Langenscheidt's standard German dictionary /. New York , 1983-1984. 1341 p. ; ***NYPL [JFC 86-781]***

Roy, P. C. (Prabhash Chandra), 1955- Indo-U. S. economic relations : trade, economic assistance, private investments, problems & future possibilities / P.C. Roy. New Delhi : Deep & Deep Publications, c1986. 206 p. : ill. ; 23 cm. Bibliography: p. [197]-204. Includes index. LC Card 86-902903 DDC 337.54073 19
1. India - Foreign economic relations - United States. 2. United States - Foreign economic relations - India. I. Title.
HF1590.15.U5 R69 1986

Roy, Ramashray. Dialogues on development : the individual, society, and political order / Ramashray Roy and R.K. Srivastava. New Delhi ; Beverly Hills : Sage Publications, 1986. 245 p. ; 23 cm. Includes bibliographical references. ISBN 0-8039-9492-3 (U. S.) LC Card 85-8368 DDC 338.954/12 19
1. Economic development - Case studies. 2. Economic policy - Case studies. 3. Bihar, India (State) - Economic conditions. I. Srivastava, R. K., 1942-. II. Title.
HD87 .R69 1986 ***NYPL [JLD 86-3196]***

Roy, Rémi, 1950- Cyr, François, 1952- Eléments d'histoire de la FTQ . [Laval] [1981] 205 p. ; ISBN 2-89035-045-2 : LC Card 82-105783 DDC 331.88/09714 19
HD8102.F43 C97 1981

Royal Asiatic Society of Great Britain and Ireland. Korea Branch.
Monograph series .
(no. 5) Cook, Harold F., 1929- Pioneer American businessman in Korea . Seoul, Korea , 1981. ix, 104 p. : LC Card 83-140523 DDC 382/.09519/0730924 B 19
HF3023.T68 C66 1981
NYPL [JFE 86-4650]

ROYAL BLUE EXPRESS SERVICES - HISTORY.
Anderson, Roy Claude. History of Royal Blue Express Services /. Newton Abbot , North Pomfret, Vt. , 1985. 216 p. : ISBN 0-7153-8654-9 : LC Card 86-136155 DDC 388.3/22/09423 19
HE5664.Z7 R63 1985

Royal Commission on Broadcasting and Related Telecommunications in New Zealand. Broadcasting and related telecommunications in New Zealand : report of the Royal Commission of Inquiry. Wellington, N.Z. : V.R. Ward, Govt. Printer, [1986] 518 p. : maps ; 24 cm. "September 1986." LC Card 87-130605 DDC 384/.068 19
1. Broadcasting policy - New Zealand. 2. Telecommunication policy - New Zealand. I. Title.
HE8620.5.Z5 R69 1986

Royal Commission on Labrador. Ten years after : progress report on the implementation of the recommendations of the Royal Commission on Labrador, 1974. [St. John's, Nfld.] : Dept. of Rural, Agricultural, and Northern Development, 1986. iv, 116 p. ; 28 cm. LC Card 86-212404 DDC 361.6/1/097182 19
1. Labrador (Nfld.) - Economic conditions. 2. Labrador (Nfld.) - Economic policy. 3. Labrador (Nfld.) - Social conditions. 4. Labrador (Nfld.) - Social policy. I. Title.
HC117.L2 R69 1986

Royal Commission on Seals and the Sealing Industry in Canada. Seals and sealing in Canada : report of the Royal Commission. [Ottawa] : Minister of Supply and Services Canada, c1986. 3 v. : ill. ; 25 cm. Includes bibliographies and index. ISBN 0-660-12127-1 (pbk.) LC Card 87-127610 DDC 338.3/729746/0971 19
1. Sealing industry - Government policy - Canada. I. Title.
HD9778.5.S423 C27 1986

Royal Commission on the Economic Union and Development Prospects for Canada.
Adapting to change . Toronto [Ont.] , Buffalo , c1986. xv, 221 p. ; ISBN 0-8020-7260-7 (pbk.) LC Card 86-673029 DDC 331.12/0971 19
HD5728 .A596 1986 ***NYPL [JLD 87-1967]***

Canadian industrial policy in action /. Toronto , Buffalo , c1985. xvii, 231 p. : ISBN 0-8020-7244-5 (pbk.) LC Card 86-672572
HD3616.C23 C36x 1985
NYPL [JLD 86-2871]

Fiscal federalism /. Toronto , Buffalo , c1986. xvi, 211 p. ; ISBN 0-8020-7312-3 (pbk.)
HJ793 .F59 1986 ***NYPL [JLE 86-3253]***

Schultz, Richard, 1945- Economic regulation and the federal system /. Toronto , Buffalo , c1985. xv, 187 p. : ISBN 0-8020-7287-9 (pbk.) LC Card 86-672574
HD3616.C23 S38x 1985
NYPL [JLD 86-2821]

Technological change in Canadian industry /. Toronto , Buffalo , c1985. xv, 233 p. ; ISBN 0-8020-7243-7 (pbk.) LC Card 86-164766 DDC 338/.06 19
HC120.T4 T42 1985 ***NYPL [JLD 87-654]***

Royal Historical Society (Great Britain)
Spufford, Peter. Handbook of medieval exchange /. London : Woodbridge, Suffolk ; xcii, 376 p., [3] leaves of plates (1 folded) : ISBN 0-86193-105-X LC Card 86-673816
HG3942 .S68x 1986

Royal Historical Society, London.
Guides and handbooks. For other vols. in this series, see Old Catalog.
(no. 13) Spufford, Peter. Handbook of medieval exchange /. London : Woodbridge, Suffolk ; xcii, 376, [3] p., [1] fold. leaf : ISBN 0-86193-105-X ***NYPL [JLE 86-4344]***

The Royal Mail Steam Packet Company /.
Migliavacca, Giorgio. [S.l.] , 1985. 41 p. : ISBN 0-934139-01-6 (pbk.) LC Card 87-149471

DDC 383/.142/09729 19
HE6939.M3 M53 1985

ROYAL MAIL STEAM PACKET COMPANY - HISTORY.
Migliavacca, Giorgio. The Royal Mail Steam Packet Company /. [S.l.] , 1985. 41 p. : ISBN 0-934139-01-6 (pbk.) LC Card 87-149471 DDC 383/.142/09729 19
HE6939.M3 M53 1985

Royal Norwegian Council for Scientific and Industrial Research. see **Norges teknisk-naturvitenskapelige forskningsråd.**

Royal Statistical Society (Great Britain)
Finance. Oxford [Oxfordshire] , New York , 1987. xiii, 495 p. ; ISBN 0-08-034780-0 : LC Card 87-7247 DDC 332/.0941 19
HG186.G7 F53 1987

Rozells, Gia L. Making dollars and cents with dollars and sense / Gia L. Rozells and James V. Bartimo. Greensboro, N.C. : Compute! Publications, c1987. ix, 207 p. : ill. ; 24 cm. (Compute! library selection) Includes index. ISBN 0-87455-101-3 (pbk.) : LC Card 87-160661 DDC 332.024/0028/55369 19
1. Finance, Personal - Data processing. 2. Dollars and Sense (Computer program). I. Bartimo, Jim, 1956-. II. Title. III. Series.
HG179 .R74 1987

Rozin, Bentsian Borisovich. Statisticheskaia otsenka normativov otraslevogo planirovaniia / B.B. Rozin, L.A. Sergeeva, M.A. IAgol'nitser ; otvetstvennyĭ redaktor V.M. Sokolov. Novosibirsk : Izd-vo "Nauka," Sibirskoe otd-nie, 1986. 188, [3] p. : ill. ; 21 cm. At head of title: Akademiia nauk SSSR. Sibirskoe otdelenie. Institut ėkonomiki i organizatsii promyshlennogo proizvodstva. Bibliography: p. 187-[189] LC Card 86-230359
1. Soviet Union - Economic policy - 1981- - Mathematical models. I. Sergeeva, L. A. (Liudmila Aleksandrovna). II. IAgol'nitser, Miron Arkad'evich. III. Sokolov, Vitaliĭ Mikhaĭlovich. IV. Title.
HC336.25 .R69 1986

Rózsa, Jánosné. Manczinger, Józsefné. Ajánlás a vállalatok stratégiai tervező munkájához /. [Budapest] [1984] 97 p. ; LC Card 86-148677
HD30.28 .M346 1984

Rózsa, Tamás. Buga, László. Biztonságos, jó utat! . [Budapest] , 1980. 95 p. : ISBN 963-316-028-6 (Magy. nemz. bibl.) LC Card 85-177784
HE5614.5.H8 B84 1980

Rozvytok kapitalistychnykh vidnosyn u promyslovosti Ukraïny XVIII st. /.
Ponomarev, Alekseĭ Mikhaĭlovich. L'viv , 1971. 181 p. ; LC Card 82-105634
HC337.U5 P58 1971

Rozwój ludności krajów socjalistycznych : praca zbiorowa / pod redakcją naukową Mikołaja Latucha i Dmitrija I. Walentieja ; [autorzy artykułów Janina Aleksińska ... et al. ; przekład artykułów autorów radzieckich Izasław Frenkel, Wiesława Zagórska].Wyd. 1. Warszawa : Państwowe Wydawn. Ekonomiczne ; Moskva : Izd-vo "Statistika", 1978. 381 p. ; 22 cm. Partly translated from Russian. Includes bibliographical references. LC Card 81-206832
1. Poland - Population. 2. Soviet Union - Population. I. Latuch, Mikołaj. II. Valenteĭ, D. I. (Dmitriĭ Ignat'evich). III. Aleksińska, Janina.
HB3608.7.A3 R69 1978

Rozwój sytuacji i polityki gospodarczej w Polsce w latach 1981-1984 / wyboru tekstów dokonał zespół pracowników Sekretariatu KRG w składzie M. Iwanek ... [et al.]. Wyd. 1. Warszawa : Krajowa Agencja Wydawnicza, 1985. 161 p. ; 22 cm. At head of title: Konsultacyjna Rada Gospodarcza. ISBN 83-03-00866-8 : LC Card 85-229473
1. Poland - Economic policy - 1981-. 2. Poland - Economic conditions - 1981-. I. Iwanek, Marian. II. Poland. Konsultacyjna Rada Gospodarcza.
HC340.3 .R69 1985

RP-Japan relations and ADB : in search of a new horizon / edited by Mamoru Tsuda & Leo A. Deocadiz. Metro Manila, Philippines : National Book Store, 1986. x, 137 p. : ill. ; 26 cm. "A Business day book"--Cover. Bibliography: p. 18-20. ISBN 971-08-3156-9 (pbk.) LC Card 86-211088 DDC 337.520599 19
1. Philippines - Foreign economic relations - Japan. 2. Japan - Foreign economic relations - Philippines. 3. Asian Development Bank. I. Tsuda, Mamoru. II. Deocadiz, Leo A.
HF1600.15.J3 R68 1986

RPM realize your power to motivate. Sanders, Mary. R.P.M. realize your power to motivate /. Farmington Hills, Mich. , c1986. 153 p., [2] p. of plates : ISBN 0-9616833-0-9 (pbk.) LC Card 87-111586 DDC 658.3/14 19
HF5549.5.M63 S26 1986

RS Wallace Station, East Peoria, Illinois. Urban Land Institute. R.S. Wallace Station, East Peoria, Illinois . Washington, D.C. (1090 Vermont Ave., N.W., Washington 20005) , c1986. 36 p. : LC Card 86-216045 DDC 333.77/17/0977352 19
HD268.E26 U73 1986

Ruanda. see **Rwanda.**

Rubalcava, Rosa María. Cortés, Fernando, 1941- Análisis del cambio en la concentración a través del coeficiente de Gini /. México, D.F. [1982] 55 leaves : LC Card 83-111847
HB523 .C67 1982

RUBBBER INDUSTRY AND TRADE - BRAZIL - BAHIA (STATE)
Borracha natural na Bahia . [Salvador] [1982] 130 p. : LC Card 87-403935 DDC 338.4/76782/098142 19
HD9161.B82 B186 1982

Rubber chemicals market in Europe. The Rubber chemicals market in the EEC. New York, N.Y. , c1983. xxi, 303 p. ; LC Card 87-142579
HD9161.E8562 R83 1983

The Rubber chemicals market in the EEC. New York, N.Y. : Frost & Sullivan, c1983. xxi, 303 p. ; 29 cm. Spine title: Rubber chemicals market in Europe. "E637." "August 1983." LC Card 87-142579
1. Rubber industry and trade - European Economic Community countries. 2. Market surveys - European Economic Community countries. I. Frost & Sullivan. II. Title: Rubber chemicals market in Europe.
HD9161.E8562 R83 1983

RUBBER GOODS INDUSTRY. see **RUBBER INDUSTRY AND TRADE.**

RUBBER GOODS - SWEDEN.
Gummivaruindustri . Stockholm , 1981. 119, [12] p. : ISBN 91-38-06243-7 LC Card 82-241338
HD9161.S82 G84 1981

RUBBER INDUSTRY AND TRADE - BRAZIL - HISTORY.
Loureiro, Antônio José Souto. A grande crise . Manaus, Amazonas, Brasil , 1986. 282 p. : LC Card 86-222988
HD9161.B8 L68 1986

RUBBER INDUSTRY AND TRADE - EUROPEAN ECONOMIC COMMUNITY COUNTRIES.
The Rubber chemicals market in the EEC. New York, N.Y. , c1983. xxi, 303 p. ; LC Card 87-142579
HD9161.E8562 R83 1983

RUBBER INDUSTRY AND TRADE - HEALTH ASPECTS - QUÉBEC (PROVINCE)
Caoutchouc et produits en matières plastiques au Québec . [Québec] , 1984. 249 p. : ISBN 2-550-10690-3 LC Card 85-155214 DDC 363.1/196684/09714 19
HD7269.R92 C23 1984

RUBBER INDUSTRY AND TRADE - HISTORY.
Coates, Austin. The commerce in rubber . Singapore , New York , 1987. xv, 380 p., [32] p. of plates : ISBN 0-19-588868-5 : LC Card 87-20332 DDC 338.1/738952 19
HD9161.A2 C62 1987

RUBBER INDUSTRY AND TRADE - INDONESIA - ABAISIAT.
Geinitz, Dedo. Entwicklungszusammenarbeit mit Indonesien . Bremen , 1985. viii, 72 p. : ISBN 3-88299-046-5 LC Card 86-204688
HD9161.I63 A244 1985

RUBBER INDUSTRY AND TRADE - SRI LANKA.
Karunaratne, S. W. Potential for foreign investment in rubber products manufacture with information on special projects and a selection of local collaborators /. [Colombo] , 1985. vii, 100 p. ; LC Card 86-902791 DDC 332.6/73/095493 19
HD9161.S752 K37 1985

RUBBER INDUSTRY AND TRADE - SWEDEN.
Gummivaruindustri . Stockholm , 1981. 119, [12] p. : ISBN 91-38-06243-7 LC Card 82-241338
HD9161.S82 G84 1981

RUBBER - PRICES - GERMANY (WEST) - ECONOMETRIC MODELS.
Borrmann, Axel. Die Wettbewerbsposition natürlicher Rohstoffe . Hamburg , 1984. 226 p. : ISBN 3-87895-250-3 LC Card 84-222130
HF1054.G4 B67 1984

RUBBER - TRADE AND STATISTICS. see **RUBBER INDUSTRY AND TRADE.**

Rubbert, Ulrich. Theoriendynamik und die Grundlagen ökonomischer Politikberatung : eine wissenschaftstheoretisch orientierte Untersuchung am Beispiel des monetaristischen Paradigmas / Ulrich Rubbert. Hamburg : Weltarchiv, 1984. 218 p. ; 24 cm. (Veröffentlichungen des HWWA-Institut für Wirtschaftsforschung-Hamburg) Originally presented as the author's thesis (doctoral)--Universität Hamburg. Bibliography: p. 207-218. ISBN 3-87895-262-7 LC Card 85-135703
1. Economic policy. 2. Monetary policy. I. Title.
HD84 .R74 1984

Rubenstein, Hymie. Coping with poverty : adaptive strategies in a Caribbean village / Hymie Rubenstein. Boulder, Colo. : Westview Press, 1987. xx, 389 p. : ill. ; 23 cm. (Westview special studies in social, political and economic development) Bibliography: p. [355]-382. Includes index. ISBN 0-8133-7387-5 (pbk. : alk. paper) : LC Card 86-32530 DDC 972.98/4400496 19
1. Poor - Saint Vincent and the Grenadines - Case studies. 2. Saint Vincent and the Grenadines - Economic conditions - Case studies. 3. Saint Vincent and the Grenadines - Social conditions - Case studies. 4. Blacks - Saint Vincent and the Grenadines - Economic conditions - Case studies. 5. Blacks - Saint Vincent and the Grenadines - Social life and customs - Case studies. I. Title.
HC156.5.Z7 S296 1987

Rubertone, Patricia E. Background study of Maine coastal life : demographic and socioeconomic patterns, Hancock County, 1790-1900 / by Patricia E. Rubertone and Leonard W. Loparto ; prepared for Cultural Resources Management Division, North Atlantic Regional Office, National Park Service, U. S. Department of Interior. [Providence, R.I.?] : Public Archaeology Laboratory, Brown University, 1983. iii, 99 leaves : ill. ; 28 cm. Bibliography: leaves 76-99. LC Card 86-601627 DDC 304.6/09741/45 19
1. Hancock County (Me.) - Population - History. 2. Hancock County (Me.) - Economic conditions. 3. Hancock County (Me.) - Social conditions. I. Loparto, Leonard W. II. United States. National Park Service. North Atlantic Regional Office. Division of Cultural Resources. III. Brown University. Public Archaeology Laboratory. IV. Title.
HB3525.M2 R82 1983

Rubery, J. (Jill)
Social security and employment /. Assen, The Netherlands , 1983. 116 p. : ISBN 90-232-2011-0 (pbk.) : LC Card 83-216203 DDC 331.12/094 19
HD7164 .S594 1983 ***NYPL [JLE 86-1107]***

Women and recession /. London , New York , 1988. xii, 294 p. ; ISBN 0-7102-0701-8 LC Card 87-20626 DDC 331.4/12 19
HD6053 .W6375 1988

Rubin, Bonnie Miller. Time out : how to take a year (or more or less) off without jeopardizing your job, your family, or your bank account / Bonnie Miller Rubin.1st ed. New York : W.W. Norton, c1987. p. cm. Includes index. LC Card 87-5723 DDC 640 19
1. Leave of absence. 2. Leisure. 3. Time management. I. Title.
HD5255 .R82 1987

Rubin, Charles, 1953- AppleWorks : boosting your business with integrated software / Charles Rubin ; foreword by R.J. Lissner.2nd ed. Redmond, Wash. : Microsoft Press ; [New York, N.Y.] : Distributed to the book trade in the U. S. by Harper & Row, c1987. xv, 299 p. : ill. ; 24 cm. Includes index. ISBN 1-556-15114-4 (pbk.) : LC Card 87-20338 DDC 650/.028/55369 19
1. AppleWorks (Computer program). 2. Business - Data

processing. I. Title.
HF5548.4.A68 R83 1987

Rubin, Donald B. Multiple imputation for nonresponse in surveys / Donald B. Rubin. New York ; Wiley, c1987. xxix, 258 p. : ill. ; 24 cm. (Wiley series in probability and mathematical statistics. Applied probability and statistics, 0271-6232) Bibliography: p. 244-250. Includes index. ISBN 0-471-08705-X : LC Card 86-28935 DDC 001.4/225 19
1. Multiple imputation (Statistics). I. Title. II. Series.
HA31.2 .R83 1987

Rubin, Harvey W. Dictionary of insurance terms / Harvey W. Rubin. New York : Barron's, c1987. ix, 371 p. ; 18 cm. (Barron's business guides) ISBN 0-8120-3772-3 (pbk.) : LC Card 87-12549 DDC 368/.003/21 19
1. Insurance - Dictionaries. I. Title. II. Series.
HG8025 .R83 1987

Rubin, Irene. New directions in budget theory /. Albany, N.Y. , 1987, c1988. p. cm. ISBN 0-88706-624-0 LC Card 87-9977 DDC 350.72/2 19
HJ2005 .N48 1987

Rubin, Laurie, 1956- Food first curriculum / by Laurie Rubin; foreword by Frances Moore Lappé. San Francisco, CA : Institute for Food and Development Policy, c1984. viii, 146 p. : ill., music ; 28 cm. (Food first books) "An integrated curriculum to help grade 6 students learn the paths of the Food they eat, the roots of hunger here and abroad, and how they can act locally on a global problem; with modifications for grades 4-5 and 7-8." Bibliography: p. 139-146. ISBN 0-935028-17-X : LC Card 84-8986 DDC 372.8/3 19
1. Food supply - Study and teaching (Elementary). 2. Nutrition - Study and teaching (Elementary). I. Institute for Food and Development Policy (San Francisco, Calif.). II. Title.
HD9000.5 .R73 1984 **NYPL [JLF 86-1436]**

Rubin, Leona G. Your 1987/88 guide to social security benefits / Leona G. Rubin. New York, N.Y. : Facts on File Publications, c1987. 194 p. ; 23 cm. Rev. ed. of: Your 1985/86 guide to social security benefits / Richard L. Rubin, Leona G. Rubin. c1985. Includes index. ISBN 0-8160-1567-8 : LC Card 86-32917 DDC 368.4/3/00973 19
1. Social security - United States - Miscellanea. I. Rubin, Richard L. Your 1985/86 guide to social security benefits. II. Title.
HD7125 .R78 1987

Rubin, Richard L.
Your 1985/86 guide to social security benefits. Rubin, Leona G. Your 1987/88 guide to social security benefits / Leona G. Rubin. New York, N.Y. , c1987. 194 p. ; ISBN 0-8160-1567-8 : LC Card 86-32917 DDC 368.4/3/00973 19
HD7125 .R78 1987

Rubin, Ronald S. Luck, David Johnston. Marketing research /. Englewood Cliffs, NJ , c1987. xvii, 683 p. : ISBN 0-13-557828-0 : LC Card 86-25255 DDC 658.8/3 19
HF5415.2 .M3555 1987

Rubin, Stanford E. Foundations of the vocational rehabilitation process / Stanford E. Rubin, Richard T. Roessler ; contributions by Charles Maria V. Arokiasamy, Ralph E. Matkin. 3rd ed. Austin, Tex. : PRO-ED, c1987. xiii, 400 p. : ill. ; 23 cm. Bibliography: p. 347-383. Includes indexes. ISBN 0-89079-147-3 (pbk.) LC Card 86-30600 DDC 362/.0425 19
1. Rehabilitation counseling. 2. Vocational rehabilitation. I. Roessler, Richard, 1944-. II. Title.
HD7255.5 .R823 1987

Rubinstein, Juan Carlos, 1928- Estructura social, estado democrático y cambio político / Juan Carlos Rubinstein. [2a ed.]. [Buenos Aires] : Editorial Universitaria de Buenos Aires, c1986. 159 p. : ill. ; 26 cm. (Temas de cátedra) Includes bibliographical references. CONTENTS. - Estructura socioeconómica y comportamiento político en la Argentina -- Urbanización, estructura de ingresos y movilidad social en la Argentina, 1960-1970 -- Estado y democracia en la economía argentina -- La proyección del estado en el desarrollo -- Un nuevo ciclo político. ISBN 950-23-0292-3 LC Card 87-114981 DDC 330.982/064 19
1. Argentina - Economic conditions - 1983-. 2. Argentina - Social conditions - 1983-. 3. Representative government and representation - Argentina. 4. Argentina - Politics and government - 1983-. I. Title. II. Series.
HC175 .R783 1986

Rubio F., Luis. A Mexican response / by Luis Rubio F. and Francisco Gil-Diaz. New York : Priority Press Publications, 1987. vi, 72 p. ; 23 cm. "A Twentieth Century Fund paper." Bibliography: p. 71-72. ISBN 0-87078-215-0 (pbk.) LC Card 87-162458 DDC 336.3/4/0972 19
1. Debts, External - Mexico. I. Gil-Díaz, Francisco, 1943-. II. Title.
HJ8519 .R83 1987

Rubner, Alex. The export cult : a global display of economic distortions / by Alex Rubner. Boulder : Westview Press, 1987, c1986. p. cm. Bibliography: p. Includes index. ISBN 0-8133-0514-4 : LC Card 86-51219 DDC 382/.6 19
1. Foreign trade promotion. I. Title.
HF1417.5 .R82 1987

Ruch robotniczy na Pomorzu Zachodnim do 1914 roku /. Głowacki, Andrzej. Warszawa , 1979. 160 p. ; ISBN 83-01-01306-0 LC Card 81-107475
HD8457.P66 G56 1979

Rucht, Dieter. Planung und Partizipation : Bürgerinitiativen als Reaktion und Herausforderung politisch-administrativer Planung / Dieter Rucht. München : Tuduv, c1982. 321 p. ; 22 cm. (Reihe Politologie-Soziologie. Bd. 9) Revision of the 1st 3 chapters of the author's thesis (doctoral--Universität München, 1979) Includes indexes. Bibliography: p. 289-310. ISBN 3-88073-105-5 LC Card 83-672501
1. Political planning - Germany, West. 2. Political participation - Germany, West. 3. Public administration - Germany (West). 4. Administrative agencies - Germany (West) - Planning. I. Title.
JN3971.A91 R82x 1982
NYPL [JLD 86-2900]

Ruddle, Kenneth. Quantitative Latin American studies . Los Angeles , 1977. xiv, 91 p. : ISBN 0-87903-227-8 LC Card 77-620011 DDC 330.9/8/003
HD5731.A6 Q36 **NYPL [JLF 80-242]**

Rudebusch, Glenn D., 1959-

Rüdel, Holger. Landarbeiter und Sozialdemokratie in Ostholstein, 1872 bis 1878 : Erfolg und Niederlage der sozialistischen Arbeiterbewegung in einem grossagrarischen Wahlkreis zwischen Reichsgründung und Sozialistengesetz / von Holger Rüdel. Neumünster : K. Wachholtz, 1986. 581 p. ; 24 cm. (Studien zur Wirtschafts- und Sozialgeschichte Schleswig-Holsteins, 0172-9152 . Bd. 9) A slight revision of the author's thesis (doctoral)--Universität Hamburg, 1984. Bibliography: p. 533-574. Includes index. ISBN 3-529-02909-2 LC Card 87-119718 DDC 331.88/13/0943512 19
1. Trade-unions - Germany (West) - Ostholstein - History. 2. Trade-unions - Agricultural laborers - Germany (West) - Ostholstein - History. 3. Socialism - Germany (West) - Ostholstein - History. 4. Peasantry - Germany (West) - Ostholstein - Political activity - History. 5. Ostholstein (Germany) - Politics and government. 6. Trade-unions - Agricultural laborers - Germany (West) - Ostholstein - Organizing - History. I. Title. II. Series.
HD6699.O88 R83 1986

Rüden, Reinhold von. Soziale Sicherung in der Bundesrepublik Deutschland / Reinhold von Rüden. Paderborn : Schöningh, c1986. 157 p. : ill. ; 24 cm. (Sozialwissenschaften . Heft 8) Includes bibliographical references and index. ISBN 3-506-23938-4 LC Card 87-127289 DDC 368.4/00943 19
1. Social security - Germany, West. I. Title. II. Series.
HD7179 .R835 1986

Rudianto, Doddy. Pembangunan ekonomi dan perkembangan bisnis di Indonesia / Doddy Rudianto. Jakarta : Golden Terayon, 1985. 53 p. ; 21 cm. Bibliography: p. 51-53. LC Card 86-944718
1. Indonesia - Economic policy. 2. Indonesia - Economic conditions - 1947-. I. Title.
HC447 .R73 1985

Rudnicki, Bohdan. Liga dwudziestu i arabska nafta / Bohdan Rudnicki. Wyd. 1. Warszawa : Krajowa Agencja Wydawnicza, 1979. 469, [3] p. : ill. ; 20 cm. Bibliography: p. 466-[470] LC Card 81-109444
1. Petroleum industry and trade - Arab countries. 2. Arab countries - Politics and government. 3. Petroleum industry and trade - Political aspects - Arab countries. I. Title.
HD9578.A55 R83 1979

Rudnicki, Leszek. Zróżnicowania wzorców konsumpcji ludności rolniczej dwuzawodowej / Leszek Rudnicki. Kraków : Akademia Ekonomiczna w Krakowie, 1985. 313 p. : ill. ; 24 cm. (Zeszyty naukowe. Seria specjalna, Monografie, 0209-1674 . nr. 66) At head of title: Akademia Ekonomiczna w Krakowie. Summary in English and Russian. Bibliography: p. 245-255. LC Card 86-174377
1. Consumption (Economics) - Poland. 2. Poland - Population, Rural. 3. Wages - Poland - Regional disparities. I. Series: Zeszyty naukowe-Akademia Ekonomiczna w Krakowie : Seria specjalna Monografie, nr. 66. II. Title.
HC340.3.Z9 C6177 1985

Rudolph, Bernd. Tagung Strategische Bankplanung (1982 : Bonn, Germany) Strategische Bankplanung . Frankfurt am Main , c1983. 345 p. : ISBN 3-7819-0293-5 LC Card 83-233043
HG1615 .T34 1982

Rudolph, Günther. Karl Rodbertus (1805-1875) und die Grundrententheorie : politische Ökonomie aus dem deutschen Vormärz / Günther Rudolph. Berlin : Akademie-Verlag, 1984. 332 p. ; 23 cm. (Schriften des Zentralinstituts für Wirtschaftswissenschaften . Nr. 21) Bibliography: p. 310-326. Includes index. LC Card 84-158301
1. Rodbertus, Karl, 1805-1875 - Views on Rent. 2. Rent (Economic theory). 3. Marxian economics. I. Series: Schriften des Zentralinstituts für Wirtschaftswissenschaften, Akademie der Wissenschaften der DDR , Nr. 21. II. Title.
HB401 .R83 1984

Rudolph, Hedwig. Workshop "Berufswege von Frauen" (1984 : Berlin, Germany) Berufsverläufe von Frauen . München , Weinheim , c1986. 291 p. : ISBN 3-87966-253-3 LC Card 87-407975 DDC 331.7/02/024042 19
HF5382.67.G3 W67 1984

Rudolph, Jürgen. Aktuelle Fragen der Theorie und Praxis der staatlichen Leitung der Landwirtschaft / Jürgen Rudolph, Edgar Seim, Rolf Steding. Potsdam-Babelsberg : Akademie für Staats- und Rechtswissenschaft der DDR, 1983. 72 p. ; 21 cm. (Aktuelle Beiträge der Staats- und Rechtswissenschaft, 0568-7551 . Heft 276) Includes bibliographical references. LC Card 83-214391
1. Agriculture and state - Germany, East. 2. Agriculture - Economic aspects - Germany, East. I. Seim, Edgar. II. Steding, Rolf. III. Title. IV. Series.
HD1960.5.Z8 R83 1983

Rudolph, Lloyd I. In pursuit of Lakshmi : the political economy of the Indian state / Lloyd I. Rudolph and Susanne Hoeber Rudolph. Chicago : University of Chicago Press, 1987. xvii, 529 p. ; 24 cm. Bibliography: p. 411-499. Includes indexes. ISBN 0-226-73138-3 : LC Card 86-24903 DDC 338.954 19
1. India - Economic policy - 1947-. 2. India - Economic conditions - 1947-. 3. India - Politics and government - 1947-. I. Rudolph, Susanne Hoeber. II. Title.
HC435 .R77 1987

Rudolph, Susanne Hoeber. Rudolph, Lloyd I. In pursuit of Lakshmi . Chicago , 1987. xvii, 529 p. ; ISBN 0-226-73138-3 : LC Card 86-24903 DDC 338.954 19
HC435 .R77 1987

Rudolphi, Michael, 1948- Aussendienststeuerung im Investitionsgütermarketing : eine Problemanalyse unter praxeologischen Gesichtspunkten / Michael Rudolphi. Frankfurt am Main : Lang, c1981. xi, 445 p. : ill. ; 21 cm. (Europäische Hochschulschriften. Reihe V, Volks- und Betriebswirtschaft . Bd. 299 = vol. 299 = vol. 299) Originally presented as the author's thesis (doctoral)--Technische Hochschule Aachen. Bibliography: p. 412-445. ISBN 3-8204-6125-6 : LC Card 81-111119
1. Selling - Industrial equipment - Management. I. Series: Europäische Hochschulschriften. Reihe V, Volks- und Betriebswirtschaft , Bd. 299. II. Title.
HF5439.I4 R83 1981

Rudra, Ashok. Agrarian relations in West Bengal : results of two surveys / Ashok Rudra & Pranab Bardhan. Bombay : Somaiya Publications, c1983. x, 104 p. ; 22 cm. Bibliography: p. [103]-104. LC Card 83-902673 DDC 338.1/0954/14 19
1. Land tenure - India - West Bengal. 2. Agricultural laborers - India - West Bengal. 3. Agricultural credit -

India - West Bengal. I. Title.
HD879.W4 R83 1983 ***NYPL [JLD 86-3785]***

Rue, Leslie W. Byars, Lloyd L. Human resource management /. Homewood, Ill. , 1987. xiii, 540 p. : ISBN 0-256-03630-6 LC Card 86-82596 DDC 658.3 19
HF5549 .B937 1987

Rueda, Germán. see **Rueda Hernanz, Germán.**

Rueda Hernanz, Germán. La desamortización de Mendizábal y Espartero en España / Germán Rueda, con la colaboración de Pablo García Colmenares, José Ramón Díez Espinosa. Madrid : Cátedra, c1986. 200 p. ; 21 cm. (Historia. Serie menor) Bibliography: p. 179-200. ISBN 84-376-0592-X LC Card 86-216590
1. Church lands - Spain - History. 2. Land tenure - Spain - History. 3. Secularization - Spain - History. 4. Alvarez y Mendizábal, Juan, 1790?-1853. 5. Espartero, Baldomero, 1793-1879. I. García Colmenares, Pablo. II. Diéz Espinosa, José Ramón. III. Series: Historia (Ediciones Cátedra). Serie menor. IV. Title.
HD774 .R84 1986

Rühli, Edwin. Strategisches Marketing und Management . Bern , c1986. 205 p. : ISBN 3-258-03566-0 : LC Card 86-159360
HF5415.135 .S77 1986

Les Rues mixtes : piétons-transports collectifs. [Bagneux] : Centre d'études des transports urbaines, [1982] 40 p. : ill. ; 30 cm. (Les Dossiers du CETUR, 0247-1159 . dossier no 18) On cover: Thème: transports collectifs. Bibliography: p. 38. ISBN 2-11-083325-4 : LC Card 84-104398
1. Pedestrian areas - France. 2. Local transit - France. 3. Urban transportation - France. I. Centre d'études des transports urbains. II. Title: Thème, transports collectifs. III. Title: Transports collectifs. IV. Series.
HE363.F72 P437 1982

Rueschemeyer, Dietrich. States versus markets in the world-system /. Beverly Hills, Calif. , c1985. 295 p. ; ISBN 0-8039-2510-7 LC Card 85-11716 DDC 338.9 19
HD3611 .S76 1985 ***NYPL [JLD 86-3227]***

Ruesga Benito, Santos, 1953- Métodos de estimación de la economía oculta : su incorporación a los sistemas de cuentas nacionales / Santos M. Ruesga Benito. Madrid : Fundación Juan March, [1985?] 55 p. : ill. ; 21 cm. (Série Universitária. 221) Bibliography: p. 53-55. ISBN 88-470-7531-18 LC Card 87-111661
1. Informal sector (Economics) - Spain. 2. National income - Spain - Accounting. I. Series: Serie universitaria (Fundación Juan March) , 221. II. Title.
HD2346.S7 R84 1985

Rüstungsexport, ein todsicheres Geschäft : Katalog zur Ausstellung / [Zusammenstellung, Projektgruppe "Rüstungsexport" im Kommunikationszentrum Idstein e.V.].1. Aufl. Idstein/Ts. : Das Kommunikationszentrum, 1984. 1 v. (various pagings) : ill. ; 30 cm. Cover title. LC Card 86-152420
1. Munitions - Developing countries - Moral and ethical aspects - Exhibitions. I. Kommunikationszentrum Idstein (Germany). Projektgruppe "Rüstungsexport.".
HD9743.D442 R87 1984

Rüstungskonversionsbemühungen in den USA in den 70iger Jahren . Braun, Axel. Frankfurt am Main , c1984. x, 379 p. : ISBN 3-88129-856-8 LC Card 85-154003
HC110.D4 B72 1984

Rüstungspolitik und Arbeiterklasse . Bonk, Heinz. Berlin , 1986. 299 p. ; LC Card 86-174039
HC79.D4 B65 1986

Rüstungspolitik und Rüstungsdynamik . Müller, Erwin, 1947- Baden-Baden , 1985. 378 p. ; ISBN 3-7890-1076-6 LC Card 85-154502
HC110.D4 M85 1985

Rüstungsproduktion und Zwangsarbeit im Volkswagenwerk, 1939-1945 . Siegfried, Klaus-Jörg, 1940- Frankfurt , New York , c1986. 239 p. : ISBN 3-593-33765-7 LC Card 87-133375 DDC 338.4/76234/0943 19
HD9743.G48 S56 1986

Die Rüstungsreferendumsinitiative--schlecht getarnter Anschlag auf unsere Landesverteidigung /. Spälti, P. Zürich , 1987. 20 p. ; LC Card 87-409331 DDC 330.9494 s 327.1/74/09494 19
HC395 .Z43 Nr. 131 HC400.D4

Ruffin, Roy, 1938- Principles of economics / Roy J. Ruffin, Paul R. Gregory. 3rd ed. Glenview, Ill. : Scott, Foresman, c1988. xxxi, 918, [42] p. : ill. (some col.) ; 27 cm.. Includes bibliographies and index. ISBN 0-673-18871-X : LC Card 87-23369 DDC 330 19
1. Economics. I. Gregory, Paul R. II. Title.
HB171.5 .R82 1988

Ruffio, Patricia. Crull, Anna W. Commercial and industrial enzymes /. Stamford, Conn., U. S.A. , c1986. xiii, 160 leaves : ISBN 0-89336-492-4 (pbk.) LC Card 87-164403 DDC 380.1/4566063 19
HD9660.E582 C783 1986

Ruffolo, Giorgio. Capitalismo riformato e sinistra . Milano , 1986. 125 p. ; ISBN 88-24-50380-2 : LC Card 86-229688
HB501 .C24265 1986

Rufus S. Lusk & Son. Lusk's Fairfax County, Virginia assessment directory . Washington, D.C. (1824 Jefferson Pl., NW, Washington 20036) , 1986. 1251, [81] p. ; LC Card 87-144674 DDC 333.33/2/09755291 19
HD266.V82 F24 1986

RUG AND CARPET INDUSTRY - INDIA - EMPLOYEES - CASE STUDIES.
Juyal, B. N. Child labour and exploitation in the carpet industry . New Delhi , c1987. 49, [1] p. ; LC Card 87-900920 DDC 331.3/1/0954 19
HD6250.I42 J87 1987

Rugbrødsbranchen : markedsstruktur, konkurrenceforhold, prisdannelse, indtjening. København : Monopoltilsynet, 1985. 112 p. : ill. ; 24 cm. (Redegørelse fra Monopoltilsynet) ISBN 87-88149-23-4 : LC Card 86-161889
1. Bread industry - Denmark. I. Denmark. Monopoltilsynet. II. Series.
HD9058.B743 D47 1985

Ruggeri, G. C. The Canadian economy . Toronto, Ont., Canada , c1987. xiii, 474 p. ; ISBN 0-7715-5515-6 (pbk.) : LC Card 87-130572 DDC 330.971/0647 19
HC115 .C2463 1987

Rugh, Jack Leighton, 1911- Channels to employment for the disabled and ex-offenders / by Jack L. Rugh ; with a major contribution to the text from John E. Kulli. San Gabriel, Calif. (5555 N. Charlotte Ave., San Gabriel 91776) : J.L. Rugh, c1987. 89 p. : ill. ; 22 cm. Bibliography: p. 41-42. LC Card 87-402897 DDC 362.4/0484/02573 19
1. Handicapped - Employment - Information services - United States. 2. Ex-convicts - Employment - Information services - United States. 3. Job hunting - United States. I. Kulli, John E. II. Title.
HD7256.U5 R75 1987

Rugman, Alan M. New theories of the multinational enterprise /. London , c1982. 303 p. : ISBN 0-7099-2224-8 LC Card 86-673671
HD2755.5 .N485x 1982

Ruhender Verkehr in Wohngebieten / [Herausgeber, Institut für Landes- und Stadtentwicklungsforschung des Landes Nordrhein-Westfalen (ILS)]. Dortmund : ILS, c1983, [1982] 121 p. : ill. ; 21 cm. (Bausteine für die Planungspraxis in Nordrhein Westfalen . 3) "Forschungsarbeit im Auftrag des Ministers für Landes- und Stadtentwicklung des Landes Nordrhein-Westfalen"--T.p. verso. LC Card 83-236251
1. Automobile parking - Germany (West) - North Rhine-Westphalia. I. Institut für Landes- und Stadtentwicklungsforschung des Landes Nordrhein-Westfalen. II. North Rhine-Westphalia (Germany). Ministerium für Landes- und Stadtentwicklung. III. Series.
HE363.G32 P377 1983

RUHR (GERMANY : REGION) - BIOGRAPHY.
Günter, Janne, 1937- Mündliche Geschichtsschreibung . Mülheim/Ruhr , 1982. 142, [1] p. : ISBN 3-923456-00-X LC Card 85-146144
HD8039.M61 G343 1982

RUHR (GERMANY : REGION) - ECONOMIC CONDITIONS.
Baroth, Hans Dieter, 1937- Das Gras wuchs ja umsonst /. Köln , c1983. 232 p. ; ISBN 3-462-01577-X LC Card 83-227195
HD8459.R82 B37 1983

Bochum, Ulrich, 1953- Industrie und Region . Frankfurt am Main , New York , c1984. 340, [38] p. : ISBN 3-8204-5550-7 LC Card 85-194544
HC288.R8 B57 1984

Günter, Janne, 1937- Mündliche Geschichtsschreibung . Mülheim/Ruhr , 1982. 142, [1] p. : ISBN 3-923456-00-X LC Card 85-146144
HD8039.M61 G343 1982

Meyer, Willm Rolf. Ressourcenumverteilung zugunsten von Problemregionen . Frankfurt/Main , New York , c1982. 262 p. : ISBN 3-593-33036-9 LC Card 82-161064 DDC 336.1/85 19
HJ1121 .M49 1982 ***NYPL [JLD 86-3292]***

Nahwanderungen im Ruhrgebiet, 1976-1984 /. Essen , c1986. 61 p. : ISBN 3-923494-67-X LC Card 87-408772 DDC 330.943/55 19
HC288.R8 N34 1986

Schlieper, Andreas. 150 Jahre Ruhrgebiet . Düsseldorf , 1986. 224 p. : ISBN 3-590-18150-8 LC Card 86-231681
HC288.R8 S34 1986

Von der Bizonengründung zur ökonomisch-politischen Westintegration . Frankfurt am Main , c1984. v, 311 p. : ISBN 3-88129-640-9 LC Card 84-154481
HC286.5 .V64 1984

Wechsel auf die Zukunft /. Essen [1984] 25 p. : LC Card 85-105225
HC288.R8 W43 1984

Wehling, Hans-Werner, 1949- Wohnstandorte und Wohnumfeldprobleme in der Kernzone des Ruhrgebietes /. Paderborn , 1984. ix, 285 p. : ISBN 3-506-72309-X LC Card 85-121205
HD7339.R79 W44 1984

RUHR (GERMANY : REGION) - ECONOMIC CONDITIONS - CONGRESSES.
Strukturanalyse Ruhrgebiet . [Essen] [1983?] 185 p. : LC Card 86-218075
HD5760.R84 S77 1983

RUHR (GERMANY : REGION) - ECONOMIC POLICY.
Programmpaket zur Verbesserung der Rahmenbedingungen für die Wirtschaft im Ruhrgebiet . Essen [197-?] 42 p. : LC Card 85-153643
HC288.R8 P76 1970z

Wechsel auf die Zukunft /. Essen [1984] 25 p. : LC Card 85-105225
HC288.R8 W43 1984

RUHR (GERMANY : REGION) - INDUSTRIES - HISTORY.
Bochum, Ulrich, 1953- Industrie und Region . Frankfurt am Main , New York , c1984. 340, [38] p. : ISBN 3-8204-5550-7 LC Card 85-194544
HC288.R8 B57 1984

Schlieper, Andreas. 150 Jahre Ruhrgebiet . Düsseldorf , 1986. 224 p. : ISBN 3-590-18150-8 LC Card 86-231681
HC288.R8 S34 1986

RUHR (GERMANY : REGION) - OCCUPATIONS - STATISTICS.
Noll, Wulf. Lokales Informationssystem Arbeitsmarkt (LISA) /. Essen , 1986. 262 p. ; ISBN 3-923494-64-5 LC Card 87-409105 DDC 331.12/5/094355 19
HD5780.R82 N65 1986

RUHR (GERMANY : REGION) - POPULATION.
Nahwanderungen im Ruhrgebiet, 1976-1984 /. Essen , c1986. 61 p. : ISBN 3-923494-67-X LC Card 87-408772 DDC 330.943/55 19
HC288.R8 N34 1986

Wehling, Hans-Werner, 1949- Wohnstandorte und Wohnumfeldprobleme in der Kernzone des Ruhrgebietes /. Paderborn , 1984. ix, 285 p. : ISBN 3-506-72309-X LC Card 85-121205
HD7339.R79 W44 1984

RUHR (GERMANY : REGION) - SOCIAL CONDITIONS.
Schlieper, Andreas. 150 Jahre Ruhrgebiet . Düsseldorf , 1986. 224 p. : ISBN 3-590-18150-8 LC Card 86-231681
HC288.R8 S34 1986

Ruhr-Universität Bochum. Institut für Entwicklungsforschung und Entwicklungspolitik. Partnerschaftliche Entwicklungspolitik im Widerstreit der Interessen . Bochum-Querenburg , 1985. i, 184 leaves ; LC Card 87-409475 DDC

332.6/7343/01724 19
HG5993 .P37 1985

Ruhrfestspiele Recklinghausen. Mein Vaterland ist international . Oberhausen , 1986. 331 p. : ISBN 3-921541-62-X LC Card 86-224091
HD7791 .M45 1986

Ruiz Avilés, Pedro. Estudio integral de la Sierra de Segura : posibilidades de desarrollo acogiendose a la política socioestructural del Mercado Común / P. Ruiz Avilés y M.L. Campillo Martín. [Jaén] : Cámara Oficial de Comercio e Industria de la Provincia de Jaén, [1985] 130 leaves : ill., maps ; 32 cm. Bibliography: leaves 127-130. ISBN 84-505-1249-2 LC Card 86-187282
1. Segura Mountains Region (Spain) - Economic conditions. 2. Agriculture - Economic aspects - Spain - Segura Mountains Region. 3. Physical geography - Spain - Segura Mountains Region. 4. Segura Mountains Region (Spain) - Economic policy. 5. European Economic Community - Spain - Segura Mountains Region. I. Campillo Martín, M. L. II. Title.
HC387.S438 R85 1985

Ruiz Castillo, Javier. El Sector vivienda . Madrid , 1982. 224 p. : ISBN 84-7088-324-0 LC Card 85-219674
HD7351.A3 S43 1982

RUIZ MATEOS, JOSÉ MARÍA.
Ekaizer, Ernesto, 1949- José María Ruiz Mateos, el ultimo magnate /. Esplugues de Llobregat, Barcelona , 1985. 833 p., [16] p. of plates : ISBN 84-01-33291-5 LC Card 86-122394 DDC 332.1/6 B 19
HG4216.R85 E38 1985
NYPL [JFD 86-6856]

Ruiz-Tagle P., Jaime.
El sindicalismo chileno después del plan laboral / Jaime Ruiz-Tagle P. Santiago, Chile : Programa de Economía del Trabajo, Academia de Humanismo Cristiano, [1985?] 211 p. ; 21 cm. Includes bibliographical references.
1. Trade-unions - Chile. 2. Syndicalism - Chile. 3. Labor and laboring classes - Chile. 4. Chile - Politics and government - 1970-. I. Academia de Humanismo Cristiano (Santiago, Chile). II. Title.
NYPL [JLD 87-1182]

Los trabajadores del Programa del Empleo Mínimo : los trabajadores del Programa de Empleo Mínimo en el capitalismo autoritario, condiciones de trabajo, comportamiento, rol sociopolítico / Jaime Ruiz-Tagle, Roberto Urmeneta. Santiago : Programa de Economía del Trabajo, Academia de Humanismo Cristiano : Programa de Investigaciones Sociales sobre Población en América Latina, 1984. 179 p. : ill. ; 21 cm. Spine title: Los trabajadores del Programa de Empleo Mínimo. Bibliography: p. 171-173. LC Card 84-234738
1. Programa de Empleo Mínimo. 2. Chile - Full employment policies. I. Urmeneta, Roberto. II. Title. III. Title: Trabajadores del Programa de Empleo Mínimo.
HD5756.A6 R86 1984

Ruíz, Vicki. Cannery women, cannery lives : Mexican women, unionization, and the California food processing industry, 1930-1950 / Vicki L. Ruíz.1st ed. Albuquerque : University of New Mexico Press, c1987. xviii, 194 p. : ill. ; 24 cm. Bibliography: p. 171-188. Includes index. ISBN 0-8263-1006-0 LC Card 87-13878 DDC 331.88/1640282/09794 19
1. United Cannery, Agricultural, Packing, and Allied Workers of America - History. 2. Women in trade-unions - California - History - Case studies. 3. Mexican American women - California - History - Case studies. 4. Women cannery workers - California - History - Case studies. I. Title.
HD6515.F72 U547 1987

Rukopozhatie druzeĭ--Arkhangel'sk-Vologda.
Ovchinnikov, V. P. (Veniamin Petrovich) Arkhangel'skiĭ avtograf /. Arkhangel'sk , 1983. 94 p. : LC Card 84-173501
HC337.R852 A746 1983

Panshev, L. V. Vologodskiĭ razbeg /. Arkhangel'sk , 1983. 93 p. : LC Card 86-195235
HC338.V58 P35 1983

Rukopozhatie piatiletok / A. Beliakov ... [et al. ; sostavitel' O.M. Shmelev]. Moskva : Izd-vo polit. lit-ry, 1981. 237 p. : ill., ports. ; 16 cm. LC Card 82-103792
1. Soviet Union - Economic policy - 1917-. 2. Central planning - Soviet Union - History. I. Beliakov, A. (Aleksandr). II. Shmelev, Oleg, 1924-.
HC335 .R76 1981

Rukosuev, P. N. (Platon Nikolaevich) Ėkonomicheskaia ėffektivnost' zhivotnovodstva v sisteme APK / P.N. Rukosuev ; otvetstvennyĭ redaktor A.I. Panchenko. Moskva : "Nauka", 1985. 127 p. ; 22 cm. At head of title: Akademiia nauk SSSR. Institut ėkonomiki. Nauchnyĭ sovet po ėkonomicheskim, sotsialisticheskim i pravovym problemam APK SSSR. Includes bibliographical references. LC Card 86-133226
1. Animal industry - Soviet Union. 2. Agricultural industries - Soviet Union. I. Panchenko, A. I. II. Title.
HD9425.S652 R86 1985

Osnovnye faktory rosta proizvoditel'nosti truda v sel'skom khoziaĭstve /. Moskva , 1986. 158 p. ; LC Card 87-163422
HD9015.S652 O85 1986

Rukovoditel'-organizator i vospitatel'. Suĭmenko, IE. I. Kerivnyk-orhanizator i vykhovatel' /. Kyïv , 1985. 189 p. ; LC Card 87-109649
HD38.2 .S85 1985

Rukovodstvo Kompartii Uzbekistana osvoeniem tselinnykh zemel' /. Ėrgashev, N. (Nazirzhon) Tashkent , 1985. 159 p. ; LC Card 86-231568
HD1741.S782 U84 1985

Rukovodstvo kompartii Uzbekistana podgotovkoĭ rabochikh kadrov v usloviiakh razvitogo sotsializma /. Shister, G. A. (Grigoriĭ Aronovich) Tashkent , 1981. 274, [2] p. ; LC Card 82-204041
HD5797.U9 S54 1981

The rule of experts . Young, S. David, 1955- Washington, D.C. , c1987. x, 99 p. ; ISBN 0-932790-62-3 (pbk.) LC Card 87-736 DDC 351.82/43046 19
HD3630.U7 Y68 1987

Ruling the waves . Cafruny, Alan W. Berkeley , c1987. xvii, 323 p. ; ISBN 0-520-05968-9 LC Card 86-30889 DDC 387.5/1 19
HE735 .C34 1987

Rullani, Enzo. Di Bernardo, Barbara. Transizione tecnologica e strategie evolutive . Padova , 1985. xiii, 432 p. : LC Card 86-214184
HD45 .D47 1985

Rumania. see **Romania.**

Rumayhī, Muḥammad Ghānim.
[Khalīj laysa nafṭ. English]
Beyond oil : unity and development in the gulf / Muhammad Rumaihi ; translated by James Dickins. London : Al Saqi Books, 1986. 156 p. : 2 maps ; 21 cm. Translation of: al-Khalīj laysa nafṭ. Bibliography: p. [143]-151. Includes index. ISBN 0-86356-120-9 : LC Card 86-200063 DDC 330.953/053 19
1. Arabian Peninsula - Economic conditions. 2. Arabian Peninsula - Social conditions. I. Title.
HC415.3 .R8613 1986

Rumberger, Russell W. The Future impact of technology on work and education /. London , New York , 1987. p. cm. ISBN 1-85000-083-2 : LC Card 87-13641 DDC 331.12/0994 19
HD6331.2.A8 F87 1987

Rumble, Greville. The politics of nuclear defence : a comprehensive introduction / Greville Rumble. Cambridge [Cambridgeshire] : Polity Press, 1985. xi, 285 p. ; 23 cm. Includes bibliographic references and index. ISBN 0-7456-0194-4 : LC Card 85-18643 DDC 355/.0217 19
1. Nuclear warfare. 2. Nuclear weapons. 3. Military policy. 4. Great Britain - Military policy. I. Title. II. Title: Nuclear defence.
U263 .R86 1985 ***NYPL [JLD 86-1092]***

Rumiantsev, A. A. Effektivnost' NTP . Leningrad , 1985. 215 p., [1] folded leaf of plates : LC Card 86-129301
HC244.Z9 T435 1985

Rumiantsev, Alekseĭ Fedorovich. Sovetskaia ėkonomika na novom ėtape /. Moskva , 1981. 223 p. : LC Card 82-118778
HC336.25 .S677 1981

Rumiantsev, Alekseĭ Matveevich. Instrumentariĭ ėkonomicheskoĭ nauki i praktiki : nauchno-populiarnyĭ spravochnik / A.M. Rumiantsev, E.G. IAkovenko, S.I. IAnaev. Moskva : Izd-vo "Znanie", 1985. 303 p. : ill. ; 21 cm. Bibliography: p. 288-[289] Includes index. LC Card 87-109217
1. Economics - Dictionaries - Russian. 2. Marxian economics - Dictionaries - Russian. I. IAkovenko, Evgeniĭ Georgievich. II. IAnaev, S. I. (Saberdzhan Ismailovich). III. Title.
HB61 .R86 1985

Rumley, Pierre-Alain. Aménagement du territoire et utilisation du sol : évolution passée et schémas prospectifs de l'utilisation du sol en Suisse = Raumplanung und Flächennutzung / Bearbeiter, Pierre-Alain Rumley. Zürich : Institut für Orts-, Regional- und Landesplanung, ETH, c1984. x, 176 p. : ill. ; 30 cm. (Berichte zur Orts-, Regional- und Landesplanung . Nr. 50) French text. Originally presented as the author's thesis (doctoral)--ETH Zürich. Summary in English and German. LC Card 85-104773
1. Land use - Switzerland. 2. Land use - Switzerland - Planning. 3. Regional planning - Switzerland. 4. Urbanization - Switzerland. I. Title. II. Title: Raumplanung und Flächennutzung. III. Series.
HD796 .R86 1984

Rummel, Julian. Narodziny żeglugi / Julian Rummel ; wybór, wstęp i przypisy Maciej Rdesiński. Wyd. 1. Gdańsk : Wydawn. Morskie, 1980. 333 p., [32] leaves of plates : ill. ; 22 cm. (Wspomnienia ludzi morza i wybrzeża) "Ważniejsze prace autora wspomnień"--p. 327-[328] Includes index. ISBN 83-215-3235-7 LC Card 80-147019
1. Merchant marine - Poland - History - 20th century. I. Rdesiński, Maciej. II. Title.
HE848.7 .R86 1980

Rumpeltes, Christiane, 1951- Arbeitslos . Reinbek bei Hamburg , 1982. 170 p. : ISBN 3-499-15024-7 (pbk.) LC Card 87-672730
HD5779 .A6x 1982

RUMRUNNING. see **SMUGGLING.**

Rumyantsev, A. M. see **Rumiantsev, Alekseĭ Matveevich.**

Rundfunk zwischen Kommerz und Politik . Bierbach, Wolf. Frankfurt am Main , New York , c1986. 2 v. (595 p.) : ISBN 3-8204-9692-0 LC Card 86-233794
HE8699.G3 B54 1986

Rundschau für Technik und Wirtschaft. Die Geschichte des Suezkanals . Prag [1912?] 26 p. ; LC Card 86-209445
HE543 .G47 1912

Runge, C. Ford (Carlisle Ford) The Future of the North American granary . Ames, Iowa , 1986. xx, 238 p. : ISBN 0-8138-0781-6 LC Card 85-23905 DDC 338.1/731/097 19
HD9036 .F87 1986 ***NYPL [JLE 86-2437]***

Runge, Harry.
Haushaltsfinanzierung durch Notendruck / von Harry Runge. Berlin : Duncker & Humblot, c1986. 69 p. ; 24 cm. (Volkswirtschaftliche Schriften. Heft 360) Bibliography: p. [68]-69. Includes index. ISBN 3-428-05984-0 LC Card 86-165742
1. Paper money - Germany (West). 2. Monetary policy - Germany, West. 3. Finance, Public - Germany, West. 4. Inflation (Finance) - Germany, West. I. Title. II. Series.
HG1004 .R75 1986

Haushaltsfinanzierung durch Notendruck / von Harry Runge. Berlin : Duncker und Humblot, c1986. 69 p. ; 24 cm. (Volkswirtschaftliche Schriften. Heft 360) Includes index. Bibliography: p. [68]-69. ISBN 3-428-05984-0
1. Fiscal policy. 2. Budget. I. Title. II. Series.
NYPL [JLE 86-2839]

Runggaldier, Ulrich. Le politiche regionali del lavoro : i casi del Tirolo, Baviera, Svezia e Francia / Ulrich Runggaldier, Lorenzo Bordogna, Pietro Kemeny ; prefazione di Antonio d'Harmant François. Milano, Italy : F. Angeli, c1986. 160 p. ; 22 cm. (Collana di politiche del lavoro . 3) Bibliography: p. [157]-160. LC Card 86-169484
1. Labor policy - Europe - Case studies. 2. Europe - Economic conditions - 1945- - Regional disparities. I. Bordogna, Lorenzo. II. Kemeny, Pietro. III. Title. IV. Series.
HD8376.5 .R93 1986

Running American business . Lamb, Robert, 1941- New York , c1987. x, 315 p. ; ISBN 0-465-07150-3 : LC Card 86-47732 DDC 658.4/03 19
HD30.28 .L355 1987

Running MS DOS . Wolverton, Van, 1939- Bellevue, Wash. [New York, NY] , c1985. xv, 423 p. : ISBN 0-914845-68-3 LC Card 85-18951

DDC 005.4/469 19
QA76.76.O63 W65 1985
NYPL [JSE 86-1760]

Running MS-DOS. Wolverton, Van, 1939- Running MS DOS . Bellevue, Wash. [New York, NY] , c1985. xv, 423 p. : ISBN 0-914845-68-3 LC Card 85-18951 DDC 005.4/469 19
QA76.76.O63 W65 1985
NYPL [JSE 86-1760]

Running the gauntlet . Townsend, John Clendenin, 1939- New York , 1986. 341 p. ; ISBN 0-8240-8298-2 (alk. paper) : LC Card 86-25632 DDC 331.88/6 19
HD8055.I56 T68 1986

Running things . Crosby, Philip B. New York , 1987, c1986. p. cm. ISBN 0-452-25915-0 LC Card 86-28508 DDC 658.4/092 19
HD57.7 .C76 1987

Runyon, Kenneth E. Consumer behavior and the practice of marketing / Kenneth E. Runyon, David W. Stewart. 3rd ed. Columbus : Merrill Pub. Co., c1987. xv, 776 p. : ill. (some col.) ; 24 cm. Includes bibliographies and indexes. ISBN 0-675-20463-1 LC Card 86-62987 DDC 658.8/342 19
1. Consumers. 2. Motivation research (Marketing). 3. Marketing research. I. Stewart, David W. II. Title.
HF5415.3 .R86 1987

Runyon, Richard P. Fundamentals of behavioral statistics / Richard P. Runyon and Audrey Haber. 6th ed. New York : Random House, c1988. p. cm. Bibliography: p. Includes index. ISBN 0-394-36619-0 LC Card 87-23066 DDC 519.5 19
1. Social sciences - Statistical methods. 2. Statistics. I. Haber, Audrey. II. Title.
HA29 .R85 1988

Ruohonen, Matti. On the use of Ventcel-Freidlin estimates in approximating the probability of ruin / Matti Ruohonen. Vaasa : Universitas Economica Wasaensis, 1979. 27 p. : ill. ; 25 cm. (Acta Wasaensia, 0355-2667 . no. 11. no. 1) Bibliography: p. 27. ISBN 951-683-103-6 (pbk.) LC Card 83-223364
1. Risk (Insurance) - Mathematical models. I. Series: Acta wasaensia, no. 11. II. Title.
HG8054.5 .R86 1979

RUPERT, ANTON.
Esterhuyse, W. P. Anton Rupert . Cape Town , c1986. 150 p. ; ISBN 0-624-02429-6 LC Card 87-122279 DDC 361.7/4/0924 B 19
HC905.R87 E88 1986

RUPERT, ANTON - VIEW ON SOCIAL ETHICS.
Esterhuyse, W. P. Anton Rupert . Cape Town , c1986. 150 p. ; ISBN 0-624-02429-6 LC Card 87-122279 DDC 361.7/4/0924 B 19
HC905.R87 E88 1986

Ruppert Karl. Maier, Jörg. Freizeitraum Oberstaufen . München , 1976. xii, 92 p. : ISBN 3-920397-13-4 LC Card 87-408421 DDC 330.94 380.1/45914337 19
HC281 .M84 Heft 13 G155.G3

Ruprecht-Karls-Universität, Heidelberg. see **Heidelberg. Universität.**

Ruprecht, Mary M.
Wagoner, Kathleen P. Integrated office systems . New York , c1987. xxi, 734 p., [4] p. of plates : ISBN 0-471-01195-9 LC Card 86-26793 DDC 651.8 19
HF5547 .W26 1987

Wagoner, Kathleen P. Office automation . New York , c1987. xvii, 432 p. : ISBN 0-471-84505-1 (pbk.) LC Card 86-26775 DDC 651.8 19
HF5547.5 .W33 1987

La Rupture : le libéralisme à l'épreuve des faits / André Fourçans, éditeur. Paris : Economica, c1986. 156 p. ; 24 cm. ISBN 2-7178-1134-6 : LC Card 87-117285
1. France - Economic policy - 1981-. 2. France - Politics and government - 1981-. I. Fourçans, André.
HC276.3 .R86 1986

RURA-URBAN MIGRATION - LATIN AMERICA - CONGRESSES.
Fachtagung "Bevölkerungsentwicklung, Bevölkerungswanderung und Urbanisierung in Lateinamerika" (1984 : Eichstätt, Germany) Desarrollo demográfico, migraciones y urbanización en América Latina . Regensburg , c1986. 432 p. : LC Card 86-181152
HB3530.5.A3 F33 1984

Rural access road programme : evaluation of roads in Bungoma / Republic of Kenya, Ministry of Works, Roads Department. Nairobi : Chief Engineer (Roads), [1977- v. : ill. ; 30 cm. Cover title. "May 1976." CONTENTS. - [1] Partl, Part 2 -- [2] Revised -- [3] Phase III. LC Card 86-981035
1. Rural roads - Kenya - Bungoma District. 2. Kenya Rural Access Roads Programme. I. Kenya. Roads Dept.
HE367.K43 R8575 1976

Rural access roads programme : evaluation of roads in Kisii / Ministry of Works, Roads Department. Nairobi : The Department, [1976- v. : ill., maps ; 30 cm. Cover title. CONTENTS. - [1] Without specific title -- [2] Revised --[3] Phase III -- [4] Phase IV. LC Card 86-981034
1. Roads - Kenya - Kisii District. 2. Kenya Rural Access Roads Programme. I. Kenya. Roads Dept.
HE367.K43 R8576 1976

Rural Access Roads Programme / Republic of Kenya, Ministry of Works, Roads Department. Nairobi : The Department, [1980?] 1 v. (various foliations) : ill. ; 30 cm. LC Card 85-981142 DDC 388.1/09676/2 19
1. Kenya Rural Access Roads Programme. 2. Rural roads - Kenya. I. Kenya. Roads Dept.
HE367.K43 R85746 1980

RURAL ACCESS ROADS PROGRAMME.
Status of evaluation of rural access roads. Nairobi , 1982. 10 leaves ; LC Card 85-981020 DDC 388.1/09676/2 19
HE367.K43 R8578 1982

Rural America, inc. A Directory of rural and specialized transit operators /. Washington, D.C. , 1986- v. <1-3 > : LC Card 86-603414 DDC 388.3/22/0973 19
HE203 .D57 1986

Rural and Allied Industries Council (W.A.) The Production, promotion, and marketing of Western Australian table grapes . Perth, WA [1985] viii, 180 p. : LC Card 87-120107 DDC 338.1/748/09941 19
HD9259.G7 A827 1985

Rural banking adrift /. Ranade, Sudhanshu, 1952- Bombay , c1984. x, 126 p. ; LC Card 84-903073 DDC 332.1/0954 19
HG3284 .R325 1984 *NYPL [JLD 87-561]*

Rural change and royal finances in Spain at the end of the old regime /. Herr, Richard. Berkeley , c1987. p. cm. ISBN 0-520-05948-4 (alk. paper) LC Card 86-25027 DDC 333.3/0946/25 19
HD779.J34 H47 1987

RURAL COMMUNITY DEVELOPMENT. see **RURAL DEVELOPMENT.**

RURAL CONDITIONS.
Peasants and peasant societies . Oxford [Oxfordshire] , New York, NY, USA , 1987. viii, 497 p. ; ISBN 0-631-15212-1 : LC Card 87-775 DDC 305.5/63 19
HD1521 .P42 1987

RURAL CREDIT. see **AGRICULTURAL CREDIT.**

Rural development administration . Tiwary, Jai Kant. Allahabad, India , 1984. xi, 248 p. ; LC Card 84-900188 DDC 307.7/2/0954 19
HN690.Z9 C68286 1984
NYPL [JLD 86-4313]

RURAL DEVELOPMENT - AFRICA.
Policies and measures to promote industrial co-operatives in Africa /. [New York] [1985] 23 p. ; LC Card 87-104469 DDC 334/.6/096 19
HD3247 .P65 1985

RURAL DEVELOPMENT - ALGERIA - CONSTANTINE (PROVINCE)
Meuleman, Johan H. Le Constantinois entre les deux guerres mondiales . Assen, Pays-Bas , 1985. 296 p., [1] folded leaf of plates : ISBN 90-232-2093-5 : LC Card 86-119662
HC815.Z7 C666 1985

Rural development and human fertility / editors, Wayne A. Schutjer and C. Shannon Stokes. New York, N.Y. : Macmillan ; London : Collier Macmillan Publishers, c1984. ix, 318 p. : ill. ; 25 cm. Includes bibliographies and index. ISBN 0-02-949680-2 : LC Card 83-26834 DDC 304.6/32/091734 19
1. Fertility, Human - Developing countries - Addresses, essays, lectures. 2. Rural development - Developing countries - Addresses, essays, lectures. 3. Developing countries - Population, Rural - Addresses, essays, lectures. I. Schutjer, Wayne A. II. Stokes, Charles Shannon, 1941-.
HB1108 .R87 1984 *NYPL [JLE 86-1084]*

Rural development and migration . Findley, Sally E. Boulder , 1987. xxiii, 308 p. : ISBN 0-8133-7326-3 (pbk. : alk. paper) : LC Card 86-33987 DDC 304.8/09599 19
HB2110.I43 F56 1987

RURAL DEVELOPMENT - ASIA - CONGRESSES.
Movement for a no poverty society . Calcutta , 1980. 78 p. ; LC Card 81-902107
HC415.P6 M68 1980

RURAL DEVELOPMENT - AUSTRALIA - SOUTH AUSTRALIA - HISTORY.
Grotz, Reinhold. Industrialisierung und Stadtentwicklung im ländlichen Südost-Australien /. Stuttgart , 1982. 299 p. : ISBN 3-88028-098-3 : LC Card 83-215667
HC607.S68 G76 1982

RURAL DEVELOPMENT - BANGLADESH.
Rahamāna, Āsahābura, 1949- Bāṅalādeśera kṛshikāṭhāmo, kṛshaka samāja, o unnaẏan /. Ḍhākā , 1986. 39, 158 p. ; LC Card 86-903304
HD2075.6 .R33 1986

Taheruddin, M. Essays on banking and development /. Dhaka , 1986. 145 p. ; LC Card 87-900643 DDC 332.1/09549/2 19
HG3290.6.A6 T35 1986

RURAL DEVELOPMENT - BENIN.
Jobs and Skills Programme for Africa. Eléments pour une stratégie d'emploi dans les zones rurales au Bénin . Addis Abeba [1980] xii, 70, 5 p. : LC Card 87-100360
HD5846.3.A6 J63 1980

RURAL DEVELOPMENT - BOLIVIA.
Segunda reforma agraria . La Paz, Bolivia [1987] 287 p. : LC Card 87-403057 DDC 333.3/1/84 19
HD1333.B5 S44 1987

RURAL DEVELOPMENT - BOLIVIA - CONGRESSES.
ACLO (Organization) "Estudio de participación campesina en la estructura y acción de ACLO" . [Sucre, Bolivia] , 1980. 94 leaves ; LC Card 83-203590
HD1531.B6 A24 1980

RURAL DEVELOPMENT - BOTSWANA.
Fones-Sundell, Melinda. Implementing rural development in Botswana . Uppsala , 1983. 75 p. : LC Card 86-215071 DDC 338.1/86811 19
HD2133 .F66 1983

Gobotswang, Z. Pilot evaluation report on Mahalapye Development Trust /. Gaborone, Botswana [1982] v leaves, 61, 3 p. ; LC Card 87-122810
HD5710.85.B59 G63 1982

RURAL DEVELOPMENT - BRAZIL, NORTHEAST.
Avaliação do polonordeste e do Projeto Sertanejo. Fortaleza , 1985. 314 p. : LC Card 87-402900 DDC 338.981/3 19
HC188.N6 A94 1985

Industrialização rural no Nordeste /. Recife , c1986. 488 p. : LC Card 87-403045 DDC 338.981/3 19
HD9014.B83 N755 1985

RURAL DEVELOPMENT - BRAZIL - PIAUÍ.
Atuação dos programas especiais no Estado do Piauí /. [Brasília] [1980] [29] leaves : LC Card 87-403685 DDC 333.91/0098122 19
HD1696.B83 P523 1980

RURAL DEVELOPMENT - BRAZIL - RIO GRANDE DO NORTE.
Rio Grande do Norte (Brazil) Programas especiais do governo, 1983-1987. Natal , 1984. [83] leaves ; LC Card 87-403924 DDC 331.12/0981/32 19
HC188.R38 P76 1984

RURAL DEVELOPMENT - BRAZIL - SERGIPE.
Projeto Tabuleiros Norte de Sergipe /. Aracaju , 1977. 521 p. : LC Card 86-131158
HD1875.S4 P76 1977

RURAL DEVELOPMENT - BURUNDI - MUGINA (COMMUNE)

Bahizi, Joseph. Monographie d'unités domestiques. [Bujumbura] [1985] 41 leaves ; LC Card 86-980542
HC880.Z7 M843 1985

RURAL DEVELOPMENT - CHINA.
On rolls the green revolution /. Beijing, China [1984] 142 p., [36] p. of plates : LC Card 86-115054 DDC 338.1/0951 19
HD2097 .O5 1984 NYPL [JLK 83-122 no.9]

RURAL DEVELOPMENT - COLOMBIA.
Rivera Cusicanqui, Silvia. Política e ideología en el movimiento campesino colombiano . [Bogotá] [s.l.] , 1982. 188 p. ; LC Card 84-155496
HD511.5.A87 R58 1982
NYPL [JLD 86-1208]

RURAL DEVELOPMENT - CONGO (BRAZZAVILLE)
N'Kaloulou, Bernard, 1952- Dynamique paysanne et développement rural au Congo /. Paris , c1984. 260 p. : ISBN 2-85802-416-X LC Card 84-246506 DDC 305.5/63 19
HD1006 .N57 1984 NYPL [JLD 87-304]

RURAL DEVELOPMENT - CONGRESSES.
Promotion of employment and incomes for the rural poor, including rural women, through non-farm activities . Geneva , 1983. 131 p. ; ISBN 92-2-103506-9 (pbk.) : LC Card 86-221308 DDC 331.12/042/091734 19
HD5710.8 .P76 1983

RURAL DEVELOPMENT - CUBA.
RURAL DEVELOPMENT - DEVELOPING COUNTRIES.
Integrated rural energy planning /. Guildford , c1985. xii, 200 p. : ISBN 0-408-22166-6
NYPL [JLF 87-3]

Integrating nutrition into agricultural and rural development projects . Rome , 1984. ix, 132 p. : ISBN 92-5-102150-3 *NYPL [JLG 86-181]*

Lombeya Bosongo L. Organisation coopérative et développement rural /. [Kinshasa] , 1985. 173 p. ; LC Card 86-185252
HD1491.5 .L66 1985

Uphoff, Norman Thomas. Local institutional development . West Hartford, CT , c1986. xv, 421 p. ; ISBN 0-931816-45-9 LC Card 86-15288 DDC 302.3/5 19
HC59.7 .U64 1986 NYPL [JLE 87-1200]

RURAL DEVELOPMENT - DEVELOPING COUNTRIES - ADDRESSES, ESSAYS, LECTURES.
Rural development and human fertility /. New York, N.Y. , London , c1984. ix, 318 p. : ISBN 0-02-949680-2 : LC Card 83-26834 DDC 304.6/32/091734 19
HB1108 .R87 1984 NYPL [JLE 86-1084]

Studies on rural development . New Delhi , 1984. viii, 96 p. ; LC Card 84-902362 DDC 307.7/2 19
HN980 .S77 1984 NYPL [JLE 86-4141]

RURAL DEVELOPMENT - DEVELOPING COUNTRIES - CONGRESSES.
Integrated rural energy planning /. Guildford, Surrey, England , 1985. xii, 200 p. : ISBN 0-408-22166-6 LC Card 87-160993 DDC 333.79/09172/4 19
HD9502.D442 I57 1985

RURAL DEVELOPMENT - ECUADOR.
Santana, Roberto. Campesinado indígena y el desafío de la modernidad /. [Quito, Ecuador] , 1983. 209 p. : LC Card 84-156117 DDC 330.9866/074/08998 19
F3721.3.E25 S26 1983
NYPL [HBC 86-2225]

RURAL DEVELOPMENT - ECUADOR - EL ORO (PROVINCE)
Informe cuatrianual, 1980-1983 /. Cuenca, Ecuador [1983] 222 p. : LC Card 86-206868
HC203.O76 I53 1983

RURAL DEVELOPMENT - ECUADOR - LOJA (PROVINCE)
Informe cuatrianual, 1980-1983 /. Cuenca, Ecuador [1983] 222 p. : LC Card 86-206868
HC203.O76 I53 1983

RURAL DEVELOPMENT - ECUADOR - ZAMORA-CHINCHIPE.
Informe cuatrianual, 1980-1983 /. Cuenca, Ecuador [1983] 222 p. : LC Card 86-206868
HC203.O76 I53 1983

RURAL DEVELOPMENT - EGYPT.
Adams, Richard H. Development and social change in rural Egypt /. Syracuse, N.Y. , 1986. xii, 231 p. : ISBN 0-8156-2362-3 (alk. paper) LC Card 85-30251 DDC 307.1/4/0962 19
HN786.Z9 C63 1986 NYPL [JLE 86-1999]

Rural development, employment and incomes in Kenya /. Livingstone, Ian. Aldershot, Hants , Brookfield, Vermont , 1986. xx, 389 p. : ISBN 0-566-00990-0 *NYPL [Sc D 86-728]*

RURAL DEVELOPMENT - ETHIOPIA.
Alemneh Dejene. Peasants, agrarian socialism, and rural development in Ethiopia /. Boulder , 1987. xiii, 162 p. : ISBN 0-8133-7247-X (pbk. : alk. paper) LC Card 86-51527 DDC 338.1/0963 19
HD2124.5 .A79 1987

Tegegne Teke. Cooperatives and national development . Addis Ababa, Ethiopia [1984] iii, 57 leaves ; LC Card 85-980411 DDC 334/.683/0963 19
HD1491.E83 T44 1984 NYPL [JLG 86-173]

RURAL DEVELOPMENT - GEORGIA.
Oliveira, Victor J. Distribution of rural employment growth by race . Washington, D.C. [1986] vii, 17 p. : LC Card 86-601118 DDC 331.6/09758 19
HD5725.G4 O56 1986

RURAL DEVELOPMENT - GHANA.
Dadson, J. A. Production co-operatives and rural development in Ghana /. [Addis Ababa] [1985] 53 p. ; LC Card 87-105501 DDC 334/.6/09667 19
HD3258.3.A4 D34 1985

RURAL DEVELOPMENT - GOVERNMENT POLICY - AUSTRIA.
Arbeitsmarktpolitik für die Landwirtschaft und den ländlichen Raum /. Graz , c1984. 138 p. : ISBN 3-900307-15-6 LC Card 85-186643
HD1536.A9 A73 1984

RURAL DEVELOPMENT - GOVERNMENT POLICY - DEVELOPING COUNTRIES.
Munasinghe, Mohan, 1945- Rural electrification for development . Boulder , 1987. xxiii, 440 p. : ISBN 0-8133-0088-6 (pbk.) LC Card 87-50130 DDC 333.79/32/091724 19
HD9688.D44 M85 1987

RURAL DEVELOPMENT - GOVERNMENT POLICY - ETHIOPIA - ADDRESSES, ESSAYS, LECTURES.
Fassil G. Kiros. Mobilizing the peasantry for rural development [microform] . [Addis Ababa , 1982] 20 leaves ; LC Card 82-980723 DDC 334/.683/0963 19
HD1538.E7 F37 1982
*NYPL [*Z-3952 no.39]*

RURAL DEVELOPMENT - GOVERNMENT POLICY - GAMBIA.
Gambia. Preparation report, rural development programme, 1980-85 /. Banjul [1979- v. <1 > : LC Card 86-203596
HD2147 .G35 1980a

RURAL DEVELOPMENT - GOVERNMENT POLICY - INDIA.
Varma, S. C. Millions in poverty grip . New Delhi , 1984. xv, 172 p. ; LC Card 84-900600 DDC 331.12/042/0954 19
HD5710.85.I4 V37 1984
NYPL [JLD 86-4236]

RURAL DEVELOPMENT - GOVERNMENT POLICY - KENYA.
Wegner, Gerhard, 1953- Bauern, Kapital und Staat in Kenia . Berlin , c1983. 94 p. : ISBN 3-88619-038-2 : LC Card 85-171380
HD1538.K4 W44 1983

RURAL DEVELOPMENT - GOVERNMENT POLICY - MALAWI.
Malawi. National rural development programme /. [Lilongwe, Malawi] , 1977. 7 v. : LC Card 85-981594
HD2133.5.Z8 M35 1977

RURAL DEVELOPMENT - GOVERNMENT POLICY - SOMALIA - CONGRESSES.
Somalia's rural development strategy, 1981-1990. Mogadishu, Somalia [1981?] vii, 45, [49] leaves : LC Card 83-980772 DDC 338.1/86773 19
HD2125.Z8 S65 1981 NYPL [JLG 86-58]

RURAL DEVELOPMENT - GOVERNMENT POLICY - UNITED STATES - STATES.
Hackett, Judith C. Managing rural infrastructure . Lexington, Ky. , c1986. iii, 36 p. : ISBN 0-87292-070-4 (pbk.) : LC Card 87-404481 DDC 363/.0973 19
HD3888 .H27 1986

RURAL DEVELOPMENT - GUINEA.
Guinea. Comité militaire de redressement national. Premières mesures de mise en application du programme du CMRN. [Conakry, R.G. , 1984] 84 p. ; LC Card 85-143345
HD2143.Z8 G85 1984

RURAL DEVELOPMENT - GUINEA-BISSAU.
Galli, Rosemary. Guinea-Bissau . London , Boulder , 1987. xvi, 217 p., [1] leaf of plates : ISBN 1-555-87025-2 (U. S. : lib. bdg.) : LC Card 86-28011 DDC 966/.5703 19
HC1080 .G35 1987

RURAL DEVELOPMENT - INDIA.
Aziz, Abdul, 1937- The rural poor . New Delhi , 1983. 92 p. ; LC Card 83-906454 DDC 330.954/052/08806942 19
HC440.P6 A98 1983 NYPL [JLD 87-544]

Bhoite, Anuradha. Women employees and rural development . Delhi, India , c1987. xiii, 135 p. ; ISBN 81-212-0085-7 : LC Card 87-900916 DDC 331.4/0954 19
HD6189 .B56 1987

Chowdhry, D. Paul. Profile of social welfare and development in India /. New Delhi , 1985. viii, 340 p. ; LC Card 85-901093 DDC 362/.954 19
HV393 .C515 1985 NYPL [JLD 86-2575]

Dubhashi, P. R. Essays in development administration /. New Delhi, India , 1987. x, 391 p. ; LC Card 87-901132 DDC 338.954 19
HC435.2 .D833 1987

Growth of agriculture and rural development in India /. New Delhi , c1987. xx, 496 p. ; LC Card 87-900250 DDC 338.1/0954 19
HD2072 .G7 1987

Lamba, S. K. Impact of land reforms on rural development . New Delhi, India , 1986 [i.e. 1985] xiv, 148 p. ; ISBN 81-85005-20-6 : LC Card 85-905086 DDC 333.3/1/54 19
HD1333.I4 L35 1986

Nanjundappa, D. M., 1930- Area planning and rural development /. New Delhi , c1981. viii, 52 p. ; LC Card 81-903723 DDC 307/.12/0954 19
HN690.Z9 C6649 1981
NYPL [JLD 86-2687]

Public administration in India . Allahabad , 1983. xii, 308 p. ; LC Card 83-907416 DDC 354.54 19
JQ224 .P75 1983 NYPL [JLE 86-4197]

Ramakrishna Sarma, K. Financial institutions and regional development in India /. Allahabad, India , 1986. xvii, 211 p. ; ISBN 81-85076-04-9 : LC Card 86-902692 DDC 332.2 19
HG3288 .R32 1986

Ranade, Sudhanshu, 1952- Rural banking adrift /. Bombay , c1984. x, 126 p. ; LC Card 84-903073 DDC 332.1/0954 19
HG3284 .R325 1984 NYPL [JLD 87-561]

Seshadri, K. Rural unrest in India /. New Delhi , 1983. xiii, 192 p. ; LC Card 83-905323 DDC 303.6/23/0954 19
HC440.P6 S47 1983 NYPL [JLD 86-3704]

Somasekhara, N. Rural energy . New Delhi , 1985. xii, 113 p. ; ISBN 81-207-0121-6 : LC Card 86-900467 DDC 333.79/0954 19
HD9502.I42 S66 1985 NYPL [JLD 86-3315]

Tiwary, Jai Kant. Rural development administration . Allahabad, India , 1984. xi, 248 p. ; LC Card 84-900188 DDC 307.7/2/0954 19
HN690.Z9 C68286 1984
NYPL [JLD 86-4313]

RURAL DEVELOPMENT - INDIA - ADDRESSES, ESSAYS, LECTURES.
Franda, Marcus F. Voluntary associations and local development in India . New Delhi , 1983. vi, 356 p. ; LC Card 83-900993 DDC 307/.14/0954 19
HN690.Z9 C6513 1983
NYPL [JLD 86-3866]

Studies on rural development . New Delhi , 1984. viii, 96 p. ; LC Card 84-902362 DDC 307.7/2 19
HN980 .S77 1984 NYPL [JLE 86-4141]

RURAL DEVELOPMENT - INDIA - ANDHRA PRADESH - CASE STUDIES.
Venkaiah, V., 1952- Impact of agro-based industries on rural economy . Bombay , 1987. xxi, 348 p. ; LC Card 86-903766 DDC 338.1/0954/84 19
HD9016.I43 A67 1987

RURAL DEVELOPMENT - INDIA - ASSAM - CASE STUDIES.
Agnihotri, S. K. Rural development through land reforms . Delhi , 1986. viii, 3, 206 p. ; LC Card 87-900356 DDC 333.3/1/54162 19
HD1333.I42 A773 1986

RURAL DEVELOPMENT - INDIA - CASE STUDIES.
Agnihotri, S. K. Rural development through land reforms . Delhi , 1986. viii, 3, 206 p. ; LC Card 87-900356 DDC 333.3/1/54162 19
HD1333.I42 A773 1986

Venkaiah, V., 1952- Impact of agro-based industries on rural economy . Bombay , 1987. xxi, 348 p. ; LC Card 86-903766 DDC 338.1/0954/84 19
HD9016.I43 A67 1987

RURAL DEVELOPMENT - INDIA - CHOTA NAGPUR.
Singh, R. S. (Rama Shankar), 1950- Changing occupational structure of scheduled tribes /. New Delhi, India , 1986. 291 p. : ISBN 81-210-0175-7 : LC Card 86-903755
HB3640.C48 S56 1986

RURAL DEVELOPMENT - INDIA - CONGRESSES.
Workshop on Promotion of Self-Employment in Rural Areas (1982 : Allahabad, India) Workshop on Promotion of Self-employment in Rural Areas, Allahabad, 26-30 November 1982 . New Delhi [1983] iii, 186 p. ; LC Card 83-906671 DDC 338.6/42 19
HD8037.I4 W67 1982

RURAL DEVELOPMENT - INDIA - ENERGY CONSUMPTION - CONGRESSES.
Energy alternatives for rural development /. Jaipur , 1985. vi, 303 p. : LC Card 86-902191 DDC 333.79/0954 19
HD9556.I42 E54 1985

RURAL DEVELOPMENT - INDIA - FINANCE.
Khemani, C. L., 1934- How and why of rural banking /. New Delhi , 1987. 255, [41] p. : LC Card 87-901033 DDC 332.1/0954 19
HG3288 .K44 1987

Ramachandra Rao, B. All about priority sector advances /. New Delhi , 1984. 350 p. : LC Card 84-901313 DDC 332.7/0954 19
HG3729.I42 R36 1984 ***NYPL [JLD 87-574]***

RURAL DEVELOPMENT - INDIA - FINANCE - CONGRESSES.
Bank finance and rural development /. Tirupati [1986] vi, 222 p. ; LC Card 86-903530 DDC 332.2 19
HG3284 .B265 1986

Command area development, successes and learnings . Hyderabad , c1980. iii, 138 p. ; LC Card 83-906246 DDC 338.1/854 19
HD1741.I29 C65 1980 ***NYPL [JLD 87-597]***

RURAL DEVELOPMENT - INDIA - GHAZIPUR (DISTRICT)
Ghate, Prabhu, 1941- Direct attacks on rural poverty . New Delhi , 1984. xvi, 597 p. : LC Card 84-902455 DDC 338.954/2 19
HC437.G48 G46 1984 ***NYPL [JLD 87-651]***

RURAL DEVELOPMENT - INDIA - HIMACHEL PRADESH.
Sharda, N. K. State finances and regional development in India /. New Delhi , c1986. 248 p. ; LC Card 86-900599 DDC 336.54/52 19
HJ1339.H55 S54 1986 ***NYPL [JLD 86-3211]***

RURAL DEVELOPMENT - INDIA - PRABHANI (DISTRICT)
Bhoite, Anuradha. Women employees and rural development . Delhi, India , c1987. xiii, 135 p. ; ISBN 81-212-0085-7 : LC Card 87-900916 DDC 331.4/0954 19
HD6189 .B56 1987

RURAL DEVELOPMENT - INDIA - PUNJAB.
Inder Pal Singh, 1959- Rural income distribution . Delhi , New Delhi, India , 1986. xvi, 123 p. : ISBN 81-7018-299-9 : LC Card 86-900514 DDC 339.2/3/0954552 19
HC440.I5 I46 1986 ***NYPL [JLD 86-3077]***

RURAL DEVELOPMENT - INDIA - RAJASTHAN - MANAGEMENT.
Kabra, Govind Das, 1943- Development of weaker sections . New Delhi , 1984, c1983. ix, 182 p. ; LC Card 84-900357 DDC 338.1/8544 19
HD1476.I42 R345 1984 ***NYPL [JLE 86-4597]***

RURAL DEVELOPMENT - INDIA - UTTAR PRADESH - FINANCE.
Mishra, M. N. (Maha Narain), 1945- Appraisal of credit facilities provided by banking institutions in rural development /. Meerut, U.P., India [1987?] x, 251, ii p. ; LC Card 87-900918 DDC 332.2 19
HG3284 .M49 1987

Rural Development Institute (U. S.) Prosterman, Roy L. Egyptian development and U. S. aid . [Seattle, Wash.?] , c1985. i, 32, A1-A10 p. ; LC Card 87-104139 DDC 338.91/73/062 19
HC830.Z9 E446 1985

RURAL DEVELOPMENT - ITALY.
Strategia dei servizi per l'agricoltura . [Roma] [1983] 158 p. : LC Card 85-155420
HD9475.I82 S77 1983

RURAL DEVELOPMENT - ITALY - PARMA (PROVINCE) - CONGRESSES.
Economia e società della montagna parmense . [Italy , 1984?] (Parma : Officina grafica artigiana) 115 p. ; LC Card 85-156635
HC307.P33 E27 1984

RURAL DEVELOPMENT - JAPAN - NAKADA-CHŌ (MIYAGI-KEN)
Moore, Richard H. Japanese agriculture . Boulder , 1987. p. cm. ISBN 0-8133-7406-5 LC Card 87-13553 DDC 338.1/0952/115 19
HD920.N33 M65 1987

RURAL DEVELOPMENT - KENYA.
Hosier, Richard. Energy use in rural Kenya . Stockholm , Uppsala , c1985. xi, 177 p. : ISBN 91-7106-241-6 ***NYPL [JLD 86-2653]***

Livingstone, Ian. Rural development, employment and incomes in Kenya /. Aldershot, Hants , Brookfield, Vermont , 1986. xx, 389 p. : ISBN 0-566-00990-0 ***NYPL [Sc D 86-728]***

RURAL DEVELOPMENT - MEXICO.
Acevedo Conde, María Luisa. Pobreza y riqueza en 378 municipios de México /. México, D.F. , 1984. 281 p. : LC Card 86-219445
HC140.P6 A25 1984

RURAL DEVELOPMENT - MEXICO - CITIZEN PARTICIPATION.
Salinas de Gortari, Carlos. Producción y participación política en el campo /. México , 1980. 320 p. : ISBN 968-582-934-9 LC Card 82-199421 DDC 338.1/0972 19
HD1792 .S287 1980 ***NYPL [JLD 86-2602]***

RURAL DEVELOPMENT - MEXICO - CONGRESSES.
U. S.-Mexico relations . Stanford, Calif. , c1987. xii, 401 p. ; ISBN 0-8047-1319-7 (alk. paper) LC Card 86-23103 DDC 338.1/872 19
HD1792 .U19 1987

RURAL DEVELOPMENT - MEXICO - JALISCO - CASE STUDIES.
Grassroots development in Latin America & the Caribbean . New York , 1985. vii, 197 p. : ISBN 0-03-001689-4 (alk. paper) : LC Card 84-18180 DDC 334/.098 19
HD3450.5.A4 G72 1985

RURAL DEVELOPMENT - MOZAMBIQUE.
Caballero, Lorenzo. Mozambique, food and agriculture sector /. Uppsala , 1984. 223, [30] p. : ISBN 91-576-2129-2 (pbk.) LC Card 86-218958 DDC 338.1/0967/9 19
HD9017.M86 C33 1984

Rural Development, National Conference on. see **National Conference on Rural Development, Des Moines, 1973.**

RURAL DEVELOPMENT - NEPAL - BAJHANG (DISTRICT) - EVALUATION.
Malla, B. C. An evaluation of development activities within Sixth Plan period in Bajhang District /. Kathmandu , 1985 [i.e. 1986] 76, [3] p. : LC Card 86-903487 DDC 338.9549/6 19
HC425.Z7 B355 1986

RURAL DEVELOPMENT - NIGERIA - ADDRESSES, ESSAYS, LECTURES.
Nigerian small farmers . Benin-City, Bendel State, Nigeria , 1980. xv, 315 p. ; LC Card 82-206979 DDC 338.1/6 19
HD1339.N5 N54 1980 ***NYPL [Sc D 86-883]***

RURAL DEVELOPMENT - PACIFIC AREA - CONGRESSES.
Movement for a no poverty society . Calcutta , 1980. 78 p. ; LC Card 81-902107
HC415.P6 M68 1980

RURAL DEVELOPMENT - PERU - AYACUCHO (DEPT.)
Gianotten, Vera. Organización campesina . Amsterdam , Cinnaminson, N.J. , c1985. ix, 531 p., [4] p. of plates : ISBN 90-6765-162-1 LC Card 85-200688
HD1531.P4 G5 1985

RURAL DEVELOPMENT - PHILIPPINES - ILOCOS NORTE - CASE STUDIES.
Findley, Sally E. Rural development and migration . Boulder , 1987. xxiii, 308 p. : ISBN 0-8133-7326-3 (pbk. : alk. paper) : LC Card 86-33987 DDC 304.8/09599 19
HB2110.I43 F56 1987

RURAL DEVELOPMENT - PLANNING.
Guidelines for the planning of rural settlements and infrastructure . Nairobi , 1985. vi, 295 p. ; ISBN 92-1-131003-2 LC Card 86-981187 DDC 363/.068 19
HD9688.A2 G85 1985

Rural development programme, 1980-85. Gambia. Preparation report, rural development programme, 1980-85 /. Banjul [1979- v. <1 > : LC Card 86-203596
HD2147 .G35 1980a

Rural Development Project (Gambia). Coordinator's Office. Gambia. Preparation report, rural development programme, 1980-85 /. Banjul [1979- v. <1 > : LC Card 86-203596
HD2147 .G35 1980a

RURAL DEVELOPMENT PROJECTS - AFRICA - ADDRESSES, ESSAYS, LECTURES.
Population and development projects in Africa /. Cambridge [Cambridgeshire] , New York , 1985. xvi, 329 p. : ISBN 0-521-30527-6 LC Card 84-29323 DDC 304.6/096 19
HB2121.A3 P67 1985 ***NYPL [JLF 86-186]***

RURAL DEVELOPMENT PROJECTS - AFRICA - CONGRESSES.
Séminaire de formation aux techniques d'élaboration de projets (1980 : Conakry, Guinea, etc.) Séminaire de formation aux techniques d'élaboration de projets . Addis-Abeba , 1982. vii, 36, [31] p. : LC Card 86-168821
HC800 .S444 1980

RURAL DEVELOPMENT PROJECTS - ASIA, SOUTHEASTERN - CASE STUDIES.
Development strategies and planning for farmers' communities . College, Laguna, Philippines , 1983. vi, 242 p. : LC Card 84-102916 DDC 338.1/859 19
HD2075.8 .D48 1983

RURAL DEVELOPMENT PROJECTS - BOLIVIA.
Diez, Rafael. Final report of the consultancy of Rafael Diez from August 3, 1982 to August 3, 1983. La Paz [1983] 1 v. (various foliations) ; LC Card 83-243264
HC182 .D49 1983

RURAL DEVELOPMENT PROJECTS - BOTSWANA.
Fones-Sundell, Melinda. Implementing rural development in Botswana . Uppsala , 1983. 75 p. : LC Card 86-215071 DDC 338.1/86811 19
HD2133 .F66 1983

RURAL DEVELOPMENT PROJECTS - DEVELOPING COUNTRIES.
Beyond bureaucracy . West Hartford, Conn. , c1986. xii, 256 p. : ISBN 0-931816-44-0 LC Card 86-34420 DDC 338.9/0068 19
HC59.72.E44 B48 1986

Kinsey, B. H. Agribusiness and rural enterprise /. London , New York , c1987. 228 p. ; ISBN 0-7099-1558-6 : LC Card 87-471 DDC 338.1/09172/4 19
HD9018.D44 K55 1987

RURAL DEVELOPMENT PROJECTS - DEVELOPING COUNTRIES - EVALUATION.
Evaluation du développement rural /. [Paris] , c1982. 201 p. : ISBN 2-11-084484-1 LC Card 84-134740
HC59.72.E44 E93 1982

RURAL DEVELOPMENT PROJECTS - DEVELOPING COUNTRIES - MANAGEMENT.
Bryant, Coralie. Managing rural development with small farmer participation /. West Hartford, CT. , c1984. xiii, 79 p. : ISBN 0-931816-52-1 (pbk.) LC Card 84-4445 DDC 307.7/2 19
HD1417 .B79 1984 ***NYPL [JLE 87-1352]***

Honadle, George. Implementation for sustainability . West Hartford, Conn. , c1985. xiv, 128 p. ; ISBN 0-931816-47-5 LC Card 85-12538 DDC 338.9/0068 19
HD1417 .H66 1985 ***NYPL [JLE 86-3888]***

RURAL DEVELOPMENT PROJECTS - DEVELOPING COUNTRIES - MANAGEMENT - CASE STUDIES.
Honadle, George. Implementation for sustainability . West Hartford, Conn. , c1985. xiv, 128 p. ; ISBN 0-931816-47-5 LC Card 85-12538 DDC 338.9/0068 19
HD1417 .H66 1985 ***NYPL [JLE 86-3888]***

RURAL DEVELOPMENT PROJECTS - GAMBIA.
Gambia. Preparation report, rural development programme, 1980-85 /. Banjul [1979- v. <1 > : LC Card 86-203596
HD2147 .G35 1980a

RURAL DEVELOPMENT PROJECTS - INDIA - GUJARAT.
Hirway, Indira. Wage employment programmes in rural development . New Delhi , c1986. vi, 112 p. ; ISBN 81-204-0072-0 : LC Card 86-903398 DDC 331.2/95475 19
HD5070.G85 H57 1986

RURAL DEVELOPMENT PROJECTS - KENYA - EVALUATION.
Bethke, Klaus W. Small projects for rural development . [Nairobi] [1983] 33, [34] leaves ; LC Card 86-981325 DDC 354.676/20082 19
HC865 .B48 1983

RURAL DEVELOPMENT PROJECTS - KENYA - PLANNING.
Bethke, Klaus W. Small projects for rural development . [Nairobi] [1983] 33, [34] leaves ; LC Card 86-981325 DDC 354.676/20082 19
HC865 .B48 1983

RURAL DEVELOPMENT PROJECTS - MALAWI.
Malawi. National rural development programme /. [Lilongwe, Malawi] , 1977. 7 v. : LC Card 85-981594
HD2133.5.Z8 M35 1977

RURAL DEVELOPMENT PROJECTS - MEXICO.
Cernea, Michael M. Measuring project impact . Washington, D.C., U. S.A. , c1979. vi, 93 p. ; LC Card 81-170764
HD1792 .C43 1979

RURAL DEVELOPMENT PROJECTS - NIGERIA - MANAGEMENT.
Eweka, J. A. (Julius A.) Village development . Ibadan, Nigeria , 1979. xvi, 194 p. ; LC Card 86-172121 DDC 338.1/9/669 19
HD2145.5 .E94 1979

RURAL DEVELOPMENT PROJECTS - SIERRA LEONE.
Büscher, Ludger. Integrated rural development . Hamburg , 1984. xx, 238 p. : ISBN 3-87895-261-9 (pbk.) LC Card 86-672442
HD2146.5 .B87x 1984 ***NYPL [JLD 86-2789]***

Okai, Matthew. Rural poverty and alleviation measures in Sierra Leone /. [Rome] , 1983. 91 p. : LC Card 87-400417 DDC 338.1/8/664 19
HC1065.Z9 P66 1983

RURAL DEVELOPMENT PROJECTS - SIERRA LEONE - BO (DISTRICT)
Yearwood, John. Storage facilities in the chiefdoms of Bo and Pujehun District /. Bo [1983] vi, 31 leaves : LC Card 87-110214 DDC 338.1/6 19
HD9017.S53 B599 1983

RURAL DEVELOPMENT PROJECTS - SIERRA LEONE - PUJEHUN (DISTRICT)
Yearwood, John. Storage facilities in the chiefdoms of Bo and Pujehun District /. Bo [1983] vi, 31 leaves : LC Card 87-110214 DDC 338.1/6 19
HD9017.S53 B599 1983

RURAL DEVELOPMENT PROJECTS - SUDAN.
ILO Identification and Programming Mission to the Republic of the Sudan. After the famine . Geneva , 1986. xi, 309 p. : ISBN 92-2-105401-2 (pbk.) LC Card 86-226792 DDC 363.8/83/09624 19
HC835.Z9 F35 1985

RURAL DEVELOPMENT PROJECTS - ZIMBABWE - EVALUATION - CASE STUDIES.
Else, John F. Planning income generating projects . Harare, Zimbabwe [1986?] 46 p. : LC Card 87-400416 DDC 338.96891/0068 19
HC910 .E43 1986

Rural development research report .
(no. 52) Morrissey, Elizabeth S. Characteristics of poverty in nonmetro counties /. Washington, D.C. , 1985. iv, 10 p. : LC Card 86-602555 DDC 362.5/0973 19
HC110.P6 M67 1985

(no. 54) Oliveira, Victor J. Distribution of rural employment growth by race . Washington, D.C. [1986] vii, 17 p. : LC Card 86-601118 DDC 331.6/09758 19
HD5725.G4 O56 1986

(no. 57) Fuller, Theodore, 1929- The Mid-Atlantic region in transition . Washington, D.C. [1986] v, 13 p. : LC Card 86-602014 DDC 331.12/0974 19
HD5725.A12 F85 1986

(no. 58) Social and economic characteristics of the population in metro and nonmetro counties, 1970-80 /. Washington, D.C. [1986] iv, 70 p. : LC Card 86-602790 DDC 304.6/0973 19
HC106.7 .S577 1986

(no. 59) Banks, Vera J. Black farmers and their farms /. Washington, D.C. , 1986. v, 27 p. : LC Card 86-602201
HD8039.F32 U616 1986

(no. 62) Ghelfi, Linda M. Poverty among black families in the nonmetro South /. Washington, D.C. , Supt. of Docs., U. S. G.P.O. [distributor, 1986] vii, 27 p. : LC Card 86-602435 DDC 330.975/043/0899607301734 19
HC107.A13 G48 1986

RURAL DEVELOPMENT - RUSSIAN S.F.S.R. - NON-CHERNOZEM REGION.
Chanturiia͡, V. K. (Vladimir Kapitonovich) Stroitsia͡ Nechernozem'e /. Moskva , 1980. 94 p. ; LC Card 81-135603
HD9715.S73 N63 1980

RURAL DEVELOPMENT - SOUTH AFRICA - TRANSKEI.
May, Julian. Development planning in Transkei . Durban , 1985. 35 p., [5] p. ; ISBN 0-86980-483-9 (pbk.) : LC Card 86-222656 DDC 338.9687/91 19
HC905.Z7 T7347 1985

RURAL DEVELOPMENT - SRI LANKA - CONGRESSES.
International Congress on New Dimensions in Population Planning and Development (1978 : Colombo, Sri Lanka) The International Congress on New Dimensions in Population Planning and Development, Bandaranaike Memorial International Conference Hall, Colombo, 26-28 March 1978 /. Colombo, Sri Lanka , 1978. 114 p., [5] leaves of plates : LC Card 84-902651 DDC 304.6/6/095493 19
HB883.5 .I57 1978 ***NYPL [JLF 86-1970]***

Rural development studies (Uppsala, Sweden) .
(no. 16) Caballero, Lorenzo. Mozambique, food and agriculture sector /. Uppsala , 1984. 223, [30] p. : ISBN 91-576-2129-2 (pbk.) LC Card 86-218958 DDC 338.1/0967/9 19
HD9017.M86 C33 1984

RURAL DEVELOPMENT - SUDAN.
ILO Identification and Programming Mission to the Republic of the Sudan. After the famine . Geneva , 1986. xi, 309 p. : ISBN 92-2-105401-2 (pbk.) LC Card 86-226792 DDC 363.8/83/09624 19
HC835.Z9 F35 1985

RURAL DEVELOPMENT - TAIWAN.
Lamba, S. K. Impact of land reforms on rural development . New Delhi, India , 1986 [i.e. 1985] xiv, 148 p. ; ISBN 81-85005-20-6 : LC Card 85-905086 DDC 333.3/1/54 19
HD1333.I4 L35 1986

RURAL DEVELOPMENT - TANZANIA.
Collier, Paul. Labour and poverty in rural Tanzania . Oxford [Oxfordhire] , New York , 1986. vii, 143 p. : ISBN 0-19-828531-0 : LC Card 86-5303 DDC 307.1/4/09678 19
HN797.Z9 C625 1986 ***NYPL [JLD 87-511]***

Employment promotion in Tanzania . Addis Ababa , 1986. ii leaves, 107 p. ; LC Card 87-980150 DDC 331.11/09678 19
HD5841.3.A6 E46 1986

RURAL DEVELOPMENT - THAILAND.
Thailand. Samnakngān Khana Kammakān Kansksā hæng Chāt. Education and employment from world capitalism to the rural Thais . Bangkok, Thailand , 1985. 46 p. : LC Card 86-915875 DDC 331.13/79593 19
HD5822.55.A6 T47 1985

Rural development through land reforms .
Agnihotri, S. K. Delhi , 1986. viii, 3, 206 p. ; LC Card 87-900356 DDC 333.3/1/54162 19
HD1333.I42 A773 1986

RURAL DEVELOPMENT - UNITED STATES - ADDRESSES, ESSAYS, LECTURES.
Rural public administration . Westport, Conn. , 1986. ix, 208 p. ; ISBN 0-313-25246-7 (lib. bdg. : alk. paper) LC Card 85-27253 DDC 352/.00722/0973 19
JS425 .R87 1986 ***NYPL [JLE 86-4005]***

RURAL DEVELOPMENT - UNITED STATES - CONGRESSES.
U. S.-Mexico relations . Stanford, Calif. , c1987. xii, 401 p. ; ISBN 0-8047-1319-7 (alk. paper) LC Card 86-23103 DDC 338.1/872 19
HD1792 .U19 1987

RURAL DEVELOPMENT - UNITED STATES - HISTORY.
West, Patrick C. Natural resource bureaucracy and rural poverty . Ann Arbor, MI , c1982. xiii, 168 p. : LC Card 83-102928 DDC 333.7/16/0973 19
HD1761 .W423 1982 ***NYPL [JLE 86-4095]***

RURAL DEVELOPMENT - ZAMBIA.
Chilivumbo, Alifeyo. Migration and uneven rural development in Africa . Lanham, MD , c1985. xx, 118 p. : ISBN 0-8191-4929-2 (alk. paper) : LC Card 85-17908 DDC 307.2 19
HB2123.6.A3 C47 1985 ***NYPL [JLD 86-1953]***

RURAL DEVELOPMENT - ZAMBIA - EASTERN PROVINCE.
Rajeswaran, K. A feasibility study on the ox-driven scotch cart project . Lusaka, Zambia [1985] vii leaves, 66 p., [3] leaves of plates : LC Card 87-980373 DDC 388.3/41/096894 19
HE153 .R35 1985

RURAL ECONOMIC DEVELOPMENT. see **RURAL DEVELOPMENT.**

RURAL EDUCATION. see **EDUCATION, RURAL.**

RURAL ELECTRIFICATION - BRAZIL.
Brazil. Grupo Executivo de Eletrificação Rural de Cooperativas. Eletrificação rural no Brasil /. Brasília, DF [1984] 93 p. : LC Card 86-200328
HD9688.B72 B74 1984

RURAL ELECTRIFICATION - DEVELOPING COUNTRIES.
Evaluating electrification experience . Washington, D.C. , 1982- v. <1 > : LC Card 86-176385 DDC 333.91/4 19
HD9688.D44 E9 1982

Munasinghe, Mohan, 1945- Rural electrification for development . Boulder , 1987. xxiii, 440 p. : ISBN 0-8133-0088-6 (pbk.) LC Card 87-50130 DDC 333.79/32/091724 19
HD9688.D44 M85 1987

Rural electrification for development .
Munasinghe, Mohan, 1945- Boulder , 1987. xxiii, 440 p. : ISBN 0-8133-0088-6 (pbk.) LC

Card 87-50130 DDC 333.79/32/091724 19
HD9688.D44 M85 1987

RURAL ELECTRIFICATION - GOVERNMENT POLICY - BRAZIL.
Brazil. Departamento Nacional de Aguas e Energia Elétrica. Pontos básicos para uma política de eletrificação rural . Brasília, D.F. , 1984. 190 p. : LC Card 86-158852
HD9688.B72 B73 1984

RURAL ELECTRIFICATION - GOVERNMENT POLICY - DEVELOPING COUNTRIES.
Munasinghe, Mohan, 1945- Rural electrification for development . Boulder , 1987. xxiii, 440 p. : ISBN 0-8133-0088-6 (pbk.) LC Card 87-50130 DDC 333.79/32/091724 19
HD9688.D44 M85 1987

RURAL ELECTRIFICATION - INDIA - BIHAR.
Sachchidananda, 1926- Electricity and social change /. Patna , 1983. xii, 264 p. ; LC Card 83-902678 DDC 303.4/83 19
HD9685.I43 B547 1983
NYPL [JLD 86-4263]

RURAL ELECTRIFICATION - ITALY, SOUTHERN.
Barone, Giuseppe, 1947- Mezzogiorno e modernizzazione . Torino , c1986. xii, 408 p. ; ISBN 88-06-59238-6 : LC Card 86-219130
HC307.S69 B37 1986

RURAL ELECTRIFICATION - NEW JERSEY - HISTORY - SOURCES.
Romeo, Mary Ellen. Darkness to daylight . Harrisburg, Pa. , c1986. 152 p. : LC Card 86-216619 DDC 621.319/09748 19
HD9688.U53 P46 1986

RURAL ELECTRIFICATION - PENNSYLVANIA - HISTORY - SOURCES.
Romeo, Mary Ellen. Darkness to daylight . Harrisburg, Pa. , c1986. 152 p. : LC Card 86-216619 DDC 621.319/09748 19
HD9688.U53 P46 1986

RURAL ELECTRIFICATION - PLANNING.
Guidelines for the planning of rural settlements and infrastructure . Nairobi , 1985. vi, 295 p. ; ISBN 92-1-131003-2 LC Card 86-981187 DDC 363/.068 19
HD9688.A2 G85 1985

RURAL ELECTRIFICATION - TEXAS - HISTORY.
Guy, Duane F. Texas 47--Deaf Smith . [Hereford, Tex.] , c1986. vii, 160 p. : LC Card 86-210662 DDC 334/.682131/09764835 19
HD9688.U54 D434 1986

RURAL ELECTRIFICATION - UNITED STATES - HISTORY.
A Brief history of the rural electric and telephone programs. [Washington, D.C.] [1986] 61 p. : LC Card 86-602412 DDC 353.0087/22 19
HD9688.U52 B75 1986

RURAL EMPLOYMENT - GOVERNMENT POLICY - INDIA.
Behari, Bepin. Unemployment, technology & rural poverty /. New Delhi , c1983. ix, 453 p. ; ISBN 0-7069-2337-5 : LC Card 83-906129 DDC 338/.06 19
HC440.I52 B43 1983 ***NYPL [JLD 87-1132]***

Gupta, Anand P. Fiscal policy and the poor /. New Delhi , c1984. 90 p. ; LC Card 84-900303 DDC 339.5/2/0954 19
HJ1331 .G87 1984 ***NYPL [JLD 87-778]***

Rural energy . Somasekhara, N. New Delhi , 1985. xii, 113 p. ; ISBN 81-207-0121-6 : LC Card 86-900467 DDC 333.79/0954 19
HD9502.I42 S66 1985 ***NYPL [JLD 86-3315]***

Rural exodus & squatter settlements in the Third World . Danesh, Abol Hassan, 1952- Lanham, MD , c1987. xii, 168 p. : ISBN 0-8191-6443-7 (alk. paper) : LC Card 87-10627 DDC 307.2 19
HB2096.4.A3 D36 1987

Rural exodus and squatter settlements in the Third World. Danesh, Abol Hassan, 1952- Rural exodus & squatter settlements in the Third World . Lanham, MD , c1987. xii, 168 p. : ISBN 0-8191-6443-7 (alk. paper) : LC Card 87-10627 DDC 307.2 19
HB2096.4.A3 D36 1987

RURAL FAMILIES - AFRICA, SUB-SAHARAN - ADDRESSES, ESSAYS, LECTURES.
Understanding Africa's rural households and farming systems /. Boulder , 1986. xiv, 234 p. : ISBN 0-8133-7175-9 : LC Card 85-32318 DDC 338.1/0967 19
HD1476.A357 U53 1986
NYPL [JLE 86-4336]

RURAL FAMILIES - COLOMBIA.
Ordóñez G., Myriam. Población y familia rural en Colombia /. Bogotá , 1986. 179 p. : LC Card 86-208940
HB2447 .O73 1986

RURAL FAMILIES - DEVELOPING COUNTRIES - CASE STUDIES.
Agricultural household models . Baltimore, Md. , 1986. xi, 335 p. : ISBN 0-8018-3149-0 LC Card 85-45102 DDC 331.7/63/091724 19
HD1542 .A34 1986 ***NYPL [JLE 86-2440]***

RURAL FAMILIES - LATIN AMERICA - CONGRESSES.
Taller "Perspectivas y Alternativas de la Agricultura Familiar" (1983 : Montevideo, Uruguay) Taller "Perspectivas y Alternativas de la Agricultura Familiar". Montevideo, Uruguay [1984] 1 v. (various pagings) : LC Card 85-203149 DDC 338.1/6 19
HD1476.L29 T35 1983 ***NYPL [JLF 86-884]***

RURAL FAMILIES - TEXAS - CONGRESSES.
Farm Crisis Workers Conference (1986 : Arlington, Tex.) Farm Crisis Workers Conference . [Austin? , 1986] 136 p. ; LC Card 87-620630 DDC 338.1/3/09764 19
HD1476.U6 T44 1986

Rural housing and the public sector /. Phillips, David R. Aldershot, Hampshire, England [Brookfield, Vt.] c1982. viii, 174 p. : ISBN 0-566-00456-9 : LC Card 82-134413 DDC 352.7/5/0941 19
HD7289.G82 S687 1982
NYPL [JLD 83-2605]

Rural housing conditions in Kisumu District, Kenya /. Sterkenburg, J. J. [Utrecht] [Nairobi] , 1982. 95 p., [6] leaves of plates : LC Card 85-981197
HD7289.K42 K67 1982

Rural housing in N.Y.S. /. Seligson, Wendy. [Albany, N.Y.] [1979] [61] p. : LC Card 82-621690 DDC 363.5/8/09747 19
HD7289.U7 N77 1979 ***NYPL [JLF 86-765]***

Rural housing in New York State. Seligson, Wendy. Rural housing in N.Y.S. /. [Albany, N.Y.] [1979] [61] p. : LC Card 82-621690 DDC 363.5/8/09747 19
HD7289.U7 N77 1979 ***NYPL [JLF 86-765]***

Rural housing in NYS. Seligson, Wendy. Rural housing in N.Y.S. /. [Albany, N.Y.] [1979] [61] p. : LC Card 82-621690 DDC 363.5/8/09747 19
HD7289.U7 N77 1979 ***NYPL [JLF 86-765]***

Rural income distribution . Inder Pal Singh, 1959- Delhi , New Delhi, India , 1986. xvi, 123 p. : ISBN 81-7018-299-9 : LC Card 86-900514 DDC 339.2/3/0954552 19
HC440.I5 I46 1986 ***NYPL [JLD 86-3077]***

Rural industrialization in Israel / edited by Raphael Bar-El with the assistance of Ariela Nesher. Boulder : Westview Press, 1987. xi, 193 p. ; 23 cm. (Westview special studies in industrial policy and development) "Published in cooperation with the Settlement Study Centre"--Cover. Includes bibliographies and index. ISBN 0-8133-7393-X (pbk. : alk. paper) : LC Card 87-2073 DDC 338.095694 19
1. Israel - Industries, Rural. I. Bar-El, Raphael. II. Nesher, Ariela. III. Merkaz le-ḥeḳer hityashvut kafrit ve-ʻironit. IV. Series.
HC415.25 .R87 1987

RURAL INDUSTRY - GREAT BRITAIN - CONGRESSES.
The Industrialization of the countryside /. Norwich [Norfolk] , c1985. xiv, 315 p. : ISBN 0-86094-202-3 LC Card 87-141251 DDC 338.9/009173/4 19
HC256.6 .I524 1985

RURAL INDUSTRY - ZAMBIA.
Milimo, J. T. Rural small enterprises in Zambia . [Lusaka] [1985] 71 p. ; LC Card 87-980231 DDC 338.6/42/096894 19
HD2346.Z29 M55 1985

The Rural integrated household survey programme : methodological report for the period of 1980-83 / the Provisional Military Government of Socialist Ethiopia, National Revolutionary Development Campaign and Central Planning Supreme Council, Central Statistical Office. Addis Abeba : The Office, [1983] 52 leaves ; 28 cm. (Statistical bulletin . 34) "February 1983." LC Card 86-980701 DDC 307.7/2/0723 19
1. Ethiopia - Population, Rural. 2. Ethiopia - Rural conditions. 3. Household surveys - Ethiopia. I. Ethiopia. Central Statistical Office. II. Series: Statistical bulletin (Ethiopia. Central Statistical Office) , 34.
HB2542.A3 R87 1983

Rural labour force survey, April 1981-April 1982 / the Provisional Military Government of Socialist Ethiopia, Office of the National Committee for Central Planning, Central Statistical Office. Addis Ababa : Central Statistical Office, 1985. xii, 170 p. ; 29 cm. (Statistical bulletin . 51) Chiefly tables. "October, 1985." Bibliography: p. 170. LC Card 86-981178 DDC 331.1/0963 19
1. Labor supply - Ethiopia - Statistics. 2. Agricultural laborers - Ethiopia - Statistics. 3. Household surveys - Ethiopia. I. Ethiopia. Central Statistical Office. II. Series: Statistical bulletin (Ethiopia. Central Statistical Office) , 51.
HD5839.7.A6 R87 1985

Rural labour market, with special reference to hired labour in Pakistan's Punjab /. Elahi, Mahboob. Lahore, Pakistan [1983] ii, ix, 186 leaves ; LC Card 86-930467
HD1537.P2 E4 1983

RURAL LIFE. see **PEASANTRY.**

RURAL MANPOWER POLICY. see **MANPOWER POLICY, RURAL.**

Rural municipality of Hanover : a background report into development and growth potential / prepared by Province of Manitoba, Dept. of Municipal Affairs, Municipal Planning Branch, in connection with the Hanover-Niverville District Advisory Planning Commission. [Winnipeg, Man.] : The Branch, [1976?] iv, 55 p. : ill. ; 35 cm. LC Card 82-219722
1. Hanover (Man.) - Economic conditions. 2. Land use - Manitoba. 3. Hanover (Man.) - Population. I. Manitoba. Municipal Planning Branch. II. Hanover-Niverville District Advisory Planning Commission.
HC118.H34 R87 1976

The rural poor . Aziz, Abdul, 1937- New Delhi , 1983. 92 p. ; LC Card 83-906454 DDC 330.954/052/08806942 19
HC440.P6 A98 1983 ***NYPL [JLD 87-544]***

RURAL POOR - BRAZIL, NORTHEAST.
Pessoa, Dirceu Murilo. Espace rural et pauvreté au nord-est du Brésil /. Paris , 1981. xvii, 288 leaves : LC Card 86-208627
HC188.N6 P47 1981

RURAL POOR - DEVELOPING COUNTRIES - ADDRESSES, ESSAYS, LECTURES.
Studies on agrarian reform and rural poverty /. Rome , New York, N.Y. , 1984. vii, 104 p. : ISBN 92-5-101371-3 (pbk.) LC Card 85-183713 DDC 338.9/009172/4 19
HD1333.5 .S78 1984 ***NYPL [JLE 86-2720]***

RURAL POOR - EAST ASIA.
Poverty in rural Asia /. Bangkok , 1984, c1983. xii, 276 p. ; ISBN 92-2-103286-8 (pbk.)
NYPL [JLE 86-1050]

RURAL POOR - EMPLOYMENT - CONGRESSES.
Promotion of employment and incomes for the rural poor, including rural women, through non-farm activities . Geneva , 1983. 131 p. ; ISBN 92-2-103506-9 (pbk.) : LC Card 86-221308 DDC 331.12/042/091734 19
HD5710.8 .P76 1983

RURAL POOR - EMPLOYMENT - GOVERNMENT POLICY - INDIA.
Varma, S. C. Millions in poverty grip . New Delhi , 1984. xv, 172 p. ; LC Card 84-900600 DDC 331.12/042/0954 19
HD5710.85.I4 V37 1984
NYPL [JLD 86-4236]

RURAL POOR - EMPLOYMENT - INDIA - ANDHRA PRADESH.
Andhra Pradesh (India). Finance and Planning (Planning Wing) Dept. Evaluation Wing. Evaluation study on the working of crash scheme for rural employment. Hyderabad , 1983. 89 p. : LC Card 86-144139 DDC 331.12/042/095484 19
HD5710.85.I42 A532 1983

RURAL POOR - EMPLOYMENT - INDIA - GUJARAT.
Hirway, Indira. Wage employment programmes in rural development . New Delhi , c1986. vi, 112 p. ; ISBN 81-204-0072-0 : LC Card 86-903398 DDC 331.2/95475 19
HD5070.G85 H57 1986

RURAL POOR - EMPLOYMENT - PAKISTAN - PUNJAB.
Elahi, Mahboob. Rural labour market, with special reference to hired labour in Pakistan's Punjab /. Lahore, Pakistan [1983] ii, ix, 186 leaves ; LC Card 86-930467
HD1537.P2 E4 1983

RURAL POOR - FRANCE.
Jégouzo, Guenhaël. Petite paysannerie en France /. Paris , c1984. 227 p. : ISBN 2-85340-610-5 LC Card 85-181759 DDC 338.1/6 19
HD1339.F8 J44 1984

RURAL POOR - GOVERNMENT POLICY - ASIA - CASE STUDIES.
The Poor in Asia . Kuala Lumpur, Malaysia , 1985- v. <1 > ; ISBN 967-99954-0-2 (v. 1) LC Card 86-944764 DDC 362.5/8/095 19
HC415.P6 P66 1985

RURAL POOR - GOVERNMENT POLICY - INDIA - STATES - CASE STUDIES.
Kohli, Atul. The state and poverty in India . Cambridge [Cambridgeshire] , New York , 1987. x, 262 p. : ISBN 0-521-32008-9 LC Card 85-25554 DDC 333.3/1/54 19
HD1333.I4 K65 1986 ***NYPL [JLD 87-1517]***

RURAL POOR - GUATEMALA.
Hintermeister, Alberto. Modernización de la agricultura y pobreza rural en Guatemala /. [Santiago, Chile] , 1982. 59 leaves : LC Card 87-403247 DDC 338.1/6/097281 19
HC144.Z9 P624 1982

RURAL POOR - HOUSING - BRAZIL - PERNAMBUCO - CONGRESSES.
Seminário Permanente de Habitação Popular (1981 : Recife, Brazil) Anais--1981 /. Recife [19]82. 178 p. ; LC Card 84-256147
HD7323.P37 S46 1981

RURAL POOR - INDIA.
Aziz, Abdul, 1937- The rural poor . New Delhi , 1983. 92 p. ; LC Card 83-906454 DDC 330.954/052/08806942 19
HC440.P6 A98 1983 ***NYPL [JLD 87-544]***

Behari, Bepin. Unemployment, technology & rural poverty /. New Delhi , c1983. ix, 453 p. ; ISBN 0-7069-2337-5 : LC Card 83-906129 DDC 338/.06 19
HC440.I52 B43 1983 ***NYPL [JLD 87-1132]***

Étienne, Gilbert. Food and poverty . New Delhi , Newbury Park, Calif. , 1987. p. cm. ISBN 0-8039-9540-7 LC Card 87-16992 DDC 338.1/0954 19
HC440.P6 E86 1987

Rural poverty in South Asia /. New York , 1988. p. cm. ISBN 0-231-06224-9 LC Card 87-9413 DDC 330.954/052/091734 19
HC440.P6 R87 1988

Seshadri, K. Rural unrest in India /. New Delhi , 1983. xiii, 192 p. ; LC Card 83-905323 DDC 303.6/23/0954 19
HC440.P6 S47 1983 ***NYPL [JLD 86-3704]***

RURAL POOR - INDIA - KARNATAKA.
Parvathamma, C., 1928- Housing, rural poor, and their living conditions /. Delhi, India [1987] vi, 135 p. ; ISBN 81-212-0088-1 : LC Card 87-900831 DDC 363.5/8 19
HD7361.K27 P37 1987

RURAL POOR - INDIA - UTTAR PRADESH.
Singh, Ajit Kumar, 1944- Agricultural development and rural poverty /. New Delhi , 1987. v, 368 p. : ISBN 81-7024-069-7 : LC Card 86-903483 DDC 338.1/8542 19
HD2075.U88 S55 1987

RURAL POOR - INDONESIA.
Poverty in rural Asia /. Bangkok , 1984, c1983. xii, 276 p. ; ISBN 92-2-103286-8 (pbk.)
NYPL [JLE 86-1050]

RURAL POOR - LATIN AMERICA - POLITICAL ACTIVITY.
Pobreza, participación y desarrollo regional /. [Bogotá, D.E., Colombia] , 1986. 536 p. : LC Card 87-103266
HC125 .P6 1986

RURAL POOR - MEXICO.
Acevedo Conde, María Luisa. Pobreza y riqueza en 378 municipios de México /. México, D.F. , 1984. 281 p. : LC Card 86-219445
HC140.P6 A25 1984

RURAL POOR - PAKISTAN.
Employment, distribution, and basic needs in Pakistan . Lahore , 1986. xxxiv, 408 p., [1] leaf of plates : LC Card 86-930280 DDC 330.9549/1 19
HD5820.5.A6 E47 1986

RURAL POOR - SIERRA LEONE.
Okai, Matthew. Rural poverty and alleviation measures in Sierra Leone /. [Rome] , 1983. 91 p. : LC Card 87-400417 DDC 338.1/8/664 19
HC1065.Z9 P66 1983

RURAL POOR - SOUTH ASIA.
Rural poverty in South Asia /. New York , 1988. p. cm. ISBN 0-231-06224-9 LC Card 87-9413 DDC 330.954/052/091734 19
HC440.P6 R87 1988

RURAL POOR - SOUTHERN STATES.
Ghelfi, Linda M. Poverty among black families in the nonmetro South /. Washington, D.C. , Supt. of Docs., U. S. G.P.O. [distributor, 1986] vii, 27 p. : LC Card 86-602435 DDC 330.975/043/0899607301734 19
HC107.A13 G48 1986

RURAL POOR - SOUTHWESTERN STATES.
Brown, F. Lee (Franklin Lee) Water and poverty in the Southwest /. Tucson , c1987. xi, 226 p. : ISBN 0-8165-1038-5 (alk. paper) : LC Card 87-19217 DDC 333.91/00979 19
HD1695.A165 B76 1987

RURAL POOR - THAILAND.
Poverty in rural Asia /. Bangkok , 1984, c1983. xii, 276 p. ; ISBN 92-2-103286-8 (pbk.)
NYPL [JLE 86-1050]

RURAL POOR - UNITED STATES.
Morrissey, Elizabeth S. Characteristics of poverty in nonmetro counties /. Washington, D.C. , 1985. iv, 10 p. : LC Card 86-602555 DDC 362.5/0973 19
HC110.P6 M67 1985

RURAL POOR - UNITED STATES - HISTORY.
West, Patrick C. Natural resource bureaucracy and rural poverty . Ann Arbor, MI , c1982. xiii, 168 p. : LC Card 83-102928 DDC 333.7/16/0973 19
HD1761 .W423 1982 ***NYPL [JLE 86-4095]***

RURAL POOR - WISCONSIN.
Saupe, William E. Rural poverty in Wisconsin counties /. Madison, WI [198-] 26 p. : LC Card 86-622097
HC107.W63 P6249 1980z

Rural poverty and alleviation measures in Sierra Leone /. Okai, Matthew. [Rome] , 1983. 91 p. : LC Card 87-400417 DDC 338.1/8/664 19
HC1065.Z9 P66 1983

Rural poverty in South Asia / T.N. Srinivasan and Pranab K. Bardhan, editors. New York : Columbia University Press, 1988. p. cm. ISBN 0-231-06224-9 LC Card 87-9413 DDC 330.954/052/091734 19
1. Rural poor - India. 2. Rural poor - South Asia. 3. India - Rural conditions. 4. South Asia - Rural conditions. I. Srinivasan, T. N., 1933-. II. Bardhan, Pranab K.
HC440.P6 R87 1988

Rural poverty in Wisconsin counties /. Saupe, William E. Madison, WI [198-] 26 p. : LC Card 86-622097
HC107.W63 P6249 1980z

Rural public administration : problems and prospects / edited by Jim Seroka. Westport, Conn. : Greenwood Press, 1986. ix, 208 p. ; 25 cm. (Contributions in political science, 0147-1066 . no. 153) Includes bibliographies and index. ISBN 0-313-25246-7 (lib. bdg. : alk. paper) LC Card 85-27253 DDC 352/.00722/0973 19
1. Local government - United States - Addresses, essays, lectures. 2. Rural development - United States - Addresses, essays, lectures. 3. United States - Rural conditions - Addresses, essays, lectures. I. Seroka, Jim. II. Series.
JS425 .R87 1986 ***NYPL [JLE 86-4005]***

Rural roads and poverty alleviation : a study prepared for the International Labour Office within the framework of the World Employment Programme / edited by John Howe and Peter Richards. London : Intermediate Technology Publications, 1984. vii, 191 p. : ill. ; 23 cm. Bibliography: p. 169-191. CONTENTS. - The economic context of rural roads / Peter Richards -- Criteria for road planning / John Howe -- The impact of rural roads on poverty alleviation / John Howe -- Rural roads and poverty alleviation in Egypt / M.A. El Hawary and T.Y. El Reedy -- Rural roads and poverty alleviation in India / P.K. Thomas -- Rural roads and poverty alleviation in Botswana / John Howe -- Rural roads and poverty alleviation in Thailand / J. Hugh Jones. ISBN 0-946688-05-2 : LC Card 86-673296
1. Rural roads - Economic aspects - Developing countries. 2. Rural development. I. Howe, J. D. G. F. II. Richards, P. J. (Peter J.). III. International Labour Office. IV. World Employment Programme.
HE336.R85 R87x 1984

RURAL ROADS - DEVELOPING COUNTRIES.
Rural transportation services . Boulder, Colo. , 1987. p. cm. ISBN 0-8133-0530-6 : LC Card 87-8226 DDC 388.1/09172/4 19
HE336.R85 R87 1987

RURAL ROADS - ECONOMIC ASPECTS - DEVELOPING COUNTRIES.
Rural roads and poverty alleviation . London , 1984. vii, 191 p. : ISBN 0-946688-05-2 : LC Card 86-673296
HE336.R85 R87x 1984

RURAL ROADS - GUATEMALA - FINANCE.
Informe de caminos rurales . [Guatemala, Guatemala] [1982] 2, [6] leaves ; LC Card 85-153481
HE359.G83 R855 1982

RURAL ROADS - KENYA.
The Framework of the impact study to monitor and evaluate rural access roads in Kenya. Nairobi , 1981. ii, 97, [97] leaves ; LC Card 85-981022
HE367.K43 R8538 1981

Rural Access Roads Programme /. Nairobi [1980?] 1 v. (various foliations) : LC Card 85-981142 DDC 388.1/09676/2 19
HE367.K43 R85746 1980

Status of evaluation of rural access roads. Nairobi , 1982. 10 leaves ; LC Card 85-981020 DDC 388.1/09676/2 19
HE367.K43 R8578 1982

RURAL ROADS - KENYA - BUNGOMA DISTRICT.
Rural access road programme . Nairobi [1977- v. : LC Card 86-981035
HE367.K43 R85755 1976

The rural settlement of Verlorenvlei in historical perspective /. Sinclair, Sharyn. Rondebosch, South Africa [1980] 234 leaves : LC Card 86-210654
HD991.Z9 V477 1980

Rural small enterprises in Zambia . Milimo, J. T. [Lusaka] [1985] 71 p. ; LC Card 87-980231 DDC 338.6/42/096894 19
HD2346.Z29 M55 1985

The Rural studies series of the Rural Sociological Society.

Rural studies series of the Rural Sociological Society.
Bonanno, Alessandro. Small farms . Boulder, Colo. , 1987. xvi, 228 p. : ISBN 0-8133-7341-7 (pbk. : alk. paper) LC Card 86-51502 DDC 338.1/6 19
HD1339.I8 B66 1987

Family farming in Europe and America /. Boulder , 1987. viii, 312 p. ; ISBN 0-8133-7340-9 (soft : alk. paper) : LC Card 87-2041 DDC 338.1/6 19
HD1476.E85 F35 1987

RURAL TELEPHONE - UNITED STATES - HISTORY.
A Brief history of the rural electric and telephone programs. [Washington, D.C.] [1986] 61 p. : LC Card 86-602412 DDC 353.0087/22 19
HD9688.U52 B75 1986

Rural to urban land conversion =. Gierman, D. M. [Ottawa] , Hull, Que. , c1977. xvii, 74 p. ; ISBN 0-662-01301-8
NYPL [JLM 80-106 no.16]

Rural to urban migration and the urban labour market . Banerjee, Biswajit. Bombay , 1986. xviii, 285 p. ; LC Card 86-900684
HD5820.D44 B36 1986
NYPL [JLD 86-4110]

RURAL TRANSIT.
Tiedtke, Hans-Ullrich. Das Bedienungsstandard-Konzept als Instrument zur Bewertung des ÖPNV in ländlichen Räumen, exemplarisch dargestellt am Einkaufsverkehr /. Bochum , 1981. viii, 274 p. ; ISBN 3-88339-192-1 : LC Card 81-205962 DDC 388/.0943 19
HE152.5 .T53 1981 NYPL [JLD 86-2578]

RURAL TRANSIT - GERMANY (WEST)
Tiedtke, Hans-Ullrich. Das Bedienungsstandard-Konzept als Instrument zur Bewertung des ÖPNV in ländlichen Räumen, exemplarisch dargestellt am Einkaufsverkehr /. Bochum , 1981. viii, 274 p. ; ISBN 3-88339-192-1 : LC Card 81-205962 DDC 388/.0943 19
HE152.5 .T53 1981 NYPL [JLD 86-2578]

RURAL TRANSIT - GOVERNMENT POLICY - NEW YORK (STATE)
New York (State). Legislature. Legislative Commission on Expenditure Review. Federal rural transportation assistance . Albany, N.Y. (111 Washington Ave., Albany 12210-2277) [1986] 5, ii, 64 p. : LC Card 86-622160 DDC 353.0087/5/009747 19
HE5633.N7 N53 1986

RURAL TRANSIT - NEW YORK (STATE)
New York (State). Legislature. Legislative Commission on Expenditure Review. Federal rural transportation assistance . Albany, N.Y. (111 Washington Ave., Albany 12210-2277) [1986] 5, ii, 64 p. : LC Card 86-622160 DDC 353.0087/5/009747 19
HE5633.N7 N53 1986

RURAL TRANSIT - UNITED STATES - DIRECTORIES.
A Directory of rural and specialized transit operators /. Washington, D.C. , 1986- v. <1-3 > : LC Card 86-603414 DDC 388.3/22/0973 19
HE203 .D57 1986

Rural transportation services : a guide to their planning and design / edited by Henri L. Beenhakker ... [et al.]. Boulder, Colo. : Westview Press, 1987. p. cm. Includes index. ISBN 0-8133-0530-6 : LC Card 87-8226 DDC 388.1/09172/4 19
1. Rural roads - Developing countries. I. Beenhakker, Henri L.
HE336.R85 R87 1987

Rural underdevelopment in Nigeria, 1900-1980. Zaria, Nigeria : Dept. of Political Science, Ahmadu Bello University, 1985. iv, 102 p. ; 25 cm. (Department of Political Science seminar series . vol. 2) Includes bibliographies. LC Card 86-154806 DDC 338.1/8669 19
1. Agriculture and state - Nigeria - History - 20th century. 2. Agriculture - Economic aspects - Nigeria - History - 20th century. 3. Agricultural innovations - Nigeria - History - 20th century. 4. Food supply - Nigeria - History - 20th century. I. Ahmadu Bello University. Dept. of Political Science. II. Series.
HD2145.5.Z8 R87 1985

Rural unrest in India /. Seshadri, K. New Delhi , 1983. xiii, 192 p. ; LC Card 83-905323 DDC 303.6/23/0954 19
HC440.P6 S47 1983 NYPL [JLD 86-3704]

RURAL-URBAN MIGRATION - AFRICA.
Sembajwe, I. S. L. (Israel Serwano Lubwama), 1947- Urban population growth rates in Africa with special reference to Lesotho /. [Roma, Lesotho] [1985] 31 leaves : LC Card 87-132328 DDC 307.2 19
HB3663.7.A3 S46 1985

Rural-urban migration and rural emigration in Pakistan . Rauf, Mohammad A. (Mohammad Abdur) Islamabad, Pakistan [1984?] 201 p. ; LC Card 86-931437 DDC 307.2 19
HB1955 .R38 1984

RURAL-URBAN MIGRATION - BRAZIL.
Muszynski, Maria Judith de Brito. O impacto político das migrações internas . São Paulo , 1986. 169 p. : LC Card 86-234794
HB2023 .M87 1986

RURAL-URBAN MIGRATION - BRAZIL - SAO PAULO.
Muszynski, Maria Judith de Brito. O impacto político das migrações internas . São Paulo , 1986. 169 p. : LC Card 86-234794
HB2023 .M87 1986

RURAL-URBAN MIGRATION - BRAZIL - SAO PAULO (STATE)
Rocha, José Carlos Rodrigues. O êxodo rural no município de Pirajuí /. Bauru-SP , 1984. iv, 66 p. : LC Card 86-158771
HB2024.P57 R62 1984

RURAL-URBAN MIGRATION - CONGO (BRAZZAVILLE)
Migrations rurales et urbanisation en République populaire du Congo. Addis Ababa , 1984. x, 168 p. : LC Card 84-980878
HB2125.A3 M54 1984

RURAL-URBAN MIGRATION - CONGO (BRAZZAVILLE) - BRAZZAVILLE.
Balandier, Georges. Sociologie des Brazzavilles noires /. Paris , c1985. xviii, 306 p., [2] leaves of plates : ISBN 2-7246-0524-1 : LC Card 86-138199
HB2125.B73 B34 1985

RURAL-URBAN MIGRATION - DEVELOPING COUNTRIES - CONGRESSES.
ASA Conference, Migrants, Workers, and the Social Order (1986 : University of Kent) Migrants, workers, and the social order /. London , New York , 1987. p. cm. ISBN 0-422-61680-X (pbk.) LC Card 87-10253
HD5856.D44 A72 1986

RURAL-URBAN MIGRATION - ECUADOR - FLORES (CHIMBORAZO) - CASE STUDIES.
Mariano, Alfonso, José, Lorenzo, Manuel . Quito, Ecuador , 1985. 128 p., [8] leaves of plates : LC Card 86-136793
HD1531.E2 M37 1985

RURAL-URBAN MIGRATION - ECUADOR - LICTO - CASE STUDIES.
Mariano, Alfonso, José, Lorenzo, Manuel . Quito, Ecuador , 1985. 128 p., [8] leaves of plates : LC Card 86-136793
HD1531.E2 M37 1985

RURAL-URBAN MIGRATION - GERMANY (WEST) - RHINELAND-PALATINATE - HISTORY.
Migration und Dorfkultur . Stuttgart , 1984. viii, 429 p. : ISBN 3-515-04199-0 LC Card 85-131269
HB2056.R53 M54 1984

RURAL-URBAN MIGRATION - INDIA - CONGRESSES.
Migrant labour and related issues /. New Delhi , c1987. xii, 334 p. : ISBN 81-204-0199-9 : LC Card 87-901172
HD5856.I4 M54 1985

RURAL-URBAN MIGRATION - INDIA - DELHI METROPOLITAN AREA.
Banerjee, Biswajit. Rural to urban migration and the urban labour market . Bombay , 1986. xviii, 285 p. ; LC Card 86-900684
HD5820.D44 B36 1986
NYPL [JLD 86-4110]

RURAL-URBAN MIGRATION - INDONESIA - CASE STUDIES.
Costello, Michael A. Mobility and employment in urban Southeast Asia . Boulder , 1987. xvi, 190 p. : ISBN 0-8133-7352-2 (pbk. : alk. paper) : LC Card 87-10649 DDC 307.2 19
HB2107 .C67 1987

RURAL-URBAN MIGRATION - IRAN.
Danesh, Abol Hassan, 1952- Rural exodus & squatter settlements in the Third World . Lanham, MD , c1987. xii, 168 p. : ISBN 0-8191-6443-7 (alk. paper) : LC Card 87-10627 DDC 307.2 19
HB2096.4.A3 D36 1987

RURAL-URBAN MIGRATION - ITALY, SOUTHERN.
Costa, Paolo. Agglomerazione urbana, localizzazione industriale e Mezzogiorno /. Milano , 1983. viii, 240 p. : LC Card 83-186216 DDC 307.2 19
HB2060.S68 C67 1983 NYPL [JLE 86-3657]

RURAL-URBAN MIGRATION - LATIN AMERICA.
Astori, Danilo. La agricultura campesina en América Latina . Montevideo, Uruguay [1985?] 35 p. ; LC Card 86-204310 DDC 338.1/098 19
HD1790.5 .A85 1985

RURAL-URBAN MIGRATION - LESOTHO.
Makatjane, Tiisetso. Internal migration and fertility in Lesotho /. [Roma, Lesotho] [1985] iii, 36 leaves ; LC Card 87-132347 DDC 304.6/32/096816 19
HB2123.7.A3 M35 1985

Sembajwe, I. S. L. (Israel Serwano Lubwama), 1947- Urban population growth rates in Africa with special reference to Lesotho /. [Roma, Lesotho] [1985] 31 leaves : LC Card 87-132328 DDC 307.2 19
HB3663.7.A3 S46 1985

RURAL-URBAN MIGRATION - PAKISTAN.
Rauf, Mohammad A. (Mohammad Abdur) Rural-urban migration and rural emigration in Pakistan . Islamabad, Pakistan [1984?] 201 p. ; LC Card 86-931437 DDC 307.2 19
HB1955 .R38 1984

RURAL-URBAN MIGRATION - PHILIPPINES - CASE STUDIES.
Costello, Michael A. Mobility and employment in urban Southeast Asia . Boulder , 1987. xvi, 190 p. : ISBN 0-8133-7352-2 (pbk. : alk. paper) : LC Card 87-10649 DDC 307.2 19
HB2107 .C67 1987

RURAL-URBAN MIGRATION - RUSSIAN S.F.S.R. - HISTORY - 18TH CENTURY.
Morrison, Daniel, 1945- "Trading peasants" and urbanization in eighteenth-century Russia . New York , 1987. 415 p. ; ISBN 0-8240-8059-9 (alk. paper) : LC Card 87-7425 DDC 307.2 19
HB2068.S65 M67 1987

RURAL-URBAN MIGRATION - SOUTH AFRICA.
Kok, P. C. Black migration to the PWV complex . Pretoria , 1985. viii, 79 p. : ISBN 0-7969-0313-1 (pbk.) : LC Card 86-232836 DDC 304.8/0968 19
HB2123.4.P68 K65 1985

RURAL-URBAN MIGRATION - SOUTH AFRICA - HISTORY - 19TH CENTURY.
Worger, William H. South Africa's city of diamonds . New Haven , c1987. xvi, 330 p. : ISBN 0-300-03716-3 (alk. paper) LC Card 86-24724 DDC 331.7/622382/0968711 19
HD9677.S63 K568 1987

RURAL-URBAN MIGRATION - SOUTH AFRICA - STATISTICS.
Cilliers, S. P. Patterns of migration and settlement in rural South Africa /. [Stellenbosch] , 1986. 19, 13 leaves, 5 folded leaves of plates : ISBN 0-908422-81-4 (pbk.) : LC Card 87-126315 DDC 304.8/0968 19
HB2123.4.A3 C56 1986

RURAL-URBAN MIGRATION - THAILAND.
Goldstein, Sidney, 1927- Urban-rural migration differentials in Thailand /. [Bangkok] , 1974. 49 p. ; LC Card 78-301310 DDC 301.36/1
HB2104.55.A3 G64
NYPL [JLM 83-719 no.12]

RURAL-URBAN MIGRATION - ZAMBIA.
Chilivumbo, Alifeyo. Migration and uneven rural development in Africa . Lanham, MD , c1985. xx, 118 p. : ISBN 0-8191-4929-2 (alk. paper) : LC Card 85-17908 DDC 307.2 19
HB2123.6.A3 C47 1985
NYPL [JLD 86-1953]

Stepwise migration. Lusaka [1981] 34, 3, 2 p. : LC Card 85-980416
HB2123.6.A3 S74 1981

Rural urban studies series .
(working paper no. 2) May, Julian. Migrant labour in Transkei . Durban , 1985. 34, vii p. ; ISBN 0-86980-467-7 (pbk.) : LC Card 86-190553 DDC 331.6/2/0968791 19
HD5856.S6 M39 1985

Rural women and development . Shobha, V.,

1952- Delhi, India , 1987. xiii, 372 p. ; LC Card 87-902500 DDC 331.4/83/095484 19
HD6073.A292 I468 1987

Rural women & development. Shobha, V., 1952- Rural women and development . Delhi, India , 1987. xiii, 372 p. ; LC Card 87-902500 DDC 331.4/83/095484 19
HD6073.A292 I468 1987

RURAL WOMEN - BANGLADESH - SOCIAL CONDITIONS.
Halim, Abdul, 1945- The effects of rice based cropping system research on women in Bangladesh /. Mymensingh , 1986. 2, 30 leaves ; LC Card 86-901954 DDC 331.4/8318/095492 19
HD1537.B3 H35 1986

RURAL WOMEN - DEVELOPING COUNTRIES.
Palmer, Ingrid. The impact of agrarian reform on women /. West Hartford, Conn. , c1985. xiv, 55 p. ; ISBN 0-931816-21-1 (pbk.) LC Card 85-5250 DDC 331.4/83/091724 19
HD6073.A292 D447 1985
NYPL [JLF 86-1633]

Palmer, Ingrid. The impact of male out-migration on women in farming /. West Hartford, Conn. , c1985. xviii, 78 p. ; ISBN 0-931816-22-X (pbk.) LC Card 85-5240 DDC 331.4/83/091724 19
HD6073.A292 D4472 1985
NYPL [JLF 86-1626]

RURAL WOMEN - DEVELOPING COUNTRIES - CASE STUDIES.
Women, work, and ideology in the Third World /. London , New York , 1985. xvii, 265 p. : ISBN 0-422-79710-3 (U. S. : pbk.) LC Card 85-17279 DDC 305.4/09172/4 19
HQ1870.9 .W657 1985
NYPL [JLD 86-2322]

RURAL WOMEN - EMPLOYMENT - AFRICA - CONGRESSES.
African and Asian Inter-regional Workshop on Strategies for Improving the Employment Conditions of Rural Women (1984 : Arusha, Tanzania) Resources, power and women . Geneva , 1985. ix, 82 p. ; ISBN 92-2-105009-2 (pbk.) : LC Card 86-208830 DDC 331.4/83/095 19
HD6207 .A78 1984

RURAL WOMEN - EMPLOYMENT - ASIA - CONGRESSES.
African and Asian Inter-regional Workshop on Strategies for Improving the Employment Conditions of Rural Women (1984 : Arusha, Tanzania) Resources, power and women . Geneva , 1985. ix, 82 p. ; ISBN 92-2-105009-2 (pbk.) : LC Card 86-208830 DDC 331.4/83/095 19
HD6207 .A78 1984

RURAL WOMEN - EMPLOYMENT - BANGLADESH.
Rahman, Rushidan Islam. The wage employment market for rural women in Bangladesh /. Dhaka, Bangladesh , 1986. xi, 97 p. ; LC Card 86-903129 DDC 331.4/295492 19
HD6061.2.B3 R34 1986

RURAL WOMEN - EMPLOYMENT - INDIA.
Bhoite, Anuradha. Women employees and rural development . Delhi, India , c1987. xiii, 135 p. ; ISBN 81-212-0085-7 : LC Card 87-900916 DDC 331.4/0954 19
HD6189 .B56 1987

RURAL WOMEN - EMPLOYMENT - INDIA - PRABHANI (DISTRICT)
Bhoite, Anuradha. Women employees and rural development . Delhi, India , c1987. xiii, 135 p. ; ISBN 81-212-0085-7 : LC Card 87-900916 DDC 331.4/0954 19
HD6189 .B56 1987

RURAL WOMEN - EMPLOYMENT - UPPER VOLTA - BOBO-DIOULASSO.
Bosch, Ellie. Marktvrouwen van Bobo . Leiden , 1983. viii, 179 p., [18] p. of plates : LC Card 86-212595
HD6217.5.Z6 B633 1983

RURAL WOMEN - EMPLOYMENT - URUGUAY.
Martorelli, Horacio. Las relaciones de trabajos de las mujeres en zonas rurales . Montevideo, Uruguay , 1981. 264 p. : LC Card 86-202374 DDC 331.4/83/09895 19
HD6132 .M375 1981

RURAL WOMEN - INDIA - NIZAMABAD (DISTRICT)
Shobha, V., 1952- Rural women and development . Delhi, India , 1987. xiii, 372 p. ; LC Card 87-902500 DDC 331.4/83/095484 19
HD6073.A292 I468 1987

RURAL WOMEN - INDIA - WARANGAL.
Shobha, V., 1952- Rural women and development . Delhi, India , 1987. xiii, 372 p. ; LC Card 87-902500 DDC 331.4/83/095484 19
HD6073.A292 I468 1987

RURAL WOMEN - INDONESIA - SLEMAN (KABUPATEN) - CASE STUDIES.
Peluso, Nancy Lee. Survival strategies of rural women traders, or, A woman's place is in the market . Geneva [1981], c1980. viii, 124 p. ; ISBN 92-2-102633-7 LC Card 83-105710 DDC 331.4/81381/095982 19
HD6194.Z6 S566 1981

RURAL WOMEN - NICARAGUA.
Revolución y mujeres del campo . Managua [1985] 46 p. : LC Card 86-231936
HD1333.N5 R48 1985

RURAL WOMEN - UPPER VOLTA - BOBO-DIOULASSO - SOCIAL CONDITIONS.
Bosch, Ellie. Marktvrouwen van Bobo . Leiden , 1983. viii, 179 p., [18] p. of plates : LC Card 86-212595
HD6217.5.Z6 B633 1983

RURAL YOUTH - EMPLOYMENT - INDIA.
Bihar (India). Rural Development Dept. Trysem . [Paṭanā] , 1980. 41 p. ; LC Card 80-908290
HD6276.I42 B54 1980

RURAL YOUTH - EMPLOYMENT - INDIA - CONGRESSES.
Training of rural youth for self-employment (TRYSEM) . Hyderabad, [India] , 1981. vii, 252 p. ; LC Card 81-904606 DDC 331.3/42492/0954 19
HD5715.5.I5 T72 1981
NYPL [JLF 86-1203]

RURAL YOUTH - HUNGARY.
Simó, Tibor. Metszetek az agrártársadalom struktúrájából /. Budapest , 1985. 167 p. ; ISBN 963-7700-25-0 : LC Card 86-232606
HD1536.H9 S56 1985

Rusch, Frank R. Competitive employment issues and strategies /. Baltimore , c1986. xvii, 363 p. : ISBN 0-933716-59-1 : LC Card 85-30929 DDC 362/.0425 19
HD7256.U5 C4655 1986 ***NYPL [JLF 87-19]***

Rusenov, Minko V. Istoriia na kooperativnoto dvizhenie v Bŭlgariia /. Sofiia , 1986- v. <1 > ; LC Card 87-158327
HD3531.5.A4 I87 1986

Rush, Howard. Hoffman, Kurt. Micro-electronics and clothing . New York , 1988. xxxii, 253 p. ; ISBN 0-275-92798-9 (alk. paper) : LC Card 87-25736 DDC 338.4/5687 19
HD9940.A2 H63 1988

Rushing, Francis W. National policies for developing high technology industries . Boulder, Colo. , c1986. xiv, 247 p. : ISBN 0-8133-7280-1 (soft : alk. paper) LC Card 86-50530 DDC 338.4/762 19
HC79.H53 N38 1986 ***NYPL [JLE 86-4504]***

Rushing, William A. Social functions and economic aspects of health insurance / William A. Rushing. Boston : Kluwer-Nijhoff Pub., c1986. vii, 226 p. ; 24 cm. (Huebner international series on risk, insurance, and economic security) Includes bibliographies and index. ISBN 0-89838-219-X LC Card 86-7297 DDC 368.3/82/00973 19
1. Insurance, Health - United States. 2. Insurance, Health - Social aspects - United States. I. Title. II. Series.
HD7102.U4 R86 1986 ***NYPL [JLE 87-1237]***

Ruske, Wilfried. Fechtel, Hans-Walter. Flächenhafte Verkehrsberuhigung . Bergisch Gladbach , 1986. 282 p. : LC Card 87-408360 DDC 388.4/0943 19
HE311.G3 F4 1986

Russ, Wolfgang, 1955- Der Anhang als dritter Teil des Jahresabschlusses : eine Analyse der bisherigen und der zukünftigen Erläuterungsvorschriften für die Aktiengesellschaft / Wolfgang Russ ; mit einem Geleitwort von Günter Sieben.1. Aufl. Bergisch Gladbach : J. Eul, 1984. xi, 332 p. : ill. ; 21 cm. (Reihe Steuer, Wirtschaft und Recht . Bd. 9) Bibliography: p. 303-332. ISBN 3-89012-013-X : LC Card 85-195717
1. Financial statements - Germany, West. 2. Financial statements - Law and legislation - Germany (West). 3. Business enterprises - Germany (West) - Accounting. I. Title. II. Series.
HF5681.B2 R817 1984

Russell, Alvin E. Moore, Carl H., 1916- Money . Jefferson, N.C. , c1987. xi, 164 p. : ISBN 0-89950-272-5 (lib. bdg.) : LC Card 87-42515 DDC 332.4/9 19
HG231 .M63 1987

Russell, Cheryl, 1953- 100 predictions for the baby boom : the next 50 years / Cheryl Russell. New York : Plenum Press, c1987. 249 p. ; 22 cm. Bibliography: p. 209-238. Includes index. ISBN 0-306-42527-0 LC Card 87-2443 DDC 338.5/443/0973 19
1. Economic forecasting - United States. 2. United States - Economic conditions - 1981-. 3. Social prediction - United States. I. Title. II. Title: One hundred predictions for the baby boom.
HC106.8 .R87 1987

Russell, George William, 1867-1935. Co-operation and nationality : a guide for rural reformers from this to the next generation / by George W. Russell (AE). Dublin : Irish Academic Press, c1982. 103 p. ; 22 cm. (Cooperative studies . 1) Reprint. Originally published: Dublin : Maunsel, 1912. ISBN 0-7165-0335-2 (pbk.) LC Card 82-192895 DDC 334/.683/09417 19
1. Agriculture, Cooperative - Ireland. 2. Nationalism - Ireland. 3. Ireland - Rural conditions. I. Title. II. Series.
HD1491.I6 R87 1982 ***NYPL [JLD 86-2358]***

Russell, J. Thomas. McGann, Anthony F. Advertising media . Homewood, Ill. , 1988. xii, 452 p. : ISBN 0-256-05988-8 LC Card 87-81340 DDC 659.1/11 19
HF5826.5 .M36 1988

Russell, Josiah Cox, 1900- The control of late ancient and medieval population / Josiah Cox Russell. Philadelphia : American Philosophical Society, 1985. xv, 272 p. ; 27 cm. (Memoirs, 0065-9738 . v. 160) Includes index. Bibliography: p. 241-264. ISBN 0-87169-160-4 LC Card 83-71298
1. Population - History. 2. Cities and towns - Europe - Growth - History. 3. Europe - Population - History. I. Series: American Philosophical Society, Philadelphia. Memoirs, v. 160. 160. II. Title.
NYPL [JLF 85-844]

Russell, Thomas, 1941- Kleppner, Otto, 1899- [Advertising procedure.] Kleppner's advertising procedure. Englewood Cliffs, N.J. , 1987, c1988. p. cm. ISBN 0-13-516451-6 LC Card 87-19346 DDC 659.1 19
HF5823 .K45 1988

Russia and America . White, Colin (Colin M.) London , New York , c1987. 268 p. ; ISBN 0-7099-5246-5 LC Card 87-13646 DDC 330.947 19
HC333 .W46 1987

RUSSIA - COMMERCE - UNITED STATES.
Rosenblatt, Samuel M. East-West trade in technology . Washington, D.C. , c1980. viii, 64 p. ; LC Card 80-81923 DDC 382/.4560973 19
HF1414.5 .R67 ***NYPL [JLD 81-233]***

RUSSIA - ECONOMIC POLICY.
Azqueta Oyarzun, Diego. Teoría económica de la acumulación socialista . Madrid , 1983. 224 p. ; ISBN 84-7214-279-5 LC Card 84-140278 DDC 332/.0415/091717 19
HC710.S3 A97 1983 ***NYPL [JLD 86-1859]***

RUSSIA - FOREIGN ECONOMIC RELATIONS - TURKEY.
Hiller, Marlene P., 1948- Krisenregion Nahost . Frankfurt am Main , New York , c1985. 335 p. : ISBN 3-8204-8249-0 LC Card 85-191941
HF1558.15.T8 H55 1985

RUSSIA - FOREIGN RELATIONS - 1917-1945.
Haigh, R. H. Soviet foreign policy, the League of Nations and Europe, 1917-39 /. Aldershot, Hants , 1986. x, 138 p. ;
NYPL [JFD 86-5778]

Russian and East European studies (Pittsburgh, Pa.)
Winiecki, Jan. The distorted world of Soviet

type economies /. Pittsburgh, Pa. , 1988. p. cm. ISBN 0-8229-1149-3 LC Card 87-25193 DDC 338.947 19
HC244 .W573 1988

Russian Communist Party (Bolshevik) see **Kommunisticheskaia partiia Sovetskogo Soiuza.**

Russian-English, English-Russian glossary of statistical terms. Kotz, Samuel. Edinburgh, 1971. vii, 87 p. ISBN 0-05-002446-9 LC Card 72-197391 DDC 519.5/01/4
HA17 .K62 NYPL [JLF 73-1241]

Russian-English phrase-book for the petrochemical and inorganic chemical industries. Kuznetsov, IU. I. (IUriĭ Igorevich) Russko-angliĭskiĭ razgovornik dlia neftekhimikov i khimikov-neorganikov /. Moskva , 1985. 359 p. ; LC Card 86-138945 DDC 660/.03/9171 19
HD9579.C32 K88 1985
*NYPL [*QAD 86-3599]*

RUSSIAN LANGUAGE - DICTIONARIES - ENGLISH.
Kotz, Samuel. Russian-English, English-Russian glossary of statistical terms. Edinburgh, 1971. vii, 87 p. ISBN 0-05-002446-9 LC Card 72-197391 DDC 519.5/01/4
HA17 .K62 NYPL [JLF 73-1241]

Kuznetsov, IU. I. (IUriĭ Igorevich) Russko-angliĭskiĭ razgovornik dlia neftekhimikov i khimikov-neorganikov /. Moskva , 1985. 359 p. ; LC Card 86-138945 DDC 660/.03/9171 19
HD9579.C32 K88 1985
*NYPL [*QAD 86-3599]*

RUSSIAN NATIONAL CHARACTERISTICS. see **NATIONAL CHARACTERISTICS, RUSSIAN.**

Russian satellites. see **Communist countries.**

RUSSIAN S.F.S.R. - COMMERCE - MATHEMATICAL MODELS.
Mezhregional'nye mezhotraslevye balansy /. Novosibirsk , 1983. 220 p. : LC Card 84-172934
HF3626.5 .M49 1983

RUSSIAN S.F.S.R. - COMMERCE - UKRAINE.
Skruten', I. S. Spivdruzhnist' u pratsi /. Kyïv , 1982. 117 p. : LC Card 83-200434
HC337.U5 S514 1982

RUSSIAN S.F.S.R. - CULTURAL POLICY.
Veselov, A. P. (Anatoliĭ Pavlovich) Bor'ba Kommunisticheskoĭ partii za provedenie kul'turnoĭ revoliutsii v derevne v gody kollektivizatsii /. Leningrad , 1978. 127 p. ; LC Card 81-166878
HD1492.S652 R878 1978

RUSSIAN S.F.S.R. - ECONOMIC CONDITIONS.
Rapoport, IU. M. (IUriĭ Mikhaĭlovich) Osushchestvlenie ėkonomicheskoĭ politiki Kommunisticheskoĭ partii v usloviiakh Evropeĭskogo Severa RSFSR, 1917-1925 gg. /. Leningrad , 1984. 216 p. ; LC Card 84-217989
HC336.9.N65 R36 1984

Solomentsev, M. S. (Mikhail Sergeevich) Rossiĭskaia Federatsiia /. Moskva , 1978. 212 p. ; LC Card 81-170399
HC337.R85 S65 1978

Zenchenko, N. S. Sotsial'naia napravlennost' planov . Moskva , 1985. 221 p. ; LC Card 86-106277
HC337.R85 Z45 1985

RUSSIAN S.F.S.R. - ECONOMIC POLICY.
Gosplan RSFSR. Metodicheskie ukazaniia k razrabotke planov ėkonomicheskogo i sotsial'nogo razvitiia RSFSR /. Moskva , 1985. 462 p. ; LC Card 85-232541
HC337.R85 G67 1985

Zenchenko, N. S. Sotsial'naia napravlennost' planov . Moskva , 1985. 221 p. ; LC Card 86-106277
HC337.R85 Z45 1985

RUSSIAN S.F.S.R. - POPULATION DENSITY.
Problemy rasseleniia v SSSR . Moskva , 1980. 254 p. : LC Card 81-135093
HB2068.S65 P76 1980

RUSSIAN S.F.S.R. - RURAL CONDITIONS.
Iz istorii krest'ianstva Evropeĭskogo Severa, Verkhnego Povolzh'ia i Urala v period Velikoĭ Oktiabr'skoĭ sotsialisticheskoĭ revoliutsii i pobedy sotsializma v SSSR, 1917-1937 gg. /. Kirov , 1979. 170 p. ; LC Card 82-103738
HD1492.S652 R8755 1979

Kolos na ladoni . Voronezh , 1985. 237 p. : LC Card 86-195464
HD1536.S65 K65 1985

Veselov, A. P. (Anatoliĭ Pavlovich) Bor'ba Kommunisticheskoĭ partii za provedenie kul'turnoĭ revoliutsii v derevne v gody kollektivizatsii /. Leningrad , 1978. 127 p. ; LC Card 81-166878
HD1492.S652 R878 1978

RUSSIAN S.F.S.R. - SOCIAL CONDITIONS.
Ivanov, E. P. (Evgeniĭ Pavlovich) Kollektivizatsiia krest'ianskikh khoziaĭstv i likvidatsiia kulachestva kak klassa na Severo-Zapade RSFSR, 1927-1937 gg. . Leningrad , 1983. 91 p. ; LC Card 84-190520
HD1492.S652 R875 1983
*NYPL [*QI 87-3170]*

RUSSIAN S.F.S.R. - SOCIAL POLICY.
Zenchenko, N. S. Sotsial'naia napravlennost' planov . Moskva , 1985. 221 p. ; LC Card 86-106277
HC337.R85 Z45 1985

Russian S.F.S.R. TSentral'noe statisticheskoe upravlenie.
Narodnoe khoziaĭstvo Karel'skoĭ ASSR . Petrozavodsk , 1985. 94 p. ; LC Card 86-124957
HA1448.K32 N37 1985

Narodnoe khoziaĭstvo Mordovskoĭ ASSR za gody odinnadtsatoĭ piatiletki, 1981-1985 gg. . Saransk , 1986. 198 p. ; LC Card 87-120800
HA1448.M59 N33 1986

Russko-angliĭskiĭ razgovornik dlia neftekhimikov i khimikov-neorganikov /. Kuznetsov, IU. I. (IUriĭ Igorevich) Moskva , 1985. 359 p. ; LC Card 86-138945 DDC 660/.03/9171 19
HD9579.C32 K88 1985
*NYPL [*QAD 86-3599]*

Russkoe geograficheskoe obschestvo. see **Geograficheskoe obshchestvo SSSR.**

Rustow, Dankwart A. Turkey, America's forgotten ally / Dankwart A. Rustow. New York, NY : Council on Foreign Relations, c1987. xv, 155 p. : ill. ; 24 cm. Bibliography: p. 138-144. Includes index. ISBN 0-87609-023-4 : LC Card 87-6712 DDC 330.9561/038 19
1. Turkey - Economic conditions - 1960-. 2. Turkey - Economic policy. 3. Turkey - Politics and government - 1960-. 4. Turkey - Foreign relations - United States. 5. United States - Foreign relations - Turkey. I. Title.
HC492 .R87 1987

La ruta transístmica y las comunicaciones marítimas hispanas, siglos XVI a XIX /. Castillero Calvo, Alfredo, 1937- Panamá , 1984. 35 p. ; LC Card 84-219993
HE326 .C37 1984

Rutake, P. (Pascal) Etude sur la petite et moyenne industrie et l'artisanat /. [Bujumbara] [1984] 7 v. in 6 : LC Card 86-980948
HD2346.B94 E78 1984

Rüter, Gert. Sicherheitsorientierte Ausbildung von Berufskraftfahren / Gert Rüter ; Batelle Institut e.V., Frankfurt am Main. Köln : Bundesanstalt für Strassenwesen, Bereich Unfallforschung, [1983] vii, 91 p. : ill. ; 21 cm. (Forschungsberichte der Bundesanstalt für Strassenwesen, Bereich Unfallforschung, 0173-7066 . 81) "Bericht zum Forschungsprojekt 8012 der Bundesanstalt für Strassenwesen, Berich Unfallforschung, Köln, Januar 1983." Bibliography: p. 79-85. LC Card 83-235527
1. Truck drivers - Training of - Germany (West). 2. Highway transport workers - Training of - Germany (West). I. Batelle-Institut. II. Bundesanstalt für Strassenwesen (Germany). Bereich Unfallforschung. III. Title. IV. Series.
HD5716.M7952 G327 1983

Rutgaĭzer, V. M. (Valeriĭ Maksovich) Kostakov, V. G. (Vladimir Georgievich) Chelovecheskiĭ faktor--zaniatost', blagosostoianie /. Moskva , 1981. 78 p. : LC Card 82-164831
HD5796 .K567 1981

Rutgers University. Center for Urban Policy Research. Hughes, James W. The dynamics of America's housing /. New Brunswick, N.J. , c1987. xiv, 224 p. ; ISBN 0-88285-122-5 : LC Card 87-4515 DDC 363.5/0973 19
HD7293 .H826 1987

Rutgers University. Graduate School of Management. Cooperative strategies in international business /. Lexington, Mass. , c1988. xxix, 513 p. : ISBN 0-669-14927-6 (alk. paper) LC Card 86-46160 DDC 338.8/8 19
HD2755.5 .C645 1988

Ruth, George E. Commercial lending / George E. Ruth. Washington, D.C. (1120 Connecticut Ave., N.W., Washington 20036) : American Bankers Association, c1987. vi, 427 p. : ill. ; 24 cm. (Education policy & development) Includes bibliographical references and index. LC Card 87-405117 DDC 332.1/753/0685 19
1. Loans - United States. 2. Loan officers - United States. I. Title. II. Series.
HG1642.U5 R88 1987

Rüther, Günther. Die Notwendige Hilfe . Melle [1986] 207 p. : ISBN 3-88368-111-3 : LC Card 86-197696
HC60 .N69 1986

Rutherford, William T. Critical employment issues facing the Southeast /. Atlanta, Ga. , 1986. xv, 156 p. ; ISBN 0-88406-191-4 LC Card 85-31410 DDC 331.12/5/0975 19
HD5725.S85 C75 1986
NYPL [JLD 86-2441]

Rutigliano, Michele. Sury, Paul de. Milano, centro finanziario internazionale /. [Milano] [1984] viii, 138 p. : ISBN 88-14-00312-2 : LC Card 86-114645
HG3090.M52 S87 1984

RUTLEDGE, ARTHUR A.
Stern, Bernard W., 1912- Rutledge unionism . Honolulu , 1986. x, 147 p. ; LC Card 86-51020 DDC 331/.041388413322/0996931 19
HD6515.T72 H37 1986

Rutledge, Marilyn.
Clay, John R. Accounting for S corporations and noncorporate entities . Fort Worth, Tex. , c1987. 1 v. (various pagings) ; LC Card 87-163295 DDC 657/.95/076 19
HF5686.C7 C58 1987

Clay, John R. Advanced compilation and review . Fort Worth, Tex. , c1987. 1 v. (various pagings) : LC Card 87-160681 DDC 657/.3 19
HF5667.65 .M42 1986 Suppl.

Clay, John R. Guide to preparing financial statements /. Fort Worth, Tex. , c1987- 2 v. (loose-leaf) ; LC Card 87-161098 DDC 657/.3 19
HF5681.B2 C565 1987

Pallais, Don. Guide to forecasts and projections /. Fort Worth, Tex. , 1986. 2 v. (loose-leaf) : LC Card 87-108778 DDC 657/.3 19
HF5681.B2 P15 1986

Rutledge unionism . Stern, Bernard W., 1912- Honolulu , 1986. x, 147 p. ; LC Card 86-51020 DDC 331/.041388413322/0996931 19
HD6515.T72 H37 1986

Rutstein, Shea Oscar. Pinto, Claudio. Fecundabilidad y edad de la mujer en las áreas rurales y semi-urbanas de cuatro países latinoamericanos /. Santiago de Chile [1978] 21, [2] p. : LC Card 83-175823
HA755 .U5 no. 151 HB940.5

Ruttan, Vernon W. Thirtle, Colin G., 1944- The role of demand and supply in the generation and diffusion of technical change /. Chur, Switzerland , New York , c1987. viii, 173 p. : ISBN 3-7186-0384-5 (U. S. : pbk.) LC Card 87-138 DDC 338/.06 19
HC79.T4 T495 1987

Rutte, Christel G. Experimental social dilemmas /. Frankfurt am Main , New York , c1986. vi, 234 p. : ISBN 3-8204-8574-0 (pbk.) : LC Card 86-10307 DDC 302 19
HM132 .E96 1986 NYPL [JLD 87-1177]

Rutterford, Janette. The securities industry : an industry note / by Janette Rutterford. [London] : City University Business School, Centre for the Study of Financial Institutions, [1986] 93 p. : ill. ; 30 cm. (Working paper . no. 83) "December 1986." Bibliography: p. 71-72. LC Card 87-160412 DDC 332.63/2/0941 19
1. Securities - Great Britain. 2. Brokers - Great Britain. I. City University (London, England). Centre for the Study of Financial Institutions. II. Series: Working paper series (City University (London, England). Business School) , no. 83. III. Title.
HG5432 .R87 1986

Ruvuma region . Salomon, Robert. Dar es

Salaam , 1981. 32 leaves : LC Card 85-981451
HD7289.T352 R897 1981

Ruz, Fidel Castro. see **Castro, Fidel, 1927-**

Rwanda . Joint UNDP/World Bank Energy Sector Assessment Program. [Washington, D.C.?] [1982] ii, 68 p., [1] folded leaf : LC Card 87-136863 DDC 333.79/0967/571 19
HD9502.R932 J65 1982

RWANDA - ECONOMIC CONDITIONS.
Rwanda, economic memorandum . [Washington, D.C.] [1983] 234 p., [2] leaves of plates : LC Card 87-116501 DDC 338.967/571 19
HC875 .R84 1983

Rwanda, economic memorandum : recent economic and sectoral developments and current policy issues : Division C, Country Programs II, Eastern Africa Region. [Washington, D.C.] : World Bank, [1983] 234 p., [2] leaves of plates : ill. (some col.) ; 28 cm. Cover title. "May 20, 1983." "Report no. 4059-RW." Includes bibliographical references. LC Card 87-116501 DDC 338.967/571 19
1. Rwanda - Economic policy. 2. Rwanda - Economic conditions. I. World Bank.
HC875 .R84 1983

RWANDA - ECONOMIC POLICY.
Rwanda, economic memorandum . [Washington, D.C.] [1983] 234 p., [2] leaves of plates : LC Card 87-116501 DDC 338.967/571 19
HC875 .R84 1983

Rwanda. Ofisi y'Igihugu yita ku Mibereho y'Abaturage. Twiyongere twongera umusaruro. Kigali [1981] 27 p. ; LC Card 82-980614
HB3662.7.A3 T88 1981

RWANDA - POPULATION.
Twiyongere twongera umusaruro. Kigali [1981] 27 p. ; LC Card 82-980614
HB3662.7.A3 T88 1981

RWANDA - POPULATION POLICY.
Twiyongere twongera umusaruro. Kigali [1981] 27 p. ; LC Card 82-980614
HB3662.7.A3 T88 1981

Rwegasira, Kami S. P. Administering management development institutions in Africa / Kami Rwegasira. Aldershot, England : Gower Pub. Co. Ltd. ; Brookfield, Vt. : Gower Pub. Co., 1988. p. cm. Bibliography: p. ISBN 0-566-05501-5 : LC Card 87-17688 DDC 658.4/07124/096 19
1. Assessment centers (Personnel management procedure). 2. Executives - Africa - Training of. 3. Personnel management - Study and teaching - Africa. I. Title.
HF5549.5.A78 R94 1988

RWI-Papiere .
(Nr. 11) Döhrn, Roland. Privater Verbrauch und Einzelhandel in der Bundesrepublik Deutschland . Essen , 1981. 280 p. ; LC Card 87-408859 DDC 338.5/28/0943 19
HB235.G3 D57 1981

(Nr. 13) Rohde, Horst. Sterbetafeln für Personenkraftwagen und Kombinationskraftwagen . Essen , 1981. 64 p. ; LC Card 87-408032 DDC 363.1/252/0943021 19
HE5614.5.G3 R64 1981

(Nr. 16) Krüger-Hemmer, Christiane. Der Staatssektor in der Input-Output-Rechnung . Essen , 1982. 175 p. ; LC Card 87-408033 DDC 339.2/3/0943 19
HC290.5.I57 K78 1982

(Nr. 8) Korthaus, E. Input-Output-Tabellen für die Bundesrepublik Deutschland, 1962 bis 1975 /. Essen , 1979. 279 p. ; LC Card 87-408858 DDC 339.2/3/0943 19
HC290.5.I57 K67 1979

Ryan, Christopher K. (Christopher Keith) Harry Gunnison Brown, economist / Christopher K. Ryan. Boulder : Westview Press, 1987. xv, 179 p. ; 22 cm. Bibliography: p. 152-168. Includes index. ISBN 0-8133-7355-7 (pbk. : alk. paper) : LC Card 86-28994 DDC 330/.092/4 B 19
1. Brown, Harry Gunnison, 1880-. 2. Economists - United States - Biography. I. Title.
HB119.B65 R93 1987

Ryans, John K. Hise, Richard T. Marketing . Houston, Tex. , 1986. xiv, 891 p. : ISBN 0-87393-038-X LC Card 83-72200 DDC 658.8 19
HF5415 .H543 1986

Rybakovskiĭ, Leonid Leonidovich. Demograficheskoe razvitie v SSSR /. Moskva , 1985. 126 p. ; LC Card 85-170633
HB3607 .D445 1985

Rybin, V. I. (Valeriĭ Ivanovich) Ėffektivnost′ i intensifikat͡sii͡a . Moskva , 1986. 161 p. ; LC Card 87-163443
HC340.I52 E33 1986

Khozi͡aĭstvennyĭ mekhanizm i povyshenie ėffektivnosti /. Moskva , 1982. 191 p. ; LC Card 84-193531
HC340.I52 K48 1982

Sovershenstvovanie planirovanii͡a i upravlenii͡a intensifikat͡sieĭ obshchestvennogo proizvodstva /. Moskva , 1984. 182 p. ; LC Card 85-240311
HC336.25 .S6735 1984

Rychetský, Jiří. Brzoň, František. Marie a František Kalkusovi /. České Budějovice , 1985. 98 p., [64] p. of plates : LC Card 86-161741
HD8420.3.A1 B78 1985

Rycroft, Robert W., 1945- Dietz, Thomas. The risk professionals /. New York , c1987. p. cm. ISBN 0-87154-214-5 : LC Card 87-19992 DDC 363.7/056/0973 19
HC110.E5 D54 1987

Rydel, M. (Maciej) Dmowski, Zygmunt. Organizacja i technika handlu zagranicznego . Gdańsk , 1979. 201 p. ; LC Card 81-181043
HF1558.7 .D59 1979

Rydings, Melanie. Ohinata, Yo. The lending procedures of commercial banks in the United States, the United Kingdom, Japan, Germany and France /. [Manchester] [1983] 138 p. ; ISBN 0-903808-34-X (pbk.) LC Card 86-132282 DDC 332.1/753 19
HG1642.U5 O35 1983

Rydzewski, J. R. Irrigation development planning . Chichester , New York , c1987. xiv, 265 p. : ISBN 0-471-91506-8 : LC Card 87-2016 DDC 333.91/3 19
HD1714 .I77 1987

Rylander, Stig, 1928- Säljande butik / Stig Rylander. Lund : Studentlitteratur, c1984. 272 p. : ill. ; 23 cm. (Bättre handel) Bibliography: p. 269-271. ISBN 91-44-99681-0 : LC Card 84-229201
1. Stores, Retail - Management. 2. Stores, Retail - Sweden - Management. I. Title. II. Series.
HF5429 .R94 1984

Rymalov, V. V. (Viktor Vladimirovich) Podryv vekovykh ustoev : protivorechii͡a mirovoĭ ėkonomicheskoĭ sistemy kapitalizma / V.V. Rymalov. Moskva : "Mysl′", 1984. 268, [3] p. : ill. ; 21 cm. At head of title: Ordena Trudovogo Krasnogo Znameni Institut mirovoĭ ėkonomiki i mezhdunarodnykh otnosheniĭ AN SSSR. Bibliography: p. 262-[269] LC Card 85-112238
1. Economic history - 1971-. 2. Capitalism. I. Title.
HC59 .R839 1984

Rymarczyk, Jan. Migracja siły roboczej do krajów EWG i jej konsekwencje społeczno-gospodarcze / Jan Rymarczyk. [Wrocław] : Wydawn. Uczelniane Akademii Ekonomicznej we Wrocławiu, 1982. 239 p., [4] folded leaves ; 24 cm. (Prace naukowe Akademii Ekonomicznej imienia Oskara Langego we Wrocławiu . nr. 218. nr. 8) Summary in German and Russian. Bibliography: p. [223]-231. LC Card 83-153742
1. Alien labor - Europe. 2. Europe - Emigration and immigration. 3. Labor supply - Europe. I. Series. II. Series: Prace naukowe Akademii Ekonomicznej imienia Oskara Langego we Wrocławiu , nr. 218. III. Title.
HB9 .B7522 nr. 218 HD8378.5.A2

Rysina, V. N. Uchastie trudi͡ashchikhsi͡a v upravlenii proizvodstvom . Moskva , 1983. 192, [2] p. : LC Card 84-210286
HD5660.S65 U26 1983

Ryther, Barbara. Tiven, Marjorie. State initiatives in elderly housing . Washington, DC , c1987. xviii, 79 p. ; LC Card 87-154352 DDC 363.5/9 19
HD7287.92.U54 T58 1987

Ryvkin, Al′bert Anatol′evich. Metodologicheskie problemy analiza dolgosrochnykh sotsial′no-ėkonomicheskikh protsessov /. Moskva , 1979. 116 p. : LC Card 87-462037
HD87 .M48 1979

Rzeczpospolita Polska. see **Poland.**

S/A Central Elétrica Rio Claro /. Marsiglia, Cecília. São Paulo , 1986. 105 p. : LC Card 87-404945 DDC 363.6/2/098161 19
HD9685.B83 C4886 1986

S. B. W. see **Saarbergwerke.**

S corporations and noncorporate entities. Clay, John R. Accounting for S corporations and noncorporate entities . Fort Worth, Tex. , c1987. 1 v. (various pagings) ; LC Card 87-163295 DDC 657/.95/076 19
HF5686.C7 C58 1987

S. E. C. see **United States. Securities and Exchange Commission.**

S. E. D. see **Sozialistische Einheitspartei Deutschlands.**

S. E. L. A. see **Sistema Económico Latinoamericano.**

S. E. N. A. I. see **Brazil. Servico Nacional de Aprendizagem Industrial.**

S. E. V. see **Sovet ėkonomicheskoĭ vzaimopomoshchi.**

S. F. I. see **International Finance Corporation.**

S. G. G. see **Schweizerische Geisteswissenschaftliche Gesellschaft.**

S. I. A. see **Securities Industry Association.**

S. I. N. D. see **Sweden. Statens industriverk.**

S. J. P. C. see **South Jersey Port Corporation.**

S T ' ông cục th Hà-N Th 1985. 234 p. : ill. ; 22 x 29 cm. Photocopy. LC Card 86-209875
1. Vietnam - Statistics. I. Vietnam. T ' ông cục th
HA4600.5 .S65 1985

S. P. D. see **Sozialdemokratische Partei Deutschlands.**

S. P. E. C. see **South Pacific Bureau for Economic Cooperation.**

S. prt. .
(100-13) Pressler, Larry, 1942- Trip report, a visit to Eastern Europe in the wake of the 27th Soviet Party Congress and the Chernobyl nuclear accident (Czechoslovakia, Hungary, Yugoslavia, and Romania) on June 28, 1986 . Washington , 1987. vi, 58 p. ; LC Card 87-601360 DDC 337.47 19
HC244 .P744 1987

(98-164) Kaplan, Marshall. Hard choices . Washington , 1984. xi, 230 p. : LC Card 84-602470 DDC 338.4/3363/0973 19
HC110.C3 K37 1984 ***NYPL [JLE 87-566]***

(98-164, App. 1-23) Hard choices . Washington , 1984. 23 v. :
NYPL [JLE 87-566 Appendix 1-23]

(99-162) Agriculture in the GATT . Washington , 1986. v, 47 p. ; LC Card 86-603393 DDC 382/.41/0973 19
HD9006 .A77 1986

(99-163) Technology and trade . Washington , 1986. x, 80 p. : LC Card 86-603362 DDC 338/.06 19
HC110.T4 T393 1986

(99-174) The Economy, small business, and the federal budget . Washington , 1986. v, 20 p. : LC Card 86-603392 DDC 338.6/42/0973 19
HC106.8 .E35 1986

(99-176) Stinson, Thomas F., 1942- Governing the heartland . Washington , 1986. xii, 159 p. : LC Card 86-603376 DDC 336/.014/77 19
HJ9181 .S75 1986

(99-177) Malone, Margaret Sahlin, 1933- Work and welfare /. Washington , 1986. ix, 162 p. ; LC Card 86-603383 DDC 362.5/84/0973 19
HD5715.2 .M34 1986

(99-180) Manchester, Paul B. Are we on the road to a balanced budget? . Washington , 1986. v, 18 p. : LC Card 86-603373 DDC 353.0072/2 19
HJ2052 .M365 1986

(99-185) Starrels, John M. The Korean economy in congressional perspective . Washington , 1986. v, 13 p. ; LC Card 87-601385 DDC 330.9519/043 19
HC467 .S724 1986

(99-191) Japanese import barriers to U. S. agricultural exports and the Common agricultural policy of the European Community and implications for U. S. agricultural trade .

Washington , 1986. vii, 65 p. : LC Card 87-601384 DDC 382/.5/0952 19
HF1601 .J363 1986

(99-199) Poverty, income distribution, the family, and public policy . Washington , 1986. viii, 125 p. : LC Card 87-601355 DDC 339.2/2/0973 19
HC110.I5 P68 1986

(99-205) Economic competitiveness promoting America's living standard /] Washington , 1986 [i.e. 1987] vii, 34 p. : LC Card 87-601340 DDC 338.973 19
HC106.8 .E2745 1987

(99-208) Ambur, Owen D. Selling out the family farm . Washington , 1986. v, 40 p. : LC Card 87-601379 DDC 338.1/6 19
HD1476.U5 A65 1986

(99-220) Earthquake insurance . Washington , 1987. ix, 61 p. : LC Card 87-601349 DDC 368.1/22 19
HG9981 .E17 1987

S. S. S. H. see **Schweizerische Geisteswissenschaftliche Gesellschaft.**

S. U. D. E. N. E. see **Brazil. Superintendência do Desenvolvimento do Nordeste.**

S. U. N. A. M. A. M. see **Brazil. Superintendência Nacional da Marinha Mercante.**

S. V. I. M. E. Z. For corporate body referred to by these initials see: **Associazione per lo sviluppo dell'industria nel Mezzogiorno.**

S. V. R. see **Siedlungsverband Ruhrkohlenbezirk.**

Das S.W.I.F.T.-System . Loh, Wolfram W. Frankfurt am Main , c1983. vii, 198 p. : ISBN 3-7819-0285-4 : LC Card 83-211180
HG1708.5 .L64 1983

S. W. O. C. see **United Steelworkers of America.**

S-165 Southern Regional Research Committee (U. S.) Food demand analysis . Blacksburg, Va. [1986] xii, 292 p. : LC Card 87-620670 DDC 339.4/86413 19
HD9000.5 .F5946 1986

S/A CENTRAL ELÉTRICA RIO CLARO (BRAZIL) - HISTORY.
Marsiglia, Cecília. S/A Central Elétrica Rio Claro /. São Paulo , 1986. 105 p. : LC Card 87-404945 DDC 363.6/2/098161 19
HD9685.B83 C4886 1986

Sa-onoy, Modesto P., 1938- The Philippine sugar trading monopoly : a historical perspective / Modesto P. Sa-onoy. Bacolod City, Philippines : Negros Occidental Historical Commission, c1984. [31] p. ; 28 cm. "A paper presented to the 6th National Conference on Local-National History, University of the Philippines, Quezon City, December 11-14, 1984"--P. [3]. "December 1984." Bibliography: p. [29]-[31]. LC Card 85-165946
1. Sugar - Philippines - Marketing. 2. Sugar trade - Philippines. I. Title.
HD9116.P61 S2 1984

Så samles vi på valen--? . Colbjørnsen, Tom. [Oslo?] [1985] 88 p. : ISBN 82-991187-5-1 LC Card 85-220350
HD6752 .C644 1985

Saage, Richard. Solidargemeinschaft und Klassenkampf . Frankfurt am Main , 1986. 382 p. ; ISBN 3-518-11363-1 ***NYPL [JLC 86-423]***

Saal, Frank E., 1947- Industrial/organizational psychology : science and practice / Frank E. Saal, Patrick A. Knight. Pacific Grove, Calif. : Brooks/Cole Pub. Co., c1988. xxx, 578 p. : ill. ; 25 cm. Bibliography: p. 522-558. Includes indexes. ISBN 0-534-08214-9 : LC Card 87-21824 DDC 158.7 19
1. Psychology, Industrial. I. Knight, Patrick A., 1954-. II. Title.
HF5548.8 .S225 1988

Saarbergwerke. Habicht, Werner. Werkssiedlung Madenfelderhof bei Landsweiler-Reden . Saarbrücken , 1985. 54 p., [52] p. of plates : LC Card 87-408673 DDC 330.943/42 19
HD7289.5.A3 G437 1985

SAARC facts and economic development /. Rahman, M. L. (Mohammad Lutfur), 1933- Dhaka , 1986. xvi, 200 p. : LC Card 87-901419 DDC 338.954 19
HC430.6 .R37 1986

SAARLAND (GERMANY) - ECONOMIC CONDITIONS.
Horch, Hans. Der Wandel der Gesellschafts- und Herrschaftsstrukturen in der Saarregion während der Industrialisierung (1740-1914) /. St. Ingbert [W. Germany] , 1985. 720 p. : ISBN 3-924555-04-4 LC Card 85-194709
HC287.S23 H67 1985

Landeszentralbank im Saarland. Landeszentralbank im Saarland . Saarbrücken , 1986. 45, xii p. : LC Card 86-176290
HC287.S23 L35 1986

SAARLAND (GERMANY) - INDUSTRIES.
Landeszentralbank im Saarland. Landeszentralbank im Saarland . Saarbrücken , 1986. 45, xii p. : LC Card 86-176290
HC287.S23 L35 1986

SAARLAND (GERMANY) - INDUSTRIES - HISTORY.
Horch, Hans. Der Wandel der Gesellschafts- und Herrschaftsstrukturen in der Saarregion während der Industrialisierung (1740-1914) /. St. Ingbert [W. Germany] , 1985. 720 p. : ISBN 3-924555-04-4 LC Card 85-194709
HC287.S23 H67 1985

SAARLAND (GERMANY) - POLITICS AND GOVERNMENT.
Horch, Hans. Der Wandel der Gesellschafts- und Herrschaftsstrukturen in der Saarregion während der Industrialisierung (1740-1914) /. St. Ingbert [W. Germany] , 1985. 720 p. : ISBN 3-924555-04-4 LC Card 85-194709
HC287.S23 H67 1985

SAARLAND (GERMANY) - SOCIAL CONDITIONS.
Horch, Hans. Der Wandel der Gesellschafts- und Herrschaftsstrukturen in der Saarregion während der Industrialisierung (1740-1914) /. St. Ingbert [W. Germany] , 1985. 720 p. : ISBN 3-924555-04-4 LC Card 85-194709
HC287.S23 H67 1985

Steffens, Horst. Autorität und Revolte . Weingarten , c1987. 419 p. : ISBN 3-924027-47-1 LC Card 87-141439 DDC 331/.0422334/094342 19
HD8039.M61 G383 1987

Saarland (Germany). Statistisches Amt. Kommunal- und Europawahl am 17. Juni 1984. Saarbrücken , 1984. 115 p. : ISBN 3-88718-020-8 : LC Card 85-130989
HA1320 .S244 Nr. 67 JN4945.S265

SABA AND CO.
The English-Arabic dictionary of professional business terms /. London , Boulder, Colo. , c1987. 210 p. ; ISBN 0-946510-33-4 : LC Card 87-163985 DDC 650/.03/21 19
HF1002 .E583 1987

Saba, Luigi, 1940- Le Iniziative locali per l'occupazione . Milano, Italy , c1985. 244 p. : LC Card 85-221711 DDC 331 s 331.12/042 19
HD85.I7 I68 no. 75 HD5713.5
NYPL [JLD 87-446]

Sabag-Vaillancourt, Carmen. Caoutchouc et produits en matières plastiques au Québec . [Québec] , 1984. 249 p. : ISBN 2-550-10690-3 LC Card 85-155214 DDC 363.1/196684/09714 19
HD7269.R92 C23 1984

Sabater, Jordi, 1958- Anarquisme i catalanisme : la CNT i el fet nacional català durant la guerra civil / Jordi Sabater.1a ed. Barcelona : Edicions 62, 1986. 231 p. ; 18 cm. (Llibres a l'abast. 216) Bibliography: p. 189-199. ISBN 84-297-2490-7 LC Card 87-108668
1. Confederación Nacional del Trabajo (Spain) - History - 20th century. 2. Syndicalism - Spain - Catalonia - History - 20th century. 3. Anarchism - Spain - Catalonia - History - 20th century. 4. Catalonia (Spain) - History - Autonomy and independence movements. I. Title.
HD8582.C583 S24 1986

Sabavala, S. A., 1918- Tata, J. R. D. (Jehangir Ratanji Dadabhoy), 1904- Keynote . Bombay , 1986. xviii, 155 p., [1] leaf of plates : ISBN 81-85110-00-X : LC Card 86-902369 DDC 338.0954
HC435.2 .T37 1986

Saboia, João, 1944-
Evolução histórica do salário mínimo no Brasil : fixação, valor real e diferenciação regional / João L.M. Saboia.Versão apresentada ao PNPE em junho/83. Rio de Janeiro : Programa Nacional de Pesquisa Econômica, 1984. 106 p. ; 30 cm. (Série Fac-símile . no. 15) Bibliography: p. 66-67. LC Card 87-403844 DDC 331.2/3 19
1. Wages - Brazil - Minimum wage - History. I. Programa Nacional de Pesquisa Econômica (Brazil). II. Title. III. Series.
HD4920.B8 S265 1984

Salário mínimo no Brasil : a experiência brasileira / João Saboia. Porto Alegre, Rio Grande do Sul : L&PM Editores, c1985. 96 p. : ill. ; 18 cm. (Coleção Universidade livre) Bibliography: p. 96. ISBN 85-25-40034-3 : LC Card 86-129265 DDC 331.2/3 19
1. Wages - Minimum wage - Brazil. I. Title.
HD4920.B8 S27 1985

Sacarto, Douglas M. Morandi, Larry B. Renewing resources . Denver, Colo. , 1984. vii, 133 p. ;
NYPL [JSF 86-712]

Sacharow, Stanley. Packaging, an introduction / by Stanley Sacharow, Aaron L. Brody. Cleveland, OH : HBJ Publications, c1986. p. cm. Bibliography: p. Includes index. ISBN 0-15-004486-0 LC Card 87-8362 DDC 658.5/64 19
1. Packaging. I. Brody, Aaron L. II. Title.
HF5770 .S274 1986

Sachchidananda, 1926- Electricity and social change / Sachchidananda, K.K. Verma. Patna : Janaki Prakashan, 1983. xii, 264 p. ; 22 cm. Includes index. Bibliography: p. [258]-260. LC Card 83-902678 DDC 303.4/83 19
1. Electric utilities - Social aspects - India - Bihar. 2. Rural electrification - India - Bihar. I. Verma, K. K. (Krishna Kumar), 1941-. II. Title.
HD9685.I43 B547 1983
NYPL [JLD 86-4263]

Sachs, Ignacy.
[Développer les champs de planification. English]
Development and planning / Ignacy Sachs ; translated by Peter Fawcett. Cambridge [Cambridgeshire] ; New York : Cambridge University Press ; ix, 134 p. ; 23 cm. Translation of: Développer les champs de planification. Bibliography: p. [112]-130. Includes index. ISBN 0-521-33454-3 LC Card 87-11780 DDC 338.9 19
1. Economic development. 2. Economic policy. 3. Central planning. I. Title.
HD82 .S23313 1987

L'Impasse Nord-Sud . Paris , c1984. 103 p. : ISBN 2-11-001207-2 : LC Card 84-163951
HC59 .I44 1984

Der Sachverständigenrat zur Begutachtung der Gesamtwirtschaftlichen Entwicklung . Schmidt, Kurt, 1924- Stuttgart , 1985. 24 p. ; ISBN 3-515-04462-0 (Deut. Bibl.) : LC Card 86-157934
HC286.7 .S353 1985

Sachverständigenrat zur Begutachtung der Gesamtwirtschaftlichen Entwicklung (Germany) Chancen für einen langen Aufschwung /. Stuttgart , 1984. xvii, 350 p. : ISBN 3-17-003288-7 : LC Card 86-178498
HC286.7 .C48 1984

SACHVERSTÄNDIGENRAT ZUR BEGUTACHTUNG DER GESAMTWIRTSCHAFTLICHEN ENTWICKLUNG (GERMANY)
Schmidt, Kurt, 1924- Der Sachverständigenrat zur Begutachtung der Gesamtwirtschaftlichen Entwicklung . Stuttgart , 1985. 24 p. ; ISBN 3-515-04462-0 (Deut. Bibl.) : LC Card 86-157934
HC286.7 .S353 1985

Sack, Manfred, 1928- Lebensraum : Strasse / Manfred Sack.1. Aufl. Bonn : Deutsches Nationalkomitee für Denkmalschutz, 1982. 81 p. : ill. (some col.) ; 24 cm. (Schriftenreihe des Deutschen Nationalkomitees für Denkmalschutz . Bd. 14) ISBN 3-922153-01-1 LC Card 85-128580
1. Roads - Germany, West. I. Title. II. Series.
HE363.G3 S23 1982

Sacks, Frank. The new IRA handbook : everyone's guide to successful investing after tax reform / by Frank Sacks, Siri Campbell & Cameron Stauth. Chicago : MCI, [1987], c1986. 126 p. : ill. ; 22 cm. Bibliography: p. 117-120. ISBN 0-911445-05-6 (pbk.) : LC Card

87-130659 DDC 332.024/01 19
1. Individual retirement accounts - United States. I. Campbell, Siri. II. Stauth, Cameron. III. Title.
HG1660.U5 S23 1987

Sacrificio de un pueblo, 15 de noviembre de 1922 /. Puig Vilazar, Carlos. [Guayaquil, Ecuador] , 1983. 88 p. ; LC Card 86-115462
HD5358.A6 P85 1983

Sacristán, Antonio.
Disertaciones sobre economía mexicana / Antonio Sacristán Colás. México, D.F. : CIDE, 1982. 39 p. ; 28 cm. LC Card 87-123937 DDC 332.1/0972 19
1. Banks and banking - Government ownership - Mexico. 2. Debts, External - Mexico. I. Centro de Investigación y Docencia Económicas. II. Title.
HG2714 .S23 1982

La situación económica mundial y México : las cuestiones que suscita el intercambio del petróleo : revisión crítica de ciertos puntos fundamentales de la teoría convencional o al uso / Antonio Sacristán Colas. México, D.F. : Centro de Investigación y Docencia Económicas, [1980] 72 p. ; 23 cm. (Ensayos. Colección Economía . núm. 1) Includes bibliographical references. LC Card 87-400921 DDC 330.972/0834 19
1. Economic history - 1971-. 2. Economic policy. 3. Petroleum industry and trade. 4. Mexico - Economic conditions - 1970-. I. Series: Ensayos. Colección Economía , 1. II. Title.
HC59 .S3122 1980

SADCC . Hanlon, Joseph. London, U.K. , c1984. 110 p. : LC Card 86-148391 DDC 332.6/732268 19
HC900 .H35 1984

The Saddlebrook papers : a reader on growth management in Florida. [Fort Lauderdale] : Florida Atlantic University/Florida International University Joint Center for Environmental and Urban Problems ; [Tallahassee] : Florida House Select Committee on Growth Management, [1985] v leaves, 177 p. : ill. ; 27 cm. Papers commissioned by the Select Committee on Growth Management, Florida House of Representatives, as background for a conference held at Saddlebrook Resort, Pasco County, Fla., Oct. 1983. Includes bibliographies. LC Card 86-621089 DDC 338.9759 19
1. Environmental policy - Florida. 2. Economic development - Environmental aspects - Florida. 3. Natural resources - Florida - Management. 4. Regional planning - Florida. 5. Local government - Florida. I. Joint Center for Environmental and Urban Problems. II. Florida. Legislature. House of Representatives. Select Committee on Growth Management.
HC107.F63 E547 1985

Sadhu, Kanan K. (Kanan Kusum)
Bio-demographic study of Kashmiris / Kanan K. Sadhu. Delhi, India : Gian Pub. House, c1987. viii, 217 p. : maps ; 23 cm. Revision of the author's thesis (Ph. D.--University of Delhi, 1983) Bibliography: p. [198]-212. Includes index. ISBN 81-212-0072-5 : LC Card 87-900298 DDC 304.6/0954/6 19
1. Jammu and Kashmir (India) - Population. 2. Fertility, Human - India - Jammu and Kashmir. I. Title.
HB3640.J36 S23 1987

Saʻdī, ʻAbd Allāh Jamʻān Saʻīd, 1954- Siyāsat al-māl fī al-Islām fī ʻahd ʻUmar ibn al-Khaṭṭāb wa-muqāranatuhā bi-al-anẓimah al-ḥadīthah / ta'līf ʻAbd Allāh Jamān Saʻīd al-Saʻdī. al-Ṭabʻah 1. al-Dawḥah, Qaṭar : Maktabat al-Madāris, 1983. 291 p. ; 24 cm. Originally presented as the author's thesis (mājistīr--Jāmiʻat al-Qāhirah, 1983). Bibliography: p. 276-286. LC Card 86-965028
1. Finance, Public - Islamic Empire. 2. Islamic Empire - History - 622-661. 3. Islam - Economic aspects. 4. Finance, Public - Islamic countries. I. Title.
HJ1438 .S23 1983

Sadka, Efraim.
Economic effects of the government budget /. Cambridge, Mass. , c1988. p. cm. ISBN 0-262-08172-5 LC Card 87-26187 DDC 338.9 19
HJ2005 .E25 1988

Nerlove, Marc, 1933- Household and economy . Boston , 1987. xiii, 155 p. : ISBN 0-12-515752-5 LC Card 86-10764 DDC 304.6/32 19
HB901 .N47 1987 ***NYPL [JLE 87-1715]***

Nerlove, Marc, 1933- Population policy and individual choice . Washington, D.C., U. S.A. , 1987. 52 p. : ISBN 0-89629-062-X (pbk.) LC Card 87-16802 DDC 363.9 19
HB901 .N474 1987

Sadolin, Pia. Regional udvikling i Danmark / Pia Sadolin, Morten Weise Olesen. [Aarhus] : Geografisk institut, Aarhus universitet, 1983. 92 p. : ill. ; 29 cm. (Notat / Geografisk institut, Aarhus universitet, 0106-9047 . 37) Bibliography: p. 90-92. LC Card 84-164625
1. Denmark - Economic conditions - 1945-. 2. Regional economics. I. Olesen, Morten Weise. II. Series: Notat (Aarhus universitet. Geografisk institut) , 37. III. Title.
HC355 .S26 1983

Sadowski, Wiesław.
Ceny detaliczne 1971-1985 /. Warszawa , 1985. 160 p. ; LC Card 86-196060
HB235.P6 C45 1985

Spis ludności i mieszkań metodą reprezentacyjną z dnia 6 XII 1984 r. . Warszawa , 1985. xx, 93 p., [2] p. of plates : LC Card 86-176185
HD7345.7.A3 S65 1985

Warunki życia ludności w 1984 r. /. Warszawa , 1985. 108 p. ; LC Card 86-225456
HD7035.7 .W35 1985

SAE Automobile Body Activity (Organization). Passenger Protection Committee. Vehicle highway infrastructure . Warrendale, PA , c1987. 208 p. : ISBN 0-89883-455-4 (pbk.) LC Card 86-63707 DDC 363.1/25 19
HE5606 .V44 1987

Saebens, Hans. Hilfe in der Not . [Bremen] [1947] 74 p. : LC Card 87-408692 DDC 338.91/73/04352 19
HC286.5 .H545 1947

Saeed, M. (Muhammad), 1950- India and East Africa : trade ties / M. Saeed and G.P. Setia. Delhi : Triveni Publications, 1986. vi, 264 p. ; 23 cm. Study on trade relations between India and Kenya, Tanzania, and Uganda. Bibliography: p. [253]-260. Includes index. LC Card 87-902493 DDC 382/.0954/0676 19
1. India - Commerce - Africa, East. 2. Africa, East - Commerce - India. I. Setia, G. P. (Guru Prasad), 1937-. II. Title.
HF3788.A45 S23 1986

Säkulare Inflation, kompetitive Geldordnung und "unbeschränkte Demokratie" . Derix, Hans-Heribert. Stuttgart , New York , 1985. xiv, 630 p. : ISBN 3-437-50284-0 LC Card 86-110730
HG229 .D46 1985

Sáenz de Buruaga, Gonzalo. La Economía china de la revolución a las cuatro modernizaciones /. Madrid [1986?] 181 p. : LC Card 86-229994
HC427.9 .E319 1986

Saes, Flávio Azevedo Marques de, 1948- Crédito e bancos no desenvolvimento da economia paulista, 1850-1930 / Flávio Azevedo Marques de Saes. São Paulo : Instituto de Pesquisas Econômicas, 1986. 238 p. : ill. ; 23 cm. (Série Ensaios econômicos . no. 56) Bibliography: p. 195-202. LC Card 87-144659 DDC 332.1/0981/61 19
1. Banks and banking - Brazil - São Paulo (State) - History. 2. Credit - Brazil - São Paulo (State) - History. 3. São Paulo, Brazil (State) - Economic conditions. I. Series: Ensaios econômicos (Universidade de São Paulo. Instituto de Pesquisas Econômicas) , 56. II. Title.
HG2889.S25 S24 1986

Säumt keine Minute! : Dokumente zur Geschichte der Arbeiterbewegung in Mannheim, 1848-1949 / herausgegeben von der Industriegewerkschaft Metall für die Bundesrepublik Deutschland, Verwaltungsstelle Mannheim ; bearbeitet von Wolfgang Brach und Fritjof Kleff. Mannheim : Edition Quadrat, c1986. xiii, 683 p. : ill. ; 24 cm. (Aus der Geschichte lernen) "Ausgewählte regionale Literatur zum Thema": p. 681-682. Includes bibliographical references and indexes. ISBN 3-923003-36-6 LC Card 87-115249 DDC 331/.0943/46 19
1. Labor and laboring classes - Germany (West) - Mannheim - History - Sources. 2. Trade-unions - Germany (West) - Mannheim - History - Sources. 3. Mannheim (Germany) - History - Sources. I. Brach, Wolfgang. II. Kleff, Fritjof, 1950-. III. Series.
HD8460.M35 S28 1986

Sáez Ch., Arturo. Cruz, María Elena. Chile--opciones y desafíos del sindicalismo rural, 1973-1985 /. Santiago, Chile , 1985. 57 p. ; LC Card 87-100897
HD6619.A29 C78 1985

Safecracking the mortgage secrets . Friedman, Janet T. (Janet Teri), 1957- Houston, Tex. , c1987. 141 p. : ISBN 0-942037-00-6 (pbk.) : LC Card 87-13357 DDC 332.7/22/0973 19
HG2040.5.U5 F75 1987

SAFETY ENGINEERING. see **INDUSTRIAL SAFETY.**

SAFETY, INDUSTRIAL. see **INDUSTRIAL SAFETY.**

Safety management in construction and industry /. Goldsmith, David, 1946- New York , c1987. viii, 120 p. : ISBN 0-07-023677-1 LC Card 86-27733 DDC 363.1/19624 19
HD7262 .G58 1987

SAFETY MEASURES. see **INDUSTRIAL SAFETY.**

Safety of aircraft under charter to the Department of Defense. United States. Congress. House. Committee on Armed Services. Subcommittee on Investigations. Report on the safety of aircraft under charter to the Department of Defense . Washington , 1986. iii, 17 p. ; LC Card 86-603401 DDC 363.1/24 19
HE9803.Z7 C538 1986

Saffady, William, 1944- The automated office : an introduction to the technology / by William Saffady. Silver Spring, Md. : National Micrographics Association, c1981. viii, 241 p. : ill. ; 24 cm. Includes bibliographical references and index. ISBN 0-89258-072-0 LC Card 81-208697 DDC 651.8/4 19
1. Office practice - Automation. 2. Business - Data processing. I. National Micrographics Association. II. Title.
HF5548.2 .S165 ***NYPL [JLE 86-3919]***

Saffer, Nirce. Clichevsky, Nora. O mercado de terra na região metropolitana de Porto Alegre /. Porto Alegre , 1982. 60 p. : LC Card 84-256219
HD500.P67 C57 1982

Safilios-Rothschild, Constantina, 1934- The policy implications of the roles of women in agriculture in Zambia / Constantina Safilios-Rothschild. [Lusaka] : National Commission for Development Planning : Ministry of Agriculture and Water Development, [1985] 49, [25] p. ; 30 cm. (Planning Division special studies . no. 20) "November, 1985." Bibliography: p. 45-49. LC Card 87-980047 DDC 331.4/83/096894 19
1. Women in agriculture - Zambia. 2. Women agricultural laborers - Zambia. 3. Women in agriculture - Government policy - Zambia. 4. Women in rural development - Government policy - Zambia. I. Title. II. Series.
HD6073.A292 Z337 1985

Safonov, F. P. (Fedor Pavlovich) Artemov, I͡U. M. (I͡Uriĭ Mikhaĭlovich) Finansovye metody material′nogo stimulirovanii͡a proizvodstva /. Moskva , 1983. 126 p. ; LC Card 84-118738
HF5549.5.I5 A69 1983

Safonova, Ė. I. (Ėleonora Ivanovna) Galkin, I. G. (Il′i͡a Grigor′evich) Sovershenstvovanie planirovanii͡a stroitel′nogo proizvodstva /. Moskva , 1986. 167 p. : LC Card 85-178938
HD9715.S72 G35 1986

Safronov, N. A. Organizat͡sii͡a i stimulirovanie truda rabotnikov transportnykh uzlov . Moskva , 1984. 96 p. ; LC Card 87-100191
HD8039.T72 S656 1984

Saftner, Donald V. Hicks, Sam A. The use of microcomputers in accounting /. St. Paul , c1985. xx, 349 p. : ISBN 0-314-87064-4 (pbk.) LC Card 85-8950 DDC 657/.028/54 19
HF5679 .H535 1985 ***NYPL [JLF 86-1720]***

Ság, László. Összehasonlító tanulmány a világ ásványi nyersanyagainak mennyiségéről, termeléséről, ár és értékrendjeinek alakulásáról /. Budapest , 1983. 57 p. : ISBN 963-671-086-4 (Magy. nemz. bibl.) LC Card 85-130135
HD9506.A2 O85 1983

Saganov, V. B. (Vladimir Biz′i͡aevich) Sistema vedenii͡a sel′skogo khozi͡aĭstva Buri͡atskoĭ ASSR . Novosibirsk , 1985. 188 p. : LC Card 86-215358
HD1995.B8 S57 1985

Sage series in neo-corporatism.
Political stability and neo-corporatism . London , Beverly Hills , 1987. x, 276 p. ; ISBN 0-8039-8028-0 LC Card 86-63492 DDC 321.9 19
HD3616.E8 P64 1987

Sage university papers series. Quantitative applications in the social sciences .
(no. 07-001) Iversen, Gudmund R. Analysis of variance /. Newbury Park , c1987. 94 p. : ISBN 0-8039-3001-1 (pbk.) LC Card 87-61276 DDC 519.5/35 19
HA31.35 .I85 1987

(no. 07-057) Schroeder, Larry D. Understanding regression analysis . Beverly Hills , c1986. 95 p. : ISBN 0-8039-2758-4 LC Card 85-63790 ***NYPL [JLK 77-39 no.57]***

(no. 07-059) Wolf, Fredric M. (Fredric Marc) Meta-analysis . Beverly Hills , c1986. 65 p. : ISBN 0-8039-2756-8 LC Card 85-52372 ***NYPL [JLK 77-39 no.59]***

Sagers, Matthew J.
The freight rate structure on Soviet railroads / by Matthew J. Sagers and Milford B. Green. Washington, D.C. : Soviet Economic Studies Branch, Center for International Research, Bureau of the Census, U. S. Dept. of Commerce, [1985] vii, 28 p. : ill. ; 28 cm. (CIR staff paper . no. 11) Bibliography: p. 26-28. "September 1985." LC Card 87-601285 DDC 385/.12/0947 19
1. Railroads - Soviet Union - Rates. I. Green, Milford B. II. Title. III. Series.
HE1895 .S25 1985

Natural gas liquids and the Soviet gas processing industry / by Matthew J. Sagers. Washington, D.C. : Soviet Economic Studies Branch, Center for International Research, Bureau of the Census, U. S. Dept. of Commerce, [1986] viii, 72, 2 p. : ill. ; 28 cm. (CIR staff paper . no. 14) "March 1986." Bibliography: p. 67-72. LC Card 87-601287 DDC 338.4/766573 19
1. Liquefied natural gas industry - Soviet Union. 2. Gas industry - Soviet Union. I. Title. II. Series.
HD9581.2.L573 S657 1986

Refinery throughput in the U. S.S.R. / by Matthew J. Sagers. Washington, D.C. : U. S.S.R. Input-Output Branch, Center for International Research, Bureau of the Census, U. S. Dept. of Commerce, [1984] v, 81, 2 p. : ill. ; 28 cm. (CIR staff paper . no. 2) "May 1984." Bibliography: p. 71-81. LC Card 87-601276 DDC 338.4/766553/0947 19
1. Petroleum industry and trade - Soviet Union. 2. Petroleum refineries - Soviet Union. I. Title. II. Series.
HD9575.S652 S25 1984

Restructuring the Soviet petroleum refining industry / by Matthew J. Sagers and Albina Tretyakova. Washington, D.C. : Soviet Economic Studies Branch, Center for International Research, Bureau of the Census, U. S. Dept. of Commerce, [1985] v, 57 p. ; 28 cm. (CIR staff paper . no. 4) "March 1985." Bibliography: p. 49-57. LC Card 87-601278 DDC 338.4/766553/0947 19
1. Petroleum industry and trade - Soviet Union. 2. Petroleum refineries - Soviet Union. I. Tretyakova, Albina. II. Title. III. Series.
HD9575.S652 S254 1985

The transportation of Soviet energy resources / Matthew J. Sagers, Milford B. Green. Totowa, N.J. : Rowman & Littlefield, 1986. xvi, 177 p. : ill., maps ; 25 cm. Includes indexes. Bibliography: p. [154]-166. ISBN 0-8476-7504-1 : LC Card 86-15508 DDC 380.5/24 19
1. Power resources - Soviet Union - Transportation. 2. Energy industries - Soviet Union - Location. I. Green, Milford B. II. Title.
HD9502.S652 S24 1986 ***NYPL [JLE 87-38]***

Saghayroun, Atif A. Rahman. Determinants of family size in rural Sudan / by Atif Abdel Rahman Saghayroun. Khartoum, Sudan : Economic and Social Research Council, National Council for Research, [1984] 36 leaves ; 32 cm. (Bulletin . no. 123) "November 1984." Bibliography: leaves 34-36. LC Card 87-119805 DDC 304.6/32/09624 19
1. Fertility, Human - Sudan. 2. Family size - Sudan. I. Series: Bulletin (Majlis al-Abḥāth al-Iqtiṣādīyah wa-al-Ijtimāʻiyah) , no. 123. II. Title.
HB1071.8.A3 S22 1984

Sagoff, Mark. The economy of the earth : philosophy, law, and the environment / Mark Sagoff. Cambridge [Cambridgeshire] ; New York : Cambridge University Press, 1988. p. cm. (Cambridge studies in philosophy and public policy) Bibliography: p. Includes index. ISBN 0-521-34113-2 LC Card 87-16091 DDC 363.7/056/0973 19
1. Environmental policy - United States. 2. United States - Economic policy. 3. United States - Social policy. 4. Environmental law - United States. 5. Social legislation - United States. I. Title. II. Series.
HC110.E5 S34 1988

SAGUNTO (SPAIN) - POPULATION.
Estructura social de la comarca "El Camp de Morvedre" /. Sagunt, Valencià [Madrid] , 1982. 2 v. (1133 p.) : ISBN 84-7231-763-3 (set) LC Card 85-188040
HB3620.S24 E87 1982

SAGUNTO (SPAIN) - SOCIAL CONDITIONS.
Estructura social de la comarca "El Camp de Morvedre" /. Sagunt, Valencià [Madrid] , 1982. 2 v. (1133 p.) : ISBN 84-7231-763-3 (set) LC Card 85-188040
HB3620.S24 E87 1982

Sah, A. K. (Anirudh Kumar) Power management in India / A.K. Sah. New Delhi : Standing Conference of Public Enterprises, [1986] x, 142, [14] p., [4] p. of plates : ill., maps ; 25 cm. LC Card 87-902432 DDC 621.4/068 19
1. Power resources - India - Management. 2. Power-plants - India - Management. I. Title.
HD9697.A3 I48 1986

Sahaf, Musadiq Amin, 1958- Marketing of horticulture industry in India / Musadiq Amin Sahaf. 1st ed. Delhi, India : Anmol Publications : Distributed by Anupama Publishers' Distributors, 1987. xiii, 151 p. ; 23 cm. Study, with reference to Jammu and Kashmir State, based on 1976-1983 data. Bibliography: p. [125]-135. Includes index. LC Card 86-903833 DDC 381/.414/0954 19
1. Horticultural products industry - India - Jammu and Kashmir. I. Title.
HD9016.I43 J367 1987

Sahateollisuus /. Juvonen, Risto. [Helsinki] . 290 p. : ISBN 951-859-690-5 LC Card 86-231276
HD9765.F4 J68 1986

Sahay, S. N. (Surendra Nath) Financial management of public enterprises / S.N. Sahay. 1st ed. New Delhi : S. Chand, 1984. xiii, 216 p. ; 22 cm. Revision of the author's thesis (Ph. D.--Patna University, 1981) Includes index. Bibliography: p. 189-193. LC Card 84-900657 DDC 354.54/12092/0681 19
1. Government business enterprises - India - Bihar - Finance. 2. Government business enterprises - India - Finance - Case studies. 3. Corporations, Government - India - Bihar - Finance. 4. Corporations, Government - India - Finance - Case studies. I. Title.
HD4295.B5 S24 1984 ***NYPL [JLD 86-4430]***

Sahel Club. L'Aide publique au développement dans les pays membres du CILSS en 1983 =. Paris , Burkina Faso [1984], c1985. v, 347 p. : LC Card 86-180117
HC1000 .A64 1985

SAHEL - ECONOMIC CONDITIONS.
Continuing the commitment . Washington, D.C. [1986] ix, 164 p. : LC Card 86-600555 DDC 338.1/8 19
HD2120.S15 C66 1986

Dumont, René, 1904- Pour l'Afrique, j'accuse . [Paris] , c1986. 457 p., [48] p. of plates : ISBN 2-259-01455-0 LC Card 86-220056
HC1002 .D85 1986

Sall, Alioune. Ressources humaines pour le développement . [Dakar, Sénégal , 1984] 51 p. : LC Card 85-129264 DDC 338.91/09624 19
HC1002 .S25 1984

SAHEL - ECONOMIC POLICY.
Somerville, Carolyn M. Drought and aid in the Sahel . Boulder , 1986. xxii, 306 p. : ISBN 0-8133-7087-6 : LC Card 86-5635 DDC 338.966 19
HC1002 .S65 1986 ***NYPL [JLD 86-4038]***

SAHEL - POLITICS AND GOVERNMENT.
Dumont, René, 1904- Pour l'Afrique, j'accuse . [Paris] , c1986. 457 p., [48] p. of plates : ISBN 2-259-01455-0 LC Card 86-220056
HC1002 .D85 1986

SAHEL - SOCIAL CONDITIONS.
Dumont, René, 1904- Pour l'Afrique, j'accuse . [Paris] , c1986. 457 p., [48] p. of plates : ISBN 2-259-01455-0 LC Card 86-220056
HC1002 .D85 1986

Sahin, Izzet. Job mobility and private pensions / Izzet Sahin. Brookfield, Wis. : International Foundation of Employee Benefit Plans, c1986. xv, 49 p. ; 28 cm. (Research report (International Foundation of Employee Benefit Plans) . rept. 86-2) "May 1986." Bibliography: p. 17. ISBN 0-89154-305-8 (pbk.) LC Card 87-129468 DDC 331.25/2/0724 19
1. Pensions - Mathematical models. 2. Occupational mobility - Mathematical models. I. Series. II. Series: Research report (International Foundation of Employee Benefit Plans) , rept. 86-2. III. Title.
HD7105 .S229 1986

Sahni, Pardeep, 1955- Public administration in India . Allahabad , 1983. xii, 308 p. ; LC Card 83-907416 DDC 354.54 19
JQ224 .P75 1983 ***NYPL [JLE 86-4197]***

Sahu, Promod K. (Promod Kumar), 1942-
Industrial economy of Orissa / Promod K. Sahu, Jagannath Panda. Delhi : B.R. Pub. Corp. ; New Delhi : Distributed by D.K. Publishers' Distributors, 1986. viii, 152 p. ; 23 cm. Includes bibliographies and index. ISBN 81-7018-401-0 : LC Card 86-903551 DDC 338.0954/13 19
1. Orissa, India - Industries. 2. Government business enterprises - India - Orissa - Finance. 3. Corporations - India - Orissa - Growth. I. Panda, Jagannath, 1952-. II. Title.
HC437.O7 S24 1986

Saibaba, G. Labour conditions in the mining industry of Andhra Pradesh : a study of interaction of unions, managements, and state / G. Saibaba. Tirupati : Sri Venkateswara University, [1985?] v, 314 p. ; 21 cm. Bibliography: p. [303]-314. LC Card 86-901021 DDC 331/.0422/095484 19
1. Miners - India - Andhra Pradesh. 2. Mineral industries - India - Andhra Pradesh. 3. Industrial relations - India - Andhra Pradesh. I. Title.
HD8039.M61 I47 1985
NYPL [JLD 87-1057]

Saidmuradov, Khabibullo Muradovich. Narodnoe khoziaĭstvo Tadzhikistana v gody Velikoĭ Otechestvennoĭ voĭny . Dushanbe , 1980. 169, [3] p. ; LC Card 81-130944
HC337.T233 D45 1980

Saieh, Alvaro. García, Valeriano F. Dinero, precios y política monetaria /. Buenos Aires, Argentina [1985] 334, [12] p. : ISBN 950-53-7077-7 LC Card 85-215884
HG221 .G3193 1985

Sail to New Zealand . Savill, David. London , 1986. 185 p., [20] p. of plates : ISBN 0-7090-2809-1 : LC Card 87-111329 DDC 387.5/065/41 19
HE945.S45 S28 1986

SAILING SHIPS - NEW ZEALAND - HISTORY.
Savill, David. Sail to New Zealand . London , 1986. 185 p., [20] p. of plates : ISBN 0-7090-2809-1 : LC Card 87-111329 DDC 387.5/065/41 19
HE945.S45 S28 1986

SAILING VESSELS. see SAILING SHIPS.

Sain, Inder, 1944- Transformation of Punjab agriculture / Inder Sain. Delhi : B.R. Pub. Corp. ; New Delhi : Distributed by D.K. Publishers' Distributors, 1987. xviii, 191 p. : maps ; 23 cm. Revision of the author's thesis (Ph. D.--Punjabi University, 1985) Bibliography: p. [179]-187. Includes index. ISBN 81-7018-451-7 : LC Card 87-900922
1. Agriculture and state - India - Punjab. 2. Agricultural innovations - India - Punjab. I. Title.
HD2075.P8 S35 1985

St. Clair . Wallace, Anthony F. C., 1923- New York , 1987. xvii, 519 p. : ISBN 0-394-52867-0 : LC Card 86-46120 DDC 307.7/66/0974817 19
HD8039.M62 U6699 1987

Saint Clair. Wallace, Anthony F. C., 1923- St. Clair . New York , 1987. xvii, 519 p. : ISBN 0-394-52867-0 : LC Card 86-46120 DDC 307.7/66/0974817 19
HD8039.M62 U6699 1987

St. Clair, David James, 1950- The motorization of American cities / David J. St. Clair. New York : Praeger, 1986. xi, 192 p. ; 25 cm. Update of thesis (doctoral)--1979. "Praeger special studies. Praeger scientific." Includes bibliographical references and index. ISBN 0-275-92126-3 (alk. paper) : LC Card 86-523 DDC 388.4/1321/0973 19
1. Transportation, Automotive - United States - History - 20th century. 2. Interstate Highway System. 3. Roads - Government policy - United States - History - 20th century. 4. Local transit - United States - History - 20th century. 5. Automobile industry and trade - United States - History - 20th century. I. Title.
HE5623 .S617 1986 ***NYPL [JLE 86-3608]***

SAINT CLAIR (SCHUYLKILL COUNTY, PA.) - SOCIAL CONDITIONS.
Wallace, Anthony F. C., 1923- St. Clair . New York , 1987. xvii, 519 p. : ISBN 0-394-52867-0 : LC Card 86-46120 DDC 307.7/66/0974817 19
HD8039.M62 U6699 1987

Saint-Etienne, Christian, 1951- The Mitterrand and Reagan economic experiments : a lesson in political economy / Christian Saint-Etienne. [Stanford, Calif.] : Hoover Institution, Stanford University, c1986. 36 p ; 23 cm. (Hoover monongraph series . 3) "April 1985." Bibliography: p. [33]-36. ISBN 0-8179-5082-6 (pbk.) LC Card 86-27776 DDC 338.944 19
1. France - Economic policy - 1945-. 2. France - Economic conditions - 1945-. 3. United States - Economic policy - 1981-. 4. United States - Economic condtions - 1981-. I. Title. II. Series.
HC276.2 .S24 1986

SAINT GALL (SWITZERLAND) - HISTORY.
Tanner, Albert. Das Schiffchen fliegt, die Maschine rauscht . Zürich , c1985. 214 p. : ISBN 3-293-00084-3 LC Card 86-124152
HD9865.S9 T36 1985

St. Hill, R. L. Labour mobility between New Zealand and Australia / R.L. St. Hill. Canterbury, N.Z. : Agricultural Economics Research Unit, Lincoln College, [1986] ix, 68 p. : ill. ; 30 cm. (Research report / Agricultural Economics Research Unit, Lincoln College, 0069-3790 . no. 180) "July 1986." Bibliography: p. 59-60. LC Card 87-109510 DDC 331.12/791 19
1. Alien labor, New Zealand - Australia. 2. Alien labor, Australian - New Zealand. 3. Wages - Australia. 4. Wages - New Zealand. I. Series: Research report (Lincoln College (University of Canterbury). Agricultural Economics Research Unit) , no. 180. II. Title.
HD8848.5.N45 S7 1986

St. John-Stevas, Norman. The omnipresence of Walter Bagehot / Norman St. John-Stevas. Oxford [Oxfordshire] ; New York : Clarendon Press, 1987. p. cm. (Romanes lecture for 1986-7) "Delivered in Oxford on 3 March 1987." ISBN 0-19-951554-9 (pbk.) : LC Card 87-13923 DDC 330/.092/4 19
1. Bagehot, Walter, 1826-1877. I. Series: Romanes lecture , 1986-7. II. Title.
HB103.B2 S29 1987

St. Louis. Federal Reserve Bank. see **Federal Reserve Bank of St. Louis.**

SAINT LUCIA - ECONOMIC CONDITIONS - STATISTICS.
Sainte-Lucie, juin 1985 . [Paris] , 1985] 120 p. : LC Card 86-209048
HC155.5.Z7 S257 1985

SAINT LUCIA - POPULATION - STATISTICS.
Sainte-Lucie, juin 1985 . [Paris] , 1985] 120 p. : LC Card 86-209048
HC155.5.Z7 S257 1985

SAINT LUCIA - STATISTICS, VITAL.
Ebanks, G. E. Mortality, fertility, and family planning . Santiago, Chile [1985] 123 p. ; LC Card 87-131697 DDC 304.6/2/09729841 19
HB1376.D65 E32 1985

SAINT VINCENT AND THE GRENADINES - ECONOMIC CONDITIONS.
St.-Vincent et les Grenadines, juin 1985 . Paris , 1985] 85 p. : LC Card 86-209310
HC156.5 .S72 1985

SAINT VINCENT AND THE GRENADINES - ECONOMIC CONDITIONS - CASE STUDIES.
Rubenstein, Hymie. Coping with poverty . Boulder, Colo. , 1987. xx, 389 p. : ISBN 0-8133-7387-5 (pbk. : alk. paper) : LC Card 86-32530 DDC 972.98/4400496 19
HC156.5.Z7 S296 1987

SAINT VINCENT AND THE GRENADINES - SOCIAL CONDITIONS.
St.-Vincent et les Grenadines, juin 1985 . Paris , 1985] 85 p. : LC Card 86-209310
HC156.5 .S72 1985

SAINT VINCENT AND THE GRENADINES - SOCIAL CONDITIONS - CASE STUDIES.
Rubenstein, Hymie. Coping with poverty . Boulder, Colo. , 1987. xx, 389 p. : ISBN 0-8133-7387-5 (pbk. : alk. paper) : LC Card 86-32530 DDC 972.98/4400496 19
HC156.5.Z7 S296 1987

St.-Vincent et les Grenadines, juin 1985 : situation économique, financière et sociale / République française, Ministère des relations extérieures, coopération et développement, Direction des politiques du développement [et] Caisse centrale de coopération économique. Paris : Le Ministère : L'Harmattan [distributor, 1985] 85 p. : ill. ; 30 cm. Cover title. Title on half t.p. : Ile de Saint Vincent. Distributor from label on half t.p. Bibliography: p. 85. LC Card 86-209310
1. Saint Vincent and the Grenadines - Economic conditions. 2. Saint Vincent and the Grenadines - Social conditions. I. France. Ministère des relations extérieurs, coopération et développement. Direction des politiques du développement. II. Caisse centrale de coopération économique (France). III. Title: Situation économique, financière et sociale. IV. Title: Ile de Saint Vincent. V. Title: Saint-Vincent et les Grenadines, juin 1985.
HC156.5 .S72 1985

Saint-Vincent et les Grenadines, juin 1985.
St.-Vincent et les Grenadines, juin 1985 . Paris , 1985] 85 p. : LC Card 86-209310
HC156.5 .S72 1985

SAINTE-FOY-TARENTAISE (FRANCE) - ECONOMIC CONDITIONS.
Bozonnet, Rémy. Sainte-Foy-Tarentaise, une montagne pour des hommes /. [Saint-Julien-Montdenis] [1984] 192 p. : LC Card 85-206948
HC278.S34 B69 1984

SAINTE-FOY-TARENTAISE (FRANCE) - HISTORY.
Bozonnet, Rémy. Sainte-Foy-Tarentaise, une montagne pour des hommes /. [Saint-Julien-Montdenis] [1984] 192 p. : LC Card 85-206948
HC278.S34 B69 1984

SAINTE-FOY-TARENTAISE (FRANCE) - INDUSTRIES - HISTORY.
Bozonnet, Rémy. Sainte-Foy-Tarentaise, une montagne pour des hommes /. [Saint-Julien-Montdenis] [1984] 192 p. : LC Card 85-206948
HC278.S34 B69 1984

Sainte-Foy-Tarentaise, une montagne pour des hommes /. Bozonnet, Rémy. [Saint-Julien-Montdenis] [1984] 192 p. : LC Card 85-206948
HC278.S34 B69 1984

Sainte-Lucie, juin 1985 : situation économique, financière et sociale / République française, Ministère des relations extérieures, coopération et développement, Direction des politiques du développement [et] Caisse centrale de coopération économique. [Paris] : La Direction : L'Harmattan [distributor, 1985] 120 p. : ill. ; 30 cm. Cover title. Title on half t.p.: Ile de Sainte-Lucie. Distributor from label on half t.p. Bibliography: p. 120. LC Card 86-209048
1. Saint Lucia - Economic conditions - Statistics. 2. Saint Lucia - Population - Statistics. I. France. Ministère des relations extérieures, coopération et développement. Direction des politiques du développement. II. Caisse centrale de coopération économique (France). III. Title: Situation économique, financière et sociale. IV. Title: Ile de Sainte-Lucie.
HC155.5.Z7 S257 1985

Sáinz, Leticia. El Sector informal en Bolivia /. [La Paz, Bolivia?] [1986] 323 p. : LC Card 87-100849
HD2346.B6 S43 1986

Sairam, T. V. (Trimurti V.), 1946- Fiscal policy and environment : a study on the role of fiscal measures with special reference to customs and central excises in forest development in India / T.V. Sairam. Delhi : Agam Prakashan, 1986. 135 p. ; 23 cm. Revision of the author's thesis (M. Phil.--Indian Institute of Public Administration, New Delhi, 1984-85) Bibliography: p. [129]-132. Includes index. LC Card 86-902779 DDC 336.2/7863498/0954 19
1. Forest products - Taxation - India. 2. Forest policy - India. I. Title.
HD9766.I62 S35 1986

A SAIS study on Africa.
The Political economy of Kenya /. New York , 1987. viii, 245 p. ; ISBN 0-275-92672-9 (alk. paper) : LC Card 87-22889 DDC 330.9676/204 19
HC865 .P65 1987

Saisonschwankungen der Bankreserven und Ultimooperationen der Schweizerischen Nationalbank /. Stuber, Barbara. Bern , c1986. 173 p. : ISBN 3-258-03653-5 : LC Card 87-130160 DDC 332.1/12/09494 19
HG1656.S9 S77 1986

Saith, Ashwani. The Re-emergence of the Chinese peasantry . London , New York , c1987. ix, 277 p. : LC Card 87-5373 DDC 305.5/63 19
HD1537.C5 R4 1987

Sajogyo. Budidaya padi di Jawa /. Jakarta , 1986. x, 339 p. : LC Card 87-941451
HD9066.I63 J3493 1986

Sakada, M. O. Suïmenko, I͡E. I. Kerivnyk-orhanizator i vykhovatel′ /. Kyïv , 1985. 189 p. ; LC Card 87-109649
HD38.2 .S85 1985

Sakombi Inongo. Regards sur Kinshasa : témoignages / Sakombi Inongo ; préface de Bolikango Akpolokaka. [Zaire] : Editions réunies, [1981?] 94 p. ; 24 cm. Bibliography: p. 91-92. LC Card 82-226585
1. Kinshasa, Zaire - Economic conditions. 2. Kinshasa, Zaire - Social conditions. 3. Kinshasa, Zaire - Politics and government. I. Title.
HC955.Z7 K497 1981

Saksena, K. D. Pricing policy and price controls in developing countries / K.D. Saksena. London : F. Pinter (Publishers) ; Boulder, Colo. : L. Rienner Publishers, c1986. x, 240 p. ; 23 cm. Spine title: Pricing policies and price controls in developing countries. Includes bibliographies and index. ISBN 0-931477-85-9 (U. S.) : LC Card 86-3287 DDC 338.5/26/091724 19
1. Price regulation - Developing countries. 2. Price regulation - India. I. Title. II. Title: Pricing policies and price controls in developing countries.
HB236.D44 S25 1986 ***NYPL [JLD 86-4069]***

Sala-Diakanda, Mpembele. Approche ethnique des phénomènes démographiques : le cas du Zaïre / Mpembele Sala-Diakanda. Louvain-la-Neuve : Cabay : Département de démographie, Université catholique de Louvain, 1980. 433 p. : ill. ; 24 cm. (Recherches démographiques . cahier no 4) "Novembre 1980." Bibliography: p. 415-433. LC Card 84-118066
1. Zaire - Population. 2. Ethnology - Zaire. I. Université catholique de Louvain (1970-). Département de démographie. II. Title. III. Series.
HB3664.5.A3 S23 1980

Sala, Edmondo. All'origine della borghesia lecchese : casa Brini nel XVIII secolo / Edmondo Sala. Lecco : Biblioteca civica Uberto Pozzoli, [1983] 83 p. : ill. ; 22 cm. (Materiali lecchesi . 3) Includes bibliographical references. LC Card 85-190056
1. Lumber trade - Italy - Lecco - History - 18th century. 2. Silk industry - Italy - Lecco - History - 18th century. 3. Brini family. I. Title. II. Series.
HD9765.I72 L437 1983

Sala Garrido, Ramón. El mercado de deuda pública / Ramón Sala Garrido. [Valencia] : Bolsa de Valencia, [1984] 163 p. : ill. ; 24 cm. Bibliography: p. 159-163. ISBN 84-505-0146-6 LC Card 86-213799
1. Debts, Public - Spain. 2. Government securities - Spain. I. Title.
HJ8739 .S25 1984

Salahdine, Mohamed. Maroc, tribus, makhzen et colons : essai d'histoire économique et sociale / Mohamed Salahdine. Paris : L'Harmattan, c1986. 337 p. : ill. ; 22 cm. (Bibliothèque du développement) Bibliography: p. 325-334. ISBN 2-85802-525-5 LC Card 86-159041
1. Morocco - Economic conditions. 2. Morocco - Social

conditions. I. Title. II. Series.
HC810 .S23 1986

Salais, Robert. Le Travail . Paris , c1986. iv, 370 p. ; ISBN 2-7178-1138-9 : LC Card 87-123294
HD8428 .T72 1986

Salam : panhā læ næothāng kækhai / dōi M Krung Thēp : Samnakphim Mahāwitthayālai Thammasāt : čhatčhamnāi dōi Sūn Nangs 2525 [1982] 16, 249 p. : ill. ; 20 cm. On problems of slum dwellers in Bangkok, Thailand, with recommendations for resolving them. Includes bibliographical references. CONTENTS. - Chumchon 'æ'at læ næothāng kieokap kānprapprung chumchon 'æ'at / dōi M LC Card 82-916400
1. Urban poor - Thailand - Bangkok. I. Akin Rabibhadana, M.R. Chumchon 'æ'at læ næothāng kieokap kānprapprung chumchon 'æ'at. 1982. II. Dirēk Tengčhamrūn. Khant
HC445.Z7 B3678 1982

SALAMANCA (SPAIN : PROVINCE) - HISTORY.
Herr, Richard. Rural change and royal finances in Spain at the end of the old regime /. Berkeley , c1987. p. cm. ISBN 0-520-05948-4 (alk. paper) LC Card 86-25027 DDC 333.3/0946/25 19
HD779.J34 H47 1987

Salamin, Pálné. Vélemények az életszínvonalról / [készült a KSH Közgazdasági Főosztálya Háztartásstatisztikai Osztályán ; összeállitotta, Salamin Pálné]. Budapest : Központi Statisztikai Hivatal, 1986. 88 p. : ill. ; 29 cm. LC Card 86-218875
1. Cost and standard of living - Hungary - Public opinion. 2. Public opinion - Hungary. I. Hungary. Központi Statisztikai Hivatal. Háztartásstatisztikai Osztály. II. Title.
HD7027.5 .S25 1986

Salamon, Lester M.
Abramson, Alan J. The nonprofit sector and the new federal budget /. Washington, D.C. , c1986. xviii, 138 p. : ISBN 0-87766-401-3 (pbk.) : LC Card 87-154012 DDC 361.7/63/0973 19
HJ2052 .A54 1986

Altschuler, David M. New York nonprofit organizations . Washington, D.C. (2100 M St., N.W., Washington 20037) , c1987. vii, 43 p. : LC Card 87-159600 DDC 658.1/5 19
HD2769.2.U6 A48 1987

Rhode Island nonprofit organizations : the challenge of retrenchment / Lester M. Salamon, Lisa A. Tunick, Carol J. De Vita ; prepared under the Urban Institute Nonprofit Sector Project. Washington, D.C. : Urban Institute ; Providence, RI : Copies available from the Rhode Island Foundation, c1987. vii, 40 p. : ill. ; 28 cm. (An Urban Institute research report) Includes bibliographical references. LC Card 87-148803 DDC 338.7/4/09745 19
1. Corporations, Nonprofit - Rhode Island - Finance. 2. Human services - Rhode Island - Finance. 3. Budget - Rhode Island. I. Tunick, Lisa A. II. De Vita, Carol J. III. Nonprofit Sector Project (Urban Institute). IV. Title. V. Series.
HD2769.2.U6 S25 1987

San Francisco Bay Area nonprofit organizations : the challenge of retrenchment / Lester M. Salamon, David M. Altschuler, Carol J. De Vita. Washington, D.C. (2100 M St., N.W., Washington 20037) : Urban Institute, c1987. vi, 26 p. : ill. (some col.) ; 28 cm. (An Urban Institute research report) "Prepared under the Urban Institute Nonprofit Sector Project." Includes bibliographical references. LC Card 87-403000 DDC 338.7/4/0979461 19
1. San Francisco Metropolitan Area (Calif.) - Appropriations and expenditures. 2. Corporations, Nonprofit - California - San Francisco Metropolitan Area - Finance. I. Altschuler, David M. II. De Vita, Carol J. III. Nonprofit Sector Project (Urban Institute). IV. Title. V. Series.
HJ9205.S3 S34 1987

Salamonné Huszty, Anna. Manczinger, Józsefné. Ajánlás a vállalatok stratégiai tervező munkájához /. [Budapest] [1984] 97 p. ; LC Card 86-148677
HD30.28 .M346 1984

I salari /. Roccella, Massimo. Bologna , c1986. 342 p. ; ISBN 88-15-01204-4 : LC Card 86-216417
HD5034 .R63 1986

Salariat. Delaunay, Jean Claude. Salariat et plus-value en France depuis la fin du XIXe siècle /. Paris , c1984. xiv, 304 p. : ISBN 2-7246-0488-1 : LC Card 84-172193 DDC 331.2/944 19
HB206 .D45 1984 ***NYPL [JLD 86-426]***

Salariat et plus-value en France depuis la fin du dix-neuvième siècle. Delaunay, Jean Claude. Salariat et plus-value en France depuis la fin du XIXe siècle /. Paris , c1984. xiv, 304 p. : ISBN 2-7246-0488-1 : LC Card 84-172193 DDC 331.2/944 19
HB206 .D45 1984 ***NYPL [JLD 86-426]***

Salariat et plus-value en France depuis la fin du XIXe siècle /. Delaunay, Jean Claude. Paris , c1984. xiv, 304 p. : ISBN 2-7246-0488-1 : LC Card 84-172193 DDC 331.2/944 19
HB206 .D45 1984 ***NYPL [JLD 86-426]***

Salariés agricoles permanents. Colliez, Jean-Paul. Les salariés agricoles permanents, leur rémunération en octobre 1982. Paris [1984] 62 p. : ISBN 2-11-083969-4 LC Card 85-108387
HD4966.A292 F73 1984

Les salariés agricoles permanents, leur rémunération en octobre 1982. Colliez, Jean-Paul. Paris [1984] 62 p. : ISBN 2-11-083969-4 LC Card 85-108387
HD4966.A292 F73 1984

El salario en México /. Bortz, Jeff. México, D.F. , 1986. 198 p. : ISBN 968-612-519-1 LC Card 87-404064 DDC 331.2/972 19
HD4981 .B677 1986

Salario humano y libertad /. Guiba (Writer) Buenos Aires , 1986. viii, 155 p. ; ISBN 950-50-3130-0 LC Card 87-101595
HD4917 .G85 1986

Salário mínimo no Brasil . Saboia, João, 1944- Porto Alegre, Rio Grande do Sul , c1985. 96 p. : ISBN 85-25-40034-3 : LC Card 86-129265 DDC 331.2/3 19
HD4920.B8 S27 1985

O salário perverso . Henrique, Luiz. Brasília , 1983. 129 p. ; LC Card 86-129394
HD5004 .H45 1983

Salarios e inflación, Argentina, 1970-1983 / Organización Internacional del Trabajo, Programa Mundial del Empleo [y] Programa Regional del Empleo para América Latina y el Caribe (PREALC). [Santiago, Chile] : PREALC, [c1984] iv, 116 p. : ill. ; 28 cm. (Documento de trabajo / PREALC . 239) LC Card 85-156959
1. Wage-price policy - Argentina. 2. Wages - Argentina. 3. Prices - Argentina. 4. Inflation (Finance) - Argentina. I. World Employment Programme. II. Regional Employment Program for Latin America and the Caribbean. III. Series: Documento de trabajo (Regional Employment Program for Latin America and the Caribbean) , 239.
HC180.W24 S25 1984

Salários indexados, preços e emprego . Garcia, Manuel Enriquez. São Paulo , 1986. 149 p. : LC Card 86-234254
HD5004 .G37 1986

Salários, inflação e moeda . Girão, José António. Lisboa , 1984. 50 p. : LC Card 85-157764
HG1145 .G57 1984

Salários, preços e câmbio . Modiano, Eduardo Marco. Rio de Janeiro, RJ , 1984. 55, [5] leaves ; LC Card 84-234066
HD5004 .M56 1984

Salary administration in Japan . Ballon, Robert J. Tokyo , 1985. 44 p. ; ISBN 4-88168-100-1 LC Card 86-115944 DDC 331.2/952 19
HD5077 .B3454 1985

Salas O'Brien, Patricia. Región sur, problemática y perspectivas /. Arequipa [1986?] 164 p. ; LC Card 87-404224 DDC 330.984/052 19
HC182 .R39 1986

Salay, David L., 1944- Hard coal, hard times . Scranton , 1984, c1983. xv, 193 p. ; ISBN 0-917445-00-7 LC Card 85-156422 DDC 331.7/622335/0974837
HD8039.M62 U633 1984
NYPL [JLE 87-1218]

Salazar, Ernesto, 1946- Pioneros de la selva : los colonos del proyecto Upano-Palora / Ernesto Salazar. Quito, Ecuador : Ediciones Abya Yala, 1986. 228 p., [11] leaves of plates : ill. ; 22 cm. Bibliography: p. 209-225. LC Card 87-400290 DDC 338.1/09866/43 19
1. Agricultural colonies - Ecuador - Morona Santiago. 2. Migration, Internal - Ecuador. 3. Migration, Internal - Andes Region. I. Title.
HD1516.E25 S25 1986

Salazar, Rebeca. Portilla, Belfor. Alimentos . México , 1983. 149, [53] p. : ISBN 968-429-384-4 LC Card 84-172348 DDC 338.1/9/1724 19
HD9018.D44 P67 1983
NYPL [JLD 86-1520]

Salazar T., Boris. Las formas de consumo en Colombia : el caso de Cali / por Boris Salazar T. [Cali, Colombia] : Universidad del Valle, Centro de Investigaciones y Documentación Socio-Económica, [1982] 118, [45] p. ; 21 cm. (Serie Monografías. monografía no. 8) Bibliography : p. [2-5] (2nd group) LC Card 85-192219 DDC 658.8/343/0986152 19
1. Consumers - Colombia - Cali. 2. Consumers' preferences - Colombia - Cali. I. Series: Serie Monografías (Universidad del Valle. Centro de Investigaciones y Documentación Socio-Económica) , monografía no. 8. II. Title.
HC200.C6 S25 1982 ***NYPL [JLD 86-1935]***

Salcedo Martín, Emilio. Esparza Cervera, José Ramón. Impuesto sobre la renta . Valencia [1982?] 1 v. (various pagings) ; ISBN 84-85672-11-9 LC Card 83-134521
HJ4744 .E86 1982

Saldru working paper .
(no. 45) Miller, Shirley. Trade unions in South Africa, 1970-1980 . Cape Town , 1982. xxxxv, 278 p. ; ISBN 0-7992-0469-2
NYPL [Sc F 86-217]

(no. 56) Ellis, George Francis Rayner. A quality of life and basic needs measurement system with application to Elsies River /. Cape Town [1983] 101, [84] p. : ISBN 0-7992-0551-6 LC Card 84-146635 DDC 338.968/00723 19
HC905.Z7 E473 1983 ***NYPL [JLF 86-1126]***

(no. 58) Schneier, Steffen. Occupational mobility among Blacks in South Africa /. Cape Town [1983] vi, 219 p. : ISBN 0-7992-0567-2 (pbk.) LC Card 84-197038 DDC 331.12/72/089968 19
HD8801 .S34 1983 ***NYPL [JLG 86-123]***

Saldu working paper .
(no. 59) Goldin, Ian. The poverty of Coloured labour preference . Cape Town [1984] ii, 97 p. : ISBN 0-7992-0570-2 (pbk.) LC Card 84-195453
HD8801.Z8 C324 1984

SALE OF BUSINESS ENTERPRISES. see **BUSINESS ENTERPRISES, SALE OF.**

The sale of liquor in New Zealand . New Zealand. Working Party on Liquor. [Wellington, N.Z. , 1986] 212, [1] p. : LC Card 87-147518 DDC 338.4/76631/09931 19
HD9390.N452 N49 1986

Saleh, Nabil A. Unlawful gain and legitimate profit in Islamic law : riba, gharar, and Islamic banking / Nabil A. Saleh. Cambridge [Cambridgeshire] ; New York : Cambridge University Press, 1986. xii, 130 p. ; 24 cm. (Cambridge studies in Islamic civilization) Includes index. Bibliography: p. ISBN 0-521-32298-7 LC Card 85-25547 DDC 297/.14 19
1. Interest (Islamic law). 2. Risk (Islamic law). 3. Sales (Islamic law). 4. Banking law (Islamic law). I. Title. II. Series.
LAW ***NYPL [JLE 86-2377]***

Sales & distribution guide to Malaysia / by Tim Allen ... [et al.]. 1st ed. Oxford ; New York : Pergamon, 1988. p. cm. ISBN 0-08-034987-0 (U. S.) : LC Card 87-21043 DDC 382/.61/09595 19
1. Investments, Foreign - Malaysia - Handbooks, manuals, etc. 2. Foreign trade promotion - Malaysia - Handbooks, manuals, etc. 3. Malaysia - Economic conditions - Handbooks, manuals, etc. I. Allen, Tim. II. Title: Sales and distribution guide to Malaysia.
HG5750.6.A3 S25 1988

Sales and distribution guide to Malaysia. Sales & distribution guide to Malaysia /. Oxford , New York , 1988. p. cm. ISBN 0-08-034987-0 (U. S.) : LC Card 87-21043 DDC 382/.61/09595 19
HG5750.6.A3 S25 1988

Sales assistant handbook. The Successful sales assistant's handbook. New York, N.Y. , c1987. xi, 268 p. : ISBN 0-13-860305-7 (pbk.) : LC Card

87-11322 DDC 332.6/2/0688 19
HG4621 .S84 1987

SALES, CONDITIONAL - INDIA.
Kothari, Vinod. Lease, financing & hire-purchase . Nagpur, India , 1986. xxvii, 799 p. ; LC Card 87-902268
HD9999.L4363 I446 1986

Sales de Bohigas, Núria, 1933- Terra, treball i propietat . Barcelona , c1986. 346 p. ; ISBN 84-7423-287-2 LC Card 86-216973
HD2025.C35 T47 1986

SALES ESTIMATES. see **SALES FORECASTING.**

SALES, EXPORT. see **EXPORT SALES.**

SALES FORECASTING.
Fritz, Wolfgang, Dipl.-Kfm. Warentest und Konsumgüter-Marketing . Wiesbaden , c1984. 596 p. : ISBN 3-409-13600-2 LC Card 84-207784
HF5415.2 .F75 1984

Maricourt, Renaud de. La prévision des ventes /. Paris , c1985. 159 p. : ISBN 2-13-039013-7 : LC Card 86-138110 DDC 658.8/18 19
HF5415 .M2794 1985

SALES FORECASTING - DATA PROCESSING.
Berry, Dick. Forecasting sales with the personal computer . New York , c1988. p. cm. ISBN 0-89930-329-3 (lib. bdg. : alk. paper) : LC Card 87-7284 DDC 658.8/18/0285416 19
HF5415.2 .B458 1988

SALES, INTERNATIONAL. see **EXPORT SALES.**

SALES (ISLAMIC LAW)
Saleh, Nabil A. Unlawful gain and legitimate profit in Islamic law . Cambridge [Cambridgeshire] , New York , 1986. xii, 130 p. ; ISBN 0-521-32298-7 LC Card 85-25547 DDC 297/.14 19
LAW ***NYPL [JLE 86-2377]***

SALES LETTER.
Werz, Edward W. Letters that sell /. Chicago , c1987. 163 p. ; ISBN 0-8092-4684-8 (pbk.) LC Card 87-20064 DDC 808/.066651 19
HF5730 .W47 1987

SALES LETTERS.
Detroy, Erich-Norbert, 1945- Wie man mit Brief, Telefon und Erstbesuch neue Kunden systematisch und dauerhaft gewinnt /. Zürich , c1982. 216 p. : ISBN 3-478-23510-3 : LC Card 82-242870
HF5446 .D47 1982

Sales management . Dalrymple, Douglas J. New York , c1988. p. cm. ISBN 0-471-62495-0 LC Card 87-23749 DDC 658.8/1 19
HF5438.4 .D34 1988

Sales management /. Futrell, Charles. Chicago , c1988. xxii, 789 p. : ISBN 0-03-010963-9 LC Card 87-8976 DDC 658.8/1 19
HF5438.4 .F87 1988

Sales management . Smith, Roger F. Englewood Cliffs, N.J. , c1987. x, 261 p. : ISBN 0-13-786534-1 LC Card 86-30299 DDC 658.8/1 19
HF5438.4 .S57 1987

Sales management and motivation /. Callanan, Joseph A. New York , 1987. xi, 204 p. : ISBN 0-531-15516-1 LC Card 86-29020 DDC 658.8/1 19
HF5438.4 .C335 1987

SALES MANAGEMENT - CASE STUDIES.
Dalrymple, Douglas J. Sales management . New York , c1988. p. cm. ISBN 0-471-62495-0 LC Card 87-23749 DDC 658.8/1 19
HF5438.4 .D34 1988

Sales management handbook / edited by Patrick Forsyth. Aldershot, Hants, England ; Brookfield, Vt., U. S.A. : Gower Pub., c1987. p. cm. Includes index. ISBN 0-566-02585-X : LC Card 87-8619 DDC 658.8/1 19
1. Sales management. I. Forsyth, Patrick.
HF5438.4 .S228 1987

Sales motivation : selling your people on selling your products. New York, N.Y., U. S.A. : Alexander Hamilton Institute, c1985. viii, 131 leaves ; 28 cm. (Modern business reports) ISBN 0-86604-150-8 (pbk.) LC Card 86-232974 DDC 658.3/14 19
1. Selling. 2. Motivation (Psychology). I. Alexander Hamilton Institute (U. S.). II. Series.
HF5438.25 .S253 1985

SALES PERSONNEL.
Garofalo, Gene. The sales professional's survival guide, or, Things your sales manager never told you /. Englewood Cliffs, NJ , c1987. p. cm. ISBN 0-13-788076-6 LC Card 86-25603 DDC 650.1/2/024381 19
HF5439.5 .G37 1987

Pfeiffer, Paul L. Counter merchandising . Chicago, Ill. (Suite 2260, 20 N. Wacker Dr., Chicago 60606) , c1986. 84 p., [1] leaf of plates : LC Card 87-404047 DDC 658.8/5 19
HF5438.25 .P49 1986

Smith, Roger F. Sales management . Englewood Cliffs, N.J. , c1987. x, 261 p. : ISBN 0-13-786534-1 LC Card 86-30299 DDC 658.8/1 19
HF5438.4 .S57 1987

SALES PERSONNEL - ABILITY TESTING.
Rosenthal, Walter, 1929- The complete portfolio of sales personnel tests with recruiting, screening, and selecting guidelines /. Westbury, N.Y. , c1987. p. cm. ISBN 0-87280-011-3 LC Card 87-17523 DDC 658.3/1125 19
HF5439.65 .R67 1987

SALES PERSONNEL - GREAT BRITAIN - SALARIES, ETC.
Tack Management Consultants. Salesmen's cars, expenses, and allowances, 1963 /. London [1963?] 163 p. ; LC Card 86-173421
HF5439.7 .T33 1963

SALES PERSONNEL - RECRUITING.
Rosenthal, Walter, 1929- The complete portfolio of sales personnel tests with recruiting, screening, and selecting guidelines /. Westbury, N.Y. , c1987. p. cm. ISBN 0-87280-011-3 LC Card 87-17523 DDC 658.3/1125 19
HF5439.65 .R67 1987

SALES PERSONNEL - SALARIES, ETC.
Garofalo, Gene. The sales professional's survival guide, or, Things your sales manager never told you /. Englewood Cliffs, NJ , c1987. p. cm. ISBN 0-13-788076-6 LC Card 86-25603 DDC 650.1/2/024381 19
HF5439.5 .G37 1987

The sales professional's advisor /. Brownstone, David M. New York , c1987. 298 p. ; ISBN 0-8144-7683-X (pbk.) : LC Card 87-47713 DDC 658.8/5 19
HF5438.25 .B747 1987

The sales professional's survival guide, or, Things your sales manager never told you /. Garofalo, Gene. Englewood Cliffs, NJ , c1987. p. cm. ISBN 0-13-788076-6 LC Card 86-25603 DDC 650.1/2/024381 19
HF5439.5 .G37 1987

SALES PROMOTION.
Farris, Paul. Advertising & promotion management . Malabar, Fla. , 1987, c1983. x, 301 p. : ISBN 0-89464-261-8 (pbk.) LC Card 87-15902 DDC 659.1 19
HF5821 .F36 1987

Foote, Cameron S. The fourth medium . Homewood, Ill. , c1986. xxix, 226 p. : ISBN 0-87094-913-6 LC Card 86-70966 DDC 658.8/2 19
HF5438.5 .F66 1986 ***NYPL [JLE 87-1433]***

Grossman, Ann. The marketer's guide to media vehicles, methods, and options . New York , 1987. xiv, 238 p. : ISBN 0-89930-266-1 (lib. bdg. : alk. paper) LC Card 87-2473 DDC 659.1 19
HF5826.5 .G76 1987

Kombinationserbjudanden. Vällingby [1984] 269, [45] p. : ISBN 91-7398-243-1 LC Card 85-115578
HF5438.5 .K66 1984

Promotional management . Englewood Cliffs, N.J. , c1988. xi, 305 p. : ISBN 0-13-731035-8 (pbk.) LC Card 87-12041 DDC 658.8 19
HF5415 .P727 1988

Rossiter, John R. Advertising and promotion management /. New York , 1987. xix, 647 p. : ISBN 0-07-053907-3 : LC Card 86-27381 DDC 659.1 19
HF5821 .R65 1987

Seltz, David D. A handbook of retail promotion ideas /. Rockville Centre, N.Y. , c1985. 256 p. ; ISBN 0-87863-220-4 LC Card 84-25969 DDC 658.8/2 19
HF5438.5 .S45 1985 ***NYPL [JLF 86-1789]***

SALES PROMOTION - CASE STUDIES.
Quelch, John A. Cases in advertising and promotion management /. Plano, Tex. , 1987. xv, 759 p. : ISBN 0-256-03713-2 LC Card 86-72244 DDC 659.1 19
HF5823 .Q44 1987

SALES PROMOTION - CONGRESSES.
Hermesiade . Essen , c1986. 182 p. ; ISBN 3-89206-143-2 LC Card 86-226901 DDC 658.8/2 19
HF5438.5 .H47 1986

Seminar on Below-the-Line and Sponsoring (1985 : Milan, Italy) Seminar on Below-the-Line and Sponsoring . Amsterdam, Netherlands [1985] vi, 270 p. : ISBN 92-831-1107-9 (pbk.) : LC Card 86-213125 DDC 658.8/2 19
HF5438.5 .S46 1985

Sales representative effectiveness to the dentist. Tustin, CA (17722 Irvine Blvd., Tustin 92680) : Biomedical Business International, c1986. 113 leaves in various foliations : ill. ; 28 cm. (Report / Biomedical Business International . #3112) LC Card 86-231841 DDC 681/.761 19
1. Dental instruments and apparatus industry - United States - Statistics. 2. Dentists - United States - Attitudes - Statistics. I. Biomedical Business International, Inc. II. Series: Report (Biomedical Business International, Inc.) , #3112.
HD9995.D43 U56 1986

SALES TAX - BRAZIL.
Longo, Carlos Alberto. Ajustamentos de impostos na fronteira e a alocação de receitas tributárias . São Paulo , 1979. 208 p. ; LC Card 80-152384
HJ5715.B8 L6617 ***NYPL [JLD 86-3846]***

SALES TAX - BRAZIL - MINAS GERAIS.
Economia mineira e o financiamento do setor público . Belo Horizonte , 1985. 126 p. : LC Card 85-207952
HJ2529.M5 E26 1985

SALES TAX - CANADA.
Robinson, Albert J., 1926- The retail sales tax in Canada /. Toronto, Ont. , c1986. viii, 165 p. ; ISBN 0-88808-025-5 (pbk.) : LC Card 86-210098 DDC 336.2/713/0971 19
HJ5715.C2 R63 1986

SALES TAX - CANADA - PROVINCES.
Robinson, Albert J., 1926- The retail sales tax in Canada /. Toronto, Ont. , c1986. viii, 165 p. ; ISBN 0-88808-025-5 (pbk.) : LC Card 86-210098 DDC 336.2/713/0971 19
HJ5715.C2 R63 1986

SALES TAX - NEW YORK (STATE)
Baynes, Peter A. Distribution of local sales tax revenue . Albany, N.Y. (119 Washington Ave., Albany 12210) [1986] 13 p. : LC Card 87-106773 DDC 336.2/713/09747 19
HJ5715.U62 N72 1986

SALES TAX - NEW YORK (STATE) - AUDITING.
An evaluation of the sales tax audit program of the New York State Department of Taxation and Finance. [Albany] [1985] 2, 75 p. : LC Card 86-621117 DDC 353.97470072/47 19
HJ5715.U6 E83 1985

SALES TAX - PERU - CERRO DE PASCO - HISTORY - 18TH CENTURY.
Espinoza Claudio, César. Alcabalas y protesta popular . Lima, Perú , 1981. iii, 111 p., [1] leaf of plates : LC Card 82-146025
HJ5715.P4 E86 1981

SALES TAX - UTAH.
Katayama, Leslee. Hotel sales, room rents, and transient room taxes in Utah, 1978-1985 /. Salt Lake City, Utah (519 Heber Wells Bldg., Salt Lake City 84134) [1985] i, 49 leaves : LC Card 86-620905 DDC 336.2/7864794 19
HJ5715.U62 U85 1985

SALES TAX - VIRGINIA - STATISTICS.
Lindsey, Donald W. Taxable sales in Virginia, 1985 /. Charlottesville, Va. (2015 Ivy Rd., Charlottesville 22903-1780) [1986] 16 p. : LC Card 86-622891 DDC 336.2/713/09755021 19
HJ5715.U62 V85 1986

Sales, the whole body approach /. Robertson, James E., 1944- Portland, Or. , 1988. p. cm. ISBN 0-943920-78-7 : LC Card 87-24679

DDC 658.8/5 19
HF5438.8.P75 R63 1988

SALESMANSHIP. see **SELLING.**

SALESMEN. see **SALES PERSONNEL.**

Salesmen's cars, expenses, and allowances, 1963 /. Tack Management Consultants. London [1963?] 163 p. ; LC Card 86-173421
HF5439.7 .T33 1963

SALESWOMEN. see **SALES PERSONNEL.**

Salgado, Germánico. Ecuador, política económica--teoría y realidad. [Guayaquil] [1986- v. <1-3 > ; LC Card 87-105005
HF1519 .E3 1986

Salhany, Roger E. The origin of rights / by Roger E. Salhany. Toronto : Carswell, 1986. viii, 175 p. ; 24 cm. Includes index. Bibliography: p. [163]-171. ISBN 0-459-38750-2 LC Card 86-177651 DDC 342.71/085 347.10285 19
1. Civil rights - Canada. 2. Civil rights - United States. I. Title.
KDZ574 .S25 1986 ***NYPL [JLE 87-1679]***

Saliba, Bonnie. Water markets in theory and practice : market transfers, water values, and public policy / by Bonnie Colby Saliba and David B. Bush. Boulder : Westview Press, 1987. viii, 273 p. : ill. ; 23 cm. (Studies in water policy and management . no. 12) Includes bibliographies and index. ISBN 0-8133-7465-0 (pbk. : alk. paper) : LC Card 87-21687 DDC 333.91/00979 19
1. Water transfer - Southwestern States. 2. Water transfer - Government policy - Southwestern States. 3. Water supply - Southwestern states. 4. Water-supply - Government policy - Southwestern States. I. Bush, David B. II. Title. III. Series.
HD1695.A165 S25 1987

Salih, Mohamed Abdel Aal. Flow of funds in the Sudan / by Mohamed Abdel Aal Salih. Khartoum, Sudan : Economic & Social Research Council, National Council for Research, [1984] 38 leaves ; 30 cm. (Bulletin / Economic and Social Research Council, National Council for Research . no. 108) "March 1984." Includes bibliographical references. LC Card 84-980837 DDC 339.2/6/09624 19
1. Flow of funds - Sudan. I. Series: Bulletin (Majlis al-Abḥāth al-Iqtiṣādīyah wa-al-Ijtimāʻīyah) , no. 108. II. Title.
HC835 .S25 1984

Salinas de Gortari, Carlos. Producción y participación política en el campo / Carlos Salinas de Gortari. 1a ed. México : Universidad Nacional Autónoma de México, Coordinación de Humanidades, 1980. 320 p. : ill. ; 23 cm. Based on the author's thesis (doctoral--Harvard University, 1978) : Political participation, public investment and system support. Bibliography: p. 313-320. ISBN 968-582-934-9 LC Card 82-199421 DDC 338.1/0972 19
1. Agriculture - Economic aspects - Mexico. 2. Rural development - Mexico - Citizen participation. 3. Political participation - Mexico. I. Title.
HD1792 .S287 1980 ***NYPL [JLD 86-2602]***

Salinas Sánchez, Javier.
García Villarejo, Avelino. Estructura financiera y actividad inversora de las administraciones públicas en Castilla y León /. Valladolid , 1984. 431 p. : ISBN 84-505-0331-0 LC Card 87-108720
HJ1249.C29 G37 1984

García Villarejo, Avelino. Manual de hacienda pública . Madrid , c1985. 686 p. : ISBN 84-309-1197-9 LC Card 87-105048
HJ1244 .G37 1985

Salinger, Sharon V. (Sharon Vineberg) "To serve well and faithfully" : labor and indentured servants in Pennsylvania, 1682-1800 / Sharon V. Salinger. Cambridge [Cambridgeshire] ; New York : Cambridge University Press, 1987. xiii, 192 p., [1] leaf of plates : facsim. ; 24 cm. Includes bibliographical references and indexes. ISBN 0-521-33442-X LC Card 87-852 DDC 306/.363/09748 19
1. Indentured servants - Pennsylvania - History. 2. Slave labor - Pennsylvania - History. I. Title.
HD4875.U5 S25 1987

Salins, Peter D. Housing America's poor /. Chapel Hill , c1987. ix, 203 p. ; ISBN 0-8078-1738-4 LC Card 86-40449 DDC 363.5/8 19
HD7287.96.U5 H68 1987

Säljande butik /. Rylander, Stig, 1928- Lund , c1984. 272 p. : ISBN 91-44-99681-0 : LC Card 84-229201
HF5429 .R94 1984

Säljledaren /. Brolin, Åke, 1924- Malmö , c1984. 140 p. : ISBN 91-38-61223-2 : LC Card 84-188808
HF5438.4 .B76 1984

Salkin, Marcia. Dowall, David E. Office automation and the implications for office development /. [Berkeley] [1986] 171 p. ; LC Card 86-622512 DDC 651.8 19
HF5547.5 .D64 1986

Sall, Alioune. Ressources humaines pour le développement : quel bilan pour le CILSS? / par Alioune Sall, Loïc Barbedette, Jean-Pierre Gontard. [Dakar, Sénégal : ENDA, 1984] 51 p. : ill. ; 22 cm. (Série Etudes et recherches . no 84-77) "Juin 1984." LC Card 85-129264 DDC 338.91/09624 19
1. Economic assistance - Sahel. 2. Sahel - Economic conditions. 3. Human capital - Sahel. 4. Permanent Inter-State Committee for Drought Control in the Sahel. I. Barbedette, Loïc. II. Gontard, Jean-Pierre. III. Series: African environment. Occasional paper , no. 77. IV. Title.
HC1002 .S25 1984

Sallandt, Peter. Burberg, Paul-Helmuth. Zielgruppenorientierte kommunale Wirtschaftsförderung . Münster , c1983. xi, 207, 16 p. : ISBN 3-88497-042-9 LC Card 84-173863
HC289.M9 B87 1983

Salles, Iraci Galvão. Trabalho, progresso e a sociedade civilizada : o Partido Republicano Paulista e a política de mão-de-obra (1870-1889) / Iraci Galvão Salles. São Paulo : HUCITEC ; [Brasília] : em convênio com o Instituto Nacional do Livro, Fundação Nacional Pró-Memória, 1986. 145 p. ; 21 cm. (Coleção Estudos históricos) Bibliography: p. 141-145. LC Card 86-224281
1. Labor policy - Brazil - São Paulo (State) - History - 19th century. 2. Partido Republicano Paulista - History - 19th century. 3. Slavery - Brazil - São Paulo (State) - History - 19th century. 4. Coffee plantation workers - Brazil - São Paulo (State) - History - 19th century. 5. São Paulo, Brazil (State) - Economic conditions. I. Title. II. Series.
HD8289.S282 S24 1986

Salles, Pierre, 1913- Problèmes économiques généraux / Pierre Salles. 5e éd. Paris : Dunod, 1984-1986 2 v. : ill. ; 24 cm. (Economie "module," 0338-6074) Includes bibliographies. "6e éd."--V. 2, t.p. CONTENTS. - 1. Microéconomie -- 2. Macroéconomie. ISBN 2-04-016910-5 (v. 1) LC Card 87-116907
1. Economics. I. Title. II. Series.
HB173 .S355 1986

Salm, Cláudio. Emprego urgente /. Curitiba , 1984. vii, 75 p. ; LC Card 86-177208
HD5713 .E47 1984

Salmen, Lawrence F., 1942- Listen to the people : participant-observer evaluation of development projects / Lawrence F. Salmen. New York : Published for the World Bank by Oxford University Press, c1987. x, 149 p. : ill. ; 23 cm. Bibliography: p. 140-144. Includes index. ISBN 0-19-520545-6 : LC Card 86-23672 DDC 338.984/12 19
1. Economic development projects - Bolivia - La Paz - Evaluation. 2. Economic development projects - Ecuador - Guayaquil - Evaluation. 3. Economic development projects - Developing countries - Evaluation. I. Title.
HC185.E44 S25 1987

Salmon, Mark. Harris, Stuart. Analysis of commodity markets for policy purposes /. London , 1978. ix, 81 p. ; ISBN 0-900842-42-3 (pbk.) LC Card 85-111455 DDC 332.64/4 19
HG6046 .H367 1978

Salmond, John A. Miss Lucy of the CIO : the life and times of Lucy Randolph Mason, 1882-1959 / John A. Salmond. Athens : University of Georgia Press, c1988. p. cm. Bibliography: p. Includes index. ISBN 0-8203-0956-7 (alk. paper) LC Card 87-5822 DDC 331.88/33/0924 B 19
1. Mason, Lucy Randolph, 1882-1959. 2. Trade-unions - United States - Officials and employees - Biography. 3. Congress of Industrial Organizations (U. S.) - Biography. 4. Feminists - United States - Biography. I. Title.
HD6509.M375 S25 1988

Salomon Brothers Center for the Study of Financial Institutions.
Black, Deborah G. Success and failure of futures contracts . New York, N.Y. (90 Trinity Pl., New York 10006) [c1986] 70 p. ; LC Card 87-129777 DDC 332.64/4 19
HG6046 .B52 1986

Smirlock, Michael. Taxes and mergers . New York, N.Y. (90 Trinity Place, New York 10006) [c1986] 42 p. : LC Card 86-210061 DDC 336.24/3 19
HD2746.5 .S64 1986

Salomon Brothers for the Study of Financial Institutions. Benston, George J. An analysis of the causes of savings and loan association failures /. New York, N.Y. (90 Trinity Place, New York 10006) [1985] 182 p. : LC Card 86-209942 DDC 332.3/2/0973 19
HG2151 .B46 1985

Salomon, Jean Jacques.
Les enjeux du changement technologique / Jean-Jacques Salomon, Geneviève Schméder. Paris : Economica : CPE, c1986. 206 p. : ill. ; 24 cm. Includes bibliographical references. ISBN 2-7178-1092-7 : LC Card 86-172778
1. Technological innovations - Economic aspects. 2. Technological innovations - Government policy. 3. Technological innovations - Economic aspects - United States. 4. Technological innovations - Government policy - United States. I. Schméder, Geneviève. II. Title.
HC79.T4 S286 1986

Le gaulois, le cow-boy, et le samouraï : la politique française de la technologie / Jean-Jacques Salomon. Paris : Economica : CPE, c1986. 209 p. : ill. ; 24 cm. Includes bibliographical references. ISBN 2-7178-1139-7 : LC Card 87-120178
1. Technological innovations - Economic aspects - France. 2. France - Economic policy - 1981-. 3. Technology and state - France. I. Title.
HC280.T4 S25 1986

Salomon, Robert. Ruvuma region : some socioeconomic data related to housing / Robert Salomon and Ali Mjella. Dar es Salaam : Building Research Unit, Ministry of Lands, Housing, and Urban Development, 1981. 32 leaves : ill., map ; 30 cm. (Working report . WR 20) Cover title: Some social economic data related to housing, Ruvuma region. "February, 1981." LC Card 85-981451
1. Housing, Rural - Tanzania - Ruvuma Region. I. Mjella, Ali. II. Title. III. Title: Some social economic data related to housing, Ruvuma region. IV. Series: Working report (Tanzania. Idara ya Utafiti wa Nyumba) , 20.
HD7289.T352 R897 1981

SALOONS. see **HOTELS, TAVERNS, ETC.**

SALT INDUSTRY AND TRADE - BRAZIL.
Duarte, Dioclécio D. A indústria extrativa do sal e a sua importância na economia do Brasil /. Rio de Janeiro, Brasil , 1941 i.e. 1942. 218 p., [24] leaves of plates : LC Card 85-222223
HD9213.B72 D83 1942

SALT INDUSTRY AND TRADE - GERMANY (WEST) - LÜBECK - HISTORY.
Heineken, Hermann. Der Salzhandel Lüneburgs mit Lübeck bis zum Anfang des 15. Jahrhunderts /. Vaduz , 1965. 150 p. ; LC Card 86-231350
HD9213.G43 L864 1965

SALT INDUSTRY AND TRADE - GERMANY (WEST) - LÜNEBURG - HISTORY.
Heineken, Hermann. Der Salzhandel Lüneburgs mit Lübeck bis zum Anfang des 15. Jahrhunderts /. Vaduz , 1965. 150 p. ; LC Card 86-231350
HD9213.G43 L864 1965

SALT INDUSTRY AND TRADE - LAW AND LEGISLATION - BRAZIL.
Duarte, Dioclécio D. A indústria extrativa do sal e a sua importância na economia do Brasil /. Rio de Janeiro, Brasil , 1941 i.e. 1942. 218 p., [24] leaves of plates : LC Card 85-222223
HD9213.B72 D83 1942

SALT (SPAIN) - ECONOMIC CONDITIONS.
Torrent, Emili. Evolució del transport a Salt /. [Salt, Spain] [1984] 32 p. : ISBN 84-85946-59-6 LC Card 87-161246
HE311.S72 S257 1984

Salter, Malcolm S. Dyer, Davis. Changing alliances /. Boston, Mass. , c1987. xvi, 333 p. ; ISBN 0-87584-175-9 LC Card 86-33619 DDC

338.4/76292/0973 19
HD9710.U52 D94 1987

Saltovskiĭ, I. A. (Ivan Aleksandrovich) Sotsialisticheskai͡a distsiplina truda i sot͡sial'nye faktory ee ukreplenii͡a v trudovykh kollektivakh / I.A. Saltovskiĭ. Kiev : Izd-vo pri Kievskom gos. universitete izdatel'skogo ob"edinenii͡a "Vyshcha shkola", 1985. 118, [2] p. ; 20 cm. Bibliography: p. [115]-[119] LC Card 86-220755
1. Labor discipline. 2. Work groups. 3. Railroads - Ukraine - Employees. I. Title.
HF5549.5.L3 S27 1985

SALTPETER INDUSTRY - CHILE - HISTORY - 20TH CENTURY. Couyoumdjian, Juan Ricardo. Chile y Gran Bretaña . [Santiago] [1986] xvi, 340 p., [4] p. of plates : LC Card 86-222403
HF1516.5.G72 C68 1986

Saltykovskai͡a, L. V. (Lilii͡a Veniaminovna) Blizhniĭ Sever Kanady : prirodnye resursy, khozi͡aĭstvo, rasselenie / L.V. Saltykovskai͡a. Moskva : Izd-vo "Nauka", 1983. 78, [2] p. : ill., maps ; 22 cm. At head of title: Akademii͡a nauk SSSR. Institut geografii. Bibliography: p. 77-[79] LC Card 83-196848
1. Canada, Northern - Economic conditions. 2. Natural resources - Canada, Northern. I. Title.
HC117.N48 S25 1983

Salum-Flecha, Antonio, 1927- Política internacional, economía e integración /. Asunción del Paraguay [1985] 178 p. ; LC Card 86-122468
HF1523 .P65 1985

Salvador Ortíz, S., 1917-1983. Comentarios económicos / S. Salvador Ortíz. 1a ed. Santo Domingo, República Dominicana : Centro de Estudios Monetarios y Bancarios, 1984- v. ; 21 cm. (Serie general) Includes bibliographical references. LC Card 85-118318 DDC 330.9 19
1. Economic history - 1971- - Addresses, essays, lectures. 2. International economic relations - Addresses, essays, lectures. 3. Latin America - Economic conditions - 1945- - Addresses, essays, lectures. 4. Dominican Republic - Economic conditions - 1961- - Addresses, essays, lectures. I. Title.
HC125 .S2615 1984 ***NYPL [JLK 85-83]***

Salvadori, Massimo L., 1908- Eurocomunismo e socialismo sovietico : problemi attuali del PCI e del movimento operaio / Massimo L. Salvadori. Torino : G. Einaudi, 1978. xxvii, 161 p. ; 18 cm. (Nuovo politecnico. 102) Includes bibliographical references. LC Card 80-497655 DDC 324.245075 19
1. Communism - Europe. 2. Communism - Soviet Union. 3. Trade-unions and communism - Italy. I. Title.
JN5657.C63 S24 ***NYPL [JLC 81-75]***

Salvaggio, Jerry Lee. The computer and telecommunications industry in Japan, 1986 / Jerry L. Salvaggio. Houston, Tex. : International Telecommunications Consultants ; Arlington, Va. : Telecom Pub. Group, [c1986] 2 v. : ill. ; 29 cm. Cover title. Bibliography: v. 1, p. 243-245. CONTENTS. - v. 1. Analysis -- v. 2. Profile. LC Card 86-214521 DDC 338.4/7004/0952 19
1. Computer industry - Japan. 2. Telecommunication - Japan. 3. Computer industry - Japan - Directories. 4. Telecommunication - Japan - Directories. I. Title.
HD9696.C63 J364 1986

Salvas-Bronsard, Lise. Bronsard, Camille. Systems of demand equations (including labour supply) for different states of the markets and for different regimes /. Montréal [198-] 28 p. ; LC Card 83-222220 DDC 338.5/212 19
HB801 .B77 1980z

Salvatore, Dominick. Schaum's outline of theory and problems of international economics / by Dominick Salvatore. 2nd ed. New York : McGraw-Hill, c1984. 231 p. : ill. ; 28 cm. (Schaum's outline series) Includes index. Spine title: International economics. ISBN 0-07-054503-0 (pbk.) LC Card 82-21666 DDC 337 19
1. International economic relations - Outlines, syllabi, etc. 2. International economic relations - Problems, exercises, etc. I. Title. II. Title: Theory and problems of international economics. III. Title: International economics.
HF1411 .S24 1984 ***NYPL [JLF 86-1845]***

Salve, Francisco García- see **García-Salve, Francisco.**

Salvucci, Richard J., 1951- Textiles and capitalism in Mexico : an economic history of the obrajes, 1539-1840 / Richard J. Salvucci. Princeton, N.J. : Princeton University Press, c1987. p. cm. Bibliography: p. Includes index. ISBN 0-691-07749-5 (alk. paper) : LC Card 87-45535 DDC 338.4/767702824/0972 19
1. Textile industry - Mexico - History. 2. Weavers - Mexico - History. I. Title. II. Title: Obrajes.
HD9864.M62 S25 1987

Der Salzhandel Lüneburgs mit Lübeck bis zum Anfang des 15. Jahrhunderts /. Heineken, Hermann. Vaduz , 1965. 150 p. ; LC Card 86-231350
HD9213.G43 L864 1965

Salzman, Marian L. Wanted, liberal arts graduates : the career guide to companies that hire smart people / Marian L. Salzman and Nancy Marx Better.1st ed. New York : Anchor Press, 1987. xvi, 341 p. ; 21 cm. "An Anchor Press/Doubleday book"--P. [4] of cover. Includes bibliographies. ISBN 0-385-24008-2 (pbk.) : LC Card 87-8846 DDC 650.1/4 19
1. Job hunting - United States. 2. Vocational guidance - United States. 3. College graduates - Employment - United States. 4. Bachelor of arts degree. 5. Master of arts degree. I. Better, Nancy Marx. II. Title.
HF5382.75.U6 S27 1987

Samabāẏa, saṃgrāma, sādhanā /. Hosena, Nājira, 1930- Ḍhākā , 1985. 8, 109 p., [7] p. of plates : LC Card 85-904909
HD3540.6.D32 H67 1985

Sămădzadă, Z. (Ziiad) Onunju beshillikdă Sovet Azărbaĭjanynyn igtisadi vă sosial inkishafy / Z. Sămădzadă, M. Musaĭev. Baky : Azărbaĭjan dȯvlăt năshriĭĭaty, 1981. 237 p. ; 21 cm. Title in colophon: Ėkonomicheskoe i sot͡sial'noe razvitie Sovetskogo Azerbaĭdzhana v desi͡atoĭ pi͡atiletke. Includes bibliographical references. LC Card 82-153126
1. Azerbaijan S.S.R. - Economic conditions. 2. Azerbaijan S.S.R. - Social conditions. I. Musaĭev, M. II. Title. III. Title: Ėkonomicheskoe i sot͡sial'noe razvitie Sovetskogo Azerbaĭdzhana v desi͡atoĭ pi͡atiletke.
HC337.A9 S32 1981

Samahang nayon . Balmores, Egmidio L., 1925- Quezon City, Philippines , c1975. x, 169 p. ; LC Card 86-132779
HD1491.P5 B34 1975

Samākhom Sangkhomsāt hæng Prathēt Thai. Rǣngngān Thai. Krung Thēp , 2528 [1985] 53 p. ; LC Card 86-915944
HD5822.55.A6 R35 1985

Samaniego, Carlos. Agricultura y alimentación . [Lima] , 1982. 536 p. : LC Card 83-174688 DDC 338.1/9/85 19
HD9014.P52 A57 1982 ***NYPL [JLD 86-268]***

Samborska-Boć, Elżbieta. Układy powiązań w kooperacji przemysłowej / Elżbieta Samborska-Boć. Wyd. 1. Wrocław : Wydawn. Uniwersytetu Wrocławskiego, 1982. 103 p. ; 24 cm. (Acta Universitatis Wratislaviensis . no 652. 113) Summary in German and Russian. Includes bibliographical references. LC Card 83-109302
1. Cooperation - Poland. I. Series: Acta Universitatis Wratislaviensis , no 652. II. Title.
HD3517.7.A4 S28 1982

Same day funds settlement for securities transactions . Financial Industry Securities Council Same Day Funds Settlement Task Force. [New York, N.Y.] [S.l.] , c1985. 61 leaves in various foliations : LC Card 85-193287 DDC 332.64 19
HG4631 .F56 1985 ***NYPL [JLF 86-919]***

Samecki, Wiesław.
Czego można oczekiwać od ekonomii / Wiesław Samecki. Systemy ekonomiczne, gospodarka rynkowa, gospodarka planowa / Wiesław Samecki. Przed kolejną reformą / Antoni Gorazd. Wyd. 1. Warszawa : Instytut Wydawniczy Związków Zawodowych, 1981. 35 p. ; 15 cm. (Biblioteczka Wszechnicy NSZZ Solidarność) Cover title. ISBN 83-202-0150-0 LC Card 86-150577
1. Poland - Economic policy - 1981-. I. Samecki, Wiesław. Systemy ekonomiczne, gospodarka rynkowa, gospodarka planowa. 1981. II. Gorazd, Antoni. Przed kolejną reformą. 1981. III. Title. IV. Title: Systemy ekonomiczne, gospodarka rynkowa, gospodarka planowa. V. Title: Przed kolejną reformą. VI. Series.
HC340.3 .S24 1981

Systemy ekonomiczne, gospodarka rynkowa, gospodarka planowa. 1981. Samecki, Wiesław. Czego można oczekiwać od ekonomii / Wiesław Samecki. Systemy ekonomiczne, gospodarka rynkowa, gospodarka planowa / Wiesław Samecki. Przed kolejną reformą / Antoni Gorazd. Wyd. 1. Warszawa , 1981. 35 p. ; ISBN 83-202-0150-0 LC Card 86-150577
HC340.3 .S24 1981

Samenwerking van Nederland met ontwikkelingslanden . (7) Wereldbevolking groeiend ontwikkelingsprobleem. Den Haag [1975] 66 p. : LC Card 87-118557
HB883.5 .W47 1975

Samfunnsøkonomiske studier. (nr. 43) Bjerkholt, Olav, 1942- MODIS IV . Oslo , 1980. 189 p. : ISBN 82-537-1014-3 (pbk.) LC Card 81-120697 DDC 330.9481/00724 19
HC365 .B46 1980

Samhällsekonomiska effekter av en kärnkraftsavveckling : rapport / från Konsekvensutredningens C-grupp. [Stockholm] : Industridepartementet : LiberFörlag, [1979] 149 p. ; 25 cm. "Ds I 1979:12." "Bilaga 3." Supplement to: Om vi avvecklar kärnkraften / Konsekvensutredningen, 1979. ISBN 91-38-05244-X LC Card 82-219542
1. Nuclear industry - Sweden. 2. Sweden - Economic conditions - 1945-. 3. Energy policy - Sweden. I. Sweden. Konsekvensutredningen. C-gruppen. II. Sweden. Konsekvensutredningen. Om vi avvecklar kärnkraften.
HD9698.S82 O42 1979

Samhällsekonomiska kalkyler vid industrinedläggningar : metod och fallstudier. Stockholm : Statens industriverk : LiberFörlag, [1982] 213 p. : ill. ; 25 cm. (SIND, 0346-5748 . 1982:10) Bibliography: p. 201-203. ISBN 91-38-07164-9 LC Card 83-219569
1. Plant shutdowns - Sweden - Case studies. 2. Unemployment - Sweden - Case studies. 3. Sweden - Economic conditions - 1945-. I. Sweden. Statens industriverk. II. Series.
HD5708.55.S8 S25 1982

Sami Uddin. Cooperative sector in India after independence / Sami Uddin, Mahfoozur Rahman. New Delhi : S. Chand, 1983. vi, 597 p. ; 23 cm. Bibliography: p. 515-524. LC Card 83-903263 DDC 334/.0954 19
1. Cooperation - India. 2. Cooperative societies - India. I. Rahman, Mahfoozur. II. Title.
HD3538 .S25 1983 ***NYPL [JLD 86-3874]***

Samir Amin. see **Amin, Samir.**

Samīr Muḥammad Raḍwān. see **Raḍwān, Samīr Muḥammad.**

Samoĭlov, L. N. (Leonid Nikolaevich) Global'nye problemy obshchestvennogo progressa : filosofskie voprosy tipologii i vzaimosvi͡azi / L.N. Samoĭlov. Moskva : Izd-vo Moskovskogo universiteta, 1985. 92 p. ; 22 cm. Includes bibliographical references. LC Card 85-170113
1. Economic development - Social aspects. 2. Social history - 20th century. 3. Communism and society. I. Title.
HD75 .S258 1985

Samokhin, I͡Uriĭ Mikhaĭlovich. T͡Selevye kompleksnye programmy . Moskva , 1984. 198 p. : LC Card 86-176369
HC336.25 .T74 1984

Samorukova, A. N. (Angara Nikolaevna) Promyshlennost' Sotsialisticheskoĭ Respubliki Rumynii / A.N. Samorukova ; otvetstvennyĭ redaktor O.R. Latsis. Moskva : "Nauka", 1986. 143 p. ; 20 cm. At head of title: Akademii͡a nauk SSSR. Institut ėkonomiki mirovoĭ sotsialisticheskoĭ sistemy. Includes bibliographical references. LC Card 86-202797
1. Romania - Industries. 2. Romania - Economic conditions - 1945-. I. Latsis, O. R. (Otto Rudol'fovich). II. Title.
HC405 .S253 1986

Samoupravljanje od ideje do stvarnosti /. Vekić, Đuro. Sarajevo [1983?] 263 p. ; LC Card 86-115347
HD5660.Y8 V44 1983

Sampaio, Maria Ruth. Abitazione e periferie urbane nei paesi in via di sviluppo . Milano, Italy , c1985. 450 p. : LC Card 86-132019
HD7287.96.L29 A25 1985
NYPL [JLD 87-1173]

Samret Siphongkun.
Botwikhro b Rǣngngān Thai. Krung Thēp , 2528 [1985] 53 p. ; LC Card 86-915944
HD5822.55.A6 R35 1985

Samsinger, Berndt R. Countertrade, eine alternative Marketing-Strategie / Berndt R. Samsinger. Bern : P. Haupt, c1986. xiii, 285 p. : ill. ; 22 cm. (Schriftenreihe des Instituts für Betriebswirtschaftliche Forschung an der Universität Zürich . Bd. 54) Originally presented as the author's thesis (doctoral)--Universität Zürich, 1986. Bibliography: p. 261-285. ISBN 3-258-03597-0 : LC Card 86-191674
1. Countertrade. I. Title. II. Series.
HF1412 .S26 1986

Samtur, Susan J. Cashing in at the checkout / Susan J. Samtur, with Tad Tuleja. New York : Stonesong Press, c1979. 152 p. : ill. ; 22 cm. "A list of refunding bulletins": p. 149-152. ISBN 0-448-15704-7 : LC Card 79-51120 DDC 381/.1 19
1. Coupons (Retail trade). 2. Rebates - United States. 3. Food prices - United States. I. Tuleja, Tad, 1944-. II. Title.
HF6127 .S25 ***NYPL [JLD 81-566]***

The Samuel Gompers papers / editor, Stuart B. Kaufman ; associate editors, Peter J. Albert ... [et al.]. Urbana : University of Illinois Press, c1986- v. : ill., plan, ports. ; 25 cm. Includes bibliographies and index. CONTENTS. - v. 1. The making of a union leader, 1850-86. ISBN 0-252-01138-4 (alk. paper : set) LC Card 84-2469 DDC 331.88/32/0924 19
1. Gompers, Samuel, 1850-1924 - Archives. 2. Trade-unions - United States - History - Sources. 3. Labor and laboring classes - United States - History - Sources. I. Gompers, Samuel, 1850-1924. II. Kaufman, Stuart Bruce.
HD6508 .S218 1986 ***NYPL [JLL 86-230]***

Samuel, Raphael. The Enemy within . London , New York , 1986. xxiii, 260 p. : ISBN 0-7102-0888-X (pbk.) : LC Card 86-12192 DDC 331.89/2822334/0941 19
HD5365.M6152 1984 .E54 1986

Samuels, Richard J. The business of the Japanese state : energy markets in comparative and historical perspective / Richard J. Samuels. Ithaca : Cornell University Press, 1987. xii, 359 p. : ill. ; 24 cm. (Cornell studies in political economy) Cornell paperbacks Bibliography: p. 331-350. Includes index. ISBN 0-8014-2022-9 (alk. paper) LC Card 87-5230 DDC 338.4/7621042/0952 19
1. Energy industries - Japan. 2. Industry and state - Japan. I. Title. II. Series.
HD9502.J32 S27 1987

Samuels, Sheldon W. The Environment of the workplace and human values /. New York , c1986. vii, 118 p. ; ISBN 0-8451-4205-4 LC Card 85-23908 DDC 174/.4 19
HD7260.5 .E58 1986 ***NYPL [JLF 87-151]***

Samuelson, Lars A. Edström, N. F. (Nils Fritiof), 1918- Ekonomiordbok . Stockholm , c1984. 145 p. : ISBN 91-1-847152-8 : LC Card 84-253890
HB61 .E29 1984 ***NYPL [JFD 87-1265]***

Samuelson, Paul Anthony 1915-
Dorfman, Robert. Linear programming and economic analysis /. New York , 1987, c1986. p. cm. ISBN 0-486-65491-5 (pbk.) LC Card 87-24382 DDC 330/.0724 19
HB135 .D67 1987

Epstein, Rachel S. Careers in the world of investments /. New York , c1988. 47 p. : ISBN 1-555-46631-1 LC Card 87-13182 DDC 332.6/023 19
HG4528 .E67 1988

Epstein, Rachel S. Investment banking /. New York , c1988. 48 p. : ISBN 1-555-46630-3 LC Card 87-18194 DDC 332.66 19
HG4534 .E67 1988

Little, Jeffrey B. Growth stocks /. New York , c1988. p. cm. ISBN 1-555-46624-9 LC Card 87-24482 DDC 332.63/22 19
HG4661 .L57 1988

Little, Jeffrey B. Investing and trading /. New York , c1988. 47 p. : ISBN 1-555-46627-3 LC Card 87-23852 DDC 332.6/78 19
HG4553 .L58 1988

Little, Jeffrey B. Understanding a company /. New York , c1988. 47 p. : ISBN 1-555-46622-2 LC Card 87-17654 DDC 657/.33 19
HG4028.B2 L57 1988

Little, Jeffrey B. Wall Street--how it works /. New York , c1988. 47 p. : ISBN 1-555-46621-4 LC Card 87-15139 DDC 332.64/273 19
HG4921 .L625 1988

Little, Jeffrey B. What is a share of stock? /. New York , c1988. 47 p. : ISBN 1-555-46620-6 LC Card 87-13788 DDC 332.63/22 19
HG4521 .L736 1988

SAMUELSON, PAUL ANTHONY 1915-
Wong, Stanley. The foundations of Paul Samuelson's revealed preference theory . London , Boston , 1978. x, 148 p. : ISBN 0-7100-8643-1 : LC Card 78-40600 DDC 339.4/7
HB801 .W594 ***NYPL [JLD 87-1092]***

Samut sathiti rāi pī, 2509 : Čhangwat Narāthiwāt = Statistical yearbook, 1966 : Changwat Narathiwat. [Bangkok] : Samnakngān Sathiti hǣng Chāt, Samnak Nāyok Ratthamontrī, [19]69. 35 p., [1] leaf of plates : map ; 24 x 37 cm. ('Ēkkasān kh B-SY chwt. no. 14-69) Thai and English. Tables. LC Card 83-921129
1. Narathiwat (Thailand : Province) - Statistics. I. Thailand. Samnakngān Sathiti hǣng Chāt. II. Title: Statistical yearbook, 1966. III. Series: 'Ēkkasān kh
HA4600.55.Z9 N3737 1969

Sanœ 'Intharasuksī. Khonrao tāi dai kī withī / Sanœ 'Intharasuksī. Phim khrang thī 1. Krung Thēp : Samnakphim 'Āthit : Chatčhamnāi dōi Sksit Sayām, 2526 [1983] 620 p. ; 20 cm. Articles on common causes of mortality among Thais. LC Card 83-916563
1. Mortality - Thailand. I. Title.
HB1474.55.A3 S36 1983

SAN (AFRICAN PEOPLE) - LAND TENURE.
Wily, Liz. The TGLP and hunter-gatherers . Gaborone, Botswana , 1981. ii, 102 p. ; LC Card 82-207525
DT797 W55 1981 ***NYPL [JLG 87-6]***

SAN (AFRICAN PEOPLE) - POLITICS AND GOVERNMENT.
Wily, Liz. The TGLP and hunter-gatherers . Gaborone, Botswana , 1981. ii, 102 p. ; LC Card 82-207525
DT797 W55 1981 ***NYPL [JLG 87-6]***

SAN ANTONIO (TEX.) - HISTORY.
Austerman, Wayne R. (Wayne Randolph), 1948- Sharps rifles and Spanish mules . College Station , c1985. x, 367 p., [8] p. of plates : ISBN 0-89096-220-0 : LC Card 84-40557 DDC 383/.49764 19
HE6376.A1 T417 1985
NYPL [JLE 85-3346]

SAN DIEGO, CALIF. - COMMERCE.
Bilbao, Elena. La frontera de San Ysidro . Tijuana, Baja California , 1986. 27 p. ; ISBN 968-607-513-5 LC Card 87-125801 DDC 330.9794/98 19
HC108.S65 B55 1986

SAN DIEGO (CALIF.) - ECONOMIC CONDITIONS.
Bilbao, Elena. La frontera de San Ysidro . Tijuana, Baja California , 1986. 27 p. ; ISBN 968-607-513-5 LC Card 87-125801 DDC 330.9794/98 19
HC108.S65 B55 1986

SAN FELICE SUL PANARO (ITALY) - RURAL CONDITIONS.
Cattini, Marco. I contadini di San Felice . Torino , c1984. xvii, 364 p., [2] leaves of plates : ISBN 88-06-05682-4 : LC Card 84-189545
HD1536.I8 C34 1984

San Francisco Bay Area nonprofit organizations . Salamon, Lester M. Washington, D.C. (2100 M St., N.W., Washington 20037) , c1987. vi, 26 p. : LC Card 87-403000 DDC 338.7/4/0979461 19
HJ9205.S3 S34 1987

SAN FRANCISCO (CALIF.) - HISTORY.
Kazin, Michael, 1948- Barons of labor . Urbana , c1987. xiv, 319 p., [14] p. of plates : ISBN 0-252-01345-X (alk. paper) LC Card 86-6967 DDC 331.88/124/0979461 19
HD6515.B9 S45 1987 ***NYPL [JLE 87-1053]***

San Francisco. Federal Home Loan Bank. see **Federal Home Loan Bank of San Francisco.**

San Francisco. Institute for Contemporary Studies. see **Institute for Contemporary Studies.**

SAN FRANCISCO METROPOLITAN AREA (CALIF.) - APPROPRIATIONS AND EXPENDITURES.
Salamon, Lester M. San Francisco Bay Area nonprofit organizations . Washington, D.C. (2100 M St., N.W., Washington 20037) , c1987. vi, 26 p. : LC Card 87-403000 DDC 338.7/4/0979461 19
HJ9205.S3 S34 1987

SAN FRANCISCO PASS (ARGENTINA AND CHILE)
Argerich, Federico Raúl. Posibilidades de intercambio compensado entre Argentina y Chile y exportaciones graníferas al area del Pacífico, ambos por el paso de San Francisco /. Córdoba , 1985. 35 p. ; LC Card 87-402749 DDC 382/.0983/082 19
HF3418.A7 A8 1985

San Francisco State University. Dept. of Sociology. Rethinking the nineteenth century . New York , c1988. p. cm. ISBN 0-313-25997-6 (lib. bdg. : alk. paper) LC Card 87-17791 DDC 330.9/034 19
HC53 .R48 1988

San Francisco State University. School of Behavioral and Social Sciences. Rethinking the nineteenth century . New York , c1988. p. cm. ISBN 0-313-25997-6 (lib. bdg. : alk. paper) LC Card 87-17791 DDC 330.9/034 19
HC53 .R48 1988

San Francisco '85 : recorded live, August 7-11, 1985, St. Francis Hotel, San Francisco, California. Florida VIII : the Eighth Annual Florida International Economic and Investment Conference, January 29-February 2, 1986, Marriott Hotel and Marina. Bethesda, Md. : Euler Enterprises, [1986] vi, 502 p. ; 26 cm. Cover title. At head of title: Investment Seminars Incorporated. Edited transcripts of two seminars presented by Investment Seminars Incorporated. LC Card 87-132666 DDC 332.6 19
1. Investments - Congresses. 2. Tax planning - Congresses. 3. Investments - United States - Congresses. 4. Tax planning - United States - Congresses. I. Investment Seminars Incorporated.
HG4508 .S215 1986

SAN JOSÉ METROPOLITAN AREA (COSTA RICA) - ECONOMIC CONDITIONS.
Algunos aspectos sociográficos del área metropolitana de San José, Costa Rica /. [Ciudad Universitaria "Rodrigo Facio"] , 1970. 105 p. : LC Card 82-196053
HC143.Z7 S3515 1970

SAN JOSÉ METROPOLITAN AREA (COSTA RICA) - POPULATION.
Algunos aspectos sociográficos del área metropolitana de San José, Costa Rica /. [Ciudad Universitaria "Rodrigo Facio"] , 1970. 105 p. : LC Card 82-196053
HC143.Z7 S3515 1970

SAN JOSÉ METROPOLITAN AREA (COSTA RICA) - SOCIAL CONDITIONS.
Algunos aspectos sociográficos del área metropolitana de San José, Costa Rica /. [Ciudad Universitaria "Rodrigo Facio"] , 1970. 105 p. : LC Card 82-196053
HC143.Z7 S3515 1970

San Pedro Amuzgos. Egli, Walter, 1945- San Pedro Amuzgos, ein mexikanisches Dorf kämpft um sein Land . Zürich , c1982. 406 p. : ISBN 3-85791-059-3 LC Card 83-139253
HD1333.M62 S264 1982

San Pedro Amuzgos, ein mexikanisches Dorf kämpft um sein Land . Egli, Walter, 1945- Zürich , c1982. 406 p. : ISBN 3-85791-059-3 LC Card 83-139253
HD1333.M62 S264 1982

San Román Rodríguez, Juan. Morón Bécquer, Pedro. El ahorro vinculado a la adquisición de viviendas . Madrid [1984?] 35 p. : ISBN 84-7196-476-7 : LC Card 85-201073
HG2156.S72 M67 1984

SAN YSIDRO (SAN DIEGO, CALIF.)
Bilbao, Elena. La frontera de San Ysidro . Tijuana, Baja California , 1986. 27 p. ; ISBN 968-607-513-5 LC Card 87-125801 DDC 330.9794/98 19
HC108.S65 B55 1986

Sánchez Alvarez, Javier. Fragoso Gutiérrez, Juan M. El mercado y los precios de los productos agropecuarios /. México , 1983. 486 p. : LC

Card 84-236815
HD9014.M62 F72 1983

Sánchez Bernal, María Isabel. Charro Valls, José María. Sociedades de garantía recíproca . Salamanca, España , 1985. 73 p. ; ISBN 84-7481-349-2 LC Card 87-133330
HG5634.5 .C47 1985

Sánchez de Toca, Joaquín, 1854-1942. Madrid (Spain). Alcaldía. Situación de crédito, hacienda y presupuesto del Municipio de Madrid en 1907 . Madrid , 1907. viii, 137 p. ; LC Card 85-131486
HJ9528.M38 M34 1907

Sánchez Enríquez, Rodrigo. Organización andina, drama y posibilidad / Rodrigo Sánchez. Huancayo, Perú : Instituto Regional de Ecología Andina, [1987] xxii, 219 p. : ill. ; 22 cm. (Serie Estudios sociales . no. 1) Bibliography: p. [215]-219. LC Card 87-404025 DDC 330.98/0038 19
1. Andes region - Economic conditions. 2. Andes region - Social conditions. 3. Peasantry - Andes Region. I. Instituto Regional de Ecología Andina. II. Title. III. Series.
HC167.A5 S26 1987

Sánchez González, Leonardo. Fundamento operacional del sistema de contabilidad general de la nación / [preparado por Leonardo Sánchez González]. 1a. ed. Santiago, Chile : Contraloría General de la República, [1986] 227 p. : ill. ; 26 cm. LC Card 87-403116 DDC 354.830072/31 19
1. Finance, Public - Chile - Accounting - Handbooks, manuals, etc. 2. Government business enterprises - Chile - Accounting - Handbooks, manuals, etc. I. Title.
HJ9923.C3 S264 1986

Sánchez González, Ramón. Los montes de Toledo en el siglo XVIII : estudio demográfico / Ramón Sánchez González. Toledo : Instituto Provincial de Investigaciones y Estudios Toledanos, Diputación Provincial, 1984. 222 p. : ill. ; 24 cm. (Instituto Provincial de Investigaciones y Estudios Toledanos (C.S.I.C.). Serie III, Estudios, catálogos, repertorios . núm. 13) Originally presented as the author's thesis (memoria de licenciatura--Universidad Complutense de Madrid, 1979) Bibliography: p. 81-86. ISBN 84-00-05873-9 LC Card 87-105458
1. Toledo Region (Spain) - Population - History - 18th century. I. Title.
HB3620.T62 S26 1984

Sánchez Holguín, Carlos Gerardo, 1952- Einige reale Aspekte der Aussenhandelsliberalisierung in Entwicklungsländern / Carlos Gerardo Sánchez Holguín. München : Florentz, c1986. 152 p. : ill. ; 21 cm. (Volkswirtschaftliche Forschung und Entwicklung . Bd. 20) Originally presented as the author's thesis (doctoral)--Universität München, 1985. Bibliography: p. 147-152. ISBN 3-88259-368-7 LC Card 86-156293
1. Tariff - Developing countries - Mathematical models. 2. Free trade and protection - Free trade - Mathematical models. I. Title. II. Series.
HF2580.9 .S25 1986

Sanchez, Joseph S., 1949- Increasing sales effectiveness : a complete guide to a successful selling program / by Joseph S. Sanchez. Lodi, N.J. : Feris-Lee Press, [c1987] 203 p. ; 23 cm. Bibliography: p. 202-203. ISBN 0-941315-14-2 : LC Card 87-8794 DDC 658.8/1 19
1. Selling. 2. Sales management. I. Title.
HF5438.25 .S26 1987

Sánchez Machado, Mario. Rovira Mas, Jorge, 1950- La crisis de Costa Rica /. San José, Costa Rica , 1986. 175 p. ; LC Card 87-125520 DDC 338.97286 19
HC143 .R667 1986

Sánchez Martínez, Hilda. Quijano, José Manuel. Finanzas, desarrollo económico y penetración extranjera /. Puebla, Pue. , 1985. 395 p. : LC Card 86-112589 DDC 332/.0972 19
HG185.M6 Q55 1985 ***NYPL [JLD 86-2195]***

Sánchez Meleán, Jorge. Reflexiones para la acción / Jorge Sánchez Meleán. 1a ed. [Venezuela?] : Fondo Editorial IRFES, 1986. xv, 322 p. : ill. ; 22 cm. Includes bibliographical references. ISBN 980-232-049-8 LC Card 87-134702 DDC 338.987 19
1. Venezuela - Economic conditions - 1958-. 2. Decentralization in government - Venezuela. 3. Coal trade - Venezuela - Zulia. 4. Socialism, Christian - Venezuela. 5. Keynesian economics. I. Title.
HC237 .S275 1986

Sánchez Muñoz, María Paloma. La dependencia tecnológica española : contratos de transferencia de tecnología entre España y el exterior / Ma. Paloma Sánchez Muñoz. [Madrid] : Ministerio de Economía y Hacienda, [1984?] xi, 591 p. : forms ; 24 cm. (Serie Economía española . 6) Originally presented as the author's thesis (doctoral--Universidad Autónoma de Madrid, 1983) Bibliography: p. [547]-591. ISBN 84-7415-170-8 : LC Card 86-212990
1. Technology transfer - Economic aspects - Spain. 2. Technology transfer - Law and legislation - Spain. I. Series: Serie Economía española (Spain. Ministerio de Economía y Hacienda. Secretaría de Estado de Comercio) , 6. II. Title.
HC390.T4 S26 1984

Sánchez, Oscar Arias. see **Arias Sánchez, Oscar.**

Sánchez Picón, Andrés. La minería del Levante almeriense, 1838-1930 : especulación, industrialización y colonización económica / Andrés Sánchez Picón. Almería : Cajal, [1983] 308 p., [14] leaves of plates : ill., facsims., ports. ; 22 cm. (Biblioteca de temas almerienses. Serie Monografías . 7) Thesis (licenciatura)--Universidad de Granada, Departamento de Historia Contemporánea, 1981. Bibliography: p. 297-307. ISBN 84-85219-49-X LC Card 85-126928
1. Mineral industries - Spain - Almería (Province). 2. Iron industry and trade - Spain - Almería (Province). 3. Lead industry and trade - Spain - Almería (Province). 4. Mines and mineral resources - Spain - Almería (Province). 5. Metallurgy - Spain - Almería (Province). I. Series: Biblioteca de temas almerienses. Serie Monografías , no. 7. II. Title.
HD9506.S762 A457 1983

Sánchez Ruiz, Enrique E. Arredondo Ramírez, Pablo. Comunicación social, poder y democracia en México /. Guadalajara, Jalisco, México , c1986. 214 p. : LC Card 86-227944
HE8689.9.M6 A77 1986

Sánchez Sánchez, Isidro. Castilla-La Mancha en la época contemporánea, 1808-1939 / Isidro Sánchez Sánchez. [Castilla-La Mancha] : Servicio de Publicaciones de la Junta de Comunidades de Castilla-La Mancha, [1986] iii, 204 p. : ill. ; 20 cm. (Monografías. 7) "Fuentes hemerográficas": p. 179-180. Bibliography: p. 183-195. ISBN 84-505-3538-7 LC Card 87-122049
1. Castilla-La Mancha (Spain) - Economic conditions. 2. Castilla-La Mancha (Spain) - Social conditions. 3. Quality of life - Spain - Castilla-La Mancha. I. Series: Monografías (Castilla-La Mancha (Spain). Junta de Comunidades) , 7. II. Title.
HC387.C245 S36 1986

Sánchez Silesky, Geovanni. Matarrita Mena, José Joaquín. Areas industriales de Costa Rica /. San José, Costa Rica, América Central [1986] 151 p. : ISBN 997-7500-01-0 LC Card 87-404258 DDC 338.097286 19
HC143 .M38 1986

Sánchez, Victorio, 1936- España 1992 : esperanza de un futuro / Victorio Sánchez.1a ed. Esplugues de Llobregat, Barcelona : Plaza & Janés, 1984. 208 p. ; 22 cm. (Hombre y sociedad) Epoca Includes bibliographical references. ISBN 84-01-33260-5 LC Card 86-205726
1. Economic forecasting - Spain. 2. Spain - Economic conditions - 1975-. I. Title.
HC385 .S26 1984

SANCTIONS, ADMINISTRATIVE - EUROPE.
Miller, Mark J. Employer sanctions in Western Europe /. Staten Island, N.Y. , 1987. viii, 67 p. ; ISBN 0-934733-20-1 (pbk.) : LC Card 86-31739 DDC 331.6/2/094 19
HD8378.5.A2 M5395 1987

Sanctity versus sovereignty . Rodman, Kenneth Aaron. New York , 1988. p. cm. ISBN 0-231-06448-9 LC Card 87-24970 DDC 332.6/7373/01724 19
HG5993 .R63 1988

SAND AND GRAVEL INDUSTRY - ITALY - SOTTOMARINA REGION.
Un Mestiere e un paese . Venezia , 1986. 172 p. : ISBN 88-317-4893-9 LC Card 86-219883
HD8039.S252 I85 1986

SAND AND GRAVEL INDUSTRY - ITALY - SOTTOMARINA REGION - EMPLOYEES.
Un Mestiere e un paese . Venezia , 1986. 172 p. : ISBN 88-317-4893-9 LC Card 86-219883
HD8039.S252 I85 1986

SAND AND GRAVEL INDUSTRY - MANAGEMENT.
Kohrs-Barrmeyer, Andrea. Die Problematik der Informationsgewinnung und -verarbeitung bei der Bewertung von Sand- und Kiesabbaugelände /. Münster [1986] xviii, 379 p. : ISBN 3-88660-330-X LC Card 86-223939 DDC 622/.3622/068 19
HD9585.S162 K64 1986

SAND - ITALY - SOTTOMARINA REGION.
Un Mestiere e un paese . Venezia , 1986. 172 p. : ISBN 88-317-4893-9 LC Card 86-219883
HD8039.S252 I85 1986

Sandalaṅkā sanda /. Subasiṃha, Vinsant. [Pannipitiya?] , 1986. viii, 269 p., [6] leaves of plates : LC Card 86-903022
HG1552.S83 A3 1986

SANDALWOOD TRADE - INDIA.
Report on the marketing of sandalwood in India. Faridabad , 1986. viii, 196 p. : LC Card 86-903266 DDC 381/.41497394/0954 19
HD9769.S33 I47 1986

Sandanger, Runar. Prosjektevaluering i u-land : eit eksempel på bruk av cost-benefit analyse / av Runar Sandanger. Oslo : Norsk utenrikspolitisk institutt, [1983] viii, 97 p. : ill. ; 30 cm. (NUPI rapport, 0800-000X . nr. 79) Summary in English. Bibliography: p. 76-78. LC Card 83-144428
1. Economic assistance, Norwegian - Developing countries - Cost effectiveness. 2. Economic development projects - Developing countries - Cost effectiveness. I. Title.
HC60 .S156 1983

Sandars, Joseph. A letter on the subject of the projected rail road between Liverpool & Manchester : pointing out the necessity for its adoption and the manifest advantages it offers to the public, with an exposure of the exorbitant & unjust charges of the water carriers / by Joseph Sandars.4th ed. Liverpool : W. Wales & Co., 1825. 46 p. ; 21 cm. LC Card 85-666157
1. Railroads - Great Britain. I. Title.
HE3018 .S36x 1825

Sandelin, Bo, 1942- Södersten, Bo. Makroekonomi och stabiliseringspolitik /. [Malmö] , c1983. 363 p. : ISBN 91-40-05037-8 : LC Card 84-166176
HB179.S8 S63 1983

Sandell, Steven H. The Problem isn't age . New York , 1987. xiii, 265 p. : ISBN 0-275-92371-1 (alk. paper) : LC Card 86-30642 DDC 331.3/94/0973 19
HD6280 .P75 1987

Sander, Otfried. Kommunale Wirtschaftsunternehmen / von Otfried Sander und Willi Weiblen. Köln : Deutscher Gemeindeverlag : W. Kohlhammer, 1982. xiv, 144 p. : ill. ; 17 cm. (Bd. 35 der Schriftenreihe Fortschrittliche Kommunalverwaltung) Includes bibliographical references and index. ISBN 3-555-00464-6 LC Card 81-192097
1. Municipal ownership - Germany, West. 2. Government business enterprises - Germany, West. I. Weiblen, Willi. II. Series: Schriftenreihe Fortschrittliche Kommunalverwaltung, Bd. 35. III. Title.
HD4659 .S26 1982

Sanders, Hyman. Chaikind, Stephen. Paying for social security . [Washington, D.C.], 1981. xix, 47 p. ; LC Card 81-601225 DDC 353.0082/56 19
HD7125 .C47 ***NYPL [JLF 86-252]***

Sanders, Mary. R.P.M. realize your power to motivate / Mary Sanders and Elizabeth Field ; edited by Jan Urban-Lurain ; cover design & illustrations by Kent Ver Planck. 1st ed. Farmington Hills, Mich. : Milestones Unltd., c1986. 153 p., [2] p. of plates : ill. ; 23 cm. ISBN 0-9616833-0-9 (pbk.) LC Card 87-111586 DDC 658.3/14 19
1. Employee motivation. 2. Achievement motivation. 3. Motivation (Psychology). I. Field, Elizabeth, 1947-. II. Urban-Lurain, Jan. III. Title. IV. Title: RPM realize your power to motivate.
HF5549.5.M63 S26 1986

Sanders, Warren H. Skinner, Hubert C. The new Dietz Confederate States catalog and handbook /. Miami, Fla. (1007 Kane Concourse, Bay Harbor Islands 33154) , 1986. viii, 270 p. : LC

Card 86-206685 DDC 769.56975/075/0973 19
HE6500 .S58 1986

Sandler, Christian Heinrich. Innovative Technologien im Vertrieb : dargestellt am Praxisfall aus der Textilindustrie / Christian Heinrich Sandler. Thun : H. Deutsch, c1986. xvii, 313 p. : ill. ; 21 cm. (Reihe Wirtschaftswissenschaften, 0253-1488 . Bd. 344) Bibliography: p. 289-313. ISBN 3-87144-926-1 LC Card 86-171131
1. Textile industry - Management. 2. Textile industry - Technological innovations. 3. Communication in management. I. Title. II. Series.
HD9850.5 .S25 1986

Sandler, Corey, 1950- Badgett, Tom. The insider's guide to Lotus 1-2-3 . Glenview, Ill. , c1987. xix, 266 p. : ISBN 0-673-18718-7 (pbk.) : LC Card 87-4864 DDC 005.36/9 19
HF5548.4.L67 B33 1987

Sandler Institutional Films.
Management--emphasize your strengths [motion picture] /. Pasadena, CA , 1985, c1986. 1 film reel (22 min.) : LC Card 86-707743 DDC 658.4 11
HD38.2

Management--emphasize your strengths [videorecording] /. Pasadena, CA , 1985, c1986. 1 videocassette (22 min.) : LC Card 86-707745 DDC 658.4 11
HD38.2

Sandole, Dennis J. D., 1941- Conflict management and problem solving . New York , 1987. x, 321 p. : ISBN 0-8147-7866-6 : LC Card 87-11072 DDC 658.4 19
HD42 .C65 1987

Sandole-Staroste, Ingrid, 1948- Conflict management and problem solving . New York , 1987. x, 321 p. : ISBN 0-8147-7866-6 : LC Card 87-11072 DDC 658.4 19
HD42 .C65 1987

Sándorné Szennyessy, Judit. Gazdaságpolitikai kézikönyv / Sándorné Szennyessy Judit, Szelecki György. [Budapest] : Reflektor, 1985. 170 p. : ill. ; 24 cm. Includes bibliographical references. LC Card 86-186314
1. Hungary - Economic policy - 1968-. 2. Hungary - Economic conditions - 1968-. I. Szelecki, György. II. Title.
HC300.28 .S26 1985

Sandoval Aguilar, Guillermo. El desarrollo costarricense y la fecundidad del hombre / responsable del proyecto, Guillermo Sandoval A. ; Abelardo Brenes C., Alfonso González O. Heredia : Universidad Nacional, "Campus Omar Dengo", Instituto de Estudios Sociales en Población, 1985. 233 p. ; 28 cm. Bibliography: p. 230-333. LC Card 86-117576
1. Fertility, Human - Costa Rica. 2. Costa Rica - Economic conditions - 1948-. 3. Costa Rica - Social conditions. I. Brenes Castro, Abelardo. II. González O., Alfonso. III. Universidad Nacional (Costa Rica). Instituto de Estudios Sociales en Población. IV. Title.
HB947 .S26 1985

Sandoval, Godofredo. Las mil caras del movimiento social boliviano / [Godofredo Sandoval]. 1a ed. La Paz, Bolivia : Librería e Impr. Offset "Panamericana", [1986] 132 p. : ill. ; 18 cm. (Colecciones Librería Imprenta Offset Panamericana) Binder's title: Caras del movimiento. "Investigación realizada en el marco del Programa de Investigación de Movimientos Sociales de la Facultad Latinoamericana de Ciencias Sociales"--Added t.p. Bibliography: p. 119-120. LC Card 86-227792
1. Trade-unions - Bolivia - Political activity. 2. Social movements - Bolivia. 3. Political participation - Bolivia. 4. Social conflict - Bolivia. 5. Central Obrera Boliviana. I. Title. II. Title: Caras del movimiento. III. Title: 1,000 caras del movimiento social boliviano.
HD6608.5 .S25 1986

Sandoval H., Orlando. Comercialización de artesanías / Orlando Sandoval H. [Quito, Ecuador] : Ediciones Coseil-Internacional, 1985. 231 p. : ill. ; 18 cm. LC Card 87-400169 DDC 331.7/94 19
1. Artisans - Ecuador. 2. Small business - Ecuador. I. Title.
HD2346.E2 S26 1985

SANDOZ AG. - HISTORY.
Riedl-Ehrenberg, Renate. Alfred Kern (1850-1893), Edouard Sandoz (1853-1928) . Zürich , c1986. 90 p. : LC Card 86-159933 DDC 338/.09494 s 338.7/66/0094943 19
HC395.5.A2 S3 no. 44 QD21

SANDOZ, EDOUARD, 1853-1928.
Riedl-Ehrenberg, Renate. Alfred Kern (1850-1893), Edouard Sandoz (1853-1928) . Zürich , c1986. 90 p. : LC Card 86-159933 DDC 338/.09494 s 338.7/66/0094943 19
HC395.5.A2 S3 no. 44 QD21

Sandström, Björn. Durö, Robert. The basic principles of marketing warfare /. Chichester [West Sussex] , New York , c1987. xi, 164 p. : ISBN 0-471-91545-9 : LC Card 87-8317 DDC 658.8 19
HF5415 .D87 1987

Sandver, Marcus H. Labor relations : process and outcomes / Marcus Hart Sandver. Boston : Little, Brown, c1987. xxii, 529 p. : ill. ; 25 cm. Includes bibliographies and index. ISBN 0-316-77024-8 LC Card 86-27314 DDC 331/.0973 19
1. Industrial relations - United States. 2. Collective bargaining - United States. 3. Labor laws and legislation - United States. I. Title.
HD8072.5 .S32 1987

Sanford, John A. The invisible partners : how the male and female in each of us affects our relationships / John A. Sanford. New York : Paulist Press, c1980. 139 p. ; 23 cm. Includes index. Bibliography: p. 129-132. ISBN 0-8091-2277-4 : LC Card 79-56604 DDC 150.19/54
1. Jung, C. G. (Carl Gustav), 1875-1961. 2. Psychoanalysis. 3. Sex differences (Psychology). I. Title.
BF175 .S24 ***NYPL [JFE 86-5093]***

Sanford, William F. The American business community and the European Recovery Program, 1947-1952 / William F. Sanford, Jr. New York : Garland Pub., 1987. xiv, 366 p. ; 23 cm. (Foreign economic policy of the United States) Originally presented as the author's thesis (Ph. D.)--University of Texas at Austin, 1980. Bibliography: p. 358-366. ISBN 0-8240-8091-2 (alk. paper) LC Card 87-23765 DDC 338.91/73/04 19
1. Marshall Plan. 2. United States - Foreign economic relations - Europe. 3. Europe - Foreign economic relations - United States. 4. Businessmen - United States - History - 20th century. I. Title. II. Series.
HC240 .S259 1987

Sang Ben, Miguel. Economía, política y sociedad : República Dominicana en transición / Miguel Sang Ben. Santo Domingo, R.D. : Editorial Argumentos, 1986. 109 p. ; 22 cm. Articles previously published in El Nuevo diario, June 1981-May 1982. ISBN 84-89529-00-0 LC Card 87-100772
1. Dominican Republic - Economic policy. 2. Dominican Republic - Economic conditions - 1961-. I. Title.
HC153.5 .S27 1986

Sang, Heng-Kang. Project evaluation : techniques and practices for developing countries / Heng-Kang Sang. New York, N.Y. : Wilson Press : Distributed to the trade by Alpha Book Distributors, c1987. p. cm. Bibliography: p. ISBN 0-9617304-0-4 : LC Card 87-6074 DDC 338.9/0068 19
1. Economic development projects - Evaluation. 2. Economic development projects - Developing countries - Evaluation. I. Title.
HD75.9 .S26 1987

Sangiovanni, Bruno. Marketing : la gestione dei prodotti / Bruno Sangiovanni.3a ed. Roma : Buffetti, c1986. 268 p. : ill. ; 24 cm. (Organizzare l'azienda. Settore marketing) Bibliography: p. 265. LC Card 85-233830 '
1. New products - Marketing. I. Title. II. Series.
HF5415.153 .S25 1986

Sangre joven . Arenal, Sandra. México, D.F. , 1986. 130 p., [2] p. of plates : ISBN 968-427-128-X LC Card 87-139058 DDC 331.4/87/0972 19
HD6073.O332 M4953 1986

Sangyō Kōgai Bōshi Kyōkai (Japan)
Environmental protection in the industrial sector in Japan . Tokyo, Japan , c1983. 168 p. : LC Card 87-672736
HC465.P55 E58x 1983

Sanín Posada, Noemí. Colombia. Ministerio de Comunicaciones. Una revolución en las comunicaciones . [Bogotá] 1986. 307 p., [5] leaves of plates : LC Card 87-401464 DDC 384/.09861 19
HE8011 .C65 1986

SANITARY AFFAIRS. see **SANITATION; PUBLIC HEALTH.**

SANITATION - DEVELOPING COUNTRIES - PLANNING - CITIZEN PARTICIPATION - PLANNING.
Whyte, Anne V. T. Guidelines for planning community participation activities in water supply and sanitation projects /. Geneva , Albany, NY , 1986. 53 p. : ISBN 92-4-170096-3 (pbk.) : LC Card 87-137091 DDC 333.91/009172/4 19
HD4465.D44 W49 1986

SANITATION - JUVENILE LITERATURE.
Johnson, Jean, 1943- Sanitation workers, A to Z /. New York, N.Y. , 1988. p. cm. ISBN 0-8027-6772-9 LC Card 87-23129 DDC 628/.4/02373 19
HD8039.S257 J64 1988

SANITATION, RURAL - DEVELOPING COUNTRIES - FINANCE.
Churchill, Anthony A., 1938- Rural water supply and sanitation . Washington, D.C. , c1987. xvi, 111 p. : ISBN 0-8213-0950-1 (pbk.) LC Card 87-23005 DDC 338.4/336361/091724 19
HD1702 .C48 1987

Sanitation workers, A to Z /. Johnson, Jean, 1943- New York, N.Y. , 1988. p. cm. ISBN 0-8027-6772-9 LC Card 87-23129 DDC 628/.4/02373 19
HD8039.S257 J64 1988

SANITATION WORKERS - JUVENILE LITERATURE.
Johnson, Jean, 1943- Sanitation workers, A to Z /. New York, N.Y. , 1988. p. cm. ISBN 0-8027-6772-9 LC Card 87-23129 DDC 628/.4/02373 19
HD8039.S257 J64 1988

SANITATION WORKERS STRIKE, MEMPHIS, TENN., 1968.
Faist, Thomas, 1959- Soziale Schliessung in rassistisch gespaltenen Arbeitsmärkten . Frankfurt am Main , New York , c1986. 161 p. ; ISBN 3-8204-9525-8 LC Card 87-407927 DDC 331.89/28136372/0976819 19
HD5325.S2572 1968 .M46 1986

Sanjaya Lall. see **Lall, Sanjaya.**

Sankar, T. L. (T. Lakshman), 1934- Public enterprises in India . Bombay , 1983. xxii, 524 p. ; LC Card 83-905617 DDC 354.5409/2 19
HD4293 .P793 1983 ***NYPL [JLD 87-723]***

Sankar, T. L. (T. Lakshmana), 1934- Public enterprise policy in India and U.K. in 1980s /. Bombay , 1987. xx, 286 p. ; LC Card 86-903771 DDC 338.6/2/0941 19
HD4293 .P775 1987

Unternehmung und Unternehmungsführung. see **Unternehmung und Unternehmungsführung.**

St. Gall, Switzerland. Hochschule für Wirtschafts- und Sozialwissenschaften. Lateinamerikanisches Institut.
Buchreihe. Veröffentlichung. For later file, which continues its numbering, see: Institut für Lateinamerikaforschung und Entwicklungszusammenarbeit. Buchreihe.
(Bd. 16) Neustadt, Peter. Wachstum und Strukturwandlungen Brasiliens in ihrer Bedeutung für die strategische Marketingplanung von Konsumgüterunternehmungen /. Diessenhofen , cop. 1979. ix, 463 p. : ISBN 3-7253-0092-5 : LC Card 80-469750
HF5415.12.B7 N48 1979
NYPL [JLD 80-3357]

Sanmarco, Philippe. Marseille, l'endroit du décor / Philippe Sanmarco, Bernard Morel. La Calade, Aix-en-Provence : Edisud, 1985. 191 p. : ill. ; 24 cm. Bibliography: p. 189-190. ISBN 2-85744-219-X : LC Card 86-168990
1. Marseille (France) - Economic conditions. 2. Marseille (France) - Politics and government. 3. Marseille (France) - Foreign population. 4. Marseille (France) - Social conditions. I. Morel, Bernard. II. Title.
HC278.M3 S26 1985

Sannerstedt, Anders, 1945- Attityder till kommunal service / Anders Sannerstedt. [Stockholm] : Kommunaldemokratiska

kommittén, [1981] vi, 166 p. : ill. ; 21 cm. (Rapport 9 från Kommunaldemokratiska forskningsgruppen) Bibliography: p. 165-166. "Ds Kn 1981:22." ISBN 91-38-06586-X LC Card 82-244101
1. Municipal services - Sweden - Public opinion. 2. Municipal government - Sweden - Public opinion. 3. Public opinion - Sweden. I. Sweden. Kommunaldemokratiska kommittén. II. Series: Rapport från Kommunaldemokratiska forskningsgruppen , 9. III. Title.
HD4485.S8 S26 1981

Sannikova, S. I. Sovershenstvovanie planirovaniia i upravleniia neftegazovym kompleksom /. Novosibirsk , 1986. 208 p. : LC Card 87-124383
HD9575.S653 S577 1986

Sano, Hans-Otto. The political economy of food in Nigeria 1960-1982 : a discussion on peasants, state, and world economy / Hans-Otto Sano. Uppsala : Scandinavian Institute of African Studies, 1983. 108 p. : maps ; 21 cm. (Research report / Scandinavian Institute of African Studies, 0080-6714 . no. 65) Bibliography: p. 102-108. ISBN 91-7106-210-6
1. Agriculture - Economic aspects - Nigeria. 2. Food supply - Nigeria. 3. Agriculture and state - Nigeria. I. Series: Nordiska Afrikainstitutet. Research report, no. 65. 65. II. Title. ***NYPL [JLD 84-860]***

Sano, Shin'ichi, 1947- Kanryō fuyu no jidai / Sano Shin'ichi. Tōkyō : Purejidentosha, 1985. 6, 255 p. ; 20 cm. In Japanese. Bibliography: p. 255. ISBN 4-8334-1266-7 : LC Card 86-179753
1. Finance, Public - Japan. 2. Bureaucracy - Japan. 3. Government executives - Japan. 4. Japan - Economic policy - 1945-. I. Title.
HC462.9 .S2534 1985 <Orien Japan>
NYPL [*OSM 87-1196]

Sanŏp Yŏn'guwŏn (Korea) KIET International Finance Conference (1985 : Seoul, Korea) International financial markets and the NICs. Seoul, Korea [1985?] viii, 144 p. : LC Card 87-129000 DDC 332/.042 19
HG205 .K54 1985

Sanson, João Rogério. A política de transportes marítimos no Brasil : o custo dos fretes nas exportações e como reduzí-lo / João Rogério Sanson, David Christopher Garlow. Rio de Janeiro : IPEA/INPES, 1986. vii, 178, 5 p. : ill. ; 30 cm. (Série Estudos de política industrial e comércio exterior . no. 9) "Tiragem 250 exemplares"--Verso t.p. Bibliography: p. 173-178. LC Card 87-403931 DDC 387.5/44/0981 19
1. Freight and freightage - Brazil - Rates. 2. Exports - Brazil. 3. Merchant marine - Brazil. 4. Merchant marine - Government policy - Brazil. I. Garlow, David Christopher. II. Title. III. Series.
HE597.B7 S26 1986

Santa Catarina, Brazil : its people, land, and production. 2nd updated ed. / published under the direction of Norberto I. Zadrozny. Florianópolis-SC-Brasil : Gaplan : CODESC, 1982. 55 p. : col. ill. ; 28 cm. LC Card 87-115191 DDC 330.981/64063 19
1. Santa Catarina (Brazil : State) - Economic conditions. I. Zadrozny, Norberto Ingo.
HC188.S26 S317 1982

SANTA CATARINA (BRAZIL : STATE) - ECONOMIC CONDITIONS.
Posição . [Florianópolis] , 1982. 135 p. ; LC Card 86-200246
HC188.S26 P67 1982

Santa Catarina, Brazil . Florianópolis-SC-Brasil , 1982. 55 p. : LC Card 87-115191 DDC 330.981/64063 19
HC188.S26 S317 1982

SANTA CATARINA (BRAZIL : STATE) - ECONOMIC CONDITIONS - STATISTICS.
Sinopse de informações dos municípios catarinenses. Florianópolis, SC , 1986. 155 leaves : LC Card 87-403943 DDC 330.981/64063 19
HC188.S26 S555 1986

SANTA CATARINA (BRAZIL : STATE) - ECONOMIC POLICY.
Luca, Walmor de. Moratória com diretas já . Brasília , 1984. 69 p. ; LC Card 86-152773
HC188.S26 L83 1984

Santa Catarina (Brazil : State). Secretaria da Indústria e do Comércio. Posição . [Florianópolis] , 1982. 135 p. ; LC Card 86-200246
HC188.S26 P67 1982

SANTA CATARINA, BRAZIL (STATE) - INDUSTRIES.
Avila, Luiz Gonçalves. Desenvolvimento industrial e rendimento da terra . Rio de Janeiro, RJ , 1985. 111 p. : LC Card 86-233493
HD1875.S26 A95 1985

Posição . [Florianópolis] , 1982. 135 p. ; LC Card 86-200246
HC188.S26 P67 1982

SANTA CLARA COUNTY, CALIF. - BIOGRAPHY.
Mahon, Thomas. Charged bodies . New York , c1985. 339 p. : ISBN 0-453-00487-3 LC Card 84-18957 DDC 338.4/76213817/0979473 19
HD9696.A3 U5666 1985
NYPL [JLD 86-1109]

SANTA CLARA COUNTY (CALIF.) - ECONOMIC CONDITIONS.
Azouaou, Alain. La Silicon Valley, un marché aux puces /. Paris , c1986. 237 p. : ISBN 2-85956-494-2 : LC Card 86-217069
HD9696.A3 U516 1986

Mahon, Thomas. Charged bodies . New York , c1985. 339 p. : ISBN 0-453-00487-3 LC Card 84-18957 DDC 338.4/76213817/0979473 19
HD9696.A3 U5666 1985
NYPL [JLD 86-1109]

SANTA CLARA COUNTY (CALIF.) - SOCIAL CONDITIONS.
Mahon, Thomas. Charged bodies . New York , c1985. 339 p. : ISBN 0-453-00487-3 LC Card 84-18957 DDC 338.4/76213817/0979473 19
HD9696.A3 U5666 1985
NYPL [JLD 86-1109]

Santa Croce sull'Arno (Italy) Il Pappagallo giallo . [Pisa] , Firenze , c1986. 194 p., [1] leaf of plates : LC Card 86-212573
HD9780.I82 P37 1986

Santa Cruz . Freitas, Benedicto. Rio de Janeiro , 1985-1987. 3 v. : LC Card 86-225964
HD1471.B72 R564 1985

SANTA CRUZ (BOLIVIA : DEPT.) - COMMERCE.
Gill, Lesley. Peasants, entrepreneurs, and social change . Boulder , 1987. xiv, 246 p. : ISBN 0-8133-7339-5 (pbk. : alk. paper) : LC Card 86-28207 DDC 303.4/0984/3 19
HD1870.S25 G54 1987

SANTA CRUZ FAZENDA (BRAZIL) - HISTORY.
Freitas, Benedicto. Santa Cruz . Rio de Janeiro , 1985-1987. 3 v. : LC Card 86-225964
HD1471.B72 R564 1985

Sánta, István. Kopcsó, István. Minőségfejlesztés az élelmiszer-termelésben . Budapest , 1984. 253 p. : ISBN 963-231-707-6 : LC Card 85-183244
HD9000.5 .K644 1984

Santa María de Cárdenas, Cecilia. El seguro agrícola como factor de desarrollo económico / Cecilia Santa María de Cárdenas, Myriam Rodríguez Daza. Bogotá : Universidad Santo Tomás de Aquino, Facultad de Economía, 1978. 168, 2, [43] p. : ill. ; 28 cm. Thesis (título de economista)--Universidad Santo Tomás de Aquino (Bogotá, Colombia), 1978. Bibliography: p. 166-168. LC Card 85-203482
1. Insurance, Agricultural. 2. Insurance, Agricultural - Colombia. 3. Agriculture - Economic aspects - Colombia. I. Rodríguez Daza, Myriam. II. Title.
HG9966 .S25 1978

Santacoloma, Juan Francisco.
Modelos macroeconómicos, ejercicios resueltos / Juan Francisco Santacoloma Sanz. Bilbao : Universidad de Deusto, 1985. 209 p. : ill. ; 23 cm. (Serie Economía. 12) ISBN 84-7485-059-2 LC Card 86-201846
1. Economics - Mathematical models - Examinations, questions, etc. 2. Macroeconomics - Mathematical models - Examinations, questions, etc. I. Series: Publicaciones de la Universidad de Deusto. Economía, 12. II. Title.
HB141 .S276 1985

Modelos macroeconómicos en economías abiertas / por Juan Francisco Santacoloma Sanz. Bilbao : Universidad de Deusto, 1983. 3 v. : ill. ; 23 cm. (Publicaciones de la Universidad de Deusto. Economía. 8-10) Vol. 3 has cover title: El sector exterior y las repercusiones internacionales. Bibliography: v. 3, p. 238-247. ISBN 84-7485-037-1 (set) LC Card 84-168556 DDC 339/.0724 19
1. Economics - Mathematical models. 2. International economic relations - Mathematical models. 3. States, Small - Economic conditions - Mathematical models. I. Title.
HB141 .S28 1983 ***NYPL [JLL 86-351]***

SANT'ALBERTO (RAVENNA, ITALY) - ECONOMIC CONDITIONS.
Cesare Zavattini presenta La civiltà delle acque . [Bologna] [1985] 272 p., 24 p. of plates : LC Card 86-105989 DDC 945/.47 19
HC308.S33 C47 1985

SANT'ALBERTO (RAVENNA, ITALY) - HISTORY.
Cesare Zavattini presenta La civiltà delle acque . [Bologna] [1985] 272 p., 24 p. of plates : LC Card 86-105989 DDC 945/.47 19
HC308.S33 C47 1985

SANT'ALBERTO (RAVENNA, ITALY) - INDUSTRIES - HISTORY.
Cesare Zavattini presenta La civiltà delle acque . [Bologna] [1985] 272 p., 24 p. of plates : LC Card 86-105989 DDC 945/.47 19
HC308.S33 C47 1985

SANT'ALBERTO (RAVENNA, ITALY) - SOCIAL CONDITIONS.
Cesare Zavattini presenta La civiltà delle acque . [Bologna] [1985] 272 p., 24 p. of plates : LC Card 86-105989 DDC 945/.47 19
HC308.S33 C47 1985

Santana, Roberto. Campesinado indígena y el desafío de la modernidad / Roberto Santana. 1a ed. [Quito, Ecuador] : Centro Andino de Acción Popular, 1983. 209 p. : ill. ; 22 cm. (Cuaderno de discusión popular . no. 7) Bibliography: p. 199-209. LC Card 84-156117 DDC 330.9866/074/08998 19
1. Indians of South America - Ecuador - Economic conditions. 2. Rural development - Ecuador. 3. Agriculture - Economic aspects - Ecuador. 4. Indians of South America - Ecuador - Loja (Province) - Economic conditions. I. Title.
F3721.3.E25 S26 1983
NYPL [HBC 86-2225]

Santarcangelo, Maria Candida Vergueiro. A situação da mulher / Maria Candida Vergueiro Santarcangelo ; prefácio, Teófilo Cavalcanti filho. São Paulo : Editora Soma, 1980. 389 p. ; 21 cm. Bibliography: p. 377-385.
1. Women - Brazil - Social conditions. 2. Women - Social conditions. I. Title. ***NYPL [JLD 86-625]***

Santen, J. van. Arbeid, plicht en vrijheid / J. van Santen. Nijmegen : SUN, c1985. 160 p. ; 22 cm. Includes bibliographical references and index. ISBN 90-6168-247-9 : LC Card 86-117515
1. Work ethic. 2. Work ethic - Netherlands. 3. Communist ethics. I. Title.
HD4905 .S26 1985

Santi, Ettore, 1948- L'Europa sindacale agli inizi degli anni '80 . Bologna , c1982. 385 p. : LC Card 84-140478 DDC 331.88/094 19
HD6657 .E89 1982

Santiago de Chile. Instituto Chileno de Educación Cooperativa. see **Instituto Chileno de Educación Cooperativa.**

Santiago de Chile. Instituto Latinoamericano del Fierro y el Acero. see **Instituto Latinoamericano del Fierro y el Acero.**

Santiago, Lilia Quindoza, 1949- Synthesis, before and beyond February 1986 . [Philippines] , 1986. xiv, 114 p. : ISBN 971-91058-0-1 (pbk.) LC Card 87-112023 DDC 338.9599 19
HC452 .S96 1986

SANTIAGO METROPOLITAN AREA (CHILE) - OCCUPATIONS.
Aldunate B., Adolfo. Análisis tipológico del trabajador del Gran Santiago e impacto sobre el ingreso de las políticas redistributivas, 1970-1971 /. [Santiago, Chile?] [1972] iv, 9, [35] p. ; LC Card 83-169296
HC193.S23 A43 1972

Santisteban, Carlos. see **Malpica Silva Santisteban, Carlos.**

Santisteban, Carlos Malpica Silva. see **Malpica Silva Santisteban, Carlos.**

SANTO DOMINGO (ANTIOQUIA, COLOMBIA) - ECONOMIC CONDITIONS.
Informe general y proyecto de parcelación,

Antioquia # 2 (Barbosa y Santo Domingo) /. Bogotá, D.E. , 1964. 2, 73, 16 leaves, [1] leaf of plates : LC Card 85-107102
HD1476.C72 B375 1964

Santoro, Vittorio. Profili funzionali e operativi delle casse rurali e artigiane / Vittorio Santoro. Milano : Giuffrè, [1984] 181 p. ; 25 cm. (Quaderni di banca, borsa e titoli di credito . 8) Includes bibliographical references and indexes. ISBN 88-14-00380-7 : LC Card 85-147834
1. Banks and banking, Cooperative - Italy. 2. Agricultural cooperative credit associations - Italy. I. Title. II. Series.
HG2039.I8 S26 1984 ***NYPL [JLE 86-3669]***

Santos, Corcino Medeiros dos. Economia e sociedade do Rio Grande do Sul : século XVIII / Corcino Medeiros dos Santos. São Paulo, SP, Brasil : Companhia Editora Nacional, 1984. xxi, 216 p. : ill. ; 21 cm. (Brasiliana. v. 379) "Em convênio com o Instituto Nacional do Livro, Fundação Nacional Pro-Memória." Bibliography: p. 209-216. ISBN 85-04-00203-9 : LC Card 85-199838
1. Rio Grande do Sul (Brazil) - Commerce - History - 18th century. 2. Land settlement - Brazil - Rio Grande do Sul - History - 18th century. 3. Rio Grande do Sul (Brazil) - History - 18th century. 4. Rio de la Plata Region - History - 18th century. 5. Colonia del Sacramento (Uruguay) - History - 18th century. I. Title.
HF3409.R56 S25 1984

Santos Graça, A. (António), 1882-1956. O poveiro / A. Santos Graça. 2a. ed. Póvoa de Varzim : Câmara Municipal da Póvoa de Varzim, 1982. 238, xvi p., [29] p. of plates : ill. ; 22 cm. Cover title. Reprint. Originally published: Póvao de Varzim : A. Santos Graça, 1932. Includes bibliographical references and index. LC Card 83-215678
1. Fishers - Portugal - Póvoa de Varzim - Social conditions. 2. Póvoa de Varzim (Portugal) - Social life and customs. I. Title.
HD8039.F66 P67 1982

Santos, José Carlos de Souza.
Demanda de fatores e ofertas na agricultura brasileira : subsídios para formulação de políticas agrícolas / José Carlos de Souza Santos. Rio de Janeiro : Programa Nacional de Pesquisa Econômica, 1983. 110 p. ; 30 cm. (Série Fac-símile . no. 11) "Versão apresentada ao PNPE en dezembro/82." Bibliography: p. 109-110. LC Card 87-403023 DDC 338.1/0981 19
1. Agriculture - Economic aspects - Brazil - Econometric models. 2. Agriculture and state - Brazil - Econometric models. 3. Elasticity (Economics) - Econometric models. I. Title. II. Series.
HD1872 .S25 1983

Demanda de fatores, energia e substituição na indústria brasileira, 1970/79 / José Carlos de Souza Santos. São Paulo : Instituto de Pesquisas Econômicas, 1986. 183 p. : ill. ; 23 cm. (Série Ensaios econômicos . no. 55) Summary in English. Bibliography: p. 171-180. LC Card 86-234783
1. Production functions (Economic theory) - Econometric models. 2. Brazil - Industries - Energy consumption - Econometric models. 3. Renewable energy sources - Brazil - Econometric models. I. Series: Ensaios econômicos (Universidade de São Paulo. Instituto de Pesquisas Econômicas) , 55. II. Title.
HB241 .S26 1986

Santos, Madalena Herculano dos. Condições de vida nos municípios paraibanos / Madalena Herculano dos Santos, Martha Gonçalves da Silva, Luiz Rodrigues Kehrle. João Pessoa (PB) : Secretaria do Planejamento e Coordenação Geral, Fundação Instituto de Planejamento da Paraíba ; Brasília, DF : Instituto de Planejamento Econômico e Social, Instituto de Planejamento : 103 p. : ill., maps ; 22 cm. (Série Instrumentos para a ação . 4) Bibliography: p. 103. LC Card 87-403990 DDC 330.981/33063 19
1. Paraíba, Brazil (State) - Economic conditions. 2. Paraíba (Brazil : State) - Social conditions. I. Silva, Martha Gonçalves da. II. Kehrle, Luiz Rodrigues. III. Fundação Instituto de Planejamento da Paraíba. IV. Instituto de Planejamento Econômico e Social. Instituto de Planejamento. V. UNICEF. VI. Title. VII. Series.
HC188.P343 S26 1986

Santos, Milton. Espaço e sociedade : ensaios / Milton Santos. Petrópolis [Brazil] : Editora Vozes, 1979. 152 p. : ill. ; 21 cm. Includes bibliographies. LC Card 80-109991
1. Urbanization - Developing countries - Addresses, essays, lectures. 2. Anthropo-geography - Addresses, essays, lectures. I. Title.
HT151 .S238 ***NYPL [JLD 81-405]***

Santos, Pedro Ribeiro dos. Génese e estrutura da Guarda Fiscal : ensaio histórico / Pedro Ribeiro dos Santos. [Lisbon] : Impr. Nacional-Casa da Moeda, [1985] 193 p., [9] leaves of plates : col. ill. ; 24 cm. Bibliography: p. 191-193. LC Card 87-400399 DDC 354.4690072/46 19
1. Portugal. Guarda Fiscal - History. 2. Customs adminsitration - Portugal - History. I. Title.
HJ6996 .A25 1985

Santos, Silvio Aparecido dos. Criação de empresas de alta tecnologia . São Paulo . 192, [1] p. ; LC Card 87-403991 DDC 338.4/362/000981 19
HC190.H53 C75 1987

Santos, Taís de Freitas. Moura, Hélio A. de (Hélio Augusto) Dinâmica demográfica recente dos estados e microrregiões do Nordeste, 1960/1980 /. Recife [Brazil] , 1986. 95 p., [6] folded p. of plates : LC Card 87-131106 DDC 304.6/0981/3 19
HB3564.N66 M68 1986

Sanyal, Bikas C. Bose, P. K. Graduate employment and higher education in West Bengal /. Paris , New Delhi , 1983. vi, 288, [1] p. : ISBN 0-85226-078-4 (pbk.) LC Card 83-163900 DDC 331.11/423 19
HD6278.I52 W473 1983
NYPL [JLD 86-2269]

Sanz de Santamaría, Alejandro. Reproducción de fuerza de trabajo, educación y migración en el sector rural colombiano /. Bogotá, Colombia , 1985. 98, [52] p. : LC Card 87-402979 DDC 331.1/09861 19
HD5757.A6 R46 1985

Sanz, Jorge Ovando. see **Ovando, Jorge.**

São mesmo nossos os minerais não-energéticos? /. Silva, Roberto Gama e. Rio de Janeiro, RJ , 1985. 164 p. : LC Card 86-153246
HD9506.B72 S55 1985

São Paulo (Brazil : State). Governor (1982- : Montoro) O orçamento de São Paulo para 1984 / André Franco Montoro. A administração governamental em 1979-82 / José Serra. São Paulo : Governo Democrático de São Paulo, Secretaria de Economia e Planejamento, 1983. 24 p. ; 22 cm. LC Card 87-130676 DDC 354.81/6100722 19
1. Budget - Brazil - São Paulo (State). I. Montoro, André Franco. II. Serra, José. Administração governamental em 1979-82. 1983. III. Title. IV. Title: Administração governamental em 1979-82.
HJ2080.5.S3 S26 1983

SÃO PAULO (BRAZIL : STATE) - INDUSTRIES - LOCATION.
Identificação e caracterização de agrupamentos industriais como subsídio à política de desenvolvimento regional. São Paulo , 1981. 134, 17, 60 p. : LC Card 86-146114
HC188.S3 I34 1981

SÃO PAULO (BRAZIL : STATE) - PUBLIC WORKS - FINANCE.
Fontes de financiamento aos municípios. São Paulo , 1984. 175 p. ; LC Card 85-221901
HJ925 .F66 1984

São Paulo (Brazil : State). Secretaria da Indústria, Comércio, Ciencia e Tecnologia. Manual básico do exportador. [São Paulo] [1985] 270 p. : LC Card 86-200367
HF3407 .M35 1985

São Paulo (Brazil : State). Secretaria de Agricultura e Abastecimento. Coordenadoria de Abastecimento. Seminário Nacional de Abastecimento Alimentar em Grandes Cidades--a Experiência de São Paulo (1984 : São Paulo, Brazil) Anais /. São Paulo, São Paulo, Brasil , 1984. xii, 421 p. : LC Card 87-404933 DDC 363.8/0981/61 19
HD9014.B83 S447 1984

São Paulo (Brazil : State). Secretaria de Estado de Relações do Trabalho. Data-base . [São Paulo] , 1986. 259 p. : LC Card 87-403668 DDC 331.88/025/8161 19
HD6615.S32 D37 1986

São Paulo (Brazil : State). Secretaria do Interior. Coordenadoria de Ação Regional. Identificação e caracterização de agrupamentos industriais como subsídio à política de desenvolvimento regional. São Paulo , 1981. 134, 17, 60 p. : LC Card 86-146114
HC188.S3 I34 1981

SÃO PAULO (BRAZIL : STATE) - SOCIAL CONDITIONS - STATISTICS.
Regiões de governo . São Paulo , 1985. [255] p. : LC Card 86-164322
HC188.S3 R44 1985

São Paulo (Brazil). Divisão de Iconografia e Museus. 1o. de maio . [São Paulo] , 1985. 80 p. : LC Card 86-200658
HD8286 .A13 1985

SÃO PAULO (BRAZIL) - POLITICS AND GOVERNMENT.
Muszynski, Maria Judith de Brito. O impacto político das migrações internas . São Paulo , 1986. 169 p. : LC Card 86-234794
HB2023 .M87 1986

São Paulo (Brazil). Secretaria Municipal do Planejamento. Cortiços em São Paulo . São Paulo , 1986. 195, [2] p. : LC Card 87-119201 DDC 363.5/8 19
HD7287.96.B62 S263 1986

SÃO PAULO, BRAZIL (STATE) - ECONOMIC CONDITIONS.
Kuznesof, Elizabeth Anne. Household economy and urban development . Boulder , 1986. 216 p. : ISBN 0-8133-7181-3 : LC Card 85-31491 DDC 307.7/64/098161 19
HC188.S3 K89 1986 ***NYPL [JLE 87-711]***

Saes, Flávio Azevedo Marques de, 1948- Crédito e bancos no desenvolvimento da economia paulista, 1850-1930 /. São Paulo , 1986. 238 p. : LC Card 87-144659 DDC 332.1/0981/61 19
HG2889.S25 S24 1986

Salles, Iraci Galvão. Trabalho, progresso e a sociedade civilizada . São Paulo [Brasília] , 1986. 145 p. ; LC Card 86-224281
HD8289.S282 S24 1986

SÃO PAULO, BRAZIL (STATE) - ECONOMIC CONDITIONS - STATISTICS.
Regiões de governo . São Paulo , 1985. [255] p. : LC Card 86-164322
HC188.S3 R44 1985

São Paulo, Brazil (State). Secretaria de Economia e Planejamento. Coordenadoria de Ação Regional.
Fontes de financiamento aos municípios. São Paulo , 1984. 175 p. ; LC Card 85-221901
HJ925 .F66 1984

Regiões de governo . São Paulo , 1985. [255] p. : LC Card 86-164322
HC188.S3 R44 1985

São Paulo, Brazil (State). Secretaria de Economia e Planejamento. Coordinating Division for Regional Action. see **São Paulo, Brazil (State). Secretaria de Economia e Planejamento. Coordenadoria de Ação Regional.**

SÃO SEBASTIÃO REGION (SÃO PAULO, BRAZIL) - ECONOMIC CONDITIONS.
Silva, Armando Corrêa da. O litoral norte do Estado de São Paulo . São Paulo , 1975. 273 p. : LC Card 85-134276
HC189.S343 S58 1975

SÃO SEBASTIÃO REGION (SÃO PAULO, BRAZIL) - POPULATION.
Silva, Armando Corrêa da. O litoral norte do Estado de São Paulo . São Paulo , 1975. 273 p. : LC Card 85-134276
HC189.S343 S58 1975

SÃO SEBASTIÃO REGION (SÃO PAULO, BRAZIL) - RURAL CONDITIONS.
Silva, Armando Corrêa da. O litoral norte do Estado de São Paulo . São Paulo , 1975. 273 p. : LC Card 85-134276
HC189.S343 S58 1975

São Vicente, Brazil (Capitania) see **São Paulo, Brazil (State)**

Saperstein, Rose, 1956- Read your way to the top with the guide / Rose Saperstein and James Joseph ; illustrations by Doug Keith. Seattle, Wash. : Bluechip Publishers, c1987. 83 p. : ill. ; 23 cm. (A Bluechip business book) Bibliography: p. [71]-73. Includes index. ISBN 0-930251-00-8 (pbk.) : LC Card 87-310 DDC 428.4/3 19
1. Business. 2. Rapid reading. 3. Reading comprehension. I. Joseph, James, 1954-. II. Title. III.

Series.
HF5351 .S34 1987

Saphāp læ 'ōkāt nai kānthamngān nai kitčhakān m rāingān phon kānsksā wičhai. [Bangkok] : Krom Rǣngngān, Krasūang Mahātthai, [2509 i.e. 1966] 2, 35 p., [5] leaves of plates : ill. ; 28 cm. ('Ēkkasān . māilēk 12) In Thai. Economic survey of employment opportunities and working conditions in mineral ore mines of southern Thailand. LC Card 80-911179
1. Tin miners - Thailand, Southern - Supply and demand. 2. Miners - Thailand, Southern - Supply and demand. 3. Tin miners - Thailand, Southern. 4. Miners - Thailand, Southern. I. Thailand. Krom Rǣngngān. II. Series: 'Ēkkasān (Thailand. Krom Rǣngngān) , māilēk 12.
HD8039.M72 T527 1966

Sapir, André.
Ekonomska reforma i migracije u Jugoslaviji : ekonometrijski model = Economic reform and migration in Yugoslavia : an econometric model / André Sapir. Zagreb : Centar za istraživanje migracija Zagreb, 1983. 56 p. ; 29 cm. (Rasprave o migracijama . br. 81 = no. 81) Translated from English into Serbo-Croatian (roman) Bibliography: p. [53]-56. LC Card 86-183906
1. Yugoslavia - Economic conditions - 1945- - Econometric models. 2. Yugoslavia - Emigration and immigration - Econometric models. I. Title. II. Title: Economic reform and migration in Yugoslavia. III. Series: Rasprave o migracijama , br. 81.
HC407 .S26 1983

Langhammer, Rolf J. Economic impact of generalized tariff preferences /. Aldershot, Hants, England , Brookfield, Vt. , 1988. p. cm. ISBN 0-566-05338-1 : LC Card 87-15045 DDC 382.7/53 19
HF1721 .L35 1988

Sapolsky, Joann. Catalogue of state shared revenue sources distributed between 1973-1986. Tallahassee, Fla. (House Office Bldg., Tallahassee 32301) : Florida Advisory Council on Intergovernmental Relations, [1986] v, 76 leaves : ill. ; 28 cm. "September 1986." "86-4." LC Card 86-623224 DDC 336.1/85/09759 19
1. Revenue sharing - Florida. 2. State-local relations - Florida. I. Florida Advisory Council on Intergovernmental Relations. II. Title.
HJ375 .S26 1986

Sapounas, Giōrgos S. Epharmosmenē analysē tēs zētēsēs : theōria, methodoi kai epharmoges / Giōrgos S. Sapounas. Athēna : Agrotikē Trapeza Hellados, 1985. 483 p. : ill. ; 24 cm. (Eidikes epistēmonikes meletes . 1) Bibliography: p. 449-483. LC Card 86-212306
1. Produce trade - Mathematical models. 2. Demand functions (Economic theory). I. Title. II. Series.
HD9000.5 .S29 1985

Sapozhnikov, A. D.
Gosudarstvenno-monopolisticheskiĭ kapitalizm i razmeshchenie proizvoditel'nykh sil /. Moskva , 1984. 182 p. ; LC Card 84-239188
HC240 .G565 1984

Sappington, David Edward Michael. Besanko, David, 1955- Designing regulatory policy with limited information /. Chur, Switzerland , New York , c1987. viii, 80 p. : ISBN 3-7186-0385-3 (pbk.) LC Card 87-277 DDC 351.82/6 19
HD3612 .B47 1987

SAR-E POL (AFGHANISTAN) - ECONOMIC CONDITIONS.
Jebens, Albrecht. Wirtschafts- und sozialgeographische Untersuchung über das Heimgewerbe in Nordafghanistan unter besonderer Berücksichtigung der Mittelstadt Sar-e-Pul . Tübingen , 1983. xii, 415 p., [2] folded leaves of plates : LC Card 86-128235
HD2346.A52 S275 1983

SAR-E POL (AFGHANISTAN) - SOCIAL CONDITIONS.
Jebens, Albrecht. Wirtschafts- und sozialgeographische Untersuchung über das Heimgewerbe in Nordafghanistan unter besonderer Berücksichtigung der Mittelstadt Sar-e-Pul . Tübingen , 1983. xii, 415 p., [2] folded leaves of plates : LC Card 86-128235
HD2346.A52 S275 1983

Saradamoni, K. (Kunjulekshmi), 1928- Women, work, and society /. Calcutta , 1985. xvi, 430 p. : LC Card 86-900827 DDC 331.4 19
HD6052 .W565 1982 ***NYPL [JLE 87-1019]***

Saraf, B. P., 1939- Capital taxation in India / B.P. Saraf. New Delhi : Deep & Deep, c1983. viii, 268 p. ; 22 cm. Includes index. Bibliography: p. [256]-266. LC Card 83-902683 DDC 343.5405/3 345.40353 19
1. Wealth tax - India. 2. Inheritance and transfer tax - India. 3. Capital levy - India. I. Title.
HJ4126.I45 S27 1983 ***NYPL [JLD 86-3821]***

Saragoza, Alex. The Monterrey elite and the Mexican State, 1880-1940 / by Alex M. Saragoza. 1st ed. Austin : University of Texas Press, c1988. p. cm. Bibliography: p. Includes index. ISBN 0-292-71113-1 LC Card 87-23779 DDC 305.5/234/097213 19
1. Capitalists and financiers - Mexico - Monterrey - History. 2. Capitalism - Mexico - Monterrey - History. 3. Monterrey (Mexico) - Industries - History. 4. Elite (Social sciences) - Mexico - Monterrey - History. 5. Garza-Sada family. I. Title.
HG185.M6 S27 1988

Sárándi, Imre. Világgazdasági korszakváltások és a mezőgazdasági termékforgalom : nemzetközi intézménytörténet, kapitalizmus, szocializmus / Sárándi Imre. [Budapest] : Szövetkezeti Kutató Intézet, [1985] 92 p. ; 29 cm. (Közlemények, 0133-4905 . 192) Includes bibliographical references. LC Card 86-218536
1. Agriculture - Economic aspects. 2. Agricultural laws and legislation. 3. Agriculture - Economic aspects - Europe, Eastern. 4. Agricultural laws and legislation - Europe, Eastern. I. Series: Közlemények / Szövetkezeti Kutató Intézet, 192. II. Title.
HD1415 .S25 1985

Sarapata, Adam. Automation and industrial workers . Oxford [Oxfordshire] , New York , 1979- v. : ISBN 0-08-023339-2 (v. 1, pt. 1) : LC Card 79-40811 DDC 331
HD6331 .A93 1979 ***NYPL [JLM 82-242]***

Sarasvati vihara series. For additional listing of contents, see Old Catalog.
(v. 35) Raghu Vira. A comprehensive English-Hindi dictionary of governmental & educational words & phrases ... /. New Delhi , 1962. 189, 1572 p. ; ***NYPL [JLF 87-203]***

Saraswathy Rao, Y. Public enterprises, a state level perspective /. Delhi , New Delhi , 1986. xix, 287 p. ; ISBN 81-7018-370-7 : LC Card 86-902715 DDC 338.6/2/095484 19
HD4295.A5 P8 1986

Saravia, Alvaro Ortíz. see **Ortíz Saravia, Alvaro.**

SARC Association, Bangladesh. Rahman, M. L. (Mohammad Lutfur), 1933- SAARC facts and economic development /. Dhaka , 1986. xvi, 200 p. : LC Card 87-901419 DDC 338.954 19
HC430.6 .R37 1986

Sardar Patel Institute of Economic and Social Research. Hirway, Indira. Wage employment programmes in rural development . New Delhi , c1986. vi, 112 p. ; ISBN 81-204-0072-0 : LC Card 86-903398 DDC 331.2/95475 19
HD5070.G85 H57 1986

Sardegna, crisi, dipendenza, alternativa : atti del convegno regionale organizzato dal PdUP, Cagliari, 28 marzo 1981. [Cagliari] : CUEC, [1984?] 223 p. ; 24 cm. LC Card 84-251167
1. Sardinia - Economic policy - Congresses. 2. Sardinia - Social policy - Congresses. 3. Sardinia - Politics and government. I. Partito di unità proletaria per il comunismo.
HC307.S3 S29 1984

Sardei-Biermann, Sabine. Jugendliche zwischen Schule und Arbeitswelt : zur Bedeutung der Schule für den Übergang in den Beruf / Sabine Sardei-Biermann. München : DJI Verlag Deutsches Jugendinstitut, c1984. v, 318 p. ; 21 cm. (DJI Forschungsbericht) Bibliography: p. 298-318. ISBN 3-87966-219-3 LC Card 84-240405
1. Occupational training - Germany, West. 2. Employees, Training of - Germany, West. 3. Youth - Employment - Germany, West. I. Title. II. Series.
HD5715.5.G4 S27 1984

Sardello, Robert J., 1942- Stirrings of culture /. Dallas, Tex. , 1986. xix, 250 p. ; ISBN 0-911005-07-2 : LC Card 86-24028 DDC 306 19
HM101 .S786 1986 ***NYPL [JFF 87-151]***

SARDINIA - ECONOMIC POLICY - CONGRESSES.
Sardegna, crisi, dipendenza, alternativa . [Cagliari] [1984?] 223 p. ; LC Card 84-251167
HC307.S3 S29 1984

SARDINIA - POLITICS AND GOVERNMENT.
Sardegna, crisi, dipendenza, alternativa . [Cagliari] [1984?] 223 p. ; LC Card 84-251167
HC307.S3 S29 1984

SARDINIA - SOCIAL POLICY - CONGRESSES.
Sardegna, crisi, dipendenza, alternativa . [Cagliari] [1984?] 223 p. ; LC Card 84-251167
HC307.S3 S29 1984

Sardoni, Claudio. Marx and Keynes on economic recession : the theory of unemployment and effective demand / Claudio Sardoni. New York : New York University Press, 1987. xiv, 152 p. ; 23 cm. Based on the author's thesis (doctoral--University of Adelaide, 1982). Bibliography: p. 144-150. Includes index. ISBN 0-8147-7871-2 : LC Card 87-13749 DDC 338.5/42 19
1. Business cycles. 2. Marxian economics. 3. Keynesian economics. 4. Unemployment. 5. Demand (Economic theory). I. Title.
HB3714 .S27 1987

Sárfalvi, Béla. Probáld, Ferenc, 1941- Az európai tőkés országok gazdaságföldrajza . Budapest , 1984. 361 p. : ISBN 963-17-7607-7 : LC Card 85-154701
HC240 .P738 1984

Sargan, John Denis. Contributions to econometrics / John Denis Sargan ; edited with an introduction by Esfandiar Maasoumi. Cambridge ; New York : Cambridge University Press, 1988- p. cm. Bibliography: v. 1, p. ISBN 0-521-32570-6 (v. 1) LC Card 87-6328 DDC 330/.028 19
1. Econometrics. I. Maasoumi, Esfandiar, 1950-. II. Title.
HB139 .S37 1988

Sargent, Alice G., 1939- Beyond sex roles /. St. Paul , c1985. xxix, 563 p. : ISBN 0-314-85293-X (pbk.) : LC Card 84-21950 DDC 305.3 19
HQ1075.5.U6 B49 1985
NYPL [JLF 86-1144]

Sargent, David R. Successful investing . New York , 1987. 529 p. : ISBN 0-671-64762-8 (pbk.) : LC Card 87-19736 DDC 332.6/78 19
HG4521 .S823 1987

Sargent, John. Fiscal and monetary policy /. Toronto , Buffalo , c1986. xviii, 339 p. : ISBN 0-8020-7263-1 (pbk.) LC Card 86-672943 DDC 336.3/0971 19
HJ793 .F55 1986 ***NYPL [JLE 87-511]***

Sargent, Thomas J.
Dynamic macroeconomic theory. Manuelli, Rodolfo E. Exercises in dynamic macroeconomic theory / Rodolfo E. Manuelli and Thomas J. Sargent. Cambridge, Mass. , 1987. xi, 223 p. ; ISBN 0-674-27476-8 (pbk. : alk. paper) LC Card 86-25767 DDC 339/.0729 19
HB172.5 .S27 1987 Suppl.

Macroeconomic theory / Thomas J. Sargent. 2nd ed. Boston : Academic Press, c1987. xxii, 510 p. : ill. ; 24 cm. (Economic theory, econometrics, and mathematical economics) Includes bibliographies and indexes. ISBN 0-12-619751-2 (alk. paper) LC Card 86-28778 DDC 339/.01 19
1. Macroeconomics. I. Title.
HB172.5 .S27 1987

Macroeconomic theory. Whiteman, Charles H. Problems in macroeconomic theory : solutions to exercises from Thomas J. Sargent's Macroeconomic theory, second editon / Charles H. Whiteman. Boston , c1987. ix, 266 p. ; ISBN 0-12-619752-0 (pbk.) LC Card 87-17398 DDC 339 19
HB172.5 .S27 1987 Suppl. 2

Manuelli, Rodolfo E. Exercises in dynamic macroeconomic theory /. Cambridge, Mass. , 1987. xi, 223 p. ; ISBN 0-674-27476-8 (pbk. : alk. paper) LC Card 86-25767 DDC 339/.0729 19
HB172.5 .S27 1987 Suppl.

Sarhan, M. E. McCoy, John Henry, 1912- Livestock and meat marketing /. New York , c1988. vii, 642 p. : ISBN 0-442-20488-4 LC Card 87-23136 DDC 381/.416/00973 19
HD9415 .M25 1988

Sarja D (Finland. Ympäristön- ja luonnonsuojeluosasto) .
(14) Wallin, Markku. Jätteiden hyötykäyttö kansantaloudessa /. [Helsinki] [1986] 87 p. :

ISBN 951-46-9505-4 LC Card 86-216953
HD9975.F52 W35 1986

Sarkar, Himansu Bhusan. Trade and commercial activities of southern India in the Malayo-Indonesian world, up to A.D. 1511 / H.B. Sarkar. Calcutta : Firma KLM, 1986- v. <1- > : maps ; 22 cm. Bibliography: v. 1, p. [363]-370. Includes index. LC Card 87-900744 DDC 382/.09548/059 19
1. India, South - Commerce - Asia, Southeastern - History. 2. Asia, Southeastern - Commerce - India, South - History. I. Title.
HF3788.A78 S25 1986

Sarkar, R. L. Tea plantation workers in the eastern Himalayas . Delhi , 1986. xxxi, 255 p. : ISBN 81-7043-055-0 : LC Card 86-903466
HD8039.T182 I48 1986

Sarlēs, Dēmētrēs. Hoi politikes pleures tēs entaxēs tēs Helladas stēn EOK : hē "eurōkommounistikē" outopia tēs "EOK tōn ergazomenōn" kai ho pragmatikos dromos tēs palēs gia tēn Ethnikē anexartēsia, tē dēmokratia kai to sosialismo / Dēmētrē Sarlē.2. ekd. Athēna : Ekdoseis "Synchronē Epochē", 1981. 212 p. ; 21 cm. LC Card 83-170595
1. European Economic Community - Greece. 2. Greece - Politics and government - 1974-. 3. Communism - Greece. 4. Communism - Europe. I. Title.
HC241.25.G8 S27 1981

Sarlis, Dimitris. see **Sarlēs, Dēmētrēs.**

Sarma, J. S. Cereal feed use in the Third World : past trends and projections to 2000 / J.S Sarma. Washington, D.C. : International Food Policy Research Institute, c1986. 68 p. : ill. ; 26 cm. (Research report . 57) "December 1986." Bibliography: p. 67-68. ISBN 0-89629-058-1 (pbk.) LC Card 86-27355 DDC 338.1/7325/091724 19
1. Flour and feed trade - Developing countries - Forecasting. 2. Grain trade - Developing countries - Forecasting. 3. Animal industry - Developing countries - Forecasting. I. Series: Research report (International Food Policy Research Institute) , 57. II. Title.
HD9052.D44 S27 1986

Sarma, N. A. International environment and India's economic development / N.A. Sarma. New Delhi : Abhinav Publications : Indian Council for Research on International Economic Relations, 1986. viii, 100 p. ; 22 cm. Includes bibliographical references and index. ISBN 81-7017-214-4 : LC Card 86-902210 DDC 338.954 19
1. India - Economic conditions - 1947-. 2. Economic development. 3. International economic relations. I. Title.
HC435.2 .S273 1986

Sarna, A. J. Boycott and blacklist : a history of Arab economic warfare against Israel / by Aaron J. Sarna. Totowa, N.J. : Rowman & Littlefield, 1986. xiv, 270 p. : 24 cm. Includes bibliographical references and index. ISBN 0-8476-7489-4 : LC Card 86-1891 DDC 337.5694/0174927 19
1. Economic sanctions, Arab countries - Israel. 2. Jewish-Arab relations - 1949-. 3. Arab countries - Foreign economic relations - Israel. 4. Israel - Foreign economic relations - Arab countries. I. Title.
HF1610.Z4 I87 1986
NYPL [*PXLB 86-6444]

SARNA KUNSTSTOFF AG - MANAGEMENT.
Kurmann, Bernadette, 1950- Firmenkultur am Beispiel der Sarna /. Bern [1985] 119 p. ; ISBN 3-258-03560-1 : LC Card 86-123837 DDC 338.7/6684/09494 19
HD9661.S94 S275 1985
NYPL [JLD 86-4028]

Sarnat, Marshall. International finance and trade /. Cambridge, Mass. , c1979. 2 v. : ISBN 0-88410-680-2 LC Card 79-11158 DDC 332.4/5 19
HG3881 .I57617 ***NYPL [JLL 80-187]***

SARNOFF, DAVID, 1891-1971.
Bilby, Kenneth. The general . New York , c1986. 326 p. ; ISBN 0-06-015568-X : LC Card 85-45621 DDC 384.54/092/4 B 19
HE8689.8 B55 1985
NYPL [MWES (Sarnoff, D.) 86-4682]

SAROAKO (INDONESIA) - ECONOMIC CONDITIONS.
Robinson, Kathryn May, 1949- Stepchildren of progress . Albany, N.Y. , c1986. xvi, 315 p. : ISBN 0-88706-119-2 LC Card 86-5847 DDC 307.7/66/095984 19
HD9539.N52 I547 1986
NYPL [JLE 86-4126]

SAROAKO (INDONESIA) - SOCIAL CONDITIONS.
Robinson, Kathryn May, 1949- Stepchildren of progress . Albany, N.Y. , c1986. xvi, 315 p. : ISBN 0-88706-119-2 LC Card 86-5847 DDC 307.7/66/095984 19
HD9539.N52 I547 1986
NYPL [JLE 86-4126]

Sarpellon, Giovanni. Understanding poverty /. Milano, Italy , c1984. 355 p. : LC Card 84-249441 DDC 339.4/6/094 19
HC240.9.P6 U53 1984 ***NYPL [JLD 86-1196]***

Sars, François de. Guide pratique du financement des industries agroalimentaires /. Paris [1986] 351 p. : LC Card 86-186921
HD9012.5 .G86 1986

Sarver, Eugene. The Eurocurrency market handbook : the global eurodeposit and related markets / Eugene Sarver. New York, N.Y. : New York Institute of Finance, c1988. xiii, 384 p. : map ; 24 cm. Bibliography: p. 358-363. Includes index. ISBN 0-13-296161-X LC Card 87-7739 DDC 332.4/5 19
1. Euro-dollar market. I. Title.
HG3897 .S27 1988

Sashkin, Marshall, 1944-
Experiencing management / Marshall Sashkin, William C. Morris. Reading, Mass. : Addison-Wesley, c1987. x, 234 p. : ill. ; 28 cm. "Designed for use with the text Management (4th ed.) by Don Hellriegel and John Slocum"--P. ix. Includes bibliographies. ISBN 0-201-11545-X (pbk.) : LC Card 86-28731 DDC 658.4/0352 19
1. Management - Simulation methods. I. Morris, William C. (William Clinton), 1928-. II. Hellriegel, Don. Management. III. Title.
HD30.26 .S27 1987

Making performance evaluation work : an M/C employee's guide to performance management. [Albany, N.Y.] : State of New York, Governor's Office of Employee Relations, c1986. 57 p. : ill. ; 23 cm. Adaptation of: A manager's guide to performance management. c1986. Bibliography: p. 55-57. ISBN 0-8144-2326-4 (pbk.) LC Card 86-209627 DDC 658.3/125 19
1. Performance standards. 2. Employees, Rating of. I. Sashkin, Marshall, 1944- Manager's guide to performance management. II. New York (State). Governor's Office of Employee Relations. III. Title.
HF5549.5.P35 S26 1986

Manager's guide to performance management. Sashkin, Marshall, 1944- Making performance evaluation work : an M/C employee's guide to performance management. [Albany, N.Y.] , c1986. 57 p. : ISBN 0-8144-2326-4 (pbk.) LC Card 86-209627 DDC 658.3/125 19
HF5549.5.P35 S26 1986

Saskatchewan Local Government Finance Commission. Final report of the Local Government Finance Commission, September 1986 / Saskatchewan Local Government Finance Commission. [Regina, Canada] : The Commission, [1986] xiii, 440 p. : ill. ; 28 cm. Includes bibliographical references. LC Card 87-163885 DDC 336/.014/7124 19
1. Local finance - Saskatchewan. I. Title.
HJ9352.S3 S37 1986

SASOLBURG (SOUTH AFRICA) - CENSUS.
Bevolkingsensus 1980 uitgesoekte statistiese streek Vereeniging/Vanderbijlpark/Sasolburg =. Pretoria [1985] xx, 301 p. : ISBN 0-621-09484-6 : LC Card 85-235498
HA4701.Z9 V474 1985

SASOLBURG (SOUTH AFRICA) - POPULATION - STATISTICS.
Bevolkingsensus 1980 uitgesoekte statistiese streek Vereeniging/Vanderbijlpark/Sasolburg =. Pretoria [1985] xx, 301 p. : ISBN 0-621-09484-6 : LC Card 85-235498
HA4701.Z9 V474 1985

Sasse, Jürgen. Deutsche Seeversicherung, 1958-1980 : Sammlung seeversicherungsrechtlicher Entscheidungen nebst Literaturverzeichnis / bearbeitet von Jürgen Sasse. Karlsruhe : Verlag Versicherungswirtschaft, 1982. 331 p. ; 21 cm. Bibliography: p. 313-318. Includes indexes. ISBN 3-88487-030-0 LC Card 83-190184
1. Insurance, Marine - Germany (West). I. Title.
HE964.5.G7 S27 1982

Sassen, Saskia. The mobility of labor and capital : a study in international investment and labor flow / Saskia Sassen. Cambridge [Cambridgeshire] ; New York : Cambridge University Press, 1988. p. cm. Includes index. ISBN 0-521-32227-8 LC Card 87-14586 DDC 331.12/791 19
1. Alien labor. 2. Capital movements. 3. Investments, Foreign. I. Title.
HD6300 .S37 1988

Sassier, Philippe. Les Français à la corbeille / Philippe Sassier, François de Witt. Paris : R. Laffont, c1985. 268 p. ; 24 cm. (Notre époque) Includes bibliographical references. ISBN 2-221-04729-X : LC Card 86-126750 DDC 332.64/244 19
1. Bourse de Paris. 2. Stock-exchange - France. 3. Stock-ownership - France. 4. Investments - France. I. Witt, François de, 1944-. II. Title.
HG4583 .S27 1985

Sassoon, David M. Bidding for projects financed by international lending agencies /. Aldershot, Hants. , c1982. vii, 345 p. : ISBN 0-566-03033-0 LC Card 82-210482 DDC 332.1/53 19
HD2365 .B52 1982 ***NYPL [JLG 85-120]***

Sassoon, Joseph. Economic policy in Iraq, 1932-1950 / Joseph Sassoon. London, England ; Totowa, N.J. : F. Cass, 1987. p. cm. Bibliography: p. Includes index. ISBN 0-7146-3305-4 : LC Card 87-6577 DDC 338.9567 19
1. Iraq - Economic policy. 2. Iraq - Foreign relations - Great Britain. 3. Great Britain - Foreign relations - Iraq. 4. Iraq - History - 1921-. I. Title.
HC415.4 .S27 1987

Sastraatmaja, Entang. Ekonomi & pembangunan : pengalaman Indonesia / Entang Sastraatmaja. Bandung : Armico, c1986. viii, 284 p. : ill. ; 21 cm. Cover title: Ekonomi pembangunan. LC Card 86-944011
1. Indonesia - Economic policy. I. Title. II. Title: Ekonomi dan pembangunan. III. Title: Ekonomi pembangunan.
HC447 .S363 1986

Sastre de Sá Torreta, Antoni. Quaderns d'història d'Algaida : Randa i les seves possessions / Antoni Sastre de Sá Torreta. Algaida : La Mata Escrita, 1983. 139 p., [8] p. of plates : ill. ; 21 cm. Bibliography: p. 135-136. LC Card 86-181627
1. Land tenure - Spain - Randa Region - History. 2. Land use - Spain - Randa Region - History. I. Title.
HD780.R36 S27 1983

Sata, Toshio, 1926- U. S.A.-Japan Conference on Manufacturing Research (1986 : Tokyo, Japan) Manufacturing research perspectives, U. S.A.-Japan . Amsterdam , New York , 1987. viii, 198 p. : ISBN 0-444-42868-2 LC Card 87-19851 DDC 338.4/767 19
HD9725 .U17 1986

SATELLITE COMMUNICATION SYSTEMS. see **ARTIFICIAL SATELLITES IN TELECOMMUNICATION.**

Satellite in revolt . McCaul, Colleen. Johannesburg, South Africa , 1987. 125 p., [11] p. of plates : ISBN 0-86982-314-0 (pbk.) LC Card 87-157406 DDC 330.9682/95063 19
HC905.Z7 K785 1987

SATELLITE INSTRUCTIONAL TELEVISION EXPERIMENT (INDIA) - CONGRESSES.
SITE to INSAT . New Delhi , 1986. viii, 165 p. : LC Card 86-902956 DDC 384.55/44/0954 19
HE8700.9.I5 S57 1986

Satellite Systems Engineering. Transponder supply & demand forecast. Bethesda, MD, U. S.A. , c1987. v, 150 p. : LC Card 87-403373 DDC 384.4/1 19
HE9721.U5 T73 1987

SATELLITES, ARTIFICIAL, IN TELECOMMUNICATION. see **ARTIFICIAL SATELLITES IN TELECOMMUNICATION.**

Sathiti thī samkhan, 2512. Čhangwat Phangngā = Some important statistics, 1969. Changwat Phang-nga. [Bangkok] : Samnakngān Sathiti hæng Chāt, Samnak Nāyok Ratthamontrī, [19]71. [11], 34 p., [1] leaf of plates : ill. (some col.), map ; 25 x 37 cm. ('Ekkasān kh S-SIS ch-no.

7-71) Chiefly tables. Thai and English. LC Card 83-921120 DDC 315.93 19
1. Phangnga (Thailand : Province) - Statistics. I. Thailand. Samnakngān Sathiti hæng Chāt. II. Title: Some important statistics, 1969. III. Series: 'Ēkkasān kh
HA4600.55.Z9 P428 1971

Sathiti thī samkhan, 2512, Čhangwat Krabī = Some important statistics, 1969, Changwat Krabi. [Bangkok] : Samnakngān Sathiti hæng Chāt, Samnak Nāyok Ratthamontrī, [19]71. [8], 36 leaves, [1] leaf of plates : col. ill., col. map ; 25 x 37 cm. ('Ēkkasān kh S-SIS ch-no. 8-71) Thai and English. LC Card 83-921122
1. Krabi (Thailand : Province) - Statistics. I. Thailand. Samnakngān Sathiti hæng Chāt. II. Title: Some important statistics, 1969, Changwat Krabi. III. Series: 'Ēkkasān kh
HA4600.55 .S275 1971

Sato, Hideo, 1942-
Japanese perspective. 1987. Canadian-Japanese economic relations in a triangular perspective / edited by Wendy Dobson. Toronto , Scarborough, Ont. [1987] vi, 54 p. : ISBN 0-88806-139-0 (pbk.) LC Card 87-169818 DDC 337.52071 19
HF1480.15.J3 C35 1987

Satō, Ryūzō, 1931- Trade friction and economic policy . Cambridge [Cambridgeshire] , New York , 1987. xii, 243 p. : ISBN 0-521-34446-8 LC Card 87-11694 DDC 382/.0952/073 19
HF3828.U5 T73 1987

Saturnino, o momento histórico do Congresso Nacional. Braga, Roberto Saturnino. Brasília , 1983. 58 p. ; LC Card 83-202638
HC187 .B76 1983

Satyanarayana. Parvathamma, C., 1928- Housing, rural poor, and their living conditions /. Delhi, India [1987] vi, 135 p. ; ISBN 81-212-0088-1 : LC Card 87-900831 DDC 363.5/8 19
HD7361.K27 P37 1987

Satzer, Rolf, 1958- Arnold, Alix, 1956- Kaputt und auch noch selber schuld . Reinbek bei Hamburg , c1986. 179, [1] p. : ISBN 3-499-15908-2 : LC Card 86-226114
HD7708 .A75 1986

Saúde e trabalho . Possas, Cristina de Albuquerque. Rio de Janeiro, RJ , 1981. xxxix, 324 p. : LC Card 82-132979 DDC 362.1/0981 19
RA418.3.B6 P68 1981 ***NYPL [JLD 86-1896]***

Saudi Arabia . Farsy, Fouad, 1946- London , New York , 1986. 264 p., [8] p. of plates : ISBN 0-7103-0128-6 LC Card 86-220645 DDC 330.953/8053 19
HC415.33 .F37 1986

SAUDI ARABIA - ECONOMIC CONDITIONS.
Farsy, Fouad, 1946- Saudi Arabia . London , New York , 1986. 264 p., [8] p. of plates : ISBN 0-7103-0128-6 LC Card 86-220645 DDC 330.953/8053 19
HC415.33 .F37 1986

A Guide to industrial investment /. Riyadh , 1986. vi, 286 p., [4] leaves of plates : LC Card 87-400301 DDC 332.6/7322538 19
HC415.33.Z9 I534 1986

SAUDI ARABIA - ECONOMIC POLICY.
Saudi Arabia. Wizārat al-Tahkṭīṭ. [Khuṭṭat al-Tanmiyah al-Rābi'ah, 1405-1410 H. English.] Fourth Development Plan, 1405-1410 A.H. (1985-1990 A.D.) [Riyadh] [1985?] xxxix, 435 p. : LC Card 86-202075 DDC 338.953/8 19
HC415.33 .S22 1985

SAUDI ARABIA - FOREIGN ECONOMIC RELATIONS - UNITED STATES.
Casillas, Rex J. Oil and diplomacy . New York , 1987. p. cm. ISBN 0-8240-8078-5 : LC Card 87-23769 DDC 337.730538 19
HF1456.5.S33 C37 1987

Saudi Arabia - Government. see **Saudi Arabia - Politics and government.**

SAUDI ARABIA - POLITICS AND GOVERNMENT.
Farsy, Fouad, 1946- Saudi Arabia . London , New York , 1986. 264 p., [8] p. of plates : ISBN 0-7103-0128-6 LC Card 86-220645 DDC 330.953/8053 19
HC415.33 .F37 1986

SAUDI ARABIA - PUBLIC LANDS.
Hajrah, Hassan Hamza. Public land distribution in Saudi Arabia /. London , New York , 1982. xxi, 280 p. : ISBN 0-582-78301-1 LC Card 83-232929 DDC 333.1/6/09538 19
HD853.Z7 H34 1982 ***NYPL [JLE 87-1566]***

Saudi Arabia. Wizārat al-Tahkṭīṭ. [Khuṭṭat al-Tanmiyah al-Rābi'ah, 1405-1410 H. English]
Fourth Development Plan, 1405-1410 A.H. (1985-1990 A.D.) [Riyadh] : Kingdom of Saudi Arabia, Ministry of Planning, [1985?] xxxix, 435 p. : col. ill. ; 29 cm. Translation of: Khuṭṭat al-Tanmiyah al-Rābi'ah, 1405-1410 H. LC Card 86-202075 DDC 338.953/8 19
1. Saudi Arabia - Economic policy. I. Title.
HC415.33 .S22 1985

Saudi oil policy and the changing world energy balance /. McHale, Thomas R. Boulder, Colo., U. S.A. , c1986. 17 p. ; ISBN 0-918714-09-5 (pbk.) : LC Card 87-119219 DDC 338.2/7282/09538 19
HD9502.A1 O28 no. 1 HD9576.S33

Sauer, Jørgen. Matthiasen, Leo. Informationsteknologi og arbejdsproces . Roskilde [1983?] 339 p. : ISBN 87-87893-19-3 LC Card 85-114664
HF5547.5 .M384 1983

Sauer, Robert L. Labor relations : structure and process / Robert L. Sauer, Keith E. Voelker. Columbus, Ohio : Merrill Pub. Co., c1987. x, 518 p. : ill. ; 25 cm. Includes bibliographies and index. ISBN 0-675-20207-8 LC Card 87-134391 DDC 331/.0973 19
1. Industrial relations - United States. 2. Collective bargaining - United States. I. Voelker, Keith E. II. Title.
HD8066 .S28 1987

Sauer, Walter, 1951- Der Dressierte Arbeiter . München , c1984. 211 p. : ISBN 3-406-09286-1 LC Card 84-181068 DDC 331.25 19
HD6331.2.G28 D74 1984

SAUERLAND (GERMANY) - COMMERCE - HISTORY.
Höher, Peter. Heimat und Fremde . Münster , 1985. viii, 414 p., [1] p. of plates : ISBN 3-88547-290-2 LC Card 85-160726 DDC 381/.0943/42 19
HF3569.S28 H64 1985

Sauermann, Heinz.
Bargaining behavior /. Tübingen , 1978. x, 383 p. : ISBN 3-16-340972-5 LC Card 86-227549 DDC 330 s 658.4 19
HB41 .B29 1967 Bd. 7 HD58.6

Beiträge zur experimentellen Wirtschaftsforschung. Tübingen, 1967- <78. v. <1-2, 4-8 > LC Card 68-85600 DDC 330 19
HB41 .B29 1967

Coalition forming behavior /. Tübingen , 1978. viii, 375 p. : ISBN 3-16-340982-2 LC Card 86-227555 DDC 330 s 658.4 19
HB41 .B29 1967 vol. 8 HD58.6

Theorie und Politik nichtregenerierbarer natürlicher Ressourcen / Heinz Sauermann. Frankfurt am Main : Haag + Herchen, c1982. viii, 251 p. : ill. ; 21 cm. Bibliography: p. 231-251. ISBN 3-88129-573-9 : LC Card 83-126048
1. Nonrenewable natural resources. I. Title.
HC55 .S26 1982

Saulitis, ĪU. ĪU. (ĪUriĭ ĪUr'evich) Kirtovskiĭ, I. Kh. Ocherki istorii marksistsko-leninskoĭ ėkonomicheskoĭ mysli Latvii, 1920-1980 /. Riga , 1985. 199 p. ; LC Card 86-176265
HB97.5 .K542 1985

Saulniers, Alfred H., 1945- Beyond management control : a systems approach to public enterprises / Alfred H. Saulniers. Austin : Office for Public Sector Studies, Institute of Latin American Studies, University of Texas at Austin, 1985. 22 p. : ill. ; 28 cm. (Technical papers series . no. 48) Bibliography; p. 17. LC Card 86-622251 DDC 354.8509/2 19
1. Government business enterprises - Peru - Management. 2. Administrative agencies - Peru. I. Title. II. Series.
HD4124 .S28 1985

Saunders, Christopher T. Industrial policies and structural change /. New York , 1987. xii, 369 p. : ISBN 0-312-00935-6 LC Card 87-9833 DDC 338.9 19
HD3611 .I377 1987

Saunders, Ronald. Aid to workers in declining industries / Ronald S. Saunders. [Toronto, Ont.] : Ontario Economic Council : Available from the Ontario Govt. Bookstore, c1984. 72 p. : ill. ; 23 cm. (Policy studies series, 0227-0005) Bibliography: p. [69]-72. ISBN 0-7743-9007-7 (pbk.) LC Card 84-174952 DDC 331.13/77/0971 19
1. Unemployment, Technological - Canada. 2. Occupational retraining - Canada. 3. Insurance, Unemployment - Canada. I. Title.
HD6331.2.C2 S28 1984
NYPL [JLD 86-1287]

Saupe, William E. Rural poverty in Wisconsin counties / William E. Saupe and John W. Belknap. Madison, WI : Research Division of the College of Agricultural and Life Sciences, University of Wisconsin-Madison, [198-] 26 p. : ill., map ; 28 cm. (Research Report / College of Agricultural & Life Sciences . R3331) Cover title. Bibliography: p. 26. LC Card 86-622097
1. Rural poor - Wisconsin. 2. Agriculture - Economic aspects - Wisconsin. I. Belknap, John W. II. University of Wisconsin--Madison. College of Agricultural and Life Sciences. Research Division. III. Series: Research report (University of Wisconsin--Madison. College of Agricultural and Life Sciences. Research Division) , R3331. IV. Title.
HC107.W63 P6249 1980z

Sauter, Franz, 1956- Transaktionskostentheorie der Organisation / Franz Sauter. München : GBI, c1985. iv, 187, 2 p. : ill. ; 21 cm. (Betriebswirtschaftliche Forschungsbeiträge . Bd. 14) Originally presented as the author's thesis (doctoral)--Universität Mannheim, 1984. Bibliography: p. 168-187. Includes index. ISBN 3-89003-013-0 LC Card 85-194969
1. Transaction costs. 2. Organizational behavior. I. Title. II. Series.
HB846.3 .S28 1985

Sautter, Christian. Les dents du géant : le Japon à la conquête du monde / Christian Sautter. Paris : O. Orban, c1987. 323 p. ; 22 cm. Bibliography: p. [294]-307. Includes index. ISBN 2-85565-362-2 : LC Card 87-169635
1. Japan - Economic policy - 1945-. 2. High technology industries - Japan. I. Title.
HC462.9 .S277 1987

Sauvant, Karl P. Trade and foreign direct investment in data services / Karl P. Sauvant. Boulder Colo. : Westview Press, 1986. xv, 223 p. : ill. ; 23 cm. (Westview special studies in international economics and business) Includes bibliographical references and index. ISBN 0-8133-7085-X : LC Card 85-22701 DDC 332.6/712 19
1. Electronic data processing - Latin America. 2. Investments, Foreign - Latin America. 3. Telecommunication policy - Latin America. I. Title.
HD9696.C63 L387 1986
NYPL [JLD 86-3043]

Savage, Ian, 1960- The deregulation of bus services / Ian Savage. Aldershot, Hampshire, England ; Brookfield, Vt., U. S.A. : Gower, c1985. xx, 267 p. : ill. ; 23 cm. (Institute for Transport Studies . 1) Bibliography: p. 257-267. ISBN 0-566-05051-X : LC Card 85-17650 DDC 388.3/22 19
1. Bus lines - Great Britain. 2. Bus lines - Government policy - Great Britain. I. Series: Institute for Transport Studies (Series) , 1. II. Title.
HE5663.A6 S33 1985 ***NYPL [JLD 87-123]***

Savage, James D., 1951- Balanced budgets and American politics / James D. Savage. Ithaca, N.Y. : Cornell University Press, c1988. p. cm. Bibliography: p. Includes index. ISBN 0-8014-2047-4 LC Card 87-25061 DDC 339.5/23/0973 19
1. Budget - United States - History. 2. Budget deficits - United States - History. 3. Deficit financing - United States - History. 4. United States - Politics and government. I. Title.
HJ2050 .S28 1988

Savage, Lon, 1928- Thunder in the mountains / by Lon Savage. Elliston, Va. : Northcross House, Publishers, 1986. iv, 160 p. : ill., ports. ; 23 cm. Bibliography: p. 156-160. ISBN 0-9617256-0-5 (pbk.) : LC Card 87-7634 DDC 331.89/2822334/097543 19
1. Coal Strike, W. Va., 1920-1921. I. Title.
HD5325.M63 1920 .W47

Savage, Michael. The dynamics of working-class politics : the Labour movement in Preston, 1880-1940 / Michael Savage. Cambridge [Cambridgeshire] ; New York : Cambridge University Press, 1987. xii, 280 p. : ill. ; 24 cm. Bibliography: p. 252-272. Includes indexes. LC Card 87-14636 DDC 322/.2/0941 19

1. Labor and laboring classes - England - Preston (Lancashire) - Political activity - History. 2. Preston (Lancashire) - Politics and government. 3. Labour Party (Great Britain) - History. I. Title.
HD8397.P74 S28 1987

Sāvanta, Śivājī, 1940- Laḍhata / Śivājī Sāvanta. 1. āvṛttī. Pravarānagara : Padmaśrī Ḍô. Viṭṭhalarāva Vikhe Pāṭīla Phaunḍeśana, 1985-1986. 2 v. : ill. ; 22 cm. In Marathi. Biography of Viṭhṭhalarāva Vikhe Pāṭila, b. 1901, pioneer of cooperative sugar factories in Maharashtra. LC Card 87-900715
1. Vikhe Pāṭila, Viṭhṭhalarāva, 1901-. 2. Sugar factories - India - Maharashtra. 3. Industrialists - India - Maharashtra - Biography. 4. Maharashtra (India) - Biography. I. Title.
HD9116.I415 M37 1985

Savara, Mira. Changing trends in women's employment : a case study of the textile industry in Bombay / Mira Savara.1st ed. Bombay : Himalaya Pub. House, 1986. xii, 137 p. ; 23 cm. Based on the author's thesis (Ph. D.--Bombay University) Bibliography: p. [133]-137. LC Card 86-902789 DDC 331.4/877/00954792 19
1. Women textile workers - India - Bombay - Case studies. 2. Women textile workers - India - Case studies. 3. Women - Employment - India - Bombay - Case studies. 4. Women - Employment - India - Case studies. I. Title.
HD6073.T42 I47 1986

Savary, Gilles. Naissance d'une région, rue Esprit-des-lois : la construction régionale en Aquitaine à travers l'action économique, 1982-1985 / Gilles Savary. [Bordeaux] : Mascaret, [1986] 274 p. : ill. ; 22 cm. ISBN 2-904506-06-5 : LC Card 86-165118
1. Aquitaine (France) - Economic policy. 2. Decentralization in government - France - Aquitaine. I. Title.
HC277.A6 S28 1986

Savary, Julien, 1944- Les conséquences économiques de l'investissement étranger en France : l'impact sur l'emploi entre 1974 et 1983 / par Julien Savary. Toulouse : Faculté des sciences économiques, Université des sciences socialies, [1984] 24 p. ; 30 cm. "Ce texte actualise une communication effectuée au colloque de l'Association française de sciences économiques le 13 juin 1983." "Mars 1984." "No 139." Includes bibliographical references. LC Card 85-143217
1. Investments, Foreign - France. I. Title.
HG5472 .S28 1984

Savchenko, P. V. (Pol′ Vi͡acheslavovich) Sotsialisticheskoe obobshchestvlenie truda /. Moskva , 1981. 166 p. ; LC Card 82-161177
HD5796 .S633 1981

Ukreplenie material′nykh osnov sotsialisticheskogo obraza zhizni /. Moskva , 1984. 156 p. ; LC Card 85-240384
HD8526.5 .U38 1984

Save your home . Porter, Steven L., 1952- Bellaire, Tex. , c1987. 167 p. : ISBN 0-941599-02-7 (pbk.) : LC Card 87-3916 DDC 332.7/22 19
HG2040.15 .P67 1987

Savenko, V. N. (Valentina Nikolaevna) Prodovol′stvennyĭ kompleks goroda : teorii͡a, praktika, problemy upravlenii͡a / V.N. Savenko. Kiev : Nauk. dumka, 1986. 173, [3] p. : ill. ; 20 cm. At head of title: Akademii͡a nauk Ukrainskoĭ SSR. Institut ėkonomiki promyshlennosti. Bibliography: p. 167-[174]. LC Card 87-161654
1. Food industry and trade - Ukraine. 2. Food supply - Ukraine. 3. Private plot agriculture - Ukraine. I. Title.
HD9015.S653 U473 1986

Savez poljoprivrednih inženjera i tehničara SRH. Kongres privrednih stručnjaka Hrvatske (1943-1944 : Otočac and Čazma, Croatia) Kongres privrednih stručnjaka Hrvatske . Zagreb , 1985. 252 p., [16] p. of plates : ISBN 86-80359-01-7 LC Card 86-176200
HC407.Z7 C7637 1943

SAVEZ SINDIKATA OPĆINE ZADAR - HISTORY.
Uranija, Valentin. 35 godina sindikata u Zadru . Zadar , 1981. 300 p., xlviii p. of plates : LC Card 86-190260
HD8632.S3433 U73 1981

Savez sindikata općine Zadar. Općinsko sindikalno vijeće. Uranija, Valentin. 35 godina sindikata u Zadru . Zadar , 1981. 300 p., xlviii p. of plates : LC Card 86-190260
HD8632.S3433 U73 1981

Savezni zavod za statistiku (Yugoslavia) [Popis stanovništva i stanova 1971. English] Population and housing census 1971 : population / Social Federal Republic of Yugoslavia, Federal Institute for Statistics. Beograd : Federal Institute for Statistics, 1974. 12 v. ; 29 cm. English, French, and Russian. Translation of: Popis stanovništva i stanova 1971. Titles on added t.p.s: Le recensement de la population et de l'habitation de 1971; Perepis′ naselenii͡a i zhilishch 1971. CONTENTS. - Bk. 1. Vital, ethnic, and migratory characteristics -- Bk. 2. Literacy status and education -- Bk. 3. Economic characteristics, pt. 1 -- Bk. 4. Economic characteristics, pt. 2 -- Bk. 5. Households and families -- Bk. 6. Ethnic, education, and economic characteristics of population and households according to number of persons -- Bk. 7. Population and households in 1948, 1953, 1961, and 1971, dwellings in 1971 -- Bk. 8. Sex and age -- Bk. 9. Migration characteristics -- Bk. 10. Industry -- Bk. 11. Agricultural population -- Bk. 12. Size of land estate and sources of household income. LC Card 83-122836
1. Yugoslavia - Census, 1971. 2. Yugoslavia - Population - Statistics. I. Title. II. Title: Recensement de la population et de l'habitation de 1971. III. Title: Perepis′ naselenii͡a i zhilishch 1971.
HA1631.5 1971 .S38 1974

Savić, Nebojša, 1951- The scenario for Yugoslav economic recovery : opportunities and challenges for the future development / Nebojša Savić. Belgrade : N. Savić, c1986. 38 p. ; 29 cm. LC Card 87-165987 DDC 338.9497 19
1. Economic forecasting - Yugoslavia. 2. Yugoslavia - Economic conditions - 1945-. 3. Yugoslavia - Economic policy - 1945-. I. Title.
HC407 .S284 1986

Savignac, Philippe. Concours publics à l'agriculture par régions ou catégories d'exploitations en 1981. Paris : République française, Ministère de l'agriculture, Service central des enquêtes et études statistiques, [1984] 81 p. : ill. ; 30 cm. (Synthèses statistiques, comptes et revenus, 0244-5271 . no 55) Chiefly tables. Cover title. Prepared by Philippe Savignac. "Juillet 1984." ISBN 2-11-083993-7 LC Card 85-168478
1. Agriculture and state - France - Statistics. 2. Agricultural price supports - France - Statistics. I. Title. II. Series.
HD1947 .S29 1984

Savill, David. Sail to New Zealand : the story of Shaw, Savill & Co., 1858-1882 / by David Savill. London : R. Hale, 1986. 185 p., [20] p. of plates : ill. (some col.) ; 24 cm. Bibliography: p. [178]-179. Includes index. ISBN 0-7090-2809-1 : LC Card 87-111329 DDC 387.5/065/41 19
1. Shaw, Savill & Co. - History. 2. Merchant marine - New Zealand - History. 3. Sailing ships - New Zealand - History. I. Title.
HE945.S45 S28 1986

Saville, John. 1848 : the British state and the Chartist movement / John Saville. Cambridge [Cambridgeshire] ; New York : Cambridge University Press, 1987. ix, 310 p. ; 24 cm. Bibliography: p. 283-301. Includes index. ISBN 0-521-33341-5 LC Card 86-29975 DDC 322/.2/0941 19
1. Chartism. 2. Great Britain - Politics and government - 1837-1901. I. Title.
HD8396 .S28 1987

Savin, V. S. Dergachev, A. F. Raschet zatrat i opredelenie ėkonomicheskoĭ ėffektivnosti avtomatizirovannykh sistem operativno-proizvodstvennogo planirovanii͡a na avtoremontnykh predprii͡atii͡akh . Moskva , 1978. 35 p. ; LC Card 81-173259
HD9710.A2 D47 1978

Saving a generation /. Bernstein, Blanche, 1912- New York , 1986. vi, 63 p. ; ISBN 0-87078-206-1 (pbk.) : LC Card 87-102738 DDC 362.5/8/0973 19
HC110.P6 B47 1986

SAVING AND INVESTMENT - AFRICA.
Hyuha, Mukwanason. Financial structure and economic development in Africa . Dar-es-Salaam, Tanzania , c1983. 43 p. : LC Card 85-981441 DDC 332/.096 19
HG187.5.A2 H98 1983

SAVING AND INVESTMENT - AMERICA - HISTORY.
García, Miguel Angel. El nacimiento de América . México, D.F. , 1984. 284 p. : ISBN 968-415-089-X LC Card 87-403199 DDC 332/.0415/091812 19
HC94.Z9 S34 1984

SAVING AND INVESTMENT - ARGENTINA.
Prebisch, Raúl. La crisis del desarrollo argentino . Buenos Aires , c1986. 195 p. ; ISBN 950-0-26293-2 LC Card 86-229773
HC180.S3 P74 1986

SAVING AND INVESTMENT - ASIA.
Improving domestic resource mobilization through financial development . Manila, Philippines , c1985. vii, 51 p. : LC Card 87-101640 DDC 332.6/72/091724 19
HC415.S3 I45 1985

SAVING AND INVESTMENT - BRAZIL, NORTHEAST.
Aspectos gerais da economia e da sociedade do Nordeste. Recife , 1984. 318 p. : LC Card 86-159446
HC188.N6 A75 1984

SAVING AND INVESTMENT - BRAZIL - PARANÁ (STATE)
Paraná, formação de capital . [Pôrto Alegre] , 1965. 185 p. : LC Card 85-131098
HC188.P35 P388 1965

SAVING AND INVESTMENT - CHILE.
Características de los instrumentos de ahorro. Santiago, Chile , 1983. 91 p. ; LC Card 84-119555 DDC 332.63/2/0983 19
HG5342 .C37 1983 ***NYPL [JLF 86-620]***

Características de los instrumentos de ahorro. Santiago, Chile , 1986. 115 p. ; LC Card 87-403226 DDC 332.63/2/0983 19
HG5342 .C37 1986

SAVING AND INVESTMENT - CHINA.
Azqueta Oyarzun, Diego. Teoría económica de la acumulación socialista . Madrid , 1983. 224 p. ; ISBN 84-7214-279-5 LC Card 84-140278 DDC 332/.0415/091717 19
HC710.S3 A97 1983 ***NYPL [JLD 86-1859]***

SAVING AND INVESTMENT - COMMUNIST COUNTRIES - CASE STUDIES.
Azqueta Oyarzun, Diego. Teoría económica de la acumulación socialista . Madrid , 1983. 224 p. ; ISBN 84-7214-279-5 LC Card 84-140278 DDC 332/.0415/091717 19
HC710.S3 A97 1983 ***NYPL [JLD 86-1859]***

SAVING AND INVESTMENT - COSTA RICA - HISTORY.
Esquivel, Francisco. El desarrollo del capital en la industria de Costa Rica, 1950-1970 /. Heredia, Costa Rica , 1985. 197 p. : ISBN 997-7650-16-0 LC Card 86-210026
HC143 .E83 1985

Villalobos Vega, Bernardo. La mesocracia de Costa Rica, 1821-1926 /. San José , c1986. 309 p. ; ISBN 997-7232-15-6 LC Card 86-231140
HC143.Z9 S38 1986

SAVING AND INVESTMENT - DEVELOPING COUNTRIES.
Chung, Shin-Yung, d. 1962. Der Zwangssparprozess als Werkzeug der Entwicklungspolitik . Bonn , c1982. xiv, 204 p., [1] leaf of plates : LC Card 83-214728
HC470.S3 C48 1982

Farm management input to rural financial systems development /. Rome , 1985. xii, 57 p. : ISBN 92-5-102191-0 (pbk.) LC Card 86-207967 DDC 332.7/1/091724 19
HD1440.D44 F37 1985

Oliva, Karl. Teilnahme ohne Teilhabe . Frankfurt am Main , New York , c1985. 285 p. : ISBN 3-593-33476-3 LC Card 85-147441
HC59.72.S3 O45 1985

SAVING AND INVESTMENT - DEVELOPING COUNTRIES - CONGRESSES.
Epargne et développement /. Paris , 1985. 410 p. : ISBN 2-7178-0855-8 : LC Card 86-149765
HC59.72.S3 E62 1985

SAVING AND INVESTMENT - DOMINICAN REPUBLIC - CONGRESSES.
La Situación y los problemas del sistema

financiero nacional. Santo Domingo, República Dominicana , 1986. 152 p. ; LC Card 86-208560
HG2817 .S57 1986

SAVING AND INVESTMENT - EFFECT OF INFLATION ON - MATHEMATICAL MODELS.
Wagner, Helmut. Inflation und Wirtschaftswachstum . Berlin , c1983. 234 p. : ISBN 3-428-05319-2 LC Card 83-219188
HG229 .W237 1983

SAVING AND INVESTMENT - ENGLAND - HISTORY.
Kenwood, A. G. Capital formation in north east England, 1800-1913 /. New York , 1985. xv, 444 p. : ISBN 0-8240-6685-5 : LC Card 84-46005 DDC 332/.0415/09428 19
HC260.S3 K46 1985 ***NYPL [JLE 86-3900]***

SAVING AND INVESTMENT - FRANCE - EFFECT OF INFLATION ON.
Susini, Jean-Jacques. A qui profite l'inflation? /. Paris , c1985. 122 p. : ISBN 2-13-039288-1 LC Card 86-153761
HG979.5 .S87 1985

SAVING AND INVESTMENT - GERMANY, WEST.
Francke, Hans-Hermann. Sparverhalten bei Unterbeschäftigung, stagnierendem oder sinkendem Realeinkommen /. Stuttgart [1985] 142 p. : LC Card 86-153649
HC290.5.S3 F69 1985

SAVING AND INVESTMENT - GERMANY (WEST) - ECONOMETRIC MODELS.
Schulze, Konrad. Ein ökonometrischer Ansatz zur Erklärung des Bausparens /. Bonn , c1985. xii, 150 p. : ISBN 3-87169-319-7 LC Card 86-231621
HC290.5.S3 S38 1985

SAVING AND INVESTMENT - GERMANY (WEST) - MATHEMATICAL MODELS.
Bock, Hartmut. Das kollektive Bausparen . Frankfurt am Main , New York , c1984. 204 p. : ISBN 3-8204-5341-5 LC Card 85-199145
HC290.5.S3 B63 1984

SAVING AND INVESTMENT - GOVERNMENT POLICY - AFRICA - CONGRESSES.
National financial policies and capital formation in Africa . Dakar, Senegal [1986] iii, 205 p. ; LC Card 87-404123 DDC 332/.096 19
HG5822 .N38 1986

SAVING AND INVESTMENT - GREAT BRITAIN - HISTORY.
Studies in capital formation in Great Britain . Oxford [Oxfordshire] , New York , c1988. p. cm. ISBN 0-19-828408-X : LC Card 87-15196 DDC 332/.0415/0941 19
HC260.S3 S78 1988

SAVING AND INVESTMENT - GREECE.
Baltas, N. K. Empeirikē diereunēsē tēs apotamieutikēs symperiphoras kai tēs zētēsēs katatheseōn apo tous idiōtes /. Athēna [1979] 128 p. ; LC Card 86-203196
HG3250.5.A6 B34 1979

SAVING AND INVESTMENT - INDIA.
Giriappa, S. Income, saving and investment patterns in rural India /. New Delhi , 1984. 82 p. ; ***NYPL [JLD 86-4357]***

Hajra, S. (Sridhar), 1936- Capital and technological progress in the Indian economy, 1950/51-1980/81 /. New Delhi , 1985. xvi, 198 p. : LC Card 85-900681 DDC 338.954 19
HC440.S3 H35 1985 ***NYPL [JLD 87-736]***

SAVING AND INVESTMENT - ITALY - STATISTICS.
Consiglio nazionale dell'economia e del lavoro (Italy) Rapporto CNEL su risparmio e borsa . Roma , 1984. 308 p. : LC Card 85-242331 DDC 332/.0415/0945021 19
HC310.S3 C66 1984

SAVING AND INVESTMENT - KOREA (SOUTH)
Chung, Shin-Yung, d. 1962. Der Zwangssparprozess als Werkzeug der Entwicklungspolitik . Bonn , c1982. xiv, 204 p., [1] leaf of plates : LC Card 83-214728
HC470.S3 C48 1982

SAVING AND INVESTMENT - LATIN AMERICA - CONGRESSES.
External debt, savings, and growth in Latin America . Washington, D.C. , Buenos Aires , 1987. xv, 207 p. ; ISBN 0-939934-95-7 (pbk.) : LC Card 87-21422 DDC 336.3/435/098 19
HJ8514.5 .E984 1987

SAVING AND INVESTMENT - MEXICO - MONTERREY - HISTORY.
Cerutti, Mario. Burguesía y capitalismo en Monterrey, 1850-1910 /. México, D.F. , 1983. 214 p. ; ISBN 968-8430-10-2 LC Card 86-221932
HC138.M6 C47 1983

SAVING AND INVESTMENT - NIGERIA.
State, oil, and agriculture in Nigeria /. Berkeley , c1987. xiv, 327 p. : ISBN 0-87725-166-5 (pbk.) : LC Card 87-2941 DDC 338.1/8669 19
HD2145.5 .S73 1987

SAVING AND INVESTMENT - NIGERIA - KANO STATE.
Bashir, Ibrahim Lawan, 1948- Sources of capital formation and accumulation among Kano entrepreneurs, 1950-1980 /. Boston, MA (270 Bay State Rd., Boston 02215) , 1986. 17 leaves ; LC Card 87-156659 DDC 332/.0415/096695 19
HC1055.Z9 S33 1986

SAVING AND INVESTMENT - PERU.
Ahorro interno y el sistema financiero /. [Lima, Peru] , 1986. 70 p. : LC Card 87-127322 DDC 332/.0985 19
HC230.S3 A38 1986

SAVING AND INVESTMENT - PORTUGAL - HISTORY.
Ferreira, António Fonseca. A acumulação capitalista em Portugal . Porto , 1977. 156 p. ; LC Card 85-194898
HF3696 .F47 1977

SAVING AND INVESTMENT - RUSSIA.
Azqueta Oyarzun, Diego. Teoría económica de la acumulación socialista . Madrid , 1983. 224 p. ; ISBN 84-7214-279-5 LC Card 84-140278 DDC 332/.0415/091717 19
HC710.S3 A97 1983 ***NYPL [JLD 86-1859]***

SAVING AND INVESTMENT - SOVIET UNION.
Puzanov, V. D. (Valeriĭ Dmitrievich) Proizvodstvennoe nakoplenie . Moskva , 1983. 109 p. ; LC Card 83-194433
HC340.S3 P89 1983

The Soviet economy on the brink of reform . Boston , 1988. p. cm. ISBN 0-04-335063-1 (alk. paper) LC Card 87-19514 DDC 338.947 19
HC335 .C626 1988

SAVING AND INVESTMENT - SPAIN.
Morón Bécquer, Pedro. El ahorro vinculado a la adquisición de viviendas . Madrid [1984?] 35 p. : ISBN 84-7196-476-7 : LC Card 85-201073
HG2156.S72 M67 1984

SAVING AND INVESTMENT - UNITED STATES.
Cohen, Jerome Bernard, 1915- Investment analysis and portfolio management. Homewood, Ill., 1973. xiv, 946 p. ISBN 0-256-01429-9 LC Card 72-98120
HG4521 .C5296 1973 ***NYPL [JLE 74-744]***

Taxes and capital formation /. Chicago , 1987. xii, 118 p. : ISBN 0-226-24079-7 LC Card 87-5898 DDC 336.2/00973 19
HJ2381 .T395 1987

SAVING AND INVESTMENT - UNITED STATES - CONGRESSES.
Conference on the Effects of Taxation on Capital Formation (1986 : Palm Beach, Fla.) Taxes and capital formation. Cambridge, Mass. (1050 Massachusetts Ave., Cambridge 02138) , 1986. 40 p. ; LC Card 87-101954 DDC 336.2/00973 19
HJ2381 .C6974 1986

SAVING AND INVESTMENT - URUGUAY.
Rocca, José. Excedentes financieros y sistema bancario, Uruguay, 1974-1982 /. Montevideo, Uruguay , 1985. 39 p. : LC Card 85-213768
HC235.S3 R63 1985

SAVING AND INVESTMENT - UZBEK S.S.R.
Chumanova, N. I. Nakoplenie i ego rol′ v obshchestvennom vosproizvodstve Uzbekskoĭ SSR /. Tashkent , 1982. 116 p. ; LC Card 83-193447
HC337.U963 S33 1982

SAVING AND INVESTMENT - ZIMBABWE - HISTORY.
Phimister, I. R. (Ian R.) An economic and social history of Zimbabwe, 1890-1948 . London , New York , 1987. p. cm. ISBN 0-582-64423-2 LC Card 87-12471 DDC 330.96891/02 19
HC910.Z9 S36 1987

SAVING AND THRIFT - ANECDOTES, FACETIAE, SATIRE, ETC.
Lowe, Mifflin. The cheapskate's handbook . Los Angeles , 1986. 104 p. : ISBN 0-8431-1246-8 (pbk.): LC Card 86-207189 DDC 332.024 19
HG7931 .L68 1986

SAVING AND THRIFT - GERMANY (WEST) - DUISBURG.
Ölçen, Ali Nejat. Türken und Rückkehr . Frankfurt a.M. , 1986. 132 p. ; ISBN 3-924320-51-9 LC Card 87-138316 DDC 331.6/2/56104355 19
HD8458.T9 O43 1986

SAVING AND THRIFT - UNITED STATES.
Krefetz, Gerald. All about saving /. New York , c1987. xvi, 224 p. : ISBN 0-471-83793-8 LC Card 86-28085 DDC 332.024/01 19
HG2491 .K74 1987

SAVING AND THRIFT - VENEZUELA.
Martín-Guédez, Rafael, 1942- Sistema financiero . Caracas [1984] (Caracas : Editorial Arte) 309 p. : LC Card 85-177967
HG2156.V42 M37 1984

Saving capitalism . Olson, James Stuart, 1946- Princeton, N.J. , c1988. p. cm. ISBN 0-691-04749-9 (alk. paper) : LC Card 87-7275 DDC 353.0082/5/09 19
HG3729.U5 O47 1988

Saving free trade . Lawrence, Robert Z., 1949- Washington, D.C. , c1986. xii, 132 p. ; ISBN 0-8157-5178-8 LC Card 86-14705 DDC 382.7/1/0973 19
HF1455 .L39 1986 ***NYPL [JLE 86-4368]***

Saving plants and jobs . Gerhart, Paul F. Kalamazoo, MI , 1987. vii, 109 p. ; ISBN 0-88099-047-3 LC Card 87-10527 DDC 331.89/15 19
HD5708.5 .G47 1987

SAVINGS ACCOUNTS - GREECE.
Baltas, N. K. Empeirikē diereunēsē tēs apotamieutikēs symperiphoras kai tēs zētēsēs katatheseōn apo tous idiōtes /. Athēna [1979] 128 p. ; LC Card 86-203196
HG3250.5.A6 B34 1979

SAVINGS AND INVESTMENT - UNITED STATES.
Taxation and the deficit economy . San Francisco, Calif. , c1986. xxvii, 554 p. : ISBN 0-936488-13-1 : LC Card 85-63549 DDC 339.5/2/0973 19
HJ257.2 .T385 1986 ***NYPL [JLE 86-4136]***

Savings and loan associations : an AICPA audit and accounting guide / prepared by the Committee on Savings and Loan Associations ; including statements of position issued by the Accounting Standards Division and special report prepared by the Special Task Force on Audits of Repurchase Securities Transactions.4th rev. ed. New York, N.Y. (1211 Avenue of the Americas, New York 10036) : American Institute of Certified Public Accountants, 1987. vii, 212 p. ; 23 cm. (Audit and accounting guide) LC Card 87-161844 DDC 657/.833 19
1. Building and loan associations - Accounting - Standards - United States. 2. Building and loan associations - Auditing - Standards - United States. I. American Institute of Certified Public Accounts. Committee on Savings and Loan Associations. II. American Institute of Certified Public Accountants. Accounting Standards Division. III. American Institute of Certified Public Accountants. Special Task Force on Audits of Repurchase Securities Transactions. Special report. 1987. IV. Series.
HF5686.B8 S27 1987

SAVINGS AND LOAN ASSOCIATIONS. see **BUILDING AND LOAN ASSOCIATIONS.**

SAVINGS-BANKS - GERMANY - HISTORY.
Emmerich, Norbert-Christian. Die deutsche Sparkassenwerbung, 1750-1981 /. Stuttgart , 1983. 344 p. : LC Card 84-119079
HF6161.B2 E64 1983

SAVINGS-BANKS - GERMANY, WEST.
Standortbestimmung . Stuttgart , c1984. 447 p. ;

ISBN 3-09-311000-9 LC Card 85-150165
HG1939.G3 S73 1984

SAVINGS-BANKS - GERMANY, WEST - HISTORY.
Emmerich, Norbert-Christian. Die deutsche Sparkassenwerbung, 1750-1981 /. Stuttgart , 1983. 344 p. : LC Card 84-119079
HF6161.B2 E64 1983

SAVINGS-BANKS - HUNGARY.
Körösényi, András. A takarékszövetkezetek banki reformjának alternativai /. Budapest [1985] 43 p. ; LC Card 87-408585
HG1939.H82 K67 1985

SAVINGS-BANKS - HUNGARY - MANAGEMENT - HANDBOOKS, MANUALS, ETC.
Galambosi, László. Takarékszövetkezeti tisztségviselők kézikönyve /. Budapest , 1986. 135 p. ; ISBN 963-7006-73-7 LC Card 87-137992
HG1939.H82 G35 1986

SAVINGS BANKS - ITALY - MANAGEMENT - CONGRESSES.
Information systems in Italian savings banks . Geneva , 1975. 93 p. : LC Card 84-247915
HG1939.I7 I54 1975

SAVINGS-BANKS - UNITED STATES.
Giesen, David. Contemporary business planning . Chicago, IL (111 E. Wacker Dr., Chicago 60601) , c1987. 128 p. : LC Card 87-401916 DDC 332.3/2/068 19
HG1897 .G54 1987

SAVINGS-BANKS - UNITED STATES - CONGRESSES.
Financial stability of the thrift industry . San Francisco, Calif. (P.O. Box 7948, San Francisco 94120) [1986?] 230 p. : LC Card 86-81012
NYPL [JLE 86-3398]

SAVINGS-BANKS - UNITED STATES - STATISTICS.
Savings institutions performance analysis /. [Raleigh, N.C.] , c1987. 159 p. ; LC Card 87-404475 DDC 332.2/1/0973021 19
HG1922 .S35 1987

Savings institutions performance analysis / Trident Financial Corporation. [Raleigh, N.C.] : The Corporation, c1987. 159 p. ; 28 cm. "June 1986." Chiefly tables. LC Card 87-404475 DDC 332.2/1/0973021 19
1. Savings-banks - United States - Statistics. 2. Building and loan associations - United States - Statistics. I. Trident Financial Corporation.
HG1922 .S35 1987

Savings performance report, fourth quarter, 1985 : including all operating savings and loan offices in California / by Market Databank, Inc. Los Angeles, Calif. (9100 Sunset Blvd., Suite 111, Los Angeles) : Market Databank, c1986. 5 v. ; 28 cm. Includes indexes. CONTENTS. - v. 1. Savings market performance report -- v. 2. Regional performance report -- v. 3. Association summary report -- v. 4. Association performance report -- v. 5. Association performance report by branch. LC Card 86-213300 DDC 332.3/2/09794021 19
1. Building and loan associations - California - Statistics. I. Market Databank.
HG2153.C3 C288 1986

Savings performance report, fourth quarter, 1985 : including all operating savings and loan offices in California / by Market Databank, Inc. Los Angeles, Calif. (9100 Sunset Blvd., Suite 111, Los Angeles) : Market Databank, c1986- v. <1 > ; 28 cm. Includes indexes. CONTENTS. - v. 1. Market performance report. LC Card 86-202354 DDC 332.3/2/09794021 19
1. Building and loan associations - California - Statistics. I. Market Databank.
HG2153.C3 S287 1986

Savings performance report, second quarter, 1986 : including all operating savings and loan offices in California / by Market Databank, Inc. Los Angeles, Calif. (9100 Sunset Blvd., Suite 111, Los Angeles) : Market Databank, c1986. 5 v. (various pagings) ; 28 cm. Includes indexes. CONTENTS. - v. 1. Market performance report -- v. 2. Regional performance report -- v. 3. Association summary report -- v. 4. Association performance report -- v. 5. Association performance report by branch. LC Card 86-224944 DDC 332.3/2/09794021 19
1. Building and loan associations - California - Statistics. I. Market Databank.
HG2153.C3 S284 1986

Saviotti, Paolo. Coombs, Rod. Economics and technological change /. Totowa, N.J. , 1987. xv, 296 p. : ISBN 0-8476-7545-9 : LC Card 86-28000 DDC 338/.06 19
HC79.T4 C67 1987

Savoie, Donald J.
The Canadian economy . Toronto , New York , c1986. 291 p. : ISBN 0-458-99950-4 (pbk.) : LC Card 86-218828 DDC 338.971 19
HC113 .C37 1986

Regional economic development . Boston , 1987. p. cm. ISBN 0-04-338155-3 (alk. paper) LC Card 87-16749 DDC 338.9 19
HD75 .R44 1987

Savoir vendre pour vendre plus /. Coureau, Serge. Paris , c1986. 147 p. ; ISBN 2-04-016534-7 LC Card 87-122332
HF5438.25 .C68 1986

Savona, Paolo, 1936- Eurodollars and international banking /. London [Miami] , 1985. xiii, 226 p. : ISBN 0-333-36553-4
NYPL [JLD 85-3068]

Savy, Michel. Atlas des Français / Michel Savy, Pierre Beckouche. Paris : Hachette, c1985. 331 p. : ill. ; 18 cm. (Collection Pluriel. 8462) Bibliography: p. [311]-312. ISBN 2-01-011512-0 LC Card 86-178635
1. France - Economic conditions - 1945- - Maps. 2. France - Economic conditions - 1945- - Regional disparities - Maps. 3. France - Social conditions - 1945- - Maps. 4. France - Statistics - Maps. I. Beckouche, Pierre, 1957-. II. Title.
HC276.2 .S325 1985

SAW FILING INDUSTRY - UNITED STATES - HISTORY - 20TH CENTURY.
Brown, Edmund D. 1594 Evans Drive, S.W. . Atlanta, Ga. (1594 Evans Dr., S.W., Atlanta 30310) , c1983. 213 p. : LC Card 82-62570 DDC 338.7/62193 19
HD9529.S294 A842 1983
NYPL [JLF 86-1803]

SAW INDUSTRY - UNITED STATES - HISTORY - 20TH CENTURY.
Brown, Edmund D. 1594 Evans Drive, S.W. . Atlanta, Ga. (1594 Evans Dr., S.W., Atlanta 30310) , c1983. 213 p. : LC Card 82-62570 DDC 338.7/62193 19
HD9529.S294 A842 1983
NYPL [JLF 86-1803]

Saw, Swee-Hock, 1931- The labour force of Singapore / by Saw Swee-Hock. Singapore : Dept. of Statistics : To be purchased from the Singapore National Printers Publication Sales Division, [1984] xi, 78 p. : ill. ; 26 cm. (Census monograph . no. 3) Study on data collected in Census of population, 1980. ISBN 997-19-1416-6 (pbk.) LC Card 86-946447 DDC 331.11/09595/7 19
1. Labor supply - Singapore - Statistics. 2. Labor supply - Singapore. I. Series: Census monograph (Singapore) , no. 3. II. Title.
HD5823.A6 S28 1984

Sawāt Sēnānarong. Barton, Thomas Frank, 1905- Phūmisāt sētthakit kh [Bangkok] 2500 [1957] 2, 5, 392 p. : LC Card 83-921251
HC445 .B36 1957

Sawhill, John C., 1936- Energy conservation . Washington, D.C. , c1986. xii, 270 p. : ISBN 0-8157-7716-7 : LC Card 85-26894 DDC 333.79/16/0973 19
HD9502.U62 E478 1986
NYPL [JLE 86-4084]

Sawyer, James E., 1943- Why Reaganomics and Keynesian economics failed / James E. Sawyer. New York : St. Martin's Press, 1987. ix, 195 p. : ill. ; 23 cm. Bibliography: p. 189-190. Includes index. ISBN 0-312-00532-6 : LC Card 87-9578 DDC 338.973 19
1. United States - Economic policy - 1981-. 2. United States - Economic conditions - 1981-. 3. Supply-side economics - United States. 4. Keynesian economics. I. Title.
HC106.8 .S28 1987

Sawyer-Lauçanno, Christopher, 1951- Case studies in international management / Christopher Sawyer-Lauçanno. Englewood Cliffs, N.J. : Prentice-Hall, c1987. xvii, 138 p. : ill. ; 24 cm. ISBN 0-13-119298-1 (pbk.) LC Card 86-22724 DDC 658/.049 19
1. International business enterprises - Management - Case studies. I. Title.
HD62.4 .S29 1987

Sawyer, Lawrence B. The practice of modern internal auditing / Lawrence B. Sawyer. 2nd ed., rev. and enl. Altamonte Springs, Fla. : Institute of Internal Auditors, 1981. xiv, 882 p. : ill. ; 24 cm. Includes bibliographies and index. ISBN 0-89413-092-7 LC Card 87-462054 DDC 657/.458 19
1. Auditing, Internal. I. Institute of Internal Auditors. II. Title.
HF5668.25 .S28 1981

Sawyer, Malcolm C.
Finance, money, and unemployment / Malcolm Sawyer. Berlin : IIM Labour Market Policy, Wissenschaftszentrum Berlin, [1985] 65 p. ; 30 cm. (Discussion papers, 0722-673X . IIM/LMP 85-11) Summary in German. Bibliography: p. 64-65. LC Card 86-205291 DDC 332 19
1. Monetary policy. 2. Unemployment. 3. Full employment policies. 4. Finance. I. Series: Discussion papers (International Institute of Management. Labour Market Policy) , IIM/LMP 85-11. II. Title.
HG230.3 .S29 1985

[Macroeconomics in question]
Macro-economics in question : the Keynesian-monetarist orthodoxies and the Kaleckian alternative / Malcolm C. Sawyer. Brighton, Sussex : Wheatsheaf Books, 1982. xiii, 190 p. : ill. ; 23 cm. Bibliography: p. [175]-187. Includes index. ISBN 0-7108-0140-8 LC Card 86-673557
1. Macroeconomics. 2. Keynesian economics. 3. Kalecki, Michał. I. Title.
HB172.5 .S28x 1982b

Saxena, P. C. (Prem Chandra), 1939- Recent advances in the techniques for demographic analysis /. Bombay , 1987. xiv, 456 p. ; LC Card 87-900498
HB849 .R42 1987

Saxena, Pradeep. Trade unionism in civil services : a study of employees' associations in the Government of Rajasthan / Pradeep Saxena. Jaipur : Aalekh Publishers, 1986. ii, 164 p. ; 22 cm. Bibliography: p. [160]-164. Based on the author's thesis (Ph. D.--University of Rajasthan) LC Card 86-903231 DDC 331.88/11354544 19
1. Trade unions - Government employees - India - Rajasthan. 2. Employee-management relations in government - India - Rajasthan. I. Title.
HD8005.2.I523 R347 1986

Saxena, R. B. IMF loan to India : an economic assessment / R.B. Saxena.1st ed. Delhi, India : Anmol Publications : Distributed by Anupama Publishers, Distributors, 1986. ix, 284 p. ; 22 cm. Bibliography: p. [259]-280. Includes index. LC Card 86-903311 DDC 332.1/52 19
1. International Monetary Fund - India. 2. Loans, Foreign - India. 3. India - Economic conditions - 1947-. I. Title.
HG3971 .S29 1986

Saxena, R. N. (Rajendra Narain), 1937- Rail transport pricing in India / R.N. Saxena. 1st ed. New Delhi : Meeranjani Publications, 1985. 549 p. : ill. ; 25 cm. Bibliography: p. 413-422. LC Card 86-903024 DDC 385/.12/0954 19
1. Railroads - India - Rates. I. Title.
HE1911 .S29 1985

Saxena, Usha, 1957- Role of multinationals in India's foreign trade / Usha Saxena. 1st ed. New Delhi : Ashish Pub. House, 1987. xx, 237 p. ; 23 cm. Revision of the author's thesis (Ph. D.--Lucknow University, Lucknow, 1986) Bibliography: p. [222]-233. Includes index. ISBN 81-7024-081-6 : LC Card 87-900766 DDC 382/.0954 19
1. International business enterprises - India. 2. India - Commerce. I. Title.
HD2899 .S29 1987

Saxenhofer, Peter. Diedrich, Wolfgang. Arbeitsbedingungen in der Schweizer Hotellerie . Bern , c1984. 185 p. : ISBN 3-258-03437-0 : LC Card 85-113566
HD5718.H82 S953 1984

Saxman, Donald. Electrochemistry . Stamford, Conn., U. S.A. , c1986. 231 leaves : ISBN 0-89336-483-5 (pbk.) LC Card 87-403910 DDC 380.1/45660297/0973 19
HD9660.E433 U544 1986

Saxonhouse, Gary R. Otsuka, Keijiro. Comparative technology choice in

development . New York , 1988. viii, 247 p. : ISBN 0-312-00516-4 : LC Card 86-29666 DDC 338.4/567721/0952 19
HD9886.I42 O87 1988

Saybrook, Conn. Collegiate School. see **Yale University.**

Sayers, Janet. Sexual contradictions : psychology, psychoanalysis, and feminism / Janet Sayers. London ; New York, NY : Tavistock Publications, 1986. x, 214 p. : ill. ; 23 cm. Includes indexes. Bibliography: p. [182]-203. ISBN 0-422-78780-9 LC Card 85-27948 DDC 155.3/3 19
1. Sex differences (Psychology). 2. Women and psychoanalysis. 3. Women - Psychology. 4. Men - Psychology. 5. Dominance (Psychology). I. Title.
BF692.2 .S29 1986 ***NYPL [JFD 86-5840]***

Sayers, Robert. The Korean onggi potter / Robert Sayers with Ralph Rinzler. Washington, D.C. : Smithsonian Institution Press, 1987. 288 p. : ill. ; 23 cm. (Smithsonian folklife studies . no. 5) Bibliography: p. 285-288. LC Card 86-600366 DDC 338.4/77382/095195 19
1. Pottery industry - Korea (South) - History. 2. Pottery, Korean. I. Rinzler, Ralph. II. Title. III. Series.
HD9617.K82 S29 1987

Saynor, Peter. Parris, Henry. Public enterprise in Western Europe /. London , Wolfeboro, N.H. , c1987. viii, 197 p. : ISBN 0-7099-0548-3 : LC Card 86-24133 DDC 338.7/4/094 19
HD4138 .P37 1987 ***NYPL [JLD 87-757]***

al-Ṣayyād, Muḥammad Maḥmūd, 1916- Majma' al-Lughah al-'Arabīyah, Cairo. Lajnat al-Jughrāfīyā. al-Mu'jam al-jughrāfī /. [al-Qāhirah] , 1974. 9,185 p. ; LC Card 77-961221
G63 .M34 1974 ***NYPL [*OEO 86-3694]***

Sazina, M. G. Rabochiĭ klass i stroitel'stvo sotsializma v stranakh TSentral'noĭ i IUgo-Vostochnoĭ Evropy /. Moskva , 1977. 382 p. ; LC Card 81-174150
HD8376.5 .R33 1977

Sāzmān-i Barnāmah (Iran) Feeder Road Programme : report on phase A : East & West Azerbaijan, Ostans 3 & 4 / Imperial Government of Iran, Plan Organisation. Tehran : ETCO, [1961?] ii, 117, 9 leaves, [59] leaves of plates (some folded) : maps (some col.) ; 30 cm. LC Card 85-211363
1. Farm roads - Iran - Āẕarbāyjan-i Khāvarī. 2. Farm roads - Iran - Āẕarbāyjān-i Bakhtarī. 3. Āẕarbāyjān-i Khāvarī (Iran) - Economic conditions. 4. Āẕarbāyjān-i Bākhtarī (Iran) - Economic conditions. 5. Āẕarbāyjān-i Khāvarī (Iran) - Population. 6. Āẕarbāyjān-i Bākhtarī (Iran) - Population. I. ETCO (Firm : Iran). II. Title.
HE365.I73 R857 1961

Sazonov, S. N. (Sergeĭ Nikolaevich) Oplata truda v sel'skom khoziaĭstve : spravochnik : voprosy i otvety / S.N. Sazonov, V.A. Chupeev. Moskva : "Kolos", 1984. 268 p. ; 21 cm. LC Card 84-244595
1. Agricultural wages - Soviet Union. I. Chupeev, V. A. (Vladimir Alekseevich). II. Title.
HD4966.A292 S6574 1984

SBA report to the administrator. United States. Small Business Administration. Office of Procurement and Technical Assistance. Report to the Administrator on the analysis of the management and administration of the Procurement and Technical Assistance programs /. [Washington, D.C.] , 1984. 1 v. (various pagings) : ***NYPL [JLF 86-1066]***

Sbalansirovannost' narodnokhoziaĭstvennogo razvitiia . Alymov, Aleksandr Nikolaevich. Kiev , 1986. 221, [3] p. ; LC Card 86-214583
HC337.U5 A793 1986

Sbalansirovannost' sotsialisticheskoĭ ėkonomiki i finansovo-kreditnyĭ mekhanizm / [nauchnyĭ redaktor, Allakhverdiān D.A.]. Moskva : Akademiia nauk SSSR, In-t ėkonomiki, Otdel planovogo upr. nar. khoziaĭstvom, Sektor finansovykh i kreditnykh otnosheniĭ, 1984. 108 p. ; 21 cm. Cover title. Includes bibliographical references. LC Card 85-240300
1. Finance - Soviet Union - Congresses. 2. Credit - Soviet Union - Congresses. 3. Soviet Union - Economic conditions - 1976- - Congresses. I. Allakhverdiān, D. A. (Derenik Akopovich). II. Institut ėkonomiki (Akademiia nauk SSSR). Sektor finansovykh i kreditnykh otnosheniĭ.
HG186.S55 S27 1984

SBB im Aaretal . Aebi, Ernst. Luzern , c1984. 111 p. : LC Card 84-234665
HE3898.A37 A42 1984

SBI report .
(# H-369) The SBI report on the market and economics of the electromedical equipment industry. Wantagh, N.Y. , c1982. iv, 157 leaves ; LC Card 87-402136 DDC 380.1/45681761 19
HD9995.E43 U58 1982

The SBI report on the market and economics of the electromedical equipment industry. Wantagh, N.Y. : Specialists in Business Information, c1982. iv, 157 leaves ; 30 cm. (SBI report . # H-369) Includes bibliographical references. LC Card 87-402136 DDC 380.1/45681761 19
1. Medical electronics equipment industry - United States - Statistics. 2. Medical instruments and apparatus industry - United States - Statistics. I. Specialists in Business Information, inc. II. Series.
HD9995.E43 U58 1982

Sbornik nauchnykh trudov (Institut ėkonomiki i organizatsii promyshlennogo proizvodstva (Akademiia nauk SSSR))
Metodologicheskie problemy formirovaniia territorial'no-proizvodstvennykh kompleksov /. Novosibirsk , 1980. 162 p. : LC Card 82-106930
HC336.25 .M46 1980

Perspektivnoe planirovanie razvitiia agrarno-promyshlennogo kompleksa /. Novosibirsk , 1979. 159 p. : LC Card 81-143730
HD9015.S652 P47 1979

Sbornik nauchnykh trudov (Vsesoiuznyĭ zaochnyĭ finansovo-ėkonomicheskiĭ institut (Soviet Union)) .
(vyp. 42) Aktual'nye problemy sotsial'no-ėkonomicheskogo razvitiia SSSR v sovremennyĭ period /. Moskva , 1984. 153 p. ; LC Card 85-205938
HC336.25 .A46 1984

Sbornik ot lektsii po aktualni problemi na sotsialno-ikonomicheskata politika na partiiata. Sofiia : Mezhduokrŭzhna partiĭna shkola pri GK na BKP, 1985. 203 p. ; 20 cm. Includes bibliographical references. LC Card 86-140158
1. Bulgaria - Economic policy - 1944-. I. Mezhduokrŭzhna partiĭna shkola (Sofia, Bulgaria).
HC403 .S27 1985

Sbornik trudov (Vsesoiuznyĭ nauchno-issledovatel'skiĭ institut sistemnykh issledovaniĭ) .
(1979, vyp. 9) Metodologicheskie problemy analiza dolgosrochnykh sotsial'no-ėkonomicheskikh protsessov /. Moskva , 1979. 116 p. : LC Card 87-462037
HD87 .M48 1979

(1982, vyp. 4) Territorial'no-proizvodstvennyĭ kompleks . Moskva , 1982. 107 p. : LC Card 83-200414
HC337.R852 K3685 1982

(1983, vyp. 1) Chislennye metody v zadachakh optimal'nogo ėkonomicheskogo planirovaniia /. Moskva , 1983. 158 p. : LC Card 84-128729
HC336.25 .C515 1983

(1983, vyp. 2) Sotsial'no-ėkonomicheskie problemy intensifikatsii obshchestvennogo proizvodstva /. Moskva , 1983. 91 p. : LC Card 84-114234
HD56 .S688 1983

(1984, vyp. 10) Renta . Moskva , 1984. 95 p. : LC Card 85-192538
HB401 .R48 1984

(1984, vyp. 7) Kompleksnye problemy obespecheniia ėkonomiki mineral'nym syr'em /. Moskva , 1984. 115 p. : LC Card 85-192528
HF1051 .K64 1984

Sbornik zadach i khoziaĭstvennykh situatsiĭ po ėkonomike i planirovaniiu mashinostroitel'noĭ promyshlennosti / pod redaktsieĭ G.A. Kraiukhina, M.I. Orlovoĭ. Moskva : "Vysshaia shkola", 1985. 246 p. ; 21 cm. Authorized for instructional purposes. LC Card 86-110747
1. Machine-tool industry - Soviet Union - Management - Problems, excercises, etc. I. Kraiukhin, G. A. II. Orlova, M. I. (Mariia Ivanovna).
HD9703.S652 S28 1985

Scaduto, Joseph V. What's it worth : a home inspection & appraisal manual / Joseph V. Scaduto.1st ed. Blue Ridge Summit, PA : Tab Books, c1985. x, 244 p. : ill. ; 25 cm. "No. 1761." Includes index. Bibliography: 223-224. ISBN 0-8306-0761-7 : LC Card 85-2801 DDC 333.33/2 19
1. Dwellings - Inspection. 2. Dwellings - Valuation. I. Title.
HD1379 .S33 1985 ***NYPL [JSE 86-1407]***

Scala, Claudio. Istituto nazionale di economia agraria. Il programma INEA per la progettazione e le analisi statistiche di un campione rappresentativo /. Roma , 1986. 122 p. : LC Card 86-213865
HD1970 .I773 1986

La scalata del mercato . Rossi, Guido. Bologna , c1986. 152 p. ; ISBN 88-15-01123-4 : LC Card 86-180921
HG5522 .R66 1986

SCALE, ECONOMIES OF. see **ECONOMIES OF SCALE.**

Scalia, Rosario, 1949- L'Osservatorio provinciale sul lavoro e sulle professioni . Milano, Italy , c1984. 143 p. : LC Card 84-190423
HD5785.N86 O87 1984
NYPL [JLD 86-1275]

Scammell, Henry. McCann, Thomas P. On the inside . Boston , c1987. p. cm. ISBN 0-933341-53-9 : LC Card 87-43040 DDC 338.7/634 19
HD9249.U6 M23 1987

Scamp, Lee C. Postal rate history of China and Hong Kong : the pre-adhesive period to the beginning of packet service from Hong Kong, 1800-1845 / by Lee C. Scamp. Houston, Tex., U. S.A. : NANCOL Enterprises with assistance from the Texas Philatelic Foundation, c1986. xx, 284 p. : ill., facsims. ; 28 cm. Bibliography: p. 201-205. LC Card 87-145274 DDC 383/.23/0951 19
1. Ship letters - Hong Kong - Rates - History - 19th century. 2. Maritime and postal hand stamps - Hong Hong - History - 19th century. 3. Postal service - China - History - 19th century. 4. Postal service - Hong Kong - History - 19th century. 5. Postal service - Macao - History - 19th century. I. Title.
HE7305.Z8 S33 1986

Scampini, Thomas J. Austin, Douglas V. Modern banking . Boston , c1985. x, 406 p. : ISBN 0-87267-053-8 LC Card 84-21754 DDC 332.1/068 19
HG1615 .A98 1985 ***NYPL [JLE 85-3956]***

SCANDINAVIA - ECONOMIC CONDITIONS.
Babashkina, M. L. Aktual'nye ėkonomicheskie i sotsial'nye problemy malykh stran Severnoĭ Evropy . Moskva , 1986. 71 p. ; LC Card 87-166353
HC343 .B34 1986

Isacson, Maths, 1948- Proto-industrialisation in Scandinavia . Leamington Spa, UK ; New York : p. cm. ISBN 0-85496-514-9 : LC Card 86-32062 DDC 338.09485 19
HC375 .I8 1987

SCANDINAVIA - ECONOMIC CONDITIONS - ECONOMETRIC MODELS.
Schneider, Friedrich. The development of the shadow economies for Denmark, Norway, and Sweden . Aarhus, Denmark [1986] 46 p. : LC Card 86-215193 DDC 381 19
HD2346.S29 S35 1986

SCANDINAVIA - ECONOMIC CONDITIONS - ECONOMETRIC MODELS - CONGRESSES.
Macroeconomic medium-term models in the Nordic countries /. Amsterdam ; New York : x, 324 p. : ISBN 0-444-70262-8 (U. S.) LC Card 87-13422 DDC 330.948/00724 19
HC345 .M33 1987

SCANDINAVIA - ECONOMIC INTEGRATION.
Almdal, Preben. Aspects of European integration . Odense C, Denmark , 1986. 108 p. ; ISBN 87-7492-578-4 : LC Card 87-114176 DDC 337.1/42 19
HC241.2 .A7344 1986

SCANDINAVIA - INDUSTRIES.
Babashkina, M. L. Aktual'nye ėkonomicheskie i sotsial'nye problemy malykh stran Severnoĭ Evropy . Moskva , 1986. 71 p. ; LC Card 87-166353
HC343 .B34 1986

SCANDINAVIA - INDUSTRIES - HISTORY - 19TH CENTURY.
Isacson, Maths, 1948- Proto-industrialisation in Scandinavia . Leamington Spa, UK ; New York : p. cm. ISBN 0-85496-514-9 : LC Card 86-32062 DDC 338.09485 19
HC375 .I8 1987

SCANDINAVIA - MANUFACTURES - ECONOMETRIC MODELS.
Dussault, François. Les modèles scandinaves et la détermination des ententes salariales des industries manufacturières canadiennes . Montréal [1982] 21, [11] p. ; LC Card 82-196710
HD4979 .D875 1982

SCANDINAVIA - OFFICIALS AND EMPLOYEES.
Den Offentliga sektorns sysselsättningsutveckling i Norden under 1970-talet =. [Oslo] [Solna] 1983. iiii, 150 p. : ISBN 91-38-07556-3 LC Card 85-184428
HD8013.S344 O35 1983

SCANDINAVIA - SOCIAL CONDITIONS.
Babashkina, M. L. Aktual'nye ėkonomicheskie i sotsial'nye problemy malykh stran Severnoĭ Evropy . Moskva , 1986. 71 p. ; LC Card 87-166353
HC343 .B34 1986

SCANDINAVIAN AIRLINES SYSTEM - MANAGEMENT.
Carlzon, Jan. Moments of truth /. Cambridge, Mass. , c1987. xiii, 135 p. ; ISBN 0-88730-200-9 LC Card 87-1070 DDC 387.7/065/485 19
HE9860.S28 C37 1987

Carlzon, Jan. Riv pyramiderna! . [Stockholm] , c19. 219 p. : ISBN 91-0-046844-4 LC Card 86-139896
HE9860.S28 C375 1986

SCANDINAVIAN COOPERATION.
Almdal, Preben. Aspects of European integration . Odense C, Denmark , 1986. 108 p. ; ISBN 87-7492-578-4 : LC Card 87-114176 DDC 337.1/42 19
HC241.2 .A7344 1986

Scandinavian Institute of African Studies. see **Nordiska Afrikainstitutet.**

Scanlan, Burt K. Management & organizational behavior / Burt Scanlan, Bernard Keys. 2nd ed. Malibar, Fla. : Krieger, 1987, c1983. xvi, 666 p. : ill. ; 24 cm. Reprint. Originally published: 2nd ed. New York : Wiley, 1983. Includes bibliographical references and index. ISBN 0-89464-246-4 LC Card 87-17035 DDC 658.4 19
1. Management. 2. Organizational behavior. I. Keys, Bernard. II. Title. III. Title: Management and organizational behavior.
HD31 .S3256 1987

Scannerdaten und Preissensitivität bei Konsumgütern /. Kucher, Eckhard. Wiesbaden , c1985. 282 p. : ISBN 3-409-13608-8 LC Card 86-128961
HB801 .K789 1985

Scanu, Salvatore. I costi dell'adempimento tributario in Italia : valutazioni sull'incidenza dei costi delle scritture contabili relative alla liquidazione dell'Iva nelle aziende del piccolo e medio dettaglio alimentare / Salvatore Scanu. [Cagliari] : Università degli studi di Cagliari, Istituto economico statistico ; Milano, Italy : F. Angeli, c1984. 153 p. ; 22 cm. Bibliography: p. [149]-150. LC Card 85-118845
1. Grocery trade - Italy - Costs. 2. Taxation - Italy - Compliance costs. 3. Groceries - Taxation - Italy. 4. Value-added tax - Italy. I. Title.
HD9326.I82 S32 1984

Scapicchio, Mark. Bingham, Julie E. HAL plain and simple . Reading, Mass. , c1988. vii, 296 p. : ISBN 0-201-08002-8 (pbk.) : LC Card 87-17524 DDC 005.36/9 19
HF5548.4.L68 B56 1988

SCARCITY.
Perelman, Michael. Marx's crises theory . New York , 1987. v, 250 p. ; ISBN 0-275-92372-X (alk. paper) : LC Card 87-6936 DDC 330.12/2 19
HB97.5 .P349 1987

Scarcity and choice in history. Court, W. H. B. (William Henry Bassano) London, 1970. viii, 256 p. LC Card 79-488977 DDC 330.9
HC253 .C675

SCARGILL, ARTHUR.
Wilsher, Peter. Strike . London [1985] xiii, 284 p., [16] p. of plates : ISBN 0-233-97825-9 : LC Card 86-221981 DDC 331.89/2822334/0941 19
HD5365.M6152 1984 .W55 1985b

Scarpello, Vida Gulbinas, 1940- Personnel/human resource management : environments and functions / Vida Gulbinas Scarpello, James Ledvinka. Boston, Mass. : PWS-Kent Pub. Co., c1988. xxii, 794 p. : ill. ; 25 cm. Includes bibliographies and indexes. ISBN 0-534-08346-3 LC Card 87-13678 DDC 658.3 19
1. Personnel management. I. Ledvinka, James. II. Title.
HF5549 .S186 1988

Scase, Richard.
Entrepreneurship in Europe . London , New York , c1987. 197 p. ; ISBN 0-7099-3849-7 LC Card 87-15425 DDC 338/.04/094 19
HD2346.E9 E57 1987

The real world of the small business owner / Richard Scase and Robert Goffee. 2nd ed. London ; New York : Croom Helm, c1987. 170 p. ; 22 cm. Includes bibliographies and index. ISBN 0-7099-5416-6 (pbk.) LC Card 87-6756 DDC 338.6/42/0941 19
1. Small business - Great Britain. 2. Businessmen - Great Britain. I. Goffee, Robert. II. Title.
HD2346.G7 S28 1987

Scelte strategiche e riorganizzazione aziendale : la grande impresa nel decennio 1975-1984 / ricerca condotta da Alberto Riva e Francesco Silva ; con la collaborazione di Alessandro Arrighetti, Luciano Consolati, Antonella Ponzi. Milano, Italy : F. Angeli, c1985. 312 p. ; 22 cm. (Collana IReR . 29) LC Card 86-146459
1. Corporate reorganizations - Italy. 2. Corporate planning - Italy. 3. Strategic planning - Italy. I. Riva, Alberto. II. Silva, Francesco, 1942-. III. Arrighetti, A. (Alessandro), 1953-. IV. Series.
HD2864 .S36 1985 ***NYPL [JLD 87-1549]***

The scenario for Yugoslav economic recovery . Savić, Nebojša, 1951- Belgrade , c1986. 38 p. ; LC Card 87-165987 DDC 338.9497 19
HC407 .S284 1986

Scenarios and strategic management /. Godet, Michel. [Prospective et planification stratégique. English.] London , Boston , 1987. xviii, 210 p. : ISBN 0-408-02890-4 LC Card 87-15774 DDC 658.4/012 19
HD30.28 .G6313 1987

Schabeck, Timothy A. Managing microcomputer security : networked/standalone : financial, engineering, management, marketing, executive / [Timothy A. Schabeck, author ; John A. Buckland, contributing author ; Joan E. Gessler, editor]. Port Jefferson Station, N.Y. (492 Old Town Rd., Port Jefferson Station 11776) : FTP Technical Library, c1986. 1 v. (various pagings) : ill. ; 40 cm. Includes bibliographical references and index. LC Card 86-216667 DDC 658.4/78 19
1. Electronic data processing departments - Security measures. 2. Microcomputers - Access control. 3. Computer crimes. 4. Electronic data processing departments - Management. 5. Disasters. I. Buckland, John A. II. Gessler, Joan E. III. Title.
HF5548.37 .S33 1986

Schabedoth, Hans-Joachim. Bittsteller oder Gegenmacht? : Perspektiven gewerkschaftlicher Politik nach der Wende / Hans-Joachim Schabedoth ; [mit einem Vorwort von Franz Steinkühler].1. Aufl. Marburg : SP-Verlag, 1985. 251 p. : ill. ; 19 cm. Bibliography: p. 240-251. ISBN 3-924800-32-4 : LC Card 86-115002 DDC 331.88/0943 19
1. Trade-unions - Germany, West. 2. Unemployment - Germany (West). I. Title.
HD6694 .S254 1985 ***NYPL [JLC 87-35]***

Schaden, Franz Henning. Entwurff und Beschreibung von der Papiermacherey, worinnen der Ursprung des Papiermachens, der Fortgang, wie heutiges Tages das Papier gemachet wird, wie solches viele Mühe und Arbeit hat, benebst denen bey den Papiermachern befindlichen Wörtern, denen Kayserlichen Verordnungen und andern dahin einschlagenden Dingen /. [Mainz , 1962] (Darmstadt : E. Roether) 1 v. (various pagings) : LC Card 87-107659
HD9820.5 .E57 1962

Schadenhofer, Leopold. Analyseinstrumente für die strategische Marketingplanung / Leopold Schadenhofer. Wien : VWGÖ, 1982. 222 p. : ill. ; 21 cm. (Dissertationen der Johannes Kepler-Universität Linz . 35) Revision of the author's thesis (doctoral)--Johannes Kepler-Universität Linz, 1981. Bibliography: p. 213-222. ISBN 3-85369-497-7 : LC Card 82-237712
1. Marketing. 2. Marketing management. I. Title. II. Series.
HF5415 .S29 1982

Schaefer, Andrew. CAL-OSHA routine compliance inspections : inspections of high hazard worksites : a Senate Industrial Relations Committee and Assembly Labor and Employment Committee oversight report / by Andrew Schaefer and Britton McFetridge. [Sacramento, CA : Senate Committee on Industrial Relations] Additional copies may be purchased from Joint Publications, [1986] 25 p. ; 28 cm. "May 1986." "079-J"--Cover. LC Card 86-622709 DDC 363.1/164/09796 19
1. California. Division of Occupational Safety and Health. 2. Industrial hygiene - California. 3. Industrial safety - California. 4. Factory inspection - California. I. McFetridge, Britton. II. California. Legislature. Senate. Committee on Industrial Relations. III. California. Legislature. General Assembly. Committee on Labor and Employment. IV. Title.
HD7262.5.U62 C573 1986

Schaefer, Felix, 1950- Muster-Stichproben-Pläne für Bevölkerungs-Stichproben in der Bundesrepublik Deutschland und West-Berlin / bearbeitet von Felix Schaefer ; Hrsg., ADM, Arbeitskreis Deutscher Marktforschungsinstitute. München : Verlag Moderne Industrie, c1979. 160 p. : ill. ; 24 cm. (MI-Wirtschaftswissenschaften) Bibliography: p. 123-124. Includes index. ISBN 3-478-39760-X; 3-478-39760-1 LC Card 84-135457
1. Germany (West) - Population - Statistical methods. 2. Sampling (Statistics). 3. Demographic surveys - Germany (West). I. Arbeitskreis Deutscher Marktforschungsinstitute. II. Title. III. Series.
HB3595 .S29 1979

Schaefer, Reinhard.
Disponibilität--Mobilität--Fluktuation / Reinhard Schaefer, Carola Schmidt, Jürgen Wahse. Berlin : Akademie-Verlag, 1982. 70 p. : ill. ; 22 cm. (Forschungsberichte / Zentralinstitut für Wirtschaftswissenschaften der Akademie der Wissenschaften der DDR . Nr. 38) Bibliography: p. 67-70. LC Card 83-225572
1. Labor mobility - Germany (East). 2. Labor turnover - Germany (East). I. Schmidt, Carola. II. Wahse, Jürgen. III. Series: Forschungsberichte (Akademie der Wissenschaften der DDR. Zentralinstitut für Wirtschaftswissenschaften) , Nr. 38. IV. Title.
HD5717.5.G35 S3 1982

Schaefer, Robert A. Starting and managing a small service business / by Robert A. Schaefer. Washington, D.C. : U. S. Small Business Administration, Office of Business Development : For sale by the Supt. of Docs., U. S. G.P.O., 1986. v, 57 p. ; 21 cm. (Starting and managing series . v. 101) Shipping list no.: 86-877-P. Bibliography: p. 55-56. S/N 045-000-00238-1 Item 074 LC Card 86-603435 DDC 658/.022 19
1. Service industries - United States - Management. 2. Small business - United States - Management. 3. New business enterprises - United States - Management. I. United States. Small Business Administration. Office of Business Development. II. Title. III. Series.
HD9981.5 .S32 1986

Schätzung von ökonometrischen Ungleichgewichtsmodellen . Bauer, Gerhard. Idstein , 1985. iii, 350 p. : ISBN 3-925196-04-8 LC Card 86-226456
HB145 .B38 1985

Schäfer, Harald. Bilanzierung von Beteiligungen an assoziierten Unternehmen nach der Equity-Methode : Untersuchung über die Anwendbarkeit der Equity-Methode in der Bundesrepublik Deutschland / Harald Schäfer. Thun : H. Deutsch, c1982. xxiii, 428 p. ; 21 cm. (Reihe Wirtschaftwissenschaften, 0253-1488 . Bd. 272) Bibliography: p. 403-428. ISBN 3-87144-714-5 LC Card 83-129280
1. Investments - Germany (West) - Accounting. I. Title. II. Series.
HF5686.I6 S33 1982

Schäfer, Wilhelm, Dr. Wirtschaftswörterbuch / von Wilhelm Schäfer. 2., völlig neubearbeitete Aufl. München : F. Vahlen, c1986- v. <1 > ; 25 cm. Introd. matter in German and English.

CONTENTS. - Bd. 1. Englisch-Deutsch. ISBN 3-8006-1100-7 (Bd. 1) LC Card 86-214220
1. Economics - Dictionaries. 2. English language - Dictionaries - German. 3. Economics - Dictionaries - German. 4. German language - Dictionaries - English. I. Title.
HB61 .S3 1986

Schäffer, Árpád. A Tagsági vagyoni hozzájárulás feltételrendszere . Budapest , 1984. 69 p. ; ISBN 963-7006-29-X : LC Card 85-185839
HD3332.5.A4 T34 1984

Schäkermann, Thomas, 1957- Umweltschutz, Umweltverschmutzung und Wirtschaftswachstum : ein Beitrag zur Umweltökonomie im Rahmen neoklassischer Wachstumsmodelle / Thomas Schäkermann. München : V. Florentz, c1986. v, 249 p. ; 21 cm. (Volkswirtschaftliche Forschung und Entwicklung . Bd. 28) Bibliography: p. 240-249. Includes index. ISBN 3-88259-404-7 LC Card 86-226458 DDC 363.7/32 19
1. Pollution - Costs. 2. Pollution - Economic aspects. 3. Environmental policy. 4. Economic development. I. Title. II. Series.
HC79.P55 S355 1986

Schalk, Hans Joachim. Differenzierte Globalsteuerung : eine empirische Analyse mit einem disaggregierten ökonometrischen Modell / Hans Joachim Schalk. Berlin ; New York : Springer-Verlag, c1985. ix, 319 p. : ill. ; 25 cm. (Studies in contemporary economics . v. 19) Bibliography: p. [304]-319. ISBN 0-387-16045-0 (U. S.) LC Card 86-141700
1. Economic stabilization - Econometric models. 2. Economic policy - Econometric models. 3. Economic development - Econometric models. I. Title. II. Series.
HB3732 .S32 1985

Schall, Lawrence D. Introduction to financial management / Lawrence D. Schall, W. Haley. 5th ed. New York : McGraw-Hill, c1988. xvii, 856 p. : ill. (some col.) ; 25 cm. (McGraw-Hill series in finance) Bibliography: p. 797-803. Includes index. ISBN 0-07-055112-X LC Card 87-21450 DDC 658.1/5 19
1. Corporations - Finance. I. Haley, Charles W. II. Title.
HG4011 .S33 1988

Schalldach, Elisabeth, 1904- Rationalisierungsmassnahmen der Nachinflationszeit im Urteil der deutschen freien Gewerkschaften, von Dr. Elisabeth Schalldach. Jena, G. Fischer, 1930. ix, [1], 186 p. 24 cm. (Abhandlungen des Wirtschaftswissenschaftlichen Seminars zu Jena .. 21. Bd., 2 Hft.) Issued in part as the author's dissertation, Jena, 1930. "Literaturverzeichnis": p. [183]-186. LC Card AC34-383
1. Industrial management - Germany. 2. Industrial organization - Germany. 3. Trade-unions - Germany. 4. Efficiency, Industrial - Germany. I. Title. II. Series.
HD70.G2 S26 1930

Schaller, Enrique C. Borrini, Héctor R. El proceso de colonización en el impenetrable chaqueño /. Corrientes , 1981. 60 leaves : LC Card 86-204205 DDC 333.3/1/8234 19
HD479.C47 B67 1981

Schamis, Graciela. Sercovich, Francisco Colman. Exportaciones de tecnología de Brasil y Argentina /. [Buenos Aires, Argentina?] , 1986. 269 p. ; LC Card 87-404009 DDC 338.981/06 19
HC190.T4 S47 1986

Schanne, Hans Günther. Kratz, Hans-Jürgen. Arbeitslosengeld /. Saarbrücken [1983] 176 p. ; ISBN 3-88968-006-2 LC Card 83-215450
HD7096.G32 S335 1983

Schanz, Günther, 1943- Mitarbeiter-Kapitalbeteiligung in der Wirtschaft Niedersachsens : eine Erhebung über praktizierte Vermögens-Beteiligungsmodelle / Günther Schanz, Hans-Christian Riekhof. Spardorf : R.F. Wilfer, c1984. 228 p. : ill. ; 21 cm. (Stiftung Sozialer Wandel in der Unternehmerischen Wirtschaft . Bd. 6) AGP-Veröffentlichungen ; Bd. 25 ISBN 3-922919-26-X : LC Card 84-162288
1. Employee ownership - Germany (West) - Lower Saxony. 2. Industrial management - Germany (West) - Lower Saxony - Employee participation. 3. Lower Saxony (Germany) - Industries. I. Riekhof, Hans-Christian. II. Series: Stiftung Sozialer Wandel in der Unternehmerischen Wirtschaft (Series) , Bd. 6. III. Title.
HD5660.G412 L687 1984

Schanz, Hermann J. Der niederrheinische Wirtschaftsraum : Standortpotential und Perspektiven / Hermann J. Schanz, Hermann Tengler. Stuttgart : C.E. Poeschel, c1986. xxii, 466 p. ; 24 cm. (Schriften zur Mittelstandsforschung . Nr. 14 NF) Bibliography: p. 459-466. ISBN 3-7910-5014-1 LC Card 87-135757 DDC 330.943/55 19
1. Duisburg Region (North Rhine-Westphalia, Germany) - Economic conditions. 2. Wesel Region (North Rhine-Westphalia, Germany) - Economic conditions. 3. Kleve Region (North Rhine-Westphalia, Germany) - Economic conditions. I. Tengler, Hermann. II. Series. III. Series: Schriften zur Mittelstandsforschung , n.F., Nr. 14. IV. Title.
HC289.D755 S32 1986

Schap, David. Municipal ownership in the electric utility industry : a centennial view / David Schap. New York : Praeger, 1986. xiii, 128 p. ; 24 cm. Includes index. Bibliography: p. 117-126. ISBN 0-03-006347-7 : LC Card 85-19418 DDC 363.6/2/0973 19
1. Electric utilities - Government ownership - United States - History. 2. Municipal ownership - United States - History. I. Title.
HD9685.U5 S3 1986 ***NYPL [JLE 86-3180]***

Schapiro, Morton Owen. Filling up America : an economic-demographic model of population growth and distribution in the nineteenth century United States / by Morton Owen Schapiro. Greenwich, Conn. : JAI Press, c1986. xiii, 149 p. : ill. ; 24 cm. (Industrial development and the social fabric. v. 8) Includes index. Bibliography: p. 137-143. ISBN 0-89232-675-1 : LC Card 86-2771 DDC 304.6/0973 19
1. Fertility, Human - United States - History - 19th century. 2. Migration, Internal - United States - History - 19th century. 3. United States - Population - History - 19th century. 4. United States - Population, Rural - History - 19th century. 5. United States - Economic conditions - To 1865. 6. United States - Economic conditions - 1865-1918. I. Title.
HB3505 .S33 1986 ***NYPL [JLE 86-3386]***

Scharf, Charles A.
Acquisitions, mergers, sales, and takeovers. Scharf, Charles A. Acquisitions, mergers, sales, buyouts, and takeovers : a handbook with forms / Charles A. Scharf, Edward E. Shea, and George C. Beck.3rd ed. Englewood Cliffs, N.J. , c1985. xi, 452 p. : ISBN 0-13-003120-8 LC Card 85-6566 DDC 658.1/6/0973 19
HD2741 .S35 1985 ***NYPL [JLF 86-611]***

Acquisitions, mergers, sales, buyouts, and takeovers : a handbook with forms / Charles A. Scharf, Edward E. Shea, and George C. Beck.3rd ed. Englewood Cliffs, N.J. : Prentice-Hall, c1985. xi, 452 p. : ill. ; 29 cm. Rev. ed. of: Acquisitions, mergers, sales, and takeovers. 1971. Includes indexes. ISBN 0-13-003120-8 LC Card 85-6566 DDC 658.1/6/0973 19
1. Consolidation and merger of corporations - United States - Handbooks, manuals, etc. 2. Business enterprises, Sale of - United States - Handbooks, manuals, etc. 3. Business enterprises - United States - Purchasing - Handbooks, manuals, etc. I. Shea, Edward E., 1932-. II. Beck, George C., 1947-. III. Scharf, Charles A. Acquisitions, mergers, sales, and takeovers. IV. Title.
HD2741 .S35 1985 ***NYPL [JLF 86-611]***

Scharff, Edward E. Worldly power : the making of the Wall Street journal / Edward E. Scharff. New York : New American Library, 1987, c1986. p. cm. "A Plume book." Bibliography: p. Includes index. ISBN 0-452-25917-7 (pbk.) LC Card 86-28562 DDC 071/.47/1 19
1. Wall Street journal - History. I. Title.
HG4910 .S3 1987

Schargott, Michael. Bartsch, Heinz. Örtliche Versorgungswirtschaft . Potsdam-Babelsberg , 1985. 79 p. : LC Card 86-121253
HD2768.G4 B27 1985

Schasse, Ulrich. Mitbestimmung, Norm und Wirklichkeit . Frankfurt , New York , c1984. 369 p. ; ISBN 3-593-33325-2 LC Card 85-128882
HD5658.A82 G35 1984

Schatan, Gilda. Schatan, Jacobo. [América Latina, deuda externa y desarrollo. English.] World debt . London , Atlantic Highlands, N.J., USA , 1987. xv, 126 p. ; ISBN 0-86232-688-5 : LC Card 87-13330 DDC 336.3/435/098 19
HJ8514.5 .S313 1987

Schatan, Jacobo.
[América Latina, deuda externa y desarrollo. English]
World debt : who is to pay? / Jacobo Schatan ; in collaboration with Gilda Schatan ; with a preface by Richard Gott. London ; Atlantic Highlands, N.J., USA : Zed Books, 1987. xv, 126 p. ; 23 cm. Translation of: América Latina, deuda externa y desarrollo. Bibliography: p. 121-124. Includes index. ISBN 0-86232-688-5 : LC Card 87-13330 DDC 336.3/435/098 19
1. Debts, External - Latin America. 2. Latin America - Economic policy. I. Schatan, Gilda. II. Title.
HJ8514.5 .S313 1987

Schattenwirtschaft . Weck-Hannemann, Hannelore. Frankfurt am Main , New York , c1983. 152 p. : ISBN 3-8204-7590-7 (pbk.) LC Card 87-672943
HD2341 .W37x 1983

Schattenwirtschaft in der Bundesrepublik . Niessen, Hans-Joachim. Opladen , 1987. 246 p. : ISBN 3-8100-0592-4 LC Card 87-131108
HD2346.G3 N545 1987

Schattenwirtschaft und alternative Ökonomie : eine politische Herausforderung für die politische Ökonomie? / Peter De Gijsel, Hans-Günther Seifert-Vogt (Hrsg.). Regensburg : Transfer Verlag, c1984. 268 p. : ill. ; 24 cm. Bibliography: p. 249-266. Includes index. ISBN 3-924956-00-6 LC Card 86-224071
1. Informal sector (Economics) - Congresses. 2. Economics - Congresses. I. De Gijsel, Peter. II. Seifert-Vogt, Hans-Günther.
HD2341 .S337 1984

Schatz, Heribert. Verbraucherinteressen im politischen Entscheidungsprozess / Heribert Schatz, unter Mitarbeit von Annemarie Bopp-Schmehl ... [et al.]. Frankfurt/Main ; New York : Campus, c1984. 275 p. ; 22 cm. (Campus Forschung. Bd. 366) Bibliography: p. 259-273. Prepared by several members of Forschungsverbund "Empirische Verbraucherforschung." ISBN 3-593-33293-0 LC Card 84-212024
1. Consumer protection - Germany, West. 2. Consumer protection - Germany, West - North Rhine-Westphalia. 3. Consumer protection - Law and legislation - Germany, West. I. Bopp-Schmehl, Annemarie, 1946-. II. Forschungsverbund "Empirische Verbraucherforschung" (Germany). III. Title.
HC290.5.C63 S33 1984

Schatz, Klaus-Werner. Die Bedeutung kleiner und mittlerer Unternehmen im Strukturwandel / von Klaus-Werner Schatz. Kiel : Institut für Weltwirtschaft, 1984. 32 p. ; 30 cm. (Kieler Diskussionsbeiträge, 0455-0420 = Kiel discussion papers . 103) Cover title. Bibliography: p. 30-32. LC Card 85-136545
1. Small business - Germany, West. 2. Germany, West - Economic conditions. 3. Germany, West - Economic policy. I. Series: Kieler Diskussionsbeiträge , 103. II. Title.
HB44 .K45 no. 103 HD2346.G3

Schatz- und Zinsverzeichnisse des fünfzehnten Jahrhunderts aus dem Fürstentum Lüneburg. Schatz- und Zinsverzeichnisse des 15. Jahrhunderts aus dem Fürstentum Lüneburg . Hildesheim , 1942. 153 p. ; LC Card 87-409521 DDC 336.2/00943/59 19
HJ2110.5.L86 S3 1942

Schatz- und Zinsverzeichnisse des 15. Jahrhunderts aus dem Fürstentum Lüneburg : Quellen zur Bevölkerungsgeschichte der Kreise Harburg, Dannenberg, Gifhorn und Ülzen, 1450-1497 / herausgegeben von Rudolf Grieser. Hildesheim : A. Lax, 1942. 153 p. ; 23 cm. (Quellen und Darstellungen zur Geschichte Niedersachsens . Bd. 50) Includes indexes. LC Card 87-409521 DDC 336.2/00943/59 19
1. Taxation - Germany (West) - Lüneburg (Principality) - Lists. 2. Lüneburg (Principality) - Genealogy. 3. Lüneburg (Principality) - History - Sources. I. Grieser, Rudolf, 1899-. II. Title: Schatz- und Zinsverzeichnisse des fünfzehnten Jahrhunderts aus dem Fürstentum Lüneburg. III. Series.
HJ2110.5.L86 S3 1942

Schatzberg, Michael G. The Political economy of Kenya /. New York , 1987. viii, 245 p. ; ISBN 0-275-92672-9 (alk. paper) : LC Card 87-22889

DDC 330.9676/204 19
HC865 .P65 1987

Schatzbuch der Grafschaft Mark, 1486 /. Mark (Grafschaft) Unna , 1986. 176 p. ; ISBN 3-87298-042-4 LC Card 87-116701 DDC 336.2/00943/55 19
HJ2110.5.M36 M37 1986

Schäublin, Lisa, 1952- Fabrikbesichtigungen /. Zürich , c1986. 206 p. : ISBN 3-85791-109-3 LC Card 87-129952 DDC 305.5/62/09494 19
HD8606.5 .F33 1986

Schauenberg, Harald. Die taktische Finanzplanung der internationalen Unternehmung / Harald Schauenberg. Königstein/Ts. : Hain, c1982. vi, 134 p. ; 23 cm. (Quantitative Methoden der Unternehmungsplanung. 18) Originally presented as the author's thesis (doctoral)--Universität Fridericiana in Karlsruhe, 1982. Bibliography: p. 129-134. ISBN 3-445-02259-3 : LC Card 82-224376
1. International business enterprises - Finance - Planning. I. Title.
HG4027.5 .S32 1982

Schauer, Donald D. Careers in trucking / by Donald D. Schauer. 1st ed. New York : Rosen Pub. Group, 1987. xii, 132 p. : ill. ; 22 cm. Includes index. Describes the opportunities, requirements, aptitudes, and regulations involved in seeking a job in the trucking industry. ISBN 0-8239-0748-1 : LC Card 87-4769 DDC 388.3/24/02373 19
1. Trucking - Vocational guidance - United States. I. Title.
HE5623 .S33 1987

Schauer, Reinbert. Die Verwaltung als betriebliches Teilsystem : Untersuchung über das Ausmass und die Ursachen der Veränderung der Funktion "Verwaltung" im Rahmen der betrieblichen Aktivitäten in der österreichischen Wirtschaft / Reinbert Schauer, unter Mitarbeit von Christian Pracher und Christina Heilbrunner. Wien : Institut für Angewandte Sozial- und Wirtschaftsforschung im Signum-Verlag, 1984. v, 258 p. : ill. ; 21 cm. Bibliography: p. 209-211. ISBN 3-85436-014-2 LC Card 84-173337
1. Management. 2. Industrial management - Austria. I. Pracher, Christian. II. Heilbrunner, Christina. III. Institut für Angewandte Sozial- und Wirtschaftsforschung (Vienna, Austria). IV. Title.
HD35 .S2655 1984

Schaum's outline of theory and problems of bookkeeping and accounting /. Lerner, Joel J. New York , c1988. 311 p. : ISBN 0-07-037231-4 (pbk.) LC Card 87-3800 DDC 657/.076 19
HF5661 .L46 1988

Schaum's outline of theory and problems of international economics /. Salvatore, Dominick. New York , c1984. 231 p. : ISBN 0-07-054503-0 (pbk.) LC Card 82-21666 DDC 337 19
HF1411 .S24 1984 ***NYPL [JLF 86-1845]***

Schaum's outline series in accounting.
Lerner, Joel J. Schaum's outline of theory and problems of bookkeeping and accounting /. New York , c1988. 311 p. : ISBN 0-07-037231-4 (pbk.) LC Card 87-3800 DDC 657/.076 19
HF5661 .L46 1988

Schechter, Peter. Bereuter, Douglas K. United States and European Community development assistance to Africa . [Washington, D.C.? , 1985?] 22, [2] leaves ; LC Card 87-108848 DDC 338.91/4/06 19
HC800 .B455 1985

Schedl, Klaus, 1949- Entwicklungsmanagement . Berlin , c1982. 192 p. : ISBN 3-428-05208-0 LC Card 83-150764 DDC 338.9/0068 19
HD84 .E56 1982 ***NYPL [JLE 87-1179]***

Scheduled castes and tribes . Parvathamma, C., 1928- New Delhi , 1984. xiii, 310 p. ;
NYPL [JLD 87-707]

SCHEDULED CASTES (INDIA) see **UNTOUCHABLES.**

Scheduled tribes (India) see **India - Scheduled tribes.**

Scheer, Christian. Verteilungswirkungen der Einkommensteuer / Christian Scheer. Göttingen : O. Schwartz, c1982. xii, 457 p. : ill. ; 21 cm. (Beiträge zur Mittelstandsforschung . Heft 56) Bibliography: p. 417-457. ISBN 3-509-01260-7 : LC Card 83-150522
1. Income tax - Germany, West. 2. Income distribution - Germany, West. 3. Germany, West - Social policy. I. Title. II. Series.
HJ4719 .S34 1982

Scheer, Harold. The multinational bank : an application of the theory of the multinational enterprise / par Harold Scheer. Genève : Institut universitaire de hautes études internationales, 1987. 131, [6] p. : ill. ; 30 cm. "Mémmoire présenté en vue de l'obtention du diplôme." Bibliography: p. [133]-[137] LC Card 87-155370 DDC 332.1/5 19
1. Banks and banking, International. 2. International finance. I. Title.
HG3881 .S338 1987

Scheer, Jens. Atomkraft am Ende? /. Göttingen , 1986. 191 p. ; ISBN 3-923478-16-X LC Card 86-228667
HD9698.A2 A795 1986

Scheetz, Thomas Edward. Peru and the International Monetary Fund / Thomas Scheetz. Pittsburgh, PA : University of Pittsburgh Press, c1986. xi, 257 p. : ill. ; 22 cm. (Pitt Latin American series) Includes index. Bibliography: p. 251-254. ISBN 0-8229-3816-2 LC Card 85-40855 DDC 332.1/52 19
1. International Monetary Fund - Peru. 2. Economic stabilization - Peru. 3. Loans, Foreign - Peru. 4. Balance of payments - Peru. I. Title.
HG3881.5.I58 S34 1986
NYPL [JLD 86-2893]

Scheffman, David T., 1943-
Empirical approaches to consumer protection economics . Washington, D.C. [1986] ii, 484 p. : LC Card 86-602207 DDC 381/.34/0973 19
HC110.C63 E46 1986

Empirical approaches to consumer protection economics . Washington, D.C. [1986] ii, 484 p. : ***NYPL [JLE 86-3552]***

Schefold, Bertram, 1943- Meyer-Abich, Klaus Michael, 1936- Die Grenzen der Atomwirtschaft . München , c1986. 230 p. : ISBN 3-406-31317-5 LC Card 86-192439
HD9698.A2 M49 1986

Scheiber, Harry N. Ohio canal era : a case study of government and the economy, 1820-1861 / Harry N. Scheiber. Athens : Ohio University Press, 1987. xxvi, 430 p. ; 23 cm. With a new preface by the author. Bibliography: p. [398]-422. Includes index. ISBN 0-8214-0048-7 LC Card 86-23800 DDC 386/.48/09771 19
1. Canals - Ohio - History - 19th century. 2. Canals - Government policy - Ohio - History - 19th century. 3. Railroads - Ohio - History - 19th century. 4. Railroads and state - Ohio - History - 19th century. 5. Ohio - Economic conditions. I. Title.
HE395.O34 S34 1987

Scheidhauer, Barbara. Recktenwald, Werner. Wie errechne ich meinen Nettolohn? Mit der Monatslohnsteuertabelle für rentenversicherungspflichtige Arbeitnehmer, 1986 und 1987, Auszug /. Saarbrücken [1987]. 128 p. ; LC Card 87-408789 DDC 343.4305/242 344.3035242 19
HJ4720.A7 R42 1987

Scheidulin, Hans. Die Häfen Bremen, Bremerhaven / Hans Scheidulin, Hermann Gutmann. Bremen : H.M. Hauschild, c1985. 160 p. : ill. (some col.) ; 29 cm. ISBN 3-920699-63-7 LC Card 86-124602 DDC 330.943/52 19
1. Bremerhaven (Germany) - Economic conditions. 2. Bremerhaven (Germany) - Commerce. I. Gutmann, Hermann. II. Title.
HC289.B72 S34 1985

Schein, Edgar H. The Art of managing human resources /. New York , 1987. xii, 307 p. : ISBN 0-19-504882-2 (alk. paper) LC Card 86-31107 DDC 658.3/01 19
HF5549.5.M3 A78 1987

Schein, Lawrence. Current issues in human-resource management / by Lawrence Schein. New York, N.Y. (845 3rd Ave., New York 10022) : Conference Board, c1986. 17 p. : ill. ; 28 cm. (Research bulletin / The Conference Board . no. 190) Includes bibliographical references. LC Card 86-212364 DDC 658.3/01 19
1. Manpower planning. I. Series: Research bulletin (Conference Board) , no. 190. II. Title.
HF5549.5.M3 S34 1986

Scheiper, Ulrich. Die sektoralen Importe und Exporte der Bundesrepublik Deutschland : eine ökonometrische Analyse unter Berücksichtigung flexibler Funktionsformen / Ulrich Scheiper. Frankfurt am Main : Haag + Herchen, c1984. v, 203 p. : ill. ; 21 cm. (Schriften zur angewandten Ökonometrie . Heft 13) Originally presented as the author's thesis (doctoral)--Christian-Albrechts-Universität zu Kiel, 1984. Bibliography: p. 198-203. ISBN 3-88129-846-0 : LC Card 85-125395
1. Germany (West) - Commerce - Econometric models. I. Title. II. Series.
HF3566.5 .S28 1984

Schelbert-Syfrig, Heidi. Makromodelle und Wirtschaftspolitik . Grüsch , c1985. 120 p. : ISBN 3-7253-0250-2 : LC Card 85-208009
HC397 .M26 1985

Schell, William, 1950- Medieval Iberian tradition and the development of the Mexican hacienda / by William Schell, Jr. Syracuse, NY : Maxwell School of Citizenship and Public Affairs, Syracuse University, 1986. 117 p. ; 23 cm. (Foreign and Comparative Studies/Latin American Series . no. 8.) Includes index. Bibliography: p. [85]-106. ISBN 0-915984-99-7 : LC Card 85-31042 DDC 307.7/2/0972 19
1. Haciendas - Mexico - History. 2. Haciendas - Spain - History. I. Series: Foreign and Comparative Studies/Latin American Series , no. 8. II. Title.
HD1471.M6 S34 1986 ***NYPL [JLE 86-1697]***

Schelle, Kurt.
Focht, Rick. Employment and gross earnings of California residents in Alaska's commercial fisheries, 1977-1982 /. Juneau, AK [1984] v, 53 p. : LC Card 86-622320 DDC 331.12/5392/09798021 19
HD4966.F652 U54 1984c

Focht, Rick. Employment and gross earnings of Oregon residents in Alaska's commercial fisheries, 1977-1982 /. Juneau, AK [1984] v, 69 p. : LC Card 86-622319 DDC 331.12/5392/09798021 19
HD4966.F652 U54 1984b

Focht, Rick. Employment and gross earnings of Washington residents in Alaska's commercial fisheries, 1977-1982 /. Juneau, AK [1984] v leaves, 126 p. ; LC Card 86-622318 DDC 331.2/8392/09797021 19
HD4966.F542 U554 1984

Schellenberger, Gerhard, 1924- Technisch rationell, sozial effektiv . Berlin , 1986. 168 p. ; ISBN 3-320-00706-8 LC Card 87-144339 DDC 338/.06 19
HC290.795.A9 T43 1986

Schellenberger, Robert Earl.
Policy formulation and strategy management.
Schellenberger, Robert Earl. Strategic management : text and cases / Glenn Boseman, Arvind Phatak, Robert E. Schellenberger. New York , c1986. xiii, 808 p. : ISBN 0-471-88059-0 : LC Card 85-9553 DDC 658.4/012 19
HD30.28 .S34 1986 ***NYPL [JLE 86-1559]***

Strategic management : text and cases / Glenn Boseman, Arvind Phatak, Robert E. Schellenberger. New York : Wiley, c1986. xiii, 808 p. : ill. ; 25 cm (Wiley series in management, 0271-6046) Rev. ed. of: Policy formulation and strategy management. 2nd ed. c1982. Includes bibliographical references and indexes. ISBN 0-471-88059-0 : LC Card 85-9553 DDC 658.4/012 19
1. Strategic planning. 2. Strategic planning - Case studies. 3. Business logistics. 4. Business logistics - Case studies. I. Boseman, F. Glenn. II. Phatak, Arvind V. III. Schellenberger, Robert Earl. Policy formulation and strategy management. IV. Title. V. Series.
HD30.28 .S34 1986 ***NYPL [JLE 86-1559]***

Schellhaass, Horst-Manfred. Schmähl, Winfried. Änderung der Beitragsfinanzierung in der Rentenversicherung? . Baden-Baden , 1984. 388 p. : ISBN 3-7890-1018-9 LC Card 84-206647
HD7179 .S324 1984

Schellinck, Douglas Anton, 1949- Marketing research : a computer assisted approach / D.A. Schellinck, R.N. Maddox. New York : Dryden Press, c1987. xii, 224 p. : ill. ; 24 cm. (The Dryden Press series in marketing) ISBN 0-03-010924-8 (pbk.) LC Card 86-29029 DDC 658.8/3/0285 19
1. Marketing research - Data processing. 2. Marketing research - Statistical methods - Data processing. I.

Maddox, R. N. (Robert Neil), 1938-. II. Title.
HF5415.2 .S32 1987

Schelsky, Helmut. Funktionäre : gefährden sie das Gemeinwohl? / Helmut Schelsky.3. Aufl. Stuttgart-Degerloch : Seewald, c1982. 310 p. ; 21 cm. Includes index. ISBN 3-512-00652-3 : LC Card 83-124834
1. Trade-unions - Germany, West - Officials and employees. 2. Bureaucracy - Germany, West. I. Title.
HD6694 .S2566 1982

Schelzel, Manfred. Hanseschiffahrt mit Norwegen / von Manfred Schelzel. Bergen : Institut für Schiffahrtswirtschaft an der Norwegischen Wirtschaftshochschule, 1979. 33 leaves ; 31 cm. Bibliography: leaf 33. LC Card 85-174193
1. Hanseatic League - Commerce - Norway - History. 2. Norway - Commerce - Hanseatic League - History. I. Title.
HF458 .S34 1979

Schendelen, M. P. C. M. van, 1944- Braakman, T. C. Sociale zekerheid in Nederland /. Utrecht , 1984. 199 p. : ISBN 90-274-5513-9 : LC Card 85-110890
HD7192 .B73 1984 ***NYPL [JLC 86-295]***

Schenk, Gerhard. Aufbereitung von Ergebnissen der Stadtverkehrsforschung . Hof/Saale , 1986. 2 v. : LC Card 87-408335 DDC 388.4/0943 19
HE4774 .A94 1986

Schenk, Hans-Otto. Die Konzentration im Handel : Ursachen, Messung, Stand, Entwicklung und Auswirkungen der Konzentration im Handel und konzentrationspolitische Konsequenzen / von Hans-Otto Schenk, Hiltrud Tenbrink, Horst Zündorf. Berlin : Duncker & Humblot, c1984. 341 p. : ill. ; 24 cm. (Schriftenreihe der Forschungsstelle für den Handel . 3. Folge, Nr. 9) Bibliography: p. [321]-341. ISBN 3-428-05618-3 LC Card 84-225438
1. Germany, West - Commerce. 2. Industrial concentration - Germany, West. I. Tenbrink, Hiltrud. II. Zündorf, Horst. III. Title. IV. Series.
HF345 .F66 Folge 3, Nr. 9 HF3566

Schenk, Karl Ernst. Bruns, Claudia. Westeuropean direct investment in Canada . Hamburg [1986] 18 p. : LC Card 86-191095
HG5152 .B78 1986

Schenker, Eric, 1931- Heilmann, Ronald L. Great Lakes transportation in the eighties /. Madison, WI , c1986. 100 p. : ISBN 0-936287-00-4 (pbk.) : LC Card 86-622259 DDC 386/.544/0977 19
HE398 .H45 1986

Schenkluhn, Brigitte, 1951- Konjunkturpolitik und Wahlen : eine fallanalytische Langzeituntersuchung der konjunkturpolitischen Regierungsentscheidungen in 7 Wahlperioden (von 1949-1976) / Brigitte Schenkluhn ; mit einem Vorwort von Peter Graf Kielmansegg und Ulrich Matz.1. Aufl. Bergisch Gladbach : J. Eul, 1985. xi, 482 p. : ill. ; 21 cm. Bibliography: p. 469-482. ISBN 3-89012-017-2 LC Card 85-153982
1. Business cycles - Germany (West) - Political aspects - Longitudinal studies. 2. Germany (West) - Economic policy - Longitudinal studies. 3. Elections - Germany (West) - Longitudinal studies. I. Title.
HB3789 .S34 1985

Schepens, Th. Vissers, A. M. C. Arbeidsmarktgedrag ten tijde van massale werkloosheid . 's-Gravenhage , 1986. 106 p. : ISBN 90-12-05302-1 LC Card 87-108930
HD5717.5.N45 V57 1986

Scheper, Wilhelm. Priebe, Hermann, 1907- Agrarpolitik in der EG . Baden-Baden , 1984. 269 p. ; ISBN 3-7890-1060-X LC Card 85-138555 DDC 338.1/84 19
HD1920.5.Z8 P74 1984

Schepers, Walter. Hübl, Lothar. Strukturwandel und Strukturpolitik . Hannover , 1983. 104 p. : LC Card 84-126938
HC286.7 .H83 1983

Scher, Carol. Scher, Les. Finding and buying your place in the country /. New York , London , c1987. p. cm. ISBN 0-02-008400-5 LC Card 87-24246 DDC 643/.2 19
HD256 .S27 1987

Scher, Les. Finding and buying your place in the country / Les Scher, Carol Scher ; art work by Roger Bayless and Pearl Hurd. New York : Collier Books ; London : Collier Macmillan, c1987. p. cm. Includes index. ISBN 0-02-008400-5 LC Card 87-24246 DDC 643/.2 19
1. Country homes - United States - Purchasing. 2. Country homes - Canada - Purchasing. 3. Vacation homes - United States - Purchasing. 4. Vacation homes - Canada - Purchasing. I. Scher, Carol. II. Title.
HD256 .S27 1987

Scherb, Margit, 1953- Stahl und Eisen bricht . Wien [1986] xi, 202 p. : ISBN 3-900351-62-7 LC Card 87-140293 DDC 330.9436/053 19
HC265 .S736 1986

Scherer, F. M. (Frederic M.) Ravenscraft, David J., 1952- Mergers, sell-offs, and economic efficiency /. Washington, D.C. , c1987. xiii, 290 p. : ISBN 0-8157-7348-X : LC Card 87-14018 DDC 338.8/3/0973 19
HD2746.5 .R38 1987

Scherer, Judy. Guide to state capital formation incentives and innovations /. [Washington, D.C. , 1983] vii, 154 p. ; LC Card 86-673432
HC110.I53 G84x 1983

Scherf, Harald. Marx und Keynes / Harald Scherf. 1. Aufl. Frankfurt am Main : Suhrkamp, 1986. 164 p. ; 18 cm. (Suhrkamp Taschenbuch Wissenschaft. 635) Includes bibliographical references. ISBN 3-518-28235-2 LC Card 87-104047 DDC 330.15/6 19
1. Marxian economics. 2. Keynesian economics. 3. Marx, Karl, 1818-1883. 4. Keynes, John Maynard, 1883-1946. I. Title.
HB97.5 .S283 1986

Schermer, A. D. (Abram D.) The Oriental challenge . Delft, the Netherlands , 1987. 281 p. : ISBN 90-70879-62-X (pbk.) LC Card 87-170212 DDC 332.6/732259 19
HC445 .O75 1987

Scherpenberg, Jens van. Öffentliche Finanzwirtschaft in Westdeutschland, 1944-1948 : Steuer- und Haushaltswesen in der Schlussphase des Krieges und den unmittelbaren Nachkriegsjahren dargestellt unter besonderer Berücksichtigung der Entwicklung in der britischen Zone / Jens van Scherpenberg. Frankfurt am Main : R.G. Fischer, c1984. 544 p. : ill. ; 21 cm. Bibliography: p. 530-544. ISBN 3-88323-502-4 LC Card 84-182435
1. Finance, Public - Germany (West) - History. I. Title.
HJ1120 .S317 1984

Scherpf, Peter, 1903- Unternehmung und Steuer . Wiesbaden , c1983. 395 p. ; ISBN 3-409-50005-7 LC Card 83-161883
HD2753.G3 U57 1983

SCHERPF, PETER, 1903-
Unternehmung und Steuer . Wiesbaden , c1983. 395 p. ; ISBN 3-409-50005-7 LC Card 83-161883
HD2753.G3 U57 1983

Schertler, Walter. Attraktivitätsanalyse von Dienstleistungen : ein empirischer Ansatz zur Entwicklung von Ausbaustrategien für Unternehmen und Staat / Walter Schertler, Wolfgang Popp. München : Minerva Publikation, c1983. 183 p. : ill. ; 21 cm. (Minerva-Fachserie Wirtschafts- und Sozialwissenschaften) Bibliography: p. 167-183. ISBN 3-597-10420-7 LC Card 83-140207
1. Service industries - Germany, West. 2. Service industries - Germany (West) - Management. I. Popp, Wolfgang. II. Title. III. Series.
HD9984.5 .S25 1983

Schettkat, Ronald.
Bevölkerungs- und Erwerbsverhaltensentwicklung in Österreich, Schweden und der Bundesrepublik Deutschland / Ronald Schettkat. Berlin : Wissenschaftszentrum Berlin, Internationales Institut für Management und Verwaltung, IIMV Arbeitsmarktpolitik, [1984] 48 p. ; 30 cm. (Discussion papers / IIM, Labour Market Policy, Wissenschaftszentrum Berlin, 0722-673X . IIM/LMP 84-12) "Juli 1984." Summary in English and German. Includes bibliographical references. LC Card 85-198691
1. Labor supply - Austria. 2. Labor supply - Sweden. 3. Labor supply - Germany, West. 4. Labor policy - Austria. 5. Labor policy - Sweden. 6. Labor policy - Germany, West. 7. Austria - Population. 8. Sweden - Population. 9. Germany, West - Population. I. Wissenschaftszentrum Berlin. II. International Institute of Management. Labour Market Policy. III. Series: Discussion papers (International Institute of Management. Labour Market Policy) , IIM/LMP 84-12. IV. Title.
HD5771 .S34 1984

Generelle Arbeitszeitverkürzung : gesamtwirtschaftliche Kosten- und Beschäftigungswirkungen / Ronald Schettkat. Berlin : Wissenschaftszentrum Berlin, 1984. iii, 108 p. : ill. ; 30 cm. (Discussion papers / International Institute of Management, 0722-673X . 84-2) Summary in English and German. Includes bibliographical references. LC Card 84-182608
1. Hours of labor - Econometric models. 2. Labor productivity - Econometric models. I. Series: Discussion papers (International Institute of Management) , 84-2. II. Title.
HD5106 .S3 1984

Scheuing, Eberhard E. (Eberhard Eugen), 1939- Johnson, Eugene M. Profitable service marketing /. Homewood, Ill. , c1986. xiv, 303 p. : ISBN 0-87094-613-7 LC Card 86-70516 DDC 658.8 19
HF5415.122 .J64 1986 ***NYPL [JLE 87-666]***

Schick, Allen. The whole and the parts : piecemeal and integrated approaches to congressional budgeting : report / prepared for the Task Force on the Budget Process by Allen Schick ; Committee on the Budget, U. S. House of Representatives. Washington : U. S. G.P.O. : For sale by the Supt. of Docs., Congressional Sales Office, U. S. G.P.O., 1987. vi, 65 p. ; 24 cm. At head of title: Committee Print. Distributed to some depository libraries in microfiche. Shipping list no.: 87-165-P. "February 1987." Bibliography: p. 61-65. "Serial no. CP-3" Item 1035-B-1, 1035-B-2 (microfiche) LC Card 87-601378 DDC 353.0072/2 19
1. Budget - United States. I. United States. Congress. House. Committee on the Budget. Task Force on Budget Process. II. Title.
HJ2052 .S335 1987

Schick, P. Charlene, 1943- Accounting fundamentals / P. Charlene Schick, Jean Gonzalez, David S. Kennedy. Englewood Cliffs, N.J. : Prentice-Hall, c1987. xviii, 509 p. : ill. (some col.) ; 25 cm. Includes index. ISBN 0-13-001918-6 LC Card 86-23732 DDC 657 19
1. Accounting. I. Gonzalez, Jean, 1945-. II. Kennedy, David S., 1938-. III. Title.
HF5635 .S3124 1987

Schieferdörfer . Bartels, Christoph. Pfaffenweiler , 1986. xiv, 370 p. : ISBN 3-89085-124-X LC Card 87-134379 DDC 338.943/43 19
HD9621.G33 R463 1986

Schier, Peter, 1950- Louven, Erhard. Shanghai, Chinas Tor zur Welt /. Hamburg , 1986. 118 p. : LC Card 86-230755
HC428.S47 L68 1986

Schiff, Maurice W. An econometric analysis of the world wheat market and simulation of alternative policies, 1960-80 / Maurice W. Schiff. Washington, DC : U. S. Dept. of Agriculture, Economic Research Service, International Economics Division, [1985] iv, 70 p. : ill. ; 28 cm. (ERS staff report . no. AGES 850827) Bibliography: p. 51-53. LC Card 85-603033 DDC 382/.41 19
1. Wheat trade - Econometric models. 2. Wheat trade - Government policy - Econometric models. I. Title.
HD9049.W4 S37 1985

Das Schiffchen fliegt, die Maschine rauscht . Tanner, Albert. Zürich , c1985. 214 p. : ISBN 3-293-00084-3 LC Card 86-124152
HD9865.S9 T36 1985

Schiffman, Leon G. Consumer behavior / Leon G. Schiffman, Leslie Lazar Kanuk. 3rd ed. Englewood Cliffs, N.J. : Prentice-Hall, c1987. xviii, 724 p. : ill. ; 25 cm. Includes bibliographies and indexes. ISBN 0-13-169020-5 LC Card 86-25224 DDC 658.8/342 19
1. Consumers. 2. Motivation research (Marketing). I. Kanuk, Leslie Lazar. II. Title.
HF5415.3 .S29 1987

Schiffmann, Dieter. Die Gewerkschaften von der Stabilisierung bis zur Weltwirtschaftskrise, 1924-1930 /. Köln , c1986. 2 v. (1586 p.) ; ISBN 3-7663-0902-1 (Bd. 1) LC Card 87-123987
HD6694 .Q44 1985 Bd. 3

SCHIFFWEILER (GERMANY) - ECONOMIC CONDITIONS.
Habicht, Werner. Werkssiedlung Madenfelderhof bei Landsweiler-Reden . Saarbrücken , 1985. 54 p., [52] p. of plates :

LC Card 87-408673 DDC 330.943/42 19
HD7289.5.A3 G437 1985

Schijnwerper op de detailhandel /. Jong, K. J. de. Deventer , 1986. 221 p. : ISBN 90-267-1058-5 : LC Card 86-177114
HF5429.6.N4 J663 1986

Schiller, Herbert I., 1919- Information and the crisis economy / Herbert I. Schiller. New York : Oxford University Press, 1986. xv, 133 p. ; 21 cm. Includes bibliographies and indexes. ISBN 0-19-520514-6 (pbk. : alk. paper) LC Card 86-2374 DDC 302.2/34 19
1. Mass media - Social aspects. 2. Economic history - 1971-. I. Title.
HE7651 .S34 1986 ***NYPL [JLD 86-3695]***

Schiller, Karl, 1911- Die Zukunft der Globalsteuerung /. Bern , c1986. 268 p. ; ISBN 3-258-03573-3 : LC Card 86-182288
HC286.7 .Z82 1986

SCHILLER, KARL, 1911-
Hahn, Jörg. Ökonomie, Politik und Krise . Würzburg , 1984. 137 p. ; ISBN 3-88479-183-4 LC Card 85-113948
HB3732 .H34 1984

Die Zukunft der Globalsteuerung /. Bern , c1986. 268 p. ; ISBN 3-258-03573-3 : LC Card 86-182288
HC286.7 .Z82 1986

Schiller, Karla, 1955- Loglineare Modellierung mit dem Abschlusstest : ein Instrument für die empirische Marketingforschung / Karla Schiller. München : V. Florentz, c1986. xiii, 226 p. : ill. ; 21 cm. (Hochschulschriften zur Betriebswirtschaftslehre . Bd. 38) Originally presented as the author's thesis (doctoral--Universität Karlsruhe (TH), 1986) Bibliography: p. 209-223. Includes index. ISBN 3-88259-397-0 LC Card 86-230772
1. Marketing - Decision making - Mathematical models. 2. Marketing research - Mathematical models. I. Title. II. Series.
HF5415.135 .S35 1986

Schiller, Robert, 1950- A comparison of Alaska's wholesale trade sector with other states / State of Alaska, Department of Commerce & Economic Development ; prepared by Robert Schiller. [Juneau, Alaska] : The Department, [1984] vi, 104 p. : ill. ; 28 cm. "December 1984." LC Card 86-620623 DDC 381/.2/09798 19
1. Wholesale trade - Alaska. 2. Wholesale trade - United States. I. Alaska. Dept. of Commerce and Economic Development. II. Title.
HF5421 .S33 1984

Schilling, Gerhard. Im Blickpunkt der Leistungsvergleich /. Berlin , 1985. 126 p. ; LC Card 85-155570
HC270.28 .I56 1985

Schimburile economice internaţionale . Iancu, Aurel. Bucureşti , 1983. 372 p. ; LC Card 85-216409
HF1411 .I24 1983 ***NYPL [JLD 87-1962]***

Schimmel, Warren T. Communicating / consulting authors, Warren T. Schimmel, Carolyn Beth Camp. New York : J. Wiley, c1987. xvi, 624 p., [32] p. of plates : ill. (some col.) ; 24 cm. Includes index. ISBN 0-471-84248-6 LC Card 87-111811 DDC 808/.066651 19
1. Communication in management. 2. English language - Business English. I. Camp, Carolyn Beth. II. Title.
HF5718 .S29 1987

Schinke, Rolf. Ursachen der Verschuldungskrise : extern oder intern bedingt? / Rolf Schinke. Göttingen : Ibero-Amerika Institut für Wirtschaftsforschung, Universität Göttingen, [1987] 33 p. : ill. ; 30 cm. (Diskussionsbeiträge . Nr. 42 =) Revised text of a lecture given on Dec. 4, 1986 at a meeting of the Göttinger Max-Eyth-Gesellschaft. Bibliography: p. 32-33. LC Card 87-409568 DDC 336.3/435/098 19
1. Debts, External - Latin America. 2. Loans, Foreign - Latin America. I. Series: Diskussionsbeiträge (Universität Göttingen. Ibero-Amerika Institut für Wirtschaftsforschung) , Nr. 42. II. Title.
HJ8514.5 .S34 1987

Schinnerer, Fritz. Unser Arbeitsgau 28 (Franken) : ein Handbuch für seine Führer, Arbeitsmänner und Freunde : ein Buch der Erinnerung für die, die in seinen Reihen standen / von Fritz Schinnerer.1. Ausg. Würzburg : Druck der Universitätsdruckerei H. Stürz ; Nürnberg : Kommissionsverlag der Fränkischen Tageszeitung, 1935. 454 p. : ill., maps ; 30 cm. LC Card 87-409298 DDC 331.3/41173/0943 19
1. Germany. Reichsarbeitsdienst. Arbeitsgau 28 (Franken). I. Title.
HD4870.G3 S35 1935

Schio e Alessandro Rossi . Convegno nazionale di studi storici (1979 : Schio, Italy) Roma , 1985-1986. 2 v. (1487 p., [1] folded leaf of plates) : LC Card 87-110167
HC302.5.R6 C66 1979

SCHIO (ITALY) - INDUSTRIES - HISTORY - 19TH CENTURY - CONGRESSES.
Convegno nazionale di studi storici (1979 : Schio, Italy) Schio e Alessandro Rossi . Roma , 1985-1986. 2 v. (1487 p., [1] folded leaf of plates) : LC Card 87-110167
HC302.5.R6 C66 1979

Şchiopu, Bucur. Gospodăriile agricole de stat / Bucur Şchiopu. Bucureşti : Editura Politică, 1966. 295 p. : ill. ; 22 cm. Bibliography: p. [291]-293. LC Card 84-183905
1. State farms - Romania. I. Title.
HD1493.R6 S35 1966

Schipper, Martin Paul. The War on poverty, 1964-1968 [microform] . Frederick, MD , c1986- microfilm reel ISBN 0-89093-495-9 (microfilm : set) : LC Card 87-10510 DDC 338.973 19
HC110 .P63

Schips, Bernd. Büttler, Hans-Jürgen. Estimation of disequilibrium models /. Berlin , New York , c1986. vi, 114 p. : ISBN 0-387-16817-6 (U. S.) : LC Card 86-22073 DDC 339.5 19
HB145 .B88 1986 ***NYPL [JLM 72-289 v.279]***

Schirmeister, Helga. Stimme und Aktion der Völker gegen das Wettrüsten . Berlin , 1985. 421 p. ; ***NYPL [JLD 86-4257]***

Schkolnik, Mariana. Sobrevivir en la población José M. Caro y en Lo Hermida / Mariana Schkolnik. [Santiago, Chile] : Programa de Economía del Trabajo, Academia de Humanismo Cristiano, [1986] 150 p., [20] p. of plates : ill. ; 22 cm. (Colección Temas sociales. 1) Bibliography: p. 131-132. LC Card 87-400080 DDC 362.5/8/098331 19
1. Poor - Chile - Santiago. 2. Basic needs - Chile - Santiago. 3. José María Caro (Santiago, Chile). 4. Lo Hermida (Santaigo, Chile). I. Programa de Economía del Trabajo (Academia de Humanismo Cristiano). II. Series: Colección Temas sociales (Santiago, Chile) , 1. III. Title.
HC193.S2 S35 1986

Schlachttier- und Fleischproduktion in Osteuropa . Pospelowa, Galina. Giessen , Berlin , 1981. 144 p. ; ISBN 3-428-04944-6 LC Card 82-167577
HD9425.B92 P67 1981

Schlager, Errol, 1950- Konjunkturzyklen : Theorie, Theoriekritik, Ideologiekritik / Errol Schlager. Augsburg : AV-Verlag, 1986. ii, 99 p. : ill. ; 21 cm. (Reihe Wissenschaft) Includes bibliographical references. ISBN 3-925274-08-1 LC Card 87-127445 DDC 338.5/42 19
1. Business cycles. I. Series: Reihe Wissenschaft (Augsburg, Germany). II. Title.
HB3716 .S35 1986

Schlagheck, James L.
Political, economic, and labor climate in Brazil. Andrade, Luis F. The labor climate in Brazil / by Luis F. Andrade. Philadelphia, Pa. , c1985. viii, 133 p. ; ISBN 0-89546-057-2 (pbk.) LC Card 85-81947 DDC 331/.0981 19
HD8286.5 .A67 1985 ***NYPL [JLF 86-1201]***

Schlangen, Gerhard. Die Systematik der unternehmerischen Sicherungsmassnahmen / Gerhard Schlangen. Münster : Lit, [1984?] vii, 179 p. : ill. ; 21 cm. (Betriebswirtschaftliche Schriftenreihe . Bd. 10) Bibliography: p. 168-177. ISBN 3-88660-063-7 LC Card 84-166733
1. Risk management. I. Title. II. Series.
HD61 .S34 1984

Schlarp, Karl-Heinz. Wirtschaft und Besatzung in Serbien, 1941-1944 : ein Beitrag zur nationalsozialistischen Wirtschaftspolitik in Südosteuropa / Karl-Heinz Schlarp. Stuttgart : F. Steiner Verlag Wiesbaden, 1986. viii, 443 p., [6] p. of plates : ill. ; 24 cm. (Quellen und Studien zur Geschichte des östlichen Europa. Bd. 25) Bibliography: p. [420]-436. Includes indexes. ISBN 3-515-04401-9 LC Card 86-181062
1. World War, 1939-1945 - Economic aspects - Yugoslavia - Serbia. 2. Serbia - Economic conditions. 3. Serbia - History - 1918-1945. 4. Serbia - Foreign economic relations - Germany. 5. Germany - Foreign economic relations - Yugoslavia - Serbia. 6. Germany - Economic policy - 1933-1945. I. Title.
HC407.Z7 S46676 1986

Schleis, Konrad, 1935- Börsengewinne dank besserer Aktienkurs-Prognose / Konrad Schleis. Niederglatt : Fortuna Finanz-Verlag, c1984. 257 p. : ill. ; 23 cm. Bibliography: p. 226-227. ISBN 3-85684-030-3 : LC Card 84-119396
1. Stocks - Germany, West. 2. Stock price forecasting. 3. Efficient market theory. I. Title.
HG5492 .S345 1984

Schlenke, Manfred. Frieden und Friedenssicherung in Vergangenheit und Gegenwart . München , 1984. 115 p. ; ISBN 3-7705-2147-1 (pbk.) :
NYPL [JFL 76-295 Bd. 7]

Schlesinger, Harris. Extending Arrow-Pratt risk premiums / by Harris Schlesinger. Berlin : IIM/Industrial Policy, Wissenschaftszentrum Berlin, [1985] 13, 4 leaves : ill. ; 30 cm. (Discussion papers / IIMV/Strukturpolitik--IIM/Industrial Policy, Wissenschaftszentrum Berlin, 0722-6748 . IIM/IP 85-18) "August 1985." Bibliography: leaf 13. LC Card 86-206602 DDC 368 19
1. Risk (Insurance) - Mathematical models. I. Series: Discussion papers (International Institute of Management. Industrial Policy) , IIM/IP 85-18. II. Title.
HG8054.5 .S35 1985

Schlesinger, James R. Organizational structures and planning / James R. Schlesinger. [Santa Monica, Calif. : Rand Corp., 1966] iii, 45 p. : ill. ; 28 cm. Cover title. "February 25, 1966." Stamped on t.p.: Rand collection. Includes bibliographical references. "P-3316." LC Card 87-404140 DDC 353.6 19
1. Organizational effectiveness. 2. Planning. 3. Communication in organizations. 4. United States. Dept. of Defense - Management. 5. United States. Dept. of Defense - Reorganization. I. Rand Corporation. II. Title.
HD58.9 .S35 1966

Schlesinger, Leonard A.
Burst, Ardis. The management game /. New York, N.Y. , 1987. 274 p. : ISBN 0-670-81225-0 LC Card 86-40617 DDC 658.4/0353 19
HD30.26 .B87 1987

Chronicles of corporate change . Lexington, Mass. , c1987. xiv, 254 p. : ISBN 0-669-13685-9 (alk. paper) LC Card 86-45555 DDC 384.6/065/73 19
HE8846.A55 C47 1987

Schlesinger, Stephen E. Stop drinking and start living / Stephen E. Schlesinger & John J. Gillick. 1st ed. Blue Ridge Summit, PA : TAB Books, 1985. xx, 133 p. : ill. ; 22 cm. Includes index. ISBN 0-8306-1937-2 : LC Card 85-14885 DDC 362.2/92 19
1. Alcoholism - United States. 2. Alcoholism - Treatment - United States. I. Gillick, John J. II. Title.
HV5033 .S34 1985 ***NYPL [JLD 86-1606]***

SCHLESWIG-HOLSTEIN (GERMANY) - ECONOMIC CONDITIONS.
Barschel, Uwe. Halbzeitbilanz '85 . Kiel [1985] 1 v. (various pagings) : LC Card 86-211699
HC287.S35 B37 1985

Schleswig-Holstein in Europa /. [Kiel] [1984?] 44 p. : LC Card 84-239599
HC287.S35 S39 1984

Schleswig-Holsteins Weg ins Industriezeitalter /. Hamburg , c1986. 175 p. : ISBN 3-7672-0965-9 LC Card 87-127674 DDC 338.0943/512 19
HC287.S35 S395 1986

SCHLESWIG-HOLSTEIN (GERMANY) - ECONOMIC POLICY.
Barschel, Uwe. Halbzeitbilanz '85 . Kiel [1985] 1 v. (various pagings) : LC Card 86-211699
HC287.S35 B37 1985

SCHLESWIG-HOLSTEIN (GERMANY) - INDUSTRIES - HISTORY.
Schleswig-Holsteins Weg ins Industriezeitalter /. Hamburg , c1986. 175 p. : ISBN 3-7672-0965-9 LC Card 87-127674 DDC 338.0943/512 19
HC287.S35 S395 1986

Schleswig-Holstein (Germany). Landtag.
Barschel, Uwe. Halbzeitbilanz '85 . Kiel [1985] 1 v. (various pagings) : LC Card 86-211699
HC287.S35 B37 1985

Schleswig-Holstein (Germany). Presse- und Informationsstelle der Landesregierung.
Barschel, Uwe. Halbzeitbilanz '85 . Kiel [1985] 1 v. (various pagings) : LC Card 86-211699
HC287.S35 B37 1985

Schleswig-Holstein in Europa / [Herausgeber, Der Beauftragte der Landesregierung für die Europawahl, Henning Schwarz, in Zusammenarbeit mit dem Landesverband Schleswig-Holstein der Europa-Union Deutschland]. [Kiel] : Der Beauftragte, [1984?] 44 p. : ill. ; 21 cm. Cover title. LC Card 84-239599
1. Schleswig-Holstein (Germany) - Economic conditions. 2. European Economic Community. 3. Europe - Economic integration. I. Schwarz, Henning. II. Europa Union Deutschland. Landesverband Schleswig-Holstein.
HC287.S35 S39 1984

Schleswig-Holsteins Weg ins Industriezeitalter / Urs J. Diederichs (Hrsg.) ; mit Beiträgen von Hans-Kai Möller ... [et al.]. Hamburg : Christians, c1986. 175 p. : ill. ; 30 cm. Bibliography: p. 172-174. Includes index. CONTENTS. - Schleswig-Holstein, ein Industrieland? / von Urs Justus Diederichs -- Die Industrialisierung der grossen Städte / von Urs Justus Diederichs -- Altona-Ottensen, blauer Dunst und rote Fahne / von Hans-Kai Möller -- Lübeck, von der Handels- zur Industriestadt / von Jenns E. Howoldt -- Neumünster, vom Tuchmacherhandwerk zur Textil- und Lederindustrie / von Klaus Tidow -- Kiel, die Stadt der Werften / von Urs Justus Diederichs -- Die Industrialisierung Flensburgs / von Gerd Vaagt -- Die Industrialisierung in den Landkreisen / von Urs Justus Diederichs -- Zwischen Landwirtschaft und Industrie, die holsteinische Unterelberegion / von Klaus-Joachim Lorenzen-Schmidt -- An der Westküste / von Nis R. Nissen -- Stormarn-Lauenburg, Industrie im Agrarbezirk / von Hansjörg Zimmermann -- Die neue Industriegesellschaft / von Urs Justus Diederichs. ISBN 3-7672-0965-9 LC Card 87-127674 DDC 338.0943/512 19
1. Schleswig-Holstein (Germany) - Economic conditions. 2. Schleswig-Holstein (Germany) - Industries - History. I. Diederichs, Urs J. (Urs Justus).
HC287.S35 S395 1986

Schlick, Manfred.
Die Haushalte der Flächenländer unter Konsolidierungszwang /. Bonn , 1986. 159 p. ; LC Card 87-409459 DDC 332 s 336.43 19
HJ1120 .B65 Nr. 262

Ziele und Möglichkeiten der Privatisierung in volkswirtschaftlicher Sicht . Bonn , 1985. 83 leaves ; LC Card 86-185728
HJ1120 .B65 Nr. 244 HD4178

Schlieper, Andreas.
Strukturanalyse Ruhrgebiet . [Essen] [1983?] 185 p. : LC Card 86-218075
HD5760.R84 S77 1983

Zimmermann, Horst, 1934- Die Gemeindefinanzen im Ruhrgebiet . Essen , 1983. xvi, 153 p. : ISBN 3-923494-28-9 LC Card 83-228289
HJ9493.5.R8 Z76 1983

150 Jahre Ruhrgebiet : ein Kapitel deutscher Wirtschaftsgeschichte / Andreas Schlieper, unter Mitarbeit von Heike Reinecke und Hans-Joachim Westholt ; mit einem Geleitwort von Johannes Rau ; herausgegeben vom Kommunalverband Ruhrgebiet.1. Aufl. Düsseldorf : Schwann, 1986. 224 p. : 50 ill. ; 22 cm. Bibliography: p. 210-216. Includes indexes. ISBN 3-590-18150-8 LC Card 86-231681
1. Ruhr (Germany : Region) - Economic conditions. 2. Ruhr (Germany : Region) - Industries - History. 3. Ruhr (Germany : Region) - Social conditions. 4. Germany, West - Economic policy. I. Reinecke, Heike. II. Westholt, Hans-Joachim. III. Kommunalverband Ruhrgebiet. IV. Title. V. Title: Einhundertfünfzig Jahre Ruhrgebiet.
HC288.R8 S34 1986

Schlotter, Hans Günther. Überwindung der Sozialstaatskrise . Baden-Baden , 1984. 317 p. : ISBN 3-7890-0925-3 LC Card 84-166713
HD7179 .U35 1984

Schlüsselgewalt : lieber instandbesetzen als kaputtbesitzen / Harry Böseke, Wolfgang Richter (Hrsg.). Dortmund : Weltkreis-Verlag, c1981. 190 p. : ill. ; 19 cm. ISBN 3-88142-261-7 : LC Card 81-206444
1. Housing policy - Germany, West. 2. Real estate development - Government policy - Germany (West). 3. Land use - Government policy - Germany (West). I. Böseke, Harry. II. Richter, Wolfgang, Dipl.-Ing.
HD7339.A3 S25 1981

Schlüpmann, Klaus. Martínez Alier, Juan. [Ecologisme i l'economia. English.] Ecological economics . Oxford [Oxfordshire] , New York, NY, USA , 1987. ix, 286 p. ; ISBN 0-631-15739-5 : LC Card 87-14512 DDC 333.7 19
HD85.S7 M363513 1987

Schmähl, Winfried. Änderung der Beitragsfinanzierung in der Rentenversicherung? : ökonomische Wirkungen des "Maschinenbeitrags" / Winfried Schmähl, Klaus-Dirk Henke, Horst M. Schellhaass.1. Aufl. Baden-Baden : Nomos, 1984. 388 p. : ill. ; 23 cm. Bibliography: p. 374-382. Includes indexes. ISBN 3-7890-1018-9 LC Card 84-206647
1. Social security - Germany, West. 2. Pensions - Germany, West. I. Henke, Klaus-Dirk. II. Schellhaass, Horst-Manfred. III. Title.
HD7179 .S324 1984

SCHMALENBACH, E. (EUGEN), 1873-1955.
Eugen Schmalenbach . Stuttgart , 1984. xvii, 478 p. : ISBN 3-8202-0295-1 LC Card 84-215889
HF5616.G3 E93 1984

Schmalenbach-Gesellschaft--Deutsche Gesellschaft für Betriebswirtschaft. Langfristiges Anlagengeschäft, Risiko-Management und Controlling /. Düsseldorf , c1986. 148 p. : ISBN 3-7754-0016-8 LC Card 86-227044
HG4534 .L36 1986

Schmalenbach-Stiftung. Eugen Schmalenbach . Stuttgart , 1984. xvii, 478 p. : ISBN 3-8202-0295-1 LC Card 84-215889
HF5616.G3 E93 1984

Schmalenbach-Tagung 1986 (1986 : Düsseldorf, Germany) Langfristiges Anlagengeschäft, Risiko-Management und Controlling /. Düsseldorf , c1986. 148 p. : ISBN 3-7754-0016-8 LC Card 86-227044
HG4534 .L36 1986

Schmalensee, Diane H. Creativity in services marketing . Chicago, IL , 1986. 175 p. : ISBN 0-87757-179-1 (pbk.) LC Card 85-26785 DDC 658.8 19
HD9980.5 .C74 1986 ***NYPL [JLF 86-1783]***

Schmalensee, Richard. Fischer, Stanley. Economics /. New York , c1988. xliii, 813 p. : ISBN 0-07-017781-3 : LC Card 87-21333 DDC 330 19
HB171.5 .F458 1988

Schmandt, Henry J.
Case studies of the impact of federal aid on major cities, city of St. Louis. Schmandt, Henry J. Federal aid to St. Louis / Henry J. Schmandt, George D. Wendel, and E. Allan Tomey. Washington, D.C. , c1983. xvii, 67 p. ; ISBN 0-8157-7727-2 (pbk.) LC Card 82-74100 DDC 336.1/85 19
HJ9268.S3 S352 1983 ***NYPL [JLE 87-1]***

Federal aid to St. Louis / Henry J. Schmandt, George D. Wendel, and E. Allan Tomey. Washington, D.C. : Brookings Institution, c1983. xvii, 67 p. ; 23 cm. Slightly condensed version of: Case studies of the impact of federal aid on major cities, city of St. Louis. ISBN 0-8157-7727-2 (pbk.) LC Card 82-74100 DDC 336.1/85 19
1. Grants-in-aid - Missouri - Saint Louis. 2. Federal-city relations - Missouri - Saint Louis. I. Wendel, George D. II. Tomey, E. Allan. III. Schmandt, Henry J. Case studies of the impact of federal aid on major cities, city of St. Louis. IV. Brookings Institution. V. Title.
HJ9268.S3 S352 1983 ***NYPL [JLE 87-1]***

Schmandt, Jurgen. Promoting high-technology industry . Boulder , 1987. 283 p. ; ISBN 0-8133-7427-8 (pbk. : alk. paper) LC Card 87-61327 DDC 338.4/762/000973 19
HC110.H53 P76 1987

Schmassmann, Norbert. Verteilungswirkungen von Erdölpreissteigerungen : Versuch einer empirischen Analyse für die Schweiz 1972-1980 / Norbert Schmassmann. Diessenhofen : Rüegger, c1983. viii, 326 p. : ill. ; 21 cm. (Basler sozialökonomische Studien. Bd. 21) "Basler Dissertation"--Verso t.p. Bibliography: p. 307-326. ISBN 3-7253-0203-0 LC Card 83-219477
1. Petroleum products - Prices - Switzerland. 2. Inflation (Finance) - Switzerland - Effect of energy costs on. 3. Income distribution - Switzerland. I. Series: Basler sozialökonomische Studien, 21. II. Title.
HD9575.S92 S27 1983

Schméder, Geneviève. Salomon, Jean Jacques. Les enjeux du changement technologique /. Paris , c1986. 206 p. : ISBN 2-7178-1092-7 : LC Card 86-172778
HC79.T4 S286 1986

Schmehl, Annemarie Bopp- see Bopp-Schmehl, Annemarie, 1946-

Schmeidler, David, 1939- Social goals and social organization . Cambridge [Cambridgeshire] , New York , 1985. xii, 365 p. : ISBN 0-521-26204-6 LC Card 85-6668 DDC 330.15/5 19
HB846 .S65 1985 ***NYPL [JLE 86-3786]***

Schmelzeisen, Hans-Michael. Bedeutung, Einsatzmöglichkeiten und -probleme des kombinierten Güterverkehrs in der Ernährungswirtschaft / Hans Michael Schmelzeisen. Münster : Lit, [1986] xii, 350 p. : ill. ; 21 cm. (Betriebswirtschaftliche Schriftenreihe . Bd. 32) Bibliography: p. 337-350. ISBN 3-88660-357-1 (Deut. Bibl.) LC Card 87-121511 DDC 380.5/24 19
1. Food - Transportation. 2. Food industry and trade - Germany, West. 3. Farm produce - Germany (West) - Transportation. I. Title. II. Series.
HE199.5.F6 S36 1986

Schmengler, Uwe. Umweltprobleme des Ballungsraums Mexiko Stadt unter besonderer Berücksichtigung der Wasserwirtschaft / vorgelegt von Uwe Schmengler. [Berlin : s.n., 1985] 120, [16] leaves : ill., maps ; 30 cm. "Wissenschaftliche Hausarbeit im Rahmen der Ersten (Wissenschaftlichen) Staatsprüfung für das Amt des Studienrats zum Thema: ..." Bibliography: leaves [121]-[136] LC Card 86-116997
1. Water quality management - Government policy - Mexico - Mexico City Metropolitan Area. 2. Water quality management - Mexico - Mexico City Metropolitan Area. I. Title.
HC138.M4 S35 1985

Schmerl, Christiane. Biermann, Ingrid, 1955- Leben mit kurzfristigem Denken . Weinheim , 1985. 224 p. ; ISBN 3-407-58260-9 LC Card 86-106693
HD6053.6.G3 B54 1985
NYPL [JLD 86-3122]

Schmid, A. Allan (Alfred Allan), 1935- Property, power, and public choice : an inquiry into law and economics / A. Allan Schmid.2nd ed. New York : Praeger, 1987. xv, 332 p. : ill. ; 24 cm. Bibliography: p. [293]-316. Includes indexes. ISBN 0-275-92797-0 (alk. paper) : LC Card 87-22893 DDC 330.1 19
1. Economics. 2. Property. 3. Social choice. 4. Welfare economics. I. Title.
HB73 .S35 1987

Schmid, Gunther, 1942-
Albrecht, Christoph, 1950- Beschäftigungsentwicklung und Qualifikationsstruktur in Berlin 1977-1983 . Berlin [1985] 2 v. : LC Card 86-204299
HD5780.B4 A43 1985

Regionalisierte Arbeitsmarkt- und Beschäftigungspolitik /. Frankfurt/Main , New York , c1983. 322 p. : ISBN 3-593-33241-8 LC Card 84-106151
HC286.7 .R44 1983

Schmid, Hanspeter, 1951- Wirtschaft, Staat und Macht : die Politik der schweizerischen Exportindustrie im Zeichen von Staats- und Wirtschaftskrise (1918-1929) / Hanspeter Schmid. Zürich : Limmat, [c1983] 432 p. : ill. ; 21 cm. (Reihe W) Revision of the author's thesis (doctoral)--Universität Basel, 1982. Bibliography: p. 415-432. ISBN 3-85791-073-9 (Schw. Buch) LC Card 83-244266
1. Switzerland - Commercial policy - History - 20th century. 2. Switzerland - Economic conditions - 1918-1945. 3. Economic history - 1918-1945. 4. Depressions - 1929 - Switzerland. 5. Depressions - 1929. I. Title.
HF1573 .S335 1983

Schmid, Josef, 1937- Bevölkerungswissenschaft . Frankfurt , New York , c1985. 227 p. ; ISBN

3-593-33461-5 LC Card 85-178756
HB849 .B48 1985

Schmid, Viola. Nicaragua . Hamburg [1986] 95 p. : ISBN 3-921620-32-5 LC Card 86-191836 DDC 330.97285/053 19
HC146 .N56 1986

Schmidt, Alfred, 1945- Korte, Hermann, 1937- Migration und ihre sozialen Folgen . Göttingen , c1983. 170 p. ; ISBN 3-525-85366-1 LC Card 84-150019
HD8458.A2 K65 1983

Schmidt, Arthur, 1943- The social and economic effect of the railroad in Puebla and Veracruz, Mexico, 1867-1911 / Arthur Schmidt. New York : Garland, 1987. 297 p. : ill. ; 24 cm. (South American and Latin American economic history) Bibliography: p. [286]-297. ISBN 0-8240-1370-0 (alk. paper) : LC Card 87-8628 DDC 385/.0972/48 19
1. Railroads - Mexico - Puebla (State) - History. 2. Railroads - Mexico - Veracruz (State) - History. 3. Ferrocarril Mexicano - History. I. Title. II. Series.
HE2819.P84 S35 1987

Schmidt, Aurel, 1935- Der Fremde bin ich selber : auf der Suche nach der verschütteten Utopie : ein Bericht / Aurel Schmidt. Basel : Lenos, c1982. 261 p. : ill. ; 20 cm. (Band 39 der Reihe Litprint) Includes bibliographies. ISBN 3-85787-103-2 : LC Card 83-109021
1. Environmental policy. 2. Utopias. 3. Human settlements. 4. Conduct of life. 5. Native races. I. Title.
HC79.E5 S284 1982

Schmidt, Axel. Betriebliche Altersversorgung in mittelständischen Unternehmen / Axel Schmidt. Stuttgart : C.E. Poeschel, c1985. xiii, 213 p. : ill. ; 24 cm. (Schriften zur Mittelstandsforschung . Nr. 3, N F) Bibliography: p. 205-212. ISBN 3-7910-5004-4 : LC Card 86-164220
1. Old age pensions - Germany, West. 2. Old age pensions - Law and legislation - Germany (West). I. Title. II. Series.
HD7105.35.G3 S35 1985
NYPL [JLL 73-505 Nr. 3]

Schmidt, Bernd, 1940- Simulation als betriebliche Entscheidungshilfe . Berlin , New York , 1987. xi, 282 p. : ISBN 0-387-17353-6 LC Card 87-121884 DDC 658.4/0352 19
HD30.23 .S56 1987

Schmidt, Brigitte. Struktur und Arbeitsweise von Arbeitsverwaltungen in EG-Ländern Frankreich, Belgien, Italien . Nürnberg , 1982. 206 p. : LC Card 83-174401
HD8431 .S77 1982

Schmidt, Carola. Schaefer, Reinhard. Disponibilität--Mobilität--Fluktuation /. Berlin , 1982. 70 p. : LC Card 83-225572
HD5717.5.G35 S3 1982

Schmidt, Christian.
The Economics of military expenditures . New York , 1987. xxiii, 391 p. : ISBN 0-312-00421-4 : LC Card 86-27886 DDC 338.4/7355 19
HC79.D4 E27 1987

Peace, defence, and economic analysis . New York , 1987. xxxiii, 450 p. : ISBN 0-312-01321-3 : LC Card 87-19708 DDC 338.4/7355 19
HC79.D4 P43 1987

Schmidt, Christian, 1950-
Essai sur l'économie ricardienne / Christian Schmidt. Paris : Economica, 1984. 168 p. ; 24 cm. Bibliography: p. [159]-163. Includes indexes. ISBN 2-7178-0693-8 : LC Card 84-218068
1. Ricardo, David, 1772-1823. 2. Classical school of economics. I. Title.
HB103.R5 S25 1984

United Nations. Secretary-General. [Economic and social consequences of the arms race and of military expenditures. French.] Conséquences économiques et sociales de la course aux armements /. Paris , 1983. 121 p. : ISBN 2-7178-0645-8 : LC Card 84-136625
HC79.D4 U52 1983

Schmidt, Gerhard, Mag. Fink, Karl, Mag. Die regionale Dynamik des Salzburger Arbeitsmarktes, 1971-1980 . Salzburg [1981?] 212 p. : LC Card 82-171635
HD5772.S24 F56 1981 ***NYPL [JLG 86-301]***

Schmidt, Helmut, Dr. rer. oec. Informationsinstrumente zur Umweltplanung : theoretische, methodische und forschungspolitische Probleme / Helmut Schmidt. Frankfurt/Main : Haag + Herchen, c1985. ix, 441 p. : ill. ; 21 cm. Originally presented as the author's thesis (doctoral)--Gesamthochschule Wuppertal, 1983. Bibliography: p. 401-441. ISBN 3-88129-947-5 LC Card 86-141873
1. Environmental policy - Mathematical models. I. Title.
HC79.E5 S285 1985

Schmidt, Ingo. Die Chicago School of Antitrust Analysis : Wettbewerbstheoretische und -politische Analyse eines Credos / Ingo Schmidt, Jan B. Rittaler.1. Aufl. Baden-Baden : Nomos Verlagsgesellschaft, 1986. 119 p. : ill. ; 23 cm. (Wirtschaftsrecht und Wirtschaftspolitik. Bd. 85) Summary in English. Bibliography: p. 115-119. ISBN 3-7890-1285-8 LC Card 87-409043 DDC 330.15/6 19
1. Chicago school of economics. 2. Laissez-faire. I. Rittaler, Jan B. II. Title.
HB98.3 .S35 1986

Schmidt, Klaus D. Business customs and protocol in the ASEAN region / Klaus D. Schmidt. Menlo Park, Calif. : Business Intelligence Program, SRI International, [c1985- v. <1 > : ill., col. maps ; 28 cm. (Report / Business Intelligence Program . no. 720-) Cover title. CONTENTS. - pt. 1. Doing business in Thailand, the Philippines, and Singapore. LC Card 87-404513 DDC 395/.52 19
1. Business etiquette - Asia, Southeastern. I. Series: Research report (Business Intelligence Program (SRI International)) , 720, etc. II. Title.
HF5387 .S36 1985

Schmidt, Klaus-Dieter. Im Anpassungsprozess zurückgeworfen : die deutsche Wirtschaft vor neuen Herausforderungen / Klaus-Dieter Schmidt et al. ; Autoren, Hugo Dicke ... [et al.]. Tübingen : J.C.B. Mohr, c1984. xx, 243 p. : 21 ill. ; 24 cm. (Kieler Studien, 0340-6989 . 185) Bibliography: p. 225-237. Includes index. ISBN 3-16-344755-4 LC Card 84-170512
1. Germany, West - Economic conditions - 1974-. 2. Germany, West - Social conditions. 3. Germany, West - Industries. I. Title. II. Series.
HC286.7 .S352 1984

Schmidt, Kurt, 1924- Der Sachverständigenrat zur Begutachtung der Gesamtwirtschaftlichen Entwicklung : Institution, Messkonzepte und wirtschaftspolitische Leitlinien / von Kurt Schmidt. Stuttgart : F. Steiner Verlag Wiesbaden, 1985. 24 p. ; 24 cm. (Sitzungsberichte der Wissenschaftlichen Gesellschaft an der Johann Wolfgang Goethe-Universität Frankfurt am Main . Bd. 21, Nr. 4) Includes bibliographical references. ISBN 3-515-04462-0 (Deut. Bibl.) : LC Card 86-157934
1. Germany, West - Economic policy - 1974-. 2. Sachverständigenrat zur Begutachtung der Gesamtwirtschaftlichen Entwicklung (Germany). I. Title. II. Series.
HC286.7 .S353 1985

Schmidt, Martin, 1953- Wechselkursrisiko, Informationsverarbeitung und Devisenterminmarkt / Martin Schmidt. Frankfurt am Main ; New York : P. Lang, c1985. 253 p. : ill. ; 21 cm. (Europäische Hochschulschriften. Reihe V, Volks- und Betriebswirtschaft, 0531-7339 . Bd. 635 = vol. 635 = vol. 635) Originally presented as the author's thesis (doctoral--Universität Giessen, 1984) Bibliography; p. 227-253. ISBN 3-8204-8882-0 : LC Card 85-209898
1. Foreign exchange - Mathematical models. I. Series: Europäische Hochschulschriften. Reihe V, Volks- und Betriebswirtschaft , Bd. 635. II. Title.
HG3823 .S35 1985

Schmidt, Peter M. Unweltthemen in der öffentlichen Diskussion / Peter M. Schmidt. 1. Aufl. Konstanz : Hartung-Gorre Verlag, 1985. ix, 296 p. : ill. ; 21 cm. (Konstanzer Dissertationen . 82) Thesis (doctoral)--Universität Konstanz, 1985. Bibliography: p. 288-296. ISBN 3-89191-001-0 LC Card 86-155948
1. Environmental policy - Germany, West. 2. Environmental protection - Germany, West. I. Title. II. Series.
HC290.5.E5 S37 1985

Schmidt-Prestin, Barbara, 1953- Bildschirmtext in Unternehmen : theoretische Ableitung von Anwendungsfeldern und Ergebnisse einer empirischen Untersuchung / Barbara Schmidt-Prestin ; mit einem Geleitwort von Norberg Szyperski. Bergisch Gladbach : J. Eul, c1986. xvi, 308 p. : ill. ; 21 cm. (Reihe Planung, Information und Unternehmungsführung . Bd. 13) Originally presented as the author's thesis (doctoral)--Universität zu Köln, 1986. Bibliography: p. 273-308. ISBN 3-89012-064-4 LC Card 87-129114 DDC 651.8/0943 19
1. Videotex systems - Germany (West). 2. Office practice - Germany (West) - Automation. 3. Business - Data processing. I. Title. II. Series.
HD9696.T463 G365 1986

Schmidt, Rainer, Dr. Offene und verdeckte Arbeitslosigkeit in der Bundesrepublik : der Einfluss der Meldequote auf die Arbeitslosenstatistik / Rainer Schmidt. Tübingen : J.C.B. Mohr, c1986. viii, 124 p. : 4 ill. ; 24 cm. (Kieler Studien, 0340-6989 . 205) Bibliography: p. 123-124. ISBN 3-16-345158-6 LC Card 87-126258 DDC 331.13/7943 19
1. Unemployment - Germany (West). 2. Unemployment - Germany (West) - Statistical methods. I. Title. II. Series.
HD5779 .S2495 1986

Schmidt, Reimer. Versicherungswirtschaftliches Studienwerk /. Wiesbaden , c1981. v. <8-10 > ; LC Card 86-171689
HG8618 .V47 1981

Schmidt, Terry. Silverman, Jerry M. Action-planning workshops for development management . Washington, D.C., U. S.A. , 1986. ix, 74 p. : ISBN 0-8213-0864-5 (pbk.) LC Card 86-28215 DDC 338.9/0068 19
HC59.7 .S4656 1986

Schmidtchen, Dieter. Property rights, Freiheit und Wettbewerbspolitik / von Dieter Schmidtchen. Tübingen : Mohr, 1983. 71 p. ; 23 cm. (Vorträge und Aufsätze, 0509-6065 . 89) "Erweiterte Fassung eines Vortrages, gehalten unter dem Titel 'Irrwege der Wettbewerbspolitik' auf Einladung des Walter Eucken Instituts am 21. Januar 1981 in Freiburg im Breisgau"--T.p. verso. Bibliography: p. 69-71. ISBN 3-16-344630-2 (Deut. Bibl.) LC Card 84-100421
1. Commercial policy - Congresses. 2. Right of property - Congresses. 3. Competition - Congresses. I. Series: Vorträge und Aufsätze (Walter Eucken Institut) , 89. II. Title.
HF1410.5 .S36 1983

Schmied, Volker. Alternativen der Arbeitsgestaltung und ihre Bewertung : Konzepte und Aktionsvariablen industrieller Arbeitsgestaltung als Gegenstand betriebswirtschaftlicher Planungsrechnung / Volker Schmied. Wiesbaden : Gabler, c1982. 423 p. : ill. ; 25 cm. (Bochumer Beiträge zur Unternehmungsführung und Unternehmensforschung. Bd. 24) Bibliography: p. 397-423. ISBN 3-409-38642-4 LC Card 83-187066
1. Quality of work life. 2. Job satisfaction. 3. Job enrichment. I. Title. II. Series.
HD6955 .S345 1982

Schmiegelow, Michèle. Japan's response to crisis and change in the world economy /. Armonk, N.Y. , c1986. xiii, 309 p. : ISBN 0-87332-405-6 LC Card 86-21907 DDC 338.952 19
HC462.9 .J355 1986 ***NYPL [JLE 87-1199]***

Schmilgun, Karl-Heinz. Wackersdorf . Passau , 1986. 75 p. : ISBN 3-88849-021-9 LC Card 86-183781
HD9698.G43 W338 1986

Schmitt, Bernard. Les pays au régime du FMI : le vice caché du système actuel des paiements internationaux / Bernard Schmitt. Albeuve, Suisse : Castella, c1984. 91 p. : ill. ; 23 cm. ISBN 2-88087-013-5 : LC Card 84-240522 DDC 382.1/7 19
1. Balance of payments. 2. International Monetary Fund. I. Title.
HG3882 .S36 1984

Schmitt, Dieter, 1939- Stromerzeugungskosten im internationalen Vergleich /. München , 1986. ca. 450 p. : ISBN 3-486-26246-7 LC Card 87-135285 DDC 338.4/336362 19
HD9685.A2 S76 1986

Schmitt, Karl. Wirtschaftlicher Wandel, religiöser Wandel und Wertwandel . Berlin , c1985. 411 p. : ISBN 3-428-05784-8 LC Card 85-218417
HC286.7 .W58 1985

Schmitt, Roland, 1954- Texte und Bildrezeption bei TV-Werbespots : eine experimentelle Untersuchung zum Einfluss von Texten auf

Bildwahrnehmung und Bildverarbeitung am Beispiel von Fernsehwerbung / Roland Schmitt. Frankfurt am Main ; New York : P. Lang, c1986. 192 p. : ill. ; 21 cm. (Europäische Hochschulschriften. Reihe I, Deutsche Sprache und Literatur, 0721-3301 . Bd. 951 = vol. 951 = vol. 951) Originally presented as Diplomarbeit, Universität Mannheim, 1984. Bibliography: p. 179-192. ISBN 3-8204-9513-4 LC Card 87-109606
1. Television advertising. 2. Television and sports. I. Title.
HF6146.T42 S29 1986

Schmitz, Andrew. Coyle, Barry. Economic gains from agricultural trade . Washington, D.C. [Springfield, VA , 1986] iii, 41 p. : LC Card 86-602417 DDC 382/.41/0973 19
HD9005 .C86 1986

Schmitz, Heinz. Vermeidung von Armut im Alter : die Mindestsicherung in Schweden, Österreich, den Niederlanden, der DDR und der Bundesrepublik Deutschland sowie denkbare Verbesserungen der bundesdeutschen gesetzlichen Rentenversicherung / Heinz Schmitz. München : Profil Verlag, c1983. 267 p. : ill. ; 21 cm. (Reihe Wissenschaft) Originally presented as the author's thesis (doctoral)--Johann Wolfgang Goethe-Universität, Frankfurt am Main, 1982. Bibliography: p. 252-267. ISBN 3-89019-099-5 LC Card 84-197886
1. Social security - Europe. 2. Old age assistance - Europe. 3. Aged - Europe - Economic conditions. 4. Poor - Europe. I. Series: Reihe Wissenschaft (Munich, Germany). II. Title.
HD7164 .S29 1983

Schmitz, Mark D. Cranfill, Steven L. Small business banking . Washington, D.C. (1120 Connecticut Ave. N.W., Washington, D.C.) , c1987. ix, 78 p. : LC Card 87-135069 DDC 332.1/753 19
HG4027.7 .C7 1987

Schmitz, Wolfgang, 1923- Marktwirtschaft und Gesellschaftsordnung . Berlin , c1983. 220 p., [1] leaf of plates : ISBN 3-428-05365-6 LC Card 83-191615
HB72 .M248 1983

SCHMITZ, WOLFGANG, 1923- Marktwirtschaft und Gesellschaftsordnung . Berlin , c1983. 220 p., [1] leaf of plates : ISBN 3-428-05365-6 LC Card 83-191615
HB72 .M248 1983

Schmitzer, Iana L. EFT : state and future of the industry / Iana L. Schmitzer. Westport, CT (P.O. Box 431, Westport 06881) : Funds Transfer Report, c1986. vi leaves, 180 p. : ill. ; 28 cm. LC Card 87-143208 DDC 332.1/028 19
1. Electronic funds transfers. 2. Electronic funds transfers - Economic aspects. I. Title.
HG1710 .S364 1986

Schmölders, Günter, 1903- Der Wohlfahrtsstaat am Ende : Adam Riese schlägt zurück / Günter Schmölders.3. Aufl. München : Wirtschaftsverlag Langen-Müller/Herbig, 1983. 283 p. ; 23 cm. Includes bibliographical references. ISBN 3-7844-7133-1 LC Card 84-138252
1. Germany, West - Economic conditions. 2. Welfare state. 3. Germany, West - Social policy. I. Title.
HC286.6 .S284 1983

Schmoller, Gustav von, 1838-1917. The mercantile system and its historical significance : illustrated chiefly from Prussian history : being a chapter from the Studien ueber die wirthschaftliche Politik Friedrichs des Grossen / by Gustav Schmoller. Fairfield, NJ : A.M. Kelley, 1988. p. cm. (Reprints of economic classics) Reprint of the 1897 translation of a chapter from the author's Studien über die wirthschaftliche Politik Friedrichs des Grossen. ISBN 0-678-00252-5 LC Card 87-17247 DDC 330.15/13/0943 19
1. Mercantile system - Prussia (Germany). 2. Prussia (Germany) - Economic policy. I. Title.
HB91 .S3 1988

Schmucker, Helga. Studien zur empirischen Haushalts- und Verbrauchsforschung / von Helga Schmucker. Berlin : Duncker & Humblot, 1980. xiv, 357 p. : ill. ; 24 cm. (Beiträge zur Ökonomie von Haushalt und Verbrauch. Heft 15) Includes bibliographies. ISBN 3-428-04657-9 LC Card 80-153661
1. Cost and standard of living - Germany, West. 2. Consumption (Economics) - Germany, West. I. Title.
TX7 .B4 Heft 15 HD7029
NYPL [JLE 86-3430]

Schneemann, Reinhard. Kretschmann, Rolf. Möglichkeiten des Berufswechsels von Haupterwerbslandwirten unter besonderer Berücksichtigung von Agrarstruktur und Arbeitsmarkt /. Göttingen , 1986. xi, 109 p. : LC Card 87-408871 DDC 331.25/924 19
HD1536.G3 K746 1986

Schneewind, Klaus A., 1939- Eltern und Kinder : Umwelteinflüsse auf das familiäre Verhalten / Klaus A. Schneewind, Michael Beckmann, Anette Engfer ; unter Mitarbeit von Antonia Hecht, Jürgen Hinderer, Rita Rinke. Stuttgart : Kohlhammer, c1983. 229 p. : ill. ; 24 cm. Includes indexes. Bibliography: p. 211-223. ISBN 3-17-007744-9 LC Card 83-150745 DDC 303.3/23/0943 19
1. Family - Germany, West. 2. Parent and child - Germany, West. 3. Human ecology - Germany (West). I. Beckmann, Michael. II. Engfer, Anette. III. Title.
HQ739 .S29 1983 ***NYPL [JLE 87-1168]***

Schneider-Barthold, Wolfgang. Industrie und Grundbedürfnisbefriedigung in Afrika : zur Förderung von Handwerk und Kleinindustrie in afrikanischen "least developed countries" am Beispiel Obervoltas / Wolfgang Schneider-Barthold. Frankfurt/Main ; New York : Campus Verlag, c1984. 264 p. ; 21 cm. (Campus Forschung. Bd. 390) Originally presented as the author's thesis (doctoral)--Freie Universität Berlin. Bibliography: p. 251-264. ISBN 3-593-33350-3 LC Card 86-125217
1. Burkina Faso - Economic conditions - Case studies. 2. Burkina Faso - Industries - Case studies. 3. Small business - Burkina Faso - Case studies. 4. Basic needs - Burkina Faso - Case studies. I. Title.
HC1040 .S35 1984

Schneider, Bertrand. La révolution aux pieds nus : rapport au Club de Rome / Bertrand Schneider. Paris : Fayard, c1985. 344 p. ; 24 cm. Bibliography: p. 340-342. ISBN 2-213-01684-4 : LC Card 86-179661
1. Non-governmental organizations - Developing countries. 2. Technical assistance - Developing countries. 3. Economic assistance - Developing countries. I. Club of Rome. II. Title.
HC60 .S314 1985

Schneider, Carlo. Convergenze tra capitalismo e socialismo . Milano , 1978. lxxi, 399 p. ; LC Card 80-478455
HB501 .C727 ***NYPL [JLD 81-646]***

Schneider, Friedrich. The development of the shadow economies for Denmark, Norway, and Sweden : a comparison / by Friedrich Schneider, Jens Lundager. Aarhus, Denmark : Institute of Economics, University of Aarhus, [1986] 46 p. : ill. ; 21 cm. (Memo . 1986-1) Bibliography: p. 41-46. LC Card 86-215193 DDC 381 19
1. Informal sector (Economics) - Scandinavia - Econometric models. 2. Scandinavia - Economic conditions - Econometric models. I. Lundager, Jens. II. Series: Memo (Aarhus universitet. Økonomisk institut) , 1986-1. III. Title.
HD2346.S29 S35 1986

Schneider, Gerhard W.
Export-import financing. Venedikian, Harry M. Export-import financing / Harry M. Venedikian and Gerald Warfield. 2nd ed. New York , c1986. xvii, 456 p. : ISBN 0-471-82449-6 : LC Card 85-29566 DDC 332.7/42 19
HG3754.U5 V46 1986 ***NYPL [JLE 86-2998]***

Schneider, Heribert M. Bankmitarbeiter und die neuen Informationstechniken . Frankfurt am Main , c1986. 240 p. ; ISBN 3-7819-0341-9 LC Card 86-228992
HG1709 .B355 1986

Schneider, Ingrid, 1953- Wende wohin? . Köln , c1983. 139 p. ; ISBN 3-921349-34-6 LC Card 84-150290
HC286.7 .W4 1983 ***NYPL [JFC 87-1258]***

Schneider, Irmgard. Der Widerstand geht weiter . Freiburg i. Br. , 1982. 261 p. : ISBN 3-921472-30-X LC Card 82-192690
HD9698.G43 W937 1982

Schneider, José Odelso. Realidade brasileira : estudo de problemas brasileiros / José Odelso Schneider, Matias Martinho Lenz, Almiro Petry.8a. ed., rev. e atualizada. Porto Alegre-RS : Editora Sulina, c1986. 438 p. : ill. ; 23 cm. (Coleção universitaria) Bibliography: p. 427-438. LC Card 87-119174
1. Brazil - Economic conditions - 1945-. 2. Brazil - Social conditions - 1964-. 3. Brazil - Politics and government - 20th century. 4. Education - Brazil. 5. Brazil - Population. I. Lenz, Matias Martinho. II. Petry, Almiro. III. Title.
HC187 .S393 1986

Schneider, Karl Josef. Das Selbstbeschränkungsabkommen zwischen Thailand und der Europäischen Gemeinschaft : Darstellungen, Auswirkungen und Folgerungen für die Umorientierung der thailändischen Landwirtschaft / von Karl Josef Schneider. Kiel : Vauk, 1986. x, 192, 30 p. ; 21 cm. Bibliography: p. 187-191. ISBN 3-922553-82-6 LC Card 87-408324 DDC 382/.413682/09593 19
1. Thailand - Commerce - European Economic Community countries. 2. European Economic Community countries - Commerce - Thailand. 3. Cassava industry - Thailand. 4. Cassava industry - European Economic Community countries. I. Title.
HF3800.55.Z7 E867 1986

Schneider, Konrad. "Banco, Species und Courant" : Untersuchungen zur hamburgischen Währung im 17. und 18. Jahrhundert / Konrad Schneider. Koblenz : Numismatischer Verlag G.M. Forneck, c1986. 136 p. : ill. ; 21 cm. Bibliography: p. 8-14. ISBN 3-923708-03-3 LC Card 87-134369 DDC 332.1/0943/515 19
1. Money - Germany (West) - Hamburg - History - 17th century. 2. Money - Germany (West) - Hamburg - History - 18th century. 3. Banks and banking - Germany (West) - Hamburg - History - 17th century. 4. Banks and banking - Germany (West) - Hamburg - History - 18th century. I. Title.
HG1010.H24 S36 1986

Schneider, Pablo R. Vides de Orive, Enna. Análisis de la situación económica de Guatemala, 1965-1984 /. Guatemala, Guatemala , 1985. ii leaves, 118 p. : LC Card 86-205265 DDC 330.97281/053 19
HC144 .V53 1985

Schneider, Pia, 1956- Finanzwirtschaftliche Nebenrechnungen : eine empirische Untersuchungen von Geschäftsberichten börsennotierter deutscher Aktiengesellschaften zum Publizitätsverhalten bei Kapitalfluss-, Umsatzüberschuss-, Wertschöpfungs- und Kapitalerhaltungsrechnungen / Pia Schneider. Frankfurt am Main ; New York : Lang, c1985. xiii, 303 p. : ill. ; 21 cm. (Europäische Hochschulschriften. Reihe V, Volks- und Betriebswirtschaft, 0531-7339 . Bd. 625 = vol. 625 = vol. 625) Bibliography: p. 279-303. ISBN 3-8204-8472-8 LC Card 85-190966
1. Corporations - Germany, West - Accounting. 2. Stock companies - Germany (West) - Accounting. 3. Cash flow - Germany, West. I. Series: Europäische Hochschulschriften. Reihe V, Volks- und Betriebswirtschaft , Bd. 625. II. Title.
HF5686.C7 S354 1985

Schneider, Sigfrid, 1915- Angewandte Fernerkundung . Hannover , 1984. x, 285 p. : ISBN 3-87870-904-8 LC Card 85-147235
HD108.8 .A54 1984

Schneider, Stephen W., 1925- The big foul up awards, 1970 through 1986 : All-American Wildcatters / by Stephen W. Schneider. Dallas, Tex. : S.W. Schneider, c1986. viii, 119 p. : ill. ; 27 cm. LC Card 87-128382
1. All-American Wildcatters. I. Title.
HD9561.W53 S36 1986

Schneider, Walter. Technologische Analyse und Prognose als Grundlage der strategischen Unternehmensplanung / Walter Schneider. Göttingen : Vandenhoeck & Ruprecht, c1984. xxii, 215 p. ; 24 cm. (Innovative Unternehmensführung. Bd. 13) Bibliography: p. [187]-215. ISBN 3-525-12561-5 LC Card 85-127182
1. Strategic planning. 2. Technological innovations. I. Title.
HD30.23 .S37 1984

Schneider, William, 1941- Lipset, Seymour Martin. The confidence gap . Baltimore , 1987. xxiv, 460 p. : ISBN 0-8018-3044-3 (pbk.) LC Card 86-27416 DDC 303.3/8/0973 19
HD2785 .L53 1987

Schneier, Craig Eric. The Performance management sourcebook /. Amherst, Mass. [1987] 393 p. : ISBN 0-87425-074-9 (pbk.) LC Card 87-153991 DDC 658.3/125 19
HF5549.5.R3 P4755 1987

Schneier, Steffen. Occupational mobility among Blacks in South Africa / Steffen Schneier. Cape Town : Southern Africa Labour and Development Research Unit, [1983] vi, 219 p. : ill. ; 30 cm. (Saldru working paper . no. 58) "November 1983." Bibliography: p. 214-219. ISBN 0-7992-0567-2 (pbk.) LC Card 84-197038 DDC 331.12/72/089968 19
1. Blacks - Employment - South Africa. 2. Occupational mobility - South Africa. I. Title. II. Series.
HD8801 .S34 1983 *NYPL [JLG 86-123]*

Schnidman, Frank.
Retention of land for agriculture : policy, practice, and potential in New England / Frank Schnidman, Michael Smiley, Eric G. Woodbury. Boston, MA : Oelgeschlager, Gunn & Hain in association with the Lincoln Institute of Land Policy, 1988. p. cm. "A Lincoln Institute of Land Policy book." Includes index. ISBN 0-89946-219-7 LC Card 87-5580 DDC 333.76/16/0974 19
1. Land use, Rural - Government policy - New England. 2. Agricultural conservation - Government policy - New England. I. Smiley, Michael. II. Woodbury, Eric G. III. Title.
HD266.A11 S36 1988

The Urban caldron /. Boston, Mass. , 1986. 152 p. ; ISBN 0-89946-207-3 LC Card 85-21641 DDC 333.73/0973 19
HD257 .U73 1986 *NYPL [JLE 86-4372]*

Schnitker, Paul. Der Goldene Boden . Stuttgart , c1987. 359 p. ; ISBN 3-421-02885-0 LC Card 87-139261 DDC 331.7/94 19
HD2346.G3 G55 1987

Schnitzler, Bert, 1933- Die Phalanx : zur Geschichte des privaten Rundfunks / Bert Schnitzler. Herford : BusseSeewald, c1986. 279 p. ; 21 cm. Includes bibliographical references and index. ISBN 3-512-00752-X LC Card 86-199408
1. Broadcasting - Germany (West) - Congresses. I. Title.
HE8689.9.G4 S36 1986

Schnütgen, Achim. Glässer, Ewald. Island /. Darmstadt , 1986. xii, 315 p., [20] p. of plates (4 folded) : ISBN 3-534-01225-9 LC Card 87-101040
HC360.5 .G57 1986

Schober, Theodor. Knöpfel, Eckehardt. Werkbuch Jugendarbeitslosigkeit . Wuppertal , c1983. 168 p. : ISBN 3-417-12855-2 (pbk.) LC Card 87-672977
HD5779 .K59x 1983

Schoch, Hans. Size and price in oligopoly / by Hans Schoch. Königstein, Ts. : Verlag A. Hain, Meisenheim ; Cambridge, Mass. : Oelgeschlager, Gunn & Hain, 1981. viii, 151 p. : ill. ; 24 cm. (Mathematical systems in economics. 63) Bibliography: p. 149-151. ISBN 3-445-12157-5 LC Card 80-84489 DDC 338.8/2/0724 19
1. Oligopolies - Mathematical models. 2. Industry, Size of - Mathematical models. 3. Price policy - Mathematical models. I. Title.
HD2757.3 .S36 1981

Schoell, William F. Marketing : contemporary concepts and practices / William F. Schoell, Joseph P. Guiltinan.3rd ed. Boston : Allyn and Bacon, 1987. p. cm. Bibliography: p. Includes index. ISBN 0-205-10569-6 LC Card 87-23178 DDC 658.8 19
1. Marketing. I. Guiltinan, Joseph P. II. Title.
HF5415 .S357 1987

Schoemaker, Paul J. H. Experiments on decisions under risk : the expected utility hypothesis / Paul J. H. Schoemaker. Boston : Martinus Nijhoff Pub., c1980. xxii, 211 p. : ill. ; 23 cm. Includes indexes. Bibliography: p. 189-203. ISBN 0-89838-035-9 LC Card 79-27948 DDC 658.4/03
1. Risk. 2. Utility theory. I. Title.
HB615 .S36 *NYPL [JLE 81-559]*

Schoen, Lothar. Goetzeler, Herbert. Wilhelm und Carl Friedrich von Siemens . Stuttgart , 1986. 131 p. : ISBN 3-515-04558-9 LC Card 86-141456
HD9695.G43 S514 1986

Schöne, Manfred, 1935-
Stammwerk Henkel, 80 Jahre in Düsseldorf-Holthausen / Manfred Schöne. Düsseldorf : Henkel, 1981. 148 p. : ill. (some col.) ; 21 cm. (Schriften des Werksarchivs der Henkel KGaA Düsseldorf . 10/11) Bibliography: p. 146-147. LC Card 86-216690
1. Henkel KGaA - History. 2. Chemical industry - Germany (West) - Düsseldorf - History. 3. Henkel family. 4. Düsseldorf-Holthausen (Düsseldorf, Germany). I. Title. II. Title: Stammwerk Henkel, achtzig Jahre in Düsseldorf-Holthausen. III. Series.
HD9654.9.H444 S36 1981

Ein Vierteljahrhundert Betriebskrankenkasse Henkel, Düsseldorf / Manfred Schöne. [Düsseldorf] : Henkel, 1977. 60 p. : ill. (some col.) ; 21 cm. (Schriften des Werksarchivs der Henkel KGaA Düsseldorf . 7) Bibliography: p. 60. LC Card 86-216782
1. Betriebskrankenkasse Henkel (Düsseldorf, Germany). 2. Insurance, Industrial - Germany (West). 3. Henkel KGaA. I. Title. II. Series.
HG9399.G33 B477 1977

Von der Leimabteilung zum grössten Klebstoffwerk Europas / Manfred Schöne. Düsseldorf : Henkel, 1979. 68 p. : ill. (some col.) ; 21 cm. (Schriften des Werkarchivs der Henkel KGaA Düsseldorf . 9) Ill. on lining papers. Bibliography: p. 68. LC Card 86-216773
1. Henkel KGaA - History. 2. Chemical industry - Germany (West) - History. 3. Lime industry - Germany (West) - History. 4. Adhesives industry - Germany (West) - History. I. Title. II. Series.
HD9654.9.H444 S37 1979

Schoenhals, Kai P. Sorge, Friedrich A. (Friedrich Adolf), 1828-1906. Friedrich A. Sorge's labor movement in the United States . New York , c1987. xiii, 196 p. ; ISBN 0-313-25518-0 (lib. bdg. : alk. paper) LC Card 86-31792 DDC 331/.0973 19
HD8072 .S7175 1987

Die Schönsten Anzeigen in den Fliegenden Blättern : Werbung zu Kaisers Zeit / mit einem Vorwort von Hans-Friedrich Müller. Hildesheim ; New York : Olms Presse, 1982. 166 p. : ill. ; 29 cm. Reprints of pages from Beiblatt der Fliegenden Blätter, Bd. 99 (1893)-Bd. 108 (1898). ISBN 3-487-08233-0 (pbk.) LC Card 87-672236
1. Advertising - Germany - History - 19th century - Sources. I. Beiblatt der Fliegenden Blätter.
HF5813.G3 S36x 1982

Schofield, Roger. The State of population theory . Oxford, OX , New York, NY, USA , 1986. 311 p. : ISBN 0-631-13975-3 : LC Card 85-26668 DDC 304.6/01 19
HB849.4 .S73 1986 *NYPL [JLE 86-2411]*

Schogt, J. C. M. De Toekomst van onze voedingsmiddelenindustrie /. Amsterdam , 1985. 156 p. : ISBN 90-10-05574-4 : LC Card 86-116607
HD9015.N42 T64 1985

Scholarly Resources, inc.
Records of the U. S. Department of State relating to commercial relations between the United States and Russia/the Soviet Union, 1910-1949 [microform]. Wilmington, DE , c1987. microfilm reel. ISBN 0-8420-3053-0 (microfilm : set) : LC Card 87-23223 DDC 337.73047 19
HF3105

Records of the U. S. Department of State relating to commercial relations between the United States and Japan, 1910-1949 [microform]. Wilmington, Del. , c1987. microfilm reel ISBN 0-8420-3061-1 (microfilm : set) : LC Card 87-23376 DDC 337.73052 19
HF3127

Scholl, Heinz. Bilderberger & Trilaterale : internationale Cliquen in der Strategie der US-Hochfinanz / Heinz Scholl. Euskirchen, Bundesrepublik Deutschland : VZD, c1977. 92 p. ; 21 cm. "Dokumentation": p. 41-86. Bibliography: p. 39-40. LC Card 85-199172
1. Corporations - United States. 2. Capitalists and financiers - United States. 3. Rockefeller family. 4. Trilateral Commission. 5. Bilderberg Meetings. 6. United States - Foreign relations - 1945-. 7. Conspiracies - United States. I. Title. II. Title: Bilderberger und Trilaterale.
HD2785 .S396 1977

Schöll, Wolfgang. Konsumentenverhalten in der Bundesrepublik Deutschland 1958-1982 : eine empirische Untersuchung der Sättigungshypothese / Wolfgang Schöll. Thun : H. Deutsch, c1985. 226, 70, [9] p. : ill. ; 21 cm. (Reihe Wirtschaftswissenschaften, 0253-1488 . Bd. 334) "D82 (Diss. TH Aachen)"--T.p. verso. Bibliography: p. [71]-[79] (2nd group) ISBN 3-87144-900-8 (Deut. Bibl.) : LC Card 85-232693
1. Consumption (Economics) - Germany, West. 2. Consumers - Germany, West. I. Title. II. Series.
HC290.5.C6 S35 1985

Schöllhammer, Hans, 1933- Entrepreneurship and small business management / Hans Schöllhammer, Arthur H. Kuriloff. Malabar, Fla. : R.E. Krieger, 1988. xvi, 608 p. : ill. ; 24 cm. Reprint. Originally published: New York : Wiley, c1979. With updating. Includes bibliographies and indexes. ISBN 0-89464-235-9 LC Card 87-14818 DDC 658/.022 19
1. New business enterprises - Management. 2. Small business - Management. 3. Entrepreneurship. I. Kuriloff, Arthur H. II. Title.
HD62.5 .S354 1988

Scholten, Ilja. Political stability and neo-corporatism . London , Beverly Hills , 1987. x, 276 p. ; ISBN 0-8039-8028-0 LC Card 86-63492 DDC 321.9 19
HD3616.E8 P64 1987

Scholz, Bernhard, 1948- Bodenschutz zwischen Datenschwemme und Informationsdefizit : politisch-administrative Lösungsansätze / Bernhard Scholz. Speyer : Forschungsinstitut für Öffentliche Verwaltung bei der Hochschule für Verwaltungswissenschaften Speyer, [1986] iii leaves, 385, 4 p. : ill. ; 30 cm. (Speyerer Forschungsberichte, 0179-2326 . 54) "Oktober 1986." Bibliography: p. 367-385. LC Card 87-126271 DDC 333.73/13/094343 19
1. Land use - Germany (West) - Rhineland-Palatinate. 2. Environmental policy - Germany (West) - Rhineland-Palatinate. 3. Environmental protection - Germany (West) - Rhineland-Palatinate. I. Title. II. Series.
HD659.R54 S36 1986

Scholz, Christian, 1952- Strategisches Management : ein integrativer Ansatz / Christian Scholz. Berlin ; New York : W. de Gruyter, 1987. xv, 305 p. ; 24 cm. Originally presented as the author's Habilitationsschrift--Universität Regensburg, 1985. Bibliography: p. [253]-287. Includes indexes. ISBN 3-11-010863-1 LC Card 87-145957 DDC 658.4/012 19
1. Strategic planning. I. Title.
HD30.28 .S346 1987

Scholz, Walter, 1920- Beiträge zur Bankaufsicht, Bankbilanz und Bankprüfung . Düsseldorf , 1985. 226 p. : ISBN 3-8021-0267-3 LC Card 85-208772
HG1605 .B44 1985

SCHOLZ, WALTER, 1920-
Beiträge zur Bankaufsicht, Bankbilanz und Bankprüfung . Düsseldorf , 1985. 226 p. : ISBN 3-8021-0267-3 LC Card 85-208772
HG1605 .B44 1985

Schomacker, Klaus. Zivile Alternativen für die Rüstungsindustrie /. Baden-Baden , 1986. 174 p. ; ISBN 3-7890-1262-9 LC Card 87-108651 DDC 338.4/76234/0943 19
HD9743.G48 Z58 1986

Schön, Wolfgang. Analyse von Unfällen motorisierter Zweiradbenutzer . [West Germany] [1976] 32 p. : LC Card 85-135424
HE5614.5.G3 A65 1976

Schonberger, Richard. World class manufacturing casebook : implementing JIT and TQC / Richard J. Schonberger. New York : Free Press ; London : Collier Macmillan, c1987. xxvi, 253 p. : ill. ; 25 cm. Bibliography: p. 251-253. ISBN 0-02-929340-5 LC Card 86-25822 DDC 658 19
1. Industrial management - Case studies. 2. Production management - Case studies. 3. Manufacturing processes - Case studies. I. Title.
HD31 .S3386 1987

Schönen, Hans G. Christliche Motive auf Briefmarken : Gabriel-Lexikon : 820 Spalten, über 8000 Stichwörter, ca. 30000 Briefmarken / Hans G. Schönen.2. Aufl. Rommerskirchen-Oekoven : H.G. Schönen, 1984, c1983. xv, 830 p. ; 21 cm. ISBN 3-9800824-0-7 : LC Card 84-208011
1. Postage-stamps - Topics - Christianity - Catalogs. I. Title. II. Title: Gabriel-Lexikon.
HE6183.C47 S36 1984

Schönfelder, Bruno. Ökonomisches Risiko und Versicherung in sozialistischen Volkswirtschaften : am Beispiel der UdSSR und der DDR unter Einbeziehung der Sozialversicherung und unter Berücksichtigung

der Versicherungstheorie / von Bruno Schönfelder. Berlin : Duncker & Humblot, c1986. 284 p. : ill. ; 24 cm. (Veröffentlichungen des Osteuropa-Institutes München. Reihe, Wirtschaft und Gesellschaft . Heft 21) Bibliography: p. [264]-282. Includes index. ISBN 3-428-05968-9 LC Card 86-185328
1. Social security - Germany, East. 2. Social security - Soviet Union. I. Title. II. Series.
HD7180.5 .S36 1986

Schönweiss, Friedrich. Mühlfeld, Claus, 1940- Konflikt und Kooperation in Arbeitgeberverbänden /. Augsburg , 1985. 403 p. ; ISBN 3-87512-138-4 : LC Card 86-152717
HD2429.G3 M84 1985

SCHOOL ATTENDANCE - BRAZIL - PARAÍBA (STATE)
Azevedo, Edilza Araújo. Causas de evasão. [Campina Grande, Brasil] , 1984. 104 leaves : LC Card 85-203901
HD5715.5.B69 P335 1984

SCHOOL BUS DRIVERS' STRIKE, DIGBY, N. S., 1979-1983.
Currie, Lawrence A., 1949- A time for change . Halifax, N.S. , c1986. 64 p. : ISBN 0-88926-031-1 (pbk.) LC Card 86-230034 DDC 331.89/281388322 19
HD5329.M82 1979 .D543 1986

SCHOOL CHILDREN - FOOD - ITALY - ROME - COSTS - ACCOUNTING - CASE STUDIES.
Mancini, Andrea, 1954- La contabilità analitica dei costi . [Torino] , 1986. 53 p. : ISBN 88-85851-00-2 : LC Card 87-114718
HF5686.C8 M265 1986

SCHOOL FINANCE. see **EDUCATION - FINANCE.**

School-leavers and their prospects . Roberts, Kenneth, 1940- Milton Keynes , 1984. viii, 133 p. ; ISBN 0-335-10418-5 (pbk.) LC Card 87-672221
HD6276.G72 R62x 1984

School of Industrial Relations research essay series .
(no. 1) Stocks, Alex M. Union raiding . Kingston, Ont., Canada , 1985. 61 p. ; ISBN 0-88886-125-7 (pbk.) LC Card 86-145321 DDC 331.87/09711 19
HD6528.B9 S86 1985 ***NYPL [JLF 87-422]***

(no. 10) Marcotte, Marilee, 1960- Equal pay for work of equal value /. Kingston, Ont., Canada , 1987. 101 p. : ISBN 0-88886-157-5 (pbk.) LC Card 87-163236 DDC 331.2/1 19
HD6061.2.C2 M37 1987

(no. 8) Venne, Rosemary Amelia, 1956- Psychological testing in personnel selection /. Kingston, Ont., Canada , 1987. 65 p. ; ISBN 0-88886-152-4 (pbk.) LC Card 87-163203 DDC 658.3/1125 19
HF5549.5.E5 V46 1987

SCHOOL TAXES. see **EDUCATION - FINANCE.**

SCHOOLS - ADMINISTRATION, FINANCIAL. see **EDUCATION - FINANCE.**

SCHOOLS, COMMERCIAL. see **BUSINESS EDUCATION.**

SCHOOLS, COUNTRY. see **EDUCATION, RURAL.**

SCHOOLS - FINANCE. see **EDUCATION - FINANCE.**

SCHOOLS - RECREATIONS. see **GAMES.**

Schoonbroodt, Jos., 1936- Etat de besoin, besoin d'Etat : l'anti-mythe politique / Jos. Schoonbroodt. Bruxelles : Vie ouvrière, c1985. 272 p. : ill. ; 22 cm. Includes bibliographical references. ISBN 2-87003-196-3 LC Card 86-146944 DDC 338.9493 19
1. Belgium - Economic policy. 2. Belgium - Economic conditions - 1945-. I. Title.
HC315 .S17 1985

SCHOONEBEEK (NETHERLANDS) - HISTORY.
Jong, H. J. de (Herman J.) Schoonebeek, olierijk in Zuidoost-Drenthe /. [Zuidwolde] , 1986. 232 p. : ISBN 90-6509-902-6 : LC Card 86-175279
HD9575.N43 N435 1986

Schoonebeek, olierijk in Zuidoost-Drenthe /. Jong, H. J. de (Herman J.) [Zuidwolde] , 1986. 232 p. : ISBN 90-6509-902-6 : LC Card 86-175279
HD9575.N43 N435 1986

Schoppe, Siegfried, 1944- Determinanten der Eigenkapitalbildung und Konsequenzen für die Wettbewerbsfähigkeit deutscher Grossunternehmen und Mittelbetriebe / von Siegfried G. Schoppe. Hamburg : Institut für Aussenhandel und Überseewirtschaft der Universität Hamburg, 1986. 24 p. : ill. ; 22 cm. (Forschungsberichte / Institut für Aussenhandel und Überseewirtschaft der Universität Hamburg . Nr. 42) Includes bibliographical references. LC Card 86-185861
1. Business enterprises - Germany, West - Finance. 2. Capital - Germany, West. I. Series: Forschungsberichte (Universität Hamburg. Institut für Aussenhandel und Überseewirtschaft) , Nr. 42. II. Title.
HG4156 .S36 1986

Schorr, John E. High performance purchasing : manufacturing resource planning for the purchasing professional / John E. Schorr, Thomas F. Wallace. Essex Junction, Vt. : O. Wight Ltd. Publications, c1986. xii, 211 p. : ill. ; 24 cm. Bibliography: p. [189]. Includes index. ISBN 0-939246-05-8 LC Card 86-201739 DDC 658.7/2 19
1. Industrial procurement. 2. Purchasing. I. Wallace, Thomas F. II. Title.
HD39.5 .S36 1986

Schors, Horst Willi, 1951- Hunziker, Peter, 1941- Lokales Bürgerfernsehen . Aarau , c1983. 192 p. ; ISBN 3-7941-2369-7 : LC Card 83-141437
HE8700.72.S95 H85 1983

Schosserer, Wolfgang.
Betriebswirtschaftliche Ergebnisse von Gartenbaubetrieben 1984 /. Wien , 1985. 13 p. ; LC Card 86-194865
HD9015.A8 B47 1985

Landeswirtschaftlicher Paritätsspiegel . Wien [1982] 11 leaves ; LC Card 86-181563
HD1935 .L325 1982

Schotten, R. Ph. Braakman, T. C. Sociale zekerheid in Nederland /. Utrecht , 1984. 199 p. : ISBN 90-274-5513-9 : LC Card 85-110890
HD7192 .B73 1984 ***NYPL [JLC 86-295]***

Schou, Bent. Stålindustri, kriseregioner og fagbevægelse . [Copenhagen] , 1983. 217 p. : LC Card 84-169019
HD9525.E752 S73 1983

Schoumacher, David. Economics U$A. Chicago, IL , 1986. 1 videocassette (28 min.) : LC Card 86-708020 DDC 330.15 11
HB99.7

Schouten, D. B. J. Het wankele evenwicht in de economie : coördinatie versus fragmentatie van nationale en internationale economische politiek / D.B.J. Schouten. Leiden : Stenfert Kroese, 1986. xiv, 189 p. ; 24 cm. ISBN 90-207-1436-8 : LC Card 86-167831
1. Economic policy. 2. Netherlands - Economic policy. 3. Economic policy - Mathematical models. I. Title.
HD85.D8 S36 1986

Schouten, J. G. (Jan Gijs)
Puyenbroek, R. (Rien) Exportgids Japan /. Amsterdam , 1985. 149 p. : ISBN 90-10-05277-X LC Card 85-236503
HF3618.J33 P89 1985

Puyenbroek, R. (Rien) Exportgids Verenigde Staten /. Amsterdam , 1985. 140 p. : ISBN 90-10-05276-1 LC Card 85-236520
HF3618.U6 P89 1985

Schrager, Ronald E. Sherman, Howard D. Junk bonds and tender offer financing /. Washington, D.C. , c1987. 22 p. ; ISBN 0-931035-15-5 (pbk.) LC Card 87-128796 DDC 332.63/2 19
HG4963 .S535 1987

Schramm, Herbert F. W. Burghagen Fachwörterbuch : Bürofach-Begriffe in vier Sprachen, Deutsch, English, français, español / bearbeitet von Herbert F.W. Schramm.1. Aufl. Hamburg : H. Burghagen, c1964. 160 p. ; 17 cm. Includes indexes. LC Card 84-256680
1. Office equipment and supplies - Dictionaries - Polyglot. 2. German language - Dictionaries - Polyglot. I. Title. II. Title: Fachwörterbuch.
HF5548 .S37 1964

Schrayer, Robert M. Opportunities in insurance careers / Robert M. Schrayer ; foreword by Bruce W. Slaughter. Lincolnwood, Ill., U. S.A. : VGM Career Horizons, c1987. xi, 145 p. : ill. ; 20 cm. (VGM career books) Bibliography: p. 145. ISBN 0-8442-6008-8 LC Card 87-60102 DDC 368/.0023/73 19
1. Insurance - United States - Vocational guidance. 2. Insurance - Study and teaching - United States. 3. Insurance - United States - Societies, etc. - Directories. I. Title. II. Series.
HG8531 .S37 1987

Schreiner, Alette. Virkninger av oljevirksomhet i Nord-Norge / av Alette Schreiner og Tor Skoglund. Oslo : Statistisk sentralbyrå : I kommisjon hos H. Aschehoug og Universitetsforlaget, 1984. 43 p. : ill. ; 29 cm. (Rapporter fra Statistisk sentralbyrå, 0332-8422 . 84/17) Bibliography: p. 40-41. ISBN 82-537-2118-8 : LC Card 85-146089
1. Petroleum industry and trade - Norway. 2. Employment forecasting - Norway. 3. Energy policy - Norway. I. Skoglund, Tor. II. Title. III. Series.
HD9575.N62 S37 1984

Schreiner, Axel T. Introduction to compiler construction with UNIX / Axel T. Schreiner, H. George Friedman, Jr. Englewood Cliffs : Prentice-Hall, c1985. viii, 194 p. : ill. ; 29 cm. Includes index. Bibliography: p. [188] ISBN 0-13-474396-2 LC Card 84-63039
1. Word processing. 2. UNIX (Computer operating system). I. Friedman, H. George. II. Title. III. Title: Introduction to compiler construction with U.N.I.X.
NYPL [JSF 86-616]

Schreuder, Gerard F. World trade in forest products, 2 /. Seattle , c1986. xi, 362 p. : ISBN 0-295-96337-9 LC Card 86-234388 DDC 382/.41498 19
HD9750.5 .W67 1986

Schreuder, H. Economische wetenschappen . Maastricht , Assen , 1985. 224 p. ; ISBN 90-232-2148-6 LC Card 86-111599
HB21 .E248 1985

Schrevel, Margreet, 1951- Op een beteren weg . Amsterdam , 1985. 239 p. : ISBN 90-6012-654-8 : LC Card 85-236523
HD8516 .O6 1985 ***NYPL [JLD 86-3427]***

Schrift- und Behördenverkehr. Seddig, Gert. Lehrbuch der Altenpflege. Hannover , c1983. 95 p. : ISBN 3-87870-204-3 LC Card 83-230557
HF5728.G3 S49 1983

Schriften der Gesellschaft zur Förderung der Westfälischen Wilhelms-Universität zu Münster .
(Heft 70) Krelle, Wilhelm. Wachstum bei Erschöpfbaren Ressourcen, gibt es das? . Münster , c1982. 59 p. : ISBN 3-402-04434-X LC Card 83-215135
HC55 .K74 1982

Schriften der Landwirtschaftskammer Rheinland .
(Heft 33) Ebel, Friedhelm. Landwirtschaft am Niederrhein . Bonn , 1976. 223 p. : LC Card 87-408419
HD1407 .L3 Heft 33 HD1960.R48

Schriften der Regio .
(8) Frey, René Leo. Die regionale Ausstrahlung der Universität Basel /. Basel , c1984. 73 p. : LC Card 84-166545 DDC 378/.103 19
HC395 .A75 no. 8 LC238.4.S92B37

Schriften der Universität Passau. Reihe Geisteswissenschaften .
(Bd. 7) Roth, Rainer A., 1942- Zur Problematik der politischen Kultur der Jungwähler in der Bundesrepublik Deutschland /. Passau , c1984. 516 p. : ISBN 3-922016-46-4
NYPL [JLE 87-703]

Schriften der Volks- und Betriebswirtschaftlichen Vereinigung im Rheinisch-Westfälischen Industriegebiet. Sonderreihe .
(Heft 9) Baum, Herbert, Dr. Wettbewerbspolitik auf dem Treibstoffmarkt /. Baden-Baden , c1983. 97 p. ; ISBN 3-7890-0881-8 LC Card 83-187053
HD9573.5 .B38 1983

Schriften der Wissenschaftlichen Gesellschaft für Marketing und Unternehmensführung e.V. Münster .
(Bd. 2) Windhorst, Karl-Götz. Wertewandel und Konsumentenverhalten . Münster , c1985. xxi, 299 p. : ISBN 3-7923-0520-8 LC Card 85-171929 DDC 338.5/21/0943 19
HB201 .W663 1985 ***NYPL [JLE 87-369]***

(Bd. 4) Schubert, Frank. Akzeptanz von

Bildschirmtext in Unternehmungen und im Markt . Münster , c1986. xxiv, 316 p. : ISBN 3-7923-0546-1 LC Card 86-227074
HD9696.T463 G37 1986

Schriften des Deutschen Instituts für Entwicklungspolitik, DIE .
(Bd. 46) Lerche, Dietrich, 1943- Grundlagen und Perspektiven des Euro-Arabischen Dialogs /. Berlin , 1977. iii, 78 p. : LC Card 85-129693
HF1532.5.Z4 A735 1977

(Bd. 70) Brandt, Hartmut. Projektplanung in der kleinbäuerlichen Produktion /. Berlin , 1982. xv, 208 p. : LC Card 83-193407
HD1476.G3 B73 1982 ***NYPL [JLE 87-2903]***

(Bd. 74) Wiemann, Jürgen. Selektiver Protektionismus und aktive Strukturanpassung . Berlin , 1983. vii, 348 p. : ISBN 3-88985-028-6 : LC Card 83-223964
HD9865.E852 W54 1983

(Bd. 81) Radke, Detlef. Auflagenpolitik und Politik-Dialog in der entwicklungspolitischen Zusammenarbeit /. Berlin , 1985. xiii, 91 p. : ISBN 3-88985-036-7 LC Card 85-134788
HC60 .R183 1985

(Bd. 81) Radke, Detlef. Auflagenpolitik und Politik-Dialog in der entwicklungspolitischen Zusammenarbeit /. Berlin , 1985. xiii, 91 p. : ISBN 3-88985-036-7 LC Card 85-134788
HC60 .R183 1985

(Bd. 85) Structural distortions and adjustment programmes in the poor countries of Africa . Berlin , 1985. xxxi, 377 p. : ISBN 3-88985-042-1 LC Card 86-226845 DDC 338.967 19
HC800 .S79 1985

(Bd. 86) Esser, Klaus. Zentralamerika, USA, EG und Bundesrepublik Deutschland /. Berlin , 1987. xi, 137 p. : ISBN 3-88985-043-X LC Card 87-401334 DDC 337.1/728 19
HC141 .E86 1987

Schriften des Forschungsinstituts der Deutschen Gesellschaft für Auswärtige Politik e.V., Bonn. Reihe, Internationale Politik und Wirtschaft .
(Bd. 50) May, Bernhard. Reagan und die Entwicklungsländer . München , 1987. xiv, 271 p. ; ISBN 3-486-53981-7 LC Card 87-139481 DDC 337.730172/4 19
HF1456.5.D44 M39 1987

Schriften des Historischen Kollegs. Kolloquien .
(7) Arbeiter und Bürger im 19. Jahrhundert . München , 1986. xiv, 342 p. ; ISBN 3-486-52871-8 LC Card 86-212379
HD8376 .A72 1986

Schriften des Instituts für Ausländisches und Internationales Finanz- und Steuerwesen der Universität Hamburg .
(Bd. 10) Nevermann, Helga. Venture Capital . Baden-Baden , 1986. 146 p. ; ISBN 3-7890-1263-7 LC Card 87-121846 DDC 332/.0415/0943 19
HG5492 .N48 1986

Schriften des Instituts für Politikwissenschaft der Westfälischen Wilhelms-Universität Münster .
(Bd. 3) Hagemann, Hermann. Die Formierung der rohstoffpolitischen Forderungen der Entwicklungsländer auf der Ebene der Vereinten Nationen bis zur ersten Konferenz für Handel und Entwicklung (UNCTAD 1) 1946 /. Münster , 1983. xix, 384, [14], 42 p. : ISBN 3-923676-11-5 LC Card 84-172079
HC59.7 .H27 1983

Schriften des Instituts für Regionalforschung der Universität Kiel .
(Bd. 9) Hermann, Hayo. Sektorale Wirtschaftsstruktur und kommunale Finanzsituation . München , c1986. xiii, 384 p. : ISBN 3-88259-405-5 LC Card 86-228161
HJ9473 .H47 1986

Schriften des Internationalen Instituts für Empirische Sozialökonomie (INIFES) .
(Bd. 8) Gestaltungsspielräume der Arbeitsmarktpolitik auf regionalen Arbeitsmärkten . Berlin , c1984. 180 p. : ISBN 3-428-05614-0 LC Card 84-218530
HD8444 .G47 1984

Schriften des Österreichischen Controller-Instituts .
(Bd. 4) Simon, Dieter. Schwache Signale . Wien , c1986. 262 p. : LC Card 87-103434 DDC 658.4/012 19
HD30.28 .S435 1986

Schriften des Vereins für Socialpolitik, Gesellschaft für Wirtschafts- und Sozialwissenschaften .
(n. F., Bd. 134) Staatsfinanzierung im Wandel . Berlin , c1983. xi, 877 p. : ISBN 3-428-05420-2
NYPL [JLL 73-186 Bd. 134]

(n.F. Bd. 153) Beiträge zur Bevölkerungsökonomie /. Berlin , c1986. 238 p. : ISBN 3-428-05969-7 LC Card 86-172600
HB3595 .B39 1986

(n.F., Bd. 122) Wert- und Präferenzprobleme in den Sozialwissenschaften /. Berlin , c1981. 268 p. : ISBN 3-428-05013-4 LC Card 86-230716
HF5415.3 .W47 1981

(n.F., Bd. 135) Finanzsysteme, Ideal- und Realtypen . Berlin , c1983. 278 p. : ISBN 3-428-05419-9 LC Card 83-240120
HJ161 .F575 1983

(n.F., Bd. 138) Geld- und Währungsordnung /. Berlin , c1983. 249 p. : ISBN 3-428-05530-6 LC Card 84-141547
HG999.5 .G4556 1983

(n.F., Bd. 141) Normengeleitetes Verhalten in den Sozialwissenschaften /. Berlin , c1984. 199 p. ; ISBN 3-428-05622-1 LC Card 86-140299
HB74.P8 N67 1984

(n.F., Bd. 142) Wachstumsverlangsamung und Konjunkturzyklen in unterschiedlichen Wirtschaftssystemen /. Berlin , c1984. 191 p. : ISBN 3-428-05626-4
NYPL [JLL 73-186 Bd. 142]

(n.F., Bd. 147) Ethik und Wirtschaftswissenschaft /. Berlin , c1985. 276 p. : ISBN 3-428-05910-7 LC Card 86-132826
HB72 .E79 1985

(n.F., Bd. 149) Geyer, Herbert, 1927- Budgetpolitik im Wandel /. Berlin , c1986. 111 p. : ISBN 3-428-05922-0 LC Card 86-165210
HJ113 .G49 1986

(n.F., Bd. 150) China im Konflikt zwischen verschiedenen Ordnungskonzeptionen /. Berlin , c1985. 157 p. : ISBN 3-428-05923-9 LC Card 86-164406
HC427.9 .C56525 1985

(n.F., Bd. 151) Strukturpolitische Probleme der Automobil-Industrie unter dem Aspekt des Wettbewerbs /. Berlin , c1985. 247 p. : ISBN 3-428-05924-7 LC Card 86-165212 DDC 338.4/76292/094 19
HD9710.E82 S77 1985

(n.F., Bd. 152) Sozialpolitik in der Beschäftigungskrise /. Berlin , c1986. 2 v. : ISBN 3-428-05949-2 (Bd. I) : LC Card 87-119211 DDC 361.6/1 19
HD5710 .S67 1986

(n.F., Bd. 154) Entwicklungstheorie, Entwicklungspraxis . Berlin , c1986. 316 p. ; ISBN 3-428-05973-5 LC Card 86-233851 DDC 338.9/009172/4 19
HC59.7 .E6473 1986

(n.F., Bd. 155) Die Internationale Schuldenkrise . Berlin , 1986. 179 p. : ISBN 3-428-05972-7 LC Card 86-172589
HJ8899 .I58 1986

(n.F., Bd. 157) Nationale Wege der Inflationsbekämpfung /. Berlin , c1986. 223 p. : ISBN 3-428-06077-6 LC Card 87-132310 DDC 332.4/1/094 19
HC240 .N315 1986

(n.F., Bd. 158) Der Einfluss des Staates auf den Wettbewerb /. Berlin , c1986. 101 p. ; ISBN 3-428-06084-9 LC Card 87-132303 DDC 338.943 19
HD3616.G35 E38 1986

Schriften des Vereins zur Wahrung der Main- und Donau-Schiffahrtsinteressen e.V. .
(Heft 4) Rhein-Main-Donau . [Nürnberg , 1937?] 195 p. : LC Card 86-216951
HE449.R38 R48 1937

Schriften des Werkarchivs der Henkel KGaA Düsseldorf .
(9) Schöne, Manfred, 1935- Von der Leimabteilung zum grössten Klebstoffwerk Europas /. Düsseldorf , 1979. 68 p. : LC Card 86-216773
HD9654.9.H444 S37 1979

Schriften des Werkarchivs der Henkel KGaA Düsseldorf, 0724-2557 .
(17) Goosmann, Cornelia. Ein Jahrhundert Wasserglas von Henkel /. Düsseldorf , c1985. 76 p. : ISBN 3-923324-67-8 LC Card 86-171258
HD9654.9.H444 G66 1985

Schriften des Werksarchivs der Henkel KGaA Düsseldorf .
(10/11) Schöne, Manfred, 1935- Stammwerk Henkel, 80 Jahre in Düsseldorf-Holthausen /. Düsseldorf , 1981. 148 p. : LC Card 86-216690
HD9654.9.H444 S36 1981

(7) Schöne, Manfred, 1935- Ein Vierteljahrhundert Betriebskrankenkasse Henkel, Düsseldorf /. [Düsseldorf] , 1977. 60 p. : LC Card 86-216782
HG9399.G33 B477 1977

Schriften des Zentralinstituts für Wirtschaftswissenschaften, Akademie der Wissenschaften der DDR .
(Nr. 21) Rudolph, Günther. Karl Rodbertus (1805-1875) und die Grundrententheorie . Berlin , 1984. 332 p. ; LC Card 84-158301
HB401 .R83 1984

Schriften des Zentrums für Regionale Entwicklungsforschung der Justus-Liebig-Universität Giessen, 0170-1614 .
(Bd. 25) Krietemeyer, Hartmut, 1955- Der Erklärungsgehalt der Exportbasistheorie /. Hamburg , 1983. 224 p. : ISBN 3-87895-240-6 : LC Card 84-147595
HC287.H4 K75 1983

(Bd. 30) Nunnenkamp, Peter. Die Rolle öffentlicher Industrieunternehmen im Exportsektor Indiens /. Hamburg , 1985. xiv, 268 p. : ISBN 3-87895-285-6 : LC Card 87-111454
HD4293 .N85 1985

Schriften zu Distribution und Handel, 0179-3608 .
(Bd. 1) Ebert, Kurt, 1954- Warenwirtschaftssysteme und Warenwirtschafts-Controlling /. Frankfurt am Main , New York , c1986. xvi, 353 p. : ISBN 3-8204-9673-4 LC Card 86-218178
HF5415.15 .E24 1986

Schriften zu Macht, Konflikt, technischem und sozialem Wandel in Organisationen .
(Bd. 6) Heinrich, Herbert, 1938- Arbeitsbewertung und Disziplinierung . Spardorf , c1985. v, 281 p. ; ISBN 3-922919-67-7 LC Card 86-162759
HF5549.5.J62 H36 1985

Schriften zu Regional- und Verkehrsproblemen in Industrie- und Entwicklungsländern. For other vols. in this series, see Old Catalog.
(Bd. 42) Pascha, Werner. Strukturanpassung in schrumpfenden Branchen . Berlin , c1986. xx, 364 p. : ISBN 3-428-05983-2 LC Card 86-151590
HB41 .S3 Bd. 42 HD9866.J32

Schriften zum Bericht der Transfer-Enquête-Kommission "Das Transfersystem in der Bundesrepublik Deutschland" .
(Bd. 2, Teilbd. 2) Haushalte mit ausgewählten staatlichen Transferzahlungen . Stuttgart , c1983. 352 p. : ISBN 3-17-007631-0 LC Card 83-117808
HC290.5.I5 H37 1983

Schriften zum bürgerlichen Recht .
(Bd. 102) Bürge, Alfons. Rechtsdogmatik und Wirtschaft . Berlin , c1987. 280 p. ; ISBN 3-428-06124-1 LC Card 87-134998 DDC 332.8/3/094 19
HB551 .B87 1987

Schriften zum Controlling, 0178-9619 .
(Bd. 1) Geiss, Wilfried. Betriebswirtschaftliche Kennzahlen . Frankfurt am Main , New York , c1986. 405 p. : ISBN 3-8204-9629-7 LC Card 87-407301 DDC 657/.42 19
HF5686.C8 G384 1986

Schriften zum Genossenschaftswesen und zur öffentlichen Wirtschaft .
(Bd. 13) Straaten, Martin. Wettbewerb und Kooperation im Landhandel . Berlin , c1985. 82 p. ; ISBN 3-428-05712-0 LC Card 85-167800
HF5429.6.G42 S77 1985

(Bd. 8) Stuchlik, Karl-Heinz. Die Arbeitsverhältnisse in deutschen Konsumgenossenschaften . Berlin , c1983. 533 p. : ISBN 3-428-05355-9 LC Card 83-191612
HD3338 .S88 1983

(Bd. 9) Jösch, Jutta. Konsumgenossenschaften und Food-Cooperatives . Berlin , c1983. 126 p. : ISBN 3-428-05423-7 LC Card 83-231020
HD3338 .J67 1983

Schriften zum gewerblichen Rechtsschutz, Urheber- und Medienrecht .
(Bd. 9) Gaul, Dieter. Rechtsprobleme der Innovation . München , 1984. xiv, 126 p. ; ISBN 3-88709-084-5 ***NYPL [JLD 85-2917]***

Schriften zum Investitionsgütermarketing, 0930-0015 .
(Bd. 1) Iske, Thorsten, 1960- Verbundgeschäfte . Frankfurt am Main , New York , c1986. v, 267 p. : ISBN 3-8204-9756-0 LC Card 86-218131
HF1019 .I85 1986

Schriften zum Marketing (Verlag Peter Lang) .
(Bd. 4) Bruhn, Manfred. Konsumentenzufriedenheit und Beschwerden . Frankfurt am Main , Bern , 1982. xiv, 211 p. ; ISBN 3-8204-5712-7 LC Card 82-131889
HF5415.3 .B78 1982

Schriften zum Steuer-, Rechnungs- und Prüfungswesen .
(Bd. 2) Georgi, Andreas A. Steuern in der Investitionsplanung . Hamburg , 1986. vii, 243, 16, xxviii p. : ISBN 3-89161-702-X LC Card 86-227290
HG4028.C4 G46 1986

Schriften zum Vergleich von Wirtschaftsordnungen. For additional listing of contents, see Old Catalog.
(Heft 32) Feucht, Martin. Theorie des Konkurrenzsozialismus . Stuttgart , New York , 1983. iv, 222 p. : ISBN 3-437-50273-5 LC Card 83-205881
HC79.S6 F48 1983

Schriften zum Vergleich von Wirtschaftsordnungen, 0582-0243 .
(Bd. 38) Zur Interdependenz von Unternehmens- und Wirtschaftsordnung /. Stuttgart , New York , 1986. x, 280 p. ; ISBN 3-437-50296-4 LC Card 87-134241 DDC 338.9 19
HB95 .Z87 1986

(Heft 35) Derix, Hans-Heribert. Säkulare Inflation, kompetitive Geldordnung und "unbeschränkte Demokratie" . Stuttgart , New York , 1985. xiv, 630 p. : ISBN 3-437-50284-0 LC Card 86-110730
HG229 .D46 1985

(Heft 39) Hartwig, Karl-Hans. Monetäre Steuerungsprobleme in sozialistischen Planwirtschaften /. Stuttgart , New York , 1987. vi, 146 p. ; ISBN 3-437-50295-6 LC Card 87-136038 DDC 339.5/3/0947 19
HG925 .H37 1987

Schriften zum Wirtschafts-, Arbeits- und Sozialrecht .
(Bd. 19) Neumann, Carl Wolfgang. Historische Entwicklung und heutiger Stand der Wettbewerbstheorie . Königstein/Ts. , 1982. 318 p. ; ISBN 3-7610-6362-8 : LC Card 83-154547
HB238 .N48 1982

Schriften zur angewandten Ökonometrie .
(Heft 13) Scheiper, Ulrich. Die sektoralen Importe und Exporte der Bundesrepublik Deutschland . Frankfurt am Main , c1984. v, 203 p. : ISBN 3-88129-846-0 : LC Card 85-125395
HF3566.5 .S28 1984

(Heft 16) Eppers, Jürgen. Zur Feinsteuerung ökonomischer Entscheidungsfolgen /. Frankfurt am Main , c1985. 87 p. : ISBN 3-88129-950-5 : LC Card 86-149502
HD30.23 .E66 1985

Schriften zur angewandten Wirtschaftsforschung, 0582-0286 .
(44) Hardes, Heinz-Dieter. Arbeitsmarktstrukturen und Beschäftigungsprobleme im internationalen Vergleich . Tübingen , 1981. xv, 484 p. : ISBN 3-16-344468-7 : LC Card 81-196609 DDC 331.13/7 19
HD5707.5 .H37 1981 ***NYPL [JLE 86-2544]***

(46) Die Input-Output-Analyse als Instrument der Strukturforschung . Tübingen , 1983. xxv, 177 p. : ISBN 3-16-344661-2 LC Card 83-206282
HB142 .I52 1983

(50) Die Bedingungen des Wirtschaftswachstums in Vergangenheit und Zukunft . Tübingen , 1984. viii, 321 p., [1] leaf of plates : ISBN 3-16-344727-9 LC Card 85-165269
HD84 .B415 1984

Schriften zur Betriebswirtschaftslehre des Verkehrs.
Brauer, Karl M. Fallstudie Haiger . Berlin , c1983. 55 p. ; ISBN 3-428-05403-2 LC Card 83-233201
HE199.G3 B73 1983

Krieger, Winfried. Computergestützte Auswahl interkontinentaler Distributionsverfahren /. Berlin , c1984. 143 p. : ISBN 3-428-05617-5 LC Card 84-219069
HF5765 .K75 1984

Seiffert, Bernd. Zahlungsmittelbewirtschaftung im Verkehrsbetrieb /. Berlin , c1986. 187 p. : ISBN 3-428-06094-6 : LC Card 87-143799 DDC 380.5/24/0943 19
HE5999.Z7 G374 1986

Schriften zur Mittelstandsforschung .
(n.F., Nr. 12) Hennicke, Martin. Zum Förderungssystem für kleine und mittlere Unternehmen . Stuttgart , c1986. 155 p. ; ISBN 3-7910-5012-5 LC Card 86-181544 DDC 338.6/42/0943 19
HD2346.G3 H44 1986

(n.F., Nr. 14) Schanz, Hermann J. Der niederrheinische Wirtschaftsraum . Stuttgart , c1986. xxii, 466 p. ; ISBN 3-7910-5014-1 LC Card 87-135757 DDC 330.943/55 19
HC289.D755 S32 1986

(n.F., Nr. 15) Albach, Horst. Finanzierung mit Risikokapital /. Stuttgart , c1986. 312 p. ; ISBN 3-7910-5015-X LC Card 87-127700 DDC 332/.0415/0943 19
HG5492 .A797 1986

(n.F., Nr. 7) Albach, Horst. Kritische Wachstumsschwellen in der Unternehmensentwicklung /. Stuttgart , c1985. xxvii, 490 p. : ISBN 3-7910-5008-7 : LC Card 86-156636
HD35 .A64 1985

(n.F., Nr. 9) Hunsdiek, Detlef. Entwicklungslinien und Entwicklungsrisiken neugegründeter Unternehmen /. Stuttgart , c1986. x, 190 p. : ISBN 3-7910-5009-5 LC Card 87-211045
HD62.5 .H86 1986

(Nr. 14 NF) Schanz, Hermann J. Der niederrheinische Wirtschaftsraum . Stuttgart , c1986. xxii, 466 p. ; ISBN 3-7910-5014-1 LC Card 87-135757 DDC 330.943/55 19
HC289.D755 S32 1986

(Nr. 15 NF) Albach, Horst. Finanzierung mit Risikokapital /. Stuttgart , c1986. 312 p. ; ISBN 3-7910-5015-X LC Card 87-127700 DDC 332/.0415/0943 19
HG5492 .A797 1986

(Nr. 2 NF) Albach, Horst. Kosten der Arbeit . Stuttgart , c1985. xi, 179 p. : ISBN 3-7910-5003-6 : LC Card 86-162885 DDC 658.3/00943 19
HD5029 .A43 1985
NYPL [JLL 73-505 Nr.2]

(Nr. 3, N F) Schmidt, Axel. Betriebliche Altersversorgung in mittelständischen Unternehmen /. Stuttgart , c1985. xiii, 213 p. : ISBN 3-7910-5004-4 : LC Card 86-164220
HD7105.35.G3 S35 1985
NYPL [JLL 73-505 Nr. 3]

(Nr. 5 NF) Weimer, Theodor. Die Bedeutung des Osthandels für mittelständische Unternehmen /. Stuttgart , c1985. 172, 7 p. : ISBN 3-7910-5006-0 LC Card 86-160626
HF3568.E35 W43 1985
NYPL [JLL 73-505 Nr.5]

(Nr. 6 NF) Behrens-Ramberg, Wolfgang. Steuerliche Anreize bei innovativen Investitionen kleiner und mittlerer Industrieunternehmen unter vergleichender Berücksichtigung nichtsteuerlicher Hilfen /. Stuttgart , c1985. 299 p. ; ISBN 3-7910-5007-9 : LC Card 86-124563 DDC 336.24/316 19
HJ2337.G3 B44 1985
NYPL [JLL 73-505 Nr.6]

(Nr. 90) Geiser, Josef. Wachstumshemmnisse mittelständischer Industriebetriebe /. Göttingen , 1983. xi, 385 p. : ISBN 3-509-01353-0 LC Card 84-221327
HD2346.G3 G372 1983

Schriften zur Ordnungspolitik .
(Bd. 2) Mitschke, Joachim. Steuer- und Transferordnung aus einem Guss . Baden-Baden , 1985. 274 p. : ISBN 3-7890-1097-9 LC Card 85-235532
HJ2687 .M57 1985

Schriften zur Personalwirtschaft.
Qualitätszirkel und Kleingruppenarbeit als praktische Organisationsentwicklung /. Frankfurt am Main , 1984. vii, 149 p. : ISBN 3-7824-0348-7 LC Card 85-131916
HD66 .Q332 1984

Schriften zur quantitativen Wirtschaftsforschung .
(Bd. 8) Meyer, Peter. Die Bedeutung wichtiger Typen von Produktionsfunktionen für die Input-Output-Analyse /. Frankfurt , c1983. 109 p. : ISBN 3-88323-438-9 LC Card 83-206578
HB241 .M49 1983

Schriften zur rheinisch-Westfälischen Wirtschaftsgeschichte. For additional listing of contents, see Old Catalog.
(Bd. 34) Wirtschaftsarchive und Kammern--Aspekte wirtschaftlicher selbstverwaltung gestern und heute . Köln , 1982. 250 p. ; LC Card 86-198576
HC286 .W59 1982

Schriften zur Staats- und Gesellschaftspolitik .
(23) Umweltschutz und Verwaltung . Bonn , c1986. 171 p. ; ISBN 3-87999-040-9 LC Card 87-136048 DDC 363.7/056/0943 19
HC290.5.E5 U645 1986

Schriften zur Textilwirtschaft, 0463-7585 .
(Bd. 37) Freitäger, Jürgen, 1959- Erwerb und Verwendung des Einkommens von Arbeitnehmerhaushalten mit erwerbstätiger Ehefrau /. Frankfurt am Main , New York , c1986. xix, 327 p. : ISBN 3-8204-9148-1 : LC Card 86-195223
HD9850.1 .M58 Bd. 37 HD6055.2.G3

(Bd. 39) Siegmann, Frank, 1956- Kurzfristprognosen für die Textilwirtschaft anhand von Bestimmungsfaktoren für Saisonschwankungen /. Frankfurt am Main , New York , c1986. xxxi, 386 p. : ISBN 3-8204-9647-5 LC Card 86-233371
HD9850.1 .M58 Bd. 39 HD9863.5

Schriften zur Umwelt- und Ressourcenökonomie, 0171-7081 .
(Bd. 5) Vogelsang, Ingo. Anreizmechanismen zur Regulierung der Elektrizitätswirtschaft . Tübingen , 1982. xii, 173 p. : ISBN 3-16-344549-7 : LC Card 83-153444
HD9685.G3 V64 1982

Schriften zur Unternehmensführung, 0582-0545 .
(33) Risiko-Management /. Wiesbaden [1986] 145 p. : ISBN 3-409-17902-X LC Card 86-161867
HD70.G2 S3 Bd. 33 HD61

Schriften zur Unternehmensplanung, 0175-8985 .
(Bd. 1) Früh, Bernhard, 1953- Entscheidungsträgermodelle bei Planungstechniken /. Frankfurt am Main , New York , c1984. 268 p. : ISBN 3-8204-5499-3 LC Card 85-197372
HD30.23 .F78 1984

Schriftenreihe Arbeitsschutz (Bundesanstalt für Arbeitsschutz und Unfallforschung) .
(Nr. 33) Meifort, J. (Joachim) Arbeitsbedingungen von Linienbus- und Strassenbahnfahrern der Dortmunder Stadtwerke Aktiengesellschaft /. Dortmund , 1983. 137 p. : ISBN 3-88314-249-2 LC Card 83-204902
HD8039.T72 G36 1983

Schriftenreihe der Bundesversicherungsanstalt für Angestellte .
(18) Germany (West) [Angestelltenversicherungsgesetz.] Angestelltenversicherungsgesetz mit Sozialgesetzbuch . Berlin [1985] 788 p. : LC Card 86-145477
HD7116.M42 G4334 Nr. 18, 1985 KK3270.5

(18) Germany (West) [Angestelltenversicherungsgesetz.] Angestelltenversicherungsgesetz mit Sozialgesetzbuch . Berlin [1986] 792 p. ; LC Card 86-229132
HD7116.M42 G4334 Nr. 18, 1986 KK3270.5

(20) Die Versichertenältesten . [Berlin] [1984]

54 p. ; LC Card 85-113867
HD7116.M42 G4334 Nr. 20, 1984 HD7179

Schriftenreihe der Deutschen Gesellschaft für Technische Zusammenarbeit .
(156) Ellenberg, Heinz, 1913- [Desarrollar sin destruir. German.] Entwicklung ohne Rückschläge . Eschborn , 1984. 139 p. : ISBN 3-88085-228-6 LC Card 86-168369
HD1131 .E4515 1984

Schriftenreihe der Deutschen Stiftung für Internationale Entwicklung. Dialog und Training.
Brodmeier, Beate. Entwicklungspolitische Fachausdrücke (Auswahl) . Baden-Baden , 1985. 48 p. ; ISBN 3-7890-1093-6 LC Card 85-186152
HD84 .B765 1985

Schriftenreihe der Deutschen Stiftung für Internationale Entwicklung. Dok. .
(Nr. 1289) Brodmeier, Beate. Entwicklungspolitische Fachausdrücke (Auswahl) . Baden-Baden , 1985. 48 p. ; ISBN 3-7890-1093-6 LC Card 85-186152
HD84 .B765 1985

Schriftenreihe der Forschungsgesellschaft für Agrarpolitik und Agrarsoziologie .
(272) Kreiten, Kurt. Gestalt und Wandel der nebenberuflichen Landwirtschaft in Nordrhein-Westfalen /. Bonn , 1985. xi, 225 p. : ISBN 3-88488-272-4 LC Card 86-205281
HD1960.N67 K74 1985

(275) Wilamowitz-Moellendorff, Ulrich von. Ansätze eines Konzepts zur Erfassung regionaler Lebensbedingungen in der Raumordnungspolitik /. Bonn , 1986. iv, 205 p. ; ISBN 3-88488-275-9 LC Card 87-407818 DDC 330.943/0878 19
HC286.7 .W54 1986

Schriftenreihe der Forschungsgesellschaft für Agrarpolitik und Agrarsoziologie e.V., 0532-2359 .
(262) Struff, Richard. Räumliche Einkommens-, Preis- und Verbrauchsunterschiede in der Bundesrepublik Deutschland /. Bonn , 1983. xi, 258 p. : ISBN 3-88488-262-7 LC Card 84-196141
HC286.7 .S836 1983

Schriftenreihe der Forschungsstelle für den Handel .
(3. Folge, Nr. 7) Handelsforschung heute . Berlin , c1979. 230 p. : ISBN 3-428-04408-8 LC Card 87-408239 DDC 380.1 s 380.1/06/04355 19
HF345 .F66 Folge 3, Nr. 7 HF308

(3. Folge, Nr. 9) Schenk, Hans-Otto. Die Konzentration im Handel . Berlin , c1984. 341 p. : ISBN 3-428-05618-3 LC Card 84-225438
HF345 .F66 Folge 3, Nr. 9 HF3566

Schriftenreihe der Gesellschaft für Deutschlandforschung e.V. .
(Bd. 16) Aussenwirtschaft der DDR und innerdeutsche Wirtschaftsbeziehungen . Berlin , c1986. 98 p. ; ISBN 3-428-06121-7 LC Card 87-137949 DDC 382/.0943/0431 19
HF3570.5.Z7 G352 1986

Schriftenreihe der Gesellschaft für Öffentliche Wirtschaft und Gemeinwirtschaft .
(Heft 27) Gesellschaft für Öffentliche Wirtschaft und Gemeinwirtschaft. Wissenschaftlicher Beirat. Zum Problem der Aufgabenverlagerung auf öffentliche Unternehmen . Baden-Baden , 1984. 73 p. ; ISBN 3-7890-1048-0 LC Card 85-143795
HD4177 .G47 1984

Schriftenreihe der Gesellschaft für Öffentliche Wirtschaft und Gemeinwirtschaft e.V. .
(Heft 14) Öffentliche Unternehmen in Rezession und Aufschwung . Berlin , 1977. 165 p. : LC Card 85-180964
HD3845 .G43 Heft 14 HD3842

Schriftenreihe der Gesellschaft für Versicherungswissenschaft und -gestaltung e. V. Köln .
(Bd. 4) Kapitalbildung und Altersvorsorge . Köln , Bergisch Gladbach [1983?] 95 p. : LC Card 84-180205
HD7105.45.G3 K37 1983

(Bd. 6) Demographische Entwicklung und kapitalbildende Altersversorgungssysteme /. Bergisch Gladbach , 1984. iii, 67 p. ; LC Card 85-154174
HD7091 .D46 1984

Schriftenreihe der Österreichischen Gesellschaft für Raumforschung und Raumplanung, 0078-3498 .
(Bd. 28) Grasberger, Helmut, 1941- Die Untersuchung des Wohnwertes von Wohngebieten /. Wien , New York , 1983. 108 p., [15] folded leaves of plates : ISBN 0-387-81752-2 (U. S.) LC Card 84-142695
HD7337.A3 G73 1983

Schriftenreihe der Otto Brenner Stiftung .
(25) Multinationale Konzerne . Köln , c1982. 478 p. : ISBN 3-7663-0506-9 LC Card 82-196963 DDC 332.6/73/0943 19
HD5710.75.G3 M84 1982
NYPL [JLD 86-2753]

(34) Metallgewerkschaften in Südafrika /. [Köln] , c1983. 217 p. ; ISBN 3-7663-0530-1 LC Card 85-232412 DDC 331.88/171/0968 19
HD6870.5.Z7 M54 1983
NYPL [JLD 87-1964]

Schriftenreihe der Stiftung Volkswagenwerk, 0172-164X .
(Bd. 23) Korte, Hermann, 1937- Migration und ihre sozialen Folgen . Göttingen , c1983. 170 p. ; ISBN 3-525-85366-1 LC Card 84-150019
HD8458.A2 K65 1983

Schriftenreihe der Studiengesellschaft für Sozialgeschichte und Arbeiterbewegung .
(Bd. 42) Lauschke, Karl. Schwarze Fahnen an der Ruhr . Marburg [/Lahn] , c1984. 400 p. : ISBN 3-921630-42-8 LC Card 84-215799
HD6698.M616 I535 1984

(Bd. 46) Roth, Bernhard. Weltökonomie oder Nationalökonomie? . Marburg , c1984. xiv, 377 p. : ISBN 3-921630-48-7 : LC Card 84-252964
HF1411 .R69 1984

(Bd. 50) Arbeitskampf um Arbeitszeit . Marburg , c1985. 218 p. : ISBN 3-921630-52-5 LC Card 86-160526
HD5378 .A73 1985

(Bd. 63) Oltmann, Joachim. Kalter Krieg und kommunale Integration . Marburg , c1987. 500 p. ; ISBN 3-921630-71-1 LC Card 87-142718 DDC 331.88/0943/52 19
HD6699.B7 O48 1987

Schriftenreihe des Bundesministers für Ernährung, Landwirtschaft und Forsten. Reihe A, Angewandte Wissenschaft. Supplement.
Gesamtkonzeption nachwachsende Rohstoffe des Bundesministeriums für Ernährung, Landwirtschaft und Forsten . Münster-Hiltrup , 1983. vi, 196 p. : ISBN 3-7843-0202-5 : LC Card 84-126491
HD9502.G42 G47 1983

Schriftenreihe des Deutschen Nationalkomitees für Denkmalschutz .
(Bd. 14) Sack, Manfred, 1928- Lebensraum . Bonn , 1982. 81 p. : ISBN 3-922153-01-1 LC Card 85-128580
HE363.G3 S23 1982

Schriftenreihe des Energiewirtschaftlichen Instituts .
(Bd. 27) Suding, Paul H. Ökonomische Ansätze zur Analyse des Energieverbrauchs der Haushalte für Rauwärmzwecke /. München , 1984. ix, 252, 10 p. : ISBN 3-486-28661-7 LC Card 84-209002
HD9502.G42 S8 1984

(Bd. 30) Angebotsentwicklung und Preisbildung natürlicher Ressourcen /. München , 1986. vii, 148, 10 p. : ISBN 3-486-26171-1 LC Card 86-182074
HC59 .A794 1986

(Bd. 31) Bozem, Karlheinz. Controlling in Versorgungsunternehmen /. München , 1986. xiv, 468, 10 p. : ISBN 3-486-26236-X LC Card 87-135246 DDC 363.6/2/0681 19
HD2763 .B66 1986

Schriftenreihe des IFO-Instituts für Wirtschaftsforschung .
(Nr. 114) Gerstenberger, Wolfgang. Strukturwandel unter verschlechterten Rahmenbedingungen . Berlin , c1984. 255 p. : ISBN 3-428-05567-5 LC Card 84-180150
HC286.7 .G46 1984

(Nr. 116) Berger, Manfred, Dipl. econ. Auslandsinvestitionen kleiner und mittlerer Unternehmen . Berlin , c1985. 164 p. : ISBN 3-428-05775-9 LC Card 85-161656
HG4538 .B4538 1985

(Nr. 117) Leibfritz, Willi. Steuerliche Investitionsförderung im internationalen Vergleich /. Berlin , c1985. 255 p. : ISBN 3-428-05776-7 LC Card 85-161706
HJ4631 .L38 1985

(Nr. 118) Laumer, Helmut. Strukturpolitik für traditionelle Industriezweige in Japan /. Berlin , c1985. 173 p. : ISBN 3-428-05920-4 LC Card 86-151482
HD3616.J32 L38 1985

(Nr. 119) Uhlmann, Luitpold. Investitionsverhalten und Unternehmensgrösse /. Berlin , c1986. 307 p. ; ISBN 3-428-06010-5 LC Card 86-216522
HG4028.C4 U37 1986

Schriftenreihe des Instituts für Allgemeine Wirtschaftsforschung der Albert-Ludwigs-Universität Freiburg i. Br. .
(Bd. 12) Enke, Harald. Konsumtive Arbeit . Freiburg im Breisgau , c1983. 354 p. : ISBN 3-448-01239-4 LC Card 83-224110
HF5549.5.J63 E54 1983

(Bd. 18) Flaig, Jürgen. Verteilungsschwankungen im Konjunkturverlauf . Freiburg im Breisgau , c1983. vi, 221 p. : ISBN 3-448-01325-0 LC Card 83-155341
HC290.5.I5 F55 1983

(Bd. 19) Horn, Christel-Margret. Feldtheorie und Konsumverhalten /. Freiburg im Breisgau , c1983. 121 p. : ISBN 3-448-01293-9 LC Card 84-136042
HF5415.3 .H65 1983

(Bd. 21) Röhling, Wolfgang. Ökonometrische Systeme mit variablen Strukturen . Freiburg im Breisgau , c1983. x, 263 p. : ISBN 3-448-01353-6 LC Card 84-132199
HB139 .R63 1983

(Bd. 23) Holzwarth, Fritz. Ordnung der Wirtschaft durch Wettbewerb . Freiburg im Breisgau , c1985. 217 p. ; ISBN 3-448-01510-5 LC Card 86-109043
HB95 .H65 1985

(Bd. 24) Pusse, Leo. Arbeitsproduktivität und Beschäftigung . Freiburg im Breisgau , c1984. viii, 311 p. : ISBN 3-448-01512-1 LC Card 85-138794
HC290.5.L3 P87 1984

Schriftenreihe des Instituts für Betriebswirtschaftliche Forschung an der Universität Zürich .
(Bd. 45) Künzli, Ernst. Forschungs- und Entwicklungsplanung . Bern , c1984. 292 p. : ISBN 3-258-03351-X : LC Card 84-178059
HD30.4 .K86 1984

(Bd. 50) Strategisches Marketing und Management . Bern , c1986. 205 p. : ISBN 3-258-03566-0 : LC Card 86-159360
HF5415.135 .S77 1986

(Bd. 54) Samsinger, Berndt R. Countertrade, eine alternative Marketing-Strategie /. Bern , c1986. xiii, 285 p. : ISBN 3-258-03597-0 : LC Card 86-191674
HF1412 .S26 1986

(Bd. 55) Staffelbach, Bruno. Strategisches Personalmanagement /. Bern [1986] x, 285 p. : ISBN 3-258-03626-8 : LC Card 86-211191
HF5549 .S842416 1986

Schriftenreihe des Instituts für Empirische Wirtschaftsforschung der Universität Zürich .
(Bd. 12) Capitelli, René. Die Zinsstruktur der Schweiz . Frankfurt am Main , c1983. ix, 221 p. : ISBN 3-88129-700-6 LC Card 84-129042
HG1623.S9 C36 1983

(Bd. 13) Karas, Thomas H. Die Nachfrage nach Ausrüstungsinvestitionen in der Schweiz 1963-1980 . Frankfurt am Main , c1984. v, 91 p. : ISBN 3-88129-798-7 : LC Card 84-208150
HC400.D4 K37 1984

Schriftenreihe des Instituts für Kredit- u. Versicherungswirtschaft, Abteilung Bankbetriebslehre .
(Bd. 4) Gach, Christian. Wirtschaftlichkeitsanalyse von Banken . Wien , c1983. iv, 75, iii, 89 p. ; ISBN 3-85428-017-3 :

LC Card 84-118578
HG3008 .G28 1983

(Bd. 6) Ippisch, Wolfgang. Bankbetriebliches Zinsspannen-Management . Wien , c1984. xxiii, 365 p. : ISBN 3-85428-022-X : LC Card 84-174308
HG1621 .I66 1984

(Bd. 7) Lehner, Susanna Walpurga. Unternehmensanalyse . Wien , c1984. 243 p. : ISBN 3-85428-023-8 : LC Card 84-173011
HG3751.5 .L44 1984

Schriftenreihe des Instituts für Kredit- und Finanzwirtschaft .
(Bd. 10) Wünsche, Gert. Grundlagen der Bankenwerbung aus verhaltenswissenschaftlicher Sicht /. Wiesbaden , c1982. 304 p. : ISBN 3-409-47003-4 LC Card 83-151107
HF6161.B2 W86 1982

(Bd. 11) Dieckhöner, Bruno. Rentabilitätsrisiken aus dem Hypothekargeschäft von Kreditinstituten in Zeiten der Geldentwertung /. Wiesbaden , c1984. xi, 395 p. : ISBN 3-409-14002-6 : LC Card 85-119494
HG2040.5.G4 D53 1984

Schriftenreihe des Instituts für Kreditwesen der Westfälischen Wilhelms-Universität Münster .
(Bd. 26) Allerkamp, Ferdinand. Tilgungsplanung . Frankfurt am Main , c1983. xii, 288 p. : ISBN 3-7819-0296-X LC Card 85-239167
HD2747 .A53 1983

(Bd. 30) Holterhus, Gerhard. Früherkennung von Bankkrisen bei der Abschlussprüfung /. Frankfurt am Main , c1985. xvi, 360 p. : ISBN 3-7819-0348-6 LC Card 86-164226
HG1768.G3 H64 1985

(Bd. 33) Kilhey, Ulrike. Die Beurteilung des Erfolgs von Bankprodukten als Grundlage produktpolitischer Entscheidungen /. Frankfurt am Main , c1987. xiv, 289 p. : ISBN 3-7819-0374-5 LC Card 87-136157 DDC 332.1/068/5 19
HF5415.15 .K55 1987

Schriftenreihe des Instituts für Städtebau, Wohnungswirtschaft und Bausparwesen e.V. (Arnold-Knoblauch-Institut) .
(Bd. 5, etc) Materialien zur Vermögensbildung in Arbeitnehmerhand. Bonn [1965-<c1985. v. <1-6 > LC Card 67-123501 DDC 368.4/00943
HD7179 .M35

Schriftenreihe des Instituts für Unternehmungsplanung .
(Bd. 3) Hölter, Erich, 1955- Computergestütztes Ertragsteuersimulationsmodell der deutschen internationalen Kapitalgesellschaft . Giessen , c1986. xxv, 383 p. : ISBN 3-922730-67-1 LC Card 87-116057 DDC 336.24/3/0943 19
HJ4720.A7 H65 1986

Schriftenreihe des Instituts für Verkehrsplanung und Verkehrswesen der Technischen Universität München, 0341-5716 .
(Heft 19) Stengel, Wolfgang. Verlagerungen der individuellen Verkehrsnachfrage bei verändertem ÖPNV-Angebot infolge neueingerichteter Stadtschnellbahnen /. Bad Honnef , 1984. iv, 210 p. : ISBN 3-88347-120-8 : LC Card 84-185940
HE311.G3 S73 1984

Schriftenreihe des Instituts für Versicherungswissenschaft an der Universität zu Köln .
(n.F., Heft 39) Reuter, Frank, Dr. Grundzüge der internationalen Unternehmenspolitik des Versicherungsunternehmens /. Berlin , c1983. 178 p. : ISBN 3-428-05308-7 LC Card 83-161541
HG8018 .C6 n.F., Heft 39 HG8059

Schriftenreihe des Instituts für Wirtschaftswissenschaften an der Rechtswissenschaftlichen Fakultät der Universität Salzburg .
(Bd. 1) Speiser, Harald. Das österreichische Foreign Debt Management, 1956-1983 . Regensburg , c1985. 120 p. : ISBN 3-924956-06-5 LC Card 86-222064
HJ8636 .S66 1985

Schriftenreihe des Lorenz-von-Stein-Instituts für Verwaltungswissenschaften Kiel .
(Bd. 3) Heilmann, Martin. Lorenz von Stein und die Grundprobleme der Steuerlehre . Heidelberg , 1984. xi, 577 p. ; ISBN 3-7685-0184-1 LC Card 84-236751
HJ2309 .H36 1984

Schriftenreihe des Rheinisch-Westfälischen Instituts für Wirtschaftsforschung Essen .
(n.F., Heft 47) Zeppernick, Ralf. Transfer-Einkommen und Einkommensverteilung /. Berlin , c1986. viii, 233, [1] p. : ISBN 3-428-05990-5 LC Card 86-178831
HC290.5.I5 Z47 1986

Schriftenreihe des Seminars für Allgemeine Betriebswirtschaftslehre der Universität Hamburg .
(Bd. 25) Stomberg, Peter. Die Probleme der Prognose des Kapitalbedarfs im Rahmen der strategischen Plannung /. Göttingen , c1984. x, 212 p. ; ISBN 0-352-51266-3 LC Card 84-240131
HD30.28 .S729 1984

(Bd. 26) Duhnkrack, Thomas. Zielbildung und strategisches Zielsystem der internationalen Unternehmung /. Göttingen , c1984. xii, 287 p. : ISBN 3-525-12664-6 (Deut. Bibl.) LC Card 85-127165
HD62.4 .D86 1984

(Bd. 27) Flohr, Bernd. Fungibilität und Elastizität von Personal /. Göttingen , c1984. xvi, 439 p. ; ISBN 3-525-12665-4 LC Card 85-125026
HF5549 .F584 1984

(Bd. 29) Feider, Josef. Konsumentenreaktion auf Preise /. Göttingen , c1985. xii, 303 p. : ISBN 3-525-12667-0 LC Card 85-203330
HF5415.3 .F39 1985

Schriftenreihe des Verbandes der Automobilindustrie e.V. (VDA) .
(Nr. 42) Kortzfleisch, Gert von. Energie für den Verkehr . Frankfurt am Main , c1984. 115 p. : LC Card 84-192683
HD9710.G4 V4 Nr. 42 HE5620.E53

(42) Kortzfleisch, Gert von. Energie für den Verkehr . Frankfurt am Main , c1984. 115 p. : LC Card 84-192683
HD9710.G4 V4 Nr. 42 HE5620.E53

Schriftenreihe des Vereins für Wirtschaftliche und Soziale Fragen e.V. Stuttgart .
(17) Verbraucherpolitik in der sozialen Marktwirtschaft . Bonn , c1984. 146 p. ; ISBN 3-922335-04-7 LC Card 85-228004
HC240.9.C63 V47 1984

(19) Ladenschluss kontrovers . Stuttgart [1984] 232 p. : ISBN 3-512-00712-0 LC Card 85-138606
HD5178 .L33 1984

Schriftenreihe des Wirtschaftswissenschaftlichen Seminars Ottobeuren, 0340-7187 .
(Bd. 15) Technologischer Wandel, Analyse und Fakten /. Tübingen , 1986. ix, 330 p. ; ISBN 3-16-345132-2 LC Card 87-109808 DDC 338/.06 19
HC79.T4 T4355 1986

Schriftenreihe "Die Arbeiterbewegung in den Rheinlanden" .
(Nr. 18) Kiefer, Rolf. Sozialdemokratische Arbeiterbewegung in der Stadt Neuss vom Sozialistengesetz bis zum Ersten Weltkrieg /. Reinbek , c1982. iv, 159 p. ; ISBN 3-88756-025-6 LC Card 83-186919
HD8460.N48 K54 1982

Schriftenreihe Europa-Forschung .
(Bd. 9) Platzer, Hans-Wolfgang. Unternehmensverbände in der EG, ihre nationale und transnationale Organisation und Politik . Kehl am Rhein , 1984. xi, 283 p. ; ISBN 3-88357-024-9 LC Card 85-131940
HD6948.G3 P58 1984

Schriftenreihe Europäisches Recht, Politik und Wirtschaft .
(Bd. 122) Western Europe in transition . Baden-Baden , 1986. 223 p. : ISBN 3-7890-1220-3 LC Card 87-136015 DDC 341.24/22 19
HC241.25.G3 W47 1986

Schriftenreihe Finanzwirtschaft und Finanzrecht.
(Bd. 39) Tinner, Hanspeter. Konzernstruktur und Steuerplanung . Bern , c1984. ix, 276 p. : ISBN 3-258-03367-6 : LC Card 84-198592
HJ4748.A3 T55 1984

(Bd. 47) Kratz, Peter. Steuerplanung internationaler Unternehmungen . Bern , c1986. xii, 344 p. : ISBN 3-258-03586-5 : LC Card 86-171030
HJ4720.A3 K73 1986

(45) Dürsteler, Urs. Kantonale Verteilung der Bundesausgaben 1983 . Bern , c1986. 55 p. ; ISBN 3-258-03577-6 : LC Card 86-149603
HJ1264.A2 D87 1986

Schriftenreihe Forum der Bundesstatistik .
(Bd. 2) Reich, Utz-Peter. Darstellungskonzepte der Input-Output-Rechnung /. Stuttgart , 1984. 185 p. : ISBN 3-17-003301-8
NYPL [JLE 86-1264]

(Bd. 5) Nutzung von anonymisierten Einzelangaben aus Daten der amtlichen Statistik . Stuttgart , 1987. 200 p. : ISBN 3-17-003338-7 LC Card 87-401358
HA29.5.G4 N88 1987

Schriftenreihe für Agrarpolitik und Agrarsoziologie. For earlier file, whose numbering continues, see: Schriftenreihe für Agrarsoziologie und Agrarrecht.
(Bd. 37) Arbeitsmarktpolitik für die Landwirtschaft und den ländlichen Raum /. Graz , c1984. 138 p. : ISBN 3-900307-15-6 LC Card 85-186643
HD1536.A9 A73 1984

Schriftenreihe für ländliche Sozialfragen, 0080-7133 .
(Heft 92) Theorie und Empirie in Wirtschaftspolitik und Wirtschaftsgeschichte . Göttingen , 1984. 245 p. : LC Card 85-111313
HC284 .T46 1984

(Heft 95) Europäische Agrarpolitik . Göttingen , 1985. 82 p. ; LC Card 86-170925
HD1920.5.Z8 E97 1985

(Heft 96) Landwirtschaft und Umweltschutz, Sozialpflichtigkeit oder Entschädigung? /. Göttingen , 1987. 116 p. : LC Card 87-401359 DDC 363.7/056/0943 19
HD1957 .L355 1987

Schriftenreihe (Germany (West). Bundesministerium für Verkehr) .
(Heft 53) Vorschläge für eine Neuordnung des organisatorischen Rahmens für den öffentlichen Personennahverkehr /. Bonn-Bad Godesberg [1977] 35 p. ; LC Card 86-173254
HE64 .A36 Heft 53 HE249

(Heft 54) Gscheidle, Kurt. Die Verkehrspolitik in der 8. Legislaturperiode /. Bonn-Bad Godesberg [1977] 29 p. : LC Card 86-173226
HE64 .A36 Heft 54 HE249

Schriftenreihe (Hans-Böckler-Stiftung) .
(11) Mitbestimmung in der Krise--Krise der Mitbestimmung? . Köln , c1984. 192 p. : ISBN 3-7663-0895-5 LC Card 85-113842
HD5660.G4 M563 1984

Schriftenreihe "Humanisierung des Arbeitslebens" .
(Bd. 28) Belastungsabbau unter Tage . Essen , 1982. 315 p. : ISBN 3-7739-0380-4 : LC Card 83-186893 DDC 363.1/1/0943 19
HD7708 .B45 1982

(Bd. 36) Qualitative Arbeitsanalyse . Frankfurt , New York , c1983. 352 p. ; ISBN 3-593-32721-X LC Card 83-161600 DDC 158.7 19
HD6955 .Q35 1983 ***NYPL [JLD 87-1014]***

(Bd. 38) Weltz, Friedrich. Innovation im Büro . Frankfurt , New York , c1983. 343 p. ; ISBN 3-593-32724-4 LC Card 83-243001
HF5548.115 .W44 1983

(Bd. 53) Arbeitsgestaltung in der Serienfertigung . Frankfurt [am Main] , New York , c1984. 315 p. : ISBN 3-593-32733-3 LC Card 84-230390
HD58.8 .A73 1984

(Bd. 55) Fricke, Werner. Beteiligung im Industriebetrieb . Frankfurt/Main , New York , c1985. 291 p. ; ISBN 3-593-32735-X LC Card 85-202742
HD5660.G4 F73 1985

(Bd. 71) Brumlop, Eva. Arbeitsbewertung bei flexiblem Personaleinsatz . Frankfurt , New York , c1986. 229 p. : ISBN 3-593-32744-9 LC Card 86-196323
HD5109.2.G3 B76 1986

Schriftenreihe (Institut "Finanzen und Steuern" (Germany)) .
(Heft 259) Zur Problematik von Subventionen als Instrument der Wirtschaftspolitik /. Bonn , 1986. 97 p. : LC Card 87-408486 DDC

336/.012/43 s 338.943 19
HJ1101 .B6 Heft 259 HD3646.G4

(Heft 73) Länderhaushalte. Bonn [1964] 112 p. ; LC Card 85-185971
HJ1101 .B6 Heft 73 HJ1120

(Heft 75) Gemeindehaushalte zur Haushaltswirtschaft der Städte Hannover, Düsseldorf, Köln, Frankfurt, Stuttgart, München. Bonn am Rhein , 1964. 148 p. ; LC Card 87-408349 DDC 336/.014/43 19
HJ9473 .G46 1964

Schriftenreihe (Institut für Angewandte Wirtschaftsforschung Tübingen) .
(Bd. 39) Aktuelle Probleme der Wirtschaftspolitik . Tübingen , 1982. vi, 69, vii, 62 p. : ISBN 3-16-344473-3 LC Card 84-125468
HJ5715.G3 A67 1982

Schriftenreihe Internationales Management .
(Bd. 1) Köpplinger, Herbert, 1954- Risiken im Auslandsgeschäft . Nürnberg , 1986. xli, 227 p. : ISBN 3-89078-005-9 LC Card 87-145527 DDC 332.6/73 19
HG4538 .K64 1986

Schriftenreihe (Österreichische Raumordnungskonferenz) .
(Nr. 38) Bauer, Helfried. Fahrradfreundliche Verkehrspolitik in Stadt und Land . Wien , 1984. 87 p. : LC Card 85-150945
HE5739.A9 B38 1984

Schriftenreihe "Raumordnung" des Bundesministers für Raumordnung, Bauwesen und Städtebau .
(06.012) Raumordnungsprognose 1990 . Bonn-Bad-Godesberg , 1977. 95 p. : LC Card 86-100310
HB3595 .R38 1977

Schriftenreihe SIB.
Moser, R. (René), 1941- Marketing-Strategie für den Detailhandel /. Münsingen , Zürich , 1981. 159 p. : ISBN 3-85681-059-5 LC Card 83-240590
HF5429.6.S92 M67 1981

Schriftenreihe Studien zu Bildung und Wissenschaft, 0175-8055 .
(37) Mädchen und Berufswahl . Bonn , Bad Honnef , 1986. 96 p. : ISBN 3-87066-631-5 LC Card 87-409396 DDC 331.4/2592/0943 19
HF5382.67.G3 M33 1986

(40) Hegelheimer, Armin. Gleichwertigkeit von allgemeiner und beruflicher Bildung /. Bonn , Bad Honnef , 1986. v, 74 p. ; ISBN 3-87066-628-5 : LC Card 87-409371 DDC 331.4/2592/0943 19
HD6059.6.G4 H42 1986

(41) Frauen und Beruf, zwischen Wunsch und Realität . Bonn , Bad Honnef , 1986. 142 p. ; ISBN 3-87066-629-3 : LC Card 87-409372 DDC 331.4/0943 19
HD6149 .F719 1986

Schriftenreihe (Universität Karlsruhe. Institut für Regionalwissenschaft) .
(Heft Nr. 22) Skutlartz, Ekkehard. Branchenportfolioanalyse und Wirtschaftsförderungsstrategien . [Karlsruhe] [1986] a-m, 205, vi p. : LC Card 87-103969
HG4529.5 .S58 1986

Schriftenreihe Unternehmung und Unternehmungsführung .
(Bd. 12) Malik, Fredmund F. Strategie des Managements komplexer Systeme . Bern , c1984. 563 p. : ISBN 3-258-03306-4 : LC Card 84-178061
HD30.28 .M334 1984

(9) Lattmann, Charles. Die verhaltenswissenschaftlichen Grundlagen der Führung des Mitarbeiters /. Bern , c1981. 565 p. : ISBN 3-258-03094-4 : LC Card 82-163528 DDC 658.3 19
HD58.7 .L36 1981 ***NYPL [JLE 86-1595]***

Schriftenreihe Verbände der Bundesrepublik Deutschland.
Fredersdorf, Hermann, 1924- Der Steuerrebell und seine Gewerkschaft . Wiesbaden , c1982. 156 p., [3] folded leaves of plates : ISBN 3-922114-02-4 LC Card 83-102197
HJ2690 .F78 1982

Schriftenreihe Wirtschaftsdidaktik Berufsbildung und Konsumentenerziehung .
(Bd. 4) Weibel, Bernd, 1951- Differenzierung der Berufsausbildung . Heidelberg , 1984. iv, 326, 6 p. : ISBN 3-88326-138-6 LC Card 85-189624
HF5381 .W43 1984

Schriftenreihe wirtschaftswissenschaftliche Forschung und Entwicklung .
(Bd. 67) Thomé, Gotthardt, 1949- Produktgestaltung und Ökologie /. München , c1981. xii, 212 p. : ISBN 3-88259-086-6 : LC Card 81-146058
HD69.N4 T54 1981 ***NYPL [JLD 86-2800]***

Schriftenreihe zur Energieforschung.
Böttges, Norbert. Rationalisierung im Energiebereich . Essen , Bielefeld , 1984. 159 p. : ISBN 3-7736-0106-9 LC Card 85-130852
HD9502.A2 B68 1984

Schrimpff, Wolfgang. Heterogene Koordinationsinstrumente im Beschäftigungssystem der DDR / von Wolfgang Schrimpff. Münster : Institut für Genossenschaftswesen der Westfälischen Wilhelms-Universität, 1983. xv, 360 p. : ill. ; 24 cm. (Kooperations- und genossenschaftswissenschaftliche Beiträge . Bd. 8) Bibliography: p. 333-349. Includes indexes. ISBN 3-7923-0505-4 LC Card 85-140056
1. Manpower policy - Germany, East. 2. Labor supply - Germany, East. I. Title. II. Series.
HD5780.5.A6 S37 1983

Schroeder, Frederick J. Compliance costs and consumer benefits of the Electronic Fund Transfer Act : recent survey evidence / Frederick J. Schroeder. Washington, D.C. : Board of Governors of the Federal Reserve System, 1985. 23 p. : ill. ; 28 cm. (Staff studies . 143) Includes bibliographical references. LC Card 86-603417 DDC 332.1/028 19
1. Electronic funds transfer - United States. 2. Electronic funds transfer - Law and legislation - United States - Compliance costs. I. Title. II. Series.
HG1710 .S38 1985

Schroeder, Ighsaan. Conditions of employment : an analysis of the conditions of employment set by the industrial councils and the wage board / Ighsaan Schroeder and Gordon Young. Cape Town : Southern Africa Labour & Development Research Unit, [1985]- 1 v. (loose-leaf) ; 32 cm. (SALDRU labour research series . v. 4-) Includes index. ISBN 0-7992-1002-1 (loose-leaf) LC Card 86-232933 DDC 331.2/0968 19
1. Employee fringe benefits - South Africa. 2. Wages - South Africa. 3. Hours of labor - South Africa. I. Young, Gordon, 1953-. II. Series: Labour research series , v. 4, etc. III. Title.
HD4927.S6 S37 1985

Schroeder, Larry D. Understanding regression analysis : an introductory guide / Larry D. Schroeder, David L. Sjoquist, Paula E. Stephan. Beverly Hills : Sage Publications, c1986. 95 p. : ill. ; 26 cm. (Sage university papers series. Quantitative applications in the social sciences . no. 07-057) Bibliography: p. 93-94. ISBN 0-8039-2758-4 LC Card 85-63790
1. Regression analysis. 2. Correlation (Statistics). I. Sjoquist, David L. II. Stephan, Paula E. III. Series. IV. Series: Quantitative applications in the social sciences, no. 57. V. Title. ***NYPL [JLK 77-39 no.57]***

Schroeter, Daniel J. Merchants of Essaouira : urban society and imperialism in southwestern Morocco, 1844-1886 / Daniel J. Schroeter. Cambridge ; New York : Cambridge University Press, 1988. p. cm. (Cambridge Middle East library) Bibliography: p. Includes index. ISBN 0-521-32455-6 LC Card 87-15163 DDC 330.964/6 19
1. Essaouira (Morocco) - Economic conditions. 2. Merchants - Morocco - Essaouira - History - 18th century. 3. Merchants - Morocco - Essaouira - History - 19th century. 4. Capitalism - Morocco - Essaouira - History - 18th century. 5. Capitalism - Morocco - Essaouira - History - 19th century. I. Title. II. Series.
HC810.Z7 E857 1988

Schroiff, Franz J. Das Binnenschiffahrt-Verkehrssystem : die Bedeutung der Wasserstrassen und der Binnenschiffahrt für die räumliche Entwicklung / Franz J. Schroiff. Hannover : C.R. Vincentz, 1984. ix, 267 p. : ill. ; 25 cm. (Veröffentlichungen der Akademie für Raumforschung und Landesplanung. Abhandlungen, 0344-0311 . Bd. 84) Bibliography: p. 262-267. ISBN 3-87870-951-X LC Card 84-221599
1. Inland water transportation - Germany (West) - History. 2. Transportation and state - Germany (West) - History. I. Title. II. Series.
HE669 .S34 1984

Schroiff, H.-W. (Hans-Willi) West European Conference on the Psychology of Work and Organization (1985 : Aachen, Germany) The psychology of work and organization . Amsterdam ; New York : xi, 407 p. : ISBN 0-444-70029-3 (U. S.) LC Card 86-8947 DDC 158.7 19
HF5548.8 .W475 1985 ***NYPL [JLE 86-4341]***

Schröter, Klaus, 1953- Die wettbewerbspolitische Behandlung der leitungsgebundenen Energiewirtschaft : dargestellt am Beispiel der Fernwärmewirtschaft der Bundesrepublik Deutschland / Klaus Schröter. Frankfurt am Main ; New York : P. Lang, c1986. viii, 300 p. ; 21 cm. (Hohenheimer volkswirtachaftliche Schriften, 0721-3085 . Bd. 3) Bibliography: p. 262-300. ISBN 3-8204-9551-7 LC Card 87-407422 DDC 363.6/2/0943 19
1. Electric utilities - Germany, West. 2. Public utilities - Germany, West. 3. Heating from central stations - Economic aspects - Germany (West). 4. Competition, Imperfect - Germany (West). I. Title. II. Series.
HD9685.G3 S375 1986

Schrumpfende Märkte : eine neue Herausforderung für den Unternehmer / Kraus ... [et al.]. Wien : Institut für Angewandte Sozial- und Wirtschaftsforschung im Signum-Verlag, 1986. vi, 241 p. : ill. ; 21 cm. Bibliography: p. 225-231. Includes index. ISBN 3-85436-037-1 LC Card 86-227304 DDC 658.8 19
1. Business. 2. Marketing. I. Kraus, Herbert, 1937-.
HF5351 .S4125 1986

Schubäus, Klaus. Das Hypothekenbankgeschäft in den Niederlanden und in der Bundesrepublik Deutschland / von Klaus Schubäus. Berlin : Duncker & Humblot, c1984. 251 p. : ill. ; 24 cm. (Untersuchungen über das Spar-, Giro- und Kreditwesen. Abteilung B: Rechtswissenschaft. Bd. 41) Bibliography: p. [243]-247. Includes index. ISBN 3-428-05569-1 LC Card 84-250906
1. Mortgage banks - Netherlands. 2. Mortgage banks - Germany, West. I. Title. II. Series.
HG2040.5.N37 S38 1984

Schubert, Frank. Akzeptanz von Bildschirmtext in Unternehmungen und im Markt : eine empirische Untersuchung über die Durchsetzung innovativer Kommunikationstechnologien im institutionellen Bereich / Frank Schubert. Münster : Regensberg, c1986. xxiv, 316 p. : ill. ; 24 cm. (Schriften der Wissenschaftlichen Gesellschaft für Marketing und Unternehmensführung e.V. Münster . Bd. 4) Originally presented as the author's thesis (doctoral)--Universität Münster. Bibliography: p. 288-316. ISBN 3-7923-0546-1 LC Card 86-227074
1. Television supplies industry - Germany (West). 2. Videotex systems - Germany (West). 3. Teletext systems - Germany (West). I. Title. II. Series.
HD9696.T463 G37 1986

Schubert, Leo. Opitz, Otto. Die EDV als Wettbewerbsinstrument des Handels /. Augsburg [1986] 37 leaves : LC Card 87-407366 DDC 650/.028/5416 19
HF5548.2 .O656 1986

Schüller, Alfred.
China im Konflikt zwischen verschiedenen Ordnungskonzeptionen /. Berlin , c1985. 157 p. : ISBN 3-428-05923-9 LC Card 86-164406
HC427.9 .C56525 1985

Wachstumsverlangsamung und Konjunkturzyklen in unterschiedlichen Wirtschaftssystemen /. Berlin , c1984. 191 p. : ISBN 3-428-05626-4
NYPL [JLL 73-186 Bd. 142]

Zur Interdependenz von Unternehmens- und Wirtschaftsordnung /. Stuttgart , New York , 1986. x, 280 p. ; ISBN 3-437-50296-4 LC Card 87-134241 DDC 338.9 19
HB95 .Z87 1986

Schüpbach, Werner. Die Bevölkerung der Stadt Luzern 1850-1914 : Demographie, Wohnverhältnisse, Hygiene und medizinische Versorgung / Werner Schüpbach. Luzern : Rex-Verlag, 1983. 323 p., [17] p. of plates : ill. ; 25 cm. (Luzerner historische Veröffentlichungen. Bd. 17) Originally presented as the author's thesis--Universität Zürich. Bibliography: p. 302-306. Includes index. ISBN 3-7252-0432-2 LC Card 83-201416

1. Lucerne (Switzerland) - Population - History. 2. Lucerne (Switzerland) - Statistics, Vital - History. 3. Lucerne (Switzerland) - Statistics, Medical - Hsitory. 4. Public health - Switzerland - Lucerne - History. I. Title. II. Series.
HB3624.L8 S38 1983

Schüssler, Gerhard. Ökonomische Strategie der 80er Jahre und Effektivität des Wirtschaftsrechts /. Berlin , 1984. 48 p. ; LC Card 84-159925
HC290.78 .O36 1984

Schuh, G. Edward (George Edward), 1930- Alexander von Humboldt Award Colloquium (1984) Technology, human capital, and the world food problem /. St. Paul, MN , 1986. x, 167 p. : LC Card 86-622216 DDC 338.1/9/1724 19
HD9018.D44 A44 1984

Schuh, J. (Jürgen) Meifort, J. (Joachim) Arbeitsbedingungen von Linienbus- und Strassenbahnfahrern der Dortmunder Stadtwerke Aktiengesellschaft /. Dortmund , 1983. 137 p. : ISBN 3-88314-249-2 LC Card 83-204902
HD8039.T72 G36 1983

Schuh, Sebastian. Möglichkeiten und Probleme der Realisierung flexibler Arbeitszeitstrukturen in Filialen der Bayerischen Vereinsbank München /. München , 1985. 67 p. : LC Card 87-401387 DDC 331.25/72 19
HD5109.2.G32 M866 1985

Schuhmair, Eugen. Sherman, Heidemarie C. Der Einfluss staatlicher Budgetdefizite auf die Zinsentwicklung in der Bundesrepublik Deutschland und den Vereinigten Staaten . München , c1986. xxiii, 190 p. : ISBN 3-88512-019-4 LC Card 86-192070
HJ2110 .S53 1986

Schulenburg, Johann-Matthias, Graf von der. Breyer, Friedrich. Family structure and intergenerational transfers in social health insurance . Berlin [1986] 24 p. : LC Card 87-156738 DDC 368.4/2016/0724 19
HD7101 .B73 1986

Schuler, Friedrich Joachim. Struktur und Dynamik der Grosshandelsbetriebe im Ballungsraum Stuttgart / Friedrich Joachim Schuler. Marburg/Lahn : Im Selbstverlag der Marburger Geographischen Gesellschaft, 1986. xiv, 156 p. : ill., maps ; 24 cm. (Marburger geographische Schriften, 0341-9290 . Heft 103) Originally presented as the author's thesis (doctoral)--Philipps-Universität Marburg/Lahn, 1986. Bibliography: p. 115-127. ISBN 3-88353-027-1 LC Card 87-116934 DDC 381/.2/094347 19
1. Wholesale trade - Germany (West) - Stuttgart Metropolitan Area. I. Title. II. Series.
HF5421.5.G4 S43 1986

Schuler, Randall S.
Canadian readings in personnel and human resource management /. St. Paul, MN , c1987. xi, 467 p. ; ISBN 0-314-32487-9 (pbk.) LC Card 87-2211 DDC 658.3/00971 19
HF5549.2.C3 C36 1987

Dolan, Shimon. Personnel and human resource management in Canada /. St. Paul, MN , c1987. xvii, 620 p. : ISBN 0-314-32486-0 LC Card 87-2207 DDC 658.3/00971 19
HF5549.2.C3 D65 1987

Readings in personnel and human resource management /. St. Paul, MN , c1988. xix, 600 p. : ISBN 0-314-33750-4 (pbk.) LC Card 86-28244 DDC 658.3 19
HF5549 .R38167 1988

Schuller, Bernd-Joachim. Ekonomi och kriminalitet : en empirisk undersökning av brottsligheten i Sverige / Bernd-Joachim Schuller. [Göteborg : Nationalekonomiska institutionen vid Göteborgs universitet, 1986] ix, 250 p. : ill. ; 25 cm. (Ekonomiska studier utgivna av Nationalekonomiska institutionen vid Göteborgs universitet . 17) Extra t.p. with thesis statement inserted. Thesis (doctoral)--Göteborgs universitet. Summary in English. Bibliography: p. 241-249. LC Card 86-212186
1. Crime and criminals - Economic aspects - Sweden. 2. Criminal justice, Administration of - Economic aspects - Sweden. I. Title. II. Series.
HB54 .G65 no. 17 HV6171

Schuller, Frank C. Drawing the line on natural gas regulation . New York , 1987. xiii, 267 p. : ISBN 0-89930-174-6 (lib. bdg. : alk. paper) LC Card 86-25769 DDC 338.2/7285/0973 19
HD9581.U5 D73 1987

Schuller, Tom. Age, capital, and democracy : member participation in pension scheme management / Tom Schuller. Aldershot, Hants., England ; Brookfield, Vt., U. S.A. : Gower, c1986. ix, 172 p. ; 23 cm. Includes index. Bibliography: p. 157-164. ISBN 0-566-00928-5 : LC Card 85-24950 DDC 332.6/7254 19
1. Pension trusts - Management. 2. Pension trusts - Investment. I. Title.
HD7105.4 .S38 1986 ***NYPL [JLD 86-2477]***

Schulte, Heinrich. Statistisch-methodische Untersuchungen zum Problem langer Wellen / Heinrich Schulte. Königstein/Ts. : Forum Academicum in der Verlagsgruppe Athenäum, Hain, Scriptor, Hanstein, 1981. x, 186 p. : ill. ; 23 cm. (Schriften zur wirtschaftswissenschaftlichen Forschung. Bd. 135) Bibliography: p. 181-186. ISBN 3-445-02189-9 LC Card 81-176113 DDC 338.9 19
1. Long waves (Economics) - Econometric models. I. Title.
HB3729 .S38 1981

Schulte, Karl-Werner. Bilanzpolitik und Publizitätsverhalten deutscher Aktiengesellschaften : derzeitige Praxis und erwartete Auswirkungen des Bilanzrichtlinien-Gesetzes / Karl-Werner Schulte. Bergisch Gladbach : J. Eul, c1986. xx, 553 p. : ill. ; 21 cm. (Reihe Steuer, Wirtschaft und Recht . Bd. 28) Bibliography: p. 508-553. ISBN 3-89012-070-9 LC Card 87-122912 DDC 658.1/5/0943 19
1. Corporations - Germany, West - Accounting. 2. Corporations - Accounting - Law and legislation - Germany (West). 3. Corporations - Germany, West - Finance. I. Title. II. Series.
HF5686.C7 S357 1986

Schultes-Jaskolla, Gabriele. Marr, Rainer, 1942- Flexibilisierung von Arbeitszeitstrukturen . [Neubiberg? , 1986] 111 leaves : LC Card 87-409556
HD5109.2.G3 M37 1986

Schultz, Gordon F. Cruise ship employment directory / by Gordon F. Schultz ; edited by Joanne Dettmering. 1987 ed. Centralia, Wash. (131 Elma Dr., Centralia 98531) : International Employment Directory, c1987. 102 p. ; 28 cm. LC Card 87-166826 DDC 385/.22/02373 19
1. Cruise ships - Vocational guidance - Directories. 2. Job hunting - Directories. I. Dettmering, Joanne. II. Title.
HE566.E9 S38 1987

Schultz, Loren A. Siegel, Eric S. The Arthur Young business plan guide /. New York , c1987. xii, 184 p. ; ISBN 0-471-85885-4 LC Card 86-32622 DDC 658.4/012 19
HD62.5 .S556 1987

Schultz, Martin, 1950- Nørrung, Per. The producing commune /. Aalborg Ø., Denmark , 1985. 39 p. ; ISBN 87-88353-11-7 (pbk.) LC Card 87-100060 DDC 334/.6/09489 19
HD3209.A4 N67 1985

Schultz, Reinhard.
Gewinn- und Kapitalbeteiligung der Arbeitnehmer (Vermögensbildung) / Reinhard Schultz. München : Minerva, c1987. 256 p. ; 21 cm. (Innenpolitik in Theorie und Praxis . 15) Bibliography: p. 246-252. Includes indexes. ISBN 3-597-10525-4 LC Card 87-127356 DDC 331.2/164 19
1. Profit-sharing - Germany, West. I. Title. II. Series.
HD3038 .S365 1987

Mein Vaterland ist international . Oberhausen , 1986. 331 p. : ISBN 3-921541-62-X LC Card 86-224091
HD7791 .M45 1986

Schultz, Richard, 1945- Economic regulation and the federal system / Richard Schultz and Alan Alexandroff. Toronto ; Buffalo : University of Toronto Press, c1985. xv, 187 p. : ill. ; 23 cm. (The Collected research studies, 0829-2396 . vol. 42) "Published ... in cooperation with the Royal Commission on the Economic Union and Development Prospects for Canada and the Canadian Government Publishing Centre, Supply and Services Canada." Bibliography: p. 172-187. ISBN 0-8020-7287-9 (pbk.) LC Card 86-672574
1. Industry and state - Canada. 2. Federal government - Canada. 3. Industrial laws and legislation - Canada. 4. Canada - Economic policy. I. Alexandroff, Alan S. II. Royal Commission on the Economic Union and Development Prospects for Canada. III. Series: Collected research studies , v. 42. IV. Title.
HD3616.C23 S38x 1985
NYPL [JLD 86-2821]

Schultz, Theodore William, 1902-
Lectures in agricultural economics . [Washington? , 1977] ix, 165 p. : LC Card 77-603242
HD1759 .L4 ***NYPL [JLE 79-149]***

Pioneers in development. New York , c1987. viii, 244 p. ; ISBN 0-19-520542-1 LC Card 86-23511 DDC 338.9 19
HD74 .P56 1987

Schultz-Wild, Rainer. Flexible Fertigung und Industriearbeit . Frankfurt Main , New York , c1986. v, 577, iii p. : ISBN 3-593-33648-0 LC Card 86-197535
HD5109.2.G3 F45 1986

Schultze, Rainer-Olaf. Ungleiche Entwicklung und Regionalpolitik in Südeuropa . Bochum , 1985. 282 p. : ISBN 3-88339-441-6 : LC Card 85-205651
HC244.5 .U48 1985

Schulz, Bernhard. Effizienzkontrolle von Umweltpolitik : eine integrierte ökonomisch-ökologische Analyse am Beispiel des Benzinbleigesetzes / Bernhard Schulz. Frankfurt am Main : Haag + Herchen, c1983. xv, 230 p. : ill. ; 21 cm. Bibliography: p. 216-230. ISBN 3-88129-744-8 LC Card 85-103230
1. Environmental policy - Germany, West. 2. Automobiles - Motors - Exhaust gas - Law and legislation - Germany (West). 3. Air - Pollution - Law and legislation - Germany (West). I. Title.
HC290.5.E5 S38 1983

Schulz, Erika, 1953- Potentielle Beschäftigungseffekte der Maschinensteuer : arbeitsmarkt-, wettbewerbs- und strukturpolitische Konsequenzen einer Neuregelung der Arbeitgeberbeiträge zur gesetzlichen Rentenversicherung / Erika Schulz. Frankfurt am Main ; New York : P. Lang, c1986. xiii, 303 p. : ill. ; 22 cm. (Europäische Hochschulschriften. Reihe V, Volks- und Betriebswirtschaft, 0531-7339 . Bd. 696 = vol. 696 = vol. 696) Bibliography: p. [287]-303. ISBN 3-8204-8483-3 LC Card 86-195650
1. Pensions - Germany (West) - Effect of inflation on. I. Series: Europäische Hochschulschriften. Reihe V, Volks- und Betriebswirtschaft , Bd. 696. II. Title.
HD7179 .S349 1986

Schulz, Knut. Handwerksgesellen und Lohnarbeiter : Untersuchungen zur oberrheinischen und oberdeutschen Stadtgeschichte des 14. bis 17. Jahrhunderts / Knut Schulz. Sigmaringen : J. Thorbecke, 1985. vii, 477 p., [20] p. of plates : ill. (some col.) ; 24 cm. Includes indexes. Bibliography: p. 457-470. ISBN 3-7995-7026-8 LC Card 85-149930
1. Apprentices - Europe - History. 2. Wages - Apprentices - Europe - History. 3. Europe - History - 1492-. I. Title.
HD4885.E8 S38 1985 ***NYPL [JLE 86-1598]***

Schulz, Wilfried. Struktur und Dynamik der Wirtschaft . Freiburg im Breisgau , c1983. 530 p. : ISBN 3-448-01348-X : LC Card 83-184564 DDC 330 19
HB44 .S77 1983

Schulze, Konrad. Ein ökonometrischer Ansatz zur Erklärung des Bausparens / Konrad Schulze. Bonn : Domus, c1985. xii, 150 p. : 27 ill. ; 21 cm. (Karlsruher Studien, 0179-2512 . Bd. 1) Bibliography: p. 149-150. ISBN 3-87169-319-7 LC Card 86-231621
1. Saving and investment - Germany (West) - Econometric models. 2. Building and loan associations - Germany, West. I. Title. II. Series.
HC290.5.S3 S38 1985

Schulze, Rolf, Prof. Dr.-Ing. Investitionsprozess . Leipzig , c1986. 432 p. : LC Card 86-193837
HG4028.C4 I534 1986

Schumacher, Egbert, 1960- Arbeitslosigkeit und psychische Gesundheit : Ergebnisse der Forschung / Egbert Schumacher. München : Profil, c1986. 231 p. ; 21 cm. Bibliography: p. 208-231. ISBN 3-89019-161-4 LC Card 87-108049 DDC 331.13/7/019 19
1. Unemployment - Psychological aspects. I. Title.
HD5708 .S38 1986

Schumacher, Horst, 1929- Geschichte der internationalen Arbeiterbewegung in Daten /. Berlin , 1986. 868 p. ; ISBN 3-320-00635-5 LC Card 86-210352
HD6475.A1 G47 1986

Schumacher, Karl-Edzard.
Entwicklungsmöglichkeiten landwirtschaftlicher Übergangsbetriebe in Niedersachsen : eine betriebswirtschaftliche Untersuchung / gefördert vom Niedersächsischen Ministerium für Ernährung, Landwirtschaft und Forsten ; erstellt im Institut für Agrarökonomie der Universität Göttingen durch Karl-Edzard Schumacher. Göttingen : Agrarsoziale Gesellschaft e.V., 1985. 234, vi p. : ill. ; 21 cm. (ASG-Materialsammlung, 0344-5712 . Nr. 171) Bibliography: p. 228-234. LC Card 86-186858
1. Agricultural industries - Germany (West) - Lower Saxony. 2. Agricultural credit corporations - Germany (West) - Lower Saxony. 3. Agriculture - Economic aspects - Germany (West) - Lower Saxony. 4. Lower Saxony (Germany) - Economic conditions. I. Agrarsoziale Gesellschaft. II. Title. III. Series.
HD9013.7.L68 S38 1985

Schuman, Nancy. Lewis, William, 1946- Fast-track careers . New York , c1987. x, 212 p. ; ISBN 0-471-83801-2 (pbk.) : LC Card 87-10045 DDC 331.7/02/0973 19
HF5382.5.U5 L45 1987

Schumann, Matthias. Eingangspostbearbeitung in Bürokommunikationssystemen : Expertensystemansatz und Standardisierung / Matthias Schumann. Berlin ; New York : Springer-Verlag, c1987. xi, 156 p. ; 25 cm. (Betriebs- und Wirtschaftsinformatik . 19) Bibliography: p. [125]-132. ISBN 0-387-17369-2 (U. S.) LC Card 87-133887 DDC 651.7/59 19
1. Office mail procedures - Germany (West). 2. Office practice - Automation. I. Title. II. Series.
HF5547 .S457 1987

Schumpeter, Joseph Alois, 1883-1950.
SCHUMPETER, JOSEPH ALOIS, 1883-1950.
Matzner, Egon, 1938- Die Soziogenese des Staates nach Elias und Schumpeter . Berlin [1979] 30, [4] p. ; LC Card 85-135122
HJ105 .M37 1979

Papachristodoulou, Christos. Inventions, innovations, and economic growth in Sweden . Uppsala , c1986. iv, 187 p. : LC Card 87-672434
HC380.T4 P36x 1986

Winterberger, Gerhard. Über Schumpeters Geschichtsdeterminismus /. Tübingen , 1983. 42 p. ; ISBN 3-16-344644-2 LC Card 83-152280 DDC 330/.092/4 19
HB119.S35 W56 1983

CAPITALISM, SOCIALISM, AND DEMOCRACY - ADDRESSES, ESSAYS, LECTURES.
Capitalism and democracy . Notre Dame, Ind. , c1985. ix, 190 p. : ISBN 0-268-00750-0 : LC Card 84-40362 DDC 335 19
HX72.S383 C36 1985 ***NYPL [JLD 85-1987]***

SCHUMPETER, JOSEPH ALOIS, 1883-1950 - ADDRESSES, ESSAYS, LECTURES.
Entrepreneurship . Wien , New York , 1984, c1983. 218 p. ; ISBN 0-387-81830-8 (U. S.) LC Card 84-26677 DDC 338/.04 19
HB615 .E635 1984 ***NYPL [JLE 85-1253]***

Schunk, Gerhard. Internationale Zusammenarbeit in hochtechnologischen Bereichen : unter besonderer Berücksichtigung von Forschung und Entwicklung in der Luftund Raumfahrt sowie der Kerntechnik / Gerhard Schunk. Baden-Baden : Nomos, 1982. 305 p. : ill. ; 24 cm. (Internationale Kooperation. 22) Summary in English. Originally presented as the author's thesis (doctoral--T. H. Aachen, 1981) Bibliography: p. 290-305. ISBN 3-7890-0760-9 LC Card 82-198815 DDC 338.4/76217 19
1. High technology industries - International cooperation. 2. High technology industries - Technological innovations. I. Title. II. Series.
HD41 .S355 1982 ***NYPL [TB (Internationale Kooperation. Bd.22)]***

Schunnesson, Torgny. Framtidsstaden : myt och verklighet i Landskrona 1982-85 / Torgny Schunnesson. [Stockholm] : Författarförlaget, c1985. 166 p. : ill. ; 21 cm. ISBN 91-7054-498-0 LC Card 86-105915
1. Landskrona (Sweden) - Economic conditions. 2. Landskrona (Sweden) - Social conditions. I. Title.
HC378.L35 S38 1985

Schurman, Rachel. Lappé, Frances Moore. Betraying the national interest /. New York , 1987, c1986. p. cm. ISBN 0-8021-0012-0 LC Card 87-12067 DDC 338.91 19
HC60 .L325 1987

Schurz, H. J. Ebel, Friedhelm. Landwirtschaft am Niederrhein . Bonn , 1976. 223 p. : LC Card 87-408419
HD1407 .L3 Heft 33 HD1960.R48

Schustack, Steve, 1952- Variations in C : programming techniques for developing efficient professional applications / Steve Schustack. Bellevue, Wash. : Microsoft Press ; [New York] : Distributed to the book trade in the U. S. by Harper & Row, c1985. xiii, 344 p. ; 24 cm. Includes index. ISBN 0-914845-48-9 : LC Card 85-5033 DDC 650/.028/5425 19
1. C (Computer program language). 2. Business - Data processing. I. Title.
HF5548.5.C12 S38 1985
NYPL [JSE 87-246]

Schuster. "Ökonomische Probleme der bedarfsorientierten Produktionsdurchführung" . Karl-Marx-Stadt , 1984. 139 p. : LC Card 84-245348
HD70.G22 O35 1984

Schuster, Fred E. The Schuster report : the proven connection between people and profits / Frederick E. Schuster. New York : Wiley, c1986. xvi, 200 p. : ill. ; 24 cm. Includes index. Bibliography: p. 167-169. ISBN 0-471-83293-6 : LC Card 86-9190 DDC 658.3/14 19
1. Organizational behavior. 2. Corporate culture. I. Title.
HD58.8 .S38 1986 ***NYPL [JLE 86-3973]***

Schuster, Helmut. Probleme der Ordnungs- und Strukturpolitik . Göttingen , c1984. viii, 311 p., [1] leaf of plates : ISBN 3-525-85925-2 LC Card 84-203472
HE152.6 .P76 1984

Schuster, Leo. Revolution des Zahlungsverkehrs durch Automation /. Frauenfeld [1984] 160 p. : ISBN 3-7193-0929-0 : LC Card 84-153299
HG1709 .R48 1984

The Schuster report . Schuster, Fred E. New York , c1986. xvi, 200 p. : ISBN 0-471-83293-6 : LC Card 86-9190 DDC 658.3/14 19
HD58.8 .S38 1986 ***NYPL [JLE 86-3973]***

Schutjer, Wayne A. Rural development and human fertility /. New York, N.Y. , London , c1984. ix, 318 p. : ISBN 0-02-949680-2 : LC Card 83-26834 DDC 304.6/32/091734 19
HB1108 .R87 1984 ***NYPL [JLE 86-1084]***

Schütt, Bernd.
Mitbestimmung in der Krise--Krise der Mitbestimmung? . Köln , c1984. 192 p. : ISBN 3-7663-0895-5 LC Card 85-113842
HD5660.G4 M563 1984

Neue Technologien und Arbeitswelt . Köln , c1984. 197 p. : ISBN 3-7663-0893-9 LC Card 85-160745
HD6331.2.G28 N475 1984
NYPL [JLD 86-3861]

Schwab, Ken, 1928- Stocks on target / Ken Schwab. Great Neck, N.Y. : Todd & Honeywell, c1986. p. cm. ISBN 0-89962-537-1 LC Card 86-30725 DDC 332.63/22 19
1. Stocks. 2. Stock-exchange. I. Title.
HG4521 .S35783 1986

Schwab, Laurent. Le Japon : réussites et incertitudes économiques / Laurent Schwab. [Paris] : Le Sycomore, c1984. 115 p. : ill. ; 21 cm. (Collection Actuels) Bibliography: p. 111-112. ISBN 2-86262-221-4 (pbk.) : LC Card 84-164308 DDC 330.952/048 19
1. Japan - Commerce. 2. Japan - Economic conditions - 1945-. 3. Japan - Social conditions - 1945-. I. Series: Actuels (Sycomore (Firm)). II. Title.
HC462.9 .S338 1984 ***NYPL [JLD 86-3612]***

Schwab, Robert, 1957- Gerston, Larry N. The deregulated society /. Pacific Grove, Calif. , c1988. xvii, 244 p. : ISBN 0-534-08208-4 (pbk.) : LC Card 87-5116 DDC 338.973 19
HD3616.U47 G47 1988

Schwache Signale . Simon, Dieter. Wien , c1986. 262 p. : LC Card 87-103434 DDC 658.4/012 19
HD30.28 .S435 1986

Schwalbach, Joachim.
Geroski, Paul A. Entrepreneurship and small firms /. Berlin [1985] 31, 2, 6 p. ; LC Card 86-213576 DDC 338.6/42 19
HD2346.E9 G47 1985

Kleindorfer, Paul R. Optimal capacity planning under stagnating demand /. Berlin [1985] 18, 4 leaves : LC Card 86-205882
HD69.C3 K49 1985

Schwammborn, Joachim. Demontage des Sozialstaats . Köln , 1986. 177 p. ; ISBN 3-8161-0107-0 LC Card 87-104505 DDC 338.943 19
HC286.7 .D455 1986

Schwanke, Dean. Mixed-use development handbook / sponsored by the Executive Group of the Urban Development/Mixed-Use Council of ULI--the Urban Land Institute. Washington, D.C. : ULI, 1987. xv, 364 p. : ill. (some col.) ; 29 cm. (Community builders handbook series) Bibliography: p. 360. Includes index. ISBN 0-08-742665-0 LC Card 86-51443 DDC 333.3/8 19
1. Real estate development. 2. Planned unit developments. I. Urban Land Institute. Urban Development/Mixed-Use Council. Executive Group. II. Title.
HD1390 .S38 1987

Schwarting, Uwe. Weimer, Theodor. Die Bedeutung des Osthandels für mittelständische Unternehmen /. Stuttgart , c1985. 172, 7 p. : ISBN 3-7910-5006-0 LC Card 86-160626
HF3568.E35 W43 1985
NYPL [JLL 73-505 Nr.5]

Schwartz, Anna Jacobson.
Money in historical perspective / Anna J. Schwartz ; with an introduction by Michael D. Bordo and Milton Friedman. Chicago : University of Chicago Press, 1987. xvii, 442 p. : ill. ; 24 cm. (A National Bureau of Economic Research monograph) "These articles were presented to Anna at a conference held in her honor in New York City on October 6, 1987"--Pref. "Appendix: publications of Anna J. Schwartz": p. 407-412. Bibliography: p. 413-428. Includes index. ISBN 0-226-74228-8 : LC Card 87-5973 DDC 332.4/9 19
1. Money - United States - History. 2. Money - Great Britain - History. 3. Monetary policy - History. 4. Gold standard - History. I. Title. II. Series.
HG538 .S354 1987

The Search for stable money . Chicago , 1987. xvii, 408 p. ; ISBN 0-226-15829-2 LC Card 86-25654 DDC 332.4/973 19
HG540 .S38 1987

Schwartz, Eli. Management policies in local government finance /. Washington, D.C. , c1987. 449 p. : ISBN 0-87326-075-9 : LC Card 87-2658 DDC 352.1 19
HJ9105 .M3 1987

Schwartz, Lawrence P., 1948- Courchene, Thomas J. Ontario's proposals for the Canadian securities industry /. Toronto , Scarborough, Ont. [1986] 39 p. : ISBN 0-88806-137-4 (pbk.) LC Card 87-133168 DDC 332.63/2 19
HG5158 .C68 1986

Schwartz, Marvin, 1948- In service to America / by Marvin Schwartz. Fayetteville, AR : University of Arkansas Press, 1988. p. cm. Bibliography: p. Includes index. ISBN 1-557-28005-3 LC Card 87-19440 DDC 361.6/09767 19
1. Volunteers in Service to America. 2. Volunteer workers in social service - Arkansas. 3. Volunteer workers in community development - Arkansas. I. Title.
HC110.P63 S34 1988

Schwartz, Michael, 1942- Intercorporate relations . Cambridge [Cambridgeshire] , New York , 1987. x, 330 p. : ISBN 0-521-33503-5 LC Card 87-6388 DDC 338.7 19
HD2741 .I585 1987

Schwartz, Moshe. Non-agricultural employment for moshav youth in the Galilee / by Moshe Schwartz, Rachel Finkel, Raphael Bar-El. Rehovot, Israel : Settlement Study Centre, c1985. 36, [2] p. ; 23 cm. (Series in memory of Isador Lubin . 4) Research report summaries / Settlement Study Centre Errata slip inserted. Bibliography: p. [37] LC Card 86-115596 DDC 331.3/4/0956945 19
1. Youth - Employment - Israel - Galilee. 2. Moshavim. I. Finkel, Rachel. II. Bar-El, Raphael. III. Series. IV. Series: Research report summaries. V. Title.
HD6276.I66 G347 1985

Schwartz, Robert A. (Robert Alan), 1937- Equity markets : structure, trading, and performance /

Robert A. Schwartz. New York : Harper & Row, c1988. xvi, 544 p. : ill. ; 25 cm. Includes bibliographies and index. ISBN 0-06-041322-0 LC Card 87-23173 DDC 332.64/0973 19
1. Securities - United States. 2. Stock-exchange - United States. I. Title.
HG4963 .S38 1988

Schwartz, Stuart B. Sugar plantations in the formation of Brazilian society : Bahaia, 1550-1835 / Stuart B. Schwartz. Cambridge [Cambridgeshire] ; New York : Cambridge University Press, 1985. xxiii, 616 p. : ill., maps ; 24 cm. (Cambridge Latin American studies. 52) Includes index. Bibliography: p. 581-592. ISBN 0-521-30934-4 LC Card 85-6716 DDC 306/.0981/42 19
1. Sugar trade - Brazil - Bahia (State) - History. 2. Plantations - Brazil - Bahia (State) - History. 3. Slavery - Brazil - Bahia (State) - History. 4. Bahia (Brazil : State) - Race relations. 5. Bahia, Brazil (State) - Social conditions. 6. Bahia, Brazil (State) - Economic conditions. I. Title.
HD9114.B7 B347 1985
NYPL [JLE 86-2276]

Schwartz, Tony, 1952- Trump, Donald, 1946- Trump . New York , 1988. p. cm. ISBN 0-394-55528-7 LC Card 87-42663 DDC 333.33/092/4 B 19
HC102.5.T78 A3 1988

Schwarz, Heino, 1936- Katholisch, proletarisch und in der Einheitsgewerkschaft / Heino Schwarz ; mit Karikaturen von Felix Mussil. Mainz : Matthias-Grünewald-Verlag, c1983. 141 p. : ill. ; 20 cm. (Reihe Arbeiterbewegung und Kirche . Nr. 7) ISBN 3-7867-1046-5 LC Card 83-193395 DDC 331.88/0943 19
1. Trade-unions - Germany, West. 2. Trade-unions, Catholic - Germany (West). I. Mussil, Felix. II. Title. III. Series.
HD6694 .S34 1983 ***NYPL [JLD 86-2783]***

Schwarz, Henning. Schleswig-Holstein in Europa /. [Kiel] [1984?] 44 p. : LC Card 84-239599
HC287.S35 S39 1984

Schwarz Kalijman, Luis M. Impuesto personal a la renta : una alternativa de reforma tributaria / Luis M. Schwarz Kalijman.1a ed. Montevideo, Uruguay : A. Monteverde, 1985. 63 p. ; 24 cm. Bibliography: verso t.p. LC Card 85-243408
1. Income tax. I. Title.
HJ4629 .S39 1985

Schwarz, Manfred, 1910- Social security in Brazil : a welfare policy based on the payroll / Manfred Schwarz. Rio de Janeiro, Brasil : ILDES, Instituto Latino-Americano de Desenvolvimento Econômico e Social, [1980] [14], 161 p. : ill. ; 22 cm. (Coleção ILDES . 1) Bibliography: 11th-14th prelim. pages. Includes index. LC Card 87-123549 DDC 368.4/00981 19
1. Social security - Brazil. I. Title. II. Series.
HD7154 .S36 1980

Schwarze Fahnen an der Ruhr . Lauschke, Karl. Marburg [/Lahn] , c1984. 400 p. : ISBN 3-921630-42-8 LC Card 84-215799
HD6698.M616 I535 1984

SCHWEDT (GERMANY) - ECONOMIC CONDITIONS.
Ein Werk des Sozialismus, der Freundschaft und der Jugend . Berlin , c1985. 296 p. : LC Card 87-112875
HD9579.C34 P4848 1985

Schwedt, Herbert. Migration und Dorfkultur . Stuttgart , 1984. viii, 429 p. : ISBN 3-515-04199-0 LC Card 85-131269
HB2056.R53 M54 1984

Schweikart, Larry. Banking in the American South from the age of Jackson to Reconstruction / Larry Schweikart. Baton Rouge : Louisiana State University Press, c1987. xiv, 367 p. : ill. ; 24 cm. Bibliography: p. [319]-351. Includes index. ISBN 0-8071-1403-0 LC Card 87-12784 DDC 332.1/0975 19
1. Banks and banking - Southern States - History. 2. Monetary policy - Southern States - History. 3. Southern States - History - 1775-1865. 4. United States - History - Civil War, 1861-1865 - Finance. I. Title.
HG2604 .S39 1987

Schweissen, Schneiden und verwandte Verfahren. Kleiber, Achim W. Fachwörterbuch, Schweissen, Schneiden und verwandte Verfahren /. Düsseldorf , 1986- , c1985- v. ; ISBN 3-87155-707-2 (Bd. 1) LC Card 86-149500 DDC 671.5/2/0331 19
TS227.5 .K54 1986 ***NYPL [JSK 86-83]***

SCHWEITZER, ALBERT, 1875-1965 - VIEWS ON ECONOMIC DEVELOPMENT.
Watzal, Ludwig, 1950- Ethik, Kultur, Entwicklung . Göttingen , c1985. 131 p. ; ISBN 3-7881-1741-9 LC Card 86-122983 DDC 338.9 19
HD75 .W37 1985

Schweitzer, Mary M. Custom and contract : household, government, and the economy in colonial Pennsylvania / Mary M. Schweitzer. New York : Columbia University Press, 1987. xii, 271 p. : ill., facsim. ; 24 cm. Bibliography: p. [255]-266. Includes index. ISBN 0-231-06288-5 LC Card 87-8003 DDC 338.9748 19
1. Pennsylvania - Economic policy. 2. Pennsylvania - Politics and government - Colonial period, ca. 1600-1775. 3. Pennsylvania - Social conditions. 4. Money - Pennsylvania - History - 18th century. 5. Land use - Pennsylvania - History - 18th century. 6. Finance, public - Pennsylvania - History - 18th century. 7. Households - Pennsylvania - History - 18th century. I. Title.
HC107.P4 S417 1987

Schweitzer, Walter. Heiratstafeln versus Familienstandstafeln : ein kritischer Vergleich / Walter Schweitzer ; Herausgeber, Bundesinstitut für Bevölkerungsforschung. Wiesbaden : Das Bundesinstitut, 1985. iii, 102 p. : ill. ; 30 cm. (Materialien zur Bevölkerungswissenschaft . Heft 44) Bibliography: p. 44. LC Card 87-408703 DDC 306.8/1/0943021 19
1. Marriage - Germany (West) - Statistics. 2. Family - Germany (West) - Statistics. 3. Germany, West - Statistics. I. Bundesinstitut für Bevölkerungsforschung (Germany). II. Title. III. Series.
HB1215 .S39 1985

SCHWEIZ. ETERNIT HOLDING.
Catrina, Werner. Der Eternit-Report . Zürich , c1985. 244 p. : ISBN 3-280-01615-0 LC Card 85-225903
HD7269.A552 S93 1985 ***NYPL [JLD 87-38]***

Schweiz UPU 1900 . Gees, René. Bern [1976?] 56 p. : LC Card 86-170456
HE6271 .G44 1976

SCHWEIZER, ALBERT, 1875-1965 - VIEWS ON ECONOMIC DEVELOPMENT.
Watzal, Ludwig, 1950- Entwicklungspolitik zwischen Immanenz und Transzendenz . Frankfurt am Main , New York , c1986. 121 p. ; ISBN 3-8204-8785-9 LC Card 86-198339
HD75 .W36 1986

Schweizer Aussenwirtschaft, Wohlstand und Entwicklungsländer /. Bluntschli, Franz. Adliswil , c1983. 38 p. : ISBN 3-7229-4032-X : LC Card 83-226336
HF1574 .B58 1983

Schweizer Banken und Schweizer Wirtschaft im Wandel der Zeit /. Staehelin, Max, 1909- Zürich , c1984. 261 p. : LC Card 84-212396
HG3204 .S77 1984

Schweizer, Max. Investieren und Finanzieren : Investitionspraxis in der Bauunternehmung / Max Schweizer. Zürich : Baufachverlag, c1984. 176 p. : ill. ; 22 cm. Bibliography: p. 167. ISBN 3-85565-209-0 : LC Card 84-244976
1. Construction industry - Switzerland - Finance. 2. Investments - Switzerland. I. Title.
HD9715.S92 S38 1984

Schweizer Pioniere der Wirtschaft und Technik. (38) Tauber, Herbert. Johann Ulrich Aebi . Zürich , c1983. 84, [2] p. : LC Card 83-192282
HC395.5.A2 S3 no. 38 HD9486.S94A36

(44) Riedl-Ehrenberg, Renate. Alfred Kern (1850-1893), Edouard Sandoz (1853-1928) . Zürich , c1986. 90 p. : LC Card 86-159933 DDC 338/.09494 s 338.7/66/0094943 19
HC395.5.A2 S3 no. 44 QD21

(45) Lang, Norbert. Johann Georg Bodmer (1786-1864) . Zürich , c1987. 92 p. : LC Card 87-134606 DDC 338/.09494 s 620/.0092/4 B 19
HC395.5.A2 S3 no. 45 TJ140.B53

Schweizer statt Sklaven . Ziegler, Béatrice. Stuttgart , c1985. 466 p., [16] p. of plates : ISBN 3-515-04174-5 : LC Card 85-133062 DDC 331.6/2/49408161 19
HD8289.S283 Z54 1985
NYPL [JLE 87-1222]

Schweizerische Bankgesellschaft. see **Union de banques suisses.**

SCHWEIZERISCHE BUNDESBAHNEN - HISTORY.
Aebi, Ernst. SBB im Aaretal . Luzern , c1984. 111 p. : LC Card 84-234665
HE3898.A37 A42 1984

Schweizerische Dividendenstatistik, 1929 bis 1932. [Bern] : Eidgenössisches Statistisches Amt, 1934. 91 p. ; 25 cm. (Beiträge zur schweizerischen Statistik . Heft 2 = 2me fasc.) LC Card 86-198072
1. Dividends - Switzerland - Statistics. I. Switzerland. Eidgenössisches Statistisches Amt. II. Series: Beiträge zur schweizerischen Statistik , Heft 2.
HA1593 .B45 Heft 2 HG4226

Schweizerische Geisteswissenschaftliche Gesellschaft. Vorträge gehalten anlässlich der Abgeordnetenversammlung vom 27. Mai 1978 =. [Bern] , 1978. 44 p. : LC Card 84-115871
HC397 .V67 1978

Schweizerische Kurse für Unternehmungsführung. Führung . Zürich , cop. 1979. 189 p. : ISBN 3-85743-841-X : LC Card 81-461814 DDC 658 19
HD35 .F8115 ***NYPL [JLE 82-593]***

SCHWEIZERISCHE KURSE FÜR UNTERNEHMUNGSFÜHRUNG.
Führung . Zürich , cop. 1979. 189 p. : ISBN 3-85743-841-X : LC Card 81-461814 DDC 658 19
HD35 .F8115 ***NYPL [JLE 82-593]***

SCHWEIZERISCHE NATIONALBANK. (Old catalog form: Banque nationale Suisse)
Stuber, Barbara. Saisonschwankungen der Bankreserven und Ultimooperationen der Schweizerischen Nationalbank /. Bern , c1986. 173 p. : ISBN 3-258-03653-5 : LC Card 87-130160 DDC 332.1/12/09494 19
HG1656.S9 S77 1986

Schweizerische Post-, Telefon- und Telegrafenbetriebe. Automobilabteilung. 75 Jahre Postauto . Bern [1981] 104 p. : LC Card 86-221362 DDC 388.3/22/09494 19
HE5683.A6 A14 1981

Schweizerische Sozialpolitik . Müller, Stefan, 1955- Bern , New York , c1984. 204 p. : ISBN 3-261-03410-6 LC Card 85-189979
HD7210 .M85 1984

Schweizerische Vereinigung für Datenverarbeitung. Berufe der Wirtschaftsinformatik in der Schweiz /. Zürich , Stuttgart , 1986. 83 p. : ISBN 3-7281-1499-5 : LC Card 86-182797
HD8039.D372 S953 1986

Schweizerische Volkssterbetafeln : 1941/50 & 1948/53 : Grundzahlen und Nettowerte : Ergänzungstabellen / herausgegeben vom Eidgenössischen Statistischen Amt. Bern : Eidgenössisches Statistisches Amt, 1955. 70 leaves ; 30 cm. LC Card 85-144744
1. Mortality - Switzerland - Tables. 2. Switzerland - Statistics, Vital. I. Switzerland. Eidgenössisches Statistisches Amt.
HB1453 .S38 1955

Schweizerische Zentralstelle für Baurationalisierung.
Liegenschaftenbuchhaltung /. Zürich , c1977. 128 p. : ISBN 3-85567-073-1 LC Card 85-141656
HF5686.R3 L54 1977

Die schweizerischen Bahnpoststempel . Müller, Alfred. Bern , 1977. 28 p. : LC Card 85-138287
HE7139.R2 M85 1977

Schweizerischer Gewerkschaftsbund. Sécurité et santé au travail . Berne [1984] 47 p. ; LC Card 85-176432 DDC 363.1/1/09494 19
HD7740 .S43 1984

Schweizerischer Nationalfonds zur Förderung der Wissenschaftlichen Forschung.
Makromodelle und Wirtschaftspolitik . Grüsch , c1985. 120 p. : ISBN 3-7253-0250-2 : LC Card 85-208009
HC397 .M26 1985

Schweizerischer Nationalfonds zur Förderung der Wissenschaftlichen Forschung. NFP "Regionalprobleme." Raumordnungspolitik im Vollzug . Grüsch , c1985. 507 p. : ISBN 3-7253-0258-8 : LC Card 86-149201
HC397 .R36 1985

Schweizerisches Institut für Aussenwirtschafts-, Struktur- und Regionalforschung an der Hochschule St. Gallen (Series) .
(Bd. 10) Genberg, Hans. External influences on the Swiss economy under fixed and flexible exchange rates /. Grüsch , c1985. ii, 182 p. : ISBN 3-7253-0249-9 (pbk.) LC Card 86-156330
HG3963 .G45 1985 *NYPL [JLD 87-539]*
(Bd. 5) Nydegger, Alfred. Investitionen und Innovationen in kleineren Industriebetrieben . Diessenhofen , c1983. viii, 317 p. : ISBN 3-7253-0196-4 LC Card 83-224277 DDC 658.1/592 19
HG4027.7 .N93 1983 *NYPL [JLD 87-633]*
(Bd. 6) Baltensperger, Ernst. Geldmengenpolitik und Inflationskontrolle . Diessenhofen , c1984. 132 p. : ISBN 3-7253-0224-3 : LC Card 84-178054 DDC 332.4/9494 19
HG1155 .B345 1984 *NYPL [JLD 87-168]*

Schwenk, Andreas. Die Kreditwürdigkeit der eingetragenen Genossenschaft / Andreas Schwenk. Göttingen : Vandenhoeck & Ruprecht, c1984. xiv, 287 p. ; 24 cm. (Hamburger Schriften zum Genossenschaftswesen . Bd. 3) A revision of the author's thesis (doctoral)--Universität Hamburg, 1978. Bibliography: p. [278]-287. ISBN 3-525-12752-9 LC Card 86-139501
1. Credit - Germany, West. 2. Credit - Law and legislation - Germany (West). 3. Cooperative societies - Germany, West. I. Title. II. Series.
HG3711.G3 S36 1984

Schwenk, Charles R. The essence of strategic decision making / Charles R. Schwenk. Lexington, Mass. : Lexington Books, c1988. xii, 138 p. : ill. ; 23 cm. Bibliography: p. [121]-133. Includes index. ISBN 0-669-13023-0 (alk. paper) LC Card 86-80040 DDC 658.4/03 19
1. Decision-making. 2. Corporate management. 3. Decision-making - Case studies. 4. Corporate management - Case studies. I. Title.
HD30.23 .S39 1988

Schwieder, Dorothy, 1933- Buxton : work and racial equality in a coal mining community / Dorothy Schwieder, Joseph Hraba, Elmer Schwieder.1st ed. Ames : Iowa State University Press, 1987. viii, 256 p. : ill. ; 23 cm. Bibliography: p. 241-246. Includes index. ISBN 0-8138-0246-6 LC Card 87-2929 DDC 305/.9622 19
1. Coal miners - Iowa - Buxton. 2. Buxton (Iowa) - Social conditions. I. Hraba, Joseph. II. Schwieder, Elmer, 1925-. III. Title.
HD8039.M62 U66825 1987

Schwieder, Elmer, 1925- Schwieder, Dorothy, 1933- Buxton . Ames , 1987. viii, 256 p. : ISBN 0-8138-0246-6 LC Card 87-2929 DDC 305/.9622 19
HD8039.M62 U66825 1987

Die schwierige Integration . Koch-Arzberger, Claudia. Opladen , c1985. 211 p. : ISBN 3-531-11785-8 LC Card 86-101159 DDC 331.6/2/0943 19
HD8458.A2 K587 1985

Schwohnke, Andreas. Teleheimarbeit als neue Rationalisierungsstrategie : Analyse und Perspektiven einer neuen Form der Arbeitsorganisation / Andreas Schwohnke, Hans-Georg Wicke. Köln : Pahl-Rugenstein, 1986. vii, 237, [14] p. : ill. ; 21 cm. (Pahl-Rugenstein Hochschulschriften Gesellschafts- und Naturwissenschaften . 220) Serie Probleme der gesellschaftlichen Arbeit Bibliography: p. [238]-[252] ISBN 3-7609-5220-8 LC Card 86-224163
1. Telecommuting - Germany (West). 2. Home labor - Germany (West) - Data processing. 3. Home-based businesses - Germany (West) - Data processing. I. Wicke, Hans-Georg. II. Series.
HD2336.G3 S38 1986

Scidà, Giuseppe. Cooperazione di credito e sviluppo sociale ed economico delle campagne in Emilia Romagna . Bologna , c1983. 173 p. : LC Card 85-156690
HG2051.I82 E433 1983

Science and Industry Forum. see **Australian Academy of Science. Science and Industry Forum.**

SCIENCE AND INDUSTRY - SOVIET UNION.
Marek, A. I. (Aleksandr Isaevich) Nauchno-proizvodstvennye kompleksy . Moskva , 1985. 141, [3] p. : LC Card 86-118921
HC340.R4 M37 1985
Raĭkom i nauchno-tekhnicheskaia͡ intelligentsii͡a /. Leningrad , 1981. 117 p. ; LC Card 82-177893
HC340.T4 R35 1981
Rodionenkov, P. A. (Petr Andreevich) Zatraty i rezulʹtaty proizvodstvennykh issledovaniĭ i razrabotok /. Leningrad , 1986. 143 p. ; LC Card 87-136354
HC340.R4 R63 1986
Sovershenstvovanie metodologii ėkonomicheskogo analiza v nauchnykh uchrezhdenii͡akh i nauchno-tekhnicheskikh kompleksakh . Kiev , 1986. 116 p. ; LC Card 87-126466
HC340.R4 S68 1986

SCIENCE AND INDUSTRY - UKRAINE.
Ėkonomizatsii͡a nauki . Kiev , 1986. 221 p. ; LC Card 87-102107
HC337.U53 R44 1986

SCIENCE AND STATE - BRAZIL - BAHIA (STATE)
Bahia, Brazil (State) Secretaria do Planejamento, Ciência e Tecnologia. Planejamento, ciência e tecnologia . [Salvador , 1983?] 93 p. : LC Card 85-136375
HC188.B3 B334 1983

SCIENCE AND STATE - GERMANY, EAST.
Innovation und Wissenschaft . Berlin , 1985. 328 p. : LC Card 86-121669
HC290.795.T4 I56 1985

Science and technology education and future human needs .
(vol. 4) Land, water, and mineral resources in science education /. Oxford , New York , 1987. xii, 312 p. : ISBN 0-08-033915-8 : LC Card 86-30527 DDC 333.7/07/101724 19
HC28 .L27 1987

Science and technology for women / editor, Malcolm S. Adiseshiah. Madras : Tamil Nadu State Council for Science & Technology, [1985] 79 p. ; 23 cm. Includes bibliographies. LC Card 85-904932 DDC 305.4/35/0954 19
1. Women in science - India. 2. Women in technology - India. 3. Women - Employment - India. I. Adiseshiah, Malcolm S. II. Tamil Nadu State Council for Science & Technology. III. Seminar on Science and technology for Women (1985 : Anna University).
Q130 .S33 1985 *NYPL [JLD 86-3369]*

SCIENCE, APPLIED. see **TECHNOLOGY.**

SCIENCE COMMUNICATION. see **COMMUNICATION IN SCIENCE.**

SCIENCE, COMMUNICATION IN. see **COMMUNICATION IN SCIENCE.**

SCIENCE - DOCUMENTATION.
Mayntz, Renate. Dokumentation und Organisation . Bergisch Gladbach , 1984. 132 p. : ISBN 3-89012-008-3 : LC Card 85-131112
HD30.3 .M394 1984

Science/earth science on stamps and banknotes [slide] / National Council for Geographic Education ; author, Robert S. Carmichael. Lincoln, Neb. : Great Plains National Instructional Television Library, 1984. 30 slides : col. + 1 script. Title from data sheet. Editor, E. Willard Miller. High school through college students. Presents a microphotographed collection of geoscience topics, as illustrated and commemorated on postage stamps and bank notes from around the world. LC Card 85-702119 DDC 551 11
1. Postage-stamps - Topics - Science. I. Carmichael, Robert S. II. National Council for Geographic Education. III. Great Plains National Instructional Television Library.
HE6183.S36

Science économique et maîtrise de l'avenir /. Delalande, Philippe, 1937- Paris , 1984. 305 p. : ISBN 2-7178-0790-X : LC Card 85-104627
HB71 .D45 1984

SCIENCE - HISTORY.
Miller, Arthur I. Imagery in scientific thought . Boston , c1984. xiv, 355 p. : ISBN 0-8176-3196-8 LC Card 83-26649 DDC 502.8 19
Q175 .M628 1984 *NYPL [JSE 86-1114]*
Miller, Arthur I. Imagery in scientific thought . Cambridge, Mass. , 1986, c1984. xiv, 355 p. : ISBN 0-262-63104-0 (pbk.) : LC Card 85-23212 DDC 502.8 19
Q175 .M628 1986 *NYPL [JSE 87-67]*
Mirowski, Philip, 1951- Against mechanism . Totowa, N.J. , 1987. p. cm. ISBN 0-8476-7436-3 : LC Card 87-21925 DDC 330/.09 19
HB71 .M635 1987

SCIENCE INFORMATION. see **COMMUNICATION IN SCIENCE.**

SCIENCE, MENTAL. see **PSYCHOLOGY.**

SCIENCE, MORAL. see **ETHICS.**

Science Museum (Great Britain) Burns, R. W. British television . London , c1986. xv, 488 p. : ISBN 0-86341-079-0 LC Card 87-160684 DDC 384.55/0941 19
HE8700.9.G7 B87 1986

SCIENCE, POLITICAL. see **POLITICAL SCIENCE.**

Science Promotion Institute (Philippines) Basic needs manual. Bicutan, Taguig, Metro Manila [1985] 58 p. : LC Card 87-118190 DDC 338.9599 19
HC460.B38 B37 1985

SCIENCE - RESEARCH. see **RESEARCH.**

SCIENCE, SOCIAL. see **SOCIOLOGY.**

SCIENCE - SOCIAL ASPECTS.
Formánek, Miloslav. Buržoazní sociálně politické teorie úlohy vědeckotechnického rozvoje /. Praha , 1980. 350 p. ;
*NYPL [*QT 87-1720]*
Governing science and technology in a democracy /. Knoxville, TN , c1986. xviii, 314 p. ; ISBN 0-87049-506-2 (alk. paper) : LC Card 86-7074 DDC 338.9/26 19
Q125 .G68 1986 *NYPL [JLD 87-462]*
Janicaud, Dominique, 1937- La puissance du rationnel /. [Paris] , c1985. 386 p. ; ISBN 2-07-070343-6 :
NYPL [JFD 86-638]
Radical science essays /. London , Atlantic Highlands, N.J. , 1986. 230 p. : LC Card 86-7425 DDC 303.4/83 19
Q175.55 .R33 1986 *NYPL [JLD 87-615]*

SCIENCES, SOCIAL. see **SOCIAL SCIENCES.**

Sciences sociales (Centre régional de publications de Toulouse)
Challier, Marie-Christine. La fécondité en France . Paris , 1985. 196 p. : ISBN 2-222-03773-5 : LC Card 86-234728
HB1003 .C46 1985

SCIENTIFIC COMMUNICATION. see **COMMUNICATION IN SCIENCE.**

SCIENTIFIC MANAGEMENT. see **INDUSTRIAL MANAGEMENT.**

Scientific reports (World Fertility Survey) .
(no. 79) Sombo, N'Cho. Enquête ivoirienne sur la fécondité, 1980-81 . Voorburg, Netherlands [1985] 63 p. : LC Card 87-132644
HB1076.A3 S65 1985

SCIENTIFIC RESEARCH. see **RESEARCH.**

Scienze regionali .
(1) L'Analisi degli insediamenti umani e produttivi /. Milano, Italy , c1984. 295 p. : LC Card 84-179265 DDC 330.945/0928 19
HC305 .A6618 1984 *NYPL [JLD 86-3298]*

SCIMA special studies.
Ghosh, A., 1921- Income distribution and the structure of production /. New Delhi , c1984. ix, 186 p. ; LC Card 83-907762 DDC 339.2/0724 19
HB523 .G46 1984 *NYPL [JLD 86-4234]*

Sčítání lidu, domů a bytů 1970. Praha : Městská správa Českého statistického úřadu, [1970?] 132, [64] p. ; 21 cm. LC Card 82-143437
1. Prague (Czechoslovakia) - Population - Statistics. 2. Czechoslovakia - Census, 1970. I. Český statistický úřad. Městská správa.
HA1198.P7 S38 1970

The SCOJA story . DeMontmollin, Richard Hall. [Columbia, S.C.] , c1986. xi, 191 p. : ISBN 0-9617613-0-X LC Card 86-62676 DDC 381/.456655/060757 19
HD9569.S663 D46 1986

The scope for sanctions . Moorsom, Richard. London , 1986. 102 p. ; ISBN 0-946848-66-1 (pbk.) : LC Card 86-226230 DDC 337.41068

19
HF1613.4 .M66 1986

Scope of C P A services. Previts, Gary John. The scope of CPA services . New York , c1985. xv, 187 p. ; ISBN 0-471-01149-5 : LC Card 85-22455 DDC 657/.09 19
HF5611 .P73 1985 ***NYPL [JLE 86-2961]***

The scope of CPA services . Previts, Gary John. New York , c1985. xv, 187 p. ; ISBN 0-471-01149-5 : LC Card 85-22455 DDC 657/.09 19
HF5611 .P73 1985 ***NYPL [JLE 86-2961]***

Scotchman. Letter to Joseph Locke, Esq. ... in reference to his bill "to regulate Sunday travelling on railways" / by a Scotchman. Glasgow : S. & T. Dunn, 1849. 16 p. ; 20 cm. LC Card 85-666156
1. Railroad law - Scotland. 2. Sunday legislation - Scotland. I. Locke, Joseph, 1805-1860. II. Title.
HE3037. S36x 1849

SCOTLAND - EMIGRATION AND IMMIGRATION.
Way of life . London [1980?] 84 p. ; ISBN 0-86226-076-0 (pbk.) LC Card 82-218547 DDC 304.8 19
HD9571.7.S36 W39 1980
NYPL [JLD 85-427]

SCOTLAND - SOCIAL CONDITIONS.
Way of life . London [1980?] 84 p. ; ISBN 0-86226-076-0 (pbk.) LC Card 82-218547 DDC 304.8 19
HD9571.7.S36 W39 1980
NYPL [JLD 85-427]

Scotland's North Sea gateway . Turner, John R. (John Raymond), 1936- Aberdeen , 1986. xvi, 228 p. : ISBN 0-08-032463-0 LC Card 87-131902 DDC 387.1/09412/35 19
HE558.A34 T87 1986

Scott, Allen, John. Production, work, territory . Boston , 1986. xix, 344 p. : ISBN 0-04-338126-X (alk. paper) LC Card 85-20006 DDC 330 19
HC59 .P682 1986 ***NYPL [JLE 86-1745]***

Scott, Christopher, 1927- World Fertility Survey . Oxford [Oxfordshire] , New York , 1986. p. cm. ISBN 0-19-828525-6 : LC Card 86-23483 DDC 304.6/32/0732 19
HB901 .H664 1986

Scott, David Logan, 1942- Wall Street words / David L. Scott. Boston : Houghton Mifflin Co., c1988. xi, 404 p. : ill. ; 24 cm. Bibliography: p. [403]-404. ISBN 0-395-43747-4 LC Card 87-21444 DDC 332.6/03/21 19
1. Investments - Dictionaries. 2. Securities - Dictionaries. 3. Stock-exchange - Dictionaries. I. Title.
HG4513 .S37 1988

Scott, F. S. (Frank Sanford), 1921- Leong, Jerrold K. (Jerrold Kim), 1947- Economic implications of import barriers to protect the U. S. sugar industry with particular reference to Hawaii /. Manoa , 1987. p. cm. LC Card 87-11855 DDC 382/.456641/09969 19
HD9107.H3 L46 1987

The Scott, Foresman series in business communication.
Bell, Arthur H. (Arthur Henry), 1946- Business communication . Glenview, Ill. , c1987. 601 p., [8] p. of plates : ISBN 0-673-18326-2 : LC Card 86-24844 DDC 808/.066651 19
HF5718 .B455 1987

Scott, Gini Graham.
Effective selling and sales management / Gini Graham Scott. Andover, Mass. : Brick House Pub. Co., c1988. p. cm. Includes index. ISBN 0-931790-76-X : LC Card 87-13829 DDC 658.8/1 19
1. Selling. 2. Sales management. I. Title.
HF5438.25 .S35 1988

It's your money! : how to collect what people owe you / Gini Graham Scott. New York, N.Y. : Avon, c1987. vii, 295 p. ; 18 cm. Bibliography: p. 295. ISBN 0-380-89979-5 (pbk.) : LC Card 85-91536 DDC 658.8/8 19
1. Collecting of accounts. I. Title.
HG3752.5 .S36 1987

Mind power : picture your way to success in business / Gini Graham Scott. Englewood Cliffs, N.J. : Prentice-Hall, c1987. xi, 183 p. ; 25 cm. Includes index. ISBN 0-13-583527-5 LC Card 87-6923 DDC 650.1 19
1. Success in business. 2. Mental discipline. I. Title.
HF5386 .S413 1987

Scott, Gregory J. Comercialización interna de los alimentos en América Latina . Ottawa, Canada , c1985. 253 p. : ISBN 0-88936-448-6 LC Card 87-118494 DDC 338.1/9/8 19
HD9014.L32 C66 1985

Scott, Hilda, 1915- Brudney, Juliet F. Forced out . New York , c1987. 208 p. ; ISBN 0-671-64411-4 (pbk.) : LC Card 87-14927 DDC 650.1/4/0240564 19
HD6280 .B78 1987

Scott, James P. Bond, Kenneth M. Essential business statistics . Boston , c1988. xiii, 332 p. : ISBN 0-534-91530-2 LC Card 87-25652 DDC 519.5/028/55369 19
HF1017 .B63 1988

Scott, Joan Wallach. Tilly, Louise. Women, work, and family /. New York , 1987. vii, 274 p. : ISBN 0-416-01681-2 (pbk.) : LC Card 87-11103 DDC 305.4/3/00941 19
HD6135 .T54 1987

Scott, John T., 1947- Baldwin, William L., 1928- Market structure and technological change /. Chur, Switzerland , New York , c1987. viii, 170 p. ; ISBN 3-7186-0375-6 (pbk.) LC Card 86-25780 DDC 338/.06 19
HD2326 .B35 1987

Scott, John, 1912- Capitalist property and financial power : a comparative study of Britain, the United States, and Japan / John Scott. Brighton, Sussex : Wheatsheaf Books, 1986. x, 230 p. ; 23 cm. Includes bibliographical references and indexes. ISBN 0-7450-0047-9
1. Corporations - Great Britain - Finance. 2. Corporations - United States - Finance. 3. Corporations - Japan - Finance. 4. Stock ownership - Great Britain. 5. Stock ownership - United States. 6. Stock ownership - Japan. I. Title.
NYPL [JLD 86-3078]

Scott, Linda F. International Scientific Forum on Changes in Energy (1981 : Mexico City, Mexico) Global energy assessment and outlook . Chur, Switzerland , New York, N.Y. , c1984. xxix, 580 p. : ISBN 3-7186-0224-5 LC Card 84-12959 DDC 333.79 19
TJ163.15 .I5678 1981 ***NYPL [JSE 86-509]***

Scott, Michael. Small firms growth and development /. Aldershot, Hampshire, England , Brookfield, Vt., U. S.A. , c1986. xix, 325 p. : ISBN 0-566-00811-4
NYPL [JLD 86-3474]

Scott, Robert Haney. Henning, Charles N. Financial markets and the economy /. Englewood Cliffs, N.J. , c1988. xvi, 638 p. : ISBN 0-13-316894-8 LC Card 87-24413 DDC 332/.0973 19
HG181 .H37 1988

Scott-Stevens, Susan. Foreign consultants and counterparts : problems in technology transfer / Susan Scott-Stevens. Boulder : Westview Press, 1987. xvii, 229 p. : ill. ; 23 cm. Bibliography: p. 203-218. Includes index. ISBN 0-8133-7370-0 (pbk. : alk. paper) LC Card 87-50750 DDC 306/.46 19
1. Technology transfer - Social aspects. 2. Community development consultants. 3. Intercultural communication. 4. Cross-cultural orientation. 5. Economic development projects - Indonesia - Case studies. I. Title.
HC79.T4 S36 1987

Scott, Terrence J. Elderly housing options / Terrence J. Scott, Robert F. Maziarka. Chicago : Pluribus Press, c1987. 235 p. : ill. ; 24 cm. Cover subtitle: Putting together a cost effective development and planning process. Includes index. ISBN 0-931028-87-6 LC Card 86-63411 DDC 363.5/9 19
1. Aged - Housing - United States. I. Maziarka, Robert F. II. Title.
HD7287.92.U54 S38 1987

Scott, Tom, 1947- Die Freiburger Enquete von 1476 . Freiburg im Breisgau , c1986. xxxiv, 102 p. : ISBN 3-923272-20-2 LC Card 87-409559 DDC 330.943/46 19
HC289.F855 F74 1986

Scott, W. F. (William F.) McCutcheon, J. J. (John J.) An introduction to the mathematics of finance /. London , 1986. x, 463 p. : ISBN 0-434-91224-7 (pbk.) : LC Card 86-219539 DDC 332/.01/51 19
HF5691 .M385 1986

Scott, W. P. The skills of communicating / Bill Scott. Aldershot, Hampshire, England : Wildwood House ; Brookfield, Vt. : Gower Pub., 1987, c1986. p. cm. ISBN 0-7045-0575-4 (pbk.) : LC Card 87-17106 DDC 658.4/5 19
1. Business communication. I. Title.
HF5718 .S38 1987

Scotti, Anthony J. Executive safety and international terrorism : a guide for travellers / Anthony J. Scotti. Englewood Cliffs, N.J. : Prentice-Hall, c1986. xv, 220 p. ; 24 cm. Includes index. Bibliography: p. 213-214. ISBN 0-13-294380-8 : LC Card 86-15079 DDC 658.4/73 19
1. Americans - Employment - Foreign countries - Protection. 2. International business enterprises - Security measures. I. Title.
HF5549.5.E45 S36 1986
NYPL [JLE 87-393]

The scourge of monetarism /. Kaldor, Nicholas, 1908- Oxford , New York , 1986. xxv, 112 p. : ISBN 0-19-877248-3 ***NYPL [JLD 86-2212]***

Scouts on stamps of the world /. Kaplan, Howard J. [Hicksville, N.Y.] , c1986. 1 v. (loose-leaf) : LC Card 86-224816 DDC 769.56/3 19
HE6183.B63 K36 1986

Scranton Anthracite Museum. Associates. Hard coal, hard times . Scranton , 1984, c1983. xv, 193 p. ; ISBN 0-917445-00-7 LC Card 85-156422 DDC 331.7/622335/0974837
HD8039.M62 U633 1984
NYPL [JLE 87-1218]

SCRANTON (PA.) - INDUSTRIES - HISTORY.
Siegenthaler, Jürg K., 1939- Konflikte der Industrialisierung . Bern , New York , c1985. 249 p. : ISBN 3-261-04012-2 LC Card 85-226977
HC398.G55 S54 1985

SCRANTON (PA.) - SOCIAL CONDITIONS.
Siegenthaler, Jürg K., 1939- Konflikte der Industrialisierung . Bern , New York , c1985. 249 p. : ISBN 3-261-04012-2 LC Card 85-226977
HC398.G55 S54 1985

Scranton, Philip.
Proprietary capitalism : the textile manufacture at Philadelphia, 1800-1885 / Philip Scranton. Philadelphia : Temple University Press, 1987. p. cm. (Technology and urban growth) Includes bibliographical references and index. ISBN 0-87722-461-7 (pbk.) : LC Card 87-488 DDC 338.4/7677/00974811 19
1. Textile industry - Pennsylvania - Philadelphia - History - 19th century. I. Title. II. Series.
HD9858.P5 S35 1987

Work sights : industrial Philadelphia, 1890-1950 / Philip Scranton, Walter Licht. Philadelphia : Temple University Press, 1986. 279 p. : chiefly ill., map ; 22 x 28 cm. Includes index. Bibliography: p. 271-275. ISBN 0-87722-341-6 : LC Card 85-26132 DDC 305.9/009748/11 19
1. Labor and laboring classes - Pennsylvania - Philadelphia - Social conditions. 2. Labor and laboring classes - Pennsylvania - Philadelphia - Social conditions - Pictorial works. 3. Philadelphia (Pa.) - Industries - History. 4. Philadelphia (Pa.) - Industries - Pictorial works. I. Licht, Walter, 1946-. II. Title.
HC108.P5 S37 1986 ***NYPL [JLF 86-1959]***

SCRANTON REGION (PA.) - SOCIAL LIFE AND CUSTOMS - ADDRESSES, ESSAYS, LECTURES.
Hard coal, hard times . Scranton , 1984, c1983. xv, 193 p. ; ISBN 0-917445-00-7 LC Card 85-156422 DDC 331.7/622335/0974837
HD8039.M62 U633 1984
NYPL [JLE 87-1218]

A scrapbook history of the Auburn Aviation Co., Inc., and the Auburn Airport at Throopsville, N.Y., 1941-1952. Ingalls, Roger W. Auburn, N.Y. , c1986. 169 p. : LC Card 87-125962
HE9803.A97 I54 1986

Scrieri, articole, cuvîntări . Pătrăşcanu, Lucreţiu, 1900-1954. Bucureşti , 1983. 415 p. ; LC Card 84-144088
HC405 .P345 1983

SCRIP. see **CURRENCY QUESTION; HOMESTEAD LAW; SECURITIES.**

The Scripophilist's guide : Southern Africa. [Johannesburg? : South African Bond and Share

Society, 1985?] 100 p. : ill. ; 30 cm. "... prepared and produced with the assistance of the South African Bond and Share Society"--P. 5. LC Card 87-100584 DDC 769.5 19
1. Stock certificates - South Africa - Catalogs. 2. Bonds - South Africa - Catalogs. 3. Stock certificates - Africa, Southern - Catalogs. 4. Bonds - Africa, Southern - Catalogs. I. South African Bond and Share Society.
HG5851.A3 S37 1985

Script for an employee flipchart presentation titled The 401(k) plan . Dunn, Pat. Chicago, Ill. , c1986. [40] p. : ISBN 0-88462-610-5 (pbk.) LC Card 86-201609 DDC 331.25/5 19
HG1660.U5 D86 1986

Scritti monetari /. Ricardo, David, 1772-1823. Roma [1985] 495 p. ; LC Card 86-207988
HG938 .R63 1985

Scrivener, Ronald. USSR economic handbook / [Ronald Scrivener]. 1st ed. London : Euromonitor Publications ; Detroit, Mich. : Distributed by Gale Research, 1986. 246 p. : ill. ; 26 cm. Distributor statement from label mounted in t.p. Includes index. ISBN 0-86338-156-1 LC Card 87-130957 DDC 330.947/0854
1. Soviet Union - Economic conditions - 1976-. 2. Soviet Union - Foreign economic relations. I. Title.
HC336.25 .S37 1986

Scruton, Roger. Sexual desire : a philosophical investigation / Roger Scruton. London : Weidenfeld and Nicolson, c1986. x, 428 p. ; 24 cm. Includes bibliographical references and indexes. ISBN 0-297-78479-X
1. Sex. 2. Sensuality. I. Title.
NYPL [JFE 86-1928]

Scudder, Mary E. D. Scudder, Thayer. An evaluation of the Gwembe South Development Project, Zambia /. Binghamton, N.Y., USA [1982] 48 p. ; LC Card 87-119502 DDC 338.96894 19
HC915.Z7 G846 1982

Scudder, Thayer. An evaluation of the Gwembe South Development Project, Zambia / Thayer Scudder, Elizabeth Colson, Mary E.D. Scudder. Binghamton, N.Y., USA : Institute for Development Anthropology, [1982] 48 p. ; 28 cm. (IDA working paper series) "August 1982." LC Card 87-119502 DDC 338.96894 19
1. Gwembe South Development Project (Zambia). 2. Economic development projects - Zambia - Gwembe District. I. Colson, Elizabeth, 1917-. II. Scudder, Mary E. D. III. Institute for Development Anthropology (Binghamton, N.Y.). IV. Title. V. Series.
HC915.Z7 G846 1982

Sculley, John. Odyssey : Pepsi to Apple--a journey of adventure, ideas, and the future / John Sculley with John A. Byrne.1st ed. New York : Harper & Row, c1987. xiv, 450 p., [16] p. of plates : ill. ; 25 cm. Bibliography: p. 431-433. Includes index. ISBN 0-06-015780-1 : LC Card 87-45142 DDC 331.7/61004165/0924 B 19
1. Sculley, John. 2. Businessmen - United States - Biography. 3. Apple Computer, Inc. 4. Computer industry - United States. I. Byrne, John A. II. Title.
HD9696.C62 S38 1987

SCULLEY, JOHN.
Sculley, John. Odyssey . New York , c1987. xiv, 450 p., [16] p. of plates : ISBN 0-06-015780-1 : LC Card 87-45142 DDC 331.7/61004165/0924 B 19
HD9696.C62 S38 1987

Scully, Michael A. The Best of This world /. Lanham, MD , c1986. x, 405 p. ; ISBN 0-8191-5605-1 (alk. paper) : LC Card 86-22411 DDC 261.8 19
HB72 .B5 1987 ***NYPL [JFE 86-5571]***

SCULPTORS - SPAIN - BARCELONA - HISTORY - 18TH CENTURY.
Martinell, César, 1888-1973. L'antic Gremi d'Escultors de Barcelona /. Valls , 1956. 68 p. ; LC Card 86-180958
HD6473.S73 B356 1956

SCULPTURE, BUDDHIST - THAILAND.
Songsan Ninkamhæng. Chotmāihēt kānsāng Phraphuttharūp phra prathān Phutthamonthon /. Krung Thēp , 2525 [1982] 172 p. : ISBN 974-7921-05-7 LC Card 83-916060
HB1912.G38 S66 1982

SCULPTURE GARDENS - THAILAND - NAKHON PATHOM (PROVINCE)
Songsan Ninkamhæng. Chotmāihēt kānsāng Phraphuttharūp phra prathān Phutthamonthon /. Krung Thēp , 2525 [1982] 172 p. : ISBN 974-7921-05-7 LC Card 83-916060
HB1912.G38 S66 1982

SCULPTURE, THAI.
Songsan Ninkamhæng. Čhotmāihēt kānsāng Phraphuttharūp phra prathān Phutthamonthon /. Krung Thēp , 2525 [1982] 172 p. : ISBN 974-7921-05-7 LC Card 83-916060
HB1912.G38 S66 1982

Scuola classica e teoria economica /. Porta, Pier Luigi. Milano , 1984. xi, 145 p. ; ISBN 88-14-00004-2 : LC Card 84-177305 DDC 330.15/3 19
HB167 .P67 1984 ***NYPL [JLE 86-4055]***

SDE .
(8) Monografi sumber daya ekonomi di bidang kehutanan Kalimantan Timur . Bogor , 1975. ix, 67 leaves : LC Card 80-941771
HD9766.173 K356 1975

The SDI and Europe /. Greenwood, David. Aberdeen, Scotland [1985] 64 p. ; LC Card 86-150232 DDC 355/.07/094 19
U395.E85 G73 1985 ***NYPL [JFG 87-57]***

Se lancer en affaires : les étapes pour bien structurer un projet d'entreprise / [recherche et rédaction, Elaine Dupont, Huguette Gaulin]. [Quebec] : Gouvernement du Québec, Ministère des communications, c1986. 450 p. : ill. (some col.) ; 19 cm. (Les Publications du Québec) Includes index. ISBN 2-551-09144-6 LC Card 86-138587 DDC 658.1/1 19
1. New business enterprises. 2. New business enterprises - Québec (Province). I. Dupont, Elaine. II. Gaulin, Huguette. III. Québec (Province). Ministère des communications.
HD62.5 .S4 1986

SEA-FISHERIES. see **FISHERIES.**

SEA FOOD.
Dore, Ian, 1941- Fresh seafood, the commercial buyer's guide . Huntington, N.Y. , c1984. 375 p. : ISBN 0-943738-07-5 : LC Card 84-5174 DDC 641.3/92/0687 19
HD9450.5 .D67 1984 ***NYPL [JSD 86-449]***

SEA FOOD - PURCHASING.
Dore, Ian, 1941- Fresh seafood, the commercial buyer's guide . Huntington, N.Y. , c1984. 375 p. : ISBN 0-943738-07-5 : LC Card 84-5174 DDC 641.3/92/0687 19
HD9450.5 .D67 1984 ***NYPL [JSD 86-449]***

SEA, FREEDOM OF THE. see **FREEDOM OF THE SEAS.**

Sea grant technical report (University of Wisconsin Sea Grant Institute) .
(no. 85-242) Heilmann, Ronald L. Great Lakes transportation in the eighties /. Madison, WI , c1986. 100 p. : ISBN 0-936287-00-4 (pbk.) : LC Card 86-622259 DDC 386/.544/0977 19
HE398 .H45 1986

Sea lane security studies : some vital issues / edited by Tun-hwa Ko & Phillip M. Chen. Taipei, Taiwan, Republic of China : Asia and World Institute, 1986. 100 p. ; 24 cm. (Asia and world monograph series . no. 39) Includes bibliographical references. LC Card 87-133640 DDC 359/.03 19
1. Trade routes - Security measures. 2. Freedom of the seas. 3. Pacific Area - Strategic aspects. I. Ko, Tun-hwa, 1921-. II. Chen, Phillip M., 1935-. III. Asia and World Institute. IV. Series.
HE327 .S435 1986

SEA LIFE. see **SEAMEN.**

SEA ROUTES. see **TRADE ROUTES.**

Sea-trading /. Packard, William V. London , c1984-c1986. 3 v. : ISBN 0-905045-64-5 (pbk.) LC Card 86-204836 DDC 387.5/44 19
HE571 .P26 1984

Seabrook, Jeremy, 1939- Landscapes of poverty / Jeremy Seabrook. Oxford, U.K. : B. Blackwell, 1985. x, 175 p. ; 24 cm. Includes bibliographical references. ISBN 0-631-14508-7 : LC Card 86-673976
1. Poverty. 2. Capitalism. 3. International economic relations. I. Title.
HC79.P6 S36x 1985

SEAFARERS' INTERNATIONAL UNION OF CANADA - BIOGRAPHY.
Edwards, Peter, 1956- Waterfront warlord . Toronto, Ont., Canada , c1987. ix, 213 p. : ISBN 1-550-13013-7 : LC Card 87-150705 DDC 331.88/113875/0924 B 19
HD6525.B36 E39 1987

SEAFARERS' INTERNATIONAL UNION OF CANADA - HISTORY.
Green, Jim. Against the tide . Toronto , 1986. xvii, 324 p., [16] p. of plates : ISBN 0-919396-49-6 (pbk.) LC Card 87-127604 DDC 331.88/113875/0971 19
HD6528.S4 G74 1986

Seafood processing & distribution market opportunities. Norwalk, Conn., U. S.A. (6 Prowitt St., Norwalk 06855) : International Resource Development Inc., c1986. vii, 244 leaves : ill. ; 28 cm. (Report / International Resource Development Inc. . #715) LC Card 87-129495 DDC 381/.4566494/0973 19
1. Fish trade. 2. Shellfish trade. 3. Market surveys. I. International Resource Development, inc. II. Title: Seafood processing and distribution market opportunities. III. Series: Report / International Resource Development Inc. , #715.
HD9450.5 .S4 1986

Seafood processing and distribution market opportunities. Seafood processing & distribution market opportunities. Norwalk, Conn., U. S.A. (6 Prowitt St., Norwalk 06855) , c1986. vii, 244 leaves : LC Card 87-129495 DDC 381/.4566494/0973 19
HD9450.5 .S4 1986

Sealander, Judith. United States. Women's Bureau. Records of the Women's Bureau of the Department of Labor, 1918-1965 [microform] /. Frederick, MD , 1987- microfilm reel ISBN 0-89093-870-9 (microfilm : pt. 1) : LC Card 87-6239 DDC 331.4/0973 19
HD6095

SEALING COMPOUNDS INDUSTRY - UNITED STATES.
Caulks & sealants market. New York, N.Y. , c1983. ix, 250 p. : LC Card 87-143824
HD9999.S44453 U53 1983

SEALING INDUSTRY - GOVERNMENT POLICY - CANADA.
Royal Commission on Seals and the Sealing Industry in Canada. Seals and sealing in Canada . [Ottawa] , c1986. 3 v. : ISBN 0-660-12127-1 (pbk.) LC Card 87-127610 DDC 338.3/729746/0971 19
HD9778.5.S423 C27 1986

SEALING (TECHNOLOGY) - EQUIPMENT AND SUPPLIES.
The U. S. market for hazardous duty liquid pumps and valves. New York, N.Y. , c1983. 2 v. (viii, 343 leaves) : LC Card 87-401677 DDC 381/.456216 19
HD9651.5 .U16 1983

SEALS AND LABELS (PHILATELY) - CATALOGS.
Granger, Louis. Catalogue des vignettes françaises de Croix-Rouge /. [Aurillac] [1964] 117 p. ; LC Card 68-39071
HE6184.S42 G7 1964

Seals and sealing in Canada . Royal Commission on Seals and the Sealing Industry in Canada. [Ottawa] , c1986. 3 v. : ISBN 0-660-12127-1 (pbk.) LC Card 87-127610 DDC 338.3/729746/0971 19
HD9778.5.S423 C27 1986

SEALS (NUMISMATICS) - UNITED STATES - CATALOGS.
Prather, Dewitt G. United States national bank notes and their seals /. Charlotte, NC , c1986. xvi, 200 p., 16 p. of plates : ISBN 0-9616836-0-0 LC Card 86-90441 DDC 769.5/5973 19
HG607 .P73 1986

Sealy, Albert H. Macro blueprint : for dialogue to shape tomorrow's economy and society with enlightened public leadership and corporate governance / Albert H. Sealy. New York : Dialogue Books, 1986. viii, 407, 232 p. ; 24 cm. "A program of the Institute for National Economic and Social Dialogue and Academy for Advancement of Corporate Governance." ISBN 0-89192-390-X LC Card 86-218989 DDC 338.973 19
1. Corporations - United States. 2. Industry - Social aspects - United States. 3. United States - Economic policy - 1981-. I. Institute for National Economic and Social Dialogue (U. S.). II. Academy for Advancement of Corporate Governance. III. Title.
HD2785 .S412 1986

SEAMEN.
Borucki, Zenon. Osobowość a przystosowanie zawodowe marynarza /. Wrocław , 1986. 174 p. : ISBN 83-04-02007-6 : LC Card 86-221057
HD8039.S4 B67 1986

SEAMEN - AZERBAIJAN S.S.R. - HISTORY - 19TH CENTURY.
Guseĭnova, D. S. Rabochie-mori͡aki Kaspii͡a . Baku , 1981. 113 p. ; LC Card 82-166385
HD8039.S42 C424 1981

SEAMEN - CASPIAN SEA - HISTORY - 19TH CENTURY.
Guseĭnova, D. S. Rabochie-mori͡aki Kaspii͡a . Baku , 1981. 113 p. ; LC Card 82-166385
HD8039.S42 C424 1981

SEAPLANES - HISTORY.
Mahoney, Lawrence. The early birds . Miami, FL , 1987. xii, 112 p. : ISBN 0-940495-07-4 (pbk.) LC Card 87-21974 DDC 387.7/065/73 19
HE9803.P36 M35 1987

SEAPRAP research report .
(no. 37) Charoon Vitiprod. Rapid population growth, living conditions, and fertility reduction implication (Bangkok metropolis) /. [Singapore] 1979. ii, 41 leaves : LC Card 82-940038
HB3644.55.B36 C48 1979

Search ACT : the guide to Advertised Computer Technologies. Louisville, Ky. : Data Courier, c1986. 1 v. (various pagings) ; 30 cm. On t.p. the registered trademark symbol "TM"is superscript following "Advertised Computer Technologies." Includes indexes. ISBN 0-914604-27-9 LC Card 86-215617 DDC 025/.06004 19
1. Computer industry - Data bases - Handbooks, manuals, etc. 2. DIALOG (Information retrieval system) - Handbooks, manuals, etc. I. Data Courier, inc.
HD9696.C62 S43 1986

Search Conference on Energy Futures for St. Lucia (1982 : Castries, Saint Lucia) The energy future for St. Lucia : a report and the recommendations submitted by the participants in the Search Conference on Energy Futures for St. Lucia, held at the Halcyon Days Hotel, June 7-10, 1982, to the government & people of St. Lucia / edited by Patricia Charles. Castries, St. Lucia : Caribbean Research Centre, St. Lucia, [1982] 23 p. ; 28 cm. "September 1982." LC Card 87-400749 DDC 333.79/097298/43 19
1. Energy policy - Saint Lucia - Congresses. I. Charles, Patricia. II. Caribbean Research Center, St. Lucia. III. Title. IV. Title: Energy future for Saint Lucia.
HD9502.S0552 S4 1982

The Search for stable money : essays on monetary reform / edited by James A. Dorn and Anna J. Schwartz. Chicago : University of Chicago Press, 1987. xvii, 408 p. ; 26 cm. Includes index. ISBN 0-226-15829-2 LC Card 86-25654 DDC 332.4/973 19
1. Monetary policy - United States. 2. Monetary policy. I. Dorn, James A. II. Schwartz, Anna Jacobson.
HG540 .S38 1987

A search for synthesis in economic theory /. Hsieh, Ching-Yao, 1917- Armonk, N.Y. , c1985. xii, 268 p. : ISBN 0-87332-328-9 LC Card 84-29816 DDC 330.1 19
HB71 .H73 1985 ***NYPL [JLE 87-315]***

SEARS, ROEBUCK AND COMPANY.
Katz, Donald R. The big store . New York , 1987. xiv, 604 p., [16] pages of plates : ISBN 0-670-80512-2 LC Card 87-40060 DDC 381/.45/000973 19
HF5467.S4 K38 1987

SEARS, ROEBUCK AND COMPANY - HISTORY.
Hoge, Cecil C. The first 100 years are the toughest /. Berkeley, Calif. , 1987. p. cm. ISBN 0-89815-221-6 LC Card 87-7077 DDC 380.1/45000/6073 19
HF5467.S4 H64 1987

Sears, Victoria Loufakis. Staffing for optimum performance / Victoria Loufakis Sears. New York, N.Y. : Executive Enterprises Publications Co., c1986. iv, 191 p. : ill. ; 28 cm. Bibliography: p. 191. ISBN 0-88057-403-8 (pbk.) LC Card 85-80707 DDC 658.3/112 19
1. Employee selection. 2. Job analysis. I. Title.
HF5549.5.S38 S4 1986

SEAS, FREEDOM OF THE. see **FREEDOM OF THE SEAS.**

Seasonal adjustment of Yugoslav time series 1971-1980. Nikolić, Miodrag M. Desezonizacija jugoslovenskih vremenskih serija 1971-1980 =. Beograd , 1982. 287 p. : LC Card 85-157587
HA37.Y8 A37 no. 109 HC407

SEASONAL LABOR - GERMANY - HISTORY.
Herbert, Ulrich, 1951- Geschichte der Ausländer, Beschäftigung in Deutschland, 1880 bis 1980 . Berlin , c1986. 272 p. : ISBN 3-8012-3019-8 LC Card 87-113703 DDC 331.6/2/0943 19
HD8458.A2 H39 1986

SEASONAL VARIATIONS (ECONOMICS) - MATHEMATICAL MODELS.
Dagum, Estela Bee. The X-II-ARIMA seasonal adjustment method /. Ottawa , c1980. 119 p. : LC Card 83-225028
HB137 .D34 1980

SEASONAL VARIATIONS (ECONOMICS) - YUGOSLAVIA.
Nikolić, Miodrag M. Desezonizacija jugoslovenskih vremenskih serija 1971-1980 =. Beograd , 1982. 287 p. : LC Card 85-157587
HA37.Y8 A37 no. 109 HC407

Seat belts are for kids, too [motion picture] / AIMS Media. Van Nuys, CA : AIMS Media, 1987. 1 film reel (10 min.) : sd., col. ; 16 mm. Title from data sheet. Ages 3-8. Issued also as videorecording. Uses puppets to urge children to use seat belts. Shows the effects of impact on a belted dummy and gives proper seat belt technique. LC Card 87-706618 DDC 363.1 11
1. Traffic accidents - United States - Juvenile films. 2. Automobiles - United States - Child restraint systems - Juvenile films. 3. Traffic safety and children - United States - Juvenile films. I. AIMS Media.
HE5614.2

Seat belts are for kids, too [videorecording] / AIMS Media. Van Nuys, CA : AIMS Media, 1987. 1 videocassette (10 min.) : sd., col. Title from data sheet. Ages 3-8. Issued as U-matic 3/4 in. or Beta 1/2 in. or VHS 1/2 in. Issued also as motion picture. Uses puppets to urge children to use seat belts. Shows the effects of impact on a belted dummy and gives proper seat belt technique. LC Card 87-706619 DDC 363.1 11
1. Traffic accidents - United States - Juvenile films. 2. Automobiles - United States - Child restraint systems - Juvenile films. 3. Traffic safety and children - United States - Juvenile films. I. AIMS Media.
HE5614.2

Seat belts, the lifesaving habit [motion picture] / AIMS Media ; producer, Michael Wright ; director, screenwriter, Barry Clark. Van Nuys, CA : AIMS Media, 1986. 1 film reel (20 min.) : sd., col. ; 16 mm. Title from data sheet. Ages 16 through adults. Issued also as videorecording. Refutes excuses for not wearing seat belts through use of convincing explanations and demonstrations. Explains that seat belts are the best protection against injury and they double the chances for survival. Stresses also the use of safety seats for children and infants. LC Card 87-705126 DDC 629.2 11
1. Traffic accidents - United States. 2. Automobiles - United States - Seat belts. 3. Automobiles - United States - Child restraint systems. I. AIMS Media.
HE5614.2

Seat belts, the lifesaving habit [videorecording] / AIMS Media ; producer, Michael Wright ; director, screenwriter, Barry Clark. Van Nuys, CA : AIMS Media, 1986. 1 videocassette (20 min.) : sd., col. Title from data sheet. Ages 16 through adults. Issued as U-matic 3/4 in. or Beta 1/2 in. or VHS 1/2 in. Issued also as motion picture. Refutes excuses for not wearing seat belts through use of convincing explanations and demonstrations. Explains that seat belts are the best protection against injury and they double the chances for survival. Stresses also the use of safety seats for children and infants. LC Card 87-705127 DDC 629.2 11
1. Traffic accidents - United States. 2. Automobiles - United States - Seat belts. 3. Automobiles - United States - Child restraint systems. I. AIMS Media.
HE5614.2

Seaton, Hugh. McCully, Al. East Prairie Metis Settlement . [Edmonton, Alta.] [1982] iii, 99 p. :Bill. ; LC Card 82-202474 DDC 333.76/17/097123 19
HD319.A4 M52 1982

SEATTLE (WASH.) - DESCRIPTION - VIEWS.
Stamets, John, 1949- Portrait of a market . Seattle , 1987. 95 p. : ISBN 0-941104-17-6 (pbk.) : LC Card 87-4746 DDC 381/.18/0979777 19
HF5472.U7 S48 1987

SEATTLE (WASH.) - SOCIAL LIFE AND CUSTOMS - PICTORIAL WORKS.
Stamets, John, 1949- Portrait of a market . Seattle , 1987. 95 p. : ISBN 0-941104-17-6 (pbk.) : LC Card 87-4746 DDC 381/.18/0979777 19
HF5472.U7 S48 1987

The seawatchers . Durrant, Lawrence L. North Ryde, NSW, Australia , 1986. xii, 248 p. : ISBN 0-207-15198-9 LC Card 86-228332 DDC 384.5/3 19
HE8683.A8 D87 1986

Sebastian, Ursula. Kolloquium 20 Jahre Weiterbildungs- und Forschungsarbeit (1987 : Leipzig, Germany) Kolloquium 20 Jahre Weiterbildungs- und Forschungsarbeit . [Leipzig] , 1986. 64 p. ; LC Card 87-408852 DDC 338.9431 19
HC290.78 .K64 1987

Sebestoimost′ i puti ee snizhenii͡a v promyshlennosti /. Igumnov, I͡U. S. (I͡Uriĭ Stepanovich) Kiev , 1986. 223 p. ; LC Card 87-126676
HC340.C7 I38 1986

Sebő, Géza. Gáti, Gábor. A munkahely-racionalizálás korszerű megközelítési módjai az élelmiszeriparban /. Budapest , 1986. 106 p. : ISBN 963-02-4171-4 LC Card 87-137979
HD9000.5 .G336 1986

Sebők, Éva, Dr. A Folyamatos árszinvonal-emelkedés társadalmi hatásai . Budapest [1985] 176 p. ; ISBN 963-608-087-9 LC Card 87-407751
HG970.5 .F65 1985

Seca . Casimiro, Liana Maria Carleial de. Fortaleza-Ceará [19]84. 63 p. ; LC Card 86-130055 DDC 330.981/31063 19
HC188.C4 C29 1984

SECA.
Avaliação do polonordeste e do Projeto Sertanejo. Fortaleza , 1985. 314 p. : LC Card 87-402900 DDC 338.981/3 19
HC188.N6 A94 1985

Brazil. Inspectoria Federal de Obras contra as Seccas. Relatorio dos trabalhos executados durante o anno de 1925 . Rio de Janeiro , 1926. xiv, 75 p. ; LC Card 85-186786
HD1696.B8 B73 1926

Guerra, Paulo de Brito, 1914- A civilização da seca . Fortaleza , 1981. 324 p. : LC Card 82-231215 DDC 361.6/0981/3 19
HT395.B72 N63 1981 ***NYPL [JLD 86-2873]***

Leite, José Alfredo A. A sócio-economia do semi-árido /. João Pessoa , 1985. 47 p. : LC Card 87-141315 DDC 330.981/33/063 19
HD1875.P34 L45 1985

Malvezzi, Roberto. Mil quatrocentos e sessenta dias no império do sol . São Paulo , 1985. 197 p. : ISBN 85-05-00296-2 : LC Card 85-200637
HC188.N6 M34 1985

Secas no Nordeste, 1979-1983 . Recife , 1983. 48 p. : LC Card 86-168746
HD1696.B84 N685 1983

SECA - CONGRESSES.
Convivência do homem com a seca e irrigação no Nordeste /. [Salvador, Brazil] [1984] 76 p. : LC Card 87-130774 DDC 333.91/3/09813 19
HD1741.B82 N624 1984

Secas no Nordeste, 1979-1983 : o longo flagelo e as ações do governo / Ministério do Interior, Superintendência do Desolvimento do Nordeste. Recife : SUDENE, 1983. 48 p. : ill. (some col.) ; 23 cm. LC Card 86-168746
1. Water resources development - Government policy - Brazil, Northeast. 2. Droughts - Brazil, Northeast. 3. Seca. I. Brazil. Superintendência do Desenvolvimento do Nordeste.
HD1696.B84 N685 1983

Sección de obras de economía (Bogotá, Colombia)
Políticas de ajuste y grupos más vulnerables en América Latina . [Bogotá, Colombia] , 1987.

278 p. : ISBN 958-9093-01-9 LC Card 87-404285 DDC 338.98 19
HC125 .P647 1987

Sección de obras de economía (Fondo de Cultura Económica (Mexico))
Cazadero, Manuel. Desarrollo, crisis e ideología en la formación del capitalismo . México , 1986. 153 p. ; ISBN 968-16-2280-4 LC Card 87-403551 DDC 330.12/2 19
HB501 .C33 1986

Kate, Adriaan ten. La política de protección en el desarrollo económico de México /. México , 1979. 376 p. ; ISBN 968-16-0352-4 LC Card 87-672671
HF1775 .K37x 1979

Seccombe, Ian J. Manpower and migration : the effects of international labor migration on agricultural development in the East Jordan Valley, 1973-1980 / by Ian J. Seccombe. [Durham, England] : University of Durham, Centre for Middle Eastern and Islamic Studies, c1981. viii, 110 p. : ill. ; 21 cm. (Occasional papers series / University of Durham, Centre for Middle Eastern and Islamic Studies, 0307-1654 . no. 11 (1981)) Bibliography: p. 105-109. LC Card 84-673623
1. Labor supply - Jordan. 2. Migrant agricultural laborers - Jordan. 3. Jordan - Emigration and immigration. 4. Agricultural development projects - Jordan. 5. Jordan - Economic conditions. I. Series: Centre for Middle Eastern and Islamic Studies. Occasional papers series, no. 11. II. Title.
HD5812.25.A6 S42x 1981 ***NYPL [JLD 86-2457]***

Un Secolo di cooperazione di credito nel Veneto : le casse rurali ed artigiane, 1883-1983 / a cura di Giovanni Zalin. Limena, Padova : Signum, c1985. 454 p., [29] p. of plates : ill. ; 25 cm. (L'Età contemporanea . 3) Includes bibliographies. LC Card 86-195743
1. Banks and banking, Cooperative - Italy - Veneto - History. 2. Agricultural cooperative credit associations - Italy - Veneto - History. I. Zalin, Giovanni.
HG2039.I8 S43 1985

SECOND BEST, THEORY OF.
Welfare economics of the second best /. Wien , New York , c1986. 280 p. ; ISBN 0-387-81942-8 (pbk. : U. S.) LC Card 86-31357 DDC 330.15/5 19
HB846.6 .W45 1986

Second century, opportunities for agriculture : proceedings : a conference for the total agricultural sector. [Edmonton] : Alberta Agriculture : Supervisor of Publications & Statutes [distributor], [1986] viii, 289 p. : ill. ; 23 cm. LC Card 87-100958 DDC 338.1/097123 19
1. Agriculture - Economic aspects - Alberta - Congresses.
HD1790.A6 S42 1986

SECOND COALITION, WAR OF THE, 1798-1801 - ECONOMIC ASPECTS - GREAT BRITAIN.
Hueckel, Glenn R. (Glenn Russell), 1945- The Napoleonic wars and their impact on factor returns and output growth in England, 1793-1815 /. New York , 1985. lvi, 212 p. ; ISBN 0-8240-6683-9 : LC Card 84-46003 DDC 330.941/073 19
HC254.5 .H78 1985 ***NYPL [JLE 86-4294]***

The Second cold war / edited by K. Subrahmanyam. New Delhi : ABC Pub. House, 1983. vi, 215 p. ; 23 cm. Includes index. LC Card 84-900004 DDC 355/.033/0047 19
1. Armed Forces - Addresses, essays, lectures. 2. World politics - 1975-1985 - Addresses, essays, lectures. 3. Arms race - History - 20th century - Addresses, essays, lectures. I. Subrahmanyam, K.
UA10 .S38 1983 ***NYPL [JFD 87-1657]***

Second conference of ambassadors/high commissioners of Sierra Leone, Freetown, 15th-21st Dec. 1978. Rapporteur's report . [Freetown , 1978?] 70 leaves ; LC Card 87-401796 DDC 338.966/4 19
HC1065 .R36 1978

"Second economy" in the USSR (trials of the 1960s). Ėvel'son, Evgeniīa. Sudebnye protsessy po ėkonomicheskim delam v SSSR . London , 1986. 370 p. ; ***NYPL [*QIX 87-4024]***

SECOND HOMES - SPAIN - CATALONIA.
Argany Comas, Isabel. La segona residència a Catalunya . [Barcelona] [1984] 71 p. ; LC Card 86-160322
HD7289.3.S72 C383 1984

Second Malaysia plan, 1971-1975. Malaysia. [Ranchangan Malaysia kedua, 1971-1975. English.] Kuala Lumpur, 1971. xv, 266 p. LC Card 76-943050 DDC 338/.09595/1 19
HC445.5 .A4 1971

Second National Forum on Issues in Vocational Assessment . National Forum on Issues in Vocational Assessment (2nd : 1986 : Dallas, Tex.) Menomonie, Wis. , c1985. vii, 236 p. : ISBN 0-916671-71-2 (pbk.) LC Card 86-217148 DDC 362/.0425 19
HD7256.U5 N336 1986

Second report of the Select Committee on Toll Financing of Roads. South Africa. Parliament. House of Assembly. Select Committee on Toll Financing of Roads. Tweede verslag van die Gekose Komitee oor Tolfinansiering van Paaie =. [Pretoria] [1982] vii p. ; ISBN 0-06-210768-3 : LC Card 83-159014
HE367.S63 T646 1982

Second to none . Smith, Steve, 1941- Missoula, Mont. , c1986. 120 p. : ISBN 0-933126-84-0 (pbk.) LC Card 86-62692 DDC 388.3/22/09786 19
HE5633.M9 S65 1986

Second underground shopper. Goldstein, Sue, 1941- The 2nd underground shopper . Kansas City , c1985. 470 p. : ISBN 0-8362-7956-5 (pbk.) : LC Card 85-620 DDC 381/.1 19
HF5466 .G6 1985 ***NYPL [JLD 86-3080]***

The second victory . Donovan, Robert J. New York , c1987. 128 p. : ISBN 0-8191-6498-4 (alk. paper) : LC Card 87-24021 DDC 338.91/73/04 19
HC240 .D65 1987

Secondary benefits associated with the Red River Waterway, Mississippi River to Shreveport, Louisiana : final report / Gulf South Research Institute ; prepared for Red River Waterway Commission. Baton Rouge, La. (P.O. Box 14787, Baton Rouge 70898) : GSRI, [1986] 2 v. : ill. ; 28 cm. "February 1986." "GSRI project no. 2400-2307." Includes bibliographical references. LC Card 87-620750 DDC 330.9766/6053 19
1. Red River Region (Tex.-La.) - Economic conditions. 2. Red River Region (Tex.-La.) - Industries. 3. Shipping - Red River Region (Tex.-La.). I. Gulf South Research Institute. II. Red River Waterway Commission.
HC107.A15 S43 1986

SECONDARY EMPLOYMENT. see **SUPPLEMENTARY EMPLOYMENT.**

The secondary market and securitization for income property mortgages /. Stevenson, Eric. Washington, D.C. (1125 15th St., N.W., Washington 20005) , c1986. xiii, 129 p. : LC Card 87-153518 DDC 332.1/753 19
HG2040.5.U5 S73 1986

The Secondary mortgage market : a handbook of strategies, techniques, and critical issues in contemporary mortgage finance / edited by Jess Lederman. Chicago, Ill. : Probus Pub. Co., c1987. xvi, 648 p. : ill. ; 24 cm. Includes index. ISBN 0-917253-74-4 : LC Card 87-2303 DDC 332.63/244 19
1. Secondary mortgage market - United States. I. Lederman, Jess.
HG2040.25 .S43 1987

SECONDARY MORTGAGE MARKET - UNITED STATES.
Mortgage-backed securities . Chicago, Ill. , c1987. xi, 474 p. : ISBN 0-917253-47-7 : LC Card 86-15087 DDC 332.63/232 19
HG4655 .M65 1987 ***NYPL [JLE 87-783]***

The Secondary mortgage market . Chicago, Ill. , c1987. xvi, 648 p. : ISBN 0-917253-74-4 : LC Card 87-2303 DDC 332.63/244 19
HG2040.25 .S43 1987

Stevenson, Eric. The secondary market and securitization for income property mortgages /. Washington, D.C. (1125 15th St., N.W., Washington 20005) , c1986. xiii, 129 p. : LC Card 87-153518 DDC 332.1/753 19
HG2040.5.U5 S73 1986

SECONDARY RECOVERY OF OIL - UNITED STATES.
The Enhanced oil recovery market, 1980-1990. New York, N.Y. , c1983. vi, 203 leaves : LC Card 87-142370 DDC 381/.45617665/0973 19
HD9565 .E53 1983

SECONDHAND TRADE - GERMANY (WEST)
Gebhardt, Peter. Der Markt gebrauchter Güter . Hamburg , c1986. xxvii, 250, [69] p. : ISBN 3-925630-10-4 LC Card 87-127354 DDC 381/.1 19
HF5482 .G42 1986

Secretaria de Estado da Fazenda . Minas Gerais (Brazil). Secretaria de Estado da Fazenda. Belo Horizonte [1983] 48 p. ; LC Card 85-207912
HJ929.M52 M55 1983

Secretariado Uruguayo de la Lana. Departamento de Información e Investigaciones Económicas. Uruguay, exportaciones cumplidas de lanas y sus productos, ovinos en pie, carne ovina y subproductos, apendice pieles lanares . [Montevideo, Uruguay] , 1984. 37 p. ; LC Card 86-164077
HD9904.U82 U78 1984

SECRETARIAL PRACTICE. see **OFFICE PRACTICE.**

Secretarial procedures and administration /. Tilton, Rita Sloan. Cincinnati , c1987. vi, 874 p. : ISBN 0-538-11790-7 LC Card 86-63074 DDC 651.3/74 19
HF5547.5 .S4 1987

Secretarial procedures and administration. Tilton, Rita Sloan. Secretarial procedures and administration /. Cincinnati , c1987. vi, 874 p. : ISBN 0-538-11790-7 LC Card 86-63074 DDC 651.3/74 19
HF5547.5 .S4 1987

SECRETARIES.
Dight, Janet. Breaking the secretary barrier . New York , c1986. xv, 303 p. ; ISBN 0-07-016905-5 LC Card 85-11360 DDC 658.4/09/024042 19
HF5547.5 .D54 1986 ***NYPL [JLE 86-1072]***

Filbert, Judith Ann. Homemaking skills go to the office . Bozeman, Mont. (P.O. Box 6244, Bozeman 59771) , c1986. 46 p. ; LC Card 86-218123 DDC 651.3/741/02373 19
HF5547.5 .F53 1986

SECRETARIES - EXAMINATIONS, QUESTIONS, ETC.
Lindsell, Sheryl L. CPS®--Certified Professional Secretary® examination /. New York, N.Y. , c1987. xxx, 286 p. : ISBN 0-13-122805-6 (pbk.) : LC Card 87-11381 DDC 651.3/741/076 19
HF5547.5 .L554 1987

SECRETARIES - JUVENILE LITERATURE.
Lillegard, Dee. I can be a secretary /. Chicago , c1987. 29 p. : ISBN 0-516-01907-4 (lib. bdg.) LC Card 86-29947 DDC 651.3/741/02373 19
HF55475 .L55 1987

The secretary's handbook /. Taintor, Sarah Augusta. New York , London , c1988. p. cm. ISBN 0-02-008830-2 LC Card 87-24960 DDC 651.7/402 19
HF5547.5 .T29 1988

The secrets of a professional futures trader /. Clasing, Henry K. Brightwaters, N.Y. , c1987. 231 p. : ISBN 0-930233-15-8 LC Card 87-166047 DDC 332.64/4 19
HG6024.A3 C58 1987

Secrets of a successful mail order guru . Tepper, Ron, 1937- New York , c1988. ix, 230 p. : ISBN 0-471-84857-3 LC Card 87-21658 DDC 658.8/72 19
HF5466 .T36 1988

Secrets of effective leadership /. Manske, Fred A., 1939- Memphis, TN , 1987. ix, 206 p. : ISBN 0-943703-00-X LC Card 87-16870 DDC 658.4/09 19
HD57.7 .M37 1987

Secrets of sales champions. 1st ed. Glendora, Calif. : Royal Pub., c1986. xix, 323 p. : ill. ; 22 cm. ISBN 0-934344-20-5 LC Card 87-120112 DDC 658.8/5 19
1. Selling.
HF5438.25 .S433 1986

The secrets of syndication . Beguelin, Richard H., 1937- Boston , c1985. xi, 287 p. : ISBN 0-316-08783-1 : LC Card 85-5157 DDC 658/.044 19
HG6021 .B4 1985 ***NYPL [JLE 85-2259]***

Secrets of the master sellers /. Henry, Porter. New York, NY , c1987. x, 294 p. : ISBN

0-8144-7688-0 (pbk.) : LC Card 87-47707 DDC 658.8/5 19
HF5438.25 .H465 1987

Secrets of the temple . Greider, William. New York , c1987. 798 p. ; ISBN 0-671-47989-X : LC Card 87-16712 DDC 332.1/1/0973 19
HG2563 .G72 1987

Le Secteur manufacturier, le commerce et le tourisme au Québec en 1983. [Québec] : Ministère de l'industrie, du commerce et du tourisme, [1984] 34 leaves : ill. ; 28 cm. Cover title. "Janvier 1984." CONTENTS. - Aperçu de la situation économique du secteur manufacturier, du commerce et du tourisme du Québec en 1983 -- Les actions du MICT en 1983. LC Card 85-127334
1. Quebec (Province) - Manufactures. 2. Quebec (Province) - Commerce. 3. Tourist trade - Quebec (Province). I. Québec (Province). Ministère de l'industrie, du commerce et du tourisme.
HD9734.C3 Q485 1984

Secteur minier dans le Nord. The Northern mineral sector . Ottawa [1985] 37, 37 p. : ISBN 0-662-53700-9 (pbk.) LC Card 85-162718 DDC 338.2/0971 19
HD9506.C23 N6758 1985
NYPL [JLF 86-175]

Le secteur non structuré d'Antananarivo . Gozo, K. M. Addis-Abéba , c1985. vi, 175 p. : LC Card 85-981181
HD2346.M282 A574 1985

Le Secteur non structuré d'Antsirabe : analyse typologique, facteurs de blocage et perspectives de promotion des activités du bois, construction métallique, garages et réparations : rapport d'une enquête / réalisée pour le compte du Gouvernement malgache.1re éd. Addis-Abéba : Bureau international du travail, Programme des emplois et des compétences techniques pour l'Afrique, 1985. iii, ii, 111, 24, 71 p. : ill. ; 30 cm. At head of title: Organisation internationale du travail. Includes bibliography. ISBN 92-2-205256-0 LC Card 87-980400
1. Informal sector (Economics) - Madagascar - Antsirabe. I. Jobs and Skills Programme for Africa. II. Madagascar.
HD2346.M282 A588 1985

Le secteur non structuré de Kinshasa . Gozo, K. M. Addis Abéba , c1985. iii, 64, [8] p. : ISBN 92-2-100538-0 LC Card 85-981182
HD2346.Z27 K54 1985

Le Secteur non structuré de Mahajanga : analyse typologique, facteurs de blocage et perspectives de promotion des activités du bois, construction métallique, garages et réparations. 1e éd. Addis Abéba : Bureau international du travail, Programme des emplois et des compétences techniques pour l'Afrique, 1985. vii, 114 p. ; 30 cm. "Rapport d'une enquête réalisée pour le compte du gouvernement malgache." ISBN 92-2-205254-4 LC Card 86-981199
1. Informal sector (Economics) - Madagascar - Mahajanga. 2. Labor supply - Madagascar - Mahajanga. I. Jobs and Skills Programme for Africa.
HD2346.M282 M347 1985

El Sector alimentario en México. México, D.F. : Instituto Nacional de Estadística, Geografía e Informática, [1984] vii, 673 p. : ill. (some col.) ; 28 cm. Includes bibliographical references. ISBN 968-8099-93-7 LC Card 85-205385
1. Food industry and trade - Mexico - Statistics. I. Instituto Nacional de Estadística, Geografía e Informática (Mexico).
HD9014.M62 S26 1984

Sector económico externo, industrialización y conflictos laborales en Venezuela /. Rangel Belis, Gonzalo. Valencia , 1985. 141 p. : ISBN 980-212-007-3 LC Card 86-226708
HF1529 .R36 1985

El sector externo de la economía salvadoreña /. Benítez Bonilla, Alberto. [San Salvador] , 1982. 21 p., [7] leaves (some folded) ; LC Card 83-154713
HF1494 .B45 1982

Sector formal de la ciudad de La Paz : los trabajadores y sus familias. La Paz, Bolivia : Ministerio de Trabajo y Desarrollo Laboral, Dirección General de Empleo, 1980. 77 leaves ; 29 cm. "Convenio Tripartito Venezuela-Bolivia--CIAT." LC Card 81-212597 DDC 331.1/0984/12 19
1. Labor supply - Bolivia - La Paz. 2. Labor and laboring classes - Bolivia - La Paz. 3. Family - Bolivia - La Paz. I. Bolivia. Dirección General de Empleo.
HD5751.L36 S42 1980 ***NYPL [JLF 87-369]***

El Sector informal en Bolivia / [edición y coordinación, Leticia Sáinz ; fotografías, Grover Hinojosa]. [La Paz, Bolivia?] : CEDLA, [1986] 323 p. : ill. ; 20 cm. Bibliography: p. 311-323. LC Card 87-100849
1. Informal sector (Economics) - Bolivia. 2. Informal sector (Economics) - Government policy - Bolivia. I. Sáinz, Leticia. II. Centrum voor Studie en Documentatie van Latijns Amerika (Amsterdam, Netherlands).
HD2346.B6 S43 1986

El Sector público colombiano, 1970-1981. Bogotá : República de Colombia, Departamento Administrativo Nacional de Estadística, 1984. 261 p. ; 28 cm. Chiefly tables. Includes bibliographical references. LC Card 87-121830 DDC 336.861 19
1. Finance, Public - Colombia - Statistics. I. Colombia. Departamento Administrativo Nacional de Estadística.
HJ945 .S43 1984

El Sector vivienda : metodología analítica / coordinador, Ramón Martín Mateo ; autores, Javier Ruiz Castillo ... [et al.]. Madrid : Instituto de Estudios de Administración Local, 1982. 224 p. : ill. ; 22 cm. Bibliography: p. 77-82. ISBN 84-7088-324-0 LC Card 85-219674
1. Housing - Spain - Mathematical models. 2. Housing - Spain - Madrid Metropolitan Area - Mathematical models. I. Martín Mateo, Ramón. II. Ruiz Castillo, Javier.
HD7351.A3 S43 1982

Sectoral studies series .
(no. 20, v. 1) The Petrochemical industry in developing countries . [Vienna] [1985] xiv, 155 p. : LC Card 86-204881 DDC 338.4/7661804/091724 19
HD9579.C33 D446 1985

Los sectores agrarios de Andalucía ante la integración en la C.E.E. /. Loring, Jaime. Madrid , 1984. 303 p. : ISBN 84-7114-149-3 LC Card 86-152628
HD2025.A5 L67 1984

SECULARIZATION - SPAIN - ANDALUSIA - HISTORY - 19TH CENTURY.
González do Molina Navarro, Manuel. Desamortización, deuda pública y crecimiento económico, Andalucía, 1820/1823 /. Granada , Córdoba :bFundación Paco Natera [1985?] 443 p. : ISBN 84-505-1053-8 LC Card 86-210676
HD779.A4 G66 1985

SECULARIZATION - SPAIN - GRANADA (PROVINCE) - HISTORY - 19TH CENTURY.
Gómez Oliver, Miguel. La desamortización de Mendizábal en Granada /. Granada [1983] 226 p. : LC Card 85-135214
HD479.G73 G65 1983

SECULARIZATION - SPAIN - HISTORY.
Rueda Hernanz, Germán. La desamortización de Mendizábal y Espartero en España /. Madrid , c1986. 200 p. ; ISBN 84-376-0592-X LC Card 86-216590
HD774 .R84 1986

SECULARIZATION - SPAIN - JAÉN (PROVINCE) - HISTORY - 18TH CENTURY.
Herr, Richard. Rural change and royal finances in Spain at the end of the old regime /. Berkeley , c1987. p. cm. ISBN 0-520-05948-4 (alk. paper) LC Card 86-25027 DDC 333.3/0946/25 19
HD779.J34 H47 1987

SECULARIZATION - SPAIN - SALAMANCA (PROVINCE) - HISTORY - 18TH CENTURY.
Herr, Richard. Rural change and royal finances in Spain at the end of the old regime /. Berkeley , c1987. p. cm. ISBN 0-520-05948-4 (alk. paper) LC Card 86-25027 DDC 333.3/0946/25 19
HD779.J34 H47 1987

Securing economic renewal : budget papers / tabled in the House of Commons by Michael H. Wilson, Minister of Finance. [Ottawa] : Dept. of Finance, Canada, [1987] 147, 161 p. : ill. ; 27 cm. English and French. Title on added t.p.: Pour assurer le renouveau économique. "February 19, 1987." CONTENTS. - The economic outlook and fiscal plan -- Supplementary information and notices of ways and means motions on the budget. LC Card 87-144360 DDC 336.71 19
1. Finance, Public - Canada. 2. Budget - Canada. 3. Canada - Economic policy. I. Wilson, Michael H. (Michael Holcombe), 1937-. II. Canada. Dept. of Finance. III. Canada. Parliament. House of Commons. IV. Title: Pour assurer le renouveau économique.
HJ793 .S43 1987

Securing economic renewal. The Agenda for economic renewal . [Ottawa] [1987] 25, 26 p. : LC Card 87-140803 DDC 338.971 19
HC115 .A624 1987

Sécurité et santé au travail : propositions de l'Union syndicale suisse pour une meilleure protection des travailleurs. 2e éd. Berne : L'Union, [1984] 47 p. ; 23 cm. (Documents de l'Union syndicale suisse) "Document ... adopté ... [1e] 29 juin 1983"--P. 3. "Mars 1984." Includes bibliographical references. LC Card 85-176432 DDC 363.1/1/09494 19
1. Industrial safety - Switzerland. 2. Industrial hygiene - Switzerland. 3. Trade-unions - Switzerland. I. Schweizerischer Gewerkschaftsbund. II. Series.
HD7740 .S43 1984

SECURITIES - ADDRESSES, ESSAYS, LECTURES.
CFA readings in fixed income securities analysis /. Charlottesville, VA (P.O. Box 3668, Charlottesville, VA 22903) , c1985. v, 255 p. :
NYPL [JLF 86-1994]

SECURITIES - ASIA.
Rowley, Anthony, 1939- Asian stockmarkets . Homewood, Ill. , 1987. 290 p. : ISBN 962-7010-29-4; 0-87094-987-X (jacket) LC Card 87-137156 DDC 332.64/25 19
HG5702 .R69 1987

SECURITIES - AUSTRALIA.
Skully, Michael T. American depositary receipts . [Melbourne] [1986] 44 leaves : LC Card 86-229206 DDC 332.6/7373/094 19
HG5892 .S58 1986

SECURITIES - BRAZIL.
Casagrande Neto, Humberto. Abertura do capital de empresas no Brasil . São Paulo , 1985. 143 p. ; ISBN 85-22-40100-4
NYPL [JLD 86-1080]

SECURITIES - BRAZIL, NORTHEAST.
Perfil de empresas. Fortaleza-CE [1984] 248 p. ; LC Card 85-191373
HG4111.5.N67 P47 1984

SECURITIES - CANADA.
Bréard, Jean-Pierre. Les contrats de souscription à forfait de valeurs mobilières /. Montréal , 1984. xv, 158 p. : ISBN 2-89266-018-1 (pbk.) :
NYPL [JLD 87-662]

Courchene, Thomas J. Ontario's proposals for the Canadian securities industry /. Toronto , Scarborough, Ont. [1986] 39 p. : ISBN 0-88806-137-4 (pbk.) LC Card 87-133168 DDC 332.63/2 19
HG5158 .C68 1986

Hunter, W. T. Canadian financial markets /. Peterborough, Canada , c1986. 193 p. : ISBN 0-921149-01-8 (pbk.) LC Card 86-206029 DDC 332.6/0973 19
HG185.C2 H86 1986

SECURITIES - CHILE.
Características de los instrumentos de ahorro. Santiago, Chile , 1983. 91 p. ; LC Card 84-119555 DDC 332.63/2/0983 19
HG5342 .C37 1983 ***NYPL [JLF 86-620]***

Características de los instrumentos de ahorro. Santiago, Chile , 1986. 115 p. ; LC Card 87-403226 DDC 332.63/2/0983 19
HG5342 .C37 1986

SECURITIES - CONGRESSES.
The Developing global securities market /. London ; Boston : viii, 192 p. ; ISBN 0-86010-979-8 LC Card 87-19086 DDC 332.6/5 19
HG4508 .D48 1987

SECURITIES - DATA BASES - DIRECTORIES.
Online databases in the securities and financial markets. New York, N.Y. , c1987. xxii, 322 p. ; ISBN 0-444-01276-1 (pbk.) LC Card 87-19954 DDC 025/.0633/0025 19
HG174 .O44 1987

SECURITIES - DICTIONARIES.
Pessin, Allan H. More words of Wall Street .

Homewood, Ill. , 1986. v, 269 p. ; ISBN 0-87094-701-X LC Card 86-70777
NYPL [JLE 86-4060]

Scott, David Logan, 1942- Wall Street words /. Boston , c1988. xi, 404 p. : ISBN 0-395-43747-4 LC Card 87-21444 DDC 332.6/03/21 19
HG4513 .S37 1988

Thomsett, Michael C. Investment and securities dictionary /. Jefferson, N.C. , 1986. vii, 328 p. : ISBN 0-89950-225-3 : LC Card 85-43594 DDC 332.6/03/21 19
HG4513 .T48 1986 *NYPL [JLE 87-450]*

SECURITIES - DIRECTORIES.
VALPORT securities index . Greenwich, Conn. (500 W. Putnam Ave., Greenwich 06830) , c1985- 1 v. (loose-leaf) ; LC Card 87-132910 DDC 332.63/2/025 19
HG4509 .V36 1985

SECURITIES EXCHANGE. see **STOCK-EXCHANGE.**

SECURITIES - GOVERNMENT POLICY - CANADA.
Courchene, Thomas J. Ontario's proposals for the Canadian securities industry /. Toronto , Scarborough, Ont. [1986] 39 p. : ISBN 0-88806-137-4 (pbk.) LC Card 87-133168 DDC 332.63/2 19
HG5158 .C68 1986

SECURITIES - GOVERNMENT POLICY - ONTARIO.
Courchene, Thomas J. Ontario's proposals for the Canadian securities industry /. Toronto , Scarborough, Ont. [1986] 39 p. : ISBN 0-88806-137-4 (pbk.) LC Card 87-133168 DDC 332.63/2 19
HG5158 .C68 1986

SECURITIES - GREAT BRITAIN.
Phillips, Patrick. Inside the new gilt-edged market /. Cambridge, England , Wolfeboro, N.H. , 1987. p. cm. ISBN 0-85941-346-2 : LC Card 86-24692 DDC 332.63/232/0941 19
HG5432 .P48 1987

Rutterford, Janette. The securities industry . [London] [1986] 93 p. : LC Card 87-160412 DDC 332.63/2/0941 19
HG5432 .R87 1986

SECURITIES - HANDBOOKS, MANUALS, ETC.
Handbook of financial markets . Homewood, Ill. , c1986. xix, 785 p. : ISBN 0-87094-600-5 LC Card 85-71920 DDC 332.6/78 19
HG4527 .H25 1986
*NYPL [*R-Econ 86-3815]*

Handbook of financial markets--securities, options, futures /. Homewood, Ill. , c1981. xxiii, 794 p. : ISBN 0-87094-216-6 LC Card 80-70448 DDC 332.6/78 19
HG4527 .H25 *NYPL [JLE 86-1500]*

The Successful sales assistant's handbook. New York, N.Y. , c1987. xi, 268 p. : ISBN 0-13-860305-7 (pbk.) : LC Card 87-11322 DDC 332.6/2/0688 19
HG4621 .S84 1987

SECURITIES - INDIA.
Structure and management of the gilt-edged securities market in India. New Delhi , 1983. v, 186 p. : LC Card 84-901424 DDC 332.63/2044 19
HG5735 .S77 1983 *NYPL [JLD 87-871]*

The securities industry . Rutterford, Janette. [London] [1986] 93 p. : LC Card 87-160412 DDC 332.63/2/0941 19
HG5432 .R87 1986

Securities Industry Association. Financial Industry Securities Council Same Day Funds Settlement Task Force. Same day funds settlement for securities transactions . [New York, N.Y.] [S.l.] , c1985. 61 leaves in various foliations : LC Card 85-193287 DDC 332.64 19
HG4631 .F56 1985 *NYPL [JLF 86-919]*

SECURITIES - ITALY.
Fabrizi, Pier Luigi. La politica degli investimenti in titoli nelle banche di deposito /. [Milano] , 1982. xii, 138 p. ; LC Card 82-165568
HG1616.I5 F33 1982

Rossi, Guido. La scalata del mercato . Bologna , c1986. 152 p. ; ISBN 88-15-01123-4 : LC Card 86-180921
HG5522 .R66 1986

SECURITIES - ITALY - STATISTICS.
Mediobanca. Indici e dati relativi ad investimenti in titoli quotati nelle borse italiane (1985) =. [Milano] [1985] v, 427 p. : LC Card 86-210524
HG5522 .M43 1985

SECURITIES - NIGERIA.
Alile, H. I. The Nigerian stock market in operation /. [Lagos, Nigeria] 1986 (Lagos, Nigeria : Jeromelaiho & Associates) 194, v p. : LC Card 87-143647 DDC 332.64/2669 19
HG5881.N6 A43 1986

SECURITIES - PERU.
Rocha C., Julio César de la (Rocha Corzo) Un análisis de la rentabilidad accionaria de la Bolsa de Valores de Lima, 1980-1983 /. Lima, Perú , 1984. ii, 56 p. ; LC Card 86-154699
HG5392 .R66 1984

SECURITIES - RATINGS.
Standard & Poor's debt ratings criteria . New York, N.Y. (25 Broadway, New York 10004) , c1986. viii, 68 p. : LC Card 87-102292 DDC 338.7/4/0973 19
HG4521 .S729 1986

SECURITIES, TAX-EXEMPT - UNITED STATES.
Howell, Dean M., 1932- How to buy tax free bonds . Denver, Colo. , 1987. 165 p. ; LC Card 86-91807 DDC 332.63/233/0973 19
HG4952 .H68 1987

SECURITIES - UNITED STATES.
Auerbach, Joseph, 1916- Investment banking and diligence . Boston, Mass. , c1986. x, 274 p. : ISBN 0-87584-171-6 (alk. paper) LC Card 86-319 DDC 332.66/0973 19
HG4910 .A94 1986 *NYPL [JLE 86-3128]*

Bréard, Jean-Pierre. Les contrats de souscription à forfait de valeurs mobilières /. Montréal , 1984. xv, 158 p. : ISBN 2-89266-018-1 (pbk.) :
NYPL [JLD 87-662]

Cohen, Jerome Bernard, 1915- Investment analysis and portfolio management. Homewood, Ill., 1973. xiv, 946 p. ISBN 0-256-01429-9 LC Card 72-98120
HG4521 .C5296 1973 *NYPL [JLE 74-744]*

Cohen, Jerome Bernard, 1915- Investment analysis and portfolio management /. Homewood, Ill. , 1977. xvi, 819 p. : ISBN 0-256-01883-9 LC Card 76-15739
HG4521 .C5296 1977
*NYPL [*R-Econ. 78-1366]*

Corporate mergers and high yield (junk) bonds . Washington , 1986. vi, 57 p. ; LC Card 87-601339 DDC 332.63/22 19
HD2746.5 .C67 1986

Currier, Chet. No cost/low cost investing /. New York , 1987. 240 p. ; ISBN 0-531-15527-7 LC Card 87-13690 DDC 332.6/78 19
HG4910 .C86 1987

The financing and regulatory capital needs of the securities industry /. [Washington, D.C.] [1985?] xiv, 69, [49] p ; *NYPL [JLF 86-863]*

Graham, Benjamin, 1894- [Security analysis.] Graham and Dodd's security analysis. New York , c1988. xiii, 656 p. : ISBN 0-07-013235-6 : LC Card 87-19990 DDC 332.63/2 19
HG4529 .G7 1988

Hillstrom, Roger. 1960-1969, a decade of corporate and international finance. New York [1972] 381 p. LC Card 72-175335 DDC 332
HG4907 .H54 *NYPL [JLG 73-17]*

The Microstructure of securities markets /. Englewood Cliffs, N.J. , c1986. ix, 254 p. ; ISBN 0-13-581794-3 LC Card 85-28265 DDC 332.64 19
HG4661 .M53 1986 *NYPL [JLE 86-2001]*

Mortgage-backed securities . Chicago, Ill. , c1987. xi, 474 p. : ISBN 0-917253-47-7 : LC Card 86-15087 DDC 332.63/232 19
HG4655 .M65 1987 *NYPL [JLE 87-783]*

The New York Institute of Finance guide to investing. New York, N.Y. , c1987. xi, 296 p. : ISBN 0-13-620436-8 (pbk.) : LC Card 87-11323 DDC 332.6/78 19
HG4921 .N53 1987

Putnam, Bluford H. The Blackwell guide to Wall Street /. Oxford, UK , New York, NY, USA , 1987. viii, 222 p. : ISBN 0-631-14183-9 : LC Card 87-10299 DDC 332.63/2 19
HG4910 .P87 1987

Schwartz, Robert A. (Robert Alan), 1937- Equity markets . New York , c1988. xvi, 544 p. : ISBN 0-06-041322-0 LC Card 87-23173 DDC 332.64/0973 19
HG4963 .S38 1988

Stevenson, Eric. The secondary market and securitization for income property mortgages /. Washington, D.C. (1125 15th St., N.W., Washington 20005) , c1986. xiii, 129 p. : LC Card 87-153518 DDC 332.1/753 19
HG2040.5.U5 S73 1986

Stocks, bonds, options, futures . New York, N.Y. [Englewood Cliffs, N.J.] , c1987. 332 p. : ISBN 0-13-846718-8 : LC Card 87-11324 DDC 332.6/78 19
HG4921 .S7945 1987

Understanding the securities markets . Jersey City, NJ (75 Montgomery St., Jersey City 07302) , c1986. 36 p. ; LC Card 87-130670 DDC 332.63/2 19
HG4910 .U53 1986

Weiss, David M., 1938- After the trade is made . New York, N.Y. , c1986. xii, 436 p. : ISBN 0-13-018581-7 : LC Card 85-30997 DDC 332.64/273 19
HG4910 .W365 1986 *NYPL [JLE 86-4304]*

SECURITIES - UNITED STATES - HANDBOOKS, MANUALS, ETC.
Fowler, Elizabeth M. Every woman's guide to profitable investing /. New York, NY , c1986. 260 p. : ISBN 0-8144-5823-8 LC Card 85-48222 DDC 332.6/78/024042 19
HG4921 .F636 1986 *NYPL [JLE 86-3339]*

Security analysis. Graham, Benjamin, 1894- [Security analysis.] Graham and Dodd's security analysis. New York , c1988. xiii, 656 p. : ISBN 0-07-013235-6 : LC Card 87-19990 DDC 332.63/2 19
HG4529 .G7 1988

SECURITY ANALYSIS. see **INVESTMENT ANALYSIS.**

Security analysis and portfolio management /. Fischer, Donald E. Englewood Cliffs, N.J. , c1987. xii, 708 p. : ISBN 0-13-798901-6 LC Card 86-25484 DDC 332.6 19
HG4529 .F57 1987

SECURITY, ECONOMIC. see **ECONOMIC SECURITY.**

Security for you and your home-- . Kelley, Clarence M. Blue Ridge Summit, Pa. , c1984. viii, 391 p. : ISBN 0-8306-0680-7 : LC Card 83-18134 DDC 643/.16 19
HV7431 .K44 1984 *NYPL [JSE 86-649]*

SECURITY, INTERNATIONAL - ADDRESSES, ESSAYS, LECTURES.
Fred och säkerhet . [Stockholm] , c1983. 385 p. : ISBN 91-7410-249-4 : LC Card 83-229846
JX1963 .F817 1983 *NYPL [JLD 84-2639]*

Nuclear proliferation and international security /. New Delhi , 1985-86 [i.e. 1985] 310 p. ; ISBN 1-85127-058-4 : LC Card 85-904278 DDC 327.1/74 19
JX1974.73 .N814 1985
NYPL [JLD 86-1334]

SECURITY, INTERNATIONAL - CONGRESSES.
Frieden und Friedenssicherung in Vergangenheit und Gegenwart . München , 1984. 115 p. ; ISBN 3-7705-2147-1 (pbk.) :
NYPL [JFL 76-295 Bd. 7]

Security management. Physical security . Boston , c1986. xii, 409 p. : ISBN 0-409-95105-6 (pbk.) LC Card 85-29083 DDC 658.4/73 19
HD38 .P49 1986 *NYPL [JLE 86-3699]*

The security of energy supplies in Western Australia /. Taylor, Neil. Murdoch, W.A. , 1986. 35 p. : ISBN 0-86905-099-0 (pbk.) : LC Card 87-118009 DDC 333.79/09941 19
HD9502.A873 W45673 1986

SECURITY PACIFIC NATIONAL BANK.
Change master companies [videorecording] . Chicago, IL , 1987. 1 videocassette (42 min.) : LC Card 87-705608 DDC 658.3 11
HD45

SECURITY PRICE FORCASTING. see **STOCK PRICE FORECASTING.**

SECURITY SYSTEMS.
Bundy, Darcie. Total coverage . New York , c1987. xiv, 224 p. ; ISBN 0-06-055077-5 : LC Card 86-46050 DDC 368/.0029 19
HG8051 .B846 1987

Henley, Ernest J. Designing for reliability and safety control /. Englewood Cliffs, N.J. , c1985. xvi, 527 p. : ISBN 0-13-201229-4 LC Card 84-17892 DDC 620/.00452 19
TA169 .H46 1985 ***NYPL [JSE 86-2491]***

Kelley, Clarence M. Security for you and your home-- . Blue Ridge Summit, Pa. , c1984. viii, 391 p. : ISBN 0-8306-0680-7 : LC Card 83-18134 DDC 643/.16 19
HV7431 .K44 1984 ***NYPL [JSE 86-649]***

Physical security . Boston , c1986. xii, 409 p. : ISBN 0-409-95105-6 (pbk.) LC Card 85-29083 DDC 658.4/73 19
HD38 .P49 1986 ***NYPL [JLE 86-3699]***

Seddig, Gert. Lehrbuch der Altenpflege. Schrift- und Behördenverkehr / Gert Seddig. Hannover : C. Vincentz Verlag, c1983. 95 p. : ill. ; 21 cm. (Manuskripte zur Altenpflege) Includes index. ISBN 3-87870-204-3 LC Card 83-230557
1. Commercial correspondence, German. 2. Office practice. 3. Old age homes - Germany (West) - Management. I. Title. II. Title: Schrift- und Behördenverkehr. III. Series.
HF5728.G3 S49 1983

Seddon, David. Nepal, a state of poverty / David Seddon. New Delhi : Vikas Pub. House, c1987. xxii, 288 p. ; 22 cm. Bibliography: p. [275]-283. Includes index. ISBN 0-7069-3414-8 : LC Card 87-900823 DDC 330.9549/6 19
1. Nepal - Economic conditions. 2. Nepal - Social conditions. I. Title.
HC425 .S43 1987

Sedemdeset i pet godini borba i sŭzidanie. 75 godini borba i sŭzidanie . Sofiia , 1985. 144 p. ; LC Card 86-195265
HD6784.M62 P762 1985

Sederberg, Kathryn. Brown, William P. The complete dictionary of media terms /. Chicago, IL , c1986. vii, 151 p. ; ISBN 0-913247-01-4 (pbk.) LC Card 86-70712 DDC 302.2/34/0321 19
HF5826.5 .B77 1986

Sedgwick, Henry D. Merrill, Ronald E. The new venture handbook . New York, NY , c1987. 356 p. : ISBN 0-8144-5895-5 LC Card 86-47818 DDC 658.1/141 19
HD62.5 .M46 1987

Sedlov, Pavel Alekseevich. Formy i metody upravleniia NTP /. Moskva , 1987. 151 p. ; LC Card 87-143073
HC340.T4 F67 1987

Sedov, A. V. (Andreĭ Vasil´evich) Agrarnaia revoliutsiia i sotsialisticheskie preobrazovaniia v sovetskoĭ derevne . Gor´kiĭ , 1980. 84 p. ; LC Card 82-141565
HD1995.R8 A68 1980

Sedov, V. I. (Vladimir Il´ich) Ladygin, Boris Nikolaevich. Istoricheskiĭ opyt sotrudnichestva stran SEV /. Moskva , 1980. 284 p. ; LC Card 81-130900
HC244 .L282 1980

Sedov, V. V. (Valentin Vasil´evich) Bartov, Vladimir Fotievich. Kontseptsii vzaimodeĭstviia ėkonomiki i prirody /. Moskva , 1984. 157 p. ; LC Card 84-225876
HC79.E5 B369 1984

Sée, N. (Norbert) Nicourt, Christian. Conditions de travail en agriculture . Paris , <1985-. v. <2 > : ISBN 2-85340-585-0 (v. 2) LC Card 86-218948
HD1536.F8 N53 1985

See- und Flusshäfen vom Hochmittelalter bis zur Industrialisierung / herausgegeben von Heinz Stoob. Köln : Böhlau, 1986. xxi, 315 p. : ill., maps ; 27 cm. (Städteforschung. Reihe A: Darstellungen. Bd. 24) Two maps in pocket. Includes index. ISBN 3-412-07585-X LC Card 87-146564 DDC 387.1/094 19
1. Harbors - Europe - History. I. Stoob, Heinz. II. Series.
HE557.A3 S37 1986

Seebeck . Mueses, Danilo A. [S.l.] , República Dominicana [1986?] 170, [5] p. : LC Card 86-177691
HE6185.L29 M84 1986

SEEBECK, NICHOLAS F., 1857-1899.
Mueses, Danilo A. Seebeck . [S.l.] , República Dominicana [1986?] 170, [5] p. : LC Card 86-177691
HE6185.L29 M84 1986

Seeberger, Jürgen. Koch, Thilo. Müllverwertung und -Beseitigung in Baden-Württemberg . Stuttgart , 1984. ii, 177 p. : LC Card 84-158868
HD4485.G32 B335 1984

SEED INDUSTRY AND TRADE - SOCIAL ASPECTS.
McMullen, Neil. Seeds and world agricultural progress /. Washington, D.C. , c1987. viii, 263 p. : ISBN 0-89068-088-4 (pbk.) : LC Card 87-60766 DDC 338.1/7 19
HD9019.S43 M36 1987

SEEDS.
(1987) McMullen, Neil. Seeds and world agricultural progress /. Washington, D.C. , c1987. viii, 263 p. : ISBN 0-89068-088-4 (pbk.) : LC Card 87-60766 DDC 338.1/7 19
HD9019.S43 M36 1987

Seeds and world agricultural progress /. McMullen, Neil. Washington, D.C. , c1987. viii, 263 p. : ISBN 0-89068-088-4 (pbk.) : LC Card 87-60766 DDC 338.1/7 19
HD9019.S43 M36 1987

Die Seehafenstädte im Weser-Jade-Raum und ihre überregionale Verflechtung /. Komp, Klaus Ulrich. Münster , 1982. x, 143 p. : LC Card 83-197866
HE558.W45 K66 1982

SEELAND, SWITZERLAND - DESCRIPTION AND TRAVEL.
Waldburger, Hans. Die Seetalbahn . Luzern , c1983. 143 p. : LC Card 84-190252
HE4918.S44 W35 1983

Die Seetalbahn . Waldburger, Hans. Luzern , c1983. 143 p. : LC Card 84-190252
HE4918.S44 W35 1983

Seetharaman, S. P. Gurdev Singh. Financing of kapas-cloth system /. New Delhi , c1987. xi, 59 p. ; ISBN 81-204-0217-0 : LC Card 87-902510 DDC 338.4/367721/0954 19
HD9886.I42 G87 1987

Segal, Paul Harold, 1946- The French state and French private investment in Czechoslovakia, 1918-1938 : a study of economic diplomacy / Paul Harold Segal. New York : Garland Pub., 1987. vi, 379 p. ; 24 cm. (Modern European history) Thesis (Ph. D.)--Columbia University, 1983. Bibliography: p. 366-379. ISBN 0-8240-8041-6 (alk. paper) : LC Card 87-252 DDC 332.6/7344/0437 19
1. Investments, French - Czechoslovakia. 2. France - Foreign economic relations - Czechoslovakia. 3. Czechoslovakia - Foreign economic relations - France. I. Title. II. Series.
HG5470.3.A3 S44 1987

Segal, Ronald, 1932- Kidron, Michael. What you need to know about business, money, and power /. New York , c1987. 187 p. : ISBN 0-671-54113-7 : LC Card 86-31571 DDC 650 19
HF5351 .K473 1987

Segale, M. Gobotswang, Z. Pilot evaluation report on Mahalapye Development Trust /. Gaborone, Botswana [1982] v leaves, 61, 3 p. ; LC Card 87-122810
HD5710.85.B59 G63 1982

Segarra, Eduardo. Local infrastructure investment in rural America /. Boulder , 1988. xxi, 291 p. ; ISBN 0-8133-7460-X (soft : alk. paper) LC Card 87-21606 DDC 332.6/7252 19
HC110.P83 L63 1988

Seger, Daniel J. Financing Illinois agricultural exports / Daniel J. Seger, David A. Lins. [Urbana?] : University of Illinois at Urbana-Champaign, College of Agriculture, Dept. of Agricultural Economics, [1985] 74 p. : ill. ; 29 cm. "June 1985; AE 4598." Bibliography: p. 63-65. LC Card 86-621070 DDC 382/.63 19
1. Produce trade - Illinois - Finance. 2. Export credit - Illinois. 3. Agricultural credit - Illinois. I. Lins, David A. II. University of Illinois at Urbana-Champaign. Dept. of Agricultural Economics. III. Title.
HD9007.I3 S44 1985

Seglin, Jeffrey L., 1956-
Bank letter writing handbook : a guide to planning and writing effective letters / Jeffrey L. Seglin.2nd ed. Boston : Bankers Pub. Co., c1987. xii, 434 p. ; 24 cm. Bibliography: p. [430]-434. ISBN 0-87267-103-8 LC Card 87-965 DDC 651.7/5/024332 19
1. Banks and banking - Records and correspondence. 2. Commercial correspondence. I. Title.
HG1616.R4 S43 1987

Personal financial planning in banks : a handbook for decision making / Jeffrey L. Seglin, Jeffrey R. Lauterbach. Boston : Bankers Pub. Co., c1986. xvii, 205 p. ; 25 cm. Includes index. Bibliography: p. [195]-199. ISBN 0-87267-059-7 LC Card 85-28738 DDC 332.1/7 19
1. Banks and banking - United States - Customer services - Handbooks, manuals, etc. 2. Finance, Personal - United States - Handbooks, manuals, etc. 3. Investment advisers - Legal status, laws, etc. - United States. I. Lauterbach, Jeffrey R. II. Title.
HG1616.C87 S44 1986 ***NYPL [JLE 87-820]***

La segmentación del mercado del crédito y sus impactos sobre la distribución del ingreso /. González, José I. (José Iván), 1944- Montevideo, Uruguay , 1984. ii, 5, 123 p. : LC Card 85-236586
HG3754.5.U8 G66 1984

Segmentationstheorien des Arbeitsmarktes und Beschäftigungsniveau . Reineke, Ulrich, 1955- Frankfurt am Main , New York , c1986. iv, 333 p. : ISBN 3-8204-9671-8 LC Card 87-407583 DDC 331.12/0943 19
HD5706 .R43 1986

Die segmentorientierte Marketingplanung im Einzelhandelsbetrieb /. Büttner, Herbert. Göttingen , 1986. 413 p. : ISBN 3-509-01424-3 LC Card 87-134581 DDC 658.8/7 19
HF5429 .B87 1986

Segnitz, Paul H.
County and postmaster postmarks of Wisconsin. Bournique, Raymond A. County & postmaster postmarks of Wisconsin. Rev. & enl. ed. / by Raymond A. Bournique. Madison, WI (5401 Raymond Rd., Madison 53711) , 1985. 12 p. : LC Card 86-174748 DDC 769.56/7/09775 19
HE6185.U7 W573 1985

La segona residència a Catalunya . Argany Comas, Isabel. [Barcelona] [1984] 71 p. ; LC Card 86-160322
HD7289.3.S72 C383 1984

SEGOVIA (SPAIN) - POPULATION DENSITY - HISTORY.
Martínez Moro, Jesús. La tierra en la comunidad de Segovia . [Valladolid] [Salamanca] , c1985. 252 p. : ISBN 84-86192-37-4 LC Card 86-211593
HD780.S44 M37 1985

SEGOVIA (SPAIN) - POPULATION - HISTORY.
Martínez Moro, Jesús. La tierra en la comunidad de Segovia . [Valladolid] [Salamanca] , c1985. 252 p. : ISBN 84-86192-37-4 LC Card 86-211593
HD780.S44 M37 1985

Séguin, Philippe, 1943- Réussir l'alternance : contre l'esprit de revanche / Philippe Séguin. Paris : R. Laffont, c1985. 220 p. ; 19 cm. (Franc-parler . 7) ISBN 2-221-04633-1 : LC Card 85-187945 DDC 944.083/8 19
1. Liberalism - France. 2. Political participation - France. 3. Political parties - France. 4. France - Politics and government - 1981-. I. Title.
JN2594.2 .S37 1985 ***NYPL [JLC 87-46]***

Seguin, Sabine Erbès- see Erbès-Seguin, Sabine.

Segunda reforma agraria : campesinos, tierra y educación popular / Miguel Urioste F. de C. La Paz, Bolivia : Centro de Estudios para el Desarrollo Laboral y Agrario, [1987] 287 p. : ill. ; 21 cm. (Talleres CEDLA . no. 1) "Contiene dos partes, la primera el trabajo realizado por Miguel Urioste ... la segunda parte comprende las reflexiones de los participantes en el primer taller organizado por el CEDLA"--P. 7. Bibliography: p. 155-157. LC Card 87-403057 DDC 333.3/1/84 19
1. Land reform - Bolivia. 2. Peasantry - Bolivia. 3. Land tenure - Bolivia. 4. Rural development - Bolivia. 5. Fundamental education - Bolivia. I. Urioste Fernández de Córdova, Miguel, 1948-. II. CEDLA (Organization). III. Title: 2a reforma agraria. IV. Series.
HD1333.B5 S44 1987

Segundo censo nacional agropecuario. II censo

nacional agropecuario. [La Paz], República de Bolivia [1986- v. <1-3 > : LC Card 87-109107
HD1867 .A14 1986

SEGURA MOUNTAINS REGION (SPAIN) - ECONOMIC CONDITIONS.
Ruiz Avilés, Pedro. Estudio integral de la Sierra de Segura . [Jaén] [1985] 130 leaves : ISBN 84-505-1249-2 LC Card 86-187282
HC387.S438 R85 1985

SEGURA MOUNTAINS REGION (SPAIN) - ECONOMIC POLICY.
Ruiz Avilés, Pedro. Estudio integral de la Sierra de Segura . [Jaén] [1985] 130 leaves : ISBN 84-505-1249-2 LC Card 86-187282
HC387.S438 R85 1985

Segurança empresarial . Hausen, Ivan Zanoni. Brasília, Distrito Federal , 1979. 157 p. : LC Card 82-100947
HD7683 .H38 1979

Segurança social em Portugal . Maia, Fernando M. Lisboa , 1985. 192 p. : LC Card 86-149393
HD7209 .M35 1985

El seguro agrícola como factor de desarrollo económico /. Santa María de Cárdenas, Cecilia. Bogotá , 1978. 168, 2, [43] p. : LC Card 85-203482
HG9966 .S25 1978

Segye Unhaeng. see **International Bank for Reconstruction and Development.**

Seibel, Hans Dieter. Management problems in Africa /. London , 1986. xviii, 395 p. ; ISBN 0-333-28992-7 ***NYPL [Sc D 86-519]***

Seibert, Georg. Zahlenbild-Almanach 1972 . Berlin , c1972. 204 p. : ISBN 3-503-00861-6 LC Card 86-133643
HC286.5 .Z225 1972

Seibert, Siegfried, 1954- Strategische Erfolgsfaktoren in mittleren Unternehmen : untersucht am Beispiel der Fördertechnikindustrie / Siegfried Seibert. Frankfurt am Main ; New York : Lang, c1987. xii, 353 p. : ill. ; 21 cm. (Europäische Hochschulschriften. Reihe V, Volks- und Betriebswirtschaft, 0531-7339 . Bd. 764 = vol. 764 = vol. 764) Bibliography: p. [290]-306. ISBN 3-8204-9828-1 LC Card 87-122289
1. Small business - Europe, German-speaking - Management. 2. Strategic planning - Europe, German-speaking. 3. Technological innovations - Europe, German-speaking - Management. 4. High technology industries - Europe, German-speaking - Management. I. Series: Europäische Hochschulschriften. Reihe V, Volks- und Betriebswirtschaft , Bd. 764. II. Title.
HD2346.G3 S38 1987

Seidel, Hans. Geldwertstabilität und Wirtschaftswachstum . Göttingen , c1984. xii, 230 p. : ISBN 3-525-13169-0 LC Card 84-232466
HG203 .G46 1984

Seidenfus, Hellmuth Stefan.
Die Bedeutung der Seehäfen für die Industrialisierung Mitteleuropas / H.St. Seidenfus. Göttingen : Vandenhoeck & Ruprecht, 1979. 20 p. ; 24 cm. (Vorträge und Studien aus dem Institut für Verkehrswissenschaft an der Universität Münster . Heft 18) Includes bibliographical references. ISBN 3-525-85769-1 LC Card 86-194319
1. Harbors - Economic aspects - Central Europe. 2. Central Europe - Industries. I. Title. II. Series.
HE131 .M84 Heft 18 HE557.A3

Probleme der Ordnungs- und Strukturpolitik . Göttingen , c1984. viii, 311 p., [1] leaf of plates : ISBN 3-525-85925-2 LC Card 84-203472
HE152.6 .P76 1984

SEIDENFUS, HELLMUTH STEFAN.
Probleme der Ordnungs- und Strukturpolitik . Göttingen , c1984. viii, 311 p., [1] leaf of plates : ISBN 3-525-85925-2 LC Card 84-203472
HE152.6 .P76 1984

Seider, Maynard, 1943- A year in the life of a factory / Maynard Seider. San Pedro, Calif. : Singlejack Books, 1984. 152 p. ; 22 cm. ISBN 0-917300-16-5 (pbk.) : LC Card 83-50914 DDC 331.89/28621381/0979466 19
1. Seider, Maynard, 1943-. 2. Electronic industry workers - California. 3. Collective bargaining - California. 4. Strikes and lockouts - California. I. Title.
HD8039.E38 U67 1984 ***NYPL [JLD 86-4400]***

SEIDER, MAYNARD, 1943-
Seider, Maynard, 1943- A year in the life of a factory /. San Pedro, Calif. , 1984. 152 p. ; ISBN 0-917300-16-5 (pbk.) : LC Card 83-50914 DDC 331.89/28621381/0979466 19
HD8039.E38 U67 1984 ***NYPL [JLD 86-4400]***

Seidl, Christian. Welfare economics of the second best /. Wien , New York , c1986. 280 p. ; ISBN 0-387-81942-8 (pbk. : U. S.) LC Card 86-31357 DDC 330.15/5 19
HB846.6 .W45 1986

Seidman, Ann Willcox, 1926-
Money, banking, and public finance in Africa / Ann Seidman. London ; Atlantic Highlands, N.J., USA : Zed Books, 1986. xv, 363 p. : ill. ; 23 cm. Bibliography: p. 330-349. Includes index. ISBN 0-86232-429-7 LC Card 87-111822 DDC 332.1/096 19
1. Finance - Africa. 2. Banks and banking - Africa. 3. Finance, Public - Africa. 4. Socialism - Africa. 5. Africa - Foreign economic relations. 6. Money - Africa. I. Title.
HG187.5.A2 S45 1986

The roots of crisis in southern Africa / Ann Seidman. Trenton, N.J. : Africa World Press, [1985] xvii, 209 p. : ill. ; 23 cm. (Impact audit . no. 4) "Oxfam America." Includes index. Bibliography: p. 175-180. ISBN 0-86543-026-8 (pbk.) : LC Card 85-72995 DDC 968.06/3 19
1. Investments, American - South Africa. 2. International business enterprises - South Africa. 3. Economic assistance, American - South Africa. 4. United States - Relations - South Africa. 5. South Africa - Relations - United States. I. Oxfam America. II. Series: Impact audit , 4. III. Title.
E183.8.S6 S45 1985 ***NYPL [Sc E 86-368]***

Seierstad, Atle. Optimal control theory with economic applications / Atle Seierstad and Knut Sydsæter. Amsterdam ; New York : North-Holland ; xvi, 445 p. : ill. ; 24 cm. (Advanced textbooks in economics. v. 24) Bibliography: p. 437-440. ISBN 0-444-87923-4 (Elsevier Science Pub. Co.) LC Card 86-16504 DDC 629.8/312 19
1. Control theory. 2. Economics - Mathematical models. I. Sydsæter, Knut. II. Title.
QA402.3 .S4 1986 ***NYPL [JLE 87-1123]***

Seiferheld, Alfredo M., 1950- Economía y petróleo durante la Guerra del Chaco : apuntes para una historia económica del conflicto paraguayo-boliviano / Alfredo M. Seiferheld. Asunción : Instituto Paraguayo de Estudios Geopolíticos e Internacionales : Lector, 1983. 535 p. : ill. ; 22 cm. (Colección histórica. 4) Includes bibliographical references. LC Card 84-121699 DDC 330.9892/071 19
1. Chaco War, 1932-1935 - Finance - Paraguay. 2. Chaco War, 1932-1935 - Finance - Bolivia. 3. Petroleum industry and trade - Political aspects - Paraguay - History. 4. Petroleum industry and trade - Political aspects - Bolivia - History. 5. Paraguay - Economic conditions - 1918-1954. 6. Bolivia - Economic conditions - 1918-1952. I. Title.
HC222 .S36 1983 ***NYPL [JLD 85-1032]***

Seifert, Eberhard. Industrielle Arbeitszeiten in Deutschland : ein wirtschafts- und sozialgeschichtlicher Abriss vom Beginn der Industrialisierung bis zum 2. Weltkrieg / Eberhard Seifert. Wuppertal : [Fachbereich Wirtschaftswissenschaft, Gesamthochschule Wuppertal], 1982. 68, [8] p. : ill. ; 21 cm. (Arbeitspapiere des Fachbereichs Wirtschaftswissenschaft der Gesamthochschule Wuppertal . Nr. 64 (1982)) Cover title. Bibliography: p. [69]-[76]. LC Card 87-672398
1. Hours of labor - Germany - History - 19th century. 2. Hours of labor - Germany - History - 20th century. I. Series: Arbeitspapiere des Fachbereichs Wirtschaftswissenschaft der Gesamthochschule Wuppertal , Nr. 64. II. Title.
HD5178 .S44x 1982

Seifert, Ekkehard. Privilegierung und Regulierung im Bankwesen : ein Beitrag zur ordnungspolitischen Problematik branchenorientierter Strukturpolitik / Ekkehard Seifert.1. Aufl. Baden-Baden : Nomos, 1984. 332 p. ; 23 cm. (Studien zum Bank- und Börsenrecht . Bd. 12) Originally presented as the author's thesis (doctoral)--Ruhr-Universität Bochum, 1982. Includes bibliographical references and index. ISBN 3-7890-0861-3 LC Card 84-186059
1. Banks and banking - Germany, West. 2. Banks and banking - Germany, West - Branch banks. 3. Banking law - Germany, West. 4. Risk - Germany, West. I. Title. II. Series.
HG3054 .S42 1984

Seifert, Hartmut, 1944- Öffentliche Arbeitsmarktpolitik in der Bundesrepublik Deutschland : zur Entwicklung der Arbeitsmarktpolitik im Verhältnis von Steuerungsaufgabe und Anpassungsfunktion / Hartmut Seifert. Köln : Bund-Verlag, [1984] ix, 288 p. ; 21 cm. (WSI-Studie zur Wirtschafts- und Sozialforschung . Nr. 54) Bibliography: p. 270-286. ISBN 3-7663-0857-2 LC Card 86-127331 DDC 331.11/0943 19
1. Manpower policy - Germany, West. 2. Germany, West - Economic conditions. I. Title. II. Series.
HD5779 .S34 1984

Seifert-Vogt, Hans-Günther. Schattenwirtschaft und alternative Ökonomie . Regensburg , c1984. 268 p. : ISBN 3-924956-00-6 LC Card 86-224071
HD2341 .S337 1984

Seiffert, Bernd.
Brauer, Karl M. Fallstudie Haiger . Berlin , c1983. 55 p. ; ISBN 3-428-05403-2 LC Card 83-233201
HE199.G3 B73 1983

Zahlungsmittelbewirtschaftung im Verkehrsbetrieb / von Bernd Seiffert. Berlin : Duncker & Humblot, c1986. 187 p. : 38 ill. ; 24 cm. (Schriften zur Betriebswirtschaftslehre des Verkehrs) Originally presented as the author's thesis (doctoral)--Technische Universität, Berlin. Bibliography: p. 177-186. Includes index. ISBN 3-428-06094-6 : LC Card 87-143799 DDC 380.5/24/0943 19
1. Freight forwarders - Germany, West. 2. Shipment of goods - Germany, West. 3. Loading and unloading. I. Title. II. Series.
HE5999.Z7 G374 1986

Seifried, Edmond J. Nevitt, Peter K. Equipment leasing for commercial bankers /. Philadelphia, Pa. , c1987. x, 123 p. ; ISBN 0-936742-37-2 (pbk.) : LC Card 87-5532 DDC 332.1/068/5 19
HD39.4 .N485 1987

Seim, Edgar. Rudolph, Jürgen. Aktuelle Fragen der Theorie und Praxis der staatlichen Leitung der Landwirtschaft /. Potsdam-Babelsberg , 1983. 72 p. ; LC Card 83-214391
HD1960.5.Z8 R83 1983

SEINING - NEW YORK (STATE) - LONG ISLAND - HISTORY.
Matthiessen, Peter. Men's lives /. New York , 1988, c1986. xvi, 335 p. ; ISBN 0-394-75560-X (pbk.) : LC Card 87-40095 DDC 338.3/72709747/21 19
HD8039.F66 U5 1988

Seira epistēmonikōn diatrivōn tēs philosophikēs scholēs .
(4) Papageōrgiou, Giōrgos. Hoi syntechnies sta Giannena kata ton 19o kai tis arches tou 20ou aiōna (arches 19ou ai. hōs 1912) /. Iōannina : Athēna : 454 p. ; LC Card 84-137611
HD2346.G752 I566 1982

Seis estudios sobre el proletariado andaluz (1868-1939). [Córdoba] : Excmo. Ayuntamiento de Córdoba, Delegación de Cultura, 1984. 247 p. ; 22 cm. Includes bibliographical references. ISBN 84-500-9584-0 LC Card 86-142680 DDC 305.5/62/09468 19
1. Proletariat - Spain - Andalusia - History - 19th century. 2. Proletariat - Spain - Andalusia - History - 20th century. 3. Labor and laboring classes - Spain - Andalusia - History - 19th century. 4. Labor and laboring classes - Spain - Andalusia - History - 20th century. I. Córdoba (Spain). Delegación de Cultura.
HD8589.A52 S45 1984 ***NYPL [JLD 87-1550]***

Seitz, John L., 1931- The politics of development : an introduction to global issues / John L. Seitz. New York, NY, USA : B. Blackwell, 1988. xiii, 194 p. : ill. ; 23 cm. Bibliography: p. [183]-188. Includes index. ISBN 0-631-15801-4 (pbk.) LC Card 87-20825 DDC 338.9 19
1. Economic development. 2. Developing countries - Economic policy. 3. Developing countries - Economic conditions. I. Title.
HD82 .S399 1988

Seja, Jürgen, 1953- Selektive Effekte der global orientierten Geldpolitik der Deutschen

Bundesbank auf die Marktstruktur im Bankensektor / Jürgen Seja. Frankfurt am Main ; New York : P. Lang, c1983. xiii, 370 p. ; 21 cm. (Europäische Hochschulschriften. Reihe V, Volks- und Betriebswirtschaft, 0531-7339 . Bd. 485 = vol. 485 = vol. 485) Originally presented as the author's thesis (doctoral--Universität Hannover, 1983) Bibliography: p. 346-370. ISBN 3-8204-5282-6 LC Card 86-119382
1. Deutsche Bundesbank. 2. Monetary policy - Germany, West. 3. Capital market - Germany, West. 4. Financial institutions - Germany, West. I. Series: Europäische Hochschulschriften. Reihe V, Volks- und Betriebswirtschaft , Bd. 485. II. Title.
HG3055 .S5 1983

Sekai Ginkō. see **International Bank for Reconstruction and Development.**

Seḳer melai ha-hon ha-ḳavu'a be-ta'aśiyah, 1.1.1982 /. Aspler, I. Yerushalayim , 1986. 80, xvii p. ; LC Card 87-128243
HA1931 .A354 no. 785 HC415.25.Z9C3

Sekiguchi, Sueo. Technology transfer through direct foreign investment / by Sueo Sekiguchi. Ibaraki, Osaka, Japan : Institute of Social and Economic Research, 1985. 61 leaves : ill. ; 29 cm. (Discussion paper . no. 131) Includes bibliographical references. LC Card 86-209818 DDC 332.6/7352 19
1. Technical assistance, Japanese - History. 2. Technology transfer - Japan - History. 3. Foreign licensing agreements - History. 4. Investments, Foreign - Government policy - History. I. Series: Discussion paper (Ōsaka Daigaku. Shakai Keizai Kenkyūjo) , no. 131. II. Title.
HC60 .S416 1985

Sektor państwowy w gospodarce Polski międzywojennej /. Gołębiowski, Jerzy. Warszawa , 1985. 366 p. ; ISBN 83-01-06292-4 : LC Card 86-108406
HD4215.7 .G65 1985

Sektorale Preisbildung und gesamtwirtschaftliche Preisstabilität /. Wied-Nebbeling, Susanne. Tübingen , 1986. xiii, 368 p. : ISBN 3-16-345102-0 LC Card 87-132436 DDC 338.5/2/0724 19
HB221 .W484 1986

Sektorale Struktur und Entwicklung der industriellen Beschäftigung in den Regionen der Bundesrepublik Deutschland /. Müller, Jürgen, 1943- Berlin , c1983. xiii, 200 p. : ISBN 3-428-05449-0 LC Card 84-109872
HC286.7 .M8 1983

Sektorale Wirtschaftsstruktur und kommunale Finanzsituation . Hermann, Hayo. München , c1986. xiii, 384 p. : ISBN 3-88259-405-5 LC Card 86-228161
HJ9473 .H47 1986

Die sektoralen Importe und Exporte der Bundesrepublik Deutschland . Scheiper, Ulrich. Frankfurt am Main , c1984. v, 203 p. : ISBN 3-88129-846-0 : LC Card 85-125395
HF3566.5 .S28 1984

Sektorberegninger for fiske og fangst /. Røgeberg, Svein Lasse. Oslo , 1979. 34 p. ; ISBN 82-537-0977-3 LC Card 86-460230
HD9465.N62 R64 1979

Sektorberegninger for samferdselssektorene og reparasjon av kjøretøyer m.v. /. Jean-Hansen, Viggo. Oslo , 1979. 56 p. ; ISBN 82-537-0968-4 LC Card 86-460231
HE259 .J4 1979

SELA. see **Sistema Económico Latinoamericano.**

Selamé, Teresita.
Barrera, Manuel. Sindicatos y estado en el Chile actual . Geneva, Switzerland , Santiago, Chile , c1985. v, 196 p. : LC Card 87-118607
HD6617 .B27 1985

Barrera, Manuel. Trade unions and the state in the present day Chile . Geneva, Switzerland , Santiago, Chile , 1986. xx, 154 p. : LC Card 87-128364 DDC 331.89/0983 19
HD6617 .B273 1986

Das Selbstbeschränkungsabkommen zwischen Thailand und der Europäischen Gemeinschaft . Schneider, Karl Josef. Kiel , 1986. x, 192, 30 p. ; ISBN 3-922553-82-6 LC Card 87-408324 DDC 382/.413682/09593 19
HF3800.55.Z7 E867 1986

Selbsthilfe zum Beispiel : eine Chronik der Genossenschaften / [Herausgeber, Dietrich Ohlmeyer ; Redaktion und Realisation, Friedrich Oehler]. Hannover : Steinbock, 1984. 264 p. : ill. (some col.) ; 27 cm. ISBN 3-921951-18-6 LC Card 85-233577
1. Producer cooperatives - Germany (West) - Lower Saxony - History. 2. Producer cooperatives - Germany (West) - Bremen Region - History. I. Ohlmeyer, Dietrich.
HD3190.A3 L687 1984

Selbstregelung und Entpolitisierung der gesetzlichen Rentenversicherung . Böckel, Thomas R., 1959- Frankfurt am Main , New York , c1986. xvi, 305 p. ; ISBN 3-8204-8847-2 LC Card 87-407917 DDC 368.4/00943 19
HD7179 .B59 1986

Seldman, Marty.
Self-talk. Seldman, Marty. Super selling through self-talk : the ultimate edge in sales success / Marty Seldman. Los Angeles, CA , 1988. p. cm. ISBN 0-89586-689-7 : LC Card 87-22581 DDC 658.8/5 19
HF5438.25 .S4375 1988

Super selling through self-talk : the ultimate edge in sales success / Marty Seldman. Los Angeles, CA : Price/Stern/Sloan, 1988. p. cm. Rev. ed. of: Self-talk. c1986. Bibliography: p. ISBN 0-89586-689-7 : LC Card 87-22581 DDC 658.8/5 19
1. Selling. I. Seldman, Marty. Self-talk. II. Title.
HF5438.25 .S4375 1988

Seleção de agregados monetários /. Melo, Valdir Ramalho de. [Brasília] [1981] 136 p. : LC Card 85-161532
HG835 .M45 1981

Selección Cultura colombiana. Sociales económicas.
Parra Peña, Isidro, 1936- El subdesarrollo y la crisis en la economía y en la teoría económica /. Bogotá , 1986. 134 p. ; ISBN 958-1-40133-4 LC Card 87-115003 DDC 338.9 19
HD85.S7 P36 1986

Select Committee on Highway Safety . Ontario. Legislative Assembly. Select Committee on Highway Safety. [Ontario, Canada] [1977] 1 v. in various pagings : LC Card 85-184813
HE5614.5.C2 O5 1977

Selected affirmative action topics in employment and business set-asides : a consultation/hearing of the United States Commission on Civil Rights, March 6-7, 1985. Washington, D.C. : The Commission, 1985- v. <1 > : ill. ; 28 cm. Includes bibliographies. Item 288-A. LC Card 85-603434 DDC 331.13/3/0973 19
1. Affirmative action programs - United States. 2. Minority business enterprises - United States. 3. Minorities - Employment - United States. 4. Affirmative action programs - Law and legislation - United States. I. United States. Commission on Civil Rights.
HF5549.5.A34 S45 1985

Selected affirmative action topics in employment and business set-asides : a consultation/hearing of the United States Commission on Civil Rights, March 6-7, 1985. Washington, D.C. : The Commission, 1985-1986. 2 v. : ill. ; 28 cm. Includes bibliographies.
1. Affirmative action programs - United States. 2. Civil rights - United States. ***NYPL [JLM 86-600]***

Selected agricultural statistics on Spain, 1970-82 / Natalie Tawil ... [et al.]. Washington, D.C. (1301 New York Ave., N.W., Washington 20005-4788) : U. S. Dept. of Agriculture, Economic Research Service, 1986. x, 142 p. : ill. ; 28 cm. (Statistical bulletin . no. 742) Cover title. "July 1986"--T.p. verso. Chiefly tables. Bibliography: p. 5-6. LC Card 86-602416 DDC 338.1/0973 s 338.1/0946/021 19
1. Agriculture - Economic aspects - Spain - Statistics. 2. Agriculture - Spain - Statistics. I. Tawil, Natalie. II. United States. Dept. of Agriculture. Economic Research Service. III. Series: Statistical bulletin (United States. Dept. of Agriculture) , no. 742.
HD1751 .A5 no. 742 HD2022

Selected basic agreements and joint declarations on labour-management relations. Geneva : International Labour Office, 1983. iv, 299 p. ; 24 cm. (Labour-management relations series, 0538-8325 . 63) Includes bibliographical references. ISBN 92-2-103460-7 (pbk.) LC Card 86-213669 DDC 331.89 s 341.7/63 19
1. Labor laws and legislation, International. I. International Labour Office. II. Series.
HD6961.A1 I73 no. 63 K1715

Selected farm machinery statistics /. Hanthorn, Michael. Washington, D.C. , 1986] ii, 54 p. : LC Card 86-602408 DDC 338.1/61/0973 19
HD1751 .A5 no. 743 HD9486.U4

Selected implications for businessmen of social responsibility in South Africa . Au, Norman. [Cape Town] [1977] ix, 141 leaves ; LC Card 81-155073
HD60.5.S7 A92 1977

Selected papers from the Charles Waldo Haskins accounting history seminars / James F. Gaertner, editor. [University, Ala.] : Academy of Accounting Historians, 1983. iv, 172 p. ; 23 cm. (Monograph / the Academy of Accounting Historians . 4) Includes bibliographies. LC Card 86-224698 DDC 657/.09 19
1. Accounting - History. 2. Haskins, Charles Waldo, 1852-1903. I. Gaertner, James F. II. Series: Monograph (Academy of Accounting Historians) , 4.
HF5611 .S45 1983

Selected radio and television criticism / edited by Anthony Slide. Metuchen, N.J. : Scarecrow Press, c1987. ix, 203 p. ; 23 cm. Includes indexes. ISBN 0-8108-1942-2 LC Card 86-27891 DDC 791.44/75/0973 19
1. Broadcasting - United States. 2. Broadcasters - United States - Biography. 3. Radio programs - United States - Reviews. 4. Television programs - United States - Reviews. I. Slide, Anthony.
PN1990.6.U5 S4 1987
NYPL [MWGI 87-1890]

Selected readings in mineral economics / edited by F.J. Anderson. New York : Pergamon Press, c1987. ix, 399 p. : ill. ; 27 cm. "Sponsored by the Mineral Economics Committee of the Canadian Institute of Mining and Metallurgy." Includes bibliographies. ISBN 0-08-035864-0 : LC Card 87-8237 DDC 338.2/0971 19
1. Mineral industries - Canada. 2. Mineral industries. I. Anderson, F. J. II. Canadian Institute of Mining and Metallurgy. Mineral Economics Committee.
HD9506.C22 S44 1987

Selected statistics on rice & corn : May 16, 1960 / Republic of the Philippines, Department of Agriculture and Natural Resources, Bureau of Agricultural Economics, Agricultural Estimates and Statistics Branch. Diliman, Quezon City : The Bureau, [1969] xxix, 306 p. : ill. ; 27 cm. Cover title: Selected statistics on rice and corn. Chiefly tables. LC Card 87-400545 DDC 338.1/7315/09599021 19
1. Rice trade - Philippines - History - Statistics. 2. Corn industry - Philippines - History - Statistics. 3. Produce trade - Philippines - History - Statistics. I. Philippines. Agricultural Estimates and Statistics Branch. II. Title: Selected statistics on rice and corn.
HD9066.P62 S45 1969

Selected statistics on rice and corn. Selected statistics on rice & corn . Diliman, Quezon City [1969] xxix, 306 p. : LC Card 87-400545 DDC 338.1/7315/09599021 19
HD9066.P62 S45 1969

Selecting and installing software packages . Breslin, Jud. New York , 1986. xviii, 242 p. : ISBN 0-89930-158-4 (lib. bdg. : alk. paper) LC Card 86-12403 DDC 658.4/038 19
QA76.754 .B74 1986 ***NYPL [JLE 87-1133]***

Selecting colour for print /. Danger, Eric P. (Eric Paxton) Aldershot, Hants, England , Brookfield, Vt., U. S. A. , c1987. x, 164 p. ; ISBN 0-291-39715-8 (U. S.) : LC Card 86-23060 DDC 659.13/23 19
HF5839 .D36 1987

Selection interviewing for managers /. Moffatt, Thomas L. Madison, Wis. , c1987. x, 196 : ISBN 0-910239-08-8 : LC Card 86-26313 DDC 658.3/112 19
HF5549.5.I6 M64 1987

SELECTION OF EMPLOYEES - UNITED STATES.
Greenwood, Reed. Employer concerns regarding workers with disabilities /. Hot Springs, Ark. [1985] xii, 170 p. ; LC Card 87-620863 DDC 658.3/045 19
HD7256.U5 G74 1985

Selections from The wealth of nations /. Smith, Adam, 1723-1790. [Inquiry into the nature and causes of the wealth of nations. Selections.] Arlington Heights, Ill. [1986], c1957. ix, 116 p. ; ISBN 0-88295-093-2 (pbk.) : LC Card 86-23951

DDC 330.1 19
HB161 .S6522 1986

Selektive Effekte der global orientierten Geldpolitik der Deutschen Bundesbank auf die Marktstruktur im Bankensektor /. Seja, Jürgen, 1953- Frankfurt am Main , New York , c1983. xiii, 370 p. ; ISBN 3-8204-5282-6 LC Card 86-119382
HG3055 .S5 1983

Selektiver Protektionismus und aktive Strukturanpassung . Wiemann, Jürgen. Berlin , 1983. vii, 348 p. : ISBN 3-88985-028-6 : LC Card 83-223964
HD9865.E852 W54 1983

Seleznev, F. (Fedor) Prodovol'stvennaîa programma SSSR . Moskva , 1986. 285 p. ; LC Card 87-110478 DDC 338.1/9/47 19
HD9015.S652 P743 1986

Seleznev, V. A. (Valeriĭ Aleksandrovich) Pervye shagi sotsialisticheskikh preobrazovaniĭ v sel'skom khozîaĭstve Severo-Zapada RSFSR, 1917-1929 gg. : deîatel'nost' Leningradskoĭ partiĭnoĭ organizatsii po osushchetvleniîu leninskogo kooperativnogo plana na pervom ego ètape / V.A. Seleznev, V.A. Smyshlîaev. Leningrad : Izd-vo Leningradskogo universiteta, 1983. 198 p. ; 22 cm. At head of title: Leningradskiĭ ordena Lenina i ordena Trudovogo Krasnogo Znameni gosudarstvennyĭ universitet imeni A.A. Zhdanova. Includes bibliographical references. LC Card 83-197523
1. Collectivization of agriculture - Russian S.F.S.R. - History. 2. Agriculture - Economic aspects - Russian S.F.S.R. - History. 3. Soviet Union - Economic policy - 1917-1928. I. Smyshlîaev, Valentin Alekseevich.
HD1492.S652 R877 1983
*NYPL [*QIP 87-1327]*

Rapoport, ÎU. M. (ÎUriĭ Mikhaĭlovich) Osushchestvlenie èkonomicheskoĭ politiki Kommunisticheskoĭ partii v usloviîakh Evropeĭskogo Severa RSFSR, 1917-1925 gg. /. Leningrad , 1984. 216 p. ; LC Card 84-217989
HC336.9.N65 R36 1984

Self-council series.
Rogers, James E., 1945- Life insurance for Canadians . Vancouver, B.C. [1980] 84 p. : ISBN 0-88908-073-9 (pbk.) LC Card 81-131363
HG8773 .R63 1980

The self-defeating organization . Matejko, Alexander. New York , 1985. xxviii, 395 p. ; ISBN 0-03-005488-5 (alk. paper) : LC Card 85-9524 DDC 302.3/5 19
HD58.9 .M38 1985 *NYPL [JLE 86-2757]*

SELF-DEFENSE.
Bundy, Darcie. Total coverage . New York , c1987. xiv, 224 p. ; ISBN 0-06-055077-5 : LC Card 86-46050 DDC 368/.0029 19
HG8051 .B846 1987

Kelley, Clarence M. Security for you and your home-- . Blue Ridge Summit, Pa. , c1984. viii, 391 p. : ISBN 0-8306-0680-7 : LC Card 83-18134 DDC 643/.16 19
HV7431 .K44 1984 *NYPL [JSE 86-649]*

SELF-DESTRUCTION. see **SUICIDE.**

Self directed IRAs for the active investor /. Heerwagen, Peter D. Chicago, Ill. , c1987. x, 233 p. : ISBN 0-917253-61-2 (pbk.) : LC Card 86-25312 DDC 332.024/01 19
HG1660.A3 H44 1987

SELF-EMPLOYED.
Delany, George. The #1 home business book . Blue Ridge Summit, PA [1987] 168 p. : ISBN 0-8306-3022-8 (pbk.) : LC Card 87-2936 DDC 658/.041 19
HD8036 .D44 1987

Edwards, Paul. Working from home . Los Angeles , New York , c1987. xii, 436 p. : ISBN 0-87477-457-8 (pbk.) LC Card 87-10188 DDC 658/.041 19
HD62.5 .E39 1987

Harrod, Jeffrey. Power, production, and the unprotected worker /. New York , 1987. xviii, 347 p. ; ISBN 0-231-05844-6 (alk. paper) LC Card 86-26374 DDC 306/.36 19
HD6971 .H287 1987

Hicks, Tyler Gregory, 1921- How to start your own business on a shoestring and make up to $500,000 a year /. Rocklin, CA , New York , c1987. xi, 225 p. ; ISBN 0-914629-12-3 (pbk.) : LC Card 86-25196 DDC 658/.041 19
HD62.5 .H527 1987

Levinson, Jay Conrad. Quit your job! . New York , c1987. 216 p. ; ISBN 0-396-08882-1 LC Card 87-15545 DDC 650.1 19
HF5384 .L48 1987

Parson, Mary Jean. Managing the one-person business /. New York , 1987. xii, 274 p. ; ISBN 0-396-09149-0 (pbk.) : LC Card 87-20069 DDC 658/.022 19
HD8036 .P37 1987

SELF-EMPLOYED - ADDRESSES, ESSAYS, LECTURES.
Survival of the small firm /. Aldershot, Hants, England , Brookfield, Vt., U. S.A. , c1986. 2 v. : ISBN 0-566-00725-8 (v. 1) : LC Card 85-27035 DDC 338.6/42 19
HD2341 .S87 1986 *NYPL [JLD 86-2643]*

SELF-EMPLOYED - CANADA.
Self-employment in Canada =. Ottawa , c1985. 33 p. : ISBN 0-660-52868-1 (pbk.) : LC Card 87-101519
HD8037.C2 S45 1985

SELF-EMPLOYED - GERMANY, WEST.
Kornhardt, Ullrich. Entwicklungstendenzen im Konsumgüterhandwerk /. Göttingen , 1986. 385 p. : ISBN 3-509-01418-9 LC Card 86-197187
HD2341.A1 G6 Bd. 37 HD2346.G3

SELF-EMPLOYED - INDIA.
Bihar (India). Rural Development Dept. Trysem . [Paṭanā] , 1980. 41 p. ; LC Card 80-908290
HD6276.I42 B54 1980

SELF-EMPLOYED - INDIA - CONGRESSES.
Training of rural youth for self-employment (TRYSEM) . Hyderabad, [India] , 1981. vii, 252 p. ; LC Card 81-904606 DDC 331.3/42492/0954 19
HD5715.5.I5 T72 1981
NYPL [JLF 86-1203]

Workshop on Promotion of Self-Employment in Rural Areas (1982 : Allahabad, India) Workshop on Promotion of Self-employment in Rural Areas, Allahabad, 26-30 November 1982 . New Delhi [1983] iii, 186 p. ; LC Card 83-906671 DDC 338.6/42 19
HD8037.I4 W67 1982

SELF-EMPLOYED - PENSIONS - UNITED STATES.
Overview of current issues relating to single-employer defined benefit pension plans and Pension Benefit Guaranty Corporation (PBGC) premiums . Washington , 1987. iii, 49 p. ; LC Card 87-601357 DDC 331.25/2/0973 19
HD7125 .O88 1987

SELF-EMPLOYED - UNITED STATES.
Riehm, Sarah, 1952- The teenage enterpreneur's guide . Chicago, IL , c1987. viii, 211 p. : ISBN 0-940625-00-8 (pbk.) : LC Card 87-1904 DDC 658/.041 19
HD6273 .R53 1987

Silliphant, Leigh. Making $70,000 a year as a self-employed manufacturer's representative /. Englewood Cliffs, N.J. , c1984. 204 p. ; ISBN 0-13-547687-9 (case) LC Card 83-16147 DDC 658.8/5 19
HF5422 .S54 1984 *NYPL [JLE 86-2636]*

Self-employed women in the peri-urban setting . Adagala, Kavetsa. Nairobi , 1985. ii, 99 leaves : LC Card 85-980984 DDC 331.4/8138118/0967625 19
HF3893.Z9 N343 1985

SELF-EMPLOYED WOMEN - KENYA - NAIROBI.
Adagala, Kavetsa. Self-employed women in the peri-urban setting . Nairobi , 1985. ii, 99 leaves : LC Card 85-980984 DDC 331.4/8138118/0967625 19
HF3893.Z9 N343 1985

SELF-EMPLOYED WOMEN - UNITED STATES.
Bohigian, Valerie. Ladybucks /. New York, N.Y. , c1987. 246 p. ; ISBN 0-396-08852-X LC Card 86-29227 DDC 650.1/024042 19
HD6072.6.U5 B64 1987

Christensen, K. (Kathleen) Women and home-based work . New York , c1988. xv, 201 p. ; ISBN 0-8050-0386-X LC Card 87-8527 DDC 305.4/3 19
HD6072.6.U5 C47 1988

Costello, Cynthia B. (Cynthia Butler) Home-based employment . Washington, D.C. (1700 18th St., N.W., Washington 20009) , 1987. iii, 20 p. ; LC Card 87-403088 DDC 331.4/0973 19
HD2336.U5 C58 1987

Self-employment in Canada = Travail autonome au Canada. Ottawa : Minister of Supply and Services Canada, c1985. 33 p. : ill. ; 28 cm. (Research series = Série recherche . 45) English and French. At head of title: Labour Force Activity Section. "July 1985." Includes bibliographical references. "Catalogue 71-582." ISBN 0-660-52868-1 (pbk.) : LC Card 87-101519
1. Self-employed - Canada. I. Statistics Canada. Labour Force Activity Section. II. Title: Travail autonome au Canada. III. Series: Research series (Statistics Canada. Labour Force Activity Section) , 45.
HD8037.C2 S45 1985

SELF-GOVERNMENT. see **DEMOCRACY; REPRESENTATIVE GOVERNMENT AND REPRESENTATION.**

SELF-HELD HOUSING - MEXICO.
Ziss, Roland. Baumaterialien und Selbsthilfe . Saarbrücken , Fort Lauderdale, Fl. , 1986. 319 p. : ISBN 3-88156-333-4 LC Card 86-197177
HD7287.96.M6 Z57 1986

SELF-HELP HOUSING - BRAZIL - FINANCE.
Economia informal, tecnologia apropriada e associativismo /. São Paulo , 1986. 176 p. : LC Card 86-233370
HC190.P6 E34 1986

SELF-HELP HOUSING - CHILE.
Bustamante G., Jaime. Algunos antecedentes estadísticos sobre las organizaciones económicas populares /. Santiago, Chile , 1986. 23 p. ; LC Card 87-101323
HD2346.C53 B87 1986

Razeto M., Luis, 1945- Las organizaciones económicas populares en la nueva coyuntura económica /. Santiago, Chile , 1984. 23 p. ; LC Card 84-227565
HD2346.C53 R39 1984

SELF-HELP HOUSING - KENYA - CASE STUDIES.
Gatabaki-Kamau, Rose. Co-operative housing development in Kenya . Nairobi, Kenya [1985] vi leaves, 131 p. : LC Card 86-980648 DDC 334/.1/096762 19
HD7287.72.K4 G37 1985

SELF-HELP HOUSING - LATIN AMERICA.
Vivienda del Tercer Mundo . Bogotá , c1986. 94 p. : ISBN 958-9054-01-3 LC Card 86-224743
HD7305.5 .V58 1986

SELF-HELP HOUSING - LATIN AMERICA - CONGRESSES.
Habitat popular . Buenos Aires , 1986. 162 p. : LC Card 87-404028 DDC 363.5/8 19
HD7305.5 .H32 1986

SELF-HELP HOUSING - MEXICO.
Legorreta, Jorge. La autoconstrucción de vivienda en México . [México, D.F.] [1984] 204 p. : LC Card 86-232442
HD7306.A3 L44 1984

SELF-INSURANCE.
Risk management and retention . Monterey, Calif. (1 Mission Plaza, Monterey 93940) , c1986. v, 71 p. : LC Card 86-202599 DDC 658 19
HD61 .R569 1986

SELF-INTEREST.
Campbell, Colin, 1940- The romantic ethic and the spirit of modern consumerism /. Oxford, UK , New York, NY, USA , 1987. 301 p. ; ISBN 0-631-15539-2 : LC Card 86-30979 DDC 339.4/7 19
HC79.C6 C36 1987

Self-made women . Jennings, Diane. Dallas , c1987. 139 p. ; ISBN 0-87833-550-1 (pbk.) : LC Card 87-16104 DDC 338/.04/088042 19
HD6054.3 .J46 1987

SELF-OPTIMIZING SYSTEMS. see **SELF-ORGANIZING SYSTEMS.**

SELF-ORGANIZING SYSTEMS.
Ritter, Wigand. Qatar, ein arabisches Erdölemirat /. Nürnberg , 1985. 201 p. : LC Card 86-205396
HC415.37 .R58 1985

SELF-ORGANIZING SYSTEMS - CONGRESSES.
Proceedings of an international conference on genetic algorithms and their applications . [S.l. , 1985] 225 p. : *NYPL [JSF 87-413]*

SELF-PUBLISHING - DATA PROCESSING.
Cavuoto, James. LaserWrite it! . Reading, Mass. , 1986. viii, 198 p. : ISBN 0-201-11327-9 : LC Card 86-3406 DDC 070.5/028/5 19
Z286.E43 C38 1986 *NYPL [JSE 86-1226]*

Self-reliance and self-sufficiency . National Workshop on Self Reliance and Self Sufficiency in the Nigerian Economy (1978 : University of Ibadan) [Ibadan, Nigeria] , 1979. 156 p. : LC Card 87-402546 DDC 338.9669 19
HC1055 .N386 1978

SELF-SERCIE STORES.
Müller, Heinz, Dipl.-Kfm. Dr. Die Warenplazierung als absatzpolitisches Instrument im Selbstbedienungseinzelhandel /. Göttingen , 1982. 479 p. : ISBN 3-509-01287-9 LC Card 84-174456
HF5845 .M964 1982

SELF-SERVICE STORAGE FACILITIES - STANDARDS - UNITED STATES.
DeGroh, Teresa. Standards for self-service storage facilities /. Chicago, IL (1313 E. 60th St., Chicago 60637) , c1986. 22 p. : LC Card 86-227124 DDC 658.7/85 19
HF5487 .D44 1986

SELF-SUFFICIENCY, ECONOMIC. see **AUTARCHY.**

Selgin, George A., 1957- The theory of free banking : money supply under competitive note issue / George A. Selgin. Totowa, N.J. : Rowman & Littlefield, c1987. p. cm. Revision of the author's thesis (doctoral--New York University). Bibliography: p. Includes index. ISBN 0-8476-7578-5 : LC Card 87-20012 DDC 332.4 19
1. Banks and banking. 2. Money supply. 3. Monetary policy. 4. Banks and banking, Central. I. Title. II. Title: Free banking: Money supply under competitive note issue.
HG1586 .S38 1987

Seligman, Barnard. Choosing an investment company / Barnard Seligman. Cambridge, Mass. : Ballinger, c1987. xvii, 174 p. : ill. ; 24 cm. Includes bibliographies and index. ISBN 0-88730-094-4 LC Card 87-1437 DDC 332.6 19
1. Mutual funds - United States. 2. Portfolio management - United States. 3. Money market funds - United States. I. Title.
HG4930 .S45 1987

Seligson, Wendy. Rural housing in N.Y.S. / New York State Assembly, Committee on Housing. [Albany, N.Y.] : The Committee, [1979] [61] p. : ill. ; 28 cm. Cover title. LC Card 82-621690 DDC 363.5/8/09747 19
1. Housing, Rural - New York (State). 2. Housing policy - New York (State). I. New York (State). Legislature. Assembly. Standing Committee on Housing. II. Title. III. Title: Rural housing in New York State. IV. Title: Rural housing in NYS.
HD7289.U7 N77 1979 *NYPL [JLF 86-765]*

Selk, Michael, 1943- Geschlecht und Berufswahl : ein Beitrag zur Theoriebildung und empirischen Erfassung geschlechtsspezifischen Berufswahlverhaltens / Michael Selk. Frankfurt am Main ; New York : P. Lang, c1984. 289 p. : ill. ; 21 cm. (Europäische Hochschulschriften. Reihe XXII, Soziologie, 0721-3379 . Bd. 96 = vol. 96 = vol. 96) Bibliography: p. 220-229. ISBN 3-8204-5375-X LC Card 85-193055
1. Occupational training for women - Germany (West). 2. Vocational guidance for women - Germany, West. 3. Sex discrimination against women - Germany, West. I. Title.
HD6059.6.G4 S45 1984

Sell, Axel. Economic structure and development of Burma / Axel Sell. Bremen : Fachbereich Wirtschaftswissenschaft der Universität Bremen, [1985] 39 p. ; 21 cm. (Berichte aus dem Weltwirtschaftlichen Colloquium der Universität Bremen . Nr. 5) "June 1985." Bibliography: p. 37-38. LC Card 86-228833 DDC 338.9591 19
1. Burma - Economic conditions - 1948-. 2. Burma - Politics and government - 1948-. 3. Burma - Economic policy. I. Title. II. Series.
HC422 .S45 1985

Sell, Friedrich L. Der Konsumcharakter der Einkommensentstehung : zur Interdependenz von Konsum- und Multiplikatortheorie / Friedrich L. Sell. Freiburg im Breisgau : R. Haufe, c1982. 221 p. : 22 ill. ; 21 cm. (Bd. 16 der Schriftenreihe des Instituts für Allgemeine Wirtschaftsforschung der Albert-Ludwigs-Universität Freiburg i. Br) Includes index. Bibliography: p. 213-218. ISBN 3-448-01269-6 LC Card 82-233541 DDC 339.4/7/0724 19
1. Consumption (Economics) - Mathematical models. 2. Multiplier (Economics). 3. Income - Mathematical models. I. Series: Freiburg i. B. Universität. Institut für Allgemeine Wirtschaftsforschung. Schriftenreihe, Bd. 16. II. Title.
HB820 .S44 1982 *NYPL [JLD 87-1580]*

Sell it by mail . Lumley, James E. A. New York , c1986. xviii, 382 p. : ISBN 0-471-87908-8 : LC Card 85-16362 DDC 658.8/4 19
HF5466 .L85 1986 *NYPL [JLE 86-3044]*

Sell your own home! . Boroson, Warren. Tucson, AZ , c1987. 238 p. : ISBN 0-89586-571-8 LC Card 87-4020 DDC 333.33/8 19
HD1379 .B645 1987

Sellars, David. Role playing the principles of selling : college and university edition / David Sellars III. Chicago : Dryden Press, c1987. xiii, 102 p. ; 28 cm. + 1 sound cassette (60 min.) ISBN 0-03-013048-4 (pbk.) LC Card 86-24073 DDC 658.8/5/071173 19
1. Selling - Study and teaching. 2. Role playing. I. Title.
HF5438.2 .S45 1987

Selleri, Luigi. L'Industria siderurgica . Milano [1986] 193 p. : ISBN 88-14-00787-X : LC Card 86-222572
HD9510.5 .I473 1986

Sellers & servants . Bunster, Ximena. New York , 1985. x, 258 p. : ISBN 0-03-060543-1 (alk. paper) : LC Card 85-6259 DDC 331.4/0985/25 19
HD6072.2.P42 L563 1985
NYPL [JLE 86-910]

Sellers and servants. Bunster, Ximena. Sellers & servants . New York , 1985. x, 258 p. : ISBN 0-03-060543-1 (alk. paper) : LC Card 85-6259 DDC 331.4/0985/25 19
HD6072.2.P42 L563 1985
NYPL [JLE 86-910]

Selles, G. (Gert) Mid career crisis / G. Selles, J. Gerrichhauzen en Ch.J. de Wolff. Deventer : Van Loghum Slaterus, [1985?] 135 p. : ill. ; 21 cm. In Dutch. Bibliography: p. 130-135. ISBN 90-6001-934-2 LC Card 86-163138
1. Career changes. 2. Age and employment. 3. Executives - Psychology. 4. Middle age - Psychological aspects. I. Gerrichhauzen, J. (John). II. Wolff, Charles J. de (Charles Johannes). III. Title.
HF5384 .S45 1985

Selling . Pederson, Carlton A. Homewood, Ill. , 1988. xvii, 644 p. : ISBN 0-256-03644-6 LC Card 87-81434 DDC 658.8/5 19
HF5438.25 .P42 1988

SELLING - AUTOMOBILES.
Hudson, Adams, 1958- How to buy or sell a car by long distance /. Osceola, Wis. , 1987. 80 p. ; ISBN 0-87938-259-7 (soft) LC Card 87-12185 DDC 629.2/222 19
HF5439.A8 H83 1987

SELLING - CASE STUDIES.
Gschwandtner, Gerhard. Supersellers . New York, N.Y. , c1986. xi, 169 p. : ISBN 0-8144-5883-1 LC Card 86-47586 DDC 658.8/5 19
HF5438.25 .G785 1986
NYPL [JLE 87-1489]

SELLING - COMPUTER PROGRAMS.
Crittenden, Vicky L. Jazz . Reading, Mass. , c1986. 62 p. : ISBN 0-201-11365-1 (pbk.) LC Card 86-211796 DDC 658.8/0028/55369 19
HF5439.C67 C75 1986

SELLING - CONGRESSES.
Hermesiade . Essen , c1986. 182 p. ; ISBN 3-89206-143-2 LC Card 86-226901 DDC 658.8/2 19
HF5438.5 .H47 1986

SELLING - DATA PROCESSING.
Collins, Rip, 1947- Double your sales commission using a personal computer /. Dubuque, Iowa , c1986. ix, 155 p. ; ISBN 0-697-00802-9 (pbk.) : LC Card 85-71486 DDC 658.8/1/00285536 19
HF5438.35 .C65 1986 *NYPL [JLE 86-1773]*

Wallis, Louis A. Computers and the sales effort . New York, N.Y. , c1986. v, 26 p. : ISBN 0-8237-0326-6 (pbk.) LC Card 87-404503 DDC 658.8/1/00285416 19
HF5438.35 .W35 1986

SELLING, DIRECT. see **DIRECT SELLING.**

Selling dreams : how advertising misleads us. Penang, Malaysia : Consumers' Association of Penang, c1986. 149 p. : ill. ; 22 cm. Includes bibliographies. ISBN 967-99502-0-4 (pbk.) LC Card 87-940287 DDC 659.1 19
1. Advertising - Psychological aspects. 2. Advertising, Fraudulent. 3. Women in advertising - Malaysia. 4. Children in advertising - Malaysia. 5. Advertising laws - Malaysia. I. Consumers Association of Penang.
HF5823 .S46 1986

SELLING - HANDICRAFT.
Long, Steve. Marketing your arts & crafts . Sandpoint, Idaho (9395 Rapid Lightning Rd., Sandpoint 83864) [c1987] iv, 188 p. : LC Card 87-401972 DDC 745.5/068/8 19
HF5439.H27 L66 1987

Smith, Allan H. How to sell your homemade creation /. Lake Park, Fla. , 1986 printing, c1985. 146 p. : ISBN 0-931113-02-4 (pbk.) : LC Card 84-52239 DDC 745.5/068/8 19
HF5439.H27 S64 1986

SELLING - HOUSEHOLD ELECTRONICS.
Adler, Stan. The magic sell . Costa Mesa, Calif. , c1986. 160 p. ; ISBN 0-937359-03-3 : LC Card 87-111850 DDC 683/.83/0688 19
HF5439.H8 A36 1986

SELLING - INDUSTRIAL EQUIPMENT - MANAGEMENT.
Rudolphi, Michael, 1948- Aussendienststeuerung im Investitionsgütermarketing . Frankfurt am Main , c1981. xi, 445 p. : ISBN 3-8204-6125-6 : LC Card 81-111119
HF5439.I4 R83 1981

SELLING - KEY ACCOUNTS.
Webster, Bryce. The power of consultative selling /. Englewood Cliffs, N.J. , c1987. xvi, 200 p. ; ISBN 0-13-685918-6 LC Card 87-2251 DDC 658.8/1 19
HF5438.25 .W287 1987

SELLING - MATHEMATICAL MODELS.
Hu, Sheng C. A game-theoretic approach to the design of an optimal sales policy /. West Lafayette, Ind. [1986] 30, 14 p. : LC Card 86-622755 DDC 658/.001/9 s 658.8/101 19
HD6483 .P8 no. 900 HF5438.25

Selling money /. Gwynne, S. C. (Samuel C.), 1953- New York , 1987, c1986. 182 p. ; ISBN 0-14-010282-5 (pbk.) LC Card 87-6969 DDC 336.3/435 19
HG3891.5 .G98 1987

The selling of British Telecom /. Newman, Karin. London , New York , c1986. viii, 176 p. : ISBN 0-03-910639-X *NYPL [JLF 86-853]*

Selling out the family farm . Ambur, Owen D. Washington , 1986. v, 40 p. : LC Card 87-601379 DDC 338.1/6 19
HD1476.U5 A65 1986

SELLING - PSYCHOLOGICAL ASPECTS.
Bel'chikov, I͡A. M. Prodavet͡s i Pokupatel', ili rasskaz o tom, kakimi mogli by stat' ikh otnoshenii͡a, bud' ri͡adom Psikholog /. Riga , 1986. 157, [3] p. : LC Card 87-129915
HF5438.8.P75 B45 1986

Marks, Ronald B., 1944- Personal selling . Boston , c1988. xvi, 607 p. : ISBN 0-205-11087-8 LC Card 87-16098 DDC 658.8/5 19
HF5438.25 .M37 1988

Robertson, James E., 1944- Sales, the whole body approach /. Portland, Or. , 1988. p. cm. ISBN 0-943920-78-7 : LC Card 87-24679 DDC 658.8/5 19
HF5438.8.P75 R63 1988

SELLING - STUDY AND TEACHING.
Sellars, David. Role playing the principles of selling . Chicago , c1987. xiii, 102 p. ; ISBN 0-03-013048-4 (pbk.) LC Card 86-24073 DDC 658.8/5/071173 19
HF5438.2 .S45 1987

Selling the rope to hang capitalism? : the debate

on West-East trade & technology transfer / edited by Charles M. Perry and Robert L. Pfaltzgraff, Jr.1st ed. Washington : Pergamon-Brassey's, 1987. viii, 246 p. ; 24 cm. "A joint publication of the International Security Studies Program, the Fletcher School of Law and Diplomacy, Tufts University, and the Institute for Foreign Policy Analysis, Inc., Cambridge, Massachusetts and Washington, D.C." Includes bibliographies and index. ISBN 0-08-034959-5 : LC Card 86-30401 DDC 382/.091713/01717 19
1. East-West trade (1945-). 2. Technology transfer - Soviet Union. 3. Technology transfer - United States. I. Perry, Charles M. II. Pfaltzgraff, Robert L. III. Fletcher School of Law and Diplomacy. International Security Studies Program. IV. Institute for Foreign Policy Analysis.
HF1412 .S45 1987

Selling through negotiation . Smith, Homer B., 1915- Alexandria, VA , c1987. 192 p. ; ISBN 0-9618228-1-3 (soft) : LC Card 87-10998 DDC 658.8/1 19
HF5438.25 .S64 1987

SELLING - VOCATIONAL GUIDANCE.
Marks, Ronald B., 1944- Personal selling . Boston , c1988. xvi, 607 p. : ISBN 0-205-11087-8 LC Card 87-16098 DDC 658.8/5 19
HF5438.25 .M37 1988

Selling your home for the best price in the shortest time : a comprehensive sales strategy and plan / prepared especially for John R. and Mary L. Smith by Ralph Ebetts in conjunction with Tom Smith. [Norwell, Mass.] : Relocation Resources, c1986. 48 leaves : ill. ; 29 cm. Fictitious home sales plan. "March 12, 1987." LC Card 87-150628 DDC 333.33/8 19
1. House selling. I. Relocation Resources (Firm).
HD1379 .S36 1986

Selling your house without a broker . Chaney, Dale. Chicago , c1986. 98 p. : ISBN 0-8092-4833-6 (pbk.) : LC Card 86-24043 DDC 333.33/8 19
HD1379 .C48 1986

Selnow, Gary W. Planning, implementing, and evaluating targeted communication programs : a manual for business communicators / Gary W. Selnow and William D. Crano. New York : Quorum Books, 1987. vi, 291 p. : ill. ; 24 cm. Includes bibliographies and index. ISBN 0-89930-208-4 (lib. bdg. : alk. paper) LC Card 86-30418 DDC 659.1 19
1. Communication in management - United States. 2. Mass media - United States - Audiences. 3. Advertising media planning - United States. I. Crano, William D., 1942-. II. Title.
HD30.3 .S46 1987

Sel'skaia͡ intelligentsiia͡ v gody Velikoĭ Otechestvennoĭ voĭny . Main, V. N. (Valentin Nikolaevich) Voronezh , 1985. 158 p. ; LC Card 84-172657
HC340.D4 M35 1985

Sel'skaia͡ obshchina v Severnoĭ Indii . Alaev, L. B. Moskva , 1981. 240 p. ; LC Card 82-101919
HD873 .A63 1981

Sel'skie kadry nechernozem'ia͡ /. Smekalov, Pavel Vasil'evich. Moskva , 1981. 190 p. ; LC Card 82-177714
HD1536.S65 S64 1981

Sel'skoe khoziaĭstvo v odinnadtsatoĭ piatiletke . Borchenko, N. (Nikolaĭ) Moskva , 1981. 93 p. ; LC Card 81-188371
HD1493.R9 B5 1981, no. 5 HD9015.S65

Seltz, David D.
Expanding your business with other people's money / David D. Seltz. New York, N.Y. : Boardroom Books, c1984. 2 v. in 1 : ill. ; 30 cm. Includes indexes. ISBN 0-932648-29-0 LC Card 83-12233 DDC 658.8/708 19
1. Franchises (Retail trade) - United States. 2. Franchises (Retail trade) - Law and legislation - United States. I. Title.
HF5429.235.U5 S442 1984
NYPL [JLF 86-664]

A handbook of retail promotion ideas / by David D. Seltz. Rockville Centre, N.Y. : Farnsworth Pub. Co., c1985. 256 p. ; 29 cm. Includes index. ISBN 0-87863-220-4 LC Card 84-25969 DDC 658.8/2 19
1. Sales promotion. 2. Small business. I. Title.
HF5438.5 .S45 1985 ***NYPL [JLF 86-1789]***

Seltz, Rüdiger. Organisation als soziales System . Berlin , c1986. 219 p. ; ISBN 3-924859-22-1 LC Card 87-137969 DDC 302.3/5 19
HD58.7 .O6687 1986

Selva adentro . Molano, Alfredo. Bogotá , 1987. 142 p. : ISBN 958-9012-02-7 LC Card 87-404301 DDC 986.1/65 19
HD519.G8 M65 1987

Selvig, Erling. Prosjektfinansiering i petroleumsvirksomheten / Erling Selvig. Oslo : Nordisk institutt for sjørett, [1983] 30, 5 p. ; 21 cm. (Marius, 0332-7868 . nr. 79) "Mars 1983." Includes bibliographical references. LC Card 84-131887
1. Petroleum industry and trade - Norway - Finance. 2. Petroleum law and legislation - Norway. I. Title. II. Series.
HD9575.N62 S44 1983

Selvityksiä ja raportteja, 0782-5277 .
(n:o 5) Pihkala, Erkki. Toisen maailmansodan aikaisesta huoltotasosta Suomessa ja analogioista 1980-luvun alun tilanteeseen /. [Helsinki] , 1986. 49 leaves ; ISBN 951-46-9497-X LC Card 86-221750
HC340.2 .P54 1986

Semana Josué de Castro e a nova geografia da fome, Rio de Janeiro, 19-24 de setembro de 1983 : aspectos da vida e da obra de Josué de Castro. [S.l. : s.n., 1983] 90 leaves : ill. ; 34 cm. Cover title. Bibliography: p. 62. LC Card 86-201115
1. Food supply. 2. Hunger. 3. Castro, Josuéde, 1908-1973. 4. Economists - Brazil - Biography. 5. Sociologists - Brazil - Biography. 6. Diplomats - Brazil - Biography. 7. Developing country specialists - Brazil - Biography.
HD9000.5 .S3968 1983

Sembajwe, I. S. L. (Israel Serwano Lubwama), 1947- Urban population growth rates in Africa with special reference to Lesotho / by Israel Sembajwe. [Roma, Lesotho] : Demography Unit, Dept. of Statistics, National University of Lesotho, [1985] 31 leaves : ill. ; 29 cm. (Working papers in demography . working paper no. 4) Cover title. "September 1985." Bibliography: leaves 28-31. LC Card 87-132328 DDC 307.2 19
1. Lesotho - Population. 2. Africa - Population. 3. Urbanization - Lesotho. 4. Urbanization - Africa. 5. Rural-urban migration - Lesotho. 6. Rural-urban migration - Africa. I. Series: Working papers in demography (National University of Lesotho. Dept. of Statistics. Demography Unit) , working paper no. 4. II. Title.
HB3663.7.A3 S46 1985

"Sēmeiōmata" Hellēnikōn kōdikōn hōs pēgē dia tēn ereunan tou oikonomikou kai koinōnikou viou tou Vyzantiou, apo tou 9ou aiōnos mechri tou etous 1204 /. Euangelatou-Notara, Phlōrentia. Athēnai , 1982. 296 p. ; LC Card 86-212063
HC294 .E9 1982

Semenov, A. I.
Marek, A. I. (Aleksandr Isaevich) Nauchno-proizvodstvennye kompleksy . Moskva , 1985. 141, [3] p. : LC Card 86-118921
HC340.R4 M37 1985

Sulitskiĭ, V. N. (Vladimir Nikolaevich) Organizatsionno-ėkonomicheskie problemy upravleniia͡ kadrami v otrasli /. Moskva , 1986. 164, [3] p. : LC Card 86-233362
HF5549.2.S65 S85 1986

SEMI-CONDUCTOR DEVICES. see **SEMICONDUCTORS.**

SEMI-CONDUCTORS. see **SEMICONDUCTORS.**

Sem'ia͡ i vosproizvodstvo struktury trudovoĭ zaniatosti : opyt sotsiologicheskogo issledovaniia͡ / [avtory V.F. Chernovolenko ... et al. ; otvetstvennyĭ redaktor V.F. Chernovolenko]. Kiev : Nauk. dumka, 1984. 238 p. : ill. ; 21 cm. At head of title: Akademiia͡ nauk Ukrainskoĭ SSR. Institut filosofii. Includes bibliographical references. LC Card 86-142706
1. Ukraine - Occupations - Case studies. 2. Kiev (Ukraine) - Occupations. 3. Labor supply - Ukraine - Kiev. 4. Labor mobility - Ukraine - Kiev. I. Chernovolenko, V. F. (Vilen Filippovich). II. Instytut filosofiï (Akademiia͡ nauk Ukraïns'koï RSR).
HB2698.U38 S46 1984

SEMICONDUCTING MATERIALS. see **SEMICONDUCTORS.**

The Semiconductor assembly equipment market in the U. S. New York, N.Y. : Frost & Sullivan, c1983. viii, 326 p. ; 29 cm. "March 1983." "(#A1085)." LC Card 87-141854 DDC 381/.4562138152 19
1. Semiconductor production equipment industry - United States. 2. Market surveys - United States. I. Frost & Sullivan.
HD9696.S43 U4955 1983

The Semiconductor industry. New York, N.Y. (500 5th Ave., New York 10110) : Find/SVP, c1984. 1 v. (various foliations) : ill. ; 29 cm. (A Business information report) Includes bibliography. LC Card 86-203040 DDC 338.4/762138152 19
1. Semiconductor industry. 2. Semiconductor industry - United States. 3. Semiconductor industry - Japan. I. Find/SVP (Firm). II. Series.
HD9696.S42 S375 1984

SEMICONDUCTOR INDUSTRY.
The Semiconductor industry. New York, N.Y. (500 5th Ave., New York 10110) , c1984. 1 v. (various foliations) : LC Card 86-203040 DDC 338.4/762138152 19
HD9696.S42 S375 1984

SEMICONDUCTOR INDUSTRY - CALIFORNIA - SANTA CLARA COUNTY - HISTORY.
Caddes, Carolyn, 1935- Portraits of success . Palo Alto, Calif. , 1986. viii, 138 p. : ISBN 0-935382-56-9 : LC Card 86-40032 DDC 338.4/7621/0979473 19
HD9696.A3 U53173 1986
NYPL [MFX (Caddes) 87-542]

SEMICONDUCTOR INDUSTRY - JAPAN.
The Semiconductor industry. New York, N.Y. (500 5th Ave., New York 10110) , c1984. 1 v. (various foliations) : LC Card 86-203040 DDC 338.4/762138152 19
HD9696.S42 S375 1984

SEMICONDUCTOR INDUSTRY - UNITED STATES.
Consolidated data base . San Jose, Calif. (1290 Ridder Park Dr., San Jose 95131-2398) , c1986. ii, 94 p. ; LC Card 87-108611 DDC 381/.45004/0973
HD9696.C63 U515626 1986

New materials for new semiconductors /. Stamford, Conn., U. S.A. , c1986. xii, 198 leaves : ISBN 0-89336-475-4 (soft) LC Card 87-404262 DDC 381/.4562138152/0973 19
HD9696.S43 U492 1986

The Semiconductor industry. New York, N.Y. (500 5th Ave., New York 10110) , c1984. 1 v. (various foliations) : LC Card 86-203040 DDC 338.4/762138152 19
HD9696.S42 S375 1984

The Semiconductor market in the U. S. New York, N.Y. , c1983. v, 207 p. : LC Card 87-143827 DDC 381/.4562138152/0973 19
HD9696.S43 U496 1983

The Semiconductor market in the U. S. New York, N.Y. : Frost & Sullivan, c1983. v, 207 p. : ill. ; 29 cm. "October 1983." "#A1225." LC Card 87-143827 DDC 381/.4562138152/0973 19
1. Semiconductor industry - United States. I. Frost & Sullivan. II. Title: Semiconductor market in the US.
HD9696.S43 U496 1983

Semiconductor market in the US. The Semiconductor market in the U. S. New York, N.Y. , c1983. v, 207 p. : LC Card 87-143827 DDC 381/.4562138152/0973 19
HD9696.S43 U496 1983

SEMICONDUCTOR PRODUCTION EQUIPMENT INDUSTRY - UNITED STATES.
The Semiconductor assembly equipment market in the U. S. New York, N.Y. , c1983. viii, 326 p. ; LC Card 87-141854 DDC 381/.4562138152 19
HD9696.S43 U4955 1983

SEMICONDUCTORS - CLEANING - EQUIPMENT AND SUPPLIES.
Cleaning and contaminant monitoring systems for the semiconductor industry . San Jose, CA (1754 Technology Dr., Suite 226, San Jose 95110) , c1986. 1 v. (various pagings) : LC Card 87-114689 DDC 380.1/4562138152
HD9999.C4862 C55 1986

SEMICONDUCTORS, COMPLEMENTARY METAL OXIDE. see **METAL OXIDE**

SEMICONDUCTORS, COMPLEMENTARY.

Séminaire de formation aux techniques d'élaboration de projets . Séminaire de formation aux techniques d'élaboration de projets (1980 : Conakry, Guinea, etc.) Addis-Abeba , 1982. vii, 36, [31] p. : LC Card 86-168821
HC800 .S444 1980

Séminaire de formation aux techniques d'élaboration de projets (1980 : Conakry, Guinea, etc.) Séminaire de formation aux techniques d'élaboration de projets : Conakry-Guinée, Abidjan-Côte d'Ivoire, Bamako-Mali, 1980. Addis-Abeba : Nations Unies, Commission économique pour l'Afrique, 1982. vii, 36, [31] p. : ill. ; 28 cm. (Série Rapports de séminaires) Cover title: Rapport. Sponsored by the African Training and Research Centre for Women and the Economic Commission for Africa of the United Nations. "ST/ECA/ATRCW/82/18." LC Card 86-168821
1. Economic development-projects - Africa - Congresses. 2. Women in rural development - Africa - Congresses. 3. Rural development projects - Africa - Congresses. I. African Training and Research Centre for Women. II. United Nations. Economic Commission for Africa. III. Title. IV. Series.
HC800 .S444 1980

Séminaire international sur la place des femmes dans l'autosuffisance et les stratégies alimentaires (1985 : Paris, France) Femmes et politiques alimentaires : actes du Séminaire international sur la place des femmes dans l'autosuffisance et les stratégies alimentaires : O.R.S.T.O.M.-C.I.E., 14-18 janvier 1985, Paris / [organisé sous la responsabilité de Jeanne Bisilliat ; actes publiés sous la responsabilité ... Jeanne Bisilliat ... et al.]. Paris : Editions de l'ORSTOM, Institut français de recherche scientifique pour le développement en coopération, 1985. 741 p. : ill. ; 24 cm. (Collection Colloques et séminaires) English and French. Summaries in English and French. Includes bibliographies and indexes. ISBN 2-7099-0763-1 LC Card 86-205282
1. Women in agriculture - Developing countries - Congresses. 2. Food supply - Developing countries - Congresses. 3. Women in development - Developing countries - Congresses. I. Bisilliat, Jeanne. II. Series: Collection Colloques et séminaires (O.R.S.T.O.M. (Agency : France)). III. Title.
HD6073.A292 D4477 1985

Seminar-cum-Study Tour on Port Development Policy (1984 : Yokohama-shi, Japan) Port development policy . Bangkok, Thailand , 1985. ix, 83 p. : LC Card 87-106926 DDC 387.1/0952 19
HE559.J3 P653 1985

Seminar "Development: Socio-cultural Dimensions" (1982 : Dept. of Sociology, Panjab University) Development, socio-cultural dimensions /. Jaipur , 1986. xxi, 264 p. ; ISBN 81-7033-020-3 : LC Card 86-902849 DDC 306/.0954 19
HC435.2 .D478 1986

Seminar Etika Pembangunan Dalam Pemikiran Islam (1985 : Yogyakarta, Indonesia) Etika pembangunan dalam pemikiran Islam di Indonesia /. Jakarta , 1986. xi, 270 p. ; ISBN 979-421-043-9 (pbk.) LC Card 86-946413
HC447 .E78 1986

Seminar für Interkulturelle Kommunikation (1986 : Universität Freiburg) Werbung in einem mehrsprachigen Land /. Freiburg, Schweiz , c1986. 152 p. : ISBN 3-7278-0382-7 LC Card 87-409238 DDC 659.1/09494 19
HF5808.S9 W47 1986

Seminar "Malaysian Agriculture--What Next?" (1985 : Kuala Lumpur, Malaysia) Options for Malaysian agriculture : proceedings of the Seminar "Malaysian Agriculture--what next?," held in Kuala Lumpur from 16 to 17 December, 1985 / organized by the Agricultural Institute of Malaysia ; edited by Wong Kai Choo ... [et al.]. [Kuala Lumpur] : Agricultural Institute of Malaysia, 1986. xxiv, 203 p. : ill. ; 30 cm. Includes speeches in Malay. Includes bibliographies. ISBN 967-99982-0-7 (pbk.) LC Card 86-943314 DDC 338.1/8595 19
1. Agriculture and state - Malaysia - Congresses. I. Wong, Kai Choo. II. Agricultural Institute of Malaysia. III. Title.
HD2080.6.Z8 S45 1985

Seminar material for understanding and using financial statements /. Chalfin, Robert J. Newark, N.J. (15 Washington St., Newark 07102) , c1987. 95, [43] leaves ; LC Card 87-402010 DDC 657/.33/024344 19
HF5681.B2 C415 1987

Seminar on Below-the-Line and Sponsoring . Seminar on Below-the-Line and Sponsoring (1985 : Milan, Italy) Amsterdam, Netherlands [1985] vi, 270 p. : ISBN 92-831-1107-9 (pbk.) : LC Card 86-213125 DDC 658.8/2 19
HF5438.5 .S46 1985

Seminar on Below-the-Line and Sponsoring (1985 : Milan, Italy) Seminar on Below-the-Line and Sponsoring : the use of promotion and sponsorship in the marketing mix, Milan, Italy, 6th-8th November 1985. Amsterdam, Netherlands : ESOMAR, [1985] vi, 270 p. : ill. ; 23 cm. Includes bibliographical references. ISBN 92-831-1107-9 (pbk.) : LC Card 86-213125 DDC 658.8/2 19
1. Sales promotion - Congresses. 2. Advertising - Congresses. 3. Marketing - Congresses. I. Title. II. Title: Sponsorship in the marketing mix.
HF5438.5 .S46 1985

Seminar on Canadian-United States Relations (1984-1985 : Harvard University Center for International Affairs) Land rites and wrongs . Boston , 1988. p. cm. ISBN 0-89946-222-7 LC Card 87-12186 DDC 333.73/13/0971 19
HD171.A15 L28 1988

Seminar on Career Planning in Bangladesh (1985 : Bangladesh Public Administration Training Centre) Career planning in Bangladesh . Dhaka , c1986. 159 p. ; LC Card 86-903477 DDC 331.7/02/095492 19
HF5382.5.B27 C37 1986

Seminar on Economic Development of the Volta Region (1983 : Ho, Ghana) The Volta Region : plans, projects, and prospects : proceedings of the Seminar on Economic Development of the Volta Region, December 5-9, 1983 / compiled by N.D. Sodzi. Accra : Published for the Volta Regional Administration, Ho, by BOARDPUB, c1986. iii, 140 p., [13] leaves of plates : ill. ; 24 cm. ISBN 996-497-032-3 LC Card 87-402835 DDC 338.9667 19
1. Volta Region (Ghana) - Economic policy - Congresses. 2. Economic development projects - Ghana - Volta Region - Congresses. 3. Infrastructure (Economics) - Ghana - Volta Region - Congresses. I. Sodzi, N. D. (Nathan D.). II. Title.
HC1060.Z7 V647 1983

Seminar on Economic Integration (1982 : Inter-American Development Bank) The economic integration process of Latin America in the 1980's : papers presented at a seminar / sponsored by the Inter-American Development Bank, September, 22-23, 1982 ; edited by José Núñez del Arco, Eduardo Margain, Rachelle Cherol. Washington, D.C. : Available from The Bank, [1984] 318 p. : ill. ; 23 cm. "Inter-American Development Bank, Institute for Latin American Integration"--Cover. "January 1984." Includes bibliographies. ISBN 0-940602-17-2 (pbk.) LC Card 87-159367
1. Latin America - Economic integration - Congresses. I. Núñez del Arco, José. II. Margain, Eduardo. III. Cherol, Rachelle. IV. Inter-American Development Bank. V. Institute for Latin American Integration. VI. Title.
HC125 .S3973 1982

Seminar on "Government Media and the Public Sector" (1983 : New Delhi, India) Government media and the public sector . New Delhi , 1983. 270 p. ; LC Card 83-907479 DDC 302.3/24/0954 19
HD59 .G62 1983 *NYPL [JLD 86-3767]*

Seminar on "Growth and Modernisation of Fertiliser Industry" (1986 : New Delhi, India) Growth and modernisation of fertiliser industry . New Delhi , 1987. 1 v. (various pagings) : LC Card 87-902183 DDC 338.4/766862/0954 19
HD9483.I42 G78 1987

Seminar on Growth of Pakistani Banking at Home & Abroad (1982 : Peshawar, Pakistan) Growth of Pakistani banking : proceedings of a seminar on growth of Pakistani banking at home and abroad, held at Peshawar June 20, 1982 / Produced by Research & Planning Division, Muslim Commercial Bank. Karachi : Research and Planning Division, MCB, 1982. 26 p. ; 24 cm. LC Card 83-931177 DDC 332.1/09549/1 19
1. Banks and banking - Pakistan - Congresses. 2. Banks and banking, Pakistani - Congresses. I. Muslim Commercial Bank. Research & Planning Division. II. Title.
HG3290.5.A6 S46 1982
NYPL [JLE 86-4582]

Seminar on Human Resources Development in the Arabian Gulf States. Nadwat Tanmiyat al-Mawārid al-Basharīyah fī al-Khalīj al-'Arabī (1975 : Bahrain) Nadwat Tanmiyat al-Mawārid al-Basharīyah fī al-Khalīj al-'Arabī . al-Kuwayt [1975?] 361, 404 p. : LC Card 86-964662
HD5715.5.P39 N33 1975

Seminar on Innovative Approaches to Projecting Migration for Integrated Rural and Urban Development Planning (1978 : Oulu, Finland) Projecting migration for integrated rural and urban development planning. Liege, Belgium , c1980. 46 p. ; LC Card 84-221919 DDC 304.8 19
HB1952 .P76 1980
NYPL [JLL 77-289 no. 16]

Seminar on Investment Policies of Arab Oil Producing Countries, 18-20 February 1974, Kuwait /. Seminar on Investment Policies of Arab Oil Producing Countries (1974 : Kuwait, Kuwait) [Kuwait] [1974?] 216 p. ; LC Card 87-400750 DDC 332.6/7353 19
HG5816.A3 S46 1974

Seminar on Investment Policies of Arab Oil Producing Countries (1974 : Kuwait, Kuwait) Seminar on Investment Policies of Arab Oil Producing Countries, 18-20 February 1974, Kuwait / the Arab Planning Institute, Kuwait Economic Society. [Kuwait] : The Institute, [1974?] 216 p. ; 27 cm. Includes bibliographical references. LC Card 87-400750 DDC 332.6/7353 19
1. Investments - Arab countries - Congresses. 2. Investments, Arab - Congresses. I. Arab Planning Institute. II. Jam'īyah al-Iqtiṣādīyah al-Kuwaytīyah. III. Title.
HG5816.A3 S46 1974

Seminar on Macroeconomic Modelling in the Nordic Countries (1984 : Fredriksdal, Lyngby, Denmark) Macroeconomic medium-term models in the Nordic countries /. Amsterdam ; New York : x, 324 p. : ISBN 0-444-70262-8 (U. S.) LC Card 87-13422 DDC 330.948/00724 19
HC345 .M33 1987

Seminar on Problem Solving in Idustrial Marketing, Lucerne (Switzerland) 26th-28th February 1986. Seminar on Problem Solving in Industrial Marketing (1986 : Lucerne, Switzerland) Amsterdam, Netherlands [1986] iv, 179 p. : ISBN 92-831-1111-7 (pbk.) : LC Card 86-213119 DDC 658.8 19
HF5415 .S3687 1986

Seminar on Problem Solving in Industrial Marketing (1986 : Lucerne, Switzerland) Seminar on Problem Solving in Idustrial Marketing, Lucerne (Switzerland) 26th-28th February 1986. Amsterdam, Netherlands : ESOMAR, [1986] iv, 179 p. : ill. ; 23 cm. Includes bibliographies. ISBN 92-831-1111-7 (pbk.) : LC Card 86-213119 DDC 658.8 19
1. Industrial marketing - Congresses. 2. Industrial marketing - Research - Congresses. I. Esomar. II. Title. III. Title: Problem solving in industrial marketing.
HF5415 .S3687 1986

Seminar on Problems of Urban Unemployment (1979 : Rabindra Bharati University) Problems of urban unemployment. Calcutta , 1981. ix, 114 p. ; LC Card 83-907262 DDC 331.13/77/0954 19
HD5819 .P76 1981 *NYPL [JLF 86-1766]*

Seminar on Retail Strategies for Profit and Growth . Seminar on Retail Strategies for Profit and Growth (1986 : Brussels, Belgium) Amsterdam, Netherlands [1986] vi, 324 p. : ISBN 92-831-1113-3 (pbk.) : LC Card 86-218316 DDC 658.8/7/0094 19
HF5429.6.E9 S45 1986

Seminar on Retail Strategies for Profit and Growth (1986 : Brussels, Belgium) Seminar on Retail Strategies for Profit and Growth : Brussels, Belgium, 4th-6th June 1986. Amsterdam, Netherlands : ESOMAR, [1986] vi, 324 p. : ill. ; 23 cm. Includes bibliographies. ISBN 92-831-1113-3 (pbk.) : LC Card 86-218316 DDC 658.8/7/0094 19
1. Retail trade - Europe - Congresses. 2. Marketing - Europe - Congresses. I. Esomar. II. Title.
HF5429.6.E9 S45 1986

Seminar on Road Transportation in the Amazon Region (1985 : Brasília and Porto Velho, Rondônia, Brazil) Tratado de cooperación amazónica . Washington, D.C. , 1986. iii, 101 p. ; ISBN 0-8270-2304-9 (pbk.) LC Card 86-152493
HE359.A5 T73 1986

Seminar on Role of Board of Directors in Corporate Governance . Seminar on Role of Board of Directors in Corporate Governance (1984 : Bombay, India) New Delhi [1984] vii, 140 p., [6] p. of plates : LC Card 87-902533 DDC 658.4/22/0954 19
HD2745 .S45 1984

Seminar on Role of Board of Directors in Corporate Governance (1984 : Bombay, India) Seminar on Role of Board of Directors in Corporate Governance : papers and proceedings. New Delhi : Associated Chambers of Commerce & Industry of India, [1984] vii, 140 p., [6] p. of plates : ill. ; 26 cm. "Organised by Assocham on May 29, 1984, at Bombay"--Pref. Includes bibliographical references. LC Card 87-902533 DDC 658.4/22/0954 19
1. Directors of corporations - Inida - Congresses. I. Associated Chambers of Commerce & Industry of India. II. Title.
HD2745 .S45 1984

Seminar on Science and technology for Women (1985 : Anna University) Science and technology for women /. Madras [1985] 79 p. ; LC Card 85-904932 DDC 305.4/35/0954 19
Q130 .S33 1985 ***NYPL [JLD 86-3369]***

Seminar on "SITE" to "INSAT": Production of Programmes for Women and Children (1984 : Space Applications Centre) SITE to INSAT . New Delhi , 1986. viii, 165 p. : LC Card 86-902956 DDC 384.55/44/0954 19
HE8700.9.I5 S57 1986

Seminar on the Effect of Internal Migration, Urbanization, and Resettlement in the IGCC Region on its Population/Family Planning Programmes . Seminar on the Effect of Internal Migration, Urbanization, and Resettlement in the IGCC Region on its Population/Family Planning Programmes (1980 : Jakarta, Indonesia) Kuala Lumpur, Malaysia [1980?] 131 p. : LC Card 81-941408
HB2101 .S45 1980

Seminar on the Effect of Internal Migration, Urbanization, and Resettlement in the IGCC Region on its Population/Family Planning Programmes (1980 : Jakarta, Indonesia) Seminar on the Effect of Internal Migration, Urbanization, and Resettlement in the IGCC Region on its Population/Family Planning Programmes : a report on the IGCC Seminar on the Effect of Internal Migration, Urbanization, and Resettlement in the IGCC Region on its Population/Family Planning Programmes, held in Jakarta, Indonesia, 18-20 March 1980 / prepared by the IGCC Secretariat ; sponsored by the Government of Japan. Kuala Lumpur, Malaysia : The Secretariat, [1980?] 131 p. : ill., maps ; 26 cm. Cover title. At head of title: Regional Organization for Inter Governmental Cooperation and Coordination in Population and Family Planning in South East Asia. Includes bibliographies. LC Card 81-941408
1. Migration, Internal - Asia, Southeastern - Congresses. 2. Urbanization - Asia, Southeastern - Congresses. 3. Land settlement - Asia, Southeastern - Congresses. 4. Asia, Southeastern - Population policy - Congresses. 5. Birth control - Asia, Southeastern - Congresses. I. IGCC Secretariat. II. Japan. III. Title.
HB2101 .S45 1980

Seminar on Trade Unions and Democracy (1st : 1986 : Kingston, Jamaica) Trade unions and democracy . [Kingston, Jamaica] [1986] iii, 52 p. : LC Card 87-133832 DDC 322/.2/09729 19
HD6571 .T72 1986

Seminar paper (Stockholms universitet. Institutet för internationell ekonomi) .
(no. 115) Herberg, Horst. Stagflation as a consequence of an expansionary monetary or fiscal policy under flexible exchange rates /. Stockholm, Sweden [1978] 34 leaves ; LC Card 81-116937
HD5710 .H47 1978
(no. 117) Gylfason, Thorvaldur. Interest, inflation, and the aggregate consumption function /. Stockholm, Sweden [1979] 44 leaves : LC Card 81-114286
HC110.C6 G95 1979

Seminar "Planung des Berufsausbildungswesens in Entwicklungsländern" vom 22. Juli bis 17. August 1965 /. Seminar "Planung des Berufsausbildungswesens in Entwicklungsländern" (1965 : Berlin, Germany) Berlin-Tegel [1965?] 1 portfolio ; LC Card 87-407604
HD5715.5.D44 S46 1965

Seminar "Planung des Berufsausbildungswesens in Entwicklungsländern" (1965 : Berlin, Germany) Seminar "Planung des Berufsausbildungswesens in Entwicklungsländern" vom 22. Juli bis 17. August 1965 / Deutsche Stiftung für Entwicklungsländer = Seminario "El Planeamiento del Sistema de Formación Professional en Países en Vías de Desarrollo" del 22 de julio al 17 de agosto de 1965 / Fundación Alemana para los Países en Vías de Desarrollo. Berlin-Tegel : Die Stiftung, [1965?] 1 portfolio ; 31 cm. Papers of a conference organized by the Deutsche Stiftung für Entwicklungsländer and held in Berlin. Spanish and German. Title from portfolio cover. LC Card 87-407604
1. Occupational training - Developing countries - Congresses. 2. Economic development - Congresses. I. Deutsche Stiftung für Entwicklungsländer. II. Title. III. Title: Seminario "El Planeamiento del Sistema de Formación Professional en Países en Vías de Desarrollo" del 22 de julio al 17 de agosto de 1965.
HD5715.5.D44 S46 1965

Seminar proceedings (University of Edinburgh. Centre of African Studies) .
(no. 25) Malawi . Edinburgh , c1985. xviii, 642 p. : LC Card 86-100522 DDC 338.96897 19
HC935 .M36 1985

Seminar: the Challenge of Sickness in the Textile Industry (1983 : Ahmadābād, India) Industrial sickness . Ahmedabad , c1984. xv, 459 p. ; LC Card 87-902007 DDC 363.1/19677/00954 19
HD9866.I63 A385 1984

Seminario ANJE '85 (7th : 1985 : Santo Domingo, Dominican Republic) Influencia del sector privado sobre la realidad nacional. [Santo Domingo] [1986] 180 p., [1] leaf of plates : LC Card 86-190331
HC153.5 .I53 1986

Seminario "Bolivia en el Año 2010" (1986 : La Paz, Bolivia?) Bolivia en el año 2010. [La Paz, Bolivia?] , 1986. ii, 325 p. : LC Card 87-101220
HC182 .B564 1986

Seminario de Análisis de la Coyuntura y las Perspectivas de la Economía en Colombia (1985 : Bogotá, Colombia?) Perspectivas de la economía mundial y colombiana /. Bogotá, Colombia , 1986. 106 p. ; ISBN 958-616-044-0 LC Card 87-115573 DDC 330.9861/0632 19
HC197 .P35 1986

Seminário de Energia de Biomassa . Seminário de Energia de Biomassa (1985? : Belo Horizonte, Brazil?) [Belo Horizonte?] , <[1986?-. v. <[1-2] > : LC Card 87-107998
HD9502.5.B543 B67 1985

Seminário de Energia de Biomassa (1985? : Belo Horizonte, Brazil?) Seminário de Energia de Biomassa : documentos básicos. [Belo Horizonte?] : Governo do Estado de Minas Gerais, Secretaria de Estado de Minas e Energia, Grupo de Trabalho de Energia de Biomassa : Companhia Energética de Minas Gerais, <[1986?- > v. <[1-2] > : ill. ; 30 cm. Includes bibliographies. CONTENTS. - [1] Produção energética a partir da cana-de-açúcar e derivados. Emprego de óleos vegetais para fins carburantes -- [2] Avaliação da produção e uso da biomassa florestal no Estado de Minas Gerais. Conservação de energia de biomassa. LC Card 87-107998
1. Biomass energy industries - Brazil - Minas Gerais. 2. Alcohol fuel industry - Brazil - Minas Gerais. 3. Sugarcane industry - Brazil - Minas Gerais. 4. Vegetable oils as fuel. I. Minas Gerais (Brazil). Grupo de Trabalho de Energia de Biomassa. II. Companhia Energética de Minas Gerais. III. Title.
HD9502.5.B543 B67 1985

Seminario de Operaciones Internacionales (1981 : Quito, Ecuador) Memorias del Seminario de Operaciones Internacionales / Banco Central del Ecuador. Quito, Ecuador : El Banco, 1981. 156 p., [2] p. of plates : ports. ; 28 cm. LC Card 86-174597
1. Ecuador - Foreign economic relations - Congresses. 2. Banks and banking - Ecuador - Congresses. I. Banco Central del Ecuador. II. Title.
HF1519 .S46 1981

Seminario di aggiornamento per i quadri sindacali della categoria (1985 : Rome, Italy) Evoluzione del processo produttivo nelle construzioni : tecniche e organizzazione : effetti sulla struttura produttiva e relazioni industriali : Seminario organizzato dalla FILLEA-CGIL nazionale, Ufficio formazione sindacale, Pomezia (Roma) 17-18 giugno 1985. Milano, Italy : F. Angeli, c1986. 142 p. : ill. ; 22 cm. (Fillea-Cgil/materiali . 1) LC Card 86-210757
1. Construction industry - Italy - Congresses. 2. Construction workers - Italy - Congresses. I. Federazione italiana lavoratori del legno dell'edilizia e industria affini. II. Confederazione generale italiana del lavoro. III. Title. IV. Series.
HD9715.I82 S46 1985

Seminario "El Planeamiento del Sistema de Formación Professional en Países en Vías de Desarrollo" del 22 de julio al 17 de agosto de 1965. Seminar "Planung des Berufsausbildungswesens in Entwicklungsländern" (1965 : Berlin, Germany) Seminar "Planung des Berufsausbildungswesens in Entwicklungsländern" vom 22. Juli bis 17. August 1965 /. Berlin-Tegel [1965?] 1 portfolio ; LC Card 87-407604
HD5715.5.D44 S46 1965

Seminario Estrategia de Desarrollo en Condiciones de Oferta Abundante de Energía Eléctrica (1980 : Asunción, Paraguay) Memoria del Seminario Estrategia de Desarrollo en Condiciones de Oferta Abundante de Energía Eléctrica : realizado desde el 28 de julio al 1o de agosto, Asunción-Itaipú, Paraguay, 1980. Asunción, Paraguay : Colegio de Graduados en Ciencias Económicas del Paraguay ; [s.l.] : Banco Interamericano de Desarrollo, 1980. 165 p., [18] leaves of plates : ill. (some col.) ; 23 cm. "El economista paraguayo : publicación del Colegio de Graduados en Ciencias Económicas del Paraguay. Asunción, octubre 1980"--Prelim. p. 1. LC Card 83-169471 DDC 363.6/2 19
1. Electric utilities - Paraguay - Congresses. 2. Industrial development projects - Paraguay - Congresses. 3. Hydroelectric power plants - Paraguay - Congresses. I. Colegio de Graduados en Ciencias Económicas del Paraguay. II. Economista paraguayo. III. Title.
HD9685.P32 S45 1980 ***NYPL [JLE 87-995]***

Seminario Interamericano Conmemorativo de los 25 Años del BID (1985 : Rio de Janeiro, Brazil) Informe del Seminario Interamericano Conmemorativo de los 25 Años del BID / Banco Interamericano de Desarrollo, Fundación Getúlio Vargas, Escuela Interamericana de Administración Pública. 1a. ed. Rio de Janeiro, RJ : FGV-Instituto de Documentação, Editora da Fundação Getúlio Vargas, 1986. 65 p. : ports. ; 21 cm. Includes bibliographical references. LC Card 87-403948 DDC 332.1/538 19
1. Inter-American Development Bank - Congresses. I. Inter-American Development Bank. II. Fundação Getúlio Vargas. III. Escola Interamericana de Administração Pública. IV. Title.
HG3881.5.I44 S46 1985

Seminario Interamericano sobre Política Tributaria (1984 : San José, Costa Rica) La Política tributaria en Latinoamérica . Washington, D.C. , 1986. ix, 180 p. ; ISBN 0-8270-2496-7 (pbk.) LC Card 87-403563 DDC 336.2/0098 19
HJ3374.5 .P65 1986

Seminario Internacional sobre "Gestión de Empresas Públicas" (1985 : Quito, Ecuador) Gestión de empresas públicas en América Latina . Quito, Ecuador , c1986. 146 p. : LC Card 87-401599 DDC 350/.0092/098 19
HD4010.5 .G47 1986

Seminario Internacional sobre Pobreza y Desarrollo Regional (1984 : Bogotá, Colombia) Pobreza, participación y desarrollo regional /. [Bogotá, D.E., Colombia] , 1986. 536 p. : LC Card 87-103266
HC125 .P6 1986

Seminario "La Opción Preferencial por los Pobres: de la Teoría a la Práctica" (1986 : Santiago, Chile?) La Opción preferencial por los pobres . [Santiago] [1987] 360 p. : LC Card 87-403060 DDC 362.5/098 19
HC130.P6 O63 1987

Seminário Nacional de Abastecimento Alimentar em Grandes Cidades--a Experiência de São Paulo (1984 : São Paulo, Brazil) Anais / Seminário Nacional de Abastecimento Alimentar em Grandes Cidades--a Experiência de São Paulo ; promoção, Secretaria de Agricultura e Abastecimento do Estado de São Paulo ; organização, Coordenadoria de Abastecimento ; colaboração, FAO-Organização de Alimentação e Agricultura das Nações Unidas, CEESP-Caixa Econômica do Estado de São Paulo, realizado no Centro Estadual de Agricultura, São Paulo, 15 a 19 de outubro de 1984. São Paulo, São Paulo, Brasil : A Coordenadoria, 1984. xii, 421 p. : ill. ; 33 cm. Includes bibliographies. LC Card 87-404933 DDC 363.8/0981/61 19
1. Food supply - Brazil - São Paulo (State) - Congresses. 2. Malnutrition - Brazil - São Paulo (State) - Congresses. I. São Paulo (Brazil : State). Secretaria de Agricultura e Abastecimento. Coordenadoria de Abastecimento. II. Food and Agriculture Organization of the United Nations. III. Caixa Econômica do Estado de São Paulo. IV. Title.
HD9014.B83 S447 1984

Seminário "Nordeste--Estrutura Econômica e Social, Desenvolvimento e Processos Políticos" (1982 : Recife, Brazil) A Questão Nordeste . Rio de Janeiro-RJ , 1984. 137 p. ; LC Card 84-191031
HC188.N6 Q47 1984

Seminário para Compatibilização da Ação Pública na Região Metropolitana de Porto Alegre . Seminário para Compatibilização da Ação Pública na Região Metropolitana de Porto Alegre (1983) Porto Alegre, RS [1983] 83 p. : LC Card 84-216956
HC189.P64 S45 1983

Seminário para Compatibilização da Ação Pública na Região Metropolitana de Porto Alegre (1983) Seminário para Compatibilização da Ação Pública na Região Metropolitana de Porto Alegre : Porto Alegre, 24 e 25 de fevereiro de 1983 / Governo do Estado do Rio Grande do Sul, Secretaria do Interior, Desenvolvimento Regional e Obras Públicas-SDO, Fundação Metropolitana de Planejamento-METROPLAN. Porto Alegre, RS : METROPLAN, [1983] 83 p. : ill. ; 30 cm. LC Card 84-216956
1. Porto Alegre Metropolitan Area (Brazil) - Economic policy - Congresses. 2. Porto Alegre Metropolitan Area (Brazil) - Social policy - Congresses. I. Rio Grande do Sul (Brazil). Fundação Metropolitana de Planejamento. II. Title.
HC189.P64 S45 1983

Seminário Permanente de Habitação Popular (1981 : Recife, Brazil) Anais--1981 / Seminário Permanente de Habitação Popular. Recife : Governo de Pernambuco, Secretaria de Habitação, [19]82. 178 p. ; 30 cm. Cover title. LC Card 84-256147
1. Housing - Brazil - Pernambuco - Congresses. 2. Rural poor - Housing - Brazil - Pernambuco - Congresses. I. Pernambuco. Secretaria de Habitação. II. Title.
HD7323.P37 S46 1981

Seminario Permanente de Problemas Colombianos. Kalmanovitz, Salomón. El desarrollo de la ganadería en Colombia, 1950-1972 . [Bogotá, Colombia] [1978] p. 195-238 : LC Card 86-157918
HD9433.C62 K35 1978

Seminario Regional Movimientos Sociales en el Noroeste de México (1984 : Culiacán, Mexico) Movimientos sociales en el noroeste de México /. México , 1985. 282 p. ; ISBN 968-590-072-8 LC Card 87-102068
HD1531.M6 M684 1985

Seminario sobre Agricultura y Alimentación (1979 : Chaclacayo, Peru) Agricultura y alimentación . [Lima] , 1982. 536 p. : LC Card 83-174688 DDC 338.1/9/85 19
HD9014.P52 A57 1982 ***NYPL [JLD 86-268]***

Seminario sobre Conceptos Teóricos de la Geografía Económica . Seminario sobre Conceptos Teóricos de la Geografía Económica (1975 : Mexico City, Mexico?) México , 1978. 78 p. ; LC Card 87-403767 DDC 330.9 19
HC13 .S46 1975

Seminario sobre Conceptos Teóricos de la Geografía Económica (1975 : Mexico City, Mexico?) Seminario sobre Conceptos Teóricos de la Geografía Económica : celebrado del 2 al 4 de julio de 1975. México : Universidad Nacional Autónoma de México, Instituto de Geografía, Departamento de Geografía Económica, 1978. 78 p. ; 28 cm. (Serie varia . núm. 4) Includes bibliographical references. LC Card 87-403767 DDC 330.9 19
1. Geography, Economic - Congresses. I. Universidad Nacional Autónoma de México. Departamento de Geografía Económica. II. Series: Serie varia (Universidad Nacional Autónoma de México. Instituto de Geografía) , t. 1, núm. 4. III. Title.
HC13 .S46 1975

Seminario sobre Consequencias para las Entidades Oficiales de Crédito de la Entrada de España en las Comunidades Europeas /. Seminario sobre Consequencias para las Entidades Oficiales de Crédito de la Entrada de España en las Comunidades Europeas (1984 : Madrid, Spain) [Madrid] [1984?] 270 p. ; ISBN 84-505-0963-7 LC Card 85-186710
HG1642.E86 S46 1984

Seminario sobre Consequencias para las Entidades Oficiales de Crédito de la Entrada de España en las Comunidades Europeas (1984 : Madrid, Spain) Seminario sobre Consequencias para las Entidades Oficiales de Crédito de la Entrada de España en las Comunidades Europeas / organizado por el Instituto de Crédito Oficial y las entidades oficiales de crédito con la colaboración del Centro Europeo de la Empresa Pública (CEEP) ; [traducciones fueron realizadas por Juan José Bosch Sintes y Ramón Profitós Rialp]. [Madrid] : El Instituto, [1984?] 270 p. ; 21 cm. ISBN 84-505-0963-7 LC Card 85-186710
1. Credit - European Economic Community countries. 2. Financial institutions - European Economic Community countries. 3. European Economic Community - Spain. I. Instituto de Crédito Oficial (Spain). II. Centre européen de l'entreprise publique. III. Title.
HG1642.E86 S46 1984

Seminário sobre Crescimento Económico e Dívida Externa, 18 e 19 de março de 1982 . Seminário sobre Crescimento Económico e Dívida Externa (1982) Lisboa , 1983. 163 p. ; LC Card 85-175819 DDC 336.3/4/09469 19
HJ8744 .S46 1982 ***NYPL [JLG 86-189]***

Seminário sobre Crescimento Económico e Dívida Externa (1982) Seminário sobre Crescimento Económico e Dívida Externa, 18 e 19 de março de 1982 : o caso de Portugal / prefácio de J. Silva Lopes.1a. ed. Lisboa : I.E.D., 1983. 163 p. ; 30 cm. (Caderno / Instituto de Estudos para o Desenvolvimento . 6) English and Portuguese. Includes bibliographical references. LC Card 85-175819 DDC 336.3/4/09469 19
1. Debts, External - Portugal - Congresses. 2. Economic development projects - Portugal - Finance - Congresses. I. Series: Caderno (Instituto de Estudos para o Desenvolvimento (Portugal)) , 6. II. Title.
HJ8744 .S46 1982 ***NYPL [JLG 86-189]***

Seminario sobre Estrategias de Desarrollo e Integración en el Grupo Andino (1984 : Lima, Peru) Estrategias de desarrollo e integración en el Grupo Andino . Lima, Perú , 1985. 414 p. : LC Card 87-125026 DDC 337.1/8 19
HC167.A5 E87 1985

Seminario "Sobre la Clase Obrera en la Argentina" (1985 : Buenos Aires, Argentina) La Clase obrera argentina . Buenos Aires , 1986. 136 p. ; LC Card 86-206788
HD8266.5 .C57 1986

Seminário sobre Política Fiscal (1984? : CGTP-IN) Contribuições para a reforma do sistema fiscal português : Seminário sobre Política Fiscal : estudos, comunicações e conclusões / CGTP-IN. Lisboa : Edições Um de Outubro, 1985. 226 p. : ill. ; 21 cm. (Colecção Manuais de fiscalidade) Includes bibliographies. LC Card 87-107879 DDC 336.469 19
1. Fiscal policy - Portugal - Congresses. 2. Finance, Public - Portugal - Congresses. I. CGTP-Intersindical. II. Title. III. Series.
HJ1252 .S46 1984

Seminário sobre Política Industrial da Bahia (1986 : Salvador, Brazil) Síntese das exposições e dos debates / Seminário sobre Política Industrial da Bahia. [Salvador] : Federação das Indústrias do Estado da Bahia, [1986] 89 p. ; 21 cm. Cover title: Política industrial da Bahia. LC Card 87-403843 DDC 338.981/42 19
1. Industry and state - Brazil - Bahia (State) - Congresses. I. Federação das Industrias do Estado da Bahia. II. Title. III. Title: Política industrial da Bahia.
HD3616.B84 B37 1986

Seminario sobre Políticas de Ajuste y Grupos Más Vulnerables en América Latina (1986 : Bogotá, Colombia) Políticas de ajuste y grupos más vulnerables en América Latina . [Bogotá, Colombia] , 1987. 278 p. : ISBN 958-9093-01-9 LC Card 87-404285 DDC 338.98 19
HC125 .P647 1987

"Seminario sobre Reforma Agraria, Cooperativismo y Autogestión en el Proceso del Agro Nacional" (1982) Reforma agraria como proceso social . Piura, Perú [1984] 163 p. : LC Card 84-232526 DDC 333.3/1/85 19
HD1333.P4 R44 1984 ***NYPL [JLD 86-2537]***

Seminario Taller "El Problema Regional y la Regionalización en Arequipa" (1986 : Arequipa, Peru?) Región sur, problemática y perspectivas /. Arequipa [1986?] 164 p. ; LC Card 87-404224 DDC 330.984/052 19
HC182 .R39 1986

Seminario-Taller La Autogestión Empresarial Urbana (1985 : Lima, Peru) Informe final / Seminario-Taller La Autogestión Empresarial Urbana, 4-5-6-7 diciembre 1985. [Lima, Perú] : INPET, [1986 or 1987] 112 p. ; 21 cm. LC Card 87-404369 DDC 338.6 19
1. Management - Peru - Employee participation - Congresses. I. INPET (Organization). II. Title.
HD5660.P4 S46 1985

Seminario Taller "Problemática del Desarrollo Regional y los Procesos de Regionalización y Microregionalización" (1986) Región sur, problemática y perspectivas /. Arequipa [1986?] 164 p. ; LC Card 87-404224 DDC 330.984/052 19
HC182 .R39 1986

Seminario Taller sobre el Decimoquinto Censo Nacional de Población y Cuarto de Vivienda, 1985. Seminario Taller sobre el XV Censo Nacional de Población y IV de Vivienda, 1985 (1986 : Girardot, Colombia) Seminario Taller sobre el XV Censo Nacional de Población y IV de Vivienda, 1985 /. Girardot [Colombia] , 1986. 327 p. : ISBN 958-608-038-2 LC Card 87-403863 DDC 304.6/0723 19
HA1011.5 1985b

Seminario Taller sobre el XV Censo Nacional de Población y IV de Vivienda, 1985 /. Seminario Taller sobre el XV Censo Nacional de Población y IV de Vivienda, 1985 (1986 : Girardot, Colombia) Girardot [Colombia] , 1986. 327 p. : ISBN 958-608-038-2 LC Card 87-403863 DDC 304.6/0723 19
HA1011.5 1985b

Seminario Taller sobre el XV Censo Nacional de Población y IV de Vivienda, 1985 (1986 : Girardot, Colombia) Seminario Taller sobre el XV Censo Nacional de Población y IV de Vivienda, 1985 / compiladores, Carmen Elisa Flórez Nieto, Rafael Echeverri Perico. Girardot [Colombia] : Departamento Nacional de Planeación, 1986. 327 p. : ill. ; 23 cm. At head of title: DNP-DANE-COLCIENCIAS-FES-CEDE. Includes bibliographies. ISBN 958-608-038-2 LC Card 87-403863 DDC 304.6/0723 19
1. Colombia - Census, 1985 - Congresses. I. Flórez Nieto, Carmen Elisa. II. Echeverri Perico, Rafael. III.

Colombia. Departamento Nacional de Planeación. IV. Title. V. Title: Seminario Taller sobre el 15o Censo Nacional de Población y 4o de Vivienda, 1985. VI. Title: Seminario Taller sobre el Decimoquinto Censo Nacional de Población y Cuarto de Vivienda, 1985.
HA1011.5 1985b

Seminario Taller sobre el 15o Censo Nacional de Población y 4o de Vivienda, 1985. Seminario Taller sobre el XV Censo Nacional de Población y IV de Vivienda, 1985 (1986 : Girardot, Colombia) Seminario Taller sobre el XV Censo Nacional de Población y IV de Vivienda, 1985 /. Girardot [Colombia] , 1986. 327 p. : ISBN 958-608-038-2 LC Card 87-403863 DDC 304.6/0723 19
HA1011.5 1985b

Seminários sobre Perspectivas dos Setores Produtivos de Minas Gerais . Seminários sobre Perspectivas dos Setores Produtivos de Minas Gerais (1986 : Belo Horizonte, Brazil) Belo Horizonte , 1986. 124 leaves ; LC Card 87-108000 DDC 338.0981/51 19
HC188.M6 S46 1986

Seminários sobre Perspectivas dos Setores Produtivos de Minas Gerais (1986 : Belo Horizonte, Brazil) Seminários sobre Perspectivas dos Setores Produtivos de Minas Gerais : sínteses. Belo Horizonte : Companhia Energética de Minas Gerais, Secretaria de Estado de Minas e Energia : Instituto de Desenvolvimento Industrial de Minas Gerais, Secretaria de Estado de Indústria e Comércio, 1986. 124 leaves ; 30 cm. LC Card 87-108000 DDC 338.0981/51 19
1. Minas Gerais (Brazil) - Industries - Congresses. I. Companhia Energética de Minas Gerais. II. Instituto de Desenvolvimento Industrial de Minas Gerais. III. Title.
HC188.M6 S46 1986

SEMINARS.
Holtz, Herman. Expanding your consulting practice with seminars /. New York , c1987. xvi, 240 p. : ISBN 0-471-85899-4 LC Card 87-14231 DDC 658.4/6 19
HD69.C6 H625 1987

SEMINARS - HANDBOOKS, MANUALS, ETC.
Lant, Jeffrey L. Money talks . Cambridge, Mass. , c1985. vii, 302 p. : ISBN 0-940374-08-0 (pbk.) LC Card 87-105725 DDC 001 19
HD69.C6 L27 1985

Semlinger, Klaus. Regionalisierte Arbeitsmarkt- und Beschäftigungspolitik /. Frankfurt/Main , New York , c1983. 322 p. : ISBN 3-593-33241-8 LC Card 84-106151
HC286.7 .R44 1983

Semotam, Josef. Sovietske skúsenosti v rozvoji tvorivej iniciatívy pracujúcich / Josef Semotam. Bratislava : Práca, 1981. 153 p. ; 21 cm. (Knižnica funkcionára . zv. 5/81) Bibliography: p. [128] LC Card 81-182787
1. Industrial productivity - Russia. 2. Socialist competition - Russia. 3. Industrial productivity - Czechoslovakia. 4. Socialist competition - Czechoslovakia. I. Title.
HC340.I52 S45 1981 ***NYPL [*QT 86-5786]***

Semyonov, Moshe. Hewers of wood and drawers of water : noncitizen Arabs in the Israeli labor market / Moshe Semyonov, Noah Lewin-Epstein. Ithaca, NY : ILR Press, c1987. xii, 152 p. : ill. ; 23 cm. (Cornell international industrial and labor relations report . no. 13) Bibliography: p. [137]-147. Includes index. ISBN 0-87546-133-6 (pbk. : alk. paper) LC Card 87-2682 DDC 331.6/99275695 19
1. Palestinian Arabs - Employment - Israel. 2. Palestinian Arabs - West Bank. 3. Palestinian Arabs - Gaza Strip. 4. Alien labor - Israel. I. Lewin-Epstein, Noah. II. Series: Cornell international industrial and labor relations reports , no. 13. III. Title.
HD8660 .S45 1987

Sen, B. R. (Binay Ranjan), 1898- Blau, Gerda. Food aid for development . Rome , Ann Arbor, MI , 1985. xi, 343 p. : ISBN 92-5-102180-5 (pbk.) LC Card 86-220906 DDC 363.8/83/091724 19
HD9018.D44 B57 1985

Sen Gupta, Amit. "All India Seminar on National Drug Policy" (1986 : New Delhi, India) Drug industry and the Indian people . New Delhi , Patna , 1986. 333 p. : LC Card 87-900874 DDC 338.4/76151/0954 19
HD9611.I52 A44 1986

Sen, P. K. (Prabhat Kumar), 1905- Purono dinera kathā / Prabhāta Sena. Kalakātā : Saumyendranātha Ṭhākura Ayākāḍemī apha Sośyāla eṇḍa Palitikyāla Thaṭa, 1985. 49 p. ; 23 cm. In Bengali. Autobiographical reminescence, up to 1934, of an Indian trade union leader and activist of the Communist Party of India. LC Card 85-904772
1. Sen, P. K. (Prabhat Kumar), 1905-. 2. Trade-unions - India - Officials and employees - Biography. 3. Communists - India - Biography. 4. Communist Party of India - Biography. I. Title.
HD6812.5.S46 A3 1985

SEN, P. K. (PRABHAT KUMAR), 1905-
Sen, P. K. (Prabhat Kumar), 1905- Purono dinera kathā /. Kalakātā , 1985. 49 p. ; LC Card 85-904772
HD6812.5.S46 A3 1985

Sen, Tapas Kumar, 1956- Corporate income tax and profit rates : short-run shifting in selected industries / Tapas Kumar Sen. New Delhi : Deep & Deep, c1984. xiii, 267 p. ; 23 cm. Based on revision of the author's thesis (Ph. D.--University of Poona) Includes indexes. Bibliography: p. [252]-263. LC Card 84-900209 DDC 336.24/3/0954 19
1. Corporations - Taxation - India. 2. Tax incidence - India. I. Title.
HJ4766.Z7 S46 1984 ***NYPL [JLD 86-4138]***

Sena, Lúcia Bastos Ribeiro de. Data-base . [São Paulo] , 1986. 259 p. : LC Card 87-403668 DDC 331.88/025/8161 19
HD6615.S32 D37 1986

O SENAI e o mercado de trabalho industrial paulista . Zingg, Rosa Lúcia. [São Paulo] , 1986. 37 leaves ; LC Card 87-402164 DDC 331.12/5/098161021 19
HD5755.S3 Z56 1986

Senaoana, M. P. Research on rural-non farm employment in Lesotho : results of a baseline survey / M.P. Senaoana, S.D. Turner, G.J. van Apeldoorn. Roma, Lesotho : District Level Planning and Rural Development Project, Institute of Southern African Studies, National University of Lesotho, [1984] 88 leaves : ill. ; 30 cm. (Research report (Institute of Southern African Studies, the National University of Lesotho) . no. 6) "September 1984." "November 1984"--Cover. Bibliography: leaves 87-88. LC Card 86-214032 DDC 331.12/5/096816 19
1. Labor supply - Lesotho. 2. Labor supply - Lesotho - Statistics. 3. Lesotho - Rural conditions. I. Turner, S. D. II. Apeldoorn, G. Jan van. III. Series: Research report (National University of Lesotho. Institute of Southern African Studies) , no. 6. IV. Title.
HD5842.7.A6 S46 1984

Senate Transportation Committee, RS 2477 Task Force report /. Roberts, Malcolm B. [Anchorage, Alaska] [1986] 121 leaves, 27 p. : LC Card 86-622718 DDC 333.78/09798 19
HE356.A4 R63 1986

Senauer, Benjamin. Food demand analysis . Blacksburg, Va. [1986] xii, 292 p. : LC Card 87-620670 DDC 339.4/86413 19
HD9000.5 .F5946 1986

Senchack, A. J. (Andrew J.)
Personal investing : techniques for successful investors / by Andrew J. Senchack. [Texas?] : Invest Publishers, c1986. 1 v. (various pagings) : ill. ; 28 cm. Includes bibliography and index. LC Card 87-104863 DDC 332.6/78 19
1. Investments - United States - Handbooks, manuals, etc. I. Title.
HG4921 .S44 1986

Smart investing : a step-by-step guide to financial security / Andrew J. Senchack. Dallas, Tex. : Taylor Pub. Co., c1987. 1 v. (various pagings) : ill. ; 28 cm. Includes a bibliography and index. ISBN 0-87833-575-7 (pbk.) : LC Card 87-1923 DDC 332.6/78 19
1. Investments - United States - Handbooks, manuals, etc. I. Title.
HG4921 .S45 1987

Senchenko, Volodymyr Ivanovych. Radians'ka Ukraïna . Kyïv , 1985. 205 p., [2] p. of plates : LC Card 87-151437
HC337.U5 R215 1985

Sendek, Robert. Shorter, Frederic Claiborne. Computational methods for population projections . New York , 1987, c1974. vii, 192 p. : ISBN 0-87834-056-4 (pbk.) LC Card 87-9303 DDC 304.6/2/0285 19
HB849.53 .S54 1987

Sénécal, Didier. Péroche, Marcel, 1907- Les mémoires de Marcel Péroche, "sénateur" du rail /. Paris , c1984. 256 p., [8] p. of plates : ISBN 2-7013-0556-X : LC Card 84-206923
HD8039.R322 F87 1984

Sénégal . Dijk, Meine Pieter van. Paris [1986] 164 p. ; ISBN 2-85802-637-8 LC Card 86-221017
HD2346.S42 D343 1986

Senegal.
International Labour Organisation. Formation professionnelle rurale, SEN/71/526 . Genève , 1976. ii, 69 p. : ISBN 92-2-201512-6 LC Card 84-125056
HD5716.A292 S385 1976

SENEGAL - ECONOMIC CONDITIONS.
ECA/UNIDO Basic Metals and Engineering Industries Development Programme Mission. Rapport de la Mission sur le programme de développement des industries métallurgiques de base et mécaniques en République du Sénégal. [S.l.] [1979] 41, 3 p. (2 fold.) ; LC Card 80-981173
HD9506.S42 E33 1979

The Political economy of risk and choice in Senegal /. London, England , Totowa, N.J. , 1987. xv, 363 p. : ISBN 0-7146-3297-X : LC Card 86-26859 DDC 338.966/3 19
HC1045 .P65 1987

Répertoire financier et monétaire du Sénégal, 1985. Le Vésinet, France [1985?] ii, 98 leaves ; LC Card 86-202435
HJ2184.5 .R46 1985

Senegal. Présidence du Conseil du gouvernement. Direction de l'animation. Bureau d'études. Problèmes d'adaptation des structures au développement socialiste /. [Dakar?] [1962] 50 leaves ; LC Card 83-113563
HC1045 .S465 1962a

SENEGAL - ECONOMIC POLICY.
ECA/UNIDO Basic Metals and Engineering Industries Development Programme Mission. Rapport de la Mission sur le programme de développement des industries métallurgiques de base et mécaniques en République du Sénégal. [S.l.] [1979] 41, 3 p. (2 fold.) ; LC Card 80-981173
HD9506.S42 E33 1979

The Political economy of risk and choice in Senegal /. London, England , Totowa, N.J. , 1987. xv, 363 p. : ISBN 0-7146-3297-X : LC Card 86-26859 DDC 338.966/3 19
HC1045 .P65 1987

Répertoire financier et monétaire du Sénégal, 1985. Le Vésinet, France [1985?] ii, 98 leaves ; LC Card 86-202435
HJ2184.5 .R46 1985

Senegal. Présidence du Conseil du gouvernement. Direction de l'animation. Bureau d'études. L'investissement-humain dans le développement socialiste /. [Dakar?] [1962] 51 leaves ; LC Card 82-206645
HC1045 .S465 1962

Senegal. Présidence du Conseil du gouvernement. Direction de l'animation. Bureau d'études. Problèmes d'adaptation des structures au développement socialiste /. [Dakar?] [1962] 50 leaves ; LC Card 83-113563
HC1045 .S465 1962a

Sourang, Abdou. Le rôle du mouvement coopératif dans le développement du Sénégal . [Dakar] [1981] 44 leaves : LC Card 85-207626
HD3567.7.A4 S67 1981

SENEGAL - INDUSTRIES.
ECA/UNIDO Basic Metals and Engineering Industries Development Programme Mission. Rapport de la Mission sur le programme de développement des industries métallurgiques de base et mécaniques en République du Sénégal. [S.l.] [1979] 41, 3 p. (2 fold.) ; LC Card 80-981173
HD9506.S42 E33 1979

Senegal. Présidence du Conseil du gouvernement. Direction de l'animation. Bureau d'études.
L'investissement-humain dans le développement socialiste / République du Sénégal, Présidence du Conseil, Commissariat général au Plan, Direction de l'animation, Bureau d'études. [Dakar?] : Le Bureau, [1962] 51 leaves ; 28 cm. "25 avril 1962." LC Card 82-206645
1. Senegal - Economic policy. 2. Senegal - Social policy.

I. Title.
HC1045 .S465 1962

Problèmes d'adaptation des structures au développement socialiste / République du Sénégal, Présidence du Conseil, Commissariat général du Plan, Direction de l'animation, Bureau d'études. [Dakar?] : Bureau d'études, [1962] 50 leaves ; 27 cm. "15 avril 1962." LC Card 83-113563
1. Senegal - Economic conditions. 2. Senegal - Economic policy. 3. Socialism - Senegal. I. Title.
HC1045 .S465 1962a

SENEGAL - SOCIAL POLICY.
Senegal. Présidence du Conseil du gouvernement. Direction de l'animation. Bureau d'études. L'investissement-humain dans le développement socialiste /. [Dakar?] [1962] 51 leaves ; LC Card 82-206645
HC1045 .S465 1962

Seng, You Poh. see **You, Poh Seng.**

Senghaas, Dieter, 1940-
Auf dem Weg zu einer neuen Weltwirtschaftsordnung? . Baden-Baden , 1983. 478 p. ; ISBN 3-7890-0919-9 LC Card 84-113581
HF1411 .A92 1983

Auf dem Weg zu einer neuen Weltwirtschaftsordnung? . Baden-Baden , 1983. 478 p. ; ISBN 3-7890-0919-9
NYPL [JLD 87-919]

Sengo rōdō kumiai undōshi . Bandō, Satoshi, 1931- Tokyo , 1975. 278 p. ; LC Card 75-804891
*HD6832 B36 NYPL [*OSM 86-2348]*

Sengoku, Tamotsu, 1928- Willing workers : the work ethics in Japan, England, and the United States / Tamotsu Sengoku ; translated by Koichi Ezaki and Yuko Ezaki. Westport, Conn. : Quorum Books, c1985. xv, 153 p. : ill. ; 24 cm. Includes bibliographical references and index. ISBN 0-89930-137-1 (lib. bdg. : alk. paper) LC Card 85-9552 DDC 306/.36 19
1. Work ethic - Japan. 2. Work ethic - England. 3. Work ethic - United States. I. Title.
HD8726.5 .S37 1985 NYPL [JLE 86-1381]

Sengupta, A. K. Ghosh, A., 1921- Income distribution and the structure of production /. New Delhi , c1984. ix, 186 p. ; LC Card 83-907762 DDC 339.2/0724 19
HB523 .G46 1984 NYPL [JLD 86-4234]

Sengupta, Jatikumar.
Econometrics of planning and efficiency /. Dordrecht , Boston , 1988. vi, 193 p., [2] p. of plates : ISBN 90-247-3602-1 LC Card 87-21305 DDC 330/.028 19
HB139 .E32 1988

Optimal decisions under uncertainty : methods, models, and management / J.K. Sengupta. Berlin ; New York : Springer-Verlag, 1985. 286 p. ; 25 cm. (Universitext) Includes bibliographical references and index. ISBN 0-387-15032-3 (U. S.) LC Card 84-26683 DDC 658.4/033 19
1. Decision-making - Mathematical models. 2. Economic policy - Mathematical models. 3. Uncertainty - Mathematical models. I. Title.
HD30.23 .S46 1985 NYPL [JLE 86-4652]

Seni, Anita. Bussière, Yves. Vieillissement de la population et demande de transport dans la région de Montréal . Montréal, Québec [1983] 83 p. : ISBN 2-89228-036-2 LC Card 84-177163
HE4509.M68 B88 1983

SENIOR CITIZENS. see **AGED.**

Senior driver facts /. Huston, Ray E. Sacramento, CA , Springfield, VA , 1986. iii, 22 p. : LC Card 86-623189 DDC 363.1/252/09794021 19
HE5614.3.C3 H87 1986

SENIORITY, EMPLOYEE - JAPAN.
Iida, Tsuneo, 1932- What is really unique about the Japanese economy? /. Nagoya, Japan , 1985. 13 leaves ; LC Card 87-109242 DDC 331.25 19
HF5549.5.S4 I35 1985

Senker, Wienfried. Doh, Rainer. Bevölkerungsentwicklung, Wirtschaftsordnung und Industrialisierungsprozess in Südosteuropa . Neuried , c1985. [12], 486, 19 p. : ISBN 3-88893-045-6 LC Card 87-140271 DDC 304.6/09498 19
HB3631 .D64 1985

Senn, Martin. Waldburger, Hans. Die Seetalbahn . Luzern , c1983. 143 p. : LC Card 84-190252
HE4918.S44 W35 1983

SENNA INDUSTRY - BRAZIL.
Tsunechiro, Alfredo. O desempenho dos mercados a termo . São Paulo , 1986. xi, 123 p. : LC Card 87-404554 DDC 332.64/4 19
HG6046 .T75 1986

SENSING, REMOTE. see **REMOTE SENSING.**

Sensor & transducers for biomedical applications. Sensors and transducers for biomedical applications. Tustin, CA, U. S.A. (17722 Irvine Blvd., Tustin 92680) , c1987. 1 v. (various foliations) : LC Card 87-403749 DDC 381/.45681761 19
HD9995.T733 U675 1987

Sensors and transducers for biomedical applications. 1st revision. Tustin, CA, U. S.A. (17722 Irvine Blvd., Tustin 92680) : Biomedical Business International, c1987. 1 v. (various foliations) : ill. ; 29 cm. (Report / Biomedical Business International . #7042) Cover title: Sensor [i.e. sensors] & transducers for biomedical applications. LC Card 87-403749 DDC 381/.45681761 19
1. Biomedical transducer industry - United States. I. Biomedical Business International, Inc. II. Title: Sensor & transducers for biomedical applications. III. Title: Sensors & transducers for biomedical applications. IV. Series: Report (Biomedical Business International, Inc.) , #7042.
HD9995.T733 U675 1987

Sensors & transducers for biomedical applications. Sensors and transducers for biomedical applications. Tustin, CA, U. S.A. (17722 Irvine Blvd., Tustin 92680) , c1987. 1 v. (various foliations) : LC Card 87-403749 DDC 381/.45681761 19
HD9995.T733 U675 1987

SENSUALITY.
Haug, Wolfgang Fritz. Kritik der Warenästhetik /. Frankfurt am Main [1983], c1971. 187 p. ; ISBN 3-518-10513-2 (pbk.) LC Card 87-673362
HF1041 .H33x 1983

Scruton, Roger. Sexual desire . London , c1986. x, 428 p. ; ISBN 0-297-78479-X
NYPL [JFE 86-1928]

Sensus van landbou- en veeteelprodouksie, 1979 = Census of agricultural and pastoral production, 1979. Pretoria : Republiek van Suid-Afrika, Sentrale Statistiekdiens : Verkrygbaar by die Staatsdrukker, [1985?] xiv, 266 p. ; 30 cm. (Verslag . no. 06-01-15 = no. 06-01-15) Afrikaans and English. ISBN 0-621-09380-7 : LC Card 86-150362 DDC 338.1/0968/021 19
1. Agricultural productivity - South Africa - Statistics. 2. Animal industry - South Africa - Statistics. I. South Africa. Central Statistical Services. II. Title: Census of agricultural and pastoral production, 1979. III. Series: Verslag (South Africa. Central Statistical Services) , no. 06-01-15.
HD2130.5 .S48 1985

Sensus van motorhandel en hersteldienste, 1977 = Census of the motor trade and repair services, 1977. Pretoria : Republiek van Suid-Afrika, Kantoor van die Eerste Minister, Sentrale Statistiekdiens : Verkrygbaar by die Staatsdrukker, [1982?] xiv, 166 p. : ill. ; 30 cm. (Verslag / Republiek van Suid-Afrika, Kantoor van die Eerste Minister, Sentrale Statistiekdiens . no. 04-16-03 = no. 04-16-03) ISBN 0-621-07034-3 : LC Card 82-240419
1. Automobile industry and trade - South Africa - Statistics. 2. Truck industry - South Africa - Statistics. 3. Motorcycle industry - South Africa - Statistics. 4. Automobile supplies industry - South Africa - Statistics. 5. Motorcycle supplies industry - South Africa - Statistics. 6. Motor vehicles - Maintenance and repair - Economic aspects - South Africa - Statistics. I. South Africa. Central Statistical Services. II. Title: Census of the motor trade and repair services, 1977. III. Series: Verslag (South Africa. Central Statistical Services) , no. 04-16-03.
HD9710.S72 S46 1982

Sensus van wassery-, skoonmaak- en kleurdienste, 1980 = Census of laundry, cleaning, and dyeing services, 1980. Pretoria : Staatsdrukker, [1984?] xiv, 59 p., [1] folded leaf of plates : ill. ; 30 cm. (Verslag . no. 18-01-02 = no. 18-01-02) ISBN 0-621-08730-0 : LC Card 86-122444
1. Laundry industry - South Africa - Statistics. 2. Cleaning and dyeing industry - South Africa - Statistics. I. South Africa. Central Statistical Services. II. Title: Census of laundry, cleaning and dyeing services, 1980. III. Series: Verslag (South Africa. Central Statistical Services) , no. 18-01-02.
HD9999.L383 S67 1984

Sepala Karunatilake, Neville. see **Karunatilake, H. N. S.**

Separatas de discursos, pareceres e projetos .
(47a) Henrique, Luiz. O salário perverso . Brasília , 1983. 129 p. ; LC Card 86-129394
HD5004 .H45 1983

(47a. Legislatura--1a. Sessão Legislativa) Tavares, José, 1949- Indústria bélica brasileira . Brasília , 1983. 44 p. ; LC Card 84-235004
HC187 .T2943 1983

(47a. Legislatura--1a. Sessão Legislativa, no. 212) Platon, Clarck. Amapá, fundamento de minha luta . Brasília , 1983. 155 p. : LC Card 86-127813
HC188.A48 P53 1983

(47a. Legislatura--2a. Sessão Legislativa, no. 114) Suplicy, Eduardo Matarazzo, 1941- Investigando o Caso Coroa-Brastel . Brasília , 1984. 215 p. ; LC Card 86-200269
HG4109 .S85 1984

(47a. Legislatura--2a. Sessão Legislativa, no. 13) Luca, Walmor de. Moratória com diretas já . Brasília , 1984. 69 p. ; LC Card 86-152773
HC188.S26 L83 1984

(47a. Legislatura--3a. Sessão Legislativa, no. 174) Pinheiro, Saramago. Reforma agrária . Brasília , 1986. 46 p. ; LC Card 86-228887
HD1333.B6 P56 1986

SEPARATION OF POWERS - UNITED STATES.
Shuman, Howard E. Politics and the budget . Englewood Cliffs, N.J. , c1988. p. cm. ISBN 0-13-684416-2 (pbk.) : LC Card 87-14521 DDC 353.0072/231 19
HJ2051 .S49 1988

SEPARATION OF POWERS - UNITED STATES - HISTORY.
Barrie, Robert W. Congress and the Executive . New York , 1987. 347 p. ; ISBN 0-8240-8071-8 (alk. paper) LC Card 87-23814 DDC 382/.3/0973 19
HF1455 .B317 1987

SEPLAN/GDF (Organization) Notícias publicadas, de março de 1977 a janeiro de 1979. [Brasília] [198-?] 116 leaves : LC Card 85-108219
HC189.B7 N68 1980z

Sepsey, György. Az 1983. évi iparstatisztikai világprogram adatai, Magyarország /. [Budapest , 1986. 289 p. ; LC Card 86-219027
HC300.28 .A14 1986

Sepúlveda, César. The U. S.-Mexico border region . [El Paso] , 1984, c1982. viii, 446 p. : ISBN 0-87404-091-4 (pbk.) LC Card 87-401861 DDC 333.7/0972/1 19
HC137.M46 U17 1984

Sepúlveda, Tomás. see **Sepúlveda Whittle, Tomás.**

Sepúlveda Whittle, Tomás. Los conceptos básicos del transporte marítimo y la situación de la actividad en América Latina. 1a ed. Santiago de Chile : Comisión Económica para América Latina y el Caribe, Naciones Unidas ; Nueva York, NY : Publicaciones de las Naciones Unidas, Sección de Ventas, 1986. 118 p. ; 23 cm. (Cuadernos de la CEPAL, 0252-2195 . 52) Prepared by Tomás Sepúlveda Whittle. "Publicación de las Naciones Unidas, no. de venta: S.86.II.G.11"--T.p. verso. Bibliography: p. 111-112. ISBN 92-1-321211-9 LC Card 87-400454 DDC 387.5/098 19
1. Shipping. 2. Merchant marine. 3. Shipping - Latin America. 4. Merchant marine - Latin America. I. United Nations. Economic Commission for Latin America. II. Series. III. Series: Cuadernos de la CEPAL , no. 52. IV. Title.
HE571 .S45 1986

SEQUENTIAL ANALYSIS.
Bakeman, Roger. Observing interaction . Cambridge [Cambridgeshire] , New York , 1986. ix, 221 p. : ISBN 0-521-25632-1 LC Card 85-22362 DDC 300/.1/51954 19
H62 .B284 1986 NYPL [JLD 86-3069]

Haumer, Heinrich. Sequentielle stochastische Investitionsplanung /. Wiesbaden , c1983. 305 p. ; ISBN 3-409-13420-4 LC Card 83-190299
HG4515.2 .H38 1983

Sequentielle stochastische Investitionsplanung /. Haumer, Heinrich. Wiesbaden , c1983. 305 p. ; ISBN 3-409-13420-4 LC Card 83-190299
HG4515.2 .H38 1983

Sequera, Armando José, 1953- Alegato contra el automóvil / Armando José Sequera. Caracas : Academia Nacional de la Historia, 1985. 157 p. ; 20 cm. (El libro menor. 73) Includes bibliographical references. ISBN 980-222-019-1 : LC Card 87-107528 DDC 388.3/21 19
1. Transportation, Automotive. 2. City and town life. I. Title.
HE5613 .S46 1985

Sequestration report for fiscal year 1986 : a summary : a joint report to the Comptroller General of the United States. Washington, D.C. : Congressional Budget Office, Congress of the U. S. : Office of Management and Budget, Executive Office of the President, [1986] 20 p. ; 26 cm. Shipping list no.: 86-212-P. "January 15, 1986." "Pursuant to the Balanced Budget and Emergency Deficit Control Act of 1985, P.L. 99-177"--Cover. Item 1005-E LC Card 87-600820 DDC 353.0072/2 19
1. Budget - United States. I. United States. Congressional Budget Office. II. United States. Office of Management and Budget.
HJ2051 .S468 1986

Ser obrero es algo relativo-- . Parodi Solari, Jorge. Lima [1986] 184 p. ; LC Card 87-405297 DDC 331.7/671/0985 19
HD8039.M52 P46 1986

Seravalli, Gilberto, 1946- Gli effetti delle integrazioni salariali sulla mobilità del lavoro / Gilberto Seravalli. Milano, Italy : F. Angeli, c1986. 119 p. : ill. ; 22 cm. (Collana di economia e politica industriale. 33) Bibliography: p. 115-119. LC Card 86-222523
1. Labor mobility - Italy. 2. Income maintenance programs - Italy. I. Title.
HD5717.5.I8 S47 1986

SERBIA - ECONOMIC CONDITIONS.
Schlarp, Karl-Heinz. Wirtschaft und Besatzung in Serbien, 1941-1944 . Stuttgart , 1986. viii, 443 p., [6] p. of plates : ISBN 3-515-04401-9 LC Card 86-181062
HC407.Z7 S46676 1986

SERBIA - FOREIGN ECONOMIC RELATIONS - GERMANY.
Schlarp, Karl-Heinz. Wirtschaft und Besatzung in Serbien, 1941-1944 . Stuttgart , 1986. viii, 443 p., [6] p. of plates : ISBN 3-515-04401-9 LC Card 86-181062
HC407.Z7 S46676 1986

SERBIA - HISTORY - 1918-1945.
Schlarp, Karl-Heinz. Wirtschaft und Besatzung in Serbien, 1941-1944 . Stuttgart , 1986. viii, 443 p., [6] p. of plates : ISBN 3-515-04401-9 LC Card 86-181062
HC407.Z7 S46676 1986

SERBIA - INDUSTRIES - STATISTICS.
Industrija SR Srbije, 1981-1982. godina /. Beograd , 1984. 76 p. ; LC Card 86-212264
HA1651 .A334 no. 239 HA1634.S47

SERBIA - STATISTICAL SERVICES.
Babić, Bogdan. Statistički informacioni sistem SR Srbije u društvenom sistemu informisanja republike . Beograd , 1986- v. <1 > ; LC Card 87-168381
HA37.Y83 S43 1986

SERBIA - STATISTICAL SERVICES - LAW AND LEGISLATION.
Babić, Bogdan. Statistički informacioni sistem SR Srbije u društvenom sistemu informisanja republike . Beograd , 1986- v. <1 > ; LC Card 87-168381
HA37.Y83 S43 1986

SERBIAN LANGUAGE. see SERBO-CROATIAN LANGUAGE.

SERBO-CROATIAN LANGUAGE - DICTIONARIES - ENGLISH.
Andrlić, Vlasta. Rječnik terminologije jugoslavenskog političko-ekonomskog sistema . Zagreb , 1985. viii, 135 p. ; LC Card 86-182784
*HB61 .A55 1985 NYPL [*QKK 87-1803]*

Bogadek, F. A. (Francis Aloysius), 1882- [New English-Croatian and Croatian-English dictionary.] Cassell's New English-Croatian and Croatian-English dictionary /. New York [c1985] vii, 531, 497, 46, 7 p. ; ISBN 0-02-512140-5 LC Card 85-23140 DDC 491.8/2321 19
*PG1377 .B72 1985 NYPL [*QAD 87-600]*

Gligorijević, Vera. Englesko-srpskohrvatski i srpskohrvatsko-engleski ekonomski rečnik =. Beograd , 1986. 549, [1] p. ; LC Card 86-196648
*HB61 .G49 1986 NYPL [*QAD 87-1743]*

Serbs, Croats and Slovenes, Kingdom of. see Yugoslavia.

Serbyn, Roman. Famine in Ukraine, 1932-1933 /. Edmonton , Downsview, Ont., Canada , 1986. 192 p. ; ISBN 0-09-286243-8 LC Card 87-148658 DDC 363.8/0947/71 19
HC337.U53 F314 1986

Sercovich, Francisco Colman. Exportaciones de tecnología de Brasil y Argentina / Francisco Sercovich, Ricardo Soifer, Graciela Schamis. [Buenos Aires, Argentina?] : Banco Interamericano de Desarrollo, Instituto para la Integración de América Latina, 1986. 269 p. ; 29 cm. Includes bibliographies. LC Card 87-404009 DDC 338.981/06 19
1. Technology transfer - Economic aspects - Brazil. 2. Technology transfer - Economic aspects - Argentina. I. Soifer, Ricardo. II. Schamis, Graciela. III. Title.
HC190.T4 S47 1986

Séréni, Jean Pierre. 150 meilleures entreprises françaises /. Paris , c1986. 313 p. ; ISBN 2-234-01894-3 : LC Card 87-107207
HF5382.75.F8 A13 1986

SERFDOM - RUSSIAN S.F.S.R. - HISTORY.
Osnovnye kategorii krest'i͡an v period pozdnego feodalizma, XVII--pervai͡a polovina XIX vv. . Smolensk , 1985. 134 p., [1] leaf of plates : LC Card 86-120158
HD1536.S65 O86 1985

Serge, Victor, 1890-1947. Los problemas del socialismo en nuestra tiempo [microform]. México, 1944. 119 p. DDC 335.082
*HX40 .P73 NYPL [*ZT-1711 no.21]*

Sergeev, I͡U. A. Medvedkov, S. I͡U. (Sergeĭ I͡Ur'evich) Mezhdunarodnyĭ marketing amerikanskoĭ tekhnologii /. Moskva , 1985. 189 p. : LC Card 85-187077
HF1009.6 .M43 1985

Sergeev, Mikhail Aleksandrovich.
Ėkonomicheskai͡a ėffektivnost' rekonstrukt͡sii deĭstvui͡ushchikh predprii͡atiĭ /. Sverdlovsk , 1981. 171 p. ; LC Card 83-192125
HD39.3 .E37 1981

Kardinal'nyĭ rost ėffektivnosti zhivogo truda--glavnyĭ faktor uskorenii͡a sot͡sial'no-ėkonomicheskogo razvitii͡a . Sverdlovsk , 1986. 2 v. ; LC Card 87-136690
HC337.R853 L35 1986

Sergeeva, L. A. (Li͡udmila Aleksandrovna) Rozin, Bent͡sian Borisovich. Statisticheskai͡a otsenka normativov otraslevogo planirovanii͡a /. Novosibirsk , 1986. 188, [3] p. : LC Card 86-230359
HC336.25 .R69 1986

Sergipe (Brazil)
Linhas de ação para o desenvolvimento de Sergipe : 1984-1987 / Estado de Sergipe, Governo João Alves Filho. [Aracaju] : O Estado, [1984] 218 p. ; 22 cm. LC Card 85-207558
1. Sergipe (Brazil) - Economic conditions. I. Title.
HC188.S45 S45 1984

SERGIPE (BRAZIL) - ECONOMIC CONDITIONS.
Sergipe (Brazil) Linhas de ação para o desenvolvimento de Sergipe . [Aracaju] [1984] 218 p. ; LC Card 85-207558
HC188.S45 S45 1984

Seri esensia .
(04) Indonesia dan masalah-masalah pembangunan /. [Jakarta] , 1986. viii, 277 p. : LC Card 87-940526
HC447 .I555936 1986

Seri monografi (Universitas/I.K.I.P. Kristen Satya Wacana. Fakultas Ekonomi) .
(no. 1) Damanik, Konta I. Kurs mata uang sebagai alat kebijakan di negara sedang berkembang (NSB) /. Salatiga , 1980. ii, 21 leaves ; LC Card 85-941470
HG1496 .D35 1980

Seri pembangunan pedesaan.
Budidaya padi di Jawa /. Jakarta , 1986. x, 339 p. : LC Card 87-941451
HD9066.I63 J3493 1986

Seri͡a Aktual'nye problemy razvitogo sot͡sializma.
Sot͡sialisticheskai͡a sobstvennost' v uslovii͡akh razvitogo sot͡sializma . Moskva , 1984. 165 p. ; LC Card 85-177805
HB701 .S59 1984

Serie A (CELADE (Organization)) .
(no. 1,045) Guatemala . [Guatemala] , San José, Costa Rica [1984] vii, 73 p. : LC Card 86-158744
HA755 .U5 no. 1045 HB949.A3

(no. 1022) Chackiel, Juan. La fuerza de trabajo en los países de la Cuenca del Plata según los censos de 1960 /. San José, Costa Rica , 1976. iv, 81 p. : LC Card 83-169596
HD5746.A6 C42 1976

(no. 151) Pinto, Claudio. Fecundabilidad y edad de la mujer en las áreas rurales y semi-urbanas de cuatro países latinoamericanos /. Santiago de Chile [1978] 21, [2] p. : LC Card 83-175823
HA755 .U5 no. 151 HB940.5

(no. 171) Ebanks, G. E. Mortality, fertility, and family planning . Santiago, Chile [1985] 123 p. ; LC Card 87-131697 DDC 304.6/2/09729841 19
HB1376.D65 E32 1985

(no. 91) Elizaga, Juan C. (Juan Carlos) Investigaciones sobre recursos humanos en América Latina . Santiago de Chile , 1972. 16 p. ; LC Card 83-103424
HA755 .U5 no. 91 HD5730.5.A6

Serie Agricultura y sociedad (Santiago, Chile) .
(85/2) Boom en el agro chileno? /. Santiago de Chile , 1985. 123 p. ; LC Card 87-401452 DDC 338.1/0983 19
HD1877 .B66 1985

Serie Anuarios.
Economía paraguaya, 1985. Asunción, Paraguay , 1986. 285 p. : LC Card 86-182987
HC222 .E27 1986

Serie Apuntes técnicos .
(no. 1) Resultados y perspectivas de la economía ecuatoriana, 1984-1985. Quito, Ecuador [1985] 27, 7 p. ; LC Card 85-215488
HC202 .R47 1985

Serie Artículos.
Fuenzalida, Valerio. Modelos de TV y radio y su influencia en la génesis cultural /. [Santiago, Chile] , 1980. 16 leaves ; LC Card 85-209582
HE8689.9.C5 F84 1980

Serie Avances de investigación (Chiclayo, Peru) .
(1) Burga, Manuel. La historia agraria /. Chiclayo, Perú , 1986. 196 p. ;
NYPL [JLD 87-1524]

Serie Avances de Investigación (Cuzco, Peru)
Cori Castro, Wilfredo. Mercados y precios en la economía campesina . [Cuzco, Peru] , 1986. 29 p. : LC Card 86-200941
HC228.C8 C59 1986

Díaz Gómez, Jorge. Deterioro de los términos de intercambio, migración eventual y pobreza campesina en el departamento del Cusco /. [Cuzco, Peru] , 1986. 17, 3 leaves, 2 leaves of plates : LC Card 86-200938
HD1531.P4 D52 1986

Serie B (CELADE (Organization)) .
(no. 48) Kayani, Ashraf K. Preparing subnational population projections . Santiago de Chile [1980] ii, 68 p. ; LC Card 84-256007 DDC 304.6/2/072 19
HB849.53 .K39 1980

Serie Bank- en effectenbedrijf.
(nr. 21) Dunnen, Emile den. Instrumenten van het geld- en valutamarktbeleid in Nederland /. Amsterdam , Deventer , 1985. 109 p. : ISBN 90-267-0955-2 : LC Card 85-115663
HG295.N4 D86 1985 NYPL [JLD 86-91]

Serie C (CELADE (Organization)) .
(no. 147) Pantelides, Edith A. El hogar como unidad de análisis de los datos censales . Santiago de Chile , 1972. ii, 48 p. : LC Card 83-169482
HA755 .U53 no. 147 HB849.49

Série Cadernos econômicos .
(29) As Cooperativas na balança comercial brasileira . [Brasília] [1986] 98 p. : LC Card 87-403826 DDC 334/.63/0981021 19
HF3401.5 .C66 1986

Série Cadernos técnicos .
(no. 24) Comercialização de alimentos na região norte, 1985 /. Brasília, DF , 1985. 51 p. ; LC Card 86-129086
HD9014.B83 N673 1985

Serie CEE.
Fernández Ordóñez, Francisco. España y la CEE . Madrid, España , 1985. 74 p. ; ISBN 84-505-4317-0 LC Card 86-151137
HG2980.5.A6 F47 1985

Serie: Ciencias económicas y empresariales.
(núm. 24) Iniciación a la economía andaluza /. [Seville, Spain] [1986] 196, [4] p. : ISBN 84-7405-343-9 LC Card 87-152155
HC387.A64 I54 1986

Serie científica (Universidad Central del Este) .
Vidal, Máximo Luis. El fin de la era del petróleo y su impacto sobre la economía mundial . San Pedro de Macorís, R.D. , 1981. 103 p. : LC Card 82-202556
HD9502.5.A433 D658 1981

Serie Cochambamba .
(3) Calderón G., Fernando. La Cancha . [Cochababma, Bolivia] , 1984. 208 p. : LC Card 85-238895
HF5473.B62 C363 1984

Serie "Comentarios sobre asuntos económicos" .
(no. [53]) Las Exportaciones y la incidencia del sector externo en el desarrollo económico. [San José] , 1984. 32, [8], [7], 4 leaves ; LC Card 87-115490 DDC 338.1/097286 19
HD9014.C772 E95 1984

(no. 55) Picado Hidalgo, Roberto. La inflación y la política económica, el caso de Costa Rica . [San José] , 1985. 16, 20 p. ; LC Card 86-219388
HC143 .P52 1985

(no. 59) Lizano Fait, Eduardo. La condicionalidad cruzada y la deuda externa /. [San José] , 1986. 16, [1] leaves : LC Card 87-127835 DDC 336.3/435/091724 19
HJ8899 .L59 1986

(no. 64) Delgado Q., Félix. Programas de estabilización y condicionalidad en Costa Rica /. San José, Costa Rica , 1986. 30, [6] leaves ; LC Card 87-404196 DDC 338.97286 19
HC143 .D45 1986

Série Comunicação & informática.
Rattner, Henrique. Informática e sociedade /. São Paulo-SP , 1985. 219 p. : LC Card 85-221850
HC79.T4 R387 1985

Serie Controversia .
(no. 105) Gallón Giraldo, Gustavo. Concertación simple y concertación ampliada /. Bogotá, Colombia [between 1982 and 1985] 62 p. ; LC Card 85-147865
HC197 .G25 1982

Serie Cooperativismo (Curitiba, Brazil) .
(1) Propostas cooperativistas /. Curitiba , 1986. 56 p. : LC Card 87-403655 DDC 334 19
HD2953 .P76 1986

Serie Cuadernos de investigación (Centro de Estudios Monetarios Latinamericanos. Departamento de Investigaciones) .
(núm. 3) Gómez de Reyes, María Teresa. Experiencias de políticas de estabilización . México, D.F. , 1985. iv, 66 leaves ; LC Card 87-122042 DDC 338.982 19
HC125 .G57 1985

Serie Cuadernos de investigación (Centro de Estudios Monetarios Latinoamericanos, Departamento de Investigaciones) .
(núm. 2) Cervantes Islas, Joel. La inflación en dos marcos cambiarios . México, D.F. , 1985. iv, 67 leaves ; LC Card 87-108752 DDC 332.4/1/098 19
HG660.5 .C43 1985

(núm. 4) Lejavitzer, Moisés. Políticas de incentivos a la exportación de manufacturas en América Latina . México, D.F. , 1985. iv, 155 leaves ; LC Card 87-122013 DDC 382/.4567/098 19
HF1480.5 .L44 1985

(núm. 5) Calderón González, Arnoldo. América Latina y el Caribe . México, D.F. , 1985. 51, [25] leaves ; LC Card 87-121714 DDC 332.4/98 19
HG660.5 .C35 1985

(núm. 8) Mántey de Anguiano, M. G. Análisis microeconómico de los factores que determinan el valor de mercado de las empresas industriales mexicanas y su tasa de expansión /. [Mexico City] [1986] iv, 63 leaves : LC Card 87-400949 DDC 658.1/5/0972 19
HG4092 .M36 1986

(núm. 9) Glower, Carlos J., 1952- América Latina y el sistema monetario internacional /. [Mexico City, Mexico] [1986] iv, 28 leaves : LC Card 87-400944 DDC 332.4/56098 29
HG3881 .G577 1986

Serie D (CELADE (Organization)) .
(no. 87) Feeney, Griffith. [Estimating infant mortality rates from child survivorship data by age of mother. Spanish.] Estimación de tasas de mortalidad infantil a partir de información de sobrevivencia de hijos clasificados por edad de la madre /. Santiago de Chile , 1977. 19 p. : LC Card 83-176243
HB1323.I42 T87418 1977

(no. 91) Arretx, Carmen. Cuatro lecciones de William Brass . Santiago de Chile , 1977. 88 p. : LC Card 83-169600
HB1321.B73 A77 1977

Serie de estudios económicos (Banco Central de Chile) .
(no. 14) Gutiérrez Urrutia, Mario. Reflexiones sobre apertura financiera . Santiago , 1982. 36 p. : LC Card 82-203323
HG845 .G87 1982

(no. 24) Valenzuela Cornejo, Ignacio. Costo real del crédito en 1984 /. Santiago , 1985. 28 p. ; LC Card 86-106375 DDC 332.7/0983 19
HG3729.C52 V35 1985

(no. 25) Rosende Ramírez, Francisco. Tipo de cambio y salarios reales . Santiago , 1985. 28 p. : LC Card 86-106380 DDC 332.4/5/0983 19
HG3934 .R67 1985

(no. 27) Rojas Ramos, Patricio. Demanda dinámica por trabajo /. Santiago , 1986. 58 p. : LC Card 87-404328 DDC 331.12/5/0983 19
HD5756.A6 R65 1986

Serie de estudios económicos (Banco Central de Chile). Documentos de investigación .
(no. 19) Toso C., Roberto. El tipo de cambio fijo en Chile . Santiago , 1983. 64 p. ; LC Card 83-192876
HG3934 .T67 1983

Serie de estudios profundos .
(no. 6) Okai, Matthew. Rural poverty and alleviation measures in Sierra Leone /. [Rome] , 1983. 91 p. : LC Card 87-400417 DDC 338.1/8/664 19
HC1065.Z9 P66 1983

Serie de historia (Madrid, Spain)
Tortella Casares, Gabriel. Introducción a la economía para historiadores /. Madrid , 1986. xv, 192 p. : ISBN 84-309-1262-2 LC Card 86-219657
HB178.5 .T693 1986

Serie de indicadores económico sociales.
Teitelboim G., Berta. Indicadores económicos y sociales [microform] . Santiago, Chile [1984] 41 p. : ***NYPL [*ZT-1711 no.26]***

Serie de indicadores económico sociales.
Teitelboim G., Berta. Indicadores económicos y sociales . Santiago, Chile , 1985. 57 p. : ***NYPL [JLD 86-2146]***

Serie de informes técnicos .
(DGSPOA/IT/109) Esquema de ordenamiento territorial de la faja petrolífera del Orinoco . Caracas , 1982. 46 p. : LC Card 86-162734
HC238.O75 E87 1982

Serie de manuales (Latin American Centre for Economic and Social Documentation) .
(no. 2) Guía conceptual y metodológica para instructores de cursos de capacitación de INFOPLAN. Santiago de Chile , 1983. iv, 70 p. : LC Card 87-108080
HC125 .G814 1983

Serie de publicaciones del Frente Democrático de Economistas, F.D.E.
Ecuador, política económica--teoría y realidad. [Guayaquil] [1986- v. <1-3 > ; LC Card 87-105005
HF1519 .E3 1986

Serie de trabajos metodológicos y sectoriales .
(no. 16 (julio de 1981)) Energía eléctrica /. [Buenos Aires] [1981] 27 p., [6] leaves of plates : LC Card 87-401272 DDC 333.79/3212/0982 19
HD9685.A72 E54 1981

(no. 16) Energía eléctrica /. [Buenos Aires] [1981] 27 p., [6] leaves of plates : LC Card 87-401272 DDC 333.79/3212/0982 19
HD9685.A72 E54 1981

(no. 20) Oferta y demanda global a precios corrientes /. [Buenos Aires, Argentina] , 1982. 115 leaves ; LC Card 87-402103 DDC 339.382 19
HC180.I5 O38 1982

(no. 22 (dic. 1982)) Agricultura, caza, silvicultura y pesca . [Buenos Aires] [1982] 57 p. : LC Card 87-401763 DDC 338.1/0982/021 19
HD1862 .A58 1982

(no. 22) Agricultura, caza, silvicultura y pesca . [Buenos Aires] [1982] 57 p. : LC Card 87-401763 DDC 338.1/0982/021 19
HD1862 .A58 1982

Série Debates (Campinas, São Paulo, Brazil)
Getúlio Vargas e a economia contemporânea /. Campinas , 1986. 179 p. ; ISBN 85-26-80033-7 LC Card 87-403048 DDC 330.981/063 19
HC187 .G45 1986

Serie Décimo aniversario.
1976-1985, diez años de la industria petrolera nacional. [Caracas] [1986- v. <1-2 > : ISBN 980-259-069-X (set) LC Card 87-403692 DDC 338.2/7282/0987 19
HD9574.V42 A56 1986

Serie del pensamiento latino americano .
Serie Departamentos académicos .
(no. 2) Román de Silgado, Manuel. Burocracia y cambio social /. [Lima] , 1975. 327 p. : LC Card 77-553812
JF1355 .R688 ***NYPL [JLC 77-327]***

Serie Desarrollo rural .
(4) Tealdo, Armando. La planificación en empresas agropecuarias . Lima, Perú [1985], c1983. 157 p. : LC Card 85-174266 DDC 630/.68 19
HD9000.5 .T4 1985 ***NYPL [JLD 86-1283]***

Série d'études par l'IRNU sur la revolution verte. see United Nations. Research Institute for Social Development. Report.

Serie di economia Boringhieri.
Marrama, Vittorio. Programmazione e sviluppo in Unione Sovietica /. Torino , c1983. 146 p. : LC Card 85-175586
HC336.25 .M358 1983

Serie Distribución del ingreso .
(1) Antecedentes estadísticos de la distribución del ingreso. Santiago de Chile , 1986. 49 p. ; LC Card 87-115916 DDC 339.2/09861 19
HC200.I5 A58 1986

(2) Antecedentes estadísticos de la distribución del ingreso. Santiago de Chile , 1986. 50 p. ; LC Card 87-115965 DDC 339.2/0981 19
HC190.I5 A57 1986

Serie Divulgación económica .
(no. 24) Trejos S., Juan Diego. Las políticas de distribución y redistribución del ingreso en Costa Rica en la década de los años setenta /. Ciudad Universitaria Rodrigo Facio , 1983. 117 p. ; LC Card 85-242016
HC143.Z9 I527 1983

Série Documentos (Brazil. Secretaria de Tecnologia Industrial) .
(17) Avaliação do Programa Nacional do Álcool /. Brasília , 1985. 175 p. : LC Card 86-146662
HD9502.5.A433 B622 1985

Serie Documentos de investigación .
(documento no. 12) Rizzo, Sócrates. Opciones de política económica, 1979-1982 /. México, D.F. [1983] 133 p. : LC Card 86-205260 DDC 338.972 19
HC135 .R44 1983

Serie Documentos de trabajo (Academia de Humanismo Cristiano (Santiago, Chile). Grupo de Investigaciones Agrarias) .
(no. 23) Cruz, María Elena. Chile--opciones y desafíos del sindicalismo rural, 1973-1985 /. Santiago, Chile , 1985. 57 p. ; LC Card 87-100897
HD6619.A29 C78 1985

Serie Documentos de trabajo (Centro de Informaciones y Estudios del Uruguay) .
(79/10) Lombardi, Nelly Niedworok de.

Algunas cifras sobre la fuerza de trabajo en el Uruguay /. [Montevideo] [1979] 18 leaves : LC Card 86-164130
HD5762.A6 L66 1979

(80/23) Apezechea, Héctor J., 1937- Tasas de participación y relaciobes multivariadas a partir e la información de la encuesta de hogares del segundo semestre de 1978 . [Montevideo, Uruguay] , 1980. 12, [44] leaves ; LC Card 86-157658
HD5762.A6 A64 1980

Serie Documentos de trabajo (Centro de Investigaciones Económicas (Instituto Torcuato Di Tella)) .
(115) Diéguez, Héctor L. Mercados de trabajo y distribución de ingresos en cuatro centros urbanos de Argentina, 1974-1981 /. Buenos Aires, Argentina , 1984. 49 p. ; ISBN 950-621-013-6 LC Card 87-401771 DDC 331.12/982 19
HD5749 .D54 1984

Serie Documentos de trabajo (Centro Interdisciplinario de Estudios sobre el Desarrollo Uruguay) .
(no. 3) Jacob, Raúl, 1946- Algunas consideraciones acerca de la formación económica del Uruguay, 1726-1930 /. Montevideo, Uruguay [1985 or 1986] 56 p. ; LC Card 86-202376 DDC 330.9895/065 19
HC232 .J287 1985

(no. 7) Astori, Danilo. La agricultura campesina en América Latina . Montevideo, Uruguay [1985?] 35 p. ; LC Card 86-204310 DDC 338.1/098 19
HD1790.5 .A85 1985

Serie Documentos de trabajo (Corporación de Estudios para el Desarrollo (Ecuador)) .
(no. 1) Análisis del presupuesto general del estado de 1986. [Quito, Ecuador] [1986] ii, 2, 26, 8 p. ; LC Card 87-115859
HJ955 .A523 1986

Série Documentos do Nordeste .
(4) Takeya, Denise Monteiro. Um outro Nordeste . Fortaleza , 1985. 137 p. : LC Card 86-232681
HD9084.B62 R568 1985

Serie Documentos (INTERCOOP, Editora Cooperativa Ltda.) .
(no. 8) La Gestión en empresas cooperativas . Buenos Aires, Argentina [1985] 146 p. ; ISBN 950-0-01257-11 LC Card 87-115117 DDC 334/.0982/54 19
HD3470.A3 C674 1985

Serie Documentos (Muller y Machicado Asociados)
Acuerdos y documentos de la nueva política económica, 1986 /. [La Paz, Bolivia?] [1987] 134 p. ; LC Card 87-403664 DDC 338.984 19
HC182 .A585 1987

Série Documentos (São Paulo (Brazil). Secretaria Municipal do Planejamento)
Cortiços em São Paulo . São Paulo , 1986. 195, [2] p. : LC Card 87-119201 DDC 363.5/8 19
HD7287.96.B62 S263 1986

Serie Documentos (Universidad de Lima. Centro de Investigaciones Económicas y Sociales) .
(no. 2) Rebolledo Soberón, Luis. Deuda externa . [Lima] , c1985. 58 p. : LC Card 86-120059
HJ8514.5 .R43 1985

(no. 3) Alcalde Cardoza, Xavier. Fondo Monetario como actor político en la escena internacional /. Lima, Perú [1986] 54 p. ; LC Card 87-400166 DDC 332.1/52 19
HG3881.5.I58 A44 1986

Serie Economía (Azcapotzalco, Mexico)
Bortz, Jeff. La estructura de salarios en México /. Azcapotzalco, México, D.F. , 1985. 371 p. : ISBN 968-8402-76-1 LC Card 87-104886
HD4981 .B67 1985

Serie Economía española (Spain. Ministerio de Economía y Hacienda. Secretaría de Estado de Comercio) .
(6) Sánchez Muñoz, María Paloma. La dependencia tecnológica española . [Madrid] [1984?] xi, 591 p. : ISBN 84-7415-170-8 : LC Card 86-212990
HC390.T4 S26 1984

Série Economie et sociologie rurales.
Berger, Alain. Les récoltants vendeurs au kilo champenois face au contrat interprofessionnel /. Paris , Epernay [1984] 45, 63 p. : ISBN 2-85340-534-6 LC Card 85-111856
HD9382.7.C5 B47 1984

Nicourt, Christian. Conditions de travail en agriculture . Paris , <1985-. v. <2 > : ISBN 2-85340-585-0 (v. 2) LC Card 86-218948
HD1536.F8 N53 1985

Série Elections sociales .
(no 2) Bon, Frédéric, 1943- Résultats des élections aux conseils de prud'hommes par département . St. Martin d'Hères [France] [1982] 303 p. ; LC Card 84-152037
HD5555 .B65 1982

Serie Ensayo (Instituto Nacional de Antropología e Historia (Mexico))
Villanueva, Eric. Crisis henequenera y movimientos campesinos en Yucatán, 1966-1983 /. México, D.F. , 1985. 220 p., [10] p. of plates : ISBN 968-603-803-5 LC Card 86-118134 DDC 304.8/0972/65 19
HD9156.H463 M67 1985
NYPL [JLD 87-342]

Serie "Esquemas" .
(no. 4) Caputo, Orlando. Notas metodológicas para el análisis de la nueva forma de funcionamiento del capitalismo . Cochabamba [1980] 33 leaves ; LC Card 83-204246
HC192 .C216 1980

Série Estatísticas básicas da economia brasileira .
(no. 2, 3) Lima, José Luiz. Estatísticas básicas do setor agrícola no Brasil /. São Paulo , 1983- v. : LC Card 83-219032 DDC 338.1/0981 19
HD9014.B82 L55 1983 ***NYPL [JLL 86-432]***

(no. 4) Costa, Iraci del Nero da. Paraná . São Paulo , 1985. 185 p. : LC Card 86-158196
HA984 .C67 1985

Serie Estudios agrarios (Asunción, Paraguay)
Fogel, Ramón B. Movimientos campesinos en el Paraguay /. Asunción, Paraguay , 1986. 230 p., [1] leaf of plates : LC Card 86-189517
HD1531.P3 F64 1986

Serie Estudios (Buenos Aires, Argentina)
Conesa, Eduardo R. Fuga de capitales . Buenos Aires , 1986. 78 p. : LC Card 87-400256 DDC 332.4/5 19
HG3931 .C66 1986

Serie Estudios (Centro de Estudios Monetarios y Bancarios (Santo Domingo, Dominican Republic))
Dauhajre, Andrés. Reforma financiera en pequeñas economías abiertas /. Santo Domingo, República Dominicana , 1986. 97 p. : LC Card 87-402920 DDC 332.4/56097293 19
HG3926.5 .D38 1986

González Vega, Claudio. Mercados financieros rurales en América Latina /. Santo Domingo, República Dominicana , 1986. 44 p. ; LC Card 87-400002 DDC 332.7/1/098 19
HG2051.L26 G66 1986

González Vega, Claudio. Mercados financieros y desarrollo /. Santo Domingo, República Dominicana , 1986. 73 p. : LC Card 87-102022
HG2817 .G66 1986

Mercados financieros y distribución del ingreso /. Santo Domingo, República Dominicana , 1986. 117 p. : LC Card 87-405027 DDC 332.1/097293 19
HG185.D65 M47 1986

Poyo, Jeffrey. Los bancos agropecuarios y la captación de depósitos /. Santo Domingo, República Dominicana , 1986. 39 p. : LC Card 87-400523 DDC 332.7/1/097293 19
HG2051.D6 P69 1986

Tejada C., Frank A. Crédito y seguro agrícola . Santo Domingo, República Dominicana , 1986. 104 p. : LC Card 87-400183 DDC 332.7/1/097293 19
HG2051.D6 T45 1986

Serie Estudios (Centro de Investigaciones en Ciencias Sociales) .
(no. 45) Balvé, Beba. De protesta a rebelión--la "subversión" (Rosario, mayo 1969) /. Buenos Aires, Argentina [1985] xvii, 123 p. ; LC Card 86-162379
HD5350.R67 B35 1985

Serie Estudios (Centro Nacional de Información y Estadísticas del Trabajo (Mexico)) .
(4) Pedrero, Mercedes. Indicadores para el estudio de la población económicamente activa basados en la información censal de 1970 /. México, D.F. [1977] 495 p. ; LC Card 85-202779
HA765 .P43 1977

Serie Estudios educativos .
(no. 20) Alaix, Ramón. Experiencias de educación y producción de fe y alegría en Oruro y Santa Cruz . La Paz, Bolivia , 1986. 191 p. ; LC Card 86-208411 DDC 331.25/92/098413 19
HD5715.5.B52 S262 1986

Serie Estudios sociales .
(no. 1) Sánchez Enríquez, Rodrigo. Organización andina, drama y posibilidad /. Huancayo, Perú [1987] xxii, 219 p. : LC Card 87-404025 DDC 330.98/0038 19
HC167.A5 S26 1987

Serie Estudios urbanos (Centro de Estudios de la Realidad Económica y Social (La Paz, Bolivia)) .
(no. 6) Calderón G., Fernando. Jatun Llajta . La Paz, Bolivia , 1982. v, 448 p., [8] leaves of plates : LC Card 83-111937 DDC 381/.1 19
HF5473.B62 C623 1982
NYPL [JLF 86-1794]

Serie Estudios y monografías.
Oyarce Pérez, Luis. Sistema de remuneraciones en la empresa /. Santiago, Chile , 1982. ix, 174 p. : LC Card 84-228804
HD4906 .O98 1982

Série Estudos de política industrial e comércio exterior .
(no. 3) Moldau, Juan Hersztajn. Custo dos recursos domésticos /. Rio de Janeiro , 1985. 94, 4 p. ; LC Card 86-200395
HC190.C7 M64 1985

(no. 8) Cavalcanti, Bianor Scelza. Administração da política industrial no Brasil . Rio de Janeiro , 1986. ii, 87, 10 p. : LC Card 87-102756 DDC 338.981 19
HD3616.B83 C28 1986

(no. 9) Sanson, João Rogério. A política de transportes marítimos no Brasil . Rio de Janeiro , 1986. vii, 178, 5 p. : LC Card 87-403931 DDC 387.5/44/0981 19
HE597.B7 S26 1986

Série Estudos e pesquisas (Fundação Instituto Brasileiro de Geografia e Estatística. Diretoria Técnica) .
(8) Força de trabalho no Brasil . Rio de Janeiro , 1982. 73 p. : ISBN 85-24-00002-3 LC Card 87-403683 DDC 331.12/72/0981 19
HD5717.5.B6 F67 1982

Série Estudos e pesquisas (Fundação Joaquim Nabuco) .
(39) Andrade, Manuel Correia de Oliveira. Classes sociais e agricultura no Nordeste /. Recife , 1985. 105 p. ; ISBN 85-7019-096-4 LC Card 87-119335
HD1875.P4 A84 1985

Série Estudos e pesquisas (Ordem dos Economistas de São Paulo)
O Perfil do economista. [São Paulo, Brazil] [1984?] 60 p. : LC Card 87-402012 DDC 330/.092/2 19
HB123.B8 P47 1984

Série Estudos e pesquisas (Projeto de Desenvolvimento Integrado da Bacia do Araguaia-Tocantins) .
(no. 10) Estudo do mercado de carne bovina /. Brasília , 1985. 89 p. : LC Card 86-197081
HD9433.B82 A74 1985

(no. 13) Perfis indicativos para a industrialização do arroz, milho e soja. Brasília , 1985. 189 p. : LC Card 86-195651
HD9066.B83 A737 1985

(no. 15) Finanças públicas municipais da região do PRODIAT /. Brasília , 1985. 420 p. ; LC Card 86-195656
HJ9388.A2 A734 1985

(no. 7) Finanças públicas dos Estados de Goiás, Maranhão, Mato Grosso e Pará /. Brasília , 1985. 114, [34] p. ; LC Card 87-404251 DDC 336.81 19
HJ929.G65 F56 1985

(no. 9) Projeto de Desenvolvimento Integrado da Bacia do Araguaia-Tocantins. Fontes de financiamento para projetos de desenvolvimento

/. Brasília , 1985. 450 p. : LC Card 86-195649
HC188.A7 P76 1985

Série Estudos e projetos (Centro de Projetos e Estudos (Bahia, Brazil)) .
(2) A Evolução dos setores secundário e terciário da economia baiana na década de 70 /. Salvador , 1985. 80 p. : LC Card 87-124067 DDC 338.4/7/00098142 19
HD9734.B73 B334 1985

Série Estudos especiais .
(5) Ness, Walter L. A influência da correção monetária no sistema financeiro /. Rio de Janeiro , 1977. 205 p. : LC Card 85-206096
HG229 .N385 1977

Série Estudos monográficos .
(1) Polary, José Henrique Braga. Reflexões sobre o quadro global e setorial da economia maranhense /. São Luís [Brazil] , 1981. 60 p. ; LC Card 87-404934 DDC 330.981/21063 19
HC188.M29 P65 1981

(4) Costa Filho, João Evangelista da. Comércio externo do Maranhão /. [São Luís, Maranhão] [1982] 72 p. : LC Card 87-404935 DDC 382/.098121 19
HF3409.M3 C67 1982

Serie Estudos para o planejamento.
(no. 24) Magalhães, Antonio Rocha. Industrialização e desenvolvimento regional . Brasília , 1983. 315 p. : LC Card 84-160221 DDC 338.981/3 19
HD3616.B84 N676 1983
NYPL [JLD 86-3120]

Série Estudos (Portugal. Ministério do Trabalho. Gabinete de Estudos, Planeamento e Organização) .
(36) Moura, João. Problemas e política de emprego no continente /. Lisboa , 1977. 56 p. ; LC Card 85-214189
HD5809.A6 M68 1977

Série Estudos regionais .
(11) Andrade, Manuel Correia de Oliveira. Sertão sul /. Recife , 1984. 648, [26] p. : LC Card 87-404838 DDC 330.981/3063 19
HC188.N6 A687 1984

(12) O Norte cearense /. Recife , 1985. 303 p. : LC Card 86-209022
HD1875.C4 N67 1985

(9) Melo, Mário Lacerda de. O meio-norte /. Recife , 1983. 474 p., [1] folded leaf of plates : LC Card 84-231900
HC188.N6 M45 1983

Série "Estudos" (Serviço de Educação Popular (Rio de Janeiro, Brazil)) .
(2) Capitalismo e classe operária no Brasil /. Petrópolis , 1984. 69 p. ; LC Card 86-222585
HC51 .C35 1984

Serie Eventos técnicos .
(no. 2) Foro . San Felipe, Venezuela , 1984. ii, 92 p. ; LC Card 85-132901 DDC 338.1/0987 19
HD1912 .F67 1984 ***NYPL [JLD 86-424]***

Série Fac-símile .
(no. 10) Werneck, Rogério L. Furquim. Desequilíbrio externo e reorientação do crescimento e dos investimentos . Rio de Janeiro-RJ [1983?] 130 p. ; LC Card 87-403024 DDC 338.981 19
HC187 .W47 1983

(no. 11) Santos, José Carlos de Souza. Demanda de fatores e ofertas na agricultura brasileira . Rio de Janeiro , 1983. 110 p. ; LC Card 87-403023 DDC 338.1/0981 19
HD1872 .S25 1983

(no. 12) Pinto, Maurício Barata de Paula. O potencial das exportações brasileiras de manufaturados /. Rio de Janeiro , 1983. 46 p. ; LC Card 87-403022 DDC 382/.4567/0981 19
HD9734.B72 P56 1983

(no. 15) Saboia, João, 1944- Evolução histórica do salário mínimo no Brasil . Rio de Janeiro , 1984. 106 p. ; LC Card 87-403844 DDC 331.2/3 19
HD4920.B8 S265 1984

Serie Historia social.
Herken Krauer, Juan Carlos, 1953- El Paraguay rural entre 1869 y 1913 . Asunción, Paraguay , 1984. 224 p., [10] p. of plates : LC Card 84-237050
HC222 .H47 1984

Serie Historia y sociedad (Valladolid, Spain) .
(no. 3) Martínez Moro, Jesús. La tierra en la comunidad de Segovia . [Valladolid] [Salamanca] , c1985. 252 p. : ISBN 84-86192-37-4 LC Card 86-211593
HD780.S44 M37 1985

Serie Indices y catálogos.
Nuevo León (Mexico : State). Archivo General del Estado. Permisos y concesiones, 1890-1912 /. [Monterrey, Mexico] [1981] 43 leaves ; LC Card 81-216459
HD3616.M44 N866 1981

Serie Informes (Centro de Informaciones y Estudios del Uruguay) .
(85/28) Argenti, Gisela. Cambio técnico, trabajo y educación . Montevideo , 1985. 91, 70 leaves : LC Card 87-124118
HC235.T4 A74 1985

Série "Initiation économique" (Yaoundé, Cameroon)
Sobgui, Gabriel Alexis. L'épreuve écrite à la capacité en droit et en économie /. Yaoundé, Cameroun , 1981. 113 p. ; LC Card 84-118988
HB74.6 .S65 1981

Serie Inspección del trabajo .
(no. 24) Galin, Pedro. Condiciones de trabajo y coordinación de las inspecciones /. Lima, Perú , 1986. 19 p. ; LC Card 87-401748 DDC 331.25 19
HD6957.L29 G35 1986

Série Instrumentos para a ação .
(4) Santos, Madalena Herculano dos. Condições de vida nos municípios paraibanos /. João Pessoa (PB) : Brasília, DF : 103 p. : LC Card 87-403990 DDC 330.981/33063 19
HC188.P343 S26 1986

Serie Investigaciones (Centro Latinoamericano de Economía Humana) .
(no. 18) Melgar, Alicia. Distribución del ingreso en el Uruguay /. Montevideo , 1981. 87 p. ; LC Card 86-160100
HC235.I5 M448 1981

Serie Investigaciones externas.
Frediani, Ramón O. El rol del empresario mediano en el desarrollo argentino . Buenos Aires, República Argentina , c1985. 123 p. : LC Card 87-101993
HD2346.A73 F73 1985

Serie Investigaciones (Montevideo, Uruguay) .
(no. 18) González, José I. (José Iván), 1944- La segmentación del mercado del crédito y sus impactos sobre la distribución del ingreso /. Montevideo, Uruguay , 1984. ii, 5, 123 p. : LC Card 85-236586
HG3754.5.U8 G66 1984

(no. 7) Martorelli, Horacio. Las relaciones de trabajos de las mujeres en zonas rurales . Montevideo, Uruguay , 1981. 264 p. : LC Card 86-202374 DDC 331.4/83/09895 19
HD6132 .M375 1981

(no. 9) Martorelli, Horacio. Nuevo estilo de desarrollo para Uruguay . Montevideo, Uruguay , 1982. 2 v. : LC Card 85-167867 DDC 338.1/09895 19
HD1907 .M376 1982 ***NYPL [JLF 86-935]***

Rocca, José. Excedentes financieros y sistema bancario, Uruguay, 1974-1982 /. Montevideo, Uruguay , 1985. 39 p. : LC Card 85-213768
HC235.S3 R63 1985

Serie investigaciones (Universidad de Costa Rica. Instituto de Investigaciones Sociales)
Aguilar Bolaños, Irene. Una caracterización socioeconómica del grupo ganaderoexportador (los casos de San Carlos y Guanacaste) 1960-1980 /. San José, Costa Rica , 1985. xiii, 260 p. ; LC Card 86-107500
HD9433.C83 S223 1985 ***NYPL [JLF 87-74]***

Serie "La Ciencia económica soviética" .
(2) Relaciones agrarias en el socialismo. Moscú , 1986. 223 p. ; LC Card 87-126164
HD9015.S652 R45 1986

Serie La Economía ecuatoriana de los últimos años .
(no. 3) La Política económica del gobierno de Febres Cordero. Quito, Ecuador [1986] 84 p. : LC Card 87-403470
HC202 .P65 1986

(no. 4) Los Grupos monopólicos en el Ecuador . Quito, Ecuador , 1986. 208 p. : LC Card 87-404236 DDC 338.8/2/09866 19
HD2838 .G78 1986

Serie La Invención.
Flores, Edmundo, 1918- Historias de Edmundo Flores. México , 1983-<c1986. v. <1-2 > : ISBN 968-471-052-6 (v. 1) LC Card 83-199689
HB123.M43 F564 1983

Serie Libros FLACSO-Chile .
(10) Lechner, Norbert, 1939- La conflictiva y nunca acabada construcción del orden deseado /. [Santiago, Chile] [1984] 204 p. ; ISBN 84-89401-05-5 LC Card 84-227472 DDC 320.982 19
JL2624 .L43 1984 ***NYPL [JLE 87-2137]***

Serie Liminar. Economía.
Outes Ruso, Xosé Luis, 1943- Introducción a la teoría del crecimiento económico /. Sada, A Coruña , 1984. 359 p. : ISBN 84-7492-320-4 LC Card 87-105223
HD75.5 .O97 1984

Serie Los Pescadores de México .
(v. 10) Alcalá, Graciela. Los pescadores de Tecolutla . México, D.F. , 1985. 215 p. : ISBN 968-496-070-0 LC Card 86-191825
HD8039.F652 M62 1985

(v. 8) Dachary, Alfredo César. El Caribe mexicano . México, D.F. , 1985. 110 p. : ISBN 968-496-069-7 LC Card 86-118335 DDC 338.3/7270972 19
HD8039.F66 M426 1985
NYPL [JLD 87-1321]

Serie Mens en ruimte .
(20) Dijk, Jouke van. Migratie en arbeidsmarkt /. Assen , 1986. 239 p. : ISBN 90-232-2213-X : LC Card 86-215033
HB2065 .D54 1986

Serie Monografías (Universidad del Valle. Centro de Investigaciones y Documentación Socio-Económica) .
(monografía no. 8) Salazar T., Boris. Las formas de consumo en Colombia . [Cali, Colombia] [1982] 118, [45] p. ; LC Card 85-192219 DDC 658.8/343/0986152 19
HC200.C6 S25 1982 ***NYPL [JLD 86-1935]***

Série Pesquisa (Instituto Brasileiro de Relações do Trabalho) .
(no. 4) Os Sindicatos e a transição democrática . São Paulo , 1986. 294 p. ; LC Card 87-153581 DDC 331.88/0981 19
HD6612 .S55 1986

Série Planejamento e programação .
(no. 3) Projeto de Desenvolvimento Integrado da Bacia do Araguaia-Tocantins. Plano de desenvolvimento das áreas-programa de Araguaína e Tocantinópolis /. Brasília , 1985. 95 p., [8] leaves of plates : LC Card 86-200369
HC189.A67 P76 1985

(no. 4) Projeto de Desenvolvimento Integrado da Bacia do Araguaia-Tocantins. Plano de desenvolvimento da área-programa do Vale do Paraná /. Brasília , 1985. 128 p., [8] folded leaves of plates : LC Card 86-199833
HC188.P36 P76 1985

Série PNPE .
(10) Barbosa, Fernando de Holanda. Microeconomia--teoria, modelos econométricos e aplicações à economia brasileira /. Rio de Janeiro , 1985. 534 p. : LC Card 87-118555 DDC 338.5 19
HB179.P75 B37 1985

(11) Araujo Júnior, José Tavares de. Tecnologia, concorrência e mudança estrutural . Rio de Janeiro , 1985. 64 p. ; LC Card 87-120280 DDC 338/.06 19
HD70.B7 A7 1985

(13) Haddad, Paulo Roberto. Dimensões do planejamento estadual no Brasil . Rio de Janeiro , 1985. 188 p. : LC Card 86-195636
HC188.M6 H33 1985

(7) Hollanda Filho, Sergio Buarque de. Estrutura industrial no Brasil . Rio de Janeiro , 1983. 275 p. : LC Card 87-119359 DDC 338.8/0981 19
HD2834 .H65 1983

(9) Mueller, Charles Curt. Das oligarquias agrárias ao predomínio urbano-industrial . Rio de Janeiro , 1983. 363 p. ; LC Card 87-403875 DDC 305.5/232/0981 19
HC187 .M76 1983

Série População e emprego .
(18) Dinâmica da economia e absorção de mão-de-obra . Recife , 1984. 79 p. ; ISBN

85-7019-063-8 LC Card 85-156612 DDC 338.981/3 19
HD5755.N63 D56 1984
NYPL [JLE 86-3545]

Serie Programa de Asesoramiento Minero .
(1) Desabastecimiento de alimentos y alternativas de solución en las minas . La Paz [Bolivia] , 1986. 128 : LC Card 87-401454 DDC 331.7/6223453/098413 19
HD8039.M72 B624 1986

Série Programas especiais .
(10) Brazil. Ministério do Interior. Subsecretaria de Programas Regionais. Programa de aproveitamento de recursos hídricos do Nordeste . Brasília [1980] [73] leaves ; LC Card 87-403686 DDC 333.91/00981/3 19
HD1696.B84 N649 1980

(34) Brazil. Ministério do Interior. Subsecretaria de Programas Regionais. Programas especiais . [Brasília] [1981] 1 v. (various foliations) ; LC Card 87-403680 DDC 338.981/1 19
HD1875.A347 B7 1981

(37) A Agricultura irrigada como estratégia de desenvolvimento regional /. Brasília [198-] 56 leaves ; LC Card 87-403682 DDC 338.1/62 19
HD1741.B82 N614 1980z

(57) Brazil. Ministério do Interior. Subsecretaria de Programas Regionais. Minutas das exposições de motivos e portarias dos programas . [Brasília] [1983?] [40] leaves ; LC Card 87-400579 DDC 333.91/15/0981 19
HD1696.B8 B75 1983

(6) Atuação dos programas especiais no Estado do Piauí /. [Brasília] [1980] [29] leaves : LC Card 87-403685 DDC 333.91/0098122 19
HD1696.B83 P523 1980

(61) Projeto sertanejo . [Brasília] [1982?] 20 leaves, [1] leaf of plates : LC Card 87-405007
HD1875.N6 P76 1982

Série Projecto Nordeste .
(vol. 2) Aspectos gerais da economia e da sociedade do Nordeste. Recife , 1984. 318 p. : LC Card 86-159446
HC188.N6 A75 1984

Série Projetos sócio-econômicos .
(no. 4) Construção de habitações na zona rural da microrregião do São Francisco /. Recife , 1982. 23 leaves ; LC Card 86-175009
HD7289.B72 S263 1982

Série Publicações misceláneas .
(no. 313) Cussianovich, Pedro. Economía y energía en Costa Rica . San José, Costa Rica , 1982. viii, 71, [10] leaves : LC Card 86-179795
HD9502.C82 C87 1982

(no. 666) Agricultural marketing handbook for Caribbean Basin products. Spanish. Manual--mercadeo de productos agrícolas de la Cuenca del Caribe /. San José, Costa Rica . x, 434 p. : ISBN 92-9039-101-4 LC Card 86-204686
HD9014.C442 A4718 1986

Série Rapports de séminaires.
Séminaire de formation aux techniques d'élaboration de projets (1980 : Conakry, Guinea, etc.) Séminaire de formation aux techniques d'élaboration de projets . Addis-Abeba , 1982. vii, 36, [31] p. : LC Card 86-168821
HC800 .S444 1980

Série Registros .
(7) 1o. de maio . [São Paulo] , 1985. 80 p. : LC Card 86-200658
HD8286 .A13 1985

Serie Relaciones internacionales .
(no. 1) Política internacional, economía e integración /. Asunción del Paraguay [1985] 178 p. ; LC Card 86-122468
HF1523 .P65 1985

Série Relatórios de pesquisa .
(no. 20) Endo, Seiti Kaneko. Pesquisa de orçamentos familiares no município de São Paulo /. São Paulo [Rio de Janeiro] , 1984. 131 p. : LC Card 85-136517
HB235.B8 E53 1984

(no. 29) O Mercado de trabalho no Brasil . São Paulo , 1986. 263 p. : LC Card 86-221361
HD5754 .M47 1986

(no. 33) Economia informal, tecnologia apropriada e associativismo /. São Paulo , 1986. 176 p. : LC Card 86-233370
HC190.P6 E34 1986

(no. 34) Milone, Paulo Cesar. População, migração e desenvolvimento econômico . São Paulo , 1986. 150 p. : LC Card 87-118486 DDC 304.6/0981 19
HB3563 .M45 1986

(no. 35) Martone, Celso L. (Celso Luiz) Mercado financeiro e ajustamento macroeconômico brasileiro, 1978-1985 /. São Paulo , 1986. 82 p. : LC Card 87-120453 DDC 332.4/981 19
HG835 .M375 1986

(v. 20) Endo, Seiti Kaneko. Pesquisa de orçamentos familiares no município de São Paulo /. São Paulo [Rio de Janeiro] , 1984. 131 p. : LC Card 85-136517
HB235.B8 E53 1984

Série Relatórios setoriais.
Jucá, Alvaro Ferraz. Gênero industrial--têxtil /. [Recife] [1985?] 34 leaves ; LC Card 86-204296
HD9864.B83 P475 1985

Serie Resultados, ponencias y recomendaciones de eventos técnicos .
(no. 337) A Mulher rural e mudanças no processo de produção agrícola . [Brasília] [1984] i, 161 p. ; LC Card 86-150197
HD6073.A292 L295 1984

Serie Seminarios y talleres .
(no. 4) Taller "Perspectivas y Alternativas de la Agricultura Familiar" (1983 : Montevideo, Uruguay) Taller "Perspectivas y Alternativas de la Agricultura Familiar". Montevideo, Uruguay [1984] 1 v. (various pagings) : LC Card 85-203149 DDC 338.1/6 19
HD1476.L29 T35 1983 ***NYPL [JLF 86-884]***

(no. 7) Taller sobre Identificación de Políticas que Permitan Dinamizar el Complejo de Producción y Comercialización de Carnes Rojas, con Enfasis en la Industria Frigorífica (1984 : Montevideo, Uruguay) Taller sobre Identificación de Políticas que Permitan Dinamizar el Complejo de Producción y Comercialización de Carnes Rojas, con Enfasis en la Industria Frigorífica. Montevideo, Uruguay [1985] 13, 18, 16 p. : LC Card 85-236237
HD9440.U82 T35 1984

Serie Simposios y seminarios internacionales .
(no. 2) El Perú frente al capital extranjero . Lima, Perú [1985] xl, 399 p. : LC Card 86-109611 DDC 332.6/73/0985 19
HG5392 .P47 1985 ***NYPL [JLD 87-384]***

Serie Técnica. Administración .
(N 1) Nociones básicas sobre cooperativismo pesquero. [Mexico City, Mexico] , 1985. 313 p. : ISBN 968-8170-25-9 LC Card 86-217319 DDC 334/.6892/0972 19
HD9464.B72 N63 1985

Série Tempo de pensar.
Política agrária /. Porto Alegre-RS , 1985. 79 p. : LC Card 86-198513
HD1531.B7 P65 1985

Série Teses e monografias .
(no. 20) Silva, Armando Corrêa da. O litoral norte do Estado de São Paulo . São Paulo , 1975. 273 p. : LC Card 85-134276
HC189.S343 S58 1975

Série Teses (Editora da UNICAMP)
Leme, Dulce M. Pompêo C. (Dulce Maria Pompêo de Camargo) Trabalhadores ferroviários em greve /. Campinas [Brazil] , 1986. 269 p. : ISBN 85-26-80007-8 : LC Card 87-102922 DDC 331.89/281385/098161 19
HD5354.R12 1906 .S365 1986

Série Teses (Escola de Pós-Graduação em Economia) .
(no. 11) Avila, Luiz Gonçalves. Desenvolvimento industrial e rendimento da terra . Rio de Janeiro, RJ , 1985. 111 p. : LC Card 86-233493
HD1875.S26 A95 1985

(no. 13) Harris, John Andrew de Oliveira. Evolução e definição da moeda /. Rio de Janeiro, RJ , 1985. 90 p. : LC Card 87-135878 DDC 332.4/981 19
HG835 .H37 1985

(no. 8) Pereira, Eduardo Novo da Costa. Bolsa de commodities . Rio de Janeiro, RJ , 1985. ix, 69 p. ; LC Card 86-129753
HG6024.B7 P47 1985

(no. 9) Lucena, José Mário Pereira de. O mercado habitacional no Brasil /. Rio de Janeiro, RJ , 1985. v, 185 p. : LC Card 85-208372
HD7323.A3 L83 1985

Serie Testimonios artesanales de Venezuela.
Naranjo M., José R. La artesanía del queso larense /. Caracas , 1985. 202 p., [16] p. of plates : ISBN 980-265-223-7 LC Card 87-403552 DDC 338.1/773/098725 19
HD9280.V43 L376 1985

Serie universitaria (Fundación Juan March) .
(209) López Alonso, Carmen. Los rostros y la realidad de la pobreza en la sociedad castellana medieval (siglos XIII-XV) /. Madrid [1983?] 54 p. ; ISBN 84-7075-284-7 LC Card 87-110606
HC387.C244 L66 1983

(209) López Alonso, Carmen. Los rostros y la realidad de la pobreza en la sociedad castellana medieval (siglos XIII-XV) /. Madrid [1983?] 54 p. ; ISBN 84-7075-284-7 LC Card 87-110606
HC387.C244 L66 1983

(221) Ruesga Benito, Santos, 1953- Métodos de estimación de la economía oculta . Madrid [1985?] 55 p. : ISBN 88-470-7531-18 LC Card 87-111661
HD2346.S7 R84 1985

(226) Izquierdo de Bartolomé, Rafael. Evolución, presente y futuro de la política común de transportes /. Madrid [1985?] 56 p. ; ISBN 84-7075-325-8 LC Card 87-111657
HE242.8 .I97 1985

(230) Fernández Alvarez, Antonio. El impacto de la política agrícola común en la integración española /. Madrid [1986?] 48 p. ; ISBN 84-7075-333-9 LC Card 87-111468
HC241.25.S6 F47 1986

(230) Fernández Alvarez, Antonio. El impacto de la política agrícola común en la integración española /. Madrid [1986?] 48 p. ; ISBN 84-7075-333-9 LC Card 87-111468
HC241.25.S6 F47 1986

(232) González Rodríguez, Juan Jesús. La patronal agraria . Madrid [1986?] 46 p. ; ISBN 84-7075-335-3 LC Card 87-111477
HD6976.A292 S74 1986

(232) González Rodríguez, Juan Jesús. La patronal agraria . Madrid [1986?] 46 p. ; ISBN 84-7075-335-3 LC Card 87-111477
HD6976.A292 S74 1986

Serie varia (Universidad Nacional Autónoma de México. Instituto de Geografía) .
(t. 1, núm. 4) Seminario sobre Conceptos Teóricos de la Geografía Económica (1975 : Mexico City, Mexico?) Seminario sobre Conceptos Teóricos de la Geografía Económica . México , 1978. 78 p. ; LC Card 87-403767 DDC 330.9 19
HC13 .S46 1975

Serie Vrouwen en ontwikkeling in Boven-Volta.
Bosch, Ellie. Marktvrouwen van Bobo . Leiden , 1983. viii, 179 p., [18] p. of plates : LC Card 86-212595
HD6217.5.Z6 B633 1983

Serie Wetenschapsfilosofie.
Klant, J. J. Filosofie van de economische wetenschappen /. Leiden , c1987. 87 p. ; ISBN 90-6890-105-2 : LC Card 87-169944
HB72 .K55 1987

Serien Kvinners levekår og livsløp.
Kvinner i arbeid . Oslo , c1984. 290 p. : ISBN 82-00-06835-8 : LC Card 85-102185
HD6170 .K85 1984

Serien om kvindeforskning .
(nr. 15) Borchorst, Anette. Arbejdsmarkedets kønsopdeling . Aalborg , 1984. 162 p. : ISBN 87-7307-252-4 LC Card 85-106008
HD6060.65.D4 B67 1984
NYPL [JFK 82-214 nr.15]

Series (American Marketing Association) .
(no. 53) 1987 AMA educators' proceedings /. Chicago, Ill. , 1987. xiv, 287 p. ; ISBN 0-87757-182-1 LC Card 87-18680 DDC 658.8 19
HF5411 .A156 1987

Series C--Political and social sciences .
(8) Business interests, organizational

development, and private interest government . Berlin , New York , 1987. viii, 232 p. ; ISBN 0-89925-380-6 (U. S.) : LC Card 87-21403 DDC 338.4/7664 19
HD9000.5 .B87 1987

Series D--Economics .
(2) Gross, Alexander, 1953- The role of the current account in asset market models of exchange rate determination /. Berlin , New York , 1987. xiii, 391 p. : ISBN 0-89925-373-3 (U. S.) : LC Card 87-8852 DDC 332.4/56 19
HG3882 .G75 1987

Series DH3, 0266-3589 .
(no. 17) Mortality statistics . London , 1986. viii, 49 p. ; ISBN 0-11-691069-0 (pbk.) : LC Card 87-147154 DDC 614.5/992 19
HB1323.I42 G764 1984

Series E (Institut řízení) .
(51) Khol, Josef, Dr. An inquiry into the perception of casual relations in problems of management /. Prague , 1976. 26 p. ; LC Card 82-210887 DDC 658.4/03 19
HD30.23 .K375 1976

(53) Smrčka, Jaroslav. Conceptual management of top-level managers /. Prague , 1977. 57 p. ; LC Card 85-139531
HD30.23 .S665 1977

Séries históricas da produção agrícola do Estado do Rio Grande do Norte, 1947-1982 : rendimento médio, área colhida, quantidade produzida, preço e valor da produção / Fundação Estadual de Planejamento Agrícola do Rio Grande do Norte, vinculada à Secretaria da Agricultura. Natal : A Fundação, 1983. 159 leaves : ill. ; 28 cm. Chiefly tables. Bibliography: leaf 159. LC Card 84-246432
1. Agriculture - Economic aspects - Brazil - Rio Grande do Norte - History - 20th century - Statistics. I. Rio Grande do Norte (Brazil). Fundação Estadual de Planejamento Agrícola.
HD1875.R48 S47 1983

Series in memory of Isador Lubin .
(4) Schwartz, Moshe. Non-agricultural employment for moshav youth in the Galilee /. Rehovot, Israel , c1985. 36, [2] p. ; LC Card 86-115596 DDC 331.3/4/0956945 19
HD6276.I66 G347 1985

Series in political economy and economic development in Latin America.
Pastor, Manuel. The International Monetary Fund and Latin America . Boulder, Colo. , 1987. xvi, 228 p. : ISBN 0-8133-7373-5 (pbk. : alk. paper) : LC Card 86-32575 DDC 332.4/98 19
HG660.5 .P33 1987

Series on econometrics and management sciences .
(v. 4) Frontiers in creative and innovative management /. Cambridge, Mass. , 1985, c1986. xxv, 391 p. : ISBN 0-88730-057-X LC Card 85-15125 DDC 658.4 19
HD53 .F76 1986 ***NYPL [JLE 86-3614]***

(v. 5) Innovation diffusion models of new product acceptance /. Cambridge, Mass. , 1986. xvi, 318 p. : ISBN 0-88730-076-6 LC Card 85-23300 DDC 658.8/343 19
HF5415.153 .I55 1986 ***NYPL [JLE 86-3235]***

(v. 7) Theil, Henri. Applied demand analysis . Cambridge, Mass. , 1987. xxi, 279 p. : ISBN 0-88730-217-3 LC Card 86-32230 DDC 338.5/212 19
HB801 .T489 1987

Series on energy conservation and energy policy.
Energy efficiency . Washington, D.C. , 1987, c1986. 333 p. : ISBN 0-918249-05-8 (pbk.) LC Card 86-28817 DDC 333.79/16/0973 19
HD9502.U52 E4883 1987

Series on public issues .
(no. 19) Hamilton, Billy. Outlook for state spending and revenues in the late '80s . College Station, Tex. , c1985. 14 p. : ISBN 0-86599-055-7 (pbk.) LC Card 86-622256 DDC 336.764 19
HJ2053.T5 H36 1985

(no. 21) Greenhut, Melvin L. Report on an income tax in Texas /. College Station, Tex. , c1986. 40 p. : ISBN 0-86599-057-3 (pbk.) LC Card 86-622258 DDC 336.24/09764 19
HJ4655.T4 G74 1986

Series on technology and social priorities.
Technology and global industry . Washington, D.C. , 1987. vi, 272 p. : ISBN 0-309-03736-0 (pbk.) LC Card 87-7765 DDC 338/.06 19
HC79.T4 T438 1987

Series PP2 .
(no. 14) Variant population projections . London , 1986. 17 p. : ISBN 0-11-690777-0 (pbk.) : LC Card 86-234516 DDC 304.6/2/0941021 19
HB3583 .V368 1986

Series 22, Uttar Pradesh. Jilā janagaṇanā hastapustikā . [Lakhanaū] [1983] xi, 174, ii p., [5] folded leaves of plates : LC Card 86-903117
HA4587.J48 J55 1983

Serieyx, Hervé. Archier, Georges. [Entreprise du 3e type. English.] The type 3 company /. New York , 1987. xiv, 123 p. : ISBN 0-89397-282-7 : LC Card 87-11203 DDC 658/.00973 19
HD58.9 .A7313 1987

Seriia Aktual'nye problemy razvitogo sotsializma.
Agropromyshlennyĭ kompleks v usloviiakh razvitogo sotsializma . Moskva , 1986. 167 p. ; LC Card 87-166350
HD9015.S652 A38 1986

Metodiki opredeleniia ėkonomicheskoĭ ėffektivnosti kapital'nykh vlozheniĭ v sotsialisticheskikh stranakh . Moskva , 1981. 101 p. ; LC Card 82-204402
HC244.Z9 C35 1981

Uchastie trudiashchikhsia v upravlenii proizvodstvom . Moskva , 1985. 69, [2] p. ; LC Card 85-224379
HD5660.S65 U27 1985

Seriia Aktual'nye problemy sovershenstvovaniia sotsializma.
Ėkonomicheskoe stimulirovanie truda v usloviiakh sotsializma . Moskva , 1986. 179 p. ; LC Card 87-166364
HD5046 .E47 1986

Seriia Ėkonomika razvivaiushchikhsia stran Azii i Afriki.
Natsionalizatsiia i gossektor v razvivaiushchikhsia stranakh . Moskva , 1986. 210 p. ; LC Card 87-165820
HD4276 .N38 1986

Perspektivy resheniia prodovol'stvennoĭ problemy v razvivaiushchikhsia stranakh . Moskva , 1985. 142 p. ; LC Card 85-188217
HD9018.D44 P47 1985

"Problema neftedollarov" . Moskva , 1984. 231 p. ; LC Card 85-189000
HC498 .P75 1984

Seriia "Ėkonomika, upravlenie i organizatsiia proizvodstva na avtomobil'nom transporte" .
(vyp. 2) Dergachev, A. F. Raschet zatrat i opredelenie ėkonomicheskoĭ ėffektivnosti avtomatizirovannykh sistem operativno-proizvodstvennogo planirovaniia na avtoremontnykh predpriiatiiakh . Moskva , 1978. 35 p. ; LC Card 81-173259
HD9710.A2 D47 1978

Seriia Mezhdunarodnye ėkonomicheskie otnosheniia.
Oskolkova, O. B. (Ol'ga Borisovna) Mirovaia prodovol'stvennaia problema i naselenie . Moskva , 1982. 77 p. ; LC Card 82-198944
HD9000.5 .O84 1982

Seriia Populiarnaia demografiia .
(vyp. 3) Naselenie Leningrada /. Moskva , 1981. 94 p. : LC Card 82-118662
HB2278.L46 N37 1981

Seriia Problemy integratsii stran Zapadnoĭ Evropy.
Murtazina, E. N. Problemy valiutnoĭ integratsii v Evropeĭskom soobshchestve . Moskva , 1985. 75 p. ; LC Card 85-224384
HG3942.8 .M87 1985

Seriia Problemy mezhdunarodnykh ėkonomicheskikh otnosheniĭ.
Mirovoe kapitalisticheskoe khoziaĭstvo v 80-e gody . Moskva , 1985. 220 p. ; LC Card 87-166175
HC59 .M549 1985

Transnatsional'nye korporatsii v sisteme gosudarstvenno-monopolisticheskogo regulirovaniia ėkonomiki . Moskva , 1985. 167 p. ; LC Card 86-187630
HD2755.5 .T714 1985

Vyvoz kapitala v 80-e gody . Moskva , 1986. 247 p. ; LC Card 87-166362
HG4538 .V93 1986

Seriia Problemy nauki i tekhnicheskogo progressa.
Slavin, S. V. (Samuil Venediktovich) Osvoenie Severa Sovetskogo Soiuza /. Moskva , 1982. 206 p. : LC Card 83-137884
HC336.9.N65 S56 1982

Seriia Problemy politicheskoĭ ėkonomii za rubezhom.
Makasheva, N. A. Sovremennyĭ monetarizm i krizis burzhuaznoĭ ėkonomicheskoĭ teorii . Moskva , 1985. 47 p. ; LC Card 86-187688
HB98.3 .M35 1985

Sovremennyĭ konservatizm i krizis burzhuaznoĭ ėkonomicheskoĭ nauki . Moskva , 1986. 175 p. ; LC Card 87-165796
HB241 .S673 1986

Seriia Problemy razvitiia sotsialisticheskikh stran.
Problemy nauchno-tekhnicheskogo progressa v bratskikh sotsialisticheskikh stranakh . Moskva , 1985. 234 p. ; LC Card 86-179196
HC244.Z9 T472 1985

Seriia Problemy upravleniia ėkonomikoĭ.
Podgotovka upravlencheskikh kadrov--opyt, problemy, perspektivy (po zarubezhnym materialam) . Moskva , 1984. 188 p. ; LC Card 85-188986
HD30.4 .P6 1984

Seriia Sotsial'no-ėkonomicheskie problemy razvitykh kapitalisticheskikh stran.
Babashkina, M. L. Aktual'nye ėkonomicheskie i sotsial'nye problemy malykh stran Severnoĭ Evropy . Moskva , 1986. 71 p. ; LC Card 87-166353
HC343 .B34 1986

Seriia Teoriia i praktika gosudarstvenno-monopolisticheskogo kapitalizma.
Dolgovremennye tendentsii v kapitalisticheskom vosproizvodstve . Moskva , 1985. 229 p. : LC Card 86-187722
HB3711 .D62 1985

Seriia "Torgovo-ėkonomicheskie otnosheniia SSSR s kapitalisticheskimi i razvivaiushchimisia stranami"
SSSR--razvivaiushchiesia strany . Moskva , 1985. 237 p. ; LC Card 86-158191
HF1558.5.D44 S77 1985

SSSR, SShA i Kanada . Moskva , 1987. 325 p. ; LC Card 86-205359
HF3628.U5 S77 1987

Seriolanti e arzenisti . Bellabarba, Marco. Cremona , 1986- v. <1 > : LC Card 86-167180
HD1676.I82 C743 1986

Serious programming for your Apple II/IIe/IIc /. Simpson, Henry. Blue Ridge Summit, PA , 1985. x, 180 p. : ISBN 0-8306-0960-1 : LC Card 85-17320 DDC 005.265 19
QA76.8.A662 S57 1985 ***NYPL [JSE 86-801]***

Serlin, Ronald C. Marascuilo, Leonard A. Statistical methods for the social and behavioral sciences /. New York , c1988. xxvi, 804 p. : ISBN 0-7167-1824-3 LC Card 87-398 DDC 519.5 19
HA29 .M2482 1988

Sermaye piyasası aracı olarak enflasyon ortamında tahvilleri değerleme /. Aşıkoğlu, Rıza. [Eskişehir, Turkey] , 1983. xii, 155 p. : LC Card 85-221546
HG5706.5.A3 A85 1983

SERMONS, ENGLISH.
Chartism and Christianity. New York , 1986. 45, 24, 90 p. ; ISBN 0-8240-5593-4 (alk. paper) : LC Card 86-25705 DDC 322/.2 19
HD8396 .C483 1986

Seroka, Jim. Rural public administration . Westport, Conn. , 1986. ix, 208 p. ; ISBN 0-313-25246-7 (lib. bdg. : alk. paper) LC Card 85-27253 DDC 352/.00722/0973 19
JS425 .R87 1986 ***NYPL [JLE 86-4005]***

Serov, V. M. (Viktor Mikhaĭlovich)
Proizvoditel'nost' truda v stroitel'stve : izmerenie, analiz, rezervy / V.M. Serov.Proizvodstvennoe izd. Moskva : Stroĭizdat, 1986. 253 p. : ill. ; 20 cm. (Proizvoditel'nost' truda--samoe vazhnoe, samoe glavnoe) Includes bibliographical references. LC Card 85-179119

1. Construction industry - Soviet Union - Labor productivity. I. Series: Proizvoditel'nost' truda--samoe vazhnoe, samoe glavnoe (Stroĭizdat (Firm)). II. Title.
HD9715.S72 S47 1986

Serra, Daniel. Monnaie, inflation et croissance / Daniel Serra ; préface de Raymond Courbis. Paris : Economica, 1982. xi, 306 p. : ill. ; 24 cm. (Collection "Modèles et macroéconomie appliquée." Série "Etudes et recherches" . no 1) Originally presented as the author's thesis (doctoral--Montpellier I, 1977) Bibliography: p. [285]-299. ISBN 2-7178-0478-1 : LC Card 82-153767 DDC 332.4/0724 19
1. Money - Mathematical models. 2. Inflation (Finance) - Mathematical models. 3. Economic development - Mathematical models. I. Title. II. Series.
HG221 .S485 1982 **NYPL [JLE 86-1903]**

Serra, José.
Administração governamental em 1979-82. 1983. São Paulo (Brazil : State). Governor (1982- : Montoro) O orçamento de São Paulo para 1984 / André Franco Montoro. A administração governamental em 1979-82 / José Serra. São Paulo , 1983. 24 p. ; LC Card 87-130676 DDC 354.81/6100722 19
HJ2080.5.S3 S26 1983

Brasil sem milagres / [José Serra] ; organização, J.A. Guilhon Albuquerque ; prefácio de Fernando H. Cardoso. São Paulo, SP : Editora Klaxon, c1986. 174 p. : ill. ; 21 cm. Author's comments taken from interviews and articles which appeared in various Brazilian journals and television programs between 1978 and 1986. LC Card 87-404803 DDC 330.981/063 19
1. Brazil - Economic conditions - 1945-. 2. Brazil - Social conditions - 1964-. I. Albuquerque, J. A. Guilhon (José Augusto Guilhon). II. Title.
HC187 .S4153 1986

A crise econômica e o flagelo do desemprego / José Serra. São Paulo : Secretaria de Economia e Planejamento, 1984. 27 p. : ill. ; 21 cm. Paper originally presented at the 36th Reunião Anual da SBPC held in São Paulo, July 6, 1984. LC Card 87-124054 DDC 331.13/704 19
1. Unemployment, Structural - Brazil. 2. Brazil - Economic conditions - 1964-1985. I. Title.
HD5708.47.B6 S47 1984

[Novo federalismo]
Um novo federalismo ; O sistema tributário "diagnóstico e reforma" / José Serra. São Paulo : Governo Democrático de São Paulo, Secretaria de Economia e Planejamento, 1984. 43 p. ; 21 cm. LC Card 87-124038 DDC 336.2/00981 19
1. Taxation - Brazil. I. Serra, José. Sistema tributário "diagnóstico e reforma. 1986. II. Title: Novo federalismo. III. Title: Sistema tributário "diagnóstico e reforma.".
HJ3424.A4 S47 1984

Sistema tributário "diagnóstico e reforma. 1986. Serra, José. [Novo federalismo.] Um novo federalismo ; O sistema tributário "diagnóstico e reforma" / José Serra. São Paulo , 1984. 43 p. ; LC Card 87-124038 DDC 336.2/00981 19
HJ3424.A4 S47 1984

Serra Pelada . Kotscho, Ricardo. São Paulo , 1984. 106 p., [16] p. of plates : LC Card 84-206686
HD8039.M732 B75 1984

Serra Puche, Jaime. García Alba Iduñate, Pascual, 1948- [Financial aspects of macroeconomic management in Mexico. Spanish.] Causas y efectos de la crisis económica en México /. México, D.F. , 1984. 124 p. : ISBN 968-12-0285-6 LC Card 86-138030
HC135 .G29818 1984

Serra Ramoneda, Antonio. Sistema económico y empresa / Antonio Serra Ramoneda. 1a ed. Barcelona : Ariel, 1986. 267 p. : ill. ; 22 cm. (Ariel economía) Includes bibliographical references. ISBN 84-344-2011-2 LC Card 87-122090
1. Industrial management. 2. Capitalism. I. Series: Ariel economía. II. Title.
HD37.S66 S46 1986

SERRANA HACIENDA (ECUADOR) - HISTORY.
Trujillo León, Jorge. La hacienda serrana, 1900-1930 /. Quito , 1986. 244 p. ; LC Card 87-115338 DDC 333.3/09866 19
HD1471.E2 T78 1986

Serrano, Francisco López. see **López Serrano, Francisco.**

Serrano Gálvez, Enrique. Economía de la actividad forestal / Enrique Serrano Gálvez. 1a ed. en español. México : Universidad Autónoma Chapingo, Dirección de Difusión Cultural, Departamento de Bosques, 1983. 139 p. : ill. ; 23 cm. (Colección Cuadernos universitarios. Serie Ciencias sociales . no. 5) Bibliography: p. 139. LC Card 86-200927
1. Forest products industry - Mexico. I. Title. II. Series.
HD9764.M62 S47 1983

Serrano Illescas, Alfonso. Pobre patria! / Alfonso Serrano Illescas. México, D.F. : Editores Asociados Mexicanos, 1982. 132 p. ; 20 cm. Includes bibliographical references. ISBN 968-409-161-3 LC Card 85-122377
1. Mexico - Economic conditions - 1918-. 2. Corruption (in politics) - Mexico. 3. Nationalism - Mexico. 4. Patriotism - Mexico. I. Title.
HC135 .S368 1982

Serrano, Julio. Exploración de la Guayana /. [Caracas] [1983] 158 p., [20] p. of plates : LC Card 85-178221 DDC 333.7/0988/1 19
HC238.G8 E98 1983 **NYPL [JSF 86-461]**

Serres, Marcel de, 1783-1862. Essai sur les arts at les manufactures de l'empire d'Autriche / par Marcel de Serres. Paris : Chaignieau aîné, 1814-1815. 3 v. : ill. ; 22 cm. Half title: Voyage dans l'empire d'Autriche, pendant les années 1809 et 1810. Vol. 1: 464 p., VIII leaves of plates (some folded); v. 2: 560 p., XV leaves of plates (some folded); v. 3: 396 p., X leaves of plates (some folded) Includes bibliographical references. LC Card 85-666370
1. Industry - Austria. 2. Austria - Manufactures. 3. Machinery. I. Title. II. Title: Voyage dans l'empire d'Autriche, pendant les années 1809 et 1810.
HC263 .S47x 1814

Sertão sul /. Andrade, Manuel Correia de Oliveira. Recife , 1984. 648, [26] p. : LC Card 87-404838 DDC 330.981/3063 19
HC188.N6 A687 1984

Servan, Roger. Dubrulle, Louis. Comptabilité analytique de gestion . [Paris] , c1985-c1987. 2 v. : ISBN 2-04-015766-2 (v. 2) : LC Card 86-149033 DDC 668/.65/0681 19
HF5642 .D74 1985

SERVANTS - ENGLAND - HISTORY.
Dawes, Frank Victor. Not in front of the servants . London , 1984. 178 p., [16] p. of plates : ISBN 0-09-155291-5 (pbk.) : LC Card 84-195925 DDC 640/.46/0942 19
HD8039.D52 G718 1984
NYPL [JLD 86-1944]

Servei de Cooperació Municipal de la Diputació de Barcelona. Manual de servicios municipales . Barcelona , 1982. 340 p. ; ISBN 84-500-5399-4 LC Card 82-214246 DDC 363/.0946 19
HD4687 .M36 1982 **NYPL [JLC 86-139]**

Service economies in Europe . Ochel, Wolfgang, 1943- Boulder , 1987. p. cm. ISBN 0-8133-0580-2 : LC Card 87-21690 DDC 338.4/6/094 19
HD9986.A2 O28 1987

SERVICE (IN INDUSTRY) see **CUSTOMER SERVICE.**

SERVICE INDUSTRIES - ACCOUNTING.
Measurement of value added at constant prices in service activities /. Paris . v. <1 > ; ISBN 92-64-02879-X (pbk.) : LC Card 87-164470 DDC 657/.45 19
HF5686.S43 M43 1987

SERVICE INDUSTRIES - ARGENTINA.
Bour, Juan Luis. La terciarización del empleo en la Argentina. El sector de servicios a las empresas /. Buenos Aires , 1985. 117 p. ; LC Card 87-123717 DDC 338.4/6/0982 19
HD9985.A72 B68 1985

SERVICE INDUSTRIES - ASIA, SOUTHEASTERN.
The Pacific challenge in international business /. Ann Arbor, Mich. , 1987. viii, 342 p. ; ISBN 0-8357-1620-1 (alk. paper) LC Card 87-5008 DDC 338.09182/3 19
HC460.5 .P32 1987

SERVICE INDUSTRIES - ASIA, SOUTHEASTERN - QUALITY CONTROL - CONGRESSES.
Quality control circle . Tokyo , 1986. x, 170 p. : ISBN 92-833-2040-3 LC Card 87-133710 DDC 658.5/62 19
HD9987.A7852 Q35 1986

SERVICE INDUSTRIES - BERLIN (GERMANY) - EMPLOYEES.
Albrecht, Christoph, 1950- Beschäftigungsentwicklung und Qualifikationsstruktur in Berlin 1977-1983 . Berlin [1985] 2 v. : LC Card 86-204299
HD5780.B4 A43 1985

SERVICE INDUSTRIES - BRAZIL - BAHIA (STATE)
A Evolução dos setores secundário e terciário da economia baiana na década de 70 /. Salvador , 1985. 80 p. : LC Card 87-124067 DDC 338.4/7/00098142 19
HD9734.B73 B334 1985

SERVICE INDUSTRIES - CONGRESSES.
Creativity in services marketing . Chicago, IL , 1986. 175 p. : ISBN 0-87757-179-1 (pbk.) LC Card 85-26785 DDC 658.8 19
HD9980.5 .C74 1986 **NYPL [JLF 86-1783]**

SERVICE INDUSTRIES - DATA PROCESSING - CONGRESSES.
Informationstechnologie im Dienstleistungsbereich . Berlin , c1985. 258 p. : ISBN 3-924859-15-9 : LC Card 86-220033 DDC 338.4/561 19
HD9980.5 .I54 1985

SERVICE INDUSTRIES - DEVELOPING COUNTRIES.
Wells, Jeremy. The export marketing of technical consulting services from developing countries /. Geneva , 1986. vi, 127 p. : LC Card 87-168669 DDC 658.4/6/091724 19
HD9989.D44 W46 1986

SERVICE INDUSTRIES - EAST ASIA.
The Pacific challenge in international business /. Ann Arbor, Mich. , 1987. viii, 342 p. ; ISBN 0-8357-1620-1 (alk. paper) LC Card 87-5008 DDC 338.09182/3 19
HC460.5 .P32 1987

SERVICE INDUSTRIES - ESTONIA.
Voprosy razvitii͡a obsluzhivanii͡a naselenii͡a . Tallin , 1985. 140 p. : LC Card 85-158428
HD9986.S683 E888 1985

SERVICE INDUSTRIES - EUROPE.
Ochel, Wolfgang, 1943- Service economies in Europe . Boulder , 1987. p. cm. ISBN 0-8133-0580-2 : LC Card 87-21690 DDC 338.4/6/094 19
HD9986.A2 O28 1987

SERVICE INDUSTRIES - GERMANY, WEST.
Schertler, Walter. Attraktivitätsanalyse von Dienstleistungen . München , c1983. 183 p. : ISBN 3-597-10420-7 LC Card 83-140207
HD9984.5 .S25 1983

Standorte von Büros im Urteil der Beschäftigten und sonstiger Nutzer /. Stuttgart , 1983. 140 p. : LC Card 83-220559
HF5547.25 .S74 1983

SERVICE INDUSTRIES - GERMANY (WEST) - HAMBURG.
Dienstleistungsmetropole Hamburg . Hamburg [1980] 27 p. ; LC Card 84-216975
HD9984.8.H3 D54 1980

SERVICE INDUSTRIES - GERMANY (WEST) - LOCATION.
Standorte und Einzugsbereiche tertiärer Einrichtungen . Damrstadt , 1985. vi, 403 p., [1] folded leaf of plates : ISBN 3-534-08402-0 LC Card 86-228150
HF5547.25 .S73 1985

Standorte von Büros im Urteil der Beschäftigten und sonstiger Nutzer /. Stuttgart , 1983. 140 p. : LC Card 83-220559
HF5547.25 .S74 1983

SERVICE INDUSTRIES - GERMANY (WEST) - MANAGEMENT.
Graumann, Jens. Die Dienstleistungsmarke . München , c1983. l, 197 p. : ISBN 3-88259-244-3 LC Card 83-180401
HD9984.5 .G7 1983

Schertler, Walter. Attraktivitätsanalyse von Dienstleistungen . München , c1983. 183 p. : ISBN 3-597-10420-7 LC Card 83-140207
HD9984.5 .S25 1983

SERVICE INDUSTRIES - GOVERNMENT POLICY.

Basche, James R., 1926- Eliminating barriers to international trade and investment in services /. New York, N.Y. (845 Third Ave., New York 10022) , c1986. 15 p. ; LC Card 87-147770 DDC 382/.45 19
HD9980.6 .B37 1986

SERVICE INDUSTRIES - GREAT BRITAIN - FORECASTING.
Rajan, Amin, 1942- Services--the second industrial revolution? . London , Boston , 1987. xviii, 257 p. : ISBN 0-408-02003-2 LC Card 86-32739 DDC 331.12/9042 19
HD9982.5 .R34 1987

SERVICE INDUSTRIES - HISTORY - JUVENILE LITERATURE.
Franck, Irene M. Helpers and aides /. New York, N.Y. , c1987. x, 182 p. : ISBN 0-8160-1445-0 LC Card 86-24370 DDC 331.7 19
HF5381.2 .F68 1987

SERVICE INDUSTRIES - INTERNATIONAL COOPERATION.
Kakabadse, Mario A. International trade in services . London , New York , c1987. 90 p. ; ISBN 0-7099-3130-1 (pbk.) LC Card 87-8951 DDC 382/.45/0009049 19
HD9980.5 .K35 1987

SERVICE INDUSTRIES - ITALY - BARI (PROVINCE)
Gatti, M. (Mario) Servizi innovativi e professionalità . Roma [1985] 231 p. : LC Card 85-237680
HD5716.S452 T84 1985

SERVICE INDUSTRIES - ITALY - PISTOIA.
Reti terziarie ed economie locali . Milano, Italy , c1983. 174 p. ; LC Card 85-215649
HD9986.I83 P577 1983

SERVICE INDUSTRIES - JAPAN - MANAGEMENT.
Shapiro, H. Jack (Harris Jack) Reviving industry in America . Cambridge, Mass. , c1987. xii, 204 p. : ISBN 0-88730-118-5 LC Card 87-17585 DDC 338.4/767/0973 19
HD9725 .S46 1987

SERVICE INDUSTRIES - KAZAKH S.S.R.
Shedenov, U. K. (Utegali Kadyrgalievich) Sotsial′no-ėkonomicheskie problemy sfery obsluzhivaniia naseleniia v usloviiakh nauchno-tekhnicheskogo progressa /. Alma-Ata , 1978. 197, [3] p. ; LC Card 81-149568
HD9986.S683 K398 1978

SERVICE INDUSTRIES - LATVIA - MATHEMATICAL MODELS.
Modelirovanie razvitiia mezhotraslevyh kompleksov Latviĭskoĭ SSR . Riga , 1985. 106 p. : LC Card 86-177817
HD9015.S653 L376 1985

SERVICE INDUSTRIES - LOCATION.
Ghosh, Avijit. Location strategies for retail and service firms /. Lexington, Mass. , c1987. x, 212 p. : ISBN 0-669-12032-4 (alk. paper) LC Card 85-45583 DDC 658.1/1 19
HF5429.275 .G47 1987

SERVICE INDUSTRIES - MANAGEMENT.
Collier, David A. Service management . Englewood Cliffs, N.J. , c1987. xiii, 300 p. : ISBN 0-13-806977-8 (pbk.) LC Card 86-30365 DDC 658.5 19
HD9980.5 .C655 1987

Corsten, Hans. Die Produktion von Dienstleistungen . Berlin , c1985. xii, 439 p. : ISBN 3-503-02523-5 LC Card 86-113978 DDC 658 19
HD9980.5 .C67 1985

Rizzo, Michael R. How to make profits with service contracts /. New York, NY , c1987. xii, 367 p. ; ISBN 0-8144-5807-6 LC Card 86-47590 DDC 658 19
HD9980.5 .R59 1987

SERVICE INDUSTRIES - MARKETING.
Ernenputsch, Margit A. Theoretische und empirische Untersuchungen zum Beschaffungsprozess von konsumtiven Dienstleistungen /. Bochum , 1986. xiii, 263 p. ; ISBN 3-88339-548-X LC Card 87-143249 DDC 658.8 19
HF5415.122 .E76 1986

Johnson, Eugene M. Profitable service marketing /. Homewood, Ill. , c1986. xiv, 303 p. : ISBN 0-87094-613-7 LC Card 86-70516 DDC 658.8 19
HF5415.122 .J64 1986 ***NYPL [JLE 87-666]***

SERVICE INDUSTRIES - MARKETING - CONGRESSES.
The Services challenge . Chicago, Ill. , 1987. vi, 108 p. : ISBN 0-87757-188-0 (pbk.) LC Card 87-12543 DDC 658.8 19
HD9980.5 .S4255 1987

SERVICE INDUSTRIES - NEW ZEALAND - STATISTICS.
Census of distribution, 1977-78 . Wellington, N.Z. [1980]-<[1981]. v. <11 > : LC Card 86-204705
HF5429.6.N47 C46 1980

SERVICE INDUSTRIES - NORWAY.
Vannebo, Olav. De tjenesteytende næringer i 80-åra /. Oslo , 1981. iii, 178 p. : ISBN 82-518-1573-8 : LC Card 83-194969
HD9986.N82 V36 1981

SERVICE INDUSTRIES - ONTARIO.
Ontario study of the service sector . [Toronto] [1986] 479 p. : ISBN 0-7729-2049-4 LC Card 87-136763 DDC 338.4/7/0009713 19
HD9985.C33 O67 1986

SERVICE INDUSTRIES - POLAND.
Funkcjonowanie rynku usług w Polsce /. Wrocław , 1986. 176 p. ; ISBN 83-7011-034-7 : LC Card 87-169457
HB9 .B7522 nr. 355 HD9986.P7

SERVICE INDUSTRIES - POLAND - ŁÓDŹ REGION.
Problemy rynku i handlu w Łodzi i regionie łódzkim /. [Łódź] , 1978. 193 p. : LC Card 80-129744
HD9986.P72 L636 1978

SERVICE INDUSTRIES - QUALITY CONTROL.
DiPrimio, Anthony. Quality assurance in service organizations /. Radnor, Pa. , c1987. xiv, 210 p. : ISBN 0-8019-7730-4 : LC Card 86-47961 DDC 658.5/62 19
HD9980.5 .D52 1987

SERVICE INDUSTRIES - SOVIET UNION.
Ukreplenie material′nykh osnov sotsialisticheskogo obraza zhizni /. Moskva , 1984. 156 p. ; LC Card 85-240384
HD8526.5 .U38 1984

SERVICE INDUSTRIES - SWEDEN.
Johnson, Anders. Släpp tjänsterna loss . [Stockholm] , c1986. 232 p. : ISBN 91-7152-374-X : LC Card 86-235064
HD9986.S82 J63 1986

SERVICE INDUSTRIES - SWEDEN - MARKETING.
Ledning, produktion & marknadsföring av tjänster . Malmö , c1981. 318 p. : ISBN 91-40-54058-8 : LC Card 81-174255
HD9986.S82 L43 1981

SERVICE INDUSTRIES - UKRAINE.
Novikov, V. N. (Valeriĭ Nikolaevich) Sovershenstvovanie ėkonomicheskogo mekhanizma v neproizvodstvennoĭ sfere . Kiev , 1986. 195 p. ; LC Card 86-233718
HD9986.S683 U3855 1986

SERVICE INDUSTRIES - UKRAINE - FORECASTING.
IUkhimenko, V. V. (Vladimir Vasil′evich) Izuchenie i prognozirovanie sprosa na bytovye uslugi /. Kiev , 1983. 103 p. ; LC Card 83-218585
HD9986.S683 U385 1983

SERVICE INDUSTRIES - UNITED STATES.
International competition in services . Washington, DC [1987] vii, 403 p. : LC Card 87-619820 DDC 382/.45/00973 19
HD9981.5 .I58 1987

Trade in services . Washington, D.C. [1986] viii, 102 p. : LC Card 86-600576 DDC 382/.45/000973 19
HD9981.5 .T7 1986

SERVICE INDUSTRIES - UNITED STATES - AUTOMATION.
Bar code markets . Norwalk, Conn., U. S.A. (6 Prowitt St., Norwalk 06855) , c1987. iv, 221 leaves : LC Card 87-401927 DDC 381/.45621399 19
HD9801.6.P763 U624 1987

SERVICE INDUSTRIES - UNITED STATES - MANAGEMENT.
Schaefer, Robert A. Starting and managing a small service business /. Washington, D.C. , 1986. v, 57 p. ; LC Card 86-603435 DDC 658/.022 19
HD9981.5 .S32 1986

Shapiro, H. Jack (Harris Jack) Reviving industry in America . Cambridge, Mass. , c1987. xii, 204 p. : ISBN 0-88730-118-5 LC Card 87-17585 DDC 338.4/767/0973 19
HD9725 .S46 1987

SERVICE INDUSTRIES - UNITED STATES - MARKETING.
Johnson, Eugene M. Profitable service marketing /. Homewood, Ill. , c1986. xiv, 303 p. : ISBN 0-87094-613-7 LC Card 86-70516 DDC 658.8 19
HF5415.122 .J64 1986 ***NYPL [JLE 87-666]***

SERVICE INDUSTRIES - WISCONSIN.
Tienda, Marta. The structural transformation of employment in Wisconsin, 1960-1980 /. Madison, WI (Rm. 245, 30 N. Murray St., Madison 53715) [1986] ii, 47 p. ; LC Card 86-623091 DDC 331.12/09775 19
HD5725.W5 T54 1986

SERVICE INDUSTRIES WORKERS - GREAT BRITAIN - SUPPLY AND DEMAND - FORECASTING.
Rajan, Amin, 1942- Services--the second industrial revolution? . London , Boston , 1987. xviii, 257 p. : ISBN 0-408-02003-2 LC Card 86-32739 DDC 331.12/9042 19
HD9982.5 .R34 1987

SERVICE INDUSTRIES WORKERS - TRAINING OF - ITALY - BARI (PROVINCE)
Gatti, M. (Mario) Servizi innovativi e professionalità . Roma [1985] 231 p. : LC Card 85-237680
HD5716.S452 T84 1985

SERVICE INDUSTRIES WORKERS - UNITED STATES.
Sheets, Robert G. The impact of service industries on underemployment in metropolitan economies /. Lexington, Mass. , c1987. xii, 185 p. ; ISBN 0-669-14575-0 (alk. paper) LC Card 86-45884 DDC 331.13 19
HD5709.2.U6 S54 1987

SERVICE INDUSTRIES WORKERS - UNITED STATES - STATISTICS.
Occupational employment in mining, construction, finance, and services. Washington, D.C. [1986] vi, 141 p. ; LC Card 86-603149 DDC 331.12/51/000973021 19
HD9506.U62 O23 1986

SERVICE INDUSTRY WORKERS - UNITED STATES - SUPPLY AND DEMAND.
The Future is now /. [Washington, D.C.] [1985] 34, xxi, [ii], leaves ; LC Card 86-211338 DDC 331.12/51/000973 19
HD5718.S452 U535 1985

Service management . Collier, David A. Englewood Cliffs, N.J. , c1987. xiii, 300 p. : ISBN 0-13-806977-8 (pbk.) LC Card 86-30365 DDC 658.5 19
HD9980.5 .C655 1987

Service national du Québec . Bisaillon, Guy. Québec [1981] 54, [4] leaves ; LC Card 82-212578
HD4870.C2 B57 1981

SERVICE RATING. see **EMPLOYEES, RATING OF.**

The Services challenge : integrating for competitive advantage / edited by John Czepiel, Carole Congram, Jim Shanahan. Chicago, Ill. : American Marketing Association, 1987. vi, 108 p. : ill. ; 28 cm. (Proceeding series / American Marketing Association) Papers presented at the 5th Annual services marketing conference held in Boston, Mass., Sept. 7-10, 1986. Includes bibliographies. ISBN 0-87757-188-0 (pbk.) LC Card 87-12543 DDC 658.8 19
1. Service industries - Marketing - Congresses. I. Czepiel, John A. II. Congram, Carole A. III. Shanahan, Jim. IV. American Marketing Association. V. Series: Proceedings series - American Marketing Association.
HD9980.5 .S4255 1987

The services economy . Nusbaumer, Jacques, économiste. [Services, nouvelle donne de

l'économie. English.] Boston , c1987. 116 p. ; ISBN 0-89838-192-4 LC Card 86-21397 DDC 338.4/6 19
HD9980.5 .N8713 1987

Services in the global market /. Nusbaumer, Jacques, économiste. Boston , c1987. ix, 245 p. ; ISBN 0-89838-198-3 LC Card 87-4053 DDC 338.4/6 19
HD9980.5 .N88 1987

Services Marketing Conference (4th : 1985 : San Francisco, Calif.) Creativity in services marketing . Chicago, IL , 1986. 175 p. : ISBN 0-87757-179-1 (pbk.) LC Card 85-26785 DDC 658.8 19
HD9980.5 .C74 1986 ***NYPL [JLF 86-1783]***

Services--the second industrial revolution? . Rajan, Amin, 1942- London , Boston , 1987. xviii, 257 p. : ISBN 0-408-02003-2 LC Card 86-32739 DDC 331.12/9042 19
HD9982.5 .R34 1987

Services World Forum (Association) The Emerging service economy /. Oxford [Oxfordshire] , New York , 1987. xii, 298 p. : ISBN 0-08-034270-1 : LC Card 86-25265 DDC 338.4/6 19
HD9980.5 .E46 1987

Servicios de transporte internacional por carretera en el GRAN : proyecto ATN/SF-2089-RE (estudio número 3). [Buenos Aires, Argentina] : Banco Interamericano de Desarrollo, Instituto para la Integración de América Latina, [1983] 3 v. : ill. ; 29 cm. CONTENTS. - [1]. Lineamientos y metodología para el proyecto de centros nacionales de frontera -- [2]. Análisis global para el mejoramiento operativo en las fronteras -- [3]. Estudio y proposición de formas organizativas para la prestación de servicios. LC Card 87-404195 DDC 388.3/21/098 19
1. Transportation, Automotive - Andes Region. 2. Transportation, Automotive - Government policy - Andes Region. I. Institute for Latin American Integration.
HE5650 .S47 1983

Serviço de Educação Popular (Rio de Janeiro, Brazil) Capitalismo e classe operária no Brasil /. Petrópolis , 1984. 69 p. ; LC Card 86-222585
HC51 .C35 1984

Serviço Social do Comércio. Departamento Regional do Ceará. Seção de Pesquisas e Estatística. Situação de saúde e lazer do comerciário de Fortaleza /. Fortaleza-CE , 1977/1978 [i.e. 1978] 66 leaves ; LC Card 83-116799
HD5755.F6 S58 1978

Serving the public, building the union . Dix, Bernard. London , 1987- v. <1 > : ISBN 0-85315-645-X (v. 1) : LC Card 87-169851 DDC 331.88/09421 19
HD8005.2.G7 D59 1987

Les servitudes de la puissance . Debeir, Jean-Claude. [Paris] , c1986. 428 p. : ISBN 2-08-211163-6 : LC Card 87-121577
HD9502.A2 D43 1986

Servizi innovativi e professionalità . Gatti, M. (Mario) Roma [1985] 231 p. : LC Card 85-237680
HD5716.S452 T84 1985

Serzhenko, V. V. (Viktor Vasil'evich) Pankova, E. A. (Evgenii͡a Afanas'evna) Vneshneėkonomicheskie svi͡azi razvivai͡ushchikhsi͡a stran . Moskva , 1985. 158 p. ; LC Card 86-130427
HF1413 .P36 1985

Seshadri, K. Rural unrest in India / K. Seshadri. 1st ed. New Delhi : Intellectual Pub. House, 1983. xiii, 192 p. ; 23 cm. Includes bibliographical references and index. LC Card 83-905323 DDC 303.6/23/0954 19
1. Rural poor - India. 2. Peasant uprisings - India. 3. Agriculture and state - India. 4. Rural development - India. I. Title.
HC440.P6 S47 1983 ***NYPL [JLD 86-3704]***

Seshadri, R. K. The Indian financial system : with particular reference to currency, government, exchange, and other connected accounts / by R.K. Seshadri. Madras : Institute for Financial Management and Research, 1985. ii, 287, v, iii p. ; 23 cm. (IFMR publication . 32) Includes index. LC Card 85-904230 DDC 336.54 19
1. Government business enterprises - India - Accounting. 2. Finance, Public - India - Accounting. I. Series: Institute for Financial Management and Research, Madras. IFMR publication, 32. II. Title.
HD4293 .S45 1985 ***NYPL [JLD 86-2433]***

Sesmarias medievais portuguesas /. Rau, Virginia. Lisboa [1982] 288 p. : LC Card 87-673341
HD784 .R3x 1982

Sessional paper (Nigeria) . (1960, no. 5) Establishment of oil refinery in Nigeria. Lagos , 1960. 6 p. ; LC Card 87-401860
HD9577.N52 E84 1960

Seth, A. N., 1914- Peasant organizations in India / A.N. Seth. Delhi : B.R. Pub. Corp. ; New Delhi, India : Distributed by D.K. Publishers' Distributors, 1984. xxxxiv, 174 p. ; 22 cm. Includes bibliographical references and index. LC Card 84-902298 DDC 305.5/63 19
1. Peasantry - India - Societies, etc. 2. Farmers - India - Societies, etc. I. Title.
HD1339.I4 S48 1984 ***NYPL [JLD 87-644]***

Seth, Satish C. India, the next 7000 days / Satish C. Seth. New Delhi : Wiley Eastern, c1985. xxiv, 312 p. [1] spolded Leaf of plates ; 23 cm. ISBN 0-85226-864-5 : LC Card 85-904799 DDC 338.5/443/0954 19
1. Economic forecasting - India. 2. Educational planning - India. 3. India - Economic policy - 1980-. I. Title.
HC435.2 .S416 1985 ***NYPL [JLD 86-3377]***

Seth, Vijay K. Industrialisation in India : spatial perspective / Vijay K. Seth. Delhi, India : Commonwealth Publishers, 1987. xii, 242 p. : 2 maps ; 22 cm. Bibliography: p. [221]-236. Includes index. ISBN 81-900026-7-8 : LC Card 87-902803 DDC 338.0954 19
1. India - Industries - Environmental aspects. 2. India - Economic conditions - 1947-. 3. Space-perception. I. Title.
HC435.2 .S418 1987

Sethi, J. D. (Jai Dev), 1924- Trusteeship, the Gandhian alternative /. New Delhi , c1986. xiii, 238 p. ; LC Card 86-903783 DDC 330.1 19
HB199 .T76 1986

Sethi, S. Prakash.
Business and society . Lexington, Mass. , c1987. xv, 654 p. : ISBN 0-669-13207-1 (pbk : alk. paper) LC Card 86-45548 DDC 658.4/08/0973 19
HD60.5.U5 B853 1987

The South African quagmire . Cambridge, Mass. , c1987. xvi, 444 p. ; ISBN 0-88730-191-6 LC Card 86-28754 DDC 320.5/6 19
HF1613.4.Z4 U67 1987

Śeti, udyoga, āṇi śikshaṇa . Desaraḍā, Eca. Ema. Auraṅgābāda , 1986. 18, 148 p. ; LC Card 87-900720
HC437.M32 D47 1986

Setia, G. P. (Guru Prasad), 1937- Saeed, M. (Muhammad), 1950- India and East Africa . Delhi , 1986. vi, 264 p. ; LC Card 87-902493 DDC 382/.0954/0676 19
HF3788.A45 S23 1986

O setor de bens de capital sob encomenda . Tadini, Venilton. São Paulo , 1986. 142 p. : LC Card 87-154239 DDC 332/.0414/0981 19
HC190.C3 T33 1986

Setor de informações técnicas / [Governo do Estado do Espírito Santo, Secretaria de Estado da Indústria e do Comércio]. [Vitória] : A Secretaria, 1983. 54 p. ; 32 cm. Cover title: Informações infra-estruturais. LC Card 85-202308
1. Espírito Santo, Brazil (State) - Economic conditions. 2. Espírito Santo (Brazil : State) - Industries. 3. Infrastructure - Brazil - Espírito Santo (State). 4. Industrial promotion - Brazil - Espírito Santo (State). I. Espírito Santo (Brazil : State). Secreria de Estado da Indústria e do Comércio. II. Title: Informações infra-estruturais.
HC188.E7 S47 1983

Setor exportador paraibano : diagnóstico. João Pessoa : CEBRAE, 1976. 72 leaves : forms ; 22 x 31 cm. Prepared by the Núcleo de Assistência Industrial, Paraíba. LC Card 84-239455
1. Paraíba, Brazil (State) - Commerce. 2. Foreign trade promotion - Brazil - Paraíba (State). I. Núcleo de Assistência Industrial (Paraíba).
HF3409.P32 S47 1976

Setor público, reordenamento e privatização / Paulo Rabello de Castro, Carlos von Doellinger. [Rio de Janeiro, RJ : Associação Nacional das Instituições do Mercado Aberto, 1986] 47 p. : ill. ; 22 cm. (Coleção Temas & teses . no. 3. 1) Cover title. Includes bibliographical references. CONTENTS. - Os novos espaços do estado na gestão econômica / Paulo Rabello de Castro -- Reordenamento do setor público / Carlos von Doellinger. LC Card 87-403308 DDC 338.981 19
1. Brazil - Economic policy. 2. Government business enterprises - Brazil. 3. Privatization - Brazil. I. Castro, Paulo Rabello de. Novos espaços do estado na gestão econômica. 1986. II. Doellinger, Carlos von. Reordenamento do setor público. 1986. III. Associação Nacional das Instituições do Mercado Aberto (Brazil). IV. Series: Coleção Temas & teses , no.3.
HC187 .S436 1986

Sett fra sjøsiden . Nielsen, Kai. [Oslo] , c1985. 88 p. : LC Card 86-205530
HE855 .N44 1985

Settembrino, Hugo O. La función gerencial en la empresa : perspectiva informática / Hugo O. Settembrino. Buenos Aires : Librería "El Ateneo" Editorial, c1985. viii, 127 p. : ill. ; 20 cm. (Biblioteca de ciencias económicas. Serie administración y dirección) Bibliography: p. 125-127. ISBN 950-0-23598-6 LC Card 85-201051
1. Management. 2. Industrial management. I. Title. II. Series.
HD37.S66 S47 1985

Sētthaph Kānwāngphǣn phatthanā khr rāingān kānsksā / dōi Sētthaph [Bangkok] : Samnakngān Khana Kammakān Phatthanākān Sētthakit lǣ Sangkhom hǣng Chāt, 2524 [1981] 8, 80 leaves ; 28 cm. A study of the production and marketing of small communication devices in Thailand. LC Card 82-920041
1. Telecommunication equipment industry - Thailand. 2. Walkie-talkies. I. Thailand. Samnakngān Khana Kammakān Phatthanākān Sētthakit lǣ Sangkhom hǣng Chāt. II. Title.
HD9696.T442 S47 1981

Setti, Eloy Olindo.
Comunicação, quale é o nosso ideal. 1986.
Propostas cooperativistas / [Organização das Cooperativas do Estado do Paraná-OCEPAR] ; colaboração, Fundação Friedrich Naumann e OCB. Curitiba , 1986. 56 p. : LC Card 87-403655 DDC 334 19
HD2953 .P76 1986

Settle, Robert B. Why they buy : American consumers inside and out / Robert B. Settle, Pamela L. Alreck. New York : Wiley, c1986. xvi, 351 p. ; 24 cm. ISBN 0-471-84457-8 : LC Card 86-13303 DDC 658.8/343/0973 19
1. Consumers - United States. 2. Consumers' preferences - United States. 3. Brand choice - United States. I. Alreck, Pamela L. II. Title.
HC110.C6 S48 1986 ***NYPL [JLE 86-4432]***

SETTLEMENT COSTS.
Bush, Vanessa A. How to buy a house when you're cash poor . Chicago , c1986. 92 p. ; ISBN 0-8092-4834-4 (pbk.) : LC Card 86-24053 DDC 332.7/22 19
HG2040.15 .B87 1986

Settore termoelettromeccanico . Tronconi, Pier Attilio. Roma , c1986. 729 p. : ISBN 88-7910-149-8 : LC Card 86-211311
HD9685.I82 T76 1986

Seusing, Ekkehart. Bibliographie der EG-Zeitschriften 1952-1980 . Kiel , 1981. ix, 280 p. ; LC Card 81-122713
HB41 .K55 Bd. 22 Z7165.E8 HC241.2

Seute, Jens. Aufbereitung von Ergebnissen der Stadtverkehrsforschung . Hof/Saale , 1986. 2 v. : LC Card 87-408335 DDC 388.4/0943 19
HE4774 .A94 1986

SĖV -- osnovnye napravlenii͡a sotrudnichestva : referativnyĭ sbornik / [redaktsionnai͡a kollegii͡a Pervushin S.P (otvetstvennyĭ redaktor) ... et al.]. Moskva : INION AN SSSR, 1984. 203 p. ; 20 cm. At head of title: Mezhdunarodnyĭ institut ėkonomicheskikh problem mirovoĭ sot͡sialisticheskoĭ sistemy. Institut nauchnoĭ informat͡sii po obshchestvennym naukam Akademii nauk SSSR. Includes bibliographies. LC Card 85-177814
1. Council for Mutual Economic Assistance. 2. Europe, Eastern - Economic integration. I. Pervushin, S. P. (Serafim Pavlovich). II. Mezhdunarodnyĭ institut ėkonomicheskikh problem mirovoĭ sot͡sialisticheskoĭ sistemy. III. Institut nauchnoĭ informat͡sii po obshchestvennym naukam (Akademii͡a nauk SSSR).
HC243.5 .S48 1984

The Seven Years War and the old regime in France . Riley, James C. Princeton, N.J. , 1986. xxii, 256 p. : ISBN 0-691-05488-6 (alk. paper) : LC Card 86-42847 DDC 330.944/034 19
HC275 .R54 1986 NYPL [JLE 87-932]

SEVEN YEARS' WAR, 1756-1763 - ECONOMIC ASPECTS - FRANCE.
Riley, James C. The Seven Years War and the old regime in France . Princeton, N.J. , 1986. xxii, 256 p. : ISBN 0-691-05488-6 (alk. paper) : LC Card 86-42847 DDC 330.944/034 19
HC275 .R54 1986 NYPL [JLE 87-932]

Sever i Sibir´ zovut molodykh /. Khlystova, E. A. (Evgeniīā Andreevna) Moskva , 1985. 109 p. : LC Card 86-153085
HF5549.5.I5 K452 1985

Sever, Michael, 1956- Der Marktanteil als Kriterium für die Produkteliminierung : eine Analyse auf der Grundlage des Erfahrungskurven-Konzeptes / Michael Sever. Frankfurt am Main ; New York : P. Lang, c1985. xv, 317 p. : ill. ; 22 cm. (Europäische Hochschulschriften. Reihe V, Volks- und Betriebswirtschaft, 0531-7339 . Bd. 657 = vol. 657 = vol. 657) Originally presented as the author's thesis (doctoral)--Johann Wolfgang Goethe-Universität, Frankfurt am Main, 1985. Bibliography: p. 281-317. ISBN 3-8204-8917-7 LC Card 86-111218
1. Product obsolescence. I. Series: Europäische Hochschulschriften. Reihe V, Volks- und Betriebswirtschaft , Bd. 657. II. Title.
HF5415.15 .S39 1985

Several papers relating to money, interest and trade, &c. /. Locke, John, 1632-1704. Fairfield, NJ , 1988. p. cm. ISBN 0-678-00334-3 LC Card 87-17243 DDC 332.4/941 19
HG937 .L74 1988

SEVERANCE TAX - LOUISIANA.
Lam, Manuel. Louisiana crude oil and natural gas report and severance and royalty sensitivity to price, second half 1985 /. Baton Rouge, La (P.O. Box 44156, Baton Rouge 70804-4156) [1986] iii, 31 p. : LC Card 86-621907 DDC 338.2/728/09763 19
HD9560.8.U53 L65 1986

Severo-Amerikanskie Shtaty. see **United States.**

Severo, Cloraldino. A política dos transportes no Brasil, 1979/85 / Cloraldino Severo. [Brasília] : Ministério dos Transportes, 1983. 91 p. : ill. ; 28 cm. "Exposição do Ministro Cloraldino Severo na Comissão de Transportes da Câmara dos Deputados"--P. [1] Cover title. Includes bibliographical references. "4." LC Card 86-153346
1. Transportation and state - Brazil. I. Brazil. Ministério dos Transportes. II. Title.
HE233 .S44 1983

Sevilla, Carlos. Información básica sobre el GATT y el desarrollo industrial y comercial de México. México , c1985. 79, 62 p. ; LC Card 87-400559 DDC 338.0972 19
HC135 .I53 1985

Sevilla Segura, Jorge. El proceso de implantación del IVA : la experiencia británica / [Jorge Sevilla Segura]. [Madrid] : Ministerio de Hacienda, Instituto de Estudios Fiscales, [1982?] iii, 182 p. ; 29 cm. (Monografía. no. 15) Bibliography: p. 178-182. LC Card 85-201954
1. Value-added tax - Great Britain. 2. Value-added tax - Spain. I. Series: Monografías (Instituto de Estudios Fiscales (Spain)) , no. 15. II. Title.
HJ5715.G7 S4 1982

Seville (Province). Diputación Provincial. Publicaciones. Sección: Historia. Seriel .
(no. 17) Herrera García, Antonio. El Aljarafe sevillano durante el antiguo régimen . [Sevilla] , 1980. 517 p., [9] leaves of plates : ISBN 84-500-4373-5 LC Card 81-173649 DDC 946/.86 19
HD779.A39 H475 1980 NYPL [JLF 86-928]

SEVILLE (SPAIN) - ECONOMIC CONDITIONS.
Morell Peguero, Blanca. Mercaderes y artesanos en la Sevilla del descubrimiento /. Sevilla , 1986. 222 p. ; ISBN 84-505-2883-6 LC Card 86-199625
HD2346.S72 S465 1986

SEVILLE (SPAIN) - SOCIAL CONDITIONS.
Morell Peguero, Blanca. Mercaderes y artesanos en la Sevilla del descubrimiento /. Sevilla , 1986. 222 p. ; ISBN 84-505-2883-6 LC Card 86-199625
HD2346.S72 S465 1986

Serie: Ciencias económicas y empresariales. see **Serie: Ciencias económicas y empresariales.**

SEWAGE DISPOSAL - AUSTRALIA - WESTERN AUSTRALIA - FINANCE.
Water Authority of Western Australia. Water Authority of Western Australia Corporate plan, 1986-1991. Appendix C, asset investment program /. Leederville, W.A. [1986] 42 p. ; LC Card 87-158833 DDC 354.9410082/325 19
HD1700.W4 W38 1986

SEWAGE DISPOSAL - DEVELOPING COUNTRIES - PLANNING - CITIZEN PARTICIPATION - PLANNING.
Whyte, Anne V. T. Guidelines for planning community participation activities in water supply and sanitation projects /. Geneva , Albany, NY , 1986. 53 p. : ISBN 92-4-170096-3 (pbk.) : LC Card 87-137091 DDC 333.91/009172/4 19
HD4465.D44 W49 1986

SEWAGE DISPOSAL - FINANCE.
Herrington, Paul. Pricing of water services /. Paris , Washington, D.C. , 1987. 145 p. : ISBN 92-64-12921-9 (pbk.) : LC Card 87-167536 DDC 338.4/336361 19
HD4456 .H47 1987

SEWERAGE - COLOMBIA - CÚCUTA.
Buenahora Febres-Cordero, Norma. Cúcuta y sus servicios públicos básicos /. Bogotá, D.E. , 1984. 136 p. ; LC Card 85-205425
HD4637.A5 B84 1984

SEWERS. see **SEWERAGE.**

SEX.
Rex-Kiss, Béla. Vizsgálatok az újszülöttek nemi arányának alakulásáról /. Budapest , 1986. 124 p. : ISBN 963-241-457-8 : LC Card 87-138601
HB1741 .R49 1986

Scruton, Roger. Sexual desire . London , c1986. x, 428 p. ; ISBN 0-297-78479-X
NYPL [JFE 86-1928]

SEX BIAS. see **SEXISM.**

Sex differences in cognitive abilities /. Halpern, Diane F. Hillsdale, N.J. , 1986. x, 189 p. : ISBN 0-89859-579-7 LC Card 86-11506 DDC 155.3/3 19
BF311 .H295 1986 NYPL [JFE 86-4001]

SEX DIFFERENCES (PSYCHOLOGY)
Fast, Irene. Gender identity . Hillsdale, N.J. , 1984. vii, 189 p. ; ISBN 0-88163-014-4 LC Card 84-6366 DDC 155.3/3 19
BF692.2 .F36 1984 NYPL [JFE 86-4829]

Halpern, Diane F. Sex differences in cognitive abilities /. Hillsdale, N.J. , 1986. x, 189 p. : ISBN 0-89859-579-7 LC Card 86-11506 DDC 155.3/3 19
BF311 .H295 1986 NYPL [JFE 86-4001]

McGee, Mark G. Human spatial abilities . New York , 1979. xiv, 144 p. : ISBN 0-03-052391-5 LC Card 79-16070 DDC 153.7/52
BF469 .M3 NYPL [JFE 84-185]

The Psychology of gender . Baltimore , c1986. vii, 293 p. : ISBN 0-8018-2974-7 (alk. paper) LC Card 85-19822 DDC 155.3/3 19
BF692.2 .P76 1986 NYPL [JFE 86-2969]

Sanford, John A. The invisible partners . New York , c1980. 139 p. ; ISBN 0-8091-2277-4 : LC Card 79-56604 DDC 150.19/54
BF175 .S24 NYPL [JFE 86-5093]

Sayers, Janet. Sexual contradictions . London , New York, NY , 1986. x, 214 p. : ISBN 0-422-78780-9 LC Card 85-27948 DDC 155.3/3 19
BF692.2 .S29 1986 NYPL [JFD 86-5840]

SEX DISCRIMINATION AGAINST WOMEN - GERMANY, WEST.
Mach mich nicht an . Berlin , c1986. [48] p. : ISBN 3-88114-313-0 : LC Card 87-118837 DDC 331.4/133/0943 19
HD6060.5.G3 M33 1986

Selk, Michael, 1943- Geschlecht und Berufswahl . Frankfurt am Main , New York , c1984. 289 p. : ISBN 3-8204-5375-X LC Card 85-193055
HD6059.6.G4 S45 1984

SEX DISCRIMINATION AGAINST WOMEN - ITALY - HISTORY.
Bettio, Francesca. The sexual division of labour . Oxford [Oxfordshire] , New York , 1988. p. cm. ISBN 0-19-828544-2 : LC Card 87-26353 DDC 305.4/3/00945 19
HD6060.65.I8 B47 1988

SEX DISCRIMINATION AGAINST WOMEN - KENYA - CASE STUDIES.
Staudt, Kathleen A. Agricultural policy implementation . West Hartford, CT , c1985. xvi, 68 p. : ISBN 0-931816-18-1 (pbk.) LC Card 84-29737 DDC 338.1/86762 19
HD2126.5.Z8 S73 1985
NYPL [JLF 86-1685]

SEX DISCRIMINATION AGAINST WOMEN - PSYCHOLOGICAL ASPECTS - CONGRESSES.
Sex role stereotyping and affirmative action policy /. Los Angeles, Calif. , c1982. 227 p. : LC Card 82-623259 DDC 331.4/133 19
HD6060 .S49 1982 NYPL [JLD 87-275]

SEX DISCRIMINATION AGAINST WOMEN - SWEDEN.
Jämställdhet i arbetsliv och samhälle. Stockholm [1985] 129 p. : ISBN 91-7168-259-7 : LC Card 86-133755
HD6060.5.S8 J36 1985

SEX DISCRIMINATION AGAINST WOMEN - UNITED STATES.
Antler, Joyce. The educated woman and professionalization . New York , 1987. x, 448 p. ; ISBN 0-8240-6839-4 (alk. paper) : LC Card 87-17604 DDC 331.4/11423 19
HD6054.2.U6 A57 1987

Benokraitis, Nijole V. (Nijole Vaicaitis) Modern sexism . Englewood Cliffs , c1986. xiii, 187 p. ; ISBN 0-13-597634-0 LC Card 85-28256
HQ1426 .B428 1986 NYPL [JLE 86-4225]

Dimen, Muriel. Surviving sexual contradictions . New York , c1986. xxi, 257 p. ; ISBN 0-02-531620-6 LC Card 86-12600 DDC 305.4/2/0973 19
HQ1426 .D56 1986 NYPL [JLE 86-4385]

For crying out loud . New York , c1986. ix, 397 p. ; ISBN 0-8298-0581-8 (pbk.) : LC Card 86-9302 DDC 305.4/2/0973 19
HQ1426 .F757 1986 NYPL [JLD 86-3989]

Morse, Roberta. The Black female professional /. Washington, D.C. [1983] i, 48 p. ; LC Card 83-80187 DDC 305.4/8896073 19
HQ1426 .M88 1983 NYPL [Sc F 86-230]

Theodore, Athena. The campus troublemakers . Houston, Tex. , c1986. xxiv, 293 p. ; ISBN 0-88105-066-0 : LC Card 85-14973 DDC 378/.12/088042 19
LB2332.3 .T44 1986 NYPL [JLE 86-4389]

SEX DISCRIMINATION AGAINST WOMEN - UNITED STATES - HISTORY.
Hidden aspects of women's work /. New York , 1987. x, 380 p. ; ISBN 0-275-92415-7 (alk. paper) : LC Card 87-2449 DDC 331.4/133/0973 19
HD6060.5.U5 H53 1987

SEX DISCRIMINATION AGAINST WOMEN - ZAMBIA.
Bardouille, R. (Raj) Women's employment patterns, discrimination, and promotion of equality in Zambia /. [Lusaka? , 1985]. ii, 160 leaves ; LC Card 87-980054 DDC 331.4/133/096894 19
HD6212.5 .B37 1985

SEX DISCRIMINATION IN CONSUMER CREDIT - KENYA - CONGRESSES.
Women and credit . [Nairobi?] [1985] 17, 2 p. ; LC Card 85-981504 DDC 332.7/088042 19
HG3756.K4 W65 1985

SEX DISCRIMINATION IN EDUCATION - AUSTRALIA.
O'Donnell, Carol. The basis of the bargain . Sydney , Boston , 1984. 186 p. ; ISBN 0-86861-497-1 LC Card 84-70146 DDC 331.4/133/0994 19
HD6060.5.A8 O36 1984
NYPL [JLD 86-2017]

SEX DISCRIMINATION IN EDUCATION - UNITED STATES.
Berger, Gilda. Women, work, and wages /. New York , 1986. 122 p. : ISBN 0-531-10074-X LC Card 85-15379 DDC 331.4/0973 19
HD6095 .B47 1986 NYPL [JLE 86-4592]

Theodore, Athena. The campus troublemakers . Houston, Tex. , c1986. xxiv, 293 p. ; ISBN 0-88105-066-0 : LC Card 85-14973 DDC 378/.12/088042 19
LB2332.3 .T44 1986 ***NYPL [JLE 86-4389]***

SEX DISCRIMINATION IN EMPLOYMENT.
Diekmann, Andreas. Einkommensunterschiede zwischen Frauen und Männern . Wien [1985] 2 v. (244, 4 p.) : LC Card 86-150241
HD6061 .D54 1985

Gender in the workplace /. Washington, D.C. , c1987. xiv, 316 p. ; ISBN 0-8157-1170-0 : LC Card 87-668 DDC 331.13/3 19
HD6060.5.U5 G46 1987

SEX DISCRIMINATION IN EMPLOYMENT - AUSTRALIA.
O'Donnell, Carol. The basis of the bargain . Sydney , Boston , 1984. 186 p. ; ISBN 0-86861-497-1 LC Card 84-70146 DDC 331.4/133/0994 19
HD6060.5.A8 O36 1984
NYPL [JLD 86-2017]

SEX DISCRIMINATION IN EMPLOYMENT - BRAZIL, NORTHEAST.
Dabat, Christine. As mulheres nas organizações profissionais /. Recife , 1985. 21 p. ; LC Card 86-177927
HD2429.B6 D33 1985

SEX DISCRIMINATION IN EMPLOYMENT - DENMARK.
Carlsen, Anne Marie Sloth. Køn og ledelse . København , 1986. 251 p. : ISBN 87-87749-29-7 (pbk.) :kr149.00 LC Card 87-145777
HD6054.4.D4 C37 1986

SEX DISCRIMINATION IN EMPLOYMENT - GERMANY, WEST.
"Was will die denn hier?" . Marburg , c1986. 156 p. ; ISBN 3-924800-82-0 LC Card 87-122751 DDC 331.4/0943 19
HD6060.65.G3 W37 1986

SEX DISCRIMINATION IN EMPLOYMENT - GERMANY (WEST) - CASE STUDIES.
Edding, Cornelia, 1943- Einbruch in den Herrenclub . Reinbek bei Hamburg , 1983. 184 p. : ISBN 3-499-15251-7 (pbk.) LC Card 87-673369
HD6054.2.G3 E33x 1983

SEX DISCRIMINATION IN EMPLOYMENT - GERMANY (WEST) - HISTORY.
Pohl, Sigrid, 1954- Entwicklung und Ursachen der Frauenlohndiskriminierung . Frankfurt am Main , New York , c1984. x, 387 p. : ISBN 3-8204-8017-X LC Card 85-189325 DDC 331.13/3/0943 19
HD6060.5.G3 P64 1984

SEX DISCRIMINATION IN EMPLOYMENT - GREAT BRITAIN.
Cockburn, Cynthia. Machinery of dominance . London , Dover, N.H. , 1985. 282 p. ; ISBN 0-7453-0065-0 (pbk.) : LC Card 86-204262 DDC 331.13/3/0941 19
HD6060.5.G7 C63 1985

Dex, Shirley. British and American women at work . Houndmills, Basingstoke, Hampshire , 1986. xii, 159 p. : ISBN 0-333-40219-7
NYPL [JLD 86-3608]

Meehan, Elizabeth M. Women's rights at work . New York , 1985. xvii, 253 p. ; ISBN 0-312-88793-0 : LC Card 84-15997 DDC 331.4/133/0941 19
HD6060 .M44 1984 ***NYPL [JLD 86-3580]***

Walby, Sylvia. Patriarchy at work . Cambridge [Cambrigeshire] , c1986. vii, 292 p. ; ISBN 0-7456-0157-X ***NYPL [JLD 87-941]***

Walby, Sylvia. Patriarchy at work . Minneapolis , c1986. vii, 292 p. ; ISBN 0-8166-1588-8 : LC Card 86-24912 DDC 331.4/133/0941 19
HD6060.65.G7 W35 1986

SEX DISCRIMINATION IN EMPLOYMENT - NETHERLANDS.
Boon, Irene. Mannen in een vrouwenberoep . Den Haag , 1984. 139 p. : ISBN 90-6252-426-5 : LC Card 84-243593
Z682.4.W65 B66 1984 ***NYPL [JLG 87-4]***

SEX DISCRIMINATION IN EMPLOYMENT - PALESTINE.
Bernstein, Deborah. The struggle for equality . New York , 1987. x, 208 p. : ISBN 0-275-92139-5 (alk. paper) : LC Card 86-8203 DDC 305.4/3/0095694 19
HD6182.2 .B47 1986 ***NYPL [JLE 87-1462]***

SEX DISCRIMINATION IN EMPLOYMENT - PSYCHOLOGICAL ASPECTS - CONGRESSES.
Sex role stereotyping and affirmative action policy /. Los Angeles, Calif. , c1982. 227 p. : LC Card 82-623259 DDC 331.4/133 19
HD6060 .S49 1982 ***NYPL [JLD 87-275]***

SEX DISCRIMINATION IN EMPLOYMENT - SWEDEN.
Granath, Erna. Kvinnoplats . Stockholm , c1985. 141 p. ; ISBN 91-38-90602-3 : LC Card 85-236327
HD6073.M392 S84 1985
NYPL [JLE 86-3898]

Jämställdhet i arbetsliv och samhälle. Stockholm [1985] 129 p. : ISBN 91-7168-259-7 : LC Card 86-133755
HD6060.5.S8 J36 1985

Towards a democratic rationality . Aldershot, Hants, England , Brookfield, Vt., USA , c1986. xi, 281 p. : ISBN 0-566-00761-4 : LC Card 86-14241 DDC 331/.09485 19
HD8576.5 .T69 1986 ***NYPL [JLD 86-3873]***

SEX DISCRIMINATION IN EMPLOYMENT - UNITED STATES.
Dex, Shirley. British and American women at work . Houndmills, Basingstoke, Hampshire , 1986. xii, 159 p. : ISBN 0-333-40219-7
NYPL [JLD 86-3608]

England, Paula. Households, employment, and gender . New York , c1986. ix, 237 p. : ISBN 0-202-30322-5 (lib. bdg.) LC Card 85-18628 DDC 304.6 19
HQ536 .E54 1986 ***NYPL [JLE 86-2828]***

Fillmore, Mary Dingee. Women MBAs . Boston, MA , 1987. xii, 233 p. ; ISBN 0-8161-8728-2 LC Card 86-32002 DDC 331.4/816584/00973 19
HD6054.4.U6 F54 1987

Gender in the workplace /. Washington, D.C. , c1987. xiv, 316 p. ; ISBN 0-8157-1170-0 : LC Card 87-668 DDC 331.13/3 19
HD6060.5.U5 G46 1987

Meehan, Elizabeth M. Women's rights at work . New York , 1985. xvii, 253 p. ; ISBN 0-312-88793-0 : LC Card 84-15997 DDC 331.4/133/0941 19
HD6060 .M44 1984 ***NYPL [JLD 86-3580]***

Morse, Roberta. The Black female professional /. Washington, D.C. [1983] i, 48 p. ; LC Card 83-80187 DDC 305.4/8896073 19
HQ1426 .M88 1983 ***NYPL [Sc F 86-230]***

Sexual harrassment and labor relations /. Washington, D.C. , c1981. iii, 100 p. : ISBN 0-87179-367-9 LC Card 81-10201 DDC 331.4/25 19
HD6060.3 S49 ***NYPL [JLD 81-2136]***

Women's work, men's work . Washington, D.C. , 1986. xii, 173 p. : ISBN 0-309-03429-9 (pbk.) LC Card 85-11541 DDC 331.1/33/0973 19
HD6060.5.U5 W66 1986
NYPL [JLF 86-1430]

SEX DISCRIMINATION IN EMPLOYMENT - UNITED STATES - ADDRESSES, ESSAYS, LECTURES.
Moore, Lynda L. Not as far as you think . Lexington, Mass. , c1986. xii, 201 p. ; ISBN 0-669-10836-7 : LC Card 85-40109 DDC 331.4/0973 19
HD6095 .M66 1986 ***NYPL [JLE 86-1878]***

SEX DISCRIMINATION IN EMPLOYMENT - UNITED STATES - CASE STUDIES.
Stolz, Barbara Ann. Still struggling . Lexington, Mass. , c1985. xviii, 205 p. ; ISBN 0-669-10930-4 (alk. paper) LC Card 85-40235 DDC 331.4/0973 19
HD6052 .S76 1985 ***NYPL [JLE 85-3704]***

SEX DISCRIMINATION IN EMPLOYMENT - UNITED STATES - HISTORY.
Hidden aspects of women's work /. New York , 1987. x, 380 p. ; ISBN 0-275-92415-7 (alk. paper) : LC Card 87-2449 DDC 331.4/133/0973 19
HD6060.5.U5 H53 1987

Working women . Washington, D.C. , c1987. xxii, 419 p. ; ISBN 0-87179-547-7 LC Card 87-9410 DDC 331.4/0973 19
HD6095 .W742 1987

SEX DISCRIMINATION IN EMPLOYMENT - UNITED STATES - HISTORY - 20TH CENTURY - CASE STUDIES.
Glazer, Penina Migdal. Unequal colleagues . New Brunswick, N.J. , c1987. xii, 295 p. : ISBN 0-8135-1187-9 (pbk.) : LC Card 86-6568 DDC 331.4/81/000973 19
HD6054.2.U6 G55 1986
NYPL [JLD 87-581]

SEX DISCRIMINATION IN EMPLOYMENT - UNITED STATES - MISCELLANEA.
Black, Beryl. Coping with sexual harassment /. New York , 1987. 149 p. ; ISBN 0-8239-0732-5 : LC Card 86-26245 DDC 331.13/3 19
HD6060.3 .B55 1987

SEX DISCRIMINATION IN EMPLOYMENT - ZAMBIA.
Bardouille, R. (Raj) Women's employment patterns, discrimination, and promotion of equality in Zambia /. [Lusaka? , 1985]. ii, 160 leaves ; LC Card 87-980054 DDC 331.4/133/096894 19
HD6212.5 .B37 1985

SEX DISCRIMINATION - LAW AND LEGISLATION - UNITED STATES.
Women's work, men's work . Washington, D.C. , 1986. xii, 173 p. : ISBN 0-309-03429-9 (pbk.) LC Card 85-11541 DDC 331.1/33/0973 19
HD6060.5.U5 W66 1986
NYPL [JLF 86-1430]

SEX DISCRIMINATION - UNITED STATES.
Helping the sexually oppressed /. Englewood Cliffs, N.J. , c1986. xix, 282 p. : ISBN 0-13-386129-5 : LC Card 85-16687 DDC 305.3 19
HN57 .H46 1986 ***NYPL [JLE 86-3217]***

Sex, drink, and fast cars . Bayley, Stephen. London , Boston , 1986. 112 p. ; ISBN 0-571-14526-4 (pbk.) : LC Card 87-672358
HD9710.U52 B34 1986

SEX IN ADVERTISING.
Nimmergut, Jörg, 1939- Werben mit Sex /. München , c1982. 383 p. : ISBN 3-453-53132-9 (pbk.) LC Card 86-673618
HF5827 .N45x 1982

SEX IN MARRIAGE.
Tarizzo, Domenico. Il nuovo amore di coppia /. Milano , 1982. 192 p. ; LC Card 82-141135 DDC 306.7 19
HQ21 .T338 1982 ***NYPL [JLD 87-1019]***

The sex of the dollar . Blau, Anne Kohn. New York , c1988. 190 p. : ISBN 0-671-60680-8 LC Card 87-23560 DDC 332.024/042 19
HG181 .B46 1988

SEX RATIO.
Rex-Kiss, Béla. Vizsgálatok az újszülöttek nemi arányának alakulásáról /. Budapest , 1986. 124 p. : ISBN 963-241-457-8 : LC Card 87-138601
HB1741 .R49 1986

SEX ROLE.
Alves, Denise. O desencontro marcado . Petrópolis , 1985. 169 p. ; LC Card 85-226159
HQ1075 .A44 1985 ***NYPL [JFD 86-7232]***

Halpern, Diane F. Sex differences in cognitive abilities /. Hillsdale, N.J. , 1986. x, 189 p. : ISBN 0-89859-579-7 LC Card 86-11506 DDC 155.3/3 19
BF311 .H295 1986 ***NYPL [JFE 86-4001]***

Lapidus, Gail Warshofsky. Women in Soviet society . Berkeley , c1978. x, 381 p. ; ISBN 0-520-02868-6 : LC Card 74-16710 DDC 305.4/0947
HQ1663 .L33 ***NYPL [JLE 80-1771]***

Tentler, Leslie Woodcock. Wage-earning women . New York , 1979. 266 p. ; ISBN 0-19-502627-6 : LC Card 79-12802 DDC 331.4/0973
HD6095 .T44 ***NYPL [JLD 86-3699]***

SEX ROLE - ADDRESSES, ESSAYS, LECTURES.
Gender and stratification /. Cambridge, CB, UK , Oxford, OX, UK , 1986. viii, 271 p. ; ISBN 0-7456-0167-7 : LC Card 85-28342 DDC 305.3 19
HQ1075 .G46 1986 ***NYPL [JLE 86-2966]***

The Social psychology of female-male

relations . Orlando , 1986. xvi, 351 p. ; ISBN 0-12-065280-3 (alk. paper) LC Card 85-9138 DDC 305.3 19
HM132 .S569 1986 *NYPL [JLE 86-1746]*

SEX ROLE - CANADA.
Wilson, S. J. (Susannah Jane) Women, the family, and the economy /. Toronto , New York , c1982. 176 p. : ISBN 0-07-548028-X (pbk.) LC Card 82-123177 DDC 305.4/0971 19
HQ1457 .W53 1982 *NYPL [JLE 86-1735]*

SEX ROLE - DENMARK.
Gydesen, Ellen. Kvinders livsgrundlag i 80-erne /. K [i.e. Copenhagen] [1985] 202 columns : LC Card 87-168500
HD6060.65.D4 G93 1985

SEX ROLE IN ADVERTISING - UNITED STATES.
Barthel, Diane L., 1949- Putting on appearances . Philadelphia , 1988. p. cm. ISBN 0-87722-528-1 (alk. paper) : LC Card 87-20010 DDC 659.1/042 19
HF5827 .B37 1988

SEX ROLE IN THE WORK ENVIRONMENT.
Gender in the workplace /. Washington, D.C. , c1987. xiv, 316 p. ; ISBN 0-8157-1170-0 : LC Card 87-668 DDC 331.13/3 19
HD6060.5.U5 G46 1987

Lewis, Diane, 1936- Why women fail in business /. Nashville , c1987. p. cm. ISBN 0-8407-4219-3 : LC Card 87-15370 DDC 658.4/09088042 19
HD6054.3 .L48 1987

Madden, Tara Roth. Women vs. women . New York, NY , c1987. xxii, 266 p. ; ISBN 0-8144-5900-5 LC Card 87-47701 DDC 658.4/095/088042 19
HD6060 .M33 1987

Melia, Jinx. [Why Jenny can't lead.] Breaking into the boardroom . New York [1987] c1986. 167 p. ; ISBN 0-399-13326-7 LC Card 87-7007 DDC 658.4/09/024042 19
HD6054.3 .M45 1987

Plogstedt, Sibylle. Übergriffe . Reinbek bei Hamburg , 1984. 157 p. ; ISBN 3-499-15353-X (pbk.) LC Card 87-672604
HD6060.3 .P56x 1984

SEX ROLE IN THE WORK ENVIRONMENT - CANADA.
Armstrong, Pat, 1945- A working majority . Ottawa, Ont. , c1983. v, 280 p. : ISBN 0-660-11314-7 (pbk.) : LC Card 83-158188 DDC 331.4/0971 19
HD6067.2.C2 A75 1983
NYPL [JLD 86-1585]

SEX ROLE IN THE WORK ENVIRONMENT - CONGRESSES.
Sex role stereotyping and affirmative action policy /. Los Angeles, Calif. , c1982. 227 p. : LC Card 82-623259 DDC 331.4/133 19
HD6060 .S49 1982 *NYPL [JLD 87-275]*

SEX ROLE IN THE WORK ENVIRONMENT - GERMANY (WEST)
"Was will die denn hier?" . Marburg , c1986. 156 p. ; ISBN 3-924800-82-0 LC Card 87-122751 DDC 331.4/0943 19
HD6060.65.G3 W37 1986

SEX ROLE IN THE WORK ENVIRONMENT - SWEDEN.
Jämställdhet i arbetsliv och samhälle. Stockholm [1985] 129 p. : ISBN 91-7168-259-7 : LC Card 86-133755
HD6060.5.S8 J36 1985

SEX ROLE IN THE WORK ENVIRONMENT - UNITED STATES.
Gender in the workplace /. Washington, D.C. , c1987. xiv, 316 p. ; ISBN 0-8157-1170-0 : LC Card 87-668 DDC 331.13/3 19
HD6060.5.U5 G46 1987

The velvet ghetto . San Francisco , 1986. 147 leaves in various foliations : LC Card 86-161157 DDC 331.4/816592/0973 19
HD6054.2.U6 V45 1986

SEX ROLE IN THE WORK ENVIRONMENT - UNITED STATES - HISTORY.
Hidden aspects of women's work /. New York , 1987. x, 380 p. ; ISBN 0-275-92415-7 (alk. paper) : LC Card 87-2449 DDC 331.4/133/0973 19
HD6060.5.U5 H53 1987

SEX ROLE - PSYCHOLOGICAL ASPECTS.
The Psychology of gender . Baltimore , c1986. vii, 293 p. : ISBN 0-8018-2974-7 (alk. paper) LC Card 85-19822 DDC 155.3/3 19
BF692.2 .P76 1986 *NYPL [JFE 86-2969]*

Sex role stereotyping and affirmative action policy / Barbara A. Gutek, editor. Los Angeles, Calif. : Institute of Industrial Relations, University of California, Los Angeles, c1982. 227 p. : ill. ; 22 cm. (Monograph and research series / Institute of Industrial Relations, University of California, Los Angeles . 32) Includes bibliographies. LC Card 82-623259 DDC 331.4/133 19
1. Sex discrimination in employment - Psychological aspects - Congresses. 2. Sex discrimination against women - Psychological aspects - Congresses. 3. Sex role in the work environment - Congresses. I. Gutek, Barbara A. II. Series: Monograph and research series (University of California, Los Angeles. Institute of Industrial Relations) , 32.
HD6060 .S49 1982 *NYPL [JLD 87-275]*

SEX ROLE - UNITED STATES.
Astrachan, Anthony. How men feel . Garden City, N.Y. , 1986. x, 444 p. ; ISBN 0-385-23333-7 : LC Card 85-22944 DDC 305.3/1 19
HQ1090.3 .A88 1986 *NYPL [JLE 86-3421]*

Beyond sex roles /. St. Paul , c1985. xxix, 563 p. : ISBN 0-314-85293-X (pbk.) : LC Card 84-21950 DDC 305.3 19
HQ1075.5.U6 B49 1985
NYPL [JLF 86-1144]

Dimen, Muriel. Surviving sexual contradictions . New York , c1986. xxi, 257 p. ; ISBN 0-02-531620-6 LC Card 86-12600 DDC 305.4/2/0973 19
HQ1426 .D56 1986 *NYPL [JLE 86-4385]*

Pleck, Joseph H. Working wives, working husbands /. Beverly Hills, Calif. , c1985. 167 p. ; ISBN 0-8039-2489-5 LC Card 85-11974 DDC 306.8/7 19
HQ536 .P59 1985 *NYPL [JLD 86-1130]*

SEXISM - UNITED STATES.
Benokraitis, Nijole V. (Nijole Vaicaitis) Modern sexism . Englewood Cliffs , c1986. xiii, 187 p. ; ISBN 0-13-597634-0 LC Card 85-28256
HQ1426 .B428 1986 *NYPL [JLE 86-4225]*

Beyond sex roles /. St. Paul , c1985. xxix, 563 p. : ISBN 0-314-85293-X (pbk.) : LC Card 84-21950 DDC 305.3 19
HQ1075.5.U6 B49 1985
NYPL [JLF 86-1144]

Dimen, Muriel. Surviving sexual contradictions . New York , c1986. xxi, 257 p. ; ISBN 0-02-531620-6 LC Card 86-12600 DDC 305.4/2/0973 19
HQ1426 .D56 1986 *NYPL [JLE 86-4385]*

Sexto censo general de población y cuarto de viviendas, 1985. Recuentos preliminares . [Montevideo] [1986] 188 p. : LC Card 87-122427 DDC 304.6/09895/021 19
HA1074 1985

Sexton, Jean. Leclerc, Claudine. La sécurité d'emploi dans l'industrie de la construction au Québec . [Quebec] , c1983. xii, 275 p. : ISBN 2-7637-7028-2 LC Card 84-126505 DDC 331.25/96 19
HD5718.B92 C248 1983
NYPL [JLE 86-3170]

Sexual contradictions . Sayers, Janet. London , New York, NY , 1986. x, 214 p. : ISBN 0-422-78780-9 LC Card 85-27948 DDC 155.3/3 19
BF692.2 .S29 1986 *NYPL [JFD 86-5840]*

Sexual desire . Scruton, Roger. London , c1986. x, 428 p. ; ISBN 0-297-78479-X
NYPL [JFE 86-1928]

SEXUAL DISCRIMINATION. see SEX DISCRIMINATION.

SEXUAL DIVISION OF LABOR.
Chabaud-Rychter, Danielle. Espace et temps du travail domestique /. Paris , 1985. 156 p. ; ISBN 2-86563-127-3 LC Card 86-165713
HD6055 .C45 1985

Houseworker's handbook. [Cambridge, Mass.] (c/o Women's Center, 46 Pleasant St., Cambridge 02139) [1974] 81 p. : LC Card 87-110536
HD6073.H84 H68 1974

Maindok, Herlinde, 1948- Frauenalltag in Männerberufen /. Frankfurt am Main , 1987. 173, [2] p. ; ISBN 3-596-23786-6 LC Card 87-164114 DDC 331.4/81 19
HD6060.6 .M35 1987

Mies, Maria. Patriarchy and accumulation on a world scale . London , Atlantic Highlands, NJ , 1986. 251 p. ; ISBN 0-86232-341-X LC Card 86-18916 DDC 305.4 19
HD6060.6 .M54 1986 *NYPL [JLD 86-3206]*

Stechert, Kathryn B. Sweet success . New York , London , c1986. xiii, 224 p. ; ISBN 0-02-614380-1 LC Card 85-30916 DDC 650.1/024/042 19
HD6053 .S724 1986 *NYPL [JLD 86-2435]*

Stechert, Kathryn B. [Sweet success.] On your own terms . New York , 1987, c1986. xvi, 314 p. ; ISBN 0-394-75301-1 (pbk.) : LC Card 86-40470 DDC 650.1/024042 19
HD6053 .S724 1987

SEXUAL DIVISION OF LABOR - ADDRESSES, ESSAYS, LECTURES.
Gender and the labour process /. Aldershot, Hampshire, Eng. , Brookfield, Vt., U. S.A. , c1986. vii, 186 p. ; ISBN 0-566-00999-4 : LC Card 85-21977 DDC 331.4 19
HD6060.6 .G45 1986 *NYPL [JLD 86-3900]*

SEXUAL DIVISION OF LABOR - BRAZIL.
Humphrey, John, 1950- Gender and work in the Third World . London , New York , 1987. p. cm. ISBN 0-422-61900-0 (cased) LC Card 87-12416 DDC 305.4/3/00981 19
HD6060.65.B6 H86 1987

SEXUAL DIVISION OF LABOR - DENMARK.
Borchorst, Anette. Arbejdsmarkedets kønsopdeling . Aalborg , 1984. 162 p. : ISBN 87-7307-252-4 LC Card 85-106008
HD6060.65.D4 B67 1984
NYPL [JFK 82-214 nr.15]

Gydesen, Ellen. Kvinders livsgrundlag i 80-erne /. K [i.e. Copenhagen] [1985] 202 columns : LC Card 87-168500
HD6060.65.D4 G93 1985

Vedel, Gitte. Om kvindearbejdets igangværende udvikling og perspektiver, i relation til den teknologiske udvikling /. Roskilde , 1982. 103 leaves : LC Card 83-172895
HD6060.65.D4 V42 1982

SEXUAL DIVISION OF LABOR - DEVELOPING COUNTRIES - CASE STUDIES.
Women, work, and ideology in the Third World /. London , New York , 1985. xvii, 265 p. : ISBN 0-422-79710-3 (U. S. : pbk.) LC Card 85-17279 DDC 305.4/09172/4 19
HQ1870.9 .W657 1985
NYPL [JLD 86-2322]

SEXUAL DIVISION OF LABOR - FRANCE - AUFFAY - HISTORY.
Gullickson, Gay L. Spinners and weavers of Auffay . Cambridge [Cambridgeshire] , New York , 1986. x, 256 p. : ISBN 0-521-32280-4 LC Card 86-6808 DDC 331.4/877/02822094425 19
HD8039.T42 F834 1986
NYPL [JLE 87-1054]

SEXUAL DIVISION OF LABOR - GAMBIA.
Nath, Kamla. Labor-saving techniques in food processing . Boston, MA (270 Bay State Rd., Boston 02215) , 1985. 26 leaves ; LC Card 87-155092 DDC 331.4/25 19
HD6073.A292 G256 1985

SEXUAL DIVISION OF LABOR - GERMANY (WEST)
Frauen und Beruf, zwischen Wunsch und Realität . Bonn , Bad Honnef , 1986. 142 p. ; ISBN 3-87066-629-3 : LC Card 87-409372 DDC 331.4/0943 19
HD6149 .F719 1986

"Was will die denn hier?" . Marburg , c1986. 156 p. ; ISBN 3-924800-82-0 LC Card 87-122751 DDC 331.4/0943 19
HD6060.65.G3 W37 1986

SEXUAL DIVISION OF LABOR - GERMANY (WEST) - HISTORY.
Pohl, Sigrid, 1954- Entwicklung und Ursachen der Frauenlohndiskriminierung . Frankfurt am Main , New York , c1984. x, 387 p. : ISBN 3-8204-8017-X LC Card 85-189325 DDC

331.13/3/0943 19
HD6060.5.G3 P64 1984

SEXUAL DIVISION OF LABOR - GREAT BRITAIN.
Armour, Hazel. New technology in the office environment /. Aldershot, Hampshire, England , Brookfield, Vt., USA , c1986. viii, 138 p. : ISBN 0-566-05031-5 LC Card 86-215701 DDC 338.4/561651 19
HF5547.5 .A786 1986

Walby, Sylvia. Patriarchy at work . Cambridge [Cambrigeshire] , c1986. vii, 292 p. ; ISBN 0-7456-0157-X *NYPL [JLD 87-941]*

Walby, Sylvia. Patriarchy at work . Minneapolis , c1986. vii, 292 p. ; ISBN 0-8166-1588-8 : LC Card 86-24912 DDC 331.4/133/0941 19
HD6060.65.G7 W35 1986

SEXUAL DIVISION OF LABOR - GREAT BRITAIN - HISTORY.
Cohn, Samuel, 1954- The process of occupational sex-typing . Philadelphia , 1985. viii, 279 p. ; ISBN 0-87722-402-1 : LC Card 85-14864 DDC 331.4/8165137/0941 19
HD6060.65.G7 C64 1985
NYPL [JLE 86-917]

SEXUAL DIVISION OF LABOR - ITALY.
Petrillo, Giovanna, 1952- Produttività e improduttività del lavoro domestico . Bologna , 1985. 139 p. ; LC Card 86-132212
HD8039.H842 I87 1985

SEXUAL DIVISION OF LABOR - ITALY - HISTORY.
Bettio, Francesca. The sexual division of labour . Oxford [Oxfordshire] , New York , 1988. p. cm. ISBN 0-19-828544-2 : LC Card 87-26353 DDC 305.4/3/00945 19
HD6060.65.I8 B47 1988

SEXUAL DIVISION OF LABOR - JAPAN.
Armour, Hazel. New technology in the office environment /. Aldershot, Hampshire, England , Brookfield, Vt., USA , c1986. viii, 138 p. : ISBN 0-566-05031-5 LC Card 86-215701 DDC 338.4/561651 19
HF5547.5 .A786 1986

SEXUAL DIVISION OF LABOR - KENYA.
Chavangi, Noel A. Culture as the basis for implementing self-sustaining wood fuel development programmes /. Nairobi, Kenya [1985] 24 leaves ; LC Card 87-111963 DDC 333.75 19
HD9769.F843 K433 1985

SEXUAL DIVISION OF LABOR - KENYA - KAKAMEGA DISTRICT.
Chavangi, Noel A. Cultural aspects of fuelwood procurement in Kakamega District /. Nairobi [1984] 13 leaves ; LC Card 87-112356 DDC 333.75 19
HD9769.F843 K43 1984

SEXUAL DIVISION OF LABOR - KENYA - STATISTICS.
Barnes, Carolyn. Kenyan smallholdings and the division of labour /. Nairobi , 1982. 39 leaves ; LC Card 87-156293
HD1476.K4 B37 1982

SEXUAL DIVISION OF LABOR - MALI.
Turrittin, Jane Sawyer. Men, women, and market trade in rural Mali, West Africa /. [East Lansing] , c1986. 17 p. ; LC Card 86-225178 DDC 331.4/8138118/096623 19
HD6060.65.M42 T87 1986

SEXUAL DIVISION OF LABOR - UNITED STATES.
Armour, Hazel. New technology in the office environment /. Aldershot, Hampshire, England , Brookfield, Vt., USA , c1986. viii, 138 p. : ISBN 0-566-05031-5 LC Card 86-215701 DDC 338.4/561651 19
HF5547.5 .A786 1986

Blau, Francine D. The economics of women, men, and work /. Englewood Cliffs, N.J. , c1986. xiv, 365 p. : ISBN 0-13-233719-3 LC Card 85-30746 DDC 305.3/0973 19
HQ1426 .B62 1986 *NYPL [JLE 86-4254]*

Pleck, Joseph H. Working wives, working husbands /. Beverly Hills, Calif. , c1985. 167 p. ; ISBN 0-8039-2489-5 LC Card 85-11974 DDC 306.8/7 19
HQ536 .P59 1985 *NYPL [JLD 86-1130]*

Women working . Mountain View, Calif. , c1988. xv, 431 p. : ISBN 0-87484-744-3 (pbk.) LC Card 87-3215 DDC 331.4/0973 19
HD6095 .W6976 1988

SEXUAL DIVISION OF LABOR - UNITED STATES - CONGRESSES.
Women, households, and the economy /. New Brunswick, N.J. , c1987. p. cm. ISBN 0-8135-1263-8 : LC Card 87-4840 DDC 331.4/0973 19
HD6060.65.U5 W65 1987

The sexual division of labour . Bettio, Francesca. Oxford [Oxfordshire] , New York , 1988. p. cm. ISBN 0-19-828544-2 : LC Card 87-26353 DDC 305.4/3/00945 19
HD6060.65.I8 B47 1988

SEXUAL HARASSMENT.
Helping the sexually oppressed /. Englewood Cliffs, N.J. , c1986. xix, 282 p. : ISBN 0-13-386129-5 : LC Card 85-16687 DDC 305.3 19
HN57 .H46 1986 *NYPL [JLE 86-3217]*

SEXUAL HARASSMENT OF WOMEN - GERMANY (WEST)
Mach mich nicht an . Berlin , c1986. [48] p. : ISBN 3-88114-313-0 : LC Card 87-118837 DDC 331.4/133/0943 19
HD6060.5.G3 M33 1986

Plogstedt, Sibylle. Übergriffe . Reinbek bei Hamburg , 1984. 157 p. ; ISBN 3-499-15353-X (pbk.) LC Card 87-672604
HD6060.3 .P56x 1984

SEXUAL HARASSMENT OF WOMEN - UNITED STATES.
Berger, Gilda. Women, work, and wages /. New York , 1986. 122 p. : ISBN 0-531-10074-X LC Card 85-15379 DDC 331.4/0973 19
HD6095 .B47 1986 *NYPL [JLE 86-4592]*

Sexual harrassment and labor relations /. Washington, D.C. , c1981. iii, 100 p. : ISBN 0-87179-367-9 LC Card 81-10201 DDC 331.4/25 19
HD6060.3 S49 *NYPL [JLD 81-2136]*

SEXUAL HARASSMENT OF WOMEN - UNITED STATES - MISCELLANEA.
Black, Beryl. Coping with sexual harassment /. New York , 1987. 149 p. ; ISBN 0-8239-0732-5 : LC Card 86-26245 DDC 331.13/3 19
HD6060.3 .B55 1987

SEXUAL HARASSMENT - UNITED STATES - MISCELLANEA.
Black, Beryl. Coping with sexual harassment /. New York , 1987. 149 p. ; ISBN 0-8239-0732-5 : LC Card 86-26245 DDC 331.13/3 19
HD6060.3 .B55 1987

Sexual harrassment and labor relations / [by the BNA editorial staff]. Washington, D.C. : BNA Books, c1981. iii, 100 p. : ill. ; 23 cm. "A BNA special report." Bibliography: p. 95-98. ISBN 0-87179-367-9 LC Card 81-10201 DDC 331.4/25 19
1. Sexual harassment of women - United States. 2. Sex discrimination in employment - United States.
HD6060.3 S49 *NYPL [JLD 81-2136]*

Seybold, John W. Dressler, Fritz R. S. The entrepreneurial age . Media, PA , c1985. ii, 228, 5 p. ; ISBN 0-918514-10-X (pbk.) LC Card 85-232719 DDC 338.04/0973 19
HB615 .D73 1985 *NYPL [JLD 86-3104]*

Seybold, Patricia B. Integrated desk-top environments : Symphony, Framework, Visi On, and DesQ / Patricia B. Seybold, co-author ; with Seybold staff writers, Ronni T. Marshak, Michael D. Millikin. New York : McGraw-Hill, c1985. ix, 181 p. : ill. ; 24 cm. (The Seybold series on professional computing) A Byte book Includes index. ISBN 0-07-056324-1 (pbk.) : LC Card 84-27841 DDC 650/.028/5425 19
1. Symphony (Computer program). 2. Framework (Computer program). 3. DESQ (Computer program). 4. Visi On (Computer program). 5. Business - Data processing. I. Marshak, Ronni T. II. Millikin, Michael D. III. Series. IV. Series: Byte books. V. Title.
HF5548.4.S95 S49 1985
NYPL [JSE 86-2011]

The Seybold series on professional computing.
O'Keeffe, Linda. Statistical packages for the IBM PC family /. New York , c1986. x, 162 p. : ISBN 0-07-056320-9 : LC Card 85-18213 DDC 658/.055365 19
HF1017 .O39 1986 *NYPL [JSE 86-1876]*

Seybold, Patricia B. Integrated desk-top environments . New York , c1985. ix, 181 p. : ISBN 0-07-056324-1 (pbk.) : LC Card 84-27841 DDC 650/.028/5425 19
HF5548.4.S95 S49 1985
NYPL [JSE 86-2011]

Seychelles : airmail history, 1938-1971 / [compiled and edited by K.B. Fitton. [Newbury, Berkshire, UK] : Indian Ocean Study Circle, [1986] iii, 41 p. : ill. ; 30 cm. Cover title. "March 1986." "No. 3." Bibliography: p. iii. LC Card 86-214104 DDC 383/.144/09696 19
1. Air mail service - Seychelles - History. I. Fitton, K. B.
HE7389.9.Z9 A47 1986

Seychelles. Statistics Division. The Household expenditure survey, 1983-1984. Mahé, Seychelles [1986] 74 p. : LC Card 86-981214 DDC 339.4/7/09696 19
HD7068.8 .H68 1986

Seyfert, Wolfgang. Zins und wirtschaftliche Entwicklung / von Wolfgang Seyfert. Köln : C. Heymann, c1985. 187 p. : ill. ; 21 cm. (Schriftenreihe Annales Universitatis Saraviensis. Rechts- und Wirtschaftswissenschaftliche Abteilung . Bd. 114) Originally presented as the author's thesis (doctoral)--Universität des Saarlandes, 1982. Bibliography: p. [183]-187. ISBN 3-452-19936-3 : LC Card 86-185586
1. Economic development. 2. Taxation. I. Title.
HD75 .S49 1985

Seyfried, Manfred, 1957- Produktivitätswachstum und Umweltschutz / Manfred Seyfried. Frankfurt am Main ; New York : P. Lang, c1986. x, 198 p. : ill. ; 21 cm. (Europäische Hochschulschriften. Reihe V, Volks- und Betriebswirtschaft, 0531-7339 . Bd. 701 = vol. 701 = vol. 701) Originally presented as the author's thesis (doctoral)--Universität Frankfurt am Main, 1985. Bibliography: p. 185-198. ISBN 3-8204-8985-1 LC Card 86-195597
1. Industrial productivity. 2. Environmental protection. I. Series: Europäische Hochschulschriften. Reihe V, Volks- und Betriebswirtschaft , Bd. 701. II. Title.
HC79.I52 S49 1986

Seymour, Edward E. An illustrated history of Canadian labour, 1800-1974 / Edward E. Seymour. 2nd ed. Ottawa : Canadian Labour Congress, 1980. xiv, 95 p. : ill. ; 28 cm. "This book is part of a series of education materials produced by the CLC Labour Education and Studies Centre for use in Labour History courses." Bibliography: p. 89-92.
1. Labor and laboring classes - Canada - History. 2. Trade-unions - Canada - History. 3. Strikes and lockouts - Canada - History. I. Title.

Seymour, Howard, 1961- The multinational construction industry / Howard Seymour. London ; New York : Croom Helm, c1987. 295 p. ; 23 cm. Bibliography: p. 276-289. Includes indexes. ISBN 0-7099-5438-7 LC Card 87-21720 DDC 338.8/87 19
1. Construction industry. 2. International business enterprises. I. Title.
HD9715.A2 S49 1987

SFAH skriftserie .
(nr. 18) Christiansen, Niels Finn. Arbejderbevægelsens forhistorie . [Copenhagen] , 1986. 188 p. : ISBN 87-87739-21-6 : LC Card 87-145749
HD6742 .C495 1986

SG Associates. Profile of the '80's /. [Washington, D.C.?] , 1980. v, 77 p. : LC Card 81-600725 DDC 380.5/0973 19
HE206.2 .P765 *NYPL [JLF 86-1445]*

Sgro, Pasquale M. The theory of duality & international trade / Pasquale M. Sgro. London : Croom Helm, c1986. 307 p. : ill. ; 23 cm. Includes indexes. Bibliography: p. 288-299. ISBN 0-7099-3307-X
1. Commerce - Mathematical models. 2. Duality theory (Mathematics). I. Title. II. Title: Theory of duality and international trade. *NYPL [JLD 86-3202]*

Shabalin, Evgeniĭ Mikhaĭlovich. Galkin, I. G. (Il'i͡a Grigor'evich) Sovershenstvovanie planirovanii͡a stroitel'nogo proizvodstva /. Moskva , 1986. 167 p. : LC Card 85-178938
HD9715.S72 G35 1986

Shabalina, G. S. Sverkhmonopolii v I͡Ugo-Vostochnoĭ Azii /. Moskva , 1983. 219 p. ; LC Card 83-223670
HD2901 .S84 1983

Shachar, A., 1935- Planning in turbulence /. Jerusalem , 1986. xii, 158 p. : ISBN 965-223-657-8 (pbk.) LC Card 87-163701 DDC 658.4/012 19
HD87.5 .P5 1986

Shackelford, John. Frank, Peter. Business opportunities for broadcasters in MDS pay television /. Washington, DC [c1982] 29 p. ; LC Card 86-201299
HE8700.72.U6 F73 1982

Shackle, G. L. S. (George Lennox Sharman), 1903-
[Selections. 1987]
Business, time, and thought : selected papers of G.L.S. Shackle / edited by Stephen F. Frowen. New York : New York University Press, 1988. p. cm. Bibliography: p. Includes index. ISBN 0-8147-2586-4 : LC Card 87-5528 DDC 330.1 19
1. Economics - Philosophy. I. Frowen, Stephen F. II. Title.
HB72 .S462 1988

Shad, John S. R., 1923- Statement of John S.R. Shad, Chairman of the Securities and Exchange Commission, before the House Subcommittee on Oversight and Investigations of the Committee on Energy and Commerce, concerning EDGAR (Electronic Data Gathering, Analysis, and Retrieval System), March 14, 1985. [Washington, D.C. : The Commission, 1985] 21, 5, 2, [12] p. : ill. ; 28 cm. Includes bibliographical references. LC Card 85-148449 DDC 353.0082/58 19
1. EDGAR (Information retrieval system). 2. United States. Securities and Exchange Commission. I. United States. Congress. House. Committee on Energy and Commerce. Subcommittee on Oversight and Investigations. II. United States. Securities and Exchange Commission. III. Title.
HG4910 .S417 1985

Shadad, Mohamed Zein. Mohamed, Yagoub Abdalla. The North Kordofan rural water supply baseline survey /. Khartoum , 1982. xv, 152 p. : LC Card 85-981166
HD1699.S82 K875 1982

Shafer, Neil. Pick, Albert. Standard catalog of world paper money /. Iola, Wis. , München , c1986. 2 v. : ISBN 0-87341-087-4 (v. 1) LC Card 86-222186 DDC 769.5/5/075 19
HG353 .P543 1986

Shaffer, Daniel N. Macro programming for 1-2-3 : new possibilities for worksheet power and control / Daniel N. Shaffer.1st ed. Indianapolis, Ind. : Hayden Books, c1987. xiv, 283 p. : ill. ; 25 cm. "For 1-2-3 Release 2"--Cover. Includes index. ISBN 0-672-46573-6 (pbk.) LC Card 86-63301 DDC 005.36/9 19
1. Lotus 1-2-3 (Computer program). 2. Macro instructions (Electronic computers). 3. Business - Data processing. I. Title.
HF5548.4.L67 S48 1987

Shaffer, R. Kent. Ferguson, Gary D. Evaluation of the small cities community development block grant program--the role of the counties [microform] /. Cambridge, Mass. , 1981. vii, vi, 186 p. ; ***NYPL [*XME-11,283]***

Shafritz, Jay M.
Dictionary of personnel management and labor relations. Shafritz, Jay M. The Facts on File dictionary of personnel management and labor relations / Jay M. Shafritz. 2nd ed., rev. and expanded. New York, N.Y. , c1985. 534 p. : ISBN 0-8160-1234-2 LC Card 85-20823 DDC 658.3/003/21 19
HF5549.A23 S52 1985
NYPL [JLE 86-4748]

The Facts on File dictionary of personnel management and labor relations / Jay M. Shafritz. 2nd ed., rev. and expanded. New York, N.Y. : Facts on File, Inc., c1985. 534 p. : ill. ; 24 cm. Rev. ed. of: Dictionary of personnel management and labor relations. 1st ed. c1980. ISBN 0-8160-1234-2 LC Card 85-20823 DDC 658.3/003/21 19
1. Personnel management - Dictionaries. 2. Industrial relations - Dictionaries. I. Shafritz, Jay M. Dictionary of personnel management and labor relations. II. Facts on File, Inc. III. Title. IV. Title: Dictionary of personnel management and labor relations.
HF5549.A23 S52 1985
NYPL [JLE 86-4748]

Shagalov, G. L. (Grigoriĭ Lazarevich) Ėkonomiko-matematicheskie metody i modeli vo vneshneėkonomicheskoĭ dei͡atel′nosti /. Moskva , 1980. 179 p. : LC Card 87-109621
HF3626.5 .E45 1980

Voprosy prognozirovanii͡a i planirovanii͡a vneshneėkonomicheskikh svi͡azeĭ /. Moskva , 1984. 93 p. ; LC Card 86-144298
HF3626.5 .V668 1984

Shagi brigadnogo podri͡ada (Kiev, Ukraine) Zakharchenko, A. G. (Alekseĭ Gavrilovich) Kollektivnyĭ podri͡ad v sel′skom khozi͡aĭstve /. Kiev , 1985. 107 p. : LC Card 86-222274
HD1492.S652 U389 1985

Shagi odinnadt͡satoĭ.
Karli͡uk, I. I͡A. (Ippolit I͡Akovlevich) Agrarno-promyshlennyĭ kompleks /. Moskva , 1981. 93 p. : LC Card 82-148305
HD9015.S652 K37 1981

Kirichenko, Vadim Nikitich. Osnovnye idei pi͡atiletki /. Moskva , 1981. 92 p. : LC Card 82-123953
HC336.25 .K569 1981

Kostakov, V. G. (Vladimir Georgievich) Chelovecheskiĭ faktor--zani͡atost′, blagosostoi͡anie /. Moskva , 1981. 78 p. : LC Card 82-164831
HD5796 .K567 1981

Shahabuddeen, M., 1931- Nationalisation of Guyana's bauxite : the case of Alcan / M. Shahabuddeen. Georgetown, Guyana : Ministry of Information, 1981. xvii, 306 p. ; 24 cm. Bibliography: p. 282-306. LC Card 82-145233 DDC 338.2/74926 19
1. Aluminum Company of Canada, ltd. 2. Aluminum industry and trade - Government ownership - Guyana. 3. International business enterprises - Guyana. I. Title.
HD9539.A63 G888 1981
NYPL [Sc E 86-189]

Shahar, A. see **Shachar, A., 1935-**

Shahi, M. A. (Muslehuddin Akhil) Money and capital markets in Nigeria : origin, growth, and development, 1959-1978 / M.A. Shahi.1st ed. Bombay : Somaiya Publications, 1983. xi [i.e. x], 60 p. ; 25 cm. Includes index. Bibliography: p. [57] LC Card 83-905358 DDC 332/.0412/09669 19
1. Capital market - Nigeria. 2. Money market - Nigeria. I. Title.
HG187.5.N6 S5 1983 ***NYPL [JLE 87-691]***

Shaikhconsultants International. Industrial democracy in India . Saddar, Karachi, Pakistan [1985] 21 p. ; LC Card 86-222345 DDC 331/.01/12095491 19
HD7262.5.P18 I53 1985

Shaikhconsults International. Why the office staff scared of time and motion study? . Saddar, Karachi, Pakistan [1985] 1 v. (various pagings) leaves ; LC Card 86-146552
HD5070.5 .W49 1985

Shailer, G. E. P. Experimental failure prediction models for small companies / by G.E.P. Shailer. [Newcastle, Australia] : Dept. of Economics and Industrial Economics, [1986] 52 p. ; 30 cm. (Discussion paper, 0812-1656 . no. 35) "August 1986." Bibliography: p. 43-47. ISBN 0-7259-0555-7 (pbk.) LC Card 87-121092 DDC 338.6/42 19
1. Business mortality - Forecasting - Mathematical models. I. Series: Discussion paper / University of Newcastle. Institute of Industrial Economics , no. 35. II. Title.
HD2747 .S42 1986

Shaked, Israel, 1948- Michel, Allen, 1945- Takeover madness . New York , c1986. xii, 397 p. : ISBN 0-471-01079-0 LC Card 85-32315 DDC 658.1/8 19
HD2746.5 .M53 1986 ***NYPL [JLE 86-2989]***

Shakhdzhakhan, Ali. Issledovanie odnoĭ matematicheskoĭ modeli ėkonomicheskogo rosta / Shakhdzhakhan Ali, A.G. Shmidt. Moskva : Vychislitel′nyĭ t͡sentr AN SSSR, 1983. 29, [2] p. : ill. ; 22 cm. (Soobshchenii͡a po prikladnoĭ matematike) Bibliography: p. [30] LC Card 83-176389
1. Economic development - Mathematical models. I. Shmidt, A. G. II. Akademii͡a nauk SSSR. Vychislitel′nyĭ t͡sentr. III. Title. IV. Series.
HD75.5 .S52 1983

Shakhmatnai͡a filatelii͡a . Voĭshko, V. B. (Vladimir Boleslavovich) Moskva , 1984. 192 p. : LC Card 84-174397
HE6183.C415 V65 1984

Shamleh, Omar. Erdölinduzierte sozioökonomische Entwicklung in den OAPEC-Staaten : der Fall Libyens / Omar Shamleh. Frankfurt am Main ; New York : P. Lang, c1986. 410 p. ; 21 cm. (Europäische Hochschulschriften. Reihe V, Volks- und Betriebswirtschaft, 0531-7339 . Bd. 681 = vol. 681 = vol. 681) Bibliography: p. 377-410. ISBN 3-8204-9097-3 LC Card 86-157642
1. Libya - Economic conditions. 2. Libya - Economic policy. 3. Libya - Social conditions. 4. Libya - Politics and government. 5. Petroleum industry and trade - Libya. I. Series: Europäische Hochschulschriften. Reihe V, Volks- und Betriebswirtschaft , Bd. 681. II. Title.
HC825 .S55 1986

Shamsutdinov, R. V. Sovershenstvovanie khozi͡aĭstvennogo mekhanizma v uslovii͡akh razvitogo sotsializma /. Tashkent , 1985. 142, [2] p. ; LC Card 86-220208
HC337.U96 S68 1985

Shanahan, Jim. The Services challenge . Chicago, Ill. , 1987. vi, 108 p. : ISBN 0-87757-188-0 (pbk.) LC Card 87-12543 DDC 658.8 19
HD9980.5 .S4255 1987

Shanbhag, V. (Vinod)
Industrial sickness . Ahmedabad , c1984. xv, 459 p. ; LC Card 87-902007 DDC 363.1/19677/00954 19
HD9866.I63 A385 1984

Issues in modernization of the textile industry . Ahmedabad , 1985. 87 p. : LC Card 87-902140 DDC 338.4/7677/00954 19
HD9866.I62 I58 1985

Shand, Richard Tregurtha. Chew, T. A. The off-farm labour supply of padi farmers in Kelantan, Malaysia [microform] /. [Canberra] , c1984. 19 p. ; ISBN 0-86784-513-9 (pbk.) LC Card 85-670027 DDC 331.12/93318/095951 19
HD5854.55.M4 C47 1984
NYPL [*ZF-1745 no.58]

Shane, Douglas R. Hoofprints on the forest : cattle ranching and the destruction of Latin America's tropical forests / Douglas R. Shane. Philadelphia : Institute for the Study of Human Issues, c1986. xvi, 159 p. ; 23 cm. Includes index. Bibliography: p. 119-143. ISBN 0-89727-054-1 : LC Card 83-26585 DDC 338.1/76213/098 19
1. Cattle trade - Latin America. 2. Beef industry - Latin America. 3. Clear-cutting - Latin America. I. Title.
HD9433.L292 S53 1984
NYPL [JLD 86-2289]

Shang yeh ching chi yen chiu so (China). Tzu liao shih. Kuo wai shang yeh yen chiu tzu liao /. [Peking] , 1984. 3, 604 p. ;
NYPL [*OVY 86-3606]

SHANGHAI (CHINA) - ECONOMIC CONDITIONS.
Louven, Erhard. Shanghai, Chinas Tor zur Welt /. Hamburg , 1986. 118 p. : LC Card 86-230755
HC428.S47 L68 1986

Shanghai, Chinas Tor zur Welt /. Louven, Erhard. Hamburg , 1986. 118 p. : LC Card 86-230755
HC428.S47 L68 1986

SHANGHAI - ECONOMIC CONDITIONS.
Honig, Emily. Sisters and strangers . Stanford, Calif. , 1986. ix, 299 p. : ISBN 0-8047-1274-3 (alk. paper) : LC Card 84-51711 DDC 331.4/87721/0951132 19
HD6073.T42 C64 1986
NYPL [JLD 86-3016]

Shanin, Teodor. Peasants and peasant societies . Oxford [Oxfordshire] , New York, NY, USA , 1987. viii, 497 p. ; ISBN 0-631-15212-1 : LC Card 87-775 DDC 305.5/63 19
HD1521 .P42 1987

Shank, William H. The amazing Pennsylvania canals / by William H. Shank. 150th anniversary ed. York, Pa. : American Canal and Transportation Center, [1986], c1981. 128 p. : ill. ; 23 cm. Bibliography: p. 126. ISBN 0-933788-37-1 (pbk.) LC Card 87-400232 DDC 386/.48/09748 19
1. Canals - Pennsylvania - History. I. Title.
HE395.P47 S5 1986

Shankar, Kripa.
Pattern of land ownership and backwardness : a study of four villages in Jaunpur District of

eastern U.P. / Kripa Shankar ; consultant, P.C. Joshi.1st ed. New Delhi : Ashish Pub. House, 1986. x, 119 p. ; 22 cm. Study based on July 1979-June 1980 data. Includes bibliographical references and index. ISBN 81-7024-021-2 : LC Card 87-900130 DDC 333.3/23/09542 19
1. Land tenure - India - Jaunpur (District). 2. Farm ownership - India - Jaunpur (District). 3. Jaunpur (India : District) - Economic conditions. I. Title.
HD879.J37 S5 1986

Uttar Pradesh in statistics /. New Delhi , 1987. viii, 82 p. ; ISBN 81-7024-071-9 : LC Card 86-903774 DDC 315.4/2 19
HA4587.U8 U87 1987

Shanker Shetty, K. Welfare state and bank nationalisation in India / K. Shanker Shetty. Delhi : Macmillan, India, 1982. xvii, 345 p. ; 23 cm. Revision of the author's thesis (Ph. D.--University of Bombay) Bibliography: p. 341-345. ISBN 0-333-90729-9 : LC Card 83-903489 DDC 332.1/0954 19
1. Banks and banking - India. 2. Banks and banking - Government ownership - India. 3. India - Economic policy - 1947-. 4. India - Social policy. I. Title.
HG3284 .S4823 1982 ***NYPL [JLD 86-4354]***

Shannon, Frank, 1947- Lotta, Raymond. America in decline . Chicago , c1984- v. : ISBN 0-916650-12-X (v. 1) : LC Card 83-22294 DDC 330.973/0927 19
HC54 .L63 1984 ***NYPL [JLL 87-106]***

SHANNON FREE AIRPORT DEVELOPMENT COMPANY.
Ireland. Oireachtas. Dáil. Committee on Public Expenditure. Review of Shannon Free Airport Development Company Limited . Dublin [1983?] 79 p. : LC Card 87-146082 DDC 387.7/36/094193 19
HE9797.5.I72 S54 1983

SHANNON'S MEASURE OF UNCERTAINTY. see **UNCERTAINTY (INFORMATION THEORY)**

Shanshieva, L. N. Problemy nauchno-tekhnicheskogo progressa v bratskikh sotsialisticheskikh stranakh . Moskva , 1985. 234 p. ; LC Card 86-179196
HC244.Z9 T472 1985

The shape of medieval monetary history /. Lopez, Robert Sabatino. London , 1986. 330 p. 1 v. (various pagings) : ISBN 0-86078-195-X LC Card 87-133292 DDC 332.4/94 19
HG243 .L67 1986

Shapiro, Alan C. International corporate finance : a survey and synthesis / Alan C. Shapiro ; sponsored by United Airlines. Tampa, FL : Financial Management Association, c1986. 79 p. : ill. ; 23 cm. (The Financial management survey and synthesis series) Bibliography: p. 78-79. ISBN 0-936795-00-X (pbk.) LC Card 86-231054 DDC 658.1/599 19
1. International business enterprises - Finance. I. United Air Lines, inc. II. Title. III. Series.
HG4027.5 .S46 1986

Shapiro, Ann-Louise, 1944- Housing the poor of Paris, 1850-1902 / Ann-Louise Shapiro. Madison, Wis. : University of Wisconsin Press, 1985. xx, 224 p. : ill. ; 24 cm. Originally presented as the author's thesis (Ph. D.)--Brown University. Includes index. Bibliography: p. 205-217. ISBN 0-299-09880-X : LC Card 84-40159 DDC 363.5/8 19
1. Public housing - France - Paris - History. 2. Public health - France - Paris - History. 3. Poor - France - Paris - History. I. Title.
HD7288.78.F82 P357 1985
NYPL [JLE 85-1534]

Shapiro, H. Jack (Harris Jack) Reviving industry in America : Japanese influences on manufacturing and the service sector / Harris Jack Shapiro, Teresa Cosenza. Cambridge, Mass. : Ballinger Pub. Co., c1987. xii, 204 p. : ill. ; 24 cm. (Ballinger series in business in a global environment) Includes bibliographies and index. ISBN 0-88730-118-5 LC Card 87-17585 DDC 338.4/767/0973 19
1. United States - Manufactures - Management. 2. Service industries - United States - Management. 3. Industrial management - United States. 4. Japan - Manufactures - Management. 5. Service industries - Japan - Management. 6. Industrial management - Japan. I. Cosenza, Teresa. II. Title. III. Series.
HD9725 .S46 1987

Shapiro, Isaac, 1957- Levitan, Sar A. Working but poor . Baltimore , c1987. ix, 142 p. : ISBN 0-8018-3583-6 (alk. paper) LC Card 87-16973 DDC 362.5/0973 19
HC110.I5 L468 1987

Shapiro, Michael E. Utility diversification : a detour with serious risks for ratepayers / prepared by Michael E. Shapiro. Sacramento, CA : Senate Office of Research : Copies from Joint Publications Office, [1986] 50 p. ; 28 cm. "January 1986." Bibliography: p. 49-50. LC Card 86-621960 DDC 338.8/3613636/0973 19
1. Public utilities - United States. 2. Diversification in industry - United States. 3. Public utilities - California. 4. Diversification in industry - California. I. California. Legislature. Senate. Office of Research. II. Title.
HD2766 .S47 1986

Sharan, Girja, 1944- Energy use in rural Gujarat /. New Delhi , c1987. iv, 186 p. : ISBN 81-204-0216-2 : LC Card 87-901949 DDC 333.79/13/095475 19
HD9502.I43 G844 1987

Sharapov, G. V. (German Vladimirovich) Istoriia sovetskogo krest'ianstva /. Moskva , 1986-<1987. v. <1-3 > : LC Card 86-230318
HD1492.S65 I88 1986

Sharda, N. K. State finances and regional development in India / N.K. Sharda. New Delhi : Deep & Deep Publications, c1986. 248 p. ; 23 cm. Includes index. Bibliography: p. [239]-246. LC Card 86-900599 DDC 336.54/52 19
1. Finance, Public - India - Himachal Pradesh. 2. Intergovernmental fiscal relations - India. 3. Federal aid to community development - India. 4. Rural development - India - Himachel Pradesh. I. Title.
HJ1339.H55 S54 1986 ***NYPL [JLD 86-3211]***

Share, Bernard. Flight of the Iolar : the Aer Lingus experience, 1936-1986 / Bernard Share. Goldenbridge, Dublin ; Dallas [Texas] : Gill and Macmillan, c1986. xii, 306 p. : ill. ; 25 cm. Bibliography: p. [294]-296. Includes index. ISBN 0-7171-1457-0 LC Card 86-223299
1. Aer Lingus - History. 2. Aeronautics, Commercial - Ireland - History. I. Title.
HE9846.A47 S42 1986

SHARE CERTIFICATES. see **STOCK CERTIFICATES.**

Share, Michael. The Central Workers' Circle of St. Petersburg, 1889-1894 : a case study of the "workers' intelligentsia" / Michael Share. New York : Garland Pub., 1987. xi, 396 p., [6] p. of plates : ill. ; 24 cm. (Modern European history) Thesis (Ph. D.)--University of Wisconsin--Madison, 1984. Bibliography: p. 372-396. ISBN 0-8240-8063-7 (alk. paper) : LC Card 87-374 DDC 305.5/62/0947453 19
1. TSentral'nyi rabochii kruzhok (Saint Petersburg, Russia). 2. Labor and laboring classes - Russian S.F.S.R. - Leningrad - History. 3. Leningrad (R.S.F.S.R.) - Social conditions. 4. Leningrad (R.S.F.S.R.) - Economic conditions. I. Title. II. Series.
HD8522.T753 S53 1987

The share-owner's guide /. Stafford, J. T. Cambridge [Cambridgeshire] , Wolfeboro, N.H., USA , 1988. p. cm. ISBN 0-85941-402-7 (pbk.) : LC Card 87-17387 DDC 332.63/22 19
HG4921 .S617 1988

SHARED HOUSING - UNITED STATES.
Horne, Jo. Homesharing and other lifestyle options /. Washington, D.C. , Glenview, Ill. , c1988. xi, 259 p. : ISBN 0-673-24886-0 (pbk.) : LC Card 87-13028 DDC 363.5/9 19
HD7287.92.U54 H65 1988

Sharenkov, S. V. (Stanislav Vasil'evich) Raikom i nauchno-tekhnicheskaia intelligentsiia /. Leningrad , 1981. 117 p. ; LC Card 82-177893
HC340.T4 R35 1981

SHARES OF STOCK. see **STOCKS.**

Sharfman, Mark P. Daft, Richard L. Organization theory . St. Paul , c1987. xxviii, 338 p. : ISBN 0-314-28488-5 (pbk.) LC Card 86-28965 DDC 658.4 19
HD31 .D136 1987

Sharif, Walid. Joint Symposium on the Energy Industries: Prospects of Co-operation Between Arab Gulf States and Japan (1984 : Tokyo, Japan) The Arab Gulf States and Japan . London , Dover, N.H. , c1986. xiv, 216 p. : ISBN 0-7099-3393-2 : LC Card 85-12819 DDC 338.2/728/0952 19
HD9576.P52 J65 1984
NYPL [JLD 86-1669]

Sharifi, Mohsen. Integrated case studies in accounting and information systems / Mohsen Sharifi, Badie Farah. Englewood Cliffs, N.J. : Prentice-Hall, c1987. ix, 229 p. : ill. ; 24 cm. Bibliography: p. 228-229. ISBN 0-13-469016-8 (pbk.) LC Card 86-30297 DDC 657/.028/5 19
1. Accounting - Data processing. 2. Information storage and retrieval systems - Accounting. I. Farah, Badie. II. Title.
HF5679 .S4754 1987

Sharikat al-Dirāsāt wa-al-Injāzāt wa-al-Irshādāt (Morocco) Les Industries mécaniques et électriques au Maroc . Casablanca [1984] 1 v. (various pagings) ; LC Card 85-206543
HD9705.M72 I53 1984

Sharing of productivity gains in Indian industry /. Singh, Nar, 1952- Delhi , 1984. x, 180 p. ;
NYPL [JLD 86-4253]

Sharing the work . Meltz, Noah M. Toronto , Buffalo , 1981. viii, 90 p. : ISBN 0-8020-2383-5
NYPL [JLD 82-233]

SHARK FISHERIES - BRAZIL - RIO GRANDE DO NORTE.
Paiva, Francisco Ismar Martins. Projeto Pesca Industrial à Vela. [Natal, Brazil] [1982 or 1983] 91 p. : LC Card 85-102872
HD9464.B73 R487 1982

Sharkansky, Ira. The political economy of Israel / Ira Sharkansky. New Brunswick, N.J., U. S.A. : Transaction Books, c1987. xi, 157 p. ; 24 cm. Includes bibliographies and index. ISBN 0-88738-117-0 : LC Card 86-25090 DDC 338.95694/054 19
1. Israel - Economic policy. I. Title.
HC415.25 .S49 1987

Sharkey, Stephen M. Evaluation of the 1984 selective speed enforcement projects in Virginia / by Stephen M. Sharkey. Charlottesville, Va. : Virginia Transportation Research Council, [1987] xii, 117, [34] p. : ill. ; 28 cm. (VTRC . 87-R13) "A report prepared by the Virginia Transportation Council under the sponsorship of the Transportation Safety Administration of the Department of Motor Vehicles." "February 1987." Bibliography: p. 117 (2nd group). LC Card 87-621546 DDC 388.3/144/09755 19
1. Speed limits - Virginia. 2. Traffic accidents - Virginia. 3. Traffic safety - Virginia. 4. Traffic accidents - Virginia - Statistics. I. Virginia Transportation Research Council. II. Virginia. Transportation Safety Administration. III. Series: VTRC (Series) , 87-R13. IV. Title.
HE5620.S6 S532 1987

Sharkovich, V. G. Lagosha, Boris Aleksandrovich. Analiz i sintez v sistemakh otraslevogo upravleniia /. Moskva , 1978. 262 p., [1] folded leaf of plates : LC Card 81-167577
HD30.25 .L335 1978

Sharma, Alakh N. Bihar, stagnation or growth /. Patna , 1987. xxix, 404 p. ; LC Card 87-902676 DDC 330.954/12052 19
HC437.B47 B49 1987

Sharma, B. D. (Banarsi Das), 1921- Art of conciliation and industrial unrest / B.D. Sharma. Bombay : Labour Consultancy Bureau, 1985. xvi, 366 p. ; 22 cm. Includes bibliographical references. LC Card 87-902679 DDC 331.89/14/0954 19
1. Mediation and conciliation, Industrial - India. 2. Labor disputes - India. 3. Trade-unions - India. I. Title.
HD5998.A3 S48 1985

Sharma, Bankey Lal. Economic ideas in ancient India before Kautilya / by Bankey Lal Sharma. New Delhi : Ramanand Vidya Bhawan, 1987. viii, 208 p. ; 23 cm. Bibliography: p. [201]-208. LC Card 86-903545 DDC 330/.0954 19
1. Economics - India - History. I. Title.
HB126.I4 S467 1987

Sharma, Dewan Chand, 1898- Kashmir agriculture & land revenue system under the Sikh rule, 1819-46 A.D. / D.C. Sharma. New Delhi, India : Rima Pub. House, 1986. xiv, 160 p., [8] p. of plates : ill. ; 23 cm. Bibliography: p. [152]-160. LC Card 86-900128
1. Agriculture - Economic aspects - India - Jammu and Kashmir - History. 2. Agriculture and state - India - Jammu and Kashmir - History. 3. Agriculture - Social aspects - India - Jammu and Kashmir - History. 4.

Land value taxation - India - Jammu and Kashmir - History. 5. Jammu and Kashmir (India) - History. I. Title. II. Title: Kashmir agriculture and land revenue system under the Sikh rule, 1819-46 A.D.
HD2075.J35 S43 1986 NYPL [JLD 86-3742]

Sharma, Dhirendra. The Indian atom . New Delhi , c1986. v, 166 p. ; LC Card 87-900288 DDC 333.79/24/0954 19
HD9698.I52 I52 1986

Sharma, Gunanidhi. Monetary structure of the Nepalese economy : policy issues in theory & practice / Gunanidhi Sharma. New Delhi : South Asian Publishers, c1987. xiv, 243 p. : ill. ; 23 cm. Revision of the author's thesis (Ph. D.--University of Rajasthan, 1986) Bibliography: p. [215]-234. Includes indexes. ISBN 81-7003-076-5 : LC Card 87-900309 DDC 332.4/95493 19
1. Monetary policy - Nepal. I. Title.
HG1220.9 .S52 1987

Sharma, Inderjit. Land revenue administration in the Punjab, 1849-1901 / Inderjit Sharma. New Delhi : Atlantic Publishers and Distributors, c1985. xi, 369 p. : 22 cm. Includes index. Bibliography: p. [353]-365. LC Card 85-904617 DDC 354.54/552007242 19
1. Land tenure - India - Punjab. 2. Landlord and tenant - India - Punjab. 3. Land value taxation - India - Punjab. I. Title.
HD879.P8 S53 1985 NYPL [JLD 87-552]

Sharma, J. V. M. Reddy, K. N. (Kaipa Narayana), 1936- Central government expenditure . New Delhi , 1984. xvi, 175 p. ; LC Card 84-901866 DDC 336.3/9/0954 19
HJ2157 .R43 1984 NYPL [JLD 87-66]

Sharma, L. R., 1934- The economy of Himachal Pradesh : growth and structure : a study in development performance / L.R. Sharma. Delhi, India : Mittal Publications, 1987. vii, 167 p. ; 23 cm. Revision of the author's thesis (Ph. D.--Himachal Pradesh University) Includes bibliographies and index. LC Card 86-903541 DDC 330.954/52 19
1. Himachal Pradesh, India - Economic conditions. I. Title.
HC437.H5 S52 1987

Sharma, O. P. Pai Panandiker, V. A., 1935- Development bureaucracy /. New Delhi , c1983. ix, 252 p. ; LC Card 83-902420 DDC 352.94/233/09542 19
HD2075.K359 P34 1983
NYPL [JLD 86-3762]

Sharma, R. D. (Ram Dutt), 1945- Development administration in a changing society /. New Delhi, India , 1987. xix, 214 p. ; ISBN 81-85135-18-5 : LC Card 87-900453 DDC 338.954/52 19
HC437.H5 D48 1987

Sharma, R. D. (Ramji Dass) Financial working of foreign multinational banks in India / R.D. Sharma. Delhi, India : Mittal Publications, 1987. 244 p. ; 22 cm. Originally presented as the author's thesis (Ph. D.--University of Jammu) Study covers the period, 1960-1980. Bibliography: p. [229]-237. Includes index. LC Card 86-903591 DDC 332.1/5 19
1. Banks and banking, Foreign - India. 2. Banks and banking, International. I. Title.
HG3284 .S487 1987

Sharma, R. K., 1947- Menon, M. S. N., 1924- No to exploitation . New Delhi , 1983. 163, xxxii p. ; LC Card 83-902131 DDC 337/.09172/4 19
HC59.7 .M445 1983 NYPL [JLE 86-4184]

Sharma, S. L. Development, socio-cultural dimensions /. Jaipur , 1986. xxi, 264 p. ; ISBN 81-7033-020-3 : LC Card 86-902849 DDC 306/.0954 19
HC435.2 .D478 1986

Sharma, Shiva Prashad. Upadhyay, Kiran Dutta. Handicrafts development in Nepal . Kathmandu, Nepal , 1985. ii, 126, [14] p. ; LC Card 86-902589 DDC 338.4/77455/095496 19
HD2346.N36 U63 1985

Sharma, Ursula, 1941- Women's work, class, and the urban household : a study of Shimla, North India / Ursula Sharma. London ; New York : Tavistock Publications, 1986. 213 p. ; 23 cm. Includes indexes. Bibliography: p. [199]-203. ISBN 0-422-79320-5 : LC Card 86-11296 DDC 305.4/3 19
1. Housewives - India - Simla - Social conditions. 2. Home economics - India - Simla - Social aspects. 3. Wages - Housewives. 4. Women - Economic conditions. I. Title.
HQ759 .S4616 1986 NYPL [JLD 87-1281]

Sharma, Yogeshwar, 1936- Energy alternatives for rural development /. Jaipur , 1985. vi, 303 p. : LC Card 86-902191 DDC 333.79/0954 19
HD9556.I42 E54 1985

Sharp, Ansel Miree, 1924- Economics of social issues / Ansel M. Sharp, Charles A. Register, Richard H. Leftwich. 8th ed. Plano, Tex. : Business Publications, 1988. xiii, 431 p. : ill. ; 24 cm. Includes bibliographies and index. ISBN 0-256-06173-4 (pbk.) LC Card 87-71674 DDC 330 19
1. Economics. 2. Social problems. I. Register, Charles A. II. Leftwich, Richard H. III. Title.
HB171.5 .S5498 1988

Sharps rifles and Spanish mules . Austerman, Wayne R. (Wayne Randolph), 1948- College Station , c1985. x, 367 p., [8] p. of plates : ISBN 0-89096-220-0 : LC Card 84-40557 DDC 383/.49764 19
HE6376.A1 T417 1985
NYPL [JLE 85-3346]

Shashua, Leon. Goldschmidt, Yaaqov. The impact of inflation on financial activity in business, with applications to the U. S. farming sector /. Totowa, N.J. , 1986. xvi, 181 p. ; ISBN 0-8476-7427-4 : LC Card 85-14196 DDC 338.1/3/0973 19
HD1761 .G645 1986 NYPL [JLE 86-3484]

Shastitko, Vladimir Mikhaĭlovich. Vneshnii͡ai͡a torgovli͡a SSSR so stranami SĖV /. Moskva , 1986. 108, [3] p. ; LC Card 86-213259
HF3628.E9 V54 1986

Shastri, Lalit. Bhopal disaster : an eye witness account / Lalit Shastri. New Delhi : Criterion Publications, [1985] 102 p. [32] p. of plates : ill. ; 22 cm. A journalist's viewpoint on the tragedy due to leakage of methyl icocyanate gas from an industrial plant in Bhopal, Madhya Pradesh, 1984. LC Card 86-902662 DDC 363.1/79 19
1. Bhopal Union Carbide Plant Disaster, Bhopal, India, 1984. 2. Union Carbide Ltd.(India) - Trials, litigation, etc. 3. Union Carbide Corporation - Trials, litigation, etc. I. Title.
HD7269.C452 I5267 1985

Shatalin, S. S. (Stanislav Sergeevich) Renta . Moskva , 1984. 95 p. : LC Card 85-192538
HB401 .R48 1984

Shaw, Christine. The A-Z of UK marketing information sources / [compiled and edited by Christine Shaw]. 1st ed. London : Euromonitor Publications, 1984. 233 p. ; 21 cm. Includes indexes. ISBN 0-86338-048-4 (pbk.) : LC Card 84-217782 DDC 330.941/0858 19
1. Marketing - Great Britain - Information services. 2. Marketing - Great Britain - Bibliography. 3. Great Britain - Economic conditions - 1945- - Information services. 4. Great Britain - Economic conditions - 1945- - Bibliography. I. Title. II. Title: AZ of UK marketing information sources.
HC256.6 .S47 1984 NYPL [JLD 86-2248]

Shaw, Frederick. The homes and homeless of post-war Britain / by Frederick Shaw. Carnforth, Lancashire, UK : Parthenon Press, c1985. viii, 288 p. : ill. ; 31 cm. Includes index. Bibliography: p. 277. ISBN 1-85070-104-0
1. Housing - Great Britain - History - 20th century. 2. Homelessness - Great Britain - History - 20th century. I. Title. NYPL [JLG 86-278]

Shaw, G. K. (Graham Keith), 1938- Greenaway, David. Macroeconomics . Oxford, OX, UK , New York, NY, USA , 1987. p. cm. ISBN 0-631-15763-8 (pbk.) : LC Card 87-20831 DDC 339/.0941 19
HB172.5 .G75 1987

Shaw, Lois Banfill. Dex, Shirley. British and American women at work . Houndmills, Basingstoke, Hampshire , 1986. xii, 159 p. : ISBN 0-333-40219-7 *NYPL [JLD 86-3608]*

SHAW, SAVILL & CO. - HISTORY.
Savill, David. Sail to New Zealand . London , 1986. 185 p., [20] p. of plates : ISBN 0-7090-2809-1 : LC Card 87-111329 DDC 387.5/065/41 19
HE945.S45 S28 1986

Shaw, Stephen, 1950-
Air transport. Shaw, Stephen, 1950- Airline marketing and management / Stephen Shaw. 2nd ed. Malabar , 1988, c1985. 296 p. ; ISBN 0-89464-256-1 LC Card 87-22639 DDC 387.7/4/0688 19
HE9781 .S35 1987

Airline marketing and management / Stephen Shaw. 2nd ed. Malabar : Krieger, 1988, c1985. 296 p. ; 24 cm. Reprint. Originally published: London : Pitman, 1985. Rev. ed. of: Air transport. 1982. Bibliography: p. 275-281. Includes indexes. ISBN 0-89464-256-1 LC Card 87-22639 DDC 387.7/4/0688 19
1. Aeronautics, Commercial - Marketing. 2. Airlines - Marketing. I. Shaw, Stephen, 1950- Air transport. II. Title.
HE9781 .S35 1987

Shaw, Timothy M. Newly industrializing countries and the political economy of south-south relations /. New York , 1988. p. cm. ISBN 0-312-01180-6 : LC Card 87-23476 DDC 337/.09172/4 19
HF1413 .N497 1988

Shawkat Ali, A. M. M. Politics and land system in Bangladesh / A.M.M. Shawkat Ali. Dhaka : National Institute of Local Government, 1986. x, 354 p. ; 22 cm. Includes index. Bibliography: p. 342-347. LC Card 86-900954 DDC 333.3/1/5492 19
1. Land settlement - Bangladesh. 2. Land settlement - Government policy - Bangladesh. I. Title.
HD880.6 .S53 1986 NYPL [JLD 86-4018]

SHAWL INDUSTRY - INDIA - JAMMU AND KASHMIR - HISTORY.
Ahad, Abdul, 1947- Kashmir to Frankfurt . New Delhi, India , 1987. xiv, 182 p., [20] p. of plates : LC Card 86-903828
HD9969.S43 I425 1987

Shaykh, Riyāḍ ʻAbd al-Ḥafīẓ. Niẓām al-iʻānah fī al-iqtiṣād al-Saʻūdī / iʻdād Riyāḍ ʻAbd al-Ḥafīẓ al-Shaykh, ʻUmar Zuhayr Ḥāfiẓ. al-Ṭabʻah 1. al-Mamlakah al-ʻArabīyah al-Suʻūdīyah : Wizārat al-Taʻlīm al-ʻĀlī, al-Majlis al-ʻIlmī bi-Jāmiʻat al-Malik ʻAbd al-ʻAzīz, 1985. 77 p. : ill. ; 25 cm. "Baḥth raqm M Q B 8-1402/1403 H." Includes bibliographies. LC Card 86-208281
1. Economic assistance, Domestic - Saudi Arabia. 2. Subsidies - Saudi Arabia. I. Ḥāfiẓ, ʻUmar Zuhayr. II. Title.
HC415.33.Z9 E447 1985

Shchedrostʹ zemli krymskoĭ : ocherki / [sostavitelʹ V.P. Terekhov]. Simferopolʹ : "Tavrii͡a", 1985. 158 p. ; 18 cm. LC Card 86-128000
1. Food industry and trade - Ukraine - Krymskai͡a oblastʹ. 2. Krymskai͡a oblastʹ (Ukraine) - Rural conditions. I. Terekhov, V. P. (Vladimir Pavlovich).
HD9015.S653 K797 1985

Shchelkanov, A. G. Prognozirovanie i ėffektivnostʹ raboty flota . Leningrad , 1985. 104 p. : LC Card 86-170274
HE847 .P77 1985

Shcherbakov, Vladimir Vasilʹevich. Rolʹ bankov v usilenii gospodstva finansovogo kapitala /. Moskva , 1985. 206 p. ; LC Card 86-102078
HG3881 .R615 1985

Shchetinin, Valentin Dmitrievich. Strukturnye sdvigi v mirovom kapitalisticheskom khozi͡aĭstve /. Kiev , 1985. 295 p. ; LC Card 86-105339
*HC59 .S8345 1985 NYPL [*QIP 87-3473]*

Shcho take stalinsʹke "tyloopolchenni͡a"? . Tersʹkyĭ, Ion. Toronto , 1969. 95 p. ; LC Card 82-105191
HD4865.S65 T47 1969

Shchukin, E. P. (Evgeniĭ Petrovich) Avrekh, G. L. (Gennadiĭ Lipanovich) Ėkonomika na urovne molekul /. Moskva , 1986. 141 p. : LC Card 86-179247
HD9656.S55 A95 1986

She hui chu i ching chi tse jen chih /. Liu, Yung-chʻeng. [Chʻang-chʻun shih] , 1985. 5, 264 p. ; LC Card 86-179707 DDC 658/.00951 19
HD70.C5 L58 1985 <Orien China>
*NYPL [*OVY 86-4140]*

She hui chu i so yu chih yen chiu /. Chiang, Hsüeh-mo. Hang-chou , 1985. [3], 211 p. ;
*NYPL [*OVL 86-3601]*

She hui chu i so yu chih yen chiu /. Liu, Shih-pai. Shang-hai , 1985. 2, 6, 223 p. ;
*NYPL [*OVY 86-3647]*

Shea, Edward E., 1932- Scharf, Charles A. Acquisitions, mergers, sales, buyouts, and

takeovers . Englewood Cliffs, N.J. , c1985. xi, 452 p. : ISBN 0-13-003120-8 LC Card 85-6566 DDC 658.1/6/0973 19
HD2741 .S35 1985 ***NYPL [JLF 86-611]***

Shea, Gordon F., 1925- Company loyalty : earning it, keeping it / Gordon F. Shea. New York, N.Y. : AMA Membership Publications Division, American Management Association, c1987. 86 p. : port. ; 23 cm. (AMA management briefing) Bibliography: p. 85-86. ISBN 0-8144-2331-0 (pbk.) : LC Card 86-28883 DDC 650.1 19
1. Organizational effectiveness. 2. Loyalty. I. Title.
HD58.9 .S48 1987

Shea, Moira M. The United States engineering plastics industry : a profile / prepared by Basic Industries, Office of Chemicals and Allied Products. Washington, D.C. : U. S. Dept. of Commerce, International Trade Administration : For sale by the Supt. of Docs., U. S. G.P.O., 1987. 51 p. : ill. ; 28 cm. Cover title: The U. S. engineering plastics industry. Shipping list no.: 87-226-P. "March 1987." S/N 003-009-00504-3 Item 231-B-1 LC Card 87-601518 DDC 338.4/76684/0973 19
1. Plastics industry and trade - United States. 2. Substitute products. I. United States. International Trade Administration. Office of Chemicals and Allied Products. II. Title. III. Title: U. S. engineering plastics industry.
HD9661.U62 S54 1987

Sheahan, John, 1923- Patterns of development in Latin America : poverty, repression, and economic strategy / John Sheahan. Princeton, N.J. : Princeton University Press, c1987. x, 399 p. : ill. ; 25 cm. Bibliography: p. [363]-393. Includes index. ISBN 0-691-07735-5 (alk. paper) : LC Card 87-2853 DDC 338.98 19
1. Latin America - Economic conditions - 1945-. 2. Latin America - Politics and government - 1948-. 3. Poor - Latin America. 4. Political rights - Latin America. 5. Foreign economic relations - Latin America. I. Title.
HC125 .S498 1987

Shear, Mel A. Property management reinvented : how to convert maintenance and energy expenses to profits / Mel A. Shear. Englewood-Cliffs, N.J. : Prentice-Hall, c1988. xiii, 306 p. : ill. ; 24 cm. Includes bibliographical references and index. ISBN 0-13-731191-5 LC Card 87-18852 DDC 333.3/068 19
1. Real estate management. I. Title.
HD1394 .S52 1988

Shedenov, U. K. (Utegali Kadyrgalievich) Sotsial′no-ėkonomicheskie problemy sfery obsluzhivaniia naseleniia v usloviiakh nauchno-tekhnicheskogo progressa / U.K. Shedenov. Alma-Ata : Izd-vo "Nauka" Kazakhskoĭ SSR, 1978. 197, [3] p. ; 21 cm. At head of title: Akademiia nauk Kazakhskoĭ SSR. Institut ėkonomiki. Bibliography: p. 195-[198] LC Card 81-149568
1. Service industries - Kazakh S.S.R. 2. Kazakh S.S.R. - Economic conditions. I. Title.
HD9986.S683 K398 1978

Sheen, Brian J., 1952- Nest egg investing : the lifelong program for financial independence / Brian J. Sheen. New York : Putnam, c1987. 224 p. : ill. ; 24 cm. ISBN 0-399-13185-X : LC Card 87-2268 DDC 332.6/78 19
1. Finance, Personal - United States. I. Title.
HG179 .S455 1987

SHEEP INDUSTRY - AUSTRALIA - EMPLOYEES - HISTORY - 20TH CENTURY.
Tsokhas, Kosmas. Shifting the burden . Canberra, Australia [1986] 61, 6 p. ; ISBN 0-86784-898-7 (pbk.) LC Card 87-151151 DDC 331.7/6363/00994 19
HD9436.A82 T75 1986

SHEEP INDUSTRY - AUSTRALIA - HISTORY - 20TH CENTURY.
Tsokhas, Kosmas. Shifting the burden . Canberra, Australia [1986] 61, 6 p. ; ISBN 0-86784-898-7 (pbk.) LC Card 87-151151 DDC 331.7/6363/00994 19
HD9436.A82 T75 1986

SHEEP INDUSTRY - AUSTRALIA - HISTORY - SOURCES.
Pemberton, P. A. Pure merinos and others . Canberra , c1986. 125 p. : ISBN 0-86784-796-4 (pbk.) LC Card 87-164515 DDC 382/.41636/0994 19
HE565.G7 P46 1986

SHEEP INDUSTRY - AUSTRALIA - VICTORIA - LOCATION.
Victoria. Saleyard Working Party. Distribution of saleyards in Victoria . [Melbourne] , 1986. 69, 7, 7 p. : LC Card 87-159450 DDC 338.1/760831 19
HD9428.A83 V538 1986

SHEEP INDUSTRY - GREAT BRITAIN - HISTORY - SOURCES.
Pemberton, P. A. Pure merinos and others . Canberra , c1986. 125 p. : ISBN 0-86784-796-4 (pbk.) LC Card 87-164515 DDC 382/.41636/0994 19
HE565.G7 P46 1986

SHEEP INDUSTRY - NEW MEXICO - HISTORY.
Baxter, John O., 1927- Las carneradas . Albuquerque , c1987. x, 198 p., [4] p. of plates : ISBN 0-8263-0961-5 LC Card 86-30906 DDC 381/.4163/009789 19
HD9436.U53 N63 1987

SHEEP INDUSTRY - SOUTHWEST, NEW - HISTORY.
Baxter, John O., 1927- Las carneradas . Albuquerque , c1987. x, 198 p., [4] p. of plates : ISBN 0-8263-0961-5 LC Card 86-30906 DDC 381/.4163/009789 19
HD9436.U53 N63 1987

SHEEP INDUSTRY - URUGUAY - STATISTICS.
Encuesta pecuaria en profundidad . Montevideo, Uruguay [1977-1978] 2 v. ; LC Card 87-402173 DDC 338.1/762/009895021 19
HD9433.U82 E53 1979

Uruguay, exportaciones cumplidas de lanas y sus productos, ovinos en pie, carne ovina y subproductos, apendice pieles lanares . [Montevideo, Uruguay] , 1984. 37 p. ; LC Card 86-164077
HD9904.U82 U78 1984

SHEEP RANCHERS - NEW MEXICO - HISTORY.
Baxter, John O., 1927- Las carneradas . Albuquerque , c1987. x, 198 p., [4] p. of plates : ISBN 0-8263-0961-5 LC Card 86-30906 DDC 381/.4163/009789 19
HD9436.U53 N63 1987

SHEEP RANCHES - NEW MEXICO - HISTORY.
Baxter, John O., 1927- Las carneradas . Albuquerque , c1987. x, 198 p., [4] p. of plates : ISBN 0-8263-0961-5 LC Card 86-30906 DDC 381/.4163/009789 19
HD9436.U53 N63 1987

SHEEP SHEARERS (PERSONS) - AUSTRALIA - HISTORY.
Merritt, John. The making of the AWU /. Melbourne , New York , 1986. x, 432 p., [16] p. of plates : ISBN 0-19-554667-9 LC Card 86-207509 DDC 331.88/13630833/0994 19
HD8842.A874 M47 1986

Sheerin, James J. The complete guide to buying, selling, and investing in undeveloped land / James J. Sheerin. Chicago, Ill. : Probus Pub. Co., c1987. xiii, 339 p. : ill. ; 24 cm. Includes index. ISBN 0-917253-57-4 : LC Card 86-25460 DDC 346.04/3 342.643 19
I. Title.
HD1382.5 .S46 1987 ***NYPL [JLE 87-1118]***

Sheets, Everett. De Old, Alan R. Transportation . Worcester, Mass. , c1986. x, 534 p. : ISBN 0-87192-126-X LC Card 86-70174 DDC 380.5 19
HE151 .D42 1986

Sheets, Robert G. The impact of service industries on underemployment in metropolitan economies / Robert G. Sheets, Stephen Nord, John J. Phelps. Lexington, Mass. : Lexington Books, c1987. xii, 185 p. ; 24 cm. Includes bibliographies and index. ISBN 0-669-14575-0 (alk. paper) LC Card 86-45884 DDC 331.13 19
1. Underemployment - United States. 2. Service industries workers - United States. 3. Metropolitan areas - United States. I. Nord, Stephen. II. Phelps, John J. III. Title.
HD5709.2.U6 S54 1987

Sheffield, John Holroyd, Earl of, 1735-1821. Observations on the commerce of the American states. By John, lord Sheffield. With an appendix ... 6th ed., enl. With a complete index ... London, J. Debrett, 1784. 2 p.l., xlvii, 345, [21] p., 1 l. XVI tab. on 30 l. 21 cm. LC Card 06-17319
1. United States - Commerce. 2. United States - Commerce - Great Britain. 3. Great Britain - Commerce - United States. I. Title.
HF3025 .S58

Shehuizhuyi suoyouzhi yanjiu. Chiang, Hsüeh-mo. She hui chu i so yu chih yen chiu /. Hang-chou , 1985. [3], 211 p. ;
NYPL [*OVL 86-3601]

Shehuizhuyi suoyouzhi yanjiu. Liu, Shih-pai. She hui chu i so yu chih yen chiu /. Shang-hai , 1985. 2, 6, 223 p. ; ***NYPL [*OVY 86-3647]***

Shein, A. I. (Aleksandr Ivanovich) Voenno-promyshlennyĭ kompleks Velikobritanii / A.I. Shein. Moskva : Izd-vo Moskovskogo universiteta, 1985. 165 p. : ill. ; 22 cm. Includes bibliographical references. LC Card 84-219560
1. War - Economic aspects - Great Britain. 2. Munitions - Great Britain. I. Title.
HC260.D4 S54 1985 ***NYPL [*QGR 87-2278]***

Sheĭnin, Ė. IA. (Ėduard IAkovlevich) Burova, S. E. (Stella Efimovna) Kritika burzhuaznykh vzgliadov na ėkonomicheskoe sotrudnichestvo stran SĖV /. Moskva , 1986. 154 p. ; LC Card 86-232355
HC243.5 .B87 1986

Sheldahl, Terry K. Beta Alpha Psi, from Omega to Zeta Omega : the making of a comprehensive accounting fraternity, 1946-1984 / Terry K. Sheldahl. New York : Garland, 1986 xxiii, 851 p., [22] p. of plates : ill., ports. ; 24 cm. (Accounting thought and practice through the years) Bibliography: p. 819-824. Includes indexes. ISBN 0-8240-7855-1 (alk. paper) : LC Card 86-31800 DDC 657/.06/073 19
1. Beta Alpha Psi - History. 2. Accounting - United States - Societies, etc. - History. I. Title. II. Series.
HF5601.B443 S54 1986

Sheldrake, John, 1944- The history of industrial training in Britain / John Sheldrake and Sarah Vickerstaff. Aldershot Hants, England ; Brookfield, Vt., USA : Avebury, c1987. v, 75 p. ; 23 cm. Bibliography: p. 66-71. Includes index. ISBN 0-566-05294-6 : LC Card 86-29601 DDC 331.25/92 19
1. Occupational training - Great Britain - History. I. Vickerstaff, Sarah, 1944-. II. Title.
HD5715.5.G7 S54 1987

Sheldrick, William F. World nitrogen survey / William F. Sheldrick. Washington, D.C. : World Bank, 1987. xxv, 227 p. : ill. ; 27 cm. (Industry and finance series . v. 20) World Bank technical paper, 0253-7494 ; no. 59 ISBN 0-8213-0895-5 LC Card 87-6203 DDC 338.4/7668624 19
1. Nitrogen industries. 2. Fertilizer industry. 3. Nitrogen. I. Title. II. Series.
HD9660.N7 S55 1987

Shelestov, D. K. (Dmitriĭ Kuz′mich) Demography in the mirror of history / Dmitry Shelestov ; [translated from the Russian by Paula Garb]. Moscow : Progress Publishers, c1987. 214 p. ; 18 cm. Title on verso t.p.: Demografiia v zerkale istorii nauki. Includes bibliographical references and index. LC Card 86-201399 DDC 304.6/0947 19
1. Demography - Soviet Union - History. 2. Demography - History. I. Title. II. Title: Demografiia v zerkale istorii nauki.
HB853.S65 S54 1983

Shell Compañía Argentina de Petróleo. Departamento de Asuntos Públicos.
Aspectos económicos de la industria petrolera. Capital Federal [1985 or 1986] 28 p. : LC Card 87-120726
HD9574.A72 A84 1985

Energía y petróleo . Capital Federal [1985 or 1986] 60 p. : LC Card 87-403778 DDC 338.2/7282 19
HD9560.5 .E525 1985

SHELL INTERNATIONAL PETROLEUM COMPANY, LTD.
Shell out of Namibia and South Africa . London [1986] 19 . : LC Card 87-138719 DDC 338.8/87 19
HD9571.9.S45 S54 1986

Shell out of Namibia and South Africa : Shell Shadow Report. London : Anti-apartheid Movement and Embargo, [1986] 19 . : ill. ; 30

cm. Cover title. LC Card 87-138719 DDC 338.8/87 19

1. Shell International Petroleum Company, ltd. 2. Petroleum industry and trade - Political aspects - South Africa. 3. Petroleum industry and trade - Political aspects - Namibia. 4. Apartheid - South Africa. 5. Namibia - International status. I. Anti-Apartheid Movement.
HD9571.9.S45 S54 1986

SHELLFISH TRADE.
Seafood processing & distribution market opportunities. Norwalk, Conn., U. S.A. (6 Prowitt St., Norwalk 06855) , c1986. vii, 244 leaves : LC Card 87-129495 DDC 381/.4566494/0973 19
HD9450.5 .S4 1986

SHELLFISH TRADE - GREAT BRITAIN.
Miller, Charlotte L. The market for seafood in the United Kingdom /. Terminal Island, CA , 1986. ii, 73 p. : LC Card 87-601563 DDC 382.1/4370941 19
HD9461.5 .M55 1986

SHELLFISH TRADE - GREAT BRITAIN - DIRECTORIES.
Miller, Charlotte L. The market for seafood in the United Kingdom /. Terminal Island, CA , 1986. ii, 73 p. : LC Card 87-601563 DDC 382.1/4370941 19
HD9461.5 .M55 1986

SHELLFISH TRADE - UNITED STATES.
Miller, Charlotte L. The market for seafood in the United Kingdom /. Terminal Island, CA , 1986. ii, 73 p. : LC Card 87-601563 DDC 382.1/4370941 19
HD9461.5 .M55 1986

Shelter, settlement, and development / edited by Lloyd Rodwin. Boston : Allen & Unwin, 1987. xvii, 476 p. : ill. ; 25 cm. "A study sponsored and financed by the United Nations/International Year of Shelter for the Homeless"--T.p. verso. Bibliography: p. [425]-462. Includes index. ISBN 0-04-711023-6 (alk. paper) LC Card 87-1038 DDC 363.5/09172/4 19

1. Housing - Developing countries. 2. Housing policy - Developing countries. I. Rodwin, Lloyd.
HD7391 .S54 1987

SHELTERED WORKSHOPS - UNITED STATES.
The Role of the sheltered workshops in the rehabilitation of the severely handicapped. New York , 1976. xxiv, 467 p. ;
NYPL [JLF 86-1287]

SHELTERED WORKSHOPS - UNITED STATES - HISTORY - 20TH CENTURY.
Weiss, Joseph W. The management of change . New York , 1986. xviii, 210 p. ; ISBN 0-275-92195-6 (alk. paper) : LC Card 86-9390 DDC 658.4 19
HD7256.U5 W38 1986
NYPL [JLE 86-4062]

Shelton, Robert D. Hazardous waste management market assessment / by Robert D. Shelton. Menlo Park, CA (333 Ravenswood Ave., Menlo Park 94025) : SRI International, Business Intelligence Program, c1986. 19 p. : ill. ; 28 cm. (Datalog file . no. 86-1055) "May 1986." LC Card 86-220787 DDC 338.4/7363728 19

1. Hazardous waste management industry - United States. 2. Market surveys - United States. I. Business Intelligence Program (SRI International). II. Title. III. Series.
HD9975.U52 S54 1986

Shemetov, P. V. (Petr Vasil'evich) KATĖK i razvitie otrasleĭ khozi͡aĭstva Sibiri /. Novosibirsk , 1984. 164 p. ; LC Card 84-167870
HC337.R852 S5246 1984

Sheng ch'an li kuei lü yen chiu / Chung-kuo sheng ch'an li ching chi hsüeh yen chiu hui pien. 880-02 Ti 1 pan. Pei-ching : Ching chi k'o hsüeh ch'u pan she : Hsin hua shu tien Pei-ching fa hsing so fa hsing, 1985. 5, 3, 466 p. : ill. ; 21 cm. Selected papers from Chung-kuo sheng ch'an li ching chi hsüeh yen chiu hui ti erh chieh nien hui, held 7-25-83 to 8-3-83 in K'un-ming shih. In Chinese. Includes bibliographies. LC Card 85-242399 DDC 335.4/12 19

1. Production (Economic theory) - Congresses. 2. Marxian economics - Congresses. I. Chung-kuo sheng ch'an li ching chi hsüeh yen chiu hui. II. Chung-kuo sheng ch'an li ching chi hsüeh yen chiu hui. Nien hui (2nd : 1983 : K'un-ming shih, China).
HB241 .S519 1985 <Orien China>
NYPL [*OVL 87-507]

Shenkman, Martin. Real estate after tax reform : a guide for investors / Martin Shenkman. New York : Wiley, c1987. xii, 307 p. ; 24 cm. Includes index. ISBN 0-471-85984-2 LC Card 87-2196 DDC 343.7305/46 347.303546 19

1. Real property and taxation - United States. 2. Real property tax - United States. I. Title.
HJ4181 .S45 1987

SHENSI PROVINCE (CHINA) - ECONOMIC CONDITIONS.
Vermeer, E. B. (Eduard B.) Economic development in provincial China . Cambridge [Cambridgeshire] , New York , 1988. p. cm. ISBN 0-521-34392-5 LC Card 87-22499 DDC 330.951/17058 19
HC428.S54 V47 1988

Shepard, Eric. Import insights . West Nyack, NY (51 Virginia Ave., West Nyack 10994) , c19. 48 p. : LC Card 86-210235 DDC 382/.4566342/0973 19
HD9397.U52 I47 1986

SHEPHARD, RONALD WILLIAM.
Teusch, Wolfgang. Aufbau und Gewinnung Shephardscher Produktionsfunktionen unter Berücksichtigung empirischer Aspekte /. Königstein/Ts. , c1983. vi, 296 p. : ISBN 3-445-02274-7 LC Card 83-195883
HB241 .T48 1983

Shepherd, A. G. Pension fund investment /. Cambridge [Cambridgeshire] , Wolfeboro, NH, U. S.A. , 1988. c. pm. ISBN 0-85941-400-0 : LC Card 87-17894 DDC 332.6/7254 19
HD7105.45.G7 P45 1988

Shepherd, Geoffrey, 1943-
Alburo, Florian A. Trade liberalization experience in the Philippines, 1960-84 /. Makati, Metro Manila [1985] 159 p. : LC Card 87-167251 DDC 382/.09599/0021 19
HF1599 .A43 1985

Managing industrial change in Western Europe /. London , New York , 1987. xii, 247 p. ; ISBN 0-86187-281-9 : LC Card 87-21875 DDC 338.94 19
HD3616.E8 M36 1987

Shepherd, Theodora B. Shepherd, William G. The ultimate deterrent . New York , 1986. x, 137 p. ; ISBN 0-275-92368-1 (alk. paper) : LC Card 86-20486 DDC 355/.03 19
UA10.5 .S524 1986 ***NYPL [JLE 87-884]***

Shepherd, William G.
Mainstreams in industrial organization /. Dordrecht , Boston , 1986. 2 v. (x, 465 p.) ; ISBN 90-247-3363-4 LC Card 86-12345 DDC 338.6 19
HD29 .M25 1986 ***NYPL [JLE 87-457]***

The ultimate deterrent : foundations of US-USSR security under stable competition / William G. Shepherd, in association with Theodora B. Shepherd. New York : Praeger, 1986. x, 137 p. ; 25 cm. Includes index. Bibliography: p. 129-133. ISBN 0-275-92368-1 (alk. paper) : LC Card 86-20486 DDC 355/.03 19

1. National security. 2. Military policy. 3. United States - Military policy. 4. Soviet Union - Military policy. 5. United States - National security. 6. Soviet Union - National security. I. Shepherd, Theodora B. II. Title.
UA10.5 .S524 1986 ***NYPL [JLE 87-884]***

Sheppard, Thomas M. Occupational outlook for New Jersey and JTPA labor market areas, 1982-1990 [microform]. Trenton, N.J. : New Jersey Dept. of Labor, Division of Planning and Research, Office of Demographic and Economic Analysis, [1984] ii leaves, 50 p. ; 28 cm. "November 1984." Includes bibliographical references. Microfilm. New York : New York Public Library, 1986. 1 microfilm reel ; 35 mm. (MN *ZZ-26,873) LC Card 84-623480 DDC 331.12/09749 19

1. Employment forecasting - New Jersey - Statistics. 2. Job vacancies - New Jersey - Statistics. 3. Labor supply - New Jersey - Statistics. 4. New Jersey - Occupations - Statistics. I. Title.
HD5725.N5 S47 1984
NYPL [*ZT-1745 no.24]

Sheriff, Abdul. Slaves, spices, & ivory in Zanzibar : integration of an East African commercial empire into the world economy, 1770-1873 / Abdul Sheriff. London : J. Currey ; Athens : Ohio University Press, 1987. xx, 297 p. : ill. ; 23 cm. (Eastern African studies) Revision of the author's thesis. Bibliography: p. 259-281. Includes index. ISBN 0-8214-0871-2 (U. S.) LC Card 87-12339 DDC 382/.096781 19

1. Zanzibar - Commerce - History - 18th century. 2. Zanzibar - Commerce - History - 19th century. 3. Slave-trade - Tanzania - Zanzibar - History. 4. Spice trade - Tanzania - Zanzibar - History. 5. Ivory industry - Tanzania - Zanzibar - History. I. Title. II. Title: Slaves, spices and ivory in Zanzibar.
HF3897 .S54 1987

Sherman, A. J. (Ari Joshua) Somary, Felix, 1881-1956. [Erinnerungen aus meinem Leben. English.] The raven of Zürich . London , New York , c1986. xii, 310 p. : ISBN 0-312-66407-9 LC Card 86-6662 DDC 330/.092/4 B 19
HB101.S6 A313 1986 ***NYPL [JFE 87-54]***

Sherman, Heidemarie C. Der Einfluss staatlicher Budgetdefizite auf die Zinsentwicklung in der Bundesrepublik Deutschland und den Vereinigten Staaten : Gutachten im Auftrag des Bundesministeriums für Wirtschaft / Bearbeiter, Heidemarie C. Sherman, Erich Langmantel, Eugen Schuhmair. München : Ifo-Institut für Wirtschaftsforschung, c1986. xxiii, 190 p. : ill. ; 21 cm. (Ifo Studien zur Finanzpolitik, 0081-7279 . 39) Bibliography: p. 185-190. ISBN 3-88512-019-4 LC Card 86-192070

1. Budget deficits - Germany (West). 2. Taxation - Germany, West. 3. Budget deficits - United States. 4. Taxation - United States. I. Langmantel, Erich. II. Schuhmair, Eugen. III. Germany (West). Bundesministerium für Wirtschaft. IV. Title. V. Series.
HJ2110 .S53 1986

Sherman, Howard D.
Heard, James E. Conflicts of interest in the proxy voting system /. Washington, D.C. , c1987. 100 p. : ISBN 0-931035-18-X (pbk.) LC Card 87-404270 DDC 338.8/3/0973 19
HD2743 .H43 1987

Junk bonds and tender offer financing / by Howard D. Sherman and Ronald E. Schrager. Washington, D.C. : IRRC's Corporate Governance Service, c1987. 22 p. ; 28 cm. Cover title. ISBN 0-931035-15-5 (pbk.) LC Card 87-128796 DDC 332.63/2 19

1. Junk bonds - United States. 2. Tender offers (Securities) - United States. I. Schrager, Ronald E. II. Title.
HG4963 .S535 1987

Sherman, Howard J. Foundations of radical political economy / Howard J. Sherman. Armonk, N.Y. : M.E. Sharpe, c1987. xi, 425 p. ; 24 cm. Bibliography: p. 393-409. Includes index. ISBN 0-87332-416-1 : LC Card 86-33849 DDC 330.1 19

1. Marxian economics. 2. Capitalism. 3. State, The. 4. Socialism. I. Title.
HB97.5 .S5117 1987

Sherman, Michael. Comprehensive compound interest tables / Michael Sherman. Newly rev. and updated ed. Chicago : Contemporary Books, c1986. 280 p. ; 21 cm. Chiefly tables. ISBN 0-8092-4875-1 (pbk.) : LC Card 86-208382 DDC 332.8/2/021 19

1. Interest - Tables. I. Title.
HG1632 .S54 1986

Sherman, Theodore A., 1899-1980. Metz, Lance E. Sherman's guide to Hugh Moore Park /. Easton, PA , 1988. p. cm. ISBN 0-930973-07-0 (pbk.) : LC Card 87-25622 DDC 338.09748/22 19
HE395 .P43 1988

Sherman, V. Clayton.
From losers to winners : how to manage problem employees-- and what to do if you can't / V. Clayton Sherman. New York, NY : American Management Association, c1987. 1 v. (various pagings) : ill., forms ; 30 cm. Bibliography: p. 165-166. Includes index. ISBN 0-8144-1146-0 (loose-leaf) LC Card 86-47823 DDC 658.3/045 19

1. Problem employees. I. Title.
HF5549.5.E42 S54 1987

From losers to winners : how to manage problem employees--and what to do if you can't / V. Clayton Sherman.Rev. ed., 1st hardcover ed. New York, NY : American Management Association, c1987. xi, 188 p. : forms ; 26 cm. Bibliography: p. 181-182. Includes index. ISBN 0-8144-5918-8 LC Card 87-47710 DDC

658.3/045 19
1. Problem employees. I. Title.
HF5549.5.E42 S54 1987b

Sherman's guide to Hugh Moore Park /. Metz, Lance E. Easton, PA , 1988. p. cm. ISBN 0-930973-07-0 (pbk.) : LC Card 87-25622 DDC 338.09748/22 19
HE395 .P43 1988

Sherrard, Michael. London Capital Group Limited (formerly British Bangladesh Trust Limited) : investigation under section 165(b) of the Companies Act 1948 : report / by Michael Sherrard and Ian Hay Davison. London : H.M.S.O., 1977. vi, 376 p. : ill. ; 30 cm. ISBN 0-11-512127-7 (pbk.) LC Card 85-164377
1. London Capital Group Ltd. 2. Corporations - Great Britain - Corrupt practices - Case studies. 3. Commercial crimes - Great Britain - Case studies. 4. Fraud - Great Britain - Case studies. 5. Stonehouse, John Thomson, 1925-. I. Davison, Ian Hay. II. Title.
HG4135 .S46 1977

Sherstobitov, Viktor Pavlovich.
Istorii͡a sovetskogo krest'i͡anstva . Moskva , 1986- v. : ***NYPL [*QG 87-3228]***

K istorii sot͡sial'no-ėkonomicheskikh ukladov Kirgizstana /. Frunze , 1972. 108 p. ; LC Card 82-171559
HC337.K545 K15 1972

Shertzer, Margaret D. Taintor, Sarah Augusta. The secretary's handbook /. New York , London , c1988. p. cm. ISBN 0-02-008830-2 LC Card 87-24960 DDC 651.7/402 19
HF5547.5 .T29 1988

Sherwood, Marika. Many struggles : West Indian workers and service personnel in Britain, (1939-45) / by Marika Sherwood. London : Karia Press, 1985, c1984. 138 p. : ill. ; 22 cm. Includes bibliographies. ISBN 0-946918-00-7 (pbk.) LC Card 86-110617 DDC 305.8/00941 19
1. Alien labor, West Indian - Great Britain - History - 20th century. 2. Blacks - Great Britain - Segregation - History - 20th century. 3. Great Britain - Race relations - History - 20th century. I. Title.
HD8398.B55 S54 1985 ***NYPL [Sc D 86-815]***

Shestopalova, Zoi͡a Vladimirovna.
Prodovol'stvennai͡a problema i perspektivy ee reshenii͡a v arabskikh stranakh : na primere Sirii, Livana i Iordanii / Z.V. Shestopalova. Moskva : Izd-vo "Nauka", Glav. red. vostochnoĭ lit-ry, 1985. 151, [4] p. : ill. ; 22 cm. At head of title: Akademii͡a nauk SSSR. Ordena Trudovogo Krasnogo Znameni Institut vostokovedenii͡a. Summary in English. Bibliography: p. 145-[152]. LC Card 86-130508
1. Food supply - Syria. 2. Food supply - Lebanon. 3. Food supply - Jordan. 4. Agriculture and state - Syria. 5. Agriculture and state - Lebanon. 6. Agriculture and state - Jordan. I. Title.
HD9016.S92 S44 1985
NYPL [*QIP 87-3413]

Shetelo, I. V. (Ivan Vasil'evich) Kryzhanovskiĭ, B. N. (Boris Nikolaevich) Spetsializatsii͡a zagotovitel'nogo proizvodstva /. Kiev , 1985. 125, [3] p. ; LC Card 87-112143
HD9703.S653 U474 1985

Sheth, Jagdish N.
Bringing innovation to market : how to break corporate and customer barriers / Jagdish N. Sheth, S. Ram. New York : Wiley, c1987. xii, 247 p. : ill. ; 24 cm. Includes bibliographies and index. ISBN 0-471-84977-4 LC Card 87-17611 DDC 658.5/78 19
1. New products. 2. Technological innovations. I. Ram, S. (Sundaresan), 1957-. II. Title.
HD69.N4 S494 1987

Contemporary views on marketing practice /. Lexington, Mass. , c1987. vi, 282 p. : ISBN 0-669-15120-3 (alk. paper) LC Card 86-46218 DDC 658.8 19
HF5411 .C66 1987

Lele, Milind M. The customer is key . New York , c1987. xii, 260 p. : ISBN 0-471-82859-9 LC Card 87-21549 DDC 658.8/12 19
HF5415.3 .L45 1987

Shetty, Y. Krishna. Quality, productivity, and innovation . New York , c1987. xx, 427 p. : ISBN 0-444-01194-3 LC Card 87-6815 DDC 658.5 19
HD58.9 .Q35 1987

Shevardnadze, Ėduard Amvrosievich. Strategii͡a uskorenii͡a--leninizm v deĭstvii : doklad na torzhestvennom zasedanii v Moskve, posvi͡ashchennom 116-ĭ godovshchine so dni͡a rozhdenii͡a V.I. Lenina, 22 apreli͡a 1986 goda / Ė.A. Shevardnadze. Moskva : Izd-vo polit. lit-ry, 1986. 29 p. ; 21 cm. Includes bibliographical references. LC Card 86-190944
1. Soviet Union - Economic policy - 1981-. 2. Soviet Union - Foreign relations - 1975-. I. Title.
HC336.25 .S524 1986

Shevchuk, L. V. (Li͡udmila Vladimirovna)
Metodicheskie osnovy analiza i prognozirovanii͡a fondootdachi : na primere stroĭindustrii BSSR / L.V. Shevchuk, L.N. Litvinova ; nauchnyĭ redaktor P.A. Kapitula. Minsk : "Nauka i tekhnika", 1983. 118 p. : ill. ; 21 cm. At head of title: Akademii͡a nauk Belorusskoĭ SSR. Institut ėkonomiki. Includes bibliographical references. LC Card 84-118665
1. Construction industry - Byelorussian S.S.R. - Capital productivity. 2. Construction industry - Byelorussian S.S.R. - Capital productivity - Econometric models. I. Litvinova, L. N. (Li͡udmila Nikolaevna). II. Kapitula, P. A. (Petr Andreevich). III. Title.
HD9715.S73 B9465 1983

Shevi͡akov, Alekseĭ I͡Ur'evich. Modelirovanie sbalansirovannosti i soglasovanii͡a planovykh resheniĭ v sfere narodnogo blagosostoi͡anii͡a / A.I͡U. Shevi͡akov, A.I͡A. Kiruta ; otvetstvennyĭ redaktor E.G. Gol'shteĭn. Moskva : "Nauka", 1986. 211 p. : ill. ; 22 cm. (Problemy sovetskoĭ ėkonomiki) At head of title: Akademii͡a nauk SSSR. T͡Sentral'nyĭ ėkonomiko-matematicheskiĭ institut. Bibliography: p. 206-[210] LC Card 86-177908
1. Soviet Union - Economic policy - 1981- - Mathematical models. 2. Central planning - Soviet Union - Mathematical models. I. Kiruta, A. I͡A. (Aleksandr I͡Akovlevich). II. Gol'shteĭn, E. G. (Evgeniĭ Grigor'evich). III. Title.
HC336.25 .S525 1986

Shevt͡sova, Valentina Efimovna. Voprosy stranovogo makromodelirovanii͡a /. Moskva , 1984. 177 p. : LC Card 86-144302
HB141 .V665 1984

Shevyrin, V. M. Davidovich, I͡A. A. Rabochai͡a molodezh' SSSR v period razvitogo sotsializma . Moskva , 1985. 37 p. ; LC Card 86-187709
HD6276.S59 D38 1985

Shiddiqi, Nourouzzaman. Etika pembangunan dalam pemikiran Islam di Indonesia /. Jakarta , 1986. xi, 270 p. ; ISBN 979-421-043-9 (pbk.) LC Card 86-946413
HC447 .E78 1986

SHIELDING (ELECTRICITY)
Mooney, Peter. Plastics EMI shielding . Stamford, Conn., U. S.A. , c1985. xxii, 297 leaves : ISBN 0-89336-409-6 (soft) LC Card 87-168832 DDC 338.4/76684 19
HD9661.U62 M654 1985

Shields, Jerry. The invisible billionaire, Daniel Ludwig / by Jerry Shields. Boston : Houghton Mifflin, 1986. xii, 401 p. : ill., port. ; 23 cm. Includes index. Illustrative matter on lining papers. Sources: p. 367-391. ISBN 0-395-35402-1 : LC Card 86-7519 DDC 387.5/092/4 B 19
1. Ludwig, Daniel Keith, 1897-. 2. Merchant marine - United States - Biography. 3. Capitalists and financiers - United States - Biography. 4. Millionaires - United States - Biography. I. Title.
HE569.L84 S55 1986 ***NYPL [JFE 86-3861]***

SHIFT-SHARE ANALYSIS - AUSTRIA - SALZBURG (LAND) - STATISTICS.
Fink, Karl, Mag. Die regionale Dynamik des Salzburger Arbeitsmarktes, 1971-1980 . Salzburg [1981?] 212 p. : LC Card 82-171635
HD5772.S24 F56 1981 ***NYPL [JLG 86-301]***

SHIFT SYSTEMS.
Quéinnec, Y. (Yvon) Le travail posté . [Toulouse-Le Mirail] , 1985. 261 p. : ISBN 2-85816-030-9 LC Card 87-133427
HD5111.5 .Q45 1985

SHIFT SYSTEMS - EUROPEAN ECONOMIC COMMUNITY COUNTRIES.
Copsey, S. M. Shiftwork review . Luxembourg , Washington, DC , 1986. xi, 122 p. : ISBN 92-825-6419-3 (pbk.) : LC Card 87-137298 DDC 331.25/72 19
HD5111.6.E86 C66 1986

SHIFT SYSTEMS - GREAT BRITAIN.
Ghobadian, Abby, 1951- The effects of new technological change on shift work in the brewing industry /. Aldershot, Hants, England , Brookfield, Vt. , c1986. xiv, 192 p. : ISBN 0-566-05132-X : LC Card 86-17536 DDC 331.25/72 19
HD8039.L62 G74 1986
NYPL [JLD 86-3864]

Shifting frontiers in financial markets / edited by Donald E. Fair ; with contributions from Marie-Christine Adam ... [et al.]. Dordrecht ; Boston : M. Nijhoff ; xii, 360 p. : ill. ; 25 cm. (Financial and monetary policy studies. 12) "Papers ... presented at the twelfth Colloquium arranged by the Société Universitaire Européenne de Recherches Financières (SUERF) which took place in Cambridge in March 1985"--P. ix. Includes bibliographies. ISBN 90-247-3225-5 LC Card 85-18821 DDC 332 19
1. Capital market - Congresses. 2. Money market - Congresses. 3. Finance - Congresses. I. Fair, Donald E.
HG4523 .S54 1986 ***NYPL [JLE 86-2694]***

Shifting gears . Katz, Harry Charles, 1951- Cambridge, Mass. , c1985. xii, 230 p. : ISBN 0-262-11098-9 LC Card 84-26105 DDC 331/.04292/0973 19
HD6976.A82 U528 1985
NYPL [JLE 85-2260]

Shifting the burden . Tsokhas, Kosmas. Canberra, Australia [1986] 61, 6 p. ; ISBN 0-86784-898-7 (pbk.) LC Card 87-151151 DDC 331.7/6363/00994 19
HD9436.A82 T75 1986

Shiftwork review . Copsey, S. M. Luxembourg , Washington, DC , 1986. xi, 122 p. : ISBN 92-825-6419-3 (pbk.) : LC Card 87-137298 DDC 331.25/72 19
HD5111.6.E86 C66 1986

Shigekawa, Marlene, 1944- Succeeding in high tech : a guide to building your career / Marlene Shigekawa. New York : Wiley, c1987. xiv, 294 p. : ill. ; 24 cm. Bibliography: p. 277-284. Includes index. ISBN 0-471-85636-3 LC Card 86-33953 DDC 650.1 19
1. High technology industries - Management. I. Title.
HD62.37 .S52 1987

Shigemori, Akira, 1942- Nihon kōkigyō no saisei /. Kyōto-shi , 1986. 4, 8, 289 p. : ISBN 4-589-01273-1 : LC Card 86-216062
HD4313 .N46 1986 <Orien Japan>
NYPL [*OSM 87-2537]

Shilling, A. Gary. The world has definitely changed : new economic forces and their implications for the next decade / A. Gary Shilling.1st ed. New York, NY (111 Broadway, Suite 1200, New York 10006) : Lakeview Press, 1986. xx, 179 p. : ill. ; 21 cm. Bibliography: p. 151-154. LC Card 86-82936 DDC 338.5/443/0973 19
1. Economic forecasting - United States. 2. United States - Economic conditions - 1981-. I. Title.
HC106.8 .S49 1986

Shilling, Dana.
Real life, real answers : earning, saving, investing, enjoying : a realistic guide to managing your money / Dana Shilling with the staff of John Hancock Financial Services. New York : Arbor House, c1988. xiv, 309 p. ; 25 cm. Includes index. ISBN 1-557-10004-7 LC Card 87-19538 DDC 332.024 19
1. Finance, Personal. 2. Investments. I. John Hancock Financial Services. II. Title.
HG179 .S465 1988

Real life, real answers : earning, saving, investing, enjoying, a realistic guide to managing your money / Dana Shilling with the staff of John Hancock Financial Services. New York : Arbor House, c1988. p. cm. Includes index. ISBN 0-87795-942-0 : LC Card 87-24380 DDC 332.024 19
1. Finance, Personal. I. Title.
HG179 .S465 1988b

Shim, Jae K. Handbook of financial analysis, forecasting, and modeling / by Jae K. Shim and Joel G. Siegel. Englewood Cliffs, NJ : Prentice-Hall, c1988. p. cm. Includes index. ISBN 0-13-377995-5 : LC Card 87-14325 DDC 658.1/5 19
1. Corporations - Finance. 2. Corporations - Finance - Mathematical models. I. Siegel, Joel G. II. Title.
HG4011 .S46 1988

Shimeles Asfaw. The economic evaluation of low traffic roads : the Kenya experience / by Shimeles Asfaw. [Nairobi? : s.n., 1980?] ii, 28, 13 leaves, [2] leaves of plates : col. maps ; 30 cm. At head of title: International Road Federation, IVth IRF African Highway Conference, Nairobi, 20th-25th January 1980. LC Card 85-981138
1. Roads - Economic aspects - Kenya. 2. Roads - Government policy - Kenya. I. International Road Federation. II. IRF African Highway Conference (4th : 1980 : Nairobi, Kenya). III. Title.
HE367.K43 E374 1980

Shimi͡alis, Ch. Nekotorye voprosy matematicheskoĭ ėkonomiki . Vil'ni͡us , 1982. 90 p. ; LC Card 83-169081
HB135 .N45 1982

Shimizu, Hiroshi. Introduction to Japan's economic and political relations with the Middle East in the inter-war period : with an annotated bibliography of the Japanese Foreign Office Archives at the Diplomatic Record Office, Tokyo / by Hiroshi Shimizu. Kent Ridge, Singapore : Dept. of Japanese Studies, National University of Singapore, [1985] v, 47 leaves ; 30 cm. (Occasional paper series / Department of Japanese Studies, National University of Singapore . no. 2) "December 1985." LC Card 87-110444 DDC 337.52056 19
1. Japan - Foreign economic relations - Middle East. 2. Middle East - Foreign economic relations - Japan. 3. Japan - Foreign relations - Middle East. 4. Middle East - Foreign relations - Japan. I. Series: Occasional paper series (National University of Singapore. Dept. of Japanese Studies) , no. 2. II. Title.
HF1602.15.M626 S56 1985

Shimomura, Mitsuko, 1938- Morita, Akio, 1921- Made in Japan . New York , c1986. viii, 309 p., [8] p. of plates : ISBN 0-525-24465-4 : LC Card 86-11479 DDC 338.7/6213/0924 B 19
HD9696.A3 J3658 1986 ***NYPL [JFE 86-5112]***

Shimov, V. N. (Vladimir Nikolaevich) Regional'nai͡a ėffektivnost' obshchestvennogo proizvodstva : problemy, metody izmereni͡ia, puti povyshenii͡a / V.N. Shimov. Minsk : Izd-vo "Universitetskoe", 1986. 167 p. ; 20 cm. Bibliography: p. 158-[164]. Includes index. LC Card 86-204677
1. Byelorussian S.S.R. - Economic conditions. 2. Byelorussian S.S.R. - Economic policy. I. Title.
HC337.B93 S55 1986

Shin, Kilman. Interest rate, risk, and income distribution / Kilman Shin. [Taegu, Korea] : Taegu University Press, c1986. v, 378 p. : ill. ; 27 cm. Includes bibliographies and index. LC Card 87-105107 DDC 330/.01/51 19
1. Inflation (Finance). 2. Interest rates. 3. Risk. 4. Income distribution. I. Title.
HG229 .S436 1986

Shinn, William T., 1936- The decline of the Russian peasant household / William T. Shinn, Jr. ; foreword by Edward L. Keenan. New York : Praeger, 1987. xvii, 122 p. ; 24 cm. (The Washington papers, 0278-937X . 124) "Published with the Center for Strategic and International Studies, Georgetown University, Washington, D.C." Bibliography: p. 66-73. Includes index. ISBN 0-275-92767-9 (alk. paper) LC Card 87-2554 DDC 338.1/0947 19
1. Agriculture - Economic aspects - Soviet Union. 2. Land tenure - Soviet Union. 3. Farmers - Soviet Union. 4. Private plot agriculture - Soviet Union. I. Center for Strategic and International Studies (Washington, D.C.). II. Title. III. Series.
HD1992 .S4735 1987

Shinwari, Ahmad Nawaz. Small scale industry in North West Frontier Province : problems and prospects : an evaluation report / by Ahmad Nawaz Shinwari. Peshawar : Sarhad Small Industries Development Board, 1983. 103 p., [3] leaves of plates : charts, maps ; 28 cm. Includes bibliographical references. LC Card 84-931673 DDC 338.6/422/0899159 19
1. Small business - Pakistan - North-west Frontier Province. 2. Refugees, Political - Afghanistan. I. Title.
HD2346.P32 N677 1983

SHIP LETTERS - HONG KONG - RATES - HISTORY - 19TH CENTURY.
Scamp, Lee C. Postal rate history of China and Hong Kong . Houston, Tex., U. S.A. , c1986. xx, 284 p. : LC Card 87-145274 DDC 383/.23/0951 19
HE7305.Z8 S33 1986

SHIP-RAILROADS - MEXICO.
United States. Congress. House. Committee on Foreign Affairs. Discussion of the Nicaragua ship canal and the Tehuantepec ship railway schemes before the Committee on Foreign Affairs of the House of Representatives. [Washington] [1882?] 80 p. ; LC Card 82-602443
HE536 .U55 1882

SHIP REGISTERS.
Mallett, Alan S. Idyll of the Kings, 1889-1979 . Kendal [Cumbria] , 1980. 64 p. : ISBN 0-905617-10-X (pbk.) LC Card 81-105772 DDC 387.5/065/41 19
HE945.K48 M35 1980

SHIP REGISTERS - GREAT BRITAIN.
Pemberton, P. A. Pure merinos and others . Canberra , c1986. 125 p. : ISBN 0-86784-796-4 (pbk.) LC Card 87-164515 DDC 382/.41636/0994 19
HE565.G7 P46 1986

SHIP REGISTERS - HISTORY.
McCusker, John J. European bills of entry and marine lists . Cambridge, Mass. , 1985. 75 p. : LC Card 86-673685
HE565.A3 M32 1985

SHIP REGISTERS - YUGOSLAVIA - CROATIA.
Regesti marittimi croati /. Padova , 1985- v. <v. 1, pt. 1 > : LC Card 86-215640
HE565.Y8 R42 1985

SHIPBUILDING - BRAZIL - FINANCE.
Estudo preliminar para o establecimento de prioridades no financiamento para construção de embarcações para a navegação interior /. [Rio de Janeiro] , 1985. [84] leaves : LC Card 87-403936 DDC 386/.0981 19
HE653 .E88 1985

SHIPBUILDING INDUSTRY - GOVERNMENT POLICY - UNITED STATES.
Hilton, Robert, 1927- U. S. maritime industries--down for the third time? /. Washington, D.C. , c1987. vi, 60 p. : ISBN 0-89206-099-9 (pbk.) LC Card 86-31768 DDC 387.5/0973 19
HE745 .H66 1987

SHIPBUILDING INDUSTRY - UNITED STATES.
Hilton, Robert, 1927- U. S. maritime industries--down for the third time? /. Washington, D.C. , c1987. vi, 60 p. : ISBN 0-89206-099-9 (pbk.) LC Card 86-31768 DDC 387.5/0973 19
HE745 .H66 1987

Ullman, Harlan. Forecasts for U. S. maritime industries in 1989 . Washington, D.C. , c1984. ix, 42 p. : ISBN 0-89206-069-7 (pbk.) LC Card 84-27501 DDC 338.4/76238/0973 19
VM299.6 .U45 1984 ***NYPL [JLD 87-155]***

SHIPBUILDING - PORTUGAL - HISTORY - 16TH CENTURY.
Solis, Duarte Gomes. Armadas da carreira da India de 1560 a 1590 . Lisboa , 1938. xvi, 20 p. : LC Card 86-140347
HF3698.I4 S65 1938

Shipilov, V. I. Metodicheskie rekomendat͡sii po issledovanii͡u proizvodstvennoĭ infrastruktury territorial'no-proizvodstvennykh kompleksov i promyshlennykh uzlov /. Sverdlovsk , 1983. 79 p. (some folded) ; LC Card 86-113572
HC340.C3 M416 1983

SHIPMENT OF GOODS - DATA PROCESSING - CASE STUDIES.
Krieger, Winfried. Computergestützte Auswahl interkontinentaler Distributionsverfahren /. Berlin , c1984. 143 p. : ISBN 3-428-05617-5 LC Card 84-219069
HF5765 .K75 1984

SHIPMENT OF GOODS - GERMANY, WEST.
Seiffert, Bernd. Zahlungsmittelbewirtschaftung im Verkehrsbetrieb /. Berlin , c1986. 187 p. : ISBN 3-428-06094-6 : LC Card 87-143799 DDC 380.5/24/0943 19
HE5999.Z7 G374 1986

SHIPMENT OF GOODS - SWEDEN - CONGRESSES.
Sverige och den internationella transportmarknaden . Stockholm [1983] 87 p. : ISBN 91-85402-64-8 : LC Card 83-223136
HE199.S77 S84 1983

SHIPMENT OF GOODS - UNITED STATES.
Barrett, Colin. Practical handbook of transportation contracting and rate negotiations /. Washington , c1987. ix, 269 p. ; ISBN 0-87408-037-1 LC Card 86-50988 DDC 380.5/24/068 19
HE199.U5 B37 1987

SHIPPING AGREEMENTS. see **SHIPPING CONFERENCES.**

SHIPPING - AMAZON RIVER REGION - CONGRESSES.
River Transportation Seminar (1986 : Iquitos, Peru) Tratado de cooperación amazónica . Washington, D.C. , 1986. iii, 110 p. ; ISBN 0-8270-2473-8 (pbk.) LC Card 87-115058
HE387.A6 R58 1986

SHIPPING - AZERBAIJAN S.S.R. - HISTORY - 19TH CENTURY.
Guseĭnova, D. S. Rabochie-mori͡aki Kaspii͡a . Baku , 1981. 113 p. ; LC Card 82-166385
HD8039.S42 C424 1981

SHIPPING - BRAZIL - ARAGUAIA RIVER - COSTS.
Estudo de custos do transporte nos rios Araguaia e Tocantins /. [Rio de Janeiro] , 1985. 95 leaves : LC Card 87-403933 DDC 386/.3/098173 19
HE424.A7 E84 1985

SHIPPING - BRAZIL - TOCANTINS RIVER - COSTS.
Estudo de custos do transporte nos rios Araguaia e Tocantins /. [Rio de Janeiro] , 1985. 95 leaves : LC Card 87-403933 DDC 386/.3/098173 19
HE424.A7 E84 1985

SHIPPING - CASPIAN SEA - HISTORY - 19TH CENTURY.
Guseĭnova, D. S. Rabochie-mori͡aki Kaspii͡a . Baku , 1981. 113 p. ; LC Card 82-166385
HD8039.S42 C424 1981

SHIPPING COMBINES. see **SHIPPING CONFERENCES.**

SHIPPING CONFERENCES - HISTORY.
Berridge, Geoff. The politics of the South Africa run . Oxford [Oxfordshire] , New York , 1987. x, 254 p. ; ISBN 0-19-827484-X : LC Card 87-1600 DDC 387.5/094 19
HE903.4 .B47 1987

SHIPPING - DANUBE RIVER.
Petrov, Vladimir. Izpolzuvaneto na reka Dunav za prevoz na tovari za i ot Sredna i Zapadna Evropa /. Sofii͡a , 1985. 71 p. ; LC Card 86-105301
HE387.D2 P36 1985

SHIPPING - DATA PROCESSING - CASE STUDIES.
Krieger, Winfried. Computergestützte Auswahl interkontinentaler Distributionsverfahren /. Berlin , c1984. 143 p. : ISBN 3-428-05617-5 LC Card 84-219069
HF5765 .K75 1984

SHIPPING - DICTIONARIES.
Brodie, Peter R., 1947- Dictionary of shipping terms /. London , New York , 1985. 155 p. ; ISBN 1-85044-069-7 (pbk.) : LC Card 86-164175 DDC 387.5/03/21 19
HE567 .B68 1985

SHIPPING - ENGLAND - HISTORY.
Ville, Simon P. English shipowning during the industrial revolution . Manchester, UK , Wolfeboro, NH, USA , c1987. x, 192 p. : ISBN 0-7190-1714-9 LC Card 87-11043 DDC 387.5/065/41 19
HE945.M49 V55 1987

SHIPPING - EUROPEAN ECONOMIC COMMUNITY COUNTRIES.
EEC maritime transport policy . Brussels [1986] 88 p., [2] leaves : LC Card 87-135615 DDC 387.5/094 19
HE822.5 .E38 1986

SHIPPING - GERMANY (WEST) - HISTORY.
Jolmes, Lothar L. V. Geschichte der Unternehmungen in der deutschen Rheinschiffahrt /. Köln , 1960. 164 p. : LC Card 85-147446
HE5 .C6 Nr. 17 HE619.R48

SHIPPING - GERMANY (WEST) - RHEIN-MAIN-DONAU-KANAL - HISTORY.
Rhein-Main-Donau . [Nürnberg , 1937?] 195 p. : LC Card 86-216951
HE449.R38 R48 1937

SHIPPING - GOVERNMENT POLICY.
Ademuni-Odeke, Dr. Protectionism and the future of international shipping . Dordrecht ; Boston : xxviii, 446 p. ; ISBN 90-247-2918-1 LC Card 83-25055 DDC 387.5/068 19
HE736 .A34 1984 ***NYPL [JLE 85-1539]***

SHIPPING - GOVERNMENT POLICY - EUROPEAN ECONOMIC COMMUNITY COUNTRIES.
EEC maritime transport policy . Brussels [1986] 88 p., [2] leaves : LC Card 87-135615 DDC 387.5/094 19
HE822.5 .E38 1986

SHIPPING - GOVERNMENT POLICY - UNITED STATES.
Hilton, Robert, 1927- U. S. maritime industries--down for the third time? /. Washington, D.C. , c1987. vi, 60 p. : ISBN 0-89206-099-9 (pbk.) LC Card 86-31768 DDC 387.5/0973 19
HE745 .H66 1987

SHIPPING - GREAT LAKES.
Heilmann, Ronald L. Great Lakes transportation in the eighties /. Madison, WI , c1986. 100 p. : ISBN 0-936287-00-4 (pbk.) : LC Card 86-622259 DDC 386/.544/0977 19
HE398 .H45 1986

SHIPPING - GREECE - CONGRESSES.
Henōsis Hellēnōn Ephoplistōn (Greece). Dioikētikon Symvoulion. Ekthesis tōn pepragmemōn tou Dioikētikou Symvouliou . Athēnai , 1957. 23 p. ; LC Card 86-235109
HE564.E3 G824 1957

SHIPPING - ICELAND.
Helgi Magnússon. Hafskip, gjörningar og gæsluvarðhald /. Reykjavík , 1986. 272 p. : LC Card 87-117447
HE945.H19 H45 1986

Shipping in international trade relations /.
Ademuni-Odeke, Dr. Brookfield, Vt. , 1988. p. cm. ISBN 0-566-05371-3 : LC Card 87-8770 DDC 387.5 19
HE571 .A34 1988

SHIPPING - INDIA - HISTORY - 16TH CENTURY.
Solis, Duarte Gomes. Armadas da carreira da India de 1560 a 1590 . Lisboa , 1938. xvi, 20 p. : LC Card 86-140347
HF3698.I4 S65 1938

SHIPPING - ITALY - GENOA - CONGRESSES.
Convegno Genova nell'economia marittimo/portuale in Europa e nel mondo (1982 : Genoa, Italy) Atti del Convegno Genova nell'economia marittimo/portuale in Europa e nel mondo . Genova [1982?] 135 p. : LC Card 86-105783
HE558.G3 C66 1982

SHIPPING - ITALY - LIGURIA.
Vallega, Adalberto. Dai porti al sistema portuale . Savona , 1985. 320 p. : LC Card 87-139096
HE558.L44 V35 1985

SHIPPING - IVORY COAST.
Gohibi, Bernard. Les incidences financières de l'assurance maritime sur l'économie ivoirienne /. Abidjan , 1984. 24 leaves ; LC Card 86-111379 DDC 368.2/2/0096668 19
HE964.5.I94 G64 1984
NYPL [JLF 86-1484]

SHIPPING - IVORY COAST - RATES.
Kouassi, Jean-Claude. Transports maritimes et balance des paiements en Côte d'Ivoire /. [Abidjan] [1982?] 23, xii leaves ; LC Card 86-111436 DDC 387.5/1 19
HE597.I9 K68 1982 ***NYPL [JLF 86-1485]***

SHIPPING - LAKE STATES - RATES.
Impact of deep-draft user charges on the six western Great Lakes states /. [Chicago, Ill.] (310 S. Michigan Ave., Chicago 60604) [1986] 3 v. : LC Card 87-404522 DDC 387.1 19
HE952.U6 I47 1986

SHIPPING - LATIN AMERICA.
Sepúlveda Whittle, Tomás. Los conceptos básicos del transporte marítimo y la situación de la actividad en América Latina. Santiago de Chile , Nueva York, NY , 1986. 118 p. ; ISBN 92-1-321211-9 LC Card 87-400454 DDC 387.5/098 19
HE571 .S45 1986

SHIPPING - MALAYSIA - HISTORY - CONGRESSES.
Kapal dan harta karam =. Kuala Lumpur , 1986. xv, 181 p. : LC Card 86-942317 DDC 387.5/09595 19
HF3800.6 .K36 1986

SHIPPING - MANAGEMENT.
Walton, Richard E. Innovating to compete . San Francisco , 1987. p. cm. ISBN 1-555-42056-7 LC Card 87-45426 DDC 658.4/06 19
HE736 .W35 1987

SHIPPING - MISSISSIPPI RIVER - HISTORY.
White, Bob. The child of an eagle . [Cape Girardeau, Mo. , c1980] v, 78 p. : LC Card 87-405068 DDC 386/.22436 19
HE630.M6 W48 1980

SHIPPING - NEW ZEALAND - ENERGY CONSUMPTION - COSTS.
Copeland, M. C. (Michael Campbell) Transport energy in New Zealand's overseas trade . Auckland, N.Z. [1982] iv, 130 p. : LC Card 84-159485 DDC 387.5/1 19
HE597.N4 C63 1982
NYPL [JSK 82-15 no.80]

SHIPPING - NEW ZEALAND - RATES.
Copeland, M. C. (Michael Campbell) Transport energy in New Zealand's overseas trade . Auckland, N.Z. [1982] iv, 130 p. : LC Card 84-159485 DDC 387.5/1 19
HE597.N4 C63 1982
NYPL [JSK 82-15 no.80]

SHIPPING - NORWAY - STAVANGER - HISTORY - 19TH CENTURY.
Grude, Egil Harald, 1944- Fra brygger til storhavn . Stavanger , c1985. 167 p. : ISBN 82-00-07235-5 : LC Card 86-148407
HE558.S67 G78 1985

SHIPPING - NORWAY - STAVANGER - HISTORY - 20TH CENTURY.
Grude, Egil Harald, 1944- Fra brygger til storhavn . Stavanger , c1985. 167 p. : ISBN 82-00-07235-5 : LC Card 86-148407
HE558.S67 G78 1985

SHIPPING - PERSONNEL MANAGEMENT.
Walton, Richard E. Innovating to compete . San Francisco , 1987. p. cm. ISBN 1-555-42056-7 LC Card 87-45426 DDC 658.4/06 19
HE736 .W35 1987

SHIPPING - POLAND.
Kwiatkowski, Eugeniusz. Pisma o rzeczypospolitej morskiej /. Szczecin , 1985. 277 p., [24] p. of plates : ISBN 83-7007-012-4 :
NYPL [*QO 86-2539]

Sójka, Zygmunt. Polska polityka morska /. Gdańsk , 1986. 237, [1] : ISBN 83-215-1646-7(pbk.) :
NYPL [*QO 87-1818]

SHIPPING - PORTUGAL - HISTORY - 16TH CENTURY.
Solis, Duarte Gomes. Armadas da carreira da India de 1560 a 1590 . Lisboa , 1938. xvi, 20 p. : LC Card 86-140347
HF3698.I4 S65 1938

SHIPPING - RED RIVER REGION (TEX.-LA.)
Secondary benefits associated with the Red River Waterway, Mississippi River to Shreveport, Louisiana . Baton Rouge, La. (P.O. Box 14787, Baton Rouge 70898) [1986] 2 v. : LC Card 87-620750 DDC 330.9766/6053 19
HC107.A15 S43 1986

SHIPPING - REGISTERS. see **SHIP REGISTERS.**

Shipping Research Bureau (Amsterdam, Netherlands) Oil tankers to South Africa, 1980-1981. Amsterdam , c1982. vi, 99 p. : ISBN 90-70331-05-5 (pbk.) LC Card 86-213340 DDC 387.5/448 19
HE595.P4 O37 1982

SHIPPING - RHINE RIVER - HISTORY.
Jolmes, Lothar L. V. Geschichte der Unternehmungen in der deutschen Rheinschiffahrt /. Köln , 1960. 164 p. : LC Card 85-147446
HE5 .C6 Nr. 17 HE619.R48

SHIPPING - SPAIN - CARTAGENA - HISTORY - 20TH CENTURY.
Egea Bruno, Pedro María. La minería cartagenera en torno a la primera guerra mundial, 1909-1923 /. [Murcia] , 1983. 76 p. : ISBN 84-86031-30-3 LC Card 85-199662
HD9506.S762 C374 1983

SHIPPING - STATISTICS.
Commodity trade (by sea) statistics . New York , 1980. v, 396 p. ; LC Card 87-112992 DDC 387.5/55/021 19
HE562.8 .C667 1980

SHIPPING TRUSTS. see **SHIPPING CONFERENCES.**

SHIPPING - UNITED STATES - HISTORY.
Bauer, K. Jack (Karl Jack), 1926- A maritime history of the United States . Columbia, S.C. , c1988. p. cm. ISBN 0-87249-519-1 LC Card 87-19190 DDC 387.5/0973 19
HE745 .B38 1988

SHIPPING - YUGOSLAVIA - CROATIA - HISTORY - SOURCES.
Regesti marittimi croati /. Padova , 1985- v. <v. 1, pt. 1 > : LC Card 86-215640
HE565.Y8 R42 1985

SHIPS.
(1984) Packard, William V. Sea-trading /. London , c1984-c1986. 3 v. : ISBN 0-905045-64-5 (pbk.) LC Card 86-204836 DDC 387.5/44 19
HE571 .P26 1984

Ships and sunken treasure. Kapal dan harta karam =. Kuala Lumpur , 1986. xv, 181 p. : LC Card 86-942317 DDC 387.5/09595 19
HF3800.6 .K36 1986

SHIPS - CARGO - PERIODICALS - HISTORY.
McCusker, John J. European bills of entry and marine lists . Cambridge, Mass. , 1985. 75 p. : LC Card 86-673685
HE565.A3 M32 1985

SHIPS - RADIO. see **RADIO IN NAVIGATION.**

SHIPS - REGISTERS. see **SHIP REGISTERS.**

Shipway, Mark. Anti-parliamentary communism : the movement for workers' councils in Britain, 1917-45 / Mark Shipway. New York : St. Martin's Press, 1988. p. cm. Bibliography: p. Includes index. ISBN 0-312-01265-9 : LC Card 87-23083 DDC 338.6 19
1. Works councils - Great Britain - History. 2. Communism - Great Britain - History. I. Title.
HD5660.G7 S48 1988

Shiriaev, A. V. (Andreĭ Vasil'evich) RAPO : opyt, problemy / A.V. Shiriaev. Moskva : "Sov. Rossiia", 1985. 155 p. ; 17 cm. (Sovety i zhizn') LC Card 86-142380
1. Agricultural industries - Russian S.F.S.R. - Management. 2. Local government - Russian S.F.S.R. I. Title. II. Series.
HD9015.S653 R8775 1985

Shiriaev, Al'bert Nikolaevich.
Steklov Seminar (1984 : Steklov Institute of Mathematics) [Statistika i upravlenie sluchaĭnykh protsessov. English.] Statistics and control of stochastic processes /. New York, N.Y. , c1985. xiii, 506 p. ; ISBN 0-911575-18-9 LC Card 85-8851 DDC 519.5 19
QA276.A1 .S7513 1984 ***NYPL [JSE 86-729]***

Stochastic optimization . Berlin , New York , c1985. x, 754 p. : ISBN 0-387-16659-9 (U. S.) LC Card 86-11865 DDC 629.8/312 19
QA402.3 .S778 1985 ***NYPL [JSE 86-1596]***

Shiriaev, IUriĭ Semenovich. Burova, S. E. (Stella Efimovna) Kritika burzhuaznykh vzgliadov na ėkonomicheskoe sotrudnichestvo stran SEV /. Moskva , 1986. 154 p. ; LC Card 86-232355
HC243.5 .B87 1986

Shirinskaia, Z. G. (Zinaida Grigor'evna) Kredit i intensifikatsiia sovkhoznogo proizvodstva / Z.G. Shirinskaia. Moskva : "Finansy", 1980. 142 p. ; 20 cm. At head of title: Moskovskiĭ finansovyĭ institut. Includes bibliographical references. LC Card 81-138434
1. State farms - Soviet Union - Finance. 2. Agricultural

productivity - Soviet Union. I. Title.
HD1493.S65 S55 1980

Shirley, Mary M., 1945- Berg, Elliot. Divestiture in developing countries /. Washington, D.C. , 1987. vii, 30 p. : ISBN 0-8213-0917-X (pbk.) LC Card 87-14235 DDC 338.9/009172/4 19
HD4420.8 .B45 1987

Shirmanov, E. P. Dergachev, A. F. Raschet zatrat i opredelenie ėkonomicheskoĭ ėffektivnosti avtomatizirovannykh sistem operativno-proizvodstvennogo planirovaniia na avtoremontnykh predpriiatiiakh . Moskva , 1978. 35 p. ; LC Card 81-173259
HD9710.A2 D47 1978

Shirokorad, L. D. (Leonid Dmitrievich) Uchenie K. Marksa ob ėtapakh razvitiia sposoba proizvodstva i problemy zrelogo sotsializma . Leningrad , 1985. 150 p. ; LC Card 86-140577
HB97.5 .U24 1985

Shirshov, V. O. (Viacheslav Osipovich) Problemy razvitiia sotsialisticheskikh finansov / V.O. Shirshov. Moskva : Moskovskiĭ in-t nar. khoziaĭstva, 1984. 87 p. ; 22 cm. Bibliography: p. 85. LC Card 85-131694
1. Finance - Soviet Union. 2. Finance, Public - Soviet Union. I. Title.
HG4186 .S47 1984

Shiryaev, Y. see **Shiriaev, IUriĭ Semenovich.**

Shishkan, N. M. (Nadezhda Mikhaĭlovna) Trud i ego problemy na sovremennom ėtape razvitiia sotsialisticheskogo obshchestva . Kishinev , 1986. 133 p. ; LC Card 87-144606
HD8529.M57 T78 1986

Shishkin, M. V. (Mikhail Vladislavovich) Genezis teoriĭ monopolii v marksistsko-leninskoĭ i burzhuaznoĭ literature (1840-1930-e gody) / M.V. Shishkin. Leningrad : Izd-vo Leningradskogo universiteta, 1985. 151 p. ; 22 cm. At head of title: Leningradskiĭ ordena Lenina i ordena Trudovogo Krasnogo Znameni gosudarstvennyĭ universitet imeni A.A. Zhdanova. Includes bibliographical references. LC Card 86-140591
1. Monopolies. 2. Lenin, Vladimir Il'ich, 1870-1924 - Views on monopolies. 3. Marxian economics. I. Title.
HD2757.2 .S49 1985

Shishkin, V. I. (Vladimir Ivanovich) Sotsialisticheskoe stroitel'stvo v sibirskoĭ derevne, noiabr' 1919-mart 1921 g. / V.I. Shishkin ; otvetstvennyĭ redaktor S.A. Krasil'nikov. Novosibirsk : Izd-vo "Nauka," Sibirskoe otd-nie, 1985. 316 p. ; 21 cm. At head of title: Akademiia nauk SSSR. Sibirskoe otdelenie. Institut istorii, filologii i filosofii. Includes bibliographical references. LC Card 86-164936
1. Agriculture and state - Russian S.F.S.R. - Siberia - History. 2. Siberia (R.S.F.S.R.) - History - Revolution, 1917-1921. 3. Siberia (R.S.F.S.R) - Rural conditions. I. Krasil'nikov, S. A. (Sergeĭ Aleksandrovich). II. Title.
HD1995.S5 S45 1985

Shishkov, IUriĭ Vital'evich. Evropeĭskoe soobshchestvo . Moskva , 1986. 270 p. : LC Card 86-202812
HC241.2 .E867 1986

Shishkov, Yuri. see **Shishkov, IUriĭ Vital'evich.**

Shishmanova, IUliia. Uzunova, IUliia. Upravlenie, marketing, uslugi /. Varna , 1986. 143 p. : LC Card 86-152606
HF5415 .U98 1986

Shister, G. A. (Grigoriĭ Aronovich) Rukovodstvo kompartii Uzbekistana podgotovkoĭ rabochikh kadrov v usloviiakh razvitogo sotsializma / G.A. Shister, M.N. Gurevich, L.G. Teteneva. Tashkent : "Uzbekistan", 1981. 274, [2] p. ; 20 cm. At head of title: Ordena Trudovogo Krasnogo Znameni Institut istorii partii pri TSK KP Uzbekistana--filial Instituta marksizma-leninizma pri TSK KPSS. Bibliography: p. 257-[275] LC Card 82-204041
1. Manpower policy - Uzbek S.S.R. 2. Employees, Training of - Uzbek S.S.R. 3. Vocational education - Uzbek S.S.R. I. Gurevich, M. N. (Maiia Naumovna). II. Teteneva, L. G. (Lidiia Georgievna). III. Title.
HD5797.U9 S54 1981

Shitov, V. N. (Vladimir Nikolaevich) Tekhnologicheskiĭ neokolonializm : istoki i sovremennaia praktika / V.N. Shitov. Moskva : Izd-vo "Nauka," Glav. red. vostochnoĭ lit-ry, 1985. 154 p. : ill. ; 20 cm. At head of title: Akademiia nauk SSSR. Ordena Trudovogo Krasnogo Znameni Institut vostokovedeniia. Bibliography: p. 146-[151] LC Card 86-130530
1. Technology transfer - Developing countries. 2. Developing countries - Dependency on foreign countries. I. Title.
HC59.72.T4 S525 1985

Shkaratan, O. I. (Ovseĭ Irmovich) Sotsial'noe upravlenie trudovym kollektivom . Moskva , 1987. 181 p. ; LC Card 87-103391
HF5549.2.S65 S675 1987

Shman'ko, G. I. Rabochiĭ klass Narodnoĭ Vengrii : povyshenie kul'turno-tekhnicheskogo urovnia v period stroitel'stva sotsializma / G.I. Shman'ko. Kiev : Nauk. dumka, 1982. 165 p. ; 21 cm. At head of title: Akademiia nauk Ukrainskoĭ SSR. Institut sotsial'nykh i ėkonomicheskikh problem zarubezhnykh stran. Includes bibliographical references. LC Card 83-143426
1. Labor and laboring classes - Hungary - History. I. Title.
HD8420.5 .S55 1982

Shmelev, Oleg, 1924- Rukopozhatie piatiletok /. Moskva , 1981. 237 p. : LC Card 82-103792
HC335 .R76 1981

Shmidt, A. G. Shakhdzhakhan, Ali. Issledovanie odnoĭ matematicheskoĭ modeli ėkonomicheskogo rosta /. Moskva , 1983. 29, [2] p. : LC Card 83-176389
HD75.5 .S52 1983

Shniper, R. I. (Ruvin Isaakovich)
Bernval'd, A. R. (Arngol'd Reĭngol'dovich) Regional'nye problemy tovarnogo obrashcheniia . Novosibirsk , 1984. 207 p. ; LC Card 85-104041
HF5415.6 .B46 1984 ***NYPL [*QIP 87-2770]***

Metodologicheskie polozheniia razrabotki krupnykh territorial'nykh programm /. Novosibirsk , 1986. 303 p. : LC Card 86-211369
HC337.R853 D56 1986

Shobha, V., 1952- Rural women and development : a study of female agricultural labourers in Telangana / V. Shobha. Delhi, India : Mittal Publications, 1987. xiii, 372 p. ; 22 cm. Cover title: Rural women & development. Originally presented as the author's thesis (doctoral--Kakatiya University) Study conducted in Warangal and Nizamabad districts, Andhra Pradesh. Bibliography: p. [345]-366. Includes index. LC Card 87-902500 DDC 331.4/83/095484 19
1. Women agricultural laborers - India - Warangal. 2. Women agricultural laborers - India - Nizamabad (District). 3. Rural women - India - Warangal. 4. Rural women - India - Nizamabad (District). I. Title. II. Title: Rural women & development.
HD6073.A292 I468 1987

Shockley-Zalabak, Pamela. Fundamentals of organizational communication : knowledge, sensitivity, skills, values / Pamela Shockley-Zalabak. New York : Longman, c1988. xii, 445 p. : ill. ; 25 cm. Includes bibliographies and indexes. ISBN 0-582-28636-0 LC Card 87-3323 DDC 658.4/5 19
1. Communication in organizations. I. Title.
HD30.3 .S55 1988

SHOE INDUSTRY - CANADA.
Profil de l'industrie canadienne de la chaussure /. [Québec] [1985] xv, 65 p. : ISBN 2-550-12407-3 LC Card 86-177298
HD9787.C23 Q436 1985

SHOE INDUSTRY - EUROPEAN ECONOMIC COMMUNITY COUNTRIES.
Hypodēmata. Athēna , 1985. 86 p. : LC Card 86-194391
HD9787.G62 H96 1985

SHOE INDUSTRY - GREECE.
Hypodēmata. Athēna , 1985. 86 p. : LC Card 86-194391
HD9787.G62 H96 1985

SHOE INDUSTRY - NEW ENGLAND - EMPLOYEES - HISTORY - 19TH CENTURY.
Blewett, Mary H. Men, women, and work . Urbana , c1988. p. cm. ISBN 0-252-01484-7 (alk. paper) LC Card 87-19039 DDC 338.4/768531/00974 19
HD8039.B72 U63 1988

SHOE INDUSTRY - NEW ENGLAND - HISTORY - 19TH CENTURY.
Blewett, Mary H. Men, women, and work . Urbana , c1988. p. cm. ISBN 0-252-01484-7 (alk. paper) LC Card 87-19039 DDC 338.4/768531/00974 19
HD8039.B72 U63 1988

SHOE INDUSTRY - QUÉBEC (PROVINCE)
Profil de l'industrie canadienne de la chaussure /. [Québec] [1985] xv, 65 p. : ISBN 2-550-12407-3 LC Card 86-177298
HD9787.C23 Q436 1985

Shofner-Hoffman, Bettye. Human resources management . Springfield, Ill., U. S.A. , c1987. xiv, 170 p. : ISBN 0-398-05296-4 LC Card 86-23016 DDC 362/.0425 19
HD7255 .H86 1987

Shohet, Jack. Disclosure checklists for banks . New York, N.Y. , c1986. 64 p. ; LC Card 86-224924 DDC 657/.833 19
HG1708 .D57 1986

Sholes, Elizabeth C., 1946- Leary, Thomas E., 1946- From fire to rust . Buffalo, N.Y. , c1987. 134 p. : ISBN 0-939032-00-7 (pbk.) LC Card 87-692 DDC 338.7/669142/0974796 19
HD9519.L2 L43 1987

Shook, Dale N. William G. McAdoo and the development of national economic policy, 1913-1918 / Dale N. Shook. New York : Garland, 1987. 427 p. ; 23 cm. (Foreign economic policy of the United States) Originally presented as the author's thesis (Ph. D.--University of Cincinnati, 1975). Bibliography: p. 415-427. ISBN 0-8240-8092-0 (alk. paper) : LC Card 87-23766 DDC 338.973 19
1. United States - Economic policy - To 1933. 2. McAdoo, William Gibbs, 1863-1941. 3. Industry and state - United States - History - 20th century. 4. United States. Treasury Dept. - History - 20th century. I. Title. II. Series.
HC106.2 .S55 1987

Shook, Robert L., 1938- Rodgers, F. G. (Francis G.) The IBM way . New York , c1986. xiv, 235 p. ; ISBN 0-06-015522-1 : LC Card 85-45223 DDC 338.7/61004/0973 19
HD9696.C64 I4875 1986
NYPL [JLE 86-1374]

SHOP COMMITTEES. see **WORKS COUNCILS.**

SHOP COUNCILS. see **WORKS COUNCILS.**

Shop-in-the-shop . Medla, Karsten, 1954- München , c1987. xxxi, 207, 6 p. ; ISBN 3-88259-428-4 LC Card 87-141864 DDC 658.8/7 19
HF5429 .M36 1987

SHOP STEWARDS - GERMANY, WEST.
Peter, Gerd, 1941- Der Arbeitsschutzbeauftragte . Frankfurt , New York , c1986. 344 p. : ISBN 3-593-33633-2 LC Card 86-160932
HD6490.S52 G365 1986

SHOP STEWARDS - ITALY.
Regalia, Ida, 1946- Eletti e abbandonati . Bologna , c1984. 355 p. : ISBN 88-15-00592-7 : LC Card 84-250543 DDC 331.87/33/0945 19
HD6490.O42 I87 1984 ***NYPL [JLD 86-211]***

The shopfloor politics of new technology /. Wilkinson, Barry. London , 1983. 120 p. ; ISBN 0-435-82950-5 : LC Card 82-236198 DDC 338/.06 19
HC260.T4 W54 1983 ***NYPL [JLD 86-1322]***

Shopov, Dimitŭr.
Kachestvoto na truda : sŭshtnost, predpostavki, problemi / Dimitŭr Shopov, Georgi Evgeniev.1. izd. Sofiia : Partizdat, 1984. 202 p. : ill. ; 20 cm. (Realniiat sotsializŭm--teoriia i praktika) Includes bibliographical references. LC Card 85-117683
1. Labor productivity - Bulgaria. I. Evgeniev, Georgi. II. Title. III. Series.
HC403.Z9 L375 1984

Nauchno-tekhnicheskiiat progres i problemite na truda . Sofiia , 1986. 297 p. : LC Card 86-196075
HD6331.2.B9 N38 1986

SHOPPERS' GUIDES. see **CONSUMER EDUCATION; SHOPPING.**

Shopping center development and investment /. Hines, Mary Alice. New York , c1987. p. cm. ISBN 0-471-62427-6 LC Card 87-26342 DDC 332.63/24 19
HF5430 .H56 1987

Shopping center development handbook / Sponsored by the Executive Group of the Commercial and Retail Development Council of ULI-the Urban Land Institute. 2nd ed.

Washington : ULI, 1985. xiii, 338 p. : ill. ; 28 cm. (Community builders handbook series) Includes bibliographical references and index. ISBN 0-87420-634-0 LC Card 85-50127
1. Shopping centers - Planning - Handbooks, manuals, etc. 2. Shopping centers - Design and construction - Handbook, manuals, etc. 3. Shopping centers - Management - Handbooks, manuals, etc. I. Urban Land Institute. Commercial and Office Development Council. Executive Group. ***NYPL [JLF 85-1243]***

Shopping center managers and retailers : working together toward increased productivity : why and how. New York : International Council of Shopping Centers, c1988. p. cm. Bibliography: p. ISBN 0-913598-73-9 (pbk.) : LC Card 87-22546 DDC 658.8/7 19
1. Shopping centers - Management. 2. Shopping centers - Marketing. 3. Retail trade - Management. I. International Council of Shopping Centers.
HF5430 .S557 1988

SHOPPING CENTERS.
Hines, Mary Alice. Shopping center development and investment /. New York , c1987. p. cm. ISBN 0-471-62427-6 LC Card 87-26342 DDC 332.63/24 19
HF5430 .H56 1987

SHOPPING CENTERS - DESIGN AND CONSTRUCTION - HANDBOOK, MANUALS, ETC.
Shopping center development handbook /. Washington , 1985. xiii, 338 p. : ISBN 0-87420-634-0 LC Card 85-50127
NYPL [JLF 85-1243]

SHOPPING CENTERS - GERMANY (WEST) - RUHR (REGION)
Heineberg, Heinz. Neue Einkaufszentren im Ruhrgebiet . Paderborn , 1986. 247 p. : ISBN 3-506-73224-2 LC Card 87-407591 DDC 381/.1/094355 19
HF5430.6.G4 H45 1986

SHOPPING CENTERS - MANAGEMENT.
Shopping center managers and retailers . New York , c1988. p. cm. ISBN 0-913598-73-9 (pbk.) : LC Card 87-22546 DDC 658.8/7 19
HF5430 .S557 1988

SHOPPING CENTERS - MANAGEMENT - HANDBOOKS, MANUALS, ETC.
Shopping center development handbook /. Washington , 1985. xiii, 338 p. : ISBN 0-87420-634-0 LC Card 85-50127
NYPL [JLF 85-1243]

SHOPPING CENTERS - MANITOBA - WINNIPEG.
Downtown and regional shopping centre retailing in Winnipeg /. Winnipeg, Man., Canada , 1985. x, 90, [8] p. : ISBN 0-920213-22-7 (pbk.) LC Card 86-137592 DDC 381/.1/0971274 19
HF5429.6.C3 D69 1985
NYPL [JLF 86-1331]

SHOPPING CENTERS - MARKETING.
Shopping center managers and retailers . New York , c1988. p. cm. ISBN 0-913598-73-9 (pbk.) : LC Card 87-22546 DDC 658.8/7 19
HF5430 .S557 1988

Wenner, S. Albert. Marketing your shopping center . New York , c1987. xi, 194 p. : ISBN 0-913598-55-0 LC Card 87-2848 DDC 658.8/7 19
HF5430 .W46 1987

SHOPPING CENTERS - PLANNING - HANDBOOKS, MANUALS, ETC.
Shopping center development handbook /. Washington , 1985. xiii, 338 p. : ISBN 0-87420-634-0 LC Card 85-50127
NYPL [JLF 85-1243]

SHOPPING CENTERS - UNITED STATES.
Dollars & cents of off-price shopping centers . Washington, D.C. , c1986. v, 78 p. : ISBN 0-87420-660-X (pbk.) LC Card 86-51102 DDC 381/.1 19
HF5430.3 .D65 1986

Hines, Mary Alice. Shopping center development and investment /. New York , c1987. p. cm. ISBN 0-471-62427-6 LC Card 87-26342 DDC 332.63/24 19
HF5430 .H56 1987

SHOPPING MALLS - MANAGEMENT.
Food courts . New York , c1987. 70 p. : ISBN 0-913598-66-6 (pbk.) LC Card 87-604 DDC 647/.9573 19
HF5430 .F66 1987

SHOPPING - UNITED STATES.
Lydenberg, Steven D. Rating America's corporate conscience . Reading, Mass. , c1986. x, 499 p. : ISBN 0-201-15886-8 : LC Card 86-8064 DDC 338.7/4/0973 19
HD60.5.U5 L93 1986
NYPL [*R-Econ. 87-1830]

SHOPS. see **STORES, RETAIL.**

Shornikov, P. M. (Petr Mikhaĭlovich) Promyshlennost′ i rabochiĭ klass Moldavskoĭ SSR v gody Velikoĭ Otechestvennoĭ voĭny / P.M. Shornikov ; otvetstvennyĭ redaktor I.E. Levit. Kishinev : "Shtiintsa", 1986. 148, [4] p. ; 20 cm. At head of title: Akademiia nauk Moldavskoĭ SSR. Institut istorii im. IA.S. Grosula. Summaries in English and French. Bibliography: p. 126-[149] LC Card 86-141169
1. World War, 1939-1945 - Economic aspects - Moldavian S.S.R. 2. Moldavian S.S.R. - Industries - History. I. Levit, I. É. (Iziaslav Élikovich). II. Title.
HC337.M553 D47 1986

A short course in gold investing . Rosenthal, Daniel M. Bethel, CT , c1986. 90 leaves : ISBN 0-938689-00-2 (pbk.) : LC Card 86-207234 DDC 332.63 19
HG295.U6 R67 1986

A short course on functional equations . Aczél, J. Dordrecht, Holland ; Boston : vi, 169 p. : ISBN 90-277-2376-1 LC Card 86-26131 DDC 515/.25 19
HB135 .A28 1987

Short, Daniel G. Welsch, Glenn A. Fundamentals of financial accounting /. Homewood, Ill. , 1987. xviii, 958 p. : ISBN 0-256-03614-4 LC Card 86-82802 DDC 657 19
HF5635 .W458 1987b

A Short introduction to the co-operative savings and credit societies and Tanzania Rural Savings and Credit Scheme / Ujamaa and Co-operative Development Division, Savings and Credit Unit. [Dar es Salaam, Tanzania] : United Republic of Tanzania, Office of the Prime Minister, [1977] 43 p. : ill. ; 32 cm. Cover title. "Prepared in December 1976." "March 1977." LC Card 77-980630 DDC 334/.2/09678 19
1. Banks and banking, Cooperative - Tanzania. 2. Agricultural cooperative credit associations - Tanzania. I. Tanzania. Ujamaa and Co-operative Development Dept. Savings and Credit Unit.
HG2039.T37 S56 1977

Short, James F. The Social fabric . Beverly Hills, Calif. , c1986. 366 p. ; ISBN 0-8039-2788-6 LC Card 86-1191 DDC 301 19
HM13 .S524 1986 ***NYPL [JLE 86-3755]***

Short, John R. The urban arena : capital, state, and community in contemporary Britain / John R. Short. London : Macmillan, 1984. viii, 202 p. : ill., maps ; 23 cm. (Critical human geography) Bibliography: p. 185-194. Includes index. ISBN 0-333-36139-3 LC Card 87-672913
1. Urban policy - Great Britain. 2. Great Britain - Economic policy - 1945-. 3. Great Britain - Economic conditions - 1945-. I. Title. II. Series.
HC256.6 .S49x 1984

Short, Joseph N. American business and foreign policy : cases in coffee and cocoa trade regulation, 1961-1974 / Joseph Short. New York : Garland, 1987. 340 p. : ill. ; 23 cm. (Foreign economic policy of the United States) Bibliography: p. 325-340. ISBN 0-8240-8093-9 (alk. paper) : LC Card 87-23792 DDC 382/.41373/0973 19
1. Coffee trade - United States. 2. Cocoa trade - United States. 3. Coffee trade - Developing countries. 4. Cocoa trade - Developing countries. 5. Foreign trade regulation - United States. 6. Business and politics - United States. I. Title. II. Series.
HD9199.U48 S46 1987

Short, K. R. M. Western broadcasting over the iron curtain /. London , 1986. 274 p. : ISBN 0-7099-4438-1 ***NYPL [MWGH 87-760]***

The short-run demand for real money balances in the Bangladesh economy . Hossain, Md. Akhtar. Bundoora, Vic., Australia [1986] 90 p. ; ISBN 0-85816-784-0 (pbk.) LC Card 86-228714 DDC 332.4/14 19
HG1240.6 .H67 1986

Short-run tax-push inflation in Finland /. Asplund, Rita. Helsinki , 1986. 65 p. : ISBN 951-46-9876-2 (pbk.) LC Card 87-163994 DDC 332.4/1/094897 19
HJ4738.3 .A86 1986

Short, Simine, 1944- Glider mail : an aerophilatelic handbook / by Simine Short ; edited by Dan Barber. Cinnaminson, NJ : American Air Mail Society, 1987. 261 p. : ill. ; 24 cm. Bibliography: p. 247-254. Includes index. ISBN 0-939429-00-4 : LC Card 86-72751 DDC 383/.144 19
1. Glider post - Handbooks, manuals, etc. 2. Postage-stamps - Topics - Gliding and soaring. 3. Postmarks - Topics - Gliding and soaring. I. Barber, Dan. II. American Air Mail Society. III. Title.
HE6239.G54 S56 1987

The short-term effects of marital disruption on the labor supply behavior of young women /. Moore, Sylvia F. Columbus, Ohio (Suite 585, 1375 Perry St., Columbus, Ohio, 43201) , 1979. v, 133 p. ; ***NYPL [JLF 86-649]***

Short-term trading in futures . Bernstein, Jacob, 1946- Chicago, Ill. , c1987. vii, 320 p. : ISBN 0-917253-66-3 (loose-leaf) : LC Card 87-4940 DDC 332.64/4 19
HG6024.3 .B477 1987

Shorter, Frederic Claiborne. Computational methods for population projections : with particular reference to development planning / Frederic C. Shorter, David Pasta, Robert Sendek.1st ed. with supplement added. New York : Population Council, 1987, c1974. vii, 192 p. : ill. ; 28 cm. ISBN 0-87834-056-4 (pbk.) LC Card 87-9303 DDC 304.6/2/0285 19
1. Population forecasting - Data processing. I. Pasta, David. II. Sendek, Robert. III. Title.
HB849.53 .S54 1987

Shoven, John B. Pensions in the U. S. economy /. Chicago , 1988. ix, 200 p. : ISBN 0-226-06285-6 LC Card 87-19987 DDC 331.25/2/0973 19
HD7105.45.U6 P46 1988

SHOW CARDS. see **ADVERTISING CARDS.**

Shpakovskaia, E. P. (Elena Petrovna) Nikitin, Sergeĭ Mikhaĭlovich. Indeksy tsen i produktsii v kapitalisticheskikh stranakh /. Moskva , 1981. 255 p. ; LC Card 86-460234
HB225 .N52 1981

Shpilevskiĭ, É.
Printsipy dinamicheskoĭ klassifikatsii stokhasticheskikh protsessov i sistem : materialy k seminaru pri Institute matematiki i kibernetiki AN Litovskoĭ SSR "Statisticheskie problemy upravleniia" / [É.K. Shpilevskiĭ] ; pod red. L. Tel′ksnis. Vil′nius : In-t matematiki i kibernetiki Akademii nauk Litovskoĭ SSR, 1978. 138 p. ; 20 cm. (Statisticheskie problemy upravleniia . vyp. 28) Titles on added t.p.: Stochastinių procesų ir sistemų dinaminės klasifikacijos principai; The principles of dynamical classification of stochastic processes and systems. At head of title: Institut matematiki i kibernetiki AN Litovskoĭ SSR. Institut fiziko-tekhnicheskikh problem ėnergetiki AN Lit. SSR. Litovskaia territorial′naia gruppa NKAU SSSR Mezhdunarodnoĭ federatsii po avtomaticheskomu upravleniiu. Summary in English and Lithuanian. Bibliography: p. 126-133. LC Card 81-173567
1. Stochastic processes - Congresses. 2. Stochastic systems - Congresses. I. Tel′ksnis, L. II. Matematikos ir kibernetikos institutas (Lietuvos TSR Mokslų akademija). III. Fizikinių-techninių energetikos problemų institutas (Lietuvos TSR Mokslų akademija). IV. Natsional′nyĭ komitet SSSR po avtomaticheskomu upravleniiu. Litovskaia territorial′naia gruppa. V. Title. VI. Title: Stochastinių procesų ir sistemų dinaminės klasifikacijos principai. VII. Title: Principles of dynamical classification of stochastic processes and systems. VIII. Series.
HD38 .S715 vyp. 28 QA274

Razrabotka i issledovanie algoritmov dinamicheskoĭ klassifikatsii protsessov . Vil′nius , 1979. 93 p. : LC Card 82-150323
HD38 .S715 vyp. 37 T57.83

Shquipni. see **Albania.**

Shquipri. see **Albania.**

Shrestha, Neeru. Cooperative development and basic needs /. Kathmandu, Nepal , 1985. iii, 238 p. ; LC Card 86-900318 DDC 338.9549/3 19
HC425 .C66 1985

SHREVEPORT METROPOLITAN AREA (LA.) - CENSUS - MAPS.
Dlin, Norman. Social atlas of Shreveport, Louisiana /. Shreveport , 1985. 1 atlas (vii, 43 p.) : LC Card 86-622543 DDC 304.6/09763/99 19
HA730.S615 D57 1985

SHREVEPORT METROPOLITAN AREA (LA.) - STATISTICS - MAPS.
Dlin, Norman. Social atlas of Shreveport, Louisiana /. Shreveport , 1985. 1 atlas (vii, 43 p.) : LC Card 86-622543 DDC 304.6/09763/99 19
HA730.S615 D57 1985

Shri Ram memorial lecture .
(1974) Dhar, D. P., 1918-1975. Enterpreneurship and development /. New Delhi [pref. 1974] 23 p., [2] p. of plates : LC Card 80-908353 DDC 338.954 19
HB615 .D49 1974

SHRIMP CULTURE - COSTS.
Marine shrimp farming . Charleston, S.C., USA (P.O. Box 16190, Charleston 29412) , c1987. vi, 90 leaves : LC Card 87-404668 DDC 338.3/71543 19
HD9472.S62 M375 1987

SHRIMP INDUSTRY.
Marine shrimp farming . Charleston, S.C., USA (P.O. Box 16190, Charleston 29412) , c1987. vi, 90 leaves : LC Card 87-404668 DDC 338.3/71543 19
HD9472.S62 M375 1987

Shrimpton, Mark. Women, work, and family in the British, Canadian, and Norwegian oilfields /. New York , 1987. p. cm. ISBN 0-312-00528-8 : LC Card 86-31393 DDC 305.4/3665 19
HD9560.5 .W66 1987

Shrivastava, Paul.
Bhopal : anatomy of a crisis / Paul Shrivastava. Cambridge, Mass. : Ballinger Pub. Co., c1987. xvi, 184 p. : ill. ; 24 cm. (Ballinger series in business in a global environment) Bibliography: p. [163]-171. Includes index. ISBN 0-88730-084-7 LC Card 86-26575 DDC 363.1/79 19
1. Bhopal Union Carbide Plant Disaster, Bhopal, India, 1984. 2. Union Carbide Ltd. (India). 3. Union Carbide Corporation. 4. Pesticides industry - India - Bhopal - Accidents. 5. Methyl isocyanate - Toxicology - India - Bhopal. I. Title. II. Series.
HD7269.C452 I5268 1987

Managing industrial crises : lessons of Bhopal / Paul Shrivastava. New Delhi, India : Vision Books, 1987. 196 p. : ill. ; 23 cm. On the Bhopal tragedy due to leakage of methyl isocyanate gas, 1984. Bibliography: p. [171]-183. Includes index. ISBN 81-7094-000-1 : LC Card 87-902160 DDC 363.1/79 19
1. Bhopal Union Carbide Plant Disaster, Bhopal, India, 1984. 2. Union Carbide Ltd. (India). 3. Methyl isocyanate - Toxicology - India - Bhopal. 4. Pesticides industry - India - Bhopal - Accidents. 5. Industrial accidents. 6. Industrial safety. I. Title.
HD7269.C452 I5269 1987

Shrivastava, S. C., 1939- Wages, profits, and productivity in selected industries of India since 1950 : an econometric study / Satish Chandra Srivastava. Bombay : Himalaya Pub. House, 1984. xii, 254 p. : ill. ; 22 cm. Spine title: Wages, profits, productivity in selected industries in India. Includes statistical tables. Bibliography: p. [251]-254. LC Card 84-900745 DDC 338/.06/0954 19
1. Wages - India - Econometric models. 2. Profit - India - Econometric models. 3. Industrial productivity - India - Econometric models. I. Title. II. Title: Wages, profits, productivity in selected industries in India.
HD5069 .S46 1984 ***NYPL [JLD 86-4260]***

Shtele, A. L. Sistema vedeniia sel'skogo i promyslovogo khoziaistva na Eniseiskom Severe . Novosibirsk , 1986. 211 p. ; LC Card 86-227282
HD1995.K73 S57 1986

Shturman, Dora, 1923- Nash novyĭ mir : teoriia, ėksperiment, rezul'tat / D. Shturman.Izd. 2-e, ispr. i dop. Ierusalim : Ėkspress, 1986. 464 p. : ill. ; 17 cm. "Spisok publikatsii D. Shturman"--p. 455-463. LC Card 87-114263
1. Marxian economics. 2. Communism. 3. Soviet Union - Economic policy - 1917-. 4. Communism - Soviet Union - History - 20th century. I. Title.
HB97.5 .S5155 1986

Shubert, Adrian, 1953- The road to revolution in Spain : the coal miners of Asturias, 1860-1934 / Adrian Shubert. Urbana : University of Illinois Press, c1987. 183 p. : map ; 24 cm. (The working class in European history) Revision of thesis (Ph. D.)--Queen Mary College, University of London, 1982. Bibliography: p. 169-175. Includes index. ISBN 0-252-01368-9 (alk. paper) LC Card 86-24998 DDC 331.7/622334/094615 19
1. Coal miners - Spain - Asturias - History - 20th century. 2. Strikes and lockouts - Coal mining - Spain - Asturias - History - 20th century. 3. Trade-unions - Coal miners - Spain - Asturias - History - 20th century. 4. Coal trade - Spain - Asturias - History - 20th century. I. Title.
HD8039.M62 S68 1987

Shubkina, I. P. Ėkonomiko-matematicheskie modeli v upravlenii proizvodstvennymi ob"edineniiami /. Moskva , 1983. 190 p. : LC Card 85-199430
HD30.25 .E397 1983

SHUDRAS. see **UNTOUCHABLES.**

Shuker, Iain G. W. Economic analysis of the cost structure of commercial sugar cane farms in Louisiana / by Iain G.W. Shuker, Arthur M. Heagler, and Brian A. Chapman. Baton Rouge, La. : Dept. of Agricultural Economics and Agribusiness, Louisiana Agricultural Experiment Station, Louisiana State University Agricultural Center, [1986] vi, 50 p. : ill. ; 28 cm. (D.A.E. research report . no. 651) "April 1986." Bibliography: p. 50. LC Card 86-622542 DDC 338.1/09763 s 338.1/7361/09763021 19
1. Sugarcane industry - Louisiana - Costs - Statistics. 2. Farms - Louisiana - Statistics. I. Heagler, Arthur M. II. Chapman, Brian A. III. Title. IV. Series.
HD1775.L8 L7 no. 651 HD9107.L8

Shukla, Surya Pal, 1939- Agriculture in north-eastern region / S.P. Shukla, A.K. Aggarwal. New Delhi, India : National Pub. House, 1986. xxvi, 223 p. : ill., map ; 22 cm. Includes bibliographies and index. LC Card 86-902178 DDC 338.1/0954/1 19
1. Agriculture - Economic aspects - India, Northeastern. I. Agarwal, A. K. (Ashok Kumar), 1949-. II. Title.
HD2075.N58 S58 1986 ***NYPL [JLD 87-938]***

Shukri Mohammed Ghanem. see **Ghanem, Shukri Mohammed.**

Shull, Steven A. Economics and politics of industrial policy . Boulder , 1986. xi, 120 p. ; ISBN 0-8133-7140-6 (pbk. : alk. paper) : LC Card 85-26478 DDC 338.94 19
HD3616.U47 E34 1986
NYPL [JLE 86-4353]

Shuman, Howard E. Politics and the budget : the struggle between the President and the Congress / Howard E. Shuman.2nd ed. Englewood Cliffs, N.J. : Prentice-Hall, c1988. p. cm. Bibliography: p. Includes index. ISBN 0-13-684416-2 (pbk.) : LC Card 87-14521 DDC 353.0072/231 19
1. Budget - United States. 2. Budget - Political aspects - United States. 3. Separation of powers - United States. I. Title.
HJ2051 .S49 1988

Shupe, Barbara, 1941- New York State population, 1790-1980 : a compilation of federal census data / Barbara Shupe, Janet Steins, Jyoti Pandit. New York : Neal-Schuman, c1987. xxvii, 333 p. : ill. ; 29 cm. Bibliography: p. xvi-xix. ISBN 1-555-70009-8 : LC Card 86-28487 DDC 304.6/2/09747 19
1. New York (State) - Population - Statistics - History. I. Steins, Janet. II. Pandit, Jyoti. III. Title.
HA545 .S58 1987

Shurgina, A. I. IUzhnaia IAkutiia, sotsial'no-ėkonomicheskiĭ aspekt . IAkutsk , 1985. 94 p. ; LC Card 86-180767
HC337.I2 I97 1985

Shurtleff, William, 1941- Tofutti® & other soy ice creams : the non-dairy frozen dessert industry and market / William Shurtleff & Akiko Aoyagi. Lafayette, CA : Soyfoods Center, c1985. 2 v. : ill. ; 28 cm. Includes index. Bibliography: p. 135-141. (v. 1) ISBN 0-933332-19-X (v. 1) : LC Card 85-10829 DDC 381/.4174 19
1. Bean curd industry - United States. 2. Soybean industry - United States. 3. Ice cream industry - United States. 4. Market surveys - United States. I. Aoyagi, Akiko, 1950-. II. Title. III. Title: Tofutti and other soy ice creams.
HD9330.B323 U 1985 ***NYPL [JLF 86-1035]***

Shusharin, A. L. (Aleksandr Leonidovich) Sootnoshenie khozraschetnoĭ ėkonomicheskoĭ ėffektivnosti sredstv proizvodstva s ikh narodno-khoziaistvennoĭ ėffektivnost'iu / A.L. Shusharin. Tomsk : Izd-vo Tomskogo universiteta, 1979. 159 p. ; 20 cm. Errata slip inserted. Includes bibliographical references. LC Card 87-462036
1. Industrial management - Soviet Union. 2. Business enterprises - Soviet Union. 3. Technological innovations - Soviet Union. I. Title.
HD70.S63 S55 1979

Shuster, Harvey L. The financial manager's guide to microsoftware / Harvey L. Shuster and Ray Dillon. New York : Wiley, 1988. p. cm. (The Wiley/Ronald-National Association of Accountants professional book series) Bibliography: p. ISBN 0-471-81176-9 LC Card 87-21663 DDC 658.1/5/0285536 19
1. Corporations - Finance - Data processing. 2. Corporations - Finance - Computer programs. I. Dillon, Ray D. II. Title. III. Series.
HG4012.5 .S47 1988

SHUTDOWN OF FACTORIES. see **PLANT SHUTDOWNS.**

Shvarts, M. A. (Mikhail Aleksandrovich) Ėkonomicheskiĭ analiz deiatel'nosti proizvodstvennogo ob"edineniia po dobyche uglia / M.A. Shvarts, G.A. Prudinskiĭ. Moskva : "Nedra", 1986. 222 p. ; 22 cm. Bibliography: p. [221] LC Card 85-236907
1. Coal mines and mining - Soviet Union - Accounting. I. Prudinskiĭ, G. A. (Grigoriĭ Aronovich). II. Title.
HF5686.M6 S48 1986

Shyam Nath, 1945- Measuring tax burden in India : a case study of Rajasthan State / Shyam Nath.1st ed. New Delhi : Ashish Pub. House, 1987. xv, 194 p. : ill. ; 23 cm. Bibliography: p. [179]-192. Includes index. ISBN 81-7024-072-7 : LC Card 87-900348 DDC 336.2/94/09544 19
1. Tax incidence - India - Rajasthan - Case studies. 2. Tax incidence - India - Case studies. I. Title.
HJ2323.I4 S59 1987

Si no hay solución a la crisis, habrá explosiones sociales generalizadas de carácter revolucionario. Castro, Fidel, 1927- [Nada podrá detener la marcha de la historia. Selections.] La Habana , 1985. 97 p. ; LC Card 87-115245 DDC 338.9 19
HC125 .C37825 1985

Siam. see **Thailand.**

Sibaja Chacón, Luis Fernando.
Encomienda de tributo en el Valle Central de Costa Rica (1569-1683). 1984. Costa Rica colonial : tres ensayos / Juan Carlos Solórzano, Luis Fernando Sibaja. [San José, Costa Rica , 1984] 83 p. ; LC Card 86-173945
HC389 .C67 1984

Siberia : problems and prospects for regional development / edited by Alan Wood. London ; New York : Croom Helm, c1987. 233 p. : maps ; 23 cm. "Published in the USA by Croom Helm in association with Methuen, Inc."--T.p. verso. Includes bibliographies and index. ISBN 0-7099-3655-9 LC Card 87-15437 DDC 330.957/0854 19
1. Siberia (R.S.F.S.R.) - Economic conditions. 2. Soviet Far East (R.S.F.S.R.) - Economic conditions. 3. Siberia (R.S.F.S.R.) - Industries. 4. Soviet Far East (R.S.F.S.R) - Industries. I. Wood, Alan, 1943-.
HC337.R852 S52697 1987

Siberia and the Soviet Far East : strategic dimensions in multinational perspective / edited by Rodger Swearingen. Stanford, Calif. : Hoover Institution Press, Stanford University, c1987. xxx, 298 p. : ill. ; 23 cm. (Hoover Press publication . 336) Includes bibliographies and index ISBN 0-8179-8362-7 (pbk.) : LC Card 86-21388 DDC 330.957/085 19
1. Siberia (R.S.F.S.R.) - Economic conditions. 2. Soviet Far East (R.S.F.S.R.) - Economic conditions. 3. Siberia (R.S.F.S.R.) - Foreign economic relations. 4. Soviet Far East (R.S.F.S.R.) - Foreign economic relations. 5. Union - Defenses. I. Swearingen, Rodger, 1923-.
HC337.R852 S5269 1987

La Siberia extremeña . Camacho Cabello, José. [Badajoz] , 1985. 201 p. : ISBN 84-505-1266-2 LC Card 86-200856
HB3620.E85 C35 1985

SIBERIA (R.S.F.S.R. AND KAZAKH S.S.R.) - ECONOMIC CONDITIONS -

CONGRESSES.
Sibirien, ein russisches und sowjetisches Entwicklungsproblem /. Berlin , c1986. 274 p. : ISBN 3-87061-260-6 LC Card 86-229174
HC336.9.S53 S53 1986

SIBERIA (R.S.F.S.R. AND KAZAKH S.S.R.) - ECONOMIC POLICY - CONGRESSES.
Sibirien, ein russisches und sowjetisches Entwicklungsproblem /. Berlin , c1986. 274 p. : ISBN 3-87061-260-6 LC Card 86-229174
HC336.9.S53 S53 1986

SIBERIA (R.S.F.S.R. AND KAZAKH S.S.R.) - INDUSTRIES - CONGRESSES.
Sibirien, ein russisches und sowjetisches Entwicklungsproblem /. Berlin , c1986. 274 p. : ISBN 3-87061-260-6 LC Card 86-229174
HC336.9.S53 S53 1986

SIBERIA (R.S.F.S.R.) - ECONOMIC CONDITIONS.
Adzhiev, M. Ė. (Murad Ėskanderovich) Sibir'--XX vek /. Moskva , 1983. 252 p., [24] p. of plates : LC Card 83-161484
HC337.R852 S522 1983

Dienes, Leslie. Soviet Asia . Boulder , 1987. xx, 289 p. ; ISBN 0-8133-7437-5 (pbk.) LC Card 87-8331 DDC 338.957 19
HC336.9.S53 D53 1987

Ėkonomicheskoe razvitie Sibiri i Dal'nego Vostoka /. Moskva , 1980. 263 p. ; LC Card 81-143669
HC337.R852 S5242 1980

Khozi͡aĭstvennoe osvoenie novykh raĭonov i ėkonomicheskiĭ rost Sibiri . Novosibirsk , 1980. 173 p. : LC Card 83-182452
HC337.R852 S5247 1980

Siberia . London , New York , c1987. 233 p. : ISBN 0-7099-3655-9 LC Card 87-15437 DDC 330.957/0854 19
HC337.R852 S52697 1987

Siberia and the Soviet Far East . Stanford, Calif. , c1987. xxx, 298 p. : ISBN 0-8179-8362-7 (pbk.) : LC Card 86-21388 DDC 330.957/085 19
HC337.R852 S5269 1987

Solov'eva, E. I., d-r ist. nauk. Promysly sibirskogo krest'i͡anstva v poreformennyĭ period /. Novosibirsk , 1981. 327 p. : LC Card 82-111175
HD2346.S652 S527 1981

Tolmachev, V. P. (Vladimir Petrovich) Ėkonomika Urala, Sibiri i Dal'nego vostoka v odinnadtsatoĭ pi͡atiletke /. Moskva , 1981. 39 p. ; LC Card 82-153584
HC337.R852 U7382 1981

SIBERIA (R.S.F.S.R.) - ECONOMIC CONDITIONS - FORECASTING.
Metody i modeli razvitii͡a regional'nykh ėkonomicheskikh sistem . Novosibirsk , 1985. 165 p. : LC Card 86-219402
HC337.R852 S52545 1985

SIBERIA (R.S.F.S.R.) - ECONOMIC CONDITIONS - MATHEMATICAL MODELS.
Metody i modeli razvitii͡a regional'nykh ėkonomicheskikh sistem . Novosibirsk , 1985. 165 p. : LC Card 86-219402
HC337.R852 S52545 1985

SIBERIA (R.S.F.S.R.) - ECONOMIC POLICY.
Dienes, Leslie. Soviet Asia . Boulder , 1987. xx, 289 p. ; ISBN 0-8133-7437-5 (pbk.) LC Card 87-8331 DDC 338.957 19
HC336.9.S53 D53 1987

Metodologicheskie polozhenii͡a razrabotki krupnykh territorial'nykh programm /. Novosibirsk , 1986. 303 p. : LC Card 86-211369
HC337.R853 D56 1986

SIBERIA (R.S.F.S.R.) - ENVIRONMENTAL POLICY.
Regional'nye osobennosti rat͡sionalizat͡sii prirodopol'zovanii͡a i okhrany sredy /. Irkutsk , 1980. 177 p. ; LC Card 82-111826
HC337.R852 S5266 1980

SIBERIA (R.S.F.S.R.) - FOREIGN ECONOMIC RELATIONS.
Siberia and the Soviet Far East . Stanford, Calif. , c1987. xxx, 298 p. : ISBN 0-8179-8362-7 (pbk.) : LC Card 86-21388 DDC 330.957/085 19
HC337.R852 S5269 1987

SIBERIA (R.S.F.S.R.) - HISTORY - REVOLUTION, 1917-1921.
Shishkin, V. I. (Vladimir Ivanovich) Sotsialisticheskoe stroitel'stvo v sibirskoĭ derevne, noi͡abr' 1919-mart 1921 g. /. Novosibirsk , 1985. 316 p. ; LC Card 86-164936
HD1995.S5 S45 1985

SIBERIA (R.S.F.S.R.) - INDUSTRIES.
De-Gennin, Vil'gel'm, 1676-1750. [Opisanie ural'skikh i sibirskikh zavodov 1735. English.] Description of Ural and Siberian factories in 1735 /. [Washington, D.C.] , 1987. p. cm. LC Card 87-600052 DDC 338.0947/87 19
HC337.R852 U733613 1987

KATĖK i razvitie otrasleĭ khozi͡aĭstva Sibiri /. Novosibirsk , 1984. 164 p. ; LC Card 84-167870
HC337.R852 S5246 1984

Rabochiĭ klass Sibiri . Novosibirsk , 1986. 355 p., [16] p. of plates : LC Card 86-211294
HD5797.S5 R33 1986

Siberia . London , New York , c1987. 233 p. : ISBN 0-7099-3655-9 LC Card 87-15437 DDC 330.957/0854 19
HC337.R852 S52697 1987

Trudovye kollektivy Sibiri . Novosibirsk , 1985. 154 p. ; LC Card 86-162191
HD5797.S5 T78 1985

SIBERIA (R.S.F.S.R.) - INDUSTRIES - HISTORY.
Voprosy istorii dorevoli͡ut͡sionnoĭ Sibiri /. Tomsk , 1983. 177 p. ; ***NYPL [*QI 87-171]***

SIBERIA (R.S.F.S.R.) - INDUSTRIES - LOCATION.
Metodologicheskie polozhenii͡a razrabotki krupnykh territorial'nykh programm /. Novosibirsk , 1986. 303 p. : LC Card 86-211369
HC337.R853 D56 1986

SIBERIA (R.S.F.S.R.) - INDUSTRIES - MATHEMATICAL MODELS.
Bostandzhi͡an, V. B. (Vardan Babkenovich) Optimizat͡sii͡a otraslevykh sistem v sostave ėkonomicheskikh programm /. Novosibirsk , 1982. 120, [1] p. : LC Card 83-107849
HC337.R852 S5234 1982

SIBERIA (R.S.F.S.R.) - INDUSTRIES - PLANNING.
Bostandzhi͡an, V. B. (Vardan Babkenovich) Optimizat͡sii͡a otraslevykh sistem v sostave ėkonomicheskikh programm /. Novosibirsk , 1982. 120, [1] p. : LC Card 83-107849
HC337.R852 S5234 1982

SIBERIA (R.S.F.S.R.) - INDUSTRIES - PLANNING - MATHEMATICAL MODELS.
Metody i modeli razvitii͡a regional'nykh ėkonomicheskikh sistem . Novosibirsk , 1985. 165 p. : LC Card 86-219402
HC337.R852 S52545 1985

SIBERIA (R.S.F.S.R) - RURAL CONDITIONS.
Shishkin, V. I. (Vladimir Ivanovich) Sotsialisticheskoe stroitel'stvo v sibirskoĭ derevne, noi͡abr' 1919-mart 1921 g. /. Novosibirsk , 1985. 316 p. ; LC Card 86-164936
HD1995.S5 S45 1985

SIBERIA (R.S.F.S.R.) - SOCIAL CONDITIONS.
Rabochiĭ klass Sibiri . Novosibirsk , 1986. 355 p., [16] p. of plates : LC Card 86-211294
HD5797.S5 R33 1986

SIBERIA, WESTERN (R.S.F.S.R.) - INDUSTRIES - PLANNING.
Optimizat͡sii͡a perspektivnykh planov razvitii͡a otraslevykh sistem . Novosibirsk , 1979. 163 p. : LC Card 81-130740
HC337.R852 S546 1979

Sibir'--dvadt͡satyĭ vek. Adzhiev, M. Ė. (Murad Ėskanderovich) Sibir'--XX vek /. Moskva , 1983. 252 p., [24] p. of plates : LC Card 83-161484
HC337.R852 S522 1983

Sibir'--XX vek /. Adzhiev, M. Ė. (Murad Ėskanderovich) Moskva , 1983. 252 p., [24] p. of plates : LC Card 83-161484
HC337.R852 S522 1983

Sibir'--20-yĭ vek. Adzhiev, M. Ė. (Murad Ėskanderovich) Sibir'--XX vek /. Moskva , 1983. 252 p., [24] p. of plates : LC Card 83-161484
HC337.R852 S522 1983

Sibirev, A. I. Material'noe stimulirovanie v khozi͡aĭstvennom mekhanizme sotsialisticheskogo obshchestva . Leningrad , 1986. 152 p. ; LC Card 86-175029
HF5549.5.I5 M3385 1986

Sibirien, ein russisches und sowjetisches Entwicklungsproblem / herausgegeben von Gert Leptin. Berlin : Berlin Verlag A. Spitz, c1986. 274 p. : ill. ; 21 cm. (Osteuropaforschung . Bd. 17) Papers presented at the 2nd Interdisziplinäre Fachtagung "Sibirien als Russisches und Sowjetisches Entwicklungsproblem" organized by the Deutsche Gesellschaft für Osteuropakunde and held June 14-15, 1984 in Vlotho. Includes bibliographical references and indexes. ISBN 3-87061-260-6 LC Card 86-229174
1. Siberia (R.S.F.S.R. and Kazakh S.S.R.) - Economic policy - Congresses. 2. Siberia (R.S.F.S.R. and Kazakh S.S.R.) - Economic conditions - Congresses. 3. Siberia (R.S.F.S.R. and Kazakh S.S.R.) - Industries - Congresses. I. Leptin, Gert, 1929-. II. Interdisziplinäre Fachtagung "Sibirien als Russisches und Sowjetisches Entwicklungsproblem" (2nd : 1984 : Vlotho, Germany). III. Deutsche Gesellschaft für Osteuropakunde. IV. Series.
HC336.9.S53 S53 1986

Sibirskiĭ ėnergeticheskiĭ institut. Kononov, I͡U. D. Vlii͡anie ėnergeticheskikh strategiĭ na ėnergopotreblenie /. Irkutsk , 1985. 106 p. : LC Card 86-233835
HD9502.S652 K65 1985

Sibitz, Bernd. Jäggle, Martin. Öffentlichkeitsarbeit 3. Welt in Österreich /. Wien , 1975- v. <1 > ; LC Card 86-234031
HC60 .J344 1975

Sibol ng Agham at Akamang Teknolohiya (Organization). National Secretariat. Cleto, Romeo B. The Ilocos and Cordillera provinces . Baguio City [Philippines] , Manila [1986] xvii, 265 p. : LC Card 87-111697 DDC 330.9599/1 19
HC457.L8 C56 1986

Sicart, Ferran. Bricall, Josep Maria, 1936- Estat autonòmic i finances públiques . [Barcelona] , 1984. 358 p. : ISBN 84-500-9868-8 LC Card 85-106586
HJ1000 .B75 1984 ***NYPL [JLE 86-3989]***

Sicherheitsorientierte Ausbildung von Berufskraftfahren /. Rüter, Gert. Köln [1983] vii, 91 p. : LC Card 83-235527
HD5716.M7952 G327 1983

Sicherung der Altersvorsorge durch Aufgabenteilung zwischen Individualversicherung und gesetzlicher Rentenversicherung : Möglichkeiten einer Neuordnung und gesamtwirtschaftliche Auswirkungen : Gutachten im Auftrag des Gesamtverbandes der Deutschen Versicherungswirtschaft (abgeschlossen 1985) / von Willi Leibfritz ... [et al.]. München : Ifo-Institut für Wirtschaftsforschung, 1986. xi, 242 p. : ill. ; 21 cm. (Ifo Studien zur Finanzpolitik, 0081-7279 . 37) Bibliography: p. 236-242. ISBN 3-88512-017-8 : LC Card 86-163171
1. Old age pensions - Germany, West. 2. Pension trusts - Germany, West. 3. Pensions - Germany, West. I. Leibfritz, Willi. II. Gesamtverband der Deutschen Versicherungswirtschaft (Germany). III. Series.
HD7105.35.G3 S53 1986

Die Sicherung des Fussgängerverkehrs. Köln : Arbeits- und Forschungsgemeinschaft für Strassenverkehr und Verkehrssicherheit, 1976. ii, 169 p. : ill. ; 21 cm. (Buchreihe der Arbeits- und Forschungsgemeinschaft für Strassenverkehr und Verkehrssicherheit, Institut an der Universität zu Köln, AFO . Bd. 29) Papers presented at a meeting sponsored jointly by the International Federation of Pedestrians and the Arbeits- und Forschungsgemeinschaft für Strassenverkehrssicherheit, Universität zu Köln, Sept. 30-Oct. 1, 1975. Includes bibliographical references. CONTENTS. - Zur Verkehrsrechtssprechung bei Fussgängerunfällen / Reinhard Beine -- Charakterisierung und Auswertung von Verkehrsunterrichtsexperimenten mit Kindern / H.H. van der Molen -- Unabwendbare Fussgängerunfälle aus verkehrssicherheitstechnischer Sicht / K. Engels -- Unvermeidbare Fussgängerunfälle aus psychologischer Sicht / L. Moser -- Neue Formen der Kooperation zwischen Wissenschaft, Verbänden und dem Staat bei der Bekämpfung von Strassenverkehrsunfällen / G. Herrmann -- Meinungen und Verhalten der Verkehrsteilnehmer am

Fussgängerstreifen / F.W. Hürlimann -- Beleuchtungsverhältnisse am Fussgängerstreifen / R. Walthert -- Fussgängerfreundliche Wohngebiete / B.W. Bolomey -- Sicherung von Schulwegen / H. Richard. LC Card 86-185084
1. Pedestrians - Germany (West) - Prevention - Congresses. 2. Traffic safety - Germany (West) - Congresses. I. International Federation of Pedestrians. II. Universität zu Köln. Arbeits- und Forschungsgemeinschaft für Strassenverkehr und Verkehrssicherheit. III. Series.
HE5614.5.G3 A7 Bd. 29

Sicherung des Sozialmietwohnungsbestandes /. Fuhrich, Manfred, 1950- Frankfurt am Main , c1986. xxiii, 180, 16 p. : ISBN 3-88129-996-3 LC Card 86-223886
HD7288.78.G3 F84 1986

Sichirollo, Livio. Morale e morali / Livio Sichirollo ; con un saggio di Eric Weil. 1a ed. Roma : Editori riuniti, 1985. 179 p. ; 22 cm. (Nuova biblioteca di cultura. 256) Includes index. "Bibliografia ragionata": p. [71]-168. ISBN 88-359-2798-6 : LC Card 85-233121 DDC 170/.9 19
1. Ethics - History. 2. Social ethics - History. I. Weil, Éric. II. Title.
BJ74 .S53 1985 ***NYPL [JFD 87-941]***

SICILY - COMMERCE - HISTORY.
Abulafia, David. Italy, Sicily, and the Mediterranean, 1100-1400 /. London , 1987. 346 p. in various pagings : ISBN 0-86078-198-4 : LC Card 87-157554 DDC 330.9182/2 19
HF3585 .A29 1987

SICILY - ECONOMIC CONDITIONS.
Bresc, Henri. Un monde méditerranéen . [Roma] , 1986. 2 v. (981 p.) : ISBN 2-7283-0103-4 (set) LC Card 87-139949
HC307.S5 B74 1986

SICILY - ECONOMIC CONDITIONS - 1945-
Busch, Angelika. Migration und psychische Belastung . Berlin , 1983. 351 p. ; ISBN 3-496-00733-8 LC Card 83-193476
HD8458.I8 B87 1983

SICILY - POPULATION - STATISTICS.
Greco, Eugenio. Storia demografica dei comuni siciliani dal 1832 al 1858 /. Palermo [1982] 60, [61] p. ; LC Card 85-103229
HB2270.S5 G74 1982

Storia demografica dei comuni siciliani dal 1862 al 1971 /. Palermo [1979] 294 p. ; LC Card 86-131917
HB2270.S5 S76 1979

SICILY - SOCIAL CONDITIONS.
Bresc, Henri. Un monde méditerranéen . [Roma] , 1986. 2 v. (981 p.) : ISBN 2-7283-0103-4 (set) LC Card 87-139949
HC307.S5 B74 1986

Sicking, Dean. Roadside concrete barriers : warrants and end treatment / by Dean L. Sicking and Hayes E. Ross, Jr. College Station, Tex. : Texas Transportation Institute, Texas A&M University System ; Springfield, Va. : Available through National Technical Information Service, [1985] vii, 60, 64, [51] p. : ill. ; 28 cm. (Research report . 346-1F) "Research study no. 2-8-83-346, concrete safety shaped barrier for roadside application." "Sponsored by Texas State Department of Highways and Public Transportation in cooperation with the U. S. Department of Transportation, Federal Highway Administration." "November 1985." Includes bibliographies. LC Card 86-622864 DDC 380.5 s 625.7/95 19
1. Roads - Guard fences. I. Ross, Hayes E. II. Texas Transportation Institute. III. Series: Research report (Texas Transportation Institute) , 346-1F. IV. Title.
HE203 .T43 no. 346-1F TE228

Sickness in small scale industrial sector /. Jyothi Rani, T. Warangal, Andhra Pradesh , 1985. xii, 258 p. ; LC Card 86-902876 DDC 338.6/42/0954 19
HD2747 .J96 1985

SICKNESS INSURANCE. see **INSURANCE, HEALTH.**

Siddayao, Corazon M.
Energy demand and economic growth : measurement and conceptual issues in policy analysis / Corazon Morales Siddayao. Boulder : Westview Press, 1986. xiv, 127 p. : ill. ; 23 cm. Includes index. Bibliography: p. 109-119. ISBN 0-8133-7154-6 : LC Card 86-906 DDC 333.79/13/091724 19
1. Energy consumption - Developing countries. 2. Energy policy - Developing countries. 3. Developing countries - Economic policy. I. Title.
HD9502.D442 S54 1986
NYPL [JLE 86-3295]

Energy Pricing Policy Workshop (1984 : Bangkok, Thailand) Criteria for energy pricing policy . London , Gaithersburg, MD, USA , 1985. 247 p. : ISBN 0-86010-618-1 : LC Card 86-147259 DDC 333.79/17 19
HD9502.D442 E56 1984

Ṣiddiqi, Muḥammad Iqbal. Model of an Islamic bank / by Muhammad Iqbal Siddiqi. 1st ed. Lahore, Pakistan : Kazi Publications, 1986. 90 p. ; 22 cm. Bibliography: p. 87. Includes index. LC Card 87-931018 DDC 332.1/0917/671 19
1. Banks and banking - Religious aspects - Islam. 2. Economics - Religious aspects - Islam. 3. Islam - Economic aspects. 4. Banks and banking - Islamic countries. I. Title.
HG3368.A6 S54 1986

Ṣiddīqī, Muḥammad Nejātullah, 1931-
Banking and monetary polic[i]es in Islamic economics / [Muhammad Nejat Allah Siddigi]. Khartoum : Faisal Islamic Bank, [between 1983 and 1986] 40 p. ; 21 cm. (Faisal Islamic Bank "Sudan" publications. English series . 2) "Annual lecture, 1983-1403, held on 21.11.1943 [i.e. 1983] at the Freindship [sic] Hall, Khartoum." LC Card 86-980021 DDC 332.1/0917/671 19
1. Banks and banking - Islamic countries. 2. Monetary policy - Islamic countries. I. Bank Fayṣal al-Islāmī al-Sūdānī. II. Series: Faisal Islamic Bank "Sudan" publications. English series , 2. III. Title.
HG3368.A6 S53 1986

Banking without interest / Muhammed Nejatullah Siddiqi. Leicester, UK : Islamic Foundation, c1983. 192 p. ; 22 cm. (Islamic economics series . 5) An English version of the author's original Urdu text: Ghair sūdi bank karī. 1969. Includes bibliographical references and indexes. ISBN 0-86037-119-0 LC Card 86-673953
1. Banks and banking. 2. Interest (Islamic law). I. Series: Islamic economic series , 5. II. Title.
HG1588 .S52x 1983

Sidebottom, Thomas O., 1956- Wortman, Leon A. C programming with business applications /. Blue Ridge Summit, PA , c1987. xii, 231 p. ; ISBN 0-8306-1457-5 : LC Card 86-23090 DDC 005.2/65 19
HF5548.5.C12 W67 1987

Sidell, Scott R. The IMF and third-world political instability : is there a connection? / Scott R. Sidell. New York : St. Martin's Press, 1988. p. cm. Includes bibliographical reference and index. ISBN 0-312-00755-8 : LC Card 87-9880 DDC 332.1/52 19
1. International Monetary Fund. 2. Developing countries - Politics and government. I. Title.
HG3881.5.I58 S53 1988

Siderēs, Euthymios G., 1957- Germanoellēniko lexiko horologias / Euthymiou G. Siderē. Athēna : [s.n.], 1984. 183 p. ; 17 cm. LC Card 86-180116
1. Labor and laboring classes - Dictionaries - German. 2. German language - Dictionaries - Greek. I. Title.
HD4839 .S56 1984

Sideri, S., 1934- Jiménez, Margarita. Historia del desarrollo regional en Colombia /. Bogotá, Colombia , 1985. 338 p. ; ISBN 958-9061-04-4 LC Card 85-242811
HC197 .J57 1985

SIDERPERÚ (ORGANIZATION) - MANAGEMENT - EVALUATION.
Ponce Vega, Luis. El propietario ausente . Lima , 1986. 80 p. ; LC Card 86-221571
HD9524.P44 S565 1986

Sidérurgie et droit de crise / L. Boy ... [et al.]. Paris : Presses universitaires de France, c1983. 207 p. ; 24 cm. (Travaux et recherches du Laboratoire associée no 301, C.N.R.S. - Université de Nice) Includes bibliographical references. CONTENTS. - Dirigisme privé et dirigisme public dans l'industrie sidérurgique / par L. Boy et A. Pirovano -- Une forme spécifique de financement de la sidérurgie / par G. Gourdet -- Nationalisation et industrie sidérurgique / par J.-J. Sueur -- Aspects sociaux de la crise sidérurgique / par M.M. Mohamed Salah -- La politique communautaire face à la crise de la sidérurgie / par P. Mottard. ISBN 2-13-038363-7 : LC Card 84-128216
1. Steel industry and trade - Government policy - France. 2. Steel industry and trade - France. 3. Steel industry and trade - Government policy - European Economic Community countries. I. Boy, L. (Laurence). II. Series.
HD9522.6 .S53 1983

Sidorov, A. I. (Alekseĭ Ivanovich) Kompleksnyĭ analiz proektnogo proizvodstva na primere promyshlennogo proektirovaniia / A.I. Sidorov. Moskva : Ėkonomika, 1985. 197, [3] p. : ill. ; 20 cm. Bibliography: p. 195-[198] LC Card 86-129875
1. Construction industry - Soviet Union - Planning. 2. Construction industry - Soviet Union - Management. I. Title.
HD9715.S72 S57 1985

Siebel, Walter. Gewerbeentwicklung und Gewerbepolitik in der Grossstadtregion /. Gerlingen , c1987. 390 p., [3] leaves of plates : ISBN 3-88350-596-X LC Card 87-146643 DDC 332.6/732243 19
HC290.5.I53 G4797 1987

Sieben, Günter. Eugen Schmalenbach . Stuttgart , 1984. xvii, 478 p. : ISBN 3-8202-0295-1 LC Card 84-215889
HF5616.G3 E93 1984

Siebert, Horst, 1938-
Angebotsentwicklung und Preisbildung natürlicher Ressourcen /. München , 1986. vii, 148, 10 p. : ISBN 3-486-26171-1 LC Card 86-182074
HC59 .A794 1986

Aussenhandelstheorie. Siebert, Horst, 1938- Aussenwirtschaft / Horst Siebert. 3., völlig neubearbeitete und wesentlich erw. Aufl. Stuttgart , c1984. xi, 303 p. : ISBN 3-437-40149-1 (pbk.) LC Card 87-672497
HF1007 .S49x 1984

Aussenwirtschaft / Horst Siebert. 3., völlig neubearbeitete und wesentlich erw. Aufl. Stuttgart : G. Fischer, c1984. xi, 303 p. : ill. ; 19 cm. (Grundwissen der Ökonomik. Volkswirtschaftslehre) Uni-Taschenbücher ; 212 Earlier eds. issued under title: Aussenhandelstheorie. Bibliography: p. 292-298. Includes index. ISBN 3-437-40149-1 (pbk.) LC Card 87-672497
1. Commerce. I. Siebert, Horst, 1938- Aussenhandelstheorie. II. Title. III. Series.
HF1007 .S49x 1984

Economics of the environment : theory and policy / Horst Siebert.2nd, rev. and enl. ed. Berlin ; New York : Springer-Verlag, c1987. xiv, 273 p. : ill. ; 24 cm. Bibliography: p. [239]-266. Includes index. ISBN 0-387-17283-1 (U. S.) LC Card 87-4703 DDC 363.7 19
1. Environmental policy - Economic aspects. I. Title.
HC79.E5 S437 1987

Regional environmental policy . New York , c1979. xii, 290 p. : ISBN 0-8147-7805-4 : LC Card 79-2058 DDC 301.31
HC79.E5 R44 ***NYPL [JLE 80-1854]***

Siebold, Thomas, 1953- Strukturelemente der Weltgesellschaft . Frankfurt am Main , 1981. v, 356 p. : ISBN 3-7875-1727-8 LC Card 83-190809
HF1411 .S845 1981

Siedlungsformen und soziale Kosten : vergleichende Analyse der sozialen Kosten unterschiedlicher Siedlungsformen / Dieter Hezel ... [et al.]. Frankfurt am Main ; New York : P. Lang, c1984. vi, 219 p., [1] folded leaf of plates : ill. ; 21 cm. (Beiträge zur kommunalen und regionalen Planung, 0721-2976 . 7) Bibliography: p. 190-215. ISBN 3-8204-5402-0 LC Card 85-190162
1. Housing - Environmental aspects - Germany (West). I. Hezel, Dieter. II. Series.
HD7339.A3 S59 1984

Siedlungsstruktur . Flückiger, Hans. Bern , c1985. 118 p. : ISBN 3-258-03529-6 : LC Card 86-134805
HN603.5 .F58 1985 ***NYPL [JLE 86-3789]***

Siedlungsverband Ruhrkohlenbezirk.
Programmpaket zur Verbesserung der Rahmenbedingungen für die Wirtschaft im Ruhrgebiet . Essen [197-?] 42 p. : LC Card 85-153643
HC288.R8 P76 1970z

Siedt, Veronika. Roesler, Jörg. Wirtschaftswachstum in der Industrie der DDR, 1945-1970 /. Berlin , 1986. 280 p. ; ISBN 3-05-000074-0 LC Card 86-196020
HC290.78 .R64 1986

Sieforth, Jeannine Morris. Medicare savings and sense : a practical, complete guide and reference manual / Jeannine Morris Sieforth.1st ed. Manzanita, Or. : Duo Associates, c1986. xviii, 181 p. : ill. ; 28 cm. Cover title: Medicare savings & sense. Bibliography: p. 171-173. Includes index. ISBN 0-9617625-0-0 (pbk.) LC Card 86-72651 DDC 344.73/0226 347.304226 19
1. Medicare - Handbooks, manuals, etc. I. Title. II. Title: Medicare savings & sense.
HD7102.U4 S525 1986

Siegel, Eric S. The Arthur Young business plan guide / Eric S. Siegel, Loren A. Schultz, Brian R. Ford ; edited by David C. Carney. New York : Wiley, c1987. xii, 184 p. ; 24 cm. Includes index. ISBN 0-471-85885-4 LC Card 86-32622 DDC 658.4/012 19
1. New business enterprises. I. Schultz, Loren A. II. Ford, Brian R. III. Carney, David C. IV. Title.
HD62.5 .S556 1987

Siegel, Joel G. Shim, Jae K. Handbook of financial analysis, forecasting, and modeling /. Englewood Cliffs, NJ , c1988. p. cm. ISBN 0-13-377995-5 : LC Card 87-14325 DDC 658.1/5 19
HG4011 .S46 1988

Siegel, Laurence. Personnel and organizational psychology / Laurence Siegel, Irving M. Lane. 2nd ed. Homewood, Ill. : Irwin, 1987. xviii, 617 p. : ill. ; 24 cm. (The Irwin series in management and the behavioral sciences) Includes bibliographies and indexes. ISBN 0-256-03369-2 LC Card 86-82591 DDC 158.7 19
1. Psychology, Industrial. I. Lane, Irving M. II. Title.
HF5548.8 .S512 1987

Siegelbaum, Lewis H. Stakhanovism and the politics of productivity in the USSR, 1935-1941 / Lewis H. Siegelbaum. Cambridge ; New York : Cambridge University Press, 1988. xv, 326 p. : ill. ; 22 cm. (Soviet and East European studies) Bibliography: p. 309-320. Includes index. ISBN 0-521-34548-0 LC Card 87-25605 DDC 331.11/8/0947 19
1. Stakhanov movement - History. 2. Industrial productivity - Soviet Union. 3. Industrial relations - Soviet Union - History. 4. Soviet Union - Economic policy - 1938-1942. I. Title.
HC340.S6 S515 1988

Siegenthaler, Jürg K., 1939- Konflikte der Industrialisierung : Industrie, Raum und Gesellschaft in Glarus und Scranton, 1840-1914 / Jürg K. Siegenthaler. Bern ; New York : P. Lang, c1985. 249 p. : ill. ; 23 cm. Includes bibliographical references. ISBN 3-261-04012-2 LC Card 85-226977
1. Glarus (Canton : Switzerland) - Industries - History. 2. Social structure - Switzerland - Glarus (Canton) - History. 3. Glarus (Canton : Switzerland) - Social conditions. 4. Scranton (Pa.) - Industries - History. 5. Social structure - Pennsylvania - Scranton - History. 6. Scranton (Pa.) - Social conditions. I. Title.
HC398.G55 S54 1985

Sieger. Zeppelinpost Spezial-Katalog / Sieger. 20. Aufl. Lorch/Württemberg : Sieger-Verlag, c1981. 384 p. : ill. ; 21 cm. Title on cover: Zeppelin Post Katalog. "Begriffsbestimmungen" also in English, French, Italian, and Spanish. LC Card 83-214233
1. Postage-stamps - Topics - Graf Zeppelin (Airship) - Catalogs. I. Title. II. Title: Zeppelin Post Katalog.
HE6183.G735 S54 1981

Sieger (Firm) Weltpostverein (UPU) : Spezial-Katalog der Sondermarken zu den Jubiläen des Weltpostvereins, der Sondermarken zu den Weltpostkongressen ... / Sieger.1. Aufl. Lorch/Württemberg : Sieger-Verlag, c1982. 408 p. : ill. ; 22 cm. LC Card 83-224689
1. Universal Postal Union. 2. Commemorative postage stamps - Catalogs. I. Title. II. Title: Spezial-Katalog der Sondermarken zu den Jubiläen des Weltpostvereins.
HE6271 .S55 1982

Siegfried, John J. The Economics of firm size, market structure, and social performance . [Washington, D.C.?] , 1980. viii, 388 p. ; LC Card 81-600757 DDC 338.6/4/0973 19
HD60.5.U5 E26 ***NYPL [JLF 86-704]***

Siegfried, Klaus-Jörg, 1940- Rüstungsproduktion und Zwangsarbeit im Volkswagenwerk, 1939-1945 : eine Dokumentation / Klaus-Jörg Siegfried. Frankfurt ; New York : Campus, c1986. 239 p. : ill. ; 21 cm. (Wolfsburger Beiträge zur Stadtgeschichte und Stadtentwicklung) Bibliography: p. 237-239. ISBN 3-593-33765-7 LC Card 87-133375 DDC 338.4/76234/0943 19
1. Munitions - Germany - History - 20th century. 2. Industrial mobilization - Germany - History - 20th century. 3. Automobile industry - Germany - Military aspects - History - 20th century. 4. World War, 1939-1945 - Germany - Equipment and supplies. 5. Volkswagenwerk - History - 20th century. 6. Forced labor - Germany - History - 20th century. 7. Prisoners of war - Germany - History - 20th century. I. Title. II. Series.
HD9743.G48 S56 1986

Siegmann, Frank, 1956- Kurzfristprognosen für die Textilwirtschaft anhand von Bestimmungsfaktoren für Saisonschwankungen / Frank Siegmann. Frankfurt am Main ; New York : P. Lang, c1986. xxxi, 386 p. : ill. ; 21 cm. (Schriften zur Textilwirtschaft, 0463-7585 . Bd. 39) Bibliography: p. 374-386. ISBN 3-8204-9647-5 LC Card 86-233371
1. Textile industry - Germany (West) - Seasonal variations. 2. Textile industry - Germany (West) - Forecasting. I. Title. II. Series.
HD9850.1 .M58 Bd. 39 HD9863.5

SIEMENS & HALSKE - HISTORY.
Goetzeler, Herbert. Wilhelm und Carl Friedrich von Siemens . Stuttgart , 1986. 131 p. : ISBN 3-515-04558-9 LC Card 86-141456
HD9695.G43 S514 1986

Peschke, Hans-Peter von, 1951- Elektroindustrie und Staatsverwaltung am Beispiel Siemens, 1847-1914 /. Frankfurt am Main , Bern , c1981. 393 p. : ISBN 3-8204-5902-2 LC Card 81-141438
HD9697.A3 G35 1981

SIEMENS, CARL FRIEDRICH, 1872-1941.
Goetzeler, Herbert. Wilhelm und Carl Friedrich von Siemens . Stuttgart , 1986. 131 p. : ISBN 3-515-04558-9 LC Card 86-141456
HD9695.G43 S514 1986

SIEMENS, WILHELM VON, 1855-1919.
Goetzeler, Herbert. Wilhelm und Carl Friedrich von Siemens . Stuttgart , 1986. 131 p. : ISBN 3-515-04558-9 LC Card 86-141456
HD9695.G43 S514 1986

Siemers, Werner, 1956- Mayer, Hans, 1951- Energie für die Armen? . Saarbrücken , Fort Lauderdale , 1984. 195 p. : ISBN 3-88156-288-5 : LC Card 85-199309
HD9502.I42 M38 1984

Siemianowski, Andrzej. Fakty, prawa, decyzje : rozprawy o konwencjonalistycznej filozofii nauki / Andrzej Siemianowski. [Wrocław] : Wydawn. Uczelniane Akademii Ekonomicznej we Wrocławiu, 1983. 103 p. ; 24 cm. (Prace naukowe Akademii Ekonomicznej im. Oskara Langego we Wrocławiu . nr. 245. nr. 17) Summary in English, French, and Russian. Limited ed. of 172 copies. Bibliography: p. [97]-100. LC Card 85-113022
1. Science - Philosophy. 2. Poincaré, Henri, 1854-1912 - Philosophy. 3. Duhem, Pierre Maurice Marie, 1861-1916 - Philosophy. I. Series: Prace naukowe Akademii Ekonomicznej imienia Oskara Langego we Wrocławiu , nr. 245. II. Title.
HB9 .B7522 nr. 245 Q175

Sierila, Pentti, 1934- Corporate planning and strategies in forest industries / by Pentti Sierila ; translated by Anna-Maija Sierila. Atlanta, GA, USA : Tappi Press, c1987. vii, 138 p. : ill. ; 23 cm. Translated from Finnish. Bibliography: p. 135-138. ISBN 0-89852-441-5 (pbk.) LC Card 87-50439 DDC 634.9/8/068 19
1. Forest products industry - Management. 2. Lumber trade - Management. 3. Forest products industry - Planning. 4. Lumber trade - Planning. I. Title.
HD9750.5 .S54 1987

Sierra Leone. Central Statistics Office. Directory of business and industry for Western Area and multiunit firms. Freetown [1968] 67 p. ; LC Card 87-112242
HC1065 .D57 1968

SIERRA LEONE - COMMERCE - DIRECTORIES.
Directory of business and industry for Western Area and multiunit firms. Freetown [1968] 67 p. ; LC Card 87-112242
HC1065 .D57 1968

SIERRA LEONE COUNCIL OF LABOUR.
Sierra Leone. Taju-Deen Commission of Inquiry. Report of the Taju-Deen Commission of Inquiry into the status, administration, and activities of the Sierra Leone Labour Congress from 1976 following the amalgamation of the then Sierra Leone Labour Congress and the Sierra Leone Council of Labour, and to inquire into all aspects of industrial relations in Sierra Leone and to make recommendations for any improvements which it may consider necessary. [Freetown] [198-] vi, 149 leaves ; LC Card 87-118833
HD8833.A5 S57 1980

SIERRA LEONE - ECONOMIC CONDITIONS.
Büscher, Ludger. Integrated rural development . Hamburg , 1984. xx, 238 p. : ISBN 3-87895-261-9 (pbk.) LC Card 86-672442
HD2146.5 .B87x 1984 ***NYPL [JLD 86-2789]***

SIERRA LEONE - ECONOMIC CONDITIONS - TO 1896.
White, E. Frances. Sierra Leone's settler women traders . Ann Arbor , c1987. xi, 168 p. : ISBN 0-472-10080-7 (alk. paper) : LC Card 86-24997 DDC 331.4/81381/09664 19
HF3933 .W47 1987

SIERRA LEONE - ECONOMIC CONDITIONS - 1961- - CONGRESSES.
National Seminar on Population, Employment, and Development Planning in Sierra Leone (1980 : Freetown, Sierra Leone) Contributed papers to the National Seminar on Population, Employment, and Development Planning in Sierra Leone . Freetown, Sierra Leone , <[1980-. v. <2 > : LC Card 87-163849 DDC 304.6/0966/4 19
HB3666.9.A3 N38 1980

SIERRA LEONE - ECONOMIC POLICY - CONGRESSES.
Rapporteur's report . [Freetown , 1978?] 70 leaves ; LC Card 87-401796 DDC 338.966/4 19
HC1065 .R36 1978

Sierra Leone. Industrial Development Dept. Implementation plan for the Growth Centre Programme. Free Town : Ministry of Trade & Industry, Industrial Development Dept., Sierra Leone Govt., [1985] 2, 57 leaves : forms ; 30 cm. LC Card 87-119663 DDC 338.6/42/09664 19
1. Small business - Government policy - Sierra Leone. I. Title.
HD2346.S5 S54 1985

SIERRA LEONE - INDUSTRIES - DIRECTORIES.
Directory of business and industry for Western Area and multiunit firms. Freetown [1968] 67 p. ; LC Card 87-112242
HC1065 .D57 1968

SIERRA LEONE LABOUR CONGRESS.
Sierra Leone. Taju-Deen Commission of Inquiry. Report of the Taju-Deen Commission of Inquiry into the status, administration, and activities of the Sierra Leone Labour Congress from 1976 following the amalgamation of the then Sierra Leone Labour Congress and the Sierra Leone Council of Labour, and to inquire into all aspects of industrial relations in Sierra Leone and to make recommendations for any improvements which it may consider necessary. [Freetown] [198-] vi, 149 leaves ; LC Card 87-118833
HD8833.A5 S57 1980

Sierra Leone. Ministry of Development and Economic Planning. Population Section.
National Seminar on Population, Employment, and Development Planning in Sierra Leone (1980 : Freetown, Sierra Leone) Contributed papers to the National Seminar on Population, Employment, and Development Planning in Sierra Leone . Freetown, Sierra Leone , <[1980-. v. <2 > : LC Card 87-163849 DDC 304.6/0966/4 19
HB3666.9.A3 N38 1980

Sierra Leone. Ministry of Foreign Affairs.
Rapporteur's report . [Freetown , 1978?] 70 leaves ; LC Card 87-401796 DDC 338.966/4 19
HC1065 .R36 1978

SIERRA LEONE - POLITICS AND GOVERNMENT - 1961- - CONGRESSES.
Rapporteur's report . [Freetown , 1978?] 70 leaves ; LC Card 87-401796 DDC 338.966/4 19
HC1065 .R36 1978

SIERRA LEONE - POPULATION - CONGRESSES.
National Seminar on Population, Employment,

and Development Planning in Sierra Leone (1980 : Freetown, Sierra Leone) Contributed papers to the National Seminar on Population, Employment, and Development Planning in Sierra Leone . Freetown, Sierra Leone , <[1980-. v. <2 > : LC Card 87-163849 DDC 304.6/0966/4 19
HB3666.9.A3 N38 1980

SIERRA LEONE - RURAL CONDITIONS.
Okai, Matthew. Rural poverty and alleviation measures in Sierra Leone /. [Rome] , 1983. 91 p. : LC Card 87-400417 DDC 338.1/8/664 19
HC1065.Z9 P66 1983

SIERRA LEONE - SOCIAL CONDITIONS - 1961- - CONGRESSES.
National Seminar on Population, Employment, and Development Planning in Sierra Leone (1980 : Freetown, Sierra Leone) Contributed papers to the National Seminar on Population, Employment, and Development Planning in Sierra Leone . Freetown, Sierra Leone , <[1980-. v. <2 > : LC Card 87-163849 DDC 304.6/0966/4 19
HB3666.9.A3 N38 1980

SIERRA LEONE - SOCIAL POLICY - CONGRESSES.
Rapporteur's report . [Freetown , 1978?] 70 leaves ; LC Card 87-401796 DDC 338.966/4 19
HC1065 .R36 1978

Sierra Leone. Taju-Deen Commission of Inquiry. Report of the Taju-Deen Commission of Inquiry into the status, administration, and activities of the Sierra Leone Labour Congress from 1976 following the amalgamation of the then Sierra Leone Labour Congress and the Sierra Leone Council of Labour, and to inquire into all aspects of industrial relations in Sierra Leone and to make recommendations for any improvements which it may consider necessary. [Freetown] : Sierra Leone Government, [198-] vi, 149 leaves ; 29 cm. "Commissions of inquiry act, cap. 54"--Cover. LC Card 87-118833
1. Sierra Leone Labour Congress. 2. Sierra Leone Council of Labour. 3. Industrial relations - Sierra Leone. I. Title.
HD8833.A5 S57 1980

Sierra Leone's settler women traders . White, E. Frances. Ann Arbor , c1987. xi, 168 p. : ISBN 0-472-10080-7 (alk. paper) : LC Card 86-24997 DDC 331.4/81381/09664 19
HF3933 .W47 1987

Siesto, Vincenzo. Barberis, Corrado. Agricoltura e strati sociali /. Milano, Italy , c1986. 269 p. ; LC Card 86-214233
HD1536.I8 B328 1986

Sieverts, Thomas. Gewerbeentwicklung und Gewerbepolitik in der Grossstadtregion /. Gerlingen , c1987. 390 p., [3] leaves of plates : ISBN 3-88350-596-X LC Card 87-146643 DDC 332.6/732243 19
HC290.5.I53 G4797 1987

Siewert, Hans-Jörg. Kunert-Schroth, Heidrun. Jugendarbeitslosigkeit, lokale Ausprägungen und kommunale Strategien . Berlin , 1987. 172 p. ; ISBN 3-88118-135-0 LC Card 87-409103 DDC 331.3/412/0943 19
HD6276.G4 K86 1987

Sigaud, Lygia. Efeitos sociais de grandes projetos hidrelétricos : as barragens de Sobradinho e Machadinho / Lygia Sigaud. [Rio de Janeiro] : Programa de Pós-Graduação em Antropologia Social, Museu Nacional--UFRJ, 1986. 116 p. ; 30 cm. (Comunicação. no. 9) Bibliography: p. 110-116. LC Card 87-120281 DDC 333.91/4 19
1. Water resources development - Social aspects - Brazil - São Francisco River Region. 2. Sobradinho Dam (Brazil) - Social aspects. 3. Electric power production - Brazil - São Francisco River Region. 4. Water resources development - Social aspects - Brazil - Uruguay River Region. 5. Machadinho (Project : Brazil) - Social aspects. 6. Electric power production - Uruguay River Region. I. Series: Comunicação (Brazil. Museu Nacional. Programa de Pós-Graduação em Antropologia Social) , no. 9. II. Title.
HD1696.B84 S346 1986

Siglo de publicidad gráfica en Colombia. 1880-1980, un siglo de publicidad gráfica en Colombia /. [Bogotá?] [1984] 286 p. : LC Card 84-202348 DDC 659.1/09861 19
HF5813.C63 A16 1984
NYPL [3-MDW+ 86-17]

Signalų apdorojimo skaitmeniniai metodai ir algoritmai. TSifrovye metody i algoritmy obrabotki signalov . Vil'nius , 1986. 120 p. : LC Card 86-232937
HD38 .S715 vyp. 73 TK5102.5

The significance of the women's movement to marketing . Venkatesh, Alladi. New York , 1985. 209 p. ; ISBN 0-03-069588-0 (alk. paper) : LC Card 85-19106 DDC 658.8/348 19
HF5415.3 .V46 1985 *NYPL [JLE 86-1081]*

Significant issues series .
(v. 6, no. 17) Ullman, Harlan. Forecasts for U. S. maritime industries in 1989 . Washington, D.C. , c1984. ix, 42 p. : ISBN 0-89206-069-7 (pbk.) LC Card 84-27501 DDC 338.4/76238/0973 19
VM299.6 .U45 1984 *NYPL [JLD 87-155]*

Significant issues series, 0736-7136 .
(v. 9, no. 4) Stoga, Alan. Breaking the economic impasse . Washington, D.C. , c1987. viii, 48 p. ; ISBN 0-89206-104-9 (pbk.) LC Card 87-14682 DDC 338.9 19
HC59 .B73 1987

Significant issues series, 0736-7146 .
(v. 9, no. 1) Hilton, Robert, 1927- U. S. maritime industries--down for the third time? /. Washington, D.C. , c1987. vi, 60 p. : ISBN 0-89206-099-9 (pbk.) LC Card 86-31768 DDC 387.5/0973 19
HE745 .H66 1987

Signora, A. (Andre) L'Industria siderurgica . Milano [1986] 193 p. : ISBN 88-14-00787-X : LC Card 86-222572
HD9510.5 .I473 1986

Šik, Ota, 1919- Ein Wirtschaftssystem der Zukunft / Ota Šik. Berlin ; New York : Springer-Verlag, c1985. 202 p. ; 25 cm. Includes bibliographical references. ISBN 0-387-15137-0 (U. S.) LC Card 85-199175
1. Comparative economics. I. Title.
HB90 .S56 1985

SIKHIM (INDIA) - CENSUS, 1981.
Census of India, 1981. Delhi , <[1982]-1985. v. in : LC Card 87-915025 DDC 304.6/0954/167021 19
HA4587.S55 C46 1982

Síklaky, István. Koncepció és kritika . Budapest , c1985. 387 p. ; ISBN 963-14-0359-9 : LC Card 86-104222
HB615 .K66 1985

Sikos, T. Tamás. Beluszky, Pál. Magyarország falutipusai /. Budapest , 1982. 167 p. : ISBN 963-7321-96-9 LC Card 84-159502
HD640.5.Z7 B44 1982

Silaev, E. D. Lipko, A. G. (Alekseĭ Gennad'evich) Proizvodstvo i potreblenie v regione /. Moskva , 1986. 142 p. : LC Card 86-211374
HC336.25 .L56 1986

Silberer, Günter. Warentest und Konsument . Frankfurt/Main , New York , c1984. 268 p. : ISBN 3-593-33295-7 LC Card 84-150919
HF1040.9.G3 W37 1984

Silbert, Alfred. Economie mondialiste et mutations politiques : dialogue sur la France du siècle / Alfred Silbert ; préface de Michel Jobert. Paris : Anthropos, c1985. 212 p. ; 23 cm. Includes bibliographical references. ISBN 2-7157-1114-X : LC Card 85-221451 DDC 330.944/08 19
1. France - Economic conditions - 20th century. 2. France - Politics and government - 20th century. I. Title.
HC276 .S52 1985

SILESIA (GERMANY) - ECONOMIC CONDITIONS.
Wolffsohn, Seew, 1916- Wirtschaftliche und soziale Entwicklungen in Brandenburg, Preussen, Schlesien und Oberschlesien in den Jahren 1640-1853, Frühindustrialisierung in Oberschlesien /. Frankfurt am Main , New York , c1985. 182 p., [2] p. of folded plates : ISBN 3-8204-8197-4 LC Card 85-219539
HC288.B68 W65 1985

SILESIA (GERMANY) - SOCIAL CONDITIONS.
Wolffsohn, Seew, 1916- Wirtschaftliche und soziale Entwicklungen in Brandenburg, Preussen, Schlesien und Oberschlesien in den Jahren 1640-1853, Frühindustrialisierung in Oberschlesien /. Frankfurt am Main , New York , c1985. 182 p., [2] p. of folded plates : ISBN 3-8204-8197-4 LC Card 85-219539
HC288.B68 W65 1985

Silgado, Manuel Román de. see **Román de Silgado, Manuel.**

SILICATE INDUSTRY - GERMANY (WEST) - HISTORY.
Goosmann, Cornelia. Ein Jahrhundert Wasserglas von Henkel /. Düsseldorf , c1985. 76 p. : ISBN 3-923324-67-8 LC Card 86-171258
HD9654.9.H444 G66 1985

La Silicon Valley, un marché aux puces /. Azouaou, Alain. Paris , c1986. 237 p. : ISBN 2-85956-494-2 : LC Card 86-217069
HD9696.A3 U516 1986

Silin, V. A. (Vladimir Andreevich) Ėkonomika--poisk, ėksperiment / V.A. Silin, A.S. Sukhov, G.T. Vlasenkov. Moskva : Izd-vo "Znanie", 1978. 109 p. ; 20 cm. Includes bibliographical references. LC Card 81-167075
1. Soviet Union - Economic conditions - 1976-. 2. Soviet Union - Economic policy - 1981-. I. Sukhov, A. S. (Alekseĭ Sergeevich). II. Vlasenkov, G. T. (Gennadiĭ Timofeevich). III. Title.
HC336.25 .S557 1978

SILK INDUSTRY - CHINA - CHUNG-SHAN HSIEN (KWANGTUNG PROVINCE) - HISTORY.
So, Alvin Y., 1953- The South China silk district . Albany, N.Y. , c1986. xii, 206 p. : ISBN 0-88706-322-5 LC Card 86-14575 DDC 338.4/7677391/095127 19
HD9926.C63 S637 1986
NYPL [JLE 87-1448]

SILK INDUSTRY - CHINA - NAN-HAI HSIEN - HISTORY.
So, Alvin Y., 1953- The South China silk district . Albany, N.Y. , c1986. xii, 206 p. : ISBN 0-88706-322-5 LC Card 86-14575 DDC 338.4/7677391/095127 19
HD9926.C63 S637 1986
NYPL [JLE 87-1448]

SILK INDUSTRY - CHINA - SHUN-TE HSIEN (KWANGTUNG PROVINCE) - HISTORY.
So, Alvin Y., 1953- The South China silk district . Albany, N.Y. , c1986. xii, 206 p. : ISBN 0-88706-322-5 LC Card 86-14575 DDC 338.4/7677391/095127 19
HD9926.C63 S637 1986
NYPL [JLE 87-1448]

SILK INDUSTRY - FRANCE - LYON - HISTORY.
Lyon, l'argent, le commerce et la soie /. Lyon , c1986. 138 p. : ISBN 2-904638-63-6 : LC Card 86-184131
HC278.L9 L96 1986

SILK INDUSTRY - ITALY - LECCO - HISTORY - 18TH CENTURY.
Sala, Edmondo. All'origine della borghesia lecchese . Lecco [1983] 83 p. : LC Card 85-190056
HD9765.I72 L437 1983

SILK INDUSTRY - SWITZERLAND - BASEL - HISTORY.
Fink, Paul. Geschichte der Basler Bandindustrie 1550-1800 /. Basel , 1983. 216 p. : ISBN 3-7190-0836-3 LC Card 83-220231 DDC 338.4/767776 19
HD9929.R6 S94 1983 *NYPL [JLE 86-2781]*

SILK WORKERS' STRIKE, PATERSON, N.J., 1913.
Golin, Steve. The fragile bridge . Philadelphia , 1988. p. cm. ISBN 0-87722-534-6 (alk. paper) : LC Card 87-24356 DDC 331.89/287739/0974924 19
HD5325.T42 1913 .P383 1988

SILK WORKERS' STRIKE, PATERSON, N.J., 1913 - HISTORY.
Tripp, Anne Huber, 1934- The I.W.W. and the Paterson silk strike of 1913 /. Urbana , c1987. xiv, 317 p., [6] p. of plates : ISBN 0-252-01382-4 LC Card 86-24989 DDC 331.89/287739/0974924 19
HD5325.T42 1913 .P387 1987

Silkman, Richard H. Subsidizing inefficiency : a study of state aid and local government productivity / by Richard H. Silkman and Dennis R. Young ; with the assistance of

Robert Lipp. New York : Praeger, 1985. xviii, 101 p.: ill. ; 25 cm. Includes index. Bibliography: p. 89-95. ISBN 0-03-000662-7 (alk. paper) : LC Card 84-26628 DDC 336.1/85 19
1. Grants-in-aid - United States - States. 2. State-local relations - United States. 3. Government productivity - United States. 4. Local government - United States. I. Young, Dennis, 1943-. II. Lipp, Robert. III. Title.
HJ275 .S53 1985 ***NYPL [JLE 85-2261]***

Sillaste, ĪU. Kh. Voprosy razvitiia obsluzhivaniia naseleniia . Tallin , 1985. 140 p. : LC Card 85-158428
HD9986.S683 E888 1985

Sillers, Donald A. Dyck, John H. South Korea . Washington, D.C. [1986] v, 74 p. : LC Card 86-602006 DDC 338.1 s 382/.41/095195 19
HD1411 .F59 no. 216 HD9005

Silliphant, Leigh. Making $70,000 a year as a self-employed manufacturer's representative / Leigh and Sureleigh Silliphant. Englewood Cliffs, N.J. : Prentice-Hall, c1984. 204 p. ; 23 cm. Includes index. ISBN 0-13-547687-9 (case) LC Card 83-16147 DDC 658.8/5 19
1. Manufacturers' agents - United States. 2. Self-employed - United States. I. Silliphant, Sureleigh. II. Title. III. Title: Making seventy thousand dollars a year as a self-employed manufacturer's representative.
HF5422 .S54 1984 ***NYPL [JLE 86-2636]***

Silliphant, Sureleigh. Silliphant, Leigh. Making $70,000 a year as a self-employed manufacturer's representative /. Englewood Cliffs, N.J. , c1984. 204 p. ; ISBN 0-13-547687-9 (case) LC Card 83-16147 DDC 658.8/5 19
HF5422 .S54 1984 ***NYPL [JLE 86-2636]***

SILOS - BOLIVIA - PLANNING - CASE STUDIES.
Estudio de factibilidad para una cadena de silos intercomunales de papa . [Sucre, Bolivia] 1982. 178 p., [2] leaves of plates : LC Card 83-202593 DDC 338.1/6 19
HD9235.P82 B525 1982
NYPL [JLF 87-711]

Silsilah-yi maṭbū'āt-i Markaz-i Taḥqīq-i Diyāl Singh Ṭrasṭ Lā'ibrerī .
(11) Khan, Muhammad Akram. Bilā sūdī bainkārī /. Lāhaur [1983] 56 p. ; LC Card 83-931274
HG3290.5.A6 K43 1983

Silsilat dalīl al-mustathmir fī al-aqṭār al-'Arabīyah / al-Mu'assasah al-'Arabīyah li-Ḍamān al-Istithmār. al-Kuwayt : al-Mu'assasah, <[1985]- > v. <2, 4-5, 7 > : col. ill. ; 24 cm. Includes bibliographical references. CONTENTS. - -- 2. Dalīl al-mustathmir fī al-Jumhūrīyah al-Tūnisīyah -- 4. Dalīl al-mustathmir fī Jumhūrīyat al-Yaman al-Dīmuqrāṭīyah al-Sha'bīyah -- 5. Dalīl al-mustathmir fī Jumhūrīyat al-Sūdān al-Dīmuqrāṭīyah -- 7.Dalīl al-mustathmir fī al-Jumhūrīyah al-'Arabīyah al Sūrīyah. LC Card 86-205217
1. Investments, Foreign - Arab countries. 2. Arab countries - Economic conditions. I. Inter-Arab Investment Guarantee Corporation.
HG5816.A3 S55 1985

Silton, Lawrence C. How to buy or sell the closely held corporation / Lawrence C. Silton. Englewood Cliffs, N.J. : Prentice-Hall, c1987. xi, 308 p. ; 25 cm. Includes index. ISBN 0-13-403064-8 LC Card 87-14433 DDC 658.1/6 19
1. Close corporations - Valuation. 2. Close corporations - Taxation - United States. 3. Close corporations - United States. I. Title.
HG4028.V3 S54 1987

Silva, Adroaldo Moura da. Emprego e preços no curto prazo / Adroaldo Moura da Silva. 2a ed. São Paulo, SP (C.P. 11474, 01000 São Paulo, SP) : IPE, USP, 1983. 94 p. ; 21 cm. (Ensaios econômicos . 02) Relatórios de pesquisa / [IPE, USP, Instituto de Pesquisas Econômicas da Faculdade de Economia e Administração da Universidade de São Paulo] Bibliography: p. 91-94.
1. Economic policy - Mathematical models. 2. Employment (Economic theory) - Mathematical models. 3. Prices - Mathematical models. I. Series: Ensaios econômicos (Universidade de São Paulo. Instituto de Pesquisas Econômicas) , 2. II. Title.
NYPL [JLD 86-3819]

Silva, Angela Inês Gandra e. Os acordos SENAI/empresa : um incentivo à formação profissional / Angela Inês Gandra e Silva. Rio de Janeiro-RJ-Brasil : Serviço Nacional de Aprendizagem Industrial, Departamento Nacional, Diretoria Técnica, Divisão de Pesquisas, Estudos e Avaliação, 1985. xvii, 97 p. ; 21 cm. (Coleção Albano Franco . 2) Summary in English. Bibliography: p. 95-97. LC Card 86-176735
1. Occupational training - Brazil. 2. Brazil. Servico Nacional de Aprendizagem Industrial. 3. Occupational training - Law and legislation - Brazil. I. Title. II. Series.
HD5715.5.B68 S55 1985

Silva, Armando Corrêa da. O litoral norte do Estado de São Paulo : (formação de uma região periférica) / Armando Corrêa da Silva. São Paulo : Instituto de Geografia, Universidade de São Paulo, 1975. 273 p. : ill., maps ; 26 cm. (Série Teses e monografias . no. 20) Originally presented as the author's thesis (doctoral)--Universidade de São Paulo. Bibliography: p. 265-273. LC Card 85-134276
1. São Sebastião Region (São Paulo, Brazil) - Economic conditions. 2. São Sebastião Region (São Paulo, Brazil) - Rural conditions. 3. Urbanization - Brazil - São Sebastião Region (São Paulo). 4. São Sebastião Region (São Paulo, Brazil) - Population. 5. Land use, Rural - Brazil - São Sebastião Region (São Paulo). I. Title. II. Series.
HC189.S343 S58 1975

Silva, Fábio Gomes da. Micro e macroeconomia : um enfoque crítico / Fábio Gomes da Silva. Petrópolis : Vozes, 1983. 125 p. : ill. ; 21 cm. Bibliography: p. 121-125. LC Card 83-202597
1. Oligopolies. 2. Prices. 3. Economic policy. I. Title.
HD2757.3 .S55 1983

Silva Fernández, Ricardo. Organización de la estadística en Cuba / Ricardo Silva Fernández. Playa, Ciudad de La Habana : Editorial Pueblo y Educación, 1985 printing, c1980. 136 p. : ill. ; 19 cm. Bibliography: p. 136. LC Card 87-115269 DDC 354.72910081/9 19
1. Cuba - Statistical services. I. Title.
HA37.C866 S55 1985

Silva, Francesco, 1942- Scelte strategiche e riorganizzazione aziendale . Milano, Italy , c1985. 312 p. ; LC Card 86-146459
HD2864 .S36 1985 ***NYPL [JLD 87-1549]***

Silva, Francisca. Junta de Andalucía. Grupo de Trabajo 14, Planificación Económica de las Corporaciones Locales y Comarcalización. Plan económico de Andalucía, 1984-1986 /. [Andalucía] , 1983. 133 p. ; ISBN 84-505-1243-3 LC Card 86-223752
HJ1249.A4 J86 1983

Silva, Gerson Augusto da. Estudos tributários / Gerson Augusto da Silva. Brasília, DF : Ministério da Fazenda, Escola de Administração Fazendária, Centro de Pesquisa, 1983. 139 p. : ill. ; 21 cm. (Coleção Gerson Augusto da Silva . 9) LC Card 84-127110
1. Taxation - Brazil. 2. Fiscal policy - Brazil. 3. Taxation - Law and legislation - Brazil. I. Title. II. Series.
HJ2525 .S49 1983

Silva Herzog, Jesús, 1892-
SILVA HERZOG, JESÚS, 1892-
Silva, J. Resende. A fronteira do sul : estudo--geographico, economico, historico e fiscal / J. Resende Silva. Rio de Janeiro : Impr. Nacional, 1922. 723 p., [1] leaf of plates : port. ; 24 cm. LC Card 85-223002
1. Rio Grande do Sul (Brazil) - Commerce - History. 2. Rio Grande do Sul (Brazil) - Politics and government. 3. Rio Grande do Sul (Brazil) - History. 4. Smuggling - Brazil - Rio Grande do Sul - History. 5. Physical geography - Brazil - Rio Grande do Sul. 6. Finance, Public - Brazil - Rio Grande do Sul. I. Title.
HF3409.R56 S55 1922

Silva, Manuela. A igualdade de oportunidades de formação profissional para as mulheres / Manuela Silva. Lisboa : Comissão da Condição Feminina : Comissão para a Igualdade no Trabalho e no Emprego, 1983. 51, [1] p. : ill. ; 21 cm. (Cadernos Condição feminina . 17) Bibliography: p. [52] LC Card 84-238349
1. Women - Employment - Portugal. 2. Occupational training - Portugal. 3. Discrimination in employment - Brazil. I. Title. II. Series.
HD6179 .S56 1983

Silva, Marcos Eugênio da. Inovação tecnológica : um estudo de caso / Marcos Eugênio da Silva. São Paulo : Instituto de Pesquisas Econômicas, 1984. 103 p. : ill. ; 21 cm. (Série Ensaios econômicos / IPE-USP . v. 31) Originally presented as the author's thesis (M.A.)--Universidade de São Paulo, 1982, under the title: Inovação tecnológica no setor de máquinas ferramentas brasileiro. Includes bibliographical references. LC Card 85-136373
1. Machine-tool industry - Brazil - Technological innovations - Case studies. I. Series: Ensaios econômicos (Universidade de São Paulo. Instituto de Pesquisas Econômicas) , 31. II. Title.
HD9703.B72 S55 1984

Silva, Maria José Oliveira e. A sociedade amazônica e o problema social da desocupação e subocupação / Maria José Oliveira e Silva. Belém : Ministério do Interior, Superintendência do Desenvolvimento da Amazônia, Coordenação de Informática, Divisão de Documentação, 1974. 42 p., 53 leaves : ill. (some col.) ; 27 cm. Summary in English. Bibliography: p. 41-42. LC Card 86-183026
1. Amazon River Region - Population. 2. Unemployment - Amazon River Region. 3. Underemployment - Amazon River Region. 4. Amazon River Region - Social conditions. I. Brazil. Superintendência do Desenvolvimento da Amazônia. Coordenação de Informática. Divisão de Documentação. II. Title.
HB3564.A73 S55 1974

Silva, Marlene Maria da. O Norte cearense /. Recife , 1985. 303 p. : LC Card 86-209022
HD1875.C4 N67 1985

Silva, Martha Gonçalves da. Santos, Madalena Herculano dos. Condições de vida nos municípios paraibanos /. João Pessoa (PB) : Brasília, DF : 103 p. : LC Card 87-403990 DDC 330.981/33063 19
HC188.P343 S26 1986

Silva, Michael A., 1951- Hickman, Craig R. The future 500 . New York, N.Y. , c1987. xiv, 274 p. ; ISBN 0-453-00544-6 LC Card 87-15204 DDC 658 19
HD31 .H4814 1987

Silva, Roberto Gama e. São mesmo nossos os minerais não-energéticos? / Roberto Gama e Silva ; prefácio de Antonio Ermírio de Moraes. Rio de Janeiro, RJ : Philobiblion, 1985. 164 p. : ill. ; 21 cm. (Coleção Visões e revisões . 3) Includes bibliographical references. LC Card 86-153246
1. Mineral industries - Brazil. 2. Mineral industries - Government policy - Brazil. I. Title.
HD9506.B72 S55 1985

Silva, Roque A. da (Roque Aparecido) Os Sindicatos e a transição democrática . São Paulo , 1986. 294 p. ; LC Card 87-153581 DDC 331.88/0981 19
HD6612 .S55 1986

Silva Ruete, Javier. La respuesta de Latinoamérica a la crisis internacional / Javier Silva Ruete, Manuel Ulloa Elías. [Lima, Peru?] : Intercampus, [1984] 99 p. ; 21 cm. Cover title. Speeches given at IX Reunión de Intercampus, Jan. 31, 1984. "9"--P. [4] of cover. LC Card 86-154728
1. Latin America - Foreign economic relations - Congresses. 2. Debts, External - Latin America - Congresses. 3. Latin America - Economic policy - Congresses. I. Ulloa Elías, Manuel. II. Title.
HF1480.5 .S55 1984

Silva Santisteban, Carlos Malpica. see **Malpica Silva Santisteban, Carlos.**

Silveira, Gilberto Borges da. Custo de produção de café /. Curitiba-Paraná [19]84. 47 p. ; LC Card 85-211612
HD9199.B7 C93 1984

Silveira, Maria Luiza Faraone. Mão-de-obra de nível médio : nível médio no processo de trabalho industrial / Maria Luiza Faraone Silveira. São Paulo : Serviço Nacional de Aprendizagem Industrial, Departamento Regional de São Paulo, 1986. 239 p. : forms ; 27 cm. "Edição patrocinada pelo Departamento Nacional do SENAI." Bibliography: p. 227-228. LC Card 87-143876 DDC 331.11/422 19
1. Skilled labor - Training of - Brazil. 2. Skilled labor - Brazil - Supply and demand. 3. Occupational training - Brazil. I. Brazil. Serviço Nacional de Aprendizagem Industrial. Departamento Regional de São Paulo. II. Title.
HD5754 .S55 1986

Silver /. Mohide, Thomas Patrick. Toronto, Ont. [1985] xiv, 406 p. : ISBN 0-7743-9897-3 (pbk.) LC Card 85-165981 DDC 338.2/7421/0971 19
HD9536.C22 M64 1985
NYPL [JLG 86-145]

Silver, A. David (Aaron David), 1941-
The Silver prescription : the eight-step action plan for entrepreneurial success / A. David Silver. New York : Wiley, c1987. xiii, 202 p. ; 24 cm. Includes index. ISBN 0-471-85637-1 LC Card 86-28135 DDC 658.1/1 19
1. New business enterprises. 2. Entrepreneurship. I. Title.
HD62.5 .S557 1987

Who's who in venture capital / A. David Silver. 3rd ed. New York : Wiley, c1987. ix, 468 p. : ill. ; 28 cm. "A Wiley-Interscience publication." Includes index. ISBN 0-471-85639-8 (pbk.) : LC Card 86-28974 DDC 332.66 19
1. Venture capital - United States - Directories. 2. Venture capital - Great Britain - Directories. 3. Venture capital - Canada - Directories. I. Title.
HG4963 .S56 1987

The silver & gold investor's profit guide . Rosenthal, Daniel M. Bethel, CT , c1986. viii, 90 leaves : ISBN 0-938689-02-9 (pbk.) : LC Card 86-232188 DDC 332.63 19
HG307.U5 R67 1986

Silver & gold report. Oweiss, Ibrahim M. What gold investors need to know about the collapse of the oil cartel /. Bethel, CT , c1986. 37 leaves : LC Card 86-209518 DDC 332.63 19
HG293 .O84 1986

SILVER INDUSTRY.
Mohide, Thomas Patrick. Silver /. Toronto, Ont. [1985] xiv, 406 p. : ISBN 0-7743-9897-3 (pbk.) LC Card 85-165981 DDC 338.2/7421/0971 19
HD9536.C22 M64 1985
NYPL [JLG 86-145]

SILVER INDUSTRY - BOLIVIA - POTOSÍ - HISTORY - 19TH CENTURY.
Mitre, Antonio. El monedero de los Andes . La Paz , 1986. 134 p. ; LC Card 87-403038 DDC 332.4/98 19
HG803 .M57 1986

SILVER INDUSTRY - CANADA.
Mohide, Thomas Patrick. Silver /. Toronto, Ont. [1985] xiv, 406 p. : ISBN 0-7743-9897-3 (pbk.) LC Card 85-165981 DDC 338.2/7421/0971 19
HD9536.C22 M64 1985
NYPL [JLG 86-145]

SILVER INDUSTRY - HONDURAS - HISTORY - 19TH CENTURY.
Finney, Kenneth V. In quest of El Dorado . New York , 1987. xii, 454 p. ; ISBN 0-8240-1359-X (alk. paper) : LC Card 87-8342 DDC 338.2/742/097283 19
HD9536.H82 F56 1987

Silver, J. Lew. Wallace, T. Dudley. Econometrics . Reading, Mass. , c1988. xviii, 440 p. : ISBN 0-201-09896-2 : LC Card 87-14492 DDC 330/.028 19
HB139 .W32 1988

The silver key to the golden treasure of Indian philately /. Jain, Manik, 1938- Calcutta , 1986. xvi, 326, [1] p. : LC Card 86-903670 DDC 769.56954 19
HE6185.I5 J35 1986

Silver, Marc L., 1950- Under construction : work and alienation in the building trades / Marc L. Silver. Albany : State University of New York Press, c1986. xi, 251 p. ; 24 cm. (SUNY series in the sociology of work) Includes indexes. Bibliography: p. 229-242. ISBN 0-88706-308-X LC Card 85-30447 DDC 331.7/624/0973 19
1. Building trades - Social aspects - United States. 2. Construction industry - Social aspects - United States. 3. Construction workers - United States. 4. Industrial sociology - United States. 5. Trade-unions - Building trades - United States. I. Title.
HD6956.B92 U67 1986
NYPL [JLE 86-4616]

SILVER MINERS - MEXICO - PACHUCA REGION - HISTORY - 18TH CENTURY.
Ladd, Doris M. The making of a strike . Lincoln , c1988. x, 205 p. ; ISBN 0-8032-2876-7 (alk. paper) LC Card 87-5897 DDC 331.8/928223423/097246 19
HD5331.M72 1766 .P325 1988

SILVER MINES AND MINING - HISTORY - 19TH CENTURY.
Finney, Kenneth V. In quest of El Dorado . New York , 1987. xii, 454 p. ; ISBN 0-8240-1359-X (alk. paper) : LC Card 87-8342 DDC 338.2/742/097283 19
HD9536.H82 F56 1987

The Silver prescription . Silver, A. David (Aaron David), 1941- New York , c1987. xiii, 202 p. ; ISBN 0-471-85637-1 LC Card 86-28135 DDC 658.1/1 19
HD62.5 .S557 1987

SILVER - UNITED STATES.
Rosenthal, Daniel M. The silver & gold investor's profit guide . Bethel, CT , c1986. viii, 90 leaves : ISBN 0-938689-02-9 (pbk.) : LC Card 86-232188 DDC 332.63 19
HG307.U5 R67 1986

SILVER - UNITED STATES - PURCHASING.
Rosenthal, Daniel M. Which 3 silver and gold dealers give you the worst prices? . Lafayette, CA , c1986. 58 leaves : ISBN 0-9615814-3-3 (pbk.) : LC Card 86-209287 DDC 332.63 19
HG307.U5 R673 1986

Silverberg, René. Le courrier des militaires belges internés aux Pays-Bas et en Suisse 1914-1919, et essai de classement des marques néerlandaises de censure et autres / René Silverberg. Bruxelles : P. de Méyère, 1978. 154 p. : ill. ; 22 cm. LC Card 80-452392 DDC 769.56/7
1. Postmarks - Belgium. 2. Postmarks - Netherlands. 3. Postmarks - Switzerland. 4. World War, 1914-1918 - Postal service. I. Title.
HE6184.C3 S55 *NYPL [JFD 81-1659]*

Silverman, Jerry M. Action-planning workshops for development management : guidelines / Jerry M. Silverman, Merlyn Kettering, and Terry D. Schmidt. Washington, D.C., U. S.A. : World Bank, 1986. ix, 74 p. : ill. ; 29 cm. (World Bank technical paper, 0253-7494 . no. 56) Bibliography: p. 49-54. ISBN 0-8213-0864-5 (pbk.) LC Card 86-28215 DDC 338.9/0068 19
1. Developing countries - Economic policy. 2. Economic development. I. Kettering, Merlyn. II. Schmidt, Terry. III. Title. IV. Series.
HC59.7 .S4656 1986

Silverman, Melvin. The art of managing technical projects / Melvin Silverman. Englewood Cliffs, N.J. : Prentice-Hall, c1987. xx, 346 p. : ill. ; 24 cm. Includes bibliographies and index. ISBN 0-13-047010-4 LC Card 87-1750 DDC 658.4/04 19
1. Industrial project management. 2. Executives. 3. Industrial management. I. Title.
HD69.P75 S54 1987

Silverstein, Jeffrey. Fleming, Maureen. Microcomputers and productivity . White Plains, NY , c1984. iii, 125 p. ; ISBN 0-86729-109-5 (pbk.) LC Card 84-164284 DDC 650/.028/54 19
HF5548.2 .F49 1984 *NYPL [JLf 87-8]*

Silvia Helena. Rastro de Cobra / Silvia Helena. [Brazil : s.n., 1984] (Rio de Janeiro, RJ : Alphaset Gráfica e Editora) 124 p., [4] p. of plates : ill. (some col.), ports. ; 23 cm. LC Card 87-130372 DDC 338.4/7004/0981 19
1. Cobra (Organization) - History. 2. Computer industry - Brazil - History. I. Title.
HD9696.C63 B77 1984

Simai, Mihály.
Az emberi tényező szerepe a világgazdaságban az 1980-as években : akadémiai székfoglaló, 1986. január 16. / Simai Mihály. Budapest : Akadémiai Kiadó, c1986. 41 p. ; 20 cm. (Értekezések, emlékezések, 0236-6258) Includes bibliographical references. ISBN 963-05-4342-7 : LC Card 87-407712
1. Human capital. 2. Economic history - 1971-. 3. Economic development. I. Title. II. Series.
HD4904.7 .S446 1986

Hatalom, technika, világgazdaság / Simai Mihály. Budapest : Közgazdasági és Jogi Könyvkiadó, 1985. 436 p. ; 21 cm. Includes bibliographical references. ISBN 963-221-548-6 : LC Card 86-187337
1. Economic history - 1971-. 2. International economic relations. 3. Technological innovations. 4. Technology transfer. I. Title.
HC59 .S529 1985

Simard, Jean-Guy. Comptabilité analytique / Jean-Guy Simard. [Bujumbura?] : République du Burundi, Ministère de la fonction publique, C.F.P., Centre de perfectionnement et de formation en cours d'emploi, [1983] 120 p. : ill. ; 32 cm. "Programme des Nations Unies pour le développement." "Mars 1983." LC Card 85-981500
1. Accounting. I. Centre de perfectionnement et de formation en cours d'emploi (Burundi). II. United Nations. Development Programme. III. Title.
HF5642 .S54 1983

Simas, José Ribamar. Subsídios para uma proposta de ocupação racional de novas áreas com agricultura de sequeiro no Nordeste brasileiro / José Ribamar Simas. Recife : Ministério do Interior, Superintendência do Desenvolvimento do Nordeste, Superintendência Adjunta de Desenvolvimento Rural, 1985 [i.e. 1986] 28, [16] p. : ill. ; 23 cm. On cover: Recife, 1986. Bibliography: p. [15]-[16] (2nd group). LC Card 87-404827 DDC 338.1/8 19
1. Land settlement - Brazil, Northeast. 2. Subsidies - Brazil, Northeast. 3. Dry farming - Brazil, Northeast. I. Title.
HD499.N67 S56 1986

Simelane, Vakashile R. Guma, Xolile P. Small farmer credit and small farmer attitudes towards co-operatives /. [Kwaluseni, Swaziland] [1982] 94 p. : LC Card 86-101161 DDC 332.7/1/096813 19
HD1491.S855 G85 1982
NYPL [JLG 86-262]

Simkin, Mark G.
Introduction to computer information systems for business / Mark G. Simkin. Dubuque, Iowa : W.C. Brown, c1987. xxvi, 678 p. : ill. (some col.) ; 28 cm. Includes index. ISBN 0-697-00125-3 LC Card 86-72218 DDC 658/.05 19
1. Business - Data processing. 2. Information storage and retrieval systems - Business. I. Title. II. Title: Computer information systems for business.
HF5548.2 .S4498 1987

Moscove, Stephen A. Accounting information systems . New York , c1987. xxi, 824 p. : ISBN 0-471-84033-5 LC Card 86-32387 DDC 657/.028/5 19
HF5679 .M62 1987

Šimko, Dušan. Strassenverkäufer und die Versorgung der Arbeiterfamilien von Kowloon (Hong Kong) im Umfeld der staatlichen Planungspolitik / Dušan Šimko. Basel : W. Gallusser und das Geographische Institut der Universität Basel in Zusammenarbeit mit der Geographisch-Ethnologischen Gesellschaft Basel : In Kommission beim Verlag Wepf, 1983. 196 p., [9] p. of plates : ill. ; 24 cm. (Basler Beiträge zur Geographie. Heft 29) Thesis (doctoral)--Universität Basel, 1982. Summary in English and German. Bibliography: p. 187-192. ISBN 3-85977-129-9 : LC Card 83-238672
1. Peddlers and peddling - Hong Kong - Kowloon - History. 2. Kowloon (Hong Kong) - Economic conditions. 3. Kowloon (Hong Kong) - Social conditions. 4. Labor and laboring classes - Hong Kong - History. I. Title. II. Series.
HF5459.H6 S56 1983

Simmert, Diethard B., 1944- Piel, Manfred, 1945- [Staatsverschuldung, Schicksalsfrage der Nation?] Staatsverschuldung, Hintergründe und Probleme /. Stuttgart [1982] 128 p. ; LC Card 83-118137
HJ8654 .P52 1982

Simmons, C. Tosco, Manuel. Aprovechamiento y dominio de las tierras en 1950-51 /. Tegucigalpa, D.C., Honduras [1952] 33 p. ; LC Card 85-197157
HD366 .T66 1952

Simmons, Colin. Development studies and colonial policy /. London , Totowa, N.J. , 1987. 292 p. : ISBN 0-7146-3231-7 : LC Card 87-6562 DDC 338.9171/241 19
HD82 .D395 1987

Simmons, Don, 1934- Post offices in the United States, 1876 /. Melber, Ky. [1986] 125 p. ; LC Card 87-400310 DDC 383/.42/0973 19
HE6366 .P67 1986

Simó, Tibor. Metszetek az agrártársadalom struktúrájából / Simó Tibor. Budapest : MSZMP KB Társadalomtudományi Intézete, 1985. 167 p. ; 20 cm. Summary in English and Russian. Includes bibliographical references. ISBN 963-7700-25-0 : LC Card 86-232606
1. Agricultural laborers - Hungary. 2. Agriculture - Social aspects - Hungary. 3. State farms - Hungary - Officials and employees. 4. Collective farms - Hungary - Officials and employees. 5. Hungary - Rural conditions.

6. Rural youth - Hungary. I. Title.
HD1536.H9 S56 1985

Simon, Dan, 1937- Das Frankreichbild der deutschen Arbeiterbewegung 1859-1865 / Dan Simon ; [aus dem Hebräischen von Leo Koppel]. 1. Aufl. [Gerlingen] : Bleicher, 1984. 334 p. ; 22 cm. (Schriftenreihe des Instituts für Deutsche Geschichte, Universität Tel-Aviv. 6) Includes index. Bibliography: p. 319-331. ISBN 3-88350-451-3 LC Card 84-173175
1. Labor and laboring classes - Germany - Attitudes - History - 19th century. 2. Press, Labor - Germany - History - 19th century. 3. Public opinion - Germany - History - 19th century. 4. France - History - Second Empire, 1852-1870 - Public opinion. I. Title.
HD8450 .S56 1984 ***NYPL [JLD 86-2711]***

Simon, David, 1957- Mackie, Peter J., 1947- The British transport industry and the European Community . Aldershot, Hampshire, England , Brookfield, Vt., U. S.A. , c1987. xvi, 184 p. : ISBN 0-566-05368-3 : LC Card 86-24186 DDC 380.5/24/0941 19
HE199.G5 M33 1987

Simon, Dieter. Schwache Signale : die Früherkennung von strategischen Diskontinuitäten durch Erfassung von "weak signals" / Dieter Simon. Wien : Service, Fachverlag an der Wirtschaftsuniversität, c1986. 262 p. : ill. ; 21 cm. (Schriften des Österreichischen Controller-Instituts . Bd. 4) Bibliography: p. 241-257. LC Card 87-103434 DDC 658.4/012 19
1. Strategic planning. 2. Industrial management. I. Title. II. Series.
HD30.28 .S435 1986

Simon, Gildas. Marchands ambulants et commerçants étrangers en France et en Allemagne fédérale /. Poitiers , 1984. 148 p. : LC Card 87-147724
HF5459.F8 M37 1984

Simon, György. Gazdasági növekedés a két világrendszerben / Simon György. [Budapest] : Kossuth, 1986. 257, [1] p. ; 20 cm. Bibliography: p. 245-[258]. ISBN 963-09-2771-3 : LC Card 87-409656
1. Economic development. 2. Comparative economics. 3. Competition, International. 4. Economic history - 1945-. I. Title.
HD85.H88 S498 1986

Simon, Hermann. Goodwill und Marketingstrategie / Hermann Simon. Wiesbaden : Gabler, c1985. 250 p. : ill. ; 25 cm. Bibliography: p. 223-241. Includes indexes. ISBN 3-409-13603-7 LC Card 85-232089 DDC 658.8/02 19
1. Marketing - Mathematical models. 2. Good-will (in business, etc.). I. Title.
HF5415 .S4958 1985

Simón, Jorge. Rocca, José. Excedentes financieros y sistema bancario, Uruguay, 1974-1982 /. Montevideo, Uruguay , 1985. 39 p. : LC Card 85-213768
HC235.S3 R63 1985

Simon, Josef, 1865-1949. Josef Simon, Schuhmacher, Gewerkschafter, Sozialist mit Ecken und Kanten / Adolf Mirkes (Hrsg.). Köln : Bund-Verlag, c1985. 465 p. : ill. ; 25 cm. Bibliography: p. 451-461. Includes index. ISBN 3-7663-0923-4 LC Card 85-186450
1. Simon, Josef, 1865-1949. 2. Zentralverband der Schuhmacher (Germany) - Biography. 3. Trade-unions - Shoemakers - Germany (West) - Biography. 4. Trade-unions - Leather workers - Germany (West) - Biography. I. Mirkes, Adolf, 1913-. II. Title.
HD6695.S55 A3 1985

SIMON, JOSEF, 1865-1949.
Simon, Josef, 1865-1949. Josef Simon, Schuhmacher, Gewerkschafter, Sozialist mit Ecken und Kanten /. Köln , c1985. 465 p. : ISBN 3-7663-0923-4 LC Card 85-186450
HD6695.S55 A3 1985

Simon, Julian Lincoln, 1932- Theory of population and economic growth / Julian L. Simon. Oxford : Basil Blackwell, 1986. xi, 232 p. : ill. ; 24 cm. Includes index. Bibliography: p. [216]-224. ISBN 0-631-14427-7 : LC Card 85-28574 DDC 338.9/00724 19
1. Population - Mathematical models. 2. Economic development - Mathematical models. I. Title.
HB849.41 .S55 1986 ***NYPL [JLE 86-3702]***

Simon, Manfred. Handwerk in Krise und Umbruch : wirtschaftliche Forderungen und sozialpolitische Vorstellungen der Handwerksmeister im Revolutionsjahr 1848/49 / Manfred Simon. Köln : Böhlau, 1983. xvii, 652 p. : ill. ; 21 cm. (Neue Wirtschaftsgeschichte. 16) Bibliography: p. 445-456. ISBN 3-412-02983-1 : LC Card 83-221725 DDC 322/.2/0943 19
1. Artisans - Germany - Political activity - History - 19th century. 2. Germany - History - Revolution, 1848-1849. 3. Germany - Economic conditions - 19th century. I. Title.
HD2346.G3 S47 1983

Simon, Péter, 1926- A magyar parasztság sorsfordulója, 1946-1949 / Simon Péter. [Budapest] : Kossuth, 1984. 212 p. : ill. ; 20 cm. (Négy évtized sorozat . 3) Includes bibliographical references. ISBN 963-09-2475-7 :
1. Land reform - Hungary - History. 2. Peasantry - Hungary - History. 3. Collective farms - Hungary - History. 4. Agriculture and state - Hungary - History. I. Title.
HD1333.H9 S57 1984 ***NYPL [JLD 86-3163]***

Simon, Richard M. Energy economics . Englewood Cliffs, N.J. , c1987. viii, 328 p. : ISBN 0-13-277245-0 : LC Card 86-25254 DDC 333.79/0973 19
HD9502.U52 E4874 1987

Simon, Sam, 1945- Phonewriting : a consumer's guide to the new world of electronic information services / Samuel A. Simon, Michael J. Whelan. [Washington, D.C.] : Telecommunications Research and Action Center, c1986. iv, 92 p., [4] p. of plates : ill. ; 22 cm. Bibliography: p. 70. ISBN 0-943444-03-9 (pbk.) LC Card 86-214171 DDC 004.6 19
1. Electronic mail systems. 2. Computer bulletin boards. I. Whelan, Michael. II. Title.
HE6239.E54 S56 1986

Simoncini, Franco. Dall'interno della UIL (1950-1985) / Franco Simoncini. Milano, Italy : F. Angeli, c1986. 274 p. ; 22 cm. (Lavoro italiano. 2, I Giorni della storia . 2) Includes bibliographical references. LC Card 86-169848
1. Unione italiana del lavoro. I. Title.
HD8473.U533 S56 1986

Simonis, Ernst Udo. Entwicklungstheorie, Entwicklungspraxis . Berlin , c1986. 316 p. ; ISBN 3-428-05973-5 LC Card 86-233851 DDC 338.9/009172/4 19
HC59.7 .E6473 1986

Simonis, Udo Ernst. Mehr Technik, weniger Arbeit? . Karlsruhe , c1984. 228 p. : ISBN 3-7880-9697-7 LC Card 85-108996
HD6331 .M384 1984

Simonoff accounting series.
Handbook of EDP auditing. Boston , c1986. 1 v. (various pagings) : ISBN 0-88712-597-2 (pbk.) LC Card 87-107300 DDC 657/.45/0285 19
HF5548.35 .H36 1986

Simons Munaro, Yehude. Lambayeque, producción ganadera, comunidades campesinas [microform] / Yehude Simons Munaro, Germán Torre Villafane. Chiclayo, Perú : Solidaridad, Centro de Estudios Sociales, 1983. 45 p. ; 33 cm. Cover title. Includes bibliographical references. Microfilm. New York : New York Public Library, 1986. 1 microfilm reel ; 35 mm. (MN *ZZ-26,374) LC Card 84-204537 DDC 338.1/76/0098514 19
1. Animal industry - Peru - Lambayeque (Dept.). 2. Agriculture, Cooperative - Peru - Lambayeque (Dept.). 3. Lambayeque, Peru (Dept.) - Rural conditions. I. Torre Villafane, Germán. II. Title.
HD9424.P43 L367 1983
NYPL [*ZT-1708 no.72]

Simonsen, Mário Henrique. A nova ordem econômica internacional e suas consequências no Brasil : conferência do Prof. Mário Henrique Simonsen, tendo como debatedores Angelo Calmon de Sá, Antônio Oliveira Santos e Antônio Porto Gonçalves no auditório de Desenbanco, em 6 de maio de 1983. Salvador : Fundação Bahiana para Estudos Econômicos e Sociais, 1983. 60 p. ; 23 cm. LC Card 87-144638 DDC 337.81 19
1. Brazil - Foreign economic relations. 2. International economic relations. I. Fundação Bahiana para Estudos Econômicas e Sociais. II. Title.
HF1513 .S55 1983

Simonson, Donald G. Pace, Edmond E. Developing a basic loan training program /. Philadelphia, Pa. , c1987. 108 p. ; ISBN 0-936742-41-0 (pbk.) : LC Card 87-7936 DDC 332.1/753/0683 19
HG1642.U5 P33 1987

Simple method for developing inexpensive & effective training. Remz, Carol L. Remz it! . Seattle, Wash. , c1987. 1 v. (various pagings) ; ISBN 0-941999-01-7 (loose-leaf) LC Card 87-80592 DDC 658.3/12404 19
HF5549.5.T7 R374 1987

Simpozium "Nauchno-tekhnicheskiĭ progress i intensifikatsiia obshchestvennogo proizvodstva" (1984 : Podol'sk, Moscow, R.S.F.S.R.) Formy i metody vzaimodeĭstviia nauki i proizvodstva / redkollegiia, Kamaev, V.D., Taksir, K.I., Mymrina, L.I. Moskva : [s.n.], 1984. 237 p. ; 21 cm. "V sbornik voshli materialy simpoziuma "Nauchno-tekhnicheskiĭ progress i intensifikatsii obshchestvennogo proizvodstva," provedennogo v 1984 godu v g. Podol'ske Moskovskoĭ oblasti."--Verso t.p. At head of title: Akademiia nauk SSSR. Ordena Trudovogo Krasnogo Znameni Institut ėkonomiki. Nauchnyĭ sovet po ėkonomicheskim problemam nauchno-tekhnicheskoĭ revoliutsii. Includes bibliographical references. LC Card 85-240380
1. Technological innovations - Soviet Union - Congresses. 2. Industrial productivity - Soviet Union - Congresses. 3. Soviet Union - Economic policy - 1981- - Congresses. I. Kamaev, V. D. (Vladimir Dorofeevich). II. Taksir, Kim Isaevich. III. Mymrina, L. I. IV. Institut ėkonomiki (Akademiia nauk SSSR). V. Nauchnyĭ sovet AN SSSR po ėkonomicheskim problemam nauchno-tekhnicheskoĭ revoliutsii. VI. Title.
HC340.T4 S48 1984

Simpson, Henry.
Programming the IBM PC user interface / Henry Simpson. New York : McGraw-Hill, c1985. vii, 228 p. : ill. ; 23 cm. Includes index. "A Byte book." ISBN 0-07-057297-6 (pbk.) : LC Card 85-7924 DDC 005.265 19
1. IBM Personal Computer - Programming. 2. IBM PCjr (Computer) - Programming. 3. Microcomputers - Programming. I. Title.
QA76.8.I2594 S575 1985
NYPL [JSE 86-1154]

Serious programming for your Apple II/IIe/IIc / by Henry Simpson. 1st ed. Blue Ridge Summit, PA : Tab Books, 1985. x, 180 p. : ill. ; 24 cm. Includes index. ISBN 0-8306-0960-1 : LC Card 85-17320 DDC 005.265 19
1. Apple II (Computer) - Programming. 2. Apple IIe (Computer) - Programming. 3. Apple IIc (Computer) - Programming. I. Title.
QA76.8.A662 S57 1985 ***NYPL [JSE 86-801]***

Simpson, Peter K., 1930- The community of cattlemen : a social history of the cattle industry in southeastern Oregon, 1869-1912 / Peter K. Simpson. Moscow, Idaho : University of Idaho Press, c1987. xiv, 228 p. ; 23 cm. Bibliography: p. [215]-223. Includes index. ISBN 0-89301-117-7 (pbk.) LC Card 87-5855 DDC 338.1/762/00979595 19
1. Cattle trade - Oregon - Harney County - History. 2. Ranchers - Oregon - Harney County - History. 3. Ranches - Oregon - Harney County - History. 4. Cattle breeders - Oregon - Harney County - History. 5. Harney County (Or.) - History. I. Title.
HD9433.U5 H277 1987

SIMPSONS LIMITED - HISTORY.
Burton, G. Allan, 1915- A store of memories /. Toronto, Ont. , c1986. 330 p., [17] p. of plates : ISBN 0-7710-1792-8 : LC Card 87-101965 DDC 381/.45/000924 B 19
HF5465.C32 B87 1986

Sims, Henry P., 1939- The thinking organization / Henry P. Sims, Jr., Dennis A. Gioia, and associates. 1st ed. San Francisco : Jossey-Bass, 1986. xxvii, 375 p. : ill. ; 24 cm. (A joint publication in the Jossey-Bass management series and the Jossey-Bass social and behavioral science series) Includes bibliographies and indexes. ISBN 0-87589-690-1 LC Card 85-45913 DDC 302.3/5 19
1. Organizational behavior. 2. Cognition. I. Gioia, Dennis A., 1947-. II. Title.
HD58.7 .S584 1986 ***NYPL [JLE 86-2921]***

Sims, Rod. Daniel, Philip. Foreign investment in Papua New Guinea . Canberra , 1986. x, 144 p. : ISBN 0-86784-761-1 (pbk.) LC Card 87-151193 DDC 332.6/7322953 19
HG5982.A3 D36 1986

Simulation als betriebliche Entscheidungshilfe : Methoden, Wer[k]zeuge, Anwendungen / herausgegeben von Jörg Biethahn und Bernd

Schmidt. Berlin ; New York : Springer, 1987. xi, 282 p. : ill. ; 25 cm. (Fachberichte Simulation . Bd. 6) Selected and revised papers originally presented at a workshop held in Erlangen, March 10-12, 1986. Includes bibliographies and index. ISBN 0-387-17353-6 LC Card 87-121884 DDC 658.4/0352 19
1. Decision-making - Simulation Methods. I. Biethahn, Jörg. II. Schmidt, Bernd, 1940-. III. Series.
HD30.23 .S56 1987

Simulation series .
(v. 12, no. 2) Computer models for production and inventory control /. La Jolla, Calif. , c1984. ix, 148 p. : LC Card 84-189641 DDC 658.5/0028/54 19
TS157 .C63 1984 *NYPL [JSF 86-930]*

SINALOA (MEXICO) - ECONOMIC CONDITIONS.
Bennholdt-Thomsen, Veronika. Bauern in Mexiko . Frankfurt [am Main] , New York , c1982. 214 p. ; ISBN 3-593-33167-5 LC Card 83-139124 DDC 305.5/63 19
HD1531.M6 B46 1982

Sinatora, Amilton. Política agrária /. Porto Alegre-RS , 1985. 79 p. : LC Card 86-198513
HD1531.B7 P65 1985

Sinavina, V. S. (Valentina Semenovna) Rezervy ėffektivnosti upravleniia proizvodstvom / V.S. Sinavina. Moskva : "Ėkonomika", 1984. 167 p. : ill. ; 20 cm. Bibliography: p. 165-[166] LC Card 84-244689
1. Industrial management - Soviet Union. 2. Industrial management - Soviet Union - Data processing. I. Title.
HD70.S63 S575 1984

Sincere, Richard E. The politics of sentiment : churches and foreign investment in South Africa / Richard E. Sincere, Jr. ; foreword by Lucy Mvubelo. Washington, D.C. : Ethics and Public Policy Center ; Lanham, MD ; xiv, 164 p. : map ; 24 cm. Bibliography: p. 153-157. Includes index. ISBN 0-89633-116-4 (alk. paper) : LC Card 87-13441 DDC 332.6/73/0968 19
1. Investments, Foreign - South Africa - Moral and ethical aspects. 2. South Africa - Race relations. 3. World Council of Churches. I. Ethics and Public Policy Center (Washington, D.C.). II. Title.
HG5851.A3 S56 1987

Sinclair, John, 1944- Images incorporated : advertising as industry and ideology / John Sinclair. London ; New York : Croom Helm, c1987. 215 p. : ill. ; 23 cm. (Media debates series) "Published in the USA by Croom Helm in association with Methuen, Inc."--T.p. verso. Bibliography: p. 194-209. Includes index. ISBN 0-7099-3388-6 LC Card 87-20040 DDC 659.1 19
1. Advertising. I. Title. II. Series.
HF5821 .S58 1987

Sinclair, P. J. N. Prices, quantities, and expectations . Oxford [Oxfordshire] , New York , 1987. xxiv, 487 p. : ISBN 0-19-828589-2 (pbk.) : LC Card 87-7770 DDC 330.15/6 19
HB99.7 .P74 1987

Sinclair, Sharyn. The rural settlement of Verlorenvlei in historical perspective / by Sharyn Sinclair. Rondebosch, South Africa : School of Environmental Studies, University of Cape Town, [1980] 234 leaves : ill. ; 30 cm. (Research report / School of Environmental Studies . no. 20) "April 1980." Bibliography: leaves 231-234. LC Card 86-210654
1. Land settlement - South Africa - Verlorevlei. 2. Land use, Rural - South Africa - Verlorevlei. I. Series: Research report (University of Cape Town. School of Environmental Studies) , no. 20. II. Title.
HD991.Z9 V477 1980

SIND PM .
(1975:7) Sweden. Statens industriverk. PU-byrån. Användarfrämjande åtgärder på dataområdet . Stockholm , 1975. 97 leaves ; ISBN 91-7318-026-2 LC Card 84-105630
HF5548.2 .S8822 1975

SIND PM, 0346-573X .
(1977:7) Tung herrkonfektion . Stockholm , 1977. 64, [11] leaves, [1] leaf of plates : ISBN 91-38-03482-4 LC Card 84-102982
HD9940.S82 T854 1977

(1978:4) Introduktion av naturgas i Sverige . Stockholm , 1978. ii, 16, 13, 11 p. ; ISBN 91-38-04192-8 LC Card 83-238196
HD9581.S82 I58 1978

(1978:7) Tung damkonfektion . Stockholm , 1978. 47, [10] p. : ISBN 91-38-04438-2 LC Card 84-106453
HD9940.S82 T85 1978

(1980:15) Sweden. Statens industriverk. Kommunal energiplanering . Stockholm , 1980. 51 p. ; ISBN 91-38-05802-2 LC Card 82-236900
HD9502.S82 S97 1980

(1980:16) Tekoindustrierna . Stockholm , 1980. 189 p. : ISBN 91-38-05813-8 LC Card 82-236884
HD9865.S86 T45 1980

(1980:2) Sweden. Statens industriverk. Ökad eldning med skogsråvara . Stockholm , 1980. 203 p. : ISBN 91-38-05361-6 LC Card 82-236954
HD9769.F843 S87 1980

(1981:19-20) Distributionsutredning. Stockholm , 1981. 2 v. : ISBN 91-38-06684-X (v. 1) LC Card 82-234445
HD9865.S86 D57 1981

(1981:4) Internationella förutsättningar för den svenska oljeförsörjningen under 1980-talet. Stockholm , 1981. 172 p. in various pagings : ISBN 91-38-06244-5 LC Card 82-241303
HD9575.S82 I57 1981

(1981:5) Gummivaruindustri . Stockholm , 1981. 119, [12] p. : ISBN 91-38-06243-7 LC Card 82-241338
HD9161.S82 G84 1981

(1982:6) Svensk gjuteriindustri . Stockholm , 1982. 62 p. : ISBN 91-38-07151-7 LC Card 83-220920
HD9506.S82 S92 1982

(1983:6) Oljeersättningsprogrammet i ett samhällsekonomiskt perspektiv. Stockholm , 1983. 39, 67, 54, 71 p. : ISBN 91-38-07618-7 LC Card 83-232276
HD9502.S82 O55 1983

Sind Sie frei? . Loeliger, Walter. Basel , 1982. 99 p. : ISBN 3-85816-043-1 : LC Card 83-100470
HD8039.T162 L64 1982

SIND, 0346-5748 .
(1981:7) De Regionala utvecklingsfonderna . Stockholm , 1981. 260 p. ; ISBN 91-38-06693-9 LC Card 82-234113
HC380.I53 R44 1981

(1982:10) Samhällsekonomiska kalkyler vid industrinedläggningar . Stockholm [1982] 213 p. : ISBN 91-38-07164-9 LC Card 83-219569
HD5708.55.S8 S25 1982

(1982:7) Lokal samverkan--fördelar för näringsliv och kommun? . Stockholm [1982] 185 p. : ISBN 91-38-07027-8 LC Card 82-236501
HC375 .L786 1982

(1982:8) Försörjningstryggheten för olja, kol och uran . Stockholm [1982] 175 p. : ISBN 91-38-07030-8 LC Card 82-240448
HD9502.S82 F68 1983

(1983:3) Sweden. Oljeersättningsdelegationen. Redovisning och analys av kommunernas oljereduktionsplaner /. Stockholm [1983] 59, [91] p. : ISBN 91-38-07458-3 LC Card 83-239703
HD9502.S82 S96 1983a

(1983:4) Olofsson, Christer. De regionala utvecklingsbolagen . Stockholm [1983] 118 p. ; ISBN 91-38-07479-6 LC Card 83-234309
HC380.I53 O46 1983

(1985:3) Exportsamverkan . [Stockholm] [1985] 261 p. : ISBN 91-38-08810-X LC Card 86-114126
HF3676.5 .E96 1985

Sindacato e crisi della democrazia . Granata, Ivano, 1949- Milano, Italy , c1986. 224 p. ; LC Card 87-103965
HD6714.M54 G724 1986

El sindicalismo internacional y la redemocratización de Chile /. Campero, Guillermo. Santiago, Chile , 1984. 77 p. ; LC Card 86-139122 DDC 331.88/0983 19
HD6617 .C357 1984

El "Sindicalismo revolucionario," 1905-1945 / selección de textos, Hugo del Campo. Buenos Aires : Centro Editor de América Latina, c1986. 153 p. ; 18 cm. (Biblioteca Política argentina . 160) Bibliography: p. 153. ISBN 950-25-1424-6 : LC Card 87-125439 DDC 335/.82/0982 19
1. Syndicalism - Argentina - History - 20th century. I. Campo, Hugo del, 1941-. II. Series.
HD6602 .S49 1986

Sindicalismo y política económica /. Gómez Buendía, Hernando. Bogotá, Colombia , 1986. 324 p. : ISBN 958-9061-16-8 LC Card 87-401441 DDC 331.88/09861 19
HD6622 .G64 1986

Sindicalismo y política en América Latina /. Godio, Julio. Caracas, Venezuela [1983] 315 p. ; LC Card 83-157510 DDC 322/.2/098 19
HD8110.5 .G64 1983 *NYPL [JLD 86-1758]*

Sindicalismo y política en Puerto Rico . Quiñones Rodríguez, Federico, 1940- [Río Piedras, P.R.] [c1977] 147 p., [4] p. of plates : ISBN 84-399-6989-9 LC Card 82-159544
HD6592 .Q56 1977

Sindicalismo y socialismo en México /. Iglesias, Severo. México, D.F. , 1985,c19. 194 p. ; ISBN 968-419-418-8 *NYPL [JLC 86-406]*

La sindicalización postal telegráfica en el Perú . Soplín E., Samuel (Soplín Escudero) Lima [1986] 57 p., [4] p. of plates : LC Card 87-145465 DDC 331.88/113834985 19
HE6899.P4 S66 1986

SINDICATO CENTRAL DE CONSTRUCTORES Y ALBAÑILES DE LA PAZ - HISTORY.
Los Constructores de la ciudad . La Paz , 1986. 84 p. : LC Card 86-234740
HD6609.B892 S563 1986

SINDICATO DE LOS OBREROS MINEROS DE ASTURIAS - HISTORY.
Moradiellos, Enrique. El Sindicato de los obreros mineros de Asturias, 1910-1930 /. Oviedo , 1986. 158 p. : ISBN 84-7468-111-1 LC Card 86-212987
HD6764.M62 O375 1986

El Sindicato de los obreros mineros de Asturias, 1910-1930 /. Moradiellos, Enrique. Oviedo , 1986. 158 p. : ISBN 84-7468-111-1 LC Card 86-212987
HD6764.M62 O375 1986

Sindicato dos Economistas do Estado de São Paulo. O Perfil do economista. [São Paulo, Brazil] [1984?] 60 p. : LC Card 87-402012 DDC 330/.092/2 19
HB123.B8 P47 1984

Sindicato Interestadual da Indústria de Máquinas (Brazil). Divisão de Economia e Estatística. Bens de produção mecânicos . São Paulo, SP, Brasil , 1982. 386 p. : LC Card 86-150156
HD9705.B72 B46 1982

SINDICATO NACIONAL DE TRABAJADORES AZUCAREROS (CUBA) - HISTORY.
García Galló, Gaspar M. Jorge. General de las cañas /. La Habana , 1983. 220 p., [18] p. of plates : LC Card 84-229562 DDC 331.88/13361/097291 19
HD6577.5.M46 G37 1983
NYPL [JFD 85-4783]

Sindicato Nacional de Trabajadores de la Construcción (Cuba). Comisión de Historia. Historia del contingente internacionalista de Granada. [Havana, Cuba] [1984] 157 p. : LC Card 85-213062
HC156.5.Z7 G844 1984

Sindicatos, democracia y crisis /. Buen L., Néstor de (Buen Lozano) México , 1985. xii, 122 p. ; ISBN 968-452-054-9 LC Card 86-209080
HD6532 .B84 1985

Os Sindicatos e a transição democrática : o que pensam os interessados? / organizador, Roque Aparecido da Silva. São Paulo : Instituto Brasileiro de Relações do Trabalho, 1986. 294 p. ; 22 cm. (Série Pesquisa / IBRART, Instituto Brasileiro de Relações do Trabalho . no. 4) LC Card 87-153581 DDC 331.88/0981 19
1. Trade-unions - Government policy - Brazil. 2. Industrial relations - Government policy - Brazil. I. Silva, Roque A. da (Roque Aparecido). II. Series: Série Pesquisa (Instituto Brasileiro de Relações do Trabalho) , no. 4.
HD6612 .S55 1986

Los Sindicatos nacionales en el México contemporáneo / coordinador, Javier Aguilar García ; autores, José Rivera Castro ... [et al.]. 1a ed. [México, D.F.] : GV Editores, 1986- v. <1 > ; 17 cm. (Ciencias sociales) Includes bibliographies. CONTENTS. - v. 1. Petroleros ISBN 968-498-020-5 (set) LC Card 87-401211 DDC 331.88/0972 19

1. Trade-unions - Mexico. I. Aguilar García, Javier. II. Rivera Castro, José. III. Series: Ciencias sociales (Mexico City, Mexico).
HD6532 .S55 1986

Sindicatos obreros y asociaciones empresarias hasta la década del centenario /. Cornblit, Oscar. Buenos Aires, Argentina , 1984. 109 p. ; LC Card 87-401262 DDC 331.88/0982 19
HD6602 .C665 1984

Sindicatos y estado en el Chile actual . Barrera, Manuel. Geneva, Switzerland , Santiago, Chile , c1985. v, 196 p. : LC Card 87-118607
HD6617 .B27 1985

Sindicatos y sistema político . Lanzaro, Jorge Luis. Montevideo, Uruguay , 1986. 132 p. ; LC Card 87-403149 DDC 322/.2/09895 19
HD3616.U72 L36 1986

Sindikatele Moldoveĭ Sovetiche. Burlaku, I. N. Sindikatele Moldoveĭ sovetiche yn konstruktsiia sochialiste /. Kishinėu , 1980. 148 p. ; LC Card 81-135331
HD6735.M56 B87 1980

Sindikatele Moldoveĭ sovetiche yn konstruktsiia sochialiste /. Burlaku, I. N. Kishinėu , 1980. 148 p. ; LC Card 81-135331
HD6735.M56 B87 1980

Sineokaia sestra Ukrainy. IUrėvich, Uladzimir Mikhaĭlavich. Syn'ooka sestra Ukraïny /. Kyïv , 1985. 158 p. ; LC Card 87-109673
HC337.B93 I97 1985

Sinetar, Marsha. Do what you love, the money will follow : discovering your right livelihood / Marsha Sinetar. New York : Paulist Press, c1986. p. cm. Bibliography: p. ISBN 0-8091-2874-8 : LC Card 86-30390 DDC 650.1 19
1. Vocational interests. 2. Job satisfaction. 3. Self-actualization (Psychology). 4. Work - Psychological aspects. I. Title.
HF5381.5 .S53 1986

SINGAPORE - ECONOMIC CONDITIONS.
The Oriental challenge . Delft, the Netherlands , 1987. 281 p. : ISBN 90-70879-62-X (pbk.) LC Card 87-170212 DDC 332.6/732259 19
HC445 .O75 1987

Singapore. Economic Development Division. Economics Section. Koh, Cher Siang. The co-operative movement in Singapore /. Singapore [1970] 26 p. ; LC Card 87-121945 DDC 334/.09595/7 19
HD3543.A4 K64 1970

SINGAPORE - ECONOMIC POLICY.
The Political economy of the new Asian industrialism /. Ithaca, N.Y. , 1987. 252 p. ; ISBN 0-8014-1948-4 (alk. paper) LC Card 86-29103 DDC 338.95 19
HC460.5 .P65 1987

SINGEN AM HOHENTWIEL (GERMANY) - APPROPRIATIONS AND EXPENDITURES.
Gebhard, Alfred. Das Dorf Singen und seine Finanzwirtschaft . Singen , 1985. 484 p. : ISBN 3-921413-23-0 LC Card 87-133391 DDC 336.43/46 19
HJ9494.S57 G4 1985

Singer, Paul Israel, 1932-
Dominação e desigualdade : estrutura de classes e repartição da renda no Brasil / Paul Singer. Rio de Janeiro, RJ : Paz e Terra, 1981. 185 p. ; 21 cm. (Coleção Estudos brasileiros. v. 49) Includes bibliographical references. LC Card 82-148154
1. Income distribution - Brazil. 2. Social classes - Brazil. 3. Brazil - Economic policy. I. Title.
HC190.I5 S55 1981 NYPL [JLD 86-3364]

Economia politica e processi di urbanizzazione / Paul Singer ; introduzione di Francesco Indovina ; [traduzione dal portoghese di Edda Barborini]. 1a ed. Venezia : Marsilio Editori, 1978. xx, 132 p. ; 22 cm. (Biblioteca Marsilio : Le scienze della nuova società. Architettura e urbanistica . 32) Translation of: Economia política da urbanização. Includes bibliographical references.
1. Urban economics - Addresses, essays, lectures. 2. Urbanization - Addresses, essays, lectures. 3. Urbanization - Latin America - Addresses, essays, lectures. 4. City planning - Addresses, essays, lectures. I. Title. NYPL [JLD 86-786]

A formação da classe operária / Paul Singer. 3a. ed. Campinas-SP : Editora da UNICAMP ; São Paulo-SP : Atual Editora, [1986] 80 p. : ill. ; 21 cm. (Discutindo a história) Bibliography: p. [75]-76. LC Card 86-224636
1. Labor and laboring classes. 2. Labor and laboring classes - Brazil. I. Title. II. Series.
HD4841 .S32 1986

Repartição da renda : pobres e ricos sob o regime militar / Paul Singer. Rio de Janeiro : J. Zahar, 1986. 95 p. ; 19 cm. (Brasil, os anos de autoritarismo) Bibliography: p. 94. ISBN 85-85061-40-5 : LC Card 86-157852
1. Income distribution - Brazil. 2. Poor - Brazil. 3. Wealth - Brazil. 4. Social classes - Brazil. I. Title. II. Series.
HC190.I5 S56 1986

Singh, Ajit Kumar, 1944- Agricultural development and rural poverty / Ajit Kumar Singh. 1st ed. New Delhi : Ashish Pub. House, 1987. v, 368 p. : maps ; 22 cm. "Based on the findings of a research project sponsored by the Indian Council of Social Science Research"--T.p. verso. With special reference to Uttar Pradesh, India, since 1951. Bibliography: p. [361]-365. Includes index. ISBN 81-7024-069-7 : LC Card 86-903483 DDC 338.1/8542 19
1. Agriculture - Economic aspects - India - Uttar Pradesh. 2. Rural poor - India - Uttar Pradesh. I. Indian Council of Social Science Research. II. Title.
HD2075.U88 S55 1987

Singh, Alok Kumar, 1958- Population and settlement in U.P. : a geographical analysis / Alok Kumar Singh. New Delhi, India : Inter-India Publications, 1985. xx, 231 p., [10] p. of plates : ill., maps ; 23 cm. Includes index. Bibliography: p. [218]-223. LC Card 86-900123 DDC 304.6/0954/2 19
1. Human settlements - India - Uttar Pradesh. 2. Land settlement - India - Uttar Predesh. 3. Uttar Pradesh, India - Population. I. Title.
HB2100.U88 S55 1985 NYPL [JLD 86-3156]

Singh, Andréa Menefee, 1943- Invisible hands . New Delhi , Newbury Park, Calif. , 1987. 273 p. ; ISBN 0-8039-9524-5 (U. S.) LC Card 87-4337 DDC 331.4/0954 19
HD6181.85 .A85 1987

Singh, Anil K., 1953- Forest resource, economy, and environment / A.K. Singh, V.K. Kumar, J. Singh. New Delhi : Concept Pub. Co., 1987. xv, 124 p. : ill., maps ; 23 cm. Study of Uttar Pradesh. Bibliography: p. [119]-121. Includes index. LC Card 87-901902 DDC 333.78/4 19
1. Forests and forestry - Economic aspects - India - Uttar Pradesh. 2. Forests and forestry - Environmental aspects - India - Uttar Pradesh. I. Kumar, V. K. (Virendra Kumar), 1954-. II. Singh, Jagadish, 1952-. III. Title.
HD9766.I63 U887 1987

Singh, Awadh Bihari Prasad, 1946- Lead bank scheme : with special reference to north Bihar / Awadh Bihari Prasad Singh. Delhi : Capital Pub. House, 1987. v, 223 p. ; 22 cm. Based on the author's thesis (Ph. D.--Bihar University, Muzaffarpur, 1984) Bibliography: p. [219]-223. LC Card 87-900328 DDC 332.1/0954/12 19
1. Banks and banking - India - Bihar. I. Title.
HG3289.B53 S57 1987

Singh, C. S. K. Pais, H. Poverty alleviation programmes . New Delhi , 1986. xii, 48, [3] p. (some folded) : LC Card 86-903597 DDC 362.5/8/09543 19
HC437.J43 P35 1986

Singh, Devi, 1952- Economics of exchange rate management / Devi Singh. New Delhi : Criterion Publications, 1986. 204 p. ; 23 cm. Evaluation of the exchange rate policy of India, since 1975. Bibliography: p. [192]-199. Includes index. LC Card 86-903032 DDC 332.4/560954 19
1. Foreign exchange - Government policy - India. 2. Foreign exchange problem - India. I. Title.
HG3971 .S56 1975

Singh, Gurdev. see **Gurdev Singh.**

Singh, H. P. Regional disparity in industrial growth / H.P. Singh. 1st ed. New Delhi, India : Anmol Publications, 1987. xvi, 304 p. : ill., maps ; 22 cm. With reference to Rajasthan. Bibliography: p. [297]-300. Includes index. ISBN 81-7041-029-0 : LC Card 87-902685 DDC 338.0954/4 19
1. Rajasthan (India) - Economic conditions - Regional disparities. 2. Rajasthan, India - Industries. I. Title.
HC437.R3 S37 1987

Singh, Inderjit, 1941- Agricultural household models . Baltimore, Md. , 1986. xi, 335 p. : ISBN 0-8018-3149-0 LC Card 85-45102 DDC 331.7/63/091724 19
HD1542 .A34 1986 NYPL [JLE 86-2440]

Singh, Jagadish, 1952- Singh, Anil K., 1953- Forest resource, economy, and environment /. New Delhi , 1987. xv, 124 p. : LC Card 87-901902 DDC 333.78/4 19
HD9766.I63 U887 1987

Singh, K. K. (Kailash Kumar), 1930- Command area development, successes and learnings . Hyderabad , c1980. iii, 138 p. ; LC Card 83-906246 DDC 338.1/854 19
HD1741.I29 C65 1980 NYPL [JLD 87-597]

Singh, Kanti. The great depression and agrarian economy : a study of an underdeveloped region of India / Kanti Singh ; foreword by S.B. Singh. Delhi, India : Mittal Publications, 1987. xii, 206 p. ; 23 cm. With special reference to Bihar, India. Bibliography: p. [195]-202. Includes index. LC Card 86-903533 DDC 338.1/0954/12 19
1. Depressions - 1929 - India. 2. Bihar (India) - Economic conditions. 3. Agriculture - Economic aspects - India - Bihar. I. Title.
HC437.B47 S53 1987

Singh, Karam, M.B.A. The Regulatory framework of accounting /. Estover, Plymouth , 1985. [12], 391 p. : ISBN 0-7121-0491-7
NYPL [JLF 87-84]

Singh, Nar, 1952- Sharing of productivity gains in Indian industry / Nar Singh. Delhi : B.R. Pub. Corp., 1984. x, 180 p. ; 21 cm. Originally presented as the author's thesis (Ph. D.--University of Lucknow, 1983) Includes index. Bibliography: p. [164]-176.
1. Profit-sharing - India. 2. Industrial productivity - India. 3. Labor productivity - India. I. Title.
NYPL [JLD 86-4253]

Singh, R. S. (Rama Shankar), 1950- Changing occupational structure of scheduled tribes / R.S. Singh. New Delhi, India : Inter-India Publications, 1986. 291 p. : ill., maps ; 23 cm. (Tribal studies of India series . T 121) With reference to Chotanagpur region of Bihar, India. Bibliography: p. [278]-286. Includes index. ISBN 81-210-0175-7 : LC Card 86-903755
1. Chota Nagpur (India) - Scheduled tribes - Employment. 2. Chota Nagpur (India) - Occupations. 3. Rural development - India - Chota Nagpur. I. Title. II. Series.
HB3640.C48 S56 1986

Singh, Ram. Mahajan, Amarjit. Problems of the aged in unorganised sector /. Delhi, India , 1987. viii, 106 p. ; LC Card 87-901315 DDC 362.6/042 19
HD7105.35.I5 M34 1987

Singh, Sita Ram. Land reforms in India / Sita Ram Singh. 1st ed. Allahabad : Kitab Mahal : Selling agents, Kitab Mahal Agencies, 1987. iv, 176 p. ; 23 cm. Originally presented as the author's thesis (Ph. D.--Magadh University) under the title: Land ceiling, a milestone in the land reform policy of Bihar. Bibliography: p. [168]-176. LC Card 87-901297 DDC 333.3/1/54 19
1. Land reform - India. I. Title.
HD1333.I4 S56 1987

Singh, V. B., 1941- Profiles of political elites in India / V.B. Singh. Delhi : Ritu Publishers, 1984. xii, 178 p. : ill. ; 22 cm. Includes index. Bibliography: p. [169]-176. LC Card 84-900272 DDC 305.5/24/0954 19
1. Elite (Social sciences) - India. 2. Politicians - India. 3. Leadership. 4. India - Politics and government - 1947-. I. Title.
JQ281 .S565 1984 NYPL [JLD 86-4319]

Singht Gill, Manohar. see **Gill, Manohar Singh, 1936-**

SINGLE PARENTS - EMPLOYMENT - AUSTRALIA.
Frey, Dianne. Survey of sole parent pensioners' workforce barriers /. Woden, ACT [1986] 40 p. : ISBN 0-642-51708-8 LC Card 87-154429 DDC 331.4/4 19
HD6220 .F74 1986

SINGLE PARENTS - GOVERNMENT POLICY - AUSTRALIA.
Frey, Dianne. Survey of sole parent pensioners' workforce barriers /. Woden, ACT [1986] 40 p. : ISBN 0-642-51708-8 LC Card 87-154429

DDC 331.4/4 19
HD6220 .F74 1986

SINGLE TAX.
George, Henry, 1839-1897. [Progress and poverty. Spanish.] Progreso y miseria /. [Madrid , 1985?] cxv, 384 p. : ISBN 84-7479-375-0 : LC Card 87-112201
HB171 .G276 1985

Singleton, Ross C. Industrial organization and antitrust : a survey of alternative perspectives / Ross C. Singleton. Columbus, Ohio : Publishing Horizons, c1986. ix, 102 p. ; 23 cm. Includes bibliographical references and indexes. ISBN 0-942280-15-6 : LC Card 85-19318 DDC 338.8/0973 19
1. Industrial organization - United States. 2. Antitrust law - Economic aspects - United States. I. Title.
HD70.U5 S54 1986 NYPL [JLD 86-3251]

Sinha, Arbind K. SITE to INSAT . New Delhi , 1986. viii, 165 p. : LC Card 86-902956 DDC 384.55/44/0954 19
HE8700.9.I5 S57 1986

Sinha, Narain. Reddy, K. N. (Kaipa Narayana), 1936- Central government expenditure . New Delhi , 1984. xvi, 175 p. ; LC Card 84-901866 DDC 336.3/9/0954 19
HJ2157 .R43 1984 NYPL [JLD 87-66]

Sinha, R. K. (Raj Kishore), 1946- Planning in India : a critique / R.K. Sinha. New Delhi : South Asian Publishers, c1987. ix, 247 p. ; 23 cm. Includes bibliographies and index. ISBN 81-7003-079-X : LC Card 87-901786 DDC 338.954 19
1. India - Economic policy - 1947-. 2. India - Social policy. I. Title.
HC435.2 .S565 1987

Sinha, Sunil Kumar. Urban growth in India, 1951-81 : a statistical analysis. New Delhi : Office of the Registrar General, India, Ministry of Home Affairs, 1986. vi, 72 p. : ill. ; 31 cm. (Census of India, 1981. Census monograph . no. 1) Bibliography: p. 71-72. "PRG.497 (N)/500-1985 (DSK.II)"--P. [4] of cover. LC Card 86-902819
1. Cities and towns - India - Growth - Statistics. 2. India - Census, 1981. I. India. Office of the Registrar General. II. Series.
HA4581.5 1981e

Sinkel, Dimitri. Computers in purchasing [microform] / Dimitri Sinkel. New York : AMA Membership Publications Division, American Management Associations, c1984. 48 p. : ill. ; 23 cm. (AMA management briefing) Microfilm. New York : New York Public Library, 1985. 1 microfilm reel ; 35 mm. (MN *ZZ-24,152) ISBN 0-8144-2305-1 : LC Card 84-9034 DDC 658.7/2/02854 19
1. Purchasing - Data processing. 2. Management - Data processing. I. Title.
*HF5437 .S52 1984 NYPL [*ZT-1565 no.12]*

Sinkovics, Alfréd. Nemzetközi tőkemozgások és a KGST / Sinkovics Alfréd. Budapest : Közgazdasági és Jogi Könyvkiadó, 1986, c1985. 336, [1] p. : ill. ; 21 cm. Bibliography: p. 328-[337]. ISBN 963-221-493-5 : LC Card 87-408509
1. Capital movements. 2. Capital movements - Europe, Eastern. 3. Europe, Eastern - Foreign economic relations. 4. Council for Mutual Economic Assistance. I. Title.
HG3891 .S57 1986

Sinn, Hans-Werner.
Kapitaleinkommensbesteuerung : eine Analyse der intertemporalen, internationalen und intersektoralen Allokationswirkungen / von Hans-Werner Sinn. Tübingen : Mohr, 1985. xv, 352 p. : ill. ; 24 cm. Bibliography: p. [330]-340. Includes indexes. ISBN 3-16-344827-5 LC Card 85-164588
1. Corporations - Taxation. I. Title.
HD2753.A3 S48 1985

[Kapitaleinkommensbesteuerung. English]
Capital income taxation and resource allocation / Hans-Werner Sinn. Amsterdam ; New York : North-Holland ; xiv, 411 p. ; 23 cm. (Studies in mathematical and managerial economics. v. 35) Translation of: Kapitaleinkommensbesteuerung. Bibliography: p. [387]-397. Includes indexes. ISBN 0-444-70208-3 LC Card 87-9126 DDC 336.24/3 19
1. Corporations - Taxation - Mathematical models. 2. Investments - Taxation - Mathematical models. 3. Capital - Mathematical models. 4. Resource allocation - Mathematical models. I. Title. II. Series.
HD2753.A3 S47413 1987

Die Sinnlichkeit der Theorie . Zellinger, Alfred, 1945- Wien , c1983. 173 p. : ISBN 3-85439-005-X LC Card 84-196565
HF1040.7 .Z45 1983

Sinopse de informações dos municípios catarinenses. 2a. ed. Florianópolis, SC : Cia. de Distritos Industriais de Santa Catarina, Secretaria da Ind. e do Comércio, 1986. 155 leaves : 1 map ; 28 cm. Cover title. LC Card 87-403943 DDC 330.981/64063 19
1. Santa Catarina (Brazil : State) - Economic conditions - Statistics. 2. Municipal services - Brazil - Santa Catarina (State) - Statistics. I. Companhia de Distritos Industriais de Sta. Catarina.
HC188.S26 S555 1986

Sinopsis (São Paulo, Brazil). Special number. Sócrates, Jodete Rios. A cidade invade as águas . [São Paulo] , 1985. 296 p., [2] folded leaves of plates : LC Card 87-118596 DDC 333.91/00981/61 19
HD1696.B84 S427 1985

Síntese das exposições e dos debates /. Seminário sobre Política Industrial da Bahia (1986 : Salvador, Brazil) [Salvador] [1986] 89 p. ; LC Card 87-403843 DDC 338.981/42 19
HD3616.B84 B37 1986

Síntesis de la economía colombiana, 1959-1974 / República de Colombia, Ministerio de Hacienda y Crédito Público, Oficina Económica. Bogotá, D.E. : La Oficina Económica, 1974. vii, 90 leaves, [6] leaves of plates : ill. ; 29 cm. Cover title. "Luis Fernando Echavarría Vélez, ministro de hacienda y crédito público." LC Card 87-403567 DDC 330.9861/0632 19
1. Colombia - Economic conditions - 1918-. I. Echavarría Vélez, Luis Fernando. II. Colombia. Ministerio de Hacienda y Crédito Públio. Oficina Económica.
HC197 .S56 1974

Sintini, Lorenzo. Cooperare e competere /. Milano , 1986. 2 v. : ISBN 88-07-10058-4 (v. 1) : LC Card 87-125969
HD2953 .C66 1986

Sinz, Manfred.
Konsequenzen der Arbeitsmarktentwicklung und des technischen Fortschritts für die Entwicklung des ländlichen Raumes. 1984. Arbeitsmarktpolitik für die Landwirtschaft und den ländlichen Raum / mit Beiträgen von Otto Lackinger, Karl Pelz, Manfred Sinz ; [Herausgeber, Hans Bach]. Graz , c1984. 138 p. : ISBN 3-900307-15-6 LC Card 85-186643
HD1536.A9 A73 1984

Sinzinger, Friedrich, 1911- Heilbronner Postgeschichte bis zur Einführung der Briefmarke 1851 / Friedrich Sinzinger. Heilbronn : Städtische Museen Heilbronn, c1984. 133 p. : ill., facsims. ; 26 cm. (Heilbronner Museumsheft . Nr. 10) Bibliography: p. 133. LC Card 87-409273 DDC 383/.494346 19
1. Postal service - Germany (West) - Heilbronn - History. 2. Heilbronn (Germany) - History. I. Series: Heilbronner Museumshefte, Nr. 10. II. Title.
HE6185.G32 H457 1984

Sipkoff, Susan Stone. Holoviak, Stephen J. Managing human productivity . New York , 1987. xiii, 216 p. : ISBN 0-275-92481-5 (alk. paper) : LC Card 86-25247 DDC 658.3/14 19
HF5549.2.U5 H65 1987

Sipos, Béla. Vállalati árelőrejelzések : módszertani kézikönyv / Sipos Béla. Budapest : Közgazdasági és Jogi Könyvkiadó, 1985. 290, [1] p. : ill. ; 24 cm. Bibliography: p. 279-[291] ISBN 963-221-515-X : LC Card 86-190915
1. Economic forecasting - Statistical methods. 2. Prices - Forecasting - Statistical methods. 3. Economic forecasting - Hungary - Statistical methods. 4. Prices - Hungary - Forecasting - Statistical methods. I. Title.
HB3730 .S495 1985

Sipos, Levente. Munkásosztályunk fejlődése 1945-ig . Győr , 1985. 126 p. ; LC Card 86-186895
HD8420.5 .M85 1985

Sipozium "Geografiia v Kirgizii" (1980 : Frunze, Kirghiz S.S.R.) Sovremennye problemy geografii Kirgizii : materialy simpoziuma "Geografiia v Kirgizii" VII S″ezda Geograficheskogo obshchestva SSSR, 22-27 sentiabria 1980 g., g. Frunze ; [readaktsionnaia kollegiia E.K. Azykova, S.U. Umurzakov (otv. red.) ... et al.]. Frunze : Izd-vo "Ilim", 1980. 167 p. : ill. ; 20 cm. At head of title: Akademiia nauk Kirgizskoĭ SSR ... Includes bibliographies. LC Card 82-121674
1. Kirghiz S.S.R. - Economic conditions - Congresses. 2. Natural resources - Kirghiz S.S.R. - Congresses. 3. Geography, Economic - Congresses. I. Azykova, E. K. II. Umurzakov, Sadybakas. III. Title.
HC337.K545 S56 1980

Siqueira, Penha. O desenvolvimento do porto de Vitória, 1870-1940 / Penha Siqueira. Vitória-ES : CODESA, 1984. 162 p. : ill. ; 22 cm. "Dissertação apresentada ao curso de pós-graduação/mestrado em história da Universidade Federal de Santa Catarina em 8 de setembro de 1980." Bibliography: p. 133-149. LC Card 85-144275
1. Harbors - Brazil - Vitória (Espírito Santo) - History. 2. Vitória (Espírito Santo, Brazil) - Commerce - History. 3. Vitória (Espírito Santo, Brazil) - Economic conditions. I. Title.
HE556.V5 S56 1984

Širdies ritmogramų atpažinimo sistema. Sistema raspoznavaniia ritmogramm serdtsa . Vil′nius , 1980. 55 p. : LC Card 81-194159
HD38 .S715 vyp. 49 QP112.5.C3

Sirenko, Vasiliĭ Fedorovich. Pravovye problemy RASU /. Kiev , 1985. 303 p. : LC Card 86-139849
HC337.U5 P65 1985

Sirey, Michel. Glück auf! . Paris [1986] 117 p. : ISBN 2-86738-115-0 : LC Card 86-178958
HD8039.M6152 F84 1986

Sirianni, Carmen. Worker participation and the politics of reform /. Philadelphia , 1987. ix, 371 p. ; ISBN 0-87722-464-1 (alk. paper) : LC Card 86-23006 DDC 658.3/152 19
HD5650 .W645 1987

Siring, Erling. To notater om sammenlikning av data fra fruktbarhetsundersøkelsen 1977 med data fra registre / av Erling Siring. Oslo : Statistisk sentralbyrå : I kommisjon hos H. Aschehoug og Universitetsforlaget, 1983. 43 p. : ill. ; 30 cm. (Rapporter fra Statistisk sentralbyrå, 0332-8422 . 83/30) Bibliography: p. 41. ISBN 82-537-2006-8 : LC Card 84-161768
1. Fertility, Human - Norway - Statistics. 2. Norway - Statistics, Vital. I. Title. II. Series.
HB1025 .S57 1983

Sirohi, A. S. (Amar Singh), 1926- Haque, T. (Tajamul), 1947- Agrarian reforms and institutional changes in India /. New Delhi , 1986, c1985. xvi, 268 p. : LC Card 86-902575 DDC 338.1/854 19
HD1333.I4 H36 1986 NYPL [JLD 87-1547]

Sirota, David. Essentials of real estate investment / David Sirota. 3rd ed. Chicago : Real Estate Education Co., 1988. xiii, 254 p. ; 28 cm. Bibliography: p. 227-228. Includes index. ISBN 0-88462-667-9 (p. 4 of cover) LC Card 87-23222 DDC 332.63/24 19
1. Real estate investment. I. Title. II. Title: Real estate management.
HD1382.5 .S52 1988

Sirota, S. M. (Simon Matveevich) Voronin, V. G. (Valeriĭ Grigor′evich) Ekonomiko-matematicheskie metody planirovaniia na predpriiatiiakh pishchevoĭ promyshlennosti /. Moskva , 1981. 270 p. : LC Card 82-103139
HD9015.S65 V67 1981

Sirs, Bill. Hard labour / Bill Sirs. London : Sidgwick & Jackson, 1985. 151 p., [8] p. of plates : ill. ; 23 cm. Includes index. ISBN 0-283-99241-7 : LC Card 86-191030 DDC 331.88/1691/0924 B 19
1. Sirs, Bill. 2. Trade unions - Great Britain - Officials and employees - Biography. 3. Iron and Steel Trades Confederation (Great Britain). 4. British Steel Corporation Strike, 1980. 5. Trade-unions - Great Britain. 6. Great Britain - Politics and government - 1945-. I. Title.
HD6665.S57 A3 1985

SIRS, BILL.
Sirs, Bill. Hard labour /. London , 1985. 151 p., [8] p. of plates : ISBN 0-283-99241-7 : LC Card 86-191030 DDC 331.88/1691/0924 B 19
HD6665.S57 A3 1985

Sirumbal, Luis Miguel. La crisis de la industria automotriz (1971-1982) / autor, Luis Miguel

Sirumbal. Lima, Perú : CEDAL, [1983] 54 p. : ill. ; 20 cm. LC Card 84-123601 DDC 338.4/76292/0985 19
1. Acuerdo de Cartagena. 2. Automobile industry and trade - Peru. 3. Automobile industry and trade - Government policy - Peru. 4. Automobile industry and trade - Andes region. 5. Automobile industry and trade - Law and legislation - Peru. I. Title.
HD9710.P382 S57 1983
NYPL [JLD 86-365]

Sisay, S. S. Budget speech / by Sheriff Saikouba Sisay. [Gambia] : Republic of the Gambia, [1986] 60 leaves ; 30 cm. Cover title. "In Parliament on Friday, 27th June, 1986." LC Card 87-403347 DDC 354.66/510072256 19
1. Budget - Gambia. 2. Gambia - Economic policy. 3. Gambia - Foreign economic relations. I. Title.
HJ2185 .S57 1986

Sisco, Carlos. Hanthorn, Michael. Selected farm machinery statistics /. Washington, D.C. , 1986] ii, 54 p. : LC Card 86-602408 DDC 338.1/61/0973 19
HD1751 .A5 no. 743 HD9486.U4

Sisler, Carol U., 1929- Enterprising families, Ithaca, New York : their houses and businesses / by Carol U. Sisler. Ithaca, N.Y. (5 Cornell Walk, Ithaca 14850) : Enterprise Publishing, 1986. 159 p. : ill. ; 28 cm. Bibliography: p. 153-157. Includes index. LC Card 86-81672 DDC 338/.092/2 B 19
1. Businessmen - New York - Ithaca - Biography. 2. Ithaca, N. Y. - Biography. 3. Businessmen - New York - Ithaca - Homes and haunts. 4. Architecture, Domestic - New York - Ithaca. I. Title.
HC102.5.A2 S55 1986

Sismondi, J.-C.-L. Simonde de (Jean-Charles-Léonard Simonde), 1773-1842. Political economy / by J.C.L. Simonde de Sismondi. Fairfield, N.J. : A.M. Kelley, 1988. p. cm. (Reprints of economic classics) "The article 'Political Economy' was composed in 1815 for David Brewster's Edinburgh Encyclopedia and is reprinted from the first American edition published by J. & E. Parker, Philadelphia, 1828". Includes index. ISBN 0-678-00120-0 LC Card 87-17084 DDC 330 19
1. Economics. 2. Political science. I. Title.
HB163 .S5853 1988

Sisson, Keith. The management of collective bargaining : an international comparison / Keith Sisson. Oxford, UK ; New York, NY, USA : Blackwell, 1987. xviii, 230 p. ; 24 cm. (Warwick studies in industrial relations) Bibliography: p. [201]-212. Includes indexes. ISBN 0-631-13439-5 : LC Card 87-6642 DDC 331.89 19
1. Collective bargaining. I. Title.
HD6971.5 .S57 1987

Sistem udruženog rada /. Milošević, Nikša. Beograd , 1985. 392 p. : LC Card 86-197428
HD5660.Y8 M55 1985

Sistem upravljanja investicijama /. Smiljanić, Slobodan. Kragujevac , 1984. 185 p. : LC Card 86-115123
HG4234.6 .S65 1984

Sistema bancario y financiero en México, 1970-1982. El Sistema bancario y financiero en México, 1970-1984. México, D.F. , c1985. 260 p. ; ISBN 968-89204-0-1 LC Card 86-223773
HG2714 .S57 1985

El Sistema bancario y financiero en México, 1970-1984. México, D.F. : Instituto Nacional de Estadística, Geografía e Informática, c1985. 260 p. ; 28 cm. Rev. ed. of: El Sistema bancario y financiero en México, 1970-1982. Chiefly tables. Bibliography: p. 1. ISBN 968-89204-0-1 LC Card 86-223773
1. Banks and banking - Mexico - Statistics. 2. Finance - Mexico - Statistics. I. Instituto Nacional de Estadística, Geografía e Informática (Mexico). II. Sistema bancario y financiero en México, 1970-1982.
HG2714 .S57 1985

Sistema de cuentas nacionales de México : estructura económica regional, producto interno bruto por entidad federativa, 1970, 1975 y 1980. México, D.F. : Instituto Nacional de Estadística Geografía e Informática : Programa de las Naciones Unidas para el Desarrollo, 1985. xiii, 577 p. : ill., col. maps ; 28 cm. Chiefly tables. ISBN 968-89200-8-8 LC Card 87-401458 DDC 339.372 19
1. Gross national product - Mexico - States - Statistics. I. Instituto Nacional de Estadística, Geografía e Informática (Mexico). II. United Nations. Development Programme.
HC140.I5 S5725 1985

El Sistema de dirección y planificación de la economía en las empresas. La Habana : Editorial de Ciencias Sociales, 1981. xi, 203 p. : ill. ; 19 cm. (Economía) Originally presented by the Dirección de Perfeccionamiento del SDPE; edited by Felino Quesada Pérez. LC Card 83-212653
1. Central planning - Cuba. 2. Cuba - Economic policy. I. Quesada Pérez, Felino. II. Cuba. Dirección de Perfeccionamiento del SDPE. III. Series: Economía / Editorial de Ciencias Sociales.
HC152.5 .S57 1981

El sistema de las relaciones políticas y económicas entre los países latinoamericanos . Kaplan, Marcos. [Buenos Aires] [1985] 62 leaves ; LC Card 86-200041
HC125 .K32 1985

Sistema de planes de desarrollo de corto plazo, 1986. Instituto Nacional de Planificación (Peru) [Lima] [1986- v. <1-35 > : LC Card 86-216851
HC227 .I529 1986

Sistema de planes de desarrollo de mediano plazo. [Lima] : República del Perú, Presidencia de la República, Sistema Nacional de Planificación, Instituto Nacional de Planificación, [1987- v. <1-2 > : ill. ; 30 cm. CONTENTS. - vol. 1. Plan nacional de desarrollo, 1986-1990 -- 2. Plan Nacional de Desarrollo, 1986-1990. Anexos. LC Card 87-404041 DDC 338.985 19
1. Peru - Economic policy. 2. Peru - Economic conditions - 1968-. I. Instituto Nacional de Planificación (Peru).
HC227 .S496 1987

Sistema de remuneraciones en la empresa /. Oyarce Pérez, Luis. Santiago, Chile , 1982. ix, 174 p. : LC Card 84-228804
HD4906 .O98 1982

Il Sistema dei trasporti nello sviluppo della cooperazione economica internazionale : l'Italia e i paesi in via di sviluppo / Achilli ... [et al.] ; a cura di Lucia Lanzanova. Milano, Italy : F. Angeli, c1985. 341 p. ; 22 cm. (Trasporti. Sezione I, Testi . 2) At head of title: ICEI, Istituto Cooperazione economica internazionale. "Convegno ... organizzato dall'Icei in collaborazione con la Cciaa di Milano dal 17 al 19 maggio 1984"--Cover p. [4] LC Card 85-218403
1. Freight and freightage - Italy - Congresses. 2. Freight and freightage - European Economic Community countries - Congresses. 3. Freight and freightage - Developing countries - Congresses. I. Achilli, Michele. II. Lanzanova, Lucia. III. Istituto per la cooperazione economica internazionale (Italy). IV. Camera di commercio, industria, artigianato e agricoltura di Milano.
HE2449 .S57 1985

Sistema Económico Latinoamericano. América Latina, Estados Unidos . México , 1986. 223 p. : ISBN 968-231-378-3 LC Card 87-128005 DDC 337.7308 19
HF1456.5.L3 A44 1986

El FMI, el Banco Mundial y la crisis latinoamericana /. México , 1986. 474 p. : ISBN 968-231-373-2 LC Card 87-127860 DDC 332.1/52 19
HG3881.5.I58 F56 1986

SISTEMA ECONÓMICO LATINOAMERICANO. Kaplan, Marcos. El sistema de las relaciones políticas y económicas entre los países latinoamericanos . [Buenos Aires] [1985] 62 leaves ; LC Card 86-200041
HC125 .K32 1985

Sistema económico y empresa /. Serra Ramoneda, Antonio. Barcelona , 1986. 267 p. : ISBN 84-344-2011-2 LC Card 87-122090
HD37.S66 S46 1986

Sistema ėkonomiko-matematicheskikh modeleĭ dli͡a analiza i prognoza urovni͡a zhizni / otvetstvennye redaktory N.P. Fedorenko, N.M. Rimashevskai͡a. Moskva : "Nauka", 1986. 262 p. : ill. ; 23 cm. At head of title: Akademii͡a nauk SSSR. T͡Sentral'nyĭ ėkonomiko-matematicheskiĭ institut. Bibliography: p. 257-[261] LC Card 86-232874
1. Cost and standard of living - Mathematical models. 2. Cost and standard of living - Czechoslovakia - Mathematical models. 3. Cost and standard of living - Soviet Union - Mathematical models. I. Fedorenko, Nikolaĭ Prokof'evich. II. Rimashevskai͡a, Natal'i͡a Mikhaĭlovna. III. T͡Sentral'nyĭ ėkonomiko-matematicheskiĭ institut (Akademii͡a nauk SSSR).
HD6978 .S56 1986

Sistema financeiro e mercado de capitais /. Galvêas, Ernane. Rio de Janeiro , 1985. 171 p. : LC Card 85-208367
HG185.B7 G35 1985

O sistema financeiro nacional . Escóssia Neto, Lauro da. [Natal] , 1985. 46, [1] p. : LC Card 86-158741
HG185.B7 E83 1985

Sistema financiero . Martín-Guédez, Rafael, 1942- Caracas [1984] (Caracas : Editorial Arte) 309 p. : LC Card 85-177967
HG2156.V42 M37 1984

Sistema financiero. La Situación y los problemas del sistema financiero nacional. Santo Domingo, República Dominicana , 1986. 152 p. ; LC Card 86-208560
HG2817 .S57 1986

Il sistema industriale del Molise /. Quintano, Claudio. Bologna , c1986. 106 p. : ISBN 88-15-01163-3 : LC Card 86-214879
HC307.M64 Q56 1986

Sistema industriale e politiche regionali . Grandinetti, Roberto, 1953- Milano, Italy , 1984. 234 p. : LC Card 85-176111 DDC 338.945/39 19
HC307.F68 G73 1984

Sistema modeleĭ narodnokhozi͡aĭstvennogo planirovanii͡a / pod redakt͡sieĭ N.P. Fedorenko, E.F. Baranova. Moskva : Izd-vo "Nauka", 1982. 375 p. ; 21 cm. (Voprosy optimal'nogo planirovanii͡a i upravlenii͡a sot͡sialisticheskoĭ ėkonomikoĭ) On page preceding t.p.: Akademii͡a nauk SSSR. T͡Sentral'nyĭ ėkonomiko-matematicheskiĭ institut. Includes bibliographies. LC Card 83-172876
1. Soviet Union - Economic policy - 1981- - Mathematical models. I. Fedorenko, Nikolaĭ Prokof'evich. II. Baranov, Ė. F. III. T͡Sentral'nyĭ ėkonomiko-matematicheskiĭ institut (Akademii͡a nauk SSSR). IV. Series.
HC336.25 .S564 1982

Sistema nacional de cadastro rural. Estatísticas cadastrais . Brasília , 1985- <v. 1-2; in 2 > : LC Card 87-117732
HD498 .E77 1985

Sistema natural'no-stoimostnykh mezhotraslevykh balansov soi͡uznoĭ respubliki . Chertan, S. E. (Sergeĭ Evgen'evich) Kishinev , 1984. 242, [6] p., [2] folded leaves of plates : LC Card 85-130960
HC337.M55 C46 1984

Sistema planirovanii͡a tekhnicheskogo urovni͡a otrasli /. Chebanenko, Vladimir Mikhaĭlovich. Moskva , 1985. 118, [7] p. : LC Card 85-241451
HD70.S63 C45 1985

Sistema raspoznavanii͡a ritmogramm serdt͡sa : materialy k seminaru pri Institute matematiki i kibernetiki AN Litovskoĭ SSR "Statisticheskie problemy upravlenii͡a" / pod redakt͡sieĭ L. Tel'ksnis. Vil'ni͡us : In-t matematiki i kibernetiki Akademii nauk Litovskoĭ SSR, 1980. 55 p. : ill. ; 20 cm. (Statisticheskie problemy upravlenii͡a . vyp. 49) Titles on added t.p.: Širdies ritmogramų atpažinimo sistema; The heart rhythmogram recognition system. At head of title: Institut matematiki i kibernetiki AN Litovskoĭ SSR. Institut fiziko-tekhnicheskikh problem ėnergetiki AN Lit.SSR. Litovskai͡a territorial'nai͡a gruppa NKAU SSSR Mezhdunarodnoĭ federat͡sii po avtomaticheskomu upravlenii͡u. Summaries in English and Lithuanian; table of contents also in English and Lithuanian. Includes bibliographies. LC Card 81-194159
1. Cardiography - Data processing - Congresses. I. Tel'ksnis, L. II. Lietuvos TSR Mokslų akademija. Matematikos ir kibernetikos institutas. III. Fizikinių-techninių energetikos problemų institutas (Lietuvos TSR Mokslų akademija). IV. Nat͡sional'nyĭ komitet SSSR po avtomaticheskomu upravlenii͡u. Litovskai͡a territorial'nai͡a gruppa. V. Title: Širdies ritmogramų atpažinimo sistema. VI. Title: Heart rhythmogram recognition system. VII. Series.
HD38 .S715 vyp. 49 QP112.5.C3

Sistema tributário "diagnóstico e reforma." Serra, José. [Novo federalismo.] Um novo federalismo ; O sistema tributário "diagnóstico e reforma" /. São Paulo , 1984. 43 p. ; LC Card

87-124038 DDC 336.2/00981 19
HJ3424.A4 S47 1984

Sistema upravleniia promyshlennost'iu KNR, 1949-1980 /. Remyga, V. N. (Vladimir Nikolaevich) Moskva , 1982. 189, [3] p. ; LC Card 82-180587
HD70.C5 R45 1982

Sistema vedeniia sel'skogo i promyslovogo khoziaistva na Eniseiskom Severe : rekomendatsii / [otvetstvennyi redaktor A.I. Solomakha ; nauchnyi redaktor A.L. Shtele]. Novosibirsk : Sibirskoe otd-nie VASKHNIL, 1986. 211 p. ; 21 cm. At head of title: Vsesoiuznaia ordena Lenina i ordena Trudovogo Krasnogo sel'skokhoziaistvennykh nauk imeni V.I. Lenina. Sibirskoe otdelenie. Nauchno-issledovatel'skii institut sel'skogo khoziaistva Krainego Severa. Upravlenie sel'skogo khoziaistva Krasnoiarskogo kraiispolkoma. LC Card 86-227282
1. Agriculture - Economic aspects - Russian S.F.S.R. - Krasnoiarskii krai. 2. Agriculture - Russian S.F.S.R. - Krasnoiarskii krai. 3. Agriculture - Arctic regions. I. Solomakha, A. I. (Aleksei Ivanovich). II. Shtele, A. L. III. Nauchno-issledovatel'skii institut sel'skogo khoziaistva Krainego Severa (Noril'sk, R.S.F.S.R.). IV. Upravlenie sel'skogo khoziaistva Krasnoiarskogo kraiispolkoma.
HD1995.K73 S57 1986

Sistema vedeniia sel'skogo khoziaistva Buriatskoi ASSR : rekomendatsii / [sostaviteli V.B. Saganov (rukovoditel') ... et al.]. Novosibirsk : Sibirskoe otd-nie VASKhNIL, 1985. 188 p. : ill. ; 20 cm. At head of title: Vsesoiuznaia ordena Lenina i ordena Trudovogo Krasnogo Znameni akademiia sel'skokhoziaistvennykh nauk imeni V.I. Lenina. Sibirskoe otdelenie. Buriatskii nauchno-issledovatel'skii institut sel'skogo khoziaistva. Ministerstvo sel'skogo khoziaistva Buriatskoi ASSR. LC Card 86-215358
1. Agriculture and state - Russian S.F.S.R. - Buriatskaia A.S.S.R. 2. Agriculture - Economic aspects - Russian S.F.S.R. - Buriatskaia A.S.S.R. I. Saganov, V. B. (Vladimir Biz'iaevich). II. Vsesoiuznaia akademiia sel'skokhoziaistvennykh nauk imeni V.I. Lenina. Sibirskoe otdelenie. III. Buriatskii nauchno-issledovatel'skii institut sel'skogo khoziaistva. IV. Buriatskaia A.S.S.R. (R.S.F.S.R.). Ministerstvo sel'skogo khoziaistva.
HD1995.B8 S57 1985

Sistema vedeniia sel'skogo khoziaistva v Litovskoi SSR. Lietuvos TSR žemės ūkio tvarkymo sistema /. Vilnius , 1985. 453 p. ; LC Card 86-215158
HD1995.L5 L535 1985

Sistemas alternativos de política salarial /. Lopes, Francisco Lafaiete. Rio de Janeiro, RJ , 1984. 51 leaves : LC Card 86-178892
HC79.W24 L66 1984

Sistemas y equipos de desmedulado en la industria del bagazo de la caña de azúcar /. Correa, Jorge Lois. Ciudad de La Habana , c1982. 77 p. : LC Card 85-198777
HD9119.B4 C83 1982

Sistemi di gestione strategica aziendale . Di Stefano, Guido, 1939- Milano, Italy , c1986. 232 p. : LC Card 86-180982
HD30.28 .D52 1986

Sistemnyi podkhod k organizatsii upravleniia /. Mil'ner, Bentsion Zakharovich. Moskva , 1983. 223 p. : LC Card 83-229946
HD70.S63 M54 1983

Sistemnyi podkhod v reshenii nekotorykh problem sotsial'no-ėkonomicheskogo optimuma / [otvetstvennyi redaktor Ovsienko IUrii Valentinovich]. Moskva : Akademiia nauk SSSR, TSentr. ėkonomiko-matematicheskii in-t, 1984. 88 p. ; 20 cm. Includes bibliographies. LC Card 86-144288
1. Industrial productivity - Soviet Union. I. Ovsienko, IU. V. II. TSentral'nyi ėkonomiko-matematicheskii institut (Akademiia nauk SSSR).
HC340.I52 S57 1984

Sistemul economic socialist. Eficiența economico-socială /. Craiova , 1983. 392 p. ; LC Card 84-152996
HC405.Z9 I523 1983

Sisterhood & solidarity . Balser, Diane. Boston, MA , c1987. vii, 247 p. ; ISBN 0-89608-278-4 : LC Card 87-4733 DDC 331.4 19
HD6079.2.U5 B34 1987

Sisterhood denied . Janiewski, Dolores E., 1948- Philadelphia , 1985. xvii, 248 p. : ISBN 0-87722-361-0 : LC Card 84-2640 DDC 305.4/2/09756563 19
HD6073.T62 U65 1985
NYPL [Sc E 86-322]

Sisters and strangers . Honig, Emily. Stanford, Calif. , 1986. ix, 299 p. : ISBN 0-8047-1274-3 (alk. paper) : LC Card 84-51711 DDC 331.4/87721/0951132 19
HD6073.T42 C64 1986
NYPL [JLD 86-3016]

Sita Ram Singh. see **Singh, Sita Ram.**

SITE to INSAT : challenges of production and research for women and children / edited by Binod C. Agrawal, Arbind K. Sinha. New Delhi : Concept Pub. Co. by arrangement with Development and Educational Communication Unit, Indian Space Research Organisation, Ahmedabad, 1986. viii, 165 p. : ill., maps ; 23 cm. Papers presented at the Seminar on "SITE" to "INSAT": Production Programmes for Women and Children, held at Space Applications Centre, Ahmedabad, Nov. 26-28, 1984. A shift from Satellite Instructional Television Experiment (SITE) to Indian National Satellite System (INSAT). Bibliography: p. 71. LC Card 86-902956 DDC 384.55/44/0954 19
1. Television programs - India - Congresses. 2. Television programs for children - India - Congresses. 3. Television in health education - India - Congresses. 4. Satellite Instructional Television Experiment (India) - Congresses. 5. Indian National Satellite System - Congresses. I. Agrawal, Binod C. II. Sinha, Arbind K. III. Indian Space Research Organisation. Development and Educational Communication Unit. IV. Seminar on "SITE" to "INSAT": Production of Programmes for Women and Children (1984 : Space Applications Centre).
HE8700.9.I5 S57 1986

Sites and services in urban housing in India /. Om Kumar, 1944- New Delhi , 1987. xii, 86 p. : ISBN 81-7000-026-2 : LC Card 87-900362 DDC 363.5/0954 19
HD7361.A3 O5 1987

Sites & services in urban housing in India. Om Kumar, 1944- Sites and services in urban housing in India /. New Delhi , 1987. xii, 86 p. : ISBN 81-7000-026-2 : LC Card 87-900362 DDC 363.5/0954 19
HD7361.A3 O5 1987

Sithanen, R. Mauritius. Commission of Inquiry into the Sugar Industry. The human factor, the sugar industry, and Mauritius . Port Louis, Mauritius [1984] 157 p. ; LC Card 85-980119 DDC 338.1/7361/096982 19
HD9118.M45 M33 1984a

Sitterly, Connie, 1953- A woman's place : management / Connie Sitterly, Beth Whitley Duke. Englewood Cliffs, N.J. : Prentice Hall, c1988. xvi, 365 p. : ill. ; 24 cm. Includes bibliographies and index. ISBN 0-13-961954-2 (pbk.) : LC Card 87-25746 DDC 658.4/09/024042 19
1. Women executives. 2. Women middle managers. I. Duke, Beth Whitley, 1954-. II. Title.
HD6054.3 .S67 1988

A situação da mulher /. Santarcangelo, Maria Candida Vergueiro. São Paulo , 1980. 389 p. ;
NYPL [JLD 86-625]

A situação das indústrias de base, TT1-39-59 /. Figueiredo, João Kubitschek de. [S.l.] [1960?] 75, [2] p. : LC Card 85-144484
HD9524.B82 F54 1960

Situação de saúde e lazer do comerciário de Fortaleza / Serviço Social do Comércio-SESC, Departamento Regional do Ceará, Assessoria Técnica, Seção de Pesquisas e Estatística. Fortaleza-CE : O Serviço, 1977/1978 [i.e. 1978] 66 leaves ; 32 cm. Cover title: Pesquisa--situação de saúde e lazer do comerciário de Fortaleza. LC Card 83-116799
1. Retail trade - Brazil - Fortaleza - Employees. 2. Businessmen - Health and hygiene - Brazil - Fortaleza. 3. Clerks - Health and hygiene - Brazil - Fortaleza. 4. Businessmen - Brazil - Fortaleza - Recreation. 5. Clerks - Brazil - Fortaleza - Recreation. I. Serviço Social do Comércio. Departamento Regional do Ceará. Seção de Pesquisas e Estatística. II. Title: Pesquisa--situação de saúde e lazer do comerciário de Fortaleza.
HD5755.F6 S58 1978

Situação e perspectivas dos recursos humanos na República da Guiné-Bissau /. Ribeiro, Sérgio. Addis Ababa [1984 or 1985] 49, 19 p., [8] leaves : LC Card 85-981187 DDC 331.11/0966/57 19
HD5849.A6 R53 1984

Situação econômica-financeira das concessionárias de energia elétrica . Eletrobrás. [Rio de Janeiro] , 1979. 64 p. ; LC Card 84-256157
HD9685.B8 E47 1979

A Situação nas antigas zonas libertadas de Cabo Delgado / Universidade Eduardo Mondlane, Centro de Estudos Africanos, Oficina de História. [Maputo, Mozambique] : A Oficina, 1983. 59 p. ; 30 cm. (CEA relatório . no. 83/4) Limited edition of 300 copies. Mimeographed. Includes bibliographical references. LC Card 86-980983 DDC 330.967/9805 19
1. Cabo Delgado (Mozambique) - Economic conditions - Case studies. 2. Cabo Delgado (Mozambique) - Politics and government - Case stidies. 3. Cabo Delgado (Mozambique) - History - Case studies. I. Universidade Eduardo Mondlane. Centro de Estudos Africanos. Oficina de História. II. Series: CEA relatório , 83/4.
HC890.Z7 C327 1983

Situación actual y perspectivas económicas, 1972 . Consejo Superior de Planificación Económica (Honduras) Tegucigalpa, D.C., Honduras, C.A. , 1972. 38, [18] leaves ; LC Card 86-158684
HC145 .C66 1972

Situación ambiental de Costa Rica /. Bonilla, Alexander. [San José] [1985] 271 p. : ISBN 997-7590-57-5 LC Card 86-156609
HC143.Z9 E52 1985

La Situación cambiaria en la República Dominicana / [editor, Frank Moya Pons]. Santo Domingo, República Dominicana : FORUM, 1984. 252 p. : ill. ; 22 cm. (Forum. 13) Papers presented at a meeting sponsored by FORUM on Sat., March 10, 1984 in the Hotel Santo Domingo Sur. LC Card 87-401265 DDC 338.97293 19
1. Dominican Republic - Economic policy - Congresses. 2. International Monetary Fund - Dominican Republic - Congresses. 3. Economic stabilization - Dominican Republic - Congresses. 4. Foreign exchange problem - Dominican Republic - Congresses. 5. Balance of payments - Dominican Republic - Congresses. I. Moya Pons, Frank, 1944-. II. FORUM (Debating society). III. Series: FORUM (Series : Santo Domingo, Dominican Republic) , 13.
HC153.5 .S575 1984

Situación de crédito, hacienda y presupuesto del Municipio de Madrid en 1907 . Madrid (Spain). Alcaldía. Madrid , 1907. viii, 137 p. ; LC Card 85-131486
HJ9528.M38 M34 1907

La situación del sector metal-mecánico en el Perú . Beltrán Alejos, Hugo. Lima, Perú , 1985. 93, [77] p. : LC Card 86-218266
HD9506.P42 B45 1985

La situación económica mundial y México . Sacristán, Antonio. México, D.F. [1980] 72 p. ; LC Card 87-400921 DDC 330.972/0834 19
HC59 .S3122 1980

Situación habitacional en Venezuela : XI censo general de población y vivienda / República de Venezuela, Presidencia de la República, Oficina Central de Estadística e Informática. [Caracas] : La Oficina, [1986- v. <1 > : ill. ; 23 cm. Vol. 1 chiefly tables. ISBN 980-280-043-0 LC Card 87-114711 DDC 363.5/1/0987/021 19
1. Housing - Venezuela - Statistics. 2. Venzuela - Census, 1981. I. Venezuela. Oficina Central de Estadística e Informática. II. Title: XI censo general de población y vivienda. III. Title: 11o censo general de población y vivienda. IV. Title: Undécimo censo general de población y vivienda.
HD7331.A3 S57 1986

Situación petrolera peruana : diagnóstico y su ubicación en el contexto internacional, Lima, Perú, febrero de 1985. [Lima, Perú] : ESAN, Instituto de Desarrollo Económico, [1985] iii, 102 leaves : ill. ; 28 cm. At head of title: Coloquio Internacional, Política Petrolera: Respuestas del Mundo. LC Card 86-193466
1. Petroleum industry and trade - Peru. I. Escuela de Administración de Negocios para Graduados. Instituto de Desarrollo Económico. II. Coloquio Internacional, Política Petrolera: Respuestas del Mundo (1985 : Lima, Peru).
HD9574.P52 S58 1985

Situación socio-económica y condiciones de vida en la Provincia de Badajoz, 1880-1902 /. Bohoyo Velázquez, Isidoro Francisco. Badajoz [1984?] 149 p., [3] p. of plates : ISBN 84-309-1055-7 LC Card 86-151914
HC387.B14 B64 1984

La Situación y los problemas del sistema financiero nacional. Santo Domingo, República Dominicana : FORUM, 1986. 152 p. ; 22 cm. (Forum. 24) Spine title: Sistema financiero. Papers presented at a meeting of FORUM, held Nov. 18, 1985, in the Hotel Santo Domingo Sur. LC Card 86-208560
1. Banks and banking - Dominican Republic - Congresses. 2. Finance - Dominican Republic - Congresses. 3. Saving and investment - Dominican Republic - Congresses. I. FORUM (Debating society). II. Title: Sistema financiero. III. Series: FORUM (Series : Santo Domingo, Dominican Republic) , 24.
HG2817 .S57 1986

Situación y posibilidades alimentarias de la población urbano marginal de Arequipa /. Pacheco S., Janette. Arequipa, Perú [1986] 38 p., 8 folded leaves of plates : LC Card 86-232480
HD9014.P53 A746 1986

Situaciones y políticas para el financiamiento industrial : Caraballeda, 8 y 9 de febrero de 1985. [Caracas, Venezuela] : Fondo de Crédito Industrial : Instituto Latinoamericano de Investigaciones Sociales, [1985?] 48 p. ; 28 cm. "Síntesis de las discusiones y conclusiones de las reuniones sostenidas en los Grupos de Reflexión"--P. [5] LC Card 86-205909
1. Finance - Venezuela - Congresses. 2. Industrial loan associations - Venezuela - Congresses. 3. Industrial loan associations - Government policy - Venezuela - Congresses. 4. Fondo de Crédito Industrial (Caracas, Venezuela) - Congresses. I. Fondo de Crédito Industrial (Caracas, Venezuela). II. Instituto Latinoamericano de Investigaciones Sociales.
HG185.V4 S58 1985

The Situation and outlook for water resource use in South Carolina, 1985-2000 : a first year interim report / prepared for South Carolina Water Resources Commission by the Strom Thurmond Institute, Clemson University. [Clemson, S.C.] : The Institute, [1985] ix, 95 leaves : ill. ; 28 cm. "November 1985." "Report no. 1"--Spine. Includes bibliographical references. LC Card 86-622603 DDC 333.91/13/09757 19
1. Water resources development - South Carolina. I. South Carolina. Water Resources Commission. II. Strom Thurmond Institute.
HD1694.S6 S57 1985

Situation économique, financière et sociale. Dominique, juin 1985 . [Paris] , c1985. 102 p. : LC Card 86-209026
HC156.5.Z7 D6626 1985

Situation économique, financière et sociale. Grenade, juin 1985 . [Paris] , 1985] 124 p. : LC Card 86-209038
HC156.5.Z7 G7465 1985

Situation économique, financière et sociale. St.-Vincent et les Grenadines, juin 1985 . Paris , 1985] 85 p. : LC Card 86-209310
HC156.5 .S72 1985

Situation économique, financière et sociale. Sainte-Lucie, juin 1985 . [Paris] , 1985] 120 p. : LC Card 86-209048
HC155.5.Z7 S257 1985

The situation of workers in Latin America /. Vargas, Ines. Oslo , 1985. 92 p. ; ISBN 82-7288-123-3 (pbk.) LC Card 86-205392 DDC 331/.098 19
HD6530.5 .V37 1985

The situation of workers in the industrialised countries with special reference to Scandinavia /. Buvollen, H. P. (Hans Petter) Oslo [1985] 24 p. ; LC Card 86-205580 DDC 331.13/7948 19
HD8540 .B86 1985

Sitzungsberichte der Akademie der Wissenschaften der DDR. Gesellschaftswissenschaften .
(Jahrg. 1979, Nr. 13/G) Herrmann, Joachim, 1932- Ökonomie und Gesellschaft an der Wende von der Antike zum Mittelalter . Berlin , 1979. 72 p. : LC Card 85-209249
HC31 .H47 1979

Sitzungsberichte der Akademie der Wissenschaften der DDR. Gesellschaftswissenschaften, 0138-4015 .
(Jahrg. 1986, Nr. 2/G) Koziolek, Helmut. Umfassende Intensivierung und Infrastruktur /. Berlin , 1986. 68 p. ; LC Card 86-169897
HC290.795.C3 K68 1986

Sitzungsberichte der Wissenschaftlichen Gesellschaft an der Johann Wolfgang Goethe-Universität Frankfurt am Main .
(Bd. 21, Nr. 4) Schmidt, Kurt, 1924- Der Sachverständigenrat zur Begutachtung der Gesamtwirtschaftlichen Entwicklung . Stuttgart , 1985. 24 p. ; ISBN 3-515-04462-0 (Deut. Bibl.) : LC Card 86-157934
HC286.7 .S353 1985

(Bd. 22, Nr. 3) Wittmann, Waldemar. Der Unternehmer /. Stuttgart , 1986. 27 p. ; ISBN 3-515-04666-6 : LC Card 87-136715 DDC 338/.04 19
HB615 .W58 1986

Siu, Paul C. P. (Paul Chan Pang), 1906- The Chinese laundryman : a study of social isolation / Paul C.P. Siu ; edited by John Kuo Wei Tchen. New York : New York University Press, c1987. xlii, 311 p. : 1 ill. ; 24 cm. Originally presented as the author's thesis (Ph. D.)--University of Chicago, 1953. Includes bibliographies and index. ISBN 0-8147-7859-3 : LC Card 87-5609 DDC 331.6/2/51073 19
1. Laundry Workers - United States. 2. Chinese Americans - Social conditions. I. Tchen, John Kuo Wei. II. Title.
HD8039.L32 U675 1987

Siuda, Wojciech. Ekonomiczne i prawne problemy przedsiębiorstwa uspołecznionego /. Poznań , 1981. 137 p. ; LC Card 83-167540
HB54 .P6 nr. 101 HD4215.7

Siva Prasad, K. Technological breakthrough in agriculture / K. Siva Prasad ; foreword by P.V. Sarma. Allahabad, India : Chugh Publications, 1987. xii, 133 p. ; 23 cm. Revision of the author's thesis (doctoral--Andhra University, 1979) Study covers Andhra Pradesh, during the period, 1957-1960, and 1976-1977. Bibliography: p. [121]-130. Includes index. ISBN 81-85076-15-4 : LC Card 86-903607 DDC 338.1/61 19
1. Agriculture - Economic aspects - India - Andhra Pradesh. 2. Agricultural innovations - India - Andhra Pradesh. I. Title.
HD2075.A5 S58 1987

Sivard, Ruth Leger. Women--a world survey / Ruth Leger Sivard. Washington, D.C. : World Priorities, c1985. 44 p. : ill. (col.) ; 28 cm. Bibliography: p. 42-43. ISBN 0-918281-00-8 (pbk.) : LC Card 85-171073 DDC 305.4 19
1. Women - History. 2. Women - Social conditions. 3. Women - Statistics. I. Title.
HQ1154 .S547 1985 ***NYPL [*R-Econ. 86-4677]***

Sivtsov, V. N. Praktikum po statistike promyshlennosti /. Moskva , 1985. 239 p. ; LC Card 85-153243
HD30.413 .P72 1985

Siwande, L. S. C. Ahmad, Nisar. Locational pattern of agricultural production/purchases . Lilongwe [Malawi] , 1984. ii, 33 leaves ; LC Card 86-980325 DDC 380.1/41/096897 19
HE199.5.F3 A38 1984

Sixel, Friedrich W. Crisis and critique : on the "logic" of late capitalism / Friedrich W. Sixel. Leiden ; New York : E.J. Brill, 1987. p. cm. (Monographs and theoretical studies in sociology and anthropology in honour of Nels Anderson, 0169-9202 . publication 22) Bibliography: p. Includes index. ISBN 90-04-08284-0 (pbk.) : LC Card 87-17217 DDC 330.12/2 19
1. Capitalism. 2. Business cycles. I. Title. II. Series.
HB501 .S618 1987

Sixième plan quinquennal de développement économique, social et culturel. Cameroon. Ministry of Planning and Land Management. VIe Plan quinquennal de développement économique, social et culturel . [Yaoundé] [1986?] lxx, 325 p., [19] leaves of plates : LC Card 87-165935
HC995 .C335 1986

Sixteen ways to profit from real estate in 1986. Turner, R. J., 1946- 16 ways to profit from real estate in 1986. Arlington, VA . 1 v. (various foliations) : ISBN 0-937583-06-5 (pbk.) LC Card 86-210837 DDC 332.63/24 19
HD1382.5 .T87 1986

Sixteenth, seventeenth, and eighteenth reports to the Parliament on tobacco bodies. Victoria. Parliament. Public Bodies Review Committee. Reports on the Tobacco Leaf Marketing Board, Tobacco Quota Committee, Tobacco Quota Appeals Tribunal . Melbourne [1986] xix, 107 p. ; LC Card 87-168528 DDC 354.9450082/332 19
HD9148.A8 V53 1986

The Sixth Five Year National Energy Plan, 1983-88. Pakistan. Planning Commission. [Islamabad] [1983 or 1984] 88 p. ; LC Card 84-932174 DDC 333.79/09549/1 19
HD9502.P272 P33 1983

Sixty-five years the realtor in Texas . Matlock, Cora Biesele. Austin, Texas , c1986. xii, 207 p. : LC Card 86-220747 DDC 333.33/06/0764 19
HD266.T4 M38 1986

Siyāsat al-māl fī al-Islām fī 'ahd 'Umar ibn al-Khaṭṭāb wa-muqāranatuhā bi-al-anẓimah al-ḥadīthah /. Sa'dī, 'Abd Allāh Jam'ān Sa'īd, 1954- al-Dawḥah, Qaṭar , 1983. 291 p. ; LC Card 86-965028
HJ1438 .S23 1983

Size and price in oligopoly /. Schoch, Hans. Königstein, Ts. , Cambridge, Mass. , 1981. viii, 151 p. : ISBN 3-445-12157-5 LC Card 80-84489 DDC 338.8/2/0724 19
HD2757.3 .S36 1981

SIZE, ECONOMIES OF. see **ECONOMIES OF SCALE.**

SIZE OF INDUSTRIES. see **INDUSTRIES, SIZE OF.**

Sjahrir, 1945-
[Political economy of basic needs in Indonesia. Indonesian]
Ekonomi politik kebutuhan pokok : sebuah tinjauan prospektif / Sjahrir.Cet. 1. Jakarta : Lembaga Penelitian, Pendidikan dan Penerangan Ekonomi dan Sosial, 1986. xxiii, 280 p. : ill. ; 23 cm. Translation of: The political economy of basic needs in Indonesia: a prospective appraisal, originally presented as the author's thesis (doctoral--Harvard University, 1983) Bibliography: p. [263]-274. ISBN 979-8015-02-9 (pbk.) LC Card 86-943050
1. Basic needs - Indonesia. I. Title.
HC450.B38 S5216 1986

Sjedinjene Američke Države. see **United States.**

Sjödal, Tage, 1928- Vald på livstid : en kritisk granskning av LO och LO-förbunden / Tage Sjödal. Stockholm : Tiden, [1984], c1983. 81 p. ; 21 cm. ISBN 91-550-2941-8 : LC Card 84-171294
1. Landsorganisationen i Sverige. 2. Trade-unions - Sweden. I. Title.
HD8572.L34 S57 1984

Sjoquist, David L. Schroeder, Larry D. Understanding regression analysis . Beverly Hills , c1986. 95 p. : ISBN 0-8039-2758-4 LC Card 85-63790 ***NYPL [JLK 77-39 no.57]***

Skagen, Anne. Workplace literacy /. New York , c1986. 74 p. : ISBN 0-8144-2325-6 LC Card 86-14013 DDC 331.25/92 19
HF5549.5.T7 W66 1986 ***NYPL [JLE 86-3510]***

Skaggs, Jimmy M. Prime cut : livestock raising and meatpacking in the United States, 1607-1983 / by Jimmy M. Skaggs.1st ed. College Station : Texas A&M University Press, c1986. xiii, 263 p., [8] p. of plates : ill. ; 24 cm. Includes index. Bibliography: p. [219]-245. ISBN 0-89096-249-9 : LC Card 85-40742 DDC 338.1/76213/0973 19
1. Meat industry and trade - United States - History. 2. Cattle trade - United States - History. 3. Stockyards - United States - History. 4. Packing-houses - United States - History. I. Title.
HD9415 .S58 1986 ***NYPL [JLE 86-3913]***

Det skal stampes halv stamp presses og klædeskæres . Andersen, Kirsten Gøgsig. København [1984] 179 columns : LC Card 85-242146
HD9999.C483 D43 1984

Skånland, Hermod, 1925- Inntektspolitikkens dilemma : kan det løses? / Hermod Skånland. [Oslo] : Cappelen, 1981 ([Oslo] : Joh. Nordahls trykkeri) 114 p., [1] leaf : ill. ; 21 cm. (Arena) ISBN 82-02-04872-9 (pbk.) : LC Card 81-199141
1. Income distribution - Norway. 2. Income - Effect of

inflation on - Norway. 3. Taxation - Norway. I. Title.
HC370.I5 S49 1981 ***NYPL [JLD 86-2672]***

Skarstein, Rune. Industrial development in Tanzania : some critical issues / Rune Skarstein, Samuel M. Wangwe. Uppsala : Scandinavian Institute of African Studies in cooperation with Tanzania Pub. House, Dar es Salaam ; Stockholm, Sweden : Distributed by Almqvist & Wiksell International, 1986. xi, 291 p. : ill. ; 24 cm. Bibliography: p. 275-291. ISBN 91-7106-254-8 (pbk.) LC Card 87-134925 DDC 338.9678 19
1. Tanzania - Industries. 2. Tanzania - Economic conditions - 1964-. 3. Industry and state - Tanzania. 4. Technology and state - Tanzania. I. Wangwe, S. M. II. Title.
HC885 .S58 1986

Skärvad, Per-Hugo. Edgren, Jan, 1940- Divisionalisering och därefter . Stockholm , c1983. 157 p. : ISBN 91-7722-013-7 : LC Card 83-186664
HD50 .E34 1983

Skatter och samhällsekonomi /. Hansson, Ingemar, 1951- Stockholm , c1986. 170 p. : ISBN 91-7150-280-7 : LC Card 86-215332
HJ2837 .H36 1986

Skattetryckets fördelning inom finländska industriföretag /. Ekholm, Bo-Göran. Helsingfors [1985] 39 p. ; ISBN 951-555-222-2 LC Card 85-214497
HD2753.F5 E38 1985

Skeeter, Sharyn. Wenschlag, Roger. The versatile salesperson . New York , c1987. viii, 205 p. : ISBN 0-471-85436-0 LC Card 87-2003 DDC 658.8/5 19
HF5438.25 .W294 1987

The skeptical economist /. Ginzberg, Eli, 1911- Boulder, Colo. , 1987. ix, 182 p. ; ISBN 0-8133-7372-7 LC Card 87-2165 DDC 330 19
HB71 .G53 1987

Skidelsky, Robert Jacob Alexander, 1939- John Maynard Keynes : a biography / by Robert Skidelsky. London : Macmillan London, 1983- v. <1 > ; 24 cm. Bibliography: v. 1, p. [403]-420. Includes index. CONTENTS. - v. 1. Hopes betrayed, 1883-1920. ISBN 0-333-11599-6 (v. 1) : LC Card 86-217586 DDC 330.15/6 B 19
1. Keynes, John Maynard, 1883-1946. 2. Economists - Great Britain - Biography. I. Title.
HB103.K47 S57 1983

Skilbred, Amy. The Watt/Clark record : environmental policies of the Reagan administration : Alaska / [Amy Skilbred ; in collaboration with Deanne Kloepfer, Susan Alexander, William C. Reffalt]. Washington, D.C. (1901 Pennsylvania Ave., N.W., Washington 20006) : Wilderness Society, c1984. iii, 63, [18] p. : ill. ; 28 cm. Errata slip laid in. LC Card 86-206945 DDC 363.7/009798 19
1. Environmental policy - Alaska. 2. National parks and reserves - Alaska - Management. 3. National parks and reserves - Alaska - Planning. 4. Alaska - Public lands - Management. 5. Alaska - Public lands - Planning. I. Title.
HC107.A47 E57 1984

SKILLED LABOR - BRAZIL - SUPPLY AND DEMAND.
Silveira, Maria Luiza Faraone. Mão-de-obra de nível médio . São Paulo , 1986. 239 p. : LC Card 87-143876 DDC 331.11/422 19
HD5754 .S55 1986

SKILLED LABOR - FRANCE.
Le Guen, René. Oxygène pour tous les cerveaux /. Paris , c1985. 204 p. : ISBN 2-209-05743-4 : LC Card 86-117864 DDC 331.7/12/0944 19
HD8038.F7 L4 1985

SKILLED LABOR - FRANCE - POLITICAL ACTIVITY - HISTORY.
Moss, Bernard H. [Origins of the French labor movement, 1830-1914. French.] Aux origines du mouvement ouvrier français . Paris , 1985. xi, 236 p. ; ISBN 2-251-60326-3
NYPL [M-10 6410 n.326]

SKILLED LABOR - GREAT BRITAIN - HISTORY - 19TH CENTURY.
Divisions of labour . Sussex [Eng.] , Urbana , 1985. ix, 254 p. ; ISBN 0-252-01189-9 LC Card 84-23988 DDC 331.7/94 19
HD8390 .D58 1985 ***NYPL [JLD 87-93]***

SKILLED LABOR - SUPPLY AND DEMAND - FORECASTING.
Forecasting skilled-manpower needs . Paris , 1985. 259 p. : ISBN 92-803-1122-3 (pbk.) LC Card 86-214025 DDC 331.12/3 19
HD5701.55 .F67 1985

SKILLED LABOR - TRAINING OF - BRAZIL.
Silveira, Maria Luiza Faraone. Mão-de-obra de nível médio . São Paulo , 1986. 239 p. : LC Card 87-143876 DDC 331.11/422 19
HD5754 .S55 1986

Skills for the changing workplace . Warmbrod, Catharine P. Columbus, Ohio (1960 Kenny Rd., Columbus 43210-1090) , 1985. ix, 93 p. ; LC Card 86-205907 DDC 651/.07/15 19
HF1106 .W36 1985

Skills for the changing workplace . Warmbrod, Catharine P. Columbus, Ohio (1960 Kenny Rd., Columbus 43210-1090) , 1985. ix, 86 p. ; LC Card 86-205842 DDC 658.8/007/15 19
HF5415 .W3155 1985

The skills of appraisal /. Slater, John, 1936- Aldershot, Hants, England , Brookfield, Vt., U. S.A. , c1988. p. cm. ISBN 0-566-02729-1 LC Card 87-22388 DDC 658.3/125 19
HF5549.5.R3 S57 1988

The skills of communicating /. Scott, W. P. Aldershot, Hampshire, England , Brookfield, Vt. , 1987, c1986. p. cm. ISBN 0-7045-0575-4 (pbk.) : LC Card 87-17106 DDC 658.4/5 19
HF5718 .S38 1987

The skills of interviewing /. Rae, Leslie. New York, N.Y. , 1988. p. cm. ISBN 0-89397-293-2 : LC Card 87-25066 DDC 658.3/1124 19
HF5549.5.I6 R34 1988

Skinner, Hubert C. The new Dietz Confederate States catalog and handbook / by Hubert C. Skinner, Erin R. Gunter, and Warren H. Sanders. Miami, Fla. (1007 Kane Concourse, Bay Harbor Islands 33154) : Bogg & Laurence Pub. Co., 1986. viii, 270 p. : ill. ; 27 cm. Spine title: Dietz Confederate States catalog. LC Card 86-206685 DDC 769.56975/075/0973 19
1. Postal service - Confederate States of America - Handbooks, manuals, etc. 2. Postage-stamps - Confederate States of America - Catalogs. I. Dietz, August, 1869-1963. II. Gunter, Erwin R. III. Sanders, Warren H. IV. Title. V. Title: Dietz Confederate States catalog.
HE6500 .S58 1986

Skipper, Harold D., 1947- Black, Kenneth. Life insurance. Englewood Cliffs, N.J. , c1987. xiii, 608 p. : ISBN 0-13-535881-7 LC Card 86-25375 DDC 368.3/2 19
HG8771 .B55 1987

Skivington, Kristen D. Daft, Richard L. Organization theory . St. Paul , c1987. xxviii, 338 p. : ISBN 0-314-28488-5 (pbk.) LC Card 86-28965 DDC 658.4 19
HD31 .D136 1987

Sklar, Martin J., 1935- The corporate reconstruction of American capitalism, 1890-1916 : the market, the law, and politics / Martin J. Sklar. Cambridge [Cambridgeshire] ; New York : Cambridge University Press, 1987. p. cm. Bibliography: p. Includes index. ISBN 0-521-30921-2 LC Card 87-9408 DDC 338.8/0973 19
1. Capital - United States - History. 2. Progressivism (United States politics). 3. Antitrust law - United States - History. 4. Business and politics - United States - History. I. Title.
HC110.C3 S58 1987

Skoglund, Tor.
Regionale strukturendringer belyst ved sysselsettingstall / av Tor Skoglund og Knut Ø. Sørensen. Oslo : Statistisk sentralbyrå : I kommisjon hos H. Aschehoug og Universitetsforlaget, 1983. 52 p. ; 30 cm. (Rapporter fra Statistisk sentralbyrå, 0332-8422 . 83/32) Bibliography: p. 50. ISBN 82-537-2003-3 : LC Card 84-161751
1. Labor supply - Norway - Regional disparities. I. Sørensen, Knut Ø. II. Title. III. Series.
HD5800.A6 S58 1983

Schreiner, Alette. Virkninger av oljevirksomhet i Nord-Norge /. Oslo , 1984. 43 p. : ISBN 82-537-2118-8 : LC Card 85-146089
HD9575.N62 S37 1984

Skogsbränsle : en utvärdering av det statliga stödet till forskning och utveckling. Stockholm : Energiforskningsnämnden : Beställs från Liber, [1986] 159 p. : ill. ; 25 cm. (Efn-rapport, 0281-0301 . nr 19) "Mars 1986." Summary in English. Bibliography: p. 145-147. ISBN 91-38-09241-7 LC Card 86-201607
1. Fuelwood industry - Sweden. 2. Fuelwood - Research - Sweden. I. Sweden. Energiforskningsnämnden. II. Series.
HD9769.F842 S57 1986

Skorov, Mikhail Sergeevich.
Nauchno-tekhnicheskiĭ progress i tiazhelaia promyshlennost′ IAponii / M.S. Skorov. Moskva : Izd-vo "Nauka", 1980. 213, [3] p. ; 20 cm. At head of title: Akademiia nauk SSSR. Institut vostokovedeniia. One folded leaf of plates inserted. Bibliography: p. 208-[214] LC Card 81-130564
1. Technological innovations - Japan. 2. Japan - Industries - 1945-. I. Title.
HC465.T4 S56 1980

Skou, Niels Holger. Teknologipolitik / Niels Holger Skou. Aarhus : Økonomisk institut, Aarhus universitet, [1981] 52 p. ; 21 cm. (Notat (Aarhus universitet. Økonomisk institut) . 1981-2) Cover title. Bibliography: p. 48-52. LC Card 82-194649
1. Technological innovations - Developing countries. 2. Technology transfer - Developing countries. 3. Technology and state - Developing countries. I. Series. II. Series: Notat (Aarhus universitet. Økonomisk institut) , 1981-2. III. Title.
HC59.72.T4 S56 1981

Skouras, Thanos, 1943- Post Keynesian economic theory . Sussex , Armonk, N.Y. , 1985. xii, 235 p. ; ISBN 0-87332-318-1 LC Card 84-23615 DDC 330/.09/04 19
HB87 .P62 1985 ***NYPL [JLD 87-1155]***

Skousen, Jo Ann. Skousen, Mark. High finance on a low budget /. Alexandria, VA , c1987. 197 p. : LC Card 87-153152 DDC 332.6/78 19
HG179 .S528 1987

Skousen, K. Fred.
Accounting . New York, N.Y. , c1987. xxvi, 1047 p. : ISBN 0-87901-338-9 LC Card 86-51180 DDC 657 19
HF5635 .S618 1987

Principles of accounting. Accounting : principles and applications / K. Fred Skousen ... [et al.].3rd ed. New York, N.Y. , c1987. xxvi, 1047 p. : ISBN 0-87901-338-9 LC Card 86-51180 DDC 657 19
HF5635 .S618 1987

Smith, Jay M. Intermediate accounting . Cincinnati , c1987. xix, 1234 p. : ISBN 0-538-01921-2 LC Card 87-60815 DDC 657/.044 19
HF5635 .S5946 1987

Skousen, Mark. High finance on a low budget / Mark and Jo Ann Skousen. 5th rev. ed. Alexandria, VA : KCI Communications, c1987. 197 p. : ill. ; 24 cm. LC Card 87-153152 DDC 332.6/78 19
1. Finance, Personal. 2. Investments. I. Skousen, Jo Ann. II. Title.
HG179 .S528 1987

Skov, Paul B. Strategy, analysis, and decisions : choosing the winning strategy / Paul B. Skov, Daniel J. Quinn. Menlo Park, Calif. (333 Ravenswood Ave., Menlo Park 94025-3476) : SRI International, Business Intelligence Program, c1985. 40 p. : ill. (some col.) ; 28 cm. (Report / SRI International, Business Intelligence Program . no. 716 (winter 1984-85)) Cover title. LC Card 87-119164 DDC 658.4/012
1. Strategic planning. 2. Decision-making. I. Quinn, Daniel J. II. Series: Research report (Business Intelligence Program (SRI International)) , no. 716. III. Title.
HD30.28 .S49 1985

Skovbro, Carsten. Andersen, René, 1936- Personaleadministration /. København , 1983. 476 p. : ISBN 87-7040-278-7 : LC Card 84-104119
HF5549.2.D45 A53 1983

Skrabka-Błotnicka, Teresa. Studencki ruch naukowy /. Wrocław , 1978. 98 p. : LC Card 81-206830
HB9 .B7522 nr. 122 HD36

Skrede, Kari. Den Norske kvinnerevolusjonen . Oslo , c1986. 166 p. : ISBN 82-00-18318-1 LC

Card 87-155462
HD6170 .N68 1986

Skrift (Forlaget Alfuff (Ålborg, Denmark)) .
(nr. 2) Nørrung, Per. The producing commune /. Aalborg Ø., Denmark , 1985. 39 p. ; ISBN 87-88353-11-7 (pbk.) LC Card 87-100060 DDC 334/.6/09489 19
HD3209.A4 N67 1985

Skrifter fra Geografisk institut ved Aarhus universitet .
(nr. 42) Søgaard, Villy. Offshoreaktiviteter i Nordsøen og basebyen Esbjerg /. [Århus] , 1983. 200 p. : ISBN 87-88615-02-2 : LC Card 84-164755
HD9575.N62 S64 1983

Skrifter fra Riksbibliotektjenesten, 0800-4129 .
(nr. 26) Engelstad, Kirsten. Viten som verktøy . Oslo , 1985. 80 p. ; ISBN 82-7195-048-7 LC Card 86-175688
HD2346.N6 E53 1985

Skrifter udgivet af det Historiske institut ved Københavns universitet .
(bd. 9) Ulrichsen, Niels. J.A.K.--en dansk krisebevægelse /. København , 1978. 202 p. ; ISBN 87-87462-13-3 LC Card 87-462108
HD2002 .U45 1978

Skrifter utgivna av Ekonomisk-historiska föreningen i Lund .
(49) Lundh, Christer. Den svenska debatten om industriell demokrati 1919-1924 /. Lund , 1987- v. <1 > ; ISBN 91-85611-17-4 LC Card 87-151790
HD5660.S9 L87 1987

Skrifter utgivna av Svenska litteratursällskapet i Finland, 0039-6842 .
(nr. 533) Finnäs, Fjalar. Den finlandssvenska befolkningsutvecklingen 1950-1980 . Helsingfors [1986] 216 p. : ISBN 951-9018-20-4 LC Card 86-232091
HB3608.3.A3 F56 1986

Skruten', I. S. Spivdruzhnist' u pratsi / I.S. Skruten'. Kyïv : "Tekhnika", 1982. 117 p. : ill. ; 22 cm. Title in colophon: Sodruzhestvo v trude. Includes bibliographical references. LC Card 83-200434
1. Ukraine - Economic conditions - 1945-. 2. Ukraine - Commerce - Russian S.F.S.R. 3. Russian S.F.S.R. - Commerce - Ukraine. I. Title. II. Title: Sodruzhestvo v trude.
HC337.U5 S514 1982

Skully, Michael T.
American depositary receipts : internationalizing Australian fund raising and securities trading / by Michael T. Skully. [Melbourne] : Committee for Economic Development in Australia, [1986] 44 leaves : ill. ; 30 cm. (CEDA information paper) "April 1986." Bibliography: p. leaves 23-24. LC Card 86-229206 DDC 332.6/7373/094 19
1. Investments, American - Australia. 2. Corporations - Australia - Finance. 3. Securities - Australia. I. Title. II. Series.
HG5892 .S58 1986

Financial institutions and markets in the South Pacific : a study of New Caledonia, Solomon Islands, Tonga, Vanuatu, and Western Samoa / Michael T. Skully. New York : St. Martin's Press, 1987. xvi, 379 p., [1] leaf of plates : maps ; 23 cm. Bibliography: p. 345-363. Includes index. ISBN 0-312-00529-6 : LC Card 87-4506 DDC 332.1/099 19
1. Financial institutions - Oceania - Case studies. 2. Finance - Oceania - Case studies. I. Title.
HG190.A2 S58 1987

Financing East Asia's success : comparative financial development in eight Asian countries / Michael T. Skully and George J. Viksnins. New York : St. Martin's Press in association with the American Enterprise Institute for Public Policy Research, 1987. xiii, 242 p. ; 23 cm. Bibliography: p. 224-235. Includes index. ISBN 0-312-00536-9 : LC Card 86-31527 DDC 332/.0959 19
1. Finance - East Asia. 2. Finance - Asia, Southeastern. 3. Financial institutions - East Asia. 4. Financial institutions - Asia, Southeastern. 5. Inflation (Finance) - East Asia. 6. Inflation (Finance) - Asia, Southeastern. I. Viksnins, George J. II. Title.
HG187.E37 S68 1987

The Skunk Camp promises /. Peters, Thomas J. New York , 1987. p. cm. ISBN 0-394-75314-3 (pbk.) : LC Card 86-46226 DDC 658.4/09 19
HD57.7 .P47 1987

Skuratova, G. F. My--khoziaeva proizvodstva . Moskva , 1984. 261 p. : LC Card 85-107808
HD5660.S65 M9 1984

Skutlartz, Ekkehard. Branchenportfolioanalyse und Wirtschaftsförderungsstrategien : anhand von Branchenportfoliomatrizen mit Verlaufspfaden dargestellt am Beispiel der Branchen des Verarbeitenden Gewerbes in Baden-Württemberg und in der Bundesrepublik Deutschland / Ekkehard Skutlartz. [Karlsruhe] : Institut für Regionalwissenschaft der Universität Karlsruhe, [1986] a-m, 205, vi p. : ill. ; 21 cm. (IfR Schriftenreihe . Heft Nr. 22 (März 1986)) Bibliography: p. i-vi. The author's rev. Lizentiatenarbeit. LC Card 87-103969
1. Portfolio management - Germany (West) - Baden-Württemberg. 2. Portfolio management - Germany (West). I. Series: Schriftenreihe (Universität Karlsruhe. Institut für Regionalwissenschaft) , Heft Nr. 22. II. Title.
HG4529.5 .S58 1986

Slack in Kenya's modern manufacturing sector /. Gershenberg, Irving. Boston, MA (270 Bay State Rd., Boston 02215) , 1985. 15 leaves ; LC Card 87-404089 DDC 338.4/767/096762 19
HD70.K4 G47 1985

Slack, Paul. Poverty and policy in Tudor and Stuart England / Paul Slack. London ; New York : Longman, 1988. p. cm. (Themes in British social history) Bibliography: p. Includes index. ISBN 0-582-48965-2 (alk. paper) LC Card 87-2657 DDC 362.5/561/0942 19
1. Great Britain - Economic policy. 2. Great Britain - Economic conditions. 3. Great Britain - Social policy. 4. Great Britain - Social conditions. 5. Poor - Great Britain - History. I. Title.
HC254.4 .S42 1988

Slade, Roger, 1941- Mergos, George, 1948- Dairy development and milk cooperatives . Washington, D.C. [1987] xiv, 140 p. : ISBN 0-8213-0932-3 (pbk.) LC Card 87-15976 DDC 334/.68371/09543 19
HD9282.I53 M286 1987

Slang dictionary English-French/French-English. Marks, Georgette A. Harrap's slang dictionary English-French/French-English /. London , 1984. 476 p. ; ISBN 0-245-54047-4
NYPL [JFC 86-640]

Släpp tjänsterna loss . Johnson, Anders. [Stockholm] , c1986. 232 p. : ISBN 91-7152-374-X : LC Card 86-235064
HD9986.S82 J63 1986

SLATE INDUSTRY - GERMANY (WEST) - RHINELAND - HISTORY.
Bartels, Christoph. Schieferdörfer . Pfaffenweiler , 1986. xiv, 370 p. : ISBN 3-89085-124-X LC Card 87-134379 DDC 338.943/43 19
HD9621.G33 R463 1986

Slater, Jeffrey, 1947-
College accounting : a practical approach, 1-10 / Jeffrey Slater. Englewood Cliffs, N.J. : Prentice Hall, c1988. p. cm. Rev. ed. of chapters 1-10 of: Practical accounting procedures. 2nd ed. c1984. Includes index. ISBN 0-13-140708-2 LC Card 87-7343 DDC 657 19
1. Accounting. I. Slater, Jeffrey, 1947- Practical accounting procedures. II. Title.
HF5635 .S6315 1988c

College accounting : a practical approach, 1-15 / Jeffrey Slater.3rd ed. Englewood Cliffs, N.J. : Prentice-Hall, c1988. p. cm. Rev ed. of: Practical accounting procedures. 2nd ed. c1984. Includes index. ISBN 0-13-140906-9 LC Card 87-21878 DDC 657 19
1. Accounting. I. Slater, Jeffrey, 1947- Practical accounting procedures. II. Title.
HF5635 .S6315 1988b

College accounting : a practical approach, 1-27 / Jeffrey Slater.3rd ed. Englewood Cliffs, N.J. : Prentice-Hall, c1988. p. cm. Rev. and enl. ed. of: Practical accounting procedures. 2nd ed. c1984. Includes index. ISBN 0-13-140716-3 LC Card 87-21879 DDC 657 19
1. Accounting. I. Slater, Jeffrey, 1947- Practical accounting procedures. II. Title.
HF5635 .S6315 1988

Practical accounting procedures.
Slater, Jeffrey, 1947- College accounting : a practical approach, 1-10 / Jeffrey Slater. Englewood Cliffs, N.J. , c1988. p. cm. ISBN 0-13-140708-2 LC Card 87-7343 DDC 657 19
HF5635 .S6315 1988c

Slater, Jeffrey, 1947- College accounting : a practical approach, 1-15 / Jeffrey Slater.3rd ed. Englewood Cliffs, N.J. , c1988. p. cm. ISBN 0-13-140906-9 LC Card 87-21878 DDC 657 19
HF5635 .S6315 1988b

Slater, Jeffrey, 1947- College accounting : a practical approach, 1-27 / Jeffrey Slater.3rd ed. Englewood Cliffs, N.J. , c1988. p. cm. ISBN 0-13-140716-3 LC Card 87-21879 DDC 657 19
HF5635 .S6315 1988

Practical business math procedures / Jeffrey Slater. 2nd ed. Homewood, Ill. : Irwin, 1987. xiv, 440 p. : ill. (some col.) ; 28 cm. Fold-out newspaper in pocket. Includes index. ISBN 0-256-03654-3 (pbk.) LC Card 85-82557 DDC 513/.93 19
1. Business mathematics - Problems, exercises, etc. I. Title.
HF5694 .S57 1987

Slater, John. Wienert, Helgard. East-West technology transfer. The trade and economic aspects /. Paris , c1986. 453 p. : ISBN 92-64-12817-4 ***NYPL [JLE 87-1561]***

Slater, John, 1936- The skills of appraisal / John Slater and Peter Packard. Aldershot, Hants, England ; Brookfield, Vt., U. S.A. : Gower Pub. Co., c1988. p. cm. Bibliography: p. ISBN 0-566-02729-1 LC Card 87-22388 DDC 658.3/125 19
1. Employess, Rating of. 2. Performance standards. 3. Interviewing. I. Packard, Peter, 1924-. II. Title.
HF5549.5.R3 S57 1988

Slater, Miriam, 1930- Glazer, Penina Migdal. Unequal colleagues . New Brunswick, N.J. , c1987. xii, 295 p. : ISBN 0-8135-1187-9 (pbk.) : LC Card 86-6568 DDC 331.4/81/000973 19
HD6054.2.U6 G55 1986
NYPL [JLD 87-581]

Slater, Robert, 1943- The titans of takeover / Robert Slater. Englewood Cliffs, N.J. : Prentice-Hall, c1987. ix, 230 p. : ports. ; 24 cm. Bibliography: p. 219-222. Includes index. ISBN 0-13-922055-0 LC Card 86-25364 DDC 338.8/3/0973 19
1. Consolidation and merger of corporations - United States. 2. Capitalists and financiers - United States. I. Title.
HD2785 .S44 1987

Slater, Roger.
Curwin, Jon. Business studies in context . London , New York , 1987. p. cm. ISBN 0-07-707034-8 : LC Card 87-22560 DDC 658.4/0352 19
HD30.25 .C87 1987

Curwin, Jon. Quantitative methods for business decisions /. New York , 1985. xii, 343 p. : ISBN 0-442-30640-7 (pbk.) LC Card 85-3267 DDC 519.5/024658 19
HF5691 .C87 1985

SLAUGHTERING AND SLAUGHTER-HOUSES - ITALY - PRATO REGION - HISTORY.
Nigro, Giampiero. Gli uomini dell'irco . Firenze , 1983. xxii, 184 p. : ISBN 88-00-86022-2 : LC Card 84-238769
HD9425.I83 P76 1983 ***NYPL [JLE 86-2127]***

SLAVE LABOR - BRAZIL - SÃO PAULO (STATE) - HISTORY - 19TH CENTURY - CASE STUDIES.
Witter, José Sebastião. A Revolta dos Parceiros /. São Paulo, SP , 1986. 77 p. : LC Card 87-102716
HD4875.B8 W58 1986

SLAVE LABOR - CROSS-CULTURAL STUDIES.
Miles, Robert, 1950- Capitalism and unfree labour . London ; New York : 250 p. : ISBN 0-422-61730-X LC Card 87-3599 DDC 331.11/734 19
HB501 .M654 1987

SLAVE LABOR - MIDDLE EAST - HISTORY.
Labor in the ancient Near East /. New Haven, Conn. , 1987. xiv, 289 p. : ISBN 0-940490-68-4

LC Card 86-32227 DDC 305.5/62/09394 19
HD8656 .L33 1987 ***NYPL [*OAC (American Oriental series)]***

SLAVE LABOR - PENNSYLVANIA - HISTORY.
Salinger, Sharon V. (Sharon Vineberg) "To serve well and faithfully" . Cambridge [Cambridgeshire] , New York , 1987. xiii, 192 p., [1] leaf of plates : ISBN 0-521-33442-X LC Card 87-852 DDC 306/.363/09748 19
HD4875.U5 S25 1987

SLAVE-TRADE - AFRICA - HISTORY.
Carreira, António. As companhias pombalinas . Lisboa [1983] 426 p. : LC Card 86-146987
HF491.C592 C37 1983

SLAVE-TRADE - BRAZIL, NORTHEAST - HISTORY.
Carreira, António. As companhias pombalinas . Lisboa [1983] 426 p. : LC Card 86-146987
HF491.C592 C37 1983

SLAVE-TRADE - TANZANIA - ZANZIBAR - HISTORY.
Sheriff, Abdul. Slaves, spices, & ivory in Zanzibar . London , Athens , 1987. xx, 297 p. : ISBN 0-8214-0871-2 (U. S.) LC Card 87-12339 DDC 382/.096781 19
HF3897 .S54 1987

SLAVEHOLDERS - BRAZIL - SÃO PAULO (STATE) - HISTORY - 19TH CENTURY.
Mello, Zélia Maria Cardoso de. Metamorfoses da riqueza, São Paulo, 1845-1895 . São Paulo , 1985. 188 p. : LC Card 85-207635
HC188.S3 M49 1985

SLAVERY - BRAZIL - BAHIA (STATE) - HISTORY.
Schwartz, Stuart B. Sugar plantations in the formation of Brazilian society . Cambridge [Cambridgeshire] , New York , 1985. xxiii, 616 p. : ISBN 0-521-30934-4 LC Card 85-6716 DDC 306/.0981/42 19
HD9114.B7 B347 1985
NYPL [JLE 86-2276]

SLAVERY - BRAZIL - SÃO PAULO (STATE) - HISTORY - 19TH CENTURY.
Salles, Iraci Galvão. Trabalho, progresso e a sociedade civilizada . São Paulo [Brasília] , 1986. 145 p. ; LC Card 86-224281
HD8289.S282 S24 1986

SLAVERY - ECUADOR - HISTORY.
Pensamiento agrario ecuatoriano /. Quito, Ecuador , 1986. 741 p. : LC Card 87-403503 DDC 333.3/1/866 19
HD1333.E2 P46 1986

SLAVERY - GUYANA - EMANCIPATION - HISTORY.
McLewin, Philip J., 1939- Power and economic change . New York , 1987. ii, 271 p. : ISBN 0-8240-1366-2 (alk. paper) : LC Card 87-8344 DDC 330.97292/04 19
HC154 .M36 1987

SLAVERY - JAMAICA - EMANCIPATION - HISTORY.
McLewin, Philip J., 1939- Power and economic change . New York , 1987. ii, 271 p. : ISBN 0-8240-1366-2 (alk. paper) : LC Card 87-8344 DDC 330.97292/04 19
HC154 .M36 1987

SLAVERY - LAW AND LEGISLATION - ECUADOR - HISTORY.
Pensamiento agrario ecuatoriano /. Quito, Ecuador , 1986. 741 p. : LC Card 87-403503 DDC 333.3/1/866 19
HD1333.E2 P46 1986

SLAVERY - MISSISSIPPI - HISTORY.
Moore, John Hebron. The emergence of the Cotton Kingdom in the Old Southwest . Baton Rouge , c1988. xii, 323 p. : ISBN 0-8071-1404-9 (pbk.) LC Card 87-2803 DDC 330.9762 19
HC107.M7 M66 1988

SLAVERY - UNITED STATES - HISTORY.
Gutman, Herbert George, 1928- Power & culture . New York, N.Y. , c1987. xi, 452 p. ; ISBN 0-394-56171-6 LC Card 87-43018 DDC 305.5/62/0973 19
HD8072 .G97 1987

Slaves of the Depression : workers' letters about life on the job / [edited by] Gerald Markowitz and David Rosner. Ithaca, N.Y. : Cornell University Press, 1987. x, 229 p. ; 23 cm. Includes bibliographical references and index. ISBN 0-8014-9464-8 (pbk. : alk. paper) LC Card 87-6671 DDC 331.25/0973 19
1. Labor and laboring classes - United States - 1914- - Sources. 2. United States - Economic conditions - 1918-1945 - Sources. 3. Depressions - 1929 - United States - Sources. I. Markowitz, Gerald E. II. Rosner, David, 1947-.
HD8072 .S6164 1987

Slaves, spices, & ivory in Zanzibar . Sheriff, Abdul. London , Athens , 1987. xx, 297 p. : ISBN 0-8214-0871-2 (U. S.) LC Card 87-12339 DDC 382/.096781 19
HF3897 .S54 1987

Slaves, spices and ivory in Zanzibar. Sheriff, Abdul. Slaves, spices, & ivory in Zanzibar . London , Athens , 1987. xx, 297 p. : ISBN 0-8214-0871-2 (U. S.) LC Card 87-12339 DDC 382/.096781 19
HF3897 .S54 1987

Slavin, S. V. (Samuil Venediktovich) Osvoenie Severa Sovetskogo Soi͡uza / S.V. Slavin. 2-e izd., dop. Moskva : Izd-vo "Nauka", 1982. 206 p. : maps ; 20 cm. (Serii͡a Problemy nauki i tekhnicheskogo progressa) At head of title: Akademii͡a nauk SSSR. Bibliography: p. 204-[205] LC Card 83-137884
1. Soviet Union, Northern - Economic conditions. I. Title. II. Series.
HC336.9.N65 S56 1982

Slavin, Sarah. The Politics of professionalism, opportunity, employment, and gender /. New York , c1987. xx, 110 p. ; ISBN 0-86656-626-0 LC Card 86-29491 DDC 331.4/81/000973 19
HD6054.2.U6 P64 1987

Sled v zhizni /. Tarasov, Ivan Gavrilovich. Frunze , 1985. 94 p. ; LC Card 87-115075
HC337.K545 T37 1985

Sleep-tight money . Krause, Lawrence A., 1940- New York , c1987. 300 p. : ISBN 0-671-64023-2 LC Card 87-14806 DDC 332.024 19
HG179 .K664 1987

Slepakov, S. S. (Sergeĭ Semenovich) Obobshchestvlenie i ėkonomicheskie interesy v sotsialisticheskom obshchestve /. Moskva , 1983. 127 p. ; LC Card 84-204638
HD3856.R9 O26 1983

Sleuwaegen, Leo. Yamawaki, Hideki. Industry competition and the formation of the European common market /. Berlin [1986] 34, 3 p. ; LC Card 87-156700 DDC 341.24/22 19
HD41 .Y35 1986

Slide, Anthony. Selected radio and television criticism /. Metuchen, N.J. , c1987. ix, 203 p. ; ISBN 0-8108-1942-2 LC Card 86-27891 DDC 791.44/75/0973 19
PN1990.6.U5 S4 1987
NYPL [MWGI 87-1890]

Slimmon, Robert F. Successful pension design for small-to medium-sized businesses / Robert F. Slimmon. 2nd ed. Englewood Cliffs, N.J. : Prentice-Hall, c1987. xix, 440 p. ; 25 cm. Includes index. ISBN 0-13-860255-7 LC Card 87-2489 DDC 658.3/253
1. Pension trusts. 2. Small business - Personnel management. 3. Profit-sharing. I. Title.
HD7105.4 .S56 1987

Sli͡usareva, I͡U. V. Pi͡atiletka, god vtoroĭ . Petrozavodsk , 1977. 101 p. ; LC Card 81-161405
HC337.K265 P52 1977

SLIVEN (BULGARIA) - ECONOMIC CONDITIONS.
Zlatanov, Zdravko Ĭordanov. 150 godini slivenska tekstilna promishlenost /. [Sofia] , 1984. 364 p., [48] p. of plates : LC Card 85-118285
HD9865.B83 S589 1984

SLIVENSKI OKRŬG (BULGARIA) - DIRECTORIES.
Slivenski okrŭg '85 =. Sofii͡a , 1985. 134 p. : LC Card 86-196443
HF5221.S56 S56 1985

Slivenski okrŭg '85 = Slivenskiĭ okrug '85 = Bezirk Sliven '85 : stopanska panorama / [sŭstavitel Elena Dikova ; avtori na tekstovete Khr. Bodurov ... et al. ; fotografi D. Dimitrov ... et al.]. Sofii͡a : Izd-vo "Reklama", 1985. 134 p. : chiefly col. ill. ; 33 cm. Bulgarian, German, and Russian. LC Card 86-196443
1. Slivenski okrŭg (Bulgaria) - Directories. I. Dikova, Elena. II. Bodurov, Khr. III. Dimitrov, D. IV. Title: Slivenskiĭ okrug '85. V. Title: Bezirk Sliven '85.
HF5221.S56 S56 1985

Slivenskiĭ okrug '85. Slivenski okrŭg '85 =. Sofii͡a , 1985. 134 p. : LC Card 86-196443
HF5221.S56 S56 1985

Sloan, Judy. Wooden, Mark. The effects of redundancy . [Bedford Park, S. Aust.] [1987] 52 p. : LC Card 87-170621 DDC 331.13/7994 19
HD5708.55.A8 W66 1987

Sloan management review.
Generating technological innovation /. New York , 1987. xii, 299 p. : ISBN 0-19-505023-1 (alk. paper) LC Card 86-33119 DDC 658.5/14 19
HD45 .G39 1987

Planning strategies that work /. New York , 1987. xii, 287 p. : ISBN 0-19-504883-0 (alk. paper) LC Card 86-31117 DDC 658.4/012 19
HD30.28 .P555 1987

The Strategic use of information technology /. New York , 1987. xiii, 206 p. : ISBN 0-19-505048-7 (alk. paper) : LC Card 87-1606 DDC 658/.05 19
HD30.2 .S79 1987

Sloan, Michael L., 1944- AppleWorks : the program for the rest of us / Michael L. Sloan.2nd ed. Glenview, Ill. : Scott, Foresman, c1988. vi, 312 p. : ill. ; 24 cm. Includes index. ISBN 0-673-18937-6 (pbk.) : LC Card 87-9775 DDC 650/.028/55369 19
1. AppleWorks (Computer program). 2. Business - Data processing. I. Title.
HF5548.4.A68 S58 1988

Sloane, Arthur A. Labor relations / Arthur A. Sloane, Fred Witney. 6th ed. Englewood Cliffs, N.J. : Prentice Hall, c1988. xiv, 543 p. : ill. ; 24 cm. Includes bibliographies and indexes. ISBN 0-13-519604-3 LC Card 87-14535 DDC 331.89/0973 19
1. Industrial relations - United States. 2. Collective bargaining - United States. I. Witney, Fred, 1917-. II. Title.
HD8072 .S6185 1988

Sloat, Warren. Williams, Bruce, 1932- The Bruce Williams book . New York , 1987. p. cm. ISBN 0-8128-3119-5 : LC Card 86-42692 DDC 658/022 19
HD62.5 .W49 1987

Slodky, Javier. Dilemas de la seguridad social en el Perú / Javier Slodky. [Lima] : Fundación Friedrich Ebert, 1985. 134 p. ; 21 cm. Bibliography: p. 129-134. LC Card 86-232616
1. Social security - Peru. I. Title.
HD7161 .S57 1985

SLOGANS.
Grinnell, J. D., 1944- The national register of advertising slogans & headlines /. Westbury, N.Y. , 1987. p. cm. ISBN 0-87280-159-4 : LC Card 87-17577 DDC 659.13/22 19
HF6135 .G74 1987

Medici Mario, 1924- La parola pubblicitaria . Pomezia , Venezia , 1986. 178 p., 40 p. of plates : ISBN 88-317-4902-1 : LC Card 86-219876
HF5813.I8 M43 1986

Sloggett, Gordon.
Energy and U. S. agriculture : irrigation pumping, 1974-83 / Gordon Sloggett. Washington, D.C. : U. S. Dept. of Agriculture, Economic Research Service : [Copies from Supt. of Docs., U. S. G.P.O., 1985] iii, 43 p. : ill. ; 28 cm. (Agricultural economic report . no. 545) Cover title. "December 1985"--P. i. Bibliography: p. 10. LC Card 86-600880 DDC 338.1 s 338.1/3 19
1. Irrigation - United States - Energy consumption - History - Statistics. 2. Pumping machinery - Fuel consumption - History - Statistics. I. United States. Dept. of Agriculture. Economic Research Service. II. Title. III. Series.
HD1751 .A91854 no. 545 S619.E53

Ground-water mining in the United States / Gordon Sloggett and Clifford Dickason. Washington, D.C : U. S. Dept. of Agriculture, Economic Research Service, 1986. iv, 19 p. : 1 map ; 28 cm. (Agricultural economic report . no. 555) Cover title. Distributed to depository libraries in microfiche. Bibliography: p. 12-14. S/N 001-019-00484-3 Item 45-C (microfiche) LC Card 86-602788 DDC 338.1 s 338.1/4 19
1. Irrigation water - United States. 2. Water,

Underground - United States. 3. Irrigation - United States - Management. 4. Irrigation farming. - United States. I. Dickason, Clifford. II. United States. Dept. of Agriculture. Economic Research Service. III. Title. IV. Series.
HD1751 .A91854 no. 555 S616.U6

Sloma, Richard S. Getting it to the bottom line : management by incremental gains / Richard S. Sloma. New York : Free Press ; London : Collier Macmillian, c1987. ix, 196 p. : ill. ; 22 cm. Includes index. ISBN 0-02-929540-8 LC Card 87-411 DDC 658.4/063 19
1. Organizational effectiveness. 2. Performance. 3. Profit. I. Title.
HD58.9 .S56 1987

Slotta, Gerd. Die Entscheidung über die Betriebspacht bzw. Betriebsverpachtung / Gerd Slotta. Hamburg : Kovač, c1986. xi, 374 p. : ill. ; 21 cm. Bibliography: p. 355-374. ISBN 3-925630-00-7 LC Card 86-152904
1. Industrial equipment leases - Germany (West) - Econometric models. 2. Commercial leases - Germany (West) - Decision making - Econometric models. 3. Lease and rental services - Germany (West) - Cost effectiveness - Econometric models. I. Title. II. Title: Entscheidung über die Betriebspacht beziehungsweise Betriebsverpachtung.
HD39.4 .S56 1986

Sloushcher, V. M. (Vitaliĭ Mironovich) Kuznetsov, ÍU. I. (ÍUriĭ Igorevich) Russko-angliĭskiĭ razgovornik dlia neftekhimikov i khimikov-neorganikov /. Moskva , 1985. 359 p. ; LC Card 86-138945 DDC 660/.03/9171 19
HD9579.C32 K88 1985 ***NYPL [*QAD 86-3599]***

SLOVENIA - ECONOMIC POLICY.
Vloga znanosti pri oblikovanju strategije razvoja SR Slovenije /. Ljubljana , 1981. 174 p. : LC Card 82-151266
HC407.Z7 S57 1981

Slovenija. see **Slovenia.**

Slović, Dragoslav. Statistika u privredi / Dragoslav Slović. Beograd : Naučna knj., 1984. 264 p. : ill. ; 24 cm. In Serbo-Croatian (roman) Bibliography: p. [263]-264. LC Card 86-115111
1. Economics, Mathematical. I. Title.
HB131 .S57 1984

Slovin, Myron B. Macroeconomics for managers / Myron B. Slovin, Marie E. Sushka. Englewood Cliffs, N.J. : Prentice-Hall, c1987. xvi, 512 p. : ill. ; 25 cm. Includes bibliographies and index. ISBN 0-13-542937-4 LC Card 86-25199 DDC 339 19
1. Macroeconomics. I. Sushka, Marie Elizabeth. II. Title.
HB172.5 .S55 1987

The slowdown in productivity growth in the 1975-83 period . Stuber, Gerald. [Ottawa] [1986] 164 p. : LC Card 87-100880 DDC 338/.06/0971 19
HC120.I52 S78 1986

Słownik handlu zagranicznego /. Białecki, Klemens. Warszawa , 1986. 359 p. ; ISBN 83-208-0112-5 : LC Card 86-221378
HF1001 .B47 1986

Slum and squatter settlements in Sub-Saharan Africa : toward a planning strategy / edited by R.A. Obudho and Constance C. Mhlanga. New York : Praeger, 1988. p. cm. Bibliography: p. Includes index. ISBN 0-275-92309-6 (alk. paper) : LC Card 87-11705 DDC 307.3/36 19
1. Urban poor - Housing - Government policy - Africa, Sub-Saharan. 2. Squatter settlements - Government policy - Africa, Sub-Saharan. 3. Slums - Government policy - Africa, Sub-Saharan. I. Obudho, Robert A. II. Mhlanga, Constance C.
HD7287.96.A438 S57 1988

SLUM CLEARANCE. see **CITY PLANNING; HOUSING; SLUMS.**

SLUMS - BRAZIL - SÃO PAULO.
Cortiços em São Paulo . São Paulo , 1986. 195, [2] p. : LC Card 87-119201 DDC 363.5/8 19
HD7287.96.B62 S263 1986

SLUMS - GOVERNMENT POLICY - AFRICA, SUB-SAHARAN.
Slum and squatter settlements in Sub-Saharan Africa . New York , 1988. p. cm. ISBN 0-275-92309-6 (alk. paper) : LC Card 87-11705 DDC 307.3/36 19
HD7287.96.A438 S57 1988

SLUMS - HONDURAS - SAN PEDRO SULA.
Estudio de diagnóstico de la población de los barrios--Chamelecón, Suyapa, Fe y Esperanza, San Antonio, San José y San Miguel /. Tegucigalpa, D.C. [1984] 1 v. (various foliations) : LC Card 85-205996
HC145.Z7 T434 1984

SLUMS - HONDURAS - TEGUCIGALPA.
Estudio de diagnóstico de la población de los barrios--Chamelecón, Suyapa, Fe y Esperanza, San Antonio, San José y San Miguel /. Tegucigalpa, D.C. [1984] 1 v. (various foliations) : LC Card 85-205996
HC145.Z7 T434 1984

SLUMS - INDIA - BOMBAY.
Brahm Prakash. The urban dead-end? . Bombay , 1983. xii, 138 p., [5] p. of plates : LC Card 84-900007 DDC 331.12/5/0954792 19
HD5820.B6 B72 1983 ***NYPL [JLD 86-3828]***

SM delrapport .
(7) Örning, Birgitta. Solidaritetsarbete . Stockholm [1978?] 66 p. : LC Card 81-140576
HD7728 .O75 1978

Smalis, I. A., 1918- Money : only a by-product / I.A. Smalis.1st ed. Santa Fe, NM, USA : Sunstone Press, 1987. 87 p. : ill. ; 23 cm. (Sunstone key business series) ISBN 0-86534-100-1 : LC Card 87-6439 DDC 650.1 19
1. Success in business. 2. Entrepreneur. I. Title. II. Series.
HF5386 .S637 1987

Small and medium-sized enterprises : keystone for a free and prosperous Europe / editors, Harry Roos ... [et al.]. Tilburg, Netherlands : Tilburg University Press, 1986. xi, 219 p. : ill. ; 24 cm. Includes bibliographies. ISBN 90-361-9711-2 (pbk.) : LC Card 86-221122 DDC 338.6/42/094 19
1. Small business - Europe. I. Roos, Harry.
HD2346.E9 S58 1986

SMALL BUSINESS.
Bayer, B. József. A kis- és középvállalatok és a gazdasági fejlődés . Budapest , 1986. 203, [1] p. : ISBN 963-221-914-7 : LC Card 87-138623
HD2341 .B29 1986

Greenfield, W. M. Successful management consulting . Englewood Cliffs, N.J. , c1987. xii, 192 p. ; ISBN 0-13-863143-3 : LC Card 86-30494 DDC 658.4/6 19
HD69.C6 G72 1987

Grover, Subhash C. (Shubash Chander), 1938- Paths to profits /. Dallas , 1985. v, 142 p. ; ISBN 0-930383-04-4 (pbk.) : LC Card 84-25548 DDC 650.1 19
HD62.7 .G75 1985 ***NYPL [JLD 86-1907]***

Hinderer, Michael. Die mittelständische Unternehmung . München , c1984. xix, 435 p. : ISBN 3-88259-328-8 LC Card 85-152951
HD2341 .H56 1984

New opportunities for entrepreneurship /. Boulder , 1987. p. cm. ISBN 0-8133-0597-7 LC Card 87-20143 DDC 338/.04 19
HD62.5 .N48 1987

The Performance of small firms . London , Wolfeboro, N.H. , c1987. 342 p. : ISBN 0-7099-4411-X : LC Card 86-29052 DDC 658/.022 19
HD2341 .P399 1987

Seltz, David D. A handbook of retail promotion ideas /. Rockville Centre, N.Y. , c1985. 256 p. ; ISBN 0-87863-220-4 LC Card 84-25969 DDC 658.8/2 19
HF5438.5 .S45 1985 ***NYPL [JLF 86-1789]***

SMALL BUSINESS - ACCOUNTING.
Guilhot, Bernard-Henri. Analyse bancaire de la P.M.E. /. Paris , c1985. 306 p. : ISBN 2-86325-035-3 : LC Card 86-152256
HG4027.7 .G85 1985

Winkler, Wigbert M. Kostenrechnung in Klein- und Mittelbetrieben . Graz , c1986. vi, 287 p. : ISBN 3-7041-0150-8 LC Card 87-409225
HF5686.C8 W683 1986

SMALL BUSINESS - ADDRESSES, ESSAYS, LECTURES.
Survival of the small firm /. Aldershot, Hants, England , Brookfield, Vt., U. S.A. , c1986. 2 v. : ISBN 0-566-00725-8 (v. 1) : LC Card 85-27035 DDC 338.6/42 19
HD2341 .S87 1986 ***NYPL [JLD 86-2643]***

SMALL BUSINESS - AFRICA.
The Informal sector in Africa. Addis Ababa [Ethiopia] , 1985. 147 p. ; ISBN 92-2-103785-1 : ***NYPL [JLE 86-1454]***

Policies and measures to promote industrial co-operatives in Africa /. [New York] [1985] 23 p. ; LC Card 87-104469 DDC 334/.6/096 19
HD3247 .P65 1985

A small business agenda . Hull, Galen. Lanham, MD , c1986. x, 128 p. ; ISBN 0-8191-5163-7 (alk. paper) : LC Card 85-26513 DDC 338.6/42/0973 19
HD2346.U5 H85 1986 ***NYPL [JLD 86-2614]***

SMALL BUSINESS - ANDES REGION.
Board of the Cartagena Agreement. Programa subregional de apoyo a la pequeña y mediana industria /. [S.l.] [between 1983 and 1986] (Lima, Perú : Europrint) 29 p. ; LC Card 87-400442 DDC 338.6/42/098 19
HD2346.A64 B63 1983

SMALL BUSINESS - ARGENTINA.
Frediani, Ramón O. El rol del empresario mediano en el desarrollo argentino . Buenos Aires, República Argentina , c1985. 123 p. : LC Card 87-101993
HD2346.A73 F73 1985

SMALL BUSINESS - ASIA - CONGRESSES.
Invisible hands . New Delhi , Newbury Park, Calif. , 1987. 273 p. ; ISBN 0-8039-9524-5 (U. S.) LC Card 87-4337 DDC 331.4/0954 19
HD6181.85 .A85 1987

Small business audit manual /. Perry, Larry L. Englewood Cliffs, N.J. , c1987- 1 v. (loose-leaf) : ISBN 0-13-813155-4 (loose-leaf) LC Card 86-63242 DDC 657/.45 19
HF5667 .P416 1987

SMALL BUSINESS - AUDITING - HANDBOOKS, MANUALS, ETC.
Perry, Larry L. Small business audit manual /. Englewood Cliffs, N.J. , c1987- 1 v. (loose-leaf) : ISBN 0-13-813155-4 (loose-leaf) LC Card 86-63242 DDC 657/.45 19
HF5667 .P416 1987

SMALL BUSINESS - AUSTRIA - FINANCE.
Aiginger, Karl. Die Grösse der Kleinen . Wien [between 1984 and 1987] 160, [1] p. : ISBN 3-85436-025-8 LC Card 87-141921 DDC 658.1/592 19
HG4027.7 .A38 1984

Pernsteiner, August W. Gestaltkonforme partnerschaftliche "Beteiligungs-" und "Kreditfinanzierung" von "Klein-" und "Mittelbetrieben" /. Wien , 1983. 355, xxx p. : ISBN 3-85369-536-1 LC Card 83-206156
HG4027.7 .P47 1983

SMALL BUSINESS - AUSTRIA - MANAGEMENT.
Aiginger, Karl. Die Grösse der Kleinen . Wien [between 1984 and 1987] 160, [1] p. : ISBN 3-85436-025-8 LC Card 87-141921 DDC 658.1/592 19
HG4027.7 .A38 1984

Holzhuber, Thomas. Strategische Unternehmensführung in Klein- und Mittelbetrieben . Wien [1984?] 198, 5 p. : ISBN 3-85436-018-5 : LC Card 84-248354
HD62.7 .H65 1984

SMALL BUSINESS - BANGLADESH - FINANCE.
Industrial investment schedule for small industry, 1982-85. Dhaka , 1982. v, 283 p. ; LC Card 84-900851 DDC 338.6/42/095492 19
HD2346.B27 I53 1982 ***NYPL [JLF 87-269]***

Small business banking . Cranfill, Steven L. Washington, D.C. (1120 Connecticut Ave. N.W., Washington, D.C.) , c1987. ix, 78 p. : LC Card 87-135069 DDC 332.1/753 19
HG4027.7 .C7 1987

SMALL BUSINESS - BIBLIOGRAPHY.
Biebel, Belle M. The small business reference guide for home-based business, small manufacturers, self-publishers, entrepreneurs, craftsmen, retailers, writers, artists /. Stratford, Conn. , c1987. viii, 63 p. ; ISBN 0-941825-02-7 (pbk.) LC Card 87-91148 DDC 016.658/022 19
HD2346.U5 B49 1987

SMALL BUSINESS - BRAZIL - ADDRESSES, ESSAYS, LECTURES.

Pequena empresa . São Paulo-Brasil [Brasília] , 1985. 2 v. : LC Card 85-180776 DDC 338.6/42/0981 19
HD9710.3.B72 P46 1985
NYPL [JLD 86-1588]

SMALL BUSINESS - BRAZIL - CEARÁ (STATE)
Ferreira, Assuéro. As pequenas e médias empresas na expansão industrial brasileira . Fortaleza-Ceará , 1985. 68 p. ; LC Card 87-102632 DDC 338.6/42/098131 19
HD2346.B72 C445 1985

SMALL BUSINESS - BURKINA FASO.
Structure et perspectives de l'artisanat et de la petite industrie du sud-ouest de la Haute-Volta . Berlin (West) [1978] xxvi, 253 p. : LC Card 85-118488
HD2346.B82 S77 1978

SMALL BUSINESS - BURKINA FASO - CASE STUDIES.
Schneider-Barthold, Wolfgang. Industrie und Grundbedürfnisbefriedigung in Afrika . Frankfurt/Main , New York , c1984. 264 p. ; ISBN 3-593-33350-3 LC Card 86-125217
HC1040 .S35 1984

SMALL BUSINESS - BURUNDI.
Etude sur la petite et moyenne industrie et l'artisanat /. [Bujumbara] [1984] 7 v. in 6 : LC Card 86-980948
HD2346.B94 E78 1984

SMALL BUSINESS - CALIFORNIA - HANDBOOKS, MANUALS, ETC.
Koch, Harry Walter, 1909- A California small business handbook /. [San Francisco] , c1986. 174 p. : ISBN 0-910553-06-8 (pbk.) : LC Card 87-167776 DDC 658/.022/09794 19
HD2346.U52 C25 1986

SMALL BUSINESS - CASE STUDIES.
Davis, Nancy Yaw. Research and consulting as a business /. Washington, D.C. , c1987. v, 41 p. : ISBN 0-913167-21-5 (pbk.) LC Card 87-20254 DDC 658.4/6 19
HD69.C6 D38 1987

SMALL BUSINESS - CASH POSITION.
Crise de liquidité et gestion de la trésorerie dans les P.M.E. Genève, Suisse , 1985. 32 p. : LC Card 87-138138
HG4027.7 .C75 1985

Goldstein, Harvey A. (Harvey Arthur), 1939- Up your cash flow . Los Angeles, Calif. , c1986. 174 p. : ISBN 0-931349-04-4 (pbk.) LC Card 86-213003 DDC 658.1/592 19
HD62.7 .G68 1986

SMALL BUSINESS - CHILE - SANTIAGO.
Corvalán Vásquez, Oscar E., 1947- Empleo y capacitación en los talleres informales de Santiago /. Montevideo , 1984. 150 p. ; LC Card 86-127324
HD2346.C54 S263 1984

SMALL BUSINESS - COLOMBIA.
Cortes, Mariluz. Success in small and medium-scale enterprises . New York , c1987. xiii, 289 p. ; ISBN 0-19-520593-6 : LC Card 86-46296 DDC 338.6/42/09861 19
HD2346.C7 C69 1987

SMALL BUSINESS - COMMUNIST COUNTRIES.
Koncepció és kritika . Budapest , c1985. 387 p. ; ISBN 963-14-0359-9 : LC Card 86-104222
HB615 .K66 1985

Popov, Nikola Grigorov. Sŭshtnost, formi i nasoki na izzhiviavane na chastnata stopanska deĭnost pri sotsializma /. Sofiia , 1985. 363 p. ; LC Card 85-169713
HC704 .P66 1985 ***NYPL [*QK 87-1471]***

The small business computer today and tomorrow /. Grieb, William E. New York, N.Y. , c1984. 287 p. : ISBN 0-671-55907-9 (pbk.) : LC Card 86-207213 DDC 658/.05416 19
HF5548.2 .G733 1984

SMALL BUSINESS - CONGRESSES.
Symposium on Linkage Between Large and Small Industries (1985 : Kuala Lumpur, Malaysia) Linkage effects and small industry development . Tokyo , 1986. iv, 191 p. : ISBN 92-833-2037-3 LC Card 87-137082 DDC 338.6/42/09595 19
HD2341 .S96 1985

SMALL BUSINESS - DATA PROCESSING.
Grieb, William E. The small business computer today and tomorrow /. New York, N.Y. , c1984. 287 p. : ISBN 0-671-55907-9 (pbk.) : LC Card 86-207213 DDC 658/.05416 19
HF5548.2 .G733 1984

Harvey, David. The electronic office in the smaller business /. Aldershot, Hants, England , Brookfield, Vt., U. S.A. , c1986. vii, 214 p. : ISBN 0-566-02578-7 LC Card 86-225568 DDC 651.8/416 19
HF5547.5 .H365 1986

Holtz, Herman. How to make money with your micro /. New York , c1984. xiv, 324 p. : ISBN 0-471-88455-3 (pbk.) : LC Card 84-3589 DDC 001.64 19
HF5548.2 .H5925 1984
NYPL [JLE 86-2074]

Hudson, R. W. Business computer systems . London , New York , c1986. x, 163 p. : ISBN 0-07-084976-5 (pbk.) : LC Card 86-10481 DDC 650/.028/5 19
HF5548.2 .H78 1986 ***NYPL [JLE 87-1038]***

Pathways through data processing, small business systems. Cherry Hill, N.J. (140 Barclay Center, Cherry Hill 08034) , c1980. 182 p. : LC Card 81-118723 DDC 001.64/04/029473 19
HF5548.2 P295 1980 ***NYPL [JLF 86-351]***

SMALL BUSINESS - DEVELOPING COUNTRIES.
Andersson, Tommy D., 1947- Profit in small firms . Aldershot, Hants, England , Brookfield, Vt., USA , c1987. 407 p. : ISBN 0-566-05468-X : LC Card 87-21321 DDC 338.6/42/091724 19
HD2346.5 .A53 1987

Hull, Galen. A small business agenda . Lanham, MD , c1986. x, 128 p. ; ISBN 0-8191-5163-7 (alk. paper) : LC Card 85-26513 DDC 338.6/42/0973 19
HD2346.U5 H85 1986
NYPL [JLD 86-2614]

Kinsey, B. H. Agribusiness and rural enterprise /. London , New York , c1987. 228 p. ; ISBN 0-7099-1558-6 : LC Card 87-471 DDC 338.1/09172/4 19
HD9018.D44 K55 1987

Little, Ian Malcolm David. Small manufacturing enterprises . New York , 1987. x, 362 p. : ISBN 0-19-520619-3 LC Card 87-12365 DDC 338.6/42/0954 19
HD9736.I52 L57 1987

SMALL BUSINESS - DEVELOPING COUNTRIES - EVALUATION.
Monitoring and evaluating small business projects . [New York, NY] , c1987. ix, 262 p. : LC Card 87-6945 DDC 361.7 19
HD2346.5 .M65 1987

Small business development : some current issues / edited by Ken O'Neill ... [et al.]. Aldershot, Hampshire ; Brookfield, Vt., U. S.A. : Avebury, c1987. xix, 276 p. : ill. ; 23 cm. Includes bibliographies. ISBN 0-566-05382-9 : LC Card 87-22386 DDC 338.6/42/0941 19
1. Small business - Great Britain. I. O'Neill, Ken, 1944-.
HD2346.G7 S58 1987

SMALL BUSINESS - ECUADOR.
Sandoval H., Orlando. Comercialización de artesanías /. [Quito, Ecuador] , 1985. 231 p. : LC Card 87-400169 DDC 331.7/94 19
HD2346.E2 S26 1985

SMALL BUSINESS - ECUADOR - DIRECTORIES.
Directorio nacional de pequeñas industrias . [Quito] , 1985. 264 p. ; LC Card 86-192239
HF3433 .D59 1985

SMALL BUSINESS - EMPLOYEES - ADDRESSES, ESSAYS, LECTURES.
Survival of the small firm /. Aldershot, Hants, England , Brookfield, Vt., U. S.A. , c1986. 2 v. : ISBN 0-566-00725-8 (v. 1) : LC Card 85-27035 DDC 338.6/42 19
HD2341 .S87 1986 ***NYPL [JLD 86-2643]***

SMALL BUSINESS - EUROPE.
Entrepreneurship in Europe . London , New York , c1987. 197 p. ; ISBN 0-7099-3849-7 LC Card 87-15425 DDC 338/.04/094 19
HD2346.E9 E57 1987

Geroski, Paul A. Entrepreneurship and small firms /. Berlin [1985] 31, 2, 6 p. ; LC Card 86-213576 DDC 338.6/42 19
HD2346.E9 G47 1985

Small and medium-sized enterprises . Tilburg, Netherlands , 1986. xi, 219 p. : ISBN 90-361-9711-2 (pbk.) : LC Card 86-221122 DDC 338.6/42/094 19
HD2346.E9 S58 1986

Small business in Europe /. Basingstoke, Hampshire , 1986. xx, 211 p. : ISBN 0-333-38405-9 : LC Card 86-673899
HD2346.E9 S62x 1986

SMALL BUSINESS - EUROPE - ADDRESSES, ESSAYS, LECTURES.
New firms and regional development in Europe /. London , Dover, N.H. , c1986. 322 p. : ISBN 0-7099-1577-2 : LC Card 85-28372 DDC 338.7/1/094 19
HD2346.E9 N48 1986 ***NYPL [JLD 86-1597]***

SMALL BUSINESS - EUROPE, GERMAN-SPEAKING - MANAGEMENT.
Seibert, Siegfried, 1954- Strategische Erfolgsfaktoren in mittleren Unternehmen . Frankfurt am Main , New York , c1987. xii, 353 p. : ISBN 3-8204-9828-1 LC Card 87-122289
HD2346.G3 S38 1987

SMALL BUSINESS - EUROPE - HISTORY.
John, Peter, 1946- Handwerkskammern im Zwielicht . Köln , 1983. 304 p. ; ISBN 3-7663-0597-2 LC Card 83-127836 DDC 338.6/425/0943 19
HD2346.E9 J63 1983 ***NYPL [JLD 87-1038]***

SMALL BUSINESS - EUROPEAN ECONOMIC COMMUNITY COUNTRIES.
P.M.E., ayudas, estímulos e instituciones especializadas en la C.E.E. . [Madrid] [1983?] 141 p. ; ISBN 84-500-8571-3 LC Card 85-135456
HD2346.E93 P16 1983

SMALL BUSINESS - EUROPEAN ECONOMIC COMMUNITY COUNTRIES - CONGRESSES.
Drexel, Ingrid. Vocational training problems in small and medium-sized enterprises . Luxembourg , Washington, DC , 1986. 279 p. : ISBN 92-825-5707-3 (pbk.) LC Card 86-213476 DDC 331.25/92/094 19
HD5715.5.E8 D74 1986

SMALL BUSINESS - FINANCE.
Aiginger, Karl. Die Grösse der Kleinen . Wien [between 1984 and 1987] 160, [1] p. : ISBN 3-85436-025-8 LC Card 87-141921 DDC 658.1/592 19
HG4027.7 .A38 1984

Crise de liquidité et gestion de la trésorerie dans les P.M.E. Genève, Suisse , 1985. 32 p. : LC Card 87-138138
HG4027.7 .C75 1985

Dible, Donald M. Up your own organizaion! . Reston, Va. , c1986. xx, 423 p. ; ISBN 0-8359-8086-3 (pbk.) : LC Card 85-8293 DDC 658/.022 19
HD62.7 .D53 1986 ***NYPL [*R-Econ. 86-288]***

Goldstein, Harvey A. (Harvey Arthur), 1939- Up your cash flow . Los Angeles, Calif. , c1986. 174 p. : ISBN 0-931349-04-4 (pbk.) LC Card 86-213003 DDC 658.1/592 19
HD62.7 .G68 1986

Guilhot, Bernard-Henri. Analyse bancaire de la P.M.E. /. Paris , c1985. 306 p. : ISBN 2-86325-035-3 : LC Card 86-152256
HG4027.7 .G85 1985

Mancuso, Joseph. How to start, finance, and manage your own small business /. Englewood Cliffs, N.J. , c1984. vi, 392 p. : ISBN 0-13-434879-6 LC Card 84-13411 DDC 658/.022 19
HD62.7 .M365 1984
NYPL [*R-Econ. 84-3832]

Milling, Bryan E. Banking strategies for businesses . Radnor, PA , c1987. viii, 231 p. : ISBN 0-8019-7651-0 (pbk.) : LC Card 86-47959 DDC 658.1/592 19
HG4027.7 .M55 1987

Owen, Robert R. (Robert Randolph) Arthur Young guide to financing for growth . New York , c1986. xiv, 298 p. ; ISBN 0-471-81946-8 : LC Card 86-1612 DDC 658.1/522 19
HG4027.7 .O94 1986 ***NYPL [JLE 86-2667]***

Rennhoff, Harley A. Get that business loan . Gretna, La. , 1987. viii, 163 p. ; ISBN 0-88289-602-4 LC Card 87-2245 DDC 658.1/5224 19
HG4027.7 .R46 1987

Veale, Stuart R. Tapping the small-business market /. New York, NY , c1987. xiii, 198 p. ; ISBN 0-13-884420-8 : LC Card 87-7732 DDC 332.6/068/8 19
HG4027.7 .V4 1987

SMALL BUSINESS - FINANCE - HANDBOOKS, MANUALS, ETC.
Feingold, S. Norman, 1914- Making it on your own /. Washington, D.C. , c1985. 300 p. ; ISBN 0-87491-779-4 (pbk.) : LC Card 85-7560 DDC 658/.022 19
HD62.7 .F44 1985 *NYPL [*R-Econ. 85-4850]*

Handbook for raising capital . Homewood, Ill. , c1987. xxiv, 666 p. : ISBN 0-87094-705-2 LC Card 86-71216 *NYPL [*R-Econ. 87-1124]*

Personal financial planning . New York, N.Y. (1211 Ave. of the Americas, New York 10036-8775) , c1987. viii, 131 p. ; LC Card 87-142958 DDC 332.024 19
HG179 .P387 1987

Small business financing : a special collection from the Journal of commercial bank lending. Philadelphia, Pa. : Robert Morris Associates, c1987. 118 p. ; 23 cm. ISBN 0-936742-40-2 (pbk.) : LC Card 87-5534 DDC 332.1/753/0685 19
1. Commercial loans - United States. 2. Banks and banking - United States. 3. Small business - United States - Finance. I. Robert Morris Associates. II. Journal of commercial bank lending. III. Title: Special collection from the Journal of commercial bank lending.
HG3754.5.U6 S6 1987

SMALL BUSINESS - FINLAND.
Neilimo, Kari, 1944- Hinnanasetanta, toiminta-analyyttinen tutkimus pienyrityksistä /. Tampere , 19. 90, [8] leaves : ISBN 951-44-1729-1 LC Card 86-140431
HF5416.5 .N45 1985

SMALL BUSINESS - GERMANY, WEST.
Albach, Horst. Kosten der Arbeit . Stuttgart , c1985. xi, 179 p. : ISBN 3-7910-5003-6 : LC Card 86-162885 DDC 658.3/00943 19
HD5029 .A43 1985 *NYPL [JLL 73-505 Nr.2]*

Die Wirksamkeit staatlicher Mittelstandsförderung im Einzelhandel /. Berlin , c1981. 223 p. : ISBN 3-428-04919-5 LC Card 82-175986 DDC 658.8 s 338.6/42/0943 19
HF5415.A2 S37 Bd. 12 HD2346.G3 *NYPL [JLE 86-3464]*

Eckstein, Werner E. Kooperative Systembildung in der Transportwirtschaft . Karlsruhe , c1985. vii, 263 p. : ISBN 3-88652-028-5 LC Card 86-135639
HE199.G3 E28 1985

Geiser, Josef. Wachstumshemmnisse mittelständischer Industriebetriebe /. Göttingen , 1983. xi, 385 p. : ISBN 3-509-01353-0 LC Card 84-221327
HD2346.G3 G372 1983

Gruhler, Wolfram. Wirtschaftsfaktor Mittelstand . Köln , c1984. 195 p. : ISBN 3-602-34845-8 (pbk.) LC Card 87-672069
HD2346.G3 G78x 1984

Hennicke, Martin. Zum Förderungssystem für kleine und mittlere Unternehmen . Stuttgart , c1986. 155 p. ; ISBN 3-7910-5012-5 LC Card 86-181544 DDC 338.6/42/0943 19
HD2346.G3 H44 1986

Hinderer, Michael. Die mittelständische Unternehmung . München , c1984. xix, 435 p. : ISBN 3-88259-328-8 LC Card 85-152951
HD2341 .H56 1984

Kornhardt, Ullrich. Entwicklungstendenzen im Konsumgüterhandwerk /. Göttingen , 1986. 385 p. : ISBN 3-509-01418-9 LC Card 86-197187
HD2341.A1 G6 Bd. 37 HD2346.G3

Laki, Mihály. A kisvállalatok állami támogatása két fejlett tőkés országban /. Budapest , 1983-1985. 62 p. ; LC Card 86-218531
HD2346.G3 L24 1983

Maier, Hans E. Das Handwerk und die Berufseingliederung Jugendlicher in der Bundesrepublik Deutschland /. Berlin [1986] 68 p. : LC Card 86-230660
HD5715.5.G4 M35 1986

Mortsiefer, Joachim. Messen und Ausstellungen als Mittel der Absatzpolitik mittelständischer Herstellerbetriebe /. Göttingen , 1986. 534 p. : ISBN 3-509-01399-9 : LC Card 86-210320 DDC 381/.18 19
HF5470 .M583 1986

Schatz, Klaus-Werner. Die Bedeutung kleiner und mittlerer Unternehmen im Strukturwandel /. Kiel , 1984. 32 p. ; LC Card 85-136545
HB44 .K45 no. 103 HD2346.G3

Weimer, Theodor. Die Bedeutung des Osthandels für mittelständische Unternehmen /. Stuttgart , c1985. 172, 7 p. : ISBN 3-7910-5006-0 LC Card 86-160626
HF3568.E35 W43 1985 *NYPL [JLL 73-505 Nr.5]*

Wünsche und Forderungen des Handwerks an Parteien, X. Deutschen Bundestag und Bundesregierung. Bonn [1983] 80 p. ; LC Card 83-220138
HD2346.G3 W86 1983

SMALL BUSINESS - GERMANY, WEST - ADDRESSES, ESSAYS, LECTURES.
Hamer, Eberhard. Mittelstand, Träger der Marktwirtschaft . Minden , c1984- v. ; ISBN 3-7907-3056-4 (Bd. 1) LC Card 85-175274 DDC 338.6/42/0943 19
HD2346.G3 H215 1984 *NYPL [JLK 86-61]*

SMALL BUSINESS - GERMANY (WEST) - BADEN-WÜRTTEMBERG.
Moosmann, Bernfried, 1957- Mittelbetriebe und Entwicklungsländer . Frankfurt am Main , New York , c1986. x, 290 p. ; ISBN 3-8204-9518-5 LC Card 86-232976
HF3569.B2 M66 1986

SMALL BUSINESS - GERMANY, WEST - FINANCE.
Berger, Manfred, Dipl. econ. Auslandsinvestitionen kleiner und mittlerer Unternehmen . Berlin , c1985. 164 p. : ISBN 3-428-05775-9 LC Card 85-161656
HG4538 .B4538 1985

Klose, Roland, 1954- Die Erschliessung des US-Marktes durch Direktinvestitionen mittelständischer deutscher Unternehmungen des Investitionsgüterbereichs /. [Würzburg? , 1983] (Würzburg : Dissertationsdruck, Schmitt & Meyer) v, 307 p. ; LC Card 84-195414
HG4910 .K56 1983

Lubitz, Karl-Joachim. Bankmarketing gegenüber mittelständischen Betrieben /. Frankfurt am Main , c1984. 299 p. ; ISBN 3-7819-3012-2 LC Card 85-153969
HG4027.7 .L83 1984

Uhlmann, Luitpold. Investitionsverhalten und Unternehmensgrösse /. Berlin , c1986. 307 p. ; ISBN 3-428-06010-5 LC Card 86-216522
HG4028.C4 U37 1986

SMALL BUSINESS - GERMANY (WEST) - HAMBURG - STATISTICS.
Das Handwerk in Hamburg . Hamburg [1979] 140 p. ; LC Card 86-133694
HA1282 .A Heft 128 HD2346.G32H3

SMALL BUSINESS - GERMANY (WEST) - LOWER SAXONY.
Menck, Karl Wolfgang. Mittelstand und Entwicklungsländer . Hamburg , 1986. 192 p. ; ISBN 3-87895-318-6 LC Card 87-407405 DDC 337.43/59/01724 19
HF1546.19.L68 M46 1986

SMALL BUSINESS - GOVERNMENT POLICY.
The Performance of small firms . London , Wolfeboro, N.H. , c1987. 342 p. : ISBN 0-7099-4411-X : LC Card 86-29052 DDC 658/.022 19
HD2341 .P399 1987

Vepa, Ram K. Small industry . New Delhi , New York, NY , c1983. xiii, 356 p. ; ISBN 0-7069-2107-0 : LC Card 83-906458 DDC 338.6/42/0954 19
HD2346.I5 V45 1983 *NYPL [JLE 87-281]*

SMALL BUSINESS - GOVERNMENT POLICY - ANDES REGION.
Board of the Cartagena Agreement. Programa subregional de apoyo a la pequeña y mediana industria /. [S.l.] [between 1983 and 1986] (Lima, Perú : Europrint) 29 p. ; LC Card 87-400442 DDC 338.6/42/098 19
HD2346.A64 B63 1983

SMALL BUSINESS - GOVERNMENT POLICY - BRAZIL, NORTHEAST.
Industrialização rural no Nordeste /. Recife , c1986. 488 p. : LC Card 87-403045 DDC 338.981/3 19
HD9014.B83 N755 1985

SMALL BUSINESS - GOVERNMENT POLICY - DEVELOPING COUNTRIES - CONGRESSES.
Promotion de la petite industrie dans les pays en développement /. Paris , c1985. 103 p. : ISBN 2-86844-008-8 LC Card 85-242526 DDC 338.6/42/0943 19
HD2346.5 .P76 1985 *NYPL [JLD 86-3171]*

SMALL BUSINESS - GOVERNMENT POLICY - EUROPE.
A Guide to small firms assistance in Europe /. Aldershot, Hants, England , Brookfield, Vt., U. S.A. , c1986. vii, 263 p. ; ISBN 0-566-05082-X : LC Card 85-27307 DDC 338.6/42/094 19
HD2346.E9 G85 1986 *NYPL [JLG 86-205]*

SMALL BUSINESS - GOVERNMENT POLICY - GERMANY (WEST)
Laki, Mihály. A kisvállalatok állami támogatása két fejlett tőkés országban /. Budapest , 1983-1985. 62 p. ; LC Card 86-218531
HD2346.G3 L24 1983

Wünsche und Forderungen des Handwerks an Parteien, X. Deutschen Bundestag und Bundesregierung. Bonn [1983] 80 p. ; LC Card 83-220138
HD2346.G3 W86 1983

SMALL BUSINESS - GOVERNMENT POLICY - GERMANY (WEST) - MATHEMATICAL MODELS.
Hull, Christopher J. Helping small firms grow . New York , c1987. 228 p. : ISBN 0-7099-4791-7 LC Card 87-15728 DDC 338.6/42 19
HD2346.G3 .H786 1987

SMALL BUSINESS - GOVERNMENT POLICY - INDIA.
Vepa, Ram K. Small industry . New Delhi , New York, NY , c1983. xiii, 356 p. ; ISBN 0-7069-2107-0 : LC Card 83-906458 DDC 338.6/42/0954 19
HD2346.I5 V45 1983 *NYPL [JLE 87-281]*

SMALL BUSINESS - GOVERNMENT POLICY - NIGERIA - KADUNA STATE.
Jaworek, Rudolf. The development of small scale industry in Kaduna State . Zaria [1980] vii, 162, [44] p., [2] leaves of plates : LC Card 84-256006
HD2356.N62 K34 1980

SMALL BUSINESS - GOVERNMENT POLICY - SIERRA LEONE.
Sierra Leone. Industrial Development Dept. Implementation plan for the Growth Centre Programme. Free Town [1985] 2, 57 leaves : LC Card 87-119663 DDC 338.6/42/09664 19
HD2346.S5 S54 1985

SMALL BUSINESS - GOVERNMENT POLICY - UNITED STATES.
Laki, Mihály. A kisvállalatok állami támogatása két fejlett tőkés országban /. Budapest , 1983-1985. 62 p. ; LC Card 86-218531
HD2346.G3 L24 1983

A Tribute to small business . [Washington, D.C.] , San Francisco , c1987. 72 p. : LC Card 87-403591 DDC 338.6/42 19
HD2346.U5 T75 1987

SMALL BUSINESS - GREAT BRITAIN.
Perry, Martin, 1956- Small factories and economic development /. Aldershot, Hants., England , Brookfield, VT, USA , c1986. xvi, 229 p. ; ISBN 0-566-05208-3 : LC Card 86-9904 DDC 338.6/42/0941 19
HC260.D5 P47 1986 *NYPL [JLD 86-3993]*

Scase, Richard. The real world of the small business owner /. London , New York , c1987. 170 p. ; ISBN 0-7099-5416-6 (pbk.) LC Card 87-6756 DDC 338.6/42/0941 19
HD2346.G7 S28 1987

Small business development . Aldershot, Hampshire , Brookfield, Vt., U. S.A. , c1987. xix, 276 p. : ISBN 0-566-05382-9 : LC Card 87-22386 DDC 338.6/42/0941 19
HD2346.G7 S58 1987

Small firms growth and development /. Aldershot, Hampshire, England , Brookfield,

Vt., U. S.A. , c1986. xix, 325 p. : ISBN 0-566-00811-4 *NYPL [JLD 86-3474]*

SMALL BUSINESS - GREAT BRITAIN - CASE STUDIES.
Chisnall, Peter M. Small firms in action . London , New York , c1987. vii, 149 p. ; ISBN 0-07-084180-2 (pbk.) : LC Card 87-21518 DDC 658/.022 19
HD2346.G7 C55 1987

SMALL BUSINESS - HANDBOOKS, MANUALS, ETC.
Kamoroff, Bernard. Small time operator . Laytonville, Calif. , c1986. 190 p. : ISBN 0-917510-06-2 (pbk.) : LC Card 84-73438 *NYPL [JLF 86-947]*

SMALL BUSINESS - HONDURAS - SAN PEDRO SULA.
Estudio de diagnóstico de la población de los barrios--Chamelecón, Suyapa, Fe y Esperanza, San Antonio, San José y San Miguel /. Tegucigalpa, D.C. [1984] 1 v. (various foliations) : LC Card 85-205996
HC145.Z7 T434 1984

SMALL BUSINESS - HONDURAS - TEGUCIGALPA.
Estudio de diagnóstico de la población de los barrios--Chamelecón, Suyapa, Fe y Esperanza, San Antonio, San José y San Miguel /. Tegucigalpa, D.C. [1984] 1 v. (various foliations) : LC Card 85-205996
HC145.Z7 T434 1984

SMALL BUSINESS - HUNGARY.
Falusné Szikra, Katalin. Az első és a második gazdaság közötti bér-, illetve jövedelem-diszparitás /. Budapest , c1986. 31 p. ; ISBN 963-05-4343-5 : LC Card 87-407713
HC300.295.I5 F35 1986

Koncepció és kritika . Budapest , c1985. 387 p. ; ISBN 963-14-0359-9 : LC Card 86-104222
HB615 .K66 1985

SMALL BUSINESS - HUNGARY - CONGRESSES.
A Kisiparosok Országos Szervezete VIII. országos küldöttgyűlése . Budapest , 1982. 167 p. : LC Card 83-229477
HD2346.H8 K58 1982

Small business in Europe / edited by Paul Burns and Jim Dewhurst. Basingstoke, Hampshire : Macmillan, 1986. xx, 211 p. : ill. ; 25 cm. (Macmillan small business series) Bibliography: p. 203-205. Includes index. ISBN 0-333-38405-9 : LC Card 86-673899
1. Small business - Europe. I. Burns, Paul, 1949-. II. Dewhurst, Jim. III. Series.
HD2346.E9 S62x 1986

Small business incubators : a how-to guide. Washington, D.C. : Community Information Exchange, National Urban Coalition, c1984. 32 p. : ill. ; 28 cm. (Technical bulletin) LC Card 86-233015 DDC 333.33/8 19
1. Commercial buildings. 2. New business enterprises. 3. Industrial promotion. 4. Buildings - Remodeling for other use. 5. Urban renewal. I. Community Information Exchange (U. S.). II. Series: Technical bulletin (Community Information Exchange (U. S.)).
HD1393.25 .S63 1984

SMALL BUSINESS - INDIA.
Jyothi Rani, T. Sickness in small scale industrial sector /. Warangal, Andhra Pradesh , 1985. xii, 258 p. ; LC Card 86-902876 DDC 338.6/42/0954 19
HD2747 .J96 1985

Little, Ian Malcolm David. Small manufacturing enterprises . New York , 1987. x, 362 p. : ISBN 0-19-520619-3 LC Card 87-12365 DDC 338.6/42/0954 19
HD9736.I52 L57 1987

Vyasulu, Vinod. Development of backward areas . New Delhi, India , 1987. xi, 188 p. : ISBN 81-85030-05-7 : LC Card 87-902689 DDC 332.6/42/0954 19
HD2346.I5 V93 1987

SMALL BUSINESS - INDIA - CASE STUDIES.
Thanulingom Nadar, N. Small scale industry . Coimbatore, Tamil Nadu , 1985. 194 p. ; LC Card 85-903280 DDC 338.6/42/095482 19
HD2346.I52 C648 1985
NYPL [JLD 86-1411]

SMALL BUSINESS - INDIA - COIMBATORE.
Thanulingom Nadar, N. Small scale industry . Coimbatore, Tamil Nadu , 1985. 194 p. ; LC Card 85-903280 DDC 338.6/42/095482 19
HD2346.I52 C648 1985
NYPL [JLD 86-1411]

SMALL BUSINESS - INDIA - CONGRESSES.
Small scale enterprises in industrial development . Newbury Park, Calif. , New Delhi , 1987. p. cm. ISBN 0-8039-9539-3 LC Card 87-23221 DDC 338.6/42/0954 19
HD2346.I5 S547 1987

SMALL BUSINESS - INDIA, NORTHEASTERN - CONGRESSES.
Industrial development in north east India /. Guwahati , 1987. xx, 179 p. : LC Card 87-902151 DDC 338.0954/1 19
HC437.N57 I55 1987

SMALL BUSINESS - INDIA - PRODUCTION STANDARDS.
Behari, Bepin. Unemployment, technology & rural poverty /. New Delhi , c1983. ix, 453 p. ; ISBN 0-7069-2337-5 : LC Card 83-906129 DDC 338/.06 19
HC440.I52 B43 1983 *NYPL [JLD 87-1132]*

SMALL BUSINESS - INDIA - UTTAR PRADESH.
Agrawal, Deepak, 1955- Prospects of industrial estates in under-developed countries /. Allahabad, India , 1987. 279 p. ; ISBN 81-85076-13-8 : LC Card 86-903605 DDC 338.6/042/09542 19
HC440.D5 A37 1987

SMALL BUSINESS - INDIA - UTTAR PRADESH - FINANCE.
Mishra, M. N. (Maha Narain), 1945- Appraisal of credit facilities provided by banking institutions in rural development /. Meerut, U.P., India [1987?] x, 251, ii p. ; LC Card 87-900918 DDC 332.2 19
HG3284 .M49 1987

SMALL BUSINESS - INDONESIA - JAKARTA.
Jakarta-Raya, Indonesia. Tenaga kerja . Jakarta [1980] 52 leaves ; LC Card 80-942103
HD5824.J27 J35 1980

SMALL BUSINESS - INFORMATION SERVICES - NORWAY.
Engelstad, Kirsten. Viten som verktøy . Oslo , 1985. 80 p. ; ISBN 82-7195-048-7 LC Card 86-175688
HD2346.N6 E53 1985

SMALL BUSINESS - INFORMATION SERVICES - UNITED STATES.
Paradis, Adrian A. The small business information source book /. White Hall, Va. , c1987. 136 p. ; ISBN 0-932620-81-7 (pbk.) LC Card 87-15925 DDC 658/.022/07073 19
HD2346.U5 P37 1987

SMALL BUSINESS - INFORMATION SERVICES - UNITED STATES - DIRECTORIES.
Biebel, Belle M. The small business reference guide for home-based business, small manufacturers, self-publishers, entrepreneurs, craftsmen, retailers, writers, artists /. Stratford, Conn. , c1987. viii, 63 p. ; ISBN 0-941825-02-7 (pbk.) LC Card 87-91148 DDC 016.658/022 19
HD2346.U5 B49 1987

The small business information source book /. Paradis, Adrian A. White Hall, Va. , c1987. 136 p. ; ISBN 0-932620-81-7 (pbk.) LC Card 87-15925 DDC 658/.022/07073 19
HD2346.U5 P37 1987

SMALL BUSINESS INVESTMENT COMPANIES - AUSTRIA.
Pernsteiner, August W. Gestaltkonforme partnerschaftliche "Beteiligungs-" und "Kreditfinanzierung" von "Klein-" und "Mittelbetrieben" /. Wien , 1983. 355, xxx p. : ISBN 3-85369-536-1 LC Card 83-206156
HG4027.7 .P47 1983

SMALL BUSINESS - IRELAND - MANAGEMENT - CASE STUDIES.
O'Connor, Nuala. Jobsuss . Cork , cl985. 96 p. ; ISBN 0-85342-748-8 (pbk.) : LC Card 86-220513 DDC 658/.022/09417 19
HD62.7 .O36 1985

SMALL BUSINESS - ITALY - EMILIA-ROMAGNA - FINANCE - HISTORY.
Cooperazione di credito e sviluppo sociale ed economico delle campagne in Emilia Romagna . Bologna , c1983. 173 p. : LC Card 85-156690
HG2051.I82 E433 1983

SMALL BUSINESS - JAPAN.
Geroski, Paul A. Entrepreneurship and small firms /. Berlin [1985] 31, 2, 6 p. ; LC Card 86-213576 DDC 338.6/42 19
HD2346.E9 G47 1985

SMALL BUSINESS - KENYA - CONGRESSES.
Exhibition and income generation for women . [Nairobi?] [1985] 17, 11 p. ; LC Card 85-981503 DDC 331.4/09676/2 19
HD6210.5 .E94 1985

SMALL BUSINESS - LAW AND LEGISLATION - UNITED STATES - CONGRESSES.
White House Conference on Small Business. The White House Conference on Small Business . Washington, D.C. , 1986. v, 76 p. : LC Card 86-603469 DDC 338.6/42/0973 19
HD2346.U5 W539 1986

SMALL BUSINESS - LESOTHO.
Crafts and small-scale industries in Lesotho . Berlin [1982] vi, 60, 16 p., [1] leaf of plates : LC Card 84-215894 DDC 338.6/42/096816 19
HD2346.L44 C73 1982 *NYPL [Sc F 86-141]*

SMALL BUSINESS - MADAGASCAR - ANTANANARIVO.
Gozo, K. M. Le secteur non structuré d'Antananarivo . Addis-Abéba , c1985. vi, 175 p. : LC Card 85-981181
HD2346.M282 A574 1985

SMALL BUSINESS - MAINE - HANDBOOKS, MANUALS, ETC.
Doing business in Maine. [Augusta, Me. , 1983] iii, 93 p. : LC Card 86-620779 DDC 346.741/07 347.41067 19
HD62.5 .D64 1983

SMALL BUSINESS - MALAWI.
Ettema, Wim. Small-scale industry in Malawi . Zomba [1983] iv, 50, [9] leaves, 9 p. : LC Card 84-980489 DDC 338.6/42/096897 19
HD2356.M3 E88 1983

SMALL BUSINESS - MANAGEMENT.
Aiginger, Karl. Die Grösse der Kleinen . Wien [between 1984 and 1987] 160, [1] p. : ISBN 3-85436-025-8 LC Card 87-141921 DDC 658.1/592 19
HG4027.7 .A38 1984

Baumback, Clifford Mason, 1915- How to organize and operate a small business /. Englewood Cliffs, NJ , c1988. xiii, 578 p. : ISBN 0-13-424987-9 LC Card 87-20455 DDC 658/.022 19
HD62.7 .B39 1988

Boehme, Joachim. Innovationsförderung durch Kooperation . Berlin , c1986. 227 p. ; ISBN 3-503-02618-5 LC Card 87-133032 DDC 338.4/762 19
HD9696.A2 B64 1986

Delany, George. The #1 home business book . Blue Ridge Summit, PA [1987] 168 p. : ISBN 0-8306-3022-8 (pbk.) : LC Card 87-2936 DDC 658/.041 19
HD8036 .D44 1987

Dible, Donald M. Up your own organizaion! . Reston, Va. , c1986. xx, 423 p. ; ISBN 0-8359-8086-3 (pbk.) : LC Card 85-8293 DDC 658/.022 19
HD62.7 .D53 1986 *NYPL [*R-Econ. 86-288]*

Frohbieter-Mueller, Jo. Stay home and mind your own business . White Hall, Va. , c1987. 280 p. : ISBN 0-932620-83-3 (pbk.) : LC Card 87-15922 DDC 658/.041 19
HD62.5 .F76 1987

Goldstein, Harvey A. (Harvey Arthur), 1939- Up your cash flow . Los Angeles, Calif. , c1986. 174 p. : ISBN 0-931349-04-4 (pbk.) LC Card 86-213003 DDC 658.1/592 19
HD62.7 .G68 1986

Harmon, Charlotte. The flea market entrepreneur /. Babylon, N.Y. , c1987. 31 p. ; ISBN 0-87576-134-8 (pbk.) : LC Card 87-2223 DDC 658.8/4 19
HF5482 .H36 1987

Husack, Glen A. More profit from your retail business . [S.l.] , c1977. 84 p. : ISBN 0-88896-066-2 (pbk.) LC Card 85-174558
HF5429 .H85 1977

Kuriloff, Arthur H. Starting and managing the small business /. New York , c1988. xxi, 663 p. : ISBN 0-07-035665-3 : LC Card 87-3832 DDC 658/.022 19
HD62.5 .K87 1988

Mancuso, Joseph. How to start, finance, and manage your own small business /. Englewood Cliffs, N.J. , c1984. vi, 392 p. : ISBN 0-13-434879-6 LC Card 84-13411 DDC 658/.022 19
HD62.7 .M365 1984
NYPL [*R-Econ. 84-3832]

Mattar, Edward Paul. Effective management techniques . Worcester, MA , 1987. p. cm. LC Card 87-15556 DDC 658.4 19
HD62.7 .M38 1987

Mucciolo, Louis. Make it yours! . New York , c1987. xiv, 269 p. ; ISBN 0-471-62585-X (pbk.) LC Card 87-8168 DDC 658.1/141 19
HD62.7 .M79 1987

O'Connor, Nuala. Jobsuss . Cork , cl985. 96 p. ; ISBN 0-85342-748-8 (pbk.) : LC Card 86-220513 DDC 658/.022/09417 19
HD62.7 .O36 1985

Schöllhammer, Hans, 1933- Entrepreneurship and small business management /. Malabar, Fla. , 1988. xvi, 608 p. : ISBN 0-89464-235-9 LC Card 87-14818 DDC 658/.022 19
HD62.5 .S354 1988

Taylor, Charlotte. The entrepreneurial workbook . New York, N.Y. , c1985. ix, 148 p. : ISBN 0-452-25660-7 : LC Card 84-29439 DDC 658/.022 19
HD62.5 .T39 1985 ***NYPL [JLF 86-795]***

Taylor, James Walter, 1933- How to create a winning business plan /. New York, NY , 1987, c1986. p. cm. ISBN 0-87280-116-0 : LC Card 87-7685 DDC 658.4/012 19
HD62.7 .T38 1987

Vanebo, Jan Ole, 1948- Systematisk ledelse i mindre bedrifter /. Kirkenær , 1980. 192 p. : ISBN 82-7048-171-8 : LC Card 82-105304
HD62.7 .V36 1980

West, Alan, 1951- A business plan . New York , 1988. xi, 196 p. : ISBN 0-89397-288-6 (pbk.) : LC Card 87-18561 DDC 658.4/012 19
HD62.7 .W47 1988

SMALL BUSINESS - MANAGEMENT - CASE STUDIES.

Kuriloff, Arthur H. Starting and managing the small business /. New York , c1988. xxi, 663 p. : ISBN 0-07-035665-3 : LC Card 87-3832 DDC 658/.022 19
HD62.5 .K87 1988

SMALL BUSINESS - MANAGEMENT - DATA PROCESSING.

Bendeich, E. (Eugen), 1945- Wirtschaftliche Datenerfassung in Klein- und Mittelbetrieben . München , c1979. 211 p. : ISBN 3-478-41740-6 LC Card 85-171162
HD62.7 .B4 1979

SMALL BUSINESS - MANAGEMENT - DECISION MAKING.

Klaes, Friedhelm, 1956- Informationsverhalten kleiner und mittlerer Unternehmen der elektrotechnischen Investitionsgüterindustrie bei strategischen Entscheidungen /. Frankfurt am Main , New York , c1986. xxii, 305 p. ; ISBN 3-8204-9713-7 LC Card 87-407575 DDC 658.4/03 19
HD62.7 .K586 1986

SMALL BUSINESS - MANAGEMENT - HANDBOOKS, MANUALS, ETC.

Feingold, S. Norman, 1914- Making it on your own /. Washington, D.C. , c1985. 300 p. ; ISBN 0-87491-779-4 (pbk.) : LC Card 85-7560 DDC 658/.022 19
HD62.7 .F44 1985
NYPL [*R-Econ. 85-4850]

SMALL BUSINESS - MANAGEMENT - STUDY AND TEACHING - UNITED STATES.

National Survey of entreprenuerial [sic] education /. [Washington, D.C.?] . v. : LC Card 86-603453 DDC 658/.022/071173 19
HF1131 .N325 1986

Small-business market. Veale, Stuart R. Tapping the small-business market /. New York, NY , c1987. xiii, 198 p. ; ISBN 0-13-884420-8 : LC Card 87-7732 DDC 332.6/068/8 19
HG4027.7 .V4 1987

Small business market factbook. Tampa, FL (P.O. Box 30168, Tampa 33630) : Payment Systems, c1986. 106 leaves : ill. ; 28 cm. Includes bibliographies. LC Card 87-100402 DDC 338.6/42/0973 19
1. Small business - United States - Finance. 2. Financial institutions - United States - Marketing. 3. Market surveys - United States. I. Payment Systems, Inc.
HG4027.7 .S64 1986

SMALL BUSINESS - MEXICO.

Pequeña y mediana empresa. [Mexico City, Mexico] [1983] 220 p. ; ISBN 968-8060-29-01 LC Card 86-144218
HD2346.M4 P47 1983

SMALL BUSINESS - MEXICO - GUADALAJARA.

Guadalajara, la gran ciudad de la pequeña industria /. Zamora, Mich. , c1985. 301 p. : ISBN 968-7230-12-6 LC Card 86-191608
HD2346.M42 G824 1985

SMALL BUSINESS - MEXICO - TAXATION.

Pequeña y mediana empresa. [Mexico City, Mexico] [1983] 220 p. ; ISBN 968-8060-29-01 LC Card 86-144218
HD2346.M4 P47 1983

SMALL BUSINESS - NETHERLANDS.

Zelfstandig werken en ondernemen in middelgrote en kleine ondernemingen /. Delft , 1985. 245 p. : ISBN 90-6275-226-8 : LC Card 86-152999
HD2346.N4 Z44 1985

SMALL BUSINESS - NETHERLANDS - TECHNOLOGICAL INNOVATIONS.

During, W. E. Innovatieproblematiek in kleine industriële bedrijven /. Assen , 1986. 242 p. : ISBN 90-232-2196-6 : LC Card 86-186964
HD2346.N4 D87 1986

Zelfstandig werken en ondernemen in middelgrote en kleine ondernemingen /. Delft , 1985. 245 p. : ISBN 90-6275-226-8 : LC Card 86-152999
HD2346.N4 Z44 1985

SMALL BUSINESS - NETHERLANDS - TECHNOLOGICAL INNOVATIONS - CASE STUDIES.

Ondernemen en vernieuwen . Delft, Netherlands , 1985. 240 p. : ISBN 90-6275-189-X LC Card 86-113900
HD2346.N4 O53 1985

SMALL BUSINESS - NEW ZEALAND - FINANCE.

Lal, Mohan. Financing small businesses /. Palmerston North, N.Z. [1977] 25, [2] p. ; LC Card 85-151230
HG4027.7 .L35 1977

SMALL BUSINESS - NIGERIA - KADUNA STATE.

Jaworek, Rudolf. The development of small scale industry in Kaduna State . Zaria [1980] vii, 162, [44] p., [2] leaves of plates : LC Card 84-256006
HD2356.N62 K34 1980

SMALL BUSINESS - NIGERIA - OYO STATE - FINANCE.

Investment opportunities in the field of small scale industries in Oyo State of Nigeria. Ibadan, Oyo State of Nigeria [1977?] v, 94 p., [15] p. of plates : LC Card 86-173553 DDC 658.1/592/096692 19
HD2346.N52 O965 1977

SMALL BUSINESS - NORWAY - MANAGEMENT.

Vanebo, Jan Ole, 1948- Systematisk ledelse i mindre bedrifter /. Kirkenær , 1980. 192 p. : ISBN 82-7048-171-8 : LC Card 82-105304
HD62.7 .V36 1980

SMALL BUSINESS - PAKISTAN - NORTH-WEST FRONTIER PROVINCE.

Shinwari, Ahmad Nawaz. Small scale industry in North West Frontier Province . Peshawar , 1983. 103 p., [3] leaves of plates : LC Card 84-931673 DDC 338.6/422/0899159 19
HD2346.P32 N677 1983

SMALL BUSINESS - PERSONNEL MANAGEMENT.

Arthur, Diane. Managing human resources in small and mid-sized companies /. New York, NY , c1987. x, 278 p. ; ISBN 0-8144-5884-X LC Card 87-47716 DDC 658.3 19
HF5549 .A955 1987

Slimmon, Robert F. Successful pension design for small-to medium-sized businesses /. Englewood Cliffs, N.J. , c1987. xix, 440 p. ; ISBN 0-13-860255-7 LC Card 87-2489 DDC 658.3/253
HD7105.4 .S56 1987

SMALL BUSINESS - PERU.

Pequeña industria, reactivación y desarrollo industrial /. [Miraflores, Lima] [1986] 127 p. : LC Card 87-127800 DDC 338.6/42/0985 19
HD2346.P4 P47 1986

SMALL BUSINESS - PERU - TECHNOLOGICAL INNOVATIONS.

Sotomayor, Octavio. Racionalidad campesina y cambio técnico /. Cusco , 1985. 23 p. ; LC Card 86-200944
HD1531.P4 S67 1985

SMALL BUSINESS - PLANNING.

Taylor, James Walter, 1933- How to create a winning business plan /. New York, NY , 1987, c1986. p. cm. ISBN 0-87280-116-0 : LC Card 87-7685 DDC 658.4/012 19
HD62.7 .T38 1987

SMALL BUSINESS - PURCHASING.

Kellogg, Douglas E. A primer for buying and selling small manufacturing companies /. New York , c1987. xiv, 225 p. : ISBN 0-471-85235-X LC Card 87-19017 DDC 658.1/6 19
HD2341 .K44 1987

Tetreault, Wilfred F., 1927- Starting right in your new business /. Reading, Mass. , c1987. ix, 226 p. ; ISBN 0-201-07795-7 (pbk.) : LC Card 87-19464 DDC 658.1/141 19
HD62.7 .T47 1987

The small business reference guide for home-based business, small manufacturers, self-publishers, entrepreneurs, craftsmen, retailers, writers, artists /. Biebel, Belle M. Stratford, Conn. , c1987. viii, 63 p. ; ISBN 0-941825-02-7 (pbk.) LC Card 87-91148 DDC 016.658/022 19
HD2346.U5 B49 1987

Small business report (Monterey, Calif.) Risk management and retention . Monterey, Calif. (1 Mission Plaza, Monterey 93940) , c1986. v, 71 p. : LC Card 86-202599 DDC 658 19
HD61 .R569 1986

SMALL BUSINESS - SOUTH AFRICA.

South Africa. National Manpower Commission. Verslag van die Nasionale Mannekragkommissie oor 'n ondersoek na die kleinsakesektor in die Republiek van Suid-Afrika, in die besonder die faktore wat die groei en ontwikkeling daarvan kan belemmer =. [Pretoria] [1983] 58 p. ; ISBN 0-620-07511-2 LC Card 85-116407 DDC 338.6/42/0968 19
HD2346.S63 S64 1983

SMALL BUSINESS - SUDAN - JŪBĀ.

Jenkins, S. J. (Susan J.) Aspects of the informal economic sector of Juba, southern Sudan /. [Jūbā, Sudan] [1981?] xiii, 217 p., [4] leaves of plates : LC Card 86-980565
HD2346.S82 J85 1981

SMALL BUSINESS - SWEDEN.

Sweden. Exportstödsutredningen. Exportfrämjande stöd till mindre och medelstora företag . [Stockholm] [1983] 8, 143, 3 p. : ISBN 91-38-08059-1 LC Card 84-218418
HF1567 .S92 1983

SMALL BUSINESS - SWEDEN - DATA PROCESSING.

Carlsson, C. (Christer), 1946- Datorstöd i mindre företag . Åbo , 1983. 248 p. : ISBN 951-648-877-3 LC Card 83-126466
HF5548.2 .C286 1983

Sweden. Statens industriverk. PU-byrån. Användarfrämjande åtgärder på dataområdet . Stockholm , 1975. 97 leaves ; ISBN 91-7318-026-2 LC Card 84-105630
HF5548.2 .S8822 1975

SMALL BUSINESS - SWITZERLAND - FINANCE.

Burkhalter, Rudolf. Die Effizienz der Finanzierungshilfen an Klein- und Mittelbetriebe im Berggebiet /. Bern [1985]

(Aarau : Cooperative Drucki) 216 p. : LC Card 86-115683
HG4027.7 .B86 1985

Nydegger, Alfred. Investitionen und Innovationen in kleineren Industriebetrieben . Diessenhofen , c1983. viii, 317 p. : ISBN 3-7253-0196-4 LC Card 83-224277 DDC 658.1/592 19
HG4027.7 .N93 1983 ***NYPL [JLD 87-633]***

SMALL BUSINESS - UNITED STATES.
The Economy, small business, and the federal budget . Washington , 1986. v, 20 p. : LC Card 86-603392 DDC 338.6/42/0973 19
HC106.8 .E35 1986

Geroski, Paul A. Entrepreneurship and small firms /. Berlin [1985] 31, 2, 6 p. ; LC Card 86-213576 DDC 338.6/42 19
HD2346.E9 G47 1985

Hull, Galen. A small business agenda . Lanham, MD , c1986. x, 128 p. ; ISBN 0-8191-5163-7 (alk. paper) : LC Card 85-26513 DDC 338.6/42/0973 19
HD2346.U5 H85 1986
NYPL [JLD 86-2614]

Laki, Mihály. A kisvállalatok állami támogatása két fejlett tőkés országban /. Budapest , 1983-1985. 62 p. ; LC Card 86-218531
HD2346.G3 L24 1983

Moore, Janice D. Thorne. A step toward independence: economic self sufficiency . Washington, D.C. , c1986. iii, 117 p. : LC Card 86-209069 DDC 362.8/3 19
HD6059.6.U6 M66 1986

National Commission on Jobs and Small Business (U. S.) Making America work again . Washington, D.C. , c1987. ix, 70 p. ; ISBN 0-9617931-0-4 (pbk.) : LC Card 86-33118 DDC 338.6/42/0973 19
HD2346.U5 N315 1987

A Tribute to small business . [Washington, D.C.] , San Francisco , c1987. 72 p. : LC Card 87-403591 DDC 338.6/42 19
HD2346.U5 T75 1987

United States. Small Business Administration. Office of Procurement and Technical Assistance. Report to the Administrator on the analysis of the management and administration of the Procurement and Technical Assistance programs /. [Washington, D.C.] , 1984. 1 v. (various pagings) : ***NYPL [JLF 86-1066]***

Williams, Bruce, 1932- The Bruce Williams book . New York , 1987. p. cm. ISBN 0-8128-3119-5 : LC Card 86-42692 DDC 658/022 19
HD62.5 .W49 1987

SMALL BUSINESS - UNITED STATES - CASE STUDIES.
Oppenheimer, Michael F. Nontariff barriers . Boulder , 1987. xiii, 203 p. ; ISBN 0-8133-7403-0 (pbk. : alk. paper) LC Card 87-50073 DDC 338.4/762/000973 19
HC110.H53 O66 1987

SMALL BUSINESS - UNITED STATES - CONGRESSES.
Small Manufacturing and Process Industry Seminar (1985 : Las Vegas, Nev.) Small Manufacturing and Process Industry Seminar proceedings, September 18-20, 1985, Las Vegas, Nevada /. Falls Church, Va. , c1985. iv, 222 p. : ISBN 0-935406-71-9 (pbk.) LC Card 85-72347 DDC 338.6/42/0973 19
HD9725 .S55 1985 ***NYPL [JLD 86-2451]***

White House Conference on Small Business. The White House Conference on Small Business . Washington, D.C. , 1986. v, 76 p. : LC Card 86-603469 DDC 338.6/42/0973 19
HD2346.U5 W539 1986

SMALL BUSINESS - UNITED STATES - EMPLOYEES.
Birch, David L. Job creation in America . New York , London , c1987. xi, 244 p. : ISBN 0-02-903610-0 LC Card 87-8523 DDC 331.12/4/0973 19
HD2346.U5 B54 1987

SMALL BUSINESS - UNITED STATES - FINANCE.
Cranfill, Steven L. Small business banking . Washington, D.C. (1120 Connecticut Ave. N.W., Washington, D.C.) , c1987. ix, 78 p. : LC Card 87-135069 DDC 332.1/753 19
HG4027.7 .C7 1987

Hellmuth, James G. Finding money . New York, N.Y. , c1983. p. cm. ISBN 0-932648-79-7 LC Card 86-31053 DDC 658.1/5224 19
HG4027.7 .H44 1983b

Small business financing . Philadelphia, Pa. , c1987. 118 p. ; ISBN 0-936742-40-2 (pbk.) : LC Card 87-5534 DDC 332.1/753/0685 19
HG3754.5.U6 S6 1987

Small business market factbook. Tampa, FL (P.O. Box 30168, Tampa 33630) , c1986. 106 leaves : LC Card 87-100402 DDC 338.6/42/0973 19
HG4027.7 .S64 1986

SMALL BUSINESS - UNITED STATES - FINANCE - DIRECTORIES.
Blum, Laurie. Free money for small businesses and entrepreneurs /. New York , c1988. ix, 229 p. ; ISBN 0-471-85803-X : LC Card 87-20978 DDC 658.1/5224 19
HG4027.7 .B58 1988

Holtz, Herman. 2001 sources of financing for small business /. New York , c1983. x, 173 p. ; ISBN 0-668-05468-9 LC Card 82-11366 DDC 658.1/522 19
HG4057 .A286 1983 ***NYPL [JLF 84-63]***

SMALL BUSINESS - UNITED STATES - FINANCE - HANDBOOKS, MANUALS, ETC.
Gladstone, David. Venture capital handbook /. Englewood Cliffs, N.J. , c1988. xv, 350 p. ; ISBN 0-13-941501-7 (pbk.) LC Card 87-61607 DDC 658.1/5224 19
HG4965 .G57 1988

Gladstone, David. Venture capital investing . Englewood Cliffs, N.J. , c1988. xiii, 400 p. ; ISBN 0-13-941428-2 LC Card 87-14414 DDC 332.6/722 19
HG4965 .G575 1988

SMALL BUSINESS - UNITED STATES - LOCATION - DIRECTORIES.
National emerging industries site selection guide /. Minneapolis, MN , c1986. 124 p. ; LC Card 86-231272 DDC 338.6/042/02573 19
HC110.D5 N38 1986

SMALL BUSINESS - UNITED STATES - MANAGEMENT.
Davidson, Jeffrey P. Look before you leap . New York , 1988. p. cm. ISBN 0-8027-1012-3 LC Card 87-23274 DDC 658.4/2 19
HD62.5 .D38 1988

Davidson, Jeffrey P. Marketing to the Fortune 500 and other corporations /. Homewood, Ill. , c1987. xv, 291 p. : ISBN 0-87094-984-5 LC Card 86-51669 DDC 658.8 19
HF5415.1 .D28 1987

Schaefer, Robert A. Starting and managing a small service business /. Washington, D.C. , 1986. v, 57 p. ; LC Card 86-603435 DDC 658/.022 19
HD9981.5 .S32 1986

SMALL BUSINESS - UNITED STATES - SOCIETIES, ETC. - DIRECTORIES.
A Tribute to small business . [Washington, D.C.] , San Francisco , c1987. 72 p. : LC Card 87-403591 DDC 338.6/42 19
HD2346.U5 T75 1987

SMALL BUSINESS - UNITED STATES - VALUATION.
Desmond, Glenn M. Handbook of small business valuation formulas /. Los Angeles , c1987. 139 p. ; ISBN 0-930458-04-4 LC Card 87-402145 DDC 658.1/522 19
HG4028.V3 D478 1987

SMALL BUSINESS - VALUATION.
Pratt, Shannon P. Valuing small businesses and professional practices /. Homewood, Ill. , c1986. xxvii, 483 p. : ISBN 0-87094-598-X LC Card 85-72255 ***NYPL [*R-Econ. 86-1421]***

Rick, Josef. Bewertung und Abgeltungskonditionen bei der Veräusserung mittelständischer Unternehmen /. Berlin , c1985. 191 p. : ISBN 3-428-05785-6 : LC Card 85-186420
HG4028.V3 R52 1985

SMALL BUSINESS - VENEZUELA.
Preliminary study report on promotion of small-medium scale industries in the Republic of Venezuela. [Tokyo] [1978] ii, 27 p. : LC Card 84-249328
HD9506.V42 P74 1978

SMALL BUSINESS - ZAMBIA.
Milimo, J. T. Rural small enterprises in Zambia . [Lusaka] [1985] 71 p. ; LC Card 87-980231 DDC 338.6/42/096894 19
HD2346.Z29 M55 1985

SMALL BUSINESS - ZIMBABWE - EVALUATION - CASE STUDIES.
Else, John F. Planning income generating projects . Harare, Zimbabwe [1986?] 46 p. : LC Card 87-400416 DDC 338.96891/0068 19
HC910 .E43 1986

SMALL COMPUTERS. see **MINICOMPUTERS.**

SMALL COUNTRIES. see **STATES, SMALL.**

Small Enterprise Evaluation Project. Monitoring and evaluating small business projects . [New York, NY] , c1987. ix, 262 p. : LC Card 87-6945 DDC 361.7 19
HD2346.5 .M65 1987

Small factories and economic development /. Perry, Martin, 1956- Aldershot, Hants., England , Brookfield, VT, USA , c1986. xvi, 229 p. ; ISBN 0-566-05208-3 : LC Card 86-9904 DDC 338.6/42/0941 19
HC260.D5 P47 1986 ***NYPL [JLD 86-3993]***

Small farm development problems and strategies /. Maharjan, Bekha L. (Bekha Lal), 1943- [Kathmandu] , 1984. 114 p. ; LC Card 84-901301 DDC 338.1/6 19
HD1476.N35 M33 1984
NYPL [JLD 86-4365]

Small farmer credit and small farmer attitudes towards co-operatives /. Guma, Xolile P. [Kwaluseni, Swaziland] [1982] 94 p. : LC Card 86-101161 DDC 332.7/1/096813 19
HD1491.S855 G85 1982
NYPL [JLG 86-262]

Small farms . Bonanno, Alessandro. Boulder, Colo. , 1987. xvi, 228 p. : ISBN 0-8133-7341-7 (pbk. : alk. paper) LC Card 86-51502 DDC 338.1/6 19
HD1339.I8 B66 1987

SMALL FARMS. see **FARMS, SMALL.**

Small firms growth and development / edited by Michael Scott ...[et al.]. Aldershot, Hampshire, England ; Brookfield, Vt., U. S.A. ; Gower Pub. Co., c1986. xix, 325 p. : ill. ; 23 cm. A selection of papers prepared for the Sixth Annual Research and Policy Conference of the Small Business Management Teachers Association, hosted by Durham University Business School, 1983. Includes bibliographies. ISBN 0-566-00811-4
1. Small business - Great Britain. 2. New business enterprises - Great Britain. I. Scott, Michael.
NYPL [JLD 86-3474]

Small firms in action . Chisnall, Peter M. London , New York , c1987. vii, 149 p. ; ISBN 0-07-084180-2 (pbk.) : LC Card 87-21518 DDC 658/.022 19
HD2346.G7 C55 1987

Small fry . Bavinck, Maarten, 1954- Amsterdam , 1984. xii, 151 p. ; ISBN 90-6256-374-0 (pbk.) LC Card 84-187330 DDC 338.3/72709549/3 19
HD9466.S723 K343 1984
NYPL [JLD 86-2668]

Small industry . Vepa, Ram K. New Delhi , New York, NY , c1983. xiii, 356 p. ; ISBN 0-7069-2107-0 : LC Card 83-906458 DDC 338.6/42/0954 19
HD2346.I5 V45 1983 ***NYPL [JLE 87-281]***

Small industry investment schedule, 1982-85. Industrial investment schedule for small industry, 1982-85. Dhaka , 1982. v, 283 p. ; LC Card 84-900851 DDC 338.6/42/095492 19
HD2346.B27 I53 1982 ***NYPL [JLF 87-269]***

Small island economies . Worrell, DeLisle. New York , 1987. xiv, 289 p. : ISBN 0-275-92795-4 (alk. paper) : LC Card 87-12495 DDC 330.9729/052 19
HC151 .W67 1987

Small Manufacturing and Process Industry Seminar proceedings, September 18-20, 1985, Las Vegas, Nevada /. Small Manufacturing and Process Industry Seminar (1985 : Las Vegas, Nev.) Falls Church, Va. , c1985. iv, 222 p. : ISBN 0-935406-71-9 (pbk.) LC Card 85-72347

DDC 338.6/42/0973 19
HD9725 .S55 1985 ***NYPL [JLD 86-2451]***

Small Manufacturing and Process Industry Seminar (1985 : Las Vegas, Nev.) Small Manufacturing and Process Industry Seminar proceedings, September 18-20, 1985, Las Vegas, Nevada / APICS. Falls Church, Va. : American Production and Inventory Control Society, c1985. iv, 222 p. : ill. ; 22 cm. "September 1985." Includes bibliographies. ISBN 0-935406-71-9 (pbk.) LC Card 85-72347 DDC 338.6/42/0973 19
1. Small business - United States - Congresses. 2. Manufacturing processes - United States - Congresses. 3. United States - Manufactures - Congresses. I. Title.
HD9725 .S55 1985 ***NYPL [JLD 86-2451]***

Small manufacturing enterprises . Little, Ian Malcolm David. New York , 1987. x, 362 p. : ISBN 0-19-520619-3 LC Card 87-12365 DDC 338.6/42/0954 19
HD9736.I52 L57 1987

SMALL NATIONS. see **STATES, SMALL.**

Small nations, giant firms /. Goodman, Louis Wolf. New York , c1987. xiii, 181 p. : ISBN 0-8419-0996-2 LC Card 87-42 DDC 338.8/888 19
HD2755.5 .G66 1987

Small projects for rural development . Bethke, Klaus W. [Nairobi] [1983] 33, [34] leaves ; LC Card 86-981325 DDC 354.676/20082 19
HC865 .B48 1983

Small scale enterprises in industrial development : the Indian experience / edited by K.B. Suri. Newbury Park, Calif. ; New Delhi : Sage Publications, 1987. p. cm. ISBN 0-8039-9539-3 LC Card 87-23221 DDC 338.6/42/0954 19
1. Small business - India - Congresses. I. Suri, K. B., 1932-.
HD2346.I5 S547 1987

Small scale industry . Thanulingom Nadar, N. Coimbatore, Tamil Nadu , 1985. 194 p. ; LC Card 85-903280 DDC 338.6/42/095482 19
HD2346.I52 C648 1985
NYPL [JLD 86-1411]

Small-scale industry in Malawi . Ettema, Wim. Zomba [1983] iv, 50, [9] leaves, 9 p. : LC Card 84-980489 DDC 338.6/42/096897 19
HD2356.M3 E88 1983

Small scale industry in North West Frontier Province . Shinwari, Ahmad Nawaz. Peshawar , 1983. 103 p., [3] leaves of plates : LC Card 84-931673 DDC 338.6/422/0899159 19
HD2346.P32 N677 1983

Small shipments and parcels guidelines to the cost-effective selection of UPS/USPS/LTL domestic ground services (and other services). NASSTRAC's 1986 small shipments and parcels guidelines to the cost-effective selection of UPS/USPS/LTL domestic ground services (and other services). Washington, D.C. (1750 Pa. Ave., NW, Suite 1105, Washington 20006-4502) , 1986. 82 p. : LC Card 87-127320 DDC 380.5/24/0973 19
HE597.U6 N37 1986

SMALL-SPACE ADVERTISING - FRANCE - HISTORY.
Petits pavés, grands bonheurs . [Paris] , c1984. 140 p. : ISBN 2-229-01400-1 : LC Card 85-104866
HF6105.F7 P48 1984

SMALL-SPACE ADVERTISING - FRANCE - HISTORY - PICTORIAL WORKS.
Petits pavés, grands bonheurs . [Paris] , c1984. 140 p. : ISBN 2-229-01400-1 : LC Card 85-104866
HF6105.F7 P48 1984

SMALL STATES. see **STATES, SMALL.**

Small time operator . Kamoroff, Bernard. Laytonville, Calif. , c1986. 190 p. : ISBN 0-917510-06-2 (pbk.) : LC Card 84-73438
NYPL [JLF 86-947]

The smart attorney's guide to accounting documents for discovery and evidence /. McNairn, William N. Redondo Beach, Calif. , 1987. x, 123 p. : ISBN 0-932621-02-3 (pbk.) LC Card 86-62954 DDC 657/.024344 19
HF5616.U5 M346 1987

The "smart card" . O'Reilly, Francis J. Stamford, Conn., U. S.A. [1986] xii, 106 leaves ; ISBN 0-89336-470-3 (soft) : LC Card 87-163972
DDC 380.1/4568 19
HD9696.O672 O74 1986

Smart contracting . Bak, Richard, 1954- Troy, Mich. , c1987. 213 p. : ISBN 0-912524-39-1 (pbk.) : LC Card 86-28327 DDC 338.4/7697 19
HD9683.A2 B35 1987

Smart investing . Senchack, A. J. (Andrew J.) Dallas, Tex. , c1987. 1 v. (various pagings) : ISBN 0-87833-575-7 (pbk.) : LC Card 87-1923 DDC 332.6/78 19
HG4921 .S45 1987

Smart questions . Leeds, Dorothy. New York , c1987. x, 309 p. ; ISBN 0-07-036996-8 LC Card 86-27469 DDC 658.4/52 19
HD38 .L3867 1987

Smart, Terry L.
Hodgetts, Richard M. Addison-Wesley economics /. Menlo Park, Calif. , c1988. vi, T1-T266, 31, 548 p. : ISBN 0-201-22775-4 LC Card 87-147565 DDC 330 19
HB171.5 .H676 1988

Hodgetts, Richard M. Essentials of economics and free enterprise /. Menlo Park, Calif. , c1987. 437 p. : ISBN 0-201-20719-2 LC Card 86-207031 DDC 330 19
HB171.5 .H677 1987

Smart, William, 1853-1915. Wieser, Friedrich, Freiherr von, 1851-1926. [Natürliche Werth. English.] Natural value /. Fairfield, NJ , 1988. p. cm. ISBN 0-678-00821-3 LC Card 87-17245 DDC 338.5/21 19
HB201 .W65 1988

Småskrifter fra Institut for udenrigshandel . (nr. 17) Kolte, Lars. Det danske valutamarked /. København , 1984, c1983. 215 p. : ISBN 87-17-03415-9 LC Card 85-127552
HG3957 .K64 1984

Lo SME e il dollaro . Martinengo, Giancarlo. [Napoli] , c1983. 84 p. ; LC Card 85-150597
HG930.5 .M27 1983

Smeal, Eleanor. Kondratas, S. Anna. Comparable worth . Washington, D.C. [c1986] 16 p. ; LC Card 86-212973 DDC 331.2/1 19
HD6061 .K66 1986

Smekal, Christian. Staatsfinanzierung und Notenbank . Wien [1984?] 211 p. : LC Card 85-198128
HG1811 .S78 1984

Smekalov, Pavel Vasil'evich. Sel'skie kadry nechernozem'i͡a / P.V. Smekalov, V.P. Tolmachev, N.N. Filippov. Moskva : "Sov. Rossii͡a", 1981. 190 p. ; 17 cm. Includes bibliographical references. LC Card 82-177714
1. Agricultural laborers - Russian S.F.S.R. - Non-Chernozem Region. 2. Labor supply - Russian S.F.S.R. - Non-Chernozem Region. I. Tolmachev, V. P. (Vladimir Petrovich). II. Filippov, N. N. III. Title.
HD1536.S65 S64 1981

Smelser, Ronald, 1942- Robert Ley, Hitler's labor leader / Ronald Smelser. New York : Berg Publishers : Distributed by St. Martin's Press, 1988. p. cm. Bibliography: p. Includes index. ISBN 0-85496-161-5 : LC Card 87-20960 DDC 331/.092/4 B 19
1. Ley, Robert, 1890-1945. 2. Deutsche Arbeitsfront. 3. Labor and laboring classes - Germany - History - 20th century. 4. National socialists - Biography. I. Title.
HD8453.L49 S64 1988

Smidt, Seymour. Bierman, Harold. The capital budgeting decision . New York , London , c1988. xvi, 557 p. : ISBN 0-02-309941-0 LC Card 87-15257 DDC 658.1/52 19
HG4028.C4 B54 1988

Smil, Vaclav. Energy in China's modernization : advances and limitations / Vaclav Smil. Armonk, N.Y. : M.E. Sharpe, c1988. xiv, 250 p. : ill., maps ; 24 cm. "An East Gate book." Bibliography: p. 229-236. Includes index. ISBN 0-87332-423-4 LC Card 87-12922 DDC 333.79/0951 19
1. Energy policy - China. 2. Power resources - China. 3. Energy industries - China. I. Title.
HD9502.C62 S644 1988

Smiley, Michael. Schnidman, Frank. Retention of land for agriculture . Boston, MA , 1988. p. cm. ISBN 0-89946-219-7 LC Card 87-5580 DDC 333.76/16/0974 19
HD266.A11 S36 1988

Smiljanić, Slobodan. Sistem upravljanja investicijama / Slobodan Smiljanić. Kragujevac : Svetlost, 1984. 185 p. : ill. ; 24 cm. In Serbo-Croatian (roman) Bibliography: p. 184-185. LC Card 86-115123
1. Corporations - Yugoslavia - Finance - Mathematical models. 2. Investments - Yugoslavia - Mathematical models. I. Title.
HG4234.6 .S65 1984

Smilor, Raymond W. Managing take-off in fast growth companies . New York , c1986. x, 191 p. : ISBN 0-03-005709-4 (alk. paper) : LC Card 85-16745 DDC 658.4/2 19
HD31 .T24 1986 ***NYPL [JLE 86-1303]***

Smirlock, Michael. Taxes and mergers : a survey / by Michael Smirlock, Randolph Beatty, Saman Majd. New York, N.Y. (90 Trinity Place, New York 10006) : Salomon Brothers Center for the Study of Financial Institutions, Graduate School of Business Administration, New York University, [c1986] 42 p. : ill. ; 23 cm. (Monograph series in finance and economics . monograph 1985-3) Bibliography: p. 39-40. LC Card 86-210061 DDC 336.24/3 19
1. Consolidation and merger of corporations - Taxation - United States. I. Beatty, Randolph. II. Majd, Saman. III. Salomon Brothers Center for the Study of Financial Institutions. IV. Title. V. Series.
HD2746.5 .S64 1986

Smirnov, A. A. (Alekseĭ Alekseevich)
Potrebitel'skai͡a kooperatsii͡a v odinnadtsatoĭ pi͡atiletke / A.A. Smirnov. Moskva : Ėkonomika, 1981. 88 p. : ill. ; 20 cm. (Ėkonomika SSSR, 1981-1985) LC Card 82-106193
1. Cooperation - Soviet Union. 2. Consumer cooperatives - Soviet Union. I. Title. II. Title: Potrebitel'skai͡a kooperatsii͡a v 11-ĭ pi͡atiletke. III. Series.
HD3355 .S65 1981

Smirnov, Aleksandr Dmitrievich, economist. Kritika antimarksistskikh ėkonomicheskikh teoriĭ v prepodavanii politicheskoĭ ėkonomii /. Moskva , 1981. 356 p. ; LC Card 82-107917
HB178 .K7 1981

Smirnov, Igor' Pavlovich. Kuzin, V. Komsomol'sko-molodezhnyĭ kollektiv /. Moskva , 1981. 157 p. ; LC Card 82-152678
HD6276.S592 K89 1981

Smirnov, V. D. (Vasiliĭ Dmitrievich)
Sotsial'no-ėkonomicheskiĭ ėksperiment v kolkhoze / V.D. Smirnov ; otvetstvennyĭ redaktor T.I. Zaslavskai͡a. Novosibirsk : Izd-vo "Nauka," Sibirskoe otd-nie, 1986. 111 p. : ill. ; 20 cm. At head of title: Akademii͡a nauk SSSR. Sibirskoe otdelenie. Institut ėkonomiki i organizat͡sii promyshlennogo proizvodstva. Includes bibliographical references. LC Card 86-171536
1. Collective farms - Russian S.F.S.R. - Siberia. I. Zaslavskai͡a, T. I. II. Title.
HD1492.S652 S527 1986

Smirnova, V. A. (Veronika Aleksandrovna)
Terekhov, I͡U. I. (I͡Uriĭ Ivanovich) Planirovanie narodnogo khozi͡aĭstva SSSR /. Khar'kov , 1985. 176 p. ; LC Card 86-102455
HC336.25 .T465 1985

Smit, Barry. Demands on rural lands . Boulder, Colo. , 1987. xvi, 336 p. : ISBN 0-8133-7361-1 (pbk. : alk. paper) LC Card 87-50751 DDC 333.76/13 19
HD105 .D43 1987

Smith, Adam, 1723-1790.
Inquiry into the nature and causes of the wealth of nations. Smith, Adam, 1723-1790. [Inquiry into the nature and causes of the wealth of nations. Selections.] Selections from The wealth of nations / Adam Smith ; edited by George J. Stigler. Arlington Heights, Ill. [1986], c1957. ix, 116 p. ; ISBN 0-88295-093-2 (pbk.) : LC Card 86-23951 DDC 330.1 19
HB161 .S6522 1986

[Inquiry into the nature and causes of the wealth of nations. German]
Der Wohlstand der Nationen : eine Untersuchung seiner Natur und seiner Ursachen / Adam Smith ; aus dem Englischen übertragen und mit einer Würdigung von Horst Claus Recktenwald. München : C.H. Beck, c1974. lxxix, 859 p., [14] p. of plates : ill. ; 23 cm. Translation of: An inquiry into the nature and causes of the wealth of nations. Bibliography: p. [831]-840. Includes indexes. ISBN 3-406-05393-9 LC Card 87-672505

1. Economics. I. Recktenwald, Horst Claus. II. Title.
HB161 .S654x 1974

[Inquiry into the nature and causes of the wealth of nations. Selections]
Selections from The wealth of nations / Adam Smith ; edited by George J. Stigler. Arlington Heights, Ill. : Harlan Davidson, [1986], c1957. ix, 116 p. ; 19 cm. (Crofts classics) Reprint. Originally published: New York : Appleton-Century-Crofts, 1957. Bibliography: p. 116. ISBN 0-88295-093-2 (pbk.) : LC Card 86-23951 DDC 330.1 19
1. Economics. I. Stigler, George Joseph, 1911-. II. Smith, Adam, 1723-1790. Inquiry into the nature and causes of the wealth of nations. III. Title.
HB161 .S6522 1986

[Selections. 1986]
The essential Adam Smith / edited and with introductory readings by Robert L. Heilbroner ; with the assistance of Laurence J. Malone. Oxford [Oxfordshire] ; New York : Oxford University Press, 1986. p. cm. Reprint. Originally published: New York : W.W. Norton. Includes index. ISBN 0-19-877270-X : LC Card 86-23856 DDC 330.15/3 19
1. Economics - Collected works. I. Heilbroner, Robert L. II. Malone, Laurence J. III. Title.
HB161 .S6522 1986b

SMITH, ADAM, 1723-1790.
Elsner, Wolfram. Ökonomische Institutionenanalyse . Berlin , c1986. xv, 469 p. : ISBN 3-428-06035-0 LC Card 86-206447
HB99.5 .E47 1986

Lange, Diedrich. Zur sozialphilosophischen Gestalt der Marktwirtschaftstheorie bei Adam Smith /. München , c1983. 230 p. : ISBN 3-88259-267-2 LC Card 84-150199
HB103.S6 L36 1983

Markt, Staat und Solidarität bei Adam Smith /. Frankfurt , New York , c1984. 238 p. ; ISBN 3-593-33338-4 LC Card 84-202891
HB103.S6 M27 1984

Recktenwald, Horst Claus. Ordnungstheorie und ökonomische Wissenschaft . Erlangen , 1985. 65 p. : ISBN 3-922135-40-4 LC Card 85-234440
HB175 .R35 1985

SMITH, ADAM, 1723-1790 - CONGRESSES.
Studien zur Entwicklung der ökonomischen Theorie /. Berlin , c1981- v. ; ISBN 3-428-04862-8 (v. 1) : LC Card 81-154218 DDC 330/.09 19
HB75 .S787 1981 ***NYPL [JLL 73-186 Bd.115]***

Smith, Allan H. How to sell your homemade creation / Allan H. Smith ; illustrations by Don Trachsler. Lake Park, Fla. : Success Pub., 1986 printing, c1985. 146 p. : ill. ; 28 cm. Includes index. ISBN 0-931113-02-4 (pbk.) : LC Card 84-52239 DDC 745.5/068/8 19
1. Selling - Handicraft. 2. Handicraft - Marketing. I. Title.
HF5439.H27 S64 1986

Smith, Barry J., 1947- How to be an effective trainer : skills for managers and new trainers / Barry J. Smith, Brian L. Delahaye.2nd ed. New York : Wiley, c1987. 404 p. : ill. ; 28 cm. (Wiley professional development programs) Bibliography: p. 395-399. Includes index. ISBN 0-471-85239-2 (pbk.) LC Card 86-26774 DDC 658.3/1243 19
1. Employees, Training of. I. Delahaye, Brian L., 1946-. II. Title. III. Series.
HF5549.5.T7 S642 1987

Smith, Ben. Harris, Stuart. Analysis of commodity markets for policy purposes /. London , 1978. ix, 81 p. ; ISBN 0-900842-42-3 (pbk.) LC Card 85-111455 DDC 332.64/4 19
HG6046 .H367 1978

Smith, Bradley F. The war's long shadow : the Second World War and its aftermath, China, Russia, Britain, America / Bradley F. Smith. New York : Simon and Schuster, c1986. 319 p. ; 23 cm.p. cm. Includes index. Bibliography: p. 303-308. ISBN 0-671-52434-8 LC Card 86-1870 DDC 940.5 19
1. World War, 1939-1945 - Diplomatic history. 2. World War, 1939-1945 - Influence. 3. World politics - 1933-1945. 4. World politics - 1945-1955. I. Title.
D749 .S65 1986 ***NYPL [JFD 86-9433]***

Smith, C. Ray (Clyde Ray), 1935- Rotch, William. The executive's guide to management accounting and control systems /. Houston, Tex. , 1987. ix, 225 p. : ISBN 0-87393-044-4 LC Card 87-163287 DDC 658.1/511 19
HF5635 .R829 1987

Smith, Chris. Disarmament and world development /. Oxford, England , New York , 1986. xiii, 306 p. ; ISBN 0-08-031309-4 : LC Card 85-19231 DDC 338.4/7355 19
JX1974 .D515 1985 ***NYPL [JLE 86-3211]***

Smith, Clayton G. Established companies diversifying into young industries : a comparison of firms with different levels of performance / by Clayton G. Smith and Arnold C. Cooper. West Lafayette, Ind. : Institute for Research in the Behavioral, Economic, and Management Sciences, Krannert Graduate School of Management, Purdue University, [1986] 27, 15 p. ; 28 cm. (Paper / Institute for Research in the Behavioral, Economic, and Management Sciences, Krannert Graduate School of Management . no. 893) Bibliography: p. 21-22. LC Card 86-621740 DDC 658/.001/9 s 338.8/3 19
1. Diversification in industry. 2. Industrial organization. 3. Industries, Size of. I. Cooper, Arnold C. II. Series: Paper (Krannert Graduate School of Management. Institute for Research in the Behavioral, Economic, and Management Sciences) , no. 893. III. Title.
HD6483 .P8 no. 893 HD2755.8

Smith, Courtney. Option strategies : profit-making techniques for stock, stock index, and commodity options / Courtney Smith. New York : Wiley, c1987. viii, 256 p. : ill. ; 24 cm. Bibliography: p. 254. Includes index. ISBN 0-471-84367-9 LC Card 87-6174 DDC 332.64/52 19
1. Financial futures. 2. Put and call transactions. I. Title.
HG6024.3 .S55 1987

Smith, D. W. Drakakis- see **Drakakis-Smith, D. W.**

Smith, Demaris C. Temporary employment : the flexible alternative / by Demaris C. Smith. White Hall, Va. : Betterway Publications, c1985. 143 p. ; 28 cm. At head of title: A complete guide and handbook to the booming temp market. Includes index. Bibliography: p. 136-138. ISBN 0-932620-56-6 (pbk.) : LC Card 85-13456 DDC 650.1/4 19
1. Temporary employment - United States. 2. Vocational guidance - United States. I. Title.
HD5854.2.U6 S6 1985 ***NYPL [JLF 86-1365]***

Smith, Edward Joseph, 1911- Impact of energy costs on manufacturing employment / Edward J. Smith. Washington, D.C. : U. S. Dept. of Agriculture, Economic Research Service, Agriculture and Rural Economics Division, [1985] iv, 16 p. : ill., 1 map ; 28 cm. (Staff report . no. AGES 850802) Distributed to depository libraries in microfiche. "For limited distribution to the research community outside the U. S. Department of Agriculture"--P. ii. "September 1985"--P. ii. Bibliography: p. 14. Item 42-W-1 (microfiche) LC Card 86-603150 DDC 331.12/57/0973 19
1. Labor supply - United States - Effect of energy costs on. 2. United States - Manufactures. I. United States. Dept. of Agriculture. Economic Research Service. Agriculture and Rural Economic Division. II. Series: ERS staff report , no. AGES 850802. III. Title.
HD5724 .S614 1985

Smith, Garry D., 1948- Business strategy and policy / Garry D. Smith, Danny R. Arnold, Bobby G. Bizzell. 2nd ed. Boston : Houghton Mifflin, c1988. xviii, 1006 p. : ill. ; 25 cm. Includes bibliographical references and index. ISBN 0-395-36946-0 LC Card 87-80879 DDC 658.4/012 19
1. Strategic planning. 2. Strategic planning - Case studies. I. Arnold, Danny R., 1948-. II. Bizzell, Bobby G. III. Title.
HD30.28 .S56 1988

Smith, Gaylord N. The Briton Manufacturing Company : a management accounting simulation : student manual / Gaylord N. Smith. New York : Harper & Row, c1988. p. cm. Includes index. ISBN 0-06-046318-X LC Card 87-15624 DDC 657/.028/55369 19
1. Management games. 2. Managerial accounting - Data processing. 3. Accounting - Data processing. I. Title.
HD30.26 .S64 1988

Smith, Geoff, 1926- Drew, Rodney. Microcomputers for financial planning /. Aldershot, Hampshire, England , Brookfield, Vt., U. S.A. , c1987. x, 105 p. : ISBN 0-566-02579-5 (pbk.) : LC Card 87-8405 DDC 658.1/5/0285416 19
HG4012.5 .D73 1987

Smith, Geoffrey N. Sweat equity : what it really takes to build America's best small companies -- by the guys who did it / Geoffrey N. Smith, Paul B. Brown. New York : Simon and Schuster, c1986. 254 p. : ill. ; 23 cm. Includes index. ISBN 0-671-55210-4 LC Card 86-6622 DDC 658/.022 19
1. New business enterprises - United States - Case studies. 2. Success in business - United States - Case studies. 3. Entrepreneur - Case studies. I. Brown, Paul B. II. Title.
HD62.5 .S625 1986 ***NYPL [JLD 86-3014]***

Smith, Gordon V., 1937- Corporate valuation : a business and professional guide / Gordon V. Smith. New York : Wiley, c1988. xiv, 224 p. : ill. ; 24 cm. (Wiley/Ronald-National Association of Accountants professional book series) Bibliography: p. 215-217. Includes index. ISBN 0-471-85826-9 LC Card 87-23114 DDC 658.1/522 19
1. Business enterprises - Valuation. I. Title. II. Series.
HG4028.V3 S58 1988

Smith, Gordon Whitford, 1934- Agricultural marketing and economic development : a Brazilian case study, 1930/1964 / Gordon W. Smith. New York : Garland, 1987. iii, 417 p. ; 24 cm. (South American and Latin American economic history) Originally presented as the author's thesis (Ph.D.)--Harvard University, Cambridge, Mass., 1965. Bibliography: p. [405]-417. ISBN 0-8240-1371-9 (alk. paper) : LC Card 87-11833 DDC 381/.41318/09816 19
1. Rice - Brazil, South - Marketing - History - 20th century. 2. Beans - Brazil, South - Marketing - History - 20th century. 3. Brazil - Economic conditions - 1918-. I. Title. II. Series.
HD9066.B84 S687 1987

Smith, Halbert C., 1934- Real estate appraisal / Halbert C. Smith and Jerry D. Belloit. 2nd ed. Dayton, Ohio : Century VII Pub. Co. ; Columbus, OH : Order from, Publishing Horizons Inc., [c1987] xii, 341 p. ; 23 cm. Includes bibliographies and index. ISBN 0-939787-01-6 (pbk.) : LC Card 86-24520 DDC 333.33/2 19
1. Real property - Valuation. I. Belloit, Jerry D. II. Title.
HD1387 .S5152 1987

Smith, Harold T., 1932- The Administrative manager : principles and strategies for the automated office / Harold T. Smith, William H. Baker, Marvin P. Evans.2nd ed. Chicago : Science Research Associates, c1987. xii, 548 p. : ill. ; 24 cm. Includes bibliographies and index. ISBN 0-574-20065-7 : LC Card 86-24881 DDC 651.8 19
1. Office management. 2. Office practice - Automation. I. Baker, William H., 1944-. II. Evans, Marvin P., 1953-. III. Title.
HF5547 .S577 1987

Smith, Homer B., 1915- Selling through negotiation : the handbook of sales negotiation / Homer B. Smith. Alexandria, VA : New Outlook, c1987. 192 p. ; 24 cm. ISBN 0-9618228-1-3 (soft) : LC Card 87-10998 DDC 658.8/1 19
1. Selling. 2. Negotiation in business. I. Title.
HF5438.25 .S64 1987

Smith, Jack L.
Financial accounting / Jack L. Smith, Robert M. Keith, William L. Stephens. New York : McGraw-Hill, c1988. xxii, 706 p. : ill. (some col.) ; 27 cm. Includes index. ISBN 0-07-059002-8 : LC Card 87-17233 DDC 657 19
1. Accounting. I. Keith, Robert M. II. Stephens, William L. III. Title.
HF5635 .S6445 1988

Managerial accounting / Jack L. Smith, Robert M. Keith, William L. Stephens. New York : McGraw-Hill, c1988. xxv, 717 p. : col. ill. ; 27 cm. Includes index. ISBN 0-07-058990-9 : LC Card 87-17223 DDC 658.1/511 19
1. Managerial accounting. I. Keith, Robert M. II. Stephens, William L. III. Title.
HF5657.4 .S55 1988

Smith, Jay M. Intermediate accounting : comprehensive volume / Jay M. Smith, Jr., K. Fred Skousen.9th ed. Cincinnati : South-Western Pub. Co., c1987. xix, 1234 p. : ill. ; 24 cm. Includes bibliographical references and

index. ISBN 0-538-01921-2 LC Card 87-60815 DDC 657/.044 19
1. Accounting. I. Skousen, K. Fred. II. Title.
HF5635 .S5946 1987

Smith, Jerald R. Airline : a strategic management simulation / Jerald R. Smith, Peggy A. Golden ; special consultant, Bryce Appleton. Englewood Cliffs, NJ : Prentice-Hall, c1987. v, 115, [38] p. : ill. ; 18 cm. ISBN 0-13-020801-9 (pbk.) LC Card 86-30488 DDC 387.7/068 19
1. Strategic planning - Simulation methods. 2. Management - Simulation methods. 3. Airlines - Management - Simulation methods. I. Golden, Peggy A. II. Title.
HD30.28 .S57 1987

Smith, Jerry D. The Warehouse management handbook /. New York , c1988. p. cm. ISBN 0-07-064952-9 : LC Card 87-16885 DDC 658.7/85 19
HF5485 .W35 1988

Smith, Kenneth, 1932- Corporate accounting systems : a software engineering approach / Kenneth Smith. Workingham, England ; Reading, Mass. : Addison-Wesley, c1988. p. cm. Bibliography: p. Includes index. ISBN 0-201-17824-9 LC Card 87-24130 DDC 657/.028/55 19
1. Accounting - Data processing. 2. Computer software - Development. 3. Software maintenance. I. Title.
HF5679 .S645 1988

Smith, Kenneth A.
Francisco, Albert K. Accounting theory and practice /. Belmont, CA , c1987. 1 v. (various pagings) : ISBN 0-932276-74-1 (pbk.) LC Card 87-62077 DDC 657/.076 19
HF5661 .F68 1987

Francisco, Albert K. Auditing /. Belmont, CA , c1987. 1 v. (various pagings) : ISBN 0-932276-76-8 (pbk.) LC Card 87-62076 DDC 657/.45/076 19
HF5667 .F68 1987

Francisco, Albert K. CPA exam questions on accounting practice /. Belmont, CA , c1987. 1 v. (various pagings) ; ISBN 0-932276-80-6 (pbk.) LC Card 87-62331 DDC 657/.076 19
HF5661 .F67 1987

Francisco, Albert K. CPA exam questions on accounting theory /. Belmont, CA. , c1987. 1 v. (various pagings) ; ISBN 0-932276-79-2 (pbk.) LC Card 87-62332 DDC 657/.076 19
HF5661 .F675 1987

Smith, Larry E. Christopher, Elizabeth M. Leadership training through gaming . New York , 1987. 187 p. : ISBN 0-89397-284-3 : LC Card 87-12362 DDC 658.4/07353 19
HD57.7 .C53 1987

Smith, Martha J. Verdier, James M. Tax expenditures . Washington, D.C. , 1982. xx, 102 p. ; ***NYPL [JLF 83-663]***

Smith, Michael J. (Michael James), 1945- Job stress and blue collar work /. Chichester [West Sussex] , New York , c1985. ix, 243 p. : ISBN 0-471-90811-8 : LC Card 85-12022 DDC 158.7 19
HF5548.85 .J64 1985 ***NYPL [JLE 86-2412]***

Smith, Milburn D. Information and records management : a decision-maker's guide to systems planning and implementation / Milburn D. Smith III. New York : Quorum Books, c1986. xiv, 285 p. : ill. ; 25 cm. Includes index. ISBN 0-89930-111-8 (lib. bdg. : alk. paper) LC Card 86-638 DDC 651.5 19
1. Records - Management. 2. Information resources management. I. Title.
HF5736 .S58 1986 ***NYPL [JLE 87-1454]***

Smith, Ralph Eugene, 1941- Imdieke, Leroy F. Financial accounting /. New York , c1987. xxii, 770, [44] p. : ISBN 0-471-80829-6 LC Card 86-28158 DDC 657 19
HF5635 .I43 1987

Smith, Ralph R. (Ralph Russell), 1947- Reischl, Dennis K. Managing for Uncle Sam . Huntsville, Ala. , c1986. ix, 271 p. : ISBN 0-936295-01-5 (pbk.) : LC Card 87-115055 DDC 353.001/7 19
HD8005.2.U5 R45 1986

Smith, Robert Stewart. Ehrenberg, Ronald G. Modern labor economics . Glenview, Ill. [1987], c1988. 721 p. : ISBN 0-673-18964-3 LC Card 87-9789 DDC 331 19
HD4901 .E34 1988

Smith, Roger F. Sales management : a practitioner's guide / Roger F. Smith. Englewood Cliffs, N.J. : Prentice-Hall, c1987. x, 261 p. : ill. ; 24 cm. Bibliography: p. 253. Includes index. ISBN 0-13-786534-1 LC Card 86-30299 DDC 658.8/1 19
1. Sales management. 2. Sales personnel. 3. Success in business. I. Title.
HF5438.4 .S57 1987

Smith, Ron, Ph. D. L'Effort économique de défense . [Grenoble] , 1985. 235 p. : LC Card 86-199399
HC280.D4 E38 1985

Smith, Shelley A. Tienda, Marta. The structural transformation of employment in Wisconsin, 1960-1980 /. Madison, WI (Rm. 245, 30 N. Murray St., Madison 53715) [1986] ii, 47 p. ; LC Card 86-623091 DDC 331.12/09775 19
HD5725.W5 T54 1986

Smith, Steve, 1941- Second to none : the story of Beach Transportation Co. and its buses. Missoula, Mont. : Pictorial Histories Pub. Co., c1986. 120 p. : ill. ; 26 cm. ISBN 0-933126-84-0 (pbk.) LC Card 86-62692 DDC 388.3/22/09786 19
1. Beach Transportation Co. 2. Bus lines - Montana. I. Title.
HE5633.M9 S65 1986

Smith, Suzanne. McGuire, Nan. Survey of private sector work and family policy . San Francisco , c1986. 41 leaves ; LC Card 87-113810 DDC 331.25/72/0979461 19
HD5126.S4 M38 1986

Smithies, Edward. The black economy in England since 1914 / Edward Smithies. London : Gill and Macmillan ; Atlantic Highlands, N.J. : Humanities Press, 1984. 165 p. ; 23 cm. Includes index. Includes bibliographical references. Bibliography: p. [160]-162. ISBN 0-391-03114-7 LC Card 84-6516 DDC 364.1/33 19
1. Black market - Great Britain - History - 20th century. 2. Employee theft - Great Britain - History - 20th century. 3. Tax evasion - Great Britain - History - 20th century. 4. Informal sector (Economics) - Great Britain - History - 20th century. I. Title.
HF5482.65.G7 S64 1984 ***NYPL [JLD 86-2509]***

Smithies, William, junior, pseud. see Defoe, Daniel, 1661?-1731.

Smithin, John N. Keynes and public policy after fifty years /. New York , <c1988-. v. <2 > : ISBN 0-8147-3444-8 (v. 1) : LC Card 87-20368 DDC 330.15/6 19
HB99.7 .K3815 1988

Smithson, C. W. (Charles W.) Hwang, Hae-Shin. Dominant firm price leadership . Toronto, Ont. [1986] 40 p. : ISBN 0-7729-2122-9 : LC Card 87-161006 DDC 338.2/3 19
HD9539.N5 H93 1986

Smithsonian folklife studies .
(no. 5) Sayers, Robert. The Korean onggi potter /. Washington, D.C. , 1987. 288 p. : LC Card 86-600366 DDC 338.4/77382/095195 19
HD9617.K82 S29 1987

Smoking out the barons : the campaign against the tobacco industry : a report of the British Medical Association Public Affairs Division. Chichester [West Sussex] ; New York : Published on behalf of the British Medical Association [by] Wiley, c1986. vii, 192 p.; 20 cm. (A Wiley medical publication) Includes bibliographical references and index. ISBN 0-471-90937-8 (pbk.) : LC Card 85-26414 DDC 659.1/967973/0941 19
1. Advertising - Cigarettes - Addresses, essays, lectures. 2. Advertising - Cigarettes - Great Britain - Addresses, essays, lectures. 3. Tobacco industry - Great Britain - Addresses, essays, lectures. I. British Medical Association. Public Affairs Division.
HF6161.C35 S66 1986 ***NYPL [JLD 86-3620]***

Smoking, Third World alert /. Nath, Uma Ram. Oxford [Oxfordshire] , New York , 1986. x, 291 p. : ISBN 0-19-261402-9 : LC Card 86-5201 DDC 363.1/9 19
HD9148.D44 N37 1986 ***NYPL [JLD 87-992]***

Smolenskiĭ gosudarstvennyĭ pedagogicheskiĭ institut imeni Karla Marksa. Osnovnye kategorii krest͡ian v period pozdnego feodalizma, XVII--pervai͡a polovina XIX vv. . Smolensk , 1985. 134 p., [1] leaf of plates : LC Card 86-120158
HD1536.S65 O86 1985

Smollan, Roy. Black advancement in the South African economy /. Braamfontein, Johannesburg , 1986. 256 p. : ISBN 0-86954-289-3 LC Card 87-119018 DDC 331.6/9968 19
HD5842.A6 B58 1986b

Smpilirēs, Giōrgos.
Archeio Dēmētriou Kallergē, 1824-1867. 1983.
Spēliōtakēs, K. K. Archeion Michaēl Iatrou, 1802-1893 / K.K. Spēliōtakēs. Archeio Dēmētriou Kallergē, 1824-1867 / Giōrgos Smpilirēs. Athēna , 1983. 189 p., [4] folded leaves of plates : LC Card 85-134031
HF3750.5.S64 A3 1983 ***NYPL [JFE 86-4131]***

Smrčka, Jaroslav. Conceptual management of top-level managers / Jaroslav Smrčka ; [translation, Štěpán Kolář]. Prague : Institute of Management Prague, 1977. 57 p. ; 24 cm. (Series E / Institute of Management Prague . 53) Translated from the Czech. Limited edition of 200 copies. LC Card 85-139531
1. Decision-making. I. Series: Series E (Institut řízení) , 53. II. Title.
HD30.23 .S665 1977

SMUGGLING - BRAZIL - RIO GRANDE DO SUL - HISTORY.
Silva, J. Resende. A fronteira do sul . Rio de Janeiro , 1922. 723 p., [1] leaf of plates : LC Card 85-223002
HF3409.R56 S55 1922

SMUGGLING - CANADA - HISTORY.
McIntosh, Dave. The collectors . Toronto, Ont., Canada , c1984. 414 p. : ISBN 0-920053-29-7 LC Card 85-162089 DDC 354.710072/46/09 19
HJ6751.A6 M35 1984 ***NYPL [JLE 86-2880]***

SMUGGLING - CHAD.
Doornbos, Paul. Some aspects of smuggling between Chad and Sudan [microform] /. Khartoum [1983] 19 leaves, [1] leaf of plates : LC Card 84-980097 DDC 364.1/33 19
HF3887.Z8 D373 1983 ***NYPL [*ZT-1646 no.52]***

SMUGGLING - COLOMBIA - CARTEGENA.
Pombo, José Ignacio de, 1761-1815. Comercio y contrabando en Cartagena de Indias, 2 de junio de 1800 /. Bogotá, Colombia , 1986. 124 p. ; LC Card 87-107126
HJ6864 .P66 1986

SMUGGLING - ITALY, NORTHERN - HISTORY - 20TH CENTURY.
Soldini, Bruno, 1939- Uomini da soma . [Lugano] , c1985. 289 p. : LC Card 86-136358
HJ6947 .S65 1985

SMUGGLING - SUDAN.
Doornbos, Paul. Some aspects of smuggling between Chad and Sudan [microform] /. Khartoum [1983] 19 leaves, [1] leaf of plates : LC Card 84-980097 DDC 364.1/33 19
HF3887.Z8 D373 1983 ***NYPL [*ZT-1646 no.52]***

SMUGGLING - SWITZERLAND - HISTORY - 20TH CENTURY.
Soldini, Bruno, 1939- Uomini da soma . [Lugano] , c1985. 289 p. : LC Card 86-136358
HJ6947 .S65 1985

Smurthwaite, A. G. Uberrima fides . [Johannesburg , 1985?] 69 p. : ISBN 0-620-08481-2 LC Card 87-146303 DDC 368/.006 19
HG8724.3.Z9 P758 1985

Smyshli͡aev, Valentin Alekseevich. Seleznev, V. A. (Valeriĭ Aleksandrovich) Pervye shagi sotsialisticheskikh preobrazovaniĭ v sel'skom khozi͡aĭstve Severo-Zapada RSFSR, 1917-1929 gg. . Leningrad , 1983. 198 p. ; LC Card 83-197523
HD1492.S652 R877 1983 ***NYPL [*QIP 87-1327]***

Smyshli͡aeva, Li͡udmila Matveevna. Rezervy intensifikatsii vosproizvodstva osnovnykh fondov i ikh ispol'zovanii͡a /. Moskva , 1984.

204 p. ; LC Card 85-240369
HC340.C3 R48 1984

Smyslov, D. V. (Dmitriĭ Vasil'evich) "Problema neftedollarov" . Moskva , 1984. 231 p. ; LC Card 85-189000
HC498 .P75 1984

Smyth, David, 1929- Currier, Chet. No cost/low cost investing /. New York , 1987. 240 p. ; ISBN 0-531-15527-7 LC Card 87-13690 DDC 332.6/78 19
HG4910 .C86 1987

Snell, Michael. Bennett, Steven J. Executive chess /. New York , c1987. xv, 256 p. ; ISBN 0-453-00550-0 LC Card 87-1723 DDC 658.4/03 19
HD30.29 .B46 1987

Snortum, John R. Social control of the drinking driver /. Chicago , 1988. p. cm. ISBN 0-226-46953-0 : LC Card 87-19111 DDC 363.1/256 19
HE5620.D7 S66 1988

Snow, Marcellus S. Telecommunications : regulation and deregulation in industrialized democracies / by Marcellus S. Snow. Amsterdam ; New York : North-Holland, 1986. xvi, 304 p. : ill. ; 24 cm. (Communications) Includes bibliographies and index. ISBN 0-444-87926-9 LC Card 86-224686 DDC 384/.041 19
1. Telecommunication policy. 2. Telecommunication - Deregulation. I. Series. II. Series: Communications (Annenberg School of Communications (University of Pennsylvania)). III. Title.
HE7645 .S58 1986

Snow, Robert T. The bourgeois opposition to export-oriented industrialization in the Philippines / by Robert T. Snow. Diliman, Quezon City, Philippines : Third World Studies Center, University of the Philippines, [1983] 45 p. ; 22 cm. (The Philippines in the Third World papers . ser. no. 39) "October 1983." Bibliography: p. 41-45. LC Card 85-196519 DDC 382/.3/09599 19
1. Philippines - Economic policy. 2. Philippines - Commercial policy. 3. Philippines - Industries. 4. Foreign trade promotion - Philippines. 5. Import substitution - Philippines. I. Title. II. Series.
HC453 .S66 1983

Snowden, Frank M. (Frank Martin), 1946- Violence and great estates in the south of Italy : Apulia, 1900-1922 / Frank M. Snowden. Cambridge [Cambridgeshire] ; New York : Cambridge University Press, 1986. x, 245 p. : ill., map ; 23 cm. Includes bibliographical references and index. ISBN 0-521-30731-7 LC Card 85-11675 DDC 322.4/4/094575 19
1. Land tenure - Italy - Puglia - History - 20th century. 2. Peasant uprisings - Italy - Puglia - History - 20th century. 3. Fascism - Italy - Puglia - History - 20th century. 4. Puglia (Italy) - Social conditions. 5. Puglia (Italy) - Economic conditions. I. Title.
HD679.P83 S66 1986 ***NYPL [JLD 86-1627]***

Snowdon, Sondra. The global edge : how your company can win in the international marketplace / Sondra Snowdon. New York : Simon and Schuster, c1986. 431 p. ; 25 cm. Includes index. ISBN 0-671-60122-9 : LC Card 86-3990 DDC 395/.22 19
1. Negotiation in business. 2. Export marketing. I. Title.
HF5387 .S59 1986 ***NYPL [JLE 86-3489]***

Snyder, Stanley G. Embezzlers' dirty tricks (and how to spot them) : the practical guide to improving business profits through the management of employee dishonesty / by Stanley G. Snyder. San Diego, CA : Westview Pub. Co., c1987. 336 p. : ill. ; 28 cm. Bibliography: p. 323-324. Includes index. ISBN 0-937535-00-1 (pbk.) : LC Card 87-50037 DDC 658.4/73 19
1. Employee theft - Prevention. 2. Embezzlement - Prevention. I. Title.
HF5549.5.E43 S59 1987

Snyder, Thomas (Thomas P.) Paying for growth : using development fees to finance infrastructure / by Thomas P. Snyder and Michael A. Stegman ; with contributions by David H. Moreau ; University of North Carolina at Chapel Hill. Washington, D.C. : ULI-the Urban Land Institute, 1986. x, 133 p. : ill. ; 28 cm. Bibliography: p. 129-133. ISBN 0-87420-663-4 (pbk.) LC Card 86-51156 DDC 338.4/3363/0973 19
1. Impact fees - United States. 2. Infrastructure (Economics) - United States - Finance. I. Stegman, Michael A. II. Moreau, David H. III. University of North Carolina at Chapel Hill. IV. Title.
HJ9156 .S69 1986

So, Alvin Y., 1953- The South China silk district : local historical transformation and world-system theory / Alvin Y. So. Albany, N.Y. : State University of New York Press, c1986. xii, 206 p. : ill. ; 24 cm. Based on the author's thesis (Ph.D.) UCLA. Includes index. Bibliography: p. [165]-189. ISBN 0-88706-322-5 LC Card 86-14575 DDC 338.4/7677391/095127 19
1. Silk industry - China - Shun-te hsien (Kwangtung Province) - History. 2. Silk industry - China - Nan-hai hsien - History. 3. Silk industry - China - Chung-shan hsien (Kwangtung Province) - History. 4. China - Economic policy. 5. China - Commerce - History. I. Title.
HD9926.C63 S637 1986 ***NYPL [JLE 87-1448]***

Só o político pode salvar o economista /. Delfim Netto, Antônio. Rio de Janeiro , 1986. xvii, 146 p. ; LC Card 87-137681 DDC 338.981 19
HC187 .D565 1986

So schaffen wir! : Gebrüder Colsman Essen-Kupferdreh / [die Bilder sind mit Agfacolor-Filmen aufgenommen von Oskar Graf]. [Germany : s.n., 193-?] (München : F. Bruckmann) [51] leaves : chiefly col. ill. ; 34 cm. Cover title. LC Card 86-213082
1. Gebrüder Colsman (Essen, Germany). 2. Copper industry and trade - Germany (West) - Essen - Employees. I. Graf, Oskar. II. Gebrüder Colsman (Essen, Germany).
HD9539.C7 G57 1930z

SOAP - MARKETING.
Promotion strategies for household cleaning products. New York, N.Y. , c1983. 2 v. (xx, 635 p.) ; LC Card 87-142358 DDC 381/.456671/0973 19
HD9999.C4863 U56 1983

SOAP TRADE - UNITED STATES.
Promotion strategies for household cleaning products. New York, N.Y. , c1983. 2 v. (xx, 635 p.) ; LC Card 87-142358 DDC 381/.456671/0973 19
HD9999.C4863 U56 1983

Soares, Fernando Brito. Prospective evolution of EEC common agricultural policy . Lisboa , Oeiras , 1985. 122 p. : LC Card 86-221785
HD1920.5.Z8 P77 1985

Soares, Nilton de Brito. Determinação de itinerários de um sistema de transporte coletivo através de ônibus : um processo aplicável em cidades de porte médio / Nilton de Brito Soares. Brasília, DF : EBTU, 1985. 98 p. : ill. ; 28 cm. (Série Teses. 7) Summary in English. Originally presented as the author's thesis (mestrado)--Universidade Federal do Rio de Janeiro, 1982. Bibliography: p. 91-92. LC Card 87-113226 DDC 388.3/22/0981 19
1. Bus lines - Brazil - Planning. I. Series: Série Teses / Empresa Brasileira dos Transportes Urbanos , 7. II. Title.
HE5653.A6 S63 1985

Sobeck, Joan m. Cyr, John E. Real estate brokerage . Chicago , c1988. xiii, 367 p. : ISBN 0-88462-674-1 (pbk.) LC Card 87-16650 DDC 333.33/068 19
HD278 .C95 1988

Sobel, Robert, 1931 (Feb. 19)-
The new game on Wall Street / Robert Sobel. New York : Wiley, c1987. xii, 244 p. : ill. ; 24 cm. Bibliography: p. 236-237. Includes index. ISBN 0-471-84527-2 LC Card 86-33986 DDC 332.6/78 19
1. Stocks - United States. 2. Investments - United States. I. Title.
HG4921 .S6156 1987

O'glove, Thornton L. Quality of earnings . New York , c1987. xviii, 204 p. : ISBN 0-02-922630-9 LC Card 86-25631 DDC 657/.33 19
HG4028.B2 O35 1987

Sobgui, Gabriel Alexis. L'épreuve écrite à la capacité en droit et en économie / Gabriel Alexis Sobgui. Yaoundé, Cameroun : Editions Lamgun, 1981. 113 p. ; 30 cm. (Série Initiation économique) Cover title. LC Card 84-118988
1. Economics - Examinations, questions, etc. I. Series: Série "Initiation économique" (Yaoundé, Cameroon). II. Title.
HB74.6 .S65 1981

SOBRADINHO DAM (BRAZIL) - SOCIAL ASPECTS.
Sigaud, Lygia. Efeitos sociais de grandes projetos hidrelétricos . [Rio de Janeiro] , 1986. 116 p. ; LC Card 87-120281 DDC 333.91/4 19
HD1696.B84 S346 1986

Sobre el surco reviven las esperanzas /. Andrión Alabarca, Aurelio, 1924- Panamá, R. de P. [1978] 84 p. : LC Card 82-100242
HD1531.P2 A53 1978

Sobrevivência, aspectos das condições de vida de menores trabalhadores de rua do Distrito Federal / Governo do Distrito Federal, Secretaria de Serviços Sociais, Fundação do Serviço Social do Distrito Federal, Coordenadoria de Planejamento e Controle, COPLAC. [Brasília] : COPLAC, 1983. 117 p. ; 21 cm. Bibliography: p. 115. LC Card 86-197113
1. Youth - Employment - Brazil - Distrito Federal. 2. Peddlers and peddling - Brazil - Distrito Federal. I. Fundação do Serviço Social do Distrito Federal. Coordenadoria de Planejamento e Controle.
HD6276.B73 D577 1983

Sobrevivir en la población José M. Caro y en Lo Hermida /. Schkolnik, Mariana. [Santiago, Chile] [1986] 150 p., [20] p. of plates : LC Card 87-400080 DDC 362.5/8/098331 19
HC193.S2 S35 1986

Sobrinho, Antonio Estevam de Lima. see **Lima Sobrinho, Antonio Estevam de.**

SOCCER - SOCIAL ASPECTS - GREAT BRITAIN.
Robins, David, 1944- We hate humans /. Harmondsworth, Middlesex, England , New York, N.Y. , 1984. 155 p. ; ISBN 0-14-007062-1
NYPL [JLD 86-4404]

Socher, Karl. Staatsfinanzierung und Notenbank . Wien [1984?] 211 p. : LC Card 85-198128
HG1811 .S78 1984

Sociaal-Economische Raad. (Old Catalog form: Netherlands (Kingdom, 1815-). Sociaal-Economische Raad)
Advies inzake het sociaal-economisch beleid op middellange termijn 1986-1990 / uitgebracht aan de ministers van Economische Zaken, Financiën en Sociale Zaken en Werkgelegenheid. Den Haag : Sociaal-Economische Raad, [1986] 142, 150 p. ; 25 cm. (Publikatie . nr. 10 (20 juni 1986) Includes bibliographical references. ISBN 90-6587-248-5 LC Card 86-234847
1. Netherlands - Economic conditions - 1945-. 2. Netherlands - Economic policy. I. Series: Publikatie (Sociaal-Economische Raad) , 86/10. II. Title.
HC321 .S63 1986, nr. 10 HC325

Advies wijziging Winkelsluitingswet . Den Haag [1986] 78 p. ; ISBN 90-6587-250-7 LC Card 86-234857
HC321 .S63 1986, nr. 11 KKM3419

Sociaal-Economische Raad. Commissie Ondernemingsraden.
Advies samenloop Wet OR en ARBO-wet . Den Haag [1986] 37 p. ; ISBN 90-6587-243-4 LC Card 87-104667
HC321 .S63 1986, nr. 6 KKM1430

Advies vereenvoudiging Wet OR : advies inzake vereenvoudiging van de Wet op de Ondernemingsraden / uitgebracht aan de ministers van Sociale Zaken en Werkgelegenheid, Justitie en Economische Zaken. Den Haag : Sociaal-Economische Raad, [1986] 61 p. ; 25 cm. (Publikatie . nr. 14 (24 okt. 1986)) ISBN 90-6587-254-X LC Card 87-165080
1. Works councils - Law and legislation - Netherlands. 2. Industrial management - Employee participation - Law and legislation - Netherlands. I. Series: Publikatie (Sociaal-Economische Raad) , 86/14. II. Title.
HC321 .S63 1986, nr. 14 KKM1350

SOCIAL ACCOUNTING. see **NATIONAL INCOME - ACCOUNTING.**

SOCIAL ACCOUNTING - DECISION MAKING.
Burke, Richard C. Decision making in complex times . Hamilton, Ont. , 1984. xii, 185 p. : ISBN 0-920212-27-1 (pbk.) LC Card 85-154342 DDC 658.4/08 19
HD60 .B86 1984 ***NYPL [JLD 86-2720]***

SOCIAL ACCOUNTING - GERMANY (WEST)
Ausländerintegration in deutschen Industriebetrieben /. Königstein/Ts. , c1985.

viii, 273 p. : ISBN 3-7756-6935-3 LC Card 85-194662 DDC 305.8/00943 19
HD8458.A2 A9265 1985
NYPL [JLD 86-2193]

SOCIAL ACCOUNTING - INFORMATION SERVICES.
Burke, Richard C. Decision making in complex times . Hamilton, Ont. , 1984. xii, 185 p. : ISBN 0-920212-27-1 (pbk.) LC Card 85-154342 DDC 658.4/08 19
HD60 .B86 1984 NYPL [JLD 86-2720]

SOCIAL ACTION.
Burns, Tom R. Man, decisions, society . New York , c1985. xiv, 342 p. : ISBN 2-88124-004-6 (France) LC Card 84-10303 DDC 301 19
HM24 .B85 1985 NYPL [JLE 86-2963]

SOCIAL ALIENATION. see **ALIENATION (SOCIAL PSYCHOLOGY)**

Social and economic characteristics of the population in metro and nonmetro counties, 1970-80 / David A. McGranahan ... [et al.]. Washington, D.C. : U. S. Dept. of Agriculture, Economic Research Service : May be purchased from the Supt. of Docs., U. S. G.P.O., [1986] iv, 70 p. : col. ill. ; 28 cm. (Rural development research report . no. 58) "September 1986." LC Card 86-602790 DDC 304.6/0973 19
1. United States - Economic conditions - 1971-1981. 2. United States - Social conditions - 1960-1980. I. McGranahan, David A. II. Series.
HC106.7 .S577 1986

The social and economic effect of the railroad in Puebla and Veracruz, Mexico, 1867-1911 /. Schmidt, Arthur, 1943- New York , 1987. 297 p. : ISBN 0-8240-1370-0 (alk. paper) : LC Card 87-8628 DDC 385/.0972/48 19
HE2819.P84 S35 1987

Social and economic effects of petroleum development in non-OPEC developing countries . McLin, Jon B. Geneva , 1986. xiii, 104 p., [4] folded leaves of plates : ISBN 92-2-105505-1 (pbk.) : LC Card 87-123328 DDC 338.2/782/091724 19
HD9578.D44 M396 1986

Social and economic formations in Bangladesh agriculture . Muqtada, M. Dacca, Bangladesh , 1986. 68 p. ; LC Card 86-902421 DDC 338.1/09549/2 19
HD2075.6 .M86 1986

Social and labour bulletin. Technological change . Geneva , 1985. 355 p. : ISBN 92-2-105162-5 (pbk.) : LC Card 86-203534 DDC 331.12 19
HD6331 .T416 1985

Social and labour practices of multinational enterprises in the textiles, clothing, and footwear industries. Geneva : International Labour Office, 1984. xii, 184 p. ; 24 cm. Includes bibliographies. ISBN 92-2-103882-3 (pbk.) : LC Card 85-183200 DDC 331.7/677 19
1. International business enterprises - Personnel management. 2. International business enterprises - Employees. 3. International business enterprises - Social aspects. 4. Textile workers. 5. Footwear industry - Employees. I. International Labour Office.
HF5549 .S83473 1984 NYPL [JLE 85-2322]

Social and vocational rehabilitation resources : an international directory = Institutions de réadaptation sociale et professionnelle : répertoire international. Geneve : International Labor Office, 1984- v. ; 24 cm. English and French. CONTENTS. - v. 1. Africa -- v. 2. Asia and the Pacific. ISBN 92-2-003776-9 (pbk. : v. 1) LC Card 86-126143 DDC 362/.0425 19
1. Vocational rehabilitation - Directories. 2. Rehabilitation - Directories. 3. Rehabilitation centers - Directories. I. Title: Institutions de réadaptation sociale et professionnelle.
HD7255 .S62 1984 NYPL [JLL 85-184]

Social aspects of mining towns of the tribal region /. Prasad, Maheshwari, 1944- New Delhi , 1986- v. <1- > ; LC Card 86-902979 DDC 307.7/66/095412 19
HD9506.I43 C486 1986

Social atlas of Shreveport, Louisiana /. Dlin, Norman. Shreveport , 1985. 1 atlas (vii, 43 p.) : LC Card 86-622543 DDC 304.6/09763/99 19
HA730.S615 D57 1985

Social behavior and natural resources series. Social science in natural resource management systems /. Boulder , 1987. xii, 265 p. : ISBN 0-8133-7485-5 (pbk. : alk. paper) LC Card 87-23138 DDC 333.7/0973 19
HC103.7 .S62 1987

SOCIAL CAPITAL. see **INFRASTRUCTURE (ECONOMICS)**

SOCIAL CHANGE - ADDRESSES, ESSAYS, LECTURES.
Entrepreneurship and social change /. Lanham, MD [S.l.] , c1986. 275 p. : ISBN 0-8191-5165-3 (alk. paper) : LC Card 85-26533 DDC 338/.04 19
HB615 .E629 1986 NYPL [JLD 86-3073]

Verwaltung und Planung im Wandel /. Köln , 1979. 112 p. ; ISBN 3-7745-6438-8 : LC Card 81-473982
HT395.G4 V48 NYPL [JLE 86-2107]

SOCIAL CHANGE - BOLIVIA - SANTA CRUZ (DEPT.)
Gill, Lesley. Peasants, entrepreneurs, and social change . Boulder , 1987. xiv, 246 p. : ISBN 0-8133-7339-5 (pbk. : alk. paper) : LC Card 86-28207 DDC 303.4/0984/3 19
HD1870.S25 G54 1987

SOCIAL CHANGE - CASE STUDIES.
Stolz, Barbara Ann. Still struggling . Lexington, Mass. , c1985. xviii, 205 p. ; ISBN 0-669-10930-4 (alk. paper) LC Card 85-40235 DDC 331.4/0973 19
HD6052 .S76 1985 NYPL [JLE 85-3704]

SOCIAL CHANGE - CONGRESSES.
Failed transitions to modern industrial society . Montreal , c1975. vii, 105 p. : ISBN 0-919958-00-1 LC Card 80-510009 DDC 303.4/094 19
HM101 .F26 NYPL [JLE 81-166]

Meissner, Hans-Günther. Werbung und gesellschaftlicher Wandel über die kommunikativen Voraussetzungen technischen, ökonomischen und sozialen Fortschritts . [Berlin] , Hamburg [1979] 23, [4] leaves ; LC Card 84-119751
HF5802.5 .M45 1979

Peasants and politics . Melbourne , c1978. 218 p. : ISBN 0-7267-2027-5
NYPL [JLE 81-1456]

Social change paper .
(10) Dogra, Bharat. Empty stomachs and packed godowns . New Delhi , 1987. viii, 126 p. ; LC Card 87-900472 DDC 338.1/9/54 19
HD9016.I42 D64 1987

Social choice and multicriterion decision-making /. Arrow, Kenneth Joseph, 1921- Cambridge, Mass. , c1986. vii, 127 p. : ISBN 0-262-01087-9 LC Card 85-19913 DDC 302/.13 19
HM271 .A73 1986 NYPL [JLD 86-3628]

Social choice and public decision making / edited by Walter P. Heller, Ross M. Starr, David A. Starrett. Cambridge [Cambridgeshire] ; New York : Cambridge University Press, 1986. xix, 215 p. : ill. ; 24 cm. (Essays in honor of Kenneth J. Arrow . v. 1) Includes bibliographies and index. ISBN 0-521-30454-7 LC Card 86-8580 DDC 339 19
1. Arrow, Kenneth Joseph, 1921-. 2. Macroeconomics. 3. Uncertainty. I. Heller, Walter P. II. Starr, Ross M. III. Starrett, David A. IV. Arrow, Kenneth Joseph, 1921-. V. Series.
HB846.8 .S59 1986 NYPL [JLE 86-4189]

SOCIAL CHOICE - CONGRESSES.
Experimental social dilemmas /. Frankfurt am Main , New York , c1986. vi, 234 p. : ISBN 3-8204-8574-0 (pbk.) : LC Card 86-10307 DDC 302 19
HM132 .E96 1986 NYPL [JLD 87-1177]

SOCIAL CHOICE - MATHEMATICAL MODELS.
Arrow, Kenneth Joseph, 1921- Social choice and multicriterion decision-making /. Cambridge, Mass. , c1986. vii, 127 p. : ISBN 0-262-01087-9 LC Card 85-19913 DDC 302/.13 19
HM271 .A73 1986 NYPL [JLD 86-3628]

Breyer, Friedrich. Family structure and intergenerational transfers in social health insurance . Berlin [1986] 24 p. : LC Card 87-156738 DDC 368.4/2016/0724 19
HD7101 .B73 1986

Social choice theory . Kelly, Jerry S. Berlin , New York , c1988. 163 p. : ISBN 0-387-17634-9 (U. S.) LC Card 87-12858 DDC 302/.13 19
HB846.8 .K44 1988

SOCIAL CLASS - SOUTH AFRICA - HISTORY.
Christie, Renfrew. Electricity, industry, and class in South Africa /. London , 1984. xiii, 241 p. : ISBN 0-333-36288-8 LC Card 87-673182
HD9685.S582 C47x 1984b

SOCIAL CLASSES - ADDRESSES, ESSAYS, LECTURES.
Gender and stratification /. Cambridge, CB, UK , Oxford, OX, UK , 1986. viii, 271 p. ; ISBN 0-7456-0167-7 : LC Card 85-28342 DDC 305.3 19
HQ1075 .G46 1986 NYPL [JLE 86-2966]

White collar workers, trade unions, and class /. London , Dover, N.H. , c1986. 215 p. : ISBN 0-7099-0571-8 : LC Card 85-28806 DDC 331.88/041 19
HD8039.M39 W45 1986
NYPL [JLD 86-1602]

SOCIAL CLASSES - AFRICA - ADDRESSES, ESSAYS, LECTURES.
Struggle for the city . Beverly Hills , c1983. 319 p. : ISBN 0-8039-2067-9 LC Card 83-11196 DDC 305.5/62/096 19
HD8774 .S87 1983 NYPL [JLD 83-3496]

SOCIAL CLASSES - BANGLADESH.
Rahman, Atiur, 1951- Peasants and classes . Dhaka , 1986. xlvi, 295 p. ; LC Card 87-900478 DDC 305.5/63 19
HD1537.B3 R32 1986

SOCIAL CLASSES - BRAZIL.
Singer, Paul Israel, 1932- Dominação e desigualdade . Rio de Janeiro, RJ , 1981. 185 p. ; LC Card 82-148154
HC190.I5 S55 1981 NYPL [JLD 86-3364]

Singer, Paul Israel, 1932- Repartição da renda . Rio de Janeiro , 1986. 95 p. ; ISBN 85-85061-40-5 : LC Card 86-157852
HC190.I5 S56 1986

SOCIAL CLASSES - BRAZIL - NOVA LIMA.
Grossi, Yonne de Souza. Mina de Morro Velho . Rio de Janeiro, RJ , 1981. 265 p. : LC Card 81-216799 DDC 338.7/6223422/098151 19
HD8039.M74 B65 1981
NYPL [JLD 86-3591]

SOCIAL CLASSES - BRAZIL - PERNAMBUCO.
Andrade, Manuel Correia de Oliveira. Classes sociais e agricultura no Nordeste /. Recife , 1985. 105 p. ; ISBN 85-7019-096-4 LC Card 87-119335
HD1875.P4 A84 1985

SOCIAL CLASSES - COLOMBIA - MEDELLÍN.
García Molina, Carlos. Mortalidad infantil y clases sociales . [Medellín, Colombia] [1986] 103 p. : ISBN 958-9127-05-3 LC Card 87-400685 DDC 304.6/4/0880542 19
HB1323.I42 C74 1986

SOCIAL CLASSES - EUROPE, EASTERN.
Matejko, Aleksander. Comparative work systems . New York , 1986. xx, 237 p. ; ISBN 0-03-004492-8 (alk. paper) : LC Card 85-6354 DDC 306/.36/0947 19
HD6957.E82 M37 1985
NYPL [JLE 86-1083]

SOCIAL CLASSES - EUROPE - HISTORY - 19TH CENTURY - CONGRESSES.
Arbeiter und Bürger im 19. Jahrhundert . München , 1986. xiv, 342 p. ; ISBN 3-486-52871-8 LC Card 86-212379
HD8376 .A72 1986

SOCIAL CLASSES - FRANCE - HISTORY.
Spurk, Jan. Soziologie der französischen Arbeiterbewegung /. Berlin , c1986. 317 p. ; ISBN 3-88619-606-2 LC Card 87-235004 DDC 331.88/0944 19
HD6684 .S68 1986

SOCIAL CLASSES - GERMANY, EAST.
Berlin. Parteihochschule "Karl Marx." Lehrstuhl Wissenschaftlicher Kommunismus. Zur Entwicklung der Klassen und Schichten in der DDR /. Berlin , 1977. 147 p. ; LC Card 78-358768
HN460.5.Z9 S62 NYPL [JLD 79-2817]

SOCIAL CLASSES - GERMANY - HISTORY.
Speier, Hans. German white-collar workers and the rise of Hitler /. New Haven , 1986. xv, 208 p. ; ISBN 0-300-03701-5 LC Card 86-9120 DDC

331.7/92/0943 19
HD8039.M4 G3639413 1986
NYPL [JLE 87-909]

SOCIAL CLASSES - GHANA.
Konings, Piet. The state and rural class formation in Ghana . London ; Boston : xvi, 391 p. : ISBN 0-7103-0117-0 LC Card 85-28109 DDC 305.5/09667 19
HN832.Z9 S65 1986 ***NYPL [Sc D 86-574]***

SOCIAL CLASSES - GREAT BRITAIN.
Class and health . London , New York , 1986. x, 223 p. : ISBN 0-422-60360-0 : LC Card 86-5972 DDC 362.1/0941 19
RA418.3.G7 C56 1986 ***NYPL [JLE 87-505]***

SOCIAL CLASSES - GREAT BRITAIN - HISTORY.
Haydu, Jeffrey. Between craft and class . Berkeley , c1988. p. cm. ISBN 0-520-06060-1 (alk. paper) LC Card 87-22169 DDC 322/.2/0941 19
HD8076 .H39 1988

SOCIAL CLASSES - GREAT BRITAIN - LONGITUDINAL STUDIES.
Class and health . London , New York , 1986. x, 223 p. : ISBN 0-422-60360-0 : LC Card 86-5972 DDC 362.1/0941 19
RA418.3.G7 C56 1986 ***NYPL [JLE 87-505]***

SOCIAL CLASSES - HAITI - HISTORY.
Mathon, Alix. [Haïti, un cas.] Haïti, un cas /. [Port-au-Prince? , 1985] (Port-au-Prince, Haïti : Impr. Le Natal) 172, 271 p. ; LC Card 86-139806 DDC 330.97294 19
HC153 .M38 1985 ***NYPL [Sc D 86-555]***

SOCIAL CLASSES - INDIA - JALPAIGURI (DISTRICT)
Bhowmik, Sharit, 1948- Class formation in the plantation system /. New Delhi , 1981. xix, 263 p. : LC Card 81-903777 DDC 305/.93633 19
HD1470.5.I42 J342 1981
NYPL [JLD 86-2612]

SOCIAL CLASSES - ITALY.
Barberis, Corrado. La società italiana . Milano, Italy [1984?] 382 p. ; LC Card 85-201583
HC305 .B365 1984

SOCIAL CLASSES - ITALY - BOLOGNA - HISTORY.
Monti, Aldino. Alle origini della borghesia urbana . Bologna , c1985. 469 p. : ISBN 88-15-00833-0 : LC Card 86-110136 DDC 333.3/0945/41 19
HD680.B65 M66 1985 ***NYPL [JLD 87-481]***

SOCIAL CLASSES - ITALY - STATISTICS.
Barberis, Corrado. Agricoltura e strati sociali /. Milano, Italy , c1986. 269 p. ; LC Card 86-214233
HD1536.I8 B328 1986

SOCIAL CLASSES - KENYA - HISTORY.
Leo, Christopher. Land and class in Kenya /. Toronto , Buffalo [N.Y.] , c1984. xii, 244 p. : ISBN 0-8020-2532-3 ***NYPL [JLE 86-1242]***

SOCIAL CLASSES - NICARAGUA.
Colburn, Forrest D. Post-revolutionary Nicaragua . Berkeley , c1986. xi, 145 p. : ISBN 0-520-05524-1 LC Card 85-5798 DDC 338.1/097285 19
HD1817 .C63 1986 ***NYPL [JLD 86-2414]***

SOCIAL CLASSES - RUSSIAN S.F.S.R. - LENINGRAD - HISTORY - 19TH CENTURY.
I͡Ukhneva, N. V. Ėtnicheskiĭ sostav i ėtnosotsial′nai͡a struktura naselenii͡a Peterburga . Leningrad , 1984. 220 p., [1] folded leaf of plates : LC Card 85-116858
HB3608.L4 I94 1984 ***NYPL [*QGK 87-925]***

SOCIAL CLASSES - SOVIET UNION - HISTORIOGRAPHY.
Cox, Terry. Peasants, class, and capitalism . Oxford [Oxfordshire] ; New York : xii, 271 p. ; ISBN 0-19-878014-1 : LC Card 86-2362 DDC 305.5/63 19
HD1536.S65 C69 1986
NYPL [JLD 86-3986]

SOCIAL CLASSES - SPAIN - TIERRA DE CAMPOS REGION - HISTORY.
Martínez Sopena, Pascual. La Tierra de Campos occidental . [Valladolid] , 1985. 843 p. : ISBN 84-505-1390-1 LC Card 86-231937
HD779.T54 M37 1985

SOCIAL CLASSES - TURKEY - HISTORY - 19TH CENTURY.
Keyder, Caglar. State and class in Turkey . London , New York , 1987. 252 p. ; ISBN 0-86091-877-7 (pbk.) : LC Card 87-14992 DDC 338.9561 19
HC492 .K497 1987

SOCIAL CLASSES - TURKEY - HISTORY - 20TH CENTURY.
Keyder, Caglar. State and class in Turkey . London , New York , 1987. 252 p. ; ISBN 0-86091-877-7 (pbk.) : LC Card 87-14992 DDC 338.9561 19
HC492 .K497 1987

SOCIAL CLASSES - UNITED STATES.
Cannon, William B., 1920- New class politics . Washington, D.C. , c1986. 137 p. ; ISBN 0-89758-042-7 (pbk.) : LC Card 86-27511 DDC 336.73 19
HJ2051 .C35 1986

Fallows, James M. Human capital . New York, N.Y. , 1988. p. cm. ISBN 0-394-56498-7 : LC Card 87-42659 DDC 306/.3 19
HC106.8 .F35 1988

Lapham, Lewis H. Money and class in America . New York , 1988, c1987. p. cm. ISBN 1-555-84109-0 LC Card 87-22515 DDC 305.5/234/0973 19
HC110.W4 L24 1988

Raines, John C. Modern work and human meaning /. Philadelphia , c1986. 150 p. ; ISBN 0-664-24703-2 (pbk.) LC Card 85-26370 DDC 241/.64 19
BJ1498 .R335 1986 ***NYPL [JLD 86-2382]***

Tigges, Leann M. Changing fortunes . New York , 1987. xvi, 174 p. : ISBN 0-275-92580-3 (alk. paper) : LC Card 87-2357 DDC 331.2/973 19
HD4975 .T5 1987

Van Sickle, Larry. The American dream and the impact of class . New York, N.Y. , c1985. 389 p. ; ISBN 0-8290-1382-2 (pbk.) LC Card 83-12613 DDC 331.3/4/0973 19
HD6273 .V36 1985 ***NYPL [JLD 86-1637]***

SOCIAL CLASSES - UNITED STATES - HISTORY.
Form, William Humbert, 1917- Divided we stand . Urbana , c1985. xviii, 306 p. ; ISBN 0-252-01168-6 (alk. paper) LC Card 85-16537 DDC 305.5/62/0973 19
HD8072.5 .F667 1985 ***NYPL [JLE 86-1940]***

Haydu, Jeffrey. Between craft and class . Berkeley , c1988. p. cm. ISBN 0-520-06060-1 (alk. paper) LC Card 87-22169 DDC 322/.2/0941 19
HD8076 .H39 1988

Social concerns for the 1980s : thought and action in social policy / Helga Nowotny (ed.). Wien : Europäisches Zentrum für Ausbildung und Forschung auf dem Gebiet der sozialen Wohlfahrt, c1984. 359 p. ; 24 cm. English and French. At head of title: European Centre for Social Welfare Training and Research. Includes bibliographies. ISBN 3-900376-18-2 (pbk.)
1. Social policy - Addresses, essays, lectures. 2. Social problems - Addresses, essays, lectures. I. Nowotny, Helga. II. Eurosocial. III. Title: Thought and action in social policy. ***NYPL [JLE 86-2856]***

SOCIAL CONFLICT - BOLIVIA.
Sandoval, Godofredo. Las mil caras del movimiento social boliviano /. La Paz, Bolivia [1986] 132 p. : LC Card 86-227792
HD6608.5 .S25 1986

SOCIAL CONFLICT - FRANCE.
Lash, Scott. The militant worker . London , 1984. vii, 264 p. ; ISBN 0-435-82516-X LC Card 87-673366
HD8076 .L37x 1984b

SOCIAL CONFLICT - GERMANY - HISTORY.
Abraham, David, 1946- The collapse of the Weimar Republic . New York , 1986. liii, 352 p. ; ISBN 0-8419-1083-9 LC Card 86-27033 DDC 338.0943 19
HD3616.G35 A27 1986

SOCIAL CONFLICT - ITALY - NAPLES (KINGDOM) - HISTORY - 18TH CENTURY.
Rao, Anna Maria, 1949- L'"Amaro della feudalità" . Napoli , c1984. 382 p. ; ISBN 88-7042-265-8 : LC Card 85-200705
HD1333.I82 N367 1984

SOCIAL CONFLICT - PERU - CERRO DE PASCO - HISTORY - 18TH CENTURY.
Espinoza Claudio, César. Alcabalas y protesta popular . Lima, Perú , 1981. iii, 111 p., [1] leaf of plates : LC Card 82-146025
HJ5715.P4 E86 1981

SOCIAL CONFLICT - ROMANIA - HISTORY - 19TH CENTURY.
Condițiile istorice ale apariției și dezvoltării clasei muncitoare din România . București , 1984. 652 p. ; LC Card 84-234192
HD8648 .C65 1984

SOCIAL CONFLICT - UNITED STATES.
Lash, Scott. The militant worker . London , 1984. vii, 264 p. ; ISBN 0-435-82516-X LC Card 87-673366
HD8076 .L37x 1984b

SOCIAL CONFLICT - UNITED STATES - HISTORY.
Hall, Gus. Working class USA . New York , 1987. 392 p. : ISBN 0-7178-0660-X : LC Card 87-3232 DDC 305.5/62/0973 19
HD8066 .H29 1987

SOCIAL CONFLICT - VENEZUELA.
Portocarrero de Guzmán, Blancanieve. El capitalismo dependiente y su incidencia en el problema agrario venezolano /. Valencia, Venezuela , c1985. 189 p. : LC Card 86-226697
HD1333.V4 P67 1985

SOCIAL CONFLICT - ZIMBABWE - HISTORY.
Phimister, I. R. (Ian R.) An economic and social history of Zimbabwe, 1890-1948 . London , New York , 1987. p. cm. ISBN 0-582-64423-2 LC Card 87-12471 DDC 330.96891/02 19
HC910.Z9 S36 1987

SOCIAL CONFORMITY. see **CONFORMITY.**

SOCIAL CONTROL.
Van Sickle, Larry. The American dream and the impact of class . New York, N.Y. , c1985. 389 p. ; ISBN 0-8290-1382-2 (pbk.) LC Card 83-12613 DDC 331.3/4/0973 19
HD6273 .V36 1985 ***NYPL [JLD 86-1637]***

Winn, Denise, 1950- The manipulated mind . London , c1983. 217 p. ; ISBN 0-86304-025-X LC Card 83-184383 DDC 302.3/3 19
BF632.5 .W56 1983 ***NYPL [JFD 87-1158]***

Social control of the drinking driver / edited by Michael D. Laurence, John R. Snortum, and Franklin E. Zimring. Chicago : University of Chicago Press, 1988. p. cm. (Studies in crime and justice) Bibliography: p. Includes index. ISBN 0-226-46953-0 : LC Card 87-19111 DDC 363.1/256 19
1. Drinking and traffic accidents. 2. Drunk driving. I. Laurence, Michael. II. Snortum, John R. III. Zimring, Franklin E.
HE5620.D7 S66 1988

SOCIAL COSTS. see **EXTERNALITIES (ECONOMICS)**

SOCIAL CREDIT - CANADA - HISTORY - 20TH CENTURY.
Osborne, Stephen. Social credit for beginners . Vancouver, Canada , c1986. 229, [1] p. : ISBN 0-88978-175-3 (pbk.) LC Card 87-122126 DDC 332.5/6/0971 19
HG355 .O83 1986

Social credit for beginners . Osborne, Stephen. Vancouver, Canada , c1986. 229, [1] p. : ISBN 0-88978-175-3 (pbk.) LC Card 87-122126 DDC 332.5/6/0971 19
HG355 .O83 1986

SOCIAL CREDIT - HISTORY - 20TH CENTURY.
Osborne, Stephen. Social credit for beginners . Vancouver, Canada , c1986. 229, [1] p. : ISBN 0-88978-175-3 (pbk.) LC Card 87-122126 DDC 332.5/6/0971 19
HG355 .O83 1986

SOCIAL DEMOCRACY. see **SOCIALISM.**

Social democracy and workers in Odessa . Weinberg, Robert. Pittsburgh, Pa. (4E23 Forbes Quad, Pittsburgh 15260) [1986] 34 p. ; LC Card 86-199472
HD8530.O32 W45 1986

Social Democratic Party of Germany. see **Sozialdemokratische Partei Deutschlands.**

Social demography.
Knodel, John E. Thailand's reproductive revolution . Madison, Wis. , c1987. xiii, 251 p. : ISBN 0-299-11050-8 LC Card 87-8172 DDC 304.6/32/09593 19
HB1054.55.A3 K576 1987

Population growth and economic development . Madison, Wis. , 1987. xiii, 702 p. ; ISBN 0-299-11130-X : LC Card 86-40447 DDC 338.9/009172/4 19
HB884 .P66547 1987

Social development, cultural change, and fertility decline . Mahadevan, K., 1940- New Delhi , Newbury Park, Calif. , 1987. p. cm. ISBN 0-8039-9536-9 LC Card 87-15001 DDC 304.6/32/095483 19
HB1050.K47 M34 1987

Social development in the Third World.
Midgley, James. Social security, inequality, and the Third world /. Chichester, [Sussex] , New York , c1984. x, 225 p. ; ISBN 0-471-90061-3 LC Card 84-5188 DDC 368.4/009172/4 19
HD7252 .M52 1984 ***NYPL [JLE 86-2165]***

SOCIAL ECOLOGY. see **HUMAN ECOLOGY.**

Social, Educational Research and Development, inc. Transitional career counseling from the Air Force to the private sector . Washington, D.C. , c1987. iv, 153 leaves : LC Card 87-401057 DDC 358.4/1154/0973 19
HF5382.75.U6 T7 1987

SOCIAL EQUALITY. see **EQUALITY.**

SOCIAL ETHICS - HISTORY.
Sichirollo, Livio. Morale e morali /. Roma , 1985. 179 p. ; ISBN 88-359-2798-6 : LC Card 85-233121 DDC 170/.9 19
BJ74 .S53 1985 ***NYPL [JFD 87-941]***

The Social fabric : dimensions and issues / editor James F. Short, Jr. Beverly Hills, Calif. : Sage Publications, c1986. 366 p. ; 23 cm. (American Sociological Association presidential series) Based on papers presented at the 79th Annual Meeting of the American Sociological Association, held in San Antonio, Tex., Aug. 27-31, 1984. Includes bibliographies and index. ISBN 0-8039-2788-6 LC Card 86-1191 DDC 301 19
1. Sociology - Congresses. 2. Social systems - Congresses. 3. Social institutions - Congresses. I. Short, James F. II. American Sociological Association. Meeting (79th : 1984 : San Antonio, Tex.). III. Series.
HM13 .S524 1986 ***NYPL [JLE 86-3755]***

Social forces and the manager : readings and cases / [edited by] William R. Allen, Louis K. Bragaw, Jr.Reprint ed. Malabar, Fla. : R.E. Krieger, 1987, c1982. xiv, 502 p. : ill. ; 24 cm. (Wiley series in management) Reprint. Originally published: New York : Wiley, c1982. Includes bibliographies. ISBN 0-89464-225-1 (pbk.) LC Card 87-3259 DDC 658.4/08/0973 19
1. Industry - Social aspects - United States. I. Allen, William Robert, 1938-. II. Bragaw, Louis K. III. Series.
HD60.5.U5 S635 1987

SOCIAL FORECASTING. see **SOCIAL PREDICTION.**

Social forecasting for company planning / edited by Brian C. Twiss. London : Macmillan, 1982. xxv, 310 p. : ill. ; 23 cm. Includes bibliographies and index. CONTENTS. - The concepts and techniques of social forecasting / Brian C. Twiss -- Macro-social forecasting and areas of ignorance / Ronald J. Brech -- Measuring change in social attitudes / Tom Punt -- Discontinuities in social attitudes / Peter M.S. Jones -- Designing and installing a system for social forecasting / Geoffrey K. Morris -- Social forecasting in Lucas / Bernard Jones -- Social forecasting in Pilkington / Philip Holroyd -- Historical perspectives of societal change and the use of scenarios at Shell / Michael Jefferson -- Socio-political forecasting / Ian H. Wilson -- The use of cross-impact analysis for social forecasting at Monsanto / J. Kenneth Craver -- Forecasts of trends in post-industrial society / Tom Stonier and Peter Thornton -- A psycho-socio-politico-economic view of the future / Ronald J. Brech. ISBN 0-333-27076-2 LC Card 86-673655
1. Corporate planning. 2. Social prediction. I. Twiss, Brian C.
HD30.28 .S65x 1982

Social formation and symbolic landscape /. Cosgrove, Denis E. Totowa, N.J. , 1985, c1984. 293 p. : ISBN 0-389-20540-0 LC Card 84-21629 DDC 304.2 19
GF90 .C67 1985 ***NYPL [JLD 86-2206]***

Social functions and economic aspects of health insurance /. Rushing, William A. Boston , c1986. vii, 226 p. ; ISBN 0-89838-219-X LC Card 86-7297 DDC 368.3/82/00973 19
HD7102.U4 R86 1986 ***NYPL [JLE 87-1237]***

SOCIAL GEOGRAPHY. see **ANTHROPO-GEOGRAPHY.**

Social goals and social organization : essays in memory of Elisha Pazner / edited by Leonid Hurwicz, David Schmeidler, Hugo Sonnenschein. Cambridge [Cambridgeshire] ; New York : Cambridge University Press, 1985. xii, 365 p. : ill. ; 24 cm. Includes bibliograhies and indexes. ISBN 0-521-26204-6 LC Card 85-6668 DDC 330.15/5 19
1. Pazner, Elisha, 1941-1979. 2. Welfare economics - Addresses, essays, lectures. 3. Distributive justice - Addresses, essays, lectures. I. Pazner, Elisha, 1941-1979. II. Hurwicz, Leonid. III. Schmeidler, David, 1939-. IV. Sonnenschein, Hugo.
HB846 .S65 1985 ***NYPL [JLE 86-3786]***

SOCIAL GROUPS - MATHEMATICAL MODELS.
Bonus, Holger. Öffentliche Güter und der Öffentlichkeitsgrad von Gütern /. Konstanz [1979] 39, 3 p. ; LC Card 85-171986
HB846.5 .B66 1979

SOCIAL HISTORY.
Wohlfarth, Karl Anton. Leistung und Ethos . Paderborn , 1984. 266 p. ; ISBN 3-506-70223-8 LC Card 84-238158
HD60 .W64 1984

SOCIAL HISTORY - MEDIEVAL, 500-1500.
Handel en wandel in de dertiende eeuw /. Amsterdam , c1986. 139 p. : ISBN 90-6707-112-9 LC Card 86-199144
HC324 .H36 1986

SOCIAL HISTORY - MODERN, 1500-
Cosgrove, Denis E. Social formation and symbolic landscape /. Totowa, N.J. , 1985, c1984. 293 p. : ISBN 0-389-20540-0 LC Card 84-21629 DDC 304.2 19
GF90 .C67 1985 ***NYPL [JLD 86-2206]***

SOCIAL HISTORY - 19TH CENTURY - ADDRESSES, ESSAYS, LECTURES.
Les Sauvages dans la cité . Seyssel , c1985. 229 p. ; ISBN 2-903528-53-5
NYPL [JLD 86-1133]

SOCIAL HISTORY - 20TH CENTURY.
Roncolini, Giuliana, 1948- La crisi della legittimità borghese . Napoli , 1978. 115 p. ; ISBN 88-20-70809-4 : LC Card 79-368996
HC54 .R64 ***NYPL [JLD 81-254]***

Samoĭlov, L. N. (Leonid Nikolaevich) Global´nye problemy obshchestvennogo progressa . Moskva , 1985. 92 p. ; LC Card 85-170113
HD75 .S258 1985

SOCIAL HISTORY - 1945-
De Vos, Wouter. Point de mire . Antwerpen, Belgiëlai 147 a , 1977. 125 p. : ISBN 90-02-01132-6 : LC Card 78-370280 DDC 309.1
HC59 .D464 ***NYPL [JLD 80-3135]***

The Limits to growth. New York [1972] 205 p. ISBN 0-87663-165-0 LC Card 73-187907 DDC 330.9/04
HC59 .L54 ***NYPL [JLD 75-167]***

Toffler, Alvin. Previews & premises /. Montréal, Québec , 1984, c1983. 230 p. ; ISBN 0-920057-37-3 (pbk.)
NYPL [JFD 86-3191]

SOCIAL HISTORY - 1970-
Jungblut, Michael. Der Wohlstand entlässt seine Kinder . Stuttgart , c1983. 303 p. ; ISBN 3-421-06164-5 LC Card 83-232938
HC59 .J78 1983

Vacca, Roberto, 1927- Rinascimento prossimo venturo /. Milano , 1986. 281 p. : LC Card 87-100469
HC59 .V24 1986

SOCIAL HISTORY - 1970- - ADDRESSES, ESSAYS, LECTURES.
Marktwirtschaft 2000 /. Krefeld , c1983. 137 p. : ISBN 3-88289-302-8 LC Card 84-229313 DDC 338.9 19
HD75.6 .M37 1983 ***NYPL [JLD 86-3124]***

SOCIAL HISTORY - 1970- - CONGRESSES.
Club of Rome Conference (1984 : Helsinki, Finland) Managing global issues . [Lahti] [1985] 216 p. : ISBN 951-45-3807-2 (pbk.) LC Card 87-140928 DDC 909.82/8 19
HC13 .C56 1984

SOCIAL HISTORY - ADDRESSES, ESSAYS, LECTURES.
Historische Anthropologie . Göttingen , c1984. 166 p. ; ISBN 3-525-33497-4 LC Card 84-203590 DDC 306/.09 19
GN345.2 .H57 1984 ***NYPL [JFC 86-1764]***

SOCIAL HISTORY - CONGRESSES.
Failed transitions to modern industrial society . Montreal , c1975. vii, 105 p. : ISBN 0-919958-00-1 LC Card 80-510009 DDC 303.4/094 19
HM101 .F26 ***NYPL [JLE 81-166]***

SOCIAL HISTORY - METHODOLOGY.
Lloyd, Christopher, 1950- Explanation in social history /. Oxford, UK , New York, NY, USA , 1986. xi, 375 p. : ISBN 0-631-13113-2 : LC Card 85-13359 DDC 301/.09 19
HN28 .L58 1986 ***NYPL [JLE 86-1677]***

SOCIAL HISTORY - PHILOSOPHY.
Lloyd, Christopher, 1950- Explanation in social history /. Oxford, UK , New York, NY, USA , 1986. xi, 375 p. : ISBN 0-631-13113-2 : LC Card 85-13359 DDC 301/.09 19
HN28 .L58 1986 ***NYPL [JLE 86-1677]***

SOCIAL HYGIENE. see **PUBLIC HEALTH.**

SOCIAL INDICATORS.
McGranahan, Donald V. Measurement and analysis of socioeconomic development . Geneva , 1985. xx, 504 p. :
NYPL [JLK 74-447 no.85.5]

SOCIAL INDICATORS - CENTRAL AMERICA.
Gallardo, María Eugenia. Centroamérica . San José, Costa Rica , 1986. 259 p. : ISBN 92-9039-110-3 LC Card 87-401731 DDC 330.9728/053 19
HC141 .G35 1986

SOCIAL INDICATORS - CHILE.
Indicadores económicos y sociales, 1960-1985 /. Santiago, Chile , c1986. xvi, 415 p. : LC Card 87-120338
HC192 .I52 1986

Teitelboim G., Berta. Indicadores económicos y sociales . Santiago, Chile , 1985. 57 p. :
NYPL [JLD 86-2146]

Teitelboim G., Berta. Indicadores económicos y sociales [microform] . Santiago, Chile [1984] 41 p. : ***NYPL [*ZT-1711 no.26]***

SOCIAL INDICATORS - GERMANY, WEST.
Wilamowitz-Moellendorff, Ulrich von. Ansätze eines Konzepts zur Erfassung regionaler Lebensbedingungen in der Raumordnungspolitik /. Bonn , 1986. iv, 205 p. ; ISBN 3-88488-275-9 LC Card 87-407818 DDC 330.943/0878 19
HC286.7 .W54 1986

SOCIAL INDICATORS - KENYA.
Kenya report of the pilot study on socio-economic indicators, 1981. [Nairobi?] [1982?] 107 leaves : LC Card 87-120114 DDC 330.9676/204 19
HC865 .K486 1982

SOCIAL INDICATORS - SOUTH AFRICA - ELSIES RIVER.
Ellis, George Francis Rayner. A quality of life and basic needs measurement system with application to Elsies River /. Cape Town [1983] 101, [84] p. : ISBN 0-7992-0551-6 LC Card 84-146635 DDC 338.968/00723 19
HC905.Z7 E473 1983 ***NYPL [JLF 86-1126]***

SOCIAL INDICATORS - UNITED STATES.
Research on the quality of life /. Ann Arbor, Mich. , 1986. xiv, 365 p. ; ISBN 0-87944-308-1 : LC Card 86-15179 DDC 305/.0973 19
HN60 .R47 1986 ***NYPL [JLE 86-3621]***

SOCIAL INFRASTRUCTURE. see **INFRASTRUCTURE (ECONOMICS)**

SOCIAL INSTITUTIONS - ADDRESSES, ESSAYS, LECTURES.
Macroeconomic conflict and social institutions /. Cambridge, Mass. , c1985. xi, 249 p. : ISBN 0-88730-034-0 LC Card 84-24376 DDC 339.2 19
HC79.I5 M225 1985 ***NYPL [JLE 86-2562]***

SOCIAL INSTITUTIONS - CONGRESSES.
The Social fabric . Beverly Hills, Calif. , c1986. 366 p. ; ISBN 0-8039-2788-6 LC Card 86-1191 DDC 301 19
HM13 .S524 1986 ***NYPL [JLE 86-3755]***

SOCIAL INSTITUTIONS - COSTA RICA - HISTORY - 20TH CENTURY.
Las Instituciones costarricenses del siglo XX /. [San José] , 1986. 376 p. ; ISBN 997-7232-96-5 LC Card 86-231789
HC143 .I54 1986

SOCIAL INSTITUTIONS - UNITED STATES.
Clark, Gordon L. Judges and the cities . Chicago , c1985. xv, 247 p. ; ISBN 0-226-10753-1 : LC Card 85-1018 DDC 306/.0973 19
HN59.2 .C57 1985 ***NYPL [JLE 86-1068]***

SOCIAL INSURANCE. see **SOCIAL SECURITY.**

SOCIAL INTEGRATION - GERMANY (WEST)
Arnold-Rösner, Regina. Berufliche Integration junger Türken . Hamburg , 1986. 122 p. : ISBN 3-925408-05-3 LC Card 86-223625
HD8458.T9 A76 1986

Ausländerintegration in deutschen Industriebetrieben /. Königstein/Ts. , c1985. viii, 273 p. : ISBN 3-7756-6935-3 LC Card 85-194662 DDC 305.8/00943 19
HD8458.A2 A9265 1985 ***NYPL [JLD 86-2193]***

Fuchs, Hans-Jürgen, 1957- Das glückliche Bewusstsein und die Krise . Frankfurt [am Main] , c1986. 133 p. ; ISBN 3-925798-25-0 LC Card 87-112965
HD8458.A2 F83 1986

SOCIAL INTEGRATION - RESEARCH - GERMANY (WEST) - HISTORY.
Korte, Hermann, 1937- Migration und ihre sozialen Folgen . Göttingen , c1983. 170 p. ; ISBN 3-525-85366-1 LC Card 84-150019
HD8458.A2 K65 1983

SOCIAL INTEGRATION - SCOTLAND.
Way of life . London [1980?] 84 p. ; ISBN 0-86226-076-0 (pbk.) LC Card 82-218547 DDC 304.8 19
HD9571.7.S36 W39 1980 ***NYPL [JLD 85-427]***

SOCIAL INTERACTION - STATISTICAL METHODS.
Bakeman, Roger. Observing interaction . Cambridge [Cambridgeshire] , New York , 1986. ix, 221 p. : ISBN 0-521-25632-1 LC Card 85-22362 DDC 300/.1/51954 19
H62 .B284 1986 ***NYPL [JLD 86-3069]***

Social investment. Bruyn, Severyn Ten Haut, 1927- The field of social investment /. Cambridge , New York , 1987. xi, 304 p. : ISBN 0-521-33292-3 LC Card 86-26393 DDC 332.6 19
HG4910 .B77 1987

Social investments and economic growth /. Valencia Roa, Carlos Alberto, 1944- 1974. xiv, 199 leaves : ***NYPL [JLD 86-2961]***

SOCIAL JUSTICE.
Baumol, William J. Superfairness . Cambridge, Mass. , c1986. xi, 266 p. : ISBN 0-262-02234-6 LC Card 85-15127 DDC 305 19
HB72 .B356 1986 ***NYPL [JLE 86-2402]***

Datta, Bhabatosh, 1911- Social justice in a mixed economy /. Calcutta , 1982. ii, 64 p. ; LC Card 82-905698 DDC 338.954 19
HC435.2 .D353 1982 ***NYPL [JLD 86-3172]***

Govil, Rishi Kumar, 1933- Agriculture planning and social justice in India /. Allahabad , 1986. vii, 214 p. ; LC Card 86-902616 DDC 338.1/854 19
HD2073 .G68 1986

Justice . New York , c1986. xii, 283 p. ; ISBN 0-306-42256-5 LC Card 86-20503 DDC 320/.01/1 19
JC578 .J89 1986 ***NYPL [JLE 87-304]***

Mower, A. Glenn (Alfred Glenn) International cooperation for social justice . Westport, Conn. , c1985. x, 271 p. ; ISBN 0-313-24702-1 (lib. bdg.) LC Card 84-27954 DDC 341.4/81 19
K3240.4 .M676 1985 ***NYPL [JLD 85-3575]***

Prakash, Om, 1927- Guided incomes policy /. New Delhi , 1983. vi, 214 p. ; LC Card 83-902415 DDC 339.5/0954 19
HC440.I5 P72 1983 ***NYPL [JLD 86-3834]***

SOCIAL JUSTICE - ADDRESSES, ESSAYS, LECTURES.
Petras, James F., 1937- Latin America . Totowa, N.J. , 1986. xi, 187 p. ; ISBN 0-8476-7505-X : LC Card 86-1885 DDC 337.8 19
HC125 .P4643 1986 ***NYPL [JLE 86-4366]***

Social justice in a mixed economy /. Datta, Bhabatosh, 1911- Calcutta , 1982. ii, 64 p. ; LC Card 82-905698 DDC 338.954 19
HC435.2 .D353 1982 ***NYPL [JLD 86-3172]***

SOCIAL LEGISLATION - GERMANY, WEST.
Germany (West) [Angestelltenversicherungsgesetz.] Angestelltenversicherungsgesetz mit Sozialgesetzbuch . Berlin [1985] 788 p. : LC Card 86-145477
HD7116.M42 G4334 Nr. 18, 1985 KK3270.5

Germany (West) [Angestelltenversicherungsgesetz.] Angestelltenversicherungsgesetz mit Sozialgesetzbuch . Berlin [1986] 792 p. ; LC Card 86-229132
HD7116.M42 G4334 Nr. 18, 1986 KK3270.5

SOCIAL LEGISLATION - UNITED STATES.
Sagoff, Mark. The economy of the earth . Cambridge [Cambridgeshire] , New York , 1988. p. cm. ISBN 0-521-34113-2 LC Card 87-16091 DDC 363.7/056/0973 19
HC110.E5 S34 1988

SOCIAL MEDICINE - BRAZIL.
Possas, Cristina de Albuquerque. Saúde e trabalho . Rio de Janeiro, RJ , 1981. xxxix, 324 p. : LC Card 82-132979 DDC 362.1/0981 19
RA418.3.B6 P68 1981 ***NYPL [JLD 86-1896]***

SOCIAL MEDICINE - GREAT BRITAIN.
Class and health . London , New York , 1986. x, 223 p. : ISBN 0-422-60360-0 : LC Card 86-5972 DDC 362.1/0941 19
RA418.3.G7 C56 1986 ***NYPL [JLE 87-505]***

SOCIAL MEDICINE - GREAT BRITAIN - LONGITUDINAL STUDIES.
Class and health . London , New York , 1986. x, 223 p. : ISBN 0-422-60360-0 : LC Card 86-5972 DDC 362.1/0941 19
RA418.3.G7 C56 1986 ***NYPL [JLE 87-505]***

SOCIAL MOBILITY - BRAZIL.
Oliveira, Lúcia Elena Garcia de. O lugar do negro na força de trabalho /. Rio de Janeiro , 1983. 86 p. ; ISBN 85-24-00024-4 LC Card 86-129924
HD8288.5.B55 O45 1983

A Transição incompleta . Rio de Janeiro-RJ , 1986. 2 v. ; LC Card 86-224684
HC187 .T72 1986

SOCIAL MOBILITY - HUNGARY - STATISTICS.
Harcsa, István. Vándorlás, mobilitás, keresetalakulás . Budapest , 1987. 86 p. ; ISBN 963-340-812-1 : LC Card 87-409641
HB2052.5.A3 H37 1987

SOCIAL MOBILITY - OMAN - BĀṬINAH.
Asche, H. (Hartmut) Mobile Lebensformgruppen Südost-Arabiens im Wandel . Berlin , 1981, c1982. xii, 344 p. : ISBN 3-496-00302-2 LC Card 86-217612
HD8039.F652 O522 1982

SOCIAL MOBILITY - POLAND.
Witkowski, Janusz. Migracje a ruchliwość społeczna ludności w Polsce /. Warszawa , 1985. 168 p. : LC Card 86-175948
HB2068.7.A3 W58 1985

SOCIAL MOBILITY - QUEBEC (PROVINCE)
Garon-Audy, Muriel. Mobilités professionnelles et géographiques au Québec, 1954-64-74 /. Montréal , 1980. 61 p. ; LC Card 81-105620 DDC 331.12/7971 19
HD5717.5.C22 Q44 1980 ***NYPL [JLM 79-970 no.22]***

SOCIAL MOVEMENTS - BOLIVIA.
Sandoval, Godofredo. Las mil caras del movimiento social boliviano /. La Paz, Bolivia [1986] 132 p. : LC Card 86-227792
HD6608.5 .S25 1986

SOCIAL MOVEMENTS - MEXICO - CONGRESSES.
Movimientos sociales en el noroeste de México /. México , 1985. 282 p. ; ISBN 968-590-072-8 LC Card 87-102068
HD1531.M6 M684 1985

SOCIAL ORGANIZATION. see **SOCIAL STRUCTURE.**

The social origins of a labor elite . Stein, Margot B. (Margot Ballou), 1945- New York , 1987. xxiv, 515 p. : ISBN 0-8240-8043-2 (alk. paper) : LC Card 87-6913 DDC 305/.9385 19
HD8039.R322 F88 1987

SOCIAL OVERHEAD CAPITAL. see **INFRASTRUCTURE (ECONOMICS)**

SOCIAL PERCEPTION - CONGRESSES.
Experimental social dilemmas /. Frankfurt am Main , New York , c1986. vi, 234 p. : ISBN 3-8204-8574-0 (pbk.) : LC Card 86-10307 DDC 302 19
HM132 .E96 1986 ***NYPL [JLD 87-1177]***

SOCIAL PLANNING. see **SOCIAL POLICY.**

SOCIAL POLICY - ADDRESSES, ESSAYS, LECTURES.
Barbara Wootton--social science and public policy . London , New York , 1986. xi, 291 p. ; ISBN 0-422-79690-5 LC Card 85-27650 DDC 330 19
HB171 .B248 1985 ***NYPL [JLE 86-1743]***

Social concerns for the 1980s . Wien , c1984. 359 p. ; ISBN 3-900376-18-2 (pbk.) ***NYPL [JLE 86-2856]***

Sozialreform und Rhetorik =. Wiesbaden , 1984. 174 p. ; ISBN 3-515-02857-9 ***NYPL [L-11 3778 Bd. 4]***

SOCIAL POLICY - CONGRESSES.
Capitalismo riformato e sinistra . Milano , 1986. 125 p. ; ISBN 88-24-50380-2 : LC Card 86-229688
HB501 .C24265 1986

Issues of the eighties . Wien , 1983. 119 p. : LC Card 83-201354 DDC 338.9 19
HD73 .I86 1983

SOCIAL POLICY - ECONOMIC ASPECTS.
Sozialpolitik in der Beschäftigungskrise /. Berlin , c1986. 2 v. : ISBN 3-428-05949-2 (Bd. I) : LC Card 87-119211 DDC 361.6/1 19
HD5710 .S67 1986

SOCIAL POLICY - EVALUATION - MATHEMATICAL MODELS - ADDRESSES, ESSAYS, LECTURES.
Microanalytic simulation models to support social and financial policy /. Amsterdam ; New York : xvii, 553 p. : ISBN 0-444-87876-9 (U. S.) LC Card 85-25231 DDC 361.6/0724 19
HD87 .M52 1986 ***NYPL [JLD 86-3485]***

Social policy in modern Britain.
Alcock, Peter, 1951- Poverty and state support /. London , New York , 1987. xi, 215 p. : ISBN 0-582-29652-8 (pbk.) LC Card 86-27857 DDC 368.4/00941 19
HD7165 .A77 1987

SOCIAL POLICY - MORAL AND ETHICAL ASPECTS.
Marktwirtschaft und Gesellschaftsordnung . Berlin , c1983. 220 p., [1] leaf of plates : ISBN 3-428-05365-6 LC Card 83-191615
HB72 .M248 1983

SOCIAL POLICY - STUDY AND TEACHING (HIGHER) - LATIN AMERICA.
Latin American Institute for Economic and Social Planning. Instituto Latinoamericano de Planificación Económica y Social (ILPES) . [Santiago, Chile] [1984] iii, 52 p. ; LC Card 84-202400
HD77.5.L29 L38 1984

SOCIAL PREDICTION - ADDRESSES, ESSAYS, LECTURES.
Marktwirtschaft 2000 /. Krefeld , c1983. 137 p. : ISBN 3-88289-302-8 LC Card 84-229313 DDC 338.9 19
HD75.6 .M37 1983 ***NYPL [JLD 86-3124]***

SOCIAL PREDICTION - NORWAY.
Ertresvåg, Per-Aslak, 1931- Ekko av fremtiden /. Oslo , c1986. 163 p. : ISBN 82-504-0815-2 LC Card 86-217931
HC365 .E77 1986

SOCIAL PREDICTION - SWEDEN.
Kommunerna och framtiden . [Stockholm] , 1984] 224 p. : ISBN 91-38-08484-8 : LC Card

85-107984
HC375 .K654 1984

SOCIAL PREDICTION - UNITED STATES.
Naisbitt, John. The year ahead, 1986 . New York, NY , c1985. 168 p. ; ISBN 0-446-38330-9 LC Card 85-17909 DDC 338.5/443/0973 19
HC106.8 .N35 1985 NYPL [JLD 86-2987]

Russell, Cheryl, 1953- 100 predictions for the baby boom . New York , c1987. 249 p. ; ISBN 0-306-42527-0 LC Card 87-2443 DDC 338.5/443/0973 19
HC106.8 .R87 1987

Van der Ryn, Sim. Sustainable communities . San Francisco [1986] xvii, 238 p. : ISBN 0-87156-800-4 LC Card 83-4676 DDC 307/.14 19
HN90.C6 V36 1986 NYPL [JLF 86-1241]

SOCIAL PROBLEMS - ADDRESSES, ESSAYS, LECTURES.
Gonella, Guido, 1905- Contestazioni /. Roma , 1983. 3 v. ; LC Card 84-237282 DDC 945.092 19
JN5451 .G57 1983 NYPL [JFE 86-1367]

Social concerns for the 1980s . Wien , c1984. 359 p. ; ISBN 3-900376-18-2 (pbk.)
NYPL [JLE 86-2856]

Sozialreform und Rhetorik =. Wiesbaden , 1984. 174 p. ; ISBN 3-515-02857-9
NYPL [L-11 3778 Bd. 4]

Wohlfahrtsstaat und soziale Probleme /. Opladen , c1984. vi, 294 p. : ISBN 3-531-11701-7 *NYPL [JLD 85-1550]*

SOCIAL PROBLEMS AND THE CHURCH. see **CHURCH AND SOCIAL PROBLEMS.**

SOCIAL PSYCHOLOGY - ADDRESSES, ESSAYS, LECTURES.
Industrial relations . Chichester , New York , c1979. xii, 412 p. ; ISBN 0-471-99701-3 LC Card 78-18452 DDC 301.5/5
HD6971 .I547 NYPL [JLE 80-1770]

The Social psychology of female-male relations : a critical analysis of central concepts / edited by Richard D. Ashmore, Frances K. Del Boca. Orlando : Academic Press, 1986. xvi, 351 p. ; 24 cm. Includes bibliographies and indexes. ISBN 0-12-065280-3 (alk. paper) LC Card 85-9138 DDC 305.3 19
1. Interpersonal relations - Addresses, essays, lectures. 2. Sex role - Addresses, essays, lectures. 3. Identity (Psychology) - Addresses, essays, lectures. 4. Men - Psychology - Addresses, essays, lectures. 5. Women - Psychology - Addresses, essays, lectures. I. Ashmore, Richard D. II. Del Boca, Frances K.
HM132 .S569 1986 NYPL [JLE 86-1746]

The social psychology of industry . Brown, J. A. C. (James Alexander Campbell), 1911-1964. Harmondsworth, Middlesex, England , New York, N.Y., U. S.A. , c1986. xviii, 335 p. ; ISBN 0-14-009109-2 (pbk.) : LC Card 87-132408 DDC 158.7 19
HF5548.8 .B7 1986

SOCIAL REFORM. see **SOCIAL PROBLEMS.**

SOCIAL REFORMERS - INDIA - BIOGRAPHY.
Ray, Renuka Mukerji, 1903- My reminiscences . New Delhi , 1982. ix, 294 p., [5] p. of plates : LC Card 82-905707 DDC 954.03/5 19
DS481.R33 A38 1982 NYPL [JFD 85-9372]

SOCIAL RESEARCH. see **SOCIAL SCIENCE RESEARCH.**

Social Research, Inc. Attitudes toward vended coffee /. [Chicago? , 1983] 1 v. (various pagings) : LC Card 86-235525 DDC 381/.4566393 19
HD9199.U48 A88 1983

Social research perspectives .
(13) Moore, Mark Harrison. Inspectors-general . New York , c1986. 120 p. ; ISBN 0-87154-605-1 : LC Card 86-6728 DDC 353.0072/32 19
HJ9801 .M66 1987 NYPL [JLE 87-1762]

(14) Dietz, Thomas. The risk professionals /. New York , c1987. p. cm. ISBN 0-87154-214-5 : LC Card 87-19992 DDC 363.7/056/0973 19
HC110.E5 D54 1987

Social science. Bagby, Wesley Marvin, 1922- Introduction to social science /. Chicago , c1987. xv, 427 p. : ISBN 0-8304-1146-1 LC Card 86-23487 DDC 306/.0973 19
HC106.8 .B34 1987

SOCIAL SCIENCE. see **SOCIAL SCIENCES; SOCIOLOGY.**

Social science approaches to business behavior / Chris Argyris ... [et al.] ; George B. Strother, editor. New York : Garland Pub., 1987. vii, 183 p. : ill. ; 23 cm. (Continuity in administrative science) Reprint. Originally published: Homewood, Ill. : Dorsey Press : R.D. Irwin, 1962. (Irwin-Dorsey series in behavioral science in business) ISBN 0-8240-8201-X (alk. paper) : LC Card 86-25802 DDC 658.4 19
1. Organizational behavior. I. Argyris, Chris, 1923-. II. Strother, George B., 1918-. III. Series. IV. Series: Irwin-Dorsey series in behavioral science in business.
HD58.7 .S66 1987

Social science classics series.
Finley, M. I. (Moses I.), 1912- Studies in land and credit in ancient Athens, 500-200 B.C. . New Brunswick, U. S.A. , c1985. xli, 332 p. ; ISBN 0-88738-066-2 : LC Card 85-14091 DDC 333.3/0938/5 19
HD134 .F5 1985 NYPL [JLE 86-4293]

Social Science History Association.
The Politics of urban fiscal policy /. Beverly Hills , c1984. 176 p. : ISBN 0-8039-2373-2 LC Card 84-13431 DDC 336/.014/73 19
HJ9144 .P64 1984 NYPL [JLD 87-126]

Soviet quantitative history /. Beverly Hills , c1984. 216 p. : ISBN 0-8039-2082-2 LC Card 83-19196 DDC 306/.072047 19
HD715 .S5956 1984 NYPL [JLD 87-841]

Social science in natural resource management systems / edited by Marc L. Miller, Richard P. Gale, and Perry J. Brown. Boulder : Westview Press, 1987. xii, 265 p. : ill. ; 23 cm. (Social behavior and natural resources series) Includes bibliographies and index. ISBN 0-8133-7485-5 (pbk. : alk. paper) LC Card 87-23138 DDC 333.7/0973 19
1. Conservation of natural resources - Government policy - United States. 2. Natural resources - Social aspects - United States. I. Miller, Marc L. II. Gale, Richard P. III. Brown, Perry J. IV. Series.
HC103.7 .S62 1987

The Social science of organization[s] : four perspectives / Henry A. Latané ... [et al.] ; edited by Harold J. Leavitt. New York : Garland Pub., 1987. ix, 182 p. : ill. ; 23 cm. (Continuity in administrative science) Reprint. Originally published: Englewood Cliffs, N.J. : Prentice-Hall, c1963. Originally published in the series: Behavioral sciences in business series. Includes bibliographies. ISBN 0-8240-8213-3 (alk. paper) : LC Card 86-27069 DDC 658.4/03 19
1. Organizational behavior. 2. Decision-making. I. Latané, Henry A. II. Leavitt, Harold J. III. Series.
HD58.7 .S67 1987

Social science research (Downsview, Ont.)
Taylor, Malcolm G. (Malcolm Gordon) Medical perspectives on Canadian Medicare . Downsview, Ont. , 1984. vii, 201 p. : ISBN 0-919762-57-3 (pbk.) LC Card 87-673411
HD7102.C2 T34x 1984

SOCIAL SCIENCE RESEARCH - NETHERLANDS - ADDRESSES, ESSAYS, LECTURES.
International dimension of development problems . Amsterdam , New York , 1984. 103 p. ; ISBN 0-444-85621-8 (pbk.) LC Card 85-209291 DDC 338.9 19
HD75 .I59 1984 NYPL [JLE 86-1391]

SOCIAL SCIENCES. Here and with local subdivisions are entered works on the discipline of social sciences.

SOCIAL SCIENCES - DATA PROCESSING.
Discovering causal structure . Orlando , 1987. xvii, 394 p. : ISBN 0-12-286962-1 (alk. paper) LC Card 87-1860 DDC 300/.1/51 19
HA29 .D495 1987

Einstein, Gilles O., 1950- Learning to use SPSSx /. Englewood Cliffs, N.J. , c1987. viii, 183 p. : ISBN 0-13-528050-8 (pbk.) LC Card 86-30263 DDC 005.3/29 19
HA32 .E45 1987

Frude, Neil. A guide to SPSS/PC+ /. New York , 1987. p. cm. ISBN 0-387-91312-2 LC Card 87-16711 DDC 300/.285416 19
HA32 .F78 1987

Norušis, M. J. (Marija J.), 1948- The SPSS guide to data analysis for SPSS with additional instructions for SPSS/PC /. Chicago, IL , c1987. xiii, 428 p. : ISBN 0-918469-42-2 (pbk.) LC Card 87-60776 DDC 001.4/22 19
HA32 .N6519 1987

Norušis, M. J. (Marija J.), 1948- SPSS/PC+ Advanced Statistics V2.0 for the IBM PC/XT/AT and PS/2 /. Chicago, Ill. , c1988. 1 v. (various pagings) : ISBN 0-918469-57-0 (pbk.) LC Card 87-62355 DDC 005.36/9 19
HA32 .N6634 1988

Norušis, M. J. (Marija J.), 1948- SPSS/PC+ V2.0 base manual for the IBM PC/XT/AT and PS/2 /. Chicago, Ill. , c1988. 606 p. in various pagings : ISBN 0-918469-55-4 (pbk.) LC Card 87-62353 DDC 300/.28/5416 19
HA32 .N6674 1988

SPSS/PC+ trends . Chicago, Ill. , c1987. 299 p. in various pagings : ISBN 0-918469-44-9 (pbk.) LC Card 87-60902 DDC 005.36/9 19
HA32 .S627 1987

SPSS-X user's guide. Chicago, Ill. , Gorinchem, Netherlands , c1988. 1072 p. : ISBN 0-918469-51-1 (pbk.) LC Card 87-62349 DDC 005.3/29 19
HA32 .S67 1988

SOCIAL SCIENCES - DICTIONARIES.
Erdsiek, Gerhard. Wörterbuch für Recht, Wirtschaft und Politik. Bleckede bei Hamburg [1964-1968] 2 v. LC Card 65-42077
NYPL [JLE 85-408]

SOCIAL SCIENCES - HISTORY. Here are entered works on the history of social sciences as a discipline.

SOCIAL SCIENCES - HISTORY - 19TH CENTURY - CONGRESSES.
Rethinking the nineteenth century . New York , c1988. p. cm. ISBN 0-313-25997-6 (lib. bdg. : alk. paper) LC Card 87-17791 DDC 330.9/034 19
HC53 .R48 1988

SOCIAL SCIENCES - MATHEMATICAL MODELS.
Discovering causal structure . Orlando , 1987. xvii, 394 p. : ISBN 0-12-286962-1 (alk. paper) LC Card 87-1860 DDC 300/.1/51 19
HA29 .D495 1987

Karakozova, Ė. V. (Ėl'vira Viktorovna) Modelirovanie v obshchestvennykh naukakh . Moskva , 1986. 101 p. ;
*NYPL [*QI 87-3444]*

SOCIAL SCIENCES - MATHEMATICS.
Aczél, J. A short course on functional equations . Dordrecht, Holland ; Boston : vi, 169 p. : ISBN 90-277-2376-1 LC Card 86-26131 DDC 515/.25 19
HB135 .A28 1987

SOCIAL SCIENCES - METHODOLOGY.
Burns, Tom R. Man, decisions, society . New York , c1985. xiv, 342 p. : ISBN 2-88124-004-6 (France) LC Card 84-10303 DDC 301 19
HM24 .B85 1985 NYPL [JLE 86-2963]

Fielding, Nigel. Linking data /. Beverly Hills , c1986. 96 p. ; ISBN 0-8039-2518-2 (pbk.) LC Card 85-62290 DDC 300/.72 19
H62 .F425 1986 NYPL [JLD 86-3863]

Karakozova, Ė. V. (Ėl'vira Viktorovna) Modelirovanie v obshchestvennykh naukakh . Moskva , 1986. 101 p. ;
*NYPL [*QI 87-3444]*

McNeill, Patrick. Research methods /. London , New York , 1985. 136 p. ; ISBN 0-422-79540-2 (pbk.) LC Card 85-4656 DDC 301/.072 19
HM24 .M37 1985 NYPL [JLD 86-4181]

Sylvan, David J., 1953- A rationalist methodology for the social sciences /. Oxford [Oxfordshire] , 1985. 188 p. : ISBN 0-631-13443-3 : LC Card 84-14480 DDC 300/.1/8 19
HM24 .S95 1985 NYPL [JLE 86-1125]

SOCIAL SCIENCES - RESEARCH.
Fielding, Nigel. Linking data /. Beverly Hills , c1986. 96 p. ; ISBN 0-8039-2518-2 (pbk.) LC Card 85-62290 DDC 300/.72 19
H62 .F425 1986 NYPL [JLD 86-3863]

SOCIAL SCIENCES - RESEARCH - AFRICA - DIRECTORIES.

Inventaire . Paris [Washington, D.C.] 1986. xxvii, 262 p. ; ISBN 92-64-02871-4 : LC Card 87-129509
HD77.5.A34 I58 1986

Organisation for Economic Co-operation and Development. Development Centre. Répertoire . Paris , Washington, D.C. , 1986. xxiv, 523 p. ; ISBN 92-64-02872-2 : LC Card 87-146730
HD77.5.A34 O75 1986

SOCIAL SCIENCES - RESEARCH - UNITED STATES.

Klinkmüller, Erich. Über interdisziplinäre, sozialwissenschaftliche Forschung in den USA und andernorts /. Berlin , 1986. 177 p. ; ISBN 3-921374-37-5 LC Card 86-211120
HC244.A1 B4 Nr. 47 H62.5.U5

Nonprofit organizations, a government management tool /. New York , 1980. xxi, 173 p. ; ISBN 0-03-053966-8 : LC Card 79-23632 DDC 350 19
JK468.R45 N66 ***NYPL [JLE 80-1874]***

SOCIAL SCIENCES - RESEARCH - UNITED STATES - METHODOLOGY - CONGRESSES.

Survey of income and program participation and related longitudinal surveys, 1984 . [Washington, D.C.] , 1985. ix, 201 p. : LC Card 85-601676 DDC 339.2/3/0973 19
HC110.I5 S89 1985 ***NYPL [JLF 86-1641]***

SOCIAL SCIENCES - STATISTICAL METHODS.

Alfred, Braxton M. Elements of statistics for the life and social sciences /. New York , c1987. xiii, 190 p. : ISBN 0-387-96500-9 : LC Card 87-4964 DDC 300/.1/5195 19
HA29 .A53 1987

Andersen, Erling B. Statistics for economics, business administration, and the social sciences /. Berlin , New York , c1987. xi, 439 p. : ISBN 0-387-17720-5 (pbk. : U. S.) LC Card 87-9423 DDC 519.5 19
HB137 .A525 1987

Bakeman, Roger. Observing interaction . Cambridge [Cambridgeshire] , New York , 1986. ix, 221 p. : ISBN 0-521-25632-1 LC Card 85-22362 DDC 300/.1/51954 19
H62 .B284 1986 ***NYPL [JLD 86-3069]***

Bruning, James L. Computational handbook of statistics /. Glenview, Ill. , c1987. 372 p. ; ISBN 0-673-18407-2 (pbk.) LC Card 86-31593 DDC 519.5 19
HA29 .B835 1987

Chesnokov, S. V. (Sergeĭ Valerianovich) Determinatsionnyĭ analiz sotsial'no-ėkonomicheskikh dannykh /. Moskva , 1982. 167, [1] p. : LC Card 83-173210
HA29.5.R9 C52 1982

Darlington, Richard B. Behavioral statistics . New York, N.Y. , London , c1987. xxiv, 628 p. : ISBN 0-02-907860-1 LC Card 87-12040 DDC 519.5 19
HA29 .D246 1987

Discovering causal structure . Orlando , 1987. xvii, 394 p. : ISBN 0-12-286962-1 (alk. paper) LC Card 87-1860 DDC 300/.1/51 19
HA29 .D495 1987

Iversen, Gudmund R. Analysis of variance /. Newbury Park , c1987. 94 p. : ISBN 0-8039-3001-1 (pbk.) LC Card 87-61276 DDC 519.5/35 19
HA31.35 .I85 1987

Lapin, Lawrence L. Statistics for modern business decisions /. San Diego , c1987. xxxiii, 825 p. : ISBN 0-15-583737-0 LC Card 85-82633 DDC 519.5/024658 19
HA29 .L2664 1987

Marascuilo, Leonard A. Statistical methods for the social and behavioral sciences /. New York , c1988. xxvi, 804 p. : ISBN 0-7167-1824-3 LC Card 87-398 DDC 519.5 19
HA29 .M2482 1988

Meddis, Ray. Statistics using ranks . Oxford, OX, UK , New York, NY, USA , 1984. vi, 449 p. : ISBN 0-631-13788-2 (pbk.) : LC Card 84-11087 DDC 519.5 19
HA29 .M43885 1984 ***NYPL [JLE 86-4708]***

Mukhin, P. A. (Pavel Aleksandrovich) Statistika kinematografii . Moskva , 1984. 103 p. : LC Card 85-203673
HA29.5.R9 M85 1984

Norušis, M. J. (Marija J.), 1948- The SPSS guide to data analysis for SPSS with additional instructions for SPSS/PC /. Chicago, IL , c1987. xiii, 428 p. : ISBN 0-918469-42-2 (pbk.) LC Card 87-60776 DDC 001.4/22 19
HA32 .N6519 1987

Phillips, John L., 1923- How to think about statistics /. New York , c1988. xiv, 198 p. : ISBN 0-7167-1923-1 (pbk.) LC Card 87-15056 DDC 519.5 19
HA29 .P517 1988

Reid, Stuart. Working with statistics . Totowa, N.J. , 1987. xiv, 183 p. ; ISBN 0-8476-7590-4 (pbk.) : LC Card 87-20508 DDC 300/.72 19
HA29 .R43 1987

Runyon, Richard P. Fundamentals of behavioral statistics /. New York , c1988. p. cm. ISBN 0-394-36619-0 LC Card 87-23066 DDC 519.5 19
HA29 .R85 1988

Stahl, Herbert. Clusteranalyse grosser Objektmengen mit problemorientierten Distanzmassen /. Thun , c1985. ii, vi, 323 p. : ISBN 3-87144-908-3 LC Card 86-112498
HA29.5.G4 S68 1985

Statistische Methoden . St. Gallen , 1983. iii, 195 p. : LC Card 83-240598
HA29.5.G4 S72 1983

vrmmon problems/proper solutions . Newbury Park, CA , 1987. p. cm. ISBN 0-8039-2806-8 : LC Card 87-20625 DDC 300/.72 19
HA29 .C7325 1987

Wilcox, Rand R. New statistical procedures for the social sciences . Hillsdale, N.J. , 1987. p. cm. ISBN 0-89859-936-9 : LC Card 87-9001 DDC 300/.1/5195 19
HA29 .W522 1987

Wolf, Fredric M. (Fredric Marc) Meta-analysis . Beverly Hills , c1986. 65 p. : ISBN 0-8039-2756-8 LC Card 85-52372
NYPL [JLK 77-39 no.59]

SOCIAL SCIENCES - STATISTICS - RESEARCH - METHODOLOGY.

Nutzung von anonymisierten Einzelangaben aus Daten der amtlichen Statistik . Stuttgart , 1987. 200 p. : ISBN 3-17-003338-7 LC Card 87-401358
HA29.5.G4 N88 1987

SOCIAL SCIENCES - STUDY AND TEACHING - AFRICA - DIRECTORIES.

Inventaire . Paris [Washington, D.C.] 1986. xxvii, 262 p. ; ISBN 92-64-02871-4 : LC Card 87-129509
HD77.5.A34 I58 1986

SOCIAL SCIENCES - UNITED STATES. Here are entered works on the discipline of social sciences in the United States.

Bagby, Wesley Marvin, 1922- Introduction to social science /. Chicago , c1987. xv, 427 p. : ISBN 0-8304-1146-1 LC Card 86-23487 DDC 306/.0973 19
HC106.8 .B34 1987

Social security : a critique of radical reform proposals / edited by Charles W. Meyer. Lexington, Mass. : Lexington Books, c1987. x, 153 p. : ill. ; 24 cm. Includes bibliographical references and index. CONTENTS. - Social security / Charles W. Meyer -- Phasing out social security : a critique of Ferrara's proposal / Bruno Stein -- Intercohort and intracohort redistribution under social security / Charles W. Meyer and Nancy L. Wolff -- Social security and private saving / Selig D. Lesnoy and Dean R. Leimer -- Labor market behavior of older workers approaching retirement / Rachel Floersheim Boaz -- The economic and political implications of a phase-out / Charles W. Meyer. ISBN 0-669-14518-1 (alk. paper) LC Card 86-45891 DDC 368.4/3/00973 19
1. Social security - United States. I. Meyer, Charles W.
HD7125 .S593 1987 ***NYPL [JLE 87-1286]***

Social Security . Bernstein, Merton C. New York , c1988. xiii, 321 p. : ISBN 0-465-07916-4 : LC Card 86-47762 DDC 368.4/3/00973 19
HD7125 .B48 1988

The Social Security Administration and information technology : special report. Washington, DC : Congress of the U. S., Office of Technology Assessment : For sale by the Supt. of Docs., U. S. G.P.O., [1986] viii, 149 p. : ill. ; 26 cm. Shipping list no.: 86-830-P. "October 1986"--P. [4] of cover. Includes bibliographical references. "OTA-CIT-311"--P. [4] of cover. S/N 052-003-01053-4 Item 1070-M LC Card 86-600567 DDC 353.0082/56 19
1. United States. Social Security Administration - Data processing. 2. United States. Social Security Administration - Procurement. I. United States. Congress. Office of Technology Assessment.
HD7125 .S5953 1986

Social security and employment / edited by Le Assen, The Netherlands : Published for the European Centre for Work and Society by Vangorcum, 1983. 116 p. : ill. ; 23 cm. (New patterns in employment . no. 5) "Contributions to a seminar on 'The Structure of the Labor Market and the Implications for the Social Security Systems in Europe,' held in Dublin, October 27-29, 1982"--Verso t.p. Sponsored by the Commission of the European Communities. Bibliography: p. 115-116. CONTENTS. - Social welfare provisions and employment / by R. Tarling, J. Rubery, and F. Wilkinson -- The effects on employment of the various possibilities for reforming social security financing / by A. and C. Euzéby -- The reconstruction of reality / by L. Lamers -- High unemployment as a challenge / by J. Volz. ISBN 90-232-2011-0 (pbk.) : LC Card 83-216203 DDC 331.12/094 19
1. Social security - Europe - Congresses. 2. Manpower policy - Europe - Congresses. 3. Income maintenance programs - Europe - Congresses. 4. Labor supply - Europe - Congresses. 5. Insurance, Unemployment - Europe - Congresses. I. Bekemans, Léonce. II. Rubery, J. (Jill). III. European Centre for Work and Society. IV. Series.
HD7164 .S594 1983 ***NYPL [JLE 86-1107]***

SOCIAL SECURITY - ARGENTINA.

Informe del gobierno argentino sobre asuntos laborales /. Buenos Aires, República Argentina , 1965. 115 leaves ; LC Card 85-115096
HD8266.5 .I53 1965

SOCIAL SECURITY - ARGENTINA - HISTORY - 20TH CENTURY.

Isuani, Ernesto A. (Ernesto Aldo) Los orígenes conflictivos de la seguridad social argentina /. Buenos Aires , c1985. 140 p. ; ISBN 950-25-0128-4 : LC Card 86-174656
HD7149 .I88 1985

SOCIAL SECURITY - AUSTRALIA - STATISTICS.

Moore, Jim. Trends in the disposable incomes of Australian families, 1964-65 to 1985-86 /. Woden, ACT [1986] vii, 103 p. ; ISBN 0-642-51700-2 (pbk.) LC Card 87-154435 DDC 339.394 19
HC610.I5 M66 1986

SOCIAL SECURITY BENEFICIARIES - GERMANY (WEST) - STATES - DIRECTORIES.

Die Versichertenältesten . [Berlin] [1984] 54 p. ; LC Card 85-113867
HD7116.M42 G4334 Nr. 20, 1984 HD7179

SOCIAL SECURITY BENEFICIARIES - UNITED STATES.

Earnings sharing options for the social security system. [Washington, D.C.?] [1986] xxv, 137 p. : LC Card 86-601147 DDC 368.4/3015/0973 19
HD7125 .E227 1986 ***NYPL [JLF 86-1058]***

SOCIAL SECURITY - BERLIN (GERMANY) - HISTORY.

Reidegeld, Eckart. Die Sozialversicherung zwischen Neuordnung und Restauration . Frankfurt am Main , c1982. 481 p. ; ISBN 3-88129-519-4 : LC Card 83-155896
HD7180.B4 R45 1982

SOCIAL SECURITY - BRAZIL.

Fonseca, Aloysio de Salles. Reorientação da assistência à saúde no âmbito da previdência social . [Brasília] , 1983. 67 p. ; LC Card 86-171863
HD7102.B7 F66 1983

Schwarz, Manfred, 1910- Social security in Brazil . Rio de Janeiro, Brasil [1980] [14], 161 p. : LC Card 87-123549 DDC 368.4/00981 19
HD7154 .S36 1980

SOCIAL SECURITY - BULGARIA.

Penkov, Petŭr. Osnovi na sotsialnoto osiguri͡avane /. Sofii͡a , 1984. 191 p. : LC Card 86-104011
HD7091 .P335 1984

Problemi na dŭrzhavnoto i obshtestvenoto

osigurīavane na rabotnitsite i sluzhitelite. Stara Zagora , 1984. 17 p. ; LC Card 86-204115
HD7211.5 .P75 1984

SOCIAL SECURITY - CASE STUDIES.
Kerans, Patrick. Welfare and worker participation . New York , 1987. p. cm. ISBN 0-312-00908-9 : LC Card 87-11878 DDC 362.8/5 19
HD7261 .K47 1987

SOCIAL SECURITY - CHILE.
Análisis de la previsión en Chile /. Santiago, Chile [1986] 309 p. : LC Card 87-115194
HD7156 .A78 1986

SOCIAL SECURITY - DENMARK.
Vesterø Jensen, Carsten. Det tvedelte pensionssystem /. Roskilde [1984] 284 p. ; LC Card 84-181865
HD7105.35.D4 J45 1984

SOCIAL SECURITY - DEVELOPING COUNTRIES.
Midgley, James. Social security, inequality, and the Third world /. Chichester, [Sussex] , New York , c1984. x, 225 p. ; ISBN 0-471-90061-3 LC Card 84-5188 DDC 368.4/009172/4 19
HD7252 .M52 1984 ***NYPL [JLE 86-2165]***

Partsch, Manfred. Prinzipien und Formen sozialer Sicherung in nicht-industriellen Gesellschaften /. Berlin , c1983. 168 p. ; ISBN 3-428-05484-9 LC Card 84-148527 DDC 368.4/009172/4 19
HD7252 .P37 1983 ***NYPL [JLE 85-1238]***

SOCIAL SECURITY - EUROPE.
Quadagno, Jill S. The transformation of old age security . Chicago , 1988. p. cm. ISBN 0-226-69923-4 : LC Card 87-18754 DDC 368.4/00973 19
HD7125 .Q46 1988

Schmitz, Heinz. Vermeidung von Armut im Alter . München , c1983. 267 p. : ISBN 3-89019-099-5 LC Card 84-197886
HD7164 .S29 1983

SOCIAL SECURITY - EUROPE - CONGRESSES.
Social security and employment /. Assen, The Netherlands , 1983. 116 p. : ISBN 90-232-2011-0 (pbk.) : LC Card 83-216203 DDC 331.12/094 19
HD7164 .S594 1983 ***NYPL [JLE 86-1107]***

SOCIAL SECURITY - EUROPE - FINANCE - CONGRESSES.
Costi e relativi finanziamenti dei sistemi pensionistici nei paesi europei . Roma , 1985. xi, 486 p. : LC Card 86-206925
HD7164 .C67 1985

SOCIAL SECURITY - EUROPEAN ECONOMIC COMMUNITY COUNTRIES.
Emerson, Michael. What model for Europe? /. Cambridge, Mass. , c1988. xi, 151 p. : ISBN 0-262-05036-6 LC Card 87-15151 DDC 331.11/094 19
HD8380.5 .E47 1988

SOCIAL SECURITY - FRANCE.
Johanet, Gilles. Contes et mécomptes de la protection sociale /. Paris , c1986. 175 p. : ISBN 2-86702-024-4 : LC Card 86-179065
HD7175 .J64 1986

SOCIAL SECURITY - FRANCE - HISTORY.
Ewald, François. L'Etat providence /. Paris , c1986. 608 p. ; ISBN 2-246-30731-7 : LC Card 86-160935
HD7175 .E93 1986

SOCIAL SECURITY - FRANCE - HISTORY - CONGRESSES.
Colloque sur l'histoire de la sécurité sociale (1980 : Caen, France) Colloque sur l'histoire de la sécurité sociale . Paris , 1981. 263 p. ; LC Card 81-201274
HD7175 .C58 1980

SOCIAL SECURITY - GERMANY, EAST.
Schönfelder, Bruno. Ökonomisches Risiko und Versicherung in sozialistischen Volkswirtschaften . Berlin , c1986. 284 p. : ISBN 3-428-05968-9 LC Card 86-185328
HD7180.5 .S36 1986

SOCIAL SECURITY - GERMANY - HISTORY.
Hennock, E. P., 1926- British social reform and German precedents . Oxford [Oxfordshire] , New York , 1987. vi, 243 p. ; ISBN 0-19-820127-3 : LC Card 87-11082 DDC 368.4/00941 19
HD7165 .H455 1987

SOCIAL SECURITY - GERMANY, WEST.
Blum, Ulrich. Raumwirkungen des Budgets der gesetzlichen Rentenversicherung . Karlsruhe , c1986. xii, 184, 35 p. : ISBN 3-88652-029-3 LC Card 87-124826 DDC 368.4/00943 19
HD7179 .B57 1986

Böckel, Thomas R., 1959- Selbstregelung und Entpolitisierung der gesetzlichen Rentenversicherung . Frankfurt am Main , New York , c1986. xvi, 305 p. ; ISBN 3-8204-8847-2 LC Card 87-407917 DDC 368.4/00943 19
HD7179 .B59 1986

Böpple, Arthur. "Sozialstaat" im Abbruch . Frankfurt/Main , c1986. 277 p. : ISBN 3-88367-062-6 LC Card 87-104497
HD7179 .B624 1986

Dinkel, Reiner. Die Auswirkungen eines Geburten- und Bevölkerungsrückgangs auf Entwicklung und Ausgestaltung von gesetzlicher Alterssicherung und Familienlastenausgleich /. Berlin , c1984. 344 p. : ISBN 3-428-05546-2 LC Card 84-186733
HD7179 .D65 1984

Holla, Michael. Die Belastung der Landwirtschaft durch Beiträge zur sozialen Sicherung im Vergleich zur Situation anderer sozialer Gruppen . Göttingen [1986] viii, 174 p. ; LC Card 87-407657 DDC 368.4/00943 19
HD7179 .H635 1986

Materialien zur Vermögensbildung in Arbeitnehmerhand. Bonn [1965-<c1985. v. <1-6 > LC Card 67-123501 DDC 368.4/00943
HD7179 .M35

Reform oder Revolution? . Bonn , 1987. vi, 241, A 140 p. : LC Card 87-409091 DDC 368.4/00943 19
HD7179 .R384 1987

Rüden, Reinhold von. Soziale Sicherung in der Bundesrepublik Deutschland /. Paderborn , c1986. 157 p. : ISBN 3-506-23938-4 LC Card 87-127289 DDC 368.4/00943 19
HD7179 .R835 1986

Schmähl, Winfried. Änderung der Beitragsfinanzierung in der Rentenversicherung? . Baden-Baden , 1984. 388 p. : ISBN 3-7890-1018-9 LC Card 84-206647
HD7179 .S324 1984

Spinnarke, Jürgen. Soziale Sicherheit in der Bundesrepublik Deutschland . Heidelberg , c1985. 142 p. : ISBN 3-8114-1085-7 : LC Card 86-103725
HD7179 .S63 1985

Strasser, Johano. Grenzen des Sozialstaats? . Köln , 1983. 206 p. ; ISBN 3-7663-0800-9 LC Card 83-142735
HC286.6 .S73 1983

Überwindung der Sozialstaatskrise . Baden-Baden , 1984. 317 p. : ISBN 3-7890-0925-3 LC Card 84-166713
HD7179 .U35 1984

SOCIAL SECURITY - GERMANY (WEST) - CONGRESSES.
Wirtschaftsentwicklung und soziale Sicherheit . Köln , 1983. viii, 146 p. : ISBN 3-452-19567-8 LC Card 84-106615
HG9399.G32 W57 1983

SOCIAL SECURITY - GERMANY, WEST - HISTORY.
Reidegeld, Eckart. Die Sozialversicherung zwischen Neuordnung und Restauration . Frankfurt am Main , c1982. 481 p. ; ISBN 3-88129-519-4 : LC Card 83-155896
HD7180.B4 R45 1982

SOCIAL SECURITY - GREAT BRITAIN.
Alcock, Peter, 1951- Poverty and state support /. London , New York , 1987. xi, 215 p. : ISBN 0-582-29652-8 (pbk.) LC Card 86-27857 DDC 368.4/00941 19
HD7165 .A77 1987

Great Britain. Equal Opportunities Commission. Green paper . Manchester [1985] 66 p. : LC Card 87-124211 DDC 368.4/00941 19
HD7165 .G725 1985

Whiteley, Paul. Pressure for the poor . London , New York , 1987. 174 p. ; ISBN 0-416-36370-9 LC Card 87-11205 DDC 362.5/8/0941 19
HC260.P63 W47 1987

SOCIAL SECURITY - GREAT BRITAIN - HISTORY.
Hennock, E. P., 1926- British social reform and German precedents . Oxford [Oxfordshire] , New York , 1987. vi, 243 p. ; ISBN 0-19-820127-3 : LC Card 87-11082 DDC 368.4/00941 19
HD7165 .H455 1987

SOCIAL SECURITY - HUNGARY.
A Lakosság jövedelme, társadalombiztosítás, családpolitika /. Budapest [1983] 82 p. : LC Card 83-206799
HC30.295.I5 L332 1983 ***NYPL [JLE 87-179]***

SOCIAL SECURITY - HUNGARY - HISTORY.
Fodor, András. A magyar társadalombiztosítás az V. ötéves terv időszakában, 1976-1980 /. Budapest , 1983. 147 p. ; ISBN 963-321-977-9 LC Card 85-129731
HD7172.5 .F62 1983

Social security in Brazil . Schwarz, Manfred, 1910- Rio de Janeiro, Brasil [1980] [14], 161 p. : LC Card 87-123549 DDC 368.4/00981 19
HD7154 .S36 1980

SOCIAL SECURITY - INDIA.
Chowdhry, D. Paul. Profile of social welfare and development in India /. New Delhi , 1985. viii, 340 p. ; LC Card 85-901093 DDC 362/.954 19
HV393 .C515 1985 ***NYPL [JLD 86-2575]***

SOCIAL SECURITY - INDIA - STATISTICS.
Statistical profile on women labour. Simla [1983] v, 224 p. ; LC Card 84-900395 DDC 331.4/0954/021 19
HD5819 .S83 1983 ***NYPL [JLF 86-1946]***

Social security, inequality, and the Third world /. Midgley, James. Chichester, [Sussex] , New York , c1984. x, 225 p. ; ISBN 0-471-90061-3 LC Card 84-5188 DDC 368.4/009172/4 19
HD7252 .M52 1984 ***NYPL [JLE 86-2165]***

SOCIAL SECURITY - IRELAND.
A National income-related pension scheme. Dublin [1976] viii, 195 p. ; LC Card 82-127069
HD7168 .N39 1976

SOCIAL SECURITY - ITALY.
La Tutela del lavoro in Italia. [Roma] [1976] 144 p. ; LC Card 86-233354
HD8481 .T85 1976

SOCIAL SECURITY - ITALY, SOUTHERN.
Boccella, Nicola Maria, 1952- Il Mezzogiorno sussidiato . Milano, Italy , c1982. 264 p. : LC Card 85-163271
HD7185.S68 B62 1982

SOCIAL SECURITY - LATIN AMERICA.
Cohen, Noemí. Trabajadores y seguridad social en América Latina /. México, D.F. [1982], c1981. 146 p. ; ISBN 968-8241-38-5 LC Card 83-140620 DDC 368.4/0098 19
HD7130.5 .C63 1982 ***NYPL [JLD 86-2768]***

SOCIAL SECURITY - LAW AND LEGISLATION - GERMANY, WEST.
Blum, Ulrich. Raumwirkungen des Budgets der gesetzlichen Rentenversicherung . Karlsruhe , c1986. xii, 184, 35 p. : ISBN 3-88652-029-3 LC Card 87-124826 DDC 368.4/00943 19
HD7179 .B57 1986

Reform oder Revolution? . Bonn , 1987. vi, 241, A 140 p. : LC Card 87-409091 DDC 368.4/00943 19
HD7179 .R384 1987

Spinnarke, Jürgen. Soziale Sicherheit in der Bundesrepublik Deutschland . Heidelberg , c1985. 142 p. : ISBN 3-8114-1085-7 : LC Card 86-103725
HD7179 .S63 1985

SOCIAL SECURITY - LAW AND LEGISLATION - NETHERLANDS.
Braakman, T. C. Sociale zekerheid in Nederland /. Utrecht , 1984. 199 p. : ISBN 90-274-5513-9 : LC Card 85-110890
HD7192 .B73 1984 ***NYPL [JLC 86-295]***

SOCIAL SECURITY - LAW AND LEGISLATION - PORTUGAL.
Maia, Fernando M. Segurança social em Portugal . Lisboa , 1985. 192 p. : LC Card

86-149393
HD7209 .M35 1985

SOCIAL SECURITY - MANITOBA - CONGRESSES.
An Inquiry into the future of public and private pension plans . Winnipeg [1976] xiii, 54 p. ; LC Card 85-103269
HD7130.M36 I56 1976

SOCIAL SECURITY - NETHERLANDS.
Braakman, T. C. Sociale zekerheid in Nederland /. Utrecht , 1984. 199 p. : ISBN 90-274-5513-9 : LC Card 85-110890
HD7192 .B73 1984 ***NYPL [JLC 86-295]***

SOCIAL SECURITY - PAKISTAN.
Qureshi, S. M. Moin. Social security scheme /. Karachi , 1984. 146 p. : LC Card 85-932136 DDC 368.4/009549/1 19
HD7220.5 .Q73 1984

SOCIAL SECURITY - PERU.
Slodky, Javier. Dilemas de la seguridad social en el Perú /. [Lima] , 1985. 134 p. ; LC Card 86-232616
HD7161 .S57 1985

SOCIAL SECURITY - PORTUGAL - HISTORY.
Maia, Fernando M. Segurança social em Portugal . Lisboa , 1985. 192 p. : LC Card 86-149393
HD7209 .M35 1985

SOCIAL SECURITY - QUÉBEC (PROVINCE)
La Compensation des charges familiales au Québec /. [Quebec] [1986] xxi, 197 p. ; ISBN 2-551-08707-4 LC Card 86-179318
HD4925.5.C2 C65 1986

Social security scheme /. Qureshi, S. M. Moin. Karachi , 1984. 146 p. : LC Card 85-932136 DDC 368.4/009549/1 19
HD7220.5 .Q73 1984

SOCIAL SECURITY - SOVIET UNION.
Razvitie obshchestvennykh fondov potrebleniia na sovremennom ėtape /. Moskva , 1984. 140 p. ; LC Card 85-240059
HD7196 .R39 1984

Schönfelder, Bruno. Ökonomisches Risiko und Versicherung in sozialistischen Volkswirtschaften . Berlin , c1986. 284 p. : ISBN 3-428-05968-9 LC Card 86-185328
HD7180.5 .S36 1986

SOCIAL SECURITY - SPAIN - CASTILLA Y LEÓN.
García Villarejo, Avelino. Estructura financiera y actividad inversora de las administraciones públicas en Castilla y León /. Valladolid , 1984. 431 p. : ISBN 84-505-0331-0 LC Card 87-108720
HJ1249.C29 G37 1984

SOCIAL SECURITY - SWITZERLAND.
Müller, Stefan, 1955- Schweizerische Sozialpolitik . Bern , New York , c1984. 204 p. : ISBN 3-261-03410-6 LC Card 85-189979
HD7210 .M85 1984

SOCIAL SECURITY TAXES - UNITED STATES.
Chaikind, Stephen. Paying for social security . [Washington, D.C.], 1981. xix, 47 p. ; LC Card 81-601225 DDC 353.0082/56 19
HD7125 .C47 ***NYPL [JLF 86-252]***

SOCIAL SECURITY - UNITED STATES.
Bernstein, Merton C. Social Security . New York , c1988. xiii, 321 p. : ISBN 0-465-07916-4 : LC Card 86-47762 DDC 368.4/3/00973 19
HD7125 .B48 1988

Boskin, Michael J. Too many promises . Homewood, Ill. , c1986. xiv, 196 p. : ISBN 0-87094-779-6 LC Card 86-70430 DDC 368.4/3/00973 19
HD7125 .B585 1986 ***NYPL [JLE 86-2970]***

Davis, Frank Green, 1913- The Black community's social security /. Washington , c1977. xiii, 189 p. : ISBN 0-8191-0282-2 LC Card 78-304298
E185.8 .D237 ***NYPL [JLD 78-1907]***

DeVol, Karen R., 1949- Income replacement for long term disability . Cambridge, Mass. , 1986. p. cm. ISBN 0-935149-04-X : LC Card 86-28264 DDC 368.4/1/00973 19
HD7103.65.U6 D484 1986

Kingson, Eric R. What you must know about Social Security & Medicare /. New York , 1987. 120 p. ; ISBN 0-88687-294-4 (pbk.) : LC Card 86-62667 DDC 368.4/3/00973 19
HD7125 .K538 1987

Lopata, Helena Znaniecka, 1925- Widows and dependent wives . New York , 1986. xxi, 242 p. ; ISBN 0-03-046301-7 (alk. paper) : LC Card 85-16753 DDC 362.8/382 19
HV699 .L67 1985 ***NYPL [JLE 86-2182]***

Pension integration . Washington, D.C. [1986] 28 p. : LC Card 86-603093 DDC 331.25/2/0973 19
HD7125 .P392 1986

Quadagno, Jill S. The transformation of old age security . Chicago , 1988. p. cm. ISBN 0-226-69923-4 : LC Card 87-18754 DDC 368.4/00973 19
HD7125 .Q46 1988

Social security . Lexington, Mass. , c1987. x, 153 p. : ISBN 0-669-14518-1 (alk. paper) LC Card 86-45891 DDC 368.4/3/00973 19
HD7125 .S593 1987 ***NYPL [JLE 87-1286]***

Wolff, Nancy, 1955- Income redistribution and the Social Security program /. Ann Arbor , c1987. vi, 181 p. : ISBN 0-8357-1807-7 LC Card 87-10791 DDC 368.4/3/00973 19
HD7105.35.U6 W65 1987

Work, health, and income among the elderly /. Washington, D.C. , c1987. xiii, 276 p. : ISBN 0-8157-1176-X : LC Card 86-26892 DDC 331.3/98 19
HD6280 .W68 1987 ***NYPL [JLE 87-960]***

SOCIAL SECURITY - UNITED STATES - EVALUATION.
Boskin, Michael J. Too many promises . Homewood, Ill. , c1986. xiv, 196 p. : ISBN 0-87094-779-6 LC Card 86-70430 DDC 368.4/3/00973 19
HD7125 .B585 1986 ***NYPL [JLE 86-2970]***

SOCIAL SECURITY - UNITED STATES - FINANCE.
Chaikind, Stephen. Paying for social security . [Washington, D.C.], 1981. xix, 47 p. ; LC Card 81-601225 DDC 353.0082/56 19
HD7125 .C47 ***NYPL [JLF 86-252]***

SOCIAL SECURITY - UNITED STATES - FORECASTING.
Andrews, George H., 1932- Actuarial projections for the old-age, survivors, and disability insurance program of social security in the United States of America /. Itasca, Ill., U. S.A. , c1987. viii, 188 p. : LC Card 87-1101 DDC 368.4/301/0973 19
HC106.8 .A56 1987

SOCIAL SECURITY - UNITED STATES - HANDBOOKS, MANUALS, ETC.
Berko, Robert L. Consumers guide to Social Security benefits . South Orange, N.J. , 1986. p. cm. ISBN 0-934873-04-6 (pbk.) : LC Card 86-23933 DDC 344.73/023 347.30423 19
HD7125 .B47 1986

Getting the most from social security . Skokie, IL (3841 W. Oakton St., Skokie 60076) , c1986. 192 p. : LC Card 86-219986 DDC 344.73/023 347.30423 19
HD7125 .G43 1986

SOCIAL SECURITY - UNITED STATES - MISCELLANEA.
Rubin, Leona G. Your 1987/88 guide to social security benefits /. New York, N.Y. , c1987. 194 p. ; ISBN 0-8160-1567-8 : LC Card 86-32917 DDC 368.4/3/00973 19
HD7125 .R78 1987

SOCIAL SECURITY - UZBEK S.S.R.
Tormysheva, T. A. (Tamara Andreevna) Okhrana truda i sotsial'noe strakhovanie trudiashchikhsia v Uzbekskoĭ SSR /. Tashkent , 1987. 131 p. ; LC Card 87-107413
HD7345.U93 T67 1987

SOCIAL SERVICE - ADMINISTRATION. see **SOCIAL WORK ADMINISTRATION.**

SOCIAL SERVICE - BRAZIL.
Brazil. Ministério do Interior. Secretaria de Planejamento. Programa nacional de apoio às migrações internas /. Brasília , 1980. 42 p. ; LC Card 86-203543 DDC 362.8/5 19
HB2023 .B73 1980

SOCIAL SERVICE - FRANCE - CASE STUDIES.
Nicolas, Jean-Pierre, 1941- La pauvreté intolérable . Toulouse [1984] 208 p. : ISBN 2-86586-026-4 : LC Card 85-118841
HC280.P6 N53 1984

SOCIAL SERVICE - GREAT BRITAIN.
Men without work . New York , 1985. xii, 447 p. ; ISBN 0-8240-7619-2 (alk. paper) : LC Card 85-13069 DDC 331.13/7941 19
HD5765.A6 M46 1985 ***NYPL [JLD 87-1031]***

Page, Robert M. Stigma /. London , Boston , 1984. xii, 207 p. ; ISBN 0-7100-9786-7 : LC Card 83-24638 DDC 302/.12 19
HM291 .P25 1984 ***NYPL [JLD 86-3113]***

SOCIAL SERVICE - INDIA.
Bulsara, Jal F. (Jal Feerose), 1899- Perspectives on social welfare in India /. New Delhi , 1984. xvi, 226 p. ; LC Card 84-900869 DDC 361/.954 19
HV40 .B886 1984 ***NYPL [JLD 86-4376]***

SOCIAL SERVICE - NEW YORK (STATE) - FINANCE.
Altschuler, David M. New York nonprofit organizations . Washington, D.C. (2100 M St., N.W., Washington 20037) , c1987. vii, 43 p. : LC Card 87-159600 DDC 658.1/5 19
HD2769.2.U6 A48 1987

SOCIAL SERVICE - SWEDEN.
Örning, Birgitta. Solidaritetsarbete . Stockholm [1978?] 66 p. : LC Card 81-140576
HD7728 .O75 1978

SOCIAL SERVICE - UNITED STATES.
Helping the sexually oppressed /. Englewood Cliffs, N.J. , c1986. xix, 282 p. : ISBN 0-13-386129-5 : LC Card 85-16687 DDC 305.3 19
HN57 .H46 1986 ***NYPL [JLE 86-3217]***

Private means--public ends . New York , 1987. xiii, 187 p. ; ISBN 0-275-92429-7 (alk. paper) : LC Card 86-25251 DDC 361.6/1/0973 19
HN65 .P69 1987 ***NYPL [JLE 87-1390]***

SOCIAL SERVICE - UNITED STATES - CASE STUDIES.
Egan, Gerard. Change agent skills in helping and human service settings /. Monterey, Calif. , c1985. xi, 306 p. : ISBN 0-534-03624-4 : LC Card 84-7804 DDC 361.3/07 19
HV11 .E43 1985 ***NYPL [JLE 86-1963]***

SOCIAL SERVICE - UNITED STATES - FINANCE - COLLECTED WORKS.
Government spending and the nonprofit sector in [name of community]. Washington, D.C. , <c1984-c1985. v. <1-11 > ; LC Card 87-168173 DDC 339.5/22/0973 19
HJ2052 .G67 1984

SOCIAL STATUS - ADDRESSES, ESSAYS, LECTURES.
Gender and stratification /. Cambridge, CB, UK , Oxford, OX, UK , 1986. viii, 271 p. ; ISBN 0-7456-0167-7 : LC Card 85-28342 DDC 305.3 19
HQ1075 .G46 1986 ***NYPL [JLE 86-2966]***

SOCIAL STRATIFICATION. see **SOCIAL CLASSES.**

SOCIAL STRUCTURE - ARGENTINA.
SOCIAL STRUCTURE - AUSTRIA - HISTORY - 18TH CENTURY.
Dickson, P. G. M. (Peter George Muir) Finance and government under Maria Theresia, 1740-1780 /. Oxford [Oxfordshire] , New York , 1987. 2 v. : ISBN 0-19-822570-9 (v. 1) : LC Card 87-1614 DDC 336.436 19
HJ1059 .D52 1987

SOCIAL STRUCTURE - CHILE.
SOCIAL STRUCTURE - EUROPE - CONGRESSES.
Periphere Räume . Paderborn , 1979. 183 p. : ISBN 3-506-73204-8 LC Card 85-209554
HC240 .P38 1979

SOCIAL STRUCTURE - EUROPE - HISTORY.
Reddy, William M. Money and liberty in modern Europe . Cambridge [Cambridgeshire] , New York , 1987. xii, 264 p. ; ISBN 0-521-30445-8 LC Card 86-11709 DDC 332.4/94 19
HG922 .R43 1987 ***NYPL [JLE 87-1346]***

SOCIAL STRUCTURE - GERMANY (WEST) - BAVARIA - HISTORY.
Hesselmann, Hans. Das Wirtschaftsbürgertum in Bayern 1890-1914 . [Stuttgart] , 1985. 419 p. :

ISBN 3-515-04565-1 LC Card 86-127555
HC287.B3 H46 1985

SOCIAL STRUCTURE - GERMANY (WEST) - RUHR (REGION) - HISTORY.
Bochum, Ulrich, 1953- Industrie und Region . Frankfurt am Main , New York , c1984. 340, [38] p. : ISBN 3-8204-5550-7 LC Card 85-194544
HC288.R8 B57 1984

SOCIAL STRUCTURE - INDIA.
Gupta, S. P. (Shiv Prakash), 1957- Structural dimensions of poverty in India /. Delhi, India , 1987. xii, 427 p. : LC Card 87-901423 DDC 362.5/0954 19
HC440.P6 G86 1987

SOCIAL STRUCTURE - ITALY - TRENTINO-ALTO ADIGE.
Penz, Hugo. Das Trentino . Innsbruck , 1984. 379 p. : ISBN 3-7030-0142-9 : LC Card 86-138251
HC307.T7 P45 1984

SOCIAL STRUCTURE - PENNSYLVANIA - SCRANTON - HISTORY.
Siegenthaler, Jürg K., 1939- Konflikte der Industrialisierung . Bern , New York , c1985. 249 p. : ISBN 3-261-04012-2 LC Card 85-226977
HC398.G55 S54 1985

SOCIAL STRUCTURE - SPAIN - SAGUNTO.
Estructura social de la comarca "El Camp de Morvedre" /. Sagunt, Valencià [Madrid] , 1982. 2 v. (1133 p.) : ISBN 84-7231-763-3 (set) LC Card 85-188040
HB3620.S24 E87 1982

SOCIAL STRUCTURE - SWITZERLAND - GLARUS (CANTON) - HISTORY.
Siegenthaler, Jürg K., 1939- Konflikte der Industrialisierung . Bern , New York , c1985. 249 p. : ISBN 3-261-04012-2 LC Card 85-226977
HC398.G55 S54 1985

SOCIAL STRUCTURE - UNITED STATES.
Clark, Gordon L. Judges and the cities . Chicago , c1985. xv, 247 p. ; ISBN 0-226-10753-1 : LC Card 85-1018 DDC 306/.0973 19
HN59.2 .C57 1985 ***NYPL [JLE 86-1068]***

SOCIAL STUDIES. see **SOCIAL SCIENCES.**

Social studies resources for secondary school librarians, teachers, and students.
Davis, James E. (James Edwin), 1940- Economics . Santa Barbara, Calif. , c1988. xv, 354 p. : ISBN 0-87436-479-5 (alk. paper) LC Card 87-18670 DDC 330/.07/1273 19
HB74.5 .D39 1988

SOCIAL SURVEYS - BOLIVIA - MOJOCOYA.
Estudio cultural y socio económico de Mojocoya--Redención Pampa. Estudio cultural socio económico, Mojocoya y Redención Pampa. Sucre, Bolivia , 1979. 266 p. : LC Card 83-204567
HC183.M65 E77 1979

SOCIAL SURVEYS - BOLIVIA - RENDENCIÓN PAMPA.
Estudio cultural y socio económico de Mojocoya--Redención Pampa. Estudio cultural socio económico, Mojocoya y Redención Pampa. Sucre, Bolivia , 1979. 266 p. : LC Card 83-204567
HC183.M65 E77 1979

SOCIAL SURVEYS - BOTSWANA.
Botswana. Central Statistics Office. Guideline for designing and executing small scale surveys in Botswana. [Gaborone] [1982] 53 p. in various pagings : LC Card 83-154943 DDC 304.6/0723 19
HB849.49 .B68 1982 ***NYPL [JLG 86-217]***

SOCIAL SURVEYS - ENGLAND - YORK (NORTH YORKSHIRE)
Rowntree, B. Seebohm (Benjamin Seebohm), 1871-1954. Poverty . New York , 1980. xxi, 426 p. : ISBN 0-8240-0120-6 (alk. paper) : LC Card 79-56969 DDC 305.5/6 19
HC258.Y6 R64 1980 ***NYPL [JLD 86-3436]***

SOCIAL SURVEYS - SOVIET UNION - METHODOLOGY.
Modelirovanie sotsial'nykh faktorov v ėkonomiko-matematicheskikh issledovaniīakh /. Moskva , 1984. 148 p. : LC Card 87-125299
HC336.25. .M636 1984

SOCIAL SURVEYS - UNITED STATES - LONGITUDINAL STUDIES.
Federal longitudinal surveys /. [Washington, D.C.?] [Springfield, VA] 1986. v, 159 p. : LC Card 86-603413 DDC 001.4/33 19
HA31.2 .F43 1986

SOCIAL SYSTEMS.
Burns, Tom R. Man, decisions, society . New York , c1985. xiv, 342 p. : ISBN 2-88124-004-6 (France) LC Card 84-10303 DDC 301 19
HM24 .B85 1985 ***NYPL [JLE 86-2963]***

Czander, William M. The application of social systems thinking to organizational consulting /. Lanham , c1986. 243 p. ; ISBN 0-8191-5183-1 (alk. paper) : LC Card 85-29508 DDC 658.4/6 19
HD69.C6 C9 1986 ***NYPL [JLE 86-3269]***

Geser, Hans. Strukturformen und Funktionsleistungen sozialer Systeme . Opladen , c1983. 275 p. : ISBN 3-531-11612-6 :
NYPL [JLE 87-1162]

Vance, A. Last chance for peace . Boulder, Colo. , c1985. xviii, 256 p. : ISBN 0-930705-01-7 (pbk.) : LC Card 84-18831 DDC 172/.24 19
BL65.P4 V36 1985 ***NYPL [JLD 86-2214]***

SOCIAL SYSTEMS - CONGRESSES.
The Social fabric . Beverly Hills, Calif. , c1986. 366 p. ; ISBN 0-8039-2788-6 LC Card 86-1191 DDC 301 19
HM13 .S524 1986 ***NYPL [JLE 86-3755]***

SOCIAL VALUES.
Mathew, Mohan, 1931- Dimensions of dialogue /. St. Louis, Mo. , c1984. 136 p. ; ISBN 0-918833-00-0 (pbk.) : LC Card 84-17009 DDC 302.5/44 19
HM291 .M392 1984 ***NYPL [JLD 86-4125]***

Sowell, Thomas, 1930- A conflict of visions /. New York , c1987. 273 p. ; ISBN 0-688-06912-6 LC Card 86-18187 DDC 303.3/72 19
HM73 .S68 1987 ***NYPL [JLD 87-823]***

Tool, Marc R. Essays in social value theory . Armonk, N.Y. , c1986. xviii, 203 p. ; ISBN 0-87332-382-3 : LC Card 86-10163 DDC 306 19
HB99.5 .T66 1986 ***NYPL [JLE 86-3931]***

SOCIAL VALUES - HISTORY.
McCracken, Grant David, 1951- Culture and consumption . Bloomington , c1988. xv, 174 p. ; ISBN 0-253-31526-3 LC Card 87-45394 DDC 339.4/7 19
HC79.C6 M385 1988

SOCIAL WELFARE. see **PUBLIC WELFARE; SOCIAL PROBLEMS; SOCIAL SERVICE; CHARITIES.**

Social Welfare Development Centre for Asia and the Pacific. Movement for a no poverty society . Calcutta , 1980. 78 p. ; LC Card 81-902107
HC415.P6 M68 1980

SOCIAL WORK. see **SOCIAL SERVICE.**

SOCIAL WORK ADMINISTRATION - UNITED STATES - CASE STUDIES.
Egan, Gerard. Change agent skills in helping and human service settings /. Monterey, Calif. , c1985. xi, 306 p. : ISBN 0-534-03624-4 : LC Card 84-7804 DDC 361.3/07 19
HV11 .E43 1985 ***NYPL [JLE 86-1963]***

SOCIAL WORK EDUCATION - UNITED STATES.
Egan, Gerard. Change agent skills in helping and human service settings /. Monterey, Calif. , c1985. xi, 306 p. : ISBN 0-534-03624-4 : LC Card 84-7804 DDC 361.3/07 19
HV11 .E43 1985 ***NYPL [JLE 86-1963]***

SOCIAL WORKERS - FRANCE - CASE STUDIES.
Nicolas, Jean-Pierre, 1941- La pauvreté intolérable . Toulouse [1984] 208 p. : ISBN 2-86586-026-4 : LC Card 85-118841
HC280.P6 N53 1984

SOCIAL WORKERS - SRI LANKA - BIOGRAPHY.
Subasiṃha, Vinsant. Sandalaṅkā sanda /. [Pannipitiya?] , 1986. viii, 269 p., [6] leaves of plates : LC Card 86-903022
HG1552.S83 A3 1986

SOCIAL WORKERS - UNITED STATES - ATTITUDES.
Reinarman, Craig. American states of mind . New Haven , c1987. x, 262 p. ; ISBN 0-300-03817-8 (alk. paper) LC Card 86-26752 DDC 330.12/2/0973 19
HD3616.U47 R1464 1987

Sociale en culturele studies .
(7) Enige aspecten van arbeid in de toekomst . 's-Gravenhage , 1986. 178 p. : ISBN 90-12-05246-7 LC Card 87-101491
HD5792 .E47 1986

(8) Fulpen, Hans van. Volkshuisvesting in demografisch en economisch perspectief /. 's-Gravenhage , 1985. 354 p. : ISBN 90-12-05159-2 LC Card 86-169936
HD7344.A3 F85 1985

Sociale zekerheid in Nederland /. Braakman, T. C. Utrecht , 1984. 199 p. : ISBN 90-274-5513-9 : LC Card 85-110890
HD7192 .B73 1984 ***NYPL [JLC 86-295]***

Socialforskningsinstituttet, Copenhagen. Publikationer.
(116) Kjær Jensen, Mogens. Unges boligsituation /. København , 1983. 139 p. : ISBN 87-7487-228-1 : LC Card 83-189408
HD7347.A3 K53 1983
NYPL [JLK 73-237 v.116]

Publkationer .
(138) Henriksen, Ingrid. Holdninger til den økonomiske fordeling =. København , 1985. 349 p. : ISBN 87-7487-265-6 : LC Card 85-186400
HC360.I5 S25 1985 vol. 1
NYPL [JLD 86-2002]

SOCIALISM - ADDRESSES, ESSAYS, LECTURES.
Bilancio della socialdemocrazia . Napoli , 1984. 156 p. ; LC Card 84-249837
HX73 .B55 1984 ***NYPL [JLD 87-1536]***

Civilizația socialistă . București , 1979. 289, [2] p., [1] leaf of plates : LC Card 80-460491
HX56 .C48 ***NYPL [JLD 81-195]***

Convergenze tra capitalismo e socialismo . Milano , 1978. lxxi, 399 p. ; LC Card 80-478455
HB501 .C727 ***NYPL [JLD 81-646]***

Demokratie . Berlin , 1981. 188 p. ; LC Card 81-149074 DDC 320.5/315 19
HX73 .D45 1981 ***NYPL [JLD 86-3341]***

SOCIALISM - AFRICA.
Seidman, Ann Willcox, 1926- Money, banking, and public finance in Africa /. London , Atlantic Highlands, N.J., USA , 1986. xv, 363 p. : ISBN 0-86232-429-7 LC Card 87-111822 DDC 332.1/096 19
HG187.5.A2 S45 1986

SOCIALISM - ALGERIA.
Lesbet, Djaffar. Les 1000 villages socialistes en Algérie /. Alger , Paris , c1983. 335 p. : ISBN 2-86738-008-1 : LC Card 84-156989 DDC 335/.00965 19
HX441.5.A6 L47 1983 ***NYPL [JLD 87-236]***

SOCIALISM - AMERICA - HISTORY.
Astesano, Eduardo. [Historia socialista de América.] Historia social de América /. Buenos Aires, Argentina [1982] 177 p. : ISBN 950-0-17004-3 LC Card 83-165516
HC94 .A83 1982

SOCIALISM AND RELIGION.
Morality of the market . Vancouver, B.C., Canada , c1985. xxv, 601 p. ; ISBN 0-88975-074-2 (pbk.) : LC Card 86-158049 DDC 174/.4 19
HB72 .M56 1985

SOCIALISM AND YOUTH - BULGARIA.
Izsledvane rolīata na proizvodstvenata sreda, trudovite kolektivi i nastavnitsite za formirane na komunisticheskо otnoshenie kŭm truda u podrastvashchtite /. Sofiīa , 1984. 150 p. ; LC Card 85-166784
HD6276.B82 I97 1984

SOCIALISM AND YOUTH - RUSSIAN S.F.S.R. - SIBERIA, EASTERN.
Sotsial'noe razvitie molodezhi v trudovykh kollektivakh novykh gorodov Sibiri . Irkutsk , 1980. 158 p. ; LC Card 82-110658
HD6276.S593 S527 1980

SOCIALISM - AUSTRALIA - HISTORY - 19TH CENTURY.
Burgmann, Verity. In our time . Sydney , Boston , 1985. xii, 236 p., [24] p. of plates : ISBN 0-86861-529-3 LC Card 84-71572 DDC 335/.00994 19
HD8846 .B87 1985 ***NYPL [JLD 86-2788]***

SOCIALISM - AUSTRIA - HISTORY - 20TH CENTURY.

Réformisme et révisionnisme dans les socialismes allemand, autrichien et français /. Paris , c1984. 195 p. ; ISBN 2-7351-0053-7 : LC Card 85-105830
HX273 .R39 1984 ***NYPL [JLE 86-4752]***

SOCIALISM - BRAZIL - MARANHÃO - HISTORY.
Corrêa, Rossini. Mudança social no Nordeste . São Luís , 1986. 176 p., [6] p. of plates : LC Card 87-152221 DDC 322/.2/098121 19
HD8289.M37 C67 1986

SOCIALISM - BULGARIA.
Georgiev, ĨAncho. Strategiia na kachestveni promeni /. Sofiia , 1986- v. <1-2 > ; LC Card 86-232319
HC403 .G465 1986

SOCIALISM - BULGARIA - VARNENSKI OKRŬG - HISTORY.
Rabotnicheskoto profsŭiuzno dvizhenie vŭv Varnenski okrŭg /. Sofiia , 1985. 348 p., [16] p. of plates : LC Card 86-111781
HD8629.V372 R37 1985

SOCIALISM - BYELORUSSIAN S.S.R. - HISTORY - 19TH CENTURY.
Bich, M. O. Rabochee dvizhenie v Belorussii v 1861-1904 gg. /. Minsk , 1983. 278 p. ; LC Card 83-182369
HD8529.B952 B52 1983
NYPL [*QM 87-2378]

SOCIALISM - CHILE.
Bossle, Lothar. Allende und der europäische Sozialismus /. Würzburg [1981?] 146 p. ; ISBN 3-88567-026-7 (pbk.) LC Card 82-149701 DDC 983/.0646/0924 19
HX197.A44 B67 1981 ***NYPL [HIF 86-2151]***

Lechner, Norbert, 1939- La conflictiva y nunca acabada construcción del orden deseado /. [Santiago, Chile] [1984] 204 p. ; ISBN 84-89401-05-5 LC Card 84-227472 DDC 320.982 19
JL2624 .L43 1984 ***NYPL [JLE 87-2137]***

Vega Tapia, Héctor. L'économie du populisme et le projet de passage au socialisme proposé par l'Unité populaire au Chili /. [Brussels] , 1984. 511 p. ; LC Card 85-146534 DDC 338.983 19
HC192 .V37 1984 ***NYPL [JLE 86-3663]***

Winn, Peter. Weavers of revolution . New York , 1986. xiv, 328 p. : ISBN 0-19-503960-2 : LC Card 85-18832 DDC 338.7/67721/098331 19
HD8039.T42 C478 1986
NYPL [JLE 86-1973]

SOCIALISM, CHRISTIAN - VENEZUELA.
Sánchez Meleán, Jorge. Reflexiones para la acción /. [Venezuela?] , 1986. xv, 322 p. : ISBN 980-232-049-8 LC Card 87-134702 DDC 338.987 19
HC237 .S275 1986

SOCIALISM - CONGRESSES.
Capitalismo riformato e sinistra . Milano , 1986. 125 p. ; ISBN 88-24-50380-2 : LC Card 86-229688
HB501 .C24265 1986

SOCIALISM - COSTA RICA.
Arias Sánchez, Oscar. Democracia, independencia y sociedad latinoamericana /. San José, Costa Rica , 1985. 100 p. ; ISBN 997-7956-09-X LC Card 87-400690 DDC 320.97286 19
HC143 .A773 1985

SOCIALISM - CUBA.
Cantón Navarro, José, 1925- Algunas ideas de José Martí en relación con la clase obrera y el socialismo /. La Habana , 1981, c1980. 174 p. ; LC Card 82-233789 DDC 320.5/31/097291 19
HX159 .C33 1981 ***NYPL [JLD 86-1423]***

SOCIALISM - DENMARK - FÅBORG (FYNS AMT) - HISTORY - 19TH CENTURY.
Venge, Mikael. Arbejdere og socialdemokrater i Faaborg omkring 1900 /. [Fåborg] , 1986. 72 p. : ISBN 87-88421-01-5 LC Card 87-144687
HD6745.F33 V46 1986

SOCIALISM - DEVELOPING COUNTRIES.
Ėkonomicheskie problemy razvitiia stran sotsialisticheskoĭ orientatsii /. Moskva , 1986. 239 p. ; LC Card 86-221922
HC59.7 .E355 1986

Rangel Guevara, Carlos. [Tercermundismo. English.] Third world ideology and Western reality . New Brunswick , c1986. xiii, 180 p. ; ISBN 0-88738-601-6 (pbk.) LC Card 85-24486 DDC 330.9172/4 19
HC59.7 .R26513 1985 ***NYPL [JLE 86-3009]***

The Socialist Third World . Oxford, UK , New York, NY , 1987. vii, 333 p. : ISBN 0-631-13442-5 : LC Card 87-5165 DDC 338.9/009172/4 19
HC59.7 .S5857 1987

SOCIALISM - DEVELOPING COUNTRIES - CONGRESSES.
Sovetsko-v'etnamskiĭ simpozium na temu "Ėkonomicheskie problemy perekhoda k sotsializmu" (1984 : Moscow, R.S.F.S.R.) Ėkonomicheskie problemy perekhoda k sotsializmu stran s nerazvitoĭ ėkonomikoĭ . [Moskva , 1986. 254 p. ; LC Card 87-108102
HC444 .S69 1984

SOCIALISM - ECUADOR - HISTORY - 20TH CENTURY.
Capelo C., J. Alejo (J. Alejo Capelo Cabello), d. 1973. El crimen del 15 de noviembre de 1922 /. [Guayaquil] , 1983. 10, 14, 19 p. : LC Card 86-114097
HD5358.A6 C36 1983

Puig Vilazar, Carlos. Sacrificio de un pueblo, 15 de noviembre de 1922 /. [Guayaquil, Ecuador] , 1983. 88 p. ; LC Card 86-115462
HD5358.A6 P85 1983

SOCIALISM - ETHIOPIA.
Alemneh Dejene. Peasants, agrarian socialism, and rural development in Ethiopia /. Boulder , 1987. xiii, 162 p. : ISBN 0-8133-7247-X (pbk. : alk. paper) LC Card 86-51527 DDC 338.1/0963 19
HD2124.5 .A79 1987

SOCIALISM - EUROPE.
Azevedo, J. Cândido de. Portugal, Europa face ao Mercado Comum . Amadora , c1978. 300 p. ; LC Card 80-121153
HC241.25.P6 A94 1978

Bossle, Lothar. Allende und der europäische Sozialismus /. Würzburg [1981?] 146 p. ; ISBN 3-88567-026-7 (pbk.) LC Card 82-149701 DDC 983/.0646/0924 19
HX197.A44 B67 1981 ***NYPL [HIF 86-2151]***

Glotz, Peter, 1939- Manifest für eine Neue Europäische Linke /. Berlin , c1985. 112, [1] p. ; ISBN 3-88680-162-4 LC Card 86-100474 DDC 320.5/31/094 19
HX238.5 .G56 1985 ***NYPL [JLD 87-1162]***

La Izquierda europea . Barcelona , 1985. 282 p. ; ISBN 84-307-7438-6 LC Card 86-186087
HX238.5 .I97 1985 ***NYPL [JLD 86-4090]***

SOCIALISM - EUROPE, EASTERN.
Rabochiĭ klass i stroitel'stvo sotsializma v stranakh TSentral'noĭ i IUgo-Vostochnoĭ Evropy /. Moskva , 1977. 382 p. ; LC Card 81-174150
HD8376.5 .R33 1977

Socialist economy and economic policy /. Wien , New York , 1985. 279 p. : ISBN 0-387-81903-7 (pbk.) LC Card 86-201536
HC704 .S557 1985

SOCIALISM - EUROPE - HISTORY.
Kloppenberg, James T. Uncertain victory . New York , 1986. x, 546 p. ; ISBN 0-19-503749-9 : LC Card 85-21636 DDC 320.5/315/094 19
JA84.E9 K57 1986 ***NYPL [JLE 86-2574]***

SOCIALISM - FRANCE.
The French socialists in power, 1981-1986 /. New York , c1987. xii, 212 p. ; ISBN 0-313-25407-9 (lib. bdg. : alk. paper) LC Card 86-33569 DDC 338.944 19
HC276.2 .F699 1987

Naville, Pierre. La maîtrise du salariat /. Paris , c1984. 153 p. ; ISBN 2-7157-1099-2 : LC Card 85-100916
HD6957.F8 N38 1984 ***NYPL [JLD 87-333]***

Poncins, Michel de. Tous capitalistes, ou, La réponse au socialisme /. Vouillé [France] , c1983. 164 p. ; LC Card 83-244442 DDC 338.944 19
HC276.2 .P63 1983 ***NYPL [JLD 86-427]***

Tuppen, John N. France under recession, 1981-1986 /. Albany , c1988. p. cm. ISBN 0-88706-580-5 LC Card 87-1980 DDC 338.944 19
HC276.3 .T86 1988

Walter, Jean Jacques, 1932- Main basse sur la France /. Paris , c1984. 252 p. ; ISBN 2-7103-0188-1 LC Card 84-231340 DDC 335/.00944 19
HX264 .W36 1984 ***NYPL [JLD 86-1773]***

SOCIALISM - FRANCE - HISTORY.
Hilden, Patricia. Working women and socialist politics in France, 1880-1914 . Oxford [Oxfordshire] , New York , 1986. viii, 307 p. ; ISBN 0-19-821935-0 : LC Card 85-15487 DDC 331.4/877/0094428 19
HD6073.T42 F84 1986
NYPL [JLD 86-1838]

Moss, Bernard H. [Origins of the French labor movement, 1830-1914. French.] Aux origines du mouvement ouvrier français . Paris , 1985. xi, 236 p. ; ISBN 2-251-60326-3
NYPL [M-10 6410 n.326]

Rice-Maximin, Edward Francis, 1941- Accomodation and resistance . New York , 1986. xi, 175 p. ; ISBN 0-313-25355-2 (lib. bdg. : alk. paper) LC Card 86-4624 DDC 959.704/1 19
DS553.1 .R53 1986 ***NYPL [JFE 87-1024]***

SOCIALISM - FRANCE - HISTORY - 20TH CENTURY.
Réformisme et révisionnisme dans les socialismes allemand, autrichien et français /. Paris , c1984. 195 p. ; ISBN 2-7351-0053-7 : LC Card 85-105830
HX273 .R39 1984 ***NYPL [JLE 86-4752]***

SOCIALISM - GERMANY.
Kautsky, Karl, 1854-1938. [Agrarfrage. English.] The agrarian question /. London , Atlantic Highlands, N.J. , 1988- p. cm. ISBN 1-85305-024-5 (v. 2) LC Card 87-20593 DDC 338.1 19
HD1306.G3 K315 1988

SOCIALISM - GERMANY (EAST)
Auf sicherem Kurs . [Berlin] [1976] 80 leaves (some folded) : LC Card 85-190579
HC290.78 .A84 1976

Florath, Walter, 1925- Der Typ ist richtig . Berlin , c1986. 151 p. : ISBN 3-355-00005-1 LC Card 86-230122
HC290.78 .F57 1986

Im Blickpunkt der Leistungsvergleich /. Berlin , 1985. 126 p. ; LC Card 85-155570
HC270.28 .I56 1985

SOCIALISM - GERMANY (EAST) - CONGRESSES.
Kolloquium 20 Jahre Weiterbildungs- und Forschungsarbeit (1987 : Leipzig, Germany) Kolloquium 20 Jahre Weiterbildungs- und Forschungsarbeit . [Leipzig] , 1986. 64 p. ; LC Card 87-408852 DDC 338.9431 19
HC290.78 .K64 1987

SOCIALISM - GERMANY - HISTORY - 20TH CENTURY.
Réformisme et révisionnisme dans les socialismes allemand, autrichien et français /. Paris , c1984. 195 p. ; ISBN 2-7351-0053-7 : LC Card 85-105830
HX273 .R39 1984 ***NYPL [JLE 86-4752]***

SOCIALISM - GERMANY - HISTORY - ADDRESSES, ESSAYS, LECTURES.
Solidargemeinschaft und Klassenkampf . Frankfurt am Main , 1986. 382 p. ; ISBN 3-518-11363-1 ***NYPL [JLC 86-423]***

SOCIALISM - GERMANY, WEST.
Ökologie und Sozialismus . Köln , c1986. 369 p. ; ISBN 3-7663-0983-8 LC Card 87-107373 DDC 363.7/056/0943 19
HC290.E5 O39 1986

SOCIALISM - GERMANY (WEST) - OSTHOLSTEIN - HISTORY.
Rüdel, Holger. Landarbeiter und Sozialdemokratie in Ostholstein, 1872 bis 1878 . Neumünster , 1986. 581 p. ; ISBN 3-529-02909-2 LC Card 87-119718 DDC 331.88/13/0943512 19
HD6699.O88 R83 1986

SOCIALISM - GREAT BRITAIN.
Cole, George Douglas Howard, 1889-1959. The next ten years in British social and economic policy /. New York , 1985. xxi, 459 p. ; ISBN 0-8240-7607-9 (alk. paper) : LC Card 85-13055 DDC 338.941 19
HC256.3 .C6 1985 ***NYPL [JLD 86-3300]***

Socialist enterprise . gottingham , Atlantic Highlands [1987] p. cm. ISBN 0-85124-460-2

LC Card 86-29699 DDC 338.941 19
HC256.6 .S629 1987

SOCIALISM - GREAT BRITAIN - HISTORY.
Hobsbawm, E. J. (Eric J.), 1917- Worlds of labour . London , c1984. x, 369 p., [4] p. of plates : ISBN 0-297-78509-5 : LC Card 86-674019
HD8388 .H63x 1984

Marx, Roland. La vie quotidienne en Angleterre au temps de l'expérience socialiste . [Paris] , c1983. 323 p. ; ISBN 2-01-008679-1 : LC Card 83-220426
HC256.5 .M3955 1983

SOCIALISM - GREAT BRITAIN - HISTORY - 19TH CENTURY.
Rothstein, Theodore. From chartism to labourism /. New York , 1984. vi, 365 p. ; ISBN 0-8240-5722-8 (alk. paper) : LC Card 83-48495 DDC 335/.1 19
HX249 .R68 1984 *NYPL [JLD 86-1828]*

SOCIALISM - GRENADA - HISTORY.
Pryor, Frederic L. Revolutionary Grenada . New York , 1986. xx, 395 p. : ISBN 0-275-92155-7 (alk. paper) : LC Card 86-8109 DDC 338.97298/45 19
HC156.5.Z7 G747 1986
NYPL [JLE 86-3969]

SOCIALISM - HISTORY.
Kautsky, Karl, 1854-1938. Die Vorläufer des neueren Sozialismus /. Stuttgart , 1895. 2 v. ;
NYPL [JLF 85-168]

Los problemas del socialismo en nuestra tiempo [microform]. México, 1944. 119 p. DDC 335.082
HX40 .P73 *NYPL [*ZT-1711 no.21]*

SOCIALISM - HUNGARY - HISTORY.
Berend, T. Iván (Tibor Iván), 1930- Szocializmus és reform /. Budapest , 1986. 194, [1] p. ; ISBN 963-05-4386-9 : LC Card 87-407684
HC300.28 .B475 1986

SOCIALISM IN BULGARIA.
Bâldescu, Emil. Din istoria legăturilor revoluţionare româno-bulgare (1909-1916) [microform]. [Bucureşti, 1966] 181 p. LC Card 81-475045
HD8646 .B34 *NYPL [*ZT-1732 no.1]*

SOCIALISM IN EAST GERMANY.
Berlin. Parteihochschule "Karl Marx." Lehrstuhl Wissenschaftlicher Kommunismus. Zur Entwicklung der Klassen und Schichten in der DDR /. Berlin , 1977. 147 p. ; LC Card 78-358768
HN460.5.Z9 S62 *NYPL [JLD 79-2817]*

SOCIALISM IN GERMANY - HISTORY.
Klönne, Arno. Die deutsche Arbeiterbewegung . Düsseldorf , Köln , 1980. 382 p. ; ISBN 3-424-00652-1 : LC Card 81-453558 DDC 322/.2/0943 19
HX276 .K547 *NYPL [JLD 81-689]*

SOCIALISM IN ROMANIA.
Bâldescu, Emil. Din istoria legăturilor revoluţionare româno-bulgare (1909-1916) [microform]. [Bucureşti, 1966] 181 p. LC Card 81-475045
HD8646 .B34 *NYPL [*ZT-1732 no.1]*

SOCIALISM - ITALY - LUNIGIANA - HISTORY - 20TH CENTURY.
Bianchi, Antonio. Lotte sociali e dittatura in Lunigiana storica e Versilia (1919-1930) /. [Firenze] , 1981. xii, 309 p. ; ISBN 88-22-23028-0 LC Card 82-125955
HD8489.L86 B5 1981

SOCIALISM - ITALY - VERSILIA PLAIN - HISTORY - 20TH CENTURY.
Bianchi, Antonio. Lotte sociali e dittatura in Lunigiana storica e Versilia (1919-1930) /. [Firenze] , 1981. xii, 309 p. ; ISBN 88-22-23028-0 LC Card 82-125955
HD8489.L86 B5 1981

SOCIALISM - LATIN AMERICA.
Arias Sánchez, Oscar. Democracia, independencia y sociedad latinoamericana /. San José, Costa Rica , 1985. 100 p. ; ISBN 997-7956-09-X LC Card 87-400690 DDC 320.97286 19
HC143 .A773 1985

Chilcote, Ronald H. Latin America . Boulder , 1986. xv, 175 p. ; ISBN 0-8133-0239-0 (pbk.) : LC Card 85-13899 DDC 338.98 19
HC125 .C487 1986 *NYPL [JLE 86-4264]*

SOCIALISM - LATIN AMERICA - HISTORY.
Godio, Julio. Sindicalismo y política en América Latina /. Caracas, Venezuela [1983] 315 p. ; LC Card 83-157510 DDC 322/.2/098 19
HD8110.5 .G64 1983 *NYPL [JLD 86-1758]*

SOCIALISM - MEXICO.
The Mexican Left, the popular movements, and the politics of austerity /. La Jolla, Calif. , 1986. vi, 96 p. ; LC Card 87-621353 DDC 322/.2/0972 19
HC135 .M525535 1986

SOCIALISM - MOLDAVIAN S.S.R. - HISTORY - SOURCES.
Rabochee dvizhenie v Moldavii, 1895-fevral' 1917 g. . Kishinev , 1985. 322 p. ; LC Card 86-100092
HD8529.M57 R32 1985

SOCIALISM - NETHERLANDS - HISTORY - 1849-
Op een beteren weg . Amsterdam , 1985. 239 p. : ISBN 90-6012-654-8 : LC Card 85-236523
HD8516 .O6 1985 *NYPL [JLD 86-3427]*

SOCIALISM - PORTUGAL.
Azevedo, J. Cândido de. Portugal, Europa face ao Mercado Comum . Amadora , c1978. 300 p. ; LC Card 80-121153
HC241.25.P6 A94 1978

SOCIALISM - SENEGAL.
Senegal. Présidence du Conseil du gouvernement. Direction de l'animation. Bureau d'études. Problèmes d'adaptation des structures au développement socialiste /. [Dakar?] [1962] 50 leaves ; LC Card 83-113563
HC1045 .S465 1962a

SOCIALISM - SOVIET UNION.
Popov, Mikhail V. Planomernoe razreshenie protivorechiĭ razvitiia sotsializma kak pervoĭ fazy kommunizma /. Leningrad , 1986. 156 p. ; LC Card 87-146874
HB97.5 .P7994 1986

Suvorova, M. I. (Mariia Il'inichna) Kritika Kominternom revizionistskikh vzgliadov na ėkonomiku sotsializma /. Moskva , 1985. 115 p. ; LC Card 84-219550
HB97.5 .S86 1985 *NYPL [*QIP 87-2751]*

SOCIALISM - SPAIN.
París Eguilaz, Higinio. España en el socialismo actual /. Madrid [1984?] 234 p. ; ISBN 84-398-2401-7 LC Card 87-120643
HC385 .P313 1984

SOCIALISM - SPAIN - HISTORY - 20TH CENTURY.
Nieto de Alba, Ubaldo, 1931- De la dictadura al socialismo democrático . Madrid , c1984. 269 p. ; ISBN 84-7209-177-5 LC Card 86-146735 DDC 338.946 19
HC385 .N49 1984 *NYPL [JLD 86-2390]*

SOCIALISM - TANZANIA.
Crouch, Susan C. (Susan Catherine), 1958- Western responses to Tanzanian socialism, 1967-83 /. Aldershot, Hants, England , Brookfield, Vt., USA , c1987. x, 194 p. ; ISBN 0-566-05455-8 : LC Card 87-15018 DDC 337.678 19
HF1612.9 .C76 1987

SOCIALISM - UKRAINE - ODESSA - HISTORY.
Weinberg, Robert. Social democracy and workers in Odessa . Pittsburgh, Pa. (4E23 Forbes Quad, Pittsburgh 15260) [1986] 34 p. ; LC Card 86-199472
HD8530.O32 W45 1986

SOCIALISM - UNITED STATES - HISTORY.
Kloppenberg, James T. Uncertain victory . New York , 1986. x, 546 p. ; ISBN 0-19-503749-9 : LC Card 85-21636 DDC 320.5/315/094 19
JA84.E9 K57 1986 *NYPL [JLE 86-2574]*

SOCIALISM - UNITED STATES - HISTORY - 20TH CENTURY.
Golin, Steve. The fragile bridge . Philadelphia , 1988. p. cm. ISBN 0-87722-534-6 (alk. paper) : LC Card 87-24356 DDC 331.89/287739/0974924 19
HD5325.T42 1913 .P383 1988

SOCIALISM - VIETNAM - CONGRESSES.
Sovetsko-v'etnamskiĭ simpozium na temu "Ėkonomicheskie problemy perekhoda k sotsializmu" (1984 : Moscow, R.S.F.S.R.) Ėkonomicheskie problemy perekhoda k sotsializmu stran s nerazvitoĭ ėkonomikoĭ . [Moskva , 1986. 254 p. ; LC Card 87-108102
HC444 .S69 1984

SOCIALISM - YUGOSLAVIA.
Lysestøl, Peder Martin. Jugoslavia . [Oslo] , c1985. 179 p. : ISBN 82-7094-421-1 LC Card 86-204691
HC407 .L97 1985

Socialismo autogestionario en marcha . Mérida, Venezuela , 1984. 377 p. ; LC Card 87-403553 DDC 335.43/09497 19
HB108.4.A2 S65 1984

Stojanović, Radmila. Na putu ka visoko industrijalizovanom socijalizmu /. Beograd , 1984. 208 p. ; LC Card 85-194079
HD3611 .S77 1984

SOCIALISM - ZAMBIA.
Chilivumbo, Alifeyo. Communal agrarian cooperative societies . Lusaka [1986] iii, 134 p. ; LC Card 86-981399 DDC 334/.683/096894 19
HD1491.Z35 C45 1986

SOCIALISM - ZIMBABWE.
Zimbabwe at 5 years of independence. [Harare?] [1984?] ix, 265 p. : LC Card 87-103323 DDC 338.96891 19
HC910 .Z3173 1984

Le socialisme dans l'entreprise . Boutefnouchet, Mostefa. Alger , c1978. 253 p. ; LC Card 84-207677
HD5660.A4 B68 1978

Socialismo autogestionario en marcha : textos-ULA en el área de las ciencias sociales / Jože Hočevar [compilador].Ed. no. 1. Mérida, Venezuela : Universidad de los Andes, Facultad de Economía, Consejo de Publicaciones, 1984. 377 p. ; 22 cm. (Textos de la Universidad de los Andes. Colección Ciencias sociales . [2].) Cover subtitle: El pensamiento económico de autores yugoslavos. Includes bibliographical references. LC Card 87-403553 DDC 335.43/09497 19
1. Economics - Yugoslavia. 2. Socialism - Yugoslavia. I. Hočevar, Jože. II. Series: Textos de la Universidad de los Andes. Colección Ciencias sociales , 2.
HB108.4.A2 S65 1984

El socialismo español y la cuestión agraria (1890-1936) /. Biglino Campos, Paloma. Madrid [1986?] 564 p. ; ISBN 84-7434-368-2 LC Card 87-136300
HD6764.A29 B54 1986

Socialismo y la dirección de la producción /. Gárciga Marrero, Rogelio, 1941- La Habana , 1986. 426 p. : LC Card 87-402070 DDC 658 19
HD37.S66 G385 1986

Socialist Agrarian reforms in Central Asia and Kazakhstan /. Tulepbaev, B. A. [Sotsialisticheskie agrarnye preobrazovaniia v Sredneĭ Azii i Kazakhstane. English.] Moscow , 1986. 231, [1] p. ; LC Card 86-171559
HD1995.C4 T8313 1986

Socialist agriculture in transition : organizational response to failing performance / edited by Josef C. Brada and Karl-Eugen Wadekin. Boulder, Colo. : Westview Press, 1986. ix, 445 p. : ill. ; 24 cm. (Westview special studies on the Soviet Union and Eastern Europe) Includes bibliographies. ISBN 0-8133-7344-1 : LC Card 86-28995 DDC 338.1/0947 19
1. Agriculture - Economic aspects - Europe, Eastern. 2. Agriculture - Economic aspects - Communist countries. 3. Agriculture and state - Communist countries. 4. Agriculture and communism. I. Brada, Josef C., 1942-. II. Wädekin, Karl Eugen.
HD1917 .S62 1986

SOCIALIST COMPETITION - BALTIC STATES.
Druzhba i sotrudnichestvo /. Tallin , 1985. 85 p. : LC Card 86-108625
HC243.Z9 S63 1985

SOCIALIST COMPETITION - BULGARIA.
Bliznakov, Ĭordan Petrov. Sotsialisticheskoto sŭrevnovanie v usloviiata na intenzifikatsiiata na proizvodstvoto /. Sofiia , 1983. 101 p. : LC Card 85-140845
HC403.Z9 S613 1983

SOCIALIST COMPETITION - BULGARIA - HANDBOOKS, MANUALS, ETC.
Narŭchnik na profsŭiuzniia aktivist po proizvodstveno-masovata rabota /. Sofiia , 1986. 200 p. ; LC Card 86-197739
HC403.Z9 S658 1986

SOCIALIST COMPETITION - BYELORUSSIAN S.S.R.
Druzhba i sotrudnichestvo /. Tallin , 1985. 85 p. : LC Card 86-108625
HC243.Z9 S63 1985

SOCIALIST COMPETITION - COMMUNIST COUNTRIES.
Utkin, Ė. A. (Ėduard Andreevich) Chemu uchit opyt druzeĭ /. Moskva , 1987. 141 p. ; LC Card 87-120824 DDC 658/.009171/7 19
HD70.C725 U85 1987

SOCIALIST COMPETITION - CZECHOSLOVAKIA.
Semotam, Josef. Sovietske skúsenosti v rozvoji tvorivej iniciatívy pracujúcich /. Bratislava , 1981. 153 p. ; LC Card 81-182787
HC340.I52 S45 1981 ***NYPL [*QT 86-5786]***

SOCIALIST COMPETITION - GERMANY (EAST)
DDR im Überblick. English. How socialist competition is run /. Berlin , 1983. 64 p. : LC Card 86-201752 DDC 338.6/048/09431 19
HC290.795.S6 D3713 1983

SOCIALIST COMPETITION - GERMANY (EAST) - CONGRESSES.
Sozialistischer Wettbewerb und umfassende Intensivierung . Berlin , 1986. 103 p. ; LC Card 86-200416
HC290.795.S6 S69 1986

SOCIALIST COMPETITION - LITHUANIA.
Antanaĭtis, I͡U. A. (I͡Ustinas Antanovich) Sotsialisticheskoe sorevnovanie i intensifikat͡sii͡a proizvodstva /. Moskva , 1987. 157 p. : LC Card 87-103350
HC337.L53 S63 1987

SOCIALIST COMPETITION - LITHUANIA - STATISTICAL METHODS.
Matematicheskie metody v organizat͡sii sotsialisticheskogo sorevnovanii͡a . Vil′ni͡us , 1986. 238 p. : LC Card 87-130668
HC337.L53 S65 1986

SOCIALIST COMPETITION - RUSSIA.
Semotam, Josef. Sovietske skúsenosti v rozvoji tvorivej iniciatívy pracujúcich /. Bratislava , 1981. 153 p. ; LC Card 81-182787
HC340.I52 S45 1981 ***NYPL [*QT 86-5786]***

SOCIALIST COMPETITION - RUSSIAN S.F.S.R. - URAL MOUNTAINS REGION - HISTORY - 20TH CENTURY.
Popov, V. (Vladimir) Razvitie promyshlennosti Urala na zavershai͡ushchem ėtape sozdanii͡a razvitogo sot͡sializma, 1951-1961 gg. . Perm′ , 1984. 70 p. ; LC Card 87-151346
HC337.R852 U73577 1984

SOCIALIST COMPETITION - SOVIET UNION.
Adresa svershenii͡ /] Moskva , 1980. 271 p., [16] p. of plates : LC Card 81-130832
HC336.25 .A35 1980

Babakov, V. M. (Viktor Mikhaĭlovich) Prot͡sent sverkh plana /. Volgograd , 1986. 45 p. : LC Card 86-220320
HC340.S6 B23 1986

Myt′ i vichnist′ rekordu . Kyïv , 1985. 124 p., [24] p. of plates : LC Card 86-178641
HC340.S6 M97 1985

Organizat͡sii͡a sorevnovanii͡a i sovershenstvovanie khozi͡aĭstvennogo mekhanizma /. Moskva , 1982. 206 p. ; LC Card 82-202826
HC340.S6 O684 1982

Preemstvennost′ stakhanovskikh tradit͡siĭ . Moskva , 1985. 222 p. ; LC Card 85-234107
HC340.S6 P68 1985

V.I. Lenin, KPSS o sot͡sialisticheskom sorevnovanii /. Moskva , 1985. 540 p. ; LC Card 86-128447
HC340.S6 V18 1985

Socialist enterprise : reclaiming the economy / by Diana Gilhespy ... [et al.] ; foreword by Larry Whitty. gottingham : New Socialist ; Atlantic Highlands : Spokesman, [1987] p. cm. Bibliography: p. ISBN 0-85124-460-2 LC Card 86-29699 DDC 338.941 19
1. Labour Party (Great Britain). 2. Socialism - Great Britain. I. Gilhespy, Diana.
HC256.6 .S629 1987

Socialist entrepreneurs . Szelényi, Iván. Madison, Wis. , 1988. p. cm. ISBN 0-299-11360-4 : LC Card 87-16085 DDC 338.1/09439 19
HD1940.5 .S94 1988

SOCIALIST PARTIES - POLAND - RADOM (VOIVODESHIP) - HISTORY.
Zdrojkowski, Józef. Rola partii robotniczych w życiu społeczno-politycznym Ziemi Radomskiej w latach 1930-1939 /. Radom , 1983. 168 p. : LC Card 86-100120
HD8539.R332 Z38 1983

Socialist Party of America. see **Socialist Party (U. S.)**

SOCIALIST PARTY (U. S.) - HISTORY.
Tripp, Anne Huber, 1934- The I.W.W. and the Paterson silk strike of 1913 /. Urbana , c1987. xiv, 317 p., [6] p. of plates : ISBN 0-252-01382-4 LC Card 86-24989 DDC 331.89/287739/0974924 19
HD5325.T42 1913 .P387 1987

SOCIALIST PROPERTY.
Sot͡sialisticheskai͡a sobstvennost′ v uslovii͡akh razvitogo sotsializma . Moskva , 1984. 165 p. ; LC Card 85-177805
HB701 .S59 1984

SOCIALIST PROPERTY - SOVIET UNION.
Napravlenii͡a i formy realizatsii obshchenarodnoĭ sobstvennosti /. Moskva , 1986. 171 p. ; LC Card 87-163156
HD4213 .N36 1986

Obshchestvennyĭ kharakter proizvodstva i sotsialisticheskai͡a sobstvennost′ /. Moskva , 1985. 286 p. ; LC Card 85-173513
HC340.I52 O27 1985

Sot͡sialisticheskai͡a sobstvennost′ v uslovii͡akh razvitogo sotsializma . Moskva , 1984. 165 p. ; LC Card 85-177805
HB701 .S59 1984

The Socialist Third World : urban development and territorial planning / edited by Dean Forbes and Nigel Thrift. Oxford, UK ; New York, NY : B. Blackwell, 1987. vii, 333 p. : ill. ; 24 cm. Bibliography: p. [303]-322. Includes index. ISBN 0-631-13442-5 : LC Card 87-5165 DDC 338.9/009172/4 19
1. Developing countries - Economic policy. 2. Developing countries - Economic conditions. 3. Regional planning - Developing countries. 4. Socialism - Developing countries. I. Forbes, D. K. (Dean K.). II. Thrift, N. J.
HC59.7 .S5857 1987

Socialist Unity Party of Germany. see **Sozialistische Einheitspartei Deutschlands.**

Socialistička Federativna Republika Jugoslavije. see **Yugoslavia.**

SOCIALISTS - BIOGRAPHY - DICTIONARIES.
Maitron, Jean. Dictionnaire biographique du mouvement ouvrier international. Paris, 1971-<c1985. <1-2, 5 > ISBN 2-7082-1955-3 (v. 2) LC Card 72-333529
HD4851 .M34

SOCIALISTS - GREAT BRITAIN - BIOGRAPHY.
Brown, J. Gordon. Maxton /. Edinburgh , 1986. 336 p., [8] p. of plates : ISBN 1-85158-042-5 ***NYPL [JFE 87-30]***

SOCIALISTS - SWITZERLAND - BIOGRAPHY.
Tschudin, Paul, 1904- Meine Ehre ist nicht die Eure! . Basel , 1986. 217 p. ; ISBN 3-85990-069-2 LC Card 87-137660 DDC 331.88/092/4 B 19
HD6772.5.T74 A3 1986

SOCIALIZATION OF INDUSTRY. see **GOVERNMENT OWNERSHIP.**

SOCIALIZATION, POLITICAL. see **POLITICAL SOCIALIZATION.**

SOCIALIZED MEDICINE. see **INSURANCE, HEALTH.**

SOCIALLY HANDICAPPED YOUTH - EMPLOYMENT - AUSTRALIA - PILBARA (W.A. : REGION)
Ladbrook, Denis A. Disadvantaged youth in an isolated region . [Pilbara, W.A.] [1985] ix, 125 p. : LC Card 87-121044 DDC 331.3/4/099413 19
HD6276.A83 P555 1985

SOCIALLY HANDICAPPED YOUTH - EMPLOYMENT - UNITED STATES.
Van Sickle, Larry. The American dream and the impact of class . New York, N.Y. , c1985. 389 p. ; ISBN 0-8290-1382-2 (pbk.) LC Card 83-12613 DDC 331.3/4/0973 19
HD6273 .V36 1985 ***NYPL [JLD 86-1637]***

SOCIALLY HANDICAPPED YOUTH - UNITED STATES.
Williams, Terry (Terry M.) Growing up poor /. Lexington, MA , c1985. xvi, 136 p. ; ISBN 0-669-09687-3 (alk. paper) LC Card 84-48564 DDC 362.7/044 19
HV1431 .W55 1985 ***NYPL [JLE 85-2236]***

Sociálno-ekonomický vývoj slovenského pol'nohospodárskeho obyvatel'stva /. Bauch, Vlastislav. Bratislava , 1986. 362, [5] p. ; LC Card 87-125324
HD1940.3.Z9 S573 1986

Sociedad de Alumnos del Doctorado en Derecho de la U.N.A.M. Mesa Redonda sobre la Carta de Punta del Este (1961 : Universidad Nacional Autónoma de México) Memoria del ciclo de conferencias de Mesa Redonda sobre la Carta de Punta del Este /. México , 1962. 224 p. : LC Card 85-105213
HC125 .M48 1961

Sociedad Mexicana de Planificación. Por una nueva política alimentaria /. [México, D.F.] , 1984. 114 p. ; LC Card 85-131176 DDC 338.1/9/72 19
HD9014.M62 P67 1984 ***NYPL [JLC 86-348]***

Sociedad soriana en el siglo XVIII. Pérez de Guinea, María del Carmen. Estudio sobre la sociedad soriana en el siglo XVIII . [Spain] [1982?] 296 p. ; LC Card 85-136714
HA1559.S65 P47 1982

Sociedad Unión Obreros Talabarteros (Argentina)
Balance general de huelga y administración, de noviembre 1904 á abril 1906 / Sociedad Unión Obreros Talabarteros. Buenos Aires : Tip. Schenone, 1906. 65 p. ; 18 cm. Chiefly tables. LC Card 85-203379
1. Sociedad Unión Obreros Talabarteros (Argentina) - Finance - Statistics. 2. Trade-unions - Harness making and trade - Argentina - Finance - Statistics. I. Title.
HD6604.H2 S63 1906

SOCIEDAD UNIÓN OBREROS TALABARTEROS (ARGENTINA) - FINANCE - STATISTICS.
Sociedad Unión Obreros Talabarteros (Argentina) Balance general de huelga y administración, de noviembre 1904 á abril 1906 /. Buenos Aires , 1906. 65 p. ; LC Card 85-203379
HD6604.H2 S63 1906

A sociedade amazônica e o problema social da desocupação e subocupação /. Silva, Maria José Oliveira e. Belém , 1974. 42 p., 53 leaves : LC Card 86-183026
HB3564.A73 S55 1974

Sociedade Anônima Central Elétrica Rio Claro. Marsiglia, Cecília. S/A Central Elétrica Rio Claro /. São Paulo , 1986. 105 p. : LC Card 87-404945 DDC 363.6/2/098161 19
HD9685.B83 C4886 1986

Sociedade Brasileira de Defesa da Tradição, Família e Propriedade. Oliveira, Plinio Corrêa de, 1908- A propriedade privada e a livre iniciativa no tufão agro-reformista /. [São Paulo] [1985] xvi, 174 p., [16] p. of plates : LC Card 87-104428
HD1333.B6 O385 1985

Sociedades cooperativas, plan de cuentas . Soto Carniago, Juan José de. Cáceres , 1984. xv, 150 p. ; ISBN 84-600-3441-0 LC Card 84-221264
HF5686.C67 S67 1984

Sociedades de garantía recíproca . Charro Valls, José María. Salamanca, España , 1985. 73 p. ; ISBN 84-7481-349-2 LC Card 87-133330
HG5634.5 .C47 1985

Società di terziario avanzato e professionalità : studio di casi su modelli imprenditoriali-organizzativi e profili professionali in tre comparti di servizio alla produzione. Roma : Istituto per lo sviluppo della formazione professionale dei lavoratori, [1984] 159 p. : ill. ; 24 cm. (Quaderni di formazione ISFOL, 0390-3532 . n. 6/84 (nov., dic. 1984)) Bibliography: p. 139-140. LC Card 85-232870
1. Business consultants - Training of - Italy - Case studies. 2. Corporate planning - Italy - Case studies. I.

Istituto per lo sviluppo della formazione professionale dei lavoratori. II. Series: Quaderni di formazione ISFOL , n. 84/6.
HD69.C6 S66 1984

SOCIETÀ EDISON.
Energia e sviluppo . Torino , c1986. xii, 346 p., [16] p. of plates : ISBN 88-06-59444-3 : LC Card 86-214309
HD9685.I84 S574 1986

La società italiana . Barberis, Corrado. Milano, Italy [1984?] 382 p. ; LC Card 85-201583
HC305 .B365 1984

Società italiana di demografia storica. La Popolazione italiana nell'Ottocento . Bologna [1985] xxv, 534 p. : LC Card 86-157672
HB3599 .P663 1985

Società svizzera di scienze morali. see **Schweizerische Geisteswissenschaftliche Gesellschaft.**

Societas Jesu. see **Jesuits.**

Societas (Privat (Firm))
Maris, Bernard. Eléments de politique économique . Toulouse , c1985. 235 p. : ISBN 2-7089-7608-7 : LC Card 85-160415 DDC 338.944 19
HC276.2 .M355 1985 ***NYPL [JLE 87-642]***

Societé américaine de psychologie. see **American Psychological Association.**

SOCIÉTÉ COTONNIÈRE DU TCHAD.
Société cotonnière du Tchad. Direction générale. Douze années de Cotontchad, 1971-1983 . N'Djaména [1984] 30 leaves ; LC Card 86-980210
HD9087.C474 S637 1984

Société cotonnière du Tchad. Direction générale.
Douze années de Cotontchad, 1971-1983 : informations et statistiques / Société cotonnière du Tchad, Présidence, Direction générale. N'Djaména : La Direction, [1984] 30 leaves ; 30 cm. Cover title. "Juillet 1984." LC Card 86-980210
1. Société cotonnière du Tchad. 2. Cotton trade - Chad. I. Title.
HD9087.C474 S637 1984

Société d'économetrie. see **Econometric Society.**

Société des baïonnettes, un regard nouveau.
Mathon, Alix. [Haïti, un cas.] Haïti, un cas /. [Port-au-Prince? , 1985] (Port-au-Prince, Haïti : Impr. Le Natal) 172, 271 p. ; LC Card 86-139806 DDC 330.97294 19
HC153 .M38 1985 ***NYPL [Sc D 86-555]***

Société d'études pour le développement économique et social (France) Evaluation du développement rural /. [Paris] , c1982. 201 p. : ISBN 2-11-084484-1 LC Card 84-134740
HC59.72.E44 E93 1982

Société d'études techniques et économiques (France) Economic transportation survey. [Paris] [Courbevoie, Seine] , 1966. 3 v. : LC Card 87-125917
HE373.I75 E36 1966

Société financière internationale. see **International Finance Corporation.**

Société List. see **List-Gesellschaft.**

Société suisse des sciences humaines. see **Schweizerische Geisteswissenschaftliche Gesellschaft.**

Société suisse des sciences morales. see **Schweizerische Geisteswissenschaftliche Gesellschaft.**

Les sociétés multinationales . Descamps, Eugène, 1922- Lyon [1985] 164 p. : ISBN 2-85008-062-4 : LC Card 86-168493
HD2755.5 .D47 1985

SOCIETIES, COOPERATIVE. see **COOPERATIVE SOCIETIES.**

SOCIETY AND ADVERTISING. see **ADVERTISING - SOCIAL ASPECTS.**

Society and family strategy . Stern, Mark J. Albany, N.Y. , c1987. xiv, 172 p. : ISBN 0-88706-495-7 LC Card 86-23121 DDC 304.6/34/0974796 19
HB935.N7 S74 1987

SOCIETY AND RELIGION. see **RELIGION AND SOCIOLOGY.**

SOCIETY AND TELECOMMUNICATION. see **TELECOMMUNICATION - SOCIAL ASPECTS.**

SOCIETY AND TRANSPORTATION. see **TRANSPORTATION - SOCIAL ASPECTS.**

Society for Economic Anthropology (U. S.)
Entrepreneurship and social change /. Lanham, MD [S.l.] , c1986. 275 p. : ISBN 0-8191-5165-3 (alk. paper) : LC Card 85-26533 DDC 338/.04 19
HB615 .E629 1986 ***NYPL [JLD 86-3073]***

Society for Ethnic Amity (Sri Lanka)
Discrimination or development?. Colombo, Sri Lanka [1985?] vii, 40 p. ; LC Card 85-904128 DDC 338.9549/3 19
HC424 .D53 1985

Society for Risk Analysis.
Risk assessment and management /. New York , c1987. xii, 740 p. : ISBN 0-306-42683-8 LC Card 87-21288 DDC 658 19
HD61 .R5684 1987

Society for Risk Analysis International Workshop on Uncertainty in Risk Assessment, Risk Management, and Decision Making (1984 : Knoxville, Tenn.) Uncertainty in risk assessment, risk management, and decision making /. New York , c1987. x, 538 p. : ISBN 0-306-42557-2 LC Card 87-2403 DDC 658 19
HD61 .S625 1984

Society for Risk Analysis International Workshop on Uncertainty in Risk Assessment, Risk Management, and Decision Making (1984 : Knoxville, Tenn.)
Uncertainty in risk assessment, risk management, and decision making / edited by Vincent T. Covello ... [et al.]. New York : Plenum Press, c1987. x, 538 p. : ill. ; 26 cm. (Advances in risk analysis . v. 4) "Proceedings of the Society for Risk Analysis International Workshop on Uncertainty in Risk Assessment, Risk Management, and Decision Making, held September 30-October 3, 1984, in Knoxville, Tennessee"--T.p. verso. Includes bibliographical references and index. ISBN 0-306-42557-2 LC Card 87-2403 DDC 658 19
1. Risk management - Congresses. 2. Risk - Congresses. 3. Uncertainty - Congresses. I. Covello, Vincent T. II. Society for Risk Analysis. III. Title. IV. Series.
HD61 .S625 1984

SOCIETY FOR WORLDWIDE INTERBANK FINANCIAL TELECOMMUNICATION.
Loh, Wolfram W. Das S.W.I.F.T.-System . Frankfurt am Main , c1983. vii, 198 p. : ISBN 3-7819-0285-4 : LC Card 83-211180
HG1708.5 .L64 1983

Society now.
McNeill, Patrick. Research methods /. London , New York , 1985. 136 p. ; ISBN 0-422-79540-2 (pbk.) LC Card 85-4656 DDC 301/.072 19
HM24 .M37 1985 ***NYPL [JLD 86-4181]***

Society of Actuaries. Actuarial mathematics /. Itasca, Ill. , 1986. xxiii, 624 p. ; ISBN 0-938959-10-7 LC Card 86-61747 DDC 368/.01 19
HG8781 .A26 1986

Society of Jesus. see **Jesuits.**

Society of Management Accountants of Canada. Accounting Principles and Practices Committee.
Brooks, Leonard J. Canadian corporate social performance . Hamilton, Ont. , 1986. xii, 267 p. : ISBN 0-920212-54-9 (pbk.) LC Card 87-100492 DDC 658.4/08/0971 19
HD60.5.C2 B76 1986

Burke, Richard C. Decision making in complex times . Hamilton, Ont. , 1984. xii, 185 p. : ISBN 0-920212-27-1 (pbk.) LC Card 85-154342 DDC 658.4/08 19
HD60 .B86 1984 ***NYPL [JLD 86-2720]***

Butterworth, John E. Financial reporting . Hamilton, Ont. , 1986. viii, 250 p. : ISBN 0-920212-52-2 (pbk.) LC Card 87-101758 DDC 657/.86203 19
HF5686.P3 B87 1986

Society of Management Accountants of Canada. Research Studies Committee. Ahmed, Mumtaz. Project management . Hamilton, Ont. [1986] xv, 254 p. : ISBN 0-920212-56-5 (pbk.) LC Card 87-158681 DDC 658.4/04 19
HF5635 .A26 1986

A socio-cultural investigation into the use and functioning of the completed shallow wells in Nyanza Province /. Kenya. Lake Basin Development Authority. Kisumu, [Kenya] , 1983. 2 v. ; LC Card 84-983298 DDC 333.91/009676/29 19
HD1699.K42 N935 1983
NYPL [JLF 86-575]

A sócio-economia do semi-árido /. Leite, José Alfredo A. João Pessoa , 1985. 47 p. : LC Card 87-141315 DDC 330.981/33/063 19
HD1875.P34 L45 1985

Socio-economic and marketing study of municipal fishing households, Bayawan, Negros Oriental, Philippines. Manila, Philippines : Ministry of Natural Resources, Bureau of Fisheries and Aquatic Resources and South China Sea Fisheries Development and Coordinating Programme, [1983] vii, 94, 7 p. : ill. ; 28 cm. (Work plan implementation (working paper) . SCS/83/WP/121) "September 1983." LC Card 86-225887
1. Fishers - Philippines - Bayawan. 2. Households - Philippines - Bayawan. 3. Cost and standard of living - Philippines - Bayawan. 4. Fish trade - Philippines - Bayawan. 5. Fishery products - Philippines - Bayawan - Marketing. I. Philippines. Bureau of Fisheries and Aquatic Resources. II. South China Sea Fisheries Development and Coordinating Programme. III. Series.
HD8039.F652 P67 1983

Socio-economic and policy implications of energy price increases /. Pereira, A. (Armand) Aldershot, Hants, England , Brookfield, Vt., USA , c1987. xxiv, 317 p. ; ISBN 0-566-05520-1 : LC Card 87-11955 DDC 338.2/3 19
HD9560.4 .P37 1987

Socio-economic aspects of integrated resource management, with special reference to the forest resources of Kassala Province, Eastern Region . Abu Sin, M. E. (Mohad E.) Khartoum , 1986. vi leaves, 109 p. : LC Card 87-980440 DDC 333.75/09629/2 19
HD9767.S843 K3724 1986

Socio-economic change in Kerala /. Verghese, K. E. New Delhi , 1986. x, 211 p. ; ISBN 81-7024-061-1 : LC Card 86-903145 DDC 330.954/83 19
HC437.K645 V47 1986

Socio-Economic Council. see **Sociaal-Economische Raad.**

Socio-economic determinants of food consumption and production in rural Sierra Leone . Strauss, John, 1951- East Lansing, Mich. , 1983. vi, 91 p. : LC Card 83-622388 DDC 339.4/8664/00724 19
HD9017.S52 S88 1983 ***NYPL [JLF 86-684]***

Socio economic fact book of Mindanao. Socio economic factbook of Mindanao. Davao City, Philippines [1985] 568 p. ; LC Card 85-234433
HA4617.M56 S63 1985

Socio economic factbook of Mindanao. Davao City, Philippines : Alternate Resource Center, [1985] 568 p. ; 22 cm. Includes bibliographies. LC Card 85-234433
1. Mindanao Island (Philippines) - Statistics. 2. Mindanao Island (Philippines) - Economic conditions - Statistics. 3. Population - Philippines - Mindanao Island. I. Alternate Resource Center (Davao City, Philippines). II. Title: Socio economic fact book of Mindanao.
HA4617.M56 S63 1985

La sociodynamique . Fauvet, Jean-Christian. Paris , 1983. 210, [5] p. : ISBN 2-7081-0524-8 : LC Card 83-152909
HF5549 .F34 1983

Socioeconomic aspects of renewable energy technologies : a study prepared for the International Labour Office within the framework of the World Employment Programme / edited by Ramesh Bhatia and Armand Pereira in collaboration with Madhura Swaminathan. New York : Praeger, 1988. p. cm. Bibliography: p. Includes index. ISBN 0-275-92851-9 (alk. paper) : LC Card 87-22890 DDC 333.7/09172/4 19
1. Renewable energy sources - Developing countries - Case studies. 2. Alcohol fuel industry - Developing countries - Case studies. 3. Irrigation pumps - Developing countries - Case studies. I. Bhatia, Ramesh, 1944-. II. Pereira, A. (Armand). III. Swaminathan, Madhura. IV. International Labour Organisation. V.

World Employment Programme.
HD9502.D442 S63 1988

Sociología del trabajo en Canet de Berenguer /. Pellicer Valero, Jesús-Agustín. Valencia , 1984. 80 p. : ISBN 84-600-3540-9 LC Card 86-216439
HD5808.C33 P45 1984

Sociologia (Franco Angeli editore) . (87) Pacifici, Giorgio. Il futuro presente . Milano, Italy , c1985. 201 p. ; LC Card 86-127322 DDC 384/.0945 19
HE8174 .P33 1985

SOCIOLOGICAL PREDICTION. see **SOCIAL PREDICTION.**

Sociologie des Brazzavilles noires /. Balandier, Georges. Paris , c1985. xviii, 306 p., [2] leaves of plates : ISBN 2-7246-0524-1 : LC Card 86-138199
HB2125.B73 B34 1985

SOCIOLOGISTS - BRAZIL - BIOGRAPHY. Semana Josué de Castro e a nova geografia da fome, Rio de Janeiro, 19-24 de setembro de 1983 . [S.l. , 1983] 90 leaves : LC Card 86-201115
HD9000.5 .S3968 1983

SOCIOLOGY. Here and with local subdivision are entered works on the discipline of sociology. Works on the social conditions of particular regions, countries, cities, etc., are entered under the name of the place subdivided by Social conditions.

SOCIOLOGY AND MEDICINE. see **SOCIAL MEDICINE.**

SOCIOLOGY AND RELIGION. see **RELIGION AND SOCIOLOGY.**

SOCIOLOGY - BIOGRAPHICAL METHODS. Deppe, Wilfried. Drei Generationen Arbeiterleben . Frankfurt/Main , New York , c1982. 419 p. ; ISBN 3-593-33018-0 LC Card 82-167833 DDC 305.5/62/0922 19
HD6957.G3 D38 1982 *NYPL [JLD 86-2569]*

Mihçiyazgan, Ursula. Wir haben uns vergessen . Hamburg , c1986. 428 p. ; ISBN 3-923002-30-0 : LC Card 87-104026
HD8458.T9 M54 1986

SOCIOLOGY, CHRISTIAN - MODERN, 1500- see **SOCIOLOGY, CHRISTIAN.**

SOCIOLOGY, CHRISTIAN (CATHOLIC) Antoncich, Ricardo. [Cristianos ante la injusticia. English.] Christians in the face of injustice . Maryknoll, N.Y. , c1987. xvi, 181 p. ; ISBN 0-88344-413-5 (pbk.) LC Card 86-23529 DDC 261.8 19
BX1753 .A5813 1987 *NYPL [JLE 87-1051]*

SOCIOLOGY, CHRISTIAN (CATHOLIC) - CONGRESSES. Soziallehre der Kirche und katholische Verbände /. Köln , 1980. 244 p. ; ISBN 3-7616-0568-4 (pbk.) : LC Card 81-122896 DDC 306/.6/0943 19
HN39.G3 S693 *NYPL [JLC 86-231]*

SOCIOLOGY, CHRISTIAN - UNITED STATES - HISTORY. Winters, Donald E. The soul of the wobblies . Westport, Conn. , 1985. 159 p. ; ISBN 0-313-24472-3 (lib. bdg.) LC Card 84-27973 DDC 331.88/6 19
HD8055.I5 W56 1985 *NYPL [JLD 87-775]*

SOCIOLOGY - COLOMBIA - HISTORY. Consuegra Higgins, José. El pensamiento económico colombiano /. Bogotá, Colombia , 1984. 216 p. ; LC Card 84-200191 DDC 330/.09861 19
HB123.C6 C662 1984 *NYPL [JLC 87-88]*

SOCIOLOGY - CONGRESSES. Normengeleitetes Verhalten in den Sozialwissenschaften /. Berlin , c1984. 199 p. ; ISBN 3-428-05622-1 LC Card 86-140299
HB74.P8 N67 1984

The Social fabric . Beverly Hills, Calif. , c1986. 366 p. ; ISBN 0-8039-2788-6 LC Card 86-1191 DDC 301 19
HM13 .S524 1986 *NYPL [JLE 86-3755]*

SOCIOLOGY, DESCRIPTIVE. see **SOCIAL HISTORY.**

SOCIOLOGY - HISTORY. Here are entered works on the history of sociology as a discipline. Works on the social history and conditions are entered under the heading Social history and under names of regions, countries, cities, etc., subdivided by Social conditions.
Korostelev, Gennadiĭ Mikhaĭlovich. Burzhuaznye kontseptsii narodonaseleniia . Moskva , 1981. 158 p. ; LC Card 82-140945
HB851 .K65 1981

Sociology in focus series. Horne, John (John D.) Work, employment, and unemployment /. London , New York , 1988. p. cm. ISBN 0-582-35499-4 (pbk.) LC Card 87-3671 DDC 306/.36 19
HD4901 .H66 1988

SOCIOLOGY, INDUSTRIAL. Borucki, Zenon. Osobowość a przystosowanie zawodowe marynarza /. Wrocław , 1986. 174 p. : ISBN 83-04-02007-6 : LC Card 86-221057
HD8039.S4 B67 1986

SOCIOLOGY, MEDICAL. see **SOCIAL MEDICINE.**

SOCIOLOGY - METHODOLOGY. Geser, Hans. Strukturformen und Funktionsleistungen sozialer Systeme . Opladen , c1983. 275 p. : ISBN 3-531-11612-6 : *NYPL [JLE 87-1162]*

McNeill, Patrick. Research methods /. London , New York , 1985. 136 p. ; ISBN 0-422-79540-2 (pbk.) LC Card 85-4656 DDC 301/.072 19
HM24 .M37 1985 *NYPL [JLD 86-4181]*

Sylvan, David J., 1953- A rationalist methodology for the social sciences /. Oxford [Oxfordshire] , 1985. 188 p. : ISBN 0-631-13443-3 : LC Card 84-14480 DDC 300/.1/8 19
HM24 .S95 1985 *NYPL [JLE 86-1125]*

SOCIOLOGY, MILITARY - CONGRESSES. Disarmament and world development /. Oxford, England , New York , 1986. xiii, 306 p. ; ISBN 0-08-031309-4 : LC Card 85-19231 DDC 338.4/7355 19
JX1974 .D515 1985 *NYPL [JLE 86-3211]*

SOCIOLOGY - PHILOSOPHY. Abercrombie, Nicholas. Class, structure, and knowledge . London , 1980. 196 p. ; ISBN 0-8147-0571-5 : *NYPL [JLD 80-2963]*

SOCIOLOGY, RELIGIOUS. see **RELIGION AND SOCIOLOGY.**

Sociology, work & industry /. Watson, Tony J. London , New York , 1987. xiv, 336 p. : ISBN 0-7102-0962-2 : LC Card 86-26035 DDC 306/.36 19
HD6955 .W38 1987

Socjologia pracy : wybór tekstów / pod redakcją Macieja Dymkowskiego, Zygmunta Gałdzickiego. Wrocław : Wydawn. Politechniki Wrocławskiej, 1978. 201 p. : ill. ; 25 cm. (Skrypty / Politechnika Wrocławska) At head of title: Politechnika Wrocławska. Bibliography: p. 196-199. LC Card 81-180007
1. Industrial sociology. 2. Work - Social aspects. I. Dymowski, Maciej. II. Gałdzicki, Zygmunt. III. Series: Skrypty / Politechnika Wrocławska.
HD6955 .S66 1978

Sócrates, Jodete Rios. A cidade invade as águas : qual a questão dos mananciais? / Jodete Rios Sócrates, Marta Dora Grostein, Marta Maria Soban Tanaka. [São Paulo] : Universidade de São Paulo, Faculdade de Arquitetura e Urbanismo, 1985. 296 p., [2] folded leaves of plates : ill., maps (some col.) ; 22 cm. Summary in English. "Sinopses, edição especial, julho de 1985." Bibliography: p. 195-229. LC Card 87-118596 DDC 333.91/00981/61 19
1. Water-supply - Brazil - São Paulo Metropolitan Area. 2. Land use - Brazil - São Paulo Metropolitan Area. 3. Water conservation - Law and legislation - Brazil - São Paulo (State). 4. Land use - Law and legislation - Brazil - São Paulo (State). I. Grostein, Marta Dora. II. Tanaka, Marta Maria Soban. III. Sinopsis (São Paulo, Brazil). Special number. IV. Title.
HD1696.B84 S427 1985

SOCRATIC METHOD. see **QUESTIONING.**

Soden, Garrett. Book, Jeffrey. The one minute maniac /. Kansas City, Mo. , c1987. 140 p. : ISBN 0-8362-1260-6 (pbk.) : LC Card 87-914 DDC 658.4/093 19
HD69.T54 B66 1987

SODERAG. Carnet d'adresses /. [Pointe-à-Pitre, Guadeloupe] [1986?] 64 p. : LC Card 87-152834
HG3729.G862 C37 1986

SODERAG. Carnet d'adresses /. [Pointe-à-Pitre, Guadeloupe] [1986?] 64 p. : LC Card 87-152834
HG3729.G862 C37 1986

Södersten, Bo. Makroekonomi och stabiliseringspolitik / Bo Södersten ; under medverkan av Lennart Berg, Sten Magnusson, Bo Sandelin. [Malmö] : Liber, c1983. 363 p. : ill. ; 25 cm. Includes bibliographies and index. ISBN 91-40-05037-8 : LC Card 84-166176
1. Macroeconomics. 2. Economic stabilization - Sweden. 3. Sweden - Economic policy. I. Berg, Lennart. II. Magnusson, Sten. III. Sandelin, Bo, 1942-. IV. Title.
HB179.S8 S63 1983

Söderström, Lars, 1940- Perspektiv på fördelningspolitiken / Lars Söderström. [Stockholm] : MAS, Stiftelsen Marknadsekonomiskt alternativ för Sverige, [1984] 83 p. : ill. ; 21 cm. (Debattserien . 6) Rapport från MAS Bibliography: p. 82-83. ISBN 91-7566-068-7 LC Card 85-108552
1. Income distribution - Sweden. I. Series: Debattserien (Stiftelsen Marknadsekonomiskt alternativ för Sverige) , 6. II. Title.
HC380.I5 S62 1984

SÖDERTÄLJE (SWEDEN) - ECONOMIC CONDITIONS. Bjessmo, Lars-Erik. Industrin i Södertälje 1920-1970 . Stockholm , 1987. 236 p. ; ISBN 91-7146-468-9 LC Card 87-151742
HC378.S7 B54 1987

SÖDERTÄLJE (SWEDEN) - INDUSTRIES - HISTORY - 20TH CENTURY. Bjessmo, Lars-Erik. Industrin i Södertälje 1920-1970 . Stockholm , 1987. 236 p. ; ISBN 91-7146-468-9 LC Card 87-151742
HC378.S7 B54 1987

Soderzhanie i struktura edinogo narodno-khoziaĭstvennogo kompleksa SSSR / otvetstvennyĭ redaktor V.V. Kulikov. Moskva : "Nauka", 1986. 229 p. ; 20 cm. (Problemy sovetskoĭ ėkonomiki) At head of title: Akademiia nauk SSSR. Ordena Trudovogo Krasnogo Znameni Institut ėkonomiki. Includes bibliographical references. LC Card 87-126348
1. Soviet Union - Economic policy - 1981-. 2. Soviet Union - Economic conditions - 1976-. I. Kulikov, V. V.
HC336.25 .S643 1986

Sodruzhestvo v trude. Skruten', I. S. Spivdruzhnist' u pratsi /. Kyïv , 1982. 117 p. : LC Card 83-200434
HC337.U5 S514 1982

Sodzi, N. D. (Nathan D.) Seminar on Economic Development of the Volta Region (1983 : Ho, Ghana) The Volta Region . Accra , c1986. iii, 140 p., [13] leaves of plates : ISBN 996-497-032-3 LC Card 87-402835 DDC 338.9667 19
HC1060.Z7 V647 1983

Soehoed, A. R. (Abdoel Raoef), 1920- Industrial development during Pelita III. [Jakarta] : Dept. of Industry, [1982] 23 p. ; 24 cm. "Paper presented by A.R. Soehoed, minister of industry at the CSIS sponsored Seminar on Industry, Jakarta, Desember 10, 1981." LC Card 83-940924 DDC 338.9598 19
1. Industry and state - Indonesia. I. Indonesia. Departemen Perindustrian. II. Title. III. Title: Industrial development during Pelita three. IV. Title: Industrial development during Pelita 3.
HD3616.I53 S629 1982

Soete, Luc. Technical change and full employment /. Oxford, UK , New York, NY, USA , 1987. vii, 279 p. : ISBN 0-631-14099-9 : LC Card 87-6637 DDC 331.12/5/0941 19
HD6331.2.G7 T39 1987

Der Sofortige Ausstieg ist möglich : das Sofort-Programm für den Ausstieg aus der Atomenergie. Bonn : Die Grünen im Bundestag, [1986] 35 cm : ill. (some col.) ; 29 cm. Cover title. Text: Matthias Küntzel. Bibliography: p. 34. LC Card 87-409511 DDC 333.79/24/0943 19
1. Nuclear energy - Government policy - Germany (West). 2. Nuclear industry - Germany (West). I. Küntzel, Matthias. II. Germany (West). Bundestag. Grünen.
HD9698.G42 S64 1986

Sofsky, Wolfgang. Löffler, Reiner. Macht, Arbeit und Humanität . Göttingen , c1986. v, 563 p. ; ISBN 3-921969-12-3 LC Card 86-227215
HD6957.G3 L64 1986

SOFT DRINK INDUSTRY - UNITED STATES.
Oliver, Thomas, 1950- The real Coke, the real story /. New York , 1986. 195 p. ; ISBN 0-394-55273-3 : LC Card 86-10151 DDC 338.7/66362/0973 19
HD9349.S634 C67 1986
NYPL [JLE 86-4489]

Oliver, Thomas, 1950- The real Coke, the real story /. New York , 1987, c1986. 234 p., [9] p. of plates : ISBN 0-14-010408-9 (pbk.) LC Card 87-11836 DDC 338.7/66362/0973 19
HD9349.S634 C67 1987

SOFT DRINK INDUSTRY - UNITED STATES - HISTORY.
Hoy, Anne H. Coca-Cola . Atlanta, Ga. , c1986. 159 p. : LC Card 86-209155 DDC 338.7/66362/0973 19
HD9349.S634 C64 1986

Oliver, Thomas, 1950- The real Coke, the real story /. New York , 1986. 195 p. ; ISBN 0-394-55273-3 : LC Card 86-10151 DDC 338.7/66362/0973 19
HD9349.S634 C67 1986
NYPL [JLE 86-4489]

Oliver, Thomas, 1950- The real Coke, the real story /. New York , 1987, c1986. 234 p., [9] p. of plates : ISBN 0-14-010408-9 (pbk.) LC Card 87-11836 DDC 338.7/66362/0973 19
HD9349.S634 C67 1987

SOFT DRINK INDUSTRY - WASHINGTON (STATE) - HISTORY.
Fowler, Ron. Washington sodas . Seattle , c1986. iv, 380 p. : LC Card 86-219084 DDC 338.4/766362/09797 19
HD9349.S633 U635 1986

The soft war . Barry, Tom, 1950- New York , 1988. xv, 304 p. ; ISBN 0-8021-0003-1 LC Card 87-13238 DDC 338.91/73/0728 19
HC141 .B375 1988

Software, a vital key to UK competitiveness /. Great Britain. Advisory Council for Applied Research and Development. London , 1986. viii, 87 p. : ISBN 0-11-630829-X (pbk.) : LC Card 86-209046 DDC 338.4/70053/0941 19
HD9696.C63 G74 1986

SOFTWARE, COMPUTER. see **COMPUTER PROGRAMS.**

SOFTWARE MAINTENANCE.
Eliason, Alan L. Program analysis and design . Chicago , c1987. ix, 134 p. : ISBN 0-574-18660-3 (pbk.) LC Card 87-4521 DDC 658/.055265 19
HF5548.2 .E4275 1987

Smith, Kenneth, 1932- Corporate accounting systems . Workingham, England , Reading, Mass. , c1988. p. cm. ISBN 0-201-17824-9 LC Card 87-24130 DDC 657/.028/55 19
HF5679 .S645 1988

Søgaard, Villy. Offshoreaktiviteter i Nordsøen og basebyen Esbjerg / Villy Søgaard, Inge Sofie Sørensen. [Århus] : Geografisk institut, Aarhus universitet, 1983. 200 p. : ill. ; 30 cm. (Skrifter / Geografisk institut, Aarhus universitet, 0106-827X . 42) "Rettelser": 4 p. inserted. Summary in English. Bibliography: p. 189-194. ISBN 87-88615-02-2 : LC Card 84-164755
1. Offshore oil industry - Social aspects - Denmark - Esbjerg (Kommun). I. Sørensen, Inge Sofie. II. Series: Skrifter fra Geografisk institut ved Aarhus universitet , nr. 42. III. Title.
HD9575.N62 S64 1983

Soglasovanie ėkonomicheskoĭ politiki stran SĖV / otvetstvennyĭ redaktor O.T. Bogomolov. Moskva : "Nauka", 1986. 287 p. ; 20 cm. At head of title: Akademiia nauk SSSR. Institut ėkonomiki mirovoĭ sotsialisticheskoĭ sistemy. Includes bibliographical references. LC Card 87-120408
1. Europe, Eastern - Economic policy. 2. Europe, Eastern - Economic integration. I. Bogomolov, Oleg Timofeevich. II. Institut ėkonomiki mirovoĭ sotsialisticheskoĭ sistemy (Akademiia nauk SSSR).
HC244 .S5925 1986

Sōgō Kenkyū Kaihatsu Kikō (Japan)
Tokyo Forum: Ethics of Human Survival (1985) Proceedings of the Tokyo Forum: Ethics of Human Survival . Tokyo, Japan , c1986. v, 88 p. : ISBN 4-7955-1024-5 LC Card 87-142747
HD73 .T65 1985

Workshop on Socio-economic Correlates of Mortality Differentials in Japan and ASEAN (1984 : Singapore) Socio-economic correlates of mortality in Japan and ASEAN /. Singapore , c1986. xxi, 295 p. : LC Card 86-945167 DDC 304.6/4/0952 19
HB1481 .W67 1984

Sohst, Wolfgang. Versicherungen in der Altbauerneuerung /. Berlin , c1985. 83 p. ; ISBN 3-433-02219-4 LC Card 86-104351
HG9986.4.G3 V47 1985

Soifer, Ricardo. Sercovich, Francisco Colman. Exportaciones de tecnología de Brasil y Argentina /. [Buenos Aires, Argentina?] , 1986. 269 p. ; LC Card 87-404009 DDC 338.981/06 19
HC190.T4 S47 1986

SOIL CONSERVATION DISTRICTS - POLAND - PRUSSIA, WEST - HISTORY.
Herrgeist, Fritz, 1895-1980. Die Wasser-, Boden- und Deichverbände in Ost- und Westpreussen, 1868 bis 1938 /. Köln , 1983. 524 p. : ISBN 3-7745-6456-6 LC Card 84-211844
HD1697.P64 P784 1983

SOIL CONSERVATION DISTRICTS - PRUSSIA, EAST (POLAND AND R.S.F.S.R.) - HISTORY.
Herrgeist, Fritz, 1895-1980. Die Wasser-, Boden- und Deichverbände in Ost- und Westpreussen, 1868 bis 1938 /. Köln , 1983. 524 p. : ISBN 3-7745-6456-6 LC Card 84-211844
HD1697.P64 P784 1983

SOIL CONSERVATION - ECONOMIC ASPECTS - UNITED STATES.
Ribaudo, Marc. Reducing soil erosion . Washington, D.C. , 1986. v, 24 p. : LC Card 86-603068 DDC 338.1 s 333.73 19
HD1751 .A91854 no. 561 S624.A1

SOIL CONSERVATION - GOVERNMENT POLICY - AUSTRALIA - CONGRESSES.
Land degradation . Cambridge [Cambridgeshire] , New York , c1987. p. cm. ISBN 0-521-34079-9 LC Card 87-13170 DDC 333.73/16 19
HD1036 .L36 1987

SOIL CONSERVATION - GOVERNMENT POLICY - UNITED STATES.
Webb, Shwu-Eng. Idling erodible cropland . Washington, D.C. [1986] iii, 31 p. : LC Card 86-601632 DDC 338.1 s 338.1/62 19
HD1751 .A91854 no. 550 HD256

SOIL CONSERVATION - GOVERNMENT POLICY - UNITED STATES - CONGRESSES.
Agriculture and the environment /. Washington, D.C. , c1986. xvii, 298 p. : ISBN 0-915707-33-0 (pbk.) : LC Card 87-43010 DDC 363.7/31 19
HD1755 .P47 1986

SOIL CONSERVATION - GREAT BRITAIN.
Countryside conflicts . Aldershot, Hants, England , Brookfield, Vt., U. S.A. , c1986. vi, 378 p. [4] leaves of plates : ISBN 0-566-05088-9 : LC Card 85-24603 DDC 333.76/17/0941 19
HD596 .C675 1986 *NYPL [JLD 86-2487]*

SOIL CONSERVATION - SOUTHERN STATES.
Healy, Robert G. Competition for land in the American South . Washington, D.C. , c1985. xxxii, 333 p. : ISBN 0-89164-094-0 (pbk.) LC Card 85-25459 DDC 333.76/13/0975 19
HD266.A13 H43 1985 *NYPL [JLE 86-2724]*

SOIL CONSERVATION - UNITED STATES.
Ribaudo, Marc. Reducing soil erosion . Washington, D.C. , 1986. v, 24 p. : LC Card 86-603068 DDC 338.1 s 333.73 19
HD1751 .A91854 no. 561 S624.A1

SOIL DEGRADATION - AUSTRALIA - CONGRESSES.
Land degradation . Cambridge [Cambridgeshire] , New York , c1987. p. cm. ISBN 0-521-34079-9 LC Card 87-13170 DDC 333.73/16 19
HD1036 .L36 1987

SOIL EROSION - ECONOMIC ASPECTS - UNITED STATES.
Ribaudo, Marc. Reducing soil erosion . Washington, D.C. , 1986. v, 24 p. : LC Card 86-603068 DDC 338.1 s 333.73 19
HD1751 .A91854 no. 561 S624.A1

SOIL EROSION - UNITED STATES.
Ribaudo, Marc. Reducing soil erosion . Washington, D.C. , 1986. v, 24 p. : LC Card 86-603068 DDC 338.1 s 333.73 19
HD1751 .A91854 no. 561 S624.A1

SOIL PRODUCTIVITY - ITALY - LAZIO - COLLECTED WORKS.
Produttività potenziale e classificazione dei terreni. Roma , 1985- v. <1 > in <5 > : LC Card 87-105342
HD679.L39 P76 1985

SOIL PRODUCTIVITY - ITALY - SACCO RIVER VALLEY.
Produttività potenziale e classificazione dei terreni. Roma , 1985- v. <1 > in <5 > : LC Card 87-105342
HD679.L39 P76 1985

Soisson, Jean Pierre, 1934- L'enjeu de la formation professionnelle / Jean-Pierre Soisson, Jean-François de Martel et Bruno Rémond ; préface de Raymond Barre. [Paris] : Fayard, c1986. iv, 315 p. : ill. ; 24 cm. Includes legislation. Bibliography: p. [297]-306. ISBN 2-213-01752-2 : LC Card 86-194690
1. Occupational training - France. I. Martel, Jean-François de, 1939-. II. Rémond, Bruno. III. Title.
HD5715.5.F8 S65 1986

Soiuz narodnoĭ molodezhi Bolgarii. see **Dimitrovski komunisticheski mladezhki sŭiuz.**

Soixante-quinze moyens qui ont fait leurs preuves d'augmenter vos rendements et diminuer vos coûts en publicité directe et en V.P.C.
Grémillard, Roger. 75 moyens qui ont fait leurs preuves d'augmenter vos rendements et diminuer vos coûts en publicité et en V.P.C. /. Créteil , c1982. 158 p. ; LC Card 82-238594
HF5466 .G718 1982

Soizmerenie zatrat i rezulʹtatov v teorii planovogo tsenoobrazovaniia /. Kirillov, S. R. (Sergeĭ Rufovich) Moskva , 1987. 188 p. ; LC Card 87-157208
HB235.S73 K57 1987

Sójka, Zygmunt. Polska polityka morska / Zygmunt Sójka, Zbigniew Kasprzyk. Wyd. 1. Gdańsk : Wydawn. Morskie, 1986. 237, [1] : ill. ; 21 cm. Bibliography: p. 228-[238]. ISBN 83-215-1646-7(pbk.) :
1. Shipping - Poland. 2. Harbors - Poland. 3. Merchant marine - Poland. I. Kasprzyk, Zbigniew. II. Title.
*NYPL [*QO 87-1818]*

Sojo, Ana, 1954- Rivera, Eugenio. Centroamérica, política económica y crisis /. San José, Costa Rica , c1986. 201 p. : ISBN 997-7904-37-5 LC Card 87-404079 DDC 338.9728 19
HC141 .R58 1986

Søkelys på mekanismene i oljemarkedet /. Austvik, Ole Gunnar. Oslo [1986?] 66 p. : LC Card 86-197742
HD9560.5 .A75 1986

Sokol Colloquium (8th : 1984 : University of Virginia) A Dance along the precipice . Lexington, Mass. , c1985. xxxii, 283 p. : ISBN 0-669-10899-5 (alk. paper) LC Card 85-5789 DDC 336.3/435/091724 19
HJ8899 .D36 1985 *NYPL [JLE 86-2308]*

Sokolin, William. Liquid assets : how to develop an enjoyable and profitable wine portfolio / William Sokolin. New York : Macmillan, c1987. 163 p. : ill. ; 24 cm. Bibliography: p. 158. Includes index. ISBN 0-02-612300-2 LC Card 86-31284 DDC 332.63 19
1. Wine as an investment. 2. Wine industry. I. Title.
HD9370.5 .S65 1987

Sokoloff, Georges.
L'économie de la détente : l'URSS et le capital occidental / Geoges Sokoloff. Paris : Presses de la Fondation nationale des sciences politiques, c1983. 255 p. : ill. ; 22 cm. Bibliography: p. [213]-235. ISBN 2-7246-0483-0 : LC Card 84-117643
1. Soviet Union - Commerce. 2. Soviet Union - Foreign economic relations. 3. East-West trade (1945-). I. Title.
HF3646.5 .S65 1983

[Economie de la détente. English]
The economy of détente : the Soviet Union and Western capital / Georges Sokoloff ; translated from the French by Jean Kirby.

Leamington Spa ; New York : Berg ; p. cm. Translation of: L'économie de la détente. Bibliography: p. Includes index. ISBN 0-907582-62-1 : LC Card 86-32627 DDC 382/.0947 19
1. Soviet Union - Commerce. 2. Soviet Union - Commercial policy. 3. Technology transfer - Soviet Union. 4. Technology transfer - United States. 5. East-West trade (1945-). I. Title.
HF3646.5 .S6513 1987

Sokoloff, Natalie J. Hidden aspects of women's work /. New York , 1987. x, 380 p. ; ISBN 0-275-92415-7 (alk. paper) : LC Card 87-2449 DDC 331.4/133/0973 19
HD6060.5.U5 H53 1987

Sokolov, D. V. (Dmitriĭ Viktorovich) Teoreticheskie i metodicheskie predposylki modelirovaniia organizatsionno-ėkonomicheskikh struktur khoziaĭstvennykh sistem / D.V. Sokolov. Leningrad : Izd-vo Leningradskogo universiteta, 1986. 134, [2] p. : ill. ; 22 cm. At head of title: Ministerstvo vysshego i srednego spetsial'nogo obrazovaniia RSFSR. Bibliography: p. 133-[135] LC Card 87-146729
1. Industrial organization. 2. Managerial economics. I. Title.
HD37.R82 S65 1986

Sokolov, M. P. (Mikhail Petrovich) Sovetskiĭ Soiuz na inostrannykh markakh /] Moskva , 1979. 286 p. : LC Card 81-136372
HE6183.S56 S68 1979

Sokolov, V. N. (Viacheslav Nikolaevich) Kursom na sotsialisticheskuiu industrializatsiiu / V.N. Sokolov. Kiev : Gol. izd-vo izdatel'skogo ob"edineniia "Vyshcha shkola", 1985. 158, [2] p. ; 20 cm. Bibliography: p. 154-[159]. LC Card 87-113771
1. Chemical industry - Ukraine - History. 2. Ukraine - Economic policy - 1917-. I. Title.
HD9656.S56 U377 1985

Sokolov, Vitaliĭ Mikhaĭlovich. Rozin, Bentsian Borisovich. Statisticheskaia otsenka normativov otraslevogo planirovaniia /. Novosibirsk , 1986. 188, [3] p. : LC Card 86-230359
HC336.25 .R69 1986

SOLAR ENERGY - GERMANY (WEST)
Ziesing, Hans-Joachim. Beurteilung der Wirtschaftlichkeitsschwelle und Analyse der Produktionskapazitäten bei neuen Technologien zur Energieeinsparung in mittel- bis längerfristiger Sicht . Berlin , 1983. 458 p. : ISBN 3-428-05497-0
NYPL [JLL 73-207 Bd. 139]

SOLAR ENERGY INDUSTRIES.
Worldwide remote power sites. New York, N.Y. , c1983. 2 v. (xx, xxvii, 500 p.) : LC Card 87-141748
HD9695.A2 W67 1983

The Worldwide solar electric generation market. New York, N.Y. , c1983. 2 v. (vii, 596 p.) : LC Card 87-401676 DDC 382/.4562131244 19
HD9681.A2 W67 1983

SOLAR ENERGY INDUSTRIES - AUSTRALIA - VICTORIA.
Andrews, John. Solar jobs in Victoria . [Victoria] [1982] xxxix p. : LC Card 87-160366
HD9681.A83 V5326 1982

SOLAR ENERGY INDUSTRIES - AUSTRALIA - VICTORIA - EMPLOYEES - SUPPLY AND DEMAND.
Andrews, John. Solar jobs in Victoria . [Victoria] [1982] xxxix p. : LC Card 87-160366
HD9681.A83 V5326 1982

Solar Energy Research Institute. Fenn, Scott. Institutional investment in renewable energy technologies /. Washington, D.C. , c1987. iii, 50 p. : ISBN 0-930135-17-1 (pbk.) LC Card 87-401940 DDC 332.6/722 19
HD9502.U52 F46 1987

Solar jobs in Victoria . Andrews, John. [Victoria] [1982] xxxix p. : LC Card 87-160366
HD9681.A83 V5326 1982

SOLAR POWER. see **SOLAR ENERGY.**

Solberg, Carl E. The prairies and the pampas : agrarian policy in Canada and Argentina, 1880-1930 / Carl E. Solberg. Stanford, Calif. : Stanford University Press, 1987. xii, 297 p. : maps ; 24 cm. (Comparative studies in history, institutions, and public policy) Bibliography: p. [264]-284. Includes index. ISBN 0-8047-1346-4 (alk. paper) : LC Card 86-27854 DDC 338.1/8 19
1. Wheat trade - Government policy - Canada - History. 2. Wheat trade - Government policy - Argentina - History. I. Title. II. Series.
HD9049.W5 C297 1987

Solberg, Ronald L., 1953- Sovereign rescheduling : risk and portfolio management / Ronald L. Solberg. London ; Boston : Allen & Unwin, 1988. p. cm. "Extension of ... PhD dissertation written at the University of California, Berkeley, from 1981 to 1984"--Acknowledgements. Bibliography: p. Includes index. ISBN 0-04-332122-4 (alk. paper) LC Card 87-18805 DDC 336.3/435 19
1. Loans, Foreign. 2. Debt relief. 3. Country risk. 4. Portfolio management. 5. Intermediation (Finance). I. Title.
HG3891.5 .S65 1988

Soldati, John M. Risk assessments : processing bond put and call features / by John M. Soldati and James G. Hilger, Jr. Washington, D.C. (1120 Connecticut Ave., N.W., Washington 20036) : American Bankers Association, c1987. 21 p. : ill. ; 28 cm. "A bankwide assessment of risks associated with traditional and nontraditional services and new business opportunities." LC Card 87-148315 DDC 332.64/52 19
1. Put and call transactions. I. Hilger, James G. II. Title.
HG6042 .S65 1987

Soldini, Bruno, 1939- Uomini da soma : contrabbando di fatica / Bruno Soldini. [Lugano] : Giornale del popolo, c1985. 289 p. : ill. ; 25 cm. Cover title: Contrabbando di fatica. LC Card 86-136358
1. Smuggling - Italy, Northern - History - 20th century. 2. Smuggling - Switzerland - History - 20th century. 3. Italy - History - German occupation, 1943-1945. 4. Reconstruction (1939-1951) - Italy, Northern. I. Title. II. Title: Contrabbando di fatica.
HJ6947 .S65 1985

Solé, Miguel José. Las condiciones de vida y de trabajo de los tamberos de la pampa húmeda : definiciones teórico metodológicas / Miguel José Solé. Stockholm : Institute of Latin American Studies, 1983. 33 p. ; 30 cm. (Research paper series . no. 38) Cover title. Summary in English. Bibliography: p. 32-33. LC Card 84-107283
1. Agriculture - Economic aspects - Argentina - Pampas. 2. Labor theory of value. 3. Rent (Economic theory). I. Series. II. Series: Research paper series (Latinamerikainstitutet i Stockholm) , paper no. 38. III. Title.
HD1865.P35 S65 1983

Soler Bordetas, Francisco Javier. Fondos de pensiones / autor, Francisco Javier Soler Bordetas. Bilbao : Ediciones Deusto, [1985?] 152 p. : port. ; 21 cm. Bibliography: p. [150]-152. ISBN 84-234-0575-3 LC Card 86-166028
1. Pension trusts - Spain. 2. Old age pensions - Spain. 3. Pension trusts. 4. Old age pensions. I. Title.
HD7105.45.S7 S57 1985

Soler, Sebastián. Temas antiliberales, marxistas y autoritarios / Sebastián Soler. Buenos Aires : Sur : [distribuidores exclusivos, Editorial Sudamericana], 1977. 179 p. ; 20 cm. Includes bibliographical references. LC Card 80-469614
1. Liberalism. 2. Authoritarianism. I. Title.
JC571 .S7173 ***NYPL [JLC 80-]***

Soley, Lawrence C. Clandestine radio broadcasting : a study of revolutionary and counterrevolutionary electronic communication / Lawrence C. Soley and John S. Nichols. New York : Prager, 1987. xiv, 384 p. ; 25 cm. Includes index. Bibliography: p. 357-368. ISBN 0-275-92259-6 (alk. paper) : LC Card 86-21169 DDC 384.54 19
1. Radio in politics. 2. Radio in propaganda. 3. Counterrevolutions. I. Nichols, John Spicer. II. Title.
HE8697.P6 S59 1986
NYPL [MWGH 87-1678]

Solid gold mail box. Weintz, Walter. The solid gold mailbox . New York , c1987. xiv, 268 p. : ISBN 0-471-85026-8 LC Card 86-28267 DDC 658.8/72 19
HF5466 .W45 1987

The solid gold mailbox . Weintz, Walter. New York , c1987. xiv, 268 p. : ISBN 0-471-85026-8 LC Card 86-28267 DDC 658.8/72 19
HF5466 .W45 1987

Solidargemeinschaft und Klassenkampf : politische Konzeptionen der Sozialdemokratie zwischen den Weltkriegen / herausgegeben von Richard Saage. Frankfurt am Main : Suhrkamp, 1986. 382 p. ; 18 cm. (Edition Suhrkamp. Neue Folge . Bd. 363) Includes bibliographical references. ISBN 3-518-11363-1
1. Socialism - Germany - History - Addresses, essays, lectures. 2. Communism - Germany - History - Addresses, essays, lectures. 3. Germany - Politics and government - 1918-1933 - Addresses, essays, lectures. 4. Germany - Politics and government - 1933-1945 - Addresses, essays, lectures. I. Saage, Richard.
NYPL [JLC 86-423]

Solidaritetsarbete . Örning, Birgitta. Stockholm [1978?] 66 p. : LC Card 81-140576
HD7728 .O75 1978

Solidarity or survival? . Lane, A. T. New York , 1987. xii, 230 p. ; ISBN 0-313-25544-X (lib. bdg. : alk. paper) LC Card 86-25735 DDC 331.6/2/0973 19
HD8081.A5 L36 1987

Solidarność . Twierdochlebow, W. J. Menlo Park, CA , 1985. 72, v leaves ; LC Card 86-221919 DDC 331.89/28238204/094382 19
HD5397.7.S512 1980 .G358 1985

SOLINGEN (GERMANY) - ECONOMIC CONDITIONS.
Lindmüller, Peter. Remscheid und Solingen im industriegeographischen Entwicklungsvergleich /. Bochum , 1986. 423 p. : ISBN 3-88339-544-7 LC Card 87-146590 DDC 330.943/55 19
HC289.R38 L56 1986

SOLINGEN (GERMANY) - INDUSTRIES - HISTORY.
Lindmüller, Peter. Remscheid und Solingen im industriegeographischen Entwicklungsvergleich /. Bochum , 1986. 423 p. : ISBN 3-88339-544-7 LC Card 87-146590 DDC 330.943/55 19
HC289.R38 L56 1986

Solis, Duarte Gomes. Armadas da carreira da India de 1560 a 1590 : relação de Duarte Gomes Solis impressa em Madrid em 1622 e reeditada com prefácio e notas de Frazão de Vasconcellos. Lisboa : Casa Portuguesa, 1938. xvi, 20 p. : ill. ; 26 cm. "125 exemplares"--P. [ii] Includes bibliographical references. LC Card 86-140347
1. Portugal - Commerce - India - History - 16th century. 2. India - Commerce - Portugal - History - 16th century. 3. Shipping - Portugal - History - 16th century. 4. Shipping - India - History - 16th century. 5. Shipbuilding - Portugal - History - 16th century. I. Vasconcellos, Frazão de. II. Title.
HF3698.I4 S65 1938

Solís, Leopoldo. see **Solís M., Leopoldo.**

Solís M., Leopoldo.
Alternativas para el desarrollo / Leopoldo Solís. 2a ed. corr. y aum. México, D.F. : Editorial J. Mortiz, 1985, c1980. 155 p. ; 21 cm. (Cuadernos de Joaquín Mortiz) Includes bibliographical references. ISBN 968-270-487-1 LC Card 86-222497
1. Mexico - Economic policy. I. Title.
HC135 .S636 1985

Rizzo, Sócrates. Opciones de política económica, 1979-1982 /. México, D.F. [1983] 133 p. : LC Card 86-205260 DDC 338.972 19
HC135 .R44 1983

Solius, G. P. Rol' bankov v usilenii gospodstva finansovogo kapitala /. Moskva , 1985. 206 p. ; LC Card 86-102078
HG3881 .R615 1985

Soljenitsyne, Alexandre. see **Solzhenitsyn, Aleksandr Isaevich, 1918-**

Sollmann, Axel, 1952- Die Massnahme-, Berichts- und Missbilligungsbeschlüsse des Parlaments im Entlastungsverfahren / Axel Sollmann. Frankfurt am Main ; New York : P. Lang, c1986. 261 p. ; 21 cm. (Europäische Hochschulschriften. Reihe II, Rechtswissenschaft, 0531-7312 . Bd. 529 = vol. 569 = vol. 569) Bibliography: p. 5-14. ISBN 3-8204-9778-1 LC Card 86-233741
1. Finance, Public - Germany, West - Accounting. 2. Finance, Public - Accounting - Law and legislation - Germany (West). I. Series: Europäische Hochschulschriften. Reihe II, Rechtswissenschaft , Bd. 529. II. Title.
HJ9925.G3 S65 1986

Solnik, Bruno H., 1944- International investments / Bruno Solnik. Reading, Mass. : Addison-Wesley, c1988. xi, 387 p. : ill. ; 25 cm. Includes bibliographies and index. ISBN 0-201-07538-5 : LC Card 87-1345 DDC 332.6/73 19
1. Investments, Foreign. I. Title.
HG4538 .S52 1988

Solodkova, S. V. (Serafima Vasil'evna) Sotsialisticheskie proizvodstvennye otnosheniia : sistemnyĭ podkhod / S.V. Solodkova, V.I. Ermakov. Moskva : "Ėkonomika", 1984. 141 p. ; 22 cm. Includes bibliographical references. LC Card 84-223476
1. Soviet Union - Economic conditions - 1976-. 2. Soviet Union - Economic policy - 1981-. I. Ermakov, V. I. (Vladimir Ivanovich). II. Title.
HC336.25 .S65 1984

Solomakha, A. I. (Alekseĭ Ivanovich) Sistema vedeniia sel'skogo i promyslovogo khoziaĭstva na Eniseĭskom Severe . Novosibirsk , 1986. 211 p. ; LC Card 86-227282
HD1995.K73 S57 1986

Solomentsev, M. S. (Mikhail Sergeevich) Rossiĭskaia Federatsiia / M.S. Solomentsev. Moskva : Izd-vo polit. lit-ry, 1978. 212 p. ; 16 cm. (Respubliki Strany Sovetov) Includes bibliographical references. LC Card 81-170399
1. Russian S.F.S.R. - Economic conditions. I. Title. II. Series.
HC337.R85 S65 1978

Solomon, Anthony M.
De Menil, George, 1940- Weltwirtschaftsgipfel /. Bonn [1983] iv, 130 p. ; ISBN 3-7713-0203-X LC Card 85-224780
HF1411 .D345 1983

The dollar, debt, and the trade deficit / Anthony M. Solomon. New York : New York University Press, 1987. 55 p. ; 22 cm. (The Joseph I. Lubin memorial lectures . no. 3) ISBN 0-8147-7863-1 : LC Card 86-23651 DDC 382.1/7/0973 19
1. Balance of trade - United States. 2. Debts, External - United States. 3. Foreign exchange problem - United States. 4. Export sales - United States. I. Title. II. Series.
HF3031 .S65 1987

Solomon, David. French, Alexander. Traffic data collection and analysis . Washington, D.C. [1986] 58 p. : ISBN 0-309-04406-5 (pbk.) : LC Card 86-51174 DDC 388.3/14/072 19
HE369 .F68 1986

Solomon Gebre. Yeraswork Admassie. Food-for-work in Ethiopia . Addis Abeba , 1985. viii, 102, [58] leaves : LC Card 86-980537 DDC 339.5/0963 19
HD5839.7.A6 Y47 1985

Solomon, George T. National Survey of entreprenuerial [sic] education /. [Washington, D.C.?] . v. : LC Card 86-603453 DDC 658/.022/071173 19
HF1131 .N325 1986

Solomon, Stephen S. Canadian mortgage payments / Stephen S. Solomon, Clifford W. Marshall, Martin Pepper. New York : Barron's Educational Series, c1987. 302 p. ; 18 cm. (Barron's financial tables for better money management) Barron's financial guides ISBN 0-8120-3939-4 (pbk.) LC Card 87-13073 DDC 332.8/0212 19
1. Interest - Canada - Tables. 2. Mortgage loans - Canada - Tables. I. Marshall, Clifford W., 1928-. II. Pepper, Martin. III. Title. IV. Title: Canadian mortgage payments. V. Series.
HG1634 .S654 1987

Solomou, Solomos. Phases of economic growth, 1850-1973 : Kondratief waves and Kuznets swings / Solomos Solomou. Cambridge [Cambridgeshire] ; New York : Cambridge University Press, 1987. p. cm. Bibliography: p. Includes index. ISBN 0-521-33457-8 LC Card 86-34324 DDC 338.9 19
1. Long waves (Economics) - Econometric models. 2. Economic development - Econometric models. I. Title.
HB3729 .S65 1987

Solórzano, Juan Carlos.
Costa Rica colonial. 1984. Costa Rica colonial : tres ensayos / Juan Carlos Solórzano, Luis Fernando Sibaja. [San José, Costa Rica , 1984] 83 p. ; LC Card 86-173945
HC389 .C67 1984

Hispanoamérica y la expansión europea, siglos XV al XVIII. 1984. Costa Rica colonial : tres ensayos / Juan Carlos Solórzano, Luis Fernando Sibaja. [San José, Costa Rica , 1984] 83 p. ; LC Card 86-173945
HC389 .C67 1984

Solov'ev, IU. P. (IUriĭ Pavlovich)
Modelirovanie i prognozirovanie ėlementov uslovno-chistoĭ produktsii i finansovykh potokov /. Moskva , 1981. 180 p. : LC Card 83-171742
HD30.25 .M635 1981

Opyt razrabotki i realizatsii sistemy ukrupnennykh modeleĭ perspektivnogo planirovaniia /. Moskva , 1984. 216 p. : LC Card 85-199888
HD75.5 .O69 1984

Voprosy postroeniia sistemy modeleĭ finansovogo aspekta vosproizvodstva /. Moskva , 1984. 154 p. : LC Card 86-144339
HG186.S55 V67 1984

Solov'eva, E. I., d-r ist. nauk. Promysly sibirskogo krest'ianstva v poreformennyĭ period / E.I. Solov'eva. Novosibirsk : Izd-vo "Nauka," Sibirskoe otd-nie, 1981. 327 p. : ill. ; 20 cm. At head of title: Akademiia nauk SSSR. Sibirskoe otdelenie. Institut istorii, filologii i filosofii. Bibliography: p. 298-[320] Includes indexes. LC Card 82-111175
1. Cottage industries - Russian S.F.S.R. - Siberia - History - 19th century. 2. Siberia (R.S.F.S.R.) - Economic conditions. I. Title.
HD2346.S652 S527 1981

Solow, Robert M. Dorfman, Robert. Linear programming and economic analysis /. New York , 1987, c1986. p. cm. ISBN 0-486-65491-5 (pbk.) LC Card 87-24382 DDC 330/.0724 19
HB135 .D67 1987

Soltan, Petr Semenovich.
Chertan, S. E. (Sergeĭ Evgen'evich) Sistema natural'no-stoimostnykh mezhotraslevykh balansov soiuznoĭ respubliki . Kishinev , 1984. 242, [6] p., [2] folded leaves of plates : LC Card 85-130960
HC337.M55 C46 1984

Optimal'noe planirovanie /. Kishinev , 1982. 166 p. : LC Card 83-149332
HD9015.S653 M64526 1982

Planirovanie ėkonomiki Moldavskoĭ SSR /. Kishinev , 1986. 161 p. ; LC Card 86-203680
HD9015.S653 M6457 1986

Solterer, Josef, 1897- Notas y material de estudio sobre el desarrollo y el sindicalismo realizado en el Instituto Americano para el Desarrollo del Sindicalismo Libre / Josef Solterer. Lima, Perú : Asociación Fomento de la Educación Laboral e Investigaciones Económicas y Sociales, [1986] xv, 76, [5] p. : port. ; 21 cm. (Economia para los trabajadores . 3) Bibliography: p. [79]-81. LC Card 86-235556
1. Economic development. 2. Trade-unions. I. Title. II. Series.
HD85.S7 S65 1986

Soltwedel, Rüdiger. Deregulierungspotentiale in der Bundesrepublik / Rüdiger Soltwedel et al. ; Autoren, Axel Busch ... [et al.]. Tübingen : Mohr, c1986. xi, 326 p. ; 24 cm. (Kieler Studien, 0340-6989 . 202) Bibliography: p. 288-326. ISBN 3-16-345145-4 (Deut. Bibl. : pbk.) LC Card 87-408380 DDC 338.6/048 19
1. Trade regulation - Germany, West. 2. Deregulation - Germany (West). I. Busch, Axel. II. Title. III. Series.
HD3616.G4 S665 1986

Solutions . Phillips, Steven R. San Diego, Calif. , c1987. xi, 127 p. ; ISBN 0-88390-205-2 (pbk.) : LC Card 87-5894 DDC 658.4/03 19
HD30.29 .P48 1987

SOLVENTS INDUSTRY - UNITED STATES.
Aliphatic solvents market. New York, N.Y. , c1983. viii, 181 leaves : LC Card 87-142189 DDC 381/.45661807 19
HD9660.S733 U525 1983

Solving world hunger. Solving world hunger, the U. S. stake /. Cabin John, MD , 1986. ix, 102 p. : ISBN 0-932020-42-9 (pbk.) : LC Card 86-17665 DDC 363.8/526/0973 19
HV696.F6 S65 1986 ***NYPL [JLF 87-531]***

Solving world hunger, the U. S. stake / E. Boyd Wennergren ... [et al.]. 1st ed. Cabin John, MD : Seven Locks Press, 1986. ix, 102 p. : ill. (some col.) ; 28 cm. "Published ... for the 'Understanding World Agriculture' project of the Consortium for International Cooperation in Higher Education (CICHE)." Bibliography: p. 98-102. ISBN 0-932020-42-9 (pbk.) : LC Card 86-17665 DDC 363.8/526/0973 19
1. Food relief, American - Developing countries. 2. Hunger. I. Wennergren, E. Boyd. II. Consortium for International Cooperation in Higher Education. III. Title: Solving world hunger.
HV696.F6 S65 1986 ***NYPL [JLF 87-531]***

Solženicins, A. I. see Solzhenitsyn, Aleksandr Isaevich, 1918-

Solženicyn, A. see Solzhenitsyn, Aleksandr Isaevich, 1918-

Solženicyn, Aleksander. see Solzhenitsyn, Aleksandr Isaevich, 1918-

Solženitsōn, Aleksander. see Solzhenitsyn, Aleksandr Isaevich, 1918-

Solzhenitsyn, Aleksandr Isaevich, 1918- RASKOLOTYĬ MIR - ADDRESSES, ESSAYS, LECTURES.
Solzhenitsyn at Harvard . Washington, D. C. , 1980. xvi, 143 p. ; ISBN 0-89633-034-6 : LC Card 79-26033 DDC 909.82
CB245.S5693 S64 ***NYPL [JFE 81-1327]***

Raskolotyĭ mir. English. Solzhenitsyn at Harvard : the address, twelve early responses , and six later reflections / Ronald Berman ... [et al.] ; edited by Ronald Berman. Washington, D. C. , 1980. xvi, 143 p. ; ISBN 0-89633-034-6 : LC Card 79-26033 DDC 909.82
CB245.S5693 S64 ***NYPL [JFE 81-1327]***

Solzhenitsyn at Harvard : the address, twelve early responses , and six later reflections / Ronald Berman ... [et al.] ; edited by Ronald Berman. Washington, D. C. : Ethics and Public Policy Center, 1980. xvi, 143 p. ; 24 cm. ISBN 0-89633-034-6 : LC Card 79-26033 DDC 909.82
1. Solzhenitsyn, Aleksandr Isaevich, 1918- Raskolotyĭ mir - Addresses, essays, lectures. 2. Civilization, Occidental - Addresses, essays, lectures. 3. Civilization, Modern - 1950- - Addresses, essays, lectures. 4. Communism - Addresses, essays, lectures. 5. Europe, Eastern - Civilization - Addresses, essays, lectures. I. Berman, Ronald. II. Solzhenitsyn, Aleksandr Isaevich, 1918- Raskolotyĭ mir. English.
CB245.S5693 S64 ***NYPL [JFE 81-1327]***

Solzhenitzyn, Aleksandr Isayevich. see Solzhenitsyn, Aleksandr Isaevich, 1918-

Somali Democratic Republic. see Somalia.

Somali Republic. see Somalia.

Somalia : a social and institutional profile / prepared by the African Studies Center ; team leader, Allan Hoben ; team members, Theodore Ahlers ... [et al.]. Boston, MA : The Center, [1983] vi, 164 p. : ill. ; 28 cm. (Working papers / African Studies Center . no. SP-1) "March 1983." "Report was prepared under Contract no. AFR 0135-c-00-2052-00 for the Agency for International Development." Bibliography: p. 113-129. LC Card 87-108393 DDC 330.967/7305 19
1. Somalia - Economic conditions - 1960-. 2. Somalia - Social conditions - 1960-. I. Hoben, Allan. II. Ahlers, Theodore H. III. Boston University. African Studies Center. IV. United States. Agency for International Development. V. Series: Working papers (Boston University. African Studies Center) , no. SP-1.
HC850 .S655 1983

Somalia.
Report of the joint Somali government and World Bank study of agricultural incentives and grain marketing in Somalia /. [Alexandria, Va. , 1984] xviii, 170, 2 p. : LC Card 87-404086 DDC 338.1/8 19
HD9047.S582 R47 1984

Somalia. Commission on National Broadcasting. Report of the Commission on National Broadcasting. Mogadishu : Somali Republic, Ministry of Information, [1966] ii, 108 leaves (2 folded) : ill. ; 33 cm. Cover title. "July 1966." LC Card 85-981107
1. Radio broadcasting - Somalia. I. Title.
HE8699.S65 S64 1966

SOMALIA - ECONOMIC CONDITIONS - 1960-
Somalia . Boston, MA [1983] vi, 164 p. : LC Card 87-108393 DDC 330.967/7305 19
HC850 .S655 1983

Somalia. Ministry of National Planning. National development strategy and programme /. Mogadishu [1985] vi, 199 p. ; LC Card 86-980272 DDC 338.967/73 19
HC850 .S653 1985

Somalia, productive sectors of the economy /. Paris , 1985. 115 leaves : ISBN 2-905760-00-1 (pbk.) LC Card 87-124493 DDC 338.967/73 19
HC850 .S658 1985

SOMALIA - ECONOMIC POLICY.
Somalia. Ministry of National Planning. National development strategy and programme /. Mogadishu [1985] vi, 199 p. ; LC Card 86-980272 DDC 338.967/73 19
HC850 .S653 1985

SOMALIA - INDUSTRIES - DIRECTORIES.
Somalia, productive sectors of the economy /. Paris , 1985. 115 leaves : ISBN 2-905760-00-1 (pbk.) LC Card 87-124493 DDC 338.967/73 19
HC850 .S658 1985

Somalia. Ministry of Local Government and Rural Development. Somalia's rural development strategy, 1981-1990. Mogadishu, Somalia [1981?] vii, 45, [49] leaves : LC Card 83-980772 DDC 338.1/86773 19
HD2125.Z8 S65 1981 ***NYPL [JLG 86-58]***

Somalia. Ministry of National Planning. National development strategy and programme / Somali Democratic Republic, Ministry of National Planning. Mogadishu : The Ministry, [1985] vi, 199 p. ; 27 cm. "September 1985." LC Card 86-980272 DDC 338.967/73 19
1. Somalia - Economic policy. 2. Somalia - Economic conditions - 1960-. I. Title.
HC850 .S653 1985

Somalia, productive sectors of the economy / [this special report has been prepared by the Documentary Survey Department of the Indian Ocean newsletter ; researched and written by Michele Miech-Chatenay ; edited by Maurice Botbol ; assisted by Martin Bennett]. 1985 ed. Paris : Banque d'information et de documention de l'ocean Indien (BIDOI), 1985. 115 leaves : maps ; 30 cm. (Indian Ocean newsletter publication) "Completed April 1985." Includes index. ISBN 2-905760-00-1 (pbk.) LC Card 87-124493 DDC 338.967/73 19
1. Somalia - Economic conditions - 1960-. 2. Agriculture - Economic aspects - Somalia. 3. Somalia - Industries - Directories. I. Miech Chatenay, Michèle. II. Botbol, Maurice. III. Bennett, Martin. IV. Indian Ocean newsletter. V. Series.
HC850 .S658 1985

SOMALIA - SOCIAL CONDITIONS - 1960-
Somalia . Boston, MA [1983] vi, 164 p. : LC Card 87-108393 DDC 330.967/7305 19
HC850 .S655 1983

Somalia. Wasaaradda Qorshaynta Qaranka. Hinzen, Eckhard. Pre-feasibility study of the integrated Ras Hafun project in north east Somalia . Kronberg [West Germany] [1981] xii, 186 leaves : LC Card 85-980733
HC850.Z9 E444 1981

Somalia's rural development strategy, 1981-1990. Mogadishu, Somalia : Ministry of Local Government and Rural Development, [1981?] vii, 45, [49] leaves : map ; 33 cm. At head of title: Somali Democratic Republic. Based on the findings and recommendations of the National Workshop on Rural Development, held in Mogadishu, Sept. 1979. Includes bibliographical references. LC Card 83-980772 DDC 338.1/86773 19
1. Agriculture and state - Somalia - Congresses. 2. Rural development - Government policy - Somalia - Congresses. I. Somalia. Ministry of Local Government and Rural Development. II. National Workshop on Rural Development (1979 : Mogadishu, Somalia).
HD2125.Z8 S65 1981 ***NYPL [JLG 86-58]***

Somary, Felix, 1881-1956.
[Erinnerungen aus meinem Leben. English] The raven of Zürich : the memoirs of Felix Somary / translated from the German by A.J. Sherman ; with a foreword by Otto von Habsburg. London : C. Hurst & Co. ; New York : St. Martin's Press, c1986. xii, 310 p. : port. ; 24 cm. Translation of: Erinnerungen aus meinem Leben. Includes index. ISBN 0-312-66407-9 LC Card 86-6662 DDC 330/.092/4 B 19
1. Somary, Felix, 1881-1956. 2. Economists - Austria - Biography. 3. Bankers - Switzerland - Biography. 4. Statesmen - Switzerland - Biography. I. Sherman, A. J. (Ari Joshua). II. Title.
HB101.S6 A313 1986 ***NYPL [JFE 87-54]***

SOMARY, FELIX, 1881-1956.
Somary, Felix, 1881-1956. [Erinnerungen aus meinem Leben. English.] The raven of Zürich . London , New York , c1986. xii, 310 p. : ISBN 0-312-66407-9 LC Card 86-6662 DDC 330/.092/4 B 19
HB101.S6 A313 1986 ***NYPL [JFE 87-54]***

Somasekhara, N. Rural energy : flows, inter-fuel substitution, and development : profile of a developing country, with special reference to India / N. Somasekhara.1st ed. New Delhi : Sterling Publishers, 1985. xii, 113 p. ; 23 cm. (Publications of the Institute of Social Studies) Includes bibliographies and index. ISBN 81-207-0121-6 : LC Card 86-900467 DDC 333.79/0954 19
1. Energy policy - India. 2. Energy development - India. 3. Rural development - India. I. Title. II. Series.
HD9502.I42 S66 1985 ***NYPL [JLD 86-3315]***

Sombo, N'Cho. Enquête ivoirienne sur la fécondité, 1980-81 : rapport d'évaluation / N'cho Sombo. Voorburg, Netherlands : International Statistical Institute, [1985] 63 p. : ill. ; 30 cm. (Scientific reports . no 79) "December 1985"--Cover. Bibliography: p. 63. LC Card 87-132644
1. Fertility, Human - Ivory Coast. I. Series: Scientific reports (World Fertility Survey) , no. 79. II. Title.
HB1076.A3 S65 1985

A sombra do cruzado . Assis, José Carlos de. Rio de Janeiro , 1986. 137 p. : LC Card 87-128261 DDC 332.4/981 19
HG835 .A88 1986

Some aspects of agricultural price and taxation policies in Pakistan / Sarfraz Khan Qureshi ... [et al.]. Islamabad, Pakistan : Pakistan Institute of Development Economics, [1985] x, 223 p. ; 29 cm. (Research report series / Pakistan Institute of Development Economics . no 146) "September 1985." Bibliography: p. 217-223. LC Card 86-930932 DDC 338.1/8 19
1. Agricultural prices - Pakistan. 2. Agriculture - Taxation - Pakistan. 3. Agriculture and state - Pakistan. I. Qureahi, Sarfraz Khan. II. Series: Research report series / Pakistan Institute of Development Economics , no. 146.
HD2075.5 .S66 1985

Some aspects of smuggling between Chad and Sudan [microform] /. Doornbos, Paul. Khartoum [1983] 19 leaves, [1] leaf of plates : LC Card 84-980097 DDC 364.1/33 19
HF3887.Z8 D373 1983
NYPL [*ZT-1646 no.52]

Some aspects of Sudanese migration to the oil-producing Arab countries, during the 1970's /. Jalāl al-Dīn, Muḥammad al-'Awaḍ. [Khartoum] [1985] 52 p. ; LC Card 86-980666 DDC 331.6/2/62409174927 19
HD8766 .J35 1985

Some factors which affect peasant motivation to work in the Ethiopian agricultural producers cooperatives /. Habtamu Wondimu. [Addis Ababa] [1983] 60 leaves : LC Card 84-980911 DDC 334/.683/0963 19
HD1491.E83 H3 1983b ***NYPL [JLG 86-163]***

Some government financial data, 1850 to 1982 /. Barnard, A. (Alan) Canberra, Australia [1986] 47, 2 p. ; ISBN 0-86784-850-2 (pbk.) LC Card 86-211320 DDC 336.94 19
HJ2193.Z7 B37 1986

Some important statistics, 1969. Sathiti thī samkhan, 2512. [Bangkok] [19]71. [11], 34 p., [1] leaf of plates : LC Card 83-921120 DDC 315.93 19
HA4600.55.Z9 P428 1971

Some important statistics, 1969, Changwat Krabi. Sathiti thī samkhan, 2512, Changwat Krabī =. [Bangkok] [19]71. [8], 36 leaves, [1] leaf of plates : LC Card 83-921122
HA4600.55 .S275 1971

Some personality determinants of the effects of participation /. Vroom, Victor Harold, 1932- New York , 1987, c1960. x, 91 p. ; ISBN 0-8240-8225-7 (alk. paper) : LC Card 86-27081 DDC 158.7 19
HF5548.8 .V695 1987

Some reflections on Nigeria's economic performance since independence, and thoughts on future prospects /. Adedeji, Adebayo. Addis Ababa [1985] 57 p. ; LC Card 86-980957 DDC 330.9669/05 19
HC1055 .A546 1985

Some social economic data related to housing, Ruvuma region. Salomon, Robert. Ruvuma region . Dar es Salaam , 1981. 32 leaves : LC Card 85-981451
HD7289.T352 R897 1981

Somensatto, Eduardo. Contemporary economic problems . Washington, D.C. , c1987. 332 p. : ISBN 0-8447-3621-X (alk. paper) LC Card 87-1395 DDC 330.973/0927 19
HC106.8 .C665 1987

Somers Islands. see Bermuda Islands.

Somerville, Carolyn M. Drought and aid in the Sahel : a decade of development cooperation / Carolyn M. Somerville. Boulder : Westview Press, 1986. xxii, 306 p. : map ; 23 cm. (Westview special studies on Africa) Includes bibliographical references and index. ISBN 0-8133-7087-6 : LC Card 86-5635 DDC 338.966 19
1. Economic assistance - Sahel. 2. Droughts - Sahel. 3. Famines - Sahel. 4. Sahel - Economic policy. I. Title.
HC1002 .S65 1986 ***NYPL [JLD 86-4038]***

Sommariva, Andrea. The ECU market . Lexington, Mass. , c1987. xiii, 246 p. : ISBN 0-669-13833-9 (alk. paper) LC Card 87-4185 DDC 332.4/56094 19
HG930.5 .E27 1987

Sommer, A. A. (Alphonse A.), 1924- Braiotta, Louis, 1943- The essential guide to effective corporate board committees /. Englewood Cliffs, N.J. , c1987. xiii, 178 p. ; ISBN 0-13-286139-9 LC Card 87-2265 DDC 658.4/22 19
HD2745 .B63 1987

Sommer, Juan. Feldman, Ernesto V. (Ernesto Víctor) Crisis financiera y endeudamiento externo en la Argentina /. [Buenos Aires] , c1986. 184 p. ; ISBN 950-25-1313-4 LC Card 86-182663
HG185.A7 F45 1986

Sommer, Manfred. Arbeitsplätze morgen /. Stuttgart , c1986. 431 p. : ISBN 3-519-02446-2 LC Card 86-171663
HD6331 .A695 1986

Somogyi, Dorottya. A fejlett tőkés országok exportpolitikája / Somogyi Dorottya. Budapest : Közgazdasági és Jogi Könyvkiadó, 1985. 277, [1] p. : ill. ; 19 cm. (Időszerű közgazdasági kérdések, 0324-3214) Bibliography: p. 275-[278] ISBN 963-221-507-9 : LC Card 85-231848
1. Foreign trade promotion. 2. Export marketing. 3. Commercial policy. 4. Hungary - Commercial policy. I. Title. II. Series.
HF1417.5 .S66 1985

Somogyi, Stefano. Storia demografica dei comuni siciliani dal 1862 al 1971 /. Palermo [1979] 294 p. ; LC Card 86-131917
HB2270.S5 S76 1979

Somwaru, Agapi. Disaggregated farm income by type of farm, 1959-82 / Agapi Somwaru. Washington, D.C. : U. S. Dept. of Agriculture, Economic Research Service : [Supt. of Docs., U. S. G.P.O., distributor], 1986. iii, 113 p. : ill. ; 28 cm. (Agricultural economic report . no. 558) Cover title. Distributed to depository libraries in microfiche. "August 1986." Bibliography: p. 79-80. S/N 001-019-00469-0 Item 42-C (microfiche) LC Card 86-602571 DDC 338.1 s 338.1/3/0973021 19
1. Farm income - United States - Statistics. 2. Farms - United States - Statistics. I. United States. Dept. of Agriculture. Economic Research Service. II. Title. III. Series.
HD1751 .A91854 no. 558 HD1769

Sønder, Ulla. Gydesen, Ellen. Kvinders livsgrundlag i 80-erne /. K [i.e. Copenhagen] [1985] 202 columns : LC Card 87-168500
HD6060.65.D4 G93 1985

Sonderforschungsbereich 3 der Universitäten Frankfurt und Mannheim "Mikroanalytische Grundlagen der Gesellschaftspolitik" (Series) Göbel, Dieter, 1949- Lebenseinkommen und Erwerbsbiographie . Frankfurt/Main , New York , c1983. xix, 364 p. : ISBN 3-593-33244-2

LC Card 84-132204
HC290.5.I5 G63 1983

Sondergutachten der Monopolkommission . (Bd. 9) Germany (West). Monopolkommission. Die Rolle der Deutschen Bundespost im Fernmeldewesen /. Baden-Baden , 1981. 110 p. ; ISBN 3-7890-0675-0(pbk.) LC Card 81-130348 DDC 383/.4943 19
HE8155 .R64 1981 *NYPL [JLE 87-312]*

Sonderveröffentlichung des Bundesinstituts für Ostwissenschaftliche und Internationale Studien.
Munkholt, Peer. The Soviet economy . Köln , 1985. iii, 79 p. ; LC Card 86-673837
HC340.D4 M86x 1985

Song, Dae-Hee. The performance evaluation of Korean public enterprises : policy, practice, and experience / Dae-Hee Song. Seoul, Korea : Korea Development Institute, [1986] 109 p. : ill. ; 28 cm. (Working paper / Korea Development Institute . 8601) "October 1986." LC Card 87-404432 DDC 354.519/5092 19
1. Government business enterprises - Korea (South) - Management - Evaluation. 2. Government business enterprises - Korea (South). I. Series: Working paper (Han'guk Kaebal Yŏn'guwŏn) , 8601. II. Title.
HD4315.5 .S65 1986

Song, Du-Yul, 1944- Sowjetunion und China : Egalisierung und Differenzierung im Sozialismus / Du-Yul Song. Frankfurt/Main ; New York : Campus-Verlag, c1984. 255 p. : ill. ; 21 cm. (Campus Forschung. Bd. 391) A revision of the author's Habilitationsschrift, Universität Münster, 1981. Bibliography: p. 239-252. ISBN 3-593-33351-1 LC Card 84-169164
1. Labor productivity - Soviet Union. 2. Labor productivity - China. 3. Agricultural productivity - Soviet Union. 4. Agricultural productivity - China. I. Title.
HC340.L3 S66 1984

Songai Hoken Jigyō Kenkyūjo (Japan) Miscellaneous casualty insurance in Japan. Tokyo, Japan [1986] xi, 315 p. ; LC Card 87-103937 DDC 368.5/00952 19
HG8705.A6 M57 1986

Songsan Ninkamhæng. Čhotmāihēt kānsāng Phraphuttharūp phra prathān Phutthamonthon / [phūriapriang, Songsan Ninkamhæng, Phannī Sunth Krung Thēp : Khana Kammakān 'Amnūaikān Chatsāng Phutthamonthon læ Krom Sinlapāk 2525 [1982] 172 p. : ill. (chiefly col.) ; 28 cm. In Thai. "Čhatphim pen thiralk nai phithī somphōt Phraphuttharūp phra prathān Phutthamonthon." On the sculpturing of the Buddha image to be erected at Phutthamonthon, Buddha Garden in Nakhon Pathom province, Thailand. Includes bibliographical references. ISBN 974-7921-05-7 LC Card 83-916060
1. Gautama Buddha - Art. 2. Sculpture, Thai. 3. Sculpture, Buddhist - Thailand. 4. Sculpture gardens - Thailand - Nakhon Pathom (Province). I. Phannī Sunth
HB1912.G38 S66 1982

SONĪ KABUSHIKI KAISHA - HISTORY.
Morita, Akio, 1921- Made in Japan . New York , c1986. viii, 309 p., [8] p. of plates : ISBN 0-525-24465-4 : LC Card 86-11479 DDC 338.7/6213/0924 B 19
HD9696.A3 J3658 1986 *NYPL [JFE 86-5112]*

Sonnberger, Harald. The IAS-System data base . Wien, Austria [1982] ii, 151, 3 p. : *NYPL [JSG 86-170]*

Sonnenschein, Hugo. Social goals and social organization . Cambridge [Cambridgeshire] , New York , 1985. xii, 365 p. : ISBN 0-521-26204-6 LC Card 85-6668 DDC 330.15/5 19
HB846 .S65 1985 *NYPL [JLE 86-3786]*

Sonnewald, Bernd, 1947- Die "Berliner Linie" und die Hausbesetzer-Szene / Bernd Sonnewald, Jürgen Raabe-Zimmermann. Berlin : Berlin Verlag, c1983. 149 p. ; 21 cm. (Politologische Studien . Bd. 27) Bibliography: p. 143-146. Includes indexes. ISBN 3-87061-170-7 LC Card 83-190228
1. Squatters - Berlin (Germany). 2. Urban poor - Housing - Berlin (Germany). 3. Housing - Berlin (Germany). I. Raabe-Zimmermann, Jürgen, 1950-. II. Title. III. Series.
HD7287.96.G32 B477 1983

SONORA (MEXICO : STATE) - HISTORY.
Radding, Cynthia. [Acumulación originaria de capital agrario en Sonora.] La acumulación originaria de capital agrario en Sonora ; Registro de los archivos del Estado de Sonora /. [Hermosillo, Sonora] , 1981. 90 p. : LC Card 82-118209
HD329.S6 R33 1981

Sonthonnax, Françoise. Chabaud-Rychter, Danielle. Espace et temps du travail domestique /. Paris , 1985. 156 p. ; ISBN 2-86563-127-3 LC Card 86-165713
HD6055 .C45 1985

Sony. see **Soni Kabushiki Kaisha.**

Sonzogni, Cristina María. La población de la ciudad de Corrientes a mediados del siglo XIX / Cristina María Sonzogni, Mirta Beatriz Ramírez. 2a ed. Corrientes : Instituto de Investigaciones Geohistóricas, 1980. 50, [4] leaves, [14] leaves of plates : ill. ; 28 cm. (Cuadernos de geohistoria regional, 0325-8246 . no. 2) Limited ed. of 200 copies. Bibliography: leaves 51-53. LC Card 85-209374
1. Corrientes (Argentina) - Population - History - 19th century. 2. Corrientes (Argentina) - Census, 1850. 3. Corrientes (Argentina) - Census, 1857. I. Ramírez, Mirta Beatriz. II. Title. III. Series.
HB3560.C67 S65 1980

Soobshcheniia po prikladnoĭ matematike.
Abdullaev, A. Kh. Zadacha razmeshcheniia sel'skokhoziaĭstvennogo proizvodstva v ob"edinenii khoziaĭstv meliorativnoĭ sistemy /. Moskva , 1985. 24, [2] p. ; LC Card 86-162160
HD9015.S652 A23 1985

Shakhdzhakhan, Ali. Issledovanie odnoĭ matematicheskoĭ modeli ėkonomicheskogo rosta /. Moskva , 1983. 29, [2] p. : LC Card 83-176389
HD75.5 .S52 1983

Zoidov, K. Kh. Ob approksimatsii makroėkonomicheskikh zavisimosteĭ posredstvom tablichnykh i splaĭnovykh proizvodstvennykh funktsiĭ /. Moskva , 1985. 25, [3] p. : LC Card 86-162091
HB142 .Z65 1985

Soom, Arnold. Der baltische Getreidehandel im 17. Jahrhundert / von Arnold Soom. Stockholm : Almqvist & Wiksell, 1961. 350 p. ; 23 cm. (Kungl. Vitterhets historie och antikvitets akademiens handlingar. Historiska serien . 8 d.) Bibliography: p. [332]-338. Includes indexes. LC Card 85-122593 DDC 380.1/4131/09474 19
1. Grain trade - Baltic States - History - 17th century. I. Title. II. Title: Baltische Getreidehandel im siebzehnten Jahrhundert. III. Series.
HD9045.S63 B37 1961

Soós, Gábor, 1922- Mit kell tudni a magyar agrártermelésről? / írta, Soós Gábor és Misi Sándor. [Budapest] : Kossuth, 1984. 218 p. ; 19 cm. (Mit kell tudni, 0324-7813) ISBN 963-09-2474-9 : LC Card 85-154641
1. Agriculture - Economic aspects - Hungary. 2. Food industry and trade - Hungary. 3. Forests and forestry - Hungary. I. Misi, Sándor. II. Title. III. Series.
HD1940.5 .S66 1984

Soós, Károly Attila. Terv, kampány, pénz : szabályozás és konjunktúraciklusok Magyarországon és Jugoszláviában / Soós Károly Attila. Budapest : Közgazdasági és Jogi Könyvkiadó, 1986. 532 p. : ill. ; 25 cm. At head of title: MTA Közgazdaságtudományi Intézet. Bibliography: p. 501-[516]. Includes indexes. ISBN 963-221-575-3 : LC Card 87-137237
1. Business cycles - Hungary. 2. Business cycles - Yugoslavia. 3. Hungary - Economic policy - 1968-. 4. Yugoslavia - Economic policy - 1945-. 5. Money - Hungary. 6. Money - Yugoslavia. 7. Capital investments - Hungary. 8. Capital investments - Yugoslavia. 9. Central planning - Europe, Eastern. I. Magyar Tudományos Akadémia. Közgazdaságtudományi Intézet. II. Title.
HB3787.5 .S66 1986

Soós, Lőrinc. Nagyné Szauter, Edit. A gazdaságilag elmaradott térségek társadalmi-gazdasági jellemzői /. Budapest , 1986. 41 p. : LC Card 86-215345
HC300.28 .N26 1986

Sootnoshenie khozraschetnoĭ ėkonomicheskoĭ ėffektivnosti sredstv proizvodstva s ikh narodno-khoziaĭstvennoĭ ėffektivnost'iu /. Shusharin, A. L. (Aleksandr Leonidovich) Tomsk , 1979. 159 p. ; LC Card 87-462036
HD70.S63 S55 1979

Sopade. see **Sozialdemokratische Partei Deutschlands.**

Soper, J. Leeds transport / by J. Soper. [Bramham, Wetherby, West Yorkshire] : Leeds Transport Historical Society, 1985- v. <1 > : ill. (some col.), maps ; 31 cm. Three folded maps in pocket. CONTENTS. - v. 1. 1830-1902. ISBN 0-9510280-0-6 (v. 1) : LC Card 87-103287 DDC 388.4/09428/19 19
1. Local transit - England - Leeds (West Yorkshire) - History. I. Title.
HE4719.L4 S67 1985

Sopher, Terry. Kloepfer, Deanne. The Watt record . Washington, D.C. [1983] ii, 66, 9, 3 p. : LC Card 86-232533 DDC 333.1/0973 19
HD183.L3 K58 1983

Soplín E., Samuel (Soplín Escudero) La sindicalización postal telegráfica en el Perú : apuntes históricos / Samuel Soplín E. Lima : Tarea, [1986] 57 p., [4] p. of plates : ill. ; 21 cm. Bibliography: p. 55-57. LC Card 87-145465 DDC 331.88/113834985 19
1. Trade-unions - Postal service - Peru - History. 2. Trade-unions - Telegraphers - Peru - History. I. Title.
HE6899.P4 S66 1986

Sorani, Silvano. Buzzetti, Luciano. Il distaccamento italiano di Palestina, 1917-1921 /. Milano , c1976. 55 p. : LC Card 86-179004
HE6185.P13 B89 1976

SORB (Series) .
(6) Konferensie Vakbondwese in Suid-Afrika (1984 : Randse Afrikaanse Universiteit) Konferensie Vakbondwese in Suid-Afrika . Johannesburg [1984] 73 p. ; ISBN 0-86970-252-1 LC Card 87-126320
HD6870.5 .K65 1984

Sorden, L. G. (Leland George) Corrigan, George A., 1896-1981. Calked boots and cant hooks /. Ashland, WI , 1986, c1976. xxi, 265 p. : ISBN 0-9613961-5-6 (pbk.) : LC Card 87-401439 DDC 331.7/634982/0924 B 19
HD8039.L92 U535 1986

Sørensen, Inge Sofie. Søgaard, Villy. Offshoreaktiviteter i Nordsøen og basebyen Esbjerg /. [Århus] , 1983. 200 p. : ISBN 87-88615-02-2 : LC Card 84-164755
HD9575.N62 S64 1983

Sorensen, John H. Impacts of hazardous technology . Albany , c1987. x, 233 p. : ISBN 0-88706-332-2 LC Card 86-1943 DDC 363.1/79 19
HD9698.U54 M475 1987 *NYPL [JLE 87-1233]*

Sørensen, Knut Ø. Skoglund, Tor. Regionale strukturendringer belyst ved sysselsettingstall /. Oslo , 1983. 52 p. ; ISBN 82-537-2003-3 : LC Card 84-161751
HD5800.A6 S58 1983

Sørensen, Peter Birch. Økonomisk politik i en åben økonomi / af Peter Birch Sørensen. København : DSF forlag : Landbohøjskolen, 1985. vi, 179 p. : ill. ; 30 cm. Bibliography: p. 178-179. LC Card 86-135751
1. Economics - Mathematical models. 2. Denmark - Economic conditions - Mathematical models. I. Title.
HB135 .S575 1985

Sorge, Friedrich A. (Friedrich Adolf), 1828-1906. Friedrich A. Sorge's labor movement in the United States : a history of the American working class from 1890 to 1896 / translated by Kai Schoenhals. New York : Greenwood Press, c1987. xiii, 196 p. ; 25 cm. (Contributions in economics and economic history, 0084-9235 . no. 73) Includes bibliographies and index. ISBN 0-313-25518-0 (lib. bdg. : alk. paper) LC Card 86-31792 DDC 331/.0973 19
1. Labor and laboring classes - United States - History - 19th century. 2. Labor disputes - United States - History - 19th century. 3. Trade-unions - United States - History - 19th century. I. Schoenhals, Kai P. II. Title. III. Title: Labor movement in the United States. IV. Series.
HD8072 .S7175 1987

SORGHUM INDUSTRY - ETHIOPIA.
Dejene Aredo. Economic study of the establishment of sorghum mill and dehuller in Ethiopia . [Addis Ababa?] [1986] 37 leaves ; LC Card 87-980144 DDC 338.1/73174/0963 19
HD9049.S6 E83 1986

SORIA (SPAIN : PROVINCE) - CIVILIZATION.
Romero, Carmelo, 1950- Historia contemporánea de Soria, 1860-1936 . [Soria] , 1982. 510 p. : ISBN 84-85792-02-5 LC Card 85-136084
HC387.S67 R66 1982

SORIA (SPAIN : PROVINCE) - ECONOMIC CONDITIONS.
Romero, Carmelo, 1950- Historia contemporánea de Soria, 1860-1936 . [Soria] , 1982. 510 p. : ISBN 84-85792-02-5 LC Card 85-136084
HC387.S67 R66 1982

SORIA (SPAIN : PROVINCE) - POLITICS AND GOVERNMENT.
Romero, Carmelo, 1950- Historia contemporánea de Soria, 1860-1936 . [Soria] , 1982. 510 p. : ISBN 84-85792-02-5 LC Card 85-136084
HC387.S67 R66 1982

SORIA (SPAIN : PROVINCE) - POPULATION - HISTORY.
Romero, Carmelo, 1950- Historia contemporánea de Soria, 1860-1936 . [Soria] , 1982. 510 p. : ISBN 84-85792-02-5 LC Card 85-136084
HC387.S67 R66 1982

SORIA (SPAIN : PROVINCE) - SOCIAL CONDITIONS.
Romero, Carmelo, 1950- Historia contemporánea de Soria, 1860-1936 . [Soria] , 1982. 510 p. : ISBN 84-85792-02-5 LC Card 85-136084
HC387.S67 R66 1982

SORIA (SPAIN) - CENSUS, 1752.
Pérez de Guinea, María del Carmen. Estudio sobre la sociedad soriana en el siglo XVIII . [Spain] [1982?] 296 p. ; LC Card 85-136714
HA1559.S65 P47 1982

SORIA (SPAIN) - CENSUS, 1787.
Pérez de Guinea, María del Carmen. Estudio sobre la sociedad soriana en el siglo XVIII . [Spain] [1982?] 296 p. ; LC Card 85-136714
HA1559.S65 P47 1982

SORIA (SPAIN) - CENSUS, 1797.
Pérez de Guinea, María del Carmen. Estudio sobre la sociedad soriana en el siglo XVIII . [Spain] [1982?] 296 p. ; LC Card 85-136714
HA1559.S65 P47 1982

SORIA (SPAIN) - POPULATION - HISTORY - 18TH CENTURY.
Pérez de Guinea, María del Carmen. Estudio sobre la sociedad soriana en el siglo XVIII . [Spain] [1982?] 296 p. ; LC Card 85-136714
HA1559.S65 P47 1982

Sorj, Bernardo. Goodman, David, 1938- From farming to biotechnology . Oxford , New York, N.Y. , 1987. 214 p. : ISBN 0-631-14405-6 : LC Card 87-687 DDC 338.1/6 19
HD1433 .G66 1987

Soros, George. The alchemy of finance : reading the mind of the market / George Soros. New York : Simon and Schuster, c1987. 351 p. : ill. (some col.) ; 25 cm. Bibliography: p. 350-351. ISBN 0-671-63455-0 LC Card 87-4745 DDC 332.6/78 19
1. Investments. I. Title.
HG4515 .S67 1987

Sorrentino, Richard M. Handbook of motivation and cognition . New York , c1986. x, 610 p. : ISBN 0-89862-667-6 LC Card 85-24916 DDC 153.8 19
BF503 .H36 1986 ***NYPL [JFE 86-2410]***

Soto Carniago, Juan José de. Sociedades cooperativas, plan de cuentas : adaptación del P.G.C. / Juan José de Soto Carniago ; prólogo de Eduardo Galán Corona. Cáceres : Universidad de Extremadura : Caja Rural Provincial de Cáceres, 1984. xv, 150 p. ; 21 cm. (Derecho) ISBN 84-600-3441-0 LC Card 84-221264
1. Cooperative societies - Spain - Accounting. I. Series: Derecho (Universidad de Extemadura (Cáceres, Spain). Servicio de Publicaciones). II. Title.
HF5686.C67 S67 1984

Soto, Hernando de, 1941- El otro sendero : la revolución informal / Hernando de Soto en colaboración con Enrique Ghersi, Mario Ghibellini y el Instituto Libertad y Democracia (ILD) ; prólogo de Mario Vargas Llosa. [Lima] : Editorial El Barranco, 1986. xxxvi, 317 p. : ill., ports. ; 24 cm. Includes bibliographical references. LC Card 87-400476 DDC 381 19
1. Informal sector (Economics) - Peru. I. Ghersi, Enrique. II. Ghibellini, Mario. III. Instituto Libertad y Democracia (Lima, Peru). IV. Title.
HD2346.P4 S67 1986

Sotomayor, Octavio. Racionalidad campesina y cambio técnico / Octavio Sotomayor. Cusco : Universidad Nacional de San Antonio Abad del Cusco, Instituto de Investigación UNSAAC-NUFFIC, 1985. 23 p. ; 31 cm. "II curso de planificación agrícola y proyectos microregiones." "Convenio de Cooperación Inter Universitaria Peruano-Holandés"--Cover. Includes bibliographical references. LC Card 86-200944
1. Peasantry - Peru. 2. Agricultural innovations - Peru. 3. Small business - Peru - Technological innovations. I. Instituto de Investigación UNSAAC-NUFFIC. II. Title.
HD1531.P4 S67 1985

Sot͡sialisticheskai͡a dist͡siplina truda i sot͡sialʹnye faktory ee ukreplenii͡a v trudovykh kollektivakh /. Saltovskiĭ, I. A. (Ivan Aleksandrovich) Kiev , 1985. 118, [2] p. ; LC Card 86-220755
HF5549.5.L3 S27 1985

Sot͡sialisticheskai͡a ėkonomicheskai͡a integrat͡sii͡a--faktor povyshenii͡a ėffektivnosti proizvodstva stran SĖV /. Zhamin, V. A. (Vitaliĭ Alekseevich) Moskva , Varna , 1978. 93 p. ; LC Card 81-149558
HC244 .Z46 1978

Sot͡sialisticheskai͡a ėkonomicheskai͡a integrat͡sii͡a--v deĭstvii.
Zhamin, V. A. (Vitaliĭ Alekseevich) Sot͡sialisticheskai͡a ėkonomicheskai͡a integrat͡sii͡a--faktor povyshenii͡a ėffektivnosti proizvodstva stran SĖV /. Moskva , Varna , 1978. 93 p. ; LC Card 81-149558
HC244 .Z46 1978

Sot͡sialisticheskai͡a integrat͡sii͡a i nauchno-tekhnicheskai͡a revoli͡ut͡sii͡a /. Bykov, A. N. (Aleksandr Naumovich) Moskva , 1981. 343 p. ; LC Card 82-101911
HC244.Z9 T43 1981

Sot͡sialisticheskai͡a sobstvennostʹ v uslovii͡akh razvitogo sot͡sializma : referativnyĭ sbornik / [redaktsionnai͡a kollegii͡a V.P. Kazakevich, M.E. Tovmosi͡an (otv. redaktor)]. Moskva : Akademii͡a nauk SSSR, In-t nauch. informat͡sii po obshchestvennym naukam, 1984. 165 p. ; 20 cm. (Seria Aktualʹnye problemy razvitogo sot͡sializma) Includes bibliographies. LC Card 85-177805
1. Socialist property. 2. Socialist property - Soviet Union. I. Kazakevich, V. P. II. Tovmosi͡an, M. E. III. Series.
HB701 .S59 1984

Sot͡sialisticheskie proizvodstvennye otnoshenii͡a . Solodkova, S. V. (Serafima Vasilʹevna) Moskva , 1984. 141 p. ; LC Card 84-223476
HC336.25 .S65 1984

Sot͡sialisticheskoe obobshchestvlenie truda / [otvetstvennyĭ redaktor P.V. Savchenko]. Moskva : Izd-vo "Nauka," 1981. 166 p. ; 20 cm. (Problemy sovetskoĭ ėkonomiki) At head of title: Akademii͡a nauk SSSR. Institut ėkonomiki. Includes bibliographical references. LC Card 82-161177
1. Labor supply - Soviet Union. 2. Labor and laboring classes - Soviet Union. I. Savchenko, P. V. (Polʹ Vi͡acheslavovich). II. Institut ėkonomiki (Akademii͡a nauk SSSR).
HD5796 .S633 1981

Sot͡sialisticheskoe sorevnovanie i intensifikat͡sii͡a proizvodstva /. Antanaĭtis, I͡U. A. (I͡Ustinas Antanovich) Moskva , 1987. 157 p. : LC Card 87-103350
HC337.L53 S63 1987

Sot͡sialisticheskoe stroitelʹstvo v sibirskoĭ derevne, noi͡abrʹ 1919-mart 1921 g. /. Shishkin, V. I. (Vladimir Ivanovich) Novosibirsk , 1985. 316 p. ; LC Card 86-164936
HD1995.S5 S45 1985

Sot͡sialisticheskoto sŭrevnovanie v uslovii͡ata na intenzifikat͡sii͡ata na proizvodstvoto /. Bliznakov, Iordan Petrov. Sofii͡a , 1983. 101 p. : LC Card 85-140845
HC403.Z9 S613 1983

Sot͡sializm--opyt, problemy, perspektivy (Izdaetlʹstvo politicheskoĭ literatury)
Agrarnai͡a politika sotsialisticheskikh stran na sovremennom ėtape /. Moskva , 1981. 366 p. ; LC Card 82-109367
HD1918 .A37 1981

Sot͡sializm--opyt, problemy, perspektivy (Izdatelʹstvo Nauka)
Maksimov, A. L. (Alekseĭ Lʹvovich) Rabochee i svobodnoe vremi͡a v uslovii͡akh razvitogo sotsializma /. Moskva , 1981. 95 p. ; LC Card 82-104233
HD5195 .M34 1981

Sot͡sialʹnai͡a napravlennostʹ planov . Zenchenko, N. S. Moskva , 1985. 221 p. ; LC Card 86-106277
HC337.R85 Z45 1985

Sot͡sialʹnai͡a struktura.
Osobennosti popolnenii͡a osnovnykh otri͡adov intelligent͡sii /. Tallin , 1981. 131 p. : LC Card 82-125732
HD8038.S652 E775 1981

Sot͡sialnata programa na partii͡ata-delo na trudovii͡a kolektiv /. Radev, Simeon. Sofii͡a , 1984. 173 p. ; LC Card 84-172433
HD8626.5 .R32 1984

Sot͡sialʹno-demograficheskai͡a struktura gorodskogo naselenii͡a i ego zani͡atostʹ /. Petrov, V. A. (Valeriĭ Arkadʹevich) Moskva , 1981. 151 p. ; LC Card 82-145197
HB2277 .P48 1981

Sot͡sialʹno-demograficheskoe razvitie krupnogo goroda /. Baranov, A. V. (Alʹbert Vasilʹevich) Moskva , 1981. 189 p. : LC Card 82-114309
HB3608.L4 B37 1981

Sot͡sialʹno-ėkonomicheskai͡a ėffektivnostʹ obshchestvennogo proizvodstva--sushchnostʹ, komponenty i voprosy ikh ot͡senki / nauchnyĭ redaktor V.I. Drits. Minsk : "Nauka i tekhnika," 1983. 158 p. ; 20 cm. At head of title: Akademii͡a nauk Belorusskoĭ SSR. Institut ėkonomiki. Includes bibliographical references. LC Card 83-206045
1. Industrial productivity - Soviet Union. 2. Basic needs - Soviet Union. I. Drits, V. I. (Valentin Ivanovich). II. Instytut ėkanomiki (Akadėmii͡a navuk Belaruskaĭ SSR).
HC340.I52 S67 1983

Sot͡sialʹno-ėkonomicheskai͡a istorii͡a Rossii . Druzhinin, N. M. (Nikolaĭ Mikhaĭlovich) Moskva , 1987. 421 p., [1] leaf of plates : LC Card 87-164847
HC334.5 .D78 1987

Sot͡sialʹno-ėkonomicheskai͡a priroda i formy neobkhodimogo produkta pri sot͡sializme /. Kurochkin, I͡U. P. (I͡Uriĭ Petrovich) Leningrad , 1984. 135 p. ; LC Card 84-218003
HC340.B38 K87 1984

Sot͡sialʹno-ėkonomicheskai͡a struktura Azerbaĭdzhana v ėpokhu imperializma /. Ismailov, Makhmud. Baku , 1982. 163 p. ; LC Card 83-189608
HC337.A9 I85 1982

Sot͡sialʹno-ėkonomicheskai͡a sushchnostʹ obshchenarodnogo khozi͡aĭstvennogo mekhanizma / pod redaktsieĭ V.P. Kornienko i L.G. Andreeva. Kiev : Gol. izd-vo izdatelʹskogo obʺedinenii͡a "Vyshcha shkola", 1985. 342 p. ; 21 cm. Includes bibliographical references. LC Card 86-197710
1. Soviet Union - Economic policy - 1981-. 2. Soviet Union - Economic conditions - 1976-. I. Kornienko, V. P. II. Andreev, L. G. (Leonid Grigorʹevich).
HC336.25 .S668 1985

Sot͡sialʹno-ėkonomicheskie problemy intensifikat͡sii obshchestvennogo proizvodstva / [otvetstvennyĭ redaktor V.G. Grebennikov]. Moskva : Vses. nauch.-issl. in-t sistemnykh issledovaniĭ, 1983. 91 p. : ill. ; 26 cm. (Sbornik trudov / VNII sistemnykh issledovaniĭ . vyp. 2) Includes bibliographies. LC Card 84-114234
1. Industrial productivity - Soviet Union. 2. Efficiency, Industrial - Soviet Union. 3. Labor and laboring classes - Soviet Union - Attitudes. 4. Labor productivity - Soviet Union. I. Grebennikov, Valeriĭ Grigorʹevich. II. Series: Sbornik trudov (Vsesoi͡uznyĭ nauchno-issledovatelʹskiĭ institut sistemnykh issledovaniĭ) , 1983, vyp. 2.
HD56 .S688 1983

Sot͡sialʹno-ėkonomicheskie problemy ispolʹzovanii͡a trudovykh resursov / [redaktory V.N. Viktorov, V.A. Alekseev]. Cheboksary : Nauchno-issl. in-t i͡azyka, lit-ry, istorii i ėkonomiki pri Sovete Ministrov Chuvashskoĭ ASSR, 1986. 70 p. ; 20 cm. Includes

bibliographies. LC Card 87-137786
1. Labor supply - Russian S.F.S.R. - Chuvashskai͡a A.S.S.R. I. Viktorov, V. N. II. Alekseev, V. A. III. Chuvashskai͡a A.S.S.R. (R.S.F.S.R.). Nauchno-issledovatel′skiĭ institut i͡azyka, literatury, istorii i ėkonomiki.
HD5797.C56 S68 1986

Sot͡sial′no-ėkonomicheskie problemy kompleksnoĭ mekhanizat͡sii sel′skokhozi͡aĭstvennogo proizvodstva /. Larkin, V. A. (Vladimir Alekseevich) Moskva , 1981. 148 p. ; LC Card 82-157096
HD1992 .L375 1981

Sot͡sial′no-ėkonomicheskie problemy sfery obsluzhivanii͡a naselenii͡a v uslovii͡akh nauchno-tekhnicheskogo progressa /. Shedenov, U. K. (Utegali Kadyrgalievich) Alma-Ata , 1978. 197, [3] p. ; LC Card 81-149568
HD9986.S683 K398 1978

Sot͡sial′no-ėkonomicheskiĭ ėksperiment v kolkhoze /. Smirnov, V. D. (Vasiliĭ Dmitrievich) Novosibirsk , 1986. 111 p. : LC Card 86-171536
HD1492.S652 S527 1986

Sot͡sial′no-ėkonomicheskoe i kul′turnoe razvitie Zabaĭkal′i͡a : materialy k "Istorii rabochego klassa Sibiri" / [redakt͡sionnai͡a kollegii͡a E.V. Vasil′evskai͡a ... I.I. Komogort͡sev (otv. redaktor) ... et al.]. Novosibirsk : Izd-vo "Nauka," Sibirskoe otd-nie, 1980. 283 p. ; 21 cm. At head of title: Akademii͡a nauk SSSR. Sibirskoe otdelenie. Institut istorii, filologii i filosofii. Includes bibliographical references. LC Card 81-132139
1. Transbaikalia (R.S.F.S.R.) - Economic conditions. 2. Transbaikalia (R.S.F.S.R.) - Social conditions. I. Vasil′evskai͡a, E. V. (Ėmilii͡a Viktorovna). II. Komogort͡sev, I. I. (Ivan Ivanovich). III. Institut istorii, filologii i filosofii (Akademii͡a nauk SSSR). IV. Title: Istorii͡a rabochego klassa Sibiri.
HC337.R852 T737 1980

Sot͡sial′no-ekonomichni ideï v zmahanni͡akh halyts′kykh ukraïnt͡siv na perelomi XIX-XX vv. /. Vytanovych, Illi͡a. Mi͡unkhen , 1970. 74 p. ; LC Card 86-214348
HC337.U52 G358 1970

Sot͡sialno-ikonomicheski problemi na izpolzuvane truda na mladezhite /. Manolov, Angel. Sofii͡a , 1984. 93 p. ; LC Card 86-226913
HD6276.B82 M36 1984

Sot͡sial′noe planirovanie na predprii͡atii͡akh NRB, GDR i ChSSR /. Kuprii͡anov, L. A. (Leonid Aleksandrovich) Leningrad , 1984. 111 p. ; LC Card 85-116781
HD7741.5 .K86 1984

Sot͡sial′noe razvitie molodezhi v trudovykh kollektivakh novykh gorodov Sibiri : sbornik nauchnykh trudov / [redakt͡sionnai͡a kollegii͡a N.K. Kuznet͡sov ... V.Kh. Kharnakhoev (otvetstvennyĭ redaktor) ... et al.]. Irkutsk : Irkutskiĭ gos. universitet im. A.A. Zhdanova, 1980. 158 p. ; 20 cm. At head of title: Ministerstvo vysshego i srednego spet͡sial′nogo obrazovanii͡a RSFSR. Irkutskiĭ gosudarstvennyĭ universitet im. A.A. Zhdanova. Includes bibliographical references. LC Card 82-110658
1. Young adults - Employment - Russian S.F.S.R. - Siberia, Eastern. 2. Young adults - Russian S.F.S.R. - Siberia, Eastern - Recreation. 3. New towns - Russian S.F.S.R. - Siberia, Eastern. 4. Socialism and youth - Russian S.F.S.R. - Siberia, Eastern. I. Kuznet͡sov, N. K. II. Kharnakhoev, V. Kh. (Viktor Kharitonovich). III. Irkutskiĭ gosudarstvennyĭ universitet im. A.A. Zhdanova.
HD6276.S593 S527 1980

Sot͡sial′noe upravlenie . Martanus, R. V. (Ri͡urik Vital′evich) Moskva , 1986. 141 p. ; LC Card 87-156789
HD38.25.S65 M35 1986

Sot͡sial′noe upravlenie trudovym kollektivom : rol′ profsoi͡uznoĭ organizat͡sii / [pod redakt͡sieĭ I͡U.E. Volkova i O.I. Shkaratana]. Moskva : Profizdat, 1987. 181 p. ; 20 cm. Includes bibliographical references. LC Card 87-103391
1. Personnel management - Soviet Union. 2. Trade-unions - Soviet Union. 3. Labor and laboring classes - Soviet Union. I. Volkov, I͡U. E. (I͡Uriĭ Evgen′evich). II. Shkaratan, O. I. (Ovseĭ Irmovich).
HF5549.2.S65 S675 1987

Sot͡sial′nye problemy truda u narodnosteĭ Severa / otvetstvennyĭ redaktor V.I. Boĭko. Novosibirsk : Izd-vo "Nauka," Sibirskoe otd-nie, 1986. 213 p. ; 21 cm. On leaf preceding t.p.: Akademii͡a nauk SSSR. Sibirskoe otdelenie. Institut istorii, filologii i filosofii. Includes bibliographies. LC Card 87-164784
1. Labor supply - Soviet Union, Northern. 2. Soviet Union, Northern - Occupations. 3. Minorities - Employment - Soviet Union, Northern. 4. Minorities - Soviet Union, Northern - Social conditions. I. Boĭko, Vladimir Ivanovich. II. Institut istorii, filologii i filosofii (Akademii͡a nauk SSR).
HD5797.N75 S67 1986

Sot͡siologii͡a na truda /. Petkov, Krŭst′o. Sofii͡a , 1985- v. <1 > : LC Card 86-232374
HD6955 .P485 1985

Sot͡siologii͡a na trudovii͡a kolektiv . Petkov, Krŭst′o. Sofii͡a , 1982. 184 p. ; LC Card 83-124278
HD6957.B85 P47 1982 ***NYPL [*QK 86-4733]***

Sottoriva, Fabio. Annullamenti del Trentino-Alto Adige, 1850-1883 = Trentino-Südtirol Abstempelungen, 1850-1883 / Fabio Sottoriva. Rovereto : Filasta, c1981. 184 p., [8] p. of plates : ill. (some col.) ; 25 cm. "300 copies"--P. [3] Bibliography: p. 183-184. LC Card 86-178380
1. Cancellations (Philately) - Italy - Trentino-Alto Adige - Catalogs. 2. Cancellations (Philately) - Italy - Trentino-Alto Adige - History - 19th century. I. Title. II. Title: Trentino-Südtirol Abstempelungen, 1850-1883.
HE6185.I72 T747 1981

Soudan. see **Sudan.**

Souden, David.
Malthus, T. R. (Thomas Robert, 1766-1834. An essay on the principle of population . London , 1986. 2 v. (18, xv, 711 p.) : ISBN 1-85196-102-X (v. 1) LC Card 87-672118
HB861 .A2x 1986 vol. 2-3

Malthus, T. R. (Thomas Robert, 1766-1834. An essay on the principle of population . London , 1986. 139 p. : ISBN 1-85196-101-1 LC Card 87-672117
HB861 .A2x 1986 vol. 1

Malthus, T. R. (Thomas Robert, 1766-1834. Essays on political economy /. London , 1986. 327 p. : ISBN 1-85196-107-0 LC Card 87-672114
HB861 .A2x 1986 vol. 7

Malthus, T. R. (Thomas Robert, 1766-1834. Essays on population /. London , 1986. 246 p. : ISBN 1-85196-104-6 LC Card 87-672116
HB861 .A2x 1986 vol. 4

Malthus, T. R. (Thomas Robert, 1766-1834. Principles of political economy . London , 1986. 2 v. (18, x, 439 p.) : ISBN 1-85196-105-4 (v. 1) LC Card 87-672115
HB861 .A2x 1986 vol. 5-6

Souder, Wm. E. (William E.) Managing new product innovations / William E. Souder. Lexington, Mass. : Lexington Books, c1987. xviii, 251 p. : ill. ; 24 cm. Includes bibliographies and index. ISBN 0-669-10809-X (alk. paper) LC Card 85-40104 DDC 658.5/75 19
1. New products - Management. I. Title.
HD69.N4 S634 1987

Sougue, Matthieu Kounabé. La pratique de l'audit financier dans les entreprises au Sénégal, à travers le cabinet Helios : mémoire de fin d'études / présenté et soutenu le 30 juin 1983 par Matthieu Kounabé Sougue. [Dakar] : Université de Dakar, Ecole nationale supérieure universitaire de technologie, Formation école supérieure de commerce, Dép. finances, comptabilité, [1983?] 194, [18] leaves : ill. ; 30 cm. Thesis (diplôme d'études supérieures de commerce et d'administration des entreprises)--Université de Dakar, 1983. Bibliography: leaves [218]-[222] LC Card 85-121418
1. Corporations - Senegal - Auditing. 2. Business enterprises - Senegal - Auditing. 3. Auditing. I. Title.
HF5686.C7 S67 1984

The soul of the wobblies . Winters, Donald E. Westport, Conn. , 1985. 159 p. ; ISBN 0-313-24472-3 (lib. bdg.) LC Card 84-27973 DDC 331.88/6 19
HD8055.I5 W56 1985 ***NYPL [JLD 87-775]***

SOUND RECORDING INDUSTRY - UNITED STATES.
The Compact disc market--phase II . New York, N.Y. (444 Madison Ave., New York 10022) , c1986. viii, 57, [13] p. : LC Card 86-227224 DDC 381/.4562138933 19
HD9697.P563 U526 1986

Wacholtz, Larry E. Inside country music /. New York , 1986. 254 p. ; ISBN 0-8230-7532-X (pbk. : alk. paper) LC Card 86-4234 DDC 784.5/2/002373 19
ML3790 .W24 1986 ***NYPL [JNE 86-18]***

Sourang, Abdou. Le rôle du mouvement coopératif dans le développement du Sénégal : mémoire de fin d'études, année académique 1980-1981 / par Abdou Sourang. [Dakar] : République du Sénégal, Ministère de l'enseignement supérieur et de la recherche scientifique, Ecole nationale d'administration et de magistrature, [1981] 44 leaves : ill. ; 30 cm. LC Card 85-207626
1. Cooperation - Senegal. 2. Senegal - Economic policy. I. Ecole nationale d'administration et de magistrature (Senegal). II. Title.
HD3567.7.A4 S67 1981

Source papers in economic history, 0813-5398 . (no. 13) Barnard, A. (Alan) Some government financial data, 1850 to 1982 /. Canberra, Australia [1986] 47, 2 p. ; ISBN 0-86784-850-2 (pbk.) LC Card 86-211320 DDC 336.94 19
HJ2193.Z7 B37 1986

Sourcebook of personal computing. Bowker's complete sourcebook of personal computing 1985. New York , c1984. lxviii, 1050 p. ; ISBN 0-8352-1931-3 (pbk.) : LC Card 84-20460 DDC 001.64 19
QA76.5 .B669 1984 ***NYPL [JSE 86-443]***

Sources : a directory of electronics information agencies outside the United States / [prepared by the Marketing Services Department, Electronic Industries Association]. Washington, D.C. (2001 Eye St., N.W., Washington 20006) : The Dept., c1987. vi, 147 p. ; 28 cm. LC Card 87-165452 DDC 016.3384/7621381 19
1. Electronic industries - Information services - Directories. I. Electronic Industries Association. Marketing Services.
HD9696.A2 S594 1987

Sources. Financial Sourcebooks' sources . Naperville, Ill. , c1987. 454 p. ; ISBN 0-942061-00-4 (pbk.) : LC Card 87-8793 DDC 332/.025/73 19
HG173 .F517 1987

Sources and methods of estimation of national income at current prices in the Gambia. [Banjul, Gambia] : Central Statistics Dept., Ministry of Economic Planning and Industrial Development, [1985] vi, 151 p. ; 30 cm. "February 1985." LC Card 87-116289 DDC 339.366/51 19
1. National income - Gambia - Statistics. I. Gambia. Central Statistics Dept.
HC1070.Z9 I57 1985

Sources et méthodes d'élaboration des comptes nationaux. Les administrations publiques. [Paris] : Ministère de l'économie, des finances et du budget, Institut national de la statistique et des études économiques : Service "Produits de diffusion", [1983] 481 p. ; 30 cm. (Nos 440-441 des Collections de l'INSEE. Série C, 0533-0793 . nos 111-112) "Octobre 1983." "INSEE, Direction de la comptabilité publique"--Cover. Includes index. LC Card 84-161813
1. Finance, Public - France - Accounting. 2. Local finance - France - Accounting. 3. National income - France - Accounting. I. France. Direction de la comptabilité publique. II. Title: Administrations publiques. III. Series: Collections de l'INSEE , no 440-441.
HC271 .A218 no. 440-441 HJ9925.F8

Sources of capital formation and accumulation among Kano entrepreneurs, 1950-1980 /. Bashir, Ibrahim Lawan, 1948- Boston, MA (270 Bay State Rd., Boston 02215) , 1986. 17 leaves ; LC Card 87-156659 DDC 332/.0415/096695 19
HC1055.Z9 S33 1986

The sources of innovation /. Hippel, Eric von. New York , c1988. xi, 218 p. : ISBN 0-19-504085-6 (alk. paper) LC Card 86-28620 DDC 338/.06 19
HC79.T4 H56 1988

Sources of population statistics in Lesotho /. Makatjane, Tiisetso. [Roma, Lesotho] [1985] iii, 29 leaves ; LC Card 87-132320 DDC

304.6/09681/6 19
HA37.L52 M35 1985

Sources of state information on corporations. How to find company intelligence in state documents /. Washington, D.C. , c1986. 110 p. ; ISBN 0-934940-38-X (pbk.) LC Card 86-218108 DDC 016.3387/4/0973 19
HD2785 .H67 1986

Sourrouille, Juan V. Inversiones extranjeras en América Latina : política económica, decisiones de inversión y comportamiento económico de las filiales / Juan V. Sourrouille, Francisco Gatto, Bernardo Kosacoff ; y la colaboración de Javier Cardozo. Buenos Aires : Instituto para la Integración de América Latina, Banco Interamericano de Desarrollo, [1984] viii, 142 p. : ill. ; 23 cm. (Cooperación empresaria--estudios) Includes bibliographical references. LC Card 86-183036
1. Investments, Foreign - Latin America - Case studies. 2. International business enterprises - Latin America - Case studies. 3. Subsidiary corporations - Latin America - Case studies. I. Gatto, Francisco. II. Kosacoff, Bernardo P. III. Title. IV. Series.
HG5160.5.A3 S64 1984

Sousa, Amaury de. A nova política salarial e as negociações coletivas de trabalho no Brasil, 1979-1982 : um estudo exploratório / Amaury de Souza. [Brazil? : s.n.], 1983. 109 leaves ; 33 cm. Cover title. LC Card 87-404781 DDC 331.2/981 19
1. Wages - Government policy - Brazil - History - 20th century. 2. Collective bargaining - Brazil - History - 20th century. I. Title.
HD5004 .S675 1983

Sousa, Fernando Freire de. A adesão de Portugal à CEE : o impacto do desarmamento aduaneiro português / [Fernando Freire de Sousa, Isabel Alves]. [Porto] : Banco Português de Atlântico, Direcção de Estudos Económicos e de Marketing, Centro de Estudos de Economia Portuguesa, [1985] 96 p. ; 29 cm. (BPA cadernos) LC Card 86-174408
1. Tariff - Portugal. 2. European Economic Community - Portugal. 3. Customs unions. I. Alves, Isabel. II. Title. III. Title: Impacto do desarmamento aduaneiro português. IV. Series.
HF2236 .S68 1985

Sousa Ferreira, Eduardo de. see **Ferreira, Eduardo de Sousa, 1936-**

Sousa, Maria das Graças de. Fernandes, Adelita Neto Carleial. Condições de vida nos bairros de Fortaleza, nov/84 a mar/85 . Fortaleza , 1986. 92 p. : LC Card 86-196902
HC189.F67 F47 1986

Sousa Neto, João Alves de. Manual de orientação sindical urbana e rural : empregados, empregadores, profissionais liberais-autônomos / João Alves de Sousa Neto. S. [i.e. São] Paulo : Publicações Associadas Paulista : Revista Imposto Fiscal, [1980?] xviii, 190 p. : form ; 21 cm. Cover title. LC Card 85-200599
1. Trade-unions - Brazil - São Paulo (State) - Directories. I. Title.
HD6615.S32 S68 1980

SOUTH AFRICA - CENSUS, 1970.
Kruger, Gudrun. Development region D . Port Elizabeth [1985] iv, 89 p. : ISBN 0-86988-274-0 (pbk.) LC Card 86-233113 DDC 304.6/09687/5 19
HA4701.Z9 C354 1985

SOUTH AFRICA - CENSUS, 1980.
Bevolkingsensus 1980 uitgesoekte statistiese streek Vereeniging/Vanderbijlpark/Sasolburg =. Pretoria [1985] xx, 301 p. : ISBN 0-621-09484-6 : LC Card 85-235498
HA4701.Z9 V474 1985

Kruger, Gudrun. Development region D . Port Elizabeth [1985] iv, 89 p. : ISBN 0-86988-274-0 (pbk.) LC Card 86-233113 DDC 304.6/09687/5 19
HA4701.Z9 C354 1985

South Africa. Central Statistical Services. Bevolkingsensus 1980, uitgesoekte statistiese streek Port Elizabeth/Uitenhage/Kirkwood =. [Pretoria] [1985] xix, 317 p. : ISBN 0-621-09480-3 : LC Card 85-241531
HA4701.Z9 P673 1985

Bevolkingsensus 1980, uitgesoekte statistiese streek, Pretoria/Wonderboom =. [Pretoria] [1985?] xx, 476 p. : ISBN 0-621-09483-8 : LC Card 85-238587
HA4701.Z9 P743 1985

Bevolkingsensus 1980 uitgesoekte statistiese streek Vereeniging/Vanderbijlpark/Sasolburg =. Pretoria [1985] xx, 301 p. : ISBN 0-621-09484-6 : LC Card 85-235498
HA4701.Z9 V474 1985

Sensus van landbou- en veeteelproduksie, 1979 =. Pretoria [1985?] xiv, 266 p. ; ISBN 0-621-09380-7 : LC Card 86-150362 DDC 338.1/0968/021 19
HD2130.5 .S48 1985

Sensus van motorhandel en hersteldienste, 1977 =. Pretoria [1982?] xiv, 166 p. : ISBN 0-621-07034-3 : LC Card 82-240419
HD9710.S72 S46 1982

Sensus van wassery-, skoonmaak- en kleurdienste, 1980 =. Pretoria [1984?] xiv, 59 p., [1] folded leaf of plates : ISBN 0-621-08730-0 : LC Card 86-122444
HD9999.L383 S67 1984

SOUTH AFRICA - COMMERCE - AUSTRALIA - STATISTICS.
Kopras, Andrew. Trading with South Africa /. [Canberra] , 1986. 14 p. ; LC Card 87-164241 DDC 382/.0968/094021 19
HF3901.A45 K66 1986

SOUTH AFRICA - COMMERCE - STATISTICS.
Kopras, Andrew. Trading with South Africa /. [Canberra] , 1986. 14 p. ; LC Card 87-164241 DDC 382/.0968/094021 19
HF3901.A45 K66 1986

South Africa. Commission of Inquiry into the Possible Introduction of a Five-Day Working Week in the Mining Industry. Report of the Commission of Inquiry into the Possible Introduction of a Five-Day Working Week in the Mining Industry of the Republic of South Africa. [Pretoria] : Dept. of Mines, Republic of South Africa, 1977. iii, 194 p. : ill. ; 30 cm. Cover title. "RP 97/1977." LC Card 85-148007
1. Hours of labor - South Africa. 2. Mineral industries - South Africa. I. Title.
HD5119.M5982 S68 1977

South Africa. Committee of Inquiry into the Textile and Clothing Industries. The policy of protection in regard to textiles and clothing : report of the Committee of Inquiry into the Textile and Clothing Industries. Pretoria : Republic of South Africa : Govt. Printer [distributor, 1982?] ix, 110, [28] p. ; 30 cm. Includes bibliographical references. ISBN 0-621-08170-1 (pbk.) : LC Card 86-207580 DDC 382/.45677/00968 19
1. Tariff on clothing - South Africa. 2. Tariff on textile fabrics - South Africa. 3. Clothing trade - South Africa. 4. Textile industry - South Africa. I. Title.
HF2651.C635 S627 1982

South Africa. Dept. of Public Works and Land Affairs. Memorandum deur die Minister van Openbare Werke en Grondsake . Pretoria [1985] 16 p. ; ISBN 0-621-09435-8 : LC Card 86-140379
HD4350.5 .M45 1985

South Africa. Dept. of Transport. Inligtingsimposium, 23 Oktober 1981 /. [Pretoria] [1981] 115 p. : LC Card 86-213181 DDC 380.5/0968 19
HE284.4.A2 I55 1981

SOUTH AFRICA. DEPT. OF TRANSPORT - CONGRESSES.
Inligtingsimposium, 23 Oktober 1981 /. [Pretoria] [1981] 115 p. : LC Card 86-213181 DDC 380.5/0968 19
HE284.4.A2 I55 1981

SOUTH AFRICA - ECONOMIC CONDITIONS.
Odén, Bertil, 1939- Sydafrika i södra Afrika /. Uppsala , 1985. 181 p. : ISBN 91-7106-236-X LC Card 85-221741
HC905 .O34 1985 ***NYPL [Sc E 86-483]***

SOUTH AFRICA - ECONOMIC CONDITIONS - TO 1918.
Wheatcroft, Geoffrey. The Randlords /. New York , 1987, c1985. xix, 314 p. : ISBN 0-671-63993-5 (pbk.) : LC Card 87-4513 DDC 338.2/0968 19
HD9536.S62 W44 1985

SOUTH AFRICA - ECONOMIC CONDITIONS - 1961-
Mansfield, W. R. (Willard Ridgway) A management crisis in Natal . [Durban, South Africa] [1985 or 1986] 26 p. ; LC Card 87-400770 DDC 338.0968 19
HC905.Z9 I526 1985

SOUTH AFRICA - ECONOMIC POLICY.
Coetzee, S. F. Regional economic development in the Southern African development area /. Sandton, Republic of South Africa , 1985. xvi, 105 p. : LC Card 87-150264 DDC 338.968 19
HC905 .C64 1985

Multilateral co-operation in southern Africa, 1984 . Pretoria , 1984. 20 p. : ISBN 0-621-09124-3 (pbk.) LC Card 86-209427 DDC 338.968 19
HC905 .M85 1984

SOUTH AFRICA - FOREIGN ECONOMIC RELATIONS - AFRICA, SOUTHERN.
Libby, Ronald T. The politics of economic power in southern Africa /. Princeton, N.J. , c1987. xxii, 361 p. : ISBN 0-691-07723-1 (alk. paper) : LC Card 87-2406 DDC 337.68 19
HF1613.3.Z4 S65 1987

SOUTH AFRICA - FOREIGN ECONOMIC RELATIONS - BELGIUM.
L'Afrique du Sud et nous . [Liège, Belgium] [1984] [69] p. : LC Card 86-200334
HF1554.5.S6 A37 1984

SOUTH AFRICA - FOREIGN ECONOMIC RELATIONS - GREAT BRITAIN.
Moorsom, Richard. The scope for sanctions . London , 1986. 102 p. ; ISBN 0-946848-66-1 (pbk.) : LC Card 86-226230 DDC 337.41068 19
HF1613.4 .M66 1986

South Africa - Government. see **South Africa - Politics and government.**

SOUTH AFRICA - INDUSTRIES - CLASSIFICATION.
Nel, P. A. The BM industrial register and its application in industrial marketing /. Pretoria , 1977. iii, 29, [34] p. ; ISBN 0-949951-74-9 (pbk.) LC Card 85-127469
HC905 .N45 1977

SOUTH AFRICA - INDUSTRIES - HISTORY.
Christie, Renfrew. Electricity, industry, and class in South Africa /. London , 1984. xiii, 241 p. : ISBN 0-333-36288-8 LC Card 87-673182
HD9685.S582 C47x 1984b

SOUTH AFRICA - INDUSTRIES - LOCATION - GOVERNMENT POLICY.
Wellings, Paul. Industrial decentralisation under apartheid . Durban , 1984. 48, xxxii p. : ISBN 0-86980-455-3 (pbk.) LC Card 87-127005 DDC 338.968 19
HC905.Z9 D59 1984

South Africa. National Manpower Commission. Verslag van die Nasionale Mannekragkommissie oor 'n ondersoek na die kleinsakesektor in die Republiek van Suid-Afrika, in die besonder die faktore wat die groei en ontwikkeling daarvan kan belemmer = Report of the National Manpower Commission on an investigation into the small business sector in the Republic of South Africa, with specific reference to the factors that may retard the growth and development thereof. [Pretoria] : Republiek van Suid-Afrika, Raad vir die Bevordering van Kleinsake, [1983] 58 p. ; 30 cm. (Verslag / Nasionale Mannekragkommissie . 1/1984 = 1/1984) Afrikaans and English. Bibliography: p. 54-58. ISBN 0-620-07511-2 LC Card 85-116407 DDC 338.6/42/0968 19
1. Small business - South Africa. 2. Informal sector (Economics) - South Africa. 3. Manpower policy - South Africa. I. Title. II. Title: Report of the National Manpower Commission on an investigation into the small business sector in the Republic of South Africa, with specific reference to the factors that may retard the growth and development thereof. III. Series: Verslag (South Africa. National Manpower Commission) , 84, 1.
HD2346.S63 S64 1983

South Africa. Parliament. House of Assembly. Select Committee on the Accounts of the South African Transport Services. First and second reports of the Select Committee on the Accounts of the South African Transport Services : (S.C.2--'83) reports, proceedings and evidence = Eerste en tweede verslae van die

Gekose Komitee oor die Rekenings van die Suid-Afrikaanse Vervoerdienste : (G.K.2--'83) verslae, verrigtings en getuienis. Pretoria : Govt. Printer, [1983] vii, 74, 7 p. ; 30 cm. Afrikaans and English. ISBN 0-06-210896-5 (pbk.) : LC Card 84-168506 DDC 354.680087/5 19
1. South African Transport Services - Auditing. I. Title. II. Title: Eerste en tweede verslae van die Gekose Komitee oor die Rekenings van die Suid-Afrikaanse Vervoerdienste.
HE284.4 .S68 1983

South Africa. Parliament. House of Assembly. Select Committee on Toll Financing of Roads.
Tweede verslag van die Gekose Komitee oor Tolfinansiering van Paaie = Second report of the Select Committee on Toll Financing of Roads. [Pretoria] : Republiek van Suid-Afrika : Staatsdrukker, [1982] vii p. ; 30 cm. Afrikaans and English. ISBN 0-06-210768-3 : LC Card 83-159014
1. Toll roads - South Africa. I. Title. II. Title: Second report of the Select Committee on Toll Financing of Roads.
HE367.S63 T646 1982

Verslag van die Gekose Komitee oor Tolfinansiering van Paaie = Report of the Select Committee on Toll Financing of Roads. [Pretoria] : Republiek van Suid-Afrika : Staatsdrukker, [1982] xix, 54 p. ; 30 cm. Afrikaans and English. ISBN 0-621-07457-8 : LC Card 83-215629
1. Toll roads - South Africa. I. Title. II. Title: Report of the Select Committee on Toll Financing of Roads.
HE367.S63 T647 1982

SOUTH AFRICA - POLITICS AND GOVERNMENT - 1961-1978.
Fatton, Robert. Black consciousness in South Africa . Albany , c1986. ix, 189 p. ; ISBN 0-88706-127-3 LC Card 85-2855 DDC 305.8/00968 19
DT763.6 .F37 1986 ***NYPL [JLE 86-2289]***

SOUTH AFRICA - POLITICS AND GOVERNMENT - 1978-
Fatton, Robert. Black consciousness in South Africa . Albany , c1986. ix, 189 p. ; ISBN 0-88706-127-3 LC Card 85-2855 DDC 305.8/00968 19
DT763.6 .F37 1986 ***NYPL [JLE 86-2289]***

Rosenthal, Daniel M. The case for South African gold mining stocks . Bethel, CT , c1987. vi, 57 p. : ISBN 0-938689-05-3 (pbk.) LC Card 87-160603 DDC 332.63/22 19
HG293 .R676 1987

SOUTH AFRICA - POPULATION, RURAL - STATISTICS.
Cilliers, S. P. Patterns of migration and settlement in rural South Africa /. [Stellenbosch] , 1986. 19, 13 leaves, 5 folded leaves of plates : ISBN 0-908422-81-4 (pbk.) : LC Card 87-126315 DDC 304.8/0968 19
HB2123.4.A3 C56 1986

SOUTH AFRICA - PUBLIC LANDS - HISTORY.
Christopher, A. J. The Crown lands of British South Africa, 1853-1914 /. Kingston, Ont., Canada , 1984. vii, 247 p., [8] p. of plates : ISBN 0-919642-04-7 LC Card 85-125786 DDC 333.1/0968 19
HD991 .C49 1984 ***NYPL [Sc E 85-373]***

SOUTH AFRICA - PUBLIC WORKS - FINANCE.
Memorandum deur die Minister van Openbare Werke en Grondsake . Pretoria [1985] 16 p. ; ISBN 0-621-09435-8 : LC Card 86-140379
HD4350.5 .M45 1985

SOUTH AFRICA - RELATIONS - ISRAEL.
Hunter, Jane, 1943- Undercutting sanctions . Washington, DC (918 16th St. NW, Suite 501, Washington 20006) , c1987. iv, 71 p. ; LC Card 87-403525 DDC 337.68 19
HF1613.4 .H86 1987

SOUTH AFRICA - RELATIONS - UNITED STATES.
Seidman, Ann Willcox, 1926- The roots of crisis in southern Africa /. Trenton, N.J. [1985] xvii, 209 p. : ISBN 0-86543-026-8 (pbk.) : LC Card 85-72995 DDC 968.06/3 19
E183.8.S6 S45 1985 ***NYPL [Sc E 86-368]***

South Africa (Republic) see South Africa.

SOUTH AFRICA - SOCIAL CONDITIONS - 1961-
Fatton, Robert. Black consciousness in South Africa . Albany , c1986. ix, 189 p. ; ISBN 0-88706-127-3 LC Card 85-2855 DDC 305.8/00968 19
DT763.6 .F37 1986 ***NYPL [JLE 86-2289]***

South Africa, the UC connection / by the UC Divestment Coalition ; with a foreword by Ron Dellums. Berkeley, Calif. : The Coalition, 1985. 39 p. : ill. ; 22 cm. Cover title. LC Card 86-201134 DDC 332.6/73794/068 19
1. Investments, American - South Africa. 2. University of California (System) - Finance. 3. Apartheid - South Africa. I. UC Divestment Coalition.
HG5851.A3 S63 1985

South African Bond and Share Society. The Scripophilist's guide . [Johannesburg? , 1985?] 100 p. : LC Card 87-100584 DDC 769.5 19
HG5851.A3 S37 1985

South African paper money trends . Hern, Brian. Braamfontein, Republic of South Africa , 1986. 172 p. : LC Card 86-201066 DDC 769.5/5968/0750968 19
HG1351.Z8 H47 1986

The South African quagmire : in search of a peaceful path to democratic pluralism / edited by S. Prakash Sethi. Cambridge, Mass. : Ballinger, c1987. xvi, 444 p. ; 24 cm. (Ballinger series in business in a global environment) Bibliography: p. [413]-444. Includes index. ISBN 0-88730-191-6 LC Card 86-28754 DDC 320.5/6 19
1. Economic sanctions, American - South Africa. 2. Economic sanctions - South Africa. 3. Investments, American - South Africa. 4. Investments, Foreign - South Africa. 5. Apartheid - South Africa. I. Sethi, S. Prakash. II. Series.
HF1613.4.Z4 U67 1987

SOUTH AFRICAN TRANSPORT SERVICES - AUDITING.
South Africa. Parliament. House of Assembly. Select Committee on the Accounts of the South African Transport Services. First and second reports of the Select Committee on the Accounts of the South African Transport Services . Pretoria [1983] vii, 74, 7 p. ; ISBN 0-06-210896-5 (pbk.) : LC Card 84-168506 DDC 354.680087/5 19
HE284.4 .S68 1983

South Africa's city of diamonds . Worger, William H. New Haven , c1987. xvi, 330 p. : ISBN 0-300-03716-3 (alk. paper) LC Card 86-24724 DDC 331.7/622382/0968711 19
HD9677.S63 K568 1987

South American and Latin American economic history.
Austin, Ruben Vargas, 1915- The development of economic policy in Mexico with special reference to economic doctrines, 1600-1958 /. New York , 1987. 336 p. ; ISBN 0-8240-1354-9 (alk. paper) : LC Card 87-8569 DDC 338.972 19
HC135 .A84 1987

Bortz, Jeff. Industrial wages in Mexico City, 1939-1975 /. New York , 1987. ix, 529 p. ; ISBN 0-8240-1355-7 (alk. paper) : LC Card 87-8341 DDC 331.2/97253 19
HD4981.Z9 M483 1987

Cardoso, Eliana A. Inflation, growth and the real exchange rate . New York , 1987. 98 p. : ISBN 0-8240-1356-5 (alk. paper) : LC Card 87-8570 DDC 330.981 19
HC187 .C218 1987

Denslow, David, 1942- Sugar production in northeastern Brazil and Cuba, 1858-1908 /. New York , 1987. 172 p. : ISBN 0-8240-1357-3 (alk. paper) : LC Card 87-8525 DDC 338.1/7361/097291 19
HD9114.C89 D45 1987

DeWind, Josh. Peasants become miners . New York , 1987. vii, 421 p. : ISBN 0-8240-1358-1 (alk. paper) LC Card 87-8361 DDC 338.2/0985/23 19
HD8039.M61 P44 1987

Finney, Kenneth V. In quest of El Dorado . New York , 1987. xii, 454 p. ; ISBN 0-8240-1359-X (alk. paper) : LC Card 87-8342 DDC 338.2/742/097283 19
HD9536.H82 F56 1987

Fleming, William J. Regional development and transportation in Argentina . New York , 1987. ii, 218 p. : ISBN 0-8240-1360-3 (alk. paper) : LC Card 87-8401 DDC 385/.065/82 19
HE2910.G64 F54 1987

García, Valeriano F. A critical inquiry into Argentine economic history, 1946-1970 /. New York , 1987. vi, 127 p. : ISBN 0-8240-1361-1 (alk. paper) : LC Card 87-7620 DDC 330.982/062 19
HG815 .G27 1987

Goizueta-Mimó, Félix. [Effects of sugar monoculture upon colonial Cuba.] Bitter Cuban sugar . New York , 1987. xvii, 287 p. : ISBN 0-8240-1362-X (alk. paper) : LC Card 87-8632 DDC 338.1/7361/097291 19
HD9114.C89 G6419 1987

Jacobstein, Helen L., 1925- The process of economic development in Costa Rica, 1948-1970 . New York , 1987. 338 p. : ISBN 0-8240-1363-8 (alk. paper) : LC Card 87-8519 DDC 338.97286 19
HC143 .J28 1987

Keremitsis, Dawn, 1921- The cotton textile industry in Porfiriato, Mexico, 1870-1910 /. New York , 1987. 232 p. : ISBN 0-8240-1364-6 (alk. paper) : LC Card 87-7619 DDC 338.4/767721/0972 19
HD9884.M42 K47 1987

Lobdell, Richard A. Economic structure and demographic performance in Jamaica, 1891-1935 /. New York , 1987. xii, 259 p. ; ISBN 0-8240-1365-4 (alk. paper) : LC Card 87-8345 DDC 304.6/097292 19
HB3553 .L63 1987

McLewin, Philip J., 1939- Power and economic change . New York , 1987. ii, 271 p. : ISBN 0-8240-1366-2 (alk. paper) : LC Card 87-8344 DDC 330.97292/04 19
HC154 .M36 1987

Pisciotta, John L. (John Lee) Development policy, inflation, and politics in Chile, 1938-1958 . New York , 1987. v, 188 p. ; ISBN 0-8240-1367-0 (alk. paper) : LC Card 87-7617 DDC 338.983 19
HC192 .P625 1987

Pitts, Mary Anne, 1927- Economic development in Chile under two growth strategies, 1925-1968 /. New York , 1987. vii, 246 p. ; ISBN 0-8240-1368-9 (alk. paper) : LC Card 87-7618 DDC 338.983 19
HC192 .P627 1987

Rounds, Christopher R., 1945- From hacienda to ejido . New York , 1987. viii, 268 p. ; ISBN 0-8240-1369-7 (alk. paper) : LC Card 87-8526 DDC 333.3/1/7249 19
HD1333.M62 Y387 1987

Schmidt, Arthur, 1943- The social and economic effect of the railroad in Puebla and Veracruz, Mexico, 1867-1911 /. New York , 1987. 297 p. : ISBN 0-8240-1370-0 (alk. paper) : LC Card 87-8628 DDC 385/.0972/48 19
HE2819.P84 S35 1987

Smith, Gordon Whitford, 1934- Agricultural marketing and economic development . New York , 1987. iii, 417 p. ; ISBN 0-8240-1371-9 (alk. paper) : LC Card 87-11833 DDC 381/.41318/09816 19
HD9066.B84 S687 1987

Stone, Irving, 1923- The composition and distribution of British investment in Latin America, 1865 to 1913 /. New York , 1987. xi, 502 p. : ISBN 0-8240-1372-7 : LC Card 87-8540 DDC 332.6/7341/08 19
HG5160.5.A3 S76 1987

Sweigart, Joseph Earl. Coffee factorage and the emergence of a Brazilian capital market, 1850-1888 /. New York , 1987. xvi, 337 p. : ISBN 0-8240-1373-5 (alk. paper) : LC Card 87-8617 DDC 338.1/3373/098153 19
HD9199.B8 R567 1987

Westfall, L. Glenn, 1943- Don Vicente Martinez Ybor, the man and his empire . New York , 1987. vii, 214 p. : ISBN 0-8240-1374-3 (alk. paper) : LC Card 87-8690 DDC 338.7/67972/0924 19
HD9149.C5 U777 1987

SOUTH AMERICAN INDIANS. see **INDIANS OF SOUTH AMERICA.**

SOUTH ASIA - COMMERCE.
Madan, B. K. (Bal Krishna), 1911- Towards monetary cooperation in South Asia /. New Delhi , 1986, c1985. 105 p. ; LC Card 86-901998 DDC 332.4/954 19
HG3881 .M2756 1986 *NYPL [JLD 87-911]*

SOUTH ASIA - ECONOMIC CONDITIONS.
Bhairav, Kalki Kaal. Populist manifesto /. Grand Forks, ND, USA (830 S. 48th St., Grand Forks 58201) [c1986] vii, 85 p. ; LC Card 86-201038 DDC 338.954 19
HC430.6 .B46 1986

Rahman, M. L. (Mohammad Lutfur), 1933- SAARC facts and economic development /. Dhaka , 1986. xvi, 200 p. : LC Card 87-901419 DDC 338.954 19
HC430.6 .R37 1986

SOUTH ASIA - FOREIGN ECONOMIC RELATIONS.
Madan, B. K. (Bal Krishna), 1911- Towards monetary cooperation in South Asia /. New Delhi , 1986, c1985. 105 p. ; LC Card 86-901998 DDC 332.4/954 19
HG3881 .M2756 1986 *NYPL [JLD 87-911]*

SOUTH ASIA - FOREIGN ECONOMIC RELATIONS - DEVELOPING COUNTRIES.
South-South economic cooperation . New Delhi , 1987. xii, 262 p. ; ISBN 81-7027-102-9 : LC Card 86-903797 DDC 337/.09172/4 19
HF1413 .S617 1987

SOUTH ASIA - INDUSTRIES - INTERNATIONAL COOPERATION - CONGRESSES.
South Asian cooperation in industry, energy, and technology /. New Delhi , Newbury Park, Calif. , 1987. p. cm. ISBN 0-8039-9538-5 (pbk.) LC Card 87-14994 DDC 337.1/54 19
HC430.6 .S675 1987

SOUTH ASIA - POPULATION - ADDRESSES, ESSAYS, LECTURES.
Population redistribution and development in South Asia /. Dordrecht , Boston , 1985. 243 p. : ISBN 90-277-1938-1 : LC Card 84-26260 DDC 304.8/0959 19
HB2096.5 .P66 1985 *NYPL [JLE 86-3852]*

SOUTH ASIA - RURAL CONDITIONS.
Rural poverty in South Asia /. New York , 1988. p. cm. ISBN 0-231-06224-9 LC Card 87-9413 DDC 330.954/052/091734 19
HC440.P6 R87 1988

SOUTH ASIAN ASSOCIATION FOR REGIONAL COOPERATION.
Rahman, M. L. (Mohammad Lutfur), 1933- SAARC facts and economic development /. Dhaka , 1986. xvi, 200 p. : LC Card 87-901419 DDC 338.954 19
HC430.6 .R37 1986

South Asian cooperation in industry, energy, and technology / edited by Arif A. Waqif. New Delhi ; Newbury Park, Calif. : Sage Publications, 1987. p. cm. Papers presented at seminar, 1984, Administrative Staff College of India, Hyderabad, sponsored by Friedrich Ebert Foundation of West Germany and Delegation of the Commission of the European Communities for South Asia. Bibliography: p. ISBN 0-8039-9538-5 (pbk.) LC Card 87-14994 DDC 337.1/54 19
1. South Asia - Industries - International cooperation - Congresses. 2. Energy industries - South Asia - International cooperation - Congresses. 3. Technology - South Asia - International cooperation - Congresses. I. Waqif, Arif A., 1943-. II. Friedrich-Ebert-Stiftung. III. Delegation of the Commission of the European Communities for South Asia.
HC430.6 .S675 1987

South Australia. Dept. of Labour. Wooden, Mark. The effects of redundancy . [Bedford Park, S. Aust.] [1987] 52 p. : LC Card 87-170621 DDC 331.13/7994 19
HD5708.55.A8 W66 1987

SOUTH AUSTRALIA - INDUSTRIES, RURAL - HISTORY.
Grotz, Reinhold. Industrialisierung und Stadtentwicklung im ländlichen Südost-Australien /. Stuttgart , 1982. 299 p. : ISBN 3-88028-098-3 : LC Card 83-215667
HC607.S68 G76 1982

South Australia. Labour, Dept. of. see **South Australia. Dept. of Labour.**

South Carolina Board of Accountancy. Roster of certified public accountants, public accountants, and accounting practitioners registered with the South Carolina Board of Accountancy. Columbia, S.C. (P.O. Box 11376, Columbia 29211) : The Board, [1986] 74 p. ; 23 cm. Cover title. "May 1986." LC Card 87-620717 DDC 657/.025/757 19
1. Accountants - South Carolina - Directories. I. Title.
HF5616.U6 S68 1986

South Carolina Council on Vocational and Technical Education. Meeting labor needs in South Carolina . Columbia, S.C. (2221 Devine St., Suite 420, Columbia 29205) [1986] 52 leaves ; LC Card 86-623031 DDC 331.12/3/09757 19
HD5725.S6 M44 1986

South Carolina. Dept. of Highways and Public Transportation. 1984 needs vs. funds expected to be available July 1983 through September 1990. [Columbia, S.C.] [1984] [49] leaves ; LC Card 86-622435 DDC 388.1/14/09757 19
HE356 .A57 1984

SOUTH CAROLINA - ECONOMIC CONDITIONS.
Piedmont Carolinas, where wealth awaits you. Charlotte, N.C. [1930?] 47 p. : LC Card 85-666462
HC107.N8 P53x 1930

South Carolina. General Assembly. Meeting labor needs in South Carolina . Columbia, S.C. (2221 Devine St., Suite 420, Columbia 29205) [1986] 52 leaves ; LC Card 86-623031 DDC 331.12/3/09757 19
HD5725.S6 M44 1986

South Carolina. Highways and Public Transportation, Dept. of. see **South Carolina. Dept. of Highways and Public Transportation.**

South Carolina. Legislature. see **South Carolina. General Assembly.**

SOUTH CAROLINA OIL JOBBERS ASSOCIATION - HISTORY.
DeMontmollin, Richard Hall. The SCOJA story . [Columbia, S.C.] , c1986. xi, 191 p. : ISBN 0-9617613-0-X LC Card 86-62676 DDC 381/.456655/060757 19
HD9569.S663 D46 1986

South Carolina Petroleum Marketers Association. DeMontmollin, Richard Hall. The SCOJA story . [Columbia, S.C.] , c1986. xi, 191 p. : ISBN 0-9617613-0-X LC Card 86-62676 DDC 381/.456655/060757 19
HD9569.S663 D46 1986

South Carolina. Water Resources Commission. The Situation and outlook for water resource use in South Carolina, 1985-2000 . [Clemson, S.C.] [1985] ix, 95 leaves : LC Card 86-622603 DDC 333.91/13/09757 19
HD1694.S6 S57 1985

South China Sea Fisheries Development and Coordinating Programme. Socio-economic and marketing study of municipal fishing households, Bayawan, Negros Oriental, Philippines. Manila, Philippines [1983] vii, 94, 7 p. : LC Card 86-225887
HD8039.F652 P67 1983

The South China silk district . So, Alvin Y., 1953- Albany, N.Y. , c1986. xii, 206 p. : ISBN 0-88706-322-5 LC Card 86-14575 DDC 338.4/7677391/095127 19
HD9926.C63 S637 1986
NYPL [JLE 87-1448]

SOUTH DAKOTA - CENSUS, 1980.
Goss, De Vee E. South Dakota county and subcounty population estimates (1980, 1982, 1984) /. Vermillion, S.D. [1985] 42 p. ; LC Card 87-620701 DDC 304.6/2/09783021 19
HA635 .G67 1985

South Dakota county and subcounty population estimates (1980, 1982, 1984) /. Goss, De Vee E. Vermillion, S.D. [1985] 42 p. ; LC Card 87-620701 DDC 304.6/2/09783021 19
HA635 .G67 1985

South Dakota county population estimates, 1984 (age by race by sex). Vermillion, S.D. : Business Research Bureau, University of South Dakota, [1986] [25] leaves ; 28 cm. Cover title. "Spring 1986." Tables. "No. 86-102." LC Card 87-620702 DDC 304.6/09783/021 19
1. South Dakota - Population - Statistics. 2. Population forecasting - South Dakota - Statistics. I. University of South Dakota. Business Research Bureau. State Data Center.
HA635 .S68 1986

SOUTH DAKOTA - ECONOMIC CONDITIONS.
South Dakota in comparison. [Aberdeen, SD] (607 North 4th St., Aberdeen 57401) , 1985. 32 p. : LC Card 87-620926 DDC 330.9783/033 19
HC107.S83 I537 1985

South Dakota employment & earnings covered by unemployment insurance, 1984. Aberdeen, S.D. : South Dakota Dept. of Labor, Labor Market Information Center, [198-] 47 p. : ill. ; 28 cm. Cover title. LC Card 87-620925
1. Labor supply - South Dakota - Statistics. 2. Wages - South Dakota - Statistics. 3. Insurance, Unemployment - South Dakota - Statistics. I. South Dakota. Labor Market Information Center.
HD5725.S8 S67 1980z

South Dakota in comparison. 1985 ed. [Aberdeen, SD] (607 North 4th St., Aberdeen 57401) : South Dakota Dept. of Labor, Labor Market Information Center, 1985. 32 p. : ill. ; 28 cm. Cover title. LC Card 87-620926 DDC 330.9783/033 19
1. Industrial promotion - South Dakota. 2. South Dakota - Economic conditions. I. South Dakota. Labor Market Information Center.
HC107.S83 I537 1985

South Dakota. Job Service Division. South Dakota occupational wage information . Aberdeen, S.D. (P.O. Box 4730, Aberdeen 57402-4730) [1986] 97 p. ; LC Card 86-622996 DDC 331.2/9783 19
HD4976.S65 S68 1986

South Dakota. Labor Market Information Center.
South Dakota employment & earnings covered by unemployment insurance, 1984. Aberdeen, S.D. [198-] 47 p. : LC Card 87-620925
HD5725.S8 S67 1980z

South Dakota in comparison. [Aberdeen, SD] (607 North 4th St., Aberdeen 57401) , 1985. 32 p. : LC Card 87-620926 DDC 330.9783/033 19
HC107.S83 I537 1985

South Dakota occupational wage information . Aberdeen, S.D. (P.O. Box 4730, Aberdeen 57402-4730) [1986] 97 p. ; LC Card 86-622996 DDC 331.2/9783 19
HD4976.S65 S68 1986

South Dakota occupational wage information : (based on job openings listed with the South Dakota Job Service) / prepared by Labor Market Information Center, South Dakota Department of Labor. Aberdeen, S.D. (P.O. Box 4730, Aberdeen 57402-4730) : The Center, [1986] 97 p. ; 22 x 28 cm. Cover title. "July 1986." Tables. LC Card 86-622996 DDC 331.2/9783 19
1. Wages - South Dakota - Statistics. 2. Job vacancies - South Dakota - Statistics. 3. South Dakota - Occupations. I. South Dakota. Job Service Division. II. South Dakota. Labor Market Information Center.
HD4976.S65 S68 1986

SOUTH DAKOTA - OCCUPATIONS.
South Dakota occupational wage information . Aberdeen, S.D. (P.O. Box 4730, Aberdeen 57402-4730) [1986] 97 p. ; LC Card 86-622996 DDC 331.2/9783 19
HD4976.S65 S68 1986

SOUTH DAKOTA - POPULATION - STATISTICS.
Goreham, Gary. South Dakotans on the move . Brookings, S.D. [1984] 24 p. : LC Card 85-620511 DDC 304.8/09783/021 19
HB1985.S8 G67 1984

Goss, De Vee E. South Dakota county and subcounty population estimates (1980, 1982, 1984) /. Vermillion, S.D. [1985] 42 p. ; LC Card 87-620701 DDC 304.6/2/09783021 19
HA635 .G67 1985

South Dakota county population estimates, 1984 (age by race by sex). Vermillion, S.D. [1986] [25] leaves ; LC Card 87-620702 DDC 304.6/09783/021 19
HA635 .S68 1986

South Dakotans on the move . Goreham, Gary. Brookings, S.D. [1984] 24 p. : LC Card

85-620511 DDC 304.8/09783/021 19
HB1985.S8 G67 1984

The south-eastern lines of the Sydney tramway system /. Keenan, David R. Sydney, N.S.W., Australia , c1982. 120 p. : ISBN 0-909338-03-5 (pbk.) LC Card 87-167855 DDC 388.4/6/09441 19
HE5179.S93 K44 1982

SOUTH-EASTERN STATE AGRICULTURAL DEVELOPMENT CORPORATION - MANAGEMENT.
South-Eastern State, Nigeria. Conclusions of the government on the report and recommendations of the committee set up to study and recommend ways of solving the financial and administrative problems of the Agricultural Development Corporation /. Calabar [Nigeria] [1971?] 5 p. ; LC Card 87-404113
HG2051.N62 C767 1971

South-Eastern State, Nigeria. Conclusions of the government on the report and recommendations of the committee set up to study and recommend ways of solving the financial and administrative problems of the Agricultural Development Corporation / South-Eastern State of Nigeria. Calabar [Nigeria] : Govt. Printer, [1971?] 5 p. ; 24 cm. "Annex to memo no. SESEC(71) 14"--P. [1]. LC Card 87-404113
1. South-Eastern State Agricultural Development Corporation - Management. 2. Agricultural credit corporations - Nigeria - Cross River State. 3. Agricultural development projects - Government policy - Nigeria - Cross River State. I. Title.
HG2051.N62 C767 1971

SOUTH JERSEY PORT CORPORATION.
Levinson, Alfred Linden, 1933- Economic impact assessment of the South Jersey Port Corporation /. Newark, N.J. (323 High St., Newark 07102) [1982] 31 leaves : LC Card 86-622073 DDC 387.1/09749/88 19
HE554.C18 L48 1982

South Korea . Dyck, John H. Washington, D.C. [1986] v, 74 p. : LC Card 86-602006 DDC 338.1 s 382/.41/095195 19
HD1411 .F59 no. 216 HD9005

South Pacific Bureau for Economic Cooperation. Directory of aid agencies. Suva, Fiji , 1985. iv, 147 p. ; LC Card 86-204497 DDC 338.91/025/9 19
HC681 .D57 1985

South Pacific focus . Buckley, K. D. (Kenneth D.) Sydney , Boston , 1986. 126 p. : ISBN 0-04-909030-5 LC Card 86-71304 DDC 387.5/065/94 19
HE945.B87 B83 1986

South-South economic cooperation : problems and prospects / Govind R. Agrawal ... [et al.]. New Delhi : Radiant Publishers, 1987. xii, 262 p. ; 22 cm. "Issued under the auspices of the Research and Information System for the Nonaligned and Other Developing Countries." Includes bibliographies and index. ISBN 81-7027-102-9 : LC Card 86-903797 DDC 337/.09172/4 19
1. Developing countries - Foreign economic relations. 2. Asia - Foreign economic relations - Developing countries. 3. South Asia - Foreign economic relations - Developing countries. 4. India - Foreign economic relations - Developing countries. I. Agrawal, Govind Ram. II. Research and Information System for the Non-aligned and Other Developing Countries.
HF1413 .S617 1987

South Tyrol. see **Trentino-Alto Adige (Italy)**

South Vietnam. see **Vietnam.**

South Vietnam, trial and experience . Nguyen, Anh Tuan. Athens, Ohio , 1987. 461 p. : ISBN 0-89680-141-1 (pbk.) : LC Card 86-23532 DDC 338.9597 19
HC444 .N43 1987

Southall, Roger. Labour and unions in Asia and Africa /. New York , 1987. p. cm. ISBN 0-312-01362-0 : LC Card 87-21475 DDC 331.88/095 19
HD6796 .L3 1987

Southeast Asia in the 1980s : the politics of economic crisis / edited by Richard Robison, Kevin Hewison, Richard Higgot. Sydney ; Boston : Allen & Unwin, 1987. p. cm. Bibliography: p. Includes index. ISBN 0-04-301289-2 LC Card 87-19550 DDC 338.959 19
1. Asia, Southeastern - Economic policy - Case studies. 2. Asia, Southeastern - Economic conditions - Case studies. I. Robison, Richard, 1943-. II. Hewison, Kevin. III. Higgott, Richard A.
HC441 .S69 1987

Southeast Asian Refugee Studies occasional papers .
(no. 4) Mason, Sarah R. Training Southeast Asian refugee women for employment . Minneapolis, Minn. , 1986. viii, 142 p. : LC Card 86-72303 DDC 331.4/2592/08995073 19
HD5715.2 .M37 1986

Southeast Asian Regional Centre for Graduate Study and Research in Agriculture.
Development strategies and planning for farmers' communities . College, Laguna, Philippines , 1983. vi, 242 p. : LC Card 84-102916 DDC 338.1/859 19
HD2075.8 .D48 1983

Southeastern Michigan minor civil divisions : births, low weight births, infant deaths, and prenatal visits by age of mother and race, 1980-1983. Detroit, Mich. (1200 Book Bldg., Detroit 48226) : Comprehensive Health Planning Council of Southeastern Michigan, c1986. i, 285 p. : ill. ; 29 cm. Chiefly ill. "June 24, 1986." LC Card 87-105776 DDC 304.6/3/09774021 19
1. Childbirth - Michigan - Statistics. 2. Infants - Michigan - Mortality - Statistics. 3. Prenatal care - Michigan - Statistics. I. Comprehensive Health Planning Council of Southeastern Michigan.
HB935.M5 S68 1986

SOUTHERN AFRICAN DEVELOPMENT COORDINATION CONFERENCE.
Hanlon, Joseph. SADCC . London, U.K. , c1984. 110 p. : LC Card 86-148391 DDC 332.6/732268 19
HC900 .H35 1984

Southern African Team for Employment Promotion.
Employment and development in Lesotho . Addis Ababa , 1983. ii, 229 p. ; ISBN 92-2-103780-0 LC Card 84-980769 DDC 331.12/09681/6 19
HD5842.7.A6 E46 1983

Kamya, Andrew, 1941- Factors affecting efficiency in the informal sector in Lusaka and Kitwe /. Lusaka , 1981. iii, 40 p. ; LC Card 87-980491
HD2346.Z292 L875 1981

The Structure of the informal sector in Mongu (Western Province) and its potential for employment creation . Lusaka, Zambia [1982] iii, 44, 10 p. ; LC Card 87-980490 DDC 331.12/51381 19
HD2346.Z292 M657 1982

SOUTHERN CONE OF SOUTH AMERICA - ECONOMIC INTEGRATION.
Estudios sobre integración económica y cooperación regional en el Cono Sur . Santiago de Chile , c1985. 283 p. ; LC Card 86-174604
HC167.S67 E78 1985

Southern Europe and the enlargement of the EEC : proceedings of a workshop held in Lisbon, June 26-28, 1980 / edited by José A. Girão. Lisboa, Portugal : Economia, 1982. 324 p. : ill. ; 24 cm. Includes bibliographies. "Workshop on "Southern Europe and the Enlargement of the EEC" was organized by Economia ... and sponsored by the Ford Foundation ... [et al.]"--P. [5] LC Card 86-201274 DDC 341.24/22 19
1. European Economic Community - Europe, Southern - Congresses. 2. European Economic Community - Greece - Congresses. 3. European Economic Community - Spain - Congresses. 4. European Economic Community - Portugal - Congresses. I. Girão, José António. II. Workshop on "Southern Europe and the Enlargement of the EEC" (1980 : Lisbon, Portugal). III. Ford Foundation.
HC241.25.E85 S68 1982

SOUTHERN PERU COPPER CORPORATION.
Alarcón Aliaga, Carlos. Privilegios y capital transnacional . [Peru?] [1985 or 1986] 168 p. : LC Card 87-127159 DDC 338.8/87 19
HD2841.Z75 S683 1985

SOUTHERN REGION, SUDAN - ECONOMIC CONDITIONS.
House, William J. Population, poverty, and basic needs in southern Sudan . [Juba, Sudan , 1985] vi, 94 leaves ; LC Card 86-981127 DDC 338.9629 19
HC835.Z7 S684 1985

SOUTHERN REGION (SUDAN) - POPULATION.
House, William J. Population, poverty, and basic needs in southern Sudan . [Juba, Sudan , 1985] vi, 94 leaves ; LC Card 86-981127 DDC 338.9629 19
HC835.Z7 S684 1985

SOUTHERN SAW SERVICE - HISTORY - 20TH CENTURY.
Brown, Edmund D. 1594 Evans Drive, S.W. . Atlanta, Ga. (1594 Evans Dr., S.W., Atlanta 30310) , c1983. 213 p. : LC Card 82-62570 DDC 338.7/62193 19
HD9529.S294 A842 1983 ***NYPL [JLF 86-1803]***

SOUTHERN STATES - ECONOMIC CONDITIONS.
Grupp, Monika. Entwicklung und sozio-ökonomische Bedeutung der holzverarbeitenden Industrien im Südosten der Vereinigten Staaten von Amerika /. Berlin , 1981, c1982. xii, 187, [30] p., [5] folded leaves of plates : ISBN 3-496-00301-4 LC Card 86-217598
HD9757.A13 G78 1982

SOUTHERN STATES - HISTORY - 1775-1865.
Schweikart, Larry. Banking in the American South from the age of Jackson to Reconstruction /. Baton Rouge , c1987. xiv, 367 p. : ISBN 0-8071-1403-0 LC Card 87-12784 DDC 332.1/0975 19
HG2604 .S39 1987

Southern States - History - Civil War, 1861-1865. see **United States - History - Civil War, 1861-1865.**

SOUTHERN STATES - POPULATION - HISTORY - 19TH CENTURY.
Steckel, Richard H. (Richard Hall), 1944- The economics of U. S. slave and southern white fertility /. New York , 1985. 253 p. ; ISBN 0-8240-6662-6 (alk. paper) : LC Card 84-48314 DDC 304.6/32/08996073075 19
HB921 .S74 1985 ***NYPL [JLE 86-2085]***

SOUTHERN STATES - SOCIAL CONDITIONS.
Like a family . Chapel Hill , c1987. xxiii, 468 p. : ISBN 0-8078-1754-6 (alk. paper) LC Card 87-40135 DDC 305/.9677 19
HD9077.A13 L55 1987

Southern timberman . Mayor, Archer H. Athens , c1988. p. cm. ISBN 0-8203-0999-0 (alk. paper) LC Card 87-22897 DDC 338.7/63498/0975 19
HD9760.B83 M39 1988

Southgate, Douglas Dewitt. Sustainable resource development in the Third World /. Boulder , 1987. vi, 177 p. : ISBN 0-8133-7522-3 (alk. paper) LC Card 87-20137 DDC 333.7/15/091724 19
HC59.7 .S8826 1987

Southwest Africa. see **Namibia.**

SOUTHWEST, NEW - HISTORY - TO 1848.
Baxter, John O., 1927- Las carneradas . Albuquerque , c1987. x, 198 p., [4] p. of plates : ISBN 0-8263-0961-5 LC Card 86-30906 DDC 381/.4163/009789 19
HD9436.U53 N63 1987

SOUTHWEST, OLD - HISTORY.
Masterson, V. V. The Katy railroad and the last frontier /. Columbia , 1988. xiv, 312 p., [24] p. of plates : ISBN 0-8262-0668-9 (pbk. : alk. paper) LC Card 87-19146 DDC 385/.0978 19
HE2791.M743 M37 1988

Souvenir, ICFTU World Conference on the Trade Union Role in Balanced Development, Vigyan Bhawan, New Delhi, India, March 18-20, 1981 / International Confederation of Free Trade Unions. New Delhi : Indian National Trade Union Congress, [1981] 68 p. : ports. ; 32 cm. Cover title. Advertising matter included in paging. Includes bibliographical references. LC Card 84-901715 DDC 331.88 19
1. International Confederation of Free Trade Unions - Congresses. 2. Trade-unions - Social aspects - Congresses. 3. Labor policy - International cooperation - Congresses. 4. International economic relations - Congresses. I. Indian National Trade Union Congress. II. ICFTU World Conference on the Trade Union Role in Balanced Development (1981 : New

Delhi, India).
HD6475.A2 I26347 1981
NYPL [JLG 86-296]

Souvenirs d'un banquier français . Morin, Jean, 1875-1969. Paris , c1983. 326 p., [8] p. of plates : ISBN 2-207-22988-2 : LC Card 84-172168
HG1552.M67 A3 1983

Souveräne Risken und internationale Verschuldung /. Löschner, Ernst. Wien , 1983. 187 p. : ISBN 3-214-06553-X : LC Card 84-152762 DDC 336.3/435/091724 19
HJ8899 .L67 1983 NYPL [JLE 86-1553]

Souza, Cláudio Alves de. Distrito Federal (Brazil). Coordenação do Sistema de Planejamento. Região geo-econômica de Brasília . [Brasília] [1980?] [28] leaves : LC Card 86-204066
HC189.B7 D57 1980

Souza Filho, José Ornellas de. Exposição do governador do Distrito Federal, José Ornellas de Souza Filho, na ADESG, em 02/09/83. [Brasília : s.n., 1983 or 1984] 40, [31 leaves] : ill. ; 31 cm. LC Card 85-148272
1. Distrito Federal (Brazil) - Economic policy. 2. Distrito Federal (Brazil) - Administrative and political divisions - Maps. 3. Municipal services - Brazil - Distrito Federal. 4. Finance, Public - Brazil - Distrito Federal. I. Escola Superior de Guerra (Brazil). Associação dos Diplomados. II. Title.
HC188.D57 S68 1983

Souza, Francisco Araújo Salles de. O estado e o cartel do leite no Brasil / Francisco Araújo Salles de Souza. 1a. ed. Brasília, Distrito Federal : Horizonte Editora, 1981. 130 p. : ill. ; 22 cm. (Movimento cultural brasileiro) Bibliography: p. 129-130. LC Card 81-217015
1. Milk trade - Brazil. 2. Industry and state - Brazil. 3. Trusts, Industrial - Brazil. I. Title.
HD9282.B72 S65 1981
NYPL [JLD 86-3366]

Souza, Mary de Melo. Castro, Paulo Furtado de. Modelo estocástico para a estimação do produto potencial "IPEA/Depto. de Economia-UnB.". [Brasília, Brazil] [1981] 12, [16] : LC Card 85-210547
HC190.I5 C37 1981

Souza, Raymundo Fonseca. Convivência do homem com a seca e irrigação no Nordeste /. [Salvador, Brazil] [1984] 76 p. : LC Card 87-130774 DDC 333.91/3/09813 19
HD1741.B82 N624 1984

Sovereign individuals of capitalism /. Abercrombie, Nicholas. London , Boston , 1986. 211 p. ; ISBN 0-04-301230-2 (alk. paper) LC Card 86-1122 DDC 330.12/2 19
HB501 .A23 1986 NYPL [JLD 86-3686]

Sovereign rescheduling . Solberg, Ronald L., 1953- London , Boston , 1988. p. cm. ISBN 0-04-332122-4 (alk. paper) LC Card 87-18805 DDC 336.3/435 19
HG3891.5 .S65 1988

Sovereign risk analysis /. Heffernan, Shelagh A., 1956- London , Boston , 1986. xvii, 181 p. : ISBN 0-04-332119-4 (alk. paper) LC Card 85-32069 DDC 332.1/5/0685 19
HG3891.5 .H44 1986 NYPL [JLD 86-2957]

Sovershenstvovanie ėkonomicheskikh metodov upravleniia sel'skokhoziaistvennym proizvodstvom / [otvetstvennyĭ redaktor A.U. Oruzbaev]. Frunze : Izd-vo "Ilim", 1982. 158 p. ; 20 cm. At head of title: Akademiia nauk Kirgizskoĭ SSR. Institut ėkonomiki. Includes bibliographical references. LC Card 83-196563
1. Agricultural industries - Kirghiz S.S.R. - Management. 2. Agriculture - Economic aspects - Kirghiz S.S.R. I. Oruzbaev, A. U. II. Institut ėkonomiki (Kyrgyz SSR ilimder akademiiasy).
HD9015.S653 K577 1982

Sovershenstvovanie ėkonomicheskogo mekhanizma v neproizvodstvennoĭ sfere . Novikov, V. N. (Valeriĭ Nikolaevich) Kiev , 1986. 195 p. ; LC Card 86-233718
HD9986.S683 U3855 1986

Sovershenstvovanie khoziaistvennogo mekhanizma i ratsional'noe ispol'zovanie resursov : tematicheskiĭ sbornik / [otvetstvennyĭ redaktor IA.I. Fel'dman]. Makhachkala : Dagestanskiĭ filial Akademii nauk SSSR, Otdel ėkonomiki, 1985. 190 p. : ill. ; 21 cm. Bibliography: p. [189] LC Card 87-136485
1. Efficiency, Industrial - Russian S.F.S.R. - Dagestanskaia A.S.S.R. 2. Labor productivity - Russian S.F.S.R. - Dagestanskaia A.S.S.R. 3. Natural resources - Russian S.F.S.R. - Dagestanskaia A.S.S.R. I. Fel'dman, IA. I., kandidat ėkonomicheskikh nauk. II. Akademiia nauk SSSR. Dagestanskiĭ filial. Otdel ėkonomiki.
HC337.D3 S655 1985

Sovershenstvovanie khoziaistvennogo mekhanizma na transporte / [otvetstvennye redaktory Leonid Vital'evich Kantorovich, Evgeniĭ Fedorovich Tikhomirov]. Moskva : Akademiia nauk SSSR, TSentr. ėkonomiko-matematicheskiĭ in-t : Nauch. sovet po kompleksnoĭ probleme edinoĭ transp. sistemy SSSR, 1983. 223 p. : ill. ; 21 cm. Includes bibliographies. LC Card 85-199829
1. Transportation - Soviet Union - Mathematical models. I. Kantorovich, L. V. (Leonid Vital'evich), 1912-. II. Tikhomirov, Evgeniĭ Fedorovich. III. TSentral'nyĭ ėkonomiko-matematicheskiĭ institut (Akademiia nauk SSSR). IV. Nauchnyĭ sovet po kompleksnoĭ probleme edinoĭ transportnoĭ sistemy SSSR.
HE255.A2 S68 1983

Sovershenstvovanie khoziaistvennogo mekhanizma v neftianoĭ i gazovoĭ promyshlennosti /. Kozlov, P. T. (Petr Tikhonovich) Alma-Ata , 1983. 134 p. : LC Card 83-194289
HD9575.S652 K69 1983

Sovershenstvovanie khoziaistvennogo mekhanizma v snabzhenii / [otvetstvennyĭ redaktor Khrutskiĭ Evgeniĭ Afanas'evich]. Moskva : Akademiia nauk SSSR, TSentr. ėkonomiko-matematicheskiĭ in-t, 1983. 127 p. : ill. ; 21 cm. Includes bibliographies. LC Card 85-180655
1. Industrial procurement - Soviet Union - Mathematical models. I. Khrutskiĭ, E. A. II. TSentral'nyĭ ėkonomiko-matematicheskiĭ institut (Akademiia nauk SSSR).
HD39.5 .S68 1983

Sovershenstvovanie khoziaistvennogo mekhanizma v stroitel'stve / [avtorskiĭ kollektiv, V.G. Evtukh (rukovoditel' avtorskogo kollektiva) ... et al.]. Minsk : "Belarus'", 1984. 111 p. : ill. ; 21 cm. (Ėkonomicheskaia zhizn' strany) LC Card 86-220340
1. Construction industry - Byelorussian S.S.R. - Technological innovations. 2. Construction industry - Byelorussian S.S.R. - Capital productivity. I. Evtukh, V. G. (Vladimir Gavrilovich). II. Series. III. Series: Ėkonomicheskaia zhizn' strany (Minsk, Byelorussian S.S.R.).
HD9715.S73 B947 1984

Sovershenstvovanie khoziaistvennogo mekhanizma v usloviiakh razvitogo sotsializma / [redaktsionnaia kollegiia, R.V. Shamsutdinov, B.M. Minbaev, IU.I. Volkov]. Tashkent : "Uzbekistan", 1985. 142, [2] p. ; 20 cm. At head of title: Tashkentskaia ordena Druzhby Narodov vysshaia partiĭnaia shkola. Bibliography: p. 141-[143] LC Card 86-220208
1. Uzbek S.S.R. - Economic policy. 2. Uzbek S.S.R. - Economic conditions. I. Shamsutdinov, R. V. II. Minbaev, B. M. III. Volkov, IU. I. IV. Tashkentskaia vysshaia partiĭnaia shkola.
HC337.U96 S68 1985

Sovershenstvovanie metodologii ėkonomicheskogo analiza v nauchnykh uchrezhdeniiakh i nauchno-tekhnicheskikh kompleksakh : sbornik nauchnykh trudov / [redaktsionnaia kollegiia V.V. Ivanov (otvetstvennyĭ redaktor), V.N. Gnoevoĭ, N.V. Kositsyna]. Kiev : IE AN USSR, 1986. 116 p. ; 21 cm. At head of title: Akademiia nauk Ukrainskoĭ SSR. Institut ėkonomiki. Includes bibliographical references. LC Card 87-126466
1. Research - Economic aspects - Soviet Union. 2. Research institutes - Soviet Union. 3. Research, Industrial - Soviet Union. 4. Science and industry - Soviet Union. I. Ivanov, V. V., k.ė.n. II. Gnoevoĭ, V. N. (Vladimir Nikolaevich). III. Kositsyn, N. S. (Nikolaĭ Stepanovich). IV. Instytut ekonomiky (Akademiia nauk Ukraïns'koï RSR).
HC340.R4 S68 1986

Sovershenstvovanie operativnogo upravleniia osnovnym proizvodstvom mashinostroitel'nogo predpriiatiia /. IUsufovich, B. E. (Boris Efimovich) Moskva , 1982. 91 p. : LC Card 82-204954
HD9705.S595 I94 1982

Sovershenstvovanie organizatsii truda i upravleniia v khimicheskoĭ promyshlennosti /. Cherednichenko, K. K. (Konstantin Konstantinovich) Moskva , 1982. 203 p. ; LC Card 83-125684
HD9656.S55 C48 1982

Sovershenstvovanie organizatsii truda na predpriiatiiakh chernoĭ metallurgii /. Bakanov, K. P. (Konstantin Pavlovich) Moskva , 1981. 47 p. ; LC Card 82-104389
HD9525.S652 B355 1981

Sovershenstvovanie planirovaniia i upravleniia intensifikatsieĭ obshchestvennogo proizvodstva / [otvetstvennyĭ redaktor Rybin V.I.]. Moskva : Akademiia nauk SSSR, In-t ėkonomiki, 1984. 182 p. ; 21 cm. Includes bibliographical references. LC Card 85-240311
1. Industrial productivity - Soviet Union. 2. Soviet Union - Economic conditions - 1976-. I. Rybin, V. I. (Valeriĭ Ivanovich). II. Institut ėkonomiki (Akademiia nauk SSSR).
HC336.25 .S6735 1984

Sovershenstvovanie planirovaniia i upravleniia neftegazovym kompleksom / otvetstvennye redaktory S.N. Starovoĭtov, S.I. Sannikova. Novosibirsk : Izd-vo "Nauka," Sibirskoe otd-nie, 1986. 208 p. : ill. ; 23 cm. At head of title: Akademiia nauk SSSR. Sibirskoe otdelenie. Institut ėkonomiki i organizatsii promyshlennogo proizvodstva. Includes bibliographies. LC Card 87-124383
1. Petroleum industry and trade - Russian S.F.S.R. - Siberia, Western - Planning. 2. Petroleum industry and trade - Russian S.F.S.R. - Siberia, Western - Management. 3. Gas industry - Russian S.F.S.R. - Siberia, Western - Planning. 4. Gas industry - Russian S.F.S.R. - Siberia, Western - Management. I. Starovoĭtov, S. N. (Sergeĭ Nikolaevich). II. Sannikova, S. I. III. Institut ėkonomiki i organizatsii promyshlennogo proizvodstva (Akademiia nauk SSSR).
HD9575.S653 S577 1986

Sovershenstvovanie planirovaniia i usilenie khoziaistvennogo mekhanizma : ėkonomicheskie voprosy narodnogo khoziaistva : mezhvuzovskiĭ sbornik / [redaktsionnaia kollegiia, I.I. Mokan (otvetstvennyĭ redaktor) ... et al.]. Kishinev : "Shtiintsa", 1983. 134 p. ; 22 cm. At head of title: Ministerstvo vysshego i srednego spetsial'nogo obrazovaniia Moldavskoĭ SSR. Kishinevskiĭ ordena Trudovogo Krasnogo Znameni gosudarstvennyĭ universitet imeni V.I. Lenina. Includes bibliographical references. LC Card 84-231201
1. Soviet Union - Economic policy - 1981-. I. Mokan, Ivan Il'ich. II. Universitatia de Stat "V.I. Lenin.".
HC336.25 .S6736 1983

Sovershenstvovanie planirovaniia stroitel'nogo proizvodstva /. Galkin, I. G. (Il'ia Grigor'evich) Moskva , 1986. 167 p. : LC Card 85-178938
HD9715.S72 G35 1986

Sovershenstvovanie proizvodstvennykh otnosheniĭ sotsializma / pod red. Ė.P. Dunaeva. Moskva : Izd-vo Moskovskogo universiteta, 1986. 203 p. ; 20 cm. Includes bibliographical references.
1. Central planning - Soviet Union. 2. Industrial productivity - Soviet Union. I. Dunaev, Ėrnst Pavlovich.
NYPL [*QIP 87-2800]

Sovershenstvovanie sistem upravleniia trudom na predpriiatiiakh mashinostroeniia /. Plaksin, V. I. (Viktor Ivanovich) Kiev , 1986. 137, [3] p. : LC Card 85-241056
HD9703.S652 P42 1986

Sovershenstvovanie sistemy narodnokhoziaistvennogo upravleniia v sotsialisticheskikh stranakh : istoriko-teoreticheskie aspekty razvitiia planirovaniia / pod redaktsieĭ V.N. Kashina, V.V. Oreshkina. Moskva : Akademiia nauk SSSR, In-t ėkonomiki, 1986. 196 p. ; 20 cm. Includes bibliographical references. LC Card 87-163453
1. Central planning - Europe, Eastern. 2. Europe, Eastern - Economic policy. I. Kashin, Valentin Nikolaevich. II. Oreshkin, V. V. (Vasiliĭ Vladimirovich). III. Institut ėkonomiki (Akademiia nauk SSSR).
HC244 .S595115 1986

Sovet ėkonomicheskoĭ vzaimopomoshchi : tseli, printsipy, struktura, deiatel'nost' / [otvetstvennyĭ za vypusk N.A. Kudriashov]. Moskva : Sekretariat SĖV, 1984. 29 p. : ill. (some col.) ; 21 cm. LC Card 86-203121
1. Council for Mutual Economic Assistance. I. Kudriashov, N. A. II. Council for Mutual Economic Assistance. Secretariat. III. Title: TSeli, printsipy,

struktura, deiatel'nost'.
HC243.5 .S683 1984

SOVET ĖKONOMICHESKOĬ VZAIMOPOMOSHCHI. (Old Catalog form: Rat für Gegenseitige Wirtschaftshilfe.)
Deutsch, Robert. The food revolution in the Soviet Union and Eastern Europe /. Boulder , 1986. xxii, 256 p. : ISBN 0-8133-7161-9 (pbk.) : LC Card 85-26625 DDC 338.1/9/47 19
HD9015.S652 D47 1986 *NYPL [JLE 86-1588]*

Sovet po izucheniiu proizvoditel'nykh sil (Soviet Union)
Gosudarstvenno-monopolisticheskiĭ kapitalizm i razmeshchenie proizvoditel'nykh sil /. Moskva , 1984. 182 p. ; LC Card 84-239188
HC240 .G565 1984

Osobennosti i problemy razmeshcheniia proizvoditel'nykh sil SSSR v period razvitogo sotsializma /. Moskva , 1980. 273 p. ; LC Card 81-143866
HC340.D5 O86 1980

Razvitie i razmeshchenie mashinostroeniia v investitsionnom komplekse /. Moskva , 1986. 128 p. : LC Card 86-232328
HD9705.S595 R39 1986

Teoreticheskie i metodologicheskie problemy regional'noĭ ėkonomiki . Moskva , 1983. 158 p. : LC Card 87-100005
HC340.D5 T437 1983

Sovetakan Hayastani banvor dasakargi dzevavorumě ev zargats'umě (1920-1940) /. Karapetian, H. S. (Hovhannes Smbati) Erevan , 1980. 272 p., [1] leaf of plates : LC Card 83-129694
HD8529.A692 K37 1980

Sovetskaia Belorussiia v odinadtsatoĭ piatiletke.
Sovetskaia Belorussiia v 11-ĭ piatiletke . Minsk , 1986. 117 p. : LC Card 87-128043
HC337.B93 S677 1986

Sovetskaia Belorussiia v 11-ĭ piatiletke : god piatyĭ, 1985 / [sostavitel' V.A. Nochevnyĭ]. Minsk : "Belarus'", 1986. 117 p. : ill. ; 20 cm. LC Card 87-128043
1. Byelorussian S.S.R. - Economic conditions - 1945-. I. Nochevnyĭ, V. A. (Vladimir Antonovich). II. Title: Sovetskaia Belorussiia v odinadtsatoĭ piatiletke.
HC337.B93 S677 1986

Sovetskaia ėkonomika na novom ėtape / [pod obshcheĭ redaktsieĭ B.I. Gosteva, A.F. Rumiantseva]. Moskva : Izd-vo "Pravda", 1981. 223 p. : ill. ; 20 cm. Includes bibliographical references. LC Card 82-118778
1. Soviet Union - Economic conditions - 1976-. 2. Soviet Union - Economic policy - 1981-. I. Gostev, B. I. II. Rumiantsev, Alekseĭ Fedorovich.
HC336.25 .S677 1981

Sovetskaia ėkonomika segodnia i zavtra /. Troshin, A. (Andreĭ) Moskva , 1981. 208 p. ; LC Card 82-144819
HC336.25 .T7 1981

Sovetskaia sotsiologicheskaia assotsiatsiia.
Nekotorye problemy internatsional'nogo vospitaniia v mnogonatsional'nom trudovom kollektive /. Moskva , 1985. 135 p. ; LC Card 86-233779
HD8526.5 .N45 1985

Sovetskaia sotsiologicheskaia assotsiatsiia. Moldavskoe otdelenie. Upravlenie sotsial'nymi protsessami v trudovykh kollektivakh /. Kishinev , 1983. 141 p. : LC Card 84-133794
HD6957.S65 U67 1983

Sovetskaia Ukraina. Radians'ka Ukraïna . Kyïv , 1985. 205 p., [2] p. of plates : LC Card 87-151437
HC337.U5 R215 1985

Sovetskiĭ Soiuz na inostrannykh markakh / M.P. Sokolov ... et al.]. Moskva : "Sviaz'", 1979. 286 p. : ill. (some col.) ; 21 cm. Includes bibliographical references. LC Card 81-136372
1. Postage-stamps - Topics - Soviet Union. I. Sokolov, M. P. (Mikhail Petrovich).
HE6183.S56 S68 1979

Sovetsko-v'etnamskiĭ simpozium na temu "Ėkonomicheskie problemy perekhoda k sotsializmu" (1984 : Moscow, R.S.F.S.R.)
Ėkonomicheskie problemy perekhoda k sotsializmu stran s nerazvitoĭ ėkonomikoĭ : materialy sovetsko-v'etnamskogo simpoziuma / [redaktsionnaia kollegiia M.E. Trigubenko, otvetstvennyĭ redaktor, Vu Khieu, E.R. Bogatova. Moskva : Izd-vo "Nauka," Glav. red. vostochnoĭ lit-ry, 1986. 254 p. ; 22 cm. At head of title: Akademiia nauk SSSR. Institut ėkonomiki mirovoĭ sotsialisticheskoĭ sistemy. Includes bibliographies. LC Card 87-108102
1. Vietnam - Economic conditions - Congresses. 2. Socialism - Vietnam - Congresses. 3. Marxian economics - Congresses. 4. Socialism - Developing countries - Congresses. I. Trigubenko, M. E. (Marina Evgen'evna). II. Vũ, Khiêu. III. Bogatova, E. R. IV. Title.
HC444 .S69 1984

Sovety i rukovodstvo ėkonomikoĭ . Avak'ian, Suren Adibekovich. Moskva , 1985. 110 p. ; LC Card 87-118114
HC336.25 .A87 1985

Sovety i zhizn'.
Shiriaev, A. V. (Andreĭ Vasil'evich) RAPO . Moskva , 1985. 155 p. ; LC Card 86-142380
HD9015.S653 R8775 1985

Soviet agriculture /. Medvedev, Zhores A., 1925- New York , c1987. xiv, 464 p. ; ISBN 0-393-02472-5 LC Card 86-31119 DDC 338.1/0947 19
HD1992 .M385 1987

Soviet Asia . Dienes, Leslie. Boulder , 1987. xx, 289 p. ; ISBN 0-8133-7437-5 (pbk.) LC Card 87-8331 DDC 338.957 19
HC336.9.S53 D53 1987

Soviet bloc. see **Communist countries.**

SOVIET CENTRAL ASIA - ECONOMIC CONDITIONS.
Dienes, Leslie. Soviet Asia . Boulder , 1987. xx, 289 p. ; ISBN 0-8133-7437-5 (pbk.) LC Card 87-8331 DDC 338.957 19
HC336.9.S53 D53 1987

SOVIET CENTRAL ASIA - ECONOMIC POLICY.
Dienes, Leslie. Soviet Asia . Boulder , 1987. xx, 289 p. ; ISBN 0-8133-7437-5 (pbk.) LC Card 87-8331 DDC 338.957 19
HC336.9.S53 D53 1987

Soviet economic assistance to the less developed countries . Bach, Quintin. Oxford [Oxfordshire] , New York , 1987. p. cm. ISBN 0-19-828572-8 : LC Card 87-20349 DDC 338.91/47/01724 19
HC60 .B23 1987

Soviet economic planning . Tesler, Edward. Falls Church, VA (7700 Leesburg Pike, #250, Falls Church 22043) , c1986. ix, 88 leaves : LC Card 87-403383 DDC 338.947 19
HC335 .T425 1986

"Soviet economic science" series .
(1) The World socialist economy. Moscow , 1986. 279 p. ; LC Card 86-231463 DDC 338.9/009171/7 19
HC704 .W67 1986

The Soviet economy . Desai, Padma. Oxford, OX, UK , 1987. viii, 281 p. : ISBN 0-631-15227-X : LC Card 86-28326 DDC 330.947/0853 19
HC336.25 .D47 1987

The Soviet economy . Munkholt, Peer. Köln , 1985. iii, 79 p. ; LC Card 86-673837
HC340.D4 M86x 1985

The Soviet economy on the brink of reform : essays in honor of Alec Nove / edited by Peter Wiles. Boston : Allen & Unwin, 1988. p. cm. Includes index. ISBN 0-04-335063-1 (alk. paper) LC Card 87-19514 DDC 338.947 19
1. Central planning - Soviet Union. 2. Soviet Union - Economic policy - 1917-. 3. Saving and investment - Soviet Union. 4. Nove, Alec. I. Nove, Alec. II. Wiles, Peter John de la Fosse.
HC335 .C626 1988

SOVIET FAR EAST (R.S.F.S.R.) - ECONOMIC CONDITIONS.
Ėkonomicheskoe razvitie Sibiri i Dal'nego Vostoka /. Moskva , 1980. 263 p. ; LC Card 81-143669
HC337.R852 S5242 1980

Siberia . London , New York , c1987. 233 p. : ISBN 0-7099-3655-9 LC Card 87-15437 DDC 330.957/0854 19
HC337.R852 S52697 1987

Siberia and the Soviet Far East . Stanford, Calif. , c1987. xxx, 298 p. : ISBN 0-8179-8362-7 (pbk.) : LC Card 86-21388 DDC 330.957/085 19
HC337.R852 S5269 1987

Tolmachev, V. P. (Vladimir Petrovich) Ėkonomika Urala, Sibiri i Dal'nego vostoka v odinnadtsatoĭ piatiletke /. Moskva , 1981. 39 p. ; LC Card 82-153584
HC337.R852 U7382 1981

SOVIET FAR EAST (R.S.F.S.R.) - ECONOMIC POLICY.
Nikitin, V. S. (Vadim Semenovich) Prognozirovanie razvitiia regional'nogo gorno-promyshlennogo kompleksa /. Moskva , 1982. 141, [3] p. : LC Card 83-154711
HD9506.S7473 S656 1982

SOVIET FAR EAST (R.S.F.S.R.) - ENVIRONMENTAL POLICY.
Regional'nye osobennosti ratsionalizatsii prirodopol'zovaniia i okhrany sredy /. Irkutsk , 1980. 177 p. ; LC Card 82-111826
HC337.R852 S5266 1980

SOVIET FAR EAST (R.S.F.S.R.) - FOREIGN ECONOMIC RELATIONS.
Siberia and the Soviet Far East . Stanford, Calif. , c1987. xxx, 298 p. : ISBN 0-8179-8362-7 (pbk.) : LC Card 86-21388 DDC 330.957/085 19
HC337.R852 S5269 1987

SOVIET FAR EAST (R.S.F.S.R) - INDUSTRIES.
Siberia . London , New York , c1987. 233 p. : ISBN 0-7099-3655-9 LC Card 87-15437 DDC 330.957/0854 19
HC337.R852 S52697 1987

SOVIET FAR EAST (R.S.F.S.R.) - INDUSTRIES - HISTORIOGRAPHY.
Istoriografiia istorii rabochego klassa Dal'nego Vostoka SSSR /. Vladivostok , 1984. 78 p. ; LC Card 85-229962
HD8529.S652 I87 1984

Soviet foreign policy, the League of Nations and Europe, 1917-39 /. Haigh, R. H. Aldershot, Hants , 1986. x, 138 p. ; *NYPL [JFD 86-5778]*

Soviet foreign trade in foodstuffs . Treml, Vladimir G. Washington, D.C. [1986] viii, 69, 2 p. ; LC Card 87-601290 DDC 382/.45664/00947 19
HD9015.S65 T74 1986

Soviet management and labor relations /. Grancelli, Bruno, 1943- Boston , c1988. xvi, 248 p. ; ISBN 0-04-497040-4 : LC Card 87-11516 DDC 331/.0947 19
HD8526.5 .G74 1988

Soviet oil and gas exports to the West . Stern, Jonathan P. Aldershot, Hants, England , Brookfield, Vt., USA , c1987. xi, 123 p. : ISBN 0-566-05124-9 : LC Card 86-32772 DDC 382/.4228/0947 19
HD9575.S652 S74 1987

Soviet quantitative history / edited by Don Karl Rowney ; foreword by Theodore K. Rabb. Beverly Hills : Sage Publications, c1984. 216 p. : ill. ; 22 cm. (New approaches to social science history . v. 4) "Published in cooperation with the Social Science History Association." Includes bibliographies and index. ISBN 0-8039-2082-2 LC Card 83-19196 DDC 306/.072047 19
1. Land tenure - Soviet Union - History - Mathematical models - Addresses, essays, lectures. 2. Peasantry - Soviet Union - History - Mathematical models - Addresses, essays, lectures. 3. Ethnology - Soviet Union - History - Mathematical models - Addresses, essays, lectures. 4. Soviet Union - Social conditions - Mathematical models - Addresses, essays, lectures. 5. Soviet Union - History - Mathematical models - Addresses, essays, lectures. I. Rowney, Don Karl, 1936-. II. Social Science History Association. III. Series.
HD715 .S5956 1984 *NYPL [JLD 87-841]*

Soviet Union.
Zakon Soiuza Sovetskikh Sotsialisticheskikh Respublik o Gosudarstvennom biudzhete SSSR na 1986 god. 1985. Dementsev, V. V. (Viktor Vladimirovich) O Gosudarstvennom biudzhete SSSR na 1986 god i ob ispolnenii Gosudarstvennogo biudzheta SSSR za 1984 god : doklad i zakliuchitel'noe slovo na sovmestnykh zasedaniiakh Soveta Soiuza i Soveta Natsional'nosteĭ chetvertoĭ sessii Verkhovnogo Soveta SSSR odinnadtsatogo

sozyva / V.V. Dementsev. Zakon Soiuza Sovetskikh Sotsialisticheskikh Respublik o Gosudarstvennom biudzhete SSSR na 1986 god. Postanovlenie Verkhovnogo Soveta SSSR ob utverzhdenii otcheta ob ispolnenii Gosudarstvennogo biudzheta SSSR za 1984 god. Moskva , 1985. 28 p. ; LC Card 86-203425
HJ2129 .D46 1985

SOVIET UNION - ARMED FORCES - FUEL.
Nikitin, V. V. (Vasiliĭ Vasil'evich) Goriuchee--frontu, 1941-1945 /. Moskva , 1984. 203 p. : LC Card 85-152473
HD9575.S652 N55 1984

SOVIET UNION - COMMERCE.
Mordasova, L. A. (Lidiia Andrianovna) Trudovye resursy v torgovle /. Moskva , 1985. 128 p. ; LC Card 86-158800
HD8526.5 .M54 1985

Sokoloff, Georges. L'économie de la détente . Paris , c1983. 255 p. : ISBN 2-7246-0483-0 : LC Card 84-117643
HF3646.5 .S65 1983

Sokoloff, Georges. [Economie de la détente. English.] The economy of détente . Leamington Spa ; New York : p. cm. ISBN 0-907582-62-1 : LC Card 86-32627 DDC 382/.0947 19
HF3646.5 .S6513 1987

SOVIET UNION - COMMERCE - EUROPE, EASTERN.
Vneshniaia torgovlia SSSR so stranami SĖV /. Moskva , 1986. 108, [3] p. ; LC Card 86-213259
HF3628.E9 V54 1986

SOVIET UNION - COMMERCE - EUROPE, EASTERN - MATHEMATICAL MODELS.
Ėkonomiko-matematicheskie metody i modeli vo vneshneėkonomicheskoĭ deiatel'nosti /. Moskva , 1980. 179 p. : LC Card 87-109621
HF3626.5 .E45 1980

SOVIET UNION - COMMERCE - FINLAND.
Neuvostoliiton-kauppa Suomen kansantaloudessa /. Helsinki , 1986. 220 p. : ISBN 951-9206-18-3 LC Card 87-127628
HF3633.S65 N48 1986

SOVIET UNION - COMMERCE - FORECASTING.
Voprosy prognozirovaniia i planirovaniia vneshneėkonomicheskikh sviazeĭ /. Moskva , 1984. 93 p. ; LC Card 86-144298
HF3626.5 .V668 1984

SOVIET UNION - COMMERCE - GERMANY (WEST) - CONGRESSES.
Clement, Hermann. Entwicklungsmöglichkeiten des deutsch-sowjetischen Handels in der zweiten Hälfte der 80er Jahre vor dem Hintergrund der sowjetischen Planung /. München , 1986. 14 leaves ; LC Card 86-167481
HF3568.S66 C58 1986

SOVIET UNION - COMMERCE - HISTORY.
Illarionov, Sergeĭ Ivanovich. Problema tovarnogo proizvodstva . Moskva , 1984. 109 p. ; LC Card 85-111933
HF3626 .I64 1984

SOVIET UNION - COMMERCE - MATHEMATICAL MODELS.
Ėkonomiko-matematicheskie metody i modeli vo vneshneėkonomicheskoĭ deiatel'nosti /. Moskva , 1980. 179 p. : LC Card 87-109621
HF3626.5 .E45 1980

Mezhregional'nye mezhotraslevye balansy /. Novosibirsk , 1983. 220 p. : LC Card 84-172934
HF3626.5 .M49 1983

SOVIET UNION - COMMERCE - SWEDEN - HISTORY - 17TH CENTURY.
Attman, Artur, 1910- Swedish aspirations and the Russian market during the 17th century /. Göteborg , Atlantic Highlands, N.J. , c1985. 41 p. : ISBN 91-85252-35-2 (pbk.) LC Card 86-214014 DDC 382/.09485/047 19
HF3678.S58 A88 1985

SOVIET UNION - COMMERCE - UNITED STATES - HISTORY - 20TH CENTURY - SOURCES.
Records of the U. S. Department of State relating to commercial relations between the United States and Russia/the Soviet Union, 1910-1949 [microform]. Wilmington, DE , c1987. microfilm reel. ISBN 0-8420-3053-0 (microfilm : set) : LC Card 87-23223 DDC 337.73047 19
HF3105

SOVIET UNION - COMMERCE - UNITED STATES - MATHEMATICAL MODELS.
Kolarik, William F. A model for the study of international trade politics . New York , 1987. 613 p. : ISBN 0-8240-8086-6 (alk. paper) : LC Card 87-23788 DDC 382/.0947/0730724 19
HF3105 .K64 1987

SOVIET UNION - COMMERCIAL POLICY.
Bubnov, Boris. Foreign trade with the USSR . Oxford , New York , c1987. p. cm. ISBN 0-08-035844-6 : LC Card 87-7167 DDC 382/.0947 19
HF1557 .B83 1987

Sokoloff, Georges. [Economie de la détente. English.] The economy of détente . Leamington Spa ; New York : p. cm. ISBN 0-907582-62-1 : LC Card 86-32627 DDC 382/.0947 19
HF3646.5 .S6513 1987

SOVIET UNION - COMMERCIAL POLICY - HISTORY - 20TH CENTURY - SOURCES.
Records of the U. S. Department of State relating to commercial relations between the United States and Russia/the Soviet Union, 1910-1949 [microform]. Wilmington, DE , c1987. microfilm reel. ISBN 0-8420-3053-0 (microfilm : set) : LC Card 87-23223 DDC 337.73047 19
HF3105

SOVIET UNION - DEFENSES.
Siberia and the Soviet Far East . Stanford, Calif. , c1987. xxx, 298 p. : ISBN 0-8179-8362-7 (pbk.) : LC Card 86-21388 DDC 330.957/085 19
HC337.R852 S5269 1987

SOVIET UNION - DEFENSES - ECONOMIC ASPECTS.
Munkholt, Peer. The Soviet economy . Köln , 1985. iii, 79 p. ; LC Card 86-673837
HC340.D4 M86x 1985

SOVIET UNION - ECONOMIC CONDITIONS.
White, Colin (Colin M.) Russia and America . London , New York , c1987. 268 p. ; ISBN 0-7099-5246-5 LC Card 87-13646 DDC 330.947 19
HC333 .W46 1987

SOVIET UNION - ECONOMIC CONDITIONS - TO 1861 - COLLECTED WORKS.
Druzhinin, N. M. (Nikolaĭ Mikhailovich) Sotsial'no-ėkonomicheskaia istoriia Rossii . Moskva , 1987. 421 p., [1] leaf of plates : LC Card 87-164847
HC334.5 .D78 1987

SOVIET UNION - ECONOMIC CONDITIONS - 1861-1917.
Küttler, Wolfgang. Lenins Formationsanalyse der bürgerlichen Gesellschaft in Russland vor 1905 . Berlin , 1978. 331 p. ; LC Card 86-102733
HC334.5 .K87 1978

McDaniel, Tim. Autocracy, capitalism, and the revolution in Russia /. Berkeley , c1987. p. cm. ISBN 0-520-05532-2 (alk. paper) LC Card 86-30790 DDC 322.4/2/0947 19
HD8526 .M385 1987

Macey, David, A. J., 1942- Government and peasant in Russia, 1861-1906 . Dekalb, Ill. , 1987. xviii, 380 p. ; ISBN 0-87580-122-6 LC Card 87-7684 DDC 338.1/847 19
HD1992 .M19 1987

SOVIET UNION - ECONOMIC CONDITIONS - 1861-1917 - COLLECTED WORKS.
Druzhinin, N. M. (Nikolaĭ Mikhailovich) Sotsial'no-ėkonomicheskaia istoriia Rossii . Moskva , 1987. 421 p., [1] leaf of plates : LC Card 87-164847
HC334.5 .D78 1987

SOVIET UNION - ECONOMIC CONDITIONS - 1918-
"Kapital" K. Marksa i ėkonomicheskie problemy razvitogo sotsializma /. Moskva , 1980. 260 p. ; LC Card 81-134413
HB501 .K248 1980

SOVIET UNION - ECONOMIC CONDITIONS - 1976-
Aktual'nye problemy sotsial'no-ėkonomicheskogo razvitiia SSSR v sovremennyĭ period /. Moskva , 1984. 153 p. ; LC Card 85-205938
HC336.25 .A46 1984

Buck, Trevor. Modern Soviet economic performance /. New York, NY , 1987. viii, 192 p. ; ISBN 0-631-14417-X : LC Card 86-24457 DDC 330.947/085 19
HC336.25 .B826 1987

Bukhval'd, E. M. Povyshenie proizvoditel'nosti truda--kliuchevaia zadacha sovetskoĭ ėkonomiki . Moskva , 1984. 63 p. ; LC Card 85-188977
HC340.L3 B85 1984

Desai, Padma. The Soviet economy . Oxford, OX, UK , 1987. viii, 281 p. : ISBN 0-631-15227-X : LC Card 86-28326 DDC 330.947/0853 19
HC336.25 .D47 1987

Ėkonomicheskaia i sotsial'naia geografiia . Leningrad , 1984. 149 p. : LC Card 85-191961
HC336.25 .E3812 1984

Ėkonomika SSSR--edinyĭ narodnokhoziaĭstvennyĭ kompleks /. Moskva , 1981. 143 p. : LC Card 82-111112
HC336.25 .E39 1981

Goldman, Marshall I. Gorbachev's challenge . New York , c1987. xvii, 296 p. : ISBN 0-393-02454-7 LC Card 86-33187 DDC 338.947 19
HC336.25 .G6365 1987

Guber, A. A. (Aleksandr Andreevich) Industry /. Moscow , 1985. 46 p., [16] p. of plates : LC Card 86-208070 DDC 338.947 19
HC336.25 .G8 1985

Khoziaĭstvennyĭ mekhanizm v sisteme optimal'nogo funktsionirovaniia sotsialisticheskoĭ ėkonomiki /. Moskva , 1985. 346 p. ; LC Card 86-114802
HC336.25 .K474 1985

Knight, Misha G. How to do business with Russians . New York , 1987. xxiv, 311 p. : ISBN 0-89930-211-4 (lib. bdg. : alk. paper) LC Card 86-30396 DDC 658.8/48/0947 19
HF1558.5.U6 K56 1987

Korop, P. N. (Petr Nikolaevich) USSR--looking at an economic map /. [Moscow] , c1985. 250 p., [3] p. of plates : LC Card 86-207488 DDC 330.947/0854 19
HC336.25 .K66 1985

Marrama, Vittorio. Programmazione e sviluppo in Unione Sovietica /. Torino , c1983. 146 p. : LC Card 85-175586
HC336.25 .M358 1983

Moiseev, Anatoliĭ Vasil'evich. Osnovy ėkonomiki vazhneĭshikh otrasleĭ narodnogo khoziaĭsva SSSR . Moskva , 1984. 191 p. : LC Card 85-113764
HC336.25 .M654 1984

Nechaev, IU. V. (IUriĭ Vasil'evich) Populiarnaia politėkonomiia /. Kiev , 1986. 246 p. : LC Card 87-169729
HC336.25 .N43 1986

Problemy ėkonomicheskogo rosta na sovremennom ėtape. Moskva , 1984. 137 p. : LC Card 85-240336
HC336.25 .P624 1984

Scrivener, Ronald. USSR economic handbook /. London , Detroit, Mich. , 1986. 246 p. : ISBN 0-86338-156-1 LC Card 87-130957 DDC 330.947/0854
HC336.25 .S37 1986

Silin, V. A. (Vladimir Andreevich) Ėkonomika--poisk, ėksperiment /. Moskva , 1978. 109 p. ; LC Card 81-167075
HC336.25 .S557 1978

Soderzhanie i struktura edinogo narodno-khoziaĭstvennogo kompleksa SSSR /. Moskva , 1986. 229 p. ; LC Card 87-126348
HC336.25 .S643 1986

Solodkova, S. V. (Serafima Vasil'evna) Sotsialisticheskie proizvodstvennye otnosheniia . Moskva , 1984. 141 p. ; LC Card 84-223476
HC336.25 .S65 1984

Sotsial'no-ėkonomicheskaia sushchnost' obshchenarodnogo khoziaĭstvennogo mekhanizma /. Kiev , 1985. 342 p. ; LC Card

86-197710
HC336.25 .S668 1985

Sovershenstvovanie planirovaniia i upravleniia intensifikatsiei obshchestvennogo proizvodstva /. Moskva , 1984. 182 p. ; LC Card 85-240311
HC336.25 .S6735 1984

Sovetskaia ėkonomika na novom ėtape /. Moskva , 1981. 223 p. : LC Card 82-118778
HC336.25 .S677 1981

Struktura narodnogo khoziaistva v usloviiakh intensifikatsii ėkonomiki /. Moskva , 1986. 267 p. ; LC Card 86-212596
HC336.25 .S795 1986

Troshin, A. (Andreĭ) Sovetskaia ėkonomika segodnia i zavtra /. Moskva , 1981. 208 p. ; LC Card 82-144819
HC336.25 .T7 1981

Ukreplenie material'nykh osnov sotsialisticheskogo obraza zhizni /. Moskva , 1984. 156 p. ; LC Card 85-240384
HD8526.5 .U38 1984

SOVIET UNION - ECONOMIC CONDITIONS - 1976- - CONGRESSES.
Sbalansirovannost' sotsialisticheskoĭ ėkonomiki i finansovo-kreditnyĭ mekhanizm /. Moskva , 1984. 108 p. ; LC Card 85-240300
HG186.S55 S27 1984

SOVIET UNION - ECONOMIC CONDITIONS - 1976- - ECONOMETRIC MODELS.
Granberg, Aleksandr Grigor'evich. Matematicheskie modeli sotsialisticheskoĭ ėkonomiki . Moskva , 1978. 350 p. : LC Card 81-160608
HC336.25 .G697 1978

Mezhotraslevye kompleksy v sisteme modeleĭ /. Moskva , 1983. 319 p. : LC Card 83-236937
HC336.25 .M49 1983

Modelirovanie mezhotraslevykh vzaimodeĭstviĭ /. Moskva , 1984. 277 p. : LC Card 84-175111
HC336.25 .M6314 1984

SOVIET UNION - ECONOMIC CONDITIONS - 1976- - MATHEMATICAL MODELS.
Matematicheskie metody v ėkonomike i narodnom khoziaistve . Moskva , 1985. 121 p. ; LC Card 87-152514
HC336.25 M377 1985

Modelirovanie sotsial'nykh faktorov v ėkonomiko-matematicheskikh issledovaniiakh /. Moskva , 1984. 148 p. : LC Card 87-125299
HC336.25. .M636 1984

SOVIET UNION - ECONOMIC CONDITIONS - 1976- - MISCELLANEA.
Guber, A. A. (Aleksandr Andreevich) Nasha ėkonomika . Moskva , 1986. 157 p. ; LC Card 87-132459 DDC 330.947/085/3 19
HC336.25 .G82 1986

SOVIET UNION - ECONOMIC CONDITIONS - 1976- - REGIONAL DISPARITIES.
Bugaev, V. K. (Vladimir Konstantinovich) Territorial'naia struktura ėkonomicheskogo raĭona . Leningrad , 1986. 164, [3] p. : LC Card 87-120624
HC336.25 .B84 1986

Lipko, A. G. (Alekseĭ Gennad'evich) Proizvodstvo i potreblenie v regione /. Moskva , 1986. 142 p. : LC Card 86-211374
HC336.25 .L56 1986

SOVIET UNION - ECONOMIC CONDITIONS - 1976- - STATISTICS.
Treml, Vladimir G. Referent USSR economic and demographic statistics for normalization of Berkeley-Duke emigre questionnaire data /. [Durham, N.C. [1986] 1 v. (various pagings) ; LC Card 86-70618 DDC 304.6/0947/021 19
HB3607 .T74 1986

SOVIET UNION - ECONOMIC POLICY.
Guber, A. A. (Aleksandr Andreevich) Industry /. Moscow , 1985. 46 p., [16] p. of plates : LC Card 86-208070 DDC 338.947 19
HC336.25 .G8 1985

Popov, Mikhail V. Planomernoe razreshenie protivorechiĭ razvitiia sotsializma kak pervoĭ fazy kommunizma /. Leningrad , 1986. 156 p. ; LC Card 87-146874
HB97.5 .P7994 1986

Tesler, Edward. Soviet economic planning . Falls Church, VA (7700 Leesburg Pike, #250, Falls Church 22043) , c1986. ix, 88 leaves : LC Card 87-403383 DDC 338.947 19
HC335 .T425 1986

SOVIET UNION - ECONOMIC POLICY - 1917-
Khoziaistvennyĭ mekhanizm funktsionirovaniia sotsialisticheskoĭ ėkonomiki /. Moskva , 1982. 358 p. ; LC Card 83-134242
HC243.5 .K47 1982

Martyniuk, S. M. (Stanislav Mikhaĭlovich) Planomernost' i ėffektivnost' sotsialisticheskogo obshchestvennogo proizvodstva /. Kiev , 1982. 141 p. ; LC Card 83-219823
HC335 .M3675 1982

Rukopozhatie piatiletok /. Moskva , 1981. 237 p. : LC Card 82-103792
HC335 .R76 1981

Shturman, Dora, 1923- Nash novyĭ mir . Ierusalim , 1986. 464 p. : LC Card 87-114263
HB97.5 .S5155 1986

The Soviet economy on the brink of reform . Boston , 1988. p. cm. ISBN 0-04-335063-1 (alk. paper) LC Card 87-19514 DDC 338.947 19
HC335 .C626 1988

SOVIET UNION - ECONOMIC POLICY - 1917-1928.
Dmitrenko, Vladimir Petrovich. Economic policy during the construction of socialism in the USSR /. Moscow , c1987. 156 p. ; LC Card 86-201129 DDC 338.947 19
HC335.2 .D56 1987

Illarionov, Sergeĭ Ivanovich. Problema tovarnogo proizvodstva . Moskva , 1984. 109 p. ; LC Card 85-111933
HF3626 .I64 1984

Rapoport, IU. M. (IUriĭ Mikhaĭlovich) Osushchestvlenie ėkonomicheskoĭ politiki Kommunisticheskoĭ partii v usloviiakh Evropeĭskogo Severa RSFSR, 1917-1925 gg. /. Leningrad , 1984. 216 p. ; LC Card 84-217989
HC336.9.N65 R36 1984

Seleznev, V. A. (Valeriĭ Aleksandrovich) Pervye shagi sotsialisticheskikh preobrazovaniĭ v sel'skom khoziaistve Severo-Zapada RSFSR, 1917-1929 gg. . Leningrad , 1983. 198 p. ; LC Card 83-197523
HD1492.S652 R877 1983
NYPL [*QIP 87-1327]

Strumilin, S. G. (Stanislav Gustavovich), 1877-1974. Na planovom fronte /. Moskva , 1980. 463 p. ; LC Card 81-135522
HC335.2 .S83 1980

SOVIET UNION - ECONOMIC POLICY - 1928-1932.
Dmitrenko, Vladimir Petrovich. Economic policy during the construction of socialism in the USSR /. Moscow , c1987. 156 p. ; LC Card 86-201129 DDC 338.947 19
HC335.2 .D56 1987

Istoriia sovetskogo krest'ianstva /. Moskva , 1986-<1987. v. <1-3 > : LC Card 86-230318
HD1492.S65 I88 1986

Kuromiya, Hiroaki. Stalin's industrial revolution . Cambridge [Cambridgeshire] , New York , 1988. p. cm. ISBN 0-521-35157-X LC Card 87-25010 DDC 338.947 19
HC335.4 .K87 1988

Strumilin, S. G. (Stanislav Gustavovich), 1877-1974. Na planovom fronte /. Moskva , 1980. 463 p. ; LC Card 81-135522
HC335.2 .S83 1980

Wilk, Marian. Pierwsza pięciolatka w Związku Radzieckim . Wrocław , 1986. 314 p., [21] p. of plates : ISBN 83-04-02190-0 : LC Card 87-110627
HC335.4 .W55 1986

SOVIET UNION - ECONOMIC POLICY - 1933-1937.
Istoriia sovetskogo krest'ianstva /. Moskva , 1986-<1987. v. <1-3 > : LC Card 86-230318
HD1492.S65 I88 1986

SOVIET UNION - ECONOMIC POLICY - 1938-1942.
Siegelbaum, Lewis H. Stakhanovism and the politics of productivity in the USSR, 1935-1941 /. Cambridge , New York , 1988. xv, 326 p. : ISBN 0-521-34548-0 LC Card 87-25605 DDC 331.11/8/0947 19
HC340.S6 S515 1988

SOVIET UNION - ECONOMIC POLICY - 1976-1980.
Efimov, A. N. (Anatoliĭ Nikolaevich) Problemy obosnovaniia gosudarstvennogo plana /. Moskva , 1980. 197, [3] p. ; LC Card 81-135658
HC336.25 .E346 1980

Khachaturov, T. S. (Tigran Sergeevich), 1906- Intensifikatsiia i ėffektivnost' v usloviiakh razvitogo sotsializma /. Moskva , 1978. 350 p. ; LC Card 81-167321
HC336.25 .K445 1978

Pavlov, V. S. (Valentin Sergeevich) Finansovye plany i balansy v sisteme ėkonomicheskogo planirovaniia /. Moskva , 1978. 238 p. ; LC Card 81-160805
HG186.S55 P38 1978

Planomernoe razvitie sotsialisticheskoĭ ėkonomiki /. Moskva , Bratislava , 1977. 262 p. ; LC Card 87-100683
HC336.25 .P448 1977

SOVIET UNION - ECONOMIC POLICY - 1976-1980 - ECONOMETRIC MODELS.
Granberg, Aleksandr Grigor'evich. Matematicheskie modeli sotsialisticheskoĭ ėkonomiki . Moskva , 1978. 350 p. : LC Card 81-160608
HC336.25 .G697 1978

SOVIET UNION - ECONOMIC POLICY - 1976-1980 - MATHEMATICAL MODELS.
Zauberman, Alfred. Planning under indeterminacy /. Bielefeld, Federal Republic of Germany [1976] 153, 5 p. ; LC Card 85-127554
HC336.25 .Z38 1976

SOVIET UNION - ECONOMIC POLICY - 1981-
Abalkin, L. I. (Leonid Ivanovich) Kursom uskoreniia /. Moskva , 1986. 213 p. ; LC Card 87-123506 DDC 338.947/009/48 19
HC336.25 .A33 1986

Ageev, V. M. (Valentin Mikhaĭlovich) Ėkonomicheskie interesy i stimuly pri sotsializme /. Moskva , 1984. 190 p. ; LC Card 85-108645
HC336.25 .A375 1984

Aktual'nye problemy planomernogo razvitiia narodnogo khoziaistva /. Moskva , 1980. 247 p. ; LC Card 81-131558
HC336.25 .A455 1980

Avak'ian, Suren Adibekovich. Sovety i rukovodstvo ėkonomikoĭ . Moskva , 1985. 110 p. ; LC Card 87-118114
HC336.25 .A87 1985

Babosov, Evgeniĭ Mikhaĭlovich. XXVII s"ezd KPSS o strategii uskoreniia sotsial'no-ėkonomicheskogo razvitiia strany /. Minsk , 1987. 124 p. ; LC Card 87-166221
HC337.B93 B33 1987

Baĭbakov, Nikolaĭ Konstantinovich. O Gosudarstvennom plane ėkonomicheskogo i sotsial'nogo razvitiia SSSR na 1981-1985 gody ... . Moskva , 1981. 44 p. ; LC Card 82-200045
HC336.25 .B33945 1981

Budaveĭ, Vsevolod IUr'evich. Dolgosrochnye narodnokhoziaistvennye programmy . Moskva , 1980. 205 p. ; LC Card 81-143196
HD45 .B792 1980

Chistiakov, E. G. (Evgeniĭ Gavrilovich) Metody sochetaniia otraslevogo i territorial'nogo planirovaniia /. Moskva , 1982. 147, [3] p. : LC Card 82-189489
HC336.25 .C516 1982

Desai, Padma. The Soviet economy . Oxford, OX, UK , 1987. viii, 281 p. : ISBN 0-631-15227-X : LC Card 86-28326 DDC 330.947/0853 19
HC336.25 .D47 1987

Ėkonomicheskie sviazi i sovershenstvovanie khoziaistvennogo mekhanizma . Kursk , 1985. 107 p. ; LC Card 86-235039
HC340.I57 E37 1985

Folom'ev, A. N. (Aleksandr Nikolaevich) Orudiia truda . Moskva , 1984. 107, [4] p. ; LC Card 85-138858
HC336.25 .F64 1984

Goldman, Marshall I. Gorbachev's challenge .

New York , c1987. xvii, 296 p. : ISBN 0-393-02454-7 LC Card 86-33187 DDC 338.947 19
HC336.25 .G6365 1987

Intensifikatsiia ėkonomiki i narodnoe potreblenie /. Moskva , 1983. 166 p. ; LC Card 84-227789
HC340.C6 I58 1983

Khoziaistvennyĭ mekhanizm v sisteme optimal'nogo funktsionirovaniia sotsialisticheskoĭ ėkonomiki /. Moskva , 1985. 346 p. ; LC Card 86-114802
HC336.25 .K474 1985

Kirichenko, Vadim Nikitich. Osnovnye idei piatiletki /. Moskva , 1981. 92 p. : LC Card 82-123953
HC336.25 .K569 1981

Makhnova, V. I. (Vera Ivanovna) Teoriia khoziaistvennykh sviazeĭ /. Moskva , 1985. 197 p. : LC Card 86-107892
HC336.25 .M347 1985

Marrama, Vittorio. Programmazione e sviluppo in Unione Sovietica /. Torino , c1983. 146 p. : LC Card 85-175586
HC336.25 .M358 1983

Material'noe stimulirovanie v khoziaistvennom mekhanizme sotsialisticheskogo obshchestva . Leningrad , 1986. 152 p. ; LC Card 86-175029
HF5549.5.I5 M3385 1986

Moiseev, Anatoliĭ Vasil'evich. Osnovy ėkonomiki vazhneĭshikh otrasleĭ narodnogo khoziaĭsva SSSR . Moskva , 1984. 191 p. : LC Card 85-113764
HC336.25 .M654 1984

Munkholt, Peer. The Soviet economy . Köln , 1985. iii, 79 p. ; LC Card 86-673837
HC340.D4 M86x 1985

Nechaev, IU. V. (IUriĭ Vasil'evich) Populiarnaia politėkonomiia /. Kiev , 1986. 246 p. : LC Card 87-169729
HC336.25 .N43 1986

Palkin, IUriĭ Ivanovich. Ėkonomicheskie zakony i ėkonomicheskaia politika KPSS /. Kiev , 1985. 245 p. ; LC Card 87-104961
HC336.25 .P35 1985

Programmno-tselevoĭ metod v planirovanii /. Moskva , 1982. 150 p. : LC Card 83-162853
HC336.25 .P6577 1982

Puzanov, V. D. (Valeriĭ Dmitrievich) Proizvodstvennoe nakoplenie . Moskva , 1983. 109 p. ; LC Card 83-194433
HC340.S3 P89 1983

Shevardnadze, Ėduard Amvrosievich. Strategiia uskoreniia--leninizm v deĭstvii . Moskva , 1986. 29 p. ; LC Card 86-190944
HC336.25 .S524 1986

Silin, V. A. (Vladimir Andreevich) Ėkonomika--poisk, ėksperiment /. Moskva , 1978. 109 p. ; LC Card 81-167075
HC336.25 .S557 1978

Soderzhanie i struktura edinogo narodno-khoziaĭstvennogo kompleksa SSSR /. Moskva , 1986. 229 p. ; LC Card 87-126348
HC336.25 .S643 1986

Solodkova, S. V. (Serafima Vasil'evna) Sotsialisticheskie proizvodstvennye otnosheniia . Moskva , 1984. 141 p. ; LC Card 84-223476
HC336.25 .S65 1984

Sotsial'no-ėkonomicheskaia sushchnost' obshchenarodnogo khoziaĭstvennogo mekhanizma /. Kiev , 1985. 342 p. ; LC Card 86-197710
HC336.25 .S668 1985

Sovershenstvovanie planirovaniia i usilenie khoziaĭstvennogo mekhanizma . Kishinev , 1983. 134 p. ; LC Card 84-231201
HC336.25 .S6736 1983

Sovetskaia ėkonomika na novom ėtape /. Moskva , 1981. 223 p. : LC Card 82-118778
HC336.25 .S677 1981

The Soviet Union under Gorbachev . London , New York , c1987. 227 p. : ISBN 0-7099-4519-1 LC Card 87-15432 DDC 338.947 19
HC336.25 .S685 1987

Struktura narodnogo khoziaĭstva v usloviiakh intensifikatsii ėkonomiki /. Moskva , 1986. 267 p. ; LC Card 86-212596
HC336.25 .S795 1986

Terekhov, IU. I. (IUriĭ Ivanovich) Planirovanie narodnogo khoziaĭstva SSSR /. Khar'kov , 1985. 176 p. ; LC Card 86-102455
HC336.25 .T465 1985

Troshin, A. (Andreĭ) Sovetskaia ėkonomika segodnia i zavtra /. Moskva , 1981. 208 p. ; LC Card 82-144819
HC336.25 .T7 1981

TSelevye kompleksnye programmy . Moskva , 1984. 198 p. : LC Card 86-176369
HC336.25 .T74 1984

SOVIET UNION - ECONOMIC POLICY - 1981- - CONGRESSES.
Clement, Hermann. Entwicklungsmöglichkeiten des deutsch-sowjetischen Handels in der zweiten Hälfte der 80er Jahre vor dem Hintergrund der sowjetischen Planung /. München , 1986. 14 leaves ; LC Card 86-167481
HF3568.S66 C58 1986

Povyshenie trudovoĭ i obshchestvenno-politicheskoĭ aktivnosti mass kak reshaiushchiĭ faktor uskoreniia sotsial'no-ėkonomicheskogo progressa sotsialisticheskogo obshchestva . Kaliningrad , 1986. 382 p. ; LC Card 87-136621
HD8526.5 .P62 1986

Simpozium "Nauchno-tekhnicheskiĭ progress i intensifikatsiia obshchestvennogo proizvodstva" (1984 : Podol'sk, Moscow, R.S.F.S.R.) Formy i metody vzaimodeĭstviia nauki i proizvodstva /. Moskva , 1984. 237 p. ; LC Card 85-240380
HC340.T4 S48 1984

SOVIET UNION - ECONOMIC POLICY - 1981- - MATHEMATICAL MODELS.
Chislennye metody v zadachakh optimal'nogo ėkonomicheskogo planirovaniia /. Moskva , 1983. 158 p. : LC Card 84-128729
HC336.25 .C515 1983

Khoziaĭstvennyĭ mekhanizm i tsenoobrazovanie /. Moskva , 1983. 77 p. ; LC Card 85-180519
HB235.S73 K47 1983

Pospelov, Germogen Sergeevich. Protsedury i algoritmy formirovaniia kompleksnykh programm /. Moskva , 1985. 422, [2] p. : LC Card 86-203758
HC336.25 .P567 1985

Problemy tselevoĭ orientatsii razvitiia resursnogo potentsiala /. Moskva , 1984. 205 p. : LC Card 86-143993
HC333.5 .P77 1984

Rozin, Bentsian Borisovich. Statisticheskaia otsenka normativov otraslevogo planirovaniia /. Novosibirsk , 1986. 188, [3] p. : LC Card 86-230359
HC336.25 .R69 1986

Sheviakov, Alekseĭ IUr'evich. Modelirovanie sbalansirovannosti i soglasovaniia planovykh resheniĭ v sfere narodnogo blagosostoianiia /. Moskva , 1986. 211 p. : LC Card 86-177908
HC336.25 .S525 1986

Sistema modeleĭ narodnokhoziaĭstvennogo planirovaniia /. Moskva , 1982. 375 p. ; LC Card 83-172876
HC336.25 .S564 1982

TSelevye kompleksnye programmy . Moskva , 1984. 198 p. : LC Card 86-176369
HC336.25 .T74 1984

SOVIET UNION - ECONOMIC POLICY - 1981-1985 - CONGRESSES.
Uskorenie sotsial'no-ėkonomicheskogo razvitiia strany--zadacha vseĭ partii, vsego naroda . Moskva , 1986. 476 p. ; LC Card 87-103200 DDC 338.947/09/048 19
HC336.25 .U748 1986

SOVIET UNION - ECONOMIC POLICY - 1981-1985 - MISCELLANEA.
Guber, A. A. (Aleksandr Andreevich) Nasha ėkonomika . Moskva , 1986. 157 p. ; LC Card 87-132459 DDC 330.947/085/3 19
HC336.25 .G82 1986

SOVIET UNION - ECONOMIC POLICY - 1986-
Danilov, L. L. (Leonid Luk'ianvich), 1914- USSR, the 12th five-year plan period /. Moscow , 1986. 55 p. : LC Card 87-123056 DDC 338.947 19
HC336.25 .D378 1986

Drits, V. I. (Valentin Ivanovich) Intensifikatsiia--opredeliaiushchee napravlenie sovremennogo ėkonomicheskogo razvitiia /. Minsk , 1986. 76, [4] p. ; LC Card 87-144484
HC336.25 .D75 1985

Egorov, A. D. (Aleksandr Dmitrievich) Khoziaĭstvennyĭ mekhanizm uskoreniia nauchno-tekhnicheskogo progressa . Minsk , 1986. 61, [3] p. ; LC Card 87-144749
HC340.Z9 T44 1986

Gorbachev, Mikhail Sergeevich, 1931- [Perestroĭka--krovnoe delo naroda. English.] Restructuring, a vital concern of the people . Moscow , 1987. 28 p. ; LC Card 87-165567 DDC 338.947 19
HC336.26 .G6713 1987

SOVIET UNION - ECONOMIC POLICY - 1986- - CONGRESSES.
Uskorenie sotsial'no-ėkonomicheskogo razvitiia strany--zadacha vseĭ partii, vsego naroda . Moskva , 1986. 476 p. ; LC Card 87-103200 DDC 338.947/09/048 19
HC336.25 .U748 1986

SOVIET UNION - ECONOMIC POLICY - 1986- - MISCELLNEA.
Guber, A. A. (Aleksandr Andreevich) Nasha ėkonomika . Moskva , 1986. 157 p. ; LC Card 87-132459 DDC 330.947/085/3 19
HC336.25 .G82 1986

SOVIET UNION - ECONOMIC POLICY - DICTIONARIES - RUSSIAN.
Moiseev, Anatoliĭ Vasil'evich. Ėkonomicheskiĭ slovar'-spravochnik . Moskva , 1978. 239 p. ; LC Card 81-165938
HB61 .M56 1978

SOVIET UNION - ECONOMIC POLICY - MATHEMATICAL MODELS.
Martynov, G. V. (Gennadiĭ Viktorovich) Mnogootraslevye kompleksy--problemy i metody optimizatsii /. Moskva , 1986. 229, [3] p. : LC Card 86-232408
HC333 .M285 1986

SOVIET UNION - ETHNIC RELATIONS.
Nekotorye problemy internatsional'nogo vospitaniia v mnogonatsional'nom trudovom kollektive /. Moskva , 1985. 135 p. ; LC Card 86-233779
HD8526.5 .N45 1985

SOVIET UNION - FOREIGN ECONOMIC RELATIONS.
Scrivener, Ronald. USSR economic handbook /. London , Detroit, Mich. , 1986. 246 p. : ISBN 0-86338-156-1 LC Card 87-130957 DDC 330.947/0854
HC336.25 .S37 1986

Sokoloff, Georges. L'économie de la détente . Paris , c1983. 255 p. : ISBN 2-7246-0483-0 : LC Card 84-117643
HF3646.5 .S65 1983

SOVIET UNION - FOREIGN ECONOMIC RELATIONS - ARAB COUNTRIES - HISTORY.
Makeev, D. A. Vneshnetorgovye sviazi SSSR so stranami Arabskogo Vostoka v 1922-1939 gg. /. Moskva , 1983. 112 p. ; LC Card 84-189987
HF1558.15.A65 M34 1983

SOVIET UNION - FOREIGN ECONOMIC RELATIONS - BULGARIA.
Zhamin, V. A. (Vitaliĭ Alekseevich) Sotsialisticheskaia ėkonomicheskaia integratsiia--faktor povysheniia ėffektivnosti proizvodstva stran SĖV /. Moskva , Varna , 1978. 93 p. ; LC Card 81-149558
HC244 .Z46 1978

SOVIET UNION - FOREIGN ECONOMIC RELATIONS - CANADA.
SSSR, SShA i Kanada . Moskva , 1987. 325 p. ; LC Card 86-205359
HF3628.U5 S77 1987

SOVIET UNION - FOREIGN ECONOMIC RELATIONS - DEVELOPING COUNTRIES.
SSSR--razvivaiushchiesia strany . Moskva , 1985. 237 p. ; LC Card 86-158191
HF1558.5.D44 S77 1985

SOVIET UNION - FOREIGN ECONOMIC RELATIONS - EGYPT - HISTORY.
Makeev, D. A. Vneshnetorgovye sviazi SSSR so stranami Arabskogo Vostoka v 1922-1939 gg. /.

Moskva , 1983. 112 p. ; LC Card 84-189987
HF1558.15.A65 M34 1983

SOVIET UNION - FOREIGN ECONOMIC RELATIONS - EUROPE.
Blinken, Antony J. Ally versus ally . New York , 1987. ix, 193 p. : ISBN 0-275-92410-6 (alk. paper) : LC Card 86-25222 DDC 388.5 19
HD9581.S652 B58 1987

SOVIET UNION - FOREIGN ECONOMIC RELATIONS - FORECASTING.
Voprosy prognozirovaniia i planirovaniia vneshneėkonomicheskikh sviazeĭ /. Moskva , 1984. 93 p. ; LC Card 86-144298
HF3626.5 .V668 1984

SOVIET UNION - FOREIGN ECONOMIC RELATIONS - INDIA.
Indo-CMEA economic relations /. New Delhi , 1987. xviii, 263 p. ; ISBN 81-7024-078-6 : LC Card 87-901620 DDC 337.54047 19
HC433 .I535 1987

Menon, M. S. N., 1924- Indo-Soviet trade and economic ties /. New Delhi , 1986. 229 p. ; LC Card 86-903273 DDC 337.54047 19
HF1590.5.S65 M46 1986

SOVIET UNION - FOREIGN ECONOMIC RELATIONS - UNITED STATES.
Boe, Jonathan E. (Jonathan Evers) American business . New York , 1987. p. cm. ISBN 0-8240-8075-0 LC Card 87-23693 DDC 337.73047 337.4 19
HF1456.5.S624 B64 1987

Knight, Misha G. How to do business with Russians . New York , 1987. xxiv, 311 p. : ISBN 0-89930-211-4 (lib. bdg. : alk. paper) LC Card 86-30396 DDC 658.8/48/0947 19
HF1558.5.U6 K56 1987

SSSR, SShA i Kanada . Moskva , 1987. 325 p. ; LC Card 86-205359
HF3628.U5 S77 1987

SOVIET UNION - FOREIGN RELATIONS.
Ratiu, Ion. Moscow challenges the world /. London , 1986. 410 p. ; ISBN 0-907671-23-5
NYPL [JLE 87-1665]

SOVIET UNION - FOREIGN RELATIONS - 1975-
Shevardnadze, Ėduard Amvrosievich. Strategiia uskoreniia--leninizm v deĭstvii . Moskva , 1986. 29 p. ; LC Card 86-190944
HC336.25 .S524 1986

SOVIET UNION - FOREIGN RELATIONS - GERMANY.
Lemke, Heinz. Finanztransaktionen und Aussenpolitik . Berlin , 1985. 215 p. ; LC Card 86-196601
HG3955 .L45 1985

SOVIET UNION - FOREIGN RELATIONS - UNITED STATES.
Kolarik, William F. A model for the study of international trade politics . New York , 1987. 613 p. : ISBN 0-8240-8086-6 (alk. paper) : LC Card 87-23788 DDC 382/.0947/0730724 19
HF3105 .K64 1987

Targ, Harry R., 1940- Strategy of an empire in decline . Minneapolis , c1986. 294 p. ; ISBN 0-930656-47-4 : LC Card 86-16338 DDC 909.82 19
D849 .T37 1986 ***NYPL [JFD 87-2032]***

SOVIET UNION - FULL EMPLOYMENT POLICIES - HISTORY - 20TH CENTURY - CONGRESSES.
Labour and employment in the USSR /. Brighton, Sussex , 1986. xviii, 280 p. : ISBN 0-7450-0038-X LC Card 86-673709
HD5796 .L33x 1986b

SOVIET UNION - HISTORY - 20TH CENTURY.
Ratiu, Ion. Moscow challenges the world /. London , 1986. 410 p. ; ISBN 0-907671-23-5
NYPL [JLE 87-1665]

SOVIET UNION - HISTORY - 1917-1936.
Altrichter, Helmut, 1945- Die Bauern von Tver . München , 1984. 373 p. : ISBN 3-486-52071-7 LC Card 84-162284
HD1536.S65 A47 1984

SOVIET UNION - HISTORY - MATHEMATICAL MODELS - ADDRESSES, ESSAYS, LECTURES.
Soviet quantitative history /. Beverly Hills , c1984. 216 p. : ISBN 0-8039-2082-2 LC Card 83-19196 DDC 306/.072047 19
HD715 .S5956 1984 ***NYPL [JLD 87-841]***

SOVIET UNION - INDUSTRIES.
Guber, A. A. (Aleksandr Andreevich) Industry /. Moscow , 1985. 46 p., [16] p. of plates : LC Card 86-208070 DDC 338.947 19
HC336.25 .G8 1985

Wilk, Marian. Pierwsza pięciolatka w Związku Radzieckim . Wrocław , 1986. 314 p., [21] p. of plates : ISBN 83-04-02190-0 : LC Card 87-110627
HC335.4 .W55 1986

SOVIET UNION - INDUSTRIES - 1957-
Khrushchev, A. T. ((Anatoliĭ Timofeevich)) Geografiia promyshlennosti SSSR /. Moskva , 1986. 415 p. : LC Card 87-117010
HC336.25 .K475 1986

Lipko, A. G. (Alekseĭ Gennad′evich) Proizvodstvo i potreblenie v regione /. Moskva , 1986. 142 p. : LC Card 86-211374
HC336.25 .L56 1986

SOVIET UNION - INDUSTRIES - 1957- - AUDITING.
Ėkonomicheskiĭ analiz khoziaĭstvennoĭ deiatel′nosti predpriiatiĭ i ob″edineniĭ /. Moskva , 1986. 406 p. : LC Card 86-227621
HC340.A8 E417 1986

SOVIET UNION - INDUSTRIES - FINANCE - PLANNING.
Cheblokov, A. T. (Andreĭ Timofeevich) Finansovoe planirovanie v promyshlennosti /. Moskva , 1983. 133, [2] p. ; LC Card 84-134674
HC336.25 .C48 1983

SOVIET UNION - INDUSTRIES - HISTORY.
Kuromiya, Hiroaki. Stalin's industrial revolution . Cambridge [Cambridgeshire] , New York , 1988. p. cm. ISBN 0-521-35157-X LC Card 87-25010 DDC 338.947 19
HC335.4 .K87 1988

SOVIET UNION - INDUSTRIES - LOCATION.
Baklanov, Petr IAkovlevich. Prostranstvennye sistemy proizvodstva . Moskva , 1986. 149 p. : LC Card 86-202803
HC340.D5 B35 1986

Khrushchev, A. T. ((Anatoliĭ Timofeevich)) Geografiia promyshlennosti SSSR /. Moskva , 1986. 415 p. : LC Card 87-117010
HC336.25 .K475 1986

Novitskiĭ, N. A. (Nikolaĭ Aleksandrovich) Faktornyĭ analiz ėffektivnosti razmeshcheniia proizvodstva /. Moskva , 1982. 126 p. : LC Card 83-193429
HC340.D5 N68 1982

Osobennosti i problemy razmeshcheniia proizvoditel′nykh sil SSSR v period razvitogo sotsializma /. Moskva , 1980. 273 p. ; LC Card 81-143866
HC340.D5 O86 1980

Teoreticheskie i metodologicheskie problemy regional′noĭ ėkonomiki . Moskva , 1983. 158 p. : LC Card 87-100005
HC340.D5 T437 1983

Territorial′naia organizatsiia proizvoditel′nykh sil SSSR /. Moskva , 1978. 124 p. : LC Card 81-149822
HC340.D5 T44 1978

Territorial′nye struktury promyshlennosti /. Moskva , 1978. 128 p. : LC Card 81-147566
HC340.D5 T464 1978

SOVIET UNION - INDUSTRIES - LOCATION - MAPS.
Territorial′naia organizatsiia proizvoditel′nykh sil SSSR /. Moskva , 1978. 124 p. : LC Card 81-149822
HC340.D5 T44 1978

SOVIET UNION - MILITARY POLICY.
Shepherd, William G. The ultimate deterrent . New York , 1986. x, 137 p. ; ISBN 0-275-92368-1 (alk. paper) : LC Card 86-20486 DDC 355/.03 19
UA10.5 .S524 1986 ***NYPL [JLE 87-884]***

SOVIET UNION - MILITARY POLICY - ECONOMIC ASPECTS.
Munkholt, Peer. The Soviet economy . Köln , 1985. iii, 79 p. ; LC Card 86-673837
HC340.D4 M86x 1985

SOVIET UNION - NATIONAL SECURITY.
Shepherd, William G. The ultimate deterrent . New York , 1986. x, 137 p. ; ISBN 0-275-92368-1 (alk. paper) : LC Card 86-20486 DDC 355/.03 19
UA10.5 .S524 1986 ***NYPL [JLE 87-884]***

SOVIET UNION, NORTHERN - ECONOMIC CONDITIONS.
Ėkonomicheskie problemy osvoeniia Ural′skogo Severa /. Sverdlovsk , 1982. 69 p. : LC Card 83-188353
HC336.9.N65 E37 1982

Rapoport, IU. M. (IUriĭ Mikhaĭlovich) Osushchestvlenie ėkonomicheskoĭ politiki Kommunisticheskoĭ partii v usloviiakh Evropeĭskogo Severa RSFSR, 1917-1925 gg. /. Leningrad , 1984. 216 p. ; LC Card 84-217989
HC336.9.N65 R36 1984

Slavin, S. V. (Samuil Venediktovich) Osvoenie Severa Sovetskogo Soiuza /. Moskva , 1982. 206 p. : LC Card 83-137884
HC336.9.N65 S56 1982

SOVIET UNION, NORTHERN - OCCUPATIONS.
Sotsial′nye problemy truda u narodnosteĭ Severa /. Novosibirsk , 1986. 213 p. ; LC Card 87-164784
HD5797.N75 S67 1986

SOVIET UNION, NORTHWESTERN - ECONOMIC CONDITIONS.
Kulibanov, V. S. (Vadim Sergeevich) Problemy razvitiia narodnogo khoziaĭstva Severo-Zapada SSSR . Leningrad , 1980. 33, [3] p. ; LC Card 82-115046
HC336.9.N65 K85 1980

SOVIET UNION, NORTHWESTERN - ECONOMIC POLICY.
Kulibanov, V. S. (Vadim Sergeevich) Problemy razvitiia narodnogo khoziaĭstva Severo-Zapada SSSR . Leningrad , 1980. 33, [3] p. ; LC Card 82-115046
HC336.9.N65 K85 1980

SOVIET UNION, NORTHWESTERN - SOCIAL CONDITIONS.
Ivanov, E. P. (Evgeniĭ Pavlovich) Kollektivizatsiia krest′ianskikh khoziaĭstv i likvidatsiia kulachestva kak klassa na Severo-Zapade RSFSR, 1927-1937 gg. . Leningrad , 1983. 91 p. ; LC Card 84-190520
HD1492.S652 R875 1983
NYPL [*QI 87-3170]

SOVIET UNION - OCCUPATIONS.
Petrov, V. A. (Valeriĭ Arkad′evich) Sotsial′no-demograficheskaia struktura gorodskogo naseleniia i ego zaniatost′ /. Moskva , 1981. 151 p. ; LC Card 82-145197
HB2277 .P48 1981

SOVIET UNION - POLITICS AND GOVERNMENT - TO 1533.
Martin, Janet, 1945- Treasure of the land of darkness . Cambridge [Cambridgeshire] , New York , 1986. x, 277 p. : ISBN 0-521-32019-4 LC Card 86-6094 DDC 380.1/456753/0947 19
HD9944.S755 M37 1986
NYPL [JLE 87-1280]

SOVIET UNION - POLITICS AND GOVERNMENT - 1917-1936.
Kuromiya, Hiroaki. Stalin's industrial revolution . Cambridge [Cambridgeshire] , New York , 1988. p. cm. ISBN 0-521-35157-X LC Card 87-25010 DDC 338.947 19
HC335.4 .K87 1988

SOVIET UNION - POLITICS AND GOVERNMENT - 1982-
The Soviet Union under Gorbachev . London , New York , c1987. 227 p. : ISBN 0-7099-4519-1 LC Card 87-15432 DDC 338.947 19
HC336.25 .S685 1987

SOVIET UNION - POPULATION.
Boiarskiĭ, Aron IAkovlevich, 1906- Praktikum po demografii /. Moskva , 1985. 141, [3] p. : LC Card 86-170070
HB3607 .B64 1985

Demograficheskoe razvitie v SSSR /. Moskva , 1985. 126 p. ; LC Card 85-170633
HB3607 .D445 1985

Detnost′ semi′i--vchera, segodnia, zavtra /. Moskva , 1986. 205 p. : LC Card 87-109456 DDC 304.6/32/0947 19
HB1017 .D47 1986

Osnovy teorii narodonaseleniia /. Moskva , 1986. 374 p. : LC Card 86-218424
HB851 .O82 1986

Petrov, V. A. (Valeriĭ Arkad'evich) Sotsial'no-demograficheskaia struktura gorodskogo naseleniia i ego zaniatost' /. Moskva , 1981. 151 p. ; LC Card 82-145197
HB2277 .P48 1981

Rozwój ludności krajów socjalistycznych . Warszawa , Moskva , 1978. 381 p. ; LC Card 81-206832
HB3608.7.A3 R69 1978

SOVIET UNION - POPULATION DENSITY.
Problemy rasseleniia v SSSR . Moskva , 1980. 254 p. : LC Card 81-135093
HB2068.S65 P76 1980

SOVIET UNION - POPULATION - MATHEMATICAL MODELS.
Iskakov, B. I. (Boris Ivanovich) Demograficheskoe modelirovanie . Moskva , 1982. 75 p. ; LC Card 83-179019
HB849.51 .I85 1982

SOVIET UNION - POPULATION POLICY.
Demograficheskaia politika sotsialisticheskogo obshchestva /. Moskva , 1986. 190 p. ;
*NYPL [*QIP 87-2842]*

Demograficheskaia politika sotsialisticheskogo obshchestva /. Moskva , 1986. 190 p. : LC Card 87-120466
HB3607 .D425 1986

SOVIET UNION - POPULATION POLICY - HISTORY.
Szabó, A. Ferenc. Fejezetek a szocialista népesedéselmélet történetéből /. [Budapest] , 1985. 94 p. ; ISBN 963-673-318-X LC Card 86-187050
HB871 .S86 1985

SOVIET UNION - POPULATION - STATISTICS.
Boiarskiĭ, Aron IAkovlevich, 1906- Praktikum po demografii /. Moskva , 1985. 141, [3] p. : LC Card 86-170070
HB3607 .B64 1985

Treml, Vladimir G. Referent USSR economic and demographic statistics for normalization of Berkeley-Duke emigre questionnaire data /. [Durham, N.C. [1986] 1 v. (various pagings) ; LC Card 86-70618 DDC 304.6/0947/021 19
HB3607 .T74 1986

SOVIET UNION - RELATIONS - UNITED STATES.
Hammer, Armand, 1897- Hammer /. New York , c1987. 544 p., [32] p. of plates : ISBN 0-399-13275-9 LC Card 86-30289 DDC 338.092/4 B 19
HC102.5.H35 A3 1987

SOVIET UNION - RURAL CONDITIONS.
Istoriia sovetskogo krest'ianstva . Moskva , 1986- v. : *NYPL [*QG 87-3228]*

Istoriia sovetskogo krest'ianstva /. Moskva , 1986-<1987. v. <1-3 > : LC Card 86-230318
HD1492.S65 I88 1986

Main, V. N. (Valentin Nikolaevich) Sel'skaia intelligentsiia v gody Velikoĭ Otechestvennoĭ voĭny . Voronezh , 1985. 158 p. ; LC Card 84-172657
HC340.D4 M35 1985

SOVIET UNION - RURAL CONDITIONS - HISTORIOGRAPHY.
Cox, Terry. Peasants, class, and capitalism . Oxford [Oxfordshire] ; New York : xii, 271 p. ; ISBN 0-19-878014-1 : LC Card 86-2362 DDC 305.5/63 19
HD1536.S65 C69 1986
NYPL [JLD 86-3986]

SOVIET UNION - SOCIAL CONDITIONS - 1801-1917 - COLLECTED WORKS.
Druzhinin, N. M. (Nikolaĭ Mikhaĭlovich) Sotsial'no-ėkonomicheskaia istoriia Rossii . Moskva , 1987. 421 p., [1] leaf of plates : LC Card 87-164847
HC334.5 .D78 1987

SOVIET UNION - SOCIAL CONDITIONS - 1945-
Matthews, Mervyn. Poverty in the Soviet Union . Cambridge [Cambridgeshire] , New York , 1986. xv, 227 p. ; ISBN 0-521-32544-7 LC Card 86-993 DDC 305.5/69/0947 19
HC340.P6 M38 1986 *NYPL [JLD 87-262]*

SOVIET UNION - SOCIAL CONDITIONS - 1970-
Aktual'nye problemy sotsial'no-ėkonomicheskogo razvitiia SSSR v sovremennyĭ period /. Moskva , 1984. 153 p. ; LC Card 85-205938
HC336.25 .A46 1984

SOVIET UNION - SOCIAL CONDITIONS - 1970- - MISCELLANEA.
Guber, A. A. (Aleksandr Andreevich) Nasha ėkonomika . Moskva , 1986. 157 p. ; LC Card 87-132459 DDC 330.947/085/3 19
HC336.25 .G82 1986

SOVIET UNION - SOCIAL CONDITIONS - ADDRESSES, ESSAYS, LECTURES.
Karpiński, Wojciech. Szkice o wolności /. Chicago, Ill. (2886 Milwaukee Ave., Chicago, Ill. 60618) , 1980. 95 p. ; LC Card 81-201974
JC585 .K32 1980 *NYPL [*QR 86-4376]*

SOVIET UNION - SOCIAL CONDITIONS - MATHEMATICAL MODELS - ADDRESSES, ESSAYS, LECTURES.
Soviet quantitative history /. Beverly Hills , c1984. 216 p. : ISBN 0-8039-2082-2 LC Card 83-19196 DDC 306/.072047 19
HD715 .S5956 1984 *NYPL [JLD 87-841]*

SOVIET UNION - SOCIAL POLICY.
Martanus, R. V. (Riurik Vital'evich) Sotsial'noe upravlenie . Moskva , 1986. 141 p. ; LC Card 87-156789
HD38.25.S65 M35 1986

SOVIET UNION - SOCIAL POLICY - CONGRESSES.
Povyshenie trudovoĭ i obshchestvenno-politicheskoĭ aktivnosti mass kak reshaiushchiĭ faktor uskoreniia sotsial'no-ėkonomicheskogo progressa sotsialisticheskogo obshchestva . Kaliningrad , 1986. 382 p. ; LC Card 87-136621
HD8526.5 .P62 1986

SOVIET UNION - STATISTICS.
Treml, Vladimir G. Referent USSR economic and demographic statistics for normalization of Berkeley-Duke emigre questionnaire data /. [Durham, N.C. [1986] 1 v. (various pagings) ; LC Card 86-70618 DDC 304.6/0947/021 19
HB3607 .T74 1986

The Soviet Union today and tomorrow.
Guber, A. A. (Aleksandr Andreevich) Industry /. Moscow , 1985. 46 p., [16] p. of plates : LC Card 86-208070 DDC 338.947 19
HC336.25 .G8 1985

The Soviet Union under Gorbachev : prospects for reform / edited by David A. Dyker. London ; New York : Croom Helm, c1987. 227 p. : ports. ; 23 cm. "Published in the USA by Croom Helm in association with Methuen, Inc."--T.p. verso. Includes bibliographies and index. ISBN 0-7099-4519-1 LC Card 87-15432 DDC 338.947 19
1. Soviet Union - Economic policy - 1981-. 2. Soviet Union - Politics and government - 1982-. I. Dyker, David A.
HC336.25 .S685 1987

Soviet Union. Verkhovnyĭ Sovet.
Postanovlenie Verkhovnogo Soveta SSSR ob utverzhdenii otcheta ob ispolnenii Gosudarstvennogo biudzheta USSR za 1984 god. 1985. Dementsev, V. V. (Viktor Vladimirovich) O Gosudarstvennom biudzhete SSSR na 1986 god i ob ispolnenii Gosudarstvennogo biudzheta SSSR za 1984 god : doklad i zakliuchitel'noe slovo na sovmestnykh zasedaniiakh Soveta Soiuza i Soveta Natsional'nosteĭ chetvertoĭ sessii Verkhovnogo Soveta SSSR odinnadtsatogo sozyva / V.V. Dementsev. Zakon Soiuza Sovetskikh Sotsialisticheskikh Respublik o Gosudarstvennom biudzhete SSSR na 1986 god. Postanovlenie Verkhovnogo Soveta SSSR ob utverzhdenii otcheta ob ispolnenii Gosudarstvennogo biudzheta SSSR za 1984 god. Moskva , 1985. 28 p. ; LC Card 86-203425
HJ2129 .D46 1985

SOVIET UNION, WESTERN - ECONOMIC CONDITIONS - CONGRESSES.
Vozrozhdenie prifrontovykh i osvobozhdennykh raĭonov SSSR v gody Velikoĭ Otechestvennoĭ voĭny 1941-1945 /. Moskva , 1986. 214 p., [24] p. of plates : LC Card 86-232256
HC336.9.W47 V69 1986

Sovietske skúsenosti v rozvoji tvorivej iniciatívy pracujúcich /. Semotam, Josef. Bratislava , 1981. 153 p. ; LC Card 81-182787
HC340.I52 S45 1981 *NYPL [*QT 86-5786]*

Sovkhozyng shu gúni ve geljegi /. Babaev, Akmyrat. Ashgabat , 1982. 55 p. : LC Card 84-126905
HD1493.S652 T873 1982

Sovremennaia pakistanskaia derevnia . Morozova, M. IU. (Marina IUr'evna) Moskva , 1986. 172 p. ; LC Card 86-174352
HD2075.5 .M67 1986

Sovremennye burzhuaznye ėkonomicheskie teorii.
Bartov, Vladimir Fotievich. Kontseptsii vzaimodeĭstviia ėkonomiki i prirody /. Moskva , 1984. 157 p. ; LC Card 84-225876
HC79.E5 B369 1984

IUdanov, A. IU. (Andreĭ IUr'evich) Teorii "otkrytoĭ ėkonomiki," doktriny i deĭstvitel'nost' /. Moskva , 1983. 190 p. ; LC Card 83-209639
HF1713 .I93 1983

Potapov, V. V. (Viktor Vladimirovich) Modifikatsii teorii "poleznosti" /. Moskva , 1984. 132 p. ; LC Card 84-247447
HB201 .P65 1984

Sovremennye problemy biosfery.
Tupytsia, IUriĭ IUr'evich. Ėkologo-ėkonomicheskaia ėffektivnost' prirodopol'zovaniia /. Moskva , 1980. 165 p. ; LC Card 81-146449
HC333.5 .T86 1980

Sovremennye problemy geografii Kirgizii . Sipozium "Geografiia v Kirgizii" (1980 : Frunze, Kirghiz S.S.R.) Frunze , 1980. 167 p. : LC Card 82-121674
HC337.K545 S56 1980

Sovremennyĭ imperializm, antogonizmy i krizisy /. Moskovtsev, I. S. (Ivan Sergeevich) Moskva , 1985. 67 p. : LC Card 85-232554
HB501 .M7219 1985

Sovremennyĭ kapitalizm : pribavochnaia stoimost', pribyl', protsent / pod redaktsieĭ S.I. Ivanova. Leningrad : Izd-vo Leningradskogo universiteta, 1985. 212 p. ; 22 cm. At head of title: Leningradskiĭ ordena Lenina i ordena Trudovogo Krasnogo Znameni gosudarstvennyĭ universitet imeni A.A. Zhdanova. Includes bibliographical references. LC Card 86-117888
1. Capitalism. I. Ivanov, Sergeĭ Ivanovich, doktor ėkonomicheskikh nauk. II. Leningradskiĭ gosudarstvennyĭ universitet imeni A.A. Zhdanova.
HB501 .S824 1985

Sovremennyĭ konservatizm i krizis burzhuaznoĭ ėkonomicheskoĭ nauki : k IX Mezhdunarodnomu kongressu po ėkonomicheskoĭ istorii : referativnyĭ sbornik / [otvetstvennyĭ redaktor i sostavitel' sbornika Makasheva N.A.]. Moskva : Akademiia nauk SSSR, In-t nauch. informatsii po obshchestvennym naukam, 1986. 175 p. ; 21 cm. (Seriia Problemy politicheskoĭ ėkonomii za rubezhom) Includes bibliographies. LC Card 87-165796
1. Supply-side economics. 2. Economics - History - 20th century. 3. Hayek, Friedrich A. von (Friedrich August), 1899-. 4. Capitalism. I. Makasheva, N. A. II. Series.
HB241 .S673 1986

Sovremennyĭ monetarizm i krizis burzhuaznoĭ ėkonomicheskoĭ teorii . Makasheva, N. A. Moskva , 1985. 47 p. ; LC Card 86-187688
HB98.3 .M35 1985

Sovremennyĭ organizator proizvodstva /.
Deĭneko, O. A. (Oleg Aleksandrovich) Moskva , 1984. 172, [2] p. : LC Card 85-112451
HD38.25.S65 D45 1984

Sovremennyĭ tarifnyĭ i netarifnyĭ protektsionizm . Diumulen, I. I. (Ippolit Ippolitovich) Moskva , 1975. 277 p. ; LC Card 82-191746
HF1713 .D62 1975

Sowell, Thomas, 1930- A conflict of visions / Thomas Sowell. 1st ed. New York : W. Morrow, c1987. 273 p. ; 22 cm. Includes bibliographical references and index. ISBN 0-688-06912-6 LC Card 86-18187 DDC 303.3/72 19
1. Social values. 2. Ideology. 3. Visions. I. Title.
HM73 .S68 1987 *NYPL [JLD 87-823]*

Sowjetunion und China . Song, Du-Yul, 1944-

Frankfurt/Main , New York , c1984. 255 p. : ISBN 3-593-33351-1 LC Card 84-169164
HC340.L3 S66 1984

SOYABEAN INDUSTRY - BRAZIL.
Desgualdo Netto, Domingos. Aspectos agroeconômicos da soja /. São Paulo , 1985. 139 p. ; LC Card 86-158570
HD9235.S62 B74 1985

SOYBEAN - BRAZIL - TRANSPORTATION.
Alternativa rodo-hidro-ferroviária para o transporte de parte da safra de soja paraguaia destinada à exportação. [Rio de Janeiro] [19]84. 65 leaves : LC Card 85-187436
HE199.5.S66 A47 1984

SOYBEAN INDUSTRY - BRAZIL.
Tsunechiro, Alfredo. O desempenho dos mercados a termo . São Paulo , 1986. xi, 123 p. : LC Card 87-404554 DDC 332.64/4 19
HG6046 .T75 1986

SOYBEAN INDUSTRY - BRAZIL - ARAGUAIA RIVER WATERSHED.
Perfis indicativos para a industrialização do arroz, milho e soja. Brasília , 1985. 189 p. : LC Card 86-195651
HD9066.B83 A737 1985

SOYBEAN INDUSTRY - BRAZIL - PARANÁ (STATE)
Estudo sobre a soja /. Curitiba , 1980. 61 leaves : LC Card 86-197070
HD9235.S62 B744 1980

SOYBEAN INDUSTRY - BRAZIL - TOCANTINS RIVER WATERSHED.
Perfis indicativos para a industrialização do arroz, milho e soja. Brasília , 1985. 189 p. : LC Card 86-195651
HD9066.B83 A737 1985

SOYBEAN INDUSTRY - PARAGUAY.
Alternativa rodo-hidro-ferroviária para o transporte de parte da safra de soja paraguaia destinada à exportação. [Rio de Janeiro] [19]84. 65 leaves : LC Card 85-187436
HE199.5.S66 A47 1984

Palau, Tomás. El cultivo del algodón y la soya en el Paraguay y sus derivaciones sociales. Santiago de Chile , 1986. 148 p. ; ISBN 92-1-321207-0 LC Card 87-400251 DDC 338.1/7351/09892 19
HD9084.P25 P35 1986

SOYBEAN INDUSTRY - UNITED STATES.
Shurtleff, William, 1941- Tofutti® & other soy ice creams . Lafayette, CA , c1985. 2 v. : ISBN 0-933332-19-X (v. 1) : LC Card 85-10829 DDC 381/.4174 19
HD9330.B323 U 1985 ***NYPL [JLF 86-1035]***

Trading in soybean complex futures /. [Chicago] , c1986. v, 53 p. ; LC Card 87-101090 DDC 332.64/4 19
HG6047.S6 T73 1986

SOYBEAN PRODUCTS - BRAZIL - PARANÁ (STATE)
Estudo sobre a soja /. Curitiba , 1980. 61 leaves : LC Card 86-197070
HD9235.S62 B744 1980

Sozdanie avtomatizirovannoĭ sistemy upravleniia ėkonomikoĭ administrativnogo raĭona : mezhvedomstvennyĭ sbornik nauchnykh trudov / pod obshcheĭ red. A. Viesisa. Riga : Latviĭskiĭ gos. universitet im. P. Stuchki, 1980. 151 p. ; 20 cm. At head of title: Ministerstvo vysshego i srednego spetsial'nogo obrazovaniia Latviĭskoĭ SSR. Latviĭskiĭ ordena Trudovogo Krasnogo Znameni gosudarstvennyĭ universitet imeni Petra Stuchki. Kafedra organizatsii mekhanizirovannoĭ obrabotki ėkonomicheskoĭ informatsii. Includes bibliographies. LC Card 81-215521
1. Accounting - Data processing. 2. Accounting - Latvia - Data processing. I. Viesis, A. P. II. Pētera Stučkas Latvijas valsts universitāte. Kafedra organizatsii mekhanizirovannoĭ obrabotki ėkonomicheskoĭ informatsii.
HF5679 .S717 1980

Sozialdemokratische Arbeiterbewegung in der Stadt Neuss vom Sozialistengesetz bis zum Ersten Weltkrieg /. Kiefer, Rolf. Reinbek , c1982. iv, 159 p. ; ISBN 3-88756-025-6 LC Card 83-186919
HD8460.N48 K54 1982

SOZIALDEMOKRATISCHE PARTEI DEUTSCHLANDS - HISTORY.
Bechtold, Hartmut. Die Kartellierung der deutschen Volkswirtschaft und die sozialdemokratische Theorie-Diskussion vor 1933 /. Frankfurt am Main , c1986. 291 p. ; ISBN 3-89228-000-2 LC Card 86-193858
HD2757.5 .B43 1986

Głowacki, Andrzej. Ruch robotniczy na Pomorzu Zachodnim do 1914 roku /. Warszawa , 1979. 160 p. ; ISBN 83-01-01306-0 LC Card 81-107475
HD8457.P66 G56 1979

Kiefer, Rolf. Sozialdemokratische Arbeiterbewegung in der Stadt Neuss vom Sozialistengesetz bis zum Ersten Weltkrieg /. Reinbek , c1982. iv, 159 p. ; ISBN 3-88756-025-6 LC Card 83-186919
HD8460.N48 K54 1982

Klönne, Arno. Die deutsche Arbeiterbewegung . Düsseldorf , Köln , 1980. 382 p. ; ISBN 3-424-00652-1 : LC Card 81-453558 DDC 322/.2/0943 19
HX276 .K547 ***NYPL [JLD 81-689]***

SOZIALDEMOKRATISCHE PARTEIDEUTSCHLANDS - PLATFORMS.
SPD wohin? . Frankfurt/Main , c1987. 114 p. ; ISBN 3-88807-047-3 LC Card 87-401340 DDC 330 s 324.243/072 19
HB97.5 .I53 Nr. 44 JN3971.A98S571712

Soziale Aspekte der Mikroelektronik / [herausgegeben im Auftrag des Vizepräsidenten und Leiters des Forschungsbereiches Gesellschaftswissenschaften ; Autoren, U. Assmann ... et al. ; verantwortlicher Bearbeiter, S. Morche]. Berlin : Akademie der Wissenschaften der DDR, Zentrum für Gesellschaftswissenschaftliche Information, 1985. 122 p. ; 21 cm. (Gesellschaftswissenschaften. GW 41) Informationen für die Leitung der Forschung "Arbeitsergebnisse der Forschungsgruppe 'Wissenschaftlich- technischer und sozialer Fortschritt' des Instituts für Soziologie und Sozialpolitik der AdW der DDR"--T.p. verso. Bibliography: p. 105-122. LC Card 87-409418 DDC 306/.46 19
1. Automation - Social aspects. 2. Microelectronics - Social aspects. 3. Communism and technology. I. Assmann, U. II. Morche, S. III. Akademie der Wissenschaften der DDR. Forschungsbereich Gesellschaftswissenschaften. IV. Forschungsgruppe "Wissenschaftlich-Technischer und Sozialer Fortschritt" des Instituts für Soziologie und Sozialpolitik der AdW der DDR. V. Series: Gesellschaftswissenschaften (Berlin, Germany) , GW 41.
HD6331 .S683 1985

Soziale Indikatoren .
(11) Ansprüche an die Arbeit . Frankfurt [am Main] , New York , c1984. 298 p. : ISBN 3-593-33390-2 LC Card 85-103333
HF5548.8 .A683 1984

(13) Arbeitsmoral und Technikfeindlichkeit . Frankfurt , New York , c1986. 274 p. : ISBN 3-593-33757-6 LC Card 86-212283
HD8444 .A73 1986

Die soziale Marktwirtschaft /. Randak, Harald, 1942- München , 1985. 143 p. : LC Card 85-216985
HC286.5 .R36 1985

Soziale Marktwirtschaft, Fundament für morgen . Kohl, Helmut, 1930- Bonn [1987] 39 p. : ISBN 3-88991-011-4 LC Card 87-409383 DDC 338.943 19
HC286.5 .K565 1987

Soziale Ordnungspolitik.
Flexible Arbeitszeit gegen starre Sozialsysteme /. Baden-Baden , 1986. 254 p. ; ISBN 3-7890-1213-0 LC Card 87-101055 DDC 331.25/72/0943 19
HD5109.2.G3 F43 1986

Überwindung der Sozialstaatskrise . Baden-Baden , 1984. 317 p. : ISBN 3-7890-0925-3 LC Card 84-166713
HD7179 .U35 1984

Soziale Schliessung in rassistisch gespaltenen Arbeitsmärkten . Faist, Thomas, 1959- Frankfurt am Main , New York , c1986. 161 p. ; ISBN 3-8204-9525-8 LC Card 87-407927 DDC 331.89/28136372/0976819 19
HD5325.S2572 1968 .M46 1986

Soziale Sicherheit in der Bundesrepublik Deutschland . Spinnarke, Jürgen. Heidelberg , c1985. 142 p. : ISBN 3-8114-1085-7 : LC Card 86-103725
HD7179 .S63 1985

Soziale Sicherung in der Bundesrepublik Deutschland /. Rüden, Reinhold von. Paderborn , c1986. 157 p. : ISBN 3-506-23938-4 LC Card 87-127289 DDC 368.4/00943 19
HD7179 .R835 1986

Sozialforschungsstelle Dortmund.
Arbeitsmarkterfahrungen und Berufsorientierungen Jugendlicher . München , c1983. 177 p. : ISBN 3-87966-202-9 LC Card 84-170074
HD6276.G4 A73 1983

Sozialgeschichtliche Bibliothek im Drumlin Verlag.
Steffens, Horst. Autorität und Revolte . Weingarten , c1987. 419 p. : ISBN 3-924027-47-1 LC Card 87-141439 DDC 331/.0422334/094342 19
HD8039.M61 G383 1987

SOZIALISTISCHE EINHEITSPARTEI DEUTSCHLANDS - CONGRESSES.
Sozialistische Einheitspartei Deutschlands. Zentralkomitee. [Bericht des Zentralkomitees der Sozialistischen Einheitspartei Deutschlands an den XI. Parteitag der SED. English.] Report of the Central Committee of the Socialist Unity Party of Germany to the 11th Congress of the SED /. Dresden [1986] 109 p. : LC Card 86-220057 DDC 338.9431 19
HC290.78 .S66 1986

Sozialistische Einheitspartei Deutschlands. Zentralkomitee.
[Bericht des Zentralkomitees der Sozialistischen Einheitspartei Deutschlands an den XI. Parteitag der SED. English]
Report of the Central Committee of the Socialist Unity Party of Germany to the 11th Congress of the SED / rapporteur, Erich Honecker. Dresden : Verlag Zeit im Bild, [1986] 109 p. : port. ; 17 cm. Translation of: Bericht des Zentralkomitees der Sozialistischen Einheitspartei Deutschlands an den XI. Parteitag der SED. LC Card 86-220057 DDC 338.9431 19
1. Sozialistische Einheitspartei Deutschlands - Congresses. 2. Economic policy - Germany (East) - Congresses. I. Honecker, Erich. II. Title.
HC290.78 .S66 1986

Mit qualitativ neuen Schritten zu höchsten Leistungen . Berlin , 1986. 80 p. ; ISBN 3-320-00807-2 LC Card 87-144292 DDC 338.9431 19
HC290.78 .M567 1986

Sozialistische Einheitspartei Deutschlands. Zentralkomitee. Akademie für Gesellschaftswissenschaften. see **Akademie für Gesellschaftswissenschaften.**

Die Sozialistische Gemeinschaft : Interessen, Zusammenarbeit, Wirtschaftswachstum / Autorenkollektiv ; [Autorenkollektiv, Hans-Georg Haupt (Leiter) ... et al., Mitarbeit, Christine Pfeiler, Hartmut Spengler ; herausgegeben im Auftrag des Rates für Wissenschaftlichen Kommunismus von einem Kollektiv, Rolf Reissig (Leiter) ... et al.]. Berlin : Dietz, 1985. 238 p. ; 18 cm. (Wissenschaftlicher Kommunismus, Theorie und Praxis) Includes bibliographical references. LC Card 86-120025 DDC 337.1/1717 19
1. Council for Mutual Economic Assistance. 2. Europe, Eastern - Economic integration. I. Haupt, Hans-Georg. II. Pfeiler, Christine. III. Spengler, Hartmut. IV. Reissig, Rolf. V. Rat für Wissenschaftlichen Kommunismus (Germany). VI. Series.
HC243.5 .S685 1985

Die sozialistische Gemeinschaft zu Beginn der 80er Jahre . Quilitzsch, Siegmar. Berlin , 1984. 141 p. : LC Card 84-180106
HC243.5 .Q55 1984

Die Sozialistische Gemeinschaftsarbeit im Territorium : Erfahrungen, Probleme, Rechtsfragen : Erfahrungsaustausch in Burg am 17. Oktober 1985. Potsdam-Babelsberg : Akademie für Staats- und Rechtswissenschaft der DDR, 1986. 175 p. ; 21 cm. (Aktuelle Beiträge der Staats- und Rechtswissenschaft, 0568-7551 . Heft 326) Papers presented at a conference sponsored by the Lehrstuhl Wirtschaftsrecht of the Akademie für Staats- und Rechtswissenschaft der DDR and the Rat des Kreises Burg. LC Card 86-212526
1. Industry and state - Germany (East) - Congresses. 2.

Industrial management - Germany (East) - Congresses. 3. Germany East - Economic policy - Congresses. I. Akademie für Staats- und Rechtswissenschaft der DDR. Lehrstuhl Wirtschaftsrecht. II. Rat des Kreises Burg. III. Series.
HD3616.G48 S68 1986

Sozialistische ökonomische Integration . Bykov, A. N. (Aleksandr Naumovich) Berlin , 1976. 218 p. ; LC Card 87-108725
HC244 .B94 1976

Sozialistischer Wettbewerb und umfassende Intensivierung : gemeinsame Tagung des Wissenschaftlichen Rates für die Wirtschaftswissenschaftliche Forschung bei der Akademie der Wissenschaften der DDR und seines Wissenschaftlichen Rates für Fragen des Sozialistischen Wettbewerbs vom 30.5.1985 / [herausgegeben im Auftrage des Präsidenten der Akademie der Wissenschaften der DDR von Heinz Stiller]. Berlin : Akademie-Verlag, 1986. 103 p. ; 30 cm. (Abhandlungen der Akademie der Wissenschaften der DDR, Abteilung Veröffentlichung der Wissenschaftlichen Räte, 0138-421X . W1, 1986) Includes bibliographies. LC Card 86-200416
1. Socialist competition - Germany (East) - Congresses. I. Stiller, Heinz. II. Akademie der Wissenschaften der DDR. Wissenschaftlicher Rat für die Wirtschaftswissenschaftliche Forschung. III. Akademie der Wissenschaften der DDR. Wissenschaftlicher Rat für Fragen des Sozialistischen Wettbewerbs. IV. Series: Abhandlungen der Akademie der Wissenschaften der DDR , Jahrg. 1986, Nr. W 1.
HC290.795.S6 S69 1986

Sozialistisches Arbeitsverhalten als Leistungsverhalten / Humboldt-Universität zu Berlin, Section Marxismus-Leninismus, Wissenschaftsbereich Politische Ökonomie ; wissenschaftliche Redaktion, Ingomar Klein. Berlin : Die Universität, [1984] 77 p. ; 21 cm. (Berichte / Humboldt-Universität zu Berlin, 0232-9123 . 11-84) Includes bibliographies. CONTENTS. - Zum Wesen und den Kriterien sozialistischen Arbeitsverhaltens / Ingomar Klein, Ruth Klein -- Die Verantwortung der leitung für die planmässige Entfaltung ... /Erika Schmidt -- Materielle und moralistische Stimulierung ... / Monika Schillat, Katja Wagner -- Die optimale Gestaltung der zeitlichen Arbeits- und Produktionsbedingungen / Inge Sauer -- Zu einigen Aufgaben bei der weiteren Entfaltung ... / Gustav Mogh, Doris Zetsche. LC Card 84-250357
1. Work ethic - Germany (East). 2. Employee morale - Germany (East). I. Klein, Ingomar. II. Humboldt-Universität zu Berlin. Wissenschaftsbereich Politische Ökonomie. III. Series: Berichte (Humboldt-Universität zu Berlin) , 84-11.
HD8460.5 .S694 1984

Soziallehre der Kirche und katholische Verbände / Anton Rauscher (Hrsg.). Köln : Bachem, 1980. 244 p. ; 19 cm. (Mönchengladbacher Gespräche . 2) Proceedings of a conference held May, 1980. Includes bibliographical references. PARTIAL CONTENTS. - Die Grundaussagen der katholischen Soziallehre zur Wirtschaftsordnung, allgemein verbindlich oder interessenbedingt? / Walter Kerber -- Programmatische Konkretisierung von Grundaussagen der katholischen Soziallehre zur Wirtschaftsordnung aus der Sicht der Katholischen Arbeitnehmerbewegung / Erwin Becker -- Programmatische Konkretisierung von Grundaussagen der katholischen Soziallehre zur Wirtschaftsordnung aus der Sicht des Bundes Katholischer Unternehmer / Cornelius Fetsch -- Verantwortung der Verbände für Werte und Verhaltensweisen in der Demokratie / Lothar Roos -- Gibt es einen unbegrenzten Pluralismus des politischen Handelns für den Katholiken und die katholischen Verbände? / Paul Hoffacker -- Die katholischen Jugendverbände und ihr Verhältnis zu den politischen Gruppierungen / Eberhard Schröder -- Was bedeutet das "Katholische" für Struktur und Engagement der katholischen Verbände? / Karl Forster -- Aus der Diskussion / Josef Oelinger. ISBN 3-7616-0568-4 (pbk.) : LC Card 81-122896 DDC 306/.6/0943 19
1. Church and social problems - Germany (West) - Catholic Church - Congresses. 2. Church and labor - Germany (West) - Congresses. 3. Sociology, Christian (Catholic) - Congresses. I. Rauscher, Anton. II. Series.
HN39.G3 S693 ***NYPL [JLC 86-231]***

Sozialökonomische Schriften zur ruralen Entwicklung .
(Bd. 57) Kirk, Michael, 1955- Ochsenanspannung in Westafrika . Göttingen , c1984. iv, 220 p. ; ISBN 3-88694-057-8 LC Card 86-202167 DDC 338.1/09688 19
HD2134 .K57 1984

Sozialpolitik in der Beschäftigungskrise / Richard Hauser ... [et al.] ; herausgegeben von Helmut Winterstein. Berlin : Duncker & Humblot, c1986. 2 v. : ill. ; 24 cm. (Schriften des Vereins für Socialpolitik, Gesellschaft für Wirtschafts- und Sozialwissenschaften . n.F., Bd. 152) Issued by the Sozialpolitischer Ausschuss of the Gesellschaft für Wirtschafts- und Sozialwissenschaften, Verein für Socialpolitik. Includes bibliographies. ISBN 3-428-05949-2 (Bd. I) : LC Card 87-119211 DDC 361.6/1 19
1. Unemployment - Effect of inflation on. 2. Social security. 3. Social policy - Economic aspects. I. Hauser, Richard, 1936-. II. Winterstein, Helmut. III. Gesellschaft für Wirtschafts- und Sozialwissenschaften, Verein für Socialpolitik. Ausschuss für Sozialpolitik. IV. Series.
HD5710 .S67 1986

Sozialpolitik und Recht .
(Bd. 6) Wirtschaftsentwicklung und soziale Sicherheit . Köln , 1983. viii, 146 p. : ISBN 3-452-19567-8 LC Card 84-106615
HG9399.G32 W57 1983

Sozialpolitische Schriften (Duncker & Humblot) .
(Heft 49) Dinkel, Reiner. Die Auswirkungen eines Geburten- und Bevölkerungsrückgangs auf Entwicklung und Ausgestaltung von gesetzlicher Alterssicherung und Familienlastenausgleich /. Berlin , c1984. 344 p. : ISBN 3-428-05546-2 LC Card 84-186733
HD7179 .D65 1984

(Heft 55) Krause, Detlef. Einkommensquellen und Lebenschancen . Berlin , c1986. 189 p. : ISBN 3-428-06114-4 LC Card 87-130932 DDC 339.2/2/0943 19
HC290.5.I5 K7 1986

Sozialreform und Rhetorik = The Rhetoric of welfare / August Bebel ... [et al.]. ; herausgegeben von Helmut Viebrock ; Kommentare von David Daiches ... [et al.]. Wiesbaden : F. Steiner, 1984. 174 p. ; 24 cm. (Studien zur Rhetorik des neunzehnten Jahrhunderts = Studies in rhetoric in the nineteenth century . Bd. 4) German or English. Includes bibliographical references. ISBN 3-515-02857-9
1. Public welfare - Addresses, essays, lectures. 2. Social policy - Addresses, essays, lectures. 3. Social problems - Addresses, essays, lectures. I. Bebel, August, 1840-1913. II. Viebrock, Helmut, 1912-. III. Daiches, David, 1912-. IV. Title: Rhetoric of welfare. V. Series: Studien zur Rhetorik des neunzehnten Jahrhunderts, Bd. 4.
NYPL [L-11 3778 Bd. 4]

Der Sozialreporter . Riesenfellner, Stefan. Wien , c1987. vi, 278 p. ; ISBN 3-900351-67-8 LC Card 87-137993 DDC 305.5/62/09436 19
HD8410 .R54 1987

"Sozialstaat" im Abbruch . Böpple, Arthur. Frankfurt/Main , c1986. 277 p. : ISBN 3-88367-062-6 LC Card 87-104497
HD7179 .B624 1986

Die Sozialversicherung zwischen Neuordnung und Restauration . Reidegeld, Eckart. Frankfurt am Main , c1982. 481 p. ; ISBN 3-88129-519-4 : LC Card 83-155896
HD7180.B4 R45 1982

Der Sozialvertrag für die Finanzierung kommunaler Einrichtungen und Gemeinschaftsaufgaben . Rickert, Heinrich. Stuttgart , c1982. 268 p. : ISBN 3-17-007760-0 : LC Card 83-152669
HJ9473 .R53 1982

Sozialverträglichkeit von Energieversorgungssystemen.
Zukünftige Energiepolitik . München , 1985. 189 p. : ISBN 3-89147-002-9 LC Card 87-104306
HD9698.G42 Z85 1985

Sozialwissenschaften .
(Heft 8) Rüden, Reinhold von. Soziale Sicherung in der Bundesrepublik Deutschland /. Paderborn , c1986. 157 p. : ISBN 3-506-23938-4 LC Card 87-127289 DDC 368.4/00943 19
HD7179 .R835 1986

Sozialwissenschaftliche Materialien .
(Bd. 13) Bauer, Fritz. Konsumenteninformation und ihre Nutzer /. Linz , 1986. ii, 113 p. : ISBN 3-85320-388-4 LC Card 87-134585 DDC 381/.3/09436 19
HC270.C6 B38 1986

(Bd. 3) Lins, Josef. Wohnungsmarkt und soziale Schicht . Linz , 1983. 89 p. : ISBN 3-85320-292-6 LC Card 84-214132 DDC 363.6/09436 19
HD7337.A3 L55 1983 ***NYPL [JLD 87-102]***

Sozialwissenschaftliche Projektgruppe München.
Weltz, Friedrich. Innovation im Büro . Frankfurt , New York , c1983. 343 p. ; ISBN 3-593-32724-4 LC Card 83-243001
HF5548.115 .W44 1983

Sozialwissenschaftliche Schriften (Duncker & Humblot) .
(Heft 13) Reheis, Fritz. Konkurrenz und Gleichgewicht als Fundamente von Gesellschaft . Berlin , c1986. xi, 401 p. : ISBN 3-428-06102-0 LC Card 87-131057 DDC 339.5 19
HB238 .R44 1986

Sozialwissenschaftliche Studien zu internationalen Problemen, 0584-603X .
(Heft 58) Peru, Kolonisation und Abhängigkeit . Saarbrücken , Fort Lauderdale , 1981. 192 p. : ISBN 3-88156-165-X : LC Card 82-104103
HD1905.O75 P47 1981

Sozialwissenschaftliche Studien zur Politik.
(Bd. 11) Die Wirtschaft der Vereinigten Staaten und der Bundesrepublik Deutschland . Bonn , c1977. 106 p. ; ISBN 3-87198-079-X LC Card 86-104673
HC106.7 .W57 1977

Sozialwissenschaftliches Forum (Cologne, Germany) .
(23) Boos, Margarete. Die Wissenschaftstheorie Carl Mengers . Wien , 1986. xiii, 252 p. ; ISBN 3-205-05044-4 LC Card 86-209140
HB101.M5 B6 1986

Die sozio-ökonomische Entwicklung der Elfenbeinküste seit der Unabhängigkeit . Jakobeit, Cord. Hamburg , 1984. viii, 132 p. : ISBN 3-923519-57-5 LC Card 84-222859
HC1025 .J35 1984

Sozio-politische Strategien multinationaler Unternehmungen . Achleitner, Paul M. Bern , c1985. ii, 334 p. : ISBN 3-258-03490-7 : LC Card 85-208760
HD62.4 .A24 1985

Die Soziogenese des Staates nach Elias und Schumpeter . Matzner, Egon, 1938- Berlin [1979] 30, [4] p. ; LC Card 85-135122
HJ105 .M37 1979

Soziologie der französischen Arbeiterbewegung /. Spurk, Jan. Berlin , c1986. 317 p. ; ISBN 3-88619-606-2 LC Card 87-235004 DDC 331.88/0944 19
HD6684 .S68 1986

Soziologie (Münster in Westfalen, Germany) .
(Bd. 7) Jacobs, Herbert. Zur Theorie und Praxis alternativer Ökonomie . Münster [1986] iii, 390 p. ; ISBN 3-88660-327-7 LC Card 87-133163 DDC 330 19
HB175 .J28 1986

SPACE IN ECONOMICS.
Energy and cities /. New Brunswick, U. S.A. , c1985. 173 p. : ISBN 0-87855-813-6 (pbk.) LC Card 84-24074 DDC 333.79/13/091732 19
HD108.2 .E525 1985 ***NYPL [JLE 86-4441]***

Greenhut, Melvin L. The economics of imperfect competition . Cambridge [Cambridgeshire] , New York , 1987. xix, 408 p. : ISBN 0-521-30552-7 LC Card 86-11707 DDC 338.6/048 19
HB238 .G74 1987 ***NYPL [JLE 87-1413]***

Ohta, H. (Hiroshi), 1940- Spatial price theory of imperfect competition /. College Station , c1988. p. cm. ISBN 0-89096-372-X : LC Card 87-22333 DDC 338.5/2 19
HB221 .O385 1988

Space-structure-economy . Karlsruhe [San Francisco, CA] c1986. vii, 311 p. : ISBN 3-88652-680-1 (pbk.) LC Card 87-129134 DDC 330.1 19
HB107.L66 S63 1986

SPACE IN ECONOMICS - ADDRESSES, ESSAYS, LECTURES.
Human behaviour in geographical space . Aldershot, Hants, England , Brookfield, Vt., U. S.A. , c1986. x, 328 p. : ISBN 0-566-00807-6 : LC Card 85-5528 DDC 338.9 19
HT391 .H785 1986 ***NYPL [JLD 86-1630]***

SPACE IN ECONOMICS - CONGRESSES.
L'Analisi degli insediamenti umani e produttivi /. Milano, Italy , c1984. 295 p. : LC Card 84-179265 DDC 330.945/0928 19
HC305 .A6618 1984 ***NYPL [JLD 86-3298]***

SPACE IN ECONOMICS - MATHEMATICAL MODELS.
Kuiper, J. H. Distribution of distances in pregeographical space /. Brookfield, Vt. , 1986. viii, 296 p. : ISBN 0-566-05214-8 : LC Card 86-7673 DDC 910 19
HT391.3 .K85 1986 ***NYPL [JSD 86-605]***

SPACE INDUSTRIALIZATION.
Logsdon, Tom, 1937- Striking it rich in space /. New York , 1988. p. cm. LC Card 87-22294 DDC 332.6/78/0919 19
HD9711.75.A2 L65 1988

SPACE INDUSTRIALIZATION - CONGRESSES.
L'Attività commerciale e industriale nello spazio . [Trieste] [1986] 192 p. : LC Card 86-215438
HD9711.75.A2 A77 1986

Gli Sviluppi delle attività commerciali nello spazio . [Trieste] [1985] 238 p. : LC Card 86-215421 DDC 338.0919 19
HD9711.75.A2 S95 1983

The space industry . Dubarle, Patrick. Paris, France [Washington, D.C.] c1985. 92 p. : ISBN 92-64-12772-0 : LC Card 86-210154 DDC 338.4/76291 19
HD9711.5.A2 D83 1985

SPACE-PERCEPTION.
McGee, Mark G. Human spatial abilities . New York , 1979. xiv, 144 p. : ISBN 0-03-052391-5 LC Card 79-16070 DDC 153.7/52
BF469 .M3 ***NYPL [JFE 84-185]***

Seth, Vijay K. Industrialisation in India . Delhi, India , 1987. xii, 242 p. : ISBN 81-900026-7-8 : LC Card 87-902803 DDC 338.0954 19
HC435.2 .S418 1987

Space-structure-economy : a tribute to August Lösch / Rolf H. Funck and Antoni Kuklinski (eds.). Karlsruhe : von Loeper : [San Francisco, CA : Kober Press, distributor], c1986. vii, 311 p. : ill. ; 25 cm. (Karlsruhe papers in economic policy research . vol. 3) Bibliography: p. 290-308. ISBN 3-88652-680-1 (pbk.) LC Card 87-129134 DDC 330.1 19
1. Lösch, August, 1906-1945. 2. Space in economics. 3. Geography, Economic. I. Lösch, August, 1906-1945. II. Funck, Rolf H. III. Kuklinski, Antoni. IV. Series.
HB107.L66 S63 1986

Spagnolo, Mario. Industria e movimento operaio a Vicenza : appunti di storia (1860-1980) / Mario Spagnolo.1a ed. Vicenza : Cooperativa libraria popolare, 1983. 107 p., [1] leaf of plate : facsim. ; 24 cm. Includes bibliographies. LC Card 85-175207
1. Trade-unions - Italy - Vicenza (Province) - History. 2. Labor disputes - Italy - Vicenza (Province) - History. 3. Labor and laboring classes - Italy - Vicenza (Province) - History. 4. Vicenza (Italy : Province) - Industries - History. I. Title.
HD6714.V53 S63 1983

Spahn, Heinz-Peter. Stagnation in der Geldwirtschaft : Dogmengeschichte, Theorie und Politik aus keynesianischer Sicht / Heinz-Peter Spahn. Frankfurt ; New York : Campus, c1986. 304 p. : ill. ; 21 cm. (Arbeitsberichte des Wissenschaftszentrums Berlin, Internationales Institut für Management und Verwaltung/Arbeitsmarktpolitik) A revision of the author's Habilitationsschrift--Freie Universität Berlin, 1986. Bibliography: p. 292-304. ISBN 3-593-33691-X LC Card 86-225253
1. Unemployment - Effect of inflation on. 2. Keynesian economics. 3. Monetary policy. I. Title. II. Series.
HD5710 .S68 1986

Spain and the telephone : a brief description of the prospects for industrial, commercial, and agricultural development in Spain with special reference to the program of the Compañía Telefónica Nacional de España. New York : International Telephone and Telegraph Corporation, 1925. 16 p., [1] folded leaf of plates : ill., map ; 23 cm. Cover title. LC Card 85-666351
1. Telephone - Spain. 2. Spain - Economic conditions. I. International Telephone and Telegraph Corporation. II. Compañía Telefónica Nacional de España.
HE9324 .S63x 1925

Spain. Biblioteca Nacional. Numeracion general de todas las personas de ambos sexos, edades y calidades q[ue] se hà hecho en esta ciudad de Lima, año de 1700 /. Lima , 1985. xv, 358 p. : LC Card 87-400680
HA1069.L7 N86 1985

SPAIN - CENSUS, 1982.
Censo agrario 1982 . Madrid , 1983. 104, 8 p. : ISBN 84-260-0803-8 LC Card 84-134551
HD2022 .C45 1983

SPAIN - COLONIES.
Bonetti, Mario. Staat und Gesellschaft im karibischen Raum im 16. Jahrhundert /. München , 1984. 668 p. : ISBN 3-7705-2162-5 LC Card 85-132458 DDC 330.9729/02 19
HC151 .B66 1984

SPAIN - COLONIES - AMERICA - COMMERCE - HISTORY.
El Comerç entre Catalunya i Amèrica (segles XVIII i XIX) /. Barcelona , 1986. 173 p. : ISBN 84-85905-24-5 LC Card 86-204187
HF3689.C3 C39 1986

Mercado, Thomas de, d. 1575. [Tratos y contratos de mercaderes. Selections.] La economia en la Andalucia del descubrimiento /. Sevilla [1985?] 276 p. ; ISBN 84-7587-047-3 LC Card 86-151225
HF1003 .M525 1985

SPAIN - COLONIES - AMERICA - ECONOMIC CONDITIONS.
Arcila Farías, Eduardo, 1913- Fundamentos económicos del Imperio Español en América /. Caracas , 1985. 133 p. : LC Card 85-242008
HC389 .A73 1985

Barrón Coral, Marcial. Perú . [Lima?] 1983 ([Lima] : General S.R.L.) 191 p. ; LC Card 84-253120
HC227 .B3365 1983

SPAIN - COLONIES - AMERICA - ECONOMIC POLICY.
Arcila Farías, Eduardo, 1913- Fundamentos económicos del Imperio Español en América /. Caracas , 1985. 133 p. : LC Card 85-242008
HC389 .A73 1985

Costa Rica colonial . [San José, Costa Rica , 1984] 83 p. ; LC Card 86-173945
HC389 .C67 1984

SPAIN - COLONIES - COMMERCE - HISTORY.
Castillero Calvo, Alfredo, 1937- La ruta transístmica y las comunicaciones marítimas hispanas, siglos XVI a XIX /. Panamá , 1984. 35 p. ; LC Card 84-219993
HE326 .C37 1984

SPAIN - COMMERCE.
Implicaciones para el sector comercio de la integración de España en el Mercado Común . [Madrid] [1979?] 106 p. ; LC Card 81-116650
HC241.25.S6 I48 1979

SPAIN - COMMERCE - CHINA.
La Economía china de la revolución a las cuatro modernizaciones /. Madrid [1986?] 181 p. : LC Card 86-229994
HC427.9 .E319 1986

SPAIN - COMMERCE - EUROPEAN ECONOMIC COMMUNITY COUNTRIES.
Alonso, José Antonio. La empresa exportadora española frente a Iberoamérica y la CEE /. Madrid , 1985. xiii, 263 p. ; ISBN 84-7232-380-3 LC Card 86-199177
HF3688.L3 A46 1985 ***NYPL [JLE 87-56]***

SPAIN - COMMERCE - FRANCE - HISTORY - CONGRESSES.
Les Communications dans la péninsule Ibérique au Moyen-Age . Paris , 1981. 208 p. : ISBN 2-222-02922-8 : LC Card 81-213698 DDC 380.5/0946 19
HE261.A5 C65 1981 ***NYPL [JLG 86-113]***

SPAIN - COMMERCE - HISTORY.
Gómez Mendoza, Antonio. Ferrocarril y mercado interior en España, 1874-1913 /. Madrid , 1984- v. : ISBN 84-500-9728-2 (v. 1) LC Card 85-215275 DDC 385/.24/0946 19
HE2469 .G66 1984 ***NYPL [JLL 86-176]***

SPAIN - COMMERCE - HISTORY - 18TH CENTURY.
Normante y Carcavilla, Lorenzo. Discurso sobre la utilidad de los conocimientos económico-políticos y la necesidad de su estudio metódico ; Proposiciones de economía civil y comercio ; Espíritu del señor Melón en su ensayo político sobre el comercio /. [Aragón] [1984?] 1 v. (various pagings) ; ISBN 84-505-0473-2 LC Card 87-104302
HC385 .N57 1984

SPAIN - COMMERCE - HISTORY - 20TH CENTURY.
SPAIN - COMMERCE - LATIN AMERICA.
Alonso, José Antonio. Efectos de la adhesión de España a la CEE sobre las exportaciones de Iberoamérica /. Madrid , 1983. 316 p. : ISBN 84-7232-299-8 LC Card 87-116624
HF3688.L3 A45 1983

Alonso, José Antonio. La empresa exportadora española frente a Iberoamérica y la CEE /. Madrid , 1985. xiii, 263 p. ; ISBN 84-7232-380-3 LC Card 86-199177
HF3688.L3 A46 1985 ***NYPL [JLE 87-56]***

SPAIN - COMMERCIAL POLICY - STUDY AND TEACHING - HISTORY - 18TH CENTURY.
Normante y Carcavilla, Lorenzo. Discurso sobre la utilidad de los conocimientos económico-políticos y la necesidad de su estudio metódico ; Proposiciones de economía civil y comercio ; Espíritu del señor Melón en su ensayo político sobre el comercio /. [Aragón] [1984?] 1 v. (various pagings) ; ISBN 84-505-0473-2 LC Card 87-104302
HC385 .N57 1984

SPAIN - ECONOMIC CONDITIONS.
Harrison, Joseph, 1944- The Spanish economy in the twentieth century /. London , c1985. 207 p. : ISBN 0-85664-721-7 : LC Card 86-674012
HC385 .H34x 1985b

Modernización económica de España, 1830-1930. English. The economic modernization of Spain, 1830-1930 /. New York , c1987. xv, 295 p. : ISBN 0-8147-7861-5 : LC Card 87-5535 DDC 330.946/07 19
HC385 .M62313 1987

Spain and the telephone . New York , 1925. 16 p., [1] folded leaf of plates : LC Card 85-666351
HE9324 .S63x 1925

SPAIN - ECONOMIC CONDITIONS - 19TH CENTURY.
La Modernización económica de España, 1830-1930 /. Madrid , c1985. 343 p. : ISBN 84-206-2431-4 LC Card 87-111312
HC385 .M623 1985

SPAIN - ECONOMIC CONDITIONS - 1918-1975.
La Modernización económica de España, 1830-1930 /. Madrid , c1985. 343 p. : ISBN 84-206-2431-4 LC Card 87-111312
HC385 .M623 1985

Nieto de Alba, Ubaldo, 1931- De la dictadura al socialismo democrático . Madrid , c1984. 269 p. ; ISBN 84-7209-177-5 LC Card 86-146735 DDC 338.946 19
HC385 .N49 1984 ***NYPL [JLD 86-2390]***

SPAIN - ECONOMIC CONDITIONS - 1975-
Gómez Fuentes, Angel, 1950- Así cambiará España . Esplugues de Llobregat, Barcelona , 1986. 333 p. ; ISBN 84-01-33317-2 LC Card 87-100798
HC241.25.S6 G65 1986

Nieto de Alba, Ubaldo, 1931- De la dictadura al socialismo democrático . Madrid , c1984. 269 p. ; ISBN 84-7209-177-5 LC Card 86-146735 DDC 338.946 19
HC385 .N49 1984 ***NYPL [JLD 86-2390]***

Nuevas tecnologías, economía y sociedad en España /. Madrid , c1986. 2 v. (xvi, 1056 p.) : ISBN 84-206-9495-9 (set) LC Card 86-205429
HC390.T4 N84 1986

París Eguilaz, Higinio. España en el socialismo actual /. Madrid [1984?] 234 p. ; ISBN 84-398-2401-7 LC Card 87-120643
HC385 .P313 1984

La Pobreza en España y sus causas /. Madrid , 1985. xx, 759 p. : ISBN 84-398-3252-4 : LC Card 86-230170
HC390.P6 P63 1985

La Reconversión industrial, la crisis y reforma agraria. [Madrid] [1984] 148 p. : ISBN

84-398-1197-7 LC Card 86-216324
HC385 .R375 1984

Sánchez, Victorio, 1936- España 1992 . Esplugues de Llobregat, Barcelona , 1984. 208 p. ; ISBN 84-01-33260-5 LC Card 86-205726
HC385 .S26 1984

SPAIN - ECONOMIC CONDITIONS - REGIONAL DISPARITIES.
La Modernización económica de España, 1830-1930 /. Madrid , c1985. 343 p. : ISBN 84-206-2431-4 LC Card 87-111312
HC385 .M623 1985

SPAIN - ECONOMIC POLICY.
Albentosa Puche, Luis. El sector exterior en España /. Madrid , c1984. 343 p. : ISBN 84-85719-40-9 LC Card 85-214668 DDC 336.3/4/0946 19
HG3883.S69 A45 1984 ***NYPL [JLC 86-251]***

Capdevila Batlles, José. Agricultura e industria española frente a la CEE . Barcelona [1985?] 252 p. : ISBN 84-7003-282-8 LC Card 86-171577
HC385 .C358 1985

Harrison, Joseph, 1944- The Spanish economy in the twentieth century /. London , c1985. 207 p. : ISBN 0-85664-721-7 : LC Card 86-674012
HC385 .H34x 1985b

Nieto de Alba, Ubaldo, 1931- De la dictadura al socialismo democrático . Madrid , c1984. 269 p. ; ISBN 84-7209-177-5 LC Card 86-146735 DDC 338.946 19
HC385 .N49 1984 ***NYPL [JLD 86-2390]***

París Eguilaz, Higinio. España en el socialismo actual /. Madrid [1984?] 234 p. ; ISBN 84-398-2401-7 LC Card 87-120643
HC385 .P313 1984

SPAIN - ECONOMIC POLICY - ECONOMETRIC MODELS.
Mauleón, Ignacio. Interest rates determinants and consequences for macroeconomic performance in Spain /. [Madrid] [1984?] 65 p. : ISBN 84-505-0648-7 (pbk.) LC Card 86-215058 DDC 332.8/2/0724 19
HG1623.S7 M38 1984

SPAIN - ECONOMIC POLICY - STUDY AND TEACHING - HISTORY - 18TH CENTURY.
Normante y Carcavilla, Lorenzo. Discurso sobre la utilidad de los conocimientos económico-políticos y la necesidad de su estudio metódico ; Proposiciones de economía civil y comercio ; Espíritu del señor Melón en su ensayo político sobre el comercio /. [Aragón] [1984?] 1 v. (various pagings) ; ISBN 84-505-0473-2 LC Card 87-104302
HC385 .N57 1984

SPAIN - EMIGRATION AND IMMIGRATION.
Emigración y retorno . [Madrid] , 1981. 325 p., [2] folded leaves of plates : ISBN 84-500-5097-9 LC Card 82-145134 DDC 325.46 19
JV8251 .E49 1981 ***NYPL [JLE 86-3179]***

SPAIN - FOREIGN ECONOMIC RELATIONS.
Punset, Eduard, 1936- La España impertinente /. Madrid , c1986. 188 p. ; ISBN 84-239-2420-3 LC Card 87-136770
HF1569 .P86 1986

SPAIN - FOREIGN ECONOMIC RELATIONS - PORTUGAL.
Dauderstädt, Michael. Las relaciones hispano-portuguesas y la integración europea /. Madrid [1987?] 36 p. ; ISBN 84-398-8593-8 LC Card 87-161277
HF1570.15.P8 D38 1987

Spain - Government. see **Spain - Politics and government.**

SPAIN - HISTORY.

SPAIN - HISTORY - 19TH CENTURY.
Modernización económica de España, 1830-1930. English. The economic modernization of Spain, 1830-1930 /. New York , c1987. xv, 295 p. : ISBN 0-8147-7861-5 : LC Card 87-5535 DDC 330.946/07 19
HC385 .M62313 1987

SPAIN - HISTORY - 20TH CENTURY.
Modernización económica de España, 1830-1930. English. The economic modernization of Spain, 1830-1930 /. New York , c1987. xv, 295 p. : ISBN 0-8147-7861-5 : LC Card 87-5535 DDC 330.946/07 19
HC385 .M62313 1987

SPAIN - HISTORY - 1939-1975.
Domínguez, Javier. Organizaciones obreras cristianas en la oposición al franquismo (1951-1975) . Bilbao [1985?] 479 p. ; ISBN 84-271-1431-1 LC Card 87-153234
HD6481.2.S7 D65 1985

Spain - Immigration. see **Spain - Emigration and immigration.**

SPAIN - INDUSTRIES.
Capdevila Batlles, José. Agricultura e industria española frente a la CEE . Barcelona [1985?] 252 p. : ISBN 84-7003-282-8 LC Card 86-171577
HC385 .C358 1985

El Ciclo industrial en España . Madrid [1984?] 436 p. : ISBN 84-7474-282-X LC Card 87-113099
HC385 .C49 1984

Maravall, Fernando. Economía y política industrial en España /. Madrid , 1987. 231 p. : ISBN 84-368-0340-X LC Card 87-121800
HC385 .M2574 1987

Nuevas tecnologías, economía y sociedad en España /. Madrid , c1986. 2 v. (xvi, 1056 p.) : ISBN 84-206-9495-9 (set) LC Card 86-205429
HC390.T4 N84 1986

SPAIN - INDUSTRIES - HISTORY - 20TH CENTURY.
Spain. Ministerio de Agricultura, Pesca y Alimentación. Secretaría General Técnica. La Agricultura y la pesca españolas en 1981. Madrid [1982?] 299 p. : ISBN 84-7479-164-2 : LC Card 83-125330 DDC 338.1/0946 19
HD2022 .A657 1982 ***NYPL [JLF 87-236]***

Spain. Ministerio de Industria y Energía. Secretaría General Técnica. El Ciclo industrial en España . Madrid [1984?] 436 p. : ISBN 84-7474-282-X LC Card 87-113099
HC385 .C49 1984

SPAIN - NOBILITY - STATISTICS - HISTORY - 18TH CENTURY.
Pérez de Guinea, María del Carmen. Estudio sobre la sociedad soriana en el siglo XVIII . [Spain] [1982?] 296 p. ; LC Card 85-136714
HA1559.S65 P47 1982

SPAIN - OCCUPATIONS.
Triadú, Joaquim, 1959- Les professions del futur /. Barcelona , 1986. 186 p. : ISBN 84-86421-20-9 LC Card 86-214981
HF5382.5.S7 T75 1986

SPAIN - OFFICIALS AND EMPLOYEES - SELECTION AND APPOINTMENT - CASE STUDIES.
Aoiz Iriarte, María Rosario. Técnicas psicosociales en la administración pública . Alcalá de Henares, Madrid, España [1984] 238 p. : ISBN 84-7351-179-4 LC Card 85-189583
HF5549.5.S38 A57 1984

SPAIN - POLITICS AND GOVERNMENT - 20TH CENTURY.
Harrison, Joseph, 1944- The Spanish economy in the twentieth century /. London , c1985. 207 p. : ISBN 0-85664-721-7 : LC Card 86-674012
HC385 .H34x 1985b

SPAIN - POLITICS AND GOVERNMENT - 1939-1975.
Punset, Eduard, 1936- La España impertinente /. Madrid , c1986. 188 p. ; ISBN 84-239-2420-3 LC Card 87-136770
HF1569 .P86 1986

SPAIN - POLITICS AND GOVERNMENT - 1975-
Punset, Eduard, 1936- La España impertinente /. Madrid , c1986. 188 p. ; ISBN 84-239-2420-3 LC Card 87-136770
HF1569 .P86 1986

SPAIN - SOCIAL CONDITIONS - 1975-
Nuevas tecnologías, economía y sociedad en España /. Madrid , c1986. 2 v. (xvi, 1056 p.) : ISBN 84-206-9495-9 (set) LC Card 86-205429
HC390.T4 N84 1986

La Pobreza en España y sus causas /. Madrid , 1985. xx, 759 p. : ISBN 84-398-3252-4 : LC Card 86-230170
HC390.P6 P63 1985

SPAIN - SOCIAL POLICY.
Nieto de Alba, Ubaldo, 1931- De la dictadura al socialismo democrático . Madrid , c1984. 269 p. ; ISBN 84-7209-177-5 LC Card 86-146735 DDC 338.946 19
HC385 .N49 1984 ***NYPL [JLD 86-2390]***

Spain. Tribunal de Cuentas. Memoria relativa a las cuentas generales del estado, 1935-1960 / Tribunal de Cuentas del Reino. Madrid : El Tribunal, 1964. 221 p. ; 30 cm. LC Card 85-104523
1. Finance, Public - Spain - History. 2. Debts, Public - Spain - History. 3. Finance, Public - Law and legislation - Spain. I. Title.
HJ1244 .S72 1964

Spälti, P. Die Rüstungsreferendumsinitiative--schlecht getarnter Anschlag auf unsere Landesverteidigung / P. Spälti. Zürich : Redressement National, 1987. 20 p. ; 22 cm. (Zeitfragen der schweizerischen Wirtschaft und Politik = Etudes d'économie et de politique suisses . Nr. 131) Cover title. LC Card 87-409331 DDC 330.9494 s 327.1/74/09494 19
1. Disarmament - Economic aspects - Switzerland. 2. Switzerland - Military policy - Economic aspects. I. Series: Zeitfragen der schweizerischen Wirtschaft und Politik , Nr. 131. II. Title.
HC395 .Z43 Nr. 131 HC400.D4

Spangenberg, Helga. Kremer, Manfred. Assimilation ausländischer Arbeitnehmer in der Bundesrepublik Deutschland . Königstein/Ts. , 1980. 203, 64 p. ; ISBN 3-7756-6934-5 LC Card 80-151671 DDC 303.4/8243 19
HD8458.A2 K73 1980 ***NYPL [JLD 86-2549]***

Spanish America. see **Latin America.**

The Spanish economy in the twentieth century /. Harrison, Joseph, 1944- London , c1985. 207 p. : ISBN 0-85664-721-7 : LC Card 86-674012
HC385 .H34x 1985b

Spanish economy in the 20th century. Harrison, Joseph, 1944- The Spanish economy in the twentieth century /. London , c1985. 207 p. : ISBN 0-85664-721-7 : LC Card 86-674012
HC385 .H34x 1985b

SPANISH LANGUAGE - DICTIONARIES - ENGLISH.
The American heritage Larousse Spanish dictionary . Boston , c1986. xxx, 532, xviii, 572 p. ; ISBN 0-395-32429-7 : LC Card 86-7202 DDC 463/.21 19
PC4640 .A54 1986
NYPL [*R-RGK 86-5942]

Glossary of the petroleum industry . Tulsa, Okla. , c1982. vi, 378 p. ; ISBN 0-87814-194-4 (pbk.) : LC Card 82-7622 DDC 665.5/03/61 19
TN865 .G63 1982 ***NYPL [JSD 86-496]***

Guiliani Cury, Hugo. Glosario de terminos de renegociación de deuda externa =. Santo Domingo, República Dominicana , 1985. 68 p. ; LC Card 86-184550
HJ8046 .G85 1985

Vox Modern Spanish and English dictionary . Lincolnwood, Ill. , c1986. xxxiv, 487, 45, 484 p. : ISBN 0-8442-7990-0 LC Card 86-61160
NYPL [*R-RGK 86-7059]

Vox new college Spanish and English dictionary . Lincolnwood, Ill., U. S.A. , c1984. xix, 1456, 60 p. : ISBN 0-8442-7998-6 (plain-edge ed.) : LC Card 84-61106 DDC 463/.21 19
PC4640 .V696 1984
NYPL [*R-RGK 85-1500]

SPANISH LANGUAGE - GLOSSARIES, VOCABULARIES, ETC.
Lozano Irueste, José María, 1920- Glosario de términos de economía y hacienda /. [Madrid] [1986] 56 p. ; ***NYPL [JLF 87-148]***

SPANISH SPEAKING PEOPLE (UNITED STATES) see **HISPANIC AMERICANS.**

SPANISH SURNAMED PEOPLE (UNITED STATES) see **HISPANIC AMERICANS.**

Sparks, Donald L. Namibia's future : the economy at independence / by Donald L. Sparks and Roger Murray. London, U.K. ; New York, N.Y., USA : Economist Intelligence Unit, c1985. 96 p., [4] p. of plates : ill., maps ; 30 cm. (Special report . no. 197) Includes bibliographical references. LC Card 87-132083 DDC 330.9688/03 19
1. Namibia - Economic conditions. 2. Namibia - Politics and government - 1946-. I. Murray, Roger. II. Series: EIU special report, no. 197. III. Title.
HC940 .S62 1985

Sparks, L. E. Investment analysis using your IBM PC and compatibles / Leslie E. Sparks. 1st ed. Blue Ridge Summit, PA : Tab Books, c1985. xi, 224 p. : ill. ; 25 cm. On t.p. the registered trademark symbol "TM" is superscript following "PC" in the title. Includes index. Bibliography: p. 219-220. ISBN 0-8306-0859-1 : LC Card 85-17322 DDC 332.6/028/55365 19
1. Investment analysis - Data processing. 2. IBM Personal Computer - Programming. I. Title.
HG4529 .S6 1985 ***NYPL [JLE 86-4621]***

Sparpolitik : ökonomische Zwänge und politische Spielräume / Heinrich Mäding, (Hrsg.) ; mit Beiträgen von Horst Eickmeyer ... [et al.]. Opladen : Westdeutscher Verlag, c1983. 152 p. ; 19 cm. Includes bibliographical references. CONTENTS. - Sparpolitik, theoretische Forderungen und politische Praxis / Heinrich Mäding -- Sparen durch Verwaltungsvereinfachung / Thomas Ellwein -- Wirtschaftsflaute--Politikflaute? / Horst Eickmeyer -- Sozialpolitik der mageren Jahre / Adrienne Windhoff-Héritier -- Das politische Dilemma der "Reaganomics" / Gerhard Lehmbruch -- Protektionismus oder neue Entwicklungspolitik / Hartmut Elsenhans. ISBN 3-531-11659-2 LC Card 84-109103
1. Supply-side economics. 2. Saving and investment. I. Mäding, Heinrich.
HB241 .S675 1983

SPARSELY SETTLED AREAS - SWEDEN.
Wolvén, Lars-Erik. Konsumenter, konsumentpolitik, rationalitet och välfärd . Umeå , 1981. 83 leaves ; LC Card 82-105540 DDC 658.8/342/09485 19
HC380.C63 W64 ***NYPL [JLM 74-106 no.61]***

Sparverhalten bei Unterbeschäftigung, stagnierendem oder sinkendem Realeinkommen /. Francke, Hans-Hermann. Stuttgart [1985] 142 p. : LC Card 86-153649
HC290.5.S3 F69 1985

Spasov, Vasil. Narŭchnik na profsŭiūzniīa aktivist . [[Sofia?] , 1985. 264 p. ; LC Card 85-216969
HC403.Z9 L366 1985

Späth, Lothar, 1937-
[Wende in die Zukunft. English]
Facing the future : Germany breaking new ground / Lothar Späth. Berlin ; New York : Springer-Verlag, c1986. xvi, 196 p. ; 24 cm. Translation of: Wende in die Zukunft. ISBN 0-387-17105-3 (U. S.) LC Card 86-25994 DDC 338.943 19
1. Germany, West - Economic conditions - 1974-. 2. Germany, West - Economic policy - 1974-. 3. Technological innovations - Economic aspects - Germany, West. 4. Europe - Economic conditions - 1945-. 5. Europe - Economic policy. 6. Technological innovations - Economic aspects - Europe. I. Title.
HC286.7 .S713 1986

SPATIAL ANALYSIS (STATISTICS)
Lierop, Wal F. J. van. Spatial interaction modelling and residential choice analysis /. Aldershot, Hants, England , Brookfield, Vt., USA , c1986. xii, 286 p. : ISBN 0-566-05036-6
NYPL [JLD 87-695]

Spatial demography. Population structures and models . London , Boston , 1986. xxii, 417 p. : ISBN 0-04-301200-0 (alk. paper) LC Card 85-30642 DDC 304.6 19
HB1951 .P67 1986 ***NYPL [JLE 86-4134]***

The Spatial impact of technological change / [edited by] John Brotchie, Peter Hall & Peter Newton. Totowa, NJ : Barnes & Noble, 1987. p. cm. Papers from an international workshop held in Melbourne in 1985 which was organized by the Working Commission 72 of the International Council for Building Research, Studies, and Documentation. Bibliography: p. ISBN 0-389-20753-5 LC Card 87-11460 DDC 338/.06 19
1. Technological innovations - Economic aspects - Congresses. 2. High technology industries - Location - Congresses. 3. Technology and state - Congresses. I. Brotchie, J. F. II. Hall, Peter Geoffrey. III. Newton, P. W. (Peter Wesley), 1948-. IV. International Council for Building Research, Studies and Documentation. Working Commission 72.
HC79.T4 S77 1987

Spatial interaction modelling and residential choice analysis /. Lierop, Wal F. J. van. Aldershot, Hants, England , Brookfield, Vt., USA , c1986. xii, 286 p. : ISBN 0-566-05036-6
NYPL [JLD 87-695]

Spatial price theory of imperfect competition /. Ohta, H. (Hiroshi), 1940- College Station , c1988. p. cm. ISBN 0-89096-372-X : LC Card 87-22333 DDC 338.5/2 19
HB221 .O385 1988

Spatial strategies in retailing /. Laulajainen, Risto. Dordrecht ; Boston : xiii, 253 p. : ISBN 90-277-2595-0 LC Card 87-20803 DDC 658.8/7 19
HF5429.275 .L38 1987

SPD wohin? : zur Analyse und Kritik des SPD-Grundsatzprogrammentwurfs / Beiträge von Eberhard Dähne ... [et al.]. Frankfurt/Main : Institut für Marxistische Studien und Forschungen (IMSF), c1987. 114 p. ; 24 cm. (Informationsbericht . Nr. 44) Includes bibliographical references. ISBN 3-88807-047-3 LC Card 87-401340 DDC 330 s 324.243/072 19
1. Sozialdemokratische ParteiDeutschlands - Platforms. I. Dähne, Eberhard. II. Series: Informationsbericht (Institut für Marxistische Studien und Forschungen (Frankfurt am Main, Germany)) , Nr. 44.
HB97.5 .I53 Nr. 44 JN3971.A98S571712

SPEAKING. see **DEBATES AND DEBATING.**

Spearhead (Eldoret, Kenya) .
(no. 84) Bread broken . Eldoret, Kenya [1984] vi, 56 p. : LC Card 85-980419 DDC 363.8/0967 19
HC800.Z9 F32 1984

SPECERIJEN-MALERIJ "DE KÖRVER" - HISTORY.
Bläsing, J. F. E. (Joachim F. E.), 1940- Op het spoor van de Körver . Leiden , 1986. xvi, 396 p. : ISBN 90-247-8065-9 : LC Card 86-214829
HD9052.N44 H453 1986

Specht, Günter. Industrielles Beschaffungsverhalten : unter besonderer Berücksichtigung der chemischen Industrie in der Bundesrepublik Deutschland und in der Volksrepublik Ungarn / Günter Specht. Frankfurt am Main ; New York : Lang, c1985. iii, 167 p. : ill. ; 21 cm. (Europäische Hochschulschriften. Reihe V, Volks- und Betriebswirtschaft, 0531-7339 . Bd. 672 = vol. 672 = vol. 672) Report on a joint program of the Technische Hochschule Darmstadt and the Veszprémi Vegyipari Egyetem. Bibliography: p. 134-135. ISBN 3-8204-8938-X LC Card 86-120719
1. Chemical industry - Germany (West). 2. Chemical industry - Hungary. I. Technische Hochschule Darmstadt. II. Veszprémi Vegyipari Egyetem. III. Series: Europäische Hochschulschriften. Reihe V, Volks- und Betriebswirtschaft , Bd. 672. IV. Title.
HD9654.5 .S64 1985

Special analysis and outlook for E.I. Du Pont De Nemours & Company (Inc.), Chemicals and Pigments Department. Boston, Mass. (7 Liberty Sq., Boston 02109) : Wainwright Forecasting Group, [1986] 17, [6] p. : ill. ; 28 cm. (The Business forecaster) Cover title. "Based on market prices as of April 30, 1986." Includes bibliographical references. LC Card 86-205857 DDC 338.4/766/00973 19
1. Paint industry and trade - United States - Forecasting. 2. Paper industry - United States - Forecasting. 3. Clothing trade - United States - Forecasting. 4. United States - Economic conditions - 1981- - Forecasting. 5. Economic forecasting - United States. I. E.I. du Pont de Nemours & Company. Chemicals and Pigments Dept. II. Wainwright Forecasting Group. III. Series.
HD9660.P253 U672 1986

Special analysis D. Supplement to special analysis D . Washington, D.C. , 1985. 1 v. (various pagings) ; ***NYPL [JLF 86-603]***

Special collection from the Journal of commercial bank lending. Small business financing . Philadelphia, Pa. , c1987. 118 p. ; ISBN 0-936742-40-2 (pbk.) : LC Card 87-5534 DDC 332.1/753/0685 19
HG3754.5.U6 S6 1987

Special Commission on a Public Agenda for Kansas. Kansas policy choices . Lawrence, Kan. , c1986. x, 210 p. : ISBN 0-7006-0302-6 (pbk.) LC Card 86-204211 DDC 338.9781 19
HC107.K2 K387 1986

Special delivery /. Brandt, Betty. Minneapolis, Minn. , c1988. 40 p. : ISBN 0-87614-312-5 (lib. bdg.) LC Card 87-15647 DDC 383/.4973 19
HE6371 .B77 1988

SPECIAL DISTRICTS - CONNECTICUT.
Tax districts. [Hartford, Conn.] [1985] 53 p. ; LC Card 86-620827 DDC 352.1/3/09746 19
HJ9210 .T39 1985

SPECIAL DISTRICTS - UNITED STATES - CORRUPT PRACTICES.
Henriques, Diana B. The machinery of greed . Lexington, Mass. , c1986. x, 161 p. ; ISBN 0-669-09809-4 (alk. paper) LC Card 85-23841 DDC 364.1/68 19
HD3885 .H45 1986 ***NYPL [JLE 86-2739]***

SPECIAL DRAWING RIGHTS.
Heinonen, Kerstin. Systemet med särskilda dragningsrätter . Helsingfors , 1985. 65 p. ; ISBN 951-686-112-1 LC Card 86-175395
HG3898 .H45 1985

The Role of the SDR in the international monetary system . Washington, D.C. , 1987. vii, 62 p. : ISBN 0-939934-81-7 (pbk.) : LC Card 87-4184 DDC 332.4/5 19
HG3898 .R65 1987

Special needs housing demonstration program report. New York (State). Division of Housing and Community Renewal. New York, N.Y. (2 World Trade Center, New York 10047) [1984] 1 v. (various foliations) : LC Card 86-622827 DDC 363.5/8 19
HD7288.85.U62 N754 1984

Special publication (International Centre for Diarrhoeal Disease Research, Bangladesh) .
(no. 24) D'Souza, S. M. (Stanislaus Michael) Mortality case study, Matlab, Bangladesh /. Dhaka, Bangladesh , 1985. 80 p. : LC Card 86-902788 DDC 304.6/4/0954923 19
HB1470.6.M37 D76 1985

Special publication (United States. Bureau of Mines)
Maas, Kenneth M. Availability of land for mineral exploration and development in northern Alaska, 1986 /. [Washington, D.C.] [1987] iv, 34 p. : LC Card 86-607920 DDC 333.73 19
HD243.A3 M32 1987

McColly, Robert A. Availability of federally owned minerals for exploration and development in western states . [Avondale, Md.] , Washington, DC [1987] iv, 27 p. : LC Card 87-600086 DDC 333.8/5/09791 19
HD243.A7 M36 1987

Special publication (University of Texas at Austin. Institute of Latin American Studies)
Pérez-López, Jorge F. Measuring Cuban economic performance /. Austin , 1987. xii, 202 p. : ISBN 0-292-75092-7 LC Card 86-24907 DDC 339.37291 19
HC152.5 .P47 1987

Special report (Economist Intelligence Unit (Great Britain)) .
(no. 174) Jones, Stephen F. North/south countertrade . London , c1984. 97 p. : LC Card 85-239985 DDC 382/.091722/01724 19
HF1414.3 .J65 1984

(no. 182) Hanlon, Joseph. SADCC . London, U.K. , c1984. 110 p. : LC Card 86-148391 DDC 332.6/732268 19
HC900 .H35 1984

Special report (National Research Council (U. S.). Transportation Research Board) .
(213) Research for public transit . Washington, D.C. , 1987. vi, 146 p. : ISBN 0-309-04461-8 (pbk.) LC Card 87-22878 DDC 388.4/0973 19
HE4451 .R47 1987

Special report of the Public Accounts Committee for the 1980 session . Mauritius. Legislative Assembly. Public Accounts Committee. Port Louis, Mauritius , 1981. 13 p. ; LC Card 82-980151 DDC 333.1/6/09697 19
HD1030.3.Z63 M38 1981

Special report on applying United States food surpluses to the problems of hunger / Select Committee on Hunger, U. S. House of Representatives. Washington : U. S. G.P.O., 1984. ii, iv, 54 p. ; 24 cm. At head of title: 99th Congress, 1st session. Committee print. Distributed to some depository libraries in microfiche. Bibliography: p. 54. Item 1009-B-11, 1009-C-11 (microfiche) LC Card 87-601529 DDC 363.8/83 19
1. Food supply. 2. Surplus agricultural commodities, American. 3. Food relief, American. 4. Food relief - United States. I. United States. Congress. House. Select

Committee on Hunger.
HD9000.5 .S666 1984

A special report to the Legislature on the 55 MPH national maximum speed limit. California. Dept. of the California Highway Patrol. [Sacramento] [1986] vi, 95, [171] p. : LC Card 86-622347 DDC 388.3/144/09794 19
HE5620.S6 C25 1986

Special reports (Institute for International Economics (U. S.)) .
(4) Global economic imbalances /. Washington, DC , 1985. x, 116 p. ; ISBN 0-88132-038-2 (pbk.) LC Card 85-8279 DDC 330.9/048 19
HD73 .G56 1985 NYPL [JLE 87-1314]

Special research report (Ontario Economic Council)
Wonnacott, Ronald J. Canada/United States free trade . Toronto, Ont. , c1985. 30 p. ; ISBN 0-7729-0036-1 (pbk.) LC Card 86-673986
HF1480.5.U57 W66x 1985

Special series (Israel. Lishkah ha-merkazit li-ṣtatisṭikah .
(no. 785) Aspler, I. Seḳer melai ha-hon ha-ḳavu'a be-ta'aśiyah, 1.1.1982 /. Yerushalayim , 1986. 80, xvii p. ; LC Card 87-128243
HA1931 .A354 no. 785 HC415.25.Z9C3

Special study (South African Institute of International Affairs)
Jenkins, Carolyn M. (Carolyn Marion) The economic implications of disinvestment for South Africa /. [Braamfontain?] , 1986. v, 100 p. ; ISBN 0-908371-51-9 (pbk.) : LC Card 87-164832 DDC 332.6/73/0968 19
HG5851.A3 J46 1986

Special study (United States. Congressional Budget Office)
Dayton, Mark R. Economic viability of Conrail. Washington, D.C. [1986] xvii, 85 p. : LC Card 86-602852 DDC 385/.1 19
HE2791.C8994 D39 1986

How federal policies affect the steel industry. Washington, D.C. [1987] xii, 66 p. : LC Card 87-601115 DDC 338.4/7669142/0973 19
HD9516 .H65 1987

The Special surgery equipment and supplies market in the U. S. New York, N.Y. : Frost & Sullivan, c1983. xxiii, 332 p. : ill. ; 29 cm. Title on spine: Special surgery instrumentation in the U. S. "June 1983." "#A1131." Bibliography: p. 321-327. LC Card 87-142345 DDC 381/.45681761 19
1. Surgical instruments and apparatus industry - United States. 2. Market surveys - United States. I. Frost & Sullivan. II. Title: Special surgery instrumentation in the U. S.
HD9995.S93 U56 1983

Special surgery instrumentation in the U. S. The Special surgery equipment and supplies market in the U. S. New York, N.Y. , c1983. xxiii, 332 p. : LC Card 87-142345 DDC 381/.45681761 19
HD9995.S93 U56 1983

Specialists in Business Information, inc. The SBI report on the market and economics of the electromedical equipment industry. Wantagh, N.Y. , c1982. iv, 157 leaves ; LC Card 87-402136 DDC 380.1/45681761 19
HD9995.E43 U58 1982

Specialty Conference on Engineering and Construction Projects (1982 : New Orleans, La.) Proceedings of the Specialty Conference on Engineering and Construction Projects : the emerging management roles : March 17-19, 1982, New Orleans, Louisiana / sponsored by the Construction Division of the American Society of Civil Engineers ; Dale R. Kern, editor. New York, N.Y. : The Society, c1982. vi, 329 p. : ill. ; 22 cm. Includes bibliographical references and indexes. ISBN 0-87262-299-1 (pbk.) LC Card 82-70492 DDC 658.5 19
1. Engineering - Management - Congresses. 2. Construction industry - Management - Congresses. I. Kern, Dale R. II. American Society of Civil Engineers. Construction Division. III. Title.
TA190 .S67 1982 NYPL [JLD 86-1905]

Specialty modeling /. Hartman, Tori. New York , c1988. x, 128 p. ; ISBN 0-525-48356-X LC Card 87-22470 DDC 659.1/52 19
HD6073.M772 U55 1988

SPECIALTY STORES.
Medla, Karsten, 1954- Shop-in-the-shop . München , c1987. xxxi, 207, 6 p. ; ISBN 3-88259-428-4 LC Card 87-141864 DDC 658.8/7 19
HF5429 .M36 1987

SPECIALTY STORES - ITALY - FLORENCE - PICTORIAL WORKS.
Le Botteghe di Firenze. Firenze , c1985. 111 p. : ISBN 88-7292-062-0 LC Card 86-183352
HF5429.6.I8 B67 1985

SPECIE. see **GOLD; MONEY; SILVER.**

SPECIE PAYMENTS. see **CURRENCY QUESTION - UNITED STATES.**

Spectacular teamwork . Blake, Robert Rogers, 1918- New York , c1987. viii, 219 p. : ISBN 0-471-85311-9 LC Card 86-28123 DDC 658.4/036 19
HD66 .B54 1987

Speculating in futures. [Chicago] : Chicago Board of Trade, c1986. v, 65 p. : ill. ; 22 cm. Bibliography: p. 64. LC Card 87-100478 DDC 332.64/4 19
1. Commodity exchanges. 2. Commodity exchanges - United States. I. Catania, Patrick J. II. Keefer, Nancy. III. Chicago. Board of Trade.
HG6046 .S63 1986

SPECULATION - CONGRESSES.
Contractual arrangements for intertemporal trade /. Minneapolis, MN , c1987. p. cm. ISBN 0-8166-1533-0 : LC Card 86-24888 DDC 332.64/4/0724 19
HB801 .C629 1987

SPECULATION - FRANCE.
Freymond, Joël. Guide du spéculateur . Paris , c1986. 175 p. : ISBN 2-226-02463-8 : LC Card 87-166254
HG6041 .F82 1986

SPECULATION - HANDBOOKS, MANUALS, ETC.
Band, Richard E. Contrary investing . New York , c1985. viii, 197 p. : ISBN 0-07-003604-7 : LC Card 85-99 DDC 332.6/78 19
HG4527 .B233 1985 NYPL [JLE 86-1234]

SPECULATION - MATHEMATICAL MODELS.
Ghosh, S. Stabilizing speculative commodity markets /. Oxford [Oxfordshire] , New York , 1987. xiii, 437 p. : ISBN 0-19-828472-1 : LC Card 86-32654 DDC 332.64/4 19
HG6046 .G485 1987

Müller, Sigrid, 1953- Arbitrage pricing of contingent claims /. Berlin , New York , 1985. viii, 151 p. ; ISBN 0-387-15973-8 (U. S.) LC Card 85-22170 DDC 332.6/0724 19
HG4515.2 .M85 1985
NYPL [JLM 72-289 no.254]

Spedale, Domenico L. L'affidamento bancario : tecniche e principe di valutazione / Domenico L. Spedale.2a ed. Milano : F. Angeli, 1985. 204 p. : ill. ; 22 cm. (Collana L'Azienda moderna. 197) Bibliography: p. [203]-204.
1. Bank examination - Italy. 2. Banks and banking - Italy - Accounting. 3. Banking law - Italy. I. Title.
NYPL [JLD 86-3241]

Spede, Edward C. Ferguson, Jerry T., 1938- Managing real estate taxes /. Westport, Conn. , 1986. x, 185 p. ; ISBN 0-89930-106-1 (lib. bdg. : alk. paper) LC Card 85-6360 DDC 343.7305/46 347.303546 19
HJ4181 .F47 1986 NYPL [JLE 86-2439]

Spedycja lądowa /. Marciniak-Neider, Danuta. Gdańsk , 1979- v. <1 > ; LC Card 81-181249
HF5780.P7 M37 1979

SPEECH PROCESSING SYSTEMS.
Krute, Stan. Commodore 64/128 graphics and sound programming /. Blue Ridge Summit, PA , 1986. xv, 253 p. : ISBN 0-8306-0440-5 : LC Card 85-14694 DDC 006.6/765 19
T385 .K77 1986 NYPL [JSE 87-266]

SPEECH PROCESSING SYSTEMS - CONGRESSES.
Pervichnoe opisanie signalov rechi . Vil'nius , 1980. 67 p. : LC Card 82-107723
HD38 .S715 vyp. 42 TK7882.S65

SPEECH PROCESSING SYSTEMS INDUSTRY.
Voice compression technology . Stamford, Conn., U. S.A. , c1985. xii, 146 leaves ; ISBN 0-89336-430-4 (soft) LC Card 87-165256 DDC 380.1/45621389 19
HD9696.T442 V65 1985

SPEECH PROCESSING SYSTEMS INDUSTRY - UNITED STATES.
Talkwriters, voice mail & speech processing in office automation. Norwalk, Conn., U. S.A. (6 Prowitt St., Norwalk 06855) , c1986. iv, 145 leaves : LC Card 86-224988 DDC 381/.45621389 19
HD9696.S643 U667 1986

The speeches and writings of Mother Jones /. Jones, Mother, 1843?-1930. [Selections. 1988.] Pittsburgh, Pa. , 1988. p. cm. ISBN 0-8229-3575-9 LC Card 87-25192 DDC 331.88/0973 19
HD8072 .J7832 1988

SPEED LIMITS - CALIFORNIA.
California. Dept. of the California Highway Patrol. A special report to the Legislature on the 55 MPH national maximum speed limit. [Sacramento] [1986] vi, 95, [171] p. : LC Card 86-622347 DDC 388.3/144/09794 19
HE5620.S6 C25 1986

SPEED LIMITS - FLORIDA.
Speed zoning for highways, roads & streets in Florida . Tallahassee, Fla. [1985] i, 43, [1] p. : LC Card 86-621262 DDC 388.3/144/09759 19
HE5620.S6 S65 1985

SPEED LIMITS - UNITED STATES.
California. Dept. of the California Highway Patrol. A special report to the Legislature on the 55 MPH national maximum speed limit. [Sacramento] [1986] vi, 95, [171] p. : LC Card 86-622347 DDC 388.3/144/09794 19
HE5620.S6 C25 1986

SPEED LIMITS - VIRGINIA.
Sharkey, Stephen M. Evaluation of the 1984 selective speed enforcement projects in Virginia /. Charlottesville, Va. [1987] xii, 117, [34] p. : LC Card 87-621546 DDC 388.3/144/09755 19
HE5620.S6 S532 1987

SPEED READING. see **RAPID READING.**

Speed zoning for highways, roads & streets in Florida : for compliance with Florida Statutes, Chapter 316. Tallahassee, Fla. : Florida Dept. of Transportation, Bureau of Traffic Engineering, [1985] i, 43, [1] p. : ill. ; 29 cm. Cover title. "April 1985." Bibliography: p. [44] LC Card 86-621262 DDC 388.3/144/09759 19
1. Speed limits - Florida. I. Florida. Bureau of Traffic Engineering.
HE5620.S6 S65 1985

Speier, Hans. German white-collar workers and the rise of Hitler / Hans Speier. New Haven : Yale University Press, 1986. xv, 208 p. ; 24 cm. Translation of: Die Angestellten vor dem Nationalsozialismus. Includes index. Bibliography: p. 191-203. ISBN 0-300-03701-5 LC Card 86-9120 DDC 331.7/92/0943 19
1. White collar workers - Germany - History. 2. Clerks - Germany - History. 3. Social classes - Germany - History. 4. White collar workers - Germany - Political activity - History. I. Title.
HD8039.M4 G3639413 1986
NYPL [JLE 87-909]

Speiser, Harald. Das österreichische Foreign Debt Management, 1956-1983 : Daten, Analyse, Ausblick / Harald Speiser. Regensburg : Transfer, c1985. 120 p. : ill. ; 24 cm. (Schriftenreihe des Instituts für Wirtschaftswissenschaften an der Rechtswissenschaftlichen Fakultät der Universität Salzburg . Bd. 1) Bibliography: p. 98. ISBN 3-924956-06-5 LC Card 86-222064
1. Debts, External - Austria. 2. Capital market - Austria. I. Title. II. Series.
HJ8636 .S66 1985

Spekner, Ágnes. Szénay, Lászlóné. A közgazdasági szabályozás és az élelmiszeripari szakágazatok gazdasági eredményeinek összefüggései és problémái az 1977-82 közötti években /. Budapest , 1984. 161 p. ; ISBN 963-491-196-X LC Card 86-199432
HD9015.H82 S935 1984

Spelet om resurserna i den svenska blandekonomin /. Höglund, Bengt. Lund , c1984. 227 p. : ISBN 91-7504-041-7 : LC Card 84-200450
HC373.5 .H64 1984

Spēliōtakēs, K. K. Archeion Michaēl Iatrou, 1802-1893 / K.K. Spēliōtakēs. Archeio Dēmētriou Kallergē, 1824-1867 / Giōrgos Smpilirēs. Athēna : Kentron Neoellēnikōn Ereunōn Ethnikou Hidrymatos Ereunōn, 1983. 189 p., [4] folded leaves of plates : ill. ; 24 cm. (Tetradia ergasias . 6) Includes bibliographical references and indexes. LC Card 85-134031
1. Spēliōtakēs, K. K. - Archives. 2. Kallergēs, Dēmētrios, 1803?-1867 - Archives. 3. Athens. Mouseion Benakē. 4. Merchants - Greece - Biography. 5. Generals - Greece - Biography. 6. Greece - History - 19th century - Sources. I. Iatros, Michaēl, 1779-1868. II. Kallergēs, Dēmetrios, 1803?-1867. III. Smpilirēs, Giōrgos. Archeio Dēmētriou Kallergē, 1824-1867. 1983. IV. Title. V. Series.
HF3750.5.S64 A3 1983 ***NYPL [JFE 86-4131]***

SPĒLIŌTAKĒS, K. K. - ARCHIVES.
Spēliōtakēs, K. K. Archeion Michaēl Iatrou, 1802-1893 /. Athēna , 1983. 189 p., [4] folded leaves of plates : LC Card 85-134031
HF3750.5.S64 A3 1983 ***NYPL [JFE 86-4131]***

Spellman, Christina. Rochell, Carlton C. Dreams betrayed . Lexington, Mass. , c1987. 138 p. ; ISBN 0-669-11105-8 (alk. paper) LC Card 85-45019 DDC 331.25 19
HD6331.2.U5 R63 1987

Spence, J. Wayne. Microcomputers in business : WordStar, dBase II and III, and Lotus 1-2-3 / J. Wayne Spence, John C. Windsor.1st ed. St. Louis : Times Mirror/Mosby College Pub., 1987. vii, 224 p. : ill. (some col.) ; 24 cm. (The Times Mirror/Mosby data processing and information systems series) Spine title: Using microcomputers in business. Includes index. ISBN 0-8016-5030-5 (pbk.) LC Card 86-30013 DDC 650/.028/5536 19
1. Business - Data processing. 2. Business - Computer programs. 3. Microcomputers. I. Windsor, John C. (John Clayton), 1946-. II. Title. III. Title: Using microcomputers in business. IV. Series.
HF5548.2 .S728 1987

Spencer, Edson W. Honeywell after 100 years / Edson W. Spencer. New York : Newcomen Society of the United States, 1985, c1986. 24 p. : ill. ; 23 cm. (Newcomen publication. no. 1258) Address delivered at a meeting of the Newcomen Society, Oct. 8, 1985, in New York City. LC Card 85-63243 DDC 338.7/62/000973 19
1. Honeywell, inc. - History. I. Title.
HD9729.H66 S66 1986

Spencer, Roger W. Lives of the laureates . Cambridge, Mass. , c1986. xii, 135 p. : ISBN 0-262-02255-9 LC Card 86-2919 DDC 330/.092/2 B 19
HB76 .L58 1986 ***NYPL [JFD 86-9827]***

Spending and deficits /. Miller, James C., III. Washington, D.C. , c1987. 18 p. ; ISBN 0-8447-1382-1 (pbk.) LC Card 87-134671 DDC 339.5/23/0973 19
HJ2052 .M54 1987

SPENDINGS TAX - CANADA.
Davies, James B., 1951- Reforming capital income taxation in Canada . [Ottawa] , c1987. ix, 153 p. : ISBN 0-660-12454-8 (pbk.) : LC Card 87-168079 DDC 336.24/24/0971 19
HJ4133.C2 .D38 1987

SPENDINGS TAX - INDIA.
Chopra, O. P. (Om Prakash), 1941- Tax ethics, unaccounted income . New Delhi , 1985, c1984. vi, 119 p. ; LC Card 85-900955 DDC 336.2/06 19
HJ2348.5 .C46 1985 ***NYPL [JLE 87-1297]***

SPENDINGS TAX - UNITED STATES.
The Consumption tax . Cambridge, Mass. , c1987. xviii, 382 p. : ISBN 0-88730-159-2 LC Card 87-17838 DDC 336.2/71/0973 19
HJ5715.U6 C658 1987

Spengler, Hartmut. Die Sozialistische Gemeinschaft . Berlin , 1985. 238 p. ; LC Card 86-120025 DDC 337.1/1717 19
HC243.5 .S685 1985

Sperber, Dan. Relevance : communication and cognition / Dan Sperber and Deirdre Wilson. Oxford [Oxfordshire] : Basil Blackwell, 1986. viii, 279 p. : ill. ; 23 cm. Includes index. Bibliography: p. [266]-274. ISBN 0-631-13756-4
1. Interpersonal communication. 2. Relevance. 3. Cognition. I. Wilson, Deirdre. II. Title.
NYPL [JFE 86-1728]

Sperline, Richard D., 1947- Brown, Constance C., 1952- Preparing documents with UNIX /. Englewood Cliffs, N.J. , c1986. xv, 206 p. : ISBN 0-13-699976-X LC Card 85-17016 DDC 652/.5 19
Z52.5.U54 B76 1986 ***NYPL [JSE 86-1215]***

Spet͡sializat͡sii͡a zagotovitel'nogo proizvodstva /. Kryzhanovskiĭ, B. N. (Boris Nikolaevich) Kiev , 1985. 125, [3] p. ; LC Card 87-112143
HD9703.S653 U474 1985

Speyerer Forschungsberichte .
(25) Protz, Michael. Administrative Zusammenarbeit in der Entwicklungspolitik . Speyer , 1982. ix, 382, 2 p. ; LC Card 86-218043
HC60 .P77 1982

Speyerer Forschungsberichte, 0179-2326 .
(54) Scholz, Bernhard, 1948- Bodenschutz zwischen Datenschwemme und Informationsdefizit . Speyer [1986] iii leaves, 385, 4 p. : LC Card 87-126271 DDC 333.73/13/094343 19
HD659.R54 S36 1986

Spezial-Katalog der Sondermarken zu den Jubiläen des Weltpostvereins. Sieger (Firm) Weltpostverein (UPU) . Lorch/Württemberg , c1982. 408 p. : LC Card 83-224689
HE6271 .S55 1982

Spezialisierung des Verkehrsangebotes und Strukturwandel in der verladenden Wirtschaft .
Offergeld, Johannes. Göttingen , 1984. 185 p. : ISBN 3-525-85690-3 (Deut. Bibl.) LC Card 84-197725
HE131 .M8 Heft 102 HE249

Spezialuntersuchung ... im Rahmen der HWWA-Strukturberichterstattung 1987 .
(1) Neue Industriepolitik oder Stärkung der Marktkräfte? . Hamburg , 1986. xiii, 221 p. ; ISBN 3-87895-315-1 LC Card 87-408234 DDC 338.9 19
HD3616.G4 N48 1986

SPICE TRADE - NETHERLANDS - HISTORY.
Bläsing, J. F. E. (Joachim F. E.), 1940- Op het spoor van de Körver . Leiden , 1986. xvi, 396 p. : ISBN 90-247-8065-9 : LC Card 86-214829
HD9052.N44 H453 1986

SPICE TRADE - TANZANIA - ZANZIBAR - HISTORY.
Sheriff, Abdul. Slaves, spices, & ivory in Zanzibar . London , Athens , 1987. xx, 297 p. : ISBN 0-8214-0871-2 (U. S.) LC Card 87-12339 DDC 382/.096781 19
HF3897 .S54 1987

Spicer, Jerry. The EAP solution . Center City, MN , 1987. 219 p. : ISBN 0-89486-405-X (pbk.) LC Card 86-82533 DDC 658.3/82 19
HF5549.5.E42 E367 1987

Spicer, Joanna. Briggs, Asa, 1921- The franchise affair . London , 1986. 226 p. ; ISBN 0-7126-1201-7 : LC Card 86-190561 DDC 384.55/453/0941 19
HE8700.9.G7 B72 1986

Spich, Robert S. Mason, R. Hal (Robert Hal), 1929- Management . Homewood, Ill. , 1987. xii, 235 p. : ISBN 0-256-05631-5 (pbk.) LC Card 86-82592 DDC 658/.049 19
HD62.4 .M373 1987

Spie, Ulrich. Der Personalmanager im Vorstand : das Berufsbild des Arbeitsdirektors im Spannungsfeld von Recht und Praxis / von Ulrich Spie. Stuttgart : Schäffer, 1985. ix, 354 p. : ill. ; 25 cm. (Schriftenreihe Der Betrieb) Bibliography: p. 317-354. ISBN 3-8202-0313-3 LC Card 86-131051
1. Personnel directors - Germany, West. 2. Personnel management - Germany, West. 3. Industrial management - Employee participation - Law and legislation - Germany (West). 4. Industrial relations - Germany, West. I. Arbeitsdirektors im Spannungsfeld von Recht und Praxis. II. Title.
HF5549.2.G3 S67 1985

Die Spielregeln für Kapitalanlagen in Mexiko . Gies, Christoph. Frankfurt , c1986. ix, 314 p. : ISBN 3-88323-603-9 LC Card 86-231145
HG5162 .G48 1986

Spies-Hankammer, Elisabeth. Lübecker Weinhandel . Lübeck , 1985. 260 p. : ISBN 3-924214-27-1 LC Card 86-145675
HD9383.8.L82 L82 1985

Spies, P. H. Perspectives on the future of Natal/KwaZulu / P.H. Spies. Pietermaritzburg : Natal Town and Regional Planning Commission, 1986. 149 p. : ill. ; 30 cm. (Natal town and regional planning report . v. 69) Bibliography: p. 146-149. ISBN 0-909232-59-8 (pbk.) : LC Card 87-166530 DDC 361.2/5/09684 s 361.6/1/09684 19
1. Political planning - South Africa - Natal. 2. Regional planning - South Africa - Natal. 3. Natal (South Africa) - Economic policy. 4. Political planning - South Africa - Kwazulu. 5. Regional planning - South Africa - Kwazulu. 6. Kwazulu (South Africa) - Economic policy. I. Series. II. Series: Natal town and regional planning reports , v. 69. III. Title.
HC517.N3 A44 vol. 69 JQ2224

Spiker, Barry K. Daniels, Tom D. Perspectives on organizational communication /. Dubuque, Iowa , c1987. xiv, 288 p. : ISBN 0-697-00444-9 LC Card 86-72711 DDC 658.4/5 19
HD30.3 .D33 1987

Spilbergs, A. Modelirovanie razvitii͡a mezhotraslevyh kompleksov Latviĭskoĭ SSR . Riga , 1985. 106 p. : LC Card 86-177817
HD9015.S653 L376 1985

Spilker, Ernst Moritz. Der Wirtschaftsraum zwischen den Wirtschaftsräumen : eine Studie über ausgewählte Kreise der rechtsrheinischen und oberhessischen Mittelgebirgslandschaft im Zeitalter der Industrialisierung von 1830 bis 1914 / Ernst Moritz Spilker. Köln : Selbstverlag Forschungsinstitut für Sozial- und Wirtschaftsgeschichte an der Universität zu Köln, 1986. 223 p. : ill. ; 24 cm. (Kölner Vorträge und Abhandlungen zur Sozial- und Wirtschaftsgeschichte . Heft 38) Bibliography: p. 211-218. LC Card 87-408201 DDC 330.943/55 19
1. Wippenfürth (Germany : Kreis) - Economic conditions. 2. Hersfeld-Rotenburg (Germany : Landkreis) - Economic conditions. 3. Altenkirchen/Westerwald (Germany : Landkreis) - Economic conditions. 4. Germany - Economic conditions - 19th century. 5. Germany - Industries - History. I. Title. II. Series.
HC288.W46 S67 1986

Spinanger, Dean.
Industrialization policies and regional economic development in Malaysia / Dean Spinanger. Singapore ; New York : Oxford University Press, 1986. xii, 197 p. : ill., maps ; 26 cm. Bibliography: p. [184]-195. Includes index. ISBN 0-19-582659-0 LC Card 86-207250 DDC 338.9595 19
1. Malaysia - Economic policy. 2. Malaysia - Industries. 3. Malaysia - Economic conditions. I. Title.
HC445.5 .S68 1986

Langhammer, Rolf J. Wirtschaftliche Zusammenarbeit zwischen den Entwicklungsländern . Tübingen , c1984. xi, 135 p. : ISBN 3-16-344889-5 : LC Card 85-143693
HF1413 .L363 1984

Spindel, Cheywa R.
Espaços de socialização e exploração do menor assalariado : família, escola e empresa / Cheywa R. Spindel. São Paulo, SP : Instituto de Estudos Econômicos, Sociais e Políticos de São Paulo, 1986. 254 p. ; 21 cm. (Monografias. 2) Bibliography: p. 234-254. LC Card 87-405001 DDC 331.3/1/0981 19
1. Youth - Employment - Brazil. 2. Children - Employment - Brazil. 3. Migration, Internal - Brazil. 4. Assimilation (Sociology). I. Series: Monografias (Instituto de Estudos Econômicos, Sociais e Políticos de São Paulo) , 2. II. Title.
HD6276.B72 S67 1986

A Mulher rural e mudanças no processo de produção agrícola . [Brasília] [1984] i, 161 p. ; LC Card 86-150197
HD6073.A292 L295 1984

Spinelli, Nicola, 1881- Dizionario commerciale, italiano-inglese e inglese-italiano : terminologia commerciale, contabile, economica, finanziaria, giuridica / Nicola Spinelli ; con un'appendice a cura del Giuseppe Motta. Torino : S. Lattes, 1957. 464, 683, 138 p. ; 21 cm.
1. Commerce - Dictionaries. 2. Commerce - Dictionaries - Italian. 3. Italian language - Dictionaries - English. 4. English language - Dictionaries - Italian. I. Title. ***NYPL [JLD 85-226]***

Spink, Frank H. Dollars & cents of off-price shopping centers . Washington, D.C. , c1986. v, 78 p. : ISBN 0-87420-660-X (pbk.) LC Card 86-51102 DDC 381/.1 19
HF5430.3 .D65 1986

Spinnarke, Jürgen. Soziale Sicherheit in der Bundesrepublik Deutschland : die Sozialversicherung, System, Rechte, Leistungen / von Jürgen Spinnarke.3., überarbeitete Aufl. Heidelberg : C.F. Müller, c1985. 142 p. : ill. ; 19 cm. (Heidelberger Wegweiser) Bibliography: p. 135-136. Includes index. ISBN 3-8114-1085-7 : LC Card 86-103725
1. Social security - Germany, West. 2. Social security - Law and legislation - Germany, West. I. Title. II. Series.
HD7179 .S63 1985

Spinners and weavers of Auffay . Gullickson, Gay L. Cambridge [Cambridgeshire] , New York , 1986. x, 256 p. : ISBN 0-521-32280-4 LC Card 86-6808 DDC 331.4/877/02822094425 19
HD8039.T42 F834 1986
NYPL [JLE 87-1054]

Spirina, N. I. Ėffektivnost′ i intensifikat͡sii͡a . Moskva , 1986. 161 p. ; LC Card 87-163443
HC340.I52 E33 1986

Spirit . Owen, Harrison, 1936- Potomac, Md. , 1987. viii, 245 p. : ISBN 0-9618205-0-0 (pbk.) LC Card 87-70469 DDC 658.4/06 19
HD58.8 .O94 1987

Spiro, Heather M. The Ilora farm settlement in Nigeria / Heather Spiro ; prepared under the auspices of the Population Council. West Hartford, Conn. : Kumarian Press, 1985. xvii, 50 p. : ill. ; 28 cm. (Women's roles and gender differences in development . 5.) On cover: Cases for planners. Bibliography: p. 48-50. ISBN 0-931816-20-3 LC Card 85-5230 DDC 331.4/83/089963 19
1. Women farmers - Nigeria. 2. Women in business - Nigeria. 3. Agricultural colonies - Nigeria. 4. Yorubas - Economic conditions. 5. Nigeria - Rural conditions. I. Population Council, New York. II. Title. III. Series.
HD6073.F3 N667 1985
NYPL [JLF 86-1629]

Spis ludności i mieszkań metodą reprezentacyjną z dnia 6 XII 1984 r. : warunki mieszkaniowe / [komitet redakcyjny Głównego Urzędu Statystycznego, przewodniczący Wiesław Sadowski ... et al. ; redaktor główny Lech Gradowski]. Warszawa : Główny Urząd Statystyczny, 1985. xx, 93 p., [2] p. of plates : col. ill. ; 29 cm. (Statystyka Polski. Seria Materiały statystyczne . 34) LC Card 86-176185
1. Housing - Poland - Statistics. 2. Poland - Population - Statistics. I. Sadowski, Wiesław. II. Gradowski, Lech. III. Poland. Główny Urząd Statystyczny. IV. Series.
HD7345.7.A3 S65 1985

Spiselman, David, 1947- A teenager's guide to money, banking, and finance / David Spiselman. New York : J. Messner, c1987. p. cm. Bibliography: p. Includes index. Gives practical advice on opening a bank account, keeping records, saving, investing, and using credit cards, as well as general information about the operation and function of banks, businesses, government, and the economy. ISBN 0-671-64345-2 LC Card 87-11059 DDC 332.024 19
1. Finance, Personal - Juvenile literature. 2. Youth - Finance, Personal - Juvenile literature. 3. Banks and banking - Juvenile literature. I. Title.
HG179 .S5554 1987

Spitálszky, Márta. Kovács, Kálmán. Tervezési szintek érdekeltségének összehangolása gazdaságszabályozási eszközökkel . Budapest , 1984. 50 p. : ISBN 963-491-189-7 LC Card 86-198789
HD1940.5.Z8 K68 1984

Spitz, P. (Pierre) Food systems and society in India : a draft interim report / Pierre Spitz. Geneva : United Nations Research Institute for Social Development, [1983] 2 v. (393 p.) : ill., maps ; 30 cm. "July 1983." Includes bibliographical references. LC Card 87-100437
1. Food supply - India. 2. Agriculture - Economic aspects - India. I. Title.
HD9016.I42 S62 1983

Spitz, Peter H. Petrochemicals : the rise of an industry / Peter H. Spitz. New York : Wiley, c1988. xxvii, 588 p. : ill. ; 24 cm. Includes bibliographies and indexes. ISBN 0-471-85985-0 : LC Card 87-23019 DDC 338.4/7661804 19
1. Petroleum chemicals industry - History. 2. Petroleum chemicals - History. I. Title.
HD9579.C32 S65 1988

Spitzenlasttarifierung, oekonomische Effizienz und Erhaltung der Eigenwirtschaftlichkeit . Meier, Kurt, Dr. Bern , c1983. viii, 202 p. : ISBN 3-258-03322-6 : LC Card 84-108545
HD9685.S92 M45 1983

Spitzer, Rudolf. Tieber, Herbert. Verstaatliche Industrie . Wien , c1983. 91 p. : LC Card 84-169053
HD4155 .T54 1983

Spitzmüller, Alexander, 1862-1953. Memoirs of Alexander Spitzmüller, Freiherr von Harmersbach (1862-1953) : former minister of trade and minister of finance in the Austro-Hungarian Empire, governor of the Austro-Hungarian Bank, director-general of the Creditanstalt Bankverein / translated and edited with introduction by Carvel de Bussy. Boulder : East European Monographs ; New York : Distributed by Columbia University Press, 1987. xi, 327 p., [5] p. of plates : ill., ports. ; 23 cm. (East European monographs. no. 228) Bibliography: p. 317-320. Includes index. ISBN 0-88033-124-0 LC Card 87-80511 DDC 332.3/2/0924 B 19
1. Spitzmüller, Alexander, 1862-1953. 2. Bankers - Austria - Biography. 3. Creditanstalt-Bankverein (Austria) - History. 4. Statesmen - Austria - Biography. I. Bussy, Carvel de. II. Title.
HG1552.S65 A3 1987

SPITZMÜLLER, ALEXANDER, 1862-1953.
Spitzmüller, Alexander, 1862-1953. Memoirs of Alexander Spitzmüller, Freiherr von Harmersbach (1862-1953) . Boulder , New York , 1987. xi, 327 p., [5] p. of plates : ISBN 0-88033-124-0 LC Card 87-80511 DDC 332.3/2/0924 B 19
HG1552.S65 A3 1987

Spivdruzhnist′ u prat͡si /. Skruten′, I. S. Kyïv , 1982. 117 p. : LC Card 83-200434
HC337.U5 S514 1982

SPOILS SYSTEMS. see **CORRUPTION (IN POLITICS)**

Spojené staty americké. see **United States.**

SPOKANE COUNTY, WASH. - HISTORY.
Prevost, Nancy M., 1953- Paradise in the Palouse . Fairfield, Wash. , c1985. 35 p. : ISBN 0-87770-365-5 (pbk.) LC Card 85-17842 DDC 338.1/09797/39 19
HD1775.W2 P74 1985 ***NYPL [JFF 86-559]***

Spółdzielczość . Boczar, Kazimierz. Warszawa , 1986. 398 p. ; ISBN 83-208-0500-7 : LC Card 86-176276
HD3057.7.A4 B63 1986

Sponsorship in the marketing mix. Seminar on Below-the-Line and Sponsoring (1985 : Milan, Italy) Seminar on Below-the-Line and Sponsoring . Amsterdam, Netherlands [1985] vi, 270 p. : ISBN 92-831-1107-9 (pbk.) : LC Card 86-213125 DDC 658.8/2 19
HF5438.5 .S46 1985

Spontaneous shelter : international perspectives and prospects / edited by Carl V. Patton. Philadelphia : Temple University Press, 1988. p. cm. Bibliography: p. Includes index. ISBN 0-87722-507-9 (alk. paper) LC Card 87-10002 DDC 363.5/8/091724 19
1. Poor - Housing - Developing countries. 2. Poor - Housing - Government policy - Developing countries. 3. Housing policy - Developing countries. I. Patton, Carl V.
HD7287.96.D44 S66 1988

SPORT FISHING. see **FISHING.**

Sport und Werbung, Präsenz und Erinnerungswirkung ausgewählter Werbeträger an Rennstrecken : Bericht über ein Studienprojekt / Hrsg. Arnold Hermanns. München : Universität der Bundeswehr München, [1986] 70, lii, [iii] p. : ill. ; 30 cm. (Arbeits- und Studienpapiere Marketing . Bd. 1/1986) Bibliography: p. [liii]-[lv]. LC Card 87-409557 DDC 659.13/42 19
1. Billboards. 2. Racetracks (Automobile racing). 3. Advertising, Outdoor. I. Hermanns, Arnold. II. Series: Arbeits- und Studienpapiere Marketing , 1986/Bd. 1.
HF5843 .S69 1986

SPORTING GOODS INDUSTRY - GERMANY (WEST)
Breitenacher, Michael. Strukturwandlungen und Entwicklungsperspektiven im Musikinstrumentenbau, in der Spielwaren- und Sportgeräteherstellung und in der Schmuckindustrie /. Berlin , c1984. 188 p. : ISBN 3-428-05566-7 LC Card 84-186644
HD9999.M83 G32 1984

Sporvejshistorisk selskab (Denmark) By i forvandling . Copenhagen , 1984. 93 p. : ISBN 87-87589-42-7 LC Card 87-155193
HE4859.C68 B92 1984

Sporvejshistorisk selskabs bogserie .
(bog nr. 18) By i forvandling . Copenhagen , 1984. 93 p. : ISBN 87-87589-42-7 LC Card 87-155193
HE4859.C68 B92 1984

Spranzi, Aldo, 1932- Calcolo dei costi nelle imprese industriali / Aldo Spranzi. 2a ed. riv. e ampliata. Milano : Giuffrè, [1986] viii, 94 p. : ill. ; 24 cm. (Università "L. Bocconi," Dipartimento di economia aziendale . 42. 8.3) Bibliography: p. [71] ISBN 88-14-00844-2 : LC Card 86-182386
1. Costs, Industrial - Econometric models. I. Series. Università "L. Bocconi," Dipartimento di economia aziendale (Series) , 42. II. Title.
HC79.C7 S67 1986

Spraos, John. IMF conditionality : ineffectual, inefficient, mistargeted / John Spraos. Princeton, N.J. : International Finance Section, Dept. of Economics, Princeton University, c1986. 34 p. ; 23 cm. (Essays in international finance, 0071-142X . no. 166 (Dec. 1986)) Pages 31-34 publishers list. Bibliography: p. 28-29. ISBN 0-88165-073-0 (pbk.) : LC Card 86-33805 DDC 332/.042 s 332.1/52 19
1. International Monetary Fund. 2. Loans, Foreign. I. Series. II. Series: Essays in international finance , no. 166. III. Title.
HG136 .P7 no. 166 HG3881.5.I58

Spravochnik po finansovo-ėkonomicheskim raschetam v sel′skokhozi͡aĭstvennykh predprii͡atii͡akh /. Val′ter, S. B. (Semen Borisovich) Moskva , 1982. 411 p. ; LC Card 83-160870
HF5686.A36 V35 1982

Spravochnik rukovoditeli͡a srednego zvena kolkhoza, sovkhoza / pod redakt͡sieĭ A.A. Cherni͡avskogo ; [sostavitel′ P.F. Pasko]. Minsk : "Uradzhaĭ," 1981. 518 p. ; 21 cm. LC Card 82-147885
1. Collective farms - Soviet Union - Management. 2. State farms - Soviet Union - Management. I. Cherni͡avskiĭ, A. A. II. Pasko, P. F.
HD1492.S65 S67 1981

Spreadsheet applications in financial accounting /. DiAntonio, Angelo E. Englewood Cliffs, N.J. , c1986. xvii, 391 p. : ISBN 0-8359-6945-2 (pbk.) : LC Card 85-14303 DDC 657/.028/553 19
HF5679 .D52 1986 ***NYPL [JLE 86-3100]***

SPREADSTAT . Ross, Steven S. New York , c1988. p. cm. ISBN 0-07-053909-X : LC Card 87-22811 DDC 005.36/9 19
HF1017 .R67 1988

Spremann, Klaus. Capital market equilibria /. Berlin , New York , c1986. x, 228 p. : ISBN 0-387-16248-8 (U. S.) LC Card 86-10104 DDC 332.6/0724 19
HG4523 .C33 1986 ***NYPL [JLE 86-4309]***

Spreter, Jürgen. Theoretische und empirische Analyse der Determinanten des Geldschöpfungsmultiplikators / Jürgen Spreter. Krefeld : G. Marchal und H.J. Matzenbacher Wissenschaftsverlag, 1983. v, 221 p. : ill. ; 21 cm. Originally presented as the author's thesis (doctoral)--Universität Stuttgart, 1982/83. Bibliography: p. 202-221. ISBN 3-88358-029-5 LC Card 83-154608
1. Money supply - Mathematical models. 2. Monetary policy - Mathematical models. I. Title.
HG226.3 .S67 1983

Springer texts in statistics.
Alfred, Braxton M. Elements of statistics for the life and social sciences /. New York , c1987. xiii, 190 p. : ISBN 0-387-96500-9 : LC Card 87-4964 DDC 300/.1/5195 19
HA29 .A53 1987

SPRINGS, ELLIOTT WHITE.
Davis, Burke, 1913- War bird . Chapel Hill , c1987. viii, 267 p., [26] p. of plates : ISBN 0-8078-1752-X (alk. paper) LC Card 87-5934

DDC 338.7/67721/0924 B 19
HD9880.S67 D38 1987

SPRINGS INDUSTRIES - HISTORY.
Davis, Burke, 1913- War bird . Chapel Hill , c1987. viii, 267 p., [26] p. of plates : ISBN 0-8078-1752-X (alk. paper) LC Card 87-5934 DDC 338.7/67721/0924 B 19
HD9880.S67 D38 1987

SPROCKHÖVEL (GERMANY) - SOCIAL CONDITIONS.
Radverkehrskonzept Sprockhövel /. Essen , c1985. 55 p., [3] folded col. leaves of plates : ISBN 3-923494-51-3 LC Card 86-113993
HE5739.G3 R33 1985

The SPSS guide to data analysis for SPSS with additional instructions for SPSS/PC /. Norušis, M. J. (Marija J.), 1948- Chicago, IL , c1987. xiii, 428 p. : ISBN 0-918469-42-2 (pbk.) LC Card 87-60776 DDC 001.4/22 19
HA32 .N6519 1987

SPSS Inc.
Norušis, M. J. (Marija J.), 1948- The SPSS guide to data analysis for SPSS with additional instructions for SPSS/PC /. Chicago, IL , c1987. xiii, 428 p. : ISBN 0-918469-42-2 (pbk.) LC Card 87-60776 DDC 001.4/22 19
HA32 .N6519 1987

Norušis, M. J. (Marija J.), 1948- SPSS/PC+ Advanced Statistics V2.0 for the IBM PC/XT/AT and PS/2 /. Chicago, Ill. , c1988. 1 v. (various pagings) : ISBN 0-918469-57-0 (pbk.) LC Card 87-62355 DDC 005.36/9 19
HA32 .N6634 1988

Norušis, M. J. (Marija J.), 1948- SPSS/PC+ V2.0 base manual for the IBM PC/XT/AT and PS/2 /. Chicago, Ill. , c1988. 606 p. in various pagings : ISBN 0-918469-55-4 (pbk.) LC Card 87-62353 DDC 300/.28/5416 19
HA32 .N6674 1988

SPSS/PC+ trends . Chicago, Ill. , c1987. 299 p. in various pagings : ISBN 0-918469-44-9 (pbk.) LC Card 87-60902 DDC 005.36/9 19
HA32 .S627 1987

SPSS-X user's guide. Chicago, Ill. , Gorinchem, Netherlands , c1988. 1072 p. : ISBN 0-918469-51-1 (pbk.) LC Card 87-62349 DDC 005.3/29 19
HA32 .S67 1988

SPSSX processing of U. S. census data. Chicago, Ill. , c1983. 79 p. : ISBN 0-918469-02-3 (pbk.) LC Card 87-160044 DDC 304.6/028/55329 19
HA37.U55 S64 1983

SPSS Inc. reports.
SPSSX processing of U. S. census data. Chicago, Ill. , c1983. 79 p. : ISBN 0-918469-02-3 (pbk.) LC Card 87-160044 DDC 304.6/028/55329 19
HA37.U55 S64 1983

SPSS/PC+ Advanced Statistics V2.0 for the IBM PC/XT/AT and PS/2 /. Norušis, M. J. (Marija J.), 1948- Chicago, Ill. , c1988. 1 v. (various pagings) : ISBN 0-918469-57-0 (pbk.) LC Card 87-62355 DDC 005.36/9 19
HA32 .N6634 1988

SPSS/PC plus version 2.0 base manual for the IBM PC/XT/AT and PS/2. Norušis, M. J. (Marija J.), 1948- SPSS/PC+ V2.0 base manual for the IBM PC/XT/AT and PS/2 /. Chicago, Ill. , c1988. 606 p. in various pagings : ISBN 0-918469-55-4 (pbk.) LC Card 87-62353 DDC 300/.28/5416 19
HA32 .N6674 1988

SPSS/PC+ trends : for the IBM PC/XT/AT / SPSS Inc. Chicago, Ill. : SPSS, c1987. 299 p. in various pagings : ill. ; 28 cm. On t.p. the registered trademark symbol "TM" is subscript following "SPSS/PC+" and "trends" in the title. Includes bibliographies and index. ISBN 0-918469-44-9 (pbk.) LC Card 87-60902 DDC 005.36/9 19
1. SPSS/PC Plus Trends (Computer system). 2. Social sciences - Data processing. I. SPSS Inc.
HA32 .S627 1987

SPSS/PC V 2.0 base manual for the IBM PC/XT/AT and PS/2. Norušis, M. J. (Marija J.), 1948- SPSS/PC+ V2.0 base manual for the IBM PC/XT/AT and PS/2 /. Chicago, Ill. , c1988. 606 p. in various pagings : ISBN 0-918469-55-4 (pbk.) LC Card 87-62353 DDC 300/.28/5416 19
HA32 .N6674 1988

SPSS X (COMPUTER SYSTEM)
Einstein, Gilles O., 1950- Learning to use SPSSx /. Englewood Cliffs, N.J. , c1987. viii, 183 p. : ISBN 0-13-528050-8 (pbk.) LC Card 86-30263 DDC 005.3/29 19
HA32 .E45 1987

Norušis, M. J. (Marija J.), 1948- The SPSS guide to data analysis for SPSS with additional instructions for SPSS/PC /. Chicago, IL , c1987. xiii, 428 p. : ISBN 0-918469-42-2 (pbk.) LC Card 87-60776 DDC 001.4/22 19
HA32 .N6519 1987

SPSS-X user's guide. Chicago, Ill. , Gorinchem, Netherlands , c1988. 1072 p. : ISBN 0-918469-51-1 (pbk.) LC Card 87-62349 DDC 005.3/29 19
HA32 .S67 1988

SPSSX processing of U. S. census data. Chicago, Ill. , c1983. 79 p. : ISBN 0-918469-02-3 (pbk.) LC Card 87-160044 DDC 304.6/028/55329 19
HA37.U55 S64 1983

SPSS-X user's guide. 3rd ed. Chicago, Ill. : SPSS ; Gorinchem, Netherlands : SPSS Europe, c1988. 1072 p. : col. ill. ; 28 cm. Ill. on p. [2]-[3] of cover. One folded reference card inserted. Bibliography: p. 1045-1048. Includes index. ISBN 0-918469-51-1 (pbk.) LC Card 87-62349 DDC 005.3/29 19
1. SPSS X (Computer system). 2. Social sciences - Data processing. I. SPSS Inc.
HA32 .S67 1988

SPSS/PC+ (COMPUTER SYSTEM)
Frude, Neil. A guide to SPSS/PC+ /. New York , 1987. p. cm. ISBN 0-387-91312-2 LC Card 87-16711 DDC 300/.285416 19
HA32 .F78 1987

Norušis, M. J. (Marija J.), 1948- SPSS/PC+ V2.0 base manual for the IBM PC/XT/AT and PS/2 /. Chicago, Ill. , c1988. 606 p. in various pagings : ISBN 0-918469-55-4 (pbk.) LC Card 87-62353 DDC 300/.28/5416 19
HA32 .N6674 1988

SPSS/PC PLUS (COMPUTER SYSTEM)
Norušis, M. J. (Marija J.), 1948- SPSS/PC+ Advanced Statistics V2.0 for the IBM PC/XT/AT and PS/2 /. Chicago, Ill. , c1988. 1 v. (various pagings) : ISBN 0-918469-57-0 (pbk.) LC Card 87-62355 DDC 005.36/9 19
HA32 .N6634 1988

SPSS/PC PLUS TRENDS (COMPUTER SYSTEM)
SPSS/PC+ trends . Chicago, Ill. , c1987. 299 p. in various pagings : ISBN 0-918469-44-9 (pbk.) LC Card 87-60902 DDC 005.36/9 19
HA32 .S627 1987

SPSSX processing of U. S. census data. Chicago, Ill. : SPSS, c1983. 79 p. : ill. ; 28 cm. (SPSS Inc. reports) On t.p. "X" is superscript. Includes index. ISBN 0-918469-02-3 (pbk.) LC Card 87-160044 DDC 304.6/028/55329 19
1. SPSS X (Computer system). 2. United States - Census - Data processing. I. SPSS Inc. II. Title: SPSSX processing of US census data. III. Series.
HA37.U55 S64 1983

SPSSX processing of US census data. SPSSX processing of U. S. census data. Chicago, Ill. , c1983. 79 p. : ISBN 0-918469-02-3 (pbk.) LC Card 87-160044 DDC 304.6/028/55329 19
HA37.U55 S64 1983

Spufford, Peter.
Handbook of medieval exchange / by Peter Spufford ; with the assistance of Wendy Wilkinson and Sarah Tolley. London : Offices of the Royal Historical Society ; Woodbridge, Suffolk ; xcii, 376 p., [3] leaves of plates (1 folded) : maps ; 24 cm. (Royal Historical Society guides and handbooks . no. 13) Bibliography: p. 323-350. Includes indexes. ISBN 0-86193-105-X LC Card 86-673816
1. Foreign exchange - History. 2. Money - Europe - History. I. Wilkinson, Wendy. II. Tolley, Sarah. III. Royal Historical Society (Great Britain). IV. Series: Guides and handbooks , no. 13. V. Title.
HG3942 .S68x 1986

Handbook of medieval exchange / by Peter Spufford with the assistance of Wendy Wilkinson and Sarah Tolley. London : Offices of the Royal Historical Society ; Woodbridge, Suffolk ; xcii, 376, [3] p., [1] fold. leaf : ill., maps ; 24 cm. (Royal Historical Society guides and handbooks . no. 13) Part of illustrative matter (1 folded leaf) inserted at back cover. Includes indexes. Bibliography: p. 323-350. ISBN 0-86193-105-X
1. Foreign exchange - History. 2. Money - Europe - History. I. Tolley, Sarah. II. Wilkinson, Wendy. III. Series: Royal Historical Society, London. Guides and handbooks, no. 13. IV. Title.
NYPL [JLE 86-4344]

Spurk, Jan. Soziologie der französischen Arbeiterbewegung / Jan Spurk. 1. Aufl. Berlin : Argument-Verlag, c1986. 317 p. ; 21 cm. (Edition Philosophie und Sozialwissenschaften . 6) Bibliography: p. 301-317. ISBN 3-88619-606-2 LC Card 87-235004 DDC 331.88/0944 19
1. Trade-unions - France - History. 2. Industrial sociology - France - History. 3. Social classes - France - History. 4. Trade-unions - Social aspects - France. I. Title. II. Series.
HD6684 .S68 1986

SQL/ORACLE (COMPUTER PROGRAM LANGUAGE)
Gane, Chris, 1938- Developing business systems in SQL . New York, NY , 1986. 1 v. (various pagings) : ISBN 0-914751-02-6 (pbk.) LC Card 87-107881 DDC 650/.028/557565 19
HF5548.5.S65 G36 1986

SQUATTER SETTLEMENTS - ARGENTINA - BUENOS AIRES.
Bellardi, Marta. Villas miseria . Buenos Aires , c1986. 157 p. : ISBN 950-25-1423-8 : LC Card 87-125510 DDC 307.3/36 19
HD7321.B9 B45 1986

SQUATTER SETTLEMENTS - BANGLADESH - DHAKA.
Choguill, Charles L. New communities for urban squatters . New York , c1987. xiv, 213 p. : ISBN 0-306-42545-9 LC Card 86-30501 DDC 307.3/36 19
HD7361.6.D57 C46 1987

SQUATTER SETTLEMENTS - GOVERNMENT POLICY - AFRICA, SUB-SAHARAN.
Slum and squatter settlements in Sub-Saharan Africa . New York , 1988. p. cm. ISBN 0-275-92309-6 (alk. paper) : LC Card 87-11705 DDC 307.3/36 19
HD7287.96.A438 S57 1988

SQUATTER SETTLEMENTS - GOVERNMENT POLICY - ARGENTINA - BUENOS AIRES.
Bellardi, Marta. Villas miseria . Buenos Aires , c1986. 157 p. : ISBN 950-25-1423-8 : LC Card 87-125510 DDC 307.3/36 19
HD7321.B9 B45 1986

SQUATTER SETTLEMENTS - IRAN.
Danesh, Abol Hassan, 1952- Rural exodus & squatter settlements in the Third World . Lanham, MD , c1987. xii, 168 p. : ISBN 0-8191-6443-7 (alk. paper) : LC Card 87-10627 DDC 307.2 19
HB2096.4.A3 D36 1987

SQUATTER SETTLEMENTS - KENYA.
Community participation for road planning in squatter settlement upgrading . Nairobi, Kenya , 1983. 56 leaves : LC Card 86-980653 DDC 388.1/09676/2 19
HE367.K43 C584 1983

SQUATTER SETTLEMENTS - LATIN AMERICA - CONGRESSES.
Abitazione e periferie urbane nei paesi in via di sviluppo . Milano, Italy , c1985. 450 p. : LC Card 86-132019
HD7287.96.L29 A25 1985
NYPL [JLD 87-1173]

SQUATTER SETTLEMENTS - MEDITERRANEAN REGION - CONGRESSES.
Abitazione e periferie urbane nei paesi in via di sviluppo . Milano, Italy , c1985. 450 p. : LC Card 86-132019
HD7287.96.L29 A25 1985
NYPL [JLD 87-1173]

SQUATTER SETTLEMENTS - PERU - LIMA METROPOLITAN AREA.
Espinoza, Néstor. El proceso de electrificación en los pueblos jóvenes . Lima, Perú [1983] 77

p. : LC Card 84-149923 DDC 363.6/2/098525 19
HD9685.P47 L54 1983
NYPL [JLD 86-3894]

SQUATTER SETTLEMENTS - SOUTH AFRICA - CAPE TOWN REGION.
Facing the squatter crisis /. Cape Town , 1977. 21 p. : LC Card 81-194960
HD7374.4.C343 F33 1977

Squatters and the roots of Mau Mau, 1905-63 /. Kanogo, Tabitha M. London , Athens , 1987. xviii, 206 p. : ISBN 0-8214-0873-9 (U.S) LC Card 87-11201 DDC 307.3/36 19
HD1538.K4 K36 1987

SQUATTERS - AUSTRALIA - QUEENSLAND - HISTORY - 19TH CENTURY.
Walker, Jan, 1954- Jondaryan station . St. Lucia , New York , 1988. p. cm. ISBN 0-7022-2093-0 (pbk.) LC Card 87-13816 DDC 333.3/09943 19
HD1039.Q43 W34 1988

SQUATTERS - BERLIN (GERMANY)
Sonnewald, Bernd, 1947- Die "Berliner Linie" und die Hausbesetzer-Szene /. Berlin , c1983. 149 p. ; ISBN 3-87061-170-7 LC Card 83-190228
HD7287.96.G32 B477 1983

Was wird in den besetzten Häusern gemacht? . Berlin [1982]. 65 p. : *NYPL [JLF 87-439]*

SQUATTERS - BRAZIL - CONCEIÇÃO DO ARAGUAIA.
Figueira, Ricardo Rezende, 1952- A justiça do lobo . Petrópolis , 1986. 115 p. ; LC Card 87-137552 DDC 305.5/63 19
HD500.C74 F54 1986

SQUATTERS - KENYA - HISTORY - 20TH CENTURY.
Kanogo, Tabitha M. Squatters and the roots of Mau Mau, 1905-63 /. London , Athens , 1987. xviii, 206 p. : ISBN 0-8214-0873-9 (U.S) LC Card 87-11201 DDC 307.3/36 19
HD1538.K4 K36 1987

Throup, David. Economic & social origins of Mau Mau 1945-53 /. London , Athens , c1988. xvi, 304 p. : ISBN 0-8214-0883-6 LC Card 87-12387 DDC 307.3/36 19
HD2126.5 .T48 1988

The squeeze /. Davidson, James Dale. New York , c1980. 281 p. ; ISBN 0-671-40084-3 LC Card 79-28411 DDC 330.973
HC106.7 .D38 *NYPL [JLE 80-1960]*

Squire, Lyn, 1946- Agricultural household models . Baltimore, Md. , 1986. xi, 335 p. : ISBN 0-8018-3149-0 LC Card 85-45102 DDC 331.7/63/091724 19
HD1542 .A34 1986 *NYPL [JLE 86-2440]*

Squire, Sanders & Dempsey. Infrastructure financing [microform] . [New York] , c1983. 22, 7, 17 p. : *NYPL [*ZT-1565 no.20]*

Sraffa, Piero.
PRODUCTION OF COMMODITIES BY MEANS OF COMMODITIES.
Franke, Reiner. Production prices and dynamical processes of the gravitation of market prices /. Frankfurt am Main , New York , c1987. 231 p. : ISBN 3-8204-9435-9 (pbk.) LC Card 87-170397 DDC 338/.01 19
HB171.S7253 F73 1987

SRAFFA, PIERO.
Ahijado, Manuel. Piero Sraffa . Madrid , 1985. 90 p. ; ISBN 84-85942-31-0 LC Card 87-104173
HB109.S73 A35 1985

Monza, Alfredo. Sraffa y sus usos /. Buenos Aires , 1985. 102 p. : ISBN 950-43-0654-3 LC Card 86-172226
HB117.S73 M66 1985

Stamatis, Georg. Sraffa und sein Verhältnis zu Ricardo und Marx /. Göttingen , Lollar , c1984. ix, 459 p. : ISBN 3-921701-04-X LC Card 84-213549
HB103.S7 S73 1984

The Value dimension . London , New York , 1986. 239 p. ; ISBN 0-7102-0766-2 (pbk.) : LC Card 87-109334 DDC 338.5/21 19
HB203 .V33 1986

Sraffa und sein Verhältnis zu Ricardo und Marx /. Stamatis, Georg. Göttingen , Lollar , c1984. ix, 459 p. : ISBN 3-921701-04-X LC Card 84-213549
HB103.S7 S73 1984

Sraffa y sus usos /. Monza, Alfredo. Buenos Aires , 1985. 102 p. : ISBN 950-43-0654-3 LC Card 86-172226
HB117.S73 M66 1985

Śramika āndolane aikya prasaṅge /. Rāẏa, Manorañjana. Kalikātā , 1986. 226 p. ; LC Card 87-900228
HD6815.W47 R39 1986

Sravnitelʹnyĭ analiz deiatelʹnosti predpriiatiĭ /. Krylov, V. F. (Vladimir Fedorovich) Moskva , 1981. 69 p. ; LC Card 82-112692
HC340.L3 K75 1981

Sredl, Henry J., 1935- The ASTD reference guide to professional training roles & competencies / Henry J. Sredl & William J. Rothwell. 1st ed. New York : Random House Professional Business Publications, c1987. 2 v. : ill. ; 25 cm. Spine title: The ASTD reference guide. Includes bibliographies and index. ISBN 0-394-55915-0 (v. 1) LC Card 86-26006 DDC 658.3/124 19
1. Employees, Training of - Handbooks, manuals, etc. 2. Personnel management - Handbooks, manuals, etc. I. Rothwell, William J., 1951-. II. American Society for Training and Development. III. Title. IV. Title: Professional training roles & competencies. V. Title: Professional training roles and competencies. VI. Title: ASTD reference guide.
HF5549.5.T7 S657 1987

Sredna Evropa i zemite po Dolniia Dunav prez XVIII-XIX v. . Paskaleva-Zakharieva, Virzhiniia. Sofiia , 1986. 317 p. : LC Card 86-219994
HC244 .P29 1986

Sredstva prodleniia navigatsii na vnutrennikh vodnykh putiakh /. Zuev, V. A. (Valeriĭ Andreevich) Leningrad , 1986. 206 p. : LC Card 86-166974
HE675 .Z84 1986

Sri Lanka Association of Economists. Structural adjustment and growth . Colombo, Sri Lanka , 1986. 170 p. ; LC Card 86-903207 DDC 338.9549/3 19
HC424 .S77 1986

Sri Lanka census of industry, 1983 : preliminary report. [Colombo] : Dept. of Census and Statistics, Ministry of Plan Implementation, [1985] viii, 17, A, 186 p. ; 23 x 28 cm. LC Card 86-903510 DDC 338.09549/3/021 19
1. Sri Lanka - Industries - Statistics. 2. Sri Lanka - Census, 1983. I. Sri Lanka. Janalēkhana hā Sankhyālēkhana Depārtamēntuva.
HD2892.8 .S68 1985

Sri Lanka census of population and housing, 1981. Volume 2, All island tables. [Colombo] : Ministry of Plan Implementation, Dept. of Census and Statistics, 1985. 3 v. in 1 ; 29 cm. CONTENTS. - pt. 1. Population -- pt. 2. Migration -- pt. 3. Housing. LC Card 86-903509 DDC 304.6/09549/3021 19
1. Sri Lanka - Population - Statistics. 2. Housing - Sri Lanka - Statistics. 3. Migration, Internal - Sri Lanka - Statistics. 4. Sri Lanka - Census, 1981. I. Sri Lanka. Janalēkhana hā Saṅkhyālēkahana Depārtamēntuva.
HA4570.8 .A4 1981b

Sri Lanka census of population and housing 1981. Census of population and housing, 1981. [Colombo] [1986] iv, 232 p. : LC Card 87-901055
HA4570.8 .A4 1981c

Sri Lanka census of population, 1963 : [all island tables]. [Colombo] : Ministry of Plan Implementation, Dept. of Census and Statistics, [1986] 250 p. ; 29 cm. LC Card 86-903270 DDC 304.6/09549/3021 19
1. Sri Lanka - Census, 1963. 2. Sri Lanka - Population - Statistics. I. Sri Lanka. Janalēkhana hā Sankhyālēkhana Depārtamēntuva.
HA4570.8 .A4 1963

SRI LANKA - CENSUS, 1963.
Sri Lanka census of population, 1963 . [Colombo] [1986] 250 p. ; LC Card 86-903270 DDC 304.6/09549/3021 19
HA4570.8 .A4 1963

SRI LANKA - CENSUS, 1981.
Census of population and housing, 1981. [Colombo] [1986] iv, 232 p. : LC Card 87-901055
HA4570.8 .A4 1981c

Sri Lanka census of population and housing, 1981. [Colombo] , 1985. 3 v. in 1 ; LC Card 86-903509 DDC 304.6/09549/3021 19
HA4570.8 .A4 1981b

SRI LANKA - CENSUS, 1983.
Sri Lanka census of industry, 1983 . [Colombo] [1985] viii, 17, A, 186 p. ; LC Card 86-903510 DDC 338.09549/3/021 19
HD2892.8 .S68 1985

SRI LANKA - COMMERCE.
Dawood, Nawaz. Tea and poverty . Kowloon, Hong Kong , 1980. xii, 166 p. ; LC Card 80-154803 DDC 338.1/7372/095493 19
HC424 .D36 1980

SRI LANKA - COMMERCE - MATHEMATICAL MODELS.
Athukoralge, Premachandra. Export instability and growth . London , Wolfeboro, N.H. , c1987. 244 p. : ISBN 0-7099-3739-3 : LC Card 86-32833 DDC 382/.6/095493 19
HF3770.8.Z5 A84 1987

Sri Lanka - Commerce - Statistics. see **Sri Lanka - Commerce.**

SRI LANKA - COMMERCIAL POLICY.
Lal, Deepak. Trade liberalization in Sri Lanka /. Aldershop, Hants, England , Brookfield, Vt. , 1988. p. cm. ISBN 0-566-05340-3 : LC Card 87-15044 DDC 382/.3/095493 19
HF1586.8 .L35 1988

SRI LANKA - DEPENDENCY ON INDIA.
Maass, Citha Doris. Indien, Nepal, Sri Lanka . Wiesbaden , 1982. xxi, 380 p. ; ISBN 3-515-03802-7 LC Card 86-214318
HF1590.15.N4 M33 1982

SRI LANKA - ECONOMIC CONDITIONS - CONGRESSES.
Structural adjustment and growth . Colombo, Sri Lanka , 1986. 170 p. ; LC Card 86-903207 DDC 338.9549/3 19
HC424 .S77 1986

SRI LANKA - ECONOMIC CONDITIONS - MATHEMATICAL MODELS.
Athukoralge, Premachandra. Export instability and growth . London , Wolfeboro, N.H. , c1987. 244 p. : ISBN 0-7099-3739-3 : LC Card 86-32833 DDC 382/.6/095493 19
HF3770.8.Z5 A84 1987

SRI LANKA - ECONOMIC POLICY.
Discrimination or development?. Colombo, Sri Lanka [1985?] vii, 40 p. ; LC Card 85-904128 DDC 338.9549/3 19
HC424 .D53 1985

Public investment, 1983-1987. Colombo , 1983. 232 p. ; LC Card 83-905444 DDC 332.6/7252/095493 19
HC424 .P82 1983 *NYPL [JLF 87-290]*

SRI LANKA - ECONOMIC POLICY - CONGRESSES.
Structural adjustment and growth . Colombo, Sri Lanka , 1986. 170 p. ; LC Card 86-903207 DDC 338.9549/3 19
HC424 .S77 1986

SRI LANKA - FOREIGN ECONOMIC RELATIONS - INDIA.
Maass, Citha Doris. Indien, Nepal, Sri Lanka . Wiesbaden , 1982. xxi, 380 p. ; ISBN 3-515-03802-7 LC Card 86-214318
HF1590.15.N4 M33 1982

Sri Lanka. Foreign Investment Advisory Committee. Karunaratne, S. W. Potential for foreign investment in rubber products manufacture with information on special projects and a selection of local collaborators /. [Colombo] , 1985. vii, 100 p. ; LC Card 86-902791 DDC 332.6/73/095493 19
HD9161.S752 K37 1985

Sri Lanka Foundation Institute. Labour standards in Sri Lanka . [Colombo] , 1981. x, 164 p. ; LC Card 83-902877 DDC 331/.09549/3 19
HD8670.8 .L32 1981 *NYPL [JLC 87-22]*

Sri Lanka Foundation Institute pocket book . (7) Labour standards in Sri Lanka . [Colombo] , 1981. x, 164 p. ; LC Card 83-902877 DDC 331/.09549/3 19
HD8670.8 .L32 1981 *NYPL [JLC 87-22]*

Sri Lanka - History, Economic. see **Sri Lanka - Economic conditions.**

SRI LANKA - INDUSTRIES - STATISTICS.
Sri Lanka census of industry, 1983 . [Colombo] [1985] viii, 17, A, 186 p. ; LC Card 86-903510

DDC 338.09549/3/021 19
HD2892.8 .S68 1985

Sri Lanka. Jalalēkhana hā Saṅkhyālēkhana Depārtamēntuva. Census of population and housing, 1981. [Colombo] [1986] iv, 232 p. : LC Card 87-901055
HA4570.8 .A4 1981c

Sri Lanka. Janalēkhana hā Saṅkhyālekahana Depārtamēntuva. Sri Lanka census of population and housing, 1981. [Colombo] , 1985. 3 v. in 1 ; LC Card 86-903509 DDC 304.6/09549/3021 19
HA4570.8 .A4 1981b

Sri Lanka. Jātika Krama Sampādana Aṃśaya. Public investment, 1983-1987. Colombo , 1983. 232 p. ; LC Card 83-905444 DDC 332.6/7252/095493 19
HC424 .P82 1983 *NYPL [JLF 87-290]*

Srī Laṅkā Maha Bāṅkuva. Central Bank of Sri Lanka . [Colombo] [1986] 238 p. : LC Card 86-903712 DDC 332.1/1/095493 19
HG3270.8.A7 C47 1986

SRĪ LAṄKĀ MAHA BĀṄKUVA.
Central Bank of Sri Lanka . [Colombo] [1986] 238 p. : LC Card 86-903712 DDC 332.1/1/095493 19
HG3270.8.A7 C47 1986

SRI LANKA - POPULATION - STATISTICS.
Census of population and housing, 1981. [Colombo] [1986] iv, 232 p. : LC Card 87-901055
HA4570.8 .A4 1981c

Sri Lanka census of population and housing, 1981. [Colombo] , 1985. 3 v. in 1 ; LC Card 86-903509 DDC 304.6/09549/3021 19
HA4570.8 .A4 1981b

Sri Lanka census of population, 1963 . [Colombo] [1986] 250 p. ; LC Card 86-903270 DDC 304.6/09549/3021 19
HA4570.8 .A4 1963

Sri Lanka. Rejistrār Janarāl Depārtamēntuva. Report of the Registrar General on vital statistics, 1981, Sri Lanka. [Colombo] [1986] viii, 178 p. ; LC Card 86-903546 DDC 304.6/09549/3021 19
HA4570.8 .R47 1986

Sri Lanka. Sālasum Kriyātmaka Kirīmē Amātyāṃśaya. Janagahana Aṃśaya. Population profile, Nuwara Eliya District. [Colombo] [1985?] viii, 35 p. : LC Card 86-902529 DDC 304.6/09549/3 19
HA4570.8.Z9 N886 1985

Sri Lanka. Sālasum Kriyātmaka Kirīmē Amātyāṃśaya. Rākirakṣā hā Minisbalaya Sālasum Aṃśaya. Foreign employment . [Colombo] [1985] x, 202 p. ; LC Card 87-900211 DDC 331.6/2/5493 19
HD8670.8 .F67 1985

SRI LANKA - SOCIAL CONDITIONS.
Dawood, Nawaz. Tea and poverty . Kowloon, Hong Kong , 1980. xii, 166 p. ; LC Card 80-154803 DDC 338.1/7372/095493 19
HC424 .D36 1980

Discrimination or development?. Colombo, Sri Lanka [1985?] vii, 40 p. ; LC Card 85-904128 DDC 338.9549/3 19
HC424 .D53 1985

SRI LANKA - STATISTICS, VITAL.
Report of the Registrar General on vital statistics, 1981, Sri Lanka. [Colombo] [1986] viii, 178 p. ; LC Card 86-903546 DDC 304.6/09549/3021 19
HA4570.8 .R47 1986

SRI LANKANS - EMPLOYMENT - FOREIGN COUNTRIES.
Foreign employment . [Colombo] [1985] x, 202 p. ; LC Card 87-900211 DDC 331.6/2/5493 19
HD8670.8 .F67 1985

Srinivasan, T. N., 1933-
General equilibrium trade policy modeling /. Cambridge, Mass. , c1986. vii, 360 p. : ISBN 0-262-19245-4 LC Card 85-19144 DDC 382/.3/0724 19
HF1410.5 .G46 1986 *NYPL [JLE 86-4456]*

Rural poverty in South Asia /. New York , 1988. p. cm. ISBN 0-231-06224-9 LC Card 87-9413 DDC 330.954/052/091734 19
HC440.P6 R87 1988

Srivastava, G. C. (Gyan Chand), 1939-
Urbanization, capital formation, and labour productivity in agriculture : a case study of Ranchi / by G.C. Srivastava. New Delhi : Radiant Publishers, 1986. xii, 205 p. : ill. ; 23 cm. Bibliography: p. [198]-205. ISBN 81-7027-097-9 : LC Card 86-902590 DDC 338.1/0954 19
1. Agriculture - Economic aspects - India - Rānchī - Case studies. 2. Agriculture - Economic aspects - India - Case studies. I. Title.
HD2075.R35 S75 1986

Srivastava, Leena. Energy policy issues . New Delhi , c1987. 146 p. : LC Card 87-900625 DDC 333.79/0954 19
HD9502.I42 E536 1987

Srivastava, R. K., 1942- Roy, Ramashray. Dialogues on development . New Delhi , Beverly Hills , 1986. 245 p. ; ISBN 0-8039-9492-3 (U. S.) LC Card 85-8368 DDC 338.954/12 19
HD87 .R69 1986 *NYPL [JLD 86-3196]*

SRS based abridged life tables, 1976-80. New Delhi : Vital Statistics Division, Office of the Registrar General, India, Ministry of Home Affairs, 1986. v, 37 p. : ill. ; 31 cm. (Occasional paper. no. 1 of 1985) At head of title: Census of India, 1981. "Printed by the Manager, Govt. of India Press, Nasik"--P. [4] of cover. Data on life expectancy, gleaned from the Sample Registration System (SRS) and arranged by urban/rural areas and males/females for India and constituent states. LC Card 87-901200
1. Life expectancy - India - Statistics. 2. India - Census, 1981. I. India. Vital Statistics Division. II. Census of India. III. Series: Occasional papers (India. Vital Statistics Division) , 1985, no. 1.
HB1470 .S77 1986

S.S.R.C. Labour Economics Study Group. Recent advances in labour economics /. London , New York , c1984. 258 p. : ISBN 0-312-66575-X (St. Martin's) : LC Card 83-40628 DDC 331 19
HD4813 .R28 1984 *NYPL [JLD 86-2455]*

SSSR--razvivaiushchiesia strany : torgovo-ėkonomicheskie otnosheniia / [avtorskiĭ kollektiv A.I. Bel'chuk ... et al.]. Moskva : "Mezhdunar. otnosheniia", 1985. 237 p. ; 21 cm. (Seriia "Torgovo-ėkonomicheskie otnosheniia SSSR s kapitalisticheskimi i razvivaiushchimisia stranami") On p. preceding t.p.: Akademiia nauk SSSR. Ordena Trudovogo Krasnogo Znameni Institut mirovoĭ ėkonomiki i mezhdunarodnykh otnosheniĭ. Bibliography: p. 230-[236] LC Card 86-158191
1. Soviet Union - Foreign economic relations - Developing countries. 2. Developing countries - Foreign economic relations - Soviet Union. I. Bel'chuk, Aleksandr Ivanovich. II. Institut mirovoĭ ėkonomiki i mezhdunarodnykh otnosheniĭ (Akademiia nauk SSSR). III. Series.
HF1558.5.D44 S77 1985

SSSR, SShA i Kanada : problemy torgovo-ėkonomicheskikh otnosheniĭ / [otvetstvennye redaktory A.V. Anikin, A.Z. Astapovich]. Moskva : "Mezhdunar. otnosheniia", 1987. 325 p. ; 21 cm. (Seriia "Torgovo-ėkonomicheskie otnosheniia SSSR s kapitalisticheskimi i razvivaiushchimisia stranami") On leaf preceding t.p.: Akademiia nauk SSSR. Ordena Trudovogo Krasnogo Znameni Institut mirovoĭ ėkonomiki i mezhdunarodnykh otnosheniĭ. Bibliography: p. 319-[324]. LC Card 86-205359
1. Soviet Union - Foreign economic relations - United States. 2. United States - Foreign economic relations - Soviet Union. 3. Soviet Union - Foreign economic relations - Canada. 4. Canada - Foreign economic relations - Soviet Union. I. Anikin, Andreĭ Vladimirovich. II. Astapovich, A. Z. (Aleksandr Zakharovich). III. Institut mirovoĭ ėkonomiki i mezhdunarodnykh otnosheniĭ (Akademiia nauk SSSR). IV. Series.
HF3628.U5 S77 1987

SSSR v XII piatiletke. Danilov, L. L. (Leonid Luk'ianvich), 1914- USSR, the 12th five-year plan period /. Moscow , 1986. 55 p. : LC Card 87-123056 DDC 338.947 19
HC336.25 .D378 1986

SSSR--bratstvo narodov.
Tarasov, Ivan Gavrilovich. Sled v zhizni /. Frunze , 1985. 94 p. ; LC Card 87-115075
HC337.K545 T37 1985

Zakariadze, M. Krepche stali /. Tbilisi , 1986. 51 p., [16] p. of plates : LC Card 85-172385
HD9525.S653 G469 1986

SSSR--bratstvo narodov (Frunze, Kirghiz S.S.R.)
Tarasov, Ivan Gavrilovich. Sled v zhizni /. Frunze , 1985. 94 p. ; LC Card 87-115075
HC337.K545 T37 1985

SSSR--bratstvo narodov (Tbilisi, Georgian S.S. R.)
Zakariadze, M. Krepche stali /. Tbilisi , 1986. 51 p., [16] p. of plates : LC Card 85-172385
HD9525.S653 G469 1986

St. Galler Forschungsgespräch (1984) Ethik und Wirtschaftswissenschaft /. Berlin , c1985. 276 p. : ISBN 3-428-05910-7 LC Card 86-132826
HB72 .E79 1985

St-Hilaire, France. Davies, James B., 1951- Reforming capital income taxation in Canada . [Ottawa] , c1987. ix, 153 p. : ISBN 0-660-12454-8 (pbk.) : LC Card 87-168079 DDC 336.24/24/0971 19
HJ4133.C2 .D38 1987

Staal, Frits. The stamps of Jammu & Kashmir / Frits Staal ; with a preface by H.D.S. Haverbeck and contributions by H. Garratt-Adams and B.P. Sharma. New York : Collectors Club, 1983. xvii, 286 p., 16 p. of plates : ill. (some col.), col. maps ; 24 cm. Other statement of responsibility from label on t.p. Col. maps on lining papers. Bibliography: p. 267-272. Includes index. Errata sheet inserted. ISBN 0-912574-37-X LC Card 87-402877 DDC 769.56954/6 19
1. Postage-stamps - India - Jammu and Kashmir - History - 19th century. 2. Postmarks - India - Jammu and Kashmir - History - 19th century. 3. Postal service - India - Jamma and Kashmir - History - 19th century. I. Title. II. Title: Stamps of Jammu and Kashmir.
HE6185.I53 J357 1983

Der Staat als Sanierer von Grossunternehmen . Sprink, Joachim. Idstein , 1986. 164 p. : ISBN 3-925196-20-X LC Card 86-229615
HD3646.G4 S67 1986

Staat, Gewerkschaft und Arbeitsprozess . Bernschneider, Wolfgang. Opladen , c1986. viii, 291 p. : ISBN 3-531-11797-1 LC Card 86-222066
HD5710.75.G3 B47 1986

Der Staat, ländliche Armutsgruppen und legale Bauernbewegung in den Philippinen /. Hanisch, Rolf, 1942- Baden-Baden , 1983. xii, 432 p. ; ISBN 3-7890-0980-6 LC Card 84-143058
HD1537.P5 H35 1983

Der Staat ohne Arbeitslose . Glaeser, Ernst, 1902-1963. Berlin , c1931. viii, 198 p. : LC Card 87-409524 DDC 305.5/62/0947 19
HD8526 .G53 1931

Staat, Steuern und Finanzausgleich : Probleme nationaler und internationaler Finanzwirtschaften im zeitlichen Wandel : Festschrift für Heinz Kolms zum 70. Geburtstag / herausgegeben von Walter A.S. Koch und Hans-Georg Petersen. Berlin : Duncker & Humblot, c1984. 452 p., [1] leaf of plates : ill. ; 24 cm. Includes bibliographical references. ISBN 3-428-05513-6 LC Card 84-166906
1. Fiscal policy - Germany, West. 2. Kolms, Heinz, 1914-. I. Kolms, Heinz, 1914-. II. Koch, Walter A. S. III. Petersen, Hans-Georg.
HJ1120 .S73 1984

Staat und Beschäftigung : Angebots- und Nachfragepolitik in Theorie und Praxis / Friedrich Buttler, Jürgen Kühl, Bernd Rahmann, Herausgeber. Nürnberg : Institut für Arbeitsmarkt- und Berufsforschung der Bundesanstalt für Arbeit, 1985. 471 p. : ill. ; 21 cm. (Beiträge zur Arbeitsmarkt- und Berufsforschung, 0173-6574 . 88) One paper in English. Papers from a seminar held in 1984. Includes bibliographies. LC Card 86-674027
1. Manpower policy - Congresses. 2. Employment (Economic theory) - Congresses. I. Buttler, Friedrich. II. Kühl, Jürgen. III. Rahmann, Bernd. IV. Series.
HD5713 .S72x 1985

Staat und Gesellschaft im karibischen Raum im 16. Jahrhundert /. Bonetti, Mario. München , 1984. 668 p. : ISBN 3-7705-2162-5 LC Card 85-132458 DDC 330.9729/02 19
HC151 .B66 1984

Staat und Wirtschaft (Berlin, Germany)
Ziegler, Wilhelm, 1891- Einführung in die Volkswirtschaft /. Berlin , 1925. 94, [1] p. ; LC Card 83-234150
HB175 .Z515 1925

Staatliche Allokationspolitik im marktwirtschaftlichen System, 0721-2860 .
(Bd. 18) Kontrolltheoretische Ansätze in makroökonometrischen Modellen /. Frankfurt am Main , New York , c1985. 170 p. : ISBN 3-8204-8314-4 LC Card 86-156081
HB3732 .K68 1985

(Bd. 19) Kempf, Theo, 1955- Theorie und Empirie betrieblicher Ausbildungsplatzangebote /. Frankfurt am Main , New York , c1985. 305 p. : ISBN 3-8204-8358-6 LC Card 86-111326
HF5549.5.T7 K42 1985

Staatliche Eingriffe in den Mietwohnungsmarkt, Erfolgskontrolle und Reformvorschläge /. Eucker-Herresthal, Waltraud. [Mainz] [1985?] v, 242 p. ; LC Card 87-407601 DDC 363.5/8 19
HD7288.85.G3 E92 1985

Staatliche Exportabsicherung . Hichert, Ingo, 1944- Köln , c1986. 302 p. : ISBN 3-602-34848-2 LC Card 87-145196 DDC 368.8/7 19
HG9977.4.G3 H53 1986

Staatliche Wirtschaftsregulierung in der Krise : Veröffentlichung der Hochschule für Wirtschaft und Politik Hamburg. Opladen : Westdeutscher Verlag, c1986. 241 p. ; 23 cm. (Jahrbuch für Sozialökonomie und Gesellschaftstheorie) Articles by Peter Beutler ... [et al.] Includes bibliographies. ISBN 3-531-11805-6 LC Card 86-228864
1. Economic policy. 2. Economic stabilization. 3. Business cycles. 4. Keynesian economics. I. Beutler, Peter. II. Hochschule für Wirtschaft und Politik Hamburg. III. Series.
HD84 .S69 1986

Staatsausgaben, Produktion und Beschäftigung . Busch, Wilfried, 1948- Frankfurt am Main , New York , c1984. viii, 304 p. : ISBN 3-8204-5352-0 LC Card 85-199154
HJ7792 .B87 1984

Staatsfinanzierung im Wandel : Verhandlungen auf der Jahrestagung des Vereins für Socialpolitik, Gesellschaft für Wirtschafts- und Sozialwissenschaften in Köln 1982 / herausgegeben von Karl-Heinrich Hansmeyer. Berlin : Duncker & Humblot, c1983. xi, 877 p. : ill. ; 24 cm. (Schriften des Vereins für Socialpolitik, Gesellschaft für Wirtschafts- und Sozialwissenschaften . n. F., Bd. 134) Includes bibliographical references. ISBN 3-428-05420-2
1. Finance, Public - Germany, West - Congresses. 2. Finance, Public - Congresses. I. Hansmeyer, Karl-Heinrich. II. Series. III. Series: Gesellschaft für Wirtschafts- und Sozialwissenschaften, Verein für Socialpolitik. Schriften, Bd. 134. 134.
NYPL [JLL 73-186 Bd. 134]

Staatsfinanzierung und Notenbank : Referate und Diskussionszusammenfassungen des Symposiums am 4./5. April 1984 in Innsbruck/Igls / Karl Socher, Christian Smekal (Hrsg.). Wien : Österreichisches Forschungsinstitut für Sparkassenwesen, [1984?] 211 p. : ill. ; 24 cm. (Dr. Stigleitner-Schriftenreihe. Bd. 24) Includes bibliographical references. CONTENTS. - Entwicklung der Staatsfinanzierung durch die Notenbank in Deutschland / Werner Ehrlicher -- Entwicklung der Staatsfinanzierung durch die Notenbank in Deutschland, Nachkriegszeit / Alois Oberhauser -- Geschichte der Staatsfinanzierung durch die Notenbank in Österreich / Hans Kernbauer, Eduard März -- Staatsfinanzierung durch die Notenbank, pro und contra / Rolf Caesar -- Staatsfinanzierung durch die Notenbank aus der Sicht der politischen Ökonomie / Peter Bernholz -- Staatsfinanzierung durch die Notenbank aus der Sicht der Geldordnung / Wolfgang Schmitz -- Staatsfinanzierung durch die Notenbank in finanzwirtschaftlicher Sicht / Otto Gandenberger -- Staastfinanzierung und Notenbank aus finanzwirtschaftlicher Sicht / Dietrich Dickertmann -- Notenbank und Stabilisierungspolitik / Ewald Nowotny -- Staatsinanzierung durch die Notenbank aus konjunktur- und strukturpolitischer Sicht / Jürgen Pahlke. LC Card 85-198128
1. Banks and banking, Central - Congresses. 2. Finance, Public - Congresses. 3. Economic policy - Congresses. 4. Banks and banking, Central - Germany (West) - Congresses. 5. Finance, Public - Germany, West - Congresses. 6. Germany, West - Economic policy - Congresses. 7. Banks and banking, Central - Austria - Congresses. 8. Finance, Public - Austria - Congresses. 9. Austria - Economic policy - Congresses. I. Socher, Karl. II. Smekal, Christian.
HG1811 .S78 1984

Staatsgrenzen : Probleme (national-) staatlichen Handelns in der alternativen Wirtschaftspolitik / herausgegeben von Michael Ernst-Poerksen ... [et al.] ; mit Beiträgen von Elmar Altvater ... [et al.]. Berlin : Argument-Verlag, c1982. 183 p. ; 19 cm. (Alternative Wirtschaftspolitik . 4) Argument-Sonderband ; AS 89 Includes bibliographies. CONTENTS. - "Das Diktat der Zahlungsbilanz" / Elmar Altvater ... [et al.] -- Aussenwirtschaftliche Aspekte einer alternativen Wirtschaftspolitik / Karl Georg Zinn -- Disproportion zwischen Realkapital und Geldkapitalakkumulation / Stephan Krüger -- Abbruch-Unternehmer-Staat / Bernd Walter Prior -- Marx und Keynes / Jörg Glombowski -- Keynesianische Fundamentalisten und die Krise der herrschenden Keynes-Interpretation / Rolf Behrens, Otto Steiger -- Zur Entmythologisierung Sraffas / Georgios Stamatis. ISBN 3-88619-089-7 LC Card 84-142799
1. Comparative economics. 2. Keynesian economics. 3. Marxian economics. 4. Germany, West - Economic policy. I. Ernst-Poerksen, Michael. II. Altvater, Elmar. III. Series. IV. Series: Argument - Sonderbände, AS 89.
HB90 .S75 1982

Staatsmonopolistische Intensivierung und Widersprüche der Reproduktion / Autorenkollektiv, Maritta Bernien ... [et al.]. Berlin : Staatsverlag der Deutschen Demokratischen Republik, [1986] 127 p. ; 22 cm. (IPW-Forschungshefte, 0322-3901 . 4/1986) Summaries in English, French, German, Russian, and Spanish. Includes bibliographical references. LC Card 87-408424 DDC 330 s 338/.06 19
1. Industrial productivity. 2. Government business enterprises. I. Bernien, Maritta. II. Series: IPW-Forschungshefte , 1986/4.
HC281 .B39 1986, Heft 4 HC79.I52

Staatsschulden und Reformpolitik . Ullmann, Hans-Peter. Göttingen , c1986. 2 v. (842 p.) ; ISBN 3-525-35398-7 LC Card 86-210338
HJ8655.B38 U55 1986

Der Staatssektor in der Input-Output-Rechnung . Krüger-Hemmer, Christiane. Essen , 1982. 175 p. ; LC Card 87-408033 DDC 339.2/3/0943 19
HC290.5.I57 K78 1982

Staatsversagen . Jänicke, Martin. München , c1986. 227 p. : ISBN 3-492-02984-1 LC Card 86-230931
HD84 .J36 1986

Staatsverschuldung . Hablützel, Peter. Basel , c1984. 96 p. : ISBN 3-7190-0864-9 LC Card 84-159813
HJ8749 .H33 1984

Staatsverschuldung, Hintergründe und Probleme /. Piel, Manfred, 1945- [Staatsverschuldung, Schicksalsfrage der Nation?] Stuttgart [1982] 128 p. ; LC Card 83-118137
HJ8654 .P52 1982

Staatsverschuldung ohne Ende? /. Ahrens, Gerhard, 1939- Hamburg [1984] 37 leaves ; LC Card 85-166341
HJ8650 .A37 1984

La stabilisation des prix des matières premières . Delmas, Philippe. Paris , 1983. vii, 359 p. : ISBN 2-7178-0657-1 : LC Card 84-116258
HF1051 .D38 1983

Stability and change in American politics . Delli Carpini, Michael X., 1953- New York , 1986. xxv, 374 p. ; ISBN 0-8147-1780-2 (alk. paper) : LC Card 85-15348 DDC 323/.042/0973 19
JK1764 .D45 1986 ***NYPL [JLE 86-2183]***

STABILIZATION, ECONOMIC. see **ECONOMIC STABILIZATION.**

STABILIZATION OF EMPLOYMENT. see **EMPLOYMENT STABILIZATION.**

Stabilization policy in France and the Federal Republic of Germany / edited by G. De Ménil and U. Westphal. Amsterdam ; New York : North Holland ; xii, 379 p. : ill. ; 24 cm. (Contributions to economic analysis. 153 153) Includes bibliographies. ISBN 0-444-87529-8 LC Card 84-28614 DDC 338.943 19
1. Economic stabilization - France - Addresses, essays, lectures. 2. Economic stabilization - Germany (West) - Addresses, essays, lectures. 3. France - Economic policy - 1945- - Addresses, essays, lectures. 4. Germany, West - Economic policy - 1974- - Addresses, essays, lectures. I. De Menil, George, 1940-. II. Westphal, Uwe. III. Series.
HC276.2 .S77 1985 ***NYPL [TB (Contributions to economic analysis. no.153)]***

Stabilizing speculative commodity markets /. Ghosh, S. Oxford [Oxfordshire] , New York , 1987. xiii, 437 p. : ISBN 0-19-828472-1 : LC Card 86-32654 DDC 332.64/4 19
HG6046 .G485 1987

Stackelberg, Friedrich von. Verkehrs- und unternehmenspolitische Anpassungsstrategien an veränderte Ressourcenbewertungen /. Göttingen , 1986. 210 p. : ISBN 3-525-85699-7 : LC Card 86-223574
HE131 .M8 Heft 109 HE249

Stadler, Manfred. Gahlen, Bernhard. Zur internationalen Wettbewerbsfähigkeit der deutschen Wirtschaft /. [Berlin] [1985] 41, 4 p. ; LC Card 86-204589
HC286.7 .G29 1985

Stadsboek Leuven / [redactie, Jaak Brepoels ... et al.]. Leuven : Kritak, c1985. 259 p. : ill. ; 21 cm. ISBN 90-6303-137-8 : LC Card 86-204792
1. Louvain (Belgium) - Economic conditions. 2. Louvain (Belgium) - Politics and government. 3. Louvain (Belgium) - Social conditions. I. Brepoels, Jaak.
HC318.L6 S73 1985

Stadt, Planung, Geschichte .
(Bd. 7) Kujath, Hans Joachim. Die Regeneration der Stadt . Hamburg , c1986. 282 p. ; ISBN 3-7672-0943-8 LC Card 87-113493 DDC 363.5/8 19
HD7339.A3 K85 1986

(1) Wohnen . Hamburg , c1983. 230 p. : ISBN 3-7672-0808-3 LC Card 83-219819 DDC 363.5/0943 19
HD7339.A3 W616 1983
NYPL [JLE 86-3338]

Stadt und Hafen : Hamburger Beiträge zur Geschichte von Handel und Schiffahrt / herausgegeben von Jürgen Ellermeyer und Rainer Postel. Hamburg : H. Christians, 1986. 209 p. : ill. ; 30 cm. (Arbeitshefte zur Denkmalpflege in Hamburg . Nr. 8) Papers presented at a meeting sponsored by the Hamburger Arbeitskreis für Regionalgeschichte, Feb. 2-4, 1984. Includes bibliographies. ISBN 3-7672-0951-9 LC Card 87-130912 DDC 387.1/0943/515 19
1. Harbors - Germany (West) - Hamburg - History. 2. Hamburg (Germany) - Commerce - History. I. Ellermeyer, Jürgen. II. Postel, Rainer. III. Hamburger Arbeitskreis für Regionalgeschichte. IV. Series.
HE558.H3 S7 1986

Stadtarchiv Unna (Germany) Mark (Grafschaft) Schatzbuch der Grafschaft Mark, 1486 /. Unna , 1986. 176 p. ; ISBN 3-87298-042-4 LC Card 87-116701 DDC 336.2/00943/55 19
HJ2110.5.M36 M37 1986

Stadtbahn für Würzburg . Naumann, Thomas. Würzburg , 1985. 237 p., [3] leaves of plates : LC Card 86-166915
HE4779.W84 N38 1985

Städte in Zahlen : ein Strukturbericht zum Thema Bevölkerung / Verfasser, Hans-Rainer Burisch ... [et al.] ; Datenerfassung und Aufbereitung, Bundesforschungsanstalt für Landeskunde und Raumordnung, Bonn-Bad Godesberg ; Redaktion, Erhard Hruschka, Egon Dheus. Hamburg : Verband Deutscher Städtestatistiker, 1985. 199 p. : ill. ; 30 cm. (Städte in Zahlen . Heft 3, Bevölkerung) ISBN 3-922421-11-3 LC Card 86-212560
1. Germany, West - Population - Statistics. I. Burisch, Hans-Rainer. II. Bundesforschungsanstalt für Landeskunde und Raumordnung. III. Series: Städte in Zahlen , Heft 3.
HB2265 .S73 1985

Städte und Steuern in der Politik Julians . Pack, Edgar. Bruxelles , 1986. 420 p. ; ISBN 2-87031-134-6 LC Card 87-105922 DDC 336.2/014/37 19
HJ9497.A3 P33 1986

Städteforschung. Reihe A: Darstellungen.
(Bd. 14) Städtewesen und Merkantilismus in Mitteleuropa /. Köln , 1983. xii, 333 p. : ISBN 3-412-00382-4 LC Card 83-155285
HF1531 .S688 1983

(Bd. 24) See- und Flusshäfen vom Hochmittelalter bis zur Industrialisierung /. Köln , 1986. xxi, 315 p. : ISBN 3-412-07585-X LC Card 87-146564 DDC 387.1/094 19
HE557.A3 S37 1986

Städtewesen und Merkantilismus in Mitteleuropa / herausgegeben von Volker Press. Köln :

Böhlau, 1983. xii, 333 p. : ill. ; 27 cm. (Städteforschung. Reihe A: Darstellungen. Bd. 14) Papers presented at a conference. Includes bibliographical references and index. CONTENTS. - Der Merkantilismus und die Städte / Volker Press -- Die Währungspolitik der grossen deutschen Handelsstädte und der fürstlichen Flächenstaaten Mitteleuropas im Zeitalter des Absolutismus / Hans Mauersberg -- Ziele und Massnahmen landesherrlicher Politik im Absolutismus gegenüber den Städten aus der Sicht des Verwaltungshistorikers / Walther Hubatsch -- Merkantilismus und zeitgenössische Rechtswissenschaft / Jürgen Weitzel -- Österreichs Städte zwischen Türkenkriegen und staatlichen Absolutismus / Karl Gutkas -- Die Stadt im süddeutschen Kleinstaat des Ancien Régime / Wolfgang Leiser -- Reichsstadt und Merkantilismus / Wolfgang Klötzer -- Die Gründung von "Hugenottenstädten" als wirtschaftspolitische Massnahme eines merkantilistischen Landesherrn / Margaret Zumstrull -- Merkantilismus und Städtewesen in Kursachsen / Richard Dietrich -- Bergstädte und Merkantilismus in Oberschlesien und Kleinpolen im XVII. Jahrhundert / Danuta Molenda -- Der preussische Spätmerkantilismus und die Manufakturstädte in den mittleren und östlichen Staatsprovinzen (1740-1806) / Gerd Heinrich. ISBN 3-412-00382-4 LC Card 83-155285
1. Central Europe - Commercial policy - History - Congresses. 2. Mercantile system - Central Europe - History - Congresses. 3. Cities and towns - Central Europe - History - Congresses. I. Press, Volker. II. Series.
HF1531 .S688 1983

Staehelin, Max, 1909- Schweizer Banken und Schweizer Wirtschaft im Wandel der Zeit / Max Staehelin. Zürich : Thomas-Verlag, c1984. 261 p. : ill. ; 22 cm. Includes bibliographical references. LC Card 84-212396
1. Banks and banking - Switzerland. 2. Switzerland - Economic conditions - 1918-. I. Title.
HG3204 .S77 1984

Staehle, Wolfgang H., 1938- Betriebswirtschaftslehre und ökonomische Krise . Wiesbaden , c1984. xxix, 412 p. : ISBN 3-409-13037-3 LC Card 85-143204
HD30.23 .B49 1984

Elias, Hermann-Josef, 1949- Gestaltung und Bewertung von Arbeitssystemen /. Frankfurt am Main , New York , c1985. 281 p. : ISBN 3-593-33444-5 LC Card 85-143343
HF5549.5.J6 E45 1985

Stände und frühmoderner Staat . Walz, Rainer. Neustadt an der Aisch , 1982. 257 p., [1] leaf of plates : ISBN 3-87707-040-9 LC Card 83-215104
HJ2675 .W35 1982

Staff report on modification no. 86-13 to New York City's FYs 1986-1989 financial plan, February 1986 / New York State Financial Control Board. [Albany, N.Y.] : The Board, [1986] 128 leaves ; 29 cm. (Staff report / New York State Financial Control Board) "February 19, 1986." LC Card 86-622416 DDC 352.1/09747/1 19
1. Finance, Public - New York (N.Y.). I. New York State Financial Control Board. II. Series: Staff report / New York State Financial Control Board.
HJ9289.N4 S734 1986

Staff report on modification no. 86-8 to New York City's FYs 1986-1989 financial plan. [Albany] : New York State Financial Control Board, [1985] 92 leaves ; 28 cm. (Staff report / New York Financial Control Board) "December 11, 1985." Includes bibliographical references. LC Card 86-622159 DDC 336.747/1 19
1. Finance, Public - New York (N.Y.). I. New York State Financial Control Board. II. Series: Staff report / New York State Financial Control Board.
HJ9289.N4 S73 1985

Staff report on proposed modification no. 86-12 to New York City's financial plan relating to the New York City Transit Authority and Staten Island Rapid Transit Operating Authority. [Albany] : New York State Financial Control Board, [1986] 27 leaves ; 29 cm. (Staff report / New York State Financial Control Board) "February 13, 1986." LC Card 86-622415 DDC 388.4/042 19
1. Local transit - New York (N.Y.) - Finance. I. New York State Financial Control Board. II. Series: Staff report / New York State Financial Control Board.
HE4491.N65 S7 1986

Staff seminar paper (Chancellor College) . (no. 51) Kandoole, B. F. Revenue and equity effects of the 1983 income tax reform in Malawi /. [Zomba, Malaŵi?] [1986] 20 p. ; LC Card 86-981440 DDC 336.2/0096897 19
HJ4791 .K36 1986

Staff studies . (143) Schroeder, Frederick J. Compliance costs and consumer benefits of the Electronic Fund Transfer Act . Washington, D.C. , 1985. 23 p. : LC Card 86-603417 DDC 332.1/028 19
HG1710 .S38 1985

Staff studies for the world economic outlook / by the Research Department of the International Monetary Fund. Washington, D.C. : The Fund, c1986. xi, 195 p. : ill. (some col.) ; 28 cm. (World economic and financial surveys, 0258-7440) "July 1986." Includes bibliographies. LC Card 86-202629 DDC 338.5/443 19
1. Economic forecasting. 2. Economic history - 1971-. I. International Monetary Fund. Research Dept. II. Series.
HC59 .S682 1986

Staffelbach, Bruno. Strategisches Personalmanagement / Bruno Staffelbach. Bern : P. Haupt, [1986] x, 285 p. : ill. ; 23 cm. (Schriftenreihe des Instituts für Betriebswirtschaftliche Forschung an der Universität Zürich . Bd. 55) Bibliography: p. 265-285. ISBN 3-258-03626-8 : LC Card 86-211191
1. Personnel management - Planning. I. Title. II. Series.
HF5549 .S842416 1986

Staffing for optimum performance /. Sears, Victoria Loufakis. New York, N.Y. , c1986. iv, 191 p. : ISBN 0-88057-403-8 (pbk.) LC Card 85-80707 DDC 658.3/112 19
HF5549.5.S38 S4 1986

Staffing patterns for manufacturing industries and hospitals / Occupational Employment Statistics Program. Little Rock, Ark. : Research and Analysis Section, Employment Security Division, [1983?] vi leaves, 249 p. ; 28 cm. LC Card 86-623216 DDC 331.12/57/09767 19
1. Labor Supply - Arkansas - Statistics. 2. Arkansas - Occupations - Statistics. 3. Arkansas - Manufactures - Employees - Statistics. 4. Hospitals - Arkansas - Staff - Statistics. I. Occupational Employment Statistics Program (Ark.).
HD5725.A8 S79 1983

Staffing the contemporary organization . Caruth, Donald L. New York , 1988. xii, 309 p. : ISBN 0-89930-236-X (lib. bdg. : alk. paper) LC Card 87-13092 DDC 658.3 19
HF5549 .C296 1988

Stafford, D. C. Albon, Robert, 1951- Rent control /. London ; New York : xi, 128 p. : ISBN 0-7099-5411-5 LC Card 87-15899 DDC 363.5/6/0941 19
HD7288.85.G7 A4 1987

Stafford, J. T. The share-owner's guide / J.T. Stafford. Cambridge [Cambridgeshire] ; Wolfeboro, N.H., USA : Woodhead-Faulkner, 1988. p. cm. (A Woodhead-Faulkner moneyguide) Includes index. ISBN 0-85941-402-7 (pbk.) : LC Card 87-17387 DDC 332.63/22 19
1. Stocks - United States - Handbooks, manuals, etc. I. Title. II. Series.
HG4921 .S617 1988

Stafford, Walter W. Closed labor markets : underrepresentation of Blacks, Hispanics, and women in New York City's core industries and jobs / by Walter W. Stafford. New York, N.Y. (105 E. 22nd St., New York 10010) : Community Service Society of New York, c1985. xvi, 203, 3, [2] p. ; 28 cm. Bibliography: p. [1]-[2] (4th group) LC Card 85-186853 DDC 331.12/09747/1 19
1. Labor supply - New York (N.Y.). 2. Afro-Americans - Employment - New York (N.Y.). 3. Hispanic Americans - Employment - New York (N.Y.). 4. Women - Employment - New York (N.Y.). 5. New York (N.Y.) - Occupations. I. Title.
HD5726.N5 S73 1985 ***NYPL [Sc F 86-274]***

Stagflation as a consequence of an expansionary monetary or fiscal policy under flexible exchange rates /. Herberg, Horst. Stockholm, Sweden [1978] 34 leaves ; LC Card 81-116937
HD5710 .H47 1978

Stagflation in the U. S.S.R. Adirim, I. G. (Itskhok Girshevich) Stagflation in the USSR /. Falls Church, VA (7700 Leesburg Pike, #212, Falls Church 22043) [1983] xi, 122 leaves ; LC Card 84-162596 DDC 332.4/1/0947 19
HC340.I5 A44 1983 ***NYPL [JLF 86-1839]***

Stagflation in the USSR /. Adirim, I. G. (Itskhok Girshevich) Falls Church, VA (7700 Leesburg Pike, #212, Falls Church 22043) [1983] xi, 122 leaves ; LC Card 84-162596 DDC 332.4/1/0947 19
HC340.I5 A44 1983 ***NYPL [JLF 86-1839]***

Stagflation, savings, and the state : perspectives on the global economy / edited by Deepak Lal and Martin Wolf. New York : Oxford University Press, 1986. xii, 402 p. : ill. ; 25 cm. (A World Bank research publication) "Published for the World Bank." Includes bibliographies and index. ISBN 0-19-520496-4 LC Card 85-31981 DDC 330.9172/4 19
1. Unemployment - Effect of inflation on - Addresses, essays, lectures. 2. Debts, External - Developing countries - Addresses, essays, lectures. 3. Developing countries - Economic conditions - Addresses, essays, lectures. I. Lal, Deepak. II. Wolf, Martin.
HG229 .S74 1986 ***NYPL [JLE 86-2621]***

Stagnation and the financial explosion /. Magdoff, Harry. New York , c1987. 208 p. : ISBN 0-85345-716-6 : LC Card 86-33129 DDC 330.973/0927 19
HC106.8 .M315 1987b

STAGNATION (ECONOMICS)
Adirim, I. G. (Itskhok Girshevich) Stagflation in the USSR /. Falls Church, VA (7700 Leesburg Pike, #212, Falls Church 22043) [1983] xi, 122 leaves ; LC Card 84-162596 DDC 332.4/1/0947 19
HC340.I5 A44 1983 ***NYPL [JLF 86-1839]***

Jones, Aubrey, 1911- Britain's economy . Cambridge [Cambridgeshire] , New York , 1985. x, 158 p. : ISBN 0-521-30816-X LC Card 85-9649 DDC 330.941/0858 19
HC256.6 .J64 1985 ***NYPL [JLD 86-1581]***

Stagnation in der Geldwirtschaft . Spahn, Heinz-Peter. Frankfurt , New York , c1986. 304 p. : ISBN 3-593-33691-X LC Card 86-225253
HD5710 .S68 1986

Stagner, Ross, 1909- Psychology of industrial conflict / Ross Stagner. New York : Garland Pub., 1987, c1956. ix, 550 p. : ill. ; 23 cm. (Continuity in administrative science) Reprint. Originally published: New York : Wiley, c1956. Bibliography: p. 515-539. Includes indexes. ISBN 0-8240-8218-4 (alk. paper) : LC Card 86-27080 DDC 158.7 19
1. Psychology, Industrial. 2. Industrial relations. I. Title. II. Series.
HF5548.8 .S713 1987

Stahl, Herbert. Clusteranalyse grosser Objektmengen mit problemorientierten Distanzmassen / Herbert Stahl. Thun : H. Deutsch, c1985. ii, vi, 323 p. : ill. ; 21 cm. (Reihe Wirtschaftswissenschaften, 0253-1488 . Bd. 338) Bibliography: p. 313-323. ISBN 3-87144-908-3 LC Card 86-112498
1. Social sciences - Statistical methods. 2. Cluster analysis. I. Title. II. Series.
HA29.5.G4 S68 1985

Stahl, Konrad, 1941- Microeconomic models of housing markets /. Berlin , New York , c1985. iv, 197 p. : ISBN 0-387-15193-1 (pbk.) LC Card 85-4648 DDC 381/.4569083/0724 19
HD7339.A3 M53 1985
NYPL [JLM 72-289 no.239]

Stahl und Eisen bricht : Industrie und staatliche Politik in Österreich / Margit Scherb, Inge Morawetz (Hg.). Wien : Verlag für Gesellschaftskritik, [1986] xi, 202 p. : ill. ; 22 cm. (Österreichische Texte zur Gesellschaftskritik . Bd. 28) Includes bibliographies. CONTENTS. - Aspekte der österreichischen Industrieentwicklung / Johanna Groinig -- Evaluierung der Effizienz der staatlichen Instrumente zur Investitionsförderung / Kurt Bayer -- Soziale Kriterien in der staatlichen Technologieförderung / Jörg Flecker -- Telekommunikation in Österreich / Johannes M. Bauer -- Personelle Verflechtungen der verstaatlichten Industrie mit der Privatindustrie / Inge Morawetz -- Die Österreichische Mineralölverwaltungs AG zwischen nationalen Aufgaben und internationalen Interessen / Rosmarie Atzenhofer -- SPÖ und verstaatlichte Industrie, oder, Die Angst vor dem Fliegen / Margit Scherb -- Schein und Wirklichkeit einer Krisenregion / Klaus Unterberger -- Abschied von der Tiefbohrtechnik / Erwin Holzer. ISBN 3-900351-62-7 LC Card 87-140293 DDC 330.9436/053 19

1. Austria - Economic conditions - 1945-. 2. Austria - Industries. 3. Industry and state - Austria. 4. Iron industry and trade - Austria - Sytria - Case studies. I. Scherb, Margit, 1953-. II. Morawetz, Inge, 1955-. III. Series.
HC265 .S736 1986

Stahl- und Leichtmetallbau, Schienenfahrzeugbau . Mayer, Ralph-Dieter. Berlin , c1985. 352 p. : ISBN 3-428-05771-6 LC Card 85-161158
HD9523.5 .M3 1985

Stahlecker, Peter. Konzentration und gesamtwirtschaftliche Stabilität : eine theoretische und empirische Analyse / Peter Stahlecker. Frankfurt am Main ; New York : P. Lang, c1984. v, 592 p. : ill. ; 21 cm. (Europäische Hochschulschriften. Reihe V, Volks- und Betriebswirtschaft, 0531-7339 . Bd. 506 = vol. 506 = vol. 506) Bibliography: p. 579-592. ISBN 3-8204-5318-0 LC Card 85-192714
1. Industrial concentration - Mathematical models. 2. Economic stabilization - Mathematical models. 3. Industrial concentration - Germany (West) - Econometric models. 4. Economic stabilization - Germany (West) - Econometric models. I. Series: Europäische Hochschulschriften. Reihe V, Volks- und Betriebswirtschaft , Bd. 506. II. Title.
HD2757 .S78 1984

Stahlknecht, Peter. Einführung in die Wirtschaftsinformatik / Peter Stahlknecht. 2., überarbeitete und erw. Aufl. Berlin ; New York : Springer-Verlag, c1985. xiv, 396 p. : ill. ; 21 cm. (Heidelberger Taschenbücher. Bd. 231) Bibliography: p. [371]-378. Includes index. ISBN 0-387-15466-3 (U. S.) LC Card 86-219262
1. Business - Data processing. I. Title.
HF5548.2 .S7725 1985

Stahmer, Carsten, 1942- Reich, Utz-Peter. Darstellungskonzepte der Input-Output-Rechnung /. Stuttgart , 1984. 185 p. : ISBN 3-17-003301-8
NYPL [JLE 86-1264]

Stai, Anette.
Crazy business : fotomodellens dagbok / Anette Stai. Oslo : Dreyer, c1984. 146 p., [48] p. of plates : ill. (some col.) ; 25 cm. ISBN 82-09-10210-9 LC Card 85-160098
1. Stai, Anette - Diaries. 2. Models, Fashion - Norway - Diaries. I. Title.
HD6073.M772 N677 1984

STAI, ANETTE - DIARIES.
Stai, Anette. Crazy business . Oslo , c1984. 146 p., [48] p. of plates : ISBN 82-09-10210-9 LC Card 85-160098
HD6073.M772 N677 1984

Staiger, Brunhild. Louven, Erhard. Shanghai, Chinas Tor zur Welt /. Hamburg , 1986. 118 p. : LC Card 86-230755
HC428.S47 L68 1986

STAKHANOV MOVEMENT.
Preemstvennost´ stakhanovskikh tradit͡siĭ . Moskva , 1985. 222 p. ; LC Card 85-234107
HC340.S6 P68 1985

STAKHANOV MOVEMENT - HISTORY.
Siegelbaum, Lewis H. Stakhanovism and the politics of productivity in the USSR, 1935-1941 /. Cambridge , New York , 1988. xv, 326 p. : ISBN 0-521-34548-0 LC Card 87-25605 DDC 331.11/8/0947 19
HC340.S6 S515 1988

Stakhanovism and the politics of productivity in the USSR, 1935-1941 /. Siegelbaum, Lewis H. Cambridge , New York , 1988. xv, 326 p. : ISBN 0-521-34548-0 LC Card 87-25605 DDC 331.11/8/0947 19
HC340.S6 S515 1988

Stalemate . Winant, Howard. New York , 1988. xv, 203 p. ; ISBN 0-275-92706-3 (alk. paper) : LC Card 87-15157 DDC 338.973 19
HC106.6 .W56 1988

STALIN, JOSEPH, 1879-1953.
Kuromiya, Hiroaki. Stalin's industrial revolution . Cambridge [Cambridgeshire] , New York , 1988. p. cm. ISBN 0-521-35157-X LC Card 87-25010 DDC 338.947 19
HC335.4 .K87 1988

Stålindustri, kriseregioner og fagbevægelse : rapport fra ekskursion til centrale industridistrikter i Vesteuropa, marts 1983 / Bue Nielsen, Bent Schou, (red.). [Copenhagen] : Geografisk centralinstitut, Københavns universitet, Laboratorium for almen kulturgeografi, 1983. 217 p. : ill. ; 30 cm. Includes bibliographies. LC Card 84-169019
1. Steel industry and trade - Europe. 2. Europe - Economic conditions - 1945-. 3. Trade-unions - Iron and steel workers - Europe. I. Nielsen, Bue. II. Schou, Bent.
HD9525.E752 S73 1983

STALINGRAD, BATTLE OF, 1942-1943.
Chuĭkov, V. I. (Vasiliĭ Ivanovich), 1900- Ot Stalingrada do Berlina /. Moskva , 1985. 699 p. : ***NYPL [*QGR 87-2179]***

Stalin's industrial revolution . Kuromiya, Hiroaki. Cambridge [Cambridgeshire] , New York , 1988. p. cm. ISBN 0-521-35157-X LC Card 87-25010 DDC 338.947 19
HC335.4 .K87 1988

Stallings, Barbara. Banker to the Third World : U. S. portfolio investment in Latin America, 1900-1986 / Barbara Stallings. Berkeley : University of California Press, c1987. xvii, 434 p. : ill. ; 22 cm. (Studies in international political economy. 18) Bibliography: p. 379-422. Includes index. ISBN 0-520-05726-0 (alk. paper) LC Card 86-24988 DDC 332.6/7373/08 19
1. Investments, American - Latin America - History. 2. Loans, American - Latin America - History. I. Title. II. Title: Banker to the 3rd World. III. Series.
HG5160.5.A3 S73 1987

Stallings, John W., 1923- Britton, Paul R., 1933- Leadership is empowering people /. Lanham, MD , c1986. xxviii, 346 p. ; ISBN 0-8191-5409-1 (alk. paper) : LC Card 86-9193 DDC 658.3/14 19
HD57.7 .B75 1986 ***NYPL [JLD 86-3818]***

Stallworthy, E. A. (Ernest A.) Kharbanda, Om Prakesh. Successful projects, with a moral for management /. Hants, England , c1986. xvii, 267 p. : ISBN 0-566-02651-1 LC Card 86-235562 DDC 658.4/04 19
HD69.P75 K55 1986

Stamatis, Georg. Sraffa und sein Verhältnis zu Ricardo und Marx / Georgios Stamatis ; mit einem Anhang, Non-basics, the standard commodity, and the uniformity of the profit rate (1982) von Spyridon Vassilakis. Göttingen : Verein zur Förderung Gesellschaftstheoretischer Studien ; Lollar : Auslieferung, Prolit-Buchvertrieb, c1984. ix, 459 p. : ill. ; 21 cm. (Göttinger Beiträge zur Gesellschaftstheorie . 5) Bibliography: p. 448-459. ISBN 3-921701-04-X LC Card 84-213549
1. Sraffa, Piero. 2. Ricardo, David, 1772-1823. 3. Marx, Karl, 1818-1883. 4. Economics. I. Vassilakis, Spyridon. Non-basics, the standard commodity, and the uniformity of the profit rate. 1984. II. Title. III. Series.
HB103.S7 S73 1984

Stamets, John, 1949- Portrait of a market : photographs of Seattle's Pike Place Market / John Stamets ; with text by Steve Dunnington.1st ed. Seattle : Real Comet Press, 1987. 95 p. : chiefly ill. ; 25 x 27 cm. ISBN 0-941104-17-6 (pbk.) : LC Card 87-4746 DDC 381/.18/0979777 19
1. Pike Place Market (Seattle, Wash.) - Pictorial works. 2. Markets - Washington (State) - Seattle - Pictorial works. 3. Seattle (Wash.) - Description - Views. 4. Seattle (Wash.) - Social life and customs - Pictorial works. I. Dunnington, Steve, 1950-. II. Title.
HF5472.U7 S48 1987

Stammer, Robert. National Conference on Microcomputers in Urban Transportation (1985 : San Diego, Calif.) Microcomputer applications within the urban transportation environment . New York, N.Y. , c1985. 824 p. : ISBN 0-87262-508-7 (pbk.) LC Card 85-73250 DDC 388.4/028/5416 19
HE305 .N33 1985 ***NYPL [JSD 86-535]***

Stammwerk Henkel, achtzig Jahre in Düsseldorf-Holthausen. Schöne, Manfred, 1935- Stammwerk Henkel, 80 Jahre in Düsseldorf-Holthausen /. Düsseldorf , 1981. 148 p. : LC Card 86-216690
HD9654.9.H444 S36 1981

Stammwerk Henkel, 80 Jahre in Düsseldorf-Holthausen /. Schöne, Manfred, 1935- Düsseldorf , 1981. 148 p. : LC Card 86-216690
HD9654.9.H444 S36 1981

Stamos, Steve, 1947-
Energy economics . Englewood Cliffs, N.J. , c1987. viii, 328 p. : ISBN 0-13-277245-0 : LC Card 86-25254 DDC 333.79/0973 19
HD9502.U52 E4874 1987
Pool, John Charles. The ABCs of international finance . Lexington, Mass. , c1987. xii, 138 p. ; ISBN 0-669-15605-1 (alk. paper) LC Card 86-45933 DDC 332/.042 19
HG3851 .P66 1987

STAMP-COLLECTING AND STAMP COLLECTORS. see POSTAGE STAMPS - COLLECTORS AND COLLECTING.

Stamp issue of 12th March 1984. Die Briefmarkenausgabe vom 12. März 1984 =. Vaduz [1984?] 41 p. : LC Card 84-248309
HE6184.F57 B75 1984

STAMPED ENVELOPES - SOVIET UNION - CATALOGS.
Orlov, V. A. (Vasiliĭ Adamovich) Khudozhestvennye markirovannye konverty SSSR . Moskva , 1984. 120 p. : LC Card 84-168398
HE6185.S652 O75 1984

Stampfl, Ronald W. Davidson, William R. Retailing management /. New York , c1988. xix, 876 p. : ISBN 0-471-85094-2 LC Card 87-10555 DDC 658.8/7 19
HF5429 .D334 1988

The stamps of Jammu & Kashmir /. Staal, Frits. New York , 1983. xvii, 286 p., 16 p. of plates : ISBN 0-912574-37-X LC Card 87-402877 DDC 769.56954/6 19
HE6185.I53 J357 1983

Stamps of Jammu and Kashmir. Staal, Frits. The stamps of Jammu & Kashmir /. New York , 1983. xvii, 286 p., 16 p. of plates : ISBN 0-912574-37-X LC Card 87-402877 DDC 769.56954/6 19
HE6185.I53 J357 1983

Stanchin, I. M. (Ivan Mikhaĭlovich) Razvitie agropromyshlennogo kompleksa Turkmenskoĭ SSR / I.M. Stanchin ; pod redakt͡sieĭ B.K. Karlieva. Ashkhabad : Ylym, 1985. 181, [3] p. : ill. ; 21 cm. At head of title: Akademii͡a nauk Turkmenskoĭ SSR. Turkmenskiĭ nauchno-issledovatel´skiĭ institut ėkonomiki sel´skogo khozi͡aĭstva. Bibliography: p. 177-[182] LC Card 85-185696
1. Agricultural industries - Turkmen S.S.R. 2. Agriculture - Economic aspects - Turkmen S.S.R. I. Karliev, B. K. II. Title.
HD9015.S653 T878 1985

Stand der grenzüberschreitenden Raumordnung am Oberrhein / herausgegeben von Kurt Becker-Marx und Werner Fricke. [Heidelberg] : Im Selbstverlag des Geographischen Institutes der Universität, 1981. 105 p. : 13 ill., maps (some col.) ; 28 cm. (Heidelberger geographische Arbeiten. Heft 71) Includes papers of a conference held June 24, 1980 at the Universität Heidelberg. Five col. maps on 5 folded leaves in pocket. Includes bibliographical references. CONTENTS. - Kolloquium zwischen Politikern, Wissenschaftlern und Praktikern über Sach- und Organisationsprobleme bei der Einrichtung einer grenzüberschreitenden Raumordnung im Oberrheingebiet -- Fallstudie Strassburg und Kehl : Untersuchung der Möglichkeiten und Beschränkungen einer kommunalen und regionalen Kooperation über die europäischen Binnengrenzen / von Kurt Becker-Marx und Sigrun Lang. ISBN 3-88570-071-9 LC Card 81-197772 DDC 361.6/0943/4 19
1. Regional planning - Germany, West - Congresses. 2. Regional planning - Switzerland - Congresses. 3. Regional planning - Rhine Valley - Congresses. I. Fricke, Werner, 1927-. II. Lang, Sigrun. III. Heidelberg. Universität. IV. Series.
HT395.G4 S735 1981
NYPL [L-10 4979 Heft 71]

Standard and Poor's Corporation. (Old Catalog form: Standard & Poor's Corporation, New York)
Standard & Poor's debt ratings criteria . New York, N.Y. (25 Broadway, New York 10004) , c1986. viii, 68 p. : LC Card 87-102292 DDC 338.7/4/0973 19
HG4521 .S729 1986

STANDARD AND POOR'S CORPORATION.
Standard & Poor's debt ratings criteria . New York, N.Y. (25 Broadway, New York 10004) , c1986. viii, 68 p. : LC Card 87-102292 DDC

338.7/4/0973 19
HG4521 .S729 1986

Standard & Poor's debt ratings criteria : industrial overview. New York, N.Y. (25 Broadway, New York 10004) : Standard & Poor's, c1986. viii, 68 p. : ill. (some col.) ; 27 cm. Includes index. LC Card 87-102292 DDC 338.7/4/0973 19
1. Standard and Poor's Corporation. 2. Securities - Ratings. I. Standard and Poor's Corporation. II. Title: Debt ratings criteria.
HG4521 .S729 1986

Standard catalog of U. S. paper money /. Krause, Chester L. Iola, WI , c1985. 192 p. : ISBN 0-87341-078-5 (pbk.) LC Card 86-223149 DDC 769.5/5973/0750973 19
HG591 .K7 1985

Standard catalog of United States paper money. Krause, Chester L. Standard catalog of U. S. paper money /. Iola, WI , c1985. 192 p. : ISBN 0-87341-078-5 (pbk.) LC Card 86-223149 DDC 769.5/5973/0750973 19
HG591 .K7 1985

Standard catalog of world paper money /. Pick, Albert. Iola, Wis. , München , c1986. 2 v. : ISBN 0-87341-087-4 (v. 1) LC Card 86-222186 DDC 769.5/5/075 19
HG353 .P543 1986

Standard Chartered Bank Zimbabwe. Investment opportunity in textiles & clothing, Zimbabwe. [Harare, Zimbabwe] [1985?] 72 p., [12] leaves of plates : LC Card 87-400412 DDC 338.4/7677/0096891 19
HD9867.Z552 I58 1985

Standard dictionary of advertising, mass media, and marketing, English-German. Koschnick, Wolfgang J., 1942- Standard-Wörterbuch für Werbung, Massenmedien und Marketing, Deutsch-Englisch /. Berlin , New York , 1987. 590 p. ; ISBN 0-89925-293-1 (U. S.) : LC Card 87-19928 DDC 659.1/03/21 19
HF5803 .K67 1987

Standard German dictionary. Klatt, Edmund. Langenscheidt's standard German dictionary /. New York , 1983-1984. 1341 p. ;
NYPL [JFC 86-781]

The Standard handbook of industrial distributors. Fairfield, CT, USA : Bergano Book Co., c1987- v. <1-2 > ; 26 cm. CONTENTS. - v. 1. The Middle East, Asia, Africa, Latin America -- v. 2. Europe. ISBN 0-917408-02-0 (pbk. : v. 1) LC Card 86-73258 DDC 380.1/456218/025 19
1. Industrial equipment industry - Directories. 2. Machinery industry - Directories. 3. Marketing channels - Directories. 4. Physical distribution of goods - Directories. I. Bergano Book Co.
HD9680.A2 S72 1987

Standard international trade classification revision 3 /. United Nations. Statistical Office. New York , 1986. xvi, 106, 31, 25 p. ; ISBN 92-1-161265-9 (pbk.) LC Card 86-226177 DDC 338/.02/012 19
HF1041 .U56 1986

Standard international trade classification revision 3. Classification by broad economic categories . New York , 1986. x, 68 p. ; ISBN 92-1-161276-4 (pbk.) LC Card 87-401426 DDC 338/.02/012 19
HF1041 .C53 1986

Standard-Lexikon für Marketing, Marktkommunikation, Markt- und Mediaforschung /. Koschnick, Wolfgang J., 1942- München , New York , 1987. vi, 940 p. : ISBN 3-598-10583-5 LC Card 87-143648 DDC 380.1/03/31 19
HF5415 .K617 1987

STANDARD OF LIVING. see **COST AND STANDARD OF LIVING.**

STANDARD OF VALUE. see **MONEY; VALUE.**

STANDARD OIL COMPANY - HISTORY.
Akin, Edward N. Flagler, Rockefeller partner and Florida baron /. Kent, Ohio , c1988. xiii, 305 p. : ISBN 0-87338-348-6 (alk. paper) LC Card 87-2070 DDC 338/.04/0924 B 19
HC102.5.F55 A75 1988

Standard Oil Company (New Jersey) see **Standard Oil Company.**

Standard-Wörterbuch für Werbung, Massenmedien und Marketing, Deutsch-Englisch /. Koschnick, Wolfgang J., 1942- Berlin , New York , 1987. 590 p. ; ISBN 0-89925-293-1 (U. S.) : LC Card 87-19928 DDC 659.1/03/21 19
HF5803 .K67 1987

Standardised unemployment rates : Quarterly labour force statistics : sources and methods / OECD Department of Economics and Statistics = Taux de chômage standardisés : sources et méthodes : Statistiques trimestrielles de la population active / Département des affaires économiques et statistiques OCDE. Paris, France : Organisation for Economic Co-operation and Development ; [Washington, D.C. : OECD Publications and Information Center], 1985. 93 p. ; 28 cm. English and French. Includes bibliographies. LC Card 86-143095 DDC 331.13/7/072 19
1. Unemployment - Statistical methods. 2. Quarterly labour force statistics. I. Organisation for Economic Co-operation and Development. Dept. of Economics and Statistics. II. Title: Taux de chômage standardisés.
HD5711 .S77 1985 ***NYPL [JLF 86-1743]***

STANDARDIZATION.
Product standardization and competitive strategy /. Amsterdam ; New York : xii, 316 p. : ISBN 0-444-70232-6(U. S.) LC Card 87-8849 DDC 338/.02 19
HD62 .P75 1987

STANDARDIZATION - CONGRESSES.
Hens, Albert T. Einige Aspekte moderner Normung unter Berücksichtigung der Produktnormung /. Dortmund , 1977. 38 p. ; LC Card 84-121721
HD30 .A7 Heft 183 HD62

STANDARDIZATION - DEVELOPING COUNTRIES - CONGRESSES.
Normungsprobleme der Dritten Welt /. Dortmund , 1979. 98 p. ; LC Card 85-239680
HD30 .A7 Heft 201 T59.A1

STANDARDIZATION - GERMANY, WEST.
Bopp-Schmehl, Annemarie, 1946- Technische Normung und Verbraucherinteressen im gesellschaftlichen Wandel /. Frankfurt am Main , c1984. iii, 269 p. ; ISBN 3-88129-834-7 : LC Card 85-119483
HC290.5.C6 B66 1984

STANDARDIZATION - GERMANY (WEST) - CONGRESSES.
Lauer, Karl Friedrich. Das Referenzbüro der Gemeinschaften /. [Dortmund?] , 1976. 76 p. ; LC Card 85-241026
HD30 .A7 Heft 171 T59.A1

Standards for self-service storage facilities /. DeGroh, Teresa. Chicago, IL (1313 E. 60th St., Chicago 60637) , c1986. 22 p. : LC Card 86-227124 DDC 658.7/85 19
HF5487 .D44 1986

Standards of practice handbook . Financial Analysts Federation. Charlottesville, Va. , New York, N.Y. , 1986. xii, 150 p. ; ISBN 0-938367-03-X (pbk.) : LC Card 87-138043 DDC 174/.9332 19
HG4921 .F38 1986

Standing, Guy.
Labour circulation and the labour process /. London [England] , Dover, N.H. , c1985. xvi, 416 p. : ISBN 0-7099-3342-8 : LC Card 84-14306 DDC 331.12/791 19
HD5856.D44 L33 1984
NYPL [JLD 86-2532]

Unemployment and labour market flexibility : the United Kingdom / Guy Standing. Geneva : International Labour Office, 1986. xi, 147 p. : ill. ; 24 cm. Includes bibliographies. ISBN 92-2-105291-5 (pbk.) : LC Card 87-114658 DDC 331.13/7941 19
1. Unemployment - Great Britain. 2. Labor mobility - Great Britain. 3. Labor supply - Great Britain. 4. Manpower policy - Great Britain. I. Title.
HD5765.A6 S72 1986

Standing up for America . Haddock, Patricia. Minneapolis, Minn. , c1987. 111 p. : ISBN 0-87518-362-X : LC Card 86-32965 DDC 338.7/6292/0924 B 92 19
HD9710.U52 I246 1987

Standish, Barry, 1954- The economic factors affecting state output and employment / by Barry Standish. Rondebosch [South Africa] : School of Economics, University of Cape Town, [1986] 86 p. : ill. ; 22 cm. (Economics learning resource . no. 8) "January 1986." Bibliography: p. 65-86. ISBN 0-7992-1016-1 (pbk.) : LC Card 87-112894 DDC 339.2/3 19
1. Welfare economics. 2. Public goods. 3. Input-output analysis. 4. Social choice. I. Title. II. Series.
HB846 .S73 1986

Standortbestimmung : Entwicklungslinien der deutschen Kreditwirtschaft / herausgegeben von Deutschen Sparkassen- und Giroverband anlässlich seines hundertjährigen Bestehens am 6. Dezember 1984, unter Mitarbeit von Günter Ashauer ... [et al.]. Stuttgart : Deutscher Sparkassenverlag, c1984. 447 p. ; 25 cm. Bibliography: p. 444-445. ISBN 3-09-311000-9 LC Card 85-150165
1. Savings-banks - Germany, West. I. Ashauer, Günter. II. Deutscher Sparkassen- und Giroverband.
HG1939.G3 S73 1984

Standorte und Einzugsbereiche tertiärer Einrichtungen : Beiträge zu einer Geographie des tertiären Sektors / herausgegeben von Günter Heinritz. Damrstadt : Wissenschaftliche Buchgesellschaft, 1985. vi, 403 p., [1] folded leaf of plates : ill., map ; 20 cm. (Wege der Forschung, 0509-9609 . Bd. 591) Bibliography: p. [381]-403. CONTENTS. - Zur Frage der Standorte für Dienstleistungen (1957) / von Walter Christaller -- Der suburbane Raum als Standort von privaten Dienstleistungseinrichtungen (1975) / von Hans Hellberg -- Die Beziehungen zwischen Einzelhandel und städtischer Zentrenstruktur (1970) / von E. Agergård, P.A. Olsen und J. Allpass -- Die Verteilung von Geschäftszentren im Verdichtungsraum (1972) / von Siegfried Lange -- Vergleichende Untersuchung der Einzelhandelsstrukturen der Städte Bursa, Kiel und London/Ontario (1974) / von Reinhard Stewig -- Zur Theorie periodischer Märkte aus der Sicht von Wirtschaftswissenschaften und Geographie (1976) / von Eugen Wirth -- Stadtzentrum und Büros (1968) / von Günter H.K. Gad -- Perspektiven bei der Untersuchung der Standorte von Bürobetrieben (1979) / von P.W. Daniels -- Der Beitrag der Geographie zur politisch-administrativen Regionalisierung (1973) / von Jürgen Deiters -- Politische Geographie und die Versorgung mit öffentlichen Dienstleistungen (1974) / von Bryan H. Massam -- Standort-Zuordnungsmodelle und ihre Anwendung in der Standortplanung zentraler öffentlicher Einrichtungen (1980) / von Gerhard Bahrenberg -- Der optimale Standort unter den Aspekten der Effizienz und Adäquanz (1977) / von Richard L. Morrill und John Symons. ISBN 3-534-08402-0 LC Card 86-228150
1. Offices - Location - Germany (West). 2. Service industries - Germany (West) - Location. I. Heinritz, Günter. II. Series.
HF5547.25 .S73 1985

Standorte von Büros im Urteil der Beschäftigten und sonstiger Nutzer / Weeber und Partner, Büro für Stadtplanung und Sozialforschung, Stuttgart. Stuttgart : Forschungsgemeinschaft Bauen und Wohnen Stuttgart, 1983. 140 p. : ill. ; 30 cm. (FBW-Veröffentlichung . Nr. 140) Bibliography: p. 136-140. LC Card 83-220559
1. Offices - Location - Germany (West). 2. Service industries - Germany (West) - Location. 3. Service industries - Germany, West. I. Weeber und Partner, Büro für Stadtplanung und Sozialforschung. II. Forschungsgemeinschaft Bauen und Wohnen. III. Series: Veröffentlichung der Forschungsgemeinschaft Bauen und Wohnen, Stuttgart , Nr. 140.
HF5547.25 .S74 1983

Die Standortfrage in der Versicherungswirtschaft . Gilles, Martina, 1956- Köln , c1987. xv, 309 p., [4] folded leaves of plates : ISBN 3-924361-26-6 LC Card 87-144415 DDC 368/.006 19
HG8618 .G55 1987

Standortpolitik multinationaler Banken /. Walter, Herbert. Thun , c1983. viii, 255 p. : ISBN 3-87144-737-4 : LC Card 83-159195
HG3881 .W273 1983

Standortprobleme von Industrieunternehmen in Ballungsräumen . Clemens, Reinhard. Göttingen , c1983. xviii, 257 p. : ISBN 3-509-01330-1 LC Card 83-198706
HC289.D6 C54 1983

Standortverlagerungen der Industrie in der Region München /. Decker, Hedwig. Kallmünz/Regensburg , 1984. xxvi, 92 p. : ISBN 3-7847-6525-4 LC Card 86-136483 DDC

304.2/0943 s 338.6/042/094336 19
HC281 .M8 Bd. 25 HC289.M86

Standpunkte (Bonn, Germany) .
(3) Kohl, Helmut, 1930- Soziale Marktwirtschaft, Fundament für morgen . Bonn [1987] 39 p. : ISBN 3-88991-011-4 LC Card 87-409383 DDC 338.943 19
HC286.5 .K565 1987

Stanfield, J. Ron, 1945- The economic thought of Karl Polanyi : lives and livelihood / J.R. Stanfield. Basingstoke, Hampshire : Macmillan, 1986. x, 162 p. ; 23 cm. Bibliography: p. 151-158. Includes index. ISBN 0-333-39629-4 LC Card 87-673390
1. Polanyi, Karl, 1886-1964. 2. Economists - Hungary. I. Title.
HB102.P64 S73x 1986b

The Stanford series on education and public policy .
(v. 5) The Future impact of technology on work and education /. London , New York , 1987. p. cm. ISBN 1-85000-083-2 : LC Card 87-13641 DDC 331.12/0994 19
HD6331.2.A8 F87 1987

Stange, Sabine. Kriegsvorbereitung im Hunsrück : der Einfluss der Raketenstationierung auf den Alltag der Menschen / Sabine Stange ; mit einem Vorwort von Robert Jungk.1. Aufl. Essen : Klartext, 1985. 157, [35] p., [4] folded leaves of plates : ill. ; 21 cm. (Reihe "Zeitgeschehen") ISBN 3-88474-409-7 : LC Card 86-148061
1. Armaments - Economic aspects - Germany (West) - Hunsrück (Region). 2. Armaments - Social aspects - Germany (West) - Hunsrück (Region). 3. Peace. I. Title. II. Series.
HC290.5.D4 S84 1985

Stanger, Robert A. How to evaluate real estate partnerships / Robert A. Stanger with Keith D. Allaire. Shrewsbury, N.J. : R.A. Stanger, c1986. xvi, 256 p. ; 24 cm. Includes index. ISBN 0-943570-10-7 LC Card 85-90539 DDC 332.63/247 19
1. Real estate investment - Syndication. 2. Limited Partnership. I. Allaire, Keith D. II. Title.
HD1382.55 .S73 1986

Stanič, Gojko. Družba, znanost, tehnologija . Ljubljana , 1982. 472 p. ; LC Card 84-235191
HC407.Z9 T434 1982

Stanis, V. F. (Vladimir Frantsevich)
Ėkonomicheskie problemy razvitiia stran sotsialisticheskoĭ orientatsii /. Moskva , 1986. 239 p. ; LC Card 86-221922
HC59.7 .E355 1986

Stanislaus, M. Sebastian. New farm technology and income distribution / M. Sebastian Stanislaus. New Delhi : Ashish, c1984. viii, 76 p. : ill. ; 23 cm. Includes index. Bibliography: p. [71]-74. LC Card 84-902272 DDC 338.1/3/095482 19
1. Farm income - India - Tiruchchirāppalli (District) - Mathematical models. 2. Income distribution - India - Tiruchchirāppalli (District) - Mathematical models. 3. Agricultural innovations - India - Tiruchchirāppalli (District). 4. Tiruchchirāppalli (India : District) - Economic conditions. I. Title.
HD2075.T57 S73 1984 ***NYPL [JLD 87-669]***

Stanley Foundation.
Occasional paper.
(27) Stevens, Charles J. Confronting the world food crisis /. Muscatine, Iowa [1981] 24 p. : LC Card 82-127279 DDC 338.1/9 19
HD9000.6 .S73 ***NYPL [JLK 75-198 no. 27]***

Stanley, Lloyd A. Guide to training needs assessment /. Ljubljana, Yugoslavia , c1984. 65 p. ; ISBN 92-9038-412-8 (pbk.) LC Card 85-242690 DDC 658.3/12404 19
HF5549.5.T7 G847 1984

STANLEY WORKS INC.
Change master companies [videorecording] . Chicago, IL , 1987. 1 videocassette (42 min.) : LC Card 87-705608 DDC 658.3 11
HD45

Stanovlenie i periody razvitiia gosudarstvenno-monopolisticheskogo kapitalizma v Anglii /. Perevozchikov, V. I. (Viktor Ivanovich) Kiev , 1982. 153 p. ; LC Card 83-102577
HC256 .P47 1982

Stanovlenie i razvitie sovetskoĭ ėkonomicheskoĭ nauki na Ukraine : 1917-1937 gody / [avtory T.I. Dereviankin ... et al. ; otvetstvennyĭ redaktor T.I. Dereviankin]. Kiev : Nauk. dumka, 1983. 285, [2] p. ; 21 cm. At head of title: Akademiia nauk Ukrainskoĭ SSR. Institut ėkonomiki. Bibliography: p. 271-[286] LC Card 84-120015 DDC 330/.072/04771 19
1. Economics - Research - Ukraine - History. 2. Marxian economics - Research - Ukraine - History. 3. Ukraine - Economic conditions - 1918-. 4. Ukraine - Economic policy. I. Derev'iankin, T. I. (Tymofiĭ Ivanovych). II. Instytut ekonomiky (Akademiia nauk Ukraïns'koï RSR).
HB74.9.S65 S72 1983 ***NYPL [*QGA 87-275]***

Stansell, Christine. City of women : sex and class in New York, 1789-1860 / Christine Stansell.Illini Books ed. Urbana : University of Illinois Press, 1987, c1986. xiv, 301 p. ; 23 cm. Bibliography: p. [229]-283. Includes index. ISBN 0-252-01481-2 (pbk.) LC Card 87-16163 DDC 305.4/2/097471 19
1. Women - Employment - New York (N.Y.) - History - 19th century. 2. Women - New York (N.Y.) - History - 19th century. 3. New York (N.Y.) - Economic conditions. 4. New York (N.Y.) - Social conditions. I. Title.
HD6096.N6 S8 1987

Stanton, B. F. (Bernard Freeland), 1925-
The cereals dilemma : surpluses in Western Europe and North America / by B.F. Stanton and E. Neville-Rolfe. Ithaca, N.Y. : Dept. of Agricultural Economics, Cornell University Agricultural Experiment Station, New York State College of Agriculture and Life Sciences, Cornell University, [1986] 50 p. : ill. ; 28 cm. (A.E. Res. . 86-13) Cover title. "May 1986." Bibliography: p. 49-50. LC Card 86-622419 DDC 338.1/731/094 19
1. Grain trade - Europe. 2. Grain trade - United States. 3. Grain trade - Canada. 4. Agricultural surpluses - Europe. 5. Agricultural surpluses - United States. 6. Agricultural surpluses - Canada. I. Neville-Rolfe, Edmund. II. Series: A.E. research , 86-13. III. Title.
HD9045.A2 S7 1986

Production costs for cereals in the European community : comparisons with the United States, 1977-1984 / by B.F. Stanton. Ithaca, N.Y. : Dept. of Agricultural Economics, Cornell University Agricultural Experiment Station, New York State College of Agriculture and Life Sciences, [1986] 178 p., 2 p. of plates : ill. ; 29 cm. (A.E. Res. . 86-2) Cover title. Bibliography: p. 173-178. LC Card 86-622607 DDC 338.1/331/094 19
1. Cereal products - European Economic Community countries - Costs. 2. Cereal products - United States - Costs. I. Series: A.E. research , 86-2. II. Title.
HD9045.E82 S73 1986

Stanton, William J. Management of the sales force / William J. Stanton, Richard H. Buskirk. 7th ed. Homewood, Ill. : Irwin, 1987. xv, 704 p. : ill., forms ; 24 cm. Includes bibliographical references and index. ISBN 0-256-03635-7 LC Card 86-82598 DDC 658.8/1 19
1. Sales management. I. Buskirk, Richard Hobart, 1927-. II. Title.
HF5438.4 .S78 1987

Stanworth, John. Survival of the small firm /. Aldershot, Hants, England , Brookfield, Vt., U. S.A. , c1986. 2 v. : ISBN 0-566-00725-8 (v. 1) : LC Card 85-27035 DDC 338.6/42 19
HD2341 .S87 1986 ***NYPL [JLD 86-2643]***

Stapleton, Charles O. California real estate principles / Charles O. Stapleton III, Thomas J. Moran, Martha R. Williams. Chicago : Real Estate Education Co., c1987. xvi, 428, 8 p. : ill. ; 28 cm. Includes index. ISBN 0-88462-569-9 (pbk.) LC Card 86-24870 DDC 333.33/09794 19
1. Real estate business - California. 2. Real property - California. I. Moran, Thomas J. II. Williams, Martha R. III. Title.
HD266.C2 S73 1987

Stapleton, John F. Sussex, Margie. The complete real estate math book /. Englewood Cliffs, N.J. , c1988. vii, 288 p. : ISBN 0-13-162298-6 (pbk.) LC Card 87-14397 DDC 513/.02433 19
HF5695.5.R3 S935 1988

STAR (COMPUTER PROGRAM)
Stringer, Kenneth W. Statistical techniques for analytical review in auditing /. New York , c1986. xii, 301 p. : ISBN 0-471-86076-X : LC Card 85-17874 DDC 657/.45/0285536 19
HF5667 .S85 1986 ***NYPL [JLE 86-2704]***

Star Spangled beer . Erickson, Jack. Reston, Va. , 1987. v, 155 p. : ISBN 0-941397-00-9 (pbk.) : LC Card 86-63993 DDC 338.7/66342/02573 19
HD9397.U52 E75 1987

Starcher, Mark L. Quantifying the impact of the Tax Reform Act of 1986 on effective corporate tax rates / by Mark L. Starcher. [Arlington, Va.] : Tax Analysts, c1986. 45, 3 leaves, 12 leaves of plates : ill. ; 28 cm. Cover title. Includes index. LC Card 87-402048 DDC 336.24/3/0973021 19
1. Corporations - Taxation - United States - Statistics. I. Title.
HJ4653.C7 S675 1986

Stark, Oded. Lucas, Robert E. B. Motivations to remit . [Tel Aviv] [1985] 27 leaves ; LC Card 86-177234
HG3984.9 .L83 1985

Stark, Robin. Encyclopedia of Lotus 1-2-3 / Robin Stark. 1st ed. Blue Ridge Summit, PA : Tab Books, c1987. x, 484 p. : ill. ; 24 cm. Includes index. Cover subtitle: A complete cross-reference to all macros, commands, functions, applications, and troubleshooting. ISBN 0-8306-7891-3 : LC Card 87-19839 DDC 005.36/9 19
1. Lotus 1-2-3 (Computer program). 2. Business - Data processing. I. Title. II. Title: Encyclopedia of Lotus one-two-three.
HF5548.4.L67 S675 1987

Stark, Walter. Untersuchungen zum Profit beim hansischen Handelskapital in der ersten Hälfte des 15. Jahrhunderts / von Walter Stark. Weimar : H. Böhlau, 1985. 147 p. ; 24 cm. (Abhandlungen zur Handels- und Sozialgeschichte, 0065-0358 . Bd. 24) Bibliography: p. [143]-147. LC Card 86-148303
1. Hansa towns - Commerce - History. 2. Profit - Hansa towns - History. I. Title. II. Series.
HF458 .S73 1985

Stark, Werner, 1909- Die Protestantische Ethik und der Verfall des Kapitalismus . [Hamburg] , 1985. 31 p. : LC Card 86-112068
HB501 .P76 1985

STARK, WERNER, 1909-
Die Protestantische Ethik und der Verfall des Kapitalismus . [Hamburg] , 1985. 31 p. : LC Card 86-112068
HB501 .P76 1985

Starovoĭtov, S. N. (Sergeĭ Nikolaevich)
Sovershenstvovanie planirovaniia i upravleniia neftegazovym kompleksom /. Novosibirsk , 1986. 208 p. : LC Card 87-124383
HD9575.S653 S577 1986

Starr, Martin Kenneth, 1927- The performance of Japanese-owned firms in America, 1982-1985 / sponsored by the Center for Operations. [New York, NY] : Graduate School of Business, Columbia University, c1987. ii, 41 leaves : ill. ; 28 cm. (Survey report . no. 2) "Martin K. Starr and Patrice A. Hall, principal investigators"--P. i. "February 1987." LC Card 87-145262 DDC 338.8/8952/073 19
1. Corporations, Japanese - United States. 2. Investments, Japanese - United States. I. Hall, Patrice A. II. Columbia University. Graduate School of Business. Center for Operations. III. Series: Survey report (Columbia University. Graduate School of Business. Center for Operations) , no. 2. IV. Title.
HD2785 .S66 1987

Starr, Philip C. Economics : principles in action / Philip C. Starr.5th ed. Belmont, Calif. : Wadsworth Pub. Co., c1988. xxii, 422 p. : ill. ; 24 cm. Includes bibliographies and index. ISBN 0-534-08496-6 (pbk.) : LC Card 87-22755 DDC 330 19
1. Economics. 2. Economics - Examinations, questions, etc. I. Title.
HB171.5 .S78 1988

Starr, Ross M. Social choice and public decision making /. Cambridge [Cambridgeshire] , New York , 1986. xix, 215 p. : ISBN 0-521-30454-7 LC Card 86-8580 DDC 339 19
HB846.8 .S59 1986 ***NYPL [JLE 86-4189]***

Starrels, John M. The Korean economy in congressional perspective : a study / prepared for the use of the Joint Economic Committee, Congress of the United States. Washington : U. S. G.P.O. : For sale by the Supt. of Docs.,

Congressional Sales Office, U. S. G.P.O., 1986. v, 13 p. ; 24 cm. (S. prt. . 99-185) At head of title: 99th Congress, 2d session. Joint committee print. Distributed to some depository libraries in microfiche. Shipping list no.: 86-867-P. "October 27, 1986." Includes bibliographical references. Item 1000-B, 1000-C (microfiche) LC Card 87-601385 DDC 330.9519/043 19
1. Korea (South) - Economic conditions - 1945-. 2. Korea (North) - Economic conditions. I. United States. Congress. Joint Economic Committee. II. Title. III. Series.
HC467 .S724 1986

Starrett, David A. Social choice and public decision making /. Cambridge [Cambridgeshire] , New York , 1986. xix, 215 p. : ISBN 0-521-30454-7 LC Card 86-8580 DDC 339 19
HB846.8 .S59 1986 ***NYPL [JLE 86-4189]***

The start-up entrepreneur . Cook, James R., 1938- New York , 1987, c1986. xii, 306 p. ; ISBN 0-06-097070-7 (pbk.) : LC Card 86-45650 DDC 658.4/2 19
HD62.5 .C664 1987

Start up telemarketing . Fidel, Stanley Leo. New York , c1987. xiv, 287 p. : ISBN 0-471-01064-2 LC Card 87-21610 DDC 658.8/5 19
HF5415.1265 .F53 1987

Start your own small business and make it succeed. Williams, Bruce, 1932- The Bruce Williams book . New York , 1987. p. cm. ISBN 0-8128-3119-5 : LC Card 86-42692 DDC 658/022 19
HD62.5 .W49 1987

Starting a labor-management committee in your organization . National Center for Productivity and Quality of Working Life. Washington , 1978. 55 p. ; LC Card 78-603560 DDC 658.31/5
HD6490.L33 N37 1978 ***NYPL [JLF 81-235]***

Starting and managing a business from your home /. Waymon, Lynne. Washington, D.C. , 1986. vi, 48 p. ; LC Card 86-602842 DDC 658/.041 19
HD62.5 .W395 1986

Starting and managing a small service business /. Schaefer, Robert A. Washington, D.C. , 1986. v, 57 p. ; LC Card 86-603435 DDC 658/.022 19
HD9981.5 .S32 1986

Starting and managing series .
(v. 101) Schaefer, Robert A. Starting and managing a small service business /. Washington, D.C. , 1986. v, 57 p. ; LC Card 86-603435 DDC 658/.022 19
HD9981.5 .S32 1986

(v. 102) Waymon, Lynne. Starting and managing a business from your home /. Washington, D.C. , 1986. vi, 48 p. ; LC Card 86-602842 DDC 658/.041 19
HD62.5 .W395 1986

(v. 2 [i.e. 102]) Waymon, Lynne. Starting and managing a business from your home /. Washington, D.C. , 1986. vi, 48 p. ; LC Card 86-602842 DDC 658/.041 19
HD62.5 .W395 1986

Starting and managing the small business /. Kuriloff, Arthur H. New York , c1988. xxi, 663 p. : ISBN 0-07-035665-3 : LC Card 87-3832 DDC 658/.022 19
HD62.5 .K87 1988

Starting at the top . Carter, John Mack. New York [1985] 252 p. ; ISBN 0-688-04520-0 LC Card 85-4826 DDC 338/.04/0922 B 19
HC102.5.A2 C37 1985
NYPL [JLD 87-1089]

Starting from scratch . Gould, J. Sutherland. New York , c1987. xiii, 366 p. ; ISBN 0-471-85024-1 LC Card 86-28136 DDC 658.1/1 19
HD62.5 .G68 1987

Starting right in your new business /. Tetreault, Wilfred F., 1927- Reading, Mass. , c1987. ix, 226 p. ; ISBN 0-201-07795-7 (pbk.) : LC Card 87-19464 DDC 658.1/141 19
HD62.7 .T47 1987

Starting your own business . Storey, M. John, 1943- New York , c1987. xv, 266 p. ; ISBN 0-471-85769-6 LC Card 87-2051 DDC 658.1/141 19
HD62.5 .S76 1987

Startzel, Donna C.
The CETA arts and humanities experience [microform] CETA Ahead project (Arts and humanities employment analysis and documentation) / prepared by Donna C. Startzel ... with A. Patrice Walker, Morgan Management Systems, Inc., Columbia, Md., ... for the Employment and Training Administration, US Dept. of Labor. Columbia, Md. : Morgan Management Systems, 1981. 197 p. ; 28 cm. "October 1981." Cover title: CETA (Comprehensive Employment and Training Act) arts and humanities experience -- CETA Ahead project ... Bibliography: p. 183-187. Microfiche. Springfield, Va. : NTIS 1984. 3 microfiches : negative ; 11 x 15 cm. (PB83-265397)
1. Employment subsidies - United States. 2. Manpower policy - United States. 3. Occupational training - United States. I. Walker, A. Patrice. II. Morgan Management Systems, Inc. III. United States. Employment and Training Administration. IV. Title. V. Title: C.E.T.A. arts and humanities experience. VI. Title: CETA (Comprehensive Employment and Training Act) arts and humanities experience -- CETA Ahead project.
NYPL [*XME-11,320]

CETA (Comprehensive Employment and Training Act) and the arts and humanities [microform] : fifteen case studies / [Donna C. Startzel and A. Patrice Walker], Morgan Management Systems, Inc., Columbia, Md. ; prepared for Employment and Training Administration, Washington, D.C. Columbia, Md. : Morgan Management Systems, 1981. 160 p. ; 28 cm. "Sep. 81." Microfiche. Springfield, Va. : NTIS, 1981. 2 microfiches : negative ; 11 x 15 cm. (PB83-265389)
1. Employment subsidies - United States. 2. Manpower policy - United States. 3. Occupational training - United States. I. Walker, A. Patrice. II. United States. Employment and Training Administration. III. Morgan Management Systems, Inc. IV. Title. V. Title: C.E.T.A. (Comprehensive Employment and Training Act) and the arts and humanities. ***NYPL [*XME-11,328]***

STARVATION.
American Jewish Joint Distribution Committee. [Choroba głodowa. English.] Hunger disease . New York , c1979. xiv, 261 p. : ISBN 0-471-05003-2 LC Card 78-26397 DDC 616.3/9
RC627.S7 A43 1979
NYPL [*PXV (Warsaw) 86-3505]

Castro, Josué de, 1908-1973. Fome, um tema proibido . Petrópolis , 1983. 154 p. ; LC Card 83-224629
HD9000.5 .C28 1983

Stasiak, Andrzej. Przestrzenne aspekty gospodarki żywnościowej do 2000 r. . Warszawa , 1986. 166 p. : ISBN 83-208-0497-3 : LC Card 86-223691
HD9015.P72 P72 1986

STATE. see **STATE, THE.**

The state and agricultural development in Egypt since 1973 /. Commander, Simon. London , Atlantic Highlands, NJ , 1988. p. cm. ISBN 0-86372-080-3 LC Card 87-3616 DDC 338.1/862 19
HD2123.Z8 C66 1988

STATE AND AGRICULTURE. see **AGRICULTURE AND STATE.**

State and class in Turkey . Keyder, Caglar. London , New York , 1987. 252 p. ; ISBN 0-86091-877-7 (pbk.) : LC Card 87-14992 DDC 338.9561 19
HC492 .K497 1987

STATE AND COMMUNINICATION. see **COMMUNICATION POLICY.**

The State and economic life.
(8) Forster, Jakob Johann Benjamin. A conjunction of interests . Toronto , Buffalo , c1986. vi, 288 p. ; ISBN 0-8020-5680-6 (alk. paper) LC Card 87-108915 DDC 382.7/0971 19
HF1765 .F67 1986

State and economy . Topik, Steven. Austin , 1985. 28 p. ; LC Card 86-622250 DDC 338.981 19
HC187 .T56 1985

STATE AND EDUCATION. see **EDUCATION AND STATE.**

STATE AND ENERGY. see **ENERGY POLICY.**

STATE AND ENVIRONMENT. see **ENVIRONMENTAL POLICY.**

STATE AND HOUSING. see **HOUSING POLICY.**

STATE AND INDUSTRY. see **INDUSTRY AND STATE.**

STATE AND INSURANCE. see **SOCIAL SECURITY.**

STATE AND LABOR. see **LABOR POLICY.**

The state and labor in modern Japan /. Garon, Sheldon. Berkeley , c1987. xvi, 326 p. ; ISBN 0-520-05983-2 (alk. paper) LC Card 86-30890 DDC 331/.0952 19
HD8726 .G37 1987

State and local finance : the pressures of the 1980s / edited by George F. Break. Madison, Wis. : Published for the Committee on Taxation, Resources and Economic Development by the University of Wisconsin Press, 1983. x, 243 p. : ill. ; 24 cm. (Publications of the Committee on Taxation, Resources and Economic Development. 12) "Proceedings of a symposium sponsored by the Committee on Taxation, Resources and Economic Development (TRED) at the Lincoln Institute of Land Policy, Cambridge, Massachusetts, 1980"--P. [ii] Includes bibliographies and index. ISBN 0-299-09340-9 : LC Card 83-47757 DDC 336.73 19
1. Finance, Public - United States - States - Congresses. 2. Finance, Public - Canada - Congresses. 3. Local finance - United States - Congresses. 4. Local finance - Canada - Congresses. I. Break, George F. II. Committee on Taxation, Resources and Economic Development.
HJ275 .S675 1983 ***NYPL [JLE 86-4001]***

State and local government . Houseman, Gerald L. Englewood Cliffs, N.J. , c1986. xvi, 272 p. : ISBN 0-13-843368-2 (pbk.) LC Card 85-16981 DDC 320.973 19
JK2408 .H79 1986 ***NYPL [JLE 86-2916]***

The State and local industrial policy / edited by Harvey A. Goldstein. Chicago, Ill. : Planners Press, American Planning Association, c1987. x, 195 p. : ill. ; 28 cm. Includes bibliographies and index. ISBN 0-918286-46-8 (pbk.) LC Card 86-72373 DDC 338.973 19
1. Industry and state - United States - States. 2. Urban policy - United States. I. Goldstein, Harvey A. II. American Planning Association.
HD3616.U47 S68 1987

State and local politics . Burns, James MacGregor. Englewood Cliffs, N.J. , c1984. xi, 266 p. : ISBN 0-13-843524-3 (pbk.) LC Card 83-21259 DDC 320.973 19
JK2408 .B87 1984 ***NYPL [JLE 87-142]***

STATE AND MEDICINE. see **MEDICAL POLICY.**

STATE AND MUSIC. see **MUSIC AND STATE.**

STATE AND NUTRITION. see **NUTRITION POLICY.**

The state and poverty in India . Kohli, Atul. Cambridge [Cambridgeshire] , New York , 1987. x, 262 p. : ISBN 0-521-32008-9 LC Card 85-25554 DDC 333.3/1/54 19
HD1333.I4 K65 1986 ***NYPL [JLD 87-1517]***

The state and province vital records guide /. Burgess, Michael, 1948- San Bernardino, Calif. , 1988. p. cm. ISBN 0-89370-815-1 : LC Card 87-6312 DDC 929/.1/02573 19
HA38 .B87 1988

The state and rural class formation in Ghana . Konings, Piet. London ; Boston : xvi, 391 p. : ISBN 0-7103-0117-0 LC Card 85-28109 DDC 305.5/09667 19
HN832.Z9 S65 1986 ***NYPL [Sc D 86-574]***

STATE AND SCIENCE. see **SCIENCE AND STATE.**

State and society in Brazil : continuity and change / edited by John D. Wirth, Edson de Oliveira Nunes, and Thomas E. Bogenschild. Boulder : Westview Press, 1987. x, 349 p. ; 23 cm. (Westview special studies on Latin America and the Caribbean) Includes bibliographies and index. CONTENTS. - Industrialization, economic growth, and balance of payments / Regis Bonelli and Pedro S. Malan -- Industrialization and economic growth / Regis Bonelli and Pedro S. Malan -- Industrialization, employment, and stratification in Brazil / Carlos A. Halsenbalg and Nelson do Valle Silva -- Dilemmas of

state-led modernization in Brazil / Edson de Oliveira Nunes and Barbara Geddes -- Novo sindicalismo and politics in Brazil / Maria Hermínia Tavares de Almeida -- Social movements and the new political order in Brazil / Renato R. Boschi -- Framing the state / Ben Ross Schneider -- Brazil's role in new world regions / John D. Wirth -- The quest for citizenship in a relational universe / Roberto da Matta. ISBN 0-8133-7401-4 (pbk. : alk. paper) : LC Card 87-2160 DDC 981/.063 19
1. Brazil - Economic conditions - 1945-. 2. Brazil - Economic policy. 3. Brazil - Politics and government - 1985-. 4. Political parties - Brazil. 5. Trade-unions - Brazil. 6. Brazil - Foreign relations. I. Wirth, John D. II. Nunes, Edson de Oliveira. III. Bogenschild, Thomas E.
HC187 .S78 1987

STATE AND TECHNOLOGY. see **TECHNOLOGY AND STATE.**

The state and the market economy . Hayward, Jack Ernest Shalom. Brighton, Sussex , 1986. xv, 267 p. : ISBN 0-7450-0012-6 LC Card 87-672693
HC276.2 .H35x 1986b

STATE AND TRANSPORTATION. see **TRANSPORTATION AND STATE.**

STATE AND URBAN TRANSPORTATION. see **URBAN TRANSPORTATION POLICY.**

State capitalism . Laux, Jeanne Kirk, 1942- Ithaca , 1988. ix, 250 p. ; ISBN 0-8014-2079-2 (alk. paper) LC Card 87-47600 DDC 338.6/2/0971 19
HD4005 .L38 1988

STATE CONTROL AND OWNERSHIP. see **GOVERNMENT OWNERSHIP.**

STATE, CORPORATE. see **CORPORATE STATE.**

STATE FARMS - CUBA.

STATE FARMS - ESTONIA - MANAGEMENT.
Luukas, Ants. [Majandi parteigrupid. Russian.] Partiĭnye gruppy v kolkhozakh i sovkhozakh /. Tallin , 1984. 77 p., [8] p. of plates : LC Card 87-115056
HD1492.S652 E85517 1984

STATE FARMS - HUNGARY.
Vályi, Éva. A mezőgazdasági vállalati szervezet fejlődésének és fejlesztésének törvényszerűségei /. Budapest , 1985. 107, [1] p. : ISBN 963-05-3468-1 : LC Card 86-137169
HD1492.H8 V33 1985

STATE FARMS - HUNGARY - FINANCE.
Kis, Pál. A mezőgazdasági nagyüzemek pénz- és hitelrendszere /. Budapest , 1985. 261 p. ; ISBN 963-232-050-6 : LC Card 85-230947
HD1440.H9 K57 1985

STATE FARMS - HUNGARY - FINANCE - STATISTICS.
A Szocialista nagyüzemek főbb ágazatainak költség- és jövedelemhelyzete 1984-ben /. Budapest , 1985. 35, [46] p. ; LC Card 85-177804
HD1492.H8 S93 1985

STATE FARMS - HUNGARY - MANAGEMENT.
A Mezőgazdasági és élelmiszeripari vállalatok gazdálkodása /. Budapest , 1984. 315, [1] p. : ISBN 963-231-968-0 : LC Card 85-230887
HD1493.H8 M48 1984

STATE FARMS - HUNGARY - OFFICIALS AND EMPLOYEES.
Simó, Tibor. Metszetek az agrártársadalom struktúrájából /. Budapest , 1985. 167 p. ; ISBN 963-7700-25-0 : LC Card 86-232606
HD1536.H9 S56 1985

STATE FARMS - IRAQ - INCOME DISTRIBUTION.
Mukhlif, Hādī Aḥmad. al-Tawzīʻ al-jughrāfī li-mazāriʻ al-dawlah fī al-ʻIrāq wa-atharihā fī al-tanmiyah al-iqtiṣādīyah /. [Baghdad] , 1985. 2 v. (607 p., 3 leaves of plates) : LC Card 86-963500
HD1493.I72 M85 1985

STATE FARMS - LATVIA - ACCOUNTING.
Vaikulis, J. (Jānis) Lauksaimniecības uzņēmumu saimnieciskās darbības analize /. Riga , 1986. 185 p. ; LC Card 86-199301
HD1492.S652 L38 1986

STATE FARMS - POLAND.
Dramowicz, Elżbieta. Przestrzenne zróżnicowanie państwowej gospodarki rolnej w Polsce /. Warszawa , 1986. 125 p. ; ISBN 83-01-05021-7 : LC Card 86-212594
HD1995.7 .D73 1986

STATE FARMS - ROMANIA.
Șchiopu, Bucur. Gospodăriile agricole de stat /. București , 1966. 295 p. : LC Card 84-183905
HD1493.R6 S35 1966

STATE FARMS - RUSSIAN S.F.S.R. - SAKHALINSKAIA OBLAST′.
Potentsial ėffektivnosti /. IUzhno-Sakhalinsk , 1985. 67 p. ; LC Card 87-100690
HD8039.F32 S656 1985

STATE FARMS - SOVIET UNION - FINANCE.
Shirinskaia, Z. G. (Zinaida Grigor′evna) Kredit i intensifikatsiia sovkhoznogo proizvodstva /. Moskva , 1980. 142 p. ; LC Card 81-138434
HD1493.S65 S55 1980

STATE FARMS - SOVIET UNION - MANAGEMENT.
Spravochnik rukovoditelia srednego zvena kolkhoza, sovkhoza /. Minsk , 1981. 518 p. ; LC Card 82-147885
HD1492.S65 S67 1981

STATE FARMS - SOVIET UNION, NORTHERN.
Mal′tsev, V. I. (Valer′ian Ivanovich) Ėkonomicheskie osnovy industrializatsii sel′skogo khoziaistva Severa /. Moskva , 1985. 142 p. ; LC Card 86-165352
HD1995.N55 M34 1985

STATE FARMS - SOVIET UNION, NORTHWESTERN.
Ivanov, V. A. (Valentin Aleksandrovich) Ėkonomicheskoe stimulirovanie povysheniia ėffektivnosti intensifikatsii sovkhoznogo proizvodstva /. Moskva , 1980. 248 p. ; LC Card 81-134017
HD1493.S652 N65 1980

STATE FARMS - TURKMEN S.S.R.
Babaev, Akmyrat. Sovkhozyn̄g shu gùni ve geljegi /. Ashgabat , 1982. 55 p. : LC Card 84-126905
HD1493.S652 T873 1982

State, finance, and industry : a comparative analysis of post-war trends in six advanced industrial economics / edited by Andrew Cox. Brighton, Sussex : Wheatsheaf, 1986. ix, 292 p. ; 23 cm. Includes bibliographies and index. ISBN 0-7108-0219-6
1. Industry and state - Case studies. 2. Industrial promotion - Case studies. I. Cox, Andrew W.
NYPL [JLD 86-2997]

State finances and regional development in India /. Sharda, N. K. New Delhi , c1986. 248 p. ; LC Card 86-900599 DDC 336.54/52 19
HJ1339.H55 S54 1986 ***NYPL [JLD 86-3211]***

STATE GOVERNMENTS.
Abney, Glenn. The politics of state and city administration /. Albany, N.Y. , c1986. xvi, 260 p. ; ISBN 0-88706-255-5 LC Card 85-14873 DDC 353.9 19
JK2408 .A26 1986 ***NYPL [JLE 86-3711]***

Bowman, Ann O'M., 1948- The resurgence of the states /. Englewood Cliffs, N.J. , c1986. x, 269 p. : ISBN 0-13-774969-4 (pbk.) LC Card 85-19213 DDC 353.9 19
JK2408 .B68 1986 ***NYPL [JLE 86-4496]***

Burns, James MacGregor. State and local politics . Englewood Cliffs, N.J. , c1984. xi, 266 p. : ISBN 0-13-843524-3 (pbk.) LC Card 83-21259 DDC 320.973 19
JK2408 .B87 1984 ***NYPL [JLE 87-142]***

Houseman, Gerald L. State and local government . Englewood Cliffs, N.J. , c1986. xvi, 272 p. : ISBN 0-13-843368-2 (pbk.) LC Card 85-16981 DDC 320.973 19
JK2408 .H79 1986 ***NYPL [JLE 86-2916]***

STATE GOVERNMENTS - UNITED STATES - ADDRESSES, ESSAYS, LECTURES.
State politics and the new federalism . White Plains, N.Y. , c1986. xv, 544 p. : ISBN 0-582-28474-0 (pbk.) LC Card 85-15956 DDC 321.02/0973 19
JK325 .S77 1986 ***NYPL [JLD 86-2766]***

The State in Caribbean society / edited by Omar Davies. New ed. Mona, Jamaica : University of the West Indies, Dept. of Economics, c1986. vii, 157 p. ; 21 cm. (Monograph / Department of Economics, UWI, Jamaica . #2) "September 1986"--T.p. verso. Proceedings of a symposium sponsored by the Dept. of Economics, University of the West Indies, Mona, Jamaica, Sept. 1985. Includes bibliographies. ISBN 976-410-001-5 (pbk.) LC Card 87-403404 DDC 330.9729/052 19
1. Caribbean Area - Economic conditions - 1945- - Congresses. 2. Caribbean area - Economic policy - Congresses. 3. Caribbean Area - Politics and government - 1945- - Congresses. I. Davies, Omar. II. University of the West Indies (Mona, Jamaica). Dept. of Economics. III. Series: Monograph (University of the West Indies (Mona, Jamaica). Dept. of Economics) , #2.
HC151 .S73 1986

The State in global perspective / edited by Ali Kazancigil. Aldershot, Hants, Eng. ; Brookfield, Vt., USA : Gower Pub. Co. ; xx, 300 p. : ill. ; 23 cm. Includes bibliographies and index. ISBN 0-566-05160-5 (U. S.) : LC Card 85-31741 DDC 320.1 19
1. State, The - Addresses, essays, lectures. 2. Comparative government - Addresses, essays, lectures. I. Kazancigil, Ali. ***NYPL [JLD 86-3236]***

State income tax consequences of retirement plan distributions /. Curatola, Anthony P. Brookfield, Wis. , c1986. 20 p. ; ISBN 0-89154-324-4 (pbk.) LC Card 87-158902 DDC 336.24/16 19
HJ4653.P5 C87 1986

State initiatives in elderly housing . Tiven, Marjorie. Washington, DC , c1987. xviii, 79 p. ; LC Card 87-154352 DDC 363.5/9 19
HD7287.92.U54 T58 1987

STATE-LOCAL FISCAL RELATIONS. see **INTERGOVERNMENTAL FISCAL RELATIONS.**

STATE-LOCAL RELATIONS - FLORIDA.
Sapolsky, Joann. Catalogue of state shared revenue sources distributed between 1973-1986. Tallahassee, Fla. (House Office Bldg., Tallahassee 32301) [1986] v, 76 leaves : LC Card 86-623224 DDC 336.1/85/09759 19
HJ375 .S26 1986

STATE-LOCAL RELATIONS - UNITED STATES.
Bowman, Ann O'M., 1948- The resurgence of the states /. Englewood Cliffs, N.J. , c1986. x, 269 p. : ISBN 0-13-774969-4 (pbk.) LC Card 85-19213 DDC 353.9 19
JK2408 .B68 1986 ***NYPL [JLE 86-4496]***

Intergovernmental relations and public policy /. New York , 1986. viii, 224 p. : ISBN 0-313-25443-5 (lib. bdg. : alk. paper) LC Card 86-3155 DDC 353.9/29 19
JK325 .I575 1986 ***NYPL [JLE 87-749]***

Silkman, Richard H. Subsidizing inefficiency . New York , 1985. xviii, 101 p.: ISBN 0-03-000662-7 (alk. paper) : LC Card 84-26628 DDC 336.1/85 19
HJ275 .S53 1985 ***NYPL [JLE 85-2261]***

State milk regulation : extent, economic effects, and legal status. [Washington, D.C.] (1301 New York Ave., N.W., Washington 20005-4788) : U. S. Dept. of Agriculture, Economic Research Service, National Economics Division, [1986] viii, 62 p. ; 28 cm. (Staff report . no. AGES860404) Bibliography: p. 51-62. LC Card 86-602413 DDC 338.1/771/0973 19
1. Milk trade - Government policy - United States. 2. Milk - Prices - Government policy - United States. 3. Dairy laws - United States - States. I. United States. Dept. of Agriculture. National Economics Division. II. Series: ERS staff report , no. AGES 860404.
HD9282.U4 S72 1986

STATE MONOPOLIES. see **GOVERNMENT MONOPOLIES.**

The State of families. Milwaukee, Wis. : Family Service America, <c1987- > v. <2 > : ill. ; 28 cm. Includes bibliographical references. CONTENTS. - -- v. 2. Work and family. ISBN 0-87304-226-3 (pbk. : v. 2) LC Card 87-24374 DDC 306.8/5/0973 19
1. Work and family - United States. 2. United States - Social conditions - 1980-. 3. Unemployment - Canada. I. Family Service America.
HD4904.25 .S83 1987

The State of population theory : from Malthus to modern times / edited by David Coleman and

Roger Schofield. Oxford, OX ; New York, NY, USA : B. Blackwell, 1986. 311 p. : ill. ; 24 cm. Includes index. ISBN 0-631-13975-3 : LC Card 85-26668 DDC 304.6/01 19
1. Population - Addresses, essays, lectures. 2. Demography - Addresses, essays, lectures. I. Coleman, David. II. Schofield, Roger.
HB849.4 .S73 1986 ***NYPL [JLE 86-2411]***

State-of-the-art and objectives of reflective raised pavement markers /. McNees, Roger W. College Station, Tex. , Springfield, Va. [1986] vii, 162 p. : LC Card 87-620643 DDC 380.5 s 625.7/97 19
HE203 .T43 no. 322-1 TE203

The state of the art in hospital advertising, 1987 /. Barnett, Ned B. Alexandria, VA , c1987. iii, 56 p. ; ISBN 0-937925-33-0 (pbk.) LC Card 87-61160 DDC 659.1/93621 19
HF6161.H7 B37 1987

State of the environment : an assessment at mid-decade : a report from the Conservation Foundation. Washington, D.C. : The Foundation, c1984. xxxiv, 586 p. : ill., maps ; 23 cm. Includes bibliographical references and index. ISBN 0-89164-084-3 LC Card 84-12651 DDC 363.7/00973 19
1. Environmental protection - United States. 2. Environmental policy - United States. I. Conservation Foundation.
TD171 .S74 1984 ***NYPL [JLD 86-3097]***

State of the environment. Agriculture and the environment in a changing world economy. Washington, D.C. , c1986. xi, 66 p. : ISBN 0-89164-099-1 (pbk.) LC Card 86-24088 DDC 338.1/873 19
HD1761 .A6228 1986

The State of the states : issues papers / The Council of State Governments. Lexington, KY : The Council, c1986. 56 p. ; 28 cm. Includes bibliographies. ISBN 0-87292-064-X (pbk.) LC Card 87-162324 DDC 330.973/0927 19
1. United States - Economic conditions - 1981-. 2. United States - Politics and government - 1981-. I. Council of State Governments.
HC106.8 .S735 1986

State of West Virginia Job Training Partnership Act : planning statistics / [prepared by Labor and Economic Research Section]. Charleston, W.Va. (112 California Ave., Charleston 25305-0112) : The Section, [1986] vi, 233 p. ; 28 cm. Chiefly tables. "June 1986." "LER-LMI-150." LC Card 86-622901 DDC 331.1/09754/021 19
1. Labor supply - West Virginia - Statistics. 2. Occupations - West Virginia - Statistics. 3. Employment forecasting - West Virginia - Statistics. 4. West Virginia - Population - Statistics. I. West Virginia. Dept. of Employment Security. Labor and Economic Research Section.
HD5725.W4 S7 1986

State of West Virginia Job Training Partnership Act planning statistics / West Virginia Department of Employment Security. Charleston, W. Va. (112 California Ave., Charleston 25305-0112) : Labor and Economic Research Section, Dept. of Employment Security, [1985] v, 122 p. ; 28 cm. "Prepared by Labor and Economic Research Section"--Cover. Chiefly tables. "LER-LMI-150. July 1985." LC Card 85-623225 DDC 331.1/09754/021 19
1. Labor supply - West Virginia - Statistics. 2. West Virginia - Population - Statistics. 3. Poor - West Virginia - Statistics. I. West Virginia. Dept. of Employment Security. Labor and Economic Research Section.
HD5725.W4 S7 1985

State, oil, and agriculture in Nigeria / Michael Watts, editor. Berkeley : Institute of International Studies, University of California, c1987. xiv, 327 p. : ill. ; 24 cm. (Research series, 0068-6093 . no. 66) Bibliography: p. 297-317. Includes index. ISBN 0-87725-166-5 (pbk.) : LC Card 87-2941 DDC 338.1/8669 19
1. Agriculture - Economic aspects - Nigeria. 2. Agriculture and state - Nigeria. 3. Petroleum industry and trade - Nigeria. 4. Saving and investment - Nigeria. 5. Nigeria - Economic policy. I. Watts, Michael. II. Series: Research series (University of California, Berkeley. Institute of International Studies) , no. 66.
HD2145.5 .S73 1987

State-owned enterprises in high technology industries . Ramamurti, Ravi. New York , 1987. xii, 306 p. ; ISBN 0-03-068767-5 (alk. paper) : LC Card 85-30751 DDC 338.4/762/00954 19
HC440.H53 R36 1986 ***NYPL [JLE 87-1514]***

State-owned multinationals /. Anastassopoulos, J. P. [Multinationales publiques. English.] Chichester [England] , New York , c1987. xii, 200 p. : ISBN 0-471-91502-5 : LC Card 87-2033 DDC 338.8/8 19
HD2755.5 .A613 1987

STATE OWNERSHIP. see **GOVERNMENT OWNERSHIP.**

STATE PLANNING. see **ECONOMIC POLICY; REGIONAL PLANNING; SOCIAL POLICY.**

State politics and the new federalism : readings and commentary / edited by Marilyn Gittell. White Plains, N.Y. : Longman, c1986. xv, 544 p. : ill., map ; 23 cm. Includes index. Bibliography: p. 533-535. ISBN 0-582-28474-0 (pbk.) LC Card 85-15956 DDC 321.02/0973 19
1. Federal government - United States - Addresses, essays, lectures. 2. State governments - United States - Addresses, essays, lectures. 3. Local government - United States - Addresses, essays, lectures. 4. Intergovernmental fiscal relations - United States - Addresses, essays, lectures. 5. United States - Politics and government - 1981- - Addresses, essays, lectures. 6. United States - Economic policy - 1981- - Addresses, essays, lectures. 7. United States - Social policy - 1980- - Addresses, essays, lectures. I. Gittell, Marilyn.
JK325 .S77 1986 ***NYPL [JLD 86-2766]***

STATE, THE - ADDRESSES, ESSAYS, LECTURES.
The Rise of the modern state /. Brighton, Sussex , 1986. viii, 255 p. ; ISBN 0-7450-0059-2
NYPL [JLD 86-2353]

The State in global perspective /. Aldershot, Hants, Eng. ; Brookfield, Vt., USA : xx, 300 p. : ISBN 0-566-05160-5 (U. S.) : LC Card 85-31741 DDC 320.1 19
NYPL [JLD 86-3236]

STATE, THE - HISTORY OF THEORIES. see **POLITICAL SCIENCE - HISTORY.**

State University of New York at Stony Brook. Institute for Technology Policy in Development. Munasinghe, Mohan, 1945- Rural electrification for development . Boulder , 1987. xxiii, 440 p. : ISBN 0-8133-0088-6 (pbk.) LC Card 87-50130 DDC 333.79/32/091724 19
HD9688.D44 M85 1987

State University of New York. Research Foundation. Institute for Traffic Safety Management and Research. Dowling, Anne M. Two years of accident experience under STOP-DWI, December 1981-November 1983 /. [Albany] [1984] xiii, 67 p. : LC Card 86-622431 DDC 363.1/251 19
HE5620.D7 D68 1984

STATE, WELFARE. see **WELFARE STATE.**

State workers' compensation. Information on the administration of workers' compensation programs in each state and the District of Columbia /. [Washington, D.C.?] [1985] iii, 426 p. ; LC Card 86-601358 DDC 368.4/1/00973 19
HD7103.65.U6 I55 1985

State workers' compensation, administration profiles. Information on the administration of workers' compensation programs in each state and the District of Columbia /. [Washington, D.C.?] [1985] iii, 426 p. ;
NYPL [JLF 86-774]

Statement of financial accounting standards . (no. 88) Public record . Stamford, Conn. (P.O. Box 3821, Stamford 06905-0821) [1986] 424 p. ; LC Card 86-81700 DDC 657/.75 19
HF5686.O5 P83 1986

Statement of John S.R. Shad, Chairman of the Securities and Exchange Commission, before the House Subcommittee on Oversight and Investigations of the Committee on Energy and Commerce, concerning EDGAR (Electronic Data Gathering, Analysis, and Retrieval System), March 14, 1985. Shad, John S. R., 1923- [Washington, D.C. , 1985] 21, 5, 2, [12] p. : LC Card 85-148449 DDC 353.0082/58 19
HG4910 .S417 1985

Statement of principles of editorial integrity in public broadcasting / developed by the Editorial Integrity Project. Columbia, S.C. (P.O. Box 5966, Columbia 29250) : The Project, [1985] 21 p. : ill. ; 22 cm. Includes bibliographical references. LC Card 87-126452 DDC 384.54/53 19
1. Public broadcasting - United States. I. Editorial Integrity Project (U. S.).
HE8689.8 .S72 1986

Statens råd för byggnadsforskning (Sweden) Byggsektorn 1990 . Stockholm [1982] 91 p. : LC Card 83-234610
HD9715.S852 B93 1982

Statens samfundsvidenskabelige forskningsråd (Denmark) Unemployment . Berlin , New York , 1987. xx, 353 p. : ISBN 0-89925-277-X : LC Card 87-24369 DDC 331.13/7 19
HD5701.3 .U53 1987

STATES, SMALL - ECONOMIC CONDITIONS - MATHEMATICAL MODELS.
Santacoloma, Juan Francisco. Modelos macroeconómicos en economías abiertas /. Bilbao , 1983. 3 v. : ISBN 84-7485-037-1 (set) LC Card 84-168556 DDC 339/.0724 19
HB141 .S28 1983 ***NYPL [JLL 86-351]***

STATES, SMALL - ECONOMIC POLICY - MATHEMATICAL MODELS.
Steingräber, Carola, 1956- Geld- und Fiskalpolitik in Portfolio-orientierten Modellen kleiner offener Volkswirtschaften . Rheinfelden , c1986. ix, 219 p. : ISBN 3-87718-532-0 LC Card 86-182509
HG230.3 .S74 1986

States versus markets in the world-system / edited by Peter Evans, Dietrich Rueschemeyer, Evelyne Huber Stephens. Beverly Hills, Calif. : Sage Publications, c1985. 295 p. ; 23 cm. (Political economy of the world-system annuals. v. 8) Includes bibliographies. ISBN 0-8039-2510-7 LC Card 85-11716 DDC 338.9 19
1. Industry and state - Case studies. 2. Comparative advantage (Commerce) - Case studies. I. Evans, Peter B., 1944-. II. Rueschemeyer, Dietrich. III. Stephens, Evelyne Huber.
HD3611 .S76 1985 ***NYPL [JLD 86-3227]***

STATESMEN - AUSTRIA - BIOGRAPHY.
Spitzmüller, Alexander, 1862-1953. Memoirs of Alexander Spitzmüller, Freiherr von Harmersbach (1862-1953) . Boulder , New York , 1987. xi, 327 p., [5] p. of plates : ISBN 0-88033-124-0 LC Card 87-80511 DDC 332.3/2/0924 B 19
HG1552.S65 A3 1987

STATESMEN - HUNGARY - INTERVIEWS.
Gáspár, Sándor. A munkásosztály szolgálatában /. [Budapest] , c1983. 326 p., [26] p. of plates : ISBN 963-322-025-4 : LC Card 84-129952
HD6680.5.Z55 G375 1983

STATESMEN - SWITZERLAND - BIOGRAPHY.
Somary, Felix, 1881-1956. [Erinnerungen aus meinem Leben. English.] The raven of Zürich . London , New York , c1986. xii, 310 p. : ISBN 0-312-66407-9 LC Card 86-6662 DDC 330/.092/4 B 19
HB101.S6 A313 1986 ***NYPL [JFE 87-54]***

STATESMEN - UNITED STATES - BIOGRAPHY.
Hammer, Armand, 1897- Hammer /. New York , c1987. 544 p., [32] p. of plates : ISBN 0-399-13275-9 LC Card 86-30289 DDC 338.092/4 B 19
HC102.5.H35 A3 1987

Hickman, Martin Berkeley, 1925- David Matthew Kennedy . Salt Lake City, Utah , c1987. xi, 403 p. : ISBN 0-87579-093-3 : LC Card 87-19898 DDC 332.1/092/4 B 19
HG2463.K46 H53 1987

Statham, Anne. The worth of women's work : a qualitative synthesis / Anne Statham, Eleanor M. Miller, and Hans O. Mauksch. Albany : State University of New York Press, c1988. xiv, 331 p. ; 24 cm. (SUNY series on women in work) Includes bibliographies and indexes. ISBN 0-88706-591-0 LC Card 87-6472 DDC 331.4/0973 19
1. Women - Employment - United States. I. Miller, Eleanor M., 1948-. II. Mauksch, Hans O. III. Title. IV. Series.
HD6095 .S73 1988

Stationary compressors in the U. S. U. S. stationary compressors market. New York, N.Y. , c1983. xi, 271 p. : LC Card 87-143527

DDC 380.1/4562153/0973 19
HD9705.5.C643 U648 1983

Stationary compressors in the US. U. S. stationary compressors market. New York, N.Y. , c1983. xi, 271 p. : LC Card 87-143527
DDC 380.1/4562153/0973 19
HD9705.5.C643 U648 1983

Stationen : Festschrift für Rudolf Eberhard zum 70. Geburtstag / herausgegeben von Theodor Maunz. Darmstadt : Wissenschaftliche Buchgesellschaft, 1984. ix, 228 p., [1] leaf of plates : ill. ; 23 cm. Includes bibliographical references. ISBN 3-534-02410-9 LC Card 85-138779
1. Germany, West - Economic policy. 2. Germany, West - Economic conditions. 3. Germany, West - Politics and government. 4. Bavaria (Germany) - Economic policy. 5. Bavaria (Germany) - Economic conditions. 6. Bavaria (Germany) - Politics and government. 7. Eberhard, Rudolf, 1914-. I. Eberhard, Rudolf, 1914-. II. Maunz, Theodor, 1901-.
HC286.5 .S825 1984

Statistica e pubblica amministrazione : ordinamento, struttura, compiti e prospettive di lavoro / a cura di Rita Perez. Milano : A. Giuffrè, 1983-1985. 2 v. ; 26 cm. Proceedings of seminars organized by the Istituto di diritto delle assicurazioni, held in Rome in 1983 and 1985. At head of title: Università degli studi di Roma "La Sapienza." Facoltà di scienze statistiche demografiche e attuariali. Istituto di diritto delle assicurazioni. CONTENTS. - [1. without special title] -- 2. I servizi pubblici. ISBN 88-14-00703-9 (v. 2) : LC Card 86-215546
1. Italy - Statistical services - Congresses. 2. Public welfare - Italy - Statistical services - Congresses. 3. Public administration - Italy - Data processing - Congresses. I. Perez, Rita. II. Università degli studi di Roma "La Sapienza." Istituto di diritto delle assicurazioni.
HA37.I9 S7 1983

Statistică industrială . Ştefan, C. Bucureşti , 1985. 223 p. ; LC Card 86-155097
HB137 .S76 1985

Statistical abstract of East-West trade and finance . Oechsler, Ronald G. Washington, D.C. [1986]. vi, 43 p. : LC Card 86-601999
DDC 382/.091713/01717021 19
HF1411 .O3455 1986

Statistical abstract of Iceland, 1984. Tölfræđihandbók 1984 =. Reykjavík , 1984. 12, 268 p. ; LC Card 87-165528
HA1491 .A4 vol. II, 82

Statistical abstract of Latin America. Supplement series .
(suppl. 6) Quantitative Latin American studies . Los Angeles , 1977. xiv, 91 p. : ISBN 0-87903-227-8 LC Card 77-620011 DDC 330.9/8/003
HD5731.A6 Q36 ***NYPL [JLF 80-242]***

(suppl. 8) Wilkie, Richard W., 1938- Latin American population and urbanization analysis . Los Angeles, Calif. , c1984. xxii, 433 p. : ISBN 0-87903-242-1 (alk. paper) : LC Card 83-620019
DDC 312/.098 19
HB3530.5 .W54 1984 ***NYPL [JLF 87-298]***

(v. 6) Quantitative Latin American studies . Los Angeles , 1977. xiv, 91 p. : ISBN 0-87903-227-8
LC Card 77-620011 DDC 330.9/8/003
HD5731.A6 Q36 ***NYPL [JLF 80-242]***

A statistical account of foreign and English railways . Bermingham, Thomas. London , 1839. 24 p. ; LC Card 85-665741
HE2271 .B47x 1839

Statistical aspects of physician payment systems : a report of the National Committee on Vital and Health Statistics. Hyattsville, Md. : U. S. Dept. of Health and Human Services, Public Health Service, National Center for Health Statistics, [1987] vii, 33 p. : ill. ; 28 cm. (Documents and committee reports, series 4 . no 24) DHHS publication ; no. (PHS) 87-1461 Prepared by the Subcommittee on Statistical Aspects of Physician Payment Systems. ISBN 0-8406-0357-6 LC Card 86-600375 DDC 362.1/0723 s 362.1/72 19
1. Ambulatory medical care - Utilization - Reporting - United States. 2. Medical record linkage - United States. I. United States. National Committee on Vital and Health Statistics. II. United States. National Committee on Vital and Health Statistics. Subcommittee on Statistical Aspects of Physician Payment Systems. III. National Center for Health Statistics (U. S.).
HA37 .U1693 no. 24 RA408.5

Statistical bulletin (Ethiopia. Central Statistical Office) .
(34) The Rural integrated household survey programme . Addis Abeba [1983] 52 leaves ;
LC Card 86-980701 DDC 307.7/2/0723 19
HB2542.A3 R87 1983

(44) Average producers' prices of agricultural commodities in rural area by region, Miazia 1973-Miazia 1974, (May 1981-April 1982) /. Addis Ababa , 1985. 14 leaves ; LC Card 85-981293 DDC 338.1/3/0963021 19
HD2124.5 .A93 1985

(51) Rural labour force survey, April 1981-April 1982 /. Addis Ababa , 1985. xii, 170 p. ; LC Card 86-981178 DDC 331.1/0963 19
HD5839.7.A6 R87 1985

Statistical bulletin (New Zealand. Dept. of Statistics)
Trends and patterns in New Zealand fertility, 1912-1983. Wellington, N.Z. , 1986. 77 p. : ISBN 0-477-06453-1 (pbk.) : LC Card 86-219193 DDC 304.6/32/09931021 19
HB1102.5.A3 T74 1986

Statistical bulletin (United States. Dept. of Agriculture) .
(no. 740) Lucier, Gary. Farm income data . Washington, DC [1986] iv, 311 p. : LC Card 86-602022 DDC 338.1/0973 s 338.1/3/0973021 19
HD1751 .A5 no. 740 HD1769

(no. 742) Selected agricultural statistics on Spain, 1970-82 /. Washington, D.C. (1301 New York Ave., N.W., Washington 20005-4788) , 1986. x, 142 p. : LC Card 86-602416 DDC 338.1/0973 s 338.1/0946/021 19
HD1751 .A5 no. 742 HD2022

(no. 743) Hanthorn, Michael. Selected farm machinery statistics /. Washington, D.C. , 1986] ii, 54 p. : LC Card 86-602408 DDC 338.1/61/0973 19
HD1751 .A5 no. 743 HD9486.U4

STATISTICAL INFERENCE. see MATHEMATICAL STATISTICS.

Statistical information on the financial services industry. 3rd ed. Washington, D.C. (1120 Connecticut Ave., N.W., Washington 20036) : American Bankers Association, c1984. xi, 272 p. : ill. ; 28 cm. Bibliography: p. 269-272. LC Card 84-253106 DDC 332.1/0973/021 19
1. Finance - United States - Statistics. 2. Financial institutions - United States - Statistics. 3. Banks and banking - United States - Statistics.
HG181 .S795 1984 ***NYPL [*R-Econ. 86-285]***

Statistical information on the financial services industry. 4th ed. Washington, D.C. (1120 Connecticut Ave., N.W., Washington 20036) : American Bankers Association, c1987. xi, 273 p. : ill. ; 28 cm. Bibliography: p. 271-273. LC Card 87-402171 DDC 332.1/0973/021 19
1. Finance - United States - Statistics. 2. Financial institutions - United States - Statistics. 3. Banks and banking - United States - Statistics. I. American Bankers Association.
HG181 .S795 1987

Statistical methods for the social and behavioral sciences /. Marascuilo, Leonard A. New York , c1988. xxvi, 804 p. : ISBN 0-7167-1824-3 LC Card 87-398 DDC 519.5 19
HA29 .M2482 1988

Statistical packages for the IBM PC family /. O'Keeffe, Linda. New York , c1986. x, 162 p. : ISBN 0-07-056320-9 : LC Card 85-18213 DDC 658/.055365 19
HF1017 .O39 1986 ***NYPL [JSE 86-1876]***

Statistical policy working paper .
(13) Federal longitudinal surveys /. [Washington, D.C.?] [Springfield, VA] 1986. v, 159 p. : LC Card 86-603413 DDC 001.4/33 19
HA31.2 .F43 1986

Statistical profile on women labour. Simla : Govt. of India, Ministry of Labour and Rehabilitation, Dept. of Labour, Labour Bureau, [1983] v, 224 p. ; 30 cm. Chiefly tables. LC Card 84-900395 DDC 331.4/0954/021 19
1. Labor supply - India - Statistics. 2. Wages - India - Statistics. 3. Social security - India - Statistics. 4. Trade-unions - India - Statistics. I. India. Labour Bureau.
HD5819 .S83 1983 ***NYPL [JLF 86-1946]***

Statistical report (Hawaii. Dept. of Planning and Economic Development) .
(190) The Population of Hawaii, 1980-1985. [Honolulu] [1986] 12 p. ; LC Card 86-622982
DDC 319.69 s 304.6/09969 19
HA329.1 .A25 no. 190 HA329.5

The Honolulu consumer price index, 1940-1986. [Honolulu] [1986] 19 p. ; LC Card 86-622085
DDC 319.69 s 338.5/28/09969 19
HA329.1 .A25 no. 187 HB235.U6

Statistical Research, Inc. Radar 33 . Westfield, N.J. (111 Prospect St., Westfield 07090) , <c1986-. <v. 2, pt. 1-2; v. 3, pt. 2 > ; LC Card 86-218886 DDC 384.54/3 19
HE8697.A8 R243 1986

Statistical techniques for analytical review in auditing /. Stringer, Kenneth W. New York , c1986. xii, 301 p. : ISBN 0-471-86076-X : LC Card 85-17874 DDC 657/.45/0285536 19
HF5667 .S85 1986 ***NYPL [JLE 86-2704]***

Statistical thinking for managers /. Hildebrand, David K., 1940- Boston, Mass. , c1987. xvii, 894 p. : ISBN 0-87150-036-1 LC Card 86-29222
DDC 519.5/024658 19
HD30.215 .H54 1987

Statistical Training Programme for Africa (United Nations)

Statistical yearbook, 1966. Samut sathiti rāi pī, 2509 . [Bangkok] [19]69. 35 p., [1] leaf of plates : LC Card 83-921129
HA4600.55.Z9 N3737 1969

Statisticheskai͡a ot͡senka faktorov khozi͡aĭstvennoĭ dei͡atel′nosti zagotovitel′nykh organizat͡siĭ /. Kulinich, Emel′i͡an Ivanovich. Moskva , 1983. 191 p. : LC Card 84-165083
HD39.5 .K84 1983

Statisticheskai͡a ot͡senka normativov otraslevogo planirovanii͡a /. Rozin, Bent͡sian Borisovich. Novosibirsk , 1986. 188, [3] p. : LC Card 86-230359
HC336.25 .R69 1986

Statisticheskie metody v issledovanii͡akh truda, dokhodov i potreblenii͡a / [redakt͡sionnai͡a kollegii͡a T.V. Ri͡abushkin (otvetstvennyĭ redaktor) ... et al.]. Moskva : Izd-vo "Nauka", 1981. 382 p. : ill. ; 21 cm. (Uchenye zapiski po statistike . t. 42) At head of title: Akademii͡a nauk SSSR. T͡Sentral′nyĭ ėkonomiko-matematicheskiĭ institut. "Bibliografii͡a osnovnykh opublikovannykh nauchnykh trudov A.I. Gozulova": p. 377-[381] Includes bibliographies. LC Card 82-155399
1. Cost and standard of living - Soviet Union - Statistical methods. 2. Quality of life - Soviet Union - Statistical methods. I. Ri͡abushkin, T. V. (Timon Vasil′evich). II. Series.
HA1.A38 A15 t. 42 HD7035

Statisticheskie problemy upravlenii͡a .
(vyp. 28) Shpilevskiĭ, Ė. Printsipy dinamicheskoĭ klassifikatsii stokhasticheskikh protsessov i sistem . Vil′ni͡us , 1978. 138 p. ;
LC Card 81-173567
HD38 .S715 vyp. 28 QA274

(vyp. 37) Razrabotka i issledovanie algoritmov dinamicheskoĭ klassifikatsii protsessov . Vil′ni͡us , 1979. 93 p. : LC Card 82-150323
HD38 .S715 vyp. 37 T57.83

(vyp. 42) Pervichnoe opisanie signalov rechi . Vil′ni͡us , 1980. 67 p. : LC Card 82-107723
HD38 .S715 vyp. 42 TK7882.S65

(vyp. 49) Sistema raspoznavanii͡a ritmogramm serdtsa . Vil′ni͡us , 1980. 55 p. : LC Card 81-194159
HD38 .S715 vyp. 49 QP112.5.C3

Statisticheskie problemy upravlenii͡a, 0132-5302 .
(vyp. 65) Obnaruzhenie izmeneniĭ svoĭstv sluchaĭnykh protsessov . Vil′ni͡us , 1984. 243 p. : LC Card 84-168819
HD38 .S715 vyp. 65 QA274.A1

(vyp. 73) T͡Sifrovye metody i algoritmy obrabotki signalov . Vil′ni͡us , 1986. 120 p. :
LC Card 86-232937
HD38 .S715 vyp. 73 TK5102.5

(vyp. 76) Kligene, Nerute. Raspoznavanie sluchaĭnykh protsessov s peremennoĭ strukturoĭ veroi͡atnostnykh raspredeleniĭ . Vil′ni͡us , 1986. 136 p. : LC Card 87-146330
HD38 .S715 vyp.76 QA274

Statisticheskoe izuchenie proizvoditel'nosti truda / [redaktsionnai͡a kollegii͡a T.V. Ri͡abushkin (otvetstvennyĭ redaktor) ... et al.]. Moskva : Izd-vo "Nauka," 1981. 407 p. ; 20 cm. (Uchenye zapiski po statistike . t. 41) At head of title: Akademii͡a nauk SSSR. T͡Sentral'nyĭ ėkonomiko-matematicheskiĭ institut. "Soderzhanie tomov 26-37 'Uchenykh zapisok po statistike AN SSSR' (1974-1980": p. 348-361. Includes bibliographies and indexes. LC Card 82-155063 DDC 330/.018 s 331.11/8/0947 19
1. Labor productivity - Soviet Union - Statistical methods. 2. Labor productivity - Statistical methods. I. Ri͡abushkin, T. V. (Timon Vasil'evich). II. T͡Sentral'nyĭ ėkonomiko-matematicheskiĭ institut (Akademii͡a nauk SSSR). III. Series.
HA1.A38 A15 t. 41 HC340.L3
NYPL [*QIP 87-1311]

Statisticheskoe upravlenie Karel'skoĭ ASSR. Narodnoe khozi͡aĭstvo Karel'skoĭ ASSR . Petrozavodsk , 1985. 94 p. ; LC Card 86-124957
HA1448.K32 N37 1985

Statisticheskoe upravlenie Kirovskoĭ oblasti. Narodnoe khozi͡aĭstvo Kirovskoĭ oblasti v desi͡atoĭ pi͡atiletke, 1976-1980 gg. . Kirov , 1981. 95 p. ; LC Card 82-146329
HC337.R852 K576 1981

Statisticheskoe upravlenie Mordovskoĭ ASSR. Narodnoe khozi͡aĭstvo Mordovskoĭ ASSR za gody odinnadtsatoĭ pi͡atiletki, 1981-1985 gg. . Saransk , 1986. 198 p. ; LC Card 87-120800
HA1448.M59 N33 1986

STATISTICIANS - UNITED STATES - DIRECTORIES.
Evinger, William R., 1943- Federal statistical directory . Phoenix, Ariz. , 1987. iv, 127 p. ; ISBN 0-89774-398-9 (pbk.) LC Card 87-12359 DDC 353.0081/9 19
HA37.U55 E85 1987

Statistički informacioni sistem SR Srbije u društvenom sistemu informisanja republike . Babić, Bogdan. Beograd , 1986- v. <1 > ; LC Card 87-168381
HA37.Y83 S43 1986

Statistics and control of stochastic processes /. Steklov Seminar (1984 : Steklov Institute of Mathematics) [Statistika i upravlenie sluchaĭnykh protsessov. English.] New York, N.Y. , c1985. xiii, 506 p. ; ISBN 0-911575-18-9 LC Card 85-8851 DDC 519.5 19
QA276.A1 .S7513 1984 ***NYPL [JSE 86-729]***

Statistics bulletin (New Zealand. Dept. of Statistics)
Census of distribution, 1977-78 . Wellington, N.Z. [1980]-<[1981]. v. <11 > : LC Card 86-204705
HF5429.6.N47 C46 1980

Statistics Canada.
Family characteristics and labour force activity . Ottawa , c1986. xxii, 131 p. ; ISBN 0-660-52240-3 (pbk.) : LC Card 86-206978
HD5728 .F36 1986

Statistics Canada [Bureau] see **Canada. Statistics Canada.**

Statistics Canada. Census and Household Surveys Field. Revised annual estimates of population for census divisions, 1971-1976 /. Ottawa , c1979. 21 p. ; LC Card 82-216681
HA745 .R473 1979

Statistics Canada. Demography Division.
Population estimation methods, Canada. Ottawa : Statistics Canada, Demography Division : Publication Sales, Statistics Canada [distributor], c1987. 117 p. : ill. ; 23 cm. Errata slip inserted. "Catalogue 91-528E." Includes bibliographical references. ISBN 0-660-12028-3 (pbk.) : LC Card 87-168812 DDC 304.6/0724 19
1. Population forecasting - Canada - Methodology. 2. Canada - Census. I. Title.
HB3529 .S73 1987

STATISTICS CANADA - HISTORY.
Cook, W. Rupert. Canadian statistical data . [Canada] [1985?] vi, 218 p. : LC Card 87-118992 DDC 354.710081/9 19
HA37.C26 C66 1985

Statistics Canada. Industrial Prices Section.
Industrial product price indexes, 1981=100 . Ottawa , c1986. 216 p. : ISBN 0-660-52876-2 (pbk.) : LC Card 87-168891
HB235.C2 I53 1986

Statistics Canada. Labour and Household Surveys Analysis Division. Rashid, A. Characteristics of high income families, 1980 /. Ottawa [1986] 97 p. : ISBN 0-660-52875-4 (pbk.) : LC Card 86-210700
HC120.I5 R36 1986

Statistics Canada. Labour Force Activity Section. Self-employment in Canada =. Ottawa , c1985. 33 p. : ISBN 0-660-52868-1 (pbk.) : LC Card 87-101519
HD8037.C2 S45 1985

Statistics Canada. Population Projections Section. Interim household and family projections for Canada, provinces, and territories to 2006 =. [Ottawa] [1987] 67 p. ; LC Card 87-162270 DDC 304.6/2/0971021 19
HA745 .I62 1987

Statistics Canada. Seasonal Adjustment and Time Series Analysis Staff. Dagum, Estela Bee. The X-II-ARIMA seasonal adjustment method /. Ottawa , c1980. 119 p. : LC Card 83-225028
HB137 .D34 1980

STATISTICS CANADA. STANDARD DIVISION.
Canadian standard industrial classification for companies and enterprises, 1980. Ottawa , c1986. xii, 381 p. ; ISBN 0-660-11945-5 : LC Card 87-120163 DDC 338/.02/0971 19
HC115 .C417 1986

Statistics Canada. Statistical Services Field. A compendium of methods of error evaluation in censuses and surveys / Statistics Canada, Statistical Services Field. Ottawa : Statistics Canada, Statistical Services Field, 1978. 25 p. ; 28 cm. "This compendium was assembled within the methodology divisions of the Statistical Services Field, Statistics Canada by a team consisting of J.-F. Gosselin, B. N. Chinnappa, P. D. Ghangurde and J. Toruigny." Bibliography: p. 25. LC Card 80-499370 DDC 001.4/225 19
1. Census. 2. Error analysis (Mathematics). I. Gosselin, J.-F. II. Title.
HA31.2 .C36 1978 ***NYPL [JLF 81-125]***

STATISTICS - CONGRESSES.
Artificial intelligence and statistics /. Reading, Mass. , c1986. xiv, 418 p. : ISBN 0-201-11568-9 : LC Card 85-28631 DDC 006.3 19
Q334 .A764 1986 ***NYPL [JSE 87-399]***

STATISTICS - DATA PROCESSING.
Bond, Kenneth M. Essential business statistics . Boston , c1988. xiii, 332 p. : ISBN 0-534-91530-2 LC Card 87-25652 DDC 519.5/028/55369 19
HF1017 .B63 1988

Bowerman, Bruce L. Computer modeling for business and industry /. New York , c1984. vii, 219 p. : ISBN 0-8247-7296-2 LC Card 84-17063 DDC 519.5/0285425 19
HF1017 .B655 1984 ***NYPL [JSE 86-623]***

Hildebrand, David K., 1940- Statistical thinking for managers /. Boston, Mass. , c1987. xvii, 894 p. : ISBN 0-87150-036-1 LC Card 86-29222 DDC 519.5/024658 19
HD30.215 .H54 1987

Levine, David M., 1946- Using Minitab with Basic business statistics /. Englewood Cliffs, N.J. , c1986. viii, 160 p. : ISBN 0-13-057779-0 (pbk.) LC Card 87-400304 DDC 519.5/028/55369 19
HF1017 .L425 1986

O'Dell, Jerry W. BASIC statistics, an introduction to problem solving with your personal computer /. Blue Ridge Summit, PA , c1984. vii, 452 p. : ISBN 0-8306-0759-5 : LC Card 84-8804 DDC 519.5/028/542 19
QA276.4 .O34 1984 ***NYPL [JSD 86-378]***

STATISTICS - DATA PROCESSING - HANDBOOKS, MANUALS, ETC.
Miller, Robert B. (Robert Burnham), 1942- Minitab handbook for business and economics /. Boston , c1988. x, 331 p. : ISBN 0-87150-092-2 (pbk.) LC Card 86-32830 DDC 519.5/02855369 19
HF1017 .M494 1988

STATISTICS - DICTIONARIES.
Kotz, Samuel. Russian-English, English-Russian glossary of statistical terms. Edinburgh, 1971. vii, 87 p. ISBN 0-05-002446-9 LC Card 72-197391 DDC 519.5/01/4
HA17 .K62 ***NYPL [JLF 73-1241]***

STATISTICS - DICTIONARIES - RUSSIAN.
Kotz, Samuel. Russian-English, English-Russian glossary of statistical terms. Edinburgh, 1971. vii, 87 p. ISBN 0-05-002446-9 LC Card 72-197391 DDC 519.5/01/4
HA17 .K62 ***NYPL [JLF 73-1241]***

Statistics for business and economics /. Albright, S. Christian. New York , London , c1987. xix, 1012, 5 p. : ISBN 0-02-301620-5 LC Card 86-23751 DDC 519.5 19
HF1017 .A43 1987

Statistics for business and economics /. Anderson, David Ray, 1941- St. Paul, MN , c1987. xxviii, 792 p. : ISBN 0-314-25873-6 : LC Card 86-24613 DDC 519.5 19
HF1017 .A6 1987

Statistics for business and economics /. Kohler, Heinz, 1934- Glenview, Ill. , c1988. 775, [153] p. : ISBN 0-673-18444-7 LC Card 87-11781 DDC 519.5/02433 19
HF1017 .K64 1988

Statistics for business and economics /. McClave, James T. San Francisco , c1988. xxii, 1267 p. : ISBN 0-02-379020-2 LC Card 87-20195 DDC 519.5 19
HF1017 .M36 1988

Statistics for business and economics /. Newbold, Paul. Englewood Cliffs, N.J. , c1988. xiii, 866 p. : ISBN 0-13-845173-7 LC Card 87-14363 DDC 519.5 19
HF1017 .N48 1988

Statistics for economics, business administration, and the social sciences /. Andersen, Erling B. Berlin , New York , c1987. xi, 439 p. : ISBN 0-387-17720-5 (pbk. : U. S.) LC Card 87-9423 DDC 519.5 19
HB137 .A525 1987

Statistics for management and economics . Keller, Gerald. Belmont, Calif. , c1988. xix, 987 p. : ISBN 0-534-08622-5 LC Card 87-19845 DDC 658.4/033 19
HD30.215 .K45 1988

Statistics for modern business decisions /. Lapin, Lawrence L. San Diego , c1987. xxxiii, 825 p. : ISBN 0-15-583737-0 LC Card 85-82633 DDC 519.5/024658 19
HA29 .L2664 1987

STATISTICS - FRANCE - HISTORY.
La Statistique en France . Bruxelles [1980] 194 p. ; LC Card 84-147748
HA19 .S73 1980

STATISTICS, MATHEMATICAL. see **MATHEMATICAL STATISTICS.**

Statistics of income : compendium of studies of international income and taxes. Washington, D.C. : Dept. of the Treasury, Internal Revenue Service : For sale by the Supt. of Docs., U. S. G.P.O., 1985. iii, 516 p. : ill., forms ; 28 cm. (Publication / Internal Revenue Service . 1267) "1979-1983"--Cover. "9-85." Includes bibliographies.
1. Corporations - Taxation - United States - Statistics. 2. Corporations, American - Taxation - United States - Statistics. 3. Corporations, Foreign - Taxation - United States - Statistics. 4. Income tax - United States - Foreign income - Statistics. 5. Foreign tax credit - United States - Statistics. I. Title: Compendium of studies of international income and taxes.
NYPL [JLF 86-833]

Statistics on external indebtedness : the debt and other external liabilities of developing, CMEA, and certain other countries and territories at end-December 1983 and end-December 1984. Paris : Organisation for Economic Co-operation and Development, 1985. 27 p. ; 30 cm. Cover title. Bibliography: p. 26. LC Card 86-204760 DDC 336.3/435/091724 19
1. Debts, External - Developing countries - Statistics. I. Organisation for Economic Co-operation and Development.
HJ8899 .S7 1985

Statistics relative to the New York State Unemployment Insurance Fund, 1936-1984. Albany, N.Y. : State of New York, Dept. of Labor, [1985] vii, 66 p. ; 28 cm. (Labor research report . 1985, no. 4) Cover title. Chiefly tables. "December 1985." LC Card 86-622164 DDC 368.4/4/009747021 19
1. Insurance, Unemployment - New York (State) -

Statistics. 2. Insurance, Unemployment - New York (State) - Finance - Statistics. I. New York (State). Dept. of Labor. II. Series.
HD7096.U6 N793 1985

STATISTICS - STUDY AND TEACHING - AFRICA - DIRECTORIES.

Statistics using ranks . Meddis, Ray. Oxford, OX, UK , New York, NY, USA , 1984. vi, 449 p. : ISBN 0-631-13788-2 (pbk.) : LC Card 84-11087 DDC 519.5 19
HA29 .M43885 1984 ***NYPL [JLE 86-4708]***

Statistiek voor marketingsbeslissingen /. Noort, W. C. J. van, 1950- Leiden , 1985. viii, 229 p. : ISBN 90-207-1351-5 : LC Card 85-214756
HF5415.2 .N66 1985

Statistik der gewerblichen Wirtschaft : Hauptergebnisse der nichtlandwirtschaftlichen Bereichszählungen 1983 / bearbeitet im Österreichischen Statistischen Zentralamt. Wien : Das Zentralamt : Kommissionsverlag, Österreichische Staatsdruckerei, 1986. 2 v. ; 30 cm. (Beiträge zur österreichischen Statistik . 790. Heft) Tables. LC Card 87-409345 DDC 314.36 s 338.09436/021 19
1. Austria - Industries - Statistics. I. Österreichisches Statistisches Zentralamt. II. Series.
HA1173 .A27 Heft 790 HC265

Statistik des Hamburgischen Staates, 0170-3064 . (Heft 128) Das Handwerk in Hamburg . Hamburg [1979] 140 p. ; LC Card 86-133694
HA1282 .A Heft 128 HD2346.G32H3

Statistik von Baden-Württemberg . (Bd. <230 >) Gemeindestatistik 1976. Stuttgart , <1976-. v. <2 > : LC Card 86-222059
HA1320.B2 A32 Bd. 230, etc. JN4939.A15

Statistik von Niedersachsen . (Bd. 387) Landwirtschaftszählung 1979, Gartenbauerhebung 1981/82 . Hannover , 1983. xv, 132 p. ; LC Card 85-117833
HD9013.7.L68 L37 1983

(Bd. 416) Agrarberichterstattung 1983 . Hannover , 1985. viii, 143 p., [3] p. of plates : LC Card 86-222908
HD1960.L68 A38 1985

Statistik von Rheinland-Pfalz . (Bd. 284) Die Wahl zum 9. Landtag in Rheinland-Pfalz am 18. März 1979 /. Bad Ems , 1979. 153, [18], 23 p. : LC Card 86-128836
HA1320 .R453 Bd. 284 JN4945.R4565

(Bd. 294) Die Unternehmen des Gastgewerbes in Rheinland-Pfalz 1979 . Bad Ems [1982] 46 p., [2] p. of plates : LC Card 83-207906 DDC 314.3/43 s 338.4/7647/944343021 19
HA1320 .R453 Bd. 294 TX910.G4

Statistika kinematografii . Mukhin, P. A. (Pavel Aleksandrovich) Moskva , 1984. 103 p. : LC Card 85-203673
HA29.5.R9 M85 1984

Statistika na t͡senite na stokite v tŭrgovii͡ata na edro i drebno. Statistika na t͡senit͡e na stokit͡e v tŭrgoviı͡ata na edro i drebno = Statistique des prix des marchandises dans le commerce de gros et de détail. Sofii͡a : Dŭrzh. pechatnitsa, 1937. 117 p. ; 28 cm. Bulgarian and French. At head of title: T͡Sarstvo Bŭlgarii͡a. Glavna direkt͡sii͡a na statistikata. LC Card 86-222130
1. Prices - Bulgaria - Statistics. I. Bulgaria. Glavna direkt͡sii͡a na statistikata. II. Title. III. Title: Statistique des prix des marchandises dans le commerce de gros et de détail.
HB235.B85 S7 1937

Statistika na t͡senit͡e na stokit͡e v tŭrgoviı͡ata na edro i drebno =. Statistika na t͡senite na stokite v tŭrgoviı͡ata na edro i drebno. Sofii͡a , 1937. 117 p. ; LC Card 86-222130
HB235.B85 S7 1937

Statistika u privredi /. Slović, Dragoslav. Beograd , 1984. 264 p. : LC Card 86-115111
HB131 .S57 1984

Statistika zarabotnoĭ platy na ugol'nykh shakhtakh . Karlin, P. I. (Pavel Ivanovich) Donetsk , 1980. 68 p. : LC Card 82-175895
HD4966.M63 S655 1980

Statistique des prix des marchandises dans le commerce de gros et de détail. Statistika na t͡senite na stokite v tŭrgoviı͡ata na edro i drebno. Statistika na tsenit͡e na stokit͡e v tŭrgoviı͡ata na edro i drebno =. Sofii͡a , 1937. 117 p. ; LC Card 86-222130
HB235.B85 S7 1937

Statistique du mouvement de la population dans les D.O.M. : 1971-1981 / INSEE. Paris : Institut national de la statistique et des études économiques, [1985] 104 p. : forms ; 30 cm. (Archives & documents . no 144) "Décembre 1985." Chiefly tables. ISBN 2-11-064898-8 : LC Card 86-216599
1. Infants (Newborn) - France - Territories and possessions - Mortality - Statistics. 2. Infants - France - Territories and possessions - Mortality - Statistics. 3. France - Statistics, Vital. 4. Marriage - France - Territories and possessions - Statistics. 5. Mortality - France - Territories and possessions - Statistics. I. Institut national de la statistique et des études économiques (France). II. Series: Archives & documents (Institut national de la statistique et des études économiques (France)) , no. 144.
HB1003 .S73 1985

Statistique du recensement de 1981 sur le lieu de naissance la citoyenneté et l'immigration. Boxhill, Walton O. 1981 Census information on place of birth, citizenship, and immigration . Ottawa , c1986. 67, [4] p. : ISBN 0-660-52864-9 (pbk.) : LC Card 86-192857
HA741.5 1981f

La Statistique en France : à l'époque napoléonienne : journée d'étude, Paris, 14 février 1980. Bruxelles : Centre Guillaume Jacquemyns, [1980] 194 p. ; 21 cm. At head of title: Ecole des hautes études en sciences sociales, Séminaire de Louis Bergeron, Paris. Includes bibliographical references. LC Card 84-147748
1. Statistics - France - History. 2. France - Statistical services - History. I. Centre Guillaume Jacquemyns. II. École des hautes études en sciences sociales.
HA19 .S73 1980

Statistiques et études générales . (no. 79) Les Logements neufs en 1978 . Paris , 1982. 40 p. : LC Card 83-176727
HD7338.A4 L64 1982

Statistisch-methodische Untersuchungen zum Problem langer Wellen /. Schulte, Heinrich. Königstein/Ts. , 1981. x, 186 p. : ISBN 3-445-02189-9 LC Card 81-176113 DDC 338.9 19
HB3729 .S38 1981

Die Statistische Differenz in der österreichischen Zahlungsbilanz / Beirat für Wirtschafts- und Sozialfragen. Wien : C. Ueberreuter, 1979. 68 p. : ill. ; 24 cm. Includes bibliographical references. LC Card 85-179826
1. Balance of payments - Austria - Statistical services. I. Beirat für Wirtschafts- und Sozialfragen.
HG3883.A9 S73 1979

Statistische Information . Liechtenstein. Amt für Volkswirtschaft. Vaduz, Fürstentum Liechtenstein [1985] 18 leaves ; LC Card 85-228548
HB3592.9.A3 L54 1985

Statistische Methoden : ihr sachgerechter Einsatz in der empirischen Wirtschafts- und Sozialforschung : ein Kompendium / von Emil Brauchlin ... [et al.]. St. Gallen : W. Surbir, 1983. iii, 195 p. : ill. ; 21 cm. Bibliography: p. 193-195. LC Card 83-240598
1. Social sciences - Statistical methods. I. Brauchlin, Emil.
HA29.5.G4 S72 1983

Statistische Methoden zur Berechnung von Preisniveauindizes integrierter Wirtschaftsräume /. Meinlschmidt, Gerhard. Göttingen , c1985. 142 p. : ISBN 3-525-11262-9 LC Card 85-213565
HB225 .M45 1985

Statistische Mitteilungen des Kantons Zürich . (Heft 107, 3. Folge) Der Grundeigentumswechsel im Kanton Zürich 1973-1980 . [Zürich] [1982] 74 p. : LC Card 85-161363
HA1608.Z6 A3 Heft 107, Folge 3 HD799.Z8

Statistische onderzoekingen . (M25) Nouwt, P. Vruchtbaarheid van geboortegeneraties gebaseerd op waarnemingen over de periode 1950-1983 /. 's-Gravenhage , 1985. 95 p. ; ISBN 90-357-0197-6 : LC Card 86-218161
HB1015 .N68 1985

(M9) Netherlands (Kingdom, 1815-). Centraal Bureau voor de Statistiek. Hoofdafdeling Bevolkingsstatistieken. De gehuwde vrouw en haar kindertal anno 1975 /. 's-Gravenhage , 1980. 78 p. : LC Card 81-100844
HB1015 .N47 1980 ***NYPL [JLM 78-1515 nr.9]***

Statistisches Amt des Kantons Zürich. Der Grundeigentumswechsel im Kanton Zürich 1973-1980 . [Zürich] [1982] 74 p. : LC Card 85-161363
HA1608.Z6 A3 Heft 107, Folge 3 HD799.Z8

Statistisches Landesamt Baden-Württemberg. Gemeindestatistik 1976. Stuttgart , <1976-. v. <2 > : LC Card 86-222059
HA1320.B2 A32 Bd. 230, etc. JN4939.A15

Landkreis Waiblingen /. [Stuttgart] [1965?] 25 p. : LC Card 85-230943
HC288.W34 L36 1965

Statistisches Landesamt Berlin. Ergebnisse der Gebäude- und Wohnungszählung in Berlin (West) am 25. Oktober 1968 . Berlin [1971] 52 p. ; LC Card 85-171262
HA1330.B6 B45 Heft 169 HD7339.B4

Ergebnisse der Gewerbesteuerstatistik in Berlin (West) 1966 /. Berlin [1972] 51 p. ; LC Card 85-171275
HA1330.B6 B45 Heft 200 HJ5627.G2

Ergebnisse der Personalstrukturerhebung in Berlin (West) am 2. Oktober 1968 /. Berlin [1971] 75 p. ; LC Card 85-171250
HA1330.B6 B45 Heft 174 HD5717.5.G32B47

Ergebnisse der Volks- und Berufszählung in Berlin (West) am 27. Mai 1970 . Berlin [1976] 4 v. : LC Card 85-171340
HA1330.B6 B45 Heft 254-257 HA1249.B47

Statistisches Landesamt Rheinland-Pfalz. Die Unternehmen des Gastgewerbes in Rheinland-Pfalz 1979 . Bad Ems [1982] 46 p., [2] p. of plates : LC Card 83-207906 DDC 314.3/43 s 338.4/7647/944343021 19
HA1320 .R453 Bd. 294 TX910.G4

Die Wahl zum 9. Landtag in Rheinland-Pfalz am 18. März 1979 /. Bad Ems , 1979. 153, [18], 23 p. : LC Card 86-128836
HA1320 .R453 Bd. 284 JN4945.R4565

Statistiske analyser . (nr. 56) Borgan, Jens-Kristian. Dødelighet i yrker og sosioøkonomiske grupper 1970-1980 /. Oslo , 1986. 217 p. : ISBN 82-537-2339-3 : LC Card 86-231576
HB1445 .B66 1986

Statistiske meddelelser . (1968:4) Danmarks areal. København , 1968. 228 p., [1] folded leaf of plates : LC Card 83-223613
HD736 .D36 1968

Statistiske undersøgelser (Danmarks statistik) . (nr. 39) Regionale dødelighedsforskelle i Danmark 1971-79. København , 1983. 136 p. : ISBN 87-501-0582-5 : LC Card 84-169325
HA1473 .A35 nr. 39 HB1441

Statisztikai idősorok a Kínai Népköztársaságról. Budapest : Központi Statisztikai Hivatal, 1986. 119 p. ; 24 cm. Tables. Bibliography: p. 119. ISBN 963-02-4495-0 LC Card 86-217703
1. China - Statistics. I. Hungary. Központi Statisztikai Hivatal.
HA4635 .S73 1986

Statisztikai időszaki közlemények . (162. köt) Az Energiatermelés és az energiafelhasználás szerkezete . Budapest , 1970. 44 p. ; LC Card 86-189699
HD9502.H92 E54 1970

(273. köt) Beruházási árindexek, 1968-1971 /. [Budapest] [1972] 56 p. ; LC Card 86-189972
HB235.H8 B48 1972

(349. köt) A Lakosság jövedelme és fogyasztása, 1960-1973 /. [Budapest] , c1975. 91 p. ; ISBN 963-340-048-1 LC Card 86-196944
HC300.295.I5 L32 1975

(448. köt) A Nemzeti vagyon és az állóeszközállomány 1970-1978 /. [Budapest] [1979] 140 p. ; LC Card 82-193609
HC300.295.W4 N454 1979

Statisztikai módszerek, témadokumentáció, 0139-1453 . (18) Szász, Kálmán. A mezőgazdaság nemzetközi összehasonlításának módszerei . Budapest , 1986. 96 p. ; ISBN 963-02-4381-4

LC Card 87-419792
HD1425 .S95 1986

Statisztikai módszertani füzetek .
(19. sz) A Mezőgazdasági és az erdőgazdálkodási árstatisztika módszere /. Budapest , 1986. 81 p. ; LC Card 87-408580
HD9015.H82 M486 1986

(20. sz) A Magyar háztartásstatisztikai megfigyelés módszertana /. Budapest , 1986. 59 p. ; LC Card 87-408579
HA37.H92 M34 1986

Statligt stöd till oljeersättning . Sweden. Oljeersättningsdelegationen. [Stockholm] [1983] 1 v. (various pagings) : ISBN 91-38-07657-8 LC Card 84-218524
HD9502.S82 S96 1983

Statsskattedirektoratet informerer. Vurderingen af landets faste ejendomme pr. 1 april 1981 . København [1982] 225 p. ; ISBN 87-503-4048-4 LC Card 82-232266
HD736 .V87 1982

STATUE OF LIBERTY (NEW YORK, N.Y.) - CENTENNIAL CELEBRATIONS, ETC.
Iacocca, Lee A. The Iacocca tapes [sound recording] . Chicago, Ill. , c1985. 6 sound cassettes : LC Card 87-750990
HD9710.U I

Status of evaluation of rural access roads. Nairobi : Chief Engineer (Roads and Aerodromes) : Permanent Secretary, Ministry of Transport and Communications, 1982. 10 leaves ; 30 cm. At head of title: Republic of Kenya, Ministry of Transport and Communications, Roads and Aerodromes Department. "A paper presented to the Joint Donors Review and Evaluation Meeting held in Nairobi on 19th-28th October, 1982." "October 1982." "P-75-82." LC Card 85-981020 DDC 388.1/09676/2 19
1. Rural Access Roads Programme. 2. Rural roads - Kenya. 3. Kenya - Rural conditions. I. Kenya. Roads and Aerodromes Dept. II. Joint Donors Review and Evaluation Meeting (1982 : Nairobi, Kenya).
HE367.K43 R8578 1982

The Status of Maine's financial institutions : a report of the bank superintendent / prepared by the staff of the Maine Bureau of Banking ; submitted to the 112th Legislature pursuant to the requirements of Title 9-B M.R.S.A. section 217. [Augusta] : The Bureau, [1985] 38 leaves ; 28 cm. Cover title. "January 15, 1985." LC Card 86-621914 DDC 332.1/09741 19
1. Banks and banking - Maine. I. Maine. Bureau of Banking.
HG2611.M2 S73 1985

The Status of Maine's financial institutions : a report of the bank superintendent / prepared by the staff of the Maine Bureau of Banking ; submitted to the 112th Legislature pursuant to the requirements of Title 9-B M.R.S.A. Section 217. [Augusta] : The Bureau, [1986] 38 leaves ; 28 cm. Cover title. "January 15, 1986." LC Card 86-621913 DDC 332.1/09741 19
1. Financial institutions - Maine. 2. Financial institutions - Maine - Statistics. I. Maine. Bureau of Banking.
HG183.M2 S7 1986

Status of women and fertility in Bangladesh /. Noman, Ayesha. Dhaka, Bangladesh , c1983. xv, 91 p. ; LC Card 83-905271 DDC 305.4/2/095492 19
HB1050.6.A3 N65 1983
NYPL [JLD 86-2056]

Status report : the debtor countries after the debt crisis. Philadelphia, PA (3624 Science Center, Philadelphia 19104) : Wharton Econometric Forecasting Associates, c1987. iii, 67 p. : ill. ; 28 cm. "January 1987." Includes bibliographical references. LC Card 87-153448 DDC 336.3/435/091724 19
1. Debts, External - Developing countries - Statistics - Forecasting. 2. Loans, Foreign - Developing countries - Statistics - Forecasting. 3. Debt relief - Developing countries - Statistics - Forecasting. I. Wharton Econometric Forecasting Associates. II. Title: Debtor countries after the debt crisis.
HJ8899 .S72 1987

Status report on concessional flows, April 1986. Washington, D.C., U. S.A. : Joint Ministerial Committee of the Boards of Governors of the World Bank and the International Monetary Fund on the Transfer of Real Resources to Developing Countries (Development Committee) : Copies from World Bank Publications Sales Unit, 1986. 25 p. ; 22 cm. (Development Committee, 0255-8807 . no. 9) Papers presented at a meeting held on Apr. 10-11, 1986 in Washington, D.C. Includes bibliographical references. ISBN 0-8213-0789-4 (pbk.) LC Card 86-214496 DDC 336.3/435/091724
1. Capital movements - Developing countries. 2. Loans, Foreign - Developing countries. 3. Economic assistance - Developing countries. 4. Investments, Foreign - Developing countries. I. Development Committee. II. Series: Development Committee (Series) , no. 9.
HG3891 .S7 1986

STATUTORY FORECLOSURE. see **FORECLOSURE.**

Statystyka i ekonometria / [zespół redakcyjny Zdzisław Hellwig, Wanda Ronka-Chmielowiec]. Wrocław : Wydawn. Uczelniane Akademii Ekonomicznej we Wrocławiu, 1978. 193 p. : ill. ; 24 cm. (Prace naukowe Akademii Ekonomicznej imienia Oskara Langego we Wrocławiu . zesz. 141) Summaries in English. Includes bibliographies. LC Card 81-206821
1. Economics, Mathematical. 2. Econometrics. I. Hellwig, Zdzisław. II. Ronka-Chmielowiec, Wanda. III. Series.
HB9 .B7522 zesz. 141 HB135

Statystyka Polski. Seria Materiały statystyczne .
(34) Spis ludności i mieszkań metodą reprezentacyjną z dnia 6 XII 1984 r. . Warszawa , 1985. xx, 93 p., [2] p. of plates : LC Card 86-176185
HD7345.7.A3 S65 1985

(37) Ceny detaliczne 1971-1985 /. Warszawa , 1985. 160 p. ; LC Card 86-196060
HB235.P6 C45 1985

Statystyka Polski. Seria Studia i prace .
(10) Warunki życia ludności w 1984 r. /. Warszawa , 1985. 108 p. ; LC Card 86-225456
HD7035.7 .W35 1985

Staud, Josef L. Online Wirtschaftsdatenbanken 1987 : mit einem Verzeichnis von Datenbanken, Anbietern und Produzenten : zweisprachig = Online business databases 1987 : with a directory of databases, hosts and producers : bilingual / Josef L. Staud. Frankfurt am Main ; New York : P. Lang, 1987. 2 v. (953 p.) : ill. ; 21 cm. English and German. Bibliography: v. 2, p. 950-953. ISBN 3-8204-9457-X LC Card 87-401300 DDC 025/.0633/025 19
1. Business - Data bases - Directories. I. Title. II. Title: Online business databases 1987.
HF5548.2 .S7737 1987

Staudinger, E. (Eduard), 1952- Auf dem Weg in die Freiheit . Graz , 1984. 356 p. : LC Card 87-672377
HD8419.S82 A93x 1984

Staudinger, Hans-Joachim, 1957- Die Überwachung der Geschäftsführung, eine betriebswirtschaftliche Betrachtung : illustriert am Beispiel der Brauindustrie / Hans-Joachim Staudinger. München : V. Florentz, c1986. lxxxvi, 340 p. ; 21 cm. (Hochschulschriften zur Betriebswirtschaftslehre . Bd. 40) Bibliography: p. lix-lxxxvi. Includes index. ISBN 3-88259-412-8 LC Card 87-125378 DDC 663/.3/0685 19
1. Industrial management. 2. Organizational behavior. 3. Brewing industry. I. Title. II. Series.
HD35 .S6745 1986

Staudt, Kathleen A. Agricultural policy implementation : a case study from western Kenya / Kathleen Staudt. West Hartford, CT : Kumarian Press, c1985. xvi, 68 p. : map ; 28 cm. (Women's roles & gender differences in development, cases for planners . 3) Bibliography: p. 65-68. ISBN 0-931816-18-1 (pbk.) LC Card 84-29737 DDC 338.1/86762 19
1. Agriculture and state - Kenya - Case studies. 2. Women farmers - Kenya - Case studies. 3. Sex discrimination against women - Kenya - Case studies. I. Series: Women's roles & gender differences in development , 3. II. Title.
HD2126.5.Z8 S73 1985
NYPL [JLF 86-1685]

Stauf, Wolfgang. Der wichtige Grund bei der personengesellschaftlichen Auflösungs- und Ausschliessungsklage : eine Untersuchung zu dem Tatbestandsmerkmal wichtiger Grund in den Paragraphen 133, 140, 142 HGB / Wolfgang Stauf. Göttingen : WiRe-Verlagsgesellschaft für Wirtschafts- und Steuerrecht, 1980. xiv, 80 p. ; 21 cm. (Abhandlungen zum Handels-, Gesellschafts- und Wirtschaftsrecht . Bd. 3) Originally presented as the author's thesis, Marburg, 1979, under title: Zum Tatbestandsmerkmal wichtiger Grund in den Paragraphen 133, 140, 142 HGB. Bibliography: p. xi-xiv. ISBN 3-88415-549-0 : LC Card 80-150978 DDC 346.73/07 347.3067 19
1. Business enterprises - Germany, West. 2. Liquidation - Germany, West. 3. Partnership - Germany, West. I. Title. II. Series.
KK2435.7 .S7 1980 ***NYPL [JLD 86-1591]***

Stauffer, Robert B. The Philippines under Marcos : failure of transnational developmentalism / Robert B. Stauffer. Sydney : Transnational Corporations Research Project, University of Sydney, [1986] 207 p. ; 21 cm. Includes bibliographies. ISBN 0-908470-69-X (pbk.) LC Card 87-123266 DDC 338.9599 19
1. Corporate state - Philippines. 2. Philippines - Politics and government - 1946-. 3. Philippines - Economic conditions - 1946-. 4. Corporations, American - Philippines. 5. Philippines - Foreign economic relations - United States. 6. United States - Foreign economic relations - Philippines. 7. Marcos, Ferdinand E. (Ferdinand Edralin), 1917-. I. Title.
HD3616.P62 S7 1986

Stauss, Connie.
Nebraska can work / by Connie Stauss. [Lincoln : Nebraska Dept. of Economic Development, 1986- v. <1 > : ill. ; 28 cm. "January 1986"--Pt. 1, t.p. Includes bibliographies. CONTENTS. - pt. 1. Policy prescriptions for solving the infrastructure problem in Nebraska. LC Card 86-622362 DDC 363/.09782 19
1. Infrastructure (Economics) - Nebraska. I. Title.
HC107.N23 C37 1986

Nebraska can work .
(pt. 1) Stauss, Connie. Policy prescriptions for solving the infrastructure problem in Nebraska /. [Lincoln , 1986] xi, 101 leaves : LC Card 87-102492 DDC 363/.09782 s 363/.09782 19
HC107.N23 C37 1986 pt. 1

Policy prescriptions for solving the infrastructure problem in Nebraska / by Connie Stauss. [Lincoln : Nebraska Dept. of Economic Development, 1986] xi, 101 leaves : ill. ; 28 cm. (Nebraska can work . pt. 1) "January 1986." Includes bibliographies. LC Card 87-102492 DDC 363/.09782 s 363/.09782 19
1. Infrastructure (Economics) - Nebraska. I. Series: Stauss, Connie. Nebraska can work , pt. 1. II. Title.
HC107.N23 C37 1986 pt. 1

Stauth, Cameron. Sacks, Frank. The new IRA handbook . Chicago [1987], c1986. 126 p. : ISBN 0-911445-05-6 (pbk.) : LC Card 87-130659 DDC 332.024/01 19
HG1660.U5 S23 1987

Stauth, Roy. A methodology for determining the socially optimum uses of estuarine resources : report 3, the Great Brak River case study / by Roy Stauth. Rondebosch, South Africa : School of Environmental Studies, University of Cape Town, [1982] v, 119 leaves : ill. ; 30 cm. (Research report / School of Environment Studies . no. 34) "March 1982." "Appendices" (13 leaves) inserted. Bibliography: leaves [7]-[9] of appendices. LC Card 86-210152
1. Great Brak River Estuary (South Africa) - Economic conditions. 2. Water resources development - Social aspects - South Africa - Great Brak River Estuary. 3. Estuarine area conservation - South Africa - Great Brak River. I. Series: Research report (University of Cape Town. School of Environmental Studies) , no. 34. II. Title.
HC905.Z7 G87 1982

Stay home and mind your own business . Frohbieter-Mueller, Jo. White Hall, Va. , c1987. 280 p. : ISBN 0-932620-83-3 (pbk.) : LC Card 87-15922 DDC 658/.041 19
HD62.5 .F76 1987

The steal . Freemantle, Brian. London , 1986. xi, 244 p. ; ISBN 0-7181-2584-3 : LC Card 87-105381 DDC 364.1/63 19
HD38.7 .F74 1986

Steam and the North Atlantic mails . Arnell, J. C. Toronto, Ont. , c1986. x, 295 p. : ISBN 0-919801-36-6 : LC Card 87-127353 DDC 383/.142/091631 19
HE6233 .A76 1986

STEAMBOAT LINES - GERMANY (WEST) - HISTORY.
Witthöft, Hans Jürgen. Hapag-Lloyd . Herford , 1979, c1974. 176 p. : ISBN 3-7822-0201-5 LC Card 85-178567
HE945.H424 W58 1979

STEAMBOAT LINES - MISSISSIPPI RIVER - HISTORY.
White, Bob. The child of an eagle . [Cape Girardeau, Mo. , c1980] v, 78 p. : LC Card 87-405068 DDC 386/.22436 19
HE630.M6 W48 1980

STEAMBOAT LINES - MISSOURI - CAPE GIRARDEAU - HISTORY.
White, Bob. The child of an eagle . [Cape Girardeau, Mo. , c1980] v, 78 p. : LC Card 87-405068 DDC 386/.22436 19
HE630.M6 W48 1980

STEAMBOAT LINES - MISSOURI - SAINT LOUIS - HISTORY.
White, Bob. The child of an eagle . [Cape Girardeau, Mo. , c1980] v, 78 p. : LC Card 87-405068 DDC 386/.22436 19
HE630.M6 W48 1980

STEAMBOATS - REGISTERS. see **SHIP REGISTERS.**

STEAMBOATS - UNITED STATES - HISTORY.
Folsom, Burton W. Entrepreneurs versus the historians /. Washington, DC , New York, NY , c1987. p. cm. ISBN 0-89526-573-7 : LC Card 87-23390 DDC 338/.04/0973 19
HG181 .F647 1987

Stechert, Kathryn B.
Sweet success : how to understand the men in your business life--and win with your own rules / Kathryn B. Stechert. New York : Macmillan ; London : Collier Macmillan, c1986. xiii, 224 p. ; 22 cm. Includes index. Bibliography: p. 207-212. ISBN 0-02-614380-1 LC Card 85-30916 DDC 650.1/024/042 19
1. Sexual division of labor. 2. Men - Psychology. 3. Success in business. I. Title.
HD6053 .S724 1986 ***NYPL [JLD 86-2435]***

[Sweet success]
On your own terms : a woman's guide to working with men / by Kathryn Stechert.1st Vintage Books ed. New York : Vintage Books, 1987, c1986. xvi, 314 p. ; 18 cm. Originally published as: Sweet success. Bibliography: p. [287]-295. Includes index. ISBN 0-394-75301-1 (pbk.) : LC Card 86-40470 DDC 650.1/024042 19
1. Women - Employment. 2. Sexual division of labor. 3. Men - Psychology. 4. Success in business. I. Title.
HD6053 .S724 1987

Steckel, Richard H. (Richard Hall), 1944- The economics of U. S. slave and southern white fertility / Richard H. Steckel. New York : Garland Pub., 1985. 253 p. ; 24 cm. (American economic history) Thesis (Ph. D.)--University of Chicago, 1977. Bibliography: p. 246-253. ISBN 0-8240-6662-6 (alk. paper) : LC Card 84-48314 DDC 304.6/32/08996073075 19
1. Fertility, Human - Southern States - History - 19th century. 2. Afro-Americans - Southern States - Population - History - 19th century. 3. Southern States - Population - History - 19th century. I. Series: American economic history (Garland Publishing, Inc.). II. Title.
HB921 .S74 1985 ***NYPL [JLE 86-2085]***

Steczkowski, Jan. Prace z zakresu planowania i ekonomiki regionu /. Kraków , 1980. 220 p. : LC Card 80-131017
HB9 .K53 nr. 116 HC340.3

Steden, Werner. Finanzpolitik und Einkommensverteilung : e. Wachstums- u. Konjunkturmodell d. Bundesrepublik Deutschland / Werner Steden. Frankfurt am Main ; Bern ; 378 p. ; 21 cm. (Finanzwissenschaftliche Schriften. Bd. 1) Bibliography: p. 367-378. ISBN 3-261-01763-5 LC Card 80-459125
1. Fiscal policy - Germany, West - Mathematical models. 2. Income tax - Germany, West - Mathematical models. 3. Income distribution - Germany, West - Mathematical models. I. Title.
HJ1120 .S74 ***NYPL [JLD 80-3205]***

Steding, Rolf. Rudolph, Jürgen. Aktuelle Fragen der Theorie und Praxis der staatlichen Leitung der Landwirtschaft /. Potsdam-Babelsberg , 1983. 72 p. ; LC Card 83-214391
HD1960.5.Z8 R83 1983

Steel . Bewlay, Simon. London [1985?] 14 p. : LC Card 87-165749 DDC 338.4/7669142/0941 19
HD9521.5 .B48 1985

Steel, Edward M. Jones, Mother, 1843?-1930. [Selections. 1988.] The speeches and writings of Mother Jones /. Pittsburgh, Pa. , 1988. p. cm. ISBN 0-8229-3575-9 LC Card 87-25192 DDC 331.88/0973 19
HD8072 .J7832 1988

STEEL INDUSTRY AND TRADE - BRAZIL.
Figueiredo, João Kubitschek de. A situação das indústrias de base, TT1-39-59 /. [S.l.] [1960?] 75, [2] p. : LC Card 85-144484
HD9524.B82 F54 1960

STEEL INDUSTRY AND TRADE - CAPITAL PRODUCTIVITY.
International Labour Organisation. Iron and Steel Committee. Productivity improvement and its effects on the level of employment and working conditions in the iron and steel industry /. Geneva , 1986. ii, 66 p. : ISBN 92-2-105498-5 (pbk.) : LC Card 86-222063 DDC 338.4/56691 19
HD9510.5 .I525 1986

STEEL INDUSTRY AND TRADE - CONGRESSES.
L'Industria siderurgica . Milano [1986] 193 p. : ISBN 88-14-00787-X : LC Card 86-222572
HD9510.5 .I473 1986

STEEL INDUSTRY AND TRADE - ENGLAND - CORBY (NORTHAMPTONSHIRE)
Maunders, A. R. A process of struggle . Aldershot, Hampshire, England , Brookfield, Vt., USA , c1987. xi, 283 p. : ISBN 0-566-05227-X : LC Card 86-25640 DDC 338.6/042 19
HD9521.8.C85 M38 1987 ***NYPL [JLD 87-1533]***

STEEL INDUSTRY AND TRADE - EUROPE.
Stålindustri, kriseregioner og fagbevægelse . [Copenhagen] , 1983. 217 p. : LC Card 84-169019
HD9525.E752 S73 1983

STEEL INDUSTRY AND TRADE - EUROPE - ADDRESSES, ESSAYS, LECTURES.
Goldberg, Walter, 1924- Ailing steel . Aldershot, England , c1986. xxiv, 535 p. : ISBN 0-566-00733-9 ***NYPL [JLD 87-399]***

STEEL INDUSTRY AND TRADE - FRANCE.
Masson, Jean Louis. Demain l'acier français /. Paris , c1986. 404 p. : ISBN 2-254-86071-1 : LC Card 86-190326
HD9522.5 .M37 1986

Sidérurgie et droit de crise /. Paris , c1983. 207 p. ; ISBN 2-13-038363-7 : LC Card 84-128216
HD9522.6 .S53 1983

STEEL INDUSTRY AND TRADE - FRANCE - HISTORY - 18TH CENTURY.
Woronoff, Denis, 1939- L'industrie sidérurgique en France pendant la Révolution et l'Empire /. Paris , c1984. 592 p. : ISBN 2-7132-0843-2 LC Card 85-138825 DDC 338.4/76691/0944 19
HD9522.5 .W64 1984 ***NYPL [JLE 86-3532]***

STEEL INDUSTRY AND TRADE - FRANCE - HISTORY - 19TH CENTURY.
Woronoff, Denis, 1939- L'industrie sidérurgique en France pendant la Révolution et l'Empire /. Paris , c1984. 592 p. : ISBN 2-7132-0843-2 LC Card 85-138825 DDC 338.4/76691/0944 19
HD9522.5 .W64 1984 ***NYPL [JLE 86-3532]***

STEEL INDUSTRY AND TRADE - GEORGIAN S.S.R.
Zakariadze, M. Krepche stali /. Tbilisi , 1986. 51 p., [16] p. of plates : LC Card 85-172385
HD9525.S653 G469 1986

STEEL INDUSTRY AND TRADE - GERMANY - BIOGRAPHY.
Blencke, Fritz. Alfred Krupp /. Leipzig , 1898. 127 p. : LC Card 85-665721
HD9523.9.K7 B53x 1898

STEEL INDUSTRY AND TRADE - GERMANY - HISTORY.
Wengenroth, Ulrich. Unternehmensstrategien und technischer Fortschritt . Göttingen , c1986. 316 p. : ISBN 3-525-36302-8
NYPL [JLE 87-917]

Wengenroth, Ulrich. Unternehmensstrategien und technischer Fortschritt . Göttingen , c1986. 316 p. : ISBN 3-525-36302-8 LC Card 87-112794 DDC 338.4/7669142/0943 19
HD9523.5 .W43 1986

STEEL INDUSTRY AND TRADE - GERMANY, WEST.
Mayer, Ralph-Dieter. Stahl- und Leichtmetallbau, Schienenfahrzeugbau . Berlin , c1985. 352 p. : ISBN 3-428-05771-6 LC Card 85-161158
HD9523.5 .M3 1985

STEEL INDUSTRY AND TRADE - GOVERNMENT POLICY - EUROPEAN ECONOMIC COMMUNITY COUNTRIES.
Sidérurgie et droit de crise /. Paris , c1983. 207 p. ; ISBN 2-13-038363-7 : LC Card 84-128216
HD9522.6 .S53 1983

STEEL INDUSTRY AND TRADE - GOVERNMENT POLICY - FRANCE.
Sidérurgie et droit de crise /. Paris , c1983. 207 p. ; ISBN 2-13-038363-7 : LC Card 84-128216
HD9522.6 .S53 1983

STEEL INDUSTRY AND TRADE - GOVERNMENT POLICY - INDIA.
Rakshit, Gangadhar, 1929- Steel industry in the public sector /. Calcutta , 1985. xii, 72 p. ; LC Card 85-904175 DDC 338.4/7669142/0954 19
HD9526.I62 R28 1985
NYPL [JLD 86-2180]

STEEL INDUSTRY AND TRADE - GOVERNMENT POLICY - UNITED STATES.
How federal policies affect the steel industry. Washington, D.C. [1987] xii, 66 p. : LC Card 87-601115 DDC 338.4/7669142/0973 19
HD9516 .H65 1987

Tiffany, Paul A. The decline of American steel . New York , 1988. p. cm. ISBN 0-19-504382-0 (alk. paper) LC Card 87-5782 DDC 338.4/7669142/0973 19
HD9515 .T54 1988

STEEL INDUSTRY AND TRADE - GREAT BRITAIN.
Bewlay, Simon. Steel . London [1985?] 14 p. : LC Card 87-165749 DDC 338.4/7669142/0941 19
HD9521.5 .B48 1985

STEEL INDUSTRY AND TRADE - GREAT BRITAIN - HISTORY.
Wengenroth, Ulrich. Unternehmensstrategien und technischer Fortschritt . Göttingen , c1986. 316 p. : ISBN 3-525-36302-8 LC Card 87-112794 DDC 338.4/7669142/0943 19
HD9523.5 .W43 1986

Wengenroth, Ulrich. Unternehmensstrategien und technischer Fortschritt . Göttingen , c1986. 316 p. : ISBN 3-525-36302-8
NYPL [JLE 87-917]

STEEL INDUSTRY AND TRADE - GREAT BRITAIN - HISTORY - 20TH CENTURY.
Tolliday, Steven. Business, banking, and politics . Cambridge, Mass. , 1987. vi, 433 p. : ISBN 0-674-08725-9 (alk. paper) LC Card 86-31944 DDC 338.4/7669142/0941 19
HD9521.5 .T64 1987

STEEL INDUSTRY AND TRADE - GREAT BRITAIN - STATISTICS.
Bewlay, Simon. Steel . London [1985?] 14 p. : LC Card 87-165749 DDC 338.4/7669142/0941 19
HD9521.5 .B48 1985

STEEL INDUSTRY AND TRADE - INDIA.
Rakshit, Gangadhar, 1929- Steel industry in the public sector /. Calcutta , 1985. xii, 72 p. ; LC Card 85-904175 DDC 338.4/7669142/0954 19
HD9526.I62 R28 1985
NYPL [JLD 86-2180]

STEEL INDUSTRY AND TRADE - INDIA - PERSONNEL MANAGEMENT.
Mathur, Reeta. Industrial relations in public enterprises /. Jaipur , 1986. vii, 226 p. ; LC Card 86-902265 DDC 331/.04135454 19
HD6976.I52 M37 1986

STEEL INDUSTRY AND TRADE - ITALY.
Moro, Domenico. Crisi e ristrutturazione dell'industria siderurgica italiana /. [Milano] [1984] 256 p. : LC Card 84-181172 DDC

338.4/76691/0945 19
HD9525.I82 M67 1984
NYPL [JLE 86-3649]

STEEL INDUSTRY AND TRADE - ITALY - CONGRESSES.
L'Industria siderurgica . Milano [1986] 193 p. : ISBN 88-14-00787-X : LC Card 86-222572
HD9510.5 .I473 1986

STEEL INDUSTRY AND TRADE - JAPAN - ADDRESSES, ESSAYS, LECTURES.
Goldberg, Walter, 1924- Ailing steel . Aldershot, England , c1986. xxiv, 535 p. : ISBN 0-566-00733-9 ***NYPL [JLD 87-399]***

STEEL INDUSTRY AND TRADE - LABOR PRODUCTIVITY.
International Labour Organisation. Iron and Steel Committee. Productivity improvement and its effects on the level of employment and working conditions in the iron and steel industry /. Geneva , 1986. ii, 66 p. : ISBN 92-2-105498-5 (pbk.) : LC Card 86-222063 DDC 338.4/56691 19
HD9510.5 .I525 1986

STEEL INDUSTRY AND TRADE - LATIN AMERICA.
Instituto Latinoamericano del Fierro y el Acero. The urgent need of Latin America to export steel [microform]. Santiago, Chile [1983?] 20 p. : LC Card 84-244660 DDC 382/.45669142/098 19
HD9524.L32 I57 1983
NYPL [*ZT-1708 no.49]

STEEL INDUSTRY AND TRADE - MONONGAHELA RIVER REGION (W. VA. AND PA.)
Hoerr, John P., 1930- And the wolf finally came . Pittsburgh, PA , 1988. p. cm. ISBN 0-8229-3572-4 LC Card 87-24932 DDC 338.4/7669142/097488 19
HD9517.M85 H64 1988

STEEL INDUSTRY AND TRADE - PENNSYLVANIA.
Hoerr, John P., 1930- And the wolf finally came . Pittsburgh, PA , 1988. p. cm. ISBN 0-8229-3572-4 LC Card 87-24932 DDC 338.4/7669142/097488 19
HD9517.M85 H64 1988

STEEL INDUSTRY AND TRADE - PENNSYLVANIA - HISTORY.
Kaufmann, Dwight W., 1919- Crucible . [Pittsburgh? Pa.] , c1986. x, 298 p. : LC Card 86-224545 DDC 338.7/669142/0973 19
HD9519.C7 K38 1986

STEEL INDUSTRY AND TRADE - RUSSIAN S.F.S.R. - MAGNITOGORSK - MANAGEMENT.
Zubets, V. M. (Vasiliĭ Mikhaĭlovich) Rezervy povysheniia ėffektivnosti proizvodstva na magnitogorskom metallurgicheskom kombinate /. Cheliabinsk , 1975. 183 p. ; LC Card 81-170397
HD9525.S653 M39 1975

STEEL INDUSTRY AND TRADE - RUSSIAN S.F.S.R. - MOSCOW - HISTORY - SOURCES.
Iz istorii razvitiia metallurgicheskoĭ promyshlennosti Moskvy, 1883-1932 gg. . Moskva , 1981. 219 p. ; LC Card 84-163581
HD9525.S653 M64 1981
NYPL [*QIP 87-3316]

STEEL INDUSTRY AND TRADE - UNITED STATES.
Causes and remedies for displacement of steel workers . [Washington, D.C.? , 1985] iv, 83, 2, 2 p. ; LC Card 86-601602 DDC 331.13/704 19
HD8039.I52 U524 1985

The Effects of semifinished steel imports on the U. S. iron and steel scrap industry . Washington, D.C. [1985] xv, 137 p. : LC Card 86-603428
HD9515 .E33 1985

Hodin, Michael W. A national policy for organized free trade . New York , 1987. 481 p. ; ISBN 0-8240-8085-8 (alk. paper) : LC Card 87-23719 DDC 382/.45669142/0973 19
HD9515 .H59 1987

Hogan, William Thomas, 1919- Minimills and integrated mills . Lexington, Mass. , c1987. 148 p. : ISBN 0-669-14021-X (alk. paper) LC Card 86-45605 DDC 338.4/7669142/0973 19
HD9515 .H599 1987

Tiffany, Paul A. The decline of American steel . New York , 1988. p. cm. ISBN 0-19-504382-0 (alk. paper) LC Card 87-5782 DDC 338.4/7669142/0973 19
HD9515 .T54 1988

The U. S. primary iron and steel industry since 1958. Washington, D.C. , 1985. xvi, 138 p. :
NYPL [JLF 86-689]

STEEL INDUSTRY AND TRADE - UNITED STATES - ADDRESSES, ESSAYS, LECTURES.
Goldberg, Walter, 1924- Ailing steel . Aldershot, England , c1986. xxiv, 535 p. : ISBN 0-566-00733-9 ***NYPL [JLD 87-399]***

STEEL INDUSTRY AND TRADE - UNITED STATES - HISTORY.
Leary, Thomas E., 1946- From fire to rust . Buffalo, N.Y. , c1987. 134 p. : ISBN 0-939032-00-7 (pbk.) LC Card 87-692 DDC 338.7/669142/0974796 19
HD9519.L2 L43 1987

Strohmeyer, John, 1924- Crisis in Bethlehem . New York, N.Y., U. S.A. , 1987, c1986. xii, 244 p. ; ISBN 0-14-010370-8 (pbk.) LC Card 87-11835 DDC 338.7/669142/0974822 19
HD9519.B4 S87 1987

STEEL INDUSTRY AND TRADE - WEST VIRGINIA.
Hoerr, John P., 1930- And the wolf finally came . Pittsburgh, PA , 1988. p. cm. ISBN 0-8229-3572-4 LC Card 87-24932 DDC 338.4/7669142/097488 19
HD9517.M85 H64 1988

STEEL INDUSTRY - COLLECTIVE BARGAINING. see **COLLECTIVE BARGAINING - STEEL INDUSTRY.**

Steel industry in the public sector /. Rakshit, Gangadhar, 1929- Calcutta , 1985. xii, 72 p. ; LC Card 85-904175 DDC 338.4/7669142/0954 19
HD9526.I62 R28 1985
NYPL [JLD 86-2180]

STEEL - MANUFACTURE. see **STEEL INDUSTRY AND TRADE.**

STEEL - MARKETING.
Reutersberg, Bernhard. Logistik als Instrument zur Steigerung der Marktleistungsfähigkeit von Stahlhandlungen /. Göttingen , 1985. 301 p. : ISBN 3-525-85697-0 : LC Card 86-162333
HE131 .M8 Heft 107 HE199.5.M4

STEEL MINIMILLS - UNITED STATES.
Hogan, William Thomas, 1919- Minimills and integrated mills . Lexington, Mass. , c1987. 148 p. : ISBN 0-669-14021-X (alk. paper) LC Card 86-45605 DDC 338.4/7669142/0973 19
HD9515 .H599 1987

STEEL STRIKE, UNITED STATES, 1919-1920.
Brody, David, 1930- Labor in crisis . Urbana , 1987, c1965. 218 p. ; ISBN 0-252-01373-5 (pbk. : alk. paper) LC Card 86-30880 DDC 331.89/269142/0973 19
HD5325.I5 1919 .B7 1987

STEEL - TRADE AND STATISTICS. see **STEEL INDUSTRY AND TRADE.**

STEEL - TRANSPORTATION - PLANNING.
Reutersberg, Bernhard. Logistik als Instrument zur Steigerung der Marktleistungsfähigkeit von Stahlhandlungen /. Göttingen , 1985. 301 p. : ISBN 3-525-85697-0 : LC Card 86-162333
HE131 .M8 Heft 107 HE199.5.M4

STEEL WORKERS. see **IRON AND STEEL WORKERS.**

Steel Workers of America, United. see **United Steelworkers of America.**

Steel Workers Organizing Committee. see **United Steelworkers of America.**

STEEL WORKERS ORGANIZING COMMITTEE (U. S.) - HISTORY - CONGRESSES.
Forging a union of steel . Ithaca, N.Y. , c1987. vii, 153 p. : ISBN 0-87546-135-2 (pbk.) LC Card 87-21508 DDC 331.88/169142/0973 19
HD6515.I5 F58 1987

Steele, Ian Kenneth. The English Atlantic, 1675-1740 : an exploration of communication and community / by Ian K. Steele. New York : Oxford University Press, 1986. xii, 400 p. maps ; 25 cm. Includes index. ISBN 0-19-503968-8 LC Card 85-25828 DDC 380.3/09171/241 19
1. Communication and traffic - North America - History. 2. Communication and traffic - West Indies, British - History. 3. Great Britain - Colonies - America - Commerce. I. Title.
HE202 .S74 1986 ***NYPL [JLE 86-4056]***

Steen, Robert. The family money game : --you can win it! / by Robert Steen ; [illustrations by Don Borie]. Longmont, Colo. : Bookmakers Guild, 1986. viii, 120 p. : ill. ; 23 cm. ISBN 0-917665-03-1 (pbk.) LC Card 85-70449
1. Finance, Personal. I. Title.
HG179 .S815 1986

Steenland, Sally. DeGooyer, Janice. Women's work, undervalued, underpaid . Washington, D.C. , 1984, c1982. 27, [4] leaves :
NYPL [*ZT-1708 no.39]

Steensma, Herman. Modern organiseren en menselijker werken /. 's-Gravenhage , 1985. 198 p. : ISBN 90-6095-314-2 : LC Card 85-214437
HF5548.8 .M55 1985

Steering Committee for the National Commuting Study. Pisarski, Alan. Commuting in America . Westport, Conn. (P.O. Box 2055, Westport 06880-2055) , c1987. 78 p. : LC Card 86-82787 DDC 388.3/14/0973 19
HD5717.5.U6 P57 1987

Steers, Richard M. Motivation and work behavior /. New York , c1987. xii, 595 p. : ISBN 0-07-060948-9 : LC Card 86-27865 DDC 658.3/14 19
HF5549.5.M63 M667 1987

Ștefan, C. Statistică industrială : metode statistice de calcul și analiză a activității întreprinderilor industriale / Constantin Ștefan. București : Editura Academiei Republicii Socialiste România, 1985. 223 p. ; 25 cm. Table of contents in English, Romanian, and Russian. Bibliography: p. 217-218. LC Card 86-155097
1. Industrial statistics. 2. Romania - Industries - Statistics. I. Title.
HB137 .S76 1985

Stefani, Xavier. Fauvet, Jean-Christian. La sociodynamique . Paris , 1983. 210, [5] p. : ISBN 2-7081-0524-8 : LC Card 83-152909
HF5549 .F34 1983

Stefany, Wallace Charles. The Department of Transportation / Wallace Charles Stefany. New York, NY : Chelsea House, c1988. p. cm. (Know your government) Bibliography: p. Includes index. Surveys the history of the Department of Transportation and describes its structure, current functions, and influence on American society. ISBN 0-87754-847-1 LC Card 87-24924 DDC 353.86 19
1. United States. Dept. of Transportation. I. Series: Know your government (New York, N.Y.). II. Title.
HE206.3 .S73 1988

Steffens, Horst. Autorität und Revolte : Alltagsleben und Streikverhalten der Bergarbeiter an der Saar im 19. Jahrhundert / Horst Steffens. Weingarten : Drumlin, c1987. 419 p. : ill. ; 22 cm. (Sozialgeschichtliche Bibliothek im Drumlin Verlag) Revision of the author's thesis (doctoral)--Universität Konstanz, 1983. Bibliography: p. 395-419. ISBN 3-924027-47-1 LC Card 87-141439 DDC 331/.0422334/094342 19
1. Miners - Germany (West) - Saarland - Economic conditions. 2. Strikes and lockouts - Germany (West) - Saarland - History - 19th century. 3. Saarland (Germany) - Social conditions. 4. Labor and laboring classes - Germany (West) - Saarland - History - 19th century. I. Title. II. Series.
HD8039.M61 G383 1987

Steger, Ulrich. Zukunft statt Wende : Wirtschaftspolitik für Hessen / Ulrich Steger ; mit einem Geleitwort von Holger Börner. Bonn : Verlag Neue Gesellschaft, c1986. 171 p. ; 21 cm. Includes bibliographical references. ISBN 3-87831-442-6 LC Card 86-226220
1. Hesse (Germany) - Economic policy. I. Title.
HC287.H4 S73 1986

Stegman, Michael A.
Housing finance and public policy : case and supplementary readings / Michael A. Stegman. New York : Van Nostrand Reinhold, c1986. xiv, 290 p. : ill. ; 23 cm. Includes bibliographical references and index. ISBN 0-442-28035-1 (pbk.) : LC Card 85-13408 DDC 332.63/24/0973 19

1. Housing - United States - Finance - Case studies. 2. Housing policy - United States - Case studies. I. Title.
HD7293.Z9 S74 1986 ***NYPL [JLE 86-3779]***

Nonfederal housing programs : how states and localities are responding to federal cutbacks in low-income housing / by Michael A. Stegman and J. David Holden.Rev. Washington, D.C. : ULI-the Urban Land Institute, 1987. viii, 231 p. ; 23 cm. Bibliography: p. 141-145. ISBN 0-87420-673-1 LC Card 87-51080 DDC 363.5/8 19
1. Housing - United States - Finance. 2. Housing policy - United States - States. 3. Housing subsidies - United States - States. 4. Local government - United States. I. Holden, J. David. II. Title.
HD7293.Z9 S75 1987

Snyder, Thomas (Thomas P.) Paying for growth . Washington, D.C. , 1986. x, 133 p. : ISBN 0-87420-663-4 (pbk.) LC Card 86-51156 DDC 338.4/3363/0973 19
HJ9156 .S69 1986

Stehl, Jan. Politik und Ökonomie als Kultur / Jan Stehl. Würzburg : Königshausen + Neumann, 1982. viii, 449 p. ; 21 cm. Includes bibliographies. ISBN 3-88479-093-5 LC Card 83-183293
1. Economics. 2. Political science. 3. Ecology. 4. Sociology, Christian. I. Title.
HB175 .S88 1982

Steidlmayer, J. Peter. Markets and market logic / J. Peter Steidlmayer and Kevin Koy. 1st ed. Chicago : Porcupine Press, c1986. 161 p. ; 24 cm. ISBN 0-941275-00-0 LC Card 87-401422 DDC 332.64 19
1. Commodity exchanges. 2. Financial futures. I. Koy, Kevin. II. Title.
HG6046 .S673 1986

Steidlmeier, Paul, 1942- The paradox of poverty : a reappraisal of economic development policy / Paul Steidlmeier. Cambridge, Mass. : Ballinger, c1987. xx, 318 p. : ill. ; 24 cm. (Ballinger series in business in a global environment) Includes bibliographies and indexes. ISBN 0-88730-184-3 LC Card 86-26589 DDC 338.9 19
1. Economic development. 2. Economic policy. 3. Poverty. I. Title. II. Series.
HD75 .S75 1987

Stein, James I. Bergman, Edward M. Cooperative forms of organization in the taxicab industry [microform] . Washington, D.C. , Springfield, Va. , 1984. 87 p. : ***NYPL [*XME-11,917]***

Stein, Judith K., 1935- Holcombe, Marya W., 1944- Writing for decision makers . New York , c1987. xi, 219 p. : ISBN 0-442-23268-3 (pbk.) : LC Card 86-24700 DDC 808/.066658 19
HF5719 .H64 1987

Stein, Lawrence M. Value investing : new strategies for stock market success / Lawrence M. Stein. New York : Wiley, c1988. xiv, 331 p. : ill. ; 23 cm. Bibliography: p. 327. ISBN 0-471-62875-1 LC Card 87-23152 DDC 332.63/22 19
1. Investments - Handbooks, manuals, etc. 2. Stocks - Handbooks, manuals, etc. I. Title.
HG4527 .S816 1988

STEIN, LORENZ VON, 1815-1890.
Heilmann, Martin. Lorenz von Stein und die Grundprobleme der Steuerlehre . Heidelberg , 1984. xi, 577 p. ; ISBN 3-7685-0184-1 LC Card 84-236751
HJ2309 .H36 1984

Stein, M. L. Divaris, Costa. Old Mutual income tax guide, 1986/87 /. [S.l.] c1987 (Cape Town : Old Mutual Print. Works) xvi, 261 p. : LC Card 87-152138 DDC 343.6805/2 346.80352 19
HJ4790.4 .D58 1987

Stein, Margot B. (Margot Ballou), 1945- The social origins of a labor elite : French engine-drivers, 1837-1917 / Margot B. Stein. New York : Garland Pub., 1987. xxiv, 515 p. : ill. ; 24 cm. (Modern European history) Originally presented as the author's thesis (Ph. D.--Harvard University, 1977) under title: Working to rule. Bibliography: p. 496-515. ISBN 0-8240-8043-2 (alk. paper) : LC Card 87-6913 DDC 305/.9385 19
1. Locomotive engineers - France - History - 19th century. 2. Railroads - France - Employees - History - 19th century. 3. France - Social conditions - 19th century. I. Title. II. Series.
HD8039.R322 F88 1987

Stein, Peter, 1953- Johansson, Mats, 1951- Frihetens idéer . [Stockholm] , c1986. 224 p. : ISBN 91-7566-106-3 LC Card 86-226727
HC106.8 .J64 1986

Steinbach, Antal. A Magyar Dolgozók Pártja Központi Vezetősége 1953. júniusi határozatának agrárpolitikai előzményei / Steinbach Antal. [Budapest] : Művelődési Minisztérium Marxizmus-Leninizmus Oktatási Főosztálya, 1985. 104 p. ; 24 cm. (Tudományos szocializmus füzetek, 0324-5683 . 83) Summary in Russian. Includes bibliographical references. ISBN 963-673-321-X LC Card 86-187055
1. Agriculture and state - Hungary - History. 2. Agriculture - Economic aspects - Hungary - History. 3. Magyar Dolgozók Pártja - History. I. Title. II. Series.
HD1940.5.Z8 S74 1985

STEINBEIS, FERDINAND VON, 1807-1893.
Müller, Fr. (Friedrich), Dr. Ferdinand von Steinbeis . Tübingen , 1907. vi, 215 p. : LC Card 85-666358
HC282.5.S67 M85x 1907

Steinberg, Eve P. Martin, Joseph H. Real estate license examinations . New York, N.Y. , 1987. p. cm. ISBN 0-668-06616-4 (pbk.) : LC Card 86-25376 DDC 333.33/076 19
HD1381.5.U5 M37 1987

Steinbrecher, Jürgen. Kockelke, Wilhelm. Untersuchung der Vorfahrtregelung "Rechts vor Links" unter dem Aspekt der Verkehrssicherheit /. Bergisch Gladbach [1983] 63, 3 p. : LC Card 84-147884
HE363.G32 U744 1983

Steiner, Manfred. Aktuelle Probleme der Marktwirtschaft in gesamt- und einzelwirtschaftlicher Sicht . Berlin , c1984. 458 p., [1] leaf of plates : ISBN 3-428-05653-1 LC Card 85-128275
HB501 .A514 1984

Steiner, Peter Otto, 1922- Lipsey, Richard G., 1928- Economics /. New York , c1987. xxvii, 942 p. : ISBN 0-06-043917-3 LC Card 86-29422 DDC 330 19
HB171.5 .L733 1987

Steingräber, Carola, 1956- Geld- und Fiskalpolitik in Portfolio-orientierten Modellen kleiner offener Volkswirtschaften : eine vergleichende Analyse / Carola Steingräber. Rheinfelden : Schäuble Verlag, c1986. ix, 219 p. : ill. ; 20 cm. (Recht, Wirtschaft, Gesellschaft. Wirtschaft . 2) Bibliography: p. 213-219. ISBN 3-87718-532-0 LC Card 86-182509
1. Monetary policy - Mathematical models. 2. Fiscal policy - Mathematical models. 3. Foreign exchange - Mathematical models. 4. States, Small - Economic policy - Mathematical models. I. Title. II. Series.
HG230.3 .S74 1986

Steinherr, Alfred. Employment and growth . Dordrecht , Boston , 1987. xii, 310 p. : ISBN 90-247-3514-9 LC Card 87-3184 DDC 331.11 19
HD73 .E46 1987

Steinisch, Irmgard. Arbeitszeitverkürzung und sozialer Wandel : der Kampf um die Achtstundenschicht in der deutschen und amerikanischen Eisen- und Stahlindustrie, 1880-1929 / Irmgard Steinisch. Berlin ; New York : W. de Gruyter, 1986. xiv, 640 p. : ill. ; 24 cm. (Veröffentlichungen der Historischen Kommission zu Berlin . Bd. 65) Beiträge zu Inflation und Wiederaufbau in Deutschland und Europa, 1914-1924 ; Bd. 6 Originally presented as the author's thesis (doctoral)--Ludwig-Maximilians-Universität München, 1981/82. Bibliography: p. [577]-620. Includes indexes. ISBN 3-11-010483-0 LC Card 87-110005 DDC 331.25/7/0973 19
1. Hours of labor - United States - History. 2. Hours of labor - Germany - History. 3. Iron industry and trade - United States - History. 4. Iron industry and trade - Germany - History. 5. Eight-hour movement - History. I. Series: Veröffentlichungen der Historischen Kommission zu Berlin beim Friedrich-Meinecke-Institut der Freien Universität Berlin , Bd. 65. II. Title.
HD5119.I52 U67 1986

Steinlin-Fritzsche, Peter. Das Versicherungswesen der Schweiz : eine Gesamtschau / von Peter Steinlin-Fritzsche. Zürich : Polygraphischer Verlag, 1961-1962. 2 v. ; 25 cm. (Veröffentlichungen des Versicherungs-Wirtschaftlichen Seminars an der Handels-Hochschule St. Gallen . 9-10) Includes bibliographies and indexes. LC Card 87-407799 DDC 368/.9494 19
1. Insurance - Switzerland. I. Title. II. Series.
HG8688 .S76 1961

Steinman, Benj. Import insights . West Nyack, NY (51 Virginia Ave., West Nyack 10994) , c19. 48 p. : LC Card 86-210235 DDC 382/.4566342/0973 19
HD9397.U52 I47 1986

Steinmetz, Thomas C. The mortgage kit : how to save $1,000s financing your home/ by Thomas C. Steinmetz. Chicago, IL : Longman Financial Services Pub., c1987. ix, 188 p. : ill. ; 28 cm. ISBN 0-88462-658-X (pbk.) : LC Card 87-3693 DDC 332.7/22 19
1. Mortgage loans - United States - Handbooks, manuals, etc. I. Title.
HG2040.5.U5 S72 1987

Steinrücke, Margareta, 1953- Generationen im Betrieb : Fallstudien zur generationenspezifischen Verarbeitung betrieblicher Konflikte / Margareta Steinrücke. Frankfurt ; New York : Campus, c1986. 343 p. ; 21 cm. (Untersuchungen des Instituts zur Erforschung Sozialer Chancen (ISO), Köln) Bibliography: p. 337-343. ISBN 3-593-33639-1 LC Card 87-137842 DDC 331.3/0943 19
1. Age and employment - Germany (West) - Case studies. 2. Conflict of generations - Germany (West) - Case studies. 3. Job security - Germany (West) - Case studies. 4. Wages - Germany (West) - Case studies. I. Series: Untersuchungen des Instituts zur Erforschung Sozialer Chancen, Köln. II. Title.
HD6283.G4 S74 1986

Steins, Janet. Shupe, Barbara, 1941- New York State population, 1790-1980 . New York , c1987. xxvii, 333 p. : ISBN 1-555-70009-8 : LC Card 86-28487 DDC 304.6/2/09747 19
HA545 .S58 1987

Steitz, Lilo. Bedürfnisse und Interessen als Triebkräfte unseres Handelns /. Berlin , 1984. 155 p. ; LC Card 84-229147
HC290.795.C3 B43 1984

Steitz, Walter. Quellen zur deutschen Wirtschafts- und Sozialgeschichte von der Reichsgründung bis zum ersten Weltkrieg /. Darmstadt , 1985. xviii, 553 p. : ISBN 3-534-07561-7 LC Card 85-229315
HC285 .Q45 1985

Steklov Seminar (1984 : Steklov Institute of Mathematics)
[Statistika i upravlenie sluchaĭnykh protsessov. English]
Statistics and control of stochastic processes / edited by N.V. Krylov, R.Sh. Liptser, and A.A. Novikov. New York, N.Y. : Optimization Software, Publications Division, c1985. xiii, 506 p. ; 25 cm. (Translations series in mathematics and engineering) "A.N. Shiryaev anniversary volume"--T.p. verso. Translation of: Statistika i upravlenie sluchaĭnykh protsessov. Includes bibliographies. ISBN 0-911575-18-9 LC Card 85-8851 DDC 519.5 19
1. Mathematical statistics - Congresses. 2. Stochastic processes - Congresses. I. Krylov, N. V. (Nikolaĭ Vladimirovich). II. Liptser, Robert Shevilevich. III. Novikov, A. A. (Anatoliĭ Aleksandrovich). IV. Shiriaev, Al'bert Nikolaevich. V. Title. VI. Series.
QA276.A1 .S7513 1984 ***NYPL [JSE 86-729]***

Steklov, Vladimir IUr'evich. V.I. Lenin i ėlektrifikatsiia / V.IU. Steklov. Izd. 3-e, perer. i dop. Moskva : Izd-vo "Nauka", 1982. 511 p., [1] leaf of plates : ill., port. ; 21 cm. At head of title: Akademiia nauk SSSR. Includes bibliographical references and index. LC Card 83-133950
1. Electrification - Economic aspects - Soviet Union - History. 2. Electric power - Soviet Union - History. 3. Lenin, Vladimir Il'ich, 1870-1924 - Views on electrification. I. Title.
HD9685.S762 S84 1982

Stellman, Caroline B. Consumer automobile leasing study / Caroline B. Stellman. Baltimore, Md. (7 N. Calvert St., Baltimore 21202) : Consumer Council of Maryland, 1986. ii, 59 p. ; 28 cm. "July 1, 1986." Bibliography: p. 58-59. LC Card 87-620899 DDC 388.3/2 19
1. Automobiles, Rental - Maryland. I. Consumer Council of Maryland. II. Title.
HE5633.M3 S74 1986

Stellner Symposium on Theories of Marketing Practice (1st : 1985 : University of Illinois at Champaign-Urbana) Contemporary views on marketing practice /. Lexington, Mass. , c1987. vi, 282 p. : ISBN 0-669-15120-3 (alk.

paper) LC Card 86-46218 DDC 658.8 19
HF5411 .C66 1987

Stelmach, Waldemar. Drugie oblicze "Solidarności" / Waldemar Stelmach. Wyd. 1. Warszawa : Instytut Wydawniczy Związków Zawodowych, 1985. 222 p. : ill. ; 21 cm. Summary in English, French, German, and Russian. Includes bibliographical references. ISBN 83-202-0391-0 : LC Card 86-208212
1. NSZZ "Solidarność" (Labor organization) - History. 2. Poland - Politics and government - 1980-. 3. Dissenters - Poland. I. Title.
HD8537.N783 S74 1985

Stelter, Thomas. Complete guide to skip tracing : the art of locating missing debtors / Thomas Stelter. Eau Claire, Wis. : Professional Education Systems, c1987. 143 p. : ill. ; 23 cm. ISBN 0-941161-16-1 (pbk.) LC Card 87-124276 DDC 658.8/8 19
1. Collecting of accounts - United States. 2. Collection laws - United States. I. Title.
HG3752.7.U6 S74 1987

Stempell, Dieter. Weltbevölkerung 2000 : Ursachen und Tendenzen der Bevölkerungsentwicklung / Dieter Stempell.1. Aufl. Leipzig : Urania-Verlag, 1985. 200 p. : ill. (some col.) ; 22 cm. (Die Menschheit an der Schwelle zum 21. Jahrhundert) Bibliography: p. 199-200. LC Card 86-166553
1. Population forecasting. I. Title. II. Series.
HB849.53 .S74 1985

Stengel, Wolfgang. Verlagerungen der individuellen Verkehrsnachfrage bei verändertem ÖPNV-Angebot infolge neueingerichteter Stadtschnellbahnen / Wolfgang Stengel. Bad Honnef : Bock + Herchen, 1984. iv, 210 p. : ill. ; 21 cm. (Schriftenreihe des Instituts für Verkehrsplanung und Verkehrswesen der Technischen Universität München, 0341-5716 . Heft 19) Bibliography: p. 208-210. ISBN 3-88347-120-8 : LC Card 84-185940
1. Urban transportation - Germany (West) - Passenger traffic - Mathematical models. 2. Subways - Germany (West) - Mathematical models. I. Title. II. Series.
HE311.G3 S73 1984

Stengos, Thanasis.
Abbott, Michael G. Alternative estimates of union-nonunion and public-private wage differentials in Ontario, 1981 /. Kingston, Ont., Canada [1986] ii, 61 p. ; LC Card 87-146006 DDC 331.2/2/09713 19
HD4980.O5 A64 1986

Abbott, Michael G. Alternative estimates of union-nonunion and public-private wage differentials in Ontario, 1981 /. Kingston, Ont., Canada , 1987. ii, 47 p. ; ISBN 0-88886-166-4 (pbk.) LC Card 87-170767 DDC 331.2/2/09713 19
HD4980.O5 A64 1987

A step-by-step guide to real estate principles in California . Calhoun, David E. Los Angeles, Calif. , c1987. 351 p. : LC Card 87-403596 DDC 333.33/09794 19
HD266.C2 C22 1987

A Step-by-step guide to resources for economic development / State of New York. 2nd ed. Albany, N.Y. : State of New York Dept. of State ; [New York, N.Y.] : New York State Urban Development Corp., 1983, c1980. 195 p. : port. ; 28 cm. Cover title. Includes index. Bibliography: p. 186-187. LC Card 85-621196 DDC 353.0082/09747 19
1. Economic assistance, Domestic - New York (State) - Handbooks, manuals, etc. 2. Community development - New York (State) - Finance - Handbooks, manuals, etc. I. Urban Development Corporation.
HC107.N73 P6353 1983 *NYPL [JLF 86-638]*

A step toward independence: economic self sufficiency . Moore, Janice D. Thorne. Washington, D.C. , c1986. iii, 117 p. : LC Card 86-209069 DDC 362.8/3 19
HD6059.6.U6 M66 1986

Stepchildren of progress . Robinson, Kathryn May, 1949- Albany, N.Y. , c1986. xvi, 315 p. : ISBN 0-88706-119-2 LC Card 86-5847 DDC 307.7/66/095984 19
HD9539.N52 I547 1986 *NYPL [JLE 86-4126]*

Stephan, David. Levine, David M., 1946- Using Minitab with Basic business statistics /. Englewood Cliffs, N.J. , c1986. viii, 160 p. : ISBN 0-13-057779-0 (pbk.) LC Card 87-400304 DDC 519.5/028/55369 19
HF1017 .L425 1986

Stephan, Gunter. Faber, Malte Michael. Entropie, Umweltschutz und Rohstoffverbrauch . Berlin , New York , 1983. ix, 181 p. : ISBN 0-387-12297-4 (U. S.) LC Card 83-193381
HC79.E5 F23 1983

Stephan, Paula E. Schroeder, Larry D. Understanding regression analysis . Beverly Hills , c1986. 95 p. : ISBN 0-8039-2758-4 LC Card 85-63790 *NYPL [JLK 77-39 no.57]*

Stephanou, K. (Kōnstantinos) Hē Hellada stēn Eurōpaikē Koinotēta . Athēna , 1987. 14, 565 p. ; LC Card 87-169443
HC241.25.G8 H43 1987

Stephens, Evelyne Huber. States versus markets in the world-system /. Beverly Hills, Calif. , c1985. 295 p. ; ISBN 0-8039-2510-7 LC Card 85-11716 DDC 338.9 19
HD3611 .S76 1985 *NYPL [JLD 86-3227]*

Stephens, William L.
Smith, Jack L. Financial accounting /. New York , c1988. xxii, 706 p. : ISBN 0-07-059002-8 : LC Card 87-17233 DDC 657 19
HF5635 .S6445 1988

Smith, Jack L. Managerial accounting /. New York , c1988. xxv, 717 p. : ISBN 0-07-058990-9 : LC Card 87-17223 DDC 658.1/511 19
HF5657.4 .S55 1988

Stephenson, Charles.
Confrontation, class consciousness, and the labor process . Westport, Conn. , 1986. viii, 261 p. ; ISBN 0-313-25140-1 (lib. bdg. : alk. paper) LC Card 85-17734 DDC 305.5/62 19
HD4851 .C63 1986 *NYPL [JLE 86-3558]*

Life and labor . Albany , c1986. x, 343 p. ; ISBN 0-88706-173-7 LC Card 86-14362 DDC 305.5/62/0973 19
HD8066 .L54 1986 *NYPL [JLE 86-4350]*

Stephenson, G. M. (Geoffrey Michael) Industrial relations . Chichester , New York , c1979. xii, 412 p. ; ISBN 0-471-99701-3 LC Card 78-18452 DDC 301.5/5
HD6971 .I547 *NYPL [JLE 80-1770]*

Stepping up to supervisor /. Haynes, Marion E. Houston, Tex. , c1987. ix, 171 p. : ISBN 0-941021-00-9 (pbk.) LC Card 87-124242 DDC 658.3/02 19
HF5549.12 .H39 1987

Stepwise migration. Lusaka : Dept. of Town and Country Planning, Research Unit, [1981] 34, 3, 2 p. : forms ; 30 cm. Field work by Mr. G. Lungwangwa, 1975. Data analysis by Miss N. Ngenda with the help of Mr. S. Kaniini. Bibliography: p. 34. LC Card 85-980416
1. Rural-urban migration - Zambia. 2. Migration, Internal - Zambia. I. Zambia. Dept. of Town and Country Planning. Research Unit.
HB2123.6.A3 S74 1981

Sterbetafeln für Personenkraftwagen und Kombinationskraftwagen . Rohde, Horst. Essen , 1981. 64 p. ; LC Card 87-408032 DDC 363.1/252/0943021 19
HE5614.5.G3 R64 1981

Sterdyniak, Henri. Pisani-Ferry, Jean. Problèmes de macroéconomie /. Paris , 1984. 452 p. : ISBN 2-7178-0801-9 : LC Card 85-100663 DDC 339 19
HB173 .P534 1984

Hē Sterea Hellas kata ton Henetotourkikon polemon, 1684-1699 kai ho Salōnōn Philotheos /. Dokos, Kōnstantinos. Athēnai , 1985. 255 p. ; LC Card 86-211599
HB2092.5.A3 D64 1985

STEREOTYPE (PSYCHOLOGY)
Venkatesh, Alladi. The significance of the women's movement to marketing . New York , 1985. 209 p. ; ISBN 0-03-069588-0 (alk. paper) : LC Card 85-19106 DDC 658.8/348 19
HF5415.3 .V46 1985 *NYPL [JLE 86-1081]*

STEREOTYPED BEHAVIOR. see **STEREOTYPE (PSYCHOLOGY)**

Sterkenburg, J. J. Rural housing conditions in Kisumu District, Kenya / J.J. Sterkenburg, J. Brandt, G.G. van Beinum. [Utrecht] : Dept. of Geography of Developing Countries, University of Utrecht ; [Nairobi] : Housing Research and Development Unit, University of Nairobi, 1982. 95 p., [6] leaves of plates : ill. ; 29 cm. Bibliography: p. 91. LC Card 85-981197
1. Housing, Rural - Kenya - Kisumu District. 2. Housing policy - Kenya - Kisumu District. I. Brandt, J. (Joke). II. Beinum, Gerlach van. III. Title.
HD7289.K42 K67 1982

Stermole, Franklin J. Economic evaluation and investment decision methods / Franklin J. Stermole and John M. Stermole. 6th ed. Golden, Colo. : Investment Evaluations Corp., c1987. vi, 479 p. : ill. ; 24 cm. Bibliography: p. 474-476. Includes index. ISBN 0-9603282-8-9 LC Card 86-83278 DDC 332.63 19
1. Capital investments - Evaluation. 2. Economic development projects - Evaluation. I. Stermole, John M. II. Title.
HG4028.C4 S714 1987

Stermole, John M. Stermole, Franklin J. Economic evaluation and investment decision methods /. Golden, Colo. , c1987. vi, 479 p. : ISBN 0-9603282-8-9 LC Card 86-83278 DDC 332.63 19
HG4028.C4 S714 1987

Stern, Bernard W., 1912- Rutledge unionism : labor relations in the Honolulu transit industry / by Bernard W. Stern ; edited by Wm. Puette. Honolulu : University of Hawaii, Center for Labor Education and Research, 1986. x, 147 p. ; 23 cm. Bibliography: p. 133-140. Includes index. LC Card 86-51020 DDC 331/.04138841322/0996931 19
1. Transit Workers Union of Hawaii - History. 2. Rutledge, Arthur A. 3. Trade-unions - Transport Workers - Hawaii - History. 4. Strikes and lockouts - Transport workers - Hawaii - History. I. Puette, William. II. Title.
HD6515.T72 H37 1986

Stern, Jonathan P. Soviet oil and gas exports to the West : commercial transaction or security threat? / Jonathan P. Stern. Aldershot, Hants, England ; Brookfield, Vt., USA : Gower Pub. Co., c1987. xi, 123 p. : ill., map ; 30 cm. (Energy papers . no. 21) Includes bibliographies. ISBN 0-566-05124-9 : LC Card 86-32772 DDC 382/.4228/0947 19
1. Petroleum industry and trade - Political aspects - Soviet Union. 2. Gas industry - Political aspects - Soviet Union. 3. East-West trade (1945-). 4. World politics - 1945-. 5. National security. I. Title. II. Series.
HD9575.S652 S74 1987

Stern, Louis W., 1935- Marketing channels / Louis W. Stern, Adel I. El-Ansary. 3rd ed. Englewood Cliffs, N.J. : Prentice-Hall, c1988. xiv, 609 p. : ill. ; 25 cm. (The Prentice-Hall series in marketing) Includes bibliographical references and indexes. ISBN 0-13-557158-8 : LC Card 87-17396 DDC 658.8/4 19
1. Marketing channels. I. Ansary, Adel I. II. Title. III. Series.
HF5415.129 .S75 1988

Stern, Mark J. Society and family strategy : Erie County, New York, 1850-1920 / Mark J. Stern. Albany, N.Y. : State University of New York Press, c1987. xiv, 172 p. : ill. ; 24 cm. Bibliography: p. 157-167. Includes index. ISBN 0-88706-495-7 LC Card 86-23121 DDC 304.6/34/0974796 19
1. Fertility, Human - New York (State) - Erie County - History - 19th century. 2. Fertility, Human - New York (State) - Erie County - History - 20th century. 3. Family - New York (State) - Erie County - History - 19th century. 4. Family - New York (State) - Erie County - History - 20th century. 5. Erie County (N.Y.) - Population - History. 6. Erie County (N.Y.) - Social conditions. I. Title.
HB935.N7 S74 1987

Stern, N. H. (Nicholas Herbert) The Theory of taxation for developing countries /. New York , c1987. xvi, 694 p. ; ISBN 0-19-520498-0 LC Card 87-11106 DDC 336.2/009172/4 19
HJ2351.7 .T47 1987

Stern, Richard Walter. Internationale Steuervorteile / Richard Walter Stern und Arthur Dan. Goldberg. 2. Aufl., geringfügig geändert. Zürich : Economic Research Institute : [Distributor], Zentral-Verlag, 1977. 56 leaves : ill. ; 30 cm. Caption title from cover. LC Card 85-173548
1. Tax incentives. I. Goldberg, Arthur Daniel. II. Title.
HJ2336 .S74 1977

Sterne, George F. Investment opportunities for the mid 1980's : wealth-building strategies in the stock market, gold, silver, diamonds ... / by George F. Sterne & Russ von Hoelscher. San Diego, Calif. : George Stern, Profit Ideas, c1985. 304 p. ; 24 cm. Bibliography: p. 283-292. ISBN 0-940398-11-7 : LC Card 78-64396
1. Investments. 2. Diamonds as an investment. I. Von Hoelscher, Russ. II. Title. ***NYPL [JLE 86-1720]***

Sterniczuk, Henryk. Decyzje w organizacjach gospodarczych / Henryk Sterniczuk. Wyd. 1. Warszawa : Państwowe Wydawn. Ekonomiczne, 1980. 167 p. ; 30 cm. (Biblioteka kadr kierowniczych) Includes bibliographical references. ISBN 83-208-0052-8 LC Card 81-109564
1. Management - Decision-making. I. Title. II. Series.
HD30.23 .S726 1980

Sternlieb, George. Hughes, James W. The dynamics of America's housing /. New Brunswick, N.J. , c1987. xiv, 224 p. ; ISBN 0-88285-122-5 : LC Card 87-4515 DDC 363.5/0973 19
HD7293 .H826 1987

Steuer- und Transferordnung aus einem Guss . Mitschke, Joachim. Baden-Baden , 1985. 274 p. : ISBN 3-7890-1097-9 LC Card 85-235532
HJ2687 .M57 1985

Steuerle, C. Eugene, 1946- Who should pay for collecting taxes? : financing the IRS / C. Eugene Steuerle. Washington, D.C. : American Enterprise Institute for Public Policy Research, 1986. p. cm. (AEI studies . 448) ISBN 0-8447-3609-0 (pbk. : alk. paper) : LC Card 86-22345 DDC 353.0072/4 19
1. United States. Internal Revenue Service. 2. Tax administration and procedure - United States. I. Title. II. Series.
HJ5018 .S84 1986

Steuerliche Anreize bei innovativen Investitionen kleiner und mittlerer Industrieunternehmen unter vergleichender Berücksichtigung nichtsteuerlicher Hilfen /. Behrens-Ramberg, Wolfgang. Stuttgart , c1985. 299 p. ; ISBN 3-7910-5007-9 : LC Card 86-124563 DDC 336.24/316 19
HJ2337.G3 B44 1985
NYPL [JLL 73-505 Nr.6]

Die steuerliche Behandlung des eigengenutzten Wohneigentums in den Ländern Bundesrepublik Deutschland, Österreich, Schweiz, Frankreich, Grossbritannien und den USA /. Hummel, Marlies. München , 1986. ii, 73 p. ; ISBN 3-88512-021-6 : LC Card 86-215255
HJ4719 .H85 1986

Steuerliche Investitionsförderung im internationalen Vergleich /. Leibfritz, Willi. Berlin , c1985. 255 p. : ISBN 3-428-05776-7 LC Card 85-161706
HJ4631 .L38 1985

Steuerliche Wirkungen des grenzüberschreitenden Mobilien-Leasing . Kieffer, Walther. Berlin , c1983. xxiv, 338 p. : ISBN 3-503-02369-0 LC Card 83-233705
HD39.4 .K54 1983

Steuern in der Investitionsplanung . Georgi, Andreas A. Hamburg , 1986. vii, 243, 16, xxviii p. : ISBN 3-89161-702-X LC Card 86-227290
HG4028.C4 G46 1986

Steuern und Reichsherrschaft . Wild, Werner. Bremen , 1984. 326 p. ; ISBN 3-88948-030-6 LC Card 85-127825
HJ2675 .W55 1984

Steuerplanung im Unternehmen mit einem computergestützten Modell /. Storz, Peter, 1954- München , c1984. vii, 657 p. : ISBN 3-88259-282-6 LC Card 84-174173 DDC 336.24/3/0943 19
HD2753.G3 S76 1984

Steuerplanung internationaler Unternehmungen . Kratz, Peter. Bern , c1986. xii, 344 p. : ISBN 3-258-03586-5 : LC Card 86-171030
HJ4720.A3 K73 1986

Steuerpolitik für die soziale Marktwirtschaft : ein Symposion der Ludwig-Erhard-Stiftung Bonn, am 17. April 1986 / mit Beiträgen von Werner Ehrlicher ... [et al.] ; Redaktion, Hartmut Pick. Stuttgart ; New York : G. Fischer, 1986. 85 p. ; 24 cm. ([Symposion] / Ludwig-Erhard-Stiftung Bonn, 0177-0659 . Bd. 21) Includes bibliographical references and indexes. CONTENTS. - Für eine marktwirtschaftliche Steuerpolitik / Hansjörg Häfele -- Für eine sozial-marktwirtschaftliche Wende in der Finanzierung des Staates / Walter Wittmann -- Möglichkeiten und Grenzen einer Steuerreform, Diskussion. ISBN 3-437-50311-1 LC Card 87-122642 DDC 336.2/00943 19
1. Taxation - Germany (West) - Congresses. 2. Taxation - Congresses. I. Ehrlicher, Werner. II. Pick, Hartmut. III. Series: Symposion (Ludwig-Erhard-Stiftung) , 21.
HJ2687 .S73 1986

Die Steuerpolitik in der Bundesrepublik Deutschland, 1949-1982 /. Muscheid, Jutta. Berlin , c1986. 212 p. : ISBN 3-428-06004-0 LC Card 86-206446
HJ2687 .M84 1986

Der Steuerrebell und seine Gewerkschaft . Fredersdorf, Hermann, 1924- Wiesbaden , c1982. 156 p., [3] folded leaves of plates : ISBN 3-922114-02-4 LC Card 83-102197
HJ2690 .F78 1982

Stevas, Norman St. John- see **St. John-Stevas, Norman.**

STEVEDORES - EFFECT OF TECHNOLOGICAL INNOVATIONS ON.
Couper, A. D. New cargo-handling techniques . Geneva , 1986. xii, 172 p., [1] folded leaf of plates : ISBN 92-2-105419-5 (pbk.) : LC Card 87-117776 DDC 331.7/61387164 19
HD6331.18.L65 C68 1986

STEVEDORES - GERMANY (WEST) - HAMBURG.
Grüttner, Michael. Arbeitswelt an der Wasserkante . Göttingen , 1984. 331 p. ; ISBN 3-525-35722-2 (Deut. Bibl.) LC Card 86-139479
HD8039.L82 G4335 1984

STEVEDORES - ITALY - RAVENNA - HISTORY.
Carli Ballola, Sandra. La Compagnia lavoratori portuali di Ravenna, 1930-1980 /. [Italy , 1981?] (Imola : Galeati) 208 p. : LC Card 83-206502
HD8039.L82 I83 1981

STEVEDORES - LOUISIANA - NEW ORLEANS - HISTORY.
Rosenberg, Daniel, 1953- New Orleans dockworkers . Albany , c1988. x, 233 p. ; ISBN 0-88706-649-6 LC Card 87-10156 DDC 331.7/61387164/0976335 19
HD8039.L82 U664 1988

STEVEDORES - WEST (U. S.) - EFFECT OF TECHNOLOGICAL INNOVATIONS ON - HISTORY.
Finlay, William. Work on the waterfront . Philadelphia , 1988. p. cm. ISBN 0-87722-523-0 (alk. paper) : LC Card 87-17976 DDC 331.88/11387164/0973 19
HD6515.L82 W474 1988

STEVEDORING. see **CARGO HANDLING.**

Stevens, Annette. Ewer, Peter. Unions and the future of Australian manufacturing /. Sydney , Boston , 1987. xi, 189 p. : ISBN 0-04-330382-X (pbk.) LC Card 87-164410 DDC 338.4/767/0994 19
HD9738.A82 E93 1987

Stevens, Barry A. Brooks, Julie K. How to write a successful business plan /. New York, NY , c1987. vii, 231 p. : ISBN 0-8144-5873-4 LC Card 86-22355 DDC 658.4/012 19
HD30.28 .B775 1987

Stevens, Brandt. Rose, Adam Zachery. Natural resource policy and income distribution /. Baltimore , c1988. xvi, 139 p. : ISBN 0-8018-3523-2 (alk. paper) LC Card 87-2788 DDC 333.7/0973 19
HC103.7 .R67 1988

Stevens, Carol Bloom. Stevens, Mark, 1947- The insiders . New York , c1987. 256 p. ; LC Card 87-2537 DDC 364.1/68 19
HG4910 .S67 1987

Stevens, Charles J. Confronting the world food crisis / Charles J. Stevens. Muscatine, Iowa : Stanley Foundation, [1981] 24 p. : ill. ; 22 cm. (Occasional paper / Stanley Foundation, 0145-8841 . 27) "December 1981." Includes bibliographical references. LC Card 82-127279 DDC 338.1/9 19
1. Food supply - Government policy. 2. Food relief - Government policy. 3. Agricultural assistance - Government policy. 4. Population policy. I. Series: Stanley Foundation. Occasional paper, 27. II. Title.
HD9000.6 .S73 ***NYPL [JLK 75-198 no. 27]***

Stevens, Christopher. Negotiating Lome III : an example of North-South bargaining / by Christopher Stevens. Sussex : IDS, [1986] 23 p. : ill. ; 21 cm. (Discussion paper, 0308-5864 . DP 215) Caption title. "May 1986." Bibliography: p. 23. LC Card 86-222421 DDC 337.406 19
1. European Economic Community - Developing countries. I. Title. II. Title: Negotiating Lome Three. III. Title: Negotiating Lome 3. IV. Series: Discussion paper (University of Sussex. Institute of Development Studies) , DP 215.
HC241.25.D44 S74 1986

Stevens, Dorothy Jo. Tice, Robert L. Hi-res graphics for the Apple II/IIe/IIc /. Blue Ridge Summit, Pa. , 1985. vii, 197 p. : ISBN 0-8306-0849-4 : LC Card 84-23954 DDC 001.64/43 19
T385 .T52 1985 ***NYPL [JSE 86-805]***

Stevens, Mark, 1947-
The insiders : the truth behind the scandal rocking Wall Street / Mark Stevens ; researched by Carol Bloom Stevens. New York : Putnam, c1987. 256 p. ; 24 cm. LC Card 87-2537 DDC 364.1/68 19
1. Insider trading in securities - United States. 2. Consolidation and merger of corporations - United States. 3. Investment banking - United States. 4. Wall Street. I. Stevens, Carol Bloom. II. Title.
HG4910 .S67 1987

Millward, Neil. British workplace industrial relations, 1980-1984 . Aldershot, England , Brookfield, Vt. , c1986. xxi, 341 p. : ISBN 0-566-05391-8 : LC Card 86-25625 DDC 331/.0941 19
HD8391 .M55 1986 ***NYPL [JLD 87-1287]***

Stevens, Paul, 1947- Energy demand . New York , 1987. 176 p. : ISBN 0-312-01361-2 : LC Card 87-21477 DDC 333.79/12 19
HD9502.A2 E54373 1987

Stevenson, David R. Davis, Nancy Yaw. Research and consulting as a business /. Washington, D.C. , c1987. v, 41 p. : ISBN 0-913167-21-5 (pbk.) LC Card 87-20254 DDC 658.4/6 19
HD69.C6 D38 1987

Stevenson, Eric. The secondary market and securitization for income property mortgages / by Eric Stevenson ; with chapters by Phillip R. Miller ... [et al.] ; edited by Ronald Rowland. Washington, D.C. (1125 15th St., N.W., Washington 20005) : Mortgage Bankers Association, c1986. xiii, 129 p. : ill. ; 25 cm. Includes bibliographical references. LC Card 87-153518 DDC 332.1/753 19
1. Mortgage loans - United States. 2. Secondary mortgage market - United States. 3. Securities - United States. I. Rowland, Ronald. II. Title.
HG2040.5.U5 S73 1986

Stevenson, H. Michael. Taylor, Malcolm G. (Malcolm Gordon) Medical perspectives on Canadian Medicare . Downsview, Ont. , 1984. vii, 201 p. : ISBN 0-919762-57-3 (pbk.) LC Card 87-673411
HD7102.C2 T34x 1984

Stevenson, Rachel. Marketing and distributive education [videorecording] /. Chicago, Ill. , 1986. 2 videocassettes (24 min. each) : LC Card 86-708241 DDC 658.8 11
HF5415

Stewart, Charles T., 1922- Technology transfer and human factors / Charles T. Stewart, Jr., Yasumitsu Nihei. Lexington, Mass. : Lexington Books, 1987. xiii, 200 p. ; 24 cm. Includes bibliographies and index. ISBN 0-669-14251-4 (alk. paper) LC Card 86-45751 DDC 338.9/26 19
1. Technology transfer - Developing countries. 2. Technology transfer - United States. 3. Technology transfer - Japan. I. Nihei, Yasumitsu, 1933-. II. Title.
T174.3 .S74 1987 ***NYPL [JLE 87-634]***

Stewart, Daisy L. Huffman, Harry. General recordkeeping /. New York , c1988. x, 564 p. : ISBN 0-07-031054-8 LC Card 87-2982 DDC 657/.2 19
HF5635 .H8834 1988

Stewart, David W.
Nonverbal communication in advertising /. Lexington, Mass. , c1988. viii, 296 p. : ISBN 0-669-14172-0 (alk. paper) LC Card 87-17143 DDC 659.1/01/9 19
HF5822 .N66 1988

Runyon, Kenneth E. Consumer behavior and the practice of marketing /. Columbus , c1987. xv, 776 p. : ISBN 0-675-20463-1 LC Card 86-62987 DDC 658.8/342 19
HF5415.3 .R86 1987

Stewart, Frances. Theory and reality in development . Basingstoke, Hampshire , 1986. xii, 291 p. : ISBN 0-333-39824-6
NYPL [JLD 86-1827]

Stewart, J. C., 1949- Corporate finance and fiscal policy in Ireland / J.C. Stewart. Aldershot, Hants, England ; Brookfield, Vt., USA : Avebury, c1987. x, 166 p. ; 23 cm. Based on the author's thesis (Ph. D.)--London School of Economics. Bibliography: p. 154-161. Includes index. ISBN 0-566-05441-8 : LC Card 87-14908 DDC 658.1/5/09415 19
1. Corporations - Ireland - Finance. 2. Corporations - Taxation - Ireland. 3. Corporate profits - Ireland - Effect of inflation on. I. Title.
HG4144 .S74 1987

Stewart, J. Richard. Campbell, Bob J. Early results of seat belt legislation in the United States of America /. Chapel Hill, N.C. [1986] 25 p. : LC Card 86-622836 DDC 363.1/2572/0973 19
HE5614.2 .C35 1986

Stewart, James C. (James Cathcart) Pioneers of a profession : chartered accountants to 1879 / Jas. C. Stewart ; with a new introductory note by T.A. Lee. New York : Garland Pub., 1986, c1977. xii, 181 p., [2] leaves of plates : ill. ; 23 cm. (Accounting thought and practice through the years) Reprint. Originally published: Edinburgh : Scottish Committee on Accounting History, Institute of Chartered Accountants of Scotland, 1977. Includes index. ISBN 0-8240-7888-8 : LC Card 86-25636 DDC 657/.092/2 B 19
1. Accountants - Scotland - Biography. 2. Accounting - Scotland - History. I. Title. II. Series.
HF5604 .S73 1986

Stewart, Jeffrey Robert, 1932- Huffman, Harry. General recordkeeping /. New York , c1988. x, 564 p. : ISBN 0-07-031054-8 LC Card 87-2982 DDC 657/.2 19
HF5635 .H8834 1988

Stewart, Michael, 1933-
Keynes and after / Michael Stewart. 3rd ed. Harmondsworth, Middlesex, England ; New York, N.Y., U. S.A. : Penguin Books, 1986. 230 p. ; 20 cm. (A Pelican book) Bibliography: p. 223-[224]. Includes index. ISBN 0-14-022646-X (pbk.) : LC Card 86-218640 DDC 330.15/6 19
1. Keynesian economics. 2. Economic history - 1918-. 3. Great Britain - Economic policy - 1945-. 4. United States - Economic policy. I. Title.
HB99.7 .S7 1986

Keynes and after / Michael Stewart. 3rd ed. Harmondsworth, England : Penguin, 1986. 230 p. ; 20 cm. Includes index. Bibliography: p. 223-[224] ISBN 0-14-022646-X
1. Keynesian economics. 2. Economic history - 1918-. I. Title. *NYPL [JLD 86-2148]*

Stewart, Olivia. The BBC and public service broadcasting /. Manchester , c1986. viii, 116 p. ; ISBN 0-7190-1964-8 : LC Card 86-209725 DDC 384.54/4/0941 19
HE8689.9.G7 B34 1986

Stewart, Shaun. Gould, Bryan. Monetarism or prosperity? /. London , 1981. x, 222 p. : ISBN 0-333-30782-8 LC Card 86-673392
HG939.5 .G65x 1981

Stewart, Trevor R. Stringer, Kenneth W. Statistical techniques for analytical review in auditing /. New York , c1986. xii, 301 p. : ISBN 0-471-86076-X : LC Card 85-17874 DDC 657/.45/0285536 19
HF5667 .S85 1986 *NYPL [JLE 86-2704]*

Stewart, Walter. Uneasy lies the head : the truth about Canada's Crown corporations / Walter Stewart. Toronto : Collins, 1987. 266 p. ; 25 cm. Bibliography: p. 232-236. Includes index. ISBN 0-00-217757-9 LC Card 87-144685 DDC 354.7109/2 19
1. Corporations, Government - Canada. 2. Corporations, Government - Canada - Provinces. I. Title.
HD4005 .S74 1987

Steyne, David. Thurcroft, a village and the miners' strike . Nottingham [Nottinghamshire] , Atlantic Highlands, NJ , 1986. 276 p. : ISBN 0-85124-441-6 LC Card 86-21887 DDC 331.89/2822334/0942823 19
HD5346.M6152 1984 .T48 1987
NYPL [JLD 87-985]

Sthanunathan, V. K. Railway economics / V.K. Sthanunathan. 1st ed. Madras : S. Viswanathan : Can be had from Ananda Book Depot, 1986. 319 p. : folded map ; 23 cm. Indian context. Bibliography: p. 319. LC Card 87-900868 DDC 385/.1 19
1. Railroads - India - Rates - History. 2. Railroads - India - Freight - History. I. Title.
HE1911 .S74 1986

Stickney, Clyde P., 1944- Davidson, Sidney, 1919- Financial accounting . Chicago , c1988. xvi, 800 p. ; ISBN 0-03-011522-1 LC Card 87-9135 DDC 657 19
HF5635 .D228 1988

Mitteilungen. see **Hamburg. Deutsches Orient-Institut. Mitteilungen.**

Stiftung Gesellschaft und Unternehmen. Engels, Wolfram. Den Staat erneuern, den Markt retten /. Köln , c1983. 228 p. ; ISBN 3-602-34836-9 LC Card 84-182378
HC286 .E54 1983

Stiftung Historisches Kolleg (Munich, Germany) Arbeiter und Bürger im 19. Jahrhundert . München , 1986. xiv, 342 p. ; ISBN 3-486-52871-8 LC Card 86-212379
HD8376 .A72 1986

Stiftung Sozialer Wandel in der Unternehmerischen Wirtschaft (Series) . (Bd. 6) Schanz, Günther, 1943- Mitarbeiter-Kapitalbeteiligung in der Wirtschaft Niedersachsens . Spardorf , c1984. 228 p. : ISBN 3-922919-26-X : LC Card 84-162288
HD5660.G412 L687 1984

STIFTUNG VOLKSWAGENWERK - HISTORY.
Korte, Hermann, 1937- Migration und ihre sozialen Folgen . Göttingen , c1983. 170 p. ; ISBN 3-525-85366-1 LC Card 84-150019
HD8458.A2 K65 1983

Stigler, George Joseph, 1911- Smith, Adam, 1723-1790. [Inquiry into the nature and causes of the wealth of nations. Selections.] Selections from The wealth of nations /. Arlington Heights, Ill. [1986], c1957. ix, 116 p. ; ISBN 0-88295-093-2 (pbk.) : LC Card 86-23951 DDC 330.1 19
HB161 .S6522 1986

Stiglitz, Joseph E.
Economics of the public sector / Joseph E. Stiglitz. 1st ed. New York : W.W. Norton, c1986. xxiii, 599 p. : ill. ; 25 cm. Accompanied by instructor's manual. Bibliography: p. [577]-586. Includes index. ISBN 0-393-01808-3 LC Card 86-211407 DDC 336.73 19
1. Finance, Public - United States. 2. Fiscal policy - United States. I. Title.
HJ257.2 .S84 1986

New developments in the analysis of market structure . Cambridge, Mass. , 1986. xxiv, 559 p. : ISBN 0-262-19241-1 LC Card 85-4246 DDC 338.8 19
HD2326 .N43 1986 *NYPL [JLD 86-3570]*

Stigma /. Page, Robert M. London , Boston , 1984. xii, 207 p. ; ISBN 0-7100-9786-7 : LC Card 83-24638 DDC 302/.12 19
HM291 .P25 1984 *NYPL [JLD 86-3113]*

STIGMA (SOCIAL PSYCHOLOGY)
Hakemulder, Roel. Subcultuur en stigma van de armoede . Leiden , 1985. 96 p. ; ISBN 90-6624-058-X LC Card 86-172398
HC79.P6 H34 1985

Page, Robert M. Stigma /. London , Boston , 1984. xii, 207 p. ; ISBN 0-7100-9786-7 : LC Card 83-24638 DDC 302/.12 19
HM291 .P25 1984 *NYPL [JLD 86-3113]*

Stigum, Marcia L.
After the trade : dealer and clearing bank operations in money market and government securities / Marcia Stigum. Homewood, Ill. : Dow Jones-Irwin, c1988. xvii, 303 p. : ill. ; 24 cm. Includes bibliographical references and index. ISBN 0-87094-937-3 LC Card 87-50773 DDC 332.63/232/0973 19
1. Government securities - United States - Handbooks, manuals, etc. 2. Money market funds - United States - Handbooks, manuals, etc. I. Title.
HG4941 .S75 1988

The Dow Jones-Irwin guide to bond and money market investments / Marcia Stigum, Frank J. Fabozzi. Homewood, Ill. : Dow Jones-Irwin, c1987. xiii, 298 p. : ill. ; 24 cm. Includes bibliographical references and index. ISBN 0-87094-892-X : LC Card 86-71921
1. Investments. 2. Money market. I. Fabozzi, Frank J. II. Title. III. Title: Guide to bond and money market investments. IV. Title: Bond and money market investments. *NYPL [*R-Econ. 87-1260]*

Still struggling . Stolz, Barbara Ann. Lexington, Mass. , c1985. xviii, 205 p. ; ISBN 0-669-10930-4 (alk. paper) LC Card 85-40235 DDC 331.4/0973 19
HD6052 .S76 1985 *NYPL [JLE 85-3704]*

Stiller, Heinz. Sozialistischer Wettbewerb und umfassende Intensivierung . Berlin , 1986. 103 p. ; LC Card 86-200416
HC290.795.S6 S69 1986

Stiller, Karl-Theodor. (joint author) Klönne, Arno. Die deutsche Arbeiterbewegung . Düsseldorf , Köln , 1980. 382 p. ; ISBN 3-424-00652-1 : LC Card 81-453558 DDC 322/.2/0943 19
HX276 .K547 *NYPL [JLD 81-689]*

Stillman, Richard Joseph, 1917- Guide to personal finance : a lifetime program of money management / Richard J. Stillman.5th ed. Englewood Cliffs, N.J. : Prentice Hall, c1988. xxii, 504 p. : ill. ; 25 cm. Bibliography: p. 486-492. Includes index. ISBN 0-13-370214-6 : LC Card 87-19298 DDC 332.024 19
1. Finance, Personal. I. Title.
HG179 .S84 1988

Stimme und Aktion der Völker gegen das Wettrüsten : Dokumente 1979-1984 / [ausgewählt und eingeleitet von Helga Schirmeister ; Auswahl der Dokumente, Helge Schirmeister u. Christa Grossmann] ; Herausgeber, Institut für Internationale Beziehungen.1. Aufl. Berlin : Staatsverlag der Deutschen Demokratischen Republik, 1985. 421 p. ; 22 cm.
1. Disarmament - Congresses. 2. Peace - Congresses. I. Grossmann, Christa. II. Schirmeister, Helga. III. Deutsche Akademie für Staats- und Rechtswissenschaft "Walter Ulbricht." Institut für Internationale Beziehungen. *NYPL [JLD 86-4257]*

Stimpson, Catharine R., 1936- Women, households, and the economy /. New Brunswick, N.J. , c1987. p. cm. ISBN 0-8135-1263-8 : LC Card 87-4840 DDC 331.4/0973 19
HD6060.65.U5 W65 1987

Stimulierung in Industriebetrieben und Kombinaten / von einem Autorenkollektiv unter der Leitung von Herbert Finger und Werner Gertich. Berlin : Die Wirtschaft, c1982. 290 p. : ill. ; 22 cm. Bibliography: p. 281-290. LC Card 83-164671
1. Employee motivation - Europe, Eastern. 2. Personnel management - Europe, Eastern. I. Finger, Herbert. II. Gertich, Werner.
HF5549.5.M63 S75 1982

Stimuly k trudu na sovremennom ėtape razvitiia sotsialisticheskogo obshchestva /. Zhelezovskaia, N. M. Moskva , 1985. 160 p. ; LC Card 86-174895
HF5549.5.I5 Z48 1985

Stine, G. Harry (George Harry), 1928- The corporate survivors / G. Harry Stine. New York, N.Y. : American Management Association, c1986. 230 p. : ill. ; 24 cm. Includes index. Bibliography: p. 215. ISBN 0-8144-5831-9 LC Card 86-47597 DDC 338.7/4/0973 19
1. Corporations - United States - History - 20th century. 2. Industrial management - United States - History - 20th century. 3. Technological innovations - Economic aspects - United States - History - 20th century. I. Title.
HD2785 .S73 1986 *NYPL [JLE 86-4469]*

Stingl, Josef, 1919- Knöpfel, Eckehardt. Werkbuch Jugendarbeitslosigkeit . Wuppertal , c1983. 168 p. : ISBN 3-417-12855-2 (pbk.) LC Card 87-672977
HD5779 .K59x 1983

Stinson, Thomas F., 1942- Governing the heartland : can rural governments survive the farm crisis : report of the Subcommittee on Intergovernmental Relations of the Committee on Governmental Affairs, United States Senate. Washington : U. S. G.P.O. : For sale by the

Supt. of Docs., Congressional Sales Office, U. S. G.P.O., 1986. xii, 159 p. : ill., 4 maps ; 24 cm. (S. prt. . 99-176) At head of title: 99th Congress, 2d session. Committee print. Distributed to some depository libraries in microfiche. Shipping list no.: 86-725-P. "July 1986." Bibliography: p. 158-159. Item 1037-B, 1037-C (microfiche) LC Card 86-603376 DDC 336/.014/77 19
1. Municipal revenue - Middle West. 2. Municipal finance - Middle West. 3. Middle West - Economic conditions. I. United States. Congress. Senate. Committee on Governmental Affairs. Subcommittee on Intergovernmental Relations. II. Title. III. Series.
HJ9181 .S75 1986

Stirrings of culture / Robert J. Sardello, editor, Gail Thomas, editor. Dallas, Tex. : Dallas Institute Publications, 1986. xix, 250 p. ; 28 cm. "The articles in this volume have all been previously published in the Institute newsletter"--P. ISBN 0-911005-07-2 : LC Card 86-24028 DDC 306 19
1. Culture. 2. City and town life - United States. 3. United States - Social conditions - 1980-. 4. Dallas (Tex.) - Social conditions. I. Sardello, Robert J., 1942-. II. Thomas, Gail. III. Institute newsletter.
HM101 .S786 1986 ***NYPL [JFF 87-151]***

Stiskin, Nahum, 1945- Huddle, Norie, 1944- Island of dreams . Cambridge, Mass. , c1987. xxiii, 355 p. : ISBN 0-87047-027-2 : LC Card 86-33842 DDC 363.7/00952 19
HC465.E5 H82 1987

Sto deset let městské hromadné dopravy v Praze. 110 let městské hromadné dopravy v Praze /. [Prague] [1985] 52 p. : LC Card 86-201750
HE4759.3.Z8 P732 1985

Sto i petdeset godini slivenska tekstilna promishlenost. Zlatanov, Zdravko Iordanov. 150 godini slivenska tekstilna promishlenost /. [Sofia] , 1984. 364 p., [48] p. of plates : LC Card 85-118285
HD9865.B83 S589 1984

Stochastic optimization : proceedings of the international conference, Kiev, 1984 / edited by I. Arkin, A. Shiraev, R. Wets. Berlin ; New York : Springer-Verlag, c1985. x, 754 p. : ill. ; 25 cm. (Lecture notes in control and information sciences. 81) Papers presented at the International Conference on Stochastic Optimization held at Kiev, USSR in Sept. 1984 and sponsored by the Committee for Systems Analysis of the USSR Academy of Sciences and others. Includes bibliographical references. ISBN 0-387-16659-9 (U. S.) LC Card 86-11865 DDC 629.8/312 19
1. Control theory - Congresses. 2. Stochastic processes - Congresses. 3. Mathematical optimization - Congresses. I. Arkin, V. I. (Vadim Iosifovich), 1937-. II. Shiriaev, Al'bert Nikolaevich. III. Wets, Roger J.-B. IV. Akademiia nauk SSSR. Komitet po sistemnomu analizu. V. International Conference on Stochastic Optimization (1984 : Kiev, Ukraine).
QA402.3 .S778 1985 ***NYPL [JSE 86-1596]***

STOCHASTIC PROCESSES - CONGRESSES.
Obnaruzhenie izmenenii svoistv sluchainykh protsessov . Vil'nius , 1984. 243 p. : LC Card 84-168819
HD38 .S715 vyp. 65 QA274.A1

Shpilevskii, E. Printsipy dinamicheskoi klassifikatsii stokhasticheskikh protsessov i sistem . Vil'nius , 1978. 138 p. ; LC Card 81-173567
HD38 .S715 vyp. 28 QA274

Steklov Seminar (1984 : Steklov Institute of Mathematics) [Statistika i upravlenie sluchainykh protsessov. English.] Statistics and control of stochastic processes /. New York, N.Y. , c1985. xiii, 506 p. ; ISBN 0-911575-18-9 LC Card 85-8851 DDC 519.5 19
QA276.A1 .S7513 1984 ***NYPL [JSE 86-729]***

Stochastic optimization . Berlin , New York , c1985. x, 754 p. : ISBN 0-387-16659-9 (U. S.) LC Card 86-11865 DDC 629.8/312 19
QA402.3 .S778 1985 ***NYPL [JSE 86-1596]***

Stochastic processes in demography and their computer implementation /. Mode, Charles J., 1927- Berlin , New York , c1985. xvii, 389 p. : ISBN 0-387-13622-3 (U. S.) LC Card 84-26707 DDC 304.6/028/54 19
HB849.51 .M635 1985 ***NYPL [JSE 86-1952]***

STOCHASTIC PROGRAMMING.
(1983) Haumer, Heinrich. Sequentielle stochastische Investitionsplanung /. Wiesbaden , c1983. 305 p. ; ISBN 3-409-13420-4 LC Card 83-190299
HG4515.2 .H38 1983

STOCHASTIC SYSTEMS - CONGRESSES.
Shpilevskii, E. Printsipy dinamicheskoi klassifikatsii stokhasticheskikh protsessov i sistem . Vil'nius , 1978. 138 p. ; LC Card 81-173567
HD38 .S715 vyp. 28 QA274

Stochastinių procesų ir sistemų dinaminės klasifikacijos principai. Shpilevskii, E. Printsipy dinamicheskoi klassifikatsii stokhasticheskikh protsessov i sistem . Vil'nius , 1978. 138 p. ; LC Card 81-173567
HD38 .S715 vyp. 28 QA274

Stochastische Modelle für die betriebliche Planung /. Hilfer, Rudolf. München , c1985. ii, 191 p. : ISBN 3-89003-015-7 LC Card 85-189343
HD30.25 .H55 1985

STOCK (ANIMALS) see LIVESTOCK.

STOCK BROKERS. see BROKERS.

STOCK CERTIFICATES - AFRICA, SOUTHERN - CATALOGS.
The Scripophilist's guide . [Johannesburg? , 1985?] 100 p. : LC Card 87-100584 DDC 769.5 19
HG5851.A3 S37 1985

STOCK CERTIFICATES - COLLECTORS AND COLLECTING.
Garrison, G. H. Haley (George H. Haley) The insider's guide to antique securities /. Williamsburg, Va. (P.O. Drawer JH, Williamsburg 23187) , c1987. 1 v. (various pagings) : LC Card 87-149140 DDC 332.63/2/0750973 19
HG4633 .G38 1987

STOCK CERTIFICATES - SOUTH AFRICA - CATALOGS.
The Scripophilist's guide . [Johannesburg? , 1985?] 100 p. : LC Card 87-100584 DDC 769.5 19
HG5851.A3 S37 1985

STOCK COMPANIES - GERMANY (WEST) - ACCOUNTING.
Faller, Eberhard. Zur Problematik der Zulässigkeit des Abweichens vom Grundsatz der Einzelerfassung und Einzelbewertung im aktienrechtlichen Jahresabschluss . Pfaffenweiler , 1985. xiv, 386 p. : ISBN 3-89085-078-2 : LC Card 86-140803
HF5681.S8 F34 1985

Schneider, Pia, 1956- Finanzwirtschaftliche Nebenrechnungen . Frankfurt am Main , New York , c1985. xiii, 303 p. : ISBN 3-8204-8472-8 LC Card 85-190966
HF5686.C7 S354 1985

STOCK COMPANIES - GERMANY (WEST) - ECONOMETRIC MODELS.
Wanik, Bernhard. Die Lohnentwicklung deutscher Industrieaktiengesellschaften /. Bonn , 1981. vii, 268 p. : LC Card 85-165602
HD5029 .W36 1981

STOCK COMPANIES - GERMANY (WEST) - TAXATION.
Faller, Eberhard. Zur Problematik der Zulässigkeit des Abweichens vom Grundsatz der Einzelerfassung und Einzelbewertung im aktienrechtlichen Jahresabschluss . Pfaffenweiler , 1985. xiv, 386 p. : ISBN 3-89085-078-2 : LC Card 86-140803
HF5681.S8 F34 1985

STOCK CONTROL. see INVENTORY CONTROL.

STOCK CORPORATIONS. see CORPORATIONS.

El stock de capital en la Argentina . Goldberg, Samuel. [Buenos Aires] , 1986. 28 leaves : LC Card 87-403996 DDC 332/.0414 19
HC180.C3 G65 1986

STOCK DIVIDENDS. see DIVIDENDS.

STOCK-EXCHANGE - ARGENTINA - ROSARIO (SANTE FE) - HISTORY.
De Marco, Miguel Ángel. 1884-1984, los cien años de la Bolsa de Comercio de Rosario /. [S.l. , 1984?] (Rosario : Escuela de Artes Gráficas del Colegio San José de Rosario) 167 p. : LC Card 87-115398 DDC 332.64/28224 19
HG5320.R67 D4 1984

STOCK-EXCHANGE - ASIA.
Rowley, Anthony, 1939- Asian stockmarkets . Homewood, Ill. , 1987. 290 p. : ISBN 962-7010-29-4; 0-87094-987-X (jacket) LC Card 87-137156 DDC 332.64/25 19
HG5702 .R69 1987

STOCK-EXCHANGE - BRAZIL - RIO DE JANEIRO - HISTORY.
Bolsa do Rio, 140 anos. Rio de Janeiro [1985] 200 p. : LC Card 87-146604 DDC 332.64/281 19
HG5340.R5 B66 1985

STOCK-EXCHANGE - CARIBBEAN AREA.
Bolsas de valores en América Latina y el Caribe. Caracas, Venezuela , 1985. 401 p. : LC Card 86-154738
HG5160.5 .B65 1985 ***NYPL [JLE 87-523]***

STOCK-EXCHANGE - CARIBBEAN AREA - DIRECTORIES.
Mercados de capital en América Latina y el Caribe . Caracas, Venezuela [1986] 114 p. ; LC Card 87-103358
HG5160.5.A3 M47 1986

STOCK-EXCHANGE - DICTIONARIES.
Scott, David Logan, 1942- Wall Street words /. Boston , c1988. xi, 404 p. : ISBN 0-395-43747-4 LC Card 87-21444 DDC 332.6/03/21 19
HG4513 .S37 1988

STOCK-EXCHANGE - EUROPEAN ECONOMIC COMMUNITY COUNTRIES - ADDRESSES, ESSAYS, LECTURES.
European equity markets . New York , 1984. 470 p. : ISBN 0-8240-6307-4 (alk. paper) : LC Card 83-49440 DDC 332.64/094
HG5430.5.A3 E84 1984
NYPL [JLE 86-4508]

STOCK-EXCHANGE - FRANCE.
Freymond, Joël. Guide du spéculateur . Paris , c1986. 175 p. : ISBN 2-226-02463-8 : LC Card 87-166254
HG6041 .F82 1986

Sassier, Philippe. Les Français à la corbeille /. Paris , c1985. 268 p. ; ISBN 2-221-04729-X : LC Card 86-126750 DDC 332.64/244 19
HG4583 .S27 1985

STOCK-EXCHANGE - GERMANY (WEST) - CONGRESSES.
Mannheimer Bankenforum (1985) Risikokapital über die Börse . Berlin , New York , c1986. x, 190 p. ; ISBN 0-387-16671-8 (U. S.) LC Card 86-225903
HG5492 .M35 1985

STOCK-EXCHANGE - INDONESIA.
Dickie, Robert B. Foreign investment and government policy in the Third World /. New York , 1988. p. cm. ISBN 0-312-00520-2 : LC Card 87-25076 DDC 332.6/7322598 19
HG5752 .D53 1988

STOCK-EXCHANGE - ITALY.
Rossi, Guido. La scalata del mercato . Bologna , c1986. 152 p. ; ISBN 88-15-01123-4 : LC Card 86-180921
HG5522 .R66 1986

STOCK-EXCHANGE - ITALY - STATISTICS.
Mediobanca. Indici e dati relativi ad investimenti in titoli quotati nelle borse italiane (1985) =. [Milano] [1985] v, 427 p. : LC Card 86-210524
HG5522 .M43 1985

STOCK-EXCHANGE - JUVENILE LITERATURE.
Little, Jeffrey B. Investing and trading /. New York , c1988. 47 p. : ISBN 1-555-46627-3 LC Card 87-23852 DDC 332.6/78 19
HG4553 .L58 1988

STOCK-EXCHANGE - LATIN AMERICA.
Bolsas de valores en América Latina y el Caribe. Caracas, Venezuela , 1985. 401 p. : LC Card 86-154738
HG5160.5 .B65 1985 ***NYPL [JLE 87-523]***

STOCK-EXCHANGE - LATIN AMERICA - DIRECTORIES.
Mercados de capital en América Latina y el Caribe . Caracas, Venezuela [1986] 114 p. ; LC Card 87-103358
HG5160.5.A3 M47 1986

STOCK EXCHANGE (LONDON, ENGLAND)
Hall, Maximilian. The city revolution . New York , 1987. xiii, 147 p. ; ISBN 0-312-00986-0 :

LC Card 87-9684 DDC 332.6/0941 19
HG186.G7 H35 1987

Thomas, William Arthur. The big bang /. Deddington, Oxford , Atlantic Highlands, N.J. , 1986. ix, 180 p. ; ISBN 0-86003-546-8 LC Card 86-226055 DDC 332.64/241 19
HG4577 .T47 1986

STOCK EXCHANGE (LONDON, ENGLAND) - HISTORY.
Michie, R. C., 1949- The London and New York stock exchanges, 1850-1914 /. London , Boston , 1987. xv, 312 p. ; ISBN 0-04-332117-8 (alk. paper) LC Card 87-1394 DDC 332.64/241 19
HG4577 .M52 1987

STOCK-EXCHANGE - NETHERLANDS.
Piller, L. Beleggen in effecten /. Utrecht , 1984. 195 p. ; ISBN 90-274-6126-0 : LC Card 85-134084
HG5562 .P55 1984

STOCK-EXCHANGE - NIGERIA.
Alile, H. I. The Nigerian stock market in operation /. [Lagos, Nigeria] 1986 (Lagos, Nigeria : Jeromelaiho & Associates) 194, v p. : LC Card 87-143647 DDC 332.64/2669 19
HG5881.N6 A43 1986

The stock exchange specialist system . Stoll, Hans R. New York, N.Y. (90 Trinity Place, New York 10006) [c1985] 53 p. : LC Card 86-210049 DDC 332.64/273 19
HG4572 .S856 1985

STOCK-EXCHANGE - UNITED STATES.
Little, Jeffrey B. Understanding Wall Street /. Blue Ridge Summit, PA , c1987. 219 p. : ISBN 0-8306-3120-8 : LC Card 87-3628 DDC 332.6/78 19
HG4910 .L54 1987

Little, Jeffrey B. [Wall Street library.] Understanding Wall Street /. Blue Ridge Summit, PA , 1986. p. cm. ISBN 0-8306-3010-4 (pbk.) : LC Card 86-27791 DDC 332.6/78 19
HG4921 .L63 1986

The Microstructure of securities markets /. Englewood Cliffs, N.J. , c1986. ix, 254 p. ; ISBN 0-13-581794-3 LC Card 85-28265 DDC 332.64 19
HG4661 .M53 1986 NYPL [JLE 86-2001]

Money guide . Kansas City, Mo. , c1987. vii, 128 p. : ISBN 0-8362-2210-5 (pbk.) : LC Card 87-1200 DDC 332.63/22 19
HG4921 .M68 1987

Schwartz, Robert A. (Robert Alan), 1937- Equity markets . New York , c1988. xvi, 544 p. : ISBN 0-06-041322-0 LC Card 87-23173 DDC 332.64/0973 19
HG4963 .S38 1988

Strebel, Paul. In the shadows of Wall Street . Englewood Cliffs, N.J. , c1988. xii, 228 p. : ISBN 0-13-455999-1 LC Card 87-42680 DDC 332.63/22 19
HG4921 .S84 1988

Weiss, David M., 1938- After the trade is made . New York, N.Y. , c1986. xii, 436 p. : ISBN 0-13-018581-7 : LC Card 85-30997 DDC 332.64/273 19
HG4910 .W365 1986 NYPL [JLE 86-4304]

STOCK-EXCHANGE - UNITED STATES - HANDBOOKS, MANUALS, ETC.
Rosenberg, Claude N. Stock market primer . New York, NY , c1987. xii, 372 p. ; ISBN 0-446-51257-5 LC Card 87-40163 DDC 332.63/22 19
HG4921 .R58 1987

STOCK-EXCHANGE - UNITED STATES - HISTORY.
Granville, Joseph Ensign, 1923- The warning . New York , c1985. xvi, 397 p. ; ISBN 0-88191-034-1 : LC Card 85-13107 DDC 332.64/273 19
HG4910 .G76 1985 NYPL [JLE 86-3122]

STOCK-EXCHANGE - UNITED STATES - JUVENILE LITERATURE.
Little, Jeffrey B. Wall Street--how it works /. New York , c1988. 47 p. : ISBN 1-555-46621-4 LC Card 87-15139 DDC 332.64/273 19
HG4921 .L625 1988

STOCK-EXCHANGES - SWITZERLAND.
The Swiss equity market . Westport, Conn. , 1985. xiv, 210 p. : ISBN 0-89930-147-9 (lib. bdg. : alk. paper) LC Card 85-12195 DDC 332.64/2494 19
HG5652 .M45 1985 NYPL [JLE 86-1965]

STOCK INDEX FUTURES.
Angell, George. West of Wall Street /. [Chicago] [1987], c1988. xxiv, 215 p. ; ISBN 0-88462-623-7 LC Card 87-3003 DDC 332.63/222 19
HG6043 .A55 1988

Byrne, B. Thomas. The stock index futures market . Chicago, Ill. , c1987. vii, 358 p. : ISBN 0-917253-28-0 LC Card 87-115177 DDC 332.63/222 19
HG6043 .B97 1987

Luskin, Donald L. Index options & futures . New York , c1987. xi, 355 p. : ISBN 0-471-85464-6 LC Card 86-28189 DDC 332.63/222 19
HG6043 .L87 1987

The stock index futures market . Byrne, B. Thomas. Chicago, Ill. , c1987. vii, 358 p. : ISBN 0-917253-28-0 LC Card 87-115177 DDC 332.63/222 19
HG6043 .B97 1987

Stock market. Alile, H. I. The Nigerian stock market in operation /. [Lagos, Nigeria] 1986 (Lagos, Nigeria : Jeromelaiho & Associates) 194, v p. : LC Card 87-143647 DDC 332.64/2669 19
HG5881.N6 A43 1986

Stock market. Money guide . Kansas City, Mo. , c1987. vii, 128 p. : ISBN 0-8362-2210-5 (pbk.) : LC Card 87-1200 DDC 332.63/22 19
HG4921 .M68 1987

The stock market /. Teweles, Richard Jack, 1924- New York , c1987. xii, 526 p. ; ISBN 0-471-82044-X LC Card 86-33950 DDC 332.64/2 19
HG4551 .T48 1987

STOCK MARKET. see **STOCK-EXCHANGE.**

Stock market anomalies / edited by Elroy Dimson. Cambridge [Cambridgeshire] ; New York : Cambridge University Press, 1988. p. cm. Includes index. ISBN 0-521-34104-3 LC Card 87-6622 DDC 332.63/2 19
1. Stock-exchange. 2. Capital market. I. Dimson, Elroy, 1947-.
HG4551 .S82 1988

Stock market investment in Malaysia and Singapore /. Neoh, Soon Kean. Kuala Lumpur , 1986. vii, 312 p. : ISBN 967-96906-6-0 (pbk.) LC Card 86-943422 DDC 332.63/22/09595 19
HG5750.6.A5 N46 1986

Stock market primer . Rosenberg, Claude N. New York, NY , c1987. xii, 372 p. ; ISBN 0-446-51257-5 LC Card 87-40163 DDC 332.63/22 19
HG4921 .R58 1987

STOCK OPTIONS. see **PUT AND CALL TRANSACTIONS.**

STOCK OWNERSHIP FOR EMPLOYEES. see **EMPLOYEE OWNERSHIP.**

STOCK-OWNERSHIP - FRANCE.
Sassier, Philippe. Les Français à la corbeille /. Paris , c1985. 268 p. ; ISBN 2-221-04729-X : LC Card 86-126750 DDC 332.64/244 19
HG4583 .S27 1985

STOCK OWNERSHIP - GREAT BRITAIN.
Scott, John, 1912- Capitalist property and financial power . Brighton, Sussex , 1986. x, 230 p. ; ISBN 0-7450-0047-9
NYPL [JLD 86-3078]

STOCK OWNERSHIP - JAPAN.
Scott, John, 1912- Capitalist property and financial power . Brighton, Sussex , 1986. x, 230 p. ; ISBN 0-7450-0047-9
NYPL [JLD 86-3078]

STOCK OWNERSHIP - UNITED STATES.
Meek, Christopher. Managing by the numbers . Reading, Mass. , c1988. ix, 293 p. : ISBN 0-201-16129-X : LC Card 87-16088 DDC 338.7/4/0973 19
HD70.U5 M413 1988

Scott, John, 1912- Capitalist property and financial power . Brighton, Sussex , 1986. x, 230 p. ; ISBN 0-7450-0047-9
NYPL [JLD 86-3078]

STOCK PRICE FORECASTING.
Chua, Jess H. Gains from stock-market timing /. New York, N.Y. (90 Trinity Pl., New York 10006) [c1986] 75 p. ; LC Card 87-129798 DDC 332.63/222 19
HG4637 .C48 1986

Griffin, Paul A. Accounting for the translation of foreign currencies . Stamford, Conn. , c1987. viii, 112 p. : ISBN 0-910065-22-5 (pbk.) LC Card 86-81640 DDC 657/.48 19
HG3853.7 .G75 1987

Haskamp, Clemens Heinrich, 1955- Aktienkursprognose auf Grundlage der Identifikation von Trend- und Saisonkomponente . Krefeld , 1985. 204 p. : ISBN 3-88358-052-1 LC Card 86-121480
HG4637 .H38 1985

Schleis, Konrad, 1935- Börsengewinne dank besserer Aktienkurs-Prognose /. Niederglatt , c1984. 257 p. : ISBN 3-85684-030-3 : LC Card 84-119396
HG5492 .S345 1984

STOCK PRICE INDEXES - ITALY.
Mediobanca. Indici e dati relativi ad investimenti in titoli quotati nelle borse italiane (1985) =. [Milano] [1985] v, 427 p. : LC Card 86-210524
HG5522 .M43 1985

STOCK PRICES. see **STOCKS - PRICES.**

STOCK TENDERS. see **TENDER OFFERS (SECURITIES)**

STOCK TRANSFER - UNITED STATES.
Financial Industry Securities Council Same Day Funds Settlement Task Force. Same day funds settlement for securities transactions . [New York, N.Y.] [S.l.] , c1985. 61 leaves in various foliations : LC Card 85-193287 DDC 332.64 19
HG4631 .F56 1985 NYPL [JLF 86-919]

Stock up on options / foreword by Richard E. Band ; by the editors of KCI Communications, Inc. Alexandria, VA (P.O. Box 1467, Alexandria 22313) : KCI Communications, c1987. 28 leaves : ill. ; 23 cm. Bibliography: leaves 24-25. LC Card 87-401634 DDC 332.64/52 19
1. Put and call transactions. I. KCI Communications, Inc.
HG6042 .S84 1987

Stock, Walter. High Technology : amerikanische Vorherrschaft und globalstrategische Absichten der USA / Walter Stock. Köln : Pahl-Rugenstein, 1986. 244 p. : ill. ; 19 cm. (Kleine Bibliothek. 390) Includes bibliographical references. ISBN 3-7609-1049-1 : LC Card 86-230225
1. High technology industries - United States. 2. United States - Economic policy - 1981-. 3. Capitalism - United States. I. Title.
HC110.H53 S76 1986

STOCKBROKERS. see **BROKERS.**

The stockbroker's guide to put and call option strategies. Gross, LeRoy. [New York, 1974] viii, 116 p. ISBN 0-13-846741-9 LC Card 74-166476 DDC 332.6/45
HG6041 .G75 NYPL [JLE 87-573]

Stockhausen, Gerard Lawrence. Threats of quotas in international trade, their effect on the exporting country / Gerard Lawrence Stockhausen. New York : Greenwood Press, 1988. 170 p. : ill. ; 25 cm. (Contributions in economics and economic history, 0084-9235 . no. 78) Bibliography: p. [155]-161. Includes index. ISBN 0-313-25785-X (lib. bdg. : alk. paper) LC Card 87-23682 DDC 382/.64 19
1. Import quotas - Mathematical models. I. Title. II. Series.
HF1430 .S86 1988

Stockhausen, Joachim von.

STOCKHOLDERS - JAPAN.
Futatsugi, Yūsaku, 1935- [Gendai Nihon no kigyō shūdan. English.] Japanese enterprise groups /. [Kobe] , 1986. 179 p. : LC Card 86-220427 DDC 338.8/0952 19
HD2756.2.J3 F8813 1986

STOCKHOLDERS' MEETINGS - UNITED STATES.
Epstein, Edward Jay, 1935- Who owns the corporation? . New York , 1986. vi, 69 p. ; ISBN 0-87078-208-8 (pbk.) : LC Card 87-101003 DDC 338.7/4/0973 19
HD2743 .E67 1986

STOCKHOLDERS - SWEDEN - REGISTERS.
Sundqvist, Sven-Ivan, 1939- Ägarna och makten

i Sveriges börsföretag 1985 =. [Stockholm] [1985] 318 p. : ISBN 91-7588-085-7 : LC Card 86-105378
HG186.S85 S86 1985 ***NYPL [JLE 86-3810]***

STOCKHOLDERS' VOTING - UNITED STATES.
Heard, James E. Conflicts of interest in the proxy voting system /. Washington, D.C. , c1987. 100 p. : ISBN 0-931035-18-X (pbk.) LC Card 87-404270 DDC 338.8/3/0973 19
HD2743 .H43 1987

Mathiasen, Karen. Corporate governance and shareholder rights . Washington, DC (1755 Massachusetts Ave., N.W., Suite 600, Washington 20036) , c1986. 96 p. ; LC Card 86-230362 DDC 346.73/0666 347.306666 19
HD2743 .M34 1986

Stockholm. Institute of Latin American Studies. see **Latinamerika-institutet i Stockholm.**

Stockholm studies in politics, 0346-6620 .
(29) Micheletti, Michele. Organizing interest and organized protest . [Stockholm] , 1985. vii, 253 p. ; ISBN 91-7146-451-4 (pbk.) LC Card 86-145828 DDC 322/.2/09481 19
HD8572.T5 M53 1985
NYPL [JLL 74-316 no.29]

Stockholmsmonografier .
(64) Grenander-Nyberg, Gertrud, 1912- En charkuterifabrik med tradition . Stockholm , c1985. 207 p. : ISBN 91-38-09206-9 LC Card 86-159511
HD9145.S88 E544 1985

STOCKKEEPING. see **INVENTORY CONTROL.**

Stockman, David Alan, 1946-
The triumph of politics : how the Reagan revolution failed / David A. Stockman.1st ed. New York : Harper & Row, c1986. 422 p. : ill. ; 24 cm. Includes index. ISBN 0-06-015560-4 : LC Card 85-45541 DDC 338.973 19
1. Government spending policy - United States. 2. Budget - United States. 3. United States - Economic policy - 1981-. 4. United States - Politics and government - 1981-. I. Title.
HC106.8 .S75 1986 ***NYPL [JLE 86-2647]***

The triumph of politics : why the Reagan revolution failed / David A. Stockman.Large print [ed.]. Boston, Mass. : G.K. Hall, 1987, c1986. xxxiii, 654 p. (large print) ; 24 cm. (G.K. Hall large print book series) Originally published: New York : Harper & Row, 1986. ISBN 0-8161-4231-9 (lg. print) : LC Card 86-22950 DDC 338.973 19
1. Government spending policy - United States. 2. Budget - United States. 3. United States - Economic policy - 1981-. 4. United States - Politics and government - 1981-. I. Title.
HC106.8 .S75 1986b

Stocks, Alex M. Union raiding : rivalry in B.C. mines, smelters, and metal industries / Alex M. Stocks. Kingston, Ont., Canada : Industrial Relations Centre, Queen's University of Kingston, 1985. 61 p. ; 29 cm. (School of Industrial Relations research essay series . no. 1) Bibliography: p. 55-61. ISBN 0-88886-125-7 (pbk.) LC Card 86-145321 DDC 331.87/09711 19
1. Trade-unions - British Columbia - Jurisdictional disputes. 2. Trade-unions - Miners - British Columbia. 3. Trade-unions - Iron and steel workers - British Columbia. 4. Trade-unions - Metal workers - British Columbia. I. Queen's University, Kingston, Ont. Industrial Relations Centre. II. Title. III. Series.
HD6528.B9 S86 1985 ***NYPL [JLF 87-422]***

Stocks, bonds, options, futures : investments and their markets / staff of the New York Institute of Finance ; edited by Stuart R. Veale. New York, N.Y. : The Institute ; [Englewood Cliffs, N.J.] : Prentice-Hall, c1987. 332 p. : ill. ; 24 cm. Includes index. ISBN 0-13-846718-8 : LC Card 87-11324 DDC 332.6/78 19
1. Investments - United States. 2. Securities - United States. 3. Commodity exchanges - United States. 4. Brokers - United States. I. Veale, Stuart R. II. New York Institute of Finance.
HG4921 .S7945 1987

STOCKS - BRAZIL - DIRECTORIES.
Guia ação . RJ [i.e. Rio de Janeiro] [1985 or 1986] 285 p. ; LC Card 87-405004 DDC 332.6/78/0981 19
HG5334.5 .G85 1985

STOCKS - CHARTS, DIAGRAMS, ETC.
Lerbinger, Paul, 1955- P & F charts . Niederglatt , c1984. 231 p. : ISBN 3-85684-031-1 : LC Card 84-119357
HG6041 .L47 1984

STOCKS - GERMANY, WEST.
Schleis, Konrad, 1935- Börsengewinne dank besserer Aktienkurs-Prognose /. Niederglatt , c1984. 257 p. : ISBN 3-85684-030-3 : LC Card 84-119396
HG5492 .S345 1984

STOCKS - HANDBOOKS, MANUALS, ETC.
Perritt, Gerald W. Expand your investment horizons and increase your stock market profits /. Chicago, IL , c1987. viii, 288 p. : ISBN 0-930369-03-3 (pbk.) LC Card 87-401495 DDC 332.63/2 19
HG4527 .P39 1987

Stein, Lawrence M. Value investing . New York , c1988. xiv, 331 p. : ISBN 0-471-62875-1 LC Card 87-23152 DDC 332.63/22 19
HG4527 .S816 1988

STOCKS - INDONESIA.
Dickie, Robert B. Foreign investment and government policy in the Third World /. New York , 1988. p. cm. ISBN 0-312-00520-2 : LC Card 87-25076 DDC 332.6/7322598 19
HG5752 .D53 1988

STOCKS - ITALY.
Rossi, Guido. La scalata del mercato . Bologna , c1986. 152 p. ; ISBN 88-15-01123-4 : LC Card 86-180921
HG5522 .R66 1986

STOCKS - ITALY - STATISTICS.
Consiglio nazionale dell'economia e del lavoro (Italy) Rapporto CNEL su risparmio e borsa . Roma , 1984. 308 p. : LC Card 85-242331 DDC 332/.0415/0945021 19
HC310.S3 C66 1984

Mediobanca. Indici e dati relativi ad investimenti in titoli quotati nelle borse italiane (1985) =. [Milano] [1985] v, 427 p. : LC Card 86-210524
HG5522 .M43 1985

STOCKS - JUVENILE LITERATURE.
Little, Jeffrey B. Growth stocks /. New York , c1988. p. cm. ISBN 1-555-46624-9 LC Card 87-24482 DDC 332.63/22 19
HG4661 .L57 1988

Little, Jeffrey B. What is a share of stock? /. New York , c1988. 47 p. : ISBN 1-555-46620-6 LC Card 87-13788 DDC 332.63/22 19
HG4521 .L736 1988

Stocks, Kevin D. McKell, Lynn J. A study of MAS practice and knowledge and bibliographic references for management advisory services . New York, N.Y. , c1987. 100, [iv], 72 p. ; ISBN 0-87051-002-9 (pbk.) : LC Card 87-19491 DDC 016.6584/6 19
HF5616.U5 M34 1987

STOCKS - MALAYSIA.
Neoh, Soon Kean. Stock market investment in Malaysia and Singapore /. Kuala Lumpur , 1986. vii, 312 p. : ISBN 967-96906-6-0 (pbk.) LC Card 86-943422 DDC 332.63/22/09595 19
HG5750.6.A5 N46 1986

STOCKS - MARKETING.
Altman, Richard M. Creating investor demand for company stock . New York , c1988. p. cm. ISBN 0-89930-173-8 (lib. bdg. : alk. paper) LC Card 86-25566 DDC 332.6/42 19
HG4661 .A57 1988

Stocks on target /. Schwab, Ken, 1928- Great Neck, N.Y. , c1986. p. cm. ISBN 0-89962-537-1 LC Card 86-30725 DDC 332.63/22 19
HG4521 .S35783 1986

STOCKS - PRICES.
Grande Esteban, Ildefonso. Modelos de valoración de acciones y metodos de constrastación /. Bilbao [1985?] 319 p. : ISBN 84-7585-025-1 LC Card 87-111240
HG4636 .G88 1985

STOCKS - PRICES - BELGIUM.
Hawawini, Gabriel A. Mandatory financial information and capital market equilibrium in Belgium /. New York , 1987. 271 p. : ISBN 0-8240-7852-7 (alk. paper) : LC Card 87-54 DDC 332.63/222/09493 19
HG5553 .H39 1987

STOCKS - PRICES - DATA BASES.
The NASDAQ handbook . Chicago, Ill. , c1987. vii, 577 p. : ISBN 0-917253-54-X : LC Card 87-12378 DDC 332.64/3/0973 19
HG4551 .N37 1987

STOCKS - PRICES - EUROPEAN ECONOMIC COMMUNITY COUNTRIES - ADDRESSES, ESSAYS, LECTURES.
European equity markets . New York , 1984. 470 p. : ISBN 0-8240-6307-4 (alk. paper) : LC Card 83-49440 DDC 332.64/094
HG5430.5.A3 E84 1984
NYPL [JLE 86-4508]

STOCKS - PRICES - GERMANY, WEST.
Haskamp, Clemens Heinrich, 1955- Aktienkursprognose auf Grundlage der Identifikation von Trend- und Saisonkomponente . Krefeld , 1985. 204 p. : ISBN 3-88358-052-1 LC Card 86-121480
HG4637 .H38 1985

STOCKS - PRICES - GERMANY (WEST) - ECONOMETRIC MODELS.
Apostolopoulos, Athanase, 1955- Aktienkurse und rationale Erwartungen . Frankfurt am Main , New York , c1986. 364 p. : ISBN 3-8204-9157-0 LC Card 86-220281
HG5494 .A66 1986

STOCKS - PRICES - GERMANY (WEST) - MATHEMATICAL MODELS.
Rothacker, Hartmut. Zeitstetige Bewertungsmodelle für Tilgungsanleihen . Heidelberg , c1986. xxiv, 350 p. : ISBN 3-7908-0343-X LC Card 86-222052
HG4523 .R68 1986

STOCKS - PRICES - GERMANY (WEST) - STATISTICS.
Index der Aktienkurse --lange Reihen. Wiesbaden , Stuttgart , 1985. 211 p. : LC Card 86-204529 DDC 332.63/222/0943 19
HG5494 .I53 1985

STOCKS - PRICES - HISTORY.
Armstrong, Martin A. The greatest bull market in history . [Princeton?] , <c1986-. v. <2 > : LC Card 87-138809 DDC 332.64 19
HG4516 .A75 1986

STOCKS - PRICES - INDIA.
Dixit, R. K. (Ramesh Kumar), 1946- Behaviour of share prices and investment in India /. New Delhi , c1986. 328 p. ; LC Card 86-902907 DDC 332.63/222/0954 19
HG5733 .D59 1986

STOCKS - PRICES - MATHEMATICAL MODELS.
Berglund, Tom. Anomalies in stock returns on a thin security market /. Helsingfors , 1986. vi, 191 p. : ISBN 951-555-239-7 (pbk.) LC Card 86-224629 DDC 332.63/222 19
HG4636 .B47 1986

STOCKS - PRICES - SWITZERLAND.
Zimmermann, Heinz, 1958- Kapitalerhöhungen und Aktienmarkt . Köln , 1986. 446 p. : ISBN 3-921471-57-5 LC Card 87-407823 DDC 332.63/222/09494 19
HG5653 .Z56 1986

STOCKS - PRICES - UNITED STATES.
Equity performance 1977-1986 . Washington, D.C. , c1987. 28, [A-Q] p. : LC Card 87-159010 DDC 332.1/754/0973 19
HG1616.I5 E68 1987

Mangold, Nancy R. (Nancy Rueyhwa), 1949- Changing auditors and the effect on earnings, auditors' opinions, and stock prices /. Ann Arbor, Mich. , c1987. viii, 165 p. ; ISBN 0-8357-1786-0 (alk. paper) LC Card 87-19128 DDC 338.7/4/0973 19
HF5686.C7 M3295 1987

Power investing . Alexandria, VA (P.O. Box 1467, Alexandria 22313) , c1987. vi, 42 leaves : LC Card 87-403629 DDC 332.63/22 19
HG4915 .P65 1987

STOCKS - PRICES - UNITED STATES - ECONOMETRIC MODELS.
Carlson, John A., 1933- Stocks, shocks, and price-output dynamics /. West Lafayette, Ind. [1984] 30, 13 p. ; LC Card 84-623131 DDC 658/.001/9 s 332.63/222/0973 19
HD6483 .P8 no. 859 HF5416.5

STOCKS - PRICES - UNITED STATES - HISTORY - CHARTS, DIAGRAMS, ETC.
Common stock price histories, 1910-1986. Morristown, N.J. , c1987. 208 p. : ISBN

0-9618454-0-6 (pbk.) LC Card 87-158025 DDC 332.63/222/0973 19
HG4916 .C65 1987

STOCKS - PRICES - UNITED STATES - STATISTICS.
Earnings surprise report, February 1987. New York, N.Y. (90 Broad St., New York 10004) , c1987. 167 p. ; LC Card 87-401689 DDC 332.63/222/0973 19
HG4915 .E275 1987

Stocks, shocks, and price-output dynamics /. Carlson, John A., 1933- West Lafayette, Ind. [1984] 30, 13 p. ; LC Card 84-623131 DDC 658/.001/9 s 332.63/222/0973 19
HD6483 .P8 no. 859 HF5416.5

STOCKS - SINGAPORE.
Neoh, Soon Kean. Stock market investment in Malaysia and Singapore /. Kuala Lumpur , 1986. vii, 312 p. : ISBN 967-96906-6-0 (pbk.) LC Card 86-943422 DDC 332.63/22/09595 19
HG5750.6.A5 N46 1986

STOCKS - SWITZERLAND.
The Swiss equity market . Westport, Conn. , 1985. xiv, 210 p. : ISBN 0-89930-147-9 (lib. bdg. : alk. paper) LC Card 85-12195 DDC 332.64/2494 19
HG5652 .M45 1985 ***NYPL [JLE 86-1965]***

STOCKS - TENDER OFFERS. see **TENDER OFFERS (SECURITIES)**

STOCKS - UNITED STATES.
Hardy, C. Colburn. The blue chip investment strategy . New York , 1987. 324 p. : ISBN 0-531-15525-0 LC Card 87-14726 DDC 332.63/22 19
HG4963 .H37 1987

Little, Jeffrey B. Understanding Wall Street /. Blue Ridge Summit, PA , c1987. 219 p. : ISBN 0-8306-3120-8 : LC Card 87-3628 DDC 332.6/78 19
HG4910 .L54 1987

Little, Jeffrey B. [Wall Street library.] Understanding Wall Street /. Blue Ridge Summit, PA , 1986. p. cm. ISBN 0-8306-3010-4 (pbk.) : LC Card 86-27791 DDC 332.6/78 19
HG4921 .L63 1986

Money guide . Kansas City, Mo. , c1987. vii, 128 p. : ISBN 0-8362-2210-5 (pbk.) : LC Card 87-1200 DDC 332.63/22 19
HG4921 .M68 1987

Sobel, Robert, 1931 (Feb. 19)- The new game on Wall Street /. New York , c1987. xii, 244 p. : ISBN 0-471-84527-2 LC Card 86-33986 DDC 332.6/78 19
HG4921 .S6156 1987

Strebel, Paul. In the shadows of Wall Street . Englewood Cliffs, N.J. , c1988. xii, 228 p. : ISBN 0-13-455999-1 LC Card 87-42680 DDC 332.63/22 19
HG4921 .S84 1988

Understanding the securities markets . Jersey City, NJ (75 Montgomery St., Jersey City 07302) , c1986. 36 p. ; LC Card 87-130670 DDC 332.63/2 19
HG4910 .U53 1986

Winter, Elmer L. Complete guide to making a public stock offering. Englewood Cliffs, N.J. [1972] 295 p. ISBN 0-13-160192-X LC Card 70-164924 DDC 658.1/52
HG4028.S7 W5 1972 ***NYPL [JLF 86-390]***

Zweig, Martin E. [Winning on Wall Street.] Martin Zweig's Winning on Wall Street /. New York , c1986. x, 293 p. : ISBN 0-446-51234-6 : LC Card 85-43167 DDC 332.63/22 19
HG6049 .Z87 1986 ***NYPL [JLE 86-2796]***

STOCKS - UNITED STATES - CHARTS, DIAGRAMS, ETC.
Fisher, Kenneth L. The Wall Street waltz . Chicago , c1987. xii, 210 p. : ISBN 0-8092-4797-6 : LC Card 87-5310 DDC 332.63/222/0973 19
HG4916 .F47 1987.

STOCKS - UNITED STATES - HANDBOOKS, MANUALS, ETC.
Rosenberg, Claude N. Stock market primer . New York, NY , c1987. xii, 372 p. ; ISBN 0-446-51257-5 LC Card 87-40163 DDC 332.63/22 19
HG4921 .R58 1987

Stafford, J. T. The share-owner's guide /. Cambridge [Cambridgeshire] , Wolfeboro, N.H., USA , 1988. p. cm. ISBN 0-85941-402-7 (pbk.) : LC Card 87-17387 DDC 332.63/22 19
HG4921 .S617 1988

STOCKS - UNITED STATES - JUVENILE LITERATURE.
Little, Jeffrey B. Wall Street--how it works /. New York , c1988. 47 p. : ISBN 1-555-46621-4 LC Card 87-15139 DDC 332.64/273 19
HG4921 .L625 1988

Stockton, Richard B. ROI, planning for profitable growth / by Richard B. Stockton. New York, N.Y., U. S.A. : Modern Business Reports, c1984. x, 141 leaves : ill. ; 28 cm. "Alexander Hamilton Institute"--Cover. ISBN 0-86604-150-8 (pbk.) LC Card 86-232254 DDC 332.63 19
1. Capital investments - Evaluation. 2. Rate of return. I. Alexander Hamilton Institute (U. S.). II. Title.
HG4028.C4 S72 1984b

STOCKYARDS - AUSTRALIA - VICTORIA - LOCATION.
Victoria. Saleyard Working Party. Distribution of saleyards in Victoria . [Melbourne] , 1986. 69, 7, 7 p. : LC Card 87-159450 DDC 338.1/760831 19
HD9428.A83 V538 1986

STOCKYARDS - UNITED STATES - HISTORY.
Skaggs, Jimmy M. Prime cut . College Station , c1986. xiii, 263 p., [8] p. of plates : ISBN 0-89096-249-9 : LC Card 85-40742 DDC 338.1/76213/0973 19
HD9415 .S58 1986 ***NYPL [JLE 86-3913]***

STOCZNIA GDAŃSKA IM. LENINA STRIKE, GDAŃSK, POLAND, 1980 - ABSTRACTS.
Twierdochlebow, W. J. Solidarność . Menlo Park, CA , 1985. 72, v leaves ; LC Card 86-221919 DDC 331.89/28238204/094382 19
HD5397.7.S512 1980 .G358 1985

Stoddard, Ellwyn R., 1927- Maquila : assembly plants in northern Mexico / by Ellwyn R. Stoddard.1st ed. El Paso, Tex. : Texas Western Press, the University of Texas at El Paso, c1987. ix, 91 p., [2] p. of plates : ill. ; 23 cm. Bibliography: p. [81]-91. ISBN 0-87404-200-3 (pbk.) LC Card 86-51646 DDC 338.4/767/09721 19
1. Offshore assembly industry - Mexico. 2. Mexican American Border Region - Industries. 3. Women offshore assembly industry workers - Health and hygiene - Mexico. I. Title.
HD9734.M42 S76 1987

Stoddart, L. Conditions of work and quality of working life . Geneva , 1986. xxi, 306 p. ; ISBN 92-2-105328-8 (pbk.) : LC Card 86-215659 DDC 306/.36/025 19
HD7260 .C64 1986

Stoeckel, John E. Fertility in Asia . London , 1986. xix, 177 p. : ISBN 0-86187-667-9 DDC 304.6/32/095 19
HB1043.A3 F47 1986b
NYPL [JLD 87-1268]

Stoffaës, Christian, 1947- French industrial policy /. Washington, D.C. , c1986. xii, 228 p. : ISBN 0-8157-0098-9 : LC Card 85-48203 DDC 338.944 19
HD3616.F82 F74 1986 ***NYPL [JLE 87-211]***

Stoffel, R. A. Internationale vergelijking loonstructuur / R.A. Stoffel. 's-Gravenhage : Centraal Planbureau, [1986] 20 p. : ill. ; 24 cm. (Onderzoeksmemorandum . no. 23) "Juli 1986." Bibliography: p. 16. LC Card 86-231311
1. Wages - Europe. 2. Wages - Netherlands. 3. Wages - United States. I. Title. II. Series.
HD5014 .S76 1986

Stöffler, Michael. Markttransparenz in der Lebensversicherung : Analyse bisheriger Erfahrungen und Empfehlungen für die Weiterentwicklung sektorspezifischer Regelungen aus wettbewerbs- und verbraucherpolitischer Sicht / wissenschaftliche Leitung, H. Diederich ... [et al.] ; Bearbeiter, Michael Stöffler. [Mainz] : Forschungsinstitut für Wirtschaftspolitik an der Universität Mainz, [1982?] vi, 248 p. : ill. ; 21 cm. Bibliography: p. 232-248. LC Card 83-202502
1. Insurance, Life - Germany (West) - State supervision. 2. Insurance, Life - Law and legislation - Germany (West). I. Diederich, Helmut, 1928-. II. Johannes Gutenberg-Universität. Forschungsinstitut für Wirtschaftspolitik. III. Title.
HG9078.Z9 S76 1982

Stoga, Alan.
Breaking the economic impasse : an urgent quadrangular agenda / contributions by Alan J. Stoga, Marina v.N. Whitman ; John N. Yochelson, editor. Washington, D.C. : Center for Strategic and International Studies, c1987. viii, 48 p. ; 23 cm. (Significant issues series, 0736-7136 . v. 9, no. 4) ISBN 0-89206-104-9 (pbk.) LC Card 87-14682 DDC 338.9 19
1. Economic history - 1971-. 2. International economic relations. 3. Economic policy. I. Whitman, Marina von Neumann. II. Yochelson, John N. III. Stoga, Alan. IV. Series.
HC59 .B73 1987

Stoga, Alan. Breaking the economic impasse . Washington, D.C. , c1987. viii, 48 p. ; ISBN 0-89206-104-9 (pbk.) LC Card 87-14682 DDC 338.9 19
HC59 .B73 1987

Stöhr, Walter B. International economic restructuring and the regional community /. Aldershot, Hants, England , Brookfield, Vt., USA , c1987. x, 404 p. : ISBN 0-566-05478-7 : LC Card 87-11841 DDC 330.9 19
HF1412 .I574 1987

Stoi͡anov, Khristo. Khumanizat͡sii͡a na truda : dva obshtestveno-istoricheski podkhoda kŭm kachestvoto na trudovii͡a zhivot / Khristo Stoi͡anov.1. izd. Sofii͡a : Izd-vo Nauka i izkustvo, 1985. 191 p. ; 22 cm. Includes bibliographical references. LC Card 85-243365
1. Quality of work life. 2. Labor and laboring classes. 3. Industrial sociology. I. Title.
HD6955 .S85 1985

Stoimostnye otnoshenii͡a v sot͡sialisticheskoĭ ėkonomike /. Nanitashvili, B. Tbilisi , 1978. 182 p. ; LC Card 81-149294
HB201 .N293 1978

Stojanović, Ivan, Dr. Pavlović, Dragiša, 1943- Ko radnike povezuje lažnim koncima . Beograd , 1984. 414 p. ; LC Card 84-178578
HC407.Z9 L36 1984

Stojanović, Radmila. Na putu ka visoko industrijalizovanom socijalizmu / Radmila Stojanović. Beograd : Savremena administracija, 1984. 208 p. ; 24 cm. In Serbo-Croatian (roman) Table of contents also in English. Bibliography: p. 197-[204] LC Card 85-194079
1. Industry and state. 2. Socialism. 3. Industry and state - Yugoslavia. 4. Socialism - Yugoslavia. I. Title.
HD3611 .S77 1984

Stoken, Dick A. Strategic investment timing : how to pinpoint & profit from short- & long-term changes in the economy / Dick A. Stoken. New York : Macmillan ; London : Collier Macmillan, c1984. x, 225 p. : ill. ; 22 cm. Includes index. ISBN 0-02-614810-2 LC Card 84-12576 DDC 332.6/78 19
1. Investments - United States - Handbooks, manuals, etc. 2. Economic forecasting - United States - Handbooks, manuals, etc. I. Title.
HG4921 .S795 1984 ***NYPL [JLD 86-2041]***

Stokes, Charles Shannon, 1941- Rural development and human fertility /. New York, N.Y. , London , c1984. ix, 318 p. : ISBN 0-02-949680-2 : LC Card 83-26834 DDC 304.6/32/091734 19
HB1108 .R87 1984 ***NYPL [JLE 86-1084]***

Stokes, Robert W. McCasland, William R. Transitway surveillance, communications, and control /. College Station, Tex. [1986] vi, 76 p. : LC Card 87-620995 DDC 380.5 s 388.3/143 19
HE203 .T43 no. 425-2F HE336.B8

Stolcke, Verena. Cafeicultura : homens, mulheres e capital (1850-1980) / Verena Stolcke ; tradução, Denise Bottmann e João R. Martins Filho. São Paulo, SP : Brasiliense, 1986. 410 p. : ill. ; 21 cm. Bibliography: p. [399]-410. LC Card 86-208925
1. Coffee trade - Brazil - History. 2. Coffee plantation workers - Brazil - History. I. Title.
HD9195.B72 S76 1986

Stølen, Nils Martin. Etterspørsel etter arbeidskraft i norske industrinæringer / av Nils Martin Stølen. Oslo : Statistisk sentralbyrå : I kommisjon hos H. Aschehoug og Universitetsforlaget, 1983. 66 p. : ill. ; 30 cm. (Rapporter fra Statistisk sentralbyrå, 0332-8422 . 83/29) Bibliography: p. 63-64. ISBN 82-537-2001-7 : LC Card 84-191739

1. Labor supply - Norway - Mathematical models. I. Title. II. Series.
HD5800.A6 S76 1983

Stoll, Edgar, 1945- Betriebswirtschaftslehre und ökonomische Krise . Wiesbaden , c1984. xxix, 412 p. : ISBN 3-409-13037-3 LC Card 85-143204
HD30.23 .B49 1984

Stoll, Hans R. The stock exchange specialist system : an economic analysis / by Hans R. Stoll. New York, N.Y. (90 Trinity Place, New York 10006) : Salomon Brothers Center for the Study of Financial Institutions, Graduate School of Business Administration, New York University, [c1985] 53 p. : ill. ; 23 cm. (Monograph series in finance and economics . monograph 1985-2) Bibliography: p. 50-51. LC Card 86-210049 DDC 332.64/273 19
1. New York Stock Exchange. 2. Brokers - New York (N.Y.). I. Title. II. Series.
HG4572 .S856 1985

Stoll, John R. Economic impact of the recreational boating industry in Texas / John R. Stoll, Lonnie L. Jones, John C. Bergstrom. College Station, TX : Texas A&M University, Sea Grant College Program, [1985] xiv, 86 p. : ill. ; 28 cm. "February 1985." Bibliography: p. 48-49. "TAMU-SG-85-604." LC Card 86-622008 DDC 330.9764/063 19
1. Boating industry - Texas. I. Jones, Lonnie L. II. Bergstrom, John C. (John Clark). III. Texas A & M University. Sea Grant College Program. IV. Title.
HD9993.B633 U58 1985

Stollberg, Gunnar. Die Rationalisierungsdebatte 1908-1933 : freie Gewerkschaften zwischen Mitwirkung und Gegenwehr / Gunnar Stollberg. Frankfurt/Main ; New York : Campus Verlag, c1981. 214 p. ; 21 cm. The author's Habilitationsschrift--TU Hannover. Includes index. Bibliography: p. 193-212. ISBN 3-593-32938-7 : LC Card 81-177695 DDC 331.88/0943 19
1. Industrial organization - Germany - History - 20th century. 2. Trade-unions - Germany - History - 20th century. 3. Industrial management - Germany - History - 20th century. 4. Labor and laboring classes - Germany - History - 20th century. I. Title.
HD70.G2 S666 1981 ***NYPL [JLD 86-1662]***

Stolleis, Michael, 1941- Pecunia nervus rerum : zur Staatsfinanzierung in der frühen Neuzeit / Michael Stolleis. Frankfurt am Main : V. Klostermann, c1983. 184 p. ; 23 cm. Bibliography: p. 176-177. Includes index. ISBN 3-465-01590-8 (Deut Bibl.) LC Card 83-183704
1. Finance, Public - Europe - History - 18th century. 2. Deficit financing - Europe - History - 18th century. 3. Sumptuary laws - Europe - History - 18th century. I. Title.
HJ1000 .S76 1983

Stolnitz, George J. Technological prospects and population trends /. Boulder, Colo. , 1987. xxiii, 211 p. ; ISBN 0-8133-7470-7 : LC Card 87-50897 DDC 304.6 19
HB871 .T3 1987

Stolovich, Luis. Compra de carteras . Montevideo [1986] 188 p. : LC Card 87-403157 DDC 332.1/09895 19
HG2954 .C66 1986

Stoltenberg, Gerhard. Unsere Verantwortung für eine gute Zukunft : ausgewählte Reden, 1982-1986 / Gerhard Stoltenberg. München : G. Olzog, c1986. 191 p. ; 20 cm. Includes index. ISBN 3-7892-7290-6 LC Card 87-130881 DDC 339.5/2/0943 19
1. Germany, West - Economic policy - 1974-. 2. Finance, Public - Germany, West. 3. Germany (West) - Politics and government - 1982-. I. Title.
HC286.7 .S767 1986

Stolz, Barbara Ann. Still struggling : America's low-income working women confronting the 1980s / Barbara Ann Stolz. Lexington, Mass. : Lexington Books, c1985. xviii, 205 p. ; 24 cm. Includes bibliographical references and index. ISBN 0-669-10930-4 (alk. paper) LC Card 85-40235 DDC 331.4/0973 19
1. Women - Employment - United States - Case studies. 2. Women - United States - Economic conditions - Case studies. 3. Sex discrimination in employment - United States - Case studies. 4. Social change - Case studies. I. Title.
HD6052 .S76 1985 ***NYPL [JLE 85-3704]***

Stomberg, Peter. Die Probleme der Prognose des Kapitalbedarfs im Rahmen der strategischen Plannung / Peter Stomberg. Göttingen : Vandenhoeck & Ruprecht, c1984. x, 212 p. ; 24 cm. (Schriftenreihe des Seminars für Allgemeine Betriebswirtschaftslehre der Universität Hamburg . Bd. 25) Bibliography: p. [202]-212. ISBN 0-352-51266-3 LC Card 84-240131
1. Strategic planning. 2. Management. 3. Industrial management. 4. Capital investments. I. Title. II. Series.
HD30.28 .S729 1984

Stone, Carl. Understanding Third World politics and economics / by Carl Stone ; [cover by Andrew McNamee]. [2nd ed.] Brown's Town P. O., St. Ann, Jamaica : Earle Pub., c1980. 105 p. ; 21 cm. Errata slip bound in book. Includes bibliographies.
1. Developing countries - Economic conditions. 2. Developing countries - Politics and government. I. Title.
NYPL [JLD 87-364]

Stone, Clarence N. (Clarence Nathan), 1935- Urban policy and politics in a bureaucratic age / Clarence N. Stone, Robert K. Whelan, William J. Murin. 2nd ed. Englewood Cliffs, N.J. : Prentice-Hall, c1986. xv, 397 p. ; 24 cm. Includes bibliographies and index. ISBN 0-13-939562-8 LC Card 85-6481 DDC 320.8/0973 19
1. Municipal government - United States. 2. Municipal officials and employees - United States. 3. Municipal services - United States. 4. Political participation - United States. I. Whelan, Robert K. II. Murin, William J. III. Title.
JS331 .S76 1986 ***NYPL [JLE 86-3158]***

Stone, Frank, 1923- Building a Canadian-American free trade area /. Washington, D.C. , c1987. xii, 217 p. ; ISBN 0-8157-2973-1 (pbk.) LC Card 87-71507 DDC 382/.0971/073 19
HF1480.15.U5 B85 1987

Stone, Gerald W. Great ideas for teaching economics /. Glenview, Ill. , c1987. xxiv, 400 p. : ISBN 0-673-17245-7 (pbk.) LC Card 87-159026 DDC 330/.07 19
HB74.5.G73 1987

Stone, Irving, 1923- The composition and distribution of British investment in Latin America, 1865 to 1913 / Irving Stone. New York : Garland Pub., 1987. xi, 502 p. : ill. ; 24 cm. (South American and Latin American economic history) Originally presented as the author's thesis (Ph. D.--Columbia University, 1962) Bibliography: p. 214-217. ISBN 0-8240-1372-7 : LC Card 87-8540 DDC 332.6/7341/08 19
1. Investments, British - Latin America - History - 19th century. 2. Investments, British - Latin America - History - 20th century. I. Title. II. Series.
HG5160.5.A3 S76 1987

Stone, Robert N. Ellefson, Paul V. U. S. wood-based industry . New York , 1984. xxv, 479 p. : ISBN 0-03-063698-1 (alk. paper) : LC Card 84-8278 DDC 338.1/7498/0973 19
HD9755 .45 1984 ***NYPL [JLE 85-706]***

STONEHOUSE, JOHN THOMSON, 1925-
Sherrard, Michael. London Capital Group Limited (formerly British Bangladesh Trust Limited) . London , 1977. vi, 376 p. : ISBN 0-11-512127-7 (pbk.) LC Card 85-164377
HG4135 .S46 1977

Stoneman, Paul. The economic analysis of technology policy / Paul Stoneman. Oxford [Oxfordshire] : Clarendon Press ; New York : Oxford University Press, 1987. x, 224 p. : ill. ; 24 cm. Includes bibliographies and index. ISBN 0-19-877260-2 (pbk.) LC Card 87-20374 DDC 338.9/26 19
1. Technological innovations - Economic aspects. 2. Diffusion of innovations. 3. Technology and state. I. Title.
HD45 .S844 1987

STONEMASONS - FRANCE - CREUSE - HISTORY.
Bandy de Nalèche, Louis. Les Maçons de la Creuse /. Limoges , 1984. 99 p., [16] p. of plates : ISBN 2-85521-059-3 : LC Card 85-169794 DDC 331.7/69321/094468 19
HB2054.C74 B36 1984

Stonfer, David. The storage battery market : profiles and trade opportunities / prepared by David Stonfer. [Washington, D.C.?] : Nonferrous Metals Division, Basic Industries Sector, International Trade Administration, U. S. Dept. of Commerce, [1985] v, 52 p. ; 28 cm. "April 1985." Item 231-B-1 LC Card 85-601888 DDC 382/.45621312424/0973 19
1. Battery industry - United States. 2. Battery industry. I. Title.
HD9697.B323 U574 1985
NYPL [JLF 87-207]

Stonham, Paul. Global stock market reforms / Paul Stonham. Aldershot, Hants, England ; Brookfield, Vt., USA : Gower Pub., c1987. x, 157 p. ; 23 cm. (Gower studies in finance and investment . 4) Includes bibliographies and index. ISBN 0-566-00821-1 : LC Card 87-276 DDC 332.64/2 19
1. Stock-exchange. I. Title. II. Series.
HG4551 .S83 1987

Stoob, Heinz. See- und Flusshäfen vom Hochmittelalter bis zur Industrialisierung /. Köln , 1986. xxi, 315 p. : ISBN 3-412-07585-X LC Card 87-146564 DDC 387.1/094 19
HE557.A3 S37 1986

Stop D.W.I. Stop DWI . Lexington, Mass. , c1986. xv, 183 p. : ISBN 0-669-12157-6 (alk. paper) LC Card 85-45676 DDC 363.1/2558 19
HE5620.D7 S89 1986 ***NYPL [JLE 86-2813]***

Stop drinking and start living /. Schlesinger, Stephen E. Blue Ridge Summit, PA , 1985. xx, 133 p. : ISBN 0-8306-1937-2 : LC Card 85-14885 DDC 362.2/92 19
HV5033 .S34 1985 ***NYPL [JLD 86-1606]***

Stop drugs at work ; implementation manual /. Gold, Mark S. New York, N.Y. , c1986. p. cm. ISBN 0-394-55091-9 LC Card 86-26168 DDC 658.3/822 19
HF5549.5.E42 G65 1986

Stop DWI : successful community responses to drunk driving / edited by Denis Foley. Lexington, Mass. : Lexington Books, c1986. xv, 183 p. : ill. ; 24 cm. Includes bibliographies and index. ISBN 0-669-12157-6 (alk. paper) LC Card 85-45676 DDC 363.1/2558 19
1. Drunk driving - United States. 2. Drunk driving - United States - Prevention. 3. Alcoholics - Rehabilitation - United States. 4. Drunk driving - United States - Prevention - Citizen participation. I. Foley, Denis. II. Title: Stop D.W.I.
HE5620.D7 S89 1986 ***NYPL [JLE 86-2813]***

Stopanska samostoi͡atelnost i stopanska otgovornost /. Petkov, Todor (Todor Iliev) Sofii͡a , 1985. 237 p. ; LC Card 85-134177
HD8626.5 .P48 1985

Stopford, John M. Britain and the multinationals / John Stopford and Louis Turner. Chichester ; New York : Wiley, c1985. xiv, 282 p. : ill. ; 24 cm. (Wiley/IRM series on multinationals) Includes bibliographical references and index. ISBN 0-471-90839-8 : LC Card 85-12352 DDC 338.8/8841 19
1. International business enterprises - Great Britain. 2. Investments, Foreign - Great Britain. 3. Great Britain - Foreign economic relations. I. Turner, Louis, 1942-. II. Title. III. Series.
HD2845 .S76 1985 ***NYPL [JLE 86-924]***

Stopford, Martin. Maritime economics / Martin Stopford. London ; Boston : Allen & Unwin, 1988. p. cm. Bibliography: p. Includes index. ISBN 0-04-623016-5 (alk. paper) LC Card 87-18802 DDC 387.5 19
1. Merchant marine. 2. Shipping. I. Title.
HE735 .S76 1988

De stora programmens tid . Wittrock, Björn. Stockholm , 1984. 186 p. ; ISBN 91-7410-200-1 : LC Card 84-189613
HD9502.S82 W58 1984

STORAGE AND MOVING TRADE - UNITED STATES - STATISTICS.
Transportation fact book. Alexandria, VA (1611 Duke St., Alexandria 22314-3482) , c1987. iii, 75 p. : LC Card 87-155218 DDC 388.3/2/0973021 19
HE5623 .T67 1987

The storage battery market . Stonfer, David. [Washington, D.C.?] [1985] v, 52 p. ; LC Card 85-601888 DDC 382/.45621312424/0973 19
HD9697.B323 U574 1985
NYPL [JLF 87-207]

Storage facilities in the chiefdoms of Bo and Pujehun District /. Yearwood, John. Bo [1983] vi, 31 leaves : LC Card 87-110214 DDC 338.1/6 19
HD9017.S53 B599 1983

STORE HOURS - GERMANY, WEST.
Ladenschluss kontrovers . Stuttgart [1984] 232 p. : ISBN 3-512-00712-0 LC Card 85-138606
HD5178 .L33 1984

STORE HOURS - LAW AND LEGISLATION - GERMANY (WEST)
Ladenschluss kontrovers . Stuttgart [1984] 232 p. : ISBN 3-512-00712-0 LC Card 85-138606
HD5178 .L33 1984

STORE HOURS - LAW AND LEGISLATION - NETHERLANDS.
Advies wijziging Winkelsluitingswet . Den Haag [1986] 78 p. ; ISBN 90-6587-250-7 LC Card 86-234857
HC321 .S63 1986, nr. 11 KKM3419

STORE LOCATION.
Laulajainen, Risto. Spatial strategies in retailing /. Dordrecht ; Boston : xiii, 253 p. : ISBN 90-277-2595-0 LC Card 87-20803 DDC 658.8/7 19
HF5429.275 .L38 1987

A store of memories /. Burton, G. Allan, 1915- Toronto, Ont. , c1986. 330 p., [17] p. of plates : ISBN 0-7710-1792-8 : LC Card 87-101965 DDC 381/.45/000924 B 19
HF5465.C32 B87 1986

STORES, COOPERATIVE. see **COOPERATIVE SOCIETIES.**

STORES, RETAIL - FRANCE - PARIS - HISTORY - 19TH CENTURY.
Nord, Philip, 1950- Paris shopkeepers and the politics of resentment /. Princeton, N.J. , c1986. xvii, 539 p. : ISBN 0-691-05454-1 : LC Card 85-42695 DDC 322/.3/0944361 19
HF5429.6.F7 N67 1986
NYPL [JLD 86-2305]

STORES, RETAIL - GREAT BRITAIN - STATISTICS.
ISBA area information, 1978 /. London , 1978. 147 p. : ISBN 0-906241-00-6 (pbk.) LC Card 83-225656 DDC 381/.1/0941021 19
HA1134 .I83 1978

STORES, RETAIL - HUNGARY - STATISTICS.
Gazdálkodási és jövedelmezőségi adatok, mutatószámok a szövetkezeti bolti kiskereskedelemben /. Budapest , 1984. 113 p. ; ISBN 963-7006-24-9 : LC Card 85-154737
HF5429.6.H8 G39 1984

STORES, RETAIL - LOCATION.
Ghosh, Avijit. Location strategies for retail and service firms /. Lexington, Mass. , c1987. x, 212 p. : ISBN 0-669-12032-4 (alk. paper) LC Card 85-45583 DDC 658.1/1 19
HF5429.275 .G47 1987

STORES, RETAIL - MANAGEMENT.
Cash, R. Patrick. Improving apparel shop profits] [New York, N.Y.] [c1986] 285 p. : ISBN 0-87102-131-5 LC Card 86-61313 DDC 687/.068/8 19
HD9940.A2 C37 1986

Husack, Glen A. More profit from your retail business . [S.l.] , c1977. 84 p. : ISBN 0-88896-066-2 (pbk.) LC Card 85-174558
HF5429 .H85 1977

Meurling, Kim. Aktiv butikk /. Oslo , 1980. 186 p. : ISBN 82-7037-129-7 : LC Card 81-174134
HF5429 .M44 1980

Rylander, Stig, 1928- Säljande butik /. Lund , c1984. 272 p. : ISBN 91-44-99681-0 : LC Card 84-229201
HF5429 .R94 1984

STORES, RETAIL - MANITOBA - WINNIPEG.
Downtown and regional shopping centre retailing in Winnipeg /. Winnipeg, Man., Canada , 1985. x, 90, [8] p. : ISBN 0-920213-22-7 (pbk.) LC Card 86-137592 DDC 381/.1/0971274 19
HF5429.6.C3 D69 1985
NYPL [JLF 86-1331]

STORES, RETAIL - NORWAY - MANAGEMENT.
Meurling, Kim. Aktiv butikk /. Oslo , 1980. 186 p. : ISBN 82-7037-129-7 : LC Card 81-174134
HF5429 .M44 1980

STORES, RETAIL - SWEDEN - MANAGEMENT.
Rylander, Stig, 1928- Säljande butik /. Lund , c1984. 272 p. : ISBN 91-44-99681-0 : LC Card 84-229201
HF5429 .R94 1984

Storey, D. J. The Performance of small firms . London , Wolfeboro, N.H. , c1987. 342 p. : ISBN 0-7099-4411-X : LC Card 86-29052 DDC 658/.022 19
HD2341 .P399 1987

Storey, M. John, 1943- Starting your own business : no money down / M. John Storey. New York : Wiley, c1987. xv, 266 p. ; 24 cm. Bibliography: p. 259. Includes index. ISBN 0-471-85769-6 LC Card 87-2051 DDC 658.1/141 19
1. New business enterprises. I. Title.
HD62.5 .S76 1987

La Storia dei poveri : pauperismo e assistenza nell'età moderna / R. Morozzo Della Rocca ... [et al.] ; a cura di Alberto Monticone. Roma : Studium, c1985. xii, 300 p. ; 21 cm. (La Cultura. 31) Bibliography: p. [296]-300. ISBN 88-382-3530-9 : LC Card 86-198943
1. Poor - Europe - History. 2. Charities - Europe - History. 3. Public welfare - Europe - History. I. Monticone, Alberto. II. Morozzo Della Rocca, Roberto, 1955-.
HC240.9.P6 S76 1985

Storia delle idee politiche e sociali .
(2) Bilancio della socialdemocrazia . Napoli , 1984. 156 p. ; LC Card 84-249837
HX73 .B55 1984 ***NYPL [JLD 87-1536]***

Storia demografica dei comuni siciliani dal 1832 al 1858 /. Greco, Eugenio. Palermo [1982] 60, [61] p. ; LC Card 85-103229
HB2270.S5 G74 1982

Storia demografica dei comuni siciliani dal 1862 al 1971 / presentazione del Stefano Somogyi. Palermo : Università di Palermo, Istituto di scienze demografiche, [1979] 294 p. ; 24 cm. (Collana di studi demografici. 12) LC Card 86-131917
1. Sicily - Population - Statistics. 2. Cities and towns - Italy - Sicily - Statistics. I. Somogyi, Stefano. II. Università di Palermo. Istituto di scienze demografiche. III. Series.
HB2270.S5 S76 1979

Storia e società (Editori Laterza)
Le Bonifiche in Italia dal '700 a oggi /. Roma , 1984. viii, 437 p. : ISBN 88-420-2429-5 : LC Card 85-173148
HD1683.I8 B66 1984 ***NYPL [JSD 87-50]***

Storia ed economia .
(18-19) Convegno nazionale di studi storici (1979 : Schio, Italy) Schio e Alessandro Rossi . Roma , 1985-1986. 2 v. (1487 p., [1] folded leaf of plates) : LC Card 87-110167
HC302.5.R6 C66 1979

Storkey, Alan. Transforming economics : a Christian way to employment / Alan Storkey. London : SPCK, 1986. xi, 212 p. : ill. ; 22 cm. (Third way books) Bibliography: p. 205-206. Includes index. ISBN 0-281-04225-X (pbk.) : LC Card 87-108686 DDC 261.8/5 19
1. Unemployment - Great Britain - Moral and ethical aspects. 2. Economics - Great Britain - Religious aspects. I. Title. II. Series.
HD5765.A6 S76 1986

STORMS - UNITED STATES.
Catastrophic losses . Oak Brook, Ill. (1200 Harger Rd., Suite 222, Oak Brook 60521) , c1986. vi, 73 p. : LC Card 87-106114 DDC 368.1/22014/0973 19
HG9979.3 .C38 1986

Storper, Michael. Production, work, territory . Boston , 1986. xix, 344 p. : ISBN 0-04-338126-X (alk. paper) LC Card 85-20006 DDC 330 19
HC59 .P682 1986 ***NYPL [JLE 86-1745]***

Storrs Agricultural Experiment Station. Groff, William H. Income variability in Connecticut, 1980 /. Storrs, CT [1987] 32 p. : LC Card 87-621355 DDC 339.2/2/09746 19
HC107.C83 I5138 1987

Story, Dale, 1950- Industry, the state, and public policy in Mexico / by Dale Story. 1st ed. Austin : University of Texas Press, 1986. xii, 275 p. ; 24 cm. (Latin American monographs / Institute of Latin American Studies, the University of Texas at Austin . no. 66) Includes index. Bibliography: p. [247]-267. ISBN 0-292-73837-4 LC Card 85-13363 DDC 338.972 19
1. Industry and state - Mexico. 2. Industrialists - Mexico. I. Series: Latin American monographs, no. 66. II. Title.
HD3616.M43 S76 1986 ***NYPL [JLE 87-656]***

Story, Joseph, 1779-1845. Commentaries on the law of promissory notes [microform], and guaranties of notes, and checks on banks and bankers. With occasional illustrations from the commercial law of the nations of continental Europe. By Joseph Story ...6th ed. Boston, Little, Brown, and company, 1868. xliv, 739 p. 25 cm. Microfilm. New York : New York Public Library, 1986. 1 microfilm reel ; 35 mm. (MN *ZZ-25,776) LC Card 12-34848
1. Promissory notes - United States. 2. Checks - United States. 3. Negotiable instruments - United States.
NYPL [*ZT-1734]

The story of Paul J. Meyer . Strain, Lois S. (Lois Smith) Hollywood, Fla. , c1986. xii, 193 p. : ISBN 0-8119-0720-1 : LC Card 86-29525 DDC 338/.04/0924 B 19
HF5386 .S8832 1986

Storz, Peter, 1954- Steuerplanung im Unternehmen mit einem computergestützten Modell / Peter Storz. München : Florentz, c1984. vii, 657 p. : ill. ; 21 cm. (Hochschulschriften zur Betriebswirtschaftslehre . Bd. 27) Originally presented as the author's thesis (doctoral)--Universität Bamberg. Bibliography: p. 636-649. Includes index. ISBN 3-88259-282-6 LC Card 84-174173 DDC 336.24/3/0943 19
1. Corporations - Taxation - Germany (West) - Data processing. I. Title. II. Series.
HD2753.G3 S76 1984

Stotter, James. Intelligent buildings : a growth industry / James Stotter. Stamford, Conn., U. S.A. : Business Communications Co., c1986. ix, 127 leaves : ill. ; 29 cm. (Business opportunity report . G-089) ISBN 0-89336-414-2 (pbk.) LC Card 87-165953 DDC 338.4/769/0973 19
1. Construction industry - United States - Forecasting. 2. Construction industry - United States - Technological innovations. 3. Technological forecasting - United States. I. Title. II. Series.
HD9715.U52 S76 1986

Stourzh, Gerald. Historische Wurzeln der Sozialpartnerschaft /. München , 1986. 368 p. ; ISBN 3-486-52971-4 LC Card 87-146580 DDC 306/.36/09436 19
HD6957.A9 H57 1986

Stout Vocational Rehabilitation Institute. Materials Development Center.
Barrett, John (John J.) The industrial work model . Menomonie, Wis. , c1987. v, 143 p. : ISBN 0-916671-73-9 (pbk.) LC Card 87-403218 DDC 362.0425 19
HD7256.U5 B37 1987

National Forum on Issues in Vocational Assessment (2nd : 1986 : Dallas, Tex.) Second National Forum on Issues in Vocational Assessment . Menomonie, Wis. , c1985. vii, 236 p. : ISBN 0-916671-71-2 (pbk.) LC Card 86-217148 DDC 362/.0425 19
HD7256.U5 N336 1986

Stover, Vergil G., 1933- Transportation and land development / Vergil G. Stover, Frank J. Koepke. Englewood Cliffs, N.J. : Prentice-Hall, c1988. xiii, 239 p. : ill. ; 29 cm. At head of title: Institute of Transportation Engineers. Includes bibliographies and index. ISBN 0-13-930413-4 : LC Card 87-11419 DDC 625.7/25 19
1. Traffic engineering. 2. Land use, Urban. 3. Building sites - Planning. I. Koepke, Frank J., 1929-. II. Institute of Transportation Engineers. III. Title.
HE335 .S76 1988

Straaten, Martin. Wettbewerb und Kooperation im Landhandel : das Konkurrenzverhältnis zwischen privatem Landhandel und den Bezugs- und Absatzgenossenschaften, am Beispiel einer Genossenschaft des Landhandels dargestellt / von Martin Straaten. Berlin : Duncker & Humblot, c1985. 82 p. ; 24 cm. (Schriften zum Genossenschaftswesen und zur öffentlichen Wirtschaft . Bd. 13) Bibliography: p. [79]-82. ISBN 3-428-05712-0 LC Card 85-167800
1. Retail trade - Germany, West. I. Title. II. Series.
HF5429.6.G42 S77 1985

Straffälligkeit und Viktimisierung ausländischer Minderheiten in der Bundesrepublik Deutschland . Pitsela, Angelika. Freiburg [i.B.] , 1986. xxvii, 479 p. ; ISBN 3-922498-16-7 LC Card 87-131111 DDC 331.6/2/495043 19
HD8458.G7 P57 1986

Straight forward managerial accounting applications . Wells, Nancy E., 1946- Burlington, VT , 1987, c1986. p. cm. ISBN 0-9612704-1-1 LC Card 87-22393 DDC 658.1/511/02855369 19
HF5657.4 .W44 1987

Strain, Lois S. (Lois Smith) The story of Paul J. Meyer : the million dollar personal success plan / by Lois S. Strain and Gladys W. Hudson. Hollywood, Fla. : F. Fell, c1986. xii, 193 p. : ill. ; 24 cm. At head of title: Success Motivation. ISBN 0-8119-0720-1 : LC Card 86-29525 DDC 338/.04/0924 B 19
1. Meyer, Paul J. 2. Businessmen - Biography. 3. Success in business. 4. Success Motivation Institute. I. Hudson, Gladys W. II. Title.
HF5386 .S8832 1986

Strain, Robert W. Property-liability insurance accounting /. Durham, N.C. , Wingdale, N.Y. , c1986. 1 v. (loose-leaf) : LC Card 86-207635 DDC 657/.836 19
HG8077 .P7 1986

Strand, Paul J., 1949- Indochinese refugees in America : problems of adaptation and assimilation / Paul J. Strand, Woodrow Jones, Jr. Durham, N.C. : Duke University Press, 1985. x, 182 p. ; 24 cm. (Duke Press policy studies) Includes index. Bibliography: p. [168]-176. ISBN 0-8223-0629-8 LC Card 84-25888 DDC 362.8/49592 19
1. Refugees - Indochina. 2. Refugees - United States. 3. Refugees - California. I. Jones, Woodrow. II. Title. III. Series.
HV640.5.I5 S77 1985 ***NYPL [JLE 86-4772]***

Strand, Stanley. Brennan, Lawrence D. (Lawrence David), 1915- Resumes for better jobs /. New York, NY , c1987. 202 p. ; ISBN 0-13-329152-9 : LC Card 87-2383 DDC 650.1/4 19
HF5383 .B68 1987

Strandell, Anne-Christine. Exportsamverkan . [Stockholm] [1985] 261 p. : ISBN 91-38-08810-X LC Card 86-114126
HF3676.5 .E96 1985

Strange, K. H. (Kathleen H.), 1904- Climbing boys : a study of sweeps' apprentices, 1773-1875 / K.H. Strange. London ; New York : Allison & Busby ; xiv, 146 p. : ill., fascims. ; 23 cm. Includes bibliographical references and index. ISBN 0-85031-431-3 : LC Card 83-143704 DDC 331.5/5 19
1. Chimney-sweeps - Great Britain - History. 2. Apprentices - Great Britain - History. I. Title.
HD8039.C482 G77 1982
NYPL [JLD 85-681]

Stránská, Ludmila. Organizačně institucionální soustava řízení MSEI / Ludmila Stránská. Praha : Ekonomický ústav ČSAV, 1985. 167 p. : ill. ; 20 cm. (Výzkum. publ. VP . č. 233) Summary in Russian. Bibliography: p. 145-150. LC Card 86-215270
1. Europe, Eastern - Economic integration. I. Series: Výzk. publ. (Ekonomicko-matematická laboratoř (Ekonomický ústav ČSAV)) , č. 233. II. Title.
HC243.5 .S88 1985

Strany razlichnogo urovni͡a razviti͡ia v mirovom khozi͡aĭstve . Zevin, Leon Zalmanovich. Moskva , 1985. 193, [4] p. ; LC Card 86-157482
HF1411 .Z43 1985

Strassenbau und Mineralölindustrie im Spiegel der Statistik : Daten und Fakten für die Bundesrepublik Deutschland / Arbeitsgemeinschaft der Bitumen-Industrie e.V. Hamburg ; [Schriftleitung, R. Urban]. Hamburg : Die Arbeitsgemeinschaft, 1976. [48] p. : col. ill. ; 20 x 21 cm. LC Card 83-126399
1. Asphalt industry - Germany (West) - Statistics. 2. Road construction - Germany (West) - Statistics. I. Urban, R. II. Arbeitsgemeinschaft der Bitumen-Industrie (Germany).
HD9582.A7 G37 1976

Strassenverkäufer und die Versorgung der Arbeiterfamilien von Kowloon (Hong Kong) im Umfeld der staatlichen Planungspolitik /. Šimko, Dušan. Basel , 1983. 196 p., [9] p. of plates : ISBN 3-85977-129-9 : LC Card 83-238672
HF5459.H6 S56 1983

Strassenverkehr zweitausend. ADAC. Strassenverkehr 2000 . München [1979] 24 p. : LC Card 85-147077
HE363.G3 A33 1979

Strassenverkehr 2000 . ADAC. München [1979] 24 p. : LC Card 85-147077
HE363.G3 A33 1979

Strassenverkehrszählung 1978 in der Bundesrepublik Deutschland : Erhebungs- und Hochrechnungsmethodik / Werner Draeger ... [et al.] ; herausgegeben im Auftrage des Bundesministers für Verkehr von der Bundesanstalt für Strassenwesen, Köln. Köln : Die Bundesanstalt, 1979. 96 p. : ill., maps ; 30 cm. (Strassenverkehrszählungen . Heft 13) Includes bibliographies. LC Card 87-408379 DDC 388/.0943 s 388.3/0943 19
1. Transportation, Automotive - Germany, West. 2. Traffic flow - Germany (West). I. Draeger, Werner. II. Germany (West). Bundesministerium für Verkehr. III. Bundesanstalt für Strassenwesen (Germany). IV. Series.
HE5601 .S89 Heft 13 HE5669.A6

Strassenverkehrszählung 1980 auf Bundesstrassen im gesamten Bundesgebiet der Republik Österreich / bearbeitet im Österreichischen Statistischen Zentralamt, unter Mitwirkung des Bundesministeriums für Bauten und Technik, Oberste Bundesstrassenverwaltung. Wien : Das Zentralamt, 1985. 288 p. : ill. ; 30 cm. (Beiträge zur österreichischen Statistik . 750. Heft) Cover title: Strassenverkehrszählung 1980--Bundesstrassen. Chiefly tables. One folded col. map in pocket. LC Card 86-170848
1. Traffic flow - Austria - Statistics. I. Österreichisches Statistisches Zentralamt. II. Austria. Bundesministerium für Bauten und Technik. Bundesstrassenverwaltung. III. Title: Strassenverkehrszählung 1980--Bundesstrassen. IV. Series.
HA1173 .A27 Heft 750 HE363.A93T7

Strassenverkehrszählung 1980--Bundesstrassen. Strassenverkehrszählung 1980 auf Bundesstrassen im gesamten Bundesgebiet der Republik Österreich /. Wien , 1985. 288 p. : LC Card 86-170848
HA1173 .A27 Heft 750 HE363.A93T7

Strassenverkehrszählungen . (Heft 13) Strassenverkehrszählung 1978 in der Bundesrepublik Deutschland . Köln , 1979. 96 p. : LC Card 87-408379 DDC 388/.0943 s 388.3/0943 19
HE5601 .S89 Heft 13 HE5669.A6

Das Strassenwesen Tirols seit der Eröffnung der Eisenbahn Innsbruck-Kufstein (1858) . Zwanowetz, Georg. Innsbruck , 1986. 163 p., 32 leaves of plates : ISBN 3-7030-0165-8 LC Card 87-142160 DDC 388.1/09436/42 19
HE247.Z7 T99 1986

Strasser, Johano. Grenzen des Sozialstaats? : soziale Sicherung in der Wachstumskrise / Johano Strasser.2., völlig überarbeitete und erheblich erw. Aufl. Köln : Bund-Verlag, 1983. 206 p. ; 21 cm. Includes bibliographical references. ISBN 3-7663-0800-9 LC Card 83-142735
1. Germany, West - Economic conditions. 2. Social security - Germany, West. 3. Germany, West - Social policy. 4. Welfare state. I. Title.
HC286.6 .S73 1983

Strasser, Stephen. Working it out® : sanity and success in the workplace / Stephen Strasser. Englewood Cliffs, N.J. : Prentice Hall, c1988. xix, 268 p. ; 24 cm. Includes bibliographical references and index. ISBN 0-13-965112-8 : LC Card 87-17197 DDC 158.7 19
1. Work. 2. Work - Psychological aspects. 3. Job satisfaction. I. Title.
HD4901 .S69 1988

La strategia aziendale /. Canziani, Arnaldo. [Milano] , 1984. xx, 288 p. ; ISBN 88-14-00283-5 : LC Card 85-105652 DDC 658.4/012 19
HD30.28 .C364 1984

Strategia aziendale e sviluppo tecnologico . Eminente, Giorgio. Bologna , c1985. 253 p. : ISBN 88-15-00917-5 : LC Card 86-176732
HD9696.A3 I733 1985

Strategia dei servizi per l'agricoltura : contributi per l'analisi / D. Lipari ... [et al.]. [Roma] : Monteverde, [1983] 158 p. : ill. ; 19 cm. At head of title: Confederazione italiana coltivatori, Centro istruzione professionale agricola e assistenza tecnica. Bibliography: p. 90. LC Card 85-155420
1. Farm supply industries - Italy. 2. Rural development - Italy. 3. Agriculture - Italy - Information services - Italy. 4. Farm produce - Italy - Marketing - Information services - Italy. 5. Communication in agriculture - Italy. I. Lipari, D. (Domenico). II. Confcoltivatori. Centro istruzione professionale agricola e assistenza tecnica.
HD9475.I82 S77 1983

Strategia generale e azione decentrata . Guidotti, Daniela. Milano, Italy , c1986. 216 p. ; LC Card 86-193797
HD6976.T42 I764 1986

Strategic behaviour and industrial competition / edited by D.J. Morris ... [et al.]. Oxford [Oxfordshire] : Clarendon Press ; New York : Oxford University Press, 1986. 243 p. ; 24 cm. Includes bibliographies. ISBN 0-19-828562-0 (pbk.) : LC Card 86-28535 DDC 338.6 19
1. Industrial organization (Economic theory). I. Morris, Derek.
HD2326 .S786 1986

Strategic change and the management process /. Johnson, Gerry. Oxford, OX, UK , New York, NY, USA , 1987. xv, 319 p. : ISBN 0-631-14717-9 : LC Card 87-5152 DDC 658.4/012 19
HD30.28 .J65 1987

STRATEGIC DEFENSE INITIATIVE.
Bryant, Richard W. The Strategic Defense Initiative, business opportunities, and technological potential /. Norwalk, Conn., U. S.A. , c1986. 1 v. (various foliations) : ISBN 0-89336-477-0 (pbk.) LC Card 87-168253 DDC 338.4/762/00973 19
HC110.H53 B79 1986

Commercializing SDI technologies /. New York , 1987. xvi, 246 p. : ISBN 0-275-92332-0 (alk. paper) : LC Card 87-18333 DDC 338.4/762 19
HC110.H53 C65 1987

Greenwood, David. The SDI and Europe /. Aberdeen, Scotland [1985] 64 p. ; LC Card 86-150232 DDC 355/.07/094 19
U395.E85 G73 1985 ***NYPL [JFG 87-57]***

The Strategic Defense Initiative, business opportunities, and technological potential /. Bryant, Richard W. Norwalk, Conn., U. S.A. , c1986. 1 v. (various foliations) : ISBN 0-89336-477-0 (pbk.) LC Card 87-168253 DDC 338.4/762/00973 19
HC110.H53 B79 1986

Strategic design and organizational change . Boschken, Herman L. Tuscaloosa, Ala. , c1989. p. cm. ISBN 0-8173-0339-1 LC Card 86-14673 DDC 387.1/0979 19
HE554.A6 B67 1989

Strategic factors in industrial relations systems. Miernyk, William H. The coalmining industry in the United States /. Geneva , 1986. 53, ix p. : ISBN 92-9014-409-2 (pbk.)
NYPL [JLE 87-1534]

Strategic human resource planning applications /. Symposium on Strategic Human Resource Planning Applications (1985 : University of Pennsylvania, Philadelphia, Pa.) New York , c1987. viii, 257 p. ; ISBN 0-306-42561-0 LC Card 87-11141 DDC 331.11 19
HF5549.5.M3 S95 1985

Strategic Information Services. Report on the coffee service industry /. Columbus, Ohio [1984] 1 v. (various foliations) : LC Card 87-100404 DDC 381/.4566393 19
HD9199.U48 R47 1984

Strategic investment timing . Stoken, Dick A. New York , London , c1984. x, 225 p. : ISBN 0-02-614810-2 LC Card 84-12576 DDC 332.6/78 19
HG4921 .S795 1984 ***NYPL [JLD 86-2041]***

Strategic management . Certo, Samuel C. New York , c1988. p. cm. ISBN 0-394-35920-8 : LC Card 87-23565 DDC 658.4/012 19
HD30.28 .C43 1988.

Strategic management . Hatten, Kenneth J. Englewood Cliffs, N.J. , c1987. xiv, 1041 p. : ISBN 0-13-850694-9 LC Card 86-30453 DDC 658.4/012 19
HD30.28 .H384 1987

Strategic management . Schellenberger, Robert Earl. New York , c1986. xiii, 808 p. : ISBN 0-471-88059-0 : LC Card 85-9553 DDC 658.4/012 19
HD30.28 .S34 1986 ***NYPL [JLE 86-1559]***

Strategic management . Thomas, Joe Gene. New York , c1988. p. cm. ISBN 0-06-046676-6 LC

Card 87-21931 DDC 658.4/012 19
HD30.28 .T47 1988

Strategic management . Thompson, Arthur A., 1940- Plano, Tex. , 1987. xviii, 1054 p. : ISBN 0-255-03717-5 LC Card 86-72250 DDC 658.4/012 19
HD30.28 .T53 1987

Strategic management and business policy /. Jauch, Lawrence R. New York , c1988. xviii, 428 p. : ISBN 0-07-032339-9 (pbk.) : LC Card 87-7191 DDC 658.4/012 19
HD30.28 .J38 1988

Strategic management and business policy. Wheelen, Thomas L. Cases in strategic management and business policy /. Reading, Mass. , c1987. xii, 530 p. : ISBN 0-201-09134-8 (pbk.) : LC Card 86-26501 DDC 658.4/012 19
HD30.28 .W428 1987

Strategic management in multinational companies /. Doz, Yves L. Oxford [Oxfordshire] , New York , 1986. xii, 243 p. : ISBN 0-08-031808-8 : LC Card 85-9282 DDC 658.4/012 19
HD62.4 .D69 1986 ***NYPL [JLE 86-1955]***

Strategic management in the United States and Japan : a comparative analysis / edited by Rosalie L. Tung. Cambridge, Mass. : Ballinger Pub. Co., c1986. xxv, 177 p. : ill. , 24 cm. "Articles ... based on papers presented at a conference held at the Wharton School, University of Pennsylvania, in Fall 1984"--Introd. Includes index. ISBN 0-88730-089-8 LC Card 86-1169 DDC 658.4/012/0952 19
1. Strategic planning - United States - Congresses. 2. Strategic planning - Japan - Congresses. I. Tung, Rosalie L. (Rosalie Lam), 1948-.
HD30.28 .S7324 1986 ***NYPL [JLE 86-3060]***

Strategic marketing for nonprofit organizations : cases and readings / [edited by] Philip Kotler, O.C. Ferrell, Charles Lamb.3rd ed. Englewood Cliffs, NJ : Prentice-Hall, c1987. x, 386 p. : ill. ; 24 cm. Rev. ed. of: Cases and readings for marketing for nonprofit organizations. c1983. Includes bibliographies. ISBN 0-13-851312-0 (pbk.) : LC Card 86-25262 DDC 658.8 19
1. Corporations, Nonprofit - Marketing. 2. Corporations, Nonprofit - Marketing - Case studies. 3. Marketing - Case studies. I. Kotler, Philip. II. Ferrell, O. C. III. Lamb, Charles W. IV. Cases and readings for marketing for nonprofit organizations.
HF5415 .C2854 1987

Strategic marketing for nonprofit organizations /. Kotler, Philip. Englewood Cliffs, N.J. , c1987. xvi, 670 p. : LC Card 86-25538 DDC 658.8 19
HF5415 .K6312 1987

Strategic marketing of hospital pharmacy products. Tustin, CA, U. S.A. (17722 Irvine Blvd., Tustin 92680) : Biomedical Business International, c1986. iii leaves, 2, 12, 134, 111 p. : ill. ; 29 cm. (Report / Biomedical Business International . #3251) LC Card 87-149442 DDC 380.1/456151 19
1. Drugs - Marketing. 2. Hospital pharmacies. I. Biomedical Business International, Inc. II. Series: Report (Biomedical Business International, Inc.) , #3251.
HD9665.5 .S77 1986

Strategic marketing of oncology products / Biomedical Business International. Tustin, CA, U. S.A. (17722 Irvine Blvd., Tustin 92680) : Biomedical Business International, c1987. 242 p. in various pagings : ill., forms ; 29 cm. (Report / Biomedical Business International . #3291) "January 1986." LC Card 87-402026 DDC 381/.45681761 19
1. Cancer diagnostic equipment industry - United States. 2. Market surveys - United States. 3. Oncologists - United States - Attitudes. I. Biomedical Business International, Inc. II. Series: Report (Biomedical Business International, Inc.) , #3291.
HD9995.C353 U67 1987

Strategic marketing of surgical products. Tustin, CA, U. S.A. (17722 Irvine Blvd., Tustin 92680) : Biomedical Business International, c1987. 1 v. (various foliations) : ill. ; 29 cm. (Report / Biomedical Business International . #3261) "May 1987." LC Card 87-168617 DDC 380.1/45681761 19
1. Surgical instruments and apparatus - Marketing. 2. Prosthesis - Equipment and supplies - Marketing. I. Biomedical Business International, Inc. II. Series: Report (Biomedical Business International, Inc.) , #3261.
HD9995.S92 S77 1987

STRATEGIC MATERIALS.
(1985) The World market for high technology industrial ceramics. New York, N.Y. [1985] 1 v. (various pagings) ; ISBN 0-931634-52-0 (pbk.) LC Card 86-201912 DDC 382/.45666 19
HD9590.5 .W67 1985

STRATEGIC MATERIALS - GOVERNMENT POLICY - UNITED STATES.
Mikesell, Raymond Frech. Nonfuel minerals . Ann Arbor , c1987. xii, 257 p. : ISBN 0-472-10083-1 : LC Card 86-27247 DDC 333.8/5/0973 19
HD9506.U62 M42 1987

STRATEGIC MATERIALS - HANDBOOKS, MANUALS, ETC.
Cavelti, Peter C., 1947- New profits in gold, silver, strategic metals . New York , 1984, c1985. 221 p. : ISBN 0-07-010288-0 LC Card 84-12268 DDC 332.63 19
HG261 .C38 1985 ***NYPL [JLE 84-2956]***

STRATEGIC MATERIALS - MIDDLE EAST.
Strategic organization design . Nadler, David. Glenview, Ill. , c1988. 209 p. : ISBN 0-673-15860-8 (pbk.) LC Card 87-9832 DDC 658.4/012 19
HD58.7 .N33 1988

STRATEGIC PLANNING.
Amler, Robert W. Analyse und Gestaltung strategischer Informationssysteme der Unternehmung . Göttingen , c1983. xx, 279 p. : ISBN 3-525-12556-9 LC Card 83-198652
HD30.28 .A45 1983

Ansoff, H. Igor. The new corporate strategy /. New York , 1988. xviii, 258 p. : ISBN 0-471-62950-2 LC Card 87-23266 DDC 658.4/012 19
HD30.28 .A535 1988

Ballance, Robert H. International industry and business . London , Boston , 1987. xxi, 357 p. ; ISBN 0-04-339037-4 (alk. paper) LC Card 86-28793 DDC 338/.09/04048 19
HC59 .B3537 1987

Barry, Bryan W. Strategic planning workbook for nonprofit organizations /. St. Paul, MN , c1986. 72 p., [8] leaves of plates : ISBN 0-940069-00-8 (pbk.) LC Card 87-153976 DDC 658.4/012 19
HD62.6 .B37 1986

Below, Patrick J. The executive guide to strategic planning /. San Francisco, Calif. , c1987. xxiii, 136 p. : ISBN 1-555-42032-X (alk. paper) LC Card 86-27863 DDC 658.4/012 19
HD30.28 .B45 1987

Bhalla, Sushil K. The effective management of technology . Columbus [Ohio] , Reading, Mass. , c1987. xiii, 205 p. : ISBN 0-201-10929-8 : LC Card 86-25847 DDC 658.5 19
HD45 .B47 1987

Boschken, Herman L. Strategic design and organizational change . Tuscaloosa, Ala. , c1989. p. cm. ISBN 0-8173-0339-1 LC Card 86-14673 DDC 387.1/0979 19
HE554.A6 B67 1989

Bryce, Herrington J. Financial and strategic management for nonprofit organizations /. Englewood Cliffs, N.J. , c1987. xviii, 395 p. : ISBN 0-13-316597-3 LC Card 86-30454 DDC 658/.049 19
HG4027.65 .B78 1987

Business policy . Oxford, UK , New York, NY, USA , 1987. viii, 208 p. : ISBN 0-631-15545-7 : LC Card 87-722 DDC 658.4/012 19
HD30.28 .B86 1987

Buzzell, Robert D. (Robert Dow), 1933- The PIMS principles . New York , London , c1987. xiii, 322 p. : ISBN 0-02-904430-8 LC Card 87-416 DDC 658.8/02 19
HF5415.13 .B893 1987

Canziani, Arnaldo. La strategia aziendale /. [Milano] , 1984. xx, 288 p. ; ISBN 88-14-00283-5 : LC Card 85-105652 DDC 658.4/012 19
HD30.28 .C364 1984

Capon, Noel. Corporate strategic planning /. New York , 1987. p. cm. ISBN 0-231-06380-6 LC Card 87-18239 DDC 658.4/012 19
HD30.28 .C375 1987

Di Stefano, Guido, 1939- Sistemi di gestione strategica aziendale . Milano, Italy , c1986. 232 p. : LC Card 86-180982
HD30.28 .D52 1986

Diskontinuitätenmanagement . Berlin , c1984. x, 320 p. : ISBN 3-503-02446-8 LC Card 85-128271
HD62.4 .D57 1984

Dögl, Rudolf. Strategisches Qualitätsmanagement im Industriebetrieb . Göttingen , c1986. xv, 267 p. : ISBN 3-525-12562-3 (Deut. Bibl.) LC Card 86-210486
HD30.28 .D64 1986

Ellis, R. Jeffery. Managing strategy in the real world . Lexington, Mass. , c1988. xviii, 340 p. : ISBN 0-669-15898-4 (alk. paper) LC Card 87-4259 DDC 658.4/012 19
HD30.28 .E45 1988

Espy, Siri N. Handbook of strategic planning for nonprofit organizations /. New York , 1986. ix, 131 p. ; ISBN 0-275-92342-8 (alk. paper) LC Card 86-21192 DDC 658.1/148 19
HD62.6 .E86 1986 ***NYPL [JLE 87-874]***

Friend, John. Planning under pressure . Oxford [Oxfordshire] , New York , 1987. xix, 338 p. : ISBN 0-08-018766-8 : LC Card 86-25219 DDC 658.4/012 19
HD30.28 .F75 1987

Fronhoff, Bernd, 1956- Die Gestaltung von Marketingstrategien . Bergisch Gladbach , 1986. ix, 369 p. : ISBN 3-89012-067-9 LC Card 87-122913 DDC 658.8/02 19
HF5415.135 .F76 1986

Godet, Michel. [Prospective et planification stratégique. English.] Scenarios and strategic management /. London , Boston , 1987. xviii, 210 p. : ISBN 0-408-02890-4 LC Card 87-15774 DDC 658.4/012 19
HD30.28 .G6313 1987

Grimm, Ulrich. Analyse strategischer Faktoren . Wiesbaden , c1983. 294 p. : ISBN 3-409-18720-0 LC Card 84-173895
HD30.28 .G76 1983

Hainzl, Martin. Konkurrenzanalyse in der strategischen Planung /. Wien , 1985. 143 p. : ISBN 3-85436-027-4 LC Card 86-127579 DDC 658.4/012 19
HD30.28 .H334 1985

Hamermesh, Richard G. Making strategy work . New York , c1986. xiii, 245 p. : ISBN 0-471-80319-7 : LC Card 85-12456 DDC 658.4/012 19
HD30.28 .H35 1986 ***NYPL [JLE 86-2018]***

Hatten, Kenneth J. Effective strategic management . Englewood Cliffs, N.J. , c1988. xiv, 338 p. : ISBN 0-13-245200-6 (pbk.) LC Card 87-20589 DDC 658.4/012 19
HD30.28 .H383 1988

Hatten, Kenneth J. Strategic management . Englewood Cliffs, N.J. , c1987. xiv, 1041 p. : ISBN 0-13-850694-9 LC Card 86-30453 DDC 658.4/012 19
HD30.28 .H384 1987

Itami, Hiroyuki, 1945- Mobilizing invisible assets /. Cambridge, Mass. , 1987. xi, 186 p. : ISBN 0-674-57770-1 (alk. paper) LC Card 86-26972 DDC 658.4/012 19
HD30.28 .I85 1987

Johnson, Gerry. Strategic change and the management process /. Oxford, OX, UK , New York, NY, USA , 1987. xv, 319 p. : ISBN 0-631-14717-9 : LC Card 87-5152 DDC 658.4/012 19
HD30.28 .J65 1987

Karlöf, Bengt, 1939- [Strategins kärnfrågor. English.] Business strategy in practice /. Chichester, England , New York , c1987. viii, 184 p. : ISBN 0-471-91620-X : LC Card 87-10452 DDC 658.4/012 19
HD30.28 .K3613 1987

Klaes, Friedhelm, 1956- Informationsverhalten kleiner und mittlerer Unternehmen der elektrotechnischen Investitionsgüterindustrie bei strategischen Entscheidungen /. Frankfurt am Main , New York , c1986. xxii, 305 p. ; ISBN 3-8204-9713-7 LC Card 87-407575 DDC 658.4/03 19
HD62.7 .K586 1986

Lamb, Robert, 1941- Running American business . New York , c1987. x, 315 p. ; ISBN 0-465-07150-3 : LC Card 86-47732 DDC 658.4/03 19
HD30.28 .L355 1987

Link, Jörg. Organisation der strategischen Planung . Heidelberg , c1985. xvii, 178 p. : ISBN 3-7908-0333-2 LC Card 86-160239 DDC 658.4/012 19
HD30.28 .L545 1985

McKenna, John F. (John Francis), 1945- Strategy, policy, and growth . Reading, Mass. , 1988. p. cm. ISBN 0-201-13987-1 : LC Card 87-1301 DDC 658.4/012 19
HD30.28 .M384 1988

Malik, Fredmund F. Strategie des Managements komplexer Systeme . Bern , c1984. 563 p. : ISBN 3-258-03306-4 : LC Card 84-178061
HD30.28 .M334 1984

Manczinger, Józsefné. Ajánlás a vállalatok stratégiai tervező munkájához /. [Budapest] [1984] 97 p. ; LC Card 86-148677
HD30.28 .M346 1984

Melcher, Horst. Aufbau eines Controllingsystems für Consulting-Unternehmen /. Darmstadt , c1982. 276 p. : ISBN 3-87820-052-8 LC Card 83-110639
HD69.C6 M45 1982

Miller, Stanley S. Competitive manufacturing . New York , c1988. ix, 245 p. : ISBN 0-442-26395-3 LC Card 87-10484 DDC 658.5/03 19
HD30.28 .M52 1988

Morrisey, George L. The executive guide to operational planning /. San Francisco , 1988. xxvii, 130 p. : ISBN 1-555-42064-8 (alk. paper) LC Card 87-45508 DDC 658.4/012 19
HD30.28 .M65 1988

Morse, Diane McGinty. Involving managers in competitive analysis /. Menlo Park, CA (333 Ravenswood Ave., Menlo Park 94025) , c1986. 11 leaves : LC Card 86-220559 DDC 658.4/012 19
HD38.7 .M67 1986

Morse, Diane McGinty. Managing competitive intelligence . Menlo Park, Calif. , c1985. 36 p. : LC Card 87-404501 DDC 658.4/7 19
HD38.7 .M674 1985

Nilsson, William P. Achieving strategic goals through executive development /. Reading, Mass. , c1987. xv, 266 p. : ISBN 0-201-12751-2 : LC Card 86-32201 DDC 658.4/012 19
HD38.2 .N54 1987

Planning strategies that work /. New York , 1987. xii, 287 p. : ISBN 0-19-504883-0 (alk. paper) LC Card 86-31117 DDC 658.4/012 19
HD30.28 .P555 1987

Pümpin, Cuno Beat. The essence of corporate strategy /. Aldershot, Hants, England , Brookfield, Vt., U. S.A. , c1987. xi, 183 p. : ISBN 0-566-02565-5 : LC Card 87-14907 DDC 658.4/012 19
HD30.28 .P85 1987

Quinn, James Brian, 1928- The strategy process . Englewood Cliffs, N.J. , c1988. p. cm. ISBN 0-13-850892-5 LC Card 87-1160 DDC 658.4/012 19
HD30.28 .Q53 1988

Robert, Michel, 1941- The strategist CEO . New York , 1988. viii, 140 p. : ISBN 0-89930-268-8 (lib. bdg. : alk. paper) LC Card 87-10945 DDC 658.4/012 19
HD30.28 .R63 1988

Schellenberger, Robert Earl. Strategic management . New York , c1986. xiii, 808 p. : ISBN 0-471-88059-0 : LC Card 85-9553 DDC 658.4/012 19
HD30.28 .S34 1986 ***NYPL [JLE 86-1559]***

Schneider, Walter. Technologische Analyse und Prognose als Grundlage der strategischen Unternehmensplanung /. Göttingen , c1984. xxii, 215 p. ; ISBN 3-525-12561-5 LC Card 85-127182
HD30.23 .S37 1984

Scholz, Christian, 1952- Strategisches Management . Berlin , New York , 1987. xv, 305 p. ; ISBN 3-11-010863-1 LC Card 87-145957 DDC 658.4/012 19
HD30.28 .S346 1987

Simon, Dieter. Schwache Signale . Wien , c1986. 262 p. : LC Card 87-103434 DDC 658.4/012 19
HD30.28 .S435 1986

Skov, Paul B. Strategy, analysis, and decisions . Menlo Park, Calif. (333 Ravenswood Ave., Menlo Park 94025-3476) , c1985. 40 p. : LC Card 87-119164 DDC 658.4/012
HD30.28 .S49 1985

Smith, Garry D., 1948- Business strategy and policy /. Boston , c1988. xviii, 1006 p. : ISBN 0-395-36946-0 LC Card 87-80879 DDC 658.4/012 19
HD30.28 .S56 1988

Stomberg, Peter. Die Probleme der Prognose des Kapitalbedarfs im Rahmen der strategischen Plannung /. Göttingen , c1984. x, 212 p. ; ISBN 0-352-51266-3 LC Card 84-240131
HD30.28 .S729 1984

Strategisches Marketing und Management . Bern , c1986. 205 p. : ISBN 3-258-03566-0 : LC Card 86-159360
HF5415.135 .S77 1986

Thomas, Joe Gene. Strategic management . New York , c1988. p. cm. ISBN 0-06-046676-6 LC Card 87-21931 DDC 658.4/012 19
HD30.28 .T47 1988

Thompson, Arthur A., 1940- Strategic management . Plano, Tex. , 1987. xviii, 1054 p. : ISBN 0-255-03717-5 LC Card 86-72250 DDC 658.4/012 19
HD30.28 .T53 1987

Thompson, Arthur A., 1940- Strategy formulation and implementation . Plano, Tex. , 1986. xvi, 452 p. : ISBN 0-256-03173-8 (pbk.) LC Card 85-73596 DDC 658.4/012 19
HD30.28 .T54 1986

Weiss, Joseph W. The management of change . New York , 1986. xviii, 210 p. ; ISBN 0-275-92195-6 (alk. paper) : LC Card 86-9390 DDC 658.4 19
HD7256.U5 W38 1986 ***NYPL [JLE 86-4062]***

STRATEGIC PLANNING - CASE STUDIES.

Bartlett, Hale C. Cases in strategic management for business /. Chicago , c1988. xiii, 784 p. : ISBN 0-03-007183-6 (pbk.) LC Card 87-20208 DDC 658.4/012 19
HD30.28 .B369 1988

Boseman, F. Glenn. Cases in strategic management /. New York , c1988. ix, 476 p. : ISBN 0-471-85463-8 (pbk.) LC Card 87-24261 DDC 658.4/012 19
HD30.28 .B67 1988

Cases in business policy /. Oxford, UK , New York , 1987. ix, 538 p. : ISBN 0-631-15544-9 (pbk.) : LC Card 87-6607 DDC 658.4/012 19
HD30.28 .C379 1987

Hatten, Kenneth J. Strategic management . Englewood Cliffs, N.J. , c1987. xiv, 1041 p. : ISBN 0-13-850694-9 LC Card 86-30453 DDC 658.4/012 19
HD30.28 .H384 1987

Pearce, John A. Company and industry cases in strategy and policy /. Homewood, IL , 1986. xiv, 711 p. : ISBN 0-256-03558-X : LC Card 85-82002 ***NYPL [JLE 87-993]***

Quinn, James Brian, 1928- The strategy process . Englewood Cliffs, N.J. , c1988. p. cm. ISBN 0-13-850892-5 LC Card 87-1160 DDC 658.4/012 19
HD30.28 .Q53 1988

Ramsey, Douglas K. The corporate warriors /. Boston , 1987. xxi, 261 p. ; ISBN 0-395-35487-0 : LC Card 86-20954 DDC 338.8/3/0973 19
HD41 .R27 1987 ***NYPL [JLE 87-1347]***

Schellenberger, Robert Earl. Strategic management . New York , c1986. xiii, 808 p. : ISBN 0-471-88059-0 : LC Card 85-9553 DDC 658.4/012 19
HD30.28 .S34 1986 ***NYPL [JLE 86-1559]***

Smith, Garry D., 1948- Business strategy and policy /. Boston , c1988. xviii, 1006 p. : ISBN 0-395-36946-0 LC Card 87-80879 DDC 658.4/012 19
HD30.28 .S56 1988

Wheelen, Thomas L. Cases in strategic management and business policy /. Reading, Mass. , c1987. xii, 530 p. : ISBN 0-201-09134-8 (pbk.) : LC Card 86-26501 DDC 658.4/012 19
HD30.28 .W428 1987

STRATEGIC PLANNING - CAST STUDIES.

Thompson, Arthur A., 1940- Strategic management . Plano, Tex. , 1987. xviii, 1054 p. : ISBN 0-255-03717-5 LC Card 86-72250 DDC 658.4/012 19
HD30.28 .T53 1987

STRATEGIC PLANNING - CONGRESSES.

Carpenter, Gregory. Business strategy and the life cycle concept . Cambridge, Mass. (1000 Massachusetts Ave., Cambridge 02138) [1985] [19] leaves ; LC Card 87-108925 DDC 658.5/038 19
HF5415.155 .C37 1985

The Management of strategic change /. Oxford [Oxfordshire] , New York, NY , 1988, c1987. p. cm. ISBN 0-631-15695-X : LC Card 87-15634 DDC 658.4/012 19
HD30.28 .M344 1988

STRATEGIC PLANNING - DATA PROCESSING.

Löffler, Reiner, 1959- STRATEGOS . Mannheim , 1986 (Darmstadt : Copy Shop) 246, [49] p. : LC Card 87-408452 DDC 658.4/0353/0285 19
HD30.26 .L64 1986

The Strategic use of information technology /. New York , 1987. xiii, 206 p. : ISBN 0-19-505048-7 (alk. paper) : LC Card 87-1606 DDC 658/.05 19
HD30.2 .S79 1987

STRATEGIC PLANNING - EUROPE, GERMAN-SPEAKING.

Seibert, Siegfried, 1954- Strategische Erfolgsfaktoren in mittleren Unternehmen . Frankfurt am Main , New York , c1987. xii, 353 p. : ISBN 3-8204-9828-1 LC Card 87-122289
HD2346.G3 S38 1987

STRATEGIC PLANNING - GERMANY (WEST)

Zörgiebel, Wilhelm W. Technologie in der Wettbewerbsstrategie . Berlin , c1983. xv, 322 p. : ISBN 3-503-02361-5 LC Card 84-158275
HD9703.G42 Z67 1983

STRATEGIC PLANNING - ITALY.

Scelte strategiche e riorganizzazione aziendale . Milano, Italy , c1985. 312 p. ; LC Card 86-146459
HD2864 .S36 1985 ***NYPL [JLD 87-1549]***

STRATEGIC PLANNING - JAPAN - CONGRESSES.

Strategic management in the United States and Japan . Cambridge, Mass. , c1986. xxv, 177 p. : ISBN 0-88730-089-8 LC Card 86-1169 DDC 658.4/012/0952 19
HD30.28 .S7324 1986 ***NYPL [JLE 86-3060]***

STRATEGIC PLANNING - SIMULATION METHODS.

Smith, Jerald R. Airline . Englewood Cliffs, NJ , c1987. v, 115, [38] p. : ISBN 0-13-020801-9 (pbk.) LC Card 86-30488 DDC 387.7/068 19
HD30.28 .S57 1987

STRATEGIC PLANNING - UNITED STATES.

The Competitive challenge . Cambridge, Mass. , c1987. xii, 256 p. : ISBN 0-88730-178-9 LC Card 87-1190 DDC 658.4/06 19
HD70.U5 C58 1987

STRATEGIC PLANNING - UNITED STATES - CONGRESSES.

Strategic management in the United States and Japan . Cambridge, Mass. , c1986. xxv, 177 p. : ISBN 0-88730-089-8 LC Card 86-1169 DDC 658.4/012/0952 19
HD30.28 .S7324 1986 ***NYPL [JLE 86-3060]***

Strategic planning workbook for nonprofit organizations /. Barry, Bryan W. St. Paul, MN , c1986. 72 p., [8] leaves of plates : ISBN 0-940069-00-8 (pbk.) LC Card 87-153976 DDC 658.4/012 19
HD62.6 .B37 1986

Strategic real estate submarkets : 147 opportunities to invest in 10 of today's overbuilt markets. Denver, Colo. (1009 Grant St., Suite 304, Denver 80203) : Gavilon Publishers, c1986. 195 p. : ill. ; 28 cm. Researched and compiled by Robert Fuller Associates, Inc. LC Card 86-228061 DDC 333.33/22/0973 19

1. Real estate investment - United States. 2. Metropolitan areas - United States. I. R. C. Fuller Associates.
HD255 .S77 1986

Strategic telemarketing . Bencin, Richard L., 1935- Philadelphia, Pa., USA , c1987. xviii, 182 p. : ISBN 0-915601-02-8 LC Card 86-30057 DDC 658.8/5 19
HF5415.1265 .B46 1987

Strategic trade policy and the new international economics / edited by Paul R. Krugman. Cambridge, Mass. : MIT Press, c1986. 313 p. ; 24 cm. Includes bibliographies and index. ISBN 0-262-11112-8 LC Card 86-2758 DDC 382/.3 19
1. Commercial policy - Addresses, essays, lectures. 2. International economic relations - Addresses, essays, lectures. I. Krugman, Paul R.
HF1411 .S82 1986 ***NYPL [JLE 86-3896]***

The Strategic use of information technology / edited by Stuart E. Madnick. New York : Oxford University Press, 1987. xiii, 206 p. : ill. ; 25 cm. (The Executive bookshelf) A selection of articles from the Sloan management review. Bibliography: p. 189-195. Includes index. ISBN 0-19-505048-7 (alk. paper) : LC Card 87-1606 DDC 658/.05 19
1. Management - Data processing. 2. Management information systems. 3. Strategic planning - Data processing. I. Madnick, Stuart E. II. Sloan management review. III. Series.
HD30.2 .S79 1987

The strategic use of regulatory investment by industry sub-groups [microform] . Oster, Sharon. New Haven, Ct. , 1980. 39 p. ;
NYPL [*XME-11,347]

La stratégie de l'Organisation de l'unité africaine pour le développement . Ndeshyo Rurihose. [Kinshasa] , 1981. 80 p. : LC Card 83-161631
HC800 .N393 1981

Strategie des Managements komplexer Systeme . Malik, Fredmund F. Bern , c1984. 563 p. : ISBN 3-258-03306-4 : LC Card 84-178061
HD30.28 .M334 1984

Strategie di marketing /. Penati, Luigi. Milano, Italy , c1986. 332 p. : LC Card 86-217663
HF5415.12.I8 P47 1986

Stratégie et communications sociales. Nicolas, Jean-Pierre, 1941- La pauvreté intolérable . Toulouse [1984] 208 p. : ISBN 2-86586-026-4 : LC Card 85-118841
HC280.P6 N53 1984

Strategie industriali e prospettive di sviluppo nel settore automobilistico / R. Argenziano ... [et al.] ; a cura di R. Argenziano e D. Velo. Milano : Giuffrè, [1985] 235 p. : ill. ; 24 cm. (Collana di diritto ed economia . 11) Includes bibliographical references. ISBN 88-14-00541-9 (pbk.) : LC Card 85-183335 DDC 338.4/76292/0945 19
1. Automobile industry and trade - Congresses. 2. Automobile industry and trade - Italy - Congresses. I. Argenziano, R. (Riccardo). II. Velo, Dario. III. Series.
HD9710.A2 S86 1985 ***NYPL [JLE 87-493]***

Strategie und Entwicklung deutscher Grossunternehmen . Massenberg, Jost A., 1956- Frankfurt am Main , New York , c1986. xi, 398 p. : ISBN 3-8204-9666-1 LC Card 86-220603
HD70.G2 M37 1986

Strategien des Personalmanagements . Wührer, Gerhard. Krefeld , 1985. 264 p. : ISBN 3-88358-054-5 LC Card 86-160291
HF5549.2.G3 W84 1985

Strategien für mehr Arbeitsplätze in Berlin . DIW-Symposion (1983 : Berlin, Germany) Berlin , c1984. 209 p. : ISBN 3-87061-277-0 LC Card 84-202956
HD5780.B4 D58 1983

Strategies and styles . Goold, Michael. Oxford, UK , New York, NY, USA , 1988, cl987. p. cm. ISBN 0-631-15829-4 : LC Card 87-12151 DDC 658/.046 19
HD2756 .G66 1988

Stratégies d'industrialisation et maîtrise du développement. Paris : Groupe de recherche et d'échanges technologiques : diffusion, Editions L'Harmattan, c1984. 115, [3] p. : ill. ; 22 cm. (Collection des ateliers Technologie et développement . no 3) "Ce texte fait suite à un séminaire ... Le compte rendu a été réalisé par Michel Leduc et Marc Ecrement." "Juin 1984." Bibliography: p. [117] ISBN 2-86844-002-9 LC Card 84-248894
1. Developing countries - Industries - Congresses. 2. Industry and state - Developing countries - Congresses. 3. Technological innovations - Economic aspects - Developing countries - Congresses. I. Leduc, Michel. II. Ecrement, Marc. III. Series.
HC59.7 .S854 1984

Strategies for integrating women into the labour market / Kirsten Hvidtfeldt, Kirsten Jørgensen, and Ruth Nielsen, eds. Copenhagen, Denmark : Women's Research Centre in Social Science, 1982. 347 p. : ill. ; 21 cm. (European women's studies in social science . no. 1 (1982)) Papers originally presented at a seminar on 'Strategies for integrating women into the labour market,' Liseleje, Denmark. Includes bibliographies. ISBN 87-88209-08-3 (pbk.) LC Card 86-673782
1. Women - Employment - Congresses. I. Hvidtfeldt, Kirsten. II. Jørgensen, Kirsten. III. Nielsen, Ruth, 1946-. IV. Series: European women's studies in social science , no. 1.
HD6052 .S77x 1982

Strategies for international industrial marketing : the management of customer relationships in European industrial markets / edited by Peter W. Turnbull and Jean-Paul Valla. London ; Dover, N.H. : Croom Helm, c1986. 310 p. : ill. ; 23 cm. Includes index. Bibliography: p. 301-305. ISBN 0-7099-2494-1 : LC Card 85-29047 DDC 658.8/48 19
1. Export marketing - Europe - Case studies. 2. Industrial marketing - Europe - Case studies. 3. Customer relations - Case studies. I. Turnbull, Peter W. II. Valla, Jean-Paul.
HF1009.7.E85 S77 1986
NYPL [JLD 86-1596]

Strategies for joint ventures in the People's Republic of China /. Mathur, Iqbal. New York , 1987. viii, 196 p. ; ISBN 0-275-92354-1 (alk. paper) : LC Card 87-7033 DDC 338.8/8851 19
HD62.47 .M38 1987

Strategies for selling underground & surface mining equipment. New York, N.Y. : Frost & Sullivan, c1983. vii, 320 p. : ill. ; 29 cm. "July 1983." "#A1125." LC Card 87-142333 DDC 381/.4568176/0973 19
1. Mining machinery industry - United States. 2. Mining machinery - Marketing. 3. Market surveys - United States. I. Frost & Sullivan. II. Title: Strategies for selling underground and surface mining equipment.
HD9506.U62 S865 1983

Strategies for selling underground and surface mining equipment. Strategies for selling underground & surface mining equipment. New York, N.Y. , c1983. vii, 320 p. : LC Card 87-142333 DDC 381/.4568176/0973 19
HD9506.U62 S865 1983

Strategies for technology-based competition . Link, Albert N. Lexington, Mass. , c1987. xii, 142 p. : ISBN 0-669-14574-2 (alk. paper) LC Card 86-45885 DDC 338.6/048 19
HF1414 .L55 1987

Strategies for the successful international investor /. Kehrer, Daniel M. New York, NY, U. S.A. , c1984. ix, 183 p. : ISBN 0-86604-174-5 (pbk.) LC Card 86-232170 DDC 332.6/73 19
HG4538 .K395 1984

Strategies-- successes-- senior executives speak out / [compiled by] J. Fred McLimore, Laurie Larwood. New York : Harper & Row, c1988. xiii, 397 p. : ill. ; 24 cm. Includes bibliographical references and index. ISBN 0-06-044354-5 (pbk.) LC Card 87-21765 DDC 658 19
1. Industrial management. 2. Industrial management - Case studies. I. McLimore, J. Fred. II. Larwood, Laurie.
HD31 .S696394 1988

Strategii͡a na kachestveni promeni /. Georgiev, I͡Ancho. Sofii͡a , 1986- v. <1-2 > ; LC Card 86-232319
HC403 .G465 1986

Strategii͡a uskoreni͡i͡a--leninizm v deĭstvii . Shevardnadze, Ėduard Amvrosievich. Moskva , 1986. 29 p. ; LC Card 86-190944
HC336.25 .S524 1986

Strategisch investeringsbeleid /. Verhaegen, P. H. A. M., 1950- Deventer , 1986. 223 p. : ISBN 90-267-1049-6 : LC Card 86-186994
HG4521 .V475 1986

Strategische Bankplanung . Tagung Strategische Bankplanung (1982 : Bonn, Germany) Frankfurt am Main , c1983. 345 p. : ISBN 3-7819-0293-5 LC Card 83-233043
HG1615 .T34 1982

Strategische Erfolgsfaktoren in mittleren Unternehmen . Seibert, Siegfried, 1954- Frankfurt am Main , New York , c1987. xii, 353 p. : ISBN 3-8204-9828-1 LC Card 87-122289
HD2346.G3 S38 1987

Strategische Unternehmensführung in Klein- und Mittelbetrieben . Holzhuber, Thomas. Wien [1984?] 198, 5 p. : ISBN 3-85436-018-5 : LC Card 84-248354
HD62.7 .H65 1984

Strategisches Management . Scholz, Christian, 1952- Berlin , New York , 1987. xv, 305 p. ; ISBN 3-11-010863-1 LC Card 87-145957 DDC 658.4/012 19
HD30.28 .S346 1987

Strategisches Marketing und Management : Konzeptionen in Theorie und Praxis / Edwin Rühli, Hans Peter Wehrli, Herausgeber. Bern : P. Haupt, c1986. 205 p. : ill. ; 23 cm. (Schriftenreihe des Instituts für Betriebswirtschaftliche Forschung an der Universität Zürich . Bd. 50) "Prof. Dr. Jan S. Krulis-Randa zum 60. Geburtstag gewidmet." "Publikationen von Prof. Dr. Jan S. Krulis-Randa": p. 204-205. Includes bibliographies. CONTENTS. - Konzeptionelle Überlegungen zur markorientierten Unternehmungsführung / Edwin Rühli -- Strategisches Marketing / Hans Peter Wehrli -- Strategie-Planung in rohstoff-bestimmter Umwelt / Peter Leumann -- Industrielles Marketing im multinationalen Unternehmen / Hans Udo Wenzel -- Kontrolle von Marketing-Aktivitäten in der Swissair / Jürg Forster -- Anpassungstendenzen im Bereich der finanziellen Führung multinational tätiger Unternehmungen aufgrund der Umweltveränderungen der letzten Jahre / Beat Baumgartner -- Personal-Marketing / Bruno Staffelbach -- Strategisches Marketing für modische Produkte / Kurt Staub -- EAN und Scanning / René Kühne -- Anmerkungen zur Lancierung einer neuen Zeitschrift / Maili Wolf. ISBN 3-258-03566-0 : LC Card 86-159360
1. Marketing - Decision making. 2. Product management. 3. Marketing management. 4. Strategic planning. I. Krulis-Randa, Jan S., 1926-. II. Rühli, Edwin. III. Wehrli, Hans-Peter. IV. Series.
HF5415.135 .S77 1986

Strategisches Personalmanagement /. Staffelbach, Bruno. Bern [1986] x, 285 p. : ISBN 3-258-03626-8 : LC Card 86-211191
HF5549 .S842416 1986

Strategisches Qualitätsmanagement im Industriebetrieb . Dögl, Rudolf. Göttingen , c1986. xv, 267 p. : ISBN 3-525-12562-3 (Deut. Bibl.) LC Card 86-210486
HD30.28 .D64 1986

The strategist CEO . Robert, Michel, 1941- New York , 1988. viii, 140 p. : ISBN 0-89930-268-8 (lib. bdg. : alk. paper) LC Card 87-10945 DDC 658.4/012 19
HD30.28 .R63 1988

STRATEGOS . Löffler, Reiner, 1959- Mannheim , 1986 (Darmstadt : Copy Shop) 246, [49] p. : LC Card 87-408452 DDC 658.4/0353/0285 19
HD30.26 .L64 1986

Strategy, analysis, and decisions . Skov, Paul B. Menlo Park, Calif. (333 Ravenswood Ave., Menlo Park 94025-3476) , c1985. 40 p. : LC Card 87-119164 DDC 658.4/012
HD30.28 .S49 1985

Strategy and structure of enterprise in a developing country /. Anyansi-Archibong, Chi. B., 1949- Aldershots, Hants, England , Brookfield, Vt., USA , c1988. xvii, 274 p. : ISBN 0-566-05471-X : LC Card 87-12020 DDC 658/.009669 19
HD70.N43 A59 1988

Strategy for export . Wild, Rolf H. Asheville, NC , c1986. 121 p. ; ISBN 0-914291-02-5 (pbk.) : LC Card 86-51529 DDC 658.8/48 19
HF1009.5 .W56 1986

A Strategy for restoration of growth in middle-income countries that face debt-servicing difficulties. Washington, D.C., U. S.A. : Joint Ministerial Committee of the Boards of Governors of the World Bank and the International Monetary Fund on the Transfer of Real Resources to Developing

Countries (Development Committee) : Copies from World Bank Publications Sales Unit, 1986. 43 p. : ill. ; 22 cm. (Development Committee, 0255-8807 . no. 10) Paper presented at meeting held Apr. 1986 in Washington, D.C. Includes bibliographical references. ISBN 0-8213-0811-4 (pbk.) LC Card 86-214478 DDC 338.9/009172/4 19
1. Debts, External - Developing countries. 2. Debt relief - Developing countries. 3. Economic development. 4. Developing countries - Economic conditions. I. Development Committee. II. Series: Development Committee (Series) , no. 10.
HJ8899 .S77 1986

Strategy formulation and implementation . Thompson, Arthur A., 1940- Plano, Tex. , 1986. xvi, 452 p. : ISBN 0-256-03173-8 (pbk.) LC Card 85-73596 DDC 658.4/012 19
HD30.28 .T54 1986

Strategy of an empire in decline . Targ, Harry R., 1940- Minneapolis , c1986. 294 p. ; ISBN 0-930656-47-4 : LC Card 86-16338 DDC 909.82 19
D849 .T37 1986 ***NYPL [JFD 87-2032]***

Strategy of socio-economic development : selected problems / [collective work edited by Jerzy Kalisiak ; authors, Andrzej Bocian ... et al. ; edited by Marian Geldner]. Warsaw : Central School of Planning and Statistics in Warsaw, Research Institute for Developing Countries, 1980. 122 p. : ill. ; 24 cm. (Teaching paper : advanced course in national economic planning . vol. 29) Includes bibliographical references. LC Card 81-107307
1. Economic development. 2. Economic policy. 3. Poland - Economic policy - 1966-1980. 4. Poland - Social conditions - 1945-. I. Kalisiak, Jerzy. II. Bocian, Andrzej. III. Geldner, Marian. IV. Title: Strategy of socioeconomic development. V. Series: Teaching paper (Szkoła Główna Planowania i Statystyki (Warsaw, Poland). Instytut Gospodarki Krajów Rozwijających się) , v. 29.
HD75 .S8 1980

Strategy of socioeconomic development. Strategy of socio-economic development . Warsaw , 1980. 122 p. : LC Card 81-107307
HD75 .S8 1980

Strategy, policy, and growth . McKenna, John F. (John Francis), 1945- Reading, Mass. , 1988. p. cm. ISBN 0-201-13987-1 : LC Card 87-1301 DDC 658.4/012 19
HD30.28 .M384 1988

The strategy process . Quinn, James Brian, 1928- Englewood Cliffs, N.J. , c1988. p. cm. ISBN 0-13-850892-5 LC Card 87-1160 DDC 658.4/012 19
HD30.28 .Q53 1988

Stratfold, Peter. BASIC business systems simulation / Peter Stratfold. London ; Boston : Butterworths, 1987. viii, 172 p. : ill. ; 22 cm. (Butterworths BASIC series) Bibliography: p. 167. Includes index. ISBN 0-408-01260-9 (pbk.) : LC Card 87-18795 DDC 650/.028/55133 19
1. Basic (Computer program language). 2. Business - Data processing. 3. Digital computer simulation. I. Title. II. Series.
HF5548.5.B3 S78 1987

Stratmann, Friedrich. Chemische Industrie unter Zwang? : staatliche Einflussnahme am Beispiel der chemischen Industrie Deutschlands, 1933-1949 / Friedrich Stratmann. Stuttgart : F. Steiner Verlag Wiesbaden, 1985. xiv, 531 p. : ill. ; 24 cm. (Zeitschrift für Unternehmensgeschichte. Beiheft . 43) "Quellen- und Literaturverzeichnis": p. 495-519. Includes index. ISBN 3-515-04399-3 LC Card 86-205409 DDC 338.4/766/0943 19
1. Chemical industry - Germany - History. 2. Chemical industry - Germany (West) - History. 3. Chemical industry - Government policy - Germany - History. 4. Chemical industry - Government policy - Germany (West) - History. I. Title. II. Series.
HD9654.5 .S77 1985

Straub, Joseph T. Introduction to business / Joseph T. Straub, Raymond F. Attner. 3rd ed. Boston, Mass. : PWS-Kent, 1988. xxi, 639, [66] p., [12] p. of plates : ill. (some col.) ; 27 cm. Bibliography: p. 667-674. Includes indexes. ISBN 0-534-87156-9 : LC Card 87-23276 DDC 658 19
1. Industrial management. 2. Business. I. Attner, Raymond F. II. Title.
HD31 .S6965 1988

Straubhaar, Thomas. Leisinger, Klaus M. Studien zur Entwicklungsökonomie /. Bern , c1986. 130 p. : ISBN 3-258-03665-9 LC Card 87-124013 DDC 338.9/009172/7 19
HC59.72.E44 L45 1986

Strauss, Beverly. Strauss, Bob. American sporting advertising /. Jefferson, Me. (Box 1060, Jefferson 04348) , 1987- v. <1 > : LC Card 87-155421 DDC 741.67/0973/074013 19
HF6161.S65 S77 1987

Strauss, Bob. American sporting advertising / [Bob and Beverly Strauss]. 1st ed. Jefferson, Me. (Box 1060, Jefferson 04348) : Circus Promotions Corp., 1987- v. <1 > : ill. ; 28 cm. CONTENTS. - v. 1. Posters and calendars. LC Card 87-155421 DDC 741.67/0973/074013 19
1. Advertising - Sporting goods - United States - Catalogs. 2. Posters, American - Catalogs. 3. Calendars - United States - Catalogs. I. Strauss, Beverly. II. Title.
HF6161.S65 S77 1987

Strauss, Carolyn. Hartman, Tori. Specialty modeling /. New York , c1988. x, 128 p. ; ISBN 0-525-48356-X LC Card 87-22470 DDC 659.1/52 19
HD6073.M772 U55 1988

Strauss, John, 1951-
Agricultural household models . Baltimore, Md. , 1986. xi, 335 p. : ISBN 0-8018-3149-0 LC Card 85-45102 DDC 331.7/63/091724 19
HD1542 .A34 1986 ***NYPL [JLE 86-2440]***

Socio-economic determinants of food consumption and production in rural Sierra Leone : application of an agricultural household model with several commodities / by John Strauss. East Lansing, Mich. : Dept. of Agricultural Economics, Michigan State University, 1983. vi, 91 p. : ill. ; 28 cm. (MSU international development paper, 0731-3438 . no. 5) Bibliography: p. 86-91. LC Card 83-622388 DDC 339.4/8664/00724 19
1. Food consumption - Sierra Leone - Mathematical models. 2. Food supply - Sierra Leone - Mathematical models. I. Title.
HD9017.S52 S88 1983 ***NYPL [JLF 86-684]***

Strawser, Robert H.
Benjamin, James J. Financial accounting /. Houston, Tex. , 1986. xii, 718 p. : ISBN 0-87393-039-8 LC Card 86-214139 DDC 657/.48 19
HF5635 .B419 1986

Francia, Arthur J. Managerial accounting /. Houston, Tex. , 1984. xiv, 651 p. : ISBN 0-931920-70-1 LC Card 83-72203 DDC 658.1/511 19
HF5657.4 .F72 1984

Strazicky, B. (Beátra), 1947- System modelling and optimization . Berlin , New York , c1986. xii, 1046 p. : ISBN 0-387-16854-0 (U. S.) LC Card 86-15637 DDC 003 19
QA402 .S95822 1986 ***NYPL [JSE 86-1775]***

STREAM POLLUTION. see WATER - POLLUTION.

STREAMS. see RIVERS.

STREAT, E. RAYMOND, SIR.
Streat, Raymond, Sir. Lancashire and Whitehall . Manchester [Greater Manchester] , c1987. 2 v. : ISBN 0-7190-2390-4 (v. 1) LC Card 87-11026 DDC 338.7/67721/0924 B 19
HD9881.5.S77 A3 1987

Streat, Raymond, Sir. Lancashire and Whitehall : the diary of Sir Raymond Streat / edited by Marguerite Dupree. Manchester [Greater Manchester] : Manchester University Press, c1987. 2 v. : ill., ports. ; 25 cm. Includes index. CONTENTS. - v. 1. 1931-39. v. 2. 1939-57. ISBN 0-7190-2390-4 (v. 1) LC Card 87-11026 DDC 338.7/67721/0924 B 19
1. Streat, E. Raymond, Sir. 2. Industrialists - Great Britain - Biography. 3. Cotton textile industry - Government policy - Great Britain - History - 20th century. 4. Cotton textile industry - England - Lancashire - History - 20th century. I. Dupree, Marguerite. II. Title.
HD9881.5.S77 A3 1987

Streatfield, K. Fertility decline in a traditional society : the case of Bali / Kim Streatfield. [Canberra, ACT] : Dept. of Demography, Australian National University : Distributed by Bibliotech, 1986. xvii, 177 p. : ill. ; 25 cm. (Indonesian population monograph series . no. 4) Bibliography: p. 161-173. ISBN 0-86784-711-5 (pbk.) LC Card 86-213262 DDC 304.6/32/095986 19
1. Fertility, Human - Indonesia - Bali (Province). 2. Birth control - Indonesia - Bali (Province). 3. Bali (Indonesia : Province) - Population. I. Title. II. Series.
HB1058.B34 S87 1986

Strebel, Paul. In the shadows of Wall Street : a guide to investing in neglected stocks / Paul Strebel, Steven Carvell. Englewood Cliffs, N.J. : Prentice-Hall, c1988. xii, 228 p. : ill. ; 24 cm. Bibliography: p. 215-220. Includes indexes. ISBN 0-13-455999-1 LC Card 87-42680 DDC 332.63/22 19
1. Stocks - United States. 2. Investments - United States. 3. Stock-exchange - United States. I. Carvell, Steven. II. Title.
HG4921 .S84 1988

Strecker, Arthur.
Normenvertrag. 1976. Lauer, Karl Friedrich. Das Referenzbüro der Gemeinschaften / Karl Friedrich Lauer. Der Normenvertrag / Arthur Strecker, Helmut Reihlen. [Dortmund?] , 1976. 76 p. ; LC Card 85-241026
HD30 .A7 Heft 171 T59.A1

Streeck, Wolfgang, 1946-
Industrial relations and technical change in the British, Italian, and German automobile industry . Berlin [1985] 1 v. (various pagings) : LC Card 86-206613 DDC 338/.04292/094 19
HD6976.A82 G75 1985

Industrial relations in West Germany : a case study of the car industry / Wolfgang Streeck. London : Heinemann, 1984. 178 p. ; 23 cm. At head of title: Policy Studies Institute. Bibliography: p. [170]-172. Includes index. ISBN 0-435-83839-3 LC Card 87-673421
1. Volkswagenwerk. 2. Trade-unions - Automobile industry workers - Germany (West). 3. Automobile industry and trade - Germany (West) - Management - Employee participation. 4. Collective bargaining - Automobile industry - Germany (West). 5. Industrial relations - Germany (West) - Case studies. I. Policy Studies Institute. II. Title.
HD6698.A8 S77x 1984b

Street fair manual : a collection of useful and valuable information about organization and management : with illustrated suggestions for the construction of carnival floats, booths, and arches. Chicago : Merchants Record Co., 1907. 79 p. : ill. ; 19 x 28 cm. LC Card 86-227641
1. Fairs. I. Merchants Record Company (Chicago, Ill.).
HF5481 .S77 1907

Street, James H. (James Harry), 1915- Latin America's economic development . Boulder , 1987. xii, 304 p. ; ISBN 1-555-87067-8 (lib. bdg. : alk. paper) : LC Card 87-10046 DDC 338.98 19
HC125 .L3536 1987

STREET-RAILROADS.
Naumann, Thomas. Stadtbahn für Würzburg . Würzburg , 1985. 237 p., [3] leaves of plates : LC Card 86-166915
HE4779.W84 N38 1985

STREET-RAILROADS - ARGENTINA - BUENOS AIRES - HISTORY.
González Podestá, Aquilino. Los tranvías de Buenos Aires /. Buenos Aires, República Argentina , c1986. 95 p. : ISBN 950-796-900-2 LC Card 87-400950 DDC 388.4/6/098211 19
HE4609.B82 G66 1986

STREET-RAILROADS - AUSTRALIA - SYDNEY (N.S.W.)
Keenan, David R. The south-eastern lines of the Sydney tramway system /. Sydney, N.S.W., Australia , c1982. 120 p. : ISBN 0-909338-03-5 (pbk.) LC Card 87-167855 DDC 388.4/6/09441 19
HE5179.S93 K44 1982

STREET-RAILROADS - CALIFORNIA - LOS ANGELES.
Bottles, Scott L. Los Angeles and the automobile . Berkeley , c1987. xiii, 301 p. : ISBN 0-520-05795-3 (alk. paper) LC Card 86-14660 DDC 388.4/1321/0979494 19
HE5634.L7 B68 1987

STREET-RAILROADS - DENMARK - COPENHAGEN - HISTORY.
By i forvandling . Copenhagen , 1984. 93 p. :

ISBN 87-87589-42-7 LC Card 87-155193
HE4859.C68 B92 1984

STREET-RAILROADS - GERMANY (WEST) - CASE STUDIES.
Hall, Peter, 1931- Can rail save the city? . Aldershot, Hants , Brookfield, Vt., U. S.A. , c1985. xii, 241 p. : ISBN 0-566-00947-1 : LC Card 85-17659 DDC 388.4/2/0943 19
HE4774 .H35 1985 ***NYPL [JLD 86-2622]***

STREET-RAILROADS - GERMANY (WEST) - WÜRZBURG.
Naumann, Thomas. Stadtbahn für Würzburg . Würzburg , 1985. 237 p., [3] leaves of plates : LC Card 86-166915
HE4779.W84 N38 1985

STREET-RAILROADS - GREAT BRITAIN - CASE STUDIES.
Hall, Peter, 1931- Can rail save the city? . Aldershot, Hants , Brookfield, Vt., U. S.A. , c1985. xii, 241 p. : ISBN 0-566-00947-1 : LC Card 85-17659 DDC 388.4/2/0943 19
HE4774 .H35 1985 ***NYPL [JLD 86-2622]***

STREET-RAILROADS - PENNSYLVANIA - HISTORY - PICTORIAL WORKS.
Berner, Allan H. Pennsylvania's street railways in early postcard views . [S.l.] , c1986. 106 p. : LC Card 86-221349 DDC 388.4/4/09748 19
HE4487.P4 B47 1986

STREET-RAILROADS - SWITZERLAND - BASEL - HISTORY.
Basler Verkehrs-Betriebe (BVB) . Villigen AG, Schweiz , c1984. 56 p., [188] p. of plates, xv p. : ISBN 3-85649-045-0 : LC Card 84-160209
HE4919.B37 B37 1984

Street talk in real estate /. West, Bill W. Alameda, Calif. [1987] vi, 216 p. : ISBN 0-934189-04-8 (pbk. : trade) : LC Card 86-50605 DDC 333.33/03/21 19
HD1365 .W47 1987

STREET TRAFFIC. see **TRAFFIC ENGINEERING.**

Streeten, Paul.
Theory and reality in development . Basingstoke, Hampshire , 1986. xii, 291 p. : ISBN 0-333-39824-6 ***NYPL [JLD 86-1827]***

What price food? : agricultural price policies in developing countries / Paul Streeten ; foreword by Michael Lipton. New York : St. Martin's Press, 1987. viii, 127 p. : ill. ; 23 cm Bibliography: p. 107-119. Includes index. ISBN 0-312-00739-6 : LC Card 87-9577 DDC 338.1/8 19
1. Agricultural prices - Government policy - Developing countries. 2. Food prices - Government policy - Developing countries. I. Title.
HD1417 .S73 1987

STREETEN, PAUL - ADDRESSES, ESSAYS, LECTURES.
Theory and reality in development . Basingstoke, Hampshire , 1986. xii, 291 p. : ISBN 0-333-39824-6 ***NYPL [JLD 86-1827]***

STREETS - EUROPE.
Grieser, Dietmar, 1934- Historische Strassen in Europa . München , c1983. 95 p. : ISBN 3-87405-160-9 (pbk.) LC Card 87-672444
HE361 .G74x 1983

STREETS - VIRGINIA - FAIRFAX COUNTY - DIRECTORIES.
Lusk's Fairfax County, Virginia assessment directory . Washington, D.C. (1824 Jefferson Pl., NW, Washington 20036) , 1986. 1251, [81] p. ; LC Card 87-144674 DDC 333.33/2/09755291 19
HD266.V82 F24 1986

Streik für fünfunddreissig Stunden. Aktive Kolleginnen und Kollegen ziehen Bilanz . Frankfurt/M. , 1984. 100 p. : ISBN 3-88332-092-7 : LC Card 85-233569 DDC 331.89/2 19
HD5378 .A64 1984

Streik für 35 Stunden. Aktive Kolleginnen und Kollegen ziehen Bilanz . Frankfurt/M. , 1984. 100 p. : ISBN 3-88332-092-7 : LC Card 85-233569 DDC 331.89/2 19
HD5378 .A64 1984

Streiks in Bayern (1889-1914) . Jüngling, Elisabeth. München , 1986. viii, 307 p., [24] p. of plates : ISBN 3-87821-214-3 LC Card 87-408637 DDC 331.89/29433 19
HD5380.B38 J86 1986

Streit, Joachim. Finanzinnovationen, Deregulierung und Geldmengensteuerung in den USA / Joachim Streit. Tübingen : Mohr, c1986. xi, 188 p. : ill. ; 24 cm. (Kieler Studien, 0340-6989 . 204) Bibliography: p. 177-188. ISBN 3-16-345156-X (pbk.) LC Card 87-408200 DDC 332/.0973 19
1. Finance - United States. 2. Banks and banking - United States - Deregulation. 3. Monetary policy - United States. I. Title. II. Series.
HG181 .S825 1986

Streit, Manfred E. Die Wirtschaft heute /. Mannheim , 1980. 638 p. : ISBN 3-411-01793-7 LC Card 86-673960
HB175 .W5934x 1980

Strengthening local linkages for socioeconomic development at regional level : a study on the rural economy of the Gwembe District, Zambia / Hans Gsänger ... [et al.]. Berlin : German Development Institute, [1986] 2 v. : ill. ; 30 cm. "Berlin, July 1986." Bibliography: v. 1, p. 125-128. LC Card 87-143388 DDC 338.96894 19
1. Gwembe District, Zambia - Economic conditions. 2. Gwembe District (Zambia) - Social conditions. 3. Gwembe District (Zambia) - Rural conditions. 4. Gwembe District (Zambia) - Politics and government. I. Gsänger, Hans. II. Deutsches Institut für Entwicklungspolitik.
HC915.Z7 G847 1986

Strengthening the international monetary system . Crockett, Andrew. Washington, D.C. , c1987. vii, 84 p. ; LC Card 86-33750 DDC 332.4/5 19
HG3881 .C694 1987

Strengthening women's participation in food and agricultural marketing : proceedings of the national seminar held at Cooperative College, Lusaka, Zambia, 16th-19th April, 1984 / Alifeyo Chilivumbo and Joyce Kanyangwa, editors. [Lusaka] : National Commission for Development Planning : University of Zambia, Rural Development Studies Bureau, [1984] 78 p. ; 30 cm. (Occasional paper / University of Zambia, Rural Development Studies Bureau . no. 21) LC Card 86-980282 DDC 331.4/83/096894 19
1. Women agricultural laborers - Zambia - Congresses. 2. Women in marketing - Zambia - Congresses. 3. Farm produce - Zambia - Marketing - Congresses. I. Chilivumbo, Alifeyo. II. Kanyangwa, Joyce. III. Series: Occasional papers (University of Zambia. Rural Development Studies Bureau) , no. 21.
HD6073.A292 Z3374 1984

Stress and the woman manager /. Davidson, Marilyn. Oxford [Oxfordshire], 1983. 230 p. ; ISBN 0-85520-623-3 ***NYPL [JLE 85-1426]***

STRESS (PSYCHOLOGY)
Ochs, Peter. Analyse und Bewertung ausgewählter sozialwissenschaftlichen Forschungen /. Dortmund , Bremerhaven , 1983. 102 p. ; ISBN 3-88314-245-X LC Card 83-207278
HD7708 .O28 1983

Stress, social support, and women /. Washington , c1986. xviii, 272 p. : ISBN 0-89116-404-9 : LC Card 84-27967 DDC 155.9 19
BF575.S75 S7739 1985 ***NYPL [JFE 86-3212]***

Witkin-Lanoil, Georgia. The female stress syndrome . New York , c1984. xi, 211 p. ; ISBN 0-937858-33-1 LC Card 83-25038 DDC 155.6/33 19
BF575.S75 W58 1984 ***NYPL [JFD 86-10468]***

Witkin-Lanoil, Georgia. The male stress syndrome . New York , c1986. 246 p. ; ISBN 0-937858-59-5 LC Card 85-61815 DDC 155.9 19
BF575.S75 W59 1986 ***NYPL [JFD 86-5693]***

Women in health & illness . Philadelphia , 1986. x, 261 p. : ISBN 0-7216-2086-8 LC Card 86-6576 DDC 155.6/33 19
RC451.4.W6 W656 1986 ***NYPL [JLF 86-1463]***

Stress, social support, and women / edited by Stevan E. Hobfoll. Washington : Hemisphere Pub. Corp., c1986. xviii, 272 p. : ill ; 24 cm. (The series in clinical and community psychology) Includes bibliographies and indexes. ISBN 0-89116-404-9 : LC Card 84-27967 DDC 155.9 19
1. Stress (Psychology). 2. Women - Psychology. I. Hobfoll, Stevan E., 1951-.
BF575.S75 S7739 1985 ***NYPL [JFE 86-3212]***

Stretch, C. The effectiveness of town planning in Natal : case studies in Pinetown and Umhlanga : a summary report / C. Stretch and C. Wright. Pietermaritzburg, Natal, South Africa : Natal Town and Regional Planning Commission, 1986. 35 p. ; 26 cm. (Natal town and regional planning report . v. 64) Bibliography: p. 33-35. LC Card 86-159747 DDC 361.2/5/09684 s 307.1/2/096845 19
1. City planning - South Africa - Pinetown. 2. City planning - South Africa - Umhlanga Rocks. I. Wright, C. II. Natal (South Africa). Town and Regional Planning Commission. III. Title. IV. Series.
HC517.N3 A44 vol. 64 HT169.S62P56

Strezhnev, A. O. Narodnoe khozi͡aĭstvo Mordovskoĭ ASSR za gody odinnadtsatoĭ pi͡atiletki, 1981-1985 gg. . Saransk , 1986. 198 p. ; LC Card 87-120800
HA1448.M59 N33 1986

Stribling, Catherine. Growing up financially : a complete guide for first-time investors to managing your hard-earned money / Catherine R. Stribling.1st ed. New York : Ballantine Books, 1987, c1986. 311 p. ; 21 cm. Includes index. ISBN 0-345-33098-6 (pbk.) : LC Card 86-90719 DDC 332.6/78 19
1. Finance, Personal - United States. 2. Investments - United States. I. Title.
HG179 .S846 1987

Strickland, Allyn D. Firm diversification, mutual forbearance behavior and price-cost margins / Allyn D. Strickland. New York : Garland Pub., 1984. 155 p. ; 24 cm. (Outstanding dissertations in economics) Originally presented as the author's thesis, University of Wisconsin-Madison, 1976. Bibliography: p. 152-155. ISBN 0-8240-4159-3 (alk. paper) LC Card 79-53209 DDC 338.8/3/0973
1. Conglomerate corporations - United States. 2. Competition - United States. 3. Diversification in industry - United States. I. Title. II. Title: Mutual forebearance behavior and price-cost margins. III. Series.
HD2756.U5 S76 1984 ***NYPL [JLE 86-3907]***

Strickland, Alonzo J.
Thompson, Arthur A., 1940- Strategic management . Plano, Tex. , 1987. xviii, 1054 p. : ISBN 0-255-03717-5 LC Card 86-72250 DDC 658.4/012 19
HD30.28 .T53 1987

Thompson, Arthur A., 1940- Strategy formulation and implementation . Plano, Tex. , 1986. xvi, 452 p. : ISBN 0-256-03173-8 (pbk.) LC Card 85-73596 DDC 658.4/012 19
HD30.28 .T54 1986

Stricklin, Wilma D. Certified professional secretary examination review series. [Kansas City, Mo.?] , New York , c1986- v. <1, 6 > : ISBN 0-471-84353-9 (pbk. : v. 1) LC Card 87-100577 DDC 651.3/74/076 19
HF5547.5 .C44 1986

Strickon, Arnold. Entrepreneurship and social change /. Lanham, MD [S.l.] , c1986. 275 p. : ISBN 0-8191-5165-3 (alk. paper) : LC Card 85-26533 DDC 338/.04 19
HB615 .E629 1986 ***NYPL [JLD 86-3073]***

STRICT FORECLOSURE. see **FORECLOSURE.**

Strigel, Werner H. Essays on the performance of leading indicators based on qualitative data /. Munich , 1985. 148 p. : ISBN 3-88512-009-7 (pbk.) : LC Card 86-181861 DDC 330/.0724 19
HB3730 .E78 1985

Strijbosch, Annemarie. Mensink, Ankie. De wording en verwording van de staat Marokko . Rotterdam , 1985. 304 p. ; ISBN 90-6330-109-X : LC Card 85-214935
HC810 .M46 1985

Strijker, D. Huizinga, W. Two lectures on the historical development of Dutch agriculture, 1600-1985 /. Den Haag [1986] 31 p. : LC Card 86-233719
HD1987 .H85 1986

Strike . Wilsher, Peter. London [1985] xiii, 284 p., [16] p. of plates : ISBN 0-233-97825-9 : LC

Card 86-221981 DDC 331.89/2822334/0941 19
HD5365.M6152 1984 .W55 1985b

Strikes /. Jackson, Michael Peart. Sussex , New York , c1987. xi, 232 p. ; ISBN 0-312-01194-6 (St. Martin's Press) : LC Card 87-14376 DDC 331.89/2 19
HD5306 .J33 1987

STRIKES AND LOCKOUTS - ARGENTINA - HISTORY - 20TH CENTURY.
Isuani, Ernesto A. (Ernesto Aldo) Los orígenes conflictivos de la seguridad social argentina /. Buenos Aires , c1985. 140 p. ; ISBN 950-25-0128-4 : LC Card 86-174656
HD7149 .I88 1985

STRIKES AND LOCKOUTS - AUSTRALIA.
Jackson, Michael Peart. Strikes /. Sussex , New York , c1987. xi, 232 p. ; ISBN 0-312-01194-6 (St. Martin's Press) : LC Card 87-14376 DDC 331.89/2 19
HD5306 .J33 1987

STRIKES AND LOCKOUTS - AUSTRALIA - DARWIN (N.T.) - HISTORY - 20TH CENTURY.
Alcorta, F. X. (Frank X.) Darwin Rebellion, 1911-1919 /. [Darwin, N.T.] , 1984. xiv, 115 p., [8] p. of plates : ISBN 0-7245-0492-3 : LC Card 84-220611 DDC 331.89/294295 19
HD5450.Z9 D373 1984 ***NYPL [JLF 87-405]***

STRIKES AND LOCKOUTS - BRAZIL.
Castro, Pedro. Greve, fatos e significados /. São Paulo , 1986. 72 p. ; ISBN 85-08-01170-9 : LC Card 86-230606
HD5353 .C37 1986

STRIKES AND LOCKOUTS - BRAZIL - SÃO PAULO (STATE)
Khoury, Yara Aun. As greves de 1917 em São Paulo e o processo de organização proletária /. São Paulo , 1981. 221 p. ; LC Card 81-210934 DDC 331.2/98161 19
HD5355.S26 K48 1981
NYPL [JLD 86-3514]

STRIKES AND LOCKOUTS - BRAZIL - SÃO PAULO (STATE) - HISTORY.
Leme, Dulce M. Pompêo C. (Dulce Maria Pompêo de Camargo) Trabalhadores ferroviários em greve /. Campinas [Brazil] , 1986. 269 p. : ISBN 85-26-80007-8 : LC Card 87-102922 DDC 331.89/281385/098161 19
HD5354.R12 1906 .S365 1986

STRIKES AND LOCKOUTS - BRITISH COLUMBIA - HISTORY - 20TH CENTURY.
Fighting heritage . Vancouver [1986?] 159 p., [32] p. of plates : ISBN 0-9692365-0-6 (pbk.) LC Card 86-231043 DDC 331.88/09711 19
HD8109.B72 F54 1986

STRIKES AND LOCKOUTS - CALIFORNIA.
Seider, Maynard, 1943- A year in the life of a factory /. San Pedro, Calif. , 1984. 152 p. ; ISBN 0-917300-16-5 (pbk.) : LC Card 83-50914 DDC 331.89/28621381/0979466 19
HD8039.E38 U67 1984
NYPL [JLD 86-4400]

STRIKES AND LOCKOUTS - CANADA.
Strikes and lockouts in Canada, 1973 /. Ottawa , 1975. 88 p. : ISBN 2-7114-5902-3 (pbk.) LC Card 82-212112
HD5328 .S77 1975

STRIKES AND LOCKOUTS - CANADA - HISTORY.
Seymour, Edward E. An illustrated history of Canadian labour, 1800-1974 /. Ottawa , 1980. xiv, 95 p. :

STRIKES AND LOCKOUTS - CHILE - HISTORY.
Pizarro, Crisóstomo. La huelga obrera en Chile, 1890-1970 /. Santiago, Chile [1986] 227 p. : LC Card 87-115190 DDC 331.89/2983 19
HD5356.A6 P59 1986

STRIKES AND LOCKOUTS - CHILE - HISTORY - 20TH CENTURY.
Gonzales Torres, Rodrigo. Los paros nacionales en Chile, 1919-1973 /. Santiago [Chile] , 1984. 234 p. ; LC Card 86-200794
HD5356.A6 G66 1984

STRIKES AND LOCKOUTS - COAL MINING - SPAIN - ASTURIAS - HISTORY - 20TH CENTURY.
Shubert, Adrian, 1953- The road to revolution in Spain . Urbana , c1987. 183 p. : ISBN 0-252-01368-9 (alk. paper) LC Card 86-24998 DDC 331.7/622334/094615 19
HD8039.M62 S68 1987

STRIKES AND LOCKOUTS - COSTA RICA - HISTORY.
Acuña Ortega, Víctor H. Los orígenes de la clase obrera en Costa Rica . San José [1986] 85 p. : LC Card 87-402904 DDC 331/.097286 19
HD8136 .A28 1986

STRIKES AND LOCKOUTS - CUBA - HISTORY.
Historia del movimiento obrero cubano, 1865-1958 /. La Habana , 1985- v. <1 > ; LC Card 87-401462
HD6577 .H57 1985

STRIKES AND LOCKOUTS - ECONOMIC ASPECTS.
Klemm, Günther. Ökonomische Analyse von Streik und Aussperrung im Rahmen einer marktwirtschaftlichen Ordnung /. Köln , 1983. viii, 214 p. : ISBN 3-921471-43-5 : LC Card 83-216635 DDC 331.89/2 19
HD5306 .K55 1983

STRIKES AND LOCKOUTS - ELECTRIC MACHINERY INDUSTRY - ITALY.
Bezza, Bruno. Le lotte degli elettromeccanici /. Milano , c1981. 179 p. : ISBN 88-20-42149-6 : LC Card 81-200954 DDC 331.89/282131/0945 19
HD5384.E3 B49 1981 ***NYPL [JLD 86-2898]***

STRIKES AND LOCKOUTS - EUROPE.
Hibbs, Douglas A., 1943- The political economy of industrial democracies /. Cambridge, Mass. , 1987. viii, 327 p. : ISBN 0-674-68580-6 LC Card 86-9799 DDC 339.5/09171/3 19
HB3743 .H53 1987 ***NYPL [JLE 87-1430]***

STRIKES AND LOCKOUTS - FINLAND.
Alasoini, Tuomo. Lakot ja yhteiskunnan muutos . Helsinki [1983] ii, 132 p. : ISBN 951-46-7101-5 LC Card 84-168540
HD5306 .A42 1983

STRIKES AND LOCKOUTS - FRANCE - HISTORY - 19TH CENTURY.
Perrot, Michelle. [Jeunesse de la grève. English.] Workers on strike . New Haven , 1987. 321 p. : ISBN 0-300-03849-6 LC Card 86-26753 DDC 331.89/2944 19
HD5374 .P4613 1987

STRIKES AND LOCKOUTS - FRANCE - VENDÉE - HISTORY.
Regourd, Florence. La Vendée ouvrière . Les Sables-d'Olonne [1981] 353 p., [16] p. of plates : ISBN 2-7188-0098-4 : LC Card 82-161939 DDC 331.89/294461 19
HD5376.V46 R43 1981
NYPL [JLF 85-1433]

STRIKES AND LOCKOUTS - GERMANY, WEST.
Aktive Kolleginnen und Kollegen ziehen Bilanz . Frankfurt/M. , 1984. 100 p. : ISBN 3-88332-092-7 : LC Card 85-233569 DDC 331.89/2 19
HD5378 .A64 1984

STRIKES AND LOCKOUTS - GERMANY (WEST) - ADDRESSES, ESSAYS, LECTURES.
Aussperrung und Streik . Mainz , 1981, c1980. 173 p. ; ISBN 3-7867-0854-1 LC Card 81-101514 DDC 331.89/2943 19
HD5378 .A97 1981 ***NYPL [JLD 86-2787]***

STRIKES AND LOCKOUTS - GERMANY (WEST) - BAVARIA - HISTORY.
Jüngling, Elisabeth. Streiks in Bayern (1889-1914) . München , 1986. viii, 307 p., [24] p. of plates : ISBN 3-87821-214-3 LC Card 87-408637 DDC 331.89/29433 19
HD5380.B38 J86 1986

STRIKES AND LOCKOUTS - GERMANY (WEST) - SAARLAND - HISTORY - 19TH CENTURY.
Steffens, Horst. Autorität und Revolte . Weingarten , c1987. 419 p. : ISBN 3-924027-47-1 LC Card 87-141439 DDC 331/.0422334/094342 19
HD8039.M61 G383 1987

STRIKES AND LOCKOUTS - GOLD MINING - RUSSIAN S.F.S.R. - SIBERIA, EASTERN - HISTORY.
Pletnev, V. Lena . Moskva , 1925. 103 p., [4] leaves of plates : LC Card 85-217266
HD9536.S653 S536 1925

STRIKES AND LOCKOUTS - GOLD MINING - SOUTH AFRICA - HISTORY.
The 1922 white mineworker's strike. Salt River [South Africa] [1986?] 44 p. : LC Card 86-195260 DDC 331.89/28223422/0968 19
HD5442.M73 A15 1986

STRIKES AND LOCKOUTS - GREAT BRITAIN.
Hain, Peter, 1950- Political strikes . Harmondsworth, Middlesex, England , New York, N.Y., U. S.A. , 1986. 357 p. ; ISBN 0-670-80601-3 : LC Card 86-216642 DDC 331.89/2941 19
HD5365.A6 H35 1986

Hain, Peter, 1950- Political strikes . Harmondsworth, Middlesex, England , New York , 1986. 357 p. ; ISBN 0-670-80601-3
NYPL [JLD 87-532]

Jackson, Michael Peart. Strikes /. Sussex , New York , c1987. xi, 232 p. ; ISBN 0-312-01194-6 (St. Martin's Press) : LC Card 87-14376 DDC 331.89/2 19
HD5306 .J33 1987

Strikes and lockouts in Canada, 1973 / Labour Data, Labour Canada = Grèves et lock-out au Canada, 1973 / Données sur le travail, Travail Canada. Ottawa : Labour Canada : Information Canada, 1975. 88 p. : ill. ; 28 cm. English and French. ISBN 2-7114-5902-3 (pbk.) LC Card 82-212112
1. Strikes and lockouts - Canada. I. Canada. Labour Data Branch. II. Title: Grèves et lock-out au Canada, 1973.
HD5328 .S77 1975

STRIKES AND LOCKOUTS - LATIN AMERICA - HISTORY - 20TH CENTURY.
Zapata, Francisco. El conflicto sindical en América Latina /. México, D.F. , 1986. 228 p. : ISBN 968-12-0323-2 LC Card 87-105269
HD5330.5.A6 Z36 1986

STRIKES AND LOCKOUTS - MEXICO - HISTORY.
Las Derrotas obreras, 1946-1952 /. México , 1984. 204 p. ; ISBN 968-580-647-0 LC Card 84-255708 DDC 331.88/0972 19
HD6532 .D36 1984 ***NYPL [JLE 86-4685]***

STRIKES AND LOCKOUTS - OFFSHORE ASSEMBLY INDUSTRY - MEXICAN-AMERICAN BORDER REGION.
Carrillo V., Jorge (Carrillo Viveros) Conflictos laborales en la industria maquiladora /. Tijuana, Baja California , 1985. 55 p. : ISBN 968-607-504-6 LC Card 87-117557 DDC 331.4/87/09721 19
HD5331.O33 C37 1985

STRIKES AND LOCKOUTS - POLAND.
A Lengyel földindulás /. Malakoff , New York , 1980. 150 p. ; LC Card 81-177379
HD8537.N783 L45 1980 ***NYPL [JLB 86-24]***

STRIKES AND LOCKOUTS - PUERTO RICO.
Quiñones Rodríguez, Federico, 1940- Sindicalismo y política en Puerto Rico . [Río Piedras, P.R.] [c1977] 147 p., [4] p. of plates : ISBN 84-399-6989-9 LC Card 82-159544
HD6592 .Q56 1977

STRIKES AND LOCKOUTS - RAILROADS - BRAZIL - SÃO PAULO (STATE) - HISTORY.
Leme, Dulce M. Pompêo C. (Dulce Maria Pompêo de Camargo) Trabalhadores ferroviários em greve /. Campinas [Brazil] , 1986. 269 p. : ISBN 85-26-80007-8 : LC Card 87-102922 DDC 331.89/281385/098161 19
HD5354.R12 1906 .S365 1986

STRIKES AND LOCKOUTS - SOUTH AFRICA - MANAGEMENT.
Botha, Henk. How to manage strikes through strategy . Moreletapark , c1986. vi, 101 p. : ISBN 0-620-10384-1 LC Card 87-148504 DDC 658.3/154 19
HD5442.A6 B68 1986

STRIKES AND LOCKOUTS - SPAIN.
Montoro Romero, Ricardo. La inserción en la actividad económica, empleo y paro juvenil /. Barcelona , Madrid , c1985. 191 p. ; ISBN 84-86434-11-4 LC Card 86-186530
HD6276.S672 M65 1985

STRIKES AND LOCKOUTS - SPAIN - CANTABRIA - HISTORY - 20TH CENTURY.
Argos Villar, José Carlos. El movimiento obrero en Cantabria (1955-1977) /. [Santander?] [1982?] 227 p. ; ISBN 84-300-6979-8 LC Card 86-203186
HD8589.C3 A74 1982

STRIKES AND LOCKOUTS - STEVEDORES - LOUISIANA - NEW ORLEANS - HISTORY.
Rosenberg, Daniel, 1953- New Orleans dockworkers . Albany , c1988. x, 233 p. ; ISBN 0-88706-649-6 LC Card 87-10156 DDC 331.7/61387164/0976335 19
HD8039.L82 U664 1988

STRIKES AND LOCKOUTS - SWITZERLAND - HISTORY.
Wandeler, Josef, 1949- Die KPS und die Wirtschaftskämpfe, 1930-1933 . Zürich , c1978. 277 p. : ISBN 3-85854-003-X LC Card 87-409249 DDC 331.89/29494 19
HD5410.A6 W36 1978

STRIKES AND LOCKOUTS - TRANSPORT WORKERS - HAWAII - HISTORY.
Stern, Bernard W., 1912- Rutledge unionism . Honolulu , 1986. x, 147 p. ; LC Card 86-51020 DDC 331/.04138841322/0996931 19
HD6515.T72 H37 1986

STRIKES AND LOCKOUTS - UKRAINE - HISTORY - 20TH CENTURY.
Ovsiîenko, O. F. Krakh zubatovshchyny na Ukraïni /. Kyïv , 1987. 137, [3] p. ; LC Card 87-161669
HD8529.U43 O97 1987

STRIKES AND LOCKOUTS - UNITED STATES.
Hibbs, Douglas A., 1943- The political economy of industrial democracies /. Cambridge, Mass. , 1987. viii, 327 p. : ISBN 0-674-68580-6 LC Card 86-9799 DDC 339.5/09171/3 19
HB3743 .H53 1987 ***NYPL [JLE 87-1430]***

Jackson, Michael Peart. Strikes /. Sussex , New York , c1987. xi, 232 p. ; ISBN 0-312-01194-6 (St. Martin's Press) : LC Card 87-14376 DDC 331.89/2 19
HD5306 .J33 1987

STRIKES AND LOCKOUTS - UNITED STATES - ADDRESSES, ESSAYS, LECTURES.
Vorse, Mary Heaton, 1874-1966. Rebel pen . New York , c1985. 345 p. : ISBN 0-85345-669-0 : LC Card 85-7130 DDC 331.4/0973 19
HD8072 .V755 1985 ***NYPL [JLD 86-2459]***

Striking a balance : the role of the Board of Trade, 1786-1986 : bicentenary lectures / edited by Susan Foreman. London : HMSO, 1986. 76 p. : ill. ; 20 x 21 cm. At head of title: Department of Trade and Industry. Includes bibliographical references. ISBN 0-11-513848-X (pbk.) : LC Card 86-231618 DDC 380.1/06/041 19
1. Great Britain. Board of Trade - History. 2. Great Britain. Dept. of Trade and Industry - History. 3. Great Britain - Commerce - History. 4. Great Britain - Industries - History. I. Foreman, Susan. II. Great Britain. Dept. of Trade and Industry.
HF73.G7 S77 1986

Striking it rich in space /. Logsdon, Tom, 1937- New York , 1988. p. cm. LC Card 87-22294 DDC 332.6/78/0919 19
HD9711.75.A2 L65 1988

Striner, Herbert E. Regaining the lead : policies for economic growth / Herbert E. Striner.2nd ed. Millwood, N.Y. : Associated Faculty Press, c1987. xvii, 205 p. ; 23 cm. Includes bibliographical references and index. ISBN 0-8046-9408-7 (pbk. : alk. paper) : LC Card 86-32218 DDC 338.973 19
1. United States - Economic policy - 1981-. 2. Germany, West - Economic policy - 1974-. 3. Japan - Economic policy - 1945-. 4. Economic policy. I. Title.
HC106.8 .S77 1987

Stringer, Kenneth W. Statistical techniques for analytical review in auditing / Kenneth W. Stringer, Trevor R. Stewart. New York : Wiley, c1986. xii, 301 p. : ill. ; 24 cm. "A Ronald Press publication." Computer program developed by Deloitte Haskins & Sells. Includes index. ISBN 0-471-86076-X : LC Card 85-17874 DDC 657/.45/0285536 19
1. STAR (Computer program). 2. Auditing - Statistical methods - Data processing. 3. Auditing, Internal - Statistical methods - Data processing. I. Stewart, Trevor R. II. Deloitte, Haskins & Sells. III. Title.
HF5667 .S85 1986 ***NYPL [JLE 86-2704]***

STRINGHER, BONALDO, 1854-1930.
Bonelli, Franco. Bonaldo Stringher . [Udine] [c1985] 169 p. : LC Card 85-220896
HJ1156.S77 B66 1985

Strittmatter, Gabriele. Kooperationsstrategien westeuropäischer und japanischer Banken in den ASEAN-Staaten / Gabriele Strittmatter. 1. Aufl. Baden-Baden : Nomos, 1984. 411 p. : ill. ; 23 cm. (Internationale Kooperation. Bd. 26) Summary in English and German. Originally presented as the author's thesis (doctoral)--TH Aachen. Bibliography: p. 389-411. ISBN 3-7890-1051-0 LC Card 86-134027
1. Banks and banking, Japanese - Southeastern Asia. 2. Banks and banking, European - Southeastern Asia. 3. International cooperation. I. Title. II. Series.
HG3324 .S77 1984

Strizek, Gisela Hammers- see Hammers-Strizek, Gisela.

Strizek, Helmut. Europäische Einigung : Bilanz und Perspektiven / Helmut Strizek, Gisela Hammers-Strizek.2., erg. und erw. Aufl. Bonn : Verlag Neue Gesellschaft, c1984. 144 p. ; 22 cm. (Reihe Praktische Demokratie) Bibliography: p. 141-143. ISBN 3-87831-274-1 LC Card 84-173216
1. Europe - Economic integration. 2. Europe - Politics and government. I. Hammers-Strizek, Gisela. II. Title.
HC241 .S72 1984

Ströbele, Wolfgang. Wirtschaftswachstum bei begrenzten Energieressourcen / von Wolfgang Ströbele. Berlin : Duncker & Humblot, c1984. 173 p. : ill. ; 24 cm. (Beiträge zur angewandten Wirtschaftsforschung. Bd. 13) Bibliography: p. 158-173. ISBN 3-428-05541-1 LC Card 84-176734
1. Economic development - Mathematical models. 2. Power resources - Mathematical models. 3. Nonrenewable natural resources - Mathematical models. 4. Production functions (Economic theory). I. Title.
HD84 .S747 1984

Strohmeyer, John, 1924- Crisis in Bethlehem : big steel's struggle to survive / by John Strohmeyer. New York, N.Y., U. S.A. : Penguin Books, 1987, c1986. xii, 244 p. ; 20 cm. Reprint. Originally published: 3rd ed. Bethesda, Md. : Adler & Adler, 1986. Includes index. ISBN 0-14-010370-8 (pbk.) LC Card 87-11835 DDC 338.7/669142/0974822 19
1. Bethlehem Steel Corporation - History. 2. Steel industry and trade - United States - History. 3. Trade-unions - Iron and steel workers - Pennsylvania - Bethlehem - History. 4. Iron and steel workers - Pennsylvania - Bethlehem - History. I. Title.
HD9519.B4 S87 1987

Stroim Kuzbass / [sostavitel´ A.M. Titova ; redaktor V.V. Bakatin]. Kemerovo : Kemerovskoe knizhnoe izd-vo, 1984. 417 p., [56] p. of plates : ill. (some col.) ; 24 cm. Bibliography: p. [415] LC Card 84-103662
1. Kuznetsk Basin (R.S.F.S.R.) - Industries. 2. Kuznetsk Basin (R.S.F.S.R.) - Economic conditions. I. Titova, A. M. (Aleksandra Mikhaĭlovna). II. Bakatin, V. V.
HC337.R852 K8975 1984

Stroitsîa Nechernozem'e /. Chanturiîa, V. K. (Vladimir Kapitonovich) Moskva , 1980. 94 p. ; LC Card 81-135603
HD9715.S73 N63 1980

Strøm, Steinar. Førsund, Finn R. Environmental economics and management . London , New York , c1988. 307 p. : ISBN 0-85664-900-7 LC Card 87-9179 DDC 363.7/0525 19
HC79.E5 F64 1988

Strom Thurmond Institute. The Situation and outlook for water resource use in South Carolina, 1985-2000 . [Clemson, S.C.] [1985] ix, 95 leaves : LC Card 86-622603 DDC 333.91/13/09757 19
HD1694.S6 S57 1985

Strombach, Manfred E., 1950- Qualitätszirkel und Kleingruppenarbeit als praktische Organisationsentwicklung /. Frankfurt am Main , 1984. vii, 149 p. : ISBN 3-7824-0348-7 LC Card 85-131916
HD66 .Q332 1984

Stromberg, Ann Helton. Women working . Mountain View, Calif. , c1988. xv, 431 p. : ISBN 0-87484-744-3 (pbk.) LC Card 87-3215 DDC 331.4/0973 19
HD6095 .W6976 1988

Stromerzeugungskosten im internationalen Vergleich / Dieter Schmitt ... [et al.] ; mit je einem Anhang von J. Klook und O. Rosenberg, sowie P.H. Suding und M. Melzer. München : R. Oldenbourg, 1986. ca. 450 p. : ill. ; 21 cm. (Aktuelle Fragen der Energiewirtschaft. Bd. 29) Bibliography: p. 305-311 (2nd group). ISBN 3-486-26246-7 LC Card 87-135285 DDC 338.4/336362 19
1. Electric utilities - Rates. I. Schmitt, Dieter, 1939-. II. Series.
HD9685.A2 S76 1986

Strong, Norman, 1954- Information and capital markets / Norman Strong and Martin Walker. Oxford, UK ; New York, NY, USA : B. Blackwell, 1987. x, 222 p. : ill. ; 24 cm. Bibliography: p. [208]-215. Includes index. ISBN 0-631-13834-X : LC Card 86-31721 DDC 332/.041 19
1. Capital market. 2. Uncertainty. 3. Rational expectations (Economic theory). I. Walker, Martin, 1953-. II. Title.
HG4523 .S77 1987

Strong Words (Firm) But the world goes on the same . Whitley Bay, Tyne & Wear , 1979. 106 p. : LC Card 81-107503
HD8399.D872 B87 1979

Strongman, John, 1947- Takeuchi, Kenji, 1932- The world copper industry . Washington, D.C., U. S.A. , c1986. xxix, 179 p. : ISBN 0-8213-0852-1 LC Card 86-26554 DDC 338.2/743 19
HD9539.C6 T35 1986

Strother, George B., 1918- Social science approaches to business behavior /. New York , 1987. vii, 183 p. : ISBN 0-8240-8201-X (alk. paper) : LC Card 86-25802 DDC 658.4 19
HD58.7 .S66 1987

STROUSBERG, BETHEL HENRY, 1823-1884.
Voigt, Wolfgang. Der Eisenbahnkönig, oder, Rumänien lag in Linden . München , 1982. 142 p. : ISBN 3-923126-15-8 (pbk.) LC Card 87-672921
HD7289.5.R1 V64x 1982

Strovskiĭ, L. E. (Leonid Evgen´evich) Bakanov, K. P. (Konstantin Pavlovich) Sovershenstvovanie organizatsii truda na predpriîatiîakh chernoĭ metallurgii /. Moskva , 1981. 47 p. ; LC Card 82-104389
HD9525.S652 B355 1981

Strub, Sean O'Brien. Lydenberg, Steven D. Rating America's corporate conscience . Reading, Mass. , c1986. x, 499 p. : ISBN 0-201-15886-8 : LC Card 86-8064 DDC 338.7/4/0973 19
HD60.5.U5 L93 1986
NYPL [*R-Econ. 87-1830]

Structural adjustment and growth : papers presented at the annual sessions, 7-8 December 1985, B.M.I.C.H.-Colombo. Colombo, Sri Lanka : Economics Dept., University of Colombo, 1986. 170 p. ; 27 cm. At head of title: The Sri Lanka Association of Economists. Includes bibliographies. LC Card 86-903207 DDC 338.9549/3 19
1. Sri Lanka - Economic policy - Congresses. 2. Sri Lanka - Economic conditions - Congresses. 3. Economic policy - Congresses. I. Sri Lanka Association of Economists. II. University of Colombo. Economics Dept.
HC424 .S77 1986

Structural adjustment and multinational enterprises. Paris : Organisation for Economic Co-operation and Development ; [Washington, D.C. : OECD Publications and Information Center, distributor], 1985. 68 p. ; 23 cm. Includes bibliographies. ISBN 92-64-12770-4 (pbk.) : LC Card 86-214254 DDC 338.8/8 19
1. International business enterprises. I. Organisation for Economic Co-operation and Development.
HD2755.5 .S85 1985

Structural analysis in the social sciences . (1) Intercorporate relations . Cambridge [Cambridgeshire] , New York , 1987. x, 330 p. : ISBN 0-521-33503-5 LC Card 87-6388 DDC 338.7 19
HD2741 .I585 1987

Structural budget deficits in the federal government : causes, consequences, and remedies / edited by Khi V. Thai. Lanham,

Md. : University Press of America, c1987. x, 294 p. : ill. ; 22 cm. Includes bibliographies. ISBN 0-8191-6138-1 (alk. paper) : LC Card 86-33961 DDC 339.5/23/0973 19
1. Budget deficits - United States. I. Thai, Khi V., 1941-.
HJ2052 .S74 1987

Structural change and interdependence. Industry in the 1980s . New York , 1985. xii, 228 p. : ISBN 92-1-106207-1 (pbk.) LC Card 86-227928 DDC 338.09 19
HD9720.5 .I53 1985

Structural change in an urban industrial region : the northeastern Ohio case / edited by David L. McKee, Richard E. Bennett. New York : Praeger, 1987. ix, 255 p. ; 25 cm. Bibliography: p. 245-250. Includes index. ISBN 0-275-92353-3 (alk. paper) : LC Card 86-30652 DDC 330.9771/3043 19
1. Ohio - Economic conditions - Congresses. 2. Ohio - Economic policy - Congresses. I. McKee, David L. II. Bennett, Richard E. (Richard Earl), 1940-.
HC107.O3 S85 1987

Structural contradictions of the colonial state . Wayne, Jack, Ph.D. [Toronto, Canada] , c1981. 23, [5] p. ; ISBN 0-7727-2825-9 (pbk.) LC Card 86-193819 DDC 330.9678/203 19
HC885 .W39 1981

Structural decoration. H.W. Johns Manufacturing Co. [New York] c1882. 32 p. : LC Card 86-224190
HD9660.P254 H174 1882

Structural dimensions of poverty in India /. Gupta, S. P. (Shiv Prakash), 1957- Delhi, India , 1987. xii, 427 p. : LC Card 87-901423 DDC 362.5/0954 19
HC440.P6 G86 1987

Structural distortions and adjustment programmes in the poor countries of Africa : a challenge for development policy / Hartmut Brandt ... [et al.]. Berlin : German Development Institute, 1985. xxxi, 377 p. : ill. ; 24 cm. (Occasional papers of the German Development Institute (GDI) . no. 85) Includes bibliographies. ISBN 3-88985-042-1 LC Card 86-226845 DDC 338.967 19
1. Africa, Sub-Saharan - Economic policy. 2. Africa, Sub-Saharan - Economic conditions - 1960-. I. Brandt, Hartmut. II. Series: Schriften des Deutschen Instituts für Entwicklungspolitik, DIE , Bd. 85.
HC800 .S79 1985

Structural dynamics of industrial policy /. Industrial policy. New Brunswick, N.J. (U. S.A.) , c1987. x, 208 p. : ISBN 0-88738-679-2 (pbk.) LC Card 87-5023 DDC 338.9 19
HD3611 .I385 1987

STRUCTURAL ENGINEERING - MANAGEMENT. see **ENGINEERING - MANAGEMENT.**

STRUCTURAL MATERIALS. see **BUILDING MATERIALS.**

The structural pest control industry . Pinto, Lawrence J. Vienna, Va. (8150 Leesburg Pike, Suite 1100, Vienna 22180) , 1981. 26, [10] p. : LC Card 86-214768 DDC 338.4/762896/0973 19
HD9718.5.P473 U663 1981

Structural reform, stabilization, and growth in Turkey /. Kopits, George. Washington, D.C. , c1987. v, 46 p. : ISBN 0-939934-84-1 (pbk.) : LC Card 87-3583 DDC 338.9561 19
HC492 .K67 1987

Structural reforms and wage setting across sectors . Riveros C., Luis. Santiago , 1984. 37, [5], 13 p. ; ***NYPL [JLF 87-136]***

The structural transformation of employment in Wisconsin, 1960-1980 /. Tienda, Marta. Madison, WI (Rm. 245, 30 N. Murray St., Madison 53715) [1986] ii, 47 p. ; LC Card 86-623091 DDC 331.12/09775 19
HD5725.W5 T54 1986

STRUCTURAL UNEMPLOYMENT. see **UNEMPLOYMENT, TECHNOLOGICAL.**

Structure /. Confédération nationale des travailleurs de Guinée. [Conakry] [1964?] 23 p. : LC Card 82-220475
HD8826.A5 C66 1964

Structure and management of the gilt-edged securities market in India. 1st ed. New Delhi : Corporate Investment Research and Consultancy Bureau, 1983. v, 186 p. : ill. ; 22 cm. Includes index. Study covers the period, 1950/1951-1980/1981. Bibliography: p. [178]-181. LC Card 84-901424 DDC 332.63/2044 19
1. Corporate Investment Research and Consultancy Bureau (India). 2. Government securities - India. 3. Securities - India.
HG5735 .S77 1983 ***NYPL [JLD 87-871]***

La structure économique et sociale d'Haïti /. Francisque, Édouard. [Port-au-Prince, Haïti] [1986] 255 p. ; LC Card 87-113952
HC153 .F72 1986

Structure et perspectives de l'artisanat et de la petite industrie du sud-ouest de la Haute-Volta : éléments d'un programme de promotion / Dorothee Fiedler ... [et al.] ; traduction, Anne-Marie Geyer. Berlin (West) : Institut allemand de développement, [1978] xxvi, 253 p. : ill. ; 30 cm. "Juillet 1978." Bibliography: p. 251-253. LC Card 85-118488
1. Artisans - Burkina Faso. 2. Small business - Burkina Faso. 3. Industrial promotion - Burkina Faso. I. Fiedler, Dorothee. II. Deutsches Institut für Entwicklungspolitik.
HD2346.B82 S77 1978

Structure industrielle et sous-traitance / C. Berthomieu ... [et al.]. Paris : Presses universitaires de France, c1983. 243 p. : ill. ; 25 cm. (Travaux et recherches du Laboratoire associé no 301, C.N.R.S. - Université de Nice, 0751-0497) Bibliography: p. 242-243. ISBN 2-13-038182-0 : LC Card 84-128203 DDC 331/.01 19
1. Subcontracting. 2. International division of labor. I. Berthomieu, Claude.
HD2381 .S77 1983 ***NYPL [JLE 86-1624]***

The Structure of British industry / edited by Peter Johnson. 2nd ed. London ; Boston : Allen & Unwin, 1988. p. cm. Includes index. ISBN 0-04-338146-4 (alk. paper) LC Card 87-18803 DDC 338.0941 19
1. Great Britain - Industries. I. Johnson, P. S.
HC256.6 .S76 1988

Structure of earnings, 1978/79 : principal results. Lønstrukturen 1978/79 . Luxembourg , Washington, D.C. , <1983-1986. v. <2-3, 6-7, 10 > ; ISBN 92-825-3817-6 (set) : LC Card 86-211360
HD5014.5 .L66 1983

Structure of employment, earnings, and assets in India . Ghadoliya, M. K. (Mahendra Kumar) Delhi , 1986. xi, 248 p. : LC Card 86-903221 DDC 331.12/5/09544 19
HD5820.U33 G47 1986

The Structure of the informal sector in Mongu (Western Province) and its potential for employment creation : report to the Government of Zambia, the Office of the Member of the Central Committee, Western Province / by the Southern African Team for Employment Promotion (SATEP) of the International Labour Office. Lusaka, Zambia : ILO, [1982] iii, 44, 10 p. ; 30 cm. Includes bibliographical references. "August 1982." LC Card 87-980490 DDC 331.12/51381 19
1. Informal sector (Economics) - Zambia - Mongu District. 2. Labor supply - Zambia - Mongu District. I. Southern African Team for Employment Promotion. II. Zambia. Office of the Member of the Central Committee, Western Province.
HD2346.Z292 M657 1982

Structured chaos : the process of productivity advance / Richard Blandy ... [et al.]. Melbourne ; New York : Oxford University Press, 1985. viii, 111 p. : ill. ; 23 cm. "Published in conjunction with the Australian Productivity Council and the National Institute of Labour Studies." Bibliography: p. 101-107. Includes index. ISBN 0-19-554687-3 LC Card 86-222312 DDC 338/.06/0994 19
1. Industrial productivity - Australia. 2. Labor productivity - Australia. 3. Industry and state - Australia. I. Blandy, Richard, 1938-. II. Australian Productivity Council. III. National Institute of Labour Studies (Australia).
HC610.I52 S77 1985

Structured COBOL with business applications /. Myers, Stanley E., 1926- Englewood Cliffs, NJ , c1988. xi, 772 p. : ISBN 0-13-854167-1 (pbk.) : LC Card 86-30646 DDC 005.13/3 19
HF5548.5.C2 M94 1988

Structured hiring : getting the right person for the right job. New York, NY, U. S.A. : Alexander Hamilton Institute, c1987. viii leaves, 144 p. : ill. ; 28 cm. (Modern business reports) ISBN 0-86604-221-0 (pbk.) LC Card 87-156398 DDC 658.3/112 19
1. Recruiting of employees. 2. Employment interviewing. 3. Employee selection. 4. Executives - Recruiting. I. Alexander Hamilton Institute (U. S.). II. Series.
HF5549.5.R44 S83 1987

Les structures économiques et sociales dans le Brionnais oriental aux XVIIe et XVIIIe siècles /. Durix, Pierre. Dijon [1983] xxxiii, 608 p. : LC Card 86-200732
HC277.B68 D87 1983

STRUCTURES, MODULAR. see **MODULAR CONSTRUCTION.**

Les Structures productives d'une région périphérique : l'est du Québec, 1896-1980 / collectif de recherche, Benoît Beaucage ... [et al.]. Rimouski : Université du Québec à Rimouski, c1984. xi, 718 p. : ill. ; 28 cm. (Documents généraux du GRIDEQ . no 11) "Juin 1984." Bibliography: p. 710-713. ISBN 2-920270-27-3 LC Card 85-132709 DDC 330.9714/77 19
1. Gaspé Peninsula (Québec) - Economic conditions. I. Beaucage, Benoît. II. Université du Québec à Rimouski. Groupe de recherche interdisciplinaire en développement de l'Est du Québec. III. Series.
HC117.G37 S78 1984

Struff, Richard. Räumliche Einkommens-, Preis- und Verbrauchsunterschiede in der Bundesrepublik Deutschland / von Richard Struff und Ulrich von Wilamowitz. Bonn : Forschungsgesellschaft für Agrarpolitik und Agrarsoziologie, 1983. xi, 258 p. : ill. ; 21 cm. (Schriftenreihe der Forschungsgesellschaft für Agrarpolitik und Agrarsoziologie e.V., 0532-2359 . 262) Bibliography: p. 237-258. ISBN 3-88488-262-7 LC Card 84-196141
1. Germany (West) - Economic conditions - 1974- - Regional disparities. I. Wilamowitz-Moellendorf, Ulrich von. II. Title. III. Series.
HC286.7 .S836 1983

The struggle for equality . Bernstein, Deborah. New York , 1987. x, 208 p. : ISBN 0-275-92139-5 (alk. paper) : LC Card 86-8203 DDC 305.4/3/0095694 19
HD6182.2 .B47 1986 ***NYPL [JLE 87-1462]***

The struggle for influence . LeMay, Michael C., 1941- Lanham , c1985. xv, 452 p. : ISBN 0-8191-4653-6 (alk. paper) : LC Card 85-6105 DDC 323.1/73 19
E184.A1 L44 1985 ***NYPL [IE 85-3562]***

Struggle for the city : migrant labor, capital, and the state in urban Africa / Frederick Cooper, editor. Beverly Hills : Sage Publications, c1983. 319 p. : ill. ; 23 cm. (Sage series on African modernization and development. v. 8) Includes bibliographies. CONTENTS. - Urban space, industrial time, and wage labor in Africa / Frederick Cooper -- Workers as criminals / William Worger -- Productivity and protest / Jeff Crisp -- Here everyone walked with fear / Jeanne Penvenne -- A colonial state and an African petty bourgeoisie / Luise White -- De la calabasse à la production en série / Gerard Salem -- Work, migration, and class in western Nigeria / Sara S. Berry -- Struggle from the margins / Colin Murray. ISBN 0-8039-2067-9 LC Card 83-11196 DDC 305.5/62/096 19
1. Labor and laboring classes - Africa - Addresses, essays, lectures. 2. Cities and towns - Africa - Addresses, essays, lectures. 3. Social classes - Africa - Addresses, essays, lectures. 4. Africa - Social conditions - Addresses, essays, lectures. I. Cooper, Frederick, 1947-.
HD8774 .S87 1983 ***NYPL [JLD 83-3496]***

Struktur ausländischer Bankensysteme. (Heft 19) Diwok, Fritz. Struktur des Bankwesens in Österreich /. Frankfurt am Main , c1982. 142 p. ; ISBN 3-7819-2771-7 LC Card 83-190921 DDC 332.1/09436 19
HG3008 .D59 1982

Die Struktur der internationalen Liquiditätskrise seit dem ersten Ölpreisschub, 1973/1974 . Dehmel, Alexander. Frankfurt am Main , New York , c1985. x, 221 p. : ISBN 3-8204-8941-X LC Card 86-108628
HG178 .D44 1985

Struktur des Bankwesens in Österreich /. Diwok, Fritz. Frankfurt am Main , c1982. 142 p. ; ISBN 3-7819-2771-7 LC Card 83-190921 DDC

332.1/09436 19
HG3008 .D59 1982

Die Struktur des von der Bundesrepublik Deutschland ausgehenden Nordatlantik-Personen-Luftverkehrs : Bericht über eine Fluggastbefragung auf Nordatlantikflügen, April 1959-März 1960. [Frankfurt am Main] : Deutsches Institut für Luftverkehrsstatistik e.V., [1963] 165 p. : ill. ; 30 cm. Summary in English and German. Questionnaire in pocket. LC Card 85-126310
1. Aeronautics, Commercial - Germany (West) - Passenger traffic. I. Deutsches Institut für Luftverkehrsstatistik.
HE9787.5.G4 S77 1963

Struktur und Arbeitsweise von Arbeitsverwaltungen in EG-Ländern Frankreich, Belgien, Italien : Studien von BA-Mitarbeitern im Rahmen von Personalaustauschprogrammen / Brigitte Schmidt ... [et al.]. Nürnberg : Institut für Arbeitsmarkt- und Berufsforschung der Bundesanstalt für Arbeit, 1982. 206 p. : ill. ; 21 cm. (Beiträge zur Arbeitsmarkt- und Berufsforschung, 0173-6574 . 69) CONTENTS. - Struktur und Arbeitsweise der französischen Arbeitsverwaltung (einschliesslich Berufsbildungssystem) / Brigitte Schmidt, Peter Schifferer -- Die Arbeitsverwaltung in Belgien / Marcel Gimbel -- Die Arbeitsverwaltung in Italien / Martha Mangelmann ... [et al.]. LC Card 83-174401
1. Labor policy - France. 2. Labor policy - Belgium. 3. Labor policy - Italy. I. Schmidt, Brigitte. II. Bundesanstalt für Arbeit (Germany). III. Series.
HD8431 .S77 1982

Struktur und Dynamik der Grosshandelsbetriebe im Ballungsraum Stuttgart /. Schuler, Friedrich Joachim. Marburg/Lahn , 1986. xiv, 156 p. : ISBN 3-88353-027-1 LC Card 87-116934 DDC 381/.2/094347 19
HF5421.5.G4 S43 1986

Struktur und Dynamik der Wirtschaft : Beiträge zum 60. Geburtstag von Karl Brandt / herausgegeben von Harald Enke, Walter Köhler, Wilfried Schulz. Freiburg im Breisgau : R. Haufe, c1983. 530 p. : ill. ; 21 cm. Includes bibliographies. "Verzeichnis der Veröffentlichungen von Karl Brandt": p. 525-530. ISBN 3-448-01348-X : LC Card 83-184564 DDC 330 19
1. Economics. 2. Microeconomics. 3. Economic development. 4. Economics - Statistical methods. 5. Brandt, Karl, 1923-. I. Brandt, Karl, 1923-. II. Enke, Harald. III. Köhler, Walter. IV. Schulz, Wilfried.
HB44 .S77 1983

Struktur- und Entwicklungsprobleme der Industrie Perus / Werner Mikus (Hrsg.). Heidelberg : Esprint, c1985. 338 p. : ill. ; 21 cm. (Heidelberger Dritte welt Studien . Bd. 20) One contribution in Spanish. Summaries in English. Includes bibliographies. CONTENTS. - Standortbedingungen der Industrie in einem Entwicklungsland /. Jürgen Gernert -- Transnationale Einflüsse auf Bergbau und Industrie Perus im Vergleich zu den übrigen Ländern des Andespaktes / Werner Mikus -- Kleinindustrie und Handwerk in Peru / Thomas Asmus -- Factores determinantes del comportamiento de la pequeña industria en la ciudad de Trujillo 1981-82 / Roberto Rodríguez Vásquez. ISBN 3-88326-165-3 LC Card 86-108518 DDC 338.0985 19
1. Peru - Industries. 2. Peru - Economic conditions - 1968-. I. Mikus, Werner. II. Series.
HC227 .S77 1985

Struktur und Wachstum: Reihe Industrie. For additional listing of contents, see Old Catalog.
(Heft 35) Breitenacher, Michael. Strukturwandlungen und Entwicklungsperspektiven im Musikinstrumentenbau, in der Spielwaren- und Sportgeräteherstellung und in der Schmuckindustrie /. Berlin , c1984. 188 p. : ISBN 3-428-05566-7 LC Card 84-186644
HD9999.M83 G32 1984

(Heft 38) Berger, Manfred, 1921- Elektrotechnische Industrie . Berlin , c1984. 261 p. : ISBN 3-428-05674-4 LC Card 85-137543
HD9696.A3 G42 1984 ***NYPL [TB (Struktur und Wachstum. Reihe Industrie. Heft 38)]***

(Heft 40) Mayer, Ralph-Dieter. Stahl- und Leichtmetallbau, Schienenfahrzeugbau . Berlin , c1985. 352 p. : ISBN 3-428-05771-6 LC Card 85-161158
HD9523.5 .M3 1985

(Heft 41) Grefermann, Klaus. Papier- und Pappeverarbeitung . Berlin , c1986. 209 p. : ISBN 3-428-06050-4 LC Card 86-233133
HD9833.5 .G73 1986

Struktur von Arbeitseinkommen . Dworschak, Franz. Idstein , 1986. ix, 408 p. : ISBN 3-925196-16-1 LC Card 86-225347
HB523 .D86 1986

Struktura narodnogo khoziaĭstva v usloviiakh intensifikatsii ėkonomiki / otvetstvennyĭ redaktor V.P. Loginov. Moskva : "Nauka", 1986. 267 p. ; 21 cm. At head of title: Akademiia nauk SSSR. Ordena Trudovogo Krasnogo Znameni Institut ėkonomiki. Includes bibliographical references. LC Card 86-212596
1. Soviet Union - Economic conditions - 1976-. 2. Soviet Union - Economic policy - 1981-. I. Loginov, V. P. II. Institut ėkonomiki (Akademiia nauk SSSR).
HC336.25 .S795 1986

Struktura obshchestvennogo proizvodstva i tendentsii ee izmeneniia : tematicheskiĭ sbornik / [otvetstvennyĭ za vypusk A.U. Khomra]. Kiev : In-t ėkonomiki AN USSR, 1979. 113 p. ; 20 cm. Includes bibliographical references. LC Card 81-130407
1. Industrial productivity - Ukraine. 2. Ukraine - Economic conditions - 1945-. I. Khomra, Aleksandr Ul'ianovich. II. Instytut ekonomiky (Akademiia nauk Ukraïns'koï RSR).
HC337.U53 I527 1979

Strukturanalyse Ruhrgebiet : Bilanz, Kritik, Perspektiven : Dokumentation einer gemeinsamen Veranstaltung des Kommunalverbandes Ruhrgebiet und des Innovationsförderungs- und Technologietransfer-Zentrum der Hochschulen des Ruhrgebiets am 23./24. März 1983 in Gelsenkirchen / Leitung, Werner Glock, Andreas Schlieper. [Essen] : Der Kommunalverband, [1983?] 185 p. : ill. ; 30 cm. LC Card 86-218075
1. Labor supply - Germany (West) - Ruhr (Region) - Congresses. 2. Labor supply - Germany (West) - Ruhr (Region) - Effect of technological innovations on - Congresses. 3. Ruhr (Germany : Region) - Economic conditions - Congresses. I. Glock, Werner. II. Schlieper, Andreas. III. Kommunalverband Ruhrgebiet. IV. Innovationsförderungs- und Technologietransfer-Zentrum der Hochschulen des Ruhrgebiets.
HD5760.R84 S77 1983

Strukturanpassung in schrumpfenden Branchen . Pascha, Werner. Berlin , c1986. xx, 364 p. : ISBN 3-428-05983-2 LC Card 86-151590
HB41 .S3 Bd. 42 HD9866.J32

Strukturberichterstattung Ruhrgebiet. Zimmermann, Horst, 1934- Die Gemeindefinanzen im Ruhrgebiet . Essen , 1983. xvi, 153 p. : ISBN 3-923494-28-9 LC Card 83-228289
HJ9493.5.R8 Z76 1983

Strukturelemente der Weltgesellschaft : Studien zu Konflikt und Kooperation in den Nord-Süd-Beziehungen / Thomas Siebold, Rainer Tetzlaff (Hrsg.). Frankfurt am Main : A. Metzner, 1981. v, 356 p. : ill. ; 24 cm. (Darstellungen zur internationalen Politik und Entwicklungspolitik, 0173-1270 . Bd. 7) Includes bibliographies. CONTENTS. - "Weltgesellschaft," Trugbild oder Wirklichkeit / Rainer Tetzlaff -- Direktinvestitionen in Länder der Dritten Welt / Uli Post, Heinz-H. Schneiders -- Die Submetropole in der Weltgesellschaft / Peter Körner -- Internationale Entwicklungsagenturen in der Weltgesellschaft / Gero Maass -- Die Auseinandersetzung über das Prinzip wirtschaftlicher Souveränität als völkerrechtlicher Ausdruck von Konflikt und Kooperation in der Weltgesellschaft / Alphons Studier -- Die Nachrichtenmedien im Nord-Süd-Konflikt / Thomas Siebold. ISBN 3-7875-1727-8 LC Card 83-190809
1. International economic relations. 2. Developing countries - Foreign economic relations. 3. Investments, Foreign - Developing countries. I. Siebold, Thomas, 1953-. II. Tetzlaff, Rainer. III. Series.
HF1411 .S845 1981

Struktureller und funktionaler Pluralismus in der öffentlichen Verwaltung /. Wersebe, Hilmar von, 1943- Frankfurt am Main , New York , c1986. 100 p. : ISBN 3-8204-9136-8 LC Card 86-229888
HD58.7 .W36 1986

Strukturen und Funktionen des informellen Sektors in Ghana . Burchards, Eckehard. Hamburg , 1983. vii, 138 p. : ISBN 3-923519-54-0 LC Card 83-214699 DDC 381 19
HD2346.G42 A243 1983

Strukturformen und Funktionsleistungen sozialer Systeme . Geser, Hans. Opladen , c1983. 275 p. : ISBN 3-531-11612-6 :
NYPL [JLE 87-1162]

Strukturnye sdvigi v mirovom kapitalisticheskom khoziaĭstve / [avtory V.I. Filippov ... et al. ; otvetstvennyĭ redaktor V.D. Shchetinin]. Kiev : Naukova dumka, 1985. 295 p. ; 21 cm. At head of title: Akademiia nauk Ukrainskoĭ SSR. Institut sotsial'nykh i ėkonomicheskikh problem zarubezhnykh stran. Includes bibliographical references and index. LC Card 86-105339
1. Economic history - 1971-. I. Filipov, Volodymyr Ivanovych. II. Shchetinin, Valentin Dmitrievich. III. Instytut sotsial'nykh i ekonomichnykh problem zarubizhnykh kraïn (Akademiia nauk Ukraïns'koï RSR).
HC59 .S8345 1985 ***NYPL [*QIP 87-3473]***

Strukturpolitik als Dimension der Vollbeschäftigungspolitik / Herausgeber, Helmut Kramer, Felix Butschek. Stuttgart : G. Fischer, c1983. 103 p. : ill. ; 24 cm. English and German. Papers presented at a Symposium organized by the Österreichisches Institut für Wirtschaftsforschung, 1981. Bibliography: p. 23-25. CONTENTS. - The world economic slowdown since the 1970's / Charles P. Kindleberger -- Options of small economies during the crisis / Erik Lundberg -- Positive Strukturanpassung als wirtschaftspolitische Herausforderung / Wolfgang Michalski -- Neo-Fordism or flexible specialization / Charles F. Sabel -- Ansätze für die Diskussion / Felix Butschek -- Ökonomische Determinanten des Strukturwandels / Kurt Rothschild, Karl Aiginger -- Möglichkeiten strukturorientierter Nachfragepolitik / Gunther Tichy, Stephan Schulmeister -- Innovationsstrategien / Arnold Schmidt, Ewald Volk -- Institutionelle und finanzielle Probleme der Strukturpolitik / Helmut Frisch, Heinz Handler. ISBN 3-437-50276-X : LC Card 83-233394
1. Full employment policies - Congresses. I. Kramer, Helmut. II. Butschek, Felix. III. Österreichisches Institut für Wirtschaftsforschung.
HD5706 .S82 1983

Strukturpolitik für traditionelle Industriezweige in Japan /. Laumer, Helmut. Berlin , c1985. 173 p. : ISBN 3-428-05920-4 LC Card 86-151482
HD3616.J32 L38 1985

Strukturpolitische Probleme der Automobil-Industrie unter dem Aspekt des Wettbewerbs / herausgegeben von Burkhardt Röper. Berlin : Duncker & Humblot, c1985. 247 p. : ill. ; 24 cm. (Schriften des Vereins für Socialpolitik, Gesellschaft für Wirtschafts- und Sozialwissenschaften . n.F., Bd. 151) Papers presented at a meeting of the Arbeitsgruppe Wettbewerb, March 31-April 1, 1982, in Salzburg. CONTENTS. - Strukturpolitische Probleme der Kfz-Industrie aus der Sicht eines in Europa in mehreren Ländern tätigen Konzerns / Robert A. Lutz -- Der Einfluss steigender Energiepreise auf Wachstums-, Struktur- und Wettbewerbsbedingungen der deutschen Automobilindustrie / Hartmut Berg -- Auswirkungen des Strukturwandels in der Automobilindustrie auf Kfz-Zulieferunternehmen / Annerose Iber-Schade -- Struktur und Wettbewerb in der Automobilindustrie aus der Sicht des Bundeskartellamtes / Ernst Niederleithinger -- Kostenrelevante Wettbewerbsfaktoren der Automobilindustrie im internationalen Vergleich / Edzard Reuter -- Herstellung und Vertrieb von Einspritzsystemen für Dieselmotoren / Georg Mosing -- Strukturpolitische Probleme in der Kfz-Industrie aus der Sicht des Bundesministeriums für Wirtschaft / Dieter Wolf. ISBN 3-428-05924-7 LC Card 86-165212 DDC 338.4/76292/094 19
1. Automobile industry and trade - Europe - Congresses. I. Röper, Burkhardt. II. Gesellschaft für Wirtschafts- und Sozialwissenschaften, Verein für Socialpolitik. Wirtschaftspolitischer Ausschuss. Arbeitsgruppe Wettbewerb. III. Series.
HD9710.E82 S77 1985

Strukturwandel des Ausländerproblems : Trends, Modelle, Perspektiven / J. Chr. Papalekas, Herausgeber. Bochum : Studienverlag N. Brockmeyer, c1986. 309 p. : ill. ; 21 cm. Includes bibliographies. ISBN 3-88339-529-3 LC Card 87-121913 DDC 331.6/2/0943 19
1. Alien labor - Germany, West. 2. Alien labor -

Government policy - Germany (West). 3. Labor supply - Germany, West. I. Papalekas, J. Chr. (Johannes Chr.).
HD8458.A2 S786 1986

Strukturwandel und realer Wechselkurs . Heitger, Bernhard. Tübingen , c1983. vii, 115 p. : ISBN 3-16-344735-X : LC Card 84-125132
HG3823 .H43 1983

Strukturwandel und Strukturpolitik . Hübl, Lothar. Hannover , 1983. 104 p. : LC Card 84-126938
HC286.7 .H83 1983

Strukturwandel unter verschlechterten Rahmenbedingungen . Gerstenberger, Wolfgang. Berlin , c1984. 255 p. : ISBN 3-428-05567-5 LC Card 84-180150
HC286.7 .G46 1984

Strukturwandlungen und Entwicklungsperspektiven im Musikinstrumentenbau, in der Spielwaren- und Sportgeräteherstellung und in der Schmuckindustrie /. Breitenacher, Michael. Berlin , c1984. 188 p. : ISBN 3-428-05566-7 LC Card 84-186644
HD9999.M83 G32 1984

Strumenti e ricerche .
(11) Rapporto ISFOL 1985 . Milano, Italy , c1985. 533 p. : LC Card 86-156267
HD5715.5.I8 R393 1985

(3) Organizzazione del lavoro, mobilità e aspetti formativi nella contrattazione . Milano, Italy , c1982. 172 p. ; LC Card 83-106874
HD6709 .O73 1982

Strumenti (Savona, Italy) .
(3) Vallega, Adalberto. Dai porti al sistema portuale . Savona , 1985. 320 p. : LC Card 87-139096
HE558.L44 V35 1985

Strumilin, S. G. (Stanislav Gustavovich), 1877-1974. Na planovom fronte / S.G. Strumilin. Moskva : Izd-vo "Nauka", 1980. 463 p. ; 27 cm. At head of title: Akademii͡a nauk SSSR. Includes bibliographical references. LC Card 81-135522
1. Soviet Union - Economic policy - 1917-1928. 2. Soviet Union - Economic policy - 1928-1932. 3. Central planning - Soviet Union - History. I. Title.
HC335.2 .S83 1980

Struminski, Julius B. Ost-Wirtschaftsreport Digest . Düsseldorf , Genève , 1977. 119 p. ; LC Card 84-154293
HC244 .O726 1977

Strumpel, Burkhard.
Gewandelte Werte, erstarrte Strukturen . Bonn , c1985. ix, 329 p. : ISBN 3-87831-423-X LC Card 86-117688 DDC 330/.0943 19
HD8451 .G54 1985

Katona, George, 1901- [Aspirations and affluence. Dutch.] Het psychologisch klimaat van de economie in de Verenigde Staten en West-Europa /. Utrecht , 1974. 247 p. ; ISBN 90-274-5826-X ***NYPL [JLD 86-295]***

Klipstein, Michael von. Der Überdruss am Überfluss . München , c1984. 212 p. : ISBN 3-7892-7194-2 LC Card 84-174408
HD6957.G35 K56 1984

Wenig Arbeit--aber viel zu tun . Opladen , c1985. 195 p. : ISBN 3-531-11724-6 ***NYPL [JLE 86-1602]***

Struttura industriale e politiche macroeconomiche in Italia / a cura di Innocenzo Cipolletta. Bologna : Il Mulino, c1986. 152 p. : ill. ; 22 cm. (Quaderni de "L'Industria" . 34) Includes bibliographical references. ISBN 88-15-01193-5 : LC Card 87-100465
1. Italy - Industries. 2. Industry and state - Italy. 3. Industrial promotion - Italy. 4. Italy - Economic policy. I. Cipolletta, Innocenzo. II. Series: Quaderni de L'Industria (Società editrice Il Mulino) , 34.
HC305 .S845 1986

Struttura produttiva e distribuzione personale del reddito . Targetti Lenti, Renata. Milano [1984] 263 p. : ISBN 88-14-00277-0 : LC Card 84-251227 DDC 339.2/2/0945 19
HC310.I5 T346 1984 ***NYPL [JLF 86-1305]***

Strutz, Henry. Talking business in German ; dictionary and reference for international business : phrases and words you need to know / by Henry Strutz. Woodbury, N.Y. : Barron's Educational Series, c1987. iv, 256 p. : ill. (some col.) ; 18 cm. (Barron's bilingual business guides) ISBN 0-8120-3747-2 (pbk.) LC Card 86-22360 DDC 650/.03/31 19
1. Commerce - Dictionaries. 2. Commerce - Dictionaries - German. 3. Business - Dictionaries. 4. Business - Dictionaries - German. 5. English language - Dictionaries - German. 6. German language - Dictionaries - English. I. Title. II. Series.
HF1002 .S79 1987

Strzelecki, Zbigniew. Migracje wewnętrzne ludności . Warszawa , 1980. xvi, 389 p. ; LC Card 86-215694
HB2068.7.A3 M54 1980

Strzoda, Joachim. Buk, Halina. Analiza ekonomiczna przedsiębiorstw przemsłowych /. Katowice , 1977. 285 p. ; LC Card 82-102080
HD36 .B775 1977

Stuart, A. A. Verrijn. see **Verrijn Stuart, A. A.**

Stuart, Charles. Bradford, David F. Issues in the measurement and interpretation of effective tax rates /. Cambridge, MA (1050 Massachusetts Ave., Cambridge 02138) [1986] 21 p. : LC Card 87-108421 DDC 336.24/26 19
HJ4631 .B73 1986

Stubborn survivors . Mortimer, Rex, 1926-1979. [Clayton, Vic.] , 1984. xvii, 180 p. : ISBN 0-86746-299-X (pbk.) LC Card 87-672646
HC59.7 .M593x 1984

Stuber, Barbara. Saisonschwankungen der Bankreserven und Ultimooperationen der Schweizerischen Nationalbank / Barbara Stuber. Bern : P. Haupt, c1986. 173 p. : ill. ; 23 cm. (Berner Beiträge zur Nationalökonomie. Bd. 39) Bibliography: p. 167-173. ISBN 3-258-03653-5 : LC Card 87-130160 DDC 332.1/12/09494 19
1. Bank reserves - Switzerland. 2. Banks and banking - Switzerland - Seasonal variations. 3. Schweizerische Nationalbank. I. Title. II. Series.
HG1656.S9 S77 1986

Stuber, Gerald. The slowdown in productivity growth in the 1975-83 period : a survey of possible explanations / Gerald Stuber. [Ottawa] : Bank of Canada, [1986] 164 p. : ill. ; 28 cm. (Technical report . 43) "October 1986." Bibliography: p. 155-164. LC Card 87-100880 DDC 338/.06/0971 19
1. Industrial productivity - Canada. 2. Canada - Economic conditions - 1945-. I. Series: Technical report (Bank of Canada) , 43. II. Title.
HC120.I52 S78 1986

Stuchevskiĭ, I. A. (Iosif Aleksandrovich)
Zemledel'tsy gosudarstvennogo khozi͡aĭstva drevnego Egipta ėpokhi Ramessidov / I.A. Stuchevskiĭ. Moskva : Izd-vo "Nauka," Glav. red. vostochnoĭ lit-ry, 1982. 254, [2] p. ; 22 cm. At head of title: Akademii͡a nauk SSSR. Ordena Trudovogo Krasnogo Znameni Institut vostokovedenii͡a. Bibliography: p. 249-[255] LC Card 82-186646
1. Agriculture and state - Egypt - History. 2. Agriculture - Taxation - Egypt - History. 3. Land tenure - Egypt - History. 4. Farmers - Egypt - History. 5. Egypt - Economic conditions - To 332 B.C. I. Title.
HD2123 .S78 1982

Stuchlik, Karl-Heinz. Die Arbeitsverhältnisse in deutschen Konsumgenossenschaften : von den Anfängen bis 1933 / von Karl-Heinz Stuchlik. Berlin : Duncker & Humblot, c1983. 533 p. : ill. ; 24 cm. (Schriften zum Genossenschaftswesen und zur öffentlichen Wirtschaft . Bd. 8) Bibliography: p. 479-533. ISBN 3-428-05355-9 LC Card 83-191612
1. Consumer cooperatives - Germany. 2. Consumer cooperatives - Germany - Employees. 3. Germany - Economic conditions. I. Title. II. Series.
HD3338 .S88 1983

Studencki ruch naukowy / [zespół redakcyjny Józef Kaleta, Teresa Skrabka-Błotnicka]. Wyd. 1. Wrocław : Wydawn. Uczelniane Akademii Ekonomicznej we Wrocławiu, 1978. 98 p. : ill., map ; 24 cm. (Prace naukowe Akademii Ekonomicznej imienia Oskara Langego we Wrocławiu . zesz. 122 (144)) Summaries in English. Includes bibliographies. LC Card 81-206830
1. Industrial management. 2. Industrial management - Poland. I. Kaleta, Józef. II. Skrabka-Błotnicka, Teresa. III. Series. IV. Series: Prace naukowe Akademii Ekonomicznej imienia Oskara Langego we Wrocławiu , nr. 122.
HB9 .B7522 nr. 122 HD36

Studenmund, A. H. Using econometrics : a practical guide / A.H. Studenmund, Henry J. Cassidy. Boston : Little, Brown, c1987. xii, 440 p. : ill. ; 24 cm. Includes bibliographical references and index. ISBN 0-316-82010-5 LC Card 86-21382 DDC 330/.028 19
1. Econometrics. 2. Regression analysis. I. Cassidy, Henry J. II. Title.
HB139 .S795 1987

Student research abstracts in population studies / editors, S. Mukerji, S. Abraham, C.P. Prakasam. 1st ed. Bombay : Himalaya Pub. House, 1986, c1985. xi, 434 p. ; 23 cm. Includes indexes. LC Card 86-902278 DDC 304.6/095 19
1. Asia - Population - Abstracts. 2. Pacific Area - Population - Abstracts. I. Mukerji, Sukumar, 1931-. II. Abraham, S. (Sarah). III. Prakasam, C. P.
HA4553 .S78 1986

Student research papers in industrial relations.
(no. 7) Christie, Alan R. An account of major activities in the Canterbury Labour and Trades Council District, 1929-1936 /. [Wellington] , 1980. 38, [3] p. ; LC Card 81-120047
HD8930.5.Z8 C3623 1980

STUDENTS AGAINST DRIVING DRUNK (ORGANIZATION)
Contract for life, the S.A.D.D. story [motion picture] /. Los Angeles, CA , 1985. 1 film reel (31 min.) : LC Card 85-700743 DDC 363.1 11
HE5620.D7

Contract for life, the S.A.D.D story [videorecording] /. Los Angeles, CA , 1985. 1 videocassette (31 min.) : LC Card 85-700744 DDC 363.1 11
HE5620.D7

STUDENTS - ARGENTINA - ROSARIO (SANTA FE) - POLITICAL ACTIVITY.
Balvé, Beba. De protesta a rebelión--la "subversión" (Rosario, mayo 1969) /. Buenos Aires, Argentina [1985] xvii, 123 p. ; LC Card 86-162379
HD5350.R67 B35 1985

STUDENTS - EMPLOYMENT.
Cohen, William A., 1937- The student's guide to finding a superior job /. San Diego , c1987. ix, 144 p. ; ISBN 0-932238-41-6 (pbk.) : LC Card 87-4487 DDC 650.1/4 19
HF5382.7 .C64 1987

STUDENTS - EMPLOYMENT - SOVIET UNION - PICTORIAL WORKS.
Molodost', trud, romantika . Moskva , 1985. 183 p., [8] p. of plates : LC Card 86-113851
HD4870.S65 M65 1985

The student's guide to finding a superior job /. Cohen, William A., 1937- San Diego , c1987. ix, 144 p. ; ISBN 0-932238-41-6 (pbk.) : LC Card 87-4487 DDC 650.1/4 19
HF5382.7 .C64 1987

STUDENTS - MEXICO - POLITICAL ACTIVITY - CONGRESSES.
Movimientos sociales en el noroeste de México /. México , 1985. 282 p. ; ISBN 968-590-072-8 LC Card 87-102068
HD1531.M6 M684 1985

Studer, Stefan. Nationalstrasse, Nationalstrafe, oder, Die Demokratie bleibt auf der Strecke / Stefan Studer. 1. Aufl. Zürich : Rotpunktverlag, 1985. 191 p. : ill. ; 21 cm. On t.p. Nationalstrasse appears with ss crossed out and f inserted above it. ISBN 3-85869-037-6 : LC Card 86-129406
1. Roads - Switzerland. 2. Transportation and state - Switzerland. I. Title. II. Title: Nationalstrasse, Nationalstrafe. III. Title: Demokratie bleibt auf der Strecke. IV. Title: Nationalstrafe.
HE363.S92 S83 1985

Studerandepopulation och arbetsmarknad : förändringar under en tjugoårsperiod : bakgrundsinformation från Studiemedelskommittén. [Stockholm] : Liber, [1986] 78 p. : ill. ; 21 cm. At head of title: Utbildningsdepartementet. "DsU 1986:11." ISBN 91-38-09464-9 LC Card 87-106834
1. College graduates - Employment - Sweden. 2. Labor supply - Sweden - Effect of education on. I. Sweden. Studiemedelskommittén.
HD6278.S75 S78 1986

Studi dell'Istituto Gramsci siciliano, 0518-4053 .
(4) La Questione meridionale oggi /. Caltanissetta , 1985. 186 p. ; LC Card 86-214162
HC307.S69 Q47 1985

Studi di economia politica.
(25) Di Nardi, Giuseppe. L'economia a una svolta critica /. Milano , 1984- v. ; LC Card

84-216905 DDC 330 19
HB177 .D48 1984 ***NYPL [JLL 73-173 v.25]***

Studi di storia monetaria e finanziaria moderna .
(4) Confalonieri, Antonio. La politica del debito pubblico in Italia, 1919-1943 /. Milano , Roma , c1986. 2 v. (536 p.) ; ISBN 88-420-2794-4 : LC Card 87-125992
HJ8678 .C64 1986

Studi e ricerche di scienze sociali. For additional listing of contents, see Old Catalog.
(60) Plan for information society-a national goal toward year 2000. Italian. Verso una società dell'informazione . Milano , 1974. 157 p. :
NYPL [TB (Studi e ricerche di scienze sociali. v.60)]

Studi e ricerche (Istituto nazionale di economia agraria) .
(3) Pieroni, Osvaldo. Agricolture a tempo parziale /. Bologna , c1983. 220 p. : ISBN 88-15-00024-0 LC Card 85-233534
HD1970 .P54 1983

Studi e ricerche (Istituto per la formazione e l'aggiornamento professionale (Rome, Italy))
Eminente, Giorgio. Strategia aziendale e sviluppo tecnologico . Bologna , c1985. 253 p. : ISBN 88-15-00917-5 : LC Card 86-176732
HD9696.A3 I733 1985

Studi economici e aziendali .
(2) Porta, Pier Luigi. Scuola classica e teoria economica /. Milano , 1984. xi, 145 p. ; ISBN 88-14-00004-2 : LC Card 84-177305 DDC 330.15/3 19
HB167 .P67 1984 ***NYPL [JLE 86-4055]***

(3) Masciocchi, Giuseppe. Crisi di impresa . Milano , 1983. viii, 112 p. ; LC Card 84-141092 DDC 657/.73 19
HD2747 .M37 1983 ***NYPL [JLE 86-4053]***

Studi NIS economia .
(10) Donzelli, Franco. Il concetto di equilibrio nella teoria economica neoclassica /. Roma , 1986. 518 p. ; LC Card 86-192826
HB145 .D65 1986

(2) Balducci, Renato, 1947- Contrattazione salariale e ciclo economico . Roma , 1982. 174 p. : ***NYPL [JLD 86-2868]***

Studi organizzativi. Teoria dell'organizzazione e realtà italiana . Milano [1980] 225 p. ; ISBN 88-20-41736-7 : LC Card 80-511472 DDC 302.3/5 19
HM131 .T4 ***NYPL [JLD 81-599]***

Studi storici (Istituto storico italiano per il Medio Evo) .
(fasc. 136-139) Conti, Elio. L'imposta diretta a Firenze nel Quattrocento (1427-1494) /. Roma , 1984. 406 p. ; LC Card 86-171245
HJ9500.F562 C65 1984

Studi sulla modernizzazione e lo sviluppo .
(2) L'Altra metà dell'economia . Napoli , 1986. 345 p. : ISBN 88-20-71420-5 : LC Card 86-214178
HD2341 .A68 1986

Studi superiori NIS. Economia.
Tani, Piero. Analisi microeconomica della produzione /. Roma , 1986. viii, 351 p. : LC Card 86-169971
HB241 .T36 1986

Studi superiori NIS. Sociologia .
(10) Manuale di ricerca sul lavoro e sulle organizzazioni /. Roma , 1985. 384 p. : LC Card 86-118313 DDC 306/.36/072 19
HD4824 .M32 1985 ***NYPL [JLD 87-1160]***

Studia folkloristica et ethnographica, 0138-9882 .
(9) Dobrossy, István. Termelés és életmód . Debrecen , 1983. 282 p. : ISBN 963-471-276-2 LC Card 86-100359
HD1492.H82 P873 1983

Studien und Arbeiten .
(1) Ölçen, Ali Nejat. Türken und Rückkehr . Frankfurt a.M. , 1986. 132 p. ; ISBN 3-924320-51-9 LC Card 87-138316 DDC 331.6/2/56104355 19
HD8458.T9 O43 1986

Studien und Dokumentationen zur deutschen Bildungsgeschichte.
(Bd. 29) Rinneberg, Karl-Jürgen. Das betriebliche Ausbildungswesen in der Zeit der industriellen Umgestaltung Deutschlands /. Köln , 1985. xvi, 481 p. : ISBN 3-412-02885-1 LC Card 86-121691
HF5549.5.T7 R486 1985

Studien und Quellen zur österreichischen Zeitgeschichte .
(Bd. 5) Garamvölgyi, Judit. Betriebsräte und sozialer Wandel in Österreich 1919/1920 . München , c1983. 296 p. ; ISBN 3-486-51721-X LC Card 83-240283
HD5660.A8 G37 1983

(Bd. 6) Loewenfeld-Russ, Hans, 1873-1945. Im Kampf gegen den Hunger . München , 1986. xxiv, 381 p., [1] leaf of plates : ISBN 3-486-52451-8 LC Card 86-224948
HC270.F3 L64 1986

Studien zum Bank- und Börsenrecht .
(Bd. 12) Seifert, Ekkehard. Privilegierung und Regulierung im Bankwesen . Baden-Baden , 1984. 332 p. ; ISBN 3-7890-0861-3 LC Card 84-186059
HG3054 .S42 1984

Studien zum Finanz- und Steuerrecht, 0170-9224 .
(Bd. 10) Heurung, Rainer-Otto, 1952- Wirken Substanzsteuern investitionshemmend? /. Frankfurt am Main , New York , c1986. xvii, 251, [93] p. : ISBN 3-8204-9800-1 LC Card 87-408762 DDC 332.63 19
HG4028.C4 H49 1986

Studien zum politischen System des Imperialismus .
(Bd. 3) Das Politische System der BRD . Berlin , 1985. 479 p. ; LC Card 86-123928 DDC 320.943 19
JN3971.A2 P59 1985 ***NYPL [JLD 86-3144]***

Studien zur angewandten Wirtschaftsforschung und Statistik.
(17) Lorenzen, Gunter. Adaptive Verfahren der Input-Output Analyse /. Göttingen , c1985. vii, 156 p. ; ISBN 3-525-11288-2 LC Card 85-221821
HB142 .L67 1985
NYPL [JLL 76-449 Heft 17]

Studien zur angewandten Wirtschaftsforschung und Statistik aus dem Institut für Statistik und Ökonometrie der Universität Hamburg .
(Heft 16) Vilks, Arnis. Aggregation und Kausalität im Modell des allgemeinen Konkurrenzgleichgewichts . Göttingen , c1984. 141 p. ; ISBN 3-525-11287-4 (Deut. Bibl.) LC Card 84-225754
HB842 .V55 1984

(Heft 17) Lorenzen, Gunter. Adaptive Verfahren der Input-Output Analyse /. Göttingen , c1985. vii, 156 p. ; ISBN 3-525-11288-2 LC Card 85-221821
HB142 .L67 1985
NYPL [JLL 76-449 Heft 17]

Studien zur empirischen Haushalts- und Verbrauchsforschung /. Schmucker, Helga. Berlin , 1980. xiv, 357 p. : ISBN 3-428-04657-9 LC Card 80-153661
TX7 .B4 Heft 15 HD7029
NYPL [JLE 86-3430]

Studien zur Entwicklung der ökonomischen Theorie / von Ernst Helmstädter ... [et al.] ; herausgegeben von Fritz Neumark. Berlin : Duncker & Humblot, c1981- v. ; 24 cm. (Schriften des Vereins für Socialpolitik . n.F., Bd. 115) Papers presented at conferences held in Giessen (1980), Salzburg (1981) and Basel (1982) Vol. 1, by Ernst Helmstädter ... [et al.]; v. 2, by Hans Christoph Binswanger ... [et al.]; v. 3, by Jürgen Backhaus ... [et al.]; v. 4, by Hajo Riese ... [et al.]; v. 5 by Hans Christoph Binswanger [et al.] Includes bibliographical references. ISBN 3-428-04862-8 (v. 1) : LC Card 81-154218 DDC 330/.09 19
1. Smith, Adam, 1723-1790 - Congresses. 2. Economics - History - Congresses. 3. Classical school of economics - Congresses. I. Helmstädter, Ernst. II. Neumark, Fritz, 1900-. III. Binswanger, Hans Christoph. IV. Backhaus, Jürgen, 1942-. V. Series: Gesellschaft für Wirtschafts- und Sozialwissenschaften, Verein für Sozialpolitik. Schriften. Neue Folge , Bd. 115.
HB75 .S787 1981
NYPL [JLL 73-186 Bd.115]

Studien zur Entwicklungsökonomie /. Leisinger, Klaus M. Bern , c1986. 130 p. : ISBN 3-258-03665-9 LC Card 87-124013 DDC 338.9/009172/7 19
HC59.72.E44 L45 1986

Studien zur Geschichte des Alltags .
(Bd. 3) Teuteberg, Hans Jürgen. Wohnalltag in Deutschland, 1850-1914 . Münster , 1985. 488 p. : ISBN 3-88547-277-5 LC Card 86-165201
HD7339.A3 T46 1985

Studien zur integrierten ländichen Entwicklung, 0177-2503 .
(4) Kireta-Katewu, Patrick R., 1953- Economic analyses of the farmer cropping system under risks and uncertainties in Sierra Leone /. Hamburg , 1985. xviii, 245 p. : ISBN 3-87895-266-X (pbk.) LC Card 87-103068 DDC 338.1/62 19
HD2146.5 .K57 1985

Studien zur integrierten ländlichen Entwicklung, 0177-2503 .
(2) Büscher, Ludger. Integrated rural development . Hamburg , 1984. xx, 238 p. : ISBN 3-87895-261-9 (pbk.) LC Card 86-672442
HD2146.5 .B87x 1984 ***NYPL [JLD 86-2789]***

Studien zur kommunalen Industrieförderung im 20. Jahrhundert . Finke, B. (Barbara) Regensburg , c1986. 125, [45], xxv p. : ISBN 3-924956-19-7 : LC Card 87-129091 DDC 338.943/34 19
HC289.R36 F56 1986

Studien zur pädagogischen Psychologie .
(Bd. 21) Kraak, Bernhard. Berufliche Motivation und berufliches Verhalten . Göttingen , c1984. i, 145 p. ; ISBN 3-8017-0218-9 LC Card 85-100278
HF5549.5.M63 K73 1984

Studien zur Politikwissenschaft (Münster in Westfalen, Germany) .
(Bd. 19) Wolfgart, Ludger. Die technische Entwicklung als Element des sozialen Wandels und ihre Auswirkungen auf den öffentlichen Sektor in der Bundesrepublik Deutschland /. Münster [1986] ii, 213 p. ; ISBN 3-88660-230-3 (cover); 3-88600-230-3 (Deut. Bibl.) LC Card 87-106473 DDC 338.943 19
HD4175 .W65 1986

(Bd. 9) Die Bundesrepublik Deutschland und die Entwicklungspolitik der Europäischen Gemeinschaft, 1957-1983 /. Münster [1986] 111 p. ; ISBN 3-88660-214-1 LC Card 86-213020
HC241.25.G3 B87 1986

Studien zur qualitativen Sozialforschung .
(Bd. 5) Norden, Gilbert. Einkommensgerechtigkeit, was darunter verstanden wird . Wien , 1985. 304 p. : ISBN 3-205-06324-4 LC Card 86-196913
HB523 .N67 1985

Studien zur Rhetorik des neunzehnten Jahrhunderts. For additional listing of contents, see Old Catalog.
(Bd. 4) Sozialreform und Rhetorik =. Wiesbaden , 1984. 174 p. ; ISBN 3-515-02857-9
NYPL [L-11 3778 Bd. 4]

Studien zur Wirtschafts- und Sozialgeschichte Schleswig-Holsteins, 0172-9152 .
(Bd. 7) Gehrmann, Rolf. Leezen 1720-1870 . Neumünster , 1984. 366 p. ; ISBN 3-529-02907-6 : LC Card 85-217552
HB3596.L44 G44 1984

(Bd. 9) Rüdel, Holger. Landarbeiter und Sozialdemokratie in Ostholstein, 1872 bis 1878 . Neumünster , 1986. 581 p. ; ISBN 3-529-02909-2 LC Card 87-119718 DDC 331.88/13/0943512 19
HD6699.O88 R83 1986

Studien zur Zeitgeschichte (Institut für Zeitgeschichte (Munich, Germany)) .
(Bd. 23) Sundhaussen, Holm. Wirtschaftsgeschichte Kroatiens im nationalsozialistischen Grossraum 1941-1945 . Stuttgart , 1983. 386 p. : ISBN 3-421-06150-5 LC Card 83-242921
HC407.Z7 C7678 1983

Studiengruppe Entwicklungsprobleme der Industriegesellschaft (Germany) Energie und Gerechtigkeit /. München , c1984. xii, 254 p. : ISBN 3-597-10259-X LC Card 84-175053
HD9502.A2 E5192 1984

Studienheft des Missionshilfe Verlages .
(Nr. 15) Nicaragua . Hamburg [1986] 95 p. : ISBN 3-921620-32-5 LC Card 86-191836 DDC 330.97285/053 19
HC146 .N56 1986

Studienprojekte der Professur für Entscheidungs- und Organisationsforschung, Personalwesen.
Möglichkeiten und Probleme der Realisierung flexibler Arbeitszeitstrukturen in Filialen der

Bayerischen Vereinsbank München /. München , 1985. 67 p. : LC Card 87-401387 DDC 331.25/72 19
HD5109.2.G32 M866 1985

Studienreihe des Instituts für Sozialforschung Frankfurt am Main (Campus Verlag)
Grenzen der Frauenlohnarbeit . Frankfurt/Main , New York , c1986. 250 p. : ISBN 3-593-33628-6 LC Card 86-228323
HD6072.2.G4 G74 1986

Teschner, Eckart, 1940- Lohnpolitik im Betrieb . Frankfurt/Main , New York , c1977. 226 p. : ISBN 3-593-32244-7 LC Card 85-134281 DDC 331.2/943 19
HD4966.M44 G48 1977

Studienzentrum Weikersheim. Umweltschutz . [Mainz] , c1984. 130 p. ; ISBN 3-7758-1086-2 LC Card 85-146233
HC290.5.E5 U64 1984

Studier i dansk merkantilisme . Glamann, Kristof. [Copenhagen] , c1983. 243 p. ; ISBN 87-500-2476-0 LC Card 85-125251
HB91 .G57 1983

Studier (Københavns universitet. Økonomiske institut) .
(nr. 30) Topp, Niels-Henrik. Udviklingen i de finanspolitiske ideer i Danmark 1930-1945 /. [Copenhagen] [1987] 437 p. ; ISBN 87-574-5100-1 : LC Card 87-149164
HB51 .C63 nr. 30 HJ1222

Studies (Centro de Estudios Monetarios Latinoamericanos)
Tamagna, Frank M. [Banca central en América Latina. English.] Central banking in Latin America /. México , 1965. xii, 285 p. ; LC Card 87-403322 DDC 332.1/1/098 19
HG2710.5.A7 T3513 1965

Studies in advertising (AEI) see **American Enterprise Institute for Public Policy Research. AEI studies.**

Studies in African political economy.
Gakou, Mohamed Lamine. [Crise de l'agriculture africaine. English.] The crisis in African agriculture /. London ; Atlantic Highlands, N.J., USA : xii, 100 p. ; ISBN 0-86232-732-6 : LC Card 87-13355 DDC 338.1/096 19
HD2117 .G3513 1987

Studies in American business and the international economy.
Behrman, Jack N. The rise of the phoenix . Boulder , 1987. xiii, 104 p. ; ISBN 0-8133-7511-8 (pbk. : alk. paper) : LC Card 87-21689 DDC 338.973 19
HC106.8 .B43 1987

Danielian, Ronald L. The forgotten deficit . Boulder , 1987. xii, 84 p. ; ISBN 0-8133-7450-2 (pbk. : alk. paper) LC Card 87-50654 DDC 332.6/7373 19
HG3883.U7 D36 1987

Studies in Asian educational and social issues .
(v. 1) Vente, Rolf E. Education and training for industrial development in Singapore and other ASEAN countries . Baden-Baden , Singapore , 1984. 175 p. : ISBN 3-7890-0941-5 LC Card 84-186381 DDC 331.25/92/0959 19
HD5715.5.S55 V46 1984
NYPL [JLD 86-2773]

Studies in capital formation in Great Britain : 1750-1920 / edited by C.H. Feinstein and Sidney Pollard with contributions by John Butt ... [et al.]. Oxford [Oxfordshire] ; New York : Clarendon Press, c1988. p. cm. Includes index. ISBN 0-19-828408-X : LC Card 87-15196 DDC 332/.0415/0941 19
1. Saving and investment - Great Britain - History. 2. Capital - Great Britain - History. 3. Great Britain - Industries - History. I. Feinstein, C. H. II. Pollard, Sidney.
HC260.S3 S78 1988

Studies in contemporary economics .
(v. 13) Illing, Gerhard. Geld und asymmetrische Information /. Berlin , New York , 1985. vi, 148 p. : ISBN 0-387-13999-0 (U. S.) LC Card 85-142939
HG220.A2 I55 1985

(v. 19) Schalk, Hans Joachim. Differenzierte Globalsteuerung . Berlin , New York , c1985. ix, 319 p. : ISBN 0-387-16045-0 (U. S.) LC Card 86-141700
HB3732 .S32 1985

(v. 20) Pfingsten, Andreas. The measurement of tax progression /. Berlin , New York , c1986. vi, 131 p. : ISBN 0-387-16072-8 (U. S. : pbk.) LC Card 86-219663 DDC 336.2/93 19
HJ2326 .P47 1986

(v. 3) Gaab, Werner. Devisenmärkte und Wechselkurse . Berlin , New York , 1983. vii, 305 p. : ISBN 0-387-12615-5 (U. S.) : LC Card 83-222336
HG3851 .G25 1983

(v. 6) Böbel, Ingo. Wettbewerb und Industriestruktur . Berlin , New York , 1984. xiv, 336 p. : ISBN 0-387-13143-4 (U. S.) LC Card 85-111698
HD2757 .B63 1984

(vol. 16) Pohmer, Karlheinz. Mikroökonomische Theorie der personellen Einkommens- und Vermögensverteilung . Berlin , New York , c1985. ix, 214 p. : ISBN 0-387-15174-5 (U. S.) LC Card 85-164096
HB523 .P64 1985

(vol. 20) Pfingsten, Andreas. The measurement of tax progression /. Berlin , New York , c1986. vi, 131 p. : ISBN 0-387-16072-8 (U. S. : pbk.) LC Card 86-219663 DDC 336.2/93 19
HJ2326 .P47 1986

(13) Illing, Gerhard. Geld und asymmetrische Information /. Berlin , New York , 1985. vi, 148 p. : ISBN 0-387-13999-0 (U. S.) LC Card 85-142939
HG220.A2 I55 1985

(17) Conrad, Klaus, 1940- Produktivitätslücken nach Wirtschaftszweigen im internationalen Vergleich . Berlin , New York , c1985. 165 p. ; ISBN 0-387-15571-6 (U. S.) LC Card 85-233665
HC110.I52 C67 1985

(6) Böbel, Ingo. Wettbewerb und Industriestruktur . Berlin , New York , 1984. xiv, 336 p. : ISBN 0-387-13143-4 (U. S.) LC Card 85-111698
HD2757 .B63 1984

Heri, Erwin W. Die Geldnachfrage . Berlin , New York , c1986. 226 p. : ISBN 0-387-17157-6 (U. S.) LC Card 86-232268
HG226.5 .H47 1986

Jäggi, Christian M. Die Makroökonomik von J.M. Keynes /. Berlin , New York , c1986. xiii, 278 p. : ISBN 0-387-16477-4 (U. S.) LC Card 86-225958
HB99.7 .J34 1986

Pimentão, Luís Nuno de Matos. Anwendungen der Variationsrechnung auf makroökonomische Modelle /. Berlin , New York , c1986. xii, 220 p. : ISBN 0-387-16484-7 (U. S.) LC Card 86-209488
HB141 .P55 1986

Studies in cybernetics, 0275-5807 .
(v. 10) Burns, Tom R. Man, decisions, society . New York , c1985. xiv, 342 p. : ISBN 2-88124-004-6 (France) LC Card 84-10303 DDC 301 19
HM24 .B85 1985 ***NYPL [JLE 86-2963]***

Studies in development management.
Hage, Jerald, 1932- Organizational change as a development strategy . Boulder, Colo. , 1987. xvi, 293 p. ; ISBN 1-555-87012-0 (lib. bdg. : alk. paper) : LC Card 87-12730 DDC 338.9/0068 19
HC59.72.E44 H34 1987

Rondinelli, Dennis A. Development administration and U. S. foreign aid policy /. Boulder , 1987. xi, 188 p. ; ISBN 0-931477-97-2 (lib. bdg.) : LC Card 87-4555 DDC 338.9/0068 19
HC59.72.E44 R66 1987

White, Louise G. Creating opportunities for change . Boulder, Colo. , 1987. xvii, 283 p. : ISBN 1-555-87031-7 (lib. bdg.) : LC Card 87-4557 DDC 338.9/0068 19
HD75.8 .W47 1987

Studies in East European and Soviet Russian agrarian policy .
(v. 2) Agriculture in inter-system comparison . Berlin , 1985. 443 p. : ISBN 3-428-05885-2 (pbk.) LC Card 86-190956 DDC 338.1/6/094 19
HD1920.E852 A37 1985

Studies in economic development and planning / Institute of Economic Growth .
(no. 39) Goldar, B. N. Productivity growth in Indian industry /. New Delhi , 1986, c1985. xvi, 206 p. ; ISBN 81-7023-062-4 : LC Card 86-902812 DDC 338/.06/0954 19
HC440.I52 G65 1986

Studies in economic history and policy.
Bernstein, Michael A. (Michael Alan), 1954- The Great Depression . Cambridge [Cambridgeshire] , New York , 1987. xvii, 269 p. : ISBN 0-521-34048-9 LC Card 87-6403 DDC 338.5/42 19
HB3717 1929 .B37 1987

Hogan, Michael J., 1943- The Marshall Plan . Cambridge [Cambridgeshire] , New York , 1987. xiv, 482 p. ; ISBN 0-521-25140-0 LC Card 86-31773 DDC 338.91/73/04 19
HC240 .H614 1987

Studies in economic policy (AEI) see **American Enterprise Institute for Public Policy Research. AEI studies.**

Studies in education and psychology (Högskolan för lärarutbildning i Stockholm. Institutionen för pedagogik) .
(13) Mattsson, Kerstin, 1946- Yrkesvalsfågan . [Malmö] , c1984. vii, 268 p. ; ISBN 91-40-05057-2 : LC Card 84-200481
HF5382.5.S8 M37 1984

Studies in energy policy (AEI) see **American Enterprise Institute for Public Policy Research. AEI studies.**

Studies in financial institutions and markets .
([4]) Pensions . London , Boston , 1987. xvi, 249 p. : ISBN 0-04-332127-5 (alk. paper) LC Card 86-32086 DDC 331.25/2/0941 19
HD7165 .P46 1987

(3) Boléat, Mark. The mortgage market /. London , Boston , 1987. x, 176 p. ; ISBN 0-04-334011-3 (alk. paper) LC Card 86-28875 DDC 332.7/22 19
HG2040.5.G7 B65 1987

Studies in government and public policy.
Browne, William Paul, 1945- Private interests, public policy, and American agriculture /. Lawrence, Kan. , c1988. p. cm. ISBN 0-7006-0334-4 : LC Card 87-23131 DDC 338.1/873 19
HD1761 .B73 1988

Jones, Bryan D. The sustaining hand . Lawrence, Kan. , c1986. xii, 247 p. : ISBN 0-7006-0278-X : LC Card 85-24631 DDC 338.4/76292/09774 19
HD9710.U53 M433 1986
NYPL [JLE 86-2386]

Studies in government regulation (AEI) see **American Enterprise Institute for Public Policy Research. AEI studies.**

Studies in historical archaeology.
Domestic pottery of the northeastern United States, 1625-1850 /. Orlando , 1985. xxi, 319 p. : ISBN 0-12-703870-1 (alk. paper) LC Card 85-9038 DDC 338.4/76663974 19
HD9611.7.A115 D66 1985
NYPL [3-MPH 86-2845]

Studies in historical archaeology (Orlando, Fla.)
Domestic pottery of the northeastern United States, 1625-1850 /. Orlando , 1985. xxi, 319 p. : ISBN 0-12-703870-1 (alk. paper) LC Card 85-9038 DDC 338.4/76663974 19
HD9611.7.A115 D66 1985
NYPL [3-MPH 86-2845]

Studies in human migration /. Khan, Najma. New Delhi , 1983. vi, 275 p. ; LC Card 83-907120 DDC 304.8/0954 19
HB3639 .K48 1983 ***NYPL [JLD 86-4136]***

Studies in human rights, 0146-3586 .
(no. 6) Mower, A. Glenn (Alfred Glenn) International cooperation for social justice . Westport, Conn. , c1985. x, 271 p. ; ISBN 0-313-24702-1 (lib. bdg.) LC Card 84-27954 DDC 341.4/81 19
K3240.4 .M676 1985 ***NYPL [JLD 85-3575]***

Studies in Indian urban development /. Mills, Edwin S. New York , 1986. viii, 214 p. ; ISBN 0-19-520507-3 : LC Card 86-2489 DDC 307.1/4/0954 19
HT147.I5 M56 1986 ***NYPL [JLE 86-3750]***

Studies in inflationary dynamics . Kapur, Basant.

Kent Ridge, Singapore , c1986. xviii, 146 p., [1] folded leaf of plates : ISBN 997-16-9099-3 (pbk.) LC Card 87-116919 DDC 332.4/1 19
HC59.7 .K276 1986

Studies in international economics (Washington, D.C.)
Bryant, Ralph C., 1938- International financial intermediation /. Washington, D.C. , c1987. xi, 181 p. : ISBN 0-8157-1138-7 : LC Card 87-10358 DDC 332/.042 19
HG3891.5 .B79 1987

Studies in international political economy.
(1) Nell, Edward J. Prosperity and public spending . Boston , 1987. p. cm. ISBN 0-04-339044-7 (alk. paper) LC Card 87-1383 DDC 339.5/22 19
HJ7451 .N44 1987

(17) Cafruny, Alan W. Ruling the waves . Berkeley , c1987. xvii, 323 p. ; ISBN 0-520-05968-9 LC Card 86-30889 DDC 387.5/1 19
HE735 .C34 1987

(18) Stallings, Barbara. Banker to the Third World . Berkeley , c1987. xvii, 434 p. : ISBN 0-520-05726-0 (alk. paper) LC Card 86-24988 DDC 332.6/7373/08 19
HG5160.5.A3 S73 1987

Broad, Robin. Unequal alliance . Berkeley , c1988. p. cm. ISBN 0-520-05905-0 LC Card 87-10745 DDC 332.1/52 19
HG3881.5.W57 B76 1988

Hampson, Fen Osler. Forming economic policy . London , 1986. x, 161 p. : ISBN 0-86187-628-8 ***NYPL [JLE 86-3813]***

Tussie, Diana. The less developed countries and the world trading system . London , 1987. viii, 162 p. ; ISBN 0-86187-614-8 ***NYPL [JLE 87-1597]***

Wood, Robert Everett, 1944- From Marshall Plan to debt crisis . Berkeley , c1986. xviii, 400 p. ; ISBN 0-520-05526-8 (alk. paper) LC Card 86-6934 DDC 338.9/009172/4 19
HC60 .W62 1986 ***NYPL [JLE 86-4443]***

Studies in international political economy (Boston, Mass.) .
(1) Nell, Edward J. Prosperity and public spending . Boston , 1987. p. cm. ISBN 0-04-339044-7 (alk. paper) LC Card 87-1383 DDC 339.5/22 19
HJ7451 .N44 1987

Studies in international political economy (Frances Pinter (Publishers))
Tussie, Diana. The less developed countries and the world trading system . London , 1987. viii, 162 p. ; ISBN 0-86187-614-8 ***NYPL [JLE 87-1597]***

Studies in labor market dynamics, 0108-2469 ; arbejdspapir.
(82-7) Pedersen, Peder J. Dynamiska processer på arbejdsmarkedet /. Aarhus [Copenhagen] [1982] 33 p. : LC Card 84-125613
HD5701.6 .P43 1982

(83-1) Westergård-Nielsen, Niels C. Overgangen fra uddannelse til erhverv . Aarhus [Copenhagen] [1983] iii, 41 p. : LC Card 84-125491
HD5701.6 .W47 1983

(83-4) Arbejdsløshed og beskæftigelse . Aarhus [Copenhagen] [1983] 34 p. ; LC Card 84-125513
HD5701.6 .A73 1983

Studies in land and credit in ancient Athens, 500-200 B.C. . Finley, M. I. (Moses I.), 1912- New Brunswick, U. S.A. , c1985. xli, 332 p. ; ISBN 0-88738-066-2 : LC Card 85-14091 DDC 333.3/0938/5 19
HD134 .F5 1985 ***NYPL [JLE 86-4293]***

Studies in law and social change .
(no. 3) The Cold war against labor . Berkeley, CA , c1987. 2 v. (xxii, 915 p.) : ISBN 0-913876-19-4 (set); 0-913876-20-4 (set) : LC Card 87-18510 DDC 331.88/0973 19
HD6508 .C62 1987

Studies in maritime history.
Bauer, K. Jack (Karl Jack), 1926- A maritime history of the United States . Columbia, S.C. , c1988. p. cm. ISBN 0-87249-519-1 LC Card 87-19190 DDC 387.5/0973 19
HE745 .B38 1988

Studies in Marxism and social theory.
Analytical Marxism /. Cambridge, CB ; New York : viii, 313 p. : ISBN 0-521-30025-8 LC Card 85-11697 DDC 335.4 19
HB97.5 .A487 1986 ***NYPL [JLE 86-1742]***

Studies in mathematical and managerial economics. For additional listing of contents, see Old Catalog.
(v. 35) Sinn, Hans-Werner. [Kapitaleinkommensbesteuerung. English.] Capital income taxation and resource allocation /. Amsterdam ; New York : xiv, 411 p. ; ISBN 0-444-70208-3 LC Card 87-9126 DDC 336.24/3 19
HD2753.A3 S47413 1987

Studies in medieval trade and finance /. Fryde, E. B. London , 1983. 1 v. (various pagings) ; ISBN 0-907628-10-9 LC Card 83-168474 DDC 382/.0942/04 19
HF3518.E85 F79 1983 ***NYPL [JLE 86-2481]***

Studies in Middle Eastern history (New York, N. Y.)
The Fertile Crescent, 1800-1914 . New York , 1987. p. cm. ISBN 0-19-504951-9 LC Card 86-33275 DDC 330.956 19
HC415.15 .F47 1987

Studies in migration : internal and international migration in India / edited by M.S.A. Rao. Delhi : Manohar, 1986. x, 400 p. : ill., map ; 23 cm. Includes bibliographies and index. ISBN 81-85054-08-8 : LC Card 86-902753 DDC 304.8/0954 19
1. Migration, Internal - India. 2. India - Emigration and immigration. I. Rao, M. S. A.
HB2099 .S78 1986

Studies in modern history (Longman(Firm))
Wright, D. G. Popular radicalism . London , New York , 1988. p. cm. ISBN 0-582-49440-0 LC Card 87-4093 DDC 322/.2/0942 19
HD8395 .W75 1988

Studies in nineteenth century rhetoric. see **Studien zur Rhetorik des neunzehnten Jahrhunderts.**

Studies in official statistics (Zambia. Central Statistical Office) .
(no. 1) Zambian official statistics . Lusaka , 1978. i, 99 p. ; LC Card 83-980761
HA37.Z352 Z36 1978

Studies in political and social processes (AEI) see **American Enterprise Institute for Public Policy Research. AEI studies.**

Studies in productivity analysis.
Measurement issues and behavior of productivity variables /. Boston , Hingham, MA, USA , c1986. ix, 262 p. : ISBN 0-89838-171-1 LC Card 85-8017 DDC 338/.06/0287 19
HD56.25 .M43 1986 ***NYPL [JLE 86-3414]***

Studies in public policy, 0140-8240 .
(no. 110) Rose, Richard, 1933- Getting by in three economies . Glasgow , 1983. 40 p. ; LC Card 83-150133 DDC 330.941/0858 19
HC256.6 .R67 1983

Studies in social welfare policies and programs, 8755-5360 .
(no. 3) Morris, Michael, 1949- Poverty and public policy . Westport, Conn. , 1986. xii, 236 p. ; ISBN 0-313-24942-3 (lib. bdg. : alk. paper) LC Card 86-398 DDC 361.6/1/0973 19
HV95 .M67 1986 ***NYPL [JLD 87-510]***

Studies in Soviet history and society (Ithaca, N. Y.)
Kaplan, Cynthia Sue. The party and agricultural crisis management in the USSR /. Ithaca , 1987. xvi, 203 p ; ISBN 0-8014-2021-0 (alk. paper) LC Card 86-32223 DDC 338.1/847 19
HD1993 .K36 1987

Studies in the modern Japanese economy.
Minami, Ryōshin, 1933- [Nihon no keizai hatten. English.] The economic development of Japan . Basingstoke, Hampshire , 1986. xxvi, 487 p. : ISBN 0-333-38582-9 LC Card 87-672411
HC462.7 .M47513x 1986b

Studies in Third World Societies .
(publication no. 29) The Economic demography of mass poverty. [Williamsburg, Va., U. S.A. , c1986] xiv, 142 p. : LC Card 85-73339 DDC 339.4/6/091724 19
HB884 .E36 1986

Studies in urban and regional policy .
(4) Henderson, J. W. (Jeffrey William), 1947- Race, class, and state housing . Aldershot, Hants, England ;Brookfield, Vt. , c1987. xxiii, 331 p. : ISBN 0-566-00785-1 : ***NYPL [JLD 87-1476]***

Studies in Venetian social and economic history /. Lane Frederic Chapin, 1900- London , 1987. 346 p. in various pagings : ISBN 0-86078-202-6 LC Card 87-160893 DDC 945/.31 19
HC308.V4 L36 1987

Studies in water policy and management .
(no. 10) Watershed resource management . Boulder , 1986. xx, 236 p. : ISBN 0-8133-7300-X (pbk. : alk. paper) : LC Card 86-18987 DDC 333.91/0095 19
HD1691 .W37 1986 ***NYPL [JLD 87-767]***

(no. 12) Saliba, Bonnie. Water markets in theory and practice . Boulder , 1987. viii, 273 p. : ISBN 0-8133-7465-0 (pbk. : alk. paper) : LC Card 87-21687 DDC 333.91/00979 19
HD1695.A165 S25 1987

(no. 7) Energy and water management in western irrigated agriculture /. Boulder, Colo. , 1986. xxiv, 415 p. : ISBN 0-8133-7086-8 (pbk. : alk. paper) LC Card 85-52184 DDC 333.91/3/0978 19
HD1735 .E54 1986 ***NYPL [JLD 87-829]***

(no. 9) Irrigation investment, technology, and management strategies for development /. Boulder , 1986. xxvii, 270 p. : ISBN 0-8133-7177-5 (pbk. : alk. paper) : LC Card 85-31523 DDC 338.4/762752/091724 19
HD1741.D44 I77 1986 ***NYPL [JLD 87-766]***

Studies (Kentron Programmatismou kai Oikonomikōn Ereunōn) .
(18) Maroulis, Dimitris. Economic development and the structure of the balance of payments . Athens , 1986. 267 p. : LC Card 87-170680 DDC 382.1/7/09495 19
HC295 .M32 1986

(4) Kazēs, D. A. (Dēmētrēs A.) [Licensing kai viomēchanikē anaptyxē. English.] Licensing and industrial development . Athens , 1986. 208 p. : LC Card 87-170691 DDC 338.09495 19
HF1429 .K3813 1986

Studies of the Harriman Institute.
Macey, David, A. J., 1942- Government and peasant in Russia, 1861-1906 . Dekalb, Ill. , 1987. xviii, 380 p. ; ISBN 0-87580-122-6 LC Card 87-7684 DDC 338.1/847 19
HD1992 .M19 1987

Studies of the Program Evaluation Division .
(56) Minnesota. Office of the Legislative Auditor. Program Evaluation Division. Tax increment financing. Saint Paul, Minn. (Veterans Service Bldg., Saint Paul 55155) , 1986. xix, 138 p. : LC Card 86-623133 DDC 336.22/09776 19
HJ9261 .M55 1986

Studies on agrarian reform and rural poverty / M.R. El Ghonemy ... [et al.]. Rome : Food and Agriculture Organization of the United Nations ; New York, N.Y. : UNIPUB [distributor], 1984. vii, 104 p. : ill. ; 23 cm. (FAO economic and social development series . no. 27) Includes bibliographies. ISBN 92-5-101371-3 (pbk.) LC Card 85-183713 DDC 338.9/009172/4 19
1. Land reform - Developing countries - Addresses, essays, lectures. 2. Rural poor - Developing countries - Addresses, essays, lectures. I. El Ghonemy, Mohamad Riad, 1924-.
HD1333.5 .S78 1984 ***NYPL [JLE 86-2720]***

Studies on rural development : experiences and issues / edited by Ajit K. Danda. New Delhi : Inter-India Publications, 1984. viii, 96 p. ; 25 cm. Includes index. Bibliography: p. [89]-93. LC Card 84-902362 DDC 307.7/2 19
1. Rural development - Developing countries - Addresses, essays, lectures. 2. Rural development - India - Addresses, essays, lectures.
HN980 .S77 1984 ***NYPL [JLE 86-4141]***

Studies on statistics .
(No. 42) Zur Neuberechnung der Indizes des Auftragseingangs und des Auftragsbestands für das Verarbeitende Gewerbe und das Bauhauptgewerbe auf Basis 1976. English. Indices of orders received and unfilled orders /. Wiesbaden , Stuttgart , 1986. 16 p. ; LC Card 86-215307
HF5437 .Z8713 1976

Studies on the structure of the industrial economy. New Delhi : Ministry of Industry, Bureau of Industrial Costs & Prices, Govt. of India, 1985- v. <1- > ; 25 cm. CONTENTS. - v. 1. Automotive tyre industry. LC Card 86-902242 DDC 338.0954 19
1. India - Industries. 2. India - Economic conditions - 1947-. I. India. Bureau of Industrial Costs & Prices.
HC435.2 .S84 1985

Studije, analize i prikazi .
(109) Nikolić, Miodrag M. Desezonizacija jugoslovenskih vremenskih serija 1971-1980 =. Beograd , 1982. 287 p. : LC Card 85-157587
HA37.Y8 A37 no. 109 HC407

Studium generale (Centro de Estudos Humanísticos (Porto, Portugal)). Estudos contemporâneos .
(no. 2/3) Perspectivas sobre o norte de Portugal. Porto , 1981. 242 p. : LC Card 83-163948
HC393.M55 P47 1981

STUDIUM Szervezésmódszertani Gazdasági Társaság (Budapest, Hungary) Baross, Jenő. A kereskedelmi hitel és a váltó gyakorlata /. Budapest , 1985. 123 p. ; LC Card 86-228454
HG3754.5.H9 B37 1985

Studium universale, 0174-7061 .
(Bd. 7) Der Bauer im Wandel der Zeit /. Bonn , 1986. x, 340 p., [1] leaf of plates : ISBN 3-416-04010-4 LC Card 86-228506
HD1521 .B37 1986

Studlar, Donley T. Political economy . Jackson , c1987. vii, 276 p. ; ISBN 0-87805-313-1 (alk. paper) LC Card 87-10425 DDC 361.6/1/0941 19
HC106 .P68 1987

Study guide for After the trade is made : an operations training manual / the New York Institute of Finance. New York, NY : The Institute, c1987. ix, 217 p. : ill. ; 24 cm. "Designed for use with David M. Weiss's After the trade is made: processing securities transactions"--P. v. ISBN 0-13-858721-3 (pbk.) : LC Card 87-14155 DDC 332.64/273 19
1. Weiss, David M., 1938- After the trade is made. 2. Stock-exchange - United States. 3. Securities - United States. 4. Commodity exchanges - United States. I. New York Institute of Finance. II. Weiss, David M., 1938- After the trade is made. III. Title: After the trade is made.
HG4910 .W365 1986 Suppl.

Study guide for Technical analysis of the futures markets . Murphy, John J. New York, NY , c1987. x, 142 p. : ISBN 0-13-858747-7 (pbk.) : LC Card 87-10991 DDC 332.64/4 19
HG6046 .M87 1986 Suppl.

A Study into the evolution and performance of the transport sector in Zambia with particular reference to the operations of the ZIMCO group of transport companies / by Abedanigo K. Banda ... [et al.]. [Lusaka?] : University of Zambia Business & Economics Association, [1980?] 89 p. : ill. ; 29 cm. (Occasional paper. no. 15) Bibliography: p. 89. LC Card 86-981420
1. Transportation - Zambia. 2. Zambia Industrial and Mining Corporation. I. Banda, Abedanigo K. II. University of Zambia. Business & Economics Association. III. Series: Occasional paper (University of Zambia. Business & Economics Association) , no. 15.
HE284.6 .S78 1980

A study of company profit-rate time series . Odagiri, Hiroyuki, 1946- Berlin [1986] 15, 5 p. ; LC Card 87-165037 DDC 338.7/4/0952 19
HG4028.P7 O33 1986

A study of housing investment and housing market behaviour /. Rantala, Olavi, 1949- Helsinki , 1986. 117 p. : ISBN 951-686-116-4 (pbk.) LC Card 86-204998 DDC 338.4/369083/0724 19
HD7287.5 .R33 1986

A study of MAS practice and knowledge and bibliographic references for management advisory services . McKell, Lynn J. New York, N.Y. , c1987. 100, [iv], 72 p. ; ISBN 0-87051-002-9 (pbk.) : LC Card 87-19491 DDC 016.6584/6 19
HF5616.U5 M34 1987

A Study of the attitudes toward and an assessment of the Financial Accounting Standards Board / prepared for the Financial Accounting Foundation ; conducted by Louis Harris and Associates, Inc. Stamford, CT : Additional copies, Order Dept., Financial Accounting Standards Board, 1985. x, 141 p. : ill. ; 28 cm. LC Card 86-230871 DDC 657/.0218 19
1. Financial Accounting Standards Board - Public opinion. 2. Accounting - Standards - United States - Public opinion. 3. Public opinion - United States. I. Financial Accounting Standards Board. II. Financial Accounting Foundation. III. Louis Harris and Associates.
HF5616.U5 S78 1985

Study of the fees and taxes which produce revenue for the construction and maintenance of the highways. Nevada. Legislature. Legislative Commission. [Carson City, Nev.] [1986] viii, 74 p. ; LC Card 86-623141 DDC 388.1/14/09793 19
HE356.N37 N42 1986

Study of the financial sector of Argentina . Tami, Felipe S. Washington, D.C. [1979] x, 146 p. : LC Card 86-673765
HG185.A7 T35x 1979

A study of the organization and coordination of electric energy planning and electric utility regulation in California . Commission on California State Government Organization and Economy. [Sacramento] (11th & L Bldg., Suite 550, Sacramento 95814) [1984] 3, x leaves, 54 p. ; LC Card 85-623154 DDC 333.79/32/09794 19
HD9685.U6 C325 1984

Study of the pleasure boat industry in the British Virgin Islands with emphasis on charter boats /. Jackson, Ivor L. [S.l. , 1981?] viii, 89 p. :
NYPL [JLF 85-543]

A Study of the Western Australian casting and forging industry. [Perth] : Dept. of Industrial Development, [1984?]-[1985] 2 v. ; 30 cm. Cover title. LC Card 86-207984 DDC 388.4/7671/09941 19
1. Metal-work - Australia - Western Australia. 2. Metal castings industry - Australia - Western Australia. 3. Forging industry - Australia - Western Australia. I. Western Australia. Dept. of Industrial Development.
HD9506.A8 W385 1984

Study of truck lane needs. Massimi, John J. Truck lane needs methodology . Austin , Springfield, Va. [1985] xii, 63 p. : LC Card 86-622425 DDC 388.1/3 19
HE336.T79 M37 1985

Study on consumption.
United States of America, tin in tinplate. London [1983] 89 p. : LC Card 84-216067 DDC 338.4/76736/0973 19
HD9529.T63 U67 1983

A Study on the improvement of the national sample censuses of agriculture in Nepal. Kathmandu : His Majesty's Govt., National Planning Commission Secretariat, Central Bureau of Statistics, Nepal, 1986. 67 p. : ill. ; 26 cm. Analytical study of the 1961/62, 1971/72, and 1981/82 censuses. LC Card 87-900372 DDC 338.1/09549/6 19
1. Agriculture - Economic aspects - Nepal - Statistics. 2. Nepal - Census. I. Nepal. Kendrīya Tathyāṅka Vibhāga.
HD2065.9 .S78 1986

Study paper (Consultative Group on International Agricultural Research) .
(no. 17) Jiggins, Janice. Gender-related impacts and the work of the international agricultural research centers /. Washington, D.C. , c1986. x, 95 p. ; ISBN 0-8213-0840-8 (pbk.) LC Card 86-24709 DDC 331.4/83/091724 19
HD6073.A292 D444 1986

Stürz, Hans. Koziolek, Helmut. Reproduktion und Infrastruktur /. Berlin , c1986. 224 p. : ISBN 3-349-00017-7 LC Card 87-130782 DDC 363/.09431 19
HC290.795.C3 K675 1986

Štuikys, V. (Vytautas) Lietuvos TSR žemės ūkio tvarkymo sistema /. Vilnius , 1985. 453 p. ; LC Card 86-215158
HD1995.L5 L535 1985

Stukolov, P. M. (Petr Mikhaĭlovich) Otraslevaia sistema planirovaniia : opyt, problemy, perspektivy / P.M. Stukolov, A.D. Gokhshtand. Moskva : "Radio i sviaz′", 1985. 71 p. : ill. ; 22 cm. Includes bibliographical references. LC Card 85-196558
1. Electronic industries - Soviet Union - Planning. I. Gokhshtand, A. D. (Abram Davidovich). II. Title.
HD9696.A3 S697 1985

Stulberg, Joseph B. Taking charge/managing conflict / Joseph B. Stulberg. Lexington, Mass. : Lexington Books, c1987. xii, 175 p. ; 25 cm. Bibliography: p. [169]. Includes index. ISBN 0-669-14014-7 (alk. paper) LC Card 86-45597 DDC 658.4 19
1. Conflict management. 2. Mediation. I. Title.
HD42 .S78 1987

Stumm, David Arthur. Developing negotiation skills in sales personnel : a guide to price realization for sales managers and sales trainers / David A. Stumm. New York : Quorum Books, 1987. xiv, 148 p. ; 25 cm. Bibliography: p. [145]. Includes index. ISBN 0-89930-279-3 (alk. paper) LC Card 87-11260 DDC 658.8/1/00683 19
1. Selling. 2. Negotiation in business. I. Title.
HF5438.25 .S773 1987

Stupin, L. P. (Leonid Pavlovich) Kadieva, D. A. Chastotnyĭ anglo-russkiĭ slovar′. Leningrad , 1986. 126 p. ; LC Card 87-146427
HB61 .K23 1986

Sturen, O. (Ole) Normungsprobleme der Dritten Welt /. Dortmund , 1979. 98 p. ; LC Card 85-239680
HD30 .A7 Heft 201 T59.A1

STUTTGART (GERMANY) - POPULATION DENSITY - CASE STUDIES.
Borcherdt, Christoph. Der "Landverbrauch," seine Erfassung und Bewertung . Stuttgart , 1985. 196 p. : ISBN 3-88028-104-1 LC Card 87-136211 DDC 333.77/13/094347 19
HD660.S83 B67 1985

Stuttgarter geographische Studien, 0343-7906 .
(Bd. 104) Borcherdt, Christoph. Der "Landverbrauch," seine Erfassung und Bewertung . Stuttgart , 1985. 196 p. : ISBN 3-88028-104-1 LC Card 87-136211 DDC 333.77/13/094347 19
HD660.S83 B67 1985

(Bd. 98) Grotz, Reinhold. Industrialisierung und Stadtentwicklung im ländlichen Südost-Australien /. Stuttgart , 1982. 299 p. : ISBN 3-88028-098-3 : LC Card 83-215667
HC607.S68 G76 1982

STYLE MANIKINS. see **MODELS, FASHION.**

STYŚ, WINCENTY.
Z Husowa po berła rektorskie . Warszawa , 1986. 340 p., [25] p. of plates : ISBN 83-205-3745-2 : LC Card 85-126839
HB114.S79 Z2 1986

Su, Wenming.
On rolls the green revolution /. Beijing, China [1984] 142 p., [36] p. of plates : LC Card 86-115054 DDC 338.1/0951 19
HD2097 .O5 1984 ***NYPL [JLK 83-122 no.9]***

The Open policy at work /. Beijing, China [1985] 281 p. ; LC Card 86-219666 DDC 337.51 19
HF1604 .O63 1985

Suárez Díaz, Reynaldo. Hombres y empresas : una visión psicosociológica de la administración / Reynaldo Suárez Díaz.1a ed. México : Editorial Trillas, 1983. 388 p. : ill. ; 23 cm. Bibliography: p. 367-373. Includes index. ISBN 968-241-155-6 LC Card 87-404869 DDC 658.3 19
1. Personnel management. 2. Psychology, Industrial. I. Title.
HF5549 .S8946 1983

Suárez San Román, Blanca.
Barkin, David. El fin de la autosuficiencia alimentaria /. México, D.F. , 1985. 249 p. : ISBN 968-493-091-7 LC Card 82-230750
NYPL [JLE 87-404]

Barkin, David. El fin de la autosuficiencia alimentaria /. México, D.F. , c1985. 249 p. : ISBN 968-493-091-7 LC Card 86-209699
HD1792 .B38 1985

Suazo, Margarita. Población y desarrollo socioeconómico en Honduras / preparado por Margarita Suazo y Rodolfo Aplícano ; con la asistencia técnica de Donald J. Bogue. Chicago, Ill., USA (1313 E. 60th St., Chicago 60637) : Centro de Desarrollo Social, c1984. 90 p., [2] leaves of plates : ill. ; 28 cm. Includes bibliographical references. LC Card 85-203746
1. Honduras - Population - Economic aspects. 2. Birth

control - Honduras. 3. Family size - Honduras. I. Aplícano, Rodolfo. II. Title.
HB3540.A3 S82 1984

Subáné Varga, Judit. Friss István emlékezete /. Budapest , 1984. 128 p. ; LC Card 86-145174
HC300.28 .F75 1984

Subasiṃha, Vinsant. Sandalaṅkā sanda / kathanaya, Vinsant Subasiṃha ; racaṇaya, Bī. Dī. Tilakaratna. [Pannipitiya?] : Sī. Āl. Ec. Subasiṃha Mānikē, 1986. viii, 269 p., [6] leaves of plates : ill., ports. ; 23 cm. Autobiographical. In Sinhalese. Autobiography of Vinsant Subasiṃha, banker and social worker from Sri Lanka. LC Card 86-903022
1. Subasiṃha, Vinsant. 2. Bankers - Sri Lanka - Biography. 3. Social workers - Sri Lanka - Biography. I. Tilakaratna, Bī. Dī. II. Title.
HG1552.S83 A3 1986

SUBASIṂHA, VINSANT.
Subasiṃha, Vinsant. Sandalaṅkā sanda /. [Pannipitiya?] , 1986. viii, 269 p., [6] leaves of plates : LC Card 86-903022
HG1552.S83 A3 1986

Subba Rao, P. Gangadhara Rao, M. Human resources management in Indian railways /. Delhi , 1986. xvi, 245 p. ; ISBN 81-7049-004-9 : LC Card 86-900747 DDC 385/.068/3 19
HD8039.R12 I437 1986
NYPL [JLE 86-4104]

Subbarao, K. De Janvry, Alain. Agricultural price policy and income distribution in India /. Delhi , New York , 1986. xi, 113 p. ; ISBN 0-19-561952-8 : LC Card 86-900015 DDC 338.1/3/0954 19
HD9016.I42 D38 1986

SUBCONTRACTING.
Männel, Wolfgang. Die Wahl zwischen Eigenfertigung und Fremdbezug . Stuttgart , c1981. xvi, 406 p. : ISBN 3-7910-0270-8 LC Card 83-167804
HD2381 .M32 1981

Structure industrielle et sous-traitance /. Paris , c1983. 243 p. : ISBN 2-13-038182-0 : LC Card 84-128203 DDC 331/.01 19
HD2381 .S77 1983 *NYPL [JLE 86-1624]*

SUBCONTRACTING - CONGRESSES.
Symposium on Linkage Between Large and Small Industries (1985 : Kuala Lumpur, Malaysia) Linkage effects and small industry development . Tokyo , 1986. iv, 191 p. : ISBN 92-833-2037-3 LC Card 87-137082 DDC 338.6/42/09595 19
HD2341 .S96 1985

SUBCONTRACTING - QUÉBEC (PROVINCE)
Lewis, Normande. Le travail à temps partiel, le partage du travail comme mesure de sécurité d'emploi et la sous-traitance . [Quebec] , c1985. 90 p. ; ISBN 2-551-08998-0 LC Card 85-213545
HD5110.2.C22 Q45 1985

SUBCONTRACTING - UNITED STATES.
The Changing workplace . Washington, D.C. [Rockville, Md.] , c1986. iv, 140 p. : ISBN 0-87179-910-3 (pbk.) LC Card 86-221689 DDC 331.25/72 19
HD5124 .C46 1986

Subcultuur en stigma van de armoede . Hakemulder, Roel. Leiden , 1985. 96 p. ; ISBN 90-6624-058-X LC Card 86-172398
HC79.P6 H34 1985

Subdesarrollo o camino al colapso . Humala Tasso, Ulises. [S.l. , 1987?] (Lima, Perú : Graphos 100 Editores) 175 p. ; LC Card 87-403093 DDC 330.985/0633 19
HC227 .H86 1987

El subdesarrollo y la crisis en la economía y en la teoría económica /. Parra Peña, Isidro, 1936- Bogotá , 1986. 134 p. ; ISBN 958-1-40133-4 LC Card 87-115003 DDC 338.9 19
HD85.S7 P36 1986

Subhas Chandra Mukhopadhyay. see **Mukhopadhyay, Subhas Chandra, 1938-**

The Subject of a moment [motion picture] / Jeffrey Gray. Provo, Utah : J. Gray, 1985. 1 film reel (ca. 27 min.) : sd., col. ; 16 mm. Title from data sheet. Ages 13 through adults. A high school senior is involved in an automobile accident in which a small girl is killed. Having been found legally drunk, the teenager must come to terms with what he has done. LC Card 85-700877 DDC 362.7 11
1. Drunk driving. 2. Youth - Alcohol use. I. Gray, Jeffrey.
HE5620.D7

SUBJECTIVISM. see **SUBJECTIVITY.**

Subjectivism, intelligibility, and economic understanding : essays in honor of Ludwig M. Lachmann on his eightieth birthday / edited by Israel M. Kirzner. Basingstoke, Hampshire : Macmillan, 1986. xi, 319 p. : ill., port. ; 23 cm. Includes bibliographies and index. ISBN 0-333-41788-7
1. Lachmann, Ludwig M. - Addresses, essays, lectures. 2. Austrian school of economists - Addresses, essays, lectures. 3. Economics - Addresses, essays, lectures. 4. Subjectivity - Addresses, essays, lectures. I. Kirzner, Israel M. II. Lachmann, Ludwig M.
NYPL [JLD 86-2215]

SUBJECTIVITY - ADDRESSES, ESSAYS, LECTURES.
Subjectivism, intelligibility, and economic understanding . Basingstoke, Hampshire , 1986. xi, 319 p. : ISBN 0-333-41788-7
NYPL [JLD 86-2215]

Submission to the Federal Commission of Inquiry on Unemployment Insurance /. Newfoundland. [St. John's] [1985] 63, vi p. : LC Card 86-215851 DDC 368.4/4/009718 19
HD7096.C2 N48 1985

Der Submissionswettbewerb . Finsinger, Jörg. Bern , c1986. 104 p. : ISBN 3-258-03617-9 : LC Card 86-224617
HD9715.S92 F56 1986

Subrahmanya, K. N. Energy problem and world economic development . New Delhi , c1983. vi, 192 p. ; LC Card 83-906441 DDC 333.79/0954 19
HD9502.I42 E54 1983 *NYPL [JLD 87-629]*

Subrahmanya, S. (Susheela) Growth of agriculture and rural development in India /. New Delhi , c1987. xx, 496 p. ; LC Card 87-900250 DDC 338.1/0954 19
HD2072 .G7 1987

Subrahmanyam, K.
Nuclear proliferation and international security /. New Delhi , 1985-86 [i.e. 1985] 310 p. ; ISBN 1-85127-058-4 : LC Card 85-904278 DDC 327.1/74 19
JX1974.73 .N814 1985
NYPL [JLD 86-1334]

The Second cold war /. New Delhi , 1983. vi, 215 p. ; LC Card 84-900004 DDC 355/.033/0047 19
UA10 .S38 1983 *NYPL [JFD 87-1657]*

Subrahmanyam, P., 1934- Organizational set-up of road transport : a focal study of APSRTC / P. Subrahmanyam. Delhi : B.R. Pub. Corp. ; New Delhi : Distributed by D.K. Publishers' Distributors, 1987. xi, 233 [i.e. 333] p. : ill. ; 23 cm. Bibliography: p. [323]-327. Includes index. ISBN 81-7018-398-7 : LC Card 86-903830 DDC 354.54/8400878/09 19
1. Andhra Pradesh State Road Transport Corporation. I. Title.
HE365.I42 S83 1987

Subrahmanyam, S. Poverty, unemployment, and perspective of development / S. Subrahmanyam. 1st ed. Allahabad, India : Chugh Publications, 1987. xi, 311 p. : map ; 23 cm. Originally presented as the author's thesis (Ph. D--Andhra University, Waltair) Study relates to East Godavari District, Andhra Pradesh. Bibliography: p. [295]-308. Includes index. ISBN 81-85076-22-7 : LC Card 87-900803 DDC 330.954/84 19
1. Poor - India - East Godavāri. 2. Unemployment - India - East Godavāri. 3. East Godavāri (India) - Economic conditions. I. Title.
HC440.P6 S9 1987

Sub-regional Symposium on Labour Inspection in Agriculture (1982 : Denpasar, Indonesia) Labour inspection in agriculture in Southeast Asia : proceedings of the Sub-regional Symposium on Labour Inspection in Agriculture, Denpasar, Bali, Indonesia, 7-11 December 1982. Bangkok : International Labour Organisation, Asian and Pacific Project for Labour Administration (ARPLA), 1983. 218 p. : ill. ; 24 cm. (ARPLA series . no. 16) Labour administration Includes bibliographies. ISBN 92-2-103533-6 LC Card 86-915732
1. Agricultural laborers - Asia, Southeastern - Congresses. 2. Agricultural laborers - Asia, Southeastern - Social conditions - Congresses. I. UNDP/ILO Regional Project for Strengthening Labour/Manpower Administration in Asia and the Pacific. II. Title. III. Series.
HD1537.A785 S8 1982

SUBSCRIPTION TELEVISION - AUSTRIA - SALZBURG (LAND)
Lenhardt, Helmut, 1923- Teure neue Medien . Salzburg , 1983. 152 p. ; ISBN 3-85015-012-7 LC Card 84-107910
HE8700.72.A9 L46 1983

SUBSCRIPTION TELEVISION - UNITED STATES.
Frank, Peter. Business opportunities for broadcasters in MDS pay television /. Washington, DC [c1982] 29 p. ; LC Card 86-201299
HE8700.72.U6 F73 1982

Subsidiariedad o intervencionismo? . Larraín P., Christian. [Santiago, Chile] [1986] 137 p. ; LC Card 87-401544 DDC 338.983 19
HC192 .L36 1986

Subsidiaritätsprinzip als Leitlinie für einen Subventionsabbau . Hummel, Marlies. München , 1985. xiii, 306 p. ; ISBN 3-88512-003-8 : LC Card 86-125424
HC290.5.S9 H85 1985

SUBSIDIARY COMPANIES. see **SUBSIDIARY CORPORATIONS.**

SUBSIDIARY CORPORATIONS - ACCOUNTING.
Goodman, Hortense. Illustrations of "push down" accounting /. New York, N.Y. (1211 Ave., of the Americas, New York 10036) , c1985. 52 p. ; LC Card 87-100703 DDC 657/.3 19
HF5681.B2 G663 1985

SUBSIDIARY CORPORATIONS - LATIN AMERICA - CASE STUDIES.
Sourrouille, Juan V. Inversiones extranjeras en América Latina . Buenos Aires [1984] viii, 142 p. : LC Card 86-183036
HG5160.5.A3 S64 1984

SUBSIDIES.
Räber, Josef. Subventionen als volkswirtschaftliche und finanzwirtschaftliche Erscheinung, mit besonderer Berücksichtigung der schweizerischen Verhältnisse in den Nachkriegsjahren /. Winterthur , 1965. xxvii, 191 p. : LC Card 85-162566
HD3646.S9 R33 1965

SUBSIDIES - BRAZIL, NORTHEAST.
Simas, José Ribamar. Subsídios para uma proposta de ocupação racional de novas áreas com agricultura de sequeiro no Nordeste brasileiro /. Recife , 1985 [i.e. 1986] 28, [16] p. : LC Card 87-404827 DDC 338.1/8 19
HD499.N67 S56 1986

SUBSIDIES - EUROPE.
Hummel, Marlies. Subsidiaritätsprinzip als Leitlinie für einen Subventionsabbau . München , 1985. xiii, 306 p. ; ISBN 3-88512-003-8 : LC Card 86-125424
HC290.5.S9 H85 1985

SUBSIDIES - GERMANY, WEST.
Fuest, Winfried, 1946- Subventionen . Köln , c1985. 40 p. : ISBN 3-602-24732-5 LC Card 85-200722
HC290.5.S9 F84 1985

Germany (West). Bundestag. Haushaltsausschuss. Fragen der Subventionspolitik . Bonn , 1982. 222 p. ; LC Card 83-190544 DDC 338.943/02 19
HD3646.G4 G47 1982

Hennicke, Martin. Zum Förderungssystem für kleine und mittlere Unternehmen . Stuttgart , c1986. 155 p. ; ISBN 3-7910-5012-5 LC Card 86-181544 DDC 338.6/42/0943 19
HD2346.G3 H44 1986

Hummel, Marlies. Subsidiaritätsprinzip als Leitlinie für einen Subventionsabbau . München , 1985. xiii, 306 p. ; ISBN 3-88512-003-8 : LC Card 86-125424
HC290.5.S9 H85 1985

Sprink, Joachim. Der Staat als Sanierer von Grossunternehmen . Idstein , 1986. 164 p. : ISBN 3-925196-20-X LC Card 86-229615
HD3646.G4 S67 1986

Zur Problematik von Subventionen als Instrument der Wirtschaftspolitik /. Bonn , 1986. 97 p. : LC Card 87-408486 DDC

336/.012/43 s 338.943 19
HJ1101 .B6 Heft 259 HD3646.G4

SUBSIDIES - GREAT BRITAIN.
Sprink, Joachim. Der Staat als Sanierer von Grossunternehmen . Idstein , 1986. 164 p. : ISBN 3-925196-20-X LC Card 86-229615
HD3646.G4 S67 1986

SUBSIDIES - ITALY.
Relazione programmatica delle partecipazioni statali per il 1984 . Roma , 1985. 563 p. ; LC Card 86-176014
HC310.I53 R45 1985

SUBSIDIES - LAW AND LEGISLATION - EUROPE.
Hummel, Marlies. Subsidiaritätsprinzip als Leitlinie für einen Subventionsabbau . München , 1985. xiii, 306 p. ; ISBN 3-88512-003-8 : LC Card 86-125424
HC290.5.S9 H85 1985

SUBSIDIES - LAW AND LEGISLATION - GERMANY (WEST)
Germany (West). Bundestag. Haushaltsausschuss. Fragen der Subventionspolitik . Bonn , 1982. 222 p. ; LC Card 83-190544 DDC 338.943/02 19
HD3646.G4 G47 1982

Hummel, Marlies. Subsidiaritätsprinzip als Leitlinie für einen Subventionsabbau . München , 1985. xiii, 306 p. ; ISBN 3-88512-003-8 : LC Card 86-125424
HC290.5.S9 H85 1985

SUBSIDIES - SAUDI ARABIA.
Shaykh, Riyāḍ ʻAbd al-Ḥafīẓ. Niẓām al-iʻānah fī al-iqtiṣād al-Saʻūdī /. al-Mamlakah al-ʻArabīyah al-Suʻūdīyah , 1985. 77 p. : LC Card 86-208281
HC415.33.Z9 E447 1985

SUBSIDIES - SWEDEN.
Lindmark, Leif. Företagsstöd och kommunalt risktagande /. Stockholm [1984] iv, 49 p. : ISBN 91-38-08297-7 LC Card 85-106839
HD3646.S8 L55 1984

Olofsson, Christer. Kommunala bolag med industriutvecklings uppgifter . Stockholm [1984] 82 p. ; ISBN 91-38-08114-8 LC Card 85-106731
HD3616.S53 O46 1984

Sweden. Oljeersättningsdelegationen. Statligt stöd till oljeersättning . [Stockholm] [1983] 1 v. (various pagings) : ISBN 91-38-07657-8 LC Card 84-218524
HD9502.S82 S96 1983

SUBSIDIES - SWEDEN - CASE STUDIES.
Icke-permanent stöd till tre industriföretag . [Stockholm] [1981] 245 p. : ISBN 91-38-06270-4 LC Card 83-245223
HD3646.S8 I25 1981

Två samhällsekonomiska utvärderingar av icke-permanent industristöd . [Stockholm] [1981] 221 p. : ISBN 91-38-06269-0 LC Card 83-245219
HD3646.S8 T85 1981

SUBSIDIES - SWITZERLAND.
Burkhalter, Rudolf. Die Effizienz der Finanzierungshilfen an Klein- und Mittelbetriebe im Berggebiet /. Bern [1985] (Aarau : Cooperative Drucki) 216 p. : LC Card 86-115683
HG4027.7 .B86 1985

Räber, Josef. Subventionen als volkswirtschaftliche und finanzwirtschaftliche Erscheinung, mit besonderer Berücksichtigung der schweizerischen Verhältnisse in den Nachkriegsjahren /. Winterthur , 1965. xxvii, 191 p. : LC Card 85-162566
HD3646.S9 R33 1965

SUBSIDIES - UNITED STATES.
Heston, Thomas J. (Thomas Janney) Sweet subsidy . New York , 1987. 544 p. ; ISBN 0-8240-8084-X (alk. paper) : LC Card 87-23776 DDC 338.1/8 19
HD9105 .H47 1987

Sprink, Joachim. Der Staat als Sanierer von Grossunternehmen . Idstein , 1986. 164 p. : ISBN 3-925196-20-X LC Card 86-229615
HD3646.G4 S67 1986

Subsídios para uma proposta de ocupação racional de novas áreas com agricultura de sequeiro no Nordeste brasileiro /. Simas, José Ribamar. Recife , 1985 [i.e. 1986] 28, [16] p. : LC Card 87-404827 DDC 338.1/8 19
HD499.N67 S56 1986

Subsidizing inefficiency . Silkman, Richard H. New York , 1985. xviii, 101 p.: ISBN 0-03-000662-7 (alk. paper) : LC Card 84-26628 DDC 336.1/85 19
HJ275 .S53 1985 ***NYPL [JLE 85-2261]***

SUBSISTENCE ECONOMY.
Lenz, Ilse. Kapitalistische Entwicklung, Subsistenzproduktion und Frauenarbeit . Frankfurt/Main , New York , c1984. 330 p. : ISBN 3-593-33407-0(pbk.)
NYPL [JLD 87-332]

SUBSISTENCE ECONOMY - MEXICO.
Bennholdt-Thomsen, Veronika. Bauern in Mexiko . Frankfurt [am Main] , New York , c1982. 214 p. ; ISBN 3-593-33167-5 LC Card 83-139124 DDC 305.5/63 19
HD1531.M6 B46 1982

SUBSISTENCE ECONOMY - PAPUA NEW GUINEA.
Philp, Norman E. The cash incentive . Canberra , 1986. xii, 135 p. : ISBN 0-86784-984-3 (pbk.) LC Card 87-150813
HD2346.P37 P46 1986

Substituição de óleo diesel : alternativas e viabilidade de diesel vegetal / elaboração, CEPED-Centro de Pesquisas e Desenvolvimento ; equipe de trabalho, coordenação, Vladmir Maretic ; equipe técnica, Leila Maria Guimarães Aguiar ... [et al.]. [Brasília, Brazil] : Ministério das Minas e Energia, Secretaria Geral, Secretaria de Tecnologia, [19]84. 84 p. : ill. ; 30 cm. LC Card 87-404960 DDC 338.4/76553 19
1. Diesel fuels industry - Brazil. 2. Vegetable oils as fuels. 3. Oil-palm - Brazil. I. Maretic, Vladmir. II. Aguiar, Leila Maria Guimarães. III. Centro de Pesquisas e Desenvolvimento (Brazil).
HD9579.D53 B737 1984

SUBSTITUTE PRODUCTS.
Plastics in business machines . Stamford, Conn. , c1986. vii, 215 leaves : ISBN 0-89336-433-6 (soft) : LC Card 87-165036 DDC 380.1/456684 19
HD9801.A2 P56 1986

Shea, Moira M. The United States engineering plastics industry . Washington, D.C. , 1987. 51 p. : LC Card 87-601518 DDC 338.4/76684/0973 19
HD9661.U62 S54 1987

Substituting agricultural materials for petroleum based industrial products /. Morris, David J. Washington, D.C. , c1986. i, 33 p. ; ISBN 0-917582-46-2 (pbk.) : LC Card 86-21350 DDC 338.4/76628 19
HD9502.5.B543 U654 1986

SUBSTITUTION (ECONOMICS)
Farzin, Yeganeh Hossein, 1950- Competition and substitutes in the market for an exhaustible resource /. Greenwich, Conn. , c1985. xvi, 209 : ISBN 0-89232-604-2 : LC Card 85-23765 DDC 338.2/7282/0724 19
HD9560.5 .F385 1985 ***NYPL [JLE 86-1585]***

SUBSTITUTION (ECONOMICS) - MATHEMATICAL MODELS.
Canto, Victor A. Currency substitution . Boston , c1987. viii, 196 p. ; ISBN 0-89838-195-9 LC Card 86-27747 DDC 332.4/56/098 19
HG3823 .C36 1987

SUBTERRANEAN WATER. see **WATER, UNDERGROUND.**

SUBTROPICAL FRUIT. see **TROPICAL FRUIT.**

Suburban gridlock /. Cervero, Robert. New Brunswick, N.J. , c1986. xxiii, 248 p. : ISBN 0-88285-115-2 : LC Card 86-2628 DDC 388.4/13142/0973 19
HE355.3.C64 C47 1986
NYPL [JLE 86-4446]

SUBURBS - FRANCE.
Lacour, Claude. Croissance urbaine . Paris , 1981. 219 p. : ISBN 2-222-02928-7 (pbk.) : LC Card 82-153821 DDC 388.4/068 19
HE4764 .L3 1981 ***NYPL [JLG 86-56]***

SUBURBS - FRANCE - CONGRESSES.
Colloque Les Périphéries urbaines (1984 : Angers, France) Actes du Colloque Les Périphéries urbaines . Caen , c1985. 270 p. : ISBN 2-905461-03-9 : LC Card 86-173712
HB2263 .C65 1984

SUBURBS - UNITED STATES.
Cervero, Robert. Suburban gridlock /. New Brunswick, N.J. , c1986. xxiii, 248 p. : ISBN 0-88285-115-2 : LC Card 86-2628 DDC 388.4/13142/0973 19
HE355.3.C64 C47 1986
NYPL [JLE 86-4446]

Subventionen . Fuest, Winfried, 1946- Köln , c1985. 40 p. : ISBN 3-602-24732-5 LC Card 85-200722
HC290.5.S9 F84 1985

Subventionen als volkswirtschaftliche und finanzwirtschaftliche Erscheinung, mit besonderer Berücksichtigung der schweizerischen Verhältnisse in den Nachkriegsjahren /. Räber, Josef. Winterthur , 1965. xxvii, 191 p. : LC Card 85-162566
HD3646.S9 R33 1965

SUBVENTIONS. see **SUBSIDIES.**

SUBWAYS.
Várszegi, Gyula. A világ metrói /. [Budapest] [1983] 250 p., [48] p. of plates : ISBN 963-02-2971-4 (Magy. nemz. bibl.) LC Card 84-219598
HE4211 .V37 1983

SUBWAYS - GERMANY (WEST) - CASE STUDIES.
Hall, Peter, 1931- Can rail save the city? . Aldershot, Hants , Brookfield, Vt., U. S.A. , c1985. xii, 241 p. : ISBN 0-566-00947-1 : LC Card 85-17659 DDC 388.4/2/0943 19
HE4774 .H35 1985 ***NYPL [JLD 86-2622]***

SUBWAYS - GERMANY (WEST) - MATHEMATICAL MODELS.
Stengel, Wolfgang. Verlagerungen der individuellen Verkehrsnachfrage bei verändertem ÖPNV-Angebot infolge neueingerichteter Stadtschnellbahnen /. Bad Honnef , 1984. iv, 210 p. : ISBN 3-88347-120-8 : LC Card 84-185940
HE311.G3 S73 1984

SUBWAYS - GREAT BRITAIN - CASE STUDIES.
Hall, Peter, 1931- Can rail save the city? . Aldershot, Hants , Brookfield, Vt., U. S.A. , c1985. xii, 241 p. : ISBN 0-566-00947-1 : LC Card 85-17659 DDC 388.4/2/0943 19
HE4774 .H35 1985 ***NYPL [JLD 86-2622]***

SUBWAYS - MISCELLANEA.
Golden tokens . Roxbury, Conn. , c1987. p. cm. ISBN 0-941067-00-9 LC Card 86-27826 DDC 388.4/28 19
HE4211 .G58 1987

Succeeding in high tech . Shigekawa, Marlene, 1944- New York , c1987. xiv, 294 p. : ISBN 0-471-85636-3 LC Card 86-33953 DDC 650.1 19
HD62.37 .S52 1987

Success and failure of futures contracts . Black, Deborah G. New York, N.Y. (90 Trinity Pl., New York 10006) [c1986] 70 p. ; LC Card 87-129777 DDC 332.64/4 19
HG6046 .B52 1986

Success guide for accountants. Half, Robert. [Success guide for accountants.] Robert Half's success guide for accountants /. New York , c1987. x, 167 p. ; ISBN 0-07-172107-X LC Card 87-16430 DDC 657/.023/72 19
HF5657 .H34 1987

SUCCESS IN BUSINESS.
Avis, Warren E. Take a chance to be first . New York , 1987, c1986. xii, 222 p. ; ISBN 0-07-002547-9 (pbk.) : LC Card 87-13236 DDC 650.1 19
HF5386 .A94 1987

Caple, John. The right work . New York, N.Y. , 1977. xvi, 269 p. ; ISBN 0-396-09064-8 LC Card 87-15734 DDC 650.1/4 19
HF5381 .C2634 1987

Crain, Sharon. Deal me in! . Boulder, Colo. , c1987. vi, 185 p. : LC Card 87-19904 DDC 650.1 19
HF5386 .C893 1987

Cunningham, Jan. All about multi-level marketing . Denver, CO (1020 15th St., Suite 41C, Denver 80202) , c1986. 173 p. : LC Card

86-213072 DDC 658.8/4 19
HF5415.126 .C85 1986

Davis, William, 1933- The corporate infighter's handbook . London , 1984. 144 p. : ISBN 0-283-99133-X (pbk.) : LC Card 85-240558 DDC 650.1 19
HF5386 .D325 1984 ***NYPL [JLE 87-618]***

Dayhoff, Signe A. Create your own career opportunities /. Andover, Mass. , c1987. x, 111 p. : ISBN 0-931790-75-1 : LC Card 86-26332 DDC 650.1/4 19
HF5549.5.C35 D38 1987

Dollé, Anne. Ça va comme un lundi . [Paris] , c1984. 237 p. ; ISBN 2-01-010177-4 : LC Card 85-143058 DDC 650.1/3 19
HF5386 .D63 1984

Gardenswartz, Lee. What it takes . New York , 1987. ix, 205 p. ; ISBN 0-385-23820-7 : LC Card 87-13657 DDC 650.1/024042 19
HF5386 .G214 1987

Godin, Seth. Business rules of thumb /. New York, NY , c1987. x, 165 p. ; ISBN 0-446-37026-6 (pbk.) LC Card 87-6262 DDC 650.1 19
HF5386 .G55 1987

Grindle, Art, 1923- I want to sell you success /. Charleston [S.C.] , c1987. p. cm. ISBN 0-931807-12-3 : LC Card 87-6962 DDC 650.1 19
HF5386 .G776 1987

Grover, Subhash C. (Shubash Chander), 1938- Paths to profits /. Dallas , 1985. v, 142 p. ; ISBN 0-930383-04-4 (pbk.) : LC Card 84-25548 DDC 650.1 19
HD62.7 .G75 1985 ***NYPL [JLD 86-1907]***

Hicks, Tyler Gregory, 1921- How to start your own business on a shoestring and make up to $500,000 a year /. Rocklin, CA , New York , c1987. xi, 225 p. ; ISBN 0-914629-12-3 (pbk.) : LC Card 86-25196 DDC 658/.041 19
HD62.5 .H527 1987

Jennings, Diane. Self-made women . Dallas , c1987. 139 p. ; ISBN 0-87833-550-1 (pbk.) : LC Card 87-16104 DDC 338/.04/088042 19
HD6054.3 .J46 1987

Job survival skills [videorecording] . Mt. Kisco, NY , 1986, c1987. 1 videocassette (50 min.) : LC Card 86-707971 DDC 650.1 11
HF5386

Kennedy, Gavin. Doing business abroad /. New York , c1985. 268 p. ; ISBN 0-671-55484-0 : LC Card 85-14416 DDC 658.4 19
HD58.6 .K45 1985 ***NYPL [JLD 86-2339]***

Korn, Errol R. Hyper-performance . New York , c1987. xi, 195 p. : ISBN 0-471-85344-5 LC Card 86-33984 DDC 650.1 19
HF5386 .K775 1987

Korn, Lester. The winning edge . New York , c1988. p. cm. ISBN 0-671-55263-5 LC Card 87-23249 DDC 658.4/09 19
HD38.2 .K67 1988

Lewis, Diane, 1936- Why women fail in business /. Nashville , c1987. p. cm. ISBN 0-8407-4219-3 : LC Card 87-15370 DDC 658.4/09088042 19
HD6054.3 .L48 1987

Molloy, John T. How to work the competition into the ground and have fun doing it . New York, NY , 1987. xiii, 206 p. ; ISBN 0-446-38499-2 (pbk.) : LC Card 86-24761 DDC 650.1 19
HF5386 .M72 1987

Norton, Hollis. How to make it when you're cash poor /. New York , 1986. 232 p. ; ISBN 0-671-62803-8 (pbk.) LC Card 86-26174 DDC 332.63/24 19
HD1382.5 .N67 1986

Peters, Roger. Practical intelligence . New York, N.Y. , c1987. x, 341 p. ; ISBN 0-06-015681-3 : LC Card 86-46096 DDC 650.1 19
HD38.2 .P47 1987

Plaschka, Gerhard. Unternehmenserfolg . Wien , c1986. viii, 228 p. ; LC Card 87-103428 DDC 658.4/09 19
HD38.2 .P55 1986

Robinson, Joe. You're the boss /. New York , c1987. x, 342 p. ; ISBN 0-312-01027-3 : LC Card 87-16149 DDC 658.4/2 19
HD62.5 .R59 1987

Rogers, David J. Waging business warfare . New York , c1987. x, 341 p. ; ISBN 0-684-18596-2 : LC Card 86-31584 DDC 658.4 19
HD38 .R5776 1987

Scott, Gini Graham. Mind power . Englewood Cliffs, N.J. , c1987. xi, 183 p. ; ISBN 0-13-583527-5 LC Card 87-6923 DDC 650.1 19
HF5386 .S413 1987

Smalis, I. A., 1918- Money . Santa Fe, NM, USA , 1987. 87 p. : ISBN 0-86534-100-1 : LC Card 87-6439 DDC 650.1 19
HF5386 .S637 1987

Smith, Roger F. Sales management . Englewood Cliffs, N.J. , c1987. x, 261 p. : ISBN 0-13-786534-1 LC Card 86-30299 DDC 658.8/1 19
HF5438.4 .S57 1987

Stechert, Kathryn B. Sweet success . New York , London , c1986. xiii, 224 p. ; ISBN 0-02-614380-1 LC Card 85-30916 DDC 650.1/024/042 19
HD6053 .S724 1986 ***NYPL [JLD 86-2435]***

Stechert, Kathryn B. [Sweet success.] On your own terms . New York , 1987, c1986. xvi, 314 p. ; ISBN 0-394-75301-1 (pbk.) : LC Card 86-40470 DDC 650.1/024042 19
HD6053 .S724 1987

Strain, Lois S. (Lois Smith) The story of Paul J. Meyer . Hollywood, Fla. , c1986. xii, 193 p. : ISBN 0-8119-0720-1 : LC Card 86-29525 DDC 338/.04/0924 B 19
HF5386 .S8832 1986

Tarkenton, Francis A. Playing to win . New York , c1984. viii, 116 p. ; ISBN 0-06-015242-7 : LC Card 83-48390 DDC 650.1 19
HF5386 .T22 1984 ***NYPL [JLD 86-3515]***

Taylor, Charlotte. The entrepreneurial workbook . New York, N.Y. , c1985. ix, 148 p. : ISBN 0-452-25660-7 : LC Card 84-29439 DDC 658/.022 19
HD62.5 .T39 1985 ***NYPL [JLF 86-795]***

Templeton, John, 1912- The Templeton plan . San Francisco , c1987. x, 181, [1] p. ; ISBN 0-06-250286-7 LC Card 86-43022 DDC 174/.4 19
HF5387 .T46 1987

Vitullo, Ray, 1925- How to get organized & increase self confidence . North Plainfield, N.J. , c1986. p. cm. ISBN 0-9607752-3-4 : LC Card 86-72854 DDC 650.1 19
HD69.T54 V58 1986

Wickham, Alexandre. Les carriéristes . Paris , c1983. 358 p. ; ISBN 2-85956-348-2 : LC Card 84-122542 DDC 650.1/4 19
HF5386 .W494 1983 ***NYPL [JLE 86-4124]***

SUCCESS IN BUSINESS - CALIFORNIA - SANTA CLARA COUNTY - CASE STUDIES.

Caddes, Carolyn, 1935- Portraits of success . Palo Alto, Calif. , 1986. viii, 138 p. : ISBN 0-935382-56-9 : LC Card 86-40032 DDC 338.4/7621/0979473 19
HD9696.A3 U53173 1986
NYPL [MFX (Caddes) 87-542]

SUCCESS IN BUSINESS - CANADA - CASE STUDIES.

Frontrunners. Chapel Hill, NC , 1987. 1 videocassette (28 min., 50 sec.) : LC Card 87-706853 DDC 338.6 11
HD9940

SUCCESS IN BUSINESS - CASE STUDIES.

Hartley, Robert F. Bullseyes and blunders . New York , c1987. vii, 253 p. : ISBN 0-471-84904-9 LC Card 86-23350 DDC 658 19
HD38 .H3487 1987 ***NYPL [JLE 87-1047]***

Heller, Robert, 1932- The supermarketers . New York , c1987. xiii, 384 p. ; ISBN 0-525-24520-0 LC Card 86-23977 DDC 658.8 19
HF5415 .H374 1987

Potts, Mark. The leading edge . New York , c1987. iv, 220 p. ; ISBN 0-07-050599-3 LC Card 86-10567 DDC 658.4/06 19
HD58.8 .P68 1987 ***NYPL [JLE 87-33]***

SUCCESS IN BUSINESS - DENMARK.

Carlsen, Anne Marie Sloth. Køn og ledelse . København , 1986. 251 p. : ISBN 87-87749-29-7 (pbk.) :kr149.00 LC Card 87-145777
HD6054.4.D4 C37 1986

SUCCESS IN BUSINESS - NETHERLANDS - CASE STUDIES.

Houweling, Marjolein. Ondernemende vrouwen /. Amsterdam , c1985. 128 p. : ISBN 90-6834-018-2 : LC Card 86-166264
HD2346.N4 H68 1985

SUCCESS IN BUSINESS - UNITED STATES.

Allen, Robert G. The challenge /. New York , c1987. 301 p. ; ISBN 0-671-52618-9 LC Card 87-4317 DDC 650.1 19
HF5386 .A543 1987

Bohigian, Valerie. Ladybucks /. New York, N.Y. , c1987. 246 p. ; ISBN 0-396-08852-X LC Card 86-29227 DDC 650.1/024042 19
HD6072.6.U5 B64 1987

Brahmstedt, W. T. (William T.), 1924- The courtiers of American business /. Palm Springs, Calif. , c1987. 190 p. : ISBN 0-88280-118-X (pbk.) : LC Card 86-29078 DDC 650.1/3 19
HF5386 .B777 1987

Kiam, Victor. Going for it! . New York , c1986. 260 p. ; ISBN 0-688-06060-9 : LC Card 85-61762 DDC 338/.04/0924 B 19
HC102.5.K53 A34 1986
NYPL [JLE 86-2954]

Lewis, William, 1946- Fast-track careers . New York , c1987. x, 212 p. ; ISBN 0-471-83801-2 (pbk.) : LC Card 87-10045 DDC 331.7/02/0973 19
HF5382.5.U5 L45 1987

Minkow, Barry. Making it in America /. [Los Angeles?] , c1985. 136 p. ; LC Card 85-51822 DDC 650.1/092/4 B 19
HC102.5.M5 A3 1985

Morrison, Ann M. Breaking the glass ceiling . Reading, Mass. , c1987. ix, 229 p. : ISBN 0-201-15787-X : LC Card 87-1853 DDC 658.4/09/024042 19
HD6054.4.U6 M67 1987

Petras, Ross. Inside track . New York , c1986. xv, 508 p. ; ISBN 0-394-74339-3 : LC Card 85-40868 DDC 650.1/4/0973 19
HF5382.U5 P44 1986
NYPL [*R-Econ. 86-3454]

Weintz, Walter. The solid gold mailbox . New York , c1987. xiv, 268 p. : ISBN 0-471-85026-8 LC Card 86-28267 DDC 658.8/72 19
HF5466 .W45 1987

Winner take all /. New York, NY , c1987. x, 222 p. ; ISBN 0-8144-7689-9 (pbk.) : LC Card 87-47708 DDC 658.4/09 19
HD38.25.U6 W56 1987

SUCCESS IN BUSINESS - UNITED STATES - CASE STUDIES.

Carter, John Mack. Starting at the top . New York [1985] 252 p. ; ISBN 0-688-04520-0 LC Card 85-4826 DDC 338/.04/0922 B 19
HC102.5.A2 C37 1985
NYPL [JLD 87-1089]

Friedman, Thomas. Up the ladder . New York, NY , 1986. xi, 203 p. ; ISBN 0-446-51291-5 LC Card 85-40655 DDC 658.4/09/0973 19
HD38.25.U6 F75 1986 ***NYPL [JLE 86-2840]***

Goldwasser, Thomas. Family pride . New York , c1986. 226 p. ; ISBN 0-396-08587-3 LC Card 86-4546 DDC 338.7/4/0973 19
HD62.25 .G64 1986 ***NYPL [JLD 87-159]***

Gschwandtner, Gerhard. Supersellers . New York, N.Y. , c1986. xi, 169 p. : ISBN 0-8144-5883-1 LC Card 86-47586 DDC 658.8/5 19
HF5438.25 .G785 1986
NYPL [JLE 87-1489]

Paul, Ronald N. The 101 best performing companies in America /. Chicago, Ill. , c1986. vii, 382 p. ; ISBN 0-917253-39-6 : LC Card 86-4947 DDC 338.7/4/0973 19
HD2785 .P38 1986 ***NYPL [JLE 86-3151]***

Risk to riche$. Washington, DC (600 Maryland Ave., S.W., Suite 700, Washington 20024) , c1986. vii, 204 p. : LC Card 87-158511 DDC 338/.04/088042 19
HD2346.U5 R57 1986

Smith, Geoffrey N. Sweat equity . New York , c1986. 254 p. : ISBN 0-671-55210-4 LC Card 86-6622 DDC 658/.022 19
HD62.5 .S625 1986 ***NYPL [JLD 86-3014]***

Wilkens, Joanne. Her own business . New York , c1987. xv, 245 p. ; ISBN 0-07-050854-2 : LC Card 86-27780 DDC 338.6/422/088042 19
HD2346.U5 W548 1987

Success in small and medium-scale enterprises . Cortes, Mariluz. New York , c1987. xiii, 289 p. ; ISBN 0-19-520593-6 : LC Card 86-46296 DDC 338.6/42/09861 19
HD2346.C7 C69 1987

SUCCESS MOTIVATION INSTITUTE.
Strain, Lois S. (Lois Smith) The story of Paul J. Meyer . Hollywood, Fla. , c1986. xii, 193 p. : ISBN 0-8119-0720-1 : LC Card 86-29525 DDC 338/.04/0924 B 19
HF5386 .S8832 1986

SUCCESS - SWITZERLAND.
Michel-Alder, Elisabeth. Männer im Glashaus . Zürich , c1986. 238 p. : ISBN 3-280-01561-8 LC Card 86-180438
HD38.25.S9 M52 1986

Successful business communication /. Treece, Malra. Boston , c1987. xv, 511 p. : ISBN 0-205-10484-3 LC Card 86-26469 DDC 808/.066651 19
HF5721 .T73 1987

Successful business computing /. Tampoe, M. London , 1982. 124 p. :
NYPL [JLD 86-2491]

Successful corporate turnarounds . Finkin, Eugene F. New York , 1987. xviii, 211 p. : ISBN 0-89930-232-7 (lib. bdg. : alk. paper) : LC Card 86-25280 DDC 658.4/063 19
HD58.8 .F52 1987

Successful investing : a complete guide to your financial future / by the staff of Babson-United Investment Advisors, Inc. ; with introductory chapters on the art of prudent investing by David R. Sargent ; editor, Carolyn M. Finnegan.4th ed., rev. and updated, 1st Fireside ed. New York : Simon & Schuster, 1987. 529 p. : ill. ; 24 cm. "A Fireside book." Includes index. ISBN 0-671-64762-8 (pbk.) : LC Card 87-19736 DDC 332.6/78 19
1. Investments. 2. Finance, Personal. I. Sargent, David R. II. Finnegan, Carolyn M. III. Babson-United Investment Advisors.
HG4521 .S823 1987

Successful investment strategy /. Craig, Malcolm. Cambridge, England , Wolfeboro, N.H., USA. , 1988. p. cm. ISBN 0-85941-383-7 : LC Card 87-8325 DDC 332.6/78 19
HG4521 .C858 1988

Successful management consulting . Greenfield, W. M. Englewood Cliffs, N.J. , c1987. xii, 192 p. ; ISBN 0-13-863143-3 : LC Card 86-30494 DDC 658.4/6 19
HD69.C6 G72 1987

The Successful office skills series.
Linkemer, Bobbi. How to run a meeting /. New York, NY , c1987. 51 p. ; ISBN 0-8144-7671-6 (pbk.) : LC Card 86-47815 DDC 658.4/563 19
HD30.3 .L55 1987

Linkemer, Bobbi. How to write an effective resume /. New York, NY , c1987. 58 p. ; ISBN 0-8144-7669-4 (pbk.) : LC Card 86-47813 DDC 650.1/4 19
HF5383 .L56 1987

Weiss, Donald H., 1936- How to deal with difficult people /. New York, N.Y. , c1987. 57 p. ; ISBN 0-8144-7674-0 (pbk.) : LC Card 86-47827 DDC 158/.2 19
HD42 .W45 1987

Weiss, Donald H., 1936- Managing stress /. New York, NY , c1987. 55 p. ; ISBN 0-8144-7673-2 (pbk.) : LC Card 86-47825 DDC 158.7 19
HF5548.85 .W39 1987

Successful oral and written presentations /. Blumenthal, Lassor A. New York, NY , c1987. 94 p. : ISBN 0-399-51330-2 (pbk.) : LC Card 87-2272 DDC 658.4/5 19
HF5718 .B57 1987

Successful pension design for small-to medium-sized businesses /. Slimmon, Robert F. Englewood Cliffs, N.J. , c1987. xix, 440 p. ; ISBN 0-13-860255-7 LC Card 87-2489 DDC 658.3/253
HD7105.4 .S56 1987

Successful projects, with a moral for management /. Kharbanda, Om Prakesh. Hants, England , c1986. xvii, 267 p. : ISBN 0-566-02651-1 LC Card 86-235562 DDC 658.4/04 19
HD69.P75 K55 1986

The Successful sales assistant's handbook. New York, N.Y. : New York Institute of Finance, c1987. xi, 268 p. : ill. ; 28 cm. Includes index. ISBN 0-13-860305-7 (pbk.) : LC Card 87-11322 DDC 332.6/2/0688 19
1. Securities - Handbooks, manuals, etc. 2. Brokers - Handbooks, manual, etc. I. New York Institute of Finance. II. Title: Sales assistant handbook.
HG4621 .S84 1987

Successful strategies for real estate agents . Wickman, Floyd. Dubuque, Iowa , c1987. xii, 226 p. ; ISBN 0-8403-4185-7 (pbk.) : LC Card 86-82782 DDC 333.33/068/8 19
HD1382 .W53 1987

Successfully developing your accounting practice . Ronald, Dana M. New York , 1987. x, 314 p. ; ISBN 0-471-84736-4 LC Card 86-32388 DDC 657/.068/8 19
HF5657 .R644 1987

SUCCESSION, INTESTATE. see **INHERITANCE AND SUCCESSION.**

Succession systems and corporate performance. Friedman, Stewart D. Leadership succession systems and corporate performance /. New York, N.Y. (316 Uris Hall, New York, N.Y. 10027) , c1985. ix, 141 p. :
NYPL [JLF 87-255]

Suchādā Waraph Thailand. Krom Sēthakit Kānphānit. Rāingān phon kānsksā wičhai . [Krung Thēp Mahā Nakh 2521 [1978] 24, [7] folded p., [7] p. of plates : LC Card 81-183926
HD9766.T52 T47 1978

Suchart Prasithrathsint. Ethnicity and fertility in Thailand / by Suchart Prasithrathsint. Singapore : Institute of Southeast Asian Studies, 1985. xviii, 270 p. : map ; 23 cm. (Research notes and discussions paper 0129-8828 . no. 51) Ethnicity and fertility in Southeast Asia series. Bibliography: p. 265-270. ISBN 997-19-8813-5
1. Fertility, Human - Thailand. 2. Ethnicity - Thailand. 3. Birth control - Thailand. I. Title.
NYPL [JLE 86-3668]

Suchāt 'Ēknarong. Thailand. Krom Sēthakit Kānphānit. Rāingān phon kānsksā wičhai . [Krung Thēp Mahā Nakh 2521 [1978] 24, [7] folded p., [7] p. of plates : LC Card 81-183926
HD9766.T52 T47 1978

Suchman, Diane R. Managing a development company : interviews with successful firms : a research report / by Diane R. Suchman, in collaboration with J. Thomas Black, Bernard J. Frieden, Ira S. Lowry. Washington, D.C. : ULI-the Urban Land Institute, [1987] v, 179 p. ; 23 cm. ISBN 0-87420-672-3 (pbk.) LC Card 87-82097 DDC 333.3/8/068 19
1. Real estate development - Management - Case studies. 2. Real estate management - Case studies. I. Title.
HD1390 .S93 1987

SUCRE (ECUADOR : CANTON) - ECONOMIC CONDITIONS.
Dueñas de Anhalzer, Carmen. Historia económica y social de Manabí /. [Quito, Ecuador] , 1986. 140 p., [4] leaves of plates : LC Card 87-107503
HC203.S83 D84 1986

SUCRE (ECUADOR : CANTON) - SOCIAL CONDITIONS.
Dueñas de Anhalzer, Carmen. Historia económica y social de Manabí /. [Quito, Ecuador] , 1986. 140 p., [4] leaves of plates : LC Card 87-107503
HC203.S83 D84 1986

Sudan . Cater, Nick. Oxford , c1986. i, 36 p. : ISBN 0-85598-075-3 (pbk.) : LC Card 86-234718 DDC 363.8/09624 19
HC835.Z9 F33 1986

Sudan. Census Office. Population of the Sudan and its regions . [Wad Medani, Sudan?] [1984?- <1 > v. : LC Card 86-980678 DDC 304.6/09624/021 19
HA4687 .A4 1983

SUDAN - CENSUS, 1983.
Population of the Sudan and its regions . [Wad Medani, Sudan?] [1984?- <1 > v. : LC Card 86-980678 DDC 304.6/09624/021 19
HA4687 .A4 1983

SUDAN - COMMERCE - HANDBOOKS, MANUALS, ETC.
Sudan, the country and its market. Paris , 1979. 145 p. : LC Card 87-112726
HC835 .S83536 1979

The Sudan demand for international reserve . Elbadawi, Ibrahim. [Khartoum] [1984] 40 leaves : LC Card 85-981026 DDC 332.4/5609624 19
HG3982.8 .E42 1984

Sudan. Economic and Social Research Council. see **Majlis al-Abḥāth al-Iqtiṣādīyah wa-al-Ijtimā'īyah.**

SUDAN - ECONOMIC CONDITIONS.
Affan, Bodour O. Abu. Industrial policies and industrialization in the Sudan /. Khartoum, Sudan , 1985. 180 p. ; ISBN 0-08-637205-44 (pbk.) LC Card 86-981076 DDC 338.9624 19
HC835 .A58 1985

Cater, Nick. Sudan . Oxford , c1986. i, 36 p. : ISBN 0-85598-075-3 (pbk.) : LC Card 86-234718 DDC 363.8/09624 19
HC835.Z9 F33 1986

SUDAN - ECONOMIC CONDITIONS - 1973-
Abu Gabal, Sayed Ahmed. Migration of Sudanese . [Khartoum] , 1984. 18, [14] p. ; LC Card 86-980176 DDC 331.6/2/6240174927 19
HD8766 .A65 1984

SUDAN - ECONOMIC CONDITIONS - HANDBOOKS, MANUALS, ETC.
Sudan, the country and its market. Paris , 1979. 145 p. : LC Card 87-112726
HC835 .S83536 1979

SUDAN - ECONOMIC POLICY.
Affan, Bodour O. Abu. Industrial policies and industrialization in the Sudan /. Khartoum, Sudan , 1985. 180 p. ; ISBN 0-08-637205-44 (pbk.) LC Card 86-981076 DDC 338.9624 19
HC835 .A58 1985

Sudan. Wizārat al-Mālīyah wa-al-Takhṭīṭ al-Iqtiṣādī. Planning. Prospects, programmes, and policies for economic development-III (PPPED-III) /. Khartoum [1984] 232 p. ; LC Card 86-980066 DDC 338.9624 19
HC835 .S8335 1984

Sudan, Egyptian. see **Sudan.**

SUDAN - EMIGRATION AND IMMIGRATION - ECONOMIC ASPECTS.
Abu Gabal, Sayed Ahmed. Migration of Sudanese . [Khartoum] , 1984. 18, [14] p. ; LC Card 86-980176 DDC 331.6/2/6240174927 19
HD8766 .A65 1984

Sudan - Government. see **Sudan - Politics and government.**

SUDAN - INDUSTRIES.
Affan, Bodour O. Abu. Industrial policies and industrialization in the Sudan /. Khartoum, Sudan , 1985. 180 p. ; ISBN 0-08-637205-44 (pbk.) LC Card 86-981076 DDC 338.9624 19
HC835 .A58 1985

Sudan. Majlis al-Abḥāth al-Igtiṣādīyah wa-al-Ijtimā'īyah. see **Majlis al-Abḥāth al-Iqtiṣādīyah wa-al-Ijtimā'īyah.**

Sudan. National Energy Administration. Sudan. National Energy Plan Committee. The national energy plan, 1985-2000 /. Khartoum, Sudan , 1985. iii, iii, 158 p. : LC Card 86-980496 DDC 333.79/09624 19
HD9502.S732 S83 1985a

Sudan. National Energy Plan Committee. The national energy plan, 1985-2000 / prepared by the National Energy Plan Committee. Khartoum, Sudan : The Committee, 1985. iii, iii, 158 p. : ill. ; 28 cm. At head of title: Democratic Republic of Sudan, Ministry of Energy and Mining, National Energy Administration. "January 1985"--Cover. LC Card 86-980496 DDC 333.79/09624 19
1. Energy policy - Sudan. I. Sudan. National Energy Administration. II. Title.
HD9502.S732 S83 1985a

SUDAN - POLITICS AND GOVERNMENT - HANDBOOKS, MANUALS, ETC.
Sudan, the country and its market. Paris , 1979.

145 p. : LC Card 87-112726
HC835 .S83536 1979

SUDAN - POPULATION - STATISTICS.
Population of the Sudan and its regions . [Wad Medani, Sudan?] [1984?- <1 > v. : LC Card 86-980678 DDC 304.6/09624/021 19
HA4687 .A4 1983

SUDAN - STATISTICS.
Regional statistical abstract, 1972-1980 /. Juba [Sudan] , 1986. xiii, 113 leaves ; LC Card 86-981387 DDC 316.24 19
HA4687 .R45 1986

Sudan, the country and its market. Paris : Groupe J.A., 1979. 145 p. : ill. ; 27 cm. (World markets, 0150-7605 . no. 19) Cover title. Bibliography: p. 131. LC Card 87-112726
1. Sudan - Economic conditions - Handbooks, manuals, etc. 2. Sudan - Commerce - Handbooks, manuals, etc. 3. Sudan - Politics and government - Handbooks, manuals, etc. I. Series: Marchés nouveaux , no 19.
HC835 .S83536 1979

Sudan. Wizārat al-Mālīyah wa-al-Takhṭīṭ al-Iqtiṣādī. Planning. Prospects, programmes, and policies for economic development-III (PPPED-III) / the Democratic Republic of Sudan, Ministry of Finance and Economic Planning (Planning). Khartoum : The Ministry, [1984] 232 p. ; 29 cm. Cover title: Prospects, programmes, and policies for economic development-III, 1984/85-1986/87 (PPPED-III). "October 1984"--Cover. LC Card 86-980066 DDC 338.9624 19
1. Public investments - Sudan. 2. Sudan - Economic policy. I. Title.
HC835 .S8335 1984

Sudan's irrigated subsector . D'Silva, Brian. Washington, D.C. , 1986. iv, 31 p. : LC Card 86-602812 DDC 333.91/3/09624 19
HD1741.S85 D75 1986

Sudarsana Rao, R. (Rokkam) Grants-in-aid and economic development in India / R. Sudarsana Rao. 1st ed. Allahabad, India : Chugh Publications, 1986. ix, 271 p. ; 23 cm. Revision of the author's thesis (Ph. D.--Andhra University, 1985) Bibliography: p. [257]-267. Includes index. ISBN 81-85076-14-6 : LC Card 86-903200 DDC 338.954
1. Grants-in-aid - India. 2. Economic assistance, Domestic - India. 3. India - Economic policy - 1947-. I. Title.
HJ1338 .S83 1986

Sudarsanam, P. S. Market and industry structure and corporate cost of capital : some U.K. evidence / by P.S. Sudarsanam. London : City University Business School, [1986] 33 p. ; 30 cm. (Working paper series, 0140-1041 . no. 80) Bibliography: p. 30-33. LC Card 86-208314 DDC 338.7/4/0941 19
1. Business enterprises - Great Britain - Finance. 2. Corporations - Great Britain - Finance. 3. Industrial organization - Great Britain. I. Series: Working paper series (City University (London, England). Business School) , no. 80. II. Title.
HG4135 .S83 1986

Sudarshan Kumari, 1924- Juyal, B. N. Child labour . Varanasi , 1985. xiii, 161 p. ; LC Card 87-901161 DDC 331.3/1/0954 19
HD6250.I42 J89 1985

Sudebnye prot͡sessy po ėkonomicheskim delam v SSSR . Evel'son, Evgenii͡a. London , 1986. 370 p. ; *NYPL [*QIX 87-4024]*

Sudene. see **Brazil. Superintendência do Desenvolvimento do Nordeste.**

Suding, Paul H. Ökonomische Ansätze zur Analyse des Energieverbrauchs der Haushalte für Rauwärmzwecke / Paul H. Suding. München : R. Oldenbourg, 1984. ix, 252, 10 p. : ill. ; 21 cm. (Schriftenreihe des Energiewirtschaftlichen Instituts . Bd. 27) Bibliography: p. 242-252. ISBN 3-486-28661-7 LC Card 84-209002
1. Households - Germany (West) - Energy consumption. 2. Energy development - Germany (West) - Econometric models. I. Title. II. Series.
HD9502.G42 S8 1984

Südwestdeutsche Schriften .
(2) Gensewich, Irmtraud. Die Tabakarbeiterin in Baden, 1870-1914 /. Mannheim , 1986. 496 p. : ISBN 3-87804-183-7 LC Card 87-121532 DDC 331.4/8797/094346 19
HD6073.T62 G34 1986

(3) Hahn, Barbara. Der geförderte Wohnungsbau in Mannheim 1850-1985 /. Mannheim , 1986. 236 p. : ISBN 3-87804-185-3 LC Card 87-121543 DDC 363.5/8/0943/46 19
HD7339.M35 H34 1986

Das Süd-Nord-Gefälle : gemeinsame Strategien für neue Strukturen / Rüdiger von Voss, Karl Friedrich (Hrsg.) ; mit Beiträgen von Eckart van Hooven ... [et al.]. Stuttgart : Bonn Aktuell, 1986. 168 p. ; 19 cm. (Bonn-aktuell) Includes bibliographical references and index. CONTENTS. - Süd-Nord-Gefälle, oder eine neue Völkerwanderung in Sicht? / Walter Tacke -- Das Süd-Nord-Gefälle, Realität und Perspektiven / Reinhart W. Wettmann -- Süd-Nord-Gefälle, Signal für politischen Handlungsbedarf? / Rüdiger Soltwedel -- Marktgerechte Massnahmen einer aktiven regionalen Strukturpolitik / Klaus-Dieter Otto -- Das Süd-Nord-Gefälle im Spiegel der Länderfinanzen / Otto Vogel -- Konferenz Norddeutschland / Uwe Lützen -- Der Norden braucht eine klare Perspektive / Eckart van Hooven. ISBN 3-87959-270-5 LC Card 87-103590 DDC 330.943/0878 19
1. Germany, Southern - Economic conditions - Regional disparities. 2. Germany, Northern - Economic conditions - Regional disparities. I. Voss, Rüdiger von, 1939-. II. Friedrich, Karl. III. Hooven, Eckart van.
HC286.7 .S9 1986

Südindische Wochenmarktsysteme . Bohle, Hans-Georg. Stuttgart , 1986. 290 p. : ISBN 3-515-04601-1 LC Card 87-136147 DDC 381/.18/09548 19
HF5475.I42 S682 1986

Südtirol. see **Trentino-Alto Adige (Italy)**

Süssmuth, Hans. Historische Anthropologie . Göttingen , c1984. 166 p. ; ISBN 3-525-33497-4 LC Card 84-203590 DDC 306/.09 19
GN345.2 .H57 1984 NYPL [JFC 86-1764]

SUEZ CANAL (EGYPT)
Die Geschichte des Suezkanals . Prag [1912?] 26 p. ; LC Card 86-209445
HE543 .G47 1912

Sufrin, Sidney C., 1910- Bhopal, its setting, responsibility, and challenge / Sidney C. Sufrin. 1st ed. Delhi : Ajanta Publications : Distributors, Ajanta Books International, 1985. 98 p. ; 23 cm. "60-9." ISBN 81-202-0135-3 : LC Card 85-903246 DDC 363.1/79 19
1. Union Carbide Ltd. (India). 2. Union Carbide Corporation. 3. Bhopal Union Carbide Plant Disaster, Bhopal, India, 1984. 4. Industrial toxicology - India - Bhopal. 5. Industrial hygiene - Government - India. 6. Methyl isocyanate - Environmental aspects - India - Bhopal. I. Title.
HD7269.C452 I527 1985
NYPL [JLD 86-1321]

Sugar and modern slavery . Plant, Roger. London , Atlantic Highlands, N.J. , 1987. xiv, 177 p. : ISBN 0-86232-572-2 : LC Card 87-13315 DDC 331.7/6361/097293 19
HD8039.S86 D652 1987

SUGAR BEET INDUSTRY - KIRGHIZ S.S.R. - PLANNING - MATHEMATICAL MODELS.
Primenenie ėkonomiko-matematicheskikh metodov v sovershenstvovanii upravlenii͡a narodnym khozi͡aĭstvom /. Frunze , 1982. 225 p. : LC Card 83-193778
HD9115.S652 P75 1982

SUGAR BEET INDUSTRY - SOVIET UNION - PLANNING - MATHEMATICAL MODELS.
Primenenie ėkonomiko-matematicheskikh metodov v sovershenstvovanii upravlenii͡a narodnym khozi͡aĭstvom /. Frunze , 1982. 225 p. : LC Card 83-193778
HD9115.S652 P75 1982

SUGAR BOUNTIES. see **SUGAR TRADE.**

SUGAR FACTORIES - INDIA - MAHARASHTRA.
Sāvanta, Śivājī, 1940- Laḍhata /. Pravarānagara , 1985-1986. 2 v. : LC Card 87-900715
HD9116.I415 M37 1985

SUGAR LAWS AND LEGISLATION - UNITED STATES.
Heston, Thomas J. (Thomas Janney) Sweet subsidy . New York , 1987. 544 p. ; ISBN 0-8240-8084-X (alk. paper) : LC Card 87-23776 DDC 338.1/8 19
HD9105 .H47 1987

SUGAR - PHILIPPINES - MARKETING.
Sa-onoy, Modesto P., 1938- The Philippine sugar trading monopoly . Bacolod City, Philippines , c1984. [31] p. ; LC Card 85-165946
HD9116.P61 S2 1984

Sugar plantations in the formation of Brazilian society . Schwartz, Stuart B. Cambridge [Cambridgeshire] , New York , 1985. xxiii, 616 p. : ISBN 0-521-30934-4 LC Card 85-6716 DDC 306/.0981/42 19
HD9114.B7 B347 1985
NYPL [JLE 86-2276]

Sugar production in northeastern Brazil and Cuba, 1858-1908 /. Denslow, David, 1942- New York , 1987. 172 p. : ISBN 0-8240-1357-3 (alk. paper) : LC Card 87-8525 DDC 338.1/7361/097291 19
HD9114.C89 D45 1987

SUGAR TRADE.
Brown, James G., 1945- The international sugar industry . Washington, D.C., U. S.A. , 1987. xii, 69 p. ; ISBN 0-8213-0884-1 (pbk.) LC Card 87-6285 DDC 338.1/736 19
HD9100.5 .B76 1987

SUGAR TRADE - BRAZIL - BAHIA (STATE) - HISTORY.
Schwartz, Stuart B. Sugar plantations in the formation of Brazilian society . Cambridge [Cambridgeshire] , New York , 1985. xxiii, 616 p. : ISBN 0-521-30934-4 LC Card 85-6716 DDC 306/.0981/42 19
HD9114.B7 B347 1985
NYPL [JLE 86-2276]

SUGAR TRADE - BRAZIL - PERNAMBUCO - HISTORY.
Pimentel, José Graciliano Alves, 1903- Memórias doces e amargas de um fabricante de açúcar /. Recife , 1980 (Recife, Pernambuco : Editora Universitária da Univ. Fed. de Pernambuco) 172 p. ; LC Card 86-158546
HD8039.S86 B755 1980

SUGAR TRADE - BRAZIL - PERNAMBUCO - HISTORY - 16TH CENTURY.
Pôrto, Josè da Costa, 1909- O açúcar num documento colonial /. Recife , 1984. 116 p. ; LC Card 87-102690
HD9114.B7 P448 1984

SUGAR TRADE - BRAZIL - PERNAMBUCO - HISTORY - 17TH CENTURY.
Pôrto, Josè da Costa, 1909- O açúcar num documento colonial /. Recife , 1984. 116 p. ; LC Card 87-102690
HD9114.B7 P448 1984

SUGAR TRADE - COSTA RICA.
Achío Tacsan, Mayra. Azúcar y política en Costa Rica /. San José , c1985. 172 p. : ISBN 997-7231-67-2 LC Card 86-209103
HD9114.C82 A24 1985

SUGAR TRADE - CUBA.
Heston, Thomas J. (Thomas Janney) Sweet subsidy . New York , 1987. 544 p. ; ISBN 0-8240-8084-X (alk. paper) : LC Card 87-23776 DDC 338.1/8 19
HD9105 .H47 1987

SUGAR TRADE - CUBA - HISTORY.
Goizueta-Mimó, Félix. [Effects of sugar monoculture upon colonial Cuba.] Bitter Cuban sugar . New York , 1987. xvii, 287 p. : ISBN 0-8240-1362-X (alk. paper) : LC Card 87-8632 DDC 338.1/7361/097291 19
HD9114.C89 G6419 1987

SUGAR TRADE - DOMINICAN REPUBLIC.
Madruga, José Manuel. Azúcar y haitianos en la República Dominicana /. Santo Domingo , 1986. 202 p. : LC Card 87-125442 DDC 331.6/2/729407293 19
HD9114.D62 M33 1986

SUGAR TRADE - GOVERNMENT POLICY.
Brown, James G., 1945- The international sugar industry . Washington, D.C., U. S.A. , 1987. xii, 69 p. ; ISBN 0-8213-0884-1 (pbk.) LC Card 87-6285 DDC 338.1/736 19
HD9100.5 .B76 1987

SUGAR TRADE - GOVERNMENT POLICY - COSTA RICA.
Achío Tacsan, Mayra. Azúcar y política en Costa Rica /. San José , c1985. 172 p. : ISBN 997-7231-67-2 LC Card 86-209103
HD9114.C82 A24 1985

SUGAR TRADE - GOVERNMENT POLICY - MAURITIUS.
Mauritius. Commission of Inquiry into the Sugar Industry. The human factor, the sugar industry, and Mauritius . Port Louis, Mauritius [1984] 157 p. ; LC Card 85-980119 DDC 338.1/7361/096982 19
HD9118.M45 M33 1984a

Mauritius. Commission of Inquiry into the Sugar Industry. Report of the Commission of Inquiry on the Sugar Industry. Port Louis, Mauritius , 1984. iii, 213 p. ; LC Card 85-980302 DDC 338.1/7361/096982 19
HD9118.M45 M33 1984

SUGAR TRADE - GOVERNMENT POLICY - UNITED STATES - MATHEMATICAL MODELS.
Leong, Jerrold K. (Jerrold Kim), 1947- Economic implications of import barriers to protect the U. S. sugar industry with particular reference to Hawaii /. Manoa , 1987. p. cm. LC Card 87-11855 DDC 382/.456641/09969 19
HD9107.H3 L46 1987

SUGAR TRADE - HAWAII - MATHEMATICAL MODELS.
Leong, Jerrold K. (Jerrold Kim), 1947- Economic implications of import barriers to protect the U. S. sugar industry with particular reference to Hawaii /. Manoa , 1987. p. cm. LC Card 87-11855 DDC 382/.456641/09969 19
HD9107.H3 L46 1987

SUGAR TRADE - LOUISIANA - TECHNOLOGICAL INNOVATIONS - HISTORY.
Heitmann, John Alfred. The modernization of the Louisiana sugar industry, 1830-1910 /. Baton Rouge , c1987. xii, 298 p. : ISBN 0-8071-1324-7 LC Card 86-27639 DDC 338.4/56641/09763 19
HD9107.L8 H45 1987

SUGAR TRADE - MAURITIUS.
Ly-Tio-Fane Pineo, Huguette. Lured away . Moka, Mauritius , 1984. 261 p. :
NYPL [JLD 87-587]

Mauritius. Commission of Inquiry into the Sugar Industry. The human factor, the sugar industry, and Mauritius . Port Louis, Mauritius [1984] 157 p. ; LC Card 85-980119 DDC 338.1/7361/096982 19
HD9118.M45 M33 1984a

Mauritius. Commission of Inquiry into the Sugar Industry. Report of the Commission of Inquiry on the Sugar Industry. Port Louis, Mauritius , 1984. iii, 213 p. ; LC Card 85-980302 DDC 338.1/7361/096982 19
HD9118.M45 M33 1984

SUGAR TRADE - MEXICO - YAUTEPEC (MORELOS) - HISTORY.
Rounds, Christopher R., 1945- From hacienda to ejido . New York , 1987. viii, 268 p. ; ISBN 0-8240-1369-7 (alk. paper) : LC Card 87-8526 DDC 333.3/1/7249 19
HD1333.M62 Y387 1987

SUGAR TRADE - PERU.
Rojas Senisse, Hugo. Azúcar . Lima [Lima?] [1984] 131 p. : LC Card 84-234204 DDC 338.1/7361/0985 19
HD9114.P52 R65 1984
NYPL [JLD 85-1982]

SUGAR TRADE - PERU - HISTORY.
Zúñiga Trelles, Washington. Las empresas azucareras y la reforma agraria /. [S.l. , 1981] ([S.l.] : EBRASA) 108 p. ; LC Card 81-204318 DDC 333.3/1/85 19
HD9114.P52 Z86 1981 ***NYPL [JLD 87-922]***

SUGAR TRADE - PERU - LAMBAYEQUE (DEPT.)

SUGAR TRADE - PHILIPPINES.
Hawes, Gary, 1950- The Philippine State and the Marcos regime . Ithaca , 1987. 196 p. ; ISBN 0-8014-2012-1 (alk. paper) LC Card 86-29237 DDC 382/.41/09599 19
HD9016.P52 H38 1987

Sa-onoy, Modesto P., 1938- The Philippine sugar trading monopoly . Bacolod City, Philippines , c1984. [31] p. ; LC Card 85-165946
HD9116.P61 S2 1984

SUGAR TRADE - UKRAINE - BIOGRAPHY.
Pamiati Abrama IUr'evicha Dobrogo. Pamiati Abrama IUr'evicha Dobrago. Parizh , 1939. 101 p., [1] leaf of plates : LC Card 83-136332
HG185.S65 P36 1939

SUGAR TRADE - UNITED STATES.
Heston, Thomas J. (Thomas Janney) Sweet subsidy . New York , 1987. 544 p. ; ISBN 0-8240-8084-X (alk. paper) : LC Card 87-23776 DDC 338.1/8 19
HD9105 .H47 1987

SUGAR TRADE - WEST INDIES - HISTORY.
Watts, David. The West Indies . Cambridge [Cambridgeshire] , New York , 1987. xxii, 609 p. : ISBN 0-521-24555-9 LC Card 87-5156 DDC 330.9729 19
HC151 .W375 1987

SUGAR WORKERS - AUSTRALIA - HISTORY.
Burrows, Geoff, 1941- The canecutters /. Carlton, Vic. , 1986. xvi, 288 p. : ISBN 0-522-84304-2 LC Card 86-215188 DDC 331.7/6361/0994 19
HD8039.S86 A83 1986

SUGAR WORKERS - BRAZIL - PERNAMBUCO - BIOGRAPHY.
Pimentel, José Graciliano Alves, 1903- Memórias doces e amargas de um fabricante de açúcar /. Recife , 1980 (Recife, Pernambuco : Editora Universitária da Univ. Fed. de Pernambuco) 172 p. ; LC Card 86-158546
HD8039.S86 B755 1980

SUGAR WORKERS - CUBA - HISTORY.
García Galló, Gaspar M. Jorge. General de las cañas /. La Habana , 1983. 220 p., [18] p. of plates : LC Card 84-229562 DDC 331.88/13361/097291 19
HD6577.5.M46 G37 1983
NYPL [JFD 85-4783]

SUGAR WORKERS - DOMINICAN REPUBLIC.
Lemoine, Maurice. [Sucre amer. English.] Bitter sugar /. London , 1985. 308 p., [17] p. of plates : ISBN 0-86232-445-9 LC Card 87-672356
HD4875.D44 L4513x 1985b

Lemoine, Maurice. [Sucre amer. English.] Bitter sugar /. London , c1985. 308 p., [17] p. of plates : ISBN 0-86232-445-9
NYPL [JLD 86-814]

Madruga, José Manuel. Azúcar y haitianos en la República Dominicana /. Santo Domingo , 1986. 202 p. : LC Card 87-125442 DDC 331.6/2/729407293 19
HD9114.D62 M33 1986

Plant, Roger. Sugar and modern slavery . London , Atlantic Highlands, N.J. , 1987. xiv, 177 p. : ISBN 0-86232-572-2 : LC Card 87-13315 DDC 331.7/6361/097293 19
HD8039.S86 D652 1987

SUGAR WORKERS - GUYANA - SUPPLY AND DEMAND - HISTORY - 19TH CENTURY.
McLewin, Philip J., 1939- Power and economic change . New York , 1987. ii, 271 p. : ISBN 0-8240-1366-2 (alk. paper) : LC Card 87-8344 DDC 330.97292/04 19
HC154 .M36 1987

SUGAR WORKERS - HAWAII - HISTORY.
Ewanchuk, Michael, 1908- Hawaiian ordeal . Winnipeg, Man. , c1986. xii, 180 p. : ISBN 0-9690768-7-8 (pbk.) : LC Card 87-156576
HD4875.U5 E93x 1986

SUGAR WORKERS - JAMAICA - SUPPLY AND DEMAND - HISTORY - 19TH CENTURY.
McLewin, Philip J., 1939- Power and economic change . New York , 1987. ii, 271 p. : ISBN 0-8240-1366-2 (alk. paper) : LC Card 87-8344 DDC 330.97292/04 19
HC154 .M36 1987

SUGAR WORKERS - MARTINIQUE - DUMAINE.
Rosélie, Roland. L'habitation sucrière au Quartier La Dumaine, Le François /. [Fort-deFrance? , 1986] ([Fort-de-France] : Impr. Désormeaux) 59 p. : LC Card 86-203128
HD8039.S86 M327 1986

SUGAR WORKERS - MARTINIQUE - LE FRANÇOIS.
Rosélie, Roland. L'habitation sucrière au Quartier La Dumaine, Le François /. [Fort-deFrance? , 1986] ([Fort-de-France] : Impr. Désormeaux) 59 p. : LC Card 86-203128
HD8039.S86 M327 1986

SUGAR WORKERS - TRINIDAD - HISTORY.
Cane farming . [San Fernando, Trinidad, West Indies , 1983?] 136 p. : LC Card 86-200484 DDC 338.1/7361/0972983 19
HD9114.T72 C36 1983

SUGARCANE - AUSTRALIA - HISTORY.
Burrows, Geoff, 1941- The canecutters /. Carlton, Vic. , 1986. xvi, 288 p. : ISBN 0-522-84304-2 LC Card 86-215188 DDC 331.7/6361/0994 19
HD8039.S86 A83 1986

SUGARCANE - BRAZIL, NORTHEAST - PROCESSING - HISTORY.
Denslow, David, 1942- Sugar production in northeastern Brazil and Cuba, 1858-1908 /. New York , 1987. 172 p. : ISBN 0-8240-1357-3 (alk. paper) : LC Card 87-8525 DDC 338.1/7361/097291 19
HD9114.C89 D45 1987

SUGARCANE - CUBA - PROCESSING - HISTORY.
Denslow, David, 1942- Sugar production in northeastern Brazil and Cuba, 1858-1908 /. New York , 1987. 172 p. : ISBN 0-8240-1357-3 (alk. paper) : LC Card 87-8525 DDC 338.1/7361/097291 19
HD9114.C89 D45 1987

SUGARCANE INDUSTRY - AUSTRALIA - HISTORY.
Burrows, Geoff, 1941- The canecutters /. Carlton, Vic. , 1986. xvi, 288 p. : ISBN 0-522-84304-2 LC Card 86-215188 DDC 331.7/6361/0994 19
HD8039.S86 A83 1986

SUGARCANE INDUSTRY - BOLIVIA - SANTA CRUZ (DEPT.)
Gill, Lesley. Peasants, entrepreneurs, and social change . Boulder , 1987. xiv, 246 p. : ISBN 0-8133-7339-5 (pbk. : alk. paper) : LC Card 86-28207 DDC 303.4/0984/3 19
HD1870.S25 G54 1987

SUGARCANE INDUSTRY - BRAZIL - MINAS GERAIS.
Seminário de Energia de Biomassa (1985? : Belo Horizonte, Brazil?) Seminário de Energia de Biomassa . [Belo Horizonte?] , <[1986?-. v. <[1-2] > : LC Card 87-107998
HD9502.5.B543 B67 1985

SUGARCANE INDUSTRY - BRAZIL, NORTHEAST.
Barbosa, Túlio. Expansión del cultivo de la caña de azúcar y de la ganadería en el Nordeste del Brasil . Santiago de Chile , Nueva York, NY, Estados Unidos de América , 1986. 170 p. : ISBN 92-1-321209-7 LC Card 87-400309 DDC 338.1/7361/09813 19
HD9114.B7 N67943 1986

SUGARCANE INDUSTRY - BRAZIL, NORTHEAST - HISTORY.
Denslow, David, 1942- Sugar production in northeastern Brazil and Cuba, 1858-1908 /. New York , 1987. 172 p. : ISBN 0-8240-1357-3 (alk. paper) : LC Card 87-8525 DDC 338.1/7361/097291 19
HD9114.C89 D45 1987

SUGARCANE INDUSTRY - BRAZIL - PERNAMBUCO - EMPLOYEES - SUPPLY AND DEMAND.
Alcool e emprego . Brasília, DF , 1983. 170 p. : LC Card 86-200307
HD5718.A4852 B63 1983

SUGARCANE INDUSTRY - BRAZIL - SÃO PAULO (STATE)
Manoel, Alvaro. Política agrícola, eficiência e concentração na agricultura brasileira . São Paulo , 1986. 180 p. : LC Card 86-234338
HD1873 .M35 1986

SUGARCANE INDUSTRY - BRAZIL - SÃO PAULO (STATE) - EMPLOYEES - SUPPLY AND DEMAND.
Alcool e emprego . Brasília, DF , 1983. 170 p. : LC Card 86-200307
HD5718.A4852 B63 1983

SUGARCANE INDUSTRY - CUBA - EQUIPMENT AND SUPPLIES.
Correa, Jorge Lois. Sistemas y equipos de desmedulado en la industria del bagazo de la caña de azúcar /. Ciudad de La Habana ,

c1982. 77 p. : LC Card 85-198777
HD9119.B4 C83 1982

SUGARCANE INDUSTRY - CUBA - HISTORY.
Denslow, David, 1942- Sugar production in northeastern Brazil and Cuba, 1858-1908 /. New York , 1987. 172 p. : ISBN 0-8240-1357-3 (alk. paper) : LC Card 87-8525 DDC 338.1/7361/097291 19
HD9114.C89 D45 1987

Goizueta-Mimó, Félix. [Effects of sugar monoculture upon colonial Cuba.] Bitter Cuban sugar . New York , 1987. xvii, 287 p. : ISBN 0-8240-1362-X (alk. paper) : LC Card 87-8632 DDC 338.1/7361/097291 19
HD9114.C89 G6419 1987

SUGARCANE INDUSTRY - DOMINICAN REPUBLIC.
Plant, Roger. Sugar and modern slavery . London , Atlantic Highlands, N.J. , 1987. xiv, 177 p. : ISBN 0-86232-572-2 : LC Card 87-13315 DDC 331.7/6361/097293 19
HD8039.S86 D652 1987

SUGARCANE INDUSTRY - DOMINICAN REPUBLIC - EMPLOYEES.
SUGARCANE INDUSTRY - GOVERNMENT POLICY - BRAZIL, NORTHEAST.
Barbosa, Túlio. Expansión del cultivo de la caña de azúcar y de la ganadería en el Nordeste del Brasil . Santiago de Chile , Nueva York, NY, Estados Unidos de América , 1986. 170 p. : ISBN 92-1-321209-7 LC Card 87-400309 DDC 338.1/7361/09813 19
HD9114.B7 N67943 1986

SUGARCANE INDUSTRY - LOUISIANA - COSTS - STATISTICS.
Shuker, Iain G. W. Economic analysis of the cost structure of commercial sugar cane farms in Louisiana /. Baton Rouge, La. [1986] vi, 50 p. : LC Card 86-622542 DDC 338.1/09763 s 338.1/7361/09763021 19
HD1775.L8 L7 no. 651 HD9107.L8

SUGARCANE INDUSTRY - MAURITIUS.
Ly-Tio-Fane Pineo, Huguette. Lured away . Moka, Mauritius , 1984. 261 p. :
NYPL [JLD 87-587]

SUGARCANE INDUSTRY - TRINIDAD - HISTORY.
Cane farming . [San Fernando, Trinidad, West Indies , 1983?] 136 p. : LC Card 86-200484 DDC 338.1/7361/0972983 19
HD9114.T72 C36 1983

Sugata Dasgupta. see **Dasgupta, Sugata, 1926-**

Sugden, Roger. Cowling, Keith. Transnational monopoly capitalism /. Sussex [England] , New York , 1987. vii, 178 p. : ISBN 0-312-00954-2 (St. Martin's) : LC Card 87-4965 DDC 338.8/8 19
HD2755.5 .C68 1987

SUGGESTION SYSTEMS - GERMANY (WEST) - NORTH RHINE-WESTPHALIA.
Stand und Entwicklung des Vorschlagswesens in Wirtschaft und Verwaltung /. Dortmund , 1978. 108 p. : ISBN 3-922104-00-2 LC Card 85-124069
HD30 .A7 Heft 193 HF5549.5.S8

Suggs, George G., 1929- Union busting in the Tri-State : the Oklahoma, Kansas, and Missouri metal workers' strike of 1935 / by George G. Suggs, Jr. Norman : University of Oklahoma Press, 1986. xiv, 282 p. : ill. ; 22 cm. Includes bibliographical references and index. ISBN 0-8061-2012-6 (alk. paper) LC Card 86-6910 DDC 331.89/2871/0973 19
1. Metal-workers' Strike, U. S., 1935 - History. 2. Trade-unions - United States - Organizing - History. I. Title.
HD5325.M52 1935 .S84 1986
NYPL [JLD 86-3971]

Suhr, Dieter.
Geld ohne Mehrwert : Entlastung der Marktwirtschaft von monetären Transaktionskosten / von Dieter Suhr. Frankfurt am Main : F. Knapp, c1983. 143 p. ; 21 cm. Includes bibliographical references. ISBN 3-7819-0302-8 LC Card 84-169137
1. Money. 2. Money supply. 3. Transaction costs. I. Title.
HG221 .S8883 1983

Optimale Liquidität : eine liquiditätstheoretische Analyse und ein kreditwirtschaftliches Wettbewerbskonzept / von Dieter Suhr und Hugo Godschalk. Frankfurt am Main : Knapp, c1986. 155 p. ; 21 cm. Includes bibliographical references. ISBN 3-7819-0349-4 LC Card 86-228333
1. Liquidity (Economics). 2. Money. I. Godschalk, Hugo T. C. II. Title.
HG178 .S84 1986

Suhrcke, Monika. Energie und Gerechtigkeit /. München , c1984. xii, 254 p. : ISBN 3-597-10259-X LC Card 84-175053
HD9502.A2 E5192 1984

The suicidal corporation /. Weaver, Paul, 1942 Oct. 18- New York , c1988. p. cm. ISBN 0-671-52378-3 LC Card 87-23468 DDC 338.7/4/0973 19
HD2785 .W38 1988

Suicide & homicide deaths, Oregon residents, 1979-1981. Suicides and homicides, Oregon residents, 1979 to 1981. Portland, OR (1400 S.W. 5th Ave., Portland 97201) [1986] 39 p. : LC Card 87-620589 DDC 614.5/985844/09795 19
HB1323.S82 U57 1986

Le suicide au Québec . Charron, Marie-France, 1952- [Quebec] , 1983. 221 p. : ISBN 2-551-05209-2 LC Card 83-168606
HB1323.S82 C352 1983

SUICIDE - MAINE - STATISTICS.
Welch, Dale E. Suicides in Maine for the 25 year period, 1958-1982 /. Augusta, Me. [1986] ii, 14, [5] p. : LC Card 86-622276 DDC 362.2 19
HB1323.S8 W45 1986

SUICIDE - OREGON - STATISTICS.
Suicides and homicides, Oregon residents, 1979 to 1981. Portland, OR (1400 S.W. 5th Ave., Portland 97201) [1986] 39 p. : LC Card 87-620589 DDC 614.5/985844/09795 19
HB1323.S82 U57 1986

SUICIDE - QUÉBEC (PROVINCE) - STATISTICS.
Charron, Marie-France, 1952- Le suicide au Québec . [Quebec] , 1983. 221 p. : ISBN 2-551-05209-2 LC Card 83-168606
HB1323.S82 C352 1983

Suicide surveillance. Centers for Disease Control suicide surveillance . Atlanta, GA [1985] ii, 33 p. : LC Card 86-602520 DDC 362.2 19
HB1323.S82 U53 1985

Suicide surveillance report, United States, 1970-1980. Centers for Disease Control suicide surveillance . Atlanta, GA [1985] ii, 33 p. : LC Card 86-602520 DDC 362.2 19
HB1323.S82 U53 1985

SUICIDE - UNITED STATES - STATISTICS.
Centers for Disease Control suicide surveillance . Atlanta, GA [1985] ii, 33 p. : LC Card 86-602520 DDC 362.2 19
HB1323.S82 U53 1985

Suicides and homicides, Oregon residents, 1979 to 1981. Portland, OR (1400 S.W. 5th Ave., Portland 97201) : Oregon Dept. of Human Resources, Health Division, Health Status Monitoring, Center for Health Statistics, [1986] 39 p. : ill. ; 28 cm. (Accidental deaths, suicides, and homicides . pt. 3) Cover title: Suicide & homicide deaths, Oregon residents, 1979-1981. "April 1986." LC Card 87-620589 DDC 614.5/985844/09795 19
1. Suicide - Oregon - Statistics. 2. Homicide - Oregon - Statistics. I. Oregon Center for Health Statistics. II. Title: Suicide & homicide deaths, Oregon residents, 1979-1981. III. Series.
HB1323.S82 U57 1986

Suicides in Maine for the 25 year period, 1958-1982 /. Welch, Dale E. Augusta, Me. [1986] ii, 14, [5] p. : LC Card 86-622276 DDC 362.2 19
HB1323.S8 W45 1986

Suïmenko, I͡E. I. Kerivnyk-orhanizator i vykhovatel′ / I͡E.I. Suïmenko, M.O. Sakada, V.A. Piddubnyĭ. Kyïv : Vyd-vo polit. lit-ry Ukraïny, 1985. 189 p. ; 20 cm. Title in colophon: Rukovoditel′-organizator i vospitatel′. Includes bibliographical references. LC Card 87-109649
1. Executives. 2. Executive ability. 3. Executives - Ukraine. 4. Industrial management - Ukraine. I. Sakada, M. O. II. Poddubnyĭ, Vladimir Andreevich. III. Title. IV. Title: Rukovoditel′-organizator i vospitatel′.
HD38.2 .S85 1985

Sŭi͡uz na bŭlgarskite filatelisti. Georgiev, Petŭr Borisov. Katalog na bŭlgarskite poshtenski marki 1979-1984 /. Sofii͡a , 1985. 119 p. : LC Card 86-112123
HE6185.B82 G47 1985

Sŭi͡uz na narodnata mladezh v Bŭlgarii͡a. see **Dimitrovski komunisticheski mladezhki sŭi͡uz.**

Sŭi͡uz po ikonomika (Bulgaria). T͡Sentralno rŭkovodstvo. Efektivnost ot teritorialnata organizatsii͡a na proizvodstvoto v uslovii͡ata na novii͡a ikonomicheski mekhanizŭm . Tŭrgovishte , 1982. 215 p. ; LC Card 84-115638
HC403.Z9 D516 1982

Sukarno, H., 1948- Mengenal administrasi dan prosedur catatan sipil pada Kantor Catatan Sipil Propinsi DKI Jakarta / H. Sukarno. Cet. 1. Jakarta : Coriena, 1985. iii, 150 p. : ill. ; 21 cm. Bibliography: p. 147-149. LC Card 86-942212
1. Jakarta Raya (Indonesia). Kantor Catatan Sipil. I. Title.
HA37.I46 J357 1985

Sukhopadhyay, Swapna. The Poor in Asia . Kuala Lumpur, Malaysia , 1985- v. <1 > ; ISBN 967-99954-0-2 (v. 1) LC Card 86-944764 DDC 362.5/8/095 19
HC415.P6 P66 1985

Sukhov, A. S. (Alekseĭ Sergeevich) Silin, V. A. (Vladimir Andreevich) Ėkonomika--poisk, ėksperiment /. Moskva , 1978. 109 p. ; LC Card 81-167075
HC336.25 .S557 1978

Sukhwal, B. L., 1929- India : economic resource base and contemporary political patterns / B.L. Sukhwal.1st ed. New York : Envoy Press, 1987. viii, 200 p. : ill. ; 23 cm. Bibliography: p. [189]-192. Includes index. ISBN 0-938719-13-0 LC Card 86-81410 DDC 333.7/0954 19
1. Natural resources - India. 2. Natural resources - Government policy - India. 3. Communication and traffic - India. 4. India - Population. I. Title.
HC433.5 .S85 1987

Sukumar Mukerji. see **Mukerji, Sukumar, 1931-**

Sukumaran Nair, M. K., 1948- Tribal economy in transition : a study of Meghalaya / M.K. Sukumaran Nair. New Delhi, India : Inter-India Publications, 1987, c1986. 159 p. ; 23 cm. (Tribal studies of India series . T 122) "Published on behalf of Indian Institute for Regional Development Studies, Kottayam." Revision of the author's thesis (Ph. D.--North Eastern Hill University, Shillong, 1983) Bibliography: p. [149]-157. Includes index. ISBN 81-210-0180-3 : LC Card 87-901406 DDC 330.954/164052 19
1. Meghalaya (India) - Scheduled tribes - Economic conditions. 2. Meghalaya (India) - Economic conditions. 3. Agriculture - Economic aspects - India - Meghalaya. I. Title. II. Series.
HC437.M4 S85 1987

Sul "movimento" della qualità della vita di lavoro / a cura di Michele Colasanto. Milano : F. Angeli, c1982. 117 p. ; 22 cm. (Collana Fondazione Giulio Pastore. Sezione Economia e sociologia del lavoro . 1) Bibliography: p. 75-76. LC Card 82-246606
1. Quality of work life. 2. Quality of work life - European Economic Community countries. 3. Quality of work life - Italy. I. Colasanto, Michele. II. Series.
HD6955 .S94 1982 ***NYPL [JLD 87-1159]***

Sulawesi Utara (Ind nesia). Gubernur. Biro Hubungan Masyarakat. Lima tahun kepemimpinan Gubernur Kepala Daerah Tingkat I Sulawesi Utara, G.H. Mantik, 1980-1985. [Manado , 1985] 2 v. : LC Card 86-940586
HC448.S785 L55 1985

SULAWESI UTARA (INDONESIA) - ECONOMIC POLICY.
Lima tahun kepemimpinan Gubernur Kepala Daerah Tingkat I Sulawesi Utara, G.H. Mantik, 1980-1985. [Manado , 1985] 2 v. : LC Card 86-940586
HC448.S785 L55 1985

Sulawesi Utara (Indonesia). Gubernur. Lima tahun kepemimpinan Gubernur Kepala Daerah Tingkat I Sulawesi Utara, G.H. Mantik, 1980-1985. [Manado , 1985] 2 v. : LC Card 86-940586
HC448.S785 L55 1985

SULAWESI UTARA (INDONESIA) - SOCIAL POLICY.
Lima tahun kepemimpinan Gubernur Kepala

Daerah Tingkat I Sulawesi Utara, G.H. Mantik, 1980-1985. [Manado , 1985] 2 v. : LC Card 86-940586
HC448.S785 L55 1985

Suleman, R. M. U. 1983-84 rabi (winter) season fertilizer review : problems of production and marketing costs / by R.M.U. Suleman. Islamabad : National Fertilizer Development Centre, Planning and Development Division, Govt. of Pakistan, [1984] iv, 28 leaves : charts ; 29 cm. (Review report / NFDC . 2) "June 1984." Bibliography: leaf 28. LC Card 85-930451 DDC 338.4/766862/095491 19
1. Fertilizer industry - Pakistan. I. Series: Review report (National Fertilizer Development Centre (Pakistan)) , 2. II. Title.
HD9483.P22 S844 1984

Sulik, Alfred. Akademia Ekonomiczna im. Karola Adamieckiego w Katowicach . Katowice , 1977. 194 p. : LC Card 82-104777
HB74.9.P7 A38 1977

Sulitskiĭ, V. N. (Vladimir Nikolaevich)
Organizatsionno-ėkonomicheskie problemy upravlenii͡a kadrami v otrasli / V.N. Sulitskiĭ ; otvetstvennyĭ redaktor A.I. Semenov. Moskva : "Nauka", 1986. 164, [3] p. : ill. ; 20 cm. (Problemy sovetskoĭ ėkonomiki) At head of title: Akademii͡a nauk SSSR. T͡Sentral'nyĭ ėkonomiko-matematicheskiĭ institut. Bibliography: p. 161-[165] LC Card 86-233362
1. Personnel management - Soviet Union - Mathematical models. I. Semenov, A. I. II. T͡Sentral'nyĭ ėkonomiko-matematicheskiĭ institut (Akademii͡a nauk SSSR).
HF5549.2.S65 S85 1986

Sulle strade ferrate nello stato pontificio . Blasi, Benedetto. Roma , 1847. 32 p. ; LC Card 85-665950
HE3098 .B52x 1847

Sullerot, Évelyne. L'âge de travailler / Evelyne Sullerot. [Paris] : Fayard, c1986. 224 p. : ill. ; 22 cm. At head of title: Centre européen Travail & société. ISBN 2-213-01597-X : LC Card 86-176051
1. Age and employment - European Economic Community countries. I. European Centre for Work and Society. II. Title.
HD6283.E86 S85 1986

Sullivan, George, 1927- Work smart, not hard / George Sullivan. New York, N.Y. : Facts on File Publications, c1987. xii, 196 p. ; 24 cm. Includes bibliographies and index. ISBN 0-8160-1393-4 : LC Card 86-24320 DDC 658.3/14 19
1. Performance. 2. Labor productivity. 3. Planning. 4. Work. I. Title.
HF5549.5.P35 S85 1987

Sullivan, Novell B. Washington, D.C. taxicab zone fare guide. [United States] : N.B. Sullivan, c1984. 86 p., [1] folded leaf of plates : ill. ; 21 cm. LC Card 86-224478 DDC 388.4/1321 19
1. Taxicabs - Washington (D.C.) - Fares. I. Title. II. Title: Taxicab zone fare guide.
HE5634.W3 S93 1984

Sullivan, Patrick J., 1929-
Blue collar, Roman collar, white collar : U. S. Catholic involvement in labor management controversies, 1960-1980 / Patrick J. Sullivan. Lanham, MD : University Press of America, c1987. xii, 346 p. ; 23 cm. Includes bibliographies. ISBN 0-8191-5704-X (alk. paper) : LC Card 86-24593 DDC 261.85 19
1. Church and labor - United States. 2. Collective bargaining - United States. 3. Industrial sociology - United States. 4. Church and social problems - Catholic Church. 5. Catholic Church - Doctrines. I. Title.
HD6338.2.U5 S85 1987

U. S. Catholic institutions and labor unions, 1960-1980 / by Patrick J. Sullivan. Lanham, MD : University Press of America, c1985. 545 p. ; 24 cm. Includes bibliographies. ISBN 0-8191-4970-5 (alk. paper) : LC Card 85-20171 DDC 331.88/1128273 19
1. Trade-unions, Catholic - United States - History - 20th century. 2. Church and labor - United States - History - 20th century. I. Title. II. Title: US Catholic institutions and labor unions, 1960-1980. III. Title: United States Catholic institutions and labor unions, 1960-1980.
HD6481.2.U6 S85 1985
NYPL [JLE 86-2407]

The Sullivan principles at Ford--audit a [microform] / by M.C. Roux, ... [et] [s.l.] : SA Institute of Race Relations, 1981. 16 p. ; 30 cm. Cover title. "February 1981." Microfilm. New York : New York Public Library, 986. 1 microfilm reel ; 35 mm. (MN *ZZ-26,873)
1. Ford Motor Company of South Africa. 2. Blacks - Employment - South Africa - Case studies. 3. Blacks - South Africa - Segregation. I. Roux, Marianne Cornelia. II. Manona, C. W. III. Title.
NYPL [*ZT-1745 no.32]

Süllow, Bernd. Korporative Repräsentation der Gewerkschaften : zur institutionellen Verbandsbeteiligung in öffentlichen Gremien / Bernd Süllow. Frankfurt ; New York : Campus, c1982. 146 p. ; 21 cm. Bibliography: p. 141-146. ISBN 3-593-33169-1 LC Card 83-153450
1. Government business enterprises - Germany (West) - Management - Employee participation. 2. Trade-unions - Germany, West. 3. Corporations, Government - Germany (West) - Management - Employee participation. I. Title.
HD4177 .S85 1982

Sulmicki, Jan. Transfer postępu naukowo-technicznego przez przedsiębiorstwa międzynarodowe a długookresowe zmiany w przedsiębiorstwa międzynarodowe a długookresowe zmiany w międzynarodowym podziale pracy / Jan Sulmicki. Wyd. 1. Warszawa : Szkoła Główna Planowania i Statystyki, 1978. 288 p. ; 24 cm. (Monografie i opracowania - Szkoła Główna Planowania i Statystyki. 65) Bibliography: p. [272]-288. LC Card 81-205742
1. International division of labor. 2. International business enterprises. 3. Technology transfer. I. Series: Monografie i opracowania (Szkoła Główna Planowania i Statystyki (Warsaw, Poland)) , 65. II. Title.
HF1411 .S876 1978

Sultanpur District, Uttar Pradesh, resource analysis for integrated development. Resource analysis for integrated development, Sultanpur District, Uttar Pradesh. New Delhi , 1986. xii, 436 p. : LC Card 87-902515
HC437.S85 R47 1986

SULTĀNPUR (INDIA) - ECONOMIC CONDITIONS.
Resource analysis for integrated development, Sultanpur District, Uttar Pradesh. New Delhi , 1986. xii, 436 p. : LC Card 87-902515
HC437.S85 R47 1986

Sulzbach, Ervino Lothar. Arroio dos Ratos, berço da indústria carbonífera nacional : esboço histórico / Ervino Lothar Sulzbach. [Rio Grande do Sul : s.n.], c1985 (Rio Grande do Sul : Flores Linotipia) 163 p. : ill. ; 21 cm. Spine title: Arroio dos Ratos. Bibliography: p. 159-160. LC Card 86-150014
1. Coal trade - Brazil - Arroio dos Ratos - History. 2. Arroio dos Ratos (Brazil) - Economic conditions. 3. Arroio dos Ratos (Brazil) - Social conditions. 4. Arroio dos Ratos (Brazil) - History. I. Title. II. Title: Arroio dos Ratos.
HD9554.B83 A777 1985

Sumangala, M. (Mahadevan) Mahadevan, K., 1940- Social development, cultural change, and fertility decline . New Delhi , Newbury Park, Calif. , 1987. p. cm. ISBN 0-8039-9536-9 LC Card 87-15001 DDC 304.6/32/095483 19
HB1050.K47 M34 1987

A summary of the American experience with the Federal Contract Compliance Program . Cohen, Leah. [Ottawa] , 1979. 72 leaves ;
NYPL [JLF 86-1657]

A summary report of the Vice President's Task Force on Youth Employment. United States. Vice President's Task Force on Youth Employment. Washington , 1980. 70 p. :
NYPL [JLF 86-214]

Summary report on a mission to southern Africa from 9 July to 21 August 1985 for the development of coal resources in Malawi, Swaziland, Mozambique, Zambia, and Zimbabwe. Lange, G. F. [Addis Ababa] [1985] ii, 60 p. ; LC Card 85-981333 DDC 338.2/724/0968 19
HD9557.A356 L36 1985

Summer, Charles Edgar. Hampton, David R. Organizational behavior and the practice of management /. Glenview, Ill. , c1987. 876 p. : ISBN 0-673-18303-3 LC Card 86-24798 DDC 658.4 19
HD58.7 .H35 1987

SUMMER EMPLOYMENT - BULGARIA - HISTORY.
40 brigadirski leta /. Sofii͡a , 1986. 173 p., [12] p. of plates : LC Card 87-103049
HD4870.B9 A15 1986

Summerfield, Penny. Braybon, Gail. Out of the cage . London , New York , 1987. xiii, 330 p. : ISBN 0-86358-046-7 : LC Card 87-13510 DDC 305.4/0941 19
HD6135 .B7 1987

Summers, Anita A.
Economic development within the Philadelphia metropolitan area / Anita A. Summers and Thomas F. Luce. Philadelphia : University of Pennsylvania Press, c1987. xiv, 268 p. : map ; 26 cm. Bibliography: p. [153]-164. Includes index. ISBN 0-8122-1231-2 (pbk.) LC Card 86-25091 DDC 338.9748/11 19
1. Philadelphia Metropolitan Area (Pa.) - Economic conditions. 2. Philadelphia Metropolitan Area (Pa.) - Economic policy. I. Luce, Thomas F. II. Title.
HC108.P5 S85 1987

Luce, Thomas F. Local fiscal issues in the Philadelphia metropolitan area /. Philadelphia , c1987. xii, 248 p., [2] p. of plates : ISBN 0-8122-1255-X (pbk.) LC Card 87-25486 DDC 336.748/11 19
HJ9307.P4 L83 1987

SUMMERS FAMILY.
Belliveau, John Edward, 1913- "Crackie" . Hantsport, N.S. , 1986. 192 p. : ISBN 0-88999-315-7 (pbk.) LC Card 87-120170 DDC 338.092/2 B 19
HC112.5.A2 B44 1986

Summers, Lawrence H. Understanding unemployment / Lawrence H. Summers. Cambridge, Mass. : MIT Press, c1988. p. cm. Bibliography: p. Includes index. ISBN 0-262-19265-9 LC Card 87-3866 DDC 331.13/7 19
1. Unemployment - Collected works. I. Title.
HD5707.5 .S85 1988

Sumner, Daniel A. (Daniel Alan), 1950- Removal of price supports and supply controls for U. S. tobacco : an economic analysis of the impact / by Daniel A. Sumner and Julian M. Alston ; with a statement by the Food and Agriculture Committee of the National Planning Association. Demoines, Iowa : Food and Agriculture Committee ; Washington, D.C. : National Planning Association, c1985. viii, 64 p. ; 26 cm. (NPA report . no. 220) FAC report ; no. 5 Bibliography: p. 44-47. ISBN 0-89068-084-1 LC Card 85-63194
1. Tobacco manufacture and trade - United States. 2. Agricultural price supports - United States. 3. Agriculture and state - United States. I. Alston, Julian M. II. NPA Committee on Food and Agriculture. III. Title. IV. Series.
NYPL [JLF 86-1014]

SUMNER, W. H. T. (WILLIAM HUNT TYLER), 1821 OR 2-1909.
Belliveau, John Edward, 1913- "Crackie" . Hantsport, N.S. , 1986. 192 p. : ISBN 0-88999-315-7 (pbk.) LC Card 87-120170 DDC 338.092/2 B 19
HC112.5.A2 B44 1986

SUMPTUARY LAWS - EUROPE - HISTORY - 18TH CENTURY.
Stolleis, Michael, 1941- Pecunia nervus rerum . Frankfurt am Main , c1983. 184 p. ; ISBN 3-465-01590-8 (Deut Bibl.) LC Card 83-183704
HJ1000 .S76 1983

Sūn Rūam Namčhai. 1982. Salam . Krung Thēp , 2525 [1982] 16, 249 p. : LC Card 82-916400
HC445.Z7 B3678 1982

Sūn Wichākān Thīyū'āsai læ Kāntang Thinthān Manut (Thailand) Chadsri Bunnag. Housing in urban development . [Bangkok] [Rotterdam] Netherlands [1985] 49, [2] leaves : LC Card 86-915989 DDC 363.5/09593 19
HD7363.55.A3 C46 1985

Sunamam. see **Brazil. Superintendência Nacional da Marinha Mercante.**

Sunburst Communications (Firm) Jobs for the '90s [videorecording] /. Pleasantville, NY , 1987. 1 videocassette (48 min.) : LC Card 87-705264 DDC 331.7 11
HF5382

SUNCORP INSURANCE AND FINANCE - HISTORY.
Thomis, Malcolm I. From SGIO to Suncorp /.

[Brisbane?] , 1986. xii, 272 p., [32] p. of plates : ISBN 0-7242-1698-7 LC Card 87-158138 DDC 368.4/009943 19
HG8220.A9 T56 1986

SUNDAY LEGISLATION - SCOTLAND.
Scotchman. Letter to Joseph Locke, Esq. ... in reference to his bill "to regulate Sunday travelling on railways" /. Glasgow , 1849. 16 p. ; LC Card 85-666156
HE3037. S36x 1849

Sunday Times of London Insight Team. Wilsher, Peter. Strike . London [1985] xiii, 284 p., [16] p. of plates : ISBN 0-233-97825-9 : LC Card 86-221981 DDC 331.89/2822334/0941 19
HD5365.M6152 1984 .W55 1985b

Sundem, Gary L.
Horngren, Charles T., 1926- Introduction to financial accounting /. Englewood Cliffs, N.J. , c1987. xx, 795 p. ; ISBN 0-13-483264-7 LC Card 86-25310 DDC 657 19
HF5635 .H813 1987

Horngren, Charles T., 1926- Introduction to management accounting /. Englewood Cliffs, N.J. , c1987. xxi, 762 p. : ISBN 0-13-487885-X LC Card 86-25138 DDC 658.1/511 19
HF5635 .H814 1987

Sundhaussen, Holm. Wirtschaftsgeschichte Kroatiens im nationalsozialistischen Grossraum 1941-1945 : das Scheitern einer Ausbeutungsstrategie / Holm Sundhaussen. Stuttgart : Deutsche Verlags-Anstalt, 1983. 386 p. : ill. ; 23 cm. (Studien zur Zeitgeschichte. Bd. 23) "Quellen- und Literaturverzeichnis": p. 348-367. Includes index. ISBN 3-421-06150-5 LC Card 83-242921
1. Croatia - Economic conditions. 2. Croatia - Commerce - History - Germany. 3. Germany - Commerce - History - Croatia. I. Series: Studien zur Zeitgeschichte (Institut für Zeitgeschichte (Munich, Germany)) , Bd. 23. II. Title.
HC407.Z7 C7678 1983

Sundin, Elisabeth. Holmquist, Carin, 1948- Förhandla mer räkna mindre /. Stockholm [1984] 124 p. : ISBN 91-38-90409-8 : LC Card 84-241380
HD30.22 .H65 1984

Sundqvist, Sven-Ivan, 1939- Ägarna och makten i Sveriges börsföretag 1985 = Owners and power in Sweden's listed companies, 1985 / Sven-Ivan Sundqvist. [Stockholm] : Marieberg, [1985] 318 p. : ill. ; 24 cm. Includes indexes. Summary in English. ISBN 91-7588-085-7 : LC Card 86-105378
1. Capitalists and financiers - Sweden - Registers. 2. Stockholders - Sweden - Registers. I. Title. II. Title: Owners and power in Sweden's listed companies 1985.
HG186.S85 S86 1985 ***NYPL [JLE 86-3810]***

Sundrum, R. M. Growth and income distribution in India : policy and performance since independence / R.M. Sundrum. New Delhi ; Beverly Hills : Sage Publications, 1986. p. cm. Bibliography: p. Includes index. ISBN 0-8039-9522-9 (U. S.) LC Card 86-26323 DDC 330.954/04 19
1. India - Economic conditions - 1947-. 2. India - Economic policy - 1947-. 3. Income distribution - India. I. Title.
HC435.2 .S883 1986

SUNDRY CIVIL APPROPRIATIONS BILLS. see **UNITED STATES - APPROPRIATIONS AND EXPENDITURES.**

Sunrise Europe . Mackintosh, Ian, 1927- Oxford, UK , New York, NY, USA , 1986. xx, 288 p. : ISBN 0-631-14406-4 : LC Card 86-6077 DDC 338.4/7004/094 19
HD9696.C63 E8547 1986
NYPL [JLE 86-3364]

A Sunset performance audit of the Pennsylvania Housing Finance Agency pursuant to Act 1981-142 / Legislative Budget and Finance Committee. Harrisburg, Pa. (Rm. 400, Finance Bldg., Harrisburg 17120) : The Committee, [1985] ii, 75 p. ; 29 cm. "Released by the Legislative Budget and Finance Committee without endorsement" "February 1985." LC Card 85-623018 DDC 353.97480086/5045 19
1. Pennsylvania Housing Finance Agency - Auditing. 2. Housing - Pennsylvania - Finance. 3. Mortgages - Pennsylvania. I. Pennsylvania. General Assembly. Legislative Budget and Finance Committee.
HD7303.P4 P425 1985
NYPL [JLF 86-1807]

Sunstone key business series.
Smalis, I. A., 1918- Money . Santa Fe, NM, USA , 1987. 87 p. : ISBN 0-86534-100-1 : LC Card 87-6439 DDC 650.1 19
HF5386 .S637 1987

SUNY series in African politics and society.
Fatton, Robert. Black consciousness in South Africa . Albany , c1986. ix, 189 p. ; ISBN 0-88706-127-3 LC Card 85-2855 DDC 305.8/00968 19
DT763.6 .F37 1986 ***NYPL [JLE 86-2289]***

SUNY series in Afro-American studies.
Dickerson, Dennis C., 1949- Out of the crucible . Albany , c1986. xiv, 323 p. : ISBN 0-88706-305-5 LC Card 85-30450 DDC 331.6/3/960730748 19
HD8039.I52 U535 1986
NYPL [JLE 86-4411]

SUNY series in American labor history.
Halpern, Martin, 1945- UAW politics in the cold war era/. Albany, N.Y. , c1988. p. cm. ISBN 0-88706-671-2 LC Card 87-13890 DDC 322/.2/0973 19
HD6515.A82 I574 1988

Peterson, Joyce Shaw, 1939- American automobile workers, 1900-1933 /. Albany , c1987. xiv, 231 p. ; ISBN 0-88706-573-2 LC Card 87-1942 DDC 331.7/6292/0973 19
HD8039.A82 U66 1987

Rosenberg, Daniel, 1953- New Orleans dockworkers . Albany , c1988. x, 233 p. ; ISBN 0-88706-649-6 LC Card 87-10156 DDC 331.7/61387164/0976335 19
HD8039.L82 U664 1988

SUNY series in environmental public policy.
Impacts of hazardous technology . Albany , c1987. x, 233 p. : ISBN 0-88706-332-2 LC Card 86-1943 DDC 363.1/79 19
HD9698.U54 M475 1987
NYPL [JLE 87-1233]

Wenz, Peter S. Environmental justice /. Albany, N.Y. , c1987. p. cm. ISBN 0-88706-644-5 LC Card 87-13206 DDC 363.7/0525 19
HB523 .W46 1987

Yeager, Rodger. Wildlife, wild death . Albany, NY , c1986. xvi, 173 p. : ISBN 0-88706-168-0 LC Card 86-5791 DDC 333.95/16/09676 19
QL84.6.K4 Y43 1986 ***NYPL [JLE 86-3870]***

SUNY series in Middle Eastern studies.
Tully, Dennis. Culture and context in Sudan . Albany, N.Y. , c1988. p. cm. ISBN 0-88706-502-3 LC Card 86-23180 DDC 338.1/09627 19
HC835.Z7 D377 1988

SUNY series in public administration.
New directions in budget theory /. Albany, N.Y. , 1987, c1988. p. cm. ISBN 0-88706-624-0 LC Card 87-9977 DDC 350.72/2 19
HJ2005 .N48 1987

SUNY series in the anthropology of work.
Robinson, Kathryn May, 1949- Stepchildren of progress . Albany, N.Y. , c1986. xvi, 315 p. : ISBN 0-88706-119-2 LC Card 86-5847 DDC 307.7/66/095984 19
HD9539.N52 I547 1986
NYPL [JLE 86-4126]

Work in market and industrial societies /. Albany , c1984. viii, 316 p. ; ISBN 0-87395-810-1 LC Card 83-9267 DDC 306/.36 19
HD4901 .A659 1984 ***NYPL [JLE 86-4483]***

SUNY series on urban public policy.
Varady, David P. Neighborhood upgrading . Albany , c1986. x, 184 p. : ISBN 0-88706-299-7 LC Card 85-30392 DDC 307.3/362/0973 19
HT175 .V37 1986 ***NYPL [JLE 87-373]***

SUNY series on women in work.
Statham, Anne. The worth of women's work . Albany , c1988. xiv, 331 p. ; ISBN 0-88706-591-0 LC Card 87-6472 DDC 331.4/0973 19
HD6095 .S73 1988

Suomalaista yhteiskuntaa rakentamassa . Mansner, Markku. Helsinki [1984] 552 p., [4] p. of plates : ISBN 951-9240-75-6 LC Card 85-130291
HD8533 .M345 1984

Suomen postimestarit 1809-1984 . Ranta, Niilo, 1914- Helsinki [1986] 144 p. : LC Card 87-101716
HE7064 .R35 1986

Suomen Tasavalta. see **Finland.**

Suomen Työnantajain Keskusliitto.
Mansner, Markku. Suomalaista yhteiskuntaa rakentamassa . Helsinki [1984] 552 p., [4] p. of plates : ISBN 951-9240-75-6 LC Card 85-130291
HD8533 .M345 1984

SUOMEN TYÖNANTAJAIN KESKUSLIITTO - HISTORY.
Mansner, Markku. Suomalaista yhteiskuntaa rakentamassa . Helsinki [1984] 552 p., [4] p. of plates : ISBN 951-9240-75-6 LC Card 85-130291
HD8533 .M345 1984

Suomi. see **Finland.**

Super marketers. Heller, Robert, 1932- The supermarketers . New York , c1987. xiii, 384 p. ; ISBN 0-525-24520-0 LC Card 86-23977 DDC 658.8 19
HF5415 .H374 1987

Super selling through self-talk . Seldman, Marty. Los Angeles, CA , 1988. p. cm. ISBN 0-89586-689-7 : LC Card 87-22581 DDC 658.8/5 19
HF5438.25 .S4375 1988

Super series. Economic and financial aspects . (no. 402) Cost reduction. Oxford , New York , 1986. ix, 65 p. : ISBN 0-08-034177-2 (pbk.) LC Card 87-100499 DDC 658.1/552 19
HD47.3 .C67 1986

Superboss . Freemantle, David. Brookfield, Vt. , 1987, c1985. p. cm. ISBN 0-7045-0551-7 (pbk.) : LC Card 87-19089 DDC 658.3 19
HF5549 .F697 1987

SUPERCALC (COMPUTER PROGRAM)
Wood, Chris. The SuperCalc program made easy /. Berkeley, Calif. , c1987. xi, 384 p. : ISBN 0-07-881002-7 (pbk.) : LC Card 86-221528 DDC 005.36/9 19
HF5548.4.S85 W66 1987

The SuperCalc program made easy /. Wood, Chris. Berkeley, Calif. , c1987. xi, 384 p. : ISBN 0-07-881002-7 (pbk.) : LC Card 86-221528 DDC 005.36/9 19
HF5548.4.S85 W66 1987

SuperCalc 3 . Willis, Jerry. Blue Ridge Summit, Pa. , 1986. vi, 248 p. : ISBN 0-8306-0494-4 : LC Card 86-5743 DDC 005.36/9 19
HF5548.4.S86 W55 1986
NYPL [JSE 87-265]

SUPERCALC 3 (COMPUTER PROGRAM)
Harvey, Greg. Mastering SuperCalc3 /. Berkeley, CA , c1986. xvi, 276 p. : ISBN 0-89588-312-0 (pbk.) : LC Card 87-119243 DDC 005.36/9 19
HF5548.4.S86 H37 1986

Willis, Jerry. SuperCalc 3 . Blue Ridge Summit, Pa. , 1986. vi, 248 p. : ISBN 0-8306-0494-4 : LC Card 86-5743 DDC 005.36/9 19
HF5548.4.S86 W55 1986
NYPL [JSE 87-265]

SUPERCALC 4.
Harvey, Greg. Mastering SuperCalc4 /. San Francisco , c1987. xix, 311 p. : ISBN 0-89588-419-4 (pbk.) : LC Card 87-60636 DDC 005.36/9 19
HF5548.4.S87 H37 1987

SUPERCALC 4 (COMPUTER PROGRAM)
Doyle, William J., 1946- Using SuperCalc 4 . New York , c1987. xvi, 382 p. : ISBN 0-471-85992-3 : LC Card 87-13804 DDC 005.36/9 19
HF5548.4.S87 D69 1987

Willis, Jerry, 1942- Working with SuperCalc 4 /. Blue Ridge Summit, PA , c1987. x, 320 p. : ISBN 0-8306-0214-3 : LC Card 86-30124 DDC 005.36/9 19
HF5548.4.S87 W54 1987

SUPERCALC3 (COMPUTER PROGRAM)
Ross, Steven C. Understanding and using SuperCalc 3 /. St. Paul , c1987. xiii, 184, [27] p. : ISBN 0-314-30123-2 (pbk.) LC Card 86-32548 DDC 005.36/9 19
HF5548.4.S86 R67 1987

Superestructuras y subdesarrollo . Guzmán Ortega, Gonzalo. Quito , 1985. 178 p. : LC Card 86-132144
HC59.7 .G86 1985

Superfairness . Baumol, William J. Cambridge, Mass. , c1986. xi, 266 p. : ISBN 0-262-02234-6 LC Card 85-15127 DDC 305 19
HB72 .B356 1986 ***NYPL [JLE 86-2402]***

Superinsulated design and construction . Lenchek, Tom. New York , c1987. ix, 172 p. : ISBN 0-442-26051-2 : LC Card 86-7089 DDC 693.8/32 19
TJ163.5.D86 L46 1987 ***NYPL [JSF 87-235]***

Superintendência do Desenvolvimento do Estado do Ceará.
Catálogo de ocupações pesquisadas em Fortaleza. [Fortaleza] . 111, [1] p. ; LC Card 83-222529
HF5382.5.B7 C38 1972

Reestudo da parte de cereais e estivas relacionado com a viabilidade técnico-econômico-financeira da Central de Abastecimento de Gêneros Alimentícios da Região Metropolitana de Fortaleza. [Fortaleza] , 1973. 72 leaves : LC Card 82-147387
HD9014.B83 F587 1973

The Superior North Shore /. Waters, Thomas F. Minneapolis , c1987. xix, 361 p. : ISBN 0-8166-1613-2 : LC Card 87-13585 DDC 333.7/09776/7 19
HC107.M6 W38 1987

The supermarketers . Heller, Robert, 1932- New York , c1987. xiii, 384 p. ; ISBN 0-525-24520-0 LC Card 86-23977 DDC 658.8 19
HF5415 .H374 1987

SUPERMARKETS - FRANCE - HISTORY.
Chavane, Laurence. Le phénomène Leclerc . Paris , c1986. 253 p., [16] p. of plates : ISBN 2-259-01481-X : LC Card 86-186372
HF5469.23.F72 L422 1986

SUPERMARKETS - UNITED STATES - DATA PROCESSING - COSTS - STATISTICS.
Information systems study, 1986. Washington, D.C. (1750 K St. N.W., Washington 20006) , c1986. v, 39 p. : LC Card 86-220211 DDC 381/.456413/00285 19
HF5469.23.U62 I543 1986

SUPERMARKETS - UNITED STATES - FINANCE - STATISTICS.
Operating results of independent supermarkets, 1984. Washington, D.C. (1750 K St., N.W., Washington 20006) , c1985. 137 p. : LC Card 86-218675 DDC 381/.456413/00973 19
HF5469.23.U62 O643 1985

SUPERMARKETS - UNITED STATES - HISTORY.
Walsh, William I. The rise and decline of the Great Atlantic & Pacific Tea Company /. Secaucus, N.J. , c1986. 254 p., [24] p. of plates : ISBN 0-8184-0382-9 : LC Card 85-24987 DDC 381/.456413/006073 19
HD9321.9.G7 W35 1986
NYPL [JLE 86-1952]

SUPERMARKETS - UNITED STATES - STATISTICS.
Operating results of independent supermarkets, 1985. Washington, D.C. (1750 K St., Washington 20006) , c1986. ix, 141 p. : LC Card 86-225218 DDC 381/.456413/00973021 19
HF5469.23.U62 O64 1986

Retail produce operations, 1986 /. Washington, D.C. (1750 K. St., N.W. Washington 20006) , Newark, Del. [1986] viii, 20 p. ; LC Card 87-101803 DDC 381/.456648/00973 19
HD9321.4 .R47 1986

Supersellers . Gschwandtner, Gerhard. New York, N.Y. , c1986. xi, 169 p. : ISBN 0-8144-5883-1 LC Card 86-47586 DDC 658.8/5 19
HF5438.25 .G785 1986
NYPL [JLE 87-1489]

SUPERTANKERS. see **TANKERS.**

The superteam solution . Hastings, Colin. San Diego, Calif. , c1987. x, 182 p. : ISBN 0-88390-206-0 (pbk.) : LC Card 87-19185 DDC 658.4/036 19
HD66 .H38 1987

Supervision . Kirkpatrick, Thomas O., 1932- Boston, Mass. , c1987. xxiii, 588 p. : ISBN 0-534-07314-X : LC Card 86-21121 DDC 658.3/02 19
HF5549 .K528 1987

Supervision . Travers, Alfred W., 1930- Englewood Cliffs, N.J. , c1988. xiv, 409 p. : ISBN 0-13-876434-4 (pbk.) LC Card 87-1173 DDC 658.3/02 19
HF5549 .T714 1988

SUPERVISION OF EMPLOYEES - UNITED STATES.
Derr, C. Brooklyn (Clyde Brooklyn) Managing the new careerists /. San Francisco , 1986. xxii, 288 p. ; ISBN 0-87589-677-4 LC Card 85-45901 DDC 658.3/02 19
HF5549.2.U5 D47 1986
NYPL [JLE 86-2427]

SUPERVISORS - FRANCE.
Le Guen, René. Oxygène pour tous les cerveaux /. Paris , c1985. 204 p. : ISBN 2-209-05743-4 : LC Card 86-117864 DDC 331.7/12/0944 19
HD8038.F7 L4 1985

SUPERVISORS - FRANCE - BIOGRAPHY.
Le Gal, André, 1920- Entre le marteau et l'enclume /. Paris , c1984. 448 p. ; ISBN 2-214-05783-8 : LC Card 85-118954 DDC 658.3/02/0924 B 19
HD8433.L4 A34 1984 ***NYPL [JLD 87-438]***

Supervisor's guide; troubled employee program. United States. Dept. of the Interior. Division of Medical and Health Services. Help for the troubled employee. Washington [1975?] 57 p. ; ***NYPL [JLF 86-1309]***

SUPERVISORS, INDUSTRIAL - HUNGARY.
Réder, Gyula. Helyzetkép az élelmiszeripari müvezetőkről /. Budapest , 1985. 81 p. ; ISBN 963-491-205-2 LC Card 86-196825
HD9015.H82 R43 1985

SUPERVISORS - TRAINING OF.
Gardner, James E. Choosing effective development programs . New York , 1987. x, 194 p. ; ISBN 0-89930-182-7 (lib. bdg. : alk. paper) LC Card 86-30604 DDC 658.4/071245 19
HF5549.15 .G36 1987

Supervivència 2000 . Garcia, Xavier, 1950- Barcelona , 1983. 267 p. ; ISBN 84-7306-196-9 LC Card 83-225437
HC59.72.E5 G37 1983
NYPL [JLD 86-2462]

Suplicy, Eduardo Matarazzo, 1941- Investigando o Caso Coroa-Brastel : discursos / pronunciados pelo Deputado Eduardo Matarazzo Suplicy. Brasília : Câmara dos Deputados, Centro de Documentação e Informação, Coordenação de Publicações, 1984. 215 p. ; 23 cm. (Separatas de discursos, pareceres e projetos . 47a. Legislatura--2a. Sessão Legislativa, no. 114) LC Card 86-200269
1. Grupo Coroa-Brastel. 2. Holding companies - Brazil - Case studies. 3. Bank holding companies - Brazil - Case studies. I. Title. II. Series.
HG4109 .S85 1984

Suppe genug, aber Seele kaputt . Kovacic, Anton. München , c1986. 185 p. ; ISBN 3-453-43075-1 : LC Card 86-230927
HC290.5.P6 K68 1986

Supplément ... à l'Annuaire Arès, défense et sécurité .
(no 3) L'Effort économique de défense . [Grenoble] , 1985. 235 p. : LC Card 86-199399
HC280.D4 E38 1985

Supplément aux Annales islamologiques, 0254-282X .
(cahier no 2, 5) Rāġib, Yūsuf. Marchands d'étoffes du Fayyoum au IIIe/IXe siècle d'après leurs archives (actes et lettres) /. Le Caire , 1982- v. : LC Card 83-156837 DDC 380.1/0962/2 19
HF366 .R34 1982 ***NYPL [*OFP 86-3324]***

Supplement to Birds of the world in philately /. Ridgely, Beverly S. Johnstown, PA , c1986. 62 p., [3] p. of plates : ISBN 0-935991-00-X (pbk.): LC Card 86-217462 DDC 769.56/4/075 769.56/432 19
HE6187 .A635 no. 106-1 HE6183.B53

Supplement to special analysis D : a report required by the Federal Capital Investment Program Information Act of 1984 (Title II of Public Law 98-501). Washington, D.C. : Office of Management and Budget, 1985. 1 v. (various pagings) ; 28 cm. "February 11, 1985." Cover title.
1. Capital budget - United States. 2. Capital investments - United States. I. United States. Federal Capital Investment Program Information Act of 1984. II. Title: Special analysis D. ***NYPL [JLF 86-603]***

SUPPLEMENTARY EMPLOYMENT.
Delany, George. The #1 home business book . Blue Ridge Summit, PA [1987] 168 p. : ISBN 0-8306-3022-8 (pbk.) : LC Card 87-2936 DDC 658/.041 19
HD8036 .D44 1987

Hoge, Cecil C. Mail order moonlighting /. Berkeley, Calif. , 1987. p. cm. ISBN 0-89815-222-4 LC Card 87-17953 DDC 658.8/72 19
HF5466 .H572 1987

SUPPLEMENTARY EMPLOYMENT - MALAYSIA - KELANTAN - CASE STUDIES.
Chew, T. A. The off-farm labour supply of padi farmers in Kelantan, Malaysia [microform] /. [Canberra] , c1984. 19 p. ; ISBN 0-86784-513-9 (pbk.) LC Card 85-670027 DDC 331.12/93318/095951 19
HD5854.55.M4 C47 1984
NYPL [*ZF-1745 no.58]

Supplementary occupations and incomes of cocoa farmers in the Suhum agricultural district of Ghana /. Nyanteng, V. K. Legon , 1979. 17 p. ; LC Card 87-402747 DDC 331.7/63374/09667 19
HD8039.C6362 G46 1979

Supplementi di studi veneziani.
Corazzol, Gigi, 1945- Livelli stipulati a Venezia nel 1591 . Pisa , c1986. 167 p., [8] leaves of plates : LC Card 86-192693
HD680.V4 C67 1986

SUPPLY AND DEMAND - MATHEMATICAL MODELS.
Aggregate supply in interlink . Paris, France , c1985. 60 p. : LC Card 86-205160 DDC 338.5/213 19
HB201 .A25 1985

Supply management . Bhote, Keki R., 1925- New York, N.Y. , c1987. 150 p. : ISBN 0-8144-2330-2 (pbk.) : LC Card 86-28795 DDC 658.7/2/0973 19
HD39.5 .B49 1987

SUPPLY OF MONEY. see **MONEY SUPPLY.**

SUPPLY-SIDE ECONOMICS.
La Nouvelle économie libérale /. Paris , c1983. 280 p. : ISBN 2-7246-0487-3 : LC Card 84-140644
HB95 .N63 1983

Sovremennyĭ konservatizm i krizis burzhuaznoĭ ėkonomicheskoĭ nauki . Moskva , 1986. 175 p. ; LC Card 87-165796
HB241 .S673 1986

Sparpolitik . Opladen , c1983. 152 p. ; ISBN 3-531-11659-2 LC Card 84-109103
HB241 .S675 1983

SUPPLY SIDE ECONOMICS - ADDRESSES, ESSAYS, LECTURES.
International monetary problems and supply-side economics . Houndmills, Basingstoke, Hampshire , 1986. viii, 162 p. : ISBN 0-333-36200-4 ***NYPL [JLD 86-4356]***

SUPPLY-SIDE ECONOMICS - CANADA.
Daly, D. J. (Donald James), 1922- On real wage unemployment /. Vancouver, B.C., Canada , 1986. vi, 117 p. : ISBN 0-88975-079-3 (pbk.) LC Card 87-142391 DDC 331.13/7971 19
HD4946.C3 D35 1986

SUPPLY-SIDE ECONOMICS - UNITED STATES.
Boskin, Michael J. Reagan and the economy . San Francisco, Calif. , New York , c1987. xvi, 301 p. : ISBN 0-917616-80-4 : LC Card 87-22544 DDC 338.973 19
HC106.8 .B656 1987

Economic report of the people /. Boston , c1986. xvii, 260 p. : ISBN 0-89608-315-2 (pbk.) : LC Card 85-30342 DDC 330.973/0927 19
HC106.8 .E29 1986 ***NYPL [JLD 87-301]***

Sawyer, James E., 1943- Why Reaganomics and Keynesian economics failed /. New York , 1987. ix, 195 p. : ISBN 0-312-00532-6 : LC Card 87-9578 DDC 338.973 19
HC106.8 .S28 1987

Supply-side portfolio strategies /. Westport, Conn. , 1988. xii, 180 p. : ISBN 0-89930-286-6 (lib. bdg. : alk. paper) LC Card 87-13091 DDC 332.6/0973 19
HG4910 .S775 1988

Tobin, James, 1918- Policies for prosperity . Cambridge, Mass. , 1987. xiv, 508 p. : ISBN 0-262-20066-X LC Card 87-2967 DDC 330.15/6 19
HB99.7 .T63 1987

SUPPLY-SIDE ECONOMICS - UNITED STATES - HISTORY - 20TH CENTURY.
Winant, Howard. Stalemate . New York , 1988. xv, 203 p. ; ISBN 0-275-92706-3 (alk. paper) : LC Card 87-15157 DDC 338.973 19
HC106.6 .W56 1988

Supply-side portfolio strategies / edited by Victor A. Canto and Arthur B. Laffer. Westport, Conn. : Quorum Books, 1988. xii, 180 p. : ill. ; 25 cm. Includes bibliographies and index. ISBN 0-89930-286-6 (lib. bdg. : alk. paper) LC Card 87-13091 DDC 332.6/0973 19
1. Investments - United States. 2. Portfolio management - United States. 3. Supply-side economics - United States. I. Canto, Victor A. II. Laffer, Arthur B.
HG4910 .S775 1988

Supported employment : a community implementation guide / by G. Thomas Bellamy ... [et al.]. Baltimore : P.H. Brookes Pub. Co., c1988. x, 287 p. : ill. ; 23 cm. Bibliography: p. 273-275. Includes index. ISBN 0-933716-83-4 (pbk.) : LC Card 87-14367 DDC 362/.0425 19
1. Handicapped - Employment - United States. 2. Vocational Rehabilitation - United States. I. Bellamy, G. Thomas.
HD7256.U5 S86 1988

Supuestos y consultas sobre licencia fiscal . Román Egea, Antonio. Madrid [1984?] 235 p. ; ISBN 84-7130-439-2 LC Card 86-149143 DDC 343.4606/8 344.60368 19
HJ5627.S7 R66 1984

Surányi, György. Bokros, Lajos. Piac és pénz a modern gazdaságban /. Budapest , 1985. 340, [1] p. ; ISBN 963-221-551-6 : LC Card 86-185991
HB95 .B65 1985

Surányi, László. A Magyar bélyegek kézikönyve /. Budapest , 1986. 551 p., viii p. of plates : ISBN 963-281-692-7 : LC Card 87-151573 DDC 769.569439 19
HE6185.H8 M32 1986

Suraphon Thamromdī.
Kānprakan sangkhom. 1985. Rǣngngān Thai. Krung Thēp , 2528 [1985] 53 p. ; LC Card 86-915944
HD5822.55.A6 R35 1985

Les Surcharges "France libre" dans les Etablissements français en Inde, 1941-1945 / éditeur, Ph. Voisin. Orléans : P. Voisin, [1984] 19 p., [4] p. of plates : ill. ; 21 cm. ISBN 2-9500569-0-3 : LC Card 86-122498
1. France - History - German occupation, 1940-1945. I. Voisin, Ph.
HE6185.F8 S87 1984

Surendar Singh, 1946- Agro-economics of dairy development in India / Surendar Singh. New Delhi : Criterion Publications, 1986. xii, 188 p. ; 22 cm. Bibliography: p. [178]-184. Includes index. LC Card 86-902764 DDC 338.1/77/0954 19
1. Dairying - Government policy - India. 2. Dairying - Economic aspects - India. 3. Dairy products - India - Marketing. I. Title.
HD9275.I52 S87 1986

Suresh Kumar, 1935- Indo-CMEA economic relations /. New Delhi , 1987. xviii, 263 p. ; ISBN 81-7024-078-6 : LC Card 87-901620 DDC 337.54047 19
HC433 .I535 1987

SURGICAL INSTRUMENTS AND APPARATUS INDUSTRY - UNITED STATES.
Cardiovascular surgery products markets in the U. S. New York, N.Y. , c1983. xxiii, 197 p. : LC Card 87-143453
HD9995.S93 U525 1983

The Special surgery equipment and supplies market in the U. S. New York, N.Y. , c1983. xxiii, 332 p. : LC Card 87-142345 DDC 381/.45681761 19
HD9995.S93 U56 1983

SURGICAL INSTRUMENTS AND APPARATUS - MARKETING.
Strategic marketing of surgical products. Tustin, CA, U. S.A. (17722 Irvine Blvd., Tustin 92680) , c1987. 1 v. (various foliations) : LC Card 87-168617 DDC 380.1/45681761 19
HD9995.S92 S77 1987

Suri, K. B., 1932- Small scale enterprises in industrial development . Newbury Park, Calif. , New Delhi , 1987. p. cm. ISBN 0-8039-9539-3 LC Card 87-23221 DDC 338.6/42/0954 19
HD2346.I5 S547 1987

Surirat Wongsangīam. Songsan Ninkamhǣng. Chotmāihēt kānsāng Phraphutthārūp phra prathān Phutthamonthon /. Krung Thēp , 2525 [1982] 172 p. : ISBN 974-7921-05-7 LC Card 83-916060
HB1912.G38 S66 1982

SURKHANDAR'INSKAI͡A OBLAST' (UZBEK S.S.R.) - ECONOMIC CONDITIONS.
Molozhavenko, Vladimir. Zharkoe solntse Surkhana /. Moskva , 1982. 189 p., [16] p. of plates : LC Card 82-177858
HC337.U962 S975 1982

Surmann, Rolf. Die Münzenberg-Legende : zur Publizistik der revolutionären deutschen Arbeiterbewegung 1921-1933 / Rolf Surmann. Köln : Prometh, c1983. 307 p. : ill. ; 21 cm. Bibliography: p. 292-300. Includes index. ISBN 3-922009-53-0 LC Card 83-155325
1. Workers' International Relief - History. 2. Labor and laboring classes - Germany - History. 3. Propaganda, German - History. 4. Münzenberg, Willi. I. Title.
HD8450 .S87 1983

Surovt͡seva, G. V. Puti razvitii͡a infrastruktury regiona /. Ufa , 1984. 117 p. : LC Card 85-199949
HE255.Z7 B377 1984

Les surplus agricoles et la pénurie alimentaire . France. Conseil économique et social. [Paris] [1986] 1 v. (various pagings) : LC Card 86-179100
HD1431 .F7 1986

SURPLUS AGRICULTURAL COMMODITIES, AMERICAN.
Special report on applying United States food surpluses to the problems of hunger /. Washington , 1984. ii, iv, 54 p. ; LC Card 87-601529 DDC 363.8/83 19
HD9000.5 .S666 1984

SURPLUS AGRICULTURAL COMMODITIES, FRENCH - DEVELOPING COUNTRIES.
France. Conseil économique et social. Les surplus agricoles et la pénurie alimentaire . [Paris] [1986] 1 v. (various pagings) : LC Card 86-179100
HD1431 .F7 1986

SURPLUS AGRICULTURAL COMMODITIES - GOVERNMENT POLICY - INDIA.
Dāśagupta, Pānnālāla, 1909- Production by the masses . Calcutta , 1983. vi, 54 p. ; LC Card 83-906787 DDC 331.11/8/0954 19
HC440.I52 D37 1983 ***NYPL [JLD 87-708]***

SURPLUS AGRICULTURAL COMMODITIES - UNITED STATES.
Embargoes, surplus disposal, and U. S. agriculture . Washington, D.C. , 1986. vi, 34 p. ; LC Card 86-603452 DDC 338.1/8 19
HD1761 .E45 1986

SURPLUS (ECONOMICS)
Gerondeau, Christian, 1938- L'énergie à revendre /. [Paris] , c1984. 333 p. : LC Card 84-166266
HD9502.A2 G47 1984

SURPLUS VALUE.
Mehrwert heute . Berlin , c1981. 285 p. ; LC Card 82-189316 DDC 338.5/21 19
HB206 .M44 1981 ***NYPL [JLD 86-2837]***

Mellár, Tamás. Az érték átalakulása termelési árrá, avagy, Az un. transzformációs probléma /. Pécs , 1982. 55 p. ; LC Card 83-179021
HB203 .M44 1982

Mugnai, Massimo, 1947- Il mondo rovesciato . Bologna , c1984. 296 p. ; ISBN 88-15-00641-9 : LC Card 86-169123
HB206 .M84 1984

SURPLUS VALUE - FRANCE - HISTORY - 20TH CENTURY.
Delaunay, Jean Claude. Salariat et plus-value en France depuis la fin du XIXe siècle /. Paris , c1984. xiv, 304 p. : ISBN 2-7246-0488-1 : LC Card 84-172193 DDC 331.2/944 19
HB206 .D45 1984 ***NYPL [JLD 86-426]***

Surrey, John. The European power plant industry : structural responses to international market pressures / by John Surrey & William Walker. [Brighton, Sussex] : Sussex European Research Centre, University of Sussex, c1981. viii, 90 p. ; 22 cm. (Sussex European papers. no. 12) Industrial adjustment and policy ; 3 Bibliography: p. 89-90. ISBN 0-903422-31-X (pbk.) : LC Card 83-130609 DDC 338.4/76213121/094 19
1. Electric power plant equipment industry - Europe. 2. Construction industry - Europe. 3. Electric power-plants - Developing countries - Design and construction. 4. Market surveys - Developing countries. I. Walker, William B. II. Title. III. Series.
HD9695.E92 S87 1981
NYPL [JLD 86-4078]

Suruagy, Divaldo. Diretrizes básicas do governo : 1983/1987 / Divaldo Suruagy. Maceió, Alagoas : Governo do Estado de Alagoas, 1983. 84 p. ; 23 cm. LC Card 85-200794
1. Alagoas (Brazil) - Economic policy. 2. Alagoas (Brazil) - Social policy. I. Title.
HC188.A46 S87 1983

Survey of advanced sales. 4th ed. Chicago : R&R Newkirk, c1987. v, 214 p. : ill. ; 28 cm. Cover title. ISBN 0-88462-703-9 (pbk.) LC Card 87-13112 DDC 368/.0068/8 19
1. Insurance - Agents. 2. Finance, Personal. 3. Investments. I. R & R Newkirk.
HG8091 .S87 1987

Survey of automation in the convenience store industry / National Association of Convenience Stores. Alexandria, Va. (1605 King St., Alexandria 22314-2792) : NACS, c1986. vii, 39, 9 p. : ill. ; 28 cm. LC Card 87-147614 DDC 381/.1 19
1. Convenience stores - United States - Automation. 2. Convenience stores - United States - Automation - Statistics. I. National Association of Convenience Stores (U. S.).
HF5469.55.U62 S87 1986

A Survey of constraints facing small-scale farmers in Mpika and Chinsali Districts, Northern Province : report. [Mpika, Zambia?] : Monitoring and Evaluation Unit, IRDP (Serenje, Mpika, and Chinsali), [1985 or 1986] 8 p., [1] leaf of plates : map ; 30 cm. Cover title. Includes bibliographical references. LC Card 86-981416 DDC 338.1/6 19
1. Farms, Small - Zambia - Mpika District. 2. Farms, Small - Zambia - Chinsali District. 3. Agriculture - Economic aspects - Zambia - Mpika District. 4. Agriculture - Economic aspects - Zambia - Chinsali District. I. Integrated Rural Development Project, Serenje-Mpika-Chinsali (Zambia). Monitoring and Evaluation Unit.
HD1476.Z352 M657 1985

Survey of employment, income distribution, and consumption patterns in Nepal. Employment, income distribution, and consumption patterns in Nepal . Kathmandu, Nepal , 1983. xiv, 122 p. ; LC Card 84-901199 DDC 330.9549/6 19
HD5812.9.A6 E47 1983
NYPL [JLF 86-1993]

Survey of fixed capital stock in industry, 1.1.1982. Aspler, I. Seḳer melai ha-hon ha-ḳavu'a be-ta'asiyah, 1.1.1982 /. Yerushalayim , 1986. 80, xvii p. ; LC Card 87-128243
HA1931 .A354 no. 785 HC415.25.Z9C3

Survey of income and program participation and related longitudinal surveys, 1984 : selected papers given at the 1984 annual meeting of the American Statistical Association in Philadelphia, Pa., August 13-16, 1984 / compiled by Daniel Kasprzyk, Delma Frankel. [Washington, D.C.] : Population Divison, Bureau of the Census, Dept. of Commerce, 1985. ix, 201 p. : ill. ; 29 cm. "January 1985." Includes bibliographies. LC Card 85-601676 DDC 339.2/3/0973 19
1. Income - United States - Congresses. 2. Transfer payments - United States - Congresses. 3. Households - United States - Congresses. 4. Social sciences - Research - United States - Methodology - Congresses. I. Kasprzyk, Daniel. II. Frankel, Delma. III. American Statistical Association. Meeting (144th : 1984 : Philadelphia, Pa.).
HC110.I5 S89 1985 ***NYPL [JLF 86-1641]***

Survey of labor relations /. Balliet, Lee. Washington, D.C. , c1981. ix, 198 p. : ISBN 0-87179-347-4 LC Card 80-26863 DDC 331/.0973
HD8072.5 .B34 *NYPL [JLE 86-4719]*

Survey of labor relations /. Balliet, Lee. Washington, D.C. , c1987. xi, 212 p. : ISBN 0-87179-544-2 (pbk.) LC Card 87-864 DDC 331/.0973 19
HD8072.5 .B34 1987

A survey of Lloyds syndicate accounts . Macve, Richard, 1940- Englewood Cliffs, NJ , 1986. xxv, 263 p. : ISBN 0-13-878273-3 : LC Card 85-12147 DDC 368/.012/094212 19
HG8039 .M33 1986 *NYPL [JLE 87-864]*

Survey of migration into the Bangkok Metropolis, the vicinity of the Bangkok Metropolis, and Khon Kaen Province, 1985. Kānsamrūat kānyāithin kh [Bangkok] [1986] 57, 165 p. ; LC Card 87-915769
HB2104.55.B36 K35 1986

Survey of New Zealand farmer intentions and opinions, November 1985-January 1986 /. Pryde, J. G. Canterbury, N.Z. [1986] 133 p. ; LC Card 87-107903 DDC 338.1/09931 19
HD8039.F32 N486 1986

Survey of private sector work and family policy . McGuire, Nan. San Francisco , c1986. 41 leaves ; LC Card 87-113810 DDC 331.25/72/0979461 19
HD5126.S4 M38 1986

A survey of recent U. S. developments in international agricultural trade models /. Thompson, Robert L. Washington, D.C. , 1981. v, 74 p. ; LC Card 81-603138 DDC 382/.41/0973 19
HD1433 .T48 *NYPL [JLF 84-568]*

Survey of sole parent pensioners' workforce barriers /. Frey, Dianne. Woden, ACT [1986] 40 p. : ISBN 0-642-51708-8 LC Card 87-154429 DDC 331.4/4 19
HD6220 .F74 1986

A survey of the economics of the retail pharmacy sector in Canada /. Maule, Christopher J., 1934- [Toronto, Ont.] , c1986. 42 p. ; ISBN 0-662-14496-1 (pbk.) LC Card 86-206188 DDC 338.4/76151/0971 19
HD9670.C22 M38 1986

Survey of the Job Training Partnership Act eight percent set-aside. 1987. Howe, Mike. Accessing private industry council funding . [Northridge, CA] (17624 Romar St., Northridge 91325) [1987?] 24, [15] leaves ; LC Card 87-401761 DDC 362.8/5 19
HD5715.2 .H69 1987

Survey report (Columbia University. Graduate School of Business. Center for Operations) . (no. 2) Starr, Martin Kenneth, 1927- The performance of Japanese-owned firms in America, 1982-1985 /. [New York, NY] , c1987. ii, 41 leaves : LC Card 87-145262 DDC 338.8/8952/073 19
HD2785 .S66 1987

Survey report (Nihon Daigaku. Sangyō Keiei Kenkyūjo) . (no. 7) A Comparative study on accounting policy between Japanese and the U. S. companies /. Tokyo, Japan , c1986. iv, 56 p. : LC Card 87-169003 DDC 657/.0952 19
HF5686.C7 C635 1986

Survey research methods /. Golden, Gary. Chicago, IL , c1982. 69 leaves : ISBN 0-8389-6753-1 (pbk.) LC Card 87-107560 DDC 300/.723 19
HA31.2 .G65 1982

SURVEYING - CONGRESSES.
The Management and development of natural resources . London [1985] 192 p. : ISBN 0-903577-33-X (pbk.) LC Card 86-206154 DDC 333.7 19
HC13 .M35 1985

SURVEYS, DEMOGRAPHIC. see **DEMOGRAPHIC SURVEYS.**

SURVEYS, ECONOMIC. see **ECONOMIC SURVEYS.**

Surveys in computer science.
Ellis, Clarence Arthur, 1943- Design of office information systems /. Berlin , New York , c1987. vi, 248 p. : ISBN 0-387-17810-4 (U. S.) : LC Card 87-9582 DDC 651.8 19
HF5548.2 .E445 1987

Surveys in development economics / edited by Norman Gemmell. Oxford, UK ; New York, NY, USA : B. Blackwell, 1987. 390 p. : ill. ; 24 cm. Bibliography: p. [373]-376. Includes index. ISBN 0-631-14713-6 : LC Card 87-5164 DDC 338.9/009172/4 19
1. Developing countries - Economic policy. 2. Developing countries - Commerce. 3. Developing countries - Industries. 4. Economic development. I. Gemmell, Norman.
HC59.7 .S882 1987

Surveys in the economics of uncertainty / edited by John D. Hey and Peter J. Lambert. Oxford, UK ; New York, NY, USA : B. Blackwell, 1987. 232 p. : ill. ; 24 cm. Includes bibliographies and index. ISBN 0-631-15335-7 LC Card 87-10366 DDC 330 19
1. Uncertainty. 2. Economics. I. Hey, John Denis. II. Lambert, Peter J.
HB615 .S97 1987

SURVEYS - LONGITUDINAL STUDIES.
Federal longitudinal surveys /. [Washington, D.C.?] [Springfield, VA] 1986. v, 159 p. : LC Card 86-603413 DDC 001.4/33 19
HA31.2 .F43 1986

Surveys on liability insurance for government entities. Oak Brook, Ill. (1200 Harger Rd., Suite 222, Oak Brook 60521) : All-Industry Research Advisory Council, c1986. vi, 66 p. ; 28 cm. "November 1986." LC Card 87-110891 DDC 368.5 19
1. Insurance, Government risks - United States. I. All-Industry Research Advisory Council. II. Title: Liability insurance for government entities.
HG8207 .S87 1986

SURVEYS, SOCIAL. see **SOCIAL SURVEYS.**

SURVEYS, TRAFFIC. see **TRAFFIC SURVEYS.**

SURVIVAL (HUMAN ECOLOGY) see **HUMAN ECOLOGY.**

Survival in the corporate fishbowl . Fernandez, John P., 1941- Lexington, Mass. , c1987. xiii, 314 p. : ISBN 0-669-10336-5 (alk. paper) LC Card 85-40021 DDC 302.3/5 19
HD6957.U6 F47 1987

Survival International. Ethiopia's bitter medicine, settling for disaster . London , 1986. 55 p. : ISBN 0-946592-01-2 (pbk.) LC Card 86-232852 DDC 333.3/1/63
HD979.Z63 E74 1986

Survival International documents .
(new ser., 3rd) Ethiopia's bitter medicine, settling for disaster . London , 1986. 55 p. : ISBN 0-946592-01-2 (pbk.) LC Card 86-232852 DDC 333.3/1/63
HD979.Z63 E74 1986

Survival models and their estimation /. London, Dick, 1943- Winsted, Conn. , c1986 (1987 printing) xii, 282 p. : ISBN 0-936031-01-8 (pbk.) LC Card 87-402847 DDC 304.6/4/015195 19
HG8782 .L57 1987

Survival of the small firm / edited by James Curran, John Stanworth, David Watkins. Aldershot, Hants, England ; Brookfield, Vt., U. S.A. : Gower Pub. Co., c1986. 2 v. : ill. ; 23 cm. Includes bibliographies. CONTENTS. - v. 1. The economics of survival and entrepreneurship -- v. 2. The employment, growth, technology, and politics. ISBN 0-566-00725-8 (v. 1) : LC Card 85-27035 DDC 338.6/42 19
1. Small business - Addresses, essays, lectures. 2. Self-employed - Addresses, essays, lectures. 3. Small business - Employees - Addresses, essays, lectures. I. Curran, James. II. Stanworth, John. III. Watkins, David, 1947-.
HD2341 .S87 1986 *NYPL [JLD 86-2643]*

Survival on the fast track /. Kovach, Barbara E. New York , c1988. xv, 240 p. ; ISBN 0-396-09027-3 LC Card 87-19940 DDC 658.4/092 19
HD57.7 .K69 1988

Survival strategies of rural women traders, or, A woman's place is in the market . Peluso, Nancy Lee. Geneva [1981], c1980. viii, 124 p. ; ISBN 92-2-102633-7 LC Card 83-105710 DDC 331.4/81381/095982 19
HD6194.Z6 S566 1981

Surviving corporate transition . Bridges, William, 1933- New York , 1988. xii, 227 p. ; ISBN 0-385-23761-8 : LC Card 87-19978 DDC 658.4/06 19
HD31 .B7395 1988

Surviving sexual contradictions . Dimen, Muriel. New York , c1986. xxi, 257 p. ; ISBN 0-02-531620-6 LC Card 86-12600 DDC 305.4/2/0973 19
HQ1426 .D56 1986 *NYPL [JLE 86-4385]*

SURVIVORS' BENEFITS (OLD AGE PENSIONS) see **OLD AGE PENSIONS.**

SURVIVORS' BENEFITS - UNITED STATES.
Lopata, Helena Znaniecka, 1925- Widows and dependent wives . New York , 1986. xxi, 242 p. ; ISBN 0-03-046301-7 (alk. paper) : LC Card 85-16753 DDC 362.8/382 19
HV699 .L67 1985 *NYPL [JLE 86-2182]*

Sury, Paul de. Milano, centro finanziario internazionale / Paul de Sury, Michele Preda, Michele Rutigliano. [Milano] : Giuffrè, [1984] viii, 138 p. : ill. ; 24 cm. (Università "L. Bocconi," Dipartimento di economia aziendale . 83. 3.38) Includes bibliographies. ISBN 88-14-00312-2 : LC Card 86-114645
1. Banks and banking - Italy - Milan. 2. Financial institutions - Italy - Milan. 3. Banks and banking, International. 4. Financial institutions, International. I. Preda, Michele. II. Rutigliano, Michele. III. Series: Università "L. Bocconi," Dipartimento di economia aziendale (Series) , 83. IV. Title.
HG3090.M52 S87 1984

Surya Prakash. Parliamentary control over public enterprises in India / Surya Prakash. 1st ed. Allahabad, India : Chugh Publications, 1985. 293 p. ; 22 cm. Includes index. Bibliography: p. [271]-278. LC Card 85-903454 DDC 354.5409/2 19
1. Government business enterprises - India. 2. Legislative oversight - India. I. Title.
HD4293 .S87 1985 *NYPL [JLD 87-325]*

Suryanarayana Raju, S. K. V. Analysis of productivity levels and economic efficiency in agriculture / S.K.V. Suryanarayana Raju. Allahabad, India : Chugh Publications, 1987 [i.e. 1986] viii, 368 p. : ill. ; 22 cm. Study conducted in Vishakhapatnam District, Andhra Pradesh. Bibliography: p. 357-366. Includes index. ISBN 81-85076-12-X : LC Card 86-903606 DDC 338.1/0954/84 19
1. Agricultural productivity - India - Vishākhapatnam District. 2. Agriculture - Economic aspects - India - Vishākhapatnam District. I. Title.
HD2075.V58 S87 1986

Suryawanshi, S. D. Dhongade, M. P. Farmers' attitude survey in the Mula Command Area, Maharashtra /. Rahuri, Maharashtra, India , 1986. vi, 69 p. ; LC Card 86-903408 DDC 338.1/0954/792 19
HD8039.F32 I44 1986

Susan Lee's ABZs of economics /. Lee, Susan, 1943- [ABZs of economics.] New York , c1987. 224 p. : ISBN 0-671-55711-4 LC Card 86-25481 DDC 330/.03 19
HB61 .L34 1987

Susanīan, K. G. (Karen Gevorkovich) Araviĭskie gosudarstva i vneshneėkonomicheskaīa strategiīa SShA / K.G. Susanīan. Moskva : "Mezhdunar. otnosheniīa", 1986. 229, [3] p. : ill. ; 20 cm. Bibliography: p. 219-[230] LC Card 86-231698 DDC 337.73053 19
1. United States - Foreign economic relations - Arabian Peninsula. 2. Arabian Peninsula - Economic conditions. 3. Petroleum industry and trade - Arabian Peninsula. 4. Arabian Peninsula - Foreign economic relations - United States. I. Title.
HF1456.5.A625 S87 1986

Susano Lucero, Aurelio Reynaldo. Liberalización financiera [microform] : posibilidades y limitaciones en el mercado bancario comercial peruano / A.R. Susano L. Lima : Universidad de Lima, c1982. [40] p. : 1 ill. ; 21 cm. (Serie Avances de investigación . no. 3) Rev. version of a report prepared for the Tercer Seminario sobre Banca y Finanzas, May 5, 1982, organized by the Centro de Investigaciones Económicas y Sociales de la Universidad de Lima. Includes bibliographical references. Microfilm. New York : New York Public Library, 1986. 1 microfilm reel ; 35 mm. (MN *ZZ-26,873) LC Card 84-227503 DDC 332.1/0985 19
1. Banks and banking - Peru - Congresses. 2. Finance - Peru - Congresses. I. Title.
HG2944 .S93 1982 *NYPL [*ZT-1745 no.6]*

Susánszky, János. Tanulmányok a szervezésről és a vezetésről / Susánszky János. Budapest : Akadémiai Kiadó, 1985. 89 p. ; 20 cm. (Tudományszervezési füzetek, 0082-6707) Includes bibliographical references. ISBN 963-05-4132-7 : LC Card 86-136320
1. Organization. 2. Management. 3. Management - Study and teaching. I. Title. II. Series.
HD37.H82 S857 1985

Sushka, Marie Elizabeth. Slovin, Myron B. Macroeconomics for managers /. Englewood Cliffs, N.J. , c1987. xvi, 512 p. : ISBN 0-13-542937-4 LC Card 86-25199 DDC 339 19
HB172.5 .S55 1987

Sŭshtnost, formi i nasoki na izzhivi͡avane na chastnata stopanska deĭnost pri sots͡ializma /. Popov, Nikola Grigorov. Sofii͡a , 1985. 363 p. ; LC Card 85-169713
HC704 .P66 1985 *NYPL [*QK 87-1471]*

Susini, Jean-Jacques. A qui profite l'inflation? / Jean-Jacques Susini ; préface de Jacques Austruy. Paris : Presses universitaires de France, c1985. 122 p. : ill. ; 24 cm. (Travaux et recherches de l'Université de droit, d'économie et de sciences sociales de Paris. Série Sciences économiques . no 13) Bibliography: p. [81]-[85] ISBN 2-13-039288-1 LC Card 86-153761
1. Inflation (Finance) - France. 2. Income distribution - France - Effect of inflation on. 3. Saving and investment - France - Effect of inflation on. I. Title. II. Series.
HG979.5 .S87 1985

Suslov, Ivan Petrovich. Val'tukh, Konstantin Kurtovich. T͡Selevai͡a funktsii͡a potreblenii͡a . Novosibirsk , 1980. 381, [3] p. ; LC Card 81-134031
HB801 .V265 1980

Sussex European papers.
(no. 12) Surrey, John. The European power plant industry . [Brighton, Sussex] , c1981. viii, 90 p. ; ISBN 0-903422-31-X (pbk.) : LC Card 83-130609 DDC 338.4/76213121/094 19
HD9695.E92 S87 1981
NYPL [JLD 86-4078]

Sussex, Margie. The complete real estate math book / Margie Sussex, John F. Stapleton. 2nd ed. Englewood Cliffs, N.J. : Prentice Hall, c1988. vii, 288 p. : ill. ; 28 cm. ISBN 0-13-162298-6 (pbk.) LC Card 87-14397 DDC 513/.02433 19
1. Business mathematics - Real estate business. I. Stapleton, John F. II. Title.
HF5695.5.R3 S935 1988

Sustainable communities . Van der Ryn, Sim. San Francisco [1986] xvii, 238 p. : ISBN 0-87156-800-4 LC Card 83-4676 DDC 307/.14 19
HN90.C6 V36 1986 *NYPL [JLF 86-1241]*

Sustainable development . Global Meeting on Environment and Development for Non-governmental Organisations (1985 : Nairobi, Kenya) [Nairobi, Kenya] [1985 or 1986] 109 p. : LC Card 86-981176 DDC 363.7/057 19
HC79.E5 G595 1985

Sustainable development . Redclift, M. R. London , New York , 1987. 221 p. : ISBN 0-416-90240-5 LC Card 87-5710 DDC 363.7 19
HD75.6 .R43 1987

Sustainable resource development in the Third World / edited by Douglas D. Southgate and John F. Disinger. Boulder : Westview Press, 1987. vi, 177 p. : ill. ; 23 cm. (Westview special studies in natural resources and energy management) Includes bibliographies and index. ISBN 0-8133-7522-3 (alk. paper) LC Card 87-20137 DDC 333.7/15/091724 19
1. Natural resources - Developing countries - Management. 2. Environmental policy - Developing countries. I. Southgate, Douglas Dewitt. II. Disinger, John F.
HC59.7 .S8826 1987

The sustaining hand . Jones, Bryan D. Lawrence, Kan. , c1986. xii, 247 p. : ISBN 0-7006-0278-X : LC Card 85-24631 DDC 338.4/76292/09774 19
HD9710.U53 M433 1986
NYPL [JLE 86-2386]

Sutcliffe, Robert B. Hard times : the world economy in turmoil / Bob Sutcliffe. London : Pluto Press, 1983. 118 p. ; 20 cm. (Arguments for socialism) Bibliography: p. [114]-118. ISBN 0-86104-505-X (pbk.) : LC Card 83-126438 DDC 330.9/04 19
1. Economic history - 1971-. 2. Capitalism. I. Title. II. Series.
HC59 .S8873 1983 *NYPL [JLD 86-4088]*

Suti͡agin, Valeriĭ Semenovich. Voprosy prognozirovanii͡a i planirovanii͡a vneshneėkonomicheskikh svi͡azeĭ /. Moskva , 1984. 93 p. ; LC Card 86-144298
HF3626.5 .V668 1984

Sutija, George, 1926- Eurodollars and international banking /. London [Miami] , 1985. xiii, 226 p. : ISBN 0-333-36553-4
NYPL [JLD 85-3068]

Sutkaĭtis, V. P. (Virgilis Povilovich) Rai͡atskas, R. L. (Raĭmundas Leonovich), 1937- Okruzhai͡ushchai͡a sreda i problemy planirovanii͡a /. Moskva , 1981. 272 p. ; LC Card 87-462039
HD75.6 .R35 1981

Sütő, Kálmánné.
Mezőgazdasági és élelmiszeripari adattár a felszabadulástól napjainkig /. Budapest , 1985. 152 p. ; ISBN 963-502-393-6 LC Card 86-202515
HD1940.5 .M497 1985

Mezőgazdasági és élelmiszeripari adattár a felszabadulástól napjainkig. English. Collection of data of agriculture and food industry from the liberation till now /. Budapest , 1985. 85 p. ; ISBN 963-502-393-6 LC Card 86-230345
HD1940.5 .M49713 1985

Sutton, Howard, 1930- Rethinking the company's selling and distribution channels / by Howard Sutton. New York, N.Y. : The Conference Board, c1986. v, 26 p. : ill. ; 28 cm. (Report / The Conference Board . no. 885) ISBN 0-8237-0328-2 (pbk.) LC Card 87-404502 DDC 658.8/4 19
1. Marketing channels - United States. 2. Direct selling - United States. 3. Telemarketing - United States. I. Series: Conference Board report, no. 885. II. Title.
HF5415.129 .S87 1986

Suvorov, B. P. (Boris Pavlovich) Optimizat͡sii͡a planirovanii͡a polimerno-neftekhimicheskogo kompleksa /. Moskva , 1984. 141 p. : LC Card 86-143987
HD9579.C33 S655 1984

Suvorova, M. I. (Marii͡a Il'inichna) Kritika Kominternom revizionistskikh vzgli͡adov na ėkonomiku sots͡ializma / M.I. Suvorova. Moskva : Izd-vo Moskovskogo universiteta, 1985. 115 p. ; 22 cm. Includes bibliographical references. LC Card 84-219550
1. Marxian economics. 2. Socialism - Soviet Union. I. Title.
HB97.5 .S86 1985 *NYPL [*QIP 87-2751]*

Suzaki, Kiyoshi. The new manufacturing challenge : techniques for continuous improvement / Kiyoshi Suzaki. New York : Free Press ; London : Collier Macmillan Publishers, c1987. xv, 255 p. : ill. ; 24 cm. Bibliography: p. 251-252. Includes index. ISBN 0-02-932040-2 LC Card 86-33715 DDC 658.5 19
1. Manufactures - Management. 2. Industrial management. 3. Manufactures - Technological innovations. 4. Manufacturing processes. I. Title.
HD9720.5 .S98 1987

Suzuki, Shigeru, 1949- Nihon no enerugī kaihatsu seisaku / Suzuki Shigeru cho. 880-03 Dai 1-han. Kyōto-shi : Mineruva Shobō, 1985. vii, 274 p. : ill. ; 22 cm. In Japanese. Includes bibliographical references and indexes. ISBN 4-623-01582-3 : LC Card 85-221878
1. Energy policy - Japan. 2. Petroleum industry and trade - Government policy - Japan. I. Title.
HD9502.J32 S89 1985 <Orien Japan>
*NYPL [*OSM 86-3954]*

Suzuki, Yoshio, 1931-
Financial innovation and monetary policy . [Tokyo] , c1986. ix, 339 p. : ISBN 4-13-047029-9 : LC Card 86-222823 DDC 332/.095 19
HG187.E37 F55 1986

[Nihon kin'yū keizairon. English]
Money, finance, and macroeconomic performance in Japan / Yoshio Suzuki ; translated by Robert Alan Feldman. New Haven : Yale University Press, c1986. xvii, 218, p. : ill. ; 24 cm. Rev. translation of: Nihon kin'yū keizairon. Includes indexes. Bibliography: p. 203-211. ISBN 0-300-03387-7 LC Card 85-26375 DDC 332/.0952 19
1. Finance - Japan. 2. Money supply - Japan. 3. Monetary policy - Japan. I. Title.
HG187.J3 S96 1986 *NYPL [JLE 86-2788]*

Svagrāyupra. Bihar (India). Rural Development Dept. Trysem . [Paṭanā] , 1980. 41 p. ; LC Card 80-908290
HD6276.I42 B54 1980

Svejnar, Jan. Economic policies and agricultural performance : the case of Nepal, 1960-1982 / by Jan Svejnar et Erik Thorbecke. Paris : Development Centre of the Organisation for Economic Co-operation and Development, 1986. 167 p. ; 23 cm. (Development Centre papers) Bibliography: p. 129-131. LC Card 87-120115 DDC 338.1/85496 19
1. Agriculture and state - Nepal. 2. Agricultural productivity - Nepal. I. Thorbecke, Erik. II. Title. III. Series.
HD2065.9.Z8 S84 1986

Svensk befolkningshistoria . Hofsten, Erland Adolf Gerhard von, 1911- [Stockholm] , c1986. 180, [1] p. : ISBN 91-29-57693-8 LC Card 86-194606
HB3617 .H768 1986

Svensk byggexport . Sveriges exportråd. [Stockholm] [1984] v, 107, [23] p. : ISBN 91-38-08107-5 LC Card 84-217971
HD9715.8.S82 S86 1984

Svensk-engelsk ordbok. Engelsk-svensk ordbok . Stockholm , 1970. 2 v. ;
NYPL [JFD 87-817]

Svensk gjuteriindustri : rapport från gjuteriutredning nr. 3. Stockholm : Statens industriverk, 1982. 62 p. : ill. ; 30 cm. (SIND PM, 0346-573X . 1982:6) ISBN 91-38-07151-7 LC Card 83-220920
1. Metal trade - Sweden - Statistics. 2. Foundries - Sweden - Statistics. I. Sweden. Statens industriverk. II. Series.
HD9506.S82 S92 1982

Svenska byggnadsentreprenörföreningen.
Byggnads- och anläggningsindustrin. [Stockholm] [1981] 84 p. : ISBN 91-38-06015-9 LC Card 84-120446
HD9715.S852 B898 1981

Svenska dagbladet/Förlagsgruppen. Vem gör vad i svenskt näringsliv . Stockholm [1983] 283 p. ; LC Card 83-225142
HF3673 .V46 1983

Den svenska debatten om industriell demokrati 1919-1924 /. Lundh, Christer. Lund , 1987- v. <1 > ; ISBN 91-85611-17-4 LC Card 87-151790
HD5660.S9 L87 1987

Den svenska ekonomins intertnationalisering . Iger, Svantc. Lund , Stockholm [1976] iv, 144 p. : ISBN 91-38-03072-1 LC Card 84-226057
HF3674 .I36 1976

Svenska Kraftverksföreningen. Personligt präglat. [Stockholm] [1985] 107 p. : LC Card 85-191053
HD9685.S854 S945 1985

SVENSKA KRAFTVERKSFÖRENINGEN.
Personligt präglat. [Stockholm] [1985] 107 p. : LC Card 85-191053
HD9685.S854 S945 1985

Svenska sparbanksföreningen. Epargne et développement /. Paris , 1985. 410 p. : ISBN 2-7178-0855-8 : LC Card 86-149765
HC59.72.S3 E62 1985

SVERDLOVSK (R.S.F.S.R.) - ECONOMIC POLICY.
Andrianov, V. V. Za slovom--delo /. Moskva , 1985. 124 p. ; LC Card 85-213388
HC338.S87 A53 1985

Sverige--EFTA--EG. Stockholm : Utrikesdepartementet, Handelsavdelningen, 1984. 145 p. ; 21 cm. English, French, German, and Swedish. LC Card 85-114840
1. European Free Trade Association - Congresses. 2. European Economic Community - Congresses. I. Sweden. Utrikesdepartementet. Handelsavdelningen.
HC241.4 .S87 1984

Sverige i imperialismens nät /. Hermansson, C. H. Stockholm , 1986. 301 p. : ISBN

91-7014-203-3 LC Card 86-225250
HD2883 .H43 1986

Sverige och den internationella transportmarknaden : konferens i samband med TFKs årsmöte den 9 november 1982. Stockholm : Transportforskningskommissionen, [1983] 87 p. : ill. ; 30 cm. (TFK rapport . 1983:2) "Februari 1983." English and Swedish. ISBN 91-85402-64-8 : LC Card 83-223136
1. Freight and freightage - Sweden. 2. Shipment of goods - Sweden - Congresses. I. Transportforskningskommissionen (Sweden). II. Series.
HE199.S77 S84 1983

Sveriges allmänna exportförening. What Sweden can do. Stockholm , 1919. 355 p. in various pagings : LC Card 85-666345
HC372.2 .W52x 1919

Sveriges arbetskraft : prognos till år 2000. Stockholm : Statistiska centralbyrån ; Örebro : SCB-Distribution [distributor, 1986] 62 p. : ill. ; 22 cm. (Information om arbetsmarknaden, 0283-3719 . 1986:7) Sveriges officiella statistik Title on verso of t.p.: The Swedish labour force. Summary in English. ISBN 91-618-0162-3 : LC Card 87-151800
1. Labor supply - Sweden. 2. Employment forecasting - Sweden. I. Sweden. Statistiska centralbyrån. II. Title: Swedish labour force. III. Series.
HD5803 .S943 1986

Sveriges exportråd. Svensk byggexport : utredning från Sveriges exportråd : förslag till åtgärder för att främja svensk byggexport. [Stockholm] : Liber, [1984] v, 107, [23] p. : ill. ; 21 cm. "Ds UD 1984:2." ISBN 91-38-08107-5 LC Card 84-217971
1. Building materials industry - Sweden. 2. Sweden - Commercial policy. 3. Foreign trade promotion - Sweden. I. Title.
HD9715.8.S82 S86 1984

Sveriges industri . Kay-Åberg, K. (Karl), 1861-1927. Stockholm , 1898. xvi p., 1054 columns, 1055-1071 p. ; LC Card 85-666356
HC372.2 .K39x 1898

Sveriges varuexport 1977-1983 : underlagsmaterial till Långtidsutredningen 1978. [Stockholm] : Ekonomidepartementet : LiberFörlag, [1979] 168 p. : ill. ; 21 cm. Prepared by Konjunkturinstitutet. Includes bibliographical references. "Ds E 1979:3." ISBN 91-38-04928-7 LC Card 83-241226
1. Sweden - Commerce. 2. Export sales - Sweden. I. Konjunkturinstitutet (Sweden). II. Sweden. Ekonomidepartementet. Långtidsutredningen 1978.
HF3676.5 .S84 1979

Sverkhmonopolii v I͡Ugo-Vostochnoĭ Azii / [otvetstvennye redaktory G.I. Chufrin, G.S. Shabalina]. Moskva : Izd-vo "Nauka," Glav. red. vostochnoĭ lit-ry, 1983. 219 p. ; 22 cm. At head of title: Akademii͡a nauk SSSR. Ordena Trudovogo Krasnogo Znameni Institut vostokovedenii͡a. Includes bibliographical references. LC Card 83-223670
1. International business enterprises - Asia, Southeastern. 2. Investments, Foreign - Asia, Southeastern. I. Chufrin, Gennadiĭ Illarionovich. II. Shabalina, G. S. III. Institut vostokovedenii͡a (Akademii͡a nauk SSSR).
HD2901 .S84 1983

Svetska dominacija krupnog kapitala /. Vojnović, Milan. Beograd , 1981. 150 p. : LC Card 85-235805
HF1411 .V655 1981

Sveuviliste u Zagrebu. Referalni centar. International directory of suppliers and agents for information handling equipment and logistical support services /. Zagreb , 1985. iii, 418 p. ; LC Card 86-220527 DDC 338.7/61004/025 19
HD9696.A2 I595 1985

Gli Sviluppi delle attività commerciali nello spazio : aspetti economici, legali e assicurativi = Developments of commercial activities in space : economic, legal and insurance aspects : 2° convegno internazionale, Roma, 3-4 marzo 1983. [Trieste] : Assicurazioni generali, [1985] 238 p. : ill. (some col.) ; 29 cm. English and Italian. Includes bibliographical references. LC Card 86-215421 DDC 338.0919 19
1. Space industrialization - Congresses. I. Title: Developments of commercial activities in space.
HD9711.75.A2 S95 1983

Sviluppo della finanza internazionale e interdipendenza dei sistemi finanziari : in onore di Riccardo Argenziano / G. Pivato ... [et al.]. [Italy] : Giuffrè, [1984] iv, 204 p. : ill. ; 25 cm. (Collana di diritto ed economia . 7) English and Italian. "Atti del Convegno 'Sviluppo della finanza internazionale e interdipendenza dei sistemi finanziari,' svoltosi nell'Aula Magna della Università di Pavia il 10 giugno 1983"--P. [iii] At head of title: Università degli studi di Pavia, Dipartimento di ricerche aziendali. Includes bibliographies. ISBN 88-14-00203-7 : LC Card 84-238589 DDC 332/.042 19
1. Argenziano, Riccardo. 2. International finance - Congresses. 3. International economic relations - Congresses. I. Argenziano, Riccardo. II. Pivato, Giorgio. III. Pavia. Università. Dipartimento di ricerche aziendali. IV. Convegno "Sviluppo della finanza internazionale e interdipendenza dei sistemi finanziari" (1983 : Università di Pavia). V. Series.
HG205.S85 S85 1984 ***NYPL [JLE 86-482]***

Swain, David, 1942- Managing public money : an introduction to public finance and budgeting / David Swain. Lanham, MD : University Press of America, c1987. x, 221 p. : ill. ; 24 cm. Bibliography: p. 207-215. Includes index. ISBN 0-8191-6505-0 (alk. paper) : LC Card 87-14261 DDC 350.72 19
1. Finance, Public. 2. Budget. 3. Finance, Public - United States. 4. Budget - United States. I. Title.
HJ141 .S93 1987

Swallow, Brent M. Cattle marketing in Lesotho / by Brent M. Swallow, None Mokitimi, and Ray F. Brokken. Maseru, Lesotho : Research Division, Ministry of Agriculture, [1986] iv, 75 leaves : ill. ; 30 cm. (Research report / Institute of Southern African Studies, National University of Lesotho . no. 13) Research Division bulletin / Ministry of Agriculture and Marketing ; RD-B-49 "September, 1986." Bibliography: leaves 71-75. LC Card 87-132309 DDC 381/.416213/096816 19
1. Beef cattle - Lesotho - Marketing. I. Mokitimi, None. II. Brokken, Ray F. III. Series: Research report (National University of Lesotho. Institute of Southern African Studies) , no. 13. IV. Title.
HD9433.L452 S9 1986

Swaminathan, Madhura. Socioeconomic aspects of renewable energy technologies . New York , 1988. p. cm. ISBN 0-275-92851-9 (alk. paper) : LC Card 87-22890 DDC 333.7/09172/4 19
HD9502.D442 S63 1988

The swamp-sago industry in West Malaysia . Tan, Koonlin. Singapore , c1983. xvi, 174 p. : ISBN 997-19-0266-4 (pbk.) LC Card 84-940373 DDC 338.1/7368 19
HD9259.S873 M37 1983

SWAMP SAGO INDUSTRY - MALAYSIA - MALAYA.
Tan, Koonlin. The swamp-sago industry in West Malaysia . Singapore , c1983. xvi, 174 p. : ISBN 997-19-0266-4 (pbk.) LC Card 84-940373 DDC 338.1/7368 19
HD9259.S873 M37 1983

Swankey, Ben. The Tory budget and the corporate plan to restructure Canada, and how the system really works / by Ben Swankey. Vancouver : Centre for Socialist Education, c1985. xi, 246 p. ; 13 cm. Includes bibliographies. ISBN 0-920879-00-4 (pbk.) LC Card 86-209703 DDC 338.971 19
1. Budget - Canada. 2. Canada - Economic policy. I. Title.
HJ2055 .S9 1985

Swann, Alan, 1946- How to understand and use design and layout / Alan Swann ; [illustrators, Mick Hill, Kevin Maddison, photographers, Rose Jones, Paul Forrester]. Cincinnati, Ohio : North Light Books, c1987. 144 p. : ill. (some col.) ; 23 cm. (A Quarto book) Includes index. ISBN 0-89134-212-5 : LC Card 87-13698 DDC 659.13/24 19
1. Advertising layout and typography. 2. Printing, Practical - Layout. 3. Newsletters. I. Title.
HF5825 .S9 1987

Swanson, Robert M. Century 21 accounting : advanced course / Robert M. Swanson, Kenton E. Ross, Robert D. Hanson.4th ed. Cincinnati : South-Western Pub. Co., c1988. xi, 653 p. : ill. (some col.) ; 24 cm. Rev. ed. of: Century 21 accounting / Robert M. Swanson ... [et al.]. 3rd ed. c1983. Includes index. ISBN 0-538-02470-4 LC Card 87-60958 DDC 657/.046 19
1. Accounting. I. Ross, Kenton E. II. Hanson, Robert D. III. Century 21 accounting. IV. Title. V. Title: Century twenty-one accounting.
HF5635 .C4228 1988

Swantz, Marja-Liisa. Women in development : a creative role denied? : the case of Tanzania / Marja-Liisa Swantz. London : C. Hurst ; New York : St. Martin's Press, c1985. ix, 177 p. : 1 map ; 23 cm. Includes index. Bibliography: p. 171-174. ISBN 0-312-88780-9 (St. Martin's Press) : LC Card 85-2120 DDC 331.4/09678 19
1. Women - Employment - Tanzania - Case studies. 2. Women - Tanzania - Social conditions - Case studies. I. Title.
HD6211.3 .S93 1985 ***NYPL [Sc D 86-104]***

Swartz, Gerald S. Meltz, Noah M. Sharing the work . Toronto , Buffalo , 1981. viii, 90 p. : ISBN 0-8020-2383-5 ***NYPL [JLD 82-233]***

Swastika Party. Arya, Dwarika Prasas, 1922- Swastika removes India's poverty and problems within 100 days . Calcutta, West Bengal , 1982. vi, 153 p. ; LC Card 82-904556 DDC 338.954 19
HC435.2 .A887 1982

SWASTIKA PARTY.
Arya, Dwarika Prasas, 1922- Swastika removes India's poverty and problems within 100 days . Calcutta, West Bengal , 1982. vi, 153 p. ; LC Card 82-904556 DDC 338.954 19
HC435.2 .A887 1982

Swastika removes India's poverty and problems within 100 days . Arya, Dwarika Prasas, 1922- Calcutta, West Bengal , 1982. vi, 153 p. ; LC Card 82-904556 DDC 338.954 19
HC435.2 .A887 1982

Swaziland /. Barendregt, J. (Jaap) Amsterdam , 's-Gravenhage , 1985. 43 p., [1] folded leaf of plates : ISBN 90-12-05175-4 LC Card 86-174569
HC925 .B37 1985

SWAZILAND - ECONOMIC CONDITIONS.
Barendregt, J. (Jaap) Swaziland /. Amsterdam , 's-Gravenhage , 1985. 43 p., [1] folded leaf of plates : ISBN 90-12-05175-4 LC Card 86-174569
HC925 .B37 1985

Swearingen, Rodger, 1923- Siberia and the Soviet Far East . Stanford, Calif. , c1987. xxx, 298 p. : ISBN 0-8179-8362-7 (pbk.) : LC Card 86-21388 DDC 330.957/085 19
HC337.R852 S5269 1987

Swearingen, Will D. (Will Davis), 1946- Moroccan mirages : agricultural dreams and deceptions, 1912-1986 / Will D. Swearingen. Princeton, N.J. : Princeton University Press, c1987. xvii, 217 p., [9] p. of plates : ill. ; 25 cm. Bibliography: p. [197]-211. Includes index. ISBN 0-691-05505-X (alk. paper) : LC Card 87-6981 DDC 338.1/0964 19
1. Agriculture - Economic aspects - Morocco - History. 2. Agriculture and state - Morocco - History. I. Title.
HD2121 .S94 1987

Sweat equity . Smith, Geoffrey N. New York , c1986. 254 p. : ISBN 0-671-55210-4 LC Card 86-6622 DDC 658/.022 19
HD62.5 .S625 1986 ***NYPL [JLD 86-3014]***

SWEATING SYSTEM - GREAT BRITAIN - HISTORY.
Morris, Jenny, 1950- Women workers and the sweated trades . Aldershot, Hants, England , Brookfield, Vt., USA , c1986. 248 p. ; ISBN 0-566-05188-5 : LC Card 86-9850 DDC 331.4/23 19
HD2339.G7 M67 1986
NYPL [JLD 86-4089]

SWEDEN - APPROPRIATIONS AND EXPENDITURES.
Hadenius, Axel, 1945- A crisis of the welfare state? . Stockholm, Sweden , c1986. 151 p. : ISBN 91-22-00821-7 (pbk.) : LC Card 87-127805 DDC 339.5/22/09485 19
HJ2837 .H34 1986

Sweden. Arkivet. see **Sweden. Riksarkivet.**

Sweden. 1980 års oljelagringskommitté. Kol, uran och gas för kristid. [Stockholm] : LiberFörlag, [1981] 192 p. : ill. ; 25 cm. "Ds H 1981:2"--Cover. ISBN 91-38-06450-2 LC Card 83-107879
1. Energy policy - Sweden. 2. Fuel - Sweden - Storage. I. Title.
HD9502.S82 S88 1981

Sweden. 1981 års energikommitté. Ny teknik för elproduktion, elanvändning . Stockholm [1983] 172 p. : LC Card 84-108404
HD9685.S852 N9 1983

Sweden. 1983 års livsmedelskommitté. Expertgruppen för produktionsmålsfrågor. 1983 års livsmedelskommitté . [Stockholm]

[1984] 255, 18 p. : ISBN 91-38-08481-3 LC Card 86-110260
HD9015.S86 A11 1984a

Sweden. 1983 års livsmedelskommitté. Expertgruppen för handels- och industrifrågor. 1983 års livsmedelskommitté : rapport / från Expertgruppen för handels- och industrifrågor. [Stockholm] : Jordbruksdepartementet, [1984] 655 p. in various pagings : ill. ; 21 cm. At head of title: Jordbruksdepartementet. "Ds Jo 1984:13." ISBN 91-38-08506-2 LC Card 86-110501
1. Food industry and trade - Sweden. I. Title.
HD9015.S86 S88 1984

Sweden. 1983 års livsmedelskommitté. Expertgruppen för prisregleringsfrågor. Prisstöd och jordbruksprisreglering : rapport / från Expertgruppen för prisregleringsfrågor. Stockholm : Jordbruksdepartementet, [1984] xvi, 260 p. ; 21 cm. "Ds Jo 1984:10." ISBN 91-38-08461-9 LC Card 86-109988
1. Food industry and trade - Sweden. 2. Price regulation - Sweden. 3. Agricultural price supports - Sweden. 4. Food prices - Sweden. I. Title.
HD9015.S86 S883 1984

Sweden. 1983 års livsmedelskommitté. Expertgruppen för prisregleringsfrågor. Vissa jordbrukspolitiska förtursfrågor. Underbilaga till rapport från 1983 års livsmedelskommittés expertgrupp för prisregleringsfrågor . [Sweden , 1983] (Jönköping . 1 v. (various pagings) : LC Card 85-191640
HD9015.S86 U47 1983

Sweden. Bostadsbidragskommittén. Bostadsbidragen . [Stockholm] [1982] 207 p. : ISBN 91-38-72586-X LC Card 83-240044
HD7350.A3 B697 1982

Sweden. Bostadsbidragskommittén. Bostadsbidragen. Bostadsbidragen . [Stockholm] [1982] 207 p. : ISBN 91-38-72586-X LC Card 83-240044
HD7350.A3 B697 1982

Sweden. Bostadsdepartementet. Energihushållning och samhällsekonomi . [Stockholm] [1980] 70, 39, 29, 58 p. : ISBN 91-38-05980-0 LC Card 84-122675
HD9502.S82 E48 1980

SWEDEN - COMMERCE.
Exportsamverkan . [Stockholm] [1985] 261 p. : ISBN 91-38-08810-X LC Card 86-114126
HF3676.5 .E96 1985

Iger, Svante. Den svenska ekonomins intertnationalisering . Lund , Stockholm [1976] iv, 144 p. : ISBN 91-38-03072-1 LC Card 84-226057
HF3674 .I36 1976

Sveriges varuexport 1977-1983 . [Stockholm] [1979] 168 p. : ISBN 91-38-04928-7 LC Card 83-241226
HF3676.5 .S84 1979

SWEDEN - COMMERCE - DIRECTORIES.
Vem gör vad i svenskt näringsliv . Stockholm [1983] 283 p. ; LC Card 83-225142
HF3673 .V46 1983

SWEDEN - COMMERCE - SOVIET UNION - HISTORY - 17TH CENTURY.
Attman, Artur, 1910- Swedish aspirations and the Russian market during the 17th century /. Göteborg , Atlantic Highlands, N.J. , c1985. 41 p. : ISBN 91-85252-35-2 (pbk.) LC Card 86-214014 DDC 382/.09485/047 19
HF3678.S58 A88 1985

SWEDEN - COMMERCIAL POLICY.
Exportsamverkan . [Stockholm] [1985] 261 p. : ISBN 91-38-08810-X LC Card 86-114126
HF3676.5 .E96 1985

Nilson, Bengt, 1952- Handelspolitik under skärpt konkurrens . Lund , c1983. 217 p. ; ISBN 91-40-04894-2 : LC Card 84-144528
HF1567 .N55 1983

Sveriges exportråd. Svensk byggexport . [Stockholm] [1984] v, 107, [23] p. : ISBN 91-38-08107-5 LC Card 84-217971
HD9715.8.S82 S86 1984

Sweden. Utredningen rörande export av teknik inom energisektorn. Ökad export av svensk energiteknik--ett handlingsprogram . [Stockholm] [1983] 171, [64] p. : ISBN 91-38-08037-0 LC Card 84-219591
HD9502.S82 S974 1983

Sweden. Data- och elektronikkommittén. Datateknik i industriproduktionen : betänkande från Data- och elektronikkommittén (DEK) : förslag till industripolitiska åtgärder. [Stockholm] : Industridepartementet : LiberFörlag, [1981] 182 p. : ill. ; 21 cm. Includes bibliographical references. "Ds I 1981:14." ISBN 91-38-06456-1 LC Card 84-113236
1. Industrial management - Sweden - Data processing. I. Title.
HD30.2 .S92 1981

Industrins datorinvesteringar 1980-1982 /. [Stockholm] [1983] 61, 2 p. : ISBN 91-38-08001-X LC Card 84-218410
HF5548.2 .I4213 1983

Investering i industrirobotar . [Stockholm] [1983] 263 p. : ISBN 91-38-07833-3 LC Card 84-218538
HD9696.R623 S845 1983

Sweden. Dataeffektutredningen. Datorer och decentralisering . [Stockholm] [1983] 52 p. : ISBN 91-38-07877-5 LC Card 84-219052
HF5548.2 .D3715 1983

Handelshögskolan i Stockholm. Ekonomiska forskningsinstitutet. Datoriseringen i försäkringsbranschen . [Stockholm] [1981] 81, [36] p. : ISBN 91-38-06574-6 LC Card 82-244714
HG8673 .H35 1981

SWEDEN - ECONOMIC CONDITIONS.
Isacson, Maths, 1948- Proto-industrialisation in Scandinavia . Leamington Spa, UK ; New York : p. cm. ISBN 0-85496-514-9 : LC Card 86-32062 DDC 338.09485 19
HC375 .I8 1987

Isacson, Maths, 1948- Vägen till fabrikerna . [Stockholm] [Uppsala] , c1983. 195, [1] p. : ISBN 91-7021-464-6 : LC Card 84-125076
HC375 .I83 1983

Magnusson, Lars, 1941- Kapitalbildning i Sverige 1750-1860 . Uppsala , Stockholm , 1983. 95 p. ; ISBN 91-554-1443-5 LC Card 83-228044
HC374 .M34 1983

SWEDEN - ECONOMIC CONDITIONS - 1945-
Ahlqvist, Berndt, 1931- I bräcklig farkost . Stockholm , c1983. 186 p. ; ISBN 91-550-2917-5 : LC Card 83-230190
HC375 .A63 1983

Andersson, Dan, 1948- Vad gör kapitalisterna? . Stockholm , c1983. 167 p. : ISBN 91-550-2919-1 : LC Card 84-143408
HG186.S85 A53 1983

Hansson, Ingemar, 1951- Skatter och samhällsekonomi /. Stockholm , c1986. 170 p. : ISBN 91-7150-280-7 : LC Card 86-215332
HJ2837 .H36 1986

Höglund, Bengt. Spelet om resurserna i den svenska blandekonomin /. Lund , c1984. 227 p. : ISBN 91-7504-041-7 : LC Card 84-200450
HC373.5 .H64 1984

Iger, Svante. Den svenska ekonomins intertnationalisering . Lund , Stockholm [1976] iv, 144 p. : ISBN 91-38-03072-1 LC Card 84-226057
HF3674 .I36 1976

Introduktion av naturgas i Sverige . Stockholm , 1978. ii, 16, 13, 11 p. ; ISBN 91-38-04192-8 LC Card 83-238196
HD9581.S82 I58 1978

Jobb i framtid? . Stockholm , c1983. 121 p. : ISBN 91-7410-270-2 : LC Card 84-103510
HC375 .J53 1983

Johnson, Anders. Släpp tjänsterna loss . [Stockholm] , c1986. 232 p. : ISBN 91-7152-374-X : LC Card 86-235064
HD9986.S82 J63 1986

Kommunerna och framtiden . [Stockholm] , 1984] 224 p. : ISBN 91-38-08484-8 : LC Card 85-107984
HC375 .K654 1984

Kommunerna och näringslivet . Stockholm , c1984. 173 p. : ISBN 91-38-90331-8 : LC Card 84-253511
HC375 .K655 1984

Konsumtion i förändring . Vällingby [1985] 87 p. : LC Card 86-224791
HC380.C6 K675 1985

Lokal samverkan--fördelar för näringsliv och kommun? . Stockholm [1982] 185 p. : ISBN 91-38-07027-8 LC Card 82-236501
HC375 .L786 1982

Oljeersättningsprogrammet i ett samhällsekonomiskt perspektiv. Stockholm , 1983. 39, 67, 54, 71 p. : ISBN 91-38-07618-7 LC Card 83-232276
HD9502.S82 O55 1983

Olofsson, Christer. De regionala utvecklingsbolagen . Stockholm [1983] 118 p. ; ISBN 91-38-07479-6 LC Card 83-234309
HC380.I53 O46 1983

Papachristodoulou, Christos. Inventions, innovations, and economic growth in Sweden . Uppsala , c1986. iv, 187 p. : LC Card 87-672434
HC380.T4 P36x 1986

De Regionala utvecklingsfonderna . Stockholm , 1981. 260 p. ; ISBN 91-38-06693-9 LC Card 82-234113
HC380.I53 R44 1981

Samhällsekonomiska effekter av en kärnkraftsavveckling . [Stockholm] [1979] 149 p. ; ISBN 91-38-05244-X LC Card 82-219542
HD9698.S82 O42 1979

Samhällsekonomiska kalkyler vid industrinedläggningar . Stockholm [1982] 213 p. : ISBN 91-38-07164-9 LC Card 83-219569
HD5708.55.S8 S25 1982

The Swedish economy /. Washington, D.C. , c1987. xvi, 338 p. : ISBN 0-8157-1042-9 : LC Card 86-29920 DDC 330.9485/058 19
HC375 .S977 1987

Trender och prognoser inför 90-talet. Stockholm , Örebro , 1985. 147 p. : ISBN 91-618-0001-5 LC Card 86-115921
LB2833 .S9 1985:2 HC375
NYPL [JLG 86-230]

SWEDEN - ECONOMIC CONDITIONS - 1945- - ECONOMETRIC MODELS.
Åberg, Yngve. Utvecklingen av produktion och produktivitet i svensk ekonomi, 1963-1981 /. [Stockholm] [1983] 83 p. : ISBN 91-38-08070-2 LC Card 84-218343
HC380.I52 A34 1983

SWEDEN - ECONOMIC POLICY.
Ahlqvist, Berndt, 1931- I bräcklig farkost . Stockholm , c1983. 186 p. ; ISBN 91-550-2917-5 : LC Card 83-230190
HC375 .A63 1983

Bäck, Kalle, 1949- Bondeopposition och bondeinflytande under frihetstiden . Stockholm , c1984. 326 p. : ISBN 91-36-02263-2 : LC Card 84-252422
HD1536.S8 B33 1984

Hur planeras Sverige? /. Stockholm , c1986. 179 p. : ISBN 91-38-90679-1 : LC Card 87-151788
HC375 .H85 1986

Kommunerna och näringslivet . Stockholm , c1984. 173 p. : ISBN 91-38-90331-8 : LC Card 84-253511
HC375 .K655 1984

Lybeck, Johan A., 1944- Konstitutionella begränsningar i Riksdagens finansmakt . [Stockholm] [1984] 147 p. : ISBN 91-38-08365-5 (Sve. bok.) : LC Card 84-240503
HJ1238 .L92 1984

Södersten, Bo. Makroekonomi och stabiliseringspolitik /. [Malmö] , c1983. 363 p. : ISBN 91-40-05037-8 : LC Card 84-166176
HB179.S8 S63 1983

The Swedish economy /. Washington, D.C. , c1987. xvi, 338 p. : ISBN 0-8157-1042-9 : LC Card 86-29920 DDC 330.9485/058 19
HC375 .S977 1987

Sweden. Ekonomidepartementet. Långtidsutredningen 1978. Sveriges varuexport 1977-1983 . [Stockholm] [1979] 168 p. : ISBN 91-38-04928-7 LC Card 83-241226
HF3676.5 .S84 1979

Sweden. Ekonomidepartementet. Långtidsutredningen 1980. Byggnads- och anläggningsindustrin. [Stockholm] [1981] 84 p. : ISBN 91-38-06015-9 LC Card 84-120446
HD9715.S852 B898 1981

Larsson, Folke. Varuhandeln. [Stockholm] [1981] 137 p. : ISBN 91-38-06014-0 LC Card 84-120411
HF5429.6.S9 L368 1981

Olsson, Hans. Industrins lönsamhet, finansiering och investeringar under 1970-talet . [Stockholm] [1981] 58 p. : ISBN 91-38-06530-4 LC Card 84-120594
HG4211 .O45 1981

Sweden. Elanvändningskommittén till restriktioner, användning och hushållning. El och olja : förslag / från Elanvändningskommittén (ELAK) till restriktioner, användning och hushållning. [Stockholm] : Industridepartementet : LiberFörlag, [1980] 265 p. : ill. ; 21 cm. "Ds I 1980:22." ISBN 91-38-05865-0 LC Card 84-102448
1. Energy policy - Sweden. 2. Energy conservation - Sweden. I. Title.
HD9502.S82 S898 1980

Sweden. Energiforskningsnämnden.
Ny teknik för elproduktion, elanvändning . Stockholm [1983] 172 p. : LC Card 84-108404
HD9685.S852 N9 1983

Skogsbränsle . Stockholm [1986] 159 p. : ISBN 91-38-09241-7 LC Card 86-201607
HD9769.F842 S57 1986

Sweden. Energihushållningsdelegationen. Program för energihushållning i befintlig bebyggelse. Energihushållning och samhällsekonomi . [Stockholm] [1980] 70, 39, 29, 58 p. : ISBN 91-38-05980-0 LC Card 84-122675
HD9502.S82 E48 1980

Sweden. Expertgruppen för internationella frågor.
De Transnationella företagens roll i världshandeln ; Gränsskydd i andra länder /. [Stockholm] [1984] 62, [36] p. ; ISBN 91-38-08406-6 LC Card 86-115056
HD9015.S86 T73 1984

Sweden. Expertgruppen för studier i offentlig ekonomi.
Administrationskostnader för våra skatter . [Stockholm] [1983] 114 p. : ISBN 91-38-08027-3 LC Card 84-219428
HJ3548 .A815 1983

Lybeck, Johan A., 1944- Konstitutionella begränsningar i Riksdagens finansmakt . [Stockholm] [1984] 147 p. : ISBN 91-38-08365-5 (Sve. bok.) : LC Card 84-240503
HJ1238 .L92 1984

Sweden. Exportstödsutredningen.
Exportfrämjande stöd till mindre och medelstora företag : betänkande / avgivet av Exportstödsutredningen. [Stockholm] : Liber, [1983] 8, 143, 3 p. : ill. ; 21 cm. "Ds UD 1983:5." Includes bibliographical references. ISBN 91-38-08059-1 LC Card 84-218418
1. Foreign trade promotion - Sweden. 2. Small business - Sweden. I. Title.
HF1567 .S92 1983

Ökad trähusexport : betänkande / avgivet av Exportstödsutredningen. [Stockholm] : Liber, [1984] 51 p. ; 21 cm. "Ds UD 1984:3." Includes bibliographical references. ISBN 91-38-08165-2 LC Card 84-219457
1. Modular construction industry - Sweden. 2. Prefabricated houses - Sweden. 3. Wood using industries - Sweden. 4. Export marketing - Sweden. I. Title.
HD9715.5.S82 S94 1984

Sweden. Finansdepartementet.
Administrationskostnader för våra skatter . [Stockholm] [1983] 114 p. : ISBN 91-38-08027-3 LC Card 84-219428
HJ3548 .A815 1983

Sweden. Foreign Affairs, Ministry of. see **Sweden. Utrikesdepartementet.**

SWEDEN - FOREIGN ECONOMIC RELATIONS.
Iger, Svante. Den svenska ekonomins intertnationalisering . Lund , Stockholm [1976] iv, 144 p. : ISBN 91-38-03072-1 LC Card 84-226057
HF3674 .I36 1976

SWEDEN - FOREIGN ECONOMIC RELATIONS - GREAT BRITAIN.
Nilson, Bengt, 1952- Handelspolitik under skärpt konkurrens . Lund , c1983. 217 p. ; ISBN 91-40-04894-2 : LC Card 84-144528
HF1567 .N55 1983

SWEDEN - FOREIGN RELATIONS - 1523-1718.
Attman, Artur, 1910- Swedish aspirations and the Russian market during the 17th century /. Göteborg , Atlantic Highlands, N.J. , c1985. 41 p. : ISBN 91-85252-35-2 (pbk.) LC Card 86-214014 DDC 382/.09485/047 19
HF3678.S58 A88 1985

SWEDEN - INDUSTRIES.
Andersson, Göran, 1944- Industrihotell och industribyar . Stockholm [1984] 150 p. : ISBN 91-38-08268-3 LC Card 85-106828
HC375 .A72 1984

Bergman, Åke. Den nya given . Stockholm [1986] 157 p. ; ISBN 91-550-3244-3 : LC Card 86-235012
HD70.S8 B48 1986

Holmlöv, Per Gunnar, 1951- Reklam i satellit-tv . Stockholm [1984] 147 p. ; ISBN 91-7258-183-2 : LC Card 84-229824
HF6146.T42 H64 1984

Lokal samverkan--fördelar för näringsliv och kommun? . Stockholm [1982] 185 p. : ISBN 91-38-07027-8 LC Card 82-236501
HC375 .L786 1982

Omfattning och erfarenheter . Stockholm [1984] 127 p. : ISBN 91-38-08319-1 LC Card 85-106802
HC375 .O39 1984

SWEDEN - INDUSTRIES - ARCHIVAL RESOURCES - SWEDEN - ADMINISTRATION.
Sweden. Riksarkivet. Att bevara företagsarkiv . [Stockholm] [1984] 119 p. ; ISBN 91-38-08403-1 LC Card 84-239019
HC375 .S965 1984

SWEDEN - INDUSTRIES - DIRECTORIES.
Vem gör vad i svenskt näringsliv . Stockholm [1983] 283 p. ; LC Card 83-225142
HF3673 .V46 1983

What Sweden can do. Stockholm , 1919. 355 p. in various pagings : LC Card 85-666345
HC372.2 .W52x 1919

SWEDEN - INDUSTRIES - HANDBOOKS, MANUALS, ETC.
Kay-Åberg, K. (Karl), 1861-1927. Sveriges industri . Stockholm , 1898. xvi p., 1054 columns, 1055-1071 p. ; LC Card 85-666356
HC372.2 .K39x 1898

SWEDEN - INDUSTRIES - HISTORY - 19TH CENTURY.
Isacson, Maths, 1948- Proto-industrialisation in Scandinavia . Leamington Spa, UK ; New York : p. cm. ISBN 0-85496-514-9 : LC Card 86-32062 DDC 338.09485 19
HC375 .I8 1987

Isacson, Maths, 1948- Vägen till fabrikerna . [Stockholm] [Uppsala] , c1983. 195, [1] p. : ISBN 91-7021-464-6 : LC Card 84-125076
HC375 .I83 1983

Sweden. Industristödsutredningen.
Icke-permanent stöd till tre industriföretag . [Stockholm] [1981] 245 p. : ISBN 91-38-06270-4 LC Card 83-245223
HD3646.S8 I25 1981

Två samhällsekonomiska utvärderingar av icke-permanent industristöd . [Stockholm] [1981] 221 p. : ISBN 91-38-06269-0 LC Card 83-245219
HD3646.S8 T85 1981

Sweden. Jordbruksdepartementet. Översyn av vissa frågor rörande jordbruksprisregleringen /. [Stockholm] [1981] iii, 104, 13, 22, 2, 9, 14 p. : ISBN 91-38-06616-5 LC Card 83-245209
HD2018 .O94 1981

Sweden. Kommunaldemokratiska kommittén.
Sannerstedt, Anders, 1945- Attityder till kommunal service /. [Stockholm] [1981] vi, 166 p. : ISBN 91-38-06586-X LC Card 82-244101
HD4485.S8 S26 1981

Sweden. Kommunikationsdepartementet.
Öresundsförbindelser . [Stockholm] [1983] 196 p. : ISBN 91-38-08123-7 LC Card 84-218397
HE256.Z7 S665 1983

Sweden. Konsekvensutredningen. C-gruppen.
Samhällsekonomiska effekter av en kärnkraftsavveckling . [Stockholm] [1979] 149 p. ; ISBN 91-38-05244-X LC Card 82-219542
HD9698.S82 O42 1979

Sweden. Konsekvensutredningen. D-gruppen.
Regionala effekter av en kärnkraftsavveckling . [Stockholm] [1979] 254 p. : ISBN 91-38-05243-1 LC Card 82-219566
HD9698.S82 O42 1979b Suppl.

Sweden. Konsekvensutredningen. Om vi avvecklar kärnkraften.
Regionala effekter av en kärnkraftsavveckling . [Stockholm] [1979] 254 p. : ISBN 91-38-05243-1 LC Card 82-219566
HD9698.S82 O42 1979b Suppl.

Samhällsekonomiska effekter av en kärnkraftsavveckling . [Stockholm] [1979] 149 p. ; ISBN 91-38-05244-X LC Card 82-219542
HD9698.S82 O42 1979

Sweden. Konsumentverket.
Kombinationserbjudanden. Vällingby [1984] 269, [45] p. : ISBN 91-7398-243-1 LC Card 85-115578
HF5438.5 .K66 1984

Konsumtion i förändring . Vällingby [1985] 87 p. : LC Card 86-224791
HC380.C6 K675 1985

Sweden. Kooperationsutredningen.
Dellenbrant, Jan Åke, 1946- Föreningsdemokrati och företagsdemokrati . [Stockholm] [1981] 85 p. ; ISBN 91-38-06488-X LC Card 83-245188
HD5660.S9 D44 1981

Fredriksson, Carl, 1947- Kooperationens industrisektor i 1980-talets industri-Sverige . [Stockholm] [1981] iv, 196, 24, 11 p. : ISBN 91-38-06535-5 LC Card 83-147552
HD3522 .F74 1981

Sweden. Malmfältsutredningen. Framtid i malmfälten : betänkande / avgivet av Malmfältsutredningen. [Stockholm] : LiberFörlag, [1984] 155, 5 p. : ill. ; 21 cm. At head of title: Industridepartementet. Bibliography: p. 153-154. "Ds I 1984:9." ISBN 91-38-08283-7 LC Card 86-111519
1. Mineral industries - Sweden. 2. Iron industry and trade - Sweden. 3. Iron mines and mining - Sweden. I. Title.
HD9506.S82 S94 1984

Sweden. Ministry of Finance. see **Sweden. Finansdepartementet.**

Sweden. Ministry of Foreign Affairs. see **Sweden. Utrikesdepartementet.**

Sweden. National Board of Health and Welfare. see **Sweden. Socialstyrelsen.**

Sweden. Oljeersättningsdelegationen.
Redovisning och analys av kommunernas oljereduktionsplaner / Oljeersättningsdelegationen. Stockholm : LiberFörlag : Statens industriverk, [1983] 59, [91] p. : ill. ; 25 cm. (SIND, 0346-5748 . 1983:3) ISBN 91-38-07458-3 LC Card 83-239703
1. Energy policy - Sweden. 2. Energy conservation - Sweden. 3. Petroleum conservation - Sweden. I. Sweden. Statens industriverk. II. Title. III. Series.
HD9502.S82 S96 1983a

Statligt stöd till oljeersättning : utvärdering av OEF's insatser och förslag till fortsatt verksamhet : rapport / från Oljeersättningsdelegationen. [Stockholm] : LiberFörlag, [1983] 1 v. (various pagings) : ill. ; 21 cm. "Ds I 1983:4." Includes bibliographical references. ISBN 91-38-07657-8 LC Card 84-218524
1. Energy policy - Sweden. 2. Renewable energy sources - Sweden. 3. Subsidies - Sweden. 4. Petroleum conservation - Sweden. I. Title.
HD9502.S82 S96 1983

Uppföljning av oljeersättningsprogrammet : delrapport / från Oljeersättningsdelegationen. [Stockholm] : Industridepartementet : Liber, [1982] 83, [74] p. : ill. ; 21 cm. "Ds I 1982:6." ISBN 91-38-07111-8 LC Card 83-217864
1. Energy policy - Sweden. 2. Power resources - Sweden. 3. Energy development - Sweden. I. Title.
HD9502.S82 S96 1982

SWEDEN - POLITICS AND GOVERNMENT - 1718-1772.
Bäck, Kalle, 1949- Bondeopposition och bondeinflytande under frihetstiden . Stockholm , c1984. 326 p. : ISBN 91-36-02263-2 : LC Card

84-252422
HD1536.S8 B33 1984

SWEDEN - POLITICS AND GOVERNMENT - 1905-1950.
Kylebäck, Hugo, 1930- Konsument- och lantbrukskooperation i Sverige . Stockholm [1984] 277 p. ; ISBN 91-85196-18-5 : LC Card 86-120646
HD3524.A1 K663 1984

SWEDEN - POLITICS AND GOVERNMENT - 1973-
Micheletti, Michele. Organizing interest and organized protest . [Stockholm] , 1985. vii, 253 p. ; ISBN 91-7146-451-4 (pbk.) LC Card 86-145828 DDC 322/.2/09481 19
HD8572.T5 M53 1985
NYPL [JLL 74-316 no.29]

SWEDEN - POPULATION.
Schettkat, Ronald. Bevölkerungs- und Erwerbsverhaltensentwicklung in Österreich, Schweden und der Bundesrepublik Deutschland /. Berlin [1984] 48 p. ; LC Card 85-198691
HD5771 .S34 1984

SWEDEN - POPULATION - HISTORY.
Hofsten, Erland Adolf Gerhard von, 1911- Svensk befolkningshistoria . [Stockholm] , c1986. 180, [1] p. : ISBN 91-29-57693-8 LC Card 86-194606
HB3617 .H768 1986

SWEDEN - POPULATION POLICY.
Kälvemark, Ann-Sofie, 1941- More children of better quality? . Uppsala , Stockholm , 1980. 160 p. : ISBN 91-554-1094-4 LC Card 81-114081
HB3617 .K34 1980

SWEDEN - POPULATION - STATISTICS.
Trender och prognoser inför 90-talet. Stockholm , Örebro , 1985. 147 p. : ISBN 91-618-0001-5 LC Card 86-115921
LB2833 .S9 1985:2 HC375
NYPL [JLG 86-230]

Sweden. Rekryteringsutredningen.
Arbetsförmedlingskontrakt : betänkande / avgivet av Rekryteringsutredningen. [Stockholm] : LiberFörlag, [1983] 195, 9, 2 p. ; 21 cm. "Ds A 1983:4." ISBN 91-38-07728-0 LC Card 84-218571
1. Contract system (Labor) - Sweden. I. Title.
HD4875.S8 S94 1983

Sweden. Riksarkivet. Att bevara företagsarkiv : betänkande / av Riksarkivet. [Stockholm] : Liber, [1984] 119 p. ; 21 cm. At head of title: Utbildningsdepartementet. "Ds U 1984:12." ISBN 91-38-08403-1 LC Card 84-239019
1. Sweden - Industries - Archival resources - Sweden - Administration. 2. Business enterprises - Archival resources - Sweden. I. Title.
HC375 .S965 1984

Sweden. Samverkanskommittén.
Arbetsanpassning : betänkande / av Samverkskommittén [sic]. [Stockholm] : Arbetsmarknadsdepartementet, [1984] 231 p. ; 25 cm. "DsA 1984:2." ISBN 91-38-08108-3 LC Card 84-193689
1. Handicapped - Employment - Sweden. 2. Vocational rehabilitation - Sweden. I. Title.
HD7256.S9 S945 1984

Sweden. Skattekreditutredningen. Kortare kredittid för skatter på energi m.m. : betänkande / av Skattekreditutredningen. [Stockholm] : LiberFörlag, [1983] 109 p. ; 21 cm. "Ds Fi 1983:23." ISBN 0-913807-27-9 LC Card 84-218594
1. Value-added tax - Sweden. 2. Energy industries - Taxation - Sweden. I. Title.
HJ5715.S84 S87 1983

Sweden. Skogsstyrelsen. Sweden. Statens industriverk. Ökad eldning med skogsråvara . Stockholm , 1980. 203 p. : ISBN 91-38-05361-6 LC Card 82-236954
HD9769.F843 S87 1980

SWEDEN - SOCIAL CONDITIONS - 1945-
Kommunerna och framtiden . [Stockholm] , 1984] 224 p. : ISBN 91-38-08484-8 : LC Card 85-107984
HC375 .K654 1984

SWEDEN - SOCIAL POLICY.
Kälvemark, Ann-Sofie, 1941- More children of better quality? . Uppsala , Stockholm , 1980. 160 p. : ISBN 91-554-1094-4 LC Card 81-114081
HB3617 .K34 1980

Sweden. Socialstyrelsen. Örning, Birgitta. Solidaritetsarbete . Stockholm [1978?] 66 p. : LC Card 81-140576
HD7728 .O75 1978

Sweden. Statens industriverk.
Distributionsutredning. Stockholm , 1981. 2 v. : ISBN 91-38-06684-X (v. 1) LC Card 82-234445
HD9865.S86 D57 1981

Exportsamverkan . [Stockholm] [1985] 261 p. : ISBN 91-38-08810-X LC Card 86-114126
HF3676.5 .E96 1985

Försörjningstryggheten för olja, kol och uran . Stockholm [1982] 175 p. : ISBN 91-38-07030-8 LC Card 82-240448
HD9502.S82 F68 1983

Gummivaruindustri . Stockholm , 1981. 119, [12] p. : ISBN 91-38-06243-7 LC Card 82-241338
HD9161.S82 G84 1981

Internationella förutsättningar för den svenska oljeförsörjningen under 1980-talet. Stockholm , 1981. 172 p. in various pagings : ISBN 91-38-06244-5 LC Card 82-241303
HD9575.S82 I57 1981

Introduktion av naturgas i Sverige . Stockholm , 1978. ii, 16, 13, 11 p. ; ISBN 91-38-04192-8 LC Card 83-238196
HD9581.S82 I58 1978

Kommunal energiplanering : slutsatser och förslag till framtida inriktning. Stockholm : Statens industriverk, 1980. 51 p. ; 30 cm. (SIND PM, 0346-573X . 1980:15) Includes bibliographical references. ISBN 91-38-05802-2 LC Card 82-236900
1. Energy policy - Sweden. 2. Local government - Sweden. I. Title. II. Series.
HD9502.S82 S97 1980

Lokal samverkan--fördelar för näringsliv och kommun? . Stockholm [1982] 185 p. : ISBN 91-38-07027-8 LC Card 82-236501
HC375 .L786 1982

Ökad eldning med skogsråvara : möjligheter och konsekvenser. Stockholm : Skogsstyrelsen : Statens industriverk, 1980. 203 p. : ill. ; 30 cm. (SIND PM, 0346-573X . 1980:2) Includes bibliographical references. ISBN 91-38-05361-6 LC Card 82-236954
1. Fuelwood industry - Sweden. 2. Forest products industry - Sweden. I. Sweden. Skogsstyrelsen. II. Title. III. Series.
HD9769.F843 S87 1980

Oljeersättningsprogrammet i ett samhällsekonomiskt perspektiv. Stockholm , 1983. 39, 67, 54, 71 p. : ISBN 91-38-07618-7 LC Card 83-232276
HD9502.S82 O55 1983

Omfattning och erfarenheter . Stockholm [1984] 127 p. : ISBN 91-38-08319-1 LC Card 85-106802
HC375 .O39 1984

De Regionala utvecklingsfonderna . Stockholm , 1981. 260 p. ; ISBN 91-38-06693-9 LC Card 82-234113
HC380.I53 R44 1981

Samhällsekonomiska kalkyler vid industrinedläggningar . Stockholm [1982] 213 p. : ISBN 91-38-07164-9 LC Card 83-219569
HD5708.55.S8 S25 1982

Svensk gjuteriindustri . Stockholm , 1982. 62 p. : ISBN 91-38-07151-7 LC Card 83-220920
HD9506.S82 S92 1982

Sweden. Oljeersättningsdelegationen. Redovisning och analys av kommunernas oljereduktionsplaner /. Stockholm [1983] 59, [91] p. : ISBN 91-38-07458-3 LC Card 83-239703
HD9502.S82 S96 1983a

Tekoindustrierna . Stockholm , 1980. 189 p. : ISBN 91-38-05813-8 LC Card 82-236884
HD9865.S86 T45 1980

Tung damkonfektion . Stockholm , 1978. 47, [10] p. : ISBN 91-38-04438-2 LC Card 84-106453
HD9940.S82 T85 1978

Tung herrkonfektion . Stockholm , 1977. 64, [11] leaves, [1] leaf of plates : ISBN 91-38-03482-4 LC Card 84-102982
HD9940.S82 T854 1977

Sweden. Statens industriverk. PU-byrån.
Användarfrämjande åtgärder på dataområdet : en studie med inriktning på mindre och medelstora företag. Stockholm : Statens industriverk, PU-byrån, 1975. 97 leaves ; 30 cm. (SIND PM . 1975:7) ISBN 91-7318-026-2 LC Card 84-105630
1. Small business - Sweden - Data processing. I. Title. II. Series.
HF5548.2 .S8822 1975

Sweden. Studiemedelskommittén.
Studerandepopulation och arbetsmarknad . [Stockholm] [1986] 78 p. : ISBN 91-38-09464-9 LC Card 87-106834
HD6278.S75 S78 1986

Sweden. Styrelsen för international utveckling.
Utvecklingssamarbetet med Tanzania 1983/84-1984/85. Stockholm, Sweden [1983] ca. 200 p. ; LC Card 86-216305
HC885 .U87 1983

Sweden. TV-reklameffektutredningen.
Effekter av TV-reklam : betänkande / av TV-reklameffektutredningen. [Stockholm] : Liber, [1986] 467 p. : ill. ; 21 cm. + 1 suppl. "Ds U 1986:2-3." ISBN 91-38-09425-8 LC Card 86-233988
1. Television advertising - Sweden. I. Title.
HF6146.T42 S94 1986

Hedman, Lowe. TV-tittandet och reklamen . [Stockholm] [1986] 83 p. : ISBN 91-38-09315-4 LC Card 86-199170
HF6146.T42 H43 1986

Sweden. Utredningen rörande export av teknik inom energisektorn. Ökad export av svensk energiteknik--ett handlingsprogram : rapport / från energiupphandlingsdelegationen, Utredningen rörande export av teknik inom energisektorn--EXTERN. [Stockholm] : Liber, [1983] 171, [64] p. : ill. ; 21 cm. At head of title: Industridepartementet. "Ds I 1983:26." ISBN 91-38-08037-0 LC Card 84-219591
1. Energy industries - Sweden. 2. Sweden - Commercial policy. 3. Foreign trade promotion - Sweden. I. Title.
HD9502.S82 S974 1983

Sweden. Utrikesdepartementet. Handelsavdelningen. Sverige--EFTA--EG. Stockholm , 1984. 145 p. ; LC Card 85-114840
HC241.4 .S87 1984

SWEDES - FINLAND - STATISTICS.
Finnäs, Fjalar. Den finlandssvenska befolkningsutvecklingen 1950-1980 . Helsingfors [1986] 216 p. : ISBN 951-9018-20-4 LC Card 86-232091
HB3608.3.A3 F56 1986

Swedish aspirations and the Russian market during the 17th century /. Attman, Artur, 1910- Göteborg , Atlantic Highlands, N.J. , c1985. 41 p. : ISBN 91-85252-35-2 (pbk.) LC Card 86-214014 DDC 382/.09485/047 19
HF3678.S58 A88 1985

SWEDISH ECONOMIC ASSISTANCE. see **ECONOMIC ASSISTANCE, SWEDISH.**

The Swedish economy / Barry P. Bosworth ... [et al.] ; Barry P. Bosworth and Alice M. Rivlin, editors. Washington, D.C. : Brookings Institution, c1987. xvi, 338 p. : ill. ; 24 cm. Includes bibliographical references and index. ISBN 0-8157-1042-9 : LC Card 86-29920 DDC 330.9485/058 19
1. Sweden - Economic conditions - 1945-. 2. Sweden - Economic policy. I. Bosworth, Barry, 1942-. II. Rivlin, Alice M.
HC375 .S977 1987

Swedish labour force. Sveriges arbetskraft . Stockholm , Örebro [1986] 62 p. : ISBN 91-618-0162-3 : LC Card 87-151800
HD5803 .S943 1986

SWEDISH LANGUAGE - DICTIONARIES - ENGLISH.
Edström, N. F. (Nils Fritiof), 1918- Ekonomiordbok . Stockholm , c1984. 145 p. : ISBN 91-1-847152-8 : LC Card 84-253890
HB61 .E29 1984 *NYPL [JFD 87-1265]*

Engelsk-svensk ordbok . Stockholm , 1970. 2 v. ; *NYPL [JFD 87-817]*

Swedish national and local government programs for conservation of energy in buildings / edited by Tage Klingberg ; with contributions from Jan Bröchner ... [et al.]. Gävle, Sweden : Distribution and sale directly from National Swedish Institute for Building Research, Information Division, [1982] 187 p. : ill. ; 30 cm. (Bulletin / The National Swedish Institute for Building Research, 0347-4348 . M82:14) Includes

bibliographies. CONTENTS. - Energy conservation policies and rental housing / by Jan Bröchner -- The targets for Swedish energy conservation, 1974-81, and some goal conflicts / by Lars Engebeck and Kurt Wickman -- Building codes as a tool for energy conservation / by Lars Engebeck -- Energy policy and the loans and grants system / by Kurt Wickman -- Societal information on energy conservation / by Jan Selmer -- "Economical boiler operation" energyrelated prototype and demonstration activities, 1975-1979 / by Christer Ericson -- Training of local instructors / by Christer Ericson -- Evaluation of EPD activities, 1979-1981 / by P.G. Holmlöv -- Historical and architectural aspects of energy conservation measures taken in existing buildings / by Olof Hirn -- The Swedish energy policy at the local government level / by Tage Klingberg and Claes Lindahl. ISBN 91-540-9134-9 (pbk.) LC Card 82-208802 DDC 333.79 19
1. Energy policy - Sweden - Addresses, essays, lectures. 2. Dwellings - Energy conservation - Government policy - Addresses, essays, lectures. I. Klingberg, Tage, 1942-. II. Bröchner, Jan, 1948-. III. Series: Bulletin (Statens institut för byggnadsforskning (Sweden)), M82:14.
HD9502.S82 S98 1982 *NYPL [JLG 86-107]*

Swee-Hock, Saw. see **Saw, Swee-Hock, 1931-**

Sweeney, Daniel J. (Daniel Joseph), 1943- Davidson, William R. Retailing management /. New York , c1988. xix, 876 p. : ISBN 0-471-85094-2 LC Card 87-10555 DDC 658.8/7 19
HF5429 .D334 1988

Sweeney, Dennis J. Anderson, David Ray, 1941- Statistics for business and economics /. St. Paul, MN , c1987. xxviii, 792 p. : ISBN 0-314-25873-6 : LC Card 86-24613 DDC 519.5 19
HF1017 .A6 1987

Sweeney, G. P. (Gerald Patrick), 1928- Innovation, entrepreneurs, and regional development / G.P. Sweeney. London : F. Pinter, 1987. xvi, 271 p. : ill. ; 23 cm. Includes bibliographies and index. ISBN 0-86187-647-4
1. Technological innovations - Economic aspects - European Economic Community countries. 2. Regional planning - European Economic Community countries. 3. European Economic Community countries - Economic conditions - Regional disparities. I. Title.
NYPL [JLD 87-1403]

Innovation, entrepreneurs, and regional development / G.P. Sweeney. New York : St. Martin's Press, c1987. xvi, 271 p. : ill., map ; 23 cm. Includes bibliographies and index. ISBN 0-312-00489-3 : LC Card 86-27999 DDC 338/.06/094 19
1. Technological innovations - Economic aspects - European Economic Community countries. 2. European Economic Community countries - Economic conditions - Regional disparities. 3. Regional planning - European Economic Community countries. 4. Entrepreneur. I. Title.
HC240.9.T4 S94 1987

Sweeney, James L. Macroeconomics [i.e. Macroeconomic] impacts of energy shocks /. Amsterdam ; New York : xvi, 331 p. : ISBN 0-444-70247-4 (U. S.) LC Card 87-9035 DDC 338.4/36655/0724 19
HG229 .M315 1987

Sweeney, Richard J. Exchange rates, trade, and the U. S. economy /. Cambridge, Mass. , c1985. xxi, 296 p. : ISBN 0-88410-948-8 LC Card 84-28328 DDC 332.4/560973 19
HG3851 .E94 1985 *NYPL [JLE 85-2269]*

Sweeney, Thomas F. Aerospace markets /. Greenwich, CT, U. S.A. (100 Northfield St., Greenwich 06830) , c1987. 1 v. (various pagings) : LC Card 87-156000 DDC 380.1/456291 19
HD9711.5.A2 A37 1987

Sweet, David C. Public utilities and the poor : rights and responsibilities / David C. Sweet and Kathryn Wertheim Hexter. New York : Praeger, 1987. xxiii, 174 p. : ill. ; 25 cm. Bibliography: p. [161]-163. Includes index. ISBN 0-275-92572-2 (alk. paper) : LC Card 87-6979 DDC 362.5/82 19
1. Economic assistance, Domestic - United States. 2. Poor - United States - Energy assistance. 3. Telephone - United States - Rates. I. Hexter, Kathryn Wertheim. II. Title.
HC110.P6 S894 1987

Sweet, Mary Elizabeth K. Taylor, John A. (John Alvin), 1930- U. S. imports of textile and apparel products under the multifiber arrangement, 1981-84 /. Washington, D.C. [1985] v, 136 p. ; LC Card 86-601665 DDC 382/.45677/00973021 19
HD9940.U4 T38 1985

Sweet Spanish onion . Idaho Oregon Onion Promotion Committee. Temple, Me. (Santa Claus Lake, Temple 04984) , 1986. ii, 46, 27 leaves : LC Card 87-120958 DDC 381/.41525/0973 19
HD9235.O62 U34 1986

Sweet subsidy . Heston, Thomas J. (Thomas Janney) New York , 1987. 544 p. ; ISBN 0-8240-8084-X (alk. paper) : LC Card 87-23776 DDC 338.1/8 19
HD9105 .H47 1987

Sweet success . Stechert, Kathryn B. New York , London , c1986. xiii, 224 p. ; ISBN 0-02-614380-1 LC Card 85-30916 DDC 650.1/024/042 19
HD6053 .S724 1986 *NYPL [JLD 86-2435]*

Sweezy, Paul Marlor, 1910- Magdoff, Harry. Stagnation and the financial explosion /. New York , c1987. 208 p. : ISBN 0-85345-716-6 : LC Card 86-33129 DDC 330.973/0927 19
HC106.8 .M315 1987b

Sweigart, Joseph Earl. Coffee factorage and the emergence of a Brazilian capital market, 1850-1888 / Joseph E. Sweigart. New York : Garland Pub., 1987. xvi, 337 p. : ill. ; 24 cm. (South American and Latin American economic history) Bibliography: p. 307-337. ISBN 0-8240-1373-5 (alk. paper) : LC Card 87-8617 DDC 338.1/3373/098153 19
1. Coffee trade - Brazil - Rio de Janeiro - History - 19th century. 2. Capital market - Brazil - Rio de Janeiro - History - 19th century. I. Title. II. Series.
HD9199.B8 R567 1987

SWIFT-System. Loh, Wolfram W. Das S.W.I.F.T.-System . Frankfurt am Main , c1983. vii, 198 p. : ISBN 3-7819-0285-4 : LC Card 83-211180
HG1708.5 .L64 1983

Swindle, Elizabeth M. Swindle, Robert E. Business mathematics . Boston, Mass. , c1987. xii, 577 p. : ISBN 0-534-07572-X : LC Card 86-27441 DDC 512/.1 19
HF5691 .S85 1987

Swindle, Robert E. Business mathematics : concepts and applications / Robert E. Swindle, Elizabeth M. Swindle. Boston, Mass. : Kent Pub. Co., c1987. xii, 577 p. : ill. ; 25 cm. Includes index. ISBN 0-534-07572-X : LC Card 86-27441 DDC 512/.1 19
1. Business mathematics. 2. Business mathematics - Problems, exercises, etc. I. Swindle, Elizabeth M. II. Title.
HF5691 .S85 1987

Swinne, Axel Hilmar. Die finanzielle Führung und Kontrolle von Auslandsgesellschaften / von Axel H. Swinne. Frankfurt am Main : A. Metzner, c1983. 422 p. : ill. ; 22 cm. (International finance management . Bd. 1) Includes bibliographical references and index. ISBN 3-7875-4200-0 LC Card 84-148375
1. International business enterprises - Finance. I. Title. II. Series.
HG4027.5 .S95 1983

Swinnerton, Guy S. Recreation on agricultural land in Alberta / prepared by Guy S. Swinnerton. Edmonton, Alta. : Environment Council of Alberta, [1982] x, 211 p. : ill., maps (some col.) ; 29 cm. "November 1982." "ECA82-17/1B27." "Recreation on agricultural land in Alberta : Summary" (7 p.) inserted. Bibliography: p. 177-211. LC Card 83-149875 DDC 333.76/17/097123 19
1. Land use, Rural - Alberta. 2. Recreation areas - Alberta. 3. Farms - Alberta - Recreational use. 4. Trespass - Alberta. I. Title.
HD319.A4 S94 1982 *NYPL [JLF 86-851]*

SWISS ECONOMIC ASSISTANCE. see **ECONOMIC ASSISTANCE SWISS.**

The Swiss equity market : a guide for investors / edited by Henri B. Meier. Westport, Conn. : Quorum Books, 1985. xiv, 210 p. : ill. ; 25 cm. Includes index. Bibliography: p. [203]-204. ISBN 0-89930-147-9 (lib. bdg. : alk. paper) LC Card 85-12195 DDC 332.64/2494 19
1. Stocks - Switzerland. 2. Stock-exchanges - Switzerland. 3. Investments - Switzerland. I. Meier, Henri B.
HG5652 .M45 1985 *NYPL [JLE 86-1965]*

SWITZERLAND - APPROPRIATIONS AND EXPENDITURES.
Boss, Alfred. Ausgabenkürzungen im öffentlichen Sektor /. Tübingen , c1987. xiii, 220 p. : ISBN 3-16-345212-4 LC Card 87-408337 DDC 336.43 19
HJ2109 .B67 1987

Switzerland. Assemblée fédérale. see **Switzerland. Bundesversammlung.**

Switzerland. Bundesamt für Aussenwirtschaft. Jolles, Paul R. Von der Handelspolitik zur Aussenwirtschaftspolitik . Bern , 1983. xix, 403 p. : ISBN 3-7272-9209-1 : LC Card 84-119428
HF1573 .J65 1983

Switzerland. Bundesamt für Forstwesen und Landschaftsschutz. Eidgenössische Betriebszählung 1985. Bern , 1986. 108 p. ; ISBN 3-303-07007-5 LC Card 87-407623 DDC 338.1/7498/09494021 19
HD9765.S92 E37 1986

Switzerland. Bundesamt für Statistik. Eidgenössische Betriebszählung 1985. Bern , 1986. 108 p. ; ISBN 3-303-07007-5 LC Card 87-407623 DDC 338.1/7498/09494021 19
HD9765.S92 E37 1986

Entwicklung der Geburtenhäufigkeit in der Schweiz nach Wochentag und Stunden /. Bern , 1984. 40 p. : LC Card 85-163580
HA1593 .B45 Heft 114 HB1033

Erhebung über die Gütertransporte auf der Strasse 1984 /. Bern , 1986. 103 p. : ISBN 3-303-11041-7 : LC Card 87-408470 DDC 388.3/24/09494/021 19
HE5683.A6 E74 1986

Switzerland. Bundesamt für Zivilluftfahrt. Mensch und Luftfahrt . Bern [1981] 177 p. : LC Card 83-116416
HE9863.A4 M45 1981

SWITZERLAND. BUNDESVERSAMMLUNG.
Grossen, Andreas. Bürger, Parlament und Steuern . Bern , c1986. vi, 134 p. : ISBN 3-7165-0510-2 LC Card 86-187534
HJ2145 .G76 1986

SWITZERLAND - CENSUS, 1980.
Leibundgut, Hansjörg, 1947- Die Bedeutung der beruflichen Mobilität als arbeitsmarktlicher Ausgleichsprozess . Bern , New York , c1986. ix, 235 p. : ISBN 3-261-03630-3 LC Card 87-122350 DDC 331.12/79494 19
HD5717.5.S9 L45 1986

SWITZERLAND - COMMERCE - CHINA.
Yang, Yuming. L'industrie horlogère suisse et ses relations avec la Chine de 1949 à 1982 /. Geneve , 1984. 186 leaves : LC Card 85-104853
HD9999.C583 S99 1984

SWITZERLAND - COMMERCIAL POLICY.
Bluntschli, Franz. Schweizer Aussenwirtschaft, Wohlstand und Entwicklungsländer /. Adliswil , c1983. 38 p. : ISBN 3-7229-4032-X : LC Card 83-226336
HF1574 .B58 1983

Jolles, Paul R. Von der Handelspolitik zur Aussenwirtschaftspolitik . Bern , 1983. xix, 403 p. : ISBN 3-7272-9209-1 : LC Card 84-119428
HF1573 .J65 1983

SWITZERLAND - COMMERCIAL POLICY - HISTORY - 20TH CENTURY.
Schmid, Hanspeter, 1951- Wirtschaft, Staat und Macht . Zürich [c1983] 432 p. : ISBN 3-85791-073-9 (Schw. Buch) LC Card 83-244266
HF1573 .S335 1983

SWITZERLAND - ECONOMIC CONDITIONS - 1918-
Borner, Silvio. Einführung in die Volkswirtschaftslehre /. Diessenhofen , c1983. 105 p. : ISBN 3-7253-0164-6 : LC Card 83-184501
HB175 .B7315 1983

Staehelin, Max, 1909- Schweizer Banken und Schweizer Wirtschaft im Wandel der Zeit /. Zürich , c1984. 261 p. : LC Card 84-212396
HG3204 .S77 1984

SWITZERLAND - ECONOMIC CONDITIONS - 1918- - REGIONAL DISPARITIES.
Raumordnungspolitik im Vollzug . Grüsch ,

c1985. 507 p. : ISBN 3-7253-0258-8 : LC Card 86-149201
HC397 .R36 1985

SWITZERLAND - ECONOMIC CONDITIONS - 1918-1945.
Schmid, Hanspeter, 1951- Wirtschaft, Staat und Macht . Zürich [c1983] 432 p. : ISBN 3-85791-073-9 (Schw. Buch) LC Card 83-244266
HF1573 .S335 1983

SWITZERLAND - ECONOMIC CONDITIONS - 1945-
Deiss, Joseph. Economie politique et politique économique de la Suisse /. Fribourg , c1979. 412 p. : LC Card 86-673870
HC397 .D387x 1979

Genberg, Hans. External influences on the Swiss economy under fixed and flexible exchange rates /. Grüsch , c1985. ii, 182 p. : ISBN 3-7253-0249-9 (pbk.) LC Card 86-156330
HG3963 .G45 1985 NYPL [JLD 87-539]

Genberg, Hans. Influences externes sur l'économie suisse en changes fixes et flottants /. Genève , c1985. ii, 202 p. : ISBN 2-8257-0127-0 : LC Card 85-235579 DDC 332.4/5609494 19
HG3963 .G46 1985 NYPL [JLD 86-2381]

Partnerschaft in der sozialen Marktwirtschaft . Bern , c1986. 367 p. ; ISBN 3-258-03604-7 LC Card 86-226613 DDC 330.943/087 19
HC286.7 .P37 1986

Zenger, Christoph. Kursschwankungen des Schweizerfrankens in ihren Auswirkungen auf Produktion, Export, Import und Fremdenverkehr . Bern , c1982. vi, 263 p. : ISBN 3-258-03172-X : LC Card 83-242397 DDC 332.4/9494 19
HG1155 .Z46 1982

SWITZERLAND - ECONOMIC CONDITIONS - 1945- - REGIONAL DISPARITIES.
Zwischen Zentren und Hinterland . Diessenhofen , c1982. 349 p. : ISBN 0-372-53017-9 : LC Card 83-129330
HC397 .Z88 1982

SWITZERLAND - ECONOMIC CONDITIONS - CONGRESSES.
Vorträge gehalten anlässlich der Abgeordnetenversammlung vom 27. Mai 1978 =. [Bern] , 1978. 44 p. : LC Card 84-115871
HC397 .V67 1978

SWITZERLAND - ECONOMIC POLICY. Here are entered works on sustained military attacks on cities, military positions, etc. with bombs, shells, rockets or other explosive missiles. Works on military bombardments by means of bombs dropped from the air are entered under Bombing, Aerial. Works on the use of explosive devices for the purposes of political terrorism, protest, etc., are entered under Bombings. See also subdivision Bombardment under names of cities, e. g. London - Bombardment, 1940.
Deiss, Joseph. Economie politique et politique économique de la Suisse /. Fribourg , c1979. 412 p. : LC Card 86-673870
HC397 .D387x 1979

Mugglin, Markus. Exportrisikogarantie, internationale Verschuldung und schweizerische Entwicklungspolitik /. Adliswil , 1985. 56 p. : ISBN 3-7229-4036-X LC Card 85-148130
HF1574.5.D44 M84 1985

SWITZERLAND - ECONOMIC POLICY - ECONOMETRIC MODELS.
Makromodelle und Wirtschaftspolitik . Grüsch , c1985. 120 p. : ISBN 3-7253-0250-2 : LC Card 85-208009
HC397 .M26 1985

Switzerland. Eidgenössisches Statistisches Amt.
Kantonale demographische Indiktoren, 1960 und 1970 =. Bern , 1977. 187 p. : LC Card 85-217076
HA1593 .B45 Heft 44 HA1604

Schweizerische Dividendenstatistik, 1929 bis 1932. [Bern] , 1934. 91 p. ; LC Card 86-198072
HA1593 .B45 Heft 2 HG4226

Schweizerische Volkssterbetafeln . Bern , 1955. 70 leaves ; LC Card 85-144744
HB1453 .S38 1955

Switzerland. Eidgenössisches Volkswirtschaftsdepartement. Abteilung für Landwirtschaft. Grundsätze für die Bewertung von Kulturland bei Güterzusammenlegungen . [Bern? , 1973?] 1 v. (loose leaf) : LC Card 86-184960
HD798 .G78 1973

SWITZERLAND - FOREIGN ECONOMIC RELATIONS.
Bluntschli, Franz. Schweizer Aussenwirtschaft, Wohlstand und Entwicklungsländer /. Adliswil , c1983. 38 p. : ISBN 3-7229-4032-X : LC Card 83-226336
HF1574 .B58 1983

Hämisegger, Kuno, 1956- Neue Formen des Auslandengagements . Bern , New York , c1986. 292 p. : ISBN 3-261-03598-6 LC Card 86-208515
HF1411 .H253 1986

Jolles, Paul R. Von der Handelspolitik zur Aussenwirtschaftspolitik . Bern , 1983. xix, 403 p. : ISBN 3-7272-9209-1 : LC Card 84-119428
HF1573 .J65 1983

SWITZERLAND - FOREIGN ECONOMIC RELATIONS - DEVELOPING COUNTRIES.
Mugglin, Markus. Exportrisikogarantie, internationale Verschuldung und schweizerische Entwicklungspolitik /. Adliswil , 1985. 56 p. : ISBN 3-7229-4036-X LC Card 85-148130
HF1574.5.D44 M84 1985

SWITZERLAND - INDUSTRIES - HISTORY.
Jaun, Rudolf, 1948- Management und Arbeiterschaft . Zürich , c1986. 505, 10 p. ; ISBN 3-905278-08-1 LC Card 87-132013 DDC 658/.009494 19
HD70.S85 J38 1986

SWITZERLAND - INDUSTRIES - LOCATION.
Flückiger, Hans. Siedlungsstruktur . Bern , c1985. 118 p. : ISBN 3-258-03529-6 : LC Card 86-134805
HN603.5 .F58 1985 NYPL [JLE 86-3789]

Hanser, Christian. Erfolgskontrolle der Industrieansiedlungspolitik . Bern , New York , c1986. 375 p. ; ISBN 3-261-03610-9 LC Card 87-407957 DDC 338.6/042/09494 19
HD58 .H36 1986

Switzerland. Informationsstelle für Steuerfragen.
Die Kalte Progression . Bern , 1982. 107 p. : LC Card 83-128720
HJ4747 .K35 1982

Switzerland. Interkantonale Kommission für Steueraufklärung. Die Kalte Progression . Bern , 1982. 107 p. : LC Card 83-128720
HJ4747 .K35 1982

SWITZERLAND - MILITARY POLICY - ECONOMIC ASPECTS.
Spälti, P. Die Rüstungsreferendumsinitiative--schlecht getarnter Anschlag auf unsere Landesverteidigung /. Zürich , 1987. 20 p. ; LC Card 87-409331 DDC 330.9494 s 327.1/74/09494 19
HC395 .Z43 Nr. 131 HC400.D4

SWITZERLAND - OFFICIALS AND EMPLOYEES.
Allenspach, Heinz. Bevorzugter Beamtenstatus, Möglichkeiten und Grenzen einer Reform . Zürich [1986] 32 p. ; LC Card 87-407830 DDC 330.9494 s 331.7/61354494 19
HC395 .Z43 Nr. 130 JN8831

SWITZERLAND - POLITICS AND GOVERNMENT - 20TH CENTURY.
Grossen, Andreas. Bürger, Parlament und Steuern . Bern , c1986. vi, 134 p. : ISBN 3-7165-0510-2 LC Card 86-187534
HJ2145 .G76 1986

SWITZERLAND - POLITICS AND GOVERNMENT - 1945-
Farago, Peter. Verbände als Träger öffentlicher Politik . Grüsch , c1987. xi, 185 p. : ISBN 3-7253-0290-1 LC Card 87-140606 DDC 322/.3/09494 19
HD2429.S92 F37 1987

Raumordnungspolitik im Vollzug . Grüsch , c1985. 507 p. : ISBN 3-7253-0258-8 : LC Card 86-149201
HC397 .R36 1985

SWITZERLAND - POPULATION.
Höpflinger, François. Bevölkerungswandel in der Schweiz . Grüsch , c1986. 179 p. : ISBN 3-7253-0269-3 LC Card 86-234328
HB3623 .H66 1986

SWITZERLAND - POPULATION - STATISTICS.
Kantonale demographische Indiktoren, 1960 und 1970 =. Bern , 1977. 187 p. : LC Card 85-217076
HA1593 .B45 Heft 44 HA1604

SWITZERLAND - SOCIAL CONDITIONS - CONGRESSES.
Vorträge gehalten anlässlich der Abgeordnetenversammlung vom 27. Mai 1978 =. [Bern] , 1978. 44 p. : LC Card 84-115871
HC397 .V67 1978

SWITZERLAND - SOCIAL LIFE AND CUSTOMS - 1895-1945.
Tschudin, Paul, 1904- Meine Ehre ist nicht die Eure! . Basel , 1986. 217 p. ; ISBN 3-85990-069-2 LC Card 87-137660 DDC 331.88/092/4 B 19
HD6772.5.T74 A3 1986

SWITZERLAND - STATISTICS, VITAL.
Höpflinger, François. Bevölkerungswandel in der Schweiz . Grüsch , c1986. 179 p. : ISBN 3-7253-0269-3 LC Card 86-234328
HB3623 .H66 1986

Kantonale demographische Indiktoren, 1960 und 1970 =. Bern , 1977. 187 p. : LC Card 85-217076
HA1593 .B45 Heft 44 HA1604

Schweizerische Volkssterbetafeln . Bern , 1955. 70 leaves ; LC Card 85-144744
HB1453 .S38 1955

Swoboda, Alexander K.
Genberg, Hans. External influences on the Swiss economy under fixed and flexible exchange rates /. Grüsch , c1985. ii, 182 p. : ISBN 3-7253-0249-9 (pbk.) LC Card 86-156330
HG3963 .G45 1985 NYPL [JLD 87-539]

Genberg, Hans. Influences externes sur l'économie suisse en changes fixes et flottants /. Genève , c1985. ii, 202 p. : ISBN 2-8257-0127-0 : LC Card 85-235579 DDC 332.4/5609494 19
HG3963 .G46 1985 NYPL [JLD 86-2381]

Threats to international financial stability /. Cambridge , New York , 1987. xviii, 307 p. : ISBN 0-521-34556-1 LC Card 87-10310 DDC 332/.042 19
HG3881 .T495 1987

Sybex ready reference series.
Harvey, Greg. Lotus 1-2-3 desktop companion /. San Francisco , c1987. ix, 976 p. : ISBN 0-89588-385-6 : LC Card 86-63454 DDC 005.36/9 19
HF5548.4.L67 H38 1987

Sych, E. N. (Evgeniia Nikolaevna)
Transportno-proizvodstvennye sistemy : razvitie i funktsionirovanie / E.N. Sych. Kiev : Nauk. dumka, 1986. 164 p. : ill. ; 20 cm. At head of title: Akademiia nauk Ukrainskoĭ SSR. Odesskoe otdelenie Instituta ėkonomiki. Bibliography: p. 157-[165] LC Card 86-233704
1. Transportation - Soviet Union. 2. Transportation - Ukraine. I. Title.
HE255 .S93 1986

Sydafrika i södra Afrika /. Odén, Bertil, 1939- Uppsala , 1985. 181 p. : ISBN 91-7106-236-X LC Card 85-221741
HC905 .O34 1985 NYPL [Sc E 86-483]

SYDKRAFT (FIRM : SWEDEN)
Bergquist, Sven, 1926- De heta åren /. [Stockholm] , 1985. 319 p. : ISBN 91-7566-089-X LC Card 85-233735
HD9698.S84 S923 1985

Sydsæter, Knut. Seierstad, Atle. Optimal control theory with economic applications /. Amsterdam ; New York : xvi, 445 p. : ISBN 0-444-87923-4 (Elsevier Science Pub. Co.) LC Card 86-16504 DDC 629.8/312 19
QA402.3 .S4 1986 NYPL [JLE 87-1123]

Syed Abdul Quddus. see **Quddus, Syed Abdul.**

Syfrig, Heidi Schelbert- see **Schelbert-Syfrig, Heidi.**

Sykes, Trevor. Two centuries of panic : a history of corporate collapses in Australia / Trevor Sykes. Sydney ; Boston : Allen & Unwin, 1987. p. cm. Bibliography: p. Includes index. ISBN 0-04-176013-1 LC Card 87-16107 DDC

338.7/4/0994 19
1. Business failures - Australia - History. 2. Corporations - Australia - History. 3. Businessmen - Australia - History. I. Title.
HD2747 .S95 1987

Sylva Charvet, Paola. Gamonalismo y lucha campesina : (estudio de la sobrevivencia y disolución de un sector terrateniente) : el caso de la Provincia de Chimborazo, 1940-1979 / Paola Sylva Charvet. [Quito] : Ediciones Abya Yala, 1986. 250 p., [3] leaves of plates : ill. ; 22 cm. "Estudio realizado durante la Maestría de Ciencias Sociales en FLACSO--Sede Quito, 1980." Bibliography: p. 239-244. LC Card 87-101122
1. Land tenure - Ecuador - Chimborazo - History. 2. Landowners - Ecuador - Chimborazo - Political activity - History. 3. Local government - Ecuador - Chimborazo - History. 4. Peasantry - Ecuador - Chimborazo - Political activity - History. 5. Oligarchy - Ecuador - Chimborazo - History. I. Title.
HD529.C47 S95 1986

Sylvan, David J., 1953- A rationalist methodology for the social sciences / David Sylvan and Barry Glassner. Oxford [Oxfordshire] : Basil Blackwell, 1985. 188 p. : ill. ; 24 cm. Includes index. Bibliography: p. [173]-183. ISBN 0-631-13443-3 : LC Card 84-14480 DDC 300/.1/8 19
1. Sociology - Methodology. 2. Political science - Methodology. 3. Social sciences - Methodology. 4. Rationalism. I. Glassner, Barry. II. Title.
HM24 .S95 1985 ***NYPL [JLE 86-1125]***

SYLVICULTURE. see **FORESTS AND FORESTRY.**

SYMBOLIC AND MATHEMATICAL LOGIC. see **LOGIC, SYMBOLIC AND MATHEMATICAL.**

SYMBOLIC INTERACTION. see **SOCIAL INTERACTION.**

SYMBOLISM IN ADVERTISING.
Rocha, Everardo P. Guimarães, 1951- Magia e capitalismo . São Paulo, SP , 1985. 162 p. : LC Card 85-199925
HF5827 .R58 1985

SYMPHONY (COMPUTER PROGRAM)
Allegretti, Enzo V. Understanding and using Symphony /. St. Paul, MN , c1987. xvii, 226, [31] p., [4] p. of plates : ISBN 0-314-34640-6 (pbk.) LC Card 87-4986 DDC 005.36/9 19
HF5548.4.S95 A45 1987

Barton, Taylor J. The illustrated Symphony (release 1.2) book /. Dallas , c1987. vii, 310 p. : ISBN 0-915381-88-5 (pbk.) LC Card 87-6135 DDC 005.36/9 19
HF5548.4.S95 B385 1987

Bolocan, David. Advanced Symphony applications . Blue Ridge Summit, PA , c1985. x, 230 p. : ISBN 0-8306-0988-1 : LC Card 85-22303 DDC 005.36/9 19
HF5548.4.S95 B64 1985
NYPL [JSE 86-2156]

Jacobson, Jay, 1946- Advanced Symphony . New York , c1985. vi, 282 p. : ISBN 0-471-82430-5 (pbk.) : LC Card 85-12202 DDC 001.64/25 19
HF5548.4.S95 J3 1985 ***NYPL [JLF 86-854]***

The Lotus guide to learning Symphony macros . Reading, Mass. , c1986. viii, 243 p. : ISBN 0-201-16684-4 (pbk.) LC Card 86-213051 DDC 005.36/9 19
HF5549.4.S95 L67 1986

Seybold, Patricia B. Integrated desk-top environments . New York , c1985. ix, 181 p. : ISBN 0-07-056324-1 (pbk.) : LC Card 84-27841 DDC 650/.028/5425 19
HF5548.4.S95 S49 1985
NYPL [JSE 86-2011]

Symposion (Ludwig-Erhard-Stiftung) .
(18) Entwicklungspolitik im Spannungsfeld von Solidarität und Eigeninteresse . Stuttgart , New York , 1986. 155 p. ; ISBN 3-437-50306-5 LC Card 87-408212 DDC 338.91/43/01724 19
HC60 .E527 1986

(21) Steuerpolitik für die soziale Marktwirtschaft . Stuttgart , New York , 1986. 85 p. ; ISBN 3-437-50311-1 LC Card 87-122642 DDC 336.2/00943 19
HJ2687 .S73 1986

Symposion "Marktwirtschaft und Umwelt" (1980 : Walter Eucken Institut) Marktwirtschaft und Umwelt : Symposion vom 26. bis 28. März 1980 / veranstaltet vom Walter Eucken Institut in Freiburg i. Br. ; Lothar Wegehenkel (Herausgeber) ; mit Beiträgen von Hans Christoph Binswanger ... [et al.]. Tübingen : Mohr, 1981. ix, 303 p. : ill. ; 23 cm. (Wirtschaftswissenschaftliche und wirtschaftsrechtliche Untersuchungen, 0083-7113 . 17) Includes bibliographical references and indexes. ISBN 3-16-343372-3 : LC Card 81-128698 DDC 363.7/0526 19
1. Environmental policy - Congresses. 2. Externalities (Economics) - Congresses. 3. Right of property - Congresses. I. Wegehenkel, Lothar. II. Binswanger, Hans Christoph. III. Walter Eucken Institut. IV. Series. V. Series: Walter Eucken Institut. Wirtschaftswissensschaftliche und wirtschaftsrechtliche Untersuchungen , 17. VI. Title.
HC79.E5 S92 1980 ***NYPL [TB (Walter Eucken Institut. Wirtschaftswissenschaftliche und wirtschaftsrechtliche Untersuchungen. Bd. 17)]***

Symposium "Issues of the Eighties" (1982 : Vienna, Austria) Issues of the eighties . Wien , 1983. 119 p. : LC Card 83-201354 DDC 338.9 19
HD73 .I86 1983

Symposium on Linkage Between Large and Small Industries (1985 : Kuala Lumpur, Malaysia) Linkage effects and small industry development : report of the Symposium on Linkage Between Large and Small Industries. Tokyo : Asian Productivity Organization, 1986. iv, 191 p. : ill. ; 26 cm. Includes bibliographies. ISBN 92-833-2037-3 LC Card 87-137082 DDC 338.6/42/09595 19
1. Small business - Congresses. 2. Subcontracting - Congresses. I. Asia Productivity Organization. II. Title.
HD2341 .S96 1985

Symposium on Logic in Computer Science (1986 : Cambridge, Mass.) Proceedings, Symposium on Logic in Computer Science, Cambridge, Massachusetts, June 16-18, 1986 / sponsored by the IEEE Computer Society Technical Committee on Mathematical Foundations of Computng in cooperation with ACM SIGACT, Association for Symbolic Logic, European Association for Theoretical Computer Science. Washington, D.C. : IEEE Computer Society Press ; Los Angeles, CA : Order from IEEE Computer Society, 1986. xi, 383 p. : ill. ; 28 cm. "IEEE Computer Society order number 720." "IEEE catalog number 86CH23218." Includes bibliographies and index. ISBN 0-8186-0720-3 (pbk.) LC Card 86-81090 DDC 004 19
1. Electronic data processing - Congresses. 2. Electronic digital computers - Programming - Congresses. 3. Logic, Symbolic and mathematical - Congresses. I. IEEE Computer Society. Technical Committee on Mathematical Foundations of Computing. II. Association for Symbolic Logic. III. European Association for Theoretical Computer Science. IV. Title. V. Title: Logic in computer science.
QA75.5 .S9813 1986 ***NYPL [JSF 86-1041]***

Symposium on Management Data Processing for PCB Manufacturing . Symposium on Management Data Processing for PCB Manufacturing (1982 : Luxembourg, Luxembourg) Lugano [1982?] 1 v. (various pagings) : LC Card 84-211066 DDC 621.381/74/0685 19
HD9696.P742 S96 1982
NYPL [JSG 86-145]

Symposium on Management Data Processing for PCB Manufacturing (1982 : Luxembourg, Luxembourg) Symposium on Management Data Processing for PCB Manufacturing : summer conference on quality assurance, quality control & economics, Hotel Holiday Inn, Luxembourg, May 13-14, 1982 : proceedings / editor, M.G. Fassini. Lugano : European Institute of Printed Circuits, [1982?] 1 v. (various pagings) : ill. ; 30 cm. Includes bibliography. LC Card 84-211066 DDC 621.381/74/0685 19
1. Printed circuits industry - Management - Data processing - Congresses. 2. Printed circuits industry - Quality control - Congresses. I. Fassini, M. G. II. European Institute of Printed Circuits. III. Title.
HD9696.P742 S96 1982
NYPL [JSG 86-145]

Symposium on Monetary Theory, January 3-8, 1986 =. Symposium on Monetary Theory (1986 : Institute of Economics, Academia Sinica) Taipei, Taiwan, Republic of China [1986?] 2 v. (iv, 630 p.) : LC Card 87-152394 DDC 332.4 19
HG203 .S96 1986

Symposium on Monetary Theory (1986 : Institute of Economics, Academia Sinica) Symposium on Monetary Theory, January 3-8, 1986 = [Huo pi li lun yen t'ao hui, Chung-hua min kuo 75 nien 1 yüeh 3 jih chih 8 jih]. Taipei, Taiwan, Republic of China : Institute of Economics, Academia Sinica, [1986?] 2 v. (iv, 630 p.) : ill. ; 26 cm. Parallel title in Chinese characters. Includes bibliographies. LC Card 87-152394 DDC 332.4 19
1. Money - Congresses. 2. Monetary policy - Congresses. I. Chung yang yen chiu yüan. Ching chi yen chiu so. II. Title. III. Title: Huo pi li lun yen t'ao hui, Chung-hua min kuo 75 nien 1 yüeh 3 jih chih 8 jih.
HG203 .S96 1986

Symposium on National Financial Policies and Capital Formation in Africa (1985 : Cairo, Egypt) National financial policies and capital formation in Africa . Dakar, Senegal [1986] iii, 205 p. ; LC Card 87-404123 DDC 332/.096 19
HG5822 .N38 1986

Symposium on Regional Development Processes and Policies and the Changing International Division of Labour (1984 : Vienna International Centre) International economic restructuring and the regional community /. Aldershot, Hants, England , Brookfield, Vt., USA , c1987. x, 404 p. : ISBN 0-566-05478-7 : LC Card 87-11841 DDC 330.9 19
HF1412 .I574 1987

Symposium on Strategic Human Resource Planning Applications (1985 : University of Pennsylvania, Philadelphia, Pa.) Strategic human resource planning applications / edited by Richard J. Niehaus. New York : Plenum Press, c1987. viii, 257 p. ; 26 cm. "Proceedings of the Symposium on Strategic Human Resource Planning Applications, held December 4-6, 1985, at the University of Pennsylvania, Philadelphia, Pennsylvania"--T.p. verso. Includes bibliographies and index. ISBN 0-306-42561-0 LC Card 87-11141 DDC 331.11 19
1. Manpower planning - Congresses. I. Niehaus, Richard J. II. Title.
HF5549.5.M3 S95 1985

Symposium on the Development of Sound Labour Relations in English-Speaking African Countries (1982 : Nairobi, Kenya) Labour-relations in Africa, English-speaking countries . Geneva , c19. 159 p. ; ISBN 92-2-103467-4 (pbk.) : LC Card 86-212930 DDC 658.3 s 331/.096 19
HD6961.A1 I73 no. 64 HD8772

Symposium on the Energy Economy (1984 : Durham, Durham) Prospects for the world oil industry : proceedings of a Symposium on the Energy Economy / co-sponsored by the Petroleum Information Committee of the Arab Gulf States and the University of Durham, England, and held in Durham, 9-10 May 1984 ; edited by Tim Niblock and Richard Lawless. London ; Dover, N.H. : C. Helm, c1985. 131 p. : ill. ; 23 cm. Includes bibliographical references and index. ISBN 0-7099-4104-8 : LC Card 85-4186 DDC 338.2/7282 19
1. Petroleum industry and trade - Congresses. 2. Gas industry - Congresses. I. Niblock, Tim. II. Lawless, Richard I. III. Petroleum Information Committee of the Arab Gulf States. IV. Durham, Eng. University. V. Title.
HD9560.5 .S96 1985 ***NYPL [JLD 85-2430]***

Symposium sur les conséquences des techniques nouvelles de l'informatique sur les conditions de vie, et de travail, sur l'emploi des travailleurs des banques et des assurances (1980 : Paris, France) Symposium sur les conséquences des techniques nouvelles de l'informatique sur les conditions de vie, et de travail, sur l'emploi des travailleurs des banques et des assurances / organisé par la Fédération nationale des employés et cadres des assurances, du crédit, de la sécurité sociale et divers (C.G.T.) et l'U.I.S. de la fonction publique et assimilés, Paris, les 25 et 26 novembre 1980. Berlin : Secrétariat de l'U.I.S.

de la fonction publique, [1983?] 96 p. : ill. ; 21 cm. LC Card 84-185736
1. Banks and banking - France - Employees - Effect of technological innovation on - Congresses. 2. Insurance companies - France - Employees - Effect of technological innovations on - Congresses. I. Fédération nationale des employés et cadres des assurances, du crédit, de la sécurité sociale et divers (France). II. Trade Unions International of Public and Allied Employees.
HD8039.B27 F77 1980

Symposium Umweltprobleme als Herausforderung der Marktwirtschaft, Neue Ideen jenseits des Dirigismus . Symposium Umweltprobleme als Herausforderung der Marktwirtschaft, Neue Ideen jenseits des Dirigismus (1983 : Stuttgart, Germany) [Köln] [Freiburg] , 1983. 300 p. ; ISBN 3-7616-0722-9 LC Card 84-152335 DDC 363.7/058 19
HC79.E5 S96 1983 ***NYPL [JLD 86-1631]***

Symposium Umweltprobleme als Herausforderung der Marktwirtschaft, Neue Ideen jenseits des Dirigismus (1983 : Stuttgart, Germany) Symposium Umweltprobleme als Herausforderung der Marktwirtschaft, Neue Ideen jenseits des Dirigismus : Referate und Diskussionsbeiträge u.a. / von Hans Ch. Binswanger ... [et al.] ; herausgegeben von Lothar Wegehenkel. [Köln] : H.M. Schleyer-Stiftung ; [Freiburg] : Walter-Eucken-Institut, 1983. 300 p. ; 21 cm. (Veröffentlichungen der Hanns Martin Schleyer-Stiftung . Bd. 11) Includes bibliographical references. ISBN 3-7616-0722-9 LC Card 84-152335 DDC 363.7/058 19
1. Environmental policy - Congresses. 2. Economic development - Environmental aspects - Congresses. I. Binswanger, Hans Christoph. II. Wegehenkel, Lothar. III. Hans Martin Schleyer-Stiftung. IV. Walter Eucken Institut. V. Title. VI. Series.
HC79.E5 S96 1983 ***NYPL [JLD 86-1631]***

SYMPTOMS. see **DIAGNOSIS.**

Ho symvoulos epicheirēseōn . Vliamos, Spyros I. Athēna , c1985. 48 p. : LC Card 86-182906
HD69.C6 V55 1985

SYNDICALISM.
García-Salve, Francisco. Con esta sangre obrera /. Madrid , 1980. 197 p., 1 leaf ; ISBN 84-85759-08-7 : LC Card 81-141428
HD6477 .G37 1980

Vasco, Neno. Concepção anarquista do sindicalismo /. Porto , 1984. 209 p. ; LC Card 84-256086 DDC 320.5/7 19
HX833 .V37 1984 ***NYPL [JLD 86-2525]***

SYNDICALISM - ARGENTINA - HISTORY - 20TH CENTURY.
El "Sindicalismo revolucionario," 1905-1945 /. Buenos Aires , c1986. 153 p. ; ISBN 950-25-1424-6 : LC Card 87-125439 DDC 335/.82/0982 19
HD6602 .S49 1986

SYNDICALISM - CHILE.
Ruiz-Tagle P., Jaime. El sindicalismo chileno después del plan laboral /. Santiago, Chile [1985?] 211 p. ; ***NYPL [JLD 87-1182]***

SYNDICALISM - GREECE.
Klōnarēs, N. G. (Nikos G.) Ho syndikalismos kai to politiko mas provlēma /. Athēnai , 1973. 78 p. ; LC Card 86-234658
HD6795.5 .K57 1973

SYNDICALISM - MEXICO - HISTORY.
Freyre Rubio, Javier. Las organizaciones sindicales, obreras y burocráticas contemporáneas en México /. Azcapotzalco [Mexico] , c1983. 265 p. : ISBN 968-597-500-0 LC Card 86-218318
HD6532 .F74 1983

SYNDICALISM - OHIO - HISTORY - 20TH CENTURY.
Wortman, Roy T., 1940- From syndicalism to trade unionism . New York , 1985. 217 p. : ISBN 0-8240-5675-2 (alk. paper) : LC Card 85-16249 DDC 331.88/6/09771 19
HD8055.I5 O38 1985 ***NYPL [JLE 86-4097]***

SYNDICALISM - SPAIN - CATALONIA - HISTORY - 20TH CENTURY.
Sabater, Jordi, 1958- Anarquisme i catalanisme . Barcelona , 1986. 231 p. ; ISBN 84-297-2490-7 LC Card 87-108668
HD8582.C583 S24 1986

Syndicalisme et politique /. Mouriaux, René. Paris , c1985. 212 p. : LC Card 86-159539
HD6687 .M68 1985

SYNDICAT DES EMPLOYÉ(E)S DE L'UQAM.
Lépine, Ginette. Vous autres au syndicat-- /. Montréal, Québec , c1984. 179 p. ; ISBN 2-89037-214-6 LC Card 85-101458
HD8005.2.C23 M665 1984

Syndicat national de l'industrie pharmaceutique (France) L'Industrie pharmaceutique, ses réalités. Paris , 1982. 54 p. : LC Card 85-124408
HD9668.4 .I53 1982

SYNDICATES (FINANCE) - ACCOUNTING.
Macve, Richard, 1940- A survey of Lloyds syndicate accounts . Englewood Cliffs, NJ , 1986. xxv, 263 p. : ISBN 0-13-878273-3 : LC Card 85-12147 DDC 368/.012/094212 19
HG8039 .M33 1986 ***NYPL [JLE 87-864]***

SYNDICATES (FINANCE) - HANDBOOKS, MANUALS, ETC.
Beguelin, Richard H., 1937- The secrets of syndication . Boston , c1985. xi, 287 p. : ISBN 0-316-08783-1 : LC Card 85-5157 DDC 658/.044 19
HG6021 .B4 1985 ***NYPL [JLE 85-2259]***

Syndicats et relations de travail dans la vie économique française /. Erbès-Seguin, Sabine. [Villeneuve d'Ascq] [1985] 137 p. ; ISBN 2-85939-262-9 : LC Card 85-226210 DDC 331/.0944 19
HD6684 .E75 1985 ***NYPL [JLE 86-2222]***

Ho syndikalismos kai to politiko mas provlēma /. Klōnarēs, N. G. (Nikos G.) Athēnai , 1973. 78 p. ; LC Card 86-234658
HD6795.5 .K57 1973

Syndikalistikē vivliothēkē .
(1) Klōnarēs, N. G. (Nikos G.) Ho syndikalismos kai to politiko mas provlēma /. Athēnai , 1973. 78 p. ; LC Card 86-234658
HD6795.5 .K57 1973

Das Syndikat . Meyer, August. Braunschweig , c1986. 348 p. ; ISBN 3-925151-18-4 LC Card 87-129940 DDC 338.2/73/0943 19
HD9523.9.R45 M49 1986

Synergy Applied Research Limited. The Private residential landlord and tenant in Christchurch . Wellington, N.Z. [1986] viii, 105 p. : ISBN 0-477-03810-7 (pbk.) LC Card 87-147647 DDC 333.33/8 19
HD7288.85.N452 C576 1986

Hoi synetairismoi stēn Hellada /. Klēmēs, Arist. N. (Aristeidēs N.), 1915- Athēna , 1985- v. <1 > : LC Card 86-228137
HD3531.83.A4 K56 1985

Synge, Richard. Energy in Nigeria / Richard Synge. London : Middle East Economic Digest, [c1986] x, 145 p. : ill. ; 30 cm. (MEED perspective) ISBN 0-946510-20-2 (pbk.) LC Card 86-215864 DDC 333.79/09669 19
1. Energy industries - Nigeria. I. Title.
HD9502.N552 S96 1986

Den synliga handen . Liedman, Sven-Eric, 1939- [Stockholm] [1986] 268 p. ; ISBN 91-7014-210-6 : LC Card 86-215138
HB116.5.B47 L54 1986

Synnott, William R. The information weapon : winning customers and markets with technology / William R. Synnott. New York : Wiley, 1987. xi, 334 p. ; 26 cm. Bibliography: p. 322. Includes index. ISBN 0-471-84557-4 LC Card 86-32393 DDC 658.4/038 19
1. Management - Communication systems. 2. Management - Data processing. 3. Information resources management. I. Title.
HD30.335 .S96 1987

Syn′ooka sestra Ukraïny /. I͡Urėvich, Uladzimir Mikhaĭlavich. Kyïv , 1985. 158 p. ; LC Card 87-109673
HC337.B93 I97 1985

A synopsis of Texas savings-and-loan associations' operations /. Born, Waldo L. College Station, Tex. [1986?] 38 p. : LC Card 86-622196 DDC 332.3/2/09764 19
HG2153.T4 B67 1986

Synov′i͡am v nasledstvo / [sostavitel′ A.A. Muzyri͡a]. Moskva : Moskovskiĭ rabochiĭ, 1986. 204 p. : ill. ; 21 cm. LC Card 86-132407
1. Labor and laboring classes - Russian S.F.S.R. - Moscow Region - Biography. I. Muzyri͡a, Aleksandra Alekseevna.
HD8529.M62 S97 1986

Syntechnies & epangelmata stē Thrakē, 1685-1920 /. Papathanasē-Mousiopoulou, Kalliopē. Athēna , 1985. 247 p. : LC Card 86-208086
HD6795.5.Z8 T56 1985

Syntechnies kai epangelmata stē Thrakē, 1685-1920. Papathanasē-Mousiopoulou, Kalliopē. Syntechnies & epangelmata stē Thrakē, 1685-1920 /. Athēna , 1985. 247 p. : LC Card 86-208086
HD6795.5.Z8 T56 1985

Hoi syntechnies sta Giannena kata ton 19o kai tis arches tou 20ou aiōna (arches 19ou ai. hōs 1912) /. Papageōrgiou, Giōrgos. Iōannina : Athēna : 454 p. ; LC Card 84-137611
HD2346.G752 I566 1982

Synthèses statistiques, comptes et revenus .
(no 68) Recettes, dépenses et revenus des exploitations agricoles en 1983 /. Paris [1986] 138 p. : LC Card 86-187878
HD1945 .R374 1986

Synthèses statistiques, comptes et revenus, 0244-5271 .
(no 55) Savignac, Philippe. Concours publics à l'agriculture par régions ou catégories d'exploitations en 1981. Paris [1984] 81 p. : ISBN 2-11-083993-7 LC Card 85-168478
HD1947 .S29 1984

Synthesis, before and beyond February 1986 : the Edgar M. Jopson memorial lectures / edited with an introduction by Lilia Quindoza Santiago. [Philippines] : Edgar M. Jopson Memorial Foundation, 1986. xiv, 114 p. : ill. ; 24 cm. English and Tagalog. "The Interdisciplinary Forum (IDF) of the University of the Philippines." ISBN 971-91058-0-1 (pbk.) LC Card 87-112023 DDC 338.9599 19
1. Philippines - Economic conditions - 1946-. 2. Philippines - Economic policy. I. Santiago, Lilia Quindoza, 1949-. II. University of the Philippines. Interdisciplinary Forum. III. Title: Edgar M. Jopson memorial lectures.
HC452 .S96 1986

Synthesis of highway practice, 0547-5570 .
(130) French, Alexander. Traffic data collection and analysis . Washington, D.C. [1986] 58 p. : ISBN 0-309-04406-5 (pbk.) : LC Card 86-51174 DDC 388.3/14/072 19
HE369 .F68 1986

A synthesis of research on competition in the financing and delivery of health services /. Langwell, Kathryn M. Hyattsville, MD. , Springfield, VA , 1982. 85 p. ; LC Card 82-600612 DDC 338.4/73621/0973 19
RA410.53 .L36 1982 ***NYPL [JLF 86-422]***

Synthesis of transit practice, 0732-1856 .
(9) MacDorman, Littleton C. Use of part-time operators /. Washington, D.C. [1986] 33 p. : ISBN 0-309-04403-0 (pbk.) LC Card 86-51175 DDC 331.25/72 19
HD8039.S82 U65 1986

Synthetic culture and development /. Constantino, Renato. Quezon City , c1985. iv, 72 p. ; ISBN 971-10-5803-0 (pbk.) LC Card 85-234601 DDC 302.2 19
HD76. C66 1985 ***NYPL [JLD 87-27]***

SYNTHETIC DETERGENTS. see **DETERGENTS, SYNTHETIC.**

SYNTHETIC DETERGENTS INDUSTRY - UNITED STATES.
Promotion strategies for household cleaning products. New York, N.Y. , c1983. 2 v. (xx, 635 p.) ; LC Card 87-142358 DDC 381/.456671/0973 19
HD9999.C4863 U56 1983

SYNTHETIC FIBER INDUSTRY. see **MAN-MADE FIBERS INDUSTRY.**

Synthetic fibers in asphalt paving mixtures /. Button, Joe W. College Station, Tex. [1984] vi, 153 p. : LC Card 86-620835 DDC 380.5 s 625.8/5 19
HE203 .T43 no. 319-1F TA443.A7

SYNTHETIC FUELS INDUSTRY - UNITED STATES.
The Unfulfilled promise of synthetic fuels . New York , 1987. xxii, 225 p. ; ISBN 0-313-25666-7 (lib. bdg. : alk. paper) LC Card

87-247 DDC 338.4/766266/0973 19
HD9502.5.S963 U5475 1987

Syrovatko, V. G. (Vitaliĭ Grigor'evich) Industrializatsiia i kadry sel'skogo khoziaistva / V.G. Syrovatko, P.F. Paramonov. Moskva : Agropromizdat, 1986. 191 p. ; 20 cm. Includes bibliographical references. LC Card 86-229171
1. Agricultural laborers - Soviet Union. 2. Employees, Training of - Soviet Union. 3. Farm mechanization - Soviet Union. I. Paramonov, P. F. (Petr Filippovich). II. Title.
HD1536.S65 S97 1986

SYSTEM ANALYSIS - CONGRESSES.
IFIP Working Conference on System Modelling and Optimization (1984 : Santiago, Chile) Recent advances in system modelling and optimization . Berlin , New York , c1986. 199 p. : ISBN 0-387-17083-9 (U. S.) LC Card 86-29770 DDC 003 19
QA402 .I43 1984 ***NYPL [JSE 87-639]***

Large-scale modelling and interactive decision analysis . Berlin , New York , c1986. vii, 362 p. : ISBN 3-540-16785-4 : LC Card 86-20205 DDC 658.4/03 19
T57.6 .L34 1986 ***NYPL [JLM 72-289 v. 273]***

System modelling and optimization . Berlin , New York , c1986. xii, 1046 p. : ISBN 0-387-16854-0 (U. S.) LC Card 86-15637 DDC 003 19
QA402 .S95822 1986 ***NYPL [JSE 86-1775]***

SYSTEM BUILDING. see **INDUSTRIALIZED BUILDING.**

SYSTEM DESIGN.
Boose, John H. Expertise transfer for expert system design /. Amsterdam , New York , 1986. viii, 312 p. : ISBN 0-444-42634-5 LC Card 86-9044 DDC 006.3/3 19
QA76.76.E95 B66 1986 ***NYPL [JSE 86-1840]***

Buhr, R. J. A. System design with Ada /. Englewood Cliffs, N.J. , c1984. xv, 256 p. : ISBN 0-13-881623-9 : LC Card 83-13673 DDC 001.64/2 19
QA76.73.A35 B83 1984 ***NYPL [JSE 86-1253]***

Building expert systems /. Reading, Mass. , 1983. xvi, 444 p. : ISBN 0-201-10686-8 LC Card 82-24511 DDC 001.64/2 19
QA76.9.E96 B84 1983 ***NYPL [JSE 87-204]***

Censo agrario 1982 . Madrid , 1983. 104, 8 p. : ISBN 84-260-0803-8 LC Card 84-134551
HD2022 .C45 1983

Hawryszkiewycz, I. T. Database analysis and design /. Chicago , c1984. xx, 578 p. : ISBN 0-574-21485-2 : LC Card 84-1341 DDC 001.64/2 19
QA76.9.D3 H386 1984 ***NYPL [JSE 86-2113]***

Henley, Ernest J. Designing for reliability and safety control /. Englewood Cliffs, N.J. , c1985. xvi, 527 p. : ISBN 0-13-201229-4 LC Card 84-17892 DDC 620/.00452 19
TA169 .H46 1985 ***NYPL [JSE 86-2491]***

How to buy an automated sales, marketing, and telemarketing system. Los Gatos, CA , c1985. 46 p. : LC Card 86-224565 DDC 658.8/0028/5 19
HF5415.1265 .H68 1985

Perkinson, Richard C. Data analysis . Wellesley, Mass. , c1984. xvii, 285 p. : ISBN 0-89435-105-2 LC Card 83-63212 DDC 001.64 19
QA76.9.D3 P46 1984 ***NYPL [JSE 85-1742]***

System design with Ada /. Buhr, R. J. A. Englewood Cliffs, N.J. , c1984. xv, 256 p. : ISBN 0-13-881623-9 : LC Card 83-13673 DDC 001.64/2 19
QA76.73.A35 B83 1984 ***NYPL [JSE 86-1253]***

A system for evaluating the performance of government-invested enterprises in Korea /. Park, Yung Chul. Washington, D.C. [1986] vi, 49 p. : ISBN 0-8213-0859-9 (pbk.) LC Card 86-28907 DDC 338.7/4/0723 19
HD4315.5 .P37 1986

System modeling and optimization. System modelling and optimization . Berlin , New York , c1986. xii, 1046 p. : ISBN 0-387-16854-0 (U. S.) LC Card 86-15637 DDC 003 19
QA402 .S95822 1986 ***NYPL [JSE 86-1775]***

System modelling and optimization : proceedings of the 12th IFIP Conference, Budapest, Hungary, September 2-6, 1985 / edited by A. Prékopa, J. Szelezsán, and B. Strazicky. Berlin ; New York : Springer-Verlag, c1986. xii, 1046 p. : ill. ; 25 cm. (Lecture notes in control and information sciences. 84) "This biannual IFIP TC-7 general conference was organized by the Jon von Neumann Society for Computer Sciences"--Pref. Includes bibliographies. ISBN 0-387-16854-0 (U. S.) LC Card 86-15637 DDC 003 19
1. System analysis - Congresses. 2. Mathematical models - Congresses. 3. Mathematical optimization - Congresses. I. Prékopa, András. II. Szelezsán, János. III. Strazicky, B. (Beátra), 1947-. IV. IFIP TC-7 (Organization). V. Neumann János Számitógéptudományu Társaság. VI. IFIP Conference on System Modeling and Optimization (12th : 1985 : Budapest, Hungary). VII. Title: System modeling and optimization.
QA402 .S95822 1986 ***NYPL [JSE 86-1775]***

SYSTEM UNCERTAINTY. see **UNCERTAINTY (INFORMATION THEORY)**

Systematic job evaluation and comparable worth /. Elizur, Dov. Aldershot, Hants, England , Brookfield, Vt., USA , c1987. xxiv, 290 p. : ISBN 0-566-05113-3 : LC Card 86-25702 DDC 658.3/06 19
HF5549.5.J62 E44 1987

Die Systematik der unternehmerischen Sicherungsmassnahmen /. Schlangen, Gerhard. Münster [1984?] vii, 179 p. : ISBN 3-88660-063-7 LC Card 84-166733
HD61 .S34 1984

Systematisk ledelse i mindre bedrifter /. Vanebo, Jan Ole, 1948- Kirkenær , 1980. 192 p. : ISBN 82-7048-171-8 : LC Card 82-105304
HD62.7 .V36 1980

Système agraire et pratiques paysannes dans les monts Dômes / G. Bazin ... [et al.]. Paris : Institut national de la recherche agronomique, 1983. xi, 318 p., [8] p. of plates : ill. ; 24 cm. Includes bibliographies. ISBN 2-85340-478-1 LC Card 84-216594
1. Agriculture - Economic aspects - France - Dômes Mountains. 2. Peasantry - France - Dômes Mountains. 3. Dômes Mountains (France) - Rural conditions. I. Bazin, G. II. Institut national de la recherche agronomique (France).
HD1950.D65 S97 1983

Système d'information sur les transports de marchandises. Les Transports routiers de marchandises effectués sur le territoire français par des véhicules étrangers /. Paris [1983] 26 p. ; LC Card 83-214677
HE5668.A6 T74 1983

Systèmes de production et transformations de l'agriculture / Didier Aubert ... [et al.]. Paris : Institut national de la recherche agronomique, 1985. 2 v. : ill. ; 25 cm. Includes bibliographies. CONTENTS. - 1. Essai de bilan des travaux du Département d'économie et sociologie rurales -- 2. Annexes : notes de lecture. ISBN 2-85340-715-2 (v. 1) LC Card 86-214407
1. Agriculture - Economic aspects - France. 2. Agricultural productivity - France. I. Aubert, Didier. II. Institut national de la recherche agronomique (France). Département d'économie et de sociologie rurales.
HD1945 .S97 1985

Systemet med särskilda dragningsrätter . Heinonen, Kerstin. Helsingfors , 1985. 65 p. ; ISBN 951-686-112-1 LC Card 86-175395
HG3898 .H45 1985

SYSTEMS ANALYSIS - CASE STUDIES.
A Casebook for systems development /. London , Baltimore, Md., USA , 1986. iv, 88, [1] p. : ISBN 0-7131-3600-6 LC Card 87-114266 DDC 658 19
HD31 .C3554 1986

A systems approach to small group interaction /. Tubbs, Stewart L., 1943- New York , 1987. p. cm. ISBN 0-394-36539-9 : LC Card 87-23394 DDC 302.3/4 19
HD66 .T82 1987

SYSTEMS BUILDING. see **INDUSTRIALIZED BUILDING.**

Systems economics : concepts, models, and multidisciplinary perspectives / edited by Karl A. Fox and Don G. Miles.1st ed. Ames : Iowa State University Press, 1987. xvii, 252 p. : ill. ; 24 cm. Includes bibliographies and indexes. ISBN 0-8138-1738-2 LC Card 86-27586 DDC 330 19
1. Economics. 2. Agriculture - Economic aspects. 3. Equilibrium (Economics). I. Fox, Karl August, 1917-. II. Miles, Don G.
HB171 .S99 1987

Systems for managing construction / edited by Peter R. Lansley and Peter A. Harlow. London ; New York : E. & F.N. Spon, 1987. p. cm. (Managing construction worldwide . v. 1) Bibliography: p. Includes index. ISBN 0-419-14000-X LC Card 87-20546 DDC 624/.068 s 624/.068 19
1. Construction industry - Management - Congresses. 2. Construction industry - Management - Case studies - Congresses. I. Lansley, Peter R. II. Harlow, P. A. (Peter Alan). III. Series.
HD9715.A2 M296 vol. 1

Systems of demand equations (including labour supply) for different states of the markets and for different regimes /. Bronsard, Camille. Montréal [198-] 28 p. ; LC Card 83-222220 DDC 338.5/212 19
HB801 .B77 1980z

Systems of profit measurement /. Baillie, John. New York , 1985. viii, 112 p. ; ISBN 0-85258-234-X (pbk.) LC Card 84-21578 DDC 657/.48 19
HF5681.I48 B34 1985

SYSTEMS OPTIMIZATION. see **MATHEMATICAL OPTIMIZATION.**

Systemy ekonomiczne, gospodarka rynkowa, gospodarka planowa. Samecki, Wiesław. Czego można oczekiwać od ekonomii /. Warszawa , 1981. 35 p. ; ISBN 83-202-0150-0 LC Card 86-150577
HC340.3 .S24 1981

Systemy organizacyjne / [zespół redakcyjny Zdzisław Hellwig, Ewa Konarzewska-Gubała]. [Wrocław] : Wydawn. Uczelniane Akademii Ekonomicznej we Wrocławiu, 1981. 75 p. : ill. ; 24 cm. (Prace naukowe Akademii Ekonomicznej imienia Oskara Langego we Wrocławiu . nr. 188) Includes bibliographical references. LC Card 83-161920
1. Organization - Addresses, essays, lectures. 2. Management - Addresses, essays, lectures. I. Hellwig, Zdzisław. II. Konarzewska-Gubała, Ewa. III. Series.
HB9 .B7522 nr. 188 HM131

Sywottek, Arnold, 1942- Arbeiter in Hamburg . Hamburg , c1983. 606 p. : ISBN 3-8103-0807-2 LC Card 86-174037
HD8460.H36 A73 1983

Szabad Európa Rádió. see **Radio Free Europe.**

Szabadfalvi, József. Árucsere és migráció . Miskolc , 1986. 237 p. : ISBN 963-01-6995-9 : LC Card 87-409685
HD5856.H9 A78 1986

Szabályozórendszer.
Hardy, Ilona. Gyakorlati útmutató a kötvény és a váltó használatához /. Budapest , 1986. 62 p. ; ISBN 963-621-315-1 LC Card 87-407776
HG5470.5.A3 H37 1986

A Szabályozórendszerre történő reagálás főbb termelőszövetkezeti tapasztalatai / Kapronczai I. ... [et al.]. Budapest : Szövetkezeti Kutató Intézet, 1985. 68 p. ; 29 cm. (Közlemények, 0133-4905 . 194) Bibliography: p. 62. LC Card 87-408583
1. Collective farms - Hungary - Management. I. Kapronczai, István. II. Series: Közlemények / Szövetkezeti Kutató Intézet, 194.
HD1492.H8 S92 1985

Szabó, A. Ferenc. Fejezetek a szocialista népesedéselmélet történetéből / Szabó A. Ferenc. [Budapest] : Művelődési Minisztérium Marxizmus-Leninizmus Oktatási Főosztálya, 1985. 94 p. ; 24 cm. (Tudományos szocializmus füzetek, 0321-5683 . 82) Summary in German and Russian. Bibliography: p. 83-91. ISBN 963-673-318-X LC Card 86-187050
1. Population. 2. Soviet Union - Population policy - History. 3. Communism and society. I. Title. II. Series.
HB871 .S86 1985

Szabó, Kálmán. Csernák, Józsefné. A családok és háztartások előreszámítása, 1981-2001 /. Budapest , 1985. 125 p. : LC Card 86-166603
HA1201 .A64 no. 59 HA1205

Szabó, László. Munkaszervezet és termelékenység a magyar parasztságnál a XIX-XX. században / Szabó László. Szolnok : [s.n.], 1968 (Debrecen : Szabadság Lapnyomda) 167 p. : ill. ; 20 cm. (A Damjanich János Múzeum közleményei . 15-18) Summary in German. Includes bibliographical references. LC Card 86-188720
1. Peasantry - Hungary - History. 2. Family farms - Hungary - History. 3. Farm management - Hungary - History. 4. Agricultural productivity - Hungary - History. I. Title. II. Series.
HD1536.H9 S89 1968

Szabó, Miklós. Lévai, Béla. Rádió-televízió anno-- /. Budapest , 1985. 94 p. : ISBN 963-223-331-X : LC Card 86-128497
HE8689.9.H8 L49 1985

Szabó, Sándor. A forgóeszköz finanszírozás elvei és gyakorlata / írta és összeállította, Szabó Sándor. [Budapest] : Állami Fejlesztési Bank, 1986. 67, [26] p. ; 30 cm. "Belső használatra." "Kapcsolódó jogszabályok jegyzéke": p. [25]-[26] (2nd group). LC Card 87-150669
1. Working capital. I. Title.
HG4028.W65 S93 1986

SZABOLCS-SZATMÁR MEGYE (HUNGARY) - INDUSTRIES - HISTORY.
Ipari üzemtörténet /. Nyíregyháza , 1979 ([Nyíregyháza] : Készült a Szabolcs-Szatmár Megyei Tanács Sokszorosító Költségvetési Üzemében) 228 p. : ISBN 963-01-2796-2 LC Card 81-173980
HC300.29.S92 I62 1979

A Szabolcs-Szatmár megyei télialma-termelés, -feldolgozás és -értékesítés rendszerének fejlesztése / [készült az Intézet Vállalati Együttműködési és Agrárszociológiai Főosztályán ; szerkesztette, Marillai Vilmos ; szerzők, Dénes Katalin ... et al.]. Budapest : Agrárgazdasági Kutató Intézet, 1985. 144 p. : ill. ; 28 cm. (Agrárgazdasági Kutató Intézet, 0209-5696 . 1985/8) Bibliography: p. 107. ISBN 963-491-208-7 LC Card 86-196831
1. Apple industry - Hungary - Szabolcs-Szatmár Megye. I. Marillai, Vilmos. II. Dénes, Katalin. III. Agrárgazdasági Kutató Intézet. Vállalati Együttműködési és Agrárszociológiai Főosztály. IV. Series: Agrárgazdasági Kutató Intézet (Series) , 1985/8.
HD9259.A6 H87 1985

Szajkó, Pál. A nyúlhústermelés és export gazdasági problémái / Szajkó Pál. Budapest : Agrárgazdasági Kutató Intézet, 1985. 57 p. : ill. ; 28 cm. (Agrárgazdasági Kutató Intézet, 0209-5696 . 1985/7) Bibliography: p. 51-52. ISBN 963-491-207-9 LC Card 86-196798
1. Rabbit meat industry - Hungary. I. Series: Agrárgazdasági Kutató Intézet (Series) , 1985/7. II. Title.
HD9438.R4 H97 1985

Szakács, Sándor. Pető, Iván. A hazai gazdaság négy évtizedének története, 1945-1985 /. Budapest , 1985- v. <1 > ; ISBN 963-221-553-2 (set) LC Card 87-105744
HC300.28 .P47 1985

Szakirodalmi Szemle (Országos Vezetőképző Központ (Hungary). Tudományos Tájékoztató Szolgálat)
Hatékony vezetői időgazdálkodás . Budapest , 1984. 62 p. ; ISBN 963-7902-09-0 (Magy. nemz. bibl.) LC Card 85-177403
HD69.T54 H38 1984

Szakmai kiskönyvtár.
Munkaügy a belkereskedelemben /. [Budapest] , 1986. 272 p. ; ISBN 963-01-7513-4 : LC Card 87-148137
HF5549.2.H85 M86 1986

Szakszervezetek Elméleti Kutató Intézete.
A Folyamatos árszinvonal-emelkedés társadalmi hatásai . Budapest [1985] 176 p. ; ISBN 963-608-087-9 LC Card 87-407751
HG970.5 .F65 1985

Héthy, Lajos. A vezetők részvétele a vezetésben /. Budapest , 1983. 87 p. : ISBN 963-608-057-7 LC Card 85-110905
HD38.25.H9 H47 1983

Szakszervezetek Elméleti Kutató Intézete. Információs- és Közvéleménykutató Részleg.
Györgypál, Katalin. A magyar szakszervezetek napjainkban . Budapest , 1984. 128 p. ; ISBN 963-608-062-3 LC Card 85-230460
HD6680.5 .G96 1984

Szakszervezetek Elméleti Kutató Intézete. Gazdaság- és Életszinvonalpolitikai Részleg.
Magyar, Lajosné. A munkaviszonyok humanizálása . Budapest [1985] 210 p. ; ISBN 963-608-075-5 LC Card 85-154632
HD6955 .M27 1985

A szakszervezetek és a tervezés /. Halmos, Csaba. Budapest , 1983. 178 p. ; ISBN 963-608-052-6 LC Card 85-108502
HD6680.5 .H34 1983

A Szakszervezetek kulturális, agitációs és propagandamunkájának kézikönyve / [szerkesztette, Roland Ferenc ; szerzők, Balog István ... et al.]. [Budapest] : Népszava, 1986. 246 p. : ill. ; 20 cm. (Szakszervezeti aktivisták kézikönyve) "A kézikönyv IV. fejezete A szakszervezetek agitációs és propagandamunkájának kézikönyve, Népszava, 1982. című kiadvány módosított változata"--T.p. verso. ISBN 963-322-335-0 : LC Card 87-409655
1. Trade-unions - Hungary. 2. Public relations - Trade-unions. I. Roland, Ferenc. II. Balog, István. III. Roland, Ferenc. Szakszervezetek agitációs és propagandamunkájának kézikönyve. 1986. IV. Series.
HD6680.5 .S874 1986

A szakszervezetek Magyarországon /. Buza, Márton. [Budapest] , 1985. 229 p. ; ISBN 963-09-2747-0 : LC Card 86-190979
HD6680.5 .B89 1985

Szakszervezetek Országos Tanácsa. A Magyar szakszervezetek feladatai a gazdaságirányítás továbbfejlesztésének segítésében . Budapest , 1984. 47 p. ; ISBN 963-322-215-X LC Card 85-176937
HC300.28 .M3297 1984

A szakszervezetek változó szerepe a gazdaság szabályozásában az európai fejlett tőkésországokban /. Forgács, Pál. Budapest , 1985. 118 p. ; ISBN 963-608-079-8 LC Card 86-228056
HD5660.E9 F67 1985

Szakszervezeti aktivisták kézikönyve.
A Szakszervezetek kulturális, agitációs és propagandamunkájának kézikönyve /. [Budapest] , 1986. 246 p. : ISBN 963-322-335-0 : LC Card 87-409655
HD6680.5 .S874 1986

Szalai, Erzsébet. Kiemelt vállalat, beruházás, érdek / Szalai Erzsébet. Budapest : Akadémiai Kiadó, 1981. 140 p. ; 24 cm. (A Szocialista vállalat . 11) ISBN 963-05-2527-5 LC Card 81-170685
1. Capital investments - Hungary - Case studies. 2. Industrial management - Hungary - Case studies. 3. Business enterprises - Hungary - Finance - Case studies. I. Title. II. Series.
HG4028.C4 S96 1981

Szalai, Júlia. Érettségizettek a munkaerőpiacon /. Budapest , 1985. 124 p. ; ISBN 963-404-026-8 LC Card 87-409614
HD6276.H82 E73 1985

A szállitási rendszer fejlesztési lehetőségeinek vizsgálata a tejiparban /. Csatorday, Géza. Budapest , 1985. 94 p. : ISBN 963-491-216-8 LC Card 86-199210
HE199.5.M5 C73 1985

A számítástechnika felhasználása a fejlődés előmozdítására . Application of computer technology for development. Hungarian. [Budapest] [1971] 95 p. : LC Card 85-178670
HD85.H88 A6615 1971

Számítógépes vállalati tervezés /. Barakonyi, Károly. Budapest , 1984. 320, [1] p. : ISBN 963-221-456-0 (Magy. nemz. bibl.) : LC Card 85-174882
HD30.2 .B36 1984

Szándékok és lehetőségek . Lugossy, Györgyi. Budapest , 1985. 85 p. : ISBN 963-491-215-X LC Card 86-199350
HD1492.H82 S665 1985

Szanton, Peter L. Baltimore 2000 : a choice of futures : a report to the Morris Goldseker Foundation / Peter L. Szanton. [Baltimore, Md.] : The Foundation, c1986. v, 51 p. : ill. ; 25 cm. LC Card 87-125975 DDC 330.9752/71043 19
1. Economic forecasting - Maryland - Baltimore. 2. Baltimore (Md.) - Economic conditions. I. Morris Goldseker Foundation (Baltimore, Md.). II. Title. III. Title: Baltimore two thousand.
HC108.B2 S9 1986

Szász, Kálmán. A mezőgazdaság nemzetközi összehasonlításának módszerei : szakirodalmi tájékoztató / Szász Kálmán. Budapest : KSH Könyvtár és Dokumentációs Szolgálat, 1986. 96 p. ; 25 cm. (Statisztikai módszerek, témadokumentáció, 0139-1453 . 18) Summary in English and Russian. Bibliography: p. 85-92. ISBN 963-02-4381-4 LC Card 87-419792
1. Agriculture - Economic aspects - Statistics - Comparative method. 2. Agriculture - Statistics - Comparative method. I. Title. II. Series.
HD1425 .S95 1986

Szathmári, Gábor. Kinek lehet igaza? : gondolatok munkáról, magánéletről és mindarról, ami elnyűheti vagy boldoggá teheti az embert / Szathmári Gábor. Budapest : Népszava, 1985. 118 p. ; 20 cm. (Fórum, 0230-8118) ISBN 963-322-273-7 : LC Card 86-156416
1. Industrial sociology. 2. Quality of work life. 3. Labor and laboring classes - Conduct of life. I. Series: Fórum (Budapest, Hungary). II. Title.
HD6955 .S975 1985

Szatmári, Tamás. Kardos, Péter. Külföldi licencek a magyar gazdaságban /. Budapest , 1984. 204, [1] p. : ISBN 963-221-396-3 : LC Card 85-157267
HF1429 .K37 1984

Szczecińskie Towarzystwo Naukowe, Wydział Nauk Społecznych (Series) .
(t. 31) Głowacki, Andrzej. Ruch robotniczy na Pomorzu Zachodnim do 1914 roku /. Warszawa , 1979. 160 p. ; ISBN 83-01-01306-0 LC Card 81-107475
HD8457.P66 G56 1979

Szegedi, Nándor. Probáld, Ferenc, 1941- Az európai tőkés országok gazdaságföldrajza . Budapest , 1984. 361 p. : ISBN 963-17-7607-7 : LC Card 85-154701
HC240 .P738 1984

Szegö, G. P. International finance and trade /. Cambridge, Mass. , c1979. 2 v. : ISBN 0-88410-680-2 LC Card 79-11158 DDC 332.4/5 19
HG3881 .I57617 ***NYPL [JLL 80-187]***

Szekér, Gyula.
A kemizálás és a magyar vegyipar / Szekér Gyula. Budapest : Műszaki Könyvkiadó, 1985. 340 p. : ill. (some col.) ; 25 cm. Bibliography: p. 317-318. ISBN 963-10-6508-1 : LC Card 86-127325
1. Chemical industry - Hungary. I. Title.
HD9656.H92 S86 1985

Műszaki fejlesztés, versenyképesség / Szekér Gyula. [Budapest] : Kossuth, 1984. 136 p. ; 20 cm. (Távlatok, 0236-8714) ISBN 963-09-2534-6 : LC Card 85-177507
1. Technological innovations - Hungary. 2. Technological innovations - Government policy - Hungary. 3. Technology and state - Hungary. I. Title.
HC300.295.T4 S97 1984

Szekfű, András. A tömegkommunikáció új útjai / Szekfű András. [Budapest] : Kossuth, 1984. 102 p. : ill. ; 20 cm. (Távlatok, 0236-8714) ISBN 963-09-2552-4 : LC Card 85-174804
1. Telecommunication. 2. Mass media. I. Title.
HE7631 .S98 1984

Szelecki, György.
Mit kell tudni a KGST-ről? / írta, Szelecki György. [Budapest] : Kossuth, 1986. 126, [5] p. : ill. ; 19 cm. (Mit kell tudni, 0324-7813) Bibliography: p. [129]-[131] ISBN 963-09-2731-4 : LC Card 86-210839
1. Council for Mutual Economic Assistance. I. Title. II. Series.
HC243.5 .S94 1986

Sándorné Szennyessy, Judit. Gazdaságpolitikai kézikönyv /. [Budapest] , 1985. 170 p. : LC Card 86-186314
HC300.28 .S26 1985

Szelényi, Iván. Socialist entrepreneurs : embourgeoisement in rural Hungary / Iván Szelényi in collaboration with Robert Manchin ... [et al.]. Madison, Wis. : University of Wisconsin Press, 1988. p. cm. Bibliography: p. ISBN 0-299-11360-4 : LC Card 87-16085 DDC 338.1/09439 19
1. Agriculture - Economic aspects - Hungary. 2. Hungary - Rural conditions. 3. Peasantry - Hungary. 4. Communism - Hungary. 5. Capitalism - Hungary. I. Title.
HD1940.5 .S94 1988

Szelezsán, János. System modelling and optimization . Berlin , New York , c1986. xii, 1046 p. : ISBN 0-387-16854-0 (U. S.) LC Card 86-15637 DDC 003 19
QA402 .S95822 1986 ***NYPL [JSE 86-1775]***

Szemelvények a szakszervezetek agitációs, propaganda- és kulturális tevékenységéből, 1948-1980 /. Kolozsvári, Ernő. Budapest , 1982. 43 p. : ISBN 963-321-957-4 LC Card 83-229170
HD6680.5.Z6 K64 1982

Személyiségfejlesztés és pályaválasztás /. Ritoók, Pálné. Budapest , 1986. 192 p. ; ISBN 963-17-8713-3 : LC Card 87-408516
HF5381 .R635 1986

A személyzeti munka gyakorlati kérdései a mezőgazdasági termelőszövetkezetekben /. Németi, László. [Budapest] , 1984. 243 p. ; ISBN 963-502-370-7 LC Card 86-147870
HD1492.H8 N43 1984

Személyzeti munka, társadalmi környezet /. Illisz, László. [Budapest] , 1986. 159 p. : ISBN 963-09-2778-0 : LC Card 87-408532
HF5549.2.H85 I44 1986

Szemere, Mátyás. A Vállalati tervezés uj módszere . [Pécs] [1985?] 167 p. : LC Card 86-187131
HD29 .V35 1985

Szénay, Lászlóné. A közgazdasági szabályozás és az élelmiszeripari szakágazatok gazdasági eredményeinek összefüggései és problémái az 1977-82 közötti években / Szénay Lászlóné, Spekner Ágnes. Budapest : Agrárgazdasági Kutató Intézet, 1984. 161 p. ; 29 cm. (Agrárgazdasági Kutató Intézet, 0209-5696 . 1984/18) Bibliography: p. 95-99. ISBN 963-491-196-X LC Card 86-199432
1. Food industry and trade - Hungary. 2. Food industry and trade - Government policy - Hungary. 3. Food industry and trade - Hungary - Finance. I. Spekner, Ágnes. II. Series: Agrárgazdasági Kutató Intézet (Series) , 1984/18. III. Title.
HD9015.H82 S935 1984

Szentiványi, Iván. Lakossági pénzügyek, pénzintézeti tevékenység / Szentiványi Iván. Budapest : Közgazdasági és Jogi Könyvkiadó, 1985. 563, [1] p. ; 21 cm. Bibliography: p. 561-[564] ISBN 963-221-602-4 : LC Card 86-186953
1. Finance - Hungary. 2. Finance, Personal - Hungary. 3. Financial institutions - Hungary. I. Title.
HG186.H8 S94 1985

Szép, György. Az Állami vállalatok szervezete, vezetése, működése és irányítása /. Budapest , 1985. 262 p. ; ISBN 963-322-140-4 : LC Card 86-202934
HD4160.5 .A78 1985

Szervezési és Vezetési Tudományos Társaság. Baranya Megyei Szervezet. A Vállalati tervezés uj módszere . [Pécs] [1985?] 167 p. : LC Card 86-187131
HD29 .V35 1985

Szervezési módszerek, 0139-262X .
(45. köt) Palicz, András. Az önálló vállalattá szervezés elméleti és módszertani megalapozása /. Budapest , 1984. 81 p. : ISBN 963-02-3351-7 : LC Card 86-126838
HD70.H8 P35 1984

Szewach, Enrique. Fundación de Investigaciones Económicas Latinoamericanas (Buenos Aires, Argentina) Gasto público . [Buenos Aires] , 1986. 6 v. in 8 : LC Card 87-403573 DDC 354.820072/252 19
HJ2075 .F86 1986

Szilagyi, Andrew D. Organizational behavior and performance / Andrew D. Szilagyi, Jr., Marc J. Wallace, Jr. 4th ed. Glenview, Ill. : Scott, Foresman, c1987. 742 p. : ill. ; 25 cm. Includes bibliographies and indexes. ISBN 0-673-16664-3 : LC Card 86-26087 DDC 658.4 19
1. Organizational behavior. I. Wallace, Marc J., 1944-. II. Title.
HD58.7 .S97 1987

Szilágyi, Klára J. A pályafejlődés vizsgálatának módszertani lehetőségei a felsőoktatásban / J. Szilágyi Klára, Völgyesy Pál. Budapest : Oktatáskutató Intézet, 1985. 110 p. ; 29 cm. Bibliography: p. 107-110. ISBN 963-404-020-9 LC Card 86-174899
1. Vocational guidance - Hungary. 2. Vocational interests - Hungary. 3. College graduates - Employment - Hungary. I. Völgyesy, Pál. II. Title.
HF5429.6.H8 S95 1985

Szilvássy, Erika. A nemzetközi pénzügyek és a külkereskedelmi fizetések gyakorlata / Szilvássy, Hidas. 2., átdolg. és bőv. kiad. Budapest : Közgazdasági és Jogi Könyvkiadó, 1985. 286 p. ; 21 cm. Bibliography: p. 262-[263] Includes index. ISBN 963-221-529-X : LC Card 86-190902
1. International finance. 2. International clearing. 3. Foreign exchange. 4. Foreign exchange problem - Hungary. I. Hidas, János. II. Title.
HG3881 .S95 1985

Szira, Tamás. A dinamikus egyensúly néhány elméleti kérdése / Szira Tamás. Budapest : Akadémiai Kiadó, 1986. 433, [1] p. ; 25 cm. Bibliography: p. 430-[434] ISBN 963-05-3987-X : LC Card 86-187062
1. Equilibrium (Economics). I. Title.
HB145 .S95 1986

Szirmai, Adam, 1946- Inequality observed : a study of attitudes towards income inequality / Adam Szirmai. Aldershot, Hants, England ; Brookfield, Vt., USA : Avebury, c1988. p. cm. Bibliography: p. ISBN 0-566-05549-X : LC Card 87-23071 DDC 339.2/09492 19
1. Income distribution - Netherlands - Public opinion. 2. Public opinion - Netherlands. I. Title.
HC329.5.I5 S96 1988

Szkice o wolności /. Karpiński, Wojciech. Chicago, Ill. (2886 Milwaukee Ave., Chicago, Ill. 60618) , 1980. 95 p. ; LC Card 81-201974
JC585 .K32 1980 ***NYPL [*QR 86-4376]***

SZKOŁA GŁÓWNA PLANOWANIA I STATYSTYKI (WARSAW, POLAND) - HISTORY.
Wyższa Szkoła Handlowa, Szkoła Głòwna Handlowa, Miejska Szkoła Handlowa, 1906-1945 /. Warszawa , 1984. 180 p. : LC Card 85-241871
HB74.9.P7 W98 1984

Szmrecsányi, Tamás, 1936- Getúlio Vargas e a economia contemporânea /. Campinas , 1986. 179 p. ; ISBN 85-26-80033-7 LC Card 87-403048 DDC 330.981/063 19
HC187 .G45 1986

A Szocialista nagyüzemek főbb ágazatainak költség- és jövedelemhelyzete 1984-ben / [készült a Költség- és Árelemzési Főosztály Mezőgazdasági Költség- és Árelemzési Osztályán ; összeállította, Tomka József]. Budapest : Mezőgazdasági és Élelmezésügyi Minisztérium Statisztikai és Gazdaságelemző Központ, 1985. 35, [46] p. ; 29 cm. (Mezőgazdasági és Élelmezésügyi Minisztérium Statisztika és Gazdaságelemző Központ . 1985-1) Chiefly tables. LC Card 85-177804
1. Collective farms - Hungary - Finance - Statistics. 2. State farms - Hungary - Finance - Statistics. 3. Agriculture - Hungary - Finance - Statistics. I. Tomka, József. II. Hungary. Statisztikai és Gazdaságelemző Központ. Mezőgazdasági Költség- és Árelemzési Osztály. III. Series: Mezőgazdasági és Élelmezésügyi Minisztérium Statisztikai és Gazdaságelemző Központ (Series) , 1985/1.
HD1492.H8 S93 1985

A Szocialista vállalat .
(11) Szalai, Erzsébet. Kiemelt vállalat, beruházás, érdek /. Budapest , 1981. 140 p. ; ISBN 963-05-2527-5 LC Card 81-170685
HG4028.C4 S96 1981

(13) Barta, Imre. A beruházások döntéselőkészítése /. Budapest , 1986. 185, [1] p. : ISBN 963-05-4182-3 : LC Card 87-408029
HG4028.C4 B335 1986

Szocialista vállalkozási szektor. Koncepció és kritika . Budapest , c1985. 387 p. ; ISBN 963-14-0359-9 : LC Card 86-104222
HB615 .K66 1985

Szocializmus és reform /. Berend, T. Iván (Tibor Iván), 1930- Budapest , 1986. 194, [1] p. ; ISBN 963-05-4386-9 : LC Card 87-407684
HC300.28 .B475 1986

Szőlőtermelés : községsoros adatok, 1873-1965 / [összeállította a Központi Statisztikai Hivatal Mezőgazdasági Statisztikai Főosztályának Összeirási Osztálya]. Budapest : Központi Statisztikai Hivatal, 1986. 519 p. ; 29 cm. (Történeti statisztikai kötetek, 0139-0279) Introductory materials in English, Hungarian and Russian. Tables. ISBN 963-340-777-X : LC Card 86-196884
1. Viticulture - Hungary - Statistics - History. 2. Wine industry - Hungary - Statistics - History. 3. Grape industry - Hungary - Statistics - History. I. Hungary. Központi Statisztikai Hivatal. Mezőgazdasági Statisztikai Főosztály. Összeirási Osztály. II. Series.
HD9385.H82 S95 1986

Szövetkezetelmélet, szövetkezetpolitika, szövetkezeti jog /. Nagy, László, 1914- Budapest , 1986. 299, [1] p. ; ISBN 963-221-904-X : LC Card 87-138020 DDC 334/.09439 19
HD3492.5.A4 N34 1986

Szövetkezeti gazdálkodás elemzése /. Lukács, Lajos. Budapest , 1983. 155 p. : ISBN 963-03-2028-2 (Magy. nemz. bibl.) LC Card 85-184472
HF5686.C67 L84 1983

Szövetkezetipolitikai, szövetkezetelméleti ismeretek /. Gyenes, Antal. Budapest , 1974. 217 p. ; LC Card 87-113832
HD3492.5.A4 G94 1974

Szpirulisz, Ildikó. Gazdaság és társadalom a nyolcvanas években Magyarországon /. Budapest , 1986- v. <1 > ; ISBN 963-7700-19-6 (set) LC Card 87-136629
HC300.28 .G265 1986

Szretter, Héctor. La terciarización del empleo en la Argentina. El sector del servicio doméstico. Buenos Aires : República Argentina, Ministerio de Trabajo y Seguridad Social : Secretaría de Planificación, 1985. iv, 82, 3 p. ; 30 cm. (Estudios y documentos de trabajo sobre empleo, remuneraciones y recursos humanos) "Proyecto Gobierno Argentino, Programa de las Naciones Unidas para el Desarrollo, Organización Internacional del Trabajo." Includes bibliographies. "ARG/84/029." LC Card 87-122558 DDC 331.7/6164046/0982 19
1. Domestics - Argentina. I. Argentina. Ministerio de Trabajo y Seguridad Social. II. Argentina. Secretaría de Planificación. III. Title. IV. Series.
HD8039.D52 A657 1985

Szűcs, Ferenc. Közgazdasági bizottságok kézikönyve /. Budapest , 1984. 324 p. ; ISBN 963-322-017-3 : LC Card 85-126303
HC300.28 .K68 1984

Szűcs, Lajos. A Magyaróvári Timföld és Műkorundgyár története, 1934-1984. 2. kiad. [Mosonmagyaróvár : MOTIM, 1984] 320 p. : ill. ; 26 cm. Summary in English, German and Russian. Includes bibliographical references. ISBN 963-02-3415-7 LC Card 86-127345
1. Magyaróvári Timföld és Műkorundgyár (Hungary) - History. 2. Aluminum industry and trade - Hungary - History. I. Title.
HD9539.A63 H858 1984

Szukicsné Serfőző, Klára. Budapest és Pest megye népességfejlődése, az ezredfordulóig várható tendenciák / [irta, Szukicsné Serfőző Klára]. Budapest : Statisztikai Kiadó, 1984. 88 p. : ill. ; 29 cm. (A Központi Statisztikai Hivatal Népességtudományi Kutató Intézetének kutatási jelentései, 0236-736X . 22) Bibliography: p. 86. LC Card 86-157549
1. Budapest (Hungary) - Population - Statistics. 2. Pest Megye (Hungary) - Population - Statistics. 3. Population forecasting - Hungary - Budapest - Statistics. 4. Population forecasting - Hungary - Pest Megye - Forecasting - Statistics. I. Title. II. Series.
HA1208.B96 S98 1984

Szymański, Kiejstut R. Kowtun, Józef. Rola, funkcje i zadania mistrza w systemie dokształcania i wychowania robotników /. Warszawa , 1979. 151, [1] p. ; LC Card 81-180277
HF5549.5.T7 K687 1979

T.G.L.P. and hunter-gatherers. Wily, Liz. The TGLP and hunter-gatherers . Gaborone, Botswana , 1981. ii, 102 p. ; LC Card 82-207525
DT797 W55 1981 ***NYPL [JLG 87-6]***

T. Ø. I. see **Transportøkonomisk institutt.**

T-one products and services. T-1 products & services. Norwalk, Conn., U. S.A. (6 Prowitt St., Norwalk 06855) , c1987. iv, 181 leaves : LC Card 87-129537 DDC 384.6/5 19
HD9697.T452 T17 1987

T.R.Y.S.E.M. Training of rural youth for self-employment (TRYSEM) . Hyderabad, [India] , 1981. vii, 252 p. ; LC Card 81-904606

DDC 331.3/42492/0954 19
HD5715.5.I5 T72 1981
NYPL [JLF 86-1203]

T. U. C. see **Trades Union Congress.**

T.U.C. overseas. Nicholson, Marjorie. The TUC overseas . London , Boston , c1986. xvi, 329 p. ; ISBN 0-04-331103-2 (alk. paper) LC Card 85-28607 DDC 331.88/0941 19
HD8383 .N52 1986 *NYPL [JLD 86-2932]*

T-1 products & services. Norwalk, Conn., U. S.A. (6 Prowitt St., Norwalk 06855) : International Resource Development, c1987. iv, 181 leaves : ill. ; 28 cm. (Report / International Resource Development Inc. . #726) "February 1987." LC Card 87-129537 DDC 384.6/5 19
1. Telephone supplies industry. 2. Telephone - Multiplex systems. 3. Market surveys. I. International Resource Development, inc. II. Title: T-one products and services. III. Series: Report / International Resource Development Inc. , #726.
HD9697.T452 T17 1987

Taarifa ya utekelezaji wa mpango wa pili wa taifa wa kujihami kiuchumi, Januari-Agosti, 1982. [Dar es Salaam] : Jamhuri ya Muungano wa Tanzania, Wizara ya Mipango na Uchumi, 1982. 46 p. ; 21 cm. In Swahili. LC Card 83-980744
1. Tanzania - Economic policy. I. Tanzania. Wizara ya Mipango na Uchumi.
HC885 .T28 1982

Tabachnikas, B. I. Ėkonomicheskie interesy i uskorenie nauchno-tekhnicheskogo progressa . Leningrad , 1984. 157 p. ; LC Card 86-186728
HC340.T4 E36 1984

TABACOS MEXICANOS, S.A. DE C.V. - HISTORY.
Chumacero, Antonio. Origen de una empresa pública . Tepic, Nayarit , 1985 [i.e. 1986] xviii, 279 p. : LC Card 87-145432 DDC 338.7/6371/0972 19
HD9144.M44 T333 1986

Die Tabakarbeiterin in Baden, 1870-1914 /. Gensewich, Irmtraud. Mannheim , 1986. 496 p. : ISBN 3-87804-183-7 LC Card 87-121532 DDC 331.4/8797/094346 19
HD6073.T62 G34 1986

TABASCO (MEXICO : STATE) - ECONOMIC CONDITIONS.
Tostado Gutiérrez, Marcela. El Tabasco porfiriano /. Villahermosa [Mexico] , 1985. 179 p. : ISBN 968-88900-7-3 LC Card 86-189960
HC137.T3 T67 1985

TABASCO (MEXICO : STATE) - POLITICS AND GOVERNMENT.
Tostado Gutiérrez, Marcela. El Tabasco porfiriano /. Villahermosa [Mexico] , 1985. 179 p. : ISBN 968-88900-7-3 LC Card 86-189960
HC137.T3 T67 1985

TABASCO (MEXICO : STATE) - SOCIAL CONDITIONS.
Tostado Gutiérrez, Marcela. El Tabasco porfiriano /. Villahermosa [Mexico] , 1985. 179 p. : ISBN 968-88900-7-3 LC Card 86-189960
HC137.T3 T67 1985

El Tabasco porfiriano /. Tostado Gutiérrez, Marcela. Villahermosa [Mexico] , 1985. 179 p. : ISBN 968-88900-7-3 LC Card 86-189960
HC137.T3 T67 1985

Tabellen zur Ermittlung der Mehrwertsteuer aus dem Brutto-Rechnungsbetrag. 9. Aufl. Stuttgart : R. Boorberg, 1983. 38 p. ; 21 cm. (Schriftenreihe "Das Recht der Wirtschaft" . Heft 138) "Die vorliegende Tabelle gilt ab 1.7.1983." ISBN 3-415-01033-3 LC Card 83-223907
1. Value-added tax - Germany, West. 2. Value-added tax - Rates and tables.
HJ5715.G3 T32 1983

Table de concertation sur l'industrie du vêtement (1985 : Montréal, Québec) Rapport de la Table de concertation sur l'industrie du vêtement : Montréal, le 29 mars 1985. [Québec] : Secrétariat permanent des Conférences socio-économiques du Québec, [1985] v, 174, 12 p. ; 28 cm. (Les Conférences socio-économiques du Québec) Cover title: Industrie du vêtement : le défi du redéveloppement. LC Card 87-103889
1. Clothing trade - Québec (Province) - Congresses. 2. Clothing trade - Canada - Congresses. I. Title. II. Title: Industrie du vêtement. III. Series.
HD9940.C22 Q847 1985

Tableaux de l'état physique et moral des salariés en France / Villermé. Paris : La Découverte, 1986. 237 p. ; 23 cm. (Cahiers libres) ISBN 2-7071-1626-2 : LC Card 87-122301
1. Labor and laboring classes - France. 2. Industrial relations - France. 3. Business enterprises - France. I. Villermé (Association).
HD8431 .T32 1986

Tableaux normalisés simplifiés par région et département . Kerromes, Armelle. Paris [1984] 273 p. ; ISBN 2-11-064692-6 : LC Card 86-176720
HA1214 1982p

Tables on houses and disabled population, series 23, West Bengal / S.N. Ghosh (Director of Census Operations, West Bengal). Delhi : Controller of Publications, 1986. v, 128 p. ; 31 cm. At head of title: Census of India, 1981. Numbered pt. VII in the scheme of the national census. "PTG.2.81 (West Bengal)/300-1986 (DSK.II)"--P. [4] of cover. LC Card 87-900630
1. Households - India - West Bengal - Statistics. 2. Handicapped - India - West Bengal - Statistics. 3. West Bengal (India) - Population - Statistics. 4. West Bengal (India) - Census, 1981. 5. India - Census, 1981. I. Ghosh, S. N., 1943-. II. India. Director of Census Operations, West Bengal.
HA4587.W47 T33 1986

Taboada, Néstor. see **Taboada Terán, Néstor.**

Taboada Terán, Néstor. Historia de las luchas sociales y el movimiento obrero en Bolivia / Néstor Taboada Terán. Cochabamba, Bolivia : Instituto de Formación y Capacitación, 1983- v. <1-3 > : ill. (some col.) ; 33 cm. (v. 2-<3 >: Historia y realidad del movimiento popular en Bolivia) Vols. <2-3 > have title: Historia de las luchas sociales y el movimiento obrero de Bolivia. Includes bibliographies. CONTENTS. - 1. De la servidumbre de los hombres comunes a la libertad -- 2. Los frutos del árbol de la libertad -- 3. La guerra de clases ha comenzado LC Card 86-203884 DDC 331.88/0984 19
1. Labor and laboring classes - Bolivia - History - Collected works. 2. Bolivia - Social conditions - Collected works. I. Instituto de Formación y Capacitación (Bolivia). II. Series: Historia y realidad del movimiento popular en Bolivia. III. Title.
HD8275 .T32 1983

Taborelli, Giorgio. Commercio in Lombardia /. Milano , c1986- v. <1 > : LC Card 87-158732
HF3589.L65 C65 1986

Tabutin, Dominique. Les transitions de mortalité dans le Tiersmonde : quelques problèmes et aspects explicatifs / Dominique Tabutin. Louvain-la-Neuve, Belgique : Ciaco éditeur, [1985] 33 p. : ill. ; 24 cm. (Working paper . no 127) "Ce texte est, à quelques nuances près, celui d'une communication sollicitée pour les Journées démographiques de l'ORSTOM qui se sont tenues à Paris du 23 au 25 septembre 1985." Summary in English. Bibliography: p. 29-32. LC Card 86-178578
1. Mortality - Developing countries. 2. Developing countries - Statistics, Vital. 3. Developing countries - Economic conditions. I. Series: Working paper (Université catholique de Louvain (1970-). Département de démographie) , no 127. II. Title.
HB1528 .T33 1985

Tachi, Ryūichirō, 1921- Japan and the United States today . New York , 1986, c1987. vii, 234 p. : ISBN 0-231-06575-2 LC Card 86-32640 DDC 332/.042/0952 19
HG3903 .J35 1987

El Táchira fronterizo . Muñoz, Arturo Guillermo. Caracas , 1985. 315 p. ; ISBN 980-265-178-8 LC Card 87-402928 DDC 330.987/120633 19
HC238.T3 M86 1985

TÁCHIRA (VENEZUELA) - ECONOMIC CONDITIONS.
Muñoz, Arturo Guillermo. El Táchira fronterizo . Caracas , 1985. 315 p. ; ISBN 980-265-178-8 LC Card 87-402928 DDC 330.987/120633 19
HC238.T3 M86 1985

Tachydromikē historia Krētikēs Politeias, 1900-1913 /. Marinakēs, Markos, 1945- Athēna , 1983. 127 p. : LC Card 85-151773
HE7180.5.Z7 C746 1983
NYPL [JFD 86-10347]

Tachydromikon Tamieutērion (Greece) Ekthesis peri tēs kinēseōs kai anaptyxeōs tou Tach. Tamieutēriou kata to etos 1934, kai kata ta proēgēthenta etē apo tēs hidryseōs tou / Hypourgeion Synkoinōnias, Tachydromikon Tamieutērion. Athēna : TTT, 1935. 67 p., [3] folded leaves of plates : ill. ; 29 cm. LC Card 87-109911
1. Tachydromikon Tamieutērion (Greece).
HG1956.G85 T33 1935

TACHYDROMIKON TAMIEUTĒRION (GREECE)
Tachydromikon Tamieutērion (Greece) Ekthesis peri tēs kinēseōs kai anaptyxeōs tou Tach. Tamieutēriou kata to etos 1934, kai kata ta proēgēthenta etē apo tēs hidryseōs tou /. Athēna , 1935. 67 p., [3] folded leaves of plates : LC Card 87-109911
HG1956.G85 T33 1935

Tack, Alfred. Marketing strategy in action / Alfred Tack. Aldershot, Hants, England : Gower, c1987. v, 245 p. ; 23 cm. ISBN 0-566-02668-6 LC Card 86-229563 DDC 658.8 19
1. Marketing. I. Title.
HF5415 .T29 1987

Tack Management Consultants. Salesmen's cars, expenses, and allowances, 1963 / compiled and published by Tack Management Consultants Ltd. London : Tack Management Consultants, [1963?] 163 p. ; 31 cm. "A Tack survey." LC Card 86-173421
1. Sales personnel - Great Britain - Salaries, etc. 2. Traveling sales personnel - Great Britain - Salaries, etc. 3. Automobiles, Company - Great Britain. I. Title.
HF5439.7 .T33 1963

Tactical military communications in Europe. The Military tactical communications switching network market in West Europe. New York, N.Y. , c1983. xvi, 232 p. ; LC Card 87-141849
HD9744.C653 E854 1983

TAD-report .
(no. 26) Kebschull, Dietrich. Transmigration in Indonesia . Hamburg , 1984. xxiv, 134 p. ; LC Card 86-223779 DDC 304.8/09598 19
HB2107 .K4 1984

Tadini, Venilton. O setor de bens de capital sob encomenda : análise do desenvolvimento recente, 1974/83 / Venilton Tadini. São Paulo : Instituto de Pesquisas Econômicas, 1986. 142 p. : ill. ; 23 cm. (Série Ensaios econômicos . no. 57) Bibliography: p. 139-142. LC Card 87-154239 DDC 332/.0414/0981 19
1. Capital investments - Brazil. 2. Industrial equipment - Brazil. 3. Industry and state - Brazil. 4. Brazil - Industries. I. Series: Ensaios econômicos (Universidade de São Paulo. Instituto de Pesquisas Econômicas) , 57. II. Title.
HC190.C3 T33 1986

Taeger, Jürgen. Die Volkszählung /. Reinbek bei Hamburg , 1983. 284 p. : ISBN 3-499-15245-2 : LC Card 84-110844
HA1234 1983

Das tägliche Duell zwischen Handel und Verbraucher . Rösch, Willi. [München-Gräfelfing] , c1975. 110 p. : LC Card 84-121903
HF5429.6.G42 R67 1975

Taehan Muyŏk Chinhŭng Kongsa. Korean parts directory. [Seoul] , 1986. 514 p. ; LC Card 86-231593
HD9705.5.P373 K676 1986

Taetzsch, Lyn. Taking charge on the job : techniques for assertive management / Lyn Taetzsch, Eileen Benson ; edited by Robert Freiberg. New York : Executive Enterprises Publications Co., c1978. 144 p. ; 24 cm. Bibliography: p. 143-144. ISBN 0-917386-22-1 : LC Card 78-111025 DDC 658.4
1. Management - Psychological aspects. 2. Assertiveness (Psychology). I. Benson, Eileen, joint author. II. Freiberg, Robert. III. Title. IV. Title: Assertive management.
HD38 .T17 *NYPL [JLE 80-1910]*

Taeuber, Cynthia Murray. Women in the American economy / by Cynthia M. Taeuber and Victor Valdisera. Washington, D.C. : U. S. Dept. of Commerce, Bureau of the Census : For sale by the Supt. of Docs., U. S. G.P.O., [1986] vi, 45 p. : col. ill. ; 28 cm. (Current population reports. Special studies. Series P-23 . no. 146) Shipping list no.: 87-242-P. "Issued November 1986." Bibliography: p. 41-43. S/N 803-005-00020-1 Item

142-C-2 LC Card 87-601515 DDC 304.6/0973/021 s 331.4/0973 19
1. Women - Employment - United States - Statistics. 2. Income - United States - Statistics. I. Valdisera, Victor M. II. United States. Bureau of the Census. III. Title.
HA203 .A218 no. 146 HD6092

Taganskiĭ, B. M. (Boris Mikhaĭlovich) Ėkonomicheskiĭ analiz v stroitel'stve / B.M. Taganskiĭ, B.M. Azbel'. Moskva : Moskovskiĭ rabochiĭ, 1986. 148, [4] p. : ill. ; 20 cm. Bibliography: p. [150]. LC Card 86-227177
1. Construction industry - Soviet Union - Labor productivity. I. Azbel', B. M. (Boris Moiseevich). II. Title.
HD9715.S72 T35 1986

Tagiuri, Renato. Organizational climate; explorations of a concept. Edited by Renato Tagiuri and George H. Litwin, with the assistance of Marilynn G. Burmeister. Contributors: Louis B. Barnes [and others] Boston, Division of Research, Graduate School of Business Administration, Harvard University, 1968. viii, 246 p. illus. 21 cm. "The papers included here were prepared for a 'Research conference on organizational climate' held at the Harvard University Graduate School of Business Administration in January 1967." Includes bibliographies and indexes. LC Card 68-8418 DDC 301.4
1. Organization - Research - Addresses, essays, lectures. 2. Research, Industrial - Addresses, essays, lectures. I. Litwin, George H. II. Barnes, Louis B. III. Title.
HM131 .T27 ***NYPL [JLD 86-684]***

Tagle Frías de Cuenca, Matilde. Historia de la Estancia "Pozo de Correa" / Matilde Tagle Frías de Cuenca. [Córdoba, Argentina] : Junta Provincial de Historia de Córdoba, 1984. 88 p. : ill. ; 21 cm. (Junta Provincial de Historia de Córdoba . 10) Bibliography: p. 83-85. LC Card 86-157022
1. Estancia Pozo de Correa - History. 2. Ranches - Argentina - Córdoba (Province) - History. I. Junta Provincial de Historia de Córdoba . II. Series: Junta Provincial de Historia de Córdoba (Series) , 10. III. Title.
HD1471.A72 C677 1984

Tagle, Jorge. Errázuriz, Enrique. Industria eléctrica, 1960-1985 . [Santiago, Chile] [1986] 243 p. : LC Card 87-403870 DDC 338.4/762131/0983 19
HD9685.C52 E77 1986

Tagliaferri, Tiziana. Albertini, Sergio. Il consolidamento strutturale dell'occupazione in specifiche aree con particolare riguardo alla provincia di Gorizia /. Milano , c1984. 184 p. ; LC Card 84-234951 DDC 331.12/0945/392 19
HD5785.G67 A42 1984

Tagliaferro, C. (Claudio) Gatti, M. (Mario) Servizi innovativi e professionalità . Roma [1985] 231 p. : LC Card 85-237680
HD5716.S452 T84 1985

A Tagsági vagyoni hozzájárulás feltételrendszere : alaprészjegy, célrészjegy, tagsági kölcsön / [összeállította, Schäffer Árpád]. Budapest : Szövetkezeti Gazdaságszervezési és Számitástechnikai Iroda, 1984. 69 p. ; 29 cm. "Jogszabálymutató": p. 69. ISBN 963-7006-29-X : LC Card 85-185839
1. Consumer cooperatives - Hungary - Finance. I. Schäffer, Árpád.
HD3332.5.A4 T34 1984

Tagtabazar raĭonynyn͡g Kirov adyndaky kolkhozynyn͡g tarykhy /. Berdiev, G. Ashgabat , 1986. 79 p. : LC Card 86-198891
HD1492.S652 T873 1986

Tagung "Energie und Gerechtigkeit" (1982 : Universität Würzburg) Energie und Gerechtigkeit /. München , c1984. xii, 254 p. : ISBN 3-597-10259-X LC Card 84-175053
HD9502.A2 E5192 1984

Tagung Strategische Bankplanung (1982 : Bonn, Germany) Strategische Bankplanung : Vorträge und Berichte der Tagung Strategische Bankplanung am 30. September 1982 / herausgegeben von Hans J. Krümmel und Bernd Rudolph. Frankfurt am Main : Knapp, c1983. 345 p. : ill. ; 21 cm. Includes bibliographies. ISBN 3-7819-0293-5 LC Card 83-233043
1. Bank management - Germany (West) - Congresses. 2. Financial institutions - Germany (West) - Management - Congresses. I. Krümmel, Hans-Jacob. II. Rudolph, Bernd. III. Title.
HG1615 .T34 1982

Tagungsberichte (Technische Hochschule Karl-Marx-Stadt) .
(Heft 4) Wissenschaftliche Konferenz "Wissenschaftlich-Technischer Fortschritt, Bedingungen, Anforderungen, Möglichkeiten der Persönlichkeitsentwicklung" (1985 : Karl-Marx-Stadt, Germany) Wissenschaftliche Konferenz "Wissenschaftlich-Technischer Fortschritt, Bedingungen, Anforderungen, Möglichkeiten der Persönlichkeitsentwicklung" am 8. und 9. Oktober 1985 in Karl-Marx-Stadt /. Karl-Marx-Stadt , 1986. 98 p. ; LC Card 87-407801 DDC 338/.06 19
HD45 .W55 1985

(Heft 4) Wissenschaftliche Konferenz "Wissenschaftlich-Technischer Fortschritt, Bedingungen, Anforderungen, Möglichkeiten der Persönlichkeitsentwicklung" (1985 : Karl-Marx-Stadt, Germany) Wissenschaftliche Konferenz "Wissenschaftlich-Technischer Fortschritt, Bedingungen, Anforderungen, Möglichkeiten der Persönlichkeitsentwicklung" am 8. und 9. Oktober 1985 in Karl-Marx-Stadt /. Karl-Marx-Stadt , 1986. 98 p. ; LC Card 87-407801 DDC 338/.06 19
HD45 .W55 1985

(Heft 9) "Ökonomische Probleme der bedarfsorientierten Produktionsdurchführung" . Karl-Marx-Stadt , 1984. 139 p. : LC Card 84-245348
HD70.G22 O35 1984

(Heft 9) "Ökonomische Probleme der bedarfsorientierten Produktionsdurchführung" . Karl-Marx-Stadt , 1984. 139 p. : LC Card 84-245348
HD70.G22 O35 1984

Taheruddin, M. Essays on banking and development / M. Taheruddin. Dhaka : Academic Publishers, 1986. 145 p. ; 23 cm. Spine title: Banking and development in Bangladesh. Includes bibliographies and index. LC Card 87-900643 DDC 332.1/09549/2 19
1. Banks and banking - Bangladesh. 2. Bank management - Bangladesh. 3. Rural development - Bangladesh. I. Title. II. Title: Banking and development in Bangladesh.
HG3290.6.A6 T35 1986

Taillefer, Bernard. Etude sur la petite et moyenne industrie et l'artisanat /. [Bujumbara] [1984] 7 v. in 6 : LC Card 86-980948
HD2346.B94 E78 1984

Taimio, Heikki. Kostiainen, Seppo. Capital controls under alternative exchange rate and monetary policy regimes /. Joensuu , 1986. 27 p. ; ISBN 951-696-619-5 (pbk.) LC Card 87-100851 DDC 332.4/5 19
HG3823 .K673 1986

Taintor, Sarah Augusta. The secretary's handbook / Sarah Augusta Taintor and Kate M. Monro. 10th ed. / revised by Margaret D. Shertzer. New York : Collier Books ; London : Collier Macmillan, c1988. p. cm. Includes index. ISBN 0-02-008830-2 LC Card 87-24960 DDC 651.7/402 19
1. Office practice. I. Monro, Kate M. II. Shertzer, Margaret D. III. Title.
HF5547.5 .T29 1988

Tairov, E. (Eri) Toshpŭlatov, Mirzapŭlat. Prevrashchenie sel'skokhozi͡aĭstvennogo truda v raznovidnost' industrial'nogo v uslovii͡akh razvitogo sotsializma. . Tashkent , 1980. 68 p. ; LC Card 81-149078
HD1536.S65 T67 1980

TAIWAN - COMMERCE - HAWAII - STATISTICS.
Hawaii's trade with Taiwan, 1976-1985 /. Honolulu, Hawaii (P.O. Box 2359, Honolulu 96804) [1986] 18 p. ; LC Card 86-622297 DDC 382/.09969/051249021 19
HF3161.H3 H378 1986

TAIWAN - ECONOMIC CONDITIONS.
Contending approaches to the political economy of Taiwan /. Armonk, N.Y. , c1988. p. cm. ISBN 0-87332-440-4 : LC Card 87-16413 DDC 338.951/249 19
HC430.5 .C75 1988

TAIWAN - ECONOMIC CONDITIONS - 1945-
Li, Kuo-ting. The evolution of policy behind Taiwan's development success /. New Haven , c1988. p. cm. ISBN 0-300-04080-6 LC Card 87-23035 DDC 338.951/249 19
HC430.5 .L4725 1988

TAIWAN - ECONOMIC CONDITIONS - 1975-
Economic development, Taiwan, Republic of China. Taipei, Taiwan, Republic of China [1986] 46 p. : LC Card 87-119341 DDC 338.951/249 19
HC430.5 .E34 1986

TAIWAN - ECONOMIC CONDITIONS - 1975- - STATISTICS.
Economic development, Taiwan, Republic of China. Taipei, Taiwan, Republic of China [1986] 46 p. : LC Card 87-119341 DDC 338.951/249 19
HC430.5 .E34 1986

TAIWAN - ECONOMIC POLICY.
The Political economy of the new Asian industrialism /. Ithaca, N.Y. , 1987. 252 p. ; ISBN 0-8014-1948-4 (alk. paper) LC Card 86-29103 DDC 338.95 19
HC460.5 .P65 1987

TAIWAN - ECONOMIC POLICY - 1945-
Li, Kuo-ting. The evolution of policy behind Taiwan's development success /. New Haven , c1988. p. cm. ISBN 0-300-04080-6 LC Card 87-23035 DDC 338.951/249 19
HC430.5 .L4725 1988

Liu, Alan P. L., 1937- Phoenix and the lame lion . Stanford, Calif. , c1987. x, 182 p. ; ISBN 0-8179-8581-6 LC Card 87-13555 DDC 338.951 19
HC430.5 .L568 1987

TAIWAN - ECONOMIC POLICY - 1975-
Economic development, Taiwan, Republic of China. Taipei, Taiwan, Republic of China [1986] 46 p. : LC Card 87-119341 DDC 338.951/249 19
HC430.5 .E34 1986

Hsing cheng yüan ching chi chien she wei yüan hui (China) Highlights of Ninth Medium-Term Economic Development Plan for Taiwan, Republic of China, 1986-1989. [Taipei? Taiwan] [1986] ii, 65 p. ; LC Card 87-400742 DDC 338.951/249 19
HC430.5 .H757 1986a

Hsing cheng yüan ching chi chien she wei yüan hui (China) Highlights of 1986 economic development plan for Taiwan, Republic of China. [Taipei] [1986] ii, 61 p. ; LC Card 87-118523 DDC 338.951/249 19
HC430.5 .H757 1986

Rabushka, Alvin. The new China . San Francisco , Boulder, Colo. , 1987. xii, 254 p. ; ISBN 0-936488-15-8 (pbk. : alk. paper) LC Card 87-10574 DDC 338.951 19
HC427.92 .R33 1987

TAIWAN - FOREIGN ECONOMIC RELATIONS - UNITED STATES.
Wheeler, Jimmy W. Beyond recrimination . Indianapolis, IN (P.O. Box 26-919, Indianapolis 46226) , c1987. xix, 218 p. : LC Card 87-165405 DDC 382/.0951249/073 19
HF1456.5.T28 W46 1987

TAJIK S.S.R. - COMMERCE.
Nazarova, N. S. (Nina Semenovna) Voprosy razvitii͡a torgovli v Tadzhikistane /. Dushanbe , 1978. 172 p. ; LC Card 81-146150
HF3629.T35 N39 1978

TAJIK S.S.R. - ECONOMIC CONDITIONS.
Narodnoe khozi͡aĭstvo Tadzhikistana v gody Velikoĭ Otechestvennoĭ voĭny . Dushanbe , 1980. 169, [3] p. ; LC Card 81-130944
HC337.T233 D45 1980

Nazarova, N. S. (Nina Semenovna) Voprosy razvitii͡a torgovli v Tadzhikistane /. Dushanbe , 1978. 172 p. ; LC Card 81-146150
HF3629.T35 N39 1978

TAJIK S.S.R. - ECONOMIC POLICY - MATHEMATICAL MODELS.
Baĭriev, B. S. Optimizatsii͡a struktur upravlenii͡a /. Ashkhabad , 1985. 169, [23] p. : LC Card 86-196466
HC337.T23 B35 1985

Takabe, Yoshinobu, 1907- Amerika shingo jiten = The Kenkyūsha dictionary of new English / Takabe Yoshinobu. Tokyo : Kenkyūsha, 1978. 717 p. ; 18 cm. In Japanese.
1. English language - Dictionaries - Japanese. 2.

Japanese language - Dictionaries - English. I. Title. II. Title: The Kenkyūsha dictionary of new English.
*NYPL [*OSG 87-2157]*

Takahashi, M. (Morio), 1892-1959. Romanized English-Japanese, Japanese-English dictionary / by M. Takahashi. Author's ed. [Tokyo] : Taiseido, 1958. 457, 1226 p. ; 19 cm.
1. English language - Dictionaries - Japanese. 2. Japanese language - Dictionaries - English. I. Title.
*NYPL [*O-*OSG 87-870]*

Takahashi, Nobuo, 1957-
A takarékszövetkezetek banki reformjának alternativái /. Körösényi, András. Budapest [1985] 43 p. ; LC Card 87-408585
HG1939.H82 K67 1985

Takarékszövetkezeti tisztségviselők kézikönyve /. Galambosi, László. Budapest , 1986. 135 p. ; ISBN 963-7006-73-7 LC Card 87-137992
HG1939.H82 G35 1986

Take a chance to be first . Avis, Warren E. New York , 1987, c1986. xii, 222 p. ; ISBN 0-07-002547-9 (pbk.) : LC Card 87-13236 DDC 650.1 19
HF5386 .A94 1987

Take command of your money and develop a winning financial plan. Kennedy, Robert A. Personal economics . Tucson, AZ , c1987. xi, 315 p. : ISBN 0-89586-517-3 (pbk.) : LC Card 86-82240 DDC 332.024 19
HG179 .K46 1987

Take control of your finances [slide] : some basics for a spending plan / produced for Cornell Cooperative Extension by Media Services ; writer, Jeanne M. Hogarth. Ithaca, NY : Cornell University Audio Visual Center, 1984. 66 slides : col. + 1 sound cassette (16 min. : analog) + 1 script + 1 teacher's guide + 2 pamphlets. Title from data sheet. Illustrator, Carlton R. Ryan. Sound accompaniment for automatic operation only. High school students through adults. Focuses on the basic steps to set up a household spending/saving plan and the tools and techniques for managing the plan. Helps to clarify values, set goals, and estimate and analyze expenses, income, and other resources. LC Card 87-705083 DDC 640 11
1. Finance, Personal. I. Cornell University. Cooperative Extension. II. Cornell University. Media Services. III. Cornell University. Audio-Visual Resource Center.
HG179

Take pride in your work and build team effectiveness /. Checketts, Darby. Provo, Utah , c1987. v, 132 p. : ISBN 0-9618170-0-3 (pbk.) LC Card 87-70380 DDC 658.4/036 19
HF5549.5.M63 C45 1987

Take your hands off my attitude! . Cornyn-Selby, Alyce, 1946- Portland, Or. , 1987. p. cm. ISBN 0-941383-02-4 : LC Card 87-15074 DDC 158.7 19
HD58.9 .C67 1987

Takenaga, Susumu. Valeur, formes de la valeur et étapes dans la pensée de Marx / Susumu Takenaga. Berne ; New York : P. Lang, c1985. 243 p. ; 21 cm. (Publications universitaires européennes. Série V, Sciences économiques . vol. 682 = Bd. 682 = vol. 682) Bibliography: p. [195]-196. ISBN 3-261-04026-2 LC Card 86-196366
1. Labor theory of value. 2. Value. I. Series: Europäische Hochschulschriften. Reihe V, Volks- und Betriebswirtschaft , Bd. 682. II. Title.
HB206 .T35 1985

Takeover . Johnston, Moira, 1934- New York , c1986. xv, 395 p. ; ISBN 0-87795-784-3 : LC Card 86-10818 DDC 338.8/3/0973 19
HD2746.5 .J64 1986 NYPL [JLE 86-3932]

Takeover /. Johnston, Moira, 1934- New York, N.Y. , 1987, c1986. xiii, 418 p. ; ISBN 0-14-010505-0 (pbk.) LC Card 87-8560 DDC 338.8/3/0973 19
HD2746.5 .J64 1987

TAKEOVER BID (SECURITIES) see **TENDER OFFERS (SECURITIES)**

Takeover defenses . Rosenbaum, Virginia. Washington, D.C. , c1987. 227 p. ; ISBN 0-931035-13-9 (pbk.) LC Card 87-400095 DDC 338.7/4/02573 19
HD2746.5 .R67 1987

The takeover game /. Brooks, John, 1920- New York , c1987. x, 390 p. ; ISBN 0-525-24586-3 : LC Card 87-5967 DDC 338.8/3/0973 19
HD2746.5 .B76 1987

Takeover madness . Michel, Allen, 1945- New York , c1986. xii, 397 p. : ISBN 0-471-01079-0 LC Card 85-32315 DDC 658.1/8 19
HD2746.5 .M53 1986 NYPL [JLE 86-2989]

Takeuchi, Kenji, 1932- The world copper industry : its changing structure and future prospects / Kenji Takeuchi, John E. Strongman, and Shunichi Maeda. Washington, D.C., U. S.A. : World Bank, c1986. xxix, 179 p. : ill. ; 28 cm. (World Bank staff commodity working papers, 0253-3537 . no. 15) Bibliography: p. 175-178. ISBN 0-8213-0852-1 LC Card 86-26554 DDC 338.2/743 19
1. Copper industry and trade. 2. Market surveys. I. Strongman, John, 1947-. II. Maeda, Shun'ichi. III. Series: World Bank staff commodity working paper , no. 15. IV. Title.
HD9539.C6 T35 1986

Takeya, Denise Monteiro. Um outro Nordeste : o algodão na economia do Rio Grande do Norte (1880-1915) / Denise Monteiro Takeya. Fortaleza : Banco do Nordeste do Brasil Escritório Técnico de Estudos Econômicos do Nordeste, 1985. 137 p. : ill. ; 21 cm. (Série Documentos do Nordeste . 4) Originally presented as the author's thesis (mestre) Pontifícia Universidade Católica de São Paulo. Bibliography: p. 127-137. LC Card 86-232681
1. Cotton trade - Brazil - Rio Grande do Norte - History. I. Title. II. Series.
HD9084.B62 R568 1985

Takezawa, Shin'ichi, 1925- In quest of human dynamism . Tokyo, Japan , 1986. viii, 552 p. : ISBN 92-833-1088-2 LC Card 86-210648 DDC 658.3/0095 19
HF5549.2.A75 Q84 1986

Taking America . Madrick, Jeffrey G. Toronto , New York , 1987. 310 p. ; ISBN 0-553-05229-2 LC Card 87-928 DDC 338.8/3/0973 19
HG4028.T4 M33 1987

Taking charge/managing conflict /. Stulberg, Joseph B. Lexington, Mass. , c1987. xii, 175 p. ; ISBN 0-669-14014-7 (alk. paper) LC Card 86-45597 DDC 658.4 19
HD42 .S78 1987

Taking charge of your career direction /. Lock, Robert D., 1930- Pacific Grove, Calif. , c1988. xv, 377 p. : ISBN 0-534-08220-3 (pbk.) : LC Card 87-11637 DDC 650.1/4 19
HF5381 .L59 1988

Taking charge on the job . Taetzsch, Lyn. New York , c1978. 144 p. ; ISBN 0-917386-22-1 : LC Card 78-111025 DDC 658.4
HD38 .T17 NYPL [JLE 80-1910]

The taking of Getty Oil . Coll, Steve. New York , 1987. xiii, 528 p. ; ISBN 0-689-11860-0 LC Card 87-11467 DDC 338.8/3622338/0973 19
HD9569.G48 C65 1987

Taking reform seriously . McCann, Michael W., 1952- Ithaca , 1986. 345 p. ; ISBN 0-8014-1952-2 LC Card 86-47647 DDC 322.4/3/0973 19
JK1118 .M37 1986 NYPL [JLE 87-1009]

Taking stock . Quarrey, Michael. Cambridge, Mass. , c1986. xxii, 176 p. ; ISBN 0-88730-131-2 LC Card 86-14045 DDC 338.7/4 19
HD5660.U5 Q37 1986 NYPL [JLE 87-49]

Taksir, Kim Isaevich. Simpozium "Nauchno-tekhnicheskiĭ progress i intensifikatsiia obshchestvennogo proizvodstva" (1984 : Podol'sk, Moscow, R.S.F.S.R.) Formy i metody vzaimodeĭstviia nauki i proizvodstva /. Moskva , 1984. 237 p. ; LC Card 85-240380
HC340.T4 S48 1984

Die taktische Finanzplanung der internationalen Unternehmung /. Schauenberg, Harald. Königstein/Ts. , c1982. vi, 134 p. ; ISBN 3-445-02259-3 : LC Card 82-224376
HG4027.5 .S32 1982

Tale er sølv, tavshed er underkastelse /. Tholstrup, Knud. [Copenhagen] [1986] 179 p. : ISBN 87-416-1329-5 : LC Card 86-215991
HC355 .T37 1986

The tale of a great sham /. Parnell, Anna, 1852-1911. Dublin , Wick, Littlehampton, West Sussex , 1986. 205 p. ; ISBN 0-905223-93-4 LC Card 86-234070 DDC 333.33/5/09415 19
HD625 .P37 1986

Tales of an old horsetrader . Daniels, Leroy Judson, 1882- Iowa City , 1987. viii, 235 p. : ISBN 0-87745-173-7 LC Card 87-10932 DDC 338.1/761/00924 B 19
HD9434.U6 D36 1987

Taliani, Enrico. Processi formativi e coscienza operaia . Pisa , c1983. 509 p. ; LC Card 86-136656 DDC 658.3/124/0945 19
HF5549.5.T7 P69 1983
NYPL [JLE 87-1466]

Talking business in German . Strutz, Henry. Woodbury, N.Y. , c1987. iv, 256 p. : ISBN 0-8120-3747-2 (pbk.) LC Card 86-22360 DDC 650/.03/31 19
HF1002 .S79 1987

Talking business in Japanese /. Akiyama, Nobuo. Hauppauge, N.Y. , c1987. p. cm. ISBN 0-8120-3848-7 LC Card 87-19601 DDC 650/.03/956 19
HF1002 .A34 1987

Talkwriters, voice mail, and speech processing in office automation. Talkwriters, voice mail & speech processing in office automation. Norwalk, Conn., U. S.A. (6 Prowitt St., Norwalk 06855) , c1986. iv, 145 leaves : LC Card 86-224988 DDC 381/.45621389 19
HD9696.S643 U667 1986

TALLÁN INDIANS - AGRICULTURE - HISTORY.
Espinoza Claudio, César. Terratenientes y campesinos en Piura, ss. XVI-XIX . Lima, Perú , 1981. xxviii, 123 p., [6] leaves of plates : LC Card 82-146131
HD559.P5 E87 1981

TALLÁN INDIANS - LAND TENURE - HISTORY.
Espinoza Claudio, César. Terratenientes y campesinos en Piura, ss. XVI-XIX . Lima, Perú , 1981. xxviii, 123 p., [6] leaves of plates : LC Card 82-146131
HD559.P5 E87 1981

Taller Alternativas de Cambio de Modelo Empresarial, San Bartolo, Valle del Santa. Taller Alternativas de Cambio de Modelo Empresarial (1985 : Cooperativa San Bartolo del Valle del Santa (Peru)) Lima, Perú [1986] 40 p. : LC Card 87-136317 DDC 334/.683/0985 19
HD1491.P4 T35 1985

Taller Alternativas de Cambio de Modelo Empresarial (1985 : Cooperativa San Bartolo del Valle del Santa (Peru)) Taller Alternativas de Cambio de Modelo Empresarial, San Bartolo, Valle del Santa. Lima, Perú : Centro de Divulgación de Historia Popular, [1986] 40 p. : ill. ; 21 cm. Cover title. LC Card 87-136317 DDC 334/.683/0985 19
1. Cooperativa San Bartolo del Valle del Santa (Peru) - Congresses. 2. Agriculture, Cooperative - Peru - Congresses. I. Centro de Divulgación de Historia Popular (Lima, Peru). II. Title.
HD1491.P4 T35 1985

Taller de Acción Cultural (Santiago, Chile) Así aprendemos . Santiago de Chile [1986] 126 p. : LC Card 87-404640 DDC 330/.07/15 19
HB74.9.C5 A85 1986

Taller de investigación .
(6) Pequeña industria, reactivación y desarrollo industrial /. [Miraflores, Lima] [1986] 127 p. : LC Card 87-127800 DDC 338.6/42/0985 19
HD2346.P4 P47 1986

(7) Empleo, salarios y distribución del ingreso . [Miraflores, Lima] , 1986. 186 p. : LC Card 87-403082 DDC 331.11/0985 19
HD5761.A6 E47 1986

(9) El Mercado de capitales como instrumento de la política económica /. [Miraflores, Lima] [1987] 111 p. ; LC Card 87-169408 DDC 332.6/0985 19
HG5392 .M43 1987

Ahorro interno y el sistema financiero /. [Lima, Peru] , 1986. 70 p. : LC Card 87-127322 DDC 332/.0985 19
HC230.S3 A38 1986

Taller de Lavandería Santa María. Así aprendemos . Santiago de Chile [1986] 126 p. : LC Card 87-404640 DDC 330/.07/15 19
HB74.9.C5 A85 1986

Taller "Perspectivas y Alternativas de la Agricultura Familiar". Taller "Perspectivas y Alternativas de la Agricultura Familiar" (1983 :

Montevideo, Uruguay) Montevideo, Uruguay [1984] 1 v. (various pagings) : LC Card 85-203149 DDC 338.1/6 19
HD1476.L29 T35 1983 ***NYPL [JLF 86-884]***

Taller "Perspectivas y Alternativas de la Agricultura Familiar" (1983 : Montevideo, Uruguay) Taller "Perspectivas y Alternativas de la Agricultura Familiar". Montevideo, Uruguay : Centro Interdisciplinario de Estudios sobre el Desarrollo, Uruguay, [1984] 1 v. (various pagings) : ill. ; 28 cm. (Serie Seminarios y talleres . no. 4) "Taller organizado por CIEDUR, se realizó en Montevideo del 27 al 30 de noviembre de 1983." "Contó con el apoyo de Inter-American Foundation." Includes bibliographies. LC Card 85-203149 DDC 338.1/6 19
1. Family farms - Latin America - Congresses. 2. Family farms - Uruguay - Congresses. 3. Rural families - Latin America - Congresses. 4. Peasantry - Latin America - Congresses. 5. Agricultural laborers - Latin America - Congresses. I. Centro Interdisciplinario de Estudios sobre el Desarrollo Uruguay. II. Title. III. Title: Perspectivas y Alternativas de la Agricultura Familiar. IV. Series.
HD1476.L29 T35 1983 ***NYPL [JLF 86-884]***

Taller sobre Identificación de Políticas que Permitan Dinamizar el Complejo de Producción y Comercialización de Carnes Rojas, con Enfasis en la Industria Frigorífica. Taller sobre Identificación de Políticas que Permitan Dinamizar el Complejo de Producción y Comercialización de Carnes Rojas, con Enfasis en la Industria Frigorífica (1984 : Montevideo, Uruguay) Montevideo, Uruguay [1985] 13, 18, 16 p. : LC Card 85-236237
HD9440.U82 T35 1984

Taller sobre Identificación de Políticas que Permitan Dinamizar el Complejo de Producción y Comercialización de Carnes Rojas, con Enfasis en la Industria Frigorífica (1984 : Montevideo, Uruguay) Taller sobre Identificación de Políticas que Permitan Dinamizar el Complejo de Producción y Comercialización de Carnes Rojas, con Enfasis en la Industria Frigorífica. Montevideo, Uruguay : Centro Interdisciplinario de Estudios sobre el Desarrollo Uruguay, [1985] 13, 18, 16 p. : ill. ; 28 cm. (Serie Seminarios y talleres . no. 7) "Taller organizado por CIEDUR, se realizó en Montevideo el 11 y 12 de setiembre de 1984." LC Card 85-236237
1. Meat industry and trade - Uruguay - Congresses. I. Centro Interdisciplinario de Estudios sobre el Desarrollo Uruguay. II. Title. III. Series.
HD9440.U82 T35 1984

Talleres CEDLA . (no. 1) Segunda reforma agraria . La Paz, Bolivia [1987] 287 p. : LC Card 87-403057 DDC 333.3/1/84 19
HD1333.B5 S44 1987

Talleristas y vendedores ambulantes en Lima /. Grompone, Romeo. Lima , 1985. 319 p. : LC Card 85-243089
HD2346.P42 L564 1985

Talley, Madelon DeVoe. The passionate investors : secrets of winning on Wall Street from Bernard Baruch to John Templeton / Madelon DeVoe Talley.1st ed. New York : Crown, c1987. 260 p. : ill. ; 24 cm. Bibliography: p. 251-252. Includes index. ISBN 0-517-56563-3 : LC Card 86-24281 DDC 332.63/22 19
1. Stocks. 2. Investments. I. Title. II. Title: Investors.
HG4521 .T29 1987

Talman, Dolf, 1952- The Computation and modelling of economic equilibria /. Amsterdam ; New York : xiv, 229 p. : ISBN 0-444-70285-7 LC Card 87-15666 DDC 339/.0724 19
HB145 .C64 1987

Taloudellinen suunnittelukeskus (Finland) Asplund, Rita. Short-run tax-push inflation in Finland /. Helsinki , 1986. 65 p. : ISBN 951-46-9876-2 (pbk.) LC Card 87-163994 DDC 332.4/1/094897 19
HJ4738.3 .A86 1986

Talukdar, Sarosh. Load management /. New York , c1987. vii, 207 p. : ISBN 0-87942-214-9 LC Card 86-33824 DDC 363.6/2 19
HD9685.U5 L58 1987

Talwar, Prem P., 1936- Recent advances in the techniques for demographic analysis /. Bombay , 1987. xiv, 456 p. ; LC Card 87-900498
HB849 .R42 1987

Tamagna, Frank M.
[Banca central en América Latina. English] Central banking in Latin America / Frank Tamagna. 1st English ed. México : Centro de Estudios Monetarios Latinoamericanos, 1965. xii, 285 p. ; 22 cm. (Studies / C.E.M.L.A) Translation and rev. ed. of: La banca central en América Latina. LC Card 87-403322 DDC 332.1/1/098 19
1. Banks and banking, Central - Latin America. 2. Monetary policy - Latin America. I. Series: Studies (Centro de Estudios Monetarios Latinoamericanos). II. Title.
HG2710.5.A7 T3513 1965

Tamames, Ramón, 1933- Guía del Mercado Común Europeo : España en la Europa de los doce / Ramón Tamames. Madrid : Alianza, c1986. xii, 309 p. ; 23 cm. Includes bibliographical references. ISBN 84-206-9524-6 LC Card 86-150515
1. European Economic Community - Spain. 2. European Economic Community. I. Title.
HC241.25.S6 T35 1986

El tamaño de las ciudades y la distribución de los ingresos (Argentina y Colombia) /. Toledo, Nora Elena. San Juan, Argentina , 1985. 63 p. : LC Card 87-400258 DDC 339.2/2/09861 19
HC200.I5 T65 1985

Tamás, Gábor. Lovassné Szecső, Judit. A kereskedelmi hitel és a váltó alkalmazásának 1985. évi tapasztalatai /. Budapest [1986] 62 p. ; ISBN 963-7202-84-6 LC Card 87-151536
HG3754.5.H9 L68 1986

Tamayo, Jesús. Espinoza Jaramillo, Frida. El estado de la investigación nacional acerca de la frontera norte de México /. [México] , 1985. 47 leaves ; LC Card 87-402765 DDC 330.972/10834 19
HC137.M46 E76 1985

Tamayo Rodríguez, Jaime E. La estructura del sindicalismo en Jalisco / Jaime E. Tamayo Rodríguez. Guadalajara, Jalisco, México : Instituto de Estudios Sociales, Universidad de Guadalajara, [1985] 224 p. ; 20 cm. (Colección Aportaciones) Includes bibliographical references. ISBN 968-570-147-4 LC Card 86-208258
1. Trade-unions - Mexico - Jalisco. I. Title. II. Series.
HD6535.J35 T36 1985

Tami, Felipe S. Study of the financial sector of Argentina : report of the consultant / Felipe S. Tami. Washington, D.C. : Economic and Social Development Dept., General Studies Division, Financial Studies Section, [1979] x, 146 p. : ill. ; 28 cm. At head of title: Inter-American Development Bank. "January 1979." LC Card 86-673765
1. Financial institutions - Argentina. 2. Finance - Argentina. I. Inter-American Development Bank. II. Title.
HG185.A7 T35x 1979

Tamil Nadu State Council for Science & Technology. Science and technology for women /. Madras [1985] 79 p. ; LC Card 85-904932 DDC 305.4/35/0954 19
Q130 .S33 1985 ***NYPL [JLD 86-3369]***

TAMILS - EMPLOYMENT - SRI LANKA. Kūriyan, Rēval. Vatukarayē kāntā śramaya surākāma . Colombo, Sri Lanka [1984] 24 p. : LC Card 86-902479
HD6182.8 .K87 1984

Tammer, Hans. Monopole, Profite, Ausbeutung / Hans Tammer. Berlin : Dietz, 1983. 237 p. : 16 ill. ; 18 cm. Includes bibliographical references. LC Card 84-142912
1. Monopolies. 2. Profit. 3. Capitalism. I. Title.
HD2757.2 .T35 1983

TAMPEREEN YLIOPISTO. YRITYKSEN TALOUSTIETEEN JA YKSITYISOIKEUDEN LAITOS. Yrityksen taloustieteet Tampereen yliopistossa /. Tampere , 1985. 47 leaves : ISBN 951-44-1859-X LC Card 87-107284
HD30.42.F5 Y74 1985

Tampoe, M. Successful business computing / M.Tampoe. London : Butterworth Scientific, 1982. 124 p. : ill.; 22cm. Includes index.
1. Business - Data processing. 2. Electronic digital computers - Purchasing. I. Title.
NYPL [JLD 86-2491]

Tan, Jing Jee. Developing managers in Asia /. Singapore , Reading, Mass. , 1986. p. cm. ISBN 0-201-13653-8 : LC Card 86-28717 DDC 658/.007/15 19
HD38.25.A78 D48 1986

Tan Kah-kee, the making of an overseas Chinese legend /. Yong, C. F. (Ching Fatt) Singapore , 1987 [i.e. 1986] xix, 391 p., [16] p. of plates : ISBN 0-19-582678-7 LC Card 86-946451 DDC 338/.04/0924 B 19
HC445.8.C47 Y66 1986

Tan, Koonlin. The swamp-sago industry in West Malaysia : a study of the Sungei Batu Pahat floodplain / Tan Koonlin. Singapore : Institute of Southeast Asian Studies, c1983. xvi, 174 p. : ill., maps ; 23 cm. Bibliography: p. 158-174. ISBN 997-19-0266-4 (pbk.) LC Card 84-940373 DDC 338.1/7368 19
1. Swamp sago industry - Malaysia - Malaya. I. Title.
HD9259.S873 M37 1983

Tan, Loong-Hoe. ASEAN-U. S. economic relations . Singapore , c1986. x, 54 p. : ISBN 997-19-8842-9 (pbk.) LC Card 87-940002 DDC 337.59073 19
HF1456.5.A7 A84 1986

Tanaka, Marta Maria Soban. Sócrates, Jodete Rios. A cidade invade as águas . [São Paulo] , 1985. 296 p., [2] folded leaves of plates : LC Card 87-118596 DDC 333.91/00981/61 19
HD1696.B84 S427 1985

Tănase, Alexandru. Civilizația socialistă . București , 1979. 289, [2] p., [1] leaf of plates : LC Card 80-460491
HX56 .C48 ***NYPL [JLD 81-195]***

Tancredo Neves na defesa do consumidor /. Neves, Tancredo, 1910- Brasília , 1985. 48 p. : LC Card 86-129214
HC190.C63 N48 1985

Taneja, Nawal K. The international airline industry : trends, issues, and challenges / Nawal K. Taneja. Lexington, Mass. : Lexington Books, c1988. xvi, 167 p. : ill., maps ; 24 cm. Bibliography: p. [161]-162. Includes index. ISBN 0-669-16167-5 (alk. paper) LC Card 87-45227 DDC 387.7 19
1. Aeronautics, Commercial. 2. Aeronautics, Commercial - United States. 3. Airlines. 4. Airlines - United States. I. Title.
HE9776 .T363 1988

Taneja, Nisha. Kathuria, Sanjay. India's exports, the challenge from China /. New Delhi , 1986. 106 p. ; LC Card 86-902526 DDC 382/.6/0954 19
HF3836.5 .K37 1986

TANGANYIKA - ECONOMIC CONDITIONS. Wayne, Jack, Ph.D. Structural contradictions of the colonial state . [Toronto, Canada] , c1981. 23, [5] p. ; ISBN 0-7727-2825-9 (pbk.) LC Card 86-193819 DDC 330.9678/203 19
HC885 .W39 1981

Tanganyika - Government. see **Tanganyika - Politics and government.**

TANGANYIKA - POLITICS AND GOVERNMENT. Wayne, Jack, Ph.D. Structural contradictions of the colonial state . [Toronto, Canada] , c1981. 23, [5] p. ; ISBN 0-7727-2825-9 (pbk.) LC Card 86-193819 DDC 330.9678/203 19
HC885 .W39 1981

Tangermann, Stefan. Welternährung und die Verantwortlichkeit der Industrieländer / von Stefan Tangermann. Kiel : Institut für Weltwirtschaft an der Universität Kiel, 1986. 27 p. ; 24 cm. (Kieler Vorträge, 0340-6970 . n.F., 111) Bibliography: p. 26-27. ISBN 3-925357-38-6 LC Card 87-126268 DDC 338.1/9/1724 19
1. Food supply - Developing countries. 2. Food relief - Developing countries. 3. Agriculture and state. 4. Agricultural assistance - Developing countries. I. Title. II. Series.
HD9018.D44 T36 1986

Tani, Piero. Analisi microeconomica della produzione / Piero Tani. 1a ed. Roma : La Nuova Italia scientifica, 1986. viii, 351 p. : ill. ; 22 cm. (Studi superiori NIS . 13.) Bibliography: p. [335]-343. Includes index. LC Card 86-169971
1. Production (Economic theory). 2. Microeconomics. I. Series: Studi superiori NIS. Economia. II. Title.
HB241 .T36 1986

TANK - VESSELS. see **TANKERS.**

Tanka, Endre. A Föld és a népgazdaság /. [Budapest] , 1985. 514 p. ; ISBN 963-03-2232-3 LC Card 86-228739
HD640.5.Z63 F65 1985

TANKER SHIPS. see **TANKERS.**

TANKERS.
Oil tankers to South Africa, 1980-1981. Amsterdam , c1982. vi, 99 p. : ISBN 90-70331-05-5 (pbk.) LC Card 86-213340 DDC 387.5/448 19
HE595.P4 O37 1982

TANKERS - STATISTICS.
Champness, Michael. Oil tanker databook, 1985 /. London ; New York : vii, 347 p. ; ISBN 0-85334-311-X LC Card 86-217414 DDC 387.5/448 19
HE566.T3 C42 1985

Tan'kov, A. V. Mezhdunarodnyĭ valiutnyĭ fond v usloviiakh sovremennogo kapitalizma / A.V. Tan'kov. Moskva : Nauchno-issl. fin. in-t, 1984. 85 p. ; 21 cm. (Aktual'nye mezhdunarodnye valiutno-finansovye problemy . vyp. 2) At head of title: Ministerstvo finansov SSSR. Nauchno-issledovatel'skiĭ finansovyĭ institut. Bibliography: p. 34-35. LC Card 87-100183
1. International Monetary Fund. I. Title. II. Series.
HG3881.5.I58 T35 1984

Tanmiyah al-'Arabīyah wa-al-'alāqāt al-dawlīyah / Jalāl Aḥmad Amīn ... [et al.]. al-Kuwayt : al-Ma'had al-'Arabī lil-Takhṭīṭ, 1983. 230, 96 p. ; 24 cm. (al-Ḥalqah al-niqāshīyah . 5) Arabic and English. Cover title. Includes bibliographies. LC Card 86-964623
1. Arab countries - Economic policy - Congresses. 2. Arab countries - Foreign economic relations - Congresses. 3. Economic development - Congresses. I. Amin, Galal A., 1935-. II. Arab Planning Institute. III. Series: Ḥalqah al-niqāshīyah , 5.
HC498 .T349 1983

Tanna, Suresh. The Regulatory framework of accounting /. Estover, Plymouth , 1985. [12], 391 p. : ISBN 0-7121-0491-7
NYPL [JLF 87-84]

Tannenbaum, Robert. Leadership and organization : a behavioral science approach / Robert Tannenbaum, Irving R. Weschler, Fred Massarik. New York : Garland, 1987, c1961. xiv, 456 p. : ill. ; 23 cm. (Continuity in administrative science) Reprint. Originally published: New York : McGraw-Hill, c1961. Bibliography: p. 431-446. Includes indexes. ISBN 0-8240-8219-2 (alk. paper) : LC Card 86-27019 DDC 303.3/4 19
1. Leadership. 2. Organization. I. Weschler, Irving R. II. Massarik, Fred. III. Title. IV. Series.
HD57.7 .T36 1987

Tanner, Albert. Das Schiffchen fliegt, die Maschine rauscht : Weber, Sticker und Unternehmer in der Ostschweiz / Albert Tanner. Zürich : Unionsverlag, c1985. 214 p. : ill. ; 28 cm. Bibliography: p. 210-213. Includes indexes. ISBN 3-293-00084-3 LC Card 86-124152
1. Textile industry - Switzerland - History. 2. Knit goods industry - Switzerland - History. 3. Textile workers - Switzerland - History. 4. Knitting, Machine - History. 5. Saint Gall (Switzerland) - History. I. Title.
HD9865.S9 T36 1985

Tanner, Ernst, Prof., Dipl. Kult.-Ing. Grundsätze für die Bewertung von Kulturland bei Güterzusammenlegungen . [Bern? , 1973?] 1 v. (loose leaf) : LC Card 86-184960
HD798 .G78 1973

Tanner, Ian, 1946- Lupton, Tom. Achieving change . Aldershots, Hants, England , Brookfield, Vt., U. S.A. , c1987. xv, 86 p. : ISBN 0-566-02526-4 : LC Card 87-17665 DDC 658.4/06 19
HD58.9 .L86 1987

Tanner, Jakob. Bundeshaushalt, Währung und Kriegswirtschaft : eine finanzsoziologische Analyse der Schweiz zwischen 1938 und 1953 / Jakob Tanner. Zürich : Limmat Verlag, c1986. 438 p. : ill. ; 21 cm. (Reihe W) Originally presented as the author's thesis (doctoral--Universität Zürich, Wintersemester 1984/85) Bibliography: p. 421-438. ISBN 3-85791-100-X : LC Card 86-199729
1. Finance, Public - Switzerland - History - 20th century. 2. Budget - Switzerland - History - 20th century. 3. Monetary policy - Switzerland - History - 20th century. 4. Armaments - Economic aspects - Switzerland - History - 20th century. 5. World War, 1939-1945 - Economic aspects - Switzerland. 6. Taxation - Switzerland - History - 20th century. I. Title.
HJ1258 .T35 1986

Tanner, Lucretia Dewey. Working women . Washington, D.C. , c1987. xxii, 419 p. ; ISBN 0-87179-547-7 LC Card 87-9410 DDC 331.4/0973 19
HD6095 .W742 1987

Tantaleán Arbulú, Javier. Metodología de evaluación y programación de sistemas de producción y consumo, MEPS /. Lima, Perú [1985]- v. <1 > : LC Card 86-215609
HD75 .M48 1985

Tanulmány (Budapest, Hungary)
Lovassné Szecső, Judit. A kereskedelmi hitel és a váltó alkalmazásának 1985. évi tapasztalatai /. Budapest [1986] 62 p. ; ISBN 963-7202-84-6 LC Card 87-151536
HG3754.5.H9 L68 1986

Tanulmányok a gazdaság irányításáról és szervezetéről .
(2. sz) Életszínvonal és közhangulat /. Budapest , 1984. 69 p. ; LC Card 86-147705
HD7027.5 .E44 1984

Tanulmányok a szervezésről és a vezetésről /. Susánszky, János. Budapest , 1985. 89 p. ; ISBN 963-05-4132-7 : LC Card 86-136320
HD37.H82 S857 1985

Tanulmányok a vezetők minősítéséről és a személyi értékelés rendszeréről. Budapest : Országos Fordító és Fordításhitelesitő Iroda, 1985. 211 p. ; 25 cm. "Kézirat gyanánt! kizárólag belső használatra!" ISBN 963-02-3494-7 (Magy. nemz. bibl.) LC Card 85-193396
1. Employees, Rating of. 2. Executives, Rating of. I. Országos Fordító és Fordításhitelesitő Iroda (Budapest, Hungary).
HF5549.5.R3 T35 1985

Tanulmányok az anyagi érdekeltség, jövedelemszabályozás témaköréből / [szerkesztette, Mihalik István]. [Budapest] : Művelődési Minisztérium Marxizmus-Leninizmus Oktatási Főosztálya, 1985. 126 p. : ill. ; 24 cm. (Politikai gazdaságtan füzetek, 0324-6396 . 48) Summary in Russian. Includes bibliographies. ISBN 963-673-308-2 LC Card 86-147619
1. Wages - Hungary. 2. Incentives in industry - Hungary. I. Mihalik, István. II. Series.
HD5022.5 .T37 1985

Tanulmányok Magyarországról, magyarokról. [Budapest] : Magyarok Világszövetsége, [1985] 280 p. ; 18 cm. On spine: Magyar Fórum. MF tanulmányok. CONTENTS. - A modern magyar gazdaság fejlődésútja / Berend T. Iván -- A mai magyar társadalom / Kulcsár Kálmán -- A népesedési folyamatok Magyarországon / Andorka Rudolf -- Magyarok a nagyvilágban / Imre Samu. ISBN 963-01-7352-2 (Magy. nemz. bibl.) LC Card 87-408505
1. Hungary - Economic conditions. 2. Hungary - Social conditions - 1945-. 3. Hungary - Population. 4. Hungarians - Foreign countries. I. Berend, T. Iván (Tibor Iván), 1930-. II. Magyar Fórum (Magyarok Világszövetsége). III. Title: MF tanulmányok.
HC300.24 .T36 1985

Tanulmny (Budapest, Hungary)
Engel, Gábor. A kereskedelmi tevékenység komplex finanszirozása /. Budapest [1985] 68 p. ; ISBN 963-7202-58-7 LC Card 86-157419
HG4026 .E517 1985

Tanzania : crisis and struggle for survival / edited by Jannik Boesen ... [et al.]. Uppsala : Scandinavian Institute of African Studies ; Stockholm, Sweden : Distributed by Almqvist & Wiksell International, 1986. 325 p. : ill. ; 24 cm. Includes bibliographies. ISBN 91-7106-257-2 (pbk.) LC Card 87-163353 DDC 330.9678/04 19
1. Agriculture - Economic aspects - Tanzania. 2. Tanzania - Economic conditions - 1964-. 3. Tanzania - Social conditions - 1964-. I. Boesen, Jannik. II. Nordiska Afrikainstitutet.
HD2128.5 .T36 1986

Tanzania. Aerodromes Division. Mkwawa, D. A. Y. A review of aerodrome statistics in Tanzania, 1970-1982. Dar es Salaam [1984] xix, 143 p. : LC Card 87-403351 DDC 387.7/36/09678021 19
HE9797.5.T34 M58 1984

Tanzania. Bureau of Statistics. Analysis of accounts of parastatals, 1966-1977. Dar Es Salaam [1979] 43 p. ; LC Card 81-142522 DDC 354.67809/2 19
HD4348.5 .A52 1979

TANZANIA - CENSUS, 1973.

TANZANIA - COLONIAL INFLUENCE.
Wayne, Jack, Ph.D. Structural contradictions of the colonial state . [Toronto, Canada] , c1981. 23, [5] p. ; ISBN 0-7727-2825-9 (pbk.) LC Card 86-193819 DDC 330.9678/203 19
HC885 .W39 1981

TANZANIA - COMMERCIAL POLICY.
East African lessons on economic liberalization /. Aldershot, Hampshire, U.K. ; Brookfield, Vt., U. S.A. : xxi, 72 p. : ISBN 0-566-05337-3 (pbk.) : LC Card 86-29602 DDC 338.967 19
HC865 .E27 1987

TANZANIA - ECONOMIC CONDITIONS - 1964-
Employment promotion in Tanzania . Addis Ababa , 1986. ii leaves, 107 p. ; LC Card 87-980150 DDC 331.11/09678 19
HD5841.3.A6 E46 1986

Skarstein, Rune. Industrial development in Tanzania . Uppsala , Stockholm, Sweden , 1986. xi, 291 p. : ISBN 91-7106-254-8 (pbk.) LC Card 87-134925 DDC 338.9678 19
HC885 .S58 1986

Tanzania . Uppsala , Stockholm, Sweden , 1986. 325 p. : ISBN 91-7106-257-2 (pbk.) LC Card 87-163353 DDC 330.9678/04 19
HD2128.5 .T36 1986

Utvecklingssamarbetet med Tanzania 1983/84-1984/85. Stockholm, Sweden [1983] ca. 200 p. ; LC Card 86-216305
HC885 .U87 1983

TANZANIA - ECONOMIC POLICY.
Crouch, Susan C. (Susan Catherine), 1958- Western responses to Tanzanian socialism, 1967-83 /. Aldershot, Hants, England , Brookfield, Vt., USA , c1987. x, 194 p. ; ISBN 0-566-05455-8 : LC Card 87-15018 DDC 337.678 19
HF1612.9 .C76 1987

East African lessons on economic liberalization /. Aldershot, Hampshire, U.K. ; Brookfield, Vt., U. S.A. : xxi, 72 p. : ISBN 0-566-05337-3 (pbk.) : LC Card 86-29602 DDC 338.967 19
HC865 .E27 1987

Luttrell, William L. Post-capitalist industrialization . New York , 1986. xv, 189 p. : ISBN 0-275-92310-X : LC Card 86-9452 DDC 338.9678 19
HD3616.T343 L88 1986
NYPL [JLE 87-351]

Nsekela, Amon J. (Amon James), 1930- A time to act . Dar es Salaam , c1984. xxi, 142 p. ; ISBN 997-660-025-9 LC Card 86-981097 DDC 338.9678 19
HC885 .N86 1984

Taarifa ya utekelezaji wa mpango wa pili wa taifa wa kujihami kiuchumi, Januari-Agosti, 1982. [Dar es Salaam] , 1982. 46 p. ; LC Card 83-980744
HC885 .T28 1982

TANZANIA - FOREIGN ECONOMIC RELATIONS.
Crouch, Susan C. (Susan Catherine), 1958- Western responses to Tanzanian socialism, 1967-83 /. Aldershot, Hants, England , Brookfield, Vt., USA , c1987. x, 194 p. ; ISBN 0-566-05455-8 : LC Card 87-15018 DDC 337.678 19
HF1612.9 .C76 1987

TANZANIA - FOREIGN RELATIONS.
Crouch, Susan C. (Susan Catherine), 1958- Western responses to Tanzanian socialism, 1967-83 /. Aldershot, Hants, England , Brookfield, Vt., USA , c1987. x, 194 p. ; ISBN 0-566-05455-8 : LC Card 87-15018 DDC 337.678 19
HF1612.9 .C76 1987

Tanzania - Government. see **Tanzania - Politics and government.**

TANZANIA - INDUSTRIES.
Luttrell, William L. Post-capitalist industrialization . New York , 1986. xv, 189 p. : ISBN 0-275-92310-X : LC Card 86-9452 DDC 338.9678 19
HD3616.T343 L88 1986
NYPL [JLE 87-351]

Skarstein, Rune. Industrial development in Tanzania . Uppsala , Stockholm, Sweden , 1986. xi, 291 p. : ISBN 91-7106-254-8 (pbk.) LC Card 87-134925 DDC 338.9678 19
HC885 .S58 1986

Tanzania. Ministry of Economic Affairs and Development Planning. Bureau of Statistics. see **Tanzania. Bureau of Statistics.**

TANZANIA - POLITICS AND GOVERNMENT - 1964-
Crouch, Susan C. (Susan Catherine), 1958- Western responses to Tanzanian socialism, 1967-83 /. Aldershot, Hants, England , Brookfield, Vt., USA , c1987. x, 194 p. ; ISBN 0-566-05455-8 : LC Card 87-15018 DDC 337.678 19
HF1612.9 .C76 1987

Nsekela, Amon J. (Amon James), 1930- A time to act . Dar es Salaam , c1984. xxi, 142 p. ; ISBN 997-660-025-9 LC Card 86-981097 DDC 338.9678 19
HC885 .N86 1984

TANZANIA - SOCIAL CONDITIONS - 1964-
Tanzania . Uppsala , Stockholm, Sweden , 1986. 325 p. : ISBN 91-7106-257-2 (pbk.) LC Card 87-163353 DDC 330.9678/04 19
HD2128.5 .T36 1986

TANZANIA - SOCIAL POLICY.
Nsekela, Amon J. (Amon James), 1930- A time to act . Dar es Salaam , c1984. xxi, 142 p. ; ISBN 997-660-025-9 LC Card 86-981097 DDC 338.9678 19
HC885 .N86 1984

Tanzania. Statistics, Bureau of. see **Tanzania. Bureau of Statistics.**

Tanzania. Ujamaa and Co-operative Development Dept. Savings and Credit Unit. A Short introduction to the co-operative savings and credit societies and Tanzania Rural Savings and Credit Scheme /. [Dar es Salaam, Tanzania] [1977] 43 p. : LC Card 77-980630 DDC 334/.2/09678 19
HG2039.T37 S56 1977

TANZANIA. WIZARA YA MALIASILLI NA UTALII - APPROPRIATIONS AND EXPENDITURES.
Ole Saibull, Solomon, 1935- Hotuba ya Ndugu S.A. ole Saibull, mbunge, waziri wa maliasili na utalii . Dar es Salaam, Tanzania , 1979. 56 p. ; LC Card 83-244807
HC885 .O44 1979

Tanzania. Wizara ya Mipango na Uchumi. Taarifa ya utekelezaji wa mpango wa pili wa taifa wa kujihami kiuchumi, Januari-Agosti, 1982. [Dar es Salaam] , 1982. 46 p. ; LC Card 83-980744
HC885 .T28 1982

Tapia Soko, Gonzalo. El problema de la recomposición de los actores campesinos en una perspectiva de democratización / Gonzalo Tapia Soko, Gonzalo Vío Grossi. Santiago [Chile] : Programa Interdisciplinario de Investigaciones en Educación, [1985] ii, 49, 5 leaves ; 27 cm. Prepared for the Seminario sobre Movimientos Sociales en Chile, organized by CLACSO, held Jan. 1985 in Santiago, Chile. Bibliography: leaves 47-49. LC Card 86-159337
1. Peasantry - Chile - Political activity. 2. Agricultural laborers - Chile - Political activity. I. Vío Grossi, Gonzalo. II. Programa Interdisciplinario de Investigaciones en Educación (Academia de Humanismo Cristiano). III. Title.
HD1531.C5 T36 1985

TAPIE, BERNARD, 1943-
Musnik, Isabelle. Tapie, les secrets de sa réussite /. Paris , c1986. 261 p. : ISBN 2-259-01546-8 : LC Card 87-167974
HC272.5.T3 M87 1986

Tapie, les secrets de sa réussite /. Musnik, Isabelle. Paris , c1986. 261 p. : ISBN 2-259-01546-8 : LC Card 87-167974
HC272.5.T3 M87 1986

Tapping the small-business market /. Veale, Stuart R. New York, NY , c1987. xiii, 198 p. ; ISBN 0-13-884420-8 : LC Card 87-7732 DDC 332.6/068/8 19
HG4027.7 .V4 1987

Tarantelli, Ezio. Economia politica del lavoro / Ezio Tarantelli. Torino : UTET, c1986. xxiv, 549 p. : ill. ; 25 cm. (Biblioteca dell'economista. Ottava serie, Sezione sesta . v. 1) Includes bibliographies. ISBN 88-02-03977-1 LC Card 86-213541
1. Labor and laboring classes. 2. Industrial relations. 3. Labor policy. I. Title. II. Series.
HD4901 .T368 1986

Tarasov, Ivan Gavrilovich. Sled v zhizni / I.G. Tarasov. Frunze : "Kyrgyzstan", 1985. 94 p. ; 20 cm. (SSSR--bratstvo narodov) LC Card 87-115075
1. Kirghiz S.S.R. - Economic conditions. 2. Kirghiz S.S.R. - Social conditions. I. Series. II. Series: SSSR--bratstvo narodov (Frunze, Kirghiz S.S.R.). III. Title.
HC337.K545 T37 1985

Tarasov, K. S. (Konstantin Sergeevich) Latinskaia͡ Amerika--problemy razvitii͡a neftı͡anoĭ promyshlennosti /. Moskva , 1984. 192 p. : LC Card 86-181028
HD9574.L3 L4 1984

Targ, Harry R., 1940- Strategy of an empire in decline : Cold War II / by Harry R. Targ. Minneapolis : MEP Publications, c1986. 294 p. ; 23 cm. (Studies in Marxism. vol. 20) Includes index. Bibliography: p. 281-287. ISBN 0-930656-47-4 : LC Card 86-16338 DDC 909.82 19
1. World politics - 1975-1985. 2. World politics - 1945-. 3. United States - Foreign relations - Soviet Union. 4. Soviet Union - Foreign relations - United States. 5. United States - Foreign relations - 1945-. I. Title.
D849 .T37 1986 ***NYPL [JFD 87-2032]***

Targeting the computer . Flamm, Kenneth, 1951- Washington, D.C. , c1987. xiii, 266 p. ; ISBN 0-8157-2852-2 : LC Card 87-11706 DDC 338.4/7004/0973 19
HD9696.C63 U516466 1987

Targets and indicators . Williamson, John, 1937- Washington, DC , 1987. xii, 108 p. : ISBN 0-88132-064-1 LC Card 87-22724 DDC 332.4/5 19
HG3881 .W4936 1987

Targett, David. The Pocket guide to business numeracy / David Targett. Oxford, OX ; New York, NY, USA : Blackwell ; x, 184 p. : ill. ; 23 cm. ISBN 0-631-15124-9 : LC Card 86-31032 DDC 513/.93/0321 19
1. Business mathematics - Dictionaries. 2. Numeracy - Dictionaries. I. Economist (London, England). II. Title.
HF5695 .T34 1987

Targetti, Ferdinando. Lezioni di economia . Milano , 1979. 195 p. ; LC Card 80-451708
HG1029.5 .L49 ***NYPL [JLC 86-357]***

Targetti Lenti, Renata. Struttura produttiva e distribuzione personale del reddito : una verifica del caso italiano / Renata Targetti Lenti. Milano : A. Giuffrè, [1984] 263 p. : ill. ; 26 cm. (Pubblicazioni dell'Istituto di studi politico-economici . 4) Includes index. Bibliography: p. 249-257. ISBN 88-14-00277-0 : LC Card 84-251227 DDC 339.2/2/0945 19
1. Income - Italy. 2. Income distribution - Italy. I. Title. II. Series.
HC310.I5 T346 1984 ***NYPL [JLF 86-1305]***

Tarifas internas na Primeira República. Bezerra, Agostinho Fernandes. As tarifas internas na 1a. República /. Brasília, DF , 1986. xv, 140 p. : LC Card 87-404990 DDC 381/.5/098134 19
HJ5101.P47 B49 1986

As tarifas internas na 1a. República /. Bezerra, Agostinho Fernandes. Brasília, DF , 1986. xv, 140 p. : LC Card 87-404990 DDC 381/.5/098134 19
HJ5101.P47 B49 1986

TARIFF - AUSTRALIA.
Rattigan, G. A. (Godfrey Alfred), 1911- Industry assistance . Carlton, Vic. , Beaverton, Or. , 1986. viii, 289 p., [4] p. of plates : ISBN 0-522-84313-1 LC Card 86-202866 DDC 338.994 19
HF2483 .R38 1986

TARIFF - BRAZIL.
Green, Ronald D. Brazilian government support for the aerospace industry /. [Washington, D.C.?] [1987] xi, 44 p. ; LC Card 87-601479 DDC 338.4/76291/0981 19
HD9711.B72 G74 1987

TARIFF - CANADA.
The Free trade papers /. Toronto , 1986. 1 [i.e. 50], 227 p. : ISBN 0-88862-972-9 LC Card 87-109310 DDC 382.7/1/0971 19
HF1479 .F74 1986

Laxer, James. Leap of faith . Edmonton , c1986. 140 p. ; ISBN 0-88830-298-3 : LC Card 87-101958 DDC 382.7/1/0971 19
HF1480.15.U5 L39 1986

TARIFF - CANADA - HISTORY.
McIntosh, Dave. The collectors . Toronto, Ont., Canada , c1984. 414 p. : ISBN 0-920053-29-7 LC Card 85-162089 DDC 354.710072/46/09 19
HJ6751.A6 M35 1984 ***NYPL [JLE 86-2880]***

TARIFF - CANADA - HISTORY - 19TH CENTURY.
Forster, Jakob Johann Benjamin. A conjunction of interests . Toronto , Buffalo , c1986. vi, 288 p. ; ISBN 0-8020-5680-6 (alk. paper) LC Card 87-108915 DDC 382.7/0971 19
HF1765 .F67 1986

TARIFF - CHILE - MATHEMATICAL MODELS.
Aedo, Cristián. Protección efectiva en Chile, 1974-1979 /. Santiago [1984] 56 leaves ; LC Card 85-152465
HF1956 .A35 1984

TARIFF - DENMARK - HISTORY.
Eliassen, Peter. Kongeåen, eller, Den gamle grænse /. [København, Amaliegade 44, 1256 K] [Esbjerg] , 1980. 357, [4] p. : ISBN 87-87796-02-3 : LC Card 81-107972
HJ6971 .E45 1980

TARIFF - DEVELOPING COUNTRIES.
Tussie, Diana. The less developed countries and the world trading system . London , 1987. viii, 162 p. ; ISBN 0-86187-614-8
NYPL [JLE 87-1597]

TARIFF - DEVELOPING COUNTRIES - MATHEMATICAL MODELS.
Sánchez Holguín, Carlos Gerardo, 1952- Einige reale Aspekte der Aussenhandelsliberalisierung in Entwicklungsländern /. München , c1986. 152 p. : ISBN 3-88259-368-7 LC Card 86-156293
HF2580.9 .S25 1986

TARIFF - EAST ASIA.
Unfair foreign trade practices . Washington , 1986. v, 27 p. ; LC Card 86-603374 DDC 382/.0973/05 19
HF3126.5 .U53 1986

TARIFF - ECONOMETRIC MODELS.
Coloma C., Fernando. Algunas consideraciones sobre los efectos distributivos del proceso de liberalización comercial /. Santiago , 1982. 31 leaves ; LC Card 87-102072
HF1713 .C617 1982

Coloma C., Fernando. Los efectos de una desgravación arancelaria en el contexto de una economía con movilidad imperfecta de trabajo /. Santiago , 1985. 46 leaves : LC Card 85-203579
HF1713 .C618 1985

TARIFF - EUROPEAN ECONOMIC COMMUNITY COUNTRIES.
Coming to grips with the internal market /. Maastricht, The Netherlands , c1986. viii, 136 p. ; ISBN 90-6779-019-2 (pbk.) LC Card 86-222624 DDC 337.1/42 19
HC241.2 .C5548 1986

TARIFF - EUROPEAN ECONOMIC COMMUNITY COUNTRIES - STATISTICS.

TARIFF - GERMANY - HISTORY.
Hahn, Hans-Werner. Geschichte des Deutschen Zollvereins /. Göttingen , c1984. 214 p. ; ISBN 3-525-33500-8 LC Card 85-129823
HF2106 .H27 1984

TARIFF - JURISPRUDENCE. see **TARIFF - LAW AND LEGISLATION.**

TARIFF - KOREA (SOUTH)
Luedde-Neurath, Richard. Import controls and export-oriented development . Boulder , 1986. xiv, 249 p. ; ISBN 0-8133-7080-9 : LC Card 85-10459 DDC 382/.3/095195 19
HF1602.5 .L84 1985 ***NYPL [JLE 86-1557]***

TARIFF - LAW AND LEGISLATION - CONGRESSES.
Tariff, legal, and credit constraints on East-West commercial relations /. Ottawa , 1975. 101 p. ; LC Card 76-379543 DDC 382.1
K3823.A55 T3 ***NYPL [JLD 86-1752]***

TARIFF - LAW AND LEGISLATION - EUROPEAN ECONOMIC COMMUNITY COUNTRIES.
Lasok, Dominik. The customs law of the European Economic Community /. Deventer, Netherlands , Boston , c1983. xxiii, 292 p. : ISBN 90-6544-077-1 (pbk.) : LC Card 84-148702 DDC 343.405/6 344.0356 19
LAW NYPL [JLE 86-2073]

McGovern, Edmond. International trade regulation . Exeter [Devon] , 1986. xliv, 629 p. ; ISBN 0-9508463-4-1 DDC 341.7/54 19
K3943 .M4 1982 NYPL [JLE 86-3637]

TARIFF - LAW AND LEGISLATION - LATIN AMERICA.
Exenciones arancelarias e integración /. [Buenos Aires] , 1986. 273 p. ; LC Card 87-400577 DDC 382.7/1/098 19
HF1733.L29 E96 1986

TARIFF - LAW AND LEGISLATION - MEXICO.
Información básica sobre el GATT y el desarrollo industrial y comercial de México. México , c1985. 79, 62 p. ; LC Card 87-400559 DDC 338.0972 19
HC135 .I53 1985

TARIFF - LAW AND LEGISLATION - UNITED STATES.
McGovern, Edmond. International trade regulation . Exeter [Devon] , 1986. xliv, 629 p. ; ISBN 0-9508463-4-1 DDC 341.7/54 19
K3943 .M4 1982 NYPL [JLE 86-3637]

Tariff, legal, and credit constraints on East-West commercial relations / edited by John P. Hardt. Ottawa : Institute of Soviet and East European Studies, Carleton University, 1975. 101 p. ; 21 cm. (East-West commercial relations series. Special study . 1) "Papers presented by members of the panel on Law and Business in East-West Trade at the international conference on the Soviet Union and Eastern Europe, held in Banff, Alberta in September 1974." Includes bibliographical references. LC Card 76-379543 DDC 382.1
1. International economic relations - Congresses. 2. Commercial law - Congresses. 3. Tariff - Law and legislation - Congresses. I. Hardt, John Pearce. II. Series.
K3823.A55 T3 NYPL [JLD 86-1752]

TARIFF LISTS. see **TARIFF - LAW AND LEGISLATION.**

TARIFF - MADEIRA ISLANDS - ACCOUNTING - HISTORY - 16TH CENTURY.
Livros de contas da ilha da Madeira, 1504-1537 /. Coimbra , 1985- v. <1 > ; LC Card 86-232733
HJ9930.3.M33 L58 1985

TARIFF - MEXICO.
Kate, Adriaan ten. La política de protección en el desarrollo económico de México /. México , 1979. 376 p. ; ISBN 968-16-0352-4 LC Card 87-672671
HF1775 .K37x 1979

Mexico. Congreso. Cámara de Senadores. Consulta sobre el GATT . México , c1986. v, 540 p. ; LC Card 87-114865 DDC 382/.0972 19
HF1481 .M45 1986

TARIFF ON AGRICULTURAL PRODUCTS. see **TARIFF ON FARM PRODUCE.**

TARIFF ON BEDDING INDUSTRY - AUSTRALIA.
Australia. Industries Assistance Commission. Interim report . Canberra , 1976. 36 p. ; ISBN 0-642-02317-4 (pbk.) LC Card 85-132707
HD9969.B433 A83 1976

TARIFF ON CANDLES - UNITED STATES.
United States. International Trade Commission. Candles from the People's Republic of China . Washington, DC [1985] 13, 37 p. ; LC Card 86-164215 DDC 382/.4574559332/0951 19
HF2651.C254 U55 1985

TARIFF ON CLOTHING.
Foreign regulations affecting U. S. textile/apparel exports. [Washington, D.C.] [1986] 283 p. ; LC Card 86-601588
HF2651.T42 F67 1986

TARIFF ON CLOTHING - SOUTH AFRICA.
South Africa. Committee of Inquiry into the Textile and Clothing Industries. The policy of protection in regard to textiles and clothing . Pretoria , 1982?] ix, 110, [28] p. ; ISBN 0-621-08170-1 (pbk.) : LC Card 86-207580 DDC 382/.45677/00968 19
HF2651.C635 S627 1982

TARIFF ON FARM PRODUCE.
Agriculture in the GATT . Washington , 1986. v, 47 p. ; LC Card 86-603393 DDC 382/.41/0973 19
HD9006 .A77 1986

Hathaway, Dale E. Agriculture and the GATT . Washington, DC , c1987. xii, 157 p. : ISBN 0-88132-052-8 LC Card 87-21430 DDC 382/.41/0973 19
HD9006 .H28 1987

TARIFF ON FARM PRODUCE - JAPAN.
Hillman, Jimmye S., 1923- Agricultural trade and protection in Japan /. Aldershot, Hants, England , Brookfield, Vt. , 1988. p. cm. ISBN 0-566-05339-X : LC Card 87-15043 DDC 382.7/3/0952 19
HD9016.J42 H55 1988

Japanese import barriers to U. S. agricultural exports and the Common agricultural policy of the European Community and implications for U. S. agricultural trade . Washington , 1986. vii, 65 p. : LC Card 87-601384 DDC 382/.5/0952 19
HF1601 .J363 1986

TARIFF ON FARM PRODUCE - LATIN AMERICA.
Basco, Carlos A. El comercio intrarregional de alimentos básicos. [S.l.] , 1986. xi, 558 p. : LC Card 87-404784 DDC 382/.41/098 19
HD9014.L32 B37 1986

TARIFF ON ORANGES - EUROPEAN ECONOMIC COMMUNITY COUNTRIES.
Dean, Gerald W. World trade in fresh oranges . Berkeley, Calif. [1967] 70 p. : LC Card 87-401008 DDC 338.1/09794 s 382/.41431 19
HD1407 .C27 no. 18 HD9259.O7

TARIFF ON PETROLEUM PRODUCTS - UNITED STATES.
Webre, Philip. The budgetary and economic effects of oil taxes. Washington, DC , 19. xvi, 55 p. ; *NYPL [JLF 86-1354]*

TARIFF ON RAW MATERIALS. see **TARIFF.**

TARIFF ON RUBBER FOOTWEAR - CANADA.
Canada. Tariff Board. Relating to the reinstatement of the general preferential tariff on imports of rubber footwear . Ottawa, Canada , c1985. vi, 88 p. ; ISBN 0-660-11961-7 (pbk.) : LC Card 87-109471 DDC 382/.0971 s 382/.4568531/00971 19
HF1762 .A3 no. 161, pt. 1 HF2651.F757C22

TARIFF ON TEXTILE FABRICS.
Foreign regulations affecting U. S. textile/apparel exports. [Washington, D.C.] [1986] 283 p. ; LC Card 86-601588
HF2651.T42 F67 1986

TARIFF ON TEXTILE FABRICS - SOUTH AFRICA.
South Africa. Committee of Inquiry into the Textile and Clothing Industries. The policy of protection in regard to textiles and clothing . Pretoria , 1982?] ix, 110, [28] p. ; ISBN 0-621-08170-1 (pbk.) : LC Card 86-207580 DDC 382/.45677/00968 19
HF2651.C635 S627 1982

TARIFF - PHILIPPINES.
Alburo, Florian A. Trade liberalization experience in the Philippines, 1960-84 /. Makati, Metro Manila [1985] 159 p. : LC Card 87-167251 DDC 382/.09599/0021 19
HF1599 .A43 1985

TARIFF - PORTUGAL.
Sousa, Fernando Freire de. A adesão de Portugal à CEE . [Porto] [1985] 96 p. ; LC Card 86-174408
HF2236 .S68 1985

TARIFF PREFERENCES.
Langhammer, Rolf J. Economic impact of generalized tariff preferences /. Aldershot, Hants, England , Brookfield, Vt. , 1988. p. cm. ISBN 0-566-05338-1 : LC Card 87-15045 DDC 382.7/53 19
HF1721 .L35 1988

TARIFF PREFERENCES - DEVELOPING COUNTRIES.
Hasse, Rolf. Ökonometrie als Instrument der Interessenpolitik . Köln , 1985. ii, 109 p. : ISBN 3-921471-52-4 : LC Card 85-216061
HF1733.D44 H37 1985

TARIFF PREFERENCES - EUROPEAN ECONOMIC COMMUNITY COUNTRIES.
Davenport, Michael, 1940- Trade policy, protectionism, and the Third World /. London , Dover, N.H. , c1986. 152 p. : ISBN 0-7099-4516-7 : LC Card 86-6192 DDC 382.7/53 19
HF2039.5.Z7 D38 1986 NYPL [JLD 86-2759]

Langhammer, Rolf J. Economic impact of generalized tariff preferences /. Aldershot, Hants, England , Brookfield, Vt. , 1988. p. cm. ISBN 0-566-05338-1 : LC Card 87-15045 DDC 382.7/53 19
HF1721 .L35 1988

TARIFF PREFERENCES - EUROPEAN ECONOMIC COMMUNITY COUNTRIES - STATISTICS.

TARIFF PREFERENCES - LATIN AMERICA.
Williamson B., Carlos. La teoría sobre preferencias arancelarias . Santiago, Chile , 1985. 35 leaves : LC Card 85-202146
HF1733.L29 W54 1985

TARIFF PREFERENCES - UNITED STATES.
Langhammer, Rolf J. Economic impact of generalized tariff preferences /. Aldershot, Hants, England , Brookfield, Vt. , 1988. p. cm. ISBN 0-566-05338-1 : LC Card 87-15045 DDC 382.7/53 19
HF1721 .L35 1988

TARIFF PREFERENCES - ZAMBIA - HISTORY.
Kanduza, Ackson M. The political economy of underdevelopment in Northern Rhodesia, 1918-1960 . Lanham, MD , c1986. x, 336 p. : ISBN 0-8191-5189-0 (alk. paper) : LC Card 85-29835 DDC 338.96894 19
HC915 .K36 1986 NYPL [JLD 86-2962]

TARIFF SCHEDULES. see **TARIFF - LAW AND LEGISLATION.**

Tariff trends in the northeast corridor. Yankee Group white paper communications systems & services . Boston, Mass. (200 Portland St., Boston 02114) , 1987. 51 leaves : LC Card 87-155249 DDC 384.6/3 19
HE8825 .Y36 1987

TARIFF UNIONS. see **CUSTOMS UNIONS.**

TARIFF - UNITED STATES.
The Free trade papers /. Toronto , 1986. l [i.e. 50], 227 p. : ISBN 0-88862-972-9 LC Card 87-109310 DDC 382.7/1/0971 19
HF1479 .F74 1986

Taylor, John, 1753-1824. Tyranny unmasked /. Cumberland, Va. , 1988. p. cm. ISBN 0-940973-05-7 (alk. paper) : LC Card 87-2957 DDC 382.7/3/0973 19
HF1754 .T4 1988

TARIFF - UNITED STATES - ECONOMETRIC MODELS.
The Protectionist threat . Philadelphia, PA (3624 Science Center, Philadelphia 19104) , c1985. 85 p. : LC Card 87-106782 DDC 382.7/3/0973 19
HF1716 .P76 1985

Tarifs routiers de marchandises. Nomenclature des marchandises : désignations usuelles et assimilations tarifaires. Paris : Lamy, [1986] 201 p. ; 30 cm. (Documents tarifaires Lamy) Title on spine: Nomenclature des marchandises, route. "Edition du 30 avril 1986." ISBN 2-7212-0295-2 LC Card 87-123802
1. Trucking - France - Rates. 2. Commercial products - France - Terminology. I. Title: Nomenclature des marchandises. II. Title: Nomenclature des marchandises, route. III. Series.
HE5668.A6 T37 1986

Tarifs routiers de marchandises. Numéros de relations. Paris : Lamy, [1986] 956 p. ; 30 cm. (Documents tarifaires Lamy) Title on spine: Numéros de relations, route. Tables. "Edition du 20 avril 1986." ISBN 2-7212-0297-9 LC Card 87-119821
1. Trucking - France - Rates. I. Title: Numéros de relations. II. Title: Numéros de relations, route. III. Series.
HE5668.A6 T38 1986

Tarify i rezhimy ėlektropotreblenii͡a /. Mikhaĭlov, V. V. (Vram Vagramovich) Moskva , 1986. 214

p. : LC Card 86-108009
HD9685.S762 M55 1986

Tarizzo, Domenico. Il nuovo amore di coppia / Domenico Tarizzo. 1a ed. Milano : Rizzoli, 1982. 192 p. ; 22 cm. Includes index. LC Card 82-141135 DDC 306.7 19
1. Sex in marriage. 2. Women - Psychology. 3. Men - Psychology. I. Title.
HQ21 .T338 1982 ***NYPL [JLD 87-1019]***

Tarkenton, Francis A. Playing to win : Fran Tarkenton's strategies for business success / by Fran Tarkenton.1st ed. New York : Harper & Row, c1984. viii, 116 p. ; 22 cm. ISBN 0-06-015242-7 : LC Card 83-48390 DDC 650.1 19
1. Success in business. 2. Leadership. I. Title.
HF5386 .T22 1984 ***NYPL [JLD 86-3515]***

Tarkka, Juha, 1954- The BOF3 quarterly model of the Finnish economy /. Helsinki , 1985. 465 p. : ISBN 951-686-108-3 (pbk.) LC Card 86-205002 DDC 330.94897/005 s 338.5/443/094897 19
HB30 .S95 no. 59 HC340.2

Tarkunda, V. M. Rationalism, humanism, and democracy . Meerut , 1985. xcii, 514 p., [2] p. of plates : LC Card 85-901252 DDC 144 19
B833 .R29 1985 ***NYPL [JFD 86-3589]***

Tarkunde, V. M. For freedom / V.M. Tarkunde. New Delhi : V.M. Tarkunde Felicitation Committee, 1984. xii, 199 p. ; 23 cm. "This volume is intended to commemorate the seventy-fifth birthday of Vithal Mahadev Tarkunde."--p. [vii] Includes bibliographical references. LC Card 84-902126 DDC 144 19
1. Tarkunde, V. M. 2. Humanism - Addresses, essays, lectures. 3. Ethics - Addresses, essays, lectures. 4. Liberty - Addresses, essays, lectures. I. Title.
B821 .T285 1984 ***NYPL [JFD 87-1740]***

TARKUNDE, V. M.
Tarkunde, V. M. For freedom /. New Delhi , 1984. xii, 199 p. ; LC Card 84-902126 DDC 144 19
B821 .T285 1984 ***NYPL [JFD 87-1740]***

Tarmisto, Vello. Izuchenie problem narodonaseleniia v Institute ėkonomiki AN Ėstonskoĭ SSR . Tallin , 1979. 78 p. ; LC Card 81-198604
HB850.5.S65 I97 1979

Tarrab, Gilbert. L'Homme d'affaires québécois des années 80 /. Montréal, Québec, Canada , c1983. 418 p., [14] p. of plates : ISBN 2-89045-585-8 LC Card 83-190776
HC117.Q4 H65 1983

Társadalmi-gazdasági fejlődés a hatodik ötéves tervidőszakban. Társadalmi-gazdasági fejlődés a VI. ötéves tervidőszakban. Budapest , 1986. 131 p. ; ISBN 963-340-800-8 : LC Card 87-408587
HC300.28 .T378 1986

Társadalmi-gazdasági fejlődés a VI. ötéves tervidőszakban. Budapest : Központi Statisztikai Hivatal, 1986. 131 p. ; 29 cm. ISBN 963-340-800-8 : LC Card 87-408587
1. Hungary - Economic conditions - 1968-. 2. Hungary - Social conditions - 1968-. I. Hungary. Központi Statisztikai Hivatal. II. Title: Társadalmi-gazdasági fejlődés a 6. ötéves tervidőszakban. III. Title: Társadalmi-gazdasági fejlődés a hatodik ötéves tervidőszakban.
HC300.28 .T378 1986

Társadalmi-gazdasági fejlődés a 6. ötéves tervidőszakban. Társadalmi-gazdasági fejlődés a VI. ötéves tervidőszakban. Budapest , 1986. 131 p. ; ISBN 963-340-800-8 : LC Card 87-408587
HC300.28 .T378 1986

A társadalmi viszonyok erőtere, a munkafolyamat /. Makó, Csaba. Budapest , 1985. 192 p. ; ISBN 963-221-528-1 : LC Card 86-187344
HF5549 .M2953 1985

Társadalmunk ingázói, az ingázók társadalma /. Bőhm, Antal. [Budapest] , 1985. 166, [I] p. ; ISBN 963-09-2654-7 : LC Card 86-185996
HD5717.5.H9 B64 1985

Társadalom statisztikai közlemények, 0133-8226. Harcsa, István. Vándorlás, mobilitás, keresetalakulás . Budapest , 1987. 86 p. ; ISBN 963-340-812-1 : LC Card 87-409641
HB2052.5.A3 H37 1987

Tarshis, Lorie. International monetary problems and supply-side economics . Houndmills, Basingstoke, Hampshire , 1986. viii, 162 p. : ISBN 0-333-36200-4 ***NYPL [JLD 86-4356]***

TARSHIS, LORIE.
International monetary problems and supply-side economics . Houndmills, Basingstoke, Hampshire , 1986. viii, 162 p. : ISBN 0-333-36200-4 ***NYPL [JLD 86-4356]***

Tartakowsky, Pierre, 1952- Les intérimeurs / Pierre Tartakowsky ; préface de Henri Krasucki. Paris : Messidor : Temps actuels, c1985. 260 p., [8] p. of plates : ill. ; 22 cm. (La Vérité vraie) Bibliography: p. 257. Includes index. ISBN 2-209-05678-0 : LC Card 85-152003 DDC 331.12/5 19
1. Temporary employment - France. I. Title.
HD5854.2.F7 T37 1985

Tarykh institutu (Kyrgyz SSR ilimder akademiiasy) K istorii sotsial'no-ėkonomicheskikh ukladov Kirgizstana /. Frunze , 1972. 108 p. ; LC Card 82-171559
HC337.K545 K15 1972

Tasa de descuento social. Coloma C., Fernando. Endeudamiento externo y tasa de descuento social . Santiago, Chile , 1986. 66 leaves : LC Card 87-102066
HJ8083 .C65 1986

Tasas de participación y relaciobes multivariadas a partir e la información de la encuesta de hogares del segundo semestre de 1978 . Apezechea, Héctor J., 1937- [Montevideo, Uruguay] , 1980. 12, [44] leaves ; LC Card 86-157658
HD5762.A6 A64 1980

Tasgian, Astrig.
La valutazione economica della vita umana : aspetti teorici ed empirici / [di] Astrig Tasgian. Torino : G. Giappichelli, 1980. 117 p. : ill. ; 24 cm. (Ricerche e contributi / Università di Torino, Laboratorio di economia politica "S. Cognetti De Martiis") Bibliography: p. [111]-117. LC Card 81-124532 DDC 331/.01/1 19
1. Public welfare - Cost effectiveness. 2. Accidents - Prevention - Cost effectiveness. I. Title.
HD4904.7 .T34 1980 ***NYPL [JLE 86-1600]***

L'imposta e il deposito previo sugli acquisti di valuta e la crisi della lira del 1976 : un caso di politica valutaria / Astrig Tasgian. Milano : F. Angeli, c1983. 139 p. : ill. ; 22 cm. (Collana Università . 14) Bibliography: p. [131]-139. LC Card 83-187693 DDC 332.4/945 19
1. Currency question - Italy. 2. Foreign exchange problem - Italy. 3. Monetary policy - Italy. 4. Balance of trade - Italy. I. Title. II. Series.
HG1029.5 .T37 1983 ***NYPL [JLD 87-813]***

Tasheva, Svetla. Khadzhiev, Stefan. Zavod "Druzhba" . Varna , 1985. 161 p., [3] leaves of plates : LC Card 86-140096
HD8039.C62 B95 1985

Tashkentskaia vysshaia partiinaia shkola. Sovershenstvovanie khoziaistvennogo mekhanizma v usloviiakh razvitogo sotsializma /. Tashkent , 1985. 142, [2] p. ; LC Card 86-220208
HC337.U96 S68 1985

Task force implementation guidelines for the development of state and community alcohol highway safety programs. [Washington, D.C.?] : U. S. Dept. of Transportation, National Highway Traffic Safety Administration, 1983. 1 v. (various pagings) ; 28 cm. Cover title. "September 1983"--P. [4] of cover. "DOT HS 806 433"--P. [4] of cover.
1. Drinking and traffic accidents - United States. 2. Traffic accidents - United States. 3. Traffic safety - United States. ***NYPL [JLF 86-245]***

Task Force on the Quality of Audits of Governmental Units. Report of the Task Force on the Quality of Audits of Governmental Units : March 1987 / American Institute of Certified Public Accountants. New York, N.Y. : The Institute, c1987. viii, 71 p. : ill. ; 22 cm. LC Card 87-149765 DDC 350.72/32 19
1. Task Force on the Quality of Audits of Governmental Units. 2. Finance, Public - United States - Auditing. I. American Institute of Certified Public Accountants. II. Title.
HJ9777.A3 T37 1987

TASK FORCE ON THE QUALITY OF AUDITS OF GOVERNMENTAL UNITS.
Task Force on the Quality of Audits of Governmental Units. Report of the Task Force on the Quality of Audits of Governmental Units . New York, N.Y. , c1987. viii, 71 p. : LC Card 87-149765 DDC 350.72/32 19
HJ9777.A3 T37 1987

Task management. Vitullo, Ray, 1925- How to get organized & increase self confidence . North Plainfield, N.J. , c1986. p. cm. ISBN 0-9607752-3-4 : LC Card 86-72854 DDC 650.1 19
HD69.T54 V58 1986

Tassey, Gregory. Link, Albert N. Strategies for technology-based competition . Lexington, Mass. , c1987. xii, 142 p. : ISBN 0-669-14574-2 (alk. paper) LC Card 86-45885 DDC 338.6/048 19
HF1414 .L55 1987

Tasso di inflazione, saggio di interesse e "nuova" macroeconomia /. Mistri, Maurizio. Padova , 1985. x, 143 p. : LC Card 86-214490
HB539 .M54 1985

A taste of freedom . Bradford, Helen. New Haven , 1987. xvi, 364 p., [2] p. of plates : ISBN 0-300-03873-9 LC Card 87-10451 DDC 331.88/0968 19
HD8801.A5 I1634 1987

Tata Energy Research Institute.
Energy policy issues . New Delhi , c1987. 146 p. : LC Card 87-900625 DDC 333.79/0954 19
HD9502.I42 E536 1987

National energy data systems . New Delhi , 1984, c1983. xxvi, 511 p. ; LC Card 84-901310 DDC 333.79/09172/4 19
HD9502.D442 N37 1984
NYPL [JLD 86-4320]

Tata Institute of Social Sciences. Unit for Child and Youth Research. Child labour and health . Bombay , c1985. xi, 287 p. ; LC Card 86-900928 DDC 331.3/1/0956 19
HD6250.I42 C46 1985
NYPL [JLD 87-1553]

Tata, J. R. D. (Jehangir Ratanji Dadabhoy), 1904- Keynote : excerpts from his speeches and chairman's statements to shareholders / J.R.D. Tata ; edited by S.A. Sabavala and R.M. Lala.1st ed. Bombay : Tata Press, 1986. xviii, 155 p., [1] leaf of plates : ill., ports. (some col.) ; 25 cm. ISBN 81-85110-00-X : LC Card 86-902369 DDC 338.0954
1. India - Economic conditions - 1947-. 2. India - Industries. 3. India - Social conditions - 1947-. I. Sabavala, S. A., 1918-. II. Lala, R. M. III. Title.
HC435.2 .T37 1986

Tatis, Antonio.
Gómez, Carmen. Población y energía en la República Dominicana, 1990-2000. Santo Domingo, República Dominicana [1985] vi, 86 p. : LC Card 86-176044
HD9502.D652 G65 1985

Gómez, Carmen. Población y vivienda en la República Dominicana . Santo Domingo, República Dominicana , 1984. 116 p. : LC Card 85-154466
HD7316.5.A3 G65 1984
NYPL [JLF 86-1146]

Tatsiĭ, G. M. (Grigoriĭ Mikhaĭlovich)
Ėkonomicheskiĭ analiz khoziaĭstvennoĭ deiatel'nosti predpriiatiĭ i ob"edineniĭ /. Moskva , 1986. 406 p. : LC Card 86-227621
HC340.A8 E417 1986

Täuber, Gudrun. Folgekosten der Besteuerung : eine theoretische und empirische Analyse / Gudrun Täuber. Spardorf : R.F. Wilfer, c1984. 204, xii p. : ill. ; 21 cm. Originally presented as the author's thesis (doctoral--Universität Erlangen-Nürnberg) Bibliography: p. v-xii. ISBN 3-922919-40-5 LC Card 85-128537
1. Tax incidence - Germany, West. 2. Tax incidence. I. Title.
HJ2323.G3 T38 1984

Tauber, Herbert. Johann Ulrich Aebi : 100 Jahre Schweizer Landmaschinen / von Herbert Tauber. Zürich : Verein für Wirtschaftshistorische Studien, c1983. 84, [2] p. : ill. ; 24 cm. (Schweizer Pioniere der Wirtschaft und Technik. 38) Bibliography: p. [86] LC Card 83-192282
1. Aebi, Johann Ulrich, 1846-1919. 2. Agricultural machinery industry - Switzerland - History. 3. Businessmen - Switzerland - Biography. 4. Aebi Maschinenfabrik (Burgdorf, Switzerland) - History. I.

Title. II. Series.
HC395.5.A2 S3 no. 38 HD9486.S94A36

Les taux de change flottants et les pays souscapitalisés . Ngirabatware, Augustin. Fribourg, Suisse , c1986. 340 p. : ISBN 2-8271-0330-3 : LC Card 86-170584
HG3877 .N48 1986

Taux de chômage standardisés. Standardised unemployment rates . Paris, France [Washington, D.C.] 1985. 93 p. ; LC Card 86-143095 DDC 331.13/7/072 19
HD5711 .S77 1985 ***NYPL [JLF 86-1743]***

Tāvare, Rāmacandra. Thāpaṭanā / Rāmacandra Tāvare. 1. āvr̥ttī. Mumbaī : Lokavāṅmaya Gr̥ha, 1986. 179 p. ; 23 cm. In Marathi. Autobiography of a member of the bonded labor class in Maharashtra. LC Card 87-900532
1. Tāvare, Rāmacandra. 2. Peonage - India - Maharashtra. 3. Maharashtra (India) - Biography. 4. Labor and laboring classes - India - Maharashtra - Biography. I. Title.
HD5820.M29 T38 1986

TĀVARE, RĀMACANDRA.
Tāvare, Rāmacandra. Thāpaṭanā /. Mumbaī , 1986. 179 p. ; LC Card 87-900532
HD5820.M29 T38 1986

Tavares de Araujo Júnior, José. see **Araujo Júnior, José Tavares de.**

Tavares, José, 1949- Indústria bélica brasileira : o homem diante da sua destruição : discursos / pronunciados pelo Deputado José Tavares. Brasília : Câmara dos Deputados, Centro de Documentação e Informação, Coordenação de Publicações, 1983. 44 p. ; 23 cm. (Separatas de discursos, pareceres e projetos . 47a. Legislatura--1a. Sessão Legislativa) Four folded p. of the Diário do Congresso Nacional inserted. LC Card 84-235004
1. Brazil - Economic policy. 2. Munitions - Brazil. I. Brazil. Congresso Nacional. Câmara dos Deputados. Centro de Documentação e Informação. Coordenação de Publicações. II. Title. III. Series.
HC187 .T2943 1983

Tavares, José Reinaldo Carneiro. Aspectos industriais da política de desenvolvimento do Nordeste : palestra do Dr. José Reinaldo Carneiro Tavares, Superintendente da SUDENE, por ocasião do I Encontro Nacional dos Empresários, dia 04 de outubro de 1985, no Centro de Convenções de Pernambuco. Recife : Ministério do Interior, Superintendência do Desenvolvimento do Nordeste, 1985. 24 leaves ; 22 cm. LC Card 87-102054 DDC 338.981/3 19
1. Industry and state - Brazil, Northeast - History - 20th century. I. Brazil. Superintendência do Desenvolvimento do Nordeste. II. Title.
HD3616.B84 N678 1985

TAVERNS. see **HOTELS, TAVERNS, ETC.**

Tavis, Lee A. Multinational managers and host government interactions /. Notre Dame, Ind. , c1987. p. cm. ISBN 0-268-01364-0 : LC Card 86-40590 DDC 658.4/08/091724 19
HD2932 .M847 1987

A távol-keleti kihívás . Hernádi, András. Budapest , 1985. 233 p. ; ISBN 963-221-545-1 : LC Card 86-186844
HC460.5 .H47 1985

Tawil, Natalie. Selected agricultural statistics on Spain, 1970-82 /. Washington, D.C. (1301 New York Ave., N.W., Washington 20005-4788) , 1986. x, 142 p. : LC Card 86-602416 DDC 338.1/0973 s 338.1/0946/021 19
HD1751 .A5 no. 742 HD2022

TAX ACCOUNTING - FRANCE - PROBLEMS, EXERCISES, ETC.
Lamorlette, Corine. 10 études de cas de fiscalité avec corrigés détaillés . Paris , 1984. 95 p. : ISBN 2-7178-0802-7 : LC Card 85-129474
HF5681.T3 L28 1984

TAX ACCOUNTING - GERMANY, WEST.
Unternehmung und Steuer . Wiesbaden , c1983. 395 p. ; ISBN 3-409-50005-7 LC Card 83-161883
HD2753.G3 U57 1983

TAX ACCOUNTING - GREAT BRITAIN.
Rankin, H. C. D. Corporation tax for students /. Wokingham, Berkshire, England , 1985. x, 230 p. : ISBN 0-85258-242-0 (pbk.) LC Card 85-3272 DDC 657/.46/0941 19
HD2753.G7 R36 1985

TAX ACCOUNTING - UNITED STATES.
Public record, FASB technical bulletin no. 86-1, Accounting for certain effects of the Tax Reform Act of 1986. Stamford, Conn. (P.O. Box 3821, Stamford 06905-0821) [1987] 172 p. ; LC Card 87-80349 DDC 657/.46 19
HF5681.T3 P83 1987

TAX ADMINISTRATION AND PROCEDURE - BRAZIL - MINAS GERAIS.
Economia mineira e o financiamento do setor público . Belo Horizonte , 1985. 126 p. : LC Card 85-207952
HJ2529.M5 E26 1985

TAX ADMINISTRATION AND PROCEDURE - GERMANY (WEST) - DATA PROCESSING.
Automatisierte Verwaltung . Frankfurt , New York , c1981. 135 p. : ISBN 3-593-32944-1 : LC Card 81-146994
HJ3484.A4 A95 1981

TAX ADMINISTRATION AND PROCEDURE - GREAT BRITAIN.
James, Simon R. The comprehensibility of taxation . Aldershot, Hants, England , Brookfield, Vt., USA , c1987. xiii, 314 p. : ISBN 0-566-05348-9 : LC Card 86-25690 DDC 336.2/00941 19
HJ2619 .J36 1987

TAX ADMINISTRATION AND PROCEDURE - HISTORY - 17TH CENTURY.
Collins, James B. Fiscal limits of absolutism . Berkeley , c1987. p. cm. ISBN 0-520-05911-5 (alk. paper) LC Card 87-19090 DDC 336.2/00944 19
HJ2648 .C65 1987

TAX ADMINISTRATION AND PROCEDURE - JAPAN.
An Outline of Japanese tax administration. [Tokyo], Japan , 1985. 85 p., [1] leaf of plates : LC Card 86-209172 DDC 354.520072/4 19
HJ3627 .O87 1985

TAX ADMINISTRATION AND PROCEDURE - SWEDEN.
Administrationskostnader för våra skatter . [Stockholm] [1983] 114 p. : ISBN 91-38-08027-3 LC Card 84-219428
HJ3548 .A815 1983

TAX ADMINISTRATION AND PROCEDURE - UNITED STATES.
Langhoff, Gary M., 1952- Assessment jurisdictions and agency resources in the United States . Chicago, Ill. , 1987. p. cm. ISBN 0-88329-061-8 : LC Card 87-4101 DDC 336.22/2 19
HJ3241 .L36 1987

Steuerle, C. Eugene, 1946- Who should pay for collecting taxes? . Washington, D.C. , 1986. p. cm. ISBN 0-8447-3609-0 (pbk. : alk. paper) : LC Card 86-22345 DDC 353.0072/4 19
HJ5018 .S84 1986

TAX ADMINISTRATION AND PROCEDURE - UNITED STATES - CONGRESSES.
Conference on Tax Administration Research Strategies (1985 : Washington, D.C.) Conference on Tax Administration Research, January 1985. Washington, D.C. [1985] 2 v. : LC Card 86-601369 DDC 353.0072/4 19
HJ3252 .C66 1985 ***NYPL [JLF 86-1791]***

Research Conference on Trends Impacting Tax Administration (1985 : Washington, D.C.) Research Conference on Trends Impacting Tax Administration, November 20-22, 1985. Washington, D.C. (1111 Constitution Ave., N.W., Washington 20224) [1985] 2 v. ; 28 cm. LC Card 87-601252 DDC 350.72/4/00973 19
HJ3252 .R357 1985

TAX ADMINISTRATION AND PROCEDURE - UNITED STATES - STATES.
Clatanoff, Robert M. Patterns of property tax administration in the United States /. Chicago, Ill. , 1986. x, 178 p. : ISBN 0-88329-145-2 (pbk.) LC Card 86-7240 DDC 353.9/37242 19
HJ4120 .C528 1986 ***NYPL [JLF 87-464]***

TAX ADMINISTRATION AND PROCEDURE - UNITED STATES - TECHNOLOGICAL INNOVATIONS - CONGRESSES.
Research Conference on Trends Impacting Tax Administration (1985 : Washington, D.C.) Research Conference on Trends Impacting Tax Administration, November 20-22, 1985. Washington, D.C. (1111 Constitution Ave., N.W., Washington 20224) [1985] 2 v. ; 28 cm. LC Card 87-601252 DDC 350.72/4/00973 19
HJ3252 .R357 1985

Tax-advantaged investments /. Windish, David F. New York, N.Y. , c1985. xii, 404 p. : ISBN 0-13-884677-4 LC Card 84-25539 DDC 332.6/042 19
HJ4653.A3 W56 1985 ***NYPL [JLE 85-3677]***

Tax-advantaged investments /. Windish, David F. New York, N.Y. , c1987. xix, 407 p. : ISBN 0-13-884693-6 : LC Card 87-11156 DDC 332.6/042 19
HJ4653.A3 W56 1987

TAX AND EXPENDITURE LIMITATIONS - CALIFORNIA.
Barbaria, Janet. The growth revolt . Sacramento, Calif. [1980] 66 p. : LC Card 81-620644 DDC 336.794 19
HJ4191 .B37 1980 ***NYPL [JLF 86-369]***

Reis, Karl Eugen. Fesseln für den Leviathan . Pfaffenweiler , 1987. xi, 338 p. ; ISBN 3-89085-159-2 LC Card 87-134876 DDC 336.973 19
HJ2381 .R356 1987

TAX AND EXPENDITURE LIMITATIONS - UNITED STATES.
Merriman, David. The control of municipal budgets . New York , c1987. x, 170 p. : ISBN 0-89930-217-3 (lib. bdg. : alk. paper) LC Card 87-2495 DDC 352.1/2/0973 19
HJ9157 .M47 1987

Reis, Karl Eugen. Fesseln für den Leviathan . Pfaffenweiler , 1987. xi, 338 p. ; ISBN 3-89085-159-2 LC Card 87-134876 DDC 336.973 19
HJ2381 .R356 1987

Tax angles and tax savings series.
Buying or selling a home . Chicago, Ill. (4025 W. Peterson Ave., Chicago 60646) , c1986. 31 p. : LC Card 86-209128 DDC 343.7305/46 347.303546 19
HJ4182.A5 B89 1986

TAX AVOIDANCE. see **TAX PLANNING.**

Tax avoision : the economic, legal, and moral inter-relationships between avoidance and evasion / A.R. Ilersic ... [et al.] ; prologue, Arthur Seldon ; epilogue, Barry Bracewell-Milnes ; with a foreword by Lord Harris of High Cross. London : Institute of Economic Affairs, 1979. x, 134 p. ; 21 cm. (IEA readings, 0305-814X . 22) Includes bibliographical references and indexes. ISBN 0-255-36126-2 (pbk.) LC Card 86-673369
1. Tax evasion - Great Britain. 2. Tax planning - Great Britain. I. Ilersic, A. R. (Alfred Roman), 1920-. II. Series.
HJ2348.5 .T39x 1979

Tax base reductions. Tax report . Springfield, Ill. (703 Stratton Office Bldg., Springfield 62706) [1986] iv, 30, 3 leaves ; LC Card 86-622596 DDC 336.2/009773 19
HJ2403 .T39 1986

TAX BURDEN. see **TAX INCIDENCE.**

Tax capacity of the states. Cohen, Carol E. 1983 tax capacity of the states . Washington, D.C. (1111 20th St., NW, Washington 20575) [1986] ix, 111 p. : LC Card 86-601628 DDC 336.2/013/73
HJ2385 .C59 1986

TAX COLLECTION - COSTA RICA - HISTORY - 16TH CENTURY.
Costa Rica colonial . [San José, Costa Rica , 1984] 83 p. ; LC Card 86-173945
HC389 .C67 1984

TAX COLLECTION - COSTA RICA - HISTORY - 17TH CENTURY.
Costa Rica colonial . [San José, Costa Rica , 1984] 83 p. ; LC Card 86-173945
HC389 .C67 1984

TAX COLLECTION - MINNESOTA.
Property tax delinquency in Minnesota . St. Paul, Minn. [1984?] iv, 84 p. : LC Card 86-622652 DDC 336.22 19
HJ4232.A25 P76 1984

TAX COLLECTION - NEW YORK (STATE)
Lost revenue . [Albany, N.Y.?] [1986] 13, 22 leaves ; LC Card 87-620567 DDC 336.2/009747 19
HJ3324 .L67 1986

TAX COLLECTION - SWEDEN.
Administrationskostnader för våra skatter . [Stockholm] [1983] 114 p. : ISBN 91-38-08027-3 LC Card 84-219428
HJ3548 .A815 1983

TAX COLLECTION - UNITED STATES - CONGRESSES.
Conference on Tax Administration Research Strategies (1985 : Washington, D.C.) Conference on Tax Administration Research, January 1985. Washington, D.C. [1985] 2 v. : LC Card 86-601369 DDC 353.0072/4 19
HJ3252 .C66 1985 ***NYPL [JLF 86-1791]***

Tax credits for low income housing . Guggenheim, Joseph. Washington, D.C. , c1986. vii, 117 p. : ISBN 0-941239-00-4 (pbk.) LC Card 87-112304 DDC 363.5/8 19
HJ4653.C73 G85 1986

TAX CREDITS - NEW YORK (STATE)
New York (State). Legislature. Legislative Commission on the Modernization and Simplification of Tax Administration and the Tax Law. Interstate business locational decisions and the effect of the state's tax structure on after-tax rates-of-return of manufacturing firms . [Albany] [1984] 121 p. : LC Card 86-621116 DDC 336.2/07 19
HJ4655.N54 N55 1984

TAX CREDITS - VIRGINIA.
Virginia's income tax age credit. [Richmond, Va.] [1984] ii, 26 leaves ; LC Card 86-622458 DDC 336.24/216 19
HJ4655.V88 A828 1984

TAX DELINQUENCY. see **TAX EVASION.**

Tax districts. [Hartford, Conn.] : State of Connecticut, Office of Policy and Management, Intergovernmental Relations Division, [1985] 53 p. ; 22 cm. Cover title. "November 1985." LC Card 86-620827 DDC 352.1/3/09746 19
1. Local taxation - Connecticut. 2. Special districts - Connecticut. I. Connecticut. Intergovernmental Relations Division.
HJ9210 .T39 1985

TAX-DODGING. see **TAX EVASION.**

Tax ethics, or, Black money. Chopra, O. P. (Om Prakash), 1941- Tax ethics, unaccounted income . New Delhi , 1985, c1984. vi, 119 p. ; LC Card 85-900955 DDC 336.2/06 19
HJ2348.5 .C46 1985 ***NYPL [JLE 87-1297]***

Tax ethics, unaccounted income . Chopra, O. P. (Om Prakash), 1941- New Delhi , 1985, c1984. vi, 119 p. ; LC Card 85-900955 DDC 336.2/06 19
HJ2348.5 .C46 1985 ***NYPL [JLE 87-1297]***

TAX EVASION - GREAT BRITAIN.
Tax avoision . London , 1979. x, 134 p. ; ISBN 0-255-36126-2 (pbk.) LC Card 86-673369
HJ2348.5 .T39x 1979

TAX EVASION - GREAT BRITAIN - HISTORY - 20TH CENTURY.
Smithies, Edward. The black economy in England since 1914 /. London , Atlantic Highlands, N.J. , 1984. 165 p. ; ISBN 0-391-03114-7 LC Card 84-6516 DDC 364.1/33 19
HF5482.65.G7 S64 1984
NYPL [JLD 86-2509]

TAX EVASION - INDIA.
Chopra, O. P. (Om Prakash), 1941- Tax ethics, unaccounted income . New Delhi , 1985, c1984. vi, 119 p. ; LC Card 85-900955 DDC 336.2/06 19
HJ2348.5 .C46 1985 ***NYPL [JLE 87-1297]***

Kabra, Kamal Nayan. Black money . New Delhi , 1985. 47 p. ; LC Card 87-900898 DDC 381 19
HJ2348.5 .K32 1985

TAX EVASION - NETHERLANDS.
Fraudenota. [Hague , 1982] 42 p. ; ISBN 90-12-04091-4 LC Card 83-197641
HJ2348.5 .F72 1982

TAX EVASION - UNITED STATES.
Cash, Adam. Guerrilla capitalism . Port Townsend, Wash. , c1984. 172 p. : ISBN 0-915179-16-4 (pbk.) LC Card 84-81910 DDC 343.7305/23 347.303523 19
HD2346.U5 C34 1984 ***NYPL [JLD 86-2946]***

Tax expenditure report for sales and use tax--Nebraska and local option, property tax, individual income tax, fiduciary income tax, corporation income tax, miscellaneous taxes : ad valorem franchise tax, alcoholic ... / prepared by Nebraska Department of Revenue ... [et al.] ; with the cooperation of the Nebraska Secretary of State ... [et al.]. Lincoln, Neb. : The Department, [1985] 245 p. ; 28 cm. Cover title: Tax expenditure report, 1985. "October 15, 1985." LC Card 86-622058 DDC 343.78204 347.8204 19
1. Taxation - Nebraska - Statistics. 2. Taxation - Law and legislation - Nebraska. I. Nebraska. Dept. of Revenue. II. Nebraska. Secretary of State. III. Title: Tax expenditure report, 1985.
HJ2419 .T39 1985

Tax expenditure report, 1985. Tax expenditure report for sales and use tax--Nebraska and local option, property tax, individual income tax, fiduciary income tax, corporation income tax, miscellaneous taxes . Lincoln, Neb. [1985] 245 p. ; LC Card 86-622058 DDC 343.78204 347.8204 19
HJ2419 .T39 1985

Tax expenditures : current issues and five-year budget projections for fiscal years 1984-1988. Washington, D.C. : Congress of the United States, Congressional Budget Office, [1983] xiv, 82 p. ; 27 cm. "A CBO report, as required by public law 93-344." Includes bibliographical references.
1. Expenditures, Public - United States. 2. Tax revenue estimating - United States. 3. Budget - United States. 4. United States - Appropriations and expenditures - Forecasting. ***NYPL [JLF 84-401]***

Tax expenditures . Verdier, James M. Washington, D.C. , 1982. xx, 102 p. ;
NYPL [JLF 83-663]

TAX EXPENDITURES - CALIFORNIA.
Analysis of the 1987-88 tax expenditure budget. Sacramento, Calif. (925 L St., Suite 650, Sacramento 95814) [1987] 2 v. ; LC Card 87-621598 DDC 353.97940072/4 19
HJ4655.C23 A53 1987

TAX EXPENDITURES - CANADA.
Jobin, Jacques. Mesure et incidence des dépenses fiscales au Québec /. Montréal [1984] 27 p. ; LC Card 85-169988
HB3 .C3 vol. 8511 HJ4662.A45

TAX EXPENDITURES - NEW ZEALAND.
Brooks, R. Inflation, tax rules, and housing in New Zealand /. Wellington, N.Z. [1986] 22, [22] p. : LC Card 87-132461 DDC 363.5/8 19
HD7387.5.A3 B76 1986

TAX EXPENDITURES - UNITED STATES.
Kettl, Donald F. Government by proxy . Washington, D.C. , c1988. x, 170 p. ; ISBN 0-87187-429-6 (pbk.) : LC Card 87-13645 DDC 353.009 19
HD3861.U6 K47 1988

TAX INCENTIVES.
Leibfritz, Willi. Steuerliche Investitionsförderung im internationalen Vergleich /. Berlin , c1985. 255 p. : ISBN 3-428-05776-7 LC Card 85-161706
HJ4631 .L38 1985

Stern, Richard Walter. Internationale Steuervorteile /. Zürich , 1977. 56 leaves : LC Card 85-173548
HJ2336 .S74 1977

Wittmann, Franz, 1933- Der Einfluss der Steuern auf die Investitionsentscheidungen der Unternehmen . Frankfurt , New York , c1986. 405 p. ; ISBN 3-593-33642-1 LC Card 86-173001
HG4028.C4 W585 1986

TAX INCENTIVES - BERLIN (GERMANY)
Hecker, Christian. Abschreibungsgesellschaften in Berlin (West) . Köln , c1982. viii, 236, xix, 78 p. : ISBN 3-921379-96-2 LC Card 83-197457
HJ4720.B45 H43 1982

TAX INCENTIVES - BRAZIL.
Harber, Richard P. Tax policy, economic development, and regional inequality [microform] . Austin , 1984. 33 p. ; LC Card 84-623077 DDC 339.5/2/09813 19
HJ2527 .H37 1984 ***NYPL [*ZT-1646 no.22]***

TAX INCENTIVES - BRAZIL, CENTRAL WEST - HANDBOOKS, MANUALS, ETC.
Centro-Oeste . [Brasília] [1983] 196 p., [3] leaves of plates : LC Card 85-208305
HC188.C46 C47 1983

TAX INCENTIVES - BRAZIL, NORTHEAST.
Incentivos fiscais e financeiros para investimentos no Nordeste do Brasil /. Recife , 1985. 92 p. ; LC Card 87-404837 DDC 332.6/7322813 19
HJ2529.N6 I53 1985

TAX INCENTIVES - FLORIDA.
Tax incentives for community revitalization in Florida /. Tallahassee, Fla. [1983] 45 p. ; LC Card 86-623222 DDC 343.75906/6 347.590366 19
HJ4655.F64 T39 1983

Tax incentives for community revitalization in Florida / prepared for the Department of Community Affairs, Division of Local Resource Management by Coopers & Lybrand. Tallahassee, Fla. : The Division, [1983] 45 p. ; 28 cm. The Florida enterprise zone program : the history and summary of the 1982, 1984, and 1986 amendments, inserted. "September 1983." LC Card 86-623222 DDC 343.75906/6 347.590366 19
1. Tax incentives - Florida. 2. Community Development - Florida. 3. Tax incentives - Law and legislation - Florida. 4. Community development - Law and legislation - Florida. I. Florida. Dept. of Community Affairs. Division of Local Resource Management. II. Cooper & Lybrand.
HJ4655.F64 T39 1983

TAX INCENTIVES - GERMANY (WEST)
Analyse der Wirksamkeit der Beschäftigungszulage . München , 1984. vii, 172 p. : LC Card 85-230164
HJ4720.A45 A53 1984

Behrens-Ramberg, Wolfgang. Steuerliche Anreize bei innovativen Investitionen kleiner und mittlerer Industrieunternehmen unter vergleichender Berücksichtigung nichtsteuerlicher Hilfen /. Stuttgart , c1985. 299 p. ; ISBN 3-7910-5007-9 : LC Card 86-124563 DDC 336.24/316 19
HJ2337.G3 B44 1985
NYPL [JLL 73-505 Nr.6]

Wittmann, Franz, 1933- Der Einfluss der Steuern auf die Investitionsentscheidungen der Unternehmen . Frankfurt , New York , c1986. 405 p. ; ISBN 3-593-33642-1 LC Card 86-173001
HG4028.C4 W585 1986

TAX INCENTIVES - GREAT BRITAIN - CASE STUDIES.
Morgan, Eleanor. Corporate taxation and investment . Haldershot, Hants Gull, England , Brookfield, Vt., USA , c1986. x, 220 p. ; ISBN 0-566-05265-2 : LC Card 86-25642 DDC 336.24/3/0941 19
HJ4708.A7 M63 1986

TAX INCENTIVES - GREAT BRITAIN - CONGRESSES.
Taxation and incentives /. [London, England] , c1976. ii, 45 p. : LC Card 85-111944
HJ2619 .T289 1976

TAX INCENTIVES - ITALY.
Politiche tributarie e struttura industriale in Italia /. Bologna , c1986. 118 p. ; ISBN 88-15-01224-9 : LC Card 86-224989
HD2753.I7 P65 1986

TAX INCENTIVES - LAW AND LEGISLATION - FLORIDA.
Tax incentives for community revitalization in Florida /. Tallahassee, Fla. [1983] 45 p. ; LC Card 86-623222 DDC 343.75906/6 347.590366 19
HJ4655.F64 T39 1983

TAX INCENTIVES - NEW YORK (STATE)
New York (State). Legislature. Legislative Commission on Public-Private Cooperation. Legislative Commission on Public-Private Cooperation second report . [Albany] [1984] 57 p. ; LC Card 86-622576 DDC 338.9747 19
HC107.N7 N3743 1984 •

New York (State). Legislature. Legislative Commission on Public-Private Cooperation. Working together for New York's economy . [Albany] [1983] 57 p. ; LC Card 86-622577 DDC 338.9747 19
HC107.N7 N3743 1983

New York (State). Legislature. Legislative Commission on the Modernization and

Simplification of Tax Administration and the Tax Law. Interstate business locational decisions and the effect of the state's tax structure on after-tax rates-of-return of manufacturing firms . [Albany] [1984] 121 p. : LC Card 86-621116 DDC 336.2/07 19
HJ4655.N54 N55 1984

TAX INCENTIVES - UNITED STATES - CONGRESSES.
Taxation and incentives /. [London, England] , c1976. ii, 45 p. : LC Card 85-111944
HJ2619 .T289 1976

TAX INCIDENCE - AUSTRALIA.
Whiteford, Peter. Issues in assistance for families . Woden, ACT [1986] iii, 56 p. ; ISBN 0-642-51604-9 (pbk.) LC Card 86-231139 DDC 362/.0425 19
HD4925.5.A8 W47 1986

TAX INCIDENCE - CANADA.
Davies, James B., 1951- Reforming capital income taxation in Canada . [Ottawa] , c1987. ix, 153 p. : ISBN 0-660-12454-8 (pbk.) : LC Card 87-168079 DDC 336.24/24/0971 19
HJ4133.C2 .D38 1987

TAX INCIDENCE - ECONOMETRIC MODELS.
Hamm, Rüdiger. Die Inzidenz sektorspezifischer Kapitalbesteuerung /. Krefeld , 1983. 296 p. : ISBN 3-88358-034-1 LC Card 83-218772
HD2753.A3 H36 1983

TAX INCIDENCE - GERMANY, WEST.
Täuber, Gudrun. Folgekosten der Besteuerung . Spardorf , c1984. 204, xii p. : ISBN 3-922919-40-5 LC Card 85-128537
HJ2323.G3 T38 1984

TAX INCIDENCE - INDIA.
Sen, Tapas Kumar, 1956- Corporate income tax and profit rates . New Delhi , c1984. xiii, 267 p. ; LC Card 84-900209 DDC 336.24/3/0954 19
HJ4766.Z7 S46 1984 ***NYPL [JLD 86-4138]***

TAX INCIDENCE - INDIA - CASE STUDIES.
Shyam Nath, 1945- Measuring tax burden in India . New Delhi , 1987. xv, 194 p. : ISBN 81-7024-072-7 : LC Card 87-900348 DDC 336.2/94/09544 19
HJ2323.I4 S59 1987

TAX INCIDENCE - INDIA - RAJASTHAN - CASE STUDIES.
Shyam Nath, 1945- Measuring tax burden in India . New Delhi , 1987. xv, 194 p. : ISBN 81-7024-072-7 : LC Card 87-900348 DDC 336.2/94/09544 19
HJ2323.I4 S59 1987

TAX INCIDENCE - MALAWI.
Kandoole, B. F. Revenue and equity effects of the 1983 income tax reform in Malawi /. [Zomba, Malaŵi?] [1986] 20 p. ; LC Card 86-981440 DDC 336.2/0096897 19
HJ4791 .K36 1986

TAX INCIDENCE - MATHEMATICAL MODELS.
Widdau, Peter, 1952- Die Quantifizierung der Steuerbelastung im internationalen Bereich . Frankfurt am Main , New York , c1984. xx, 413 p. : ISBN 3-8204-8044-7 : LC Card 85-191946
HJ2321 .W46 1984

TAX INCIDENCE - NEW YORK (STATE)
Interstate tax comparisons . [Albany, N.Y.] [1985] 106 p. ; LC Card 86-621354 DDC 336.2/009747 19
HJ2424 .I57 1985

Who pays New York taxes? . [Albany, N.Y.] [1985] 2, 101 p. : LC Card 86-621353 DDC 336.2/94/09747 19
HJ2322.N7 W48 1985

TAX INCIDENCE - QUÉBEC (PROVINCE)
White paper on the personal tax and transfer systems /. Québec , 1984. 380 p. : ISBN 2-551-08967-0 (pbk.) : LC Card 85-150790 DDC 336.24/215/09714 19
HJ4663.Q8 W47 1984 ***NYPL [JLF 87-360]***

TAX INCIDENCE - UNITED STATES.
Interstate tax comparisons . [Albany, N.Y.] [1985] 106 p. ; LC Card 86-621354 DDC 336.2/009747 19
HJ2424 .I57 1985

Tax increment financing. Minnesota. Office of the Legislative Auditor. Program Evaluation Division. Saint Paul, Minn. (Veterans Service Bldg., Saint Paul 55155) , 1986. xix, 138 p. : LC Card 86-623133 DDC 336.22/09776 19
HJ9261 .M55 1986

TAX INCREMENT FINANCING - LAW AND LEGISLATION - MINNESOTA.
Minnesota. Office of the Legislative Auditor. Program Evaluation Division. Tax increment financing. Saint Paul, Minn. (Veterans Service Bldg., Saint Paul 55155) , 1986. xix, 138 p. : LC Card 86-623133 DDC 336.22/09776 19
HJ9261 .M55 1986

TAX INCREMENT FINANCING - MINNESOTA.
Minnesota. Office of the Legislative Auditor. Program Evaluation Division. Tax increment financing. Saint Paul, Minn. (Veterans Service Bldg., Saint Paul 55155) , 1986. xix, 138 p. : LC Card 86-623133 DDC 336.22/09776 19
HJ9261 .M55 1986

Tax letters : sample correspondence for income tax professionals. 2nd ed. Calabasas, CA (5115 Douglas Fir, Suite H, Calabasas 91302) : IPS, Professional Tax Products Division, c1986. 1 v. (various pagings) : forms ; 28 cm. Cover title. Includes index. LC Card 87-132645 DDC 651.7/52 19
1. Income tax - United States. 2. Form letters.
HJ4652 .T374 1986

TAX PLANNING - CONGRESSES.
San Francisco '85 . Bethesda, Md. [1986] vi, 502 p. ; LC Card 87-132666 DDC 332.6 19
HG4508 .S215 1986

TAX PLANNING - GERMANY (WEST)
Kratz, Peter. Steuerplanung internationaler Unternehmungen . Bern , c1986. xii, 344 p. : ISBN 3-258-03586-5 : LC Card 86-171030
HJ4720.A3 K73 1986

TAX PLANNING - GREAT BRITAIN.
Durkacz, Victor Edward. Financial planning for new businesses /. Chichester [West Sussex] , New York , c1985. 257 p. : ISBN 0-471-90843-6 (pbk.) : LC Card 85-17927 DDC 658.1/5 19
HG4027.6 .D87 1985 ***NYPL [JLE 86-929]***

Tax avoision . London , 1979. x, 134 p. ; ISBN 0-255-36126-2 (pbk.) LC Card 86-673369
HJ2348.5 .T39x 1979

TAX PLANNING - SWITZERLAND.
Tinner, Hanspeter. Konzernstruktur und Steuerplanung . Bern , c1984. ix, 276 p. : ISBN 3-258-03367-6 : LC Card 84-198592
HJ4748.A3 T55 1984

TAX PLANNING - UNITED STATES.
Ferguson, Jerry T., 1938- Managing real estate taxes /. Westport, Conn. , 1986. x, 185 p. ; ISBN 0-89930-106-1 (lib. bdg. : alk. paper) LC Card 85-6360 DDC 343.7305/46 347.303546 19
HJ4181 .F47 1986 ***NYPL [JLE 86-2439]***

Reed, John T. Aggressive tax avoidance for real estate investors . Danville, CA , 1986. 267 p. : ISBN 0-939224-13-5 (pbk.) :
NYPL [JLF 86-1562]

Robinson, Gerald J. Federal income taxation of real estate . Boston, Mass. , c1984. ca. 750 p. in various pagings ; ISBN 0-88712-081-4 LC Card 83-50925 DDC 343.7305/2 347.30352 19
KF6535 .R6 1984 ***NYPL [JLL 87-136]***

Robinson, Gerald J. Federal income taxation of real estate . Boston, Mass. , c1987. ca. 480 p. in various pagings ; ISBN 0-88712-743-6 LC Card 83-50925
NYPL [JLL 87-136 Suppl. 1987/1]

Robinson, Gerald J. Federal income taxation of real estate : text, forms, and tax planning ideas : 4th ed. Cumulative supplement /. Boston, Mass. , c1985- v. ISBN 0-88712-305-8 (pbk.) LC Card 83-50925
NYPL [*R-Econ. 85-1660 Suppl.]

TAX PLANNING - UNITED STATES - CONGRESSES.
San Francisco '85 . Bethesda, Md. [1986] vi, 502 p. ; LC Card 87-132666 DDC 332.6 19
HG4508 .S215 1986

Tax policy, economic development, and regional inequality [microform] . Harber, Richard P. Austin , 1984. 33 p. ; LC Card 84-623077 DDC 339.5/2/09813 19
HJ2527 .H37 1984 ***NYPL [*ZT-1646 no.22]***

TAX PRACTICE. see **TAX ADMINISTRATION AND PROCEDURE.**

TAX PROCEDURE. see **TAX ADMINISTRATION AND PROCEDURE.**

The Tax Reform Act of 1986 . Block, Stanley B. Homewood, Ill. , 1987. v, 26 p. ; ISBN 0-256-06055-X (pbk.) LC Card 87-403584 DDC 658.1/5 19
HG4026 .B589 1987 Suppl.

Tax reform and the U. S. economy : papers : presented at a conference at the Brookings Institution, December 2, 1986 / by Henry J. Aaron ... [et al.] ; edited by Joseph A. Pechman. Washington, D.C. : Brookings Institution, c1987. ix, 107 p. : ill. ; 26 cm. (Brookings dialogues on public policy) Includes bibliographical references. ISBN 0-8157-6959-8 (pbk.) LC Card 87-70178 DDC 330.973/0927 19
1. Taxation - Law and legislation - Economic aspects - United States - Congresses. I. Aaron, Henry J. II. Pechman, Joseph A., 1918-. III. Brookings Institution. IV. Series.
HJ2381 .T387 1987

Tax report : tax base reductions : the fiscal impact of recent changes in federal and state tax law / Illinois Economic and Fiscal Com[m]ission. Springfield, Ill. (703 Stratton Office Bldg., Springfield 62706) : The Commission, [1986] iv, 30, 3 leaves ; 28 cm. "May 1986." LC Card 86-622596 DDC 336.2/009773 19
1. Taxation - Illinois. 2. Revenue - Illinois. 3. Taxation - United States. 4. Intergovernmental tax relations - Illinois. 5. Taxation - Law and legislation - Economic aspects - Illinois. I. Illinois. Economic and Fiscal Commission. II. Title: Tax base reductions.
HJ2403 .T39 1986

TAX RETURNS - COMPUTER PROGRAMS.
Thompson, Gary J. 1986 tax software report /. Green Bay, Wis. (P.O. Box 12470, Green Bay, 54307-2470) : ii, 54 leaves ; LC Card 87-102387 DDC 343.7305/2044/0285536 347.303520440285536 19
HJ3252 .T47 1986

TAX RETURNS - UNITED STATES - DATA PROCESSING.
Thompson, Gary J. 1986 tax software report /. Green Bay, Wis. (P.O. Box 12470, Green Bay, 54307-2470) : ii, 54 leaves ; LC Card 87-102387 DDC 343.7305/2044/0285536 347.303520440285536 19
HJ3252 .T47 1986

TAX REVENUE ESTIMATING - AUSTRIA.
Budgetvorschau 1986-1990. Wien , 1986. 45 p. : LC Card 86-227246
HJ2101 .B83 1986

TAX REVENUE ESTIMATING - UNITED STATES.
Tax expenditures . Washington, D.C. [1983] xiv, 82 p. ; ***NYPL [JLF 84-401]***

Verdier, James M. Tax expenditures . Washington, D.C. , 1982. xx, 102 p. ;
NYPL [JLF 83-663]

Tax, S.E.C., and accounting aspects of corporate acquisitions, 1984. Tax, SEC, and accounting aspects of corporate acquisitions, 1984 /. New York, N.Y. (810 Seventh Ave., New York 10019) , c1984. 584 p. : LC Card 84-231882 DDC 343.7306/7 347.30367 19
KF6499.M4 T39 1984 ***NYPL [JLD 87-57]***

Tax saver. Knepp, Jay. Tax[s]aver. Menlo Park, Calif. , c1987. 143 p. : ISBN 0-376-07015-3 (pbk.) : LC Card 86-80874 DDC 343.7305/23 347.303523 19
HJ4653.D4 K56 1987

TAX SAVINGS. see **TAX PLANNING.**

Tax, SEC, and accounting aspects of corporate acquisitions, 1984 / Jack S. Levin, chairman. New York, N.Y. (810 Seventh Ave., New York 10019) : Practising Law Institute, c1984. 584 p. : ill. ; 22 cm. (Corporate law and practice course handbook series. no. 444) "Prepared for distribution at the tax, SEC, and accounting aspects of corporate acquisitions program, April-May 1984"--P. 5. "B4-6674." Includes bibliographical references. LC Card 84-231882 DDC 343.7306/7 347.30367 19
1. Consolidation and merger of corporations - Taxation - United States. 2. Consolidation and merger of corporations - United States. I. Levin, Jack S., 1936-. II. Practising Law Institute. III. Title: Tax, S.E.C., and accounting aspects of corporate acquisitions, 1984.
KF6499.M4 T39 1984 ***NYPL [JLD 87-57]***

Tax shelters . Farrell, Michael D. Chicago, Ill. , c1985. x, 250 p. : ISBN 0-930369-04-1 : LC Card 85-207994 DDC 343.7305/23 347.303523 19
KF6297.5 .F37 1985 ***NYPL [JLE 86-1019]***

TAX SHELTERS - LAW AND LEGISLATION - UNITED STATES.
Farrell, Michael D. Tax shelters . Chicago, Ill. , c1985. x, 250 p. : ISBN 0-930369-04-1 : LC Card 85-207994 DDC 343.7305/23 347.303523 19
KF6297.5 .F37 1985 ***NYPL [JLE 86-1019]***

TAX SHELTERS - UNITED STATES.
Cook, Wade. Pay no taxes with real estate /. Orem, Utah , c1982. xvii, 152, [7] p. : ISBN 0-910019-09-6 (pbk.) LC Card 86-228579 DDC 343.7305/46 347.303546 19
HJ4181 .C66 1982

Farrell, Michael D. Tax shelters . Chicago, Ill. , c1985. x, 250 p. : ISBN 0-930369-04-1 : LC Card 85-207994 DDC 343.7305/23 347.303523 19
KF6297.5 .F37 1985 ***NYPL [JLE 86-1019]***

Windish, David F. Tax-advantaged investments /. New York, N.Y. , c1985. xii, 404 p. : ISBN 0-13-884677-4 LC Card 84-25539 DDC 332.6/042 19
HJ4653.A3 W56 1985 ***NYPL [JLE 85-3677]***

Windish, David F. Tax-advantaged investments /. New York, N.Y. , c1987. xix, 407 p. : ISBN 0-13-884693-6 : LC Card 87-11156 DDC 332.6/042 19
HJ4653.A3 W56 1987

The Tax system in Lebanon / Beirut Chamber of Commerce and Industry. 1st ed. Beirut, Lebanon : Economical Studies and Documentation Center, Beirut Chamber of Commerce and Industry, 1983. 14 p. ; 24 cm. Cover title. LC Card 87-402832 DDC 343.569204 345.692034 19
1. Taxation - Lebanon. I. Ghurfat al-Tijārah wa-al-Ṣināʻah fī Bayrūt.
HJ2909 .T39 1983

Taxable sales in Virginia, 1985 /. Lindsey, Donald W. Charlottesville, Va. (2015 Ivy Rd., Charlottesville 22903-1780) [1986] 16 p. : LC Card 86-622891 DDC 336.2/713/09755021 19
HJ5715.U62 V85 1986

TAXATION - ADMINISTRATION. see **TAX ADMINISTRATION AND PROCEDURE.**

Taxation and fiscal administration in ancient India . Tripāṭhi, Oṅkāranātha, 1934- Lucknow, U.P. , 1985. xii, 152 p. ; LC Card 85-903145 DDC 336.34 19
HJ2932 .T75 1985 ***NYPL [JLD 86-1318]***

Taxation and incentives / IFS. [London, England] : Institute for Fiscal Studies, c1976. ii, 45 p. : ill. ; 29 cm. Cover title. Papers presented at a one-day conference arranged by the Institute for Fiscal Studies. LC Card 85-111944
1. Taxation - Great Britain - Congresses. 2. Taxation - United States - Congresses. 3. Labor supply - Great Britain - Effect of taxation on - Congresses. 4. Labor supply - United States - Effect of taxation on - Congresses. 5. Tax incentives - Great Britain - Congresses. 6. Tax incentives - United States - Congresses. I. Institute for Fiscal Studies (Great Britain).
HJ2619 .T289 1976

TAXATION AND REAL PROPERTY. see **REAL PROPERTY AND TAXATION.**

Taxation and the deficit economy : fiscal policy and capital formation in the United States / edited by Dwight R. Lee ; foreword by Michael J. Boskin. San Francisco, Calif. : Pacific Research Institute for Public Policy, c1986. xxvii, 554 p. : ill. ; 23 cm. (Pacific studies in public policy) Includes bibliographies and index. ISBN 0-936488-13-1 : LC Card 85-63549 DDC 339.5/2/0973 19
1. Fiscal policy - United States. 2. Savings and investment - United States. 3. Government spending policy - United States. I. Lee, Dwight R.
HJ257.2 .T385 1986 ***NYPL [JLE 86-4136]***

TAXATION - AUSTRALIA - STATISTICS - HISTORY.
Barnard, A. (Alan) Some government financial data, 1850 to 1982 /. Canberra, Australia [1986] 47, 2 p. ; ISBN 0-86784-850-2 (pbk.) LC Card 86-211320 DDC 336.94 19
HJ2193.Z7 B37 1986

TAXATION - BOLIVIA.
Ovando, Jorge. El tributo indígena en las finanzas bolivianas del siglo XIX /. La Paz, Bolivia [1985] 565 p. : ***NYPL [JLC 86-407]***

TAXATION - BRAZIL.
Alagoas (Brazil). Secretaria da Fazenda. Posicionamento das finanças de Alagoas na atual crise /. [Maceió] , 1983. 97 p. : LC Card 86-201070
HJ929.A52 A42 1983

Baptista, Lourival. Reforma tributária, federalismo e desenvolvimento nacional /. Brasília , 1983. 255 p. : LC Card 86-210783
HJ2525 .B36 1983

Biava, Adriano Henrique Rebelo. Contribuição de melhoria . São Paulo-SP , 1987. 243 p. : LC Card 87-404978 DDC 339.5/2/0981 19
HJ2525 .B5 1987

Franco, Luiz L. O Brasil que temos, o país que queremos /. Guarulhos, S.P. [Brazil] , c1985. 87 p. ; LC Card 86-223053
HC187 .F7315 1985

Nunes, Helvídio. Reforma tributária . Brasília , 1982. 108 p. ; LC Card 86-128083
HJ2527 .N85 1982

Serra, José. [Novo federalismo.] Um novo federalismo ; O sistema tributário "diagnóstico e reforma" /. São Paulo , 1984. 43 p. ; LC Card 87-124038 DDC 336.2/00981 19
HJ3424.A4 S47 1984

Silva, Gerson Augusto da. Estudos tributários /. Brasília, DF , 1983. 139 p. : LC Card 84-127110
HJ2525 .S49 1983

Taxation by political inertia . Rose, Richard, 1933- London , Boston , 1987. viii, 264 p. : ISBN 0-04-320197-0 (alk. paper) LC Card 87-11478 DDC 336.2/00941 19
HJ2619 .R68 1987

TAXATION - CAMEROON.
Répertoire financier et fiscal du Cameroun . Le Vésinet, France [1987?] 147 p. ; LC Card 87-124445
HJ1489 .R46 1987

TAXATION - CANADA.
Comparative tax systems . Arlington, Va. , 1987. xiv, 447 p. : ISBN 0-918255-05-8 (pbk.) : LC Card 87-50143 DDC 336.2 19
HJ2599.5 .C65 1987

TAXATION - CENTRAL EUROPE - HISTORY.
Wealth and taxation in Central Europe . Leamington Spa, UK ; New York, N.Y., USA : 162 p. ; ISBN 0-85496-523-8 : LC Card 86-24490 DDC 336.43 19
HJ1000 .W4 1987

TAXATION - COMPLIANCE COSTS.
Tiebel, Christoph. Überwälzte Kosten der Gesetze . Göttingen , c1986. xv, 256 p. : ISBN 3-525-11333-1 (Deut. Bibl.) LC Card 87-135628 DDC 336.2/4 19
HJ2309 .T48 1986

TAXATION - CONGRESSES.
London Conference on Taxes and Growth (1986) London Conference on Taxes and Growth . New York, NY [1986] 61 p. ; LC Card 87-404887 DDC 339.5/25 19
HJ2279 .L655 1986

Steuerpolitik für die soziale Marktwirtschaft . Stuttgart , New York , 1986. 85 p. ; ISBN 3-437-50311-1 LC Card 87-122642 DDC 336.2/00943 19
HJ2687 .S73 1986

Taxation in developed countries . Paris , Washington, D.C. , 1987. 99 p. ; ISBN 92-64-12929-4 (pbk.) : LC Card 87-163512 DDC 336.24 19
HJ4621 .T28 1987

TAXATION - DEVELOPING COUNTRIES.
The Theory of taxation for developing countries /. New York , c1987. xvi, 694 p. ; ISBN 0-19-520498-0 LC Card 87-11106 DDC 336.2/009172/4 19
HJ2351.7 .T47 1987

TAXATION - DICTIONARIES - TURKISH.
Akdoğan, Abdurrahman. Açıklamalı maliye ve vergi sözlüğü /. [Ankara?] , Yenişehir, Ankara , 1986. 229 p. ; LC Card 87-968120
HJ129.T9 A43 1986

TAXATION, DOUBLE - GERMANY, WEST.
Ausländische Investitionen in U. S.-Grundvermögen /. Herne , 1984, c1983. 86 p. ; ISBN 3-482-69041-3 LC Card 84-203818 DDC 346.43/07 344.3067 19
K3830.4 .A97 1984 ***NYPL [JLD 86-2326]***

TAXATION - EFFECT OF INFLATION ON.
Naust, Hermann. Direkte Steuern und intertemporale Allokation . Köln , c1983. xiv, 374 p. : ISBN 3-452-19402-7 : LC Card 83-163600 DDC 336.2 19
HJ3851 .N38 1983

TAXATION - EUROPE.
Comparative tax systems . Arlington, Va. , 1987. xiv, 447 p. : ISBN 0-918255-05-8 (pbk.) : LC Card 87-50143 DDC 336.2 19
HJ2599.5 .C65 1987

TAXATION - EVASION. see **TAX EVASION.**

TAXATION - FINLAND - EFFECT OF INFLATION ON.
Asplund, Rita. Short-run tax-push inflation in Finland /. Helsinki , 1986. 65 p. : ISBN 951-46-9876-2 (pbk.) LC Card 87-163994 DDC 332.4/1/094897 19
HJ4738.3 .A86 1986

TAXATION - FRANCE - EXAMINATIONS, QUESTIONS, ETC.
Cozian, Maurice. Annales de fiscalité . Paris , 1981. 127 p. ; ISBN 2-7111-0289-0 : LC Card 81-150065
HJ2659 .C65 1981

TAXATION - FRANCE - HISTORY - 17TH CENTURY.
Collins, James B. Fiscal limits of absolutism . Berkeley , c1987. p. cm. ISBN 0-520-05911-5 (alk. paper) LC Card 87-19090 DDC 336.2/00944 19
HJ2648 .C65 1987

TAXATION - GERMANY - HISTORY.
Wild, Werner. Steuern und Reichsherrschaft . Bremen , 1984. 326 p. ; ISBN 3-88948-030-6 LC Card 85-127825
HJ2675 .W55 1984

TAXATION - GERMANY, WEST.
Fuest, Winfried, 1946- Irrtümer in der aktuellen Steuerdiskussion /. Köln , c1987. 54 p. : ISBN 3-602-24749-X LC Card 87-409547 DDC 336.2/00943 19
HJ2687 .F834 1987

Krätke, Michael. Kritik der Staatsfinanzen . Hamburg , 1984. 297 p. ; ISBN 3-87975-247-8 LC Card 84-186778
HJ2687 .K67 1984

Mann, Hugo, 1954- Theorie und Politik der Steuerreform in der Demokratie /. Frankfurt am Main , New York , c1987. vi, 264 p. ; ISBN 3-8204-9464-2 LC Card 87-407788 DDC 336.2/00943 19
HJ2687 .M3 1987

Mitschke, Joachim. Steuer- und Transferordnung aus einem Guss . Baden-Baden , 1985. 274 p. : ISBN 3-7890-1097-9 LC Card 85-235532
HJ2687 .M57 1985

Sherman, Heidemarie C. Der Einfluss staatlicher Budgetdefizite auf die Zinsentwicklung in der Bundesrepublik Deutschland und den Vereinigten Staaten . München , c1986. xxiii, 190 p. : ISBN 3-88512-019-4 LC Card 86-192070
HJ2110 .S53 1986

Unternehmung und Steuer . Wiesbaden , c1983. 395 p. ; ISBN 3-409-50005-7 LC Card 83-161883
HD2753.G3 U57 1983

Zahn, Joachim, Professor Dr. Eine Finanzpolitik des langen Atems erforderlich /. Bonn [1984] 31 leaves ; LC Card 86-198580
HJ1120 .B65 Nr. 234

TAXATION - GERMANY (WEST) - CONGRESSES.
Steuerpolitik für die soziale Marktwirtschaft . Stuttgart , New York , 1986. 85 p. ; ISBN 3-437-50311-1 LC Card 87-122642 DDC 336.2/00943 19
HJ2687 .S73 1986

TAXATION - GERMANY (WEST) - ECONOMETRIC MODELS.

Francke, Hans-Hermann. Zinswirkungen der Staatsverschuldung . Berlin , c1984. 138 p. : ISBN 3-428-05727-9 LC Card 86-107232
HJ8654 .F73 1984

TAXATION - GERMANY, WEST - HISTORY.
Fredersdorf, Hermann, 1924- Der Steuerrebell und seine Gewerkschaft . Wiesbaden , c1982. 156 p., [3] folded leaves of plates : ISBN 3-922114-02-4 LC Card 83-102197
HJ2690 .F78 1982

Muscheid, Jutta. Die Steuerpolitik in der Bundesrepublik Deutschland, 1949-1982 /. Berlin , c1986. 212 p. : ISBN 3-428-06004-0 LC Card 86-206446
HJ2687 .M84 1986

TAXATION - GERMANY (WEST) - JÜLICH-BERG - HISTORY - 16TH CENTURY.
Walz, Rainer. Stände und frühmoderner Staat . Neustadt an der Aisch , 1982. 257 p., [1] leaf of plates : ISBN 3-87707-040-9 LC Card 83-215104
HJ2675 .W35 1982

TAXATION - GERMANY (WEST) - JÜLICH-BERG - HISTORY - 17TH CENTURY.
Walz, Rainer. Stände und frühmoderner Staat . Neustadt an der Aisch , 1982. 257 p., [1] leaf of plates : ISBN 3-87707-040-9 LC Card 83-215104
HJ2675 .W35 1982

TAXATION - GERMANY (WEST) - LÜNEBURG (PRINCIPALITY) - LISTS.
Schatz- und Zinsverzeichnisse des 15. Jahrhunderts aus dem Fürstentum Lüneburg . Hildesheim , 1942. 153 p. ; LC Card 87-409521 DDC 336.2/00943/59 19
HJ2110.5.L86 S3 1942

TAXATION - GERMANY (WEST) - MARK (GRAFSCHAFT) - LISTS.
Mark (Grafschaft) Schatzbuch der Grafschaft Mark, 1486 /. Unna , 1986. 176 p. ; ISBN 3-87298-042-4 LC Card 87-116701 DDC 336.2/00943/55 19
HJ2110.5.M36 M37 1986

TAXATION - GREAT BRITAIN.
Hannington, Wal, 1895- The problem of the distressed areas /. New York , 1985. 286 p. : ISBN 0-8240-7613-3 : LC Card 85-14663 DDC 338.941 19
HC256.3 .H265 1985 ***NYPL [JLD 86-3420]***

James, Simon R. The comprehensibility of taxation . Aldershot, Hants, England , Brookfield, Vt., USA , c1987. xiii, 314 p. : ISBN 0-566-05348-9 : LC Card 86-25690 DDC 336.2/00941 19
HJ2619 .J36 1987

Rose, Richard, 1933- Taxation by political inertia . London , Boston , 1987. viii, 264 p. : ISBN 0-04-320197-0 (alk. paper) LC Card 87-11478 DDC 336.2/00941 19
HJ2619 .R68 1987

TAXATION - GREAT BRITAIN - CONGRESSES.
London Conference on Taxes and Growth (1986) London Conference on Taxes and Growth . New York, NY [1986] 61 p. ; LC Card 87-404887 DDC 339.5/25 19
HJ2279 .L655 1986

Taxation and incentives /. [London, England] , c1976. ii, 45 p. : LC Card 85-111944
HJ2619 .T289 1976

TAXATION - HISTORY.
Adams, Charles, 1930- Fight, flight, fraud . Curaçao , c1982. iv, 307 p. : LC Card 83-80155 DDC 336.2/009 19
HJ2250 .A32 1982 ***NYPL [JLG 86-104]***

Webber, Carolyn. A history of taxation and expenditure in the Western world /. New York , c1986. 734 p. ,[16] p. of plates : ISBN 0-671-54617-1 LC Card 86-3863 DDC 336.2/009 19
HJ2250 .W42 1986 ***NYPL [JLE 86-3474]***

TAXATION - ILLINOIS.
Tax report . Springfield, Ill. (703 Stratton Office Bldg., Springfield 62706) [1986] iv, 30, 3 leaves ; LC Card 86-622596 DDC 336.2/009773 19
HJ2403 .T39 1986

Taxation in ancient India. Tripāṭhī, Oṅkāranātha, 1934- Taxation and fiscal administration in ancient India . Lucknow, U.P. , 1985. xii, 152 p. ; LC Card 85-903145 DDC 336.34 19
HJ2932 .T75 1985 ***NYPL [JLD 86-1318]***

Taxation in developed countries : an international symposium / organised by the French Ministry of Finance in association with the Committee on Fiscal Affairs of the OECD, Paris, 12th and 13th January 1987. Paris : Organisation for Economic Co-operation and Development ; Washington, D.C. : OECD Publications and Information Centre, [distributor], 1987. 99 p. ; 23 cm. ISBN 92-64-12929-4 (pbk.) : LC Card 87-163512 DDC 336.24 19
1. Income tax - Congresses. 2. Taxation - Congresses. I. France. Ministère des finances. II. Organisation for Economic Co-operation and Development. Committee on Fiscal Affairs.
HJ4621 .T28 1987

TAXATION, INCIDENCE OF. see **TAXATION.**

TAXATION - INDIA.
Dhawan, O. P. Non resident Indians . New Delhi , 1984. xvi, 428 p. ; LC Card 85-900577 DDC 346.54/07 345.4067 19
HG5732 .D43 1984 ***NYPL [JLE 86-1363]***

TAXATION - INDIA - HISTORY.
Tripāṭhī, Oṅkāranātha, 1934- Taxation and fiscal administration in ancient India . Lucknow, U.P. , 1985. xii, 152 p. ; LC Card 85-903145 DDC 336.34 19
HJ2932 .T75 1985 ***NYPL [JLD 86-1318]***

TAXATION - ITALY - ADDRESSES, ESSAYS, LECTURES.
Per una ristrutturazione e riconversione dell'industria italiana /. Bologna , 1980. 244 p. ; LC Card 82-102594 DDC 338.945 19
HD3616.I83 P43 ***NYPL [JLD 86-599]***

TAXATION - ITALY - COMPLIANCE COSTS.
Scanu, Salvatore. I costi dell'adempimento tributario in Italia . [Cagliari] , Milano, Italy , c1984. 153 p. ; LC Card 85-118845
HD9326.I82 S32 1984

TAXATION - ITALY - FLORENCE - HISTORY.
Conti, Elio. L'imposta diretta a Firenze nel Quattrocento (1427-1494) /. Roma , 1984. 406 p. ; LC Card 86-171245
HJ9500.F562 C65 1984

TAXATION - ITALY - NAPLES (KINGDOM) - LISTS.
Cozzetto, Fausto. Mezzogiorno e demografia nel XV secolo /. Soveria M.lli, CZ , c1986. ix, 202 p. ; LC Card 86-213782
HB3600.N37 C69 1986

TAXATION - JAPAN.
Comparative tax systems . Arlington, Va. , 1987. xiv, 447 p. : ISBN 0-918255-05-8 (pbk.) : LC Card 87-50143 DDC 336.2 19
HJ2599.5 .C65 1987

An Outline of Japanese tax administration. [Tokyo], Japan , 1985. 85 p., [1] leaf of plates : LC Card 86-209172 DDC 354.520072/4 19
HJ3627 .O87 1985

TAXATION - LATIN AMERICA - CONGRESSES.
La Política tributaria en Latinoamérica . Washington, D.C. , 1986. ix, 180 p. ; ISBN 0-8270-2496-7 (pbk.) LC Card 87-403563 DDC 336.2/0098 19
HJ3374.5 .P65 1986

TAXATION - LAW AND LEGISLATION - BRAZIL.
Silva, Gerson Augusto da. Estudos tributários /. Brasília, DF , 1983. 139 p. : LC Card 84-127110
HJ2525 .S49 1983

TAXATION - LAW AND LEGISLATION - CAMEROON.
Répertoire financier et fiscal du Cameroun . Le Vésinet, France [1987?] 147 p. ; LC Card 87-124445
HJ1489 .R46 1987

TAXATION - LAW AND LEGISLATION - COMPLIANCE COSTS.
Tiebel, Christoph. Überwälzte Kosten der Gesetze . Göttingen , c1986. xv, 256 p. : ISBN 3-525-11333-1 (Deut. Bibl.) LC Card 87-135628 DDC 336.2/4 19
HJ2309 .T48 1986

TAXATION - LAW AND LEGISLATION - CRIMINAL PROVISIONS. see **TAX EVASION.**

TAXATION - LAW AND LEGISLATION - ECONOMIC ASPECTS - ILLINOIS.
Tax report . Springfield, Ill. (703 Stratton Office Bldg., Springfield 62706) [1986] iv, 30, 3 leaves ; LC Card 86-622596 DDC 336.2/009773 19
HJ2403 .T39 1986

TAXATION - LAW AND LEGISLATION - ECONOMIC ASPECTS - UNITED STATES - CONGRESSES.
Tax reform and the U. S. economy . Washington, D.C. , c1987. ix, 107 p. : ISBN 0-8157-6959-8 (pbk.) LC Card 87-70178 DDC 330.973/0927 19
HJ2381 .T387 1987

TAXATION - LAW AND LEGISLATION - GERMANY, WEST.
Mitschke, Joachim. Steuer- und Transferordnung aus einem Guss . Baden-Baden , 1985. 274 p. : ISBN 3-7890-1097-9 LC Card 85-235532
HJ2687 .M57 1985

TAXATION - LAW AND LEGISLATION - NEBRASKA.
Tax expenditure report for sales and use tax--Nebraska and local option, property tax, individual income tax, fiduciary income tax, corporation income tax, miscellaneous taxes . Lincoln, Neb. [1985] 245 p. ; LC Card 86-622058 DDC 343.78204 347.8204 19
HJ2419 .T39 1985

TAXATION - LAW AND LEGISLATION - SPAIN.
García Villarejo, Avelino. Manual de hacienda pública . Madrid , c1985. 686 p. : ISBN 84-309-1197-9 LC Card 87-105048
HJ1244 .G37 1985

TAXATION - LEBANON.
The Tax system in Lebanon /. Beirut, Lebanon , 1983. 14 p. ; LC Card 87-402832 DDC 343.569204 345.692034 19
HJ2909 .T39 1983

TAXATION - MAINE - STATISTICS.
Compendium of state fiscal information /. [Augusta?] [1985] 40 leaves : LC Card 86-621730 DDC 336.741/021 19
HJ2410 .C65 1985

TAXATION - MEXICO - HISTORY - 19TH CENTURY.
Tenenbaum, Barbara, 1946- The politics of penury . Albuquerque , c1986. xviii, 250 p. ; ISBN 0-8263-0890-2 : LC Card 86-16027 DDC 336.72 19
HJ802 .T46 1986 ***NYPL [JLE 87-482]***

TAXATION - MINNESOTA.
Minnesota tax handbook . [St. Paul] [1985] iii, 70 p. ; LC Card 86-620842 DDC 343.77604 347.76034 19
HJ2415 .M49 1985

TAXATION - MONTANA.
House, Verne W. Trends in the Montana economy and taxation /. Bozeman [1986] 19 p. : LC Card 87-620963 DDC 330.9786/033 19
HC107.M9 H68 1986

TAXATION - MOROCCO.
Zemrani, Anas Bensalah. La fiscalité face au développement économique et social du Maroc /. Rabat , 1982. 395 p. ; LC Card 83-183254
HJ3032 .Z34 1982

TAXATION - NEBRASKA - STATISTICS.
Tax expenditure report for sales and use tax--Nebraska and local option, property tax, individual income tax, fiduciary income tax, corporation income tax, miscellaneous taxes . Lincoln, Neb. [1985] 245 p. ; LC Card 86-622058 DDC 343.78204 347.8204 19
HJ2419 .T39 1985

TAXATION - NEVADA.
Nevada. Legislature. Legislative Commission. Study of the fees and taxes which produce revenue for the construction and maintenance of the highways. [Carson City, Nev.] [1986] viii, 74 p. ; LC Card 86-623141 DDC 388.1/14/09793 19
HE356.N37 N42 1986

TAXATION - NEW YORK (N.Y.)
Citizens Budget Commission (New York, N.Y.) Municipal tax policy in New York City . New York, N.Y. (110 E. 42nd St., New York 10017) [1986] iii leaves, 25 p. ; LC Card 87-110053

DDC 336.2/0097471 19
HJ9289.N4 C54 1986

TAXATION - NEW YORK (STATE)
Interstate tax comparisons . [Albany, N.Y.] [1985] 106 p. ; LC Card 86-621354 DDC 336.2/009747 19
HJ2424 .I57 1985

The President's tax reform proposal . [Albany, N.Y.] [1985] 48 leaves : LC Card 86-622434 DDC 336.2/009747 19
HJ2424 .P84 1985

The United States Senate's tax reform proposal . [Albany, N.Y.?] [1986] 18, 6, 2 leaves ; LC Card 87-620727 DDC 336.2/009747 19
HJ2424 .U55 1986

Who pays New York taxes? . [Albany, N.Y.] [1985] 2, 101 p. : LC Card 86-621353 DDC 336.2/94/09747 19
HJ2322.N7 W48 1985

TAXATION - NEW ZEALAND.
Brooks, R. Inflation, tax rules, and housing in New Zealand /. Wellington, N.Z. [1986] 22, [22] p. : LC Card 87-132461 DDC 363.5/8 19
HD7387.5.A3 B76 1986

TAXATION - NORWAY.
Skånland, Hermod, 1925- Inntektspolitikkens dilemma . [Oslo] , 1981 ([Oslo] : Joh. Nordahls trykkeri) 114 p., [1] leaf : ISBN 82-02-04872-9 (pbk.) : LC Card 81-199141
HC370.I5 S49 1981 NYPL [JLD 86-2672]

TAXATION OF ARTICLES OF CONSUMPTION.
Naust, Hermann. Direkte Steuern und intertemporale Allokation . Köln , c1983. xiv, 374 p. : ISBN 3-452-19402-7 : LC Card 83-163600 DDC 336.2 19
HJ3851 .N38 1983

TAXATION OF ARTICLES OF CONSUMPTION - INDIA.
Agarwala, N. L. (Natwar Lal) Commodity taxation and India's fiscal policy /. New Delhi , c1985. 294 p. ; LC Card 85-904360 DDC 339.5/25/0954 19
HJ5715.I4 A73 1985 NYPL [JLD 87-610]

TAXATION OF BONDS, SECURITIES, ETC. - DENMARK.
Beskatningen af aktieafkast i Danmark og i det øvrige Vesteuropa /. København [1986] 23 p. ; ISBN 87-7353-047-6 LC Card 87-144435
HJ5913.D4 B47 1986

TAXATION OF BONDS, SECURITIES, ETC. - EUROPE.
Beskatningen af aktieafkast i Danmark og i det øvrige Vesteuropa /. København [1986] 23 p. ; ISBN 87-7353-047-6 LC Card 87-144435
HJ5913.D4 B47 1986

TAXATION OF CONSUMER GOODS. see **TAXATION OF ARTICLES OF CONSUMPTION.**

TAXATION OF FOREIGN INVESTMENTS. see **INVESTMENTS, FOREIGN - LAW AND LEGISLATION.**

TAXATION OF FRANCHISES. see **CORPORATIONS - TAXATION.**

TAXATION OF INCOME. see **INCOME TAX.**

Taxation of Lloyd's underwriters /. Carmichael, K. S. (Keith Stanley) London , 1980. xvi, 107 p. : ISBN 0-372-30027-8 (pbk.) : LC Card 81-107459
HG8123.G7 C37 1980

TAXATION OF REAL PROPERTY. see **REAL PROPERTY TAX.**

TAXATION - PAKISTAN - CONGRESSES.
Workshop: Middle Management and the Fisc. (1983 : Lahore, Pakistan) Miscellany II . Lahore [1984?] 251 p. : LC Card 86-930242 DDC 354.549/10072 19
HJ3611.5 .W67 1983

TAXATION, PROGRESSIVE - AUSTRALIA.
Kakwani, Nanak. Analyzing redistribution policies . Cambridge [Cambridgeshire] , New York , 1986. ix, 293 p. : ISBN 0-521-30838-0 LC Card 85-31342 DDC 339.5/2 19
HC610.I5 K35 1986 NYPL [JLE 86-3491]

TAXATION, PROGRESSIVE - GERMANY (WEST) - MATHEMATICAL MODELS.
Pfingsten, Andreas. The measurement of tax progression /. Berlin , New York , c1986. vi, 131 p. : ISBN 0-387-16072-8 (U. S. : pbk.) LC Card 86-219663 DDC 336.2/93 19
HJ2326 .P47 1986

TAXATION, PROGRESSIVE - MATHEMATICAL MODELS.
Pfingsten, Andreas. The measurement of tax progression /. Berlin , New York , c1986. vi, 131 p. : ISBN 0-387-16072-8 (U. S. : pbk.) LC Card 86-219663 DDC 336.2/93 19
HJ2326 .P47 1986

TAXATION - SOVIET UNION - HISTORY.
Menz, Gertraud. Die Entwicklung der sowjetischen Besteuerung unter besonderer Berücksichtigung der ordnungspolitischen Funktionen /. Berlin , 1960. 247 p. : LC Card 86-161289
HJ2802 .M46 1960

TAXATION - SPAIN.
García Villarejo, Avelino. Manual de hacienda pública . Madrid , c1985. 686 p. : ISBN 84-309-1197-9 LC Card 87-105048
HJ1244 .G37 1985

TAXATION - SPAIN - AUTONOMOUS COMMUNITIES.
Gimeno Ullastres, Juan Antonio. El nuevo Estado fiscal español . Madrid , 1981. xx, 315 p. : ISBN 84-7214-219-1 LC Card 85-176738
HJ1249.A1 G56 1981

TAXATION, STATE - UNITED STATES - STATES.

TAXATION - SWEDEN.
Hadenius, Axel, 1945- A crisis of the welfare state? . Stockholm, Sweden , c1986. 151 p. : ISBN 91-22-00821-7 (pbk.) : LC Card 87-127805 DDC 339.5/22/09485 19
HJ2837 .H34 1986

Hansson, Ingemar, 1951- Skatter och samhällsekonomi /. Stockholm , c1986. 170 p. : ISBN 91-7150-280-7 : LC Card 86-215332
HJ2837 .H36 1986

TAXATION - SWEDEN - MATHEMATICAL MODELS.
Agell, Jonas. The effects of capital taxation . Uppsala , Stockholm, Sweden , 1986. 123 p. : ISBN 91-554-1938-0 (pbk.) LC Card 87-100538 DDC 330 s 336.2/009481 19
HB51 .S7 no. 9 HJ2838

TAXATION - SWITZERLAND - BASEL-STADT - HISTORY.
Rosen, Josef. Verwaltung und Ungeld in Basel, 1360-1535 . Stuttgart , 1986. 231 p. ; ISBN 3-515-03348-3 : LC Card 86-184510
HG1160.B37 R67 1986

TAXATION - SWITZERLAND - HISTORY - 20TH CENTURY.
Tanner, Jakob. Bundeshaushalt, Währung und Kriegswirtschaft . Zürich , c1986. 438 p. : ISBN 3-85791-100-X : LC Card 86-199729
HJ1258 .T35 1986

TAXATION - TURKEY.
Özer, İlhan. Kamu alacaklarının tahsili teorisi ve Türkiye'de uygulaması /. Ankara , 1979. xv, 236 p. ; LC Card 85-968002
HJ2906.5 .O93 1979

TAXATION - UNITED STATES - CONGRESSES.
Conference on the Effects of Taxation on Capital Formation (1986 : Palm Beach, Fla.) Taxes and capital formation. Cambridge, Mass. (1050 Massachusetts Ave., Cambridge 02138) , 1986. 40 p. ; LC Card 87-101954 DDC 336.2/00973 19
HJ2381 .C6974 1986

London Conference on Taxes and Growth (1986) London Conference on Taxes and Growth . New York, NY [1986] 61 p. ; LC Card 87-404887 DDC 339.5/25 19
HJ2279 .L655 1986

Taxation and incentives /. [London, England] , c1976. ii, 45 p. : LC Card 85-111944
HJ2619 .T289 1976

TAXATION - UNITED STATES - HISTORY.
Adams, Charles, 1930- Fight, flight, fraud . Curaçao , c1982. iv, 307 p. : LC Card 83-80155 DDC 336.2/009 19
HJ2250 .A32 1982 NYPL [JLG 86-104]

TAXATION - UNITED STATES - STATES. see **TAXATION, STATE.**

TAXATION - VIRGINIA.
The Treasury's tax reform proposal. [Richmond?] [1985] 22 leaves ; LC Card 86-622457 DDC 336.2/05 19
HJ2381 .T74 1985

Ware, Peggy M. Virginia, an outline of the state and local taxes /. Richmond, Va. (1000 Washington Bldg., Richmond 23219) [1986] iv, 26 p. ; LC Card 86-622876 DDC 343.75504/3 347.550343 19
HJ2438 .W37 1986

Taxe d'habitation . France. Service de la législation fiscale. [Paris] [1984] 192 p. in various pagings ; LC Card 85-103723
HJ4346 .F73 1984

Taxe professionelle : rapport au Parlement sur l'application des articles 13 à 20 de la Loi de finances, rectificative du 28 juin 1982 / Ministère de l'économie, des finances et du budget, Direction générale des impôts, Service de la législation fiscale. [Paris] : Le Service, [1983] v, 80, [23] p. ; 30 cm. LC Card 85-129298
1. Licenses - France. I. France. Service de la législation fiscale. II. France. Parlement (1946-).
HJ5412 .T39 1983

TAXES. see **TAXATION.**

Taxes and capital formation / edited by Martin Feldstein. Chicago : University of Chicago Press, 1987. xii, 118 p. : ill. ; 24 cm. (A National Bureau of Economic Research project report) Includes bibliographies and index. ISBN 0-226-24079-7 LC Card 87-5898 DDC 336.2/00973 19
1. Taxation - United States. 2. Saving and investment - United States. 3. Taxation. 4. Saving and investment. I. Feldstein, Martin S. II. Series.
HJ2381 .T395 1987

Taxes and capital formation. Conference on the Effects of Taxation on Capital Formation (1986 : Palm Beach, Fla.) Cambridge, Mass. (1050 Massachusetts Ave., Cambridge 02138) , 1986. 40 p. ; LC Card 87-101954 DDC 336.2/00973 19
HJ2381 .C6974 1986

Taxes and mergers . Smirlock, Michael. New York, N.Y. (90 Trinity Place, New York 10006) [c1986] 42 p. : LC Card 86-210061 DDC 336.24/3 19
HD2746.5 .S64 1986

TAXES, SCHOOL. see **EDUCATION - FINANCE.**

TAXICAB DRIVERS - SWITZERLAND - BASEL - BIOGRAPHY.
Loeliger, Walter. Sind Sie frei? . Basel , 1982. 99 p. : ISBN 3-85816-043-1 : LC Card 83-100470
HD8039.T162 L64 1982

Taxicab zone fare guide. Sullivan, Novell B. Washington, D.C. taxicab zone fare guide. [United States] , c1984. 86 p., [1] folded leaf of plates : LC Card 86-224478 DDC 388.4/1321 19
HE5634.W3 S93 1984

TAXICABS - UNITED STATES.
Bergman, Edward M. Cooperative forms of organization in the taxicab industry [microform] . Washington, D.C. , Springfield, Va. , 1984. 87 p. : NYPL [*XME-11,917]

TAXICABS - WASHINGTON (D.C.) - FARES.
Sullivan, Novell B. Washington, D.C. taxicab zone fare guide. [United States] , c1984. 86 p., [1] folded leaf of plates : LC Card 86-224478 DDC 388.4/1321 19
HE5634.W3 S93 1984

TAXPAYER COMPLIANCE - UNITED STATES - CONGRESSES.
Conference on Tax Administration Research Strategies (1985 : Washington, D.C.) Conference on Tax Administration Research, January 1985. Washington, D.C. [1985] 2 v. : LC Card 86-601369 DDC 353.0072/4 19
HJ3252 .C66 1985 NYPL [JLF 86-1791]

Tax[s]aver. Knepp, Jay. Menlo Park, Calif. , c1987. 143 p. : ISBN 0-376-07015-3 (pbk.) : LC Card 86-80874 DDC 343.7305/23 347.303523 19
HJ4653.D4 K56 1987

Taya, Teizo. Floating exchange rates and the state of world trade payments /. Cambridge, Mass. , 1984. xxvi, 309 p. ; ISBN 0-88410-998-4 (pbk.) LC Card 84-2905 DDC 332.4/562 19
HG3852 .F56 1984 NYPL [JLD 86-2709]

Tayeng, J. Household population by religion of head of household, up to C.D. block and town level, series 14, Meghalaya . New Delhi , 1986. iii, 70 p. ; LC Card 87-901361 DDC 304.6/0954/164021 19
HA4587.M43 H68 1986

Tayloe Murphy Institute. Lindsey, Donald W. Taxable sales in Virginia, 1985 /. Charlottesville, Va. (2015 Ivy Rd., Charlottesville 22903-1780) [1986] 16 p. : LC Card 86-622891 DDC 336.2/713/09755021 19
HJ5715.U62 V85 1986

Taylor, Charlotte. The entrepreneurial workbook : a step-by-step guide to starting and operating your own small business / by Charlotte Taylor. New York, N.Y. : New American Library, c1985. ix, 148 p. : forms ; 28 cm. "A Plume book". ISBN 0-452-25660-7 : LC Card 84-29439 DDC 658/.022 19
1. New business enterprises - Management. 2. Small business - Management. 3. Success in business. I. Title.
HD62.5 .T39 1985 ***NYPL [JLF 86-795]***

Taylor, J. Edward. The Design of alternative development strategies /. Rohtak, India , 1986. xiv, 330 p. : LC Card 86-901301 DDC 338.9 19
HD82 .D383 1986 ***NYPL [JLE 86-4232]***

Taylor, James Walter, 1933-
How to create a winning business plan / by James W. Taylor. New York, NY : Modern Business Reports, 1987, c1986. p. cm. ISBN 0-87280-116-0 : LC Card 87-7685 DDC 658.4/012 19
1. Small business - Management. 2. Small business - Planning. I. Title.
HD62.7 .T38 1987

Paul, Ronald N. The 101 best performing companies in America /. Chicago, Ill. , c1986. vii, 382 p. ; ISBN 0-917253-39-6 : LC Card 86-4947 DDC 338.7/4/0973 19
HD2785 .P38 1986 ***NYPL [JLE 86-3151]***

Taylor, Jeffrey R., 1954- Employment outlook for China to the year 2000 / by Jeffrey R. Taylor. Washington, D.C. : Center for International Research, U. S. Bureau of the Census, [1986] 43 leaves, 2 p. ; 28 cm. (CIR staff paper . no. 16) "March 1986." Bibliography: leaves 41-43. LC Card 87-601289 DDC 331.12/3/0951021 19
1. Employment forecasting - China. 2. Labor supply - China. I. Title. II. Series.
HD5830.A6 T375 1986

Taylor, John, 1753-1824. Tyranny unmasked / by John Taylor of Caroline ; introduction by Forrest McDonald. Cumberland, Va. : James River Press, 1988. p. cm. Reprint. Originally published: Washington City : Davis and Force, 1822. Includes index. ISBN 0-940973-05-7 (alk. paper) : LC Card 87-2957 DDC 382.7/3/0973 19
1. Tariff - United States. 2. United States - Politics and government - 1817-1825. I. Title.
HF1754 .T4 1988

Taylor, John A. (John Alvin), 1930- U. S. imports of textile and apparel products under the multifiber arrangement, 1981-84 / [prepared principally by John A. Taylor, Elaine T. Freeman, and Mary Elizabeth Sweet]. Washington, D.C. : U. S. International Trade Commission, [1985] v, 136 p. ; 28 cm. (USITC publication. 1767) Cover title. "October 1985." Chiefly tables. LC Card 86-601665 DDC 382/.45677/00973021 19
1. Clothing trade - United States - Statistics. 2. Textile industry - United States - Statistics. I. Freeman, Elaine T. II. Sweet, Mary Elizabeth K. III. United States. International Trade Commission. IV. Title. V. Title: US imports of textile and apparel products under the multifiber arrangement, 1981-84. VI. Title: United States imports of textile and apparel products under the multifiber arrangement, 1981-84.
HD9940.U4 T38 1985

Taylor, John, of Caroline. see **Taylor, John, 1753-1824.**

Taylor, Kent F. Holland in Australia . Melbourne , 1986. xxii, 229 p. : ISBN 0-86431-032-3 LC Card 87-164636 DDC 331.7/02/0994 19
HF5381.H56693 H65 1986

Taylor, Laurie, 1935- Uninvited guests : the intimate secrets of television and radio / Laurie Taylor and, Bob Mullan ; photographs by Nigel Inglis ; qualitative research by The Research Business. London : Chatto & Windus, 1986. 218 p. : ill. ; 24 cm. Bibliography: p. 209-212. Includes index. ISBN 0-7011-2973-5 : LC Card 86-183414 DDC 791.44/75/0941 19
1. Television audiences - Great Britain. 2. Television broadcasting - Social aspects - Great Britain. 3. Radio audiences - Great Britain. 4. Radio broadcasting - Social aspects - Great Britain. I. Mullan, Bob. II. Title.
HE8689.7.A8 T39 1986

Taylor, Malcolm G. (Malcolm Gordon) Medical perspectives on Canadian Medicare : attitudes of Canadian physicians to policies and problems of the Medical Care Insurance Program / Malcolm G. Taylor, H. Michael Stevenson, A. Paul Williams. Downsview, Ont. : Institute for Behavioural Research, York University, 1984. vii, 201 p. : ill. ; 28 cm. (Social science research (Downsview, Ont.)) Includes bibliographical references. ISBN 0-919762-57-3 (pbk.) LC Card 87-673411
1. Medicare - Canada - Public opinion. 2. Insurance, Health - Canada - Public opinion. 3. Physicians - Canada - Attitudes. I. Stevenson, H. Michael. II. Williams, A. Paul (Alan Paul), 1951-. III. York University, Toronto, Ont. Institute for Behavioural Research. IV. Title. V. Series.
HD7102.C2 T34x 1984

Taylor, Mark P., 1958- Cuthbertson, Keith. Macroeconomic systems /. Oxford, UK , New York, NY, USA , 1987. ix, 278 p. : ISBN 0-631-14341-6 : LC Card 87-10332 DDC 339 19
HB172.5 .C87 1987

Taylor, Mary Sue, 1938- Clear & simple filing and records management / Mary Sue Taylor. New York, NY : Prentice Hall, c1987. 171 p. : ill. ; 28 cm. Cover title: Monarch's clear & simple filing and records management. "A Monarch book." ISBN 0-671-62397-4 (pbk.) : LC Card 86-28534 DDC 651.5 19
1. Filing systems. 2. Records - Management. I. Title. II. Title: Clear and simple filing and records management. III. Title: Monarch's clear & simple filing and records management.
HF5736 .T388 1987

Taylor, Michael, 1946- Multinationals and the restructuring of the world economy /. London , Dover, N.H. , c1986- viii, 389 p. : ISBN 0-7099-2457-7 (v. 2) : LC Card 85-29081 DDC 338.8/81 19
HD2755.5 .M8442 1986
NYPL [JLD 86-2089]

Taylor, Neil.
Collie, coal, and energy policy in Western Australia / by Neil Taylor. Murdoch, W.A. : Murdoch University, [1985] 56 p. : charts, maps ; 30 cm. (Discussion paper . no. 1/85) "March, 1985." Bibliography: p. 47-53. ISBN 0-86905-080-X (pbk.) LC Card 87-116549 DDC 333.8/22/099412 19
1. Coal trade - Government policy - Australia - Collie (W.A.). 2. Energy policy - Australia - Western Australia. I. Series: Discussion paper (Murdoch University) , 85/1. II. Title.
HD9558.A83 C657 1985

The security of energy supplies in Western Australia / by Neil Taylor. Murdoch, W.A. : School of Social Inquiry, Murdoch University, 1986. 35 p. : ill. ; 30 cm. (Discussion paper . no. 5/86) Bibliography: p. 34-35. ISBN 0-86905-099-0 (pbk.) : LC Card 87-118009 DDC 333.79/09941 19
1. Energy policy - Australia - Western Australia. 2. Power resources - Australia - Western Australia. I. Series: Discussion paper (Murdoch University) , n. 86/5. II. Title.
HD9502.A873 W45673 1986

Taylor, Richard F. Previts, Gary John. John Raymond Wildman . University, Ala. , 1978. viii, 84 p. ; LC Card 86-224716
HF5604.5.W55 P74 1978

Taylor, William, 1959- Nader, Ralph. The big boys . New York , c1986. xix, 571 p. ; ISBN 0-394-53338-0 : LC Card 85-25979 DDC 338.6/44/0973 19
HD2785 .N33 1986 ***NYPL [JLE 86-2421]***

Tazwīr al-mustanadāt wa-tazyīf al-ʻumlāt wa-al-asālīb al-ʻilmīyah lil-kashf ʻanhā. [Cairo] : Jāmiʻat al-Duwal al-ʻArabīyah, al-Munaẓẓamah al-ʻArabīyah lil-Difāʻ al-Ijtimāʻī ḍidda al-Jarīmah, [1978] 296 p., [1] leaf of plates : ill. (some col.) ; 25 cm. (Majmūʻah ʻilmīyah / tuṣdiruhā al-Munaẓẓamah al-ʻArabīyah lil-Difāʻ al-Ijtimāʻī ḍidda al-Jarīmah . al-kitāb 1. (sanat 1978)) Bibliography: p. 293-294. ISBN 977-7049-73-0 LC Card 79-961630
1. Counterfeits and counterfeiting. 2. Forgery. 3. Criminal investigation - Arab countries. I. Arab Organization for Social Defense against Crime. II. Series: Majmūʻah ʻilmīyah , al-kitāb 1.
HG335 .T3 1978

T.C. Anadolu Üniversitesi yayınları. İktisadi ve İdari Bilimler Fakültesi yayınları .
(no. 13) Aşıkoğlu, Rıza. Sermaye piyasası aracı olarak enflasyon ortamında tahvilleri değerleme /. [Eskişehir, Turkey] , 1983. xii, 155 p. : LC Card 85-221546
HG5706.5.A3 A85 1983

TCA, Seminario sobre Transporte Fluvial. River Transportation Seminar (1986 : Iquitos, Peru) Tratado de cooperación amazónica . Washington, D.C. , 1986. iii, 110 p. ; ISBN 0-8270-2473-8 (pbk.) LC Card 87-115058
HE387.A6 R58 1986

Tchad. see **Chad.**

Tchen, John Kuo Wei. Siu, Paul C. P. (Paul Chan Pang), 1906- The Chinese laundryman . New York , c1987. xlii, 311 p. : ISBN 0-8147-7859-3 : LC Card 87-5609 DDC 331.6/2/51073 19
HD8039.L32 U675 1987

TCOs förslag till forskning.
Jämställdhet i arbetsliv och samhälle. Stockholm [1985] 129 p. : ISBN 91-7168-259-7 : LC Card 86-133755
HD6060.5.S8 J36 1985

Tea and poverty . Dawood, Nawaz. Kowloon, Hong Kong , 1980. xii, 166 p. ; LC Card 80-154803 DDC 338.1/7372/095493 19
HC424 .D36 1980

TEA PLANTATION WORKERS - EMPLOYMENT - INDIA - DARJILING (DISTRICT)
Tea plantation workers in the eastern Himalayas . Delhi , 1986. xxxi, 255 p. : ISBN 81-7043-055-0 : LC Card 86-903466
HD8039.T182 I48 1986

TEA PLANTATION WORKERS - EMPLOYMENT - NEPAL.
Kansakar, Vidya Bir Singh. Migration and employment in the tea estates of Nepal /. Kathmandu , 1985. vii, 87, iv, xvii p. ; LC Card 86-903522 DDC 331.12/5372/095496 19
HD8039.T182 N355 1985

Tea plantation workers in the eastern Himalayas : a study on wages, employment, and living standards / edited by R.L. Sarkar, Mahendra P. Lama.1st ed. Delhi : Atma Ram, 1986. xxxi, 255 p. : ill., maps (some folded) ; 23 cm. "This study was sponsored by Ambekar Institute of Labour Studies, Bombay, and Friedrich Ebert Foundation, New Delhi"--P. [v] Study covers Darjeeling District, West Bengal, 1930-1983, sponsored by Ambekar Institute of Labour Studies, Bombay, and Friedrich Ebert Foundation, New Delhi. Bibliography: p. [231]-245. ISBN 81-7043-055-0 : LC Card 86-903466
1. Tea plantation workers - India - Darjiling (District). 2. Tea plantation workers - Employment - India - Darjiling (District). I. Sarkar, R. L. II. Lama, Mahendra P. III. Ambekar Institute for Labour Studies. IV. Friedrich-Ebert-Stiftung.
HD8039.T182 I48 1986

TEA PLANTATION WORKERS - INDIA - DARJILING (DISTRICT)
Tea plantation workers in the eastern Himalayas . Delhi , 1986. xxxi, 255 p. : ISBN 81-7043-055-0 : LC Card 86-903466
HD8039.T182 I48 1986

TEA PLANTATION WORKERS - INDIA - JALPAIGURI (DISTRICT)
Bhowmik, Sharit, 1948- Class formation in the plantation system /. New Delhi , 1981. xix, 263 p. : LC Card 81-903777 DDC 305/.93633 19
HD1470.5.I42 J342 1981
NYPL [JLD 86-2612]

TEA PLANTATION WORKERS - NEPAL.
Kansakar, Vidya Bir Singh. Migration and employment in the tea estates of Nepal /. Kathmandu , 1985. vii, 87, iv, xvii p. ; LC Card 86-903522 DDC 331.12/5372/095496 19
HD8039.T182 N355 1985

TEA PLANTATION WORKERS - SRI LANKA.
Kūriyan, Rēval. Vatukarayē kāntā śramaya surākāma . Colombo, Sri Lanka [1984] 24 p. :

LC Card 86-902479
HD6182.8 .K87 1984

TEA ROOMS. see **RESTAURANTS, LUNCH ROOMS, ETC.**

TEA TRADE - BURUNDI.
Les Cultures industrielles du Burundi . Bujumbura [1985] 63 p. : LC Card 85-981329
HD9195.B942 C85 1985

TEA TRADE - INDIA - JALPAIGURI (DISTRICT)
Bhowmik, Sharit, 1948- Class formation in the plantation system /. New Delhi , 1981. xix, 263 p. : LC Card 81-903777 DDC 305/.93633 19
HD1470.5.I42 J342 1981
NYPL [JLD 86-2612]

TEA TRADE - MATHEMATICAL MODELS.
Akiyama, T. (Takamasa), 1944- A new global tea model . Washington, D.C. , 1987. vi, 130 p. ; ISBN 0-8213-0868-8 LC Card 87-6238 DDC 382/.41372 19
HD9198.A2 A424 1987

TEACHERS - GERMANY (WEST) - SUPPLY AND DEMAND.
Pieper, Beate. Vom Lehrermangel zur Lehrerarbeitslosigkeit . Münster , 1984. ix, 265 p. : ISBN 3-923881-11-8 : LC Card 85-195712 DDC 331.12 19
LB2833.4.G4 P54 1984
NYPL [JLD 87-1161]

Teaching paper (Szkoła Główna Planowania i Statystyki (Warsaw, Poland). Instytut Gospodarki Krajów Rozwijających się) . (v. 29) Strategy of socio-economic development . Warsaw , 1980. 122 p. : LC Card 81-107307
HD75 .S8 1980

Tealdo, Armando. La planificación en empresas agropecuarias : plan operativo / Armando Tealdo. Lima, Perú : Centro de Estudios para el Desarrollo y la Participación, [1985], c1983. 157 p. : ill. ; 21 cm. (Serie Desarrollo rural . 4) LC Card 85-174266 DDC 630/.68 19
1. Agricultural industries - Planning. 2. Agricultural industries - Peru - Planning. I. Title. II. Series.
HD9000.5 .T4 1985 ***NYPL [JLD 86-1283]***

Team theory /. Kim, Ki Hang. Chichester , New York , 1987. viii, 246 p. ; ISBN 0-7458-0154-4 : LC Card 87-4137 DDC 658.4/036 19
HD30.23 .K396 1987

TEAM WORK IN INDUSTRY. see **WORK GROUPS.**

Teamsters, Chauffeurs, Warehousemen and Helpers of America, International Brotherhood of. see **International Brotherhood of Teamsters, Chauffeurs, Warehousemen and Helpers of America.**

Teamsters Union. see **International Brotherhood of Teamsters, Chauffeurs, Warehousemen and Helpers of America.**

Teamwork, joint labor-management programs in America / edited by Jerome M. Rosow. New York : Pergamon Press, 1986. xvi, 199 p. : ill. ; 24 cm. (Pergamon Press/Work in America Institute series) Includes bibliographies and index. ISBN 0-08-032799-0 : LC Card 85-28397 DDC 331.01/12/0973 19
1. Industrial relations - United States. 2. Industrial management - United States - Employee participation. I. Rosow, Jerome M.
HD8072.5 .T43 1986 ***NYPL [JLE 86-3139]***

TEAROOMS. see **RESTAURANTS, LUNCH ROOMS, ETC.**

Tebhāgā āndolana /. Datta, Śekhara. Ḍhākā , 1985. 103, [1] p. ; LC Card 86-902072
HD1537.I4 D34 1985

Technical Advisory Corporation (New York, N. Y.) A Plan for an industrial survey for Kalamazoo, August 1, 1926. New York , 1926. 30 p. ; LC Card 85-666471
HC108.K34 P52x 1926

TECHNICAL ASSISTANCE - AFRICA.
Proceedings of second (special) general conference . Accra, Ghana [1985?] 73 p. ; LC Card 86-220781 DDC 338.96 19
HC800 .P77 1985

TECHNICAL ASSISTANCE AGREEMENTS. see **FOREIGN LICENSING AGREEMENTS.**

TECHNICAL ASSISTANCE, AMERICAN - AFRICA.
Diversity in development . New York, NY , c1985. 49 p. : ISBN 0-932140-06-8 (pbk.) LC Card 86-231753 DDC 361.7/096 19
HC800.Z9 E444 1985

TECHNICAL ASSISTANCE, AMERICAN - AFRICA - DIRECTORIES.
Diversity in development . New York, NY , c1986. xvii, 620 p. : ISBN 0-932140-07-6 (pbk.) LC Card 86-231757 DDC 361.7/025/73 19
HC800.Z9 E444 1986

TECHNICAL ASSISTANCE, AMERICAN - CENTRAL AMERICA.
An Evaluation of ROCAP activities in marketing, 1965-71 /. Washington, D.C. (1200 18th St., N.W., Washington 20036) [1971] xvii, 82, 3 leaves, [1] leaf of plates : LC Card 81-146599
HC141 .E93 1971

TECHNICAL ASSISTANCE, AMERICAN - EUROPE. see **TECHNICAL ASSISTANCE, AMERICAN.**

Technical assistance and training services of the International Monetary Fund. International Monetary Fund. Washington, D.C. , 1985. iii, 31 p. : LC Card 86-202820 DDC 332.1/52 19
HG3881.5.I58 I568 1985

TECHNICAL ASSISTANCE, AUSTRIAN - DEVELOPING COUNTRIES.
Höll, Otmar. Österreichische Entwicklungshilfe, 1970-1983 . Wien , Laxenburg, Austria , c1986. 187 p. : ISBN 3-7003-0659-8 LC Card 86-192362
HC60 .H6643 1986

TECHNICAL ASSISTANCE, CANADIAN - DEVELOPING COUNTRIES.
With our own hands . Ottawa, Canada , c1986. 206 p. : ISBN 0-88936-460-5 (pbk.) LC Card 86-212405 DDC 338.91/71/01724 19
HC59.72.F44 W58 1986

TECHNICAL ASSISTANCE, CUBAN - GRENADA.
Historia del contingente internacionalista de Granada. [Havana, Cuba] [1984] 157 p. : LC Card 85-213062
HC156.5.Z7 G844 1984

TECHNICAL ASSISTANCE - DEVELOPING COUNTRIES.
Commission of the European Communities. Directorate-General of Information. A Community research policy for development. Brussels [1983] 21 p. ; LC Card 85-166173 DDC 338.91/4/01724 19
HC60 .C584 1983

Does aid work? . Oxford [Oxfordshire] , New York , 1986. xv, 381 p. ; ISBN 0-19-877250-5 : LC Card 86-12621 DDC 338.91/09172/4 19
HC60 .D53 1986 ***NYPL [JLE 86-4563]***

Höll, Otmar. Österreichische Entwicklungshilfe, 1970-1983 . Wien , Laxenburg, Austria , c1986. 187 p. : ISBN 3-7003-0659-8 LC Card 86-192362
HC60 .H6643 1986

Information note on the technical cooperation programme /. Rome [1985?] 29 p. : LC Card 87-122600 DDC 338.9/26/091724 19
HC60 .I477 1985

International Monetary Fund. Technical assistance and training services of the International Monetary Fund. Washington, D.C. , 1985. iii, 31 p. : LC Card 86-202820 DDC 332.1/52 19
HG3881.5.I58 I568 1985

Kress, Roland, 1961- Die politischen Stiftungen in der Entwicklungspolitik . Bochum , 1985. iv, 224 p. ; ISBN 3-88339-426-2 : LC Card 85-175519
HC60 .K727 1985

Neundörfer, Konrad. Wir und die Dritte Welt . Köln , c1985. x, 214 p. ; ISBN 3-452-20304-2 LC Card 85-164555
HC59.7 .N375 1985

Oteiza, Enrique. Technical co-operation among Third World countries and the international order /. Mexico, D.F. , 1978. 72 p. ; LC Card 86-223022 DDC 338.9/26 19
HC60 .O838 1978

Schneider, Bertrand. La révolution aux pieds nus . Paris , c1985. 344 p. ; ISBN 2-213-01684-4 : LC Card 86-179661
HC60 .S314 1985

Stockhausen, Joachim von. Theorie und Politik der Entwicklungshilfe . München , c1986. viii, 324 p. ; ISBN 3-8039-0332-1 LC Card 86-225372
HC60 .S7977 1986

TECHNICAL ASSISTANCE - DEVELOPING COUNTRIES - CASE STUDIES.
Information note on the technical cooperation programme /. Rome [1985?] 29 p. : LC Card 87-122600 DDC 338.9/26/091724 19
HC60 .I477 1985

TECHNICAL ASSISTANCE - DEVELOPING COUNTRIES - MANAGEMENT.
Neun, Hansjörg, 1953- Projektübergabe bei der technischen Zusammenarbeit mit Entwicklungsländer /. Augsburg [1985] viii, 315 p. : ISBN 3-87512-135-X : LC Card 86-228570
HD84 .N43 1985

TECHNICAL ASSISTANCE, FRENCH - DEVELOPING COUNTRIES.
France. Mission "Recherche, technologie et progrès en coopération." Recherche et coopération avec le Tiers Monde . Paris , c1983. 120 p. ; ISBN 2-11-001071-1 : LC Card 83-196852
HC60 .F727 1983

TECHNICAL ASSISTANCE IN UNDERDEVELOPED AREAS. see **TECHNICAL ASSISTANCE.**

TECHNICAL ASSISTANCE - ISLANDS OF THE PACIFIC - DIRECTORIES.
Directory of aid agencies. Suva, Fiji , 1985. iv, 147 p. ; LC Card 86-204497 DDC 338.91/025/9 19
HC681 .D57 1985

TECHNICAL ASSISTANCE, ITALIAN - PERU.
Aumento del ingreso y mejoramiento de las condiciones de trabajo del sector informal urbano en sietes ciudades del Perú /. [Lima, Perú?] , 1986. ii, 69, [25] leaves : LC Card 87-106249
HD2346.P4 A85 1986

TECHNICAL ASSISTANCE, JAPANESE - HISTORY.
Sekiguchi, Sueo. Technology transfer through direct foreign investment /. Ibaraki, Osaka, Japan , 1985. 61 leaves : LC Card 86-209818 DDC 332.6/7352 19
HC60 .S416 1985

TECHNICAL ASSISTANCE - PAKISTAN.
Cooperation in development and humanitarian assistance. Islamabad, Pakistan [1985] 50 p. : LC Card 86-930251 DDC 338.91/09549/1 19
HC440.5 .C66 1985

TECHNICAL ASSISTANCE - PERU.
Buroz Castillo, Eduardo. Programa de cooperación técnica Perú-Venezuela-OEA . Caracas , 1976. [11], 62 p. ; LC Card 84-136478
HD1696.P5 B87 1976

TECHNICAL ASSISTANCE - SAHEL.
Berg, Elliot. Absorptive capacity in the Sahel countries. [Paris] [Ouagadougou, Burkina Faso] [1983] xi, 133 p. ; LC Card 87-402541 DDC 338.91/0966 19
HC1002 .B47 1983

TECHNICAL ASSISTANCE - SAHEL - DIRECTORIES.
L'Aide publique au développement dans les pays membres du CILSS en 1983 =. Paris , Burkina Faso [1984], c1985. v, 347 p. : LC Card 86-180117
HC1000 .A64 1985

TECHNICAL ASSISTANCE, SWISS - DEVELOPING COUNTRIES.
Glinz, Ferdinand N. Entwicklungsförderung am Wendepunkt . Zürich , c1986. 320 p. ; ISBN 3-280-01676-2 LC Card 86-227950
HC59.7 .G55 1986

TECHNICAL ASSISTANCE - TOGO.
Kjellstrom, Sven B., 1945- Institutional development and technical assistance in macro-economic policy formulation . Washington, D.C., U. S.A. [1987] 69 p. ; ISBN 0-8213-0919-6 (pbk.) LC Card 87-14021 DDC 339.5/0966/81 19
HC1015 .K58 1987

TECHNICAL ASSISTANCE, UNITED NATIONS. see **UNITED NATIONS - TECHNICAL ASSISTANCE.**

TECHNICAL ASSISTANCE - VENEZUELA.
Buroz Castillo, Eduardo. Programa de cooperación técnica Perú-Venezuela-OEA . Caracas , 1976. [11], 62 p. ; LC Card 84-136478
HD1696.P5 B87 1976

TECHNICAL ASSISTANCE, WEST GERMAN - DEVELOPING COUNTRIES.
Entwicklungspolitik, Bilanz und Perspektiven . Bonn , 1986. 256 p. ; LC Card 87-409363 DDC 338.91/43/01724 19
HC60 .E523 1986

Kress, Roland, 1961- Die politischen Stiftungen in der Entwicklungspolitik . Bochum , 1985. iv, 224 p. ; ISBN 3-88339-426-2 : LC Card 85-175519
HC60 .K727 1985

Neundörfer, Konrad. Wir und die Dritte Welt . Köln , c1985. x, 214 p. ; ISBN 3-452-20304-2 LC Card 85-164555
HC59.7 .N375 1985

Die Notwendige Hilfe . Melle [1986] 207 p. : ISBN 3-88368-111-3 : LC Card 86-197696
HC60 .N69 1986

Stockhausen, Joachim von. Theorie und Politik der Entwicklungshilfe . München , c1986. viii, 324 p. ; ISBN 3-8039-0332-1 LC Card 86-225372
HC60 .S7977 1986

TECHNICAL ASSISTANCE, WEST GERMAN - DEVELOPING COUNTRIES - CONGRESSES.
Germany (West). Bundestag. Ausschuss für Wirtschaftliche Zusammenheit. Entwicklungspolitik, Bilanz und Perspektiven . Bonn , 1986. 256 p. ; LC Card 87-409259 DDC 339.91/43/01724 19
HC60 .G467 1986

TECHNICAL ASSISTANCE - ZIMBABWE - CONGRESSES.
Zimbabwe Conference on Reconstruction and Development (1981 : Salisbury, Zimbabwe) Zimbabwe Conference on Reconstruction and Development, Salisbury, 23rd to 27th March 1981 . Causeway, Zimbabwe [1981?] vi, 194 p. : LC Card 86-980955 DDC 338.96891 19
HC910 .Z318 1981a

Technical bulletin (Community Information Exchange (U. S.))
Corporate support for community development. Washington, D.C. , c1984. 15 p. ; LC Card 87-100348 DDC 361.7/65/0973 19
HD60.5.U5 C689 1984

Guggenheim, Joseph. HUD's rental rehabilitation program, HUD's housing development grant program /. Washington, D.C. [c1984] 13 p. ; LC Card 87-100358 DDC 363.5/8 19
HD7288.85.U6 G84 1984

Small business incubators . Washington, D.C. , c1984. 32 p. : LC Card 86-233015 DDC 333.33/8 19
HD1393.25 .S63 1984

Technical bulletin (International Fertilizer Development Center) .
(T-33) Mudahar, Mohinder S. Fertilizer marketing systems and policies in the developing world /. Muscle Shoals, Ala. , 1987. 43 p. : ISBN 0-88090-059-8 (pbk.) LC Card 87-3152 DDC 381/.4566862/091724 19
HD9483.D44 K36 1987

Technical change and full employment / edited by Christopher Freeman and Luc Soete. Oxford, UK ; New York, NY, USA : B. Blackwell, 1987. vii, 279 p. : ill. ; 24 cm. Bibliography: p. 265-273. Includes index. ISBN 0-631-14099-9 : LC Card 87-6637 DDC 331.12/5/0941 19
1. Labor supply - Great Britain - Effect of technological innovations on. I. Freeman, Christopher. II. Soete, Luc.
HD6331.2.G7 T39 1987

Technical co-operation among Third World countries and the international order /. Oteiza, Enrique. Mexico, D.F. , 1978. 72 p. ; LC Card 86-223022 DDC 338.9/26 19
HC60 .O838 1978

TECHNICAL EDUCATION - EUROPE.
Poppe, Johann Heinrich Moritz von, 1776-1854. Ausführliche Volks-Gewerbslehre, oder, Allgemeine und besondere Technologie zur Belehrung und zum Nutzen für alle Stände /. Stuttgart , Wien , 1833- v. <1 > : LC Card 87-409525 DDC 331.7/02/024042 19
HF5382.5.E84 P66 1833

TECHNICAL EDUCATION - FRANCE - HISTORY - 19TH CENTURY.
Edmonson, James M. From Mecanicien to ingenieur . New York, NY , 1987. x, 631 p. ; ISBN 0-8240-8036-X (alk. paper) : LC Card 87-300 DDC 338.4/76218/0944 19
HD9705.F7 E35 1987

TECHNICAL EDUCATION - GREAT BRITAIN.
Grant, Pamela, 1944- Youth employment and technological change . Aldershot, [England] , Brookfield, USA , c1987. xii, 393 p. : ISBN 0-566-05423-X : LC Card 86-33659 DDC 331.3/4125/0941 19
HD6276.G7 G66 1987

The technical enterprise . Fusfeld, Herbert I. Cambridge, Mass. , 1986. xiii, 312 p. ; ISBN 0-88730-033-2 LC Card 86-3340 DDC 338/.06 19
HC79.T4 F87 1986 ***NYPL [JLE 86-3344]***

Technical information for practitioners series .
(1) Other comprehensive bases of accounting /. New York, N.Y. (1211 Ave. of the Americas, New York 10036-8775) , c1986. vii, 52 p. ; LC Card 86-206776 DDC 657/.0218 19
HF5616.U5 O88 1986

TECHNICAL INNOVATIONS. see TECHNOLOGICAL INNOVATIONS.

TECHNICAL INSTITUTES. see TECHNICAL EDUCATION.

Technical Marketing Associates. An evaluation of industrial purchasing and distribution trends . Cleveland, Ohio (1230 Keith Bldg., Cleveland 44115) , c1985. 173 p. : LC Card 86-219582 DDC 658.7 19
HD39.5 .E93 1985

Technical memoranda (United States. Congress. Office of Technology Assessment)
Commercial newsgathering from space. Washington, DC [1987] ix, 51 p. : LC Card 87-619818 DDC 070.4/3 19
HE9721.U5 C65 1987

Research funding as an investment--can we measure the returns? Washington, D.C. [1986] vi, 72 p. : LC Card 86-600525 DDC 338/.06 19
HC110.R4 R47 1986

A Review of U. S. competitiveness in agricultural trade. Washington, D.C. [1986] ix, 101 p. : LC Card 86-600586 DDC 382/.41/0973 19
HD1761 .R48 1986

Technical paper (United States. Bureau of the Census) .
(54) Cleveland, Robert W. Income nonresponses . [Washington] [1985] iv, 87 p. : LC Card 85-603179 DDC 339.2/2/0973021 19
HC110.I5 C44 1985

(56) Estimates of poverty, including the value of noncash benefits, 1985. Washington, D.C. [1986] v, 86 p. ; LC Card 86-603442 DDC 362.5/8/0973 19
HC110.P63 E783 1986

Technical papers series .
(no. 39 39) Kennedy, Peter, 1954- Food and agricultural policy in Peru, 1960-1977 [microform] /. Austin (Sid Richardson Hall 1.310, Austin 78712) , 1983. 22 p. ; LC Card 83-623239 DDC 338.1/885 19
HD1903 .K46 1983 ***NYPL [*ZT-1646 no.20]***

(no. 40 40) Harber, Richard P. Tax policy, economic development, and regional inequality [microform] . Austin , 1984. 33 p. ; LC Card 84-623077 DDC 339.5/2/09813 19
HJ2527 .H37 1984 ***NYPL [*ZT-1646 no.22]***

(no. 47) Topik, Steven. State and economy . Austin , 1985. 28 p. ; LC Card 86-622250 DDC 338.981 19
HC187 .T56 1985

(no. 48) Saulniers, Alfred H., 1945- Beyond management control . Austin , 1985. 22 p. : LC Card 86-622251 DDC 354.8509/2 19
HD4124 .S28 1985

(no. 49) Collins, Paul D. Brazil in Africa . Austin , 1986. 16 p. ; LC Card 86-622252 DDC 337.8106 19
HF1514.5.A35 C65 1986

(no. 50) Boneo, Horacio. Interlinkages, concept, characteristics, and determining factors /. Austin , 1986. 17 p. : LC Card 86-622253 DDC 338.7/4/091724 19
HD4420.8 .B67 1986

(no. 51) Hallauer, Robert. Export promotion policies in Costa Rica . Austin , 1985. 17 p. ; LC Card 86-622254 DDC 382/.63/097286 19
HF1487 .H35 1985

Technical publication series (University of Ghana. Institute of Statistical, Social, and Economic Research) .
(no. 49) Ewusi, Kodwo. The development and resettlement of oncho-freed zones in the Volta River Basin of West Africa . [Legon, Ghana] [1985] 89 p. ; LC Card 87-127503 DDC 333.3/1/667 19
HD1022.Z8 V654 1985

Technical report (Bank of Canada) .
(43) Stuber, Gerald. The slowdown in productivity growth in the 1975-83 period . [Ottawa] [1986] 164 p. : LC Card 87-100880 DDC 338/.06/0971 19
HC120.I52 S78 1986

(46) Kuszczak, John. A VAR analysis of economic interdependence . [Ottawa] [1987] ii, 55 p. : LC Card 87-167407 DDC 338.5/42/0971 19
HB3755 .K87 1987

Technical report (Kenya Rangeland Ecological Monitoring Unit) .
(no. 72) Agatsiva, J. L. Land use mapping of Kenya using remote sensing techniques /. [Nairobi] , 1982. iv, 39 p. : LC Card 84-980919 DDC 333.73/13/028 19
HD983.Z7 A38 1982

(no. 93) Peden, D. G. The use of resource survey data in decision-making with special reference to Kitui District in Kenya /. Nairobi, Kenya , 1982. 12 leaves ; LC Card 85-980593 DDC 333.74/09676/24 19
HD983.Z8 K587 1982

Technical report (Texas Transportation Institute) .
(1082-1F) Bullard, Diane L. Texas public transit reference manual /. College Station, Tex. [1985] xv, 279 p. : LC Card 86-623065 DDC 388.4/09764 19
HE4426.T4 B84 1985

TECHNICAL SCHOOLS. see TECHNICAL EDUCATION.

Technical services monograph .
(LMEP-14) High technology employment . Augusta, Me. (20 Union St., Augusta 04330) [1985] iii, 23 p. : LC Card 85-623118 DDC 331.12/57/09741 19
HD5718.H542 U635 1985

TECHNICIANS IN INDUSTRY - FRANCE.
Le Guen, René. Oxygène pour tous les cerveaux /. Paris , c1985. 204 p. : ISBN 2-209-05743-4 : LC Card 86-117864 DDC 331.7/12/0944 19
HD8038.F7 L4 1985

TECHNICIANS IN INDUSTRY - FRANCE - HISTORY - 19TH CENTURY.
Edmonson, James M. From Mecanicien to ingenieur . New York, NY , 1987. x, 631 p. ; ISBN 0-8240-8036-X (alk. paper) : LC Card 87-300 DDC 338.4/76218/0944 19
HD9705.F7 E35 1987

TECHNICIANS IN INDUSTRY - GREAT BRITAIN.
Cockburn, Cynthia. Machinery of dominance . London , Dover, N.H. , 1985. 282 p. ; ISBN 0-7453-0065-0 (pbk.) : LC Card 86-204262 DDC 331.13/3/0941 19
HD6060.5.G7 C63 1985

Grant, Pamela, 1944- Youth employment and technological change . Aldershot, [England] , Brookfield, USA , c1987. xii, 393 p. : ISBN 0-566-05423-X : LC Card 86-33659 DDC 331.3/4125/0941 19
HD6276.G7 G66 1987

TECHNICIANS IN INDUSTRY - SALARIES, ETC. - GERMANY (WEST) - HESSE - STATISTICS.
Gehalts- und Lohnstrukturerhebung 1978 . Wiesbaden , 1983. 285, [3] p. ; LC Card 84-217477
HA1320 .H529 n.F., Nr. 152 HD5030.H47

TECHNICIANS IN INDUSTRY - UNITED STATES - VOCATIONAL GUIDANCE.
Paradis, Adrian A. Opportunities in vocational & technical careers /. Lincolnwood, Ill., U. S.A. , c1987. xi, 147 p. : ISBN 0-8442-6018-5 LC Card 87-60104 DDC 371.4/25/02373 19
HF5382.5.U5 P28 1987

Technico-economic analysis of the role of road freight transport : report / prepared by an OECD scientific expert group. Paris : Organisation for Economic Co-operation and Development ; [Washington, D.C. : OECD Publications and Information Centre, distributor], 1986. 135 p. : ill. ; 27 cm. (Road transport research) Includes bibliographies. ISBN 92-64-12843-3 (pbk.) : LC Card 86-215619 DDC 388.3/24 19
1. Trucking. I. Series.
HE5611 .T43 1986

Technik auf dem Prüfstand : Methoden und Massstäbe der Technologiebewertung / [Herausgeber], Erwin Münch, Ortwin Renn, Thomas Roser. Essen : W. Girardet ; Gräfelfing : Energiewirtschaft und Technik Verlagsgesellschaft, [1982] 183 p. : ill. ; 23 cm. "Ein Grossteil der hier vorgelegten Beiträge stammt aus einem Seminar zum Thema Technologiebewertung, das das Deutsche Atomforum im Frühjahr 1981 in Düsseldorf veranstaltet hat"--P. 10. Includes bibliographical references and index. ISBN 3-7736-0340-1 LC Card 83-187518
1. Nuclear industry - Germany (West) - Congresses. 2. Nuclear industry - Environmental aspects - Germany (West) - Congresses. I. Münch, Erwin. II. Renn, Ortwin. III. Roser, Thomas. IV. Deutsches Atomforum.
HD9698.G42 T43 1982

Technik und internationale Politik / Beate Kohler-Koch (Hrsg.). 1. Aufl. Baden-Baden : Nomos, 1986. 520 p. ; 23 cm. Papers presented at a conference held at Technische Hochschule Darmstadt on June 20-22, 1985. Includes bibliographical references. ISBN 3-7890-1239-4 (Deut. Bibl.) LC Card 87-103890 DDC 338/.06 19
1. Technological innovations - Economic aspects - Congresses. 2. Technology transfer - Economic aspects - Congresses. 3. International economic relations - Congresses. I. Kohler-Koch, Beate, 1941-. II. Technische Hochschule Darmstadt.
HC79.T4 T422 1986

Technik von gestern für die Ziele von morgen? : energiepolitische Orientierungen auf dem Weg zur postmaterialistischen Gesellschaft / Martin Held, Walter Molt (Hrsg.). Opladen : Westdeutscher Verlag, c1986. 153 p. ; 21 cm. Bibliography: p. [141]-150. ISBN 3-531-11713-0 LC Card 86-230906
1. Energy development - Social aspects. 2. Energy policy. I. Held, Martin, Dr. II. Molt, Walter, 1932-.
HD9502.A2 T43 1986

Die Technikwahl bei linearer Einzelproduktion, oder, Die dritte Krise der Profitrate /. Helmedag, Fritz, 1953- Frankfurt am Main , New York , c1986. viii, 301 p. : ISBN 3-8204-9645-9 LC Card 86-219002
HB601 .H44 1986

Technique & documentation.
Guide pratique du financement des industries agroalimentaires /. Paris [1986] 351 p. : LC Card 86-186921
HD9012.5 .G86 1986

Roux, Pierre, docteur en sciences économiques. Economie agricole /. Paris , c1986- v. <1 > : ISBN 2-85206-353-0 (set) LC Card 87-106675
HD1415 .R62 1986

Technique comptable algérienne /. Benaïssa, Younès. Alger , 1985- v. <1 > : LC Card 86-966696
HF5616.A4 B46 1985

Les techniques de banque et de crédit au Maroc /. Barrādah, Muḥammad. Casablanca , 1985. 590 p. : LC Card 86-967115
HG3382.A6 B37 1985

Techniques in training and performance development series.
Mink, Oscar G. Groups at work /. Englewood Cliffs, N.J. , c1987. xiii, 279 p. : ISBN 0-87778-196-6 LC Card 87-9081 DDC 658.4/036 19
HD66 .M55 1987

Rossett, Allison. Training needs assessment /. Englewood Cliffs, N.J. , c1987. xvi, 294 p. : ISBN 0-87778-195-8 LC Card 87-9070 DDC 658.3/124 19
HF5549.5.T7 R65 1987

Techniques of financial analysis /. Helfert, Erich A. Homewood, Ill. , 1987. xiii, 458 p. : ISBN 0-256-03625-X (pbk.) LC Card 86-82589 DDC 658.1/51 19
HG4026 .H44 1987

Techniques of structured problem solving /. VanGundy, Arthur B. New York , c1988. xiv, 386 p. : ISBN 0-442-28847-6 LC Card 87-6168 DDC 658.4/03 19
HD30.29 .V36 1988

Techniques vivantes. Développement en zones arides.
Funel, Jean Marie. Politiques d'aménagement hydro-agricole /. Paris , c1980. 212 p. : ISBN 2-85319-083-8 LC Card 86-112826
HD1699.S37 F86 1980

Technisch rationell, sozial effektiv : soziale Komponenten technischer Entwicklung / Autorenkollektiv unter der Leitung von Gerhard Schellenberger ; [herausgegeben vom Wissenschaftlichen Rat für Soziologische Forschung in der DDR]. Berlin : Dietz, 1986. 168 p. ; 18 cm. (Schriftenreihe "Soziologie.") Includes bibliographical references. ISBN 3-320-00706-8 LC Card 87-144339 DDC 338/.06 19
1. Automation - Economic aspects - Germany (East). 2. Automation - Social aspects - Germany (East). 3. Technological innovations - Economic aspects - Germany (East). 4. Technological innovations - Social aspects - Germany, East. I. Schellenberger, Gerhard, 1924-. II. Wissenschaftlicher Rat für Soziologische Forschung in der DDR.
HC290.795.A9 T43 1986

Technisch-Wirtschaftlicher Dienst der Ländervereine. Kooperationsführer Kamerun /. Köln , 1986. 70 p. : LC Card 87-408425 DDC 330.967/1104 19
HC995 .K66 1986

Kontakt & Studium. see **Kontakt & Studium.**

Die technische Entwicklung als Element des sozialen Wandels und ihre Auswirkungen auf den öffentlichen Sektor in der Bundesrepublik Deutschland /. Wolfgart, Ludger. Münster [1986] ii, 213 p. ; ISBN 3-88660-230-3 (cover); 3-88600-230-3 (Deut. Bibl.) LC Card 87-106473 DDC 338.943 19
HD4175 .W65 1986

Technische Hochschule Darmstadt.
Specht, Günter. Industrielles Beschaffungsverhalten . Frankfurt am Main , New York , c1985. iii, 167 p. : ISBN 3-8204-8938-X LC Card 86-120719
HD9654.5 .S64 1985

Technik und internationale Politik /. Baden-Baden , 1986. 520 p. ; ISBN 3-7890-1239-4 (Deut. Bibl.) LC Card 87-103890 DDC 338/.06 19
HC79.T4 T422 1986

Technische Hochschule Karl-Marx-Stadt. Forschungsgruppe "Politökonomische Probleme des Wissenschaftlich-Technischen Fortschritts." Politökonomische Probleme des Gebrauchswerts, der Nützlichkeit und der Bewertung von Gebrauchswerten /. Karl-Marx-Stadt [1983] 92 p. ; LC Card 84-167577
HB201 .P63 1983

Technische Hochschule Karl-Marx-Stadt. Forschungsgruppe Soziologie.
Wissenschaftliche Konferenz "Wissenschaftlich-Technischer Fortschritt, Bedingungen, Anforderungen, Möglichkeiten der Persönlichkeitsentwicklung" (1985 : Karl-Marx-Stadt, Germany) Wissenschaftliche Konferenz "Wissenschaftlich-Technischer Fortschritt, Bedingungen, Anforderungen, Möglichkeiten der Persönlichkeitsentwicklung" am 8. und 9. Oktober 1985 in Karl-Marx-Stadt /. Karl-Marx-Stadt , 1986. 98 p. ; LC Card 87-407801 DDC 338/.06 19
HD45 .W55 1985

Technische Hochschule Karl-Marx-Stadt. Sektion Wirtschaftswissenschaften. "Ökonomische Probleme der bedarfsorientierten Produktionsdurchführung" . Karl-Marx-Stadt , 1984. 139 p. : LC Card 84-245348
HD70.G22 O35 1984

Technische Hochschule Karl-Marx-Stadt. Wissenschaftsbereich "Leitung und Organisation des Sozialistischen Industriebetriebes." Wissenschaftliche Tagung "Nutzung Ökonomisch-Mathematischer Methoden und der Elektronischen Rechentechnik zur Erhöhung der Reaktionsfähigkeit der Industriekombinate gegenüber der Bedarfsdynamik" (1983 : Technische Hochschule Karl-Marx Stadt) Wissenschaftliche Tagung "Nutzung Ökonomisch-Mathematischer Methoden und der Elektronischen Rechentechnik zur Erhöhung der Reaktionsfähigkeit der Industriekombinate gegenüber der Bedarfsdynamik," 8. Juni 1983 . Karl-Marx-Stadt [1983] iii, 56 p. ; LC Card 84-117572
HD30.25 .W56 1983

Technische Hochschule Leipzig. Institut für Sozialistische Wirtschaftsführung.
Kolloquium 20 Jahre Weiterbildungs- und Forschungsarbeit (1987 : Leipzig, Germany) Kolloquium 20 Jahre Weiterbildungs- und Forschungsarbeit . [Leipzig] , 1986. 64 p. ; LC Card 87-408852 DDC 338.9431 19
HC290.78 .K64 1987

Technische Normung und Verbraucherinteressen im gesellschaftlichen Wandel /. Bopp-Schmehl, Annemarie, 1946- Frankfurt am Main , c1984. iii, 269 p. ; ISBN 3-88129-834-7 : LC Card 85-119483
HC290.5.C6 B66 1984

Technische Universität Berlin. Institut für Arbeitswissenschaft. Arbeitsgestaltung in der Serienfertigung . Frankfurt [am Main] , New York , c1984. 315 p. : ISBN 3-593-32733-3 LC Card 84-230390
HD58.8 .A73 1984

Technische Universität Braunschweig. Institut für Stadtbauwesen. Fechtel, Hans-Walter. Flächenhafte Verkehrsberuhigung . Bergisch Gladbach , 1986. 282 p. : LC Card 87-408360 DDC 388.4/0943 19
HE311.G3 F4 1986

Technischer Fortschritt und Arbeitslosigkeit / Harald Hagemann, Peter Kalmbach (Hg.). Frankfurt/Main ; New York : Campus Verlag, c1983. 372 p. : ill. ; 21 cm. (Campus Forschung. Bd. 344) Includes bibliographies. CONTENTS. - Ansichten zur Maschinerie / Albert Jeck und Heinz D. Kurz, David Ricardo -- Technischer Fortschritt, Reallohn und Beschäftigung in einem Marxschen Modell langfristigen Wachstums / Jörg Glombowski -- Lederers Theorie der strukturellen Arbeitslosigkeit und lange Wellen / Robert A. Dickler -- Der Beitrag der "Kieler Schule" zur Freisetzungs- und Kompensationstheorie / Bernd Mettelsiefen -- Wachstumsgleichgewicht, Traverse und technologische Unterbeschäftigung / Harald Hagemann -- Die Berechnung der Freisetzung und Einsparung von Arbeitskräften / Peter Kalmbach -- Konsequenzen technologischen Wandels / Hans-Dieter Feser und Thomas Lärm -- Mikroelektronik und Beschäftigung / Alexander Gerybadze -- Technischer Wandel, Weltmarkt und Beschäftigung / Joachim Wagner -- Technologieverträge als gewerkschaftliches Instrument der Einflussnahme auf Investitionsentscheidungen / Hans Peter Widmaier. ISBN 3-593-33246-9 LC Card 84-143045
1. Unemployment, Technological - Addresses, essays, lectures. 2. Machinery in industry - Addresses, essays, lectures. I. Hagemann, Harald. II. Kalmbach, Peter.
HD6331 .T39 1983 ***NYPL [JLD 87-331]***

TECHNOCRACY.
Citizen participation in public decision making /. Westport, Conn. , 1987. xii, 237 p. ; ISBN 0-313-25478-8 (lib. bdg. : alk. paper) : LC Card 86-7571 DDC 323/.042/0973 19
JK1764 .C525 1987 ***NYPL [JLD 87-932]***

Technologia / [zespół redakcyjny Władysław Błaszków, Jerzy Ziobrowski]. [Wrocław] : Wydawn. Uczelniane Akademii Ekonomicznej we Wrocławiu, 1982. 188 p. : ill. ; 24 cm. (Prace naukowe Akademii Ekonomicznej imienia Oskara Langego we Wrocławiu . nr. 191) Summaries in English; table of contents also in English. Includes bibliographies. LC Card 83-176194
1. Chemistry, Technical. I. Błaszków, Władysław. II. Ziobrowski, Jerzy. III. Series.
HB9 .B7522 nr. 191 TP185

Technological breakthrough in agriculture /. Siva Prasad, K. Allahabad, India , 1987. xii, 133 p. ;

ISBN 81-85076-15-4 : LC Card 86-903607 DDC 338.1/61 19
HD2075.A5 S58 1987

Technological change : the tripartite response, 1982-85. Geneva : International Labour Office, 1985. 355 p. : ill. ; 24 cm. "The articles included in this volume were originally published in the Social and Labour Bulletin"--T.p. verso. Includes bibliographies and index. ISBN 92-2-105162-5 (pbk.) : LC Card 86-203534 DDC 331.12 19
1. Labor supply - Effect of technological innovations on. 2. Industrial relations - Effect of technological innovations on. I. International Labour Office. II. Social and labour bulletin.
HD6331 .T416 1985

Technological change, collective bargaining, and industrial efficiency /. Willman, Paul. Oxford , New York , c1986. xvi, 282 p. : ISBN 0-19-827262-6 : LC Card 86-5104 DDC 331.88/0941 19
HD6664 .W56 1986 ***NYPL [JLD 87-994]***

Technological change, employment, and spatial dynamics . International Symposium on Technological Change and Employment: Urban and Regional Dimensions (1985 : Zandvoort, Netherlands) Berlin , New York , c1986. vii, 466 p. : ISBN 0-387-16478-2 (U. S. : pbk.) LC Card 86-10081 DDC 331.12 19
HD6331 .I6 1985
NYPL [JLM 72-289 v.270]

Technological change in Canadian industry / D.G. McFetridge. Toronto ; Buffalo : University of Toronto Press, c1985. xv, 233 p. ; 23 cm. (The Collected research studies, 0829-2396 . vol. 3) "Published by the University of Toronto Press in cooperation with the Royal Commission on the Economic Union and Development Prospects for Canada and the Canadian Government Publishing Centre, Supply and Services Canada." Includes bibliographies. ISBN 0-8020-7243-7 (pbk.) LC Card 86-164766 DDC 338/.06 19
1. Technological innovations - Economic aspects - Canada. 2. Technology transfer - Canada. 3. Canada - Industries. I. McFetridge, D. G., 1945-. II. Royal Commission on the Economic Union and Development Prospects for Canada. III. Series: Collected research studies , v. 3.
HC120.T4 T42 1985 ***NYPL [JLD 87-654]***

Technological change in economy and society. Technologischer Wandel in Wirtschaft und Gesellschaft =. Freiburg, Schweiz , 1985. 316 p., [1] leaf of plates : ISBN 3-7278-0347-9 : LC Card 86-129382
HC79.T4 T436 1985

Technological economics .
(Bd. 10) Zörgiebel, Wilhelm W. Technologie in der Wettbewerbsstrategie . Berlin , c1983. xv, 322 p. : ISBN 3-503-02361-5 LC Card 84-158275
HD9703.G42 Z67 1983

(Bd. 16) Nosko, Herbert. Rationelle Energieverwendung im Industriebetrieb . Berlin , c1986. xiii, 289 p. : ISBN 3-503-02547-2 LC Card 86-192206
HD9502.A2 N67 1986

(Bd. 22) Boehme, Joachim. Innovationsförderung durch Kooperation . Berlin , c1986. 227 p. ; ISBN 3-503-02618-5 LC Card 87-133032 DDC 338.4/762 19
HD9696.A2 B64 1986

TECHNOLOGICAL FORECASTING - UNITED STATES.
Stotter, James. Intelligent buildings . Stamford, Conn., U. S.A. , c1986. ix, 127 leaves : ISBN 0-89336-414-2 (pbk.) LC Card 87-165953 DDC 338.4/769/0973 19
HD9715.U52 S76 1986

TECHNOLOGICAL INNOVATION - UNITED STATES - STATES.
Corporation for Enterprise Development. Building the new economy . Washington, D.C. , 1986. iv, 178 p. ; ISBN 0-9605804-2-5 (pbk.) LC Card 86-61273 DDC 338.973 19
HC110.I53 C67 1986

TECHNOLOGICAL INNOVATIONS - ADDRESSES, ESSAYS, LECTURES.
(1972) Heyel, Carl, 1908- John Diebold on management. Englewood Cliffs, N.J. [1972] ix, 282 p. ISBN 0-13-510214-6 LC Card 75-170643 DDC 658
HD45 .H42 ***NYPL [JLF 73-1242]***

(1983) The Trouble with technology . London , 1983. x, 224 p. : ISBN 0-86187-285-1
NYPL [JLE 86-1128]

(1984) Entrepreneurship . Wien , New York , 1984, c1983. 218 p. ; ISBN 0-387-81830-8 (U. S.) LC Card 84-26677 DDC 338/.04 19
HB615 .E635 1984 ***NYPL [JLE 85-1253]***

(1985) The Uneasy alliance . Boston, Mass. , c1985. x, 485 p. : ISBN 0-87584-172-4 LC Card 85-8709 DDC 658.5 19
HD56 .U53 1985 ***NYPL [JLE 86-2361]***

(1986) Design, innovation, and long cycles in economic development /. London , 1986. 248 p. : ISBN 0-86187-616-4
NYPL [JLE 86-3312]

(1986) Okonomische und soziale Wirksamkeit des wissenschaftlich-technischen Fortschritts /. Berlin , 1986. 314 p. : ISBN 3-320-00713-0
NYPL [JLD 86-4381]

TECHNOLOGICAL INNOVATIONS - AUSTRALIA.
Markey, Ray. The trade union response to technological change in Australia /. Kensington, N.S.W. , 1983. iii, 56 p. ;
NYPL [JLE 87-904]

TECHNOLOGICAL INNOVATIONS - BULGARIA.
Aktivizirane na mladezhkoto nauchno i tekhnichesko tvorchestvo /. Sofiia , 1985. 135 p. : LC Card 86-220354
HC403.Z9 T419 1985

Nauchno-tekhnicheskiiat progress--delo na vsichki. Varna , 1985. 187 p. : LC Card 86-198872
HC403.Z9 T46 1985

Trendafilov, Toncho. Nauchno-tekhnicheskata revoliutsiia--zakonomernost na uskorenoto razvitie na sotsialisticheskoto obshtestvo /. Sofiia , 1985. 93 p. : LC Card 86-163246
HC403.Z9 T477 1985

TECHNOLOGICAL INNOVATIONS - COMMUNIST COUNTRIES.
Bykov, A. N. (Aleksandr Naumovich) Sotsialisticheskaia integratsiia i nauchno-tekhnicheskaia revoliutsiia /. Moskva , 1981. 343 p. ; LC Card 82-101911
HC244.Z9 T43 1981

TECHNOLOGICAL INNOVATIONS - COMMUNIST COUNTRIES - MANAGEMENT - CONGRESSES.
Organization of innovation . Berlin , New York , 1987. x, 238 p. : ISBN 0-89925-167-6 (U. S.) : LC Card 87-19936 DDC 658.4/06 19
HD45 .O73 1987

TECHNOLOGICAL INNOVATIONS - CONGRESSES.
International Symposium on Technological Change and Employment: Urban and Regional Dimensions (1985 : Zandvoort, Netherlands) Technological change, employment, and spatial dynamics . Berlin , New York , c1986. vii, 466 p. : ISBN 0-387-16478-2 (U. S. : pbk.) LC Card 86-10081 DDC 331.12 19
HD6331 .I6 1985
NYPL [JLM 72-289 v.270]

Technology management '85 . London , c1985. 160 p. : ISBN 0-903748-61-4
NYPL [JLG 87-124]

TECHNOLOGICAL INNOVATIONS - CZECHOSLOVAKIA - MANAGEMENT.
Formy i metody upravleniia NTP /. Moskva , 1987. 151 p. ; LC Card 87-143073
HC340.T4 F67 1987

TECHNOLOGICAL INNOVATIONS - DEVELOPING COUNTRIES.
Bentabet, Mohamed. Auto économie . Casablanca [1985] 106 p. ; LC Card 86-198953
HC59.72.T4 B46 1985

Fransman, Martin. Technology and economic development /. Brighton, Sussex , 1986. xi, 161 p. : ISBN 0-7450-0104-1 ***NYPL [JLD 87-320]***

Skou, Niels Holger. Teknologipolitik /. Aarhus [1981] 52 p. ; LC Card 82-194649
HC59.72.T4 S56 1981

TECHNOLOGICAL INNOVATIONS - ECONOMIC ASPECTS.
Amendola, Mario. The innovative choice . Oxford [Oxfordshire] , New York, NY, USA , 1988. p. cm. ISBN 0-631-15791-3 : LC Card 87-25004 DDC 338/.06 19
HC79.T4 A46 1988

Baldwin, William L., 1928- Market structure and technological change /. Chur, Switzerland , New York , c1987. viii, 170 p. ; ISBN 3-7186-0375-6 (pbk.) LC Card 86-25780 DDC 338/.06 19
HD2326 .B35 1987

Coombs, Rod. Economics and technological change /. Totowa, N.J. , 1987. xv, 296 p. : ISBN 0-8476-7545-9 : LC Card 86-28000 DDC 338/.06 19
HC79.T4 C67 1987

Fusfeld, Herbert I. The technical enterprise . Cambridge, Mass. , 1986. xiii, 312 p. ; ISBN 0-88730-033-2 LC Card 86-3340 DDC 338/.06 19
HC79.T4 F87 1986 ***NYPL [JLE 86-3344]***

Hanson, Philip. The comparative economics of research development in East and West . Chur, Switzerland , New York , c1987. viii, 101 ; ISBN 3-7186-0419-1 (pbk.) LC Card 87-23623 DDC 338/.06 19
HC79.T4 H355 1987

Hippel, Eric von. The sources of innovation /. New York , c1988. xi, 218 p. : ISBN 0-19-504085-6 (alk. paper) LC Card 86-28620 DDC 338/.06 19
HC79.T4 H56 1988

Industrial change in advanced economies /. London , Wolfeboro, N.H. , c1987. 319 p. : ISBN 0-7099-3828-4 : LC Card 86-19661 DDC 338.09 19
HC79.T4 H35 1987 ***NYPL [JLD 87-410]***

Nelson, Richard R. Understanding technical change as an evolutionary process /. Amsterdam ; New York : viii, 125 p. ; ISBN 0-444-70207-5 (pbk.) LC Card 87-9109 DDC 338/.06 19
HC79.T4 N45 1987

Nouvelles technologies et enjeux sociaux . Lyon , c1986. 230 p. : ISBN 2-7297-0279-2 : LC Card 86-187357
HC79.T4 N68 1986

Pontones S., Jaime. Condicionantes estructurales del desarrollo tecnológico /. [Mexico City, Mexico] [1982] 27, [2] leaves ; LC Card 85-203882
HC79.T4 P66 1982

Rattner, Henrique. Informática e sociedade /. São Paulo-SP , 1985. 219 p. : LC Card 85-221850
HC79.T4 R387 1985

Salomon, Jean Jacques. Les enjeux du changement technologique /. Paris , c1986. 206 p. : ISBN 2-7178-1092-7 : LC Card 86-172778
HC79.T4 S286 1986

Stoneman, Paul. The economic analysis of technology policy /. Oxford [Oxfordshire] , New York , 1987. x, 224 p. : ISBN 0-19-877260-2 (pbk.) LC Card 87-20374 DDC 338.9/26 19
HD45 .S844 1987

Technologischer Wandel in Wirtschaft und Gesellschaft =. Freiburg, Schweiz , 1985. 316 p., [1] leaf of plates : ISBN 3-7278-0347-9 : LC Card 86-129382
HC79.T4 T436 1985

Teubal, Morris. Innovation performance, learning, and government policy . Madison, Wis. , 1987. xvi, 308 p. : ISBN 0-299-10950-X : LC Card 86-40448 DDC 338/.06 19
HC79.T4 T485 1987

Thirtle, Colin G., 1944- The role of demand and supply in the generation and diffusion of technical change /. Chur, Switzerland , New York , c1987. viii, 173 p. : ISBN 3-7186-0384-5 (U. S. : pbk.) LC Card 87-138 DDC 338/.06 19
HC79.T4 T495 1987

TECHNOLOGICAL INNOVATIONS - ECONOMIC ASPECTS - AUSTRALIA - CONGRESSES.
An Industrial research and development and marketing package for Australia . [Canberra?] [1984] 48, 4 leaves : LC Card 87-153477 DDC 338/.06 19
HC610.T4 I53 1984

TECHNOLOGICAL INNOVATIONS - ECONOMIC ASPECTS - CANADA.
Technological change in Canadian industry /. Toronto , Buffalo , c1985. xv, 233 p. ; ISBN 0-8020-7243-7 (pbk.) LC Card 86-164766 DDC 338/.06 19
HC120.T4 T42 1985 ***NYPL [JLD 87-654]***

TECHNOLOGICAL INNOVATIONS - ECONOMIC ASPECTS - CANADA - CONGRESSES.
Twentieth joint conference . [Charlottetown, P.E.I. , 1986] 94 p. ; LC Card 87-147512 DDC 338/.06 19
HC120.T4 T84 1986

TECHNOLOGICAL INNOVATIONS - ECONOMIC ASPECTS - CANADA - STATISTICS.
Betcherman, Gordon. Working with technology . [Ottawa] , 1986. 43 p. : ISBN 0-660-12174-3 (pbk.) : LC Card 86-224095 DDC 338/.06 19
HC120.A9 B47 1986

TECHNOLOGICAL INNOVATIONS - ECONOMIC ASPECTS - CONGRESSES.
The Spatial impact of technological change /. Totowa, NJ , 1987. p. cm. ISBN 0-389-20753-5 LC Card 87-11460 DDC 338/.06 19
HC79.T4 S77 1987

Technik und internationale Politik /. Baden-Baden , 1986. 520 p. ; ISBN 3-7890-1239-4 (Deut. Bibl.) LC Card 87-103890 DDC 338/.06 19
HC79.T4 T422 1986

Technologischer Wandel, Analyse und Fakten /. Tübingen , 1986. ix, 330 p. ; ISBN 3-16-345132-2 LC Card 87-109808 DDC 338/.06 19
HC79.T4 T4355 1986

Technology and global industry . Washington, D.C. , 1987. vi, 272 p. : ISBN 0-309-03736-0 (pbk.) LC Card 87-7765 DDC 338/.06 19
HC79.T4 T438 1987

TECHNOLOGICAL INNOVATIONS - ECONOMIC ASPECTS - CZECHOSLOVAKIA - FORECASTING.
Formy i metody upravleniia NTP /. Moskva , 1987. 151 p. ; LC Card 87-143073
HC340.T4 F67 1987

TECHNOLOGICAL INNOVATIONS - ECONOMIC ASPECTS - DEVELOPING COUNTRIES.
Fuenzalida Faivovich, Edmundo. [América Latina y la concentración del poder en la arena política.] América Latina y la concentración del poder en la arena política ; El impacto social del cambio tecnológico actual en los países menos desarrollados /. [Santiago de Chile] [between 1974 and 1979] 24, 25 leaves ; LC Card 82-180082
HD2810.5 .F84 1974

TECHNOLOGICAL INNOVATIONS - ECONOMIC ASPECTS - DEVELOPING COUNTRIES - CONGRESSES.
Stratégies d'industrialisation et maîtrise du développement. Paris , c1984. 115, [3] p. : ISBN 2-86844-002-9 LC Card 84-248894
HC59.7 .S854 1984

TECHNOLOGICAL INNOVATIONS - ECONOMIC ASPECTS - EUROPE.
A High technology gap? . New York, N.Y. , c1987. xii, 114 p. : ISBN 0-87609-021-8 (pbk.) : LC Card 87-6713 DDC 338/.06 19
HC240.9.T4 H54 1987

Nauchno-tekhnicheskiĭ progress i strukturnye sdvigi v ėkonomike sovremennogo kapitalizma . Moskva , 1987. 168 p. ; LC Card 87-165811
HC240.9.T4 N38 1987

Poniatowski, Michel. Les technologies nouvelles . Paris , c1986. 334 p. ; ISBN 2-259-01439-9 : LC Card 86-182131
HC240.9.T4 P65 1986

Späth, Lothar, 1937- [Wende in die Zukunft. English.] Facing the future . Berlin , New York , c1986. xvi, 196 p. ; ISBN 0-387-17105-3 (U. S.) LC Card 86-25994 DDC 338.943 19
HC286.7 .S713 1986

Technologie nouvelle et ruptures régionales /. Paris , c1986. 216 p. : ISBN 2-7178-1133-8 : LC Card 86-224660
HC240.9.T4 T42 1986

TECHNOLOGICAL INNOVATIONS - ECONOMIC ASPECTS - EUROPEAN ECONOMIC COMMUNITY COUNTRIES.
Sweeney, G. P. (Gerald Patrick), 1928- Innovation, entrepreneurs, and regional development /. London , 1987. xvi, 271 p. : ISBN 0-86187-647-4 ***NYPL [JLD 87-1403]***

Sweeney, G. P. (Gerald Patrick), 1928- Innovation, entrepreneurs, and regional development /. New York , c1987. xvi, 271 p. : ISBN 0-312-00489-3 : LC Card 86-27999 DDC 338/.06/094 19
HC240.9.T4 S94 1987

Working towards European unification . [Luxembourg] , 1986. 60 p. ; LC Card 87-149629 DDC 338/.06 19
HC240.9.T4 W67 1986

TECHNOLOGICAL INNOVATIONS - ECONOMIC ASPECTS - FRANCE.
Salomon, Jean Jacques. Le gaulois, le cow-boy, et le samouraï . Paris , c1986. 209 p. : ISBN 2-7178-1139-7 : LC Card 87-120178
HC280.T4 S25 1986

TECHNOLOGICAL INNOVATIONS - ECONOMIC ASPECTS - GERMANY (EAST)
Innovation und Wissenschaft . Berlin , 1985. 328 p. : LC Card 86-121669
HC290.795.T4 I56 1985

Neuererbewegung und wissenschaftliche Arbeitsorganisation (WAO) in der DDR /. Bonn , c1980. 49 p. ; LC Card 86-170039
HD45 .N415 1980

Technisch rationell, sozial effektiv . Berlin , 1986. 168 p. ; ISBN 3-320-00706-8 LC Card 87-144339 DDC 338/.06 19
HC290.795.A9 T43 1986

TECHNOLOGICAL INNOVATIONS - ECONOMIC ASPECTS - GERMANY, WEST.
Gruhler, Wolfram. Die grosse Denkverbiegung . Köln , c1987. 159 p. ; ISBN 3-87427-657-0 LC Card 87-152206 DDC 338.943 19
HC286.5 .G715 1987

Krause, Hans-Ulrich. Gewinnung, Verarbeitung und Aufbereitung von Informationen für die Geschäftsfeldplanung . Giessen , c1984. xii,324 p. ; ISBN 3-922730-52-3 LC Card 85-150146
HD35 .K71215 1984

Pieper, Antje, 1943- Forschung und Entwicklung, eine Chance für die Wirtschaft /. Köln , c1984. 56 p. : ISBN 3-602-24853-4 LC Card 85-217568
HC290.5.T4 P54 1984

Späth, Lothar, 1937- [Wende in die Zukunft. English.] Facing the future . Berlin , New York , c1986. xvi, 196 p. ; ISBN 0-387-17105-3 (U. S.) LC Card 86-25994 DDC 338.943 19
HC286.7 .S713 1986

Technologische Entwicklung und Beschäftigung /. Bonn [1985] 10 p. ; LC Card 86-154491
HC290.5.T4 T44 1985

TECHNOLOGICAL INNOVATIONS - ECONOMIC ASPECTS - GREAT BRITAIN.
The Challenge of new technology . Aldershot, Hants, England , Brookfield, Vt., U. S.A. , c1988. x, 155 p. : ISBN 0-566-05147-8 : LC Card 87-8592 DDC 338/.06 19
HC260.T4 C46 1988

Wilkinson, Barry. The shopfloor politics of new technology /. London , 1983. 120 p. ; ISBN 0-435-82950-5 : LC Card 82-236198 DDC 338/.06 19
HC260.T4 W54 1983 ***NYPL [JLD 86-1322]***

TECHNOLOGICAL INNOVATIONS - ECONOMIC ASPECTS - HUNGARY.
Farkas, János. Az innováció társadalmi-gazdasági akadályai /. Budapest , 1984. 350 p. ; ISBN 963-221-453-6 : LC Card 85-157214
HC300.295.T4 F36 1984

TECHNOLOGICAL INNOVATIONS - ECONOMIC ASPECTS - IRELAND.
Innovation policy . Paris , Washington, D.C. , 1987. 75 p. ; ISBN 92-64-12918-9 (pbk.) : LC Card 87-164488 DDC 338/.06 19
HC260.5.Z9 T45 1987

TECHNOLOGICAL INNOVATIONS - ECONOMIC ASPECTS - ITALY - LOMBARDY.
Gario, Giuseppe. Discontinuità e permanenza . Milano, Italy , c1986. 262 p. : LC Card 87-149940
HC307.L8 G37 1986

TECHNOLOGICAL INNOVATIONS - ECONOMIC ASPECTS - JAPAN.
Freeman, Christopher. Technology, policy, and economic performance . London , New York , 1987. 155 p. : ISBN 0-86187-928-7 : LC Card 87-18553 DDC 338.952 19
HC465.T4 F74 1987

A High technology gap? . New York, N.Y. , c1987. xii, 114 p. : ISBN 0-87609-021-8 (pbk.) : LC Card 87-6713 DDC 338/.06 19
HC240.9.T4 H54 1987

The Japanese challenge . Stamford, Conn., U. S.A. , c1986. xii, 108 leaves : ISBN 0-89336-489-4 (pbk.) LC Card 87-404570 DDC 338/.06 19
HC465.T4 J365 1986

TECHNOLOGICAL INNOVATIONS - ECONOMIC ASPECTS - KOREA (SOUTH) - CASE STUDIES.
Enos, John L. (John Lawrence), 1924- The adoption and diffusion of imported technology . New York , c1988. 272 p. : ISBN 0-7099-2030-X LC Card 87-19894 DDC 338.9519/506 19
HC470.T4 E56 1987

TECHNOLOGICAL INNOVATIONS - ECONOMIC ASPECTS - NIGERIA.
Fadahunsi, Akin. The development process and technology . Uppsala , 1986. 41 p. ; ISBN 91-7106-257-2 (pbk.) LC Card 87-119156 DDC 338.9669/07 19
HC1055.Z9 T43 1986

TECHNOLOGICAL INNOVATIONS - ECONOMIC ASPECTS - PHILIPPINES.
Basic needs manual. Bicutan, Taguig, Metro Manila [1985] 58 p. : LC Card 87-118190 DDC 338.9599 19
HC460.B38 B37 1985

TECHNOLOGICAL INNOVATIONS - ECONOMIC ASPECTS - SOVIET UNION.
Egorov, A. D. (Aleksandr Dmitrievich) Khoziaĭstvennyĭ mekhanizm uskoreniia nauchno-tekhnicheskogo progressa . Minsk , 1986. 61, [3] p. ; LC Card 87-144749
HC340.Z9 T44 1986

Kritika antimarksistskikh vzgliadov po problemam NTR /. Moskva , 1987. 157 p. ; LC Card 87-164887
HC340.T4 K75 1987

Rasshirenie samostoiatel'nosti predpriiatiĭ i nauchno-tekhnicheskoe razvitie proizvodstva /. Moskva , 1986. 205 p. ; LC Card 87-162795
HG4186 .R37 1986

Rol' nauchno-tekhnicheskogo progressa v intensifikatsii obshchestvennogo proizvodstva /. Moskva , 1986. 177 p. : LC Card 87-163537
HC340.T4 R65 1986

TECHNOLOGICAL INNOVATIONS - ECONOMIC ASPECTS - SOVIET UNION - FORECASTING.
Formy i metody upravleniia NTP /. Moskva , 1987. 151 p. ; LC Card 87-143073
HC340.T4 F67 1987

TECHNOLOGICAL INNOVATIONS - ECONOMIC ASPECTS - SOVIET UNION - REPUBLICS - CONGRESSES.
Upravlenie nauchno-tekhnicheskim progressom v soiuznykh respublikakh /. Tallin , 1986. 158 p. ; LC Card 87-123175
HC340.T4 U77 1986

TECHNOLOGICAL INNOVATIONS - ECONOMIC ASPECTS - SPAIN.
Nuevas tecnologías, economía y sociedad en España /. Madrid , c1986. 2 v. (xvi, 1056 p.) : ISBN 84-206-9495-9 (set) LC Card 86-205429
HC390.T4 N84 1986

TECHNOLOGICAL INNOVATIONS - ECONOMIC ASPECTS - UNITED STATES.
A High technology gap? . New York, N.Y. , c1987. xii, 114 p. : ISBN 0-87609-021-8 (pbk.) : LC Card 87-6713 DDC 338/.06 19
HC240.9.T4 H54 1987

Nauchno-tekhnicheskiĭ progress i strukturnye sdvigi v ėkonomike sovremennogo kapitalizma . Moskva , 1987. 168 p. ; LC Card 87-165811
HC240.9.T4 N38 1987

Salomon, Jean Jacques. Les enjeux du changement technologique /. Paris , c1986. 206 p. : ISBN 2-7178-1092-7 : LC Card 86-172778
HC79.T4 S286 1986

TECHNOLOGICAL INNOVATIONS - ECONOMIC ASPECTS - UNITED STATES - ECONOMETRIC MODELS.
Ács, Zoltán J. The determinants of innovation in large and small firms /. Berlin [1986] 39 p. ; LC Card 87-156684 DDC 338.6/4 19
HC110.T4 A59 1986

TECHNOLOGICAL INNOVATIONS - ECONOMIC ASPECTS - UNITED STATES - HISTORY - 20TH CENTURY.
Stine, G. Harry (George Harry), 1928- The corporate survivors /. New York, N.Y. , c1986. 230 p. : ISBN 0-8144-5831-9 LC Card 86-47597 DDC 338.7/4/0973 19
HD2785 .S73 1986 ***NYPL [JLE 86-4469]***

TECHNOLOGICAL INNOVATIONS - ECONOMIC ASPECTS - URUGUAY.
Argenti, Gisela. Cambio técnico, trabajo y educación . Montevideo , 1985. 91, 70 leaves : LC Card 87-124118
HC235.T4 A74 1985

TECHNOLOGICAL INNOVATIONS - ECONOMIC ASPECTS - YUGOSLAVIA.
Družba, znanost, tehnologija . Ljubljana , 1982. 472 p. ; LC Card 84-235191
HC407.Z9 T434 1982

TECHNOLOGICAL INNOVATIONS - EUROPE - CONGRESSES.
Technology and work . London , Dover, N.H. , c1986. 304 p. : ISBN 0-7099-3801-2 : LC Card 86-4202 DDC 303.4/83 19
HC244.Z9 T475 1986 ***NYPL [JLD 86-2160]***

TECHNOLOGICAL INNOVATIONS - EUROPE, EASTERN.
Bykov, A. N. (Aleksandr Naumovich) Sotsialisticheskai͡a integratsii͡a i nauchno-tekhnicheskai͡a revoli͡utsii͡a /. Moskva , 1981. 343 p. ; LC Card 82-101911
HC244.Z9 T43 1981

Effektivnost′ NTP . Leningrad , 1985. 215 p., [1] folded leaf of plates : LC Card 86-129301
HC244.Z9 T435 1985

Poznański, Kazimierz. Technology, competition, & the Soviet bloc in the world market /. Berkeley , c1987. ix, 226 p. ; ISBN 0-87725-170-3 (pbk.) : LC Card 87-3505 DDC 338/.06 19
HC244.Z9 T4716 1987

Problemy nauchno-tekhnicheskogo progressa v bratskikh sotsialisticheskikh stranakh . Moskva , 1985. 234 p. ; LC Card 86-179196
HC244.Z9 T472 1985

Vneshneėkonomicheskie otnoshenii͡a sotsialisticheskikh stran v uslovii͡akh NTR /. Moskva , 1985. 215 p. ; LC Card 84-219529
HF1531 .V62 1985 ***NYPL [*QIP 87-2072]***

TECHNOLOGICAL INNOVATIONS - EUROPE, EASTERN - CONGRESSES.
Technology and work . London , Dover, N.H. , c1986. 304 p. : ISBN 0-7099-3801-2 : LC Card 86-4202 DDC 303.4/83 19
HC244.Z9 T475 1986 ***NYPL [JLD 86-2160]***

TECHNOLOGICAL INNOVATIONS - EUROPE, GERMAN-SPEAKING - MANAGEMENT.
Seibert, Siegfried, 1954- Strategische Erfolgsfaktoren in mittleren Unternehmen . Frankfurt am Main , New York , c1987. xii, 353 p. : ISBN 3-8204-9828-1 LC Card 87-122289
HD2346.G3 S38 1987

TECHNOLOGICAL INNOVATIONS - EUROPE - HISTORY - 18TH CENTURY - CONGRESSES.
Technologischer Wandel im 18. Jahrhundert /. Wolfenbüttel , c1981. 246 p. ; ISBN 3-88373-018-1 LC Card 84-116829 DDC 338/.06 19
HC240.9.T4 T43 1981 ***NYPL [JLE 86-927]***

TECHNOLOGICAL INNOVATIONS - FRANCE.
Le Renouvellement du tissu industriel . Paris [1986] 130 p. ; ISBN 2-11-001568-3 : LC Card 86-191910
HD3616.F83 R46 1986

TECHNOLOGICAL INNOVATIONS - GERMANY, EAST.
Intensivierung des wissenschaftlich-technischen Arbeitsprozesses /. Jena , 1985. 200 p. : LC Card 86-132567 DDC 338/.06/09431 19
HC290.795.I52 I57 1985

Ökonomische und soziale Wirksamkeit des wissenschaftlich-technischen Fortschritts /. Berlin , 1986. 314 p. ; ISBN 3-320-00713-0 LC Card 87-100866 DDC 338/.06 19
HC290.795.T4 O38 1986

TECHNOLOGICAL INNOVATIONS - GERMANY (EAST) - EMPLOYEE PARTICIPATION - CONGRESSES.
Wissenschaftliche Konferenz "Wissenschaftlich-Technischer Fortschritt, Bedingungen, Anforderungen, Möglichkeiten der Persönlichkeitsentwicklung" (1985 : Karl-Marx-Stadt, Germany) Wissenschaftliche Konferenz "Wissenschaftlich-Technischer Fortschritt, Bedingungen, Anforderungen, Möglichkeiten der Persönlichkeitsentwicklung" am 8. und 9. Oktober 1985 in Karl-Marx-Stadt /. Karl-Marx-Stadt , 1986. 98 p. ; LC Card 87-407801 DDC 338/.06 19
HD45 .W55 1985

TECHNOLOGICAL INNOVATIONS - GERMANY (EAST) - MANAGEMENT.
Opyt khozi͡aĭstvovanii͡a v ob″edinenii͡akh promyshlennosti sotsialisticheskikh stran /. Moskva , 1985. 157 p. : LC Card 87-152292
HD70.E7 O69 1985

TECHNOLOGICAL INNOVATIONS - GERMANY, WEST.
Gaul, Dieter. Rechtsprobleme der Innovation . München , 1984. xiv, 126 p. ; ISBN 3-88709-084-5 ***NYPL [JLD 85-2917]***

TECHNOLOGICAL INNOVATIONS - GOVERNMENT POLICY.
Coombs, Rod. Economics and technological change /. Totowa, N.J. , 1987. xv, 296 p. : ISBN 0-8476-7545-9 : LC Card 86-28000 DDC 338/.06 19
HC79.T4 C67 1987

Salomon, Jean Jacques. Les enjeux du changement technologique /. Paris , c1986. 206 p. : ISBN 2-7178-1092-7 : LC Card 86-172778
HC79.T4 S286 1986

TECHNOLOGICAL INNOVATIONS - GOVERNMENT POLICY - HUNGARY.
Szekér, Gyula. Műszaki fejlesztés, versenyképesség /. [Budapest] , 1984. 136 p. ; ISBN 963-09-2534-6 : LC Card 85-177507
HC300.295.T4 S97 1984

TECHNOLOGICAL INNOVATIONS - GOVERNMENT POLICY - IRELAND.
Innovation policy . Paris , Washington, D.C. , 1987. 75 p. ; ISBN 92-64-12918-9 (pbk.) : LC Card 87-164488 DDC 338/.06 19
HC260.5.Z9 T45 1987

TECHNOLOGICAL INNOVATIONS - GOVERNMENT POLICY - UNITED STATES.
Salomon, Jean Jacques. Les enjeux du changement technologique /. Paris , c1986. 206 p. : ISBN 2-7178-1092-7 : LC Card 86-172778
HC79.T4 S286 1986

TECHNOLOGICAL INNOVATIONS - GREAT BRITAIN.
Batstone, Eric. Unions, unemployment and innovation /. Oxford [Oxfordshire] , New York, N.Y., USA , 1986. viii, 320 p. ; ISBN 0-631-14961-9 : LC Card 85-30679 DDC 331.88/0941 19
HD6664 .B335 1986 ***NYPL [JLE 86-4031]***

Willman, Paul. Technological change, collective bargaining, and industrial efficiency /. Oxford , New York , c1986. xvi, 282 p. : ISBN 0-19-827262-6 : LC Card 86-5104 DDC 331.88/0941 19
HD6664 .W56 1986 ***NYPL [JLD 87-994]***

TECHNOLOGICAL INNOVATIONS - GREAT BRITAIN - HISTORY - 19TH CENTURY.
Divisions of labour . Sussex [Eng.] , Urbana , 1985. ix, 254 p. ; ISBN 0-252-01189-9 LC Card 84-23988 DDC 331.7/94 19
HD8390 .D58 1985 ***NYPL [JLD 87-93]***

TECHNOLOGICAL INNOVATIONS - GREAT BRITAIN - MANAGEMENT.
Clark, Peter A. Anglo-American innovation /. Berlin , New York , 1987. ix, 404 p. : ISBN 0-89925-164-1 (U. S.) : LC Card 87-22221 DDC 338/.06 19
HD45 .C52 1987

TECHNOLOGICAL INNOVATIONS - HUNGARY.
Szekér, Gyula. Műszaki fejlesztés, versenyképesség /. [Budapest] , 1984. 136 p. ; ISBN 963-09-2534-6 : LC Card 85-177507
HC300.295.T4 S97 1984

TECHNOLOGICAL INNOVATIONS - HUNGARY - BARANYA MEGYE - CONGRESSES.
Múlt, jelen, jövő a műszaki haladás szolgálatában . Pécs , 1985. 305 p. : LC Card 87-408539
HC300.29.B37 M86 1985

TECHNOLOGICAL INNOVATIONS - INDIA.
Hajra, S. (Sridhar), 1936- Capital and technological progress in the Indian economy, 1950/51-1980/81 /. New Delhi , 1985. xvi, 198 p. : LC Card 85-900681 DDC 338.954 19
HC440.S3 H35 1985 ***NYPL [JLD 87-736]***

TECHNOLOGICAL INNOVATIONS - ITALY.
Tre incognite per lo sviluppo . Milano, Italy , c1986. 383 p. : LC Card 86-198933
HC310.I53 T74 1986

TECHNOLOGICAL INNOVATIONS - ITALY - FINANCE - CONGRESSES.
Il Finanziamento dell'innovazione nelle imprese industriali /. Milano, Italy , c1985. 271 p. : LC Card 86-157239
HC310.T4 F55 1985

TECHNOLOGICAL INNOVATIONS - ITALY - HISTORY - 20TH CENTURY.
Maione, Giuseppe, 1942- Tecnocrati e mercanti . Milano, Italia , c1986. 354 p. ; LC Card 86-194293
HC305 .M274 1986

TECHNOLOGICAL INNOVATIONS - JAPAN.
Gijutsu kakushin to joshi rōdō /. Tōkyō , 1985. x, 219 p. : ISBN 4-13-051068-1 ***NYPL [*OSL 87-1658]***

Skorov, Mikhail Sergeevich. Nauchno-tekhnicheskiĭ progress i ti͡azhelai͡a promyshlennost′ I͡Aponii /. Moskva , 1980. 213, [3] p. ; LC Card 81-130564
HC465.T4 S56 1980

TECHNOLOGICAL INNOVATIONS - JAPAN - ADDRESSES, ESSAYS, LECTURES.
R & D management systems in Japanese industry /. Amsterdam ; New York : ix, 331 p. : ISBN 0-444-86808-9 (U. S.) LC Card 83-20489 DDC 658.5/7/0952 19
HD45 .R2 1984 ***NYPL [JLD 87-107]***

TECHNOLOGICAL INNOVATIONS - LATIN AMERICA.
Wionczek, Miguel S. Capital y tecnología en México y América Latina /. México , 1981. 413 p. ; ISBN 968-470-018-0 ***NYPL [JLE 87-377]***

TECHNOLOGICAL INNOVATIONS - MANAGEMENT.
Bhalla, Sushil K. The effective management of technology . Columbus [Ohio] , Reading, Mass. , c1987. xiii, 205 p. : ISBN 0-201-10929-8 : LC Card 86-25847 DDC 658.5 19
HD45 .B47 1987

Davis, Donald D., 1950- Managing technological innovation /. San Francisco , 1986. xxi, 302 p. : ISBN 1-555-42008-7 LC Card 86-15378 DDC 658.5/14 19
HD45 .D34 1986 ***NYPL [JLE 87-862]***

Foster, Richard N. Innovation . New York , c1986. 316 p. : ISBN 0-671-62250-1 : LC Card 86-1945 DDC 658.4/062 19
HD45 .F67 1986 ***NYPL [JLE 86-1899]***

Generating technological innovation /. New York , 1987. xii, 299 p. : ISBN 0-19-505023-1 (alk. paper) LC Card 86-33119 DDC 658.5/14 19
HD45 .G39 1987

New technology as organizational innovation . Cambridge, Mass. , c1987. xvi, 308 p. : ISBN 0-88730-186-X LC Card 86-32110 DDC

658.5/14 19
HD45 .N43 1987

The process of technological change . Cambridge [Cambridgeshire] , New York , 1988. p. cm. ISBN 0-521-32303-7 LC Card 87-6641 DDC 658.5/14 19
HD45 .P757 1988

Quality, productivity, and innovation . New York , c1987. xx, 427 p. : ISBN 0-444-01194-3 LC Card 87-6815 DDC 658.5 19
HD58.9 .Q35 1987

TECHNOLOGICAL INNOVATIONS - MANAGEMENT - CASE STUDIES.
Dean, James W., 1956- Deciding to innovate . Cambridge, Mass. , c1987. xviii, 165 p. ; ISBN 0-88730-189-4 LC Card 87-17432 DDC 658.5/14 19
HD9725 .D35 1987

TECHNOLOGICAL INNOVATIONS - MANAGEMENT - CONGRESSES.
Innovation and entrepreneurship in organizations . Amsterdam ; New York : vii, 207 p. : ISBN 0-444-42716-3 (U. S.) : LC Card 86-24207 DDC 658.4/012 19
HD41 .I56 1986

Organization of innovation . Berlin , New York , 1987. x, 238 p. : ISBN 0-89925-167-6 (U. S.) : LC Card 87-19936 DDC 658.4/06 19
HD45 .O73 1987

TECHNOLOGICAL INNOVATIONS - MEXICO.
Wionczek, Miguel S. Capital y tecnología en México y América Latina /. México , 1981. 413 p. ; ISBN 968-470-018-0
NYPL [JLE 87-377]

TECHNOLOGICAL INNOVATIONS - NETHERLANDS.
Kleinknecht, A. Industriële innovatie in Nederland . Assen , 1987. viii, 140 p. ; ISBN 90-232-2261-X : LC Card 87-157579
HC329.5.T4 K58 1987

TECHNOLOGICAL INNOVATIONS - RUSSIAN S.F.S.R. - ĪAKUTSKAĪA A.S.S.R.
Ėffektivnost′ kapital′nykh vlozheniĭ i novoĭ tekhniki v narodnom khoziaĭstve ĪAkutskoĭ ASSR . ĪAkutsk , 1981. 91 p. ; LC Card 82-217455
HC337.I23 C34 1981

TECHNOLOGICAL INNOVATIONS - RUSSIAN S.F.S.R. - LENINGRAD.
Raĭkom i nauchno-tekhnicheskaia intelligentsiia /. Leningrad , 1981. 117 p. ; LC Card 82-177893
HC340.T4 R35 1981

TECHNOLOGICAL INNOVATIONS - RUSSIAN S.F.S.R. - URAL MOUNTAINS REGION - CONGRESSES.
Kardinal′nyĭ rost ėffektivnosti zhivogo truda--glavnyĭ faktor uskoreniia sotsial′no-ėkonomicheskogo razvitiia . Sverdlovsk , 1986. 2 v. ; LC Card 87-136690
HC337.R853 L35 1986

TECHNOLOGICAL INNOVATIONS - SOCIAL ASPECTS.
Francis, Arthur. New technology at work /. Oxford [Oxfordshire] , New York , 1986. vi, 216 p. ; ISBN 0-19-878016-8 : LC Card 86-12705 DDC 338/.06 19
HD6331 .F66 1987 *NYPL [JLD 87-912]*

Nouvelles technologies et enjeux sociaux . Lyon , c1986. 230 p. : ISBN 2-7297-0279-2 : LC Card 86-187357
HC79.T4 N68 1986

Vasil′chuk, ĪU. A. Nauchno-tekhnicheskaia revoliutsiia i rabochiĭ klass pri kapitalizme . Moskva , 1980. 295 p. : LC Card 81-130590
HD6331 .V22 1980

Von der Bereitschaft zum technischen Wandel /. Berlin , 1981. 278 p. : ISBN 3-8009-1339-9 LC Card 83-194263
HC79.T4 V66 1981

TECHNOLOGICAL INNOVATIONS - SOCIAL ASPECTS - CONNECTICUT.
Asher, Robert. Connecticut workers and technological change . Storrs , c1983. 100 p. : LC Card 83-62409 DDC 306/.3/09746 19
HD8083.C7 A83 1983 *NYPL [JLE 86-1507]*

TECHNOLOGICAL INNOVATIONS - SOCIAL ASPECTS - EUROPEAN ECONOMIC COMMUNITY COUNTRIES.
Working towards European unification . [Luxembourg] , 1986. 60 p. ; LC Card 87-149629 DDC 338/.06 19
HC240.9.T4 W67 1986

TECHNOLOGICAL INNOVATIONS - SOCIAL ASPECTS - GERMANY, EAST.
Technisch rationell, sozial effektiv . Berlin , 1986. 168 p. ; ISBN 3-320-00706-8 LC Card 87-144339 DDC 338/.06 19
HC290.795.A9 T43 1986

TECHNOLOGICAL INNOVATIONS - SOCIAL ASPECTS - GERMANY (EAST) - CONGRESSES.
Wissenschaftliche Konferenz "Wissenschaftlich-Technischer Fortschritt, Bedingungen, Anforderungen, Möglichkeiten der Persönlichkeitsentwicklung" (1985 : Karl-Marx-Stadt, Germany) Wissenschaftliche Konferenz "Wissenschaftlich-Technischer Fortschritt, Bedingungen, Anforderungen, Möglichkeiten der Persönlichkeitsentwicklung" am 8. und 9. Oktober 1985 in Karl-Marx-Stadt /. Karl-Marx-Stadt , 1986. 98 p. ; LC Card 87-407801 DDC 338/.06 19
HD45 .W55 1985

TECHNOLOGICAL INNOVATIONS - SOCIAL ASPECTS - GREAT BRITAIN.
Wilkinson, Barry. The shopfloor politics of new technology /. London , 1983. 120 p. ; ISBN 0-435-82950-5 : LC Card 82-236198 DDC 338/.06 19
HC260.T4 W54 1983 *NYPL [JLD 86-1322]*

TECHNOLOGICAL INNOVATIONS - SOCIAL ASPECTS - HUNGARY.
Farkas, János. Az innováció társadalmi-gazdasági akadályai /. Budapest , 1984. 350 p. ; ISBN 963-221-453-6 : LC Card 85-157214
HC300.295.T4 F36 1984

TECHNOLOGICAL INNOVATIONS - SOVIET UNION.
Chebanenko, Vladimir Mikhaĭlovich. Sistema planirovaniia tekhnicheskogo urovnia otrasli /. Moskva , 1985. 118, [7] p. : LC Card 85-241451
HD70.S63 C45 1985

Lazurenko, S. G. (Serafima Grigor′evna) Izmerenie vliianiia nauchno-tekhnicheskogo progressa na rost natsional′nogo dokhoda /. Moskva , 1981. 127 p. ; LC Card 82-115905
HC340.T4 L39 1981

Marek, A. I. (Aleksandr Isaevich) Nauchno-proizvodstvennye kompleksy . Moskva , 1985. 141, [3] p. : LC Card 86-118921
HC340.R4 M37 1985

Printsipy ėkonomicheskogo upravleniia nauchno-tekhnicheskim progressom . Kiev , 1982. 122 p. ; LC Card 83-143870
HC340.T4 P67 1982

Problemy sovershenstvovaniia material′no-tekhnicheskoĭ bazy otrasleĭ obshchestvennogo proizvodstva . Moskva , 1983. 167 p. : LC Card 84-211670
HD70.S63 P753 1983

Raĭkom i nauchno-tekhnicheskaia intelligentsiia /. Leningrad , 1981. 117 p. ; LC Card 82-177893
HC340.T4 R35 1981

Rodionenkov, P. A. (Petr Andreevich) Zatraty i rezul′taty proizvodstvennykh issledovaniĭ i razrabotok /. Leningrad , 1986. 143 p. ; LC Card 87-136354
HC340.R4 R63 1986

Shusharin, A. L. (Aleksandr Leonidovich) Sootnoshenie khozraschetnoĭ ėkonomicheskoĭ ėffektivnosti sredstv proizvodstva s ikh narodno-khoziaĭstvennoĭ ėffektivnost′iu /. Tomsk , 1979. 159 p. ; LC Card 87-462036
HD70.S63 S55 1979

Tekhniko-ėkonomicheskie raschety na predpriiatii /. Kiev , 1984. 126 p. : LC Card 84-234261
HD70.S63 T45 1984

TECHNOLOGICAL INNOVATIONS - SOVIET UNION - CONGRESSES.
Simpozium "Nauchno-tekhnicheskiĭ progress i intensifikatsiia obshchestvennogo proizvodstva" (1984 : Podol′sk, Moscow, R.S.F.S.R.) Formy i metody vzaimodeĭstviia nauki i proizvodstva /. Moskva , 1984. 237 p. ; LC Card 85-240380
HC340.T4 S48 1984

TECHNOLOGICAL INNOVATIONS - SOVIET UNION - COSTS - ACCOUNTING.
Borodkin, Alekseĭ Sergeevich. Uchet zatrat na osvoenie novoĭ tekhniki /. Moskva , 1985. 142 p. : LC Card 86-219761
HF5686.C8 B597 1985

TECHNOLOGICAL INNOVATIONS - SOVIET UNION - EVALUATION - MATHEMATICAL MODELS.
Ėkonomicheskoe izmerenie i otsenka ėffektivnosti nauchno-tekhnicheskogo progressa /. Moskva , 1982. 172 p. ; LC Card 84-209110
HC79.T4 E55 1982

TECHNOLOGICAL INNOVATIONS - SOVIET UNION - FINANCE.
Ėkonomicheskie interesy i uskorenie nauchno-tekhnicheskogo progressa . Leningrad , 1984. 157 p. ; LC Card 86-186728
HC340.T4 E36 1984

TECHNOLOGICAL INNOVATIONS - SOVIET UNION - MANAGEMENT.
Budaveĭ, Vsevolod ĪUr′evich. Dolgosrochnye narodnokhoziaĭstvennye programmy . Moskva , 1980. 205 p. ; LC Card 81-143196
HD45 .B792 1980

Formy i metody upravleniia NTP /. Moskva , 1987. 151 p. ; LC Card 87-143073
HC340.T4 F67 1987

Upravlenie nauchno-tekhnicheskim progressom na predpriiatii /. Novosibirsk , 1986. 222 p. ; LC Card 87-124400
HD45 .U52 1986

TECHNOLOGICAL INNOVATIONS - SWEDEN.
Papachristodoulou, Christos. Inventions, innovations, and economic growth in Sweden . Uppsala , c1986. iv, 187 p. : LC Card 87-672434
HC380.T4 P36x 1986

TECHNOLOGICAL INNOVATIONS - UKRAINE.
Pliushch, M. R. Vklad robitnychoho klasu Ukraïns′koï RSR u pryskorenniа naukovo-tekhnichnoho prohresu v promyslovosti, 50-70-i roky /. Kyïv , 1981. 244 p. ; LC Card 82-200854
HC337.U53 T465 1981

Povyshenie ėffektivnosti proizvodstva v usloviiakh sovershenstvovaniia khoziaĭstvennogo mekhanizma . Kiev , 1982. 106 p. ; LC Card 83-145049
HC337.U5 T46 1982

TECHNOLOGICAL INNOVATIONS - UNITED STATES.
Dressler, Fritz R. S. The entrepreneurial age . Media, PA , c1985. ii, 228, 5 p. ; ISBN 0-918514-10-X (pbk.) LC Card 85-232719 DDC 338.04/0973 19
HB615 .D73 1985 *NYPL [JLD 86-3104]*

Lund, Robert T. Keeping America at work . New York , c1986. xi, 260 p. : ISBN 0-471-81563-2 LC Card 85-17900 DDC 331.12/0973 19
HD45 .L86 1985 *NYPL [JLD 86-2101]*

Technology and trade . Washington , 1986. x, 80 p. : LC Card 86-603362 DDC 338/.06 19
HC110.T4 T393 1986

Willman, Paul. Technological change, collective bargaining, and industrial efficiency /. Oxford , New York , c1986. xvi, 282 p. : ISBN 0-19-827262-6 : LC Card 86-5104 DDC 331.88/0941 19
HD6664 .W56 1986 *NYPL [JLD 87-994]*

TECHNOLOGICAL INNOVATIONS - UNITED STATES - EMPLOYEE PARTICIPATION.
Change master companies [videorecording] . Chicago, IL , 1987. 1 videocassette (42 min.) : LC Card 87-705608 DDC 658.3 11
HD45

The Change masters [motion picture] . Chicago, Ill. , 1987. 1 film reel (29 min.) : LC Card 87-705269 DDC 658.3 11
HD45

The Change masters [videorecording] . Chicago, Ill. , 1987. 1 videocassette (29 min.) : LC Card 86-707881 DDC 658.3 11
HD45

TECHNOLOGICAL INNOVATIONS - UNITED STATES - HISTORY.
Filippelli, Ronald L. Labor in the USA . New York , c1984. xii, 315 p. ; ISBN 0-394-34149-X LC Card 83-23458 DDC 331/.0973 19
HD8066 .F54 1984 ***NYPL [JFE 86-5130]***

TECHNOLOGICAL INNOVATIONS - UNITED STATES - MANAGEMENT.
Clark, Peter A. Anglo-American innovation /. Berlin , New York , 1987. ix, 404 p. : ISBN 0-89925-164-1 (U. S.) : LC Card 87-22221 DDC 338/.06 19
HD45 .C52 1987

The Competitive challenge . Cambridge, Mass. , c1987. xii, 256 p. : ISBN 0-88730-178-9 LC Card 87-1190 DDC 658.4/06 19
HD70.U5 C58 1987

TECHNOLOGICAL INNOVATIONS - UZBEK S.S.R.
Ergashev, A. (Atakul) Dialektika ob″ektivnogo i sub″ektivnogo v razvitii nauchno-tekhnicheskoĭ revoli͡utsii /. Tashkent , 1980. 185 p. ; LC Card 81-143159
HC337.U963 T44 1980

Technological prospects and population trends / edited by Thomas J. Espenshade and George J. Stolnitz. Boulder, Colo. : Westview Press, 1987. xxiii, 211 p. ; 22 cm. (AAAS selected symposium . 103) Includes bibliographies. ISBN 0-8133-7470-7 : LC Card 87-50897 DDC 304.6 19
1. Population. 2. Technological innovations. I. Espenshade, Thomas J. II. Stolnitz, George J. III. Series.
HB871 .T3 1987

TECHNOLOGICAL TRANSFER. see **TECHNOLOGY TRANSFER.**

TECHNOLOGICAL UNEMPLOYMENT. see **UNEMPLOYMENT, TECHNOLOGICAL.**

Technologie in der Wettbewerbsstrategie . Zörgiebel, Wilhelm W. Berlin , c1983. xv, 322 p. : ISBN 3-503-02361-5 LC Card 84-158275
HD9703.G42 Z67 1983

Technologie nouvelle et ruptures régionales / textes réunis et présentés par Jacques Federwisch, Henry G. Zoller. Paris : Economica, c1986. 216 p. : ill. ; 24 cm. Includes bibliographies. ISBN 2-7178-1133-8 : LC Card 86-224660
1. Technological innovations - Economic aspects - Europe. 2. Europe - Economic conditions - Regional disparities. 3. High technology industries - Europe. I. Federwisch, Jacques. II. Zoller, Henry.
HC240.9.T4 T42 1986

Les technologies nouvelles . Poniatowski, Michel. Paris , c1986. 334 p. ; ISBN 2-259-01439-9 : LC Card 86-182131
HC240.9.T4 P65 1986

Technologische Analyse und Prognose als Grundlage der strategischen Unternehmensplanung /. Schneider, Walter. Göttingen , c1984. xxii, 215 p. ; ISBN 3-525-12561-5 LC Card 85-127182
HD30.23 .S37 1984

Technologische Entwicklung und Beschäftigung / [herausgegeben vom Bundesministerium für Wirtschaft, Referat Öffentlichkeitsarbeit]. Bonn : Das Bundesministerium, [1985] 10 p. ; 29 cm. (BMWI Dokumentation, 0342-9288 . Nr. 268) Cover title. "Juli 1985." LC Card 86-154491
1. Technological innovations - Economic aspects - Germany, West. 2. Manpower policy - Germany, West. 3. Labor supply - Germany (West) - Effect of technological innovations on. I. Germany (West). Bundesministerium für Wirtschaft. Referat Öffentlichkeitsarbeit. II. Series.
HC290.5.T4 T44 1985

Technologischer Wandel, Analyse und Fakten / herausgegeben von Gottfried Bombach, Bernhard Gahlen, Alfred E. Ott. Tübingen : J.C.B. Mohr, 1986. ix, 330 p. ; 24 cm. (Schriftenreihe des Wirtschaftswissenschaftlichen Seminars Ottobeuren, 0340-7187 . Bd. 15) Proceedings of the 15th Wirtschaftswissenschaftliches Seminar Ottobeuren, held Sept. 23-27, 1985. Includes bibliographies. ISBN 3-16-345132-2 LC Card 87-109808 DDC 338/.06 19
1. Technological innovations - Economic aspects - Congresses. I. Bombach, Gottfried. II. Gahlen, Bernhard. III. Ott, Alfred Eugen. IV. Wirtschaftswissenschaftliches Seminar Ottobeuren (15th : 1985). V. Series.
HC79.T4 T4355 1986

Technologischer Wandel im achzehnten Jahrhundert. Technologischer Wandel im 18. Jahrhundert /. Wolfenbüttel , c1981. 246 p. ; ISBN 3-88373-018-1 LC Card 84-116829 DDC 338/.06 19
HC240.9.T4 T43 1981 ***NYPL [JLE 86-927]***

Technologischer Wandel in Wirtschaft und Gesellschaft = Changement de technologie en économie et société = Technological change in economy and society / herausgegeben von Heinrich Bortis und Louis Bosshart. Freiburg, Schweiz : Universitätsverlag, 1985. 316 p., [1] leaf of plates : ill. ; 23 cm. German, English, and French. "Wissenschaftliches Kolloquium veranstaltet aus Anlass des 60. Geburtstages von Professor Dr. rer. oec. Florian Fleck." Includes bibliographies and indexes. ISBN 3-7278-0347-9 : LC Card 86-129382
1. Technological innovations - Economic aspects. 2. Economic policy. 3. Fleck, Florian H. I. Bortis, Heinrich. II. Bosshart, Louis. III. Fleck, Florian H. IV. Title: Changement de technologie en économie et société. V. Title: Technological change in economy and society.
HC79.T4 T436 1985

Technologischer Wandel und internationaler Handel im 18. und 19. Jahrhundert. Fremdling, Rainer. Berlin , c1986. 493 p. ; ISBN 3-428-06042-3 LC Card 87-127793 DDC 382/.456691/094 19
HD9525.A2 F74 1986

TECHNOLOGY - ADDRESSES, ESSAYS, LECTURES.
(1983) The Trouble with technology . London , 1983. x, 224 p. : ISBN 0-86187-285-1
NYPL [JLE 86-1128]

(1986) Competitiveness through technology . Lexington, Mass. , c1986. xix, 215 p. : ISBN 0-669-11604-1 (alk. paper) LC Card 85-45379 DDC 338.97306 19
T185 .C67 1986 ***NYPL [JLE 86-1968]***

TECHNOLOGY AND CIVILIZATION - CONGRESSES.
Cambio cultural e imagen del hombre /. Bilbao, España , c1984. 248 p. ; ISBN 84-271-1384-6 LC Card 85-234026
CB245 .C29 1984 ***NYPL [JFD 86-6394]***

TECHNOLOGY AND CIVILIZATION - FORECASTING.
Hegedüs, Zsuzsa. Il presente è l'avvenire . Milano, Italy , c1985. 126 p. : LC Card 85-215705
HD85.I7 I68 no. 77 HD6955
NYPL [JLD 87-427]

Technology and commodity trade [microform] / Statistics Canada, Sciences and Technology Statistics Division. Ottawa : The Division, c1984. 40 p. : ill. ; 28 cm. Bibliography: p. [31]-33. Microfilm. New York : New York Public Library, 1986. 1 microfilm reel ; 35 mm. (MN *ZZ-26,873) ISBN 0-660-11447-X (pbk.) : LC Card 85-132672 DDC 382/.4562/000971 19
1. Technology transfer - Canada. 2. Balance of trade - Canada. 3. High technology industries - Canada. 4. Canada - Commerce. I. Canada. Statistics Canada. Sciences and Technology Statistics Division.
HC120.T4 T43 1984
NYPL [*ZT-1745 no.16]

Technology and economic development /. Fransman, Martin. Brighton, Sussex , 1986. xi, 161 p. : ISBN 0-7450-0104-1
NYPL [JLD 87-320]

Technology and employment : innovation and growth in the U. S. economy / Panel on Technology and Employment, Committee on Science, Engineering, and Public Policy [of the] National Academy of Sciences, National Academy of Engineering [and] Institute of Medicine ; Richard M. Cyert and David C. Mowery, editors. Washington, D.C. : National Academy Press, 1987. xiii, 225 p. : ill. ; 23 cm. Bibliography: p. 194-208. Includes index. ISBN 0-309-03744-1 (pbk.) : LC Card 87-42807 DDC 331.12/0973 19
1. Labor supply - United States - Effect of technological innovations on - Congresses. 2. United States - Full employment policies - Congresses. 3. United States - Economic conditions - 1981- - Congresses. I. Cyert, Richard Michael, 1921-. II. Mowery, David C. III. Committee on Science, Engineering, and Public Policy (U. S.). Panel on Technology and Employment.
HD6331.2.U5 T43 1987

Technology and global industry : companies and nations in the world economy / Bruce R. Guile and Harvey Brooks, editors. Washington, D.C. : National Academy Press, 1987. vi, 272 p. : ill. ; 23 cm. (Series on technology and social priorities) At head of title: National Academy of Engineering. "Most of the material in this book was presented at a National Academy of Engineering symposium titled 'World Technologies and National Sovereignty' held on February 13 and 14, 1986"--Pref. Includes bibliographies and index. ISBN 0-309-03736-0 (pbk.) LC Card 87-7765 DDC 338/.06 19
1. Technological innovations - Economic aspects - Congresses. 2. Technology and state - Congresses. I. Guile, Bruce R. II. Brooks, Harvey. III. National Academy of Engineering. IV. Series.
HC79.T4 T438 1987

TECHNOLOGY AND STATE - ADDRESSES, ESSAYS, LECTURES.
Competitiveness through technology . Lexington, Mass. , c1986. xix, 215 p. : ISBN 0-669-11604-1 (alk. paper) LC Card 85-45379 DDC 338.97306 19
T185 .C67 1986 ***NYPL [JLE 86-1968]***

TECHNOLOGY AND STATE - BRAZIL.
Araujo Júnior, José Tavares de. Tecnologia, concorrência e mudança estrutural . Rio de Janeiro , 1985. 64 p. ; LC Card 87-120280 DDC 338/.06 19
HD70.B7 A7 1985

TECHNOLOGY AND STATE - BRAZIL - BAHIA (STATE)
Bahia, Brazil (State) Secretaria do Planejamento, Ciência e Tecnologia. Planejamento, ciência e tecnologia . [Salvador , 1983?] 93 p. : LC Card 85-136375
HC188.B3 B334 1983

TECHNOLOGY AND STATE - CASE STUDIES.
National policies for developing high technology industries . Boulder, Colo. , c1986. xiv, 247 p. : ISBN 0-8133-7280-1 (soft : alk. paper) LC Card 86-50530 DDC 338.4/762 19
HC79.H53 N38 1986 ***NYPL [JLE 86-4504]***

TECHNOLOGY AND STATE - CITIZEN PARTICIPATION.
Coombs, Rod. Economics and technological change /. Totowa, N.J. , 1987. xv, 296 p. : ISBN 0-8476-7545-9 : LC Card 86-28000 DDC 338/.06 19
HC79.T4 C67 1987

TECHNOLOGY AND STATE - COMMUNIST COUNTRIES - CONGRESSES.
Organization of innovation . Berlin , New York , 1987. x, 238 p. : ISBN 0-89925-167-6 (U. S.) : LC Card 87-19936 DDC 658.4/06 19
HD45 .O73 1987

TECHNOLOGY AND STATE - CONGRESSES.
Organization of innovation . Berlin , New York , 1987. x, 238 p. : ISBN 0-89925-167-6 (U. S.) : LC Card 87-19936 DDC 658.4/06 19
HD45 .O73 1987

The Spatial impact of technological change /. Totowa, NJ , 1987. p. cm. ISBN 0-389-20753-5 LC Card 87-11460 DDC 338/.06 19
HC79.T4 S77 1987

Technology and global industry . Washington, D.C. , 1987. vi, 272 p. : ISBN 0-309-03736-0 (pbk.) LC Card 87-7765 DDC 338/.06 19
HC79.T4 T438 1987

TECHNOLOGY AND STATE - DEVELOPING COUNTRIES.
Skou, Niels Holger. Teknologipolitik /. Aarhus [1981] 52 p. ; LC Card 82-194649
HC59.72.T4 S56 1981

TECHNOLOGY AND STATE - FRANCE.
Dussauge, Pierre. L'industrie française de l'armement . Paris , c1985. xi, 179 p. : ISBN 2-7178-0999-6 : LC Card 86-216731
HD9743.F82 D87 1985

Salomon, Jean Jacques. Le gaulois, le cow-boy, et le samouraï . Paris , c1986. 209 p. : ISBN 2-7178-1139-7 : LC Card 87-120178
HC280.T4 S25 1986

TECHNOLOGY AND STATE - HUNGARY.
Szekér, Gyula. Műszaki fejlesztés, versenyképesség /. [Budapest] , 1984. 136 p. ;

ISBN 963-09-2534-6 : LC Card 85-177507
HC300.295.T4 S97 1984

TECHNOLOGY AND STATE - JAPAN.
Freeman, Christopher. Technology, policy, and economic performance . London , New York , 1987. 155 p. : ISBN 0-86187-928-7 : LC Card 87-18553 DDC 338.952 19
HC465.T4 F74 1987

TECHNOLOGY AND STATE - SOVIET UNION.
Kritika antimarksistskikh vzgli͡adov po problemam NTR /. Moskva , 1987. 157 p. ; LC Card 87-164887
HC340.T4 K75 1987

TECHNOLOGY AND STATE - TANZANIA.
Skarstein, Rune. Industrial development in Tanzania . Uppsala , Stockholm, Sweden , 1986. xi, 291 p. : ISBN 91-7106-254-8 (pbk.) LC Card 87-134925 DDC 338.9678 19
HC885 .S58 1986

TECHNOLOGY AND STATE - UNITED STATES.
Research funding as an investment--can we measure the returns? Washington, D.C. [1986] vi, 72 p. : LC Card 86-600525 DDC 338/.06 19
HC110.R4 R47 1986

TECHNOLOGY AND STATE - UNITED STATES - CASE STUDIES.
DiFilippo, Anthony, 1950- Military spending and industrial decline . Westport, Conn. , c1986. x, 199 p. ; ISBN 0-313-25179-7 (lib bdg. : alk. paper) LC Card 85-27144 DDC 338.4/7621902/0973 19
HD9703.U5 D54 1986
NYPL [JLD 86-2930]

TECHNOLOGY AND STATE - UNITED STATES - STATES.
Promoting high-technology industry . Boulder , 1987. 283 p. ; ISBN 0-8133-7427-8 (pbk. : alk. paper) LC Card 87-61327 DDC 338.4/762/000973 19
HC110.H53 P76 1987

Technology and the transformation of white-collar work / edited by Robert E. Kraut. Hillsdale, N.J. : L. Erlbaum Associates, 1987. x, 281 p. : ill. ; 24 cm. Presented at a conference sponsored by Bell Communications Research, June 1984. Bibliography: p. 253-267. Includes indexes. ISBN 0-89859-633-5 : LC Card 86-29039 DDC 331.7/92/0973 19
1. White collar workers - United States - Effect of technological innovations on - Congresses. 2. Office practice - Automation - Congresses. I. Kraut, Robert E. II. Bell Communications Research, Inc.
HD8039.M4 U577 1987

Technology and trade : indicators of U. S. industrial innovation : a study / prepared for the use of the Joint Economic Committee, Congress of the United States. Washington : U. S. G.P.O. : For sale by the Supt. of Docs., Congressional Sales Office, U. S. G.P.O., 1986. x, 80 p. : ill. ; 24 cm. (S. prt. . 99-163) At head of title: 99th Congress, 2d session. Joint committee print. Distributed to some depository libraries in microfiche. Shipping list no.: 86-660-P. "July 14, 1986." Includes bibliographical references. LC Card 86-603362 DDC 338/.06 19
1. Technological innovations - United States. 2. High technology industries. 3. Competition, International. 4. United States - Commerce. 5. Research, Industrial - United States. 6. High technology industries - United States. 7. Research, Industrial. I. United States. Congress. Joint Economic Committee. II. Series.
HC110.T4 T393 1986

Technology and urban growth.
Scranton, Philip. Proprietary capitalism . Philadelphia , 1987. p. cm. ISBN 0-87722-461-7 (pbk.) : LC Card 87-488 DDC 338.4/7677/00974811 19
HD9858.P5 S35 1987

Technology and work : East West comparison / edited by Peter Grootings. London ; Dover, N.H. : Croom Helm in association with European Co-ordination Centre for Research and Documentation in Social Sciences, c1986. 304 p. : ill. ; 23 cm. Chiefly papers derived from an international seminar held in Bled, Yugoslavia in late 1981, organized by the Vienna Centre and the Yugoslav Center for Theory and Practice of Self-Management Edvard Kardelj. Includes bibliographies. ISBN 0-7099-3801-2 : LC Card 86-4202 DDC 303.4/83 19
1. Technological innovations - Europe, Eastern - Congresses. 2. Technological innovations - Europe - Congresses. 3. Labor and laboring classes - Europe, Eastern - Congresses. 4. Labor and laboring classes - Europe - Congresses. I. Grootings, Peter, 1951- . II. European Centre for the Co-ordination of Research and Documentation in Social Sciences. III. Jugoslovenski centar za teoriju i praksu samoupravljanja Edvard Kardelj.
HC244.Z9 T475 1986 ***NYPL [JLD 86-2160]***

TECHNOLOGY ASSESSMENT - FORMS.
Metodología de evaluación y programación de sistemas de producción y consumo, MEPS /. Lima, Perú [1985]- v. <1 > : LC Card 86-215609
HD75 .M48 1985

TECHNOLOGY - AUSTRALIA - MARKETING - CONGRESSES.
An Industrial research and development and marketing package for Australia . [Canberra?] [1984] 48, 4 leaves : LC Card 87-153477 DDC 338/.06 19
HC610.T4 I53 1984

Technology-based training. Oxford ; New York : Pergamon Infotech, c1986. ix, 357 p. : ill., ports. ; 31 cm. (State of the art report . 14:8) Bibliography: p. 333-345. Includes indexes. ISBN 0-08-034097-0 LC Card 87-160178 DDC 658.3/12404 19
1. Employees, Training of - Computer-assisted instruction. 2. Occupational training - Computer-assisted instruction. I. Pergamon Infotech. II. Series: State of the art report , ser. 14, no. 8.
HF5549.5.T7 T39 1986

Technology, competition, & the Soviet bloc in the world market /. Poznański, Kazimierz. Berkeley , c1987. ix, 226 p. ; ISBN 0-87725-170-3 (pbk.) : LC Card 87-3505 DDC 338/.06 19
HC244.Z9 T4716 1987

Technology, competition, and the Soviet bloc in the world market. Poznański, Kazimierz. Technology, competition, & the Soviet bloc in the world market /. Berkeley , c1987. ix, 226 p. ; ISBN 0-87725-170-3 (pbk.) : LC Card 87-3505 DDC 338/.06 19
HC244.Z9 T4716 1987

The technology connection . Gerstein, Marc Saul. Reading, Mass. , c1987. xiv, 194 p. : ISBN 0-201-12188-3 (pbk.) : LC Card 86-22343 DDC 658.4/012 19
HD30.28 .G47 1987

TECHNOLOGY - EUROPEAN ECONOMIC COMMUNITY COUNTRIES - INTERNATIONAL COOPERATION.
Coming to grips with the internal market /. Maastricht, The Netherlands , c1986. viii, 136 p. ; ISBN 90-6779-019-2 (pbk.) LC Card 86-222624 DDC 337.1/42 19
HC241.2 .C5548 1986

Technology Exchange Program (1986 : Washington, D.C.) Plastics recycling as a future business opportunity, Friday, June 20, 1986 at the Sheraton-Carlton Hotel, Washington, D.C. : proceedings, Technology Exchange Program / Plastics Institute of America, Inc. Lancaster, Pa., U. S.A. : Technomic Pub., c1986. iii, 139 p. : ill. ; 28 cm. Bibliography: p. 40-42. ISBN 0-87762-510-7 (pbk.) LC Card 86-51296 DDC 668.4/192 19
1. Plastics industry and trade - United States - Congresses. 2. Plastic scrap - United States - Recycling - Congresses. 3. Plastics industry and trade - Congresses. 4. Plastic scrap - Recycling - Congresses. I. Plastics Institute of America. II. Title.
HD9661.U62 T39 1986

TECHNOLOGY - EXHIBITIONS. see **EXHIBITIONS.**

Technology, human capital, and the world food problem /. Alexander von Humboldt Award Colloquium (1984) St. Paul, MN , 1986. x, 167 p. : LC Card 86-622216 DDC 338.1/9/1724 19
HD9018.D44 A44 1984

TECHNOLOGY - INTERNATIONAL COOPERATION.
Nouvelles technologies et enjeux sociaux . Lyon , c1986. 230 p. : ISBN 2-7297-0279-2 : LC Card 86-187357
HC79.T4 N68 1986

Technology management '85 : the Grand Hotel, Eastbourne, 2nd-4th October, 1985. London : Institution of Electronic and Radio Engineers, c1985. 160 p. : ill. ; 30 cm. (Publication / Institution of Electronic and Radio Engineers . 64) Title on half t.p.: "Diamond jubilee conference on technology management '85." Includes bibliographical references and index. ISBN 0-903748-61-4
1. Technological innovations - Congresses. 2. Industrial management - Congresses. 3. Employees, Training of - Congresses. 4. Marketing management - Congresses. 5. Research, Industrial - Management - Congresses. I. Institution of Electronic and Radio Engineers. II. Title: Diamond jubilee conference on technology management '85. III. Series: Publication / Institution of Electronic and Radio Engineers , 64. ***NYPL [JLG 87-124]***

TECHNOLOGY - NIGERIA.
Nambudiri, C. N. S. Third World multinationals . Geneva , 1983. iv, 41 p. ; ISBN 92-2-103386-4 (pbk.) LC Card 86-213622 DDC 338.8/88669 19
HD2928 .N35 1983

Technology, policy, and economic performance . Freeman, Christopher. London , New York , 1987. 155 p. : ISBN 0-86187-928-7 : LC Card 87-18553 DDC 338.952 19
HC465.T4 F74 1987

Technology, public policy, and the changing structure of American agriculture. Washington, D.C. : Congress of the U. S., Office of Technology Assessment : For sale by the Supt. of Docs., U. S. G.P.O., [1986] vi, 374 p. : ill., maps ; 26 cm. Shipping list no.: 86-250-P. "March 1986"--P. [4] of cover. "OTA-F-285"--P. [4] of cover. S/N 052-003-01018-6 Item 1070-M Includes bibliographies and index. LC Card 85-600632 DDC 338.1/0973 19
1. Agriculture - Economic aspects - United States. 2. Agriculture and state - United States. 3. Agricultural innovations - United States.
HD1761 .T37 1986 ***NYPL [JLF 86-1376]***

Technology, regions, and policy / edited by John Rees. Totowa, N.J. : Rowman and Littlefield, 1986. xiv, 322 p. : ill. ; 24 cm. Includes bibliographies and index. ISBN 0-8476-7409-6 LC Card 85-24970 DDC 338.4/76213817/0973 19
1. High technology industries - Government policy - United States. 2. High technology industries - United States - Location. 3. United States - Economic conditions - 1981- - Regional disparities. 4. United States - Economic policy - 1981-. I. Rees, John, 1948-.
HC110.H53 T43 1986 ***NYPL [JLE 86-3327]***

Technology Sharing Program (U. S.)
Gilbert, Gorman, 1943- The management and regulation of ground transportation at U. S. airports . Washington, D.C. [1986] 153 p. : LC Card 87-600652 DDC 387.7/362 19
HE9797.4.A2 G55 1986

Weiner, Edward. Urban transportation planning in the United States . [Washington, D.C.] [1986] vii, 149 p. : LC Card 87-601522 DDC 388.4/068 19
HE308 .W45 1986

TECHNOLOGY - SOCIAL ASPECTS.
Formánek, Miloslav. Buržoazní sociálně politické teorie úlohy vědeckotechnického rozvoje /. Praha , 1980. 350 p. ;
NYPL [*QT 87-1720]

Gorz, André. [Chemins du paradis. English.] Paths to paradise . London , 1985. vii, 120 p. ; ISBN 0-86104-762-1 (pbk.) :
NYPL [JLD 86-3006]

Governing science and technology in a democracy /. Knoxville, TN , c1986. xviii, 314 p. ; ISBN 0-87049-506-2 (alk. paper) : LC Card 86-7074 DDC 338.9/26 19
Q125 .G68 1986 ***NYPL [JLD 87-462]***

Janicaud, Dominique, 1937- La puissance du rationnel /. [Paris] , c1985. 386 p. ; ISBN 2-07-070343-6 : ***NYPL [JFD 86-638]***

Radical science essays /. London , Atlantic Highlands, N.J. , 1986. 230 p. : LC Card 86-7425 DDC 303.4/83 19
Q175.55 .R33 1986 ***NYPL [JLD 87-615]***

TECHNOLOGY - SOCIAL ASPECTS - DEVELOPING COUNTRIES.
The AT reader . London , 1985. xvii, 468 p. : ISBN 0-946688-10-9 ***NYPL [JLE 86-2305]***

TECHNOLOGY - SOCIAL ASPECTS - HISTORY.
Pernoud, Régine, 1909- Le Moyen Age pour quoi faire? /. [Paris] , c1986. 315 p. : ISBN

2-234-01940-0 : LC Card 86-189820
HC41 .P46 1986

TECHNOLOGY - SOUTH ASIA - INTERNATIONAL COOPERATION - CONGRESSES.
South Asian cooperation in industry, energy, and technology /. New Delhi , Newbury Park, Calif. , 1987. p. cm. ISBN 0-8039-9538-5 (pbk.) LC Card 87-14994 DDC 337.1/54 19
HC430.6 .S675 1987

Technology, trade, and the U.S residential construction industry : special report. Washington, D.C. : U. S. Congress, Office of Technology Assessment : For sale by the Supt. of Docs., U. S. G.P.O., 1986. x, 91 p. : ill. ; 26 cm. Shipping list no.: 86-777-P. "September 1986"--P. [4] of cover. "OTA-TET-315"--P. [4] of cover. Includes bibliographical references. S/N 052-003-01050-0 Item 1070-M LC Card 86-600575 DDC 338.4/769083/0973 19
1. Construction industry - United States. 2. Construction industry - United States - Technological innovations. 3. Industrialized building - United States - Technological innovations. 4. House construction - United States - Technological innovations. 5. Building laws - United States. I. United States. Congress. Office of Technology Assessment. II. Title: Technology, trade, and the US residential construction industry, special report.
HD9715.U52 T43 1986

Technology, trade, and the US residential construction industry, special report.
Technology, trade, and the U.S residential construction industry . Washington, D.C. , 1986. x, 91 p. : LC Card 86-600575 DDC 338.4/769083/0973 19
HD9715.U52 T43 1986

Technology trade with the Middle East /. Emery, James J. Boulder , 1986. xvii, 302 p. : ISBN 0-8133-7043-4 : LC Card 85-3215 DDC 338.9/26 19
HC415.15.Z9 H533 1986
NYPL [JLE 86-2460]

TECHNOLOGY TRANSFER - ADDRESSES, ESSAYS, LECTURES.
The Political economy of international technology transfer /. Westport, Conn. , c1986. viii, 267 p. : ISBN 0-89930-128-2 (lib. bdg. : alk. paper) LC Card 85-28128 DDC 338.9/26 19
HD45 .P574 1986 *NYPL [JLE 86-3313]*

Technology transfer and human factors /.
Stewart, Charles T., 1922- Lexington, Mass. , 1987. xiii, 200 p. ; ISBN 0-669-14251-4 (alk. paper) LC Card 86-45751 DDC 338.9/26 19
T174.3 .S74 1987 *NYPL [JLE 87-634]*

TECHNOLOGY TRANSFER - ARGENTINA.
La Cooperación empresarial argentino-brasileña . [Buenos Aires] ,. 1983. viii, 160 p. ; LC Card 87-125370 DDC 338.8/8/0981 19
HD2829 .C66 1983

TECHNOLOGY TRANSFER - AUSTRALIA.
Gannicott, K. G. (Ken G.) Australia's dependence on foreign technology /. [Canberra, Australia] [1982] 38 p. ; LC Card 84-197120 DDC 338.994/06 19
HC610.T4 G36 1982

TECHNOLOGY TRANSFER - BRAZIL.
La Cooperación empresarial argentino-brasileña . [Buenos Aires] , 1983. viii, 160 p. ; LC Card 87-125370 DDC 338.8/8/0981 19
HD2829 .C66 1983

TECHNOLOGY TRANSFER - CANADA.
Technological change in Canadian industry /. Toronto , Buffalo , c1985. xv, 233 p. ; ISBN 0-8020-7243-7 (pbk.) LC Card 86-164766 DDC 338/.06 19
HC120.T4 T42 1985 *NYPL [JLD 87-654]*

Technology and commodity trade [microform] /. Ottawa , c1984. 40 p. : ISBN 0-660-11447-X (pbk.) : LC Card 85-132672 DDC 382/.4562/000971 19
HC120.T4 T43 1984
*NYPL [*ZT-1745 no.16]*

TECHNOLOGY TRANSFER - COMMUNIST COUNTRIES.
Wienert, Helgard. East-West technology transfer. The trade and economic aspects /. Paris , c1986. 453 p. : ISBN 92-64-12817-4
NYPL [JLE 87-1561]

TECHNOLOGY TRANSFER - CONGRESSES.
Varna Forum (2nd : 1985 : Varna, Bulgaria) Varna Forum II . [Varna?] [s.n.] [1985] 166 p. ; LC Card 86-220415 DDC 382/.091713/01717 19
HF1410.5 .V37 1985

TECHNOLOGY TRANSFER - DEVELOPING COUNTRIES.
Lambert, Denis Clair. Le mimétisme technologique des Tiers-Mondes . Paris , 1983. 223 p. : ISBN 2-7178-0597-4 : LC Card 83-233513
HC59.72.T4 L35 1983

Marton, Katherin. Multinationals, technology, and industrialization . Lexington, Mass. , c1986. xiii, 304 p. ; ISBN 0-669-13209-8 (alk. paper) LC Card 86-7218 DDC 338.8/881724 19
HD2932 .M37 1986 *NYPL [JLE 86-3372]*

Partnerschaftliche Entwicklungspolitik im Widerstreit der Interessen . Bochum-Querenburg , 1985. i, 184 leaves ; LC Card 87-409475 DDC 332.6/7343/01724 19
HG5993 .P37 1985

Shitov, V. N. (Vladimir Nikolaevich) Tekhnologicheskiĭ neokolonializm . Moskva , 1985. 154 p. : LC Card 86-130530
HC59.72.T4 S525 1985

Skou, Niels Holger. Teknologipolitik /. Aarhus [1981] 52 p. ; LC Card 82-194649
HC59.72.T4 S56 1981

Stewart, Charles T., 1922- Technology transfer and human factors /. Lexington, Mass. , 1987. xiii, 200 p. ; ISBN 0-669-14251-4 (alk. paper) LC Card 86-45751 DDC 338.9/26 19
T174.3 .S74 1987 *NYPL [JLE 87-634]*

TECHNOLOGY TRANSFER - ECONOMIC ASPECTS.
Hartmann, Wolf-Dietrich, 1946- Internationaler Technologieaustausch--Kooperation oder Konfrontation? . Frankfurt/Main , 1984. 153 p. ; ISBN 3-88012-633-X LC Card 85-155132 DDC 338.9/26 19
HC79.T4 H36 1984

Wienert, Helgard. East-West technology transfer. The trade and economic aspects /. Paris , c1986. 453 p. : ISBN 92-64-12817-4
NYPL [JLE 87-1561]

TECHNOLOGY TRANSFER - ECONOMIC ASPECTS - ARGENTINA.
Sercovich, Francisco Colman. Exportaciones de tecnología de Brasil y Argentina /. [Buenos Aires, Argentina?] , 1986. 269 p. ; LC Card 87-404009 DDC 338.981/06 19
HC190.T4 S47 1986

TECHNOLOGY TRANSFER - ECONOMIC ASPECTS - BRAZIL.
Sercovich, Francisco Colman. Exportaciones de tecnología de Brasil y Argentina /. [Buenos Aires, Argentina?] , 1986. 269 p. ; LC Card 87-404009 DDC 338.981/06 19
HC190.T4 S47 1986

TECHNOLOGY TRANSFER - ECONOMIC ASPECTS - CHINA.
Rode, Reinhard, 1947- US-Technologietransferpolitik gegenüber der UdSSR und der VR China . Frankfurt am Main [1986] 39 p. : ISBN 3-926197-01-3 LC Card 87-120584 DDC 338.9/26 19
HC340.T4 R63 1986

TECHNOLOGY TRANSFER - ECONOMIC ASPECTS - CONGRESSES.
Technik und internationale Politik /. Baden-Baden , 1986. 520 p. ; ISBN 3-7890-1239-4 (Deut. Bibl.) LC Card 87-103890 DDC 338/.06 19
HC79.T4 T422 1986

TECHNOLOGY TRANSFER - ECONOMIC ASPECTS - DEVELOPING COUNTRIES.
Osterkamp, Rigmar. Die Investitionsgüterindustrie . München , c1986. v, 199 p. ; ISBN 3-8039-0334-3 LC Card 87-401371 DDC 338.4/76218/091724 19
HD9705.D462 O88 1986

TECHNOLOGY TRANSFER - ECONOMIC ASPECTS - EUROPE.
A High technology gap? . New York, N.Y. , c1987. xii, 114 p. : ISBN 0-87609-021-8 (pbk.) : LC Card 87-6713 DDC 338/.06 19
HC240.9.T4 H54 1987

TECHNOLOGY TRANSFER - ECONOMIC ASPECTS - HANDBOOKS, MANUALS, ETC.
Grant, Land. High-tech exporter's sourcebook . Brooklyn, N.Y. , 1987. viii, 263 p. ; LC Card 87-157599 DDC 382/.6/02573 19
HC79.T4 G68 1987

TECHNOLOGY TRANSFER - ECONOMIC ASPECTS - JAPAN.
A High technology gap? . New York, N.Y. , c1987. xii, 114 p. : ISBN 0-87609-021-8 (pbk.) : LC Card 87-6713 DDC 338/.06 19
HC240.9.T4 H54 1987

The Japanese challenge . Stamford, Conn., U. S.A. , c1986. xii, 108 leaves : ISBN 0-89336-489-4 (pbk.) LC Card 87-404570 DDC 338/.06 19
HC465.T4 J365 1986

TECHNOLOGY TRANSFER - ECONOMIC ASPECTS - SOVIET UNION.
Rode, Reinhard, 1947- US-Technologietransferpolitik gegenüber der UdSSR und der VR China . Frankfurt am Main [1986] 39 p. : ISBN 3-926197-01-3 LC Card 87-120584 DDC 338.9/26 19
HC340.T4 R63 1986

TECHNOLOGY TRANSFER - ECONOMIC ASPECTS - SPAIN.
Sánchez Muñoz, María Paloma. La dependencia tecnológica española . [Madrid] [1984?] xi, 591 p. : ISBN 84-7415-170-8 : LC Card 86-212990
HC390.T4 S26 1984

TECHNOLOGY TRANSFER - ECONOMIC ASPECTS - UNITED STATES.
Hartmann, Wolf-Dietrich, 1946- Internationaler Technologieaustausch--Kooperation oder Konfrontation? . Frankfurt/Main , 1984. 153 p. ; ISBN 3-88012-633-X LC Card 85-155132 DDC 338.9/26 19
HC79.T4 H36 1984

A High technology gap? . New York, N.Y. , c1987. xii, 114 p. : ISBN 0-87609-021-8 (pbk.) : LC Card 87-6713 DDC 338/.06 19
HC240.9.T4 H54 1987

Rode, Reinhard, 1947- US-Technologietransferpolitik gegenüber der UdSSR und der VR China . Frankfurt am Main [1986] 39 p. : ISBN 3-926197-01-3 LC Card 87-120584 DDC 338.9/26 19
HC340.T4 R63 1986

TECHNOLOGY TRANSFER - EUROPE.
Ilgen, Thomas L. Trading technology . New York , 1987. x, 203 p. ; ISBN 0-275-92483-1 (alk. paper) : LC Card 86-21197 DDC 338.94/06 19
HC415.15 .I45 1986 *NYPL [JLE 87-832]*

TECHNOLOGY TRANSFER - EUROPE - HISTORY - 18TH CENTURY - CONGRESSES.
Technologischer Wandel im 18. Jahrhundert /. Wolfenbüttel , c1981. 246 p. ; ISBN 3-88373-018-1 LC Card 84-116829 DDC 338/.06 19
HC240.9.T4 T43 1981 *NYPL [JLE 86-927]*

TECHNOLOGY TRANSFER - EUROPEAN ECONOMIC COMMUNITY COUNTRIES.
Urban, Sabine M.-L. Entreprises allemandes et coopération industrielle à l'échelle européenne . Paris , c1986. 162 p. : ISBN 2-11-001580-2 : LC Card 86-175800
HD2844 .U7 1986

TECHNOLOGY TRANSFER - GOVERNMENT POLICY - UNITED STATES.
Committee on Science, Engineering, and Public Policy (U. S.). Panel on the Impact of National Security Controls on International Technology Transfer. Balancing the national interest . Washington, D.C. , 1987. xiii, 321 p. : ISBN 0-309-03738-7 LC Card 87-60020 DDC 337.73 19
HF1456 .C65 1987

TECHNOLOGY TRANSFER - GREECE.
Kazēs, D. A. (Dēmētrēs A.) [Licensing kai viomēchanikē anaptyxē. English.] Licensing and industrial development . Athens , 1986. 208 p. : LC Card 87-170691 DDC 338.09495 19
HF1429 .K3813 1986

TECHNOLOGY TRANSFER - HUNGARY.
Kardos, Péter. Külföldi licencek a magyar gazdaságban /. Budapest , 1984. 204, [1] p. : ISBN 963-221-396-3 : LC Card 85-157267
HF1429 .K37 1984

TECHNOLOGY TRANSFER - JAPAN.
Ilgen, Thomas L. Trading technology . New York , 1987. x, 203 p. ; ISBN 0-275-92483-1 (alk. paper) : LC Card 86-21197 DDC 338.94/06 19
HC415.15 .I45 1986 ***NYPL [JLE 87-832]***

Stewart, Charles T., 1922- Technology transfer and human factors /. Lexington, Mass. , 1987. xiii, 200 p. ; ISBN 0-669-14251-4 (alk. paper) LC Card 86-45751 DDC 338.9/26 19
T174.3 .S74 1987 ***NYPL [JLE 87-634]***

TECHNOLOGY TRANSFER - JAPAN - HISTORY.
Sekiguchi, Sueo. Technology transfer through direct foreign investment /. Ibaraki, Osaka, Japan , 1985. 61 leaves : LC Card 86-209818 DDC 332.6/7352 19
HC60 .S416 1985

TECHNOLOGY TRANSFER - KOREA (SOUTH) - CASE STUDIES.
Enos, John L. (John Lawrence), 1924- The adoption and diffusion of imported technology . New York , c1988. 272 p. : ISBN 0-7099-2030-X LC Card 87-19894 DDC 338.9519/306 19
HC470.T4 E56 1987

TECHNOLOGY TRANSFER - LATIN AMERICA.
Wionczek, Miguel S. Capital y tecnología en México y América Latina /. México , 1981. 413 p. ; ISBN 968-470-018-0
NYPL [JLE 87-377]

TECHNOLOGY TRANSFER - LAW AND LEGISLATION - SPAIN.
Sánchez Muñoz, María Paloma. La dependencia tecnológica española . [Madrid] [1984?] xi, 591 p. : ISBN 84-7415-170-8 : LC Card 86-212990
HC390.T4 S26 1984

TECHNOLOGY TRANSFER - NEAR EAST.
Emery, James J. Technology trade with the Middle East /. Boulder , 1986. xvii, 302 p. : ISBN 0-8133-7043-4 : LC Card 85-3215 DDC 338.9/26 19
HC415.15.Z9 H533 1986
NYPL [JLE 86-2460]

Ilgen, Thomas L. Trading technology . New York , 1987. x, 203 p. ; ISBN 0-275-92483-1 (alk. paper) : LC Card 86-21197 DDC 338.94/06 19
HC415.15 .I45 1986 ***NYPL [JLE 87-832]***

Technology transfer to the Middle East [microform] . Washington, D.C. [1984] 27 p. :
NYPL [*ZT-1554 no.18]

TECHNOLOGY TRANSFER - SOCIAL ASPECTS.
Scott-Stevens, Susan. Foreign consultants and counterparts . Boulder , 1987. xvii, 229 p. : ISBN 0-8133-7370-0 (pbk. : alk. paper) LC Card 87-50750 DDC 306/.46 19
HC79.T4 S36 1987

TECHNOLOGY TRANSFER - SOVIET UNION.
Goldman, Marshall I. Gorbachev's challenge . New York , c1987. xvii, 296 p. : ISBN 0-393-02454-7 LC Card 86-33187 DDC 338.947 19
HC336.25 .G6365 1987

Multinational corporations, OPEC, cartels, foreign investment, and technology transfer [microform] . Frederick, MD , 1987. microfilm reel ISBN 0-89093-552-1 (microfilm) : LC Card 87-6249 DDC 338.8 19
HD2755.5

Selling the rope to hang capitalism? . Washington , 1987. viii, 246 p. ; ISBN 0-08-034959-5 : LC Card 86-30401 DDC 382/.091713/01717 19
HF1412 .S45 1987

Sokoloff, Georges. [Economie de la détente. English.] The economy of détente . Leamington Spa ; New York : p. cm. ISBN 0-907582-62-1 : LC Card 86-32627 DDC 382/.0947 19
HF3646.5 .S6513 1987

Technology transfer through direct foreign investment /. Sekiguchi, Sueo. Ibaraki, Osaka, Japan , 1985. 61 leaves : LC Card 86-209818 DDC 332.6/7352 19
HC60 .S416 1985

Technology transfer to the Middle East [microform] : summary. Washington, D.C. : Congress of the United States, Office of Technology Assessment : For sale by the Supt. of Docs., U. S. G.P.O., [1984] 27 p. : ill. ; 23 cm. Cover title. "OTA-ISC-174"--P. [4] of cover. "September 1984"--P. [4] of cover. Microfilm. New York : New York Public Library, 1985. 1 microfilm reel ; 35 mm. (MN *ZZ-24,952)
1. Technology transfer - Near East. 2. Technology transfer - United States.
NYPL [*ZT-1554 no.18]

TECHNOLOGY TRANSFER - UNITED STATES.
Medvedkov, S. IU. (Sergeĭ IUr'evich) Mezhdunarodnyĭ marketing amerikanskoĭ tekhnologii /. Moskva , 1985. 189 p. : LC Card 85-187077
HF1009.6 .M43 1985

Multinational corporations, OPEC, cartels, foreign investment, and technology transfer [microform] . Frederick, MD , 1987. microfilm reel ISBN 0-89093-552-1 (microfilm) : LC Card 87-6249 DDC 338.8 19
HD2755.5

Selling the rope to hang capitalism? . Washington , 1987. viii, 246 p. ; ISBN 0-08-034959-5 : LC Card 86-30401 DDC 382/.091713/01717 19
HF1412 .S45 1987

Sokoloff, Georges. [Economie de la détente. English.] The economy of détente . Leamington Spa ; New York : p. cm. ISBN 0-907582-62-1 : LC Card 86-32627 DDC 382/.0947 19
HF3646.5 .S6513 1987

Stewart, Charles T., 1922- Technology transfer and human factors /. Lexington, Mass. , 1987. xiii, 200 p. ; ISBN 0-669-14251-4 (alk. paper) LC Card 86-45751 DDC 338.9/26 19
T174.3 .S74 1987 ***NYPL [JLE 87-634]***

Technology transfer to the Middle East [microform] . Washington, D.C. [1984] 27 p. :
NYPL [*ZT-1554 no.18]

Technology's crucible . Martin, James, 1933- Englewood Cliffs, N.J. , 1987. xii, 206 p. : ISBN 0-13-902024-1 : LC Card 86-91492 DDC 303.4/9 19
T20 .M348 1987 ***NYPL [JLE 87-228]***

Técnicas presupuestarias en la administración pública /. Herrero Suazo, Santiago. Alcalá de Henares-Madrid, España [1984?] 382 p. : ISBN 84-7351-173-5 LC Card 85-185202
HJ1248 .H47 1984

Técnicas psicosociales en la administración pública . Aoiz Iriarte, María Rosario. Alcalá de Henares, Madrid, España [1984] 238 p. : ISBN 84-7351-179-4 LC Card 85-189583
HF5549.5.S38 A57 1984

Le tecniche esecutive nell'edilizia residenziale degli anni '80 . Bianchi, Roberto, 1954- Milano, Italy , c1986. 144 p. : LC Card 87-126093
HD9715.5.I83 L653 1986

Tecnici, ricercatori, quadri e sindacato / F. Vigevani ... [et al.] ; Luigi Pallotta, Aldo Rossi. Roma : Ediesse, 1985. 126 p. : ill. ; 19 cm. (Collana Riquadri) LC Card 86-169979
1. Professional employees - Italy - Congresses. 2. Middle managers - Italy - Congresses. 3. Trade-unions - Professional employees - Italy - Congresses. 4. Trade-unions - Middle managers - Italy - Congresses. I. Vigevani, F. (Fausto). II. Pallotta, Luigi, 1951-. III. Rossi, Aldo, 1931-.
HD8038.I8 T43 1985

Tecnocrati e mercanti . Maione, Giuseppe, 1942- Milano, Italia , c1986. 354 p. ; LC Card 86-194293
HC305 .M274 1986

Tecnologia, concorrência e mudança estrutural . Araujo Júnior, José Tavares de. Rio de Janeiro , 1985. 64 p. ; LC Card 87-120280 DDC 338/.06 19
HD70.B7 A7 1985

Tecnologia e impresa.
Il Robot italiano . Milano , 1984. 194 p. : LC Card 86-129858
HD9696.R623 I837 1984
NYPL [JLD 87-1277]

Tecnologia e racionalização da agro-pecuária, com o aproveitamento das bacias hidrográficas sergipanas. Almeida, Edimilson Machado de, 1937- Tecnologia e racionalização da agropecuária, com o aproveitamento das bacias hidrográficas /. Aracaju [1971] 100 leaves : LC Card 85-203218
HD1875.S4 A65 1971

Tecnologia e racionalização da agropecuária, com o aproveitamento das bacias hidrográficas /. Almeida, Edimilson Machado de, 1937- Aracaju [1971] 100 leaves : LC Card 85-203218
HD1875.S4 A65 1971

Tecnologías pesqueras en el trópico húmedo de México /. Ortiz de Montellano, Ana. México, D.F. , 1985. 146 p. : LC Card 86-208331
HD9464.M42 O77 1985

TECNOLOGICAL INNOVATIONS - SOCIAL ASPECTS.
Rattner, Henrique. Informática e sociedade /. São Paulo-SP , 1985. 219 p. : LC Card 85-221850
HC79.T4 R387 1985

TECOLUTLA (MEXICO) - SOCIAL CONDITIONS.
Alcalá, Graciela. Los pescadores de Tecolutla . México, D.F. , 1985. 215 p. : ISBN 968-496-070-0 LC Card 86-191825
HD8039.F652 M62 1985

Tedesco, Eleanor Hollis.
Administrative office management. Tedesco, Eleanor Hollis. Administrative office systems management / Eleanor Hollis Tedesco, Robert B. Mitchell. 2nd ed. New York , c1987. xii, 736 p. : ISBN 0-471-01201-7 LC Card 86-26800 DDC 651.3 19
HF5547 .T37 1987

Administrative office systems management / Eleanor Hollis Tedesco, Robert B. Mitchell. 2nd ed. New York : Wiley, c1987. xii, 736 p. : ill. (some col.), forms ; 26 cm. Rev. ed. of: Administrative office management. c1984. Includes bibliographies and index. ISBN 0-471-01201-7 LC Card 86-26800 DDC 651.3 19
1. Office management. 2. Office practice - Automation. I. Mitchell, Robert B., 1952-. II. Tedesco, Eleanor Hollis. Administrative office management. III. Title.
HF5547 .T37 1987

Tedlow, Richard S.
Chandler, Alfred Dupont. The coming of managerial capitalism . Homewood, Ill. , 1985. xiv, 877 p. : ISBN 0-256-03285-8 LC Card 84-82470 DDC 338.6/44/0973 19
HD2785 .C47 1985 ***NYPL [JLE 86-4418]***

Managing big business . Boston, Mass. , c1986. xxvii, 425 p. ; ISBN 0-87584-142-2 LC Card 86-7683 DDC 338.6/44/0973 19
HD2785 .M353 1986 ***NYPL [JLE 87-1360]***

Teece, David J. The Competitive challenge . Cambridge, Mass. , c1987. xii, 256 p. : ISBN 0-88730-178-9 LC Card 87-1190 DDC 658.4/06 19
HD70.U5 C58 1987

TEEN-AGE PREGNANCY. see **PREGNANCY, ADOLESCENT.**

TEEN-AGERS. see **YOUTH.**

The teenage enterpreneur's guide . Riehm, Sarah, 1952- Chicago, IL , c1987. viii, 211 p. : ISBN 0-940625-00-8 (pbk.) : LC Card 87-1904 DDC 658/.041 19
HD6273 .R53 1987

TEENAGERS - EMPLOYMENT - WYOMING.
Wyoming. Dept. of Labor and Statistics. Wyoming child labor, 1986. Cheyenne, Wyo. (Herschler Bldg., Cheyenne 82002) [1986] vi, 74 p. : LC Card 87-622019 DDC 331.3/4/09787 19
HD6274.W8 W96 1986

A teenager's guide to money, banking, and finance /. Spiselman, David, 1947- New York , c1987. p. cm. ISBN 0-671-64345-2 LC Card 87-11059 DDC 332.024 19
HG179 .S5554 1987

Tegegne Teke. Cooperatives and national development : the Ethiopian experience / by Tegegne Teka. Addis Ababa, Ethiopia : Institute of Development Research, Addis Ababa University, [1984] iii, 57 leaves ; 30 cm. (IDR working paper . no. 18) "August 1984." Bibliography: leaves 56-57. LC Card 85-980411 DDC 334/.683/0963 19
1. Agriculture, Cooperative - Ethiopia. 2. Producer cooperatives - Ethiopia. 3. Peasantry - Ethiopia. 4. Agriculture - Ethiopia - Societies, etc. 5. Rural development - Ethiopia. I. Title. II. Series.
HD1491.E83 T44 1984 ***NYPL [JLG 86-173]***

Tegler, Eugeniusz. Polityka finansowa PRL : wstęp do nauki polityki finansowej : skrypt dla

studentów Studium Administracyjnego / Eugeniusz Tegler.Wyd. 2., zmienione. Szczecin : Wydawnictwa Nauk. Wyższej Szkoły Pedagogicznej w Szczecinie, 1984. 128 p. ; 24 cm. Bibliography: p. 123-127. LC Card 86-100923
1. Finance, Public - Poland. I. Title.
HJ1213.Z6 T44 1984

Tegtmeier, Andre P. Politik gegen die Krise . Marburg , 1985. 157 p. : ISBN 3-924800-01-4 : LC Card 86-119259 DDC 338.9 19
HC59 .P584 1985

Tehnilis-majandusliku ja sotsiaalse arengu planeerimine tootmiskoondistes (tööstusettevõtetes) /. Kull, Eduard. Tallinn , 1985. 277 p. : LC Card 86-221274
HD70.E68 K85 1985

TEHUANTEPEC RAILWAY.
United States. Congress. House. Committee on Foreign Affairs. Discussion of the Nicaragua ship canal and the Tehuantepec ship railway schemes before the Committee on Foreign Affairs of the House of Representatives. [Washington] [1882?] 80 p. ; LC Card 82-602443
HE536 .U55 1882

Teichgraeber, Richard F. The Boundaries of economics /. Cambridge , New York , 1988. xi, 122 p. ; ISBN 0-521-34450-6 LC Card 87-17772 DDC 330 19
HB33 .B68 1988

Teichman, Judith A., 1947- Policymaking in Mexico : from boom to crisis / Judith A. Teichman. Boston : Allen & Unwin, c1988. p. cm. (Thematic studies in Latin America) Bibliography: p. Includes index. ISBN 0-04-445033-8 : LC Card 87-18704 DDC 338.2/7282/0972 19
1. Petroleum industry and trade - Government policy - Mexico. 2. Mexico - Economic policy 1970-. 3. Banks and banking - Government ownership - Mexico. I. Title. II. Series.
HD9574.M6 T45 1988

Teichmann, Ulrich, 1942- Der Entscheidungsprozess in der Wirtschaftspolitik / Ulrich Teichmann. Darmstadt : Wissenschaftliche Buchgesellschaft, 1983. vi, 135 p. ; 20 cm. (Erträge der Forschung. Bd. 197) Bibliography: p. 131-312. Includes index. ISBN 3-534-08177-3 LC Card 83-206492
1. Economic policy - Citizen participation. 2. Economic policy. I. Title.
HD84 .T39 1983

Teichova, Alice. International business and Central Europe, 1918-1939 /. [Leicester, Leicestershire] , New York , 1983. xxvii, 459 p. : ISBN 0-312-41982-1 : LC Card 83-13956 DDC 338.8/8843 19
HD2844 .I57 1983 ***NYPL [JLE 86-3697]***

Teiger, Catherine. Quéinnec, Y. (Yvon) Le travail posté . [Toulouse-Le Mirail] , 1985. 261 p. : ISBN 2-85816-030-9 LC Card 87-133427
HD5111.5 .Q45 1985

Teilnahme ohne Teilhabe . Oliva, Karl. Frankfurt am Main , New York , c1985. 285 p. : ISBN 3-593-33476-3 LC Card 85-147441
HC59.72.S3 O45 1985

Teitelboim G., Berta.
Indicadores económicos y sociales : series anuales, 1960-1984 / Berta Teitelboim G. Santiago, Chile : Programa de Economía del Trabajo, Academia de Humanismo Cristiano, 1985. 57 p. : ill. ; 22 cm. (Serie de indicadores económico sociales) "Junio 1985." Chiefly tables.
1. Economic indicators - Chile. 2. Social indicators - Chile. I. Title. II. Series. ***NYPL [JLD 86-2146]***

Indicadores económicos y sociales [microform] : series anuales, 1960-1982 / Berta Teitelboim G. Santiago, Chile : Programa de Economía del Trabajo, Academia de Humanismo Cristiano, [1984] 41 p. : ill. ; 22 cm. At head of title: Serie de indicadores económico sociales. Jan. 1984. Chiefly tables. Microfilm. New York : New York Public Library, 1986. 1 microfilm reel ; 35 mm. (MN *ZZ-26,232)
1. Economic indicators - Chile. 2. Social indicators - Chile. I. Title. II. Title: Serie de indicadores económico sociales. ***NYPL [*ZT-1711 no.26]***

Teixeira Werneck Vianna, Maria Lúcia. see Vianna, Maria Lúcia Teixeira Werneck.

Teja, Ana María. Análisis de la encuesta sobre cambio técnico en la industria del cuero en Uruguay / Ana María Teja. Montevideo, Uruguay : Centro de Investigaciones Económicas, [1980] 56 p., [60] leaves ; 28 cm. (III. Serie Estudios . no. 11) Includes bibliographical references. LC Card 86-157655
1. Leather industry and trade - Uruguay. 2. Leather industry and trade - Uruguay - Technological innovations. I. Series: III. Serie, Estudios (Centro de Investigaciones Económicas (Uruguay)) , no. 11. II. Title.
HD9780.U82 T45 1980

Tejada C., Frank A. Crédito y seguro agrícola : incidencia en el desarrollo económico de la República Dominicana / Frank A. Tejada C.1a ed. Santo Domingo, República Dominicana : Centro de Estudios Monetarios y Bancarios, 1986. 104 p. : ill. ; 21 cm. (Serie Estudios) Bibliography: p. 103-104. LC Card 87-400183 DDC 332.7/1/097293 19
1. Agricultural credit - Dominican Republic. 2. Insurance, Agricultural - Dominican Republic. 3. Agriculture - Economic aspects - Dominican Republic. 4. Agriculture and state - Dominican Republic. I. Series: Serie Estudios (Centro de Estudios Monetarios y Bancarios (Santo Domingo, Dominican Republic)). II. Title.
HG2051.D6 T45 1986

Tekhnicheskie perspektivy zheleznodorozhnogo transporta v blizhaĭshee vremi͡a. Lomonosov, I͡U. (I͡Uriĭ), 1876-1952. Moskva, 1924. 67 p. LC Card 60-59178
HE3135 .L6

Tekhniko-ėkonomicheskie raschety na predprii͡atii / [avtory, V.I. Gab ... et al.]. Kiev : "Tekhnika", 1984. 126 p. : ill. ; 20 cm. Bibliography: p. 124-[125] LC Card 84-234261
1. Industrial management - Soviet Union - Mathematical models. 2. Technological innovations - Soviet Union. I. Gab, V. I. (Valentin Ivanovich).
HD70.S63 T45 1984

Tekhniko-ėkonomicheskoe i sot͡sial'noe planirovanie v proizvodstvennykh ob"edinenii͡akh, na predprii͡atii͡akh. Kull, Eduard. Tehnilis-majandusliku ja sotsiaalse arengu planeerimine tootmiskoondistes (tööstusettevõtetes) /. Tallinn , 1985. 277 p. : LC Card 86-221274
HD70.E68 K85 1985

Tekhnologicheskiĭ neokolonializm . Shitov, V. N. (Vladimir Nikolaevich) Moskva , 1985. 154 p. : LC Card 86-130530
HC59.72.T4 S525 1985

Tekhunot demografiyot shel ha-ukhlusiyah : nitunim kelal-artsiyim meha-peḳidah ha-mele'ah. Yerushalayim : Medinat Yiśra'el, ha-Lishkah ha-merkazit li-sṭaṭisṭiḳah, 1985. 31, 175, xxxiv p. : ill. ; 29 cm. (Pirsume mifḳad ha-ukhlusin veha-diyur, 1983, 0334-1305 . mis. 7) English and Hebrew. Title on added t.p.: Demographic characteristics of the population. Tables. LC Card 86-204169
1. Israel - Census, 1983. 2. Israel - Population - Statistics. 3. Housing - Israel - Statistics. I. Israel. Lishkah ha-merkazit li-sṭaṭisṭiḳah. II. Title: Demographic characteristics of the population. III. Series: Pirsume mifḳad ha-ukhlusin veha-diyur, 1983 , mis. 7.
HA4560 .A4 1983

Teknisk-økonomisk-organisatorisk analyse / udarbejdet af I. Krüger A/S. København : Miljøministeriet, [1983] 131 p. : ill. ; 24 cm. "Rapportbilag I til Vandprisudvalgets betænkning." "Oktober 1983." Bibliography: p. 130-131. ISBN 87-503-4561-3 LC Card 84-169883
1. Municipal water supply - Denmark - Rates. 2. Water consumption - Denmark. I. Denmark. Udvalget til undersøgelse af vandforsyningernes økonomiske baggrund. Vandpriser. II. I. Krüger A/S.
HD4465.D4 T44 1983

Tekniske rapporter, 0106-9039 .
(39) Nordisk arealklassifikation /. København [1985] 19 p. ; ISBN 87-88083-23-3 LC Card 86-162708
HD730 .N67 1985

Teknologipolitik /. Skou, Niels Holger. Aarhus [1981] 52 p. ; LC Card 82-194649
HC59.72.T4 S56 1981

Teknowledge series in knowledge engineering .
(v. 1) Building expert systems /. Reading, Mass. , 1983. xvi, 444 p. : ISBN 0-201-10686-8 LC Card 82-24511 DDC 001.64/2 19
QA76.9.E96 B84 1983 ***NYPL [JSE 87-204]***

Tekoindustrierna : förutsättningar på kort och lång sikt. Stockholm : Statens industriverk, 1980. 189 p. : ill. ; 30 cm. (SIND PM, 0346-573X . 1980:16) Includes bibliographical references. ISBN 91-38-05813-8 LC Card 82-236884
1. Textile industry - Sweden. 2. Clothing trade - Sweden. I. Sweden. Statens industriverk. II. Series.
HD9865.S86 T45 1980

Tel-Aviv. University. Institute for German History.
Jahrbuch Beiheft .
(7. 7) Frieden und Friedenssicherung in Vergangenheit und Gegenwart . München , 1984. 115 p. ; ISBN 3-7705-2147-1 (pbk.) :
NYPL [JFL 76-295 Bd. 7]

TELECOM AUSTRALIA.
Albon, Robert, 1951- The Telecom monopoly . Perth, W.A. , 1986. 56 p. : ISBN 0-949186-10-4 (pbk.) : LC Card 86-213521 DDC 384/.0994 19
HE8540.T44 A42 1986

The Telecom monopoly . Albon, Robert, 1951- Perth, W.A. , 1986. 56 p. : ISBN 0-949186-10-4 (pbk.) : LC Card 86-213521 DDC 384/.0994 19
HE8540.T44 A42 1986

TELECOMMUNICATION - ADDRESSES, ESSAYS, LECTURES.
Telecommunications . Dedham, MA , c1984. xxii, 687 p. : ISBN 0-89006-140-8 LC Card 84-70225 DDC 384 19
HE7631 .T443 1984 ***NYPL [JLE 86-1167]***

TELECOMMUNICATION - ALBERTA.
W.J. Page & Associates. Telecommunications in Northern Alberta /. [Edmonton, Alta. , 1986?] 39, [96] p. : LC Card 86-235313 DDC 384/.068 19
HE7819.A43 W15 1986

TELECOMMUNICATION AND STATE.
Jussawalla, Meheroo, 1923- The calculus of international communications . Littleton, Colo. , 1987. xiv, 159 p. ; ISBN 0-87287-503-2 : LC Card 87-2640 DDC 384/.068 19
HE7645 .J87 1987

TELECOMMUNICATION - AUSTRALIA.
Albon, Robert, 1951- The Telecom monopoly . Perth, W.A. , 1986. 56 p. : ISBN 0-949186-10-4 (pbk.) : LC Card 86-213521 DDC 384/.0994 19
HE8540.T44 A42 1986

TELECOMMUNICATION - COLOMBIA.
Colombia. Ministerio de Comunicaciones. Una revolución en las comunicaciones . [Bogotá] 1986. 307 p., [5] leaves of plates : LC Card 87-401464 DDC 384/.09861 19
HE8011 .C65 1986

TELECOMMUNICATION - DEREGULATION.
Snow, Marcellus S. Telecommunications . Amsterdam , New York , 1986. xvi, 304 p. : ISBN 0-444-87926-9 LC Card 86-224686 DDC 384/.041 19
HE7645 .S58 1986

TELECOMMUNICATION - EMPLOYEES - TRAINING OF - ITALY - MILAN.
Le 150 ore e la formazione professionale in azienda . Milano, Italy , c1985. 178 p. : LC Card 86-141990
HD5716.T242 I82 1985
NYPL [JFD 87-3739]

TELECOMMUNICATION - ENGLAND - LINCOLNSHIRE.
Clark, David, Ph. D. Information services in rural areas . Norwich [Norfolk] , c1980. x, 122 p. : ISBN 0-86094-058-6 (pbk.) LC Card 81-149488
HE8109.L55 C55 1980

TELECOMMUNICATION EQUIPMENT INDUSTRY.
Blatherwick, David E. S. The international politics of telecommunications /. [Berkeley, Calif.] , c1987. ix, 107 p. ; ISBN 0-87725-168-1 (pbk.) : LC Card 87-3509 DDC 384/.068 19
HE7645 .B57 1987

Fiber optic telecommunications opportunities. Norwalk, Conn., U. S.A. (6 Prowitt St., Norwalk 06855) , c1986. viii, 205 leaves ; LC Card 87-129456 DDC 381/.456213692/0973 19
HD9696.F522 F5 1986

International telecommunications markets, production & trade /. New York, N.Y. , 1986.

317 p. : ISBN 0-935859-11-X (pbk.) LC Card 86-23052 DDC 338.7/62138 19
HD9696.T442 I578 1986

Poppel, Harvey L. Information technology . New York , c1987. xx, 207 p. : ISBN 0-07-050511-X : LC Card 86-27782 DDC 338.4/7004/0973 19
HD9696.C62 P623 1987

Voice compression technology . Stamford, Conn., U. S.A. , c1985. xii, 146 leaves ; ISBN 0-89336-430-4 (soft) LC Card 87-165256 DDC 380.1/45621389 19
HD9696.T442 V65 1985

Wideband communications services & equipment markets. Norwalk, Conn., U. S.A. (6 Prowitt St., Norwalk 06855) , c1986. iii, 198 leaves : LC Card 87-129548 DDC 384/.0973 19
HD9696.T442 W53 1986

TELECOMMUNICATION EQUIPMENT INDUSTRY - JAPAN.
Japanese penetration into the United States communications data processing and office equipment markets. New York, N.Y. , c1983. v, 308 p. ; LC Card 87-143908 DDC 381/.45004/0973 19
HD9696.D383 U635 1983

TELECOMMUNICATION EQUIPMENT INDUSTRY - QUÉBEC (PROVINCE)
Lapointe, Alain. Les industries québécoises de services télématiques . Montréal [1984] x, 305 p. : ISBN 2-551-06190-3 LC Card 84-230415 DDC 384/.09714 19
HE7818.Q4 L36 1984 ***NYPL [JLF 86-1397]***

TELECOMMUNICATION EQUIPMENT INDUSTRY - THAILAND.
Sētthaph Kānwāngphæn phatthanā khr [Bangkok] , 2524 [1981] 8, 80 leaves ; LC Card 82-920041
HD9696.T442 S47 1981

TELECOMMUNICATION EQUIPMENT INDUSTRY - UNITED STATES.
Consolidated data base . San Jose, Calif. (1290 Ridder Park Dr., San Jose 95131-2398) , c1986. ii, 94 p. ; LC Card 87-108611 DDC 381/.45004/0973
HD9696.C63 U515626 1986

Japanese penetration into the United States communications data processing and office equipment markets. New York, N.Y. , c1983. v, 308 p. ; LC Card 87-143908 DDC 381/.45004/0973 19
HD9696.D383 U635 1983

The Market for advanced business communications in the United States. New York, N.Y. , c1983. 2 v. (x, 365 leaves) : LC Card 87-144924 DDC 384/.041 19
HD9696.T443 U5465 1983

Telecommunications opportunities for colleges and universities /. McLean, Va. (1355 Beverly Rd., Suite 100, McLean 22101) , c1986. 208 p. ; LC Card 86-231086 DDC 384.6/3 19
HD9696.T443 U572 1986

TELECOMMUNICATION EQUIPMENT INDUSTRY - UNITED STATES - CONSOLIDATION.
Huber, Peter W. (Peter William), 1952- The geodesic network . Washington, D.C. , 1987. 1 v. (various pagings) : LC Card 87-601031 DDC 384/.041 19
HE8819 .H76 1987

TELECOMMUNICATION - EUROPE.
Tydeman, John. New media in Europe . London , New York , c1986. xii, 260 p. : ISBN 0-07-084799-1 : LC Card 85-19839 DDC 384.55/094 19
HE8700.9.E8 T93 1986
NYPL [JLE 86-3209]

TELECOMMUNICATION - FRANCE.
Darmon, Jacques. Le grand dérangement . [Paris] , c1985. 269 p. : LC Card 85-242541 DDC 384/.068 19
HE8144 .D37 1985 ***NYPL [JLE 87-363]***

TELECOMMUNICATION - FRANCE - NORD-PAS-DE-CALAIS - HISTORY - CONGRESSES.
Histoire de la poste et des télécommunications dans la région Nord-Pas-de-Calais . [Lille] , c1983. 156 p. : LC Card 86-115052
HE6986.N67 H57 1983

TELECOMMUNICATION - GERMANY, WEST.
Germany (West). Monopolkommission. Die Rolle der Deutschen Bundespost im Fernmeldewesen /. Baden-Baden , 1981. 110 p. ; ISBN 3-7890-0675-0(pbk.) LC Card 81-130348 DDC 383/.4943 19
HE8155 .R64 1981 ***NYPL [JLE 87-312]***

Knieps, Günter. Entstaatlichung im Telekommunikationsbereich . Tübingen , 1985. xi, 205 p. : ISBN 3-16-344955-7 LC Card 86-156485
HE8154 .K55 1985

TELECOMMUNICATION - GERMANY (WEST) - MANAGEMENT.
Detjen, Günther, 1930- Betriebswirtschaftslehre des Post- und Fernmeldewesens /. Gelsenkirchen-Buer , c1984-c1985. 2 v. : ISBN 3-87333-070-9 (Bd. 1) LC Card 87-104294 DDC 383/.4943 19
HE6995 .D37 1984

TELECOMMUNICATION - GERMANY (WEST) - RATES.
Die Gebührenpolitik der Deutschen Bundespost im Kleingut- und Fernmeldebereich . [Mainz] [1984?] xi, 300 p. ; LC Card 87-407592 DDC 383/.23/0943 19
HE6998 .G42 1984

Neumann, Karl-Heinz. Gebührenpolitik im Telekommunikationsbereich /. Baden-Baden , 1984. 348 p. : ISBN 3-7890-1049-9 : LC Card 86-166218
HE8157 .N48 1984

TELECOMMUNICATION - GREAT BRITAIN.
Newman, Karin. The selling of British Telecom /. London , New York , c1986. viii, 176 p. : ISBN 0-03-910639-X ***NYPL [JLF 86-853]***

TELECOMMUNICATION - INFORMATION SERVICES - UNITED STATES - DIRECTORIES.
How to find information about companies in the telecommunications, data processing, and office automation industries /. Washington, DC , c1987. ii, 130 p. ; ISBN 0-934940-48-7 (pbk.) LC Card 86-51630 DDC 338.7/61004/072073 19
HD9696.A3 U559 1987

TELECOMMUNICATION - ITALY.
Il Gigante nano . Torino , c1985. 382 p. : LC Card 86-128171 DDC 384.54/0945 19
HE8689.9.I8 G54 1985
NYPL [MWGK (Italy) 86-2853]

Pacifici, Giorgio. Il futuro presente . Milano, Italy , c1985. 201 p. ; LC Card 86-127322 DDC 384/.0945 19
HE8174 .P33 1985

TELECOMMUNICATION - JAPAN.
Salvaggio, Jerry Lee. The computer and telecommunications industry in Japan, 1986 /. Houston, Tex. , Arlington, Va. [c1986] 2 v. : LC Card 86-214521 DDC 338.4/7004/0952 19
HD9696.C63 J364 1986

TELECOMMUNICATION - JAPAN - DIRECTORIES.
Salvaggio, Jerry Lee. The computer and telecommunications industry in Japan, 1986 /. Houston, Tex. , Arlington, Va. [c1986] 2 v. : LC Card 86-214521 DDC 338.4/7004/0952 19
HD9696.C63 J364 1986

TELECOMMUNICATION - JURISPRUDENCE. see **TELECOMMUNICATION - LAW AND LEGISLATION.**

TELECOMMUNICATION - LAW AND LEGISLATION - GERMANY, WEST.
Knieps, Günter. Entstaatlichung im Telekommunikationsbereich . Tübingen , 1985. xi, 205 p. : ISBN 3-16-344955-7 LC Card 86-156485
HE8154 .K55 1985

TELECOMMUNICATION - LAW AND LEGISLATION - UNITED STATES.
Issues in international telecommunications policy . Washington, D.C. , c1983. xviii, 260 p. ; ISBN 0-9612072-0-5 (pbk.) LC Card 83-82231 DDC 343.73/0994 347.303994 19
KF2765 .I85 1983 ***NYPL [JLF 86-1125]***

Tunstall, Jeremy. Communications deregulation . Oxford, UK , New York, NY, USA , 1986. xi, 324 p. ; ISBN 0-631-14819-1 : LC Card 85-22983 DDC 343.73/0994 347.303994 19
KF2765 .T86 1986 ***NYPL [JLE 86-2991]***

TELECOMMUNICATION POLICY.
Blatherwick, David E. S. The international politics of telecommunications /. [Berkeley, Calif.] , c1987. ix, 107 p. ; ISBN 0-87725-168-1 (pbk.) : LC Card 87-3509 DDC 384/.068 19
HE7645 .B57 1987

Martin, James, 1933- The wired world . Carnforth, Lancashire, England , 1986. xiii, 140 p. : ISBN 0-906774-49-7 (pbk.) LC Card 87-157689 DDC 384 19
HE7631 .M373 1986

Snow, Marcellus S. Telecommunications . Amsterdam , New York , 1986. xvi, 304 p. : ISBN 0-444-87926-9 LC Card 86-224686 DDC 384/.041 19
HE7645 .S58 1986

Trends of change in telecommunications policy. Paris , Washington, D.C. , 1987. 353 p. : ISBN 92-64-12940-5 (pbk.) : LC Card 87-163585 DDC 384/.068 19
HE7645 .T74 1987

TELECOMMUNICATION POLICY - ADDRESSES, ESSAYS, LECTURES.
Telecommunications . Dedham, MA , c1984. xxii, 687 p. : ISBN 0-89006-140-8 LC Card 84-70225 DDC 384 19
HE7631 .T443 1984 ***NYPL [JLE 86-1167]***

TELECOMMUNICATION POLICY - AFRICA.
Plan général de développement du réseau régional en Afrique =. Genève , 1983. 134 p. : ISBN 92-71-02066-9 LC Card 85-146412
HE8465 .P54 1983

United Nations transport and communications decade in Africa (1978-1988) . [S.l.] [1983?] iii, 32 p. ; LC Card 87-115721 DDC 380.3/096 19
HE8465 .U55 1983

TELECOMMUNICATION POLICY - ALBERTA.
W.J. Page & Associates. Telecommunications in Northern Alberta /. [Edmonton, Alta. , 1986?] 39, [96] p. : LC Card 86-235313 DDC 384/.068 19
HE7819.A43 W15 1986

TELECOMMUNICATION POLICY - AUSTRALIA.
Albon, Robert, 1951- The Telecom monopoly . Perth, W.A. , 1986. 56 p. : ISBN 0-949186-10-4 (pbk.) : LC Card 86-213521 DDC 384/.0994 19
HE8540.T44 A42 1986

TELECOMMUNICATION POLICY - COLOMBIA.
Colombia. Ministerio de Comunicaciones. Una revolución en las comunicaciones . [Bogotá] 1986. 307 p., [5] leaves of plates : LC Card 87-401464 DDC 384/.09861 19
HE8011 .C65 1986

TELECOMMUNICATION POLICY - FRANCE.
Darmon, Jacques. Le grand dérangement . [Paris] , c1985. 269 p. : LC Card 85-242541 DDC 384/.068 19
HE8144 .D37 1985 ***NYPL [JLE 87-363]***

TELECOMMUNICATION POLICY - GERMANY (WEST)
Neumann, Karl-Heinz. Gebührenpolitik im Telekommunikationsbereich /. Baden-Baden , 1984. 348 p. : ISBN 3-7890-1049-9 : LC Card 86-166218
HE8157 .N48 1984

TELECOMMUNICATION POLICY - LATIN AMERICA.
Sauvant, Karl P. Trade and foreign direct investment in data services /. Boulder Colo. , 1986. xv, 223 p. : ISBN 0-8133-7085-X : LC Card 85-22701 DDC 332.6/712 19
HD9696.C63 L387 1986
NYPL [JLD 86-3043]

TELECOMMUNICATION POLICY - NEW ZEALAND.
Royal Commission on Broadcasting and Related Telecommunications in New Zealand. Broadcasting and related telecommunications in New Zealand . Wellington, N.Z. [1986] 518 p. : LC Card 87-130605 DDC 384/.068 19
HE8620.5.Z5 R69 1986

TELECOMMUNICATION POLICY - UNITED STATES.
Tunstall, Jeremy. Communications deregulation . Oxford, UK , New York, NY, USA , 1986. xi, 324 p. ; ISBN 0-631-14819-1 : LC Card 85-22983 DDC 343.73/0994 347.303994 19
KF2765 .T86 1986 NYPL [JLE 86-2991]

Wenders, John T. The economics of telecommunications . Cambridge, Mass. , c1987. x, 284 p. : ISBN 0-88730-119-3 LC Card 86-17280 DDC 384/.041/0973 19
HE7787 .W47 1986 NYPL [JLE 87-1593]

TELECOMMUNICATION POLICY - WASHINGTON (STATE)
Washington (State). Governor's Citizens Utility and Telecommunication Advisory Committee. Utilities in transition . [Olympia, Wash.] [1984] 61, 18, [20] p. ; LC Card 85-622797 DDC 363.6/09797 19
HE7791.W2 W37 1984 NYPL [JLF 86-1773]

TELECOMMUNICATION - QUÉBEC (PROVINCE)
Lapointe, Alain. Les industries québécoises de services télématiques . Montréal [1984] x, 305 p. : ISBN 2-551-06190-3 LC Card 84-230415 DDC 384/.09714 19
HE7818.Q4 L36 1984 NYPL [JLF 86-1397]

TELECOMMUNICATION - QUÉBEC (PROVINCE) - CONGRESSES.
Conférence sur les communications (1983 : Montréal, Québec) La Conférence sur les communications . [Québec] [1984] ix, 489 p. ; ISBN 2-551-06176-8 LC Card 85-103400
HE7818.Q4 C46 1983

TELECOMMUNICATION - SOCIAL ASPECTS - GERMANY (WEST)
Mettler-Meibom, Barbara E. Breitbandtechnologie . Opladen , c1986. xxiv, 477, [60] p. : ISBN 3-531-11782-3 LC Card 86-184911
HE8154 .M47 1986

TELECOMMUNICATION - SOCIAL ASPECTS - ITALY.
Pacifici, Giorgio. Il futuro presente . Milano, Italy , c1985. 201 p. ; LC Card 86-127322 DDC 384/.0945 19
HE8174 .P33 1985

TELECOMMUNICATION SWITCHING SYSTEMS EQUIPMENT INDUSTRY - UNITED STATES.
A Competitive assessment of the U. S. digital central office switch industry /. Washington, D.C. , 1986. xv, 106 p. : LC Card 86-603064 DDC 382/.456321387 19
HD9696.T443 U5225 1986

The Digital telecommunications market. New York, N.Y. , c1983. 2 v. (vii, 269 leaves) : LC Card 87-143942 DDC 384 19
HD9697.T453 U525 1983

Packet switching equipment markets /. Stamford, Conn., U. S.A. , c1985. v, 205 leaves : ISBN 0-89336-465-7 (pbk.) LC Card 87-403884 DDC 381/.456213878 19
HD9696.T443 U556 1985

TELECOMMUNICATION SWTICHING SYSTEMS EQUIPMENT INDUSTRY - EUROPE.
The Military tactical communications switching network market in West Europe. New York, N.Y. , c1983. xvi, 232 p. ; LC Card 87-141849
HD9744.C653 E854 1983

TELECOMMUNICATION SYSTEMS.
Business guide to communications systems /. London , 1987. x, 230 p. : ISBN 0-273-02671-2 (pbk.) : LC Card 87-147021 DDC 651.7 19
HD30.335 .B85 1987

Grover, Kenneth C. Foundations of business telecommunications management /. New York , c1986. xvi, 196 p. ; ISBN 0-306-42249-2 (pbk.) LC Card 86-5063 DDC 384 19
HF5541.T4 G76 1986 NYPL [JLE 86-3270]

Heldman, Robert K. Telecommunications management planning . Blue Ridge Summit, PA , c1987. xviii, 734 p. : ISBN 0-8306-2864-9 : LC Card 86-30002 DDC 658.4/038 19
HD30.335 .H45 1987

Vignault, Walter L. Worldwide telecommunications guide for the business manager /. New York , c1987. xvi, 417 p. : ISBN 0-471-85828-5 LC Card 87-2002 DDC 384 19
HF5541.T4 V54 1987

TELECOMMUNICATION SYSTEMS - ADDRESSES, ESSAYS, LECTURES.
Telecommunications . Dedham, MA , c1984. xxii, 687 p. : ISBN 0-89006-140-8 LC Card 84-70225 DDC 384 19
HE7631 .T443 1984 NYPL [JLE 86-1167]

TELECOMMUNICATION SYSTEMS - UNITED STATES.
New RHC strategies /. Boston, MA (200 Portland St., Boston 02114) , c1987. iii, 117 p. ; LC Card 87-147694 DDC 384.6/065/73 19
HE8846.A55 N497 1987

TELECOMMUNICATION - UNITED STATES.
Beyond private lines . Boston, MA (200 Portland St., Boston 02114) , c1987. iv, 117 p. : LC Card 87-144067 DDC 384.3/0973 19
HE7775 .B46 1987

Chronicles of corporate change . Lexington, Mass. , c1987. xiv, 254 p. : ISBN 0-669-13685-9 (alk. paper) LC Card 86-45555 DDC 384.6/065/73 19
HE8846.A55 C47 1987

The Enhanced data network (van) market. New York, N.Y. , c1983. v, 258 p. : LC Card 87-143825
HD9696.D383 U6344 1983

Faulhaber, Gerald R. Telecommunications in turmoil . Cambridge, Mass. , c1987. xviii, 186 p. ; ISBN 0-88730-157-6 LC Card 87-1377 DDC 384/.068 19
HE8846.A55 F38 1987

Huber, Peter W. (Peter William), 1952- The geodesic network . Washington, D.C. , 1987. 1 v. (various pagings) : LC Card 87-601031 DDC 384/.041 19
HE8819 .H76 1987

Industry basics . Washington, D.C. (2000 M St., N.W., Suite 550, Washington 20036) , c1986. 53 p. : LC Card 86-208618 DDC 384.6/0973 19
HE8731 .I53 1986

The Market for advanced business communications in the United States. New York, N.Y. , c1983. 2 v. (x, 365 leaves) : LC Card 87-144924 DDC 384/.041 19
HD9696.T443 U5465 1983

TELECOMMUNICATION - UNITED STATES - APPARATUS AND SUPPLIES - MARKETING.
Telecommunications opportunities for colleges and universities /. McLean, Va. (1355 Beverly Rd., Suite 100, McLean 22101) , c1986. 208 p. ; LC Card 86-231086 DDC 384.6/3 19
HD9696.T443 U572 1986

TELECOMMUNICATION - UNITED STATES - RATES.
Wenders, John T. The economics of telecommunications . Cambridge, Mass. , c1987. x, 284 p. : ISBN 0-88730-119-3 LC Card 86-17280 DDC 384/.041/0973 19
HE7787 .W47 1986 NYPL [JLE 87-1593]

Telecommunications : an interdisciplinary text / edited by Leonard Lewin. Dedham, MA : Artech House, c1984. xxii, 687 p. : ill. ; 24 cm. Rev. and expanded edition of: Telecommunications, an interdisciplinary survey. c1979. Includes bibliographies and index. ISBN 0-89006-140-8 LC Card 84-70225 DDC 384 19
1. Telecommunication - Addresses, essays, lectures. 2. Telecommunication policy - Addresses, essays, lectures. 3. Telecommunication systems - Addresses, essays, lectures. I. Lewin, Leonard, 1919-. II. Telecommunications, an interdisciplinary survey.
HE7631 .T443 1984 NYPL [JLE 86-1167]

Telecommunications . Snow, Marcellus S. Amsterdam , New York , 1986. xvi, 304 p. : ISBN 0-444-87926-9 LC Card 86-224686 DDC 384/.041 19
HE7645 .S58 1986

Telecommunications, an interdisciplinary survey. Telecommunications . Dedham, MA , c1984. xxii, 687 p. : ISBN 0-89006-140-8 LC Card 84-70225 DDC 384 19
HE7631 .T443 1984 NYPL [JLE 86-1167]

TELECOMMUNICATIONS - CONGRESSES.
NTG-Fachtagung (1986 : Nuremberg, Germany) Von der Nachrichtentechnik zur Informationstechnik . Berlin , c1986. 104 p. : ISBN 3-8007-1485-X LC Card 87-136748 DDC 384 19
HE7604 .N74 1986

Telecommunications in Northern Alberta /. W.J. Page & Associates. [Edmonton, Alta. , 1986?] 39, [96] p. : LC Card 86-235313 DDC 384/.068 19
HE7819.A43 W15 1986

Telecommunications in turmoil . Faulhaber, Gerald R. Cambridge, Mass. , c1987. xviii, 186 p. ; ISBN 0-88730-157-6 LC Card 87-1377 DDC 384/.068 19
HE8846.A55 F38 1987

Telecommunications management planning . Heldman, Robert K. Blue Ridge Summit, PA , c1987. xviii, 734 p. : ISBN 0-8306-2864-9 : LC Card 86-30002 DDC 658.4/038 19
HD30.335 .H45 1987

Telecommunications opportunities for colleges and universities / Arvind D. Bhandari, editor ; Alan Pearce, contributing editor, Mark L. Wolsky, contributing editor. McLean, Va. (1355 Beverly Rd., Suite 100, McLean 22101) : TeleStrategies Pub., c1986. 208 p. ; 28 cm. LC Card 86-231086 DDC 384.6/3 19
1. Telecommunication equipment industry - United States. 2. Telecommunication - United States - Apparatus and supplies - Marketing. 3. Telephone supplies industry - United States. 4. Telephone - United States - Equipment and supplies - Marketing. 5. College students as consumers - United States. 6. Universities and colleges - United States - Communication systems. 7. Market surveys - United States. I. Bhandari, Arvind D. II. Pearce, Alan. III. Wolsky, Mark L. IV. Telestrategies Publishing (McLean, Va.).
HD9696.T443 U572 1986

TELECOMMUTING - GERMANY (WEST)
Schwohnke, Andreas. Teleheimarbeit als neue Rationalisierungsstrategie . Köln , 1986. vii, 237, [14] p. : ISBN 3-7609-5220-8 LC Card 86-224163
HD2336.G3 S38 1986

TELECONFERENCING.
Rogers, Everett M. Communication technology . New York , London , c1986. xii, 273 p. : ISBN 0-02-927110-X LC Card 85-27555 DDC 621.38 19
TK5102.5 .R55 1986 NYPL [JSE 86-1913]

TELECONFERENCING EQUIPMENT INDUSTRY - UNITED STATES.
The Market for advanced business communications in the United States. New York, N.Y. , c1983. 2 v. (x, 365 leaves) : LC Card 87-144924 DDC 384/.041 19
HD9696.T443 U5465 1983

The Teleconferencing market. New York, N.Y. (106 Fulton St., New York 10038) , c1983. 288 p. : LC Card 87-143433
HD9696.T443 U574 1983

The Teleconferencing market. New York, N.Y. (106 Fulton St., New York 10038) : Frost & Sullivan, c1983. 288 p. : ill. ; 29 cm. Spine title: Teleconferencing market in the U. S. "September 1983." "#1112." LC Card 87-143433
1. Teleconferencing equipment industry - United States. 2. Market surveys - United States. I. Frost & Sulivan. II. Title: Teleconferencing market in the U. S.
HD9696.T443 U574 1983

Teleconferencing market in the U. S. The Teleconferencing market. New York, N.Y. (106 Fulton St., New York 10038) , c1983. 288 p. : LC Card 87-143433
HD9696.T443 U574 1983

TELEFACSIMILE. see FACSIMILE TRANSMISSION.

TELEFAX. see FACSIMILE TRANSMISSION.

TELEGRAMS. see TELEGRAPH.

TELEGRAPH CODE ADDRESSES - DIRECTORIES.
Catálogo de tarifas postales y telegráficas. Madrid [1964?] 256, [42] p. : LC Card 85-106223
HE8277 .C37 1964

TELEGRAPH - SPAIN - RATES.
Catálogo de tarifas postales y telegráficas. Madrid [1964?] 256, [42] p. : LC Card 85-106223
HE8277 .C37 1964

TELEGRAPHERS - UNITED STATES - HISTORY - 19TH CENTURY.
Gabler, Edwin, 1949- The American telegrapher . New Brunswick, NJ , c1988. p. cm. ISBN 0-8135-1284-0 : LC Card 87-19878 DDC 331.89/2813841/0973 19
HD5325 .T252 1883

Telemarketing : a business start-up manual. [S.l.] : National Telemarketing Center, c1987. [64] p. ; 28 cm. LC Card 87-154058 DDC 658.8/5 19
1. Telemarketing. I. National Telemarketing Center.
HF5415.1265 .T44 1987

TELEMARKETING.
Bencin, Richard L., 1935- Strategic telemarketing . Philadelphia, Pa., USA , c1987. xviii, 182 p. : ISBN 0-915601-02-8 LC Card 86-30057 DDC 658.8/5 19
HF5415.1265 .B46 1987

Fidel, Stanley Leo. Start up telemarketing . New York , c1987. xiv, 287 p. : ISBN 0-471-01064-2 LC Card 87-21610 DDC 658.8/5 19
HF5415.1265 .F53 1987

Goodman, Gary S. [Breakthroughs in telemarketing.] Gary Goodman's breakthroughs in telemarketing /. New York , c1987. ix, 148 p. ; ISBN 0-13-346891-7 (pbk.) : LC Card 86-43170 DDC 658.8/5 19
HF5415.1265 .G66 1987

Grossman, Ann. The marketer's guide to media vehicles, methods, and options . New York , 1987. xiv, 238 p. : ISBN 0-89930-266-1 (lib. bdg. : alk. paper) LC Card 87-2473 DDC 659.1 19
HF5826.5 .G76 1987

Heldman, Robert K. Telecommunications management planning . Blue Ridge Summit, PA , c1987. xviii, 734 p. : ISBN 0-8306-2864-9 : LC Card 86-30002 DDC 658.4/038 19
HD30.335 .H45 1987

An Introduction to communication on the telephone [videorecording] /. Del Mar, CA , 1987. 1 videocassette (7 min.) : LC Card 87-700082 DDC 658.8 11
HF5415.1265

McCafferty, Thomas. In-house t-e-l-e marketing . Chicago, Ill. , c1987. x, 337 p. : ISBN 0-917253-51-5 (pbk.) LC Card 86-63991 DDC 658.8/5 19
HF5415.1265 .M34 1987

McHatton, Robert J. Total telemarketing /. New York , c1988. x, 246 p. : ISBN 0-471-62755-0 (pbk.) : LC Card 87-21547 DDC 658.8/5 19
HF5415.1265 .M38 1988

Questions and recommendations on the telephone [videorecording] /. Del Mar, CA , 1987. 1 videocassette (13 min.) : LC Card 87-700084 DDC 658.8 11
HF5415.1265

Telemarketing . [S.l.] , c1987. [64] p. ; LC Card 87-154058 DDC 658.8/5 19
HF5415.1265 .T44 1987

TELEMARKETING - DATA PROCESSING.
How to buy an automated sales, marketing, and telemarketing system. Los Gatos, CA , c1985. 46 p. : LC Card 86-224565 DDC 658.8/0028/5 19
HF5415.1265 .H68 1985

TELEMARKETING - MANAGEMENT.
Ford, Wayne, 1944- Telemarketing management for business /. Walnut Creek, Calif. , c1987. 125 p. ; ISBN 0-943995-01-9 (pbk.) LC Card 87-18050 DDC 658.8/5 19
HF5415.1265 .F67 1987

McCafferty, Thomas. In-house t-e-l-e marketing . Chicago, Ill. , c1987. x, 337 p. : ISBN 0-917253-51-5 (pbk.) LC Card 86-63991 DDC 658.8/5 19
HF5415.1265 .M34 1987

Telemarketing management for business /. Ford, Wayne, 1944- Walnut Creek, Calif. , c1987. 125 p. ; ISBN 0-943995-01-9 (pbk.) LC Card 87-18050 DDC 658.8/5 19
HF5415.1265 .F67 1987

TELEMARKETING - UNITED STATES.
Sutton, Howard, 1930- Rethinking the company's selling and distribution channels /. New York, N.Y. , c1986. v, 26 p. : ISBN 0-8237-0328-2 (pbk.) LC Card 87-404502 DDC 658.8/4 19
HF5415.129 .S87 1986

Wallis, Louis A. Computers and the sales effort . New York, N.Y. , c1986. v, 26 p. : ISBN 0-8237-0326-6 (pbk.) LC Card 87-404503 DDC 658.8/1/00285416 19
HF5438.35 .W35 1986

Telematica . Glücksmann, Riccardo. Milano , 1982. xii, 273 p., [4] p. of plates : ISBN 88-7056-120-8 LC Card 84-184344
HD9696.D383 I84 1982

TELEPHONE.
Industry basics . Washington, D.C. (2000 M St., N.W., Suite 550, Washington 20036) , c1986. 53 p. : LC Card 86-208618 DDC 384.6/0973 19
HE8731 .I53 1986

TELEPHONE - CALIFORNIA.
California. Public Utilities Commission. Report to the Legislature . [San Francisco] [1984] 40 leaves ; LC Card 86-622236 DDC 384.6/09794 19
HE8840.C2 C35 1984

Telephone call accounting market in the U. S.
The Call accounting market in the United States. New York, N.Y. , c1983. x, 275 p. : LC Card 87-143500 DDC 381/.45621387 19
HD9697.T453 U522 1983

TELEPHONE - DIRECTORIES - YELLOW PAGES.
Berdie, Douglas R. The Yellow Pages report . St. Paul, Minn. (905 Raymond Ave., St. Paul 55114) , c1986. 109 p. ; LC Card 86-209709 DDC 659.13/2 19
HF6146.T4 B45 1986

Wagner, W. F., 1944- Advertising in the yellow pages . Los Angeles, CA , c1986. viii, 174 p. : ISBN 0-940969-00-9 (pbk.) : LC Card 86-83085 DDC 659.13/2 19
HF6146.T4 W34 1986

TELEPHONE ETIQUETTE.
An Introduction to communication on the telephone [videorecording] /. Del Mar, CA , 1987. 1 videocassette (7 min.) : LC Card 87-700082 DDC 658.8 11
HF5415.1265

Klein, Jean H., 1938- The phone book . Norfolk , c1987. p. cm. ISBN 0-89865-542-0 (pbk.) : LC Card 87-20897 DDC 651.7/3 19
HF5541.T4 K56 1987

Lapp, Robert. Developing effective telephone skills /. Eau Claire, WI , c1987. 56 p. : ISBN 0-941161-20-X (pbk.) LC Card 87-403090 DDC 651.7/3 19
HF5541.T4 L36 1987

Questions and recommendations on the telephone [videorecording] /. Del Mar, CA , 1987. 1 videocassette (13 min.) : LC Card 87-700084 DDC 658.8 11
HF5415.1265

Winston, Arthur. Complete guide to tested telephone collection techniques /. Englewood Cliffs, N.J. , c1988. p. cm. ISBN 0-13-160185-7 : LC Card 87-22321 DDC 658.8/8 19
HG3752.7.U6 W56 1988

TELEPHONE - GERMANY (WEST) - RATES.
Neumann, Karl-Heinz. Gebührenpolitik im Telekommunikationsbereich /. Baden-Baden , 1984. 348 p. : ISBN 3-7890-1049-9 : LC Card 86-166218
HE8157 .N48 1984

TELEPHONE - GOVERNMENT POLICY - CALIFORNIA.
California. Public Utilities Commission. Report to the Legislature . [San Francisco] [1984] 40 leaves ; LC Card 86-622236 DDC 384.6/09794 19
HE8840.C2 C35 1984

TELEPHONE IN BUSINESS.
Dordick, Herbert S., 1925- Innovative management using telecommunications . New York , c1986. x, 226 p. : ISBN 0-471-81296-X : LC Card 86-7797 DDC 658.4/5 19
HF5541.T4 D67 1986 ***NYPL [JLE 86-4425]***

Grover, Kenneth C. Foundations of business telecommunications management /. New York , c1986. xvi, 196 p. ; ISBN 0-306-42249-2 (pbk.) LC Card 86-5063 DDC 384 19
HF5541.T4 G76 1986 ***NYPL [JLE 86-3270]***

Klein, Jean H., 1938- The phone book . Norfolk , c1987. p. cm. ISBN 0-89865-542-0 (pbk.) : LC Card 87-20897 DDC 651.7/3 19
HF5541.T4 K56 1987

Lapp, Robert. Developing effective telephone skills /. Eau Claire, WI , c1987. 56 p. : ISBN 0-941161-20-X (pbk.) LC Card 87-403090 DDC 651.7/3 19
HF5541.T4 L36 1987

Parker, Martin F. The practical guide to voice mail /. Berkeley, Calif. , c1987. xiv, 306 p. : ISBN 0-07-881243-7 (pbk.) LC Card 86-210772 DDC 621.385 19
HF5541.T4 P37 1987

Using new communications technologies . Washington, D.C. , c1986. ix, 57 p. : ISBN 0-937790-30-3 (pbk.) : LC Card 85-63320 DDC 384 19
HF5541.T4 U75 1986

Vignault, Walter L. Worldwide telecommunications guide for the business manager /. New York , c1987. xvi, 417 p. : ISBN 0-471-85828-5 LC Card 87-2002 DDC 384 19
HF5541.T4 V54 1987

Winston, Arthur. Complete guide to tested telephone collection techniques /. Englewood Cliffs, N.J. , c1988. p. cm. ISBN 0-13-160185-7 : LC Card 87-22321 DDC 658.8/8 19
HG3752.7.U6 W56 1988

TELEPHONE - LONG DISTANCE - UNITED STATES.
Fiber optics after long distance /. Boston, Mass. (89 Broad St., Boston 02110) , c1986. vii, 114 p. : LC Card 86-220473 DDC 381/.456213692/0973 19
HD9696.F523 U5429 1986

TELEPHONE - MULTIPLEX SYSTEMS.
T-1 products & services. Norwalk, Conn., U. S.A. (6 Prowitt St., Norwalk 06855) , c1987. iv, 181 leaves : LC Card 87-129537 DDC 384.6/5 19
HD9697.T452 T17 1987

TELEPHONE - NEW JERSEY - EMERGENCY REPORTING SYSTEMS.
New Jersey. Legislature. Emergency Response System Study Commission. Public hearing before Emergency Response System Study Commission on implementation of a statewide enhanced 911 service . [Trenton, N.J.] [1986] 49 p. ; LC Card 87-621252 DDC 384.6/42 19
HE8840.N5 N48 1986

TELEPHONE - NORTHEASTERN STATES - RATES.
Yankee Group white paper communications systems & services . Boston, Mass. (200 Portland St., Boston 02114) , 1987. 51 leaves : LC Card 87-155249 DDC 384.6/3 19
HE8825 .Y36 1987

TELEPHONE - SPAIN.
Spain and the telephone . New York , 1925. 16 p., [1] folded leaf of plates : LC Card 85-666351
HE9324 .S63x 1925

TELEPHONE SUPPLIES INDUSTRY.
International telecommunications markets, production & trade /. New York, N.Y. , 1986. 317 p. : ISBN 0-935859-11-X (pbk.) LC Card 86-23052 DDC 338.7/62138 19
HD9696.T442 I578 1986

Optical fiber in the local loop. Norwalk, Conn. (6 Prowitt St., Norwalk 06855) , c1986. iv, 208 leaves : LC Card 87-127281 DDC 381/.456213692/0973 19
HD9696.F522 O67 1986

T-1 products & services. Norwalk, Conn., U. S.A. (6 Prowitt St., Norwalk 06855) , c1987. iv, 181 leaves : LC Card 87-129537 DDC 384.6/5 19
HD9697.T452 T17 1987

TELEPHONE SUPPLIES INDUSTRY - UNITED STATES.
The Call accounting market in the United States. New York, N.Y. , c1983. x, 275 p. : LC Card 87-143500 DDC 381/.45621387 19
HD9697.T453 U522 1983

The Digital telecommunications market. New York, N.Y. , c1983. 2 v. (vii, 269 leaves) : LC Card 87-143942 DDC 384 19
HD9697.T453 U525 1983

The Market for advanced business communications in the United States. New York, N.Y. , c1983. 2 v. (x, 365 leaves) : LC

Card 87-144924 DDC 384/.041 19
HD9696.T443 U5465 1983

Payphone magazine (formerly Private payphone news) presents the Payphone magazine reference guide. Houston, Tex. (P.O. Box 42371, Houston 77042) , c1986. 1 v. (loose-leaf) ; LC Card 87-112738 DDC 338.4/7621386 19
HD9697.T453 U557 1986

Telecommunications opportunities for colleges and universities /. McLean, Va. (1355 Beverly Rd., Suite 100, McLean 22101) , c1986. 208 p. ; LC Card 86-231086 DDC 384.6/3 19
HD9696.T443 U572 1986

TELEPHONE SYSTEMS.
Huber, Peter W. (Peter William), 1952- The geodesic network . Washington, D.C. , 1987. 1 v. (various pagings) : LC Card 87-601031 DDC 384/.041 19
HE8819 .H76 1987

TELEPHONE - UNITED STATES.
Beyond private lines . Boston, MA (200 Portland St., Boston 02114) , c1987. iv, 117 p. : LC Card 87-144067 DDC 384.3/0973 19
HE7775 .B46 1987

Chronicles of corporate change . Lexington, Mass. , c1987. xiv, 254 p. : ISBN 0-669-13685-9 (alk. paper) LC Card 86-45555 DDC 384.6/065/73 19
HE8846.A55 C47 1987

Faulhaber, Gerald R. Telecommunications in turmoil . Cambridge, Mass. , c1987. xviii, 186 p. ; ISBN 0-88730-157-6 LC Card 87-1377 DDC 384/.068 19
HE8846.A55 F38 1987

Industry basics . Washington, D.C. (2000 M St., N.W., Suite 550, Washington 20036) , c1986. 53 p. : LC Card 86-208618 DDC 384.6/0973 19
HE8731 .I53 1986

Integrated voice/data PBXs /. Boston, MA (200 Portland St., Boston 02114) , c1987. iv, 102 p. : LC Card 87-402843 DDC 381/.45621385 19
HE8817 .I57 1987

Leibowitz, Dennis. The cellular communications industry /. New York, N.Y. (140 Broadway, New York 10005) , c1985. ii, 67 p. : LC Card 86-201572 DDC 384.5/33/0973 19
HD9696.R363 U65 1985

New RHC strategies /. Boston, MA (200 Portland St., Boston 02114) , c1987. iii, 117 p. ; LC Card 87-147694 DDC 384.6/065/73 19
HE8846.A55 N497 1987

Payphone magazine (formerly Private payphone news) presents the Payphone magazine reference guide. Houston, Tex. (P.O. Box 42371, Houston 77042) , c1986. 1 v. (loose-leaf) ; LC Card 87-112738 DDC 338.4/7621386 19
HD9697.T453 U557 1986

TELEPHONE - UNITED STATES - ACCOUNTING - EQUIPMENT AND SUPPLIES.
The Call accounting market in the United States. New York, N.Y. , c1983. x, 275 p. : LC Card 87-143500 DDC 381/.45621387 19
HD9697.T453 U522 1983

TELEPHONE - UNITED STATES - CONSOLIDATION.
Huber, Peter W. (Peter William), 1952- The geodesic network . Washington, D.C. , 1987. 1 v. (various pagings) : LC Card 87-601031 DDC 384/.041 19
HE8819 .H76 1987

TELEPHONE - UNITED STATES - EQUIPMENT AND SUPPLIES - MARKETING.
Telecommunications opportunities for colleges and universities /. McLean, Va. (1355 Beverly Rd., Suite 100, McLean 22101) , c1986. 208 p. ; LC Card 86-231086 DDC 384.6/3 19
HD9696.T443 U572 1986

TELEPHONE - UNITED STATES - HISTORY.
Coll, Steve. The deal of the century . New York , 1988, c1986. xv, 400 p. : ISBN 0-671-64592-7 (pbk.) : LC Card 87-23410 DDC 384.6/065/73 19
HE8846.A55 C58 1988

Temin, Peter. The fall of the Bell system . Cambridge , New York , 1987. xviii, 378 p. : ISBN 0-521-34557-X LC Card 87-10293 DDC 384.6/065/73 19
HE8846.A55 T44 1987

Weinhaus, Carol L. Behind the telephone debates /. Norwood, N.J. , 1987. p. cm. ISBN 0-89391-452-5 LC Card 87-19459 DDC 384.6/0973 19
HE8815 .W45 1987

TELEPHONE - UNITED STATES - LONG DISTANCE - HISTORY.
Kahaner, Larry. On the line . New York, NY , 1987, c1986. 344 p., [8] p. of plates : ISBN 0-446-38550-6 (pbk.) LC Card 87-10561 DDC 384.6/065/73 19
HE8846.M375 K34 1987

TELEPHONE - UNITED STATES - MULTIPLEX SYSTEMS.
Beyond private lines . Boston, MA (200 Portland St., Boston 02114) , c1987. iv, 117 p. : LC Card 87-144067 DDC 384.3/0973 19
HE7775 .B46 1987

TELEPHONE - UNITED STATES - PRIVATE BRANCH EXCHANGES.
Integrated voice/data PBXs /. Boston, MA (200 Portland St., Boston 02114) , c1987. iv, 102 p. : LC Card 87-402843 DDC 381/.45621385 19
HE8817 .I57 1987

TELEPHONE - UNITED STATES - RATES.
Sweet, David C. Public utilities and the poor . New York , 1987. xxiii, 174 p. : ISBN 0-275-92572-2 (alk. paper) : LC Card 87-6979 DDC 362.5/82 19
HC110.P6 S894 1987

Wenders, John T. The economics of telecommunications . Cambridge, Mass. , c1987. x, 284 p. : ISBN 0-88730-119-3 LC Card 86-17280 DDC 384/.041/0973 19
HE7787 .W47 1986 ***NYPL [JLE 87-1593]***

TELEPHONE - UNITED STATES - RATES - PEAK-LOAD PRICING - MATHEMATICAL MODELS.
Park, Rolla Edward. Optimal peak-load pricing for local telephone calls /. Santa Monica, CA , 1986. xiii, 37 p. : ISBN 0-8330-0741-6 (pbk.) LC Card 86-204468 DDC 384.6/3 19
HE8825 .P369 1986

Park, Rolla Edward. Optimal peak-load pricing for local telephone calls . Santa Monica, CA , c1986. x, 72 p. : ISBN 0-8330-0747-5 (pbk.) LC Card 86-203146 DDC 384.6/3 19
HE8825 .P369 1986 Suppl.

Park, Rolla Edward. Optimal peak-load pricing for local telephone calls . Santa Monica, CA , c1987. x, 75 p. : ISBN 0-8330-0857-9 (pbk.) LC Card 87-154411 DDC 384.6/3 19
HE8825 .P37 1987

Park, Rolla Edward. Optimal peak-load pricing for local telephone calls /. Santa Monica, CA , c1987. xiii, 41 p. : ISBN 0-8330-0856-X (pbk.) LC Card 87-410013 DDC 384.6/3 19
HE8825 .P369 1987

TELEPHONING. see **TELEPHONE ETIQUETTE.**

TELEPROCESSING NETWORKS. see **COMPUTER NETWORKS.**

Telestrategies Publishing (McLean, Va.)
Telecommunications opportunities for colleges and universities /. McLean, Va. (1355 Beverly Rd., Suite 100, McLean 22101) , c1986. 208 p. ; LC Card 86-231086 DDC 384.6/3 19
HD9696.T443 U572 1986

TELETEXT SYSTEMS.
Alber, Antone F. Videotex/teletext . New York , c1985. xiii, 498 p., [4] p. of plates : ISBN 0-07-000957-0 : LC Card 84-23319 DDC 384 19
TK5105 .A42 1985 ***NYPL [JSE 86-1907]***

TELETEXT SYSTEMS - GERMANY (WEST)
Schubert, Frank. Akzeptanz von Bildschirmtext in Unternehmungen und im Markt . Münster , c1986. xxiv, 316 p. : ISBN 3-7923-0546-1 LC Card 86-227074
HD9696.T463 G37 1986

A Televisão em Portugal. [Lisbon] : Instituto Progresso Social e Democracia Francisco Sá Carneiro, [1985] 95 p. : ill. ; 23 cm. (Portugal--desafios e soluções . 5) LC Card 87-102704 DDC 384.55/4/09469 19
1. Television broadcasting - Portugal - Congresses. I. Instituto Progresso Social e Democracia Francisco Sá Carneiro. II. Series.
HE8700.9.P8 T45 1985

Televisió, federalisme. Barcelona : Diputació de Barcelona, Institut de Ciències Socials, [1986] 209 p. ; 24 cm. (Quaderns de ciències socials . núm. 7-1986) Text in Spanish. Includes bibliographies. LC Card 86-210066
1. Television broadcasting - Spain. 2. Public relations - Spain. I. Instituto de Ciencias Sociales (Barcelona, Spain). II. Title: Federalisme. III. Series: Quaderns de ciències socials , núm. 1986-7.
HE8700.9.S63 T44 1986

TELEVISION ADAPTATIONS.
Gebrewold, Kiflemariam. Fernsehexport der Bundesrepublik Deutschland . Bochum , 1983. xiv, 316 p. : ISBN 3-88339-317-7 LC Card 83-232957
HE8700.66.G3 G43 1983

TELEVISION ADVERTISING - EUROPE.
Tydeman, John. New media in Europe . London , New York , c1986. xii, 260 p. : ISBN 0-07-084799-1 : LC Card 85-19839 DDC 384.55/094 19
HE8700.9.E8 T93 1986
NYPL [JLE 86-3209]

TELEVISION ADVERTISING - GREAT BRITAIN - HISTORY.
British television advertising . London , 1986. 528 p., xxxii p. of plates : ISBN 0-09-165800-4 : LC Card 87-120167 DDC 659.14/3/0941 19
HF6146.T42 B675 1986

TELEVISION ADVERTISING - RESEARCH - UNITED STATES - TECHNOLOGICAL INNOVATIONS - CONGRESSES.
Advertising Research Foundation Key Issues Workshop (1985 : New York, N.Y.) Transcript proceedings . New York, NY (3 E. 54th St., New York 10022-3180) , c1985. 174 p. : LC Card 86-214476 DDC 659.14/3/0973 19
HF6146.T42 A27 1985a

Advertising Research Foundation Key Issues Workshop (1986 : New York, N.Y.) Transcript proceedings . New York, NY (3 E. 54th St., New York 10022-3180) , c1986. 214 p. : LC Card 87-404527 DDC 659.14/3/0973 19
HF6146.T42 A27 1986

TELEVISION ADVERTISING - SWEDEN.
Hedman, Lowe. TV-tittandet och reklamen . [Stockholm] [1986] 83 p. : ISBN 91-38-09315-4 LC Card 86-199170
HF6146.T42 H43 1986

Sweden. TV-reklameffektutredningen. Effekter av TV-reklam . [Stockholm] [1986] 467 p. : ISBN 91-38-09425-8 LC Card 86-233988
HF6146.T42 S94 1986

TELEVISION ADVERTISING - UNITED STATES.
Himmelstein, Hal. Television myth and the American mind /. New York , 1984. xii, 336 p. : ISBN 0-03-062134-8 (alk. paper) : LC Card 84-11621 DDC 302.2/345 19
PN1992.3.U5 H55 1984
NYPL [MWGT 85-394]

TELEVISION ADVERTISING - UNITED STATES - CONGRESSES.
Advertising Research Foundation Key Issues Workshop (1985 : New York, N.Y.) Transcript proceedings . New York, NY (3 E. 54th St., New York 10022-3180) , c1985. 161 p. : LC Card 86-211136 DDC 659.14/3/0973 19
HF6146.T42 A27 1985

TELEVISION AND SPORTS.
Schmitt, Roland, 1954- Texte und Bildrezeption bei TV-Werbespots . Frankfurt am Main , New York , c1986. 192 p. : ISBN 3-8204-9513-4 LC Card 87-109606
HF6146.T42 S29 1986

TELEVISION AUDIENCES.
Winn, Marie. Unplugging the plug-in drug /. New York, N.Y., U. S.A. , 1987. xviii, 206 p. : ISBN 0-14-008895-4 (pbk.) : LC Card 86-30655 DDC 302.2/345 19
HE8700.65 .W56 1987

TELEVISION AUDIENCES - BRAZIL - STATISTICS.
Atlas de cobertura 1985/86. [Rio de Janeiro]

[1985?] ca. 100 p. : LC Card 86-201241
HE8700.66.B7 A74 1985

TELEVISION AUDIENCES - GREAT BRITAIN.
Taylor, Laurie, 1935- Uninvited guests . London , 1986. 218 p. : ISBN 0-7011-2973-5 : LC Card 86-183414 DDC 791.44/75/0941 19
HE8689.7.A8 T39 1986

TELEVISION AUDIENCES - ITALY.
Il Consumo dell'audiovisivo /. Milano, Italy , c1984. 173 p. : LC Card 85-178903
HE8700.66.I8 C66 1984

TELEVISION AUDIENCES - QUÉBEC (PROVINCE) - CASE STUDIES.
Caron, André H. Les télévisions étrangères . [Montréal] , 1983. ix, 166 p., 12 leaves : ISBN 2-920396-86-2 : LC Card 83-157210 DDC 302.2/345/09714 19
HE8700.9.C2 C37 1983
NYPL [MWGS 86-2473]

TELEVISION BROADCASTING.
Winn, Marie. Unplugging the plug-in drug /. New York, N.Y., U. S.A. , 1987. xviii, 206 p. : ISBN 0-14-008895-4 (pbk.) : LC Card 86-30655 DDC 302.2/345 19
HE8700.65 .W56 1987

TELEVISION BROADCASTING - AUDIENCES. see **TELEVISION AUDIENCES.**

TELEVISION BROADCASTING - BRAZIL - STATISTICS.
Atlas de cobertura 1985/86. [Rio de Janeiro] [1985?] ca. 100 p. : LC Card 86-201241
HE8700.66.B7 A74 1985

TELEVISION BROADCASTING - DENMARK.
Denmark. Mediekommissionen. Betænkning om et øget dansk tv-udbud. [København] , 1983. 168 p. : ISBN 87-503-4624-5 LC Card 85-128700
HE8700.9.D4 D45 1983

TELEVISION BROADCASTING - EUROPE.
Tydeman, John. New media in Europe . London , New York , c1986. xii, 260 p. : ISBN 0-07-084799-1 : LC Card 85-19839 DDC 384.55/094 19
HE8700.9.E8 T93 1986
NYPL [JLE 86-3209]

TELEVISION BROADCASTING - FRANCE.
Frèches, José. La guerre des images /. Paris , c1986. 173 p. : ISBN 2-207-23215-8 : LC Card 86-141723
HE8700.9.F7 F77 1986

TELEVISION BROADCASTING - GERMANY, WEST.
Gebrewold, Kiflemariam. Fernsehexport der Bundesrepublik Deutschland . Bochum , 1983. xiv, 316 p. : ISBN 3-88339-317-7 LC Card 83-232957
HE8700.66.G3 G43 1983

Mettler-Meibom, Barbara E. Breitbandtechnologie . Opladen , c1986. xxiv, 477, [60] p. : ISBN 3-531-11782-3 LC Card 86-184911
HE8154 .M47 1986

Nach fünfundzwanzig Jahren . Köln , 1980. 399 p. : ISBN 3-7745-6465-5
NYPL [MWGK (Germany) 74-75 Bd.4]

TELEVISION BROADCASTING - GHANA.
Golden jubilee, July 1935-1985 /. Accra [Ghana] [1985] 64 p. : LC Card 86-155961 DDC 384.54/06/0667 19
HE8689.9.G45 G65 1985

TELEVISION BROADCASTING - GOVERNMENT POLICY - CANADA.
Canada. Task Force on Broadcasting Policy. Report of the Task Force on Broadcasting Policy. [Toronto] , c1986. 730 p. : ISBN 0-660-12164-6 (pbk.) : LC Card 86-231885 DDC 384.54/0971 19
HE8689.9.C3 C37 1986

TELEVISION BROADCASTING - GREAT BRITAIN.
Briggs, Asa, 1921- The franchise affair . London , 1986. 226 p. ; ISBN 0-7126-1201-7 : LC Card 86-190561 DDC 384.55/453/0941 19
HE8700.9.G7 B72 1986

TELEVISION BROADCASTING - GREAT BRITAIN - FEES.
Two studies concerning the British Broadcasting Corporation /. London , 1979. 48 p. : ISBN 0-11-340763-7 (pbk.) LC Card 83-221765
HE8689.9.G7 T85 1979

TELEVISION BROADCASTING - GREAT BRITAIN - HISTORY.
Burns, R. W. British television . London , c1986. xv, 488 p. : ISBN 0-86341-079-0 LC Card 87-160684 DDC 384.55/0941 19
HE8700.9.G7 B87 1986

Moss, Nicholas. BBC TV presents . London , 1986. 120 p. : ISBN 0-946358-29-X LC Card 87-146728 DDC 384.55/4/06041 19
HE8700.9.G7 M67 1986

TELEVISION BROADCASTING - GREAT BRITAIN - PLANNING.
Two studies concerning the British Broadcasting Corporation /. London , 1979. 48 p. : ISBN 0-11-340763-7 (pbk.) LC Card 83-221765
HE8689.9.G7 T85 1979

TELEVISION BROADCASTING - HUNGARY - PÉCS - HISTORY.
Békés, Sándor. Az első évtized . Pécs , 1986. 221 p. : LC Card 87-148227
HE8700.9.H8 B45 1986

TELEVISION BROADCASTING - ITALY.
Il Gigante nano . Torino , c1985. 382 p. : LC Card 86-128171 DDC 384.54/0945 19
HE8689.9.I8 G54 1985
NYPL [MWGK (Italy) 86-2853]

Martini, Paolo. TV, sorrisi e milioni . Milano , 1985. 243 p. ; ISBN 88-345-0020-2 : LC Card 86-129631 DDC 384.55/0945 19
HE8700.9.I8 M37 1985

TELEVISION BROADCASTING - MEXICO.
Arredondo Ramírez, Pablo. Comunicación social, poder y democracia en México /. Guadalajara, Jalisco, México , c1986. 214 p. : LC Card 86-227944
HE8689.9.M6 A77 1986

Esparza Oteo T., Luis. La política cultural del estado mexicano y el desarrollo de la T.V. /. México, D.F. , 1984. 116 p. ; LC Card 87-404017 DDC 384.55/4/0972 19
HE8700.9.M6 E84 1984

TELEVISION BROADCASTING POLICY - UNITED STATES.
Baughman, James L., 1952- Television's guardians . Knoxville , c1985. xvi, 311 p. : ISBN 0-87049-448-1 : LC Card 84-13178 DDC 384.55/4 19
HE8700.8 .B38 1985
NYPL [MWGT 85-1604]

TELEVISION BROADCASTING - POLITICAL ASPECTS. see **TELEVISION IN POLITICS.**

TELEVISION BROADCASTING - PORTUGAL - CONGRESSES.
A Televisão em Portugal. [Lisbon] [1985] 95 p. : LC Card 87-102704 DDC 384.55/4/09469 19
HE8700.9.P8 T45 1985

TELEVISION BROADCASTING - SOCIAL ASPECTS - GREAT BRITAIN.
Root, Jane. Open the box . London , 1986. 126 p. : ISBN 0-906890-78-0 (pbk.) : LC Card 86-206072 DDC 302.2/345/0941 19
HE8700.9.G7 R66 1986

Taylor, Laurie, 1935- Uninvited guests . London , 1986. 218 p. : ISBN 0-7011-2973-5 : LC Card 86-183414 DDC 791.44/75/0941 19
HE8689.7.A8 T39 1986

TELEVISION BROADCASTING - SOCIAL ASPECTS - QUÉBEC (PROVINCE) - CASE STUDIES.
Caron, André H. Les télévisions étrangères . [Montréal] , 1983. ix, 166 p., 12 leaves : ISBN 2-920396-86-2 : LC Card 83-157210 DDC 302.2/345/09714 19
HE8700.9.C2 C37 1983
NYPL [MWGS 86-2473]

TELEVISION BROADCASTING - SPAIN.
La Televisión en España mañana . Madrid , 1986. 331 p. ; ISBN 84-323-0563-X LC Card 86-199326
HE8700.9.S63 T45 1986
NYPL [MWGV (Spain) 87-2054]

Televisió, federalisme. Barcelona [1986] 209 p. ; LC Card 86-210066
HE8700.9.S63 T44 1986

TELEVISION BROADCASTING - UNITED STATES.
Bortz, Paul I. Great expectations . Washington, D.C. , c1986. vii, 137 p., [3] folded leaves : ISBN 0-89324-012-5 (pbk.) LC Card 87-401854 DDC 384.55/453/068 19
HE8700.8 .B66 1986

Himmelstein, Hal. Television myth and the American mind /. New York , 1984. xii, 336 p. : ISBN 0-03-062134-8 (alk. paper) : LC Card 84-11621 DDC 302.2/345 19
PN1992.3.U5 H55 1984
NYPL [MWGT 85-394]

TELEVISION BROADCASTING - VOCATIONAL GUIDANCE.
Levinson, Richard. Off camera . New York, N.Y. , c1986. 279 p. ; ISBN 0-452-25873-1 LC Card 86-18089 DDC 384.55/023/73 19
HE8700.4 .L48 1986
NYPL [MWGR 87-881]

TELEVISION COMMERCIAL FILMS.
Grandi, Roberto. Come parla la pubblicità . Milano , 1987. 175 p. ; LC Card 87-168680
HF6146.T42 G7 1987

TELEVISION COMMERCIALS. see **TELEVISION ADVERTISING.**

TELEVISION FREQUENCY ALLOCATION - GREAT BRITAIN.
CSP International (Firm) Deregulation of the radio spectrum in the UK /. London , 1987. vi, 182, [30] p. : ISBN 0-11-513979-6 (pbk.) : LC Card 87-170465 DDC 384.54/52 19
HE8689.9.G7 C76 1987

TELEVISION - GREAT BRITAIN - HISTORY.
Burns, R. W. British television . London , c1986. xv, 488 p. : ISBN 0-86341-079-0 LC Card 87-160684 DDC 384.55/0941 19
HE8700.9.G7 B87 1986

Television History Workshop (Great Britain)
Making cars . London , Boston , c1985. ix, 131 p. : ISBN 0-7102-0272-5 : LC Card 84-13398 DDC 338.4/76292/0942574 19
HD8039.A82 G75 1984
NYPL [JLE 86-2303]

TELEVISION IN ADVERTISING. see **TELEVISION ADVERTISING.**

TELEVISION IN HEALTH EDUCATION - INDIA - CONGRESSES.
SITE to INSAT . New Delhi , 1986. viii, 165 p. : LC Card 86-902956 DDC 384.55/44/0954 19
HE8700.9.I5 S57 1986

Television in India . Acharya, Rabi Narayan, 1960- Delhi , 1987. vi, 166 p. : ISBN 81-7049-015-4 : LC Card 87-900915 DDC 384.55/0954 19
HE8700.9.I5 A24 1987

TELEVISION IN MANAGEMENT.
Bunyan, John A. Why video works . White Plains, NY , c1987. x, 203 p. : ISBN 0-86729-079-X : LC Card 86-21106 DDC 658/.0028 19
HD30.34 .B86 1987

TELEVISION IN POLITICS - UNITED STATES.
Broh, C. Anthony. A horse of a different color . Washington, D.C. , 1987. xiv, 93 p. : ISBN 0-941410-54-4 (pbk.) : LC Card 87-2869 DDC 324.973/0927 19
HE8700.76.U6 B76 1987

Hollander, Richard S. Video democracy . Mt. Airy, Md. , c1985. ix, 161 p. : ISBN 0-912338-51-2 LC Card 85-81818 DDC 384.55/5 19
HE8700.76.U6 H65 1985
NYPL [MWGT 86-1503]

Political broadcast catechism. Washington , c1984. 61 p. : *NYPL [MWGH 85-3267]*

TELEVISION - INDIA.
Acharya, Rabi Narayan, 1960- Television in India . Delhi , 1987. vi, 166 p. : ISBN 81-7049-015-4 : LC Card 87-900915 DDC 384.55/0954 19
HE8700.9.I5 A24 1987

TELEVISION INDUSTRY - FRANCE.
Frèches, José. La guerre des images /. Paris , c1986. 173 p. : ISBN 2-207-23215-8 : LC Card 86-141723
HE8700.9.F7 F77 1986

TELEVISION INDUSTRY - ITALY.
Il Consumo dell'audiovisivo /. Milano, Italy ,

c1984. 173 p. : LC Card 85-178903
HE8700.66.I8 C66 1984

TELEVISION INDUSTRY - VOCATIONAL GUIDANCE.
Levinson, Richard. Off camera . New York, N.Y. , c1986. 279 p. ; ISBN 0-452-25873-1 LC Card 86-18089 DDC 384.55/023/73 19
HE8700.4 .L48 1986
NYPL [MWGR 87-881]

TELEVISION - ITALY.
Martini, Paolo. TV, sorrisi e milioni . Milano , 1985. 243 p. ; ISBN 88-345-0020-2 : LC Card 86-129631 DDC 384.55/0945 19
HE8700.9.I8 M37 1985

TELEVISION - ITALY - ADDRESSES, ESSAYS, LECTURES.
Il Territorio immaginario /. Milano [1980] 106 p. ; ISBN 88-20-41848-7 : LC Card 81-123209 DDC 302.2/34/0945 19
HE8700.9.I8 T47 1980
NYPL [JFD 86-8337]

TELEVISION - LAW AND LEGISLATION - MEXICO.
Esparza Oteo T., Luis. La política cultural del estado mexicano y el desarrollo de la T.V. /. México, D.F. , 1984. 116 p. ; LC Card 87-404017 DDC 384.55/4/0972 19
HE8700.9.M6 E84 1984

TELEVISION - LAW AND LEGISLATION - UNITED STATES.
Baughman, James L., 1952- Television's guardians . Knoxville , c1985. xvi, 311 p. : ISBN 0-87049-448-1 : LC Card 84-13178 DDC 384.55/4 19
HE8700.8 .B38 1985
NYPL [MWGT 85-1604]

Television myth and the American mind /.
Himmelstein, Hal. New York , 1984. xii, 336 p. : ISBN 0-03-062134-8 (alk. paper) : LC Card 84-11621 DDC 302.2/345 19
PN1992.3.U5 H55 1984
NYPL [MWGT 85-394]

La télévision par cable commence demain /.
Pigeat, Henri, 1939- Paris , c1983. 239 p. ; ISBN 2-259-01062-8 : LC Card 83-237808
HE8700.72.F8 P54 1983

TELEVISION PROGRAMS FOR CHILDREN - INDIA - CONGRESSES.
SITE to INSAT . New Delhi , 1986. viii, 165 p. : LC Card 86-902956 DDC 384.55/44/0954 19
HE8700.9.I5 S57 1986

TELEVISION PROGRAMS, FOREIGN - QUÉBEC (PROVINCE)
Caron, André H. Les télévisions étrangères . [Montréal] , 1983. ix, 166 p., 12 leaves : ISBN 2-920396-86-2 : LC Card 83-157210 DDC 302.2/345/09714 19
HE8700.9.C2 C37 1983
NYPL [MWGS 86-2473]

TELEVISION PROGRAMS - GERMANY (WEST) - HAMBURG.
Renckstorf, Karsten. Landesprogramme von Hörfunk und Fernsehen in Hamburg . Hamburg , c1985. xlvii, vi, 388 p. : ISBN 3-87296-067-9 (pbk.) LC Card 86-109817 DDC 384.54/43/0943515 19
HE8700.9.G4 R45 1985 *NYPL [MWGK (Germany, West) 86-4239]*

TELEVISION PROGRAMS - INDIA - CONGRESSES.
SITE to INSAT . New Delhi , 1986. viii, 165 p. : LC Card 86-902956 DDC 384.55/44/0954 19
HE8700.9.I5 S57 1986

TELEVISION PROGRAMS - RATINGS.
Beville, Hugh Malcolm. Audience ratings . Hillsdale, N.J. , 1987. p. cm. ISBN 0-8058-0175-8 LC Card 87-21001 DDC 384.54/3 19
HE8697.A8 B46 1987

TELEVISION PROGRAMS - UNITED STATES - HISTORY AND CRITICISM.
Himmelstein, Hal. Television myth and the American mind /. New York , 1984. xii, 336 p. : ISBN 0-03-062134-8 (alk. paper) : LC Card 84-11621 DDC 302.2/345 19
PN1992.3.U5 H55 1984
NYPL [MWGT 85-394]

TELEVISION PROGRAMS - UNITED STATES - REVIEWS.
Selected radio and television criticism /. Metuchen, N.J. , c1987. ix, 203 p. ; ISBN 0-8108-1942-2 LC Card 86-27891 DDC 791.44/75/0973 19
PN1990.6.U5 S4 1987
NYPL [MWGI 87-1890]

TELEVISION SCRIPTS.
Katins, Sabine. All you need is freedom . Berlin [1977] 35 p. : LC Card 86-207107 DDC 968.91/05 19
HC910 .K37 1977

TELEVISION - SOCIAL ASPECTS - INDIA.
Bhat, Vighnesh N., 1951- Mind managers and defiled doordarshan /. Jalandhar , 1987. 208 p. ; ISBN 81-7072-011-7 : LC Card 87-900504 DDC 302.2/345/0954 19
HE8700.9.I5 B53 1987

TELEVISION STATIONS - UNITED STATES - MANAGEMENT.
Marcus, Norman, 1934- Broadcast and cable management /. Englewood Cliffs, N.J. , c1986. xii, 308 p. : ISBN 0-13-083577-3 LC Card 85-3565 DDC 384.54/068 19
HE8700.8 .M37 1986 *NYPL [JLE 86-3127]*

TELEVISION SUPPLIES INDUSTRY - GERMANY (WEST)
Schubert, Frank. Akzeptanz von Bildschirmtext in Unternehmungen und im Markt . Münster , c1986. xxiv, 316 p. : ISBN 3-7923-0546-1 LC Card 86-227074
HD9696.T463 G37 1986

TELEVISION - TERMINOLOGY.
Benigni, Glauco. Do you speak televisionese? /. Milano [1985] 141 p. : LC Card 85-241850
HE8700.6 .B46 1985

Television's guardians . Baughman, James L., 1952- Knoxville , c1985. xvi, 311 p. : ISBN 0-87049-448-1 : LC Card 84-13178 DDC 384.55/4 19
HE8700.8 .B38 1985
NYPL [MWGT 85-1604]

Tel′ksnis, L.
Kligene, Nerute. Raspoznavanie sluchaĭnykh protsessov s peremennoĭ strukturoĭ veroi͡atnostnykh raspredeleniĭ . Vil′ni͡us , 1986. 136 p. : LC Card 87-146330
HD38 .S715 vyp.76 QA274

Obnaruzhenie izmeneniĭ svoĭstv sluchaĭnykh protsessov . Vil′ni͡us , 1984. 243 p. : LC Card 84-168819
HD38 .S715 vyp. 65 QA274.A1

Shpilevskiĭ, Ė. Printsipy dinamicheskoĭ klassifikatsii stokhasticheskikh protsessov i sistem . Vil′ni͡us , 1978. 138 p. ; LC Card 81-173567
HD38 .S715 vyp. 28 QA274

Sistema raspoznavanii͡a ritmogramm serdt͡sa . Vil′ni͡us , 1980. 55 p. : LC Card 81-194159
HD38 .S715 vyp. 49 QP112.5.C3

Tell it to the world . Halpern, Burton M. Jerusalem , New York, N.Y. [c1982] 152 p. ; ISBN 965-229-004-1 LC Card 86-214902 DDC 659.2 19
HD59 .H25 1982

Telser, Lester G., 1931- A theory of efficient cooperation and competition / Lester G. Telser. Cambridge ; New York : Cambridge University Press, 1987. xii, 306 p. : ill. ; 25 cm. Bibliography: p. 296-300. Includes index. ISBN 0-521-30619-1 LC Card 87-5114 DDC 338.6/042/0724 19
1. Competition - Mathematical models. I. Title.
HD41 .T43 1987

TELSTAR SATELLITES. see **ARTIFICIAL SATELLITES IN TELECOMMUNICATION.**

Temas antiliberales, marxistas y autoritarios /. Soler, Sebastián. Buenos Aires , 1977. 179 p. ; LC Card 80-469614
JC571 .S7173 *NYPL [JLC 80-]*

Temas de cátedra.
Rubinstein, Juan Carlos, 1928- Estructura social, estado democrático y cambio político /. [Buenos Aires] , c1986. 159 p. : ISBN 950-23-0292-3 LC Card 87-114981 DDC 330.982/064 19
HC175 .R783 1986

Temas del siglo XX .
(37) Compra de carteras . Montevideo [1986] 188 p. : LC Card 87-403157 DDC 332.1/09895 19
HG2954 .C66 1986

Temas nacionales.
(14) Lanzaro, Jorge Luis. Sindicatos y sistema político . Montevideo, Uruguay , 1986. 132 p. ; LC Card 87-403149 DDC 322/.2/09895 19
HD3616.U72 L36 1986

Temática jalisciense .
(no. 12) Gutiérrez Zermeño, Rodolfo, 1953- Movimiento obrero en Jalisco, período 1925-1930 /. Guadalajara, Jalisco, México , 1985. 64 p. ; ISBN 968-8322-01-6 LC Card 86-208368
HD6535.J35 G88 1985

Temin, Peter. The fall of the Bell system : a study in prices and politics / Peter Temin with Louis Galambos. Cambridge ; New York : Cambridge University Press, 1987. xviii, 378 p. : ill. ; 24 cm. Includes bibliographical references and index. ISBN 0-521-34557-X LC Card 87-10293 DDC 384.6/065/73 19
1. American Telephone and Telegraph Company - Reorganization - History. 2. Telephone - United States - History. I. Galambos, Louis. II. Title.
HE8846.A55 T44 1987

Templ, Franz. Osteuropa im Blickpunkt . Linz [1985?] 168 p. ; LC Card 87-142952 DDC 382/.091713/01717 19
HF1411 .O687 1985

Temple University Press. Noble, Charles, 1948- Liberalism at work . Philadelphia , 1986. x, 292 p. : ISBN 0-87722-421-8 (alk. paper) : LC Card 86-1766 DDC 353.0083/0289 19
HD7654 .N63 1986 *NYPL [JLE 86-4426]*

Templeton, Jane Farley. Focus groups : a guide for marketing & advertising professionals / Jane Farley Templeton. Chicago, Ill. : Probus Pub. Co., c1987. xiii, 315 p. ; 24 cm. Includes bibliographies and index. ISBN 0-917253-78-7 : LC Card 87-4977 DDC 658.8/3 19
1. Marketing research. 2. Advertising research. I. Title.
HF5415.2 .T43 1987

Templeton, John, 1912- The Templeton plan : 21 steps to success and happiness / as described by John Marks Templeton to James Ellison.1st ed. San Francisco : Harper & Row, c1987. x, 181, [1] p. ; 22 cm. "A Giniger book." Bibliography: p. [182]. ISBN 0-06-250286-7 LC Card 86-43022 DDC 174/.4 19
1. Business ethics. 2. Christian ethics. 3. Business - Religious aspects - Christianity. 4. Success in business. I. Ellison, James, 1930-. II. Title.
HF5387 .T46 1987

The Templeton plan . Templeton, John, 1912- San Francisco , c1987. x, 181, [1] p. ; ISBN 0-06-250286-7 LC Card 86-43022 DDC 174/.4 19
HF5387 .T46 1987

Tempo da vendere, tempo da usare . Ravaioli, Carla. Milano, Italy , c1986. 142 p. ; LC Card 86-182560
HD5106 .R357 1986

Il tempo e il lavoro /. Gasparini, Giovanni, 1940- Milano, Italy , c1986. 178 p. ; LC Card 86-180970
HD5106 .G37 1986

Temporale Entwicklungstheorie /. Pychlau, Matthias. Pfaffenweiler , 1986. viii, 79 p. ; ISBN 3-89085-110-X LC Card 87-409006 DDC 338.9 19
HD84 .P9 1986

Temporary employment . Smith, Demaris C. White Hall, Va. , c1985. 143 p. ; ISBN 0-932620-56-6 (pbk.) : LC Card 85-13456 DDC 650.1/4 19
HD5854.2.U6 S6 1985 *NYPL [JLF 86-1365]*

TEMPORARY EMPLOYMENT - FRANCE.
Tartakowsky, Pierre, 1952- Les intérimeurs /. Paris , c1985. 260 p., [8] p. of plates : ISBN 2-209-05678-0 : LC Card 85-152003 DDC 331.12/5 19
HD5854.2.F7 T37 1985

TEMPORARY EMPLOYMENT - UNITED STATES.
The Changing workplace . Washington, D.C. [Rockville, Md.] , c1986. iv, 140 p. : ISBN 0-87179-910-3 (pbk.) LC Card 86-221689 DDC 331.25/72 19
HD5124 .C46 1986

Smith, Demaris C. Temporary employment .

White Hall, Va. , c1985. 143 p. ; ISBN 0-932620-56-6 (pbk.) : LC Card 85-13456 DDC 650.1/4 19
HD5854.2.U6 S6 1985 NYPL [JLF 86-1365]

Temporary equilibrium : selected readings / edited by Jean-Michel Grandmont. Boston : Acadmeic Press, c1987. p. cm. (Economic theory, econometrics, and mathematical economics) Bibliography: p. Includes index. ISBN 0-12-295145-X (alk. paper) LC Card 87-1128 DDC 339.5 19
1. Equilibrium (Economics). I. Grandmont, Jean-Michel.
HB145 .T45 1987

Le Temps des initiatives / "Echange et projets" ; préface de François Bloch-Lainé. Paris : A. Michel, c1983. 187 p. ; 24 cm. ISBN 2-226-01647-3 : LC Card 83-212781
1. Industry and state - France. 2. France - Economic policy - 1945-. 3. France - Industries. I. Échange et projets (Association).
HD3616.F83 T46 1983

Ten biggest mistakes buyers make and how to avoid them. Yokl, Robert T. The 10 biggest mistakes buyers make and how to avoid them /. Willow Grove, PA (1834 Fleming Ave., Willow Grove 19090) , c1987. 26 p. : LC Card 87-61507 DDC 658.7/2 19
HF5437 .Y65 1987

Ten years after . Royal Commission on Labrador. [St. John's, Nfld.] , 1986. iv, 116 p. ; LC Card 86-212404 DDC 361.6/1/097182 19
HC117.L2 R69 1986

Tenaga kerja . Jakarta-Raya, Indonesia. Jakarta [1980] 52 leaves ; LC Card 80-942103
HD5824.J27 J35 1980

The Tenant movement in New York City, 1904-1984 / edited by Ronald Lawson, with the assistance of Mark Naison. New Brunswick, N.J. : Rutgers University Press, c1986. xiv, 289 p. : ill. ; 24 cm. Includes bibliographies and indexes. ISBN 0-8135-1203-4 (pbk.) : LC Card 85-27894 DDC 333.33/8 19
1. Rental housing - New York (N.Y.) - History - 20th century. 2. Landlord and tenant - New York (N.Y.) - History - 20th century. 3. New York (N.Y.) - Social conditions. I. Lawson, Ronald, 1940-. II. Naison, Mark, 1946-.
HD7288.85.U62 N58 1986 NYPL [JLE 86-4565]

Tenbrink, Hiltrud. Schenk, Hans-Otto. Die Konzentration im Handel . Berlin , c1984. 341 p. : ISBN 3-428-05618-3 LC Card 84-225438
HF345 .F66 Folge 3, Nr. 9 HF3566

Tendencias sindicales después del VI Congreso de la C.O.B. / Ramiro Carrasco ... [et al.]. 1a ed. La Paz : Ed. "CINCO", c1985. 111 p. ; 21 cm. Papers presented at a meeting organized by the Centro de Investigación y Consultoría and held in Jan. 1985. Includes bibliographical references. LC Card 86-137172
1. Congreso de la COB (6th : 1984 : Cochabamba, Bolivia) - Congresses. 2. Central Obrera Boliviana - Congresses. 3. Trade-unions - Bolivia - Political activity - Congresses. I. Carrasco, Ramiro. II. Centro de Investigación y Consultoría (La Paz, Bolivia).
HD8272.C65 T45 1985

Tendentsii razvitiia passazhirskikh perevozok v Litovskoĭ SSR : metodicheskie ukazaniia / [redaktsionnaia kollegiia, A.N. Gul'binskas (otvetstvennyĭ redaktor) ... et al.]. Vil'nius : Akademiia nauk Litovskoĭ SSR, In-t ėkonomiki, 1985. 179 p. : ill. ; 21 cm. Includes bibliographies. LC Card 86-199868
1. Transportation - Lithuania - Passenger traffic. I. Gul'binskas, A. N. (Al'binas Nikodemovich). II. Ekonomikos institutas (Lietuvos TSR Mokslų akademija).
HE255.Z7 L577 1985

TENDER OFFERS (SECURITIES)
Knights, raiders, and targets . New York , 1987. p. cm. ISBN 0-19-504405-3 (alk. paper) LC Card 86-33293 DDC 338.8/3 19
HD2746.5 .K58 1987

Madrick, Jeffrey G. Taking America . Toronto , New York , 1987. 310 p. ; ISBN 0-553-05229-2 LC Card 87-928 DDC 338.8/3/0973 19
HG4028.T4 M33 1987

Mathiasen, Karen. Corporate governance and shareholder rights . Washington, DC (1755 Massachusetts Ave., N.W., Suite 600, Washington 20036) , c1986. 96 p. ; LC Card 86-230362 DDC 346.73/0666 347.306666 19
HD2743 .M34 1986

TENDER OFFERS (SECURITIES) - CASE STUDIES.
Michel, Allen, 1945- Takeover madness . New York , c1986. xii, 397 p. : ISBN 0-471-01079-0 LC Card 85-32315 DDC 658.1/8 19
HD2746.5 .M53 1986 NYPL [JLE 86-2989]

TENDER OFFERS (SECURITIES) - UNITED STATES.
Combating takeover attempts. Washington, D.C. , c1986. xi, 12 p. : LC Card 86-224303 DDC 658.1/6 19
HD2746.5 .C645 1986

Johnston, Moira, 1934- Takeover . New York , c1986. xv, 395 p. ; ISBN 0-87795-784-3 : LC Card 86-10818 DDC 338.8/3/0973 19
HD2746.5 .J64 1986 NYPL [JLE 86-3932]

Johnston, Moira, 1934- Takeover /. New York, N.Y. , 1987, c1986. xiii, 418 p. ; ISBN 0-14-010505-0 (pbk.) LC Card 87-8560 DDC 338.8/3/0973 19
HD2746.5 .J64 1987

Sherman, Howard D. Junk bonds and tender offer financing /. Washington, D.C. , c1987. 22 p. ; ISBN 0-931035-15-5 (pbk.) LC Card 87-128796 DDC 332.63/2 19
HG4963 .S535 1987

TENDER OFFERS (SECURITIES) - UNITED STATES - DIRECTORIES.
Rosenbaum, Virginia. Takeover defenses . Washington, D.C. , c1987. 227 p. ; ISBN 0-931035-13-9 (pbk.) LC Card 87-400095 DDC 338.7/4/02573 19
HD2746.5 .R67 1987

Tenenbaum, Barbara, 1946- The politics of penury : debt and taxes in Mexico, 1821-1856 / Barbara A. Tenenbaum. Albuquerque : University of New Mexico Press, c1986. xviii, 250 p. ; 24 cm. Originally presented as the author's thesis (doctoral--Harvard) Includes index. Bibliography: p. 217-240. ISBN 0-8263-0890-2 : LC Card 86-16027 DDC 336.72 19
1. Finance, Public - Mexico - History - 19th century. 2. Debts, Public - Mexico - History - 19th century. 3. Taxation - Mexico - History - 19th century. 4. Mexico - Politics and government - 1821-1861. I. Title.
HJ802 .T46 1986 NYPL [JLE 87-482]

Tenencia de la tierra y desarrollo socio-económico del sector agrícola. Ecuador / Comité Interamericano de Desarrollo Agrícola. [Guayaquil] : Departamento de Publicaciones de la Facultad de Ciencias Económicas de la Universidad de Guayaquil, [1981] xxv, 539 p., [16] leaves of plates : ill., map ; 28 cm. (Biblioteca ecuatoriana . 27) Reprint. Originally published: Washington, D.C. : Unión Panamericana, Secretaría General de la Organización de los Estados Americanos, 1965. Bibliography: p. [533]-539. LC Card 87-673171
1. Land tenure - Ecuador. 2. Ecuador - Rural conditions. 3. Agriculture - Economic aspects - Ecuador. 4. Agriculture and state - Ecuador. I. Inter-American Committee for Agricultural Development. II. Title: Ecuador, tenencia de la tierra y desarrollo socio-económico del sector agrícola. III. Series: Biblioteca ecuatoriana (Guayaquil, Ecuador) , 27.
HD526 .T46x 1981

Tenencia de la tierra y movimiento campesino en el Ecuador /. Farrell, Gilda. Quito, Ecuador , 1981. 158 p., [2] leaves of plates : LC Card 86-174088
HD529.C67 F37 1981

TENEZ INDIANS. see **CHINANTEC INDIANS.**

Tenfelde, Klaus.
Arbeit und Arbeitserfahrung in der Geschichte /. Göttingen , 1986. 128 p. ; ISBN 3-525-33516-4 *NYPL [JLC 87-12]*

Arbeit und Arbeitserfahrung in der Geschichte /. Göttingen , c1986. 128 p. ; ISBN 3-525-33516-4 LC Card 86-226588
HD4904 .A6644 1986

Bis vor die Stufen des Throns . München , c1986. 530 p. : ISBN 3-406-31297-7 LC Card 87-103686 DDC 331.7/622334/0943 19
HD8039.M61 G32 1986

Proletarische Provinz : Radikalisierung und Widerstand in Penzberg/Oberbayern, 1900-1945 / Klaus Tenfelde.Durchgesehene und erw. Ausg. München : R. Oldenbourg, 1982. xvii, 409 p. : 50 ill. ; 24 cm. The author's Habilitationsschrift--Ludwig-Maximilians-Universität, Munich, 1980/81. First published in: Bayern in der NS-Zeit. [Bd.] 4. Herrschaft und Gesellschaft im Konflikt, Teil C. 1981. Bibliography: p. [383]-399. Includes index. ISBN 3-486-50701-X : LC Card 83-124119
1. Labor and laboring classes - Germany (West) - Penzberg - Political activity - History - 20th century. 2. Coal miners - Germany (West) - Penzberg - History - 20th century. 3. Anti-Nazi movement - Germany (West) - Penzberg. 4. Penzberg (Germany) - History. I. Title.
HD8460.P452 T46 1982

Tengler, Hermann.
Clemens, Reinhard. Standortprobleme von Industrieunternehmen in Ballungsräumen . Göttingen , c1983. xviii, 257 p. : ISBN 3-509-01330-1 LC Card 83-198706
HC289.D6 C54 1983

Schanz, Hermann J. Der niederrheinische Wirtschaftsraum . Stuttgart , c1986. xxii, 466 p. ; ISBN 3-7910-5014-1 LC Card 87-135757 DDC 330.943/55 19
HC289.D755 S32 1986

Tennent, James C. The oil scouts : reminiscences of the night riders of the hemlocks / by James C. Tennent ; with introduction by P.C. Boyle. [Pennsylvania? : s.n., 1986] 85 p. : ill., ports. ; 24 cm. Reprint. Originally published: [Oil City, Pa.] : Derrick Pub. Co., 1915. Includes foreword of 1931 1st reprint ed. LC Card 87-404148 DDC 338.2/7282/09748 19
1. Petroleum industry and trade - Pennsylvania - History - 19th century. 2. Oil wells - Pennsylvania - History - 19th century. 3. Petroleum industry and trade - Pennsylvania - Corrupt practices - History - 19th century. 4. Tennent, James C. I. Title.
HD9567.P4 T46 1986

TENNENT, JAMES C.
Tennent, James C. The oil scouts . [Pennsylvania? , 1986] 85 p. : LC Card 87-404148 DDC 338.2/7282/09748 19
HD9567.P4 T46 1986

Tennessee. Dept. of Public Health. State Center for Health Statistics. see **Tennessee. State Center for Health Statistics.**

Tennessee. State Center for Health Statistics.
Infant mortality in Tennessee, 1979-1982 . Nashville, Tenn. [1986] vii, 23 p. : LC Card 86-622027 DDC 304.6/4/0880542 19
HB1323.I42 U6385 1986

The M. L. Seidman memorial town hall lecture series. see **The M. L. Seidman memorial town hall lecture series.**

The Tennessee Valley Authority /. Van Fleet, Alanson A. New York , c1987. 92 p. : ISBN 1-555-46123-9 : LC Card 86-31738 DDC 353.0082/3/09768 19
HD9685.U7 T385 1987

Tennstedt, Florian. Politik der Armut und die Spaltung des Sozialstaats /. Frankfurt am Main , 1985. 474 p. : ISBN 3-518-11233-3 : LC Card 85-183026
HC290.5.P6 P65 1985

Tenth report on public undertakings, delays in commencement of production business, under utilisation of capacity and related matters, Ministry of Finance (Bureau of Public Enterprises) . India. Parliament. Committee on Public Undertakings. New Delhi , c1981. vii, 50 p. ; LC Card 81-902947 DDC 354.5409/2 19
HD4293 .I515 1981

Tentler, Leslie Woodcock. Wage-earning women : industrial work and family life in the United States, 1900-1930 / Leslie Woodcock Tentler. New York : Oxford University Press, 1979. 266 p. ; 22 cm. Includes index. Bibliography: p. 241-260. ISBN 0-19-502627-6 : LC Card 79-12802 DDC 331.4/0973
1. Women - Employment - United States - History. 2. Women - United States - History. 3. Sex role. I. Title.
HD6095 .T44 NYPL [JLD 86-3699]

TENURE OF LAND. see **LAND TENURE.**

TENURE OF OFFICE. see **CIVIL SERVICE.**

Tények, adatok a szakszervezeti mozgalomról. Kolozsvári, Ernő. Szemelvények a szakszervezetek agitációs, propaganda- és kulturális tevékenységéből, 1948-1980 /.

Budapest , 1982. 43 p. : ISBN 963-321-957-4 LC Card 83-229170
HD6680.5.Z6 K64 1982

Teoreticheskie i metodicheskie predposylki modelirovaniia organizatsionno-ėkonomicheskikh struktur khoziaistvennykh sistem /. Sokolov, D. V. (Dmitriĭ Viktorovich) Leningrad , 1986. 134, [2] p. : LC Card 87-146729
HD37.R82 S65 1986

Teoreticheskie i metodologicheskie problemy regional'noĭ ėkonomiki : sbornik nauchnykh trudov / [redaktsionnaia kollegiia V.P. Mozhin (otv. redaktor) ... et al.]. Moskva : Sovet po izucheniiu proizvoditel'nykh sil pri Gosplane SSSR, 1983. 158 p. : ill. ; 21 cm. Includes bibliographical references. LC Card 87-100005
1. Soviet Union - Industries - Location. 2. Regional planning - Soviet Union. I. Mozhin, V. P. II. Sovet po izucheniiu proizvoditel'nykh sil (Soviet Union).
HC340.D5 T437 1983

Teoreticheskie issledovaniia regional'nykh faktorov razmeshcheniia khoziaistva /. Egengel'dyev, Ė. (Ėsengel'dy) Ashkabad , 1985. 227 p. : LC Card 86-172008
HC337.T853 D53 1985

Teoretické otázky formování plánovitého řízení národního hospodářství ČSSR /. Klusoň, Václav. Praha , 1986- v. <1 > ; LC Card 87-167771
HC270.28 .K58 1986

Teoría de la democracia social . Figuerola, Francisco José. Buenos Aires , 1986. xxv, 492 p. ; ISBN 950-43-0832-5 LC Card 86-184525
HD2081 .F54 1986

Teoría de la renta capitalista de la tierra. Mendoza, Carlos. Teoría de la renta capitalista de la tierra ; y, Génesis de la renta capitalista de la tierra y del arrendatario /. Buenos Aires , 1985. 108 p. : ISBN 950-9478-11-3 LC Card 86-101927
HB401 .M38 1985

Teoría de los precios sociales /. Azqueta Oyarzun, Diego. Alcala de Henares-Madrid, España [1985?] 250 p. : ISBN 84-7351-181-6 : LC Card 87-105447
HB846.3 .A97 1985

Teoria dell'organizzazione e realtà italiana : problemi e contributi / a cura di P. Bontadini e G. Gasparini ; scritti di A. Anfossi ... [et al.]. Milano : F. Angeli, [1980] 225 p. ; 22 cm. (Sociologia del lavoro e delle organizzazioni. 4) Previously published in Studi organizzativi, 1979, n. 1-2. Includes bibliographies. ISBN 88-20-41736-7 : LC Card 80-511472 DDC 302.3/5 19
1. Organization - Addresses, essays, lectures. 2. Management - Addresses, essays, lectures. 3. Italy - Economic conditions - Addresses, essays, lectures. 4. Italy - Social conditions - Addresses, essays, lectures. I. Bontadini, Piero. II. Gasparini, Giovanni, 1940-. III. Anfossi, Anna. IV. Studi organizzativi. V. Series: Sociologia del lavoro e dell'organizzazione, 4.
HM131 .T4 ***NYPL [JLD 81-599]***

Teoría económica de la acumulación socialista . Azqueta Oyarzun, Diego. Madrid , 1983. 224 p. ; ISBN 84-7214-279-5 LC Card 84-140278 DDC 332/.0415/091717 19
HC710.S3 A97 1983 ***NYPL [JLD 86-1859]***

Teoria ekonomiczna : metodologia i rekonstrukcje / [redakcja naukowa Piotr Buczkowski, Leszek Nowak].Wyd. 1. Poznań : Wydawn. Akademii Ekonomicznej, 1978. 147 p. : ill. ; 24 cm. (Zeszyty naukowe / Akademia Ekonomiczna w Poznaniu. Seria I . zesz. nr. 76) Includes bibliographies. LC Card 81-206275
1. Economics. I. Buczkowski, Piotr. II. Nowak, Leszek. III. Series: Zeszyty naukowe / Akademia Ekonomiczna w Poznaniu. Seria I , zesz. nr. 76.
HB54 .P6 nr. 76 HB179.P7

La teoría sobre preferencias arancelarias . Williamson B., Carlos. Santiago, Chile , 1985. 35 leaves : LC Card 85-202146
HF1733.L29 W54 1985

Teoría y práctica de la indexación . Oría, Gerardo J. (Gerardo Juan) Buenos Aires , 1985. 216 p. ; ISBN 950-9209-28-7 LC Card 86-151154
HG815 .O75 1985

Teorie dell'organizzazione . Grandori, Anna. [Milano] , 1984. xxiii, 213 p. : ISBN 88-14-00411-0 : LC Card 85-162760
HD37.I8 G73 1984

Teorii "otkrytoĭ ėkonomiki," doktriny i deĭstvitel'nost' /. IUdanov, A. IU. (Andreĭ IUr'evich) Moskva , 1983. 190 p. ; LC Card 83-209639
HF1713 .I93 1983

Teoriia i metody sistemnogo analiza. Chesnokov, S. V. (Sergeĭ Valerianovich) Determinatsionnyĭ analiz sotsial'no-ėkonomicheskikh dannykh /. Moskva , 1982. 167, [1] p. : LC Card 83-173210
HA29.5.R9 C52 1982

Teoriia i praktika ėkonomiki demoprotsessa : sbornik nauchnykh trudov / [otvetstvennye redaktory V.S. Steshenko, V.K. Cherniak]. Kiev : IĖ AN USSR, 1982. 181 p., [2] folded leaves of plates : ill. ; 20 cm. At head of title: Akademiia nauk Ukrainskoĭ SSR. Institut ėkonomiki. Includes bibliographical references. LC Card 83-145373
1. Population policy. 2. Ukraine - Population policy. 3. Ukraine - Population. I. Steshenko, Valentina Sergeevna. II. Cherniak, V. K. III. Instytut ekonomiky (Akademiia nauk Ukraïns'koï RSR).
HB883.5 .T46 1982

Teoriia i praktika optimizatsii proizvodstvennykh moshchnosteĭ morskikh portov /. Gorbatyĭ, M. M. (Mark Moiseevich) Moskva , 1981. 167 p. : LC Card 82-162836
HE551 .G625 1981

Teoriia khoziaistvennykh sviazeĭ /. Makhnova, V. I. (Vera Ivanovna) Moskva , 1985. 197 p. : LC Card 86-107892
HC336.25 .M347 1985

Teorija i praksa domaćih i medunarodnih plaćanja /. Vrsaljko, Krešimir. Zagreb , 1982. xiv, 460 p. ; LC Card 84-160248
HG2341.Y82 V77 1982

Teorijski spisi.
Čelenković, Teodosije. Radna snaga u samoupravnom društvu . Beograd , 1980. 241 p. ; LC Card 82-166188
HD5811.6.A6 C45 1980

Korać, Slobodan. Konflikti razvojnih ciljeva u samoupravnom društvu /. Beograd , 1981. 304 p. : LC Card 82-166028
HD42 .K67 1981

TEPIC (MEXICO) - ECONOMIC CONDITIONS.
López González, Pedro. La población de Tepic bajo la organización regional, 1530-1821 /. Tepic, Nay. , 1984. 80 p. : LC Card 86-119610
HB3532.T47 L66 1984

TEPIC (MEXICO) - GENEALOGY.
López González, Pedro. La población de Tepic bajo la organización regional, 1530-1821 /. Tepic, Nay. , 1984. 80 p. : LC Card 86-119610
HB3532.T47 L66 1984

TEPIC (MEXICO) - POPULATION - HISTORY.
López González, Pedro. La población de Tepic bajo la organización regional, 1530-1821 /. Tepic, Nay. , 1984. 80 p. : LC Card 86-119610
HB3532.T47 L66 1984

Tepper, August. Mambrey, Peter. Computer und Partizipation . Opladen , c1986. xiv, 271 p. : ISBN 3-531-11851-X LC Card 87-122986 DDC 650/.028/5 19
HF5548.2 .M27 1986

Tepper, Ron, 1937-
The consultant's problem solving workbook / Ron Tepper. New York : Wiley, c1987. xiv, 323 p. : ill. ; 29 cm. Includes index. ISBN 0-471-84682-1 LC Card 86-24728 DDC 658.4/6 19
1. Business consultants. I. Title.
HD69.C6 T47 1987

Secrets of a successful mail order guru : Chase Revel / Ron Tepper. New York : J. Wiley, c1988. ix, 230 p. : ill. ; 24 cm. Includes index. ISBN 0-471-84857-3 LC Card 87-21658 DDC 658.8/72 19
1. Mail-order business. 2. Revel, Chase. I. Title.
HF5466 .T36 1988

Terán, Néstor Taboada. see **Taboada Terán, Néstor.**

Terasawa, Katsuaki. Quirk, James P. The choice of discount rate applicable to government resource use . Santa Monica, CA [1987] xviii, 52 p. : ISBN 0-8330-0849-8 (pbk.) LC Card 87-9867 DDC 336.3/9 19
HJ7451 .Q57 1987

Terbócs, László. Halmos, Csaba. A szakszervezetek és a tervezés /. Budapest , 1983. 178 p. ; ISBN 963-608-052-6 LC Card 85-108502
HD6680.5 .H34 1983

Tercer informe de gobierno. Zacatecas (Mexico : State). Governor (1980- : Cervantes Corona) Zacatecas , 1983. 350 p. : LC Card 86-202257
HJ15.Z3 Z33 1980

La terciarización del empleo en la Argentina. Cimillo, Elsa. [Buenos Aires] [1985] 23, [41], 3 p. ; LC Card 87-123708 DDC 381/.1/0982 19
HF5429.6.A7 C56 1985

La terciarización del empleo en la Argentina. Lindenboim, Javier. Buenos Aires , 1985. vi, 59, 50, 3 p. ; LC Card 87-122527 DDC 381 19
HD2346.A73 L56 1985

La terciarización del empleo en la Argentina. Szretter, Héctor. Buenos Aires , 1985. iv, 82, 3 p. ; LC Card 87-122558 DDC 331.7/6164046/0982 19
HD8039.D52 A657 1985

La terciarización del empleo en la Argentina. El sector de servicios a las empresas /. Bour, Juan Luis. Buenos Aires , 1985. 117 p. ; LC Card 87-123717 DDC 338.4/6/0982 19
HD9985.A72 B68 1985

Terekhov, A. I. Romanov, A. K. (Arnol'd Konstantinovich) Matematicheskoe modelirovanie dvizheniia kadrov v organizatsiiakh /. Moskva , 1986. 154 p. : LC Card 87-158073
HF5549.5.T8 R56 1986

Terekhov, IU. I. (IUriĭ Ivanovich) Planirovanie narodnogo khoziaistva SSSR / IU.I. Terekhov, V.A. Smirnova. Khar'kov : Izd-vo pri Khar'kovskom gos. universitete izdatel'skogo ob"edineniia "Vyshcha shkola", 1985. 176 p. ; 23 cm. Authorized for instructional purposes. Includes bibliographies. LC Card 86-102455
1. Soviet Union - Economic policy - 1981-. I. Smirnova, V. A. (Veronika Aleksandrovna). II. Title.
HC336.25 .T465 1985

Terekhov, V. P. (Vladimir Pavlovich) Shchedrost' zemli krymskoĭ . Simferopol' , 1985. 158 p. ; LC Card 86-128000
HD9015.S653 K797 1985

A terhességmegszakításon átesett 18 éven aluli hajadonok társadalmi-demográfiai jellemzői /. Pongrácz, Tiborné. Budapest , c1986. 115 p. ; LC Card 87-409645
HA1201 .A64 no. 62 HQ767.5.H8

Terkla, David G. Doeringer, Peter B. Invisible factors in local economic development /. New York , 1987. vii, 144 p. : ISBN 0-19-504965-9 (alk. paper) LC Card 87-13550 DDC 338.9744/3 19
HC107.M42 W674 1987

The term structure of interest rates in New Zealand, 1977-1985 /. LLoyd, K. A. Wellington, N.Z. [1986] 41, 3 p. : LC Card 86-212755 DDC 332.8/2/09931 19
HG1623.N48 L56 1986

Termelés és életmód . Dobrossy, István. Debrecen , 1983. 282 p. : ISBN 963-471-276-2 LC Card 86-100359
HD1492.H82 P873 1983

Termelőszövetkezeti szakemberek munkahelyváltoztatása . Meszticzky, András. [Budapest] , 1985. 165 p. : LC Card 86-218526
HD1492.H8 M37 1985

A termelőszövetkezeti termelésirányítókról . Ivanics, András. Budapest , 1984. 83 p. ; ISBN 963-491-179-X LC Card 86-198816
HD1492.H82 B675 1984

TERMINALS, COMPUTER. see **COMPUTER TERMINALS.**

TERMINALS, DATA (COMPUTERS) see **COMPUTER TERMINALS.**

Terminologie des échanges et paiements internationaux et de la comptabilité nationale. Organisation for European Economic Co-operation. Paris [1958] 146, [6] p. LC Card

58-47135 DDC 382.03
HF1002 .O7 *NYPL [JLF 87-128]*

The terms of trade and Third World countries /. Mannur, H. G. Pulau Pinang , 1978. ii, 35 p. ; LC Card 84-940687
HF4055 .M36 1978

Ternovoĭ, O. I. V.I. Lenin, KPSS o sotsialisticheskom sorevnovanii /. Moskva , 1985. 540 p. ; LC Card 86-128447
HC340.S6 V18 1985

Terny, Guy. Le Financement des équipements publics de demain /. Paris , c1986. 432 p. : ISBN 2-7178-1186-9 : LC Card 87-117264
HC280.C3 F56 1986

Terol Esteban, Alberto. Lampreave Pérez, José Luis. La empresa española ante el impuesto sobre el valor añadido, medidas de adaptación y ajuste /. Madrid, España , 1985. 493 p. : ISBN 84-7196-571-2 : LC Card 86-208329
HJ5715.S7 L36 1985

Terra de Deus, terra de irmãos : manual. Brasília-DF : CNBB, [1986] 190 p. : ill. ; 23 cm. At head of title: Campanha da fraternidade, 1986. Bibliography: p. 189-190. LC Card 86-233600
1. Land reform - Brazil. 2. Land tenure - Brazil. 3. Church and social problems - Catholic Church. 4. Church and social problems - Brazil. 5. Indians of South America - Brazil - Land tenure. I. Catholic Church. Conferência Nacional dos Bispos do Brasil. II. Title: Campanha da fraternidade, 1986.
HD1333.B6 T47 1986

A terra era liberta . Luna, Regina Celi Miranda Reis. São Luís, MA , 1985. xxvii, 146 p. : LC Card 87-135907 DDC 333.3/0981/21 19
HD499.P46 L86 1985

Terra, Juan Pablo, 1924. Proceso y significado del cooperativismo uruguayo / Juan Pablo Terra. Montevideo : Arca : Banda Oriental, [1986] 171 p. ; 19 cm. At head of title: Comisión Económica para América Latina y el Caribe (CEPAL). Bibliography: p. [163]-171. LC Card 87-403179 DDC 334/.09885 19
1. Cooperation - Uruguay - History. I. United Nations. Economic Commission for Latin America and the Caribbean. II. Title.
HD3482.A4 T47 1986

A terra, o homem, as reformas /. Vinhas, M. Rio de Janeiro (R. Hermenegildo de Barros, 31-A Glória, Rio de Janeiro) , 1980. xiii, 151 p. ;
NYPL [JLD 86-783]

Terra, treball i propietat : classes agràries i règim senyorial als països catalans / Núria Sales ... [et al.] ; pròleg de Ramon Garrabou. Barcelona : Centre de Treball i Documentació : Crítica, c1986. 346 p. ; 20 cm. Includes bibliographical references. ISBN 84-7423-287-2 LC Card 86-216973
1. Agriculture - Economic aspects - Spain - Catalonia - History. 2. Peasantry - Spain - Catalonia - History. 3. Land tenure - Spain - Catalonia - History. 4. Farm tenancy - Economic aspects - Spain - Catalonia - History. I. Sales de Bohigas, Núria, 1933-. II. Centre de Treball i Documentació (Barcelona, Spain).
HD2025.C35 T47 1986

TERRAIN SESING, REMOTE. see **REMOTE SENSING.**

Terratenientes y campesinos en Piura, ss. XVI-XIX . Espinoza Claudio, César. Lima, Perú , 1981. xxviii, 123 p., [6] leaves of plates : LC Card 82-146131
HD559.P5 E87 1981

El terremoto de octubre de 1986 en San Salvador y la situación habitacional de los sectores populares /. Lungo, Mario. Ciudad Universitaria Rodrigo Facio [Costa Rica] , 1987. 26 leaves ; LC Card 87-125001 DDC 363.3/495 19
HD7287.96.S22 S265 1987

Terremoto del diecinueve de septiembre y los trabajadores mexicanos. El Terremoto del 19 de septiembre y los trabajadores mexicanos. [Mexico City, Mexico?] [1985] 114 p. ; LC Card 86-144990
HC138.M4 T47 1985 *NYPL [JLC 87-130]*

Terremoto e crisi urbana : le forze intellettuali e la ricostruzion e: 3 proposte di ricerca-intervento dagli atti del seminario organizzato dal C.R.E.S.M. di Napoli su localizzazione residenziale e produttiva nel dopo-terremoto [e] aspetti sociali, economici e territoriali nell'opera di recostruzione, Napoli, Castel Sant'Elmo, 15/20 giugno 1981. Napoli : Cooperativa sintesi editrice, 1981. 207 p. ; 24 cm. (Ricostruire e/o trasformare . 2) "Contributi di: V. Andriello, [et al.] ... ."
1. Earthquakes - Italy, Southern. 2. Disaster relief - Italy, Southern. 3. City planning - Italy - Naples. 4. Naples (Italy) - Earthquake, 1980. I. Andriello, Vincenzo. II. Centro ricerche economiche e sociali per il Meridionale (Naples, Italy). III. Series.
NYPL [JLE 86-4532]

Terres australes et antarctiques françaises : catalogue spécialisé 1982 / Gérard Dupraz ... [et al.]. [France] : Editions du Pôle sud, 1982. 216 p. : ill. (some col.) ; 22 cm. LC Card 82-171424
1. Postage-stamps - Terres australes et antarctiques françaises - Catalogs. I. Dupraz, Gérard.
HE6185.F83 T477 1982

TERRITORIAL INDUSTRIAL COMPLEXES - SOVIET UNION, NORTHERN.
Kaplan, L. M. (Lev Moiseevich) Ėkonomicheskie problemy upravleniia stroitel'nym proizvodstvom na Severe /. Leningrad , 1983. 167 p. : LC Card 84-113191
HD9715.S73 N675 1983

TERRITORIAL PRODUCTION COMPLEXES - KAZAKH S.S.R.
Ėffektivnost' territorial'noĭ organizatsii promyshlennogo proizvodstva v Kazakhstane /. Alma-Ata , 1980. 190 p. ; LC Card 82-164638
HC337.K33 D53 1980

TERRITORIAL PRODUCTION COMPLEXES - RUSSIAN S.F.S.R. - KANSK-ACHINSK BASIN.
Territorial'no-proizvodstvennyĭ kompleks . Moskva , 1982. 107 p. : LC Card 83-200414
HC337.R852 K3685 1982

TERRITORIAL PRODUCTION COMPLEXES - RUSSIAN S.F.S.R. - MANAGEMENT.
Territorial'no-proizvodstvennye kompleksy . Novosibirsk , 1986. 263 p. : LC Card 86-231926
HC336.25 .T467 1986

TERRITORIAL PRODUCTION COMPLEXES - RUSSIAN S.F.S.R. - SIBERIA.
KATĖK i razvitie otrasleĭ khoziaĭstva Sibiri /. Novosibirsk , 1984. 164 p. ; LC Card 84-167870
HC337.R852 S5246 1984

Metodologicheskie polozheniia razrabotki krupnykh territorial'nykh programm /. Novosibirsk , 1986. 303 p. : LC Card 86-211369
HC337.R853 D56 1986

Metodologicheskie problemy formirovaniia territorial'no-proizvodstvennykh kompleksov /. Novosibirsk , 1980. 162 p. : LC Card 82-106930
HC336.25 .M46 1980

Territorial'no-proizvodstvennye kompleksy--voprosy struktury i razvitiia . Novosibirsk , 1981. 152 p. ; LC Card 82-160051
HC337.R852 S5276 1981

TERRITORIAL PRODUCTION COMPLEXES - SOVIET UNION.
Ėkonomika SSSR--edinyĭ narodnokhoziaĭstvennyĭ kompleks /. Moskva , 1981. 143 p. : LC Card 82-111112
HC336.25 .E39 1981

Metodologicheskie problemy formirovaniia territorial'no-proizvodstvennykh kompleksov /. Novosibirsk , 1980. 162 p. : LC Card 82-106930
HC336.25 .M46 1980

TERRITORIAL PRODUCTION COMPLEXES - SOVIET UNION - CAPITAL PRODUCTIVITY.
Problemy povysheniia ėkonomicheskoĭ ėffektivnosti kapital'nykh vlozheniĭ v territorial'nye promyshlennye kompleksy. Moskva , 1983. 170 p. : LC Card 84-202808
HC340.C3 P747 1983

TERRITORIAL PRODUCTION COMPLEXES - SOVIET UNION - MANAGEMENT.
Territorial'no-proizvodstvennye kompleksy . Novosibirsk , 1986. 263 p. : LC Card 86-231926
HC336.25 .T467 1986

TERRITORIAL PRODUCTION COMPLEXES - SOVIET UNION - METHODOLOGY.
Metodicheskie rekomendatsii po issledovaniiu proizvodstvennoĭ infrastruktury territorial'no-proizvodstvennykh kompleksov i promyshlennykh uzlov /. Sverdlovsk , 1983. 79 p. (some folded) ; LC Card 86-113572
HC340.C3 M416 1983

TERRITORIAL PRODUCTION COMPLEXES - SOVIET UNION, NORTHERN.
Krasnopol'skiĭ, B. Kh. (Boris Khananovich) Infrastruktura v sisteme regional'nogo khoziaĭstvennogo kompleksa Severa . Moskva , 1980. 143, [2] p. ; LC Card 81-131391
HC336.9.N65 K73 1980

TERRITORIAL PRODUCTION COMPLEXES - TAJIK S.S.R. - MATHEMATICAL MODELS.
Baĭriev, B. S. Optimizatsiia struktur upravleniia /. Ashkhabad , 1985. 169, [23] p. : LC Card 86-196466
HC337.T23 B35 1985

Territoriale Probleme der ökonomischen Integration der EG-Länder /. Oelke, Eckhard. Gotha , 1986. 118 p. : ISBN 3-7301-0872-7 LC Card 87-118872 DDC 337.1/42 19
HC241.2 .O32 1986

Territorial'naia organizatsiia prodovol'stvennogo kompleksa : sbornik nauchnykh trudov / [redkol. A.T. Velikokhat'ko ... P.P. Marakulin (otv. red.) ... et al.]. Kiev : Akademiia nauk Ukr. SSR, Sovet po izucheniiu proizvoditel'nykh sil USSR, 1985. 163 p. ; 20 cm. Includes bibliographical references. LC Card 86-175134
1. Food industry and trade - Ukraine - Location. 2. Agricultural industries - Ukraine - Location. I. Velikokhat'ko, A. T. II. Marakulin, P. P. (Pavel Pavlovich). III. Rada po vyvchenniu produktyvnykh syl URSR.
HD9015.S653 U4755 1985

Territorial'naia organizatsiia proizvoditel'nykh sil SSSR / [redaktsionnaia kollegiia, O.A. Kibal'chich ... et al.]. Moskva : Moskovskiĭ filial geogr. ob-va SSSR, 1978. 124 p. : ill. ; 20 cm. Includes bibliographical references. LC Card 81-149822
1. Soviet Union - Industries - Location. 2. Soviet Union - Industries - Location - Maps. I. Kibal'chich, Oleg Alekseevich. II. Geograficheskoe obshchestvo SSSR. Moskovskiĭ filial.
HC340.D5 T44 1978

Territorial'naia struktura ėkonomicheskogo raĭona . Bugaev, V. K. (Vladimir Konstantinovich) Leningrad , 1986. 164, [3] p. : LC Card 87-120624
HC336.25 .B84 1986

Territorial'no-proizvodstvennye kompleksy : sovershenstvovanie protsessa formirovaniia / otvetstvennyĭ redaktor M.K. Bandman. Novosibirsk : Izd-vo "Nauka," Sibirskoe otd-nie, 1986. 263 p. : ill. ; 23 cm. At head of title: Akademiia nauk SSSR. Sibirskoe otdelenie. Institut ėkonomiki i organizatsii promyshlennogo proizvodstva. Includes bibliographies. LC Card 86-231926
1. Territorial production complexes - Soviet Union - Management. 2. Territorial production complexes - Russian S.F.S.R. - Management. I. Bandman, Mark Konstantinovich. II. Institut ėkonomiki i organizatsii promyshlennogo proizvodstva (Akademiia nauk SSSR).
HC336.25 .T467 1986

Territorial'no-proizvodstvennye kompleksy--voprosy struktury i razvitiia : sbornik nauchnykh trudov / pod redaktsieĭ M.K. Bandmana. Novosibirsk : Akademiia nauk SSSR, Sibirskoe otd-nie, In-t ėkonomiki i organizatsii promyshlennogo proizvodstva, 1981. 152 p. ; 20 cm. Includes bibliographies. LC Card 82-160051
1. Territorial production complexes - Russian S.F.S.R. - Siberia. I. Bandman, Mark Konstantinovich. II. Institut ėkonomiki i organizatsii promyshlennogo proizvodstva (Akademiia nauk SSSR).
HC337.R852 S5276 1981

Territorial'no-proizvodstvennyĭ kompleks : problemy sotsial'nogo razvitiia i upravleniia (na primere KATĖKa) / [otvetstvennye redaktory A.V. Kochetkov, O.S. Pchelintsev]. Moskva : Vses. nauchno-issl. in-t sistemnykh issledovaniĭ, 1982. 107 p. : ill. ; 26 cm. (Sbornik trudov . vyp. 4) Includes bibliographies. LC Card 83-200414
1. Territorial production complexes - Russian S.F.S.R. - Kansk-Achinsk Basin. 2. Energy industries - Russian S.F.S.R. - Kansk-Achinsk Basin. I. Kochetkov, Andreĭ Vasil'evich. II. Pchelintsev, Oleg Sergeevich. III. Series:

Sbornik trudov (Vsesoiūznyĭ nauchno-issledovatel'skiĭ institut sistemnykh issledovaniĭ) , 1982, vyp. 4.
HC337.R852 K3685 1982

Territorial'nye osobennosti razmeshcheniīa pishchevoĭ promyshlennosti USSR / [avtory IU.P. Lebedinskiĭ ... et al. ; otvetstvennyĭ redaktor IU.P. Lebedinskiĭ]. Kiev : Nauk. dumka, 1982. 282 p. ; 21 cm. At head of title: Akademiīa nauk Ukrainskoĭ SSR. Sovet po izucheniīu proizvoditel'nykh sil USSR. Bibliography: p. 282-[283] LC Card 83-197067
1. Food industry and trade - Ukraine - Location. I. Lebedinskiĭ, IUriĭ Petrovich. II. Rada po vyvchenniū produktyvnykh syl URSR.
HD9015.S653 U476 1982

Territorial'nye struktury promyshlennosti / [redaktsionnaīa kollegiīa O.A. Kibal'chich ... et al.]. Moskva : Moskovskiĭ filial Geograficheskogo obshchestva SSSR, 1978. 128 p. : ill. ; 20 cm. LC Card 81-147566
1. Soviet Union - Industries - Location. 2. Europe, Eastern - Industries - Location. 3. Industry - Location. I. Kibal'chich, Oleg Aleksandrovich. II. Geograficheskoe obshchestvo SSSR. Moskovskiĭ filial.
HC340.D5 T464 1978

Terror in the skies /. Ashwood, Thomas M. New York , 1987. p. cm. ISBN 0-8128-3125-X : LC Card 86-42779 DDC 363.2/876 19
HE9779 .A74 1987

TERROR, REIGN OF. see **FRANCE - HISTORY - REVOLUTION, 1789-1799.**

Ters'kyĭ, Ĭon. Shcho take stalins'ke "tyloopolchenniīa"? : spohady / Ĭon Ters'kyĭ. Toronto : Basilian Press, 1969. 95 p. ; 21 cm. Bibliography: p. 94-95. LC Card 82-105191
1. Forced labor - Ukraine. 2. Forced labor - Russian S.F.S.R. I. Title.
HD4865.S65 T47 1969

Terssac, G. de (Gilbert) Quéinnec, Y. (Yvon) Le travail posté . [Toulouse-Le Mirail] , 1985. 261 p. : ISBN 2-85816-030-9 LC Card 87-133427
HD5111.5 .Q45 1985

TERUEL (SPAIN : PROVINCE) - ECONOMIC CONDITIONS.
Estudio para el desarrollo de las zonas económicas de la Provincia de Teruel /. [Teruel] , 1965. 75, 61, 63, 65, 74, 61 p. ; LC Card 85-110389
HC387.T4 E886 1965

Infante Díaz, Jorge. Aproximación a la estructura económica de la provincia de Teruel /. [Teruel] , 1986. 59 p. : ISBN 84-505-3546-8 LC Card 87-105066
HC387.T4 I53 1986

TERUEL, SPAIN (PROVINCE) - ECONOMIC POLICY.
Estudio para el desarrollo de las zonas económicas de la Provincia de Teruel /. [Teruel] , 1965. 75, 61, 63, 65, 74, 61 p. ; LC Card 85-110389
HC387.T4 E886 1965

Területfejlesztési közlemények, 0139-0376 .
(13. sz) A Magyarországi településrendszer strukturális változása /. Budapest , 1984. 155 p., [1] folded leaf of plates : ISBN 963-03-2079-7 (Magy. nemz. bibl.) LC Card 85-231254
HD640.5 .M343 1984

Terushkin, Anatoliĭ Georgievich. Voprosy postroeniīa sistemy modeleĭ finansovogo aspekta vosproizvodstva /. Moskva , 1984. 154 p. : LC Card 86-144339
HG186.S55 V67 1984

Terv, kampány, pénz . Soós, Károly Attila. Budapest , 1986. 532 p. : ISBN 963-221-575-3 : LC Card 87-137237
HB3787.5 .S66 1986

Tervezési szintek érdekeltségének összehangolása gazdaságszabályozási eszközökkel . Kovács, Kálmán. Budapest , 1984. 50 p. : ISBN 963-491-189-7 LC Card 86-198789
HD1940.5.Z8 K68 1984

Teschner, Eckart, 1940- Lohnpolitik im Betrieb : eine empirische Untersuchung in der Metall-, Chemie-, Textil- und Tabakindustrie / Eckart Teschner. Frankfurt/Main ; New York : Campus, c1977. 226 p. : ill. ; 21 cm. (Studienreihe des Instituts für Sozialforschung Frankfurt am Main) Bibliography: p. 221-226. "D 30"--T.p. verso. ISBN 3-593-32244-7 LC Card 85-134281 DDC 331.2/943 19
1. Wages - Metal-workers - Germany (West) - Case studies. 2. Wages - Chemical workers - Germany (West) - Case studies. 3. Wages - Textile workers - Germany (West) - Case studies. 4. Wages - Tobacco workers - Germany (West) - Case studies. I. Series: Studienreihe des Instituts für Sozialforschung Frankfurt am Main (Campus Verlag). II. Title.
HD4966.M44 G48 1977

Tese, Vincent. Rebuilding New York--the next phase, from recovery to resurgence : a strategic plan for expanding economic and job development in New York State / Vincent Tese. [New York, NY (1515 Broadway, New York 10036) : Office of Director of Economic Development, 1985] 74 leaves ; 29 cm. "September 30, 1985." LC Card 86-622413 DDC 338.9747 19
1. New York (State) - Economic conditions. 2. New York (State) - Economic policy. I. New York (State). Office of Economic Development. II. Title.
HC107.N7 T47 1985

Teses (Editora da UNICAMP)
Barreiro, José Carlos. Campesinato e capitalismo /. Campinas-SP [1986] 128 p. ; LC Card 86-229683
HD1531.B7 B37 1986

Teses (Rio Grande do Sul (Brazil). Fundação de Economia e Estatística) .
(n. 8) Carrion, Rosinha Machado. Participação ou manipulação . Porto Alegre, RS , 1984. 111 p. : LC Card 84-209842 DDC 658 19
HD37.P63 C29 1984 ***NYPL [JLE 86-2263]***

Teses (Rio Grande do Sul (Brazil). Fundação de Economica e Estatística) .
(n. 7) Pereira, José Maria Dias. A participação da alimentação na inflação brasileira nos anos 70 . Porto Alegre, RS , 1984. 139 p. : LC Card 85-128694 DDC 338.4/36413/00981 19
HD9014.B82 P47 1984
NYPL [JLE 86-2264]

Tesis doctorales (Institución "Fernando el Católico") .
(58) Biescas, José Antonio, 1946- El proceso de industrialización en la región aragonesa en el período 1900-1920 /. Zaragoza , 1985. 335 p. : ISBN 84-00-06130-6 LC Card 87-111810
HC387.A68 B536 1985

Tesler, Edward. Soviet economic planning : theory and practice / Edward Tesler. Falls Church, VA (7700 Leesburg Pike, #250, Falls Church 22043) : Delphic Associates, c1986. ix, 88 leaves : ill. ; 28 cm. (Monograph series on Soviet Union) LC Card 87-403383 DDC 338.947 19
1. Central planning - Soviet Union. 2. Soviet Union - Economic policy. I. Title. II. Series.
HC335 .T425 1986

Test of the Chilean labor market efficiency.
Riveros C., Luis. Structural reforms and wage setting across sectors . Santiago , 1984. 37, [5], 13 p. ; ***NYPL [JLF 87-136]***

Testaments of radicalism : memoirs of working class politicians 1790-1885 / edited and introduced by David Vincent. London : Europa Publications, c1977. vii, 246 p., [3] leaves of plates : ill. ; 25 cm. Includes bibliographical references and index. ISBN 0-905118-01-4 : LC Card 77-377253 DDC 322/.2/0922 B
1. Labor and laboring classes - Great Britain - Biography. 2. Labor and laboring classes - Great Britain - Political activity - History. I. Vincent, David, 1949-.
HD8383.7.A1 T47 ***NYPL [JLE 86-4274]***

Testfahrer und Autospione . Maxeiner, Dirk, 1953- Stuttgart , 1985. 214 p. : ISBN 3-613-01022-4 : LC Card 85-170273
HD9710.A2 M385 1985

Testi e contributi di economia .
(6) Leccisotti, Mario. Politiche dell'impresa e sistema tributario /. Napoli , 1984. 174 p. : ISBN 88-20-70883-3 :
NYPL [JLD 86-3651]

TESTING EQUIPMENT INDUSTRY - UNITED STATES.
The Microwave test equipment market in the U. S. New York, N.Y. , c1983. iii, 223 p. ; LC Card 87-143814
HD9696.M533 U56 1983

TESTS, PSYCHOLOGICAL. see **PSYCHOLOGICAL TESTS.**

Teteneva, L. G. (Lidiīa Georgievna)
Akhunova, M. A. Rabochiĭ klass Uzbekistana v usloviīakh nauchno-tekhnicheskoĭ revoliūtsii /. Tashkent , 1984. 181 p. ; LC Card 85-232015
HD6331.2.S652 U93 1984

Shister, G. A. (Grigoriĭ Aronovich) Rukovodstvo kompartii Uzbekistana podgotovkoĭ rabochikh kadrov v usloviīakh razvitogo sotsializma /. Tashkent , 1981. 274, [2] p. ; LC Card 82-204041
HD5797.U9 S54 1981

Tetradia ergasias .
(6) Spēliōtakēs, K. K. Archeion Michaēl Iatrou, 1802-1893 /. Athēna , 1983. 189 p., [4] folded leaves of plates : LC Card 85-134031
HF3750.5.S64 A3 1983
NYPL [JFE 86-4131]

Tétreault, Mary Ann, 1942- Dependency theory and the return of high politics /. Westport, Conn. , 1986. xii, 270 p. : ISBN 0-313-24860-5 (lib. bdg. : alk. paper) LC Card 85-17745 DDC 337 19
HF1411 .D35 1986 ***NYPL [JLE 86-2911]***

Tetreault, Wilfred F., 1927- Starting right in your new business / Wilfred Tetreault, Robert W. Clements. Rev. ed. Reading, Mass. : Addison-Wesley Pub. Co., c1987. ix, 226 p. ; 24 cm. "Business opportunities, general resources, and references": p. 223-226. ISBN 0-201-07795-7 (pbk.) : LC Card 87-19464 DDC 658.1/141 19
1. Small business - Purchasing. 2. Business enterprises, Sale of. I. Clements, Robert W. II. Title.
HD62.7 .T47 1987

Tetzel, Manfred. Philosophie und Ökonomie, oder, Das Exempel Bernstein / Manfred Tetzel ; [herausgegeben von der Akademie für Gesellschaftswissenschaften beim Zentralkomitee der Sozialistischen Einheitspartei Deutschlands]. Berlin : Dietz, 1984. 187 p. : ill. ; 20 cm. Bibliography: p. 177-182. Includes index. LC Card 84-166815
1. Bernstein, Eduard, 1850-1932. 2. Marxian economics. 3. Historical materialism. I. Akademie für Gesellschaftswissenschaften. II. Title.
HB107.B52 T48 1984

Tetzlaff, Rainer. Strukturelemente der Weltgesellschaft . Frankfurt am Main , 1981. v, 356 p. : ISBN 3-7875-1727-8 LC Card 83-190809
HF1411 .S845 1981

Teubal, Morris. Innovation performance, learning, and government policy : selected essays / Morris Teubal. Madison, Wis. : University of Wisconsin Press, 1987. xvi, 308 p. : ill. ; 24 cm. (The Economics of technological change) Includes bibliographies and index. ISBN 0-299-10950-X : LC Card 86-40448 DDC 338/.06 19
1. Technological innovations - Economic aspects. 2. Technology and state. I. Title. II. Series.
HC79.T4 T485 1987

Teufelsbauer, Werner. Richter, Josef. Energiekosten und Anpassungsverhalten der Wirtschaft /. Wien , 1985. iv, 184 p. : ISBN 3-85436-031-2 LC Card 86-154099
HD9502.A92 R53 1985

Teure neue Medien . Lenhardt, Helmut, 1923- Salzburg , 1983. 152 p. ; ISBN 3-85015-012-7 LC Card 84-107910
HE8700.72.A9 L46 1983

Teusch, Wolfgang. Aufbau und Gewinnung Shephardscher Produktionsfunktionen unter Berücksichtigung empirischer Aspekte / von Wolfgang Teusch. Königstein/Ts. : Verlagsgruppe Athenäum, Hain, Hanstein, c1983. vi, 296 p. : ill. ; 23 cm. (Mathematical systems in economics. 78) Bibliography: p. 288-296. ISBN 3-445-02274-7 LC Card 83-195883
1. Production functions (Economic theory). 2. Shephard, Ronald William. I. Title.
HB241 .T48 1983

Teuteberg, Hans Jürgen. Wohnalltag in Deutschland, 1850-1914 : Bilder, Daten, Dokumente / Hans J. Teuteberg, Clemens Wischermann. Münster : F. Coppenrath, 1985. 488 p. : ill. ; 28 cm. (Studien zur Geschichte des Alltags . Bd. 3) Bibliography: p. 483-485. ISBN 3-88547-277-5 LC Card 86-165201
1. Housing - Germany - History. 2. Housing policy - Germany - History. I. Wischermann, Clemens. II. Title. III. Series.
HD7339.A3 T46 1985

TEUTECAS INDIANS. see **CHINANTEC INDIANS.**

Teweles, Richard Jack, 1924- The stock market / Richard J. Teweles, Edward S. Bradley. 5th ed. New York : Wiley, c1987. xii, 526 p. ; 24 cm. (Wiley professional banking and finance series, 0733-8945) "A revision of earlier editions by the late George L. Leffler and Loring C. Farwell." Includes bibliographical references and index. ISBN 0-471-82044-X LC Card 86-33950 DDC 332.64/2 19
1. Stock-exchange. I. Bradley, Edward S. II. Leffler, George Leland, 1899- Stock market. III. Title. IV. Series.
HG4551 .T48 1987

Tews, Hans Peter. Abbrüche beruflicher Rehabilitationsmassnahmen : ein Forschungsprojekt der Arbeitsgemeinschaft Deutscher Berufsförderungswerke / Hans Peter Tews ; unter Mitwirkung von J.P. Foit ... [et al.].1. Aufl. Hamburg : Hamburger Buchwerkstatt, 1986. 277 p. ; 21 cm. (Arbeit, Bildung, Gesellschaft . Bd. 3) Includes bibliographical references. ISBN 3-925408-04-5 LC Card 87-127427 DDC 362/.0425 19
1. Rehabilitation - Germany, West. 2. Rehabilitation counseling. I. Arbeitsgemeinschaft Deutscher Berufsförderungswerke. II. Title. III. Series.
HD7256.G3 T48 1986

TEXACO, INC.
Petzinger, Thomas. Oil & honor . New York , c1987. 495 p., [8] p. of plates : ISBN 0-399-13276-7 LC Card 87-2255 DDC 338.8/3622338/0973 19
HD9569.T4 P48 1987

Texas A & M University. Center for Education and Research in Free Enterprise. Hamilton, Billy. Outlook for state spending and revenues in the late '80s . College Station, Tex. , c1985. 14 p. : ISBN 0-86599-055-7 (pbk.) LC Card 86-622256 DDC 336.764 19
HJ2053.T5 H36 1985

Texas. A & M University, College Station. Agricultural Extension Service. see **Texas Agricultural Extension Service.**

Texas A & M University. Dept. of Agricultural Economics. Economic status of Texas agriculture /. College Station, Tex. [1985] ii, 30 leaves : LC Card 87-620640 DDC 338.1/09764 19
HD1775.T4 E28 1985

Texas A & M University economic series . (no. 8) Ohta, H. (Hiroshi), 1940- Spatial price theory of imperfect competition /. College Station , c1988. p. cm. ISBN 0-89096-372-X : LC Card 87-22333 DDC 338.5/2 19
HB221 .O385 1988

Texas A & M University. Sea Grant College Program. Stoll, John R. Economic impact of the recreational boating industry in Texas /. College Station, TX [1985] xiv, 86 p. : LC Card 86-622008 DDC 330.9764/063 19
HD9993.B633 U58 1985

Texas. Agricultural and Mechanical College, College Station. Extension Service. see **Texas Agricultural Extension Service.**

Texas Agricultural Experiment Station. Dept. of Agricultural Economics. Knutson, Ronald D. Cooperative involvement in issues of domestic farm policy /. College Station, Tex. , 1986. 59 p. : LC Card 86-623063 DDC 338.1/8764 19
HD1491.U6 T45 1986

Texas Agricultural Extension Service. (Old Catalog form: Texas. Agricultural and Mechanical College, College Station. Extension Service).
Economic status of Texas agriculture /. College Station, Tex. [1985] ii, 30 leaves : LC Card 87-620640 DDC 338.1/09764 19
HD1775.T4 E28 1985

The Farm credit crisis . College Station, Tex. [1986] ii, 57 p. : LC Card 86-622188 DDC 332.7/1/0973 19
HG2051.U5 F26 1986

Texas. Agriculture, Dept. of. see **Texas. Dept. of Agriculture.**

TEXAS - APPROPRIATIONS AND EXPENDITURES.
Hamilton, Billy. Outlook for state spending and revenues in the late '80s . College Station, Tex. , c1985. 14 p. : ISBN 0-86599-055-7 (pbk.) LC Card 86-622256 DDC 336.764 19
HJ2053.T5 H36 1985

TEXAS ASSOCIATION OF REALTORS - HISTORY.
Matlock, Cora Biesele. Sixty-five years the realtor in Texas . Austin, Texas , c1986. xii, 207 p. : LC Card 86-220747 DDC 333.33/06/0764 19
HD266.T4 M38 1986

TEXAS - COMMERCE.
Doing business in Texas. [Austin, Tex.] [1986], c1985. 52, [64] p. : LC Card 87-621557 DDC 332.6/7322764 19
HC107.T4 D65 1986

Paggi, Mechel S. Impact of agricultural exports for Texas /. College Station, Tex. [1986] 20 leaves, [1] leaf of plates : LC Card 87-620821 DDC 382/.41/09764 19
HD1775.T4 P34 1986

Texas. Dept. of Agriculture. (Old Catalog form: Texas. Agriculture Dept.)
Farm Crisis Workers Conference (1986 : Arlington, Tex.) Farm Crisis Workers Conference . [Austin? , 1986] 136 p. ; LC Card 87-620630 DDC 338.1/3/09764 19
HD1476.U6 T44 1986

Texas. Dept. of Highways and Public Transportation. see **Texas. State Dept. of Highways and Public Transportation.**

TEXAS - DESCRIPTION AND TRAVEL - 1981-
Doing business in Texas. [Austin, Tex.] [1986], c1985. 52, [64] p. : LC Card 87-621557 DDC 332.6/7322764 19
HC107.T4 D65 1986

TEXAS - ECONOMIC CONDITIONS.
Doing business in Texas. [Austin, Tex.] [1986], c1985. 52, [64] p. : LC Card 87-621557 DDC 332.6/7322764 19
HC107.T4 D65 1986

The Gulf Intracoastal Waterway in Texas . [Austin] , 1982. 1 v. (various pagings) : LC Card 83-620632
HE631.T4 G44 1982

Hamilton, Billy. Outlook for state spending and revenues in the late '80s . College Station, Tex. , c1985. 14 p. : ISBN 0-86599-055-7 (pbk.) LC Card 86-622256 DDC 336.764 19
HJ2053.T5 H36 1985

Hodgetts, Richard M. Addison-Wesley economics /. Menlo Park, Calif. , c1988. vi, T1-T266, 31, 548 p. : ISBN 0-201-22775-4 LC Card 87-147565 DDC 330 19
HB171.5 .H676 1988

Paggi, Mechel S. Impact of agricultural exports for Texas /. College Station, Tex. [1986] 20 leaves, [1] leaf of plates : LC Card 87-620821 DDC 382/.41/09764 19
HD1775.T4 P34 1986

Texas Economic Development Commission.
Doing business in Texas. [Austin, Tex.] [1986], c1985. 52, [64] p. : LC Card 87-621557 DDC 332.6/7322764 19
HC107.T4 D65 1986

TEXAS - ECONOMIC POLICY.
Doing business in Texas. [Austin, Tex.] [1986], c1985. 52, [64] p. : LC Card 87-621557 DDC 332.6/7322764 19
HC107.T4 D65 1986

Texas forty-seven. Guy, Duane F. Texas 47--Deaf Smith . [Hereford, Tex.] , c1986. vii, 160 p. : LC Card 86-210662 DDC 334/.682131/09764835 19
HD9688.U54 D434 1986

TEXAS. GENERAL LAND OFFICE - HISTORY.
The Land commissioners of Texas . Austin (1700 N. Congress Ave., Austin 78701) , 1986. vii, 133 p., [2] leaves of plates : LC Card 87-620990 DDC 353.97640071/32/0922 B 19
HD243.T4 L28 1986

TEXAS. GENERAL LAND OFFICE - OFFICIALS AND EMPLOYEES - BIOGRAPHY.
The Land commissioners of Texas . Austin (1700 N. Congress Ave., Austin 78701) , 1986. vii, 133 p., [2] leaves of plates : LC Card 87-620990 DDC 353.97640071/32/0922 B 19
HD243.T4 L28 1986

Texas. Highways and Public Transportation, State Dept. of. see **Texas. State Dept. of Highways and Public Transportation.**

The Texas housing affordability index /. Wright, A. L. (Arthur L.) College Station, TX [1986] 5, [17] p. : LC Card 86-622195 DDC 338.4/369083/09764021 19
HD7303.T4 W748 1986

Texas Instruments Incorporated. Proceedings of an international conference on genetic algorithms and their applications . [S.l. , 1985] 225 p. : ***NYPL [JSF 87-413]***

Texas. Land Office. see **Texas. General Land Office.**

TEXAS - OCCUPATIONS.
Mercer, Kent. Directory of licensed occupations and apprenticeship programs in Texas. [Austin, Tex.] [1985] iv, 102 p. ; LC Card 86-622006 DDC 331.7/02/09764 19
HF5382.5.U6 T45 1985

Texas public transit reference manual /. Bullard, Diane L. College Station, Tex. [1985] xv, 279 p. : LC Card 86-623065 DDC 388.4/09764 19
HE4426.T4 B84 1985

Texas real estate finance / Richard L. Chumbley ... [et al.]. New York : Wiley, c1987. xviii, 365 p. : ill. ; 29 cm. (The John Wiley Texas real estate series) Includes index. ISBN 0-471-82300-7 (pbk.) LC Card 86-29004 DDC 332.7/2/09764 19
1. Real estate business - Texas - Finance. 2. Mortgage loans - Texas. I. Chumbley, Richard L. II. Series.
HD266.T4 T5 1987

Texas Real Estate Research Center.
Born, Waldo L. A synopsis of Texas savings-and-loan associations' operations /. College Station, Tex. [1986?] 38 p. : LC Card 86-622196 DDC 332.3/2/09764 19
HG2153.T4 B67 1986

Harris, Jack C., 1945- 1985-86 real estate review and outlook /. College Station, Tex. [1985?] 22 p. ; LC Card 86-621364 DDC 333.33/09764 19
HD266.T4 H37 1985

Wright, A. L. (Arthur L.) The Texas housing affordability index /. College Station, TX [1986] 5, [17] p. : LC Card 86-622195 DDC 338.4/369083/09764021 19
HD7303.T4 W748 1986

Texas. State Dept. of Highways and Public Transportation.
Benson, Fred C. Hot-mix pavement stability performance versus laboratory test results /. College Station, Tex. [1985] xi, 225 p. : LC Card 86-620969 DDC 380.5 s 625.8/5 19
HE203 .T43 no. 285-1 TE200

Button, Joe W. Synthetic fibers in asphalt paving mixtures /. College Station, Tex. [1984] vi, 153 p. : LC Card 86-620835 DDC 380.5 s 625.8/5 19
HE203 .T43 no. 319-1F TA443.A7

Lomax, Timothy J. Guidelines for estimating the cost effectiveness of high-occupancy vehicle lanes /. College Station, Tex. , Springfield, Va. [1985] xiii, 55 p. : LC Card 86-622240 DDC 380.5 s 388.3/142 19
HE203 .T43 no. 339-5 HE356.T4

Lomax, Timothy J. Relative mobility in Texas cities, 1975 to 1984 /. College Station, Tex. [1986] xiii, 30, 9 p. : LC Card 87-620994 DDC 380.5 s 388.4/1314/09764 19
HE203 .T43 no. 339-8 HE356.T4

McCasland, William R. Transitway surveillance, communications, and control /. College Station, Tex. [1986] vi, 76 p. : LC Card 87-620995 DDC 380.5 s 388.3/143 19
HE203 .T43 no. 425-2F HE336.B8

McFarland, William F. New approaches to project ranking . College Station, Tex. , Springfield, Va. [1985] xvii, 116 p. : LC Card 86-622422 DDC 380.5 s 388.1/12/09764 19
HE203 .T43 no. 337-1F HE356.T4

McNees, Roger W. State-of-the-art and objectives of reflective raised pavement markers /. College Station, Tex. , Springfield, Va. [1986] vii, 162 p. : LC Card 87-620643 DDC

380.5 s 625.7/97 19
HE203 .T43 no. 322-1 TE203

Mason, John M. (John Michael), 1950- Operational and geometric evaluation of exclusive truck lanes /. College Station, Tex. , Springfield, Va. [1986] vii, 156 p. : LC Card 86-622239 DDC 380.5 s 388.3/14 19
HE203 .T43 no. 331-3F HE356.T4

Massimi, John J. Truck lane needs methodology . Austin , Springfield, Va. [1985] xii, 63 p. : LC Card 86-622425 DDC 388.1/3 19
HE336.T79 M37 1985

Noel, James S. Retention of reflective raised pavement markers /. College Station, Tex. , Springfield, Va. [1986] xiii, 170 p. : LC Card 87-620642 DDC 380.5 s 625.7/042 19
HE203 .T43 no. 322-3 TE203

Roberts, Freddy L. Establishing material properties for thin asphalt concrete surfaces on granular bases /. College Station, Tex. [1985] xvi, 141 p. : LC Card 86-620971 DDC 380.5 s 625.8/5 19
HE203 .T43 no. 345-1 TE270

Texas State Library. Information Services Division. Mercer, Kent. Directory of licensed occupations and apprenticeship programs in Texas. [Austin, Tex.] [1985] iv, 102 p. ; LC Card 86-622006 DDC 331.7/02/09764 19
HF5382.5.U6 T45 1985

Texas State Occupational Information Coordinating Committee. Mercer, Kent. Directory of licensed occupations and apprenticeship programs in Texas. [Austin, Tex.] [1985] iv, 102 p. ; LC Card 86-622006 DDC 331.7/02/09764 19
HF5382.5.U6 T45 1985

Texas Transportation Institute.
Benson, Fred C. Hot-mix pavement stability performance versus laboratory test results /. College Station, Tex. [1985] xi, 225 p. : LC Card 86-620969 DDC 380.5 s 625.8/5 19
HE203 .T43 no. 285-1 TE200

Bullard, Diane L. Texas public transit reference manual /. College Station, Tex. [1985] xv, 279 p. : LC Card 86-623065 DDC 388.4/09764 19
HE4426.T4 B84 1985

The Effect of tire pressures on flexible pavements /. College Station, Tex. , Springfield, Va. , 1985. viii, 235 p. : LC Card 86-622241 DDC 380.5 s 625.8 19
HE203 .T43 no. 372-1F TE270

Lomax, Timothy J. Relative mobility in Texas cities, 1975 to 1984 /. College Station, Tex. [1986] xiii, 30, 9 p. : LC Card 87-620994 DDC 380.5 s 388.4/1314/09764 19
HE203 .T43 no. 339-8 HE356.T4

McCasland, William R. Transitway surveillance, communications, and control /. College Station, Tex. [1986] vi, 76 p. : LC Card 87-620995 DDC 380.5 s 388.3/143 19
HE203 .T43 no. 425-2F HE336.B8

Roberts, Freddy L. Establishing material properties for thin asphalt concrete surfaces on granular bases /. College Station, Tex. [1985] xvi, 141 p. : LC Card 86-620971 DDC 380.5 s 625.8/5 19
HE203 .T43 no. 345-1 TE270

Sicking, Dean. Roadside concrete barriers . College Station, Tex. , Springfield, Va. [1985] vii, 60, 64, [51] p. : LC Card 86-622864 DDC 380.5 s 625.7/95 19
HE203 .T43 no. 346-1F TE228

Texas. Transportation Planning Division. The Gulf Intracoastal Waterway in Texas . [Austin] , 1982. 1 v. (various pagings) : LC Card 83-620632
HE631.T4 G44 1982

Texas. University at Austin. Lyndon Baines Johnson Library. see **Lyndon Baines Johnson Library.**

Texas. University. Business Administration School. see **Texas. University. College of Business Administration.**

Texas. University. College of Business Administration. (Old Catalog form: Texas. University. Business Administration School)
The Role of affect in consumer behavior . Lexington, Mass. , c1986. ix, 196 p. : ISBN 0-669-12874-0 (alk. paper) LC Card 85-46042 DDC 658.8/342 19
HF5415.3 .R65 1986 ***NYPL [JLE 86-3376]***

Texas 47--Deaf Smith . Guy, Duane F. [Hereford, Tex.] , c1986. vii, 160 p. : LC Card 86-210662 DDC 334/.682131/09764835 19
HD9688.U54 D434 1986

A Textbook of insurance broking / edited by Roderick Clews. 2nd ed. Wolfeboro, N.H., USA : Woodhead-Faulkner in association with the British Insurance Brokers' Association, 1988. p. cm. Includes index. ISBN 0-85941-386-1 : LC Card 87-21036 DDC 368/.941 19
1. Insurance - Great Britain.
HG8597 .T49 1988

Texte und Bildrezeption bei TV-Werbespots . Schmitt, Roland, 1954- Frankfurt am Main , New York , c1986. 192 p. : ISBN 3-8204-9513-4 LC Card 87-109606
HF6146.T42 S29 1986

The Textile and apparel trade crisis : a study prepared for the Fiber, Fabric, and Apparel Coalition for Trade (FFACT) / by Thomas R. Howell ... [et al.]. Washington, D.C. (1775 Pennsylvania Ave., N.W., Washington 20006) : Dewey, Ballantine, Bushby, Palmer & Wood, c1985. vi, 200, [23] p. : ill. ; 28 cm. Cover title. "August 1985." Includes bibliographical references. LC Card 87-122082 DDC 382/.45677 19
1. Textile industry - Government policy. 2. Clothing trade - Government policy. 3. Textiles - Commerce. 4. Free trade and protection. 5. International economic relations. I. Howell, Thomas R., 1949-. II. Fiber, Fabric and Apparel Coalition for Trade (U. S.). III. Dewey, Ballantine, Bushby, Palmer & Wood.
HD9850.6 .T475 1985

TEXTILE FABRICS - INDIA.
Report on development of India's handloom fabrics for export to the United States of America, September 1957 /. [S.l. , 1957] (Delhi : Albion Press) ii, ii, 108 p., [8] p. of plates : LC Card 81-911063
HD9866.I62 R46 1957

TEXTILE FABRICS - PURCHASING.
Planning & implementing an apparel sourcing strategy . Arlington, Va. (2500 Wilson Blvd., Suite 301, Arlington 22209) , c1986. 41 p. : LC Card 87-107327 DDC 687/.068/7 19
HD9940.U4 P52 1986

TEXTILE FABRICS - TARIFF. see **TARIFF ON TEXTILE FABRICS.**

TEXTILE FACTORIES - SOUTHERN STATES - HISTORY.
Like a family . Chapel Hill , c1987. xxiii, 468 p. : ISBN 0-8078-1754-6 (alk. paper) LC Card 87-40135 DDC 305/.9677 19
HD9077.A13 L55 1987

TEXTILE INDUSTRY - BRAZIL - ADDRESSES, ESSAYS, LECTURES.
Pequena empresa . São Paulo-Brasil [Brasília] , 1985. 2 v. : LC Card 85-180776 DDC 338.6/42/0981 19
HD9710.3.B72 P46 1985 ***NYPL [JLD 86-1588]***

TEXTILE INDUSTRY - BRAZIL - PERNAMBUCO.
Jucá, Alvaro Ferraz. Gênero industrial--têxtil /. [Recife] [1985?] 34 leaves ; LC Card 86-204296
HD9864.B83 P475 1985

TEXTILE INDUSTRY - BRAZIL - RIO GRANDE DO SUL - DIRECTORIES.
Catálogo da indústria têxtil e do vestuário do Rio Grande do Sul /. [Porto Alegre] , 1985. 96 p. ; LC Card 86-209398
HD9864.B83 R593 1985

TEXTILE INDUSTRY - BULGARIA - SLIVEN - HISTORY.
Zlatanov, Zdravko Ĭordanov. 150 godini slivenska tekstilna promishlenost /. [Sofia] , 1984. 364 p., [48] p. of plates : LC Card 85-118285
HD9865.B83 S589 1984

TEXTILE INDUSTRY - DEVELOPING COUNTRIES.
Emerging textile-exporting countries, 1984 . Washington, D.C. [1985] vii, 520 p. ; LC Card 86-603429 DDC 382/.456770091724 19
HD9868.D44 E54 1985

TEXTILE INDUSTRY - ETHIOPIA - MANAGEMENT - EMPLOYEE PARTICIPATION.
Regessa Kebede. The effect of leader behavior on worker job satisfaction and job performance in Ethiopian textile factories . [Turku] , c1987. 138 p. : LC Card 87-170154 DDC 677/.0068 19
HD5658.T42 E87 1987

TEXTILE INDUSTRY - EUROPE, EASTERN.
Die Textilindustrie im Ostblock . Frankfurt/Main , 1967. 88, 17 p., [3] leaves of plates : LC Card 85-116763
HD9865.E79 T49 1967

TEXTILE INDUSTRY - GERMANY (WEST) - CAPITAL INVESTMENTS.
Hergeth, Helmut H. A., 1956- Investitionsstrategien für stagnierende Branchen . Münster [1986?] xii, 261 p. : ISBN 3-88660-338-5 LC Card 87-134812 DDC 338.4/3677/00943 19
HD9863.5 .H39 1986

TEXTILE INDUSTRY - GERMANY (WEST) - FINANCE.
Hergeth, Helmut H. A., 1956- Investitionsstrategien für stagnierende Branchen . Münster [1986?] xii, 261 p. : ISBN 3-88660-338-5 LC Card 87-134812 DDC 338.4/3677/00943 19
HD9863.5 .H39 1986

TEXTILE INDUSTRY - GERMANY (WEST) - FORECASTING.
Siegmann, Frank, 1956- Kurzfristprognosen für die Textilwirtschaft anhand von Bestimmungsfaktoren für Saisonschwankungen /. Frankfurt am Main , New York , c1986. xxxi, 386 p. : ISBN 3-8204-9647-5 LC Card 86-233371
HD9850.1 .M58 Bd. 39 HD9863.5

TEXTILE INDUSTRY - GERMANY (WEST) - NORTH RHINE-WESTPHALIA - STATISTICS.
Das Textilgewerbe in Nordrhein-Westfalen 1977 bis 1980. Düsseldorf [1982] 109 p. : LC Card 87-407312 DDC 943/.55 s 338.4/7677/0094355021 19
HA1320.N6 A32 Heft 477 HD9863.7.N67

TEXTILE INDUSTRY - GERMANY (WEST) - SEASONAL VARIATIONS.
Siegmann, Frank, 1956- Kurzfristprognosen für die Textilwirtschaft anhand von Bestimmungsfaktoren für Saisonschwankungen /. Frankfurt am Main , New York , c1986. xxxi, 386 p. : ISBN 3-8204-9647-5 LC Card 86-233371
HD9850.1 .M58 Bd. 39 HD9863.5

TEXTILE INDUSTRY - GOVERNMENT POLICY.
The Textile and apparel trade crisis . Washington, D.C. (1775 Pennsylvania Ave., N.W., Washington 20006) , c1985. vi, 200, [23] p. : LC Card 87-122082 DDC 382/.45677 19
HD9850.6 .T475 1985

TEXTILE INDUSTRY - GOVERNMENT POLICY - DEVELOPING COUNTRIES.
Howell, Thomas R., 1949- The EEC and the third Multifiber Arrangement . Washington, DC , 1986. [14], 126, [12] p. : LC Card 86-224652 DDC 382/.45677/0094 19
HD9865.E852 H68 1986

Wiemann, Jürgen. Selektiver Protektionismus und aktive Strukturanpassung . Berlin , 1983. vii, 348 p. : ISBN 3-88985-028-6 : LC Card 83-223964
HD9865.E852 W54 1983

TEXTILE INDUSTRY - GOVERNMENT POLICY - EUROPEAN ECONOMIC COMMUNITY COUNTRIES.
Howell, Thomas R., 1949- The EEC and the third Multifiber Arrangement . Washington, DC , 1986. [14], 126, [12] p. : LC Card 86-224652 DDC 382/.45677/0094 19
HD9865.E852 H68 1986

Wiemann, Jürgen. Selektiver Protektionismus und aktive Strukturanpassung . Berlin , 1983. vii, 348 p. : ISBN 3-88985-028-6 : LC Card 83-223964
HD9865.E852 W54 1983

TEXTILE INDUSTRY - GOVERNMENT POLICY - UNITED STATES.
Cline, William R. The future of world trade in textiles and apparel /. Washington, DC , 1987. xiv, 325 p. : ISBN 0-88132-025-0 (pbk.) : LC Card 87-17068 DDC 382/.45677 19
HD9850.5 .C55 1987

TEXTILE INDUSTRY - INDIA - AHMADĀBĀD - CONGRESSES.
Industrial sickness . Ahmedabad , c1984. xv, 459 p. ; LC Card 87-902007 DDC 363.1/19677/00954 19
HD9866.I63 A385 1984

TEXTILE INDUSTRY - INDIA - CONGRESSES.
Issues in modernization of the textile industry . Ahmedabad , 1985. 87 p. : LC Card 87-902140 DDC 338.4/7677/00954 19
HD9866.I62 I58 1985

TEXTILE INDUSTRY - INDIA - GUJARAT - MANAGEMENT.
Dave, Nalini V. Industrial sickness and key areas of management . New Delhi , c1987. 523 p. : LC Card 87-901105 DDC 658/.00954/75 19
HD2747 .D32 1987

TEXTILE INDUSTRY - INDIA - PUNJAB.
Asdhir, Vijay, 1947- Industrial relations in India . New Delhi , c1987. 376 p. ; LC Card 86-903540 DDC 331.89/2877/00954552 19
HD8686.5 .A85 1987

TEXTILE INDUSTRY - ITALY - SCHIO - HISTORY - 19TH CENTURY - CONGRESSES.
Convegno nazionale di studi storici (1979 : Schio, Italy) Schio e Alessandro Rossi . Roma , 1985-1986. 2 v. (1487 p., [1] folded leaf of plates) : LC Card 87-110167
HC302.5.R6 C66 1979

TEXTILE INDUSTRY - JAPAN. .
Pascha, Werner. Strukturanpassung in schrumpfenden Branchen . Berlin , c1986. xx, 364 p. : ISBN 3-428-05983-2 LC Card 86-151590
HB41 .S3 Bd. 42 HD9866.J32

TEXTILE INDUSTRY - LAW AND LEGISLATION - UNITED STATES.
International trade in textiles & apparel . [Washington, D.C.] , c1987. 1 v. (various foliations) : LC Card 87-404516 DDC 382/.45677/00973 19
HD9850.5 .I43 1987

TEXTILE INDUSTRY - MANAGEMENT.
Sandler, Christian Heinrich. Innovative Technologien im Vertrieb . Thun , c1986. xvii, 313 p. : ISBN 3-87144-926-1 LC Card 86-171131
HD9850.5 .S25 1986

TEXTILE INDUSTRY - MASSACHUSETTS - LOWELL - HISTORY - 19TH CENTURY.
Dalzell, Robert F. Enterprising elite . Cambridge, Mass. , 1987. xviii, 298 p., [11] p. of plates : ISBN 0-674-25765-0 (alk. paper) LC Card 86-33649 DDC 338.4/7677/0097444 19
HD9858.L9 D35 1987

TEXTILE INDUSTRY - MASSACHUSETTS - WALTHAM - HISTORY - 19TH CENTURY.
Dalzell, Robert F. Enterprising elite . Cambridge, Mass. , 1987. xviii, 298 p., [11] p. of plates : ISBN 0-674-25765-0 (alk. paper) LC Card 86-33649 DDC 338.4/7677/0097444 19
HD9858.L9 D35 1987

TEXTILE INDUSTRY - MEXICO - HISTORY.
Salvucci, Richard J., 1951- Textiles and capitalism in Mexico . Princeton, N.J. , c1987. p. cm. ISBN 0-691-07749-5 (alk. paper) : LC Card 87-45535 DDC 338.4/767702824/0972 19
HD9864.M62 S25 1987

TEXTILE INDUSTRY - MEXICO - STATISTICS.
La Industria textil y del vestido en México, 1970-1982. México, D.F. , 1984. 77 p. : ISBN 968-8097-69-1 LC Card 85-203070 DDC 338.4/7677/00972021 19
HD9864.M62 I53 1984 ***NYPL [JLF 87-363]***

TEXTILE INDUSTRY - NETHERLANDS - HISTORY.
Buter, Adriaan. De kadans van de getouwen . Amsterdam , 1985. 160 p. : ISBN 90-10-05573-6 LC Card 86-110698
HD9865.N65 B88 1985

TEXTILE INDUSTRY - PARAGUAY.
Morínigo, José N. Las artesanías de cuero y tejido en el Paraguay . Asunción , 1979. 106, [1] p. : LC Card 83-219583
HD9780.P373 A866 1979
NYPL [JLF 86-1810]

TEXTILE INDUSTRY - PARAGUAY - ASUNCIÓN REGION.
Morínigo, José N. Las artesanías de cuero y tejido en el Paraguay . Asunción , 1979. 106, [1] p. : LC Card 83-219583
HD9780.P373 A866 1979
NYPL [JLF 86-1810]

TEXTILE INDUSTRY - PENNSYLVANIA - PHILADELPHIA - HISTORY - 19TH CENTURY.
Scranton, Philip. Proprietary capitalism . Philadelphia , 1987. p. cm. ISBN 0-87722-461-7 (pbk.) : LC Card 87-488 DDC 338.4/7677/00974811 19
HD9858.P5 S35 1987

TEXTILE INDUSTRY - PORTUGAL - HISTORY.
Mónica, Maria Filomena, 1943- Artesãos e operários . Lisboa [1986] 228 p., [24] p. of plates : LC Card 86-229921
HD8596 .M65 1986

TEXTILE INDUSTRY - SOUTH AFRICA.
South Africa. Committee of Inquiry into the Textile and Clothing Industries. The policy of protection in regard to textiles and clothing . Pretoria , 1982?] ix, 110, [28] p. ; ISBN 0-621-08170-1 (pbk.) : LC Card 86-207580 DDC 382/.45677/00968 19
HF2651.C635 S627 1982

TEXTILE INDUSTRY - SOVIET UNION - LABOR PRODUCTIVITY.
Denisova, N. F. (Nina Fedorovna) Planirovanie otdelochnogo proizvodstva s primeneniem matematicheskikh metodov i ĖVM . Moskva , 1984. 59, [5] p. : LC Card 85-131509
HD9865.S652 D46 1984

TEXTILE INDUSTRY - SOVIET UNION - MANAGEMENT.
Nogaĭ, A. I. (Anatoliĭ Il'ich) Ėkonomicheskiĭ analiz raboty predpriiatiĭ legkoĭ promyshlennosti /. Moskva , 1982. 175 p. : LC Card 83-142136
HD9865.S652 N64 1982

TEXTILE INDUSTRY - SOVIET UNION - PLANNING - DATA PROCESSING.
Denisova, N. F. (Nina Fedorovna) Planirovanie otdelochnogo proizvodstva s primeneniem matematicheskikh metodov i ĖVM . Moskva , 1984. 59, [5] p. : LC Card 85-131509
HD9865.S652 D46 1984

TEXTILE INDUSTRY - SOVIET UNION - PLANNING - MATHEMATICAL MODELS.
Denisova, N. F. (Nina Fedorovna) Planirovanie otdelochnogo proizvodstva s primeneniem matematicheskikh metodov i ĖVM . Moskva , 1984. 59, [5] p. : LC Card 85-131509
HD9865.S652 D46 1984

TEXTILE INDUSTRY - STATISTICS.
La Industria textil y del vestido en México, 1970-1982. México, D.F. , 1984. 77 p. : ISBN 968-8097-69-1 LC Card 85-203070 DDC 338.4/7677/00972021 19
HD9864.M62 I53 1984 ***NYPL [JLF 87-363]***

TEXTILE INDUSTRY - SWEDEN.
Distributionsutredning. Stockholm , 1981. 2 v. : ISBN 91-38-06684-X (v. 1) LC Card 82-234445
HD9865.S86 D57 1981

Tekoindustrierna . Stockholm , 1980. 189 p. : ISBN 91-38-05813-8 LC Card 82-236884
HD9865.S86 T45 1980

TEXTILE INDUSTRY - SWEDEN - MARKS HÄRAD - HISTORY - 19TH CENTURY.
Andersson-Palmqvist, Lena. Decentraliserad textilindustri . Stockholm , 1979/80 [i.e. 1980] 68 p. : ISBN 91-86016-06-7 LC Card 81-138133
HD9865.S87 M373 1980

TEXTILE INDUSTRY - SWEDEN - STATISTICS.
Distributionsutredning. Stockholm , 1981. 2 v. : ISBN 91-38-06684-X (v. 1) LC Card 82-234445
HD9865.S86 D57 1981

TEXTILE INDUSTRY - SWITZERLAND - DIRECTORIES.
Handbuch der schweizerischen Textil-, Bekleidungs- und Lederwirtschaft =. Zürich , 1986. 214 p. : ISBN 3-909214-07-X LC Card 86-221803
HD9940.S93 H36 1986

TEXTILE INDUSTRY - SWITZERLAND - HISTORY.
Tanner, Albert. Das Schiffchen fliegt, die Maschine rauscht . Zürich , c1985. 214 p. : ISBN 3-293-00084-3 LC Card 86-124152
HD9865.S9 T36 1985

TEXTILE INDUSTRY - TECHNOLOGICAL INNOVATIONS.
Sandler, Christian Heinrich. Innovative Technologien im Vertrieb . Thun , c1986. xvii, 313 p. : ISBN 3-87144-926-1 LC Card 86-171131
HD9850.5 .S25 1986

TEXTILE INDUSTRY - UNITED STATES.
Emerging textile-exporting countries, 1984 . Washington, D.C. [1985] vii, 520 p. ; LC Card 86-603429 DDC 382/.456770091724 19
HD9868.D44 E54 1985

Foreign regulations affecting U. S. textile/apparel exports. [Washington, D.C.] [1986] 283 p. ; LC Card 86-601588
HF2651.T42 F67 1986

Ghadar, Fariborz. U. S. industrial competitiveness . Lexington, Mass. , c1987. x, 114 p. : ISBN 0-669-15689-2 (alk. paper) LC Card 86-46341 DDC 338.4/7677/00973 19
HD9855 .G47 1987

International trade in textiles & apparel . [Washington, D.C.] , c1987. 1 v. (various foliations) : LC Card 87-404516 DDC 382/.45677/00973 19
HD9850.5 .I43 1987

TEXTILE INDUSTRY - UNITED STATES - STATISTICS.
Taylor, John A. (John Alvin), 1930- U. S. imports of textile and apparel products under the multifiber arrangement, 1981-84 /. Washington, D.C. [1985] v, 136 p. ; LC Card 86-601665 DDC 382/.45677/00973021 19
HD9940.U4 T38 1985

TEXTILE INDUSTRY - VIRGINIA - DIRECTORIES.
Haigh, Robert William, 1926- Leading Virginia industries . Charlottesville, Va. [1986] 161 p. : LC Card 87-620837 DDC 338.4/7677/009755 19
HD9857.V8 H35 1986

TEXTILE INDUSTRY - VIRGINIA - FINANCE - STATISTICS.
Haigh, Robert William, 1926- Leading Virginia industries . Charlottesville, Va. [1986] 161 p. : LC Card 87-620837 DDC 338.4/7677/009755 19
HD9857.V8 H35 1986

TEXTILE INDUSTRY - VIRGINIA - STATISTICS.
Haigh, Robert William, 1926- Leading Virginia industries . Charlottesville, Va. [1986] 161 p. : LC Card 87-620837 DDC 338.4/7677/009755 19
HD9857.V8 H35 1986

TEXTILE INDUSTRY - ZIMBABWE.
Investment opportunity in textiles & clothing, Zimbabwe. [Harare, Zimbabwe] [1985?] 72 p., [12] leaves of plates : LC Card 87-400412 DDC 338.4/7677/0096891 19
HD9867.Z552 I58 1985

TEXTILE MACHINERY INDUSTRY - EGYPT.
Economical study of spare parts consumption in textile industry in Egypt. Cairo, Egypt [1984?] 2 v. : LC Card 86-960234 DDC 338.4/76817677/0962 19
HD9705.5.P373 E34 1984

TEXTILE TRADE AND STATISTICS. see **TEXTILE FABRICS; TEXTILE INDUSTRY.**

Textile worker. Fitz-Gerald, Christine Maloney. I can be a textile worker /. Chicago , c1987. 29 p. : ISBN 0-516-01912-0 (lib bdg.) LC Card 87-10716 DDC 677/.0023/73 19
HD8039.C6 F57 1987

TEXTILE WORKERS.
Social and labour practices of multinational enterprises in the textiles, clothing, and footwear industries. Geneva , 1984. xii, 184 p. ; ISBN 92-2-103882-3 (pbk.) : LC Card 85-183200 DDC 331.7/677 19
HF5549 .S83473 1984 ***NYPL [JLE 85-2322]***

TEXTILE WORKERS - CHILE.
Winn, Peter. Weavers of revolution . New York , 1986. xiv, 328 p. : ISBN 0-19-503960-2 : LC Card 85-18832 DDC 338.7/67721/098331 19
HD8039.T42 C478 1986
NYPL [JLE 86-1973]

TEXTILE WORKERS - ECUADOR - QUITO REGION.
Pérez Sáinz, Juan Pablo. Entre la fábrica y la ciudad /. Quito, Ecuador , 1986, c1985. 87, [6] p. ; LC Card 87-403298 DDC 331.7/677/00986613 19
HD8039.T42 E26 1986

TEXTILE WORKERS - EGYPT - POLITICAL ACTIVITY.
Goldberg, Ellis. Tinker, tailor, and textile worker . Berkeley , 1986. xiii, 234 p. : ISBN 0-520-05353-2 (alk. paper) LC Card 85-16472 DDC 322.4/4/0962 19
HD8786 .G65 1986 *NYPL [JLE 87-500]*

TEXTILE WORKERS - ENGLAND - LANCASHIRE - HISTORY.
Fleischman, Richard K. Conditions of life among the cotton workers of southeastern Lancashire, 1780-1850 /. New York , 1985. 475 p. ; ISBN 0-8240-6681-2 (alk. paper) : LC Card 84-46001 DDC 305/.9677/094276 19
HD8039.T42 G74 1985
NYPL [JLE 86-3899]

TEXTILE WORKERS - ETHIOPIA.
Regessa Kebede. The effect of leader behavior on worker job satisfaction and job performance in Ethiopian textile factories . [Turku] , c1987. 138 p. : LC Card 87-170154 DDC 677/.0068 19
HD5658.T42 E87 1987

TEXTILE WORKERS - GERMANY (WEST) - NORTH RHINE-WESTPHALIA - STATISTICS.
Das Textilgewerbe in Nordrhein-Westfalen 1977 bis 1980. Düsseldorf [1982] 109 p. : LC Card 87-407312 DDC 943/.55 s 338.4/7677/0094355021 19
HA1320.N6 A32 Heft 477 HD9863.7.N67

TEXTILE WORKERS - JUVENILE LITERATURE.
Fitz-Gerald, Christine Maloney. I can be a textile worker /. Chicago , c1987. 29 p. : ISBN 0-516-01912-0 (lib bdg.) LC Card 87-10716 DDC 677/.0023/73 19
HD8039.C6 F57 1987

TEXTILE WORKERS - NETHERLANDS - HISTORY.
Buter, Adriaan. De kadans van de getouwen . Amsterdam , 1985. 160 p. : ISBN 90-10-05573-6 LC Card 86-110698
HD9865.N65 B88 1985

TEXTILE WORKERS - SWITZERLAND - HISTORY.
Tanner, Albert. Das Schiffchen fliegt, die Maschine rauscht . Zürich , c1985. 214 p. : ISBN 3-293-00084-3 LC Card 86-124152
HD9865.S9 T36 1985

Textiles and capitalism in Mexico . Salvucci, Richard J., 1951- Princeton, N.J. , c1987. p. cm. ISBN 0-691-07749-5 (alk. paper) : LC Card 87-45535 DDC 338.4/767702824/0972 19
HD9864.M62 S25 1987

TEXTILES - COMMERCE.
The Textile and apparel trade crisis . Washington, D.C. (1775 Pennsylvania Ave., N.W., Washington 20006) , c1985. vi, 200, [23] p. : LC Card 87-122082 DDC 382/.45677 19
HD9850.6 .T475 1985

Textiles in transition . Kane, Nancy Frances, 1954- New York , c1988. p. cm. ISBN 0-313-25529-6 (lib. bdg. : alk. paper) LC Card 87-24950 DDC 338.4/767721/0973 19
HD9875 .K3 1988

Das Textilgewerbe in Nordrhein-Westfalen 1977 bis 1980. Düsseldorf : Landesamt für Datenverarbeitung und Statistik Nordrhein-Westfalen, [1982] 109 p. : ill. ; 30 cm. (Beiträge zur Statistik des Landes Nordrhein-Westfalen . Heft 477) Chiefly tables. LC Card 87-407312 DDC 943/.55 s 338.4/7677/0094355021 19
1. Textile industry - Germany (West) - North Rhine-Westphalia - Statistics. 2. Textile workers - Germany (West) - North Rhine-Westphalia - Statistics. I. Landesamt für Datenverarbeitung und Statistik Nordrhein-Westfalen. II. Series.
HA1320.N6 A32 Heft 477 HD9863.7.N67

Die Textilindustrie im Ostblock : ein West-Ost-Vergleich. Frankfurt/Main : Arbeitgeberkreis Gesamttextil, 1967. 88, 17 p., [3] leaves of plates : ill. ; 17 x 24 cm. Includes bibliographical references. LC Card 85-116763
1. Textile industry - Europe, Eastern. I. Arbeitgeberkreis Gesamttextil (Germany).
HD9865.E79 T49 1967

Texto para discussão (Pontifícia Universidade Católica do Rio de Janeiro. Departamento de Economia) .
(no. 66) Lopes, Francisco Lafaiete. Sistemas alternativos de política salarial /. Rio de Janeiro, RJ , 1984. 51 leaves : LC Card 86-178892
HC79.W24 L66 1984

(no. 70) Modiano, Eduardo Marco. Salários, preços e câmbio . Rio de Janeiro, RJ , 1984. 55, [5] leaves ; LC Card 84-234066
HD5004 .M56 1984

Texto para discussão (Universidade de Brasília. Departamento de Economia) .
(no. 72) Castro, Paulo Furtado de. Modelo estocástico para a estimação do produto potencial "IPEA/Depto. de Economia-UnB.". [Brasília, Brazil] [1981] 12, [16] : LC Card 85-210547
HC190.I5 C37 1981

(no. 83) Roland, Marcos M. O valor de uso em Marx /. [Brasília] [19]81. 52, [2] leaves ; LC Card 85-228336
HB206 .R65 1981

Textos de contrapunto .
(3) Jiménez, Félix. Perú, economía no-neoclásica, modelo de acumulación, crisis y alternativa de desarrollo no-monetarista /. Lima, Perú , 1986. 107 p. : LC Card 87-404229 DDC 338.985 19
HC227 .J53 1986

Textos de la Universidad de los Andes. Colección Ciencias sociales. Serie Economía.
Socialismo autogestionario en marcha . Mérida, Venezuela , 1984. 377 p. ; LC Card 87-403553 DDC 335.43/09497 19
HB108.4.A2 S65 1984

Textos fiscales.
Román Egea, Antonio. Supuestos y consultas sobre licencia fiscal . Madrid [1984?] 235 p. ; ISBN 84-7130-439-2 LC Card 86-149143 DDC 343.4606/8 344.60368 19
HJ5627.S7 R66 1984

Textos (Pontifícia Universidade Católica do Rio de Janeiro. Instituto de Relações Internacionais) .
(no. 2) Hirst, Mônica. As relações dos Estados Unidos com as potências médias na América Latina, México e Brasil /. [Rio de Janeiro] , 1985. 48 leaves ; LC Card 87-143873 DDC 337.73072 19
HF1456.5.M6 H57 1985

Teytaud, A. Robert. Towle, Edward L. Final report . St. Thomas, U. S.V.I. [1982] 17, 15, 4 leaves : LC Card 86-185489 DDC 333.7/097297/22 19
HC155.Z9 E56 1982

TFK rapport .
(1983:2) Sverige och den internationella transportmarknaden . Stockholm [1983] 87 p. : ISBN 91-85402-64-8 : LC Card 83-223136
HE199.S77 S84 1983

The TGLP and hunter-gatherers . Wily, Liz. Gaborone, Botswana , 1981. ii, 102 p. ; LC Card 82-207525
DT797 W55 1981 *NYPL [JLG 87-6]*

TGV atlantique : rapports sur le projet de desserte de l'ouest et du sud-ouest de la France par trains à grande vitesse / Ministère des transports, Direction des transports terrestres. Paris : Documentation française, [1984] 410 p., [8] folded leaves of plates : ill. (some col.) ; 30 cm. "Avril 1984." ISBN 2-11-001253-6 : LC Card 85-103473 DDC 385/.22 19
1. High speed trains - France. I. France. Direction des transports terrestres.
HE3065 .T34 1984

Thai, Khi V., 1941- Structural budget deficits in the federal government . Lanham, Md. , c1987. x, 294 p. : ISBN 0-8191-6138-1 (alk. paper) : LC Card 86-33961 DDC 339.5/23/0973 19
HJ2052 .S74 1987

THAI SCULPTURE. see **SCULPTURE, THAI.**

THAILAND - CENSUS, 1960.
Luther, Norman Y., 1936- Consistent correction of census and vital registration data for Thailand, 1960-80 /. Honolulu, Hawaii [1986] vii, 39 p. ; ISBN 0-86638-089-2 (pbk.) : LC Card 86-32807 DDC 304.6/0723 19
HA39.T4 L87 1986

THAILAND - CENSUS, 1970.
Luther, Norman Y., 1936- Consistent correction of census and vital registration data for Thailand, 1960-80 /. Honolulu, Hawaii [1986] vii, 39 p. ; ISBN 0-86638-089-2 (pbk.) : LC Card 86-32807 DDC 304.6/0723 19
HA39.T4 L87 1986

THAILAND - CENSUS, 1980.
Luther, Norman Y., 1936- Consistent correction of census and vital registration data for Thailand, 1960-80 /. Honolulu, Hawaii [1986] vii, 39 p. ; ISBN 0-86638-089-2 (pbk.) : LC Card 86-32807 DDC 304.6/0723 19
HA39.T4 L87 1986

THAILAND - COMMERCE - EUROPEAN ECONOMIC COMMUNITY COUNTRIES.
Schneider, Karl Josef. Das Selbstbeschränkungsabkommen zwischen Thailand und der Europäischen Gemeinschaft . Kiel , 1986. x, 192, 30 p. ; ISBN 3-922553-82-6 LC Card 87-408324 DDC 382/.413682/09593 19
HF3800.55.Z7 E867 1986

Thailand Correspondenz .
(9) Föste, Wolfgang. Verkaufte Träume . München , c1982. 53 p. : ISBN 3-88676-011-1 (pbk.) LC Card 87-672593
HD6250.T52 F67x 1982

Thailand. Dept. of Fine Arts. see **Thailand. Krom Sinlapākōn.**

THAILAND - ECONOMIC CONDITIONS.
Barton, Thomas Frank, 1905- Phūmisāt sĕtthakit kh [Bangkok] 2500 [1957] 2, 5, 392 p. : LC Card 83-921251
HC445 .B36 1957

Donner, Wolf. Thailand ohne Tempel . Frankfurt [am Main] , c1984. 202 p. : ISBN 3-88323-499-0 LC Card 85-157332
HC445 .D67 1984

The Oriental challenge . Delft, the Netherlands , 1987. 281 p. : ISBN 90-70879-62-X (pbk.) LC Card 87-170212 DDC 332.6/732259 19
HC445 .O75 1987

THAILAND - ECONOMIC POLICY.
Donner, Wolf. Thailand ohne Tempel . Frankfurt [am Main] , c1984. 202 p. : ISBN 3-88323-499-0 LC Card 85-157332
HC445 .D67 1984

Thailand. Samnakngān Khana Kammakān Phatthanākān Sĕtthakit læ Sangkhom hæng Chāt. Phon kānphatthanā nai raya khrng Phæn Phatthanā-- Chabap thī 5, Ph [Bangkok] [2529 i.e. 1986] 2, 215, 25 p. ; LC Card 86-915872
HC445 .T448 1986

THAILAND - ECONOMIC POLICY - HANDBOOKS, MANUALS, ETC.
Khrōngkān 'an n [Bangkok] [2526 i.e. 1983] 221 p. (some folded), [1] leaf of plates : LC Card 83-916454
HC445 .K53 1983

Thailand, its economic products. 3rd ed. [Bangkok] : Dept. of Commercial Intelligence, 1961, 1962 printing. 68 p. : ill. ; 27 cm. LC Card 82-122480
1. Commercial products - Thailand - Directories. I. Thailand. Krom Kānsonthēt.
HF1040.9.T5 T53 1962

Thailand. Khana Kammakān 'Amnūaikān Chatsāng Phutthamonthon. Songsan Ninkamhæng. Chotmāihēt kānsāng Phraphuttharūp phra prathān Phutthamonthon /. Krung Thēp , 2525 [1982] 172 p. : ISBN 974-7921-05-7 LC Card 83-916060
HB1912.G38 S66 1982

Thailand. Krom Kānsonthēt. Thailand, its economic products. [Bangkok] , 1961, 1962 printing. 68 p. : LC Card 82-122480
HF1040.9.T5 T53 1962

Thailand. Krom Ræŋngān. Saphāp læ 'ōkāt nai kānthamngān nai kitčhakān m [Bangkok] [2509 i.e. 1966] 2, 35 p., [5] leaves of plates : LC Card 80-911179
HD8039.M72 T527 1966

Thailand. Krom Sĕtthakit Kānphānit. Rāingān phon kānsksā wičhai : Panhā bāng prakān

kieokap mai læ kānpramœn phon kānkhūapkhum kānsong mai læ mai prærūp ' [Krung Thēp Mahā Nakh Krom Sētthakit Kānphānit, Krasūang Phānit, 2521 [1978] 24, [7] folded p., [7] p. of plates : ill. ; 22 cm. In Thai. Report signed: Suchādā Warāph LC Card 81-183926
1. Forest products industry - Thailand. I. Suchādā Warāph
HD9766.T52 T47 1978

Thailand. Krom Şinlapākōn. Songsan Ninkamhæng. Chotmāihēt kānsāng Phraphutthārūp phra prathān Phutthamonthon /. Krung Thēp , 2525 [1982] 172 p. : ISBN 974-7921-05-7 LC Card 83-916060
HB1912.G38 S66 1982

Thailand ohne Tempel . Donner, Wolf. Frankfurt [am Main] , c1984. 202 p. : ISBN 3-88323-499-0 LC Card 85-157332
HC445 .D67 1984

Thailand. Samnakngān Khana Kammakān Kansksā hæng Chāt. Education and employment from world capitalism to the rural Thais : summary of research report. Bangkok, Thailand : National Education Commission, Office of the Prime Minister : Institute of Human Resources, Thammasat University, 1985. 46 p. : ill. ; 27 cm. LC Card 86-915875 DDC 331.13/79593 19
1. Unemployment - Thailand. 2. Unemployed - Education - Thailand. 3. Rural development - Thailand. I. Mahāwitthayālai Thammasāt. Institute of Human Resources. II. Title.
HD5822.55.A6 T47 1985

Thailand. Samnakngān Khana Kammakān Phatthanākān Sētthakit læ Sangkhom hæng Chāt.
Phon kānphatthanā nai raya khrng Phæn Phatthanā-- Chabap thī 5, Ph [Bangkok] : K [2529 i.e. 1986] 2, 215, 25 p. ; 28 cm. In Thai. Mid-term review of the Fifth National Economic and Social Development Five Year Plan, 1982-1984, Thailand. Includes bibliographical references. LC Card 86-915872
1. Thailand - Economic policy. 2. Thailand - Social policy. I. Title.
HC445 .T448 1986

Sētthaph Kānwāngphæn phatthanā khr [Bangkok] , 2524 [1981] 8, 80 leaves ; LC Card 82-920041
HD9696.T442 S47 1981

THAILAND - SOCIAL CONDITIONS.
Donner, Wolf. Thailand ohne Tempel . Frankfurt [am Main] , c1984. 202 p. : ISBN 3-88323-499-0 LC Card 85-157332
HC445 .D67 1984

THAILAND - SOCIAL POLICY.
Thailand. Samnakngān Khana Kammakān Phatthanākān Sētthakit læ Sangkhom hæng Chāt. Phon kānphatthanā nai raya khrng Phæn Phatthanā-- Chabap thī 5, Ph [Bangkok] [2529 i.e. 1986] 2, 215, 25 p. ; LC Card 86-915872
HC445 .T448 1986

THAILAND - STATISTICAL SERVICES.
Luther, Norman Y., 1936- Consistent correction of census and vital registration data for Thailand, 1960-80 /. Honolulu, Hawaii [1986] vii, 39 p. ; ISBN 0-86638-089-2 (pbk.) : LC Card 86-32807 DDC 304.6/0723 19
HA39.T4 L87 1986

Thailand's reproductive revolution . Knodel, John E. Madison, Wis. , c1987. xiii, 251 p. : ISBN 0-299-11050-8 LC Card 87-8172 DDC 304.6/32/09593 19
HB1054.55.A3 K576 1987

Thaker, B. C. Fiscal policy, monetary analysis, and debt management : with special reference to India / B.C. Thaker.1st ed. New Delhi : Ashish Pub. House, 1985. xvi, 356 p. : ill. ; 23 cm. Includes index. Bibliography: p. [340]-353. LC Card 85-903636 DDC 339.5/2/0954 19
1. Monetary policy - India. 2. Debt. 3. Debt - India. 4. Fiscal policy - India. I. Title.
HG230.3 .T46 1985 ***NYPL [JLD 86-1324]***

Thakur, Baleshwar. Urban settlements in eastern India : entropy changes and pattern analysis / Baleshwar Thakur. New Delhi : Concept, 1980. 222 p. : maps ; 23 cm. Originally presented as the author's thesis, Patna University. Includes index. Bibliography: p. [194]-216. LC Card 80-900438 DDC 307.7/6/09541
1. Urbanization - India. 2. Entropy (Information theory). I. Title.
HT147.I5 T53 1980 ***NYPL [JLD 80-3943]***

Thames essay .
(no. 45) Banks, Gary. Economic policy and the adjustment problem /. Aldershot, Hants., England , Brookfield, Vt. , 1986. x, 101 p. ; ISBN 0-566-05332-2 : LC Card 86-14934 DDC 338.9 19
HF1421 .B36 1987
NYPL [JLL 74-802 no.45]

(no. 49) Langhammer, Rolf J. Economic impact of generalized tariff preferences /. Aldershot, Hants, England , Brookfield, Vt. , 1988. p. cm. ISBN 0-566-05338-1 : LC Card 87-15045 DDC 382.7/53 19
HF1721 .L35 1988

(no. 51) Lal, Deepak. Trade liberalization in Sri Lanka /. Aldershop, Hants, England , Brookfield, Vt. , 1988. p. cm. ISBN 0-566-05340-3 : LC Card 87-15044 DDC 382/.3/095493 19
HF1586.8 .L35 1988

(no. 52) Hillman, Jimmye S., 1923- Agricultural trade and protection in Japan /. Aldershot, Hants, England , Brookfield, Vt. , 1988. p. cm. ISBN 0-566-05339-X : LC Card 87-15043 DDC 382.7/3/0952 19
HD9016.J42 H55 1988

(no. 53) Hayes, J. P. (John Philip), 1924- Economic effects of sanctions on southern Africa /. Aldershot, Hampshire, England , Brookfield, Vt., USA , 1987. xii, 100 p. : ISBN 0-566-05539-2 (pbk.) : LC Card 87-11674 DDC 337.68 19
HF1413.5 .H39 1987

Thames essay, 0306-6991 .
(no. 17) Harris, Stuart. Analysis of commodity markets for policy purposes /. London , 1978. ix, 81 p. ; ISBN 0-900842-42-3 (pbk.) LC Card 85-111455 DDC 332.64/4 19
HG6046 .H367 1978

(no. 46) Pryke, Richard. Competition among international airlines /. Aldershot , Brookfield, USA , 1987. xi, 113 p. : ISBN 0-566-05333-0 : LC Card 86-31877 DDC 387.7/1 19
HE9780 .P79 1987

(no. 47) Riedel, James. Myths and reality of external constraints on development /. Aldershot, Hampshire, U.K. , Brookfield, Vt., USA , 1987. xvi, 111 p. : ISBN 0-566-05336-5 (pbk.) : LC Card 86-31801 DDC 330.9172/4 19
HC59.7 .R494 1987

Thames essays.
(no. 49) Langhammer, Rolf J. Economic impact of generalized tariff preferences /. Aldershot, Hants, England , Brookfield, Vt. , 1988. p. cm. ISBN 0-566-05338-1 : LC Card 87-15045 DDC 382.7/53 19
HF1721 .L35 1988

Thames essays, 0306-6991 .
(no. 48) East African lessons on economic liberalization /. Aldershot, Hampshire, U.K. ; Brookfield, Vt., U. S.A. : xxi, 72 p. : ISBN 0-566-05337-3 (pbk.) : LC Card 86-29602 DDC 338.967 19
HC865 .E27 1987

Thammasat University, Bangkok, Thailand. see **Mahāwitthayālai Thammasāt.**

Thana statistics. [Dacca] : Bangladesh Bureau of Statistics, Statistics Division, Ministry of Planning, Govt. of the People's Republic of Bangladesh, 1981- v. ; 30 cm. CONTENTS. - v. 1. Basic information, land utilisation, & irrigation, 1974-75 to 1978-79 -- v. 2. Major crops, 1974-75 to 1979-80 -- v. 3. Minor crops, 1970-71 to 1979-80. LC Card 82-903357 DDC 333.73/13/095492021 19
1. Land use - Bangladesh - Statistics. 2. Irrigation - Bangladesh - Statistics. I. Bangladesh. Parisaṃkhyāna Bibhāga.
HD880.6.Z63 T46 1981
NYPL [JLM 87-178]

Thanākhar Krungdēp Chākat. see **Bangkok Bank Limited.**

Thanner, Benedikt. Leibfritz, Willi. Berücksichtigung der zentralen Orte im kommunalen Finanzausgleich Bayern . München , 1986. vi, 151 p. : ISBN 3-88512-018-6 LC Card 86-172605
HJ9493.5.B38 L45 1986

Thanulingom Nadar, N. Small scale industry : interrelationship with large scale industry / by N. Thanulingom Nadar.1st ed. Coimbatore, Tamil Nadu : Rainbow Publications, 1985. 194 p. ; 22 cm. Bibliography: p. [165]-173. LC Card 85-903280 DDC 338.6/42/095482 19
1. Small business - India - Coimbatore. 2. Small business - India - Case studies. 3. Industries, Size of - India - Coimbatore. 4. Industries, Size of - India - Case studies. 5. Coimbatore, India (District) - Industries. I. Title.
HD2346.I52 C648 1985
NYPL [JLD 86-1411]

Thāpaṭanā /. Tāvare, Rāmacandra. Mumbaī , 1986. 179 p. ; LC Card 87-900532
HD5820.M29 T38 1986

THAR DESERT (INDIA AND PAKISTAN) - ECONOMIC CONDITIONS.
Mann, H. S. (Haracharan Singh), 1922- Halting the march . [New Delhi] [1983] 35, [1] p., [4] p. of plates : LC Card 86-204352 DDC 338.1/0954/4 19
HC437.T47 M36 1983

Tharakan, P. K. Mathew. Imperfect competition and international trade . Brighton, Sussex , Atlantic Highlands, N.J. , c1986. xiv, 242 p. : ISBN 0-391-03403-0 (Humanities Press) LC Card 86-660 DDC 382 19
HF1411 .I354 1986 ***NYPL [JLD 86-2120]***

THATCHER, MARGARET.
Wilsher, Peter. Strike . London [1985] xiii, 284 p., [16] p. of plates : ISBN 0-233-97825-9 : LC Card 86-221981 DDC 331.89/2822334/0941 19
HD5365.M6152 1984 .W55 1985b

Thatcherism at work . MacInnes, John. Milton Keynes, England , Philadelphia , 1987. p. cm. ISBN 0-335-15517-0 LC Card 87-24722 DDC 338.941 19
HD8391 .M26 1987

That's a great idea /. Husch, Tony, 1943- Berkeley, Calif. , 1987, c1986. p. cm. ISBN 0-89815-218-6 LC Card 87-13891 DDC 658.5/75 19
HD69.N4 H87 1987

Thayer, Lee O. Organization--communication . Norwood, N.J. , c1986- v. : ISBN 0-89391-274-3 (v. 1) LC Card 85-6159 DDC 302.3/5 19
HD31 .O727 1986 ***NYPL [JLL 86-382]***

Thaysen, Uwe, 1940- Die Deutschen Länder und die Europäischen Gemeinschaften . Baden-Baden , 1986. 294 p. ; ISBN 3-7890-1350-1 LC Card 87-141896 DDC 341.24/22 19
HC241.25.G3 D48 1986

The Future is Now: A Home Equity Conversion Conference (1985 : Washington, D.C.)
Proceedings from The Future is Now, A Home Equity Conversion Conference. Washington, D.C. : U. S. Dept. of Health and Human Services, Office of Human Development Services, Administration on Aging : U. S. Dept. of Housing and Urban Development, Office of Intergovernmental Relations, [1985?] ix, 76 p. ; 28 cm. Conference held Jan. 10-11, 1985; sponsored by the U. S. Administration on Aging, U. S. Dept. of Housing and Urban Development, and the Federal Council on Aging. LC Card 86-601425 DDC 332.7/22 19
1. Home equity conversion - United States - Congresses. 2. Aged - United States - Housing - Congresses. I. United States. Administration on Aging. II. United States. Dept. of Housing and Urban Development. III. Federal Council on Aging (U. S.). IV. Title. V. Title: Future is Now, A Home Equity Conversion Conference.
HG2040.45 .F87 1985

Thebes, Manfred. Jansen, Paul Günter. Arbeitsmarktatlas . [Düsseldorf] [1977] 206, A19 p. : LC Card 85-173256
HD5780.A76 J36 1977

Theil, Henri. Applied demand analysis : results from system-wide approaches / Henri Theil, Kenneth W. Clements. Cambridge, Mass. : Ballinger Pub. Co., 1987. xxi, 279 p. : ill. ; 24 cm. (Series on econometrics and management sciences . v. 7) Includes bibliographies and index. ISBN 0-88730-217-3 LC Card 86-32230 DDC 338.5/212 19
1. Demand functions (Economic theory). 2.

Consumption (Economics) - Econometric models. 3. Econometrics. I. Clements, Kenneth W., 1950-. II. Title. III. Series.
HB801 .T489 1987

Thematic studies in Latin America.
Brockett, Charles D., 1946- Land, power, and poverty . Boston , c1988. p. cm. ISBN 0-04-497027-7 LC Card 87-22746 DDC 338.1/09728 19
HD1797 .B76 1988

Teichman, Judith A., 1947- Policymaking in Mexico . Boston , c1988. p. cm. ISBN 0-04-445033-8 : LC Card 87-18704 DDC 338.2/7282/0972 19
HD9574.M6 T45 1988

Thème.
Raumordnungspolitik im Vollzug . Grüsch , c1985. 507 p. : ISBN 3-7253-0258-8 : LC Card 86-149201
HC397 .R36 1985

Thème, transports collectifs. Les Rues mixtes . [Bagneux] [1982] 40 p. : ISBN 2-11-083325-4 : LC Card 84-104398
HE363.F72 P437 1982

Theodore, Athena. The campus troublemakers : academic women in protest / Athena Theodore. Houston, Tex. : Cap and Gown Press, c1986. xxiv, 293 p. ; 24 cm. Includes index. Bibliography: p.275-286. ISBN 0-88105-066-0 : LC Card 85-14973 DDC 378/.12/088042 19
1. Women college teachers - United States. 2. Women college graduates - Employment - United States. 3. Sex discrimination in education - United States. 4. Sex discrimination against women - United States. I. Title.
LB2332.3 .T44 1986 ***NYPL [JLE 86-4389]***

Theoretical studies in Islamic banking and finance / edited by Mohsin S. Khan, Abbas Mirakhor. Houston, Tex. : Institute for Research and Islamic Studies, 1987. xvi, 245 p. : ill. ; 22 cm. Bibliography: p. 221-239. Includes index. ISBN 0-932625-07-X : LC Card 86-83221 DDC 332.1/0917/4927 19
1. Banks and banking - Islamic countries. 2. Banks and banking - Religious aspects - Islam. 3. Interest (Islamic law). I. Khan, Mohsin S. II. Mirakhor, Abbas.
HG3368.A6 T47 1987

Theoretische und empirische Analyse der Determinanten des Geldschöpfungsmultiplikators /. Spreter, Jürgen. Krefeld , 1983. v, 221 p. : ISBN 3-88358-029-5 LC Card 83-154608
HG226.3 .S67 1983

Theoretische und empirische Untersuchungen zum Beschaffungsprozess von konsumtiven Dienstleistungen /. Ernenputsch, Margit A. Bochum , 1986. xiii, 263 p. ; ISBN 3-88339-548-X LC Card 87-143249 DDC 658.8 19
HF5415.122 .E76 1986

La théorie de la régulation . Boyer, Robert. Paris , 1986. 142 p. : ISBN 2-7071-1628-9 : LC Card 87-108410
HC276.3.B69 1986

La théorie de l'échange international de produits différenciés /. Caille, Pierre. Fribourg, Suisse , c1986. 267 p. : ISBN 2-8271-0337-0 LC Card 86-210742
HF1008 .C35 1986

Theorie der säkularen Nachwuchsbeschränkung 1800 bis 2000 /. Linde, Hans. Frankfurt [am Main] , New York , c1984. 201 p. ; ISBN 3-593-33385-6 LC Card 85-131521
HB901 .L55 1984

Theorie des Konkurrenzsozialismus . Feucht, Martin. Stuttgart , New York , 1983. iv, 222 p. : ISBN 3-437-50273-5 LC Card 83-205881
HC79.S6 F48 1983

Théorie des marchés d'assurance /. Cresta, Jean-Paul. Paris , 1984. vii, 231 p. : ISBN 2-7178-0696-2 : LC Card 84-235141
HG8054.5 .C74 1984

La théorie des transferts internationaux /. Berthélemy, Jean-Claude. Paris , c1986. ix, 225 p. : ISBN 2-7178-0982-1 : LC Card 86-176393
HG3882 .B48 1986

Théorie du déséquilibre et politique économique /. Picard, Pierre. Paris , 1985. 253 p. : ISBN 2-7178-0877-9 : LC Card 86-109716 DDC 339.5 19
HB145 .P53 1985

Die Theorie erschöpfbarer natürlicher Ressourcen bei wachsender Bevölkerung /. Müller, Karl-Wilhelm, 1953- Frankfurt am Main , New York , c1984. 191 p. : ISBN 3-8204-5315-6 LC Card 85-197540
HD75.6 .M85 1984

Theorie und Empirie betrieblicher Ausbildungsplatzangebote /. Kempf, Theo, 1955- Frankfurt am Main , New York , c1985. 305 p. : ISBN 3-8204-8358-6 LC Card 86-111326
HF5549.5.T7 K42 1985

Theorie und Empirie flexibler Wechselkurse . Bischofberger, Karlheinz. Berlin , c1986. 248 p. : ISBN 3-428-05988-3 LC Card 86-206335
HG3823 .B57 1986

Theorie und Empirie in Wirtschaftspolitik und Wirtschaftsgeschichte : Wilhelm Abel zum 80. Geburtstag / mit Beiträgen von P. von Blanckenburg ... [et al.]. Göttingen : Agrarsoziale Gesellschaft, 1984. 245 p. : ill. ; 21 cm. (Schriftenreihe für ländliche Sozialfragen, 0080-7133 . Heft 92) Bibliography of works by W. Abel: p. 241-242. Includes bibliographical references. CONTENTS. - Sozialkulturelle Aspekte des Ernährungsverhaltens / Peter von Blanckenburg -- Das Wirtschaftssystem als Subsystem / Hans-Günther Schlotter -- Wandlungen der Arbeitsmarktstruktur in Deutschland im ausgehenden 19. und beginnenden 20. Jahrhundert / Karl-Heinz Schmidt -- Soziale Sicherung zwischen Theorie und Empirie / Detlev Zöllner -- Der Monatsbilderzyklus zweier Salburger Handschriften des frühen 9. Jahrhunderts in agrarhistorischer Sicht / Walter Achilles -- Das Raster der sozialpolitischen Massnahmen in Deutschland in der vorindustriellen Zeit / Friedrich-Wilhelm Henning -- Münzverschlechterung, Geldmengenwachstum und Bevölkerungsvermehrung als Einflussgrössen der sogenannten Preisrevolution im 16. und beginnenden 17. Jahrhundert in Deutschland / Bernd Sprenger -- Eisenmarkt und Eisenpreise im Kurfürstentum Braunschweig-Lüneburg 1733-1807 / Hans-Jürgen Gerhard -- Handwerkliche Tradition und industrielle Revolution / Karl Heinrich Kaufhold -- Die sozialökonomischen Lebensbedingungen der Untersichten Deutschlands im 19. Jahrhundert / Diedrich Saalfeld -- Über Armenfürsorge und Arme in Göttingen im 18. und frühen 19. Jahrhundert / Wieland Sachse. LC Card 85-111313
1. Germany - Economic conditions. 2. Europe - Economic conditions. 3. Economic history. 4. Abel, Wilhelm, 1904-. I. Abel, Wilhelm, 1904-. II. Blanckenburg, Peter von. III. Series.
HC284 .T46 1984

Theorie und Empirie in Wirtschaftspolitik und Wirtschaftsgeschichte : Festschrift für Wilhelm Abel zum 80. Geburtstag / herausgegeben von Karl Heinrich Kaufhold und Friedrich Riemann. Göttingen : O. Schwartz, 1984. 242 p. : ill. ; 23 cm. (Göttinger Beiträge zur Wirtschafts- und Sozialgeschichte. Bd. 11) Includes bibliographical references. ISBN 3-509-01366-2 : LC Card 85-120064
1. Europe - Economic conditions. 2. Europe - Social conditions. 3. Agriculture - Economic aspects - Europe - History. 4. Europe - Industries - History. 5. Abel, Wilhelm, 1904-. I. Abel, Wilhelm, 1904-. II. Kaufhold, Karl Heinrich. III. Riemann, Friedrich.
HC240 .T45 1984

Theorie und Forschung. Psychologie .
(Bd. 6) Neppl, Rainer. Zur Wahrnehmung und Bewertung der Gerechtigkeit der Einkommens-Verteilung /. Regensburg , 1986. 310 p. : ISBN 3-89073-362-X LC Card 87-121773 DDC 339.2 19
HB523 .N47 1986

Theorie und Politik der Entwicklungshilfe .
Stockhausen, Joachim von. München , c1986. viii, 324 p. ; ISBN 3-8039-0332-1 LC Card 86-225372
HC60 .S7977 1986

Theorie und Politik der Steuerreform in der Demokratie /. Mann, Hugo, 1954- Frankfurt am Main , New York , c1987. vi, 264 p. ; ISBN 3-8204-9464-2 LC Card 87-407788 DDC 336.2/00943 19
HJ2687 .M3 1987

Theorie und Politik nichtregenerierbarer natürlicher Ressourcen /. Sauermann, Heinz. Frankfurt am Main , c1982. viii, 251 p. : ISBN 3-88129-573-9 : LC Card 83-126048
HC55 .S26 1982

Theorie und Praxis des Marxismus-Leninismus (Vienna, Austria) .
(78/Nr. 2) Türkiye Komünist Partisi/Marksist-Leninist. Kritik der "Drei Welten Theorie" durch die TKP/ML . Wien [1978] 1 v. (various pagings) ; LC Card 85-134265
HC59.7 .T867 1978

Theoriendynamik und die Grundlagen ökonomischer Politikberatung . Rubbert, Ulrich. Hamburg , 1984. 218 p. ; ISBN 3-87895-262-7 LC Card 85-135703
HD84 .R74 1984

Theories of income distribution / edited by Athanasios Asimakopulos. Boston : Kluwer Academic Publishers, c1988. x, 255 p. : ill. ; 24 cm. (Recent economic thought series) Includes bibliographies and indexes. CONTENTS. - The classical theory of distribution / J.C. Weldon -- Marx's theory of income distribution / David P. Levine -- Distribution / Allan J. Braff -- The distribution theory of Marshall's Principles / John K. Whitaker -- Post-Keynesian theories of distribution / Athanasios Asimakopulos -- The neo-Ricardian approach and the distribution of income / Alessandrio Roncaglia -- The general equilibrium theory of distribution / Michael C. Howard -- Factor shares in Canada, the United States, and the United Kindgom / Camilo Dagum -- Economic development and income distribution / Robin Rowley. ISBN 0-89838-232-7 LC Card 87-3248 DDC 339.2 19
1. Income distribution. I. Asimakopulos, A., 1930-. II. Series.
HB523 .T44 1988

Theories of industrial organization /. Reid, Gavin C. Oxford, UK , New York, NY, USA , 1987. 234 p. : ISBN 0-631-15172-9 : LC Card 86-31007 DDC 338.7 19
HD2326 .R45 1987

Theories of the labor movement / edited by Simeon Larson and Bruce Nissen. Detroit, Mich. : Wayne State University Press, 1987. xi, 395 p. ; 26 cm. Bibliography: p. 379-383. Includes index. ISBN 0-8143-1815-0 : LC Card 86-32414 DDC 331.88/09 19
1. Trade-unions - History. I. Larson, Simeon, 1925-. II. Nissen, Bruce, 1948-.
HD6476 .T47 1987

Théories ordinaires de la pauvreté /. Ogien, Ruwen. Paris , 1983. 176 p. ; ISBN 2-13-037937-0 : LC Card 84-151584
HC79.P6 O47 1983

Theory and practice of urban land values in India /. Dange, Manohar N. Bombay , 1983. xii, 132 p. ; LC Card 83-903969 DDC 333.33/2/0954 19
HD878 .D36 1983 ***NYPL [JLD 87-729]***

Theory and problems of international economics. Salvatore, Dominick. Schaum's outline of theory and problems of international economics /. New York , c1984. 231 p. : ISBN 0-07-054503-0 (pbk.) LC Card 82-21666 DDC 337 19
HF1411 .S24 1984 ***NYPL [JLF 86-1845]***

Theory and reality in development : essays in honour of Paul Streeten / edited by Sanjaya Lall and Frances Stewart. Basingstoke, Hampshire : Macmillan, 1986. xii, 291 p. : port. ; 23 cm. "Publications by Paul Streeten": p. 270-278. Includes bibliographies and index. ISBN 0-333-39824-6
1. Streeten, Paul - Addresses, essays, lectures. 2. Economic development - Addresses, essays, lectures. 3. Developing countries - Economic conditions - Addresses, essays, lectures. I. Streeten, Paul. II. Lall, Sanjaya. III. Stewart, Frances.
NYPL [JLD 86-1827]

Theory I . Thompson, Richard E. San Antonio, Tex. , c1986. 105 p. : ISBN 0-940555-00-X (pbk.) LC Card 86-90531 DDC 658.4/00207 19
HD70.U5 T48 1986

The theory of duality & international trade /. Sgro, Pasquale M. London , c1986. 307 p. : ISBN 0-7099-3307-X ***NYPL [JLD 86-3202]***

Theory of duality and international trade. Sgro, Pasquale M. The theory of duality & international trade /. London , c1986. 307 p. : ISBN 0-7099-3307-X ***NYPL [JLD 86-3202]***

A theory of efficient cooperation and competition /. Telser, Lester G., 1931- Cambridge , New York , 1987. xii, 306 p. : ISBN 0-521-30619-1 LC Card 87-5114 DDC 338.6/042/0724 19
HD41 .T43 1987

The theory of environmental policy /. Baumol, William J. Cambridge [Cambridgeshire] , New York , 1988. x, 299 p. : ISBN 0-521-32224-3 LC Card 87-24975 DDC 363.7/001 19
HC79.E5 B375 1988

The theory of finance . Martin, John D., 1945- Chicago , c1988. xxvi, 709 p. : ISBN 0-03-063854-2 LC Card 87-496 DDC 332/.01 19
HG173 .M353 1988

The theory of financial markets and information /. Ohlson, James A. New York , c1987. xiii, 181 p. ; ISBN 0-444-01161-7 LC Card 87-9100 DDC 332.6 19
HG173 .O34 1987

The theory of free banking . Selgin, George A., 1957- Totowa, N.J. , c1987. p. cm. ISBN 0-8476-7578-5 : LC Card 87-20012 DDC 332.4 19
HG1586 .S38 1987

THEORY OF GAMES. see **GAME THEORY.**

The theory of inertial inflation . Pereira, Luiz Carlos Bresser. [Inflação e recessão. English.] Boulder, Colo. , 1987. xiii, 206 p. : ISBN 1-555-87007-4 (alk. paper) : LC Card 86-29832 DDC 332.4/1/0981 19
HG835 .P4413 1987

The theory of monopoly capitalism . Foster, John Bellamy. New York , 1986. 280 p. ; ISBN 0-85345-688-7 : LC Card 85-32097 DDC 330.12/2 19
HB501 .F66 1986 ***NYPL [JLD 86-2415]***

Theory of population and economic growth /. Simon, Julian Lincoln, 1932- Oxford , 1986. xi, 232 p. : ISBN 0-631-14427-7 : LC Card 85-28574 DDC 338.9/00724 19
HB849.41 .S55 1986 ***NYPL [JLE 86-3702]***

The Theory of taxation for developing countries / edited by David Newbery, Nicholas Stern. New York : Published for the World Bank [by] Oxford University Press, c1987. xvi, 694 p. ; 26 cm. Includes bibliographies and index. ISBN 0-19-520498-0 LC Card 87-11106 DDC 336.2/009172/4 19
1. Taxation - Developing countries. I. Newbery, David M. G. II. Stern, N. H. (Nicholas Herbert).
HJ2351.7 .T47 1987

Therapie in der Berufsschule? . Kornblum, Hans-Joachim. München , c1984. x, 458 p. : ISBN 3-597-10503-3 : LC Card 85-105593
HD5715.5.G4 K67 1984

Therborn, Göran, 1941- Why some peoples are more unemployed than others / Göran Therborn. London : Verso, 1986. 181 p. ; 22 cm. Includes index. Bibliography: p. 163-178. ISBN 0-86091-109-8 : LC Card 86-673385
1. Unemployment. I. Title.
HD5707.5 .T53x 1986 ***NYPL [JLD 86-3537]***

Theroux, David J. Friedman, Milton, 1912- Politics and tyranny . San Francisco, Calif. , c1984. 68 p. ; ISBN 0-936488-00-X (pbk.) : LC Card 84-61364 DDC 330 19
HB98.3 .F75 1984 ***NYPL [JLE 87-857]***

Thévenot, Laurent. Le Travail . Paris , c1986. iv, 370 p. ; ISBN 2-7178-1138-9 : LC Card 87-123294
HD8428 .T72 1986

Thielen, Helmut, 1941- Agrarreformen in Lateinamerika zwischen Ökonomie und Ökologie : Modellfall Nicaragua / Helmut Thielen. Frankfurt am Main : Haag + Herchen, c1985. 518 p. : ill. ; 21 cm. Bibliography: p. 484-503. ISBN 3-88129-958-0 LC Card 86-153251 DDC 333.3/1/7285 19
1. Land reform - Nicaragua. 2. Agriculture - Economic aspects - Nicaragua. 3. Agricultural conservation - Nicaragua. 4. Agricultural pollution - Nicaragua. I. Title.
HD1333.N5 T48 1985 ***NYPL [JLD 87-467]***

Thiemeyer, Theo. Öffentliche Unternehmen in Rezession und Aufschwung . Berlin , 1977. 165 p. : LC Card 85-180964
HD3845 .G43 Heft 14 HD3842

Thien, Hans-Günter, 1947- Herrschaft, Krise, Überleben . Münster , 1986. 396 p. : ISBN 3-924550-19-0 LC Card 86-229590
HC286.7 .H48 1986

Thierauf, Robert J. A problem-finding approach to effective corporate planning / Robert J. Thierauf. New York : Quorum Books, c1987. p. cm. Bibliography: p. Includes index. ISBN 0-89930-262-9 (lib. bdg. : alk. paper) LC Card 87-5971 DDC 658.4/012 19
1. Corporate planning. 2. Problem solving. I. Title.
HD30.28 .T45 1987

Thierry, François. Monnaies d'Extrême Orient / par François Thierry. Paris : Administration des monnaies et médailles, <[1986- v. <2 > : ill. ; 30 cm. (Les Collections monétaires . VII, 2) Bibliography: v. 2, p. 91-92. CONTENTS. - -- 2. Vietnam-Japon. ISBN 2-11-080873-X (v. 2) : LC Card 86-218568
1. Numismatics - Asia - Catalogs. 2. Money - Asia - History. I. Title. II. Series.
HG1250.5 .T45 1986

Thigpen, M. Elton, 1932- World demand prospects for jute / M. Elton Thigpen, Paula Marongiu, and Saidur R. Lasker. Washington, D.C. : World Bank ; Rome : FAO, 1987. vi, 178 p. ; 28 cm. (World Bank staff commodity working papers, 0253-3537 . no. 16) "A joint study by the Commodities and Trade Division of the Food and Agriculture Organization (FAO) of the United Nations and the Commodity Studies and Projections Division of the World Bank." Includes bibliographical references. ISBN 0-8213-0867-X (pbk.) LC Card 86-32522 DDC 338.4/767713 19
1. Jute industry - Forecasting. I. Marongiu, Paula, 1940-. II. Lasker, Saidur R., 1940-. III. Food and Agriculture Organization of the United Nations. Commodities and Trade Division. IV. International Bank for Reconstruction and Development. Commodity Studies and Projections Division. V. Series: World Bank staff commodity working paper , no. 16. VI. Title.
HD9156.J7 T46 1987

THIMBLEMAKERS - GERMANY (WEST) - NUREMBERG - HISTORY.
Greif, Helmut. Nuremberg thimblemakers /. [Des Moines, Iowa] , c1986. 30 p. : LC Card 86-209810 DDC 338.4/76878 19
HD8039.T522 G34 1986

Thimm, Heinz-Ulrich. Kireta-Katewu, Patrick R., 1953- Economic analyses of the farmer cropping system under risks and uncertainties in Sierra Leone /. Hamburg , 1985. xviii, 245 p. : ISBN 3-87895-266-X (pbk.) LC Card 87-103068 DDC 338.1/62 19
HD2146.5 .K57 1985

Thimmaiah, G.
Inequality and poverty : a case study of Karnataka / G. Thimmaiah.1st ed. Bombay : Himalaya Pub. House, 1983. xiv, 106 p. ; 23 cm. Includes bibliographical references. LC Card 83-903408 DDC 339.4/6/095487 19
1. Poor - India - Karnataka. 2. Income distribution - India - Karnataka. 3. Karnataka, India - Economic conditions. 4. Karnataka, India - Social conditions. I. Title.
HC437.K27 T47 1983 ***NYPL [JLD 86-3792]***

The political economy of land reforms / by G. Thimmaiah and Abdul Aziz. New Delhi : Ashish Pub. House, [1983?] xiii, 94 p. ; 22 cm. With reference to Karnataka. Includes bibliographical references and index. LC Card 84-900237 DDC 333.3/1/5487 19
1. Land reform - India - Karnataka. 2. Land reform - Government policy - India - Karnataka. 3. Land reform - Law and legislation - India - Karnataka. 4. Karnataka, India - Economic conditions. I. Aziz, Abdul, 1937-. II. Title.
HD1333.I42 K3778 1983
NYPL [JLD 87-752]

Thimrén, Claes. Imperfectly competitive markets for exhaustible resources : a game-theoretic approach / Claes Thimrén. Stockholm, Sweden : Stockholm School of Economics, the Economic Research Institute, [1986] 94 p. : ill. ; 30 cm. (Research report) "April 1986." Bibliography: p. 93-94. ISBN 91-7258-212-X (pbk.) LC Card 87-151530 DDC 333.7/0724 19
1. Competition, Imperfect - Mathematical models. 2. Nonrenewable natural resources - Mathematical models. I. Series: Research report (Handelshögskolan i Stockholm. Ekonomiska forskningsinstitutet). II. Title.
HB238 .T54 1986

Thin security market. Berglund, Tom. Anomalies in stock returns on a thin security market /. Helsingfors , 1986. vi, 191 p. : ISBN 951-555-239-7 (pbk.) LC Card 86-224629 DDC 332.63/222 19
HG4636 .B47 1986

Things that go bump in the flight . Welch, Robert, 1932- White Hall, Va. , c1987. 156 p. ; ISBN 0-932620-75-2 (pbk.) : LC Card 87-1418 DDC 629.13/0028 19
HE9787 .W45 1987

Things your sales manager never told you. Garofalo, Gene. The sales professional's survival guide, or, Things your sales manager never told you /. Englewood Cliffs, NJ , c1987. p. cm. ISBN 0-13-788076-6 LC Card 86-25603 DDC 650.1/2/024381 19
HF5439.5 .G37 1987

Think about our population . Nam, Charles B. New York City, NY , 1988. viii, 117 p. : ISBN 0-8027-6753-2 LC Card 87-21601 DDC 304.6/0973 19
HB3505 .N29 1988

The Think series.
Nam, Charles B. Think about our population . New York City, NY , 1988. viii, 117 p. : ISBN 0-8027-6753-2 LC Card 87-21601 DDC 304.6/0973 19
HB3505 .N29 1988

THINK TANKS. see **PROBLEM SOLVING, GROUP.**

THINKING, ARTIFICIAL. see **ARTIFICIAL INTELLIGENCE.**

Thinking on your feet . Woodall, Marian K., 1941- Lake Oswego, Or. , 1987. xv, 100 p. ; ISBN 0-941159-01-9 (pbk.) : LC Card 86-63594 DDC 658.4/5 19
HF5718 .W65 1987

The thinking organization /. Sims, Henry P., 1939- San Francisco , 1986. xxvii, 375 p. : ISBN 0-87589-690-1 LC Card 85-45913 DDC 302.3/5 19
HD58.7 .S584 1986 ***NYPL [JLE 86-2921]***

Third Congress of Working People of Romania. Congress of Working People of Romania (3rd : 1986 : Bucharest, Romania) Bucharest [1986?] ii, 56 p. ; LC Card 86-225999 DDC 331/.09498 19
HD8642 .C59 1986

The third man . Komons, Nick A. Washington, D.C. , 1987. iv, 162 p. : LC Card 87-21267 DDC 363.1/2475 19
HD8039.A42 U54 1987

Third-party maintenance of computer and datacom equipment. Norwalk, Conn., U. S.A. (6 Prowitt St., Norwalk 06855) : International Resource Development, c1987. vi, 180 leaves ; 28 cm. (Report / International Resource Development Inc. . #724) "January 1987." LC Card 87-129551 DDC 381/.45004/0973 19
1. Computer service industry. 2. Data processing service centers. 3. Market surveys. I. International Resource Development, inc. II. Series: Report / International Resource Development Inc. , #724.
HD9696.C62 T45 1987

Third party maintenance of computers and data terminals in the United States. New York, N.Y. : Frost & Sullivan, c1983. vi, 269 leaves ; 29 cm. "#A1209." "April 1983." LC Card 87-142515 DDC 381/.4562139/0973 19
1. Computer service industry - United States. 2. Computer service industry - United States - Directories. 3. Market surveys - United States. I. Frost & Sullivan.
HD9696.C63 U5874 1983

Third underground shopper. Goldstein, Sue, 1941- The 3rd underground shopper . Kansas City , 1986. x, 532 p. ; ISBN 0-8362-7937-9 (pbk.) : LC Card 86-28758 DDC 381/.1 19
HF5466 .G6 1986

Third way books.
Storkey, Alan. Transforming economics . London , 1986. xi, 212 p. : ISBN 0-281-04225-X (pbk.) : LC Card 87-108686 DDC 261.8/5 19
HD5765.A6 S76 1986

The Third World and the world economic system / V.R. Panchamukhi ... [et al.]. New Delhi : Radiant Publishers ; Atlantic Highlands, N.J. : Distributed in the U. S.A. by Humanities Press, 1986. viii, 309 p. ; 22 cm. Includes bibliographies. ISBN 81-7027-092-8 : LC Card 86-900419 DDC 330.9172/4 19
1. Economic history - 1945-1971. 2. Developing countries - Economic conditions.
HC59.7 .T744 1986 ***NYPL [JLD 86-3145]***

Third World books.
Lemoine, Maurice. [Sucre amer. English.] Bitter sugar /. London , c1985. 308 p., [17] p. of

plates : ISBN 0-86232-445-9
NYPL [JLD 86-814]

Mies, Maria. Patriarchy and accumulation on a world scale . London , Atlantic Highlands, NJ , 1986. 251 p. ; ISBN 0-86232-341-X LC Card 86-18916 DDC 305.4 19
HD6060.6 .M54 1986 NYPL [JLD 86-3206]

Third World countries in the international cotton economy / by the Egyptian Institute of National Planning. [Nyon, Switzerland?] : Third World Forum, 1979. i, 61 p. : ill. ; 22 cm. (Third World Forum occasional paper . no. 6) Includes bibliographical references. LC Card 86-223016
1. Cotton trade - Developing countries. I. Ma'had al-Takhṭit al-Qawmi (Egypt). II. Series: Occasional paper (Third World Forum) , no. 6.
HD9088.D44 T47 1979

Third world development / [editor-in-chief, Enver Carim]. London ; New York : Grosvenor Press International, 1985. 3 v. : ill. (some col.) ; 30 cm. Includes advertising matter. Includes index. CONTENTS. - Vol. Industrial development & agriculture -- v. 2. High technology & communication -- v. 3. Health & education. ISBN 0-946027-65-X (v. 1)
1. Developing countries. 2. Developing countries - Economic conditions. I. Carim, Enver.
NYPL [JLF 86-626]

Third World economy . Joshi, Navin Chandra. New Delhi , 1983. x, 134 p. ; LC Card 83-904473 DDC 330.9172/4 19
HC59.7 .J645 1983 NYPL [JLD 86-3794]

Third world ideology and Western reality . Rangel Guevara, Carlos. [Tercermundismo. English.] New Brunswick , c1986. xiii, 180 p. ; ISBN 0-88738-601-6 (pbk.) LC Card 85-24486 DDC 330.9172/4 19
HC59.7 .R26513 1985 NYPL [JLE 86-3009]

Third World minerals and global pricing . Nwoke, Chibuzo. London [Atlantic Highlands] N.J. , 1987. x, 229 p. : ISBN 0-86232-441-6 : LC Card 87-12621 DDC 338.2/3 19
HD9506.D452 N86 1986

Third World multinationals . Nambudiri, C. N. S. Geneva , 1983. iv, 41 p. ; ISBN 92-2-103386-4 (pbk.) LC Card 86-213622 DDC 338.8/88669 19
HD2928 .N35 1983

The Third world, premises of U. S. policy / W. Scott Thompson, editor ; Dennis Austin ... [et al.]. San Francisco : Institute for Contemporary Studies, c1978. xv, 332 p. : graph ; 21 cm. Includes index. Bibliography: p. 305-311. ISBN 0-917616-30-8 : LC Card 78-67593 DDC 309.1/172/4
1. International economic relations - Addresses, essays, lectures. 2. Developing countries - Foreign economic relations - Addresses, essays, lectures. 3. United States - Foreign economic relations - Developing countries - Addresses, essays, lectures. 4. Developing countries - Foreign economic relations - United States - Addresses, essays, lectures. I. Thompson, W. Scott (Willard Scott), 1942-. II. Austin, Dennis, 1922-. III. Institute for Contemporary Studies.
HC59.7 .T456 NYPL [JLD 81-653]

Third World studies.
Beckford, George L. Persistent poverty . London , Totowa, N.J. , c1983. xxv, 244 p. : ISBN 0-86232-207-3 (pbk.) LC Card 85-149825 DDC 338.1/09172/4 19
HC59.72.P6 B43 1983 NYPL [JLD 87-628]

Thiriez, Sebastien, 1958- Armstrong-Wright, Alan, 1929- Bus services . Washington, D.C. , 1987. x, 97 p. ; ISBN 0-8213-0943-9 (pbk.) LC Card 87-17183 DDC 388.4/1322/091724 19
HE5725 .A76 1987

Thirlwall, A. P. Nicholas Kaldor / Anthony P. Thirlwall ; with a foreword by Sir Douglas Wass. Washington Square, NY : New York University Press, 1987. xvii, 360 p., [8] pages of plates : ill. ; 25 cm. Bibliography: p. 338-347. Includes indexes. ISBN 0-8147-8177-2 : LC Card 87-22065 DDC 330/.092/4 B 19
1. Kaldor, Nicholas, 1908-1986. 2. Economists - Great Britain - Biography. I. Title.
HB103.K36 T45 1987

Thirtle, Colin G., 1944- The role of demand and supply in the generation and diffusion of technical change / Colin G. Thirtle and Vernon W. Ruttan. Chur, Switzerland ; New York : Harwood Academic Publications, c1987. viii, 173 p. : ill. ; 22 cm. (Fundamentals of pure and applied economics, 0191-1708 . v. 21.) Bibliography: p. 133-161. Includes index. ISBN 3-7186-0384-5 (U. S. : pbk.) LC Card 87-138 DDC 338/.06 19
1. Technological innovations - Economic aspects. 2. Supply and demand. I. Ruttan, Vernon W. II. Series: Fundamentals of pure and applied economics , v. 21. III. Title.
HC79.T4 T495 1987

THIRTY-FIVE HOUR WEEK - AUSTRIA.
Marzen, Walter. Ist die 35-Stunden-Woche ein Mittel zur Beseitigung der Arbeitslosigkeit? . Innsbruck , 1980. 29 leaves ; LC Card 85-170048
HD5108.2.A9 M37 1980

THIRTY-FIVE HOUR WEEK - GERMANY (WEST)
Aktive Kolleginnen und Kollegen ziehen Bilanz . Frankfurt/M. , 1984. 100 p. : ISBN 3-88332-092-7 : LC Card 85-233569 DDC 331.89/2 19
HD5378 .A64 1984

Arbeitskampf um Arbeitszeit . Marburg , c1985. 218 p. : ISBN 3-921630-52-5 LC Card 86-160526
HD5378 .A73 1985

Memorandum '84 . Köln , c1984. 475 p. : ISBN 3-7609-0883-7 : LC Card 85-128558
HC286.7 .M465 1984

This is the North Eastern State of Nigeria. The North-Eastern State of Nigeria. [Nigeria? , 1968?] (Zaria : Gaskiya Corp.) 83 p. : LC Card 86-235207
HC1055.Z9 N676 1968

This world. The Best of This world /. Lanham, MD , c1986. x, 405 p. ; ISBN 0-8191-5605-1 (alk. paper) : LC Card 86-22411 DDC 261.8 19
HB72 .B5 1987 NYPL [JFE 86-5571]

Thody, Philip Malcolm Waller, 1928-
Faux amis & key words : a dictionary-guide to French language, culture, and society through lookalikes and confusables / Philip Thody & Howard Evans ; with Gwilym Rees. London : Athlone Press, 1985. 224 p. ; 23 cm. English and French. Includes index. Bibliography: p. [209]-212. ISBN 0-485-11243-4 : LC Card 84-108125 DDC 443/.21 19
1. French language - Paronyms - Dictionaries. 2. English language - Paronyms - Dictionaries. 3. French language - Dictionaries - English. 4. English language - Dictionaries - French. 5. French language - Synonyms and antonyms - Dictionaries. 6. French language - Errors of usage. I. Evans, Howard. II. Rees, Gwilym. III. Title. IV. Title: Faux amis and key words.
PC2593 .T45 1985 NYPL [JFD 86-5704]

Mistakable French : a dictionary of words & phrases easily confused / Philip Thody & Howard Evans with Gwilym Rees.1st U. S. ed. New York : Scribner, 1985. 224 p. ; 23 cm. Text in English and French. Includes index. Bibliography: p. [209]-212. ISBN 0-684-18324-2 : LC Card 84-51853 DDC 443/.21 19
1. French language - Paronyms - Dictionaries. 2. English language - Paronyms - Dictionaries. 3. French language - Dictionaries - English. 4. English language - Dictionaries - French. 5. French language - Synonyms and antonyms - Dictionaries. 6. French language - Errors of usage. I. Evans, Howard. II. Rees, Gwilym. III. Title.
PC2593 .T46 1985 NYPL [JFD 86-5781]

Tholstrup, Knud. Tale er sølv, tavshed er underkastelse / Knud Tholstrup. [Copenhagen] : Vendelkær, [1986] 179 p. : ill. ; 22 cm. ISBN 87-416-1329-5 : LC Card 86-215991
1. Denmark - Economic conditions - 1945-. I. Title.
HC355 .T37 1986

Thom, DeCourcy W. (DeCourcy Wright), 1858-1932. Juglar, Clément, 1819-1905. [Des crises commerciales. English.] A brief history of panics and their periodical occurrence in the United States /. New York, NY , 1988. p. cm. ISBN 0-678-00168-5 LC Card 87-17069 DDC 338.5/42 19
HB3743 .J8513 1988

Thom, Norbert.
Stand und Entwicklung des Vorschlagswesens in Wirtschaft und Verwaltung /. Dortmund , 1978. 108 p. : ISBN 3-922104-00-2 LC Card 85-124069
HD30 .A7 Heft 193 HF5549.5.S8

Zukunftsaspekte der anwendungsorientierten Betriebswirtschaftslehre . Stuttgart , c1986. xii, 641 p. : ISBN 3-7910-0402-6 LC Card 86-202268
HD35 .Z84 1986

Thomas, Dale F. Fees for services : principles and practices among state vocational rehabilitation agencies and facilities / Dale F. Thomas. Menomonie, WI : Research and Training Center, Stout Vocational Rehabilitation Institute, School of Education and Human Services, University of Wisconsin-Stout, [1986] v, 90 p. : ill. ; 28 cm. (Research report) Bibliography: p. 63-64. LC Card 86-622897 DDC 338.4/33620425 19
1. Rehabilitation centers - United States - Fees. 2. Rehabilitation centers - United States - Cost control. I. Series: Research report (Stout Vocational Rehabilitation Institute. Research and Training Center). II. Title.
HD7256.U5 T47 1986

Thomas, David Allen, 1939- Business communication today! / David A. Thomas, Maridell Fryar ; consultant, Juanita Fleming Harman. 2nd ed. Lincolnwood, Ill., U. S.A. : National Textbook Co., c1988. xi, 532 p. : ill. ; 24 cm. Bibliography: p. [521]-525. Includes index. ISBN 0-8442-5595-5 LC Card 87-60193 DDC 651.7 19
1. Business communication. I. Fryar, Maridell. II. Title.
HF5718 .T46 1988

The Thomas Davis lecture series.
Ireland in transition /. Cork , 1986. 178 p. ; ISBN 0-85342-786-0 (pbk.) : LC Card 87-111629 DDC 306/.09417 19
HC260.5 .I735 1986

Thomas, Earl. A history of Adolf Hitler and the Third Reich in postage stamps and postal stationery / by Earl Thomas, Jr. Silver Spring, Md. : Bibliophile Legion Books, c1987. p. cm. Bibliography: p. ISBN 0-918184-06-1 LC Card 87-755 DDC 769.56/3 19
1. Postage-stamps - Topics - Hitler, Adolf, 1889-1945 - History. 2. Postal stationery - Germany - History - 20th century. I. Title.
HE6183.H53 T46 1987

Thomas, Gail. Stirrings of culture /. Dallas, Tex. , 1986. xix, 250 p. ; ISBN 0-911005-07-2 : LC Card 86-24028 DDC 306 19
HM101 .S786 1986 NYPL [JFF 87-151]

Thomas, Joe Gene. Strategic management : concepts, practice, and cases / Joe G. Thomas. New York : Harper & Row, c1988. p. cm. Includes bibliographies and index. ISBN 0-06-046676-6 LC Card 87-21931 DDC 658.4/012 19
1. Strategic planning. I. Title.
HD30.28 .T47 1988

Thomas, O. Tom. Trimming float to build earnings : a handbook of strategies, analyses, and applications / O. Tom Thomas. Chicago, Ill. (111 E. Wacker Dr., Chicago 60601) : U. S. League of Savings Institutions, c1986. iv, 104 p. : ill. ; 28 cm. Bibliography: p. 104. LC Card 86-233102 DDC 332.1/752 19
1. Check float - United States. I. United States League of Savings Institutions. II. Title.
HG1692 .T46 1986

Thomas, R. E. (Raymond Elliott) The government of business / R.E. Thomas. 3rd ed. Oxford, UK ; Atlantic Highlands, NJ, USA : P. Allan, 1987. viii, 277 p. : ill. ; 22 cm. Includes bibliographies and index. ISBN 0-86003-548-4 LC Card 87-12647 DDC 338.0941 19
1. Industrial management - Great Britain. 2. Industry and state - Great Britain. I. Title.
HD70.G7 T48 1987

Thomas Robert Malthus, critical assessments / edited by John Cunningham Wood. London ; Dover, N.H. : Croom Helm, c1986. 4 v. : ill., ports. ; 24 cm. (The Croom Helm critical assessments of leading economists) Includes bibliographies. Includes bibliographies. CONTENTS. - v. 1. The life of Thomas Robert Malthus and perspectives on his thought -- v. 2. Malthus's principle of population and theory of political economy -- v. 3. Malthusian economic analysis -- v. 4. Specialised topics. ISBN 0-7099-3650-8 (set) : LC Card 85-22412 DDC 304.6/092/4 19
1. Malthus, Thomas Robert, 1766-1834. 2. Demographers - Great Britain - Biography. 3. Economists - Great Britain - Biography. I. Wood, John Cunningham. II. Series.
HB863 .T38 1986 NYPL [JFF 86-588]

Thomas, S. D. (Steve D.) The realities of nuclear power : international economic and regulatory experience / S.D. Thomas. Cambridge ; New York : Cambridge University Press, 1988. p. cm. Bibliography: p. Includes index. ISBN

0-521-32750-4 LC Card 87-22488 DDC 338.4/7621483 19
1. Nuclear industry. I. Title.
HD9698.A2 T53 1988

Thomas, Sue. Family finance : how to make your money go further / Sue Thomas. Cambridge [Cambridgeshire] ; Wolfeboro, NH, U. S.A. : Woodhead-Faulkner, 1988. p. cm. (A Woodhead-Faulkner moneyguide) ISBN 0-85941-420-5 (pbk.) : LC Card 87-17386 DDC 332.024 19
1. Finance, Personal. 2. Family. I. Title. II. Series.
HG179 .T457 1988

Thomas, Ulrike. 100 Jahre im Dienst der Gesundheit, 1886-1986 /. Ludwigshafen am Rhein , c1986. 159 p. : LC Card 87-408744 DDC 338.7/616151/0943 19
HD9669.9.K56 A15 1986

Thomas, Vinod, 1949- Linking macroeconomic and agricultural policies for adjustment with growth : the Colombian experience / Vinod Thomas with contributions from Sebastian Edwards ... [et al.]. Baltimore : Published for the World Bank [by] the Johns Hopkins University Press, c1985. xv, 252 p. ; 24 cm. "A World Bank publication." Includes bibliographical references and index. ISBN 0-8018-3121-0 : LC Card 85-45105 DDC 338.9861 19
1. Agriculture and state - Colombia - Addresses, essays, lectures. 2. Price policy - Colombia - Addresses, essays, lectures. 3. Coffee trade - Colombia - Addresses, essays, lectures. 4. Colombia - Economic policy - Addresses, essays, lectures. 5. Colombia - Commercial policy - Addresses, essays, lectures. I. Title.
HC197 .T38 1985 ***NYPL [JLE 86-1438]***

Thomas, William Arthur. The big bang / W.A. Thomas. Deddington, Oxford : P. Allan ; Atlantic Highlands, N.J. : Distributed in the U. S.A. and Canada by Humanities Press, 1986. ix, 180 p. ; 23 cm. Distributor from label on t.p. Bibliography: p. 175-176. Includes index. ISBN 0-86003-546-8 LC Card 86-226055 DDC 332.64/241 19
1. Stock Exchange (London, England). I. Title.
HG4577 .T47 1986

Thomason, Michael. Flynt, J. Wayne, 1940- Mine, mill & microchip . Northridge, Calif. , 1987. 376 p. : ISBN 0-89781-215-8 LC Card 87-9192 DDC 338.09761 19
HC107.A4 F57 1987

Thomé, Gotthardt, 1949- Produktgestaltung und Ökologie / Gotthardt Thomé. München : Florentz, c1981. xii, 212 p. : ill. ; 21 cm. (Schriftenreihe wirtschaftswissenschaftliche Forschung und Entwicklung . Bd. 67) Includes index. Bibliography: p. 189-212. ISBN 3-88259-086-6 : LC Card 81-146058
1. New products - Environmental aspects. 2. Product management - Environmental aspects. 3. Industry - Environmental aspects. 4. Industry - Social aspects. I. Title. II. Series.
HD69.N4 T54 1981 ***NYPL [JLD 86-2800]***

Thomée, Friedrich, 1920- Dynamische Preisbildungsprozesse in Monopol / Friedrich M. Thomée. Wiesbaden : Gabler, c1983. 247 p. : ill. ; 24 cm. (Betriebswirtschaftliche Forschung zur Unternehmensführung. Bd. 16) Bibliography: p. [225]-247. ISBN 3-409-13035-7 : LC Card 84-116637
1. Prices - Mathematical models. 2. Monopolies - Mathematical models. I. Title.
HB221 .T465 1983

Thomis, Malcolm I. From SGIO to Suncorp / Malcolm I. Thomis & Murdoch Wales. [Brisbane?] : Suncorp Insurance and Finance, 1986. xii, 272 p., [32] p. of plates : ill. ; 26 cm. Bibliography: p. 234-264. Includes index. ISBN 0-7242-1698-7 LC Card 87-158138 DDC 368.4/009943 19
1. Insurance, Government - Australia - Queensland - History. 2. Workers' compensation - Australia - Queensland - History. 3. Queensland. State Government Insurance Office - History. 4. Suncorp Insurance and Finance - History. I. Wales, Murdoch, 1925-. II. Title.
HG8220.A9 T56 1986

Thompson, A. M. Coetzee, S. F. Regional economic development in the Southern African development area /. Sandton, Republic of South Africa , 1985. xvi, 105 p. : LC Card 87-150264 DDC 338.968 19
HC905 .C64 1985

Thompson, Allen R.
Economics / Allen R. Thompson. 2nd ed. Reading, Mass. : Addison-Wesley, c1988. xxxii, 888, [46] p. : ill. ; 26 cm. Includes index. ISBN 0-201-09682-X : LC Card 87-912 DDC 330 19
1. Economics. I. Title.
HB171.5 .T33 1988

Macroeconomics / Allen R. Thompson. 2nd ed. Reading, Mass. : Addison-Wesley Pub., c1988. xxx, 888, [38] p. : ill. (some col.) ; 26 cm. Includes index. ISBN 0-201-09684-6 (pbk.) LC Card 87-916 DDC 339 19
1. Macroeconomics. I. Title.
HB172.5 .T48 1988

Microeconomics / Allen R. Thompson. 2nd ed. Reading, Mass. : Addison-Wesley Pub., c1988. xxx, 888, [35] p. : ill. (some col.) ; 26 cm. Includes bibliographical references and index. ISBN 0-201-09683-8 (pbk.) LC Card 87-910 DDC 338.5 19
1. Microeconomics. I. Title.
HB172 .T49 1988

Thompson, Arthur A., 1940-
Strategic management : concepts and cases / Arthur A. Thompson, Jr., and A.J. Strickland III.4th ed. Plano, Tex. : Business Publications, 1987. xviii, 1054 p. : ill. ; 25 cm. Includes bibliographies and index. ISBN 0-255-03717-5 LC Card 86-72250 DDC 658.4/012 19
1. Strategic planning. 2. Strategic planning - Cast studies. I. Strickland, Alonzo J. II. Title.
HD30.28 .T53 1987

Strategy formulation and implementation : tasks of the general manager / Arthur A. Thompson, Jr., and A.J. Strickland III.3rd ed. Plano, Tex. : Business Publications, 1986. xvi, 452 p. : ill. ; 24 cm. Includes bibliographies and index. ISBN 0-256-03173-8 (pbk.) LC Card 85-73596 DDC 658.4/012 19
1. Strategic planning. I. Strickland, Alonzo J. II. Title.
HD30.28 .T54 1986

Thompson, David R. Thompson, Richard E. Theory I . San Antonio, Tex. , c1986. 105 p. : ISBN 0-940555-00-X (pbk.) LC Card 86-90531 DDC 658.4/00207 19
HD70.U5 T48 1986

Thompson, Dennis L. The Private exercise of public functions /. Port Washington, N.Y. , 1985. 251 p. ; ISBN 0-8046-9368-4 LC Card 84-9254 DDC 361.6/1 19
H97 .P76 1985 ***NYPL [JLE 86-2611]***

Thompson, Frank. The American farmer book . [Smithshire, Ill.] (Box 181, Smithshire 61478) [c1986] 192 p. : LC Card 86-203314 DDC 338.1/0973 19
HD8039.F32 U614 1986

Thompson G., Roberto. Problemática agraria y política petrolera en Chiapas / Roberto Thompson G. Tuxtla Gutiérrez, Chiapas : H. Congreso del Estado de Chiapas : Centro de Investigaciones Ecológicas del Sureste, 1983. 37 p., [1] leaf of plates : ill. ; 22 cm. Synthesis of a larger study entitled "Expansión petrolera y problemática agraria en el sureste de México; el caso de la llamada Area Petrolera de Reforma, noroeste de Chiapas y Tabasco central, 1970-1980." LC Card 84-243074
1. Petroleum industry and trade - Government policy - Mexico - Chiapas. 2. Agriculture - Economic aspects - Mexico - Chiapas. 3. Labor supply - Mexico - Chiapas. I. Chiapas (Mexico). Congreso. II. Centro de Investigaciones Ecológicas del Sureste (San Cristóbal de Las Casas, Mexico). III. Title.
HD9574.M63 C457 1983

Thompson, Gary J. 1986 tax software report / prepared by Gary J. Thompson. Green Bay, Wis. (P.O. Box 12470, Green Bay, 54307-2470) : Form Systems & Services, c1986. ii, 54 leaves ; 28 cm. LC Card 87-102387 DDC 343.7305/2044/0285536 347.303520440285536 19
1. Tax returns - United States - Data processing. 2. Tax returns - Computer programs. I. Title.
HJ3252 .T47 1986

Thompson, George (George H.) Zenz, Gary Joseph. Purchasing and the management of materials /. New York , c1987. xvi, 542 p. : ISBN 0-471-81802-X LC Card 86-32589 DDC 658.7/2 19
HD39.5 .W47 1987

Thompson, Grahame. Managing the UK economy . Cambridge, UK , 1987. xxvii, 328 p. : ISBN 0-7456-0316-5 : LC Card 86-26860 DDC 338.941 19
HC256.5 .M392 1987

Thompson, James D. Comparative studies in administration /. New York , 1987. xiv, 224, 40 p. : ISBN 0-8240-8220-6 (alk. paper) : LC Card 86-27017 DDC 658 19
HD30.55 .C66 1987

Thompson, Jera L. ALM on micros . York, PA (P.O. Box 1508, York 17405) , c1986. 86 p. : LC Card 87-108676 DDC 332.1/028/5416 19
HG1615.25 .A46 1986

Thompson, Kenneth, 1937- Beliefs and ideology / Kenneth Thompson. Chichester, West Sussex : Ellis Horwood ; London ; 135 p. ; 20 cm. (Key ideas) Includes index. Bibliography: p. [129]-131. ISBN 0-85312-858-8 : LC Card 86-2984 DDC 306/.4 19
1. Ideology. 2. Culture. I. Title. II. Series.
BL60 .T49 1986 ***NYPL [JLD 86-2479]***

Thompson, Paul M. Parker, Dennis J. Urban flood protection benefits . Aldershot, Hants, England , Brookfield, Vt., U. S.A. , c1987. xvii, 284 p. : ISBN 0-291-39707-7 LC Card 87-147842 DDC 363.3/49372 19
HD1676.G7 P37 1987

Thompson, Pauline J. Up and running in real estate sales / by P.J. Thompson. Santa Barbara, Calif. : Kricket Publications, c1987. vi, 202 p. : ill., forms ; 23 cm. Includes index. ISBN 0-918785-02-2 (pbk.) : LC Card 87-16916 DDC 333.33 19
1. Real estate business - United States. 2. Real estate agents - United States. I. Title.
HD255 .T49 1987

Thompson, Richard E. Theory I : end your one-minute search for excellence / Richard E. Thompson and David R. Thompson. San Antonio, Tex. : SENSS, c1986. 105 p. : ill. ; 21 cm. ISBN 0-940555-00-X (pbk.) LC Card 86-90531 DDC 658.4/00207 19
1. Industrial management - United States. I. Thompson, David R. II. Title.
HD70.U5 T48 1986

Thompson, Robert L. A survey of recent U. S. developments in international agricultural trade models / Robert L. Thompson. Washington, D.C. : U. S. Dept. of Agriculture, Economic Research Service, 1981. v, 74 p. ; 28 cm. (Bibliographies and literature of agriculture . no. 21) Cover title. "September 1981"--P. [i] Item 32-B-1 Bibliography: p. 52-74. LC Card 81-603138 DDC 382/.41/0973 19
1. Agriculture - Economic aspects - Mathematical models. 2. Produce trade - Mathematical models. 3. Export sales - Mathematical models. I. United States. Dept. of Agriculture. Economic Research Service. II. Title. III. Series.
HD1433 .T48 ***NYPL [JLF 84-568]***

Thompson, W. Scott (Willard Scott), 1942- The Third world, premises of U. S. policy /. San Francisco , c1978. xv, 332 p. : ISBN 0-917616-30-8 : LC Card 78-67593 DDC 309.1/172/4
HC59.7 .T456 ***NYPL [JLD 81-653]***

Thomsen, Stephen E.
Danielian, Ronald L. The forgotten deficit . Boulder , 1987. xii, 84 p. ; ISBN 0-8133-7450-2 (pbk. : alk. paper) LC Card 87-50654 DDC 332.6/7373 19
HG3883.U7 D36 1987

International capital flows and the United States : pallative [i.e. palliative], panacea, or Pandora's box? : a special report / by Stephen E. Thomsen. Washington, D.C. (1400 Eye St., N.W., Suite 510, Washington 20005) : International Economic Policy Association, [1985] vi, 62 p. : ill. ; 23 cm. "October 1985"--Cover. Errata slip inserted. Bibliography: p. 60-62. LC Card 87-108428 DDC 332/.042/0973 19
1. Investments, Foreign - United States. 2. Investments, American. 3. Balance of payments - United States. I. International Economic Policy Association. II. Title.
HG4910 .T47 1985

Thomsen, Thomas. Caballero, Lorenzo. Mozambique, food and agriculture sector /. Uppsala , 1984. 223, [30] p. : ISBN 91-576-2129-2 (pbk.) LC Card 86-218958 DDC 338.1/0967/9 19
HD9017.M86 C33 1984

Thomsen, Veronika Bennholdt- see **Bennholdt-Thomsen, Veronika.**

Thomsett, Michael C.
Builder's guide to accounting / by Michael C. Thomsett. Rev., 2nd ed. Carlsbad, CA : Craftsman Book Co., c1987. 302 p. : ill. ; 28 cm. Includes index. ISBN 0-934041-18-0 (pbk.) : LC Card 87-6817 DDC 657/.869 19
1. Construction industry - Accounting. I. Title.
HF5686.B7 T47 1987

Homeowners money management : a guide to realizing your life dreams by controlling your financial plan / by Michael C. Thomsett. Emmaus, Pa. : Rodale Press, c1987. xiii, 238 p. : ill. ; 24 cm. Includes index. ISBN 0-87857-673-8 (alk. paper) : LC Card 86-26096 DDC 332.024 19
1. Home ownership - United States. 2. Investments - United States. 3. Finance, Personal - United States. 4. Homeowners - United States - Finance, Personal. I. Title.
HD7287.82.U6 T47 1987

Investment and securities dictionary / compiled by Michael C. Thomsett. Jefferson, N.C. : McFarland, 1986. vii, 328 p. : ill. ; 24 cm. ISBN 0-89950-225-3 : LC Card 85-43594 DDC 332.6/03/21 19
1. Investments - Dictionaries. 2. Securities - Dictionaries. I. Title.
HG4513 .T48 1986 *NYPL [JLE 87-450]*

Thon, Wolfgang, 1956- Peter, Gerd, 1941- Der Arbeitsschutzbeauftragte . Frankfurt , New York , c1986. 344 p. : ISBN 3-593-33633-2 LC Card 86-160932
HD6490.S52 G365 1986

Thorbecke, Erik. Svejnar, Jan. Economic policies and agricultural performance . Paris , 1986. 167 p. ; LC Card 87-120115 DDC 338.1/85496 19
HD2065.9.Z8 S84 1986

Thorbecke, Erik, 1929- Greer, Joel William, 1948- Food poverty and consumption patterns in Kenya /. Geneva , 1986. xii, 170 p. : ISBN 92-2-105374-1 (pbk.) : LC Card 87-115091 DDC 338.1/9/6762 19
HD9017.K42 G74 1986

Thorndike, David, 1925- Thorndike encyclopedia of banking and financial tables / by David Thorndike. 3rd ed. Boston : Warren, Gorham & Lamont, c1987. 1737 p. in various pagings ; 29 cm. Includes index. ISBN 0-88712-883-1 LC Card 87-50721 DDC 332.8/0212 19
1. Interest - Tables. 2. Interest rates - Tables. 3. Investments - Tables. 4. Banks and banking - Tables. I. Title.
HG1626 .T49 1987

Thorndike encyclopedia of banking and financial tables /. Thorndike, David, 1925- Boston , c1987. 1737 p. in various pagings ; ISBN 0-88712-883-1 LC Card 87-50721 DDC 332.8/0212 19
HG1626 .T49 1987

Thornton, John H. Block, Stanley B. Personal financial management /. New York , c1988. xvii, 603 p. : ISBN 0-06-040789-1 LC Card 87-19088 DDC 332.024 19
HG179 .B555 1988

Thornton, Robert J. Forging new relationships among business, labor, and government /. Greenwich, Conn. , c1986. xiii, 210 p. ; ISBN 0-89232-656-5 : LC Card 86-2839 DDC 338.973 19
HD3616.U47 F583 1986
NYPL [JLE 86-3452]

Thorsen, Harry D., 1913-
Scouts on stamps of the world. Kaplan, Howard J. Scouts on stamps of the world / by Howard J. Kaplan and William E. Hoffmann ; assistant editors, William Parkin, John B. Adams, William C. Cowan. 7th ed. [Hicksville, N.Y.] , c1986. 1 v. (loose-leaf) : LC Card 86-224816 DDC 769.56/3 19
HE6183.B63 K36 1986

Thorsen, Thorkil. Alkoholforbrug og trafikulykker : en analyse af forholdet mellem alkoholforbrug og alkoholproblemets omfang i trafikken i Danmark 1930-1983 / Thorkil Thorsen og Jógvan Petersen. København : Alkohol- og narkotikarådet, 1986. 69 p. : ill. ; 24 cm. (Alkohol- og narkotikarådets skriftserie, 0109-8918 . 6) Summary in English. Bibliography: p. 47-49. ISBN 87-88225-38-3 LC Card 86-209934
1. Drinking and traffic accidents - Denmark. I. Petersen, Jógvan, 1947-. II. Title. III. Series.
HE5620.D7 T49 1986

Thost, Per. Larsen, Flemming. Parkeringsbehov i ældre tætte bydele . København , 1985. 250 p. : LC Card 86-165642
HE336.P37 L37 1985

Thott, Otto, 1703-1785. Glamann, Kristof. Studier i dansk merkantilisme . [Copenhagen] , c1983. 243 p. ; ISBN 87-500-2476-0 LC Card 85-125251
HB91 .G57 1983

THOTT, OTTO, 1703-1785.
Glamann, Kristof. Studier i dansk merkantilisme . [Copenhagen] , c1983. 243 p. ; ISBN 87-500-2476-0 LC Card 85-125251
HB91 .G57 1983

Thought and action in social policy. Social concerns for the 1980s . Wien , c1984. 359 p. ; ISBN 3-900376-18-2 (pbk.)
NYPL [JLE 86-2856]

THRACE - OCCUPATIONS - HISTORY.
Papathanasē-Mousiopoulou, Kalliopē. Syntechnies & epangelmata stē Thrakē, 1685-1920 /. Athēna , 1985. 247 p. : LC Card 86-208086
HD6795.5.Z8 T56 1985

Threats of quotas in international trade, their effect on the exporting country /. Stockhausen, Gerard Lawrence. New York , 1988. 170 p. : ISBN 0-313-25785-X (lib. bdg. : alk. paper) LC Card 87-23682 DDC 382/.64 19
HF1430 .S86 1988

Threats to international financial stability / edited by Richard Portes and Alexander K. Swoboda. Cambridge ; New York : Cambridge University Press, 1987. xviii, 307 p. : ill. ; 24 cm. Proceedings of an international conference held in Geneva, September 11-13, 1986 and organized by the International Center for Monetary and Banking Studies. Includes bibliographies and index. CONTENTS. - The anatomy of financial crises / Barry Eichengreen and Richard Portes -- The role of public policy in ensuring financial stability / Ernst Baltensperger and Jean Dermine -- The design of bank regulation and supervision / Stephen M. Schaefer -- Competitive financial reregulation / Edward J. Kane -- Emergency liquidity assistance for international banks / Jack Guttentag and Richard Herring -- The interbank market, contagion effects, and international financial crises / Anthony Saunders -- Public policy and international financial stability / Joan Pearce -- Policy and financial innovation / Markus Lusser. ISBN 0-521-34556-1 LC Card 87-10310 DDC 332/.042 19
1. International finance. I. Portes, Richard. II. Swoboda, Alexander K. III. International Center for Monetary and Banking Studies.
HG3881 .T495 1987

Threats to private enterprise in Australia /. Tsung, Stephen. [Melbourne] , 1976. 80 p. ; LC Card 82-127568
HD3616.A83 T78 1976

Three essays on money, wealth, and the exchange rate /. Puumanen, Kari. Helsinki , 1986. 143 p. : ISBN 951-686-119-9 (pbk.) LC Card 86-235460 DDC 332.4/0724 19
HG221 .P97 1986

Three-interval polynomial approximation for continuous univariate distribution functions. Tsai, Hsien-Tang. A 3-interval polynomial approximation for continuous univariate distribution functions /. West Lafayette, Ind. [1986] 7, 14 p. : LC Card 86-622753 DDC 658/.001/9 s 519/.2 19
HD6483 .P8 no. 898 QA273.6

THREE MILE ISLAND NUCLEAR POWER PLANT, PA.
Impacts of hazardous technology . Albany , c1987. x, 233 p. : ISBN 0-88706-332-2 LC Card 86-1943 DDC 363.1/79 19
HD9698.U54 M475 1987
NYPL [JLE 87-1233]

Thri Shṭāra Ko-apāreṭibha Mālaṭipārapāsa Sosaiṭi. Hosena, Nājira, 1930- Samabāya, saṃgrāma, sādhanā /. Ḍhākā , 1985. 8, 109 p., [7] p. of plates : LC Card 85-904909
HD3540.6.D32 H67 1985

THRI SHṬĀRA KO-APĀREṬIBHA MĀLAṬIPĀRAPĀSA SOSAIṬI.
Hosena, Nājira, 1930- Samabāya, saṃgrāma, sādhanā /. Ḍhākā , 1985. 8, 109 p., [7] p. of plates : LC Card 85-904909
HD3540.6.D32 H67 1985

Thrift industry. Financial stability of the thrift industry . San Francisco, Calif. (P.O. Box 7948, San Francisco 94120) [1986?] 230 p. : LC Card 86-81012 *NYPL [JLE 86-3398]*

Thrift, N. J.
Multinationals and the restructuring of the world economy /. London , Dover, N.H. , c1986- viii, 389 p. : ISBN 0-7099-2457-7 (v. 2) : LC Card 85-29081 DDC 338.8/81 19
HD2755.5 .M8442 1986
NYPL [JLD 86-2089]

The Socialist Third World . Oxford, UK , New York, NY , 1987. vii, 333 p. : ISBN 0-631-13442-5 : LC Card 87-5165 DDC 338.9/009172/4 19
HC59.7 .S5857 1987

Thriving on chaos . Peters, Thomas J. New York , 1987. xii, 561 p. : ISBN 0-394-56784-6 LC Card 87-45575 DDC 658 19
HD70.U5 P426 1987

Thro, Ellen. Blau, Anne Kohn. The sex of the dollar . New York , c1988. 190 p. : ISBN 0-671-60680-8 LC Card 87-23560 DDC 332.024/042 19
HG181 .B46 1988

Throup, David. Economic & social origins of Mau Mau 1945-53 / David Throup. London : J. Currey ; Athens : Ohio University Press, c1988. xvi, 304 p. : maps ; 23 cm. (Eastern African studies) Bibliography: p. 285-295. Includes index. ISBN 0-8214-0883-6 LC Card 87-12387 DDC 307.3/36 19
1. Agriculture and state - Kenya - History - 20th century. 2. Kenya - Economic conditions - To 1963. 3. Kenya - Social conditions. 4. Kenya - Politics and government - To 1963. 5. Squatters - Kenya - History - 20th century. 6. Mau Mau - History. 7. Kikuyu (African people) - History - 20th century. I. Title. II. Title: Economic and social origins of Mau Mau. III. Series: Eastern African studies (London, England).
HD2126.5 .T48 1988

Thunder in the mountains /. Savage, Lon, 1928- Elliston, Va. , 1986. iv, 160 p. : ISBN 0-9617256-0-5 (pbk.) : LC Card 87-7634 DDC 331.89/2822334/097543 19
HD5325.M63 1920 .W47

Thurcroft, a village and the miners' strike : an oral history / the people of Thurcroft. Nottingham [Nottinghamshire] ; Atlantic Highlands, NJ : Spokesman, 1986. 276 p. : ill. ; 23 cm. Contains some short linking and explanatory passages written by Peter Gibbon and David Steyne. Includes index. ISBN 0-85124-441-6 LC Card 86-21887 DDC 331.89/2822334/0942823 19
1. Coal Strike, Great Britain, 1984-1985. 2. Coal miners - England - Thurcroft (South Yorkshire) - Interviews. 3. Thurcroft (South Yorkshire) - Social conditions. I. Gibbon, Peter. II. Steyne, David.
HD5346.M6152 1984 .T48 1987
NYPL [JLD 87-985]

THURCROFT (SOUTH YORKSHIRE) - SOCIAL CONDITIONS.
Thurcroft, a village and the miners' strike . Nottingham [Nottinghamshire] , Atlantic Highlands, NJ , 1986. 276 p. : ISBN 0-85124-441-6 LC Card 86-21887 DDC 331.89/2822334/0942823 19
HD5346.M6152 1984 .T48 1987
NYPL [JLD 87-985]

Thürmer, Lothar. Bürokratie und Effizienz staatlichen Handelns : der Beitrag der ökonomischen Theorie der Politik zur Erklärung des Verhaltens demokratisch gesteuerter Verwaltungen / von Lothar Thürmer. Berlin : Duncker & Humblot, c1984. 177 p. : ill. ; 24 cm. (Volkswirtschaftliche Schriften. Heft 338) Bibliography: p. [146]-177. ISBN 3-428-05543-8 LC Card 84-156948
1. Bureaucracy - Europe. 2. Government business enterprises - Europe. I. Title. II. Series.
HD38.4 .T47 1984

Thurn und Taxis, Kurhessen 1816-1867 . Köhler, H. (Heinz) Kassel [1970?]- v. <1 > : LC Card 86-235280
HE6185.G32 H474 1970

Thurow, Lester C. Heilbroner, Robert L. Economics explained /. New York , 1987. 250 p. : ISBN 0-671-64556-0 (pbk.) LC Card 87-12807

DDC 330 19
HB171 .H479 1987

Thweatt, William O. Classical political economy . Boston , c1988. viii, 275 p. : ISBN 0-89838-229-7 : LC Card 87-3394 DDC 330.15/3 19
HB94 .C42 1988

Tibbitts, Samuel J. Bennett, Addison C. Making innovation practical /. Chicago, Ill. , c1986. vi, 238 p. : ISBN 0-931028-79-5 LC Card 86-62191 DDC 658.4/06 19
HD58.8 .B46 1986

Tibiriçá, Luiz Caldas. Brasil : corrupção e incompetência / Luiz Caldas Tibiriçá.1a. ed. São Paulo, SP : Edições Populares, 1984. 159 p. ; 21 cm. LC Card 84-215785
1. Corruption (in politics) - Brazil. 2. Brazil - Economic conditions - 1964-1985. 3. Brazil - Social conditions - 1964-. 4. Brazil - Politics and government - 1965-1984. I. Title.
HC187 .T5 1984 ***NYPL [JLD 87-507]***

Tice, Robert L. Hi-res graphics for the Apple II/IIe/IIc / by Robert L. Tice and Dorothy Jo Stevens. Blue Ridge Summit, Pa. : Tab Books, 1985. vii, 197 p. : ill. ; 24 cm. Includes index. ISBN 0-8306-0849-4 : LC Card 84-23954 DDC 001.64/43 19
1. Apple II (Computer) - Programming. 2. Apple IIe (Computer) - Programming. 3. Apple IIc (Computer) - Programming. I. Stevens, Dorothy Jo. II. Title.
T385 .T52 1985 ***NYPL [JSE 86-805]***

Tichelman, Fritjof. Op een beteren weg . Amsterdam , 1985. 239 p. : ISBN 90-6012-654-8 : LC Card 85-236523
HD8516 .O6 1985 ***NYPL [JLD 86-3427]***

Tichy, Gunther. Aiginger, Karl. Die Grösse der Kleinen . Wien [between 1984 and 1987] 160, [1] p. : ISBN 3-85436-025-8 LC Card 87-141921 DDC 658.1/592 19
HG4027.7 .A38 1984

TICINO (SWITZERLAND) - ECONOMIC CONDITIONS.
Un Paese che cambia /. Locarno , 1985. 293 p. : LC Card 85-195116 DDC 330.9494/7 19
HC398.T5 P34 1985

TICINO (SWITZERLAND) - SOCIAL CONDITIONS.
Un Paese che cambia /. Locarno , 1985. 293 p. : LC Card 85-195116 DDC 330.9494/7 19
HC398.T5 P34 1985

TIDAL POWER INDUSTRY.
Worldwide remote power sites. New York, N.Y. , c1983. 2 v. (xx, xxvii, 500 p.) : LC Card 87-141748
HD9695.A2 W67 1983

Tidrick, Gene, 1942- China's industrial reform /. New York , c1987. xii, 378 p. ; ISBN 0-19-520592-8 : LC Card 87-5616 DDC 338.951 19
HD3616.C63 C495 1987

Tiebel, Christoph. Überwälzte Kosten der Gesetze : eine empirische Analyse der Folgekosten für den Markt / Christoph Tiebel ; mit einer Einführung von H.C. Recktenwald. Göttingen : Vandenhoek & Ruprecht, c1986. xv, 256 p. : 53 ill. ; 24 cm. (Abhandlungen zu den wirtschaftlichen Staatswissenschaften. Bd. 27) Bibliography: p. [235]-256. ISBN 3-525-11333-1 (Deut. Bibl.) LC Card 87-135628 DDC 336.2/4 19
1. Taxation - Compliance costs. 2. Taxation - Law and legislation - Compliance costs. I. Title. II. Series.
HJ2309 .T48 1986

Tieber, Herbert. Verstaatliche Industrie : was gesagt und was verschwiegen wird-- : eine kommentierte Dokumentation / Herbert Tieber, Rudolf Spitzer. Wien : Jugend und Volk, c1983. 91 p. : ill. ; 21 cm. (Schriftenreihe der Gemeinwirtschaft) LC Card 84-169053
1. Government ownership - Austria. 2. Government business enterprises - Austria. 3. Industry and state - Austria. I. Spitzer, Rudolf. II. Title.
HD4155 .T54 1983

Tiedtke, Hans-Ullrich. Das Bedienungsstandard-Konzept als Instrument zur Bewertung des ÖPNV in ländlichen Räumen, exemplarisch dargestellt am Einkaufsverkehr / Hans-Ullrich Tiedtke. Bochum : Brockmeyer, 1981. viii, 274 p. ; 21 cm. (Bochumer wirtschaftswissenschaftliche Studien. Nr. 77) Originally presented as the author's thesis (doctoral)--Ruhr-Universität Bochum, 1980. Bibliography: p. 243-274. ISBN 3-88339-192-1 : LC Card 81-205962 DDC 388/.0943 19
1. Rural transit. 2. Rural transit - Germany (West). I. Title.
HE152.5 .T53 1981 ***NYPL [JLD 86-2578]***

Tiempo de Venezuela.
Gabaldón, Arnoldo. Política ambiental y sociedad /. Caracas, Venezuela , 1986. 225 p. : ISBN 980-01-0034-2 LC Card 87-115207 DDC 363.7/056/0987 19
HC239.5.E5 G32 1986

Tienda, Marta. The structural transformation of employment in Wisconsin, 1960-1980 / Marta Tienda, Shelley A. Smith. Madison, WI (Rm. 245, 30 N. Murray St., Madison 53715) : Research Division of the Agricultural and Life Sciences University of Wisconsin-Madison, [1986] ii, 47 p. ; 28 cm. (Research Report / College of Agricultural & Life Sciences . R3377) Bibliography: p. 36-37. LC Card 86-623091 DDC 331.12/09775 19
1. Labor supply - Wisconsin. 2. Service industries - Wisconsin. 3. Wisconsin - Occupations. 4. Wisconsin - Industries. I. Smith, Shelley A. II. Series: Research report (University of Wisconsin--Madison. College of Agricultural and Life Sciences. Research Division) , R3377. III. Title.
HD5725.W5 T54 1986

La Tierra de Campos occidental . Martínez Sopena, Pascual. [Valladolid] , 1985. 843 p. : ISBN 84-505-1390-1 LC Card 86-231937
HD779.T54 M37 1985

TIERRA DE CAMPOS REGION (SPAIN) - POPULATION - HISTORY.
Martínez Sopena, Pascual. La Tierra de Campos occidental . [Valladolid] , 1985. 843 p. : ISBN 84-505-1390-1 LC Card 86-231937
HD779.T54 M37 1985

La tierra en la comunidad de Segovia . Martínez Moro, Jesús. [Valladolid] [Salamanca] , c1985. 252 p. : ISBN 84-86192-37-4 LC Card 86-211593
HD780.S44 M37 1985

Tierra y ganado en Pacajes . Birbuet D., Gustavo. La Paz, Bolivia , 1986. 86 p. : LC Card 87-403087 DDC 333.3/0984/12 19
HD490.C34 B57 1986

Las tierras comunales en el Ecuador /. González S., Víctor A. Guayaquil, Ecuador , 1982. 109 p. ; LC Card 87-672596
HD1289.E2 G66x 1982

Tierras para asentamientos populares : criterios de selección y desarrollo / CIUDAD, Jorge García, Diego Carrión (coordinación CIUDAD) ; ALAHUA, Fernando Luis Chaves, Jorge Di Paula (coordinación ALAHUA).1a ed. Quito, Ecuador : CIUDAD : ALAHUA, 1985. 378 p. : ill. ; 21 cm. "Programa regional ALAHUA: selección de tierras para asentamientos populares." Bibliography: p. 251-266. LC Card 87-400165 DDC 333.77/13/0986613 19
1. Land use, Urban - Ecuador - Quito Region. 2. Community development, Urban - Ecuador - Quito Region - Citizen participation. I. García, Jorge. II. Carrión, Diego. III. Chaves, Fernando Luis. IV. Di Paula, Jorge. V. Centro de Investigaciones CIUDAD (Quito, Ecuador). VI. ALAHUA (Association).
HD530.Q58 T54 1985

Le Tiers-mondisme en question / sous la direction de Rony Brauman. Paris : O. Orban, c1986. 225 p. ; 22 cm. (Collection Liberté sans frantières) "Actes du colloques organisé par la Fondation Liberté sans frontières les 23 et 24 janvier 1985"--P. 9. Includes bibliographical references. PARTIAL CONTENTS. - L'héritage colonial français / Jacques Marseill -- Le tiers-mondisme, de Lénine à nos jours / Ilios Yannakakis -- La fin des mythes révolutionnaires / Gérard Chaliand -- Tiers-Monde, culpabilité, haine de soi / Pascal Bruckner -- Les pénuries dans les pays les moins avancés / Jacques Giri -- Comment réduire la pauvreté / Gilbert Etienne -- La nouvelle Asie industrielle / Michel Fouquin -- Les controverses démographiques / Alfred Sauvy. ISBN 2-85565-299-5 : LC Card 86-185503
1. Developing countries - Economic policy - Congresses. 2. Developing countries - Economic conditions - Congresses. 3. Economic assistance - Developing countries - Congresses. I. Brauman, Rony. II. Fondation Liberté sans frontières. III. Series.
HC60 .T518 1986

Tietenberg, Thomas H. Environmental and natural resource economics / Tom Tietenberg. 2nd ed. Glenview, Ill. : Scott, Foresman, c1988. 559 p. : ill. ; 24 cm. Includes bibliographies and indexes. ISBN 0-673-18945-7 LC Card 87-23250 DDC 333.7 19
1. Environmental policy. 2. Natural resources - Government policy. 3. Raw materials - Government policy. I. Title.
HC79.E5 T525 1988

Tietz, Reinhard. Wert- und Präferenzprobleme in den Sozialwissenschaften /. Berlin , c1981. 268 p. : ISBN 3-428-05013-4 LC Card 86-230716
HF5415.3 .W47 1981

Tietzel, Manfred. Wirtschaftstheorie und Unwissen : Überlegungen zur Wirtschaftstheorie jenseits von Risiko und Unsicherheit / von Manfred Tietzel. Tübingen : Mohr, 1985. viii, 208 p. ; 24 cm. (Die Einheit der Gesellschaftswissenschaften, 0424-6985 . Bd. 39) Bibliography: p. [178]-195. Includes indexes. ISBN 3-16-944919-2 LC Card 86-147807
1. Economics. 2. Risk. 3. Uncertainty. I. Title. II. Series.
HB175 .T55 1985

Tiffany, Paul A. The decline of American steel : how management, labor, and government went wrong / Paul A. Tiffany. New York : Oxford University Press, 1988. p. cm. Revision of thesis (Ph. D.)--University of California at Berkeley. Bibliography: p. Includes index. ISBN 0-19-504382-0 (alk. paper) LC Card 87-5782 DDC 338.4/7669142/0973 19
1. Steel industry and trade - United States. 2. Steel industry and trade - Government policy - United States. 3. Trade-unions - Iron and steel workers - United States. I. Title.
HD9515 .T54 1988

Tiffen, Rodney. Mortimer, Rex, 1926-1979. Stubborn survivors . [Clayton, Vic.] , 1984. xvii, 180 p. : ISBN 0-86746-299-X (pbk.) LC Card 87-672646
HC59.7 .M593x 1984

Tiffin, Joseph, 1905- Industrial psychology / Joseph Tiffin. New York : Garland Pub., 1987, [c1942] xvi, 386 p. : ill. ; 23 cm. (Continuity in administrative science) Reprint. Originally published: New York : Prentice-Hall, 1942. Includes bibliographical references and index. ISBN 0-8240-8221-4 (alk. paper) : LC Card 86-25803 DDC 158.7 19
1. Psychology, Industrial. I. Title. II. Series.
HF5548.8 .T5 1987

Tiger, Henri. Restructuration industrielle et filières de main-d'œuvre : l'agglomération grenobloise des origines de la grande industrie aux firmes multinationales / Henri Tiger, avec la participation de Maud Fontaine, Farid Paya pour L'élaboration du modèle de traitement, Carmen Yanez pour le redressement des données et le calcul des indicateurs. Paris : Centre de sociologie urbaine, 1979. 389 p. : ill. ; 24 cm. Includes bibliographical references and appendices. LC Card 85-126419
1. Labor supply - France - Grenoble Metropolitan Area - History. 2. Grenoble Metropolitan Area (France) - Industries - History. I. Title.
HD5776.G74 T54 1979

Tigges, Leann M. Changing fortunes : industrial sectors and workers' earnings / Leann M. Tigges. New York : Praeger, 1987. xvi, 174 p. : ill. ; 25 cm. Bibliography: p. [161]-170. Includes index. ISBN 0-275-92580-3 (alk. paper) : LC Card 87-2357 DDC 331.2/973 19
1. Wages - United States. 2. Age and employment - United States. 3. Industrial organization - United States. 4. Social classes - United States. I. Title.
HD4975 .T5 1987

Tikhomirov, E. F.
Organizatsionno-ėkonomicheskie problemy sovershenstvovaniia funktsionirovaniia transportnykh sistem /. Moskva , 1984. 144 p. : LC Card 85-199422
HE5675.A6 O765 1984

Tikhomirov, Evgeniĭ Fedorovich.
Sovershenstvovanie khoziaĭstvennogo mekhanizma na transporte /. Moskva , 1983. 223 p. : LC Card 85-199829
HE255.A2 S68 1983

Tikhomirov, N. P. (Nikolaĭ Petrovich) Iskakov, B. I. (Boris Ivanovich) Demograficheskoe modelirovanie . Moskva , 1982. 75 p. ; LC

Card 83-179019
HB849.51 .I85 1982

Tikhonov, Vladimir Aleksandrovich. Obobshchestvlenie sel'skokhoziaistvennogo proizvodstva /. Moskva , 1986. 159 p. ; LC Card 86-177899
HD9015.S652 O26 1986

TIKHVIN REGION (R.S.F.S.R.) - ECONOMIC POLICY.
Dolgosrochnoe sotsial'no-ėkonomicheskoe planirovanie /. Leningrad , 1986. 165 p. : LC Card 87-146872
HC338.T5 D65 1986

Tilakaratna, Bī. Ḍī. Subasiṃha, Vinsant. Sandalaṅkā sanda /. [Pannipitiya?] , 1986. viii, 269 p., [6] leaves of plates : LC Card 86-903022
HG1552.S83 A3 1986

Tilastoja. A, Väestö, työvoima, asuminen .
(1984:2) Kinturi, Jorma. Väestö, asunnot ja asuntorakentaminen suur- ja peruspiireittäin Helsingissä 1970-1983 =. Helsinki , 1984. 36 p., [1] folded leaf of plates : LC Card 85-156678
HD7345.3.H5 K563 1984

(1985:2) Lankinen, Leila. Asuminen Helsingissä 1950-1983 =. Helsinki , 1985. 80 p. : LC Card 86-148571
HD7345.3.H5 L35 1985

Tilastotiedotus (Finland. Työsuojeluhallitus) .
(84/2) Metsä- ja uittotöiden työtapaturmat vuonna 1982 =. Tampere , Helsinki , 1984. 50 p. : ISBN 951-46-7685-8 LC Card 85-149625
HD7269.F7262 F56 1984

Tilgungsplanung . Allerkamp, Ferdinand. Frankfurt am Main , c1983. xii, 288 p. : ISBN 3-7819-0296-X LC Card 85-239167
HD2747 .A53 1983

Tilley, Marcia L. Plaxico, James Sam, 1924- Financial status of Oklahoma farmers and ranchers, 1985 . [Stillwater] [1986] 42 p. ; LC Card 86-622478 DDC 338.1/3/09766021 19
HD1775.O5 P57 1986

Tilli, Maria Grazia. Vino e olio in Toscana =. Firenze , c1985. 386 p. : LC Card 86-138958 DDC 338.4/76632/009455 19
HD9385.I82 T858 1985 ***NYPL [JSF 87-35]***

Tilly, Louise.
National Research Council (U. S.). Committee on Women's Employment and Related Social Issues. Panel on Technology and Women's Employment. Computer chips and paper clips . Washington, D.C. , 1986. v. : ISBN 0-309-03688-7 (v. 1) LC Card 86-18113 DDC 331.4/8165137/0973 19
HD6331.18.M39 N38 1986 ***NYPL [JLL 87-129]***

Women, work, and family / Louise A. Tilly and Joan W. Scott. New York : Methuen, 1987. vii, 274 p. : ill. ; 23 cm. Originally published: New York : Holt, Rinehart and Winston, 1978. Bibliography: p. 233-268. Includes index. ISBN 0-416-01681-2 (pbk.) : LC Card 87-11103 DDC 305.4/3/00941 19
1. Women - Employment - Great Britain - History. 2. Women - Employment - France - History. 3. Work and family - Great Britain - History. 4. Work and family - France - History. I. Scott, Joan Wallach. II. Title.
HD6135 .T54 1987

Tilly, Richard H. Beiträge zur quantitativen vergleichenden Unternehmensgeschichte /. Stuttgart , c1985. 206 p. : ISBN 3-608-91325-4 LC Card 85-233589
HD2734 .B32 1985

Tilton, Rita Sloan. Secretarial procedures and administration / Rita Sloan Tilton, J. Howard Jackson, Estelle L. Popham. 9th ed. Cincinnati : South-Western Pub. Co., c1987. vi, 874 p. : ill., forms ; 24 cm. Rev. ed. of: Secretarial procedures and administration / Estelle L. Popham ... [et al.]. 8th ed. c1983. Includes bibliographies and index. ISBN 0-538-11790-7 LC Card 86-63074 DDC 651.3/74 19
1. Office practice. I. Jackson, J. Howard (James Howard), 1928-. II. Popham, Estelle L. III. Secretarial procedures and administration. IV. Title.
HF5547.5 .S4 1987

Timber Corps (Great Britain)
Meet the members . [London?] [194-?] (Bristol : Bennett Bros.) 76 p., [12] p. of plates : LC Card 84-190854
HD6073.L92 G76 1940z

TIMBER CORPS (GREAT BRITAIN) - HISTORY.
Meet the members . [London?] [194-?] (Bristol : Bennett Bros.) 76 p., [12] p. of plates : LC Card 84-190854
HD6073.L92 G76 1940z

The timber industries of New Hampshire and Vermont . Nevel, Robert L. Broomall, Pa. , 1986. 56 p. : LC Card 86-601144 DDC 338.1/7498/09742 19
HD9757.N4 N48 1986

The timber industry in interior Alaska . Pierce, Brad. [Juneau] [1986] 65 p. ; LC Card 86-621755 DDC 338.1/7498/09798 19
HD9757.A7 P54 1986

TIMBER - NEW HAMPSHIRE.
Nevel, Robert L. The timber industries of New Hampshire and Vermont . Broomall, Pa. , 1986. 56 p. : LC Card 86-601144 DDC 338.1/7498/09742 19
HD9757.N4 N48 1986

TIMBER - VERMONT.
Nevel, Robert L. The timber industries of New Hampshire and Vermont . Broomall, Pa. , 1986. 56 p. : LC Card 86-601144 DDC 338.1/7498/09742 19
HD9757.N4 N48 1986

Timberlake, Lloyd. Africa in crisis : the causes, the cures of environmental bankruptcy / y Lloyd Timberlake; edited by Jon Tinker. Philadelphia : New Society Publishers, 1986. 232 p. : ill., maps ; 21 cm. (An Earthscan book) Bibliography: p. [233] ISBN 0-86571-082-1
1. Environmental policy - Africa. 2. Land use - Africa. I. Tinker, Jon. II. Title. ***NYPL [Sc D 87-100]***

Time and money . Crowe, Robert M. Homewood, Ill. , c1987. 1 v. (various pagings) : ISBN 1-556-23051-6 (pbk.) LC Card 87-70621 DDC 332.024 19
HG1621 .C76 1987

A time for change . Currie, Lawrence A., 1949- Halifax, N.S. , c1986. 64 p. : ISBN 0-88926-031-1 (pbk.) LC Card 86-230034 DDC 331.89/281388322 19
HD5329.M82 1979 .D543 1986

Time-Life Books. Jackson, Donald Dale, 1935- Flying the mail /. Alexandria, Va. , c1982. 176 p. : ISBN 0-8094-3329-X LC Card 82-2020 DDC 383/.144/09 19
HE6496 .J3 1982 ***NYPL [JLF 87-386]***

TIME MANAGEMENT.
Delden, P. J. van, 1949- De toekomst van de vrije tijd /. [Deventer] , c1986. 102 p. ; ISBN 90-6001-973-3 : LC Card 86-199367
HD4904.6 .D45 1986

Henry, Lauchland. The professional's guide to working smarter /. Tenafly, N.J. , 1988. xv, 208 p. : ISBN 0-935310-03-7 LC Card 87-23868 DDC 650.1 19
HD8038.A1 H47 1988

Hobbs, Charles R. Time power /. New York , c1987. ix, 209 p. : ISBN 0-06-015589-2 : LC Card 86-46072 DDC 650.1 19
HD69.T54 H62 1987

Rubin, Bonnie Miller. Time out . New York , c1987. p. cm. LC Card 87-5723 DDC 640 19
HD5255 .R82 1987

Vitullo, Ray, 1925- How to get organized & increase self confidence . North Plainfield, N.J. , c1986. p. cm. ISBN 0-9607752-3-4 : LC Card 86-72854 DDC 650.1 19
HD69.T54 V58 1986

TIME MANAGEMENT - ANECDOTES, FACETIAE, SATIRE, ETC.
Book, Jeffrey. The one minute maniac /. Kansas City, Mo. , c1987. 140 p. : ISBN 0-8362-1260-6 (pbk.) : LC Card 87-914 DDC 658.4/093 19
HD69.T54 B66 1987

TIME MANAGEMENT - NETHERLANDS.
Delden, P. J. van, 1949- De toekomst van de vrije tijd /. [Deventer] , c1986. 102 p. ; ISBN 90-6001-973-3 : LC Card 86-199367
HD4904.6 .D45 1986

TIME MANAGEMENT - UNITED STATES.
Pleck, Joseph H. Working wives, working husbands /. Beverly Hills, Calif. , c1985. 167 p. ; ISBN 0-8039-2489-5 LC Card 85-11974 DDC 306.8/7 19
HQ536 .P59 1985 ***NYPL [JLD 86-1130]***

Time out . Rubin, Bonnie Miller. New York , c1987. p. cm. LC Card 87-5723 DDC 640 19
HD5255 .R82 1987

Time power /. Hobbs, Charles R. New York , c1987. ix, 209 p. : ISBN 0-06-015589-2 : LC Card 86-46072 DDC 650.1 19
HD69.T54 H62 1987

TIME-SERIES ANALYSIS - MATHEMATICAL MODELS.
Dagum, Estela Bee. The X-II-ARIMA seasonal adjustment method /. Ottawa , c1980. 119 p. : LC Card 83-225028
HB137 .D34 1980

TIME STUDY.
Mundel, Marvin Everett, 1916- Motion and time study . Englewood Cliffs, N.J. , c1985. xvi, 752 p. : ISBN 0-13-603044-0 LC Card 84-18173 DDC 658.5/42 19
T60.7 .M86 1985 ***NYPL [JSE 86-2187]***

Why the office staff scared of time and motion study? . Saddar, Karachi, Pakistan [1985] 1 v. (various pagings) leaves ; LC Card 86-146552
HD5070.5 .W49 1985

A time to act . Nsekela, Amon J. (Amon James), 1930- Dar es Salaam , c1984. xxi, 142 p. ; ISBN 997-660-025-9 LC Card 86-981097 DDC 338.9678 19
HC885 .N86 1984

A time to be rich . Hunt, Lacy H. New York , c1987. xvi, 282 p. : ISBN 0-89256-325-7 : LC Card 87-9431 DDC 332.6/78 19
HG4910 .H86 1987

Times Mirror/Mosby data processing and information systems series.

The Times Mirror/Mosby data processing and information systems series.
Cohen, Eli B. Business BASIC for the IBM PC with cases /. St. Louis , 1987. xxiv, 634 p. : ISBN 0-8016-1244-6 (pbk.) LC Card 86-23100 DDC 005.2/165 19
HF5548.5.B3 C64 1987

Lientz, Bennet P. Data communications for business /. St. Louis , 1987. xx, 326 p. : ISBN 0-8016-3013-4 LC Card 86-23012 DDC 650/.028/546 19
HF5548.2 .L535 1987

Spence, J. Wayne. Microcomputers in business . St. Louis , 1987. vii, 224 p. : ISBN 0-8016-5030-5 (pbk.) LC Card 86-30013 DDC 650/.028/5536 19
HF5548.2 .S728 1987

Timm, Paul R. Business communication : getting results / Paul R. Timm, Christopher G. Jones ; with a guide to basic language usage by Ray L. Young.2nd ed. Englewood Cliffs, N.J. : Prentice-Hall, c1987. xvi, 509 p. : ill. ; 25 cm. Includes bibliographies and index. ISBN 0-13-091779-6 LC Card 86-30650 DDC 658.4/5 19
1. Communication in management. I. Jones, Christopher G. II. Young, Ray L. III. Title.
HF5718 .T53 1987

Timm, Willy. Mark (Grafschaft) Schatzbuch der Grafschaft Mark, 1486 /. Unna , 1986. 176 p. ; ISBN 3-87298-042-4 LC Card 87-116701 DDC 336.2/00943/55 19
HJ2110.5.M36 M37 1986

Timmer, C. Peter. Getting prices right : the scope and limits of agricultural price policy / C. Peter Timmer. Ithaca : Cornell University Press, 1986. 160 p. : ill. ; 23 cm. Includes index. Bibliography: p. 151-155. ISBN 0-8014-9441-9 (pbk. : alk. paper) LC Card 86-47649 DDC 338.1/8 19
1. Food prices - Government policy - United States. 2. Agricultural prices - Government policy - United States. I. Title.
HD9006 .T58 1986 ***NYPL [JLE 86-4488]***

Timmer, Reinhard. Raumordnung und Industrialisierung / Reinhard Timmer. Hannover : Niedersächsische Landeszentrale für Politische Bildung, 1977. 103 p. : ill. ; 21 cm. Bibliography: p. 99-103. LC Card 84-150907
1. Germany, West - Economic conditions. 2. Regional planning - Germany, West. I. Title.
HC286.5 .T55 1977

Timofeev, Timur Timofeevich. Rabochiĭ klass v proshlom i nastoiashchem . Moskva , 1984,

c1983. 255 p. ; LC Card 84-169518
HD4854 .R273 1984

Timor Timur, Indonesia.
East Timor develops. [Dili] [1984] 45 p. : LC Card 85-942048 DDC 338.9598/6 19
HC448.T513 E2 1984

TIMOR TIMUR, INDONESIA - DESCRIPTION AND TRAVEL.
East Timor develops. [Dili] [1984] 45 p. : LC Card 85-942048 DDC 338.9598/6 19
HC448.T513 E2 1984

TIMOR TIMUR (INDONESIA) - ECONOMIC CONDITIONS.
East Timor develops. [Dili] [1984] 45 p. : LC Card 85-942048 DDC 338.9598/6 19
HC448.T513 E2 1984

Martinez, José Fernando Trindade. Recursos económicos do Ultramar Português, sua valorização e perspectivas futuras . Lisboa , 1960. 113 p. ; LC Card 86-169892
HC890 .M37 1960

Timpe, A. Dale.
Creativity /. New York, N.Y. , c1987. xvi, 383 p. : ISBN 0-8160-1463-9 : LC Card 86-29320 DDC 650.1 19
HD53 .C745 1987

Leadership /. New York, N.Y. , c1987. xi, 368 p. : ISBN 0-8160-1462-0 : LC Card 86-24167 DDC 658.4/092 19
HD57.7 .L43 1987

Tims, Wouter. Pereira, A. (Armand) Socio-economic and policy implications of energy price increases /. Aldershot, Hants, England , Brookfield, Vt., USA , c1987. xxiv, 317 p. ; ISBN 0-566-05520-1 : LC Card 87-11955 DDC 338.2/3 19
HD9560.4 .P37 1987

Timush, Andreĭ Ivanovich. Upravlenie sotsial′nymi protsessami v trudovykh kollektivakh /. Kishinev , 1983. 141 p. : LC Card 84-133794
HD6957.S65 U67 1983

TIN INDUSTRY - BOLIVIA - CONGRESSES.
Bolivia frente a la crisis del estaño . La Paz, Bolivia [1986] 62 p. ; LC Card 86-189109
HD9539.T6 B646 1986 ***NYPL [JLC 87-146]***

TIN INDUSTRY - CONGRESSES.
Bolivia frente a la crisis del estaño . La Paz, Bolivia [1986] 62 p. ; LC Card 86-189109
HD9539.T6 B646 1986 ***NYPL [JLC 87-146]***

TIN INDUSTRY - INDONESIA.
Profile of the primary commodity sector in Malaysia. [Kuala Lumpur] [1984] 77 p. : LC Card 86-945653 DDC 338.09595 19
HD9016.M32 P76 1984

TIN INDUSTRY - MEXICO - HISTORY.
Barrett, Elinore M. The Mexican colonial copper industry /. Albuquerque , c1987. xi, 143 p. : ISBN 0-8263-0929-1 LC Card 86-24991 DDC 338.2/743/0972 19
HD9539.C7 M417 1987

TIN MINERS - BOLIVIA - BUSTILLO.
Desabastecimiento de alimentos y alternativas de solución en las minas . La Paz [Bolivia] , 1986. 128 : LC Card 87-401454 DDC 331.7/6223453/098413 19
HD8039.M72 B624 1986

TIN MINERS - THAILAND, SOUTHERN.
Saphāp læ ʻōkāt nai kānthamngān nai kitčhakān m [Bangkok] [2509 i.e. 1966] 2, 35 p., [5] leaves of plates : LC Card 80-911179
HD8039.M72 T527 1966

TIN MINERS - THAILAND, SOUTHERN - SUPPLY AND DEMAND.
Saphāp læ ʻōkāt nai kānthamngān nai kitčhakān m [Bangkok] [2509 i.e. 1966] 2, 35 p., [5] leaves of plates : LC Card 80-911179
HD8039.M72 T527 1966

TIN - TRADE AND STATISTICS. see **TIN INDUSTRY.**

Tınar, Mustafa Yaşar, 1955- Humanisierung der Arbeit und Produktivität : Auswirkungen einer Erweiterung des Entscheidungsspielraums der Arbeitnehmer auf Fehlzeiten, Fluktuation und Arbeitsproduktivität in Wirtschaftsorganisationen / Mustafa Yaşar Tınar. Frankfurt am Main ; New York : P. Lang, c1986. xiii, 296 p. : ill. ; 21 cm. (Europäische Hochschulschriften. Reihe V, Volks- und Betriebswirtschaft, 0531-7339 . Bd. 754 = vol. 754 = vol. 754) Originally presented as the author's thesis (doctoral--Johann Wolfgang Goethe-Universität in Frankfurt am Main, 1986) under the title: Auswirkungen einer Erweiterung des Entscheidungsspielraums der Arbeitnehmer auf Fehlzeiten, Fluktuation und Arbeitsproduktivität in Wirtschaftsorganisationen. Bibliography: p. 255-296. ISBN 3-8204-9542-8 LC Card 86-233418
1. Job satisfaction - Germany, West. 2. Labor productivity - Germany, West. 3. Hours on labor, Flexible - Germany (West). I. Series: Europäische Hochschulschriften. Reihe V, Volks- und Betriebswirtschaft , Bd. 754. II. Title.
HF5549.5.J63 T55 1986

Tinbergen, Jan, 1903- Warfare and welfare : integrating security policy into socio-economic policy / Jan Tinbergen, Dietrich Fischer. Brighton, Sussex : Wheatsheaf Books ; New York : St. Martin's Press, 1987. xiv, 189 p. ; 25 cm. Includes bibliographies and index. ISBN 0-312-00957-7 (St. Martin's) : LC Card 87-9625 DDC 361.6/1 19
1. Welfare economics. 2. Economic security. 3. National security. 4. International organization. I. Fischer, Dietrich, 1941-. II. Title.
HB846 .T55 1987

Tiner, John I. Accounting for treasury products : a practical guide to accounting and taxation aspects of risk control / John I. Tiner and Joe M. Conneely. Cambridge, England ; Wolfeboro, N.H., USA : Woodhead-Faulkner, 1988. p. cm. Includes index. ISBN 0-85941-389-6 : LC Card 87-12531 DDC 657/.833 19
1. Banks and banking - Great Britain - Accounting. 2. Banks and banking - Taxation - Great Britain. 3. Financial futures - Great Britain - Accounting. 4. Financial futures - Taxation - Great Britain. I. Conneely, Joe M. II. Title. III. Title: Treasury products.
HG1708 .T56 1988

Ting, Wenlee. Multinational risk assessment and management : strategies for investment and marketing decisions / Wenlee Ting. New York : Quorum Books, c1987. p. cm. Bibliography: p. Includes index. ISBN 0-89930-175-4 (lib. bdg. : alk. paper) LC Card 87-5970 DDC 658 19
1. Risk management - Political aspects. 2. International business enterprises - Management. 3. Investments, Foreign - Political aspects - Evaluation. 4. Political stability - Evaluation. 5. Country risk. I. Title.
HD61 .T56 1987

Tinker, Jon. Timberlake, Lloyd. Africa in crisis . Philadelphia , 1986. 232 p. : ISBN 0-86571-082-1
NYPL [Sc D 87-100]

Tinker, tailor, and textile worker . Goldberg, Ellis. Berkeley , 1986. xiii, 234 p. : ISBN 0-520-05353-2 (alk. paper) LC Card 85-16472 DDC 322.4/4/0962 19
HD8786 .G65 1986 ***NYPL [JLE 87-500]***

TINKERS - IRELAND - ECONOMIC CONDITIONS.
Rottman, David B. The population structure and living circumstances of Irish travellers . Dublin , 1986. 134 p. : ISBN 0-7070-0084-X (pbk.) : LC Card 86-215759 DDC 330.9417 s 305.5/68 19
HC257.I6 E3 no. 131 DX217

TINKERS - IRELAND - SOCIAL CONDITIONS.
Rottman, David B. The population structure and living circumstances of Irish travellers . Dublin , 1986. 134 p. : ISBN 0-7070-0084-X (pbk.) : LC Card 86-215759 DDC 330.9417 s 305.5/68 19
HC257.I6 E3 no. 131 DX217

Tinner, Hanspeter. Konzernstruktur und Steuerplanung : Strukturierung und Umstrukturierung von schweizerischen internationalen Konzernen aus steuerlicher Sicht / von Hanspeter Tinner. Bern : P. Haupt, c1984. ix, 276 p. : ill. ; 23 cm. (Schriftenreihe Finanzwirtschaft und Finanzrecht. Bd. 39) Bibliography: p. 260-276. ISBN 3-258-03367-6 : LC Card 84-198592
1. International business enterprises - Taxation - Switzerland. 2. Tax planning - Switzerland. I. Title. II. Series.
HJ4748.A3 T55 1984

TINPLATE INDUSTRY - UNITED STATES.
United States of America, tin in tinplate. London [1983] 89 p. : LC Card 84-216067 DDC 338.4/76736/0973 19
HD9529.T63 U67 1983

Tiozzo, Piergiorgio. Un Mestiere e un paese . Venezia , 1986. 172 p. : ISBN 88-317-4893-9 LC Card 86-219883
HD8039.S252 I85 1986

El tipo de cambio fijo en Chile . Toso C., Roberto. Santiago , 1983. 64 p. ; LC Card 83-192876
HG3934 .T67 1983

Tipo de cambio y salarios reales . Rosende Ramírez, Francisco. Santiago , 1985. 28 p. : LC Card 86-106380 DDC 332.4/5/0983 19
HG3934 .R67 1985

Tipton, Frank B., 1943-
An economic and social history of Europe from 1939 to the present / Frank B. Tipton and Robert Aldrich. Baltimore, Md. : Johns Hopkins University Press, 1987. vii, 297 p. : maps ; 23 cm. Bibliography: p. 280-286. Includes index. ISBN 0-8018-3538-0 LC Card 87-3870 DDC 330.94/055 19
1. Europe - Economic conditions - 1918-1945. 2. Europe - Economic conditions - 1945-. 3. Europe - Social conditions - 20th century. I. Aldrich, Robert, 1954-. II. Title.
HC240 .T563 1987

An economic and social history of Europe, 1890-1939 / Frank B. Tipton and Robert Aldrich. Baltimore : Johns Hopkins University Press, 1987. vii, 323 p. : maps ; 23 cm. Bibliography: p. 308-313. Includes index. ISBN 0-8018-3537-2 LC Card 87-3869 DDC 330.94/028 19
1. Europe - Economic conditions - 19th century. 2. Europe - Economic conditions - 20th century. 3. Europe - Social conditions - 1789-1900. 4. Europe - Social conditions - 20th century. I. Aldrich, Robert, 1954-. II. Title.
HC240 .T56 1987

TIRE INDUSTRY WORKERS - FRANCE - CLERMONT-FERRAND.
Barrière, Antoine. Michelin . Nonette , 1983. 289 p. ; ISBN 2-902894-20-1
NYPL [JLD 86-4467]

TIRES, RUBBER.
The Effect of tire pressures on flexible pavements /. College Station, Tex. , Springfield, Va. , 1985. viii, 235 p. : LC Card 86-622241 DDC 380.5 s 625.8 19
HE203 .T43 no. 372-1F TE270

Tiret, Edmond. Witcomb, Henry, 1822- Dictionnaire des termes de marine français-anglais & anglais-français. Paris, 1883. 2 v. LC Card 29-23644
V24 .W5 ***NYPL [JSE 86-1965]***

Tiroler Wirtschaftsstudien. For additional listing of contents, see Old Catalog.
(11. Folge) Zwanowetz, Georg. Das Strassenwesen Tirols seit der Eröffnung der Eisenbahn Innsbruck-Kufstein (1858) . Innsbruck , 1986. 163 p., 32 leaves of plates : ISBN 3-7030-0165-8 LC Card 87-142160 DDC 388.1/09436/42 19
HE247.Z7 T99 1986

(37. Folge) Penz, Hugo. Das Trentino . Innsbruck , 1984. 379 p. : ISBN 3-7030-0142-9 : LC Card 86-138251
HC307.T7 P45 1984

Tiroler Wirtschaftsstudien; Schriftenreihe der Jubiläumsstiftung der Kammer der Gewerblichen Wirtschaft für Tirol. see **Tiroler Wirtschaftsstudien.**

TIRUCHCHIRĀPPALLI (INDIA : DISTRICT) - ECONOMIC CONDITIONS.
Stanislaus, M. Sebastian. New farm technology and income distribution /. New Delhi , c1984. viii, 76 p. : LC Card 84-902272 DDC 338.1/3/095482 19
HD2075.T57 S73 1984 ***NYPL [JLD 87-669]***

Tirumalai, R., 1924- The voice of enterprise : 150 years of the Madras Chamber of Commerce & Industry / R. Tirumalai.1st ed. Bangalore : Macmillan India, 1986. xxii, 464 p., [41] p. of plates : ill., facsims., maps ; 23 cm. Maps on lining papers. Bibliography: p. 433-449. Includes index. ISBN 0-333-90907-0 : LC Card 86-903465 DDC 380.1/06/05482 19
1. Madras Chamber of Commerce and Industry - History. 2. Madras (India : State) - Economic

conditions. 3. Madras (India : State) - Commerce - History. I. Madras Chamber of Commerce and Industry. II. Title.
HF331.I4 T57 1986

Tishkov, I. E. (Ivan Efremovich) Uchet i kal'kulirovanie sebestoimosti produktsii vspomogatel'nykh proizvodstv / I.E. Tishkov. Moskva : "Finansy", 1980. 110 p. ; 20 cm. Includes bibliographical references. LC Card 81-143226
1. Costs, Industrial - Soviet Union. 2. Factories - Soviet Union - Accounting. I. Title.
HC340.C7 T57 1980

T.I.S.S. series .
(no. 54) Child labour and health . Bombay , c1985. xi, 287 p. ; LC Card 86-900928 DDC 331.3/1/0956 19
HD6250.I42 C46 1985 *NYPL [JLD 87-1553]*

(53) Ranadive, K. R. Accumulation, employment, and labour aristocracy . Bombay [1982] 55 p. ; LC Card 83-903051 DDC 305.5/62/0954 19
HD8686.5 .R325 1982 *NYPL [JLF 87-500]*

Tisul' . Karmanov, V. A. (Vladimir Andreevich) Kemerovo , 1983. 93 p., [8] p. of plates : LC Card 84-103652
HC337.R852 T575 1983

TISUL' REGION (R.S.F.S.R.) - ECONOMIC CONDITIONS.
Karmanov, V. A. (Vladimir Andreevich) Tisul' . Kemerovo , 1983. 93 p., [8] p. of plates : LC Card 84-103652
HC337.R852 T575 1983

The titans of takeover /. Slater, Robert, 1943- Englewood Cliffs, N.J. , c1987. ix, 230 p. : ISBN 0-13-922055-0 LC Card 86-25364 DDC 338.8/3/0973 19
HD2785 .S44 1987

TITHES - SPAIN - ZAMORA (PROVINCE) - HISTORY - STATISTICS.
Alvarez Vázquez, J. A. (José Antonio) Los diezmos en Zamora (1500-1840) /. Salamanca, España [Zamora] , 1984. ii, 318 p. ; ISBN 84-7481-296-8 LC Card 85-123559
HJ2287.S74 A58 1984

Titlestad, Kirstin Dale, 1951- Kvinner i arbeid . Oslo , c1984. 290 p. : ISBN 82-00-06835-8 : LC Card 85-102185
HD6170 .K85 1984

Titma, M. Kh. Osobennosti popolneniia osnovnykh otriadov intelligentsii /. Tallin , 1981. 131 p. : LC Card 82-125732
HD8038.S652 E775 1981

Titorenko, G. A. (Galina Anton'evna) Proektirovanie mashinnoĭ obrabotki ėkonomicheskoĭ informatsii /. Moskva , 1979. 287 p. : LC Card 81-159368
HF5548.2 .P79 1979

Titova, A. M. (Aleksandra Mikhaĭlovna) Stroim Kuzbass /. Kemerovo , 1984. 417 p., [56] p. of plates : LC Card 84-103662
HC337.R852 K8975 1984

Tiumenskiĭ gosudarstvennyĭ universitet.
Kooperativnoe dvizhenie v Sibiri . Tiumen' , 1984. 72 p. ; LC Card 85-179545
HD3517.A3 R875 1984

Tiutiukin, S. V. (Stanislav Vasil'evich) Rabochee dvizhenie v Rossii v period imperializma . Moskva , 1982. 144 p. ; LC Card 83-174879
HD8526 .R3112 1982

Tiutkov, O. V.
Aktual'nye problemy prirodopol'zovaniia v promyshlennom regione /. Sverdlovsk , 1985. 151 p. : LC Card 86-126638
HC337.R852 U732 1985

Ėkonomicheskie problemy osvoeniia Ural'skogo Severa /. Sverdlovsk , 1982. 69 p. : LC Card 83-188353
HC336.9.N65 E37 1982

Tiven, Marjorie. State initiatives in elderly housing : what's new, what's tried and true / project director, Ronne Thielen ; authors, Marjorie Tiven and Barbara Ryther. Washington, DC : Council of State Housing Agencies : National Association of State Units on Aging, c1987. xviii, 79 p. ; 28 cm. "December 1986." Bibliography: p. 77. LC Card 87-154352 DDC 363.5/9 19
1. Aged - Housing - Government policy - United States - States. I. Ryther, Barbara. II. Council of State Housing Agencies (U. S.). III. National Association of State Units on Aging. IV. Title.
HD7287.92.U54 T58 1987

Tiwary, Jai Kant. Rural development administration : perspectives and prospects / Jai Kant Tiwary. Allahabad, India : Chugh, 1984. xi, 248 p. ; 22 cm. Includes indexes. Bibliography: p. [230]-238. LC Card 84-900188 DDC 307.7/2/0954 19
1. Rural development - India. 2. Agriculture and state - India. I. Title.
HN690.Z9 C68286 1984 *NYPL [JLD 86-4313]*

Tixier, Maud. Dictionnaire américain-anglais-français du management / Maud Tixier. Paris : Dalloz, 1985. 381 p. ; 23 cm. (Dalloz gestion. Management) ISBN 2-247-00647-7 : LC Card 86-160705
1. Management - Dictionaries. 2. Management - Dictionaries - French. 3. English language - Dictionaries - French. 4. French language - Dictionaries - English. I. Title. II. Title: Dictionnaire du management. III. Series.
HD30.15 .T59 1985 *NYPL [JLD 86-3975]*

Tjänstesverige.
Johnson, Anders. Släpp tjänsterna loss . [Stockholm] , c1986. 232 p. : ISBN 91-7152-374-X : LC Card 86-235064
HD9986.S82 J63 1986

De tjenesteytende næringer i 80-åra /. Vannebo, Olav. Oslo , 1981. iii, 178 p. : ISBN 82-518-1573-8 : LC Card 83-194969
HD9986.N82 V36 1981

Tjenesteytende næringer i 80-årene. Vannebo, Olav. De tjenesteytende næringer i 80-åra /. Oslo , 1981. iii, 178 p. : ISBN 82-518-1573-8 : LC Card 83-194969
HD9986.N82 V36 1981

Tkachenko, P. G. (Pavel Grigor'evich) Ėkonomicheskiĭ mekhanizm ėksperimenta /. Kiev , 1985. 166 p. : LC Card 86-220234
HC337.U53 I524 1985

To die by inches . Garner, Edward. Fermoy, Co. Cork, Ireland , c1986. 133 p. : ISBN 0-907568-03-3 (pbk.) : LC Card 87-111519 DDC 363.5/85/094195 19
HC260.5.Z7 F474 1986

To do good and do well [microform] . Haley, Charles T. 1980. x, 233 leaves ;
NYPL [Sc Micro R-4654]

To no privileged class . Layton, Stanford J., 1941- Provo, Utah , Salt Lake City, Utah , c1987. p. cm. ISBN 0-941214-59-1 : LC Card 87-14299 DDC 333.1/6/0978 19
HD1339.U5 L39 1987

To notater om sammenlikning av data fra fruktbarhetsundersøkelsen 1977 med data fra registre /. Siring, Erling. Oslo , 1983. 43 p. : ISBN 82-537-2006-8 : LC Card 84-161768
HB1025 .S57 1983

"To serve well and faithfully" . Salinger, Sharon V. (Sharon Vineberg) Cambridge [Cambridgeshire] , New York , 1987. xiii, 192 p., [1] leaf of plates : ISBN 0-521-33442-X LC Card 87-852 DDC 306/.363/09748 19
HD4875.U5 S25 1987

To the Columbia gateway . Lewty, Peter J., 1934- Pullman, Wash. , 1987. p. cm. ISBN 0-87422-030-0 (alk. paper) : LC Card 87-21041 DDC 385/.09795 19
HE2791.N855 L48 1987

To the last drop . Keating, Michael, 1943- Toronto, Ont., Canada , c1986. xviii, 265 p. : ISBN 0-7715-9704-5 LC Card 86-224945 DDC 363.7/394/0971 19
HC120.W32 K43 1986

To their own soil . Atack, Jeremy. Ames , 1987. xi, 322 p. : ISBN 0-8138-0086-2 LC Card 86-21349 DDC 338.1/0974 19
HD1773.A4 A86 1987

"To toil the livelong day" : America's women at work, 1780-1980 / edited by Carol Groneman and Mary Beth Norton. Ithaca, N.Y. : Cornell University Press, 1987. xi, 312 p. ; 23 cm. Papers presented at the Sixth Berkshire Conference on the History of Women held at Smith College June 1-3, 1984. Includes bibliographical references and index. ISBN 0-8014-1847-X (alk. paper) LC Card 86-47975 DDC 331.4/0973 19
1. Women - Employment - United States - History - 19th century - Congresses. 2. Women - Employment - United States - History - 20th century - Congresses. 3. Women - United States - Economic conditions - Congresses. I. Groneman, Carol. II. Norton, Mary Beth. III. Berkshire Conference on the History of Women (6th : 1984 : Smith College).
HD6095 .T6 1987

A to Z of industrial relations practices at the workplace. Phillip, George J. A-Z of industrial relations practices at the workplace /. Kingston, Jamaica , 1987. xiii, 122 p. : ISBN 976-625-009-X (pbk.) LC Card 87-403438 DDC 331/.097292 19
HD6971 .P46 1987

TOBACCO HABIT - DEVELOPING COUNTRIES.
Nath, Uma Ram. Smoking, Third World alert /. Oxford [Oxfordshire] , New York , 1986. x, 291 p. : ISBN 0-19-261402-9 : LC Card 86-5201 DDC 363.1/9 19
HD9148.D44 N37 1986 *NYPL [JLD 87-992]*

TOBACCO INDUSTRY.
United States. International Trade Commission. Certain tobacco . Washington, DC [1985] 1 v. (various pagings) ; LC Card 87-600640 DDC 338.1/7371/0973 19
HD9136 .U55 1985

TOBACCO INDUSTRY - CUBA - HISTORY - 19TH CENTURY.
Westfall, L. Glenn, 1943- Don Vicente Martinez Ybor, the man and his empire . New York , 1987. vii, 214 p. : ISBN 0-8240-1374-3 (alk. paper) : LC Card 87-8690 DDC 338.7/67972/0924 19
HD9149.C5 U777 1987

TOBACCO INDUSTRY - DEVELOPING COUNTRIES.
Nath, Uma Ram. Smoking, Third World alert /. Oxford [Oxfordshire] , New York , 1986. x, 291 p. : ISBN 0-19-261402-9 : LC Card 86-5201 DDC 363.1/9 19
HD9148.D44 N37 1986 *NYPL [JLD 87-992]*

TOBACCO INDUSTRY - FLORIDA - HISTORY - 19TH CENTURY.
Westfall, L. Glenn, 1943- Don Vicente Martinez Ybor, the man and his empire . New York , 1987. vii, 214 p. : ISBN 0-8240-1374-3 (alk. paper) : LC Card 87-8690 DDC 338.7/67972/0924 19
HD9149.C5 U777 1987

TOBACCO INDUSTRY - GOVERNMENT POLICY - AUSTRALIA - VICTORIA.
Victoria. Parliament. Public Bodies Review Committee. Reports on the Tobacco Leaf Marketing Board, Tobacco Quota Committee, Tobacco Quota Appeals Tribunal . Melbourne [1986] xix, 107 p. ; LC Card 87-168528 DDC 354.9450082/332 19
HD9148.A8 V53 1986

TOBACCO INDUSTRY - GOVERNMENT POLICY - KENTUCKY.
Kentucky. General Assembly. Tobacco Task Force. Final report of the Kentucky Tobacco Task Force /. Frankfort, Ky. [1986] vii, 91 p. : LC Card 86-622267 DDC 338.1/7371/09769 19
HD9137.K4 K45 1986

TOBACCO INDUSTRY - GOVERNMENT POLICY - UNITED STATES.
United States. International Trade Commission. Certain tobacco . Washington, DC [1985] 1 v. (various pagings) ; LC Card 87-600640 DDC 338.1/7371/0973 19
HD9136 .U55 1985

TOBACCO INDUSTRY - GREAT BRITAIN - ADDRESSES, ESSAYS, LECTURES.
Smoking out the barons . Chichester [West Sussex] , New York , c1986. vii, 192 p.; ISBN 0-471-90937-8 (pbk.) : LC Card 85-26414 DDC 659.1/967973/0941 19
HF6161.C35 S66 1986 *NYPL [JLD 86-3620]*

TOBACCO INDUSTRY - KENTUCKY.
Kentucky. General Assembly. Tobacco Task Force. Final report of the Kentucky Tobacco Task Force /. Frankfort, Ky. [1986] vii, 91 p. : LC Card 86-622267 DDC 338.1/7371/09769 19
HD9137.K4 K45 1986

TOBACCO INDUSTRY - MEXICO - HISTORY.
Chumacero, Antonio. Origen de una empresa pública . Tepic, Nayarit , 1985 [i.e. 1986] xviii, 279 p. : LC Card 87-145432 DDC 338.7/6371/0972 19
HD9144.M44 T333 1986

TOBACCO INDUSTRY - STATISTICS.
Korb, Penelope. U. S. and world food, beverages, and tobacco expenditures, 1970-83 /. Washington, D.C. , 1986. iv, 84 p. : LC Card 86-603160 DDC 339.4/8664/0021 19
HD9000.4 .K67 1986

TOBACCO INDUSTRY - UNITED STATES - STATISTICS.
Korb, Penelope. U. S. and world food, beverages, and tobacco expenditures, 1970-83 /. Washington, D.C. , 1986. iv, 84 p. : LC Card 86-603160 DDC 339.4/8664/0021 19
HD9000.4 .K67 1986

TOBACCO INDUSTRY - ZAMBIA.
A Report on the resources, activities, and constraints in tobacco schemes . Lusaka , 1985. iii, 37 p. ; LC Card 85-981599 DDC 338.1/7371/096894 19
HD9147.Z34 R46 1985

TOBACCO MANUFACTURE AND TRADE - UNITED STATES.
Sumner, Daniel A. (Daniel Alan), 1950- Removal of price supports and supply controls for U. S. tobacco . Demoines, Iowa , Washington, D.C. , c1985. viii, 64 p. ; ISBN 0-89068-084-1 LC Card 85-63194
NYPL [JLF 86-1014]

TOBACCO WORKERS INTERNATIONAL UNION - HISTORY.
Kaufman, Stuart Bruce. Challenge & change . Kensington, Md. , c1986. ix, 163 p. : LC Card 86-229223 DDC 331.88/1797/0973 19
HD6515.T6 K38 1986

Tobias, Andrew P.
The only other investment guide you'll ever need / Andrew Tobias. New York : Simon and Schuster, c1987. 271 p. ; 23 cm. Includes index. ISBN 0-671-64166-2 LC Card 87-20494 DDC 332.6/78 19
1. Investments. 2. Finance, Personal. I. Title.
HG4521 .T6 1987

Treating malpractice : report of the Twentieth Century Fund Task Force on Medical Malpractice Insurance / background paper by Andrew Tobias. New York : Priority Press Publications, 1986. ix, 70 p. ; 23 cm. Bibliography: p. 69-70. ISBN 0-87078-173-1 (pbk.) : LC Card 86-217256 DDC 368.5 19
1. Insurance, Physicians' liability - United States. I. Twentieth Century Fund. Task Force on Medical Malpractice Insurance. II. Title.
HG8054 .T63 1986

Tobin, James, 1918-
Essays in economics. Volume 2, Consumption and econometrics /1st MIT Press ed. Cambridge, Mass. : MIT Press, 1987. vii, 492 p. : ill. ; 24 cm. (The Papers of James Tobin . v. 2) Includes bibliographies and index. ISBN 0-262-20064-3 LC Card 87-3913 DDC 330/.028 19
1. Consumption (Economics) - Econometric models. 2. Econometrics. 3. Rationing, Consumer - Econometric models. 4. Unemployment - Effect of inflation on - Econometric models. I. Series: Tobin, James, 1918- Essays. v. 2. II. Title.
HB801 .T6 1987

Essays in economics : macroeconomics / James Tobin.1st MIT Press ed. Cambridge, Mass. : MIT Press, 1987. xvi, 526 p. : ill. ; 24 cm. (The Papers of James Tobin . v. 1) Reprint. Originally published: Amsterdam ; New York : North-Holland, 1971. Includes bibliographies and index. ISBN 0-262-20062-7 LC Card 86-21157 DDC 339 19
1. Economics. 2. Macroeconomics. I. Series: Tobin, James, 1918- Essays. v. 1. II. Title.
HB34 .T622 1987

Essays. Selections .
(v. 1) Tobin, James, 1918- Essays in economics . Cambridge, Mass. , 1987. xvi, 526 p. : ISBN 0-262-20062-7 LC Card 86-21157 DDC 339 19
HB34 .T622 1987

(v. 2) Tobin, James, 1918- Essays in economics. Cambridge, Mass. , 1987. vii, 492 p. : ISBN 0-262-20064-3 LC Card 87-3913 DDC 330/.028 19
HB801 .T6 1987

Policies for prosperity : essays in a Keynesian mode / James Tobin ; edited by P.M. Jackson.1st MIT Press ed. Cambridge, Mass. : MIT Press, 1987. xiv, 508 p. : ill. ; 24 cm. Includes bibliographies and index. ISBN 0-262-20066-X LC Card 87-2967 DDC 330.15/6 19
1. Keynesian economics. 2. Supply-side economics - United States. 3. United States - Economic policy - 1981-. I. Jackson, P. M. (Peter McLeod). II. Title.
HB99.7 .T63 1987

Tobin's q and industry investment in West Germany /. Funke, Michael, 1956- Berlin [1986] 36 p. : LC Card 87-156645 DDC 332.63 19
HC290.5.C3 F86 1986

TOCANTINÓPOLIS REGION (BRAZIL) - ECONOMIC POLICY.
Projeto de Desenvolvimento Integrado da Bacia do Araguaia-Tocantins. Plano de desenvolvimento das áreas-programa de Araguaína e Tocantinópolis /. Brasília , 1985. 95 p., [8] leaves of plates : LC Card 86-200369
HC189.A67 P76 1985

TOCANTINÓPOLIS REGION (BRAZIL) - SOCIAL POLICY.
Projeto de Desenvolvimento Integrado da Bacia do Araguaia-Tocantins. Plano de desenvolvimento das áreas-programa de Araguaína e Tocantinópolis /. Brasília , 1985. 95 p., [8] leaves of plates : LC Card 86-200369
HC189.A67 P76 1985

Tochilin, Viktor Aleksandrovich.
Modelirovanie i optimizatsionnye raschety . Kiev , 1986. 222, [2] p. : LC Card 86-233713
HD9015.S652 M62 1986

Problemy optimizatsii mezhotraslevykh sviazeĭ . Kiev , 1976. 135 p. : LC Card 87-100694
HD9015.S653 U4547 1976

Toçi, V. Fishta, Iljaz. Ekonomia e Shqipërisë në vitet e para të ndërtimit socialist, 1944-1948 /. Tiranë , 1984. 489 p. ; LC Card 85-163026
HC402 .F55 1984

Todaro C., Rosalba. Gálvez, Thelma. Yo trabajo así-- en casa particular /. Santiago, Chile , 1985. 113 p. : LC Card 86-208887
HD6072.2.C5 G35 1985

Today's marketing research. Advertising Research Foundation Key Issues Workshop (1986 : New York, N.Y.) Transcript proceedings . New York, NY (3 E. 54th St., New York 10022-3180) , c1986. 268 p. : LC Card 87-149342 DDC 658.8/3 19
HF5802.5 .A3826 1986

Todd, Daniel. World aerospace : a statistical handbook / Daniel Todd and Ronald D. Humble. London ; New York : Croom Helm, c1987. 226 p. : ill. ; 30 cm. Includes index. ISBN 0-7099-4325-3 LC Card 86-29368 DDC 338.4/76291/021 19
1. Aerospace industries - Statistics. I. Humble, Ronald. II. Title.
HD9711.5.A2 T629 1987

Todd, I. A. The Organisation in its environment /. London , 1984. xiii, 624 p. : ISBN 0-421-32290-X (pbk.) : LC Card 84-242095 DDC 302.3/5 19
HD31 .O7217 1984 ***NYPL [JLD 86-2539]***

Todd, Jean Elizabeth. Changing the definition of a household : a study based on the 1981 Labour force survey in England to estimate the effect on housing data of a change in the definition of a household / Jean Todd, David Griffiths. London : H.M.S.O., 1986. viii, 43 p. : ill. ; 30 cm. At head of title: Office of Population Censuses and Surveys. Social Survey Division. Includes bibliographical reference. ISBN 0-11-691071-2 (pbk.) : LC Card 87-132272
1. Household surveys - Great Britain. 2. Households - Great Britain. 3. Population surveys - Great Britain. I. Griffiths, David. II. Great Britain. Office of Population Censuses and Surveys. Social Survey Division. III. Title.
HB849.49 .T63 1986

Todd, John D. Courchene, Thomas J. Ontario's proposals for the Canadian securities industry /. Toronto , Scarborough, Ont. [1986] 39 p. : ISBN 0-88806-137-4 (pbk.) LC Card 87-133168 DDC 332.63/2 19
HG5158 .C68 1986

Todo lo que usted quería saber sobre los bancos, pero temía preguntar /. Bouzas, Carlos, 1937- [Montevideo, Uruguay?] , 1986. 75 p. : LC Card 87-403156 DDC 332.1/09895 19
HG2954 .B68 1986

Todo para la G.M. : un ejemplo de desordenación territorial, la GM en Zaragoza / Javier Bascones ... [et al.] ; edición preparada por José Luis García Cano. Madrid : Ediciones Miraguano, [1981?] 174 p. : ill. ; 17 cm. (Colección Amigos de la tierra . 7) Bibliography: p. 170-174. ISBN 84-85639-19-7 LC Card 82-134601 DDC 338.8/87 19
1. General Motors Corporation. 2. Automobile industry and trade - Environmental aspects - Spain - Zaragoza. 3. International business enterprises - Spain - Zaragoza. I. Bascones, Javier. II. García Cano, José Luis.
HD9710.S754 G467 1981
NYPL [JLC 86-300]

Todorovski, Vladimir. Lekov, Kostadin. Nasoki za usŭvŭrshenstvuvane na sistemata za upravlenie na truda /. Sofiia , 1985. 103 p. ; LC Card 86-230344
HF5549.2.B9 L46 1985

Todt, Horst. Normengeleitetes Verhalten in den Sozialwissenschaften /. Berlin , c1984. 199 p. ; ISBN 3-428-05622-1 LC Card 86-140299
HB74.P8 N67 1984

Tödtling, Franz. Unions in crisis and beyond . Dover, Mass. , c1986. xii, 340 p. : ISBN 0-86569-127-4 : LC Card 85-26646 DDC 331.88 19
HD6508 .U45 1986 ***NYPL [JLE 86-1936]***

Todyka, IUriĭ Nikolaevich. Gosudarstvennyĭ apparat i problemy okhrany prirody v usloviiakh APK / IU.N. Todyka, V.N. Vinnik ; pod redaktsieĭ V.I. Mokriaka. Kishinev : "Shtiintsa", 1986. 179, [5] p. ; 17 cm. At head of title: Akademiia nauk Moldavskoĭ SSR. Otdel filosofii i prava. Summary in English. Bibliography: p. 170-[180] LC Card 86-141430
1. Agriculture and state - Environmental aspects - Moldavian S.S.R. 2. Environmental protection - Moldavian S.S.R. 3. Agricultural industries - Environmental aspects - Moldavian S.S.R. I. Vinnik, V. N. (Viktor Nikolaevich). II. Mokriak, V. I. (Vladimir Il'ich). III. Title.
HD1995.M5 T63 1986

De toekomst van de vrije tijd /. Delden, P. J. van, 1949- [Deventer] , c1986. 102 p. ; ISBN 90-6001-973-3 : LC Card 86-199367
HD4904.6 .D45 1986

De Toekomst van onze voedingsmiddelenindustrie / redactie, J.C.M. Schogt en W.J. Beek. Amsterdam : Elsevier, 1985. 156 p. : ill. ; 21 cm. (Toekomstbeeld der techniek. 41) Bibliography: p. [152]-153. ISBN 90-10-05574-4 : LC Card 86-116607
1. Food industry and trade - Netherlands. I. Schogt, J. C. M. II. Beek, W. J. III. Series.
HD9015.N42 T64 1985

Toekomstbeeld der techniek.
(41) De Toekomst van onze voedingsmiddelenindustrie /. Amsterdam , 1985. 156 p. : ISBN 90-10-05574-4 : LC Card 86-116607
HD9015.N42 T64 1985

Toekomstverkenning volkshuisvesting : bijdrage aan de toekomst van de volkshuisvesting, een inventarisatie en programmeringsstudie / F.M. Dieleman, red. ; J.B. Burie ... [et al.]. Delft : Delftse Universitaire Pers, 1985. 100 p. : ill. ; 24 cm. Bibliography: p. 91-100. ISBN 90-6275-193-8 : LC Card 86-157352
1. Public housing - Netherlands. 2. Housing policy - Netherlands. 3. Housing - Netherlands. I. Dieleman, F. M. II. Burie, J. B.
HD7288.78.N4 T64 1985

Toffler, Alvin. Previews & premises / by Alvin Toffler. 1st Canadian ed. Montréal, Québec : Black Rose Books, 1984, c1983. 230 p. ; 22 cm. Includes index. ISBN 0-920057-37-3 (pbk.)
1. Toffler, Alvin. 2. Social history - 1945-. 3. Civilization, Modern - 1950-. I. Title. II. Title: Previews and premises. ***NYPL [JFD 86-3191]***

TOFFLER, ALVIN.
Toffler, Alvin. Previews & premises /. Montréal, Québec , 1984, c1983. 230 p. ;

ISBN 0-920057-37-3 (pbk.)
NYPL [JFD 86-3191]

Toffler, Betsy-Ann. Imber, Jane. Dictionary of advertising and direct mail terms /. New York , c1987. xi, 514 p. : ISBN 0-8120-3765-0 (pbk.) : LC Card 87-1197 DDC 659.1/03/21 19
HF5803 .I46 1987

Toft, Lise. Carlsen, Anne Marie Sloth. Køn og ledelse . København , 1986. 251 p. : ISBN 87-87749-29-7 (pbk.) :kr149.00 LC Card 87-145777
HD6054.4.D4 C37 1986

Tofutti® & other soy ice creams . Shurtleff, William, 1941- Lafayette, CA , c1985. 2 v. : ISBN 0-933332-19-X (v. 1) : LC Card 85-10829 DDC 381/.4174 19
HD9330.B323 U 1985 NYPL [JLF 86-1035]

Tofutti and other soy ice creams. Shurtleff, William, 1941- Tofutti® & other soy ice creams . Lafayette, CA , c1985. 2 v. : ISBN 0-933332-19-X (v. 1) : LC Card 85-10829 DDC 381/.4174 19
HD9330.B323 U 1985 NYPL [JLF 86-1035]

TOGO - CENSUS, 1981.
Aperçu des résultats d'ensemble du recensement général de la population et de l'habitat au Togo de novembre 1981 . [Lomé] [1986] 70 p. : LC Card 87-126698 DDC 304.6/0966/81021 19
HA4723 .A4 1981

TOGO - COMMERCE - STATISTICS.
Annuaire rétrospectif des statistiques du commerce extérieur du Togo, 1968-1978 /. Lomé [1982] 37 leaves, [3] leaves of plates : LC Card 86-130147 DDC 382/.096681/0021 19
HF3923.A45 A56 1982

Togo. Direction de la statistique.
Annuaire rétrospectif des statistiques du commerce extérieur du Togo, 1968-1978 /. Lomé [1982] 37 leaves, [3] leaves of plates : LC Card 86-130147 DDC 382/.096681/0021 19
HF3923.A45 A56 1982

Togo. Direction de la statistique. Bureau central du recensement. Aperçu des résultats d'ensemble du recensement général de la population et de l'habitat au Togo de novembre 1981 . [Lomé] [1986] 70 p. : LC Card 87-126698 DDC 304.6/0966/81021 19
HA4723 .A4 1981

Togo. Direction de la statistique. Division Documentation et publications. Annuaire rétrospectif des statistiques du commerce extérieur du Togo, 1968-1978 /. Lomé [1982] 37 leaves, [3] leaves of plates : LC Card 86-130147 DDC 382/.096681/0021 19
HF3923.A45 A56 1982

TOGO - ECONOMIC CONDITIONS.
Gozo, K. M. Effets de la récession sur l'économie togolaise . Addis Abéba , 1985. 50, 24 p. ; ISBN 92-2-205044-4 LC Card 86-159834 DDC 330.966/8104 19
HC1015 .G69 1985

Gù-Konu, E. Y. Population et progrès socio-économique au Togo /. Lome , 1980. 291 p. : LC Card 87-148380
HB3665.8.A3 G8 1980

Kjellstrom, Sven B., 1945- Institutional development and technical assistance in macro-economic policy formulation . Washington, D.C., U. S.A. [1987] 69 p. ; ISBN 0-8213-0919-6 (pbk.) LC Card 87-14021 DDC 339.5/0966/81 19
HC1015 .K58 1987

TOGO - ECONOMIC POLICY.
Dovi-Sodemekou, Folly B. (Folly Bebey) Emploi et éducation dans le 2e plan de développement économique et social du Togo /. Lomé, Togo [1985] 89, 52, 9, 2 p. : LC Card 87-131183
HD5846.5.A6 D68 1985

Kjellstrom, Sven B., 1945- Institutional development and technical assistance in macro-economic policy formulation . Washington, D.C., U. S.A. [1987] 69 p. ; ISBN 0-8213-0919-6 (pbk.) LC Card 87-14021 DDC 339.5/0966/81 19
HC1015 .K58 1987

TOGO - FOREIGN ECONOMIC RELATIONS.
Gozo, K. M. Effets de la récession sur l'économie togolaise . Addis Abéba , 1985. 50, 24 p. ; ISBN 92-2-205044-4 LC Card 86-159834 DDC 330.966/8104 19
HC1015 .G69 1985

Togo. Ministère de l'éducation nationale et de la recherche scientifique. Locoh, Thérèse. La fécondité en Afrique noire /. Lomé [1985] 36, 22 leaves : LC Card 87-126644
HB1071 .L63 1985

TOGO - POPULATION.
Akakpo-Ahianyo, Anani. Contribution à l'étude des migrations au Togo /. Lomé , 1976. 108 p., [5] p. of plates : LC Card 87-150756
HB2125.8.A3 A38 1976

Gù-Konu, E. Y. Population et progrès socio-économique au Togo /. Lome , 1980. 291 p. : LC Card 87-148380
HB3665.8.A3 G8 1980

Locoh, Thérèse. Comprendre les problèmes de population . Lomé, Togo , 1984. 72, [3], 3 p. : LC Card 87-131146
HB871 .L57 1984

TOGO - POPULATION - STATISTICS.
Aperçu des résultats d'ensemble du recensement général de la population et de l'habitat au Togo de novembre 1981 . [Lomé] [1986] 70 p. : LC Card 87-126698 DDC 304.6/0966/81021 19
HA4723 .A4 1981

TOGO - SOCIAL CONDITIONS.
Gù-Konu, E. Y. Population et progrès socio-économique au Togo /. Lome , 1980. 291 p. : LC Card 87-148380
HB3665.8.A3 G8 1980

TOGO - SOCIAL POLICY.
Dovi-Sodemekou, Folly B. (Folly Bebey) Emploi et éducation dans le 2e plan de développement économique et social du Togo /. Lomé, Togo [1985] 89, 52, 9, 2 p. : LC Card 87-131183
HD5846.5.A6 D68 1985

TOGO - STATISTICS, VITAL.
Locoh, Thérèse. La fécondité en Afrique noire /. Lomé [1985] 36, 22 leaves : LC Card 87-126644
HB1071 .L63 1985

Togolezskaya Respublika. see **Togo.**

TOILET PREPARATIONS - EUROPE - MARKETING.
Marketing strategies for selling cosmetics & toiletries in Europe. New York, N.Y. , c1983. 381 p. ; LC Card 87-141847 DDC 380.1/456685/094 19
HD9970.5.C673 E8555 1983

TOILET PREPARATIONS INDUSTRY - EUROPE.
Marketing strategies for selling cosmetics & toiletries in Europe. New York, N.Y. , c1983. 381 p. ; LC Card 87-141847 DDC 380.1/456685/094 19
HD9970.5.C673 E8555 1983

TOILET PREPARATIONS INDUSTRY - UNITED STATES.
Geriatrics OTC health aid and toiletries products market-U. S. New York, N.Y. , c1983. 2 v. (viii, 352 leaves) ; LC Card 87-144078 DDC 381/.456151/0973 19
HD9666.5 .G47 1983

Toisen maailmansodan aikaisesta huoltotasosta Suomessa ja analogioista 1980-luvun alun tilanteeseen /. Pihkala, Erkki. [Helsinki] , 1986. 49 leaves ; ISBN 951-46-9497-X LC Card 86-221750
HC340.2 .P54 1986

Tokareva, N. A. (Nadezhda Andreevna)
Denisova, N. F. (Nina Fedorovna) Planirovanie otdelochnogo proizvodstva s primeneniem matematicheskikh metodov i EVM . Moskva , 1984. 59, [5] p. : LC Card 85-131509
HD9865.S652 D46 1984

Tokman, Víctor E.
Desarrollo desigual y absorción de empleo : América Latina, 1950-80 / Víctor E. Tokman. [Santiago, Chile] : Organización Internacional del Trabajo, Programa Mundial del Empleo, Programa Regional del Empleo para América Latina y el Caribe, 1982. 34 p. ; 27 cm. (Trabajo ocasional . 44) "Original: español." Cover title. Bibliography: p. [33]-34. LC Card 87-403246 DDC 330.98/0038 19
1. Latin America - Economic conditions - 1945- - Regional disparaties. 2. Labor supply - Latin America. I. Series: Occasional paper (Regional Employment Program for Latin America and the Caribbean) , 44. II. Title.
HC125 .T57 1982

Toksanbaeva, M. S. Bukhval'd, E. M. Povyshenie proizvoditel'nosti truda--klīūchevaīā zadacha sovetskoĭ ėkonomiki . Moskva , 1984. 63 p. ; LC Card 85-188977
HC340.L3 B85 1984

Tokyo Forum: Ethics of Human Survival (1985)
Proceedings of the Tokyo Forum: Ethics of Human Survival : Monday, 10 June 1985 / co-sponsors, Independent Commission on International Humanitarian Issues (ICIHI), United Nations University (UNU), National Institute for Research Advancement (NIRA). Tokyo, Japan : NIRA, c1986. v, 88 p. : ill. ; 26 cm. (International conference report series . 1) ISBN 4-7955-1024-5 LC Card 87-142747
1. Economic development - Moral and ethical aspects - Congresses. 2. Economic policy - Moral and ethical aspects - Congresses. I. Independent Commission on International Humanitarian Issues. II. United Nations University. III. Sōgō Kenkyū Kaihatsu Kikō (Japan). IV. Title. V. Series.
HD73 .T65 1985

Tokyo. Nomura Sōgō Kenkyūjo. see **Nomura Sōgō Kenkyūjo.**

TOKYO ROUND (1973-1979)
Hasse, Rolf. Ökonometrie als Instrument der Interessenpolitik . Köln , 1985. ii, 109 p. : ISBN 3-921471-52-4 : LC Card 85-216061
HF1733.D44 H37 1985

Tokyo Trade Symposium (1985) Trade routes to sustained economic growth : report of a study group of the Trade Policy Research Centre / Amnuay Viravan ... [et al.]. New York : St. Martin's Press for the United Nations, 1987. lii, 178 p. ; 23 cm. "Tokyo Trade Symposium to mark the fortieth anniversary of the United Nations." Includes bibliographies and index. ISBN 0-312-01263-2 : LC Card 87-3494 DDC 382 19
1. International economic relations. 2. Commercial policy. 3. Economic development. I. 'Amnūai Wīrawan. II. United Nations. III. Title.
HF1411 .T577 1985

Tolchin, Martin. Buying into America : how foreign money is changing the face of our nation / by Martin and Susan Tolchin. New York : Times Books, 1988. p. cm. Includes index. ISBN 0-8129-1667-0 : LC Card 87-40198 DDC 332.6/73/0973 19
1. Investments, Foreign - United States. I. Tolchin, Susan J. II. Title.
HG4910 .T65 1988

Tolchin, Susan J. Tolchin, Martin. Buying into America . New York , 1988. p. cm. ISBN 0-8129-1667-0 : LC Card 87-40198 DDC 332.6/73/0973 19
HG4910 .T65 1988

Toledano Laredo, Armando. Intégration et démocratie / par Armando Toledano Laredo ; préface de Jean-Victor Louis. Bruxelles, Belgique : Editions de l'Université de Bruxelles, 1982. 192 p. ; 24 cm. At head of title: Institut d'études européennes, Université libre de Bruxelles. Bibliography: p. 190. ISBN 2-8004-0777-8 :c275F LC Card 83-163343
1. International economic integration. 2. Europe - Economic integration. 3. European Economic Community. 4. Latin America - Economic integration. I. Université libre de Bruxelles. Institut d'études européennes. II. Title.
HF1418.5 .T65 1982

Toledo, Nora Elena. El tamaño de las ciudades y la distribución de los ingresos (Argentina y Colombia) / Nora Elena Toledo. 1a ed. San Juan, Argentina : [s.n.], 1985. 63 p. : ill. ; 23 cm. (Cuadernos de ciencias sociales. Serie Testeos teóricos . 1) Includes bibliographical references. LC Card 87-400258 DDC 339.2/2/09861 19
1. Income distribution - Colombia - Case studies. 2. Income distribution - Argentina - Case studies. 3. Wages - Colombia - Case studies. 4. Wages - Argentina - Case studies. 5. Cities and towns - Colombia - Growth - Case studies. 6. Cities and towns - Argentina - Growth - Case studies. I. Title. II. Series.
HC200.I5 T65 1985

TOLEDO REGION (SPAIN) - POPULATION - HISTORY - 18TH CENTURY.
Sánchez González, Ramón. Los montes de Toledo en el siglo XVIII . Toledo , 1984. 222

p. : ISBN 84-00-05873-9 LC Card 87-105458
HB3620.T62 S26 1984

Tölfræðihandbók 1984 = Statistical abstract of Iceland, 1984. Reykjavík : Hagstofu Íslands, 1984. 12, 268 p. ; 25 cm. (Hagskýrslur Íslands = Statistics of Iceland . II, 82) LC Card 87-165528
1. Iceland - Statistics - Periodicals. I. Iceland. Hagstofa. II. Title: Statistical abstract of Iceland, 1984. III. Series: Hagskýrslur Íslands , II, 82.
HA1491 .A4 vol. II, 82

TOLL-FREE TELEPHONE CALLS - UNITED STATES - DIRECTORIES.
Bly, Amy Sprecher. Information hotline U. S.A. /. New York , c1987. xviii, 286 p. ; ISBN 0-452-25921-5 (pbk.) : LC Card 87-5687 DDC 384.6/025/73 19
HE8811 .B49 1987

TOLL ROADS - SOUTH AFRICA.
South Africa. Parliament. House of Assembly. Select Committee on Toll Financing of Roads. Tweede verslag van die Gekose Komitee oor Tolfinansiering van Paaie =. [Pretoria] [1982] vii p. ; ISBN 0-06-210768-3 : LC Card 83-159014
HE367.S63 T646 1982

South Africa. Parliament. House of Assembly. Select Committee on Toll Financing of Roads. Verslag van die Gekose Komitee oor Tolfinansiering van Paaie =. [Pretoria] [1982] xix, 54 p. ; ISBN 0-621-07457-8 : LC Card 83-215629
HE367.S63 T647 1982

Tolley, Sarah.
Spufford, Peter. Handbook of medieval exchange /. London : Woodbridge, Suffolk ; xcii, 376, [3] p., [1] fold. leaf : ISBN 0-86193-105-X ***NYPL [JLE 86-4344]***

Spufford, Peter. Handbook of medieval exchange /. London : Woodbridge, Suffolk ; xcii, 376 p., [3] leaves of plates (1 folded) : ISBN 0-86193-105-X LC Card 86-673816
HG3942 .S68x 1986

Tolliday, Steven.
The Automobile industry and its workers . New York , 1987. viii, 335 p. : ISBN 0-312-00553-9 : LC Card 86-29815 DDC 331/.04292 19
HD9710.A2 A865 1987

Business, banking, and politics : the case of British Steel, 1918-1939 / Steven Tolliday. Cambridge, Mass. : Harvard University Press, 1987. vi, 433 p. : ill. ; 25 cm. (Harvard studies in business history. 39) Bibliography: p. 356-421. Includes index. ISBN 0-674-08725-9 (alk. paper) LC Card 86-31944 DDC 338.4/7669142/0941 19
1. Steel industry and trade - Great Britain - History - 20th century. I. Title. II. Series.
HD9521.5 .T64 1987

Tollison, Robert D.
Ekelund, Robert B. (Robert Burton), 1940- Economics /. Glenview, Ill. , c1988. xl, 942, [33] p. : ISBN 0-673-39717-3 LC Card 87-23306 DDC 330 19
HB171.5 .E47 1988

Ekelund, Robert B. (Robert Burton), 1940- Macroeconomics /. Glenview, Ill. , c1988. xxix, 592 p. : ISBN 0-673-39768-8 (pbk.) LC Card 87-23513 DDC 339 19
HB172.5 .E42 1988

Ekelund, Robert B. (Robert Burton), 1940- Microeconomics /. Glenview, Ill. , c1988. xxx, 619 p. : ISBN 0-673-39769-6 (pbk.) LC Card 87-23514 DDC 338.5 19
HB172 .E39 1988

The Political economy of rent-seeking /. Boston , c1988. xvi, 492 p. : ISBN 0-89838-241-6 LC Card 87-16887 DDC 333/.012 19
HB401 .P64 1988

TOLLS - EUROPEAN ECONOMIC COMMUNITY COUNTRIES.
Heute Grenzen-- morgen Europa /. Bonn , c1984. 107 p. : ISBN 3-7713-0227-7 LC Card 85-146220
HE197.E86 H48 1984

Tolmachev, V. P. (Vladimir Petrovich)
Ėkonomika Urala, Sibiri i Dal'nego vostoka v odinnadtsatoĭ pi͡atiletke / V.P. Tolmachev. Moskva : Ob-vo "Znanie" RSFSR, 1981. 39 p. ; 20 cm. (V pomoshch' lektoru) At head of title: Obshchestvo "Znanie" RSFSR, Nauchno-metodicheskiĭ sovet po propagande konkretnoĭ ėkonomiki, ėffektivnosti i upravlenii͡a proizvodstvom. Bibliography: p. 39. LC Card 82-153584
1. Ural Mountains Region (R.S.F.S.R.) - Economic conditions. 2. Siberia (R.S.F.S.R.) - Economic conditions. 3. Soviet Far East (R.S.F.S.R.) - Economic conditions. I. Title.
HC337.R852 U7382 1981

Smekalov, Pavel Vasil'evich. Sel'skie kadry nechernozem'i͡a /. Moskva , 1981. 190 p. ; LC Card 82-177714
HD1536.S65 S64 1981

Tolstikov, S. A. Uchastie trudi͡ashchikhsi͡a v upravlenii proizvodstvom . Moskva , 1985. 69, [2] p. ; LC Card 85-224379
HD5660.S65 U27 1985

Tolvaly, Anikó. Németh, Ernő. A bér- és keresetszabályozás müködése 1983-ban /. [Budapest] [1984] 245 p. : ISBN 963-02-3277-4 LC Card 85-231744
HD5022.5 .N46 1984

Toma, Eugenia Froedge. Central bankers, bureaucratic incentives, and monetary policy /. Dordrecht ; Boston : xiv, 251 p. : ISBN 90-247-3366-9 LC Card 86-12572 DDC 332.1/12/0973 19
HG2565 .C33 1986 ***NYPL [JLE 87-394]***

Toma, Mark. Central bankers, bureaucratic incentives, and monetary policy /. Dordrecht ; Boston : xiv, 251 p. : ISBN 90-247-3366-9 LC Card 86-12572 DDC 332.1/12/0973 19
HG2565 .C33 1986 ***NYPL [JLE 87-394]***

Tomar, J. S., 1943- Lamba, S. K. Impact of land reforms on rural development . New Delhi, India , 1986 [i.e. 1985] xiv, 148 p. ; ISBN 81-85005-20-6 : LC Card 85-905086 DDC 333.3/1/54 19
HD1333.I4 L35 1986

Tomasko, Robert M. Downsizing : reshaping the corporation for the future / Robert M. Tomasko. New York : AMACOM, c1987. p. cm. Bibliography: p. Includes index. ISBN 0-8144-5907-2 LC Card 87-47709 DDC 338.6/4 19
1. Industries, Size of - United States. 2. Middle managers - United States. 3. Industrial organization - United States. 4. Corporations - United States. I. Title.
HD69.S5 T59 1987

Tomaszewski, Jerzy, 1930-
Kostrowicka, Irena. Historia gospodarcza Polski XIX i XX wieku /. Warszawa , 1984. 583 p., [3] folded leaves of plates : ISBN 83-05-11411-2 : LC Card 85-218322
HC340.3 .K67 1984

Landau, Zbigniew. The Polish economy in the twentieth century /. London , c1985. vi, 346 p. ; ISBN 0-7099-1607-8 LC Card 86-673496
HC340.3 .L36x 1985b

Landau, Zbigniew. Wirtschaftsgeschichte Polens im 19. und 20. Jahrhundert /. Berlin , 1986. vi, 300 p. : LC Card 86-223591
HC340.3 .L367 1986

A tömegkommunikáció új útjai /. Szekfű, András. [Budapest] , 1984. 102 p. : ISBN 963-09-2552-4 : LC Card 85-174804
HE7631 .S98 1984

Tomer, John F. Organizational capital : the path to higher productivity and well-being / John F. Tomer. New York : Praeger, 1987. xvi, 188 p. : ill. ; 25 cm. Bibliography: p. [167]-179. Includes index. ISBN 0-275-92582-X (alk. paper) : LC Card 87-16828 DDC 338.5 19
1. Industrial organization. 2. Industrial management. 3. Industrial productivity. 4. Business enterprises. I. Title.
HD31 .T635 1987

Tomey, E. Allan. Schmandt, Henry J. Federal aid to St. Louis /. Washington, D.C. , c1983. xvii, 67 p. ; ISBN 0-8157-7727-2 (pbk.) LC Card 82-74100 DDC 336.1/85 19
HJ9268.S3 S352 1983 ***NYPL [JLE 87-1]***

Tomić, Danilo. Jugoslovenska agrarna teorija i politika : rezultati, problemi i ocene / Danilo Tomić. Bačka Topola : Centar za kulturu, obrazovanje i informisanje, JUR Izdavačka delatnost, 1985. 211 p. : ill. ; 21 cm. (Biblioteka Naša praksa) In Serbo-Croatian (roman) Revised version of the author's thesis (doctoral--Poljoprivredni fakultet u Novom Sadu, 1984) Bibliography: p. 191-204. LC Card 85-195818
1. Agriculture and state - Yugoslavia. I. Title. II. Series.
HD2045.5.Z8 T62 1985

Tomioka, Ellen Miller. Tomioka, Seishiro. Planned unit developments . New York , c1984. xviii, 192 p. : ISBN 0-471-08595-2 : LC Card 82-13419 DDC 307/.12/0973 19
HD257 .T65 1984 ***NYPL [JLF 86-1316]***

Tomioka, Seishiro. Planned unit developments : design and regional impact / Seshiro Tomioka, Ellen Miller Tomioka. New York : Wiley, c1984. xviii, 192 p. : ill. ; 29 cm. "A Wiley-Interscience publication." Includes bibliographical references and index. ISBN 0-471-08595-2 : LC Card 82-13419 DDC 307/.12/0973 19
1. Planned unit developments - United States. 2. City planning - United States. 3. Regional planning - United States. I. Tomioka, Ellen Miller. II. Title.
HD257 .T65 1984 ***NYPL [JLF 86-1316]***

Tomita, Teruhiko, 1937- Transferability of Japanese-style management to Britain / by Teruhiko Tomita. Hikone, Japan : Faculty of Economics Shiga University, [1986] 63 leaves : ill. ; 30 cm. (Working paper . no. 16) "September 1986." Bibliography: leaves 49-50. LC Card 87-168468 DDC 331.25 19
1. Industrial management - Japan. 2. Industrial management - Great Britain. I. Series: Working paper (Shiga Daigaku. Keizai Gakubu) , no. 16. II. Title.
HD70.J3 T585 1986

Tomka, József. A Szocialista nagyüzemek főbb ágazatainak költség- és jövedelemhelyzete 1984-ben /. Budapest , 1985. 35, [46] p. ; LC Card 85-177804
HD1492.H8 S93 1985

Tomlinson, Gerald, 1933-
Brief, Arthur P., 1946- Managing smart . Lexington, Mass. , c1987. x, 164 p. ; ISBN 0-669-12654-3 (alk. paper) LC Card 85-45978 DDC 658.3 19
HD31 .B7396 1987

Hakoun, Mitchell. Accountant's complete model letter book /. Englewood Cliffs, N.J. , c1987. xxi, 424 p. : ISBN 0-13-001199-1 : LC Card 87-11548 DDC 657 19
HF5726 .H3257 1987

Tomlinson, Jim. Employment policy : the crucial years, 1939-1955 / Jim Tomlinson. Oxford [Oxfordshire] : Clarendon Press ; New York : Oxford University Press, 1987. xi, 185 p. ; 23 cm. Bibliography: p. [176]-182. Includes index. ISBN 0-19-828564-7 : LC Card 87-7837 DDC 339.5/0941 19
1. Great Britain - Economic policy - 1918-1945. 2. Great Britain - Economic policy - 1945-. 3. Great Britain - Full employment policies. I. Title.
HC256.4 .T586 1987

Tomorrow's global executive /. Ferguson, Henry. Homewood, Ill. , c1988. xiii, 265 p. : ISBN 1-15-562305-75 LC Card 87-71259 DDC 658/.049 19
HD62.4 .F47 1988

Tomov, Mitko. Pŭtishta za podobri͡avane na kachestvoto / Mitko Tomov. Pleven : Druzhestvo za razprostranenie na nauch. znanii͡a "Georgi Kirkov", Okrŭzhen sŭvet, 1984. 68, [4] p. ; 20 cm. Bibliography: p. 69-[70] LC Card 85-179053
1. Labor productivity - Bulgaria. 2. Industrial productivity - Bulgaria. 3. Quality of products - Bulgaria. I. Title.
HC403.Z9 L38 1984

Tompkins, James A. The Warehouse management handbook /. New York , c1988. p. cm. ISBN 0-07-064952-9 : LC Card 87-16885 DDC 658.7/85 19
HF5485 .W35 1988

Toncré, Emery. Maximizing cash flow : practical financial controls for your business / Emery Toncré. New York : Wiley, c1986. ix, 210 p. : ill. ; 24 cm. (Wiley series on small business management) Includes bibliographical references and index. ISBN 0-471-80744-3 : LC Card 85-29643 DDC 658.1/5244 19
1. Cash management. 2. Cash flow. I. Title.
HG4028.C45 T66 1986
NYPL [JLE 86-3140]

Tongren, Hale N., 1921- Cases in consumer behavior / Hale N. Tongren. Englewood Cliffs, N.J. : Prentice-Hall, c1987. xiii, 224 p. : ill. ; 23 cm. ISBN 0-13-115346-3 (pbk.) LC Card 86-25547 DDC 658.8/342 19
1. Consumers - Case studies. 2. Consumers - United

States - Case studies. I. Title.
HF5415.3 .T64 1987

Tonini, Alicia del Carmen. Angueira, María del Carmen. Capitalismo de estado, 1927-1956 /. Buenos Aires , c1986. 116 p. : ISBN 950-25-1416-5 LC Card 87-100705
HD9711.A72 A54 1986

TONNAGE FEES - LAKE STATES.
Impact of deep-draft user charges on the six western Great Lakes states /. [Chicago, Ill.] (310 S. Michigan Ave., Chicago 60604) [1986] 3 v. : LC Card 87-404522 DDC 387.1 19
HE952.U6 I47 1986

Too many promises . Boskin, Michael J. Homewood, Ill. , c1986. xiv, 196 p. : ISBN 0-87094-779-6 LC Card 86-70430 DDC 368.4/3/00973 19
HD7125 .B585 1986 ***NYPL [JLE 86-2970]***

Too old for a job, too young for a pension? . Crompton, Cathy. Canberra , 1986. x, 69 p. ; ISBN 0-644-05599-5 LC Card 87-150775 DDC 368.4/4/00880564 19
HD6283.A8 C76 1986

Tööjõu kasutamise probleeme Eesti NSV-s / koostanud Vambola Türk. Tallinn : "Eesti Raamat", 1986. 179 p. ; 21 cm. Title in colophon: Nekotorye problemy ispol'zovaniia trudovykh rezervov v Ėstonskoĭ SSR. Bibliography: p. 172-[178] LC Card 87-107003
1. Labor supply - Estonia. I. Türk, V. (Vambola). II. Title: Nekotorye problemy ispol'zovaniia trudovykh rezervov v Ėstonskoĭ SSR.
HD5797.E75 T66 1986

Tool, Marc R. Essays in social value theory : a neoinstitutionalist contribution / Marc R. Tool. Armonk, N.Y. : M.E. Sharpe, c1986. xviii, 203 p. ; 24 cm. Includes bibliographies. ISBN 0-87332-382-3 : LC Card 86-10163 DDC 306 19
1. Institutional economics. 2. Social values. I. Title.
HB99.5 .T66 1986 ***NYPL [JLE 86-3931]***

Toole, John H. Men, money, and power : the story of the First Interstate Bank of Missoula / by John H. Toole. Missoula, Mont. : [First Interstate Bank of Missoula], c1986. xiv, 97 p. : ill., ports. ; 29 cm. Bibliography: p. viii. ISBN 0-87842-210-2 LC Card 86-23569 DDC 332.1/224/0978685 19
1. First Interstate Bank of Missoula (Mont.) - History. I. Title.
HG2613.M634 F5737 1986

Toomey, Robert R., 1949- Vivian and Sons, 1809-1924 : a study of the firm in the copper and related industries / Robert R. Toomey. New York : Garland, 1985. 427 p. ; 24 cm. (British economic history) Originally presented as the author's thesis (doctoral)--University of Wales, 1979. Includes bibliographies. ISBN 0-8240-6692-8 (alk. paper) : LC Card 84-46012 DDC 338.7/622343/0941 19
1. Vivian and Sons (Firm) - History. 2. Copper industry and trade - Great Britain - History. 3. Nonferrous metal industries - Great Britain - History. I. Title. II. Series.
HD9539.C7 G778 1985
NYPL [JLE 86-4440]

Tootelian, Dennis H. Cases and classics in marketing management /. San Diego , c1986. ix, 513 p. : ISBN 0-15-505775-8 LC Card 85-80071 DDC 658.8/00973 19
HF5415.13 .C28 1986 ***NYPL [JLE 86-3101]***

Tooze, Michael J., 1942- Chapman, Paul G., 1952- The youth training scheme in the United Kingdom /. Aldershot, Hants, England , Brookfield, Vt., U. S.A. , c1987. x, 124 p. ; ISBN 0-566-05360-8 : LC Card 86-29604 DDC 331.3/42592/0941 19
HD5715.5.G7 C47 1987

Top emerging private companies. Tustin, CA, U. S.A. (17722 Irvine Blvd., Tustin 92680) : Biomedical Business International, c1987. iv, 8, 144, [112] leaves : ill. ; 29 cm. (Report / Biomedical Business International . #7079) "April 1987." LC Card 87-402028 DDC 681/.761/029473 19
1. Medical instruments and apparatus industry - United States - Directories. 2. Pharmaceutical industry - United States - Directories. I. Biomedical Business International, Inc. II. Series: Report (Biomedical Business International, Inc.) , #7079.
HD9994.U52 T66 1987

Top five hundred RDT&E companies. Top 500 RDT&E companies /. Greenwich, CT, U. S.A. (100 Northfield St., Greenwich 06830) , c1986. 721, [50] p. : LC Card 87-120786 DDC 338.7/6234/02573 19
HD9743.U6 T66 1986

Top level advice to aspirant black managers /. Mcunu, Ernest. Braamfontein [1985] 48 p. ; LC Card 87-152084 DDC 658.4/09 19
HD38.2 .M395 1985

Top 500 RDT&E companies / Richard Ford, project director. 1st ed. Greenwich, CT, U. S.A. (100 Northfield St., Greenwich 06830) : Defense Marketing Services, c1986. 721, [50] p. : ill. ; 29 cm. Includes index. LC Card 87-120786 DDC 338.7/6234/02573 19
1. Munitions - United States - Directories. I. Ford, Richard, 1923-. II. Defense Marketing Services, inc. III. Title: Top 500 research, development, testing, & evaluation companies. IV. Title: Top five hundred RDT&E companies.
HD9743.U6 T66 1986

Top 500 research, development, testing, & evaluation companies. Top 500 RDT&E companies /. Greenwich, CT, U. S.A. (100 Northfield St., Greenwich 06830) , c1986. 721, [50] p. : LC Card 87-120786 DDC 338.7/6234/02573 19
HD9743.U6 T66 1986

Topakian, Gregory. Doeringer, Peter B. Invisible factors in local economic development /. New York , 1987. vii, 144 p. : ISBN 0-19-504965-9 (alk. paper) LC Card 87-13550 DDC 338.9744/3 19
HC107.M42 W674 1987

Topham, Anthony. Coates, Ken. Trade unions and politics /. Oxford, OX, UK , New York, NY, USA , 1986. ix, 268 p. : ISBN 0-631-13752-1 : LC Card 85-22959 DDC 322/.2/0941 19
HD6667 .C63 1986 ***NYPL [JLE 86-1729]***

Topham, Tony. Coates, Ken. Trade unions in Britain /. Nottingham , 1980. xii, 385 p. : ISBN 0-85124-293-6 LC Card 86-673477 DDC 331.88/0941 19
HD6664 .C38765 1980

Topical law reports (Commerce Clearing House) Jarnagin, Bill D. Financial accounting standards . Chicago, Ill. (4025 W. Peterson Ave., Chicago 60646) , 1986. xv, 1253 p. : LC Card 87-116311 DDC 657/.0218 19
HF5616.U5 B66 1986

Topics in regulatory economics and policy . (1) The Political economy of rent-seeking /. Boston , c1988. xvi, 492 p. : ISBN 0-89838-241-6 LC Card 87-16887 DDC 333/.012 19
HB401 .P64 1988

Topics in regulatory economics and policy series. Frantz, Roger S. X-efficiency . Boston , c1988. xviii, 227 p. : ISBN 0-89838-242-4 LC Card 87-17071 DDC 338/.06 19
HD56 .F725 1988

Topik, Steven.
The political economy of the Brazilian State, 1889-1930 / by Steven Topik. 1st ed. Austin : University of Texas Press, 1987. xii, 241 p. : ill. ; 24 cm. (Latin American monographs / Institute of Latin American Studies, the University of Texas at Austin . no. 71) Bibliography: p. [207]-228. Includes index. ISBN 0-292-76500-2 LC Card 87-5835 DDC 338.981 19
1. Brazil - Economic policy. 2. Finance - Brazil - History. 3. Coffee trade - Brazil - History. 4. Railroads - Brazil - History. 5. Brazil - Industries - History. 6. Brazil - History - 1889-1930. I. Series: Latin American monographs (University of Texas at Austin. Institute of Latin American Studies) , no. 71. II. Title.
HC187 .T558 1987

State and economy : Brazil under the empire and the republic / Steven Topik. Austin : Office for Public Sector Studies, Institute of Latin American Studies, University of Texas at Austin, 1985. 28 p. ; 28 cm. (Technical papers series . no. 47) Bibliography: p. 23-28. LC Card 86-622250 DDC 338.981 19
1. Brazil - Economic policy. 2. Brazil - History - 1822-. I. Title. II. Series.
HC187 .T56 1985

Topp, Niels-Henrik. Udviklingen i de finanspolitiske ideer i Danmark 1930-1945 / Niels-Henrik Topp. [Copenhagen] : Jurist- og økonomforbundet forlag, [1987] 437 p. ; 23 cm. (Studier / Københavns universitets økonomiske institut, 0589-672X . nr. 30) Thesis (doctoral)--Københavns universitet, 1986. Summary in English. Bibliography: p. 383-432. Includes index. ISBN 87-574-5100-1 : LC Card 87-149164
1. Fiscal policy - Denmark - History - 20th century. 2. Denmark - Economic conditions - 1918-1945. I. Series: Studier (Københavns universitet. Økonomiske institut) , nr. 30. II. Title.
HB51 .C63 nr. 30 HJ1222

Topritzhofer, Edgar, 1944- Das Exportgeschäft : seine Abwicklung und Absicherung / von Edgar Topritzhofer, Reinhard Moser.2., verb. und erw. Aufl. Wien : Service Fachverlag an der Wirtschaftsuniversität Wien, 1984. 250 p. : ill. ; 30 cm. Bibliography: p. 249-250. ISBN 3-85428-025-4 LC Card 84-232997
1. Export marketing. I. Moser, Reinhard. II. Title.
HF1009.5 .T665 1984

Topsøe-Jensen, Hanne. Christoffersen, Mads. Fysisk planlægning og samfundsmæssige reproduktionsproblemer . København , 1980, c1979. 317 p. ; ISBN 87-500-1922-8
NYPL [JLD 86-2303]

Torbert, William R., 1944- Managing the corporate dream : restructuring for long-term success / William R. Torbert. Homewood, Ill. : Dow Jones-Irwin, c1987. xxiv, 250 p. ; 24 cm. Includes bibliographies and index. ISBN 0-87094-922-5 LC Card 86-72274
I. Title. ***NYPL [JLE 87-1258]***

Torchelli, Juan Carlos. Franz, Paulo Renato Ferreira. Região geoeconômica de Brasília . Planaltina-DF [Brazil] , 1985. 70 p. : LC Card 87-143606 DDC 338.1/3/098174 19
HD1875.B7 F7 1985

Torgovlia i kupechestvo v doreformennoĭ Gruzii. Ordzhonikidze, Ė. A. (Ėteri Aleksandrovna) Vačroba da vačart'a p'ena rep'ormamdeli xanis Sak'art'veloši /. T'bilisi , 1974. 158 p. ; LC Card 86-168874
HF3629.G4 O73 1974

Torkanovskiĭ, E. P. (Evgeniĭ Petrovich) Organizatsiia sorevnovaniia i sovershenstvovanie khoziaĭstvennogo mekhanizma /. Moskva , 1982. 206 p. ; LC Card 82-202826
HC340.S6 O684 1982

Tormysheva, T. A. (Tamara Andreevna) Okhrana truda i sotsial'noe strakhovanie trudiashchikhsia v Uzbekskoĭ SSR / T.A. Tormysheva, M.G. Zakirov ; pod redaktsieĭ N.M. Makhmudovoĭ. Tashkent : "Meditsina" UzSSR, 1987. 131 p. ; 20 cm. Bibliography: p. 125. LC Card 87-107413
1. Industrial hygiene - Uzbek S.S.R. 2. Industrial hygiene - Law and legislation - Uzbek S.S.R. 3. Social security - Uzbek S.S.R. I. Zakirov, M. G. (Mustafa Gazizovich). II. Makhmudova, N. M. III. Title.
HD7345.U93 T67 1987

Tornes, Kristin. Den Norske kvinnerevolusjonen . Oslo , c1986. 166 p. : ISBN 82-00-18318-1 LC Card 87-155462
HD6170 .N68 1986

Toro Agudelo, Hernán. Hacia una reforma social urbana en Colombia : el pensamiento liberal en la solución del problema de vivienda popular / Hernán Toro Agudelo.1a ed. Bogotá, Colombia : Ediciones Tercer Mundo, 1986. 342 p. : ill. ; 22 cm. ISBN 958-601-100-3 LC Card 87-107055
1. Housing policy - Colombia. 2. Urban policy - Colombia. 3. Liberalism - Colombia. I. Title.
HD7325.A3 T67 1986

Törőcsik, Frigyes. Az Ország közúthálózatának müszaki minősitése és nyilvántartása /. [Budapest] , 1983. 2 v. : LC Card 84-253458
HE363.H82 O76 1983

Török, Ádám. Komparatív előnyök : nemzetközi példák, hazai tapasztalatok / Török Ádám. Budapest : Közgazdasági és Jogi Könyvkiadó, 1986, c1985. 225, [1] p. ; 21 cm. Bibliography: p. 215-[226] ISBN 963-221-579-6 : LC Card 87-105362
1. Comparative advantage (Commerce). 2. Hungary - Commerce. I. Title.
HF1412 .T67 1986

Toronto, Ont. University. see **University of Toronto.**

Torras de la Luz, Jacinto, 1909-1963. [Selections. 1984]
Obras escogidas / Jacinto Torras. La

Habana : Editora Politica, 1984- v. <1 > : ill. ; 23 cm. At head of title, v. <1 >: Instituto de Historia del Movimiento Comunista y de la Revolución Socialista de Cuba, anexo al Comité Central del Partido Comunista de Cuba. CONTENTS. - t. 1. 1939-1945 LC Card 87-125434 DDC 338.97291 19
1. Cuba - Economic conditions - 1918-1959. 2. Cuba - Economic conditions - 1959-. 3. Cuba - Economic policy. 4. Marxian economics. I. Instituto de Historia del Movimiento Comunista y de la Revolución Socialista de Cuba. II. Title.
HC152.5 .T662 1984

TORRE DEL GRECO (ITALY) - ECONOMIC CONDITIONS.
Pavanello, Mariano, 1944- Antropologia ed economia dell'artigianato artistico . Milano, Italy , c1984. 183 p. : LC Card 84-147193
HD2346.I82 T676 1984

Torre, Germán. see **Torre Villafane, Germán.**

Torre, Hugo O. de la. Lazzati, Santiago. Análisis de normas sobre contabilidad e inflación . Buenos Aires [1981] 157 p. ; LC Card 82-216941
HF5658.5 .L39 1981

Torre Villafane, Germán. Simons Munaro, Yehude. Lambayeque, producción ganadera, comunidades campesinas [microform] /. Chiclayo, Perú , 1983. 45 p. ; LC Card 84-204537 DDC 338.1/76/0098514 19
HD9424.P43 L367 1983 *NYPL [*ZT-1708 no.72]*

Torrent, Emili. Evolució del transport a Salt / Emili Torrent. [Salt, Spain] : Servei Municipal de Publicacions, [1984] 32 p. : ill. ; 21 cm. (Monografies d'estudis locals. Història . 1) ISBN 84-85946-59-6 LC Card 87-161246
1. Transportation - Spain - Salt - History. 2. Salt (Spain) - Economic conditions. I. Title. II. Series.
HE311.S72 S257 1984

Torres, Gilma Mosquera. see **Mosquera Torres, Gilma.**

Torres y Torres Lara, Carlos. Las cooperativas en el Perú, su situación actual y legislación vigente / Carlos Torres y Torres Lara. Lima, Perú : Asesorandina, 1985. 144 p. ; 22 cm. Bibliography: p. 59-60. LC Card 86-110544 DDC 346.85/0668 348.506668 19
1. Cooperative societies - Law and legislation - Peru. 2. Cooperative societies - Peru. I. Title.
KHQ1370 .T67 1985 *NYPL [JLD 86-2183]*

Tórrez G. O., José Guillermo (Torrez Gómez Ortega) Minería e integración boliviana / José Guillermo Tórrez G.O. 1a ed. La Paz, Bolivia : Librería y Editorial Juventud, 1986. 181 p., [8] leaves of plates : ill., maps ; 22 cm. LC Card 87-400195 DDC 338.2/0984 19
1. Corporación Minera de Bolivia - History. 2. Mineral industries - Government ownership - Bolivia - History. 3. Bolivia - Economic policy. I. Title.
HD9506.B64 C67 1986

Tortella Casares, Gabriel. Introducción a la economía para historiadores / Gabriel Tortella. Madrid : Tecnos, 1986. xv, 192 p. : ill. ; 24 cm. (Serie de historia) Bibliography: p. [187]-189. Includes index. ISBN 84-309-1262-2 LC Card 86-219657
1. Economics. I. Series: Serie de historia (Madrid, Spain). II. Title.
HB178.5 .T693 1986

Tortella, Gabriel. see **Tortella Casares, Gabriel.**

Történeti statisztikai kötetek, 0139-0279.
Szőlőtermelés . Budapest , 1986. 519 p. ; ISBN 963-340-777-X : LC Card 86-196884
HD9385.H82 S95 1986

The Tory budget and the corporate plan to restructure Canada, and how the system really works /. Swankey, Ben. Vancouver , c1985. xi, 246 p. ; ISBN 0-920879-00-4 (pbk.) LC Card 86-209703 DDC 338.971 19
HJ2055 .S9 1985

Tosato, G. (Giancarlo) Energy after the eighties . Amsterdam , New York , 1984. xxii, 298 p. : ISBN 0-444-42404-0 : LC Card 84-13742 DDC 333.79 19
HD9502.A2 E537 1984 *NYPL [JLE 86-1572]*

Tosco, Manuel. Aprovechamiento y dominio de las tierras en 1950-51 / preparado por M. Tosco y R. Cabañas ; en colaboración con C. Simmons y J. Joosten. Tegucigalpa, D.C., Honduras : Talleres Tipo-Litográficos "Aristón", [1952] 33 p. ; 32 cm. Tables. Includes bibliographical references. LC Card 85-197157
1. Land use, Rural - Honduras - Statistics. 2. Land tenure - Honduras - Statistics. I. Cabañas, R. II. Simmons, C. III. Joosten, J. IV. Title.
HD366 .T66 1952

Toshpŭlatov, Mirzapŭlat. Prevrashchenie sel'skokhoziaistvennogo truda v raznovidnost' industrial'nogo v usloviiakh razvitogo sotsializma. : sotsial'nye problemy / M. Tashpulatov, Kh. Pulatov, E. Tairov. Tashkent : Izd-vo "Fan" Uzbekskoĭ SSR, 1980. 68 p. ; 20 cm. At head of title: Ministerstvo prosveshcheniia Uzbekskoĭ SSR. Ferganskiĭ gosudarstvennyĭ pedagogicheskiĭ institut im. Ulugbeka. Bibliography: p. 63-[66] LC Card 81-149078
1. Agricultural laborers - Uzbek S.S.R. I. Pulatov, Kh. II. Tairov, E. (Eri). III. Title.
HD1536.S65 T67 1980

Toso C., Roberto. El tipo de cambio fijo en Chile : la experiencia en el período 1979-1982 / Roberto Toso C. Santiago : Banco Central de Chile, 1983. 64 p. ; 27 cm. (Serie de estudios económicos : documentos de investigación . no. 19) Includes bibliographical references. LC Card 83-192876
1. Foreign exchange - Chile. 2. Foreign exchange administration - Chile. I. Series: Serie de estudios económicos (Banco Central de Chile). Documentos de investigación , no. 19. II. Title.
HG3934 .T67 1983

Tostado Gutiérrez, Marcela. El Tabasco porfiriano / Marcela Tostado Gutiérrez. 1a ed. Villahermosa [Mexico] : Gobierno del Estado de Tabasco, 1985. 179 p. : ill. ; 22 cm. (Colección Arqueología, antropología e historia. Serie Historia) Bibliography: p. 177-179. ISBN 968-88900-7-3 LC Card 86-189960
1. Tabasco (Mexico : State) - Economic conditions. 2. Capitalism - Mexico - Tabasco (State) - History. 3. Tabasco (Mexico : State) - Social conditions. 4. Tabasco (Mexico : State) - Politics and government. I. Title. II. Series.
HC137.T3 T67 1985

TOT füzetek .
(4) A Mezőgazdasági szövetkezetek szabályozó rendszere /. [Budapest] , 1979. 119 p. ; LC Card 86-187443
HD1492.H8 M417 1979

TOT füzetek, 0139-4851 .
(16) Németi, László. A személyzeti munka gyakorlati kérdései a mezőgazdasági termelőszövetkezetekben /. [Budapest] , 1984. 243 p. ; ISBN 963-502-370-7 LC Card 86-147870
HD1492.H8 N43 1984

Total coverage . Bundy, Darcie. New York , c1987. xiv, 224 p. ; ISBN 0-06-055077-5 : LC Card 86-46050 DDC 368/.0029 19
HG8051 .B846 1987

Total needs selling. 3rd ed. Chicago : R & R Newkirk, c1986. viii, 174 p. : ill. ; 28 cm. ISBN 0-88462-564-8 (pbk.) LC Card 86-23542 DDC 368.3/2/00688 19
1. Insurance, Life - Agents. 2. Selling. I. R & R Newkirk.
HG8877 .T68 1986

Total quality control for management . Nemoto, Masao. [TQC to toppu bu-kachō no yakuwari. English.] Englewood Cliffs, N.J. , c1987. xix, 238 p. : ISBN 0-13-925637-7 : LC Card 87-2329 DDC 658.4/036 19
HD66 .N4613 1987

Total telemarketing /. McHatton, Robert J. New York , c1988. x, 246 p. : ISBN 0-471-62755-0 (pbk.) : LC Card 87-21547 DDC 658.8/5 19
HF5415.1265 .M38 1988

Tóth, Béláné. Gazdálkodási és jövedelmezőségi adatok, mutatószámok a szövetkezeti bolti kiskereskedelemben /. Budapest , 1984. 113 p. ; ISBN 963-7006-24-9 : LC Card 85-154737
HF5429.6.H8 G39 1984

TOTZENBACH REGION (AUSTRIA) - HISTORY.
Landskron, Ferdinand. Von der Bauernfaust zur Bauernkammer /. Totzenbach [1983] 194 p. ; LC Card 84-168829
HD1536.A9 L36 1983

Touche Ross & Co. Touche Ross guide to personal financial management /. Englewood Cliffs, N.J. , c1987. xviii, 332 p. ; ISBN 0-13-925413-7 : LC Card 87-2470 DDC 332.024 19
HG179 .P5729 1987

Touche Ross guide to personal financial management / John R. Connell ... [et al.]. Rev. ed. Englewood Cliffs, N.J. : Prentice-Hall, c1987. xviii, 332 p. ; 29 cm. Includes index. ISBN 0-13-925413-7 : LC Card 87-2470 DDC 332.024 19
1. Finance, Personal. I. Connell, John R. II. Touche Ross & Co.
HG179 .P5729 1987

TOULOUSE REGION (FRANCE) - ECONOMIC CONDITIONS.
Marconis, Robert. Midi-Pyrénées XIXe-XXe siècles . [Toulouse?] [1985?] 2 v. : ISBN 2-86726-084-7 (set) LC Card 87-112330
HC277.M54 M37 1985

Touraine, Alain.
Le mouvement ouvrier / Alain Touraine, Michel Wieviorka, François Dubet. [Paris] : Fayard, c1984. 438 p. : ill. ; 24 cm. (Mouvements . 2) Includes indexes. Bibliography: p. [419]-432. ISBN 2-213-01361-6 : LC Card 84-202370 DDC 322/.2/0944 19
1. Trade-unions - France. 2. Trade-unions - France - Political activity. 3. Trade-unions - Europe. 4. Trade-unions - Europe - Political activity. I. Wieviorka, Michel. II. Dubet, François. III. Series: Mouvements (Paris, France) , 2. IV. Title.
HD6684 .T655 1984 *NYPL [JLE 86-279]*

[Mouvement ouvrier. English]
The workers' movement / Alain Touraine, Michel Wieviorka, François Dubet ; translated by Ian Patterson. Cambridge [Cambridgeshire] ; New York : Cambridge University Press ; xx, 322 p. ; 24 cm. Translation of: Le mouvement ouvrier. Bibliography: p. 295-319. Includes index. ISBN 0-521-30852-6 LC Card 87-8010 DDC 322/.2/0944 19
1. Trade-unions - France. 2. Trade-unions - France - Political activity. I. Wieviorka, Michel. II. Dubet, François. III. Title.
HD6684 .T65513 1987

TOURISM. see **TOURIST TRADE.**

TOURIST INDUSTRY. see **TOURIST TRADE.**

TOURIST TRADE - AUSTRIA - HISTORY.
Otruba, Gustav. A. Hitler's "Tausend-Mark-Sperre" und die Folgen für Österreichs Fremdenverkehr (1933-1938) /. Linz , c1983. iii, 205 p. ; ISBN 3-85320-308-6 LC Card 84-213145
HG999 .O87 1983

TOURIST TRADE - BRAZIL.
Brazil. Congresso Nacional. Câmara dos Deputados. Comissão de Esporte e Turismo. Vôos "charters" e as empresas de aviação civil . Brasília , 1986. 98 p. ; LC Card 87-405035 DDC 387.7/0981 19
HE9833.A4 B7 1986

TOURIST TRADE - GERMANY (WEST) - OBERSTAUFEN.
Maier, Jörg. Freizeitraum Oberstaufen . München , 1976. xii, 92 p. : ISBN 3-920397-13-4 LC Card 87-408421 DDC 330.94 380.1/45914337 19
HC281 .M84 Heft 13 G155.G3

TOURIST TRADE - QUEBEC (PROVINCE)
Le Secteur manufacturier, le commerce et le tourisme au Québec en 1983. [Québec] [1984] 34 leaves : LC Card 85-127334
HD9734.C3 Q485 1984

TOURIST TRADE - SPAIN - AMPURDÁN (REGION)
El Baix Empordà . Barcelona , c1984. xii, 303 p. : ISBN 84-505-0289-6 LC Card 85-186183
HC387.A636 B35 1984

TOURIST TRADE - TANZANIA.
Ole Saibull, Solomon, 1935- Hotuba ya Ndugu S.A. ole Saibull, mbunge, waziri wa maliasili na utalii . Dar es Salaam, Tanzania , 1979. 56 p. ; LC Card 83-244807
HC885 .O44 1979

TOURIST TRAFFIC. see **TOURIST TRADE.**

TOURISTS. see **TOURIST TRADE.**

Tourret, Jean-Claude. Dacier, Pierre. Les dossiers noirs de l'industrie française /. [Paris] , c1985. 414 p. ; ISBN 2-213-01659-3 : LC Card 86-178468
HC276.2 .D2 1985

Tous capitalistes. Poncins, Michel de. Tous capitalistes, ou, La réponse au socialisme /. Vouillé [France] , c1983. 164 p. ; LC Card 83-244442 DDC 338.944 19
HC276.2 .P63 1983 ***NYPL [JLD 86-427]***

Tous capitalistes, ou, La réponse au socialisme /. Poncins, Michel de. Vouillé [France] , c1983. 164 p. ; LC Card 83-244442 DDC 338.944 19
HC276.2 .P63 1983 ***NYPL [JLD 86-427]***

Toussaint, Marcel. China market atlas / by Marcel Toussaint. Hong Kong : Business International, c1986. ix, 222 p. : chiefly ill. (some col.) ; 42 cm. Includes index. LC Card 86-218633 DDC 330.951/058 19
1. China - Economic conditions - 1976- - Statistics. I. Business International Asia/Pacific Ltd. II. Title.
HC427.92 .T69 1986

Tout sur la France en 100 graphiques / [réalisé par une équipe de chercheurs, de journalistes et de graphistes ; conception et rédaction, Brigitte Trillat et Laurent Chemineau, avec Yan de Kérorguen ... et al.]. Paris : Autrement, c1986. 113 p. : chiefly col. ill. ; 22 cm. ISBN 2-86260-154-3 : LC Card 87-106635
1. France - Statistics. 2. France - Population - Statistics. 3. France - Economic conditions - 1981- - Statistics. I. Trillat, Brigitte. II. Chemineau, Laurent.
HA1224 .T68 1986

Tovarnoe obrashchenie . Levin, A. I. (Aleksandr Ivanovich) Moskva , 1980. 286 p. ; LC Card 81-141540
HF1040.9.S65 L48 1980

Tovarovedenie vkusovykh tovarov /. Korobkina, Z. V. (Zoi͡a Vasil′evna) Moskva , 1986. 207 p. ; LC Card 86-220308
HD9015.S652 K67 1986

Tovmosi͡an, M. E.
Agropromyshlennyĭ kompleks v uslovii͡akh razvitogo sotsializma . Moskva , 1986. 167 p. ; LC Card 87-166350
HD9015.S652 A38 1986

Bukhval′d, E. M. Povyshenie proizvoditel′nosti truda--kli͡uchevai͡a zadacha sovetskoĭ ėkonomiki . Moskva , 1984. 63 p. ; LC Card 85-188977
HC340.L3 B85 1984

Ėkonomicheskoe stimulirovanie truda v uslovii͡akh sotsializma . Moskva , 1986. 179 p. ; LC Card 87-166364
HD5046 .E47 1986

Metodiki opredelenii͡a ėkonomicheskoĭ ėffektivnosti kapital′nykh vlozheniĭ v sotsialisticheskikh stranakh . Moskva , 1981. 101 p. ; LC Card 82-204402
HC244.Z9 C35 1981

Sotsialisticheskai͡a sobstvennost′ v uslovii͡akh razvitogo sotsializma . Moskva , 1984. 165 p. ; LC Card 85-177805
HB701 .S59 1984

Uchastie trudi͡ashchikhsi͡a v upravlenii proizvodstvom . Moskva , 1985. 69, [2] p. ; LC Card 85-224379
HD5660.S65 U27 1985

Toward a new economics . Eichner, Alfred S. Armonk, N.Y. , c1985. ix, 240 p. : ISBN 0-87332-326-2 LC Card 84-27724 DDC 330 19
HB171 .E35 1985 ***NYPL [JLE 86-1977]***

Toward a new Iron Age? : quantitative modeling of resource exhaustion / Robert B. Gordon ... [et al.]. Cambridge, Mass. : Harvard University Press, 1987. vi, 173 p. : ill. ; 25 cm. Bibliography: p. [163]-168. Includes index. ISBN 0-674-89818-4 (alk. paper) LC Card 86-22923 DDC 333.8/5 19
1. Nonrenewable natural resources - Mathematical models. 2. Resource allocation - Mathematical models. 3. Copper industry and trade - Mathematical models. I. Gordon, Robert B. (Robert Boyd), 1929-.
HC59 .T63 1987

Toward a political economy of development : a rational choice perspective / edited by Robert H. Bates. Berkeley : University of California Press, c1988. p. cm. (California series on social choice and political economy . 14) Bibliography: p. Includes index. ISBN 0-520-06051-2 (alk. paper) LC Card 87-10870 DDC 338.9/009172/4 19
1. Developing countries - Economic policy. 2. Developing countries - Economic conditions. 3. Developing countries - Politics and government. 4. Social choice. I. Bates, Robert H. II. Series.
HC59.7 .T7376 1988

Toward a profile of Soviet behavior in international financial markets /. Neu, C. R. (Carl Richard), 1949- Santa Monica, CA [1987] xv, 58 p. : ISBN 0-8330-0865-X (pbk.) LC Card 87-13084 DDC 332/.042/0947 19
HG3955 .N48 1987

Toward an alternative security system . Johansen, Robert C. New York, N.Y. , c1983. 57 p. ; ISBN 0-911646-12-5 (pbk.) : LC Card 83-215670 DDC 355/.03 19
UA10.5 .J64 1983

Towards a democratic rationality : making the case for Swedish labour / [edited by] John Fry. Aldershot, Hants, England ; Brookfield, Vt., USA : Gower, c1986. xi, 281 p. : ill. ; 23 cm. Bibliography: p. 271-281. ISBN 0-566-00761-4 : LC Card 86-14241 DDC 331/.09485 19
1. Labor and laboring classes - Sweden. 2. Sex discrimination in employment - Sweden. 3. Industrial management - Sweden - Employee participation. 4. Labor policy - Sweden. 5. Industrial relations - Sweden. I. Fry, John, 1942-.
HD8576.5 .T69 1986 ***NYPL [JLD 86-3873]***

Towards a new United Nations development strategy . Rist, Gilbert, 1938- Nyon , 1977. 74 p. ; LC Card 81-118524
HC60 .R539 1977

Towards a viable and vibrant public sector in India : a plaidoyer for change in government policies, in managerial practices within the public sector, and in overall environment in the country concerning the public sector / [edited] by Raj K. Nigam ; foreword by P.N. Haksar. New Delhi : Documentation Centre for Corporate & Business Policy Research, 1986. xiii, 188, 163, 8, 103 p. ; 24 cm. Bibliography: p. 164. Comprises keynote papers and documents. LC Card 86-903205 DDC 338.6/2/0954
1. Government business enterprises - India. I. Nigam, Raj Kumar, 1923-. II. Documentation Centre for Corporate & Business Policy Research (India).
HD4293 .T667 1986

Towards an African economic community : (lessons of experience from ECOWAS) : proceedings of an international conference / edited by Akinola A. Owosekun. [Ibadan, Nigeria] : Nigerian Institute of Social and Economic Research, 1986. 401 p. ; 25 cm. Papers from a seminar on "ECOWAS and Lagos Plan of Action" co-sponsored by the Nigerian Institute of Social and Economic Research and the Friedrich Ebert Foundation. Includes bibliographies. ISBN 978-18-1040-8 LC Card 87-143033 DDC 337.1/66 19
1. Economic Community of West African States - Congresses. 2. Africa, West - Economic integration - Congresses. I. Owosekun, Akinola Adeniyi. II. Nigerian Institute of Social and Economic Research. III. Friedrich-Ebert-Stiftung.
HC1000 .T69 1986

Towards an interest-free Islamic economic system . Khan, Waqar Masood. Leicester , Islamabad , c1985. 126 p. ; ISBN 0-86037-155-7
NYPL [JLD 87-381]

Towards forecasting manpower requirements. Wellington [N.Z.] : Research and Planning Division, Dept. of Labour, [1977] 90 p. : ill. ; 30 cm. "November 1977." LC Card 85-184797
1. Employment forecasting - New Zealand. I. New Zealand. Dept. of Labour. Research and Planning Division.
HD5850.4.A6 T69 1977

Towards full employment . Driver, Ciaran. London , New York , 1987. xii, 238 p. : ISBN 0-7102-0918-5 LC Card 87-9814 DDC 339.5 19
HD5713.2 .D75 1987

Towards increasing self-reliance . Mauritius. Ministry of Economic Planning and Development. Port Louis [1983] 33 p. ; LC Card 86-980675 DDC 338.969/82 19
HC597.5 .M39 1983

Towards monetary cooperation in South Asia /. Madan, B. K. (Bal Krishna), 1911- New Delhi , 1986, c1985. 105 p. ; LC Card 86-901998 DDC 332.4/954 19
HG3881 .M2756 1986 ***NYPL [JLD 87-911]***

Towards poverty alleviation programmes in Nagaland and Manipur /. Roy Burman, B. K. Delhi , 1984. xxxi, 123 p. ; LC Card 84-902780 DDC 338.954/165 19
HC437.N25 R69 1984 ***NYPL [JLD 87-903]***

Towards recovery and sustainable growth / by Florian A. Alburo ... [et al.]. [Quezon] : School of Economics, University of the Philippines, [1985] 71 leaves ; 29 cm. "September 1985." LC Card 86-147888 DDC 338.9599 19
1. Philippines - Economic policy. I. Alburo, Florian A. II. University of the Philippines. School of Economics.
HC453 .T68 1985

Towards reducing the dependence on capital imports . Ahrens, Heinz-Dietmar. Wiesbaden , 1982. xvi, 337 p. : ISBN 3-515-03853-1 (pbk.) LC Card 86-214363 DDC 338.9549/1 19
HC440.5 .A726 1982

Towards self sufficiency . Lusaka Province (Zambia). Provincial Planning Unit. [Lusaka, Zambia?] [1984] 100 p., [14] leaves of plates : LC Card 86-980293 DDC 338.1/86894 19
HD2131.5 .L87 1984

Towarzystwo jezusowe. see **Jesuits.**

TOWERS, GRAHAM F., 1897-1975.
Fullerton, Douglas H. Graham Towers and his times . Toronto, Ont. , c1986. 348 p., [16] p. of plates : ISBN 0-7710-3218-8 : LC Card 86-231010 DDC 332.1/1/092 B 19
HG1552.T68 F85 1986

Towle, Edward L. Final report : island resource management, the Virgin Islands experience : a planning study for a workshop on environmental assessment, resource allocation, carrying capacity, growth management, and enhancing information transfer for decision-making in smaller islands / prepared for the U. S. National Commission for UNESCO, Man and the Biosphere Program, MAB 7B Directorate ; prepared by Edward L. Towle ; with the assistance of Jerome McElroy, A. Robert Teytaud. St. Thomas, U. S.V.I. : Island Resources Foundation, [1982] 17, 15, 4 leaves : ill. ; 29 cm. "October 1982." Bibliography: leaves 14-17 (1st group) "Contract #1021-010583." LC Card 86-185489 DDC 333.7/097297/22 19
1. Environmental policy - Virgin Islands of the United States. I. McElroy, Jerome L. II. Teytaud, A. Robert. III. United States National Commission for Unesco. MAB 7B Directorate. IV. Island Resources Foundation (Virgin Islands of the United States). V. Title.
HC155.Z9 E56 1982

Towle, Philip, 1945- Protest and perish : a critique of unilateralism / by Philip Towle, Iain Elliot, and Gerald Frost. London : Alliance Publishers for the Institute for European Defence and Strategic Studies, 1982. 121 p. ; 21 cm. Includes bibliographical references. ISBN 0-907967-02-7 (pbk.) : LC Card 83-198296 DDC 355/.0217/0941 19
1. Atomic weapons and disarmament. 2. Antinuclear movement - Great Britain. 3. World politics - 1945-. 4. Great Britain - Military policy. I. Elliot, Iain F. II. Frost, Gerald. III. Title.
UA647 .T69 1982 ***NYPL [JLD 86-1904]***

TOWN LIFE. see **CITY AND TOWN LIFE.**

TOWN MEETING. see **LOCAL GOVERNMENT.**

TOWN PLANNING. see **CITY PLANNING.**

TOWNS. see **CITIES AND TOWNS.**

Townsend, Carl, 1938- Exploring word processors : CP/M edition / Carl Townsend. Beaverton, Or. : Dilithium Press, c1984. viii, 239 p. : ill. ; 23 cm. Includes index. Bibliography: p. [235] ISBN 0-88056-104-1 (pbk.) : LC Card 83-26259 DDC 652 19
1. Word processing. 2. CP/M (Computer operating system). I. Title.
Z52.5.C65 T68 1984 ***NYPL [JSD 86-495]***

Townsend, John Clendenin, 1939- Running the gauntlet : cultural sources of violence against the I.W.W. / John Clendenin Townsend. New York : Garland, 1986. 341 p. ; 24 cm. (American legal and constitutional history) Bibliography: p. 311-341. ISBN 0-8240-8298-2 (alk. paper) : LC Card 86-25632 DDC 331.88/6 19
1. Industrial Workers of the World. I. Title. II. Series.
HD8055.I56 T68 1986

Townsend, Patrick L. Commit to quality / Patrick L. Townsend with Joan E. Gebhardt. New York : Wiley, c1986. xvii, 189 p. : ill. ; 24 cm. Includes index. ISBN 0-471-83953-1 LC Card

85-29639 DDC 658.5/62 19
1. Quality assurance. 2. Quality circles. I. Gebhardt, Joan E. II. Title.
HD66 .T65 1986 *NYPL [JLE 86-3004]*

TOWNSEND, WALTER DAVIS, 1856-1918.
Cook, Harold F., 1929- Pioneer American businessman in Korea . Seoul, Korea , 1981. ix, 104 p. : LC Card 83-140523 DDC 382/.09519/0730924 B 19
HF3023.T68 C66 1981
NYPL [JFE 86-4650]

TOWNSHIP FINANCE. see **LOCAL FINANCE.**

TOWNSHIP GOVERNMENT. see **LOCAL GOVERNMENT.**

Townsley, Joe. Wood, Frank. Finance /. London , 1986. 410 p. : ISBN 0-273-02587-2 (pbk.) : LC Card 86-224835 DDC 332/.0941 19
HG186.G7 W66 1986

TOXIC AND INFLAMMABLE GOODS. see **HAZARDOUS SUBSTANCES.**

TOXICOLOGY.
Bellini, James. High tech holocaust /. Newton Abbot , c1986. 255 p. ; ISBN 0-7153-8812-6
NYPL [JLE 87-827]

TOY INDUSTRY - GERMANY, WEST.
Breitenacher, Michael. Strukturwandlungen und Entwicklungsperspektiven im Musikinstrumentenbau, in der Spielwaren- und Sportgeräteherstellung und in der Schmuckindustrie /. Berlin , c1984. 188 p. : ISBN 3-428-05566-7 LC Card 84-186644
HD9999.M83 G32 1984

Toye, J. F. J. Dilemmas of development : reflections on the counter-revolution in development theory and policy / John Toye. Oxford, [Oxfordshire], UK ; New York, NY, USA : Blackwell, 1987. ix, 177 p. ; 23 cm. Bibliography: p. [162]-170. Includes index. ISBN 0-631-14569-9 (U. S.) : LC Card 86-30955 DDC 338.9/009172/4 19
1. Economic development. 2. Developing countries - Economic policy. I. Title.
HD82 .T65 1987

Tozzi, Michel. Militer autrement / Michel Tozzi. Bruxelles, Belgique : Vie ouvrière ; Lyon, France : Chronique sociale, [1985] 162 p. ; 22 cm. (Collection "Nouvelles pratiques sociales", 0762-0810) Bibliography: p. 161-162. ISBN 2-85008-067-5 : LC Card 86-178750
1. Trade-unions - France. 2. France - Social conditions - 1945-. I. Title. II. Series.
HD6684 .T66 1985

Trng, H Ch Trng H Hà N Khoa học xã h 1982-1983. 2 v. ; 19 cm. Includes bibliographies. CONTENTS. - t LC Card 87-142403
1. Land tenure - Vietnam - History. I. Title.
HD890.5 .T78 1982

Trabajadores del Programa de Empleo Mínimo. Ruiz-Tagle P., Jaime. Los trabajadores del Programa del Empleo Mínimo . Santiago , 1984. 179 p. : LC Card 84-234738
HD5756.A6 R86 1984

Los trabajadores del Programa del Empleo Mínimo . Ruiz-Tagle P., Jaime. Santiago , 1984. 179 p. : LC Card 84-234738
HD5756.A6 R86 1984

Trabajadores urbanos . Duarte, Isis. Santo Domingo, República Dominicana , c1986. 314 p. ; LC Card 87-402153 DDC 331/.097293 19
HD8218.5 .D83 1986

Trabajadores y seguridad social en América Latina /. Cohen, Noemí. México, D.F. [1982], c1981. 146 p. ; ISBN 968-8241-38-5 LC Card 83-140620 DDC 368.4/0098 19
HD7130.5 .C63 1982 *NYPL [JLD 86-2768]*

Trabajo docente (Pontificia Universidad Católica de Chile. Instituto de Economía) .
(no. 46) Rosende Ramírez, Francisco. Consideraciones acerca del estado del debate en teoría macroeconómica /. Santiago , 1986. 51 leaves ; LC Card 87-116226 DDC 339 19
HB178.5 .R67 1986

Trabajo docente (Universidad Católica de Chile. Instituto de Economía) .
(no. 40) Williamson B., Carlos. La teoría sobre preferencias arancelarias . Santiago, Chile , 1985. 35 leaves : LC Card 85-202146
HF1733.L29 W54 1985

Trabajo familiar, conducta reproductiva y estratificación social : un estudio en las áreas rurales de México / Elena Zúñiga ... [et al.] ; editor, Jorge Martínez Manautou.1a ed. México, D.F. : Instituto Mexicano del Seguro Social, 1986. 226 p. ; 22 cm. Errata slip inserted. Bibliography: p. 223-226. ISBN 968-8241-06-7 LC Card 87-400355 DDC 304.6/32/0972 19
1. Fertility, Human - Mexico. 2. Peasantry - Mexico. 3. Mexico - Rural conditions. I. Zúñiga, Elena. II. Martínez Manautou, Jorge. III. Instituto Mexicano del Seguro Social.
HB941 .T7 1986

El trabajo infantil urbano en Managua /. D'Ciófalo V., Giovanni. Managua , 1986. ii, 76, 3, [33] leaves ; LC Card 87-403894 DDC 331.3/1/09728513 19
HD6250.N5 M363 1986

Trabajo (Instituto Nacional de Carnes (Uruguay)) .
(no. 11) Uruguay, producción y comercialización de ganado y carnes. [Montevideo, Uruguay] , 1985. 90 p. : LC Card 87-403154 DDC 338.1/760883/09895 19
HD9424.U8 U783 1985

Trabajo, una nueva civilización y cultura del trabajo. Máspero, Emilio. Importancia y significado de la encíclica sobre el trabajo humano del papa Juan Pablo II para el movimiento obrero latinoamericano /. [Caracas, Venezuela] [1984] 159 p. : LC Card 87-404543 DDC 261.8/5 19
HD6338 .M425 1984

Los trabajos de las mujeres entre el campo y la ciudad, 1920-1982 . Mack, Macarena. [Santiago, Chile] [1986] 108 p. ; LC Card 86-217673
HD6126 .M33 1986

O trabalhador e a produção hoje . Costa, Beatriz B. Petrópolis , Rio de Janeiro, RJ, Brasil , 1985. 78 p. ; LC Card 86-150042 DDC 331.11/8 19
HC79.L3 C67 1985

Trabalhadores ferroviários em greve /. Leme, Dulce M. Pompêo C. (Dulce Maria Pompêo de Camargo) Campinas [Brazil] , 1986. 269 p. : ISBN 85-26-80007-8 : LC Card 87-102922 DDC 331.89/281385/098161 19
HD5354.R12 1906 .S365 1986

Trabalho cooperativo em duas aldeias de Trás-os-Montes /. Portela, José, 1950- Porto , 1986. 79 p., [4] p. of plates : LC Card 87-400109 DDC 334/.683/094692 19
HD1491.P82 T736 1986

Trabalho, progresso e a sociedade civilizada . Salles, Iraci Galvão. São Paulo [Brasília] , 1986. 145 p. ; LC Card 86-224281
HD8289.S282 S24 1986

Trabis, Roland. Industrie et politique à la frontière Mexique-U. S.A. : le cas de Nuevo Laredo, 1966-1984 / Roland Trabis. Paris : Editions du CNRS, c1985. 241 p., [1] p. of plates : ill. ; 24 cm. (Amérique latine--pays ibériques) Bibliography: p. [229]-239. Includes index. ISBN 2-222-03772-7 : LC Card 86-175728
1. Nuevo Laredo (Mexico) - Economic conditions. 2. Mexican American Border Region - Industries. I. Title. II. Series.
HC138.N84 T73 1985

Tracey, Mrs. Organisation for Economic Co-operation and Development. Library. L'emploi des jeunes =. [Paris] , 1980. [6], 119 p. ; LC Card 81-122004 DDC 016.3313/4 19
HD6270 .O72 1980

Tracking America's economy /. Frumkin, Norman. Armonk, N.Y. , c1987. 250 p. : ISBN 0-87332-437-4 : LC Card 87-9694 DDC 338.5/44/0973 19
HC106.8 .F78 1987

Tracking and testing advertising and other marketing effects. Donius, James F. Marketplace measurement . New York, NY (155 E. 44th St., New York 11710) , c1986. xiii, 206 p. : LC Card 87-120244 DDC 659.1/11 19
HF5823 .D655 1986

Tractor industry in India. New Delhi : Research Consultancy Bureau, [1982?]. 3 v. ; 29 cm. LC Card 83-906487 DDC 338.4/7629225 19
1. Tractor industry - India. 2. Agricultural machinery industry - India. I. Research Consultancy Bureau (India).
HD9710.4.I42 T73 1982
NYPL [JLM 86-469]

TRACTOR INDUSTRY - INDIA.
Tractor industry in India. New Delhi [1982?]. 3 v. ; LC Card 83-906487 DDC 338.4/7629225 19
HD9710.4.I42 T73 1982
NYPL [JLM 86-469]

TRACTOR INDUSTRY - UNITED STATES.
Zinman, Michael. The history of the decline and fall of the Raterpillar Tractor Company . Ardsley, N.Y. , c1986. 231 p. : ISBN 0-937704-03-2 (pbk.) : LC Card 86-82887 DDC 338.7/629225 19
HD9710.4.U64 R388 1986

TRADE. see **BUSINESS; COMMERCE.**

Trade adjustment assistance : new ideas for an old program : special report. Washington, DC : Congress of the U. S., Office of Technology Assessment : For sale by the Supt. of Docs., U. S. G.P.O., [1987] viii, 69 p. : ill. ; 26 cm. Shipping list no.: 87-347-P. Includes bibliographical references. "June 1987"--P. [4] of cover. "OTA-ITE-346"--P. [4] of cover. S/N 052-003-01073-9 Item 1070-M LC Card 87-619836 DDC 362.8/5 19
1. Trade adjustment assistance - United States. I. United States. Congress. Office of Technology Assessment.
HF1421 .T73 1987

TRADE ADJUSTMENT ASSISTANCE.
Banks, Gary. Economic policy and the adjustment problem /. Aldershot, Hants., England , Brookfield, Vt. , 1986. x, 101 p. ; ISBN 0-566-05332-2 : LC Card 86-14934 DDC 338.9 19
HF1421 .B36 1987
NYPL [JLL 74-802 no.45]

TRADE ADJUSTMENT ASSISTANCE - AUSTRALIA.
Anderson, Kym. Australian protectionism . Sydney , Boston , 1987. xii, 160 p. : ISBN 0-04-330383-8 (pbk.) LC Card 86-47990 DDC 382.7/3/0994 19
HF1625 .A53 1987

TRADE ADJUSTMENT ASSISTANCE - UNITED STATES.
Causes and remedies for displacement of steel workers . [Washington, D.C.? , 1985] iv, 83, 2, 2 p. ; LC Card 86-601602 DDC 331.13/704 19
HD8039.I52 U524 1985

Gray, H. Peter. International trade, employment, and structural adjustment . Geneva , 1986. x, 108 p. ; ISBN 92-2-105325-3 (pbk.) : LC Card 87-119470 DDC 331.12/0973 19
HD5710.75.U6 G73 1986

Lawrence, Robert Z., 1949- Saving free trade . Washington, D.C. , c1986. xii, 132 p. ; ISBN 0-8157-5178-8 LC Card 86-14705 DDC 382.7/1/0973 19
HF1455 .L39 1986 *NYPL [JLE 86-4368]*

Trade adjustment assistance . Washington, DC [1987] viii, 69 p. : LC Card 87-619836 DDC 362.8/5 19
HF1421 .T73 1987

TRADE ADJUSTMENT ASSISTANCE - UNITED STATES - CASE STUDIES.
Kaplan, Daniel P. Has trade protection revitalized domestic industries? Washington, D.C. [1986] xvi, 111 p. : LC Card 86-603423 DDC 382.7/3/0973 19
HF1421 .K36 1986

TRADE AGREEMENTS (COMMERCE) see **COMMERCIAL TREATIES.**

TRADE AGREEMENTS (LABOR) see **COLLECTIVE LABOR AGREEMENTS.**

Trade, aid, and democracy in the Caribbean : report of seminar for youth leaders held in Antigua, May 29-30, 1986. [S.l.] : Bustamante Institute of Public and International Affairs, [1986] 68 p. : ill. ; 21 cm. Cover title. LC Card 87-400829 DDC 338.91/09729 19
1. Economic assistance - Caribbean Area - Congresses. 2. Caribbean Area - Commerce - Congresses. I. Bustamante Institute of Public and International Affairs.
HC151 .T73 1986

Trade among multinationals . MacCharles, Donald C. (Donald Clare), 1935- London , New York , c1987. xiv, 207 p. ; ISBN 0-7099-4618-X LC Card 87-9077 DDC 382/.3

19
HF1411 .M2325 1987

Trade and commerce in Rajasthan during the 18th century /. Gupta, B. L. (Babu Lal), 1949- Jaipur , 1987. iv, 274 p. : LC Card 87-902534 DDC 380.1/0954/4 19
HF3789.R33 G86 1987

Trade and commercial activities of southern India in the Malayo-Indonesian world, up to A.D. 1511 /. Sarkar, Himansu Bhusan. Calcutta , 1986- v. <1- > : LC Card 87-900744 DDC 382/.09548/059 19
HF3788.A78 S25 1986

Trade and foreign direct investment in data services /. Sauvant, Karl P. Boulder Colo. , 1986. xv, 223 p. : ISBN 0-8133-7085-X : LC Card 85-22701 DDC 332.6/712 19
HD9696.C63 L387 1986 *NYPL [JLD 86-3043]*

Trade and investment in Zimbabwe. Whitsun Foundation. Project 1.07 . Harare, Zimbabwe [1983?] 2 v. ; ISBN 0-7974-0597-6 LC Card 84-981092 DDC 380.1/096891 19
HF3902 .W48 1983 *NYPL [JLM 87-272]*

TRADE AND PROFESSIONAL ASSOCIATIONS - AUSTRIA.
Traxler, Franz. Interessenverbände der Unternehmer . Frankfurt am Main , New York , c1986. xv, 410 p. ; ISBN 3-593-33584-0 LC Card 86-156435
HD2429.A9 T73 1986

TRADE AND PROFESSIONAL ASSOCIATIONS - BRAZIL, NORTHEAST.
Dabat, Christine. As mulheres nas organizações profissionais /. Recife , 1985. 21 p. ; LC Card 86-177927
HD2429.B6 D33 1985

TRADE AND PROFESSIONAL ASSOCIATIONS - DENMARK.
Due, Jesper. Hva' nu Larsen . [Copenhagen] , c1984. 152 p. ; ISBN 87-574-4410-2 : LC Card 84-229467
HD2429.D4 D84 1984

TRADE AND PROFESSIONAL ASSOCIATIONS - GERMANY - HISTORY.
Vereinswesen und bürgerliche Gesellschaft in Deutschland /. München , 1984. 180 p. ; ISBN 3-486-52081-4 LC Card 84-205111
HD2429.G3 V46 1984

TRADE AND PROFESSIONAL ASSOCIATIONS - GERMANY, WEST.
Mühlfeld, Claus, 1940- Konflikt und Kooperation in Arbeitgeberverbänden /. Augsburg , 1985. 403 p. ; ISBN 3-87512-138-4 : LC Card 86-152717
HD2429.G3 M84 1985

TRADE AND PROFESSIONAL ASSOCIATIONS - GREAT BRITAIN - DIRECTORIES.
Trade associations and professional bodies of the United Kingdom /. Oxford , New York , 1987. vii, 513 p. ; ISBN 0-08-033390-7 LC Card 87-132682 DDC 062/.025 19
HD2429.G7 T73 1987

TRADE AND PROFESSIONAL ASSOCIATIONS - JAPAN.
Lynn, Leonard H. Organizing business . Washington, D.C. , c1988. xviii, 191 p. ; ISBN 0-8447-3629-5 (alk. paper) LC Card 87-17468 DDC 061/.3 19
HD2425 .L96 1988

TRADE AND PROFESSIONAL ASSOCIATIONS - MEXICO.
Cleaves, Peter S. Professions and the state . Tucson , c1987. xv, 147 p. : ISBN 0-8165-1016-4 (alk. paper) LC Card 87-5911 DDC 331.7/12/0972 19
HD8038.M6 C55 1987

TRADE AND PROFESSIONAL ASSOCIATIONS - POLAND - HISTORY.
Ajzner, Seweryn. Związek Związków Zawodowych, 1931-1939 /. Warszawa , 1979. 458 p. ; LC Card 81-172691
HD8537.Z873 A38 1979

TRADE AND PROFESSIONAL ASSOCIATIONS - SPAIN.
Pascual, Julio, 1944- En defensa de la empresa . Madrid , c1984. 242 p. ; ISBN 84-7209-175-9 LC Card 85-215607
HD3616.S49 P34 1984 *NYPL [JLD 87-1507]*

TRADE AND PROFESSIONAL ASSOCIATIONS - SWITZERLAND - POLITICAL ACTIVITY.
Farago, Peter. Verbände als Träger öffentlicher Politik . Grüsch , c1987. xi, 185 p. : ISBN 3-7253-0290-1 LC Card 87-140606 DDC 322/.3/09494 19
HD2429.S92 F37 1987

Wirtschaftsverbände in der Schweiz . Grüsch , c1986. xv, 294 p. : ISBN 3-7253-0260-X : LC Card 86-136455 DDC 322/.3/09494 19
HD2429.S92 W57 1986 *NYPL [JLD 86-2919]*

TRADE AND PROFESSIONAL ASSOCIATIONS - UNITED STATES.
The Corporate view . Washington, DC , c1982. vii, 92 p. ; *NYPL [JLF 87-940]*

Lynn, Leonard H. Organizing business . Washington, D.C. , c1988. xviii, 191 p. ; ISBN 0-8447-3629-5 (alk. paper) LC Card 87-17468 DDC 061/.3 19
HD2425 .L96 1988

TRADE AND PROFESSIONAL ASSOCIATIONS - UNITED STATES - DIRECTORIES.
A Tribute to small business . [Washington, D.C.] , San Francisco , c1987. 72 p. : LC Card 87-403591 DDC 338.6/42 19
HD2346.U5 T75 1987

Trade associations and professional bodies of the United Kingdom / edited by Patricia Millard. 8th ed. (rev. and enl.). Oxford ; New York : Pergamon Press, 1987. vii, 513 p. ; 24 cm. Includes indexes. ISBN 0-08-033390-7 LC Card 87-132682 DDC 062/.025 19
1. Trade and professional associations - Great Britain - Directories. I. Millard, Patricia.
HD2429.G7 T73 1987

TRADE, BALANCE OF. see **BALANCE OF TRADE.**

TRADE BARRIERS. see **COMMERCIAL POLICY.**

The trade card in nineteenth-century America /. Jay, Robert. Columbia , 1987. 112 p. : ISBN 0-8262-0619-0 (alk. paper) LC Card 86-30902 DDC 769.5 19
HF5851 .J39 1987

Trade card in 19th-century America. Jay, Robert. The trade card in nineteenth-century America /. Columbia , 1987. 112 p. : ISBN 0-8262-0619-0 (alk. paper) LC Card 86-30902 DDC 769.5 19
HF5851 .J39 1987

Trade catalogs in the Hagley Museum and Library /. Hagley Museum and Library. Wilmington, Del. , 1987. 104 p. : ISBN 0-914650-26-2 (pbk.) LC Card 87-146349 DDC 016.3801/029/4 19
HF5861 .H234 1987

The Trade deficit in manufactured goods : effects on industrial construction / prepared by the Basic Industries Sector Group, International Trade Administration, U. S. Department of Commerce. [Washington] : The Administration ; Washington, D.C. : For sale by Supt. of Docs., U. S. G.P.O., [1986] vi, 79 p. : ill. ; 28 cm. "January 1986." Bibliography: p. 74-76. LC Card 86-601142 DDC 382/.4567/0973 19
1. United States - Manufactures - Capital investments. 2. Industrial buildings - United States - Finance. 3. Balance of trade - United States. I. United States. International Trade Administration. Basic Industries Sector.
HD9725 .T73 1986

Trade deficit of the 1980's. Carvounis, Chris C. The United States trade deficit of the 1980s . New York , 1987. vi, 190 p. ; ISBN 0-89930-219-X (lib. bdg. : alk. paper) LC Card 87-2561 DDC 382.1/7/0973 19
HF3031 .C37 1987

Trade, development and the world economy . Díaz Alejandro, Carlos Federico. Oxford, OX, UK , New York, NY, USA , 1988. p. cm. ISBN 0-631-15687-9 : LC Card 87-20836 DDC 337.8 19
HF1480.5 .D52 1988

TRADE FAIRS. see **FAIRS.**

Trade friction and economic policy : problems and prospects for Japan and the United States / edited by Ryuzo Sato and Paul Wachtel. Cambridge [Cambridgeshire] ; New York : Cambridge University Press, 1987. xii, 243 p. : ill. ; 24 cm. Includes bibliographies and index. ISBN 0-521-34446-8 LC Card 87-11694 DDC 382/.0952/073 19
1. Japan - Commerce - United States. 2. United States - Commerce - Japan. 3. Japan - Economic policy - 1945-. 4. United States - Economic policy - 1981-. I. Satō, Ryūzō, 1931-. II. Wachtel, Paul.
HF3828.U5 T73 1987

The Trade gap : regaining the competitive edge / prepared by the Public Agenda Foundation. Dayton, Ohio (100 Commons Rd., Dayton 45459-2777) : Domestic Policy Association, c1987. 35 p. : ill. (some col.) ; 28 cm. (National issues forums) Bibliography: p. 34. LC Card 87-71294 DDC 382.1/7/0973 19
1. Balance of trade - United States. 2. United States - Commerce. 3. Competition, International. I. Public Agenda Foundation. II. Series.
HF3031 .T7 1987

Trade in services : exports and foreign revenues : special report. Washington, D.C. : Congress of the U. S., Office of Technology Assessment : For sale by the Supt. of Docs., U. S. G.P.O., [1986] viii, 102 p. : ill. ; 26 cm. "September 1986"--P. [4] of cover. Includes bibliographical references. "OTA-ITE-316"--P. [4] of cover. LC Card 86-600576 DDC 382/.45/000973 19
1. Service industries - United States. 2. United States - Commerce. 3. Balance of trade - United States. I. United States. Congress. Office of Technology Assessment.
HD9981.5 .T7 1986

TRADE JOURNALISM. see **JOURNALISM, COMMERCIAL.**

Trade liberalization experience in the Philippines, 1960-84 /. Alburo, Florian A. Makati, Metro Manila [1985] 159 p. : LC Card 87-167251 DDC 382/.09599/0021 19
HF1599 .A43 1985

Trade liberalization in Sri Lanka /. Lal, Deepak. Aldershop, Hants, England , Brookfield, Vt. , 1988. p. cm. ISBN 0-566-05340-3 : LC Card 87-15044 DDC 382/.3/095493 19
HF1586.8 .L35 1988

Trade policies for a better future : the Leutwiler report, the GATT, and the Uruguay Round / with an introduction by Arthur Dunkel. Dordrecht ; Boston : M. Nijhoff ; vii, 174 p. : ill. ; 25 cm. Revision and expansion of: Trade policies for a better future. 1985. Bibliography: p. 173-174. ISBN 0-89838-925-9 LC Card 87-22126 DDC 382.9/2 19
1. Commercial policy. 2. Tariff. 3. General Agreement on Tariffs and Trade (Organization). I. Dunkel, Arthur, 1932-.
HF1411 .T712 1987

Trade policy and U. S. competitiveness / edited by Claude E. Barfield and John H. Makin. Washington, D.C. : American Enterprise Institute for Public Policy Research ; Lanham, Md. : Distributed by arrangement with UPA, c1987. xvi, 144 p. ; 24 cm. ISBN 0-8447-3633-3 (alk. paper) LC Card 87-18831 DDC 382/.3/0973 19
1. United States - Commercial policy. 2. Competition - United States. 3. Competition, International. I. Barfield, Claude E. II. Makin, John H. III. Title: Trade policy and US competitiveness.
HF1455 .T65 1987

Trade policy and US competitiveness. Trade policy and U. S. competitiveness /. Washington, D.C. , Lanham, Md. , c1987. xvi, 144 p. ; ISBN 0-8447-3633-3 (alk. paper) LC Card 87-18831 DDC 382/.3/0973 19
HF1455 .T65 1987

Trade policy, protectionism, and the Third World /. Davenport, Michael, 1940- London , Dover, N.H. , c1986. 152 p. : ISBN 0-7099-4516-7 : LC Card 86-6192 DDC 382.7/53 19
HF2039.5.Z7 D38 1986 *NYPL [JLD 86-2759]*

Trade Policy Research Centre.
East African lessons on economic liberalization /. Aldershot, Hampshire, U.K. ; Brookfield, Vt., U. S.A. : xxi, 72 p. : ISBN 0-566-05337-3 (pbk.) : LC Card 86-29602 DDC 338.967 19
HC865 .E27 1987

Hayes, J. P. (John Philip), 1924- Economic effects of sanctions on southern Africa /. Aldershot, Hampshire, England , Brookfield, Vt., USA , 1987. xii, 100 p. : ISBN 0-566-05539-2 (pbk.) : LC Card 87-11674 DDC 337.68 19
HF1413.5 .H39 1987

Hillman, Jimmye S., 1923- Agricultural trade and protection in Japan /. Aldershot, Hants, England , Brookfield, Vt. , 1988. p. cm. ISBN 0-566-05339-X : LC Card 87-15043 DDC 382.7/3/0952 19
HD9016.J42 H55 1988

Pryke, Richard. Competition among international airlines /. Aldershot , Brookfield, USA , 1987. xi, 113 p. : ISBN 0-566-05333-0 : LC Card 86-31877 DDC 387.7/1 19
HE9780 .P79 1987

Riedel, James. Myths and reality of external constraints on development /. Aldershot, Hampshire, U.K. , Brookfield, Vt., USA , 1987. xvi, 111 p. : ISBN 0-566-05336-5 (pbk.) : LC Card 86-31801 DDC 330.9172/4 19
HC59.7 .R494 1987

TRADE PREFERENCES. see **TARIFF PREFERENCES.**

Trade price list . H.W. Johns Manufacturing Co. New York , c1898. 15 p. ; LC Card 86-223003
HD9715.8.U52 H14 1898

TRADE REGULATION - ADDRESSES, ESSAYS, LECTURES.
Hundert Jahre Rechts- und Wirtschaftsgeschichte an der Rechts-, Wirtschafts- und Sozialwissenschaftlichen Fakultät der Universität Freiburg =. Freiburg, Schweiz , 1982. 96 p., [6] p. of plates : ISBN 3-7278-0277-4 : LC Card 83-108855 DDC 340 19
K296 .H86 1982 ***NYPL [JLD 86-676]***

TRADE REGULATION - CONGRESSES.
Innovation and entrepreneurship in organizations . Amsterdam ; New York : vii, 207 p. : ISBN 0-444-42716-3 (U. S.) : LC Card 86-24207 DDC 658.4/012 19
HD41 .I56 1986

Mainstreams in industrial organization /. Dordrecht , Boston , 1986. 2 v. (x, 465 p.) ; ISBN 90-247-3363-4 LC Card 86-12345 DDC 338.6 19
HD29 .M25 1986 ***NYPL [JLE 87-457]***

Public regulation . Cambridge, Mass. , c1987. xiv, 404 p. ; ISBN 0-262-02258-3 LC Card 86-21302 DDC 338.973 19
HD3616.U47 P83 1987

TRADE REGULATION - ECONOMIC ASPECTS - MATHEMATICAL MODELS.
Besanko, David, 1955- Designing regulatory policy with limited information /. Chur, Switzerland , New York , c1987. viii, 80 p. : ISBN 3-7186-0385-3 (pbk.) LC Card 87-277 DDC 351.82/6 19
HD3612 .B47 1987

TRADE REGULATION - GERMANY - HISTORY - 20TH CENTURY.
Holzwarth, Fritz. Ordnung der Wirtschaft durch Wettbewerb . Freiburg im Breisgau , c1985. 217 p. ; ISBN 3-448-01510-5 LC Card 86-109043
HB95 .H65 1985

TRADE REGULATION - GERMANY, WEST.
Soltwedel, Rüdiger. Deregulierungspotentiale in der Bundesrepublik /. Tübingen , c1986. xi, 326 p. ; ISBN 3-16-345145-4 (Deut. Bibl. : pbk.) LC Card 87-408380 DDC 338.6/048 19
HD3616.G4 S665 1986

TRADE REGULATION - GERMANY (WEST) - CASE STUDIES.
Vogelsang, Ingo. Anreizmechanismen zur Regulierung der Elektrizitätswirtschaft . Tübingen , 1982. xii, 173 p. : ISBN 3-16-344549-7 : LC Card 83-153444
HD9685.G3 V64 1982

TRADE REGULATION - SAUDI ARABIA.
A Guide to industrial investment /. Riyadh , 1986. vi, 286 p., [4] leaves of plates : LC Card 87-400301 DDC 332.6/7322538 19
HC415.33.Z9 I534 1986

TRADE REGULATION - SWITZERLAND.
Weber, Rolf H. Wirtschaftsregulierung in wettbewerbspolitischen Ausnahmebereichen . Baden-Baden , 1986. 710 p. : ISBN 3-7890-1288-2 LC Card 87-128141
HD3616.S93 W425 1986

TRADE REGULATION - UNITED STATES.
Adams, Walter, 1922 (Aug. 27)- The bigness complex . New York , 1986. xiii, 426 p. ; ISBN 0-394-54721-7 : LC Card 86-42624 DDC 338.6/44/0973 19
HD2785 .A68 1986 ***NYPL [JLE 87-1432]***

Bain, Joe Staten, 1912- Industrial organization . Greenwich, Conn. , c1987. 2 v. ; ISBN 0-89232-702-2 (set) LC Card 87-2618 DDC 338.6 19
HD2326 .B34 1987

Chamber of Commerce of the United States of America. Council on Trends and Perspective. Government regulation of business . Washington, D.C. , c1979. x, 108 p. ; ISBN 0-89834-018-7(pbk.) : LC Card 79-91604 DDC 338.973
HD3616.U46 C44 1979
NYPL [JLE 80-2446]

Dunfee, Thomas W. Legal aspects of government regulation of business /. New York , c1984. viii, 335 p. ; ISBN 0-471-87029-3 (pbk.) : LC Card 83-21879 DDC 346.73/07 347.3067 19
KF1600 .D86 1984 ***NYPL [JLE 86-3511]***

Goodman, Marshall R. Managing regulatory reform . New York , 1987. xvi, 236 p. : ISBN 0-275-92472-5 (alk. paper) : LC Card 87-2436 DDC 338.973 19
HD3616.U47 G67 1987

Howell, Rate A. The legal environment of business /. Chicago , c1987. xiv, 783 p. : ISBN 0-03-008369-9 LC Card 86-4503 DDC 346.73/07 347.3067 19
KF1600 .H68 1987 ***NYPL [JLE 87-911]***

Issues after a century of federal competition policy /. Lexington, Mass. , c1987. vii, 387 p. ; ISBN 0-669-13320-5 (alk. paper) LC Card 86-45377 DDC 338.6/048/0973 19
HD3616.U47 I77 1987

Kettl, Donald F. Government by proxy . Washington, D.C. , c1988. x, 170 p. ; ISBN 0-87187-429-6 (pbk.) : LC Card 87-13645 DDC 353.009 19
HD3861.U6 K47 1988

Leone, Robert A. Who profits . New York , 1986. xiii, 248 p. ; ISBN 0-465-09183-0 : LC Card 85-47992 DDC 338.973 19
HD3616.U47 L44 1986
NYPL [JLD 86-2410]

McAdams, Tony. Law, business, and society /. Plano, Tex. , 1986. xvi, 662, 52 p. : ISBN 0-256-03070-7 LC Card 85-73323 DDC 346.73/065 347.30665 19
KF1355 .M28 1986 ***NYPL [JLE 87-891]***

Oster, Sharon. The strategic use of regulatory investment by industry sub-groups [microform] . New Haven, Ct. , 1980. 39 p. ;
NYPL [*XME-11,347]

Weber, Rolf H. Wirtschaftsregulierung in wettbewerbspolitischen Ausnahmebereichen . Baden-Baden , 1986. 710 p. : ISBN 3-7890-1288-2 LC Card 87-128141
HD3616.S93 W425 1986

TRADE REGULATION - UNITED STATES - CONGRESSES.
Public regulation . Cambridge, Mass. , c1987. xiv, 404 p. ; ISBN 0-262-02258-3 LC Card 86-21302 DDC 338.973 19
HD3616.U47 P83 1987

TRADE REGULATION - UNITED STATES - PUBLIC OPINION.
Lipset, Seymour Martin. The confidence gap . Baltimore , 1987. xxiv, 460 p. : ISBN 0-8018-3044-3 (pbk.) LC Card 86-27416 DDC 303.3/8/0973 19
HD2785 .L53 1987

Reinarman, Craig. American states of mind . New Haven , c1987. x, 262 p. ; ISBN 0-300-03817-8 (alk. paper) LC Card 86-26752 DDC 330.12/2/0973 19
HD3616.U47 R1464 1987

Trade report (Hawaii. International Services Branch) .
(no. 57) Hawaii's trade with Taiwan, 1976-1985 /. Honolulu, Hawaii (P.O. Box 2359, Honolulu 96804) [1986] 18 p. ; LC Card 86-622297 DDC 382/.09969/051249021 19
HF3161.H3 H378 1986

(no. 58) Hawaii's trade with Japan, 1976-1985 /. Honolulu, Hawaii (P.O. Box 2359, Honolulu 96804) [1986] 20 p. : LC Card 86-623207 DDC 382/.09969/052 19
HF3161.H3 H38733 1986

(no. 59) Hawaii's trade with New Zealand, 1976-1985 /. Honolulu, Hawaii (P.O. Box 2359, Honolulu 96804) [1986] 14 p. : LC Card 87-620878 DDC 382/.09931/0969021 19
HF3161.H3 H3878 1986

TRADE, RESTRAINT OF. see **RESTRAINT OF TRADE.**

TRADE ROUTES - PANANA - CANAL ZONE - HISTORY.
Castillero Calvo, Alfredo, 1937- La ruta transístmica y las comunicaciones marítimas hispanas, siglos XVI a XIX /. Panamá , 1984. 35 p. ; LC Card 84-219993
HE326 .C37 1984

TRADE ROUTES - SECURITY MEASURES.
Sea lane security studies . Taipei, Taiwan, Republic of China , 1986. 100 p. ; LC Card 87-133640 DDC 359/.03 19
HE327 .S435 1986

Trade routes to sustained economic growth . Tokyo Trade Symposium (1985) New York , 1987. lii, 178 p. ; ISBN 0-312-01263-2 : LC Card 87-3494 DDC 382 19
HF1411 .T577 1985

Trade union action to stop oil to South Africa /. Turner, Terisa. Port Harcourt , c1985. v, 35 p. ; LC Card 87-673464
HF1613.4 .T87x 1985

Trade Union Congress. see **Trades Union Congress.**

The trade union directory . Eaton, Jack. London , 1981. xii, 323 p. ; ISBN 0-86104-350-2 (pbk.) LC Card 86-673635
HD6663 .E27x 1981

Trade union handbook . Marsh, Arthur Ivor. Aldershot, Hants, England , 1984. x, 415 p. : ISBN 0-566-02426-8 : LC Card 84-236090 DDC 331.88/0941 19
HD6663 .M37 1984
NYPL [*R-Econ. 86-3335]

Trade union handbook . Marsh, Arthur Ivor. Aldershot, Hants, England , Brookfield, Vt., U. S.A. , c1988. x, 387 p. : ISBN 0-566-02749-6 : LC Card 87-13408 DDC 331.88/0941 19
HD6663 .M37 1988

The trade union response to technological change in Australia /. Markey, Ray. Kensington, N.S.W. , 1983. iii, 56 p. ;
NYPL [JLE 87-904]

The Trade union situation and industrial relations in Austria : report of an ILO mission. Geneva : International Labour Office, 1986. xiii, 107 p. ; 24 cm. Includes bibliographies. ISBN 92-2-105659-7 (pbk.) : LC Card 87-123441 DDC 331/.09436 19
1. Trade-unions - Austria. 2. Industrial relations - Austria. I. International Labour Office.
HD6674 .T72 1986

The Trade union situation and industrial relations in Hungary : report of an ILO mission. Geneva : International Labour Office, 1984. 100 p. ; 24 cm. Includes bibliographies. ISBN 92-2-103894-7
1. Trade-unions - Hungary. 2. Industrial relations - Hungary. I. International Labor Office.
NYPL [JLE 85-1780]

The Trade union situation and industrial relations in Spain : report of an ILO mission. Geneva : International Labour Office, 1985. xiii, 138 p. : ill. ; 25 cm. Includes bibliographical references. ISBN 92-2-105202-8 (pbk.) : LC Card 86-207841 DDC 331.88/0946 19
1. Trade-unions - Spain. 2. Industrial relations - Spain. I. International Labour Office.
HD6762 .T68 1985

Trade union situations in PTT services. Matthew, J. Purchasing power of PTT personnel, 1965 /. Brussels [1966] 1 v. (various pagings) ; LC Card 87-165119
HE6241 .M37 1966

Trade unionism and politics in Niger. Martens, George R. Lome, Togo [1986] 93 p. ; LC Card

86-172446 DDC 322/.2/09669 19
HD6882.Z65 M37 1986

Trade unionism in civil services . Saxena, Pradeep. Jaipur , 1986. ii, 164 p. ; LC Card 86-903231 DDC 331.88/11354544 19
HD8005.2.I523 R347 1986

Trade unionism in the republic of Mali : case study. [Lome, Togo] : Regional Economic Research and Documentation Center, [1983] 78 p. : ill. ; 30 cm. Cover title. "A special issue of Labor and development, July 1983." Bibliography: p. 68-78.
LC Card 87-107028 DDC 331.88/0966/23 19
1. Union nationale des travailleurs du Mali - History. 2. Trade-unions - Mali - History. I. Centre régional d'études et de documentation économiques. II. Labor and development. Special issue.
HD8827.A5 U557 1983

TRADE-UNIONS - AFRICA.
African-American Labor Center. African-American Labor Center, 1965-1970 [microform]. New York, N.Y. [1970] 16 p. : *NYPL [*ZT-1646 no.23]*

Geiss, Imanuel. Gewerkschaften in Afrika /. Hannover , 1965. 233 p. : LC Card 85-125305
HD6857 .G45 1965

Labour and unions in Asia and Africa /. New York , 1987. p. cm. ISBN 0-312-01362-0 : LC Card 87-21475 DDC 331.88/095 19
HD6796 .L3 1987

TRADE-UNIONS - AGRICULTURAL LABORERS - CHILE.
Cruz, María Elena. Chile--opciones y desafíos del sindicalismo rural, 1973-1985 /. Santiago, Chile , 1985. 57 p. ; LC Card 87-100897
HD6619.A29 C78 1985

TRADE-UNIONS - AGRICULTURAL LABORERS - GERMANY (WEST) - OSTHOLSTEIN - HISTORY.
Rüdel, Holger. Landarbeiter und Sozialdemokratie in Ostholstein, 1872 bis 1878 . Neumünster , 1986. 581 p. ; ISBN 3-529-02909-2 LC Card 87-119718 DDC 331.88/13/0943512 19
HD6699.O88 R83 1986

TRADE-UNIONS - AGRICULTURAL LABORERS - GERMANY (WEST) - OSTHOLSTEIN - ORGANIZING - HISTORY.
Rüdel, Holger. Landarbeiter und Sozialdemokratie in Ostholstein, 1872 bis 1878 . Neumünster , 1986. 581 p. ; ISBN 3-529-02909-2 LC Card 87-119718 DDC 331.88/13/0943512 19
HD6699.O88 R83 1986

TRADE-UNIONS - AGRICULTURAL LABORERS - SPAIN - HISTORY.
Biglino Campos, Paloma. El socialismo español y la cuestión agraria (1890-1936) /. Madrid [1986?] 564 p. ; ISBN 84-7434-368-2 LC Card 87-136300
HD6764.A29 B54 1986

TRADE UNIONS AND BOLSHEVISM. see **TRADE-UNIONS AND COMMUNISM.**

TRADE-UNIONS AND CHRISTIANITY.
Markiewicz, Stanisław. Chrześcijaństwo a związki zawodowe /. Warszawa , 1985. 618 p. : ISBN 83-202-0352-X (pbk.) : *NYPL [*QO 86-2625]*

TRADE-UNIONS AND CHRISTIANITY - GERMANY - HISTORY.
Roder, Hartmut, 1951- Der christlich-nationale Deutsche Gewerkschaftsbund (DGB) im politisch-ökonomischen Kräftefeld der Weimarer Republik . Frankfurt am Main , New York , c1986. 804 p. : ISBN 3-8204-9325-5 LC Card 86-194815
HD8443.D457 R63 1986

TRADE-UNIONS AND COMMUNISM - BULGARIA - GABROVSKI OKRŬG - HISTORY.
Revoli͡ut͡sionnoto profsi͡uzno dvizhenie v Gabrovski okrŭg /. Sofii͡a , 1986. 305 p., [16] p. of plates : LC Card 86-232088
HD6785.G32 R48 1986

TRADE-UNIONS AND COMMUNISM - BULGARIA - HISTORY.
Vŭznikvane, razvitie i zalez na oporti͡unizma v bŭlgarskoto rabotnichesko dvizhenie, 1891/1948 /. Sofii͡a , 1986. 696 p. ; LC Card 86-200229
HD8628 .V89 1986

TRADE-UNIONS AND COMMUNISM - GERMANY (EAST) - CONGRESSES.
Kolloquium zur Gewerkschaftlichen Interessenvertretung beim Umfassenden Aufbau des Sozialismus in der Deutschen Demokratischen Republik (1964) Protokoll über das Kolloquium zur Gewerkschaftlichen Interessenvertretung beim Umfassenden Aufbau des Sozialismus in der Deutschen Demokratischen Republik am 31. Januar 1964. [Bernau] [1964] iv, 246 p. ; LC Card 85-125499
HD6700.5 .K65 1964

TRADE-UNIONS AND COMMUNISM - HISTORY - 20TH CENTURY.
Mezhdunarodnoe rabochee dvizhenie . Moskva , 1980. 412 p. ; LC Card 81-143888
HD4854 .M474 1980

TRADE-UNIONS AND COMMUNISM - ITALY.
Salvadori, Massimo L., 1908- Eurocomunismo e socialismo sovietico . Torino , 1978. xxvii, 161 p. ; LC Card 80-497655 DDC 324.245075 19
JN5657.C63 S24 *NYPL [JLC 81-75]*

TRADE-UNIONS AND COMMUNISM - MEXICO.
Iglesias, Severo. Sindicalismo y socialismo en México /. México, D.F. , 1985,c19. 194 p. ; ISBN 968-419-418-8 *NYPL [JLC 86-406]*

TRADE-UNIONS AND COMMUNISM - UNITED STATES.
Boulware, Lemuel Richetts, 1895- What to do about communism in unions . [Schenectady, N.Y.?] [1952?] 62 p. ; *NYPL [JLD 86-247]*

TRADE-UNIONS AND COMMUNISM - UNITED STATES - HISTORY - CASE STUDIES.
Halpern, Martin, 1945- UAW politics in the cold war era/. Albany, N.Y. , c1988. p. cm. ISBN 0-88706-671-2 LC Card 87-13890 DDC 322/.2/0973 19
HD6515.A82 I574 1988

Trade unions and democracy : a seminar held in Kingston, Jamaica, February 28-29, 1986. [Kingston, Jamaica] : Bustamante Institute of Public & International Affairs, [1986] iii, 52 p. : ill. ; 21 cm. Cover title: Trade unions & democracy. "May 1986." "First Seminar on Trade Unions and Democracy in Kingston from February 27 to 29"--Foreword. LC Card 87-133832 DDC 322/.2/09729 19
1. Trade-unions - Caribbean Area - Congresses. 2. Democracy - Congresses. I. Bustamante Institute of Public and International Affairs. II. Seminar on Trade Unions and Democracy (1st : 1986 : Kingston, Jamaica). III. Title: Trade unions & democracy.
HD6571 .T72 1986

Trade unions & democracy. Trade unions and democracy . [Kingston, Jamaica] [1986] iii, 52 p. : LC Card 87-133832 DDC 322/.2/09729 19
HD6571 .T72 1986

TRADE-UNIONS AND FASCISM - GERMANY - HISTORY - 20TH CENTURY.
40 Jahre danach . Frankfurt/Main , 1985. 96 p. ; ISBN 3-88367-060-X : LC Card 86-109007 DDC 322/.2/0943 19
HD6490.F582 G316 1985

TRADE-UNIONS AND FOREIGN POLICY - GERMANY - HISTORY - 20TH CENTURY.
40 Jahre danach . Frankfurt/Main , 1985. 96 p. ; ISBN 3-88367-060-X : LC Card 86-109007 DDC 322/.2/0943 19
HD6490.F582 G316 1985

Trade unions and politics /. Coates, Ken. Oxford, OX, UK , New York, NY, USA , 1986. ix, 268 p. : ISBN 0-631-13752-1 : LC Card 85-22959 DDC 322/.2/0941 19
HD6667 .C63 1986 *NYPL [JLE 86-1729]*

Trade unions and politics in the 1980s . Fatchett, D. J. (Derek John), 1945- London , New York , c1987. p. cm. ISBN 0-7099-4903-0 LC Card 87-14092 DDC 322/.2/0941 19
HD6667 .F37 1987

Trade unions and the economic crisis of the 1980s / edited by William Brierley. Aldershot, Hants, England ; Brookfield, Vt., U. S.A. : Gower, c1987. x, 210 p. ; 23 cm. Includes bibliographies. CONTENTS. - Trade unions, industrial change, and the effects of recession in West Germany and the United Kingdom / by Rob Atkinson -- Italian trade unions / by Bill Brierley / Labour confederations and socialist governments in France, 1981-1986 / by Jeff Bridgford and Peter Morris / Trade unions and industrial relations in Spain / by Richard Hawkesworth and Lluis Fina / Trade unions and economic crisis in Poland / by Frances Millard / Reality versus theory in the Yugoslav self-management system / by Mica Jovanovic / Economic crisis and stability of employment in the Brazilian motor industry / by John Humphrey / Labour, the oil boom and economic recession in Ecuador / by David Corkill / Trade unionism on the periphery / by Gail Martin / The crisis of trade unionism in Turkey / Hüseyin Ramazanoglu / South Africa in crisis / by Mark Mitchell and Dave Russell. ISBN 0-566-05245-8 :
LC Card 86-25641 DDC 331.88/094 19
1. Trade-unions - Economic aspects - Europe. 2. Europe - Economic conditions - 20th century. 3. Trade-unions - Economic aspects - Developing countries. 4. Developing countries - Economic conditions. I. Brierley, William, 1951-.
HD6657 .T68 1987

Trade unions and the state in the present day Chile . Barrera, Manuel. Geneva, Switzerland , Santiago, Chile , 1986. xx, 154 p. : LC Card 87-128364 DDC 331.89/0983 19
HD6617 .B273 1986

TRADE-UNIONS - ARGENTINA - CONGRESSES.
La Clase obrera argentina . Buenos Aires , 1986. 136 p. ; LC Card 86-206788
HD8266.5 .C57 1986

TRADE-UNIONS - ARGENTINA - DIRECTORIES.
Guía de organizaciones gremiales, 1984 /. Capital Federal, República Argentina [between 1984 and 1986] [12], 651 p. : LC Card 87-123823 DDC 331.88/025/82 19
HD6601.5 .G85 1984

TRADE-UNIONS - ARGENTINA - HISTORY.
Cornblit, Oscar. Sindicatos obreros y asociaciones empresarias hasta la década del centenario /. Buenos Aires, Argentina , 1984. 109 p. ; LC Card 87-401262 DDC 331.88/0982 19
HD6602 .C665 1984

Falcón, Ricardo. El mundo del trabajo urbano, 1890-1914 /. Buenos Aires , c1986. 141 p. ; ISBN 950-25-1414-2 : LC Card 87-101423
HD8266 .F35 1986

TRADE-UNIONS - ARGENTINA - HISTORY - 20TH CENTURY.
Isuani, Ernesto A. (Ernesto Aldo) Los orígenes conflictivos de la seguridad social argentina /. Buenos Aires , c1985. 140 p. ; ISBN 950-25-0128-4 : LC Card 86-174656
HD7149 .I88 1985

TRADE-UNIONS - ARGENTINA - OFFICIALS AND EMPLOYEES - POLITICAL ACTIVITY - HISTORY.
Fernández, Arturo. Ideologías de los grupos dirigentes sindicales /. Buenos Aires , c1986. 2 v. ; ISBN 950-25-1403-3 (v. 1) LC Card 86-205687
HD6603.5 .F47 1986

TRADE-UNIONS - ARGENTINA - ROSARIO (SANTA FE)
Balvé, Beba. De protesta a rebelión--la "subversión" (Rosario, mayo 1969) /. Buenos Aires, Argentina [1985] xvii, 123 p. ; LC Card 86-162379
HD5350.R67 B35 1985

TRADE-UNIONS - ASIA.
Labour and unions in Asia and Africa /. New York , 1987. p. cm. ISBN 0-312-01362-0 : LC Card 87-21475 DDC 331.88/095 19
HD6796 .L3 1987

TRADE-UNIONS - AUSTRALIA.
Ewer, Peter. Unions and the future of Australian manufacturing /. Sydney , Boston , 1987. xi, 189 p. : ISBN 0-04-330382-X (pbk.) LC Card 87-164410 DDC 338.4/767/0994 19
HD9738.A82 E93 1987

Markey, Ray. The trade union response to technological change in Australia /. Kensington, N.S.W. , 1983. iii, 56 p. ; *NYPL [JLE 87-904]*

TRADE-UNIONS - AUSTRALIA - DARWIN (N.T.) - HISTORY - 20TH CENTURY.
Alcorta, F. X. (Frank X.) Darwin Rebellion, 1911-1919 /. [Darwin, N.T.] , 1984. xiv, 115 p., [8] p. of plates : ISBN 0-7245-0492-3 : LC

Card 84-220611 DDC 331.89/294295 19
HD5450.Z9 D373 1984 ***NYPL [JLF 87-405]***

TRADE-UNIONS - AUSTRALIA - DIRECTORIES.
Rawson, Donald William. Australian unions, 1984 /. Sydney , c1985. 123 p. ; ISBN 0-949614-13-0 LC Card 85-169297 DDC 331.88/025/94 19
HD6891 .R35 1985 ***NYPL [JLD 86-1566]***

TRADE-UNIONS - AUSTRALIA - HISTORY.
Merritt, John. The making of the AWU /. Melbourne , New York , 1986. x, 432 p., [16] p. of plates : ISBN 0-19-554667-9 LC Card 86-207509 DDC 331.88/13630833/0994 19
HD8842.A874 M47 1986

TRADE-UNIONS - AUSTRALIA - HISTORY - SOURCES.
Hagan, Jim. Australian trade unionism in documents /. Melbourne, Australia , 1986. xvi, 289 p. ; ISBN 0-582-71146-0 (pbk.) LC Card 86-223615 DDC 331.88/0994 19
HD6892 .H34 1986

TRADE-UNIONS - AUSTRALIA - STATISTICS.
Rawson, Donald William. Australian unions, 1984 /. Sydney , c1985. 123 p. ; ISBN 0-949614-13-0 LC Card 85-169297 DDC 331.88/025/94 19
HD6891 .R35 1985 ***NYPL [JLD 86-1566]***

TRADE-UNIONS - AUSTRIA.
The Trade union situation and industrial relations in Austria . Geneva , 1986. xiii, 107 p. ; ISBN 92-2-105659-7 (pbk.) : LC Card 87-123441 DDC 331/.09436 19
HD6674 .T72 1986

TRADE-UNIONS - AUSTRIA - HISTORY - 20TH CENTURY.
Garamvölgyi, Judit. Betriebsräte und sozialer Wandel in Österreich 1919/1920 . München , c1983. 296 p. ; ISBN 3-486-51721-X LC Card 83-240283
HD5660.A8 G37 1983

TRADE-UNIONS - AUSTRIA - POLITICAL ACTIVITY - HISTORY.
Misslbeck, Johannes, 1954- Der Österreichische Gewerkschaftsbund . Frankfurt/M. [1983] iii, 197 p. : ISBN 3-89038-000-X (pbk.) LC Card 84-191049
HD8403 .M57 1983

TRADE-UNIONS - AUSTRIA - VORARLBERG - HISTORY.
Im Prinzip, Hoffnung . Bregenz , c1984. 368 p. : ISBN 3-900438-07-9 LC Card 86-120542 DDC 331.88/09436/45 19
HD6679.V67 I4 1984 ***NYPL [JLD 87-1568]***

TRADE-UNIONS - AUTOMOBILE INDUSTRY WORKERS.
The Automobile industry and its workers . New York , 1987. viii, 335 p. : ISBN 0-312-00553-9 : LC Card 86-29815 DDC 331/.04292 19
HD9710.A2 A865 1987

TRADE-UNIONS - AUTOMOBILE INDUSTRY WORKERS - GERMANY (WEST)
Streeck, Wolfgang, 1946- Industrial relations in West Germany . London , 1984. 178 p. ; ISBN 0-435-83839-3 LC Card 87-673421
HD6698.A8 S77x 1984b

TRADE-UNIONS - AUTOMOBILE INDUSTRY WORKERS - GREAT BRITAIN.
The Car industry . London , New York , 1985. viii, 210 p. : ISBN 0-422-79550-X LC Card 85-14742 DDC 331/.04292/0941 19
HD6976.A82 G72 1985
NYPL [JLD 87-403]

TRADE-UNIONS - BANK EMPLOYEES - GREAT BRITAIN.
Morris, Timothy, 1953- Innovations in banking . London , Wolfeboro, N.H. , c1986. 137 p. : ISBN 0-7099-4607-4 : LC Card 86-13400 DDC 332.1/068/3 19
HG2988 .M675 1986 ***NYPL [JLD 87-81]***

TRADE-UNIONS - BARBADOS - DIRECTORIES.
Blondel, Eaulin. Credit unions, co-operatives, trade unions, and friendly societies in Barbados . St. Augustine, Trinidad, Trinidad and Tobago [1986] v, 102 p. ; LC Card 87-403330 DDC 334/.025/72981 19
HD3464.9.A6 B353 1986

TRADE-UNIONS - BELGIUM.
Arcq, Etienne. La C.S.C. et le programme gouvernemental de mars 1984 /. Bruxelles [1984] 23 leaves ; LC Card 84-171486
HD8502.C62 A73 1984

TRADE-UNIONS - BELGIUM - OFFICIALS AND EMPLOYEES - BIOGRAPHY.
Victor Michel . Bruxelles , c1985. 263 p., [8] p. of plates : ISBN 2-87003-189-0 : LC Card 86-163882
HD6722.5.M52 V52 1985

TRADE-UNIONS - BESSARABIA (MOLDAVIAN S.S.R. AND UKRAINE) - HISTORY.
Burlaku, I. N̦. Sindikatele Moldoveĭ sovetiche yn konstruktsii͡a sochialistė /. Kishinėu , 1980. 148 p. ; LC Card 81-135331
HD6735.M56 B87 1980

TRADE-UNIONS, BLACK - AFRICA.
Geiss, Imanuel. Gewerkschaften in Afrika /. Hannover , 1965. 233 p. : LC Card 85-125305
HD6857 .G45 1965

TRADE-UNIONS, BLACK - SOUTH AFRICA.
African worker under apartheid. Brussels [1984]. 109 p. : ***NYPL [Sc D 86-730]***

Webster, Eddie. Cast in a racial mould . Johannesburg , 1985. xv, 299 p., [8] p. of plates : ISBN 0-86975-285-5
NYPL [JLD 87-780]

TRADE-UNIONS, BLACK - SOUTH AFRICA - CONGRESSES.
Black labor unions in South Africa . Washington, D.C. , 1987. vi, 63 p. ; LC Card 86-600599 DDC 331.6/9/968 19
HD6870.5 .B53 1987

TRADE-UNIONS, BLACK - SOUTH AFRICA - HISTORY.
Bradford, Helen. A taste of freedom . New Haven , 1987. xvi, 364 p., [2] p. of plates : ISBN 0-300-03873-9 LC Card 87-10451 DDC 331.88/0968 19
HD8801.A5 I1634 1987

Webster, Eddie. Cast in a racial mould . Johannesburg , 1985. xv, 299 p., [6] p. of plates : ISBN 0-86975-285-5 (pbk.) : LC Card 86-213551 DDC 331.88/1712/0968 19
HD6870.5.Z7 F758 1985

TRADE-UNIONS - BOLIVIA - HISTORY.
Alvarez España, Waldo. Memorias del primer ministro obrero . La Paz, Bolivia , 1986. 300 p., [6] leaves of plates : LC Card 87-403477 DDC 331.88/0984 19
HD6608.5.A55 A3 1986

TRADE-UNIONS - BOLIVIA - OFFICIALS AND EMPLOYEES - BIOGRAPHY.
Alvarez España, Waldo. Memorias del primer ministro obrero . La Paz, Bolivia , 1986. 300 p., [6] leaves of plates : LC Card 87-403477 DDC 331.88/0984 19
HD6608.5.A55 A3 1986

TRADE-UNIONS - BOLIVIA - POLITICAL ACTIVITY.
Sandoval, Godofredo. Las mil caras del movimiento social boliviano /. La Paz, Bolivia [1986] 132 p. : LC Card 86-227792
HD6608.5 .S25 1986

TRADE-UNIONS - BOLIVIA - POLITICAL ACTIVITY - CONGRESSES.
Tendencias sindicales después del VI Congreso de la C.O.B. /. La Paz , c1985. 111 p. ; LC Card 86-137172
HD8272.C65 T45 1985

TRADE-UNIONS - BRAZIL.
Andrade, Luis F. The labor climate in Brazil /. Philadelphia, Pa. , c1985. viii, 133 p. ; ISBN 0-89546-057-2 (pbk.) LC Card 85-81947 DDC 331/.0981 19
HD8286.5 .A67 1985 ***NYPL [JLF 86-1201]***

Lula, 1945- Lula sem censura . Petrópolis [Brazil] , 1981. 101 p. ; ***NYPL [JLC 86-389]***

State and society in Brazil . Boulder , 1987. x, 349 p. ; ISBN 0-8133-7401-4 (pbk. : alk. paper) : LC Card 87-2160 DDC 981/.063 19
HC187 .S78 1987

TRADE-UNIONS - BRAZIL - HISTORY - PICTORIAL WORKS.
1o. de maio . [São Paulo] , 1985. 80 p. : LC Card 86-200658
HD8286 .A13 1985

TRADE-UNIONS - BRAZIL - POLITICAL ACTIVITY - HISTORY.
Roio, José Luiz del. 1o. de maio /. São Paulo , 1986. 152, [16] p. : LC Card 86-197367
HD7791 .R59 1986

TRADE-UNIONS - BRAZIL - RIO GRANDE DO NORTE - HISTORY - 20TH CENTURY.
Oliveira, Geraldo Sabino de. História do sindicalismo no Rio Grande do Norte /. Natal [Brazil] , 1985. 68 p., [6] leaves of plates : LC Card 87-403987 DDC 331.88/0981/32 19
HD6615.R54 O45 1985

TRADE-UNIONS - BRAZIL - SÃO PAULO (STATE) - DIRECTORIES.
Data-base . [São Paulo] , 1986. 259 p. : LC Card 87-403668 DDC 331.88/025/8161 19
HD6615.S32 D37 1986

Sousa Neto, João Alves de. Manual de orientação sindical urbana e rural . S. [i.e. São] Paulo [1980?] xviii, 190 p. : LC Card 85-200599
HD6615.S32 S68 1980

TRADE-UNIONS - BRICKLAYERS - BOLIVIA - LA PAZ - HISTORY.
Los Constructores de la ciudad . La Paz , 1986. 84 p. : LC Card 86-234740
HD6609.B892 S563 1986

TRADE-UNIONS - BRITISH COLUMBIA - HISTORY - 20TH CENTURY.
Fighting heritage . Vancouver [1986?] 159 p., [32] p. of plates : ISBN 0-9692365-0-6 (pbk.) LC Card 86-231043 DDC 331.88/09711 19
HD8109.B72 F54 1986

TRADE-UNIONS - BRITISH COLUMBIA - JURISDICTIONAL DISPUTES.
Stocks, Alex M. Union raiding . Kingston, Ont., Canada , 1985. 61 p. ; ISBN 0-88886-125-7 (pbk.) LC Card 86-145321 DDC 331.87/09711 19
HD6528.B9 S86 1985 ***NYPL [JLF 87-422]***

TRADE-UNIONS - BUILDING TRADES - CALIFORNIA - SAN FRANCISCO - HISTORY.
Kazin, Michael, 1948- Barons of labor . Urbana , c1987. xiv, 319 p., [14] p. of plates : ISBN 0-252-01345-X (alk. paper) LC Card 86-6967 DDC 331.88/124/0979461 19
HD6515.B9 S45 1987 ***NYPL [JLE 87-1053]***

TRADE-UNIONS - BUILDING TRADES - UNITED STATES.
Silver, Marc L., 1950- Under construction . Albany , c1986. xi, 251 p. ; ISBN 0-88706-308-X LC Card 85-30447 DDC 331.7/624/0973 19
HD6956.B92 U67 1986
NYPL [JLE 86-4616]

TRADE-UNIONS - BULGARIA.
Profsŭi͡uzno stroitelstvo . Sofii͡a , 1985. 310 p. : LC Card 86-209854
HD6782 .P78 1985

TRADE-UNIONS - BULGARIA - DATA PROCESSING.
Zhecheva, Marii͡a. Informat͡sionno osiguri͡avane na profsŭi͡uznite organi . Sofii͡a , 1985. 138 p. : LC Card 86-192068
HD6782 .Z44 1985

TRADE-UNIONS - BULGARIA - GABROVSKI OKRŬG - HISTORY.
Revoli͡ut͡sionnoto profsŭi͡uzno dvizhenie v Gabrovski okrŭg /. Sofii͡a , 1986. 305 p., [16] p. of plates : LC Card 86-232088
HD6785.G32 R48 1986

TRADE-UNIONS - BULGARIA - MANAGEMENT.
Zhecheva, Marii͡a. Informat͡sionno osiguri͡avane na profsŭi͡uznite organi . Sofii͡a , 1985. 138 p. : LC Card 86-192068
HD6782 .Z44 1985

TRADE-UNIONS - BULGARIA - VARNENSKI OKRŬG - HISTORY.
Rabotnicheskoto profsŭi͡uzno dvizhenie vŭv Varnenski okrŭg /. Sofii͡a , 1985. 348 p., [16] p. of plates : LC Card 86-111781
HD8629.V372 R37 1985

TRADE-UNIONS - CALIFORNIA - POLITICAL ACTIVITY - ADDRESSES, ESSAYS, LECTURES.
Zur Haltung der herrschenden Klasse und der Arbeiterbewegung zur Beschäftigung ausländischer Arbeiter. [Rostock] , 1980. 64 p. ;

LC Card 82-209919 DDC 331.6/2/0943 19
HD8458.A2 Z87 1980 NYPL [JLD 87-143]

TRADE-UNIONS - CANADA.
Unions in transition . San Francisco, Calif. , c1986. xviii, 506 p. : ISBN 0-917616-74-X : LC Card 86-10256 DDC 331.88 19
HD .U46 1986 NYPL [JLE 86-4238]

TRADE-UNIONS - CANADA - CORRUPT PRACTICES.
Edwards, Peter, 1956- Waterfront warlord . Toronto, Ont., Canada , c1987. ix, 213 p. : ISBN 1-550-13013-7 : LC Card 87-150705 DDC 331.88/113875/0924 B 19
HD6525.B36 E39 1987

TRADE-UNIONS - CANADA - HISTORY.
Seymour, Edward E. An illustrated history of Canadian labour, 1800-1974 /. Ottawa , 1980. xiv, 95 p. :

TRADE-UNIONS - CANADA - OFFICIALS AND EMPLOYEES - BIOGRAPHY.
Edwards, Peter, 1956- Waterfront warlord . Toronto, Ont., Canada , c1987. ix, 213 p. : ISBN 1-550-13013-7 : LC Card 87-150705 DDC 331.88/113875/0924 B 19
HD6525.B36 E39 1987

TRADE-UNIONS - CARIBBEAN AREA - CONGRESSES.
Trade unions and democracy . [Kingston, Jamaica] [1986] iii, 52 p. : LC Card 87-133832 DDC 322/.2/09729 19
HD6571 .T72 1986

TRADE-UNIONS, CATHOLIC - GERMANY - HISTORY.
Roder, Hartmut, 1951- Der christlich-nationale Deutsche Gewerkschaftsbund (DGB) im politisch-ökonomischen Kräftefeld der Weimarer Republik . Frankfurt am Main , New York , c1986. 804 p. : ISBN 3-8204-9325-5 LC Card 86-194815
HD8443.D457 R63 1986

TRADE-UNIONS, CATHOLIC - GERMANY (WEST)
Schwarz, Heino, 1936- Katholisch, proletarisch und in der Einheitsgewerkschaft /. Mainz , c1983. 141 p. : ISBN 3-7867-1046-5 LC Card 83-193395 DDC 331.88/0943 19
HD6694 .S34 1983 NYPL [JLD 86-2783]

TRADE-UNIONS, CATHOLIC - GERMANY (WEST) - BIOGRAPHY.
Wittkamp, Heinrich, 1903- Achtzig Jahre kritischer Bürger im 20. Jahrhundert . Mannheim , c1986. 232 p., [16] p. of plates : ISBN 3-87804-182-9 (Deut. Bibl.) LC Card 86-230657
HD6695.W58 A3 1986

TRADE-UNIONS, CATHOLIC - NETHERLANDS - MAASTRICHT - HISTORY.
Perry, Jos. Roomsche kinine tegen roode koorts . Amsterdam , 1983. 334 p. : ISBN 90-6012-571-1 : LC Card 83-240733
HD6481.2.N4 P47 1983
NYPL [JLD 86-3418]

TRADE-UNIONS, CATHOLIC - SPAIN - POLITICAL ACTIVITY - HISTORY.
Domínguez, Javier. Organizaciones obreras cristianas en la oposición al franquismo (1951-1975) . Bilbao [1985?] 479 p. ; ISBN 84-271-1431-1 LC Card 87-153234
HD6481.2.S7 D65 1985

TRADE-UNIONS, CATHOLIC - UNITED STATES - HISTORY - 20TH CENTURY.
Sullivan, Patrick J., 1929- U. S. Catholic institutions and labor unions, 1960-1980 /. Lanham, MD , c1985. 545 p. ; ISBN 0-8191-4970-5 (alk. paper) : LC Card 85-20171 DDC 331.88/1128273 19
HD6481.2.U6 S85 1985
NYPL [JLE 86-2407]

TRADE-UNIONS - CHILE.
Barrera, Manuel. Sindicatos y estado en el Chile actual . Geneva, Switzerland , Santiago, Chile , c1985. v, 196 p. : LC Card 87-118607
HD6617 .B27 1985

Campero, Guillermo. El sindicalismo internacional y la redemocratización de Chile /. Santiago, Chile , 1984. 77 p. ; LC Card 86-139122 DDC 331.88/0983 19
HD6617 .C357 1984

Clases sociales y acción obrera en Chile /. México, D.F. , 1986. 230 p. ; ISBN 968-12-0326-7 LC Card 87-404023 DDC 331/.0983 19
HD8296.5 .C57 1986

Ruiz-Tagle P., Jaime. El sindicalismo chileno después del plan laboral /. Santiago, Chile [1985?] 211 p. ; *NYPL [JLD 87-1182]*

TRADE-UNIONS - CHILE - HISTORY.
Pizarro, Crisóstomo. La huelga obrera en Chile, 1890-1970 /. Santiago, Chile [1986] 227 p. : LC Card 87-115190 DDC 331.89/2983 19
HD5356.A6 P59 1986

TRADE-UNIONS - CHILE - POLITICAL ACTIVITY.
Frías F., Patricio. Prácticas y orientaciones del movimiento sindical en la lucha por la democracia /. Santiago, Chile , 1986. 57 p. ; LC Card 87-101389
HD6618.5 .F75 1986

TRADE-UNIONS - CHINA - HISTORY - 20TH CENTURY.
Chung-kuo kung jen yün tung ti hsien ch'ü. Pei-ching , 1983- v. : LC Card 84-231479 DDC 322/.2/0951 19
HD8736 .C496 1983 <Orien China>
*NYPL [*OVY 87-4134]*

TRADE-UNIONS - CHINA - SHANGHAI - POLITICAL ACTIVITY - HISTORY - 20TH CENTURY.
Honig, Emily. Sisters and strangers . Stanford, Calif. , 1986. ix, 299 p. : ISBN 0-8047-1274-3 (alk. paper) : LC Card 84-51711 DDC 331.4/87721/0951132 19
HD6073.T42 C64 1986
NYPL [JLD 86-3016]

TRADE-UNIONS - COAL MINERS - BRAZIL - CRICIÚMA.
Volpato, Terezinha Gascho. A pirita humana . Florianópolis , 1984. 159 p. : LC Card 85-150574
HD8039.M62 B78 1984

TRADE-UNIONS - COAL MINERS - GERMANY (WEST) - HISTORY.
Lauschke, Karl. Schwarze Fahnen an der Ruhr . Marburg [/Lahn] , c1984. 400 p. : ISBN 3-921630-42-8 LC Card 84-215799
HD6698.M616 L535 1984

TRADE-UNIONS - COAL MINERS - INDIA.
Basurāẏa, Sunīla. Kaẏalā śramika, jībana o saṃgrāma /. Durgāpura , Kalikātā , 1986. 239 p. ; LC Card 86-903821
HD8039.M62 I394 1986

TRADE-UNIONS - COAL MINERS - SPAIN - ASTURIAS - HISTORY - 20TH CENTURY.
Shubert, Adrian, 1953- The road to revolution in Spain . Urbana , c1987. 183 p. : ISBN 0-252-01368-9 (alk. paper) LC Card 86-24998 DDC 331.7/622334/094615 19
HD8039.M62 S68 1987

TRADE-UNIONS - COLOMBIA.
Gómez Buendía, Hernando. Sindicalismo y política económica /. Bogotá, Colombia , 1986. 324 p. : ISBN 958-9061-16-8 LC Card 87-401441 DDC 331.88/09861 19
HD6622 .G64 1986

TRADE-UNIONS - CONGO (BRAZZAVILLE) - HISTORY.
Etonokani, Jean-René. Genèse et évolution du mouvement syndical congolais /. [Brazzaville? , between 1982 and 1986] (Brazzaville : Service polycopie de la Conférence épiscopale du Congo) 180 p., [20] p. of plates : LC Card 86-179682
HD6878 .E86 1982

TRADE-UNIONS - CONGRESSES.
Recent advances in labour economics /. London , New York , c1984. 258 p. : ISBN 0-312-66575-X (St. Martin's) : LC Card 83-40628 DDC 331 19
HD4813 .R28 1984 NYPL [JLD 86-2455]

TRADE-UNIONS - CONSTRUCTION WORKERS - BOLIVIA - LA PAZ - HISTORY.
Los Constructores de la ciudad . La Paz , 1986. 84 p. : LC Card 86-234740
HD6609.B892 S563 1986

TRADE-UNIONS - CONSTRUCTION WORKERS - LAW AND LEGISLATION - UNITED STATES.
Northrup, Herbert Roof, 1918- Doublebreasted operations and pre-hire agreements in construction . Philadelphia, Penn., USA , c1987. viii, 127 p. : ISBN 0-89546-067-X (pbk.) LC Card 87-81475 DDC 331.88/92 19
HD9715.U52 N67 1984 Suppl.

TRADE-UNIONS - CUBA - HISTORY.
Historia del movimiento obrero cubano, 1865-1958 /. La Habana , 1985- v. <1 > ; LC Card 87-401462
HD6577 .H57 1985

Riesgo, Rodolfo. Cuba, el movimiento obrero y su entorno socio-politico, 1865-1983 /. Miami , 1985. 251 p. ; ISBN 0-917049-02-0 (pbk.) LC Card 86-673864
HD6578.5 .R53x 1985

TRADE-UNIONS - CUBA - OFFICIALS AND EMPLOYEES - BIOGRAPHY.
García Galló, Gaspar M. Jorge. General de las cañas /. La Habana , 1983. 220 p., [18] p. of plates : LC Card 84-229562 DDC 331.88/13361/097291 19
HD6577.5.M46 G37 1983
NYPL [JFD 85-4783]

TRADE-UNIONS - CUBA - POLITICAL ACTIVITY.
Riesgo, Rodolfo. Cuba, el movimiento obrero y su entorno socio-politico, 1865-1983 /. Miami , 1985. 251 p. ; ISBN 0-917049-02-0 (pbk.) LC Card 86-673864
HD6578.5 .R53x 1985

TRADE-UNIONS - CUBA - POLITICAL ACTIVITY - HISTORY.
Córdova, Efrén. Castro and the Cuban labor movement . Lanham, MD , c1987. xii, 341 p. ; ISBN 0-8191-5952-2 (alk. paper) : LC Card 86-28159 DDC 322/.2/097291 19
HD6578.5 .C67 1987

TRADE-UNIONS - DENMARK - FÅBORG (FYNS AMT) - HISTORY - 19TH CENTURY.
Venge, Mikael. Arbejdere og socialdemokrater i Faaborg omkring 1900 /. [Fåborg] , 1986. 72 p. : ISBN 87-88421-01-5 LC Card 87-144687
HD6745.F33 V46 1986

TRADE-UNIONS - DENMARK - HISTORY - 19TH CENTURY.
Christiansen, Niels Finn. Arbejderbevægelsens forhistorie . [Copenhagen] , 1986. 188 p. : ISBN 87-87739-21-6 : LC Card 87-145749
HD6742 .C495 1986

TRADE-UNIONS - DEVELOPING COUNTRIES.
International labour and the Third World . Aldershot, Hants, England , c1987. xii, 283 p. ; ISBN 0-566-00971-4 : LC Card 86-31791 DDC 331/.09172/4 19
HD8943 .I55 1987

TRADE-UNIONS - DOMINICAN REPUBLIC - HISTORY.
Orbe, Justino José del. Mauricio Báez y la clase obrera /. Santo Domingo, República Dominicana , 1981. 158 p. : LC Card 82-138627 DDC 331.88/092/4 B 19
HD6584.Z55 B346 1981
NYPL [JLE 86-3246]

TRADE-UNIONS - DOMINICAN REPUBLIC - OFFICIALS AND EMPLOYEES - BIOGRAPHY.
Orbe, Justino José del. Mauricio Báez y la clase obrera /. Santo Domingo, República Dominicana , 1981. 158 p. : LC Card 82-138627 DDC 331.88/092/4 B 19
HD6584.Z55 B346 1981
NYPL [JLE 86-3246]

TRADE-UNIONS - ECONOMIC ASPECTS - DEVELOPING COUNTRIES.
Trade unions and the economic crisis of the 1980s /. Aldershot, Hants, England , Brookfield, Vt., U. S.A. , c1987. x, 210 p. ; ISBN 0-566-05245-8 : LC Card 86-25641 DDC 331.88/094 19
HD6657 .T68 1987

TRADE-UNIONS - ECONOMIC ASPECTS - EUROPE.
Trade unions and the economic crisis of the 1980s /. Aldershot, Hants, England , Brookfield, Vt., U. S.A. , c1987. x, 210 p. ; ISBN 0-566-05245-8 : LC Card 86-25641 DDC 331.88/094 19
HD6657 .T68 1987

TRADE-UNIONS - ECONOMIC ASPECTS - UNITED STATES.
Kelso, Louis O. Democracy and economic power . Cambridge, Mass. , 1986. xii, 175 p. : ISBN 0-88730-115-0 : LC Card 86-14027 DDC 338.6 19
HD5660.U5 K45 1986 ***NYPL [JLE 86-4658]***

TRADE-UNIONS - ECUADOR.
Ycaza, Patricio. Movimiento obrero, estado y modernización capitalista en el Ecuador, 1960-1983 /. Ecuador [1985 or 1986] 38 p. ; LC Card 86-171415
HC202 .Y35 1985

TRADE-UNIONS - ECUADOR - HISTORY.
Ycaza, Patricio. Historia del movimiento obrero ecuatoriano . Quito , 1984. 371 p. :
NYPL [JLB 86-21]

TRADE-UNIONS - ECUADOR - HISTORY - 20TH CENTURY.
Capelo C., J. Alejo (J. Alejo Capelo Cabello), d. 1973. El crimen del 15 de noviembre de 1922 /. [Guayaquil] , 1983. 10, 14, 19 p. : LC Card 86-114097
HD5358.A6 C36 1983

Masas, luchas, solidaridad /. [S.l. , 1985] ([Guayaquil] : Litografía e Impr. de la Universidad de Guayaquil) 298 p. : LC Card 86-177888
HD8316 .M37 1985

TRADE-UNIONS - ECUADOR - HISTORY - SOURCES.
Movimiento obrero del Ecuador, 1970-1979 . Guayaquil, Ecuador [1985] 300 p. ; LC Card 86-105256 DDC 331.88/09866 19
HD6627 .M68 1985 ***NYPL [JLD 86-3140]***

TRADE-UNIONS - EGYPT - HISTORY.
Beinin, Joel, 1948- Workers on the Nile . Princeton, N.J. , c1987. xix, 488 p. : ISBN 0-691-05506-8 (alk. paper) : LC Card 87-45510 DDC 305.5/62/0962 19
HD8786 .B45 1987

TRADE-UNIONS - ELECTRIC INDUSTRIES WORKERS - CHILE.
Errázuriz, Enrique. Industria eléctrica, 1960-1985 . [Santiago, Chile] [1986] 243 p. : LC Card 87-403870 DDC 338.4/762131/0983 19
HD9685.C52 E77 1986

TRADE-UNIONS - ELECTRIC INDUSTRY WORKERS - ITALY.
Bezza, Bruno. Le lotte degli elettromeccanici /. Milano , c1981. 179 p. : ISBN 88-20-42149-6 : LC Card 81-200954 DDC 331.89/282131/0945 19
HD5384.E3 B49 1981 ***NYPL [JLD 86-2898]***

TRADE-UNIONS - ENGLAND - NOTTINGHAM (NOTTINGHAMSHIRE) - HISTORY.
Wyncoll, Peter, 1939-1982. The Nottingham labour movement, 1880-1939 /. London , Atlantic Highlands, N.J. , 1985. 256 p. ; ISBN 0-85315-613-1 (pbk.) : LC Card 86-213667 DDC 331.88/09425/27 19
HD6669.N68 W96 1985

TRADE-UNIONS - EUROPE.
Forgács, Pál. A szakszervezetek változó szerepe a gazdaság szabályozásában az európai fejlett tőkésországokban /. Budapest , 1985. 118 p. ; ISBN 963-608-079-8 LC Card 86-228056
HD5660.E9 F67 1985

Touraine, Alain. Le mouvement ouvrier /. [Paris] , c1984. 438 p. : ISBN 2-213-01361-6 : LC Card 84-202370 DDC 322/.2/0944 19
HD6684 .T655 1984 ***NYPL [JLE 86-279]***

TRADE UNIONS - EUROPE - ADDRESSES, ESSAYS, LECTURES.
Economic crisis, trade unions, and the state /. London , Dover, N.H. , c1986. 295 p. ; ISBN 0-7099-1447-4 : LC Card 85-28055 DDC 331/.094 19
HD8391 .E26 1986 ***NYPL [JLD 86-1301]***

Unions in crisis and beyond . Dover, Mass. , c1986. xii, 340 p. : ISBN 0-86569-127-4 : LC Card 85-26646 DDC 331.88 19
HD6508 .U45 1986 ***NYPL [JLE 86-1936]***

TRADE UNIONS - EUROPE - CASE STUDIES.
L'Europa sindacale agli inizi degli anni '80 . Bologna , c1982. 385 p. : LC Card 84-140478 DDC 331.88/094 19
HD6657 .E89 1982

TRADE-UNIONS - EUROPE - HISTORY.
Markiewicz, Stanisław. Chrześcijaństwo a związki zawodowe /. Warszawa , 1985. 618 p. : ISBN 83-202-0352-X (pbk.) :
NYPL [*QO 86-2625]

TRADE-UNIONS - EUROPE - POLITICAL ACTIVITY.
Touraine, Alain. Le mouvement ouvrier /. [Paris] , c1984. 438 p. : ISBN 2-213-01361-6 : LC Card 84-202370 DDC 322/.2/0944 19
HD6684 .T655 1984 ***NYPL [JLE 86-279]***

TRADE-UNIONS - EUROPE - POLITICAL ACTIVITY - ADDRESSES, ESSAYS, LECTURES.
Industrial relations in Europe . London , Dover, N.H. , c1985. ix, 277 p. ; ISBN 0-7099-4212-5 : LC Card 85-21321 DDC 331/.094 19
HD8376.5 .I54 1985 ***NYPL [JLD 86-1065]***

TRADE-UNIONS - EUROPEAN ECONOMIC COMMUNITY COUNTRIES.
L'Association des travailleurs aux choix technologiques . Luxembourg , Washington, D.C. , 1986. 45 p. : ISBN 92-825-5880-0 : LC Card 86-179382
HD6331.2.E86 A88 1986

La Formation des syndicalistes aux nouvelles technologies de l'information et à leur introduction dans les entreprises . Luxembourg , Washington, D.C. , 1986. 52, 13, 7 p. : ISBN 92-825-5881-9 : LC Card 86-179989
HD6331.2.E86 F67 1986

TRADE-UNIONS - EUROPEAN ECONOMIC COMMUNITY COUNTRIES - POLITICAL ACTIVITY.
Barnouin, Barbara. The European labour movement and European integration /. London , Wolfeboro, N.H. , 1986. viii, 172 p. ; ISBN 0-86187-650-4 : LC Card 86-5901 DDC 331.88/091 19
HD8372.E86 B37 1986
NYPL [JLE 86-4058]

Debunne, Georges. Vakbonden en Europa . Leuven , c1987. 206 p. ; ISBN 90-6303-228-5 : LC Card 87-157537
HD8372.E86 D43 1987

TRADE-UNIONS - FOUNDRYMEN - SOUTH AFRICA - HISTORY.
Webster, Eddie. Cast in a racial mould . Johannesburg , 1985. xv, 299 p., [6] p. of plates : ISBN 0-86975-285-5 (pbk.) : LC Card 86-213551 DDC 331.88/1712/0968 19
HD6870.5.Z7 F758 1985

TRADE-UNIONS - FRANCE.
Erbès-Seguin, Sabine. Syndicats et relations de travail dans la vie économique française /. [Villeneuve d'Ascq] [1985] 137 p. ; ISBN 2-85939-262-9 : LC Card 85-226210 DDC 331/.0944 19
HD6684 .E75 1985 ***NYPL [JLE 86-2222]***

Mothé-Gautrat, Daniel, 1924- Pour une nouvelle culture d'entreprise /. Paris , 1986. 173 p. ; ISBN 2-7071-1596-7 : LC Card 86-185142
HD8431 .M63 1986

Touraine, Alain. Le mouvement ouvrier /. [Paris] , c1984. 438 p. : ISBN 2-213-01361-6 : LC Card 84-202370 DDC 322/.2/0944 19
HD6684 .T655 1984 ***NYPL [JLE 86-279]***

Touraine, Alain. [Mouvement ouvrier. English.] The workers' movement /. Cambridge [Cambridgeshire] ; New York : xx, 322 p. ; ISBN 0-521-30852-6 LC Card 87-8010 DDC 322/.2/0944 19
HD6684 .T65513 1987

Tozzi, Michel. Militer autrement /. Bruxelles, Belgique , Lyon, France [1985] 162 p. ; ISBN 2-85008-067-5 : LC Card 86-178750
HD6684 .T66 1985

TRADE-UNIONS - FRANCE - HISTORY.
Bron, Jean. La lutte des classes aujourd'hui, 1950-1981 /. Paris , 1982. 318 p. ; ISBN 2-7082-0349-5 ***NYPL [JLD 86-1408]***

Spurk, Jan. Soziologie der französischen Arbeiterbewegung /. Berlin , c1986. 317 p. ; ISBN 3-88619-606-2 LC Card 87-235004 DDC 331.88/0944 19
HD6684 .S68 1986

Validire, Jean-Louis. André Bergeron, une force ouvrière /. Paris , c1984. 244 p. ; ISBN 2-259-01206-X : LC Card 85-105625 DDC 331.88/0944 19
HD6684 .V35 1984

TRADE-UNIONS - FRANCE - POLITICAL ACTIVITY.
Mouriaux, René. Syndicalisme et politique /. Paris , c1985. 212 p. : LC Card 86-159539
HD6687 .M68 1985

Touraine, Alain. Le mouvement ouvrier /. [Paris] , c1984. 438 p. : ISBN 2-213-01361-6 : LC Card 84-202370 DDC 322/.2/0944 19
HD6684 .T655 1984 ***NYPL [JLE 86-279]***

Touraine, Alain. [Mouvement ouvrier. English.] The workers' movement /. Cambridge [Cambridgeshire] ; New York : xx, 322 p. ; ISBN 0-521-30852-6 LC Card 87-8010 DDC 322/.2/0944 19
HD6684 .T65513 1987

TRADE-UNIONS - FRANCE - POLITICAL ACTIVITY - HISTORY.
Moss, Bernard H. [Origins of the French labor movement, 1830-1914. French.] Aux origines du mouvement ouvrier français . Paris , 1985. xi, 236 p. ; ISBN 2-251-60326-3
NYPL [M-10 6410 n.326]

TRADE-UNIONS - GERMANY.
Schalldach, Elisabeth, 1904- Rationalisierungsmassnahmen der Nachinflationszeit im Urteil der deutschen freien Gewerkschaften. Jena, 1930. ix, [1], 186 p. LC Card AC34-383
HD70.G2 S26 1930

TRADE-UNIONS - GERMANY, EAST.
How much say do the trade unions have? . Berlin [1986] 61 p., [16] p. of plates : LC Card 87-117720 DDC 331.88/09431 19
HD6700.5.Z6 H69 1986

TRADE-UNIONS - GERMANY (EAST) - CONGRESSES.
Kolloquium zur Gewerkschaftlichen Interessenvertretung beim Umfassenden Aufbau des Sozialismus in der Deutschen Demokratischen Republik (1964) Protokoll über das Kolloquium zur Gewerkschaftlichen Interessenvertretung beim Umfassenden Aufbau des Sozialismus in der Deutschen Demokratischen Republik am 31. Januar 1964. [Bernau] [1964] iv, 246 p. ; LC Card 85-125499
HD6700.5 .K65 1964

TRADE-UNIONS - GERMANY (EAST) - HISTORY - CHRONOLOGY.
Geschichte des FDGB . Berlin , c1985. 364 p. ; LC Card 86-124681 DDC 331.88/0943 19
HD8460.5.A5 F7326 1985

TRADE-UNIONS - GERMANY - HISTORY.
Klönne, Arno. Die deutsche Arbeiterbewegung . Düsseldorf , Köln , 1980. 382 p. ; ISBN 3-424-00652-1 : LC Card 81-453558 DDC 322/.2/0943 19
HX276 .K547 ***NYPL [JLD 81-689]***

TRADE-UNIONS - GERMANY - HISTORY - 19TH CENTURY.
Eisenberg, Christiane, 1956- Deutsche und englische Gewerkschaften . Göttingen , c1986. 391 p. ; ISBN 3-525-35733-8 LC Card 87-127078 DDC 331.88/0941 19
HD6694 .E27 1986

TRADE-UNIONS - GERMANY - HISTORY - 20TH CENTURY.
Stollberg, Gunnar. Die Rationalisierungsdebatte 1908-1933 . Frankfurt/Main , New York , c1981. 214 p. ; ISBN 3-593-32938-7 : LC Card 81-177695 DDC 331.88/0943 19
HD70.G2 S666 1981 ***NYPL [JLD 86-1662]***

TRADE-UNIONS - GERMANY - HISTORY - 20TH CENTURY - SOURCES.
Die Gewerkschaften von der Stabilisierung bis zur Weltwirtschaftskrise, 1924-1930 /. Köln , c1986. 2 v. (1586 p.) ; ISBN 3-7663-0902-1 (Bd. 1) LC Card 87-123987
HD6694 .Q44 1985 Bd. 3

TRADE-UNIONS - GERMANY - POLITICAL ACTIVITY - ADDRESSES, ESSAYS, LECTURES.
Wozu noch in die Parlamente? /. [Reutlingen] , 1978. 81 p. : LC Card 82-223081 DDC 322/.2/0943 19
HD6697 .W69 1978 ***NYPL [JLD 87-886]***

TRADE-UNIONS - GERMANY - POLITICAL ACTIVITY - HISTORY - 20TH CENTURY - ADDRESSES, ESSAYS, LECTURES.
Zur Haltung der herrschenden Klasse und der Arbeiterbewegung zur Beschäftigung ausländischer Arbeiter. [Rostock] , 1980. 64 p. ; LC Card 82-209919 DDC 331.6/2/0943 19
HD8458.A2 Z87 1980 *NYPL [JLD 87-143]*

TRADE-UNIONS - GERMANY, WEST.
Berghahn, Volker Rolf. Unternehmer und Politik in der Bundesrepublik /. Frankfurt am Main , 1985. 363 p. : ISBN 3-518-11265-1 LC Card 85-235608
HC286.5 .B37 1985

Grumbach, Jürgen. Energieforschung und Arbeitnehmerinteressen . Frankfurt , New York , c1986. 307 p. ; ISBN 3-593-33655-3 LC Card 87-127360 DDC 331.1/0943 19
HC290.5.E5 G74 1986

Kontos, Maria. Verbandsstrategien zur Ausländerbeschäftigung in der Bundesrepublik . Königstein/Ts. , c1983. viii, 235 p. ; ISBN 3-7756-6938-8 LC Card 83-190064 DDC 331.6/2/0943 19
HD8458.A2 K598 1983
NYPL [JLD 86-2465]

Krack, Jürgen. Lieber besser statt mehr? . Köln , c1985. 306, [2] p. : ISBN 3-7663-0569-7 LC Card 85-125869
HD5029 .K72 1985

Kulke, Ulrich. Betriebsnahe Tarifpolitik zur Stärkung der gewerkschaftlichen Basis /. Berlin , 1977. 108 p. ; ISBN 3-88114-215-0 : LC Card 80-489437
HD6694 .K82 *NYPL [JLD 81-350]*

Müller-Vogg, Hugo. Die Krise der deutschen Gewerkschaften . Stuttgart , c1986. 96 p. ; ISBN 3-87959-284-5 LC Card 87-104011
HD6694 .M847 1986

Schabedoth, Hans-Joachim. Bittsteller oder Gegenmacht? . Marburg , 1985. 251 p. : ISBN 3-924800-32-4 : LC Card 86-115002 DDC 331.88/0943 19
HD6694 .S254 1985 *NYPL [JLC 87-35]*

Schwarz, Heino, 1936- Katholisch, proletarisch und in der Einheitsgewerkschaft /. Mainz , c1983. 141 p. : ISBN 3-7867-1046-5 LC Card 83-193395 DDC 331.88/0943 19
HD6694 .S34 1983 *NYPL [JLD 86-2783]*

Süllow, Bernd. Korporative Repräsentation der Gewerkschaften . Frankfurt , New York , c1982. 146 p. ; ISBN 3-593-33169-1 LC Card 83-153450
HD4177 .S85 1982

Welsch, Johann. Gewerkschaften und Strukturwandel . Köln , c1986. iii, 114 p. ; ISBN 3-7663-3011-X LC Card 86-223645 DDC 331.13/704 19
HD6694 .W37 1986

TRADE-UNIONS - GERMANY, WEST - ADDRESSES, ESSAYS, LECTURES.
Ausstieg? . Hamburg , 1985. 159 p. : ISBN 3-87975-289-3 LC Card 85-219857 DDC 331/.0943 19
HD6694 .A97 1985 *NYPL [JLD 87-710]*

TRADE-UNIONS - GERMANY (WEST) - BAVARIA - HISTORY.
Jüngling, Elisabeth. Streiks in Bayern (1889-1914) . München , 1986. viii, 307 p., [24] p. of plates : ISBN 3-87821-214-3 LC Card 87-408637 DDC 331.89/29433 19
HD5380.B38 J86 1986

TRADE-UNIONS - GERMANY (WEST) - BREMEN - HISTORY - 20TH CENTURY.
Oltmann, Joachim. Kalter Krieg und kommunale Integration . Marburg , c1987. 500 p. ; ISBN 3-921630-71-1 LC Card 87-142718 DDC 331.88/0943/52 19
HD6699.B7 O48 1987

TRADE-UNIONS - GERMANY (WEST) - CORRUPT PRACTICES.
Kusch, Franz. Macht, Profit & Kollegen . Stuttgart [1986] 184 p. : ISBN 3-87959-272-1 LC Card 86-182407
HD6490.C642 G35 1986

TRADE-UNIONS - GERMANY (WEST) - DÜSSELDORF - HISTORY - 19TH CENTURY.
Lenger, Friedrich. Zwischen Kleinbürgertum und Proletariat . Göttingen , c1986. 332 p. ; ISBN 3-525-35731-1 LC Card 87-134322 DDC 331/.0943/55 19
HD8460.D872 L46 1986

TRADE-UNIONS - GERMANY (WEST) - HISTORY - 20TH CENTURY.
Reese, Hartmut. Arbeiterbewegung in der Zusammenbruchsgesellschaft . Münster [1984?] 209 p. ; ISBN 3-88660-133-1 LC Card 85-128699
HD6694 .R35 1984

TRADE-UNIONS - GERMANY (WEST) - MANNHEIM - HISTORY - SOURCES.
Säumt keine Minute! . Mannheim , c1986. xiii, 683 p. : ISBN 3-923003-36-6 LC Card 87-115249 DDC 331/.0943/46 19
HD8460.M35 S28 1986

TRADE-UNIONS - GERMANY, WEST - OFFICIALS AND EMPLOYEES.
Schelsky, Helmut. Funktionäre . Stuttgart-Degerloch , c1982. 310 p. ; ISBN 3-512-00652-3 : LC Card 83-124834
HD6694 .S2566 1982

TRADE-UNIONS - GERMANY (WEST) - OSTHOLSTEIN - HISTORY.
Rüdel, Holger. Landarbeiter und Sozialdemokratie in Ostholstein, 1872 bis 1878 . Neumünster , 1986. 581 p. ; ISBN 3-529-02909-2 LC Card 87-119718 DDC 331.88/13/0943512 19
HD6699.O88 R83 1986

TRADE-UNIONS - GERMANY, WEST - POLITICAL ACTIVITY.
Bernschneider, Wolfgang. Staat, Gewerkschaft und Arbeitsprozess . Opladen , c1986. viii, 291 p. : ISBN 3-531-11797-1 LC Card 86-222066
HD5710.75.G3 B47 1986

TRADE-UNIONS - GERMANY, WEST - POLITICAL ACTIVITY - ADDRESSES, ESSAYS, LECTURES.
Wozu noch in die Parlamente? /. [Reutlingen] , 1978. 81 p. : LC Card 82-223081 DDC 322/.2/0943 19
HD6697 .W69 1978 *NYPL [JLD 87-886]*

TRADE-UNIONS - GERMANY (WEST) - RHINE RIVER VALLEY - HISTORY - CONGRESSES.
Der I. Kongress der Revolutionären Gewerkschafts-Opposition (RGO) im Bezirk Mittelrhein (Raum Aachen-Köln-Koblenz) im Jahre 1930 /. Reinbek , c1982. 136 p. : ISBN 3-88756-024-8 : LC Card 84-135308
HD6699.R47 I18 1982

TRADE UNIONS - GOVERNMENT EMPLOYEES - INDIA - RAJASTHAN.
Saxena, Pradeep. Trade unionism in civil services . Jaipur , 1986. ii, 164 p. ; LC Card 86-903231 DDC 331.88/11354544 19
HD8005.2.I523 R347 1986

TRADE-UNIONS - GOVERNMENT EMPLOYEES - QUÉBEC (PROVINCE) - MONTRÉAL.
Lépine, Ginette. Vous autres au syndicat-- /. Montréal, Québec , c1984. 179 p. ; ISBN 2-89037-214-6 LC Card 85-101458
HD8005.2.C23 M665 1984

TRADE-UNIONS - GOVERNMENT EMPLOYEES - UNITED STATES.
Public sector labor relations . Lexington, Mass. , c1988. xi, 648 p. ; ISBN 0-669-12893-7 (alk. paper) LC Card 82-64038 DDC 331.89/041353 19
HD8005.6.U5 P83 1988

Reischl, Dennis K. Managing for Uncle Sam . Huntsville, Ala. , c1986. ix, 271 p. : ISBN 0-936295-01-5 (pbk.) : LC Card 87-115055 DDC 353.001/7 19
HD8005.2.U5 R45 1986

TRADE-UNIONS - GOVERNMENT POLICY - ARGENTINA.
Informe del gobierno argentino sobre asuntos laborales /. Buenos Aires, República Argentina , 1965. 115 leaves ; LC Card 85-115096
HD8266.5 .I53 1965

TRADE-UNIONS - GOVERNMENT POLICY - BRAZIL.
Costa, Sérgio Amad, 1958- Estado e controle sindical no Brasil . São Paulo , 1986. xiv, 192 p. : ISBN 85-85008-48-2 : LC Card 87-154269 DDC 331.88/0981 19
HD6612 .C67 1986

Os Sindicatos e a transição democrática . São Paulo , 1986. 294 p. ; LC Card 87-153581 DDC 331.88/0981 19
HD6612 .S55 1986

TRADE-UNIONS - GOVERNMENT POLICY - CHILE.
Barrera, Manuel. Trade unions and the state in the present day Chile . Geneva, Switzerland , Santiago, Chile , 1986. xx, 154 p. : LC Card 87-128364 DDC 331.89/0983 19
HD6617 .B273 1986

TRADE-UNIONS - GREAT BRITAIN.
Batstone, Eric. Unions, unemployment and innovation /. Oxford [Oxfordshire] , New York, N.Y., USA , 1986. viii, 320 p. ; ISBN 0-631-14961-9 : LC Card 85-30679 DDC 331.88/0941 19
HD6664 .B335 1986 *NYPL [JLE 86-4031]*

Burns, Patrick. Democracy at work /. London , 1981. 164 p. : ISBN 0-330-26478-8 (pbk.) LC Card 86-673620
HD6664 .B845x 1981

Coates, Ken. Trade unions in Britain /. Nottingham , 1980. xii, 385 p. : ISBN 0-85124-293-6 LC Card 86-673477 DDC 331.88/0941 19
HD6664 .C38765 1980

Freedom and fairness . Nottingham, England , Atlantic Highlands, N.J. , 1986. 157 p. ; ISBN 0-85124-440-8 LC Card 86-28038 DDC 331.88/0942 19
HD6664 .F763 1986

Sirs, Bill. Hard labour /. London , 1985. 151 p., [8] p. of plates : ISBN 0-283-99241-7 : LC Card 86-191030 DDC 331.88/1691/0924 B 19
HD6665.S57 A3 1985

Willman, Paul. Technological change, collective bargaining, and industrial efficiency /. Oxford , New York , c1986. xvi, 282 p. : ISBN 0-19-827262-6 : LC Card 86-5104 DDC 331.88/0941 19
HD6664 .W56 1986 *NYPL [JLD 87-994]*

TRADE-UNIONS - GREAT BRITAIN - COLONIES - HISTORY - 20TH CENTURY.
Nicholson, Marjorie. The TUC overseas . London , Boston , c1986. xvi, 329 p. ; ISBN 0-04-331103-2 (alk. paper) LC Card 85-28607 DDC 331.88/0941 19
HD8383 .N52 1986 *NYPL [JLD 86-2932]*

TRADE-UNIONS - GREAT BRITAIN - DIRECTORIES.
Eaton, Jack. The trade union directory . London , 1981. xii, 323 p. ; ISBN 0-86104-350-2 (pbk.) LC Card 86-673635
HD6663 .E27x 1981

Marsh, Arthur Ivor. Trade union handbook . Aldershot, Hants, England , 1984. x, 415 p. : ISBN 0-566-02426-8 : LC Card 84-236090 DDC 331.88/0941 19
HD6663 .M37 1984
*NYPL [*R-Econ. 86-3335]*

Marsh, Arthur Ivor. Trade union handbook . Aldershot, Hants, England , Brookfield, Vt., U. S.A. , c1988. x, 387 p. : ISBN 0-566-02749-6 : LC Card 87-13408 DDC 331.88/0941 19
HD6663 .M37 1988

TRADE-UNIONS - GREAT BRITAIN - FINANCE.
Fatchett, D. J. (Derek John), 1945- Trade unions and politics in the 1980s . London , New York , c1987. p. cm. ISBN 0-7099-4903-0 LC Card 87-14092 DDC 322/.2/0941 19
HD6667 .F37 1987

TRADE-UNIONS - GREAT BRITAIN - HANDBOOKS, MANUALS, ETC.
Marsh, Arthur Ivor. Trade union handbook . Aldershot, Hants, England , 1984. x, 415 p. : ISBN 0-566-02426-8 : LC Card 84-236090 DDC 331.88/0941 19
HD6663 .M37 1984
*NYPL [*R-Econ. 86-3335]*

Marsh, Arthur Ivor. Trade union handbook . Aldershot, Hants, England , Brookfield, Vt., U. S.A. , c1988. x, 387 p. : ISBN 0-566-02749-6 : LC Card 87-13408 DDC 331.88/0941 19
HD6663 .M37 1988

TRADE-UNIONS - GREAT BRITAIN - HISTORY.
Clegg, Hugh Armstrong. A history of British

trade unions since 1889 /. Oxford , New York , <1987- c1985-. p. cm. ISBN 0-19-828307-5 (pbk. : v. 2) : LC Card 87-15229 DDC 331.88/0941 19
HD6664 .C3864 1987

Marrocu, Luciano. Laburismo e trade unions . Bari , 1981. 183 p. ; LC Card 81-137615 DDC 331.88/0941 19
HD6664 .M24 ***NYPL [JLD 86-3453]***

Richardson, William, Sir, 1909- A union of many trades . Manchester [197-?] xv, 388 p., [16] p. of plates : ISBN 0-906957-01-X : LC Card 83-222175
HD8383.U553 R53 1970z

TRADE-UNIONS - GREAT BRITAIN - HISTORY - 18TH CENTURY.
British trade unionism, 1750-1850 . London , New York , 1988. p. cm. ISBN 0-582-49459-1 LC Card 87-22614 DDC 331.88/0941 19
HD6664 .B83 1988

TRADE-UNIONS - GREAT BRITAIN - HISTORY - 19TH CENTURY.
British trade unionism, 1750-1850 . London , New York , 1988. p. cm. ISBN 0-582-49459-1 LC Card 87-22614 DDC 331.88/0941 19
HD6664 .B83 1988

TRADE-UNIONS - GREAT BRITAIN - MINORITY MEMBERSHIP.
Wrench, John. Unequal comrades . Coventry , 1986. 30 p. ; ISBN 0-948303-65-4 (pbk.) : LC Card 87-146518 DDC 331.6 19
HD6490.R22 G78 1986

TRADE UNIONS - GREAT BRITAIN - OFFICIALS AND EMPLOYEES - BIOGRAPHY.
Sirs, Bill. Hard labour /. London , 1985. 151 p., [8] p. of plates : ISBN 0-283-99241-7 : LC Card 86-191030 DDC 331.88/1691/0924 B 19
HD6665.S57 A3 1985

TRADE-UNIONS - GREAT BRITAIN - POLITICAL ACTIVITY.
Coates, Ken. Trade unions and politics /. Oxford, OX, UK , New York, NY, USA , 1986. ix, 268 p. : ISBN 0-631-13752-1 : LC Card 85-22959 DDC 322/.2/0941 19
HD6667 .C63 1986 ***NYPL [JLE 86-1729]***

Fatchett, D. J. (Derek John), 1945- Trade unions and politics in the 1980s . London , New York , c1987. p. cm. ISBN 0-7099-4903-0 LC Card 87-14092 DDC 322/.2/0941 19
HD6667 .F37 1987

Hain, Peter, 1950- Political strikes . Harmondsworth, Middlesex, England , New York , 1986. 357 p. ; ISBN 0-670-80601-3
NYPL [JLD 87-532]

TRADE-UNIONS - GREAT BRITAIN - POLITICAL ACTIVITY - HISTORY.
Marrocu, Luciano. Laburismo e trade unions . Bari , 1981. 183 p. ; LC Card 81-137615 DDC 331.88/0941 19
HD6664 .M24 ***NYPL [JLD 86-3453]***

TRADE-UNIONS - GREAT BRITAIN - POLITICAL ACTIVITY - HISTORY - 19TH CENTURY.
Rothstein, Theodore. From chartism to labourism /. New York , 1984. vi, 365 p. ; ISBN 0-8240-5722-8 (alk. paper) : LC Card 83-48495 DDC 335/.1 19
HX249 .R68 1984 ***NYPL [JLD 86-1828]***

TRADE-UNIONS - GREATBRITAIN - HISTORY - 19TH CENTURY.
Eisenberg, Christiane, 1956- Deutsche und englische Gewerkschaften . Göttingen , c1986. 391 p. ; ISBN 3-525-35733-8 LC Card 87-127078 DDC 331.88/0941 19
HD6694 .E27 1986

TRADE-UNIONS - GREECE - CONGRESSES.
Hellēniko syndikalistiko kinēma . Athēna , 1984. 215 p. ; LC Card 86-193159
HD6795.5 .H44 1984

TRADE-UNIONS - GUINEA.
Confédération nationale des travailleurs de Guinée. Structure /. [Conakry] [1964?] 23 p. : LC Card 82-220475
HD8826.A5 C66 1964

TRADE-UNIONS - HARNESS MAKING AND TRADE - ARGENTINA - FINANCE - STATISTICS.
Sociedad Unión Obreros Talabarteros (Argentina) Balance general de huelga y administración, de noviembre 1904 á abril 1906 /. Buenos Aires , 1906. 65 p. ; LC Card 85-203379
HD6604.H2 S63 1906

TRADE-UNIONS - HISTORY.
Theories of the labor movement /. Detroit, Mich. , 1987. xi, 395 p. ; ISBN 0-8143-1815-0 : LC Card 86-32414 DDC 331.88/09 19
HD6476 .T47 1987

TRADE-UNIONS - HISTORY - 20TH CENTURY.
Mezhdunarodnoe rabochee dvizhenie . Moskva , 1980. 412 p. ; LC Card 81-143888
HD4854 .M474 1980

TRADE-UNIONS - HOTELS, TAVERNS, ETC.
IUF Mediterranean Hotel and Restaurant Workers' Conference (1978 : Palermo, Sicily) IUF Mediterranean Hotel and Restaurant Workers' Conference, Palermo, November 15-17, 1978. Petit-Lancy, Switzerland [1978?] 1 v. (various pagings) ; LC Card 83-225538
HD6475.A2 I7836 1978

TRADE-UNIONS - HUNGARY.
Buza, Márton. A szakszervezetek Magyarországon /. [Budapest] , 1985. 229 p. ; ISBN 963-09-2747-0 : LC Card 86-190979
HD6680.5 .B89 1985

A Gazdaságirányítás és a szakszervezetek /. Budapest , 1985. 191 p. ; ISBN 963-322-253-2 : LC Card 86-104573
HC300.28 .G349 1985

Györgypál, Katalin. A magyar szakszervezetek napjainkban . Budapest , 1984. 128 p. ; ISBN 963-608-062-3 LC Card 85-230460
HD6680.5 .G96 1984

Halmos, Csaba. A szakszervezetek és a tervezés /. Budapest , 1983. 178 p. ; ISBN 963-608-052-6 LC Card 85-108502
HD6680.5 .H34 1983

Juhász, Ottó. A népgazdasági szintü gazdaságpolitikai döntések végrehajtását segitő szakszervezeti munka . [Budapest] [1984] 136 p. ; ISBN 963-608-064-X LC Card 86-126615
HD6680.5 .J84 1984

Kolozsvári, Ernő. Szemelvények a szakszervezetek agitációs, propaganda- és kulturális tevékenységéből, 1948-1980 /. Budapest , 1982. 43 p. : ISBN 963-321-957-4 LC Card 83-229170
HD6680.5.Z6 K64 1982

Közgazdasági bizottságok kézikönyve /. Budapest , 1984. 324 p. ; ISBN 963-322-017-3 : LC Card 85-126303
HC300.28 .K68 1984

A Magyar szakszervezetek feladatai a gazdaságirányítás továbbfejlesztésének segítésében . Budapest , 1984. 47 p. ; ISBN 963-322-215-X LC Card 85-176937
HC300.28 .M3297 1984

A Szakszervezetek kulturális, agitációs és propagandamunkájának kézikönyve /. [Budapest] , 1986. 246 p. : ISBN 963-322-335-0 : LC Card 87-409655
HD6680.5 .S874 1986

The Trade union situation and industrial relations in Hungary . Geneva , 1984. 100 p. ; ISBN 92-2-103894-7 ***NYPL [JLE 85-1780]***

TRADE-UNIONS - HUNGARY - HISTORY.
Ez az a munkásság-- /. Budapest , 1984. 225 p., [40] p. of plates : ISBN 963-322-103-X LC Card 85-184724
HD6680.5 .E95 1984

TRADE-UNIONS - HUNGARY - OFFICIALS AND EMPLOYEES - INTERVIEWS.
Gáspár, Sándor. A munkásosztály szolgálatában /. [Budapest] , c1983. 326 p., [26] p. of plates : ISBN 963-322-025-4 : LC Card 84-129952
HD6680.5.Z55 G375 1983

Trade unions in Britain /. Coates, Ken. Nottingham , 1980. xii, 385 p. : ISBN 0-85124-293-6 LC Card 86-673477 DDC 331.88/0941 19
HD6664 .C38765 1980

Trade unions in South Africa, 1970-1980 . Miller, Shirley. Cape Town , 1982. xxxxv, 278 p. ; ISBN 0-7992-0469-2 ***NYPL [Sc F 86-217]***

TRADE-UNIONS - INDIA.
Anonymous struggles . New Delhi , 1983. 24 p. ; LC Card 83-904576 DDC 344.54/01 345.4041 19
LAW ***NYPL [JLD 86-3877]***

Sharma, B. D. (Banarsi Das), 1921- Art of conciliation and industrial unrest /. Bombay , 1985. xvi, 366 p. ; LC Card 87-902679 DDC 331.89/14/0954 19
HD5998.A3 S48 1985

TRADE-UNIONS - INDIA - OFFICIALS AND EMPLOYEES.
Madhusudhana Rao, M. Labour management relations and trade union leadership . New Delhi , c1986. 392 p. ; LC Card 86-903198 DDC 331/.0954 19
HD6812 .M23 1986

TRADE-UNIONS - INDIA - OFFICIALS AND EMPLOYEES - BIOGRAPHY.
Sen, P. K. (Prabhat Kumar), 1905- Purono dinera kathā /. Kalakātā , 1985. 49 p. ; LC Card 85-904772
HD6812.5.S46 A3 1985

TRADE-UNIONS - INDIA - STATISTICS.
Statistical profile on women labour. Simla [1983] v, 224 p. ; LC Card 84-900395 DDC 331.4/0954/021 19
HD5819 .S83 1983 ***NYPL [JLF 86-1946]***

TRADE-UNIONS - INDIA - WEST BENGAL - HISTORY.
Rāya, Manorañjana. Śramika āndolane aikya prasaṅge /. Kalikātā , 1986. 226 p. ; LC Card 87-900228
HD6815.W47 R39 1986

Trade Unions International of Food, Tobacco, Hotel and Allied Industries' Workers.
Problems of workers in the meat, dairy, edible oils, and fats industries . Sofia , 1986. 43 p. ; LC Card 86-222996 DDC 338.4/7664 19
HD8039.F7 P76 1986

Trade Unions International of Public and Allied Employees. Symposium sur les conséquences des techniques nouvelles de l'informatique sur les conditions de vie, et de travail, sur l'emploi des travailleurs des banques et des assurances (1980 : Paris, France) Symposium sur les conséquences des techniques nouvelles de l'informatique sur les conditions de vie, et de travail, sur l'emploi des travailleurs des banques et des assurances /. Berlin [1983?] 96 p. : LC Card 84-185736
HD8039.B27 F77 1980

TRADE-UNIONS - IRON AND STEEL WORKERS - BRITISH COLUMBIA.
Stocks, Alex M. Union raiding . Kingston, Ont., Canada , 1985. 61 p. ; ISBN 0-88886-125-7 (pbk.) LC Card 86-145321 DDC 331.87/09711 19
HD6528.B9 S86 1985 ***NYPL [JLF 87-422]***

TRADE-UNIONS - IRON AND STEEL WORKERS - EUROPE.
Stålindustri, kriseregioner og fagbevægelse . [Copenhagen] , 1983. 217 p. : LC Card 84-169019
HD9525.E752 S73 1983

TRADE-UNIONS - IRON AND STEEL WORKERS - PENNSYLVANIA - BETHLEHEM - HISTORY.
Strohmeyer, John, 1924- Crisis in Bethlehem . New York, N.Y., U. S.A. , 1987, c1986. xii, 244 p. ; ISBN 0-14-010370-8 (pbk.) LC Card 87-11835 DDC 338.7/669142/0974822 19
HD9519.B4 S87 1987

TRADE-UNIONS - IRON AND STEEL WORKERS - UNITED STATES.
Tiffany, Paul A. The decline of American steel . New York , 1988. p. cm. ISBN 0-19-504382-0 (alk. paper) LC Card 87-5782 DDC 338.4/7669142/0973 19
HD9515 .T54 1988

TRADE-UNIONS - IRON AND STEEL WORKERS - UNITED STATES - HISTORY.
Brody, David, 1930- Labor in crisis . Urbana , 1987, c1965. 218 p. ; ISBN 0-252-01373-5 (pbk. : alk. paper) LC Card 86-30880 DDC 331.89/269142/0973 19
HD5325.I5 1919 .B7 1987

TRADE-UNIONS - IRON AND STEEL WORKERS - UNITED STATES - HISTORY - CONGRESSES.
Forging a union of steel . Ithaca, N.Y. , c1987. vii, 153 p. : ISBN 0-87546-135-2 (pbk.) LC Card

87-21508 DDC 331.88/169142/0973 19
HD6515.I5 F58 1987

TRADE-UNIONS - ITALY.
Cos'e il sindacato. Roma , c1986. 76 p. : ISBN 88-7910-145-5 : LC Card 86-163777
HD6709 .C675 1986

Esposito, Gennaro, 1956- Decentramento produttivo, lavoro a domicilio e sindacato /. Milano [1983] 109 p. ; LC Card 85-150186
HD2336.I8 E86 1983

Il Futuro del sindacato /. Roma , c1986. xxvii, 347 p. ; LC Card 86-223517
HD6709 .F88 1986

Nacamulli, Raoul C. D. La razionalità contrattata . Bologna , c1986. 166 p. : ISBN 88-15-01189-7 : LC Card 87-122104
HD6709 .N296 1986

Pirzio Ammassari, Gloria. I sindacalisti . Bari , c1982. 155 p. ; LC Card 82-131644 DDC 331.87/33/0945 19
HD6709 .P57 1982 ***NYPL [JLD 86-2840]***

Scheggi Merlini, Lorenzo, 1944- Il ritorno del gigante /. Milano, Italy , c1985. 140 p. ; LC Card 86-137491 DDC 331.88/0945 19
HD6709 .S39 1985

TRADE-UNIONS - ITALY - HISTORY - 20TH CENTURY.
Piccioni, Alessandro. La Cgil nei suoi congressi /. Roma , c1986. 168 p. ; LC Card 87-103188
HD8473 .P53 1986

TRADE-UNIONS - ITALY - MILAN - HISTORY - 20TH CENTURY.
Granata, Ivano, 1949- Sindacato e crisi della democrazia . Milano, Italy , c1986. 224 p. ; LC Card 87-103965
HD6714.M54 G724 1986

TRADE-UNIONS - ITALY - NOVARA (PROVINCE) - HISTORY.
Bermani, Cesare, 1937- Dalla grande associazione degli operai di Novara al Circolo operaio agricolo della Bicocca . Novara [1983] 345 p., [31] p. of plates : LC Card 85-148843
HD6714.N68 B47 1983

TRADE-UNIONS - ITALY - OFFICIALS AND EMPLOYEES.
Regalia, Ida, 1946- Eletti e abbandonati . Bologna , c1984. 355 p. : ISBN 88-15-00592-7 : LC Card 84-250543 DDC 331.87/33/0945 19
HD6490.O42 I87 1984 ***NYPL [JLD 86-211]***

TRADE-UNIONS - ITALY - OFFICIALS AND EMPLOYEES - CORRESPONDENCE.
Lama, Luciano. Cari compagni . Roma , c1986. vii, 184 p. ; LC Card 87-155314
HD6710.L35 A4 1986

TRADE-UNIONS - ITALY - POLITICAL ACTIVITY.
Carrieri, Mimmo. Il mestiere politico del sindacato /. Roma , 1986. 218 p. ; ISBN 88-359-2930-X : LC Card 86-200898
HD8485 .C37 1986

Keszthelyi, Csaba. Az autonómia kérdése az olasz szakszervezeti egységért folytatott küzdelemben /. [Budapest] , 1985. 75 p. ; ISBN 963-673-322-8 LC Card 86-185901
HD6680.5.Z65 K47 1985

TRADE-UNIONS - ITALY - TRIESTE REGION - HISTORY - 20TH CENTURY.
--Anche l'uomo doveva essere di ferro . Milano, Italy , c1986. 441 p. : LC Card 86-213675
HD8490.T742 A53 1986

TRADE-UNIONS - ITALY - VICENZA (PROVINCE) - HISTORY.
Spagnolo, Mario. Industria e movimento operaio a Vicenza . Vicenza , 1983. 107 p., [1] leaf of plate : LC Card 85-175207
HD6714.V53 S63 1983

TRADE-UNIONS - JAPAN.
Bandō, Satoshi, 1931- Sengo rōdō kumiai undōshi . Tokyo , 1975. 278 p. ; LC Card 75-804891
HD6832 B36 ***NYPL [*OSM 86-2348]***

Labor unions and labor-management relations. Tokyo, Japan , 1986. 48 p. : ISBN 4-538-74002-0 : LC Card 86-220438 DDC 331/.0952 19
HD8726.5 .L33 1986

TRADE-UNIONS - KENYA.
Kongstad, Per. Industri, fagbevægelse og lønarbejde i Kenya . Roskilde [1983] 76 p. ; LC Card 85-238103
HC865 .K66 1983

TRADE-UNIONS - LATIN AMERICA.
Cohen, Noemí. Trabajadores y seguridad social en América Latina /. México, D.F. [1982], c1981. 146 p. ; ISBN 968-8241-38-5 LC Card 83-140620 DDC 368.4/0098 19
HD7130.5 .C63 1982 ***NYPL [JLD 86-2768]***

Vargas, Ines. The NIEO and the situatuon of workers . Oslo [1985] xiv, 290 p. ; ISBN 82-7288-121-7 (pbk.) LC Card 86-205407 DDC 331/.098 19
HD6530.5 .V36 1985

Vargas, Ines. The situation of workers in Latin America /. Oslo , 1985. 92 p. ; ISBN 82-7288-123-3 (pbk.) LC Card 86-205392 DDC 331/.098 19
HD6530.5 .V37 1985

TRADE-UNIONS - LATIN AMERICA - HISTORY.
Godio, Julio. Sindicalismo y política en América Latina /. Caracas, Venezuela [1983] 315 p. ; LC Card 83-157510 DDC 322/.2/098 19
HD8110.5 .G64 1983 ***NYPL [JLD 86-1758]***

Lateinamerikanische Gewerkschaften zwischen staatlicher Gängelung und Autonomie . Saarbrücken , Fort Lauderdale , 1985. 306 p. ; ISBN 3-88156-315-6 LC Card 87-135045 DDC 331.88/098 19
HD6571 .L38 1985

Latin American labor organizations /. New York , 1987. xiv, 929 p. ; ISBN 0-313-22834-5 (lib. bdg. : alk. paper) LC Card 86-33613 DDC 331.88/098 19
HD6530.5 .L38 1987

TRADE-UNIONS - LATIN AMERICA - HISTORY - 20TH CENTURY.
Zapata, Francisco. El conflicto sindical en América Latina /. México, D.F. , 1986. 228 p. : ISBN 968-12-0323-2 LC Card 87-105269
HD5330.5.A6 Z36 1986

TRADE-UNIONS - LAW AND LEGISLATION - BRAZIL.
Costa, Sérgio Amad, 1958- Estado e controle sindical no Brasil . São Paulo , 1986. xiv, 192 p. : ISBN 85-85008-48-2 : LC Card 87-154269 DDC 331.88/0981 19
HD6612 .C67 1986

TRADE-UNIONS - LAW AND LEGISLATION - FRANCE.
Ortscheidt, Pierre. L'entreprise face au nouveau droit de travail /. Paris , c1985. 221 p. ; ISBN 2-7178-0915-5 : LC Card 85-191518
KJV3399 .O78 1985 ***NYPL [JLE 87-358]***

TRADE-UNIONS - LAW AND LEGISLATION - ITALY.
Balducci, Cataldo. Il sindacato /. Torino , c1984. 2 v. ; ISBN 88-02-03818-X (set) : LC Card 85-158972 DDC 344.45/0188 344.504188 19
LAW ***NYPL [JLE 86-3250]***

TRADE-UNIONS - LAW AND LEGISLATION - UNITED STATES - HISTORY - 20TH CENTURY.
The Cold war against labor . Berkeley, CA , c1987. 2 v. (xxii, 915 p.) : ISBN 0-913876-19-4 (set); 0-913876-20-4 (set) : LC Card 87-18510 DDC 331.88/0973 19
HD6508 .C62 1987

TRADE-UNIONS - LEATHER WORKERS - GERMANY (WEST) - BIOGRAPHY.
Simon, Josef, 1865-1949. Josef Simon, Schuhmacher, Gewerkschafter, Sozialist mit Ecken und Kanten /. Köln , c1985. 465 p. : ISBN 3-7663-0923-4 LC Card 85-186450
HD6695.S55 A3 1985

TRADE-UNIONS - MALI - HISTORY.
Trade unionism in the republic of Mali . [Lome, Togo] [1983] 78 p. : LC Card 87-107028 DDC 331.88/0966/23 19
HD8827.A5 U557 1983

TRADE-UNIONS - MAURITIUS - HISTORY.
Allgoo, Rajpalsingh. Le mouvement syndical à l'île Maurice /. Port Louis, Ile Maurice , 1985. 110 p., [14] leaves of plates : LC Card 87-119075
HD8840.3.A5 A7825 1985

TRADE-UNIONS - METAL-WORKERS - BRAZIL.
Lula, 1945- Lula sem censura . Petrópolis [Brazil] , 1981. 101 p. ; ***NYPL [JLC 86-389]***

TRADE-UNIONS - METAL-WORKERS - BRAZIL - SANTA LUZIA (MINAS GERAIS)
Franco, José Ronaldo de Mello. O movimento sindical metalúrgico em Santa Luzia /. [Santa Luzia, Minas Gerais, Brazil?] 1985. 111 p. ; LC Card 87-404244 DDC 331.88/171/098151 19
HD6614.M5 F73 1985

TRADE-UNIONS - METAL-WORKERS - BRAZIL - SÃO PAULO (STATE) - HISTORY - 20TH CENTURY.
O Movimento sindical no interior . Piracicaba, SP [19]84. 38, [10] p. : LC Card 86-200279
HD6615.S32 M68 1984

TRADE-UNIONS - METAL WORKERS - BRITISH COLUMBIA.
Stocks, Alex M. Union raiding . Kingston, Ont., Canada , 1985. 61 p. ; ISBN 0-88886-125-7 (pbk.) LC Card 86-145321 DDC 331.87/09711 19
HD6528.B9 S86 1985 ***NYPL [JLF 87-422]***

TRADE-UNIONS - METAL-WORKERS - SOUTH AFRICA - ADDRESSES, ESSAYS, LECTURES.
Metallgewerkschaften in Südafrika /. [Köln] , c1983. 217 p. ; ISBN 3-7663-0530-1 LC Card 85-232412 DDC 331.88/171/0968 19
HD6870.5.Z7 M54 1983
NYPL [JLD 87-1964]

TRADE-UNIONS - MEXICO.
Buen L., Néstor de (Buen Lozano) Sindicatos, democracia y crisis /. México , 1985. xii, 122 p. ; ISBN 968-452-054-9 LC Card 86-209080
HD6532 .B84 1985

Los Sindicatos nacionales en el México contemporáneo /. [México, D.F.] , 1986- v. <1 > ; ISBN 968-498-020-5 (set) LC Card 87-401211 DDC 331.88/0972 19
HD6532 .S55 1986

TRADE-UNIONS - MEXICO - CONGRESSES.
Movimientos sociales en el noroeste de México /. México , 1985. 282 p. ; ISBN 968-590-072-8 LC Card 87-102068
HD1531.M6 M684 1985

TRADE-UNIONS - MEXICO - GUADALAJARA.
Guadalajara, la gran ciudad de la pequeña industria /. Zamora, Mich. , c1985. 301 p. : ISBN 968-7230-12-6 LC Card 86-191608
HD2346.M42 G824 1985

TRADE-UNIONS - MEXICO - HISTORY.
Freyre Rubio, Javier. Las organizaciones sindicales, obreras y burocráticas contemporáneas en México /. Azcapotzalco [Mexico] , c1983. 265 p. : ISBN 968-597-500-0 LC Card 86-218318
HD6532 .F74 1983

Iglesias, Severo. Sindicalismo y socialismo en México /. México, D.F. , 1985,c19. 194 p. ; ISBN 968-419-418-8 ***NYPL [JLC 86-406]***

Las Derrotas obreras, 1946-1952 /. México , 1984. 204 p. ; ISBN 968-580-647-0 LC Card 84-255708 DDC 331.88/0972 19
HD6532 .D36 1984 ***NYPL [JLE 86-4685]***

TRADE-UNIONS - MEXICO - JALISCO.
Tamayo Rodríguez, Jaime E. La estructura del sindicalismo en Jalisco /. Guadalajara, Jalisco, México [1985] 224 p. ; ISBN 968-570-147-4 LC Card 86-208258
HD6535.J35 T36 1985

TRADE-UNIONS - MEXICO - JALISCO - HISTORY - 20TH CENTURY.
Gutiérrez Zermeño, Rodolfo, 1953- Movimiento obrero en Jalisco, período 1925-1930 /. Guadalajara, Jalisco, México , 1985. 64 p. ; ISBN 968-8322-01-6 LC Card 86-208368
HD6535.J35 G88 1985

TRADE-UNIONS - MEXICO - JALISCO - POLITICAL ACTIVITY - HISTORY - 20TH CENTURY.
Gutiérrez Zermeño, Rodolfo, 1953- Movimiento obrero en Jalisco, período 1925-1930 /. Guadalajara, Jalisco, México , 1985. 64 p. ; ISBN 968-8322-01-6 LC Card 86-208368
HD6535.J35 G88 1985

TRADE-UNIONS - MEXICO - MEXICO - HISTORY.
García Luna O., Margarita (García Luna

Ortega) El movimiento obrero en el Estado de México . Toluca, Estado de México , 1984. 302 p. : ISBN 968-514-014-6 LC Card 86-173738
HC137.M473 G37 1984

TRADE-UNIONS - MEXICO - POLITICAL ACTIVITY.
The Mexican Left, the popular movements, and the politics of austerity /. La Jolla, Calif. , 1986. vi, 96 p. ; LC Card 87-621353 DDC 322/.2/0972 19
HC135 .M525535 1986

TRADE-UNIONS - MIDDLE MANAGERS - ITALY - CONGRESSES.
Tecnici, ricercatori, quadri e sindacato /. Roma , 1985. 126 p. : LC Card 86-169979
HD8038.I8 T43 1985

TRADE-UNIONS - MINERS - BOLIVIA.
Calla, Ricardo. La derrota de Lechín . La Paz, Bolivia , 1986. 79 p. : LC Card 87-105127
HD6609.M62 F433 1986

Lazarte, Jorge. Crisis de identidad y centralidad minera . [La Paz, Bolivia] [1986] 37 p. : LC Card 87-401455 DDC 331.88/122/0984 19
HD8039.M61 B586 1986

TRADE-UNIONS - MINERS - BRAZIL - NOVA LIMA.
Grossi, Yonne de Souza. Mina de Morro Velho . Rio de Janeiro, RJ , 1981. 265 p. : LC Card 81-216799 DDC 338.7/6223422/098151 19
HD8039.M74 B65 1981
NYPL [JLD 86-3591]

TRADE-UNIONS - MINERS - BRITISH COLUMBIA.
Stocks, Alex M. Union raiding . Kingston, Ont., Canada , 1985. 61 p. ; ISBN 0-88886-125-7 (pbk.) LC Card 86-145321 DDC 331.87/09711 19
HD6528.B9 S86 1985 ***NYPL [JLF 87-422]***

TRADE-UNIONS - MINERS - COLORADO - HISTORY.
Neuschatz, Michael. The golden sword . New York , 1986. xii, 301 p. ; ISBN 0-313-25104-5 (lib. bdg. : alk. Paper) LC Card 85-27026 DDC 331.88/122334/09788 19
HD8039.M61 U48 1986
NYPL [JLE 87-766]

TRADE-UNIONS - MINERS - HUNGARY - HISTORY.
Gergely, Ernő. A Bányaipari Dolgozók Szakszervezetének története /. [Budapest] , 1983. 218 p. ; ISBN 963-00-0667-7 (Magy. nemz. bibl.) LC Card 85-109054
HD6680.5.Z7 M6113 1983

TRADE-UNIONS - MINERS - SPAIN - ASTURIAS - HISTORY.
Moradiellos, Enrique. El Sindicato de los obreros mineros de Asturias, 1910-1930 /. Oviedo , 1986. 158 p. : ISBN 84-7468-111-1 LC Card 86-212987
HD6764.M62 O375 1986

TRADE-UNIONS - MOLDAVIAN S.S.R. - HISTORY.
Burlaku, I. N. Sindikatele Moldoveĭ sovetiche yn konstruktsiia sochialiste /. Kishinëu , 1980. 148 p. ; LC Card 81-135331
HD6735.M56 B87 1980

TRADE-UNIONS - MOZAMBIQUE - MAPUTO - HISTORY.
Capela, José. O movimento operário em Lourenço Marques, 1898-1927 /. [Porto?] [1981?] 281, [1] p. ; LC Card 87-401260 DDC 331.88/0967/9 19
HD6869.Z8 M363 1981

TRADE-UNIONS - MUNICIPAL EMPLOYEES - NEW YORK (N.Y.)
Maier, Mark. City unions . New Brunswick [N.J.] , c1987. xii, 221 p. ; ISBN 0-8135-1229-8 (pbk.) : LC Card 86-26031 DDC 331.88/113520747/1 19
HD8005.2.U53 N46 1987

TRADE-UNIONS - NETHERLANDS.
Arbeidsmarkt op drift . [Amsterdam] , 1986. 190 p. : ISBN 90-6287-549-1 : LC Card 86-154853
HD5792 .A72 1986 ***NYPL [JLD 86-4417]***

Niessen, Jan. Emancipatie in internationaal perspectief . Amsterdam , 1987. 282 p. ; ISBN 90-6256-460-7 : LC Card 87-158046
HD8518.5.M6 N54 1987

TRADE-UNIONS - NETHERLANDS - HISTORY - 20TH CENTURY.
Hueting, Ernest. Naar groter eenheid . Amsterdam , 1983, c1982. 432 p. : ISBN 90-6012-531-2 : LC Card 83-184649
HD6727 .H83 1983 ***NYPL [JLG 87-188]***

Vakbeweging in verandering . Deventer , 1986. 191 p. : ISBN 90-267-1082-8 : LC Card 86-224831
HD6727 .V29 1986

TRADE-UNIONS - NICARAGUA - HISTORY.
Pérez Bermúdez, Carlos. El movimiento obrero en Nicaragua . [S.l. , 1985] ([Managua, Nicaragua?] : Editorial "El Amanecer") 2 v. in 1 : LC Card 86-174663
HD6557 .P473 1985

TRADE-UNIONS - NICARAGUA - POLITICAL ACTIVITY.
Vilas, Carlos María. Democracia y participación obrera en la Revolución Sandinista /. Morelia, Michoacán , 1985. 44 p., [6] p. of plates : LC Card 87-128110 DDC 322/.2/097285 19
HD8168 .V55 1985

TRADE-UNIONS - NIGER - HISTORY.
Martens, George R. Trade unionism and politics in Niger. Lome, Togo [1986] 93 p. ; LC Card 86-172446 DDC 322/.2/09669 19
HD6882.Z65 M37 1986

TRADE-UNIONS - NIGER - POLITICAL ACTIVITY.
Martens, George R. Trade unionism and politics in Niger. Lome, Togo [1986] 93 p. ; LC Card 86-172446 DDC 322/.2/09669 19
HD6882.Z65 M37 1986

TRADE-UNIONS - NIGERIA - POLITICAL ACTIVITY - HISTORY.
Offiong, Daniel A. Organised labour and political development in Nigeria /. Calabar, Nigeria , 1983. x, 362 p. ; ISBN 978-231-601-6 (pbk.) LC Card 86-173440 DDC 322/.2/09669 19
HD6885.5.Z65 O36 1983

TRADE-UNIONS - NORWAY - HISTORY - 19TH CENTURY.
Arbeiderbevegelsens historie i Norge /. Oslo , 1985-<1987. v. <1, 5 > : ISBN 82-10-02750-6 : LC Card 87-116315
HD6752 .A74 1985

TRADE-UNIONS - NORWAY - HISTORY - 20TH CENTURY.
Arbeiderbevegelsens historie i Norge /. Oslo , 1985-<1987. v. <1, 5 > : ISBN 82-10-02750-6 : LC Card 87-116315
HD6752 .A74 1985

TRADE-UNIONS - NORWAY - PUBLIC OPINION.
Colbjørnsen, Tom. Så samles vi på valen--? . [Oslo?] [1985] 88 p. : ISBN 82-991187-5-1 LC Card 85-220350
HD6752 .C644 1985

TRADE-UNIONS - OFFICIALS AND EMPLOYEES - ITALY.
Pirzio Ammassari, Gloria. I sindacalisti . Bari , c1982. 155 p. ; LC Card 82-131644 DDC 331.87/33/0945 19
HD6709 .P57 1982 ***NYPL [JLD 86-2840]***

TRADE-UNIONS - OFFICIALS AND EMPLOYEES - TRAINING OF - MAURITIUS - CONGRESSES.
National Programme on Worker's Participation and Development (1983 : Mauritius) Report on the National Programme on Worker's Participation and Development, 3-14 October, 1983, Mauritius. [Mauritius? , between 1983 and 1985] 33 p. ; LC Card 86-980341 DDC 658.3/152/096982 19
HD6890.5 .N37 1983

TRADE-UNIONS - OHIO - HISTORY - 20TH CENTURY.
Wortman, Roy T., 1940- From syndicalism to trade unionism . New York , 1985. 217 p. : ISBN 0-8240-5675-2 (alk. paper) : LC Card 85-16249 DDC 331.88/6/09771 19
HD8055.I5 O38 1985 ***NYPL [JLE 86-4097]***

TRADE-UNIONS - ONTARIO - ECONOMETRIC MODELS.
Abbott, Michael G. Alternative estimates of union-nonunion and public-private wage differentials in Ontario, 1981 /. Kingston, Ont., Canada , 1987. ii, 47 p. ; ISBN 0-88886-166-4 (pbk.) LC Card 87-170767 DDC 331.2/2/09713 19
HD4980.O5 A64 1987

TRADE-UNIONS - PAINTERS, INDUSTRIAL - SWEDEN - HISTORY.
Böethius, Erland, 1951- Målarettan 100 år /. [Stockholm] , c1984. 448 p. : ISBN 91-7810-054-2 : LC Card 84-239262
HD6759.P26 B64 1984

TRADE-UNIONS - PAPER INDUSTRY WORKERS - QUÉBEC (PROVINCE) - HISTORY.
Vanasse, Gilbert, 1948- Histoire de la Fédération des travailleurs du papier et de la forêt /. Montréal, Québec , 1986- v. <1 > : ISBN 2-89035-122-X (t. 1) LC Card 86-231295
HD6528.P332 F438 1986

TRADE-UNIONS - PENNSYLVANIA - HISTORY - 20TH CENTURY.
Meyerhuber, Carl I., 1940- Less than forever . Selinsgrove , London , c1987. 235 p. ; ISBN 0-941664-27-9 (alk. paper) LC Card 86-62504 DDC 331.88/09748 19
HD6517.P4 M49 1987

TRADE-UNIONS - PERU.
Parodi Solari, Jorge. Ser obrero es algo relativo-- . Lima [1986] 184 p. ; LC Card 87-405297 DDC 331.7/671/0985 19
HD8039.M52 P46 1986

TRADE-UNIONS - PERU - HISTORY.
Marín Taborda, Iván. María Cano en el amanecer de la clase obrera /. Bogotá , 1985. 103 p. : LC Card 86-165616
HD6642 .M37 1985 ***NYPL [JLD 86-3540]***

TRADE-UNIONS - PERU - HISTORY - SOURCES.
Marín Taborda, Iván. María Cano en el amanecer de la clase obrera /. Bogotá , 1985. 103 p. : LC Card 86-165616
HD6642 .M37 1985 ***NYPL [JLD 86-3540]***

TRADE UNIONS - PETROLEUM WORKERS.
Turner, Terisa. Trade union action to stop oil to South Africa /. Port Harcourt , c1985. v, 35 p. ; LC Card 87-673464
HF1613.4 .T87x 1985

TRADE-UNIONS - PETROLEUM WORKERS - COLOMBIA.
La Ocupación y su remuneración en las empresas petroleras en Colombia, 1977-1984. Bogotá, D.E. [1986] 37 p. : LC Card 87-402964 DDC 331.12/5223382/09861 19
HD8039.P42 V446 1986

TRADE-UNIONS - PHILIPPINES - HANDBOOKS, MANUALS, ETC.
Del Rosario, Rody. Unyon! /. Malate, Manila [1985] 65 p. : LC Card 85-184386
HD6828 .D45 1985

TRADE-UNIONS - POLAND.
A Lengyel földindulás /. Malakoff , New York , 1980. 150 p. ; LC Card 81-177379
HD8537.N783 L45 1980 ***NYPL [JLB 86-24]***

TRADE-UNIONS - POLAND - OFFICIALS AND EMPLOYEES - BIOGRAPHY.
Wałęsa, Lech, 1943- [Chemin d'espoir. English.] A way of hope /. New York , c1987. 325 p., [17] p. of plates : ISBN 0-8050-0668-0 LC Card 87-21194 DDC 322/.2/0924 B 19
HD6735.7.Z55 W34813 1987

TRADE-UNIONS - POLAND - POLITICAL ACTIVITY.
Markiewicz, Stanisław. Chrześcijaństwo a związki zawodowe /. Warszawa , 1985. 618 p. : ISBN 83-202-0352-X (pbk.) :
NYPL [*QO 86-2625]

TRADE-UNIONS - POLICE - UKRAINE - HISTORY - 20TH CENTURY.
Ovsiienko, O. F. Krakh zubatovshchyny na Ukraïni /. Kyïv , 1987. 137, [3] p. ; LC Card 87-161669
HD8529.U43 O97 1987

TRADE-UNIONS - PORTUGAL - HISTORY.
Goodolphim, Costa, 1842-1910. A associação . Lisboa, Portugal , 1974. 206 p. ; LC Card 87-401116 DDC 334/.09494 19
HD3529.A4 G66 1974

TRADE-UNIONS - POSTAL SERVICE - CONGRESSES.
Matthew, J. Purchasing power of PTT personnel, 1965 /. Brussels [1966] 1 v. (various pagings) ; LC Card 87-165119
HE6241 .M37 1966

TRADE-UNIONS - POSTAL SERVICE - PERU - HISTORY.

Soplín E., Samuel (Soplín Escudero) La sindicalización postal telegráfica en el Perú . Lima [1986] 57 p., [4] p. of plates : LC Card 87-145465 DDC 331.88/113834985 19
HE6899.P4 S66 1986

TRADE-UNIONS - PROFESSIONAL EMPLOYEES - ITALY - CONGRESSES.
Tecnici, ricercatori, quadri e sindacato /. Roma , 1985. 126 p. : LC Card 86-169979
HD8038.I8 T43 1985

TRADE-UNIONS - PROFESSIONAL EMPLOYEES - MEXICO.
Cleaves, Peter S. Professions and the state . Tucson , c1987. xv, 147 p. : ISBN 0-8165-1016-4 (alk. paper) LC Card 87-5911 DDC 331.7/12/0972 19
HD8038.M6 C55 1987

TRADE-UNIONS - PROFESSIONAL EMPLOYEES - SWEDEN.
Micheletti, Michele. Organizing interest and organized protest . [Stockholm] , 1985. vii, 253 p. ; ISBN 91-7146-451-4 (pbk.) LC Card 86-145828 DDC 322/.2/09481 19
HD8572.T5 M53 1985
NYPL [JLL 74-316 no.29]

TRADE-UNIONS - PUERTO RICO.
Quiñones Rodríguez, Federico, 1940- Sindicalismo y política en Puerto Rico . [Río Piedras, P.R.] [c1977] 147 p., [4] p. of plates : ISBN 84-399-6989-9 LC Card 82-159544
HD6592 .Q56 1977

TRADE-UNIONS - PUERTO RICO - POLITICAL ACTIVITY.
Quiñones Rodríguez, Federico, 1940- Sindicalismo y política en Puerto Rico . [Río Piedras, P.R.] [c1977] 147 p., [4] p. of plates : ISBN 84-399-6989-9 LC Card 82-159544
HD6592 .Q56 1977

TRADE UNIONS - QUÉBEC (PROVINCE) - QUÉBEC.
Cyr, François, 1952- Eléments d'histoire de la FTQ . [Laval] [1981] 205 p. ; ISBN 2-89035-045-2 : LC Card 82-105783 DDC 331.88/09714 19
HD8102.F43 C97 1981

TRADE-UNIONS - RAILROADS - HUNGARY - HISTORY.
Gadanecz, Béla. A vasutas munkásmozgalom története . Budapest , 1985. 351 p. ; ISBN 963-322-262-1 LC Card 86-227921
HD8039.R12 H93 1985

TRADE-UNIONS - SHOEMAKERS - GERMANY (WEST) - BIOGRAPHY.
Simon, Josef, 1865-1949. Josef Simon, Schuhmacher, Gewerkschafter, Sozialist mit Ecken und Kanten /. Köln , c1985. 465 p. : ISBN 3-7663-0923-4 LC Card 85-186450
HD6695.S55 A3 1985

TRADE-UNIONS - SOCIAL ASPECTS - CONGRESSES.
Souvenir, ICFTU World Conference on the Trade Union Role in Balanced Development, Vigyan Bhawan, New Delhi, India, March 18-20, 1981 /. New Delhi [1981] 68 p. : LC Card 84-901715 DDC 331.88 19
HD6475.A2 I26347 1981
NYPL [JLG 86-296]

TRADE-UNIONS - SOCIAL ASPECTS - FRANCE.
Spurk, Jan. Soziologie der französischen Arbeiterbewegung /. Berlin , c1986. 317 p. ; ISBN 3-88619-606-2 LC Card 87-235004 DDC 331.88/0944 19
HD6684 .S68 1986

TRADE-UNIONS - SOUTH AFRICA.
African worker under apartheid. Brussels [1984]. 109 p. : *NYPL [Sc D 86-730]*

Jones, Robert A., MSc. Collective bargaining in South Africa /. Johannesburg , 1984. 104 p. ; ISBN 0-86954-173-0 *NYPL [JLD 85-1003]*

Webster, Eddie. Cast in a racial mould . Johannesburg , 1985. xv, 299 p., [8] p. of plates : ISBN 0-86975-285-5
NYPL [JLD 87-780]

TRADE-UNIONS - SOUTH AFRICA - ADDRESSES, ESSAYS, LECTURES.
Metallgewerkschaften in Südafrika /. [Köln] , c1983. 217 p. ; ISBN 3-7663-0530-1 LC Card 85-232412 DDC 331.88/171/0968 19
HD6870.5.Z7 M54 1983
NYPL [JLD 87-1964]

TRADE-UNIONS - SOUTH AFRICA - CONGRESSES.
Konferensie Vakbondwese in Suid-Afrika (1984 : Randse Afrikaanse Universiteit) Konferensie Vakbondwese in Suid-Afrika . Johannesburg [1984] 73 p. ; ISBN 0-86970-252-1 LC Card 87-126320
HD6870.5 .K65 1984

TRADE UNIONS - SOUTH AFRICA - DIRECTORIES.
Miller, Shirley. Trade unions in South Africa, 1970-1980 . Cape Town , 1982. xxxxv, 278 p. ; ISBN 0-7992-0469-2 *NYPL [Sc F 86-217]*

TRADE-UNIONS - SOUTH AFRICA - HISTORY.
Webster, Eddie. Cast in a racial mould . Johannesburg , 1985. xv, 299 p., [6] p. of plates : ISBN 0-86975-285-5 (pbk.) : LC Card 86-213551 DDC 331.88/1712/0968 19
HD6870.5.Z7 F758 1985

TRADE UNIONS - SOUTH AFRICA - STATISTICS.
Miller, Shirley. Trade unions in South Africa, 1970-1980 . Cape Town , 1982. xxxxv, 278 p. ; ISBN 0-7992-0469-2 *NYPL [Sc F 86-217]*

TRADE-UNIONS - SOUTH AMERICA - HISTORY.
Bergquist, Charles W. Labor in Latin America . Stanford, Calif. , 1986. xiv, 397, [8] p. of plates : ISBN 0-8047-1253-0 (alk. paper) : LC Card 84-51648 DDC 331/.0968 19
HD8256 .B47 1986 *NYPL [JLE 86-2972]*

TRADE-UNIONS - SOUTHERN STATES - ORGANIZING - HISTORY.
Griffith, Barbara S. The crisis of American labor . Philadelphia , 1988. xvi, 239 p. : ISBN 0-87722-503-6 (alk. paper) : LC Card 87-9998 DDC 331.88/33/0975 19
HD8055.C75 G75 1988

TRADE-UNIONS - SOVIET UNION.
Report of the Union Delegation to the U. S.S.R. . London [1946?] iii, 40 p. : LC Card 87-100506
HD8526.5 .R46 1946

Sotsial'noe upravlenie trudovym kollektivom . Moskva , 1987. 181 p. ; LC Card 87-103391
HF5549.2.S65 S675 1987

Voprosy ukreplenii͡a trudovoĭ i proizvodstvennoĭ distsipliny v deiatel'nosti profsoiuznykh organizatsiĭ . Moskva , 1984. 77 p. ; LC Card 86-181312
HF5549.5.L3 V67 1984

TRADE-UNIONS - SOVIET UNION - HISTORY - 20TH CENTURY.
Reznikov, Iosif Emmanuilovich. Die Organisation der Gewerkschaften der Sowjetunion /. Moskau , 1927. 76 p. ; LC Card 86-231829
HD6732 .R398 1927

TRADE-UNIONS - SPAIN.
Baranova, T. N. (Tat'iana Nikolaevna) Rabochiĭ klass Ispanii boretsia . Moskva , 1978. 151 p. ; LC Card 81-147187
HD8586.5 .B37 1978

The Trade union situation and industrial relations in Spain . Geneva , 1985. xiii, 138 p. : ISBN 92-2-105202-8 (pbk.) : LC Card 86-207841 DDC 331.88/0946 19
HD6762 .T68 1985

TRADE-UNIONS - SPAIN - CANTABRIA - HISTORY - 20TH CENTURY.
Argos Villar, José Carlos. El movimiento obrero en Cantabria (1955-1977) /. [Santander?] [1982?] 227 p. ; ISBN 84-300-6979-8 LC Card 86-203186
HD8589.C3 A74 1982

TRADE-UNIONS - SPAIN - MONTIJO - HISTORY - 19TH CENTURY.
Introducción a la historia del movimiento obrero en Montijo . [Montijo?] [1982?] 103 p., 48 p. of plates : ISBN 84-300-6966-6 LC Card 85-177027
HD8590.M65 I57 1982

TRADE-UNIONS - SPAIN - PAÍS VASCO - RECOGNITION - ELECTIONS.
Kaiero Uria, Andoni. Las elecciones sindicales en Euskadi, representación de los trabajadores en la empresa e implantación de los sindicatos . Vitoria , 1985. 629 p. : ISBN 84-7542-199-7 LC Card 87-146467
HD6490.R42 S74 1985

TRADE-UNIONS - SPAIN - PAÍS VASCO - RECOGNITION - ELECTIONS - STATISTICS.
Kaiero Uria, Andoni. Las elecciones sindicales en Euskadi, representación de los trabajadores en la empresa e implantación de los sindicatos . Vitoria , 1985. 629 p. : ISBN 84-7542-199-7 LC Card 87-146467
HD6490.R42 S74 1985

TRADE-UNIONS - SPAIN - VALLADOLID (PROVINCE) - HISTORY.
Prado Moura, Angel de. El movimiento obrero en Valladolid durante la II República, 1931-1936 /. [Castilla y León] , 1985. 234 p. : ISBN 84-505-2341-9 LC Card 86-214605
HD8119.V34 P72 1985

TRADE-UNIONS - STEVEDORES - GERMANY (WEST) - HAMBURG - HISTORY.
Grüttner, Michael. Arbeitswelt an der Wasserkante . Göttingen , 1984. 331 p. ; ISBN 3-525-35722-2 (Deut. Bibl.) LC Card 86-139479
HD8039.L82 G4335 1984

TRADE-UNIONS - STEVEDORES - LOUISIANA - NEW ORLEANS - HISTORY.
Rosenberg, Daniel, 1953- New Orleans dockworkers . Albany , c1988. x, 233 p. ; ISBN 0-88706-649-6 LC Card 87-10156 DDC 331.7/61387164/0976335 19
HD8039.L82 U664 1988

TRADE-UNIONS - STEVEDORES - WEST (U. S.) - HISTORY.
Finlay, William. Work on the waterfront . Philadelphia , 1988. p. cm. ISBN 0-87722-523-0 (alk. paper) : LC Card 87-17976 DDC 331.88/11387164/0973 19
HD6515.L82 W474 1988

TRADE-UNIONS - SUGAR WORKERS - BRAZIL - PARAÍBA (STATE) - CONGRESSES.
Canavieiros em greve . São Paulo , 1985. 105 p. : LC Card 87-104183 DDC 331.88/1361/098134 19
HD6614.S85 C36 1985

TRADE-UNIONS - SUGAR WORKERS - BRAZIL - PERNAMBUCO (STATE) - CONGRESSES.
Canavieiros em greve . São Paulo , 1985. 105 p. : LC Card 87-104183 DDC 331.88/1361/098134 19
HD6614.S85 C36 1985

TRADE-UNIONS - SUGAR WORKERS - BRAZIL - SÃO PAULO (STATE) - CONGRESSES.
Canavieiros em greve . São Paulo , 1985. 105 p. : LC Card 87-104183 DDC 331.88/1361/098134 19
HD6614.S85 C36 1985

TRADE-UNIONS - SWEDEN.
Inte bara ord-- . Stockholm , c1984. 120 p., [8] p. of plates : ISBN 91-550-3086-6 : LC Card 85-120867
HD6758 .I58 1984

Meidner, Rudolf. I arbetets tjänst /. Stockholm , 1984. 473 p. : ISBN 91-550-2932-9 : LC Card 84-229372
HD5803 .M45 1984

Sjödal, Tage, 1928- Vald på livstid . Stockholm [1984], c1983. 81 p. ; ISBN 91-550-2941-8 : LC Card 84-171294
HD8572.L34 S57 1984

TRADE-UNIONS - SWITZERLAND.
Sécurité et santé au travail . Berne [1984] 47 p. ; LC Card 85-176432 DDC 363.1/1/09494 19
HD7740 .S43 1984

TRADE-UNIONS - SWITZERLAND - BASEL - HISTORY.
Degen, Bernard, 1952- Das Basel der andern . Basel , 1986. 199 p. : ISBN 3-85990-073-6 LC Card 87-137650 DDC 331.88/09494/3 19
HD6775.B29 D44 1986

TRADE-UNIONS - SWITZERLAND - BIOGRAPHY.
Tschudin, Paul, 1904- Meine Ehre ist nicht die Eure! . Basel , 1986. 217 p. ; ISBN

3-85990-069-2 LC Card 87-137660 DDC 331.88/092/4 B 19
HD6772.5.T74 A3 1986

TRADE-UNIONS - SWITZERLAND - HISTORY.
Wandeler, Josef, 1949- Die KPS und die Wirtschaftskämpfe, 1930-1933 . Zürich , c1978. 277 p. : ISBN 3-85854-003-X LC Card 87-409249 DDC 331.89/29494 19
HD5410.A6 W36 1978

TRADE-UNIONS - SWITZERLAND - OFFICIALS AND EMPLOYEES - BIOGRAPHY.
Tschudin, Paul, 1904- Meine Ehre ist nicht die Eure! . Basel , 1986. 217 p. ; ISBN 3-85990-069-2 LC Card 87-137660 DDC 331.88/092/4 B 19
HD6772.5.T74 A3 1986

TRADE-UNIONS - TELEGRAPHERS - PERU - HISTORY.
Soplín E., Samuel (Soplín Escudero) La sindicalización postal telegráfica en el Perú . Lima [1986] 57 p., [4] p. of plates : LC Card 87-145465 DDC 331.88/113834985 19
HE6899.P4 S66 1986

TRADE-UNIONS - TELEGRAPHERS - UNITED STATES - HISTORY - 19TH CENTURY.
Gabler, Edwin, 1949- The American telegrapher . New Brunswick, NJ , c1988. p. cm. ISBN 0-8135-1284-0 : LC Card 87-19878 DDC 331.89/2813841/0973 19
HD5325 .T252 1883

TRADE-UNIONS - TEXTILE WORKERS - BRAZIL - SÃO PAULO (STATE) - HISTORY - 20TH CENTURY.
O Movimento sindical no interior . Piracicaba, SP [19]84. 38, [10] p. : LC Card 86-200279
HD6615.S32 M68 1984

TRADE-UNIONS - THRACE - HISTORY.
Papathanasē-Mousiopoulou, Kalliopē. Syntechnies & epangelmata stē Thrakē, 1685-1920 /. Athēna , 1985. 247 p. : LC Card 86-208086
HD6795.5.Z8 T56 1985

TRADE-UNIONS - TRANSPORT WORKERS - GERMANY (WEST)
Berger, Axel. Mitgliederförderung in Strassenverkehrsgenossenschaften /. Münster , 1985. 455 p. ; ISBN 3-7923-0537-2 (Deut. Bibl.) LC Card 86-148185
HD6698.T72 B863 1985

TRADE-UNIONS - TRANSPORT WORKERS - HAWAII - HISTORY.
Stern, Bernard W., 1912- Rutledge unionism . Honolulu , 1986. x, 147 p. ; LC Card 86-51020 DDC 331/.04138841322/0996931 19
HD6515.T72 H37 1986

TRADE-UNIONS - TURKEY.
Esin, Pars. Türkiye'de işveren sendikacılığı /. Ankara , 1974. xii, 288 p. ; LC Card 83-103059
HD6796.7 .E85 1974

TRADE-UNIONS - UKRAINE.
Kondratiuk, K. K. (Konstantin Konstantinovich) Profsoiuzy Ukrainy na zavershaiushchem ėtape stroitel′stva sotsializma /. L′vov , 1985. 173 p. ; LC Card 87-165263
HD6735.U5 K65 1985

TRADE-UNIONS - UNITED STATES.
Balliet, Lee. Survey of labor relations /. Washington, D.C. , c1981. ix, 198 p. : ISBN 0-87179-347-4 LC Card 80-26863 DDC 331/.0973
HD8072.5 .B34 ***NYPL [JLE 86-4719]***

Balliet, Lee. Survey of labor relations /. Washington, D.C. , c1987. xi, 212 p. : ISBN 0-87179-544-2 (pbk.) LC Card 87-864 DDC 331/.0973 19
HD8072.5 .B34 1987

Boulware, Lemuel Richetts, 1895- What to do about communism in unions . [Schenectady, N.Y.?] [1952?] 62 p. ; ***NYPL [JLD 86-247]***

Lehr, Richard I. The new unionism . New York, N.Y. , c1987. 114 p. ; ISBN 0-88057-672-3 (pbk.) LC Card 86-82864 DDC 331.88/0973 19
HD6508 .L427 1987

O'Reilly, James T., 1947- Unions' rights to company information /. Philadelphia, Pa. , c1987. xiii, 312 p. ; ISBN 0-89546-060-2 LC Card 85-82257 ***NYPL [JLL 74-174 no.21]***

Reynolds, Morgan O., 1942- Making America poorer . Washington, D.C. , c1987. ix, 218 p. ; ISBN 0-932790-63-1 LC Card 87-6569 DDC 338.5/1/0973 19
HD6508 .R435 1987

Unions in transition . San Francisco, Calif. , c1986. xviii, 506 p. : ISBN 0-917616-74-X : LC Card 86-10256 DDC 331.88 19
HD .U46 1986 ***NYPL [JLE 86-4238]***

Willman, Paul. Technological change, collective bargaining, and industrial efficiency /. Oxford , New York , c1986. xvi, 282 p. : ISBN 0-19-827262-6 : LC Card 86-5104 DDC 331.88/0941 19
HD6664 .W56 1986 ***NYPL [JLD 87-994]***

TRADE-UNIONS - UNITED STATES - ADDRESSES, ESSAYS, LECTURES.
Unions in crisis and beyond . Dover, Mass. , c1986. xii, 340 p. : ISBN 0-86569-127-4 : LC Card 85-26646 DDC 331.88 19
HD6508 .U45 1986 ***NYPL [JLE 86-1936]***

TRADE-UNIONS - UNITED STATES - ELECTIONS.
Benson, Herman W., 1910 (ca.)- How to get an honest union election /. Brooklyn, N.Y. [c1987] 65 p. : ISBN 0-9602244-4-0 (pbk.) LC Card 86-73217 DDC 331.87/4/0973 19
HD6490.E42 U62 1987

TRADE-UNIONS - UNITED STATES - HISTORY.
Balfour, Alan. Union-management relations in a changing economy /. Englewood Cliffs, N.J. , c1987. xiv, 482 p. : ISBN 0-13-938804-4 LC Card 86-30495 DDC 331/.0973 19
HD8066 .B34 1987

Brody, David. Workers in industrial America . New York , 1981, 1980. ix, 257 p. ; ISBN 0-19-502491-5 (pbk.) LC Card 78-27157
NYPL [JLD 86-3729]

Filippelli, Ronald L. Labor in the USA . New York , c1984. xii, 315 p. ; ISBN 0-394-34149-X LC Card 83-23458 DDC 331/.0973 19
HD8066 .F54 1984 ***NYPL [JFE 86-5130]***

How mighty a force? . Los Angeles , c1983. ix, 369 p. ; ***NYPL [JLD 87-277]***

Jones, Mother, 1843?-1930. [Selections. 1988.] The speeches and writings of Mother Jones /. Pittsburgh, Pa. , 1988. p. cm. ISBN 0-8229-3575-9 LC Card 87-25192 DDC 331.88/0973 19
HD8072 .J7832 1988

Life and labor . Albany , c1986. x, 343 p. ; ISBN 0-88706-173-7 LC Card 86-14362 DDC 305.5/62/0973 19
HD8066 .L54 1986 ***NYPL [JLE 86-4350]***

TRADE-UNIONS - UNITED STATES - HISTORY - 19TH CENTURY.
Sorge, Friedrich A. (Friedrich Adolf), 1828-1906. Friedrich A. Sorge's labor movement in the United States . New York , c1987. xiii, 196 p. ; ISBN 0-313-25518-0 (lib. bdg. : alk. paper) LC Card 86-31792 DDC 331/.0973 19
HD8072 .S7175 1987

TRADE-UNIONS - UNITED STATES - HISTORY - 20TH CENTURY.
The Cold war against labor . Berkeley, CA , c1987. 2 v. (xxii, 915 p.) : ISBN 0-913876-19-4 (set); 0-913876-20-4 (set) : LC Card 87-18510 DDC 331.88/0973 19
HD6508 .C62 1987

Fantasia, Rick. Cultures of solidarity . Berkeley , c1988. p. cm. ISBN 0-520-06053-9 (alk. paper) LC Card 87-16748 DDC 331.8/0973 19
HD8072.5 .F36 1988

Goldfield, Michael. The decline of organized labor in the United States /. Chicago , 1987. xv, 294 p. : ISBN 0-226-30102-8 LC Card 86-24890 DDC 331.88/0973 19
HD6508 .G683 1987

Pesotta, Rose, 1896- Bread upon the waters /. Ithaca, N.Y. , c1987. xxiv, 435 p., [10] p. of plates : ISBN 0-87546-127-1 (pbk. : alk. paper) LC Card 87-2953 DDC 331.88/0973 19
HD8072 .P375 1987

TRADE-UNIONS - UNITED STATES - HISTORY - SOURCES.
The Samuel Gompers papers /. Urbana , c1986- v. : ISBN 0-252-01138-4 (alk. paper : set) LC Card 84-2469 DDC 331.88/32/0924 19
HD6508 .S218 1986 ***NYPL [JLL 86-230]***

TRADE-UNIONS - UNITED STATES - MINORITY MEMBERSHIP - CASE STUDIES.
Copeland, Vincent. The blast furnace brothers /. New York, N.Y. , 1973. iv, 33 p. : LC Card 87-125932 DDC 331.13/3 19
HD4903.3.B582 U63 1973

TRADE-UNIONS - UNITED STATES - OFFICIALS AND EMPLOYEES.
Wells, Don, 1946- Empty promises . New York , c1987. xviii, 167 p. ; ISBN 0-85345-710-7 : LC Card 87-24687 DDC 331.25 19
HD6957.U6 W34 1987

TRADE-UNIONS - UNITED STATES - OFFICIALS AND EMPLOYEES - BIOGRAPHY.
Dubofsky, Melvyn, 1934- "Big Bill" Haywood /. New York , 1987. viii, 184 p. ; ISBN 0-312-01272-1 : LC Card 87-17355 DDC 331.88/6 B 19
HD6509.H3 D82 1987

Franco, Joseph. Hoffa's man . New York , c1987. xv, 332 p., [8] p. of plates : ISBN 0-13-517764-2 : LC Card 87-42675 DDC 331.88/11388324/0924 B 19
HD6509.F69 A3 1987

Salmond, John A. Miss Lucy of the CIO . Athens , c1988. p. cm. ISBN 0-8203-0956-7 (alk. paper) LC Card 87-5822 DDC 331.88/33/0924 B 19
HD6509.M375 S25 1988

TRADE-UNIONS - UNITED STATES - OFFICIALS AND EMPLOYEES - CORRUPT PRACTICES.
United States. President's Commission on Organized Crime. The edge . Washington, D.C. , 1985. 356 p. ; ***NYPL [JLE 87-41]***

United States. President's Commission on Organized Crime. The edge . Washington, D.C. , 1986. xxii, 393 p. ;
NYPL [JLE 86-2671]

TRADE-UNIONS - UNITED STATES - ORGANIZING.
New York (State). Legislature. Assembly. Standing Committee on Labor. A report on the plight of the collective bargaining system /. [Albany] [1984] 64 p. ; LC Card 86-622572 DDC 331.89/0973 19
HD6508 .N49 1984

Perry, Charles R. Union corporate campaigns /. Philadelphia, Pa. , c1987. viii, 211 p. : ISBN 0-89546-065-3 : LC Card 86-82727 DDC 331.89/12 19
HD6490.O72 U665 1987

TRADE-UNIONS - UNITED STATES - ORGANIZING - CASE STUDIES.
Grenier, Guillermo J. Inhuman relations . Philadelphia , 1988. xx, 232 p. ; ISBN 0-87722-502-8 (alk. paper) : LC Card 87-10116 DDC 331.25 19
HD6490.O72 U645 1988

Perry, Charles R. Union corporate campaigns /. Philadelphia, Pa. , c1987. viii, 211 p. : ISBN 0-89546-065-3 : LC Card 86-82727 DDC 331.89/12 19
HD6490.O72 U665 1987

TRADE-UNIONS - UNITED STATES - ORGANIZING - HISTORY.
Suggs, George G., 1929- Union busting in the Tri-State . Norman , 1986. xiv, 282 p. : ISBN 0-8061-2012-6 (alk. paper) LC Card 86-6910 DDC 331.89/2871/0973 19
HD5325.M52 1935 .S84 1986
NYPL [JLD 86-3971]

TRADE-UNIONS - UNITED STATES - POLITICAL ACTIVITY.
Lane, A. T. Solidarity or survival? . New York , 1987. xii, 230 p. ; ISBN 0-313-25544-X (lib. bdg. : alk. paper) LC Card 86-25735 DDC 331.6/2/0973 19
HD8081.A5 L36 1987

Rosenblum, Gerald. Immigrant workers; their impact on American labor radicalism. New

York [1973] vi, 189 p. ISBN 0-465-03207-9 LC Card 72-89280
HD8081.A5 R67 ***NYPL [JLE 73-3033]***

TRADE-UNIONS - UNITED STATES - POLITICAL ACTIVITY - HISTORY - 20TH CENTURY.
Vittoz, Stanley. New Deal labor policy and the American industrial economy /. Chapel Hill , c1987. 241 p. ; ISBN 0-8078-1729-5 LC Card 86-24911 DDC 331/.0973 19
HD8072 .V715 1987

TRADE-UNIONS - UNITED STATES - PUBLIC OPINION.
Lipset, Seymour Martin. The confidence gap . Baltimore , 1987. xxiv, 460 p. : ISBN 0-8018-3044-3 (pbk.) LC Card 86-27416 DDC 303.3/8/0973 19
HD2785 .L53 1987

A View of unions /. [Washington? D.C.] [1985] 25 p. ; LC Card 86-211350 DDC 331.88/0973 19
HD6508 .V39 1985

TRADE-UNIONS - URUGUAY.
Lucha y polémica sindical, 1968-1973. [Montevideo?] , 1985. 4 v. ; LC Card 86-107744 DDC 322/.2/09895 19
HD6647 .L83 1985 ***NYPL [JLC 86-368]***

TRADE-UNIONS - URUGUAY - HISTORY - 20TH CENTURY.
Lanzaro, Jorge Luis. Sindicatos y sistema político . Montevideo, Uruguay , 1986. 132 p. ; LC Card 87-403149 DDC 322/.2/09895 19
HD3616.U72 L36 1986

TRADE-UNIONS - URUGUAY - POLITICAL ACTIVITY.
Lucha y polémica sindical, 1968-1973. [Montevideo?] , 1985. 4 v. ; LC Card 86-107744 DDC 322/.2/09895 19
HD6647 .L83 1985 ***NYPL [JLC 86-368]***

TRADE-UNIONS - VENEZUELA - HISTORY - 20TH CENTURY.
Godio, Julio. 50 años de la C.T.V., 1936-1986 . Caracas, Venezuela [1986] 149 p. ; ISBN 980-607-709-1 LC Card 87-401745 DDC 331.88/0987 19
HD8362.C68 G63 1986

TRADE-UNIONS - VENEZUELA - STATISTICS.
Estadísticas sociales . Caracas, Venezuela , 1983. 2 v. ; LC Card 84-183391 DDC 312/.0987 19
HA1095 .E88 1983 ***NYPL [JLM 85-550]***

TRADE-UNIONS - VIETNAM.
Đ ' ang c Hà N 1985. 88 p. ; LC Card 87-153845
HD6820.5 .D36 1985

TRADE-UNIONS - WEST INDIES, BRITISH.
Lewis, W. Arthur (William Arthur), 1915- Labour in the West Indies . London , 1977. 104 p., [12] p. of plates : ISBN 0-901241-25-3 (pbk.) LC Card 86-232414
HD6595.4 .L49 1977

TRADE-UNIONS - WEST (U. S.) - HISTORY - 20TH CENTURY.
Labor in the West /. Manhattan, Kan., USA , c1986. 88 p. : ISBN 0-89745-090-6 (pbk.) LC Card 87-400877 DDC 331/.0978 19
HD8083.A17 L32 1986

TRADE-UNIONS - WHITE COLLAR WORKERS - ADDRESSES, ESSAYS, LECTURES.
White collar workers, trade unions, and class /. London , Dover, N.H. , c1986. 215 p. : ISBN 0-7099-0571-8 : LC Card 85-28806 DDC 331.88/041 19
HD8039.M39 W45 1986
NYPL [JLD 86-1602]

TRADE-UNIONS - WOODWORKERS - AUSTRIA.
Czasny, Karl. Lehrjahre bei Bau-Holz . Wien , c1985. ix, 148 p. ; ISBN 3-900351-34-1 LC Card 86-227367 DDC 331.88/174/09436 19
HD6678.W62 G493 1985

TRADE-UNIONS - WOODWORKERS - GERMANY (WEST) - BIOGRAPHY.
Wittkamp, Heinrich, 1903- Achtzig Jahre kritischer Bürger im 20. Jahrhundert . Mannheim , c1986. 232 p., [16] p. of plates : ISBN 3-87804-182-9 (Deut. Bibl.) LC Card 86-230657
HD6695.W58 A3 1986

TRADE-UNIONS - YUGOSLAVIA - ZADAR (CROATIA) - HISTORY.
Uranija, Valentin. 35 godina sindikata u Zadru . Zadar , 1981. 300 p., xlviii p. of plates : LC Card 86-190260
HD8632.S3433 U73 1981

Trade wars . Conybeare, John A. C. New York , 1987. xv, 319 p. ; ISBN 0-231-06234-6 LC Card 87-8097 DDC 382 19
HF1414 .C665 1987

TRADEMARKS.
Napoles, Veronica, 1951- Corporate identity design /. New York , c1988. 144 p. : ISBN 0-442-26844-0 (pbk.) : LC Card 87-6190 DDC 659.2/85 19
HD59.2 .N36 1988

TRADES. see **OCCUPATIONS.**

TRADES UNION CONGRESS - DIRECTORIES.
Eaton, Jack. The trade union directory . London , 1981. xii, 323 p. ; ISBN 0-86104-350-2 (pbk.) LC Card 86-673635
HD6663 .E27x 1981

TRADES UNION CONGRESS - HISTORY - 20TH CENTURY.
Nicholson, Marjorie. The TUC overseas . London , Boston , c1986. xvi, 329 p. ; ISBN 0-04-331103-2 (alk. paper) LC Card 85-28607 DDC 331.88/0941 19
HD8383 .N52 1986 ***NYPL [JLD 86-2932]***

TRADES-WASTE. see **FACTORY AND TRADE WASTE.**

Tradesmen and traders . Mackenney, Richard. London , c1987. xv, 289 p. : ISBN 0-7099-1763-5 LC Card 87-672566
HD6472.V4 M33x 1987b

TRADESMEN'S CARDS. see **ADVERTISING CARDS.**

Trading companies . Colaiácovo, Juan Luis. Rio de Janeiro, RJ , c1986. 448 p. : ISBN 85-85037-07-5; 85-05-37070-5 LC Card 87-135895 DDC 382/.06/01 19
HF1009.5 .C575 1986

TRADING COMPANIES.
Colaiácovo, Juan Luis. Trading companies . Rio de Janeiro, RJ , c1986. 448 p. : ISBN 85-85037-07-5; 85-05-37070-5 LC Card 87-135895 DDC 382/.06/01 19
HF1009.5 .C575 1986

TRADING COMPANIES - CASE STUDIES.
Colaiácovo, Juan Luis. Trading companies . Rio de Janeiro, RJ , c1986. 448 p. : ISBN 85-85037-07-5; 85-05-37070-5 LC Card 87-135895 DDC 382/.06/01 19
HF1009.5 .C575 1986

TRADING COMPANIES - CZECHOSLOVAKIA - DIRECTORIES.
Your trade partners in Czechoslovakia /. Praha , 1986. 187 p. : LC Card 87-127524 DDC 382/.025/437 19
HF3550.3.A48 Y58 1986

TRADING COMPANIES - DEVELOPING COUNTRIES - DIRECTORIES.
Handbook of state trading organizations of developing countries =. New York , 1985. clxxxix, 542 p. : ISBN 92-1-012014-0 (pbk.) LC Card 86-233995
HF1009.7.D44 H35 1985

TRADING COMPANIES - DEVELOPING COUNTRIES - HANDBOOKS, MANUALS, ETC.
Handbook of state trading organizations of developing countries =. New York , 1985. clxxxix, 542 p. : ISBN 92-1-012014-0 (pbk.) LC Card 86-233995
HF1009.7.D44 H35 1985

TRADING COMPANIES - HUNGARY.
Hegyi, Anna. A külkereskedő vállalat /. Budapest , 1985. 213, [1] p., [1] folded leaf of plates : ISBN 963-221-531-1 : LC Card 86-187063
HF1009.7.H8 H44 1985

The Hungarian enterprise in the context of intra-CMEA relations /. Budapest , 1986. 93 p. ; ISBN 963-301-138-8 (pbk.) LC Card 87-101284 DDC 337.439 19
HF1542.5.H8 H85 1986

TRADING COMPANIES - MACAO - HISTORY - 18TH CENTURY.
Diário da navegação de Macau, 1759-1761 . Lisboa , 1970. 274 p. ; LC Card 86-201114
HF1009.7.M25 D53 1970

As "Trading companies" no comércio exterior brasileiro. 3a. ed. aum. Rio de Janeiro-RJ : Associação Brasileira das Empresas Comerciais Exportadoras, 1984. 148 p. : ill. ; 31 cm. Includes bibliographical references. LC Card 85-208188
1. Export trading companies - Brazil. I. Associação Brasileira das Empresas Comerciais Exportadoras.
HF1009.7.B8 T73 1984

Trading gold and silver with futures and options / by the editors of Personal finance. 1st ed. Alexandria, VA (1101 King St., Suite 400, Alexandria 22314) : KCI, c1986. 149, 10 p. : ill. ; 28 cm. "Material ... taken from a seminar presented by Personal finance in New York City on September 9, 1986"--Prelim. p. [5] LC Card 87-110004 DDC 332.64/52 19
1. Gold. 2. Silver. 3. Commodity exchanges. I. Personal finance.
HG293 .T73 1986

Trading in banking : the impact of technology and deregulation on competition : preliminary report. [New York?] : Wilke Organization, c1986. iv ; 24 cm. Bibliography: p. 23. LC Card 87-128754 DDC 332.1/0973 19
1. Banks and banking - United States - Technological innovations. 2. Investment banking - United States - Technological innovations. 3. Bank investments - United States. 4. Banks and banking - United States - Deregulation. 5. Bankers - United States - Attitudes. I. Wilke Organization.
HG2491 .T7 1986

Trading in banking : the impact of technology and deregulation on competition. New York : Wilke Organization, c1987. x, 137 p. ; 28 cm. Bibliography: p. 123. Includes index. ISBN 0-939853-00-0 (pbk.) LC Card 87-404278 DDC 332.1/0973 19
1. Banks and banking - United States - Technological innovations. 2. Investment banking - United States - Technological innovations. 3. Bank investments - United States. 4. Banks and banking - United States - Deregulation. 5. Banks and banking - United States - Statistics. I. Wilke Organization.
HG2491 .T697 1987

Trading in soybean complex futures / [prepared by the Education and Publication Services Department of the Chicago Board of Trade]. [Chicago] : The Board, c1986. v, 53 p. ; 22 cm. LC Card 87-101090 DDC 332.64/4 19
1. Soybean industry - United States. 2. Commodity exchanges - United States. I. Chicago Board of Trade. Education and Publication Services Dept.
HG6047.S6 T73 1986

Trading markets and entry costs /. Holler, Manfred Joseph, 1946- Aarhus, Denmark [1986] 15 p. ; LC Card 86-219580 DDC 382.1 19
HD2756.5 .H64 1986

"Trading peasants" and urbanization in eighteenth-century Russia . Morrison, Daniel, 1945- New York , 1987. 415 p. ; ISBN 0-8240-8059-9 (alk. paper) : LC Card 87-7425 DDC 307.2 19
HB2068.S65 M67 1987

Trading secrets /. Winans, R. Foster. New York , c1986. xiv, 320 p., [8] p. of plates : ISBN 0-312-81227-2 : LC Card 86-12700 DDC 364.1/68 19
HG4572 .W547 1986 ***NYPL [JLE 86-4323]***

Trading technology . Ilgen, Thomas L. New York , 1987. x, 203 p. ; ISBN 0-275-92483-1 (alk. paper) : LC Card 86-21197 DDC 338.94/06 19
HC415.15 .I45 1986 ***NYPL [JLE 87-832]***

Trading up /. Goldstone, Nancy Bazelon. New York , c1988. viii, 262 p. ; ISBN 0-525-24621-5 : LC Card 87-19975 DDC 332.4/5/0924 B 19
HG3853 .G65 1988

Trading with South Africa /. Kopras, Andrew. [Canberra] , 1986. 14 p. ; LC Card 87-164241 DDC 382/.0968/094021 19
HF3901.A45 K66 1986

Tradition och reform i västra Södermanlands jordbruk, 1810-1890 . Köll, Anu-Mai. Stockholm , 1983. 252 p. : ISBN 91-22-00633-8 LC Card 84-114628
HD2020.S63 K65 1983

Traditsii krest'ianskogo zemlepol'zovaniia v Pomor'e i Zapadnoi Sibiri v XVII-XVIII vv. /. Vlasova, I. V. (Irina Vladimirovna) Moskva , 1984. 230 p. : LC Card 85-174592
HD719.W45 V55 1984

TRAFFIC. see **COMMUNICATION AND TRAFFIC.**

TRAFFIC ACCIDENTS AND ALCOHOLISM. see **DRINKING AND TRAFFIC ACCIDENTS.**

TRAFFIC ACCIDENTS - AUSTRALIA - FAIRFIELD (N.S.W.)
Fairfield on-scene study of collisions . [Sydney?] [1977] 120 p. : LC Card 85-170609
HE5614.5.A8 F37 1977

TRAFFIC ACCIDENTS - BRITISH COLUMBIA.
Rethinking young drivers /. [North Vancouver, B.C.] , c1987. ii, 291 p. : ISBN 0-7726-0588-2 (pbk.) LC Card 87-167603 DDC 363.1/251 19
HE5620.J8 R47 1987

Rothe, John Peter, 1948- Young drivers involved in injury producing crashes . North Vancouver, B.C. , c1986. ii, 77 p. : ISBN 0-7726-0530-0 (pbk.) LC Card 87-167610 DDC 363.1/251 19
HE5620.J8 R67 1986

TRAFFIC ACCIDENTS - CALIFORNIA - STATISTICS.
Huston, Ray E. Senior driver facts /. Sacramento, CA , Springfield, VA , 1986. iii, 22 p. : LC Card 86-623189 DDC 363.1/252/09794021 19
HE5614.3.C3 H87 1986

TRAFFIC ACCIDENTS - GERMANY (WEST) - BAVARIA.
Untersuchung der Unfälle auf Bundesautobahnen . [München?] [1976] 84 p. : LC Card 85-135444
HE5614.5.G3 U58 1976

TRAFFIC ACCIDENTS - GERMANY (WEST) - BAVARIA - ACCIDENTS.
Analyse von Unfällen motorisierter Zweiradbenutzer . [West Germany] [1976] 32 p. : LC Card 85-135424
HE5614.5.G3 A65 1976

TRAFFIC ACCIDENTS - GERMANY (WEST) - COLOGNE REGION.
Echterhoff, Wilfried. Einfluss von Verkehrssicherheitsinformationen auf unfallbeteiligte Kraftfahrer /. Köln [1983], c1981. 112 p. : LC Card 84-147580
HE5614.5.G3 E34 1983

TRAFFIC ACCIDENTS - GERMANY (WEST) - HESSE.
Untersuchung der Unfälle auf Bundesautobahnen . [München?] [1976] 84 p. : LC Card 85-135444
HE5614.5.G3 U58 1976

TRAFFIC ACCIDENTS - GERMANY (WEST) - NORTH RHINE-WESTPHALIA.
Untersuchung der Unfälle auf Bundesautobahnen . [München?] [1976] 84 p. : LC Card 85-135444
HE5614.5.G3 U58 1976

TRAFFIC ACCIDENTS - GERMANY (WEST) - STATISTICS.
Rohde, Horst. Sterbetafeln für Personenkraftwagen und Kombinationskraftwagen . Essen , 1981. 64 p. ; LC Card 87-408032 DDC 363.1/252/0943021 19
HE5614.5.G3 R64 1981

TRAFFIC ACCIDENTS - GREAT BRITAIN.
Grime, G. (Geoffrey) Handbook of road safety research /. London , Boston , 1987. ix, 149 p. : ISBN 0-408-02780-0 : LC Card 86-26427 DDC 363.1/25/0941 19
HE5614.5.G7 G77 1987

TRAFFIC ACCIDENTS - HUNGARY - BUDAPEST.
Buga, László. Biztonságos, jó utat! . [Budapest] , 1980. 95 p. : ISBN 963-316-028-6 (Magy. nemz. bibl.) LC Card 85-177784
HE5614.5.H8 B84 1980

TRAFFIC ACCIDENTS - ILLINOIS - STATISTICS.
Motorcycle accident facts, 1984. [Springfield, Ill.] , 1984. 15 p. : LC Card 86-622490 DDC 363.1/259 19
HE5614.3.I4 M674 1984

TRAFFIC ACCIDENTS - NEW YORK (STATE)
Dowling, Anne M. Two years of accident experience under STOP-DWI, December 1981-November 1983 /. [Albany] [1984] xiii, 67 p. : LC Card 86-622431 DDC 363.1/251 19
HE5620.D7 D68 1984

TRAFFIC ACCIDENTS - PREVENTION. see **TRAFFIC SAFETY.**

TRAFFIC ACCIDENTS - RUSSIAN S.F.S.R.
Osnovnye prichiny i usloviia vozniknoveniia PTP s tiazhelymi posledstviiami, puti i metody ikh ustraneniia. Bulgarian. Osnovni prichini i usloviia za vŭznikvane na PTP s tezhki posledstviia, pŭtishta i metodi za tiakhnoto otstraniavane /. Sofiia , 1985. 95 p. : LC Card 87-101607
HF5614.5.S62 O7516 1985

TRAFFIC ACCIDENTS - UNITED STATES.
Comparison of the insurance loss experience of unibody and frame construction cars after a collision repair, 1981-82 models. Washington, D.C. (Watergate 600, Washington 20037) , c1985. 10 p. : LC Card 87-107697 DDC 368.5/72/00973 19
HG9970.3 .C65 1985

Consistency of model year injury claim frequency results for selected 1981-1983 models. Washington, D.C (Watergate 600, Washington 20037) , c1986. 11 p. ; LC Card 87-107714 DDC 368.5/72/00973 19
HG9970.3 .C66 1986

Relationships between losses and vehicle density, 1982-84 models. Washington, D.C. (Watergate 600, Washington 20037) , c1985. 24 p. : LC Card 87-107842 DDC 368.5/72/00973 19
HG9970.3 .R45 1985

Seat belts, the lifesaving habit [motion picture] /. Van Nuys, CA , 1986. 1 film reel (20 min.) : LC Card 87-705126 DDC 629.2 11
HE5614.2

Seat belts, the lifesaving habit [videorecording] /. Van Nuys, CA , 1986. 1 videocassette (20 min.) : LC Card 87-705127 DDC 629.2 11
HE5614.2

Task force implementation guidelines for the development of state and community alcohol highway safety programs. [Washington, D.C.?] , 1983. 1 v. (various pagings) ;
NYPL [JLF 86-245]

TRAFFIC ACCIDENTS - UNITED STATES - COSTS - STATISTICS.
Highway Loss Data Institute insurance collision report . Washington, D.C. (Watergate 600, Washington 20037) , c1986. 51 p. : LC Card 86-210266 DDC 368.5/72/00973021 19
HG9970.3 .H536 1986

Highway Loss Data Institute insurance collision report . Washington, DC (Watergate 600, Washington 20037) , c1986. 24 p. ; LC Card 87-107636 DDC 368.5/72/00973021 19
HG9970.3 .H5365 1986

Highway Loss Data Institute insurance injury report . Washington, D.C. (Watergate 600, Washington 20037) , c1986. 30 p. : LC Card 87-107645 DDC 368.5/72/00973021 19
HG9970.3 .H537 1986

TRAFFIC ACCIDENTS - UNITED STATES - JUVENILE FILMS.
Seat belts are for kids, too [motion picture] /. Van Nuys, CA , 1987. 1 film reel (10 min.) : LC Card 87-706618 DDC 363.1 11
HE5614.2

Seat belts are for kids, too [videorecording] /. Van Nuys, CA , 1987. 1 videocassette (10 min.) : LC Card 87-706619 DDC 363.1 11
HE5614.2

TRAFFIC ACCIDENTS - UNITED STATES - STATISTICS.
Injury and collision losses by engine option, selected 1983 models. Washington, D.C. (Watergate 600, Washington 20037) , c1985. 11 p. ; LC Card 87-115471 DDC 368.5/72/00973 19
HG9970.3 .I524 1985

TRAFFIC ACCIDENTS - VIRGINIA.
Sharkey, Stephen M. Evaluation of the 1984 selective speed enforcement projects in Virginia /. Charlottesville, Va. [1987] xii, 117, [34] p. : LC Card 87-621546 DDC 388.3/144/09755 19
HE5620.S6 S532 1987

TRAFFIC ACCIDENTS - VIRGINIA - STATISTICS.
Sharkey, Stephen M. Evaluation of the 1984 selective speed enforcement projects in Virginia /. Charlottesville, Va. [1987] xii, 117, [34] p. : LC Card 87-621546 DDC 388.3/144/09755 19
HE5620.S6 S532 1987

Traffic and public transport in metropolitan Khartoum . Affan, Bodour O. Abu. Khartoum [1985] iv, 73 leaves ; LC Card 86-980566 DDC 388.4/1/096262 19
HE311.S742 K472 1985

Traffic and transportation report, 1986. Washington, D.C. (1750 K St., NW, Washington 20006) : Food Marketing Institute, Research Division, c1986. vi, 25 p. : ill. ; 28 cm. LC Card 86-232133 DDC 388.3/24 19
1. Food - Transportation. 2. Trucking - United States. I. Food Marketing Institute. Research Division.
HE199.5.F6 T715 1986

TRAFFIC CENSUS. see **TRAFFIC SURVEYS.**

TRAFFIC, CITY. see **TRAFFIC ENGINEERING.**

TRAFFIC CONGESTION - GERMANY (WEST)
Feuchtinger, Max Erich. Planungsbeispiele für Knotenpunkte des Strassenverkehrs /. Bad Godesberg [1960] 93 p., [2] folded leaves of plates : LC Card 86-191612
HE363.G3 F48 1960

TRAFFIC CONGESTION - TEXAS.
Lomax, Timothy J. Relative mobility in Texas cities, 1975 to 1984 /. College Station, Tex. [1986] xiii, 30, 9 p. : LC Card 87-620994 DDC 380.5 s 388.4/1314/09764 19
HE203 .T43 no. 339-8 HE356.T4

TRAFFIC CONGESTION - UNITED STATES.
Cervero, Robert. Suburban gridlock /. New Brunswick, N.J. , c1986. xxiii, 248 p. : ISBN 0-88285-115-2 : LC Card 86-2628 DDC 388.4/13142/0973 19
HE355.3.C64 C47 1986
NYPL [JLE 86-4446]

TRAFFIC CONTROL. see **TRAFFIC ENGINEERING.**

Traffic data collection and analysis . French, Alexander. Washington, D.C. [1986] 58 p. : ISBN 0-309-04406-5 (pbk.) : LC Card 86-51174 DDC 388.3/14/072 19
HE369 .F68 1986

TRAFFIC ENGINEERING.
Koller, Sándor. Forgalomtechnika és közlekedéstervezés /. Budapest , 1986. 291 p. : ISBN 963-10-6412-3 : LC Card 87-148352
HE333 .K575 1986

Stover, Vergil G., 1933- Transportation and land development /. Englewood Cliffs, N.J. , c1988. xiii, 239 p. : ISBN 0-13-930413-4 : LC Card 87-11419 DDC 625.7/25 19
HE335 .S76 1988

TRAFFIC ENGINEERING - GERMANY, WEST.
ADAC. Strassenverkehr 2000 . München [1979] 24 p. : LC Card 85-147077
HE363.G3 A33 1979

Feuchtinger, Max Erich. Planungsbeispiele für Knotenpunkte des Strassenverkehrs /. Bad Godesberg [1960] 93 p., [2] folded leaves of plates : LC Card 86-191612
HE363.G3 F48 1960

TRAFFIC ENGINEERING - GERMANY (WEST) - MÜNSTER IN WESTFALEN.
Busse, Dieter. Die Wirkungen von Sonderfahrstreifen für Busse auf die Fahrzeiten im Individualverkehr und öffentlichen Personenahverkehr . Münster [1985?] xii, 274 p. : ISBN 3-88660-264-8 LC Card 86-138804
HE363.G34 M933 1985

TRAFFIC ENGINEERING - HUNGARY.
Az Ország közuthálózatának müszaki minősitése és nyilvántartása /. [Budapest] , 1983. 2 v. : LC Card 84-253458
HE363.H82 O76 1983

TRAFFIC ESTIMATION - PAKISTAN - KARACHI.
Afghani, Abdus Sattar. Traffic growth in

Karachi . [Karachi] [1985] [25] leaves : LC Card 85-931413 DDC 388.4/13142/09549183 19
HE373.P183 K372 1985

TRAFFIC ESTIMATION - WASHINGTON METROPOLITAN AREA.
Kaufmann, Elizabeth Irwin. Traffic growth resulting from future development . Washington, D.C. (1875 Eye St., N.W., Washington 20006-5454) , c1987. ix, 53, 15 p. : LC Card 87-161086 DDC 388.4/13142/09753 19
HE356.5.W3 K38 1987

TRAFFIC FLOW - AUSTRIA - STATISTICS.
Strassenverkehrszählung 1980 auf Bundesstrassen im gesamten Bundesgebiet der Republik Österreich /. Wien , 1985. 288 p. : LC Card 86-170848
HA1173 .A27 Heft 750 HE363.A93T7

TRAFFIC FLOW - DENMARK - RANDERS.
Trafikanalyse Randers 1.-2. december 1982. [Copenhagen] [1983] 64 p. : LC Card 84-169856
HE373.D43 R368 1983

TRAFFIC FLOW - GERMANY (WEST)
Strassenverkehrszählung 1978 in der Bundesrepublik Deutschland . Köln , 1979. 96 p. : LC Card 87-408379 DDC 388/.0943 s 388.3/0943 19
HE5601 .S89 Heft 13 HE5669.A6

TRAFFIC FLOW - MATHEMATICAL MODELS.
Leutzbach, Wilhelm. [Einführung in die Theorie des Verkehrsflusses. English.] Introduction to the theory of traffic flow /. Berlin , New York , c1988. xi, 204 p. : ISBN 0-387-17113-4 (U. S.) : LC Card 87-9839 DDC 388.3/143 19
HE336.T7 L4813 1988

TRAFFIC FLOW - STATISTICAL METHODS.
Leutzbach, Wilhelm. [Einführung in die Theorie des Verkehrsflusses. English.] Introduction to the theory of traffic flow /. Berlin , New York , c1988. xi, 204 p. : ISBN 0-387-17113-4 (U. S.) : LC Card 87-9839 DDC 388.3/143 19
HE336.T7 L4813 1988

TRAFFIC FLOW - TEXAS.
Lomax, Timothy J. Relative mobility in Texas cities, 1975 to 1984 /. College Station, Tex. [1986] xiii, 30, 9 p. : LC Card 87-620994 DDC 380.5 s 388.4/1314/09764 19
HE203 .T43 no. 339-8 HE356.T4

TRAFFIC FLOW - TEXAS - EVALUATION.
Mason, John M. (John Michael), 1950- Operational and geometric evaluation of exclusive truck lanes /. College Station, Tex. , Springfield, Va. [1986] vii, 156 p. : LC Card 86-622239 DDC 380.5 s 388.3/14 19
HE203 .T43 no. 331-3F HE356.T4

TRAFFIC FLOW - UNITED STATES.
Cervero, Robert. Suburban gridlock /. New Brunswick, N.J. , c1986. xxiii, 248 p. : ISBN 0-88285-115-2 : LC Card 86-2628 DDC 388.4/13142/0973 19
HE355.3.C64 C47 1986
NYPL [JLE 86-4446]

Traffic growth in Karachi . Afghani, Abdus Sattar. [Karachi] [1985] [25] leaves : LC Card 85-931413 DDC 388.4/13142/09549183 19
HE373.P183 K372 1985

Traffic growth resulting from future development . Kaufmann, Elizabeth Irwin. Washington, D.C. (1875 Eye St., N.W., Washington 20006-5454) , c1987. ix, 53, 15 p. : LC Card 87-161086 DDC 388.4/13142/09753 19
HE356.5.W3 K38 1987

TRAFFIC MANAGEMENT, INDUSTRIAL. see **SHIPMENT OF GOODS.**

TRAFFIC NOISE - GERMANY (WEST)
Fechtel, Hans-Walter. Flächenhafte Verkehrsberuhigung . Bergisch Gladbach , 1986. 282 p. : LC Card 87-408360 DDC 388.4/0943 19
HE311.G3 F4 1986

Franz, Lothar. Verkehrsberuhigung in Städten und Gemeinden /. Grafenau , c1982. 134 p. : ISBN 3-88508-780-4 : LC Card 82-204794
HE311.G3 F73 1982

TRAFFIC REGULATION. see **TRAFFIC ENGINEERING.**

TRAFFIC SAFETY AND CHILDREN - UNITED STATES - JUVENILE FILMS.
Seat belts are for kids, too [motion picture] /. Van Nuys, CA , 1987. 1 film reel (10 min.) : LC Card 87-706618 DDC 363.1 11
HE5614.2

Seat belts are for kids, too [videorecording] /. Van Nuys, CA , 1987. 1 videocassette (10 min.) : LC Card 87-706619 DDC 363.1 11
HE5614.2

TRAFFIC SAFETY - BERLIN (GERMANY)
Homfeld, Wolfgang. Verkehrsberuhigung in Berlin (West) . Berlin , c1984. 306 p. : ISBN 3-496-00782-6 LC Card 84-212018
HE311.G32 B4753 1984

TRAFFIC SAFETY - CONGRESSES.
International Seminar on "Road Safety" (1986 : Srinagar, India) International Seminar on "Road Safety", Srinagar, September 17-18, 1986 /. New Delhi [1986] 1 v. (various pagings) : LC Card 87-901986 DDC 363.1/25 19
HE5614 .I5717 1986

Road Traffic Safety Seminar (1984 : Wellington, N.Z.) Road Traffic Safety Seminar, 15-17 August, 1984 . Wellington, N.Z. [1985?] 2 v. : LC Card 87-101217 DDC 363.1/25/09931 19
HE5614.5.N45 R62 1984

Vehicle highway infrastructure . Warrendale, PA , c1987. 208 p. : ISBN 0-89883-455-4 (pbk.) LC Card 86-63707 DDC 363.1/25 19
HE5606 .V44 1987

TRAFFIC SAFETY - DENMARK - RESEARCH.
Virksomheden i årene 1981-1983 . Gentofte , København , 1984. 80 p. : ISBN 87-7327-022-9 LC Card 86-100414
HE5614.5.D4 V57 1984

TRAFFIC SAFETY - EUROPE.
TRAFFIC SAFETY - GERMANY, WEST.
ADAC. Strassenverkehr 2000 . München [1979] 24 p. : LC Card 85-147077
HE363.G3 A33 1979

Fechtel, Hans-Walter. Flächenhafte Verkehrsberuhigung . Bergisch Gladbach , 1986. 282 p. : LC Card 87-408360 DDC 388.4/0943 19
HE311.G3 F4 1986

Grosse-Berndt, Gisela. Wirksamkeitsuntersuchung zum ADAC-Motorrad-Sicherheitstraining. Köln [1983] iii, 160, ii, 112, 27 p. : LC Card 84-147564
HE5614.5.G3 G75 1983

TRAFFIC SAFETY - GERMANY (WEST) - COLOGNE.
Haas, Ingrid. Funktion und Wirkung von Aufklebern an Personenkraftwagen /. Köln [1983] 101, [13] p. : LC Card 84-147451
HE5614.5.G3 H28 1983

Kockelke, Wilhelm. Untersuchung der Vorfahrtregelung "Rechts vor Links" unter dem Aspekt der Verkehrssicherheit /. Bergisch Gladbach [1983] 63, 3 p. : LC Card 84-147884
HE363.G32 U744 1983

TRAFFIC SAFETY - GERMANY (WEST) - CONGRESSES.
Die Sicherung des Fussgängerverkehrs. Köln , 1976. ii, 169 p. : LC Card 86-185084
HE5614.5.G3 A7 Bd. 29

TRAFFIC SAFETY - GOVERNMENT POLICY - GREAT BRITAIN.
Irwin, Alan. Risk and the control of technology . Manchester [Greater Manchester] , Dover, N.H., USA , c1985. vii, 265 p. : ISBN 0-7190-1723-8 : LC Card 84-17153 DDC 363.1/25561/0941 19
HE5614.2 .I79 1985 ***NYPL [JLD 87-929]***

TRAFFIC SAFETY - GOVERNMENT POLICY - UNITED STATES.
Irwin, Alan. Risk and the control of technology . Manchester [Greater Manchester] , Dover, N.H., USA , c1985. vii, 265 p. : ISBN 0-7190-1723-8 : LC Card 84-17153 DDC 363.1/25561/0941 19
HE5614.2 .I79 1985 ***NYPL [JLD 87-929]***

TRAFFIC SAFETY - GREAT BRITAIN.
Grime, G. (Geoffrey) Handbook of road safety research /. London , Boston , 1987. ix, 149 p. : ISBN 0-408-02780-0 : LC Card 86-26427 DDC 363.1/25/0941 19
HE5614.5.G7 G77 1987

TRAFFIC SAFETY - HUNGARY.
Az OKBT Tudományos Kutatási Szakbizottság kezdeményezése, illetve megbízása alapján készült kutatások, 1973-1983 /. [Budapest] , 1983. 124 p. : ISBN 963-02-3169-7 (Magy. nemz. bibl.) LC Card 85-126922
HE5614.5.H8 O38 1983
NYPL [JLD 87-1181]

TRAFFIC SAFETY - HUNGARY - BUDAPEST.
Buga, László. Biztonságos, jó utat! . [Budapest] , 1980. 95 p. : ISBN 963-316-028-6 (Magy. nemz. bibl.) LC Card 85-177784
HE5614.5.H8 B84 1980

TRAFFIC SAFETY - NEW MEXICO.
New Mexico. Traffic Safety Bureau. Highway safety plan, fiscal year 1987 /. Santa Fe, N.M. (P.O. Box 1028, Santa Fe 87504-1028) [1986] 190 leaves : LC Card 86-622688 DDC 363.1/256/09789 19
HE5614.3.N47 N49 1986

TRAFFIC SAFETY - NEW ZEALAND - CONGRESSES.
Road Traffic Safety Seminar (1984 : Wellington, N.Z.) Road Traffic Safety Seminar, 15-17 August, 1984 . Wellington, N.Z. [1985?] 2 v. : LC Card 87-101217 DDC 363.1/25/09931 19
HE5614.5.N45 R62 1984

TRAFFIC SAFETY - ONTARIO.
Ontario. Legislative Assembly. Select Committee on Highway Safety. Select Committee on Highway Safety . [Ontario, Canada] [1977] 1 v. in various pagings : LC Card 85-184813
HE5614.5.C2 O5 1977

TRAFFIC SAFETY - RESEARCH.
OECD road safety research . Paris [Washington, D.C.] 1986. 106 p. : ISBN 92-64-12814-X (pbk.) : LC Card 86-212506 DDC 363.1/25 19
HE5614 .O34 1986

TRAFFIC SAFETY - RESEARCH - HUNGARY.
Az OKBT Tudományos Kutatási Szakbizottság kezdeményezése, illetve megbízása alapján készült kutatások, 1973-1983 /. [Budapest] , 1983. 124 p. : ISBN 963-02-3169-7 (Magy. nemz. bibl.) LC Card 85-126922
HE5614.5.H8 O38 1983
NYPL [JLD 87-1181]

TRAFFIC SAFETY - RUSSIAN S.F.S.R.
Osnovnye prichiny i usloviia vozniknoveniia PTP s tiazhelymi posledstviiami, puti i metody ikh ustraneniia. Bulgarian. Osnovni prichini i usloviia za vŭznikvane na PTP s tezhki posledstviia, pŭtishta i metodi za tiakhnoto otstraniavane /. Sofiia , 1985. 95 p. : LC Card 87-101607
HF5614.5.S62 O7516 1985

TRAFFIC SAFETY - STUDY AND TEACHING - EVALUATION.
Effectiveness of road safety education programmes . Paris [Washington, D.C.] 1986. 134 p. : ISBN 92-64-12881-6 : LC Card 87-119891 DDC 363.1/2575/07 19
HE5613.5 .E33 1986

TRAFFIC SAFETY - STUDY AND TEACHING - GERMANY (WEST)
Methoden und Kriterien zur Überprüfung des Erfolgs von Aufklärungskampagnen . Köln , 1982. 99, [93] p. : LC Card 83-178796
HE5614.5.G3 M37 1982

TRAFFIC SAFETY - STUDY AND TEACHING - HUNGARY - CONGRESSES.
Budapesti pedagógusok közlekedési oktatási és nevelési konferenciája . [Budapest , 1978] ([Budapest] :fKészült az MTI Sokszorosító Üzemében) 100 p. ; LC Card 82-204792
HE5614 .B78 1978

TRAFFIC SAFETY - UNITED STATES.
Task force implementation guidelines for the development of state and community alcohol highway safety programs. [Washington, D.C.?] , 1983. 1 v. (various pagings) ;
NYPL [JLF 86-245]

TRAFFIC SAFETY - VIRGINIA.
Sharkey, Stephen M. Evaluation of the 1984 selective speed enforcement projects in Virginia /. Charlottesville, Va. [1987] xii, 117, [34] p. : LC Card 87-621546 DDC 388.3/144/09755 19
HE5620.S6 S532 1987

TRAFFIC SIGNS AND SIGNALS.
Are you reading me? [motion picture] /. Falls Church, VA , 1985. 1 film reel (9 min.) : LC Card 85-702717 DDC 388.3 11
HE5614

Are you reading me? [videorecording] /. Falls Church, VA , 1985. 1 videocassette (9 min.) : LC Card 85-702718 DDC 388.3 11
HE5614

TRAFFIC SURVEYS - DATA PROCESSING.
French, Alexander. Traffic data collection and analysis . Washington, D.C. [1986] 58 p. : ISBN 0-309-04406-5 (pbk.) : LC Card 86-51174 DDC 388.3/14/072 19
HE369 .F68 1986

TRAFFIC SURVEYS - DENMARK.
60-punkts tællinger 1983. [Copenhagen] , 1984. 36 p. : LC Card 85-156478
HE373.D4 A6 1984

TRAFFIC SURVEYS - DENMARK - RANDERS.
Trafikanalyse Randers 1.-2. december 1982. [Copenhagen] [1983] 64 p. : LC Card 84-169856
HE373.D43 R368 1983

TRAFFIC SURVEYS - EQUIPMENT AND SUPPLIES.
French, Alexander. Traffic data collection and analysis . Washington, D.C. [1986] 58 p. : ISBN 0-309-04406-5 (pbk.) : LC Card 86-51174 DDC 388.3/14/072 19
HE369 .F68 1986

TRAFFIC SURVEYS - ILLINOIS.
Illinois travel statistics, 1985. [Springfield, Ill.] [1986] 19 leaves : LC Card 86-622775 DDC 388.3/142/09773 19
HE371.I3 I47 1986

TRAFFIC SURVEYS - ISRAEL.
Economic transportation survey. [Paris] [Courbevoie, Seine] , 1966. 3 v. : LC Card 87-125917
HE373.I75 E36 1966

TRAFFIC SURVEYS - KENYA.
Trends in road use in Kenya . Nairobi , 1981. viii, 158 p. : LC Card 87-980482 DDC 388.3/142/096762 19
HE373.K4 T73 1981

TRAFFIC SURVEYS - UNITED STATES.
Lau, Lorrie A. Y. Analysis of national and regional travel trends /. Washington, D.C. , 1986. iii, 78, 32 p. : LC Card 87-601033 DDC 388.3/14/0973 19
HE370.T74 L38 1986

TRAFFIC SURVEYS - WASHINGTON METROPOLITAN AREA.
1986 D.C. Core Cordon Count of vehicular and passenger volumes /. [Washington, D.C.] , c1986. iv, 34 p., [66] p. : LC Card 87-105302 DDC 388.4/13142/09753 19
HE372.W3 A15 1986

TRAFFIC SURVEYS - WASHINGTON METROPOLITAN AREA - STATISTICS.
1986 Beltway cordon count of vehicular and passenger volumes. [Washington, D.C.] [1986] iv, 35 p., [109] p. : LC Card 87-119314 DDC 388.4/1314/09753021 19
HE5634.W3 A17 1986

TRAFFIC VIOLATIONS - UNITED STATES.
Reducing highway crashes through administrative license revocation. [Washington, D.C.?] , 1986. 89 p. : ***NYPL [JLF 86-1382]***

Il traffico nei centri storici /. Bortoli, Michele. [Lucca, Italy] , 1986. 236 p. : LC Card 87-151755
HE311.I82 L843 1986

El Tráfico de perfeccionamiento : admisión temporal, reposición con franquicia, draw back. 2a ed. rev. Madrid, España : Servicio de Estudios Económicos, Banco Exterior de España, 1983. 96 p. : forms ; 19 cm. (Manuales Extebank. Serie Comercio exterior . 1) ISBN 84-500-9221-3 LC Card 85-193715
1. Drawbacks - Spain. I. Banco Exterior de España. Servicio de Estudios Económicos. II. Series.
HF1717.S7 T73 1983

Trafikanalyse Randers 1.-2. december 1982. [Copenhagen] : Vejdirektoratet, Økonomisk-statistisk afd., [1983] 64 p. : ill. (some col.) ; 30 cm. "September 1983." LC Card 84-169856
1. Traffic surveys - Denmark - Randers. 2. Traffic flow - Denmark - Randers. I. Denmark. Vejdirektoratet. Økonomisk-statistisk afdeling.
HE373.D43 R368 1983

Tragediia millionov. Lapitskiĭ, Mark Isaakovich. The tragedy of millions . Moscow , 1985. 54 p., [8] p. of plates : LC Card 87-100047 DDC 331.13/7 19
HD5708 .L36 1985

The tragedy of black lung . Barth, Peter S., 1937- Kalamazoo, MI , 1987. xi, 292 p. ; ISBN 0-88099-044-9 (pbk.) LC Card 87-8332 DDC 368.4/1 19
HD7264 .B37 1987

The tragedy of millions . Lapitskiĭ, Mark Isaakovich. Moscow , 1985. 54 p., [8] p. of plates : LC Card 87-100047 DDC 331.13/7 19
HD5708 .L36 1985

Träger, Manfred Georg. Entwicklung und Funktion des britischen und deutschen Systems der Arbeitsvermittlungs- und Berufsberatungsdienste : ein Vergleich unter besonderer Berücksichtigung aktueller Beschäftigungsprobleme / Manfred Georg Träger. Nürnberg : Institut für Arbeitsmarkt- und Berufsforschung der Bundesanstalt für Arbeit, 1981. ii, 80, 48 p. ; 21 cm. (Beiträge zur Arbeitsmarkt- und Berufsforschung, 0173-6574 . 58) "Glossarium, Wörterverzeichnis Deutsch-Englisch": p. 1-48 (2nd group) Bibliography: p. 79-80. LC Card 82-200262 DDC 331.11/0941 19
1. Manpower policy - Great Britain. 2. Manpower policy - Germany, West. I. Title. II. Series.
HD5765.A6 T72 1981 ***NYPL [JLD 87-905]***

TRAILS - ALASKA.
Roberts, Malcolm B. Senate Transportation Committee, RS 2477 Task Force report /. [Anchorage, Alaska] [1986] 121 leaves, 27 p. : LC Card 86-622718 DDC 333.78/09798 19
HE356.A4 R63 1986

Train, John. The midas touch : the strategies that have made Warren Buffet America's pre-eminent investor / John Train.1st ed. New York : Harper & Row, c1987. xi, 207 p. ; 24 cm. Bibliography: p. [193]-195. Includes index. ISBN 0-06-015643-0 : LC Card 86-45157 DDC 332.6/092/4 B 19
1. Buffet, Warren. 2. Capitalists and financiers - United States - Biography. 3. Investments - United States. I. Title.
HG172.B84 T72 1987

The trainer's handbook . Mitchell, Garry. New York , c1987. ix, 351 p. : ISBN 0-8144-5875-0 LC Card 86-47819 DDC 658.3/124 19
HF5549.5.T7 M58 1987

The Trainer's library / developed by the Learning and Development Organization of the American Telephone and Telegraph Company in conjunction with Addison-Wesley Training Systems. Reading, Mass. : Addison-Wesley, <1987- > p. cm. Includes bibliographies and indexes. CONTENTS. - -- [2] Planning and analysis -- [3] Techniques of instructional development. ISBN 0-201-12633-8 (v. 2) : LC Card 87-11415 DDC 658.3/124 19
1. Employees, Training of. I. American Telephone and Telegraph Company. Learning and Development Organization. II. Addison-Wesley Training Systems (Firm).
HF5549.5.T7 T663 1987

The Trainer's professional development handbook / Ray Bard ... [et al.], with Sheila C. Henderson ... [et al.]. 1st ed. San Francisco : Jossey-Bass, 1987. xix, 327 p. : ill. ; 26 cm. (Jossey-Bass management series) Bibliography: p. 291-302. Includes index. ISBN 1-555-42067-2 (alk. paper) LC Card 87-45507 DDC 658.3/124 19
1. Employees, Training of. I. Bard, Ray. II. Series.
HF5549.5.T7 T6633 1987

Training and development handbook : a guide to human resource development / Robert L. Craig, editor in chief.3rd ed. New York : McGraw-Hill, c1987. xiv, 878 p. : ill. ; 24 cm. "Sponsored by the American Society for Training and Development." Includes bibliographies and index. ISBN 0-07-013353-0 : LC Card 87-2629 DDC 658.3/124 19
1. Employees, Training of. I. Craig, Robert L. II. American Society for Training and Development.
HF5549.5.T7 T6648 1987

Training and employment programs for Americans with disabilities. National directory, training and employment programs for Americans with disabilities /. Washington, D.C. [1985] vii, 374 p. : LC Card 85-602984 DDC 362.4/0484/02573 19
HD7256.U5 N335 1985 ***NYPL [JLF 87-466]***

Training and technology . Kearsley, Greg, 1951- Reading, Ma. , c1984. vii, 198 p. : ISBN 0-201-10335-4 : LC Card 83-22336 DDC 658.3/12404 19
HF5549.5.T7 K343 1984
NYPL [JLE 86-2641]

Training and technology. Kearsley, Greg, 1951- Training and technology . Reading, Ma. , c1984. vii, 198 p. : ISBN 0-201-10335-4 : LC Card 83-22336 DDC 658.3/12404 19
HF5549.5.T7 K343 1984
NYPL [JLE 86-2641]

Training for new technology /. Bushnell, David S. New York , c1983. 41 p. ; ISBN 0-08-029508-8 : LC Card 83-17341 DDC 658.3/124 19
HD5715.2 .B87 1983
NYPL [JLM 83-380 no.27]

Training for work in the computer age . Goldstein, Harold. Washington, D.C. , 1986. iv, 109 p. ; LC Card 86-601422 DDC 331.25/92 19
HD5715.2 .G63 1986

Training in organizations . Goldstein, Irwin L., 1937- Monterey, Calif. , c1986. xv, 315 p. : ISBN 0-534-05604-0 : LC Card 85-21348 DDC 658.3/12404 19
HF5549.5.T7 G543 1985
NYPL [JLE 86-1519]

Training in the automated office . Goldfield, Randy J. New York , 1987. ix, 190 p. ; ISBN 0-89930-112-6 (lib. bdg. : alk. paper) LC Card 86-30605 DDC 658.3/1245 19
HF5547.5 .G655 1987

Training needs . Richter, Lothar. Geneva , 1986. viii, 83 p. : ISBN 92-2-105458-6 (pbk.) : LC Card 86-222104 DDC 331.25/92 19
HD5715 .R53 1986

TRAINING NEEDS.
Guide to training needs assessment /. Ljubljana, Yugoslavia , c1984. 65 p. ; ISBN 92-9038-412-8 (pbk.) LC Card 85-242690 DDC 658.3/12404 19
HF5549.5.T7 G847 1984

Rossett, Allison. Training needs assessment /. Englewood Cliffs, N.J. , c1987. xvi, 294 p. : ISBN 0-87778-195-8 LC Card 87-9070 DDC 658.3/124 19
HF5549.5.T7 R65 1987

Training needs assessment /. Rossett, Allison. Englewood Cliffs, N.J. , c1987. xvi, 294 p. : ISBN 0-87778-195-8 LC Card 87-9070 DDC 658.3/124 19
HF5549.5.T7 R65 1987

TRAINING NEEDS - EVALUATION.
Hawthorne, Elizabeth M. Evaluating employee training programs . New York , 1987. xiv, 196 p. : ISBN 0-89930-242-4 (lib. bdg. : alk. paper) LC Card 87-5984 DDC 658.3/12404 19
HF5549.5.T7 H36 1987

Training needs for co-operative movement staff : a quantitative survey, Kenya, 1983. [Nairobi?] : Ministry of Co-operative Development, Training and Manpower Development Section, [1984] [166] p. : ill. ; 29 cm. LC Card 86-980729 DDC 331.12/51334/096762 19
1. Cooperative societies - Kenya - Employees - Training of. 2. Kenya - Officials and employees - In-service training. 3. Manpower policy - Kenya. I. Kenya. Ministry of Co-operative Development. Training and Manpower Development Section.
HD3560.5.A4 T73 1984

TRAINING, OCCUPATIONAL. see **OCCUPATIONAL TRAINING.**

TRAINING OF EMPLOYEES. see **EMPLOYEES, TRAINING OF.**

TRAINING OF EXECUTIVES. see **EXECUTIVES, TRAINING OF.**

Training of rural youth for self-employment (TRYSEM) : proceedings of seminars, July 7-9, 1980 & September 8-10, 1980. Hyderabad,

[India] : National Institute of Rural Development, 1981. vii, 252 p. ; 24 cm. Spine title: TRYSEM. LC Card 81-904606 DDC 331.3/42492/0954 19
1. Occupational training - India - Congresses. 2. Self-employed - India - Congresses. 3. Rural youth - Employment - India - Congresses. 4. Manpower policy, Rural - India - Congresses. I. Title: TRYSEM. II. Title: T.R.Y.S.E.M.
HD5715.5.I5 T72 1981 *NYPL [JLF 86-1203]*

Training Southeast Asian refugee women for employment . Mason, Sarah R. Minneapolis, Minn. , 1986. viii, 142 p. : LC Card 86-72303 DDC 331.4/2592/08995073 19
HD5715.2 .M37 1986

TRAINING, VOCATIONAL. see **OCCUPATIONAL TRAINING.**

The training wheel . Rogoff, Rosalind Louise. New York , c1987. 151 p. : ISBN 0-471-83467-X LC Card 86-32409 DDC 658.3/12404 19
HF5549.5.T7 R565 1987

TRAINING WITHIN INDUSTRY. see **EMPLOYEES, TRAINING OF.**

Trainor, Lois. (joint author) Davis, Charlotte. Ports of California. Los Angeles [1970] 80 p. LC Card 79-114863 DDC 387.1/09794
HE554.C16 D3

Trăistaru, Ion. Eficienţa economico-socială /. Craiova , 1983. 392 p. ; LC Card 84-152996
HC405.Z9 I523 1983

Traité marxiste d'économie politique. Le Capitalisme monopoliste d'État. Paris [1971] 2 v. LC Card 75-585406
HC59 .C26 *NYPL [JLC 71-28]*

La trama secreta de la radiodifusión argentina . Horvath, Ricardo. Cap. Fed. [i.e. Buenos Aires, Argentina] [1986] 153 p. ; ISBN 950-9458-13-9 LC Card 86-226636
HE8699.A7 H67 1986

Tramontana, Antonino. La Potestà impositiva dei comuni e delle province /. Rimini , c1985. 109 p. ; LC Card 85-194391 DDC 336.2/014/45 19
HJ9498 .P68 1985 *NYPL [JLE 86-4120]*

The trampling of the grass . Ramphal, S. S. [Addis Ababa?] [1985] 41 p. : LC Card 85-981035 DDC 338.96 19
HC800 .R36 1985

TRAMPS - ENGLAND - HISTORY.
Pound, John. Poverty and vagrancy in Tudor England /. London , New York , 1986. xii, 116 p. ; ISBN 0-582-35508-7 : LC Card 85-19747 DDC 305.5/69/0942 19
HC260.P6 P68 1986 *NYPL [JLD 86-2366]*

TRAMWAYS. see **STREET-RAILROADS.**

Tran, Van Hoa. National income and economic progress . New York , 1988. p. cm. ISBN 0-312-01566-6 : LC Card 87-24063 DDC 339.3 19
HB141.5 .N375 1988

Tranquillitas ordinis . Weigel, George. Oxford , New York , 1987. xiii, 489 p. ; ISBN 0-19-504193-3 (alk. paper) : LC Card 86-12742 DDC 261.8/73/08822 19
BX1795.P43 W45 1987
NYPL [JFE 87-1638]

Trans Atlantik. Kampe, Dieter, 1953- Die Macher . Pfaffenweiler , 1986. 191 p. ; ISBN 3-89085-143-6 LC Card 87-133889 DDC 338.0943 19
HC286.7 .K36 1986

TRANSACTION COSTS.
Becker, Hans, Dr. Eine Transaktionskostentheoretische Interpretation interner Arbeitsmärkte /. Berlin , c1985. 156 p. ; ISBN 3-428-05848-8 LC Card 85-218635 DDC 331.12 19
HD5706 .B4 1985

Sauter, Franz, 1956- Transaktionskostentheorie der Organisation /. München , c1985. iv, 187, 2 p. : ISBN 3-89003-013-0 LC Card 85-194969
HB846.3 .S28 1985

Suhr, Dieter. Geld ohne Mehrwert . Frankfurt am Main , c1983. 143 p. ; ISBN 3-7819-0302-8 LC Card 84-169137
HG221 .S8883 1983

Transactions of the American Philosophical Society, 0065-9746 .
(v. 76, pt. 3) Morrison, Rodney J., 1934- Henry C. Carey and American economic development /. Philadelphia , 1986. ix, 91 p. : ISBN 0-87169-763-7 (pbk.) LC Card 86-71420 DDC 338.973/0092/4 19
HB119.C3 M67 1986

Eine Transaktionskostentheoretische Interpretation interner Arbeitsmärkte /. Becker, Hans, Dr. Berlin , c1985. 156 p. ; ISBN 3-428-05848-8 LC Card 85-218635 DDC 331.12 19
HD5706 .B4 1985

Transaktionskostentheorie der Organisation /. Sauter, Franz, 1956- München , c1985. iv, 187, 2 p. : ISBN 3-89003-013-0 LC Card 85-194969
HB846.3 .S28 1985

Transamerica Corporation. The Competitive challenge . Cambridge, Mass. , c1987. xii, 256 p. : ISBN 0-88730-178-9 LC Card 87-1190 DDC 658.4/06 19
HD70.U5 C58 1987

TRANSBAIKALIA (R.S.F.S.R.) - ECONOMIC CONDITIONS.
Sotsial′no-ėkonomicheskoe i kul′turnoe razvitie Zabaĭkal′i͡a . Novosibirsk , 1980. 283 p. ; LC Card 81-132139
HC337.R852 T737 1980

TRANSBAIKALIA (R.S.F.S.R.) - SOCIAL CONDITIONS.
Sotsial′no-ėkonomicheskoe i kul′turnoe razvitie Zabaĭkal′i͡a . Novosibirsk , 1980. 283 p. ; LC Card 81-132139
HC337.R852 T737 1980

Transborder data flows. Jussawalla, Meheroo, 1923- The calculus of international communications . Littleton, Colo. , 1987. xiv, 159 p. ; ISBN 0-87287-503-2 : LC Card 87-2640 DDC 384/.068 19
HE7645 .J87 1987

TRANSCAUCASIA - COMMERCE - MATHEMATICAL MODELS.
Mezhregional′nye mezhotraslevye balansy /. Novosibirsk , 1983. 220 p. : LC Card 84-172934
HF3626.5 .M49 1983

Transcript proceedings . Advertising Research Foundation Key Issues Workshop (1985 : New York, N.Y.) New York, NY (3 E. 54th St., New York 10022-3180) , c1985. 174 p. : LC Card 86-214476 DDC 659.14/3/0973 19
HF6146.T42 A27 1985a

Transcript proceedings . Advertising Research Foundation Key Issues Workshop (1985 : New York, N.Y.) New York, NY (3 E. 54th St., New York 10022-3180) , c1985. 161 p. : LC Card 86-211136 DDC 659.14/3/0973 19
HF6146.T42 A27 1985

Transcript proceedings . Advertising Research Foundation Key Issues Workshop (1986 : New York, N.Y.) New York, NY (3 E. 54th St., New York 10022-3180) , c1986. 268 p. : LC Card 87-149342 DDC 658.8/3 19
HF5802.5 .A3826 1986

Transcript proceedings . Advertising Research Foundation Key Issues Workshop (1986 : New York, N.Y.) New York, NY (3 E. 54th St., New York 10022-3180) , c1986. 214 p. : LC Card 87-404527 DDC 659.14/3/0973 19
HF6146.T42 A27 1986

A Transcription of key addresses at San Antonio's Bio-Medical Seminar / sponsored by National Association of Office and Industrial Parks, San Antonio Chapter, October 24, 1985, Wyndham Hotel. San Antonio, TX (8961 Tesoro Dr., Suite 308, San Antonio 78217) : The Chapter, c1985. v, 104, [4] leaves of plates : ill. ; 28 cm. Cover title: Development opportunities for the 80's. LC Card 87-144092 DDC 338.4/7681761/09764351 19
1. Biotechnology industries - Texas - San Antonio - Congresses. 2. Medical instruments and apparatus industry - Texas - San Antonio - Congresses. 3. Pharmaceutical industry - Texas - San Antonio - Congresses. 4. Medical centers - Texas - San Antonio - Congresses. 5. Health facilities - Texas - San Antonio - Congresses. I. National Association of Office and Industrial Parks. San Antonio Chapter. II. Title: Development opportunities for the 80's.
HD9999.B443 U667 1985

Transfer-Einkommen und Einkommensverteilung /. Zeppernick, Ralf. Berlin , c1986. viii, 233, [1] p. : ISBN 3-428-05990-5 LC Card 86-178831
HC290.5.I5 Z47 1986

Transfer-Enquête-Kommission (Germany) Haushalte mit ausgewählten staatlichen Transferzahlungen . Stuttgart , c1983. 352 p. : ISBN 3-17-007631-0 LC Card 83-117808
HC290.5.I5 H37 1983

TRANSFER OF TECHNOLOGY. see **TECHNOLOGY TRANSFER.**

TRANSFER PAYMENTS - AUSTRALIA.
Kakwani, Nanak. Analyzing redistribution policies . Cambridge [Cambridgeshire] , New York , 1986. ix, 293 p. : ISBN 0-521-30838-0 LC Card 85-31342 DDC 339.5/2 19
HC610.I5 K35 1986 *NYPL [JLE 86-3491]*

TRANSFER PAYMENTS - EUROPEAN ECONOMIC COMMUNITY COUNTRIES.
Hackenbroch, Inge. Zur Theorie und Politik eines supranationalen Finanzausgleichs . München , c1983. xvi, 350 p. ; ISBN 3-8039-0259-2 LC Card 83-167962
HJ1000.5 .H33 1983

TRANSFER PAYMENTS - GERMANY, WEST.
Haushalte mit ausgewählten staatlichen Transferzahlungen . Stuttgart , c1983. 352 p. : ISBN 3-17-007631-0 LC Card 83-117808
HC290.5.I5 H37 1983

Mitschke, Joachim. Steuer- und Transferordnung aus einem Guss . Baden-Baden , 1985. 274 p. : ISBN 3-7890-1097-9 LC Card 85-235532
HJ2687 .M57 1985

Zeppernick, Ralf. Transfer-Einkommen und Einkommensverteilung /. Berlin , c1986. viii, 233, [1] p. : ISBN 3-428-05990-5 LC Card 86-178831
HC290.5.I5 Z47 1986

TRANSFER PAYMENTS - GERMANY (WEST) - RUHR (REGION)
Meyer, Willm Rolf. Ressourcenumverteilung zugunsten von Problemregionen . Frankfurt/Main , New York , c1982. 262 p. : ISBN 3-593-33036-9 LC Card 82-161064 DDC 336.1/85 19
HJ1121 .M49 1982 *NYPL [JLD 86-3292]*

TRANSFER PAYMENTS - QUÉBEC (PROVINCE)
White paper on the personal tax and transfer systems /. Québec , 1984. 380 p. : ISBN 2-551-08967-0 (pbk.) : LC Card 85-150790 DDC 336.24/215/09714 19
HJ4663.Q8 W47 1984 *NYPL [JLF 87-360]*

TRANSFER PAYMENTS - UNITED STATES.
The Distributional impacts of public policies /. New York , 1988. xvii, 257 p. ; ISBN 0-312-00749-3 : LC Card 87-11877 DDC 339.2/0973 19
HC110.I5 D535 1988

TRANSFER PAYMENTS - UNITED STATES - CONGRESSES.
Survey of income and program participation and related longitudinal surveys, 1984 . [Washington, D.C.] , 1985. ix, 201 p. : LC Card 85-601676 DDC 339.2/3/0973 19
HC110.I5 S89 1985 *NYPL [JLF 86-1641]*

Transfer postępu naukowo-technicznego przez przedsiębiorstwa międzynarodowe a długookresowe zmiany w przedsiębiorstwa międzynarodowe a długookresowe zmiany w międzynarodowym podziale pracy /. Sulmicki, Jan. Warszawa , 1978. 288 p. ; LC Card 81-205742
HF1411 .S876 1978

TRANSFER PRICING.
Andersson, Per Magnus, 1951- Internprissättning inom offentlig förvaltning . Lund [1984] xii, 357 p. ; ISBN 91-44-43971-7 : LC Card 84-210334
HD62.45 .A53 1984

Winter, Richard, 1946- Pretiale Lenkung bei sicheren und unsicheren Erwartungen /. Frankfurt am Main , New York , c1986. 243 p. ; ISBN 3-8204-9816-8 LC Card 87-407541 DDC 658.8/16 19
HD62.45 .W56 1986

TRANSFER PRICING - DEVELOPING COUNTRIES.
Essays from the Ghana-Valco renegotiations, 1982-85 /. [Accra, Ghana] 1986 (Accra : Printed by the Ghana Pub. Corp.) viii, 163 p. ;

ISBN 996-490-120-8 (pbk.) LC Card 87-127499 DDC 338.8/87 19
HD9539.A63 G44 1986

Transferability of Japanese-style management to Britain /. Tomita, Teruhiko, 1937- Hikone, Japan [1986] 63 leaves : LC Card 87-168468 DDC 331.25 19
HD70.J3 T585 1986

TRANSFERS OF FUNDS, ELECTRONIC. see **ELECTRONIC FUNDS TRANSFERS.**

The transformation of American industrial relations /. Kochan, Thomas A. New York , c1986. viii, 287 p. ; ISBN 0-465-08696-9 : LC Card 85-47502 DDC 331/.0973 19
HD8072 .K67 1986

The transformation of an Indian labor market . Lambert, Richard D. Amsterdam , Philadelphia , 1986. ix, 249 p. ; ISBN 0-915027-63-1 (alk. paper) : LC Card 86-26900 DDC 331.11/0954/792 19
HD5820.P78 L36 1986

The transformation of industrial organization . Hearn, Frank. Belmont, Calif. , c1988. xii, 370 p. ; ISBN 0-534-08160-6 (pbk.) LC Card 87-17755 DDC 306/.3 19
HD70.U5 H42 1988

The transformation of old age security . Quadagno, Jill S. Chicago , 1988. p. cm. ISBN 0-226-69923-4 : LC Card 87-18754 DDC 368.4/00973 19
HD7125 .Q46 1988

Transformation of Punjab agriculture /. Sain, Inder, 1944- Delhi , New Delhi , 1987. xviii, 191 p. : ISBN 81-7018-451-7 : LC Card 87-900922
HD2075.P8 S35 1985

TRANSFORMERS, ELECTRIC. see **ELECTRIC TRANSFORMERS.**

Transforming economics . Storkey, Alan. London , 1986. xi, 212 p. : ISBN 0-281-04225-X (pbk.) : LC Card 87-108686 DDC 261.8/5 19
HD5765.A6 S76 1986

A Transição incompleta : Brasil desde 1945 / organizada por Edmar Bacha e Herbert S. Klein ; Edmar Lisboa Bacha ... [et al.]. Rio de Janeiro-RJ : Paz e Terra, 1986. 2 v. ; 21 cm. (Coleção Estudos brasileiros. vol. 93-94) Includes bibliographies. CONTENTS. - v. 1. População, emprego, agricultura e urbanização -- v. 2. Desigualdade social, educação, saúde e previdência. LC Card 86-224684
1. Brazil - Economic conditions - 1945-1964. 2. Brazil - Economic conditions - 1964-1985. 3. Brazil - Social conditions - 1945-1964. 4. Brazil - Social conditions - 1964-. 5. Brazil - Population. 6. Labor supply - Brazil. 7. Brazil - Rural conditions. 8. Urbanization - Brazil. 9. Social mobility - Brazil. 10. Poor - Brazil. 11. Education - Brazil. 12. Public health - Brazil. I. Bacha, Edmar Lisboa. II. Klein, Herbert S. III. Series: Coleção Estudos brasileiros (Paz e Terra (Firm)) , v. 93-94.
HC187 .T72 1986

La transición del feudalismo al capitalismo y la revolución industrial /. Cartay Angulo, Rafael, 1941- [Mérida? , 1983] (Mérida, Venezuela : Tall. Gráf. Universitarios) 258 p. ; LC Card 84-188666
HC51 .C363 1983

Transición demográfica y oferta de fuerza de trabajo en Colombia / Servicio Nacional de Empleo--SENALDE, Oficina Intenacional del Trabajo--OIT, Fondo de las Naciones Unidas para Actividades en Materia de Población--UNFPA. 1a ed. [Bogotá], República de Colombia : Ministerio de Trabajo y Seguridad Social, Dirección General del Servicio Nacional de Empleo, 1986. 2 v. : ill. ; 24 cm. (Colección Biblioteca SENALDE . v. 3-4) Bibliography: v. 1, p. 373-374. ISBN 958-95096-0-6 (set) LC Card 87-113652 DDC 331.11/09861 19
1. Labor supply - Colombia. 2. Demographic transition - Colombia. 3. Colombia - Population. 4. Manpower policy - Colombia. I. Colombia. Servicio Nacional de Empleo. Dirección General. II. International Labour Office. III. United Nations Fund for Population Activities. IV. Series.
HD5757.A6 T7 1986

TRANSIENT LABOR. see **MIGRANT LABOR.**

TRANSIT, INTERNATIONAL - BULGARIA.
Petrov, Milan, k.i.n. Mezhdunarodnite pŭtnicheski prevozi i tekhnite valutno-finansovi problemi /. Sofiīa , 1984. 95, [1] p. ; LC Card 85-167160
HE265.A2 P48 1984

TRANSIT, INTERNATIONAL - BURUNDI - CONGRESSES.
Enclavement et sous-développement au Burundi . Bujumbura, Burundi [1983] xi, 448 p. : LC Card 85-980729 DDC 338.967/572 19
HE283.8 .E53 1983

TRANSIT SYSTEMS. see **LOCAL TRANSIT.**

TRANSIT WORKERS UNION OF HAWAII - HISTORY.
Stern, Bernard W., 1912- Rutledge unionism . Honolulu , 1986. x, 147 p. ; LC Card 86-51020 DDC 331/.04138841322/0996931 19
HD6515.T72 H37 1986

Transition and development : problems of Third World socialism / edited by Richard R. Fagen, Carmen Diana Deere, and José Luis Coraggio. New York, NY : Monthly Review Press ; [Berkeley, Calif.] : Center for the Study of the Americas, c1986. 352 p. ; 21 cm. (MR/Censa series on the Americas) Includes index. Bibliography: p. 331-344. ISBN 0-85345-705-0 (pbk.) : LC Card 86-12579 DDC 335.43/09172/4 19
1. Communism - Developing countries. 2. Communism - Latin America. 3. Communism - Nicaragua. I. Fagen, Richard R. II. Deere, Carmen Diana. III. Coraggio, José Luis. IV. Series.
HX517.8 .T73 1986 ***NYPL [JLD 86-3907]***

Transition in agriculture : a strategic assessment of agriculture and banking / prepared for the American Bankers Association by Hopkin and Associates. Washington, D.C. (1120 Connecticut Ave. N.W., Washington 20036) : The Association, c1986. 2 v. : ill. ; 28 cm. Includes bibliographies. CONTENTS. - [1] Research report -- [2] Strategic planning guide. LC Card 86-233848 DDC 332.7/1/0973 19
1. Agricultural credit corporations - United States. 2. Agricultural credit - United States. 3. Agriculture - United States - Finance. I. American Bankers Association. II. Hopkin and Associates.
HG2051.U5 T68 1986

The transition in reproductive behavior in the third world /. Bongaarts, John, 1945- New York, N.Y. [1986] 29 p. : LC Card 87-154566 DDC 304.6/32/091724 19
HB1108 .B65 1986

Transition in the nuclear industry : proceedings of the symposium / sponsored by the Construction and Energy Divisions of the American Society of Civil Engineers in conjunction with the ASCE Convention in Denver, Colorado, April 29-30, 1985 ; edited by James H. Olyniec. New York, N.Y. : The Society, c1985. iii, 233 p. : ill. ; 22 cm. Includes bibliographies and indexes. ISBN 0-87262-443-9 (pbk.) LC Card 85-70499 DDC 338.4/762148/0973 19
1. Nuclear industry - United States - Congresses. 2. Nuclear engineering - United States - Congresses. I. Olyniec, James H. II. American Society of Civil Engineers. Construction Division. III. American Society of Civil Engineers. Energy Division. IV. ASCE National Convention (1985 : Denver, Colo.).
HD9698.U52 T73 1985 ***NYPL [JSD 86-173]***

The transition to an industrial economy in monsoon Asia /. Oshima, Harry T. (Harry Tatsumi) Manila, Philippines , c1983. 111 p. ; LC Card 87-105003 DDC 338.095 19
HC412 .O694 1983

Transition to nowhere . Liu, William Thomas, 1930- Nashville , c1979. 214 p., [2] leaves of plates : ISBN 0-8202-0189-8 : LC Card 78-21129 DDC 361.5/3/09597
HV640.5.V5 L58 ***NYPL [JLD 87-670]***

The transition to retirement . Morrison, Malcolm H. Washington, D.C. (1990 M St., N.W., Washington 20036) , c1985. 85 p. : LC Card 85-169472 DDC 306/.38/0973 19
HQ1062 .M64 1985 ***NYPL [JLE 86-2236]***

Transitional career counseling from the Air Force to the private sector : a job search training program for Air Force retirees / prepared by Social, Educational Research and Development, Inc. Washington, D.C. : SERD, c1987. iv, 153 leaves : ill. ; 28 cm. "January 1987." Includes bibliographical references. LC Card 87-401057 DDC 358.4/1154/0973 19
1. Job hunting - Study and teaching - United States. 2. Career changes - Study and teaching - United States. 3. Retired military personnel - Employment - United States. 4. United States. Air Force - Personnel management. I. Social, Educational Research and Development, inc.
HF5382.75.U6 T7 1987

Les transitions de mortalité dans le Tiersmonde . Tabutin, Dominique. Louvain-la-Neuve, Belgique [1985] 33 p. : LC Card 86-178578
HB1528 .T33 1985

Transitway surveillance, communications, and control /. McCasland, William R. College Station, Tex. [1986] vi, 76 p. : LC Card 87-620995 DDC 380.5 s 388.3/143 19
HE203 .T43 no. 425-2F HE336.B8

Transizione tecnologica e strategie evolutive . Di Bernardo, Barbara. Padova , 1985. xiii, 432 p. : LC Card 86-214184
HD45 .D47 1985

TRANSKEI (SOUTH AFRICA) - ECONOMIC CONDITIONS - STATISTICS.
Kruger, Gudrun. Development region D . Port Elizabeth [1985] iv, 89 p. : ISBN 0-86988-274-0 (pbk.) LC Card 86-233113 DDC 304.6/09687/5 19
HA4701.Z9 C354 1985

TRANSKEI (SOUTH AFRICA) - ECONOMIC POLICY.
May, Julian. Development planning in Transkei . Durban , 1985. 35 p., [5] p. ; ISBN 0-86980-483-9 (pbk.) : LC Card 86-222656 DDC 338.9687/91 19
HC905.Z7 T7347 1985

TRANSKEI (SOUTH AFRICA) - POPULATION - STATISTICS.
Kruger, Gudrun. Development region D . Port Elizabeth [1985] iv, 89 p. : ISBN 0-86988-274-0 (pbk.) LC Card 86-233113 DDC 304.6/09687/5 19
HA4701.Z9 C354 1985

Translations series in mathematics and engineering.
Steklov Seminar (1984 : Steklov Institute of Mathematics) [Statistika i upravlenie sluchaĭnykh protsessov. English.] Statistics and control of stochastic processes /. New York, N.Y. , c1985. xiii, 506 p. ; ISBN 0-911575-18-9 LC Card 85-8851 DDC 519.5 19
QA276.A1 .S7513 1984 ***NYPL [JSE 86-729]***

Transmigrasi . Otten, Mariël. Copenhagen , c1986. 254 p. : LC Card 87-144670 DDC 333.3/1/598 19
HD896 .O88 1986

Transmigration in Indonesia . Kebschull, Dietrich. Hamburg , 1984. xxiv, 134 p. ; LC Card 86-223779 DDC 304.8/09598 19
HB2107 .K4 1984

TRANSMISSION OF DATA. see **DATA TRANSMISSION SYSTEMS.**

Transnacionales y nación . Granado Cosio, Hugo del. [La Paz, Bolivia] , 1986. 24 p. ; LC Card 87-115866 DDC 338.8/87 19
HD9574.B82 G73 1986

Transnational banks and the dynamics of the Peruvian foreign debt and inflation /. Uriarte, J. Manuel. New York , c1986. x, 195 p. : ISBN 0-03-002599-0 (alk. paper) : LC Card 84-26307 DDC 336.3/4/0985 19
HJ8604 .U75 1985 ***NYPL [JLE 86-1384]***

Transnational corporations and uneven development . Jenkins, Rhys Owen, 1948- London , New York , 1987. p. cm. ISBN 0-416-73340-9 LC Card 87-12351 DDC 338.8/83 19
HD2932 .J45 1987

Transnational corporations in South Africa and Namibia : United Nations public hearings / United Nations Centre on Transnational Corporations. New York : United Nations, 1986-<1987 > v. <1-2, 4 > ; 28 cm. Includes bibliographies. "ST/CTC/68." "United Nations publication. Sales no. E.86.II.A.6"--V. 1, t.p. verso. CONTENTS. - v. 1. Reports of the Panel of Eminent Persons and of the Secretary-General -- v. 2. Verbatim records --v. 4. Policy instruments and statements. ISBN 92-1-104190-2 (pbk. : set) LC Card 87-403059 DDC 338.8/8868 19
1. International business enterprises - South Africa. 2. International business enterprises - Namibia. I. Centre

on Transnational Corporations (United Nations).
HD2922 .T72 1986

TransNational, Inc.
A Basic guide to exporting. Washington, D.C. [1986] viii, 148 p. : LC Card 86-603426 DDC 658.8/48 19
HF1009.6 .B38 1986

A Basic guide to exporting. Washington, D.C. [1986] viii, 148 p. : ***NYPL [*R-Econ. 87-422]***

Transnational monopoly capitalism /. Cowling, Keith. Sussex [England] , New York , 1987. vii, 178 p. : ISBN 0-312-00954-2 (St. Martin's) : LC Card 87-4965 DDC 338.8/8 19
HD2755.5 .C68 1987

Transnationals and development. Manchester, England : University of Manchester, Dept. of Administrative Studies, 1984. i, 64 p. ; 21 cm. (Manchester papers on development / University of Manchester, Department of Administrative Studies, 0260-8235 . issue no. 9 (May 1984)) Cover title. "May 1984." Includes bibliographies. CONTENTS. - Food and agricultural exports from less-developed countries / David Colman -- The state, foreign enterprise and industrial capitalism in West Africa / Paul Collins.
1. Food industry and trade - Developing countries. 2. Investments, Foreign - Africa, West. 3. Industry and state - Africa, West. 4. Capital - Africa, West. 5. Developing countries - Commerce. I. Colman, David. Food and agricultural exports from less-developed countries. II. Cook, P. (Paul). State, foreign enterprise and industrial capitalism in West Africa. III. Series.
NYPL [JLD 86-3224]

De Transnationella företagens roll i världshandeln ; Gränsskydd i andra länder / 1983 års livsmedelskommitté, Expertgruppen för internationella frågor. [Stockholm] : Jordbruksdepartementet : Liber, [1984] 62, [36] p. ; 21 cm. "Ds Jo 1984:8." Bibliography: p. 21. ISBN 91-38-08406-6 LC Card 86-115056
1. Food industry and trade - Sweden. 2. International business enterprises - Sweden. I. Sweden. Expertgruppen för internationella frågor.
HD9015.S86 T73 1984

Transnat͡sional'nye korporat͡sii v sisteme gosudarstvenno-monopolisticheskogo regulirovanii͡a ėkonomiki : referativnyĭ sbornik / [otvetstvennyĭ redaktor-sostavitel' sbornika Bezrukov A.I.]. Moskva : Akademii͡a nauk SSSR, In-t nauch. informat͡sii po obshchestvennym naukam, 1985. 167 p. ; 20 cm. (Serii͡a Problemy mezhdunarodnykh ėkonomicheskikh otnosheniĭ) Includes bibliographical references. LC Card 86-187630
1. International business enterprises. 2. Industry and state. I. Bezrukov, A. I. II. Institut nauchnoĭ informat͡sii po obshchestvennym naukam (Akademii͡a nauk SSSR). III. Series.
HD2755.5 .T714 1985

Transponder supply & demand forecast. Bethesda, MD, U. S.A. : Satellite Systems Engineering, c1987. v, 150 p. : ill. ; 28 cm. "May 1987." Bibliography: p. 149. "(SSE/R-86/018)." LC Card 87-403373 DDC 384.4/1 19
1. Artificial satellites in telecommunication - United States. 2. Market surveys - United States. I. Satellite Systems Engineering. II. Title: Transponder supply and demand forecast.
HE9721.U5 T73 1987

Transponder supply and demand forecast. Transponder supply & demand forecast. Bethesda, MD, U. S.A. , c1987. v, 150 p. : LC Card 87-403373 DDC 384.4/1 19
HE9721.U5 T73 1987

TRANSPORT AND GENERAL WORKERS' UNION (GREAT BRITAIN) - HISTORY.
Fuller, Ken. Radical aristocrats . London , Atlantic Highlands, N.J. , 1985. 256 p. : ISBN 0-85315-649-2 (pbk.) : LC Card 86-214586 DDC 331.88/1138841322/09421 19
HD8039.M82 G74 1985

Transport energy in New Zealand's overseas trade . Copeland, M. C. (Michael Campbell) Auckland, N.Z. [1982] iv, 130 p. : LC Card 84-159485 DDC 387.5/1 19
HE597.N4 C63 1982
NYPL [JSK 82-15 no.80]

Le Transport fluvial : schéma de développement du transport fluvial et schéma directeur des voies navigables : rapport au ministre d'Etat, ministre des Transports et au ministre d'Etat, ministre du Plan et de l'aménagement du territoire / commission présidée par Roger Grégoire. Paris : Documentation française, c1983. 108 p. : ill. ; 24 cm. (Collection des rapports officiels) "Mars 1983." Bibliography: p. 105. ISBN 2-11-001087-8 : LC Card 83-170808
1. Inland navigation - Government policy - France. I. Grégoire, Roger, 1913-. II. France. Ministère des transports. III. France. Ministère du plan et de l'aménagement du territoire. IV. Series.
HE668 .T73 1983

Transport geography of India . Raza, Moonis. New Delhi , 1986. xii, 299 p. : LC Card 86-903251 DDC 380.5/0954 19
HE3298 .R39 1986

Transport in India. 1st ed. New Delhi : Lok Sabha Secretariat, 1986. v, 64 p. ; 26 cm. The study is largely based on published sources and is primarily intended to serve as background material for members of Parliament"--Pref. Bibliography: p. 63-64. "PRIS-A(BRO-3)/86"--T.p. verso. LC Card 87-900171 DDC 380.5/0954 19
1. Transportation - India. I. India. Parliament. Lok Sabha. Secretariat.
HE271.A2 T73 1986

Transport Sector I (Road Maintenance) (633-0073) Botswana Transport Sector I (Road Maintenance) (633-0073). [Botswana? , 1979?] 1 v. (various pagings) : LC Card 86-148788
HE367.B652 B67 1979

TRANSPORT WORKERS - GERMANY (WEST) - DORTMUND.
Meifort, J. (Joachim) Arbeitsbedingungen von Linienbus- und Strassenbahnfahrern der Dortmunder Stadtwerke Aktiengesellschaft /. Dortmund , 1983. 137 p. : ISBN 3-88314-249-2 LC Card 83-204902
HD8039.T72 G36 1983

TRANSPORT WORKERS - SOVIET UNION - LABOR PRODUCTIVITY.
Organizat͡sii͡a i stimulirovanie truda rabotnikov transportnykh uzlov . Moskva , 1984. 96 p. ; LC Card 87-100191
HD8039.T72 S656 1984

Transportation . De Old, Alan R. Worcester, Mass. , c1986. x, 534 p. : ISBN 0-87192-126-X LC Card 86-70174 DDC 380.5 19
HE151 .D42 1986

Transportation . Petersen, Sybil. Arlington, Va. (P.O. Box 926, Arlington 22216) [1986] [8], 40 p. : LC Card 87-401670 DDC 363.1/7 19
HE199.5.D3 P48 1986

TRANSPORTATION.
Bell, G. J. (Graham J.) The business of transport /. Plymouth [Devon] , 1984. viii, 344 p. : ISBN 0-7121-2406-3 (pbk.) LC Card 84-170770 DDC 380.5 19
HE151 .B436 1984 ***NYPL [JLD 87-86]***

De Old, Alan R. Transportation . Worcester, Mass. , c1986. x, 534 p. : ISBN 0-87192-126-X LC Card 86-70174 DDC 380.5 19
HE151 .D42 1986

Moavenzadeh, Fred, 1935- Transportation, energy, and economic development . Amsterdam ; New York : viii, 529 p. : ISBN 0-444-42338-9 (U. S.) : LC Card 84-5954 DDC 333.79 19
HE148 .M6 1984 ***NYPL [JLE 86-1569]***

Owen, Wilfred. Transportation and world development /. Baltimore , c1987. xiv, 156 p. : ISBN 0-8018-3495-3 (alk. paper) LC Card 87-4154 DDC 380.5 19
HE151 .O94 1987

Perspektiven verkehrswissenschaftlicher Forschung . Berlin , c1985. 606 p., [1] leaf of plates : ISBN 3-428-05738-4 LC Card 85-155542
HE151 .P44 1985

Probleme der Ordnungs- und Strukturpolitik . Göttingen , c1984. viii, 311 p., [1] leaf of plates : ISBN 3-525-85925-2 LC Card 84-203472
HE152.6 .P76 1984

Wolkowitsch, Maurice. Géographie des transports /. Paris , 1982, c1973. 383 p. : ISBN 2-200-31188-5 LC Card 83-147243
HE151 .W63 1982

TRANSPORTATION - ADDRESSES, ESSAYS, LECTURES.
Readings in contemporary transportation /. Tulsa, OK , c1983. x, 325 p. : ISBN 0-87814-215-0 (pbk.) LC Card 82-22379 DDC 380.5 19
HE151 .R37 1983 ***NYPL [JLF 86-2000]***

TRANSPORTATION - AMAZON RIVER REGION.
Estudio de transportes en la Región Amazónica y en el Alto Paraguay. Buenos Aires [1983- v. <1 > : LC Card 87-400601 DDC 380.5/0981/1 19
HE230 .E85 1983

Transportation and land development /. Stover, Vergil G., 1933- Englewood Cliffs, N.J. , c1988. xiii, 239 p. : ISBN 0-13-930413-4 : LC Card 87-11419 DDC 625.7/25 19
HE335 .S76 1988

Transportation and marketing of natural gas. Mogel, William A. New York, N.Y. , c1986. iii, 165 p. : ISBN 0-88057-466-6 (pbk.) LC Card 86-220986 DDC 388.5 19
HD9580.U5 M64 1985 Suppl.

TRANSPORTATION AND STATE - BRAZIL.
Alternativa rodo-hidro-ferroviária para o transporte de parte da safra de soja paraguaia destinada à exportação. [Rio de Janeiro] [19]84. 65 leaves : LC Card 85-187436
HE199.5.S66 A47 1984

Severo, Cloraldino. A política dos transportes no Brasil, 1979/85 /. [Brasília] , 1983. 91 p. : LC Card 86-153346
HE233 .S44 1983

TRANSPORTATION AND STATE - BRAZIL - CONGRESSES.
Conferência do Ministro dos Transportes na Escola Superior de Guerra . [Brasília] [198-] [61] p. : LC Card 86-193198
HE233 .C59 1980z

TRANSPORTATION AND STATE - CHILE - SANTIAGO METROPOLITAN AREA.
Matas, Jaime. Los problemas ambientales del sistema de transporte urbano /. Santiago de Chile , 1981. 30 leaves : LC Card 82-201768
HE234.Z7 S355 1981

TRANSPORTATION AND STATE - COLOMBIA.
Latorre, Emilio. Transporte y crecimiento regional en Colombia /. Bogotá, Colombia , 1986. 137 p. : ISBN 958-9061-14-1 LC Card 87-115019 DDC 380.5/09861 19
HE235 .L37 1986

TRANSPORTATION AND STATE - COSTA RICA.
Hernández C., Alexandra. Encuesta de consumo energético en el sector transporte /. San José, Costa Rica , 1985. 68, [137] p. : LC Card 86-218227
HE5638 .H37 1985

TRANSPORTATION AND STATE - DEVELOPING COUNTRIES.
Armstrong-Wright, Alan, 1929- Bus services . Washington, D.C. , 1987. x, 97 p. ; ISBN 0-8213-0943-9 (pbk.) LC Card 87-17183 DDC 388.4/1322/091724 19
HE5725 .A76 1987

United Nations Centre for Human Settlements. Transportation strategies for human settlements in developing countries. Nairobi , 1984. v, 79 p. ; LC Card 85-980241 DDC 380.5/068 19
HE148.5 .U55 1984

TRANSPORTATION AND STATE - EUROPE - CONGRESSES.
The Regionalisation of transport and regional planning in practice . Paris, France [Washington, D.C.] c1984. 199 p. : ISBN 92-821-1091-5 (pbk.) : LC Card 85-180250 DDC 380.5/068 19
HE242 .R44 1984 ***NYPL [JLG 86-138]***

TRANSPORTATION AND STATE - EUROPEAN ECONOMIC COMMUNITY COUNTRIES.
Izquierdo de Bartolomé, Rafael. Evolución, presente y futuro de la política común de transportes /. Madrid [1985?] 56 p. ; ISBN 84-7075-325-8 LC Card 87-111657
HE242.8 .I97 1985

TRANSPORTATION AND STATE - FRANCE.
France. Groupe de politique des transports. Rapport du Groupe de politique des transports. Paris , c1984. 246 p. : ISBN 2-11-001216-1 : LC Card 84-163968
HE248 .F716 1984

Villette, Jean. Transports, décentralisation 9o

plan /. Paris , c1986. 161 p. : ISBN 2-11-001549-7 : LC Card 86-181094
HE248.A2 V55 1986

TRANSPORTATION AND STATE - GERMANY, WEST.
Bode, Peter M. Alptraum Auto . München , 1986. 237 p. : ISBN 3-922696-46-5 LC Card 87-107197 DDC 303.4/832 19
HE5613 .B63 1986

Bundesverband des Deutschen Gross- und Aussenhandels. Vorschläge und Beiträge des Bundesverbandes des Deutschen Gross- und Aussenhandels e.V. für die X. Legislaturperiode des Deutschen Bundestages. Bonn [1983] 56 p. ; LC Card 83-243234
HF1545 .B83 1983

Clauss, Rüdiger, 1952- Marketing der Unternehmen des öffentlichen Personen, nahverkehrs im Spannungsfeld erwerbswirtschaftlicher und gemeinwirtschaftlicher Ziele /. Bergisch Gladbach , 1985. xiii, 308 p. : ISBN 3-89012-019-9 LC Card 85-175468
HE249 .C42 1985

Gscheidle, Kurt. Die Verkehrspolitik in der 8. Legislaturperiode /. Bonn-Bad Godesberg [1977] 29 p. : LC Card 86-173226
HE64 .A36 Heft 54 HE249

Michelbach, Roger. Probleme der Sanierung der Deutschen Bundesbahn durch die Änderung institutioneller Rahmenbedingungen /. Thun , c1984. xi, 450 p. : ISBN 3-87144-865-6 LC Card 85-137676
HE3080.D4 M53 1984

Oettle, Karl. Ökonomische Probleme des öffentlichen Verkehrs . Baden-Baden , 1981. 373 p. ; ISBN 3-7890-0568-1 : LC Card 82-159141 DDC 380.5/068 19
HE249 .O33 1981 ***NYPL [JLD 86-2588]***

Offergeld, Johannes. Spezialisierung des Verkehrsangebotes und Strukturwandel in der verladenden Wirtschaft . Göttingen , 1984. 185 p. : ISBN 3-525-85690-3 (Deut. Bibl.) LC Card 84-197725
HE131 .M8 Heft 102 HE249

Verkehrs- und unternehmenspolitische Anpassungsstrategien an veränderte Ressourcenbewertungen /. Göttingen , 1986. 210 p. : ISBN 3-525-85699-7 : LC Card 86-223574
HE131 .M8 Heft 109 HE249

Vorschläge für eine Neuordnung des organisatorischen Rahmens für den öffentlichen Personennahverkehr /. Bonn-Bad Godesberg [1977] 35 p. ; LC Card 86-173254
HE64 .A36 Heft 53 HE249

TRANSPORTATION AND STATE - GERMANY (WEST) - HISTORY.
Schroiff, Franz J. Das Binnenschiffahrt-Verkehrssystem . Hannover , 1984. ix, 267 p. : ISBN 3-87870-951-X LC Card 84-221599
HE669 .S34 1984

TRANSPORTATION AND STATE - GERMANY (WEST) - SCHLESWIG-HOLSTEIN - CONGRESSES.
Gestaltung künftiger Raumstrukturen durch veränderte Verkehrskonzepte . Hannover , 1986. xii, 173 p. : ISBN 3-87870-767-3 LC Card 87-401351 DDC 380.5/0943/512 19
HE249.Z7 S343 1986

TRANSPORTATION AND STATE - JAPAN.
Nihon kōkigyō no saisei /. Kyōto-shi , 1986. 4, 8, 289 p. : ISBN 4-589-01273-1 : LC Card 86-216062
HD4313 .N46 1986 <Orien Japan> ***NYPL [*OSM 87-2537]***

TRANSPORTATION AND STATE - KENYA - NAIROBI.
Mogridge, M. C. Project identification . Nairobi [1971] 81 leaves in various pagings : LC Card 87-118674
HE283.5.Z7 N456 1971

TRANSPORTATION AND STATE - MEXICO - CONGRESSES.
Reunión Nacional para el Desarrollo de la Industria, el Comercio, la Distribución y Otros Servicios (1981 : Mexico City, Mexico) Memoria /. [Mexico City] , 1981. 428 p., [4] folded leaves of plates : LC Card 84-228700
HD3616.M42 R46 1981

TRANSPORTATION AND STATE - NIGERIA - CONGRESSES.
Transportation in Nigerian national development . Ibadan , c1981. xi, 602 p. : ISBN 978-18-1010-6 (pbk.) LC Card 82-196087 DDC 380.5/09669 19
HE287.7 .T72 1981 ***NYPL [Sc E 86-178]***

TRANSPORTATION AND STATE - SWITZERLAND.
Studer, Stefan. Nationalstrasse, Nationalstrafe, oder, Die Demokratie bleibt auf der Strecke /. Zürich , 1985. 191 p. : ISBN 3-85869-037-6 : LC Card 86-129406
HE363.S92 S83 1985

TRANSPORTATION AND STATE - TURKEY.
Devlet Planlama Teşkilatı (Turkey) 1983-1993 Ulaştırma Ana Planı. [Ankara] [1982] 1 v. (various pagings) : LC Card 85-226492
HE268.25 .D48 1982

TRANSPORTATION AND STATE - UNITED STATES.
Profile of the '80's /. [Washington, D.C.?] , 1980. v, 77 p. : LC Card 81-600725 DDC 380.5/0973 19
HE206.2 .P765 ***NYPL [JLF 86-1445]***

Transportation and world development /. Owen, Wilfred. Baltimore , c1987. xiv, 156 p. : ISBN 0-8018-3495-3 (alk. paper) LC Card 87-4154 DDC 380.5 19
HE151 .O94 1987

TRANSPORTATION, AUTOMOTIVE.
Sequera, Armando José, 1953- Alegato contra el automóvil /. Caracas , 1985. 157 p. ; ISBN 980-222-019-1 : LC Card 87-107528 DDC 388.3/21 19
HE5613 .S46 1985

TRANSPORTATION, AUTOMOTIVE - AMAZON RIVER REGION - CONGRESSES.
Tratado de cooperación amazónica . Washington, D.C. , 1986. iii, 101 p. ; ISBN 0-8270-2304-9 (pbk.) LC Card 86-152493
HE359.A5 T73 1986

TRANSPORTATION, AUTOMOTIVE - ANDES REGION.
Servicios de transporte internacional por carretera en el GRAN . [Buenos Aires, Argentina] [1983] 3 v. : LC Card 87-404195 DDC 388.3/21/098 19
HE5650 .S47 1983

TRANSPORTATION, AUTOMOTIVE - CALIFORNIA - LOS ANGELES.
Bottles, Scott L. Los Angeles and the automobile . Berkeley , c1987. xiii, 301 p. : ISBN 0-520-05795-3 (alk. paper) LC Card 86-14660 DDC 388.4/1321/0979494 19
HE5634.L7 B68 1987

TRANSPORTATION, AUTOMOTIVE - COSTA RICA - ENERGY CONSERVATION.
Hernández C., Alexandra. Encuesta de consumo energético en el sector transporte /. San José, Costa Rica , 1985. 68, [137] p. : LC Card 86-218227
HE5638 .H37 1985

TRANSPORTATION, AUTOMOTIVE - COSTA RICA - ENERGY CONSUMPTION.
Hernández C., Alexandra. Encuesta de consumo energético en el sector transporte /. San José, Costa Rica , 1985. 68, [137] p. : LC Card 86-218227
HE5638 .H37 1985

TRANSPORTATION, AUTOMOTIVE - DENMARK - PLANNING.
Hansen, Christian Overgård. Forbedring og rationalisering af rutebilkørsel /. Esbjerg , 1986. 259 p. : ISBN 87-88521-37-0 LC Card 86-205999
HE5677.A6 H36 1986

TRANSPORTATION, AUTOMOTIVE - DICTIONARIES - POLYGLOT.
Dictionary of road transport terminology in four languages, English, French, German, and Spanish /. Amsterdam , New York , 1988. xxviii, 351 p. ; ISBN 0-444-42819-4 : LC Card 87-13397 DDC 388/.03 19
HE5613 .D53 1988

TRANSPORTATION, AUTOMOTIVE - GERMANY, WEST.
ADAC. Strassenverkehr 2000 . München [1979] 24 p. : LC Card 85-147077
HE363.G3 A33 1979

Strassenverkehrszählung 1978 in der Bundesrepublik Deutschland . Köln , 1979. 96 p. : LC Card 87-408379 DDC 388/.0943 s 388.3/0943 19
HE5601 .S89 Heft 13 HE5669.A6

TRANSPORTATION, AUTOMOTIVE - GERMANY (WEST) - ENERGY CONSERVATION.
Kortzfleisch, Gert von. Energie für den Verkehr . Frankfurt am Main , c1984. 115 p. : LC Card 84-192683
HD9710.G4 V4 Nr. 42 HE5620.E53

TRANSPORTATION, AUTOMOTIVE - GOVERNMENT POLICY - ANDES REGION.
Servicios de transporte internacional por carretera en el GRAN . [Buenos Aires, Argentina] [1983] 3 v. : LC Card 87-404195 DDC 388.3/21/098 19
HE5650 .S47 1983

TRANSPORTATION, AUTOMOTIVE - HISTORY.
Wolf, Winfried. Eisenbahn und Autowahn . Hamburg , c1987. 565 p. : ISBN 3-89136-105-X LC Card 87-167400 DDC 388/.09 19
HE151 .W58 1987

TRANSPORTATION, AUTOMOTIVE - MALAWI - STATISTICS.
Growth of road traffic densities in Malaŵi. Lilongwe , 1985. 88 leaves ; LC Card 86-980330 DDC 388.3/142/096897 19
HE367.M32 G76 1985

TRANSPORTATION, AUTOMOTIVE - POLAND - MANAGEMENT.
Krasucka, Alicja. Organizacja transportu samochodowego /. Gdańsk , 1984. 181 p., [8] leaves of plates (7 folded) : ISBN 83-7017-058-7 : LC Card 86-173836
HE5675.7.A6 K7 1984

TRANSPORTATION, AUTOMOTIVE - RUSSIAN S.F.S.R. - SAFETY MEASURES.
Osnovnye prichiny i uslovii͡a vozniknovenii͡a PTP s ti͡azhelymi posledstvii͡ami, puti i metody ikh ustranenii͡a. Bulgarian. Osnovni prichini i uslovii͡a za vŭznikvane na PTP s tezhki posledstvii͡a, pŭtishta i metodi za ti͡akhnoto otstrani͡avane /. Sofii͡a , 1985. 95 p. : LC Card 87-101607
HF5614.5.S62 O7516 1985

TRANSPORTATION, AUTOMOTIVE - SOVIET UNION - DATA PROCESSING.
Kaftani͡uk, I͡U. A. (I͡Uriĭ Anatol′evich) Vychislitel′nai͡a tekhnika na avtomobil′nom transporte . Moskva , 1985. 183 p. : LC Card 86-163666
HE5613 .K36 1985

TRANSPORTATION, AUTOMOTIVE - SOVIET UNION - MANAGEMENT - MATHEMATICAL MODELS.
Organizat͡sionno-ėkonomicheskie problemy sovershenstvovanii͡a funktsionirovanii͡a transportnykh sistem /. Moskva , 1984. 144 p. : LC Card 85-199422
HE5675.A6 O765 1984

TRANSPORTATION, AUTOMOTIVE - SOVIET UNION - SAFETY MEASURES.
Luk′i͡anov, V. V. Bezopasnost′ dorozhnogo dvizhenii͡a /. Moskva , 1978. 244, [4] p. ; LC Card 81-166116
HE5675.A6 L84 1978

TRANSPORTATION, AUTOMOTIVE - SWITZERLAND - STATISTICS.
Erhebung über die Gütertransporte auf der Strasse 1984 /. Bern , 1986. 103 p. : ISBN 3-303-11041-7 : LC Card 87-408470 DDC 388.3/24/09494/021 19
HE5683.A6 E74 1986

TRANSPORTATION, AUTOMOTIVE - TAXATION - EUROPEAN ECONOMIC COMMUNITY COUNTRIES.
González Blanch, Francisco. Implantación en España de un sistema de tarificación por el uso de la infraestructura viaria /. Madrid [1984?] 204 p. ; ISBN 84-7196-470-8 : LC Card 85-201965
HJ5956.E86 G66 1984

TRANSPORTATION, AUTOMOTIVE - TAXATION - SPAIN.

González Blanch, Francisco. Implantación en España de un sistema de tarificación por el uso de la infraestructura viaria /. Madrid [1984?] 204 p. ; ISBN 84-7196-470-8 : LC Card 85-201965
HJ5956.E86 G66 1984

TRANSPORTATION, AUTOMOTIVE - TAXATION - UNITED STATES.
Highway finance . [Washington] [1983] iii, 96 p. ; *NYPL [JLF 87-431]*

TRANSPORTATION, AUTOMOTIVE - UNITED STATES.
Lau, Lorrie A. Y. Analysis of national and regional travel trends /. Washington, D.C. , 1986. iii, 78, 32 p. : LC Card 87-601033 DDC 388.3/14/0973 19
HE370.T74 L38 1986

TRANSPORTATION, AUTOMOTIVE - UNITED STATES - HISTORY - 20TH CENTURY.
St. Clair, David James, 1950- The motorization of American cities /. New York , 1986. xi, 192 p. ; ISBN 0-275-92126-3 (alk. paper) : LC Card 86-523 DDC 388.4/1321/0973 19
HE5623 .S617 1986 NYPL [JLE 86-3608]

TRANSPORTATION, AUTOMOTIVE - UNITED STATES - STATISTICS.
Briggs, Dwight. Journey-to-work trends . Washington, D.C. , Springfield, VA [1986] 1 v. (various pagings) : LC Card 86-602387 DDC 388.4/1314/0973 19
HE371.A3 B75 1986

TRANSPORTATION - BRAZIL.
Carvalho, Osvaldo Ferraro de. Ensaio sôbre a problemática dos transportes /. Rio de Janeiro , 1957. 324 p., [5] folded leaves of plates : LC Card 85-197985
HE233 .C345 1957

TRANSPORTATION, CHOICE OF. see **CHOICE OF TRANSPORTATION.**

TRANSPORTATION - COLOMBIA.
Latorre, Emilio. Transporte y crecimiento regional en Colombia /. Bogotá, Colombia , 1986. 137 p. : ISBN 958-9061-14-1 LC Card 87-115019 DDC 380.5/09861 19
HE235 .L37 1986

TRANSPORTATION - COST EFFECTIVENESS.
Adler, Hans A. Economic appraisal of transport projects . Baltimore , 1987. xii, 235 p. : ISBN 0-8018-3411-2 : LC Card 86-21348 DDC 380.5/068/1 19
HE151 .A32 1987

TRANSPORTATION - COST EFFECTIVENESS - CASE STUDIES.
Adler, Hans A. Economic appraisal of transport projects . Baltimore , 1987. xii, 235 p. : ISBN 0-8018-3411-2 : LC Card 86-21348 DDC 380.5/068/1 19
HE151 .A32 1987

Transportation data book : demographics, highways, transit, air / prepared by North Central Texas Council of Governments. Arlington, Tex. (P.O. Drawer COG, Arlington 76005-5888) : The Council, c1987. 101 leaves in various foliations : ill. ; 30 cm. "January 1987." LC Card 87-152338 DDC 380.5/09764/2812 19
1. Urban transportation - Texas - Dallas Metropolitan Area - Statistics. 2. Urban transportation - Texas - Fort Worth Metropolitan Area - Statistics. I. North Central Texas Council of Governments.
HE310.D25 T73 1987

TRANSPORTATION - DENMARK - PASSENGER TRAFFIC.
Persontrafik i 1975 og 1981 . [Copenhagen] [1983] 94 p. : ISBN 87-88453-06-5 LC Card 84-169450
HE257 .P47 1983

Transportation, energy, and economic development . Moavenzadeh, Fred, 1935- Amsterdam ; New York : viii, 529 p. : ISBN 0-444-42338-9 (U. S.) : LC Card 84-5954 DDC 333.79 19
HE148 .M6 1984 NYPL [JLE 86-1569]

TRANSPORTATION - ENERGY CONSERVATION.
Moavenzadeh, Fred, 1935- Transportation, energy, and economic development . Amsterdam ; New York : viii, 529 p. : ISBN 0-444-42338-9 (U. S.) : LC Card 84-5954 DDC 333.79 19
HE148 .M6 1984 NYPL [JLE 86-1569]

TRANSPORTATION - ENERGY CONSUMPTION.
Moavenzadeh, Fred, 1935- Transportation, energy, and economic development . Amsterdam ; New York : viii, 529 p. : ISBN 0-444-42338-9 (U. S.) : LC Card 84-5954 DDC 333.79 19
HE148 .M6 1984 NYPL [JLE 86-1569]

TRANSPORTATION - ENVIRONMENTAL ASPECTS - CHILE - SANTIAGO METROPOLITAN AREA.
Matas, Jaime. Los problemas ambientales del sistema de transporte urbano /. Santiago de Chile , 1981. 30 leaves : LC Card 82-201768
HE234.Z7 S355 1981

TRANSPORTATION - EUROPE - CONGRESSES.
The Regionalisation of transport and regional planning in practice . Paris, France [Washington, D.C.] c1984. 199 p. : ISBN 92-821-1091-5 (pbk.) : LC Card 85-180250 DDC 380.5/068 19
HE242 .R44 1984 NYPL [JLG 86-138]

TRANSPORTATION - EUROPE, EASTERN - RATES.
Konovalova, N. A. (Nina Alekseevna) Mezhdunarodnye transportnye tarify /. Moskva , 1985. 278 p. ; LC Card 86-127719
HE195.5.E852 K65 1985

Transportation fact book. Alexandria, VA (1611 Duke St., Alexandria 22314-3482) : Household Goods Carriers Bureau, c1987. iii, 75 p. : ill. ; 28 cm. Cover title. LC Card 87-155218 DDC 388.3/2/0973021 19
1. Storage and moving trade - United States - Statistics. 2. Moving, Household - United States - Statistics. I. Household Goods Carriers Bureau (U. S.).
HE5623 .T67 1987

TRANSPORTATION - FRANCE - HISTORY - CONGRESSES.
Les Communications dans la péninsule Ibérique au Moyen-Age . Paris , 1981. 208 p. : ISBN 2-222-02922-8 : LC Card 81-213698 DDC 380.5/0946 19
HE261.A5 C65 1981 NYPL [JLG 86-113]

TRANSPORTATION - FRANCE - MIDI-PYRÉNÉES.
Marconis, Robert. Midi-Pyrénées XIXe-XXe siècles . [Toulouse?] [1985?] 2 v. : ISBN 2-86726-084-7 (set) LC Card 87-112330
HC277.M54 M37 1985

TRANSPORTATION - FRANCE - TOULOUSE REGION.
Marconis, Robert. Midi-Pyrénées XIXe-XXe siècles . [Toulouse?] [1985?] 2 v. : ISBN 2-86726-084-7 (set) LC Card 87-112330
HC277.M54 M37 1985

TRANSPORTATION - FREIGHT. see **FREIGHT AND FREIGHTAGE.**

TRANSPORTATION - GERMANY (EAST) - SONDERSHAUSEN (LANDKREIS)
Fieber, Joachim. Die effektivere Gestaltung des Personennahverkehrs im Kreis Sondershausen . Potsdam-Babelsberg , Leipzig , 1983. 75 p. : LC Card 83-241076
HE249.5.Z7 S664 1983

TRANSPORTATION - GERMANY, WEST.
Oettle, Karl. Ökonomische Probleme des öffentlichen Verkehrs . Baden-Baden , 1981. 373 p. ; ISBN 3-7890-0568-1 : LC Card 82-159141 DDC 380.5/068 19
HE249 .O33 1981 NYPL [JLD 86-2588]

Offergeld, Johannes. Spezialisierung des Verkehrsangebotes und Strukturwandel in der verladenden Wirtschaft . Göttingen , 1984. 185 p. : ISBN 3-525-85690-3 (Deut. Bibl.) LC Card 84-197725
HE131 .M8 Heft 102 HE249

TRANSPORTATION - GERMANY, WEST - FINANCE.
Vorschläge für eine Neuordnung des organisatorischen Rahmens für den öffentlichen Personennahverkehr /. Bonn-Bad Godesberg [1977] 35 p. ; LC Card 86-173254
HE64 .A36 Heft 53 HE249

TRANSPORTATION - GERMANY (WEST) - HAIGER - CASE STUDIES.
Brauer, Karl M. Fallstudie Haiger . Berlin , c1983. 55 p. ; ISBN 3-428-05403-2 LC Card 83-233201
HE199.G3 B73 1983

TRANSPORTATION - GERMANY (WEST) - MANAGEMENT - EMPLOYEE PARTICIPATION.
Ehinger, Jürgen. Erfahrungen mit der Mitbestimmung in kommunalen Unternehmen . Baden-Baden , 1986. 147 p. ; ISBN 3-7890-1289-0 LC Card 87-118963 DDC 350.87/00943 19
HD2768.G44 E38 1986

TRANSPORTATION - GERMANY (WEST) - MARKETING.
Clauss, Rüdiger, 1952- Marketing der Unternehmen des öffentlichen Personen, nahverkehrs im Spannungsfeld erwerbswirtschaftlicher und gemeinwirtschaftlicher Ziele /. Bergisch Gladbach , 1985. xiii, 308 p. : ISBN 3-89012-019-9 LC Card 85-175468
HE249 .C42 1985

TRANSPORTATION - GERMANY (WEST) - MÜNSTER IN WESTFALEN.
Busse, Dieter. Die Wirkungen von Sonderfahrstreifen für Busse auf die Fahrzeiten im Individualverkehr und öffentlichen Personenahverkehr . Münster [1985?] xii, 274 p. : ISBN 3-88660-264-8 LC Card 86-138804
HE363.G34 M933 1985

TRANSPORTATION - GERMANY, WEST - PASSENGER TRAFFIC.
Clauss, Rüdiger, 1952- Marketing der Unternehmen des öffentlichen Personen, nahverkehrs im Spannungsfeld erwerbswirtschaftlicher und gemeinwirtschaftlicher Ziele /. Bergisch Gladbach , 1985. xiii, 308 p. : ISBN 3-89012-019-9 LC Card 85-175468
HE249 .C42 1985

Michelbach, Roger. Probleme der Sanierung der Deutschen Bundesbahn durch die Änderung institutioneller Rahmenbedingungen /. Thun , c1984. xi, 450 p. : ISBN 3-87144-865-6 LC Card 85-137676
HE3080.D4 M53 1984

Regionale Struktur des Personenverkehrs in der Bundesrepublik Deutschland im Jahre 1980 /. Berlin , 1985. ix, 320 p. : ISBN 3-428-05961-1 LC Card 86-165242
HC281 .B33 Heft 88 HE249

Vorschläge für eine Neuordnung des organisatorischen Rahmens für den öffentlichen Personennahverkehr /. Bonn-Bad Godesberg [1977] 35 p. ; LC Card 86-173254
HE64 .A36 Heft 53 HE249

TRANSPORTATION - GERMANY (WEST) - SCHLESWIG-HOLSTEIN - CONGRESSES.
Gestaltung künftiger Raumstrukturen durch veränderte Verkehrskonzepte . Hannover , 1986. xii, 173 p. : ISBN 3-87870-767-3 LC Card 87-401351 DDC 380.5/0943/512 19
HE249.Z7 S343 1986

TRANSPORTATION - GREAT BRITAIN.
Bell, G. J. (Graham J.) The business of transport /. Plymouth [Devon] , 1984. viii, 344 p. : ISBN 0-7121-2406-3 (pbk.) LC Card 84-170770 DDC 380.5 19
HE151 .B436 1984 NYPL [JLD 87-86]

TRANSPORTATION - HISTORY.
Wolf, Winfried. Eisenbahn und Autowahn . Hamburg , c1987. 565 p. : ISBN 3-89136-105-X LC Card 87-167400 DDC 388/.09 19
HE151 .W58 1987

Transportation in Nigerian national development : proceedings of a conference held at the University of Ibadan, Ibadan, July 4th-9th, 1977 / edited by S.O. Onakomaiya and N.F. Ekanem. Ibadan : Nigerian Institute of Social and Economic Research, c1981. xi, 602 p. : ill. ; 25 cm. Includes bibliographical references. ISBN 978-18-1010-6 (pbk.) LC Card 82-196087 DDC 380.5/09669 19
1. Transportation - Nigeria - Congresses. 2. Transportation and state - Nigeria - Congresses. I. Onakomaiya, S. O. II. Ekanam, N. F. (Nkanta F.). III. Nigerian Institute of Social and Economic Research. IV. Conference on Transportation in Nigeria (1977 : University of Ibadan).
HE287.7 .T72 1981 NYPL [Sc E 86-178]

TRANSPORTATION - INDIA.
Raza, Moonis. Transport geography of India . New Delhi , 1986. xii, 299 p. : LC Card 86-903251 DDC 380.5/0954 19
HE3298 .R39 1986

Transport in India. New Delhi , 1986. v, 64 p. ; LC Card 87-900171 DDC 380.5/0954 19
HE271.A2 T73 1986

TRANSPORTATION - INDIA - PASSENGER TRAFFIC.
Patankar, P. G. Road passenger transport in India /. Pune [1985?] xi, 226 p., [4] p. of plates : LC Card 85-905215 DDC 388/.042/0954 19
HE365.I43 B86 1985 ***NYPL [JLE 86-4230]***

TRANSPORTATION INSURANCE. see **INSURANCE, MARINE.**

TRANSPORTATION - ITALY - LIGURIA.
Vallega, Adalberto. Dai porti al sistema portuale . Savona , 1985. 320 p. : LC Card 87-139096
HE558.L44 V35 1985

TRANSPORTATION - KAZAKH S.S.R.
Bekkulov, A. B. (Ablkaĭ Bekkulovich) Problemy razvitii͡a transporta Kazakhstana . Alma-Ata , 1984. 229 p. ; LC Card 84-226651
HE255.Z7 K393 1984

TRANSPORTATION - KENYA - NAIROBI.
Mitullah, W. V. Management of urban services in Nairobi . Nairobi, Kenya , 1985. 109, 106, vi p., [6] leaves of plates : LC Card 87-116360 DDC 388.4/09676/25 19
HD4720.5.N35 M57 1985

Mogridge, M. C. Project identification . Nairobi [1971] 81 leaves in various pagings : LC Card 87-118674
HE283.5.Z7 N456 1971

TRANSPORTATION - LITHUANIA - PASSENGER TRAFFIC.
Tendent͡sii razvitii͡a passazhirskikh perevozok v Litovskoĭ SSR . Vil′ni͡us , 1985. 179 p. : LC Card 86-199868
HE255.Z7 L577 1985

TRANSPORTATION - NEW JERSEY.
New Jersey. Legislature. General Assembly. Transportation, Communications & High Technology Committee. Public hearing before the Assembly Transportation, Communications & High Technology Committee on transportation infrastructure . [Trenton, N.J.] [1986]. 95 p. ;
NYPL [JLF 86-1583]

TRANSPORTATION - NIGERIA - CONGRESSES.
Transportation in Nigerian national development . Ibadan , c1981. xi, 602 p. : ISBN 978-18-1010-6 (pbk.) LC Card 82-196087 DDC 380.5/09669 19
HE287.7 .T72 1981 ***NYPL [Sc E 86-178]***

TRANSPORTATION - NIGERIA - KADUNA STATE.
Ogwude, Innocent C. (Innocent Chuka) Industrial demand for freight transport in Kaduna State /. Zaria [Nigeria] [1984] 101 p. : LC Card 86-152627 DDC 380.5/24/096695 19
HE287.7.Z7 K336 1984

TRANSPORTATION - NORWAY - FINANCE.
Jean-Hansen, Viggo. Sektorberegninger for samferdselssektorene og reparasjon av kjøretøyer m.v. /. Oslo , 1979. 56 p. ; ISBN 82-537-0968-4 LC Card 86-460231
HE259 .J4 1979

TRANSPORTATION - NORWAY - HISTORY.
Bjørnland, Dag, 1935- Fra dampmaskin til jetfly . [Oslo] , c1982. 104 p. : ISBN 82-508-0180-6 : LC Card 83-134968
HE259 .B5 1982

TRANSPORTATION - NORWAY - OSLO - HISTORY.
Winge, Harald. Føringaredskaper i Aker fogderi . Oslo , 1976. 105 p. : LC Card 86-460271
HE259.Z7 A48 1976

Transportation of imports and exports : modal split. Lilongwe : Transport Planning Unit, Economic Planning Division, Office of the President and Cabinet, 1984. i, 23 leaves ; 30 cm. Cover title. LC Card 86-980329 DDC 385/.24/096897 19
1. Railroads - Malawi - Freight. 2. Trucking - Malawi. 3. Malawi - Commerce. I. Malawi. Transport Planning Unit.
HE3432 .T7 1984

The transportation of Soviet energy resources /. Sagers, Matthew J. Totowa, N.J. , 1986. xvi, 177 p. : ISBN 0-8476-7504-1 : LC Card 86-15508 DDC 380.5/24 19
HD9502.S652 S24 1986 ***NYPL [JLE 87-38]***

TRANSPORTATION - PARAGUAY.
Estudio de transportes en la Región Amazónica y en el Alto Paraguay. Buenos Aires [1983- v. <1 > : LC Card 87-400601 DDC 380.5/0981/1 19
HE230 .E85 1983

TRANSPORTATION - PENNSYLVANIA - EASTON REGION - HISTORY - 19TH CENTURY.
Metz, Lance E. Sherman's guide to Hugh Moore Park /. Easton, PA , 1988. p. cm. ISBN 0-930973-07-0 (pbk.) : LC Card 87-25622 DDC 338.09748/22 19
HE395 .P43 1988

TRANSPORTATION - POLAND.
Blotko, Kazimierz. Racjonalny podział przewozów ładunków między gałęzie transportu /. Warszawa , 1978. 126 p. ; LC Card 81-206824
HF5780.P7 B57 1978

TRANSPORTATION POLICY. see **TRANSPORTATION AND STATE.**

TRANSPORTATION - RATES.
Konovalova, N. A. (Nina Alekseevna) Mezhdunarodnye transportnye tarify /. Moskva , 1985. 278 p. ; LC Card 86-127719
HE195.5.E852 K65 1985

TRANSPORTATION - RESEARCH - UNITED STATES.
Killi, Egil.
Transportproblemer, -politikk, -forskning og -undervisning i USA. Slemdal, 1968. 65, 3, 5 l. LC Card 75-408744
HE203 .K5 ***NYPL [JLF 86-617]***

Research for public transit . Washington, D.C. , 1987. vi, 146 p. : ISBN 0-309-04461-8 (pbk.) LC Card 87-22878 DDC 388.4/0973 19
HE4451 .R47 1987

TRANSPORTATION - RUSSIAN S.F.S.R. - BASHKIRSKAI͡A A.S.S.R.
Puti razvitii͡a infrastruktury regiona /. Ufa , 1984. 117 p. : LC Card 85-199949
HE255.Z7 B377 1984

TRANSPORTATION - RUSSIAN S.F.S.R. - MOSCOW - MATHEMATICAL MODELS.
Matematicheskie metody v upravlenii gorodskimi transportnymi sistemami /. Leningrad , 1979. 150 p. : LC Card 81-163008
HE311.S652 M675 1979

TRANSPORTATION - SOCIAL ASPECTS.
Reichman, Shalom, 1935- Les transports, servitude ou liberté? /. Paris , c1983. 197 p. ; ISBN 2-13-037934-6 : LC Card 83-230014
HE151 .R44 1983

TRANSPORTATION - SOUND, THE (DENMARK AND SWEDEN)
Öresundsförbindelser . [Stockholm] [1983] 196 p. : ISBN 91-38-08123-7 LC Card 84-218397
HE256.Z7 S665 1983

TRANSPORTATION - SOUTH AFRICA - CONGRESSES.
Inligtingsimposium, 23 Oktober 1981 /. [Pretoria] [1981] 115 p. : LC Card 86-213181 DDC 380.5/0968 19
HE284.4.A2 I55 1981

TRANSPORTATION - SOUTHERN CONE OF SOUTH AMERICA.
Estudios sobre integración económica y cooperación regional en el Cono Sur . Santiago de Chile , c1985. 283 p. ; LC Card 86-174604
HC167.S67 E78 1985

TRANSPORTATION - SOVIET UNION.
Ėkonomicheskie problemy transporta SSSR /. Moskva , 1985. 181, [3] p. ; LC Card 86-100790
HE255.A2 E38 1985

Rezer, Semen Moiseevich. Vzaimodeĭstvie transportnykh sistem /. Moskva , 1985. 243 p. : LC Card 85-223225
HE255 .R493 1985

Sych, E. N. (Evgenii͡a Nikolaevna) Transportno-proizvodstvennye sistemy . Kiev , 1986. 164 p. : LC Card 86-233704
HE255 .S93 1986

TRANSPORTATION - SOVIET UNION - MANAGEMENT - MATHEMATICAL MODELS.
Avtomatizat͡sii͡a upravlenii͡a transportnymi sistemami /. Moskva , 1984. 271 p. : LC Card 84-195421
HE255 .A93 1984

TRANSPORTATION - SOVIET UNION - MATHEMATICAL MODELS.
Sovershenstvovanie khozi͡aĭstvennogo mekhanizma na transporte /. Moskva , 1983. 223 p. : LC Card 85-199829
HE255.A2 S68 1983

TRANSPORTATION - SPAIN - HISTORY - CONGRESSES.
Les Communications dans la péninsule Ibérique au Moyen-Age . Paris , 1981. 208 p. : ISBN 2-222-02922-8 : LC Card 81-213698 DDC 380.5/0946 19
HE261.A5 C65 1981 ***NYPL [JLG 86-113]***

TRANSPORTATION - SPAIN - SALT - HISTORY.
Torrent, Emili. Evolució del transport a Salt /. [Salt, Spain] [1984] 32 p. : ISBN 84-85946-59-6 LC Card 87-161246
HE311.S72 S257 1984

Transportation strategies for human settlements in developing countries. United Nations Centre for Human Settlements. Nairobi , 1984. v, 79 p. ; LC Card 85-980241 DDC 380.5/068 19
HE148.5 .U55 1984

TRANSPORTATION - STUDY AND TEACHING (SECONDARY) - FRANCE - LYON.
Transports et échanges . [Lyon] , 1979. 64 p. ; LC Card 80-125866
HE192.F8 T73 1979

TRANSPORTATION - SUDAN - KHARTOUM METROPOLITAN AREA.
Affan, Bodour O. Abu. Traffic and public transport in metropolitan Khartoum . Khartoum [1985] iv, 73 leaves ; LC Card 86-980566 DDC 388.4/1/096262 19
HE311.S742 K472 1985

TRANSPORTATION - SWITZERLAND - BASEL - HISTORY.
Basler Verkehrs-Betriebe (BVB) . Villigen AG, Schweiz , c1984. 56 p., [188] p. of plates, xv p. : ISBN 3-85649-045-0 : LC Card 84-160209
HE4919.B37 B37 1984

TRANSPORTATION TO AIRPORTS. see **ACCESS TO AIRPORTS.**

TRANSPORTATION - UKRAINE.
Sych, E. N. (Evgenii͡a Nikolaevna) Transportno-proizvodstvennye sistemy . Kiev , 1986. 164 p. : LC Card 86-233704
HE255 .S93 1986

TRANSPORTATION - UNITED STATES.
Farley, H. W. Cheaper transportation . Yorkville, Ill. , 1874. 10 p. ; LC Card 85-665909
HE199.U6 F3x 1874

Killi, Egil.
Transportproblemer, -politikk, -forskning og -undervisning i USA. Slemdal, 1968. 65, 3, 5 l. LC Card 75-408744
HE203 .K5 ***NYPL [JLF 86-617]***

TRANSPORTATION - UNITED STATES - ADDRESSES, ESSAYS, LECTURES.
Readings in contemporary transportation /. Tulsa, OK , c1983. x, 325 p. : ISBN 0-87814-215-0 (pbk.) LC Card 82-22379 DDC 380.5 19
HE151 .R37 1983 ***NYPL [JLF 86-2000]***

TRANSPORTATION - UNITED STATES - PASSENGER TRAFFIC.
Klinger, Dieter. Personal travel in the U. S. . Washington, D.C. , Springfield, Va. [1986] 2 v. : LC Card 86-603072 DDC 380.5/22/0973021 19
HE199.9 .K535 1986

Meyer, John Robert. Deregulation and the future of intercity passenger travel /. Cambridge, Mass. , c1987. xviii, 294 p. : ISBN 0-262-13225-7 LC Card 86-27308 DDC 387.7/42/0973 19
HE9803.A35 M49 1987

TRANSPORTATION - YEMEN.
Becker, Fritz, 1947- Entwicklungseffekte durch Verkehrserschliessung in der Arabischen Republik Jemen . Bochum , 1984. 50 p. : LC Card 84-241945
HE268.7 .B4 1984 *NYPL [JLH 86-2]*

TRANSPORTATION - YEMEN - MAPS.
Becker, Fritz, 1947- Entwicklungseffekte durch Verkehrserschliessung in der Arabischen Republik Jemen . Bochum , 1984. 50 p. : LC Card 84-241945
HE268.7 .B4 1984 *NYPL [JLH 86-2]*

TRANSPORTATION - ZAMBIA.
A Study into the evolution and performance of the transport sector in Zambia with particular reference to the operations of the ZIMCO group of transport companies /. [Lusaka?] [1980?] 89 p. : LC Card 86-981420
HE284.6 .S78 1980

TRANSPORTATIONS - BRAZIL - STATISTICS.
Inquéritos especiais /. Rio de Janeiro, Brasil , 1984. 4 v. in 5. ; *NYPL [JLF 86-202]*

Transporte urbano em questão /. Brinco, Ricardo. Porto Alegre , 1985. 114 p. ; LC Card 87-404831 DDC 388.4 19
HE305 .B75 1985

Transporte y crecimiento regional en Colombia /. Latorre, Emilio. Bogotá, Colombia , 1986. 137 p. : ISBN 958-9061-14-1 LC Card 87-115019 DDC 380.5/09861 19
HE235 .L37 1986

Transporte y servicios urbanos en América Latina. Transports urbains et services en Amérique latine . Arcueil, France , Quito [1985- v. <1 > : ISBN 2-85782-137-9 (set) LC Card 87-153020
HE311.L29 T73 1985

Transportforskningskommissionen (Sweden) Sverige och den internationella transportmarknaden . Stockholm [1983] 87 p. : ISBN 91-85402-64-8 : LC Card 83-223136
HE199.S77 S84 1983

Transportno-proizvodstvennye sistemy . Sych, E. N. (Evgeniia Nikolaevna) Kiev , 1986. 164 p. : LC Card 86-233704
HE255 .S93 1986

Transportøkonomisk institutt. Killi, Egil. Transportproblemer, -politikk, -forskning og -undervisning i USA. Slemdal, 1968. 65, 3, 5 l. LC Card 75-408744
HE203 .K5 *NYPL [JLF 86-617]*

Transportproblemer, -politikk, -forskning og -undervisning i USA. Killi, Egil. Slemdal, 1968. 65, 3, 5 l. LC Card 75-408744
HE203 .K5 *NYPL [JLF 86-617]*

Transports. Reichman, Shalom, 1935- Les transports, servitude ou liberté? /. Paris , c1983. 197 p. ; ISBN 2-13-037934-6 : LC Card 83-230014
HE151 .R44 1983

Transports & communication, 0760-9922 . (4) Darbéra, Richard. Le planificateur et le cyclopousse . Caen , 1986. xiii, 190 p. : ISBN 2-86878-015-6 : LC Card 86-192929
HE311.I4 D36 1986

Transports collectifs. Les Rues mixtes . [Bagneux] [1982] 40 p. : ISBN 2-11-083325-4 : LC Card 84-104398
HE363.F72 P437 1982

Transports, décentralisation, neuvième plan. Villette, Jean. Transports, décentralisation 9o plan /. Paris , c1986. 161 p. : ISBN 2-11-001549-7 : LC Card 86-181094
HE248.A2 V55 1986

Transports, décentralisation 9o plan /. Villette, Jean. Paris , c1986. 161 p. : ISBN 2-11-001549-7 : LC Card 86-181094
HE248.A2 V55 1986

Transports et échanges : dans la région lyonnaise, de l'antiquité à nos jours : livret du professeur / commentaires établies par Annie Charnay ... [et al.]. [Lyon] : Centre régional de documentation pédagogique de Lyon : Service éducatif des Archives départementales du Rhône, 1979. 64 p. ; 27 cm. Includes bibliographies. LC Card 80-125866
1. Transportation - Study and teaching (Secondary) - France - Lyon. I. Charnay, Annie. II. Centre régional de documentation pédagogique de Lyon. III. Archives départementales du Rhône. Service éducatif.
HE192.F8 T73 1979

Transports maritimes et balance des paiements en Côte d'Ivoire /. Kouassi, Jean-Claude. [Abidjan] [1982?] 23, xii leaves ; LC Card 86-111436 DDC 387.5/1 19
HE597.I9 K68 1982 *NYPL [JLF 86-1485]*

Les Transports routiers de marchandises effectués sur le territoire français par des véhicules étrangers / rédaction, Département des statistiques des transports. Paris : Le Département, [1983] 26 p. ; 30 cm. Cover title: Système d'information sur les transports de marchandises. "ISSN 0181-5334"--Cover. "Février 1983"--Cover. LC Card 83-214677
1. Trucking - France - Statistics. I. France. Département des statistiques des transports. II. Title: Système d'information sur les transports de marchandises.
HE5668.A6 T74 1983

Les transports, servitude ou liberté? /. Reichman, Shalom, 1935- Paris , c1983. 197 p. ; ISBN 2-13-037934-6 : LC Card 83-230014
HE151 .R44 1983

Transports urbains et services en Amérique latine : actes de l'atelier de recherche, Quito, 8-12 juillet 1985 / publication préparée et présentée par Etienne Henry & Oscar Figueroa = Transporte y servicios urbanos en América Latina : actas del taller de investigación, Quito, 8-12 de julio de 1985 / publicación preparada y presentada por Etienne Henry & Oscar Figueroa. Arcueil, France : INRETS ; Quito : CIUDAD, [1985- v. <1 > : ill. ; 21 x 30 cm. Text in French and Spanish; summaries in French, Spanish, English, and Portuguese. Includes bibliographies. CONTENTS. - t. 1. Transports et citadins. ISBN 2-85782-137-9 (set) LC Card 87-153020
1. Urban transportation - Latin America - Congresses. I. Henry, Etienne. II. Figueroa, Oscar. III. INRETS (Institute : France). IV. Centro de Investigaciones CIUDAD. V. Title: Transporte y servicios urbanos en América Latina.
HE311.L29 T73 1985

Transpress Lexikon Stadtverkehr / Hans Glissmeyer, Leiter des Autorenkollektivs ; [Autoren, Hans Glissmeyer ... et al.]. 1. Aufl. Berlin : Transpress VEB Verlag für Verkehrswesen, 1985. 487 p., 33 p. of plates : ill. ; 22 cm. Bibliography: p. 487. LC Card 86-166711
1. Urban transportation - Dictionaries - German. I. Glissmeyer, Hans. II. Title: Lexikon Stadtverkehr.
HE305 .T78 1985

Transtec (Firm ; Brussels, Belgium) Bauwens, Jan G., 1924- Industrial co-operation and investment in Yugoslavia /. Luxembourg , Washington, D.C. , 1986. viii, 161 p. : ISBN 92-825-6410-X (pbk.) : LC Card 86-216364 DDC 332.6/73/09497 19
HG5682 .B38 1986

TRANSYLVANIA (ROMANIA) - INDUSTRIES - HISTORY.
Vajda, Lajos. Erdélyi bányák, kohók, emberek, századok . Bukarest , 1981. 544 p. : LC Card 83-124763
HD8039.M61 R68 1981

Transzformációs probléma. Mellár, Tamás. Az érték átalakulása termelési árrá, avagy, Az un. transzformációs probléma /. Pécs , 1982. 55 p. ; LC Card 83-179021
HB203 .M44 1982

Los tranvías de Buenos Aires /. González Podestá, Aquilino. Buenos Aires, República Argentina , c1986. 95 p. : ISBN 950-796-900-2 LC Card 87-400950 DDC 388.4/6/098211 19
HE4609.B82 G66 1986

Traoré, Aminata. La mine d'argile est notre champ / Aminata Traoré. [Abidjan?] : Diffusion, CEDA, [1985] (Abidjan : Société d'impr. ivoirienne) [36] p. : ill. ; 25 cm. Cover title. LC Card 86-200373
1. Women potters - Ivory Coast - Katiola (Centre). 2. Women - Employment - Ivory Coast - Katiola (Centre). 3. Pottery - Ivory Coast - Katiola (Centre). I. Title.
HD6073.P82 I967 1985

TRASH. see **REFUSE AND REFUSE DISPOSAL.**

Trasporti marittimi di linea /. Ogliari, Francesco. Milano , 1975- v. : LC Card 76-507610
HE839 .O35 *NYPL [JSK 86-35]*

Tratado de cooperación amazónica : seminario realizado en la[s] ciudades de Brasilia y Porto Velho, Brasil, del 8 al 16 de octubre de 1985, en el ámbito del Tratado de cooperación amazónica. Washington, D.C. : Secretaría Ejecutiva para Asuntos Económicos y Sociales, Departamento de Desarrollo Regional, 1986. iii, 101 p. ; 23 cm. English, Portuguese, and Spanish. "Seminario sobre Transporte por Carreteras en la Amazonia"--Cover. ISBN 0-8270-2304-9 (pbk.) LC Card 86-152493
1. Transportation, Automotive - Amazon River Region - Congresses. 2. Road construction - Amazon River Region - Congresses. I. Seminar on Road Transportation in the Amazon Region (1985 : Brasília and Porto Velho, Rondônia, Brazil). II. Organization of American States. Dept. of Regional Development.
HE359.A5 T73 1986

Tratado de cooperación amazónica . River Transportation Seminar (1986 : Iquitos, Peru) Washington, D.C. , 1986. iii, 110 p. ; ISBN 0-8270-2473-8 (pbk.) LC Card 87-115058
HE387.A6 R58 1986

Trattato di economia pubblica .
(4) Forte, Francesco, 1929- Il bilancio nell'economia pubblica /. Milano [1985] 2 v. ; ISBN 88-14-00636-9 : LC Card 86-151358 DDC 350.72/2 19
HJ2005 .F67 1985 *NYPL [JLE 86-2653]*

Trautman, James M. Bortz, Paul I. Great expectations . Washington, D.C. , c1986. vii, 137 p., [3] folded leaves : ISBN 0-89324-012-5 (pbk.) LC Card 87-401854 DDC 384.55/453/068 19
HE8700.8 .B66 1986

Trautwein, Hans-Michael, 1957-
Arbeitnehmerfonds in Schweden, der dritte Weg? : Entwicklung und Kritik eines aktuellen Modells zur Demokratisierung der Wirtschaft / Hans-Michael Trautwein. Frankfurt am Main ; New York : P. Lang, c1986. 353, 39, [116] p. : ill. ; 21 cm. (Europäische Hochschulschriften. Reihe V, Volks- und Betriebswirtschaft, 0531-7339 . Bd. 706 = vol. 706 = vol. 706) Originally presented as the author's thesis (doctoral)--Universität Bremen, 1985. Bibliography: p. [97]-[116] ISBN 3-8204-9336-0 LC Card 86-203867
1. Gain sharing - Sweden. 2. Industrial management - Sweden - Employee participation. I. Series: Europäische Hochschulschriften. Reihe V, Volks- und Betriebswirtschaft , Bd. 706. II. Title.
HD4928.G342 S88 1986

Le Travail : marchés, règles, conventions / Robert Salais et Laurent Thévenot, éds. ; introductions, Robert Boyer et Jean-Jacques Silvestre. Paris : INSEE : Economica, c1986. iv, 370 p. ; 24 cm. "Une première version des textes publiés dans cet ouvrage a été présentée lors d'une table-ronde organisée conjointement par le C.N.R.S. et l'I.N.S.E.E. les 22 et 23 novembre 1984 et intitulée: 'Les outils de gestion du travail'"--Avertissement. Includes bibliographies. ISBN 2-7178-1138-9 : LC Card 87-123294
1. Industrial relations - France. 2. Industrial management - France. I. Salais, Robert. II. Thévenot, Laurent. III. Centre national de la recherche scientifique (France). IV. Institut national de la statistique et des études économiques (France).
HD8428 .T72 1986

Le travail à domicile dans le vêtement pour dames . Jean, Diane. [Montréal] [1982] xi, 146, [1] p. : ISBN 2-550-02847-3 LC Card 83-242834
HD6073.C62 C25 1982

Travail autonome au Canada. Self-employment in Canada =. Ottawa , c1985. 33 p. : ISBN 0-660-52868-1 (pbk.) : LC Card 87-101519
HD8037.C2 S45 1985

Travail et automatisation dans l'industrie automobile / Groupe d'études et de recherches permanent sur l'industrie et les salariés de l'automobile. [France] : Gerpisa ; Grenoble : Diffusion, Service des publications, IREP-Développement, 1986. 141 p. ; 21 cm. (Actes du Gerpisa . no 2) Bibliography: p. 127-134. ISBN 2-86561-070-5 : LC Card 87-151670
1. Automobile industry and trade - France - Technological innovations. 2. Automobile industry workers - France - Effect of technological innovations on. I. Groupe d'études et de recherches permanent sur

l'industrie et les salariés de l'automobile. II. Series.
HD9710.F72 T72 1986

Travail et sa sociologie. English. Industrial sociology : work in the French tradition / edited by Michael Rose ; translated by Alan Raybould. London ; Newbury Park, Calif. : Sage Publications, 1987. xvi, 184 p. ; 23 cm. Translation of: Travail et sa sociologie. "Original French text edited by Claude Durand and the Groupe de Sociologie du Travail." Includes bibliographies and index. ISBN 0-8039-8053-1 LC Card 87-50308 DDC 306/.36/0944 19
1. Industrial sociology - France. I. Rose, Michael, 1937-. II. Durand, Claude, 1927-. III. Title.
HD6957.F8 T7313 1987

Travail, loisirs, culture. Relations et interactions. Symposium international organisé par la Fondation Industrie-Université à l'occasion du 90e anniversaire de la S.A. Bekaert, mercredi 2 décembre 1970, Palais des Congrés, Bruxelles. [Bruxelles], Fondation Industrie-Université, [r. de la Concorde, 53]; [Zwevegem], Bekaertstr., 1,] 1970. ix, 163 p. diagrs., tables. 26 cm. Includes bibliographical references. LC Card 71-856101
1. Leisure - Congresses. 2. Work - Congresses. 3. Culture - Congresses. I. Fondation industrie-université (Brussels, Belgium). II. Bekaert, s. a.
HD4904.7 .T7 1970

Le travail posté . Quéinnec, Y. (Yvon) [Toulouse-Le Mirail] , 1985. 261 p. : ISBN 2-85816-030-9 LC Card 87-133427
HD5111.5 .Q45 1985

Les Travailleurs antillais, guyanais, réunionnais en lutte contre le colonialisme et le racisme, pour le droit à la différence et l'unité des travailleurs. Paris : Editions caribéennes, c1980. 89 p., [4] p. of plates : ill. ; 21 cm. At head of title: C.F.D.T. (union régionale) "Meeting du 4 avril 1979"--P. 11. ISBN 2-903033-10-2 LC Card 84-164737
1. Labor and laboring classes - Martinique - Congresses. 2. Labor and laboring classes - Guadeloupe - Congresses. 3. Labor and laboring classes - French Guiana - Congresses. 4. Labor and laboring classes - Réunion - Congresses. I. Confédération française démocratique du travail.
HD8250 .T73 1980

Les travailleurs sous-prolétaires face aux mutations de l'emploi /. Godinot, Xavier, 1951- Paris [1985] 155 p. ; ISBN 2-904972-04-08 LC Card 86-166442
HD5775 .G63 1985

Travancore and Cochin (India)
Five year plan : explanatory memorandum and detailed estimates for the year 1954-55 / Government of Travancore-Cochin. Trivandrum : Printed by the Superintendent of Govt. Presses at the Govt. Central Press, 1954. iii, 45 p. ; 34 cm. LC Card 83-238882
1. Budget - India - Travancore and Cochin. 2. Finance, Public - India - Travancore and Cochin. 3. Travancore and Cochin (India) - Economic policy. I. Title.
HJ2158.T7 T73 1954

TRAVANCORE AND COCHIN (INDIA) - ECONOMIC POLICY.
Travancore and Cochin (India) Five year plan . Trivandrum , 1954. iii, 45 p. ; LC Card 83-238882
HJ2158.T7 T73 1954

Travaux & mémoires de l'Institut des hautes études de l'Amérique latine .
(34) Les Phénomènes de "frontière" dans les pays tropicaux . Paris , 1981. vii, 456 p. : LC Card 83-122397
HD1131 .P47 1981

Travaux de droit, d'économie, de sciences politiques, de sociologie et d'anthropologie .
(no. 148) Loubergé, Henri. Financement et assurance des crédits à l'exportation . Genève , 1985. 502 p. : ***NYPL [JLD 86-2109]***

Travaux d'étudiants .
(no 1) Bahizi, Joseph. Monographie d'unités domestiques. [Bujumbura] [1985] 41 leaves ; LC Card 86-980542
HC880.Z7 M843 1985

Travaux du Centre de géographie humaine et sociale, 0223-9272 .
(no 7) Colloque "Poitiers 1981" (1981 : Université de Poitiers) Actes du Colloque "Poitiers 1981" . Poitiers [France] [1983] 472 p. : LC Card 84-119227
HB3594.P65 C65 1981

Travaux du GRIR .
(5) Analyse socio-économique comparée des coopératives d'habitation en France et au Québec . [Chicoutimi] [1985] xvi, 391 p. : ISBN 2-920730-04-5 LC Card 86-181851
HD7287.72.F8 A53 1985

Travaux et documents de l'ORSTOM .
(no 172) Trincaz, Pierre Xavier. Colonisation et régionalisme . Paris , 1984. 270 p. : ISBN 2-7099-0713-5 LC Card 86-148748 DDC 330.966/3 19
HC1045.Z7 Z548 1984

Travaux et recherches de l'Université de droit, d'économie et de sciences sociales de Paris. Série Sciences économiques .
(no 13) Susini, Jean-Jacques. A qui profite l'inflation? /. Paris , c1985. 122 p. : ISBN 2-13-039288-1 LC Card 86-153761
HG979.5 .S87 1985

Travaux et recherches du Laboratoire associée no 301, C.N.R.S. - Université de Nice.
Sidérurgie et droit de crise /. Paris , c1983. 207 p. ; ISBN 2-13-038363-7 : LC Card 84-128216
HD9522.6 .S53 1983

Travaux scientifiques de la Faculté européenne des sciences du foncier-Strasbourg .
(Bd. 3) Weimar, Robert. Die Umweltvorsorge im Rahmen der Landesplanung Nordrhein-Westfalen . Frankfurt am Main , New York , c1983. xxiii, 313 p. : ISBN 3-8204-7669-5 LC Card 83-206670
HC287.N6 W44 1983

TRAVEL TIME (TRAFFIC ENGINEERING) - UNITED STATES.
Lau, Lorrie A. Y. Analysis of national and regional travel trends /. Washington, D.C. , 1986. iii, 78, 32 p. : LC Card 87-601033 DDC 388.3/14/0973 19
HE370.T74 L38 1986

TRAVELER'S CHECKS.
Reproducciones de billetes y cheques de viaje extranjeros /. [Madrid] [1972?] 140 p. : LC Card 85-140130
HG353 .R44 1972

TRAVELING SALES PERSONNEL.
Bishop, Howard, 1938- Master guide to field sales management tactics and techniques /. Englewood Cliffs, N.J. , c1987. xxii, 306 p. : ISBN 0-13-559840-0 LC Card 87-17425 DDC 658.8/1 19
HF5438.4 .B57 1987

TRAVELING SALES PERSONNEL - GREAT BRITAIN - SALARIES, ETC.
Tack Management Consultants. Salesmen's cars, expenses, and allowances, 1963 /. London [1963?] 163 p. ; LC Card 86-173421
HF5439.7 .T33 1963

Travers, Alfred W., 1930- Supervision : techniques and new dimensions / Alfred W. Travers. Englewood Cliffs, N.J. : Prentice-Hall, c1988. xiv, 409 p. : ill. ; 24 cm. Includes bibliographies and index. ISBN 0-13-876434-4 (pbk.) LC Card 87-1173 DDC 658.3/02 19
1. Supervision of employees. 2. Personnel management. I. Title.
HF5549 .T714 1988

Travis, A. B., 1929- Davis, Steve, 1953- The electric mailbox /. Dallas, Tex. , c1986. 286 p. ; ISBN 0-911061-14-2 (pbk.) LC Card 84-91756 DDC 384.3/4 19
HE6239.E54 D38 1986

Traxler, Franz. Interessenverbände der Unternehmer : Konstitutionsbedingungen und Steuerungskapazitäten, analysiert am Beispiel Österreichs / Franz Traxler ; Vorwort von Claus Offe. Frankfurt am Main ; New York : Campus, c1986. xv, 410 p. ; 21 cm. Bibliography: p. 382-409. ISBN 3-593-33584-0 LC Card 86-156435
1. Trade and professional associations - Austria. I. Title.
HD2429.A9 T73 1986

Trayectoria de una crítica. Modelo económico chileno . Santiago, Chile [1982] 606 p. ; LC Card 83-201307
HC192 .M63 1982

Traylor, Harlon D. An analysis of grain elevator bankruptcies in Louisiana / by Harlon D. Traylor and Susan D. Harper. [Baton Rouge?] : Dept. of Agricultural Economics and Agribusiness, Louisiana Agricultural Experiment Station, Louisiana State University Agricultural Center, [1986] iii, 77 p. ; 28 cm. (D.A.E. research report . no. 661) "November 1986." Bibliography: p. 70-72. LC Card 87-620885 DDC 338.1/09763 s 338.1/6 19
1. Grain - Storage - Economic aspects - Louisiana. 2. Grain elevators - Economic aspects - Louisiana. 3. Bankruptcy - Louisiana. I. Harper, Susan D. II. Title. III. Series.
HD1775.L8 L7 no. 661 HD9037.L6

Tre incognite per lo sviluppo : strutture di mercato, scelte tecnologiche e ruolo delle istituzioni nell'ultimo decennio / E. Altvater ... [et al.] ; presentazione di Roberto Panizza : introduzione e cura di Angelo Michelsons. Milano, Italy : F. Angeli, c1986. 383 p. : ill. ; 22 cm. (Collana di economia e politica industriale. 34) Includes bibliographical references and index. LC Card 86-198933
1. Industrial promotion - Italy. 2. Italy - Commercial policy. 3. Export marketing - Italy. 4. Technological innovations - Italy. 5. Industry and state - Italy. I. Altvater, Elmer. II. Michelsons, Angelo.
HC310.I53 T74 1986

Treasure of the land of darkness . Martin, Janet, 1945- Cambridge [Cambridgeshire] , New York , 1986. x, 277 p. : ISBN 0-521-32019-4 LC Card 86-6094 DDC 380.1/456753/0947 19
HD9944.S755 M37 1986
NYPL [JLE 87-1280]

TREASURE-TROVE - MALAYSIA - HISTORY - CONGRESSES.
Kapal dan harta karam =. Kuala Lumpur , 1986. xv, 181 p. : LC Card 86-942317 DDC 387.5/09595 19
HF3800.6 .K36 1986

Treasury products. Tiner, John I. Accounting for treasury products . Cambridge, England , Wolfeboro, N.H., USA , 1988. p. cm. ISBN 0-85941-389-6 : LC Card 87-12531 DDC 657/.833 19
HG1708 .T56 1988

Treasury Strategies, Inc. Financial Industry Securities Council Same Day Funds Settlement Task Force. Same day funds settlement for securities transactions . [New York, N.Y.] [S.l.] , c1985. 61 leaves in various foliations : LC Card 85-193287 DDC 332.64 19
HG4631 .F56 1985 ***NYPL [JLF 86-919]***

The Treasury's tax reform proposal.
[Richmond?] : Research Division, Virginia Dept. of Taxation, [1985] 22 leaves ; 28 cm. (Issue paper / Research Division, Virginia Department of Taxation . no. 1) "January 1985." LC Card 86-622457 DDC 336.2/05 19
1. Taxation - United States. 2. Taxation - Virginia. I. Virginia. Dept. of Taxation. Research Division. II. Series. III. Series: Issue paper (Virginia. Dept. of Taxation. Research Division) , no. 1.
HJ2381 .T74 1985

Treated wood update . Fuller, Bernard. Lexington, Mass., USA (24 Hartwell Ave., Lexington 02173) , c1985. iii, 121 p. : LC Card 86-201219 DDC 381/.45674/0973 19
HD9754 .F85 1985

Treating malpractice . Tobias, Andrew P. New York , 1986. ix, 70 p. ; ISBN 0-87078-173-1 (pbk.) : LC Card 86-217256 DDC 368.5 19
HG8054 .T63 1986

A treatise on the law of bankruptcy and insolvency [microform] /. Hilliard, Francis, 1808?-1878. Philadelphia , London , 1872. xxxiii, 564, 84, xxiii p. ; ***NYPL [*ZT-1689]***

Treatise on the law of private corporations aggregate [microform] /. Angell, Joseph Kinnicut, 1794-1857. Boston , 1855. lv, 939 p. ; ***NYPL [*ZT-1731]***

Trebici, Vladimir. Demografia teritorială a României / Vladimir Trebici, Ilie Hristache. București : Editura Academiei Republicii Socialiste România, 1986. 160 p. : ill. ; 24 cm. Tables of contents in English, French, and Russian. Includes bibliographical references. LC Card 87-151036
1. Romania - Population. I. Hristache, Ilie. II. Title.
HB3631 .T72 1986

Treble, John. Recent advances in labour economics /. London , New York , c1984. 258 p. : ISBN 0-312-66575-X (St. Martin's) : LC Card

83-40628 DDC 331 19
HD4813 .R28 1984 ***NYPL [JLD 86-2455]***

Trecciola, Antonio. Mattei, Enrico. Enrico Mattei, 1945-1953 . [Matelica] [1982] 199 p. : LC Card 84-190191
HD9575.I84 E585 1982

TREE PLANTING - KENYA.
Chavangi, Noel A. Culture as the basis for implementing self-sustaining wood fuel development programmes /. Nairobi, Kenya [1985] 24 leaves ; LC Card 87-111963 DDC 333.75 19
HD9769.F843 K433 1985

TREE PLANTING - KENYA - KAKAMEGA DISTRICT.
Chavangi, Noel A. Cultural aspects of fuelwood procurement in Kakamega District /. Nairobi [1984] 13 leaves ; LC Card 87-112356 DDC 333.75 19
HD9769.F843 K43 1984

Treece, Malra.
Successful business communication / Malra Treece. 3rd ed. Boston : Allyn and Bacon, c1987. xv, 511 p. : ill. ; 25 cm. Rev. ed. of: Successful business writing. c1980. Includes index. ISBN 0-205-10484-3 LC Card 86-26469 DDC 808/.066651 19
1. Commercial correspondence. 2. Communication in management. I. Treece, Malra. Successful business writing. II. Title.
HF5721 .T73 1987

Successful business writing. Treece, Malra. Successful business communication / Malra Treece. 3rd ed. Boston , c1987. xv, 511 p. : ISBN 0-205-10484-3 LC Card 86-26469 DDC 808/.066651 19
HF5721 .T73 1987

Tregubov, A. L. Voprosy ukrepleniia trudovoĭ i proizvodstvennoĭ distsipliny v deiatel'nosti profsoiuznykh organizatsiĭ . Moskva , 1984. 77 p. ; LC Card 86-181312
HF5549.5.L3 V67 1984

Trejos S., Juan Diego. Las políticas de distribución y redistribución del ingreso en Costa Rica en la década de los años setenta / Juan Diego Trejos S. Ciudad Universitaria Rodrigo Facio : Universidad de Costa Rica, Instituto de Investigaciones en Ciencias Económicas, 1983. 117 p. ; 28 cm. (Serie Divulgación económica . no. 24) Bibliography: p. [112]-117. LC Card 85-242016
1. Income distribution - Costa Rica. I. Title. II. Series.
HC143.Z9 I527 1983

Trelles Aréstegui, Efraín. Las Crisis económicas en la historia del Perú /. [Lima, Perú] [s.l.] , 1986. 376 p. : LC Card 87-400306 DDC 330.985 19
HC227 .C744 1986

Treml, Vladimir G.
Referent USSR economic and demographic statistics for normalization of Berkeley-Duke emigre questionnaire data / Vladimir G. Treml ; editors, Gregory Grossman, Vladimir G. Treml ; technical editor, Nikolai Malyshev. [Durham, N.C. : V.G. Treml, [1986] 1 v. (various pagings) ; 29 cm. (Berkeley-Duke occassional papers on the second economy in the USSR . paper no. 7, June 1986) LC Card 86-70618 DDC 304.6/0947/021 19
1. Soviet Union - Population - Statistics. 2. Soviet Union - Statistics. 3. Soviet Union - Economic conditions - 1976- - Statistics. I. Grossman, Gregory. II. Valyshev, Nikolai. III. Series: Berkeley-Duke occasional papers on the second economy in the USSR , paper no. 7. IV. Title.
HB3607 .T74 1986

Soviet foreign trade in foodstuffs : a measure / by Vladimir G. Treml. Washington, D.C. : Center for International Research, Bureau of the Census, U. S. Dept. of Commerce, [1986] viii, 69, 2 p. ; 28 cm. (CIR staff paper . no. 17) Cover title: Soviet foreign trade in foodstuffs : a calorie measure. "April 1986." Bibliography: p. 65-69. LC Card 87-601290 DDC 382/.45664/00947 19
1. Food industry and trade - Soviet Union. 2. Food consumption - Soviet Union. I. Title. II. Series.
HD9015.S65 T74 1986

Trenbeth, Richard P. The membership mystique : how to create income and influence with membership programs / by Richard P. Trenbeth. Ambler, PA : Fund-Raising Institute, c1986. xi, 280 p. : ill. ; 24 cm. ISBN 0-930807-01-4 (pbk.) LC Card 85-70785 DDC 060/.68 19
1. Fund raising. 2. Membership campaigns. 3. Corporations, Nonprofit. 4. Associations, institutions, etc. I. Title.
HG177 .T74 1986

Trendafilov, Toncho. Nauchno-tekhnicheskata revoliutsiia--zakonomernost na uskorenoto razvitie na sotsialisticheskoto obshtestvo / [Toncho Trendafilov, Ogniân Panov]. Sofiia : In-t za propaganda na marksizma-leninizma pri Sofiiskiia GK na BKP, 1985. 93 p. : ill. ; 21 cm. Includes bibliographical references. LC Card 86-163246
1. Technological innovations - Bulgaria. I. Panov, Ogniân. II. Institut za propaganda na marksizma-leninizma. III. Title.
HC403.Z9 T477 1985

Trender och prognoser inför nittio-talet. Trender och prognoser inför 90-talet. Stockholm , Örebro , 1985. 147 p. : ISBN 91-618-0001-5 LC Card 86-115921
LB2833 .S9 1985:2 HC375
NYPL [JLG 86-230]

Trender och prognoser inför 90-talet. Stockholm : Statistiska centralbyrån ; Örebro : SCB distributionen, 1985. 147 p. : ill. ; 30 cm. (Information i prognosfrågor, 0082-0180 . 1985:2) Sveriges officiella statistik Title on added t.p.: Trends and forecasts, population, education and labour market in Sweden. ISBN 91-618-0001-5 LC Card 86-115921
1. Economic forecasting - Sweden. 2. Employment forecasting - Sweden. 3. Population forecasting - Sweden. 4. Education - Sweden - Forecasting. 5. Sweden - Economic conditions - 1945-. 6. Sweden - Population - Statistics. I. Title: Trends and forecasts, population, education and labour market in Sweden. II. Title: Trender och prognoser inför nittio-talet. III. Series.
LB2833 .S9 1985:2 HC375
NYPL [JLG 86-230]

Trends. Hern, Brian. South African paper money trends . Braamfontein, Republic of South Africa , 1986. 172 p. : LC Card 86-201066 DDC 769.5/5968/0750968 19
HG1351.Z8 H47 1986

Trends and forecasts, population, education and labour market in Sweden. Trender och prognoser inför 90-talet. Stockholm , Örebro , 1985. 147 p. : ISBN 91-618-0001-5 LC Card 86-115921
LB2833 .S9 1985:2 HC375
NYPL [JLG 86-230]

Trends and patterns in New Zealand fertility, 1912-1983. Wellington, N.Z. : Dept. of Statistics, 1986. 77 p. : charts ; 30 cm. (Statistical bulletin) Bibliography: p. 23. ISBN 0-477-06453-1 (pbk.) : LC Card 86-219193 DDC 304.6/32/09931021 19
1. Fertility, Human - New Zealand - Statistics. 2. New Zealand - Population - Statistics. I. New Zealand. Dept. of Statistics. II. Series: Statistical bulletin (New Zealand. Dept. of Statistics).
HB1102.5.A3 T74 1986

Trends and patterns of internal migration in the Philippines, 1970-1980 /. Nguiagain, Titus, 1953- [Quezon] [1986] 41 p. ; LC Card 87-120929 DDC 304.8/09599 19
HB2109 .N48 1986

Trends in capital expenditure on fixed assets /. Van Zyl, S. J. J. Pretoria , 1985. ix, 100 p. : ISBN 0-908408-49-8 (pbk.) LC Card 86-206341 DDC 658.8/3968 s 332/.0414/0968 19
HC517.S7 S48 no. 125 HG4028.C4

Trends in corporate education and training /. Lusterman, Seymour. New York, N.Y. , c1985. vii, 23 p. ; ISBN 0-8237-0311-8 (pbk.) LC Card 87-106076 DDC 331.25/92/0973 19
HF5549.5.T7 L86 1985

Trends in employee counseling programs /. McGowan, Brenda G. New York , c1984. 55 p. ; ISBN 0-08-032361-8 (pbk.) : LC Card 84-22820 DDC 658.3/82 19
HF5549.5.C8 M34 1984
NYPL [JLM 83-380 no.37]

Trends in foreign aid, 1977-86 : study / prepared by the Foreign Affairs and National Defense Division, Congressional Research Service, for them Select Committee on Hunger, U. S. House of Representatives. Washington : U. S. G.P.O. : For sale by the Supt. of Docs., Congressional Sales Office, U. S. G.P.O., 1986. vii, 21 p. : ill. ; 24 cm. At head of title: 99th Congress, 2d session. Committee print. Distributed to some depository libraries in microfiche. Shipping list no.: 86-933-P. Includes bibliographical references. Item 1009-B-11, 1009-C-11 (microfiche) LC Card 87-601358 DDC 338.91/73 19
1. Economic assistance, American. 2. Military assistance, American. 3. Food relief, American. I. Library of Congress. Foreign Affairs and National Defense Division. II. United States. Congress. House. Select Committee on Hunger.
HC60 .T69 1986

Trends in international trade and Australia's performance /. Lougheed, A. L. Canberra, Australia , 1986. 16, [4] p. : ISBN 0-909992-18-5 (pbk.) LC Card 87-107912 DDC 382/.0994 19
HF3946.5 .L68 1986

Trends in Kenyan short wave listening : research for Radio FEBA Seychelles / project directors, Randolph Nunnelee, Robert J. Oehrig, Jr. Nairobi, Kenya : Daystar Communications, c1979. vii, 87 [26] leaves : ill. ; 30 cm. Survey conducted for the Far East Broadcasting Association. Bibliography: leaves [25]-[26] LC Card 85-980967 DDC 384.54/3 19
1. Radio audiences - Kenya. 2. Radio, Shortwave - Kenya. 3. Radio FEBA Seychelles (Mahé Island). I. Nunnelee, Randolph. II. Oehrig, Robert J. III. Far East Broadcasting Association.
HE8697.A8 T74 1979

Trends in occupational mobility among migrants /. Pande, Sunanda. Jaipur , 1986. xii, 232 p. ; ISBN 81-7033-023-8 : LC Card 86-902816 DDC 331.5/44/0954 19
HD5856.I4 P36 1986

Trends in road use in Kenya : a focus on the GBC and RAR programmes. Nairobi : Chief Engineer (Roads and Aerodromes), Ministry of Transport and Communications, 1981. viii, 158 p. : ill. ; 30 cm. At head of title: Republic of Kenya, Ministry of Transport and Communications, Roads and Aerodromes Department. LC Card 87-980482 DDC 388.3/142/096762 19
1. Traffic surveys - Kenya. 2. Kenya. Roads and Aerodromes Dept.
HE373.K4 T73 1981

Trends in the construction of dwelling units in the Port Elizabeth/Uitenhage and East London/King William's town regions, 1970-1984, including additions and alterations /. Erwee, Johannes Albertus. Port Elizabeth [South Africa] [1985] 44 leaves : ISBN 0-86988-244-9 (pbk.) LC Card 86-229280 DDC 363.5/1/096875 19
HD7374.4.P6 E735 1985

Trends in the disposable incomes of Australian families, 1964-65 to 1985-86 /. Moore, Jim. Woden, ACT [1986] vii, 103 p. ; ISBN 0-642-51700-2 (pbk.) LC Card 87-154435 DDC 339.394 19
HC610.I5 M66 1986

Trends in the Montana economy and taxation /. House, Verne W. Bozeman [1986] 19 p. : LC Card 87-620963 DDC 330.9786/033 19
HC107.M9 H68 1986

Trendwende im Osthandel /. Wolff von Amerongen, Otto, 1918- Bonn , 1977. 23 p. ; LC Card 85-141570
HF1411 .W583 1977

Trenkler, Dietrich. Verallgemeinerte Ridge Regression : eine Untersuchung von theoretischen Eigenschaften und der Operationalität verzerrter Schätzer im linearen Modell / Dietrich Trenkler. Frankfurt am Main : A. Hain, c1986. viii, 255 p. ; 21 cm. (Mathematical systems in economics. 104) Bibliography: p. 246-255. ISBN 3-445-02406-5 LC Card 87-104568 DDC 330/.01/51 19
1. Economics, Mathematical. I. Title.
HB135 .T74 1986

Trenta mesos de col·lectivisme a Catalunya, cinquanta anys després /. Pérez Baró, Albert. Barcelona , 1986. 283 p. : ISBN 84-297-2412-5 LC Card 86-186185
HD4245.C3 P45 1986

Das Trentino . Penz, Hugo. Innsbruck , 1984. 379 p. : ISBN 3-7030-0142-9 : LC Card 86-138251
HC307.T7 P45 1984

Trentino. Alto Adige. see **Trentino-Alto Adige (Italy)**

TRENTINO-ALTO ADIGE (ITALY) - ECONOMIC CONDITIONS - REGIONAL DISPARITIES.
Penz, Hugo. Das Trentino . Innsbruck , 1984. 379 p. : ISBN 3-7030-0142-9 : LC Card 86-138251
HC307.T7 P45 1984

TRENTINO-ALTO ADIGE, ITALY - POPULATION.
Penz, Hugo. Das Trentino . Innsbruck , 1984. 379 p. : ISBN 3-7030-0142-9 : LC Card 86-138251
HC307.T7 P45 1984

Trentino-Südtirol Abstempelungen, 1850-1883. Sottoriva, Fabio. Annullamenti del Trentino-Alto Adige, 1850-1883 =. Rovereto , c1981. 184 p., [8] p. of plates : LC Card 86-178380
HE6185.I72 T747 1981

Trentino-Tiroler Etschland. see **Trentino-Alto Adige (Italy)**

Trepelkov, V. P. (Vasiliĭ Petrovich) Zarubezhnyĭ biznes amerikanskikh monopoliĭ / V.P. Trepelkov. Moskva : "Mezhdunar. otnosheniia," 1982. 239 p ; 21 cm. Includes bibliographical references. LC Card 83-114503
1. Investments, American. I. Title.
HG4538 .T7 1982

Tres-punkts tællinger 1983. 60-punkts tællinger 1983. [Copenhagen] , 1984. 36 p. : LC Card 85-156478
HE373.D4 A6 1984

TRESPASS - ALBERTA.
Swinnerton, Guy S. Recreation on agricultural land in Alberta /. Edmonton, Alta. [1982] x, 211 p. : LC Card 83-149875 DDC 333.76/17/097123 19
HD319.A4 S94 1982 ***NYPL [JLF 86-851]***

Tress, Roland. Das Güterverkehrszentrum als infrastrukturelle Schnittstelle des Güterverkehrs / von Roland Tress. Düsseldorf : J. Fischer, 1984. xv, 288 p. : ill. ; 24 cm. (Buchreihe des Instituts für Verkehrswissenschaft an der Universität zu Köln, 0341-5767 . Nr. 45) Bibliography: p. 273-287. LC Card 86-140143
1. Freight forwarders - Germany (West) - Ruhr River. 2. Freight forwarders - Rhine River. 3. Inland water transportation - Germany (West) - Ruhr River. 4. Inland water transportation - Rhine River. I. Title. II. Series.
HE5 .C6 Nr. 45 HE5999.Z7G2

Tretiak, Lois Dougan. Joint ventures in the People's Republic of China . Hong Kong , New York, N.Y., U. S.A. , c1985. 347 p. ; LC Card 87-404122 DDC 658.1/8 19
HD2910 .J65 1985

Tret'iak, V. P. (Vladimir Petrovich) Priamye khoziaĭstvennye sviazi v sotsialisticheskoĭ ėkonomike / V.P. Tret'iak. Leningrad : Izd-vo Leningradskogo universiteta, 1986. 141 p. : ill. ; 22 cm. At head of title: Ministerstvo vysshego i srednego spetsial'nogo obrazovaniia RSFSR. Includes bibliographical references. LC Card 87-146709
1. Physical distribution of goods - Soviet Union. 2. Consumption (Economics) - Soviet Union. 3. Industrial procurement - Soviet Union. I. Title.
HF5415.6 .T74 1986

Tretyakova, Albina.
Cost estimates for the Soviet gas industry, 1970 to 1990 / by Albina Tretyakova and Meredith Heinemeier ; edited by Jeanine Braithwaite. Washington, D.C. : Center for International Research, Bureau of the Census, U. S. Dept. of Commerce, [1986] vii, 116 p. ; 28 cm. (CIR staff paper . no. 19) "June 1986." Bibliography: p. 99-116. LC Card 87-601292 DDC 338.2/3 19
1. Gas industry - Soviet Union - Costs - Forecasting. 2. Gas industry - Soviet Union - Costs - Statistics. I. Heinemeier, Meredith M. II. Braithwaite, Jeanine. III. Title. IV. Series.
HD9581.S652 T74 1986

Sagers, Matthew J. Restructuring the Soviet petroleum refining industry /. Washington, D.C. [1985] v, 57 p. ; LC Card 87-601278 DDC 338.4/766553/0947 19
HD9575.S652 S254 1985

Treue, Wilhelm, 1909- Goetzeler, Herbert. Wilhelm und Carl Friedrich von Siemens . Stuttgart , 1986. 131 p. : ISBN 3-515-04558-9 LC Card 86-141456
HD9695.G43 S514 1986

Trevisan, Edilberto. Ao apito do trem : antecedentes e construção da ferrovia de Paranaguá a Curitiba / Edilberto Trevisan. [Curitiba] : Rede Ferroviária Federal, 1985-1986 [i.e. 1986] 123 p. : ill. ; 28 cm. LC Card 87-121016 DDC 385/.0981/62 19
1. Ferrovia Paranaguá-Curitiba - History. 2. Railroads - Brazil - Parana (State) - History. I. Rede Ferroviária Federal (Brazil). II. Title.
HE2930.P34 T74 1986

Trevor, Malcolm, 1932- The Internationalization of Japanese business . Boulder , 1986. p. cm. ISBN 0-8133-0531-4 : LC Card 87-8186 DDC 338.8/8952/04 19
HD2844.5 .I567 1986

Trezise, Philip H., 1912- Building a Canadian-American free trade area /. Washington, D.C. , c1987. xii, 217 p. ; ISBN 0-8157-2973-1 (pbk.) LC Card 87-71507 DDC 382/.0971/073 19
HF1480.15.U5 B85 1987

Triadú, Joaquim, 1959- Les professions del futur / Joaquim Triadú. 1a ed. Barcelona : Tibidabo Edicions, 1986. 186 p. : ill. ; 19 cm. (Colección Conocer a tiempo) Bibliography: p. [185]-186. ISBN 84-86421-20-9 LC Card 86-214981
1. Vocational guidance - Spain. 2. Occupational training - Spain. 3. Spain - Occupations. I. Title.
HF5382.5.S7 T75 1986

Triana, Santiago Pérez. see **Pérez Triana, Santiago, 1858-1916.**

Triangle papers .
(33) Restoring growth in the debt-laden Third World . New York , 1987. x, 82 p. : ISBN 0-930503-02-3 : LC Card 87-23778 DDC 336.3/435/091724 19
HJ8899 .R47 1987

Tribal economy in transition . Sukumaran Nair, M. K., 1948- New Delhi, India , 1987, c1986. 159 p. ; ISBN 81-210-0180-3 : LC Card 87-901406 DDC 330.954/164052 19
HC437.M4 S85 1987

Tribal peasantry dynamics of development /. Pathy, Jaganath, 1948- New Delhi , 1984, c1983. xiii, 233 p. : LC Card 84-900095 DDC 330.954/75052 19
HD879.G8 P37 1984 ***NYPL [JLD 87-724]***

Tribal studies of India series .
(T 121) Singh, R. S. (Rama Shankar), 1950- Changing occupational structure of scheduled tribes /. New Delhi, India , 1986. 291 p. : ISBN 81-210-0175-7 : LC Card 86-903755
HB3640.C48 S56 1986

(T 122) Sukumaran Nair, M. K., 1948- Tribal economy in transition . New Delhi, India , 1987, c1986. 159 p. ; ISBN 81-210-0180-3 : LC Card 87-901406 DDC 330.954/164052 19
HC437.M4 S85 1987

TRIBES - INDIA - CHOTA NĀGPUR.
Prasad, Maheshwari, 1944- Social aspects of mining towns of the tribal region /. New Delhi , 1986- v. <1- > ; LC Card 86-902979 DDC 307.7/66/095412 19
HD9506.I43 C486 1986

TRIBES - INDIA - KORAPUT (DISTRICT) - ECONOMIC CONDITIONS.
Mahapatro, Prafulla Ch. Economic development of tribal India /. New Delhi , 1987. xvi, 408 p. : ISBN 81-7024-077-8 : LC Card 87-900212 DDC 338.954/13 19
HC437.K63 M34 1987

A Tribute to small business : America's growth industry. [Washington, D.C.] : U. S. Small Business Administration ; San Francisco : Pacific Bell Directory, c1987. 72 p. : ill., ports. ; 28 cm. LC Card 87-403591 DDC 338.6/42 19
1. Small business - United States. 2. Small business - Government policy - United States. 3. White House Conference on Small Business. 4. Small business - United States - Societies, etc. - Directories. 5. Trade and professional associations - United States - Directories. I. United States. Small Business Administration. II. Pacific Bell Directory (Firm).
HD2346.U5 T75 1987

Trident Financial Corporation. Savings institutions performance analysis /. [Raleigh, N.C.] , c1987. 159 p. ; LC Card 87-404475 DDC 332.2/1/0973021 19
HG1922 .S35 1987

Triebler, Stephan Ferdinand, 1950-
Verkehrskriminalität und Alkohol in einer Grossstadt : eine Untersuchung über Aspekte der polizeilichen Kontrolltätigkeit im Bereich der Kreispolizeibehörde Köln im Zeitraum von 1970 bis 1980 / vorgelegt von Stephan Ferdinand Triebler. [West Germany : s.n., 1983?] (Köln : Copy-Star) xv, 190 p. : ill. ; 21 cm. Thesis (doctoral)--Universität Bielefeld, 1983. Bibliography: p. vii-xiv. LC Card 84-240261
1. Drinking and traffic accidents - Germany (West) - Cologne - Case studies. 2. Drunk driving - Germany (West) - Cologne - Case studies. I. Title.
HE5620.D7 T75 1983

Trierer historische Forschungen, 0720-9096 .
(Bd. 7) International Congress on Economic History (8th : 1982 : Budapest, Hungary) Münzprägung, Geldumlauf und Wechselkurse . Trier , 1984. 421 p. : ISBN 3-923087-06-3 (pbk.)
HG205 1982 .I53 ***NYPL [JLE 86-3176]***

Trieste. Università. Istituto di statistica. Pubblicazioni. For additional listing of contents, see Old Catalog.
(n.17) Umani, Mario. Un procedimento per la ripartizione ottimale di una collettività in classi . [Trieste] , 1978. 19 p. ; LC Card 81-111875 DDC 368/.092 19
HG9970 .U46 1978 ***NYPL [TB (Triesta. Università Istituto do statistica. Pubblicazioni. n.17)]***

Trifonov, D. (Dimitŭr) 40 brigadirski leta /. Sofiia , 1986. 173 p., [12] p. of plates : LC Card 87-103049
HD4870.B9 A15 1986

Trigubenko, M. E. (Marina Evgen'evna)
Sovetsko-v'etnamskiĭ simpozium na temu "Ėkonomicheskie problemy perekhoda k sotsializmu" (1984 : Moscow, R.S.F.S.R.) Ėkonomicheskie problemy perekhoda k sotsializmu stran s nerazvitoĭ ėkonomikoĭ . [Moskva , 1986. 254 p. ; LC Card 87-108102
HC444 .S69 1984

Trilateral Commission. Restoring growth in the debt-laden Third World . New York , 1987. x, 82 p. : ISBN 0-930503-02-3 : LC Card 87-23778 DDC 336.3/435/091724 19
HJ8899 .R47 1987

TRILATERAL COMMISSION.
Scholl, Heinz. Bilderberger & Trilaterale . Euskirchen, Bundesrepublik Deutschland , c1977. 92 p. ; LC Card 85-199172
HD2785 .S396 1977

Trilla i Bellart, Carme.
Finançament del l'accés a l'habitatge a Catalunya en els darrers anys / Carme Trilla i Bellart. [1a ed.]. [Barcelona] : Generalitat de Catalunya, Departament de Política Territorial i Obres Públiques, Direcció General d'Arquitectura i Habitatge : Cambra Oficial de la Propietat Urbana de Barcelona, [1984] 58 p. : ill. ; 25 cm. "1"--Spine. Includes bibliographical references. LC Card 86-160332
1. Housing - Spain - Catalonia - Finance. 2. Mortgage loans - Spain - Catalonia. 3. Real property - Spain - Catalonia - Finance. I. Title.
HD7351.C37 T75 1984

La financiación del acceso a la vivienda de España, 1976-1981 / Carme Trilla i Bellart. [1a ed.]. [Barcelona] : Generalitat de Catalunya, Departament de Política Territorial i Obres Públiques, Direcció General d'Arquitectura i Habitatge : Cambra Oficial de la Propietat Urbana de Barcelona, [1984] 56 p. : ill. ; 25 cm. "4"--Spine. LC Card 86-160004
1. Housing - Spain - Finance. 2. Mortgage loans - Spain. I. Title.
HD7351.A4 T75 1984

Trillat, Brigitte. Tout sur la France en 100 graphiques /. Paris , c1986. 113 p. : ISBN 2-86260-154-3 : LC Card 87-106635
HA1224 .T68 1986

Trillitzsch, Uwe. Radverkehrskonzept Sprockhövel /. Essen , c1985. 55 p., [3] folded col. leaves of plates : ISBN 3-923494-51-3 LC Card 86-113993
HE5739.G3 R33 1985

Trimble, William F., 1947- Lewis, W. David (Walter David), 1931- The airway to everywhere . Pittsburgh, PA [1988] p. cm.

ISBN 0-8229-3579-1 LC Card 87-25176 DDC 387.7/065/73 19
HE9803.A944 L48 1988

Trimestre económico. Lecturas .
(49) Autoafirmación colectiva . México , 1983. 327 p. ; ISBN 968-16-1335-X LC Card 86-159023
HC59.7 .A92 1983

(57) Bacha, Edmar Lisboa. El milagro y la crisis . México , 1986. 468 p. : ISBN 968-16-2152-2 LC Card 87-400019 DDC 338.981 19
HC187 .B128 1986

Trimming float to build earnings . Thomas, O. Tom. Chicago, Ill. (111 E. Wacker Dr., Chicago 60601) , c1986. iv, 104 p. : LC Card 86-233102 DDC 332.1/752 19
HG1692 .T46 1986

Trincaz, Pierre Xavier. Colonisation et régionalisme : Ziguinchor en Casamance / Pierre Xavier Trincaz. Paris : Editions de l'ORSTOM : Institut français de recherche scientifique pour le développement en coopération, 1984. 270 p. : ill. ; 24 cm. (Collection Travaux et documents . no 172) "Thèse de troisième cycle, soutenue en 1979 à l'Université de Paris V"--Verso of t.p. Bibliography: p. 231-243. ISBN 2-7099-0713-5 LC Card 86-148748 DDC 330.966/3 19
1. Ziguinchor (Senegal) - Economic conditions. 2. Ziguinchor (Senegal) - Social conditions. I. Series: Travaux et documents de l'ORSTOM , no 172. II. Title.
HC1045.Z7 Z548 1984

Trindade Martinez, José Fernando. see **Martinez, José Fernando Trindade.**

Trinidad and Tobago . Mitchell, Nikola. London , 19. 92 p. : ISBN 0-333-31482-4 (pbk.) LC Card 85-187281 DDC 300/.7/1272983 19
HC157.T83 M58 1985

TRINIDAD AND TOBAGO - ADMINISTRATIVE AND POLITICAL DIVISIONS.
1980 population and housing census . Trinidad and Tobago , c1986. 15 p. : LC Card 87-402815 DDC 304.6/097298/3 19
HA867 .A4 1980b

TRINIDAD AND TOBAGO - CENSUS, 1980.
1980 population and housing census . Trinidad and Tobago , c1986. 15 p. : LC Card 87-402815 DDC 304.6/097298/3 19
HA867 .A4 1980b

TRINIDAD AND TOBAGO - ECONOMIC CONDITIONS - STUDY AND TEACHING (SECONDARY) - TRINIDAD AND TOBAGO.
Mitchell, Nikola. Trinidad and Tobago . London , 19. 92 p. : ISBN 0-333-31482-4 (pbk.) LC Card 85-187281 DDC 300/.7/1272983 19
HC157.T83 M58 1985

TRINIDAD AND TOBAGO - POPULATION - STATISTICS.
Population abstract, 1970-1981. Trinidad and Tobago , c1986. ix, 48 p. : LC Card 87-125348 DDC 304.6/097298/3021 19
HA867 .P66 1986

1980 population and housing census . Trinidad and Tobago , c1986. 15 p. : LC Card 87-402815 DDC 304.6/097298/3 19
HA867 .A4 1980b

TRINIDAD AND TOBAGO - SOCIAL CONDITIONS - STUDY AND TEACHING (SECONDARY) - TRINIDAD AND TOBAGO.
Mitchell, Nikola. Trinidad and Tobago . London , 19. 92 p. : ISBN 0-333-31482-4 (pbk.) LC Card 85-187281 DDC 300/.7/1272983 19
HC157.T83 M58 1985

Trinidad busway. Joefield-Napier, Wallace. Financial integration and interest rate linkages between North Atlantic and Caribbean economies, January 1968 to December 1976 /. St. Augustine, Trinidad [1980] vii, 82 p. : LC Card 81-132125 DDC 332.8/2/0724 19
HG1623.C27 J64 1980 ***NYPL [Sc E 86-329]***

Trinidad Island-Wide Cane Farmers Association. Centenary Committee. Cane farming . [San Fernando, Trinidad, West Indies , 1983?] 136 p. : LC Card 86-200484 DDC 338.1/7361/0972983 19
HD9114.T72 C36 1983

Trinidad-Tobago. see **Trinidad and Tobago.**

Trinity University (San Antonio, Tex.) Lives of the laureates . Cambridge, Mass. , c1986. xii, 135 p. : ISBN 0-262-02255-9 LC Card 86-2919 DDC 330/.092/2 B 19
HB76 .L58 1986 ***NYPL [JFD 86-9827]***

Trip report, a visit to Eastern Europe in the wake of the 27th Soviet Party Congress and the Chernobyl nuclear accident (Czechoslovakia, Hungary, Yugoslavia, and Romania) on June 28, 1986 . Pressler, Larry, 1942- Washington , 1987. vi, 58 p. ; LC Card 87-601360 DDC 337.47 19
HC244 .P744 1987

Tripartite Technical Meeting for the Food Products and Drink Industries, 2d, Geneva, 1978. Labour and social problems arising out of seasonal fluctuations of the food products and drink industries / second Tripartite Technical Meeting for the Food Products and Drink Industries, Geneva, 1978. Geneva : International Labour Office, 1978. ii, 51 p. ; 24 cm. At head of title: International Labour Organisation, Programme of Industrial Activities, Report II. Includes bibliographical references. ISBN 92-2-101879-2 (pbk.) : LC Card 80-477150 DDC 331.2/0464
1. Food industry and trade - Seasonal variations - Congresses. 2. Beverage industry - Seasonal variations - Congresses. 3. Labor supply - Congresses. 4. Wages - Congresses. I. Title.
HD9000.1 .T75 1978a ***NYPL [JLE 80-1039]***

Tripathi, B. B. Govil, Rishi Kumar, 1933- Agriculture planning and social justice in India /. Allahabad , 1986. vii, 214 p. ; LC Card 86-902616 DDC 338.1/854 19
HD2073 .G68 1986

Tripāṭhī, Oṅkāranātha, 1934- Taxation and fiscal administration in ancient India : from the Vedic times to the end of the Mauryan period / by O.N. Tripathi. Lucknow, U.P. : Upper India Pub. House, 1985. xii, 152 p. ; 22 cm. Spine title: Taxation in ancient India. Originally presented as the author's thesis (Ph. D.--Lucknow University) "56-9." Bibliography: p. [151]-152. LC Card 85-903145 DDC 336.34 19
1. Taxation - India - History. 2. Fiscal policy - India - History. I. Title. II. Title: Taxation in ancient India.
HJ2932 .T75 1985 ***NYPL [JLD 86-1318]***

Tripcovici, Nicolae. Filatelia : pasiune, competiție, studiu / Nicolae Tripcovici. București : Editura Sport-Turism, 1985. 213 p., [16] p. of plates : ill. (some col.) ; 24 cm. Bibliography: p. 209-[210]. LC Card 87-164874
1. Postage stamps - Collectors and collecting. I. Title.
HE6213 .T75 1985

Tripp, Anne Huber, 1934- The I.W.W. and the Paterson silk strike of 1913 / Anne Huber Tripp. Urbana : University of Illinois Press, c1987. xiv, 317 p., [6] p. of plates : ill., ports. ; 25 cm. Bibliography: p. 283-305. Includes index. ISBN 0-252-01382-4 LC Card 86-24989 DDC 331.89/287739/0974924 19
1. Silk Workers' Strike, Paterson, N.J., 1913 - History. 2. Industrial Workers of the World - History. 3. Socialist Party (U. S.) - History. 4. Paterson (N.J.) - Economic conditions. I. Title.
HD5325.T42 1913 .P387 1987

TRIPS, BUSINESS. see **BUSINESS TRAVEL.**

TRIPURA (INDIA) - CENSUS, 1981.
Census of India, 1981. Gangtok, Sikkim , <1983-1986. v. in : LC Card 87-915028 DDC 315.4/15 19
HA4587.T74 C46 1983

Trischler, Helmuth. Bis vor die Stufen des Throns . München , c1986. 530 p. : ISBN 3-406-31297-7 LC Card 87-103686 DDC 331.7/622334/0943 19
HD8039.M61 G32 1986

Trito Ektakto Schedio Oikonomikēs Draseōs, 1979-1981. Leukōsia : Grapheio Programmatismou, Epitropē Programmatismou, [1981?] xv, 398 p. ; 25 cm. At head of title: Kypriakē Dēmokratia. LC Card 86-192190
1. Cyprus - Economic policy. 2. Cyprus - Economic conditions. I. Cyprus. Grapheio Programmatismou. Epitropē Programmatismou.
HC415.2 .T75 1981

The triumph of politics . Stockman, David Alan, 1946- New York , c1986. 422 p. : ISBN 0-06-015560-4 : LC Card 85-45541 DDC 338.973 19
HC106.8 .S75 1986 ***NYPL [JLE 86-2647]***

The triumph of politics . Stockman, David Alan, 1946- Boston, Mass. , 1987, c1986. xxxiii, 654 p. (large print) ; ISBN 0-8161-4231-9 (lg. print) : LC Card 86-22950 DDC 338.973 19
HC106.8 .S75 1986b

Trivedi, P. K. Akiyama, T. (Takamasa), 1944- A new global tea model . Washington, D.C. , 1987. vi, 130 p. ; ISBN 0-8213-0868-8 LC Card 87-6238 DDC 382/.41372 19
HD9198.A2 A424 1987

Troiano, Alberto C. (Alberto Carlos) Los revalúos técnicos de bienes : un estudio acerca de la normativa vigente : tecnología de preparación y tratamiento contable / Alberto C. Troiano. Buenos Aires : Ediciones Macchi, [1982] 63, [2] p. : ill. ; 23 cm. Bibliography: p. [65] ISBN 950-0-37018-2 LC Card 84-237340
1. Accounting - Argentina - Effect of inflation on. 2. Indexation (Economics) - Law and legislation - Argentina. I. Title.
HF5658.5 .T76 1982

Troitzsch, Ulrich. Technologischer Wandel im 18. Jahrhundert /. Wolfenbüttel , c1981. 246 p. ; ISBN 3-88373-018-1 LC Card 84-116829 DDC 338/.06 19
HC240.9.T4 T43 1981 ***NYPL [JLE 86-927]***

Trolle, Ulf af, 1919- Markedsføring : markedsforhold, analysemetoder, planlegging og strategi / Ulf af Trolle, Svein-Erik Blom.2. utg. °slo] : Universitetsforlaget, 1982. 496 p. : ill. ; 25 cm. Bibliography: p. 483-488. Includes index. ISBN 82-00-05931-6 : LC Card 83-184229
1. Marketing - Denmark. I. Blom, Svein-Erik. II. Title.
HF5415.12.D4 T76 1982

Tromlakova, E. M. (Elena Mikhaĭlovna) Ėffektivnost′ proizvodstva v evropeĭskikh stranakh SĖV / E.M. Tromlakova ; otvetstvennyĭ redaktor K.I. Mikul′skiĭ. Moskva : "Nauka", 1986. 157 p. ; 20 cm. Bibliography: p. 153-157. LC Card 86-233225
1. National income - Europe, Eastern. I. Mikul′skiĭ, Konstantin Ivanovich. II. Title.
HC244.Z9 I5188 1986

Tronconi, Pier Attilio. Settore termoelettromeccanico : crisi e processi di trasformazione : un caso per la politica industriale / Pier Attilio Tronconi. Roma : Lavoro, c1986. 729 p. : ill. ; 21 cm. (Contributi . 20) ISBN 88-7910-149-8 : LC Card 86-211311
1. Electric utilities - Government policy - Italy. I. Title.
HD9685.I82 T76 1986

Tron′ko, Petro Tymofiĭovych. Istoriia kolhospu "Zdobutok ZHovtnia" /. Kyïv , 1986. 188 p., [8] p. of plates : LC Card 87-161618
HD1492.S652 U3835 1986

Tronstad, Roger, 1955- Finnmarkshandelen i 1680-åra / Roger Tronstad. [Oslo : T. Roger, 1981] ix, 244 p., [20] p. of plates : ill. ; 21 cm. "Hovedfagsoppgave i historie til historisk-filosofisk embetseksamen, Universitetet i Oslo, våren 1981." Bibliography: p. 241-244. LC Card 83-152832
1. Finnmark fylke (Norway) - Commerce - History. I. Title.
HF3669.F5 T76 1981

TROPICAL FRUIT INDUSTRY - LATIN AMERICA.
El Mercado regional de frutas . [Montevideo] , 1983. 63 p. ; LC Card 86-171763
HD9259.T753 L295 1983

TROPICAL FRUIT - LATIN AMERICA - MARKETING.
El Mercado regional de frutas . [Montevideo] , 1983. 63 p. ; LC Card 86-171763
HD9259.T753 L295 1983

TROPICAL RAIN FOREST ECOLOGY. see **RAIN FOREST ECOLOGY.**

Troshin, A. (Andreĭ) Sovetskaia ėkonomika segodnia i zavtra / A. Troshin. Moskva : "Molodaia gvardiia", 1981. 208 p. ; 17 cm. (Universitet molodogo marksista) Includes bibliographical references. LC Card 82-144819
1. Soviet Union - Economic conditions - 1976-. 2. Soviet Union - Economic policy - 1981-. I. Title. II. Series.
HC336.25 .T7 1981

Trotzdem-Kollektiv (Reutlingen, Germany) Wozu noch in die Parlamente? /. [Reutlingen] , 1978.

81 p. : LC Card 82-223081 DDC 322/.2/0943 19
HD6697 .W69 1978 *NYPL [JLD 87-886]*

Trouble brewing . Waddington, David P. Aldershot , Brookfield, U. S.A. , c1987. x, 164 p. : ISBN 0-566-05374-8 : LC Card 86-31849 DDC 331.89/28633/0942496 19
HD5366.L62 1981 .B578 1987

The Trouble with technology : explorations in the process of technological change / edited by Stuart Macdonald, D. McL. Lamberton, Thomas Mandeville. London : F. Pinter, 1983. x, 224 p. : ill. ; 24 cm. Includes bibliograpical references and indexes. ISBN 0-86187-285-1
1. Technology - Addresses, essays, lectures. 2. Technological innovations - Addresses, essays, lectures. I. Lamberton, Donald Mclean. II. Macdonald, Stuart. III. Mandeville, T. D. *NYPL [JLE 86-1128]*

Troubled employee program. United States. Dept. of the Interior. Division of Medical and Health Services. Help for the troubled employee. Washington [1975?] 57 p. ;
NYPL [JLF 86-1309]

TROUBLED EMPLOYEE PROGRAMS. see **EMPLOYEE ASSISTANCE PROGRAMS.**

Troubled passage . Preston, Edmund, 1941- Washington, D.C. , 19. vii, 340 p. ; LC Card 87-25500 DDC 353.0087/77 19
HE9803.A35 P74 1987

TROUBLESHOOTING IN COMPUTER SCIENCE. see **DEBUGGING IN COMPUTER SCIENCE.**

Trouet, Klaus. US-Administration . Frankfurt (M) , 1976. 153 p. : LC Card 85-224662
HD9654.9.H64 U7 1976

Trouillot, Michel-Rolph. Peasants and capital : Dominica in the world economy / Michel-Rolph Trouillot. Baltimore : Johns Hopkins University Press, c1988. xiv, 344 p. : ill. ; 24 cm. (Johns Hopkins studies in Atlantic history and culture) Based on the author's thesis (doctoral). Bibliography: p. 317-337. Includes index. ISBN 0-8018-3481-3 (alk. paper) LC Card 87-20018 DDC 305.5/63 19
1. Peasantry - Dominica - History. 2. Capitalism - Dominica - History. 3. Dominica - Economic conditions. I. Title.
HD1531.D58 T76 1988

Les trous du commerce extérieur /. Chatelain, Jacky. Paris , c1984. 170 p. : ISBN 2-86738-031-1 : LC Card 84-241861
HF3556.5 .C42 1984

Troy, Kathryn. Meeting human needs : corporate programs and partnerships / by Kathryn Troy. New York, NY : Conference Board, c1986. vii, 55 p. ; 28 cm. (The Conference Board report . no. 881) ISBN 0-8237-0323-1 (pbk.) LC Card 86-207649 DDC 658.3/8 19
1. Welfare work in industry - United States. 2. Industry - Social aspects - United States. I. Title. II. Series.
HD7654 .T73 1986

Trube, Achim. Arbeitslosigkeit und Neue Armut in Düsseldorf . Bochum , c1986. 65 p. : ISBN 3-925222-03-0 LC Card 87-409036 DDC 331.13/794355 19
HD5780.D85 A73 1986

Truchon, Michel. Balfet, Michel. Les 50 mots clefs de la consommation /. Toulouse , c1985. 310 p. : ISBN 2-7089-1969-5 : LC Card 86-140639 DDC 339.4/7 19
HB801 .B276 1985

Truchot, Didier. Benoit, Philippe. Affiches de pub, 1983/85 /. Paris , c1986. 237 p. : ISBN 2-85108-429-1 : LC Card 86-192339
HF5843 .B44 1986

TRUCK DRIVERS - AUSTRALIA - HISTORY.
Maddock, John, 1917- Mail for the back of beyond /. Kenthurst , 1986. 160 p. : ISBN 0-86417-063-7 LC Card 86-207558 DDC 383/.143/0994 19
HE5709.A6 M33 1986

TRUCK DRIVERS - GERMANY (WEST)
Plänitz, Günther. Das bisschen Fahren-- . Hamburg , 1983. 317 p. : ISBN 3-87975-248-6 LC Card 84-187043
HD8039.M7952 G37 1983

TRUCK DRIVERS - HUNGARY - ANECDOTES, FACETIAE, SATIRE, ETC.
Cserhalmi, Imre. Ha nincs fék, gáz van . [Budapest] , 1984. 294 p. ; LC Card 85-183756
HE5667.5.A6 C74 1984

TRUCK DRIVERS - ICELAND - BIOGRAPHY.
Indriði G. Þorsteinsson, 1926- Fimmtán gírar áfram . Reykjavík , 1981. 178 p., [16] p. of plates : LC Card 83-185502
HD8039.M7952 I25 1981

TRUCK DRIVERS - JUVENILE LITERATURE.
Bourne, Miriam Anne. A day in the life of a cross-country trucker /. Mahwah, N.J. , c1988. 32 p. : ISBN 0-8167-1117-8 (lib. bdg.) : LC Card 87-13582 DDC 388.3/24/02373 19
HD8039.M795 B68 1988

TRUCK DRIVERS - TRAINING OF - GERMANY (WEST)
Rüter, Gert. Sicherheitsorientierte Ausbildung von Berufskraftfahren /. Köln [1983] vii, 91 p. : LC Card 83-235527
HD5716.M7952 G327 1983

TRUCK DRIVERS - UNITED STATES - ATTITUDES.
Reinarman, Craig. American states of mind . New Haven , c1987. x, 262 p. ; ISBN 0-300-03817-8 (alk. paper) LC Card 86-26752 DDC 330.12/2/0973 19
HD3616.U47 R1464 1987

TRUCK INDUSTRY - SOUTH AFRICA - STATISTICS.
Sensus van motorhandel en hersteldienste, 1977 =. Pretoria [1982?] xiv, 166 p. : ISBN 0-621-07034-3 : LC Card 82-240419
HD9710.S72 S46 1982

Truck lane needs methodology . Massimi, John J. Austin , Springfield, Va. [1985] xii, 63 p. : LC Card 86-622425 DDC 388.1/3 19
HE336.T79 M37 1985

TRUCK LANES - TEXAS.
Massimi, John J. Truck lane needs methodology . Austin , Springfield, Va. [1985] xii, 63 p. : LC Card 86-622425 DDC 388.1/3 19
HE336.T79 M37 1985

TRUCK LANES - TEXAS - EVALUATION.
Mason, John M. (John Michael), 1950- Operational and geometric evaluation of exclusive truck lanes /. College Station, Tex. , Springfield, Va. [1986] vii, 156 p. : LC Card 86-622239 DDC 380.5 s 388.3/14 19
HE203 .T43 no. 331-3F HE356.T4

TRUCKING.
Technico-economic analysis of the role of road freight transport . Paris [Washington, D.C.] 1986. 135 p. : ISBN 92-64-12843-3 (pbk.) : LC Card 86-215619 DDC 388.3/24 19
HE5611 .T43 1986

TRUCKING - AUSTRALIA - HISTORY.
Maddock, John, 1917- Mail for the back of beyond /. Kenthurst , 1986. 160 p. : ISBN 0-86417-063-7 LC Card 86-207558 DDC 383/.143/0994 19
HE5709.A6 M33 1986

TRUCKING - BRAZIL - STATISTICS.
Estudo sobre o transporte rodioviário de carga. [Brasília] , 1984- v. <1- > : LC Card 87-403695 DDC 388.3/24/0981021 19
HE5653.A6 E85 1984

TRUCKING - FRANCE - RATES.
Tarifs routiers de marchandises. Paris [1986] 201 p. ; ISBN 2-7212-0295-2 LC Card 87-123802
HE5668.A6 T37 1986

Tarifs routiers de marchandises. Paris [1986] 956 p. ; ISBN 2-7212-0297-9 LC Card 87-119821
HE5668.A6 T38 1986

TRUCKING - FRANCE - STATISTICS.
Les Transports routiers de marchandises effectués sur le territoire français par des véhicules étrangers /. Paris [1983] 26 p. ; LC Card 83-214677
HE5668.A6 T74 1983

TRUCKING - GERMANY (WEST) - SAFETY MEASURES.
Plänitz, Günther. Das bisschen Fahren-- . Hamburg , 1983. 317 p. : ISBN 3-87975-248-6 LC Card 84-187043
HD8039.M7952 G37 1983

TRUCKING - GOVERNMENT POLICY - UNITED STATES.
Tye, William B. Encouraging cooperation among competitors . New York , 1987. xix, 202 p. : ISBN 0-89930-246-7 (lib. bdg. : alk. paper) LC Card 86-25554 DDC 388.3/24 19
HE5623 .T94 1987

TRUCKING - HUNGARY - ANECDOTES, FACETIAE, SATIRE, ETC.
Cserhalmi, Imre. Ha nincs fék, gáz van . [Budapest] , 1984. 294 p. ; LC Card 85-183756
HE5667.5.A6 C74 1984

TRUCKING - ICELAND.
Indriði G. Þorsteinsson, 1926- Fimmtán gírar áfram . Reykjavík , 1981. 178 p., [16] p. of plates : LC Card 83-185502
HD8039.M7952 I25 1981

TRUCKING - MALAWI.
Transportation of imports and exports . Lilongwe , 1984. i, 23 leaves ; LC Card 86-980329 DDC 385/.24/096897 19
HE3432 .T7 1984

TRUCKING - SWITZERLAND - STATISTICS.
Erhebung über die Gütertransporte auf der Strasse 1984 /. Bern , 1986. 103 p. : ISBN 3-303-11041-7 : LC Card 87-408470 DDC 388.3/24/09494/021 19
HE5683.A6 E74 1986

TRUCKING - UNITED STATES.
Traffic and transportation report, 1986. Washington, D.C. (1750 K St., NW, Washington 20006) , c1986. vi, 25 p. : LC Card 86-232133 DDC 388.3/24 19
HE199.5.F6 T715 1986

TRUCKING - UNITED STATES - DEREGULATION.
Glaskowsky, Nicholas A. Effects of deregulation on motor carriers /. Westport, Conn. (P.O. Box 2055, Westport 06880) , 1986. viii, 86 p. : LC Card 86-80416 DDC 388.3/24/0973 19
HE5623 .G55 1986

TRUCKING - UNITED STATES - RATES.
Tye, William B. Encouraging cooperation among competitors . New York , 1987. xix, 202 p. : ISBN 0-89930-246-7 (lib. bdg. : alk. paper) LC Card 86-25554 DDC 388.3/24 19
HE5623 .T94 1987

TRUCKING - VOCATIONAL GUIDANCE - UNITED STATES.
Schauer, Donald D. Careers in trucking /. New York , 1987. xii, 132 p. : ISBN 0-8239-0748-1 : LC Card 87-4769 DDC 388.3/24/02373 19
HE5623 .S33 1987

TRUCKS - FRANCE - STATISTICS.
Enquête sur l'utilisation des véhicules utilitaires légers . Paris [1983] 58 p. : LC Card 84-191337
HE5668.A6 E56 1983

TRUCKS - LICENSES - MAINE.
Pease, Allen. Appendix for the feasibility report of implementing the International Registration Plan in the State of Maine . [Augusta, Me.] [1985] 39 leaves : LC Card 85-622841 DDC 388.3/24 19
HE5633.M2 P39 1985

Pease, Allen. Report on the feasibility of implementing the International Registration Plan in the State of Maine . [Augusta, Me.] [1985] ii, 24 leaves ; LC Card 85-622840 DDC 388.3/24 19
HE5633.M2 P4 1985

TRUCKS - REGISTRATION AND TRANSFER - MAINE.
Pease, Allen. Appendix for the feasibility report of implementing the International Registration Plan in the State of Maine . [Augusta, Me.] [1985] 39 leaves : LC Card 85-622841 DDC 388.3/24 19
HE5633.M2 P39 1985

Pease, Allen. Report on the feasibility of implementing the International Registration Plan in the State of Maine . [Augusta, Me.] [1985] ii, 24 leaves ; LC Card 85-622840 DDC 388.3/24 19
HE5633.M2 P4 1985

Trud i ego problemy na sovremennom ėtape razvitii͡a sotsialisticheskogo obshchestva : voprosy politicheskoĭ ėkonomii : mezhvuzovskiĭ sbornik / [redaktsionnai͡a kollegii͡a N.M. Shishkan (otvetstvennyĭ redaktor) ... et al.]. Kishinev : "Shtiintsa", 1986. 133 p. ; 22 cm. At head of title: Ministerstvo vysshego i srednego spet͡sialʹnogo obrazovanii͡a MSSR. Kishinevskiĭ ordena

Trudovogo Krasnogo Znameni gosudarstvennyĭ universitet imeni V.I. Lenina. Includes bibliographical references. LC Card 87-144606
1. Labor and laboring classes - Moldavian S. S. R. I. Shishkan, N. M. (Nadezhda Mikhaĭlovna). II. Universitati͡a de Stat "V.I. Lenin.".
HD8529.M57 T78 1986

Trudova slava / [sŭstavitel i redaktor Todor Gigov]. Sofii͡a : Profizdat, <1986- > v. <4 > : ill. ; 21 cm. CONTENTS. - -- t. 4. Khudozhestveno-dokumentalni razkazi za proslaveni min'ori, metalurzi, energetit͡si i geolozi. LC Card 86-228746
1. Miners - Bulgaria - Biography. 2. Metal-workers - Bulgaria - Biography. 3. Energy industries - Bulgaria - Employees - Biography. 4. Geologists - Bulgaria - Biography. I. Gigov, Todor.
HD8039.M62 B88 1986

Trudovoe pravo i povyshenie kachestva truda / pod red. S.A. Ivanova. Moskva : Nauka, 1987. 270 p. ; 22 cm. At head of title: Akademii͡a nauk SSSR. Institut gosudarstva i prava. Includes bibliographical references.
1. Labor laws and legislation - Soviet Union. 2. Labor productivity - Soviet Union. I. Ivanov, Semen Aleksandrovich. *NYPL [*QIX 87-3357]*

Trudovoĭ vklad krest'i͡anstva v pobedu i uprochnenie sotsializma . Kosti͡uk, Mikhail Pavlovich. Minsk , 1986. 236 p. ; LC Card 86-136452
HD1492.S652 B9252 1986

Trudovye kollektivy Sibiri : problemy formirovanii͡a i razvitii͡a / otvetstvennyĭ redaktor V.V. Alekseev. Novosibirsk : Izd-vo "Nauka," Sibirskoe otd-nie, 1985. 154 p. ; 22 cm. At head of title: Akademii͡a nauk SSSR. Sibirskoe otdelenie. Institut istorii, filologii i filosofii. Includes bibliographical references. LC Card 86-162191
1. Labor supply - Russian S.F.S.R. - Siberia. 2. Siberia (R.S.F.S.R.) - Industries. I. Alekseev, Veniamin Vasil'evich. II. Institut istorii, filologii i filosofii (Akademii͡a nauk SSSR).
HD5797.S5 T78 1985

Trudovye resursy i ikh ispol'zovanie /. Korolev, L. P. (Leonid Pavlovich) Moskva , 1982. 139 p. ; LC Card 82-158161
HD5797.M66 K67 1982

Trudovye resursy v torgovle /. Mordasova, L. A. (Lidii͡a Andrianovna) Moskva , 1985. 128 p. ; LC Card 86-158800
HD8526.5 .M54 1985

Trudovye resursy Vostoka : demografo-ėkonomicheskie problemy / [otvetstvennyĭ redaktor I͡A.N. Guzevatyĭ]. Moskva : Izd-vo "Nauka," Glav. red. vostochnoĭ lit-ry, 1987. 319 p. ; 23 cm. At head of title: Akademii͡a nauk SSSR. Ordena Trudovogo Krasnogo Znameni Institut votokovedenii͡a. Summary in English. Bibliography: p. 295-[311]. LC Card 87-142995
1. Labor supply - Asia. 2. Asia - Population - Economic aspects. 3. Asia - Economic conditions - 1945-. I. Guzevatyĭ, I͡Aropolk Nikolaevich. II. Institut vostokovedenii͡a (Akademii͡a nauk SSSR).
HD5811.85.A6 T78 1987

True Value . Kantowicz, Edward R. Chicago , 1986. 270 p., [16] p. of plates : ISBN 0-89526-580-X : LC Card 86-42795 DDC 381/.45683/0924 B 19
HD9745.U5 C655 1986
NYPL [JLE 87-1449]

Trueblood, Michael A. The Ivory Coast : an export market profile / Michael A. Trueblood, Nadine R. Horenstein ; in cooperation with the Foreign Agricultural Service. Washington, DC : U. S. Dept. of Agriculture, Economic Research Service : [Supt. of Docs., U. S. G.P.O., distributor], 1986. iv, 32 p. : ill., 1 map ; 28 cm. (Foreign agricultural economic report . no. 223) Cover title. Distributed to depository libraries in microfiche. "September 1986"--P. i. Bibliography: p. 29-30. S/N 001-019-00471-1 Item 42-B (microfiche) LC Card 86-602806 DDC 338.1 s 382/.41/096668 19
1. Produce trade - Ivory Coast. 2. Produce trade - United States. 3. Agriculture - Economic aspects - Ivory Coast. 4. Ivory Coast - Commerce - United States. 5. United States - Commerce - Ivory Coast. I. Horenstein, Nadine R., 1954-. II. United States. Dept. of Agriculture. Economic Research Service. III. United States. Foreign Agricultural Service. IV. Title. V. Series.
HD1411 .F59 no. 223 HD9017.I912

Truett, Dale B.
Truett, Lila J. Macroeconomics /. St. Louis , 1987. xxii, 531, [44] p. : ISBN 0-8016-5158-1 (pbk.) LC Card 86-23879 DDC 339 19
HB172.5 .T78 1987

Truett, Lila J. (Lila Jane) Economics /. St. Louis , 1987. xxviii, 859, [57] p. : ISBN 0-8016-5149-2 LC Card 86-23102 DDC 330 19
HB171.5 .T69 1987

Truett, Lila J. (Lila Jane) Managerial economics . Cincinnati , c1988. xi, 564 p. : ISBN 0-538-08890-7 LC Card 87-60268 DDC 338.5/024658 19
HD30.22 .T78 1988

Truett, Lila J. (Lila Jane) Microeconomics /. St. Louis , 1987. xx, 533, [33] p. : ISBN 0-8016-5151-4 (pbk.) LC Card 86-30029 DDC 338.5 19
HB172 .T784 1987

Truett, Lila J. Macroeconomics / Lila J. Truett, Dale B. Truett. St. Louis : Times Mirror/Mosby College Pub., 1987. xxii, 531, [44] p. : ill. ; 26 cm. Includes bibliographical references and index. ISBN 0-8016-5158-1 (pbk.) LC Card 86-23879 DDC 339 19
1. Macroeconomics. I. Truett, Dale B. II. Title.
HB172.5 .T78 1987

Truett, Lila J. (Lila Jane)
Economics / Lila J. Truett, Dale B. Truett. St. Louis : Times Mirror/Mosby College Pub., 1987. xxviii, 859, [57] p. : ill. (some col.) ; 27 cm. Includes bibliographical references and index. ISBN 0-8016-5149-2 LC Card 86-23102 DDC 330 19
1. Economics. I. Truett, Dale B. II. Title.
HB171.5 .T69 1987

Managerial economics : analysis, problems, cases / Lila J. Truett, Dale B. Truett.3rd ed. Cincinnati : South-Western Pub. Co., c1988. xi, 564 p. : ill. ; 24 cm. Includes bibliographies and index. ISBN 0-538-08890-7 LC Card 87-60268 DDC 338.5/024658 19
1. Managerial economics. I. Truett, Dale B. II. Title.
HD30.22 .T78 1988

Microeconomics / Lila J. Truett, Dale B. Truett. St. Louis : Times Mirror/Mosby College Pub., 1987. xx, 533, [33] p. : ill. (some col.) ; 26 cm. Supplementary materials include a study guide, a test bank, transparency acetates and masters, an instructor's manual, and a software package. Includes bibliographical references and index. ISBN 0-8016-5151-4 (pbk.) LC Card 86-30029 DDC 338.5 19
1. Microeconomics. I. Truett, Dale B. II. Title.
HB172 .T784 1987

Trujillo León, Jorge. La hacienda serrana, 1900-1930 / Jorge Trujillo León. Quito : Instituto de Estudios Ecuatorianos : Abya Yala, 1986. 244 p. ; 22 cm. Bibliography: p. 231-237. LC Card 87-115338 DDC 333.3/09866 19
1. Haciendas - Ecuador - History. 2. Serrana Hacienda (Ecuador) - History. I. Title.
HD1471.E2 T78 1986

TRUMAN, HARRY S., 1884-1972.
Rogulev, I͡U. N. (I͡Uriĭ Nikolaevich) Krakh rabocheĭ politiki administrat͡sii Trumėna . Moskva , 1981. 135 p. ; LC Card 82-155486
HD8072.5 .R64 1981

Trump . Trump, Donald, 1946- New York , 1988. p. cm. ISBN 0-394-55528-7 LC Card 87-42663 DDC 333.33/092/4 B 19
HC102.5.T78 A3 1988

Trump, Donald, 1946- Trump : the art of the deal / by Donald Trump with Tony Schwartz. New York : Random House, 1988. p. cm. ISBN 0-394-55528-7 LC Card 87-42663 DDC 333.33/092/4 B 19
1. Trump, Donald, 1946-. 2. Businessmen - United States - Biography. 3. Real estate developers - United States - Biography. I. Schwartz, Tony, 1952-. II. Title.
HC102.5.T78 A3 1988

TRUMP, DONALD, 1946-
Trump, Donald, 1946- Trump . New York , 1988. p. cm. ISBN 0-394-55528-7 LC Card 87-42663 DDC 333.33/092/4 B 19
HC102.5.T78 A3 1988

Trumper, James D., 1958- Eliason, Alan L. Program analysis and design . Chicago , c1987. ix, 134 p. : ISBN 0-574-18660-3 (pbk.) LC Card 87-4521 DDC 658/.055265 19
HF5548.2 .E4275 1987

Trunskiĭ, I͡U. G. Frant͡suzskai͡a derevni͡a v XIX-XX vekakh : tendent͡sii razvitii͡a / I͡U.G. Trunskiĭ ; otvetstvennyĭ redaktor V.M. Dalin. Moskva : "Nauka", 1986. 283 p. ; 21 cm. At head of title: Akademii͡a nauk SSSR. Institut vseobshcheĭ istorii. Summary in French. Includes bibliographical references. LC Card 86-201573
1. Agriculture - Economic aspects - France - History. 2. France - Rural conditions. I. Dalin, V. M. (Viktor Moiseevich). II. Title. III. Title: Frant͡suzskai͡a derevni͡a v 19-om-20-om vekakh. IV. Title: Frant͡suzskai͡a derevni͡a v devi͡atnadt͡satom-dvadt͡satom vekakh.
HD1945 .T78 1986

Trusova, V. F. Krasnai͡a linii͡a . Moskva , 1986. 382 p. : LC Card 86-112685
HD8526.5 .K73 1986

Trusteeship, the Gandhian alternative / editor, J.D. Sethi. New Delhi : Gandhi Peace Foundation, c1986. xiii, 238 p. ; 24 cm. Comprises mostly contributed articles and selected papers presented at a seminar held at the Gandhi Peace Foundation, November 1985. Includes bibliographical references. LC Card 86-903783 DDC 330.1 19
1. Economics - Social aspects - Congresses. 2. India - Economic conditions - Congresses. I. Sethi, J. D. (Jai Dev), 1924-. II. Gandhi Peace Foundation (New Delhi, India).
HB199 .T76 1986

TRUSTS, INDUSTRIAL - BRAZIL.
Souza, Francisco Araújo Salles de. O estado e o cartel do leite no Brasil /. Brasília, Distrito Federal , 1981. 130 p. : LC Card 81-217015
HD9282.B72 S65 1981
NYPL [JLD 86-3366]

TRUSTS, INDUSTRIAL - EUROPE.
Jacquemin, Alex. Economie industrielle européenne . [Paris] , c1979. xxii, 376 p. : ISBN 2-04-010465-8 LC Card 86-673881
HD70.E8 J3x 1979

TRUSTS, INDUSTRIAL - GERMANY, WEST.
Werner, Horst S. Der aktienrechtliche Abhängigkeitstatbestand . Göttingen , 1979. xxxix, 214 p. ; ISBN 3-88415-560-1 : LC Card 80-452340 DDC 346.43/066
LAW *NYPL [JLD 86-1592]*

TRUSTS, INDUSTRIAL - LAW AND LEGISLATION. see **ANTITRUST LAW.**

TRUSTS, INDUSTRIAL - UNITED STATES.
Asch, Peter. Economic theory and the antitrust dilemma /. Malabar, Fla. , 1984, c1970. x, 414 p. : ISBN 0-89874-699-X LC Card 83-19947 DDC 338.8/0973 19
HD2785 .A78 1984 *NYPL [JLE 86-4132]*

Trysem . Bihar (India). Rural Development Dept. [Paṭanā] , 1980. 41 p. ; LC Card 80-908290
HD6276.I42 B54 1980

TRYSEM. Training of rural youth for self-employment (TRYSEM) . Hyderabad, [India] , 1981. vii, 252 p. ; LC Card 81-904606 DDC 331.3/42492/0954 19
HD5715.5.I5 T72 1981
NYPL [JLF 86-1203]

T͡Sagolova, R. S. (Ruf' Sergeevna)
Leksiko-semanticheskie osobennosti politiko-ėkonomicheskoĭ terminologii / R.S. T͡Sagolova. Moskva : Izd-vo Moskovskogo universiteta, 1985. 146 p. ; 23 cm. Includes bibliographical references. LC Card 86-106188
1. Economics - Terminology. 2. English language - Terms and phrases. I. Title.
HB62 .T76 1985

Tsao, James T. H. China's development strategies and foreign trade / James T.H. Tsao ; foreword by Lawrence R. Klein. Lexington, Mass. : Lexington Books, c1987. xii, 209 p. : ill. ; 24 cm. Bibliography: p. [199]-203. Includes index. ISBN 0-669-13954-8 (alk. paper) LC Card 86-45590 DDC 338.951 19
1. China - Economic policy - 1949-. 2. China - Commerce. 3. China - Commercial policy. 4. China - Commerce - United States. 5. United States - Commerce - China. I. Title.
HC427.9 .T689 1987

T͡Sarevski, Nesho Vŭlev. The People's Republic of Bulgaria : an active participant in socialist economic integration / Nesho Tsarevski. Sofia : Sofia Press, 1986. 102 p. ; 20 cm. Title from colophon: Narodna Republika Bŭlgarii͡a. Includes

bibliographical references. LC Card 87-123346 DDC 337.1/4977 19
1. Bulgaria - Economic policy - 1944-. 2. Bulgaria - Economic conditions - 1944-. 3. Council for Mutual Economic Assistance. 4. Europe, Eastern - Economic integration. I. Title. II. Title: Narodna Republika Bŭlgariia.
HC403 .T748 1986

T͡Saritsina, G. A. Rasshirenie samostoiatel'nosti predpriiatiĭ i nauchno-tekhnicheskoe razvitie proizvodstva /. Moskva , 1986. 205 p. ; LC Card 87-162795
HG4186 .R37 1986

Tschechoslowakei 1984/85 . Altmann, Franz-Lothar. München , 1985. 31 leaves ; LC Card 85-179408
HC270.28 .A415 1985

Die tschechoslowakische Volkswirtschaft und der Rat für gegenseitige Wirtschaftshilfe (RGW) /. Altmann, Franz-Lothar. München [1986] 31 leaves ; LC Card 86-203484
HF3550.3.Z7 E8523 1986

Tschernobyl hat unser Leben verändert : vom Ausstieg der Frauen / Marina Gambaroff ... [et al.]. Reinbek bei Hamburg : Rowohlt, 1986. 203 p. : ill. ; 19 cm. (Rororo aktuell) Includes bibliographies. ISBN 3-499-15922-8 : LC Card 87-123041 DDC 363.1/79 19
1. Antinuclear movement - Germany (West). 2. Nuclear energy - Political aspects - Germany (West). 3. Women in politics - Germany, West. 4. Chernobyl Nuclear Accident, Chernobyl', Ukraine, 1986. I. Gambaroff, Marina, 1943-.
HD9698.G42 T73 1986

Tschiersch, Joachim E. Appropriate mechanization for small farmers in developing countries / Joachim E. Tschiersch. Saarbrücken : Verlag Breitenbach, 1978. iii, 106 p. ; 23 cm. (Publications of the Research Centre for International Agrarian Development ; 8) Includes bibliographical references. ISBN 3-88156-112-9 LC Card 80-472522 DDC 338.1/61/091724
1. Farm mechanization - Developing countries. 2. Farms, Small - Developing countries. I. Series: Research Centre for International Agrarian Development. Publications, 8. II. Title.
S675 .T72 ***NYPL [JLE 80-1482]***

Tschudin, Paul, 1904- Meine Ehre ist nicht die Eure! : eine Lebensgeschichte von unten / Paul Tschudin.1. Aufl. Basel : Z-Verlag, 1986. 217 p. ; 20 cm. ISBN 3-85990-069-2 LC Card 87-137660 DDC 331.88/092/4 B 19
1. Tschudin, Paul, 1904-. 2. Trade-unions - Switzerland - Biography. 3. Socialists - Switzerland - Biography. 4. Switzerland - Social life and customs - 1895-1945. 5. Trade-unions - Switzerland - Officials and employees - Biography. I. Title.
HD6772.5.T74 A3 1986

TSCHUDIN, PAUL, 1904-
Tschudin, Paul, 1904- Meine Ehre ist nicht die Eure! . Basel , 1986. 217 p. ; ISBN 3-85990-069-2 LC Card 87-137660 DDC 331.88/092/4 B 19
HD6772.5.T74 A3 1986

Tsegaye, Mebratu. Dublin, Jack. Mid-term evaluation of the Malawi Union of Savings and Credit Co-operatives Project (612-0205) /. Lilongwe, Malawi , 1983. x, 84, [29] leaves ; LC Card 85-981350 DDC 334/.22/096897 19
HG2039.M29 D83 1983

T͡Selevaia funkt͡siia potrebleniia . Val'tukh, Konstantin Kurtovich. Novosibirsk , 1980. 381, [3] p. ; LC Card 81-134031
HB801 .V265 1980

T͡Selevye kompleksnye programmy : voprosy razrabotki, modelirovaniia, ispol'zovaniia / [nauchnye redaktory IUriĭ Mikhaĭlovich Samokhin, Andreĭ Georgievich Fonotov]. Moskva : Akademiia nauk SSSR, T͡Sentr. ėkonomiko-matematicheskiĭ in-t, 1984. 198 p. : ill. ; 21 cm. Includes bibliographies. LC Card 86-176369
1. Soviet Union - Economic policy - 1981-. 2. Soviet Union - Economic policy - 1981- - Mathematical models. I. Samokhin, IUriĭ Mikhaĭlovich. II. Fonotov, A. G. III. T͡Sentral'nyĭ ėkonomiko-matematicheskiĭ institut (Akademiia nauk SSSR).
HC336.25 .T74 1984

T͡Seli, print͡sipy, struktura, deiatel'nost'. Sovet ėkonomicheskoĭ vzaimopomoshchi . Moskva , 1984. 29 p. : LC Card 86-203121
HC243.5 .S683 1984

T͡Sena i khozraschet / pod redakt͡sieĭ A.A. Deriabina. Moskva : In-t ėkonomiki AN SSSR, 1986. 144 p. ; 20 cm. Includes bibliographical references. LC Card 87-163568
1. Prices - Soviet Union. 2. Costs, Industrial - Soviet Union. 3. Profit - Soviet Union. 4. Industrial management - Soviet Union. I. Deriabin, Anatoliĭ Aleksandrovich. II. Institut ėkonomiki (Akademiia nauk SSSR).
HB235.S73 T72 1986

T͡Senoobrazovanie v voennom proizvodstve SShA /. Vasiutovich, V. P. (Vladimir Petrovich) Moskva , 1980. 221 p. ; LC Card 81-143903
HD9743.U6 V37 1980

T͡Senov, Kiril. 75 godini borba i sŭzidanie . Sofiia , 1985. 144 p. ; LC Card 86-195265
HD6784.M62 P762 1985

T͡Sentralen komitet na DKMS. Zadachite na DKMS vŭv VUZ za povishavane na ikonomicheskata podgotovka na studentite i mladite khora ot drugite otriadi na mladezhta . Svishtov , 1985. 91 p. ; LC Card 86-159994
HB74.9.B9 Z33 1985

Tsentralen kooperativen sŭiuz. Istoriia na kooperativnoto dvizhenie v Bŭlgariia /. Sofiia , 1986- v. <1 > ; LC Card 87-158327
HD3531.5.A4 I87 1986

T͡Sentral'naia Evropa i zemli vdol' Nizhnego Dunaia v XVIII i XIX vekakh.
Paskaleva-Zakharieva, Virzhiniia. Sredna Evropa i zemite po Dolniia Dunav prez XVIII-XIX v. . Sofiia , 1986. 317 p. : LC Card 86-219994
HC244 .P29 1986

T͡Sentral'noe filatelisticheskoe agenstvo "Soiuzpechat'."
Katalog konvertov pervogo dnia i kartmaksimumov, 1980-1983 /. Moskva , 1985. 221 p. : LC Card 86-102861
HE6184.F57 K38 1985

Pochtovye marki . Moskva , 1984. 223 p. : LC Card 85-185295
HE6185.C92 P63 1984

Podvig na pochtovoĭ marke . Moskva , 1985. 135 p. : LC Card 86-113767
HE6183.G47 P63 1985

T͡Sentral'nyĭ ėkonomiko-matematicheskiĭ institut (Akademiia nauk SSSR)
Demograficheskaia politika sot͡sialisticheskogo obshchestva /. Moskva , 1986. 190 p. ;
NYPL [*QIP 87-2842]

Demograficheskaia politika sot͡sialisticheskogo obshchestva /. Moskva , 1986. 190 p. : LC Card 87-120466
HB3607 .D425 1986

Ėkonomicheskie problemy prirodopol'zovaniia /. Moskva , 1985. 137 p. : LC Card 86-119089
HC340.E5 E395 1985

Ėkonomicheskoe izmerenie i ot͡senka ėffektivnosti nauchno-tekhnicheskogo progressa /. Moskva , 1982. 172 p. ; LC Card 84-209110
HC79.T4 E55 1982

Ėkonomiko-matematicheskie metody i modeli vo vneshneėkonomicheskoĭ deiatel'nosti /. Moskva , 1980. 179 p. : LC Card 87-109621
HF3626.5 .E45 1980

Ėkonomiko-matematicheskie modeli v upravlenii proizvodstvennymi ob"edineniiami /. Moskva , 1983. 190 p. : LC Card 85-199430
HD30.25 .E397 1983

Ėksperimental'naia razrabotka natural'no-stoimostnykh mezhotraslevykh balansov soiuznoĭ respubliki /. Moskva , 1980. 137 p. : LC Card 85-199427
HC337.E7 E49 1980

Instrumental'nye sistemy modelirovaniia /. Moskva , 1983. 97 p. : LC Card 84-210491
HB143.5 .I57 1983

Khoziaĭstvennyĭ mekhanizm i povyshenie ėffektivnosti proizvodstva /. Moskva , 1986. 252 p. ; LC Card 86-232347
HC340.I52 K49 1986

Khoziaĭstvennyĭ mekhanizm i t͡senoobrazovanie /. Moskva , 1983. 77 p. ; LC Card 85-180519
HB235.S73 K47 1983

Khoziaĭstvennyĭ mekhanizm v sisteme optimal'nogo funkt͡sionirovaniia sotsialisticheskoĭ ėkonomiki /. Moskva , 1985. 346 p. ; LC Card 86-114802
HC336.25 .K474 1985

Kompleksnaia organizat͡siia issledovaniĭ . Moskva , 1981. 191 p. : LC Card 82-130582
HC340.R4 K66 1981

Metodologiia prognozirovaniia vosproizvodstva i ispol'zovaniia resursov v ėkonomike SSSR /. Moskva , 1984. 201 p. : LC Card 85-199435
HC340.I52 M485 1984

Mezhotraslevye kompleksy v sisteme modeleĭ /. Moskva , 1983. 319 p. : LC Card 83-236937
HC336.25 .M49 1983

Modelirovanie ėkonomicheskogo povedeniia sotsialisticheskogo predpriiatiia /. Moskva , 1984. 131 p. : LC Card 86-144437
HD30.25 .M623 1984

Modelirovanie i prognozirovanie ėlementov uslovno-chistoĭ produktsii i finansovykh potokov /. Moskva , 1981. 180 p. : LC Card 83-171742
HD30.25 .M635 1981

Modelirovanie mezhotraslevykh vzaimodeĭstviĭ /. Moskva , 1984. 277 p. : LC Card 84-175111
HC336.25 .M6314 1984

Modelirovanie sot͡sial'nykh faktorov v ėkonomiko-matematicheskikh issledovaniiakh /. Moskva , 1984. 148 p. : LC Card 87-125299
HC336.25. .M636 1984

Optimizat͡siia planirovaniia polimerno-neftekhimicheskogo kompleksa /. Moskva , 1984. 141 p. : LC Card 86-143987
HD9579.C33 S655 1984

Opyt razrabotki i realizat͡sii sistemy ukrupnennykh modeleĭ perspektivnogo planirovaniia /. Moskva , 1984. 216 p. : LC Card 85-199888
HD75.5 .O69 1984

Organizat͡sionno-ėkonomicheskie problemy sovershenstvovaniia funktsionirovaniia transportnykh sistem /. Moskva , 1984. 144 p. : LC Card 85-199422
HE5675.A6 O765 1984

Priniatie resheniĭ v upravlenii khoziaĭstvennymi sviaziami /. Moskva , 1982. 80 p. : LC Card 85-180526
HD30.23 .P745 1982

Problemy t͡selevoĭ orientat͡sii razvitiia resursnogo potentsiala /. Moskva , 1984. 205 p. : LC Card 86-143993
HC333.5 .P77 1984

Programmno-t͡selevoĭ metod v planirovanii /. Moskva , 1982. 150 p. : LC Card 83-162853
HC336.25 .P6577 1982

Programmnoe obespechenie ėkonomiko-matematicheskikh issledovaniĭ /. Moskva , 1982. 142 p. : LC Card 84-209065
HD30.25 .P76 1982

Realizat͡siia na ĖVM uchetno-planovykh rabot material'no-tekhnicheskogo snabzheniia /. Moskva , 1983. 63 p. : LC Card 84-210458
HD39.5 .R43 1983

Sistema ėkonomiko-matematicheskikh modeleĭ dlia analiza i prognoza urovnia zhizni /. Moskva , 1986. 262 p. : LC Card 86-232874
HD6978 .S56 1986

Sistema modeleĭ narodnokhoziaĭstvennogo planirovaniia /. Moskva , 1982. 375 p. ; LC Card 83-172876
HC336.25 .S564 1982

Sistemnyĭ podkhod v reshenii nekotorykh problem sotsial'no-ėkonomicheskogo optimuma /. Moskva , 1984. 88 p. ; LC Card 86-144288
HC340.I52 S57 1984

Sovershenstvovanie khoziaĭstvennogo mekhanizma na transporte /. Moskva , 1983. 223 p. : LC Card 85-199829
HE255.A2 S68 1983

Sovershenstvovanie khoziaĭstvennogo mekhanizma v snabzhenii /. Moskva , 1983. 127 p. : LC Card 85-180655
HD39.5 .S68 1983

Statisticheskoe izuchenie proizvoditel'nosti truda /. Moskva , 1981. 407 p. ; LC Card 82-155063 DDC 330/.018 s 331.11/8/0947 19
HA1.A38 A15 t. 41 HC340.L3
NYPL [*QIP 87-1311]

Sulitskiĭ, V. N. (Vladimir Nikolaevich) Organizatsionno-ėkonomicheskie problemy upravleniia kadrami v otrasli /. Moskva , 1986. 164, [3] p. : LC Card 86-233362
HF5549.2.S65 S85 1986

TSelevye kompleksnye programmy . Moskva , 1984. 198 p. : LC Card 86-176369
HC336.25 .T74 1984

Voprosy postroeniia sistemy modeleĭ finansovogo aspekta vosproizvodstva /. Moskva , 1984. 154 p. : LC Card 86-144339
HG186.S55 V67 1984

Voprosy stranovogo makromodelirovaniia /. Moskva , 1984. 177 p. : LC Card 86-144302
HB141 .V665 1984

TSentral'nyĭ nauchno-issledovatel'skiĭ institut morskogo flota (Leningrad, R.S.F.S.R.)
Prognozirovanie i ėffektivnost' raboty flota . Leningrad , 1985. 104 p. : LC Card 86-170274
HE847 .P77 1985

TSENTRAL'NYĬ RABOCHIĬ KRUZHOK (SAINT PETERSBURG, RUSSIA)
Share, Michael. The Central Workers' Circle of St. Petersburg, 1889-1894 . New York , 1987. xi, 396 p., [6] p. of plates : ISBN 0-8240-8063-7 (alk. paper) : LC Card 87-374 DDC 305.5/62/0947453 19
HD8522.T753 S53 1987

TSeny i tarify / [avtory uchebnogo posobiia G.A. Gorina ... et al.]. Moskva : Ėkonomika, 1983. 150 p. : ill. ; 22 cm. Authorized for instructional purposes. Includes bibliographical references. LC Card 84-117348
1. Prices - Soviet Union. I. Gorina, G. A. (Galina Anatol'evna).
HB235.S73 T735 1983

Tshibaka, Tshikala B., 1949- The effects of trade and exchange rate policies on agriculture in Zaire / Tshikala B. Tshibaka. Washington, D.C., USA : International Food Policy Research Institute, 1986. 65 p. : ill. ; 26 cm. (Research report (International Food Policy Research Institute) . 56) Bibliography: p. 63-65. ISBN 0-89629-057-3 LC Card 86-27449 DDC 338.1/09675/1 19
1. Agriculture - Economic aspects - Zaire. 2. Agriculture and state - Zaire. 3. Foreign exchange problem - Zaire. 4. Zaire - Economic policy. I. International Food Policy Research Institute. II. Series. III. Series: Research report (International Food Policy Research Institute) , 56. IV. Title.
HD2135.5 .T75 1986

Tsichritzis, Dionysios C. IFIP TC 8/WG 8.4 Working Conference on Methods and Tools for Office Systems (1986 : Pisa, Italy) Office systems . Amsterdam ; New York : xi, 347 p. : ISBN 0-444-70241-5 (U. S.) LC Card 87-8916 DDC 651.8 19
HF5548.2 .I285 1986

TSifrovye metody i algoritmy obrabotki signalov : materialy k seminaru pri Institute matematiki i kibernetiki AN Litovskoĭ SSR "Statisticheskie problemy upravleniia / pod redaktsieĭ TS. Paulauskasa. Vil'nius : In-t matematiki i kibernetiki Akademii nauk Litovskoĭ SSR, 1986. 120 p. : ill. ; 20 cm. (Statisticheskie problemy upravleniia, 0132-5302 . vyp. 73) Titles on added t.p.: Signalu apdorojimo skaitmeniniai metodai ir algoritmai; Digital methods and algorithms i.e. algorithms of signal processing. At head of title: Institut matematiki i kibernetiki AN Litovskoĭ SSR. Institut fiziko-tekhnicheskikh problem ėnergetiki AN LITSSR. Litovskaia territorial'naia gruppa NKAU SSSR Mezhdunarodnoĭ federatsii po avtomaticheskomu upravleniiu. Includes bibliographies. LC Card 86-232937
1. Signal processing - Digital techniques. I. Paulauskas, TS. II. Matematikos ir kibernetikos institutas (Lietuvos TSR Mokslų akademija). III. Fizikinių-techninių energetikos problemų institutas (Lietuvos TSR Mokslų akademija). IV. Natsional'nyĭ komitet SSSR po avtomaticheskomu upravleniiu. Litovskaia territorial'naia gruppa. V. Title: Signalų apdorojimo skaitmeniniai metodai ir algoritmai. VI. Title: Digital methods and algorithms of signal processing. VII. Series.
HD38 .S715 vyp. 73 TK5102.5

Tsikata, Fui S. Essays from the Ghana-Valco renegotiations, 1982-85 /. [Accra, Ghana] 1986 (Accra : Printed by the Ghana Pub. Corp.) viii, 163 p. ; ISBN 996-490-120-8 (pbk.) LC Card 87-127499 DDC 338.8/87 19
HD9539.A63 G44 1986

Tsokhas, Kosmas. Shifting the burden : social relations of production in the Australian pastoral industry, 1929-36 / Kosmas Tsokhas. Canberra, Australia : Australian National University, [1986] 61, 6 p. ; 21 cm. (Working paper, 0728-6090 . no. 77) "December 1986." Includes bibliographical references. ISBN 0-86784-898-7 (pbk.) LC Card 87-151151 DDC 331.7/6363/00994 19
1. Sheep industry - Australia - Employees - History - 20th century. 2. Sheep industry - Australia - History - 20th century. I. Series: Working papers in economic history , working paper no. 77. II. Title.
HD9436.A82 T75 1986

Tsokopoulos, Vasias. Peiraias, 1835-1870 : eisagōgē stēn historia tou Hellēnikou Mantsester / Vasias Tsokopoulos. Athēna : Ekdoseis Kastaniōtē, 1984. 280 p., [8] p. of plates : ill. ; 21 cm. "Hetaireia Oikonomikēs kai Koinōnikēs Historias tēs Helladas." Includes index. Bibliography: p. 267-272. LC Card 86-128354
1. Piraeus (Greece) - Economic conditions. 2. Piraeus (Greece) - Social conditions. 3. Piraeus (Greece) - History. I. Hetaireia Oikonomikēs kai Koinōnikēs Historias tēs Helladas. II. Title.
HC298.P57 T77 1984 ***NYPL [JLD 86-171]***

Tsuda, Mamoru. RP-Japan relations and ADB . Metro Manila, Philippines , 1986. x, 137 p. : ISBN 971-08-3156-9 (pbk.) LC Card 86-211088 DDC 337.520599 19
HF1600.15.J3 R68 1986

Tsunechiro, Alfredo. O desempenho dos mercados a termo : os casos do café, soja e boi gordo na Bolsa de Mercadorias de São Paulo / Alfredo Tsunechiro. São Paulo : Governo do Estado de São Paulo, Secretaria de Agricultura e Abastecimento, Instituto de Economia Agrícola, 1986. xi, 123 p. : ill. ; 23 cm. (Relatório de pesquisa, 0101-5109 . 18/86) Originally presented as the author's thesis (mestre en economia)--Universidade de São Paulo, 1983. Summary also in English. Bibliography: p. 107-113. LC Card 87-404554 DDC 332.64/4 19
1. Commodity exchanges. 2. Commodity exchanges - Brazil - São Paulo. 3. Coffee industry - Brazil. 4. Soybean industry - Brazil. 5. Senna industry - Brazil. I. Series: Relatório de pesquisa (São Paulo (Brazil : State). Instituto de Economia Agrícola) , no. 86/18. II. Title.
HG6046 .T75 1986

Tsung, Stephen. Threats to private enterprise in Australia / by Stephen Tsung. [Melbourne] : Committee for Economic Development of Australia, 1976. 80 p. ; 30 cm. "A CEDA study"--Cover. "December 1976." Includes bibliographical references. "M 46." LC Card 82-127568
1. Industry and state - Australia. I. Title.
HD3616.A83 T78 1976

TSvetkov, V. V. Pravovye problemy RASU /. Kiev , 1985. 303 p. : LC Card 86-139849
HC337.U5 P65 1985

TSygankov, P. A. (Pavel Afanas'evich) V bor'be protiv vsevlastiia kapitala / P. TSygankov, S. Luchinova. Moskva : Moskovskiĭ rabochiĭ, 1986. 139 p. ; 17 cm. (Bibliotechka propagandista i politinformatora) Includes bibliographical references. LC Card 86-132423
1. Capitalism. 2. Economic history - 1971-. 3. Communism - 1945-. I. Luchinova, S. (Svetlana). II. Title. III. Series.
HB501 .T78 1986

TSymek, A. A. Valentik, I. IA. (Ivan IAkovlevich) Ėkonomicheskie osnovy intensifikatsii lesnogo khoziaĭstva Karel'skoĭ ASSR /. Leningrad , 1986. 135, [1] p. : LC Card 87-125199
HD9765.S653 K378 1986

TSyrkin, E. B. (Efim Borisovich) Avrekh, G. L. (Gennadiĭ Lipanovich) Ėkonomika na urovne molekul /. Moskva , 1986. 141 p. : LC Card 86-179247
HD9656.S55 A95 1986

Tu, Pierre N. V. (Pierre Ninh Van) Introductory optimization dynamics : optimal control with economics and management science applications / Pierre N.V. Tu. Berlin ; New York : Springer-Verlag, 1984. xiii, 387 p. : ill. ; 25 cm. Bibliography: p.[373]-387. ISBN 0-387-13305-4 (U. S.)
1. Control theory. 2. Management - Mathematical models. I. Title. ***NYPL [JSE 86-1520]***

Tubbs, Stewart L., 1943- A systems approach to small group interaction / Stewart L. Tubbs. 3rd ed. New York : Random House, 1987. p. cm. Bibliography: p. Includes index. ISBN 0-394-36539-9 : LC Card 87-23394 DDC 302.3/4 19
1. Work groups. 2. Small groups. 3. Organizational behavior. I. Title.
HD66 .T82 1987

TUBE WELL. see **WELLS.**

Tübinger geographische Studien, 0564-4232 .
(Heft 87) Jebens, Albrecht. Wirtschafts- und sozialgeographische Untersuchung über das Heimgewerbe in Nordafghanistan unter besonderer Berücksichtigung der Mittelstadt Sar-e-Pul . Tübingen , 1983. xii, 415 p., [2] folded leaves of plates : LC Card 86-128235
HD2346.A52 S275 1983

Tübinger wirtschaftswissenschaftliche Abhandlungen (Tübingen, Germany) .
(Bd. 29) Wied-Nebbeling, Susanne. Sektorale Preisbildung und gesamtwirtschaftliche Preisstabilität /. Tübingen , 1986. xiii, 368 p. : ISBN 3-16-345102-0 LC Card 87-132436 DDC 338.5/2/0724 19
HB221 .W484 1986

Tubol'tsev, M. N. Khoziaĭstvovat' umelo i ėffektivno /. Moskva , 1985. 267, [5] p. ; LC Card 85-148146
HC338.M6 K47 1985

The TUC overseas . Nicholson, Marjorie. London , Boston , c1986. xvi, 329 p. ; ISBN 0-04-331103-2 (alk. paper) LC Card 85-28607 DDC 331.88/0941 19
HD8383 .N52 1986 ***NYPL [JLD 86-2932]***

Tüchter, Ulrich. Cash Management : eine elektronische Bankdienstleistung für die Unternehmung / Ulrich Tüchter. Köln : Wison, c1985. 122 p. : ill. ; 21 cm. (Kölner bankwirtschaftliche Studien. Bd. 8) Bibliography: p. 105-115. ISBN 3-87951-126-8 LC Card 87-152212 DDC 332.1/2/0681 19
1. Cash management. 2. Banks and banking - Automation. I. Title. II. Series.
HG4028.C45 T83 1985

Tuchtfeldt, Egon, 1923- Leisinger, Klaus M. Studien zur Entwicklungsökonomie /. Bern , c1986. 130 p. : ISBN 3-258-03665-9 LC Card 87-124013 DDC 338.9/009172/7 19
HC59.72.E44 L45 1986

Tucker, Ken. Firms and markets . London , c1986. xiii, 271 p. : ISBN 0-7099-2446-1
NYPL [JLD 86-2134]

Tucker, Lewis R., 1943- International marketing . Boston, Mass. , c1986. xii, 466 p. : ISBN 0-534-06270-9 (pbk.) : LC Card 85-19820 DDC 658.8/48 19
HF1009.5 .I545 1986 ***NYPL [JLE 86-3023]***

Tucker, Scott. Barton, Taylor J. The illustrated Symphony (release 1.2) book /. Dallas , c1987. vii, 310 p. : ISBN 0-915381-88-5 (pbk.) LC Card 87-6135 DDC 005.36/9 19
HF5548.4.S95 B385 1987

Tucoo-Chala, Pierre. Les Communications dans la péninsule Ibérique au Moyen-Age . Paris , 1981. 208 p. : ISBN 2-222-02922-8 : LC Card 81-213698 DDC 380.5/0946 19
HE261.A5 C65 1981 ***NYPL [JLG 86-113]***

Tudo é história .
(109) Moura, Gerson. A campanha do petróleo /. São Paulo-SP , 1986. 92 p. : LC Card 86-190721
HD9574.B84 P445 1986

(110) Witter, José Sebastião. A Revolta dos Parceiros /. São Paulo, SP , 1986. 77 p. : LC Card 87-102716
HD4875.B8 W58 1986

(75) Brandão, Carlos Rodrigues. Os caipiras de São Paulo /. São Paulo-Brasil , 1983. 92, [4] p. : LC Card 84-179661
HD1531.B7 B72 1983

Tudo é história (1981) .
(75) Brandão, Carlos Rodrigues. Os caipiras de São Paulo /. São Paulo-Brasil , 1983. 92, [4] p. : LC Card 84-179661
HD1531.B7 B72 1983

Tudomány és közlekedés .
(8) Az OKBT Tudományos Kutatási Szakbizottság kezdeményezése, illetve megbízása alapján készült kutatások, 1973-1983 /. [Budapest] , 1983. 124 p. : ISBN 963-02-3169-7 (Magy. nemz. bibl.) LC Card

85-126922
HE5614.5.H8 O38 1983 *NYPL [JLD 87-1181]*

Tudományos szocializmus füzetek, 0321-5683 . (82) Szabó, A. Ferenc. Fejezetek a szocialista népesedéselmélet történetéből /. [Budapest] , 1985. 94 p. ; ISBN 963-673-318-X LC Card 86-187050
HB871 .S86 1985

Tudományos szocializmus füzetek, 0324-5683 . (76) Görög, Tibor. Ökopesszimizmus, technooptimizmus és korunk globális problémái /. [Budapest] , 1984. 85 p. : ISBN 963-673-290-6 LC Card 85-130717
HC59 .G6226 1984

(83) Steinbach, Antal. A Magyar Dolgozók Pártja Központi Vezetősége 1953. júniusi határozatának agrárpolitikai előzményei /. [Budapest] , 1985. 104 p. ; ISBN 963-673-321-X LC Card 86-187055
HD1940.5.Z8 S74 1985

(84) Keszthelyi, Csaba. Az autonómia kérdése az olasz szakszervezeti egységért folytatott küzdelemben /. [Budapest] , 1985. 75 p. ; ISBN 963-673-322-8 LC Card 86-185901
HD6680.5.Z65 K47 1985

Tudományszervezési füzetek, 0082-6707. Susánszky, János. Tanulmányok a szervezésről és a vezetésről /. Budapest , 1985. 89 p. ; ISBN 963-05-4132-7 : LC Card 86-136320
HD37.H82 S857 1985

Tudor, Gheorghe. Pagini din gîndirea economică militară românească /. București , 1983. 219 p. ; LC Card 84-116220
HC405.Z9 D443 1983

Türken und Rückkehr . Ölçen, Ali Nejat. Frankfurt a.M. , 1986. 132 p. ; ISBN 3-924320-51-9 LC Card 87-138316 DDC 331.6/2/56104355 19
HD8458.T9 O43 1986

Tuffs, V. Norway number one : the 4 Sk Lion of 1855 / by V. Tuffs. York, England : J. Barefoot, c1983. 52 p. : ill. ; 30 cm. (European philately . 13) Bibliography: p. 52. ISBN 0-906845-26-2 (pbk.) LC Card 87-100273 DDC 769.569481 19
1. Postage-stamps - Norway - Topics - Kings and rulers. 2. Postage-stamps - Norway - Topics - Regalia (Insignia). I. Title. II. Title: 4 Sk Lion of 1855. III. Series.
HE6183.K56 T83 1983

Tugendhat, Christopher, 1937- Making sense of Europe / Christopher Tugendhat. New York : Columbia University Press, 1988. p. cm. Bibliography: p. Includes index. ISBN 0-231-06682-1 (alk. paper) LC Card 87-15871 DDC 337.1/42 19
1. European Economic Community. I. Title.
HC241.2 .T83 1988

TUITION. see **EDUCATION - FINANCE.**

Tuleja, Tad, 1944-
Miller, Robert B. (Robert Bruce), 1931- Conceptual selling . Berkeley, Calif. , New York, N.Y. , c1987. 320 p. : ISBN 0-8050-0410-6 LC Card 86-29428 DDC 658.8/5 19
HF5438.25 .M566 1987

Samtur, Susan J. Cashing in at the checkout /. New York , c1979. 152 p. : ISBN 0-448-15704-7 : LC Card 79-51120 DDC 381/.1 19
HF6127 .S25 *NYPL [JLD 81-566]*

Tulepbaev, B. A.
[Sotsialisticheskie agrarnye preobrazovaniia v Sredneĭ Azii i Kazakhstane. English]
Socialist Agrarian reforms in Central Asia and Kazakhstan / B. Tulepbayev. Moscow : General Editorial Board for Foreign Publications, Nauka Publishers, 1986. 231, [1] p. ; 22 cm. Translation of: Sotsialisticheskie agrarnye preobrazovaniia v Sredneĭ Azii i Kazakhstane. Bibliography: p. 213-[232] LC Card 86-171559
1. Agriculture and state - Soviet Central Asia - History. 2. Agriculture and state - Kazakh S.S.R. - History. 3. Collectivization of agriculture - Soviet Central Asia - History. 4. Collectivization of agriculture - Kazakh S.S.R. - History. I. Title.
HD1995.C4 T8313 1986

Tulin, K. see **Lenin, Vladimir Il'ich, 1870-1924.**

Tullis, F. LaMond, 1935-
Food, the state, and international political economy . Lincoln , c1986. xxiii, 351 p. : ISBN 0-8032-4413-4 (alk. paper) LC Card 85-30893 DDC 338.1/9/1724 19
HD9018.D44 F67 1986 *NYPL [JLD 86-3440]*

Pursuing food security . Boulder , 1987. xv, 357 p. : ISBN 1-555-87032-5 (lib. bdg. : alk. paper) : LC Card 87-4524 DDC 337/.05 s 338.1/9/1724 19
HF1410 .I579 vol. 3 HD9018.D44

Tullock, Gordon.
Democracy and public choice . Oxford [Oxfordshire] , New York, NY, USA , 1987. x, 265 p. : ISBN 0-631-15029-3 : LC Card 87-6402 DDC 302/.13 19
HB846.8 .D46 1987

The Political economy of rent-seeking /. Boston , c1988. xvi, 492 p. : ISBN 0-89838-241-6 LC Card 87-16887 DDC 333/.012 19
HB401 .P64 1988

Private wants, public means : an economic analysis of the desirable scope of government / Gordon Tullock. Lanham : University Press of America, c1987. viii, 262 p. : ill. ; 22 cm. Reprint. Originally published: New York : Basic Books, 1970. Includes bibliographical references and index. ISBN 0-8191-6370-8 (pbk. : alk. paper) : LC Card 87-8273 DDC 330.15/5 19
1. Welfare economics. 2. Welfare state. 3. Public administration. I. Title.
HB99.3 .T8 1987

TULLOCK, GORDON.
Democracy and public choice . Oxford [Oxfordshire] , New York, NY, USA , 1987. x, 265 p. : ISBN 0-631-15029-3 : LC Card 87-6402 DDC 302/.13 19
HB846.8 .D46 1987

Tully, Dennis. Culture and context in Sudan : the process of market incorporation in Dar Masalit / by Dennis Tully. Albany, N.Y. : State University of New York Press, c1988. p. cm. (SUNY series in Middle Eastern studies) Bibliography: p. Includes index. ISBN 0-88706-502-3 LC Card 86-23180 DDC 338.1/09627 19
1. Dar Masalit (Sudan) - Economic conditions. 2. Agriculture - Sudan - Dar Masalit. 3. Economic anthropology - Sudan - Dar Masalit. I. Title. II. Series.
HC835.Z7 D377 1988

Tumlir, Jan. Banks, Gary. Economic policy and the adjustment problem /. Aldershot, Hants., England , Brookfield, Vt. , 1986. x, 101 p. ; ISBN 0-566-05332-2 : LC Card 86-14934 DDC 338.9 19
HF1421 .B36 1987 *NYPL [JLL 74-802 no.45]*

TUNA INDUSTRY - ISLANDS OF THE PACIFIC.
Doulman, David J., 1950- Options for U. S. fisheries investment in the Pacific Islands region /. Honolulu, Hawaii, U. S.A. , 1987. vi, 30 p. ; ISBN 0-86638-097-3 (pbk.) LC Card 87-9198 DDC 338.3/72758 19
HD9469.T83 I743 1987

TUNA INDUSTRY - ISLANDS OF THE PACIFIC - FINANCE.
Doulman, David J., 1950- Options for U. S. fisheries investment in the Pacific Islands region /. Honolulu, Hawaii, U. S.A. , 1987. vi, 30 p. ; ISBN 0-86638-097-3 (pbk.) LC Card 87-9198 DDC 338.3/72758 19
HD9469.T83 I743 1987

TUNA INDUSTRY - MEXICO.
Hudgins, Linda Lucas, 1946- Development of the Mexican tuna industry, 1976-86 /. Honolulu, Hawaii , 1987. p. cm. ISBN 0-86638-091-4 LC Card 87-505 DDC 338.3/72758 19
HD9469.T83 M64 1987

TUNA INDUSTRY - PACIFIC AREA.
The Development of the tuna industry in the Pacific islands region . [Honolulu, Hawaii] , c1987. xviii, 416 p. : ISBN 0-86638-096-5 (pbk.) LC Card 87-6818 DDC 338.3/72758 19
HD9469.T83 P163 1987

Tunesien . Bolz, Reinhardt. Hamburg , 1976. xxiii, 471 p. : LC Card 86-177615
HC820 .B66 1976

Tung damkonfektion : omvärldsanalys. Stockholm : Statens industriverk, 1978. 47, [10] p. : ill. ; 30 cm. (SIND PM, 0346-573X . 1978:7) ISBN 91-38-04438-2 LC Card 84-106453
1. Women's clothing industry - Sweden. I. Sweden. Statens industriverk. II. Series.
HD9940.S82 T85 1978

Tung herrkonfektion : omvärldsanalys. Stockholm : Statens industriverk, 1977. 64, [11] leaves, [1] leaf of plates : ill. ; 30 cm. (SIND PM, 0346-573X . 1977:7) ISBN 91-38-03482-4 LC Card 84-102982
1. Men's clothing industry - Sweden. I. Sweden. Statens industriverk. II. Series.
HD9940.S82 T854 1977

Tung, Rosalie L. (Rosalie Lam), 1948-
The new expatriates : managing human resources abroad / Rosalie L. Tung. Cambridge, Mass. : Ballinger Pub. Co., c1988. xiii, 200 p. : ill., forms ; 24 cm. Bibliography: p. [187]-189. Includes index. ISBN 0-88730-133-9 LC Card 87-17835 DDC 658.3/1 19
1. International business enterprises - Personnel management. 2. International business enterprises - Case studies. I. Title.
HF5549 .T82 1988

Strategic management in the United States and Japan . Cambridge, Mass. , c1986. xxv, 177 p. : ISBN 0-88730-089-8 LC Card 86-1169 DDC 658.4/012/0952 19
HD30.28 .S7324 1986 *NYPL [JLE 86-3060]*

Tunick, Lisa A. Salamon, Lester M. Rhode Island nonprofit organizations . Washington, D.C. , Providence, RI , c1987. vii, 40 p. : LC Card 87-148803 DDC 338.7/4/09745 19
HD2769.2.U6 S25 1987

TUNISIA - ECONOMIC CONDITIONS - 1956-
Bolz, Reinhardt. Tunesien . Hamburg , 1976. xxiii, 471 p. : LC Card 86-177615
HC820 .B66 1976

Jedidi, Mohammed. Croissance économique et espace urbain dans le Sahel tunisien depuis l'indépendance /. [Tunis] , 1986. 2 v. : LC Card 87-123401
HC820 .J43 1986

TUNISIA - ECONOMIC POLICY.
Bolz, Reinhardt. Tunesien . Hamburg , 1976. xxiii, 471 p. : LC Card 86-177615
HC820 .B66 1976

TUNISIA - SOCIAL CONDITIONS.
Bolz, Reinhardt. Tunesien . Hamburg , 1976. xxiii, 471 p. : LC Card 86-177615
HC820 .B66 1976

The Tunnel : the Channel and beyond / editor, Bronwen Jones ; contributing authors, John Ardill ... [et al.]. Chichester : Ellis Horwood ; New York : Halsted Press, 1987. xxxi, 334 p. : ill. ; 24 cm. Includes bibliographies and index. ISBN 0-7458-0277-X : LC Card 87-17025 DDC 385/.312/0916336 19
1. Tunnels - English Channel. I. Jones, Bronwen. II. Ardill, John.
HE380.G73 E547 1987

TUNNELS - ENGLISH CHANNEL.
The Tunnel . Chichester , New York , 1987. xxxi, 334 p. : ISBN 0-7458-0277-X : LC Card 87-17025 DDC 385/.312/0916336 19
HE380.G73 E547 1987

Tunstall, Jeremy. Communications deregulation : the unleashing of America's communicationsindustry / Jeremy Tunstall. Oxford, UK ; New York, NY, USA : B. Blackwell, 1986. xi, 324 p. ; 24 cm. Includes index. Bibliography: p. [296]-315. ISBN 0-631-14819-1 : LC Card 85-22983 DDC 343.73/0994 347.303994 19
1. Telecommunication - Law and legislation - United States. 2. Telecommunication policy - United States. I. Title.
KF2765 .T86 1986 *NYPL [JLE 86-2991]*

Tuovila, Olavi. Optimal financing policy of the firm : a control-theoretic approach applied to selected oil-product distribution firms / Olavi Tuovila. Vaasa : Universitas Wasaensis, 1983. 127 p. : ill. ; 25 cm. (Acta Wasaensia, 0355-2667 . no. 19. no. 5.) Bibliography: p. 109-114. ISBN 951-683-199-0 (pbk.) LC Card 84-204398
1. Corporations - Finance - Mathematical models. 2. Petroleum industry and trade - Finance - Mathematical

models. I. Series: Acta wasaensia, no. 19. II. Title.
HG4012 .T86 1983

Tuppen, John N. France under recession, 1981-1986 / John Tuppen. Albany : State University of New York Press, c1988. p. cm. Bibliography: p. ISBN 0-88706-580-5 LC Card 87-1980 DDC 338.944 19
1. France - Economic conditions - 1981-. 2. France - Economic policy - 1981-. 3. France - Social conditions - 1945-. 4. France - Politics and government - 1981-. 5. Socialism - France. 6. Privatization - France. 7. Local government - France. I. Title.
HC276.3 .T86 1988

Tupytsia, IUrii IUr'evich. Ekologo-ekonomicheskaia effektivnost' prirodopol'zovaniia / IU.IU. Tupytsia. Moskva : Izd-vo "Nauka," 1980. 165 p. ; 21 cm. (Sovremennye problemy biosfery) On page preceding t.p.: Akademiia nauk SSSR. Nauchnyi sovet po problemam biosfery. Bibliography: p. 151-[164] LC Card 81-146449
1. Natural resources - Soviet Union. 2. Environmental protection - Soviet Union. I. Title. II. Series.
HC333.5 .T86 1980

Turani, Giuseppe.
Briganti e gentiluomini della finanza italiana / Giuseppe Turani. [Milano] : Sperling & Kupfer, c1987. 394 p. ; 22 cm. ("E & M," economia e management . 28.) Includes index. ISBN 88-20-00657-X : LC Card 87-168620
1. Finance - Italy. 2. Capitalists and financiers - Italy. 3. Commercial crimes - Italy. I. Series: "E & M," economia e management , 28. II. Title.
HG186.I8 T86 1987

1985-1995, il secondo miracolo economico italiano : istruzioni per l'uso / Giuseppe Turani. Milano : Sperling & Kupfer, c1986. 147 p. : ill. ; 22 cm. ("E & M," economia e management . 18.) ISBN 88-20-00586-7 : LC Card 86-202136
1. Italy - Economic conditions - 1976-. 2. Economic forecasting - Italy. I. Series: "E & M," economia e management , 18. II. Title.
HC305 .T85 1986

Turban, Efraim. Decision support and expert systems : managerial perspectives / Ephraim Turban. New York : Macmillan ; London : Collier Macmillan, c1988. xxi, 697 p. : ill. ; 26 cm. (Macmillan series in information systems) Includes bibliographies and index. ISBN 0-02-421650-X LC Card 87-23911 DDC 658.4/03 19
1. Management - Data processing. 2. Decision support systems. 3. Expert systems (Computer science). I. Title. II. Series.
HD30.2 .T87 1988

TURBO PASCAL (COMPUTER PROGRAM)
Wortman, Leon A. Turbo Pascal for the Mac . Blue Ridge Summit, PA , c1987. x, 274 p. : ISBN 0-8306-2927-0 (pbk.) : LC Card 87-7134 DDC 650/.028/5416 19
HF5548.5.P14 W67 1987

Turbo Pascal for the Mac . Wortman, Leon A. Blue Ridge Summit, PA , c1987. x, 274 p. : ISBN 0-8306-2927-0 (pbk.) : LC Card 87-7134 DDC 650/.028/5416 19
HF5548.5.P14 W67 1987

Túri vásár /. Varga, Lajos. Mezőtúr , 1983. 188 p. ; ISBN 963-7612-04-1 LC Card 85-109670
HF5474.H82 M498 1983

Turk, Ivan. Iskazivanje i ocjenjivanje rezultata poslovanja organizacija udruženog rada / Ivan Turk. Zagreb : Informator, 1982. x, 171 p. ; 24 cm. (Organizacija i ekonomika) In Serbo-Croatian (Roman) Includes bibliographical references and index. LC Card 83-110726
1. Industrial management - Yugoslavia. 2. Government business enterprises - Yugoslavia. 3. Yugoslavia - Economic policy - 1945-. I. Title.
HD70.Y8 T87 1982

Türk Sanayicileri ve İş Adamları Derneği.
An Econometric model for Turkey, 1965-1984. Istanbul, Turkey [1986] x, 84 p. : LC Card 87-142603 DDC 330.9561/038/0151 19
HC492 .E28 1986

The Turkish economy, 1981. Istanbul [1981] 256 p. : LC Card 87-404163 DDC 330.9561/038 19
HC492 .T876 1981

Türk, V. (Vambola) Tööjõu kasutamise probleeme Eesti NSV-s /. Tallinn , 1986. 179 p. ; LC Card 87-107003
HD5797.E75 T66 1986

Turkey, America's forgotten ally /. Rustow, Dankwart A. New York, NY , c1987. xv, 155 p. : ISBN 0-87609-023-4 : LC Card 87-6712 DDC 330.9561/038 19
HC492 .R87 1987

TURKEY - COMMERCE.
Karluk, S. Rıdvan. Türkiye'de ihracata yönelik dış ticaret politikası ve ihracatın yapısal analizi /. Eskişehir , 1981. xx, 454 p. ; LC Card 82-241650
HF1583.4 .K37 1981

TURKEY - COMMERCE - EUROPEAN ECONOMIC COMMUNITY COUNTRIES.
Hale, William M. Turkish agriculture and Community enlargement /. [Ankara] , 1984. 37 p. ; LC Card 87-113782 DDC 338.9561 s 338.1/09561 19
HC401 .A356 no. 1949 HD9016.T82

TURKEY - COMMERCE - HISTORY - 19TH CENTURY.
Pamuk, Şevket. The Ottoman empire and European capitalism, 1820-1913 . Cambridge [Cambridgeshire] , New York , 1987. xii, 278 p. : ISBN 0-521-33194-3 LC Card 86-28386 DDC 330.956/01 19
HF1583.4 .P36 1987

TURKEY - COMMERCIAL POLICY.
Karluk, S. Rıdvan. Türkiye'de ihracata yönelik dış ticaret politikası ve ihracatın yapısal analizi /. Eskişehir , 1981. xx, 454 p. ; LC Card 82-241650
HF1583.4 .K37 1981

1971 yılı ithalât rejimi ve programı hakkında görüşler. Ankara , 1971. 15 p. ; LC Card 86-156490
HF1583.4 .A14 1971

TURKEY - ECONOMIC CONDITIONS.
Ceylan, Sadi, 1951- Die geschichtliche Umwandlung der ökonomischen Gesellschaftsformation der Türkei /. Berlin , c1985. 270 p. ; ISBN 3-88548-482-X LC Card 86-221332
HC492 .C49 1985

Doh, Rainer. Bevölkerungsentwicklung, Wirtschaftsordnung und Industrialisierungsprozess in Südosteuropa . Neuried , c1985. [12], 486, 19 p. : ISBN 3-88893-045-6 LC Card 87-140271 DDC 304.6/09498 19
HB3631 .D64 1985

Keyder, Caglar. State and class in Turkey . London , New York , 1987. 252 p. ; ISBN 0-86091-877-7 (pbk.) : LC Card 87-14992 DDC 338.9561 19
HC492 .K497 1987

TURKEY - ECONOMIC CONDITIONS - 1960-
Kopits, George. Structural reform, stabilization, and growth in Turkey /. Washington, D.C. , c1987. v, 46 p. : ISBN 0-939934-84-1 (pbk.) : LC Card 87-3583 DDC 338.9561 19
HC492 .K67 1987

Rustow, Dankwart A. Turkey, America's forgotten ally /. New York, NY , c1987. xv, 155 p. : ISBN 0-87609-023-4 : LC Card 87-6712 DDC 330.9561/038 19
HC492 .R87 1987

The Turkish economy, 1981. Istanbul [1981] 256 p. : LC Card 87-404163 DDC 330.9561/038 19
HC492 .T876 1981

TURKEY - ECONOMIC CONDITIONS - 1960- - ECONOMETRIC MODELS.
Conway, Patrick J. Economic shocks and structural adjustments . Amsterdam ; New York : xiv, 219 p. : ISBN 0-444-70281-4 LC Card 87-15667 DDC 338.9561 19
HC492 .C65 1987

An Econometric model for Turkey, 1965-1984. Istanbul, Turkey [1986] x, 84 p. : LC Card 87-142603 DDC 330.9561/038/0151 19
HC492 .E28 1986

TURKEY - ECONOMIC CONDITIONS - CONGRESSES.
Osmanistische Studien zur Wirtschafts- und Sozialgeschichte . Wiesbaden , 1986. xi, 206 p., iv p. of plates : ISBN 3-477-02652-9 (Deut. Bibl.) LC Card 86-224062
HC492 .O85 1986

TURKEY - ECONOMIC POLICY.
Devlet Planlama Teşkilatı (Turkey) Dördüncü Beş Yıllık Kalkınma Planı, 1979-1983. Ankara [1979] xiv, 692 p. ; LC Card 83-228455
HC401 .A356 no. 1664 HC492

Heper, Metin. Development administration in Turkey . Bebek, Istanbul [1980] vi, 116 p. ; LC Card 87-400032 DDC 338.9561 19
HC492 .H47 1980

Hiller, Marlene P., 1948- Krisenregion Nahost . Frankfurt am Main , New York , c1985. 335 p. : ISBN 3-8204-8249-0 LC Card 85-191941
HF1558.15.T8 H55 1985

Kopits, George. Structural reform, stabilization, and growth in Turkey /. Washington, D.C. , c1987. v, 46 p. : ISBN 0-939934-84-1 (pbk.) : LC Card 87-3583 DDC 338.9561 19
HC492 .K67 1987

Planned development in Turkey and the State Planning Organization. [Ankara] [1986] 47 p. : LC Card 87-151757 DDC 338.9561 19
HC492 .P63 1986

Rustow, Dankwart A. Turkey, America's forgotten ally /. New York, NY , c1987. xv, 155 p. : ISBN 0-87609-023-4 : LC Card 87-6712 DDC 330.9561/038 19
HC492 .R87 1987

The Turkish economy, 1981. Istanbul [1981] 256 p. : LC Card 87-404163 DDC 330.9561/038 19
HC492 .T876 1981

TURKEY - ECONOMIC POLICY - ECONOMETRIC MODELS.
Conway, Patrick J. Economic shocks and structural adjustments . Amsterdam ; New York : xiv, 219 p. : ISBN 0-444-70281-4 LC Card 87-15667 DDC 338.9561 19
HC492 .C65 1987

TURKEY - FOREIGN ECONOMIC RELATIONS.
Pamuk, Şevket. The Ottoman empire and European capitalism, 1820-1913 . Cambridge [Cambridgeshire] , New York , 1987. xii, 278 p. : ISBN 0-521-33194-3 LC Card 86-28386 DDC 330.956/01 19
HF1583.4 .P36 1987

TURKEY - FOREIGN ECONOMIC RELATIONS - RUSSIA.
Hiller, Marlene P., 1948- Krisenregion Nahost . Frankfurt am Main , New York , c1985. 335 p. : ISBN 3-8204-8249-0 LC Card 85-191941
HF1558.15.T8 H55 1985

TURKEY - FOREIGN RELATIONS - UNITED STATES.
Rustow, Dankwart A. Turkey, America's forgotten ally /. New York, NY , c1987. xv, 155 p. : ISBN 0-87609-023-4 : LC Card 87-6712 DDC 330.9561/038 19
HC492 .R87 1987

Turkey - Government. see **Turkey - Politics and government.**

TURKEY - HISTORY - 1453-1683 - CONGRESSES.
Osmanistische Studien zur Wirtschafts- und Sozialgeschichte . Wiesbaden , 1986. xi, 206 p., iv p. of plates : ISBN 3-477-02652-9 (Deut. Bibl.) LC Card 86-224062
HC492 .O85 1986

TURKEY - INDUSTRIES - HISTORY.
Ceylan, Sadi, 1951- Die geschichtliche Umwandlung der ökonomischen Gesellschaftsformation der Türkei /. Berlin , c1985. 270 p. ; ISBN 3-88548-482-X LC Card 86-221332
HC492 .C49 1985

TURKEY - INDUSTRIES - HISTORY - 19TH CENTURY.
Pamuk, Şevket. The Ottoman empire and European capitalism, 1820-1913 . Cambridge [Cambridgeshire] , New York , 1987. xii, 278 p. : ISBN 0-521-33194-3 LC Card 86-28386 DDC 330.956/01 19
HF1583.4 .P36 1987

TURKEY INDUSTRY - CALIFORNIA - ECONOMETRIC MODELS.
Eidman, Vernon R., 1936- Decision models for California turkey growers /. Berkeley, Calif. [1968] ii, 80 p. : LC Card 87-401009 DDC 338.1/09794 s 636.5/92/0068 19
HD1407 .C27 no. 21 HD9437.U63C3

TURKEY - POLITICS AND GOVERNMENT - 1960-
Rustow, Dankwart A. Turkey, America's forgotten ally /. New York, NY , c1987. xv, 155 p. : ISBN 0-87609-023-4 : LC Card 87-6712 DDC 330.9561/038 19
HC492 .R87 1987

TURKEY - POPULATION.
Doh, Rainer. Bevölkerungsentwicklung, Wirtschaftsordnung und Industrialisierungsprozess in Südosteuropa . Neuried , c1985. [12], 486, 19 p. : ISBN 3-88893-045-6 LC Card 87-140271 DDC 304.6/09498 19
HB3631 .D64 1985

TURKEY - SOCIAL CONDITIONS.
Ceylan, Sadi, 1951- Die geschichtliche Umwandlung der ökonomischen Gesellschaftsformation der Türkei /. Berlin , c1985. 270 p. ; ISBN 3-88548-482-X LC Card 86-221332
HC492 .C49 1985

TURKEY - SOCIAL POLICY.
Devlet Planlama Teşkilatı (Turkey) Dördüncü Beş Yıllık Kalkınma Planı, 1979-1983. Ankara [1979] xiv, 692 p. ; LC Card 83-228455
HC401 .A356 no. 1664 HC492

Planned development in Turkey and the State Planning Organization. [Ankara] [1986] 47 p. : LC Card 87-151757 DDC 338.9561 19
HC492 .P63 1986

Turkin, V. G. (Vladimir Gavrilovich) Povyshat' ėffektivnost' partiĭnoĭ raboty / V.G. Turkin. Moskva : Moskovskiĭ rabochiĭ, 1978. 63 p. ; 20 cm. LC Card 81-170148
1. Employee motivation - Soviet Union. 2. Kommunisticheskaia partiia Sovetskogo Soiuza - Party work. I. Title.
HF5549.5.M63 T87 1978

Turkish agriculture and Community enlargement /. Hale, William M. [Ankara] , 1984. 37 p. ; LC Card 87-113782 DDC 338.9561 s 338.1/09561 19
HC401 .A356 no. 1949 HD9016.T82

The Turkish economy, 1981. Istanbul : Turkish Industrialists and Businessmen's Association, [1981] 256 p. : ill. ; 30 cm. "Edited by Ertuğrul İhsan Özol, Dr. Hayri Ürgüplü"--T.p. verso. "July 27, 1980 [i.e. 1981]"--T.p. verso. LC Card 87-404163 DDC 330.9561/038 19
1. Turkey - Economic conditions - 1960-. 2. Turkey - Economic policy. I. Özol, Ertuğrul İhsan. II. Ürgüplü, Hayri Suat. III. Türk Sanayicileri ve İş Adamları Derneği.
HC492 .T876 1981

Turkish workers in Europe : an interdisciplinary study / editors, İlhan Başgöz, Norman Furniss ; [photography by İbrahim Demirel. Bloomington, Ind. (143 Goodbody Hall, Indiana University, Bloomington 47405) : Indiana University Turkish Studies, c1985. 191 p. : ill. ; 23 cm. (Indiana University Turkish studies . v. 5) Includes bibliographies. LC Card 85-71750 DDC 331.6/2/56104 19
1. Alien labor, Turkish - Europe. 2. Alien labor, Turkish - Germany, West. I. Başgöz, M. İlhan. II. Furniss, Norman, 1944-. III. Series.
HD8378.5.T8 T87 1985
NYPL [JLE 86-2980]

TÜRKIVE KOMÜNIST PARTISI/MARKSIST-LENINIST.
Türkiye Komünist Partisi/Marksist-Leninist. Kritik der "Drei Welten Theorie" durch die TKP/ML . Wien [1978] 1 v. (various pagings) ; LC Card 85-134265
HC59.7 .T867 1978

Türkiye Komünist Partisi/Marksist-Leninist. Kritik der "Drei Welten Theorie" durch die TKP/ML : (Auslandsorganisation). Wien : G. Strobl, [1978] 1 v. (various pagings) ; 21 cm. (Theorie und Praxis des Marxismus-Leninismus . Nr. 2/78 = 21) Cover title. LC Card 85-134265
1. Developing countries - Dependency on foreign countries. 2. Imperialism. 3. Communism. 4. Türkive Komünist Partisi/Marksist-Leninist. I. Series: Theorie und Praxis des Marxismus-Leninismus (Vienna, Austria) , 78/Nr. 2. II. Title.
HC59.7 .T867 1978

Türkiye Ticaret Odaları, Sanayi Odaları ve Ticaret Borsaları Birliği. 1971 yılı ithalât rejimi ve programı hakkında görüşler. Ankara , 1971. 15 p. ; LC Card 86-156490
HF1583.4 .A14 1971

Türkiye ve Orta-Doğu Âmme İdaresi Enstitüsü. Yayınları.
(no. 187) Özer, İlhan. Kamu alacaklarının tahsili teorisi ve Türkiye'de uygulaması /. Ankara , 1979. xv, 236 p. ; LC Card 85-968002
HJ2906.5 .O93 1979

Türkiye'de ihracata yönelik dış ticaret politikası ve ihracatın yapısal analizi /. Karluk, S. Rıdvan. Eskişehir , 1981. xx, 454 p. ; LC Card 82-241650
HF1583.4 .K37 1981

Türkiye'de işveren sendikacılığı /. Esin, Pars. Ankara , 1974. xii, 288 p. ; LC Card 83-103059
HD6796.7 .E85 1974

Türkiye'de tarımsal kooperatiflerin toplumsal değişmeye etkileri . Ürper, Yılmaz. Eskişehir , 1985. xvi, 109, xxxiii p. ; LC Card 86-161567
HG2051.T92 I48 1985

TURKMEN S.S.R. - INDUSTRIES - LOCATION.
Egengel'dyev, E. (Esengel'dy) Teoreticheskie issledovaniia regional'nykh faktorov razmeshcheniia khoziaistva /. Ashkabad , 1985. 227 p. : LC Card 86-172008
HC337.T853 D53 1985

Turku, Finland. Akademi (1918-). Statsvetenskapliga facultaten. Meddelanden. Serie A. .
(181) Nyberg, Peter. On the choice of optimal central bank currency baskets /. Åbo , 1982. 24 p. ;
NYPL [JLL 77-251 no. 181]

Turku, Finland. Akademi (1918-). Statsvetenskapliga fakulteten.
(187) Willner, Johan. Economic policy under imperfect competition /. Åbo [Finland] 1983. 34 p. ; ISBN 951-648-926-5 (pbk.) LC Card 84-137942 DDC 338.9/00724 19
HB238 .W539 1983
NYPL [JLL 77-251 no.187]

Meddelanden. Ser. A .
Turn-around . Davis, Marvin A. Chicago , c1987. 194 p. ; ISBN 0-8092-4780-1 : LC Card 86-29285 DDC 658.4/06 19
HD58.8 .D38 1987

Turnbaugh, Sarah Peabody. Domestic pottery of the northeastern United States, 1625-1850 /. Orlando , 1985. xxi, 319 p. : ISBN 0-12-703870-1 (alk. paper) LC Card 85-9038 DDC 338.4/76663974 19
HD9611.7.A115 D66 1985
NYPL [3-MPH 86-2845]

Turnbull, Peter W.
Research in international marketing /. London , Dover, N.H. , c1986. 376 p. : ISBN 0-7099-4313-X : LC Card 85-29052 DDC 382/.6 19
HF1009.5 .R46 1986 NYPL [JLD 86-2264]

Strategies for international industrial marketing . London , Dover, N.H. , c1986. 310 p. : ISBN 0-7099-2494-1 : LC Card 85-29047 DDC 658.8/48 19
HF1009.7.E85 S77 1986
NYPL [JLD 86-1596]

Turner, Bryan S. Abercrombie, Nicholas. Sovereign individuals of capitalism /. London , Boston , 1986. 211 p. ; ISBN 0-04-301230-2 (alk. paper) LC Card 86-1122 DDC 330.12/2 19
HB501 .A23 1986 NYPL [JLD 86-3686]

Turner, Dennis E. Niland, John R. Control, consensus, or chaos? . Sydney , Boston , 1985. xiv, 330 p. : ISBN 0-86861-447-5 (pbk.) LC Card 85-70461 DDC 331.89/0994 19
HD8846.5 .N55 1985 NYPL [JLD 87-354]

Turner, John R. (John Raymond), 1936-
Scotland's North Sea gateway : Aberdeen Harbour, AD 1136-1986 / John R. Turner. Aberdeen : Aberdeen University Press, 1986. xvi, 228 p. : ill. ; 22 cm. Bibliography: p. 222. Includes index. ISBN 0-08-032463-0 LC Card 87-131902 DDC 387.1/09412/35 19
1. Harbors - Scotland - Aberdeen (Grampian) - History. I. Title.
HE558.A34 T87 1986

Turner, Louis, 1942-
Industrial collaboration with Japan / Louis Turner ; with a foreword by Hiroshi Takeuchi, in association with Ayako Asakura ... [et al.]. London ; New York : Routledge & K. Paul, 1987. 117 p. ; 22 cm. (Chatham House paper . 34) "The Royal Institute of International Affairs." Bibliography: p. 112-117. ISBN 0-7102-1109-0 (pbk.) : LC Card 86-26048 DDC 338.8/8 19
1. Joint ventures - Japan. 2. Joint ventures - United States. 3. Joint ventures - Europe. I. Title. II. Series.
HD62.47 .T87 1987

Stopford, John M. Britain and the multinationals /. Chichester , New York , c1985. xiv, 282 p. : ISBN 0-471-90839-8 : LC Card 85-12352 DDC 338.8/8841 19
HD2845 .S76 1985 NYPL [JLE 86-924]

Turner, Lowell. Wilensky, Harold L. Democratic corporatism and policy linkages . Berkeley , c1987. ix, 97 p. ; ISBN 0-87725-169-X (pbk.) : LC Card 87-3525 DDC 338.9 19
HD3616.E8 W54 1987

Turner, Michael Edward. Enclosures in Britain, 1750-1830 / prepared for the Economic History Society by Michael Turner. London : Macmillan, 1984. 96 p. : ill., map ; 22 cm. (Studies in economic and social history) Bibliography: p. 84-93. Includes index. ISBN 0-333-31682-7 (pbk.) LC Card 86-673799
1. Inclosures - Great Britain - History. I. Economic History Society. II. Title.
HD594.6 .T84x 1984

Turner, R. J., 1946- 16 ways to profit from real estate in 1986. Arlington, VA : Alexandria House Books, [c1986] 1 v. (various foliations) : ill. ; 28 cm. Includes bibliography. ISBN 0-937583-06-5 (pbk.) LC Card 86-210837 DDC 332.63/24 19
1. Real estate investment. I. Title. II. Title: Sixteen ways to profit from real estate in 1986.
HD1382.5 .T87 1986

Turner, S. D. Senaoana, M. P. Research on rural-non farm employment in Lesotho . Roma, Lesotho [1984] 88 leaves : LC Card 86-214032 DDC 331.12/5/096816 19
HD5842.7.A6 S46 1984

Turner, Terisa. Trade union action to stop oil to South Africa / Terisa Turner ; Organization of African Trade Union Unity. Port Harcourt : Publication Committee, University of Port Harcourt, c1985. v, 35 p. ; 23 cm. "This booklet reflects the views of its author and the International Oil Working Group .... [It] reprints a review of Trade union action to stop oil to South Africa which was presented by the Organization of African Trade Union Unity to the June 1983 International Conference of Trade Unions on Sanctions and Other Actions Against the Apartheid Regime in South Africa, held in Geneva"--P. i, iv. LC Card 87-673464
1. Economic sanctions - South Africa. 2. Embargo. 3. Trade unions - Petroleum workers. I. Organisation of African Trade Union Unity. II. International Oil Working Group. III. Title.
HF1613.4 .T87x 1985

Turnier, Alain.
Société des baïonnettes, un regard nouveau. 1985. Mathon, Alix. [Haïti, un cas.] Haïti, un cas / Alix Mathon. La société des baïonnettes, un regard nouveau / Alain Turnier. [Port-au-Prince? , 1985] (Port-au-Prince, Haïti : Impr. Le Natal) 172, 271 p. ; LC Card 86-139806 DDC 330.97294 19
HC153 .M38 1985 NYPL [Sc D 86-555]

TURNKEY COMPUTER SYSTEMS - UNITED STATES.
The Mini-microcomputer turnkey engineering systems market. New York, N.Y. , c1983. vi, 228 p. ; LC Card 87-142400 DDC 381/.4500416 19
HD9696.C63 U5262 1983

TURNOVER OF LABOR. see **LABOR TURNOVER.**

TURNOVER TAX - GERMANY (WEST)
Aktuelle Probleme der Wirtschaftspolitik . Tübingen , 1982. vi, 69, vii, 62 p. : ISBN 3-16-344473-3 LC Card 84-125468
HJ5715.G3 A67 1982

TURNOVER TAX - HUNGARY.
Turnover tax-system in Hungary /. Budapest , 1985. 21 p. ; ISBN 963-621-208-2 (pbk.) : LC Card 86-202548 DDC 336.2/7 19
HJ5715.H9 T87 1985

TURNOVER TAX - SOVIET UNION.
Penkaitis, Norbert. Volkswirtschaftliche Aspekte

der sowjetischen Umsatzsteuer /. Berlin , 1986. 121 p. : ISBN 3-428-06108-X LC Card 87-408633 DDC 336.2/7 19
HJ5715.S65 P46 1986

Turnover tax-system in Hungary / [editorial board ... O. Gadó (president) ... et al.]. Budapest : Ministry of Finance, 1985. 21 p. ; 20 cm. (Public finance in Hungary, 0230-9718 . 24) ISBN 963-621-208-2 (pbk.) : LC Card 86-202548 DDC 336.2/7 19
1. Turnover tax - Hungary. I. Gadó, Ottó. II. Series.
HJ5715.H9 T87 1985

TURNPIKE ROADS. see **TOLL ROADS.**

TURNPIKE THEORY (ECONOMICS) - CASE STUDIES.
De Castro, Steve. "Turnpikes for small open economies . [Brasília] [1982] 22 leaves ; LC Card 83-156613 DDC 339.2/3/091724 19
HD82 .D376 1982

"Turnpikes for small open economies . De Castro, Steve. [Brasília] [1982] 22 leaves ; LC Card 83-156613 DDC 339.2/3/091724 19
HD82 .D376 1982

Turos, Wiesław. Migracje wewnętrzne ludności . Warszawa , 1980. xvi, 389 p. ; LC Card 86-215694
HB2068.7.A3 M54 1980

Turra, Flávio Enir. Custo de produção de café /. Curitiba-Paraná [19]84. 47 p. ; LC Card 85-211612
HD9199.B7 C93 1984

Turrell, Robert Vicat. Capital and labour on the Kimberley diamond fields, 1871-1890 / Robert Vicat Turrell. Cambridge [Cambridgeshire] ; New York : Cambridge University Press, 1987. xviii, 297 p. : ill. ; 24 cm. (African studies series. 54) Bibliography: p. 278-290. Includes index. ISBN 0-521-33354-7 LC Card 86-32740 DDC 331.7/622382/0968711 19
1. Diamond industry and trade - South Africa - Kimberley - History. 2. Diamond miners - South Africa - Kimberley - History. 3. Blacks - Employment - South Africa - Kimberley - History. 4. Industrial relations - South Africa - Kimberley - History. 5. Capitalism - South Africa - Kimberley - History. I. Title. II. Series.
HD9677.S63 K567 1987

Turrittin, Jane Sawyer. Men, women, and market trade in rural Mali, West Africa / by Jane Sawyer Turrittin. [East Lansing] : Michigan State University, c1986. 17 p. ; 28 cm. (Working paper / Women in International Development . #114) Bibliography: p. 14-15. LC Card 86-225178 DDC 331.4/8138118/096623 19
1. Sexual division of labor - Mali. 2. Markets - Mali. 3. Women - Mali. 4. Women merchants - Mali. I. Series: Working paper (Michigan State University. Office of Women in International Development) , #114. II. Title.
HD6060.65.M42 T87 1986

Tushman, Michael. Nadler, David. Strategic organization design . Glenview, Ill. , c1988. 209 p. : ISBN 0-673-15860-8 (pbk.) LC Card 87-9832 DDC 658.4/012 19
HD58.7 .N33 1988

Tussie, Diana. The less developed countries and the world trading system : a challenge to the GATT / Diana Tussie. London : Frances Pinter, 1987. viii, 162 p. ; 24 cm. (Studies in international political economy) Includes index. Bibliography: p. [147]-153. ISBN 0-86187-614-8
1. Tariff - Developing countries. 2. Developing countries - Commerce. 3. Latin America - Economic integration. I. Series. II. Series: Studies in international political economy (Frances Pinter (Publishers)). III. Title. ***NYPL [JLE 87-1597]***

Tussing, A. Dale. Rottman, David B. The population structure and living circumstances of Irish travellers . Dublin , 1986. 134 p. : ISBN 0-7070-0084-X (pbk.) : LC Card 86-215759 DDC 330.9417 s 305.5/68 19
HC257.I6 E3 no. 131 DX217

La Tutela del lavoro in Italia. [Roma] : Presidenza del Consiglio dei ministri, Servizi informazioni e proprietà letteraria, [1976] 144 p. ; 24 cm. (Quaderno . n. 21) "Supplemento alla rivista 'Vita italiana - Documenti e informazioni,' n. 9/76"--Cover. LC Card 86-233354
1. Labor policy - Italy. 2. Right to labor - Italy. 3. Employee rights - Italy. 4. Labor bureaus - Italy. 5. Industrial hygiene - Italy. 6. Social security - Italy. 7. Workers' compensation - Italy. 8. Labor laws and legislation - Italy. I. Italy. Servizi delle informazioni e della proprietà letteraria, artistica e scientifica. II. Vita italiana. N. 9/76 (Supplement). III. Series: Quaderno (Italy. Servizi delle informazioni e della proprietà letteraria, artistica e scientifica) , n. 21.
HD8481 .T85 1976

Tuthill, Janet C., 1949- Brinkerhoff, Derick W. La gestion efficace des projets de développement . West Hartford, Conn. , c1987. vi, 186 p. : ISBN 0-931816-06-8 (pbk.) LC Card 86-33733 DDC 338.9/0068 19
HD75.8 .B75 1987

Tuths, Donna M. Oppenheimer, Michael F. Nontariff barriers . Boulder , 1987. xiii, 203 p. ; ISBN 0-8133-7403-0 (pbk. : alk. paper) LC Card 87-50073 DDC 338.4/762/000973 19
HC110.H53 O66 1987

Tutkimusraportti (Finland. Työsuojeluhallitus) . (50) Riikonen, Eila. Työnteon turvallisuus . Tampere , 19. x, 131, [66] p. : ISBN 951-860-009-0 LC Card 86-222051
HD7262.5.F5 R55 1986

TV. see **TELEVISION.**

TV Ontario. Frontrunners. Chapel Hill, NC , 1987. 1 videocassette (28 min., 50 sec.) : LC Card 87-706853 DDC 338.6 11
HD9940

TV, sorrisi e milioni . Martini, Paolo. Milano , 1985. 243 p. ; ISBN 88-345-0020-2 : LC Card 86-129631 DDC 384.55/0945 19
HE8700.9.I8 M37 1985

TV-tittandet och reklamen . Hedman, Lowe. [Stockholm] [1986] 83 p. : ISBN 91-38-09315-4 LC Card 86-199170
HF6146.T42 H43 1986

Två samhällsekonomiska utvärderingar av icke-permanent industristöd : fallstudier / utförda för Industristödsutredningen. [Stockholm] : LiberFörlag, [1981] 221 p. : ill. ; 21 cm. At head of title: Industridepartementet. Bibliography: p. 219-221. ISBN 91-38-06269-0 LC Card 83-245219
1. Subsidies - Sweden - Case studies. 2. Industry and state - Sweden - Case studies. I. Sweden. Industristödsutredningen.
HD3646.S8 T85 1981

Det tvedelte pensionssystem /. Vesterø Jensen, Carsten. Roskilde [1984] 284 p. ; LC Card 84-181865
HD7105.35.D4 J45 1984

De tweede taakdimensie . Wijvekate, M. L. (Maren L.) Naarden , c1986. 343 p. : ISBN 90-6010-628-8 : LC Card 86-199762
HD53 .W55 1986

Tweede verslag van die Gekose Komitee oor Tolfinansiering van Paaie =. South Africa. Parliament. House of Assembly. Select Committee on Toll Financing of Roads. [Pretoria] [1982] vii p. ; ISBN 0-06-210768-3 : LC Card 83-159014
HE367.S63 T646 1982

TWENTIETH CENTURY - FORECASTS.
Baade, Fritz, 1893- [Wettlauf zum Jahre 2000. English.] The race to the year 2000, our future. Garden City, N.Y., 1962. xix, 246 p. LC Card 62-7600 DDC 330.9/04 19
HC59 .B2513 1962

Global 2000 Study (United States) The global 2000 report to the President--entering the twenty-first century . Washington, D.C. , 1980-1981. 3 v. : LC Card 80-602859 DDC 333.7
HC79.E5 G59 1980b ***NYPL [JLF 87-206]***

Grün, Josef, 1951- Global denken, vor Ort handeln . Freiburg i. Br. , 1984. 373 p. : ISBN 3-921472-73-3 LC Card 84-246414
HC79.E5 G77 1984

Martin, James, 1933- Technology's crucible . Englewood Cliffs, N.J. , 1987. xii, 206 p. : ISBN 0-13-902024-1 : LC Card 86-91492 DDC 303.4/9 19
T20 .M348 1987 ***NYPL [JLE 87-228]***

Twentieth Century Fund.
Bernstein, Blanche, 1912- Saving a generation /. New York , 1986. vi, 63 p. ; ISBN 0-87078-206-1 (pbk.) : LC Card 87-102738 DDC 362.5/8/0973 19
HC110.P6 B47 1986

Destler, I. M. American trade politics . Washington, DC , New York, NY , 1986. xiii, 366 p. : ISBN 0-88132-058-7 : LC Card 86-27168 DDC 380.1/3/0973 19
HF1455 .D48 1986

A Twentieth Century Fund report.
Boskin, Michael J. Too many promises . Homewood, Ill. , c1986. xiv, 196 p. : ISBN 0-87094-779-6 LC Card 86-70430 DDC 368.4/3/00973 19
HD7125 .B585 1986 ***NYPL [JLE 86-2970]***

Twentieth Century Fund. Task Force on Medical Malpractice Insurance. Tobias, Andrew P. Treating malpractice . New York , 1986. ix, 70 p. ; ISBN 0-87078-173-1 (pbk.) : LC Card 86-217256 DDC 368.5 19
HG8054 .T63 1986

Twentieth joint conference : facing technology : Confederation Centre, Charlottetown, P.E.I., Wednesday, November 5, 1986 / sponsors, Prince Edward Island Labour Management Relations Council and Labour Canada. [Charlottetown, P.E.I. : The Council, 1986] 94 p. ; 28 cm. Cover title. LC Card 87-147512 DDC 338/.06 19
1. Technological innovations - Economic aspects - Canada - Congresses. 2. Industrial management - Canada - Congresses. 3. Unemployment - Canada - Congresses. I. Prince Edward Island Labour-management Relations Council. II. Canada. Labour Canada. III. Title: Facing technology.
HC120.T4 T84 1986

Twenty activities for developing managerial effectiveness. Lewis, Mike. 20 activities for developing managerial effectiveness . Aldershot, Hants, England , c1986. xii, 276 p. : ISBN 0-566-02515-9 LC Card 87-147860 DDC 658.4/07124 19
HD31 .L387 1986

TWENTY-FIRST CENTURY - FORECASTS.
Bennett, Georgette. Crimewarps . Garden City, N.Y. , 1987. xix, 435 p. ; ISBN 0-385-23090-7 : LC Card 86-10885 DDC 364/.973 19
HV6791 .B45 1987 ***NYPL [JLE 87-1261]***

Chant, Verne G. Two global scenarios . Laxenburg, Austria , c1981. vi, 75 p. : ISBN 3-7045-0026-7 (pbk.) LC Card 83-130587 DDC 333.79/12 19
HD9502.A2 C45 1981 ***NYPL [JLE 86-595]***

Global 2000 Study (United States) The global 2000 report to the President--entering the twenty-first century . Washington, D.C. , 1980-1981. 3 v. : LC Card 80-602859 DDC 333.7
HC79.E5 G59 1980b ***NYPL [JLF 87-206]***

Görög, Tibor. Ökopesszimizmus, technooptimizmus és korunk globális problémái /. [Budapest] , 1984. 85 p. : ISBN 963-673-290-6 LC Card 85-130717
HC59 .G6226 1984

Grün, Josef, 1951- Global denken, vor Ort handeln . Freiburg i. Br. , 1984. 373 p. : ISBN 3-921472-73-3 LC Card 84-246414
HC79.E5 G77 1984

Johnston, William B., 1945- Workforce 2000 . Indianapolis, Ind. [Washington, D.C.?] , 1987. xxvii, 117 p. : LC Card 87-601910 DDC 331.12/5/0973 19
HD8072.5 .J64 1987

Martin, James, 1933- Technology's crucible . Englewood Cliffs, N.J. , 1987. xii, 206 p. : ISBN 0-13-902024-1 : LC Card 86-91492 DDC 303.4/9 19
T20 .M348 1987 ***NYPL [JLE 87-228]***

Pousset, Henri, 1914- Mögliche globale Wirtschaftsstrategie im 3. Jahrtausend /. Frankfurt am Main , c1986. 190 p. : ISBN 3-88129-956-4 LC Card 86-160350
HD84 .P65 1986

Twenty-five years manufacturing pure foods. The Burt Olney Canning Company (factories-Oneida, Albion, and Medina, N.Y.). [Oneida, N.Y. , 1911?] (Oneida, N.Y. : Ryan & Burkhart) [63] p. : LC Card 87-115754
HD9321.9.B85 B87 1911

Twenty five years of merchant banking in Nigeria /. Adewunmi, Wole. Akoka , 1985. xvi, 136 p. ; ISBN 978-226-475-X : LC Card 87-142907 DDC 332.66/09669 19
HG1971.N6 A34 1985

Twierdochlebow, W. J. Solidarność : a biblio-historiography of the Gdansk strike and birth of Solidarity movement / W.J. Twierdochlebow.2nd ed. Menlo Park, CA : Center for the Study of Opposition in Poland, 1985. 72, v leaves ; 28 cm. (Monographic publications) Cover title. Bibliography: leaf v. Includes indexes. LC Card 86-221919 DDC 331.89/28238204/094382 19
1. Stocznia Gdańska im. Lenina Strike, Gdańsk, Poland, 1980 - Abstracts. 2. NSZZ "Solidarność" (Labor organization) - Abstracts. I. Center for the Study of Opposition in Poland. II. Title. III. Series.
HD5397.7.S512 1980 .G358 1985

Twiss, Brian C. Social forecasting for company planning /. London , 1982. xxv, 310 p. : ISBN 0-333-27076-2 LC Card 86-673655
HD30.28 .S65x 1982

Twiyongere twongera umusaruro. Kigali : Republika y'u Rwanda, Ofisi y'Igihugu yita ku Mibereho y'Abaturage, [1981] 27 p. ; 22 cm. In Ruanda. "Avril 1981." LC Card 82-980614
1. Rwanda - Population. 2. Food supply - Rwanda. 3. Rwanda - Population policy. I. Rwanda. Ofisi y'Igihugu yita ku Mibereho y'Abaturage.
HB3662.7.A3 T88 1981

Two centuries of panic . Sykes, Trevor. Sydney , Boston , 1987. p. cm. ISBN 0-04-176013-1 LC Card 87-16107 DDC 338.7/4/0994 19
HD2747 .S95 1987

Two essays. Röpke, Wilhelm, 1899-1966. [Problem of economic order.] 2 essays /. Lanham, MD , c1987. x, 103 p. ; ISBN 0-8191-6125-X (alk. paper) : LC Card 86-33982 DDC 338.9 19
HD82 .R682 1987

Two feet to tidewater . Jones, Robert C., 1934- Boulder, Colo. , c1987. xvi, 269 p., [1] leaf of plates : ISBN 0-87108-729-4 LC Card 87-2428 DDC 385/.065/741 19
HE2791.W76647 J66 1987

Two global scenarios . Chant, Verne G. Laxenburg, Austria , c1981. vi, 75 p. : ISBN 3-7045-0026-7 (pbk.) LC Card 83-130587 DDC 333.79/12 19
HD9502.A2 C45 1981 ***NYPL [JLE 86-595]***

Two hundred twenty best franchises to buy. Jones, Constance. The 220 best franchises to buy . Toronto , New York , 1987. xi, 459 p. ; ISBN 0-553-34385-8 (pbk.) : LC Card 86-47887 DDC 658.8/708 19
HF5429.235.U5 J66 1987

Two lectures on the historical development of Dutch agriculture, 1600-1985 /. Huizinga, W. Den Haag [1986] 31 p. : LC Card 86-233719
HD1987 .H85 1986

Two new investment reports from Doug Casey. Casey, Douglas R. Arlington, VA (1300 N. 17th St., Suite 1660, Arlington 22209) , c1985. 64, 65 p. : LC Card 86-230393 DDC 332.6/78 19
HG4921 .C35 1985

Two studies concerning the British Broadcasting Corporation / Home Office. London : H.M.S.O., 1979. 48 p. : ill. ; 25 cm. Includes bibliographical references. CONTENTS. - 1. The BBC's forward planning -- 2. Methods of payment of the television license fee. ISBN 0-11-340763-7 (pbk.) LC Card 83-221765
1. British Broadcasting Corporation - Planning. 2. British Broadcasting Corporation - Finance. 3. Radio broadcasting - Great Britain - Planning. 4. Radio broadcasting - Great Britain - Fees. 5. Television broadcasting - Great Britain - Planning. 6. Television broadcasting - Great Britain - Fees. I. British Broadcasting Corporation. II. Great Britain. Home Office. III. Title: 2 studies concerning the British Broadcasting Corporation.
HE8689.9.G7 T85 1979

Two thousand and one sources of financing for small businesses. Holtz, Herman. 2001 sources of financing for small business /. New York , c1983. x, 173 p. ; ISBN 0-668-05468-9 LC Card 82-11366 DDC 658.1/522 19
HG4057 .A286 1983 ***NYPL [JLF 84-63]***

Two thousand one sources of financing for small businesses. Holtz, Herman. 2001 sources of financing for small business /. New York , c1983. x, 173 p. ; ISBN 0-668-05468-9 LC Card 82-11366 DDC 658.1/522 19
HG4057 .A286 1983 ***NYPL [JLF 84-63]***

Two years of accident experience under STOP-DWI, December 1981-November 1983 /. Dowling, Anne M. [Albany] [1984] xiii, 67 p. : LC Card 86-622431 DDC 363.1/251 19
HE5620.D7 D68 1984

Twose, Nigel. Fighting the famine / text by Nigel Twose ; photographs by Mike Goldwater. London : Pluto Press, 1985. 96 p. : ill. ; 20 x 21 cm. Bibliography: p. 94. ISBN 0-7453-0131-2 (pbk.) : LC Card 86-135675 DDC 363.8/83/0966 19
1. Famines - Africa, Sub-Saharan. 2. Famines - Sahel. 3. Famines - Ethiopia. I. Goldwater, Mike. II. Title.
HC800.Z9 F385 1985 ***NYPL [JLD 87-768]***

Tycoon . Wansell, Geoffrey, 1945- New York , 1987. 396 p., [16] p. of plates : ISBN 0-689-11817-1 LC Card 87-11473 DDC 338/.04/0924 B 19
HC252.5.G64 W36 1987

Tydeman, John. New media in Europe : satellites, cable, VCRs and videotex / John Tydeman, Ellen Jakes Kelm. London : New York : McGraw-Hill, c1986. xii, 260 p. : maps ; 24 cm. Includes bibliographies and index. ISBN 0-07-084799-1 : LC Card 85-19839 DDC 384.55/094 19
1. Television broadcasting - Europe. 2. Television advertising - Europe. 3. Moving-picture industry - Europe. 4. Video tape recorder industry - Europe. 5. Telecommunication - Europe. I. Kelm, Ellen Jakes. II. Title.
HE8700.9.E8 T93 1986
NYPL [JLE 86-3209]

Tye, William B. Encouraging cooperation among competitors : the case of motor carrier deregulaton and collective ratemaking / William B. Tye. New York : Quorum Books, 1987. xix, 202 p. : ill. ; 24 cm. Bibliography: p. [181]-196. Includes index. ISBN 0-89930-246-7 (lib. bdg. : alk. paper) LC Card 86-25554 DDC 388.3/24 19
1. Trucking - United States - Rates. 2. Trucking - Government policy - United States. I. Title.
HE5623 .T94 1987

Tymes, Elna.
Lotus 1-2-3 financial models / Elna R. Tymes and Tony Dowden ; with Charles E. Prael. Rev. ed. Indianapolis, Ind. : Hayden Books, c1988. vi, 307 p. ; 28 cm. Rev. ed. of 1-2-3 from A to Z. c1985. Includes indexes. ISBN 0-672-48410-2 (pbk.) LC Card 87-72205 DDC 005.36/9 19
1. Lotus 1-2-3 (Computer program). 2. Business - Data processing. I. Dowden, Tony. II. Prael, Charles E. III. Tymes, Elna. 1-2-3 from A to Z. IV. Title. V. Title: Lotus one-two-three financial models.
HF5548.4.L67 T95 1988

Mastering AppleWorks / Elna Tymes. 2nd ed. San Francisco : SYBEX, c1987. xxii, 479 p. : ill. ; 23 cm. Includes index. ISBN 0-89588-398-8 (pbk.) : LC Card 87-60799 DDC 650/.028/55369 19
1. AppleWorks (Computer program). 2. Apple II (Computer) - Programming. 3. Business - Data processing. I. Title.
HF5548.4.A68 T95 1987

Mastering First Choice / Elna Tymes. Glenview, Ill. : Scott, Foresman, c1987. ix, 301 p. : ill. ; 24 cm. Bibliography: p. 293-294. Includes index. ISBN 0-673-18767-5 (pbk.) : LC Card 86-26098 DDC 650/.028/55369 19
1. First Choice (Computer program). 2. Business - Data processing. I. Title.
HF5548.4.F57 T96 1987

1-2-3 from A to Z. Tymes, Elna. Lotus 1-2-3 financial models / Elna R. Tymes and Tony Dowden ; with Charles E. Prael. Rev. ed. Indianapolis, Ind. , c1988. vi, 307 p. ; ISBN 0-672-48410-2 (pbk.) LC Card 87-72205 DDC 005.36/9 19
HF5548.4.L67 T95 1988

Tyner, Wallace E. McKinzie, Lance. A perspective on U. S. farm problems and agricultural policy /. Boulder , 1987. xvii, 189 p. : ISBN 0-8133-7376-X (pbk. : alk. paper) LC Card 86-51501 DDC 338.1/873 19
HD1470.5.U6 M35 1987

Työelämän suhteiden neuvottelukunta (Series) . (1983/4) Alasoini, Tuomo. Lakot ja yhteiskunnan muutos . Helsinki [1983] ii, 132 p. : ISBN 951-46-7101-5 LC Card 84-168540
HD5306 .A42 1983

Työnteon turvallisuus . Riikonen, Eila. Tampere , 19. x, 131, [66] p. : ISBN 951-860-009-0 LC Card 86-222051
HD7262.5.F5 R55 1986

Työsuojelu kunnissa ja kuntainliitoissa. Swedish. Arbetarskyddet inom kommuner och kommunalförbund / [redaktionskommitté, Lea Alasilta-Hagman ... et al. ; översättning, Carl-Gustav Zilliacus]. [Helsinki] : Arbetarskyddscentralen, [1983] 137 p. : ill. ; 21 cm. Translation of: Työsuojelu kunnissa ja kuntainliitoissa. LC Card 83-229126
1. Industrial safety - Finland. I. Alasilta-Hagman, Lea, 1946-. II. Title.
HD7727.3 .T94618 1983

Työväenkulttuuriprojektin julkaisu .
(4) Metsänkylä, Antti. Metallityön tallennus . Helsinki , 1986. 77 p. : ISBN 951-9074-93-7 LC Card 87-101629
HD9506.F52 M43 1986

Der Typ ist richtig . Florath, Walter, 1925- Berlin , c1986. 151 p. : ISBN 3-355-00005-1 LC Card 86-230122
HC290.78 .F57 1986

Type three company. Archier, Georges. [Entreprise du 3e type. English.] The type 3 company /. New York , 1987. xiv, 123 p. : ISBN 0-89397-282-7 : LC Card 87-11203 DDC 658/.00973 19
HD58.9 .A7313 1987

The type 3 company /. Archier, Georges. [Entreprise du 3e type. English.] New York , 1987. xiv, 123 p. : ISBN 0-89397-282-7 : LC Card 87-11203 DDC 658/.00973 19
HD58.9 .A7313 1987

TYPEWRITING.
College keyboarding/typewriting . Cincinnati , c1985. 396, xvi p. : ISBN 0-538-20750-7 LC Card 84-50474 DDC 652.3 19
Z49 .C65 1985 ***NYPL [JSF 86-1142]***

Typoskript-Edition Hieronymus. Wirtschafts- und Sozialwissenschaften .
(Bd. 15) Dietrich, Bernhard R. Inkasso Unternehmungen /. Neuried , c1986. xxxv, 200 p. ; ISBN 3-88893-050-2 LC Card 87-133343 DDC 658.8/8 19
HG3752.5 .D54 1986

TYRANNY. see **DESPOTISM.**

Tyranny unmasked /. Taylor, John, 1753-1824. Cumberland, Va. , 1988. p. cm. ISBN 0-940973-05-7 (alk. paper) : LC Card 87-2957 DDC 382.7/3/0973 19
HF1754 .T4 1988

Tyrol, South. see **Trentino-Alto Adige (Italy)**

Tyson, Kirk W. M., 1952- Business intelligence--putting it all together / Kirk W.M. Tyson. Lombard, Ill. : Leading Edge Publications, c1986. vi, 275 p. : ill. ; 24 cm. Bibliography: p. 265-270. Includes index. ISBN 0-941101-00-2 : LC Card 86-27309 DDC 658.4/7 19
1. Business intelligence. I. Title.
HD38.7 .T95 1986

Tyson, S. (Shaun) Appraising and exploring organizations /. London , New York , c1988. p. cm. ISBN 0-7099-4340-7 : LC Card 87-20063 DDC 658.3/14 19
HF5549.5.A83 A66 1988

Tysse, G. John. Responding to comparable worth in today's environment . [Washington, D.C.] , c1986. xi, 160 leaves ; ISBN 0-916559-07-6 (loose-leaf) : LC Card 86-63777 DDC 658.3/2 19
HD6061.2.U6 R47 1986

Tzamtzēs, A. I. Hē nautilia tou Pēliou stēn Tourkokratia : mia agnōstē ptychē tēs neōterēs nautikēs mas historias / A.I. Tzamtzēs. [Athēnai] : Vivliopōleio tēs "Hestias", [198-] 103 p., [20] p. of plates : ill. ; 21 cm. Bibliography: p. 92-94. Includes index. LC Card 87-111965
1. Merchant marine - Greece - Magnesia - History - 18th century. 2. Merchant marine - Greece - Magnesia - History - 19th century. 3. Pelion Mountains Region (Greece) - History. I. Title.
HE872.5.Z6 T98 1980z

U. C. L. A. see **California. University. University at Los Angeles.**

U-hjelp og handel . Kristiansen, Stein. Bergen [1982] iv, 325 p. : LC Card 83-139901
HC60 .K76 1982

U. I. S. A. E. see **International Union of Anthropological and Ethnological Sciences.**

U.K. banking after deregulation /. Mullineux, A. W. London , New York , c1987. 180 p. ; ISBN 0-7099-4689-9 LC Card 87-6742 DDC 332.1/0941 19
HG2988 .M85 1987

U.K. consumer electronics. Norwalk, Conn., U. S.A. (6 Prowitt St., Norwalk 06855) : International Resource Development, c1986. vi, 198 leaves ; 28 cm. (Report / International Resource Development Inc. . #699) "June 1986." LC Card 86-228422 DDC 381/.45621381/0941 19
1. Electronic industries - Great Britain. 2. Market surveys - Great Britain. I. International Resource Development, inc. II. Title: United Kingdom consumer electronics. III. Title: UK consumer electronics. IV. Series: Report / International Resource Development Inc. , #699.
HD9696.A3 G785 1986

U.K. occupation and employment trends to 1990. UK occupation and employment trends to 1990 . London , Boston , 1986. xxiv, 249 p. : ISBN 0-408-02980-3 : LC Card 86-13617 DDC 331.12/0941 19
HD5765.A6 U38 1986 ***NYPL [JLE 86-4156]***

U. L. I. see **Urban Land Institute.**

U. N. For corporate body represented by these initials see: **United Nations.**

U. N. C. T. A. D. see **United Nations. Conference on Trade and Development.**

U. N. O. For corporate body represented by these initials see: **United Nations.**

UNRISD studies on the green revolution. see **United Nations. Research Institute for Social Development. Report.**

U nas dole i niedole / [autorzy ... Krystian Brodacki ... et al. ; wstęp Marcina Czerwińskiego]. Wyd. 1. Warszawa : Czytelnik, 1978. 283 p. ; 20 cm. LC Card 81-208722
1. Professions - Poland. 2. Occupational prestige - Poland. I. Brodacki, Krystian.
HD8038.P6 U25 1978

U. R. S. R. see **Ukraine.**

U. S. A. I. D. see **United States. Agency for International Development.**

U. S. agriculture & Third World development : the critical linkage / edited by Randall B. Purcell & Elizabeth Morrison. Boulder : L. Rienner Publishers, 1987. xi, 258 p. ; 25 cm. Includes bibliographies and index. ISBN 1-555-87011-2 (lib. bdg.) : LC Card 86-29860 DDC 338.1/09172/4 19
1. Agriculture - Economic aspects - United States. 2. Produce trade - United States. 3. Agriculture - Developing countries. 4. Agriculture and state - United States. 5. United States - Commerce - Developing countries. 6. Developing countries - Commerce - United States. I. Purcell, Randall B. II. Morrison, Elizabeth, 1959-.
HD1765 .U15 1987

U. S. agriculture and Third World economic development : critical interdependency. Washington, D.C. : National Planning Association, c1987. xv, 103 p. : ill. ; 22 cm. (FAC report . #6) NPA report ; #223 Based on papers presented at a meeting sponsored by the NPA Food and Agricultural Committee and the Winrock International Institute for Agricultural Development, Oct. 1-3, 1986. Includes bibliographical references. ISBN 0-89068-086-8 (pbk.): LC Card 86-62757 DDC 338.9/009172/4 19
1. Agriculture - Economic aspects - United States - Congresses. 2. Agriculture - Economic aspects - Developing countries - Congresses. 3. Produce trade - United States - Congresses. 4. Produce trade - Developing countries - Congresses. 5. Agriculture and state - United States - Congresses. 6. Agriculture and state - Developing countries - Congresses. 7. United States - Foreign economic relations - Developing countries - Congresses. 8. Developing countries - Foreign economic relations - United States - Congresses. 9. Competition, International - Congresses. I. NPA Committee on Food and Agriculture. II. Series.
HD1755 .U173 1987

U. S. aid to Israel . Laufer, Leopold Yehuda. [Jerusalem] [1983] 55 p. : LC Card 87-400279 DDC 338.91/73/05694 19
HC415.25 .L38 1983

U. S. aid to the West Bank and Gaza . Laufer, Leopold Yehuda. [Jerusalem] [1985] 54 p. ; LC Card 87-400340 DDC 338.91/73/056951 19
HC415.25.Z7 W4735 1985

U. S. aid to Zimbabwe . Wasserman, Gary, 1944- [Washington, D.C.?] [1983] ix, 20, [71] p. ; LC Card 87-109216 DDC 338.91/73/06891 19
HC910 .W37 1983

U. S. and Canadian investment in South Africa and Namibia . Bowers, Cathy. Washington, D.C. , c1986. xiii, 238 p. ; ISBN 0-931035-10-4 (pbk.) LC Card 86-209149 DDC 338.8/8973/068025 19
HG5851.A3 B69 1986

U. S. and world food, beverages, and tobacco expenditures, 1970-83 /. Korb, Penelope. Washington, D.C. , 1986. iv, 84 p. : LC Card 86-603160 DDC 339.4/8664/0021 19
HD9000.4 .K67 1986

U. S. arms exports . Ferrari, Paul L. Washington, DC , c1987. xii, 342 p. : ISBN 0-931035-12-0 (pbk.) LC Card 87-80032 DDC 382/.456234/0971 19
HD9743.U6 F47 1987

U. S. ASEAN relations : prospects for the 1990s, March 31-April 2, 1986, Kuala Lumpur, Malaysia : report, proceedings of a conference / sponsored by Center for Strategic and International Studies, Georgetown University, Washington, D.C. in association with Institute of Strategic and International Studies, Malaysia ; edited by Ray S. Cline. Washington, D.C. : United States Global Strategy Council, 1987. xxii, 222 p. ; 28 cm. Includes bibliographies. ISBN 0-943057-00-0 (pbk.) LC Card 87-50526 DDC 337.59073 19
1. United States - Foreign economic relations - Asia, Southeastern - Congresses. 2. Asia, Southeastern - Foreign economic relations - United States - Congresses. 3. United States - Foreign relations - Asia, Southeastern - Congresses. 4. Asia, Southeastern - Foreign relations - United States - Congresses. 5. Military assistance, American - Asia, Southeastern - Congresses. I. Cline, Ray S. II. Georgetown University. Center for Strategic and International Studies. III. Institute of Strategic and International Studies (Malaysia).
HF1456.5.A7 U72 1987

U. S. Catholic institutions and labor unions, 1960-1980 /. Sullivan, Patrick J., 1929- Lanham, MD , c1985. 545 p. ; ISBN 0-8191-4970-5 (alk. paper) : LC Card 85-20171 DDC 331.88/1128273 19
HD6481.2.U6 S85 1985
NYPL [JLE 86-2407]

U. S. clinical testing market / Biomedical Business International. 3rd revision. Tustin, CA, U. S.A. (17722 Irvine Blvd., Tustin 92680) : BBI, c1987. 223 leaves in various foliations ; 29 cm. (Report / Biomedical Business International . #7040) "March 1987." LC Card 87-402039 DDC 381/.45681761 19
1. Medical laboratory equipment industry - United States. 2. Market surveys - United States. I. Biomedical Business International, Inc. II. Title: US clinical testing market. III. Series: Report (Biomedical Business International, Inc.) , #7040.
HD9995.L33 U5484 1987

U. S. corporate withdrawal from South Africa . Hauck, David. Washington, D.C. (Suite 600, 1755 Massachusetts Ave., N.W., Washington 20036) [1986] 22 p. ; LC Card 86-209299 DDC 332.6/7373/068 19
HG5851.A3 H39 1986

U. S. decennial life tables for 1979-81. Hyattsville, Md. : U. S. Dept. of Health and Human Services, Public Health Service, National Center for Health Statistics ; Washington, D.C. : For sale by the Supt. of Docs., U. S. G.P.O., 1985-<1986 > v. ; 28 cm. + 1 supplement. (DHHS publication. no. (PHS) 85-1150-1-) Errata leaf inserted in v. 2, no. 5. CONTENTS. - v. 1, no. 1. United States life tables. no. 2. United States life tables, eliminating certain causes of death. no. 3. Methodology of the national and state life tables. no. 4. Some trends and comparison of United States life table data, 1900-1981 -- v. 2. State life tables, Alabama-Wyoming (51 v.) LC Card 85-600190 DDC 304.6/4/0973021 19
1. Mortality - United States - Tables - Collected works. 2. Mortality - United States - Tables - Methodology - Collected works. 3. Mortality - United States - States - Tables - Collected works. 4. United States - Statistics, Vital - Collected works. I. National Center for Health Statistics (U. S.). II. Title: US decennial life tables for 1979-81.
HB1335 .U17 1985 ***NYPL [JLM 86-491]***

U. S. direct investment abroad : balance of payments and direct investment position estimates, 1977-81. Washington, D.C. : U. S. Dept. of Commerce, Bureau of Economic Analysis : For sale by the Supt. of Docs., U. S. G.P.O., 1986. x, 41 p. ; 28 cm. Shipping list no.: 86-1011-P. "November 1986." Chiefly tables. S/N 003-010-00175-5 Item 130-D-1 LC Card 87-600815
1. Investments, American - Statistics. I. United States. Bureau of Economic Analysis. II. Title: US direct investment abroad, balance of payments and direct investment position estimates, 1977-81.
HG4538 .U22 1986

The U. S. dollar . Pick, Franz. Bethel, CT , c1986. xvi, 103 p., [1] folded leaf of plates : ISBN 0-916373-04-5 (pbk.): LC Card 86-210094 DDC 332.4/973 19
HG539 .P5 1986

U. S.-EC relations : protecting the world's open trading system : report of the twenty-sixth meeting of members of Congress and of the European Parliament, January 6-9, 1986, pursuant to H. Res. 981, authorizing the Committee on Foreign Affairs to conduct thorough studies and investigations of all matters coming within the jurisdiction of the committee. Washington : U. S. G.P.O. : For sale by the Supt. of Docs., Congressional Sales Office, U. S. G.P.O., 1986. vii, 78 p. ; 24 cm. At head of title: 99th Congress, 2d session. Committee print. "Printed for the use of the Committee on Foreign Affairs." "June 1986." "59-582 O." LC Card 86-603395 DDC 337.4073 19
1. United States - Foreign economic relations - European Economic Community countries. 2. European Economic Community countries - Foreign economic relations - United States. I. United States. Congress. II. European Parliament. III. United States. Congress. House. Committee on Foreign Affairs.
HF1456.5.E825 U17 1986

U. S. economic history /. Niemi, Albert W. Lanham, MD [1987], c1980. xiii, 475 p. : ISBN 0-8191-6335-X (pbk. : alk. paper) : LC Card 87-10730 DDC 330.973 19
HC103 .N5 1987

U. S. economic review : perspective and prospects. Bala Cynwyd, Pa., USA (150 Monument Rd., Bala Cynwyd 19004-1790) : Chase Econometrics, c1985. 7, 28 p. : ill. ; 28 cm. "December 1986"--Cover. LC Card 87-145506 DDC 338.5/443/0973 19
1. Economic forecasting - United States. 2. United States - Economic conditions - 1981-. 3. United States - Economic conditions - 1981-. 4. Economic history - 1971-. I. Chase Econometrics (Firm). II. Title: US economic review.
HC106.8 .U18 1985

The U. S. economy to 1990 /. Collins, Lora S. New York, N.Y. , c1985. 21 p. : ISBN 0-8237-0307-X (pbk.) LC Card 86-200284 DDC 338.5/443/0973 19
HC106.8 .C636 1985

U. S. engineering plastics industry. Shea, Moira M. The United States engineering plastics industry . Washington, D.C. , 1987. 51 p. : LC Card 87-601518 DDC 338.4/76684/0973 19
HD9661.U62 S54 1987

U. S. errors. Datz, Stephen R. Errors . Loveland, Colo. (P.O. Box 402, Loveland 80537) , 1986. vi, 100 p. : LC Card 87-128178 DDC 769.56973 19
HE6184.E7 D38 1986

U. S. essential air services study /. Lin, Leesha. Ottawa-Hull , c1986. viii, 118 p. : ISBN 0-662-14800-2 (pbk.) LC Card 87-102545 DDC 387.7/1 19
HE9803.A4 L55 1986

The U. S. Hispanic market. Valencia, Humberto. New York, N.Y. [1984] 1 v. (various foliations) : ISBN 0-931634-48-2 (pbk.) LC Card 86-203027 DDC 658.8/348 19
HC110.C6 V35 1984

U. S. imports of textile and apparel products under the multifiber arrangement, 1981-84 /. Taylor, John A. (John Alvin), 1930- Washington, D.C. [1985] v, 136 p. ; LC Card

86-601665 DDC 382/.45677/00973021 19
HD9940.U4 T38 1985

U. S. industrial competitiveness . Ghadar, Fariborz. Lexington, Mass. , c1987. x, 114 p. : ISBN 0-669-15689-2 (alk. paper) LC Card 86-46341 DDC 338.4/7677/00973 19
HD9855 .G47 1987

The U. S. international payments crisis : debt, jobs, and politics : a briefing paper / prepared by the International Economic Policy Association. Washington, D.C. (1400 Eye St., N.W., Suite 510, Washington 20005) : IEPA, [1986] 31 p. : ill. ; 28 cm. Cover title. "January, 1986." Includes bibliographical references. LC Card 87-108567 DDC 382.1/7/0973 19
1. Balance of payments - United States. 2. Balance of trade - United States. I. International Economic Policy Association.
HG3883.U7 U18 1986

U. S. investments and bank loans in South Africa (supplemental material to the hearings and markups of January 31 and February 7, 1984, serial no. 98-14, on District of Columbia South Africa divestment) : staff report for the Committee on the District of Columbia, House of Representatives, Ninety-ninth Congress, first session. Washington : U. S. G.P.O., 1985. vi, 24 p.: 24 cm. Distributed to some depository libraries in microfiche. "April 25, 1985." "Serial no. S-3." Item 1014-A, 1014-B (microfiche) LC Card 85-602615 DDC 332.6/7373/068 19
1. Investments, American - South Africa. 2. Bank loans - South Africa. 3. Bank loans - United States. 4. Bank investments - South Africa. 5. Bank investments - United States. I. United States. Congress. House. Committee on the District of Columbia. II. Title: US investments and bank loans in South Africa.
HG5851.A3 U17 1985

U. S. labor policy in postwar Japan /. Park, Sung-Jo. [Berlin] [c1985] 157 p. : ISBN 3-88548-424-2 LC Card 86-200166 DDC 331.11/0952 19
HD5827.A6 P37 1985

U. S. maritime industries--down for the third time? /. Hilton, Robert, 1927- Washington, D.C. , c1987. vi, 60 p. : ISBN 0-89206-099-9 (pbk.) LC Card 86-31768 DDC 387.5/0973 19
HE745 .H66 1987

The U. S. market for hazardous duty liquid pumps and valves. New York, N.Y. : Frost & Sullivan, c1983. 2 v. (viii, 343 leaves) : ill. ; 29 cm. "August 1983." LC Card 87-401677 DDC 381/.456216 19
1. Chemical plant equipment industry - United States. 2. Pumping machinery industry - United States. 3. Valve industry - United States. 4. Sealing (Technology) - Equipment and supplies. 5. Hazardous substances. 6. Market surveys - United States. I. Frost & Sullivan. II. Title: US market for hazardous duty liquid pumps and valves.
HD9651.5 .U16 1983

The U. S. market for intelligent terminals. New York, N.Y. : Frost & Sullivan, c1983. vi, 195 p. : ill. ; 29 cm. "July 1983." "A1166." LC Card 87-143740 DDC 381/.456213985/0973 19
1. Computer industry - United States. 2. Artificial intelligence. 3. Computer terminals. 4. Market surveys - United States. I. Frost & Sullivan.
HD9696.C63 U5885 1983

The U. S.-Mexico border region : anticipating resource needs and issues to the year 2000 / edited by César Sepúlveda & Albert E. Utton. [El Paso] : Texas Western Press : Center for Inter-American and Border Studies, University of Texas at El Paso, 1984, c1982. viii, 446 p. : ill., maps ; 24 cm. Articles in English and Spanish, each with a summary in the other language. "Papers ... prepared for two conferences on the topic of 'Anticipating transboundary resource needs and issues in the U. S.-Mexico border region to the year 2000' held at San Padre Island, Texas, April 23-24, 1981, and at Querétarp, Mexico, January 28-29, 1982"--P. vii. Sponsored by the Instituto Mexicano Matías Romero de Estudios Diplomáticos, and others. Published also as v. 22, no. 4 of Natural resources journal. Includes bibliographical references. ISBN 0-87404-091-4 (pbk.) LC Card 87-401861 DDC 333.7/0972/1 19
1. Natural resources - Mexican-American Border Region. 2. Mexican-American Border Region - Economic conditions. 3. Mexican-American Border Region - Economic policy. 4. Economic forecasting - Mexican-American Border Region. I. Sepúlveda, César. II. Utton, Albert E., 1931-. III. Instituto Mexicano Matías Romero de Estudios Diplomáticos. IV. Title: US-Mexico border region.
HC137.M46 U17 1984

U. S.-Mexico relations : agriculture and rural development / edited by Bruce F. Johnston ... [et al.]. Stanford, Calif. : Stanford University Press, c1987. xii, 401 p. ; 24 cm. This volume produced during a series of conferences sponsored by the U. S.-Mexico Project between 1981 and 1985. Includes bibliographical references and index. ISBN 0-8047-1319-7 (alk. paper) LC Card 86-23103 DDC 338.1/872 19
1. Agriculture - Economic aspects - Mexico - Congresses. 2. Agriculture - Economic aspects - United States - Congresses. 3. Mexico - Commerce - United States - Congresses. 4. United States - Commerce - Mexico - Congresses. 5. Rural development - Mexico - Congresses. 6. Rural development - United States - Congresses. 7. Agriculture and state - Mexico - Congresses. 8. Agriculture and state - United States - Congresses. I. Johnston, Bruce F., 1919-. II. Project on United States-Mexico Relations. III. Title: US-Mexico relations.
HD1792 .U19 1987

The U. S. Mint /. Wolman, Paul. New York , c1987. 92 p. : ISBN 0-87754-829-3 (lib. bdg.) : LC Card 86-31720 DDC 353.0082/2 19
HG459 .W65 1987

The U. S. mobile radio communications equipment market. New York, N.Y. : Frost & Sullivan, c1983. viii, 253 p. : ill. ; 29 cm. "April 1983." "#A1133." LC Card 87-142226 DDC 384.5/3 19
1. Radio supplies industry - United States. 2. Cellular radio equipment industry - United States. 3. Market surveys - United States. I. Frost & Sullivan. II. Title: United States mobile radio communications equipment market. III. Title: US mobile radio communications equipment market.
HD9696.R363 U684 1983

U. S. national economic policy, 1917-1985 /. Campagna, Anthony S. New York , 1987. xix, 642 p. : ISBN 0-275-92426-2 (alk. paper) : LC Card 86-30316 DDC 338.973 19
HC106.2 .C26 1987

U. S. News & World Report, inc. see **United States News & World Report, inc.**

U. S. News investment guide / edited by John H. Harms. 1st ed. Washington, D.C. (2400 N. St., N.W., Washington 20037-1196) : U. S. News & World Report, c1987. iv, 60 p. : ill. ; 27 cm. LC Card 87-143438 DDC 332.6/78 19
1. Investments - United States. I. Harms, John H. II. United States News & World Report, inc. III. Title: United States News investment guide. IV. Title: US News investment guide.
HG4910 .U25 1987

The U. S. non telecommunications fiber optic component market in the U. S. New York, N.Y. : Frost & Sullivan, c1982. vi, 255 leaves : ill. ; 29 cm. LC Card 87-143641 DDC 381/.456213692/0973 19
1. Fiber optics industry - United States. 2. Market surveys - United States. I. Frost & Sullivan. II. Title: US non telecommunications fiber optic component market in the US.
HD9696.F523 U557 1982

U. S. Postal Service bicentennial postmarks, 1972-1984 /. Rothenberg, Bertram. Johnstown, PA, USA , c1986. 42 p. : ISBN 0-935991-01-8 (pbk.): LC Card 86-224991 DDC 769.56/7/0973 19
HE6187 .A635 no. 110 HE6183.A45

The U. S. primary iron and steel industry since 1958. Washington, D.C. : U. S. Dept. of Commerce, Economic Affairs, Office of Business Analysis, 1985. xvi, 138 p. : ill. ; 28 cm. (Studies in the economics of production) "May 1985." Includes bibliographical references.
1. Iron industry and trade - United States. 2. Steel industry and trade - United States. I. United States. Dept. of Commerce. Office of Business Analysis. II. Title: US primary iron and steel industry since 1958.
NYPL [JLF 86-689]

The U. S. professional/executive workstations market. New York, N.Y. : Frost & Sullivan, c1983. vi, 284 p. : ill. ; 29 cm. "June 1983." "#A1230." Spine title: Professional/executive workstations. LC Card 87-142071 DDC 381/.4500416/0973 19
1. Electronic office machine industry - United States. 2. Market surveys - United States. I. Frost & Sullivan. II. Title: United States professional/executive workstations market. III. Title: US professional/executive workstations market. IV. Title: Professional/executive workstations.
HD9801.U542 U18 1983

U. S. S. R. see **Ukraine.**

U. S.S.R.--looking at an economic map. Korop, P. N. (Petr Nikolaevich) USSR--looking at an economic map /. [Moscow] , c1985. 250 p., [3] p. of plates : LC Card 86-207488 DDC 330.947/0854 19
HC336.25 .K66 1985

U. S. stationary compressors market. New York, N.Y. : Frost & Sullivan, c1983. xi, 271 p. : ill. ; 29 cm. Spine title: Stationary compressors in the U. S. "#A1110." "March 1983." LC Card 87-143527 DDC 380.1/4562153/0973 19
1. Compressor industry - United States. 2. Market surveys - United States. I. Frost & Sullivan. II. Title: Stationary compressors in the U. S. III. Title: US stationary compressors market. IV. Title: Stationary compressors in the US.
HD9705.5.C643 U648 1983

U. S. trade relations in the Pacific Rim : emerging trade problems and commercial opportunities : a report / prepared by the Committee on Energy and Commerce of the U. S. House of Representatives. Washington : U. S. G.P.O. : For sale by the Supt. of Docs., Congressional Sales Office, U. S. G.P.O., 1987. v, 57 p. ; 24 cm. At head of title: 100th Congress, 1st session, Committee print. Distributed to some depository libraries in microfiche. Shipping list no.: 87-175-P. "March 1987." Bibliography: p. 57. "Committee print 100-D." Item 1019-A, 1019-B (microfiche) LC Card 87-601361 DDC 382/.0973/09 19
1. United States - Commerce - Pacific area. 2. Pacific area - Commerce - United States. 3. United States - Commerce - East Asia. 4. East Asia - Commerce - United States. I. United States. Congress. House. Committee on Energy and Commerce. II. Title: US trade relations in the Pacific Rim.
HF3126.5 .U17 1987

U. S. trade relations with Asia : report of a staff study mission to Korea, Taiwan, Hong Kong, China, Thailand, Singapore, and Indonesia, November 30 to December 27, 1986 to the Committee on Foreign Affairs, U. S. House of Representatives. Washington : U. S. G.P.O. : For sale by the Supt. of Docs., Congressional Sales Office, U. S. G.P.O., 1987. vii, 85 p. ; 24 cm. At head of title: 100th Congress, 1st session. Committee print. Distributed to some depository libraries in microfiche. Shipping list no.: 87-121-P. "February 1987." Item 1017-A, 1017-B (microfiche) LC Card 87-601359 DDC 382/.0973/05 19
1. United States - Commerce - Asia - Statistics. 2. Asia - Commerce - United States - Statistics. 3. Competition, Unfair - Asia. 4. United States - Foreign economic relations - Asia. 5. Asia - Foreign economic relations - United States. I. United States. Congress. House. Committee on Foreign Affairs. II. Title: US trade relations with Asia.
HF3118 .U15 1987

U. S. wood-based industry . Ellefson, Paul V. New York , 1984. xxv, 479 p. : ISBN 0-03-063698-1 (alk. paper) : LC Card 84-8278 DDC 338.1/7498/0973 19
HD9755 .45 1984 ***NYPL [JLE 85-706]***

U. S.A.-Japan Conference on Manufacturing Research (1986 : Tokyo, Japan)
Manufacturing research perspectives, U. S.A.-Japan : proceedings of the U. S.A.-Japan Conference on Manufacturing Research, October 27-28, 1986, Tokyo, Japan / edited by Arthur Gerstenfeld, Carole Ganz, Toshio Sata. Amsterdam ; New York : Elsevier, 1987. viii, 198 p. : ill. ; 25 cm. (Advances in industrial engineering . 7) Conference sponsored by the National Science Foundation's Division of International Programs and the Japan Society for the Promotion of Science. Includes bibliographies and indexes. ISBN 0-444-42868-2 LC Card 87-19851 DDC 338.4/767 19
1. United States - Manufactures - Congresses. 2. Japan - Manufactures - Congresses. 3. United States - Industries - Congresses. 4. Japan - Industries - Congresses. I. Gerstenfeld, Arthur, 1927-. II. Ganz, Carole, 1941-. III. Sata, Toshio, 1926-. IV. Title. V. Series.
HD9725 .U17 1986

U. S.-Japan Automotive Industry Conference (6th : 1987? : University of Michigan) The Japanese competition . Ann Arbor, MI , 1987. xii, 124 p. ; ISBN 0-939512-30-0 LC Card 86-31756 DDC 338.4/76292/0952 19
HD9710.J32 J374 1987
NYPL [JFL 81-188 no.15]

U. S.-Third World policy perspectives .
(no. 1) Adjustment crisis in the Third World /. New Brunswick, USA , c1984. x, 186 p. ; ISBN 0-88738-040-9 LC Card 84-8690 DDC 337/.09172/4 19
HC59.7 .A733 1984 ***NYPL [JLE 86-2491]***
(no. 2) Uncertain future . New Brunswick, N.J. , c1984. x, 129 p. ; ISBN 0-88738-041-7 : LC Card 84-16240 DDC 332.1/5 19
HG3891.5 .U53 1984 ***NYPL [JLE 86-2494]***
(no. 5) Development strategies reconsidered /. New Brunswick, N.J., U. S.A. , c1986. viii, 190 p. ; ISBN 0-87855-991-4 (pbk.) : LC Card 85-24582 DDC 338.9/009172/4 19
HC59.7 .D482 1986 ***NYPL [JLE 86-2976]***

U.T.B. Uhlands international directory of technical branches. Uhlands Internationales Technisches Branchen-Adressbuch =. Leipzig , 1926. 22, 767 p. ; LC Card 85-666352
HC282.2 .U45x 1926

UA-CNRS 915 Espaces géographiques et sociétés localisées dans la France de l'Ouest. Colloque Les Périphéries urbaines (1984 : Angers, France) Actes du Colloque Les Périphéries urbaines . Caen , c1985. 270 p. : ISBN 2-905461-03-9 : LC Card 86-173712
HB2263 .C65 1984

UAW politics in the cold war era/. Halpern, Martin, 1945- Albany, N.Y. , c1988. p. cm. ISBN 0-88706-671-2 LC Card 87-13890 DDC 322/.2/0973 19
HD6515.A82 I574 1988

Ubach i Soler, Tomàs M., 1955- El ferrocarril : la xarxa catalana / Tomàs M. Ubach i Soler.1a ed. Barcelona : Ketres, 1984. 232 p. : ill. ; 20 cm. (Col·lecció Ventall . 3) Includes index. Bibliography: p. 223-224. ISBN 84-85256-39-5 LC Card 84-254098
1. Railroads - Spain - Catalonia. 2. Railroads - Spain. I. Title.
HE3199.C38 U23 1984 ***NYPL [JSD 86-434]***

UBATUBA (SÃO PAULO, BRAZIL) - POPULATION.
Marcilio, Maria Luiza. Caiçara . São Paulo-SP (Brasil) , c1986. 244 p. : ISBN 85-05-00523-6 LC Card 87-404833 DDC 304.6/0981/61 19
HD1531.B7 M34 1986

Uberrima fides : Priceforbes Federale Volkskas : a brief history of the group to commemorate the opening of PFV's new headquarters in Johannesburg's Centenary Year of 1986 and to celebrate their 50 years of insurance broking in South Africa / [compiled, J.W. Redding ; written, A.G. Smurthwaite ; researched, D.A. Barker, J.W. Redding, R.R. Rumbelow]. [Johannesburg : P.F.V., 1985?] 69 p. : ill. (some col.) ; 31 cm. ISBN 0-620-08481-2 LC Card 87-146303 DDC 368/.006 19
1. Priceforbes Federale Volkskas (Firm) - History. 2. Insurance companies - South Africa - History. I. Redding, J. W. (John W.). II. Smurthwaite, A. G.
HG8724.3.Z9 P758 1985

Übersee-Museum Bremen. Indonesien-Abteilung. Geinitz, Dedo. Entwicklungszusammenarbeit mit Indonesien . Bremen , 1985. viii, 72 p. : ISBN 3-88299-046-5 LC Card 86-204688
HD9161.I63 A244 1985

Ubezpieczenia komunikacyjne . Zelwiański, Ryszard. Warszawa , 1979. 177, [3] p. : ISBN 83-219-0031-3 LC Card 81-181561
HG9905.P7 Z45 1979

Ubezpieczenia morskie /. Kamiński, Zenon. Gdańsk , 1980. 191 p. ; LC Card 80-129098
HE965 .K26 1980

UC Divestment Coalition. South Africa, the UC connection /. Berkeley, Calif. , 1985. 39 p. : LC Card 86-201134 DDC 332.6/73794/068 19
HG5851.A3 S63 1985

Uchastie trudi͡ashchikhsi͡a v upravlenii proizvodstvom : materialy soveshchanii͡a / [otvetstvennye redaktory V.N. Rysina, V.A. Kikot']. Moskva : Vses. nauchno-issl. in-t sistemnykh issledovaniĭ, 1983. 192, [2] p. : ill. ; 26 cm. Bibliography: p. 192-[193] LC Card 84-210286
1. Industrial management - Soviet Union - Employee participation - Congresses. 2. Industrial management - Employee participation - Congresses. I. Rysina, V. N. II. Kikot', V. A. (Vil' Alekseevich). III. Vsesoi͡uznyĭ nauchno-issledovatel'skiĭ institut sistemnykh issledovaniĭ.
HD5660.S65 U26 1983

Uchastie trudi͡ashchikhsi͡a v upravlenii proizvodstvom : sovetskiĭ opyt : nauchno-analiticheskiĭ obzor / [avtory obzora, A.M. Eremin, S.A. Tolstikov ; otvetstvennyĭ redaktor M.E. Tovmosi͡an]. Moskva : Akademii͡a nauk SSSR, In-t nauch. informat͡sii po obshchestvennym naukam, 1985. 69, [2] p. ; 20 cm. (Serii͡a Aktual'nye problemy razvitogo sot͡sializma) Bibliography: p. 64-[70] LC Card 85-224379
1. Industrial management - Soviet Union - Employee participation. I. Eremin, A. M. (Al'bert Mikhaĭlovich). II. Tolstikov, S. A. III. Tovmosi͡an, M. E. IV. Series.
HD5660.S65 U27 1985

Uchenie K. Marksa ob ėtapakh razviti͡a sposoba proizvodstva i problemy zrelogo sot͡sializma : mezhvuzovskiĭ sbornik / pod redaktsieĭ L.D. Shirokorada. Leningrad : Izd-vo Leningradskogo universiteta, 1985. 150 p. ; 22 cm. At head of title: Ministerstvo vysshego i srednego spet͡sial'nogo obrazovanii͡a RSFSR. Includes bibliographical references. LC Card 86-140577
1. Marxian economics - Congresses. 2. Production (Economic theory) - Congresses. 3. Communism - Soviet Union - Congresses. 4. Marx, Karl, 1818-1883 - Congresses. I. Shirokorad, L. D. (Leonid Dmitrievich). II. Nauchnai͡a konferent͡sii͡a "Uchenie K. Marksa ob ėtapakh razviti͡a sposoba proizvodstva i kontsept͡sii͡a razvitogo sot͡sializma" (1983 : Leningrad, R.S.F.S.R.).
HB97.5 .U24 1985

Uchenye zapiski po statistike .
(t. 41) Statisticheskoe izuchenie proizvoditel'nosti truda /. Moskva , 1981. 407 p. ; LC Card 82-155063 DDC 330/.018 s 331.11/8/0947 19
HA1.A38 A15 t. 41 HC340.L3
NYPL [*QIP 87-1311]
(t. 42) Statisticheskie metody v issledovanii͡akh truda, dokhodov i potreblenii͡a /. Moskva , 1981. 382 p. : LC Card 82-155399
HA1.A38 A15 t. 42 HD7035

Uchet i kal'kulirovanie sebestoimosti produkt͡sii vspomogatel'nykh proizvodstv /. Tishkov, I. E. (Ivan Efremovich) Moskva , 1980. 110 p. ; LC Card 81-143226
HC340.C7 T57 1980

Uchet zatrat na osvoenie novoĭ tekhniki /. Borodkin, Alekseĭ Sergeevich. Moskva , 1985. 142 p. : LC Card 86-219761
HF5686.C8 B597 1985

UCSD PASCAL (COMPUTER PROGRAM LANGUAGE)
McKelvey, James. The debugger's handbook . Belmont, Calif. , c1986. xvi, 138 p. : ISBN 0-534-06432-9 LC Card 85-22628 DDC 005.13/3 19
QA76.73.U25 M34 1986 ***NYPL [JSE 87-65]***

Udal't͡sova, Zinaida Vladimirovna. Istorii͡a krest'i͡anstva v Evrope, Ėpokha feodalizma . Moskva , 1985- v. : ***NYPL [*QGS 86-1566]***

Udenrigsøkonomi i Østeuropa . Nielsen, Margit, 1950- Esbjerg , 1985. 99 p. ; ISBN 87-88521-19-2 LC Card 85-227937
HF1531 .N54 1985

Udviklingen i de finanspolitiske ideer i Danmark 1930-1945 /. Topp, Niels-Henrik. [Copenhagen] [1987] 437 p. ; ISBN 87-574-5100-1 : LC Card 87-149164
HB51 .C63 nr. 30 HJ1222

Udviklingslandenes økonomi /. Laursen, Karsten. Århus [1986] ii, 203 p. : LC Card 86-215996
HC59.7 .L3243 1986

Udyoga kāryālaya (utpādana garne) ko nāma sūcī = Manufacturing establishments directory. [Kathmandu] : Śrī 5 ko Sarakāra, Rāshṭriya Yojāna Āyogako Sacivālaya, Kendriya Tathyāṅka Vibhāga, [1985] 202 p. ; 29 cm. In Nepali. LC Card 87-901652
1. Nepal - Manufactures - Directories. 2. Nepal - Industries - Directories. I. Nepal. Kendriya Tathyāṅka Vibhāga. II. Title: Manufacturing establishments directory.
HD9736.N382 U39 1985

Über interdisziplinäre, sozialwissenschaftliche Forschung in den USA und andernorts /. Klinkmüller, Erich. Berlin , 1986. 177 p. ; ISBN 3-921374-37-5 LC Card 86-211120
HC244.A1 B4 Nr. 47 H62.5.U5

Über Schumpeters Geschichtsdeterminismus /. Winterberger, Gerhard. Tübingen , 1983. 42 p. ; ISBN 3-16-344644-2 LC Card 83-152280 DDC 330/.092/4 19
HB119.S35 W56 1983

Der Überdruss am Überfluss . Klipstein, Michael von. München , c1984. 212 p. : ISBN 3-7892-7194-2 LC Card 84-174408
HD6957.G35 K56 1984

Die Übergangsperiode : sozialökonomische und ideologisch-kulturelle Prozesse im internationalen Vergleich / [Redaktion, Walter Markov ... et al. ; Autoren, Maria Anders ... et al.]. [Leipzig] : Karl-Marx-Universität Leipzig, Interdisziplinäres Zentrum für Vergleichende Revolutionsforschung, 1986. 80 p. ; 21 cm. (Leipziger Beiträge zur Revolutionsforschung, 0323-6714 . Lehrheft 15) "Lehrhefte für Weiterbildung." Includes bibliographies. CONTENTS. - Ergebnisse und Typen der sozialistischen Industrialisierung in der UdSSR und im Mittel- und Südosteuropa / Gerhard Fuchs, Hartmut Kästner, Michael Laschke -- Ansatzpunkte für die Bestimmung des Industrialisierungsweges in heute wenig entwickelten sozialistischen Ländern / Angela Wagener -- Zahlenmässiges Wachstum der Arbeiterklasse sozialistischer Länder Europas während der Übergangsperiode im stadialen historischen Vergleich / Gottfried Dittrich -- Die Überwindung der Dorfbourgeoisie als Klasse in der UdSSR und in den sozialistischen Ländern Mittel- und Südosteuropas / Maria Anders, Lutz-Dieter Behrendt -- Gemeinsamkeiten und Besonderheiten der Entwicklung des Volksbildungswesens in der Übergangsperiode zum Sozialismus / Gottfried Uhlig. LC Card 87-407523 DDC 338.9/009171/7 19
1. Communist countries - Economic policy. 2. Central planning - Communist countries. I. Markov, Walter M. II. Anders, Maria, Dr. sc. phil. III. Series.
HC704 .U24 1986

Übergriffe . Plogstedt, Sibylle. Reinbek bei Hamburg , 1984. 157 p. ; ISBN 3-499-15353-X (pbk.) LC Card 87-672604
HD6060.3 .P56x 1984

Überlebenslesebuch : Wettrüsten, Nord-Süd-Konflikt, Umweltzerstörung / [Autoren, Hans Dietz, Wolfgang Emer, Klaus Schutz ; Redaktion, Wolfgang Müller].Originalausg. Reinbek bei Hamburg : Rowohlt, [1984], c1983. 316 p. : ill. ; 19 cm. (Kulturen und Ideen) Rororo Sachbuch ; 7672 Includes bibliographies and filmographies. ISBN 3-499-17672-6 : LC Card 85-168871
1. Armaments - Economic aspects. 2. International economic relations. 3. Developing countries - Economic conditions. 4. Human ecology. I. Dietz, Hans. II. Series.
HC79.D4 U24 1984

Überprüfung von Aufklärungskampagnen. Methoden und Kriterien zur Überprüfung des Erfolgs von Aufklärungskampagnen . Köln , 1982. 99, [93] p. : LC Card 83-178796
HE5614.5.G3 M37 1982

Die Überwachung der Geschäftsführung, eine betriebswirtschaftliche Betrachtung . Staudinger, Hans-Joachim, 1957- München , c1986. lxxxvi, 340 p. ; ISBN 3-88259-412-8 LC Card 87-125378 DDC 663/.3/0685 19
HD35 .S6745 1986

Ueberwachung kommerzieller Bankkredite /. Zellweger, Bruno. Bern , c1983. xx, 330 p. : ISBN 3-258-03246-7 : LC Card 83-214274
HG1526 .B27 Bd. 77 HG1642.S95

Überwachung kommerzieller Bankkredite. Zellweger, Bruno. Ueberwachung kommerzieller Bankkredite /. Bern , c1983. xx, 330 p. : ISBN 3-258-03246-7 : LC Card 83-214274
HG1526 .B27 Bd. 77 HG1642.S95

Überwälzte Kosten der Gesetze . Tiebel, Christoph. Göttingen , c1986. xv, 256 p. : ISBN 3-525-11333-1 (Deut. Bibl.) LC Card 87-135628 DDC 336.2/4 19
HJ2309 .T48 1986

Überwindung der Sozialstaatskrise : ordnungspolitische Ansätze / Philipp Herder-Dorneich, Helmut Klages, Hans-Günther Schlotter (Hrsg.).1. Aufl.

Baden-Baden : Nomos Verlagsgesellschaft, 1984. 317 p. : ill. ; 23 cm. (Soziale Ordnungspolitik) Summary in English and German. Includes bibliographical references. CONTENTS. - Sozialstaatskrise und soziale Ordnungspolitik / Philipp Herder-Dorneich -- Die Grenzen des Sozialstaates als normatives Problem / Hans-Günther Schlotter -- Gesellschaftliche Probleme des Sozialstaates / Helmut Klages -- Der Beiträg der Gesundheitsökonomie zur Ordnungspolitik des Gesundheitswesens / Gérard Gäfgen -- Konkurrenz der Steuerungssysteme in der gesetzlichen Krankenversicherung / Günter Neubauer -- Aspekte einer demografisch akzentuierten Gesellschaftspolitik / Max Wingen -- Soziale Alterssicherung in ordnungspolitischer Sicht / Hans-Günther Schlotter -- Soziale Sicherung und institutionale Effizienz / Horst Hanusch -- Überlegungen zur Ausgestaltung der Alterssicherung in der Bundesrepublik / Günter Buttler, Helmut Winterstein. ISBN 3-7890-0925-3 LC Card 84-166713
1. Social security - Germany, West. 2. Welfare state. I. Herder-Dorneich, Philipp, 1928-. II. Klages, Helmut. III. Schlotter, Hans Günther. IV. Series.
HD7179 .U35 1984

Uffelmann, Maris. Eglington, Peter. An economic analysis of oilsands policy in Canada . Ottawa, Ont. [1984] 1 v. (various pagings) : LC Card 84-213823 DDC 333.8/232 19
HD9574.C23 W654 1984

Ugarte Ochoa, Marco Aurelio. La Convención, el trabajo y sus luchas sociales /. [Peru? , 1983] (Cusco, Perú : Impr. AMAUTA) 152, vii p., [12] leaves of plates : LC Card 87-127171 DDC 330.985/3 19
HC228.C65 C66 1983

UGC monograph series in economics. Pakistan's development priorities . Karachi , 1984. 390 p. ; LC Card 85-930745 DDC 338.9549/1 19
HC440.5 .P3624 1984b

Ühiskonnateaduste Informatsioonikeskus (Eesti NSV Teaduste Akadeemia)
Issledovaniia Instituta ėkonomiki Akademii nauk Ėstonskoĭ SSR v X piatiletke . Tallin , 1983. 233 p. ; LC Card 86-181279
HB74.9.S65 I86 1983

Izuchenie problem narodonaseleniia v Institute ėkonomiki AN Ėstonskoĭ SSR . Tallin , 1979. 78 p. ; LC Card 81-198604
HB850.5.S65 I97 1979

Uspekhi ėkonomicheskogo i kul′turnogo razvitiia Ėstonskoĭ SSR za gody sovetskoĭ vlasti . Tallin , 1980. 222 p. ; LC Card 81-198881
HC337.E7 U86 1980

Uhl, Joseph N. Kohls, Richard L. Marketing of agricultural products /. New York , London , c1985. xi, 624 p. : ISBN 0-02-365670-0 LC Card 84-817 DDC 381/.41 19
HD9000.5 .K57 1985 ***NYPL [JLE 86-4145]***

Uhlands guide internazionale per tutti i rami tecnici. Uhlands Internationales Technisches Branchen-Adressbuch =. Leipzig , 1926. 22, 767 p. ; LC Card 85-666352
HC282.2 .U45x 1926

Uhlands internationaal technisch branchen-adresboek. Uhlands Internationales Technisches Branchen-Adressbuch =. Leipzig , 1926. 22, 767 p. ; LC Card 85-666352
HC282.2 .U45x 1926

Uhlands international directory of technical branches. Uhlands Internationales Technisches Branchen-Adressbuch =. Leipzig , 1926. 22, 767 p. ; LC Card 85-666352
HC282.2 .U45x 1926

Uhlands internationales technisches branchadressbok. Uhlands Internationales Technisches Branchen-Adressbuch =. Leipzig , 1926. 22, 767 p. ; LC Card 85-666352
HC282.2 .U45x 1926

Uhlands Internationales Technisches Branchen-Adressbuch = Uhlands internationales technisches branchadressbok = Uhlands internationaal technisch branchen-adresboek = Guide international des branches techniques par Uhland = Uhlands international directory of technical branches = Uhlands guida internazionale per tutti i rami tecnici / herausgegeben unter Mitwirkung der Deutschen Polytechnischen Gesellschaft E.V., Leipzig. Leipzig : Uhlands Technische Bibliothek, 1926. 22, 767 p. ; 23 cm. Cover title: U.T.B. Uhlands international directory of technical branches. "Index of the technical terms": 22 p. at beginning. LC Card 85-666352
1. Germany - Industries - Directories. I. Deutsche Polytechnische Gesellschaft e.V. II. Title: Uhlands internationales technisches branchadressbok. III. Title: Uhlands internationaal technisch branchen-adresboek. IV. Title: Guide international des branches techniques par Uhland. V. Title: Uhlands international directory of technical branches. VI. Title: Uhlands guide internazionale per tutti i rami tecnici. VII. Title: U.T.B. Uhlands international directory of technical branches.
HC282.2 .U45x 1926

Uhle-Fassing, Marion. Meissner, Werner, 1937- Weiche Modelle und iterative Schätzung . Frankfurt , New York , c1982. 114 p. : ISBN 3-593-33105-5 : LC Card 83-126780
HB141 .M415 1982

Uhlig, Christian.
Internationale Produktionskooperation im Vorderen Orient : joint ventures und andere Formen unternehmerischer Zusammenarbeit / Christian Uhlig, Michael Lange. Stuttgart : Edition Erdmann, c1983. xvi, 338 p. : ill. ; 21 cm. (Bochumer Materialien zur Entwicklungsforschung und Entwicklungspolitik, 0170-1916 . Bd. 24) Includes bibliographical references. ISBN 3-522-68000-6 LC Card 83-217029
1. International business enterprises - Middle East. 2. Joint ventures - Middle East. 3. International cooperation. I. Lange, Michael. II. Title. III. Series.
HD2891.9 .U44 1983

Die Zukunft der Globalsteuerung /. Bern , c1986. 268 p. ; ISBN 3-258-03573-3 : LC Card 86-182288
HC286.7 .Z82 1986

Uhlig, Karl-Heinz. Internationales Konzernmarketing / Karl-Heinz Uhlig, Hans-Jürgen Hartig. Berlin : Verlag Die Wirtschaft, c1986. 143 p. : ill. ; 19 cm. Includes bibliographical references. ISBN 3-349-00001-0 LC Card 87-118692 DDC 658.8/48 19
1. Export marketing. 2. International business enterprises. I. Hartig, Hans-Jürgen. II. Title.
HF1009.5 .U36 1986

Uhlmann, Luitpold.
Berger, Manfred, Dipl. econ. Auslandsinvestitionen kleiner und mittlerer Unternehmen . Berlin , c1985. 164 p. : ISBN 3-428-05775-9 LC Card 85-161656
HG4538 .B4538 1985

Instrumentelle Aspekte der Investitionsförderung : Gutachten im Auftrag der Kreditanstalt für Wiederaufbau, Frankfurt/Main / von Luitpold Uhlmann, Manfred Berger. München : Ifo-Institut für Wirtschaftsforschung, 1986. vii, 270 p. : ill. ; 21 cm. (Ifo Studien zur Finanzpolitik, 0081-7279 . 41) Includes bibliographical references. ISBN 3-88512-024-0 LC Card 86-215244 DDC 332.63 19
1. Capital investments - Germany, West. I. Berger, Manfred, Dipl. econ. II. Kreditanstalt für Wiederaufbau. III. Title. IV. Series.
HG4028.C4 U367 1986

Investitionsverhalten und Unternehmensgrösse / von Luitpold Uhlmann, Manfred Berger. Berlin : Duncker & Humblot, c1986. 307 p. ; 24 cm. (Schriftenreihe des IFO-Instituts für Wirtschaftsforschung . Nr. 119) Bibliography: p. [157]-158. ISBN 3-428-06010-5 LC Card 86-216522
1. Capital investments - Germany, West. 2. Corporations - Germany, West - Finance. 3. Small business - Germany, West - Finance. I. Berger, Manfred, Dipl. econ. II. Title. III. Series.
HG4028.C4 U37 1986

Uhlmann, Rolf. Andres, Willy. Finanzbuchhaltung /. Zürich , 1983. 179 p. : ISBN 3-286-50261-8 LC Card 83-225439
HF5645 .A64 1983

Uibopuu, Henn-Jüri, 1929- Osteuropa im Blickpunkt . Linz [1985?] 168 p. ; LC Card 87-142952 DDC 382/.091713/01717 19
HF1411 .O687 1985

Uil′iam Petti /. Anikin, Andreĭ Vladimirovich. Moskva , 1986. 92, [3] p. ; LC Card 86-206468 DDC 330.15/3 19
HB103.P5 A83 1986

UITENHAGE (SOUTH AFRICA) - CENSUS, 1980.
Bevolkingsensus 1980, uitgesoekte statistiese streek Port Elizabeth/Uitenhage/Kirkwood =. [Pretoria] [1985] xix, 317 p. : ISBN 0-621-09480-3 : LC Card 85-241531
HA4701.Z9 P673 1985

Az új növekedési pálya feltételei és követelményei /. Hoós, János. Budapest , 1985. 227, [2] p. : ISBN 963-221-508-7 : LC Card 86-128355
HC300.28 .H664 1985

UJAMAA VILLAGES - TANZANIA.
Collier, Paul. Labour and poverty in rural Tanzania . Oxford [Oxfordhire] , New York , 1986. vii, 143 p. : ISBN 0-19-828531-0 : LC Card 86-5303 DDC 307.1/4/09678 19
HN797.Z9 C625 1986 ***NYPL [JLD 87-511]***

UK banking after deregulation. Mullineux, A. W. U.K. banking after deregulation /. London , New York , c1987. 180 p. ; ISBN 0-7099-4689-9 LC Card 87-6742 DDC 332.1/0941 19
HG2988 .M85 1987

UK companies and their subsidiary or related companies in South Africa and Namibia. London : Anti Apartheid Movement, [1986] [18] p. ; 20 x 31 cm. "September 1986." Cover title. LC Card 87-138700 DDC 338./8941/068 19
1. Investments, British - South Africa. 2. Investments, British - Namibia. I. Anti-Apartheid Movement.
HG5851.A3 U39 1986

UK consumer electronics. U.K. consumer electronics. Norwalk, Conn., U. S.A. (6 Prowitt St., Norwalk 06855) , c1986. vi, 198 leaves ; LC Card 86-228422 DDC 381/.45621381/0941 19
HD9696.A3 G785 1986

UK occupation and employment trends to 1990 : an employer-based study of the trends and their underlying causes / [by the Institute of Manpower Studies for the Occupations Study Group] ; edited by Amin Rajan and Richard Pearson. London ; Boston : Butterworths, 1986. xxiv, 249 p. : ill., forms ; 25 cm. Bibliography: p. 201. ISBN 0-408-02980-3 : LC Card 86-13617 DDC 331.12/0941 19
1. Employment forecasting - Great Britain. 2. Manpower planning - Great Britain. 3. Great Britain - Occupations - Forecasting. I. Rajan, Amin, 1942-. II. Pearson, Richard. III. Institute of Manpower Studies (Great Britain). IV. Occupations Study Group (Great Britain). V. Title: U.K. occupation and employment trends to 1990.
HD5765.A6 U38 1986 ***NYPL [JLE 86-4156]***

UK tax savings for the higher paid (1979) /. Blackstone, L. R. (Lance R.) London , c1979. 10 p. ; LC Card 81-112830
HJ4708.A7 B533 1979

Układy powiązań w kooperacji przemysłowej /. Samborska-Boć, Elżbieta. Wrocław , 1982. 103 p. ; LC Card 83-109302
HD3517.7.A4 S28 1982

Ukraïna. see **Ukraine.**

UKRAINE - COMMERCE - RUSSIAN S.F.S. R.
Skruten′, I. S. Spivdruzhnist′ u pratsi /. Kyïv , 1982. 117 p. : LC Card 83-200434
HC337.U5 S514 1982

UKRAINE - ECONOMIC CONDITIONS - 1918-
Rabochiĭ klass Ukrainskoĭ SSR . Kiev , 1986. 238 p. ; LC Card 86-155918
HD8529.U42 R33 1986

Stanovlenie i razvitie sovetskoĭ ėkonomicheskoĭ nauki na Ukraine . Kiev , 1983. 285, [2] p. ; LC Card 84-120015 DDC 330/.072/04771 19
HB74.9.S65 S72 1983 ***NYPL [*QGA 87-275]***

UKRAINE - ECONOMIC CONDITIONS - 1945-
Alymov, Aleksandr Nikolaevich. Sbalansirovannost′ narodnokhoziaistvennogo razvitiia . Kiev , 1986. 221, [3] p. ; LC Card 86-214583
HC337.U5 A793 1986

Ekonomiko-statystychne vyvchenniia mizhhaluzevykh narodnohospodars′kykh kompleksiv . Kyïv , 1985. 95 p. ; LC Card 86-194555
HC337.U53 I573 1985

Gorbachev, Mikhail Sergeevich, 1931- Aktivno

deĭstvovat′, ne teri͡at′ vremeni . Moskva , 1985. 45 p. ; LC Card 86-181428
HC337.U53 I525 1985

Narodno-khozi͡aĭstvennye proport͡sii, ikh planirovanie i prognozirovanie /. Kiev , 1985. 318 p. : LC Card 86-210651
HC337.U5 P5 1985 t. 1

Radi͡ans′ka Ukraïna . Kyïv , 1985. 205 p., [2] p. of plates : LC Card 87-151437
HC337.U5 R215 1985

Skruten′, I. S. Spivdruz͡hnist′ u prat͡si /. Kyïv , 1982. 117 p. : LC Card 83-200434
HC337.U5 S514 1982

Struktura obshchestvennogo proizvodstva i tendent͡sii ee izmenenii͡a . Kiev , 1979. 113 p. ; LC Card 81-130407
HC337.U53 I527 1979

V i͡edynomu narodnohospodars′komu kompleksi /. Uzhhorod , 1982. 179 p. : LC Card 83-180335
HC337.U52 W485 1982

Vosproizvodstvo trudovykh resursov /. Kiev , 1984. 177, [3] p. ; LC Card 86-189052
HD5797.U37 V67 1984

UKRAINE - ECONOMIC POLICY.
Stanovlenie i razvitie sovetskoĭ ėkonomicheskoĭ nauki na Ukraine . Kiev , 1983. 285, [2] p. ; LC Card 84-120015 DDC 330/.072/04771 19
*HB74.9.S65 S72 1983 NYPL [*QGA 87-275]*

UKRAINE - ECONOMIC POLICY - 1917-
Sokolov, V. N. (Vi͡acheslav Nikolaevich) Kursom na sotsialisticheskui͡u industrializat͡sii͡u /. Kiev , 1985. 158, [2] p. ; LC Card 87-113771
HD9656.S56 U377 1985

UKRAINE - ECONOMIC POLICY - DATA PROCESSING.
Pravovye problemy RASU /. Kiev , 1985. 303 p. : LC Card 86-139849
HC337.U5 P65 1985

UKRAINE - HISTORY - 1921-1944.
UKRAINE - HISTORY - 1921-1944 - CONGRESSES.
Famine in Ukraine, 1932-1933 /. Edmonton , Downsview, Ont., Canada , 1986. 192 p. ; ISBN 0-09-286243-8 LC Card 87-148658 DDC 363.8/0947/71 19
HC337.U53 F314 1986

UKRAINE - INDUSTRIES - HISTORY.
V bitvakh za sovetskui͡u Ukrainu . Kiev , 1985. 172 p. ; LC Card 85-170194
HC337.U53 D48 1985

UKRAINE - INDUSTRIES - HISTORY - 18TH CENTURY.
Ponomarev, Alekseĭ Mikhaĭlovich. Rozvytok kapitalistychnykh vidnosyn u promyslovosti Ukraïny XVIII st. /. L′viv , 1971. 181 p. ; LC Card 82-105634
HC337.U5 P58 1971

UKRAINE - MANUFACTURES - HISTORY - 18TH CENTURY.
Ponomarev, Alekseĭ Mikhaĭlovich. Rozvytok kapitalistychnykh vidnosyn u promyslovosti Ukraïny XVIII st. /. L′viv , 1971. 181 p. ; LC Card 82-105634
HC337.U5 P58 1971

UKRAINE - OCCUPATIONS - CASE STUDIES.
Sem′i͡a i vosproizvodstvo struktury trudovoĭ zani͡atosti . Kiev , 1984. 238 p. : LC Card 86-142706
HB2698.U38 S46 1984

UKRAINE - POPULATION.
Teorii͡a i praktika ėkonomiki demoprot͡sessa . Kiev , 1982. 181 p., [2] folded leaves of plates : LC Card 83-145373
HB883.5 .T46 1982

UKRAINE - POPULATION POLICY.
Teorii͡a i praktika ėkonomiki demoprot͡sessa . Kiev , 1982. 181 p., [2] folded leaves of plates : LC Card 83-145373
HB883.5 .T46 1982

UKRAINE - SOCIAL CONDITIONS - 1945-
Radi͡ans′ka Ukraïna . Kyïv , 1985. 205 p., [2] p. of plates : LC Card 87-151437
HC337.U5 R215 1985

UKRAINE - SOCIAL POLICY.
Kondrati͡uk, K. K. (Konstantin Konstantinovich) Profspi͡lky Ukraïny na zavershai͡ushchem ėtape stroitel′stva sotsializma /. L′vov , 1985. 173 p. ; LC Card 87-165263
HD6735.U5 K65 1985

UKRAINE, WESTERN - ECONOMIC CONDITIONS.
V i͡edynomu narodnohospodars′komu kompleksi /. Uzhhorod , 1982. 179 p. : LC Card 83-180335
HC337.U52 W485 1982

Ukrainian Soviet Socialist Republic. see **Ukraine.**

UKRAINIANS - HAWAII - HISTORY.
Ewanchuk, Michael, 1908- Hawaiian ordeal . Winnipeg, Man. , c1986. xii, 180 p. : ISBN 0-9690768-7-8 (pbk.) : LC Card 87-156576
HD4875.U5 E93x 1986

Ukraïns′ka Radi͡ans′ka Sot͡sialistychna Respublika. see **Ukraine.**

Ukraïns′ka respublikans′ka rada profesiĭnykh spilok. Rekomendat͡sii po ukreplenii͡u trudovoĭ i proizvodstvennoĭ distsipliny /. Kiev , 1984. 41 p. ; LC Card 86-181301
HF5549.5.L3 R45 1984

Ukrainskai͡a Sovet͡skai͡a Sot͡sialisticheskai͡a Respublika. see **Ukraine.**

Ukreplenie material′nykh osnov sotsialisticheskogo obraza zhizni / pod redakt͡sieĭ Savchenko P.V. Moskva : In-t ėkonomiki Akademii nauk SSSR, 1984. 156 p. ; 21 cm. Includes bibliographical references. LC Card 85-240384
1. Labor and laboring classes - Soviet Union. 2. Service industries - Soviet Union. 3. Soviet Union - Economic conditions - 1976-. I. Savchenko, P. V. (Pol′ Vi͡acheslavovich). II. Institut ėkonomiki (Akademii͡a nauk SSSR).
HD8526.5 .U38 1984

Ulack, Richard, 1942- Costello, Michael A. Mobility and employment in urban Southeast Asia . Boulder , 1987. xvi, 190 p. : ISBN 0-8133-7352-2 (pbk. : alk. paper) : LC Card 87-10649 DDC 307.2 19
HB2107 .C67 1987

Ulbrich, Wolfgang. Kenya : Voraussetzungen und Möglichkeiten der industriellen Entwicklung / Wolfgang Ulbrich. Hamburg : Afrika-Verein, 1971. 308 p., [1] folded leaf of plates : map ; 21 cm. (Afrika Industrieberichte. 16) Bibliography: p. 306-307. LC Card 85-163190
1. Kenya - Economic conditions - 1963-. 2. Kenya - Industries. 3. Infrastructure (Economics) - Kenya. 4. Kenya - Commerce. I. Title. II. Series.
HC865 .U43 1971

Ulbricht, Mechthild, 1938- Von der Bereitschaft zum technischen Wandel /. Berlin , 1981. 278 p. : ISBN 3-8009-1339-9 LC Card 83-194263
HC79.T4 V66 1981

ULI-UMTA Policy Forum on Joint Development of Rail Transit Facilities . ULI/UMTA Policy Forum on Joint Development of Rail Transit Facilities (1986 : Washington, D.C.] [Washington, D.C.] [1987] iv, 107 p. : ISBN 0-87420-671-5 (pbk.) LC Card 87-82098 DDC 333.3/8 19
HD257 .U43 1986

Ul′i͡anov, Vladimir Il′ich. see **Lenin, Vladimir Il′ich, 1870-1924.**

Ul′i͡anovskiĭ, R. A. (Rostislav Aleksandrovich) Agrarnai͡a Indii͡a mezhdu mirovymi voĭnami : opyt issledovanii͡a kolonial′no-feodal′nogo kapitalizma / R.A. Ul′i͡anovskiĭ. Moskva : Izd-vo "Nauka," Glav. red. vostochnoĭ lit-ry, 1981. 342, [2] p. ; 21 cm. Bibliography: p. 334-[343] LC Card 82-102795 DDC 338.1/0954 19
1. Agriculture - Economic aspects - India. 2. India - Rural conditions. 3. India - Economic conditions - 1918-1947. I. Title.
HD2072 .U44 1981

Ulinder, Daniel D. Hamilton, S. W. (Stanley William), 1939- Foundations of real estate financing . Vancouver , c1982. xv, 319 p. : ISBN 0-409-98843-X LC Card 87-143264
HF5695.5.R3 H36 1982

Ulit͡skiĭ, L. I. (Lazar′ Ioakhimovich) K organizatsii koksokhimicheskoĭ promyshlennosti v Sredneĭ Azii. Tashkent, Izd-vo AN UzSSR, 1945. 63 p. diagrs. 23 cm. At head of title: Akademii͡a nauk Uzbekskoĭ SSR. Institut ėkonomiki. Bibliography: p. 61-63. LC Card 51-55383
1. Coke industry - Soviet Central Asia. 2. Coal-tar industry - Soviet Central Asia. I. Title.
HD9559 .C7S68

ULI/UMTA Policy Forum on Joint Development of Rail Transit Facilities (1986 : Washington, D.C.) ULI-UMTA Policy Forum on Joint Development of Rail Transit Facilities : June 11-12, 1986. [Washington, D.C.] : Urban Land Institute, [1987] iv, 107 p. : ill. ; 28 cm. "ULI catalog number U01"--P. iii. ISBN 0-87420-671-5 (pbk.) LC Card 87-82098 DDC 333.3/8 19
1. Real estate development - United States - Congresses. 2. Land use, Urban - United States - Congresses. 3. Local transit - United States - Congresses. I. Urban Land Institute. II. United States. Urban Mass Transportation Administration. III. Title.
HD257 .U43 1986

Ullah, Philip. Unemployed people . Milton Keynes, England , Philadelphia, PA, USA , 1987. 292 p. ; ISBN 0-335-15507-3 LC Card 87-5792 DDC 305/.90694 19
HD5708 .U57 1987

Ullman, Harlan.
Forecasts for U. S. maritime industries in 1989 : balancing national security and economic considerations / by Harlan K. Ullman, Paula J. Pettavino. Washington, D.C. : Center for Strategic and International Studies, Georgetown University, c1984. ix, 42 p. : ill. ; 22 cm. (Significant issues series . v. 6, no. 17) Bibliography: p. 37-42. ISBN 0-89206-069-7 (pbk.) LC Card 84-27501 DDC 338.4/76238/0973 19
1. United States. Navy - Reserve fleets. 2. Shipbuilding industry - United States. 3. Merchant marine - United States. I. Pettavino, Paula J. II. Title. III. Series.
VM299.6 .U45 1984 NYPL [JLD 87-155]

Hilton, Robert, 1927- U. S. maritime industries--down for the third time? /. Washington, D.C. , c1987. vi, 60 p. : ISBN 0-89206-099-9 (pbk.) LC Card 86-31768 DDC 387.5/0973 19
HE745 .H66 1987

Ullmann, Hans-Peter. Staatsschulden und Reformpolitik : die Entstehung moderner öffentlicher Schulden in Bayern und Baden, 1780-1820 / von Hans-Peter Ullmann. Göttingen : Vandenhoeck & Ruprecht, c1986. 2 v. (842 p.) ; 25 cm. (Veröffentlichungen des Max-Planck-Instituts für Geschichte . 82) Bibliography: p. 754-824. Includes index. ISBN 3-525-35398-7 LC Card 86-210338
1. Debts, Public - Germany (West) - Bavaria - History. 2. Finance, Public - Germany, West - Bavaria - History. 3. Debts, Public - Germany (West) - Baden - History. 4. Finance, Public - Germany (West) - Baden - History. I. Title. II. Series.
HJ8655.B38 U55 1986

Ullmo, Pierre-Antoine. Epargne et développement /. Paris , 1985. 410 p. : ISBN 2-7178-0855-8 : LC Card 86-149765
HC59.72.S3 E62 1985

Ulloa Elías, Manuel. Silva Ruete, Javier. La respuesta de Latinoamérica a la crisis internacional /. [Lima, Peru?] [1984] 99 p. ; LC Card 86-154728
HF1480.5 .S55 1984

Ul′masov, Akhmed Ul′masovich.
Uzbekistan--ėkonomicheskiĭ rost i blagosostoi͡anie naselenii͡a / A. Ul′masov. Tashkent : Izd-vo "Uzbekistan", 1978. 182 p. ; 20 cm. Includes bibliographical references. LC Card 81-145788
1. Uzbek S.S.R. - Economic conditions. 2. Cost and standard of living - Uzbek S.S.R. I. Title.
HC337.U96 U95 1978

Ulph, Alistair.
Demand, equilibrium, and trade . London , 1984. xx, 256 p. : ISBN 0-333-33184-2 LC Card 87-673439
HB34 .D45x 1984b

Oligopoly, competition, and welfare /. Oxford, OX, UK , New York, NY, USA , 1985. 191 p. : ISBN 0-631-14479-X (pbk.) LC Card 85-11200 DDC 338.8/2 19
HD2757.3 .O44 1985 NYPL [JLE 86-1961]

Pereira, A. (Armand) Socio-economic and policy implications of energy price increases /. Aldershot, Hants, England , Brookfield, Vt., USA , c1987. xxiv, 317 p. ; ISBN 0-566-05520-1 : LC Card 87-11955 DDC 338.2/3 19
HD9560.4 .P37 1987

Ulph, David, 1946- Economics, growth, and sustainable environments . New York , 1988.

viii, 205 p. : ISBN 0-312-01240-3 : LC Card 87-12520 DDC 363.7 19
HC79.E5 E2774 1988

Ulrichsen, Niels. J.A.K.--en dansk krisebevægelse / af Niels Ulrichsen. København : Den danske historiske forening, 1978. 202 p. ; 24 cm. (Skrifter udgivet af det Historiske institut ved Københavns universitet . bd. 9) Bibliography: p. 155-157. ISBN 87-87462-13-3 LC Card 87-462108
1. Agriculture - Economic aspects - Denmark - History. 2. J.A.K. - History. 3. Denmark - Economic conditions - 1918-1945. 4. Kristiansen, Kristian Engelbrecht, 1882-. I. Title. II. Series.
HD2002 .U45 1978

Ultanbaev, R. R. (Rafaėl′ Rafil′benovich) Ladygin, Boris Nikolaevich. Istoricheskiĭ opyt sotrudnichestva stran SĖV /. Moskva , 1980. 284 p. ; LC Card 81-130900
HC244 .L282 1980

The ultimate benefit book . Brentlinger, Marilyn E., 1925- Cleveland, Ohio , c1987. 231 p. : ISBN 0-940601-01-X : LC Card 87-12171 DDC 361.7/068/1 19
HG177 .B74 1987

The ultimate deterrent . Shepherd, William G. New York , 1986. x, 137 p. ; ISBN 0-275-92368-1 (alk. paper) : LC Card 86-20486 DDC 355/.03 19
UA10.5 .S524 1986 ***NYPL [JLE 87-884]***

Ulymzhiev, D. B. (Dashi Batuevich) Put′ mongol′skogo aratstva k sotsializmu / D.B. Ulymzhiev ; otvetstvennye redaktory I.I. Kuznetsov, Sh.B. Chimitdorzhiev. Novosibirsk : Izd-vo "Nauka," Sibirskoe otd-nie, 1987. 283, [5] p. ; 21 cm. At head of title: Akademiia nauk SSSR. Sibirskoe otdelenie. Buriatskiĭ filial. Buriatskiĭ institut obshchestvennykh nauk. Bibliography: p. 267-[284]. LC Card 87-159668
1. Agriculture, Cooperative - Mongolia - History. 2. Collectivization of agriculture - Mongolia - History. 3. Agriculture and state - Mongolia - History. I. Kuznetsov, I. I. (Il′ia Innokent′evich). II. Chimitdorzhiev, Sh. B. III. Title.
HD1491.M55 U49 1987

Uma Vasudev. see Vasudev, Uma.

Umani, Mario. Un procedimento per la ripartizione ottimale di una collettività in classi : applicazioni in campo assicurativo / Mario Umani. [Trieste] : Università degli studi di Trieste, Facoltà di economia e commercio, Istituto di statistica, 1978. 19 p. ; 24 cm. (Pubblicazione / Università degli studi di Trieste, Facoltà di economia e commercio, Istituto di statistica . n. 17) Summary in English. Bibliography: p. 19. LC Card 81-111875 DDC 368/.092 19
1. Insurance, Automobile - Risks - Econometric models. 2. Cluster analysis. I. Series: Trieste. Università. Istituto di statistica. Pubblicazioni, n.17. II. Title.
HG9970 .U46 1978 ***NYPL [TB (Triesta. Università Istituto do statistica. Pubblicazioni. n.17)]***

Umapathy, Srinivasan. Current budgeting practices in U. S. industry : the state of the art / Srinivasan Umapathy ; foreword by John Leslie Livingstone. New York : Quorum Books, 1987. xxxix, 176 p. ; 22 cm. Bibliography: p. [167]-171. Includes index. ISBN 0-89930-250-5 (lib. bdg. : alk. paper) LC Card 87-5969 DDC 658.1/54 19
1. Budget in business. 2. Corporations - United States - Finance - Planning. I. Title.
HG4028.B8 U46 1987

Umbach, Eberhard. Leben im Jahr 2000 und danach . Berlin , c1984. 213 p. : ISBN 3-7605-8571-X LC Card 85-128359
HB3595 .L43 1984

Umeå, Sweden. Universitetet. Sociologiska institutionen.
Research reports.
(no. 61) Wolvén, Lars-Erik. Konsumenter, konsumentpolitik, rationalitet och välfärd . Umeå , 1981. 83 leaves ; LC Card 82-105540 DDC 658.8/342/09485 19
HC380.C63 W64 ***NYPL [JLM 74-106 no.61]***

Umfassende Intensivierung und Infrastruktur /. Koziolek, Helmut. Berlin , 1986. 68 p. ; LC Card 86-169897
HC290.795.C3 K68 1986

Die Umrechnung der Jahresabschlüsse ausländischer Konzernunternehmen und die Verrechnung der daraus resultierenden Umrechnungsdifferenzen . Müller, Herbert, 1948- Bochum , 1986. x, 348 p. ; ISBN 3-88339-547-1 LC Card 87-143252 DDC 657/.48 19
HG3853.7 .M84 1986

Umsetzung organisatorischer Neuerungen . Kempf, Thomas. Berlin , 1986. 237 p. : ISBN 3-88118-133-4 LC Card 87-114986
HD58.8 .K46 1986

Umstot, Denis D. Understanding organizational behavior / Denis D. Umstot. 2nd ed. St. Paul : West Pub. Co., c1988. xviii, 532 p. : ill. ; 27 cm. Includes bibliographies and indexes. ISBN 0-314-62488-0 LC Card 87-25255 DDC 658.3 19
1. Organizational behavior. I. Title.
HD58.7 .U47 1988

Umurzakov, Sadybakas. Sipozium "Geografiia v Kirgizii" (1980 : Frunze, Kirghiz S.S.R.) Sovremennye problemy geografii Kirgizii . Frunze , 1980. 167 p. : LC Card 82-121674
HC337.K545 S56 1980

Umwegproduktion und Positivität des Zinses . Reiss, Winfried, 1941- Berlin , c1981. 152 p. : ISBN 3-428-05009-6 LC Card 82-146836 DDC 332.8/2/0724 19
HB539 .R423 1981 ***NYPL [JLE 86-2623]***

Umweltaussenpolitik . Prittwitz, Volker. Frankfurt , New York , c1984. vii, 211 p. : ISBN 3-593-33369-4 LC Card 84-202897
HC240.9.A4 P75 1984

Das umweltbewusste Konsumentenverhalten . Balderjahn, Ingo. Berlin , c1986. ix, 277 p. ; ISBN 3-428-06107-1 LC Card 87-113640 DDC 658.8/34/0724 19
HF5415.3 .B316 1986

Die Umweltpolitik im Spannungsfeld politischer und wirtschaftlicher Interessen /. Aeberhardt, Werner. Köln , 1985. 134, [9] p. : ISBN 3-921471-55-9 : LC Card 86-145456
HC400.E5 A33 1985

Umweltpolitik in Bayern / [Herausgeber, Bayerisches Staatsministerium für Landesentwicklung und Umweltfragen]. München : Das Ministerium, [1986] 176 p. : ill. (chiefly col.) ; 19 cm. LC Card 86-204249
1. Environmental policy - Germany, West - Bavaria. 2. Environmental protection - Germany (West) - Bavaria. I. Bavaria (Germany). Bayerisches Staatsministerium für Landesentwicklung und Umweltfragen.
HC287.B3 U48 1986

Umweltpolitisches Gespräch (1983 : Bad Godesberg, Bonn, Germany) Ökonomische Instrumente der Umweltpolitik : neuer Weg oder Sackgasse? : Symposium der Deutschen Stiftung für Umweltpolitik / Umweltpolitisches Gespräch ; Schirmherr, Axel Wernitz ; Leitung, K.-H. Hansmeyer. Berlin : E. Schmidt, c1984. 108 p. ; 21 cm. (Beiträge zur Umweltgestaltung. Bd. A 93) Includes bibliographical references. ISBN 3-503-02401-8 LC Card 86-152141
1. Environmental policy - Germany (West) - Congresses. 2. Environmental protection - Germany (West) - Congresses. I. Hansmeyer, Karl-Heinrich. II. Deutsche Stiftung für Umweltpolitik. III. Title.
HC290.5.E5 U625 1983

Umweltprobleme des Ballungsraums Mexiko Stadt unter besonderer Berücksichtigung der Wasserwirtschaft /. Schmengler, Uwe. [Berlin , 1985] 120, [16] leaves : LC Card 86-116997
HC138.M4 S35 1985

Umweltprobleme und Umweltbewusstsein in der DDR / Beiträge von Werner Gruhn ... [et al.] ; [herausgegeben von der Redaktion Deutschland Archiv]. Köln : Verlag Wissenschaft und Politik, c1985. 252 p. : ill. ; 21 cm. Includes bibliographical references. CONTENTS. - Die Entwicklung der Umwelt in der DDR / Cord Schwartau -- Landwirtschaft und Umwelt in der DDR / Andreas Kurjo -- Zum nuklearen Umweltschutz in der DDR / Manfred Melzer -- Umweltschutz als ökonomischer Faktor / Werner Gruhn -- Die offizielle Ökologiedebatte in der DDR / Gerhard Timm -- Die Gesellschaft für Natur und Umwelt / Peter Wensierski -- Gesellschaftlicher Dissens im Wandel / Hubertus Knabe -- Zweifel an der Industriegesellschaft / Hubertus Knabe. ISBN 3-8046-8649-4 LC Card 86-119841
1. Environmental policy - Germany, East. 2. Environmental protection - Germany, East. I. Gruhn, Werner. II. Redaktion Deutschland Archiv (Germany).
HC290.795.E5 U585 1985

Umweltschutz : Herausforderung unserer Generation / Hans J. Elster ... [et al.] ; mit einem Vorwort von Heinz Riesenhuber. [Mainz] : v. Hase & Koehler, c1984. 130 p. ; 21 cm. (Dokumentation / Studienzentrum Weikersheim e.V. . 10) Papers from a meeting sponsored by the Studienzentrum Weikersheim e.V. and held Nov. 12-13, 1983. Bibliography: p. 123-127. ISBN 3-7758-1086-2 LC Card 85-146233
1. Environmental policy - Germany (West) - Congresses. 2. Environmental policy - Congresses. 3. Environmental protection - Germany (West) - Congresses. 4. Environmental protection - Congresses. 5. Human ecology - Germany (West) - Congresses. 6. Human ecology - Congresses. I. Elster, Hans-Joachim, 1908-. II. Studienzentrum Weikersheim. III. Series: Dokumentation (Studienzentrum Weikersheim) , 10.
HC290.5.E5 U64 1984

Umweltschutz in öffentlichen Budgets /. Roloff, Otto, 1937- Regensburg , c1986. 278 p. : ISBN 3-924956-14-6 LC Card 87-129127 DDC 363.7/00943 19
HC290.5.E5 R65 1986

Umweltschutz, Umweltverschmutzung und Wirtschaftswachstum . Schäkermann, Thomas, 1957- München , c1986. v, 249 p. ; ISBN 3-88259-404-7 LC Card 86-226458 DDC 363.7/32 19
HC79.P55 S355 1986

Umweltschutz und industrielle Standortentscheidung /. Knödgen, Gabriele, 1949- Frankfurt/Main , New York , c1982. 219 p. : ISBN 3-593-33158-6 LC Card 83-110653
HC59.72.P55 K58 1982

Umweltschutz und Verwaltung : der öffentliche Dienst zwischen politischem Anspruch und Realisierungsnot / Hartkopf ... [et al.]. Bonn : Godesberger Taschenbuch-Verlag, c1986. 171 p. ; 18 cm. (Schriften zur Staats- und Gesellschaftspolitik . 23) Godesberger Taschenbücher Papers presented at the 27th Beamtenpolitische Arbeitstagung, held in Bad Kissingen, Jan. 7-8, 1986. CONTENTS. - Umweltschutz und Verwaltung / Friedrich Zimmermann -- Umweltschutz, Anforderung an die Verwaltung / Heinrich von Lersner -- Umweltgestaltung, Verwaltung im Dialog mit den Betroffenen / Jürgen Salzwedel -- Umweltinformation, Verwaltung zwischen Datenhunger und Datenwust / Klaus Töpfer -- Umweltverwaltung, eine organisatorische Herausforderung / Günter Hartkopf -- Umweltschutz im Interessenkonflikt (Forum) ISBN 3-87999-040-9 LC Card 87-136048 DDC 363.7/056/0943 19
1. Environmental policy - Germany (West) - Congresses. 2. Environmental protection - Germany (West) - Congresses. 3. Environmental law - Germany (West) - Congresses. I. Hartkopf, Günter. II. Beamtenpolitische Arbeitstagung (27th : 1986 : Bad Kissingen, Germany). III. Series.
HC290.5.E5 U645 1986

Umweltverbände . Leonhard, Martin. Opladen , c1986. xiii, 352 p. ; ISBN 3-531-11820-X LC Card 86-192568
HC290.5.E5 L46 1986

Die Umweltvorsorge im Rahmen der Landesplanung Nordrhein-Westfalen . Weimar, Robert. Frankfurt am Main , New York , c1983. xxiii, 313 p. : ISBN 3-8204-7669-5 LC Card 83-206670
HC287.N6 W44 1983

Umzugsverhalten der Bevölkerung in ausgewählten ländlichen Teilräumen am Beispiel der Region Neckar-Alb . Heinzmann, Ute. Tübingen , 1985. 69, [4] p. : LC Card 86-195573
HB2056.N43 H45 1985

Un capitalisme idéal /. Marrey, Bernard. Paris , c1984. 236 p., [24] p. of plates : ISBN 2-86215-060-6 : LC Card 84-252196 DDC 338.7/6413374/0944 19
HD9200.F74 M356 1984
NYPL [JLD 87-1579]

UN End of Decade Conference on Women (1985 : Nairobi, Kenya) Women and employment in Kenya . [Nairobi] [1985] iii, 46 p. ; LC Card 85-981502 DDC 331.4/09676/2 19
HD6210.5 .W65 1985

Un procedimento per la ripartizione ottimale di una collettività in classi . Umani, Mario. [Trieste] , 1978. 19 p. ; LC Card 81-111875 DDC 368/.092 19
HG9970 .U46 1978 *NYPL [TB (Triesta. Università Istituto do statistica. Pubblicazioni. n.17)]*

Un semáforo en rojo . Betancur, Belisario, 1923- [Bogotá] [1984] 12, 12, 12 p. ; LC Card 87-125515 DDC 338.98 19
HC125 .B42 1984

Una caracterización socioeconómica del grupo ganaderoexportador (los casos de San Carlos y Guanacaste) 1960-1980 /. Aguilar Bolaños, Irene. San José, Costa Rica , 1985. xiii, 260 p. ; LC Card 86-107500
HD9433.C83 S223 1985 *NYPL [JLF 87-74]*

Unbalanced accounts . Lieberman, Annette. New York , c1987. xx, 281 p. ; ISBN 0-87113-141-2 LC Card 86-28845 DDC 332.4/01/9 19
HG179 .L49 1987

Unbewusst dagegen . Wünschmann, Andreas, 1942- Stuttgart , 1984, c1980. 177 p. : ISBN 3-87959-214-4 (pbk.) LC Card 87-673462
HD9698.A2 W86x 1984

Unblocking organizational communication . Francis, Dave. Aldershot, Hants, England , Brookfield, Vt. , c1987. xiv, 185 p. ; ISBN 0-566-02572-8 : LC Card 87-14836 DDC 658.4/5 19
HD30.3 .F73 1987

**Uncertain future : **commercial banks and the Third World / Richard E. Feinberg and Valeriana Kallab, editors ; contributors, Lawrence J. Brainard ... [et al.]. New Brunswick, N.J. : Transaction Books, c1984. x, 129 p. ; 23 cm. (U. S.-Third World policy perspectives / Overseas Development Council . no. 2) Includes bibliographical references. ISBN 0-88738-041-7 : LC Card 84-16240 DDC 332.1/5 19
1. Loans, Foreign - Developing countries - Addresses, essays, lectures. 2. Debts, External - Developing countries - Addresses, essays, lectures. 3. Banks and banking, International - Developing countries - Addresses, essays, lectures. I. Feinberg, Richard E. II. Kallab, Valeriana. III. Brainard, Lawrence J. IV. Series: U. S.-Third World policy perspectives , no. 2.
HG3891.5 .U53 1984 *NYPL [JLE 86-2494]*

Uncertain returns : the multimillion dollar market in reimported pharmaceuticals : a staff report / prepared for the use of the Subcommittee on Oversight and Investigations of the Committee on Energy and Commerce, U. S. House of Representatives. Washington : U. S. G.P.O. : For sale by the Supt. of Docs., Congressional Sales Office, U. S. G.P.O., 1986. v, 210 p. ; 24 cm. At head of title: 99th Congress, 2d session. Committee print. Distributed to some depository libraries in microfiche. Shipping list no.: 86-657-P. "July 1986." Includes bibliographical references. "Committee print 99-GG." Item 1019-A, 1019-B (microfiche) LC Card 86-603379 DDC 364.1/42 19
1. Drug trade - Corrupt practices. 2. Drug trade - United States. I. United States. Congress. House. Committee on Energy and Commerce. Subcommittee on Oversight and Investigations.
HD9665.5 .U53 1986

Uncertain victory . Kloppenberg, James T. New York , 1986. x, 546 p. ; ISBN 0-19-503749-9 : LC Card 85-21636 DDC 320.5/315/094 19
JA84.E9 K57 1986 *NYPL [JLE 86-2574]*

UNCERTAINTY.
Aiginger, Karl. Production and decision theory under uncertainty /. Oxford [Oxfordshire] , New York, NY, USA , 1987. p. cm. ISBN 0-631-14792-6 : LC Card 87-23854 DDC 338.5 19
HB241 .A52 1987

Ford, J. L. Economic choice under uncertainty . New York , c1987. ix, 146 p. ; ISBN 0-312-01244-6 : LC Card 87-18806 DDC 330.1 19
HB615 .F674 1987

Galts, Helmut. Ungewissheit und Planungsmethodik . Münster [1983] vi, 234 p. : ISBN 3-88660-143-9 LC Card 84-178712
HB615 .G35 1983

Hanuscheck, Randolf. Investitionsplanung auf der Grundlage vager Daten . Idstein , 1986. xiii, 196 p. : ISBN 3-925196-19-6 LC Card 86-230117
HG4521 .H2385 1986

Laux, Helmut. Grundfragen der Erfolgskontrolle /. Berlin , New York , c1986. x, 161 p. : ISBN 0-387-17037-5 LC Card 86-232406
HD30.23 .L39 1986

Planning in turbulence /. Jerusalem , 1986. xii, 158 p. : ISBN 965-223-657-8 (pbk.) LC Card 87-163701 DDC 658.4/012 19
HD87.5 .P5 1986

Quick, Rolf H. Informationsprozesse auf spekulativen Märkten . Thun , c1984. vii, 291 p. : ISBN 3-87144-790-0 : LC Card 84-159793
HG3853 .Q53 1984

Social choice and public decision making /. Cambridge [Cambridgeshire] , New York , 1986. xix, 215 p. : ISBN 0-521-30454-7 LC Card 86-8580 DDC 339 19
HB846.8 .S59 1986 *NYPL [JLE 86-4189]*

Strong, Norman, 1954- Information and capital markets /. Oxford, UK , New York, NY, USA , 1987. x, 222 p. : ISBN 0-631-13834-X : LC Card 86-31721 DDC 332/.041 19
HG4523 .S77 1987

Surveys in the economics of uncertainty /. Oxford, UK , New York, NY, USA , 1987. 232 p. : ISBN 0-631-15335-7 LC Card 87-10366 DDC 330 19
HB615 .S97 1987

Tietzel, Manfred. Wirtschaftstheorie und Unwissen . Tübingen , 1985. viii, 208 p. ; ISBN 3-16-944919-2 LC Card 86-147807
HB175 .T55 1985

Winter, Richard, 1946- Pretiale Lenkung bei sicheren und unsicheren Erwartungen /. Frankfurt am Main , New York , c1986. 243 p. ; ISBN 3-8204-9816-8 LC Card 87-407541 DDC 658.8/16 19
HD62.45 .W56 1986

Uncertainty and the labor market . McKenna, C. J. New York , c1985. viii, 165 p. : ISBN 0-312-82861-6 : LC Card 85-1988 DDC 331.11 19
HD5707 .M39 1985 *NYPL [JLD 86-3666]*

UNCERTAINTY - CONGRESSES.
Society for Risk Analysis International Workshop on Uncertainty in Risk Assessment, Risk Management, and Decision Making (1984 : Knoxville, Tenn.) Uncertainty in risk assessment, risk management, and decision making /. New York , c1987. x, 538 p. : ISBN 0-306-42557-2 LC Card 87-2403 DDC 658 19
HD61 .S625 1984

Uncertainty in risk assessment, risk management, and decision making /. Society for Risk Analysis International Workshop on Uncertainty in Risk Assessment, Risk Management, and Decision Making (1984 : Knoxville, Tenn.) New York , c1987. x, 538 p. : ISBN 0-306-42557-2 LC Card 87-2403 DDC 658 19
HD61 .S625 1984

UNCERTAINTY (INFORMATION THEORY)
Hopf, Michael. Informationen für Märkte und Märkte für Informationen /. Frankfurt am Main , 1983. iv, 237 p. : ISBN 3-922182-14-3 : LC Card 84-180866
HB133 .H66 1983

UNCERTAINTY - MATHEMATICAL MODELS.
Ball, Helmut. Zukunftsvorsorge und ökonomische Entwicklung . Frankfurt [am Main] , New York , c1984. 263 p. : ISBN 3-593-33318-X LC Card 84-175872
HD75.5 .B35 1984

Sengupta, Jatikumar. Optimal decisions under uncertainty . Berlin , New York , 1985. 286 p. ; ISBN 0-387-15032-3 (U. S.) LC Card 84-26683 DDC 658.4/033 19
HD30.23 .S46 1985 *NYPL [JLE 86-4652]*

UNCERTAINTY - MATHEMATICAL MODELS - CONGRESSES.
Monetary policy and uncertainty . Baden-Baden , 1986. 262 p. : ISBN 3-7890-1257-2 (pbk.) LC Card 86-225786 DDC 332.4/0724 19
HG230.3 .M655 1986

UNCTAD statistical pocketbook / United Nations Conference on Trade and Development. New York : United Nations, 1984. xv, 96 p. : ill. (some col.) ; 21 cm. LC Card 86-200987 DDC 330.9172/4 19
1. Developing countries - Commerce - Statistics. 2. Developing countries - Economic conditions - Statistics. I. United Nations. Conference on Trade and Development.
HF4055 .U53 1984

La UNCTAD y los problemas de transporte marítimo de los países en desarrollo . Hoyos Lascano, Fernando. Bogotá, D.E. , 1975 ([Bogotá] : Gráficas Venus) 99 p. ; LC Card 85-205214
HE807 .H69 1975

--und heute die ganze Welt . Köhler, Otto, 1935- Hamburg , c1986. 350 p. : ISBN 3-89136-081-9 LC Card 87-116787
HD9654.9.I5 K64 1986

Undécimo censo general de población y vivienda. Situación habitacional en Venezuela . [Caracas] [1986- v. <1 > : ISBN 980-280-043-0 LC Card 87-114711 DDC 363.5/1/0987/021 19
HD7331.A3 S57 1986

Under construction . Silver, Marc L., 1950- Albany , c1986. xi, 251 p. ; ISBN 0-88706-308-X LC Card 85-30447 DDC 331.7/624/0973 19
HD6956.B92 U67 1986 *NYPL [JLE 86-4616]*

Under the influence [motion picture] / National Highway Traffic Safety Administration, Dept. of Transportation. Washington, DC : The Administration : Distributed by National Audiovisual Center, 1983. 1 film reel (25 min.) : sd., col. ; 16 mm. Title from data sheet. Made in 1975. General public, police officers, and police trainees. Issued also as videorecording. Shows the results of experiments conducted to determine whether .1 percent alcohol in the bloodstream impairs an individual's driving abilities. LC Card 84-700613 DDC 362.2 11
1. Drinking and traffic accidents. 2. Alcohol - Physiological effect. I. United States. National Highway Traffic Safety Administration. II. National Audiovisual Center.
HE5620.D7

Under the influence [videorecording] / National Highway Traffic Safety Administration, Dept. of Transportation. Washington, DC : The Administration : Distributed by National Audiovisual Center, 1983. 1 videocassette (25 min.) : sd., col. Title from data sheet. Made in 1975. General public, police officers, and police trainees. Issued as U-matic 3/4 in. or Beta 1/2 in. or VHS 1/2 in. Issued also as motion picture. Shows the results of experiments conducted to determine whether .1 percent alcohol in the bloodstream impairs an individual's driving abilitites. LC Card 84-706720 DDC 362.2 11
1. Drinking and traffic accidents. 2. Alcohol - Physiological effect. I. United States. National Highway Traffic Safety Administration. II. National Audiovisual Center.
HE5620.D7

Underbilaga till rapport från 1983 års livsmedelskommittés expertgrupp för prisregleringsfrågor : vissa jordbrukspolitiska förtursfrågor : kompensationssystem. [Sweden : s.n., 1983] (Jönköping : Lbs offset) 1 v. (various pagings) : ill. ; 21 cm. LC Card 85-191640
1. Food industry and trade - Sweden. 2. Food prices - Sweden. 3. Price regulation - Sweden. I. Sweden. 1983 års livsmedelskommitté. Expertgruppen för prisregleringsfrågor. Vissa jordbrukspolitiska förtursfrågor.
HD9015.S86 U47 1983

Undercutting sanctions . Hunter, Jane, 1943- Washington, DC (918 16th St. NW, Suite 501, Washington 20006) , c1987. iv, 71 p. ; LC Card 87-403525 DDC 337.68 19
HF1613.4 .H86 1987

UNDERDEVELOPED AREAS - ECONOMIC ASSISTANCE. see **ECONOMIC ASSISTANCE.**

UNDERDEVELOPED AREAS - RURAL DEVELOPMENT. see **RURAL DEVELOPMENT.**

UNDERDEVELOPED AREAS - TECHNICAL ASSISTANCE. see **TECHNICAL ASSISTANCE.**

Underdevelopment and choices in agriculture . Chakrabarti, Rajendra M. New Delhi , 1986.

xv, 322 p. : LC Card 86-903184 DDC 338.1/0954 19
HC435.2 .C466 1986

Underdevelopment is a state of mind . Harrison, Lawrence E. [Cambridge, Mass.] , Lanham, MD , 1988, c1985. p. cm. ISBN 0-8191-6490-9 (pbk. : alk. paper) : LC Card 87-24678 DDC 330.98/0038 19
HC125 .H384 1988

UNDEREMPLOYMENT - AMAZON RIVER REGION.
Silva, Maria José Oliveira e. A sociedade amazônica e o problema social da desocupação e subocupação /. Belém , 1974. 42 p., 53 leaves : LC Card 86-183026
HB3564.A73 S55 1974

UNDEREMPLOYMENT - AUSTRALIA.
Bosworth, Derek L. Labour utilisation in Australia . [Bedford Park, S. Aust.] [1986] i, 205 p. : LC Card 86-229498 DDC 331.12/5/0994 19
HD5850.A6 B67 1986

UNDEREMPLOYMENT - BRAZIL - RIO GRANDE DO SUL.
O Emprego no Rio Grande do Sul . Porto Alegre , 1985. 163 p. : LC Card 85-207909
HD5755.R54 E46 1985

UNDEREMPLOYMENT - COLOMBIA.
Hopkins, Mike. Alternatives to unemployment and underemployment . Boulder , 1985. xiv, 129 p. : ISBN 0-8133-0200-5 (pbk.) LC Card 85-45007 DDC 331.13/79861 19
HD5757.A6 H67 1985 ***NYPL [JLD 86-2149]***

UNDEREMPLOYMENT - FRANCE.
Godinot, Xavier, 1951- Les travailleurs sous-prolétaires face aux mutations de l'emploi /. Paris [1985] 155 p. ; ISBN 2-904972-04-08 LC Card 86-166442
HD5775 .G63 1985

UNDEREMPLOYMENT - GERMANY (WEST) - ECONOMETRIC MODELS.
Busch, Wilfried, 1948- Staatsausgaben, Produktion und Beschäftigung . Frankfurt am Main , New York , c1984. viii, 304 p. : ISBN 3-8204-5352-0 LC Card 85-199154
HJ7792 .B87 1984

UNDEREMPLOYMENT - INDIA.
Mehta, Vadilal Lallubhai, 1903- Unemployment, inequality, parallel economy . Ahmedabad , 1982. viii, 141 p., [1] leaf of plates : LC Card 82-900764 DDC 331.13/7954 19
HD5819 .M43 1982 ***NYPL [JLD 85-2751]***

UNDEREMPLOYMENT - MATHEMATICAL MODELS.
Eichberger, Jürgen, 1952- Geld und Kredit in einer Ökonomie mit festen Preisen . Frankfurt am Main , New York , c1984. 152 p. : ISBN 3-8204-5441-1 LC Card 85-191492
HG230.3 .E53 1984

UNDEREMPLOYMENT - UNITED STATES.
Dumas, Lloyd J. The overburdened economy . Berkeley , c1986. xiv, 297 p. ; ISBN 0-520-05686-8 (alk. paper) LC Card 85-20856 DDC 331.13/7973 19
HD5724 .D775 1986 ***NYPL [JLD 86-2582]***

Sheets, Robert G. The impact of service industries on underemployment in metropolitan economies /. Lexington, Mass. , c1987. xii, 185 p. ; ISBN 0-669-14575-0 (alk. paper) LC Card 86-45884 DDC 331.13 19
HD5709.2.U6 S54 1987

UNDERGROUND RAILROADS. see **SUBWAYS.**

UNDERGROUND WATER. see **WATER, UNDERGROUND.**

Undersøkelse av personer som var med i en del av arbeidsmarkedsetatens tiltak pr. 31. mars 1978. Oslo : Arbeidsdirektoratet, 1979. iv, 68, 4 p. ; 30 cm. LC Card 83-109890
1. Unemployment - Norway. 2. Unemployment - Norway - Statistics. I. Norway. Arbeidsdirektoratet.
HD5800.A6 U53 1979

Undersøkelser for mastergraden i etnologi . (nr. 1) Winge, Harald. Føringaredskaper i Aker fogderi . Oslo , 1976. 105 p. : LC Card 86-460271
HE259.Z7 A48 1976

Understanding a company /. Little, Jeffrey B. New York , c1988. 47 p. : ISBN 1-555-46622-2 LC Card 87-17654 DDC 657/.33 19
HG4028.B2 L57 1988

Understanding Africa's rural households and farming systems / edited by Joyce Lewinger Moock ; foreword by Bede N. Okigbo. Boulder : Westview Press, 1986. xiv, 234 p. : ill. ; 23 cm. (Westview special studies on Africa) Bibliography: p. 217-232. ISBN 0-8133-7175-9 : LC Card 85-32318 DDC 338.1/0967 19
1. Family farms - Africa, Sub-Saharan - Addresses, essays, lectures. 2. Households - Africa, Sub-Saharan - Addresses, essays, lectures. 3. Rural families - Africa, Sub-Saharan - Addresses, essays, lectures. I. Moock, Joyce Lewinger.
HD1476.A357 U53 1986 ***NYPL [JLE 86-4336]***

Understanding and using financial statements. Chalfin, Robert J. Seminar material for understanding and using financial statements /. Newark, N.J. (15 Washington St., Newark 07102) , c1987. 95, [43] leaves ; LC Card 87-402010 DDC 657/.33/024344 19
HF5681.B2 C415 1987

Understanding and using Lotus one-two-three. Ross, Steven C. Understanding and using Lotus 1-2-3 . St. Paul , c1987. xv, 232, [34] p. : ISBN 0-314-34741-0 (pbk.) LC Card 86-33964 DDC 650/.028/55369 19
HF5548.4.L67 R673 1987

Understanding and using Lotus 1-2-3 . Ross, Steven C. St. Paul , c1987. xv, 232, [34] p. : ISBN 0-314-34741-0 (pbk.) LC Card 86-33964 DDC 650/.028/55369 19
HF5548.4.L67 R673 1987

Understanding and using microcomputers /. Zimmerman, Steven M. St. Paul , c1988. xxvi, 371 p. : ISBN 0-314-60096-5 (pbk.) LC Card 87-19044 DDC 650/.028/5416 19
HF5548.2 .Z58 1988

Understanding and using SuperCalc 3 /. Ross, Steven C. St. Paul , c1987. xiii, 184, [27] p. : ISBN 0-314-30123-2 (pbk.) LC Card 86-32548 DDC 005.36/9 19
HF5548.4.S86 R67 1987

Understanding and using Symphony /. Allegretti, Enzo V. St. Paul, MN , c1987. xvii, 226, [31] p., [4] p. of plates : ISBN 0-314-34640-6 (pbk.) LC Card 87-4986 DDC 005.36/9 19
HF5548.4.S95 A45 1987

Understanding business /. Nickels, William G. St. Louis , 1987. xxix, 721, 115, 2 p. : ISBN 0-8016-3627-2 LC Card 86-23080 DDC 650 19
HF5351 .N53 1987

Understanding Capital . Foley, Duncan K. Cambridge, Mass. , 1986. viii, 183 p. : ISBN 0-674-92087-2 (alk. paper) LC Card 86-4736 DDC 335.4/1 19
HB501 .F644 1986 ***NYPL [JLE 86-4606]***

Understanding factoring and trade credit /. Crichton, Susan. London , 1986. xv, 199 p. : ISBN 0-08-039204-0 (pbk.) : LC Card 87-122377 DDC 658.8/8 19
HG3752.3 .C75 1986

Understanding first-time recreation vehicle buyers : a research report / by Burson-Marsteller Research. Reston, VA (P.O. Box 2999, 1896 Preston White Dr., Reston 22090) : Prepared for Recreation Vehicle Industry Association, c1986. xxvi, 80 p. ; 28 cm. LC Card 87-108982 DDC 381/45629226/0973 19
1. Recreational vehicle industry - United States. 2. Consumers - United States - Attitudes. 3. Consumers' preferences - United States. 4. Market surveys - United States. I. Burson-Marsteller (Firm). II. Recreation Vehicle Industry Association (U. S.).
HD9710.37.U62 U53 1986

Understanding hazardous waste crime . Rebovich, Donald. [Trenton?] [1986] viii, 70 p. : LC Card 86-622805 DDC 364.1/42 19
HD9975.U53 A1157 1986

Understanding hospitality accounting I /. Cote, Raymond. East Lansing, Mich. , c1987. p. cm. ISBN 0-86612-035-1 : LC Card 87-15724 DDC 657/.837 19
HF5686.H75 C63 1987

Understanding industrial relations in modern Japan /. Koike, Kazuo, 1932- New York , 1987. p. cm. ISBN 0-312-01301-9 : LC Card 87-24068 DDC 331/.0952 19
HD8726.5 .K548 1987

Understanding organizational behavior /. Umstot, Denis D. St. Paul , c1988. xviii, 532 p. : ISBN 0-314-62488-0 LC Card 87-25255 DDC 658.3 19
HD58.7 .U47 1988

Understanding peasant agriculture . Astroth, Joseph H., 1955- Chicago, Ill. , 1987. p. cm. ISBN 0-89065-127-2 (pbk.) : LC Card 87-15099 DDC 333.76/13/0724 19
HD879.P8 A77 1987

Understanding people in organizations /. Dailey, Robert C. St. Paul, MN , c1988. xviii, 525 p. : ISBN 0-314-24254-6 LC Card 86-32460 DDC 658.4 19
HD58.7 .D34 1988

Understanding poverty / edited by Giovanni Sarpellon. Milano, Italy : F. Angeli, c1984. 355 p. : ill. ; 22 cm. (Persona e società . 2) Includes bibliographies. LC Card 84-249441 DDC 339.4/6/094 19
1. Poor - European Economic Community countries - Addresses, essays, lectures. 2. Poverty - Addresses, essays, lectures. I. Sarpellon, Giovanni. II. Series.
HC240.9.P6 U53 1984 ***NYPL [JLD 86-1196]***

Understanding regression analysis . Schroeder, Larry D. Beverly Hills , c1986. 95 p. : ISBN 0-8039-2758-4 LC Card 85-63790
NYPL [JLK 77-39 no.57]

Understanding technical change as an evolutionary process /. Nelson, Richard R. Amsterdam ; New York : viii, 125 p. ; ISBN 0-444-70207-5 (pbk.) LC Card 87-9109 DDC 338/.06 19
HC79.T4 N45 1987

Understanding the equalization rate / New York State Div[i]sion of Equalization and Assessment. Albany, N.Y. (Governor Nelson A. Rockefeller Empire State Plaza, Albany 12223) : The Division, [1986] 28 p. : ill. ; 28 cm. "October, 1986." LC Card 87-620729 DDC 336.22/2 19
1. Real property tax - New York (State) - Rates and tables. 2. Assessment - New York (State). I. New York (State). Division of Equalization and Assessment.
HJ4249 .U53 1986

Understanding the futures markets. New York, NY (100 Church St., Suite 1850 New York 10007) : Commodity Research Bureau, c1987. 61 p. ; 22 cm. LC Card 87-129996 DDC 332.64/4 19
1. Financial futures. 2. Forward exchange. 3. Commodity exchanges. I. Commodity Research Bureau (New York, N.Y.).
HG6024.A3 U64 1987

Understanding the language of banking. Washington, D.C. (1120 Connecticut Ave., N.W., Washington 20036) : American Institute of Banking, American Bankers Association, c1986. v, 258 p. : ill. ; 24 cm. "Catalog #624700"--Cover. LC Card 87-111196 DDC 332.1/014 19
1. Banks and banking - Dictionaries. I. American Institute of Banking.
HG151 .U53 1986

Understanding the securities markets : the fundamentals of trading in stocks and bonds. Jersey City, NJ (75 Montgomery St., Jersey City 07302) : Commodity Research Bureau, c1986. 36 p. ; 22 cm. LC Card 87-130670 DDC 332.63/2 19
1. Securities - United States. 2. Stocks - United States. 3. Bonds - United States. I. Commodity Research Bureau (Chicago, Ill.).
HG4910 .U53 1986

Understanding Third World politics and economics /. Stone, Carl. Brown's Town P. O., St. Ann, Jamaica , c1980. 105 p. ;
NYPL [JLD 87-364]

Understanding unemployment /. Summers, Lawrence H. Cambridge, Mass. , c1988. p. cm. ISBN 0-262-19265-9 LC Card 87-3866 DDC 331.13/7 19
HD5707.5 .S85 1988

Understanding United States government growth . Berry, William Dale. New York , 1987. xiv, 212 p. : ISBN 0-275-92509-9 (alk.

paper) : LC Card 87-11818 DDC 336.73 19
HJ257.2 .B47 1987

Understanding Wall Street /. Little, Jeffrey B. Blue Ridge Summit, PA , c1987. 219 p. : ISBN 0-8306-3120-8 : LC Card 87-3628 DDC 332.6/78 19
HG4910 .L54 1987

Understanding Wall Street /. Little, Jeffrey B. [Wall Street library.] Blue Ridge Summit, PA , 1986. p. cm. ISBN 0-8306-3010-4 (pbk.) : LC Card 86-27791 DDC 332.6/78 19
HG4921 .L63 1986

Underwood, John.
Trinidad busway. 1980. Joefield-Napier, Wallace. Financial integration and interest rate linkages between North Atlantic and Caribbean economies, January 1968 to December 1976 / by W. Joefield-Napier. Trinidad busway : a user survey / by J.R. Underwood and L.G. Cadan. St. Augustine, Trinidad [1980] vii, 82 p. : LC Card 81-132125 DDC 332.8/2/0724 19
HG1623.C27 J64 1980 ***NYPL [Sc E 86-329]***

Underwood, Lorraine A. How to find information about executives /. Washington, DC , c1986. 72 p. ; ISBN 0-934940-44-4 (pbk.) : LC Card 86-51569 DDC 658.4/0072 19
HD38.25.U6 H69 1986

UNDERWRITING. see **INSURANCE; SECURITIES.**

UNDP/ILO Regional Project for Strengthening Labour/Manpower Administration in Asia and the Pacific. Sub-regional Symposium on Labour Inspection in Agriculture (1982 : Denpasar, Indonesia) Labour inspection in agriculture in Southeast Asia . Bangkok , 1983. 218 p. : ISBN 92-2-103533-6 LC Card 86-915732
HD1537.A785 S8 1982

The Uneasy alliance : managing the productivity-technology dilemma / edited by Kim B. Clark, Robert H. Hayes, Christopher Lorenz. Boston, Mass. : Harvard Business School Press, c1985. x, 485 p. : ill. ; 24 cm. (Research colloquium / Harvard Business School) Includes bibliographies and index. ISBN 0-87584-172-4 LC Card 85-8709 DDC 658.5 19
1. Industrial productivity - Addresses, essays, lectures. 2. Efficiency, Industrial - Addresses, essays, lectures. 3. Technological innovations - Addresses, essays, lectures. I. Clark, Kim B. II. Hayes, Robert H. III. Lorenz, Christopher, 1946-. IV. Series: Research colloquium (Harvard University. Graduate School of Business Administration).
HD56 .U53 1985 ***NYPL [JLE 86-2361]***

Uneasy lies the head . Stewart, Walter. Toronto , 1987. 266 p. ; ISBN 0-00-217757-9 LC Card 87-144685 DDC 354.7109/2 19
HD4005 .S74 1987

UNEMPLOYED - AUSTRALIA - CASE STUDIES.
Wooden, Mark. The effects of redundancy . [Bedford Park, S. Aust.] [1987] 52 p. : LC Card 87-170621 DDC 331.13/7994 19
HD5708.55.A8 W66 1987

UNEMPLOYED - AUSTRIA - CASE STUDIES.
Entlassen ins Nichts . Berlin , c1983. 255 p. ; ISBN 3-8012-0089-2 (pbk.) LC Card 87-672743
HD5779 .E57x 1983

UNEMPLOYED - BELGIUM.
Chômage des jeunes . Bruxelles [1984] 49 p. : LC Card 84-222918
HD6276.B42 C48 1984

UNEMPLOYED - COSTA RICA - STATISTICS.
Encuesta nacional de hogares, empleo y desempleo . San José, Costa Rica , 1982. xi, xi, 86 p. ; LC Card 82-202317
HD5734.A6 E53 1982

UNEMPLOYED - EDUCATION - THAILAND.
Thailand. Samnakngān Khana Kammakān Kansksā hæng Chāt. Education and employment from world capitalism to the rural Thais . Bangkok, Thailand , 1985. 46 p. : LC Card 86-915875 DDC 331.13/79593 19
HD5822.55.A6 T47 1985

UNEMPLOYED - GERMANY - CASE STUDIES.
Entlassen ins Nichts . Berlin , c1983. 255 p. ; ISBN 3-8012-0089-2 (pbk.) LC Card 87-672743
HD5779 .E57x 1983

UNEMPLOYED - GERMANY - HISTORY - 20TH CENTURY.
The German unemployed . Beckenham, Kent , 1987. xviii, 314 p. : ISBN 0-7099-0941-1
NYPL [JLD 87-801]

UNEMPLOYED - GERMANY, WEST.
Kovacic, Anton. Suppe genug, aber Seele kaputt . München , c1986. 185 p. ; ISBN 3-453-43075-1 : LC Card 86-230927
HC290.5.P6 K68 1986

Weissbuch Arbeitszeitverkürzung /. Stuttgart , 1983. 152 p. : ISBN 3-87959-212-8 LC Card 84-163631
HD5108.2.G47 W45 1983

UNEMPLOYED - GERMANY (WEST) - INTERVIEWS.
Alheit, Peter. Beschädigtes Leben . Frankfurt[/Main] , New York , c1986. 361 p. ; ISBN 3-593-33606-5 LC Card 86-148737
HD6276.G4 A44 1986

Arbeitslos . Reinbek bei Hamburg , 1982. 170 p. : ISBN 3-499-15024-7 (pbk.) LC Card 87-672730
HD5779 .A6x 1982

UNEMPLOYED - GERMANY (WEST) - RUHR (REGION)
Fokkink, Manfred, 1955- Denk ja nicht, Du bist selber schuld . Gelsenkirchen-Buer , 1980. 180 p. : LC Card 82-114713
HD6276.G4 F6 1980 ***NYPL [JLE 86-1457]***

UNEMPLOYED - GOVERNMENT POLICY - INDIA - CONGRESSES.
Problems of urban unemployment. Calcutta , 1981. ix, 114 p. ; LC Card 83-907262 DDC 331.13/77/0954 19
HD5819 .P76 1981 ***NYPL [JLF 86-1766]***

UNEMPLOYED - GREAT BRITAIN.
Men without work . New York , 1985. xii, 447 p. ; ISBN 0-8240-7619-2 (alk. paper) : LC Card 85-13069 DDC 331.13/7941 19
HD5765.A6 M46 1985
NYPL [JLD 87-1031]

UNEMPLOYED - GREECE.
Phrankos, Dionysios M., 1926- Hoi makrochronies exelixeis tou oikonomika mē energou plēthysmou tēs Hellados /. Athēna , 1983. 148 p. : LC Card 85-152730
HD5811.83.A6 P47 1983

UNEMPLOYED - INDIA - BOMBAY.
Brahm Prakash. The urban dead-end? . Bombay , 1983. xii, 138 p., [5] p. of plates : LC Card 84-900007 DDC 331.12/5/0954792 19
HD5820.B6 B72 1983 ***NYPL [JLD 86-3828]***

UNEMPLOYED - MATHEMATICAL MODELS.
Hodeige, Christian H., 1958- Job-Search im strukturierten Arbeitsmarkt . Freiburg , c1985. 166 p. ; ISBN 3-7930-0113-1 LC Card 86-142859
HD5701.6 .H62 1985

McKenna, C. J. Uncertainty and the labor market . New York , c1985. viii, 165 p. : ISBN 0-312-82861-6 : LC Card 85-1988 DDC 331.11 19
HD5707 .M39 1985 ***NYPL [JLD 86-3666]***

Unemployed people : social and psychological perspectives / edited by David Fryer and Philip Ullah. Milton Keynes, England ; Philadelphia, PA, USA : Open University Press, 1987. 292 p. ; 24 cm. Includes bibliographies and indexes. ISBN 0-335-15507-3 LC Card 87-5792 DDC 305/.90694 19
1. Unemployment - Social aspects. 2. Unemployment - Psychological aspects. 3. Unemployed. I. Fryer, David. II. Ullah, Philip.
HD5708 .U57 1987

UNEMPLOYED - SERVICES FOR - AUSTRALIA - WESTERN AUSTRALIA.
Wiechec, Jane. Employment, the community link /. Perth, W.A. [1986] 108 p. ; LC Card 87-158082 DDC 331.12/5/09941 19
HD5850.W4 W54 1986

UNEMPLOYED - SERVICES FOR - UNITED STATES.
United States. Secretary of Labor's Task Force on Economic Adjustment and Worker Dislocation. Economic adjustment and worker dislocation in a competitive society . Washington, D.C. [1986] 189 p. in various pagings : LC Card 87-601034 DDC 331.13/7973 19
HC106.8 .U545 1986

UNEMPLOYED - SPAIN - CANET DE BERENGUER.
Pellicer Valero, Jesús-Agustín. Sociología del trabajo en Canet de Berenguer /. Valencia , 1984. 80 p. : ISBN 84-600-3540-9 LC Card 86-216439
HD5808.C33 P45 1984

UNEMPLOYED - SWEDEN.
Arbetslöshetens offer. Stockholm , 1983. 56 p. : ISBN 91-38-07637-3 LC Card 83-181664
HD5803 .A72 1983

UNEMPLOYED - SWEDEN - STATISTICS.
Arbetslöshetens offer. Stockholm , 1983. 56 p. : ISBN 91-38-07637-3 LC Card 83-181664
HD5803 .A72 1983

UNEMPLOYED - UNITED STATES.
Bernick, Michael, 1953- Urban illusions . New York , 1987. x, 243 p. ; ISBN 0-275-92804-7 (alk. paper) : LC Card 87-7208 DDC 331.13/7973 19
HD5708.85.U6 B47 1987

UNEMPLOYED - UNITED STATES - STATISTICS.
Barnes, William R. Employment problems and America's cities /. [Washington, D.C.] , 1984. xiii, 66, 33 p. ; ***NYPL [JLF 86-1]***

Linking employment problems to economic status . Washington, D.C. [1986] vi, 56 p. ; LC Card 86-603148 DDC 331.13/7973 19
HD5724 .L425 1986

UNEMPLOYED - WALES, SOUTH.
Harris, C. C. (Christopher Charles) Redundancy and recession in South Wales /. Oxford, OX, UK , New York, NY, USA , 1987. p. cm. ISBN 0-631-15106-0 : LC Card 87-6301 DDC 331.13/794294 19
HD5766.A6 H37 1987

Unemployment : theory, policy, and structure / editors, Peder J. Pederson and Reinhard Lund. Berlin ; New York : W. de Gruyter, 1987. xx, 353 p. : ill. ; 24 cm. (De Gruyter studies in organization . 10) Papers presented at a conference sponsored by the Danish Social Science Research Council, held in Rønne, Denmark, Sept. 1985. Includes bibliographies. ISBN 0-89925-277-X : LC Card 87-24369 DDC 331.13/7 19
1. Unemployment - Congresses. 2. Employment (Economic theory) - Congresses. I. Pedersen, Peder J. II. Lund, Reinhard. III. Statens samfundsvidenskabelige forskningsråd (Denmark). IV. Series.
HD5701.3 .U53 1987

Unemployment . Minford, Patrick. Oxford, UK , New York, NY, USA , 1985. x, 214 p. : ISBN 0-631-14506-0 : LC Card 85-13511 DDC 331.13/7941 19
HD5765.A6 M55 1985
NYPL [JLE 86-2297]

UNEMPLOYMENT.
Arndt, Helmut, 1911- Vollbeschäftigung . Berlin , c1984. 196 p. : ISBN 3-428-05602-7 LC Card 84-209024
HD5706 .A855 1984

Degrotte, Jean-André, 1947- L'économie bafouée, ou, Les hommes politiques au créneau /. Paris , c1985. 130, [11] p. : ISBN 2-7266-0074-3 LC Card 85-230533
HD5106 .D42 1985

Driver, Ciaran. Towards full employment . London , New York , 1987. xii, 238 p. : ISBN 0-7102-0918-5 LC Card 87-9814 DDC 339.5 19
HD5713.2 .D75 1987

Freyssinet, Jacques. Le chômage /. Paris , 1984. 128 p. : ISBN 2-7071-1478-2 LC Card 85-115448 DDC 331.13/7 19
HD5707.5 .F74 1984

Hardes, Heinz-Dieter. Arbeitsmarktstrukturen und Beschäftigungsprobleme im internationalen Vergleich . Tübingen , 1981. xv, 484 p. : ISBN 3-16-344468-7 : LC Card 81-196609 DDC 331.13/7 19
HD5707.5 .H37 1981 ***NYPL [JLE 86-2544]***

Hobson, J. A. (John Atkinson), 1858-1940. The economics of unemployment /. New York , 1985. 157 p. ; ISBN 0-8240-7615-X : LC Card 85-13053 DDC 331.13/7 19
HB822 .H63 1985 ***NYPL [JLC 86-452]***

Horne, John (John D.) Work, employment, and unemployment /. London , New York , 1988. p. cm. ISBN 0-582-35499-4 (pbk.) LC Card 87-3671 DDC 306/.36 19
HD4901 .H66 1988

Labour market flexibility . Paris , Washington, D.C. , 1986. 23 p. ; LC Card 86-215799 DDC 331.12 19
HD5707 .L28 1986

Lapitskiĭ, Mark Isaakovich. The tragedy of millions . Moscow , 1985. 54 p., [8] p. of plates : LC Card 87-100047 DDC 331.13/7 19
HD5708 .L36 1985

Marquis, Benoît, 1932- Victoire définitive sur le chômage . [Montréal] , c1984. 176, [3] p. : ISBN 2-9800322-0-4 LC Card 84-191778 DDC 331.13/77 19
HD5707.5 .M37 1984 ***NYPL [JLD 86-2652]***

Osmond, John. Work in the future . Wellingborough, Northamptonshire , Rochester, Vt. , 1986. 144 p. : ISBN 0-7225-1245-7 (pbk.) : LC Card 87-100557 DDC 306/.36 19
HD5707.5 .O84 1986

Priewe, Jan, 1949- Zur Kritik konkurrierender Arbeitsmarkt- und Beschäftigungstheorien und ihrer politischen Implikationen . Frankfurt am Main , New York , c1984. 385 p. ; ISBN 3-8204-8033-1 LC Card 85-198523
HD5707.5 .P75 1984

The Rise in unemployment /. Oxford, UK , New York, NY, USA , 1987, c1986. 382 p. : ISBN 0-631-15419-1 (pbk.) : LC Card 87-699 DDC 331.13/7 19
HD5707.5 .R57 1987

Sardoni, Claudio. Marx and Keynes on economic recession . New York , 1987. xiv, 152 p. ; ISBN 0-8147-7871-2 : LC Card 87-13749 DDC 338.5/42 19
HB3714 .S27 1987

Sawyer, Malcolm C. Finance, money, and unemployment /. Berlin [1985] 65 p. ; LC Card 86-205291 DDC 332 19
HG230.3 .S29 1985

Therborn, Göran, 1941- Why some peoples are more unemployed than others /. London , 1986. 181 p. ; ISBN 0-86091-109-8 : LC Card 86-673385
HD5707.5 .T53x 1986 ***NYPL [JLD 86-3537]***

Unemployment and the right to work /. Edinburgh , New York , c1982. x, 98 p. ; ISBN 0-8164-2391-1 (Seabury Press : pbk.) LC Card 87-150638
HD5707.5 .U544 1982

Unemployment and the structure of labor markets /. New York, NY, USA , 1987. vi, 253 p. : ISBN 0-631-15378-0 : LC Card 86-24478 DDC 331.13/7 19
HD5707.5 .U545 1987

Unemployment, hysteresis, and the natural rate hypothesis . Oxford, UK , New York, NY, USA , 1987. p. cm. ISBN 0-631-15688-7 : LC Card 87-14071 DDC 331.13/7 19
HD5707.5 .U555 1987

Welzk, Stefan. Boom ohne Arbeitsplätze /. Köln , c1986. 250 p. ; ISBN 3-462-01787-X LC Card 86-230211
HD5710.75.G3 W44 1986

Wooden, Mark. The personal consequences of redundancy . [Bedford Park, South Australia] [1987] 102 p. : LC Card 87-155519 DDC 331.13/7 19
HD5707.5 .W66 1987

UNEMPLOYMENT - ADDRESSES, ESSAYS, LECTURES.

Unemployment and growth in the Western economies /. New York, N.Y. , c1984. x, 142 p. ; ISBN 0-87609-001-3 (pbk.) : LC Card 84-9415 DDC 331.13/791812 19
HD5707.5 .U54 1984 ***NYPL [JLE 86-1564]***

UNEMPLOYMENT - AMAZON RIVER REGION.

Silva, Maria José Oliveira e. A sociedade amazônica e o problema social da desocupação e subocupação /. Belém , 1974. 42 p., 53 leaves : LC Card 86-183026
HB3564.A73 S55 1974

Unemployment and growth in the Western economies / Andrew J. Pierre, editor ; Marina v.N. Whitman ... [et al.] ; introduction by Robert D. Hormats. New York, N.Y. : Council on Foreign Relations, c1984. x, 142 p. ; 23 cm. (Europe/America . 2) Includes bibliographical references. ISBN 0-87609-001-3 (pbk.) : LC Card 84-9415 DDC 331.13/791812 19
1. Unemployment - Addresses, essays, lectures. 2. Economic policy - Addresses, essays, lectures. 3. Full employment policies - Addresses, essays, lectures. 4. Economic history - 1971- - Addresses, essays, lectures. I. Pierre, Andrew J. II. Whitman, Marina von Neumann. III. Council on Foreign Relations. IV. Series.
HD5707.5 .U54 1984 ***NYPL [JLE 86-1564]***

Unemployment and labour market flexibility . Standing, Guy. Geneva , 1986. xi, 147 p. : ISBN 92-2-105291-5 (pbk.) : LC Card 87-114658 DDC 331.13/7941 19
HD5765.A6 S72 1986

Unemployment and the right to work / edited by Jacques Pohier and Dietmar Mieth ; English language editor, Marcus Lefébure. Edinburgh : T. & T. Clark ; New York : Seabury Press, c1982. x, 98 p. ; 22 cm. (Concilium . 160) ISBN 0-8164-2391-1 (Seabury Press : pbk.) LC Card 87-150638
1. Unemployment. 2. Right to labor. I. Pohier, Jacques. II. Mieth, Dietmar Marie. III. Lefébure, Marcus. IV. Series: Concilium (Glen Rock, N.J.) , v. 160.
HD5707.5 .U544 1982

Unemployment and the search for work in Transkei . Muller, N. D. Umtata, Transkei [1982] 19 leaves ; LC Card 86-206957 DDC 331.13/7968791 19
HD5842.T73 M85 1982

Unemployment and the structure of labor markets / edited by Kevin Lang and Jonathan S. Leonard. New York, NY, USA : B. Blackwell, 1987. vi, 253 p. : ill. ; 24 cm. Cover title: Unemployment & the structure of labor markets. Bibliography: p. [234]-243. Includes index. ISBN 0-631-15378-0 : LC Card 86-24478 DDC 331.13/7 19
1. Unemployment. 2. Wage-price policy. I. Lang, Kevin. II. Leonard, Jonathan S. (Jonathan Shawn). III. Title: Unemployment & the structure of labor markets.
HD5707.5 .U545 1987

Unemployment & the structure of labor markets. Unemployment and the structure of labor markets /. New York, NY, USA , 1987. vi, 253 p. : ISBN 0-631-15378-0 : LC Card 86-24478 DDC 331.13/7 19
HD5707.5 .U545 1987

UNEMPLOYMENT - AUSTRALIA.

Bosworth, Derek L. Labour utilisation in Australia . [Bedford Park, S. Aust.] [1986] i, 205 p. : LC Card 86-229498 DDC 331.12/5/0994 19
HD5850.A6 B67 1986

UNEMPLOYMENT - AUSTRIA.

Amanshauser, Wilfried. Jugendarbeitsmarktförderung in Österreich /. Wien [1985] ii, 71, 3 p. ; LC Card 86-165982
HD6276.A9 A43 1985

Marzen, Walter. Ist die 35-Stunden-Woche ein Mittel zur Beseitigung der Arbeitslosigkeit? . Innsbruck , 1980. 29 leaves ; LC Card 85-170048
HD5108.2.A9 M37 1980

UNEMPLOYMENT - AUSTRIA - ECONOMETRIC MODELS.

Böhm, Walter. Längsschnittanalyse des österreichischen Arbeitsmarktes . Wien , 1986. 138 p. : ISBN 3-85369-654-6 LC Card 87-142156 DDC 331.12/5/09436 19
HD5771 .B64 1986

UNEMPLOYMENT - AUSTRIA - HISTORY - 20TH CENTURY - SOURCES.

Entlassen ins Nichts . Berlin , c1983. 255 p. ; ISBN 3-8012-0089-2 (pbk.) LC Card 87-672743
HD5779 .E57x 1983

UNEMPLOYMENT - BRAZIL.

Garcia, Manuel Enriquez. Salários indexados, preços e emprego . São Paulo , 1986. 149 p. : LC Card 86-234254
HD5004 .G37 1986

Unemployment by occupation, 1985 : State of Iowa. Des Moines, Iowa (1000 E. Grand Ave., Des Moines 50319) : Dept. of Employment Services, Audit and Analysis Section, Labor Market Information Unit, [1986] [12] leaves ; 28 cm. "August 1986." Chiefly tables. LC Card 86-622759 DDC 331.13/79777 19
1. Unemployment - Iowa - Statistics. 2. Iowa - Occupations - Statistics. 3. Labor supply - Iowa - Statistics. I. Iowa. Labor Market Information Unit.
HD5725.I8 U54 1986

UNEMPLOYMENT - CANADA.

Bellan, Ruben C., 1918- The unnecessary evil . Toronto, Ont. , c1986. 173 p. : ISBN 0-7710-1153-9 : LC Card 86-222233 DDC 331.13/7971 19
HD5728 .B43 1986

Daly, D. J. (Donald James), 1922- On real wage unemployment /. Vancouver, B.C., Canada , 1986. vi, 117 p. : ISBN 0-88975-079-3 (pbk.) LC Card 87-142391 DDC 331.13/7971 19
HD4946.C3 D35 1986

Foot, David K. A challenge of the 1980s . [Toronto] , c1981. 99 p. in various pagings :
NYPL [JLF 86-1304]

The State of families. Milwaukee, Wis. , <c1987-. v. <2 > : ISBN 0-87304-226-3 (pbk. : v. 2) LC Card 87-24374 DDC 306.8/5/0973 19
HD4904.25 .S83 1987

UNEMPLOYMENT - CANADA - CONGRESSES.

Twentieth joint conference . [Charlottetown, P.E.I. , 1986] 94 p. ; LC Card 87-147512 DDC 338/.06 19
HC120.T4 T84 1986

UNEMPLOYMENT - CHILE.

Rojas Ramos, Patricio. Demanda dinámica por trabajo /. Santiago , 1986. 58 p. : LC Card 87-404328 DDC 331.12/5/0983 19
HD5756.A6 R65 1986

UNEMPLOYMENT - CHILE - ECONOMETRIC MODELS.

Coeymans, Juan Eduardo. Determinants of sectoral annual real wages in a developing economy /. Santiago , 1986. 32, [4] leaves : LC Card 87-404007 DDC 331.12/5/0983 19
HD5006 .C64 1986

UNEMPLOYMENT - COLLECTED WORKS.

Summers, Lawrence H. Understanding unemployment /. Cambridge, Mass. , c1988. p. cm. ISBN 0-262-19265-9 LC Card 87-3866 DDC 331.13/7 19
HD5707.5 .S85 1988

UNEMPLOYMENT - COLOMBIA.

Hopkins, Mike. Alternatives to unemployment and underemployment . Boulder , 1985. xiv, 129 p. : ISBN 0-8133-0200-5 (pbk.) LC Card 85-45007 DDC 331.13/79861 19
HD5757.A6 H67 1985
NYPL [JLD 86-2149]

UNEMPLOYMENT COMPENSATION. see **INSURANCE, UNEMPLOYMENT.**

UNEMPLOYMENT - CONGRESSES.

Unemployment . Berlin , New York , 1987. xx, 353 p. : ISBN 0-89925-277-X : LC Card 87-24369 DDC 331.13/7 19
HD5701.3 .U53 1987

Wage rigidity and unemployment /. Baltimore , 1986. viii, 221 p. : ISBN 0-8018-3400-7 LC Card 86-45446 DDC 331.2/1 19
HD4909 .W26 1986 ***NYPL [JLD 86-4077]***

UNEMPLOYMENT - DENMARK.

Ungdomsarbejdsløshed og beskæftigelsesforanstaltninger . København [1984] 100 leaves : LC Card 85-124463
HD6276.D4 U54 1984

UNEMPLOYMENT - DENMARK - MATHEMATICAL MODELS.

Arbejdsløshed og beskæftigelse . Aarhus [Copenhagen] [1983] 34 p. ; LC Card 84-125513
HD5701.6 .A73 1983

UNEMPLOYMENT - ECONOMETRIC MODELS.

Paldam, Martin. How much does one percent of growth change the unemployment? . Aarhus, Denmark [1986] 35 p. : LC Card 86-221448 DDC 331.13/7 19
HD5707.5 .P34 1986

Riese, Martin. Die Messung der Arbeitslosigkeit /. Berlin , c1986. 199 p. : ISBN 3-428-06034-2 LC Card 86-215265 DDC 331.12/0724 19
HD5707.5 .R54 1986

UNEMPLOYMENT - EFFECT OF INFLATION ON.

Gröschel, Ulrich. Inflation und Beschäftigung in

Volkswirtschaften mit Güter- und Arbeitsmarktkontrakten /. Berlin , c1986. 252 p. ; ISBN 3-428-06149-7 LC Card 87-120985 DDC 331.13/72 19
HD5710.2 .G76 1986

Marquis, Benoît, 1932- Victoire définitive sur le chômage . [Montréal] , c1984. 176, [3] p. : ISBN 2-9800322-0-4 LC Card 84-191778 DDC 331.13/77 19
HD5707.5 .M37 1984 ***NYPL [JLD 86-2652]***

Sozialpolitik in der Beschäftigungskrise /. Berlin , c1986. 2 v. : ISBN 3-428-05949-2 (Bd. I) : LC Card 87-119211 DDC 361.6/1 19
HD5710 .S67 1986

Spahn, Heinz-Peter. Stagnation in der Geldwirtschaft . Frankfurt , New York , c1986. 304 p. : ISBN 3-593-33691-X LC Card 86-225253
HD5710 .S68 1986

Willke, Gerhard. Globalsteuerung und gespaltene Konjunktur . Leyden ; Boston : xiii, 243 p. : ISBN 3-12-915020-X LC Card 84-181249
HD5779 .W55 1978

UNEMPLOYMENT - EFFECT OF INFLATION ON - ADDRESSES, ESSAYS, LECTURES.

Stagflation, savings, and the state . New York , 1986. xii, 402 p. : ISBN 0-19-520496-4 LC Card 85-31981 DDC 330.9172/4 19
HG229 .S74 1986 ***NYPL [JLE 86-2621]***

UNEMPLOYMENT - EFFECT OF INFLATION ON - COLLECTED WORKS.

Meade, J. E. (James Edward), 1907- [Works. 1988.] The collected papers of James Meade /. London , Boston , 1988- p. cm. ISBN 0-04-445073-7 (v. 1. : alk. paper) LC Card 87-15288 DDC 330.1 19
HD5710 .M43 1988

UNEMPLOYMENT - EFFECT OF INFLATION ON - ECONOMETRIC MODELS.

Tobin, James, 1918- Essays in economics. Cambridge, Mass. , 1987. vii, 492 p. : ISBN 0-262-20064-3 LC Card 87-3913 DDC 330/.028 19
HB801 .T6 1987

UNEMPLOYMENT - EFFECT OF INFLATION ON - MATHEMATICAL MODELS.

Herberg, Horst. Stagflation as a consequence of an expansionary monetary or fiscal policy under flexible exchange rates /. Stockholm, Sweden [1978] 34 leaves ; LC Card 81-116937
HD5710 .H47 1978

Kudiss, Reinhard, 1952- Die Bestimmung des Produktionspotentials in Theorie und Empirie . Frankfurt am Main , New York , c1984. xvi, 198 p. : ISBN 3-8204-5579-5 LC Card 85-189908
HB3730 .K766 1984

Meade, James Edward, 1907- Alternative systems of business organization and of worker's remuneration /. London , Boston , 1986. x, 144 p. : ISBN 0-04-331112-1 (alk. paper) LC Card 85-26734 DDC 330/.1 19
HB238 .M4 1986 ***NYPL [JLD 86-2943]***

UNEMPLOYMENT - EUROPE.

The Changing experience of employment . Houndmills, Basingstoke, Hampshire , 1986. x, 230 p. ; ISBN 0-333-39695-2
NYPL [JLD 87-933]

The Fight against unemployment . Cambridge, Mass. , 1987. xii, 204 p. : ISBN 0-262-12122-0 LC Card 87-5356 DDC 339.5/094 19
HD5764.A6 F54 1987

UNEMPLOYMENT - EUROPE - CONGRESSES.

Convegno "Il lavoro si crea" (1985 : Ravenna, Italy) Il lavoro si crea . Milano, Italy , c1986. 305 p. : LC Card 86-232529
HD5764.A6 C68 1985

Employment forecasting . London , New York , c1988. p. cm. ISBN 0-86187-938-4 : LC Card 87-21882 DDC 331.12/094 19
HD5764 .E47 1988

Job generation . Salt Lake City, Utah , c1986. xiv, 138 p. ; ISBN 0-913420-89-1 (pbk.) LC Card 86-31285 DDC 331.12/094 19
HD5724 .J63 1986

UNEMPLOYMENT - EUROPEAN ECONOMIC COMMUNITY COUNTRIES.

Minford, Patrick. Unemployment . Oxford, UK , New York, NY, USA , 1985. x, 214 p. : ISBN 0-631-14506-0 : LC Card 85-13511 DDC 331.13/7941 19
HD5765.A6 M55 1985
NYPL [JLE 86-2297]

UNEMPLOYMENT - EUROPEAN ECONOMIC COMMUNITY COUNTRIES - COSTS - CASE STUDIES.

Junankar, P. N. Programme of research and actions on the development of the labour market . Luxembourg [Washington, DC] 1986. vi, 76, 35 p. : ISBN 92-825-6084-8 (pbk.) : LC Card 86-220947
HD5764.5.A6 J85 1986

UNEMPLOYMENT - FRANCE.

Godinot, Xavier, 1951- Les travailleurs sous-prolétaires face aux mutations de l'emploi /. Paris [1985] 155 p. ; ISBN 2-904972-04-08 LC Card 86-166442
HD5775 .G63 1985

Vasseur, Philippe. Le chômage, c'est les autres /. Paris , c1985. 224 p. ; ISBN 2-7144-1867-8 : LC Card 86-120821 DDC 331.13/7944 19
HD5775 .V37 1985

UNEMPLOYMENT - FRANCE - PSYCHOLOGICAL ASPECTS.

Arbeitslosigkeit in der Arbeitsgesellschaft /. Frankfurt am Main , 1984. 350 p. ; ISBN 3-518-11212-0 : LC Card 84-192978
HD5708 .A72 1984

UNEMPLOYMENT - GERMANY - HISTORY - 20TH CENTURY.

The German unemployed . Beckenham, Kent , 1987. xviii, 314 p. : ISBN 0-7099-0941-1
NYPL [JLD 87-801]

UNEMPLOYMENT - GERMANY - HISTORY - 20TH CENTURY - SOURCES.

Entlassen ins Nichts . Berlin , c1983. 255 p. ; ISBN 3-8012-0089-2 (pbk.) LC Card 87-672743
HD5779 .E57x 1983

UNEMPLOYMENT - GERMANY (WEST)

Arbeitslose Jugendliche, eine Zielgruppe für Fernsehen und Hörfunk? /. München , New York , 1985. 157 p. : ISBN 3-598-20759-X LC Card 86-153843
HD6276.G39 A73 1985

Hardes, Heinz-Dieter. Arbeitsmarktstrukturen und Beschäftigungsprobleme im internationalen Vergleich . Tübingen , 1981. xv, 484 p. : ISBN 3-16-344468-7 : LC Card 81-196609 DDC 331.13/7 19
HD5707.5 .H37 1981 ***NYPL [JLE 86-2544]***

Hof, Bernd. Arbeitsmarktstrukturen im Wandel /. Köln , c1985. 56 p. : ISBN 3-602-24737-6 LC Card 86-119065 DDC 331.12/5/0943 19
HD5779 .H638 1985

Knöpfel, Eckehardt. Werkbuch Jugendarbeitslosigkeit . Wuppertal , c1983. 168 p. : ISBN 3-417-12855-2 (pbk.) LC Card 87-672977
HD5779 .K59x 1983

Krisenverschärfung durch Angebotspolitik . Köln , c1984. 104 p. ; ISBN 3-7663-0877-7 LC Card 84-215633
HC286.7 .K75 1984

Kunert-Schroth, Heidrun. Jugendarbeitslosigkeit, lokale Ausprägungen und kommunale Strategien . Berlin , 1987. 172 p. ; ISBN 3-88118-135-0 LC Card 87-409103 DDC 331.3/412/0943 19
HD6276.G4 K86 1987

Pieper, Beate. Vom Lehrermangel zur Lehrerarbeitslosigkeit . Münster , 1984. ix, 265 p. : ISBN 3-923881-11-8 : LC Card 85-195712 DDC 331.12 19
LB2833.4.G4 P54 1984
NYPL [JLD 87-1161]

Politik der Armut und die Spaltung des Sozialstaats /. Frankfurt am Main , 1985. 474 p. : ISBN 3-518-11233-3 : LC Card 85-183026
HC290.5.P6 P65 1985

Schabedoth, Hans-Joachim. Bittsteller oder Gegenmacht? . Marburg , 1985. 251 p. : ISBN 3-924800-32-4 : LC Card 86-115002 DDC 331.88/0943 19
HD6694 .S254 1985 ***NYPL [JLC 87-35]***

Schmidt, Rainer, Dr. Offene und verdeckte Arbeitslosigkeit in der Bundesrepublik . Tübingen , c1986. viii, 124 p. : ISBN 3-16-345158-6 LC Card 87-126258 DDC 331.13/7943 19
HD5779 .S2495 1986

Welzk, Stefan. Boom ohne Arbeitsplätze /. Köln , c1986. 250 p. ; ISBN 3-462-01787-X LC Card 86-230211
HD5710.75.G3 W44 1986

UNEMPLOYMENT - GERMANY (WEST) - DÜSSELDORF - PSYCHOLOGICAL ASPECTS.

Arbeitslosigkeit und Neue Armut in Düsseldorf . Bochum , c1986. 65 p. : ISBN 3-925222-03-0 LC Card 87-409036 DDC 331.13/794355 19
HD5780.D85 A73 1986

UNEMPLOYMENT - GERMANY (WEST) - EFFECT OF INFLATION ON.

Francke, Hans-Hermann. Sparverhalten bei Unterbeschäftigung, stagnierendem oder sinkendem Realeinkommen /. Stuttgart [1985] 142 p. : LC Card 86-153649
HC290.5.S3 F69 1985

Willke, Gerhard. Globalsteuerung und gespaltene Konjunktur . Leyden ; Boston : xiii, 243 p. : ISBN 3-12-915020-X LC Card 84-181249
HD5779 .W55 1978

UNEMPLOYMENT - GERMANY (WEST) - EFFECT OF INFLATION ON - ECONOMETRIC MODELS.

Kudiss, Reinhard, 1952- Die Bestimmung des Produktionspotentials in Theorie und Empirie . Frankfurt am Main , New York , c1984. xvi, 198 p. : ISBN 3-8204-5579-5 LC Card 85-189908
HB3730 .K766 1984

UNEMPLOYMENT - GERMANY (WEST) - NORTH RHINE-WESTPHALIA - HISTORY - 20TH CENTURY.

Bremicker, Burckhardt. Analyse der Arbeitslosigkeit in den Regionen Nordrhein-Westfalens . Bochum , 1984. xx, 381 p. : ISBN 3-88339-362-2 LC Card 84-196621 DDC 331.13/794355 19
HD5780.N6 B74 1984 ***NYPL [JLD 86-2367]***

UNEMPLOYMENT - GERMANY (WEST) - PSYCHOLOGICAL ASPECTS.

Arbeitslosigkeit in der Arbeitsgesellschaft /. Frankfurt am Main , 1984. 350 p. ; ISBN 3-518-11212-0 : LC Card 84-192978
HD5708 .A72 1984

Arend, Brigitte, 1953- Vom Lohnarbeiter zum Klienten . Frankfurt am Main , c1986. 206 p. ; ISBN 3-445-02490-1 LC Card 86-231993
HD5708 .A74 1986

Biermann, Ingrid, 1955- Leben mit kurzfristigem Denken . Weinheim , 1985. 224 p. ; ISBN 3-407-58260-9 LC Card 86-106693
HD6053.6.G3 B54 1985
NYPL [JLD 86-3122]

Brandt, Franz. Ursachen für die Schwierigkeiten bei der Eingliederung von Schwerbehinderten auf dem allgemeinen Arbeitsmarkt /. Bonn [1984] 410 p. ; LC Card 87-408829 DDC 331.5/9/0943 19
HD7256.G3 B7 1984

UNEMPLOYMENT - GERMANY (WEST) - PSYCHOLOGICAL ASPECTS - INTERVIEWS.

Ohne Arbeit geh'ste kaputt . Köln , c1983. 183 p. : ISBN 3-7609-0798-9 LC Card 84-176249
HD5779 .O355 1983

UNEMPLOYMENT - GERMANY (WEST) - REGIONAL DISPARITIES - CONGRESSES.

Gestaltungsspielräume der Arbeitsmarktpolitik auf regionalen Arbeitsmärkten . Berlin , c1984. 180 p. : ISBN 3-428-05614-0 LC Card 84-218530
HD8444 .G47 1984

UNEMPLOYMENT - GERMANY (WEST) - RUHR (REGION)

Fokkink, Manfred, 1955- Denk ja nicht, Du bist selber schuld . Gelsenkirchen-Buer , 1980. 180 p. : LC Card 82-114713
HD6276.G4 F6 1980 ***NYPL [JLE 86-1457]***

UNEMPLOYMENT - GERMANY (WEST) - STATISTICAL METHODS.

Schmidt, Rainer, Dr. Offene und verdeckte Arbeitslosigkeit in der Bundesrepublik . Tübingen , c1986. viii, 124 p. : ISBN 3-16-345158-6 LC Card 87-126258 DDC

331.13/7943 19
HD5779 .S2495 1986

UNEMPLOYMENT - GREAT BRITAIN.
Ashton, D. N. Unemployment under capitalism . Brighton, Sussex , 1986. xiv, 225 p. : ISBN 0-7108-0163-7
NYPL [JLD 86-1049]

Batstone, Eric. Unions, unemployment and innovation /. Oxford [Oxfordshire] , New York, N.Y., USA , 1986. viii, 320 p. ; ISBN 0-631-14961-9 : LC Card 85-30679 DDC 331.88/0941 19
HD6664 .B335 1986 ***NYPL [JLE 86-4031]***

Changing places . London , Baltimore, Md., USA , 1987. xv, 144 p. : ISBN 0-7131-6498-0 (pbk.) : LC Card 87-148942 DDC 331.12/5/0941 19
HD5765.A6 C49 1987

Coates, Ken. Trade unions and politics /. Oxford, OX, UK , New York, NY, USA , 1986. ix, 268 p. : ISBN 0-631-13752-1 : LC Card 85-22959 DDC 322/.2/0941 19
HD6667 .C63 1986 ***NYPL [JLE 86-1729]***

Fattigdom i England . København [1986] 24 columns : ISBN 87-7296-008-6 : LC Card 87-168467
HC260.P6 F37 1986

Hannington, Wal, 1895- The problem of the distressed areas /. New York , 1985. 286 p. : ISBN 0-8240-7613-3 : LC Card 85-14663 DDC 338.941 19
HC256.3 .H265 1985 ***NYPL [JLD 86-3420]***

Hardes, Heinz-Dieter. Arbeitsmarktstrukturen und Beschäftigungsprobleme im internationalen Vergleich . Tübingen , 1981. xv, 484 p. : ISBN 3-16-344468-7 : LC Card 81-196609 DDC 331.13/7 19
HD5707.5 .H37 1981 ***NYPL [JLE 86-2544]***

Hart, P. E. (Peter Edward) Youth unemployment in Great Britain /. Cambridge [Cambridgeshire] , New York, NY, USA , 1988. p. cm. ISBN 0-521-35348-3 LC Card 87-25597 DDC 331.3/4137941 19
HD6276.G72 H37 1988

Keane, John, 1949- After full employment /. London , Dover, N.H., USA , 1986. 198 p. ; ISBN 0-09-164091-1 (pbk.) : LC Card 86-213691 DDC 339.5/0941 19
HD5765.A6 K42 1986

Minford, Patrick. Unemployment . Oxford, UK , New York, NY, USA , 1985. x, 214 p. : ISBN 0-631-14506-0 : LC Card 85-13511 DDC 331.13/7941 19
HD5765.A6 M55 1985
NYPL [JLE 86-2297]

Standing, Guy. Unemployment and labour market flexibility . Geneva , 1986. xi, 147 p. : ISBN 92-2-105291-5 (pbk.) : LC Card 87-114658 DDC 331.13/7941 19
HD5765.A6 S72 1986

UNEMPLOYMENT - GREAT BRITAIN - EFFECT OF INFLATION ON.
Dobrovolny, Jiri, 1943- Preis- und Lohndirigismen im Dienste der Stabilisierungspolitik . Bern , New York , c1985. xi, 433 p. : ISBN 3-261-03517-X LC Card 86-105626 DDC 338.5/2/0945 19
HB236.G7 D63 1985

Jones, Aubrey, 1911- Britain's economy . Cambridge [Cambridgeshire] , New York , 1985. x, 158 p. : ISBN 0-521-30816-X LC Card 85-9649 DDC 330.941/0858 19
HC256.6 .J64 1985 ***NYPL [JLD 86-1581]***

Managing the UK economy . Cambridge, UK , 1987. xxvii, 328 p. : ISBN 0-7456-0316-5 : LC Card 86-26860 DDC 338.941 19
HC256.5 .M392 1987

UNEMPLOYMENT - GREAT BRITAIN - EFFECT OF INFLATION ON - COLLECTED WORKS.
Meade, J. E. (James Edward), 1907- [Works. 1988.] The collected papers of James Meade /. London , Boston , 1988- p. cm. ISBN 0-04-445073-7 (v. 1. : alk. paper) LC Card 87-15288 DDC 330.1 19
HD5710 .M43 1988

UNEMPLOYMENT - GREAT BRITAIN - HISTORY - 20TH CENTURY.
Jones, Russell, 1959- Wages and employment policy, 1936-1985 /. London , Boston , 1987. xvii, 175 p. ; ISBN 0-04-331110-5 (alk. paper) LC Card 86-14143 DDC 339.5/0941 19
HD5015 .J66 1987 ***NYPL [JLD 87-831]***

UNEMPLOYMENT - GREAT BRITAIN - MORAL AND ETHICAL ASPECTS.
Storkey, Alan. Transforming economics . London , 1986. xi, 212 p. : ISBN 0-281-04225-X (pbk.) : LC Card 87-108686 DDC 261.8/5 19
HD5765.A6 S76 1986

UNEMPLOYMENT - GREECE.
Phrankos, Dionysios M., 1926- Hoi makrochronies exelixeis tou oikonomika mē energou plēthysmou tēs Hellados /. Athēna , 1983. 148 p. : LC Card 85-152730
HD5811.83.A6 P47 1983

UNEMPLOYMENT - HISTORY.
Unemployment, hysteresis, and the natural rate hypothesis . Oxford, UK , New York, NY, USA , 1987. p. cm. ISBN 0-631-15688-7 : LC Card 87-14071 DDC 331.13/7 19
HD5707.5 .U555 1987

Unemployment, hysteresis, and the natural rate hypothesis : proceedings of a conference held at the University of St. Andrews, Scotland, July 1986 / edited by Rod Cross, with the assistance of A. Chawluk and M. Malek. Oxford, UK ; New York, NY, USA : Blackwell, 1987. p. cm. Bibliography: p. Includes index. ISBN 0-631-15688-7 : LC Card 87-14071 DDC 331.13/7 19
1. Unemployment. 2. Unemployment - History. 3. Employment (Economic theory). I. Cross, Rod. II. Chawluk, A. III. Malek, M.
HD5707.5 .U555 1987

UNEMPLOYMENT - INDIA.
Chaudhary, S. K. Planning and employment trends in India /. New Delhi , c1987. 300 p. ; LC Card 86-903543 DDC 331.11/0954/12 19
HD5819 .C47 1987

Mehta, Vadilal Lallubhai, 1903- Unemployment, inequality, parallel economy . Ahmedabad , 1982. viii, 141 p., [1] leaf of plates : LC Card 82-900764 DDC 331.13/7954 19
HD5819 .M43 1982 ***NYPL [JLD 85-2751]***

UNEMPLOYMENT - INDIA - BIHAR.
Chaudhary, S. K. Planning and employment trends in India /. New Delhi , c1987. 300 p. ; LC Card 86-903543 DDC 331.11/0954/12 19
HD5819 .C47 1987

UNEMPLOYMENT - INDIA - EAST GODAVARI.
Subrahmanyam, S. Poverty, unemployment, and perspective of development /. Allahabad, India , 1987. xi, 311 p. : ISBN 81-85076-22-7 : LC Card 87-900803 DDC 330.954/84 19
HC440.P6 S9 1987

UNEMPLOYMENT - INDIA - KARNATAKA.
Prabhakara, N. R. Population growth and unemployment in India /. New Delhi , 1986. ix, 102 p. ; ISBN 81-7024-041-7 : LC Card 86-902156 DDC 331.13/795487 19
HD5820.K37 P7 1986

UNEMPLOYMENT - INDIANA.
Wynne, John, 1961- The Indiana economy . Indianapolis, IN [1986] 22, [2] p. : LC Card 86-622749 DDC 330.9772/043 19
HD5725.I6 W96 1986

Unemployment, inequality, parallel economy .
Mehta, Vadilal Lallubhai, 1903- Ahmedabad , 1982. viii, 141 p., [1] leaf of plates : LC Card 82-900764 DDC 331.13/7954 19
HD5819 .M43 1982 ***NYPL [JLD 85-2751]***

UNEMPLOYMENT INSURANCE. see **INSURANCE, UNEMPLOYMENT.**

Unemployment insurance monographs .
(3) Malisoff, Harry. The insurance character of unemployment insurance /. Kalamazoo, Mich. [1961] 44 p. ; LC Card 87-401793 DDC 368.4/4/0973 19
HD7096.U5 M266 1961

UNEMPLOYMENT - IOWA - STATISTICS.
Unemployment by occupation, 1985 . Des Moines, Iowa (1000 E. Grand Ave., Des Moines 50319) [1986] [12] leaves ; LC Card 86-622759 DDC 331.13/79777 19
HD5725.I8 U54 1986

UNEMPLOYMENT - ITALY.
Palazzi, Paolo. Domanda di lavoro e produttività nell'industria italiana /. Bologna , c1980. 177 p. ; LC Card 82-156294 DDC 331.13/7945 19
HD5784 .P28 1980 ***NYPL [JLD 86-2811]***

UNEMPLOYMENT - ITALY - NUORO (SARDINIA : PROVINCE)
L'Osservatorio provinciale sul lavoro e sulle professioni . Milano, Italy , c1984. 143 p. : LC Card 84-190423
HD5785.N86 O87 1984
NYPL [JLD 86-1275]

UNEMPLOYMENT - ITALY - REGIONAL DISPARITIES.
Magni, Carlo. I mercati regionali del lavoro e il problema degli indicatori . Milano [1981] 133, [3] p. : ISBN 88-20-42109-7 : LC Card 81-194409
HD5784 .M3 1981 ***NYPL [JLD 87-815]***

UNEMPLOYMENT - ITALY - STATISTICAL METHODS.
Magni, Carlo. I mercati regionali del lavoro e il problema degli indicatori . Milano [1981] 133, [3] p. : ISBN 88-20-42109-7 : LC Card 81-194409
HD5784 .M3 1981 ***NYPL [JLD 87-815]***

UNEMPLOYMENT - MARYLAND - STATISTICS.
Zoned employment and unemployment statistics . Baltimore, Md. (1100 N. Eutaw St., Baltimore 21201) [1986] [51] p. : LC Card 86-622109 DDC 331.12/5/09752021 19
HD5725.M35 Z67 1986

UNEMPLOYMENT - MATHEMATICAL MODELS.
Arbejdsløshed og beskæftigelse . Aarhus [Copenhagen] [1983] 34 p. ; LC Card 84-125513
HD5701.6 .A73 1983

Cuddington, John T. Budget deficits and the current account in the presence of classical unemployment /. [Madrid] [1984] 47 p. : ISBN 84-505-0847-9 (pbk.) LC Card 86-215031 DDC 339.5/23/0724 19
HJ2005 .C83 1984

Pedersen, Peder J. Dynamiska processer på arbejdsmarkedet /. Aarhus [Copenhagen] [1982] 33 p. : LC Card 84-125613
HD5701.6 .P43 1982

Westergård-Nielsen, Niels C. Overgangen fra uddannelse til erhverv . Aarhus [Copenhagen] [1983] iii, 41 p. : LC Card 84-125491
HD5701.6 .W47 1983

UNEMPLOYMENT - NETHERLANDS.
Enige aspecten van arbeid in de toekomst . 's-Gravenhage , 1986. 178 p. : ISBN 90-12-05246-7 LC Card 87-101491
HD5792 .E47 1986

Kloosterman, Robert. Werkloosheid in Nederland, 1920-1939 . Utrecht , 1985. xiv, 351 p. : ISBN 90-6194-315-9 : LC Card 86-150980
HD5792 .K56 1985 ***NYPL [JLD 86-3407]***

Vissers, A. M. C. Arbeidsmarktgedrag ten tijde van massale werkloosheid . 's-Gravenhage , 1986. 106 p. : ISBN 90-12-05302-1 LC Card 87-108930
HD5717.5.N45 V57 1986

UNEMPLOYMENT - NETHERLANDS - REGIONAL DISPARITIES.
Kloosterman, Robert. Werkloosheid in Nederland, 1920-1939 . Utrecht , 1985. xiv, 351 p. : ISBN 90-6194-315-9 : LC Card 86-150980
HD5792 .K56 1985 ***NYPL [JLD 86-3407]***

UNEMPLOYMENT - NORWAY.
Undersøkelse av personer som var med i en del av arbeidsmarkedsetatens tiltak pr. 31. mars 1978. Oslo , 1979. iv, 68, 4 p. ; LC Card 83-109890
HD5800.A6 U53 1979

UNEMPLOYMENT - NORWAY - STATISTICS.
Undersøkelse av personer som var med i en del av arbeidsmarkedsetatens tiltak pr. 31. mars 1978. Oslo , 1979. iv, 68, 4 p. ; LC Card 83-109890
HD5800.A6 U53 1979

UNEMPLOYMENT - PSYCHOLOGICAL ASPECTS.
Arbeitslosigkeit in der Arbeitsgesellschaft /. Frankfurt am Main , 1984. 350 p. ; ISBN 3-518-11212-0 : LC Card 84-192978
HD5708 .A72 1984

Lapit͡skiĭ, Mark Isaakovich. The tragedy of millions . Moscow , 1985. 54 p., [8] p. of

plates : LC Card 87-100047 DDC 331.13/7 19
HD5708 .L36 1985

Schumacher, Egbert, 1960- Arbeitslosigkeit und psychische Gesundheit . München , c1986. 231 p. ; ISBN 3-89019-161-4 LC Card 87-108049 DDC 331.13/7/019 19
HD5708 .S38 1986

Unemployed people . Milton Keynes, England , Philadelphia, PA, USA , 1987. 292 p. ; ISBN 0-335-15507-3 LC Card 87-5792 DDC 305/.90694 19
HD5708 .U57 1987

Wooden, Mark. The personal consequences of redundancy . [Bedford Park, South Australia] [1987] 102 p. : LC Card 87-155519 DDC 331.13/7 19
HD5707.5 .W66 1987

UNEMPLOYMENT - PSYCHOLOGICAL ASPECTS - CONGRESSES.
Individuelle und gesellschaftliche Kosten der Massenarbeitslosigkeit . Weinheim , 1985. xxvi, 506 p. : ISBN 3-407-54689-0 LC Card 86-118545 DDC 331.13/7/019 19
HD5708 .I53 1985 ***NYPL [JLD 87-387]***

UNEMPLOYMENT - QUÉBEC (PROVINCE)
Fortin, Pierre. [Unemployment, inflation, and economic stabilization in Quebec. French.] Chômage, inflation et régulation de la conjoncture au Québec /. Montréal, Québec [1980] viii, 144 p. : ISBN 0-88806-063-7 (pbk.) LC Card 87-673448
HC117.Q4 F63x 1980

UNEMPLOYMENT - SCANDINAVIA.
Buvollen, H. P. (Hans Petter) The situation of workers in the industrialised countries with special reference to Scandinavia /. Oslo [1985] 24 p. ; LC Card 86-205580 DDC 331.13/7948 19
HD8540 .B86 1985

UNEMPLOYMENT - SOCIAL ASPECTS.
Unemployed people . Milton Keynes, England , Philadelphia, PA, USA , 1987. 292 p. ; ISBN 0-335-15507-3 LC Card 87-5792 DDC 305/.90694 19
HD5708 .U57 1987

UNEMPLOYMENT - SOCIAL ASPECTS - CONGRESSES.
Individuelle und gesellschaftliche Kosten der Massenarbeitslosigkeit . Weinheim , 1985. xxvi, 506 p. : ISBN 3-407-54689-0 LC Card 86-118545 DDC 331.13/7/019 19
HD5708 .I53 1985 ***NYPL [JLD 87-387]***

UNEMPLOYMENT - SOUTH AFRICA - DURBAN.
Padayachee, Vishnu. An analysis of some aspects of employment and unemployment in the African townships of Umlazi and Lamontville . Durban [South Africa] [1985] iii, 49 p. ; ISBN 0-949947-75-X (pbk.) LC Card 87-404149 DDC 331.12/5/0968455 19
HD5842.D87 P33 1985

UNEMPLOYMENT - SOUTH AFRICA - TRANSKEI.
Muller, N. D. Unemployment and the search for work in Transkei . Umtata, Transkei [1982] 19 leaves ; LC Card 86-206957 DDC 331.13/7968791 19
HD5842.T73 M85 1982

UNEMPLOYMENT - SPAIN.
Albentosa Puche, Luis. El paro en España /. Madrid , c1983. 349 p. : ISBN 84-85719-34-4 LC Card 86-121124 DDC 331.11/0946 19
HD5807 .A44 1983 ***NYPL [JLC 87-37]***

UNEMPLOYMENT - STATISTICAL METHODS.
Standardised unemployment rates . Paris, France [Washington, D.C.] 1985. 93 p. ; LC Card 86-143095 DDC 331.13/7/072 19
HD5711 .S77 1985 ***NYPL [JLF 86-1743]***

UNEMPLOYMENT, STRUCTURAL - BRAZIL.
Serra, José. A crise econômica e o flagelo do desemprego /. São Paulo , 1984. 27 p. : LC Card 87-124054 DDC 331.13/704 19
HD5708.47.B6 S47 1984

UNEMPLOYMENT, STRUCTURAL - BRAZIL - RIO GRANDE DO SUL.
Carrion Júnior, Francisco M. (Francisco Machado), 1944- O Rio Grande em busca de novos caminhos por um projeto regional /. Porto Alegre, RS , 1986. 78 p. : LC Card 87-129162 DDC 330.981/65063 19
HC188.R4 C35 1986

UNEMPLOYMENT, STRUCTURAL - CHILE.
Reactivación con transformación . [Santiago, Chile] [c1984] 29 leaves ; LC Card 85-156967
HD5708.47.C5 R43 1984

UNEMPLOYMENT, STRUCTURAL - ECUADOR.
El Ecuador en la encrucijada . Quito , 1986. 307 p. : LC Card 87-400394 DDC 331.12/09866 19
HD5758.A6 E28 1986

UNEMPLOYMENT, STRUCTURAL - GERMANY (WEST)
Welsch, Johann. Gewerkschaften und Strukturwandel . Köln , c1986. iii, 114 p. ; ISBN 3-7663-3011-X LC Card 86-223645 DDC 331.13/704 19
HD6694 .W37 1986

UNEMPLOYMENT, STRUCTURAL - KENYA.
Population, economics, and unemployment . [Nairobi] [1982] 55 leaves ; LC Card 85-980190
HD5708.47.K4 P67 1982

UNEMPLOYMENT, STRUCTURAL - LATIN AMERICA.
García, Norberto E. Absorción creciente con subempleo persistente (América Latina, 1950-80) /. [Santiago, Chile] , 1982. 35 p. ; LC Card 87-403250 DDC 331.12/098 19
HD5730.5.A6 G355 1982

UNEMPLOYMENT - SWEDEN.
Arbetslöshetens offer. Stockholm , 1983. 56 p. : ISBN 91-38-07637-3 LC Card 83-181664
HD5803 .A72 1983

UNEMPLOYMENT - SWEDEN - CASE STUDIES.
Samhällsekonomiska kalkyler vid industrinedläggningar . Stockholm [1982] 213 p. : ISBN 91-38-07164-9 LC Card 83-219569
HD5708.55.S8 S25 1982

UNEMPLOYMENT - SWEDEN - ECONOMETRIC MODELS.
Åberg, Yngve. The impact of working hours and other factors on production and employment /. Aldershot, Hants, England , Brookfield, Vt., U. S.A. , c1987. viii, 166 p. : ISBN 0-566-05480-9 : LC Card 87-8393 DDC 331.25/7/09485 19
HD5202 .A64 1987

UNEMPLOYMENT - SWEDEN - MATHEMATICAL MODELS.
Edin, Per-Anders. Individuella sysselsättningskonsekvenser av nedläggningar /. Helsingfors [1984] 20 leaves ; ISBN 951-555-208-7 LC Card 85-151846
HD5803 .E33 1984

UNEMPLOYMENT - SWEDEN - STATISTICS.
Arbetslöshetens offer. Stockholm , 1983. 56 p. : ISBN 91-38-07637-3 LC Card 83-181664
HD5803 .A72 1983

UNEMPLOYMENT, TECHNOLOGICAL - ADDRESSES, ESSAYS, LECTURES.
Technischer Fortschritt und Arbeitslosigkeit /. Frankfurt/Main , New York , c1983. 372 p. : ISBN 3-593-33246-9 LC Card 84-143045
HD6331 .T39 1983 ***NYPL [JLD 87-331]***

UNEMPLOYMENT, TECHNOLOGICAL - CANADA.
Saunders, Ronald. Aid to workers in declining industries /. [Toronto, Ont.] , c1984. 72 p. : ISBN 0-7743-9007-7 (pbk.) LC Card 84-174952 DDC 331.13/77/0971 19
HD6331.2.C2 S28 1984
NYPL [JLD 86-1287]

UNEMPLOYMENT, TECHNOLOGICAL - FRANCE.
France. Conseil économique et social. Informatique et emploi . [Paris] [1984] 24, 4 p., 8 leaves, 187, 13 p. : LC Card 84-218059
HD6331.2.F8 F73 1984

Pastré, Olivier. L'informatisation et l'emploi /. Paris , 1983. 127 p. : ISBN 2-7071-1387-5 LC Card 83-161919 DDC 331.12/0944 19
HD6331.2.F8 P37 1983

UNEMPLOYMENT, TECHNOLOGICAL - GERMANY, WEST.
Poppe, Jürgen. Mikroelektronik, Jobkiller oder Jobknüller? . Pfaffenweiler , 1984. 93 p. : ISBN 3-89085-027-8 : LC Card 85-129494
HD6331.2.G28 P66 1984

UNEMPLOYMENT, TECHNOLOGICAL - GREAT BRITAIN.
Grant, Pamela, 1944- Youth employment and technological change . Aldershot, [England] , Brookfield, USA , c1987. xii, 393 p. : ISBN 0-566-05423-X : LC Card 86-33659 DDC 331.3/4125/0941 19
HD6276.G7 G66 1987

Unemployment, technology & rural poverty /.
Behari, Bepin. New Delhi , c1983. ix, 453 p. ; ISBN 0-7069-2337-5 : LC Card 83-906129 DDC 338/.06 19
HC440.I52 B43 1983 ***NYPL [JLD 87-1132]***

UNEMPLOYMENT - THAILAND.
Thailand. Samnakngān Khana Kammakān Kansksā hæng Chāt. Education and employment from world capitalism to the rural Thais . Bangkok, Thailand , 1985. 46 p. : LC Card 86-915875 DDC 331.13/79593 19
HD5822.55.A6 T47 1985

Unemployment under capitalism . Ashton, D. N. Brighton, Sussex , 1986. xiv, 225 p. : ISBN 0-7108-0163-7 ***NYPL [JLD 86-1049]***

UNEMPLOYMENT - UNITED STATES.
Ashton, D. N. Unemployment under capitalism . Brighton, Sussex , 1986. xiv, 225 p. : ISBN 0-7108-0163-7
NYPL [JLD 86-1049]

Dumas, Lloyd J. The overburdened economy . Berkeley , c1986. xiv, 297 p. ; ISBN 0-520-05686-8 (alk. paper) LC Card 85-20856 DDC 331.13/7973 19
HD5724 .D775 1986 ***NYPL [JLD 86-2582]***

Hardes, Heinz-Dieter. Arbeitsmarktstrukturen und Beschäftigungsprobleme im internationalen Vergleich . Tübingen , 1981. xv, 484 p. : ISBN 3-16-344468-7 : LC Card 81-196609 DDC 331.13/7 19
HD5707.5 .H37 1981 ***NYPL [JLE 86-2544]***

Keane, John, 1949- After full employment /. London , Dover, N.H., USA , 1986. 198 p. ; ISBN 0-09-164091-1 (pbk.) : LC Card 86-213691 DDC 339.5/0941 19
HD5765.A6 K42 1986

Williams, Terry (Terry M.) Growing up poor /. Lexington, MA , c1985. xvi, 136 p. ; ISBN 0-669-09687-3 (alk. paper) LC Card 84-48564 DDC 362.7/044 19
HV1431 .W55 1985 ***NYPL [JLE 85-2236]***

UNEMPLOYMENT - UNITED STATES - ABSTRACTS.
Kotli͡arov, Vladimir Fedorovich. Bezraboti͡tsa v SShA i ee gosudarstvenno-monopolisticheskoe regulirovanie v sovremennykh uslovii͡akh /. Leningrad , 1977. 18 p. ; LC Card 81-166000
HD5724 .K67 1977

UNEMPLOYMENT - UNITED STATES - CONGRESSES.
The Black youth employment crisis /. Chicago , 1986. viii, 469 p. : ISBN 0-226-26164-6 LC Card 85-20989 DDC 331.3/46396073 19
HD6273 .B57 1986 ***NYPL [JLE 86-3726]***

Job generation . Salt Lake City, Utah , c1986. xiv, 138 p. ; ISBN 0-913420-89-1 (pbk.) LC Card 86-31285 DDC 331.12/094 19
HD5724 .J63 1986

UNEMPLOYMENT - UNITED STATES - EFFECT OF INFLATION ON.
Magdoff, Harry. Stagnation and the financial explosion /. New York , c1987. 208 p. : ISBN 0-85345-716-6 : LC Card 86-33129 DDC 330.973/0927 19
HC106.8 .M315 1987b

UNEMPLOYMENT - UNITED STATES - HISTORY.
Bernstein, Irving, 1916- A caring society . Boston , 1985. 338 p., [24] p. of plates : ISBN 0-395-33116-1 : LC Card 84-25129 DDC 362.8/5/0973 19
HD8072 .B365 1985 ***NYPL [JLD 86-2102]***

UNEMPLOYMENT - WALES, SOUTH.
Harris, C. C. (Christopher Charles) Redundancy and recession in South Wales /. Oxford, OX, UK , New York, NY, USA , 1987. p. cm. ISBN 0-631-15106-0 : LC Card 87-6301 DDC 331.13/794294 19
HD5766.A6 H37 1987

UNEMPLOYMENT - WYOMING - STATISTICS.
Wyoming income and employment report /. Cheyenne, Wyo. [1986] 54, [33], iii p. : LC Card 86-623087 DDC 331.12/5/09787021 19
HD5725.W9 W97 1986

UNEP regional seas reports and studies . (no. 69) Environment and resources in the Pacific /. Geneva, Switzerland , 1985. iv, 294 p. : LC Card 86-217776 DDC 333.7/2/099 19
HC681.3.E5 E58 1985

Unequal alliance . Broad, Robin. Berkeley , c1988. p. cm. ISBN 0-520-05905-0 LC Card 87-10745 DDC 332.1/52 19
HG3881.5.W57 B76 1988

Unequal colleagues . Glazer, Penina Migdal. New Brunswick, N.J. , c1987. xii, 295 p. : ISBN 0-8135-1187-9 (pbk.) : LC Card 86-6568 DDC 331.4/81/000973 19
HD6054.2.U6 G55 1986 ***NYPL [JLD 87-581]***

Unequal comrades . Wrench, John. Coventry , 1986. 30 p. ; ISBN 0-948303-65-4 (pbk.) : LC Card 87-146518 DDC 331.6 19
HD6490.R22 G78 1986

Unequal exchange and the evolution of the world system . Raffer, Kunibert, 1951- New York , 1987. ix, 301 p. ; ISBN 0-312-00440-0 : LC Card 86-31306 DDC 337 19
HF1411 .R26 1987

Unesco.
International directory of suppliers and agents for information handling equipment and logistical support services /. Zagreb , 1985. iii, 418 p. ; LC Card 86-220527 DDC 338.7/61004/025 19
HD9696.A2 I595 1985

Regional Meeting on Socio-economic and Policy Aspects of Water Resources Management in Africa (1986 : Addis Ababa, Ethiopia) Regional Meeting on Socio-economic and Policy Aspects of Water Resources Management in Africa, 2-7 June 1986, Addis Ababa, Ethiopia /. [Addis Ababa?] [1986] 19 v. : LC Card 86-981006 DDC 333.91/0096 19
HD1699.A1 R44 1986

Unesco. Regional Office for Education in Asia and the Pacific. Manual for repackaging of information on population education. Bangkok : Unesco Regional Office for Education in Asia and the Pacific, 1986. 94 p. : ill. ; 32 cm. (Population education programme service) Bibliography: p. 94. LC Card 86-915865 DDC 304.6/07/1 19
1. Population - Studying and teaching - Handbooks, manuals, etc. 2. Population - Informational services - Handbooks, manuals, etc. 3. Population - Documentation - Handbooks, manuals, etc. I. Title. II. Series.
HB850 .U57 1986

Unexpected Japan . Riccomini, Donald R., 1952- New York , 1985. iv, 132 p. ; ISBN 0-8027-0858-7 : LC Card 85-7313 DDC 658/.00952 19
HD70.J3 R53 1985 ***NYPL [JLD 86-1348]***

UNFAIR COMPETITION. see **COMPETITION, UNFAIR.**

Unfair foreign trade practices : selected problems in five Far East countries : staff report / by the Subcommittee on Oversight and Investigations of the Committee on Energy and Commerce, U. S. House of Representatives. Washington : U. S. G.P.O. : For sale by the Supt. of Docs., Congressional Sales Office, U. S. G.P.O., 1986. v, 27 p. ; 24 cm. At head of title: 99th Congress, 2d session. Committee print. Distributed to some depository libraries in microfiche. Shipping list no.: 86-545-P. "June 1986." "Committee print 99-CC." Item 1019-A, 1019-B (microfiche) LC Card 86-603374 DDC 382/.0973/05 19
1. United States - Commerce - East Asia. 2. East Asia - Commerce - United States. 3. Competition, Unfair - East Asia. 4. Tariff - East Asia. 5. Nontariff trade barriers - East Asia. I. United States. Congress. House. Committee on Energy and Commerce. Subcommittee on Oversight and Investigations.
HF3126.5 .U53 1986

UNFAIR TRADE PRACTICES. see **COMPETITION, UNFAIR.**

Unfit to manage! . Lieberman, Ernest D. New York , c1988. xvii, 301 p. ; ISBN 0-07-037815-0 : LC Card 87-20891 DDC 658/.00973 19
HD70.U5 L54 1988

The Unfulfilled promise of synthetic fuels : technological failure, policy immobilism, or commercial illusion / edited by Ernest J. Yanarella and William C. Green. New York : Greenwood Press, 1987. xxii, 225 p. ; 24 cm. (Contributions in political science, 0147-1066 . no. 179) Bibliography: p. [213]-215. Includes index. ISBN 0-313-25666-7 (lib. bdg. : alk. paper) LC Card 87-247 DDC 338.4/766266/0973 19
1. Synthetic fuels industry - United States. I. Yanarella, Ernest J. II. Green, William C., 1941-. III. Series.
HD9502.5.S963 U5475 1987

Ungarische Akademie der Wissenschaften. see **Magyar Tudományos Akadémia, Budapest.**

Ungarische Nationalbank. see **Magyar Nemzeti Bank.**

Ungdomsarbejdsløshed og beskæftigelsesforanstaltninger : en analyse af udstødning fra arbejdsmarkedet, det offentliges rolle i selektionsprocesserne samt mulighederne for konstruktive modforanstaltninger / Kirsten Marie Bruun ... [et al.]. København : Sociale højskolers årskursus, [1984] 100 leaves : ill. ; 30 cm. "Hovedopgave"--Cover. Includes bibliographies. LC Card 85-124463
1. Youth - Employment - Denmark. 2. Unemployment - Denmark. I. Bruun, Kirsten Marie.
HD6276.D4 U54 1984

Unger, Fritz. Konsumentenpsychologie und Markenartikel /. Heidelberg , c1986. xiii, 238 p. ; ISBN 3-7908-0353-7 LC Card 87-127600 DDC 658.8/342 19
HF5415 .K598 1986

Unger, Maurice Albert, 1917-
Real estate finance / Maurice A. Unger, Ronald W. Melicher. 2nd ed. Cincinnati : South-Western Pub. Co., c1984. vi, 426 p. : ill. ; 24 cm. Includes index. Bibliography: p. 385-395. ISBN 0-538-19630-0 LC Card 83-61343 DDC 332.7/2 19
1. Leases. 2. Construction industry - Finance. 3. Housing - Finance. I. Melicher, Ronald W. II. Title.
HG2040 .U53 1984 ***NYPL [JLE 86-4718]***

Real estate, principles, and practices / Maurice A. Unger, George R. Karvel. 8th ed. Cincinnati : South-Western Pub. Co., c1987. ix, 650 p. : ill. (some col.) ; 24 cm. Rev. ed. of: Real estate, principles & practices. 7th ed. c1983. Includes bibliographical references and index. ISBN 0-538-19761-7 LC Card 86-61595 DDC 333.33 19
1. Real estate business. I. Karvel, George R. II. Unger, Maurice Albert, 1917- Real estate, principles & practices. III. Title.
HD1375 .U6 1987

Real estate, principles & practices. Unger, Maurice Albert, 1917- Real estate, principles, and practices / Maurice A. Unger, George R. Karvel. 8th ed. Cincinnati , c1987. ix, 650 p. : ISBN 0-538-19761-7 LC Card 86-61595 DDC 333.33 19
HD1375 .U6 1987

Ungerer, Horst. The European monetary system . Washington, D.C. , c1986. vii, 75 p. : ISBN 0-939934-79-5 (pbk.) : LC Card 86-21432 DDC 332.4/5/094 19
HG930.5 .E86863 1986

Ungern-Sternberg, Thomas R. von.
Unges boligsituation /. Kjær Jensen, Mogens. København , 1983. 139 p. : ISBN 87-7487-228-1 : LC Card 83-189408
HD7347.A3 K53 1983
NYPL [JLK 73-237 v.116]

Ungewissheit und Planungsmethodik . Galts, Helmut. Münster [1983] vi, 234 p. : ISBN 3-88660-143-9 LC Card 84-178712
HB615 .G35 1983

Ungleiche Entwicklung und Regionalpolitik in Südeuropa : Italien, Spanien, Portugal = Desarrollo desigual y politica regional en Europa del Sur : Italia, España, Portugal / Dieter Nohlen und Rainer-Olaf Schultze unter Mitwirkung von Wolfgang Merkel. Bochum : Studienverlag N. Brockmeyer, 1985. 282 p. : ill. ; 21 cm. (Politikwissenschaftliche Paperbacks . Bd. 6) In English, German, Portuguese, and Spanish. Papers presented at the Arbeitstagung Regionalpolitik und Politische Dezentralisierung in Südeuropa held in Heidelberg/Rauenberg on July 19-21, 1984. Includes bibliographies. ISBN 3-88339-441-6 : LC Card 85-205651
1. Europe, Southern - Economic conditions - Regional disparities - Congresses. 2. Regional planning - Europe, Southern - Congresses. I. Nohlen, Dieter. II. Schultze, Rainer-Olaf. III. Merkel, Wolfgang. IV. Arbeitstagung Regionalpolitik und Politische Dezentralisierung in Südeuropa. V. Title: Desarrollo desigual y política regional en Europa del Sur. VI. Series.
HC244.5 .U48 1985

Unheard voices . Marshall, F. Ray. New York , c1987. xi, 339 p. : ISBN 0-465-08869-4 : LC Card 83-46084 DDC 338.6 19
HD5660.U5 M36 1987

Unicamp. see **Universidade Estadual de Campinas.**

UNICEF.
Bureau de zone UNICEF de Yaoundé. Eléments du rapport annuel de la zone de Yaoundé /. N'Djaména [1984] [43] leaves : LC Card 86-980240
HC990 .B87 1984

Eu preciso trabalhar . Rio de Janeiro [between 1983 and 1986] 85 p. ; LC Card 86-150189
HD6276.B72 E9 1983

Política x técnica no planejamento . São Paulo [Brasília] , 1982. 251 p. ; LC Card 86-150182
HD85.P65 P65 1982

Políticas de ajuste y grupos más vulnerables en América Latina . [Bogotá, Colombia] , 1987. 278 p. : ISBN 958-9093-01-9 LC Card 87-404285 DDC 338.98 19
HC125 .P647 1987

Santos, Madalena Herculano dos. Condições de vida nos municípios paraibanos /. João Pessoa (PB) : Brasília, DF : 103 p. : LC Card 87-403990 DDC 330.981/33063 19
HC188.P343 S26 1986

Unidad Agrícola Industrial para la Mujer / Secretaría de la Reforma Agraria, Instituto de Capacitación Agraria. [Mexico City] : El Instituto, 1981. 45 p. : ill. ; 23 cm. Cover title: Manual Unidad Agrícola Industrial para la Mujer. LC Card 84-228117
1. Unidad Agrícola Industrial para la Mujer (Mexico). 2. Women agricultural laborers - Mexico. I. Instituto de Capacitación Agraria (Mexico). II. Title: Manual Unidad Agrícola Industrial para la Mujer.
HD6073.A29 M68 1981

UNIDAD AGRÍCOLA INDUSTRIAL PARA LA MUJER (MEXICO)
Unidad Agrícola Industrial para la Mujer /. [Mexico City] , 1981. 45 p. : LC Card 84-228117
HD6073.A29 M68 1981

Unificación de deudas . Pérez Triana, Santiago, 1858-1916. Londres , 1912. 81 p. ; LC Card 85-111033
HJ8589 .P47 1912

A unified theory of estimation and inference for nonlinear dynamic models /. Gallant, A. Ronald, 1942- Oxford [Oxfordshire] , New York, NY, USA. , 1988. p. cm. ISBN 0-631-15765-4 : LC Card 87-25602 DDC 330/.028 19
HB141 .G33 1988

Uniform system of accounts for hotels. 8th rev. ed. New York, N.Y. (40 W. 38th St., New York 10018) : Hotel Association of New York City, 1986. x, 139 p. : forms ; 24 cm. "Prepared by International Association of Hospitality Accountants"--P. v. "As recommended and prescribed by the Hotel Association of New York City, Inc., and adopted by the American Hotel and Motel Association"--Cover. LC Card 86-220845 DDC 657/.837 19
1. Hotels, taverns, etc. - United States - Accounting. I. Hotel Association of New York City. II. International Association of Hospitality Accountants. III. American Hotel & Motel Association.
HF5686.H75 U55 1986

Uninvited guests . Taylor, Laurie, 1935- London , 1986. 218 p. : ISBN 0-7011-2973-5 : LC Card 86-183414 DDC 791.44/75/0941 19
HE8689.7.A8 T39 1986

UNION AGREEMENTS. see **COLLECTIVE LABOR AGREEMENTS.**

Union Bank of Switzerland. see **Union de banques suisses.**

Union busting in the Tri-State . Suggs, George G., 1929- Norman , 1986. xiv, 282 p. : ISBN 0-8061-2012-6 (alk. paper) LC Card 86-6910 DDC 331.89/2871/0973 19
HD5325.M52 1935 .S84 1986
NYPL [JLD 86-3971]

UNION CARBIDE CORPORATION.
Everest, Larry. Behind the poison cloud . Chicago , 1986. 192 p. : ISBN 0-916650-26-X : LC Card 85-26863 DDC 363.1/79 19
HD7269.C452 I524 1986
NYPL [JSD 86-425]

Shrivastava, Paul. Bhopal . Cambridge, Mass. , c1987. xvi, 184 p. : ISBN 0-88730-084-7 LC Card 86-26575 DDC 363.1/79 19
HD7269.C452 I5268 1987

Sufrin, Sidney C., 1910- Bhopal, its setting, responsibility, and challenge /. Delhi , 1985. 98 p. ; ISBN 81-202-0135-3 : LC Card 85-903246 DDC 363.1/79 19
HD7269.C452 I527 1985
NYPL [JLD 86-1321]

UNION CARBIDE CORPORATION - TRIALS, LITIGATION, ETC.
Shastri, Lalit. Bhopal disaster . New Delhi [1985] 102 p. [32] p. of plates : LC Card 86-902662 DDC 363.1/79 19
HD7269.C452 I5267 1985

UNION CARBIDE LTD. (INDIA)
Everest, Larry. Behind the poison cloud . Chicago , 1986. 192 p. : ISBN 0-916650-26-X : LC Card 85-26863 DDC 363.1/79 19
HD7269.C452 I524 1986
NYPL [JSD 86-425]

Kurzman, Dan. A killing wind . New York , c1987. xvi, 297 p., [16] p. of plates : ISBN 0-07-035687-4 LC Card 87-3398 DDC 363.1/79 19
HD7269.C452 I525 1987

Shrivastava, Paul. Bhopal . Cambridge, Mass. , c1987. xvi, 184 p. : ISBN 0-88730-084-7 LC Card 86-26575 DDC 363.1/79 19
HD7269.C452 I5268 1987

Shrivastava, Paul. Managing industrial crises . New Delhi, India , 1987. 196 p. : ISBN 81-7094-000-1 : LC Card 87-902160 DDC 363.1/79 19
HD7269.C452 I5269 1987

Sufrin, Sidney C., 1910- Bhopal, its setting, responsibility, and challenge /. Delhi , 1985. 98 p. ; ISBN 81-202-0135-3 : LC Card 85-903246 DDC 363.1/79 19
HD7269.C452 I527 1985
NYPL [JLD 86-1321]

UNION CARBIDE LTD.(INDIA) - TRIALS, LITIGATION, ETC.
Shastri, Lalit. Bhopal disaster . New Delhi [1985] 102 p. [32] p. of plates : LC Card 86-902662 DDC 363.1/79 19
HD7269.C452 I5267 1985

UNION-CASTLE MAIL STEAMSHIP COMPANY - HISTORY.
Berridge, Geoff. The politics of the South Africa run . Oxford [Oxfordshire] , New York , 1987. x, 254 p. ; ISBN 0-19-827484-X : LC Card 87-1600 DDC 387.5/094 19
HE903.4 .B47 1987

Union corporate campaigns /. Perry, Charles R. Philadelphia, Pa. , c1987. viii, 211 p. : ISBN 0-89546-065-3 : LC Card 86-82727 DDC 331.89/12 19
HD6490.O72 U665 1987

UNION COUNTY (OR.) - HISTORY.
Barklow, Irene. From trails to rails . Enterprise, Or. , c1987. ix, 300 p. : ISBN 0-9618185-2-2 : LC Card 87-15709 DDC 383/.4979571 19
HE6376.A1 O727 1987

UNION DE BANQUES SUISSES.
Gross, Peter, Dr. Logistik einer Grossbank . Bern , c1983. 52 p. : ISBN 3-258-03274-2 : LC Card 83-181853
HG1526 .B27 Bd. 80 HG3208.U54

Union der Anthropologischen und Ethnologischen Wissenschaften. see **International Union of Anthropological and Ethnological Sciences.**

UNIÓN GENERAL DE TRABAJADORES DE ESPAÑA - HISTORY.
Biglino Campos, Paloma. El socialismo español y la cuestión agraria (1890-1936) /. Madrid [1986?] 564 p. ; ISBN 84-7434-368-2 LC Card 87-136300
HD6764.A29 B54 1986

Unión Internacional de las Sciencias Antropológicas y Etnológicas. see **International Union of Anthropological and Ethnological Sciences.**

Union Internacional para el Estudio Científico de la Población. see **International Union for the Scientific Study of Population.**

Union internationale des sciences anthropologiques et ethnologiques. see **International Union of Anthropological and Ethnological Sciences.**

Union internationale des télécommunications. see **International Telecommunication Union.**

Union internationale des transports routiers. see **International Road Transport Union.**

Unión internationale pour l'étude scientifique de la population. see **International Union for the Scientific Study of Population.**

UNION-MANAGEMENT COMMITTEES. see **LABOR-MANAGEMENT COMMITTEES.**

Union-management relations in a changing economy /. Balfour, Alan. Englewood Cliffs, N.J. , c1987. xiv, 482 p. : ISBN 0-13-938804-4 LC Card 86-30495 DDC 331/.0973 19
HD8066 .B34 1987

Unión Nacional de Instituciones para el Trabajo de Acción Social (Bolivia) Desabastecimiento de alimentos y alternativas de solución en las minas . La Paz [Bolivia] , 1986. 128 : LC Card 87-401454 DDC 331.7/6223453/098413 19
HD8039.M72 B624 1986

UNION NATIONALE DES TRAVAILLEURS DU MALI - HISTORY.
Trade unionism in the republic of Mali . [Lome, Togo] [1983] 78 p. : LC Card 87-107028 DDC 331.88/0966/23 19
HD8827.A5 U557 1983

A union of many trades . Richardson, William, Sir, 1909- Manchester [197-?] xv, 388 p., [16] p. of plates : ISBN 0-906957-01-X : LC Card 83-222175
HD8383.U553 R53 1970z

Union of People's Youth of Bulgariia. see **Dimitrovski komunisticheski mladezhki súiuz.**

UNION OF SHOP, DISTRIBUTIVE AND ALLIED WORKERS - HISTORY.
Richardson, William, Sir, 1909- A union of many trades . Manchester [197-?] xv, 388 p., [16] p. of plates : ISBN 0-906957-01-X : LC Card 83-222175
HD8383.U553 R53 1970z

Union of South Africa. see **South Africa.**

Union raiding . Stocks, Alex M. Kingston, Ont., Canada , 1985. 61 p. ; ISBN 0-88886-125-7 (pbk.) LC Card 86-145321 DDC 331.87/09711 19
HD6528.B9 S86 1985 *NYPL [JLF 87-422]*

Union syndicale suisse. see **Schweizerischer Gewerkschaftsbund.**

Unione degli industriali della provincia di Bergamo (Italy) Le Condizioni industriali della provincia di Bergamo, 1891 . Bologna [1983] 130 p., [1] leaf of plates : LC Card 85-235349
HC307.B5 C59 1983

Unione di banche svizzere. see **Union de banques suisses.**

UNIONE ITALIANA DEL LAVORO.
Simoncini, Franco. Dall'interno della UIL (1950-1985) /. Milano, Italy , c1986. 274 p. ; LC Card 86-169848
HD8473.U533 S56 1986

Unione sindicale svizzero. see **Schweizerischer Gewerkschaftsbund.**

Unions and the future of Australian manufacturing /. Ewer, Peter. Sydney , Boston , 1987. xi, 189 p. : ISBN 0-04-330382-X (pbk.) LC Card 87-164410 DDC 338.4/767/0994 19
HD9738.A82 E93 1987

Unions in crisis and beyond : perspectives from six countries / edited by Richard Edwards, Paolo Garonna, Franz Tödtling. Dover, Mass. : Auburn House Pub. Co., c1986. xii, 340 p. : ill. ; 25 cm. Includes index. Bibliography: p. 309-324. ISBN 0-86569-127-4 : LC Card 85-26646 DDC 331.88 19
1. Trade-unions - United States - Addresses, essays, lectures. 2. Trade unions - Europe - Addresses, essays, lectures. I. Edwards, Richard, 1944-. II. Garonna, P., 1948-. III. Tödtling, Franz.
HD6508 .U45 1986 *NYPL [JLE 86-1936]*

Unions in transition : entering the second century / edited by Seymour Martin Lipset. San Francisco, Calif. : ICS Press, c1986. xviii, 506 p. : ill. ; 24 cm. Includes bibliographical references and index. ISBN 0-917616-74-X : LC Card 86-10256 DDC 331.88 19
1. Trade-unions - United States. 2. Trade-unions - Canada. I. Lipset, Seymour Martin.
HD .U46 1986 *NYPL [JLE 86-4238]*

Unions' rights to company information /. O'Reilly, James T., 1947- Philadelphia, Pa. , c1987. xiii, 312 p. ; ISBN 0-89546-060-2 LC Card 85-82257 *NYPL [JLL 74-174 no.21]*

UNIONS, TRADE. see **TRADE-UNIONS.**

Unions, unemployment and innovation /. Batstone, Eric. Oxford [Oxfordshire] , New York, N.Y., USA , 1986. viii, 320 p. ; ISBN 0-631-14961-9 : LC Card 85-30679 DDC 331.88/0941 19
HD6664 .B335 1986 *NYPL [JLE 86-4031]*

UNIT-CONTAINER SYSTEMS. see **UNITIZED CARGO SYSTEMS.**

UNIT TRUSTS. see **INVESTMENT TRUSTS.**

United Air Lines, inc. Shapiro, Alan C. International corporate finance . Tampa, FL , c1986. 79 p. : ISBN 0-936795-00-X (pbk.) LC Card 86-231054 DDC 658.1/599 19
HG4027.5 .S46 1986

United Arab Republic (al-Iqlīm al Misri) see **Egypt.**

United Arab Republic (Egyptian region) see **Egypt.**

United Arab Republic (Southern region) see **Egypt.**

UNITED CANNERY, AGRICULTURAL, PACKING, AND ALLIED WORKERS OF AMERICA - HISTORY.
Ruíz, Vicki. Cannery women, cannery lives . Albuquerque , c1987. xviii, 194 p. : ISBN 0-8263-1006-0 LC Card 87-13878 DDC 331.88/1640282/09794 19
HD6515.F72 U547 1987

United Dairy Industry Association (U. S.) Butter and margarine attitude & usage . Rosemont, Ill. (6300 N. River Rd., Rosemont 60018) , c1986. 234 p. : LC Card 87-404035 DDC 338.1/772/0973 19
HD9278.U4 B87 1986

UNITED FRUIT COMPANY.
Colombia. Congreso. Cámara de Representantes. Comisión Nombrada para Estudiar el Conflicto Surgido entre la United Fruit Company y la Cooperativa Bananera Colombiana. Informe de la Comisión Nombrada para Estudiar el Conflicto Surgido entre la United Fruit Company y la Cooperativa Bananera Colombiana. Bogotá , 1930. 32 p. ; LC Card 83-189629
HD9259.B3 C728 1930

McCann, Thomas P. On the inside . Boston , c1987. p. cm. ISBN 0-933341-53-9 : LC Card 87-43040 DDC 338.7/634 19
HD9249.U6 M23 1987

United Kingdom consumer electronics. U.K. consumer electronics. Norwalk, Conn., U. S.A. (6 Prowitt St., Norwalk 06855) , c1986. vi, 198 leaves ; LC Card 86-228422 DDC 381/.45621381/0941 19
HD9696.A3 G785 1986

United Nations. Africa, Economic commission for. see **United Nations. Economic Commission for Africa.**

United Nations Association of the United States of America. Economic Policy Council.
America's new competitors . Cambridge, Mass. , c1988. xiv, 290 p. ; ISBN 0-88730-135-5 LC Card 87-19295 DDC 337.730172/4 19
HF1456.5.D44 A44 1988

The Jobs challenge . Cambridge, Mass. , 1986. xvi, 304 p. : ISBN 0-88410-990-9 LC Card

85-7547 DDC 331.12 19
HD5707 .J63 1985 ***NYPL [JLE 86-2190]***

United Nations. Caribbean Development and Co-operation Committee. Informe final del octavo período de sesiones del Comité de Desarrollo y Cooperación del Caribe (Puerto Príncipe, Haití, 6 al 12 de junio de 1984). [Port-au-Prince?] : CDCC, 1984. iv, 36 p. ; 28 cm. At head of title: Comisión Económica para América Latina, Subsede Regional para el Caribe. "Español. Original: inglés." "Lista de los documentos principales": p. 36. "E/CEPAL/G.1317, E/CEPAL/CDCC/G.118." LC Card 85-187058
1. Caribbean area - Economic policy. 2. Caribbean area - Economic integration. I. Title.
HC151 .U54 1984

United Nations Centre for Human Settlements. Community participation for road planning in squatter settlement upgrading . Nairobi, Kenya , 1983. 56 leaves : LC Card 86-980653 DDC 388.1/09676/2 19
HE367.K43 C584 1983

Energy requirements and utilization in rural and urban low-income settlements. Nairobi , 1984. iii, 76 p. : LC Card 86-980596 DDC 333.79/13/091724 19
HD9502.D442 E57 1984

Guidelines for the planning of rural settlements and infrastructure . Nairobi , 1985. vi, 295 p. ; ISBN 92-1-131003-2 LC Card 86-981187 DDC 363/.068 19
HD9688.A2 G85 1985

Moavenzadeh, Fred, 1935- The construction industry in developing countries. Nairobi , 1984. 2 v. ; LC Card 85-980242 DDC 338.4/767/091724 19
HD9715.D44 M63 1984

Population distribution and urbanization . Nairobi, Kenya , 1985. 95 p. ; LC Card 85-980971 DDC 304.6/1 19
HB2160 .P67 1985

The Promotion of non-conventional approaches to housing finance for low-income groups. Nairobi , 1984. ii, 54 p. ; LC Card 86-980642 DDC 363.5/8 19
HD7287.95 .P76 1984

A Review of technologies for the provision of basic infrastructure in low-income settlements. Nairobi , 1984. viii, 82 p. ; LC Card 86-980643 DDC 363/.09172/4 19
HC59.72.C3 R47 1984

Transportation strategies for human settlements in developing countries. Nairobi : United Nations Centre for Human Settlements (Habitat), 1984. v, 79 p. ; 30 cm. Bibliography: p. 72-79. LC Card 85-980241 DDC 380.5/068 19
1. Transportation and state - Developing countries. I. Title.
HE148.5 .U55 1984

United Nations. Comisión Económica para Europa. see **United Nations. Economic Commission for Europe.**

United Nations. Commission économique pour l'Europe. see **United Nations. Economic Commission for Europe.**

United Nations. Committee on the Exercise of the Inalienable Rights of the Palestinian People. Israeli settlements in Gaza and the West Bank (including Jerusalem) . New York , 1982. 66 p. : LC Card 82-232749 DDC 307.7/2/08992405695 19
HD850.Z8 W474 1982
NYPL [*PXLB 86-5156]

UNITED NATIONS CONFERENCE ON THE HUMAN ENVIRONMENT, STOCKHOLM, 1972 - ADDRESSES, ESSAYS, LECTURES.
Diez años después de Estocolmo . Madrid [1983?] 285 p. : ISBN 84-85633-26-3 LC Card 84-122682 DDC 304.2 19
GF49 .D54 1983 ***NYPL [JLE 86-1307]***

United Nations. Conference on Trade and Development. (Old Catalog form: United Nations Conference on Trade and Development)

UNITED NATIONS CONFERENCE ON TRADE AND DEVELOPMENT - HISTORY.
The History of UNCTAD, 1964-1984 /. New York , 1985. ix, 294 p. ; ISBN 92-1-112189-2 (pbk.) LC Card 86-202097 DDC 341.7/54 19
HF1411 .H516 1985

United Nations. Conférence sur le commerce et le développement. see **United Nations. Conference on Trade and Development.**

United Nations. Conferencia sobre Comercio y Desarrollo. see **United Nations. Conference on Trade and Development.**

United Nations. Conferentie inzake Handel en Ontwikkeling. see **United Nations. Conference on Trade and Development.**

United Nations definitive & airmail stamps issued & reprinted 1958-1985 /. Lamers, Duane E. Chicago, IL, USA (Box 1674, Chicago 60690) , c1985. 52 p. : LC Card 87-146520 DDC 769.56/1 19
HE6246 .L36 1985

United Nations definitive and airmail stamps issued and reprinted 1958-1985. Lamers, Duane E. United Nations definitive & airmail stamps issued & reprinted 1958-1985 /. Chicago, IL, USA (Box 1674, Chicago 60690) , c1985. 52 p. : LC Card 87-146520 DDC 769.56/1 19
HE6246 .L36 1985

United Nations. Dept. of Economic and Social Affairs. Application of computer technology for development. Hungarian. A számítástechnika felhasználása a fejlődés előmozdítására . [Budapest] [1971] 95 p. : LC Card 85-178670
HD85.H88 A6615 1971

United Nations. Dept. of Economic and Social Affairs. Statistical Office. see **United Nations. Statistical Office.**

United Nations. Dept. of International Economic and Social Affairs.
Acsádi, György. Policy relevance of findings of the world fertility survey for developing countries /. New York , 1986. vi, 160 p. ; LC Card 85-37681 DDC 304.6/32/091724 19
HB1108 .A28 1986

Age structure of mortality in developing countries . New York , 1986. vi, 267 p. : LC Card 87-401611 DDC 304.6/4 19
HB1528 .A36 1986

Methodologies for assessing the impact of deep sea-bed minerals on the world economy /. New York , 1986. ix, 153 p. : LC Card 87-118207 DDC 338.2 19
HD9506.A2 M47 1986

Review and appraisal of the World Population Plan of Action : 1984 report. New York : United Nations, 1986. vi, 169 p. : ill. ; 23 cm. (Population studies / Department of International and Social Affairs . no. 99) Includes bibliographical references. "ST/ESA/SER.A/99." "United Nations publication. Sales no. E.86.XIII.2"--T.p. verso. ISBN 92-1-151158-5 (pbk.) LC Card 87-105369 DDC 304.6 19
1. Population policy. 2. Population. I. Series: Population studies (New York, N.Y.) , no. 99. II. Title.
HB883.5 .U55 1986

United Nations. Economic and Social Council. Committee for Development Planning. The challenge to multilateralism . New York , 1985. ix, 39 p. : ISBN 92-1-109109-8 (pbk.) LC Card 86-105993 DDC 382.9/1 19
HF1411 .U5383 1985

United Nations. Economic and Social Council. Committee for Development Planning. Doubling development finance . New York , 1986. v, 47 p. ; ISBN 92-1-104185-6 (pbk.) LC Card 87-103015 DDC 338.91/09172/4 19
HG3881 .U646 1986

World population prospects . New York , 1986. x, 330 p. : ISBN 92-1-151159-3 (pbk.) LC Card 87-104085 DDC 304.6/2/021 19
HA155 .W693 1986

United Nations. Dept. of International Economic and Social Affairs. Population Division. Population policy briefs . New York , 1986. viii, 49 p. ; LC Card 87-117649 DDC 304.6/09172/4 19
HB884 .P66557 1986

United Nations. Dept. of Technical Cooperation for Development.
Economic performance of public enterprises . New York , 1986. vii, 264 p. : ISBN 92-1-123103-5 (pbk.) LC Card 87-108199 DDC 338.6/2/091724 19
HD4420.8 .E28 1986

United Nations. Dept. of Technical Cooperation for Development. Development Administration Division. Pricing policy and investment criteria in public enterprises . Ljubljana, Yugoslavia , 1982. 297 p. : ISBN 92-9038-024-1 (pbk.) LC Card 85-242542 DDC 338.7/4 19
HD3842 .P75 1985 ***NYPL [JLE 87-547]***

United Nations. Dept. of Technical Cooperation of Development. Uses of census data for demographic research and development planning in Africa . New York , 1986. iv, 24 p. ; LC Card 87-118612 DDC 304.6/096 19
HB3661 .U94 1986

United Nations. Economic and Social Affairs, Dept. of. see **United Nations. Dept. of Economic and Social Affairs.**

United Nations. Economic and Social Commission for Asia and the Pacific.
An Integrated approach to population, food, and nutrition policies and programmes for national development . Bangkok, Thailand [1979 or 1980] 39 p. ; LC Card 82-169080
HA4553 .I58 1979

Port development policy . Bangkok, Thailand , 1985. ix, 83 p. : LC Card 87-106926 DDC 387.1/0952 19
HE559.J3 P653 1985

Re-orientation of industrial policies . [Bangkok] [1979. iii, 196 p. ; LC Card 83-187259
HD3616.A772 R46 1979

United Nations. Economic and Social Council. Committee for Development Planning.
The challenge to multilateralism : a time for renewal : views and recommendations of the Committee for Development Planning. New York : United Nations, 1985. ix, 39 p. : ill. ; 23 cm. At head of title: Department of International Economic and Social Affairs. "ST/ESA/169." "United Nations publication sales no. E.85.II.C.2"--T.p. verso. Bibliography: p. 32. ISBN 92-1-109109-8 (pbk.) LC Card 86-105993 DDC 382.9/1 19
1. International economic relations. I. United Nations. Dept. of International Economic and Social Affairs. II. Title.
HF1411 .U5383 1985

Doubling development finance : meeting a global challenge : views and recommendations of the Committee for Development Planning. New York : United Nations, 1986. v, 47 p. ; 22 cm. At head of title: Department of International Economic and Social Affairs. "United Nations publication sales no. E.86.II.A. 10"--Verso t.p. "ST/ESA/187." Bibliography: p. 45. ISBN 92-1-104185-6 (pbk.) LC Card 87-103015 DDC 338.91/09172/4 19
1. International finance. 2. International economic relations. 3. Economic assistance - Developing countries. 4. International cooperation. I. United Nations. Dept. of International Economic and Social Affairs. II. Title.
HG3881 .U646 1986

United Nations. Economic and Social Council. Economic commission for Africa. see **United Nations. Economic Commission for Africa.**

United Nations. Economic and Social Council. Economic Commission for Europe. see **United Nations. Economic Commission for Europe.**

United Nations. Economic and Social Council. Economic Commission for Latin America. see **United Nations. Economic Commission for Latin America.**

UNITED NATIONS - ECONOMIC ASSISTANCE.
Cooperation in development and humanitarian assistance. Islamabad, Pakistan [1985] 50 p. : LC Card 86-930251 DDC 338.91/09549/1 19
HC440.5 .C66 1985

Rist, Gilbert, 1938- Towards a new United Nations development strategy . Nyon , 1977. 74 p. ; LC Card 81-118524
HC60 .R539 1977

United Nations. Economic Commission for Africa and Near East. see **United Nations. Economic Commission for Africa.**

United Nations. Economic Commission for Africa. Population Division. Interrelationships among infant and childhood mortality, socio-economic factors and fertility in Zambia . Lusaka , Addis Ababa [1984?] 300 p. : LC Card 87-105950 DDC 304.6/32/096894 19
HB1323.I42 Z335 1984

United Nations. Economic Commission for Europe. Timber Committee. Forestry and the forest industries . Dordrecht ; Boston : xi, 428 p. : ISBN 90-247-3592-0 LC Card 87-20400 DDC 338.1/749 19
HD9765.A2 F64 1987

United Nations. Economic Commission for Latin America and the Caribbean.
Debt, adjustment, and renegotiation in Latin America . Boulder, Colo. , 1986. x, 171 p. : ISBN 0-931477-72-7 : LC Card 85-30098 DDC 336.3/435/098 19
HJ8514.5 .D44 1986 ***NYPL [JLE 87-781]***

Devlin, Robert. External debt in Bolivia /. Boulder, Colo. , 1987. p. cm. ISBN 0-8133-7366-2 : LC Card 87-2088 DDC 336.3/4/0984 19
HJ8574 .D48 1987

The Economic crisis . Santiago, Chile , New York, NY, USA , 1986. 132 p. : ISBN 92-1-121132-8 (pbk.) LC Card 87-404540 DDC 338.98 19
HC125 .E368 1986

Economic panorama of Latin America, 1986 . Santiago, Chile [1986] 82 p. : LC Card 87-107353 DDC 330.98/0038 19
HC125 .E373 1986

Las Empresas transnacionales en el desarrollo colombiano. Santiago de Chile , Nueva York, NY , 1986. 218 p. : ISBN 92-1-321213-5 LC Card 87-402186 DDC 338.8/88861 19
HD2837 .E47 1986

Escenarios políticos y sociales del desarrollo latinoamericano /. [S.l.] [Buenos Aires] , c1986. 231 p. ; ISBN 950-23-0274-5 LC Card 87-400175 DDC 338.98 19
HC125 .E82 1986

Protectionism in the European community against Brazilian exports . Brasília , 1985. 125 p. ; LC Card 86-119107 DDC 382.7/3/094 19
HF3499.5.Z7 B76 1985

Terra, Juan Pablo, 1924. Proceso y significado del cooperativismo uruguayo /. Montevideo [1986] 171 p. ; LC Card 87-403179 DDC 334/.09885 19
HD3482.A4 T47 1986

Uruguay . Montevideo [1986] 103 p. : LC Card 87-403165 DDC 330.9895/065 19
HC232 .U78 1986

United Nations. Economic Commission for Latin America and the Caribbean. División de Estadísticas y Análisis Cuantitativo. Antecedentes estadísticos de la distribución del ingreso. Santiago de Chile , 1986. 49 p. ; LC Card 87-115916 DDC 339.2/09861 19
HC200.I5 A58 1986

United Nations. Economic Commission for Latin America and the Caribbean. División de Estadísticos y Análisis Cuantitativo. Antecedentes estadísticos de la distribución del ingreso. Santiago de Chile , 1986. 50 p. ; LC Card 87-115965 DDC 339.2/0981 19
HC190.I5 A57 1986

United Nations. Economic Commission for Latin America. International Trade and Development Division. América Latina y la economía mundial del algodón. Santiago de Chile , 1985. 128 p. : ISBN 92-1-321189-9 LC Card 85-230001 DDC 338.1/7351/098 19
HD9884.L3 A46 1985 ***NYPL [JLE 86-3341]***

United Nations Educational Scientific and Cultural Organization. International Institute for Educational Planning. see **International Institute for Educational Planning.**

United Nations Educational Scientific and Cultural Organization - Technical assistance. see **United Nations - Technical assistance.**

United Nations. Europäische Wirtschaftskommission. see **United Nations. Economic Commission for Europe.**

United Nations. Europe, Economic Commission for. see **United Nations. Economic Commission for Europe.**

United Nations. European Economic Commission. see **United Nations. Economic Commission for Europe.**

United Nations. Evropeĭskaya Ekonomicheskaya Komissiya. see **United Nations. Economic Commission for Europe.**

United Nations. FAO/ECE Agriculture and Timber Division. General review /. New York , 1986. iii, 81 p. ; ISBN 92-1-116361-7 (pbk.) LC Card 87-120391 DDC 338.1/094 19
HD1917 .U5 no. 28, vol. 1

United Nations Fund for Population Activities. Pendidikan kependudukan untuk perwira. [Jakarta] [1981] vi, 120 p. : LC Card 85-940192
HB850.5 .P46 1981

Transición demográfica y oferta de fuerza de trabajo en Colombia /. [Bogotá], República de Colombia , 1986. 2 v. : ISBN 958-95096-0-6 (set) LC Card 87-113652 DDC 331.11/09861 19
HD5757.A6 T7 1986

United Nations. General Assembly. United Nations. Secretary-General. [Economic and social consequences of the arms race and of military expenditures. French.] Conséquences économiques et sociales de la course aux armements /. Paris , 1983. 121 p. : ISBN 2-7178-0645-8 : LC Card 84-136625
HC79.D4 U52 1983

United Nations. General Assembly. Conference on Trade and Development. see **United Nations. Conference on Trade and Development.**

United Nations. Group of Consultant Experts on the Economic and Social Consequences of the Arms Race and Military Expenditures. United Nations. Secretary-General. [Economic and social consequences of the arms race and of military expenditures. French.] Conséquences économiques et sociales de la course aux armements /. Paris , 1983. 121 p. : ISBN 2-7178-0645-8 : LC Card 84-136625
HC79.D4 U52 1983

United Nations. Industrial Development Organization.
Aizawa, Minoru. Review on the development of antibiotics industry in selected countries . [Vienna, Austria] , 1985. 92 p. : LC Card 86-151674 DDC 338.4/7615329/0952 19
HD9675.A63 J33 1985

Industry in the 1980s . New York , 1985. xii, 228 p. : ISBN 92-1-106207-1 (pbk.) LC Card 86-227928 DDC 338.09 19
HD9720.5 .I53 1985

International comparative advantage in manufacturing . Vienna , 1986. xii, 226 p. : ISBN 92-1-106210-1 (pbk.) LC Card 86-214978 DDC 382.1/042 19
HF1412 .I57 1986

Wong, John, 1939- Regional industrial co-operation . Vienna , 1986. xi, 102 p. : ISBN 92-1-106204-7 (pbk.) LC Card 86-214910 DDC 337.1/5 19
HC441 .W66 1986

United Nations Industrial Development Organization. Division for Industrial Studies. Statistics and Survey Unit.
Africa in figures /. [Vienna] [1985] iv, 153 p. ; LC Card 87-402813 DDC 338.096/021 19
HD9737.A2 A38 1985

Industry in the 1980s . New York , 1985. xii, 228 p. : ISBN 92-1-106207-1 (pbk.) LC Card 86-227928 DDC 338.09 19
HD9720.5 .I53 1985

United Nations Industrial Development Organization. Regional and Country Studies Branch.
International economic restructuring and the regional community /. Aldershot, Hants, England , Brookfield, Vt., USA , c1987. x, 404 p. : ISBN 0-566-05478-7 : LC Card 87-11841 DDC 330.9 19
HF1412 .I574 1987

Policies and measures to promote industrial co-operatives in Africa /. [New York] [1985] 23 p. ; LC Card 87-104469 DDC 334/.6/096 19
HD3247 .P65 1985

United Nations Industrial Development Organization. Regional Expert Consultation on the Role of Rural Co-operatives in the Productive Sectors in Africa.
Dadson, J. A. Production co-operatives and rural development in Ghana /. [Addis Ababa] [1985] 53 p. ; LC Card 87-105501 DDC 334/.6/09667 19
HD3258.3.A4 D34 1985

Policies and measures to promote industrial co-operatives in Africa /. [New York] [1985] 23 p. ; LC Card 87-104469 DDC 334/.6/096 19
HD3247 .P65 1985

United Nations Industrial Development Organization. Sectoral Studies Branch. The Petrochemical industry in developing countries . [Vienna] [1985] xiv, 155 p. : LC Card 86-204881 DDC 338.4/7661804/091724 19
HD9579.C33 D446 1985

United Nations Institute for Namibia.
Development studies and management secondment programme / United Nations Institute for Namibia. Lusaka, Zambia : The Institute, 1985. v, 26 p. ; 30 cm. LC Card 87-980229 DDC 338.9/007/15 19
1. Economic development - Study and teaching (Higher) - Namibia. I. Title.
HD77.5.N3 U55 1985

United Nations International Comparison Project. World comparisons of purchasing power and real product for 1980 . New York , 1986- v. <1 > ; LC Card 86-225798 DDC 339.3 19
HC79.I5 W675 1986

United Nations. International Labor Office. see **International Labor Office.**

United Nations. International Labor Organization. see **International Labor Organization.**

United Nations. Konferent͡siia po torgovle i razvitiiu. see **United Nations. Conference on Trade and Development.**

United Nations. Latin America, Economic Commission for. see **United Nations. Economic Commission for Latin America.**

United Nations Organization. see **United Nations.**

UNITED NATIONS - POPULATION ASSISTANCE.
Johnson, Stanley, 1940- World population and the United Nations . Cambridge [Cambridgeshire] , New York , 1987. xxxviii, 357 p. ; ISBN 0-521-32207-3 LC Card 87-5126 DDC 363.9 19
HB884.5 .J64 1987

UNITED NATIONS - POSTAL SERVICE.
Lamers, Duane E. United Nations definitive & airmail stamps issued & reprinted 1958-1985 /. Chicago, IL, USA (Box 1674, Chicago 60690) , c1985. 52 p. : LC Card 87-146520 DDC 769.56/1 19
HE6246 .L36 1985

United Nations Regional Housing Centre for the E.S.C.A.P. Region. Dholakia, Bakul H. 1947- The economics of housing in India . Delhi , 1982. xviii, 274 p. ; LC Card 83-905798 DDC 363.5/0954 19
HD7361.A3 D47 1982
NYPL [JLD 85-2908]

United Nations. Research Institute for Social Development.
Rello, Fernando. Estado y ejidos en México . Ginebra , 1986. xxvi, 122 p. : LC Card 86-210274
HG2051.M62 L37 1986

Report.
(no. 85.5) McGranahan, Donald V. Measurement and analysis of socioeconomic development . Geneva , 1985. xx, 504 p. :
NYPL [JLK 74-447 no.85.5]

United Nations. Secretariat. Statistical Office. see **United Nations. Statistical Office.**

United Nations. Secretary-General.
The Economic and social consequences of disarmament . Washington, D.C. [1961] ii leaves, 89 p. ; LC Card 85-115648
HC110.D4 E37 1961

[Economic and social consequences of the arms race and of military expenditures. French]

Conséquences économiques et sociales de la course aux armements / préface et étude par Christian Schmidt. Paris : Economica, 1983. 121 p. : ill. ; 24 cm. At head of title: Nations Unies. "Par une lettre datée du 30 juillet 1982, le Président du Groupe d'experts consultants a transmis au Secrétaire général le rapport qui est soumis dans le présent document à l'Assemblée générale"--P. after t.p. Translation of: Economic and social consequences of the arms race and of military expenditures. ISBN 2-7178-0645-8 : LC Card 84-136625
1. Armed Forces - Appropriations and expenditures. 2. War - Economic aspects. 3. Disarmament - Economic aspects. I. Schmidt, Christian, 1950-. II. United Nations. Group of Consultant Experts on the Economic and Social Consequences of the Arms Race and Military Expenditures. III. United Nations. General Assembly. IV. Title.
HC79.D4 U52 1983

United Nations. Statistical Office. (Old Catalog form: United Nations. Secretariat. Statistical Office.)
Classification by broad economic categories . New York , 1986. x, 68 p. ; ISBN 92-1-161276-4 (pbk.) LC Card 87-401426 DDC 338/.02/012 19
HF1041 .C53 1986

Commodity trade (by sea) statistics . New York , 1980. v, 396 p. ; LC Card 87-112992 DDC 387.5/55/021 19
HE562.8 .C667 1980

Handbook of national accounting . New York , 1986. xi, 180 p. : ISBN 92-1-161264-0 (pbk.) LC Card 87-106896 DDC 339.3/2 19
HC79.I5 H36 1986

Standard international trade classification revision 3 / Department of International Economic and Social Affairs, Statistical Office. New York : United Nations, 1986. xvi, 106, 31, 25 p. ; 28 cm. (Statistical papers. Series M . no. 34, rev. 3) "ST/ESA/STAT/SER.M/34/REV.3" "United Nations publication sales no. E.86.XVII.12"--T.p. verso. Includes bibliographical references. ISBN 92-1-161265-9 (pbk.) LC Card 86-226177 DDC 338/.02/012 19
1. Commercial products - Classification. I. Title.
HF1041 .U56 1986

UNITED NATIONS - TECHNICAL ASSISTANCE.
Cooperation in development and humanitarian assistance. Islamabad, Pakistan [1985] 50 p. : LC Card 86-930251 DDC 338.91/09549/1 19
HC440.5 .C66 1985

United Nations transport and communications decade in Africa : technical consultative meeting on railways / prepared by the Economic Commission for Africa. [Addis Ababa?] : ECA, [1985?- v. <1 > : maps ; 28 cm. "DEC/TRANSCOM/TCT/85/RAIL/2." Cover title: United Nations transport and communications decade in Africa, 1978-1988 : Railways. CONTENTS. - v. A. Economic and railway problems in Africa. LC Card 86-981012 DDC 385/.096 19
1. Railroads - Africa. 2. Africa - Economic conditions - 1960-. I. United Nations. Economic Commission for Africa.
HE3395 .U65 1985

United Nations transport and communications decade in Africa (1978-1988) : review of the programme of the first phase (1980-1983). [S.l.] : Economic Commission for Africa, [1983?] iii, 32 p. ; 34 x 42 cm. "Economic Commission for Africa, third conference of ministers of transport, communications, and planning, Cairo, Egypt, 8 to 11 March 1983." LC Card 87-115721 DDC 380.3/096 19
1. United Nations Transport and Communications Decade in Africa, 1978-1988. 2. Telecommunication policy - Africa. 3. Postal service - Africa. 4. Economic development projects - Africa. I. United Nations. Economic Commission for Africa.
HE8465 .U55 1983

United Nations transport and communications decade in Africa, 1978-1988. Port guide on African major ports. [Addis Ababa, Ethiopia] [1986?] ii, 256 p. ; LC Card 86-980946 DDC 387.1/096 19
HE559.5 .P68 1986

UNITED NATIONS TRANSPORT AND COMMUNICATIONS DECADE IN AFRICA, 1978-1988.
United Nations transport and communications decade in Africa (1978-1988) . [S.l.] [1983?] iii, 32 p. ; LC Card 87-115721 DDC 380.3/096 19
HE8465 .U55 1983

United Nations University Symposium on Energy and Agriculture Futures--Policy Implications of Global Models (1982 : Paris, France)
Energy and agriculture : their interacting futures : policy implications of global models : proceedings of The United Nations University Symposium on Energy and Agriculture Futures--Policy Implications of Global Models, held in Paris, February 22-25, 1982 / edited by Maurice Lévy, John L. Robinson. [Chur, Switzerland ; New York] : Harwood Academic Publishers for the United Nations University, c1984. xii, 370 p. : ill. ; 23 cm. (Global modelling and applications, 0739-5671 . v. 1) Includes bibliographies and index. ISBN 3-7186-0187-7 LC Card 83-18363 DDC 333.79 19
1. Agriculture and state - Congresses. 2. Food supply - Government policy - Congresses. 3. Energy policy - Congresses. 4. Agriculture - Energy consumption - Congresses. I. Levy, Maurice, 1922-. II. Robinson, John L. III. Title. IV. Series.
HD1405 .E53 1983 ***NYPL [JLD 86-1837]***

United Nations. Welthandels- und Entwicklungskonferenz. see **United Nations. Conference on Trade and Development.**

United Nations. World Health Organization. see **World Health Organization.**

United Nations World Security Organization. see **United Nations.**

United Nations/International Year of Shelter for the Homeless. Housing and Urban Development Corporation. HUDCO's initiatives for IYSH. New Delhi [1987?] 49 p. : LC Card 87-902550 DDC 363.5/8 19
HD7287.96.I4 H67 1987

United States.
Federal Capital Investment Program Information Act of 1984. Supplement to special analysis D : a report required by the Federal Capital Investment Program Information Act of 1984 (Title II of Public Law 98-501). Washington, D.C. , 1985. 1 v. (various pagings) ; ***NYPL [JLF 86-603]***

FEDERAL-STATE TAX COLLECTION ACT OF 1972.
Ware, Ray M. Piggybacking--the federal-state collection act of 1972 /. Lexington, Ky. , 1980. ix leaves, 35 p. ; ***NYPL [JLM 79-1230 no.10]***

TAX REFORM ACT OF 1986.
Highlights of the Tax Reform Act of 1986 /. Boston [1986] xi, 94 p. ; ***NYPL [JLE 87-761]***

United States. Agency for International Development. (Old Catalog form: United States. International Development, Agency for)

United States. Agency for International Development. Agribusiness Division. Kinsey, B. H. Agribusiness and rural enterprise /. London , New York , c1987. 228 p. ; ISBN 0-7099-1558-6 : LC Card 87-471 DDC 338.1/09172/4 19
HD9018.D44 K55 1987

United States. Agency for International Development. Directorate for Energy and Natural Resources. Energy programs in the Agency for International Development. [Washington, D.C.] : Agency for International Development, Bureau for Science and Technology, Directorate for Energy and Natural Resources, [1986] 38 p. ; 28 cm. "August 1986." LC Card 86-603136 DDC 333.79/15/091724 19
1. Energy development - Developing countries. 2. Energy policy - Developing countries. 3. Economic assistance, American. 4. Technical assistance, American. 5. United States. Agency for International Development. I. Title.
HD9502.D442 U55 1986

United States. Agency for International Development. Regional Office for Central America and Panama Affairs. An Evaluation of ROCAP activities in marketing, 1965-71 /. Washington, D.C. (1200 18th St., N.W., Washington 20036) [1971] xvii, 82, 3 leaves, [1] leaf of plates : LC Card 81-146599
HC141 .E93 1971

United States. Agricultural Cooperative Service. Knutson, Ronald D. Cooperative involvement in issues of domestic farm policy /. College Station, Tex. , 1986. 59 p. : LC Card 86-623063 DDC 338.1/8764 19
HD1491.U6 T45 1986

United States. Agricultural Research Service. Western Regional Research Center. Proyecto harinas compuestas . La Paz, Bolivia , 1982. 272, [2], 3 p., [9] p. of plates : LC Card 83-195592
HD9044.B52 P76 1982

United States. Agriculture and Forestry, Committee on (Senate) see **United States. Congress. Senate. Committee on Agriculture and Forestry.**

United States. Agriculture, Dept. of. see **United States. Dept. of Agriculture.**

United States aid to Israel. Laufer, Leopold Yehuda. U. S. aid to Israel . [Jerusalem] [1983] 55 p. : LC Card 87-400279 DDC 338.91/73/05694 19
HC415.25 .L38 1983

United States aid to the West Bank and Gaza. Laufer, Leopold Yehuda. U. S. aid to the West Bank and Gaza . [Jerusalem] [1985] 54 p. ; LC Card 87-400340 DDC 338.91/73/056951 19
HC415.25.Z7 W4735 1985

UNITED STATES. AIR FORCE - PERSONNEL MANAGEMENT.
Transitional career counseling from the Air Force to the private sector . Washington, D.C. , c1987. iv, 153 leaves : LC Card 87-401057 DDC 358.4/1154/0973 19
HF5382.75.U6 T7 1987

The United States and Canada . Wonnacott, Paul. Washington, DC , 1987. xii, 173 p. : ISBN 0-88132-056-0 (pbk.) : LC Card 87-2660 DDC 382.71073 19
HF1456.5.C2 W65 1987

United States and European Community development assistance to Africa . Bereuter, Douglas K. [Washington, D.C.? , 1985?] 22, [2] leaves ; LC Card 87-108848 DDC 338.91/4/06 19
HC800 .B455 1985

United States and Foreign Commercial Service. A Basic guide to exporting. Washington, D.C. [1986] viii, 148 p. : LC Card 86-603426 DDC 658.8/48 19
HF1009.6 .B38 1986

The United States and Japan in the international monetary system, 1946-1985 /. Roosa, Robert V. New York , 1986. ii, 76 p. ; LC Card 86-230043 DDC 332.4/560952 19
HG3881 .R66 1986

UNITED STATES - APPROPRIATIONS AND EXPENDITURES - FORECASTING.
Tax expenditures . Washington, D.C. [1983] xiv, 82 p. ; ***NYPL [JLF 84-401]***

Verdier, James M. Tax expenditures . Washington, D.C. , 1982. xx, 102 p. ; ***NYPL [JLF 83-663]***

UNITED STATES - ARMED FORCES - APPROPRIATIONS AND EXPENDITURES.
Weida, William J. The political economy of national defense /. Boulder , 1987. xvii, 230 p. ; ISBN 0-8133-0432-6 (alk. paper) : LC Card 86-19015 DDC 355.6/22/0973 19
UA23 .W3694 1987 ***NYPL [JLE 87-1043]***

UNITED STATES - ARMED FORCES - FINANCE, PERSONAL.
Pillsbury, Hobart B. Armed forces guide to personal financial planning . Harrisburg, PA , c1987. p. cm. ISBN 0-8117-2123-X LC Card 86-30201 DDC 332.024/355 19
HG179 .P55 1987

UNITED STATES - ARMED FORCES - PROCUREMENT.
Coalition of Northeast Governors. Policy Research Center. A case of inequity [microform] . [New York] , 1977. 39 p. ; ***NYPL [*ZT-1564 no.21]***

United States. Armed Services, Committee on (House) see **United States. Congress. House. Committee on Armed Services.**

United States. Arms Control and Disarmament Agency. The Economic and social consequences of disarmament . Washington, D.C. [1961] ii leaves, 89 p. ; LC Card 85-115648
HC110.D4 E37 1961

United States Army in World War II. History of the War Department.
Fairchild, Byron. The Army and industrial manpower /. Westport, Conn. , 1987. xiv, 291 p. : ISBN 0-313-25480-X (lib. bdg. : alk. paper) LC Card 86-25738 DDC 331.11/0973 19
HD5724 .F25 1987

United States. Banking, Housing and Urban Affairs, Committee on. (Senate) see United States. Congress. Senate. Committee on Banking, Housing and Urban Affairs.

UNITED STATES - BIOGRAPHY.
Goldman, Peter Louis, 1933- The end of the world that was . New York , c1986. xiv, 129 p., [8] p. of plates : ISBN 0-525-24428-X LC Card 85-31223 DDC 920/.073 19
CT220 .G6 1986 ***NYPL [JFD 86-6015]***

United States. Board of Engineers for Rivers and Harbors. (Old Catalog form: United States. Rivers and Harbors, Board of Engineers for.)
Port of Mobile, Alabama. The Port of Mobile, Alabama / prepared by the Water Resources Support Center. Rev. 1986. Washington , Fort Belvoir, Va. , 1986. vi, 99 p. : LC Card 86-603154 DDC 387.1/09761/22 19
HE554.M7 P67 1986

United States. Board of Governors of the Federal Reserve System. (Old Catalog form: United States. Federal Reserve Board.)

UNITED STATES. BOARD OF GOVERNORS OF THE FEDERAL RESERVE SYSTEM - HISTORY.
Livingston, James, 1949- Origins of the Federal Reserve System . Ithaca , 1986. 250 p. ; ISBN 0-8014-1844-5 (alk. paper) LC Card 85-48199 DDC 332.1/1/0973 19
HG2563 .L58 1986 ***NYPL [JLE 86-2522]***

United States. Bureau of Economic Analysis. U. S. direct investment abroad . Washington, D.C. , 1986. x, 41 p. ; LC Card 87-600815
HG4538 .U22 1986

United States. Bureau of Employment Security. Unemployment Insurance Service. see United States. Unemployment Insurance Service.

United States. Bureau of Internal Revenue. see **United States. Internal Revenue Service.**

United States. Bureau of Mines. (Old Catalog form: United States. Mines Bureau.)
An Appraisal of minerals availability for 34 commodities /. [Pittsburgh, Pa.] , 1987. iii, 300 p. : LC Card 87-600244 DDC 333.8/5 19
HD9506.A2 A72 1987

Financing foreign development of non-fuel mineral resources . [Washington, D.C.] [1986] 308 p. : LC Card 86-602175 DDC 332.1/5 19
HD9506.D452 F56 1986

Mineral industries of Latin America /. Washington, D.C. , 1987. p. cm. LC Card 87-600334 DDC 338.2/098 19
HD9506.L252 M37 1987

United States. Bureau of the Mint. (Old Catalog form: United States. Mint Bureau)
World coinage report, 1980-1984. Washington, D.C. [1986?] vi, 114 p. : LC Card 86-602440 DDC 737.4/021 19
HG327 .W67 1986

UNITED STATES. BUREAU OF THE MINT - HISTORY.
Wolman, Paul. The U. S. Mint /. New York , c1987. 92 p. : ISBN 0-87754-829-3 (lib. bdg.) : LC Card 86-31720 DDC 353.0082/2 19
HG459 .W65 1987

United States Catholic Conference. Administrative Board. Divestment, disinvestment, and South Africa : a policy statement of the USCC Administrative Board. Washington, D.C. : U. S. Catholic Conference, c1986. 36 p. ; 22 cm. (Publication / Office of Publishing and Promotion Services, United States Catholic Conference . no. 137-7) ISBN 1-555-86137-7 (pbk.) LC Card 87-136857 DDC 332.6/7373/068 19
1. Investments, American - South Africa. 2. Disinvestment - South Africa. 3. Economic sanctions, American - South Africa. 4. Apartheid - South Africa. 5. Race relations - Religious aspects - Catholic Church. I. Title.
HG5851.A3 U55 1986

United States Catholic institutions and labor unions, 1960-1980. Sullivan, Patrick J., 1929- U. S. Catholic institutions and labor unions, 1960-1980 /. Lanham, MD , c1985. 545 p. ; ISBN 0-8191-4970-5 (alk. paper) : LC Card 85-20171 DDC 331.88/1128273 19
HD6481.2.U6 S85 1985
NYPL [JLE 86-2407]

UNITED STATES - CENSUS.
Briggs, Dwight. Journey-to-work trends . Washington, D.C. , Springfield, VA [1986] 1 v. (various pagings) : LC Card 86-602387 DDC 388.4/1314/0973 19
HE371.A3 B75 1986

UNITED STATES - CENSUS - DATA PROCESSING.
SPSSX processing of U. S. census data. Chicago, Ill. , c1983. 79 p. : ISBN 0-918469-02-3 (pbk.) LC Card 87-160044 DDC 304.6/028/55329 19
HA37.U55 S64 1983

UNITED STATES - CENSUS, 20TH, 1980.
Census '80 . Baltimore, Md. (2225 N. Charles St., Baltimore 21218) [1983] xv, 106 leaves : LC Card 83-622347 DDC 339.2/2/097526 19
HC108.B2 C46 1983 ***NYPL [JLF 86-1594]***

Crowley, Charles. Income and poverty in New Jersey [microform] . Trenton, N.J. [1982] 32 p. ; LC Card 83-620831 DDC 339.2/2/09749 19
HC107.N53 I5113 1982
NYPL [*ZT-1712 no.31]

UNITED STATES - CENSUS, 20TH, 1980 - EVALUATION.
Census of population and housing (1980). Evaluation and research reports. Programs to improve coverage in the 1980 census. 1980 census of population and housing. Washington, D.C. [1987] 83 p. : LC Card 87-601259
HA201 1980aa

United States Chamber of Commerce. see **Chamber of Commerce of the United States of America.**

United States - Civil service. see **Civil service - United States.**

United States civilian nuclear power policy, 1954-1984 . Holl, Jack M. Washington, D.C. , Springfield, Va. [1986] 46 p., [1] leaf of plates : LC Card 86-601137 DDC 333.79/24 19
HD9698.U52 H65 1986

UNITED STATES - COLONIES - ASIA - ECONOMIC POLICY.
Giesecke, Leonard F. (Leonard Frederick) History of American economic policy in the Philippines during the American colonial period, 1900-1935 /. New York , 1987. 279 p. ; ISBN 0-8240-8082-3 (alk. paper) : LC Card 87-23786 DDC 337.730599 19
HF1456.5.P6 G53 1987

UNITED STATES - COMMERCE - ASIA - CONGRESSES.
Vision of the future . Washington, D.C. , 1986. x, 189 p. : LC Card 87-125235 DDC 382/.0973/05 19
HF3118 .V57 1986

UNITED STATES - COMMERCE - ASIA - STATISTICS.
U. S. trade relations with Asia . Washington , 1987. vii, 85 p. ; LC Card 87-601359 DDC 382/.0973/05 19
HF3118 .U15 1987

UNITED STATES - COMMERCE - BRAZIL.
Matz, Viktor, 1947- Entwicklungsländer im internationalen Konjunkturzusammenhang . Bergisch Gladbach , c1986. 199, lxxvi p. ; ISBN 3-89012-052-0 LC Card 86-227998
HF3408.U5 M37 1986

UNITED STATES - COMMERCE - CANADA.
Wonnacott, Ronald J. Canada/United States free trade . Toronto, Ont. , c1985. 30 p. ; ISBN 0-7729-0036-1 (pbk.) LC Card 86-673986
HF1480.5.U57 W66x 1985

UNITED STATES - COMMERCE - CARIBBEAN AREA.
Mukerjee, Dilip. Lessons from the Caribbean Basin initiative /. Kuala Lumpur, Malaysia , c1985. 36 p. ; ISBN 967-99974-6-4 (pbk.) LC Card 87-101396 DDC 338.91/73/0729 19
HF1456.5.C27 M85 1985

UNITED STATES - COMMERCE - CENTRAL AMERICA.
Mukerjee, Dilip. Lessons from the Caribbean Basin initiative /. Kuala Lumpur, Malaysia , c1985. 36 p. ; ISBN 967-99974-6-4 (pbk.) LC Card 87-101396 DDC 338.91/73/0729 19
HF1456.5.C27 M85 1985

UNITED STATES - COMMERCE - CHINA.
Lardy, Nicholas R. China's entry into the world economy . Lanham, MD , New York, N.Y. , c1987. xviii, 57 p. : ISBN 0-8191-6371-6 (alk. paper) : LC Card 87-10625 DDC 382/.0951 19
HF3820.5 .L37 1987

Tsao, James T. H. China's development strategies and foreign trade /. Lexington, Mass. , c1987. xii, 209 p. : ISBN 0-669-13954-8 (alk. paper) LC Card 86-45590 DDC 338.951 19
HC427.9 .T689 1987

UNITED STATES - COMMERCE - COLOMBIA.
Matz, Viktor, 1947- Entwicklungsländer im internationalen Konjunkturzusammenhang . Bergisch Gladbach , c1986. 199, lxxvi p. ; ISBN 3-89012-052-0 LC Card 86-227998
HF3408.U5 M37 1986

UNITED STATES - COMMERCE - CONGRESSES.
Proceedings of a symposium on competitiveness of U. S. grains in international markets /. Fargo, N.D. [1986] ii leaves, 67 p. : LC Card 86-622839 DDC 382/.4131/0973 19
HD9035 .P76 1986

United States. Commerce, Dept. of. see **United States. Dept. of Commerce.**

UNITED STATES - COMMERCE - DEVELOPING COUNTRIES.
Der Neue Protektionismus . Bonn , c1983. 195 p. : ISBN 3-87831-370-5 LC Card 83-198686
HF1756 .N58 1983

U. S. agriculture & Third World development . Boulder , 1987. xi, 258 p. ; ISBN 1-555-87011-2 (lib. bdg.) : LC Card 86-29860 DDC 338.1/09172/4 19
HD1765 .U15 1987

UNITED STATES - COMMERCE - EAST ASIA.
U. S. trade relations in the Pacific Rim . Washington , 1987. v, 57 p. ; LC Card 87-601361 DDC 382/.0973/09 19
HF3126.5 .U17 1987

Unfair foreign trade practices . Washington , 1986. v, 27 p. ; LC Card 86-603374 DDC 382/.0973/05 19
HF3126.5 .U53 1986

UNITED STATES - COMMERCE - GREAT BRITAIN.
Sheffield, John Holroyd, Earl of, 1735-1821. Observations on the commerce of the American states. London, 1784. 2 p.l., xlvii, 345, [21] p., 1 l. LC Card 06-17319
HF3025 .S58

UNITED STATES - COMMERCE - HANDBOOKS, MANUALS, ETC.
A Basic guide to exporting /. [Reno, Nev.] [198-] 68 leaves ; LC Card 86-622819
HF3035 .B37 1980z

Importing into the United States . Washington, D.C. [1985] 84 p. : LC Card 85-603032 DDC 343.73/087 347.30387 19
HF3035 .I46 1985

Importing into the United States. Rocklin, Calif. , c1987. 83 p. : ISBN 0-914629-35-2 (pbk.) : LC Card 87-16931 DDC 343.73/087 347.30387 19
HF3055 .I46 1987

UNITED STATES - COMMERCE - HISTORY.
Dobson, John M. A history of American enterprise /. Englewood Cliffs, N.J. , c1988. p. cm. ISBN 0-13-389081-3 LC Card 87-18679 DDC 338.0973 19
HF3021 .D6 1988

UNITED STATES - COMMERCE - INDIA.
Report on development of India's handloom fabrics for export to the United States of America, September 1957 /. [S.l. , 1957]

(Delhi : Albion Press) ii, ii, 108 p., [8] p. of plates : LC Card 81-911063
HD9866.I62 R46 1957

UNITED STATES - COMMERCE - IVORY COAST.
Trueblood, Michael A. The Ivory Coast . Washington, DC , 1986. iv, 32 p. : LC Card 86-602806 DDC 338.1 s 382/.41/096668 19
HD1411 .F59 no. 223 HD9017.I912

UNITED STATES - COMMERCE - JAMAICA.
Lyn-Cook, Marlene. Marketing guidelines for Jamaica's non-traditional exports. [Miami, FL] [1986] 83 leaves : LC Card 87-156503 DDC 382/.097292/073 19
HF1009.7.J25 L96 1986

UNITED STATES - COMMERCE - JAPAN.
De Mente, Boye. How to do business with the Japanese . Lincolnwood, Ill., U. S.A. , c1987. vi, 269 p. ; ISBN 0-8442-8509-9 (pbk.) LC Card 86-62724 DDC 395/.52 19
HF5387 .D3835 1987

Krasner, Stephen D., 1942- Asymmetries in Japanese-American trade . Berkeley , c1987. vii, 80 p. ; ISBN 0-87725-532-6 (pbk.) : LC Card 87-81842 DDC 382/.0973/052 19
HF3127 .K73 1987

McCreary, Don R. Japanese-U. S. business negotiations . New York , 1986. viii, 121 p. ; ISBN 0-275-92006-2 (alk. paper) : LC Card 86-554 DDC 658 19
HD58.6 .M38 1986 ***NYPL [JLE 86-3074]***

Trade friction and economic policy . Cambridge [Cambridgeshire] , New York , 1987. xii, 243 p. : ISBN 0-521-34446-8 LC Card 87-11694 DDC 382/.0952/073 19
HF3828.U5 T73 1987

UNITED STATES - COMMERCE - JAPAN - CONGRESSES.
Bergsten, C. Fred, 1941- The United States-Japan economic problem /. Washington, D.C. , c1985. x, 164 p. : ISBN 0-262-52108-3 LC Card 85-18106 DDC 382/.0973/052 19
HF3127 .B47 1985 ***NYPL [JLE 87-19]***

UNITED STATES - COMMERCE - JAPAN - ECONOMETRIC MODELS.
Audretsch, David B. Industrial policy, R&D, and U. S.-Japanese trade /. Berlin [1986] 39 p. ; LC Card 87-156721 DDC 382/.0952/073 19
HF3127 .A93 1986

UNITED STATES - COMMERCE - JAPAN - HISTORY - 20TH CENTURY.
Bauge, Kenneth L. (Kenneth LeRoy) Voluntary export restriction as a foreign commercial policy with special reference to Japanese cotton textiles, 1930-1962 /. New York , 1987. 277 p. ; ISBN 0-8240-8072-6 LC Card 87-23717 DDC 382/.4567721/0952 19
HD9886.J3 B38 1987

UNITED STATES - COMMERCE - JAPAN - HISTORY - 20TH CENTURY - SOURCES.
Records of the U. S. Department of State relating to commercial relations between the United States and Japan, 1910-1949 [microform]. Wilmington, Del. , c1987. microfilm reel ISBN 0-8420-3061-1 (microfilm : set) : LC Card 87-23376 DDC 337.73052 19
HF3127

UNITED STATES - COMMERCE - KOREA (SOUTH)
Dyck, John H. South Korea . Washington, D.C. [1986] v, 74 p. : LC Card 86-602006 DDC 338.1 s 382/.41/095195 19
HD1411 .F59 no. 216 HD9005

Kim, Chungsoo. Effects of neo-protectionism on the Korean exports /. [Seoul] , 1986. 203 p. : LC Card 86-234427 DDC 382/.095195/073 19
HF3830.5.Z7 U54 1986

UNITED STATES - COMMERCE - LATIN AMERICA.
Instituto Latinoamericano del Fierro y el Acero. The urgent need of Latin America to export steel [microform]. Santiago, Chile [1983?] 20 p. : LC Card 84-244660 DDC 382/.45669142/098 19
HD9524.L32 I57 1983
NYPL [*ZT-1708 no.49]

UNITED STATES - COMMERCE - MEXICO.
Matz, Viktor, 1947- Entwicklungsländer im internationalen Konjunkturzusammenhang . Bergisch Gladbach , c1986. 199, lxxvi p. ; ISBN 3-89012-052-0 LC Card 86-227998
HF3408.U5 M37 1986

UNITED STATES - COMMERCE - MEXICO - CONGRESSES.
U. S.-Mexico relations . Stanford, Calif. , c1987. xii, 401 p. ; ISBN 0-8047-1319-7 (alk. paper) LC Card 86-23103 DDC 338.1/872 19
HD1792 .U19 1987

UNITED STATES - COMMERCE - NIGERIA.
Mabbs-Zeno, Carl. Nigeria . Washington, D.C. [1986] vi, 54 p. : LC Card 86-601597 DDC 382/.41/09669 19
HD9017.N52 M3 1986

UNITED STATES - COMMERCE - PACIFIC AREA.
U. S. trade relations in the Pacific Rim . Washington , 1987. v, 57 p. ; LC Card 87-601361 DDC 382/.0973/09 19
HF3126.5 .U17 1987

UNITED STATES - COMMERCE - RUSSIA.
Rosenblatt, Samuel M. East-West trade in technology . Washington, D.C. , c1980. viii, 64 p. ; LC Card 80-81923 DDC 382/.4560973 19
HF1414.5 .R67 ***NYPL [JLD 81-233]***

UNITED STATES - COMMERCE - SOVIET UNION - HISTORY - 20TH CENTURY - SOURCES.
Records of the U. S. Department of State relating to commercial relations between the United States and Russia/the Soviet Union, 1910-1949 [microform]. Wilmington, DE , c1987. microfilm reel. ISBN 0-8420-3053-0 (microfilm : set) : LC Card 87-23223 DDC 337.73047 19
HF3105

UNITED STATES - COMMERCE - SOVIET UNION - MATHEMATICAL MODELS.
Kolarik, William F. A model for the study of international trade politics . New York , 1987. 613 p. : ISBN 0-8240-8086-6 (alk. paper) : LC Card 87-23788 DDC 382/.0947/0730724 19
HF3105 .K64 1987

United States - Commerce - Statistics. see **United States - Commerce.**

UNITED STATES - COMMERCIAL POLICY.
Auction quotas and United States trade policy /. Washington, DC , c1987. xiii, 241 p. : ISBN 0-88132-050-1 (pbk.) LC Card 87-12948 DDC 382/.52/0973 19
HF1455 .A83 1987

Barber, Clarence L., 1917- Manitoba's interest in and attitude towards a proposed Canada-United States free trade area . [Winnipeg , 1985] 35 leaves : LC Card 86-175828 DDC 382/.0971/073 19
HF1479 .B37 1985

Destler, I. M. American trade politics . Washington, DC , New York, NY , 1986. xiii, 366 p. : ISBN 0-88132-058-7 : LC Card 86-27168 DDC 380.1/3/0973 19
HF1455 .D48 1986

Destler, I. M. Anti-protection . Washington, DC , c1987. xii, 204 p. ; ISBN 0-88132-065-X (pbk.) LC Card 87-22545 DDC 382/.3/0973 19
HF1455 .D482 1987

Economic choices . Arlington, Va. , c1987. 73 p. : ISBN 0-932765-08-4 (pbk.) : LC Card 87-686 DDC 338.973 19
HC106 .E24 1987

Economic competitiveness promoting America's living standard /] Washington , 1986 [i.e. 1987] vii, 34 p. : LC Card 87-601340 DDC 338.973 19
HC106.8 .E2745 1987

The Free trade papers /. Toronto , 1986. l [i.e. 50], 227 p. : ISBN 0-88862-972-9 LC Card 87-109310 DDC 382.7/1/0971 19
HF1479 .F74 1986

Gold, Kenneth A. (Kenneth Alan) United States foreign economic policy-making . New York , 1987. 349 p. ; ISBN 0-8240-8083-1 : LC Card 87-23785 DDC 382/.456413/00973 19
HD9006 .G64 1987

Hodin, Michael W. A national policy for organized free trade . New York , 1987. 481 p. ; ISBN 0-8240-8085-8 (alk. paper) : LC Card 87-23719 DDC 382/.45669142/0973 19
HD9515 .H59 1987

Lawrence, Robert Z., 1949- Saving free trade . Washington, D.C. , c1986. xii, 132 p. ; ISBN 0-8157-5178-8 LC Card 86-14705 DDC 382.7/1/0973 19
HF1455 .L39 1986 ***NYPL [JLE 86-4368]***

Lovett, William Anthony. World trade rivalry . Lexington, Mass. , c1987. xxxv, 260 p. : ISBN 0-669-11027-2 (alk. paper) LC Card 85-40388 DDC 382/.3 19
HF1008 .L68 1987

Mukerjee, Dilip. Lessons from the Caribbean Basin initiative /. Kuala Lumpur, Malaysia , c1985. 36 p. ; ISBN 967-99974-6-4 (pbk.) LC Card 87-101396 DDC 338.91/73/0729 19
HF1456.5.C27 M85 1985

Der Neue Protektionismus . Bonn , c1983. 195 p. : ISBN 3-87831-370-5 LC Card 83-198686
HF1756 .N58 1983

Paarlberg, Robert L. Fixing farm trade . Cambridge, Mass. , c1988. xiv, 159 p. ; ISBN 0-88730-196-7 LC Card 87-24118 DDC 382/.41/0973 19
HD9006 .P27 1988

Putting America first . Washington, D.C. , c1987. 87 p. ; ISBN 0-944468-00-4 (pbk.) : LC Card 87-50998 DDC 382/.3/0973 19
HF1455 .P87 1987

Rosenblatt, Samuel M. East-West trade in technology . Washington, D.C. , c1980. viii, 64 p. ; LC Card 80-81923 DDC 382/.4560973 19
HF1414.5 .R67 ***NYPL [JLD 81-233]***

Trade policy and U. S. competitiveness /. Washington, D.C. , Lanham, Md. , c1987. xvi, 144 p. ; ISBN 0-8447-3633-3 (alk. paper) LC Card 87-18831 DDC 382/.3/0973 19
HF1455 .T65 1987

US economic expansion . Moscow , 1986. 216 p. ; LC Card 87-112029 DDC 337.7308 19
HF1456.5.L3 U8 1986

Vargish, George. What's made in the U. S.A.? /. New Brunswick, U. S.A. , c1988. 160 p. : ISBN 0-88738-187-1 LC Card 87-19164 DDC 382/.3/0973 19
HF1716 .V37 1988

Wheeler, Jimmy W. Beyond recrimination . Indianapolis, IN (P.O. Box 26-919, Indianapolis 46226) , c1987. xix, 218 p. : LC Card 87-165405 DDC 382/.0951249/073 19
HF1456.5.T28 W46 1987

Wonnacott, Paul. The United States and Canada . Washington, DC , 1987. xii, 173 p. : ISBN 0-88132-056-0 (pbk.) : LC Card 87-2660 DDC 382.71073 19
HF1456.5.C2 W65 1987

Wonnacott, Ronald J. Canada/United States free trade . Toronto, Ont. , c1985. 30 p. ; ISBN 0-7729-0036-1 (pbk.) LC Card 86-673986
HF1480.5.U57 W66x 1985

UNITED STATES - COMMERCIAL POLICY - CONGRESSES.
Current U. S. trade policy . Cambridge, Mass. (1050 Massachusetts Ave., Cambridge 02138) , 1986. iii, 128 p. ; LC Card 86-201110 DDC 382/.3/0973 19
HF1455 .C87 1986

UNITED STATES - COMMERCIAL POLICY - HANDBOOKS, MANUALS, ETC.
Importing into the United States . Washington, D.C. [1985] 84 p. : LC Card 85-603032 DDC 343.73/087 347.30387 19
HF3035 .I46 1985

Importing into the United States. Rocklin, Calif. , c1987. 83 p. : ISBN 0-914629-35-2 (pbk.) : LC Card 87-16931 DDC 343.73/087 347.30387 19
HF3055 .I46 1987

UNITED STATES - COMMERCIAL POLICY - HISTORY.
Barrie, Robert W. Congress and the Executive . New York , 1987. 347 p. ; ISBN 0-8240-8071-8 (alk. paper) LC Card 87-23814 DDC 382/.3/0973 19
HF1455 .B317 1987

Olnek, Jay I. The invisible hand . Riverdale, N.Y. , c1984. 176 p. : ISBN 0-938538-01-2 LC Card 82-24634 DDC 382.7/1/0973 19
HF1455 .O49 1984 ***NYPL [JLE 87-21]***

UNITED STATES - COMMERCIAL POLICY - HISTORY - 20TH CENTURY.

Mayer, Robert Stanley. The influence of Frank A. Vanderlip and the National City Bank on American commerce and foreign policy, 1910-1920 /. New York , 1987. viii, 221 p. ; ISBN 0-8240-8087-4 : LC Card 87-23793 DDC 332.1/5/097471 19
HG2613.N54 N3555 1987

UNITED STATES - COMMERCIAL POLICY - HISTORY - 20TH CENTURY - SOURCES. Records of the U. S. Department of State relating to commercial relations between the United States and Russia/the Soviet Union, 1910-1949 [microform]. Wilmington, DE , c1987. microfilm reel. ISBN 0-8420-3053-0 (microfilm : set) : LC Card 87-23223 DDC 337.73047 19
HF3105

Records of the U. S. Department of State relating to commercial relations between the United States and Japan, 1910-1949 [microform]. Wilmington, Del. , c1987. microfilm reel ISBN 0-8420-3061-1 (microfilm : set) : LC Card 87-23376 DDC 337.73052 19
HF3127

United States. Commission on Neighborhoods, National. see **United States. National Commission on Neighborhoods.**

United States Conference of Mayors. Meyers, Edward M. Rebuilding America's cities . Cambridge, Mass. , c1986. xxi, 290 p. : ISBN 0-88730-051-0 LC Card 85-30780 DDC 307.3/4/0973 19
HT175 .U59 1986 ***NYPL [JLE 86-2874]***

United States. Congress.
Causes and remedies for displacement of steel workers . [Washington, D.C.? , 1985] iv, 83, 2, 2 p. ; LC Card 86-601602 DDC 331.13/704 19
HD8039.I52 U524 1985

U. S.-EC relations . Washington , 1986. vii, 78 p. ; LC Card 86-603395 DDC 337.4073 19
HF1456.5.E825 U17 1986

United States. Congress. Commission on Security and Cooperation in Europe. Implementation of the Helsinki accords : hearing before the Commission on Security and Cooperation in Europe, Ninety-ninth Congress, first session, Soviet forced labor practices, August 15, 1985, Buffalo, NY. Washington : U. S. G.P.O., 1986. iii, 85 p. ; 24 cm. Distributed to some depository libraries in microfiche. Shipping list no.: 86-207-P. Includes bibliographical references. Item 1089-C, 1089-D (microfiche) LC Card 86-601286 DDC 331.11/732/0947 19
1. Forced labor - Soviet Union. 2. Foreign trade regulation - United States. I. Title.
HD4875.S59 U55 1986

United States. Congress. House. (Old Catalog form: United States. House of Representatives)
Report .
(no. 99-1009) United States. Congress. House. Committee on Science and Technology. Prospects for sustainable development in Sub-Saharan Africa . Washington , 1986. vii, 88 p. ; LC Card 86-603140 DDC 338.967 19
HD2117 .U48 1986

United States. Congress. House. Aging, Select Committee on. see **United States. Congress. House. Select Committee on Aging.**

United States. Congress. House. Budget, Committee on the. see **United States. Congress. House. Committee on the Budget.**

United States. Congress. House. Committee on Armed Services. (Old Catalog form: United States. Armed Services, Committee on // Hearings printed in 1978 and later are available only in microform. Please consult the librarians in the Economic and Public Affairs Division.

United States. Congress. House. Committee on Armed Services. Subcommittee on Investigations. Report on the safety of aircraft under charter to the Department of Defense : report of the Investigations Subcommittee of the Committee on Armed Services, House of Representatives, Ninety-ninth Congress, second session. Washington : U. S. G.P.O. : For sale by the Supt. of Docs., Congressional Sales Office, 1986. iii, 17 p. ; 23 cm. At head of title: 99th Congress, 2d session. Committee print. Distributed to some depository libraries in microfiche. Shipping list no.: 86-725-P. "July 1986." "No. 22." Item 1012-A, 1012-B (microfiche) LC Card 86-603401 DDC 363.1/24 19
1. Aeronautics, Commercial - Chartering - United States - Safety measures. 2. Air charter contracts - Government policy - United States. I. Title. II. Title: Safety of aircraft under charter to the Department of Defense.
HE9803.Z7 C538 1986

United States. Congress. House. Committee on Banking, Currency and Housing. Subcommittee on Historic Preservation and Coinage. Preservation programs of the Federal government in the area of housing and community development / staff report to the Subcommittee on Historic Preservation and Coinage of the Committee on Banking, Currency and Housing, House of Representatives, 94th Congress, second session. Washington : U. S. Govt. Print. Off., 1976. vi, 86 p. ; 24 cm. Includes bibliographical references. LC Card 77-601749
1. Urban renewal - United States. 2. Buildings - Repair and reconstruction. 3. Community development - United States. I. Title: Preservation programs of the Federal government in the area of housing ...
HT175 .U583 1976 ***NYPL [JLE 78-1181]***

United States. Congress. House. Committee on Education and Labor. (Old Catalog form: United States. Education and Labor, Committee on // Hearings printed in 1978 and later are available only in microform. Please consult the librarians in the Economic and Public Affairs Division.

United States. Congress. House. Committee on Education and Labor. Subcommittee on Employment Opportunities. Job training under the new federalism . [Chicago?] , 1986. ii, 299 p. : LC Card 86-203209 DDC 331.25/92/0973 19
HD5715.2 .J63 1986

United States. Congress. House. Committee on Energy and Commerce.
U. S. trade relations in the Pacific Rim . Washington , 1987. v, 57 p. ; LC Card 87-601361 DDC 382/.0973/09 19
HF3126.5 .U17 1987

United States. Congress. House. Committee on Energy and Commerce. Subcommittee on Oversight and Investigations.
The Competitiveness of American metal mining and processing . Washington , 1986. x, 186 p. ; LC Card 86-603391 DDC 338.2/74/0973 19
HD9506.U62 C63 1986

Dangerous medicine : the risk to American consumers from prescription drug diversion and counterfeiting : report by the Subcommittee on Oversight and Investigations of the Committee on Energy and Commerce, U. S. House of Representatives. Washington : U. S. G.P.O. : For sale by the Supt. of Docs., U. S. G.P.O., Congressional Sales Office, 1986. v, 31 p. ; 24 cm. At head of title: 99th Congress, 2d session. Committee print, 99-Z. Distributed to some depository libraries in microfiche. Shipping list no.: 86-376-P. "April 1986." Includes bibliographical references. S/N 052-070-06106-5 1019-A, 1019-B (microfiche) LC Card 86-602099 DDC 363.1/942/0973 19
1. Drug adulteration - United States. 2. Consumer protection - United States. 3. Counterfeits and counterfeiting - United States. I. Title.
HD9665.9.U6 U55 1986

Shad, John S. R., 1923- Statement of John S.R. Shad, Chairman of the Securities and Exchange Commission, before the House Subcommittee on Oversight and Investigations of the Committee on Energy and Commerce, concerning EDGAR (Electronic Data Gathering, Analysis, and Retrieval System), March 14, 1985. [Washington, D.C. , 1985] 21, 5, 2, [12] p. : LC Card 85-148449 DDC 353.0082/58 19
HG4910 .S417 1985

Uncertain returns . Washington , 1986. v, 210 p. ; LC Card 86-603379 DDC 364.1/42 19
HD9665.5 .U53 1986

Unfair foreign trade practices . Washington , 1986. v, 27 p. ; LC Card 86-603374 DDC 382/.0973/05 19
HF3126.5 .U53 1986

United States. Congress. House. Committee on Energy and Commerce. Subcommittee on Telecommunications, Consumer Protection, and Finance.
Corporate debt . Washington , 1986. v, 31 p. : LC Card 86-603382 DDC 338.7/4/0973 19
HG4028.D3 C67 1986

Corporate mergers and high yield (junk) bonds . Washington , 1986. vi, 57 p. ; LC Card 87-601339 DDC 332.63/22 19
HD2746.5 .C67 1986

United States. Congress. House. Committee on Foreign Affairs. (Old Catalog form: United States. Foreign Affairs, Committee on (House))
Discussion of the Nicaragua ship canal and the Tehuantepec ship railway schemes before the Committee on Foreign Affairs of the House of Representatives. [Washington] : The Committee, [1882?] 80 p. ; 26 cm. LC Card 82-602443
1. Nicaragua Canal (Nicaragua). 2. Tehuantepec Railway. 3. Canals, Interoceanic - Central America. 4. Ship-railroads - Mexico. I. Title.
HE536 .U55 1882

Feeding the world's population . Washington , 1984. xii, 779 p. : LC Card 86-602524 DDC 363.8 19
HD9000.5 .F35 1986

Implications of population trends for U. S. foreign policy in Central America . Washington , 1984. iii, 16 p. : LC Card 86-602534 DDC 304.6/09728 19
HB3533 .I55 1984

U. S.-EC relations . Washington , 1986. vii, 78 p. ; LC Card 86-603395 DDC 337.4073 19
HF1456.5.E825 U17 1986

U. S. trade relations with Asia . Washington , 1987. vii, 85 p. ; LC Card 87-601359 DDC 382/.0973/05 19
HF3118 .U15 1987

United States. Congress. House. Committee on Foreign Affairs. Subcommittee on Europe and the Middle East. Poland's renewal and U. S. options . Washington , 1987. xv, 41 p. : LC Card 87-601374 DDC 337.438073 19
HC340.3 .P646 1987

United States. Congress. House. Committee on Foreign Affairs. Subcommittee on International Organizations and Movements.
Modern communications and foreign policy. Report no. 5 together with part X of the Hearings on winning the cold war: the U. S. ideological offensive ... pursuant to H. Res. 179 ... Washington, U. S. Govt. Print. Off., 1967. vii, 13R, iv, 216 p. illus. 24 cm. (90th Congress, 1st session. House report. no. 362) Bibliographical footnotes. LC Card 67-61749
1. Public opinion - United States. 2. Mass media - United States. 3. United States - Relations (general) with foreign countries. 4. United States - Foreign opinion. I. Title.
E744 .U45 1967 ***NYPL [JLE 73-233]***

United States. Congress. House. Committee on Science and Technology. Hearings printed in 1978 and later are available only in microform. Please consult the librarians in the Economic and Public Affairs Division.
Prospects for sustainable development in Sub-Saharan Africa : report / by the Committee on Science and Technology, House of Representatives, Ninety-ninth Congress, second session. Washington : U. S. G.P.O., 1986. vii, 88 p. ; 24 cm. (House report / 99th Congress, 2d session . 99-1009) Distributed to some depository libraries in microfiche. Shipping list no.: 86-867-P. "October 16, 1986." Union calendar no. 599. Includes bibliographical references. Item 1008-C, 1008-D (microfiche) LC Card 86-603140 DDC 338.967 19
1. Agricultural assistance, American - Africa, Sub-Saharan. 2. Agriculture - Africa, Sub-Saharan. 3. Natural resources - Africa, Sub-Saharan - Management. 4. Africa, Sub-Saharan - Population policy. I. Series. II. Series: United States. Congress. House. Report , no. 99-1009. III. Title.
HD2117 .U48 1986

United States. Congress. House. Committee on the Budget. Hearings printed in 1978 and later are available only in microform. Please consult the librarians in the Economic and Public Affairs Division.

United States. Congress. House. Committee on the Budget. Task Force on Budget Process.
Schick, Allen. The whole and the parts . Washington , 1987. vi, 65 p. ; LC Card 87-601378 DDC 353.0072/2 19
HJ2052 .S335 1987

United States. Congress. House. Committee on the District of Columbia. (Old Catalog form: United States. District of Columbia, Committee on // Hearings printed in 1978 and later are available only in microform. Please consult the librarians in the Economic and Public Affairs Division.
Changing the course . Washington , 1986. xvii, 142 p. : LC Card 86-603365 DDC 336.1/85 19
HJ275 .C455 1986

U. S. investments and bank loans in South Africa (supplemental material to the hearings and markups of January 31 and February 7, 1984, serial no. 98-14, on District of Columbia South Africa divestment) . Washington , 1985. vi, 24 p.: LC Card 85-602615 DDC 332.6/7373/068 19
HG5851.A3 U17 1985

United States. Congress. House. Committee on Ways and Means. (Old Catalog form: United States. Ways and Means, Committee on (House) Hearings printed in 1978 and later are available only in microform. Please consult the librarians in the Economic and Public Affairs Division.

United States. Congress. House. Committee on Ways and Means. Subcommittee on Oversight. Overview of current issues relating to single-employer defined benefit pension plans and Pension Benefit Guaranty Corporation (PBGC) premiums . Washington , 1987. iii, 49 p. ; LC Card 87-601357 DDC 331.25/2/0973 19
HD7125 .O88 1987

United States. Congress. House of Representatives. see **United States. Congress. House.**

United States. Congress. House. Science and Technology, Committee on. see **United States. Congress. House. Committee on Science and Technology.**

United States. Congress. House. Select Committee on Aging.
America's uninsured and underinsured . Washington , 1986. vi, 13 p. ; LC Card 86-603377 DDC 368.3/8/00973 19
HD7102.U4 A755 1986

United States. Congress. House. Select Committee on Aging. Subcommittee on Health and Long-Term Care. Catastrophic health insurance . Washington , 1986. iii, 278 p. : LC Card 86-603399 DDC 368.3/82/00973 19
HD7102.U4 C37 1986

United States. Congress. House. Select Committee on Hunger.
Foreign indebtedness and basic human needs in four African countries . Washington , 1986. ii, 54 p. : LC Card 86-603396 DDC 336.3/435/0967
HC800 .F67 1986

Special report on applying United States food surpluses to the problems of hunger /. Washington , 1984. ii, iv, 54 p. ; LC Card 87-601529 DDC 363.8/83 19
HD9000.5 .S666 1984

Trends in foreign aid, 1977-86 . Washington , 1986. vii, 21 p. : LC Card 87-601358 DDC 338.91/73 19
HC60 .T69 1986

United States. Congress. House. Subcommittee on Employment Opportunities. see **United States. Congress. House. Committee on Education and Labor. Subcommittee on Employment Opportunities.**

United States. Congress. House. Subcommittee on Health and Long-Term Care. see **United States. Congress. House. Select Committee on Aging. Subcommittee on Health and Long-Term Care.**

United States. Congress. House. Subcommittee on Historic Preservation and Coinage. see **United States. Congress. House. Committee on Banking, Currency and Housing. Subcommittee on Historic Preservation and Coinage.**

United States. Congress. House. Subcommittee on International Organizations and Movements. see **United States. Congress. House. Committee on Foreign Affairs. Subcommittee on International Organizations and Movements.**

United States. Congress. House. Subcommittee on Investigations. see **United States. Congress. House. Committee on Armed Services. Subcommittee on Investigations.**

United States. Congress. House. Subcommittee on Oversight. see **United States. Congress. House. Committee on Ways and Means. Subcommittee on Oversight.**

United States. Congress. House. Task Force on Budget Process. see **United States. Congress. House. Committee on the Budget. Task Force on Budget Process.**

United States. Congress. Joint Committee on Taxation. Overview of current issues relating to single-employer defined benefit pension plans and Pension Benefit Guaranty Corporation (PBGC) premiums . Washington , 1987. iii, 49 p. ; LC Card 87-601357 DDC 331.25/2/0973 19
HD7125 .O88 1987

United States. Congress. Joint Economic Committee. Hearings printed in 1978 and later are available only in microform. Please consult the librarians in the Economic and Public Affairs Division.

United States. Congress. Joint Economic Committee. Subcommittee on Agriculture and Transportation. Ambur, Owen D. Selling out the family farm . Washington , 1986. v, 40 p. : LC Card 87-601379 DDC 338.1/6 19
HD1476.U5 A65 1986

United States. Congress. Joint Economic Committee. Subcommittee on Economic Goals and Intergovernmental Policy.
Hard choices . Washington , 1984. 23 v. :
NYPL [JLE 87-566 Appendix 1-23]

Kaplan, Marshall. Hard choices . Washington , 1984. xi, 230 p. : LC Card 84-602470 DDC 338.4/3363/0973 19
HC110.C3 K37 1984 ***NYPL [JLE 87-566]***

United States. Congress. Joint Economic Committee. Subcommittee on Economic Resources, Competitiveness, and Security Economics. Manchester, Paul B. Are we on the road to a balanced budget? . Washington , 1986. v, 18 p. : LC Card 86-603373 DDC 353.0072/2 19
HJ2052 .M365 1986

United States. Congress. Joint Economic Committee. Subcommittee on Trade, Productivity, and Economic Growth. Poverty, income distribution, the family, and public policy . Washington , 1986. viii, 125 p. : LC Card 87-601355 DDC 339.2/2/0973 19
HC110.I5 P68 1986

United States. Congress. Library. see **United States. Library of Congress.**

United States. Congress. Senate.
S. hrg. .
(99-1052) United States. Congress. Senate. Committee on Agriculture, Nutrition, and Forestry. Review of the implementation of the Food Security Act of 1985 . Washington , 1987. iv, 180 p. : LC Card 87-601199 DDC 338.1/9/73 19
HD1761 .U515 1987

United States. Congress. Senate. Agriculture, Nutrition, and Forestry, Committee on. see **United States. Congress. Senate. Committee on Agriculture, Nutrition, and Forestry.**

United States. Congress. Senate. Commerce, Science, and Transportation, Committee on. see **United States. Congress. Senate. Committee on Commerce, Science, and Transportation.**

United States. Congress. Senate. Committee on Agriculture and Forestry. (Old Catalog form: United States. Agriculture and Forestry, Committee on (Senate)) // Hearings printed in 1978 and later are available only in microform. Please consult the librarians in the Economic and Public Affairs Division.

United States. Congress. Senate. Committee on Agriculture and Forestry. Subcommittee on Foreign Agricultural Policy. The World Food Conference . Washington , 1974. xv, 377 p. : LC Card 74-603025
TX345 .W58 ***NYPL [JLF 78-685]***

United States. Congress. Senate. Committee on Agriculture and Forestry. Subcommittee on Rural Development. National Conference on Rural Development, Des Moines, 1973. Proceedings. Washington, 1974. iii, 108 p. LC Card 74-600918 DDC 309.2/63/0973
HN65 .N35 1973 ***NYPL [JLE 81-564 no.2]***

United States. Congress. Senate. Committee on Agriculture, Nutrition, and Forestry.
Agriculture in the GATT . Washington , 1986. v, 47 p. ; LC Card 86-603393 DDC 382/.41/0973 19
HD9006 .A77 1986

Review of the implementation of the Food Security Act of 1985 : hearing before the Committee on Agriculture, Nutrition, and Forestry, United States Senate, Ninety-ninth Congress, second session, August 28, 1986, Lincoln, NE. Washington : U. S. G.P.O. : For sale by the Supt. of Docs., Congressional Sales Office, U. S. G.P.O., 1987. iv, 180 p. : ill. ; 24 cm. (S. hrg. . 99-1052) Distributed to some depository libraries in microfiche. Shipping list no.: 87-162-P. Item 1032-C, 1032-D (microfiche) LC Card 87-601199 DDC 338.1/9/73 19
1. Agriculture and state - United States. 2. Agriculture - Economic aspects - United States. 3. Nutrition policy - United States. I. Series: United States. Congress. Senate. S. hrg. , 99-1052. II. Title.
HD1761 .U515 1987

United States. Congress. Senate. Committee on Banking, Housing and Urban Affairs. (Old Catalog form: United States. Banking, Housing and Urban Affairs, Committee on (Senate)) // Hearings printed in 1978 and later are available only in microform. Please consult the librarians in the Economic and Public Affairs Division.

United States. Congress. Senate. Committee on Commerce, Science, and Transportation. Hearings printed in 1978 and later are available only in microform. Please consult the librarians in the Economic and Public Affairs Division.
Earthquake insurance . Washington , 1987. ix, 61 p. : LC Card 87-601349 DDC 368.1/22 19
HG9981 .E17 1987

United States. Congress. Senate. Committee on Finance. (Old Catalog form: United States. Finance, Committee on (Senate) // Hearings printed in 1978 and later are available only in microform. Please consult the librarians in the Economic and Public Affairs Division.
Ludwick, David E. The competitive position of U. S. and European Community pork and the United States and third-country markets . Washington, DC [1985] xxiii, 341 p. : LC Card 86-601366 DDC 380.1/4566492/0973 19
HD9435.U52 L83 1985

United States. Congress. Senate. Committee on Finance. Subcommittee on Social Security and Income Maintenance Programs. Malone, Margaret Sahlin, 1933- Work and welfare /. Washington , 1986. ix, 162 p. ; LC Card 86-603383 DDC 362.5/84/0973 19
HD5715.2 .M34 1986

United States. Congress. Senate. Committee on Foreign Relations. (Old Catalog form: United States. Foreign Relations, Committee on (Senate)) // Hearings printed in 1978 and later are available only in microform. Please consult the librarians in the Economic and Public Affairs Division.

United States. Congress. Senate. Committee on Foreign Relations. Subcommittee on Multinational Corporations. A Documentary history of the Petroleum Reserves Corporation, 1943-1944 . Washington , 1974. v, 119 p. : LC Card 74-602382
HD9566 .D6 ***NYPL [JLE 78-1181]***

United States. Congress. Senate. Committee on Governmental Affairs. Subcommittee on Intergovernmental Relations. Stinson, Thomas F., 1942- Governing the heartland . Washington , 1986. xii, 159 p. : LC Card 86-603376 DDC 336/.014/77 19
HJ9181 .S75 1986

United States. Congress. Senate. Committee on Labor and Human Resources. Subcommittee on Employment and Productivity. Malone, Margaret Sahlin, 1933- Work and welfare /. Washington , 1986. ix, 162 p. ; LC Card 86-603383 DDC 362.5/84/0973 19
HD5715.2 .M34 1986

United States. Congress. Senate. Democratic Policy Committee. Democratic Working Group on Economic Competitiveness. Economic competitiveness promoting America's living standard /] Washington , 1986 [i.e. 1987] vii, 34 p. : LC Card 87-601340 DDC 338.973 19
HC106.8 .E2745 1987

United States. Congress. Senate. Governmental Affairs, Committee on. see **United States. Congress. Senate. Committee on Governmental Affairs.**

United States. Congress. Senate. Subcommittee on Foreign Agricultural Policy. see **United States. Congress. Senate. Committee on Agriculture and Forestry. Subcommittee on Foreign Agricultural Policy.**

United States. Congress. Senate. Subcommittee on Intergovernmental Relations. see **United States. Congress. Senate. Committee on Governmental Affairs. Subcommittee on Intergovernmental Relations.**

United States. Congress. Senate. Subcommittee on Multinational Corporations. see **United States. Congress. Senate. Committee on Foreign Relations. Subcommittee on Multinational Corporations.**

United States. Congress. Senate. Subcommittee on Rural Development. see **United States. Congress. Senate. Committee on Agriculture and Forestry. Subcommittee on Rural Development.**

United States. Congress. Taxation, Joint Committee on. see **United States. Congress. Joint Committee on Taxation.**

UNITED STATES. CONGRESS - VOTING.
West, Darrell M., 1954- Congress and economic policymaking /. Pittsburgh, Pa. , c1987. xiv, 203 p. ; ISBN 0-8229-5396-X (pbk.) LC Card 87-40160 DDC 338.973 19
HC106.8 .W45 1987

United States. Congress (98th, 2nd session : 1984). Senate.
S. prt. .
(98-164) Kaplan, Marshall. Hard choices . Washington , 1984. xi, 230 p. : LC Card 84-602470 DDC 338.4/3363/0973 19
HC110.C3 K37 1984 ***NYPL [JLE 87-566]***

(98-164, App. 1-23) Hard choices . Washington , 1984. 23 v. :
NYPL [JLE 87-566 Appendix 1-23]

United States. Congressional Delegation to the World Food Conference. The World Food Conference . Washington , 1974. xv, 377 p. : LC Card 74-603025
TX345 .W58 ***NYPL [JLF 78-685]***

United States. Congressional Research Service. see **United States. Library of Congress. Congressional Research Service.**

UNITED STATES - CONSTITUTIONAL HISTORY.
Alexander, Albert. The economic world of 1787 and the Constitution /. New York (150 Nassau St., Rm. 1625, New York 10038) [1987] 18 p. ; LC Card 87-403433 DDC 330.973/0318 19
HC105.6 .A44 1987

United States. Consumer Finance, National Commission on. see **United States. National Commission on Consumer Finance.**

United States. Council on Environmental Quality. Global 2000 Study (United States) The global 2000 report to the President--entering the twenty-first century . Washington, D.C. , 1980-1981. 3 v. : LC Card 80-602859 DDC 333.7
HC79.E5 G59 1980b ***NYPL [JLF 87-206]***

United States - Currency question. see **Currency question - United States.**

United States. Customs Service.
A biographical directory of the United States Customs Service, 1771-1989 / compiled, edited, and produced by United States Customs Service, Department of the Treasury, Washington, D.C. 1st ed. Washington, D.C. : The Service, [1985] ca. 350 p. ; 28 cm. Cover title: A biographical directory of the U. S. Customs Service, 1771-1989. "August 1985." LC Card 85-603304 DDC 353.0072/46/025 19
1. United States Customs Service - Officials and employees - Registers. 2. United States Customs Service - Officials and employees - Biography. I. Title. II. Title: Biographical directory of the U. S. Customs Service, 1771-1989.
HJ6731 .U18 1985

Importing into the United States . Washington, D.C. [1985] 84 p. : LC Card 85-603032 DDC 343.73/087 347.30387 19
HF3035 .I46 1985

Importing into the United States. Rocklin, Calif. , c1987. 83 p. : ISBN 0-914629-35-2 (pbk.) : LC Card 87-16931 DDC 343.73/087 347.30387 19
HF3055 .I46 1987

UNITED STATES CUSTOMS SERVICE - OFFICIALS AND EMPLOYEES - BIOGRAPHY.
United States. Customs Service. A biographical directory of the United States Customs Service, 1771-1989 /. Washington, D.C. [1985] ca. 350 p. ; LC Card 85-603304 DDC 353.0072/46/025 19
HJ6731 .U18 1985

UNITED STATES CUSTOMS SERVICE - OFFICIALS AND EMPLOYEES - REGISTERS.
United States. Customs Service. A biographical directory of the United States Customs Service, 1771-1989 /. Washington, D.C. [1985] ca. 350 p. ; LC Card 85-603304 DDC 353.0072/46/025 19
HJ6731 .U18 1985

United States. Defense Dept. see **United States. Dept. of Defense.**

United States. Dept. of Agriculture. (Old Catalog form: United States. Agriculture Dept.

United States. Dept. of Agriculture. Agricultural Research Service. see **United States. Agricultural Research Service.**

United States. Dept. of Agriculture. Economic Research Service. (Old Catalog form: United States. Agriculture Dept. Economic Research Service.)
Banks, Vera J. Black farmers and their farms /. Washington, D.C. , 1986. v, 27 p. : LC Card 86-602201
HD8039.F32 U616 1986

Coyle, Barry. Economic gains from agricultural trade . Washington, D.C. [Springfield, VA , 1986] iii, 41 p. : LC Card 86-602417 DDC 382/.41/0973 19
HD9005 .C86 1986

Dyck, John H. South Korea . Washington, D.C. [1986] v, 74 p. : LC Card 86-602006 DDC 338.1 s 382/.41/095195 19
HD1411 .F59 no. 216 HD9005

Embargoes, surplus disposal, and U. S. agriculture . Washington, D.C. , 1986. vi, 34 p. ; LC Card 86-603452 DDC 338.1/8 19
HD1761 .E45 1986

Florida and Mexico competition for the winter fresh vegetable market /. Washington, D.C. [1986] v, 101 p. : LC Card 86-602381 DDC 338.1 s 381/.415/0973 19
HD1751 .A91854 no. 556 HD9225.U53F5

Fuller, Theodore, 1929- The Mid-Atlantic region in transition . Washington, D.C. [1986] v, 13 p. : LC Card 86-602014 DDC 331.12/0974 19
HD5725.A12 F85 1986

Ghelfi, Linda M. Poverty among black families in the nonmetro South /. Washington, D.C. , Supt. of Docs., U. S. G.P.O. [distributor, 1986] vii, 27 p. : LC Card 86-602435 DDC 330.975/043/0899607301734 19
HC107.A13 G48 1986

Hanthorn, Michael. Selected farm machinery statistics /. Washington, D.C. , 1986] ii, 54 p. : LC Card 86-602408 DDC 338.1/61/0973 19
HD1751 .A5 no. 743 HD9486.U4

Lectures in agricultural economics . [Washington? , 1977] ix, 165 p. : LC Card 77-603242
HD1759 .L4 ***NYPL [JLE 79-149]***

Mabbs-Zeno, Carl. Nigeria . Washington, D.C. [1986] vi, 54 p. : LC Card 86-601597 DDC 382/.41/09669 19
HD9017.N52 M3 1986

Morrissey, Elizabeth S. Characteristics of poverty in nonmetro counties /. Washington, D.C. , 1985. iv, 10 p. : LC Card 86-602555 DDC 362.5/0973 19
HC110.P6 M67 1985

Ribaudo, Marc. Reducing soil erosion . Washington, D.C. , 1986. v, 24 p. : LC Card 86-603068 DDC 338.1 s 333.73 19
HD1751 .A91854 no. 561 S624.A1

Selected agricultural statistics on Spain, 1970-82 /. Washington, D.C. (1301 New York Ave., N.W., Washington 20005-4788) , 1986. x, 142 p. : LC Card 86-602416 DDC 338.1/0973 s 338.1/0946/021 19
HD1751 .A5 no. 742 HD2022

Sloggett, Gordon. Energy and U. S. agriculture . Washington, D.C. , 1985] iii, 43 p. : LC Card 86-600880 DDC 338.1 s 338.1/3 19
HD1751 .A91854 no. 545 S619.E53

Sloggett, Gordon. Ground-water mining in the United States /. Washington, D.C , 1986. iv, 19 p. : LC Card 86-602788 DDC 338.1 s 338.1/4 19
HD1751 .A91854 no. 555 S616.U6

Somwaru, Agapi. Disaggregated farm income by type of farm, 1959-82 /. Washington, D.C. , 1986. iii, 113 p. : LC Card 86-602571 DDC 338.1 s 338.1/3/0973021 19
HD1751 .A91854 no. 558 HD1769

Thompson, Robert L. A survey of recent U. S. developments in international agricultural trade models /. Washington, D.C. , 1981. v, 74 p. ; LC Card 81-603138 DDC 382/.41/0973 19
HD1433 .T48 ***NYPL [JLF 84-568]***

Trueblood, Michael A. The Ivory Coast . Washington, DC , 1986. iv, 32 p. : LC Card 86-602806 DDC 338.1 s 382/.41/096668 19
HD1411 .F59 no. 223 HD9017.I912

United States. Dept. of Agriculture. Economic Research Service. Agriculture and Rural Economic Division. Smith, Edward Joseph, 1911- Impact of energy costs on manufacturing employment /. Washington, D.C. [1985] iv, 16 p. : LC Card 86-603150 DDC 331.12/57/0973 19
HD5724 .S614 1985

United States. Dept. of Agriculture. Economic Research Service. International Economic Division. D'Silva, Brian. Sudan's irrigated subsector . Washington, D.C. , 1986. iv, 31 p. : LC Card 86-602812 DDC 333.91/3/09624 19
HD1741.S85 D75 1986

United States. Dept. of Agriculture. Economic Research Service. International Economics Division.
Grigsby, S. Elaine. Alternative export strategies and U. S. agricultural policies for grains and oilseeds, 1950-83 /. [Washington, D.C.] , 1986. v., 37 p. : LC Card 86-602816 DDC 382/.4131/0973 19
HD9036 .G83 1986

Haley, Stephen L. The value of the dollar and competitiveness of U. S. wheat exports /. [Washington, D.C.] [1986] iv, 28 p. : LC Card 86-602853 DDC 382/.41311/0973 19
HD9049.W5 U4288 1986

Korb, Penelope. U. S. and world food, beverages, and tobacco expenditures, 1970-83 /. Washington, D.C. , 1986. iv, 84 p. : LC Card 86-603160 DDC 339.4/8664/0021 19
HD9000.4 .K67 1986

United States. Dept. of Agriculture. Farmers Home Administration. see **United States. Farmers Home Administration.**

United States. Dept. of Agriculture. National Economics Division. State milk regulation . [Washington, D.C.] (1301 New York Ave., N.W., Washington 20005-4788) [1986] viii, 62 p. ; LC Card 86-602413 DDC 338.1/771/0973 19
HD9282.U4 S72 1986

United States. Dept. of Agriculture. Rural Electrification Administration. see **United States. Rural Electrification Administration.**

United States. Dept. of Commerce. (Old Catalog form: United States. Commerce Dept.)
Lieberthal, Kenneth. Bureaucratic politics and Chinese energy development /. [Washington, D.C.] [1986] xii, 405 p. ; LC Card 86-602422

DDC 333.79/0951 19
HD9502.C62 L54 1986

United States. Dept. of Commerce. Bureau of Economic Analysis. see **United States. Bureau of Economic Analysis.**

United States. Dept. of Commerce. Bureau of Mines. see **United States. Bureau of Mines.**

United States. Dept. of Commerce. Office of Business Analysis. The U. S. primary iron and steel industry since 1958. Washington, D.C. , 1985. xvi, 138 p. : *NYPL [JLF 86-689]*

United States. Dept. of Defense. (Old Catalog form: United States. Defense Dept.)

UNITED STATES. DEPT. OF DEFENSE - MANAGEMENT.
Schlesinger, James R. Organizational structures and planning /. [Santa Monica, Calif. , 1966] iii, 45 p. : LC Card 87-404140 DDC 353.6 19
HD58.9 .S35 1966

UNITED STATES. DEPT. OF DEFENSE - REORGANIZATION.
Schlesinger, James R. Organizational structures and planning /. [Santa Monica, Calif. , 1966] iii, 45 p. : LC Card 87-404140 DDC 353.6 19
HD58.9 .S35 1966

United States. Dept. of Energy. Office of Minority Economic Impact. Occupations in energy-related industries [microform] . Washington, D.C. , 1981. ca. 300 p. ; *NYPL [*XME-11,557]*

United States. Dept. of Energy. Office of Policy, Planning, and Analysis. National energy policy plan projections to 2010 : a technical report in support of the National Energy Policy Plan. Washington, D.C. : U. S. Dept. of Energy, Office of Policy, Planning, and Analysis, [1985] 1 v. (various pagings) : ill. ; 28 cm. "December 1985." Includes bibliography. "DOE/PE-0029/3." LC Card 86-601637 DDC 333.79/0973 19
1. Energy industries - United States - Forecasting. 2. Energy consumption - United States - Forecasting. 3. Power resources - United States - Forecasting. I. Title.
HD9502.U52 U5125 1985

United States. Dept. of Health, Education, and Welfare. Social Security Administration. see **United States. Social Security Administration.**

United States. Dept. of Housing and Urban Development. (Old Catalog form: United States. Housing and Urban Development, Dept. of.)

United States. Dept. of Housing and Urban Development. Office of Policy Development and Research. Division of Policy Studies. The conversion of rental housing to condominiums and cooperatives : impacts on housing costs / Division of Policy Studies. [Washington, D.C.] : Dept. of Housing and Urban Development, Office of Policy Development and Research, 1982. 95 p. : ill. ; 28 cm. "HUD-PDR-692." "August 1981." "January 1982" -- Cover. Includes bibiliographical references.
1. Condominium (Housing) - United States. 2. Rental housing - United States. 3. Housing, Cooperative - United States. 4. Housing - United States - Costs. I. Title. *NYPL [JLF 86-442]*

United States. Dept. of Housing and Urban Development. Policy Development and Research, Office of. see **United States. Dept. of Housing and Urban Development. Office of Policy Development and Research.**

United States. Dept. of Labor. (Old Catalog form: United States. Labor Dept.)

United States. Dept. of Labor. Bureau of Labor-Management Relations and Cooperative Programs. Labor-management cooperation . [Washington, D.C.?] , 1984. v, 77 p. ; LC Card 85-602044 DDC 331.01/12/0973 19
HD6490.L332 U55 1984
NYPL [JLF 86-559]

United States. Dept. of Labor. Employment and Training Administration. see **United States. Employment and Training Administration.**

United States. Dept. of Labor. Employment Service. see **United States Employment Service.**

UNITED STATES. DEPT. OF LABOR - HISTORY - JUVENILE LITERATURE.
Cutrona, Cheryl. The Department of Labor /. [New York] , c1988. 95 p. : ISBN 0-87754-844-7 LC Card 87-24906 DDC 353.83 19
HD8066 .C85 1988

United States. Dept. of Labor. Manpower Administration. (Old Catalog form: United States. Manpower Administration)
Breakthrough for disadvantaged youth. [Washington] 1969. iii, 256 p. LC Card 79-604757 DDC 331.3/4/0973
HD6273 .B7 *NYPL [JLF 86-435]*

United States. Dept. of Labor. Wage and Hour and Public Contracts Divisons. see **United States. Wage and Hour and Public Contracts Divisions.**

United States. Dept. of Labor. Women's Bureau. see **United States. Women's Bureau.**

United States. Dept. of State. (Old Catalog form: United States. State Dept.)

United States. Dept. of State. Agency for International Development. see **United States. Agency for International Development.**

UNITED STATES. DEPT. OF STATE - ARCHIVES.
Records of the U. S. Department of State relating to commercial relations between the United States and Japan, 1910-1949 [microform]. Wilmington, Del. , c1987. microfilm reel ISBN 0-8420-3061-1 (microfilm : set) : LC Card 87-23376 DDC 337.73052 19
HF3127

Records of the U. S. Department of State relating to commercial relations between the United States and Russia/the Soviet Union, 1910-1949 [microform]. Wilmington, DE , c1987. microfilm reel. ISBN 0-8420-3053-0 (microfilm : set) : LC Card 87-23223 DDC 337.73047 19
HF3105

United States. Dept. of the Interior. (Old Catalog form: United States. Interior Dept.)

United States. Dept. of the Interior. Bureau of Mines. see **United States. Bureau of Mines.**

United States. Dept. of the Interior. Division of Medical and Health Services. Help for the troubled employee. Washington : U. S. Dept. of the Interior, Office of Organization and Personnel Management, Division of Medical and Health Services, [1975?] 57 p. ; 27 cm. Cover title. At head of title: Supervisor's guide; troubled employee program.
1. Personnel management - United States. 2. Alcoholism and employment - United States. 3. Drugs and employment - United States. I. Title. II. Title: Supervisor's guide; troubled employee program. III. Title: Troubled employee program.
NYPL [JLF 86-1309]

United States. Dept. of the Interior. National Park Service. see **United States. National Park Service.**

United States. Dept. of the Interior. Office of Inspector General. The Financial condition of the government of the Virgin Islands as of September 30, 1981 /. Washington, D.C. [1983] 129 p. ; LC Card 84-603162 DDC 354.7297/22007231 19
HJ9923.V6 F56 1983

United States. Dept. of the Treasury.
Estimate of the expenditure ... of the United States, for the year 1789. New York : Printed by Thomas Greenleaf, [1789] 26, [2] p. (the last 2 pages blank) ; 35 cm. (fol.) Title from caption on p. 2. Page [1] begins: Treasury Department. September 19, 1789. The Secretary of the Treasury, in obedience to the order of the House of Representatives, of the 17th instant, respectfully reports ... "General account of anticipations" (p. 16-26) has covering letter (p. 14) dated Sept. 25, 1789. Evans 22213; Papers of the Bibl. Soc. of Amer., v. 58 (1964), p. 123. LC Card 87-109324 DDC n-us 19
1. United States - Appropriations and expenditures. 2. Budget - United States. I. Title.
HJ2050 .U55 1789

United States. Dept. of the Treasury. Office of State and Local Finance. Federal-state-local fiscal relations . Washington, D.C. [1986] 2 v. (viii, 1118 p.) : LC Card 86-603179 DDC 336.73 19
HJ275 .F427 1986

United States. Dept. of Transportation. (Old Catalog form: United States. Transportation Dept.)

United States. Dept. of Transportation. Federal Highway Administration. see **United States. Federal Highway Administration.**

United States. Dept. of Transportation. Office of the Assistant Secretary for Policy and International Affairs.
Profile of the '80's /. [Washington, D.C.?] , 1980. v, 77 p. : LC Card 81-600725 DDC 380.5/0973 19
HE206.2 .P765 *NYPL [JLF 86-1445]*

Weiner, Edward. Urban transportation planning in the United States . [Washington, D.C.] [1986] vii, 149 p. : LC Card 87-601522 DDC 388.4/068 19
HE308 .W45 1986

United States. Dept. of Transportation. Office of the Secretary. Contracting with the United States Department of Transportation [microform]. Rev. 11-84. Washington, D.C. : U. S. Dept. of Transportation, Office of the Secretary of Transportation, 1984. iii, 40 p. : ill. ; 23 cm. Cover title. "November 1984"--P. i. "DOT 518"--P. [4] of cover. Microfilm. New York : New York Public Library, 1986. 1 microfilm reel ; 35 mm. (MN *ZZ-26,232)
1. Public contracts - United States. 2. Research and development contracts, Government - United States. I. Title. *NYPL [*ZT-1711 no.25]*

United States. Dept. of Transportation. Research and Special Programs Administration. Bloch, Arnold J. Interstate highway trade-in process. Vol. 1. Assessment /. New York , 1982. [45] p. : *NYPL [*XME-11,324]*

United States. Dept. of Transportation. Urban Mass Transportation Administration. see **United States. Urban Mass Transportation Administration.**

United States. District of Columbia, Committee on the (House) see **United States. Congress. House. Committee on the District of Columbia.**

United States. Economic Analysis, Bureau of. see **United States. Bureau of Economic Analysis.**

United States - Economic conditions. Here are entered works on the economic history or conditions of the United States. Works on the discipline of economics in the United States are entered under: Economics - United States.

UNITED STATES - ECONOMIC CONDITIONS - TO 1865.
Alexander, Albert. The economic world of 1787 and the Constitution /. New York (150 Nassau St., Rm. 1625, New York 10038) [1987] 18 p. ; LC Card 87-403433 DDC 330.973/0318 19
HC105.6 .A44 1987

Huston, James L., 1947- The panic of 1857 and the coming of the Civil War /. Baton Rouge , c1987. xviii, 315 p. ; ISBN 0-8071-1368-9 LC Card 87-2705 DDC 338.5/42 19
HB3717 1857 .H87 1987

Schapiro, Morton Owen. Filling up America . Greenwich, Conn. , c1986. xiii, 149 p. : ISBN 0-89232-675-1 : LC Card 86-2771 DDC 304.6/0973 19
HB3505 .S33 1986 *NYPL [JLE 86-3386]*

UNITED STATES - ECONOMIC CONDITIONS - TO 1865 - REGIONAL DISPARITIES.
The Economy of early America . Charlottesville , 1988. xvi, 334 p. : ISBN 0-8139-1139-7 LC Card 87-6169 DDC 330.973/02 19
HC104 .E26 1988

UNITED STATES - ECONOMIC CONDITIONS - 1865-1918.
Schapiro, Morton Owen. Filling up America . Greenwich, Conn. , c1986. xiii, 149 p. : ISBN 0-89232-675-1 : LC Card 86-2771 DDC 304.6/0973 19
HB3505 .S33 1986 *NYPL [JLE 86-3386]*

UNITED STATES - ECONOMIC CONDITIONS - 1918-1945.
Bernstein, Michael A. (Michael Alan), 1954-

The Great Depression . Cambridge [Cambridgeshire] , New York , 1987. xvii, 269 p. : ISBN 0-521-34048-9 LC Card 87-6403 DDC 338.5/42 19
HB3717 1929 .B37 1987

Fearon, Peter. War, prosperity, and depression . Lawrence, Kan. , 1987. p. cm. ISBN 0-7006-0348-4 : LC Card 87-21571 DDC 330.973/091 19
HC106.2 .F42 1987

Vittoz, Stanley. New Deal labor policy and the American industrial economy /. Chapel Hill , c1987. 241 p. ; ISBN 0-8078-1729-5 LC Card 86-24911 DDC 331/.0973 19
HD8072 .V715 1987

UNITED STATES - ECONOMIC CONDITIONS - 1918-1945 - SOURCES.
Slaves of the Depression . Ithaca, N.Y. , 1987. x, 229 p. ; ISBN 0-8014-9464-8 (pbk. : alk. paper) LC Card 87-6671 DDC 331.25/0973 19
HD8072 .S6164 1987

UNITED STATES - ECONOMIC CONDITIONS - 1945-
Easterlin, Richard A., 1926- Birth and fortune . Chicago , 1987. xii, 228 p. : ISBN 0-226-18032-8 (pbk.) : LC Card 86-30724 DDC 304.6/0973 19
HB3505 .E247 1987

Heilbroner, Robert L. Economics explained /. New York , 1987. 250 p. : ISBN 0-671-64556-0 (pbk.) LC Card 87-12807 DDC 330 19
HB171 .H479 1987

Hutchinson, Harry D. Money, banking, and the United States economy /. Englewood Cliffs, NJ , 1988. p. cm. ISBN 0-13-600156-4 LC Card 87-19299 DDC 332.1/0973 19
HG2491 .H8 1988

Jorgenson, Dale Weldeau, 1933- Productivity and U. S. economic growth /. Cambridge, Mass. , 1987. 567 p. : ISBN 0-674-71175-0 (alk. paper) LC Card 87-12098 DDC 338/.06/0973 19
HC110.I52 J67 1987

Levy, Frank, 1941- Dollars and dreams . New York , 1987. p. cm. ISBN 0-87154-523-3 : LC Card 86-42952 DDC 339.2/0973 19
HC110.I5 L47 1987

Political economy . Jackson , c1987. vii, 276 p. ; ISBN 0-87805-313-1 (alk. paper) LC Card 87-10425 DDC 361.6/1/0941 19
HC106 .P68 1987

UNITED STATES - ECONOMIC CONDITIONS - 1961- - STATISTICS.
Morin, André, analyste en rémunération. Analyse de l'évolution des principaux indicateurs économiques au Québec, en Ontario, au Canada et aux Etats-Unis . [Québec] [1982] 209 p. ; ISBN 2-551-04641-6 LC Card 83-103355
HC117.Q4 M66 1982

UNITED STATES - ECONOMIC CONDITIONS - 1971- - ADDRESSES, ESSAYS, LECTURES.
Marcy, Sam, 1911- Anatomy of the economic crisis /. Atlanta , c1982. viii, 120 p. : ISBN 0-89567-077-1 (pbk.) ***NYPL [JLD 86-1329]***

UNITED STATES - ECONOMIC CONDITIONS - 1971-1981.
Bowman, Thomas F. Finding your best place to live in America /. New York , c1981. xiii, 337 p. : ISBN 0-940162-00-8 (pbk.) : LC Card 81-51506 DDC 973.927 19
HT123 .B665 ***NYPL [Pub. Cat. 86-574]***

Davidson, James Dale. The squeeze /. New York , c1980. 281 p. ; ISBN 0-671-40084-3 LC Card 79-28411 DDC 330.973
HC106.7 .D38 ***NYPL [JLE 80-1960]***

Profile of the '80's /. [Washington, D.C.?] , 1980. v, 77 p. : LC Card 81-600725 DDC 380.5/0973 19
HE206.2 .P765 ***NYPL [JLF 86-1445]***

Social and economic characteristics of the population in metro and nonmetro counties, 1970-80 /. Washington, D.C. [1986] iv, 70 p. : LC Card 86-602790 DDC 304.6/0973 19
HC106.7 .S577 1986

UNITED STATES - ECONOMIC CONDITIONS - 1971-1981 - CONGRESSES.
Die Wirtschaft der Vereinigten Staaten und der Bundesrepublik Deutschland . Bonn , c1977. 106 p. ; ISBN 3-87198-079-X LC Card 86-104673
HC106.7 .W57 1977

UNITED STATES - ECONOMIC CONDITIONS - 1981-
Andrews, George H., 1932- Actuarial projections for the old-age, survivors, and disability insurance program of social security in the United States of America /. Itasca, Ill., U. S.A. , c1987. viii, 188 p. : LC Card 87-1101 DDC 368.4/301/0973 19
HC106.8 .A56 1987

Bagby, Wesley Marvin, 1922- Introduction to social science /. Chicago , c1987. xv, 427 p. : ISBN 0-8304-1146-1 LC Card 86-23487 DDC 306/.0973 19
HC106.8 .B34 1987

Batra, Raveendra N. The great depression of 1990 /. Dallas, Tex. , c1985. xv, 175 p. : ISBN 0-939352-02-8 : LC Card 85-50275 DDC 338.5/42 19
HC106.8 .B39 1985 ***NYPL [JLD 86-4007]***

Batra, Raveendra N. The great depression of 1990 /. New York , c1987. 235 p. ; ISBN 0-671-64022-4 LC Card 87-4816 DDC 338.5/42 19
HC106.8 .B39 1987

Behrman, Jack N. The rise of the phoenix . Boulder , 1987. xiii, 104 p. ; ISBN 0-8133-7511-8 (pbk. : alk. paper) : LC Card 87-21689 DDC 338.973 19
HC106.8 .B43 1987

Boskin, Michael J. Reagan and the economy . San Francisco, Calif. , New York , c1987. xvi, 301 p. : ISBN 0-917616-80-4 : LC Card 87-22544 DDC 338.973 19
HC106.8 .B656 1987

Capitalismes fin de siècle /. Paris , c1986. 268 p. : ISBN 2-13-039425-6 : LC Card 86-231136
HC106.8 .C364 1986

Collins, Lora S. The U. S. economy to 1990 /. New York, N.Y. , c1985. 21 p. : ISBN 0-8237-0307-X (pbk.) LC Card 86-200284 DDC 338.5/443/0973 19
HC106.8 .C636 1985

Contemporary economic problems . Washington, D.C. , c1987. 332 p. : ISBN 0-8447-3621-X (alk. paper) LC Card 87-1395 DDC 330.973/0927 19
HC106.8 .C665 1987

Dumas, Lloyd J. The overburdened economy . Berkeley , c1986. xiv, 297 p. ; ISBN 0-520-05686-8 (alk. paper) LC Card 85-20856 DDC 331.13/7973 19
HD5724 .D775 1986 ***NYPL [JLD 86-2582]***

Economic competitiveness promoting America's living standard /] Washington , 1986 [i.e. 1987] vii, 34 p. : LC Card 87-601340 DDC 338.973 19
HC106.8 .E2745 1987

Economic report of the people /. Boston , c1986. xvii, 260 p. : ISBN 0-89608-315-2 (pbk.) : LC Card 85-30342 DDC 330.973/0927 19
HC106.8 .E29 1986 ***NYPL [JLD 87-301]***

The Economy, small business, and the federal budget . Washington , 1986. v, 20 p. : LC Card 86-603392 DDC 338.6/42/0973 19
HC106.8 .E35 1986

Evans, David Michael, 1955- Economic cancer /. Saratoga, CA [1987], c1986. 119 p. ; ISBN 0-88247-764-1 (pbk.) : LC Card 86-62711 DDC 338.973 19
HC106.8 .E93 1987

Fallows, James M. Human capital . New York, N.Y. , 1988. p. cm. ISBN 0-394-56498-7 : LC Card 87-42659 DDC 306/.3 19
HC106.8 .F35 1988

Für einen anhaltenden Aufschwung . Kiel [1986] 29 p. : ISBN 3-925357-33-5 (Deut. Bibl.) : LC Card 86-234971
HB44 .K45 no. 123 HC286.7

Gordon, Sanford D. Introductory economics /. Lexington, Mass. , c1987. xviii, 490 p. : ISBN 0-669-09119-7 LC Card 86-80503 DDC 330.973/092 19
HB171.5 .G648 1987

Granville, Joseph Ensign, 1923- The warning . New York , c1985. xvi, 397 p. ; ISBN 0-88191-034-1 : LC Card 85-13107 DDC 332.64/273 19
HG4910 .G76 1985 ***NYPL [JLE 86-3122]***

Grayson, C. Jackson (Charles Jackson), 1923- American business, a two-minute warning . New York , London , c1988. xvii, 368 p. : ISBN 0-02-912680-0 LC Card 87-19391 DDC 658/.00973 19
HD70.U5 G69 1988

Hibbs, Douglas A., 1944- The American political economy . Cambridge, Mass. , 1987. xiii, 404 p. : ISBN 0-674-02735-3 (alk. paper) LC Card 87-155 DDC 338.973 19
HB3743 .H52 1987

Hollingsworth, J. Rogers (Joseph Rogers), 1932- The governance of the American economy . Berlin [1985] 60 p. ; LC Card 86-205784 DDC 330.973 19
HC106.8 .H635 1985

Johansson, Mats, 1951- Frihetens idéer . [Stockholm] , c1986. 224 p. : ISBN 91-7566-106-3 LC Card 86-226727
HC106.8 .J64 1986

Kiplinger forecasts . Washington, DC , New York, NY , c1986. vi, 330 p. ; ISBN 0-938721-01-1 (pbk.) : LC Card 86-203273 DDC 338.5/443/0973 19
HC106.8 .K56 1986

Levitan, Sar A. Working but poor . Baltimore , c1987. ix, 142 p. : ISBN 0-8018-3583-6 (alk. paper) LC Card 87-16973 DDC 362.5/0973 19
HC110.I5 L468 1987

Magdoff, Harry. Stagnation and the financial explosion /. New York , c1987. 208 p. : ISBN 0-85345-716-6 : LC Card 86-33129 DDC 330.973/0927 19
HC106.8 .M315 1987b

Making the grade . Washington, D.C. , c1987. ii, 142 p. : ISBN 0-9605804-4-1 (pbk.) LC Card 87-70671 DDC 330.973/0927 19
HC106.8 .M318 1987

Malkin, Lawrence. The national debt /. New York , c1987. ix, 309 p. ; ISBN 0-8050-0382-7 LC Card 86-27347 DDC 336.3/4/0973 19
HJ8119 .M34 1987

Manchester, Paul B. Are we on the road to a balanced budget? . Washington , 1986. v, 18 p. : LC Card 86-603373 DDC 353.0072/2 19
HJ2052 .M365 1986

Milton, Arthur, 1922- Milton on America . Secaucus, N.J. , 1987. 192 p., [8] p. of plates : ISBN 0-8065-1039-0 : LC Card 87-401577 DDC 330.973/0927 19
HC106.8 .M55 1987

Naisbitt, John. The year ahead, 1986 . New York, NY , c1985. 168 p. ; ISBN 0-446-38330-9 LC Card 85-17909 DDC 338.5/443/0973 19
HC106.8 .N35 1985 ***NYPL [JLD 86-2987]***

Nevaer, Louis E. V. Corporate financial planning and management in a deficit economy /. New York , 1987. 171 p. : ISBN 0-89930-202-5 (lib. bdg. : alk. paper) LC Card 86-25582 DDC 658.1/145 19
HG4063 .N48 1987

Poniachek, Harvey A. Direct foreign investment in the United States /. Lexington, Mass. , c1986. xiii, 256 p. : ISBN 0-669-11076-0 (alk. paper) LC Card 85-40457 DDC 332.6/73/0973 19
HG4910 .P66 1986 ***NYPL [JLE 86-4295]***

Poverty, income distribution, the family, and public policy . Washington , 1986. viii, 125 p. : LC Card 87-601355 DDC 339.2/2/0973 19
HC110.I5 P68 1986

Promoting high-technology industry . Boulder , 1987. 283 p. ; ISBN 0-8133-7427-8 (pbk. : alk. paper) LC Card 87-61327 DDC 338.4/762/000973 19
HC110.H53 P76 1987

Rivière, Jean, professeur. Les Etats-Unis à l'horizon de la troisième révolution industrielle /. Nancy , c1986. 207 p. : ISBN 2-86480-174-4 LC Card 86-202607
HC106.8 .R57 1986

Rose, Stephen J., (Stephen Jay), 1947- The American economy poster and fact book /. New York , c1987. vi, 56 p. : ISBN 0-394-74390-3 (pbk.) : LC Card 86-43119

DDC 338.973 19
HC106.8 .R658 1987

Russell, Cheryl, 1953- 100 predictions for the baby boom . New York , c1987. 249 p. ; ISBN 0-306-42527-0 LC Card 87-2443 DDC 338.5/443/0973 19
HC106.8 .R87 1987

Sawyer, James E., 1943- Why Reaganomics and Keynesian economics failed /. New York , 1987. ix, 195 p. : ISBN 0-312-00532-6 : LC Card 87-9578 DDC 338.973 19
HC106.8 .S28 1987

Shilling, A. Gary. The world has definitely changed . New York, NY (111 Broadway, Suite 1200, New York 10006) , 1986. xx, 179 p. : LC Card 86-82936 DDC 338.5/443/0973 19
HC106.8 .S49 1986

The State of the states . Lexington, KY , c1986. 56 p. ; ISBN 0-87292-064-X (pbk.) LC Card 87-162324 DDC 330.973/0927 19
HC106.8 .S735 1986

U. S. economic review . Bala Cynwyd, Pa., USA (150 Monument Rd., Bala Cynwyd 19004-1790) , c1985. 7, 28 p. : LC Card 87-145506 DDC 338.5/443/0973 19
HC106.8 .U18 1985

U. S. economic review . Bala Cynwyd, Pa., USA (150 Monument Rd., Bala Cynwyd 19004-1790) , c1985. 7, 28 p. : LC Card 87-145506 DDC 338.5/443/0973 19
HC106.8 .U18 1985

UNITED STATES - ECONOMIC CONDITIONS - 1981- - CASE STUDIES.
Richards, Eugene. Below the line . Mount Vernon, N.Y. , c1987. 218 p. : ISBN 0-89043-062-4 LC Card 86-70834 DDC 305.5/69/0973 19
HC110.P6 R52 1987

UNITED STATES - ECONOMIC CONDITIONS - 1981- - CHARTS, DIAGRAMS, ETC.
Rose, Stephen J., (Stephen Jay), 1947- The American economy poster and fact book /. New York , c1987. vi, 56 p. : ISBN 0-394-74390-3 (pbk.) : LC Card 86-43119 DDC 338.973 19
HC106.8 .R658 1987

UNITED STATES - ECONOMIC CONDITIONS - 1981- - CONGRESSES.
Community energy management as an economic development strategy . [Lincoln, Neb.] (Box 95085, Lincoln 68509-5085) [1984 or 1985] iv, 396 p. : LC Card 86-622211 DDC 333.79/0973 19
HD9502.U52 C656 1984

Research Conference on Trends Impacting Tax Administration (1985 : Washington, D.C.) Research Conference on Trends Impacting Tax Administration, November 20-22, 1985. Washington, D.C. (1111 Constitution Ave., N.W., Washington 20224) [1985] 2 v. ; 28 cm. LC Card 87-601252 DDC 350.72/4/00973 19
HJ3252 .R357 1985

Technology and employment . Washington, D.C. , 1987. xiii, 225 p. : ISBN 0-309-03744-1 (pbk.) : LC Card 87-42807 DDC 331.12/0973 19
HD6331.2.U5 T43 1987

The 1986-87 outlook . New York, N.Y. (845 3rd Ave., New York 10022) , c1986. 18 p. : LC Card 86-212392 DDC 338.5/443/0973 19
HC106.8 .A14 1986

UNITED STATES - ECONOMIC CONDITIONS - 1981- - FORECASTING.
Special analysis and outlook for E.I. Du Pont De Nemours & Company (Inc.), Chemicals and Pigments Department. Boston, Mass. (7 Liberty Sq., Boston 02109) [1986] 17, [6] p. : LC Card 86-205857 DDC 338.4/766/00973 19
HD9660.P253 U672 1986

UNITED STATES - ECONOMIC CONDITIONS - 1981- - PICTORIAL WORKS.
Richards, Eugene. Below the line . Mount Vernon, N.Y. , c1987. 218 p. : ISBN 0-89043-062-4 LC Card 86-70834 DDC 305.5/69/0973 19
HC110.P6 R52 1987

UNITED STATES - ECONOMIC CONDITIONS - 1981- - PUBLIC OPINION.
The American dream . [New York] , c1987. 103 p. : LC Card 87-404096 DDC 330.973/0927 19
HC106.8 .A437 1987

UNITED STATES - ECONOMIC CONDITIONS - 1981- - REGIONAL DISPARITIES.
Technology, regions, and policy /. Totowa, N.J. , 1986. xiv, 322 p. : ISBN 0-8476-7409-6 LC Card 85-24970 DDC 338.4/76213817/0973 19
HC110.H53 T43 1986 ***NYPL [JLE 86-3327]***

UNITED STATES - ECONOMIC CONDITIONS - FORECASTING.
Johnston, William B., 1945- Workforce 2000 . Indianapolis, Ind. [Washington, D.C.?] , 1987. xxvii, 117 p. : LC Card 87-601910 DDC 331.12/5/0973 19
HD8072.5 .J64 1987

UNITED STATES - ECONOMIC CONDITIONS - REGIONAL DISPARITIES.
Agnew, John A. The United States in the world-economy . Cambridge , New York , 1987. xvii, 264 p. : ISBN 0-521-30410-5 LC Card 86-32743 DDC 337.73 19
HC103 .A37 1987

Booth, Douglas E. Regional long waves, uneven growth, and the cooperative alternative /. New York , 1987. 121 p. ; ISBN 0-275-92567-6 (alk. paper) : LC Card 87-2348 DDC 338.973 19
HB3729 .B66 1987

UNITED STATES - ECONOMIC CONDTIONS - 1981-
Saint-Etienne, Christian, 1951- The Mitterrand and Reagan economic experiments . [Stanford, Calif.] , c1986. 36 p ; ISBN 0-8179-5082-6 (pbk.) LC Card 86-27776 DDC 338.944 19
HC276.2 .S24 1986

United States. Economic Opportunity, Office of. see **United States. Office of Economic Opportunity.**

United States economic penetration of Venezuela and its effects on diplomacy, 1895-1906 /.
Carreras, Charles. New York , 1987. 252 p. : ISBN 0-8240-8077-7 (alk. paper) : LC Card 87-23723 DDC 332.6/7373/087 19
HG5412 .C45 1987

UNITED STATES - ECONOMIC POLICY.
Campagna, Anthony S. U. S. national economic policy, 1917-1985 /. New York , 1987. xix, 642 p. : ISBN 0-275-92426-2 (alk. paper) : LC Card 86-30316 DDC 338.973 19
HC106.2 .C26 1987

Committee for Economic Development. Research and Policy Committee. Leadership for dynamic state economies . New York, N.Y. , 1986. xii, 104 p. ; ISBN 0-87186-782-6 LC Card 86-20760 DDC 338.973 19
HC103 .C734 1986 ***NYPL [JLF 86-1832]***

Economic choices . Arlington, Va. , c1987. 73 p. : ISBN 0-932765-08-4 (pbk.) : LC Card 87-686 DDC 338.973 19
HC106 .E24 1987

Hodgetts, Richard M. Essentials of economics and free enterprise /. Menlo Park, Calif. , c1987. 437 p. : ISBN 0-201-20719-2 LC Card 86-207031 DDC 330 19
HB171.5 .H677 1987

Niemi, Albert W. U. S. economic history /. Lanham, MD [1987], c1980. xiii, 475 p. : ISBN 0-8191-6335-X (pbk. : alk. paper) : LC Card 87-10730 DDC 330.973 19
HC103 .N5 1987

Political economy . Jackson , c1987. vii, 276 p. ; ISBN 0-87805-313-1 (alk. paper) LC Card 87-10425 DDC 361.6/1/0941 19
HC106 .P68 1987

The Politics of American economic policy making /. Armonk, N.Y. , c1987. 455 p. : ISBN 0-87332-406-4 : LC Card 87-12827 DDC 338.973 19
HJ257 .P59 1987

Sagoff, Mark. The economy of the earth . Cambridge [Cambridgeshire] , New York , 1988. p. cm. ISBN 0-521-34113-2 LC Card 87-16091 DDC 363.7/056/0973 19
HC110.E5 S34 1988

Stewart, Michael, 1933- Keynes and after /. Harmondsworth, Middlesex, England , New York, N.Y., U. S.A. , 1986. 230 p. ; ISBN 0-14-022646-X (pbk.) : LC Card 86-218640 DDC 330.15/6 19
HB99.7 .S7 1986

Weaver, Paul, 1942 Oct. 18- The suicidal corporation /. New York , c1988. p. cm. ISBN 0-671-52378-3 LC Card 87-23468 DDC 338.7/4/0973 19
HD2785 .W38 1988

Withers, William, 1905-1987. Politics and economic policy . New York, N.Y. , c1986. 240 p. : ISBN 0-8062-2722-2 : LC Card 86-201185 DDC 338.973 19
HC106 .W82 1986

UNITED STATES - ECONOMIC POLICY - TO 1933.
Morrison, Rodney J., 1934- Henry C. Carey and American economic development /. Philadelphia , 1986. ix, 91 p. : ISBN 0-87169-763-7 (pbk.) LC Card 86-71420 DDC 338.973/0092/4 19
HB119.C3 M67 1986

Nelson, John R., 1952- Liberty and property . Baltimore , c1987. xv, 221 p. : ISBN 0-8018-3440-6 (alk. paper) LC Card 86-21373 DDC 338.973 19
HC105 .N45 1987

Shook, Dale N. William G. McAdoo and the development of national economic policy, 1913-1918 /. New York , 1987. 427 p. ; ISBN 0-8240-8092-0 (alk. paper) : LC Card 87-23766 DDC 338.973 19
HC106.2 .S55 1987

UNITED STATES - ECONOMIC POLICY - 1933-1945.
Olson, James Stuart, 1946- Saving capitalism . Princeton, N.J. , c1988. p. cm. ISBN 0-691-04749-9 (alk. paper) : LC Card 87-7275 DDC 353.0082/5/09 19
HG3729.U5 O47 1988

UNITED STATES - ECONOMIC POLICY - 1961-1971.
Winant, Howard. Stalemate . New York , 1988. xv, 203 p. ; ISBN 0-275-92706-3 (alk. paper) : LC Card 87-15157 DDC 338.973 19
HC106.6 .W56 1988

UNITED STATES - ECONOMIC POLICY - 1971-
The Prospects for economic recovery. Washington, D.C. , 1982. xx, 120 p. :
NYPL [JLF 86-1215]

UNITED STATES - ECONOMIC POLICY - 1971-1981.
Müller, Ronald E. National economic growth and stabilization policy in the age of multinational corporations . [Sydney] , 1979. vi, 45 p. : ISBN 0-908470-00-2 (pbk.) LC Card 87-672345
HC106.7 .M84x 1979

Neikirk, William. Volcker, portrait of the money man /. New York , Chicago, Ill. , c1987. xvi, 222 p. ; ISBN 0-86553-178-1 LC Card 87-19953 DDC 332.1/1/0924 B 19
HB119.V6 N45 1987

Winant, Howard. Stalemate . New York , 1988. xv, 203 p. ; ISBN 0-275-92706-3 (alk. paper) : LC Card 87-15157 DDC 338.973 19
HC106.6 .W56 1988

UNITED STATES - ECONOMIC POLICY - 1971-1981 - CONGRESSES.
Die Wirtschaft der Vereinigten Staaten und der Bundesrepublik Deutschland . Bonn , c1977. 106 p. ; ISBN 3-87198-079-X LC Card 86-104673
HC106.7 .W57 1977

UNITED STATES - ECONOMIC POLICY - 1981-
América Latina, Estados Unidos . México , 1986. 223 p. : ISBN 968-231-378-3 LC Card 87-128005 DDC 337.7308 19
HF1456.5.L3 A44 1986

America's changing role in the world-system /. New York , 1987. xi, 300 p. : ISBN 0-275-92417-3 (alk. paper) : LC Card 86-25245 DDC 337.73 19
HC106.8 .A455 1987

Anderson, Martin, 1936- An economic bill of rights /. Stanford, Calif. , 1984. 22 p. ; ISBN 0-8179-5122-9 (pbk.) LC Card 86-21394 DDC

338.973 19
HC106.8 .A55 1984

Arbeit, Entropie, Apokalypse . Zürich , 1982. 134 p. : LC Card 83-128724
HC106.8 .A73 1982

Arndt, Sven W. Competitiveness . Washington, D.C. , Lanham, MD , c1987. 120 p. : ISBN 0-8447-3625-2 (alk. paper) LC Card 87-1250 DDC 382/.0973 19
HF3031 .A83 1987

Behrman, Jack N. The rise of the phoenix . Boulder , 1987. xiii, 104 p. ; ISBN 0-8133-7511-8 (pbk. : alk. paper) : LC Card 87-21689 DDC 338.973 19
HC106.8 .B43 1987

Beyond Reagan . Washington, D.C. , c1987. v, 209 p. : ISBN 0-87187-437-7 (pbk.) : LC Card 87-3057 DDC 338.973 19
HC106.8 .B47 1987

Boskin, Michael J. Reagan and the economy . San Francisco, Calif. , New York , c1987. xvi, 301 p. : ISBN 0-917616-80-4 : LC Card 87-22544 DDC 338.973 19
HC106.8 .B656 1987

Bull-Berg, Hans Jacob. American international oil policy . New York , 1987. xvi, 209 p. : ISBN 0-312-00465-6 : LC Card 86-31583 DDC 333.8/232/0973 19
HD9566 .B87 1987

Capitalismes fin de siècle /. Paris , c1986. 268 p. : ISBN 2-13-039425-6 : LC Card 86-231136
HC106.8 .C364 1986

Contemporary economic problems . Washington, D.C. , c1987. 332 p. : ISBN 0-8447-3621-X (alk. paper) LC Card 87-1395 DDC 330.973/0927 19
HC106.8 .C665 1987

Corporation for Enterprise Development. Building the new economy . Washington, D.C. , 1986. iv, 178 p. ; ISBN 0-9605804-2-5 (pbk.) LC Card 86-61273 DDC 338.973 19
HC110.I53 C67 1986

Economic choices 1987 /. Washington, D.C. , 1986. xii, 126 p. ; ISBN 0-8157-1040-2 LC Card 85-48278 ***NYPL [JLE 86-2737]***

Economic competitiveness promoting America's living standard /] Washington , 1986 [i.e. 1987] vii, 34 p. : LC Card 87-601340 DDC 338.973 19
HC106.8 .E2745 1987

Economic report of the people /. Boston , c1986. xvii, 260 p. : ISBN 0-89608-315-2 (pbk.) : LC Card 85-30342 DDC 330.973/0927 19
HC106.8 .E29 1986 ***NYPL [JLD 87-301]***

Evans, David Michael, 1955- Economic cancer /. Saratoga, CA [1987], c1986. 119 p. ; ISBN 0-88247-764-1 (pbk.) : LC Card 86-62711 DDC 338.973 19
HC106.8 .E93 1987

Frumkin, Norman. Tracking America's economy /. Armonk, N.Y. , c1987. 250 p. : ISBN 0-87332-437-4 : LC Card 87-9694 DDC 338.5/44/0973 19
HC106.8 .F78 1987

Für einen anhaltenden Aufschwung . Kiel [1986] 29 p. : ISBN 3-925357-33-5 (Deut. Bibl.) : LC Card 86-234971
HB44 .K45 no. 123 HC286.7

Henning, C. Randall. Macroeconomic diplomacy in the 1980s . London , New York , c1987. x, 76 p. ; ISBN 0-7099-3794-6 (pbk.) LC Card 87-20041 DDC 337/.09171/3 19
HF1455 .H46 1987

Hibbs, Douglas A., 1944- The American political economy . Cambridge, Mass. , 1987. xiii, 404 p. : ISBN 0-674-02735-3 (alk. paper) LC Card 87-155 DDC 338.973 19
HB3743 .H52 1987

Hines, Lawrence Gregory. The market, energy, and the environment /. Boston , c1988. xii, 305 p. : ISBN 0-205-10568-8 : LC Card 87-1037 DDC 333.7/0973 19
HC110.E5 H57 1988

Johansson, Mats, 1951- Frihetens idéer . [Stockholm] , c1986. 224 p. : ISBN 91-7566-106-3 LC Card 86-226727
HC106.8 .J64 1986

Kozlova, K. B. Institut͡sionalizm v amerikanskoĭ politėkonomii . Moskva , 1987. 214, [2] p. ; LC Card 87-159642
HB99.5 .K69 1987

Magdoff, Harry. Stagnation and the financial explosion /. New York , c1987. 208 p. : ISBN 0-85345-716-6 : LC Card 86-33129 DDC 330.973/0927 19
HC106.8 .M315 1987b

Malkin, Lawrence. The national debt /. New York , c1987. ix, 309 p. ; ISBN 0-8050-0382-7 LC Card 86-27347 DDC 336.3/4/0973 19
HJ8119 .M34 1987

Nathan, Richard P. Reagan and the States /. Princeton, N.J. , c1987. xv, 375 p. : ISBN 0-691-07748-7 (alk. paper) : LC Card 87-45529 DDC 353.0072/5 19
HJ2051 .N167 1987

Neikirk, William. Volcker, portrait of the money man /. New York , Chicago, Ill. , c1987. xvi, 222 p. ; ISBN 0-86553-178-1 LC Card 87-19953 DDC 332.1/1/0924 B 19
HB119.V6 N45 1987

The New economic role of American states . New York , 1988. x, 370 p. ; ISBN 0-19-505003-7 LC Card 87-12499 DDC 338.973 19
HC106.8 .N495 1988

Poverty, income distribution, the family, and public policy . Washington , 1986. viii, 125 p. : LC Card 87-601355 DDC 339.2/2/0973 19
HC110.I5 P68 1986

Protecting the environment . Washington, D.C. , c1986. iii, 88 p. ; ISBN 0-89195-040-0 (pbk.) : LC Card 86-82962 DDC 363.7/056/0973 19
HC110.E5 P77 1986

Rose, Adam Zachery. Natural resource policy and income distribution /. Baltimore , c1988. xvi, 139 p. : ISBN 0-8018-3523-2 (alk. paper) LC Card 87-2788 DDC 333.7/0973 19
HC103.7 .R67 1988

Rose, Stephen J., (Stephen Jay), 1947- The American economy poster and fact book /. New York , c1987. vi, 56 p. : ISBN 0-394-74390-3 (pbk.) : LC Card 86-43119 DDC 338.973 19
HC106.8 .R658 1987

Saint-Etienne, Christian, 1951- The Mitterrand and Reagan economic experiments . [Stanford, Calif.] , c1986. 36 p ; ISBN 0-8179-5082-6 (pbk.) LC Card 86-27776 DDC 338.944 19
HC276.2 .S24 1986

Sawyer, James E., 1943- Why Reaganomics and Keynesian economics failed /. New York , 1987. ix, 195 p. : ISBN 0-312-00532-6 : LC Card 87-9578 DDC 338.973 19
HC106.8 .S28 1987

Sealy, Albert H. Macro blueprint . New York , 1986. viii, 407, 232 p. ; ISBN 0-89192-390-X LC Card 86-218989 DDC 338.973 19
HD2785 .S412 1986

Stock, Walter. High Technology . Köln , 1986. 244 p. : ISBN 3-7609-1049-1 : LC Card 86-230225
HC110.H53 S76 1986

Stockman, David Alan, 1946- The triumph of politics . New York , c1986. 422 p. : ISBN 0-06-015560-4 : LC Card 85-45541 DDC 338.973 19
HC106.8 .S75 1986 ***NYPL [JLE 86-2647]***

Stockman, David Alan, 1946- The triumph of politics . Boston, Mass. , 1987, c1986. xxxiii, 654 p. (large print) ; ISBN 0-8161-4231-9 (lg. print) : LC Card 86-22950 DDC 338.973 19
HC106.8 .S75 1986b

Striner, Herbert E. Regaining the lead . Millwood, N.Y. , c1987. xvii, 205 p. ; ISBN 0-8046-9408-7 (pbk. : alk. paper) : LC Card 86-32218 DDC 338.973 19
HC106.8 .S77 1987

Technology, regions, and policy /. Totowa, N.J. , 1986. xiv, 322 p. : ISBN 0-8476-7409-6 LC Card 85-24970 DDC 338.4/76213817/0973 19
HC110.H53 T43 1986 ***NYPL [JLE 86-3327]***

Tobin, James, 1918- Policies for prosperity . Cambridge, Mass. , 1987. xiv, 508 p. : ISBN 0-262-20066-X LC Card 87-2967 DDC 330.15/6 19
HB99.7 .T63 1987

Trade friction and economic policy . Cambridge [Cambridgeshire] , New York , 1987. xii, 243 p. : ISBN 0-521-34446-8 LC Card 87-11694 DDC 382/.0952/073 19
HF3828.U5 T73 1987

United States. Secretary of Labor's Task Force on Economic Adjustment and Worker Dislocation. Economic adjustment and worker dislocation in a competitive society . Washington, D.C. [1986] 189 p. in various pagings : LC Card 87-601034 DDC 331.13/7973 19
HC106.8 .U545 1986

West, Darrell M., 1954- Congress and economic policymaking /. Pittsburgh, Pa. , c1987. xiv, 203 p. ; ISBN 0-8229-5396-X (pbk.) LC Card 87-40160 DDC 338.973 19
HC106.8 .W45 1987

Winant, Howard. Stalemate . New York , 1988. xv, 203 p. ; ISBN 0-275-92706-3 (alk. paper) : LC Card 87-15157 DDC 338.973 19
HC106.6 .W56 1988

UNITED STATES - ECONOMIC POLICY - 1981- - ADDRESSES, ESSAYS, LECTURES.

State politics and the new federalism . White Plains, N.Y. , c1986. xv, 544 p. : ISBN 0-582-28474-0 (pbk.) LC Card 85-15956 DDC 321.02/0973 19
JK325 .S77 1986 ***NYPL [JLD 86-2766]***

UNITED STATES - ECONOMIC POLICY - 1981- - CHARTS, DIAGRAMS, ETC.

Rose, Stephen J., (Stephen Jay), 1947- The American economy poster and fact book /. New York , c1987. vi, 56 p. : ISBN 0-394-74390-3 (pbk.) : LC Card 86-43119 DDC 338.973 19
HC106.8 .R658 1987

UNITED STATES - ECONOMIC POLICY - 1981- - CONGRESSES.

Carson, Carol S. The use of national income and product accounts for public policy . Washington, D.C. , 1986. 26 p. : LC Card 86-601338 DDC 339.5/0973 19
HC110.I5 C37 1986

Japan and the United States today . New York , 1986, c1987. vii, 234 p. : ISBN 0-231-06575-2 LC Card 86-32640 DDC 332/.042/0952 19
HG3903 .J35 1987

UNITED STATES - ECONOMIC POLICY - 1981- - DECISION MAKING.

West, Darrell M., 1954- Congress and economic policymaking /. Pittsburgh, Pa. , c1987. xiv, 203 p. ; ISBN 0-8229-5396-X (pbk.) LC Card 87-40160 DDC 338.973 19
HC106.8 .W45 1987

United States. Education and Labor, Committee on (House) see **United States. Congress. House. Committee on Education and Labor.**

United States. Embassy (Germany : West) Die Wirtschaft der Vereinigten Staaten und der Bundesrepublik Deutschland . Bonn , c1977. 106 p. ; ISBN 3-87198-079-X LC Card 86-104673
HC106.7 .W57 1977

UNITED STATES - EMIGRATION AND IMMIGRATION - ADDRESSES, ESSAYS, LECTURES.

Los Factores del cambio demográfico en México /. México, D.F. , 1984. 422 p. : ISBN 968-231-281-7 LC Card 85-231767
HB1361 .F33 1984 ***NYPL [JLE 87-753]***

UNITED STATES - EMIGRATION AND IMMIGRATION - GOVERNMENT POLICY.

The Hands that feed us . Washington, D.C. , c1986. iii leaves, 150, 2 p., [3] leaves of plates : ISBN 0-86566-039-5 (pbk.) : LC Card 87-154337 DDC 331.5/44/09759 19
HD1527.F6 H36 1986

UNITED STATES - EMIGRATION AND IMMIGRATION - HISTORY.

Lane, A. T. Solidarity or survival? . New York , 1987. xii, 230 p. ; ISBN 0-313-25544-X (lib. bdg. : alk. paper) LC Card 86-25735 DDC 331.6/2/0973 19
HD8081.A5 L36 1987

Muller, Thomas, 1933- The fourth wave .

Washington , c1985. xvii, 217 p. ; ISBN 0-87766-349-1 LC Card 85-22646 DDC 331.6/2/720794 19
HD8081.M6 M85 1985 ***NYPL [JLE 86-3014]***

United States - Employees. see **United States - Officials and employees.**

United States. Employment and Training Administration.
Startzel, Donna C. The CETA arts and humanities experience [microform] CETA Ahead project (Arts and humanities employment analysis and documentation) /. Columbia, Md. , 1981. 197 p. ; ***NYPL [*XME-11,320]***

Startzel, Donna C. CETA (Comprehensive Employment and Training Act) and the arts and humanities [microform] . Columbia, Md. , 1981. 160 p. ; ***NYPL [*XME-11,328]***

United States. Employment and Training Administration. Office of Youth Program.
Completing the youth agenda : a plan for knowledge development, dissemination and application for fiscal 1980. Washington : Dept. of Labor, Employment and Training Administration, Office of Youth Programs, 1979. 73 p. ; 28 cm. "October 1979."
1. Youth - Employment - United States. 2. Vocational guidance - United States. 3. Occupational training - United States. I. Title. ***NYPL [JLF 86-454]***

United States. Employment and Training Administration. Office of Youth Programs.
United States. Vice President's Task Force on Youth Employment. A summary report of the Vice President's Task Force on Youth Employment. Washington , 1980. 70 p. : ***NYPL [JLF 86-214]***

United States. Employment and Training Administration. Youth Programs, Office of. see **United States. Employment and Training Administration. Office of Youth Programs.**

United States. Employment of the Handicapped, President's Committee on. see **United States. President's Committee on Employment of the Handicapped.**

United States Employment Service. Division of Occupational Analysis. Guide for occupational exploration /. [Washington, D.C.] , Circle Pines, Minn. , c1984. vii, 984 p. : LC Card 87-402857 DDC 331.7/02/0973 19
HF5382.5.U5 G83 1984

United States Employment Service. Division of Testing. Guide for occupational exploration /. [Washington, D.C.] , Circle Pines, Minn. , c1984. vii, 984 p. : LC Card 87-402857 DDC 331.7/02/0973 19
HF5382.5.U5 G83 1984

United States. Employment Standards Administration. Division of State Workers' Compensation Programs.
Information on the administration of workers' compensation programs in each state and the District of Columbia /. [Washington, D.C.?] [1985] iii, 426 p. ; ***NYPL [JLF 86-774]***

Information on the administration of workers' compensation programs in each state and the District of Columbia /. [Washington, D.C.?] [1985] iii, 426 p. ; LC Card 86-601358 DDC 368.4/1/00973 19
HD7103.65.U6 I55 1985

United States. Energy, Dept. of. see **United States. Dept. of Energy.**

United States. Energy Information Administration. Office of Oil and Gas. An Economic analysis of natural gas resources and supply /. Washington, D.C. [1986] xx, 179 p. : LC Card 86-603066 DDC 338.2/7285/0973 19
HD9581.U5 E26 1986

The United States engineering plastics industry . Shea, Moira M. Washington, D.C. , 1987. 51 p. : LC Card 87-601518 DDC 338.4/76684/0973 19
HD9661.U62 S54 1987

United States. Engineers for Rivers and Harbors, Board of. see **United States. Board of Engineers for Rivers and Harbors.**

United States. Environmental Quality, Council on. see **United States. Council on Environmental Quality.**

UNITED STATES - EXECUTIVE DEPARTMENTS - AUDITING.
Moore, Mark Harrison. Inspectors-general . New York , c1986. 120 p. ; ISBN 0-87154-605-1 : LC Card 86-6728 DDC 353.0072/32 19
HJ9801 .M66 1987 ***NYPL [JLE 87-1762]***

United States. Executive Office of the President. Council on Environmental Quality. see **United States. Council on Environmental Quality.**

United States. Executive Office of The President. Office of Management and Budget. see **United States. Office of Management and Budget.**

UNITED STATES. FARMERS HOME ADMINISTRATION.
FmHA guaranteed lending manual /. Washington, D.C. (1120 Connecticut Ave., N.W., Washington 20036) , c1986. xi, 88, [59] p. : LC Card 86-226067 DDC 332.1/753 19
HG2051.U5 F55 1986

United States. Federal Committee on Statistical Methodology. Subcommittee on Federal Longitudinal Surveys. Federal longitudinal surveys /. [Washington, D.C.?] [Springfield, VA] 1986. v, 159 p. : LC Card 86-603413 DDC 001.4/33 19
HA31.2 .F43 1986

United States. Federal Highway Administration. Office of Highway Information Management.
Briggs, Dwight. Journey-to-work trends . Washington, D.C. , Springfield, VA [1986] 1 v. (various pagings) : LC Card 86-602387 DDC 388.4/1314/0973 19
HE371.A3 B75 1986

United States. Federal Highway Administration. Office of Highway Planning. see **United States. Office of Highway Planning.**

United States. Federal Reserve Board. see **United States. Board of Governors of the Federal Reserve System.**

United States. Federal Reserve System. see **United States. Board of Governors of the Federal Reserve System.**

United States. Finance, Committee on (Senate) see **United States. Congress. Senate. Committee on Finance.**

United States. Foreign Affairs, Committee on (House) see **United States. Congress. House. Committee on Foreign Affairs.**

United States. Foreign Agricultural Service.
Dyck, John H. South Korea . Washington, D.C. [1986] v, 74 p. : LC Card 86-602006 DDC 338.1 s 382/.41/095195 19
HD1411 .F59 no. 216 HD9005

Mabbs-Zeno, Carl. Nigeria . Washington, D.C. [1986] vi, 54 p. : LC Card 86-601597 DDC 382/.41/09669 19
HD9017.N52 M3 1986

Trueblood, Michael A. The Ivory Coast . Washington, DC , 1986. iv, 32 p. : LC Card 86-602806 DDC 338.1 s 382/.41/096668 19
HD1411 .F59 no. 223 HD9017.I912

United States foreign economic policy-making . Gold, Kenneth A. (Kenneth Alan) New York , 1987. 349 p. ; ISBN 0-8240-8083-1 : LC Card 87-23785 DDC 382/.456413/00973 19
HD9006 .G64 1987

United States foreign economic policy toward China, 1943-1946 . Cosgrove, Julia Fukuda. New York , 1987. 235 p. ; ISBN 0-8240-8079-3 (alk. paper) : LC Card 87-23791 DDC 337.73051 19
HF1456.5.C6 C67 1987

UNITED STATES - FOREIGN ECONOMIC RELATIONS.
Agnew, John A. The United States in the world-economy . Cambridge , New York , 1987. xvii, 264 p. : ISBN 0-521-30410-5 LC Card 86-32743 DDC 337.73 19
HC103 .A37 1987

América Latina, Estados Unidos . México , 1986. 223 p. : ISBN 968-231-378-3 LC Card 87-128005 DDC 337.7308 19
HF1456.5.L3 A44 1986

America's changing role in the world-system /. New York , 1987. xi, 300 p. : ISBN 0-275-92417-3 (alk. paper) : LC Card 86-25245 DDC 337.73 19
HC106.8 .A455 1987

Bull-Berg, Hans Jacob. American international oil policy . New York , 1987. xvi, 209 p. : ISBN 0-312-00465-6 : LC Card 86-31583 DDC 333.8/232/0973 19
HD9566 .B87 1987

Cohen, Stephen D. The making of United States international economic policy . New York , 1987. p. cm. ISBN 0-275-92334-7 (alk. paper) : LC Card 87-24082 DDC 382/.3/0973 19
HF1455 .C576 1987

Committee on Science, Engineering, and Public Policy (U. S.). Panel on the Impact of National Security Controls on International Technology Transfer. Balancing the national interest . Washington, D.C. , 1987. xiii, 321 p. : ISBN 0-309-03738-7 LC Card 87-60020 DDC 337.73 19
HF1456 .C65 1987

Danielian, Ronald L. The forgotten deficit . Boulder , 1987. xii, 84 p. ; ISBN 0-8133-7450-2 (pbk. : alk. paper) LC Card 87-50654 DDC 332.6/7373 19
HG3883.U7 D36 1987

Foreign regulations affecting U. S. textile/apparel exports. [Washington, D.C.] [1986] 283 p. ; LC Card 86-601588
HF2651.T42 F67 1986

Gold, Kenneth A. (Kenneth Alan) United States foreign economic policy-making . New York , 1987. 349 p. ; ISBN 0-8240-8083-1 : LC Card 87-23785 DDC 382/.456413/00973 19
HD9006 .G64 1987

Hathaway, Dale E. Agriculture and the GATT . Washington, DC , c1987. xii, 157 p. : ISBN 0-88132-052-8 LC Card 87-21430 DDC 382/.41/0973 19
HD9006 .H28 1987

Henning, C. Randall. Macroeconomic diplomacy in the 1980s . London , New York , c1987. x, 76 p. ; ISBN 0-7099-3794-6 (pbk.) LC Card 87-20041 DDC 337/.09171/3 19
HF1455 .H46 1987

Heston, Thomas J. (Thomas Janney) Sweet subsidy . New York , 1987. 544 p. ; ISBN 0-8240-8084-X (alk. paper) : LC Card 87-23776 DDC 338.1/8 19
HD9105 .H47 1987

UNITED STATES - FOREIGN ECONOMIC RELATIONS - AFRICA.
Die Wirtschaftliche Expansion der USA . Moskau , 1986. 175 p. ; LC Card 87-408806 DDC 337.7305 19
HF1456.5.A64 W57 1986

UNITED STATES - FOREIGN ECONOMIC RELATIONS - AFRICA, SUB-SAHARAN.
Ozadovskiĭ, A. A. (Andreĭ Andreevich) Uoll-strit protiv Afriki /. Kiev , 1985. 228, [4] p. ; LC Card 86-219442
HF1611.Z4 U556 1985

UNITED STATES - FOREIGN ECONOMIC RELATIONS - ARABIAN PENINSULA.
Susanīān, K. G. (Karen Gevorkovich) Araviĭskie gosudarstva i vneshneēkonomicheskaīa strategiīa SShA /. Moskva , 1986. 229, [3] p. : LC Card 86-231698 DDC 337.73053 19
HF1456.5.A625 S87 1986

UNITED STATES - FOREIGN ECONOMIC RELATIONS - ASIA.
Das Dreieck Europa-Amerika-Asien /. [Diessenhofen] , 1986. 154 p. : ISBN 3-7253-0272-3 LC Card 86-231548
HC412 .D7 1986

U. S. trade relations with Asia . Washington , 1987. vii, 85 p. ; LC Card 87-601359 DDC 382/.0973/05 19
HF3118 .U15 1987

Die Wirtschaftliche Expansion der USA . Moskau , 1986. 175 p. ; LC Card 87-408806 DDC 337.7305 19
HF1456.5.A64 W57 1986

UNITED STATES - FOREIGN ECONOMIC RELATIONS - ASIA - CONGRESSES.
Vision of the future . Washington, D.C. , 1986. x, 189 p. : LC Card 87-125235 DDC

382/.0973/05 19
HF3118 .V57 1986

UNITED STATES - FOREIGN ECONOMIC RELATIONS - ASIA, SOUTHEASTERN - CONGRESSES.

ASEAN-U. S. economic relations . Singapore , c1986. x, 54 p. : ISBN 997-19-8842-9 (pbk.) LC Card 87-940002 DDC 337.59073 19
HF1456.5.A7 A84 1986

U. S. ASEAN relations . Washington, D.C. , 1987. xxii, 222 p. ; ISBN 0-943057-00-0 (pbk.) LC Card 87-50526 DDC 337.59073 19
HF1456.5.A7 U72 1987

UNITED STATES - FOREIGN ECONOMIC RELATIONS - AUSTRIA.

Einwitschläger, Arno. Amerikanische Wirtschaftspolitik in Österreich, 1945-1949 /. Wien , 1986. 206 p. : ISBN 3-205-08814-X LC Card 87-112406
HF1456.5.A9 E39 1986

UNITED STATES - FOREIGN ECONOMIC RELATIONS - BOLIVIA.

La Nueva política económica . La Paz, Bolivia , 1986. 57 p. : LC Card 87-403839 DDC 338.984 19
HC182 .N84 1986

UNITED STATES - FOREIGN ECONOMIC RELATIONS - BRAZIL.

Coes, Donald V., 1943- O Brasil na economia internacional. [Salvador, Brazil] [1984?] 55 p. : LC Card 86-234065
HF1513 .C64 1984

Hirst, Mônica. As relações dos Estados Unidos com as potências médias na América Latina, México e Brasil /. [Rio de Janeiro] , 1985. 48 leaves ; LC Card 87-143873 DDC 337.73072 19
HF1456.5.M6 H57 1985

UNITED STATES - FOREIGN ECONOMIC RELATIONS - CANADA.

Canadian-Japanese economic relations in a triangular perspective /. Toronto , Scarborough, Ont. [1987] vi, 54 p. : ISBN 0-88806-139-0 (pbk.) LC Card 87-169818 DDC 337.52071 19
HF1480.15.J3 C35 1987

Laxer, James. Leap of faith . Edmonton , c1986. 140 p. ; ISBN 0-88830-298-3 : LC Card 87-101958 DDC 382.7/1/0971 19
HF1480.15.U5 L39 1986

Wonnacott, Paul. The United States and Canada . Washington, DC , 1987. xii, 173 p. : ISBN 0-88132-056-0 (pbk.) : LC Card 87-2660 DDC 382.71073 19
HF1456.5.C2 W65 1987

UNITED STATES - FOREIGN ECONOMIC RELATIONS - CANADA - CONGRESSES.

Building a Canadian-American free trade area /. Washington, D.C. , c1987. xii, 217 p. ; ISBN 0-8157-2973-1 (pbk.) LC Card 87-71507 DDC 382/.0971/073 19
HF1480.15.U5 B85 1987

UNITED STATES - FOREIGN ECONOMIC RELATIONS - CARIBBEAN AREA.

Notas críticas sobre el plan Reagan para la cuenca del Caribe /. La Habana , 1982. 84 p. ; LC Card 87-400638 DDC 337.729073 19
HF1456.5.C27 N67 1982

UNITED STATES - FOREIGN ECONOMIC RELATIONS - CHINA.

Cosgrove, Julia Fukuda. United States foreign economic policy toward China, 1943-1946 . New York , 1987. 235 p. ; ISBN 0-8240-8079-3 (alk. paper) : LC Card 87-23791 DDC 337.73051 19
HF1456.5.C6 C67 1987

UNITED STATES - FOREIGN ECONOMIC RELATIONS - COLLECTED WORKS.

Lotta, Raymond. America in decline . Chicago , c1984- v. : ISBN 0-916650-12-X (v. 1) : LC Card 83-22294 DDC 330.973/0927 19
HC54 .L63 1984 ***NYPL [JLL 87-106]***

UNITED STATES - FOREIGN ECONOMIC RELATIONS - DEVELOPING COUNTRIES.

America's new competitors . Cambridge, Mass. , c1988. xiv, 290 p. ; ISBN 0-88730-135-5 LC Card 87-19295 DDC 337.730172/4 19
HF1456.5.D44 A44 1988

Godfried, Nathan. Bridging the gap between rich and poor . New York , 1987. xii, 225 p. ; ISBN 0-313-25648-9 (lib. bdg. : alk. paper) LC Card 87-8471 DDC 338.91/73/056 19
HC415.15 .G63 1987

May, Bernhard. Reagan und die Entwicklungsländer . München , 1987. xiv, 271 p. ; ISBN 3-486-53981-7 LC Card 87-139481 DDC 337.730172/4 19
HF1456.5.D44 M39 1987

Portilla, Belfor. Alimentos . México , 1983. 149, [53] p. : ISBN 968-429-384-4 LC Card 84-172348 DDC 338.1/9/1724 19
HD9018.D44 P67 1983
NYPL [JLD 86-1520]

UNITED STATES - FOREIGN ECONOMIC RELATIONS - DEVELOPING COUNTRIES - ADDRESSES, ESSAYS, LECTURES.

The Third world, premises of U. S. policy /. San Francisco , c1978. xv, 332 p. : ISBN 0-917616-30-8 : LC Card 78-67593 DDC 309.1/172/4
HC59.7 .T456 ***NYPL [JLD 81-653]***

UNITED STATES - FOREIGN ECONOMIC RELATIONS - DEVELOPING COUNTRIES - CONGRESSES.

U. S. agriculture and Third World economic development . Washington, D.C. , c1987. xv, 103 p. : ISBN 0-89068-086-8 (pbk.): LC Card 86-62757 DDC 338.9/009172/4 19
HD1755 .U173 1987

UNITED STATES - FOREIGN ECONOMIC RELATIONS - EUROPE.

Hogan, Michael J., 1943- The Marshall Plan . Cambridge [Cambridgeshire] , New York , 1987. xiv, 482 p. ; ISBN 0-521-25140-0 LC Card 86-31773 DDC 338.91/73/04 19
HC240 .H614 1987

Pullen, William George. World War debts and United States foreign policy, 1919-1929 /. New York , 1987. 157 p. ; ISBN 0-8240-8088-2 : LC Card 87-23789 DDC 337.7304 19
HF1456.5.E8 P84 1987

Sanford, William F. The American business community and the European Recovery Program, 1947-1952 /. New York , 1987. xiv, 366 p. ; ISBN 0-8240-8091-2 (alk. paper) LC Card 87-23765 DDC 338.91/73/04 19
HC240 .S259 1987

US economic expansion . Moscow , 1986. 172 p. ; LC Card 86-204071 DDC 337.7304 19
HF3092 .U8 1986

UNITED STATES - FOREIGN ECONOMIC RELATIONS - EUROPEAN ECONOMIC COMMUNITY COUNTRIES.

U. S.-EC relations . Washington , 1986. vii, 78 p. ; LC Card 86-603395 DDC 337.4073 19
HF1456.5.E825 U17 1986

UNITED STATES - FOREIGN ECONOMIC RELATIONS - EUROPEAN ECONOMIC COMMUNITY COUNTRIES - CONGRESSES.

Confrontation or negotiation . Millwood, N.Y. , 1985. xvi, 303 p. : ISBN 0-8046-9397-8 : LC Card 85-18667 DDC 382/.41/094 19
HD9015.E82 C67 1985
NYPL [JLE 86-4594]

UNITED STATES - FOREIGN ECONOMIC RELATIONS - GERMANY.

McNeil, William C. American money and the Weimar Republic . New York , 1986. x, 352 p. : ISBN 0-231-06236-2 LC Card 85-29962 DDC 336.3/4/0943 19
HG3949 .M38 1986 ***NYPL [JLE 86-3268]***

UNITED STATES - FOREIGN ECONOMIC RELATIONS - GERMANY, WEST.

Berghahn, Volker Rolf. [Unternehmer und Politik in der Bundesrepublik. English.] The Americanisation of West German industry, 1945-1973 /. Leamington Spa , New York , c1986. viii, 344 p. : ISBN 0-907582-55-9 : LC Card 86-222514
HC286.5 .B37x 1986b

UNITED STATES - FOREIGN ECONOMIC RELATIONS - GREAT BRITAIN.

Rowland, Benjamin M. Commercial conflict and foreign policy . New York , 1987. 431 p. ; ISBN 0-8240-8090-4 (alk. paper) : LC Card 87-23787 DDC 337.73041 19
HF1456.5.G7 R68 1987

UNITED STATES - FOREIGN ECONOMIC RELATIONS - INDIA.

Roy, P. C. (Prabhash Chandra), 1955- Indo-U. S. economic relations . New Delhi , c1986. 206 p. : LC Card 86-902903 DDC 337.54073 19
HF1590.15.U5 R69 1986

UNITED STATES - FOREIGN ECONOMIC RELATIONS - JAPAN.

Canadian-Japanese economic relations in a triangular perspective /. Toronto , Scarborough, Ont. [1987] vi, 54 p. : ISBN 0-88806-139-0 (pbk.) LC Card 87-169818 DDC 337.52071 19
HF1480.15.J3 C35 1987

The Japanese challenge . Stamford, Conn., U. S.A. , c1986. xii, 108 leaves : ISBN 0-89336-489-4 (pbk.) LC Card 87-404570 DDC 338/.06 19
HC465.T4 J365 1986

Ōmae, Ken'ichi, 1943- Beyond national borders . Homewood, Ill. , c1987. xi, 128 p. : ISBN 1-556-23017-6 LC Card 86-72864 DDC 337.52 19
HF1602.15.U6 O4 1987

Wheeler, Jimmy W. Beyond recrimination . Indianapolis, IN (P.O. Box 26-919, Indianapolis 46226) , c1987. xix, 218 p. : LC Card 87-165405 DDC 382/.0951249/073 19
HF1456.5.T28 W46 1987

UNITED STATES - FOREIGN ECONOMIC RELATIONS - JAPAN - CONGRESSES.

Japan and the United States today . New York , 1986, c1987. vii, 234 p. : ISBN 0-231-06575-2 LC Card 86-32640 DDC 332/.042/0952 19
HG3903 .J35 1987

UNITED STATES - FOREIGN ECONOMIC RELATIONS - KOREA (SOUTH)

Wheeler, Jimmy W. Beyond recrimination . Indianapolis, IN (P.O. Box 26-919, Indianapolis 46226) , c1987. xix, 218 p. : LC Card 87-165405 DDC 382/.0951249/073 19
HF1456.5.T28 W46 1987

UNITED STATES - FOREIGN ECONOMIC RELATIONS - LATIN AMERICA.

América Latina, Estados Unidos . México , 1986. 223 p. : ISBN 968-231-378-3 LC Card 87-128005 DDC 337.7308 19
HF1456.5.L3 A44 1986

Clayton, Lawrence A. Grace . Ottawa, Ill. , c1985. xiii, 403 p., [32] p. of plates : ISBN 0-915463-25-3 LC Card 85-14856 DDC 338.8/8885 19
HD9505.P4 C43 1986 ***NYPL [JLE 86-3892]***

Rosenberg, Emily S., 1944- World War I and the growth of United States predominance in Latin America /. New York , 1987. p. cm. ISBN 0-8240-8089-0 : LC Card 87-23683 DDC 337.7308 19
HF1456.5.L3 R67 1987

US economic expansion . Moscow , 1986. 216 p. ; LC Card 87-112029 DDC 337.7308 19
HF1456.5.L3 U8 1986

UNITED STATES - FOREIGN ECONOMIC RELATIONS - MEXICO.

Baldridge, Donald C. (Donald Carl) Mexican petroleum and United States-Mexican relations, 1919-1923 /. New York , 1987. 255 p. ; ISBN 0-8240-8070-X (alk. paper) LC Card 87-23817 DDC 338.2/7282/0972 19
HD9574.M6 B324 1987

Beelen, George D. Harding and Mexico . New York , 1987. xiii, 200 p., [16] p. of plates : ISBN 0-8240-8073-4 (alk. paper) LC Card 87-23724 DDC 337.72073 19
HF1456.5.M6 B44 1987

Bodayla, Stephen D. Financial diplomacy . New York , 1987. x, 216 p. ; ISBN 0-8240-8074-2 (alk. paper) LC Card 87-23790 DDC 337.73072 19
HF1456.5.M6 B63 1987

González-Aréchiga, Bernardo. Vinculación fronteriza a Estados Unidos y su cambio con la crisis /. Tijuana, Baja California , 1985. 54 p. ; ISBN 968-607-500-3 LC Card 86-187758
HF3239.M49 G66 1985

Hirst, Mônica. As relações dos Estados Unidos com as potências médias na América Latina, México e Brasil /. [Rio de Janeiro] , 1985. 48 leaves ; LC Card 87-143873 DDC 337.73072 19
HF1456.5.M6 H57 1985

UNITED STATES - FOREIGN ECONOMIC RELATIONS - MIDDLE EAST.

Godfried, Nathan. Bridging the gap between rich and poor . New York , 1987. xii, 225 p. ; ISBN 0-313-25648-9 (lib. bdg. : alk. paper) LC Card 87-8471 DDC 338.91/73/056 19
HC415.15 .G63 1987

Painter, David S. [Oil and the American century.] Private power and public policy . London , c1986. xii, 302 p. : ISBN 1-85043-021-7 LC Card 87-673320
HD9566 .P24x 1986b

UNITED STATES - FOREIGN ECONOMIC RELATIONS - PHILIPPINES.
Giesecke, Leonard F. (Leonard Frederick) History of American economic policy in the Philippines during the American colonial period, 1900-1935 /. New York , 1987. 279 p. ; ISBN 0-8240-8082-3 (alk. paper) : LC Card 87-23786 DDC 337.730599 19
HF1456.5.P6 G53 1987

Stauffer, Robert B. The Philippines under Marcos . Sydney [1986] 207 p. ; ISBN 0-908470-69-X (pbk.) LC Card 87-123266 DDC 338.9599 19
HD3616.P62 S7 1986

UNITED STATES - FOREIGN ECONOMIC RELATIONS - POLAND.
Poland's renewal and U. S. options . Washington , 1987. xv, 41 p. : LC Card 87-601374 DDC 337.438073 19
HC340.3 .P646 1987

UNITED STATES - FOREIGN ECONOMIC RELATIONS - SAUDI ARABIA.
Casillas, Rex J. Oil and diplomacy . New York , 1987. p. cm. ISBN 0-8240-8078-5 : LC Card 87-23769 DDC 337.730538 19
HF1456.5.S33 C37 1987

UNITED STATES - FOREIGN ECONOMIC RELATIONS - SOVIET UNION.
Boe, Jonathan E. (Jonathan Evers) American business . New York , 1987. p. cm. ISBN 0-8240-8075-0 LC Card 87-23693 DDC 337.73047 337.4 19
HF1456.5.S624 B64 1987

SSSR, SShA i Kanada . Moskva , 1987. 325 p. ; LC Card 86-205359
HF3628.U5 S77 1987

UNITED STATES - FOREIGN ECONOMIC RELATIONS - TAIWAN.
Wheeler, Jimmy W. Beyond recrimination . Indianapolis, IN (P.O. Box 26-919, Indianapolis 46226) , c1987. xix, 218 p. : LC Card 87-165405 DDC 382/.0951249/073 19
HF1456.5.T28 W46 1987

UNITED STATES - FOREIGN ECONOMIC RELATIONS - VENEZUELA.
Carreras, Charles. United States economic penetration of Venezuela and its effects on diplomacy, 1895-1906 /. New York , 1987. 252 p. : ISBN 0-8240-8077-7 (alk. paper) : LC Card 87-23723 DDC 332.6/7373/087 19
HG5412 .C45 1987

UNITED STATES - FOREIGN OPINION.
United States. Congress. House. Committee on Foreign Affairs. Subcommittee on International Organizations and Movements. Modern communications and foreign policy. Washington, 1967. vii, 13R, iv, 216 p. LC Card 67-61749
E744 .U45 1967 ***NYPL [JLE 73-233]***

UNITED STATES - FOREIGN RELATIONS - 1897-1901.
Carreras, Charles. United States economic penetration of Venezuela and its effects on diplomacy, 1895-1906 /. New York , 1987. 252 p. : ISBN 0-8240-8077-7 (alk. paper) : LC Card 87-23723 DDC 332.6/7373/087 19
HG5412 .C45 1987

UNITED STATES - FOREIGN RELATIONS - 20TH CENTURY.
Bodayla, Stephen D. Financial diplomacy . New York , 1987. x, 216 p. ; ISBN 0-8240-8074-2 (alk. paper) LC Card 87-23790 DDC 337.73072 19
HF1456.5.M6 B63 1987

Heston, Thomas J. (Thomas Janney) Sweet subsidy . New York , 1987. 544 p. ; ISBN 0-8240-8084-X (alk. paper) : LC Card 87-23776 DDC 338.1/8 19
HD9105 .H47 1987

UNITED STATES - FOREIGN RELATIONS - 1909-1913.
Mayer, Robert Stanley. The influence of Frank A. Vanderlip and the National City Bank on American commerce and foreign policy, 1910-1920 /. New York , 1987. viii, 221 p. ; ISBN 0-8240-8087-4 : LC Card 87-23793 DDC 332.1/5/097471 19
HG2613.N54 N3555 1987

UNITED STATES - FOREIGN RELATIONS - 1913-1921.
Mayer, Robert Stanley. The influence of Frank A. Vanderlip and the National City Bank on American commerce and foreign policy, 1910-1920 /. New York , 1987. viii, 221 p. ; ISBN 0-8240-8087-4 : LC Card 87-23793 DDC 332.1/5/097471 19
HG2613.N54 N3555 1987

Rosenberg, Emily S., 1944- World War I and the growth of United States predominance in Latin America /. New York , 1987. p. cm. ISBN 0-8240-8089-0 : LC Card 87-23683 DDC 337.7308 19
HF1456.5.L3 R67 1987

UNITED STATES - FOREIGN RELATIONS - 1921-1923.
Beelen, George D. Harding and Mexico . New York , 1987. xiii, 200 p., [16] p. of plates : ISBN 0-8240-8073-4 (alk. paper) LC Card 87-23724 DDC 337.72073 19
HF1456.5.M6 B44 1987

UNITED STATES - FOREIGN RELATIONS - 1933-1945.
Cosgrove, Julia Fukuda. United States foreign economic policy toward China, 1943-1946 . New York , 1987. 235 p. ; ISBN 0-8240-8079-3 (alk. paper) : LC Card 87-23791 DDC 337.73051 19
HF1456.5.C6 C67 1987

Rowland, Benjamin M. Commercial conflict and foreign policy . New York , 1987. 431 p. ; ISBN 0-8240-8090-4 (alk. paper) : LC Card 87-23787 DDC 337.73041 19
HF1456.5.G7 R68 1987

UNITED STATES - FOREIGN RELATIONS - 1945-
Scholl, Heinz. Bilderberger & Trilaterale . Euskirchen, Bundesrepublik Deutschland , c1977. 92 p. ; LC Card 85-199172
HD2785 .S396 1977

Targ, Harry R., 1940- Strategy of an empire in decline . Minneapolis , c1986. 294 p. ; ISBN 0-930656-47-4 : LC Card 86-16338 DDC 909.82 19
D849 .T37 1986 ***NYPL [JFD 87-2032]***

UNITED STATES - FOREIGN RELATIONS - 1945-1953.
Cosgrove, Julia Fukuda. United States foreign economic policy toward China, 1943-1946 . New York , 1987. 235 p. ; ISBN 0-8240-8079-3 (alk. paper) : LC Card 87-23791 DDC 337.73051 19
HF1456.5.C6 C67 1987

UNITED STATES - FOREIGN RELATIONS - 1981-
Bagby, Wesley Marvin, 1922- Introduction to social science /. Chicago , c1987. xv, 427 p. : ISBN 0-8304-1146-1 LC Card 86-23487 DDC 306/.0973 19
HC106.8 .B34 1987

UNITED STATES - FOREIGN RELATIONS - ASIA, SOUTHEASTERN - CONGRESSES.
U. S. ASEAN relations . Washington, D.C. , 1987. xxii, 222 p. ; ISBN 0-943057-00-0 (pbk.) LC Card 87-50526 DDC 337.59073 19
HF1456.5.A7 U72 1987

UNITED STATES - FOREIGN RELATIONS - CENTRAL AMERICA.
Barry, Tom, 1950- The soft war . New York , 1988. xv, 304 p. ; ISBN 0-8021-0003-1 LC Card 87-13238 DDC 338.91/73/0728 19
HC141 .B375 1988

Implications of population trends for U. S. foreign policy in Central America . Washington , 1984. iii, 16 p. : LC Card 86-602534 DDC 304.6/09728 19
HB3533 .I55 1984

Williams, Robert G. (Robert Gregory), 1948- Export agriculture and the crisis in Central America /. Chapel Hill , c1986. xvi, 257 p. : ISBN 0-8078-1693-0 LC Card 85-20978 DDC 382/.41/09728 19
HD9884.C352 W55 1986
NYPL [JLE 86-3412]

United States. Foreign Relations, Committee on (Senate) see United States. Congress. Senate. Committee on Foreign Relations.

UNITED STATES - FOREIGN RELATIONS - EUROPE.
Blinken, Antony J. Ally versus ally . New York , 1987. ix, 193 p. : ISBN 0-275-92410-6 (alk. paper) : LC Card 86-25222 DDC 388.5 19
HD9581.S652 B58 1987

UNITED STATES - FOREIGN RELATIONS - GREAT BRITAIN.
Helmreich, Jonathan E. Gathering rare ores . Princeton, N.J. , c1986. xiv, 303 p. : ISBN 0-691-04738-3 (alk. paper) : LC Card 86-4862 DDC 327.1/11 19
HD9698.U52 H45 1986
NYPL [JLE 86-4584]

UNITED STATES - FOREIGN RELATIONS - ITALY.
Harper, John Lamberton. America and the reconstruction of Italy, 1945-1948 /. Cambridge [Cambridgeshire] , New York , 1986. x, 213 p. ; ISBN 0-521-32518-8 LC Card 85-30915 DDC 338.91/73/045 19
HC305 .H36 1986 ***NYPL [JLE 86-3600]***

Ortona, Egidio. Anni d'America /. Bologna , c1984- v. ; ISBN 88-15-00531-5 (v. 1) : LC Card 84-240652 DDC 338.91/73/045 19
HC305 .O78 1984 ***NYPL [JLL 86-503]***

UNITED STATES - FOREIGN RELATIONS - POLAND.
Poland's renewal and U. S. options . Washington , 1987. xv, 41 p. : LC Card 87-601374 DDC 337.438073 19
HC340.3 .P646 1987

UNITED STATES - FOREIGN RELATIONS - SOVIET UNION.
Knight, Misha G. How to do business with Russians . New York , 1987. xxiv, 311 p. : ISBN 0-89930-211-4 (lib. bdg. : alk. paper) LC Card 86-30396 DDC 658.8/48/0947 19
HF1558.5.U6 K56 1987

Kolarik, William F. A model for the study of international trade politics . New York , 1987. 613 p. : ISBN 0-8240-8086-6 (alk. paper) : LC Card 87-23788 DDC 382/.0947/0730724 19
HF3105 .K64 1987

Targ, Harry R., 1940- Strategy of an empire in decline . Minneapolis , c1986. 294 p. ; ISBN 0-930656-47-4 : LC Card 86-16338 DDC 909.82 19
D849 .T37 1986 ***NYPL [JFD 87-2032]***

UNITED STATES - FOREIGN RELATIONS - TURKEY.
Rustow, Dankwart A. Turkey, America's forgotten ally /. New York, NY , c1987. xv, 155 p. : ISBN 0-87609-023-4 : LC Card 87-6712 DDC 330.9561/038 19
HC492 .R87 1987

UNITED STATES - FULL EMPLOYMENT POLICIES.
Cook, Robert F., 1943- Public service employment . Kalamazoo, Mich. , 1985. xiii, 131 p. ; ISBN 0-88099-031-7 (pbk.) LC Card 85-22495 DDC 331.13/77/0973 19
HD5713.6.U54 C66 1985
NYPL [JLE 86-3877]

Light, John J. Realistic economics /. Indianapolis, IN (P.O. Box 1606, Indianapolis 46206) , c1984. 111 p. ; ISBN 0-933021-00-3 : LC Card 84-249506 DDC 331.12/0973 19
HD5724 .L4236 1984 ***NYPL [JLE 86-4650]***

UNITED STATES - FULL EMPLOYMENT POLICIES - CONGRESSES.
Technology and employment . Washington, D.C. , 1987. xiii, 225 p. : ISBN 0-309-03744-1 (pbk.) : LC Card 87-42807 DDC 331.12/0973 19
HD6331.2.U5 T43 1987

United States-Fusionsrichtlinien, 1984.
US-Fusionsrichtlinien, 1984 /. Köln , c1985. 83 p. ; ISBN 3-452-20248-8 : LC Card 86-100251
HB41 .F63 Heft 6 KF1477

UNITED STATES - GENEALOGY - HANDBOOKS, MANUALS, ETC.
Burgess, Michael, 1948- The state and province

vital records guide /. San Bernardino, Calif. , 1988. p. cm. ISBN 0-89370-815-1 : LC Card 87-6312 DDC 929/.1/02573 19
HA38 .B87 1988

United States - Government. see **United States - Politics and government.**

United States - Government employees. see **United States - Officials and employees.**

United States. Handicapped, President's Committee on Employment of the. see **United States. President's Committee on Employment of the Handicapped.**

United States. Health Resources Administration. National Center for Health Services Research. see **National Center for Health Services Research.**

United States. Highway Administration. see **United States. Federal Highway Administration.**

United States. Highway Planning, Office of. see **United States. Office of Highway Planning.**

UNITED STATES - HISTORY - CONSTITUTIONAL PERIOD, 1789-1809.
Alexander, Albert. The economic world of 1787 and the Constitution /. New York (150 Nassau St., Rm. 1625, New York 10038) [1987] 18 p. ; LC Card 87-403433 DDC 330.973/0318 19
HC105.6 .A44 1987

UNITED STATES - HISTORY - CIVIL WAR, 1861-1865 - ECONOMIC ASPECTS.
O'Brien, Patrick Karl. The economic effects of the American Civil War /. Atlantic Highlands, NJ , 1988. p. cm. ISBN 0-391-03561-4 : LC Card 87-18631 DDC 330.973/07 19
HC105.6 .O27 1988

UNITED STATES - HISTORY - CIVIL WAR, 1861-1865 - FINANCE.
Schweikart, Larry. Banking in the American South from the age of Jackson to Reconstruction /. Baton Rouge , c1987. xiv, 367 p. : ISBN 0-8071-1403-0 LC Card 87-12784 DDC 332.1/0975 19
HG2604 .S39 1987

United States - History, Economic. see **United States - Economic conditions.**

United States - History, Political. see **United States - Politics and government.**

United States. House of Representatives. see **United States. Congress. House.**

United States. Housing and Development Dept. see **United States. Dept. of Housing and Urban Development.**

United States. Housing and Urban Development, Dept. of. see **United States. Dept. of Housing and Urban Development.**

United States - Immigration. see **United States - Emigration and immigration.**

United States imports of textile and apparel products under the multifiber arrangement, 1981-84. Taylor, John A. (John Alvin), 1930- U. S. imports of textile and apparel products under the multifiber arrangement, 1981-84 /. Washington, D.C. [1985] v, 136 p. ; LC Card 86-601665 DDC 382/.45677/00973021 19
HD9940.U4 T38 1985

United States in foreign opinion. see **United States - Foreign opinion.**

The United States in the world-economy . Agnew, John A. Cambridge , New York , 1987. xvii, 264 p. : ISBN 0-521-30410-5 LC Card 86-32743 DDC 337.73 19
HC103 .A37 1987

United States. Income Maintenance Programs, President's Commission on. see **United States. President's Commission on Income Maintenance Programs.**

United States - Income tax. see **Income tax - United States.**

United States industrial competitiveness. Ghadar, Fariborz. U. S. industrial competitiveness . Lexington, Mass. , c1987. x, 114 p. : ISBN 0-669-15689-2 (alk. paper) LC Card 86-46341 DDC 338.4/7677/00973 19
HD9855 .G47 1987

UNITED STATES - INDUSTRIES - CONGRESSES.
U. S.A.-Japan Conference on Manufacturing Research (1986 : Tokyo, Japan) Manufacturing research perspectives, U. S.A.-Japan . Amsterdam , New York , 1987. viii, 198 p. : ISBN 0-444-42868-2 LC Card 87-19851 DDC 338.4/767 19
HD9725 .U17 1986

UNITED STATES - INDUSTRIES - HANDBOOKS, MANUALS, ETC.
Mattera, Philip. Inside U. S. business . Homewood, Ill. , c1987. xiv, 424 p. ; ISBN 0-87094-950-0 LC Card 87-70392 DDC 338.0973 19
HC106.8 .M337 1987

UNITED STATES - INDUSTRIES - HISTORY.
Blackford, Mansel G., 1944- The rise of modern business in Great Britain, the United States, and Japan /. Chapel Hill , c1988. xi, 176 p. : ISBN 0-8078-1760-0 (alk. paper) LC Card 87-10022 DDC 338.09 19
HC255 .B59 1988

DiBacco, Thomas V. Made in the U. S.A. . New York , c1987. xii, 290 p. ; ISBN 0-06-015624-4 : LC Card 86-45652 DDC 338.0973 19
HC103 .D46 1987 ***NYPL [JLD 87-1292]***

Dobson, John M. A history of American enterprise /. Englewood Cliffs, N.J. , c1988. p. cm. ISBN 0-13-389081-3 LC Card 87-18679 DDC 338.0973 19
HF3021 .D6 1988

Weaver, Paul, 1942 Oct. 18- The suicidal corporation /. New York , c1988. p. cm. ISBN 0-671-52378-3 LC Card 87-23468 DDC 338.7/4/0973 19
HD2785 .W38 1988

Yates, W. Ross (Willard Ross) Joseph Wharton . Bethlehem , London , c1987. 413 p. : ISBN 0-934223-00-9 (alk. paper) LC Card 86-81983 DDC 338.7/6691/0924 B 19
HC102.5.W47 Y38 1987

UNITED STATES - INDUSTRIES - INFORMATION SERVICES - DIRECTORIES.
Who knows about industries and markets /. Washington, D.C. , c1986. 54 p. ; ISBN 0-934940-33-9 (pbk.) LC Card 86-217691 DDC 338/.06/072073 19
HC102.2 .W48 1986

UNITED STATES - INDUSTRIES - LOCATION - DIRECTORIES.
National emerging industries site selection guide /. Minneapolis, MN , c1986. 124 p. ; LC Card 86-231272 DDC 338.6/042/02573 19
HC110.D5 N38 1986

United States - Industries - Statistics. see **United States - Industries.**

UNITED STATES - INSULAR POSSESSIONS - MANAGEMENT.
Integrated renewable resource management for U. S. insular areas. Washington, DC [1987] vi, 443 p. : LC Card 86-600595 DDC 333.7 19
HC154.5 .I58 1987

United States. Interior Dept. see **United States. Dept. of the Interior.**

United States. Internal Revenue Office. see **United States. Internal Revenue Service.**

United States. Internal Revenue Service. (Old Catalog form: United States. Internal Revenue Office)

United States. Internal Revenue Service. Office of Investigations. Multi-agency financial investigative task forces [microform] Washington, D.C. [1983] 1 v. (various pagings) : ***NYPL [*ZT-1708 no.61]***

United States. Internal Revenue Service. Office of the Assistant Commissioner (Planning, Finance, and Research) Conference on Tax Administration Research Strategies (1985 : Washington, D.C.) Conference on Tax Administration Research, January 1985. Washington, D.C. [1985] 2 v. : LC Card 86-601369 DDC 353.0072/4 19
HJ3252 .C66 1985 ***NYPL [JLF 86-1791]***

United States. Internal Revenue Service. Statistics of Income Division. Workshop on Exact Matching Methodologies (May 9-10, 1985 : Arlington, Va.) Record linkage techniques--1985 . [Washington, D.C.] , 1985. vii, 397 p. : ***NYPL [JLF 86-1723]***

United States. International Development Agency. see **United States. Agency for International Development.**

United States. International Trade Administration.
A Basic guide to exporting. Washington, D.C. , 1981. vii, 133 p. : LC Card 82-601093 DDC 658.8/48 19
HF1009.5 .B344 1981 ***NYPL [JLF 87-351]***

A Basic guide to exporting. Washington, D.C. [1986] viii, 148 p. : ***NYPL [*R-Econ. 87-422]***

Green, Ronald D. Brazilian government support for the aerospace industry /. [Washington, D.C.?] [1987] xi, 44 p. ; LC Card 87-601479 DDC 338.4/76291/0981 19
HD9711.B72 G74 1987

The Robotics industry. Washington, D.C. , 1983. 54 p. : ***NYPL [JLF 86-713]***

United States. International Trade Administration. Assistant Secretary for Trade Development. A Competitive assessment of the United States equipment leasing industry. Washington, D.C. [1985] xvi, 116 p. : LC Card 85-601661 DDC 382/.45 19
HD9999.L4363 U63 1985
NYPL [JLF 86-1710]

United States. International Trade Administration. Basic Industries Sector. The Trade deficit in manufactured goods . [Washington] , Washington, D.C. [1986] vi, 79 p. : LC Card 86-601142 DDC 382/.4567/0973 19
HD9725 .T73 1986

United States. International Trade Administration. Capital Goods and International Construction Sector Group.
A Competitive assessment of the U. S. computer-aided design and manufacturing industry /. Washington, D.C. [1987] xi, 58 p. ; LC Card 87-601120 DDC 338.4/7670427 19
HD9696.C63 U514932 1987

A Competitive assessment of the U. S. robotics industry /. Washington, D.C. [1987] xiii, 85 p. ; LC Card 87-601316 DDC 338.4/7629892 19
HD9696.R623 U615 1987

A Competitive assessment of the U. S. transformer industry /. Washington, D.C. [1986] xii, 82 p. : ***NYPL [JSF 86-672]***

United States. International Trade Administration. Market Expansion Division. Foreign regulations affecting U. S. textile/apparel exports. [Washington, D.C.] [1986] 283 p. ; LC Card 86-601588
HF2651.T42 F67 1986

United States. International Trade Administration. Nonferrous Metals Division.
Aluminum mill products . Washington, D.C. [1986] xvi, 111 p. : LC Card 86-602432 DDC 382/.45673722/0973 19
HD9539.A63 U5126 1986

The End-use markets for 13 nonferrous metals /. Washington, D.C. [1986] vii, 52 p. ; LC Card 86-602419 DDC 381/.45673/0973 19
HD9539.A3 U44 1986

United States. International Trade Administration. Office of Chemicals and Allied Products. Shea, Moira M. The United States engineering plastics industry . Washington, D.C. , 1987. 51 p. : LC Card 87-601518 DDC 338.4/76684/0973 19
HD9661.U62 S54 1987

United States. International Trade Administration. Office of Computers and Business Equipment.
A Competitive assessment of the United States microcomputer industry . Washington, D.C. [1986] xiv, 123 p. : ***NYPL [JLF 87-251]***

A Competitive assessment of the United States microcomputer industry . Washington, D.C. [1986] xiv, 123 p. : LC Card 86-602781 DDC 338.4/700416/0973 19
HD9696.C63 U514937 1986

United States. International Trade Administration Office of Service Industries. A Competitive assessment of the United States equipment leasing industry. Washington, D.C. [1985] xvi, 116 p. : LC Card 85-601661 DDC

382/.45 19
HD9999.L4363 U63 1985 *NYPL [JLF 86-1710]*

United States. International Trade Administration. Office of Telecommunications. A Competitive assessment of the U. S. digital central office switch industry /. Washington, D.C. , 1986. xv, 106 p. : LC Card 86-603064 DDC 382/.456321387 19
HD9696.T443 U5225 1986

United States. International Trade Administration. Office of Trade and Investment Analysis.
Davis, Lester A. Contribution of exports to U. S. employment . Washington, D.C. , 1986. 33 p. : LC Card 86-602848 DDC 331.12/0973 19
HD5710.75.U6 D38 1986

Oechsler, Ronald G. Statistical abstract of East-West trade and finance . Washington, D.C. [1986]. vi, 43 p. : LC Card 86-601999 DDC 382/.091713/01717021 19
HF1411 .O3455 1986

United States. International Trade Commission.
Candles from the People's Republic of China : determination of the commission in investigation no. 731-TA-282 (preliminary) under the Tariff Act of 1930, together with the information obtained in the investigation. Washington, DC : U. S. International Trade Commission, [1985] 13, 37 p. ; 28 cm. (USITC publication. 1768) Cover title. "October 1985." LC Card 86-164215 DDC 382/.4574559332/0951 19
1. Tariff on candles - United States. 2. Candle industry - China. I. Title.
HF2651.C254 U55 1985

Certain tobacco : report to the President on investigation no. 22-47 under section 22 of the Agricultural Adjustment Act. Washington, DC : U. S. International Trade Commission, [1985] 1 v. (various pagings) ; 28 cm. (USITC publication. 1644) Cover title. Distributed to depository libraries in microfiche. "February 1985." Includes bibliographical references. Item 980-E (microfiche) LC Card 87-600640 DDC 338.1/7371/0973 19
1. Tobacco industry - Government policy - United States. 2. Tobacco industry. I. Title.
HD9136 .U55 1985

The Effects of semifinished steel imports on the U. S. iron and steel scrap industry . Washington, D.C. [1985] xv, 137 p. : LC Card 86-603428
HD9515 .E33 1985

Emerging textile-exporting countries, 1984 . Washington, D.C. [1985] vii, 520 p. ; LC Card 86-603429 DDC 382/.456770091724 19
HD9868.D44 E54 1985

Ludwick, David E. The competitive position of U. S. and European Community pork and the United States and third-country markets . Washington, DC [1985] xxiii, 341 p. : LC Card 86-601366 DDC 380.1/4566492/0973 19
HD9435.U52 L83 1985

Taylor, John A. (John Alvin), 1930- U. S. imports of textile and apparel products under the multifiber arrangement, 1981-84 /. Washington, D.C. [1985] v, 136 p. ; LC Card 86-601665 DDC 382/.45677/00973021 19
HD9940.U4 T38 1985

The United States-Japan economic problem /. Bergsten, C. Fred, 1941- Washington, D.C. , c1985. x, 164 p. : ISBN 0-262-52108-3 LC Card 85-18106 DDC 382/.0973/052 19
HF3127 .B47 1985 *NYPL [JLE 87-19]*

United States. Joint Economic Committee. see **United States. Congress. Joint Economic Committee.**

United States. Labor, Dept. of. see **United States. Dept. of Labor.**

United States labor policy in postwar Japan. Park, Sung-Jo. U. S. labor policy in postwar Japan /. [Berlin] [c1985] 157 p. : ISBN 3-88548-424-2 LC Card 86-200166 DDC 331.11/0952 19
HD5827.A6 P37 1985

United States. Laws, statutes, etc. (Old Catalog form: United States. Statutes)
FAIR LABOR STANDARDS ACT.
United States. Wage and Hour and Public Contracts Divisions. Laundry and cleaning services. [Washington, 1969] iii, 31, A-ii, A-67p. *NYPL [JLF 86-586]*

United States League of Savings Institutions.
Thomas, O. Tom. Trimming float to build earnings . Chicago, Ill. (111 E. Wacker Dr., Chicago 60601) , c1986. iv, 104 p. : LC Card 86-233102 DDC 332.1/752 19
HG1692 .T46 1986

United States. Library of Congress. Congressional Research Service. Handbook of alternative energy technology development and policy /. [Washington, D.C.] , 1983. xiv, 341 p. : *NYPL [JLF 86-1486]*

United States. Library of Congress. Congressional Research Service. Environment and Natural Resources Policy Division. see **United States. Library of Congress. Environment and Natural Resources Policy Division.**

United States. Library of Congress. Environment and Natural Resources Policy Division.
Pollution taxes, effluent charges, and other alternatives for pollution control : a report / prepared by the Environment and Natural Resources Policy Division of the Congressional Research Service of the Library of Congress for the Committee on Environment and Public Work, U. S. Senate, at the request of Edmund S. Muskie. Washington : U. S. Govt. Print. Off., 1977 iv, 869 p. : ill. ; 23 cm. At head of title: 95th Congress, 1st session. Committe print. "Serial no. 95-5." Includes bibliographical references. LC Card 78-602626
1. Environmental policy - United States - Addresses, essays, lectures. 2. Environmental law - United States - Addresses, essays, lectures. 3. Pollution - Economic aspects - Addresses, essays, lectures. 4. Pollution - Law and legislation - Economic aspects - United States - Addresses, essays, lectures. I. Title.
HC110.E5 U58 1977a *NYPL [JLE 79-2372]*

United States. Manpower Administration. see **United States. Dept. of Labor. Manpower Administration.**

UNITED STATES - MANUFACTURES.
Cohen, Stephen S. Manufacturing matters . New York , c1987. xiv, 297 p. : ISBN 0-465-04384-4 : LC Card 86-47737 DDC 338.4/767/0973 19
HD9725 .C58 1987

Gray, Wayne B. (Wayne Burger), 1955- Productivity versus OSHA and EPA regulations /. Ann Arbor, Mich. , c1986. xii, p. : ISBN 0-8357-1721-6 (alk. paper) LC Card 85-28873 DDC 338/.06/0973 19
HC110.I52 G73 1986 *NYPL [JLE 86-2375]*

Smith, Edward Joseph, 1911- Impact of energy costs on manufacturing employment /. Washington, D.C. [1985] iv, 16 p. : LC Card 86-603150 DDC 331.12/57/0973 19
HD5724 .S614 1985

Vargish, George. What's made in the U. S.A.? /. New Brunswick, U. S.A. , c1988. 160 p. : ISBN 0-88738-187-1 LC Card 87-19164 DDC 382/.3/0973 19
HF1716 .V37 1988

UNITED STATES - MANUFACTURES - CAPITAL INVESTMENTS.
The Trade deficit in manufactured goods . [Washington] , Washington, D.C. [1986] vi, 79 p. : LC Card 86-601142 DDC 382/.4567/0973 19
HD9725 .T73 1986

UNITED STATES - MANUFACTURES - CONGRESSES.
Small Manufacturing and Process Industry Seminar (1985 : Las Vegas, Nev.) Small Manufacturing and Process Industry Seminar proceedings, September 18-20, 1985, Las Vegas, Nevada /. Falls Church, Va. , c1985. iv, 222 p. : ISBN 0-935406-71-9 (pbk.) LC Card 85-72347 DDC 338.6/42/0973 19
HD9725 .S55 1985 *NYPL [JLD 86-2451]*

U. S.A.-Japan Conference on Manufacturing Research (1986 : Tokyo, Japan) Manufacturing research perspectives, U. S.A.-Japan . Amsterdam , New York , 1987. viii, 198 p. : ISBN 0-444-42868-2 LC Card 87-19851 DDC 338.4/767 19
HD9725 .U17 1986

UNITED STATES - MANUFACTURES - MANAGEMENT.
Gunn, Thomas G. Manufacturing for competitive advantage . Cambridge, Mass. , c1987. xvi, 221 p. ; ISBN 0-88730-154-1 LC Card 87-1093 DDC 658 19
HD9725 .G85 1987

Shapiro, H. Jack (Harris Jack) Reviving industry in America . Cambridge, Mass. , c1987. xii, 204 p. : ISBN 0-88730-118-5 LC Card 87-17585 DDC 338.4/767/0973 19
HD9725 .S46 1987

UNITED STATES - MANUFACTURES - MANAGEMENT - DATA PROCESSING.
Manufacturing database management systems /. Boston, MA (89 Broad St., Boston 02110) , c1986. vii, 216 p. : LC Card 86-210661 DDC 381/.4500574/0973 19
HD9696.C63 U5226 1986

UNITED STATES - MANUFACTURES - TECHNOLOGICAL INNOVATIONS - DECISION MAKING - CASE STUDIES.
Dean, James W., 1956- Deciding to innovate . Cambridge, Mass. , c1987. xviii, 165 p. ; ISBN 0-88730-189-4 LC Card 87-17432 DDC 658.5/14 19
HD9725 .D35 1987

United States maritime industries--down for the third time? Hilton, Robert, 1927- U. S. maritime industries--down for the third time? /. Washington, D.C. , c1987. vi, 60 p. : ISBN 0-89206-099-9 (pbk.) LC Card 86-31768 DDC 387.5/0973 19
HE745 .H66 1987

UNITED STATES - MILITARY POLICY.
Assessing the nuclear age . Chicago, Ill. , c1986. xvii, 382 p. ; ISBN 0-941682-07-2 LC Card 85-82511 DDC 355/.0217 19
U264 .A79 1986 *NYPL [JLE 87-11]*

Hough, Richard L. Economic assistance and security . Fort Lesley J. McNair, Washington, D.C. , 1982. xii, 139 p. : LC Card 82-600548 DDC 338.91/73/01724 19
HC60 .H675 1982

Poklad, B. I. (Boris Iosifovich) Real′nosti sovremennogo mira i politika konfrontatsii /. Moskva , 1985. 157 p. ; LC Card 85-170137
JX1974.7 .P585 1985 *NYPL [*QIK 87-1550]*

Shepherd, William G. The ultimate deterrent . New York , 1986. x, 137 p. ; ISBN 0-275-92368-1 (alk. paper) : LC Card 86-20486 DDC 355/.03 19
UA10.5 .S524 1986 *NYPL [JLE 87-884]*

Weida, William J. The political economy of national defense /. Boulder , 1987. xvii, 230 p. ; ISBN 0-8133-0432-6 (alk. paper) : LC Card 86-19015 DDC 355.6/22/0973 19
UA23 .W3694 1987 *NYPL [JLE 87-1043]*

UNITED STATES - MILITARY POLICY - ECONOMIC ASPECTS.
Bryant, Richard W. The Strategic Defense Initiative, business opportunities, and technological potential /. Norwalk, Conn., U. S.A. , c1986. 1 v. (various foliations) : ISBN 0-89336-477-0 (pbk.) LC Card 87-168253 DDC 338.4/762/00973 19
HC110.H53 B79 1986

United States. Minerals Management Service. Pacific OCS Region. Webster, Frank L. Pacific OCS lease sale, October 1, 1964, Oregon and Washington /. [Washington] [1985] iii, 36 p. : LC Card 86-601138 DDC 333.33/9 19
HD243.A18 W43 1985

United States. Mines Bureau. see **United States. Bureau of Mines.**

United States mobile radio communications equipment market. The U. S. mobile radio communications equipment market. New York, N.Y. , c1983. viii, 253 p. : LC Card 87-142226 DDC 384.5/3 19
HD9696.R363 U684 1983

United States. National Archives and Records Service. National Audiovisual Center. see **National Audiovisual Center.**

United States. National Audiovisual Center. see **National Audiovisual Center.**

United States national bank notes and their seals /. Prather, Dewitt G. Charlotte, NC , c1986.

xvi, 200 p., 16 p. of plates : ISBN 0-9616836-0-0 LC Card 86-90441 DDC 769.5/5973 19
HG607 .P73 1986

United States. National Center for Health Sciences Research. see **National Center for Health Services Research.**

United States. National Center for Productivity and Quality of Working Life. see **National Center for Productivity and Quality of Working Life.**

United States. National Commission for Employment Policy. Goldstein, Harold. Training for work in the computer age . Washington, D.C. , 1986. iv, 109 p. ; LC Card 86-601422 DDC 331.25/92 19
HD5715.2 .G63 1986

United States National Commission for Unesco. MAB 7B Directorate. Towle, Edward L. Final report . St. Thomas, U. S.V.I. [1982] 17, 15, 4 leaves : LC Card 86-185489 DDC 333.7/097297/22 19
HC155.Z9 E56 1982

United States. National Commission on Consumer Finance. Consumer credit in the United States; report. [Washington; for sale by the Supt. of Docs., U. S. Govt. Print. Off.] 1972 [i.e. 1973] xxv, 294 p. illus. 27 cm. Includes bibliographical references. LC Card 72-600335 DDC 332.7/43
1. Consumer credit - United States. 2. Consumer protection - United States. I. Title.
HG3755 .U59 1972 ***NYPL [JLF 74-435]***

United States. National Commission on Neighborhoods. People, building neighborhoods : final report to the President and the Congress of the United States / the National Commission on Neighborhoods. [Washington?] : The Commission ; Washington : for sale by the Supt. of Docs., U. S. Govt. Print. Off., [1979] xi, 358 p. : ill. ; 28 cm. Includes bibliographies. LC Card 79-602955 DDC 307.7/6/0973
1. Community development - United States. 2. Neighborhood. I. Title.
HN90.C6 U66 1979 ***NYPL [JLM 81-194]***

United States. National Committee on Vital and Health Statistics.
Statistical aspects of physician payment systems . Hyattsville, Md. [1987] vii, 33 p. : ISBN 0-8406-0357-6 LC Card 86-600375 DDC 362.1/0723 s 362.1/72 19
HA37 .U1693 no. 24 RA408.5

United States. National Committee on Vital and Health Statistics. Subcommittee on Statistical Aspects of Physician Payment Systems. Statistical aspects of physician payment systems . Hyattsville, Md. [1987] vii, 33 p. : ISBN 0-8406-0357-6 LC Card 86-600375 DDC 362.1/0723 s 362.1/72 19
HA37 .U1693 no. 24 RA408.5

United States. National Marine Fisheries Service. Southwest Region.
Miller, Charlotte L. The French market for U. S. seafood products /. Terminal Island, CA , 1986. ii, 63 p. ; LC Card 86-602854 DDC 382/.4566494/0944 19
HD9462.5 .M54 1986

Miller, Charlotte L. The market for seafood in the United Kingdom /. Terminal Island, CA , 1986. ii, 73 p. : LC Card 87-601563 DDC 382.1/4370941 19
HD9461.5 .M55 1986

United States. National Park Service. Denver Service Center. Clemensen, A. Berle. Illinois and Michigan Canal National Heritage Corridor, Illinois . [Denver, Colo.] [1985] ix, 109 p. : LC Card 85-603278 DDC 386/.48/097732 19
HE396.I4 C56 1985

United States. National Park Service. North Atlantic Regional Office. Division of Cultural Resources.
Rubertone, Patricia E. Background study of Maine coastal life . [Providence, R.I.?] , 1983. iii, 99 leaves : LC Card 86-601627 DDC 304.6/09741/45 19
HB3525.M2 R82 1983

Weinbaum, Paul O. Hoosac docks . Boston, Mass. , 1985. vi, 95 p. : LC Card 85-603289 DDC 387.1/64/0974461 19
HE554.B6 W45 1985

UNITED STATES - NATIONAL SECURITY.
Bull-Berg, Hans Jacob. American international oil policy . New York , 1987. xvi, 209 p. : ISBN 0-312-00465-6 : LC Card 86-31583 DDC 333.8/232/0973 19
HD9566 .B87 1987

Committee on Science, Engineering, and Public Policy (U. S.). Panel on the Impact of National Security Controls on International Technology Transfer. Balancing the national interest . Washington, D.C. , 1987. xiii, 321 p. : ISBN 0-309-03738-7 LC Card 87-60020 DDC 337.73 19
HF1456 .C65 1987

Hough, Richard L. Economic assistance and security . Fort Lesley J. McNair, Washington, D.C. , 1982. xii, 139 p. : LC Card 82-600548 DDC 338.91/73/01724 19
HC60 .H675 1982

Losoncz, Miklós. Erők és érdekek . Budapest , 1986. 191 p. : ISBN 963-326-966-0 : LC Card 87-148142
HF1414.5 .L67 1986

Shepherd, William G. The ultimate deterrent . New York , 1986. x, 137 p. ; ISBN 0-275-92368-1 (alk. paper) : LC Card 86-20486 DDC 355/.03 19
UA10.5 .S524 1986 ***NYPL [JLE 87-884]***

Wiarda, Howard J., 1939- Population, internal unrest, and U. S. security in Latin America /. [Amherst] , 1986. 50 p. ; LC Card 87-621399 DDC 304.6/098 19
HB3530.5.A3 W5 1986

United States. Navy Center for Applied Research in Artificial Intelligence. Proceedings of an international conference on genetic algorithms and their applications . [S.l. , 1985] 225 p. : ***NYPL [JSF 87-413]***

UNITED STATES. NAVY - HISTORY.
Bauer, K. Jack (Karl Jack), 1926- A maritime history of the United States . Columbia, S.C. , c1988. p. cm. ISBN 0-87249-519-1 LC Card 87-19190 DDC 387.5/0973 19
HE745 .B38 1988

UNITED STATES. NAVY - RESERVE FLEETS.
Ullman, Harlan. Forecasts for U. S. maritime industries in 1989 . Washington, D.C. , c1984. ix, 42 p. : ISBN 0-89206-069-7 (pbk.) LC Card 84-27501 DDC 338.4/76238/0973 19
VM299.6 .U45 1984 ***NYPL [JLD 87-155]***

United States. Neighborhoods, National Commissioon on. see **United States. National Commission on Neighborhoods.**

United States News & World Report, inc. U. S. News investment guide /. Washington, D.C. (2400 N. St., N.W., Washington 20037-1196) , c1987. iv, 60 p. : LC Card 87-143438 DDC 332.6/78 19
HG4910 .U25 1987

United States News investment guide. U. S. News investment guide /. Washington, D.C. (2400 N. St., N.W., Washington 20037-1196) , c1987. iv, 60 p. : LC Card 87-143438 DDC 332.6/78 19
HG4910 .U25 1987

United States - Noncontiguous possessions. see **United States - Insular possessions.**

UNITED STATES - OCCUPATIONS.
Chronicle occupational briefs and occupational reprints. Moravia, NY [1986- 4 v. (loose-leaf) : LC Card 86-231523 DDC 331.7/02/0973 19
HF5382.5.U5 C49 1986

Chronicle occupational briefs and occupational reprints. Moravia, NY [1987]- 4 v. (loose-leaf) : LC Card 87-403954 DDC 331.7/02/0973 19
HF5382.5.U5 C49 1987

Dictionary of occupational titles /. [Washington] , 1977. xli, 1371 p. ; LC Card 78-601723 DDC 331.7/003
HB2595 .U543 1977
NYPL [*R-TMH 78-1740]

Guide for occupational exploration /. [Washington, D.C.] , Circle Pines, Minn. , c1984. vii, 984 p. : LC Card 87-402857 DDC 331.7/02/0973 19
HF5382.5.U5 G83 1984

Kerns, Allen F. Dictionary of worker traits /. Philadelphia, PA , 1987- p. cm. ISBN 0-9618599-9-7 LC Card 87-12478 DDC 331.7/02/0973 19
HB2595 .K43 1987

Paradis, Adrian A. Opportunities in vocational & technical careers /. Lincolnwood, Ill., U. S.A. , c1987. xi, 147 p. : ISBN 0-8442-6018-5 LC Card 87-60104 DDC 371.4/25/02373 19
HF5382.5.U5 P28 1987

Ritzer, George. Working, conflict and change /. Englewood Cliffs, N.J. , c1986. xii, 451 p. ; ISBN 0-13-967589-2 : LC Card 85-28135 DDC 306/.36/0973 19
HD6957.U6 R5 1986 ***NYPL [JLE 86-3160]***

VGM's careers encyclopedia /. Lincolnwood, Ill., U. S.A. , c1988. xi, 484 p. ; ISBN 0-8442-6132-7 LC Card 87-62404 DDC 331.7/02/0973 19
HF5382.5.U5 C337 1988

UNITED STATES - OCCUPATIONS - LICENSES.
Young, S. David, 1955- The rule of experts . Washington, D.C. , c1987. x, 99 p. ; ISBN 0-932790-62-3 (pbk.) LC Card 87-736 DDC 351.82/43046 19
HD3630.U7 Y68 1987

United States of America, tin in tinplate. London : International Tin Council, [1983] 89 p. : ill. ; 30 cm. (Study on consumption) LC Card 84-216067 DDC 338.4/76736/0973 19
1. Tinplate industry - United States. 2. Market surveys - United States. I. International Tin Council. II. Series.
HD9529.T63 U67 1983

United States of Colombia. see **Colombia.**

UNITED STATES OF EUROPE (PROPOSED) see **EUROPEAN FEDERATION.**

United States. Office of Economic Opportunity. (Old Catalog form: United States. Economic Opportunity, Office of)
Cooperative League of the U. S. A. How to organize a co-op . Washington , 1969. 53 p. : ***NYPL [JLF 86-590]***

United States. Office of Highway Planning. Highway finance . [Washington] [1983] iii, 96 p. ; ***NYPL [JLF 87-431]***

United States. Office of Highway Planning. Urban Planning and Transportation Management Division. Review of Federal-Aid Urban System program. [Washington, D.C.?] : Federal Highway Administration, Office of Highway Planning, Urban Planning and Transportation Management Division, [1985] 55 p. : ill. ; 28 cm. "January 1985."
1. Urban transportation - United States. 2. Local transit - United States - Finance. I. Title.
NYPL [JLF 86-340]

United States. Office of Human Development. Rehabilitation Services Administration. see **United States. Rehabilitation Services Administration.**

United States. Office of Management and Budget. Statistical Policy Office. Federal longitudinal surveys /. [Washington, D.C.?] [Springfield, VA] 1986. v, 159 p. : LC Card 86-603413 DDC 001.4/33 19
HA31.2 .F43 1986

United States. Office of Military Government for Germany. see **Germany (Territory under Allied Occupation, 1945-1955. U. S. Zone). Office of Military Government.**

United States. Office of National Parks, Buildings and Reservations. see **United States. National Park Service.**

United States. Office of Revenue Sharing. An Alphabetical guide to Office of Revenue Sharing account numbers /. Washington, D.C. , 1981. iii, 187 p. ; ***NYPL [JLF 87-470]***

United States. Office of Tax Analysis. Report to Congress on the capital gains tax reductions of 1978. [Washington, D.C.] : Office of the Secretary of the Treasury, Office of Tax Analysis : For sale by Supt. of Doc., U. S. G.P.O., [1985] xix, 199 p. ; 28 cm. "September, 1985." Includes bibliographies. LC Card 85-602710 DDC 336.24/3 19

1. Capital gains tax - United States. I. Title. II. Title: Capital gains tax reductions of 1978.
HJ4653.C3 U55 1985

United States. Office of the Assistant Secretary of Defense (Program Analysis and Evaluation) Quirk, James P. The choice of discount rate applicable to government resource use . Santa Monica, CA [1987] xviii, 52 p. : ISBN 0-8330-0849-8 (pbk.) LC Card 87-9867 DDC 336.3/9 19
HJ7451 .Q57 1987

United States. Office of the Under Secretary of Defense for Policy.
Henry, Donald Putnam, 1957- The financial cost of export credit guarantee programs /. Santa Monica, CA , 1987. ix, 37 p. ; ISBN 0-8330-0794-7 (pbk.) LC Card 87-4630 DDC 382/.63 19
HG3754.5.U6 H46 1987

Neu, C. R. (Carl Richard), 1949- Toward a profile of Soviet behavior in international financial markets /. Santa Monica, CA [1987] xv, 58 p. : ISBN 0-8330-0865-X (pbk.) LC Card 87-13084 DDC 332/.042/0947 19
HG3955 .N48 1987

United States. Office of Vocational and Adult Education. Education and training for older persons . [Washington, D.C.?] , 1981. iii, 64 p. :
NYPL [JLF 86-1274]

UNITED STATES - OFFICIALS AND EMPLOYEES - RATING OF.
Morrisey, George L. Performance appraisals in the public sector . Reading, Mass. , 1983. xiii, 172 p. ; ISBN 0-201-04847-7 (pbk.) : LC Card 83-6049 DDC 353.001/42 19
JK766.6 .M67 1983 ***NYPL [JLE 83-3164]***

United States - Outlying possessions. see **United States - Insular possessions.**

UNITED STATES - POLITICS AND GOVERNMENT - 1789-1815.
Nelson, John R., 1952- Liberty and property . Baltimore , c1987. xv, 221 p. : ISBN 0-8018-3440-6 (alk. paper) LC Card 86-21373 DDC 338.973 19
HC105 .N45 1987

UNITED STATES - POLITICS AND GOVERNMENT - 1817-1825.
Taylor, John, 1753-1824. Tyranny unmasked /. Cumberland, Va. , 1988. p. cm. ISBN 0-940973-05-7 (alk. paper) : LC Card 87-2957 DDC 382.7/3/0973 19
HF1754 .T4 1988

UNITED STATES - POLITICS AND GOVERNMENT - 1857-1861.
Huston, James L., 1947- The panic of 1857 and the coming of the Civil War /. Baton Rouge , c1987. xviii, 315 p. ; ISBN 0-8071-1368-9 LC Card 87-2705 DDC 338.5/42 19
HB3717 1857 .H87 1987

UNITED STATES - POLITICS AND GOVERNMENT - 1933-1945.
Vittoz, Stanley. New Deal labor policy and the American industrial economy /. Chapel Hill , c1987. 241 p. ; ISBN 0-8078-1729-5 LC Card 86-24911 DDC 331/.0973 19
HD8072 .V715 1987

UNITED STATES - POLITICS AND GOVERNMENT - 1945-
Delli Carpini, Michael X., 1953- Stability and change in American politics . New York , 1986. xxv, 374 p. ; ISBN 0-8147-1780-2 (alk. paper) : LC Card 85-15348 DDC 323/.042/0973 19
JK1764 .D45 1986 ***NYPL [JLE 86-2183]***

LeMay, Michael C., 1941- The struggle for influence . Lanham , c1985. xv, 452 p. : ISBN 0-8191-4653-6 (alk. paper) : LC Card 85-6105 DDC 323.1/73 19
E184.A1 L44 1985 ***NYPL [IE 85-3562]***

Malone, Margaret Sahlin, 1933- Work and welfare /. Washington , 1986. ix, 162 p. ; LC Card 86-603383 DDC 362.5/84/0973 19
HD5715.2 .M34 1986

Neuman, W. Russell. The paradox of mass politics . Cambridge, Mass. , 1986. 241 p. : ISBN 0-674-65455-2 (alk. paper) LC Card 86-288 DDC 324.973 19
JK1967 .N48 1986 ***NYPL [JLE 86-4140]***

Wilensky, Harold L. Democratic corporatism and policy linkages . Berkeley , c1987. ix, 97 p. ; ISBN 0-87725-169-X (pbk.) : LC Card 87-3525 DDC 338.9 19
HD3616.E8 W54 1987

UNITED STATES - POLITICS AND GOVERNMENT - 1945- - ECONOMETRIC MODELS.
Berry, William Dale. Understanding United States government growth . New York , 1987. xiv, 212 p. : ISBN 0-275-92509-9 (alk. paper) : LC Card 87-11818 DDC 336.73 19
HJ257.2 .B47 1987

UNITED STATES - POLITICS AND GOVERNMENT - 1945-1953.
Rogulev, ĪU. N. (ĪUriĭ Nikolaevich) Krakh rabocheĭ politiki administratsii Trumėna . Moskva , 1981. 135 p. ; LC Card 82-155486
HD8072.5 .R64 1981

UNITED STATES - POLITICS AND GOVERNMENT - 1977-
Rabochee dvizhenie v razvitykh kapitalisticheskikh stranakh . Moskva , 1987. 268 p. ; LC Card 87-164460
HD8378 .R29 1987

UNITED STATES - POLITICS AND GOVERNMENT - 1981-
Bagby, Wesley Marvin, 1922- Introduction to social science /. Chicago , c1987. xv, 427 p. : ISBN 0-8304-1146-1 LC Card 86-23487 DDC 306/.0973 19
HC106.8 .B34 1987

Cannon, William B., 1920- New class politics . Washington, D.C. , c1986. 137 p. ; ISBN 0-89758-042-7 (pbk.) : LC Card 86-27511 DDC 336.73 19
HJ2051 .C35 1986

Goodman, Marshall R. Managing regulatory reform . New York , 1987. xvi, 236 p. : ISBN 0-275-92472-5 (alk. paper) : LC Card 87-2436 DDC 338.973 19
HD3616.U47 G67 1987

Johansson, Mats, 1951- Frihetens idéer . [Stockholm] , c1986. 224 p. : ISBN 91-7566-106-3 LC Card 86-226727
HC106.8 .J64 1986

The State of the states . Lexington, KY , c1986. 56 p. ; ISBN 0-87292-064-X (pbk.) LC Card 87-162324 DDC 330.973/0927 19
HC106.8 .S735 1986

Stockman, David Alan, 1946- The triumph of politics . New York , c1986. 422 p. : ISBN 0-06-015560-4 : LC Card 85-45541 DDC 338.973 19
HC106.8 .S75 1986 ***NYPL [JLE 86-2647]***

Stockman, David Alan, 1946- The triumph of politics . Boston, Mass. , 1987, c1986. xxxiii, 654 p. (large print) ; ISBN 0-8161-4231-9 (lg. print) : LC Card 86-22950 DDC 338.973 19
HC106.8 .S75 1986b

Weida, William J. The political economy of national defense /. Boulder , 1987. xvii, 230 p. ; ISBN 0-8133-0432-6 (alk. paper) : LC Card 86-19015 DDC 355.6/22/0973 19
UA23 .W3694 1987 ***NYPL [JLE 87-1043]***

West, Darrell M., 1954- Congress and economic policymaking /. Pittsburgh, Pa. , c1987. xiv, 203 p. ; ISBN 0-8229-5396-X (pbk.) LC Card 87-40160 DDC 338.973 19
HC106.8 .W45 1987

UNITED STATES - POLITICS AND GOVERNMENT - 1981- - ADDRESSES, ESSAYS, LECTURES.
State politics and the new federalism . White Plains, N.Y. , c1986. xv, 544 p. : ISBN 0-582-28474-0 (pbk.) LC Card 85-15956 DDC 321.02/0973 19
JK325 .S77 1986 ***NYPL [JLD 86-2766]***

UNITED STATES - POLITICS AND GOVERNMENT - 1981- - PUBLIC OPINION.
Poole, Keith T. Women, public opinion, and politics . New York , c1985. xii, 196 p. : ISBN 0-582-28274-8 LC Card 84-7155 DDC 305.4/0973 19
HQ1410 .P66 1985 ***NYPL [JLE 85-1580]***

UNITED STATES - POPULATION.
Easterlin, Richard A., 1926- Birth and fortune . Chicago , 1987. xii, 228 p. : ISBN 0-226-18032-8 (pbk.) : LC Card 86-30724 DDC 304.6/0973 19
HB3505 .E247 1987

Nam, Charles B. Think about our population . New York City, NY , 1988. viii, 117 p. : ISBN 0-8027-6753-2 LC Card 87-21601 DDC 304.6/0973 19
HB3505 .N29 1988

Pol, Louis G. Business demography . New York , c1987. p. cm. ISBN 0-89930-218-1 (lib. bdg. : alk. paper) LC Card 87-2494 DDC 304.6 19
HB849.41 .P63 1987

Promoting high-technology industry . Boulder , 1987. 283 p. ; ISBN 0-8133-7427-8 (pbk. : alk. paper) LC Card 87-61327 DDC 338.4/762/000973 19
HC110.H53 P76 1987

UNITED STATES - POPULATION - CONGRESSES.
Population change, natural resources, and regionalism /. Milford, Pa. , c1986. viii, 104 p. : ISBN 0-938549-00-6 (pbk.) LC Card 86-25682 DDC 304.6/0973 19
HB3505 .P62 1986

Research Conference on Trends Impacting Tax Administration (1985 : Washington, D.C.) Research Conference on Trends Impacting Tax Administration, November 20-22, 1985. Washington, D.C. (1111 Constitution Ave., N.W., Washington 20224) [1985] 2 v. ; 28 cm. LC Card 87-601252 DDC 350.72/4/00973 19
HJ3252 .R357 1985

UNITED STATES - POPULATION DENSITY - CONGRESSES.
Population change, natural resources, and regionalism /. Milford, Pa. , c1986. viii, 104 p. : ISBN 0-938549-00-6 (pbk.) LC Card 86-25682 DDC 304.6/0973 19
HB3505 .P62 1986

UNITED STATES - POPULATION - HISTORY - 19TH CENTURY.
Schapiro, Morton Owen. Filling up America . Greenwich, Conn. , c1986. xiii, 149 p. : ISBN 0-89232-675-1 : LC Card 86-2771 DDC 304.6/0973 19
HB3505 .S33 1986 ***NYPL [JLE 86-3386]***

UNITED STATES - POPULATION POLICY - CONGRESSES.
Population change, natural resources, and regionalism /. Milford, Pa. , c1986. viii, 104 p. : ISBN 0-938549-00-6 (pbk.) LC Card 86-25682 DDC 304.6/0973 19
HB3505 .P62 1986

UNITED STATES - POPULATION, RURAL - HISTORY - 19TH CENTURY.
Schapiro, Morton Owen. Filling up America . Greenwich, Conn. , c1986. xiii, 149 p. : ISBN 0-89232-675-1 : LC Card 86-2771 DDC 304.6/0973 19
HB3505 .S33 1986 ***NYPL [JLE 86-3386]***

United States - Presidents. see **Presidents - United States.**

United States. President's Commission on Income Maintenance Programs. Poverty amid plenty, the American paradox; report. [Washington; For sale by the Supt. of Docs., U. S. Govt. Print. Off.] 1969. ix, 155 p. illus. 25 cm. Commonly known as the Heineman report. Includes bibliographical references. LC Card 71-605334 DDC 362.5/0973
1. Income - United States. 2. Poor - United States. I. Title. II. Title: Heineman report on income maintenance.
HC110.P63 A59 ***NYPL [JLF 86-478]***

United States. President's Commission on Organized Crime.
America's habit : drug abuse, drug trafficking, and organized crime : report to the President and the Attorney General / President's Commission on Organized Crime. Washington, D.C. : The Commission : For sale by the Supt. of Docs., U. S. G.P.O., 1986. 486, [312] p. ; 23 cm. "March 1986"--Cover. Includes bibliographical references.
1. Narcotics, Control of - United States. 2. Narcotic laws - United States. 3. Drug abuse - United States. 4. Organized crime - United States. I. Title. II. Title: Drug abuse, drug trafficking, and organized crime.
NYPL [JLE 86-3348]

The edge : organized crime, business, and labor unions. Appendix : [report to the President and the Attorney General] / President's Commission on Organized Crime. Washington,

D.C. : The Commission : For sale by the Supt. of Docs., U. S. G.P.O., 1985. 356 p. ; 23 cm. "October 1985"--Cover. Includes bibliographical references.
1. Organized crime - United States. 2. Trade-unions - United States - Officials and employees - Corrupt practices. 3. Racketeering - United States. I. Title. II. Title: Organized crime, business, and labor unions.
NYPL [JLE 87-41]

The edge : organized crime, business and labor unions : report to the President and the Attorney General / President's Commission on Organized Crime. Washington, D.C. : The Commission : For sale by the Supt. of Docs., U. S. G.P.O., 1986. xxii, 393 p. ; 23 cm. "March 1986"--Cover. Includes bibliographical references.
1. Organized crime - United States. 2. Trade-unions - United States - Officials and employees - Corrupt practices. 3. Racketeering - United States. I. Title. II. Title: Organized crime, business and labor unions.
NYPL [JLE 86-2671]

Organized crime : federal law enforcement perspective : record of hearing I, November 29, 1983, Washington, D.C. / President's Commission on Organized Crime. Washington, D.C. : The Commission : For sale by the Supt. of Docs, U. S. G.P.O., 1983. vi, 159 p. : ill., ports. ; 23 cm. Spine title: Record of hearing I, federal perspective. "November 1983."--Cover.
1. Organized crime - United States. 2. Law enforcement - United States. I. Title. II. Title: Record of hearing I, federal perspective.
NYPL [JLE 86-1587]

Organized crime and money laundering : record of hearing II, March 14, 1984, New York, New York / President's Commission on Organized Crime. Washington, D.C. : The Commission : For sale by the Supt. of Docs., U. S. G.P.O., [1985]. vi, 189 p. : ill. ; 23 cm. Spine title: Record of hearing II, money laundering. "March 1984."
1. Organized crime - United States. 2. Banks and banking - United States. 3. Money - United States - Criminal provisions. I. Title. II. Title: Record of hearing II, money laundering. ***NYPL [JLE 86-1282]***

United States. President's Committee on Employment of the Handicapped. Joint Seminar on Designing Jobs for Handicapped Workers (1985 : Chicago, Ill.) Designing jobs for handicapped workers . Hot Springs, Ark. (P.O. Box 1358, Hot Spring 71902) [1986] 66 p. : LC Card 86-622317 DDC 658.3/045 19
HD7256.U5 J65 1985

United States professional/executive workstations market. The U. S. professional/executive workstations market. New York, N.Y. , c1983. vi, 284 p. : LC Card 87-142071 DDC 381/.4500416/0973 19
HD9801.U542 U18 1983

UNITED STATES - PUBLIC LANDS.
Kloepfer, Deanne. The Watt record . Washington, D.C. [1983] ii, 66, 9, 3 p. : LC Card 86-232533 DDC 333.1/0973 19
HD183.L3 K58 1983

UNITED STATES - PUBLIC WORKS - ACCOUNTING.
Van Daniker, Relmond P., 1942- Infrastructure assets . Stamford, Conn. (High Ridge Park, P.O. Box 3821, Stamford 06905-0821) , c1986. xii, 155 p. ; LC Card 86-90661 DDC 657/.835 19
HJ9816 .V35 1986

UNITED STATES - PUBLIC WORKS - FINANCE.
Hackett, Judith C. Managing rural infrastructure . Lexington, Ky. , c1986. iii, 36 p. : ISBN 0-87292-070-4 (pbk.) : LC Card 87-404481 DDC 363/.0973 19
HD3888 .H27 1986

Petersen, John E. Innovative capital financing /. Chicago, IL (1313 E. 60th St., Chicago 60637) , 1985. ii, 38 p. : LC Card 86-175368 DDC 336.73 19
HG4936 .P424 1985

UNITED STATES - RACE RELATIONS - HISTORY.
Andolsen, Barbara Hilkert. "Daughters of Jefferson, daughters of bootblacks" . Macon, GA , c1986. xiv, 130 p. ; ISBN 0-86554-204-X : LC Card 86-816 DDC 305.4/2/0973 19
HQ1426 .A6827 1986 ***NYPL [JLE 86-3359]***

Denby, Charles. Indignant heart . Montréal , 1979. 295 p. : ISBN 0-919618-93-6 LC Card 87-672793
HD8039.A82 U633x 1979

United States. Rehabilitation Services Administration. The Role of the sheltered workshops in the rehabilitation of the severely handicapped. New York , 1976. xxiv, 467 p. ;
NYPL [JLF 86-1287]

UNITED STATES - RELATIONS (GENERAL) WITH FOREIGN COUNTRIES.
United States. Congress. House. Committee on Foreign Affairs. Subcommittee on International Organizations and Movements. Modern communications and foreign policy. Washington, 1967. vii, 13R, iv, 216 p. LC Card 67-61749
E744 .U45 1967 ***NYPL [JLE 73-233]***

UNITED STATES - RELATIONS - ISRAEL.
Hunter, Jane, 1943- Undercutting sanctions . Washington, DC (918 16th St. NW, Suite 501, Washington 20006) , c1987. iv, 71 p. ; LC Card 87-403525 DDC 337.68 19
HF1613.4 .H86 1987

UNITED STATES - RELATIONS - LATIN AMERICA - ADDRESSES, ESSAYS, LECTURES.
Petras, James F., 1937- Latin America . Totowa, N.J. , 1986. xi, 187 p. ; ISBN 0-8476-7505-X : LC Card 86-1885 DDC 337.8 19
HC125 .P4643 1986 ***NYPL [JLE 86-4366]***

UNITED STATES - RELATIONS - MIDDLE EAST.
Laufer, Leopold Yehuda. U. S. aid to the West Bank and Gaza . [Jerusalem] [1985] 54 p. ; LC Card 87-400340 DDC 338.91/73/056951 19
HC415.25.Z7 W4735 1985

UNITED STATES - RELATIONS - SOUTH AFRICA.
Seidman, Ann Willcox, 1926- The roots of crisis in southern Africa /. Trenton, N.J. [1985] xvii, 209 p. : ISBN 0-86543-026-8 (pbk.) : LC Card 85-72995 DDC 968.06/3 19
E183.8.S6 S45 1985 ***NYPL [Sc E 86-368]***

UNITED STATES - RELATIONS - SOVIET UNION.
Hammer, Armand, 1897- Hammer /. New York , c1987. 544 p., [32] p. of plates : ISBN 0-399-13275-9 LC Card 86-30289 DDC 338.092/4 B 19
HC102.5.H35 A3 1987

United States - Revenue. see **Tariff - United States; Taxation - United States.**

United States. Revenue Sharing, Office of. see **United States. Office of Revenue Sharing.**

United States. Rivers and Harbors, Board of Engineers for. see **United States. Board of Engineers for Rivers and Harbors.**

UNITED STATES - RURAL CONDITIONS.
Atack, Jeremy. To their own soil . Ames , 1987. xi, 322 p. : ISBN 0-8138-0086-2 LC Card 86-21349 DDC 338.1/0974 19
HD1773.A4 A86 1987

Is there a moral obligation to save the family farm? /. Ames , 1987. xxvii, 427 p. : ISBN 0-8138-1000-0 (pbk.) LC Card 87-13399 DDC 338.1/0973 19
HD1476.U5 I8 1987

Local infrastructure investment in rural America /. Boulder , 1988. xxi, 291 p. ; ISBN 0-8133-7460-X (soft : alk. paper) LC Card 87-21606 DDC 332.6/7252 19
HC110.P83 L63 1988

Waterfield, Larry W. Conflict and crisis in rural America /. New York , 1986. iv, 235 p. : ISBN 0-03-006074-5 (alk. paper) : LC Card 85-19366 DDC 333.76/0973 19
HD256 .W35 1986 ***NYPL [JLE 86-2792]***

UNITED STATES - RURAL CONDITIONS - ADDRESSES, ESSAYS, LECTURES.
Rural public administration . Westport, Conn. , 1986. ix, 208 p. ; ISBN 0-313-25246-7 (lib. bdg. : alk. paper) LC Card 85-27253 DDC 352/.00722/0973 19
JS425 .R87 1986 ***NYPL [JLE 86-4005]***

UNITED STATES - RURAL CONDITIONS - CONGRESSES.
National Conference on Rural Development, Des Moines, 1973. Proceedings. Washington, 1974. iii, 108 p. LC Card 74-600918 DDC 309.2/63/0973
HN65 .N35 1973 ***NYPL [JLE 81-564 no.2]***

United States. Rural Electrification Administration.
A Brief history of the rural electric and telephone programs. [Washington, D.C.] [1986] 61 p. : LC Card 86-602412 DDC 353.0087/22 19
HD9688.U52 B75 1986

UNITED STATES. RURAL ELECTRIFICATION ADMINISTRATION - HISTORY.
A Brief history of the rural electric and telephone programs. [Washington, D.C.] [1986] 61 p. : LC Card 86-602412 DDC 353.0087/22 19
HD9688.U52 B75 1986

United States. Science Policy Researc Division. Alternative Energy Technology Group. Handbook of alternative energy technology development and policy /. [Washington, D.C.] , 1983. xiv, 341 p. : ***NYPL [JLF 86-1486]***

United States. Secretary of Labor's Task Force on Economic Adjustment and Worker Dislocation. Economic adjustment and worker dislocation in a competitive society : report of the Secretary of Labor's Task Force on Economic Adjustment and worker Dislocation. Washington, D.C. : The Task Force, [1986] 189 p. in various pagings : ill. ; 28 cm. "Malcolm R. Lovell, Jr., Task Force chairman"--P. [1] Shipping list no.: 87-108-P. "December 1986." Bibliography: p. [183]-[184] Item 754 LC Card 87-601034 DDC 331.13/7973 19
1. United States - Economic policy - 1981-. 2. Unemployed - Services for - United States. 3. Plant shutdowns - United States. 4. Layoffs. 5. Plant shutdowns. 6. Unemployed. I. Lovell, Malcolm Read, 1921-. II. Title.
HC106.8 .U545 1986

United States. Secretary of Transportation. see **United States. Dept. of Transportation.**

United States. Securities and Exchange Commission. Directorate of Economic and Policy Analysis. The financing and regulatory capital needs of the securities industry /. [Washington, D.C.] [1985?] xiv, 69, [49] p ;
NYPL [JLF 86-863]

United States. Senate. Committee on Agriculture and Forestry. National Agricultural Outlook Conference (U. S.) (1976 : Washington, D.C.) 1977 U. S. agricultural outlook . Washington , 1976. vi, 445 p. : LC Card 86-602345
HD1765 .N37 1976

The United States Senate's tax reform proposal : the impact on New York State. [Albany, N.Y.?] : New York State Dept. of Taxation and Finance, New York State Division of the Budget, [1986] 18, 6, 2 leaves ; 18 cm. Cover title. "June, 1986." LC Card 87-620727 DDC 336.2/009747 19
1. Taxation - New York (State). 2. Income tax - New York (State). 3. Taxation - United States. 4. Income tax - United States. 5. Intergovernmental tax relations - New York (State). I. New York (State). Dept. of Taxation and Finance. II. New York (State). Division of the Budget.
HJ2424 .U55 1986

United States - Shipping. see **Shipping - United States.**

United States. Small Business Administration.
National Survey of entreprenuerial [sic] education /. [Washington, D.C.?] . v. : LC Card 86-603453 DDC 658/.022/071173 19
HF1131 .N325 1986

A Tribute to small business . [Washington, D.C.] , San Francisco , c1987. 72 p. : LC Card 87-403591 DDC 338.6/42 19
HD2346.U5 T75 1987

United States. Small Business Administration. Office of Business Development.
Schaefer, Robert A. Starting and managing a small service business /. Washington, D.C. , 1986. v, 57 p. ; LC Card 86-603435 DDC 658/.022 19
HD9981.5 .S32 1986

Waymon, Lynne. Starting and managing a business from your home /. Washington, D.C. , 1986. vi, 48 p. ; LC Card 86-602842 DDC 658/.041 19
HD62.5 .W395 1986

United States. Small Business Administration. Office of Economic Research / Advocacy.
Oster, Sharon. The strategic use of regulatory investment by industry sub-groups [microform] . New Haven, Ct. , 1980. 39 p. ;
*NYPL [*XME-11,347]*

United States. Small Business Administration. Office of Procurement and Technical Assistance. Report to the Administrator on the analysis of the management and administration of the Procurement and Technical Assistance programs / [compiled and edited by Bill Warner, Hattie L. Dorman]. [Washington, D.C.] : U. S. Small Business Administration, 1984. 1 v. (various pagings) : ill. ; 28 cm. Title from cover. Spine title: SBA report to the Administrator. "March 5, 1984-May 18, 1984." Includes bibliographies.
1. United States. Small Business Administration. Office of Procurement and Technical Assistance. 2. Small business - United States. 3. Minority business enterprises - United States. I. Warner, Bill. II. Dorman, Hattie L. III. Title. IV. Title: SBA report to the administrator. *NYPL [JLF 86-1066]*

UNITED STATES. SMALL BUSINESS ADMINISTRATION. OFFICE OF PROCUREMENT AND TECHNICAL ASSISTANCE.
United States. Small Business Administration. Office of Procurement and Technical Assistance. Report to the Administrator on the analysis of the management and administration of the Procurement and Technical Assistance programs /. [Washington, D.C.] , 1984. 1 v. (various pagings) : *NYPL [JLF 86-1066]*

United States. Social and Rehabilitation Service. Rehabilitation Services Administration. see **United States. Rehabilitation Services Administration.**

United States - Social conditions. Here are entered works on the Social history or conditions of the United States. Works on the discipline of sociology in the United States are entered under Sociology - United States.

UNITED STATES - SOCIAL CONDITIONS - 1865-1918.
Winters, Donald E. The soul of the wobblies . Westport, Conn. , 1985. 159 p. ; ISBN 0-313-24472-3 (lib. bdg.) LC Card 84-27973 DDC 331.88/6 19
HD8055.I5 W56 1985 *NYPL [JLD 87-775]*

UNITED STATES - SOCIAL CONDITIONS - 1933-1945.
Hodges, James A., 1932- New deal labor policy and the southern cotton textile industry, 1933-1941 /. Knoxville , c1986. xii, 252 p. : ISBN 0-87049-496-1 (alk. paper) : LC Card 85-20368 DDC 338.4/767721/0975 19
HD8039.T42 U652 1986
NYPL [JLE 86-3477]

UNITED STATES - SOCIAL CONDITIONS - 1945-
Easterlin, Richard A., 1926- Birth and fortune . Chicago , 1987. xii, 228 p. : ISBN 0-226-18032-8 (pbk.) : LC Card 86-30724 DDC 304.6/0973 19
HB3505 .E247 1987

UNITED STATES - SOCIAL CONDITIONS - 1960-
Bowman, Thomas F. Finding your best place to live in America /. New York , c1981. xiii, 337 p. : ISBN 0-940162-00-8 (pbk.) : LC Card 81-51506 DDC 973.927 19
HT123 .B665 *NYPL [Pub. Cat. 86-574]*

UNITED STATES - SOCIAL CONDITIONS - 1960-1980.
Social and economic characteristics of the population in metro and nonmetro counties, 1970-80 /. Washington, D.C. [1986] iv, 70 p. : LC Card 86-602790 DDC 304.6/0973 19
HC106.7 .S577 1986

UNITED STATES - SOCIAL CONDITIONS - 1980-
Bagby, Wesley Marvin, 1922- Introduction to social science /. Chicago , c1987. xv, 427 p. : ISBN 0-8304-1146-1 LC Card 86-23487 DDC 306/.0973 19
HC106.8 .B34 1987

Fallows, James M. Human capital . New York, N.Y. , 1988. p. cm. ISBN 0-394-56498-7 : LC Card 87-42659 DDC 306/.3 19
HC106.8 .F35 1988

Levitan, Sar A. Working but poor . Baltimore , c1987. ix, 142 p. : ISBN 0-8018-3583-6 (alk. paper) LC Card 87-16973 DDC 362.5/0973 19
HC110.I5 L468 1987

The State of families. Milwaukee, Wis. , <c1987-. v. <2 > : ISBN 0-87304-226-3 (pbk. : v. 2) LC Card 87-24374 DDC 306.8/5/0973 19
HD4904.25 .S83 1987

Stirrings of culture /. Dallas, Tex. , 1986. xix, 250 p. ; ISBN 0-911005-07-2 : LC Card 86-24028 DDC 306 19
HM101 .S786 1986 *NYPL [JFF 87-151]*

UNITED STATES - SOCIAL CONDITIONS - 1980- - CASE STUDIES.
Richards, Eugene. Below the line . Mount Vernon, N.Y. , c1987. 218 p. : ISBN 0-89043-062-4 LC Card 86-70834 DDC 305.5/69/0973 19
HC110.P6 R52 1987

UNITED STATES - SOCIAL CONDITIONS - 1980- - PICTORIAL WORKS.
Richards, Eugene. Below the line . Mount Vernon, N.Y. , c1987. 218 p. : ISBN 0-89043-062-4 LC Card 86-70834 DDC 305.5/69/0973 19
HC110.P6 R52 1987

UNITED STATES - SOCIAL POLICY.
Beyond Reagan . Washington, D.C. , c1987. v, 209 p. : ISBN 0-87187-437-7 (pbk.) : LC Card 87-3057 DDC 338.973 19
HC106.8 .B47 1987

Haveman, Robert H. Poverty policy and poverty research . Madison, Wis. , 1987. xi, 307 p. : ISBN 0-299-11150-4 : LC Card 86-40453 DDC 362.5/8/0973 19
HC110.P6 H38 1987

The Mean season . New York, c1987. xvi, 205 p. ; ISBN 0-394-55338-1 : LC Card 86-43126 DDC 361/.973 19
HC110.P63 M42 1987

Morris, Michael, 1949- Poverty and public policy . Westport, Conn. , 1986. xii, 236 p. ; ISBN 0-313-24942-3 (lib. bdg. : alk. paper) LC Card 86-398 DDC 361.6/1/0973 19
HV95 .M67 1986 *NYPL [JLD 87-510]*

Moynihan, Daniel P. (Daniel Patrick), 1927- The politics of a guaranteed income. New York [1973] xiii, 579 p. ISBN 0-394-46354-4 LC Card 77-37069 DDC 362.5
HC110.I5 M65 *NYPL [JLE 74-384]*

Noble, Charles, 1948- Liberalism at work . Philadelphia , 1986. x, 292 p. : ISBN 0-87722-421-8 (alk. paper) : LC Card 86-1766 DDC 353.0083/0289 19
HD7654 .N63 1986 *NYPL [JLE 86-4426]*

Private means--public ends . New York , 1987. xiii, 187 p. ; ISBN 0-275-92429-7 (alk. paper) : LC Card 86-25251 DDC 361.6/1/0973 19
HN65 .P69 1987 *NYPL [JLE 87-1390]*

Sagoff, Mark. The economy of the earth . Cambridge [Cambridgeshire] , New York , 1988. p. cm. ISBN 0-521-34113-2 LC Card 87-16091 DDC 363.7/056/0973 19
HC110.E5 S34 1988

UNITED STATES - SOCIAL POLICY - 1980- - ADDRESSES, ESSAYS, LECTURES.
State politics and the new federalism . White Plains, N.Y. , c1986. xv, 544 p. : ISBN 0-582-28474-0 (pbk.) LC Card 85-15956 DDC 321.02/0973 19
JK325 .S77 1986 *NYPL [JLD 86-2766]*

United States. Social Security Administration. (Old Catalog form: United States. Social Security board)

UNITED STATES. SOCIAL SECURITY ADMINISTRATION - DATA PROCESSING.
The Social Security Administration and information technology . Washington, DC [1986] viii, 149 p. : LC Card 86-600567 DDC 353.0082/56 19
HD7125 .S5953 1986

UNITED STATES. SOCIAL SECURITY ADMINISTRATION - PROCUREMENT.
The Social Security Administration and information technology . Washington, DC [1986] viii, 149 p. : LC Card 86-600567 DDC 353.0082/56 19
HD7125 .S5953 1986

United States. State Dept. see **United States. Dept. of State.**

UNITED STATES - STATISTICAL SERVICES - DIRECTORIES.
Evinger, William R., 1943- Federal statistical directory . Phoenix, Ariz. , 1987. iv, 127 p. ; ISBN 0-89774-398-9 (pbk.) LC Card 87-12359 DDC 353.0081/9 19
HA37.U55 E85 1987

UNITED STATES - STATISTICS, VITAL - COLLECTED WORKS.
U. S. decennial life tables for 1979-81. Hyattsville, Md. , Washington, D.C. , 1985-<1986. v. ; LC Card 85-600190 DDC 304.6/4/0973021 19
HB1335 .U17 1985 *NYPL [JLM 86-491]*

United States. Statutes. see **United States. Laws, statutes, etc.**

United States - Tariff. see **Tariff - United States.**

United States. Tax Analysis, Office of. see **United States. Office of Tax Analysis.**

United States - Taxation. see **Taxation - United States.**

The United States trade deficit of the 1980s . Carvounis, Chris C. New York , 1987. vi, 190 p. ; ISBN 0-89930-219-X (lib. bdg. : alk. paper) LC Card 87-2561 DDC 382.1/7/0973 19
HF3031 .C37 1987

United States. Trade Development. Office of Aerospace. A Competitive assessment of the U. S. general aviation aircraft industry /. Washington, D.C. , 1986. xix, 69 p. : LC Card 86-602548 DDC 338.4/762913334/0973 19
HD9711.U6 C636 1986

The United States, transnational business, and the law . International Law Symposium (1984 : Cambridge, Cambridgeshire) New York , c1985. x, 132 p. ; ISBN 0-379-20783-4 LC Card 85-61594 DDC 346/.07 342.67 19
K1004.6 1984 *NYPL [JLF 86-1046]*

United States. Transportation, Dept. of. see **United States. Dept. of Transportation.**

United States. Treasury Dept. Bureau of the Mint. see **United States. Bureau of the Mint.**

United States. Treasury Dept. Customs Service. see **United States. Customs Service.**

UNITED STATES. TREASURY DEPT. - HISTORY - 20TH CENTURY.
Shook, Dale N. William G. McAdoo and the development of national economic policy, 1913-1918 /. New York , 1987. 427 p. ; ISBN 0-8240-8092-0 (alk. paper) : LC Card 87-23766 DDC 338.973 19
HC106.2 .S55 1987

United States. Treasury Dept. Internal Revenue Service. see **United States. Internal Revenue Service.**

United States. Treasury Dept. Office of Revenue Sharing. see **United States. Office of Revenue Sharing.**

United States. Treasury Dept. Office of Tax Analysis. see **United States. Office of Tax Analysis.**

United States. Unemployment Insurance Service.
Rosbrow, James M. Fifty years of unemployment insurance--a legislative history, 1935-1985. Washington, D.C. , 1986. vii, 97 p. ; LC Card 87-601117 DDC 368.4/4/00973 s 344.73/024/0262 368.4/4/00973 s 347.304240262 19
HD7096.U5 U637 no. 86-5 KF3675

United States. United States Dept. of Housing and Urban Development. Office of Policy Development and Research. The Fair Housing Assistance Program evaluation /. Washington, D.C. [1985] 1 v. (various pagings) : *NYPL [JLF 87-17]*

United States. Urban Mass Transportation Administration. Office of Grants Management. A Directory of rural and specialized transit operators /. Washington, D.C. , 1986- v. <1-3 > : LC Card 86-603414

DDC 388.3/22/0973 19
HE203 .D57 1986

United States. Urban Mass Transportation Administration. Office of Service and Management Demonstrations. Gilbert, Gorman, 1943- The management and regulation of ground transportation at U. S. airports . Washington, D.C. [1986] 153 p. : LC Card 87-600652 DDC 387.7/362 19
HE9797.4.A2 G55 1986

United States. Vice President's Task Force on Youth Employment. A summary report of the Vice President's Task Force on Youth Employment. Washington : The Task Force, 1980. 70 p. : ill. ; 28 cm. Supported by a contract from the U. S. Dept. of Labor, Office of Youth Programs. Feb. 1980; reprinted Aug. 1980. Bibliography: p. 68-70.
1. Youth - Employment - United States. 2. High school dropouts - Employment - United States. 3. Manpower policy - United States. I. United States. Employment and Training Administration. Office of Youth Programs. II. Title. ***NYPL [JLF 86-214]***

United States - Vital statistics. see United States - Statistics, Vital.

United States. Wage and Hour and Public Contracts Divisions. (Old Catalog form: United States. Labor Dept. Wage and Hour Division)
Laundry and cleaning services; a study of the economic effects of the $1.15 minimum wage and 42 hour maximum workweek standards under the Fair labor standards act. Submitted to the Congress, 1969. [Washington, 1969] iii, 31, A-ii, A-67p. 27cm. (Economic effects studies) Cover title.
1. United States. Laws, statutes, etc. Fair labor standards act. 2. Wages - Laundry workers - United States. 3. Wages - Minimum wage - United States. 4. Hours of labor - United States. 5. Wages - Cleaning and dyeing industry - United States. I. Title. ***NYPL [JLF 86-586]***

United States. War Assets Corporation. see War Assets Corporation.

United States. Ways and Means, Committee on (House) see United States. Congress. House. Committee on Ways and Means.

United States. Woman in Industry Service. see United States. Women's Bureau.

United States. Women's Bureau.
The Business of caring [videorecording] /. Washington, DC , 1984. 1 videocassette (23 min.) : LC Card 84-707513 DDC 362.7 11
HF5549.5.D39

Records of the Women's Bureau of the Department of Labor, 1918-1965 [microform] / advisory editor, Judith Sealander ; edited by Dale Grinder. Frederick, MD : University Publications of America, 1987- microfilm reel (Research collections in women's studies) Research collections in labor studies Accompanied by a printed reel guide, compiled by Blair Hydrick. CONTENTS. - pt. 1. Reports of the director, annual summaries, major conferences, speeches, and articles. ISBN 0-89093-870-9 (microfilm : pt. 1) : LC Card 87-6239 DDC 331.4/0973 19
1. Women - Employment - United States - History - Sources. 2. United States. Women's Bureau - Archives. I. Sealander, Judith. II. Grinder, Dale. III. Hydrick, Blair. IV. University Publications of America, Inc. V. Title. VI. Series.
HD6095

Women, clerical work, and office automation . Washington, D.C. , 1986. vi, 64 p. ; LC Card 86-602559 DDC 331.4/8165137/0973 19
HD6095 .W685 1986

UNITED STATES. WOMEN'S BUREAU - ARCHIVES.
United States. Women's Bureau. Records of the Women's Bureau of the Department of Labor, 1918-1965 [microform] /. Frederick, MD , 1987- microfilm reel ISBN 0-89093-870-9 (microfilm : pt. 1) : LC Card 87-6239 DDC 331.4/0973 19
HD6095

UNITED STEELWORKERS OF AMERICA.
Whyte, William Foote, 1914- Pattern for industrial peace /. New York , 1987, c1951. ix, 245 p. : ISBN 0-8240-8227-3 (alk. paper) : LC Card 86-25790 DDC 331.89/0469142/0977/311 19
HD6515.I52 C48 1987

UNITED STEELWORKERS OF AMERICA - HISTORY - CONGRESSES.
Forging a union of steel . Ithaca, N.Y. , c1987. vii, 153 p. : ISBN 0-87546-135-2 (pbk.) LC Card 87-21508 DDC 331.88/169142/0973 19
HD6515.I5 F58 1987

United Workers' Party (Hungary) see Magyar Dolgozók Pártja.

UNITIZED CARGO SYSTEMS.
Koch, Hasso B. Funktions- und Sozialstrukturen auf Containerschiffen /. Frankfurt am Main , New York , c1986. vi, 542 p. : ISBN 3-8204-9334-4 LC Card 86-194048
HE566.C6 K63 1986

UNIVERSAL POSTAL UNION.
Gees, René. Schweiz UPU 1900 . Bern [1976?] 56 p. : LC Card 86-170456
HE6271 .G44 1976

Sieger (Firm) Weltpostverein (UPU) . Lorch/Württemberg , c1982. 408 p. : LC Card 83-224689
HE6271 .S55 1982

Universidad Autónoma de Santo Domingo. Duarte, Isis. Trabajadores urbanos . Santo Domingo, República Dominicana , c1986. 314 p. ; LC Card 87-402153 DDC 331/.097293 19
HD8218.5 .D83 1986

Universidad Boliviana Mayor de San Simón. Facultad de Ciencias Económicas. Producción y comercialización de la coca . Cochabamba, Bolivia , 1972. 92 leaves in various foliations, [3] folded leaves of plates : LC Card 85-138614
HD9019.C632 B646 1972

Universidad Central de Ecuador. Instituto de Investigaciones Económicas. Ecuador, pasado y presente /. Quito, Ecuador , 1982. 273 p. ; LC Card 83-156158
HC202 .E28 1982

Universidad de Antioquia. Centro de Investigaciones Económicas. López Castaño, Hugo. El comercio callejero en la ciudad de Medellín . Medellín , 1983. xv, 194 leaves : LC Card 85-131765
HF5459.C7 L67 1983

Universidad de Buenos Aires. Escenarios políticos y sociales del desarrollo latinoamericano /. [S.l.] [Buenos Aires] , c1986. 231 p. ; ISBN 950-23-0274-5 LC Card 87-400175 DDC 338.98 19
HC125 .E82 1986

Universidad de Costa Rica. Cátedra de Historia de las Instituciones de Costa Rica. Las Instituciones costarricenses del siglo XX /. [San José] , 1986. 376 p. ; ISBN 997-7232-96-5 LC Card 86-231789
HC143 .I54 1986

Universidad de Costa Rica. Escuela de Economía Agrícola. Rojas Rojas, Edgar. Indices de eficiencia económica para la industria beneficiadora de café . San José, Costa Rica , 1986. 14 leaves : LC Card 87-403520 DDC 338.1/6 19
HD9199.C82 R65 1986

Universidad de Costa Rica. Instituto de Investigaciones en Ciencias Económicas. Pacheco O., Amparo. Préstamo del BID al sector pesquero . [San José] , 1984. 50 p. : LC Card 86-185463
HD9464.A2 P33 1984

Universidad de Costa Rica. Instituto de Investigaciones Sociales. Propuesta para el desarrollo de un programa de investigación sobre propiedad social con énfasis en cooperativismo /. San José, Costa Rica , 1986. ii, 70 p. : LC Card 87-125056 DDC 334/.097286 19
HD3454.A4 P76 1986

Universidad de Cuenca. Instituto de Investigaciones Sociales. La Crisis de la economía ecuatoriana . Quito , 1986. 232 p. : LC Card 87-400395 DDC 330.9866/074 19
HC202 .C755 1986

Universidad de Granada. Instituto de Desarrollo Regional. Martín Rodríguez, Manuel. Las haciendas locales de la Provincia de Granada, 1940-1983 . Granada [1985?] 369 p. ; ISBN 84-338-0266-6 LC Card 86-230887
HJ9527.G7 M37 1985

Universidad de Guadalajara. Instituto de Geografía y Estadística. Municipio de Poncitlán. Guadalajara, Jal., México [1979] 71 p. : LC Card 86-188934
HC138.P63 M85 1979

Universidad de la República (Uruguay). Instituto de Economía. Medina Spangenberg, Ernesto. "Algunas consideraciones sobre el tipo real de cambio en el Uruguay, período 1.78-12.82" /. Montevideo, Uruguay [1984] 39 p. : LC Card 84-253583
HG3940 .M43 1984

Universidad de la República (Uruguay). Instituto de Estadísticas. Protasi, Juan Carlos. La flotación cambiaría . Montevideo, Uruguay [1985] 33 leaves : LC Card 86-160085
HG3940 .P76 1985

Universidad de Lima. Centro de Investigaciones Económicas y Sociales.
Migraciones laborales en el Perú . [Monterrico] [c1984] 47 p. : LC Card 84-235623 DDC 331.12/7985 19
HD5761 .M53 1984 ***NYPL [JLF 86-799]***

Rebolledo Soberón, Luis. Deuda externa . [Lima] , c1985. 58 p. : LC Card 86-120059
HJ8514.5 .R43 1985

Universidad de los Andes (Bogotá, Colombia). Centro de Estudios sobre Desarrollo Económico. Flórez Nieto, Carmen Elisa. The existence of a Latin American mortality pattern . Bogotá, Colombia , 1985. 153 p. : LC Card 87-145922
HB1397 .F56 1985

Universidad de los Andes (Bogotá, Colombia). Centro Interdisciplinario de Estudios Regionales. Pobreza, participación y desarrollo regional /. [Bogotá, D.E., Colombia] , 1986. 536 p. : LC Card 87-103266
HC125 .P6 1986

Universidad de los Andes (Bogotá, Colombia). Facultad de Arquitectura. Vivienda del Tercer Mundo . Bogotá , c1986. 94 p. : ISBN 958-9054-01-3 LC Card 86-224743
HD7305.5 .V58 1986

Universidad de los Andes (Mérida, Venezuela). Instituto de Investigaciones Económicas.
Plan de desarrollo regional / Instituto de Investigaciones Económicas, U.L.A.--CORPOANDES. Mérida : El Instituto : CORPOANDES, 1973- v. <1-5 > : maps ; 27 cm. Vols. <4-5 > cover title. Includes bibliographical references. CONTENTS. - [1] Programas subregionales, Alto Llano Occidental, Grita-Torbes -- [2] Programas subregionales, Chama-Mocotíes, Motatán-Cenizo -- [3] Diagnóstico, anexo estadístico -- [4] Diagnóstico del sector público en la Región de los Andes -- [5] Formulación macroeconómica de la Región Andina. LC Card 86-202604
1. Andes Region - Economic policy. 2. Venezuela - Economic policy. I. Corporación de los Andes. II. Title.
HC238.A683 U55 1973

Universidad de Murcia. Facultad de Filosofía y Letras. Egea Bruno, Pedro María. La minería cartagenera en torno a la primera guerra mundial, 1909-1923 /. [Murcia] , 1983. 76 p. : ISBN 84-86031-30-3 LC Card 85-199662
HD9506.S762 C374 1983

Universidad de Salamanca, Colegio Universitario de Zamora (Series) .
(3) Alvarez Vázquez, J. A. (José Antonio) Los diezmos en Zamora (1500-1840) /. Salamanca, España [Zamora] , 1984. ii, 318 p. ; ISBN 84-7481-296-8 LC Card 85-123559
HJ2287.S74 A58 1984

Universidad de São Paulo. Instituto de Pesquisas Econômicas.
Avaliação global do programa de nutrição Brasil-BIRD . [São Paulo, SP] [Brasília] , 1981- v. <1 > : LC Card 87-123819 DDC 363.8/56/0981 19
HD9014.B82 A82 1981

O Mercado de trabalho no Brasil . São Paulo , 1986. 263 p. : LC Card 86-221361
HD5754 .M47 1986

Universidad del Zulia. Centro Programa de Estudios Latinoamericanos. Crisis y control de cambio /. Maracaibo, Venezuela , 1984. 101

p. ; LC Card 87-400572 DDC 332.4/560987 19
HG3941 .C74 1984

Universidad Externado de Colombia. Perspectivas de la economía mundial y colombiana /. Bogotá, Colombia , 1986. 106 p. ; ISBN 958-616-044-0 LC Card 87-115573 DDC 330.9861/0632 19
HC197 .P35 1986

Universidad Mayor de San Andrés. Facultad de Derecho. Conferencias sobre desarrollo económico, presupuesto, estabilización y nacionalización de empresas económicas. La Paz, Bolivia , 1955. 180 p. : LC Card 86-167406
HC182 .C54 1955

Universidad Mayor de San Andrés. Taller de Historia Oral Andina. Los Constructores de la ciudad . La Paz , 1986. 84 p. : LC Card 86-234740
HD6609.B892 S563 1986

Universidad Nacional Agraria. Estrategias para el desarrollo de la Sierra /. Cusco , c1986. 418 p. : LC Card 86-199393
HC228.A54 E87 1986

Universidad Nacional Autónoma de México. Departamento de Geografía Económica. Quintana Roo . Puerto Morelos, Q.R. , 1980. iv, 203 p., [32] leaves of plates : LC Card 84-222175
HC137.Q5 Q55 1980

Seminario sobre Conceptos Teóricos de la Geografía Económica (1975 : Mexico City, Mexico?) Seminario sobre Conceptos Teóricos de la Geografía Económica . México , 1978. 78 p. ; LC Card 87-403767 DDC 330.9 19
HC13 .S46 1975

Universidad Nacional Autónoma de México. Facultad de Derecho. Mesa Redonda sobre la Carta de Punta del Este (1961 : Universidad Nacional Autónoma de México) Memoria del ciclo de conferencias de Mesa Redonda sobre la Carta de Punta del Este /. México , 1962. 224 p. : LC Card 85-105213
HC125 .M48 1961

Universidad Nacional Autónoma de México. Instituto de Investigaciones Sociales. Las Derrotas obreras, 1946-1952 /. México , 1984. 204 p. ; ISBN 968-580-647-0 LC Card 84-255708 DDC 331.88/0972 19
HD6532 .D36 1984 ***NYPL [JLE 86-4685]***

Movimientos sociales en el noroeste de México /. México , 1985. 282 p. ; ISBN 968-590-072-8 LC Card 87-102068
HD1531.M6 M684 1985

Universidad Nacional (Costa Rica). Instituto de Estudios Sociales en Población. Sandoval Aguilar, Guillermo. El desarrollo costarricense y la fecundidad del hombre /. Heredia , 1985. 233 p. ; LC Card 86-117576
HB947 .S26 1985

Universidad Nacional (Costa Rica). Unidad Coordinadora de Investigación y Documentación. Paz Cárcamo, Guillermo. El universo del café /. Heredia [1983] 145 p. ; LC Card 87-400683 DDC 338.1/7373/097286 19
HD9195.C82 P39 1983

Universidad Nacional "José Faustino Sánchez Carrión." Facultad de Sociología. Pacheco B., Gabriel (Pacheco Bustamante) Apuntes sobre el problema parcelario en la Provincia de Chancay /. Huacho, Perú , 1984. 49 p. ; LC Card 86-124478
HD1491.P42 C56 1984

Universidad Técnica de Machala. Departamento de Investigaciones Socioeconómicas. Maldonado Calderón, Arturo. Actividad económica del hombre del suburbio /. Machala, Ecuador , 1985. 168 p., [3] folded leaves of plates : LC Card 87-110202 DDC 330.9866/31 19
HC203.M33 M35 1985

Universidade de Brasília. Departamento de Economia. Castro, Paulo Furtado de. Modelo estocástico para a estimação do produto potencial "IPEA/Depto. de Economia-UnB.". [Brasília, Brazil] [1981] 12, [16] : LC Card 85-210547
HC190.I5 C37 1981

Universidade de Brasília. Departamento de Sociologia. Cidadão, estado e políticas no Brasil contemporâneo /. Brasília-Distrito Federal , c1986. 290 p. : ISBN 85-23-00214-6 LC Card 87-405054 DDC 338.981 19
HD1873 .C53 1986

Universidade de Coimbra. Biblioteca Geral. Livros de contas da ilha da Madeira, 1504-1537 /. Coimbra , 1985- v. <1 > ; LC Card 86-232733
HJ9930.3.M33 L58 1985

Universidade de Lisboa. Centro de Estudos Geográficos. Madeira em mapas e em números. [Lisboa] , 1984. iii, 61 leaves : LC Card 85-144457
HA2285 .M33 1984

Universidade de Lisboa. Faculdade de Direito. Liberalismo, intervencionismo e o caso português . [Lisbon] [1982] 44 p. ; LC Card 86-132673
HJ1252 .L52 1982

Universidade de São Paulo. Faculdade de Economia e Administração. História empresarial vivida /. São Paulo , 1986-<1987. v. <1-3 > ; LC Card 86-226035
HD70.B7 H57 1986

Universidade de São Paulo. Instituto de Administração. Criação de empresas de alta tecnologia . São Paulo . 192, [1] p. ; LC Card 87-403991 DDC 338.4/362/000981 19
HC190.H53 C75 1987

Universidade de São Paulo. Instituto de Estudos Brasileiros. Marsiglia, Cecília. S/A Central Elétrica Rio Claro /. São Paulo , 1986. 105 p. : LC Card 87-404945 DDC 363.6/2/098161 19
HD9685.B83 C4886 1986

Universidade Eduardo Mondlane. Centro de Estudos Africanos. Wuyts, Marc. Camponeses e economia rural em Moçambique [microform] /. Maputo , 1978. 31, A1-A6 p. ; LC Card 80-980386 DDC 338.1/0967/9 19
HD2129 .W89 1978
NYPL [*ZT-1564 no.14]

Universidade Eduardo Mondlane. Centro de Estudos Africanos. Oficina de História. A Situação nas antigas zonas libertadas de Cabo Delgado /. [Maputo, Mozambique] , 1983. 59 p. ; LC Card 86-980983 DDC 330.967/9805 19
HC890.Z7 C327 1983

Universidade Estadual de Campinas. Departamento de Política e História Econômica. Getúlio Vargas e a economia contemporânea /. Campinas , 1986. 179 p. ; ISBN 85-26-80033-7 LC Card 87-403048 DDC 330.981/063 19
HC187 .G45 1986

Universidade Federal de Minas Gerais. Centro de Desenvolvimento e Planejamento Regional. Plano Cruzado . Rio de Janeiro , 1987. xii, 203 p. : LC Card 87-127770 DDC 338.981 19
HC187 .P59 1987

Universidade Federal do Rio Grande do Sul. Centro de Estudos e Pesquisas Econômicas. Michel, Nelson Emílio. Evolução dos índices do número e do valor de cheques compensados no Rio Grande do Sul, período de 1960-7, e sua análise estatística /. Porto Alegre , 1976. 79 leaves : LC Card 82-159893
HG1692 .M53 1976

Università degli studi di Roma "La Sapienza." Istituto di diritto delle assicurazioni. Statistica e pubblica amministrazione . Milano , 1983-1985. 2 v. ; ISBN 88-14-00703-9 (v. 2) : LC Card 86-215546
HA37.I9 S7 1983

Università di Palermo. Istituto di scienze demografiche. Storia demografica dei comuni siciliani dal 1862 al 1971 /. Palermo [1979] 294 p. ; LC Card 86-131917
HB2270.S5 S76 1979

Università di Palermo. Istituto di statistica sociale e scienze demografiche e biometriche. Greco, Eugenio. Storia demografica dei comuni siciliani dal 1832 al 1858 /. Palermo [1982] 60, [61] p. ; LC Card 85-103229
HB2270.S5 G74 1982

Vizzini, Sergio. Indagine socio-demografica sugli immigrati stranieri in Sicilia . Palermo [1983] 108 p. ; LC Card 86-131931
HB3600.M39 V58 1983

Università di Pisa. Istituto di sociologia. Processi formativi e coscienza operaia . Pisa , c1983. 509 p. ; LC Card 86-136656 DDC 658.3/124/0945 19
HF5549.5.T7 P69 1983
NYPL [JLE 87-1466]

Università "L. Bocconi," Dipartimento di economia aziendale (Series) .
(38) Fabrizi, Pier Luigi. La politica degli investimenti in titoli nelle banche di deposito /. [Milano] , 1982. xii, 138 p. ; LC Card 82-165568
HG1616.I5 F33 1982

(42) Spranzi, Aldo, 1932- Calcolo dei costi nelle imprese industriali /. Milano [1986] viii, 94 p. : ISBN 88-14-00844-2 : LC Card 86-182386
HC79.C7 S67 1986

(55) Brondoni, Silvio M. Politiche di mercato dei beni industriali /. [Milano] [1983] ix, 279 p. : LC Card 83-234353
HD9680.A2 B76 1983

(81) Canziani, Arnaldo. La strategia aziendale /. [Milano] , 1984. xx, 288 p. ; ISBN 88-14-00283-5 : LC Card 85-105652 DDC 658.4/012 19
HD30.28 .C364 1984

(83) Sury, Paul de. Milano, centro finanziario internazionale /. [Milano] [1984] viii, 138 p. : ISBN 88-14-00312-2 : LC Card 86-114645
HG3090.M52 S87 1984

(90) Grandori, Anna. Teorie dell'organizzazione . [Milano] , 1984. xxiii, 213 p. : ISBN 88-14-00411-0 : LC Card 85-162760
HD37.I8 G73 1984

(96) La Gestione degli istituti di credito industriale /. Milano [1985] xviii, 868 p. : ISBN 88-14-00665-2 : LC Card 86-170383
HG3726 .G47 1985

(97) Frattini, Giovanni. Contabilità e bilancio . Milano [1986] xiii, 317 p. : ISBN 88-14-00831-0 : LC Card 86-182373
HF5625 .F73 1986

Universiṭah ha-ʻIvrit bi-Yerushalayim. Programme of Canadian Studies. Planning in turbulence /. Jerusalem , 1986. xii, 158 p. : ISBN 965-223-657-8 (pbk.) LC Card 87-163701 DDC 658.4/012 19
HD87.5 .P5 1986

Universitas Gadjah Mada. Pusat Penelitian dan Studi Pedesaan & Kawasan. Kredit pedesaan di Indonesia /. Yogyakarta , 1986. xii, 160 p. ; LC Card 86-943011
HG2051.I65 K74 1986

Universitas Indonesia. Lembaga Demografi. Ananta, Aris. Perilaku fertilitas di beberapa daerah di Jawa /. Jakarta , 1986. vi, 56, 26 p. ; LC Card 86-946460
HB1058.J38 A52 1986

Universität Bamberg. Lehrstuhl für Bevölkerungswissenschaft. Bevölkerungswissenschaft . Frankfurt , New York , c1985. 227 p. ; ISBN 3-593-33461-5 LC Card 85-178756
HB849 .B48 1985

UNIVERSITÄT BASEL - FINANCE.
Frey, René Leo. Die regionale Ausstrahlung der Universität Basel /. Basel , c1984. 73 p. : LC Card 84-166545 DDC 378/.103 19
HC395 .A75 no. 8 LC238.4.S92B37

UNIVERSITÄT BASEL - PUBLIC RELATIONS.
Frey, René Leo. Die regionale Ausstrahlung der Universität Basel /. Basel , c1984. 73 p. : LC Card 84-166545 DDC 378/.103 19
HC395 .A75 no. 8 LC238.4.S92B37

Universität Bielefeld. Evaluation der Berufsberatung der Bundesanstalt für Arbeit . Nürnberg , 1983. vii, 282 p. : LC Card 85-107586
HF5382.5.G3 E9 1983

Universität Bonn. Institut für Agrarpolitik, Marktforschung und Wirtschaftssoziologie. Einkommenswirkungen von Getreidepreissenkungen /. Münster-Hiltrup , 1985. viii, 158 p. : ISBN 3-7843-0315-3 LC Card 87-408928 DDC 338.1/0943 s 338.1/331/094 19
HD1920.5 .E37 1985

Universität Essen. Fachbereich Architektur, Bio- und Geowissenschaften. Arbeitersiedlungen im 19. Jahrhundert . Bochum , c1985. 189 p. :

ISBN 3-88339-427-0 LC Card 85-164690
HD7289.5.A3 G42 1985

Universität Frankfurt am Main. Internationaler Kapitalverkehr und Devisenhandel /. Frankfurt am Main , c1986. 133 p. ; ISBN 3-7819-0347-8 LC Card 87-164156 DDC 332/.042 19
HG3891 .I58 1986

Universität Hamburg. Fachbereich Wirtschaftswissenschaften. Die Protestantische Ethik und der Verfall des Kapitalismus . [Hamburg] , 1985. 31 p. : LC Card 86-112068
HB501 .P76 1985

Universität Heidelberg. Südasien-Institut. Grundbedürfnisse als Gegenstand der Entwicklungspolitik . Wiesbaden , 1982. viii, 220 p. : ISBN 3-515-03838-8 (Deut. Bibl.) LC Card 85-134671
HC59.72.B38 G78 1982

Universität Karlsruhe. Institut für Regionalwissenschaft. Heinzmann, Ute. Umzugsverhalten der Bevölkerung in ausgewählten ländlichen Teilräumen am Beispiel der Region Neckar-Alb . Tübingen , 1985. 69, [4] p. : LC Card 86-195573
HB2056.N43 H45 1985

Universität Karlsruhe. Institut für Soziologie. Arbeitsgestaltung in der Serienfertigung . Frankfurt [am Main] , New York , c1984. 315 p. : ISBN 3-593-32733-3 LC Card 84-230390
HD58.8 .A73 1984

Universität Kiel. Institut für Landwirtschaftliche Betriebs- und Arbeitslehre. Intrasektorale Einkommensstreuung in der Landwirtschaft /. Münster-Hiltrup , 1983. 177 p. : ISBN 3-7843-0281-5 : LC Card 83-236007
HD1955 .I57 1983

Kühl, Rainer. Wettbewerbstheoretische Analyse des Landwarenmarktes in der Bundesrepublik Deutschland . Kiel , 1986. 77 p. : ISBN 3-922553-79-6 LC Card 86-172903
HD9013.5 .K84 1986

Universität Kiel. Institut für Weltwirtschaft. Fels, Gerhard. Mehr Flexibilität am Arbeitsmarkt /. Kiel , 1986. 21 p. ; ISBN 3-925357-37-8 LC Card 87-126264 DDC 331.25/72/0943 19
HD5109.2.G3 F4 1986

Free trade in the world economy . Boulder , 1987. p. cm. ISBN 0-8133-0596-9 LC Card 87-20148 DDC 382.7/1 19
HF1703 .F74 1987

Für einen anhaltenden Aufschwung . Kiel [1986] 29 p. : ISBN 3-925357-33-5 (Deut. Bibl.) : LC Card 86-234971
HB44 .K45 no. 123 HC286.7

The International debt problem . Tübingen , 1986. vi, 193 p. : ISBN 3-16-345084-9 (pbk.) LC Card 86-201893 DDC 336.3/435 19
HG3891.5 .I557 1986

The International debt problem . Boulder , 1987. p. cm. ISBN 0-8133-0595-0 LC Card 87-20149 DDC 336.3/435 19
HG3891.5 .I557 1987

Reassessing the role of government in the mixed economy /. Boulder , 1987. p. cm. ISBN 0-8133-0598-5 : LC Card 87-20142 DDC 338.9 19
HD73 .R43 1987

Universität Kiel. Institut für Weltwirtschaft. Bibliothek. Bibliographie der EG-Zeitschriften 1952-1980 . Kiel , 1981. ix, 280 p. ; LC Card 81-122713
HB41 .K55 Bd. 22 Z7165.E8 HC241.2

Universität Mannheim. Fakultät für Betriebswirtschaftslehre. Betriebswirtschaftliche Erkenntnisse für Regierung, Verwaltung und öffentliche Unternehmen . Baden-Baden , 1985. 266 p. : ISBN 3-7890-1104-5 LC Card 85-213984
HJ9705 .B48 1985

Universität Mannheim. Forschungsgruppe Konsumenteninformation. Warentest und Konsument . Frankfurt/Main , New York , c1984. 268 p. : ISBN 3-593-33295-7 LC Card 84-150919
HF1040.9.G3 W37 1984

Universität Mannheim. Industrieseminar. Kortzfleisch, Gert von. Energie für den Verkehr . Frankfurt am Main , c1984. 115 p. : LC Card 84-192683
HD9710.G4 V4 Nr. 42 HE5620.E53

Universität München. Institut für Psychologie. Qualitative Arbeitsanalyse . Frankfurt , New York , c1983. 352 p. ; ISBN 3-593-32721-X LC Card 83-161600 DDC 158.7 19
HD6955 .Q35 1983 ***NYPL [JLD 87-1014]***

Universität Münster. Gesellschaft zur Förderung der Verkehrswissenschaft. Studienkreis. Verkehrs- und unternehmenspolitische Anpassungsstrategien an veränderte Ressourcenbewertungen /. Göttingen , 1986. 210 p. : ISBN 3-525-85699-7 : LC Card 86-223574
HE131 .M8 Heft 109 HE249

Universität Münster. Institut für Verkehrswissenschaft. Verkehrs- und unternehmenspolitische Anpassungsstrategien an veränderte Ressourcenbewertungen /. Göttingen , 1986. 210 p. : ISBN 3-525-85699-7 : LC Card 86-223574
HE131 .M8 Heft 109 HE249

Universität Stuttgart. Institut für Kernenergetik und Energiesysteme. Friedrich, R. (Rainer) Energie und Umwelt . Stuttgart [1985] 115 p. : LC Card 87-409534 DDC 333.79/0943/46 19
HD9502.G43 B324 1985

Friedrich, R. (Rainer) Energie und Umwelt . Stuttgart [1985] 124 p. : LC Card 87-409533 DDC 333.79/0943/46 19
HD9502.G43 B3238 1985

Universität Tübingen. Wirtschaftswissenschaftliche Fakultät. 150 Jahre Promotion an der Wirtschaftswissenschaftlichen Fakultät der Universität Tübingen . Stuttgart , c1984. xxxvi, 809 p. : ISBN 3-8062-0409-8 LC Card 85-140557
HB74.9.G3 A15 1984 ***NYPL [JFE 87-1673]***

UNIVERSITÄT TÜBINGEN. WIRTSCHAFTSWISSENSCHAFTLICHE FAKULTÄT - ALUMNI - BIOGRAPHY. 150 Jahre Promotion an der Wirtschaftswissenschaftlichen Fakultät der Universität Tübingen . Stuttgart , c1984. xxxvi, 809 p. : ISBN 3-8062-0409-8 LC Card 85-140557
HB74.9.G3 A15 1984 ***NYPL [JFE 87-1673]***

Universität zu Köln. Arbeits- und Forschungsgemeinschaft für Strassenverkehr und Verkehrssicherheit. Die Sicherung des Fussgängerverkehrs. Köln , 1976. ii, 169 p. : LC Card 86-185084
HE5614.5.G3 A7 Bd. 29

Universität Zurich. Institut für Schweizerisches Bankwesen. Internationale Wettbewerbsfähigkeit des Finanzplatzes Schweiz /. Bern , c1987. 131 p. : ISBN 3-258-03806-6 LC Card 87-114764 DDC 332.1 s 332.1/09494 19
HG1526 .B27 Bd. 101 HG3206

Universität Zürich. Soziologisches Institut. Zwischen Zentren und Hinterland . Diessenhofen , c1982. 349 p. : ISBN 0-372-53017-9 : LC Card 83-129330
HC397 .Z88 1982

Universitatia de Stat "V.I. Lenin." Burlaku, I. N. Sindikatele Moldoveĭ sovetiche yn konstruktsiia sochialiste /. Kishinėu , 1980. 148 p. ; LC Card 81-135331
HD6735.M56 B87 1980

Otsenka ėffektivnosti proizvodstva i rezervy ee rosta . Kishinev , 1982. 130 p. : LC Card 83-179279
HD9015.S653 M6454 1982

Sovershenstvovanie planirovaniia i usilenie khoziaistvennogo mekhanizma . Kishinev , 1983. 134 p. ; LC Card 84-231201
HC336.25 .S6736 1983

Trud i ego problemy na sovremennom ėtape razvitiia sotsialisticheskogo obshchestva . Kishinev , 1986. 133 p. ; LC Card 87-144606
HD8529.M57 T78 1986

Université catholique de Louvain (1970-). Département de démographie. Sala-Diakanda, Mpembele. Approche ethnique des phénomènes démographiques . Louvain-la-Neuve , 1980. 433 p. : LC Card 84-118066
HB3664.5.A3 S23 1980

Université de Bordeaux I. Institut d'économie régionale du Sud-Ouest. Lacour, Claude. Croissance urbaine . Paris , 1981. 219 p. : ISBN 2-222-02928-7 (pbk.) : LC Card 82-153821 DDC 388.4/068 19
HE4764 .L3 1981 ***NYPL [JLG 86-56]***

Université de Lausanne. Ecole des hautes études commerciales. International banking /. New York , 1988. p. cm. ISBN 0-312-00862-7 : LC Card 87-21276 DDC 332.1/5 19
HG3881 .I57513 1988

Université de Moncton. Canadian Institute for Research on Regional Development. Regional economic development . Boston , 1987. p. cm. ISBN 0-04-338155-3 (alk. paper) LC Card 87-16749 DDC 338.9 19
HD75 .R44 1987

Université de Montréal. Centre de recherches en développement économique.
Cahier .
(no 22) Garon-Audy, Muriel. Mobilités professionnelles et géographiques au Québec, 1954-64-74 /. Montréal , 1980. 61 p. ; LC Card 81-105620 DDC 331.12/7971 19
HD5717.5.C22 Q44 1980
NYPL [JLM 79-970 no.22]

Université de Paris III. Institut des hautes études de l'Amérique latine. Les Phénomènes de "frontière" dans les pays tropicaux . Paris , 1981. vii, 456 p. : LC Card 83-122397
HD1131 .P47 1981

Université de Paris. Institut des hautes études de l'Amérique latine.
Travaux et mémoires.
(26) Marchand, Bernard. Vénézuela. Paris, 1971. ix, 218 p. LC Card 74-856272
HD9574.V42 M276 ***NYPL [JLE 71-452]***

Université de Poitiers. Centre de géographie humaine et sociale. Colloque "Poitiers 1981" (1981 : Université de Poitiers) Actes du Colloque "Poitiers 1981" . Poitiers [France] [1983] 472 p. : LC Card 84-119227
HB3594.P65 C65 1981

Études méditerranéennes. see **Études méditerranéennes.**

Université des sciences sociales de Grenoble. Institut de recherche économique et de planification du développement. Chaponnière, R. Les fonctions des agents économiques exportant des biens d'équipement, dans le cadre des relations est-ouest et nord-sud, depuis 1970 /. [Paris] [1981] 159 leaves : LC Card 82-180468 DDC 382/.456817 19
HD9705.A2 C55 1981 ***NYPL [JLG 86-212]***

Université du Burundi. Centre universitaire de recherche pour le développement économique et social. Coopératives et populations rurales . [Bujumbura] [1986] ix, 64 leaves : LC Card 86-981185
HD3561.A4 C66 1986

Etude sur la petite et moyenne industrie et l'artisanat /. [Bujumbara] [1984] 7 v. in 6 : LC Card 86-980948
HD2346.B94 E78 1984

Université du Burundi. Faculté des sciences économiques et administratives. Enclavement et sous-développement au Burundi . Bujumbura, Burundi [1983] xi, 448 p. : LC Card 85-980729 DDC 338.967/572 19
HE283.8 .E53 1983

Université du Burundi. Laboratoire Logique paysanne et pratiques sociales. Coopératives et populations rurales . [Bujumbura] [1986] ix, 64 leaves : LC Card 86-981185
HD3561.A4 C66 1986

Université du Québec à Chicoutimi. Groupe de recherche et d'intervention régionales. Analyse socio-économique comparée des coopératives d'habitation en France et au Québec . [Chicoutimi] [1985] xvi, 391 p. : ISBN 2-920730-04-5 LC Card 86-181851
HD7287.72.F8 A53 1985

UNIVERSITÉ DU QUÉBEC À MONTRÉEAL - EMPLOYEES. Lépine, Ginette. Vous autres au syndicat-- /. Montréal, Québec , c1984. 179 p. ; ISBN 2-89037-214-6 LC Card 85-101458
HD8005.2.C23 M665 1984

Université du Québec à Rimouski. Groupe de recherche interdisciplinaire en développement de l'Est du Québec. Les Structures productives d'une région périphérique . Rimouski , c1984. xi, 718 p. : ISBN 2-920270-27-3 LC Card 85-132709 DDC 330.9714/77 19
HC117.G37 S78 1984

Université libre de Bruxelles, Faculté de philosophie et lettres (Series) .
(90) Nieuwenhuysen, A. van (Andrée) Les finances du duc de Bourgogne, Philippe le Hardi (1384-1404) . Bruxelles, Belgique , 1984. 556 p. ; ISBN 2-8004-0838-3 : LC Card 85-160639
HJ1099.B85 N54 1984

Université libre de Bruxelles. Institut d'études europééenes. International trade and exchange rates in the late eighties /. Amsterdam ; New York : xii, 418 p. : ISBN 2-8004-0892-8
NYPL [JLE 87-120]

Université libre de Bruxelles. Institut d'études européennes.
International trade and exchange rates in the late eighties /. Amsterdam ; New York : xii, 418 p. : ISBN 0-444-87941-2 LC Card 86-223111 DDC 382.4/5 19
HG203 .I58 1985

Toledano Laredo, Armando. Intégration et démocratie /. Bruxelles, Belgique , 1982. 192 p. ; ISBN 2-8004-0777-8 :c275F LC Card 83-163343
HF1418.5 .T65 1982

Université Paul Valery. Centre d'histoire contemporaine du Languedoc méditerranéen et du Roussillon. see **Centre d'histoire contemporaine du Languedoc méditerranéen et du Roussillon.**

Universiteit van de Nederlandse Antillen. Nos futuro . Curaçao, NA , Zutphen , c1986. 496 p. : ISBN 90-6011-512-0 : LC Card 86-220862
HC157.5 .N67 1986

Universiteit van Suriname. Instituut voor Economisch en Sociaal Onderzoek.
Onderzoek naar werkgelegenheid, inkomen en de structuur van de stedelijke economie van Paramaribo . Paramaribo, Suriname [1978] 69 leaves : LC Card 87-115836
HD5759.5.P37 O53 1978

Universitet druzhby narodov imeni Patrisa Lumumby. Ėkonomicheskie problemy razvitiia stran sotsialisticheskoĭ orientatsii /. Moskva , 1986. 239 p. ; LC Card 86-221922
HC59.7 .E355 1986

Universitet molodogo marksista.
Troshin, A. (Andreĭ) Sovetskaia ėkonomika segodnia i zavtra /. Moskva , 1981. 208 p. ; LC Card 82-144819
HC336.25 .T7 1981

Universiti Malaya. Jabatan Sejarah. Kapal dan harta karam =. Kuala Lumpur , 1986. xv, 181 p. : LC Card 86-942317 DDC 387.5/09595 19
HF3800.6 .K36 1986

UNIVERSITIES AND COLLEGES - ASIA, SOUTHEASTERN - CONGRESSES.
IGCC Workshop on Linkages Between University Based Population Activities and National Population/Family Planning Programmes (1978 : Bangkok, Thailand) IGCC Workshop on Linkages Between University Based Population Activities and National Population/Family Planning Programmes . Kuala Lumpur, Selangor [1978?] 111 p. : LC Card 81-941403
HB3641 .I35 1978

UNIVERSITIES AND COLLEGES - BRAZIL.
A Renda da terra . [São Paulo, Brazil] , Petrópolis , c1980. 152 p. : LC Card 81-214665
HC186 .C36a no. 27 HB401

UNIVERSITIES AND COLLEGES - BUSINESS MANAGEMENT.
Fulton, Patsy J. General office procedures for colleges /. Cincinnati , c1988. viii, 399 p. : ISBN 0-538-11732-X (pbk.) LC Card 86-63580 DDC 651 19
HF5547.5 .F84 1988

UNIVERSITIES AND COLLEGES - GRADUATE WORK.
Lento-McGovern, Diane, 1956- Life after college . White Hall, Va. , c1987. 179 p. ; ISBN 0-932620-77-9 (pbk.) : LC Card 87-6412 DDC 331.7/02 19
HF5381 .L354 1987

UNIVERSITIES AND COLLEGES - GRADUATES. see **COLLEGE GRADUATES.**

UNIVERSITIES AND COLLEGES - UNITED STATES - COMMUNICATION SYSTEMS.
Telecommunications opportunities for colleges and universities /. McLean, Va. (1355 Beverly Rd., Suite 100, McLean 22101) , c1986. 208 p. ; LC Card 86-231086 DDC 384.6/3 19
HD9696.T443 U572 1986

UNIVERSITIES AND COLLEGES - UNITED STATES - GRADUATE WORK.
Johnston, Robert F. Entrepreneurial science . New York , 1987. 157 p. ; ISBN 0-89930-260-2 (lib. bdg. : alk. paper) LC Card 87-2518 DDC 338/.06 19
HC110.H53 J65 1987

University College of Swansea. Centre for Development Studies (Series) .
(new ser., no. 1) Landivar, Jorge F. The role of housing in development models . Swansea, U.K. , 1986. 60 p. ; ISBN 0-906250-12-9 (pbk.) LC Card 87-166136 DDC 363.5/8 19
HD7287.96.E2 L36 1986

University Consortium for Research on North America. Land rites and wrongs . Boston , 1988. p. cm. ISBN 0-89946-222-7 LC Card 87-12186 DDC 333.73/13/0971 19
HD171.A15 L28 1988

UNIVERSITY GRADUATES. see **COLLEGE GRADUATES.**

University of Birmingham. Centre for Russian and East European Studies. Batt, Judy. Economic reform and political change in eastern Europe . New York , 1987. p. cm. ISBN 0-312-01196-2 : LC Card 87-24065 DDC 338.9437 19
HC270.28 .B37 1987

University of California. see **California. University.**

University of California, Los Angeles. Institute of Industrial Relations. Human resource management in high-technology firms /. Lexington, Mass. , 1986, c1987. x, 243 p. : ISBN 0-669-13686-7 (alk. paper) LC Card 86-45556 DDC 658.3 19
HF5549 .H875 1987 ***NYPL [JLE 87-1100]***

UNIVERSITY OF CALIFORNIA (SYSTEM) - FINANCE.
South Africa, the UC connection /. Berkeley, Calif. , 1985. 39 p. : LC Card 86-201134 DDC 332.6/73794/068 19
HG5851.A3 S63 1985

University of Chemical Engineering, Veszprém, Hungary. see **Veszprémi Vegyipari Egyetem.**

University of College of Swansea. School of Social Studies. Redundancy and Unemployment Research Group. Harris, C. C. (Christopher Charles) Redundancy and recession in South Wales /. Oxford, OX, UK , New York, NY, USA , 1987. p. cm. ISBN 0-631-15106-0 : LC Card 87-6301 DDC 331.13/794294 19
HD5766.A6 H37 1987

University of Colombo. Economics Dept.
Structural adjustment and growth . Colombo, Sri Lanka , 1986. 170 p. ; LC Card 86-903207 DDC 338.9549/3 19
HC424 .S77 1986

University of Connecticut. Center for Oral History. Palmer, Michele. Catalogue of interviews . [Storrs, Conn.] , 1983. ii, 79 p. ; LC Card 86-621476 DDC 331.12/09746 19
HD6331.2.U52 C86 1983

University of Connecticut. Project on Women and Technology. Women, work, and technology . Ann Arbor , c1987. viii, 387 p. ; ISBN 0-472-06373-1 (pbk. : alk. paper) : LC Card 87-16236 DDC 331.4 19
HD6052 .W566 1987

University of Delhi. Agricultural Economics Research Centre. Gupta, D. P. (Dharm Pall), 1932- Agricultural development in Haryana /. New Delhi, India , 1985. xiii, 120 p. : LC Card 85-901427 DDC 338.1/854558 19
HD2075.H3 G85 1985
NYPL [JLD 86-3862]

University of Durham. Centre for Middle Eastern and Islamic Studies. Hajrah, Hassan Hamza. Public land distribution in Saudi Arabia /. London , New York , 1982. xxi, 280 p. : ISBN 0-582-78301-1 LC Card 83-232929 DDC 333.1/6/09538 19
HD853.Z7 H34 1982 ***NYPL [JLE 87-1566]***

University of Edinburgh. Centre of African Studies. Malawi . Edinburgh , c1985. xviii, 642 p. : LC Card 86-100522 DDC 338.96897 19
HC935 .M36 1985

University of Florida. Institute of Food and Agricultural Sciences. Economic efficiency in agricultural and food marketing /. Ames , 1987. xii, 315 p. ; ISBN 0-8138-0533-3 LC Card 87-2821 DDC 381/.41/0973 19
HD9000.5 .E26 1987

University of Florida. Real Estate Research Center. Real estate appraisal, finance, investment, and business management . [Tallahassee] , c1986. ix, 441, iv, 86 p. : LC Card 87-159867 DDC 333.33 19
HD1375 .R375 1986

University of Ghana. Institute of Statistical, Social, and Economic Research. Nyanteng, V. K. Yam production, marketing, and prices in Ghana /. Legon , 1978. vii leaves, 159 p. : LC Card 87-400731 DDC 338.1/7523/09667 19
HD9235.S92 G46 1978

University of Houston-University Park. Center for Public Policy. Handbook on the Houston economy. [Houston, Tex. , 1986?] 36 p. : LC Card 86-622198 DDC 330.9764/1411063 19
HC108.H8 H36 1986

University of Ibadan. Centre for Agricultural and Rural Development.
Eweka, J. A. (Julius A.) Village development . Ibadan, Nigeria , 1979. xvi, 194 p. ; LC Card 86-172121 DDC 338.1/9/669 19
HD2145.5 .E94 1979

Nigerian small farmers . Benin-City, Bendel State, Nigeria , 1980. xv, 315 p. ; LC Card 82-206979 DDC 338.1/6 19
HD1339.N5 N54 1980 ***NYPL [Sc D 86-883]***

University of Ibadan. Urban and Regional Planning Programme. Physical planning inputs in national and state development plans . Ibadan [1984?] v, 312 p. : LC Card 87-400745 DDC 338.9669 19
HC1055 .P488 1984

University of Illinois at Urbana-Champaign. African Studies Program. Brazil and the Ivory Coast . Greenwich, Conn. , c1987. p. cm. ISBN 0-89232-819-3 : LC Card 87-3667 DDC 332/.042/0981 19
HG3891.5 .B72 1987

University of Illinois at Urbana-Champaign. Center for Latin American and Caribbean Studies. Brazil and the Ivory Coast . Greenwich, Conn. , c1987. p. cm. ISBN 0-89232-819-3 : LC Card 87-3667 DDC 332/.042/0981 19
HG3891.5 .B72 1987

University of Illinois at Urbana-Champaign. Dept. of Agricultural Economics. Seger, Daniel J. Financing Illinois agricultural exports /. [Urbana?] [1985] 74 p. : LC Card 86-621070 DDC 382/.63 19
HD9007.I3 S44 1985

University of Kansas. Division of Continuing Education. Making do and doing without . [Lawrence, Kan.] , 1985, c1983. 98 p. ; LC Card 86-622703 DDC 330.9781/032 19
HC107.K2 M35 1985

University of Kentucky. College of Business and Economics. Office for Research and Extension. Hultman, Charles W. An examination of issues related to multibank holding companies /. [Frankfort, Ky. , 1983] [8], 56 leaves ; LC Card 86-620545 DDC 332.1/6 19
HG2567 .H85 1983

University of London. Australian Studies Centre. Australian industrial relations . London [1986] 24 p. ; ISBN 0-902499-56-4 (pbk.) : LC Card 86-233230 DDC 331/.0994 19
HD8846.5 .A96 1986

University of London. School of Oriental and African Studies. Conference on Africa and the Market Economy (1985 : University of

London) Conference on Africa and the Market Economy. London , 1985. 1 v. (various pagings) ; LC Card 86-218280 DDC 330.96/0328 19
HC800 .C657 1985

University of Malawi. Centre for Social Research. Ettema, Wim. Small-scale industry in Malawi . Zomba [1983] iv, 50, [9] leaves, 9 p. : LC Card 84-980489 DDC 338.6/42/096897 19
HD2356.M3 E88 1983

University of Mauritius. School of Administration. Pochun, Malati J. Determinants of import prices in Mauritius /. Réduit, Mauritius , 1981. 15 p. ; LC Card 82-980680
HB235.M38 P63 1981

University of Miami. Law and Economics Center. The Role of privatization in Florida's growth /. [Tallahassee?] , c1987. iv, 474 p. ; LC Card 87-403210 DDC 338.9 19
HD3865.F6 R65 1987

University of Michigan. Environmental Conflict Project. Alternative environmental conflict management approaches . [Ann Arbor, MI] (Dana Bldg., Ann Arbor 48109-1115) [1986] 252 p. : LC Card 86-225219 DDC 363.7/058/0973 19
HC110.E5 A643 1986

University of Minnesota. Southeast Asian Refugee Studies Project. Mason, Sarah R. Training Southeast Asian refugee women for employment . Minneapolis, Minn. , 1986. viii, 142 p. : LC Card 86-72303 DDC 331.4/2592/08995073 19
HD5715.2 .M37 1986

University of Nairobi. Housing Research and Development Unit. Gatabaki-Kamau, Rose. Co-operative housing development in Kenya . Nairobi, Kenya [1985] vi leaves, 131 p. : LC Card 86-980648 DDC 334/.1/096762 19
HD7287.72.K4 G37 1985

University of Nairobi. Population Studies and Research Institute.
Population, economics, and unemployment . [Nairobi] [1982] 55 leaves ; LC Card 85-980190
HD5708.47.K4 P67 1982

Proceedings of the workshop on the "Interrelationship between agricultural settlement, agricultural development, and population change" in selected Eastern Africa Countries, Ethiopia, Kenya, Sudan, and Tanzania, held at the Population Studies and Research Institute, University of Nairobi, April 13-16, 1981. Nairobi [1981] 304 p. : LC Card 85-980248 DDC 338.1/09676 19
HD982.Z63 P76 1981

University of Nebraska--Lincoln. Community Resource and Research Center. Community energy management as an economic development strategy . [Lincoln, Neb.] (Box 95085, Lincoln 68509-5085) [1984 or 1985] iv, 396 p. : LC Card 86-622211 DDC 333.79/0973 19
HD9502.U52 C656 1984

University of Nebraska--Lincoln. Dept. of Community and Regional Planning.
Community energy management as an economic development strategy . [Lincoln, Neb.] (Box 95085, Lincoln 68509-5085) [1984 or 1985] iv, 396 p. : LC Card 86-622211 DDC 333.79/0973 19
HD9502.U52 C656 1984

University of New Orleans. Institute for the Comparative Study of Public Policy.
Economics and politics of industrial policy . Boulder , 1986. xi, 120 p. ; ISBN 0-8133-7140-6 (pbk. : alk. paper) : LC Card 85-26478 DDC 338.94 19
HD3616.U47 E34 1986
NYPL [JLE 86-4353]

University of New South Wales. Industrial Relations Research Centre. Markey, Ray. The trade union response to technological change in Australia /. Kensington, N.S.W. , 1983. iii, 56 p. ; ***NYPL [JLE 87-904]***

University of North Carolina. see **University of North Carolina at Chapel Hill.**

University of North Carolina at Chapel Hill. Dept. of City and Regional Planning. Bergman, Edward M. Cooperative forms of organization in the taxicab industry [microform] . Washington, D.C. , Springfield, Va. , 1984. 87 p. : ***NYPL [*XME-11,917]***

University of North Carolina (System). Highway Safety Research Center. Campbell, Bob J. Early results of seat belt legislation in the United States of America /. Chapel Hill, N.C. [1986] 25 p. : LC Card 86-622836 DDC 363.1/2572/0973 19
HE5614.2 .C35 1986

University of Nottingham. Dept. of Manuscripts. Miscellaneous lace records / University of Nottingham, Manuscripts Department. [Nottingham] : The Dept., [c1985] 12 p. ; 30 cm. "L/." LC Card 87-116493 DDC 016.3384/7677653/0942527 19
1. Lace industry - England - Nottingham - History - Sources - Bibliography - Catalogs. 2. University of Nottingham. Dept. of Manuscripts - Catalogs. I. Title.
HD9933.G73 N688 1985

UNIVERSITY OF NOTTINGHAM. DEPT. OF MANUSCRIPTS - CATALOGS.
University of Nottingham. Dept. of Manuscripts. Miscellaneous lace records /. [Nottingham] [c1985] 12 p. ; LC Card 87-116493 DDC 016.3384/7677653/0942527 19
HD9933.G73 N688 1985

University of Oregon. Bureau of Governmental Research and Service. Oregon county finances, fiscal 1984. Eugene, OR [1985] 17, [12] p. ; LC Card 86-622281 DDC 336/.014/795 19
HJ9302 .O725 1985

University of Oregon. Bureau of Municipal Research and Service. Population trends, Linn County, Oregon . [Eugene] [1964] 20 leaves : LC Card 85-209473
HA597.L56 P66 1964

University of Pennsylvania. Center for Risk and Decision Processes. Insuring and managing hazardous risks--from Seveso to Bhopal and beyond /. Berlin , New York , c1987. ix, 534 p. : ISBN 0-387-17732-9 (U. S.) LC Card 87-4963 DDC 346.03/8 342.638 19
HG9994 .I57 1987

University of Pennsylvania studies on South Asia, 0169-0361 .
(v. 3) Lambert, Richard D. The transformation of an Indian labor market . Amsterdam , Philadelphia , 1986. ix, 249 p. ; ISBN 0-915027-63-1 (alk. paper) : LC Card 86-26900 DDC 331.11/0954/792 19
HD5820.P78 L36 1986

University of Pretoria. Bureau of Financial Analysis. Ontleding van genoteerde maatskappye JEB industriële afdelingsgemiddeldes . Pretoria , 1984. iv, 163 p. ; ISBN 0-86979-588-0 LC Card 85-156278
HD2922 .O57 1984

University of Queensland Press scholars' library. Logan, William Stewart, 1942- The Gentrification of inner Melbourne . St. Lucia, Qld., Australia ; New York : xxxiii, 328 p. : ISBN 0-7022-1729-8 LC Card 84-17382 DDC 307/.2 19
HD7379.M45 L64 1985
NYPL [JLD 87-798]

University of Rochester. Center for Research in Government Policy and Business. Rasche, Robert H. Controlling the growth of monetary aggregates /. Boston , c1987. xviii, 212 p. : ISBN 0-89838-226-2 : LC Card 87-3737 DDC 332.4/6 19
HG230.3 .R37 1987

University of South Carolina. College of Business Administration. International countertrade /. New York , 1987. xii, 191 p. : ISBN 0-89930-213-0 (lib. bdg. : alk. paper) LC Card 86-25319 DDC 382 19
HF1410.5 .I5716 1987

University of South Dakota. Business Research Bureau. State Data Center. South Dakota county population estimates, 1984 (age by race by sex). Vermillion, S.D. [1986] [25] leaves ; LC Card 87-620702 DDC 304.6/09783/021 19
HA635 .S68 1986

University of Swaziland. Social Science Research Unit. Guma, Xolile P. Small farmer credit and small farmer attitudes towards co-operatives /. [Kwaluseni, Swaziland] [1982] 94 p. : LC Card 86-101161 DDC 332.7/1/096813 19
HD1491.S855 G85 1982
NYPL [JLG 86-262]

University of the Philippines. Interdisciplinary Forum. Synthesis, before and beyond February 1986 . [Philippines] , 1986. xiv, 114 p. : ISBN 971-91058-0-1 (pbk.) LC Card 87-112023 DDC 338.9599 19
HC452 .S96 1986

University of the Philippines. School of Economics. Towards recovery and sustainable growth /. [Quezon] [1985] 71 leaves ; LC Card 86-147888 DDC 338.9599 19
HC453 .T68 1985

University of the West Indies (Mona, Jamaica). Dept. of Economics.
The Debt problem in Jamaica . Mona, Jamaica , c1986. viii, 125 p. : ISBN 976-410-002-3 (pbk.) LC Card 87-403413 DDC 336.3/4/097292 19
HJ8552 .D43 1986

The State in Caribbean society /. Mona, Jamaica , c1986. vii, 157 p. ; ISBN 976-410-001-5 (pbk.) LC Card 87-403404 DDC 330.9729/052 19
HC151 .S73 1986

University of Toronto. Institute for Policy Analysis. Foot, David K. A challenge of the 1980s . [Toronto] , c1981. 99 p. in various pagings : ***NYPL [JLF 86-1304]***

University of Toronto. Institute of Environmental Studies. Mitullah, W. V. Management of urban services in Nairobi . Nairobi, Kenya , 1985. 109, 106, vi p., [6] leaves of plates : LC Card 87-116360 DDC 388.4/09676/25 19
HD4720.5.N35 M57 1985

University of Warwick. Centre for Corporate Strategy and Change. The Management of strategic change /. Oxford [Oxfordshire] , New York, NY , 1988, c1987. p. cm. ISBN 0-631-15695-X : LC Card 87-15634 DDC 658.4/012 19
HD30.28 .M344 1988

University of Wisconsin--Madison. College of Agricultural and Life Sciences. Research Division. Saupe, William E. Rural poverty in Wisconsin counties /. Madison, WI [198-] 26 p. : LC Card 86-622097
HC107.W63 P6249 1980z

University of Wisconsin--Madison. Institute for Research on Poverty. Fighting poverty . Cambridge, Mass. , 1986. viii, 418 p. : ISBN 0-674-30085-8 (alk. paper) LC Card 85-24848 DDC 362.5/8/0973 19
HC110.P63 F54 1986 ***NYPL [JLE 86-4089]***

University of Zambia.
Chilivumbo, Alifeyo. Communal agrarian cooperative societies . Lusaka [1986] iii, 134 p. ; LC Card 86-981399 DDC 334/.683/096894 19
HD1491.Z35 C45 1986

National Workshop on Project Evaluation (1984 : National Institute for Public Administration, Lusaka, Zambia) Collected papers of the National Workshop on Project Evaluation, held at the National Institute for Public Administration, 10-14 December, 1984. [Lusaka] , 1985. 1 v. in various pagings ; LC Card 85-981123 DDC 338.96894/0068 19
HC915.Z9 E446 1984

University of Zambia. Business & Economics Association. A Study into the evolution and performance of the transport sector in Zambia with particular reference to the operations of the ZIMCO group of transport companies /. [Lusaka?] [1980?] 89 p. : LC Card 86-981420
HE284.6 .S78 1980

University of Zambia. Rural Development Studies Bureau. Milimo, J. T. Rural small enterprises in Zambia . [Lusaka] [1985] 71 p. ; LC Card 87-980231 DDC 338.6/42/096894 19
HD2346.Z29 M55 1985

University of Zimbabwe. Dept. of Land Management. Accelerating food production in Sub-Saharan Africa /. Baltimore , c1987. xix, 417 p. ; ISBN 0-8018-3390-6 (alk. paper) LC Card 86-10684 DDC 338.1/9/67 19
HD2117 .A33 1987 ***NYPL [JLE 87-1366]***

University Publications of America, Inc.
International trade [microform] . Frederick, MD , 1987. microfilm reel ISBN 0-89093-551-3

(microfilm) : LC Card 87-6240 DDC 382 19
HF1008

Multinational corporations, OPEC, cartels, foreign investment, and technology transfer [microform] . Frederick, MD , 1987. microfilm reel ISBN 0-89093-552-1 (microfilm) : LC Card 87-6249 DDC 338.8 19
HD2755.5

United States. Women's Bureau. Records of the Women's Bureau of the Department of Labor, 1918-1965 [microform] /. Frederick, MD , 1987- microfilm reel ISBN 0-89093-870-9 (microfilm : pt. 1) : LC Card 87-6239 DDC 331.4/0973 19
HD6095

The War on poverty, 1964-1968 [microform] . Frederick, MD , c1986- microfilm reel ISBN 0-89093-495-9 (microfilm : set) : LC Card 87-10510 DDC 338.973 19
HC110 .P63

University series (Park Ridge, Ill.)
Baehr, Melany E. Experience and background inventory . [Park Ridge, Ill.] (1550 Northwest Highway, Park Ridge 60068) [c1986] 48 p. ; LC Card 87-404267 DDC 658.3/112 19
HF5549.5.S38 B34 1986

Baehr, Melany E. Experience and background questionnaire . [Park Ridge, Ill.] (1550 Northwest Highway, Park Ridge 60068) , c1986. 20 p. ; LC Card 87-404268 DDC 658.3/1125 19
HF5381.7 .B327 1986

El universo del café /. Paz Cárcamo, Guillermo. Heredia [1983] 145 p. ; LC Card 87-400683 DDC 338.1/7373/097286 19
HD9195.C82 P39 1983

Uniwersytet Łódzki. Instytut Ekonometrii i Statystyki. Macromodels and forecasts of national economy . Warszawa , 1986. 284 p. : ISBN 83-01-06464-1 (pbk.) : LC Card 86-226942 DDC 338.947 19
HC244 .M227 1986

UNIX Ada programming /. Gehani, Narain, 1947- Englewood Cliffs, NJ , c1987. xix, 310 p. : ISBN 0-13-938325-5 LC Card 86-22547 DDC 005.4/465 19
QA76.73.A35 G437 1987 ***NYPL [JSE 87-568]***

UNIX and XENIX demystified /. Clukey, Lee Paul. Blue Ridge Summit, Pa. , 1985. xii, 243 p. ; ISBN 0-8306-0874-5 : LC Card 85-2658 DDC 001.64/2 19
QA76.6 .C57 1985 ***NYPL [JSE 86-1905]***

UNIX (COMPUTER OPERATING SYSTEM)
Brown, Constance C., 1952- Preparing documents with UNIX /. Englewood Cliffs, N.J. , c1986. xv, 206 p. : ISBN 0-13-699976-X LC Card 85-17016 DDC 652/.5 19
Z52.5.U54 B76 1986 ***NYPL [JSE 86-1215]***

Clukey, Lee Paul. UNIX and XENIX demystified /. Blue Ridge Summit, Pa. , 1985. xii, 243 p. ; ISBN 0-8306-0874-5 : LC Card 85-2658 DDC 001.64/2 19
QA76.6 .C57 1985 ***NYPL [JSE 86-1905]***

Gehani, Narain, 1947- UNIX Ada programming /. Englewood Cliffs, NJ , c1987. xix, 310 p. : ISBN 0-13-938325-5 LC Card 86-22547 DDC 005.4/465 19
QA76.73.A35 G437 1987 ***NYPL [JSE 87-568]***

Moore, F. Richard. Programming in C with a bit of UNIX /. Englewood Cliffs, NJ , 1985. vii, 193 p. : ISBN 0-13-730102-2 : LC Card 84-26642 DDC 001.64/24 19
QA76.73.C15 M66 1985 ***NYPL [JSE 86-1377]***

Schreiner, Axel T. Introduction to compiler construction with UNIX /. Englewood Cliffs , c1985. viii, 194 p. : ISBN 0-13-474396-2 LC Card 84-63039 ***NYPL [JSF 86-616]***

The unknown Iacocca /. Wyden, Peter. New York , c1987. 416 p. : ISBN 0-688-06616-X LC Card 87-15240 DDC 338.7/6292/0924 B 19
HD9710.U52 I28 1987

Unlawful gain and legitimate profit in Islamic law . Saleh, Nabil A. Cambridge [Cambridgeshire] , New York , 1986. xii, 130 p. ; ISBN 0-521-32298-7 LC Card 85-25547 DDC 297/.14 19
LAW ***NYPL [JLE 86-2377]***

UNLOADING. see **LOADING AND UNLOADING.**

UNMARRIED MOTHERS - GREAT BRITAIN - CASE STUDIES.
Page, Robert M. Stigma /. London , Boston , 1984. xii, 207 p. ; ISBN 0-7100-9786-7 : LC Card 83-24638 DDC 302/.12 19
HM291 .P25 1984 ***NYPL [JLD 86-3113]***

Unmittelbare Versorgungszusage und Direktversicherung als Gestaltungsformen der betrieblichen Altersversorgung /. Haueisen, Peter, 1955- Frankfurt am Main , New York , c1983. xx, 297 p. : ISBN 3-8204-7592-3 LC Card 86-107083 DDC 331.25/2/0943 19
HD7105.35.G3 H38 1983

The unnecessary evil . Bellan, Ruben C., 1918- Toronto, Ont. , c1986. 173 p. : ISBN 0-7710-1153-9 : LC Card 86-222233 DDC 331.13/7971 19
HD5728 .B43 1986

Uno-dos-tres en el mundo de las finanzas. Person, Ron, 1948- [1-2-3 business formula handbook. Spanish.] 1-2-3 en el mundo de las finanzas . Miami, Fla., E.U.A. , 1988. p. cm. ISBN 0-939573-02-4 LC Card 87-20916 DDC 005.36/9 19
HF5548.4.L67 P4718 1988

Uno, Kimio. Japanese industrial performance / Kimio Uno. Amsterdam ; New York : North-Holland ; xix, 439 p. : ill. ; 25 cm. + 1 computer disk (5 1/4 in.) System requirements for computer disk: IBM PC, XT, or AT. Bibliography: p. 417-426. Includes index. ISBN 0-444-70274-1 LC Card 87-15452 DDC 338.0952 19
1. Japan - Industries. 2. Japan - Economic conditions - 1945-. 3. Industrial productivity - Japan. 4. Japan - Foreign economic relations. I. Title.
HC462.9 .U56 1987

The Unofficial economy : consequences and perspectives in different economic systems / edited by Sergio Alessandrini and Bruno Dallago. Aldershot, Hants, England ; Brookfield, Vt., USA : Gower, c1987. 345 p. : ill. ; 23 cm. Includes bibliographies. ISBN 0-566-05131-1 : LC Card 86-25634 DDC 381 19
1. Informal sector (Economics). 2. Comparative economics. I. Alessandrini, Sergio. II. Dallago, Bruno, 1950-.
HD2341 .U56 1987

UNP monograph .
(5) Lamers, Duane E. United Nations definitive & airmail stamps issued & reprinted 1958-1985 /. Chicago, IL, USA (Box 1674, Chicago 60690) , c1985. 52 p. : LC Card 87-146520 DDC 769.56/1 19
HE6246 .L36 1985

Unplugging the plug-in drug /. Winn, Marie. New York, N.Y., U. S.A. , 1987. xviii, 206 p. : ISBN 0-14-008895-4 (pbk.) : LC Card 86-30655 DDC 302.2/345 19
HE8700.65 .W56 1987

The unpublished David Ogilvy /. Ogilvy, David, 1911- New York , c1986. 178 p., [6] p. of plates : ISBN 0-517-56609-5 : LC Card 87-13583 DDC 659.1/092/4 B 19
HF5810.O34 A3 1986

Unser Arbeitsgau 28 (Franken) . Schinnerer, Fritz. Würzburg , Nürnberg , 1935. 454 p. : LC Card 87-409298 DDC 331.3/41173/0943 19
HD4870.G3 S35 1935

Unsere Verantwortung für eine gute Zukunft . Stoltenberg, Gerhard. München , c1986. 191 p. ; ISBN 3-7892-7290-6 LC Card 87-130881 DDC 339.5/2/0943 19
HC286.7 .S767 1986

UNSKILLED LABOR.
Kraft, Kornelius. Wettbewerbssituation und Marktzutrittsbarrieren bei spezifischen Qualifikationen /. Berlin [1985] 35, 6 p. : LC Card 86-211574
HD5707 .K73 1985

Unstable at the top . Kets de Vries, Manfred F. R. New York , 1988, c1987. xiv, 221 p. ; ISBN 0-453-00562-4 LC Card 87-23182 DDC 158.7 19
HD58.7 .K475 1988

Unterdrückung, Hunger, Krieg : die Folgen imperialistischer Politik : Materialien gegen den Weltwirtschaftsgipfel vom 2.-4. Mai in Bonn / [Herausgeber, Göttinger Arbeitskreis gegen Atomenergie, und Anti-Mil Kommission, KB Göttingen]. Göttingen : Der Arbeitskreis, [1985?] 73 p. : ill. ; 30 cm. Cover title. Bibliography: p. 61. LC Card 86-152237
1. Developing countries - Economic conditions - Congresses. 2. Developing countries - Social conditions - Congresses. 3. Developing countries - Dependency on foreign countries - Congresses. 4. Imperialism - Congresses. 5. Germany (West) - Foreign economic relations - Developing countries - Congresses. 6. Developing countries - Foreign economic relations - Germany (West) - Congresses. I. Göttinger Arbeitskreis Gegen Atomenergie. II. KB Göttingen (Germany). Anti-Mil Kommission.
HC59.7 .U55 1985

Das Unternehmen als Grösse der Arbeitswelt : der Arbeiter als Gesellschafter? / herausgegeben für die Internationale Stiftung Humanum von Arthur F. Utz. Bonn : WBV : Scientia Humana Institut, 1984. 291 p. ; 19 cm. (Humanum) Papers presented at a conference sponsored by the Internationale Stiftung Humanum. Bibliography: p. 209-214. Includes index. CONTENTS. - Der Weg des Arbeitnehmers in die Disposition des Kapitals / Arthur F. Utz -- Das Arbeitsverhältnis in der geltenden Rechtsordnung / Theo Mayer-Maly -- Unternehmensverfassung / Peter Hanau -- Unternehmensgebundene Verfügungsrechte im Spannungsfeld zwischen marktwirtschaftlichen Funktionserfordernissen und sozialstaatlichen Bindungen / Alfred Schüller. ISBN 3-923202-02-4 LC Card 85-119845
1. Industrial sociology - Germany (West) - Congresses. 2. Industrial management - Germany (West) - Employee participation - Congresses. I. Utz, Arthur Fridolin, 1908-. II. International Foundation Humanum. III. Series.
HD6957.G3 U58 1984

Unternehmen Braunkohle . Kleinebeckel, Arno. Köln , 1986. 287 p. : ISBN 3-7743-0225-1 LC Card 86-193426
HD9559.L6 G36 1986

Die Unternehmen des Gastgewerbes in Rheinland-Pfalz 1979 : Ergebnisse der Handels- und Gaststättenzählung 1979 / Herausgeber, Statistisches Landesamt Rheinland-Pfalz. Bad Ems : Das Landesamt, [1982] 46 p., [2] p. of plates : ill. ; 30 cm. (Statistik von Rheinland-Pfalz . Bd. 294) Chiefly tables. LC Card 83-207906 DDC 314.3/43 s 338.4/7647/944343021 19
1. Hotels, taverns, etc. - Germany (West) - Rhineland-Palatinate - Statistics. 2. Restaurants, lunch rooms, etc. - Germany (West) - Rhineland-Palatinate - Statistics. I. Statistisches Landesamt Rheinland-Pfalz. II. Series.
HA1320 .R453 Bd. 294 TX910.G4

Unternehmensanalyse . Lehner, Susanna Walpurga. Wien , c1984. 243 p. : ISBN 3-85428-023-8 : LC Card 84-173011
HG3751.5 .L44 1984

Unternehmenserfolg . Plaschka, Gerhard. Wien , c1986. viii, 228 p. ; LC Card 87-103428 DDC 658.4/09 19
HD38.2 .P55 1986

Unternehmensführung und Logistik / Schriftleitung, Horst Albach und Hans-Christian Pfohl. Wiesbaden : Gabler, c1984. 151 p. : ill. ; 24 cm. (ZfB-Ergänzungsheft . 2/84) Summaries in English and German. Includes bibliographies. CONTENTS. - Die Bedeutung der betriebswirtschaftlichen Logistik für die Unternehmensführung / Udo Schulten und Klaus Blümel -- Rationalisierungsreserven im Umlaufvermögen / Dietmar Meyersiek, Michael Perraudin und Michael Roever -- Zentralisationsgrad der Materialbeschaffung und Bestellpolitik / Joachim Reese -- Logistik-Controlling / Hans-Christian Pfohl und Heinz Hoffmann -- Materialflussorientierte Logistik / Horst Wildemann -- Bestandscontrolling aus der Sicht der Unternehmensleitung / Alfred F. Kellermann -- Bestandscontrolling in der Praxis / Klaus Nührich -- Modell- und computergestützte Gestaltung physischer Distributionssysteme / Günther Diruf -- Verbesserung der Zusammenarbeit an Logistikschnittstellen zwischen Verlader und Spediteur / Uwe Nitzinger. ISBN 3-409-13038-1 LC Card 85-126091
1. Industrial management. 2. Business logistics. I. Albach, Horst. II. Pfohl, Hans-Christian. III. Series: ZfB-Ergänzungsheft , 84/2.
HD28 .Z46 nr. 84/2 HD30.28

Unternehmenskonzentration, Marktmacht und Lohnniveau . Feldmann, Berthold. Göttingen , c1984. xii, 260 p. : ISBN 3-525-12269-1 LC Card 85-162393
HD2746.5 .F45 1984

Unternehmensökonomie . Braun, Wolfram. Wiesbaden , c1985. 246 p. : ISBN 3-409-13316-X LC Card 85-239244 DDC 330.15/5 19
HB98.2 .B74 1985

Unternehmensstrategien und technischer Fortschritt . Wengenroth, Ulrich. Göttingen , c1986. 316 p. : ISBN 3-525-36302-8 LC Card 87-112794 DDC 338.4/7669142/0943 19
HD9523.5 .W43 1986

Unternehmensstrategien und technischer Fortschritt . Wengenroth, Ulrich. Göttingen , c1986. 316 p. : ISBN 3-525-36302-8
NYPL [JLE 87-917]

Unternehmenstheorie als Entscheidungshilfe /. Koch, Helmut, 1919- Wiesbaden , c1987. 199 p. : ISBN 3-409-13908-7 LC Card 87-143813 DDC 658.4/2 19
HB615 .K63 1987

Unternehmensverbände in der EG, ihre nationale und transnationale Organisation und Politik . Platzer, Hans-Wolfgang. Kehl am Rhein , 1984. xi, 283 p. ; ISBN 3-88357-024-9 LC Card 85-131940
HD6948.G3 P58 1984

Der Unternehmer /. Wittmann, Waldemar. Stuttgart , 1986. 27 p. ; ISBN 3-515-04666-6 : LC Card 87-136715 DDC 338/.04 19
HB615 .W58 1986

Unternehmer und Politik in der Bundesrepublik /. Berghahn, Volker Rolf. Frankfurt am Main , 1985. 363 p. : ISBN 3-518-11265-1 LC Card 85-235608
HC286.5 .B37 1985

Die Unternehmerlücke /. Hamer, Eberhard. Stuttgart , 1984. 238 p. ; ISBN 3-87959-223-3 LC Card 85-128353
HB615 .H235 1984

Unternehmung und Steuer : Festschrift zur Vollendung des 80. Lebensjahres von Peter Scherpf / herausgegeben von Lutz Fischer ; mit Beiträgen von Kuno Barth ... [et al.]. Wiesbaden : Gabler, c1983. 395 p. ; 25 cm. Includes bibliographical references. ISBN 3-409-50005-7 LC Card 83-161883
1. Business enterprises - Taxation - Germany, West. 2. Tax accounting - Germany, West. 3. Taxation - Germany, West. 4. International finance. 5. Scherpf, Peter, 1903-. I. Scherpf, Peter, 1903-. II. Fischer, Lutz. III. Barth, Kuno.
HD2753.G3 U57 1983

Unternehmung und Unternehmungsführung. (9) Lattmann, Charles. Die verhaltenswissenschaftlichen Grundlagen der Führung des Mitarbeiters /. Bern , c1981. 565 p. : ISBN 3-258-03094-4 : LC Card 82-163528 DDC 658.3 19
HD58.7 .L36 1981 NYPL [JLE 86-1595]

Unternehmungsbewertung von Kreditinstituten /. Zessin, Axel, 1953- Göttingen , 1982. 296 p. : ISBN 3-509-01313-1 LC Card 84-109138
HG4028.V3 Z47 1982

Unternehmungsführung und Mitbestimmung /. Hentze, Joachim. Würzburg , 1985. 297 p. : ISBN 3-7908-0268-9 LC Card 85-186054
HD5660.G4 H43 1985

Unterschiede in der Beschäftigungsentwicklung zwischen den USA, Japan und der EG . Wohlers, Eckhardt. Hamburg , 1986. 294 p. : ISBN 3-87895-307-0 LC Card 86-233505
HD5724 .W57 1986

Untersuchung der Unfälle auf Bundesautobahnen : Verkehr und Unfälle auf den Autobahnen im gesamten Bundesgebiet, 1969-1976 : Detailuntersuchung der Bundesautobahn-Unfälle in den Ländern Bayern, Hessen und Nordrhein-Westfalen, 1975/76 / bearbeitet von ADAC-Zentrale, Abteilung Verkehrstechnik, Ulrich Heuber ... [et al.]. [München?] : ADAC : Auto Motor und Sport, [1976] 84 p. : ill. ; 30 cm. (Verkehrsunfälle . 4) LC Card 85-135444
1. Traffic accidents - Germany (West) - Bavaria. 2. Traffic accidents - Germany (West) - Hesse. 3. Traffic accidents - Germany (West) - North Rhine-Westphalia. I. Heuber, Ulrich. II. ADAC. Abteilung Verkehrstechnik. III. Series.
HE5614.5.G3 U58 1976

Untersuchung der Vorfahrtregelung "Rechts vor Links" unter dem Aspekt der Verkehrssicherheit /. Kockelke, Wilhelm. Bergisch Gladbach [1983] 63, 3 p. : LC Card 84-147884
HE363.G32 U744 1983

Die Untersuchung des Wohnwertes von Wohngebieten /. Grasberger, Helmut, 1941- Wien , New York , 1983. 108 p., [15] folded leaves of plates : ISBN 0-387-81752-2 (U. S.) LC Card 84-142695
HD7337.A3 G73 1983

Untersuchungen des Ludwig-Uhland-Instituts der Universität Tübingen .
(66. Bd) Beyrer, Klaus. Die Postkutschenreise /. Tübingen , 1985. 284 p. : ISBN 3-925340-35-1 LC Card 86-198761
HE6995 .B49 1985

Untersuchungen über das Spar-, Giro- und Kreditwesen. Abteilung B: Rechtswissenschaft.
(Bd. 41) Schubäus, Klaus. Das Hypothekenbankgeschäft in den Niederlanden und in der Bundesrepublik Deutschland /. Berlin , c1984. 251 p. : ISBN 3-428-05569-1 LC Card 84-250906
HG2040.5.N37 S38 1984

Untersuchungen (Universität zu Köln. Institut für Wirtschaftspolitik) .
(41) Panek, Hans-Thomas. Die Währungskrisen vom November 1968 bis Mai 1971 im politischen Prozess der Bundesrepublik Deutschland /. Köln , 1977. 293 p. ; ISBN 3-921471-29-X LC Card 86-184843
HG999.5 .P35 1977

(55) Klemm, Günther. Ökonomische Analyse von Streik und Aussperrung im Rahmen einer marktwirtschaftlichen Ordnung /. Köln , 1983. viii, 214 p. : ISBN 3-921471-43-5 : LC Card 83-216635 DDC 331.89/2 19
HD5306 .K55 1983

Untersuchungen zu Handel und Verkehr der vor- und frühgeschichtlichen Zeit in Mittel- und Nordeuropa .
(T. 3) Der Handel des frühen Mittelalters . Göttingen , 1985. 510 p. : ISBN 3-525-82433-5 (Deut. Bibl.) LC Card 86-209040
HF3495 .U57 1985 t. 3

Untersuchungen zum Profit beim hansischen Handelskapital in der ersten Hälfte des 15. Jahrhunderts /. Stark, Walter. Weimar , 1985. 147 p. ; LC Card 86-148303
HF458 .S73 1985

Untersuchungen zur Verbesserung der betrieblichen Arbeitssituation unter Verwendung der Akzeptanz im Rahmen von Arbeitsanalyse und Arbeitsentwicklung /. Pankow, Michael. Hamburg , c1986. 1 v. (various pagings) ; ISBN 3-925630-13-9 LC Card 87-146606 DDC 658.3/14 19
HF5549.5.J63 P345 1986

Untersuchungen zur Wirtschaftspolitik, 0175-7458 .
(62) Killat, Gerhard. Kommunalisierung der Wohnungspolitik? . Köln , 1984. xiii, 291 p. : ISBN 3-921471-50-8 : LC Card 85-137757
HD7339.A3 K49 1984

(64) Hasse, Rolf. Ökonometrie als Instrument der Interessenpolitik . Köln , 1985. ii, 109 p. : ISBN 3-921471-52-4 : LC Card 85-216061
HF1733.D44 H37 1985

(67) Aeberhardt, Werner. Die Umweltpolitik im Spannungsfeld politischer und wirtschaftlicher Interessen /. Köln , 1985. 134, [9] p. : ISBN 3-921471-55-9 : LC Card 86-145456
HC400.E5 A33 1985

(69) Zimmermann, Heinz, 1958- Kapitalerhöhungen und Aktienmarkt . Köln , 1986. 446 p. : ISBN 3-921471-57-5 LC Card 87-407823 DDC 332.63/222/09494 19
HG5653 .Z56 1986

(70) Kotios, Angelos, 1957- Die neuere Diskussion über den Zusammenhang von Wechselkursflexibilität und Inflation /. Köln , 1986. 384 p. ; ISBN 3-921471-58-3 LC Card 87-407838 DDC 332.4/5 19
HG3821 .K67 1986

Untiet, Charles J. Competition in the oil pipeline industry : a preliminary report. [Washington, D.C.] : Antitrust Division, Dept. of Justice, [1984] iii leaves, 73, [332] p., [10] p. of plates : ill., maps ; 28 cm. "May 1984." Includes bibliographical references. LC Card 84-602723 DDC 388.5 19
1. Petroleum pipeline industry - United States. 2. Competition - United States. I. Title.
HD9580.U5 U58 1984 NYPL [JLF 85-864]

UNTOUCHABLES - ECONOMIC CONDITIONS.
Parvathamma, C., 1928- Scheduled castes and tribes . New Delhi , 1984. xiii, 310 p. ;
NYPL [JLD 87-707]

Punjab (India). Economic and Statistical Organisation. Report on the evaluation study of working of the Punjab Scheduled Castes Land Development and Finance Corporation. Chandigarh [pref. 1978] viii, 98 p. ; LC Card 79-903307
HC437.P8 P85 1978a

UNTOUCHABLES - INDIA - PRADESH.
Prasad, R. R., 1955- Change and continuity among the scheduled caste leather workers /. Hyderabad , 1986. 132 p., [4] leaves of plates : LC Card 87-902216
HD8039.L42 I575 1986

UNTOUCHABLES - SOCIAL CONDITIONS.
Parvathamma, C., 1928- Scheduled castes and tribes . New Delhi , 1984. xiii, 310 p. ;
NYPL [JLD 87-707]

Unweltpolitik / [Beirat für Wirtschafts- und Sozialfragen]. Wien : Der Beirat ; Korneuburg : Hersteller und Kommissionsverlag, C. Ueberreuter, 1986. 277 p. : ill. ; 24 cm. Includes bibliographies. LC Card 86-191881
1. Environmental policy. 2. Environmental protection. I. Beirat für Wirtschafts- und Sozialfragen.
HC79.E5 U57 1986

Unweltthemen in der öffentlichen Diskussion /. Schmidt, Peter M. Konstanz , 1985. ix, 296 p. : ISBN 3-89191-001-0 LC Card 86-155948
HC290.5.E5 S37 1985

Unwin, K. I. Clark, David, Ph. D. Information services in rural areas . Norwich [Norfolk] , c1980. x, 122 p. : ISBN 0-86094-058-6 (pbk.) LC Card 81-149488
HE8109.L55 C55 1980

Unyon! /. Del Rosario, Rody. Malate, Manila [1985] 65 p. : LC Card 85-184386
HD6828 .D45 1985

Uoll-strit protiv Afriki /. Ozadovskiĭ, A. A. (Andreĭ Andreevich) Kiev , 1985. 228, [4] p. ; LC Card 86-219442
HF1611.Z4 U556 1985

Uomini, collina e vigneto in Piemonte, da metà Ottocento agli anni trenta /. Rapetti, Vittorio, 1955- Alessandria , 1984. 342 p., [16] p. of plates : LC Card 86-151345
HD9385.I82 P547 1984

Uomini da soma . Soldini, Bruno, 1939- [Lugano] , c1985. 289 p. : LC Card 86-136358
HJ6947 .S65 1985

Up and running! . Popyk, Marilyn K., 1945- Reading, Mass. , c1987. xxv, 647, [28] p. : ISBN 0-201-06274-7 (pbk.) : LC Card 86-26620 DDC 650/.028/5536 19
HF5548.2 .P614 1987

Up and running in real estate sales /. Thompson, Pauline J. Santa Barbara, Calif. , c1987. vi, 202 p. : ISBN 0-918785-02-2 (pbk.) : LC Card 87-16916 DDC 333.33 19
HD255 .T49 1987

Up the down escalator . Manley, Michael, 1924- Washington, D.C , 1987. xv, 332 p. ; ISBN 0-88258-112-0 : LC Card 87-3872 DDC 338.97292 19
HC154 .M34 1987

Up the ladder . Friedman, Thomas. New York, NY , 1986. xi, 203 p. ; ISBN 0-446-51291-5 LC Card 85-40655 DDC 658.4/09/0973 19
HD38.25.U6 F75 1986 NYPL [JLE 86-2840]

Up your cash flow . Goldstein, Harvey A. (Harvey Arthur), 1939- Los Angeles, Calif. , c1986. 174 p. : ISBN 0-931349-04-4 (pbk.) LC Card 86-213003 DDC 658.1/592 19
HD62.7 .G68 1986

Up your own organizaion! . Dible, Donald M.

Reston, Va. , c1986. xx, 423 p. ; ISBN 0-8359-8086-3 (pbk.) : LC Card 85-8293 DDC 658/.022 19
*HD62.7 .D53 1986 NYPL [*R-Econ. 86-288]*

Upadhyay, Kiran Dutta. Handicrafts development in Nepal : past efforts and future possibilities / Kiran Dutta Upadhyay, Shiva Prasad Sharma.1st ed. Kathmandu, Nepal : K. Bhattarai and M. Sharma, 1985. ii, 126, [14] p. ; 29 cm. Bibliography: p. [127]-[131] LC Card 86-902589 DDC 338.4/77455/095496 19
1. Handicraft - Economic aspects - Nepal. I. Sharma, Shiva Prashad. II. Title.
HD2346.N36 U63 1985

Upadhyaya, Kamal Prasad. External debt and debt servicing in Nepal / Kamal Prasad Upadhyaya. Kathmandu : Centre for Economic Development and Administration, Tribhuvan University, Kirtipur, 1985. ii, 67, [1] p. ; 29 cm. "June 1985." Bibliography: p. [68] LC Card 86-902874 DDC 336.3/4/095496 19
1. Debts, External - Nepal. I. Title.
HJ8777.9 .U62 1985

Upadhyaya, Murari Prasad. Malla, B. C. An evaluation of development activities within Sixth Plan period in Bajhang District /. Kathmandu , 1985 [i.e. 1986] 76, [3] p. : LC Card 86-903487 DDC 338.9549/6 19
HC425.Z7 B355 1986

Upadhyaya, P. K. (Pratap Krishna), 1916- Distribution and consumption of diesel oil in agriculture / P.K. Upadhyaya ; assistance in project, P. Subrahmanyam ; assistance in field investigation, Rajesh and Rameshwar, M.V. Nadkarni. Delhi, India : Mittal Publications, 1985. xii, 150 p. : maps ; 22 cm. Bibliography: p. [149]-150. Includes index. LC Card 86-902439 DDC 333.79 19
1. Diesel fuels - India. 2. Agricultural machinery - India - Fuel consumption. I. Title.
HD9579.D53 I68 1985

Update series C229 . (no. 14) Goreham, Gary. South Dakotans on the move . Brookings, S.D. [1984] 24 p. : LC Card 85-620511 DDC 304.8/09783/021 19
HB1985.S8 G67 1984

Update the transportation problem /. Nakhla, Afaf Fouad. Cairo [1985- v. <1 > ; LC Card 87-401510 DDC 361.6/0962 s 380.5/24 19
HD82 .C23 no. 1415 HE199.A2

Updated load forecast of energy and peak demand on the Delmarva Peninsula /. Estomin, Steven. Bethesda, Md. (4550 Montgomery Ave., Bethesda 20814) [1986] iv, 4, 53, [18] p. : LC Card 87-620907 DDC 333.79/3212/097521 19
HD9685.U6 A123 1986

Uphoff, Norman Thomas. Local institutional development : an analytical sourcebook with cases / Norman Uphoff for the Rural Development Committee, Cornell University. West Hartford, CT : Kumarian Press, c1986. xv, 421 p. ; 24 cm. (Kumarian Press library of management for development) Includes indexes. Bibliography: p. [367]-407. ISBN 0-931816-45-9 LC Card 86-15288 DDC 302.3/5 19
1. Rural development - Developing countries. 2. Agricultural development projects - Developing countries. 3. Natural resources - Developing countries - Management. 4. Medical care - Developing countries. 5. Developing countries - Economic conditions. I. Cornell University. Rural Development Committee. II. Title. III. Series.
HC59.7 .U64 1986 NYPL [JLE 87-1200]

UPPER CLASSES - ENGLAND - HISTORY. Dawes, Frank Victor. Not in front of the servants . London , 1984. 178 p., [16] p. of plates : ISBN 0-09-155291-5 (pbk.) : LC Card 84-195925 DDC 640/.46/0942 19
HD8039.D52 G718 1984
NYPL [JLD 86-1944]

UPPER CLYDE SHIPBUILDERS - EMPLOYEES. Foster, John. The politics of the UCS work-in . London , Atlantic Highlands, N.J. , 1986. 446 p. : ISBN 0-85315-663-8 (pbk.) : LC Card 86-235159 DDC 331.89/282383/094141 19
HD5365.S512 1971 .C584 1986

Uppföljning av oljeersättningsprogrammet . Sweden. Oljeersättningsdelegationen. [Stockholm] [1982] 83, [74] p. : ISBN 91-38-07111-8 LC Card 83-217864
HD9502.S82 S96 1982

Uppsala. Universitet. Nordiska Afrikainstitutet. see **Nordiska Afrikainstitutet.**

Uppsala. Universitet. Scandinavian Institute of African Studies. see **Nordiska Afrikainstitutet.**

Upravlencheskie novovvedenii͡a v SShA : problema vnedrenii͡a / otvetstvennyĭ redaktor I͡U.A. Ushanov ; [avtorskiĭ kollektiv V.P. Averchev ... et al.]. Moskva : "Nauka", 1986. 244, [3] p. : ill. ; 22 cm. At head of title: Akademii͡a nauk SSSR. Institut SShA i Kanady. Bibliography: p. 235-[245] LC Card 85-231514
1. Management - United States. I. Ushanov, I͡Uriĭ Aleksandrovich. II. Averchev, V. P. III. Institut Soedinennykh Shtatov Ameriki i Kanady (Akademii͡a nauk SSSR).
HD70.U5 U67 1986

Upravlenie agropromyshlennymi ob˝edinenii͡ami v usloviiakh integrirovannoĭ ėkonomiki /. Kulish, N. E. (Nikolaĭ Efimovich) Kiev , 1985. 174 p. : LC Card 87-104750
HD9015.S653 U4425 1985
*NYPL [*QIP 87-4125]*

Upravlenie ėffektivnost´i͡u proizvodstva / [avtory V.A. Podsolonko ... et al.]. Kiev : Nauk. dumka, 1985. 125 p. : ill. ; 20 cm. At head of title: Akademii͡a nauk Ukrainskoĭ SSR. Dnepropetrovskoe otdelenie Instituta ėkonomiki promyshlennosti. Bibliography: p. 123-[124] LC Card 85-181580
1. Industrial management - Ukraine - Decision making. I. Podsolonko, Vladimir Andreevich. II. Instytut ekonomiky promyslovosti (Akademii͡a nauk Ukraïns´koï RSR). Dnipropetrovs´kyĭ viddil.
HD30.23 .U67 1985

Upravlenie, marketing, uslugi /. Uzunova, I͡Ulii͡a. Varna , 1986. 143 p. : LC Card 86-152606
HF5415 .U98 1986

Upravlenie mezhdunarodnoĭ spet͡sializat͡sieĭ proizvodstva stran SĖV /. Leznik, A. D. (Aleksandr Davidovich) Moskva , 1982. 143 p. ; LC Card 83-123508
HC244 .L466 1982

Upravlenie na narodnoto potreblenie / Atanas Li͡utov ... [et al.]. Sofii͡a : Izd-vo na Bŭlgarskata akademii͡a na naukite, 1984. 235 p. : ill. ; 21 cm. Titles on added t.p.: Management of national consumption; Upravlenie narodnym potrebleniem. At head of title: Bŭlgarska akademii͡a na naukite. Ikonomicheski institut. Errata slip inserted. Summary in English and Russian. Includes bibliographical references. LC Card 85-212359
1. Consumption (Economics) - Bulgaria. I. Li͡utov, Atanas N. II. Ikonomicheski institut (Bŭlgarska akademii͡a na naukite). III. Title: Management of national consumption. IV. Title: Upravlenie narodnym potrebleniem.
HC403.Z9 C628 1984

Upravlenie narodnym potrebleniem. Upravlenie na narodnoto potreblenie /. Sofii͡a , 1984. 235 p. : LC Card 85-212359
HC403.Z9 C628 1984

Upravlenie nauchno-tekhnicheskim progressom na predprii͡atii / otvetstvennye redaktory A.G. Aganbegi͡an, V.D. Rechin. Novosibirsk : Izd-vo "Nauka," Sibirskoe otd-nie, 1986. 222 p. ; 23 cm. At head of title: Akademii͡a nauk SSSR. Sibirskoe otdelenie. Institut ėkonomiki i organizat͡sii promyshlennogo proizvodstva. Includes bibliographies. LC Card 87-124400
1. Technological innovations - Soviet Union - Management. I. Aganbegi͡an, Abel Gezevich. II. Rechin, V. D. III. Institut ėkonomiki i organizat͡sii promyshlennogo proizvodstva (Akademii͡a nauk SSSR).
HD45 .U52 1986

Upravlenie nauchno-tekhnicheskim progressom v soi͡uznykh respublikakh / [otvetstvennye redaktory A.A. Këërna, N.G. Chumachenko]. Tallin : "Valgus", 1986. 158 p. ; 20 cm. At head of title: Akademii͡a nauk SSSR. Nauchnyĭ sovet po ėkonomicheskim problemam nauchno-tekhnicheskoĭ revoli͡ut͡sii. Problemnai͡a komissii͡a territorial´nogo upravlenii͡a nauchno-tekhnicheskim progressom. Akademii͡a nauk ĖSSR. Institut ėkonomiki. Includes bibliographical references. LC Card 87-123175
1. Technological innovations - Economic aspects - Soviet Union - Republics - Congresses. 2. Research, Industrial - Soviet Union - Republics - Congresses. I. Kõõrna, A. II. Chumachenko, Nikolaĭ Grigor´evich. III. Nauchnyĭ sovet AN SSSR po ėkonomicheskim problemam nauchno-tekhnicheskoĭ revoli͡ut͡sii. IV. Akademii͡a nauk SSSR. Problemnai͡a komissii͡a territorial´nogo upravlenii͡a nauchno-tekhnicheskim progressom. V. Majanduse Instituut (Eesti NSV Teaduste Akadeemia).
HC340.T4 U77 1986

Upravlenie prot͡sessom novovvedeniĭ. Upravlenie prot͡sessom novovvedeniĭ v kapitalisticheskoĭ firme /. Moskva , 1985. 228 p. : LC Card 86-151912
HD58.8 .U67 1985

Upravlenie prot͡sessom novovvedeniĭ v kapitalisticheskoĭ firme / [avtorskiĭ kollektiv, Sterlin A.P. ... et al. ; nauchnyĭ rukovoditel´ kollektiva i otvetstvennyĭ redaktor, Klimov N.A.]. Moskva : [IMĖMO AN SSSR], 1985. 228 p. : ill. ; 20 cm. Title on cover: Upravlenie prot͡sessom novovvedeniĭ. At head of title: Akademii͡a nauk SSSR. Ordena Trudovogo Krasnogo Znameni Institut mirovoĭ ėkonomiki i mezhdunarodnykh otnosheniĭ. Includes bibliographical references. LC Card 86-151912
1. Organizational change. 2. Business enterprises. 3. Industrial management. 4. Technological innovations. 5. Capitalism. I. Klimov, N. A. (Nikolaĭ Andreevich). II. Institut mirovoĭ ėkonomiki i mezhdunarodnykh otnosheniĭ (Akademii͡a nauk SSSR). III. Title: Upravlenie prot͡sessom novovvedeniĭ.
HD58.8 .U67 1985

Upravlenie sel´skogo khozi͡aĭstva Krasnoi͡arskogo kraĭispolkoma. Sistema vedenii͡a sel´skogo i promyslovogo khozi͡aĭstva na Eniseĭskom Severe . Novosibirsk , 1986. 211 p. ; LC Card 86-227282
HD1995.K73 S57 1986

Upravlenie sot͡sialisticheskoĭ torgovleĭ . Bel´chikov, I͡A. M. Riga , 1978. 170, [2] p. ; LC Card 82-106625
HF2546.5 .B44 1978

Upravlenie sot͡sial´nymi prot͡sessami v trudovykh kollektivakh / otvetstvennyĭ redaktor A.I. Timush. Kishinev : "Shtiint͡sa", 1983. 141 p. : ill. ; 22 cm. At head of title: Akademii͡a nauk Moldavskoĭ SSSR. Otdel filosofii i prava. Moldavskoe otdelenie Sovetskoĭ sot͡siologicheskoĭ assot͡siat͡sii Akademii nauk SSSR. Includes bibliographical references. LC Card 84-133794
1. Industrial sociology - Soviet Union. 2. Personnel management - Soviet Union. I. Timush, Andreĭ Ivanovich. II. Akademii͡a de Shtiint͡se a RSSM. Sekt͡sii͡a de Filozofie shi Drept. III. Sovetskai͡a sot͡siologicheskai͡a assot͡siat͡sii͡a. Moldavskoe otdelenie.
HD6957.S65 U67 1983

Upravlenie trudom v uslovii͡akh nauchno-tekhnicheskogo progressa /. Nemt͡sev, F. L. (Fedor Logvinovich) Minsk , 1985. 125 p. ; LC Card 85-231066
HF5549.2.S65 N45 1985

Upravlenie trudovymi resursami : territorial´no-otraslevoĭ aspekt / [avtory A.I. Frydynskiĭ ... et al. ; otvetstvennyĭ redaktor A.N. Zolotarev]. Kiev : Nauk. dumka, 1986. 238 p. ; 21 cm. At head of title: Akademii͡a nauk Ukrainskoĭ SSR. Khar´kovskoe otdelenie Instituta ėkonomiki. Bibliography: p. 231-[237] LC Card 86-233715
1. Manpower policy - Ukraine. 2. Labor supply - Ukraine. I. Frydynskiĭ, A. I. (Aleksandr Ignat´evich). II. Zolotarev, Anatoliĭ Nikolaevich. III. Instytut ekonomiky (Akademii͡a nauk Ukraïns´koï RSR). Kharkivs´ke viddilenni͡a.
HD5797.U37 U67 1986

Upravlenie v sisteme proizvodstvennykh otnosheniĭ / [redaktsionnai͡a kollegii͡a P.P. Luzan (otv. redaktor), V.G. Istomin, I.A. Revinskiĭ]. Novosibirsk : Pedinstitut, 1974. 82 p. ; 20 cm. (Nauchnye trudy. vyp. 100) At head of title: Ministerstvo prosveshchenii͡a RSFSR. Novosibirskiĭ gosudarstvennyĭ pedagogicheskiĭ institut. Includes bibliographical references. LC Card 83-120398
1. Industrial management - Soviet Union. I. Luzan, P. P. II. Istomin, V. G. III. Revinskiĭ, I. A. IV. Novosibirskiĭ gosudarstvennyĭ pedagogicheskiĭ institut. V. Series: Nauchnye trudy / Novosibirskiĭ gosudarstvennyĭ pedagogicheskiĭ institut , vyp. 100.
HD70.S63 U68 1974

Ural i problemy regional´noĭ istoriografii. Period kapitalizma : informat͡sionnye materialy / Sverdlovsk : UNT͡S AN SSSR, 1986. 83 p. ; 20 cm. At head of title: Akademii͡a nauk SSSR. Ural´skiĭ nauchnyĭ t͡sentr. Institut ėkonomiki. Includes bibliographical references. LC Card 87-159699

1. Ural Mountains Region (R.S.F.S.R.) - Industries - Historiography. 2. Ural Mountains Region (R.S.F.S.R.) - Social conditions - Historiography. 3. Capitalism - Russian S.F.S.R. - Ural Mountains Region - Historiography. I. Gavrilov, D. V. (Dmitriĭ Vasil'evich). II. Allaiarova, Vera Stepanovna. III. Ol'khovaia, L. V. IV. Institut ėkonomiki (Akademiia nauk SSSR. Ural'skiĭ nauchnyĭ tsentr).
HC337.R852 U73853 1986

URAL MOUNTAINS REGION (R.S.F.S.R.) - ECONOMIC CONDITIONS.
Ėkonomicheskie problemy osvoeniia Ural'skogo Severa /. Sverdlovsk , 1982. 69 p. : LC Card 83-188353
HC336.9.N65 E37 1982

Popov, V. (Vladimir) Razvitie promyshlennosti Urala na zavershaiushchem ėtape sozdaniia razvitogo sotsializma, 1951-1961 gg. . Perm' , 1984. 70 p. ; LC Card 87-151346
HC337.R852 U73577 1984

Tolmachev, V. P. (Vladimir Petrovich) Ėkonomika Urala, Sibiri i Dal'nego vostoka v odinnadtsatoĭ piatiletke /. Moskva , 1981. 39 p. ; LC Card 82-153584
HC337.R852 U7382 1981

URAL MOUNTAINS REGION (R.S.F.S.R.) - ECONOMIC POLICY.
Deiatel'nost' partiĭnykh organizatsiĭ po razvitiiu promyshlennosti Urala v period razvitogo sotsializma . Perm' , 1984. 96 p. ; LC Card 86-181271
HC337.R852 U734 1984

URAL MOUNTAINS REGION (R.S.F.S.R.) - INDUSTRIES.
De-Gennin, Vil'gel'm, 1676-1750. [Opisanie ural'skikh i sibirskikh zavodov 1735. English.] Description of Ural and Siberian factories in 1735 /. [Washington, D.C.] , 1987. p. cm. LC Card 87-600052 DDC 338.0947/87 19
HC337.R852 U733613 1987

Deiatel'nost' partiĭnykh organizatsiĭ po razvitiiu promyshlennosti Urala v period razvitogo sotsializma . Perm' , 1984. 96 p. ; LC Card 86-181271
HC337.R852 U734 1984

URAL MOUNTAINS REGION (R.S.F.S.R.) - INDUSTRIES - ENVIRONMENTAL ASPECTS.
Aktual'nye problemy prirodopol'zovaniia v promyshlennom regione /. Sverdlovsk , 1985. 151 p. : LC Card 86-126638
HC337.R852 U732 1985

URAL MOUNTAINS REGION (R.S.F.S.R.) - INDUSTRIES - HISTORIES - 20TH CENTURY.
Popov, V. (Vladimir) Razvitie promyshlennosti Urala na zavershaiushchem ėtape sozdaniia razvitogo sotsializma, 1951-1961 gg. . Perm' , 1984. 70 p. ; LC Card 87-151346
HC337.R852 U73577 1984

URAL MOUNTAINS REGION (R.S.F.S.R.) - INDUSTRIES - HISTORIOGRAPHY.
Ural i problemy regional'noĭ istoriografii. Sverdlovsk , 1986. 83 p. ; LC Card 87-159699
HC337.R852 U73853 1986

URAL MOUNTAINS REGION (R.S.F.S.R.) - INDUSTRIES - HISTORY.
Formirovanie i razvitie rabochego klassa i promyshlennosti Urala v period stroitel'stva sotsializma, 1917-1937 . Sverdlovsk , 1982. 138 p. ; LC Card 84-211723
HD8529.U7 F67 1982

Vasil'ev, A. F. (Aleksandr Filippovich) Promyshlennost' Urala v gody Velikoĭ Otechestvennoĭ voĭny 1941-1945 /. Moskva , 1982. 279 p., [1] folded leaf of plates : LC Card 83-165021
HC337.R852 U7387 1982

URAL MOUNTAINS REGION (R.S.F.S.R.) - INDUSTRIES - MATHEMATICAL MODELS.
Matematicheskie metody v prilozhenii k resheniiu ėkonomicheskikh zadach /. Sverdlovsk , 1985. 116 p. : LC Card 86-135187
HC337.R852 U7355 1985

URAL MOUNTAINS REGION (R.S.F.S.R.) - SOCIAL CONDITIONS - HISTORIOGRAPHY.
Ural i problemy regional'noĭ istoriografii. Sverdlovsk , 1986. 83 p. ; LC Card 87-159699
HC337.R852 U73853 1986

Uranija, Valentin. 35 godina sindikata u Zadru : u povodu 40-godišnjice ustanka i socijalističke revolucije naroda i narodnosti SFR Jugoslavije, 35 godina Saveza sindikata Jugoslavije i 30 godina radničkog samoupravljanja u SFRJ / [tekst priredio Valentin Uranija]. Zadar : Općinsko sindikalno vijeće Zadar, 1981. 300 p., xlviii p. of plates : ill. ; 24 cm. In Serbo-Croatian (roman) Summary in English. Bibliography: p. 292. Includes index. LC Card 86-190260
1. Savez sindikata općine Zadar - History. 2. Trade-unions - Yugoslavia - Zadar (Croatia) - History. 3. Works councils - Yugoslavia - Zadar (Croatia) - History. I. Savez sindikata općine Zadar. Općinsko sindikalno vijeće. II. Title.
HD8632.S3433 U73 1981

URANIUM INDUSTRY - ENVIRONMENTAL ASPECTS - AUSTRALIA - BROKEN HILL (N.S.W.)
Honeymoon uranium mine occupation [sound recording]. Los Angeles, Calif. , p1983. 1 sound cassette (53 min.) : LC Card 87-752867
HD9539.U72

URANIUM INDUSTRY - FORECASTING.
The Uranium market, 1986-2000 /. London , c1986. xii, 123 p. : LC Card 87-162222 DDC 338.2/74932/021 19
HD9539.U7 U73 1986

URANIUM INDUSTRY - POLITICAL ASPECTS - HISTORY.
Helmreich, Jonathan E. Gathering rare ores . Princeton, N.J. , c1986. xiv, 303 p. : ISBN 0-691-04738-3 (alk. paper) : LC Card 86-4862 DDC 327.1/11 19
HD9698.U52 H45 1986 ***NYPL [JLE 86-4584]***

URANIUM INDUSTRY - SOCIAL ASPECTS - AUSTRALIA - BROKEN HILL (N.S.W.)
Honeymoon uranium mine occupation [sound recording]. Los Angeles, Calif. , p1983. 1 sound cassette (53 min.) : LC Card 87-752867
HD9539.U72

URANIUM INDUSTRY - STATISTICS.
The Uranium market, 1986-2000 /. London , c1986. xii, 123 p. : LC Card 87-162222 DDC 338.2/74932/021 19
HD9539.U7 U73 1986

Uranium Institute. Supply and Demand Committee. The Uranium market, 1986-2000 /. London , c1986. xii, 123 p. : LC Card 87-162222 DDC 338.2/74932/021 19
HD9539.U7 U73 1986

The Uranium market, 1986-2000 / Uranium Institute, the Supply and Demand Committee. London : The Institute, c1986. xii, 123 p. : ill. ; 23 cm. "December 1986." Bibliography: p. 119-120. LC Card 87-162222 DDC 338.2/74932/021 19
1. Uranium industry - Forecasting. 2. Uranium industry - Statistics. I. Uranium Institute. Supply and Demand Committee.
HD9539.U7 U73 1986

Urban and regional policy and development studies.
Housing America's poor /. Chapel Hill , c1987. ix, 203 p. ; ISBN 0-8078-1738-4 LC Card 86-40449 DDC 363.5/8 19
HD7287.96.U5 H68 1987

The urban arena . Short, John R. London , 1984. viii, 202 p. : ISBN 0-333-36139-3 LC Card 87-672913
HC256.6 .S49x 1984

The Urban caldron / edited by Joseph DiMento, LeRoy Graymer, Frank Schnidman ; cosponsored by University of California, Los Angeles, Extensioon, the Public Policy Program and the Lincoln Institute of Land Policy. Boston, Mass. : Oelgeschlager, Gunn & Hain, 1986. 152 p. ; 24 cm. "The Second Annual Donald Hagman Memorial Conference"--Table of contents. "A Lincoln Institute of Land Policy Book." Includes bibliographies and index. ISBN 0-89946-207-3 LC Card 85-21641 DDC 333.73/0973 19
1. Land use, Urban - Government policy - United States - Congresses. 2. Urban policy - United States - Congresses. 3. Housing policy - United States - Congresses. I. DiMento, Joseph F. II. Graymer, LeRoy, 1932-. III. Schnidman, Frank. IV. Donald Hagman Memorial Conference (2nd).
HD257 .U73 1986 ***NYPL [JLE 86-4372]***

The urban dead-end? . Brahm Prakash. Bombay , 1983. xii, 138 p., [5] p. of plates : LC Card 84-900007 DDC 331.12/5/0954792 19
HD5820.B6 B72 1983 ***NYPL [JLD 86-3828]***

URBAN DESIGN. see CITY PLANNING.

Urban Development Corporation. A Step-by-step guide to resources for economic development /. Albany, N.Y. [New York, N.Y.] , 1983, c1980. 195 p. : LC Card 85-621196 DDC 353.0082/09747 19
HC107.N73 P6353 1983
NYPL [JLF 86-638]

Urban dynamics and urban externalities /. Miyao, Takahiro. Chur, Switzerland , New York , c1987. viii, 107 p. : ISBN 3-7186-0333-0 (pbk.) LC Card 86-25629 DDC 330.9173/2 19
HB2161 .M595 1987

URBAN ECOLOGY - POLAND.
Bonenberg, Wojciech. Przemysł w mieście . Gliwice , 1985. 181 p., [8] folded leaves of plates : LC Card 86-219523
HC340.3.Z9 D52 1985

URBAN ECONOMICS - ADDRESSES, ESSAYS, LECTURES.
Singer, Paul Israel, 1932- Economia politica e processi di urbanizzazione /. Venezia , 1978. xx, 132 p. ; ***NYPL [JLD 86-786]***

URBAN ECONOMICS - CONGRESSES.
L'Analisi degli insediamenti umani e produttivi /. Milano, Italy , c1984. 295 p. : LC Card 84-179265 DDC 330.945/0928 19
HC305 .A6618 1984 ***NYPL [JLD 86-3298]***

Urbanisation in the developing world /. London , Dover, N.H. , c1986. 265 p. ; ISBN 0-7099-0884-9 : LC Card 86-4551 DDC 307.7/6/091724 19
HT149.5 .U74 1986 ***NYPL [JLD 86-2402]***

Urban flood protection benefits . Parker, Dennis J. Aldershot, Hants, England , Brookfield, Vt., U. S.A. , c1987. xvii, 284 p. : ISBN 0-291-39707-7 LC Card 87-147842 DDC 363.3/49372 19
HD1676.G7 P37 1987

URBAN HOMESTEADING - UNITED STATES.
Varady, David P. Neighborhood upgrading . Albany , c1986. x, 184 p. : ISBN 0-88706-299-7 LC Card 85-30392 DDC 307.3/362/0973 19
HT175 .V37 1986 ***NYPL [JLE 87-373]***

URBAN HOUSING. see HOUSING.

Urban illusions . Bernick, Michael, 1953- New York , 1987. x, 243 p. ; ISBN 0-275-92804-7 (alk. paper) : LC Card 87-7208 DDC 331.13/7973 19
HD5708.85.U6 B47 1987

Urban innovation abroad.
Choguill, Charles L. New communities for urban squatters . New York , c1987. xiv, 213 p. : ISBN 0-306-42545-9 LC Card 86-30501 DDC 307.3/36 19
HD7361.6.D57 C46 1987

Urban Institute.
Government spending and the nonprofit sector in [name of community]. Washington, D.C. , <c1984-c1985. v. <1-11 > ; LC Card 87-168173 DDC 339.5/22/0973 19
HJ2052 .G67 1984

Profile of the '80's /. [Washington, D.C.?] , 1980. v, 77 p. : LC Card 81-600725 DDC 380.5/0973 19
HE206.2 .P765 ***NYPL [JLF 86-1445]***

Urban Institute research report.
An Urban Institute research report.
Altschuler, David M. New York nonprofit organizations . Washington, D.C. (2100 M St., N.W., Washington 20037) , c1987. vii, 43 p. : LC Card 87-159600 DDC 658.1/5 19
HD2769.2.U6 A48 1987

The [Name of community] nonprofit sector in a time of government retrenchment. Washington, D.C. , c1984-<c1986. v. <1-2, 5-6, 9-11, 13-15 > : LC Card 87-167661 DDC 338.7/4/0973 19
HG4061 .N36 1984

Salamon, Lester M. Rhode Island nonprofit organizations . Washington, D.C. , Providence, RI , c1987. vii, 40 p. : LC Card 87-148803 DDC 338.7/4/09745 19
HD2769.2.U6 S25 1987

Salamon, Lester M. San Francisco Bay Area nonprofit organizations . Washington, D.C. (2100 M St., N.W., Washington 20037) , c1987. vi, 26 p. : LC Card 87-403000 DDC 338.7/4/0979461 19
HJ9205.S3 S34 1987

Urban Land Institute.
The Development trends, 1986 /. Washington, D.C. , c1986. 48 p. : ISBN 0-87420-657-X (pbk.) LC Card 86-227316 DDC 333.3/8/0973 19
HD1390 .D485 1986

Dollars & cents of off-price shopping centers . Washington, D.C. , c1986. v, 78 p. : ISBN 0-87420-660-X (pbk.) LC Card 86-51102 DDC 381/.1 19
HF5430.3 .D65 1986

Dowden, C. James. Creating a community association . Washington, D.C. , Alexandria, Va. , 1986. vii, 76 p. : ISBN 0-87420-659-6 (pbk.) LC Card 86-50785 DDC 643/.2 19
HD7287.67.U5 C73 1986

Employment and parking in suburban business parks . Washington, D.C. , c1986. iv, 31 p. : ISBN 0-87420-662-6 (pbk.) LC Card 86-219885 DDC 338.6/042 19
HD255 .E45 1986

R.S. Wallace Station, East Peoria, Illinois : an evaluation of land use potential and development strategies for CILCORP Inc. Washington, D.C. (1090 Vermont Ave., N.W., Washington 20005) : ULI-the Urban Land Institute, c1986. 36 p. : ill. (some col.) ; 28 cm. (A Panel Advisory Service report) "June 22-27, 1986." An evaluation of the development potential of Wallace Generating Station closed by the Central Illinois Light Company in Oct. 1985. LC Card 86-216045 DDC 333.77/17/0977352 19
1. Real estate development - Illinois - East Peoria. 2. Land use - Illinois - East Peoria - Planning. 3. Electric power-plants - Illinois - East Peoria - Remodeling for other use. I. Central Illinois Light Company (East Peoria, Ill.). II. Title. III. Title: RS Wallace Station, East Peoria, Illinois. IV. Series.
HD268.E26 U73 1986

ULI/UMTA Policy Forum on Joint Development of Rail Transit Facilities (1986 : Washington, D.C.) ULI-UMTA Policy Forum on Joint Development of Rail Transit Facilities . [Washington, D.C.] [1987] iv, 107 p. : ISBN 0-87420-671-5 (pbk.) LC Card 87-82098 DDC 333.3/8 19
HD257 .U43 1986

Urban Land Institute. Commercial and Office Development Council. Executive Group.
Shopping center development handbook /. Washington , 1985. xiii, 338 p. : ISBN 0-87420-634-0 LC Card 85-50127
NYPL [JLF 85-1243]

Urban Land Institute. Panel Advisory Service.
Bedford Properties, Lenexa, Kansas . Washington, D.C. (1090 Vermont Ave., N.W., Washington 20005) [1986?] 37 p. : LC Card 87-141440 DDC 333.3/8/09781675 19
HD268.L46 B43 1986

Urban Land Institute. Urban Development/Mixed-Use Council. Executive Group. Schwanke, Dean. Mixed-use development handbook /. Washington, D.C. , 1987. xv, 364 p. : ISBN 0-08-742665-0 LC Card 86-51443 DDC 333.3/8 19
HD1390 .S38 1987

URBAN LAND USE. see **LAND USE, URBAN.**

Urban land use and planning /. Chaurasia, B. P. (Bhanu Pratap) Allahabad, India , 1987. xxiii, 347 p. : ISBN 81-85076-20-0 : LC Card 87-900386 DDC 333.77/17/09542 19
HD879.U8 C53 1987

Urbán, László. A földmüvesszövetkezetek, fogyasztási szövetkezetek négy évtizede Szolnok megyében / Urbán László. Szolnok : [s.n.], 1985 ([Szolnok] : Készült a Damjanich János Múzeum Rota Gépén) 435 p. ; 21 cm. Continuation of: Demokratikus agrárszövetkezetek Szolnok megyében, 1945-1949, published in 1977. Bibliography: p. 427-434. ISBN 963-01-6642-9 LC Card 87-407748
1. Consumer cooperatives - Hungary - Szolnok Megye - History. 2. Agriculture, Cooperative - Hungary - Szolnok Megye - History. I. Title. II. Title: Földmüvesszövetkezetek, fogyasztási szövetkezetek 4 évtizede Szolnok megyében.
HD3332.5.A6 S98 1985

URBAN LIFE. see **CITY AND TOWN LIFE.**

Urban-Lurain, Jan. Sanders, Mary. R.P.M. realize your power to motivate /. Farmington Hills, Mich. , c1986. 153 p., [2] p. of plates : ISBN 0-9616833-0-9 (pbk.) LC Card 87-111586 DDC 658.3/14 19
HF5549.5.M63 S26 1986

Urban policy and politics in a bureaucratic age /. Stone, Clarence N. (Clarence Nathan), 1935- Englewood Cliffs, N.J. , c1986. xv, 397 p. ; ISBN 0-13-939562-8 LC Card 85-6481 DDC 320.8/0973 19
JS331 .S76 1986 ***NYPL [JLE 86-3158]***

URBAN POLICY - BANGLADESH - DHAKA.
Choguill, Charles L. New communities for urban squatters . New York , c1987. xiv, 213 p. : ISBN 0-306-42545-9 LC Card 86-30501 DDC 307.3/36 19
HD7361.6.D57 C46 1987

URBAN POLICY - COLOMBIA.
Toro Agudelo, Hernán. Hacia una reforma social urbana en Colombia . Bogotá, Colombia , 1986. 342 p. : ISBN 958-601-100-3 LC Card 87-107055
HD7325.A3 T67 1986

URBAN POLICY - GREAT BRITAIN.
Herington, John. The outer city /. London , New York , 1984. 205 p. : ISBN 0-06-318237-8
NYPL [JLE 86-1465]

Short, John R. The urban arena . London , 1984. viii, 202 p. : ISBN 0-333-36139-3 LC Card 87-672913
HC256.6 .S49x 1984

URBAN POLICY - INDIA - CONGRESSES.
Problems of urban unemployment. Calcutta , 1981. ix, 114 p. ; LC Card 83-907262 DDC 331.13/77/0954 19
HD5819 .P76 1981 ***NYPL [JLF 86-1766]***

Urban policy problems : federal policy and institutional change / edited by Mark S. Rosentraub. New York : Praeger, 1986. vi, 261 p. : ill. ; 25 cm. "Praeger special studies, Praeger scientific." "Published in cooperation with the Policy Studies Organization."--t.p. Includes bibliographies and index. ISBN 0-03-004218-6 (alk. paper) : LC Card 86-596 DDC 307.7/6/0973 19
1. Urban policy - United States. 2. Federal-city relations - United States. I. Rosentraub, Mark S., 1950-. II. Policy Studies Organization.
HT123 .U7466 1986 ***NYPL [JLE 86-3613]***

URBAN POLICY - UNITED STATES.
Clark, Gordon L. Judges and the cities . Chicago , c1985. xv, 247 p. ; ISBN 0-226-10753-1 : LC Card 85-1018 DDC 306/.0973 19
HN59.2 .C57 1985 ***NYPL [JLE 86-1068]***

Drennan, Matthew P., 1937- Modeling metropolitan economies for forecasting and policy analysis /. New York , 1985. x, 242 p. ; ISBN 0-8147-1781-0 (alk. paper) : LC Card 85-13784 DDC 330.9173/2 19
HT321 .D74 1985 ***NYPL [JLE 86-1102]***

Meyers, Edward M. Rebuilding America's cities . Cambridge, Mass. , c1986. xxi, 290 p. : ISBN 0-88730-051-0 LC Card 85-30780 DDC 307.3/4/0973 19
HT175 .U59 1986 ***NYPL [JLE 86-2874]***

Pagano, Michael A. How the public works . Washington, D.C. , c1986. ix, 68, 6 p. : ISBN 0-933729-13-8 (pbk.) : LC Card 87-129719 DDC 338.4/3363/0973 19
HJ9145 .P343 1986

The State and local industrial policy /. Chicago, Ill. , c1987. x, 195 p. : ISBN 0-918286-46-8 (pbk.) LC Card 86-72373 DDC 338.973 19
HD3616.U47 S68 1987

Urban policy problems . New York , 1986. vi, 261 p. : ISBN 0-03-004218-6 (alk. paper) : LC Card 86-596 DDC 307.7/6/0973 19
HT123 .U7466 1986 ***NYPL [JLE 86-3613]***

Varady, David P. Neighborhood upgrading . Albany , c1986. x, 184 p. : ISBN 0-88706-299-7 LC Card 85-30392 DDC 307.3/362/0973 19
HT175 .V37 1986 ***NYPL [JLE 87-373]***

URBAN POLICY - UNITED STATES - CONGRESSES.
The Urban caldron /. Boston, Mass. , 1986. 152 p. ; ISBN 0-89946-207-3 LC Card 85-21641 DDC 333.73/0973 19
HD257 .U73 1986 ***NYPL [JLE 86-4372]***

URBAN POLICY - ZIMBABWE.
Report on housing and urban development in Zimbabwe . [Harare, Zimbabwe , 1986] vi, 46 p., [1] folded leaf of plates : LC Card 87-980381 DDC 363.5/8 19
HD7374.5.A3 R46 1986

URBAN POOR - BRAZIL - HISTORY.
Hahner, June Edith, 1940- Poverty and politics . Albuquerque , 1986. xvi, 415 p. : ISBN 0-8263-0878-3 : LC Card 86-1258 DDC 305.5/69/0981 19
HC190.P6 H34 1986 ***NYPL [JLE 86-4407]***

URBAN POOR - EMPLOYMENT - UNITED STATES.
Bernick, Michael, 1953- Urban illusions . New York , 1987. x, 243 p. ; ISBN 0-275-92804-7 (alk. paper) : LC Card 87-7208 DDC 331.13/7973 19
HD5708.85.U6 B47 1987

URBAN POOR - HOUSING - BERLIN (GERMANY)
Sonnewald, Bernd, 1947- Die "Berliner Linie" und die Hausbesetzer-Szene /. Berlin , c1983. 149 p. ; ISBN 3-87061-170-7 LC Card 83-190228
HD7287.96.G32 B477 1983

URBAN POOR - HOUSING - BRAZIL - SÃO PAULO.
Cortiços em São Paulo . São Paulo , 1986. 195, [2] p. : LC Card 87-119201 DDC 363.5/8 19
HD7287.96.B62 S263 1986

URBAN POOR - HOUSING - DEVELOPING COUNTRIES.
Durand-Lasserve, Alain. L'exclusion des pauvres dans les villes du Tiers-Monde . Paris , c1986. 198 p. : ISBN 2-85802-613-8 LC Card 87-111461
HD7391 .D79 1986

URBAN POOR - HOUSING - GOVERNMENT POLICY - AFRICA, SUB-SAHARAN.
Slum and squatter settlements in Sub-Saharan Africa . New York , 1988. p. cm. ISBN 0-275-92309-6 (alk. paper) : LC Card 87-11705 DDC 307.3/36 19
HD7287.96.A438 S57 1988

URBAN POOR - HOUSING - LATIN AMERICA - CONGRESSES.
Abitazione e periferie urbane nei paesi in via di sviluppo . Milano, Italy , c1985. 450 p. : LC Card 86-132019
HD7287.96.L29 A25 1985
NYPL [JLD 87-1173]

URBAN POOR - HOUSING - MEDITERRANEAN REGION - CONGRESSES.
Abitazione e periferie urbane nei paesi in via di sviluppo . Milano, Italy , c1985. 450 p. : LC Card 86-132019
HD7287.96.L29 A25 1985
NYPL [JLD 87-1173]

URBAN POOR - NETHERLANDS - ALKMAAR - HISTORY.
Loo, L. Frank van, 1945- Armelui . Bergen (NH) , 1986. 285 p. ; ISBN 90-70805-10-3 : LC Card 86-205672
HC328.A44 L66 1986

URBAN POOR - THAILAND - BANGKOK.
Salam . Krung Thēp , 2525 [1982] 16, 249 p. : LC Card 82-916400
HC445.Z7 B3678 1982

Urban population growth rates in Africa with special reference to Lesotho /. Sembajwe, I. S. L. (Israel Serwano Lubwama), 1947- [Roma, Lesotho] [1985] 31 leaves : LC Card 87-132328 DDC 307.2 19
HB3663.7.A3 S46 1985

URBAN POPULATION MOVEMENTS. see **RESIDENTIAL MOBILITY.**

URBAN PROBLEMS. see **URBAN POLICY.**

Urban Programme (Great Britain) Assessment of the employment effects of economic development projects funded under the Urban Programme /. London , 1986. vi, 52 p. : ISBN 0-11-751859-X (pbk.) : LC Card 86-197217 DDC 331.12/0941 19
HD5765.A6 A87 1986

URBAN PROGRAMME (GREAT BRITAIN)
Assessment of the employment effects of economic development projects funded under the Urban Programme /. London , 1986. vi, 52 p. : ISBN 0-11-751859-X (pbk.) : LC Card 86-197217 DDC 331.12/0941 19
HD5765.A6 A87 1986

Urban, R. Strassenbau und Mineralölindustrie im Spiegel der Statistik . Hamburg , 1976. [48] p. : LC Card 83-126399
HD9582.A7 G37 1976

URBAN REDEVELOPMENT. see **URBAN RENEWAL.**

URBAN RENEWAL - AUSTRALIA - MELBOURNE (VIC.)
Logan, William Stewart, 1942- The Gentrification of inner Melbourne . St. Lucia, Qld., Australia ; New York : xxxiii, 328 p. : ISBN 0-7022-1729-8 LC Card 84-17382 DDC 307/.2 19
HD7379.M45 L64 1985 *NYPL [JLD 87-798]*

URBAN RENEWAL - DENMARK.
Denmark. Udvalget vedrørende byfornyelse og støtte til ejerboliger. Redegørelse om støtte til ejerboliger i forbindelse med byfornyelse . København [1981] 128 p. : ISBN 87-503-3873-0 LC Card 82-194685
HD7347.A4 D455 1981

URBAN RENEWAL - INDIA.
Housing and Urban Development Corporation. HUDCO's initiatives for IYSH. New Delhi [1987?] 49 p. : LC Card 87-902550 DDC 363.5/8 19
HD7287.96.I4 H67 1987

URBAN RENEWAL - MINNESOTA.
Minnesota. Office of the Legislative Auditor. Program Evaluation Division. Tax increment financing. Saint Paul, Minn. (Veterans Service Bldg., Saint Paul 55155) , 1986. xix, 138 p. : LC Card 86-623133 DDC 336.22/09776 19
HJ9261 .M55 1986

URBAN RENEWAL - NEW YORK (N.Y.)
New York City Partnership. The Partnership. New York, N.Y. , c1986. 44 p. : LC Card 86-223138 DDC 380.1/06/07471 19
HF296.N4 N48 1986

URBAN RENEWAL - UNITED STATES.
Frieden, Bernard J. The politics of neglect . Cambridge, Mass. [1975] x, 281 p. ; ISBN 0-262-06061-2 LC Card 75-6792 DDC 309.2/62/0973
HT167 .F74 *NYPL [JLE 80-1135]*

Industrial democracy . Beverly Hills , c1985. 308 p. : ISBN 0-8039-2476-3 LC Card 85-11741 DDC 338.973/009173/2 19
HT321 .I53 1985 *NYPL [JLD 86-3621]*

Meyers, Edward M. Rebuilding America's cities . Cambridge, Mass. , c1986. xxi, 290 p. : ISBN 0-88730-051-0 LC Card 85-30780 DDC 307.3/4/0973 19
HT175 .U59 1986 *NYPL [JLE 86-2874]*

Rosen, Christine Meisner, 1951- The limits of power . Cambridge [Cambridgeshire] , New York , 1986. xii, 395 p. : ISBN 0-521-30319-2 LC Card 85-7753 DDC 307.7/6/0973 19
HT371 .R67 1986 *NYPL [JLE 86-2388]*

United States. Congress. House. Committee on Banking, Currency and Housing. Subcommittee on Historic Preservation and Coinage. Preservation programs of the Federal government in the area of housing and community development /. Washington , 1976. vi, 86 p. ; LC Card 77-601749
HT175 .U583 1976 *NYPL [JLE 78-1181]*

Varady, David P. Neighborhood upgrading . Albany , c1986. x, 184 p. : ISBN 0-88706-299-7 LC Card 85-30392 DDC 307.3/362/0973 19
HT175 .V37 1986 *NYPL [JLE 87-373]*

URBAN RENEWAL - UNITED STATES - FINANCE.
United States. Office of Urban Rehabilitation and Community Reinvestment. FHA Title I property improvement loan insurance [microform] . Washington , 1978. 19 p. ;
*NYPL [*ZT-1564 no.11]*

Urban-rural migration differentials in Thailand /. Goldstein, Sidney, 1927- [Bangkok] , 1974. 49 p. ; LC Card 78-301310 DDC 301.36/1
HB2104.55.A3 G64
NYPL [JLM 83-719 no.12]

URBAN-RURAL MIGRATION - IRAN.
Danesh, Abol Hassan, 1952- Rural exodus & squatter settlements in the Third World . Lanham, MD , c1987. xii, 168 p. : ISBN 0-8191-6443-7 (alk. paper) : LC Card 87-10627 DDC 307.2 19
HB2096.4.A3 D36 1987

URBAN-RURAL MIGRATION - RUSSIAN S. F.S.R. - NON-CHERNOZEM REGION.
Vasil'ev, Ivan Afanas'evich. Korennye i priezzhie /. Moskva , 1980. 86 p. ; LC Card 81-178115
HD1536.S65 V375 1980

URBAN-RURAL MIGRATION - WASHINGTON METROPOLITAN AREA.
Gale, Dennis E. Black and white urban-to-suburban outmigrants . Washington, D.C. [1986] 46 p. : LC Card 87-404424 DDC 307.2 19
HB1987.W34 G35 1986

URBAN-RURAL MIGRATION - ZAMBIA.
Chilivumbo, Alifeyo. Migration and uneven rural development in Africa . Lanham, MD , c1985. xx, 118 p. : ISBN 0-8191-4929-2 (alk. paper) : LC Card 85-17908 DDC 307.2 19
HB2123.6.A3 C47 1985
NYPL [JLD 86-1953]

Urban, Sabine M.-L. Entreprises allemandes et coopération industrielle à l'échelle européenne : étude / réalisée par Sabine Urban et Serge Vendemini. Paris : Documentation française, c1986. 162 p. : ill. ; 30 cm. (Etudes et recherches / Commissariat général du plan . no 2) Includes bibliographical references. ISBN 2-11-001580-2 : LC Card 86-175800
1. Corporations, West German - European Economic Community countries. 2. European Economic Community countries - Economic integration. 3. Technology transfer - European Economic Community countries. I. Vendemini, Serge. II. Series: Etudes et recherches (France. Commissariat général du plan) , no 2. III. Title.
HD2844 .U7 1986

Urban settlements in eastern India . Thakur, Baleshwar. New Delhi , 1980. 222 p. : LC Card 80-900438 DDC 307.7/6/09541
HT147.I5 T53 1980 *NYPL [JLD 80-3943]*

Urban, Stanisław. Z Husowa po berła rektorskie . Warszawa , 1986. 340 p., [25] p. of plates : ISBN 83-205-3745-2 : LC Card 85-126839
HB114.S79 Z2 1986

Urban Systems Research & Engineering.
Ferguson, Gary D. Evaluation of the small cities community development block grant program--the role of the counties [microform] /. Cambridge, Mass. , 1981. vii, vi, 186 p. ;
*NYPL [*XME-11,283]*

Newman & Hermanson Company. Evaluation of the small cities component of the community development block grant program [microform] . Cambridge, Mass. , 1981. viii, xvii, 147 p. ;
*NYPL [*XME-11,274]*

URBAN TRAFFIC. see **TRAFFIC ENGINEERING.**

URBAN TRANSIT. see **LOCAL TRANSIT.**

URBAN TRANSPORTATION.
Brinco, Ricardo. Transporte urbano em questão /. Porto Alegre , 1985. 114 p. ; LC Card 87-404831 DDC 388.4 19
HE305 .B75 1985

Rallis, Tom. City transport in developed and developing countries /. New York , 1988. xiv, 202 p. : ISBN 0-312-00450-8 : LC Card 86-29789 DDC 388.4 19
HE305 .R35 1988

URBAN TRANSPORTATION AND STATE. see **URBAN TRANSPORTATION POLICY.**

URBAN TRANSPORTATION - CALIFORNIA - LOS ANGELES.
Bottles, Scott L. Los Angeles and the automobile . Berkeley , c1987. xiii, 301 p. : ISBN 0-520-05795-3 (alk. paper) LC Card 86-14660 DDC 388.4/1321/0979494 19
HE5634.L7 B68 1987

URBAN TRANSPORTATION - DATA PROCESSING - CONGRESSES.
National Conference on Microcomputers in Urban Transportation (1985 : San Diego, Calif.) Microcomputer applications within the urban transportation environment . New York, N.Y. , c1985. 824 p. : ISBN 0-87262-508-7 (pbk.) LC Card 85-73250 DDC 388.4/028/5416 19
HE305 .N33 1985 *NYPL [JSD 86-535]*

URBAN TRANSPORTATION - DICTIONARIES - GERMAN.
Transpress Lexikon Stadtverkehr /. Berlin , 1985. 487 p., 33 p. of plates : LC Card 86-166711
HE305 .T78 1985

URBAN TRANSPORTATION - ENERGY CONSUMPTION.
Energy and cities /. New Brunswick, U. S.A. , c1985. 173 p. : ISBN 0-87855-813-6 (pbk.) LC Card 84-24074 DDC 333.79/13/091732 19
HD108.2 .E525 1985 *NYPL [JLE 86-4441]*

URBAN TRANSPORTATION - FINANCE.
Co-ordinated urban transport pricing . Paris [Washington, D.C.] 1985. 151 p. : ISBN 92-64-12692-9 (pbk.) : LC Card 86-125699 DDC 388.4/042 19
HE305 .C58 1985

URBAN TRANSPORTATION - FRANCE.
Les Rues mixtes . [Bagneux] [1982] 40 p. : ISBN 2-11-083325-4 : LC Card 84-104398
HE363.F72 P437 1982

URBAN TRANSPORTATION - FRANCE - TOULOUSE REGION.
Marconis, Robert. Midi-Pyrénées XIXe-XXe siècles . [Toulouse?] [1985?] 2 v. : ISBN 2-86726-084-7 (set) LC Card 87-112330
HC277.M54 M37 1985

URBAN TRANSPORTATION - GERMANY, WEST.
Fechtel, Hans-Walter. Flächenhafte Verkehrsberuhigung . Bergisch Gladbach , 1986. 282 p. : LC Card 87-408360 DDC 388.4/0943 19
HE311.G3 F4 1986

Franz, Lothar. Verkehrsberuhigung in Städten und Gemeinden /. Grafenau , c1982. 134 p. : ISBN 3-88508-780-4 : LC Card 82-204794
HE311.G3 F73 1982

URBAN TRANSPORTATION - GERMANY (WEST) - PASSENGER TRAFFIC - MATHEMATICAL MODELS.
Stengel, Wolfgang. Verlagerungen der individuellen Verkehrsnachfrage bei verändertem ÖPNV-Angebot infolge neueingerichteter Stadtschnellbahnen /. Bad Honnef , 1984. iv, 210 p. : ISBN 3-88347-120-8 : LC Card 84-185940
HE311.G3 S73 1984

URBAN TRANSPORTATION - INDIA.
Darbéra, Richard. Le planificateur et le cyclopousse . Caen , 1986. xiii, 190 p. : ISBN 2-86878-015-6 : LC Card 86-192929
HE311.I4 D36 1986

URBAN TRANSPORTATION - ITALY - LUCCA - PLANNING.
Bortoli, Michele. Il traffico nei centri storici /. [Lucca, Italy] , 1986. 236 p. : LC Card 87-151755
HE311.I82 L843 1986

URBAN TRANSPORTATION - LATIN AMERICA - CONGRESSES.
Transports urbains et services en Amérique latine . Arcueil, France , Quito [1985- v. <1 > : ISBN 2-85782-137-9 (set) LC Card 87-153020
HE311.L29 T73 1985

URBAN TRANSPORTATION - MANAGEMENT.
Fielding, Gordon J. Managing public transit strategically . San Francisco , 1987. xxii, 270 p. : ISBN 1-555-42068-0 (alk. paper) LC Card 87-45497 DDC 388.4/068 19
HE4301 .F54 1987

URBAN TRANSPORTATION - MATHEMATICAL MODELS.
Pauck, Reinhard. Mikroökonomische Modelle des städtischen Verkehrs . Baden-Baden , 1983. 295 p. : ISBN 3-7890-0779-X LC Card 83-157997 DDC 388.4/0724 19
HE305 .P39 1983 *NYPL [JLD 87-977]*

URBAN TRANSPORTATION - PAKISTAN.
Quddus, Syed Abdul. Rail transport in Pakistan

/. Lahore [1984?] 277 p. ; LC Card 85-932263 DDC 385/.09549/1 19
HE3300.5 .Q33 1984

URBAN TRANSPORTATION - PLANNING.
Bortoli, Michele. Il traffico nei centri storici /. [Lucca, Italy] , 1986. 236 p. : LC Card 87-151755
HE311.I82 L843 1986

Urban transportation planning in the United States . Weiner, Edward. [Washington, D.C.] [1986] vii, 149 p. : LC Card 87-601522 DDC 388.4/068 19
HE308 .W45 1986

Urban transportation planning in the United States . Weiner, Edward. New York , 1987. xii, 122 p. : ISBN 0-275-92493-9 (alk. paper) : LC Card 86-30343 DDC 388.4/068 19
HE308 .W45 1987 *NYPL [JLE 87-1506]*

URBAN TRANSPORTATION POLICY.
Co-ordinated urban transport pricing . Paris [Washington, D.C.] 1985. 151 p. : ISBN 92-64-12692-9 (pbk.) : LC Card 86-125699 DDC 388.4/042 19
HE305 .C58 1985

URBAN TRANSPORTATION POLICY - GERMANY, WEST.
Fechtel, Hans-Walter. Flächenhafte Verkehrsberuhigung . Bergisch Gladbach , 1986. 282 p. : LC Card 87-408360 DDC 388.4/0943 19
HE311.G3 F4 1986

Franz, Lothar. Verkehrsberuhigung in Städten und Gemeinden /. Grafenau , c1982. 134 p. : ISBN 3-88508-780-4 : LC Card 82-204794
HE311.G3 F73 1982

URBAN TRANSPORTATION POLICY - INDIA.
Darbéra, Richard. Le planificateur et le cyclopousse . Caen , 1986. xiii, 190 p. : ISBN 2-86878-015-6 : LC Card 86-192929
HE311.I4 D36 1986

URBAN TRANSPORTATION POLICY - UNITED STATES.
Bloch, Arnold J. Interstate highway trade-in process. Vol. 1. Assessment /. New York , 1982. [45] p. : *NYPL [*XME-11,324]*

URBAN TRANSPORTATION - SOVIET UNION - MATHEMATICAL MODELS.
Matematicheskie metody v upravlenii gorodskimi transportnymi sistemami /. Leningrad , 1979. 150 p. : LC Card 81-163008
HE311.S652 M675 1979

URBAN TRANSPORTATION - TAXATION.
Co-ordinated urban transport pricing . Paris [Washington, D.C.] 1985. 151 p. : ISBN 92-64-12692-9 (pbk.) : LC Card 86-125699 DDC 388.4/042 19
HE305 .C58 1985

URBAN TRANSPORTATION - TEXAS - DALLAS METROPOLITAN AREA - STATISTICS.
Transportation data book . Arlington, Tex. (P.O. Drawer COG, Arlington 76005-5888) , c1987. 101 leaves in various foliations : LC Card 87-152338 DDC 380.5/09764/2812 19
HE310.D25 T73 1987

URBAN TRANSPORTATION - TEXAS - FORT WORTH METROPOLITAN AREA - STATISTICS.
Transportation data book . Arlington, Tex. (P.O. Drawer COG, Arlington 76005-5888) , c1987. 101 leaves in various foliations : LC Card 87-152338 DDC 380.5/09764/2812 19
HE310.D25 T73 1987

URBAN TRANSPORTATION - UNITED STATES.
United States. Office of Highway Planning. Urban Planning and Transportation Management Division. Review of Federal-Aid Urban System program. [Washington, D.C.?] [1985] 55 p. : *NYPL [JLF 86-340]*

URBAN TRANSPORTATION - UNITED STATES - PLANNING - HISTORY.
Weiner, Edward. Urban transportation planning in the United States . [Washington, D.C.] [1986] vii, 149 p. : LC Card 87-601522 DDC 388.4/068 19
HE308 .W45 1986

URBAN TRANSPORTATION - UNITED STATES - STATISTICS.
Briggs, Dwight. Journey-to-work trends . Washington, D.C. , Springfield, VA [1986] 1 v. (various pagings) : LC Card 86-602387 DDC 388.4/1314/0973 19
HE371.A3 B75 1986

URBAN TRANSPORTATION - WASHINGTON METROPOLITAN AREA - PASSENGER TRAFFIC - STATISTIC.
1986 Beltway cordon count of vehicular and passenger volumes. [Washington, D.C.] [1986] iv, 35 p., [109] p. : LC Card 87-119314 DDC 388.4/1314/09753021 19
HE5634.W3 A17 1986

Urbanisation des terres rurales. Gierman, D. M. Rural to urban land conversion =. [Ottawa] , Hull, Que. , c1977. xvii, 74 p. ; ISBN 0-662-01301-8 *NYPL [JLM 80-106 no.16]*

Urbanisation in the developing world / edited by David Drakakis-Smith. London ; Dover, N.H. : Croom Helm, c1986. 265 p. ; 23 cm. Includes index. Bibliography: p. 221-249. ISBN 0-7099-0884-9 : LC Card 86-4551 DDC 307.7/6/091724 19
1. Cities and towns - Developing countries - Congresses. 2. Cities and towns - Developing countries - Growth - Congresses. 3. Economic development - Congresses. 4. Urbanization - Developing countries - Congresses. 5. Urban economics - Congresses. I. Drakakis-Smith, D. W.
HT149.5 .U74 1986 *NYPL [JLD 86-2402]*

URBANISM. see **CITIES AND TOWNS.**

Urbanização e custo de reprodução da força de trabalho /. Vieira, Cláudio Afonso. São Paulo , 1984. 175 p., [5] folded leaves ; LC Card 85-136502
HD5755.S3 V54 1984

Urbanização e custo de reprodução da força de trabalho /. Vieira, Cláudio Afonso. São Paulo , 1984. 175 p., [5] folded leaves of plates :

Urbanización, migraciones y cambios en la sociedad peruana.
(6) Galin, Pedro. Asalariados y clases populares en Lima /. Lima [1986] 127 p. ; LC Card 87-400199 DDC 331/.0985/25 19
HD8350.L562 G35 1986

(7) Parodi Solari, Jorge. Ser obrero es algo relativo-- . Lima [1986] 184 p. ; LC Card 87-405297 DDC 331.7/671/0985 19
HD8039.M52 P46 1986

URBANIZATION - ADDRESSES, ESSAYS, LECTURES.
Singer, Paul Israel, 1932- Economia politica e processi di urbanizzazione /. Venezia , 1978. xx, 132 p. ; *NYPL [JLD 86-786]*

World patterns of modern urban change . Chicago , 1986. x, 479 p. : ISBN 0-89065-122-1 : LC Card 85-23231 DDC 910 s 307.7/6 19
H31 .C514 no.217-218
NYPL [JFM 72-132 no.217-218]

URBANIZATION - AFRICA.
Population distribution and urbanization [in] ECA member states. [Addis Ababa?] , 1983. ix, 81 p. : LC Card 86-980945 DDC 304.6/1 19
HB2121 .P66 1983

Sembajwe, I. S. L. (Israel Serwano Lubwama), 1947- Urban population growth rates in Africa with special reference to Lesotho /. [Roma, Lesotho] [1985] 31 leaves : LC Card 87-132328 DDC 307.2 19
HB3663.7.A3 S46 1985

Die Verplante Wohnmisere . Saarbrücken , Fort Lauderdale , 1986. 334 p. : ISBN 3-88156-329-6 LC Card 87-408292 DDC 363.5/1/096 19
HD7287.96.A4 V47 1986

URBANIZATION - AFRICA, SUB-SAHARAN.
Nourrir les villes en Afrique sub-saharienne /. Paris , c1985. 421 p. : ISBN 2-85802-562-X LC Card 86-222243
HD9017.S82 N68 1985

URBANIZATION - ASIA, SOUTHEASTERN - CONGRESSES.
Seminar on the Effect of Internal Migration, Urbanization, and Resettlement in the IGCC Region on its Population/Family Planning Programmes (1980 : Jakarta, Indonesia) Seminar on the Effect of Internal Migration, Urbanization, and Resettlement in the IGCC Region on its Population/Family Planning Programmes . Kuala Lumpur, Malaysia [1980?] 131 p. : LC Card 81-941408
HB2101 .S45 1980

URBANIZATION - BRAZIL.
Estudos e propostas para a organização territorial e desenvolvimento urbano do Brasil. Brasilia , 1981. 126 leaves, [7] folded leaves of plates : *NYPL [JLG 86-151]*

A Transição incompleta . Rio de Janeiro-RJ , 1986. 2 v. ; LC Card 86-224684
HC187 .T72 1986

URBANIZATION - BRAZIL - HISTORY.
Hahner, June Edith, 1940- Poverty and politics . Albuquerque , 1986. xvi, 415 p. : ISBN 0-8263-0878-3 : LC Card 86-1258 DDC 305.5/69/0981 19
HC190.P6 H34 1986 *NYPL [JLE 86-4407]*

URBANIZATION - BRAZIL - SÃO PAULO.
Vieira, Cláudio Afonso. Urbanização e custo de reprodução da força de trabalho /. São Paulo , 1984. 175 p., [5] folded leaves ; LC Card 85-136502
HD5755.S3 V54 1984

URBANIZATION - BRAZIL - SÃO PAULO (STATE)
Identificação e caracterização de agrupamentos industriais como subsídio à política de desenvolvimento regional. São Paulo , 1981. 134, 17, 60 p. : LC Card 86-146114
HC188.S3 I34 1981

URBANIZATION - BRAZIL - SÃO SEBASTIÃO REGION (SÃO PAULO)
Silva, Armando Corrêa da. O litoral norte do Estado de São Paulo . São Paulo , 1975. 273 p. : LC Card 85-134276
HC189.S343 S58 1975

URBANIZATION - CANADA.
Gierman, D. M. Rural to urban land conversion =. [Ottawa] , Hull, Que. , c1977. xvii, 74 p. ; ISBN 0-662-01301-8
NYPL [JLM 80-106 no.16]

Urbanization, capital formation, and labour productivity in agriculture . Srivastava, G. C. (Gyan Chand), 1939- New Delhi , 1986. xii, 205 p. : ISBN 81-7027-097-9 : LC Card 86-902590 DDC 338.1/0954 19
HD2075.R35 S75 1986

URBANIZATION - CONGO (BRAZZAVILLE)
Migrations rurales et urbanisation en République populaire du Congo. Addis Ababa , 1984. x, 168 p. : LC Card 84-980878
HB2125.A3 M54 1984

URBANIZATION - DEVELOPING COUNTRIES.
Cubukgil, Adil. Urbanization in developing countries . [Toronto] , 1981. ii, 77 p. ;
NYPL [JLF 87-277]

URBANIZATION - DEVELOPING COUNTRIES - ADDRESSES, ESSAYS, LECTURES.
Santos, Milton. Espaço e sociedade . Petrópolis [Brazil] , 1979. 152 p. : LC Card 80-109991
HT151 .S238 *NYPL [JLD 81-405]*

URBANIZATION - DEVELOPING COUNTRIES - CONGRESSES.
Urbanisation in the developing world /. London , Dover, N.H. , c1986. 265 p. ; ISBN 0-7099-0884-9 : LC Card 86-4551 DDC 307.7/6/091724 19
HT149.5 .U74 1986 *NYPL [JLD 86-2402]*

URBANIZATION - FRANCE.
Lacour, Claude. Croissance urbaine . Paris , 1981. 219 p. : ISBN 2-222-02928-7 (pbk.) : LC Card 82-153821 DDC 388.4/068 19
HE4764 .L3 1981 *NYPL [JLG 86-56]*

URBANIZATION - GOVERNMENT POLICY - DEVELOPING COUNTRIES.
Population distribution and urbanization . Nairobi, Kenya , 1985. 95 p. ; LC Card 85-980971 DDC 304.6/1 19
HB2160 .P67 1985

Urbanization in developing countries . Cubukgil, Adil. [Toronto] , 1981. ii, 77 p. ;
NYPL [JLF 87-277]

URBANIZATION - INDIA.
Thakur, Baleshwar. Urban settlements in eastern India . New Delhi , 1980. 222 p. : LC Card 80-900438 DDC 307.7/6/09541
HT147.I5 T53 1980 *NYPL [JLD 80-3943]*

URBANIZATION - INDONESIA - CASE STUDIES.
Costello, Michael A. Mobility and employment

in urban Southeast Asia . Boulder , 1987. xvi, 190 p. : ISBN 0-8133-7352-2 (pbk. : alk. paper) : LC Card 87-10649 DDC 307.2 19
HB2107 .C67 1987

URBANIZATION - IRAN.
Danesh, Abol Hassan, 1952- Rural exodus & squatter settlements in the Third World . Lanham, MD , c1987. xii, 168 p. : ISBN 0-8191-6443-7 (alk. paper) : LC Card 87-10627 DDC 307.2 19
HB2096.4.A3 D36 1987

URBANIZATION - ISLAMIC COUNTRIES.
Muslim world . Lanham, MD , c1987. viii, 190 p. : ISBN 0-8191-6558-1 (alk. paper) : LC Card 87-14087 DDC 330.917/671 19
HC499 .M875 1987

URBANIZATION - ITALY - MILAN REGION.
Metropoli e agricoltura /. Milano , c1982. 319 p. : LC Card 82-246692 DDC 333.76/13/094521 19
HD680.M54 M47 1982
NYPL [JLD 86-3678]

URBANIZATION - ITALY, SOUTHERN.
Costa, Paolo. Agglomerazione urbana, localizzazione industriale e Mezzogiorno /. Milano , 1983. viii, 240 p. : LC Card 83-186216 DDC 307.2 19
HB2060.S68 C67 1983 NYPL [JLE 86-3657]

URBANIZATION - LATIN AMERICA.
Gwynne, Robert N. Industrialization and urbanization in Latin America /. Baltimore, Md. , 1986. xiv, 259 p. : ISBN 0-8018-3113-X LC Card 85-10079 DDC 338.098 19
HC125 .G96 1986 NYPL [JLD 86-2200]

Die Verplante Wohnmisere . Saarbrücken , Fort Lauderdale , 1986. 334 p. : ISBN 3-88156-329-6 LC Card 87-408292 DDC 363.5/1/096 19
HD7287.96.A4 V47 1986

URBANIZATION - LATIN AMERICA - ADDRESSES, ESSAYS, LECTURES.
Singer, Paul Israel, 1932- Economia politica e processi di urbanizzazione /. Venezia , 1978. xx, 132 p. ; *NYPL [JLD 86-786]*

URBANIZATION - LATIN AMERICA - CONGRESSES.
Fachtagung "Bevölkerungsentwicklung, Bevölkerungswanderung und Urbanisierung in Lateinamerika" (1984 : Eichstätt, Germany) Desarrollo demográfico, migraciones y urbanización en América Latina . Regensburg , c1986. 432 p. : LC Card 86-181152
HB3530.5.A3 F33 1984

URBANIZATION - LATIN AMERICA - MAPS.
Wilkie, Richard W., 1938- Latin American population and urbanization analysis . Los Angeles, Calif. , c1984. xxii, 433 p. : ISBN 0-87903-242-1 (alk. paper) : LC Card 83-620019 DDC 312/.098 19
HB3530.5 .W54 1984 NYPL [JLF 87-298]

URBANIZATION - LATIN AMERICA - STATISTICS.
Wilkie, Richard W., 1938- Latin American population and urbanization analysis . Los Angeles, Calif. , c1984. xxii, 433 p. : ISBN 0-87903-242-1 (alk. paper) : LC Card 83-620019 DDC 312/.098 19
HB3530.5 .W54 1984 NYPL [JLF 87-298]

URBANIZATION - LESOTHO.
Sembajwe, I. S. L. (Israel Serwano Lubwama), 1947- Urban population growth rates in Africa with special reference to Lesotho /. [Roma, Lesotho] [1985] 31 leaves : LC Card 87-132328 DDC 307.2 19
HB3663.7.A3 S46 1985

URBANIZATION - MEXICO - MEXICO CITY - HISTORY.
López Monjardín, Adriana. Hacia la ciudad del capital--México, 1790-1870 /. México, D.F. , 1985. 193 p. : LC Card 87-124857 DDC 330.972/53 19
HC138.M4 L66 1985

URBANIZATION - PHILIPPINES - CASE STUDIES.
Costello, Michael A. Mobility and employment in urban Southeast Asia . Boulder , 1987. xvi, 190 p. : ISBN 0-8133-7352-2 (pbk. : alk. paper) : LC Card 87-10649 DDC 307.2 19
HB2107 .C67 1987

URBANIZATION - QATAR.
Ritter, Wigand. Qatar, ein arabisches Erdölemirat /. Nürnberg , 1985. 201 p. : LC Card 86-205396
HC415.37 .R58 1985

URBANIZATION - RUSSIAN S.F.S.R. - HISTORY - 18TH CENTURY.
Morrison, Daniel, 1945- "Trading peasants" and urbanization in eighteenth-century Russia . New York , 1987. 415 p. ; ISBN 0-8240-8059-9 (alk. paper) : LC Card 87-7425 DDC 307.2 19
HB2068.S65 M67 1987

URBANIZATION - SWITZERLAND.
Rumley, Pierre-Alain. Aménagement du territoire et utilisation du sol . Zürich , c1984. x, 176 p. : LC Card 85-104773
HD796 .R86 1984

URBANIZATION - THAILAND.
Chadsri Bunnag. Housing in urban development . [Bangkok] [Rotterdam] Netherlands [1985] 49, [2] leaves : LC Card 86-915989 DDC 363.5/09593 19
HD7363.55.A3 C46 1985

URBANIZATION - UNITED STATES.
Rosen, Christine Meisner, 1951- The limits of power . Cambridge [Cambridgeshire] , New York , 1986. xii, 395 p. : ISBN 0-521-30319-2 LC Card 85-7753 DDC 307.7/6/0973 19
HT371 .R67 1986 NYPL [JLE 86-2388]

URBANIZATION - VENEZUELA - HISTORY.
Estaba, Rosa M. Geografía de los paisajes urbanos e industriales de Venezuela /. Caracas , c1985. 291 p., [4] folded leaves : ISBN 980-271-006-7 LC Card 86-148810 DDC 307.7/6/0987 19
HC237 .E766 1985 NYPL [JLD 86-2340]

URBANIZATION - ZAMBIA - LUSAKA REGION.
Van den Berg, L. M. Anticipating urban growth in Africa . Lusaka, Zambia , 1984. viii, 167 p., [4] p. of plates : LC Card 86-980297 DDC 307.7/6/096894 19
HD993.Z9 L88 1984

URBANIZATION - ZIMBABWE.
Report on housing and urban development in Zimbabwe . [Harare, Zimbabwe , 1986] vi, 46 p., [1] folded leaf of plates : LC Card 87-980381 DDC 363.5/8 19
HD7374.5.A3 R46 1986

Urbas, Helmut, 1951- Die wirtschaftliche Betrachtungsweise im Steuerrecht / Helmut Urbas. Frankfurt am Main ; New York : P. Lang, c1987. viii, 392 p. : ill. ; 21 cm. (Europäische Hochschulschriften. Reihe V, Volks- und Betriebswirtschaft, 0531-7339 . Bd. 785 = vol. 785 = vol. 785) Bibliography: p. 285-391. ISBN 3-8204-0915-7 LC Card 87-409061 DDC 336.24/0943 19
1. Income tax - Germany, West. 2. Income tax - Law and legislation - Germany, West. I. Series: Europäische Hochschulschriften. Reihe V, Volks- und Betriebswirtschaft , Bd. 785. II. Title.
HJ4719 .U7 1987

Urferer, Wilhelm. Das Wohnungswesen in Oberösterreich seit Beginn dieses Jahrhunderts im Vergleich zu seiner gesamtstaatlichen Entwicklung / Wilhelm Urferer. Linz : R. Trauner, c1986. viii, 235 p. : ill. ; 24 cm. (Linzer Schriften zur Sozial- u. Wirtschaftsgeschichte . Bd. 18) Bibliography: p. 217-235. ISBN 3-85320-384-1 LC Card 87-127729 DDC 363.5/8/094362 19
1. Housing - Austria - Upper Austria - History. 2. Housing policy - Austria - Upper Austria - History. 3. Housing subsidies - Austria - Upper Austria - History. I. Title. II. Series.
HD7337.U6 U74 1986

Urff, Winfried von. Priebe, Hermann, 1907- Agrarpolitik in der EG . Baden-Baden , 1984. 269 p. ; ISBN 3-7890-1060-X LC Card 85-138555 DDC 338.1/84 19
HD1920.5.Z8 P74 1984

The urgent need of Latin America to export steel [microform]. Instituto Latinoamericano del Fierro y el Acero. Santiago, Chile [1983?] 20 p. : LC Card 84-244660 DDC 382/.45669142/098 19
HD9524.L32 I57 1983
*NYPL [*ZT-1708 no.49]*

Ürgüplü, Hayri Suat. The Turkish economy, 1981. Istanbul [1981] 256 p. : LC Card 87-404163 DDC 330.9561/038 19
HC492 .T876 1981

Uriarte, J. Manuel. Transnational banks and the dynamics of the Peruvian foreign debt and inflation / J. Manuel Uriarte. New York : Praeger, c1986. x, 195 p. : ill. ; 24 cm. Includes index. Bibliography: p. 185-189. ISBN 0-03-002599-0 (alk. paper) : LC Card 84-26307 DDC 336.3/4/0985 19
1. Debts, External - Peru. 2. Loans, Foreign - Peru. 3. Inflation (Finance) - Peru. 4. Banks and banking, Foreign - Peru. I. Title.
HJ8604 .U75 1985 NYPL [JLE 86-1384]

Uriarte, Pedro. Psicosociología de la organización : un enfoque sistémico / Pedro Uriarte. Bilbao : Universidad de Deusto, 1985. 284 p. : ill. ; 23 cm. (Publicaciones de la Universidad de Deusto. Sociología . v. 5) ISBN 84-7485-049-5 LC Card 86-151352
1. Industrial sociology. 2. Psychology, Industrial. 3. Industrial organization. 4. Industrial management. I. Title. II. Series.
HD6955 .U75 1985

Uribe-Echevarría, Francisco. Pobreza, participación y desarrollo regional /. [Bogotá, D.E., Colombia] , 1986. 536 p. : LC Card 87-103266
HC125 .P6 1986

Uribe, Jorge Restrepo. see **Restrepo Uribe, Jorge.**

Urien, Julio César. Un aporte para la liberación / Julio César Urien. Buenos Aires, Argentina : Ediciones Temática, c1985. 51 p. ; 20 cm. ISBN 950-9235-13-X LC Card 85-201095
1. Latin America - Economic policy. 2. Latin America - Dependency on foreign countries. 3. Economics - History - 20th century. 4. Developing countries - Dependency on foreign countries. I. Title.
HC125 .U75 1985

URINARY INCONTINENCE PRODUCTS INDUSTRY.
Urology and incontinence products /. Tustin, CA (17722 Irvine Blvd., Tustin 92680) , c1986. 1 v. (various foliations) : LC Card 86-235104
HD9995.U742 U76 1986a

URINE - ANALYSIS.
Drug abuse . New York, N.Y. , c1987. 132 p. : ISBN 0-8144-3511-4 (pbk.) LC Card 86-32254 DDC 658.3/822 19
HF5549.5.D7 D7 1987

Urioste Fernández de Córdova, Miguel, 1948- Segunda reforma agraria . La Paz, Bolivia [1987] 287 p. : LC Card 87-403057 DDC 333.3/1/84 19
HD1333.B5 S44 1987

Uris, Auren. The executive deskbook / Auren Uris. 3rd ed. New York : Van Nostrand Reinhold Co., c1988. xiv, 427 p. : ill. ; 23 cm. Includes index. ISBN 0-442-28790-9 (pbk.) LC Card 87-10597 DDC 658.4 19
1. Management. I. Title.
HD31 .U66 1988

Urmeneta, Roberto. Ruiz-Tagle P., Jaime. Los trabajadores del Programa del Empleo Mínimo . Santiago , 1984. 179 p. : LC Card 84-234738
HD5756.A6 R86 1984

UROLOGICAL EQUIPMENT INDUSTRY.
Urology and incontinence products /. Tustin, CA (17722 Irvine Blvd., Tustin 92680) , c1986. 1 v. (various foliations) : LC Card 86-235104
HD9995.U742 U76 1986a

Urology and incontinence products / Biomedical Business International. 1st revision. Tustin, CA (17722 Irvine Blvd., Tustin 92680) : Biomedical Business International, c1986. 1 v. (various foliations) : ill. ; 29 cm. (Report / Biomedical Business International . #7062) "August 1986." LC Card 86-235104
1. Urinary incontinence products industry. 2. Urological equipment industry. 3. Market surveys. I. Biomedical Business International, Inc. II. Series: Report (Biomedical Business International, Inc.) , #7062.
HD9995.U742 U76 1986a

Ürper, Yılmaz. Türkiye'de tarımsal kooperatiflerin toplumsal değişmeye etkileri : Eskişehir İli tarım kredi kooperatifleri üzerinde bir uygulama / Yılmaz Ürper. Eskişehir : Anadolu Üniversitesi, 1985. xvi, 109, xxxiii p. ; 24 cm. (Anadolu Üniversitesi yayınları . no. 94. no. 24) Bibliography: p. i-xvi (2nd group) LC Card 86-161567

1. Agricultural cooperative credit associations - Turkey - Eskişehir İli. I. Series: Anadolu Üniversitesi yayınları. İktisadi ve İdari Bilimler Fakültesi yayınları , 24. II. Title.
HG2051.T92 I48 1985

Urquidi, Víctor L. Basic issues in Latin American development prospects / Victor L. Urquidi. Coral Gables, Fla. : Institute of Interamerican Studies, Graduate School of International Studies, University of Miami, [between 1983 and 1986] 27 p. ; 22 cm. (Occasional papers / Institute of Interamerican Studies, Graduate School of International Studies, University of Miami) The basis of a lecture delivered at the University of Miami, Mar. 2, 1982. Brought up to date with a postscript dated July 1983. Bibliography: p. 26-27. LC Card 87-118247 DDC 338.98 19
1. Latin America - Economic policy. I. Series: Occasional papers (University of Miami. Institute of Interamerican Studies) . II. Title.
HC125 .U765 1983

Urry, John. Lash, Scott. The end of organized capitalism /. Madison, Wis. , c1987. 383 p. : ISBN 0-299-11670-0 : LC Card 87-14248 DDC 330.12/2 19
HB501 .L278 1987

Ursachen der Verschuldungskrise . Schinke, Rolf. Göttingen [1987] 33 p. : LC Card 87-409568 DDC 336.3/435/098 19
HJ8514.5 .S34 1987

Ursachen für die Schwierigkeiten bei der Eingliederung von Schwerbehinderten auf dem allgemeinen Arbeitsmarkt /. Brandt, Franz. Bonn [1984] 410 p. ; LC Card 87-408829 DDC 331.5/9/0943 19
HD7256.G3 B7 1984

Ursachen, Umfang und Auswirkungen der Abwanderung im ländlichen Bereich Galiciens am Beispiel der Provinz Orense /. Azcárate, Blanca, 1954- Frankfurt am Main , New York , c1985. 213 p. : ISBN 3-8204-8166-4 LC Card 85-190546
HD8589.O74 A92 1985

Ursachen- und Krisenanalyse der Verschuldung von Entwicklungsländern . Fuchs, Nikolaus, 1955- Berlin , c1986. 258 p. : ISBN 3-925410-05-8 LC Card 87-124994 DDC 336.3/435/091724 19
HJ8899 .F83 1986

Uruguay : informe económico 1985 / Comisión Económica para América Latina y el Caribe. Montevideo : Arca, [1986] 103 p. : ill. ; 19 cm. LC Card 87-403165 DDC 330.9895/065 19
1. Uruguay - Economic conditions - 1973-. I. United Nations. Economic Commission for Latin America and the Caribbean.
HC232 .U78 1986

URUGUAY. ADMINISTRACIÓN NACIONAL DE COMBUSTIBLES, ALCOHOL Y PORTLAND.
Uruguay. Asemblea General. Cámara de Representantes. Investigación en la Administración, Nacional de Combustibles, Alcohol y Portland /. [Montevideo] , 1935. 352 p. ; LC Card 85-105071
HD9574.U72 U78 1935

Uruguay. Asemblea General. Cámara de Representantes. Investigación en la Administración, Nacional de Combustibles, Alcohol y Portland / Cámara de Representantes. [Montevideo] : La Cámara, 1935. 352 p. ; 29 cm. "Repartido 239 de 1935." Spine title: Investigacion en la A.N.C.A.P. LC Card 85-105071
1. Uruguay. Administración Nacional de Combustibles, Alcohol y Portland. 2. Petroleum industry and trade - Uruguay. 3. Distilling industries - Uruguay. 4. Cement industries - Uruguay. 5. Governmental investigations - Uruguay. I. Title. II. Title: Investigacion en la A.N.C.A.P. III. Title: Investigacion en la ANCAP.
HD9574.U72 U78 1935

URUGUAY - CENSUS, 1960.
Chackiel, Juan. La fuerza de trabajo en los países de la Cuenca del Plata según los censos de 1960 /. San José, Costa Rica , 1976. iv, 81 p. : LC Card 83-169596
HD5746.A6 C42 1976

URUGUAY - CENSUS, 1985.
Recuentos preliminares . [Montevideo] [1986] 188 p. : LC Card 87-122427 DDC 304.6/09895/021 19
HA1074 1985

Uruguay. Combustibles, Alcohol y Portland, Administración Nacional de. see Uruguay. Administración Nacional de Combustibles, Alcohol y Portland.

Uruguay. Comercio Exterior, Dirección General de. see Uruguay. Dirección General de Comercio Exterior.

Uruguay. Dirección de Investigaciones Económicas Agropecuarias. Encuesta pecuaria en profundidad . Montevideo, Uruguay [1977-1978] 2 v. ; LC Card 87-402173 DDC 338.1/762/009895021 19
HD9433.U82 E53 1979

Uruguay. Dirección General de Comercio Exterior. (Old Catalog form: Uruguay. Comercio Exterior, Dirección General de) Producción y exportación de lácteos /. Montevideo, Uruguay , 1977. 21 p. ; LC Card 85-205438
HD9275.U92 P76 1977

Uruguay. Dirección General de Estadística y Censos. (Old Catalog form: Uruguay. Estadística y Censos, Dirección General de) Encuesta de gastos e ingresos de los hogares, 1982-1983 . [Montevideo] [1986] 76, 96, 120 p. : LC Card 87-403151 DDC 339.4/2/09895 19
HD7020 .E53 1986

Recuentos preliminares . [Montevideo] [1986] 188 p. : LC Card 87-122427 DDC 304.6/09895/021 19
HA1074 1985

Uruguay. Dirección Nacional de Recursos Humanos.
Empleo y estructura ocupacional en grandes establecimientos industriales /. Montevideo , 1984. 51 leaves ; LC Card 86-174021
HB2667 .E46 1984

Estimación de las necesidades de formación profesional en el Uruguay . Montevideo , 1981. 98 leaves ; LC Card 86-174016
HD5715.5.U8 E86 1981

Informe sobre el mercado de empleo, 1983 /. Montevideo , 1984. 8, [19] leaves ; LC Card 86-174013
HD5762.A6 I54 1984

URUGUAY - ECONOMIC CONDITIONS.
Jacob, Raúl, 1946- Algunas consideraciones acerca de la formación económica del Uruguay, 1726-1930 /. Montevideo, Uruguay [1985 or 1986] 56 p. ; LC Card 86-202376 DDC 330.9895/065 19
HC232 .J287 1985

URUGUAY - ECONOMIC CONDITIONS - 1918- - ADDRESSES, ESSAYS, LECTURES.
El Primer batllismo . Montevideo [1985] 159 p. : LC Card 85-233561 DDC 338.9895 19
HC232 .P75 1985 ***NYPL [JLC 86-259]***

URUGUAY - ECONOMIC CONDITIONS - 1945-
Bensión, Alberto. Las opciones de política económica en Uruguay /. Montevideo, Uruguay , 1986. 106 p., [48] leaves ; LC Card 87-121223 DDC 338.9895 19
HC232 .B44 1986

Fortuna, Juan Carlos. Las bases de un desarrollo social diferente . Montevideo [1985] 117 p. ; LC Card 86-131906
HC232 .F76 1985

URUGUAY - ECONOMIC CONDITIONS - 1973-
Cancela Vilanova, Walter, 1948- El programa de la CONAPRO y las perspectivas económicas inmediatas /. [Montevideo, Uruguay] [1985] 39 p. ; LC Card 85-235957 DDC 338.9895 19
HC232 .C283 1985

Uruguay . Montevideo [1986] 103 p. : LC Card 87-403165 DDC 330.9895/065 19
HC232 .U78 1986

URUGUAY - ECONOMIC CONDITIONS - ADDRESSES, ESSAYS, LECTURES.
El Primer batllismo . Montevideo [1985] 159 p. : LC Card 85-233561 DDC 338.9895 19
HC232 .P75 1985 ***NYPL [JLC 86-259]***

URUGUAY - ECONOMIC POLICY.
Bensión, Alberto. Las opciones de política económica en Uruguay /. Montevideo, Uruguay , 1986. 106 p., [48] leaves ; LC Card 87-121223 DDC 338.9895 19
HC232 .B44 1986

Cancela Vilanova, Walter, 1948- El programa de la CONAPRO y las perspectivas económicas inmediatas /. [Montevideo, Uruguay] [1985] 39 p. ; LC Card 85-235957 DDC 338.9895 19
HC232 .C283 1985

Gómez de Reyes, María Teresa. Experiencias de políticas de estabilización . México, D.F. , 1985. iv, 66 leaves ; LC Card 87-122042 DDC 338.982 19
HC125 .G57 1985

Peirano, Ricardo. El rol del empresario privado en el desarrollo económico y social en democracia /. Montevideo, Uruguay , 1986. 79 leaves ; LC Card 87-404359 DDC 338.9895 19
HC232 .P45 1986

URUGUAY - ECONOMIC POLICY - ADDRESSES, ESSAYS, LECTURES.
El Primer batllismo . Montevideo [1985] 159 p. : LC Card 85-233561 DDC 338.9895 19
HC232 .P75 1985 ***NYPL [JLC 86-259]***

URUGUAY - ECONOMIC POLICY - CASE STUDIES.
Cartas, José María. Precondiciones para la implementación de la economía social de mercado en América Latina . Buenos Aires, República Argentina , c1985. 80 p. ; LC Card 87-101628
HC125 .C374 1985

Uruguay. Estadística y Censos, Dirección General de. see Uruguay. Dirección General de Estadística y Censos.

Uruguay, exportaciones cumplidas de lanas y sus productos, ovinos en pie, carne ovina y subproductos, apendice pieles lanares : zafra 83-84 (completa). [Montevideo, Uruguay] : Secretariado Uruguayo de la Lana, Departamento de Información e Investigaciones Económicas, 1984. 37 p. ; 23 x 34 cm. Cover title. Chiefly tables. "Acumulados y comparación con la zafra 82-83." LC Card 86-164077
1. Wool trade and industry - Uruguay - Statistics. 2. Sheep industry - Uruguay - Statistics. I. Secretariado Uruguayo de la Lana. Departamento de Información e Investigaciones Económicas.
HD9904.U82 U78 1984

URUGUAY - INDUSTRIES.
Fortuna, Juan Carlos. Las bases de un desarrollo social diferente . Montevideo [1985] 117 p. ; LC Card 86-131906
HC232 .F76 1985

Uruguay. Ministerio de Economía y Finanzas. Dirección General de Estadística y Censos. see Uruguay. Dirección General de Estadística y Censos.

Uruguay. Ministerio de Hacienda. Dirección General de Estadística y Censos. see **Uruguay. Dirección General de Estadística y Censos.**

URUGUAY - OCCUPATIONS - STATISTICS.
Empleo y estructura ocupacional en grandes establecimientos industriales /. Montevideo , 1984. 51 leaves ; LC Card 86-174021
HB2667 .E46 1984

URUGUAY - POLITICS AND GOVERNMENT - 1904-1973.
Lanzaro, Jorge Luis. Sindicatos y sistema político . Montevideo, Uruguay , 1986. 132 p. ; LC Card 87-403149 DDC 322/.2/09895 19
HD3616.U72 L36 1986

URUGUAY - POLITICS AND GOVERNMENT - 1904-1973 - ADDRESSES, ESSAYS, LECTURES.
El Primer batllismo . Montevideo [1985] 159 p. : LC Card 85-233561 DDC 338.9895 19
HC232 .P75 1985 ***NYPL [JLC 86-259]***

URUGUAY - POLITICS AND GOVERNMENT - 1973-
Lanzaro, Jorge Luis. Sindicatos y sistema político . Montevideo, Uruguay , 1986. 132 p. ; LC Card 87-403149 DDC 322/.2/09895 19
HD3616.U72 L36 1986

URUGUAY - POPULATION - STATISTICS.
Recuentos preliminares . [Montevideo] [1986] 188 p. : LC Card 87-122427 DDC 304.6/09895/021 19
HA1074 1985

Uruguay, producción y comercialización de ganado y carnes. [Montevideo, Uruguay] : Dirección de Comercialización : Dirección de Estudios Económicos, Instituto Nacional de Carnes, 1985. 90 p. : ill. ; 29 cm. (Trabajo . no. 11) A paper presented at the IX Reunión de Juntas de Carnes, held in Buenos Aires, Argentina, Sept. 12-13, 1985. LC Card 87-403154 DDC 338.1/760883/09895 19
1. Meat industry and trade - Uruguay. 2. Animal industry - Uruguay. I. Instituto Nacional de Carnes (Uruguay). Dirección de Comercialización. II. Instituto Nacional de Carnes (Uruguay). Dirección de Estudios Económicos. III. Series: Trabajo (Instituto Nacional de Carnes (Uruguay)) , no. 11.
HD9424.U8 U783 1985

Uruguay. Secretaría de Planeamiento, Coordinación y Difusión. Dirección General de Estadística y Censos. see Uruguay. Dirección General de Estadística y Censos.

URUGUAY - SOCIAL POLICY.
Peirano, Ricardo. El rol del empresario privado en el desarrollo económico y social en democracia /. Montevideo, Uruguay , 1986. 79 leaves ; LC Card 87-404359 DDC 338.9895 19
HC232 .P45 1986

Urundi. see **Burundi.**

Urzúa, Raúl. La Opción preferencial por los pobres . [Santiago] [1987] 360 p. : LC Card 87-403060 DDC 362.5/098 19
HC130.P6 O63 1987

US-Administration : die Verwaltung des Werkes Hoechst, 1945-1953 / [herausgegeben von] Klaus Trouet. Frankfurt (M) : Hoechst, 1976. 153 p. : ill. ; 21 cm. (Dokumente aus Hoechst-Archiven . 48) Compilation of documents. Bibliography: p. 153. LC Card 85-224662
1. Hoechst AG - Archives. 2. Chemical industry - Germany (West) - History - Sources. I. Trouet, Klaus. II. Series.
HD9654.9.H64 U7 1976

US aid to Israel. Laufer, Leopold Yehuda. U. S. aid to Israel . [Jerusalem] [1983] 55 p. : LC Card 87-400279 DDC 338.91/73/05694 19
HC415.25 .L38 1983

US aid to the West Bank and Gaza. Laufer, Leopold Yehuda. U. S. aid to the West Bank and Gaza . [Jerusalem] [1985] 54 p. ; LC Card 87-400340 DDC 338.91/73/056951 19
HC415.25.Z7 W4735 1985

US and world food, beverages, and tobacco expenditures, 1970-1983. Korb, Penelope. U. S. and world food, beverages, and tobacco expenditures, 1970-83 /. Washington, D.C. , 1986. iv, 84 p. : LC Card 86-603160 DDC 339.4/8664/0021 19
HD9000.4 .K67 1986

US-Asia Institute (Washington, D.C.) Vision of the future . Washington, D.C. , 1986. x, 189 p. : LC Card 87-125235 DDC 382/.0973/05 19
HF3118 .V57 1986

US-Australia Joint Seminar on the Future Impact of technology on Work and Education (1984 : Monash University) The Future impact of technology on work and education /. London , New York , 1987. p. cm. ISBN 1-85000-083-2 : LC Card 87-13641 DDC 331.12/0994 19
HD6331.2.A8 F87 1987

US Catholic institutions and labor unions, 1960-1980. Sullivan, Patrick J., 1929- U. S. Catholic institutions and labor unions, 1960-1980 /. Lanham, MD , c1985. 545 p. ; ISBN 0-8191-4970-5 (alk. paper) : LC Card 85-20171 DDC 331.88/1128273 19
HD6481.2.U6 S85 1985
NYPL [JLE 86-2407]

US clinical testing market. U. S. clinical testing market /. Tustin, CA, U. S.A. (17722 Irvine Blvd., Tustin 92680) , c1987. 223 leaves in various foliations ; LC Card 87-402039 DDC 381/.45681761 19
HD9995.L33 U5484 1987

US corporate withdrawal from South Africa. Hauck, David. U. S. corporate withdrawal from South Africa . Washington, D.C. (Suite 600, 1755 Massachusetts Ave., N.W., Washington 20036) [1986] 22 p. ; LC Card 86-209299 DDC 332.6/7373/068 19
HG5851.A3 H39 1986

US decennial life tables for 1979-81. U. S. decennial life tables for 1979-81. Hyattsville, Md. , Washington, D.C. , 1985-<1986. v. ; LC Card 85-600190 DDC 304.6/4/0973021 19
HB1335 .U17 1985 ***NYPL [JLM 86-491]***

US direct investment abroad, balance of payments and direct investment position estimates, 1977-81. U. S. direct investment abroad . Washington, D.C. , 1986. x, 41 p. ; LC Card 87-600815
HG4538 .U22 1986

US dollar. Pick, Franz. The U. S. dollar . Bethel, CT , c1986. xvi, 103 p., [1] folded leaf of plates : ISBN 0-916373-04-5 (pbk.): LC Card 86-210094 DDC 332.4/973 19
HG539 .P5 1986

US economic expansion : Western Europe. Moscow : "Social Sciences Today" Editorial Board, 1986. 172 p. ; 21 cm. (Problems of the contemporary world . 120) Title in colophon: Ėkonomicheskaia ėkspansiia SShA. Edited by I.R. Grigulevich. Includes bibliographies. LC Card 86-204071 DDC 337.7304 19
1. United States - Foreign economic relations - Europe. 2. Europe - Foreign economic relations - United States. I. Grigulevich, Iosif Romual'dovich. II. Izdatel'stvo Nauka. Redaktsiia "Obshchestvennye nauki i sovremennost'.". III. Title: Ėkonomicheskaia ėkspansiia SShA. IV. Series: Problems of the contemporary world , no. 120.
HF3092 .U8 1986

US economic expansion : Latin America. Moscow : "Social Sciences Today" Editorial Board, 1986. 216 p. ; 21 cm. (Problems of the contemporary world . 121) Title in colophon: Ėkonomicheskaia ėkspansiia SShA. Bibliography: p. 209-[214]. At head of title: USSR Academy of Sciences. LC Card 87-112029 DDC 337.7308 19
1. United States - Foreign economic relations - Latin America. 2. Latin America - Foreign economic relations - United States. 3. United States - Commercial policy. 4. Banks and banking, American - Latin America. I. Akademiia nauk SSSR. II. Title: Ėkonomicheskaia ėkspansiia SShA.
HF1456.5.L3 U8 1986

US economic history. Niemi, Albert W. U. S. economic history /. Lanham, MD [1987], c1980. xiii, 475 p. : ISBN 0-8191-6335-X (pbk. : alk. paper) : LC Card 87-10730 DDC 330.973 19
HC103 .N5 1987

US economic review. U. S. economic review . Bala Cynwyd, Pa., USA (150 Monument Rd., Bala Cynwyd 19004-1790) , c1985. 7, 28 p. : LC Card 87-145506 DDC 338.5/443/0973 19
HC106.8 .U18 1985

US economy to 1990. Collins, Lora S. The U. S. economy to 1990 /. New York, N.Y. , c1985. 21 p. : ISBN 0-8237-0307-X (pbk.) LC Card 86-200284 DDC 338.5/443/0973 19
HC106.8 .C636 1985

US essential air services study. Lin, Leesha. U. S. essential air services study /. Ottawa-Hull , c1986. viii, 118 p. : ISBN 0-662-14800-2 (pbk.) LC Card 87-102545 DDC 387.7/1 19
HE9803.A4 L55 1986

US-Fusionsrichtlinien, 1984 / [Herausgeber, Forschungsinstitut für Wirtschaftsverfassung und Wettbewerb e.V.]. Köln : Heymann, c1985. 83 p. ; 23 cm. (FIW-Dokumentation, 0071-769X . Heft 6) German and English. ISBN 3-452-20248-8 : LC Card 86-100251
1. Consolidation and merger of corporations - United States. I. Forschungsinstitut für Wirtschaftsverfassung und Wettbewerb (Cologne, Germany). II. Title: United States-Fusionsrichtlinien, 1984. III. Series.
HB41 .F63 Heft 6 KF1477

US imports of textile and apparel products under the multifiber arrangement, 1981-84. Taylor, John A. (John Alvin), 1930- U. S. imports of textile and apparel products under the multifiber arrangement, 1981-84 /. Washington, D.C. [1985] v, 136 p. ; LC Card 86-601665 DDC 382/.45677/00973021 19
HD9940.U4 T38 1985

US industrial competitiveness. Ghadar, Fariborz. U. S. industrial competitiveness . Lexington, Mass. , c1987. x, 114 p. : ISBN 0-669-15689-2 (alk. paper) LC Card 86-46341 DDC 338.4/7677/00973 19
HD9855 .G47 1987

US investments and bank loans in South Africa. U. S. investments and bank loans in South Africa (supplemental material to the hearings and markups of January 31 and February 7, 1984, serial no. 98-14, on District of Columbia South Africa divestment) . Washington , 1985. vi, 24 p.: LC Card 85-602615 DDC 332.6/7373/068 19
HG5851.A3 U17 1985

US maritime industries--down for the third time? Hilton, Robert, 1927- U. S. maritime industries--down for the third time? /. Washington, D.C. , c1987. vi, 60 p. : ISBN 0-89206-099-9 (pbk.) LC Card 86-31768 DDC 387.5/0973 19
HE745 .H66 1987

US market for hazardous duty liquid pumps and valves. The U. S. market for hazardous duty liquid pumps and valves. New York, N.Y. , c1983. 2 v. (viii, 343 leaves) : LC Card 87-401677 DDC 381/.456216 19
HD9651.5 .U16 1983

US-Mexico border region. The U. S.-Mexico border region . [El Paso] , 1984, c1982. viii, 446 p. : ISBN 0-87404-091-4 (pbk.) LC Card 87-401861 DDC 333.7/0972/1 19
HC137.M46 U17 1984

US-Mexico relations. U. S.-Mexico relations . Stanford, Calif. , c1987. xii, 401 p. ; ISBN 0-8047-1319-7 (alk. paper) LC Card 86-23103 DDC 338.1/872 19
HD1792 .U19 1987

US mobile radio communications equipment market. The U. S. mobile radio communications equipment market. New York, N.Y. , c1983. viii, 253 p. : LC Card 87-142226 DDC 384.5/3 19
HD9696.R363 U684 1983

US national economic policy, 1917-1985. Campagna, Anthony S. U. S. national economic policy, 1917-1985 /. New York , 1987. xix, 642 p. : ISBN 0-275-92426-2 (alk. paper) : LC Card 86-30316 DDC 338.973 19
HC106.2 .C26 1987

US News investment guide. U. S. News investment guide /. Washington, D.C. (2400 N. St., N.W., Washington 20037-1196) , c1987. iv, 60 p. : LC Card 87-143438 DDC 332.6/78 19
HG4910 .U25 1987

US non telecommunications fiber optic component market in the US. The U. S. non telecommunications fiber optic component market in the U. S. New York, N.Y. , c1982. vi, 255 leaves : LC Card 87-143641 DDC 381/.456213692/0973 19
HD9696.F523 U557 1982

US primary iron and steel industry since 1958. The U. S. primary iron and steel industry since 1958. Washington, D.C. , 1985. xvi, 138 p. :
NYPL [JLF 86-689]

US professional/executive workstations market. The U. S. professional/executive workstations market. New York, N.Y. , c1983. vi, 284 p. : LC Card 87-142071 DDC 381/.4500416/0973 19
HD9801.U542 U18 1983

US stationary compressors market. U. S. stationary compressors market. New York, N.Y. , c1983. xi, 271 p. : LC Card 87-143527 DDC 380.1/4562153/0973 19
HD9705.5.C643 U648 1983

US-Technologietransferpolitik gegenüber der UdSSR und der VR China . Rode, Reinhard, 1947- Frankfurt am Main [1986] 39 p. : ISBN 3-926197-01-3 LC Card 87-120584 DDC 338.9/26 19
HC340.T4 R63 1986

US trade relations in the Pacific Rim. U. S. trade relations in the Pacific Rim . Washington , 1987. v, 57 p. ; LC Card 87-601361 DDC 382/.0973/09 19
HF3126.5 .U17 1987

US trade relations with Asia. U. S. trade relations with Asia . Washington , 1987. vii, 85 p. ; LC Card 87-601359 DDC 382/.0973/05 19
HF3118 .U15 1987

US wood-based industry. Ellefson, Paul V. U. S. wood-based industry . New York , 1984. xxv, 479 p. : ISBN 0-03-063698-1 (alk. paper) : LC

Card 84-8278 DDC 338.1/7498/0973 19
HD9755 .45 1984 **NYPL [JLE 85-706]**

USAID-Bolivia (Mission)
Diez, Rafael. Final report of the consultancy of Rafael Diez from August 3, 1982 to August 3, 1983. La Paz [1983] 1 v. (various foliations) ; LC Card 83-243264
HC182 .D49 1983

Proyecto harinas compuestas . La Paz, Bolivia , 1982. 272, [2], 3 p., [9] p. of plates : LC Card 83-195592
HD9044.B52 P76 1982

USAID/Tanzania. Program and background materials for Tanzania/USAID bilateral talks, November 30 and December 1, 1983. [Dar es Salaam, Tanzania] : USAID, [1983?] 1 v. (various pagings) ; 34 cm. Title from label on cover. LC Card 86-980179 DDC 338.91/73/0678 19
1. Economic assistance, American - Tanzania. I. Title.
HC885 .U8 1983

USE OF LAND. see **LAND USE.**

The use of microcomputers in accounting /. Hicks, Sam A. St. Paul , c1985. xx, 349 p. : ISBN 0-314-87064-4 (pbk.) LC Card 85-8950 DDC 657/.028/54 19
HF5679 .H535 1985 **NYPL [JLF 86-1720]**

The use of national income and product accounts for public policy . Carson, Carol S. Washington, D.C. , 1986. 26 p. : LC Card 86-601338 DDC 339.5/0973 19
HC110.I5 C37 1986

Use of part-time operators /. MacDorman, Littleton C. Washington, D.C. [1986] 33 p. : ISBN 0-309-04403-0 (pbk.) LC Card 86-51175 DDC 331.25/72 19
HD8039.S82 U65 1986

The use of resource survey data in decision-making with special reference to Kitui District in Kenya /. Peden, D. G. Nairobi, Kenya , 1982. 12 leaves ; LC Card 85-980593 DDC 333.74/09676/24 19
HD983.Z8 K587 1982

USE TAX - NEW YORK (STATE) - AUDITING.
An evaluation of the sales tax audit program of the New York State Department of Taxation and Finance. [Albany] [1985] 2, 75 p. : LC Card 86-621117 DDC 353.97470072/47 19
HJ5715.U6 E83 1985

USED BUSES - UNITED STATES - PRICES.
Plachno, Larry, 1943. Used intercity bus pricing, 1978-1986 /. Polo, Ill. , c1987. 40 p. : ISBN 0-933449-03-8 (pbk.) LC Card 87-19189 DDC 629.2/2233/029473 19
HD9710.33.U52 P42 1987

Used intercity bus pricing, 1978-1986 /. Plachno, Larry, 1943. Polo, Ill. , c1987. 40 p. : ISBN 0-933449-03-8 (pbk.) LC Card 87-19189 DDC 629.2/2233/029473 19
HD9710.33.U52 P42 1987

USEFUL ARTS. see **TECHNOLOGY.**

Usefulness to investors and creditors of information provided by financial reporting /. Griffin, Paul A. Stamford, Conn. , c1987. xii, 294 p. ; ISBN 0-910065-24-1 (pbk.) LC Card 87-81637 DDC 657/.3 19
HF5681.B2 G79 1987

Uses of census data for demographic research and development planning in Africa : aspects of technical co-operation / Department of Technical Co-operation for Development. New York : United Nations, 1986. iv, 24 p. ; 28 cm. "ST/TCD/SER.E/3." "United Nations publication. Sales no. E.86.II.H.1"--T.p. verso. Bibliography: p. 23-24. LC Card 87-118612 DDC 304.6/096 19
1. Population forecasting - Africa - Case studies. 2. Africa - Economic policy - Case studies. I. United Nations. Dept. of Technical Cooperation of Development.
HB3661 .U94 1986

Usha, M. N. Prabhakara, N. R. Population growth and unemployment in India /. New Delhi , 1986. ix, 102 p. ; ISBN 81-7024-041-7 : LC Card 86-902156 DDC 331.13/795487 19
HD5820.K37 P7 1986

Ushanov, I͡Uriĭ Aleksandrovich. Upravlencheskie novovvedenii͡a v SShA . Moskva , 1986. 244, [3] p. : LC Card 86-231514
HD70.U5 U67 1986

Usherov, I. G. (Il'i͡a Grigor'evich) Zubet͡s, V. M. (Vasiliĭ Mikhaĭlovich) Rezervy povyshenii͡a ėffektivnosti proizvodstva na magnitogorskom metallurgicheskom kombinate /. Cheli͡abinsk , 1975. 183 p. ; LC Card 81-170397
HD9525.S653 M39 1975

Using AppleWorks /. Aron, Arthur. Indianapolis, Ind. , c1987. xviii, 458 p. : ISBN 0-88022-280-8 (pbk.) LC Card 86-63838 DDC 005.36/9 19
HF5548.4.A68 A76 1987

Using Dollars and Sense on the IBM /. Adams, Steve, 1948- Indianapolis, Ind. , c1987. xviii, 439 p. : ISBN 0-88022-287-5 (pbk.) : LC Card 86-63981 DDC 332.024/0028/55369 19
HG179 .A34 1987

Using econometrics . Studenmund, A. H. Boston , c1987. xii, 440 p. : ISBN 0-316-82010-5 LC Card 86-21382 DDC 330/.028 19
HB139 .S795 1987

Using HAL . Postman, Andrew. Berkeley, Calif. , c1987. xvi, 557 p. : ISBN 0-07-881268-2 (pbk.) : LC Card 87-403738 DDC 005.36/9 19
HF5548.4.L68 P67 1987

Using Lotus Manuscript /. Nelson, Kay Yarborough. Berkeley, Calif. , c1987. xvii, 410 p. : ISBN 0-07-881003-5 (pbk.) : LC Card 87-401628 DDC 652/.5 19
HF5548.115 .N45 1987

Using Managing Your Money /. Weinberg, Mark D. Indianapolis, Ind. , c1987. xviii, 422 p. : ISBN 0-88022-277-8 (pbk.) : LC Card 86-62530 DDC 332.024/0028/55369 19
HG179 .W42 1987

Using microcomputers in business. Spence, J. Wayne. Microcomputers in business . St. Louis , 1987. vii, 224 p. : ISBN 0-8016-5030-5 (pbk.) LC Card 86-30013 DDC 650/.028/5536 19
HF5548.2 .S728 1987

Using microcomputers in marketing /. Parsons, Leonard J. [Boston, Mass.?] , c1986. xi, 141 p. : LC Card 86-216432 DDC 658.8/0028/5416 19
HF5415.125 .P37 1986

Using Minitab with Basic business statistics /. Levine, David M., 1946- Englewood Cliffs, N.J. , c1986. viii, 160 p. : ISBN 0-13-057779-0 (pbk.) LC Card 87-400304 DDC 519.5/028/55369 19
HF1017 .L425 1986

Using new communications technologies : a guide for organizations. Washington, D.C. : Media Institute, c1986. ix, 57 p. : ill. ; 23 cm. Includes bibliographical references. ISBN 0-937790-30-3 (pbk.) : LC Card 85-63320 DDC 384 19
1. Business - Communication systems. 2. Telephone in business. I. Media Institute (Washington, D.C.).
HF5541.T4 U75 1986

Using one-two-three. Using 1-2-3 /. Carmel, Ind. , c1987. xxviii, 905 p. : ISBN 0-88022-332-4 (pbk.) LC Card 87-61897 DDC 005.36/9 19
HF5548.4.L67 U85 1987

Using SuperCalc 4 . Doyle, William J., 1946- New York , c1987. xvi, 382 p. : ISBN 0-471-85992-3 : LC Card 87-13804 DDC 005.36/9 19
HF5548.4.S87 D69 1987

Using the microcomputer in cost accounting . Lehman, Mark W. St. Paul , c1988. x, 396 p. : ISBN 0-314-34729-1 (pbk.) LC Card 87-10632 DDC 657/.42/02855369 19
HF5686.C8 L34 1988

Using the microcomputer in managerial accounting . Lehman, Mark W. St. Paul , c1987. x, 406 p. : ISBN 0-314-98515-8 (pbk.) LC Card 87-2194 DDC 658.1/511/02855369 19
HF5657.4 .L44 1987

Using the microcomputer in marketing /. Parkinson, Lynn K. London , New York , c1987. ix, 158 p. : ISBN 0-07-084163-2 (pbk.) : LC Card 86-27364 DDC 658.8/0028/5416 19
HF5415.125 .P36 1987

Using 1-2-3 / developed by Que Corporation. Special ed. Carmel, Ind. : Que Corp., c1987. xxviii, 905 p. : ill. ; 24 cm. Includes index. ISBN 0-88022-332-4 (pbk.) LC Card 87-61897 DDC 005.36/9 19
1. Lotus 1-2-3 (Computer program). 2. Business - Data processing. I. Que Corporation. II. Title: Using one-two-three.
HF5548.4.L67 U85 1987

Uskorenie sot͡sial'no-ėkonomicheskogo razvitii͡a strany--zadacha vseĭ partii, vsego naroda : dokumenty i materialy : dli͡a sistemy politicheskoĭ ucheby. Moskva : Izd-vo polit. lit-ry, 1986. 476 p. ; 21 cm. Includes bibliographical references and index. LC Card 87-103200 DDC 338.947/09/048 19
1. Soviet Union - Economic policy - 1981-1985 - Congresses. 2. Soviet Union - Economic policy - 1986- - Congresses.
HC336.25 .U748 1986

Uslovii͡a truda pri sot͡sializme . Prigarin, V. S. (Valentin Stepanovich) Leningrad , 1985. 125 p. ; LC Card 86-124818
HD7725 .P83 1985

Uslovii͡a truda v regione / [avtory A.I. Amosha ... et al. ; otvetstvennyĭ redaktor A.I. Amosha]. Kiev : Naukova dumka, 1985. 252 p. : ill. ; 21 cm. At head of title: Akademii͡a nauk Ukrainskoĭ SSR. Institut ėkonomiki promyshlennosti. Includes index. Bibliography: p. 239-[251]. LC Card 86-105167
1. Work environment - Ukraine - Donetskai͡a oblast'. 2. Industrial hygiene - Ukraine - Donetskai͡a oblast'. I. Amosha, Aleksandr Ivanovich. II. Instytut ekonomiky promyslovosti (Akademii͡a nauk Ukraïns'koï RSR).
HD7726.U39 U85 1985 **NYPL [*QGA 87-3379]**

Usmanov, Kh. F. Razvitie kapitalizma v sel'skom khozi͡aĭstve Bashkirii v poreformennyĭ period, 60-90-e gody XIX v. / Kh.F. Usmanov. Moskva : Izd-vo "Nauka", 1981. 368 p. ; 21 cm. At head of title: Akademii͡a nauk SSSR. Bashkirskiĭ filial. Institut istorii, i͡azyka i literatury. Includes bibliographical references. LC Card 82-118144
1. Agriculture - Economic aspects - Russian S.F.S.R. - Bashkirskai͡a A.S.S.R. - History - 19th century. 2. Peasantry - Russian S.F.S.R. - Bashkirskaia A.S.S.R. - History - 19th century. I. Title.
HD1995.B38 U86 1981

Uso de energia na indústria de cimento em Minas Gerais, 1980-1983. [Belo Horizonte] : Companhia Energética de Minas Gerais : Conselho Estadual de Energia, Secretaria de Estado de Minas E Energia, 1985. 146 p. : ill. ; 30 cm. Cover title. At head of title: Governo do Estado de Minas Gerais. Bibliography: p. 145-146. LC Card 86-152639
1. Cement industries - Brazil - Minas Gerais - Energy consumption. I. Companhia Energética de Minas Gerais. II. Minas Gerais (Brazil). Conselho Estadual de Energia.
HD9622.B73 M569 1985

Uspekhi ėkonomicheskogo i kul'turnogo razvitii͡a Ėstonskoĭ SSR za gody sovetskoĭ vlasti : referativnyĭ sbornik / [redakt͡sionnai͡a kollegii͡a I͡U. Kakhk (gl. red.) ... L.I. Apananskiĭ (sostavitel')]. Tallin : Akademii͡a nauk Ėstonskoĭ SSR, 1980. 222 p. ; 20 cm. At head of title: Akademii͡a nauk Ėstonskoĭ SSR. T͡Sentr nauchnoĭ informat͡sii po obshchestvennym naukam. Errata slip inserted. LC Card 81-198881
1. Estonia - Economic conditions - 1944- - Abstracts. 2. Estonia - Social conditions - Abstracts. I. Kahk, Juhan. II. Apananskiĭ, L. III. Ühiskonnateaduste Informatsioonikeskus (Eesti NSV Teaduste Akadeemia).
HC337.E7 U86 1980

USSR economic handbook /. Scrivener, Ronald. London , Detroit, Mich. , 1986. 246 p. : ISBN 0-86338-156-1 LC Card 87-130957 DDC 330.947/0854
HC336.25 .S37 1986

USSR--looking at an economic map /. Korop, P. N. (Petr Nikolaevich) [Moscow] , c1985. 250 p., [3] p. of plates : LC Card 86-207488 DDC 330.947/0854 19
HC336.25 .K66 1985

USSR, the 12th five-year plan period /. Danilov, L. L. (Leonid Luk'i͡anvich), 1914- Moscow , 1986. 55 p. : LC Card 87-123056 DDC 338.947 19
HC336.25 .D378 1986

Ústav pro filozofii a sociologii ČSAV. Migrace a osídlení v socialistických zemích =. Praha , 1984- v. <1 > : LC Card 87-160334
HB2041 .M526 1984

Usteri, Martin. Bodenrecht in Bewegung : Referate, gehalten anlässlich einer Arbeitstagung des Redressement national am 25. September

1985 in Zürich / Martin Usteri, Martin Lendi, Heinz Rey. Zürich : Redressement national, [1985] 27 p. ; 23 cm. (Zeitfragen der schweizerischen Wirtschaft und Politik . Nov. 1985, Nr. 126 =) Cover title. CONTENTS. - Aushöhlung der Eigentumsgarantie durch den Richter? / Martin Usteri -- Nutzungsbeschränkungen, Sinn und Problematik / Martin Lendi -- Wem darf der Boden gehören? / Heinz Rey. LC Card 86-195037
1. Real property - Switzerland. I. Lendi, Martin. II. Rey, Heinz, 1943-. III. Redressement national (Society : Switzerland). IV. Series. V. Series: Zeitfragen der schweizerischen Wirtschaft und Politik , Nr. 126. VI. Title.
HC395 .Z43 Nr. 126 KKW683

USURY - GREAT BRITAIN.
Locke, John, 1632-1704. Several papers relating to money, interest and trade, &c. /. Fairfield, NJ , 1988. p. cm. ISBN 0-678-00334-3 LC Card 87-17243 DDC 332.4/941 19
HG937 .L74 1988

USURY LAWS - ECONOMIC ASPECTS - EUROPE.
Bürge, Alfons. Rechtsdogmatik und Wirtschaft . Berlin , c1987. 280 p. ; ISBN 3-428-06124-1 LC Card 87-134998 DDC 332.8/3/094 19
HB551 .B87 1987

USURY - MORAL AND ETHICAL ASPECTS - HISTORY.
Langholm, Odd Inge, 1928- The Aristotelian analysis of usury /. Bergen [Norway] , New York, NY , c1984. 153 p. ; ISBN 82-00-07290-8 LC Card 85-167906 DDC 332.8/3/09 19
HB551 .L36 1984 ***NYPL [JLD 86-2545]***

Utah affirmative action information, 1985. Jensen, Kenneth E. [Salt Lake City] [1986] i, 253 p. ; LC Card 86-622873 DDC 331.11/43 19
HD5725.U8 J46 1986

Utah. Dept. of Employment Security. (Old Catalog form: Utah. Employment Security Dept.)
Jensen, Kenneth E. Utah personal income, 1929-1985 /. [Salt Lake City] [1986] 114 p. : LC Card 87-621301 DDC 339.2/2/09792 19
HC107.U83 I515 1986

Utah. Employment Security, Dept. of. see **Utah. Dept. of Employment Security.**

Utah personal income, 1929-1985 /. Jensen, Kenneth E. [Salt Lake City] [1986] 114 p. : LC Card 87-621301 DDC 339.2/2/09792 19
HC107.U83 I515 1986

Utah State Tax Commission. Economic & Statistical Unit. Katayama, Leslee. Hotel sales, room rents, and transient room taxes in Utah, 1978-1985 /. Salt Lake City, Utah (519 Heber Wells Bldg., Salt Lake City 84134) [1985] i, 49 leaves : LC Card 86-620905 DDC 336.2/7864794 19
HJ5715.U62 U85 1985

'Utaybah, Mānī' Sa'īd, 1946- The economy of Abu Dhabi : ancient & modern / by Mana Saeed Al-Otaiba. [S.l. : s.n., 197-?] (Beirut, Lebanon : Commercial & Industrial Press) 247 p. ; 21 cm. Bibliography: p. 245. LC Card 86-965159
1. Abū Ẓaby (United Arab Emirates : Emirate) - Economic conditions. 2. Abū Ẓaby (United Arab Emirates : Emirate) - Industries - History. I. Title.
HC415.36.Z7 A288 1970z

UTILITARIANISM.
Penz, G. Peter. Consumer sovereignty and human interests /. Cambridge [Cambridgeshire] , New York , 1986. xiv, 242 p. ; ISBN 0-521-26571-1 LC Card 85-22407 DDC 330.15/5 19
HB846 .P46 1986 ***NYPL [JLE 86-3311]***

Riley, Jonathan, 1955- Liberal utilitarianism . Cambridge [Cambridgeshire] , New York , 1987. p. cm. ISBN 0-521-30692-2 LC Card 87-6598 DDC 302/.13 19
HB846.8 .R55 1987

Utilities in transition . Washington (State). Governor's Citizens Utility and Telecommunication Advisory Committee. [Olympia, Wash.] [1984] 61, 18, [20] p. ; LC Card 85-622797 DDC 363.6/09797 19
HE7791.W2 W37 1984
NYPL [JLF 86-1773]

Utility diversification . Shapiro, Michael E. Sacramento, CA [1986] 50 p. ; LC Card 86-621960 DDC 338.8/3613636/0973 19
HD2766 .S47 1986

UTILITY THEORY.
Maierbeck, Marianne. Nutzen- und Zielprobleme privater Haushalte . Berlin , 1978. 203 p. : ISBN 3-428-04220-4 : LC Card 79-356181
TX7 .B4 Heft 13 HB201
NYPL [JLE 86-3431]

Politökonomische Probleme des Gebrauchswerts, der Nützlichkeit und der Bewertung von Gebrauchswerten /. Karl-Marx-Stadt [1983] 92 p. ; LC Card 84-167577
HB201 .P63 1983

Potapov, V. V. (Viktor Vladimirovich) Modifikatsii teorii "poleznosti" /. Moskva , 1984. 132 p. ; LC Card 84-247447
HB201 .P65 1984

Schoemaker, Paul J. H. Experiments on decisions under risk . Boston , c1980. xxii, 211 p. : ISBN 0-89838-035-9 LC Card 79-27948 DDC 658.4/03
HB615 .S36 ***NYPL [JLE 81-559]***

UTILITY THEORY - MATHEMATICAL MODELS.
Wagener, Martin. Kardinalität in der Nutzentheorie /. Königstein/Ts. , c1983. xii, 160 p. ; ISBN 3-445-02289-5 LC Card 83-195855
HB201 .W17 1983

UTILIZATION OF LAND. see **LAND USE.**

Utilization of medicaid paid health services by Medicaid recipients in New York City, Nassau, Monroe, and western central counties, 1980-1981 / Cesar A. Perales ... [et al.]. Albany, N.Y. (1 Commerce Plaza, Albany 12210) : New York State Dept. of Social Services, Division of Medical Assistance, [1985] ii, 31, 17 p. : ill. ; 29 cm. (Program analysis and utilization review report . 2) "January, 1985." Bibliography: p. 29-31. LC Card 86-622554 DDC 362.1/04252/09747 19
1. Medicaid - New York (State). I. Perales, Cesar A., 1940-. II. New York (State). Dept. of Social Services. Division of Medical Assistance. III. Series.
HD7102.U5 N684 1985

Utkal University. Dept. of Rural Economics, Sociology, and Applied Economics. Regulated markets in Orissa . Bhubaneswar, Orissa [1973] 56 p. ; LC Card 82-903827
HF5415.12.I5 R44 1973

Utkin, Ė. A. (Ėduard Andreevich) Chemu uchit opyt druzeĭ / Ė.A. Utkin. Moskva : Izd-vo polit. lit-ry, 1987. 141 p. ; 20 cm. LC Card 87-120824 DDC 658/.009171/7 19
1. Industrial management - Communist countries. 2. Efficiency, Industrial - Communist countries. 3. Socialist competition - Communist countries. I. Title.
HD70.C725 U85 1987

Utmutató és példatár az 1985. január 1-től érvényes jövedelem- és keresetszabályozási rendszer alkalmazásához /. László, Gyula, Dr. Budapest , 1985. 153 p. ; ISBN 963-621-216-3 LC Card 85-138648
HJ4715 .L37 1985

Utopie et les Verts. Dumont, René, 1904- Les raisons de la colère, ou, L'utopie et les Verts /. Paris , c1986. 137 p. ; ISBN 2-7266-0075-1 LC Card 86-158407
HC59.72.E5 D85 1986

Uttar Pradesh in statistics / compiled by Kripa Shankar. 1st ed. New Delhi : Ashish Pub. House, 1987. viii, 82 p. ; 25 cm. Covers the period 1970-71 to 1984-85. ISBN 81-7024-071-9 : LC Card 86-903774 DDC 315.4/2 19
1. Uttar Pradesh, India - Statistics. 2. Uttar Pradesh, India - Economic conditions. I. Shankar, Kripa.
HA4587.U8 U87 1987

UTTAR PRADESH, INDIA - ECONOMIC CONDITIONS.
Uttar Pradesh in statistics /. New Delhi , 1987. viii, 82 p. ; ISBN 81-7024-071-9 : LC Card 86-903774 DDC 315.4/2 19
HA4587.U8 U87 1987

UTTAR PRADESH (INDIA) - INDUSTRIES, RURAL.
Agrawal, Deepak, 1955- Prospects of industrial estates in under-developed countries /. Allahabad, India , 1987. 279 p. ; ISBN 81-85076-13-8 : LC Card 86-903605 DDC 338.6/042/09542 19
HC440.D5 A37 1987

UTTAR PRADESH, INDIA - POPULATION.
Singh, Alok Kumar, 1958- Population and settlement in U.P. . New Delhi, India , 1985. xx, 231 p., [10] p. of plates : LC Card 86-900123 DDC 304.6/0954/2 19
HB2100.U88 S55 1985
NYPL [JLD 86-3156]

UTTAR PRADESH, INDIA - STATISTICS.
Uttar Pradesh in statistics /. New Delhi , 1987. viii, 82 p. ; ISBN 81-7024-071-9 : LC Card 86-903774 DDC 315.4/2 19
HA4587.U8 U87 1987

Uttarākhaṇḍa meṃ kulī begāra prathā . Pāṭhaka, Śekhara, 1951- Naī Dillī , 1987, c1986. 339 p., [16] p. of plates : LC Card 87-902810
HD1537.I4 P38 1987

Utter, Werner. Aufbruch zum Himmel . Dortmund , c1982. 99 p. : ISBN 3-88379-328-0 : LC Card 83-125566
HE6184.A4 A84 1982

Utton, Albert E., 1931- The U. S.-Mexico border region . [El Paso] , 1984, c1982. viii, 446 p. : ISBN 0-87404-091-4 (pbk.) LC Card 87-401861 DDC 333.7/0972/1 19
HC137.M46 U17 1984

Utton, Michael A. Profits and stability of monopoly / M.A. Utton. Cambridge [Cambridgeshire] ; New York : Cambridge University Press, 1986. vii, 96 p. ; 24 cm. (Occasional papers / the National Institute of Economic and Social Research . 38) Includes index. Bibliography: p. 91-93. ISBN 0-521-32550-1 LC Card 86-4226 DDC 338.8/2/0941 19
1. Profit. 2. Oligopolies - Great Britain. 3. Profit - Great Britain. I. Series: National Institute of Economics and Social Research. Occasional papers , 38. II. Title.
HD2757.3 .U88 1986 ***NYPL [TB (National Institute of Economic and Social Research. Occasional papers. v.38)]***

Utvecklingen av produktion och produktivitet i svensk ekonomi, 1963-1981 /. Åberg, Yngve. [Stockholm] [1983] 83 p. : ISBN 91-38-08070-2 LC Card 84-218343
HC380.I52 A34 1983

Utvecklingssamarbetet med Tanzania 1983/84-1984/85. Stockholm, Sweden : Styrelsen för internationell utveckling, [1983] ca. 200 p. ; 30 cm. LC Card 86-216305
1. Economic assistance, Swedish - Tanzania. 2. Tanzania - Economic conditions - 1964-. I. Sweden. Styrelsen för international utveckling.
HC885 .U87 1983

Utz, Arthur Fridolin, 1908- Das Unternehmen als Grösse der Arbeitswelt . Bonn , 1984. 291 p. ; ISBN 3-923202-02-4 LC Card 85-119845
HD6957.G3 U58 1984

UUDENMAAN LÄÄNI (FINLAND) - ECONOMIC CONDITIONS.
Uudenmaan lääni (Finland). Teollisuuden aluerakennetyöryhmä. Uudenmaan läänin teollisuuden alueellinen kehitys ja kehitysedellytykset /. Helsinki , 1983. ii, ix, x, 101, 2, 5 p. : ISBN 951-46-6843-X LC Card 84-180431
HC340.2.Z7 U938 1983

UUDENMAAN LÄÄNI (FINLAND) - INDUSTRIES.
Uudenmaan lääni (Finland). Teollisuuden aluerakennetyöryhmä. Uudenmaan läänin teollisuuden alueellinen kehitys ja kehitysedellytykset /. Helsinki , 1983. ii, ix, x, 101, 2, 5 p. : ISBN 951-46-6843-X LC Card 84-180431
HC340.2.Z7 U938 1983

Uudenmaan lääni (Finland). Teollisuuden aluerakennetyöryhmä. Uudenmaan läänin teollisuuden alueellinen kehitys ja kehitysedellytykset / Uudenmaan läänin teollisuustoimikunta, Teollisuuden aluerakennetyöryhmä. Helsinki : [Uudenmaan lääninhallitus] : Valtion painatuskeskus, 1983. ii, ix, x, 101, 2, 5 p. : ill. ; 30 cm. (Uudenmaan lääninhallituksen julkaisusarja = Länsstyrelsens i Nylands län publikationsserie . 1983:1) Summary in Swedish. ISBN 951-46-6843-X LC Card 84-180431
1. Uudenmaan lääni (Finland) - Industries. 2. Uudenmaan lääni (Finland) - Economic conditions. I. Series: Uudenmaan lääninhallituksen julkaisusarja .

1983:1. II. Title.
HC340.2.Z7 U938 1983

Uudenmaan läänin teollisuuden alueellinen kehitys ja kehitysedellytykset /. Uudenmaan lääni (Finland). Teollisuuden aluerakennetyöryhmä. Helsinki , 1983. ii, ix, x, 101, 2, 5 p. : ISBN 951-46-6843-X LC Card 84-180431
HC340.2.Z7 U938 1983

Uudenmaan lääninhallituksen julkaisusarja . (1983:1) Uudenmaan lääni (Finland). Teollisuuden aluerakennetyöryhmä. Uudenmaan läänin teollisuuden alueellinen kehitys ja kehitysedellytykset /. Helsinki , 1983. ii, ix, x, 101, 2, 5 p. : ISBN 951-46-6843-X LC Card 84-180431
HC340.2.Z7 U938 1983

Uvarov, V. P. (Vladimir Pavlovich) Ėkonomicheskoe soupravlenie : politėkonomicheskiĭ analiz sotsial-demokraticheskoĭ teorii i burzhuaznoĭ praktiki / V.P. Uvarov, L.F. Zaiko. Minsk : Izd-vo "Universitetskoe", 1985. 159 p. ; 20 cm. Includes bibliographical references. LC Card 85-217045
1. Industrial management - Germany (West) - Employee participation. 2. Industrial sociology - Germany, West. I. Zaiko, L. F. (Leonid Fedorovich). II. Title.
HD5660.G4 U93 1985

UWIST/Croom Helm series on management and new information technology.
Long, Richard J. New office information technology . London , New York , c1987. xix, 333 p. : ISBN 0-7099-4103-X (jacket); 0-7099-4130-X LC Card 87-3601 DDC 651.8 19
HF5547.5 .L65 1987

Uxpanapa . Ewell, Peter T., 1947- Ithaca, N.Y. [1982] xiv, 218 p., [35] leaves of plates : LC Card 84-621492 DDC 338.1/0972/6 19
HD1795.P3 E94 1982

UZBEK S.S.R. - ECONOMIC CONDITIONS.
Ergashev, A. (Atakul) Dialektika ob″ektivnogo i sub″ektivnogo v razvitii nauchno-tekhnicheskoĭ revoliutsii /. Tashkent , 1980. 185 p. ; LC Card 81-143159
HC337.U963 T44 1980

Sovershenstvovanie khoziaĭstvennogo mekhanizma v usloviiakh razvitogo sotsializma /. Tashkent , 1985. 142, [2] p. ; LC Card 86-220208
HC337.U96 S68 1985

Ul′masov, Akhmed Ul′masovich. Uzbekistan--ėkonomicheskiĭ rost i blagosostoianie naseleniia /. Tashkent , 1978. 182 p. ; LC Card 81-145788
HC337.U96 U95 1978

UZBEK S.S.R. - ECONOMIC POLICY.
Sovershenstvovanie khoziaĭstvennogo mekhanizma v usloviiakh razvitogo sotsializma /. Tashkent , 1985. 142, [2] p. ; LC Card 86-220208
HC337.U96 S68 1985

Uzbekistan--ėkonomicheskiĭ rost i blagosostoianie naseleniia /. Ul′masov, Akhmed Ul′masovich. Tashkent , 1978. 182 p. ; LC Card 81-145788
HC337.U96 U95 1978

Uzbekskaia Sovetskaia Sotsialisticheskaia Respublika. see **Uzbek S. S. R.**

Uzoaga, William Okefie. Money and banking in Nigeria / by W. Okefie Uzoaga. Enugu, Nigeria : Fourth Dimension Publishers, 1981. xiv, 304 p. ; 21 cm. Includes index. Bibliography: p. 285-290. ISBN 978-15-6175-0
1. Banks and banking - Nigeria. 2. Money - Nigeria. 3. Nigeria - Economic conditions - 1970-. I. Title.
NYPL [Sc D 84-373]

Uzunova, IUliia. Upravlenie, marketing, uslugi / IUliia Uzunova, IUliia Shishmanova. 1. izd. Varna : Kn-vo "Georgi Bakalov", 1986. 143 p. : ill. ; 20 cm. Bibliography: p. 138-[142] LC Card 86-152606
1. Marketing. 2. Marketing research. I. Shishmanova, IUliia. II. Title.
HF5415 .U98 1986

V bitvakh za sovetskuiu Ukrainu : ratnyĭ i trudovoĭ podvig narodov SSSR v gody Velikoĭ Otechestvennoĭ voĭny : istoriia i sovremennost′ / [avtorskiĭ kollektiv L.G. Mel′nik ... et al.]. Kiev : Izd-vo pri Kievskom gos. universitete izdatel′skogo ob″edineniia "Vyshcha shkola", 1985. 172 p. ; 21 cm. Bibliography: p. 163-[173] LC Card 85-170194
1. World war, 1939-1945 - Economic aspects - Ukraine. 2. Reconstruction (1939-1951) - Ukraine. 3. Ukraine - Industries - History. 4. World War, 1939-1945 - Ukraine. I. Mel′nik, L. G. (Leonid Gerasimovich).
HC337.U53 D48 1985

V bor′be protiv vsevlastiia kapitala /. TSygankov, P. A. (Pavel Afanas′evich) Moskva , 1986. 139 p. ; LC Card 86-132423
HB501 .T78 1986

V edinom narodnokhoziaĭstvennom komplekse. V iedynomu narodnohospodars′komu kompleksi /. Uzhhorod , 1982. 179 p. : LC Card 83-180335
HC337.U52 W485 1982

V.I. Lenin i ėlektrifikatsiia /. Steklov, Vladimir IUr′evich. Moskva , 1982. 511 p., [1] leaf of plates : LC Card 83-133950
HD9685.S762 S84 1982

V.I. Lenin, KPSS o sotsialisticheskom sorevnovanii / [sostavitel′ O.I. Ternovoĭ]. Izd. 3-e, perer. i dop. Moskva : Izd-vo polit. lit-ry, 1985. 540 p. ; 21 cm. Includes bibliographical references. LC Card 86-128447
1. Socialist competition - Soviet Union. I. Ternovoĭ, O. I. II. Lenin, Vladimir Il′ich, 1870-1924. III. Kommunisticheskaia partiia Sovetskogo Soiuza.
HC340.S6 V18 1985

V iedynomu narodnohospodars′komu kompleksi / [uporiadkuvannia i vstupna stattia I.F. Popovycha]. Uzhhorod : Vyd-vo "Karpaty", 1982. 179 p. : ill. (some col.) ; 21 cm. Title in colophon: V edinom narodnokhoziaĭstvennom komplekse. LC Card 83-180335
1. Ukraine, Western - Economic conditions. 2. Ukraine - Economic conditions - 1945-. I. Popovych, I. F. II. Title: V edinom narodnokhoziaĭstvennom komplekse.
HC337.U52 W485 1982

V. K. U. see **Verband Kommunaler Unternehmen.**

V tvorcheskoĭ laboratorii Karla Marksa . Kogan, A. M. (Al′bert Moiseevich) Moskva , 1983. 172, [4] p. ; LC Card 83-166605
HB501 .K57 1983

v. <2, 4, 5, 8, 9, 11 > : An Urban Institute research report.
Government spending and the nonprofit sector in [name of community]. Washington, D.C. , <c1984-c1985. v. <1-11 > ; LC Card 87-168173 DDC 339.5/22/0973 19
HJ2052 .G67 1984

Vaasan Kauppakorkeakoulu. Julkaisuja. Tutkimuksia.
(n:o 85) Karhu, Veli. Akseleraatioteoriaan perustuvia investointifunktiokokeiluja yritystason aineistolla /. Vaasa , 1982. 43, [1] leaves ; ISBN 951-683-160-5 LC Card 83-100841 DDC 332/.0415 19
HG4028.C4 K349 1982
NYPL [JLM 73-601 n:o 85]

Vaasan korkeakoulun julkaisuja. Tutkimuksia, 0358-9080 .
(n:o 85) Karhu, Veli. Akseleraatioteoriaan perustuvia investointifunktiokokeiluja yritystason aineistolla /. Vaasa , 1982. 43, [1] leaves ; ISBN 951-683-160-5 LC Card 83-100841 DDC 332/.0415 19
HG4028.C4 K349 1982
NYPL [JLM 73-601 n:o 85]

(9) Karhu, Veli. Akseleraatioteoriaan perustuvia investointifunktiokokeiluja yritystason aineistolla /. Vaasa , 1982. 43, [1] leaves ; ISBN 951-683-160-5 LC Card 83-100841 DDC 332/.0415 19
HG4028.C4 K349 1982
NYPL [JLM 73-601 n:o 85]

Vaca Narvaja, Fernando. Perdía, Roberto Cirilo. Existe otra Argentina posible /. Buenos Aires , 1986. 276 p. : ISBN 950-97640-0-0 LC Card 87-139879 DDC 336.3/4/0982 19
HG3881.5.I58 P47 1986

VACATION HOMES - CANADA - PURCHASING.
Scher, Les. Finding and buying your place in the country /. New York , London , c1987. p. cm. ISBN 0-02-008400-5 LC Card 87-24246 DDC 643/.2 19
HD256 .S27 1987

VACATION HOMES - UNITED STATES - PURCHASING.
Scher, Les. Finding and buying your place in the country /. New York , London , c1987. p. cm. ISBN 0-02-008400-5 LC Card 87-24246 DDC 643/.2 19
HD256 .S27 1987

Vacca, Roberto, 1927- Rinascimento prossimo venturo / Roberto Vacca. 1a ed. Milano : Bompiani, 1986. 281 p. : ill. ; 23 cm. Includes index. LC Card 87-100469
1. Economic history - 1971-. 2. Social history - 1970-. I. Title.
HC59 .V24 1986

Vacca, Susan M., 1954- Leape, Martha P. The Harvard guide to careers /. Cambridge, Mass. , 1987. ix, 181 p. ; ISBN 0-674-37564-5 (pbk.) LC Card 87-8409 DDC 331.7/02 19
HF5382.5.U5 L36 1987

Vačroba da vačart‘a p‘ena rep‘ormamdeli xanis Sak‘art‘veloši /. Ordzhonikidze, Ė. A. (Ėteri Aleksandrovna) T‘bilisi , 1974. 158 p. ; LC Card 86-168874
HF3629.G4 O73 1974

Vad gör kapitalisterna? . Andersson, Dan, 1948- Stockholm , c1983. 167 p. : ISBN 91-550-2919-1 : LC Card 84-143408
HG186.S85 A53 1983

Vad kostade det? . Lagerqvist, Lars O. Stockholm , c18. 115 p. : ISBN 91-36-02399-X : LC Card 86-158743
HD7040 .L34 1985

Vadilal Lallubhai Mehta. see **Mehta, Vadilal Lallubhai, 1903-**

Väestö, asunnot ja asuntorakentaminen suur- ja peruspiireittäin Helsingissä 1970-1983 =. Kinturi, Jorma. Helsinki , 1984. 36 p., [1] folded leaf of plates : LC Card 85-156678
HD7345.3.H5 K563 1984

VAGABONDS. see **TRAMPS.**

Vägen till fabrikerna . Isacson, Maths, 1948- [Stockholm] [Uppsala] , c1983. 195, [1] p. : ISBN 91-7021-464-6 : LC Card 84-125076
HC375 .I83 1983

Vaggi, Gianni. The economics of François Quesnay / Gianni Vaggi. Durham : Duke University Press, 1987. xv, 247 p. : ill. ; 23 cm. Originally presented as the author's thesis (doctoral--Cambridge) Bibliography: p. 221-229. Includes index. ISBN 0-8223-0757-X LC Card 87-3549 DDC 330.15/2 19
1. Quesnay, François, 1694-1774. 2. Economics - France - History - 18th century. 3. Physiocrats. I. Title.
HB105.Q5 V34 1987

The vagrant peasant . Nag Chowdhury-Zilly, Aditee. Wiesbaden , 1982. xv, 196 p. : ISBN 3-515-03855-8 (pbk.) LC Card 86-214350
HD1537.I4 N327 1982

VAGRANTS. see **TRAMPS.**

Vahlne, Jan-Erik, 1941- Multinationella förtag . Lund , 1985. 196 p. : ISBN 91-578-0210-6 : LC Card 86-216456
HD2755.5 .M864 1985

Vahtre, S. Eesti ala mõisate nimestik /. Tallinn , 1981. 191 p. ; LC Card 82-143283
HD1329.E75 E37 1981
NYPL [JFD 86-6806]

Vaigerṭ, R. (Re'uven) Yaḳir, E. (Eli), 1929- Milon munaḥim be-khalkalah ve-nihul 'asaḳim /. Tel-Aviv , 1986. 414, 38 p. : LC Card 87-162041
HB61 .Y25 1986

Vaikulis, J. (Jānis) Lauksaimniecības uzņēmumu saimnieciskās darbības analīze / J. Vaikulis. Riga : Avots, 1986. 185 p. ; 21 cm. Title in colophon: Analiz khoziaĭstvennoĭ deiatel′nosti sel′skokhoziaĭstvennykh predpriiatiĭ. LC Card 86-199301
1. Collective farms - Latvia - Accounting. 2. State farms - Latvia - Accounting. 3. Agricultural productivity - Latvia. I. Title. II. Title: Analiz khoziaĭstvennoĭ deiatel′nosti sel′skokhoziaĭstvennykh predpriiatiĭ.
HD1492.S652 L38 1986

Vaillancourt, François. Income distribution and economic security in Canada /. Toronto , Buffalo , c1985. xv, 321 p. : ISBN 0-8020-7241-0 (pbk.) LC Card 85-227851 DDC 330.971/064 19
HC120.I5 I53 1985 NYPL [JLE 86-1881]

Vajc, Klaus, 1958- Ausgliederung des Zahlungsverkehrs aus dem Universalbankbereich / Klaus Vajc. Frankfurt am Main ; New York : P. Lang, c1986. viii, 238 p. : ill. ; 21 cm. (Europäische Hochschulschriften. Reihe V, Volks- und Betriebswirtschaft, 0531-7339 . Bd. 734 = vol. 734 = vol. 734) Bibliography: p. 211-238. ISBN 3-8204-8825-1 LC Card 86-220359
1. Check collection systems - Germany (West). 2. Banks and banking - Germany (West) - Automation. I. Series: Europäische Hochschulschriften. Reihe V, Volks- und Betriebswirtschaft , Bd. 734. II. Title.
HG1692 .V34 1986

Vajda, János. Lányfalvi, Sándor. Adalékok a tartósítóipar hosszútávu fejlesztésének megalapozásához /. Budapest , 1984. 115 p. ; ISBN 963-491-199-4 LC Card 86-199120
HD9326.H82 L36 1984

Vajda, Lajos. Erdélyi bányák, kohók, emberek, századok : gazdaság-, társadalom- és munkásmozgalomtörténet a XVIII. század második felétől 1918-ig / Vajda Lajos. Bukarest : Politikai Könyvkiadó, 1981. 544 p. : ill. ; 20 cm. Errata slip inserted. Includes bibliographical references and indexes. LC Card 83-124763
1. Miners - Romania - Transylvania - History. 2. Metal-workers - Romania - Transylvania - History. 3. Transylvania (Romania) - Industries - History. I. Title.
HD8039.M61 R68 1981

Vajna, Thomas. Das Kaufkraftargument / Thomas Vajna. Köln : Deutscher Instituts-Verlag, c1982. 52 p. ; 21 cm. (Beiträge zur Wirtschafts- und Sozialpolitik . 110 = 11/1982) Includes bibliographical references. ISBN 3-602-24710-4 : LC Card 83-193844
1. Wages - Germany, West. 2. Purchasing power - Germany, West. 3. Collective bargaining - Germany, West. I. Series: Beiträge zur Wirtschafts- und Sozialpolitik , 110. II. Title.
HD5029 .V35 1982

Vakbeweging in verandering : dilemma's en uitdagingen / onder redactie van J.C. Looise, J. Paauwe, H.J. van Zuthem ; met medewerking van W. Albeda ... [et al.]. Deventer : Kluwer, 1986. 191 p. : ill. ; 25 cm. "Bundel ter gelegenheid van het afscheid van ... Harm van der Meulen"--P. [2] Summary in English. Includes bibliographies. ISBN 90-267-1082-8 : LC Card 86-224831
1. Trade-unions - Netherlands - History - 20th century. 2. Christelijk Nationaal Vakverbond in Nederland. 3. Meulen, Harm van der. I. Looise, J. C., 1949-. II. Paauwe, J., 1953-. III. Zuthem, H. J. van, 1929-. IV. Albeda, W., 1925-. V. Meulen, Harm van der.
HD6727 .V29 1986

Vakbonden en Europa . Debunne, Georges. Leuven , c1987. 206 p. ; ISBN 90-6303-228-5 : LC Card 87-157537
HD8372.E86 D43 1987

Vakbondwese in Suid-Afrika. Konferensie Vakbondwese in Suid-Afrika (1984 : Randse Afrikaanse Universiteit) Konferensie Vakbondwese in Suid-Afrika . Johannesburg [1984] 73 p. ; ISBN 0-86970-252-1 LC Card 87-126320
HD6870.5 .K65 1984

Válaszúton az Európai Gazdasági Közösség /. Inotai, András. [Budapest] , 1985. 369 p. ; ISBN 963-09-2587-7 : LC Card 86-228244
HC241.2 .I583 1985

Vald på livstid . Sjödal, Tage, 1928- Stockholm [1984], c1983. 81 p. ; ISBN 91-550-2941-8 : LC Card 84-171294
HD8572.L34 S57 1984

Valdés, Alberto, 1935- Crop insurance for agricultural development . Baltimore , c1986. xviii, 322 p. ISBN 0-8018-2673-X (alk. paper) LC Card 85-9810 DDC 368.1/22 19
HG9968 .C76 1985 ***NYPL [JLE 86-1082]***

Valdés Paz, Juan. Notas críticas sobre el plan Reagan para la cuenca del Caribe /. La Habana , 1982. 84 p. ; LC Card 87-400638 DDC 337.729073 19
HF1456.5.C27 N67 1982

Valdés, Ximena. Mack, Macarena. Los trabajos de las mujeres entre el campo y la ciudad, 1920-1982 . [Santiago, Chile] [1986] 108 p. ; LC Card 86-217673
HD6126 .M33 1986

Valdisera, Victor M. Taeuber, Cynthia Murray. Women in the American economy /. Washington, D.C. [1986] vi, 45 p. : LC Card 87-601515 DDC 304.6/0973/021 s 331.4/0973 19
HA203 .A218 no. 146 HD6092

Vale, Philip A., 1955- Financial management handbook /. Aldershot, Hants, England , c1987. p. cm. ISBN 0-566-02623-6 : LC Card 87-40 DDC 658.1/5 19
HG4027.3 .F53 1987

Valencia Correa, Hernando. Isaza Tobón, Gabriela. El IDEMA, hacia una pérdida de los objetivos sociales. [Colombia? , between 1984 and 1987] ([Colombia?] : Litoarte) 126 p., [1] leaf of plates : LC Card 87-404223 DDC 381/.41/09861 19
HD9014.C72 I8 1984

Valencia, Humberto. The U. S. Hispanic market. New York, N.Y. : Find/SVP, [1984] 1 v. (various foliations) : ill. ; 29 cm. (A Business information report) "November 1984." ISBN 0-931634-48-2 (pbk.) LC Card 86-203027 DDC 658.8/348 19
1. Hispanic Americans as consumers. 2. Hispanic Americans - Economic conditions. I. Find/SVP (Firm). II. Title. III. Series.
HC110.C6 V35 1984

Valencia Roa, Carlos Alberto, 1944- Social investments and economic growth / by Carlos Alberto Valencia Roa. 1974. xiv, 199 leaves : ill. Thesis (Ph. D.) -- Stanford University, 1974. Bibliography: leaves 194-199. Photocopy. Ann Arbor, Mich. : University Microfilms International, 1977. 21 cm.
1. Human capital - Mathematical models. 2. Economic policy - Mathematical models. 3. Education and state - Mathematical models. I. Title.
NYPL [JLD 86-2961]

VALENCIA (SPAIN) - COMMERCE - HISTORY - 18TH CENTURY.
Franch Benavent, Ricardo, 1956- Crecimiento comercial y enriquecimiento burgués en la Valencia del siglo XVIII /. Valencia [1986?] 340 p. : ISBN 84-505-4154-9 LC Card 87-110614
HF3690.V3 F7 1986

Valenta, John A. Born, Waldo L. A synopsis of Texas savings-and-loan associations' operations /. College Station, Tex. [1986?] 38 p. : LC Card 86-622196 DDC 332.3/2/09764 19
HG2153.T4 B67 1986

Valenteĭ, D. I. (Dmitriĭ Ignat'evich)
Nechernozem'e . Moskva , 1977. 94 p. ; LC Card 82-107146
HB3608.N57 N43 1977

Osnovy teorii narodonaseleniia /. Moskva , 1986. 374 p. : LC Card 86-218424
HB851 .O82 1986

Rozwój ludności krajów socjalistycznych . Warszawa , Moskva , 1978. 381 p. ; LC Card 81-206832
HB3608.7.A3 R69 1978

Valentik, I. IA. (Ivan IAkovlevich)
Ekonomicheskie osnovy intensifikatsii lesnogo khoziaistva Karel'skoĭ ASSR / I.IA. Valentik, A.F. Kozlov, M.D. Nekrasov ; pod redaktsieĭ A.A. TSymeka. Leningrad : Izd-vo "Nauka," Leningradskoe otd-nie, 1986. 135, [1] p. : maps ; 22 cm. At head of title: Akademiia nauk SSSR. Karel'skiĭ filial. Bibliography: p. 133-[136]. LC Card 87-125199
1. Forest products industry - Russian S.F.S.R. - Karel'skaia A.S.S.R. I. Kozlov, A. F. II. Nekrasov, M. D. III. TSymek, A. A. IV. Title.
HD9765.S653 K378 1986

Valenzuela C. Pecci, Antonio. Morínigo, José N. Las artesanías de cuero y tejido en el Paraguay . Asunción , 1979. 106, [1] p. : LC Card 83-219583
HD9780.P373 A866 1979
NYPL [JLF 86-1810]

Valenzuela Cornejo, Ignacio. Costo real del crédito en 1984 / Ignacio Valenzuela Cornejo. Santiago : Departamento de Informaciones, Estadísticas y Publicaciones del Banco Central de Chile, 1985. 28 p. ; 27 cm. (Serie de estudios económicos . no. 24) "Edición de 300 ejemplares"--T.p. verso. Includes bibliographical references. LC Card 86-106375 DDC 332.7/0983 19
1. Credit - Chile - Econometric models. I. Series: Serie de estudios económicos (Banco Central de Chile) , no. 24. II. Title.
HG3729.C52 V35 1985

Valenzuela Ruiz, Armando. Yepes C., Alfonso. Del caos al orden . [S.l. , 1986] ([S.l.] : Editorial Nomos) 239 p., [1] leaf of plates : LC Card 87-400255 DDC 331.1/1/09861 19
HD5757.A6 Y46 1986

Valeur, formes de la valeur et étapes dans la pensée de Marx /. Takenaga, Susumu. Berne , New York , c1985. 243 p. ; ISBN 3-261-04026-2 LC Card 86-196366
HB206 .T35 1985

Validire, Jean-Louis. André Bergeron, une force ouvrière / Jean-Louis Validire. Paris : Plon, c1984. 244 p. ; 20 cm. Bibliography: p. [243]-244. ISBN 2-259-01206-X : LC Card 85-105625 DDC 331.88/0944 19
1. Trade-unions - France - History. 2. Front populaire - History. 3. CGT-FO (Union) - History. 4. Bergeron, André, 1922-. I. Title.
HD6684 .V35 1984

Valiutnye otnosheniia kapitalizma . Korolev, I. S. (Ivan Sergeevich) Moskva , 1986. 228 p. ; LC Card 86-232369
HG6230.3 .K66 1986

Valla, Jean-Paul. Strategies for international industrial marketing . London , Dover, N.H. , c1986. 310 p. : ISBN 0-7099-2494-1 : LC Card 85-29047 DDC 658.8/48 19
HF1009.7.E85 S77 1986
NYPL [JLD 86-1596]

VALLADOLID (SPAIN : PROVINCE) - ECONOMIC CONDITIONS.
Prado Moura, Angel de. El movimiento obrero en Valladolid durante la II República, 1931-1936 /. [Castilla y León] , 1985. 234 p. : ISBN 84-505-2341-9 LC Card 86-214605
HD8119.V34 P72 1985

A vállalat rendszerképe /. Koblencz, József. Budapest , 1984. 179 p. : ISBN 963-512-143-1 : LC Card 86-186873
HD37.H82 K63 1984

Vállalatgazdaságtani ismeretek vezetők számára. Ábel, István. A vállalatok pénzügyi szabályozása . Budapest , 1984. 32, [1] p. ; LC Card 85-175023
HG4149.5 .A54 1984

Vállalati árelőrejelzések . Sipos, Béla. Budapest , 1985. 290, [1] p. : ISBN 963-221-515-X : LC Card 86-190915
HB3730 .S495 1985

A vállalati bértarifarendszer /. Ott, György. [Budapest] , 1984. 110 p. ; ISBN 963-322-158-7 : LC Card 85-176915
HD5022.5 .O77 1984

A Vállalati magatartást motiváló gazdasági és társadalmi tényezők című konferencia előadásai : [Pécs, 1985. május 9-10]. Pécs : [Pécsi Janus Pannonius Tudományegyetem Közgazdaságtudományi Kar], 1985. 2 v. : ill. ; 27 cm. One contribution in English. Includes bibliographies. LC Card 87-408547
1. Industrial management - Hungary - Congresses. 2. Hungary - Economic policy - 1968- - Congresses. 3. Food industry and trade - Hungary - Congresses. 4. Marketing - Hungary - Congresses. 5. Environmental policy - Hungary - Congresses. 6. Language and languages - Study and teaching - Hungary - Congresses. I. Pécsi Janus Pannonius Tudományegyetem. Közgazdaságtudományi Kar.
HD70.H8 V334 1985

A Vállalati tervezés uj módszere : a pécsi konferencia tanulmánykötete : Pécs, 1985. IV. 11-12 / [szerkesztők, Kéri István, Szemere Mátyás]. [Pécs] : SZVT Baranya Megyei Szervezete, [1985?] 167 p. : ill. ; 29 cm. Organized by the Szervezési és Vezetési Tudományos Társaság Baranya Megyei Szervezete. LC Card 86-187131
1. Industrial management - Congresses. 2. Industrial management - Hungary - Congresses. 3. Corporate planning - Congresses. I. Kéri, István. II. Szemere, Mátyás. III. Szervezési és Vezetési Tudományos Társaság. Baranya Megyei Szervezet.
HD29 .V35 1985

Vállalatok környezete, céljai, szervezete /. Antal, Iván. Budapest , 1986. 270 p. : ISBN 963-221-567-2 : LC Card 87-149512
HD70.H8 A536 1986

A vállalatok pénzügyi szabályozása . Ábel, István. Budapest , 1984. 32, [1] p. ; LC Card

85-175023
HG4149.5 .A54 1984

El Valle de Alcudia . Gascón Bueno, Francisco. Bilbao , 1978. xvi, 609 p., [10] folded leaves of plates : ISBN 84-400-5486-6 LC Card 85-227628
HD2025.C54 G37 1978

El Valle de Alcudia durante el siglo XVIII. Gascón Bueno, Francisco. El Valle de Alcudia . Bilbao , 1978. xvi, 609 p., [10] folded leaves of plates : ISBN 84-400-5486-6 LC Card 85-227628
HD2025.C54 G37 1978

VALLE DEL CAUCA, COLOMBIA - ECONOMIC CONDITIONS.
Perfiles económicos del Valle del Cauca, Colombia. Cali, Colombia [1981?] 40 p. : LC Card 86-120381 DDC 330.9861/520632 19
HC198.V3 P47 1981

Valle, Silvia del. Portilla, Belfor. Alimentos . México , 1983. 149, [53] p. : ISBN 968-429-384-4 LC Card 84-172348 DDC 338.1/9/1724 19
HD9018.D44 P67 1983 *NYPL [JLD 86-1520]*

Vallega, Adalberto. Dai porti al sistema portuale : teoria generale e caso ligure / Adalberto Vallega. Savona : Camera di commercio, industria, artigianato, agricoltura di Savona, 1985. 320 p. : ill. ; 23 cm. (Strumenti. 3) Bibliography: p. 311-320. LC Card 87-139096
1. Harbors - Italy - Liguria. 2. Transportation - Italy - Liguria. 3. Shipping - Italy - Liguria. 4. Freight and freightage - Italy - Liguria. I. Series: Strumenti (Savona, Italy) , 3. II. Title.
HE558.L44 V35 1985

Vallés Ferrer, José. Iniciación a la economía andaluza /. [Seville, Spain] [1986] 196, [4] p. : ISBN 84-7405-343-9 LC Card 87-152155
HC387.A64 I54 1986

Vallès i Sanchis, Ismael. Pérez Planelles, Francisco, fl. 1774-1807. Plan estatístico de la villa de Alcoy /. [València] [Alcoi] , 1983. xiii, 31 p. ; LC Card 86-150151
HC388.A44 P47 1983

Vallés, José. see **Vallés Ferrer, José.**

Valli, Linda, 1947- Becoming clerical workers / Linda Valli. Boston : Routledge & Kegan Paul, 1986. xv, 261 p. ; 23 cm. (Critical social thought) Includes index. Bibliography: p. 248-257. ISBN 0-7102-0336-5
1. Women clerks - United States. 2. Women clerks - Training of - United States. I. Title. II. Series.
NYPL [JLD 86-1147]

Valli, Vittorio, 1941- L'Economia tedesca . Milano , c1981. 273 p. : LC Card 87-673286
HC286.7 .E29x 1981

Vallin, Jacques. Methodologies for the collection and analysis of mortality data . Liège, Belgium , 1984. vi, 510 p. : ISBN 2-87040-032-2 (pbk.) LC Card 86-205582 DDC 304.6/4/072 19
HB1321 .M48 1984

El valor añadido /. Queréndez, Francisco. Bilbao [1985?] 167 p. ; ISBN 84-234-0582-6 LC Card 87-105408
HD47 .Q38 1985

O valor de uso em Marx /. Roland, Marcos M. [Brasília] [19]81. 52, [2] leaves ; LC Card 85-228336
HB206 .R65 1981

VALPORT securities index : May 31, 1985. Greenwich, Conn. (500 W. Putnam Ave., Greenwich 06830) : Business Information Services, c1985- 1 v. (loose-leaf) ; 28 cm. "Form no. SJO74-32." LC Card 87-132910 DDC 332.63/2/025 19
1. Securities - Directories.
HG4509 .V36 1985

VALS report .
(no. 63) Index, 1978-1985 and survey methodology. Menlo Park, CA (333 Ravenswood Ave., Menlo Park 94025) [1986] vi, 45 leaves ; LC Card 86-220307 DDC 305/.0973 19
HF5415.3 .I47 1986

(no. 66) Christen, François G. Buying by mail . Menlo Park, CA (333 Ravenswood Ave., Menlo Park 94025) , c1986. v, 2, 59, 6 leaves : LC Card 86-209563 DDC 658.8/4 19
HF5415.126 .C48 1986

Val'ter, S. B. (Semen Borisovich) Spravochnik po finansovo-ėkonomicheskim raschetam v sel'skokhoziaĭstvennykh predpriiatiiakh / S.B. Val'ter, S.I. Kovanov. Moskva : "Finansy i statistika", 1982. 411 p. ; 21 cm. LC Card 83-160870
1. Agriculture - Soviet Union - Accounting. 2. Agricultural industries - Soviet Union - Accounting. I. Kovanov, S. I. (Stanislav Ivanovich). II. Title.
HF5686.A36 V35 1982

Val'tukh, Konstantin Kurtovich.
Matematicheskiĭ i statisticheskiĭ analiz funktsii potrebleniia / K.K. Val'tukh, N.P. Dement'ev, I.A. Itskovich ; otvetstvennyĭ redaktor V.P. Busygin. Novosibirsk : Izd-vo "Nauka," Sibirskoe otd-nie, 1986. 165, [3] p. : ill. ; 20 cm. At head of title: Akademiia nauk SSSR. Sibirskoe otdelenie. Institut ėkonomiki i organizatsii promyshlennogo proizvodstva. Bibliography: p. 163-[166] LC Card 86-230310
1. Consumption (Economics) - Mathematical models. 2. Consumption (Economics) - Soviet Union - Mathematical models. I. Dement'ev, N. P. II. Itskovich, I. A. (Iosif Aleksandrovich). III. Busygin, Vladimir Petrovich. IV. Title.
HB801 .V26 1986

TSelevaia funktsiia potrebleniia : analiz i prakticheskoe ispol'zovanie / K.K. Val'tukh ; otvetstvennyĭ redaktor I.P. Suslov. Novosibirsk : Izd-vo "Nauka," Sibirskoe otd-nie, 1980. 381, [3] p. ; 20 cm. (Problemy narodno-khoziaĭstvennogo optimuma) On leaf preceding t.p.: Akademiia nauk SSSR. Sibirskoe otdelenie. Institut ėkonomiki i organizatsii promyshlennogo proizvodstva. Bibliography: p. 381-[382] LC Card 81-134031
1. Consumption (Economics) - Mathematical models. 2. Consumption (Economics) - Soviet Union - Mathematical models. I. Suslov, Ivan Petrovich. II. Title. III. Series.
HB801 .V265 1980

Valuation and selection of convertible bonds . Gepts, Stefaan J. New York, NY , 1987. xiii, 177 p. : ISBN 0-275-92466-1 (alk. paper) : LC Card 87-14606 DDC 332.63/23 19
HG4651 .G46 1987

Valuation of a closely held business. New York, N.Y. (1211 Ave. of the Americas, New York 10036-8775) : American Institute of Certified Public Accountants, c1987. 44 p. : forms ; 23 cm. (Management advisory services practice aids. Small business consulting practice aid . 8) Bibliography: p. 43-44. LC Card 87-402129 DDC 658.1/522 19
1. Close corporations - United States - Valuation. I. American Institute of Certified Public Accountants. II. Series.
HF5681.V3 V35 1987

VALUATION OF LAND. see **REAL PROPERTY - VALUATION.**

Valuation reference manual . Martin, Thomas John, 1942- [Hicksville, N.Y. (383 S. Broadway, Hicksville 11801) , c1986] ix, 134 leaves ; LC Card 86-233027 DDC 658.1/522 19
HG4028.V3 M33 1986

VALUATION - SPAIN.
Poveda Blanco, Francisco. La valoración de bases imponibles en los impuestos sobre la renta y el patrimonio /. [Alicante] [1984?] 395 p. ; LC Card 84-216651 DDC 333.33/2/0946 19
HJ4125.S8 P68 1984 *NYPL [JLE 86-1461]*

VALUE. Here are entered works on the theory of value in economics. Works on moral and esthetic values, etc. are entered under Values.

VALUE ADDED.
Queréndez, Francisco. El valor añadido /. Bilbao [1985?] 167 p. ; ISBN 84-234-0582-6 LC Card 87-105408
HD47 .Q38 1985

VALUE ADDED - ACCOUNTING.
Measurement of value added at constant prices in service activities /. Paris . v. <1 > ; ISBN 92-64-02879-X (pbk.) : LC Card 87-164470 DDC 657/.45 19
HF5686.S43 M43 1987

The value-added tax . McLure, Charles E. Washington, D.C. : Lanham, MD ; xi, 184 p. : ISBN 0-8447-3613-9 (alk. paper) LC Card 86-28905 DDC 339.5/25/0973 19
HJ5715.U6 M364 1987

VALUE-ADDED TAX - BRAZIL.
Longo, Carlos Alberto. Ajustamentos de impostos na fronteira e a alocação de receitas tributárias . São Paulo , 1979. 208 p. ; LC Card 80-152384
HJ5715.B8 L6617 *NYPL [JLD 86-3846]*

VALUE-ADDED TAX - EUROPE.
National Economic Development Office. Value added tax. London, 1971. vi, 113 p. ISBN 0-11-700550-9 LC Card 72-180346 DDC 336.2/71
HJ5715.G7 N36 1971 *NYPL [JLE 74-313]*

VALUE-ADDED TAX - GERMANY, WEST.
Tabellen zur Ermittlung der Mehrwertsteuer aus dem Brutto-Rechnungsbetrag. Stuttgart , 1983. 38 p. ; ISBN 3-415-01033-3 LC Card 83-223907
HJ5715.G3 T32 1983

VALUE-ADDED TAX - GREAT BRITAIN.
National Economic Development Office. Value added tax. London, 1971. vi, 113 p. ISBN 0-11-700550-9 LC Card 72-180346 DDC 336.2/71
HJ5715.G7 N36 1971 *NYPL [JLE 74-313]*

Sevilla Segura, Jorge. El proceso de implantación del IVA . [Madrid] [1982?] iii, 182 p. ; LC Card 85-201954
HJ5715.G7 S4 1982

VALUE-ADDED TAX - INDIA.
Chopra, O. P. (Om Prakash), 1941- Tax ethics, unaccounted income . New Delhi , 1985, c1984. vi, 119 p. ; LC Card 85-900955 DDC 336.2/06 19
HJ2348.5 .C46 1985 *NYPL [JLE 87-1297]*

VALUE-ADDED TAX - ITALY.
Scanu, Salvatore. I costi dell'adempimento tributario in Italia . [Cagliari] , Milano, Italy , c1984. 153 p. ; LC Card 85-118845
HD9326.I82 S32 1984

VALUE-ADDED TAX - LAW AND LEGISLATION - SPAIN - CATALONIA.
L'IVA en els sectors agrari i pesquer catalans. [Barcelona] , 1985. 49 p. ; ISBN 84-393-0632-6 LC Card 86-165858
HJ5715.S7 L58 1985

VALUE-ADDED TAX - RATES AND TABLES.
Tabellen zur Ermittlung der Mehrwertsteuer aus dem Brutto-Rechnungsbetrag. Stuttgart , 1983. 38 p. ; ISBN 3-415-01033-3 LC Card 83-223907
HJ5715.G3 T32 1983

VALUE-ADDED TAX - SPAIN.
Lampreave Pérez, José Luis. La empresa española ante el impuesto sobre el valor añadido, medidas de adaptación y ajuste /. Madrid, España , 1985. 493 p. : ISBN 84-7196-571-2 : LC Card 86-208329
HJ5715.S7 L36 1985

Sevilla Segura, Jorge. El proceso de implantación del IVA . [Madrid] [1982?] iii, 182 p. ; LC Card 85-201954
HJ5715.G7 S4 1982

VALUE-ADDED TAX - SPAIN - ACCOUNTING.
Queréndez, Francisco. El valor añadido /. Bilbao [1985?] 167 p. ; ISBN 84-234-0582-6 LC Card 87-105408
HD47 .Q38 1985

VALUE-ADDED TAX - SPAIN - CATALONIA.
L'IVA en els sectors agrari i pesquer catalans. [Barcelona] , 1985. 49 p. ; ISBN 84-393-0632-6 LC Card 86-165858
HJ5715.S7 L58 1985

VALUE-ADDED TAX - SWEDEN.
Sweden. Skattekreditutredningen. Kortare kredittid för skatter på energi m.m. . [Stockholm] [1983] 109 p. ; ISBN 0-913807-27-9 LC Card 84-218594
HJ5715.S84 S87 1983

VALUE-ADDED TAX - UNITED STATES.
McLure, Charles E. The value-added tax . Washington, D.C. : Lanham, MD ; xi, 184 p. : ISBN 0-8447-3613-9 (alk. paper) LC Card 86-28905 DDC 339.5/25/0973 19
HJ5715.U6 M364 1987

VALUE - CONGRESSES.
Wert- und Präferenzprobleme in den Sozialwissenschaften /. Berlin , c1981. 268 p. : ISBN 3-428-05013-4 LC Card 86-230716
HF5415.3 .W47 1981

The Value dimension : Marx versus Ricardo and Sraffa / edited by Ben Fine. London ; New York : Routledge & Kegan Paul, 1986. 239 p. ; 24 cm. (Economy and society paperbacks) Includes

bibliographies. ISBN 0-7102-0766-2 (pbk.) : LC Card 87-109334 DDC 338.5/21 19
1. Value - History. 2. Value. 3. Marxian economics. 4. Ricardo, David, 1772-1823. 5. Sraffa, Piero. I. Fine, Ben. II. Series: Economy & society paperbacks.
HB203 .V33 1986

VALUE - HISTORY.
The Value dimension . London , New York , 1986. 239 p. ; ISBN 0-7102-0766-2 (pbk.) : LC Card 87-109334 DDC 338.5/21 19
HB203 .V33 1986

Value investing . Stein, Lawrence M. New York , c1988. xiv, 331 p. : ISBN 0-471-62875-1 LC Card 87-23152 DDC 332.63/22 19
HG4527 .S816 1988

The value of the dollar and competitiveness of U. S. wheat exports /. Haley, Stephen L. [Washington, D.C.] [1986] iv, 28 p. : LC Card 86-602853 DDC 382/.41311/0973 19
HD9049.W5 U4288 1986

VALUES. Here are entered works on moral and esthetic values, etc. Works on the economic theory of value are entered under: Value.

Values and Lifestyles Program (SRI International)
Christen, François G. Buying by mail . Menlo Park, CA (333 Ravenswood Ave., Menlo Park 94025) , c1986. v, 2, 59, 6 leaves : LC Card 86-209563 DDC 658.8/4 19
HF5415.126 .C48 1986

VALUES AND LIFESTYLES PROGRAM (SRI INTERNATIONAL) - INDEXES.
Index, 1978-1985 and survey methodology. Menlo Park, CA (333 Ravenswood Ave., Menlo Park 94025) [1986] vi, 45 leaves ; LC Card 86-220307 DDC 305/.0973 19
HF5415.3 .I47 1986

VALUES - CONGRESSES.
Cambio cultural e imagen del hombre /. Bilbao, España , c1984. 248 p. ; ISBN 84-271-1384-6 LC Card 85-234026
CB245 .C29 1984 ***NYPL [JFD 86-6394]***

Valuing small businesses and professional practices /. Pratt, Shannon P. Homewood, Ill. , c1986. xxvii, 483 p. : ISBN 0-87094-598-X LC Card 85-72255 ***NYPL [*R-Econ. 86-1421]***

Una valutazione intersettoriale costi benefici estesa al territorio . Piazzo, Pietrenzo, 1935- Roma , c1984. viii, 224 p., 6 folded leaves of plates : LC Card 84-250428
HC307.A2 P53 1984

La valutazione, simulazione e previsione nella gestione d'impresa . Gambel, Edoardo L. Milano, Italy , c1986. 190 p. : LC Card 86-217652
HF5679 .G36 1986

VALVE INDUSTRY - UNITED STATES.
The U. S. market for hazardous duty liquid pumps and valves. New York, N.Y. , c1983. 2 v. (viii, 343 leaves) : LC Card 87-401677 DDC 381/.456216 19
HD9651.5 .U16 1983

Valvo, Tino, 1948- Retribuzioni a confronto : indagine empirica sulle strutture e sui differenziali retributivi, condotta nell'area torinese / di Tino Valvo. Milano, Italy : F. Angeli, c1986. 247 p. : ill. ; 22 cm. (Collana Ires/Cgil . 9) Bibliography: p. 157. LC Card 86-170001
1. Wages - Italy - Turin Region - Statistics. I. Series: Collana Ires/Cgil (Milan, Italy) , 9. II. Title.
HD5035.T87 V34 1986

Vályi, Éva. A mezőgazdasági vállalati szervezet fejlődésének és fejlesztésének törvényszerűségei / Vályi Éva. Budapest : Akadémiai Kiadó, 1985. 107, [1] p. : ill. ; 19 cm. (A Nagyüzemi gazdálkodás kérdései, 0077-2658) Bibliography: p. 107-[108] ISBN 963-05-3468-1 : LC Card 86-137169
1. Collective farms - Hungary. 2. State farms - Hungary. I. Title. II. Series.
HD1492.H8 V33 1985

Valyshev, Nikolai. Treml, Vladimir G. Referent USSR economic and demographic statistics for normalization of Berkeley-Duke emigre questionnaire data /. [Durham, N.C. [1986] 1 v. (various pagings) ; LC Card 86-70618 DDC 304.6/0947/021 19
HB3607 .T74 1986

Van Damme, J. A. see **Vandamme, J.**

Van Daniker, Relmond P., 1942- Infrastructure assets : an assessment of user needs and recommendations for financial reporting / Relmond P. Van Daniker and Vernon Kwiatkowski. Stamford, Conn. (High Ridge Park, P.O. Box 3821, Stamford 06905-0821) : Governmental Accounting Standards Board of the Financial Accounting Foundation, c1986. xii, 155 p. ; 23 cm. (Research report) Bibliography: p. 147-155. LC Card 86-90661 DDC 657/.835 19
1. United States - Public works - Accounting. 2. Infrastructure (Economics) - United States - Accounting. 3. Finance, Public - United States - States - Accounting. 4. Local finance - United States - Accounting. I. Kwiatkowski, Vernon. II. Financial Accounting Foundation. Governmental Accounting Standards Board. III. Series: Research report (Financial Accounting Foundation. Governmental Accounting Standards Board). IV. Title.
HJ9816 .V35 1986

Van den Berg, L. M. Anticipating urban growth in Africa : land use and land values in the rurban fringe of Lusaka, Zambia / door Leonardus Marinus van den Berg. Lusaka, Zambia : Available from Zambia Geographical Association, 1984. viii, 167 p., [4] p. of plates : ill., maps ; 30 cm. (Zambia Geographical Association occassional study, 0250-8109 . no. 13) Summary in Dutch. Thesis (Ph. D.)--Universiteit van Amsterdam, 1984. Bibliography: p. 154-162. Includes indexes. LC Card 86-980297 DDC 307.7/6/096894 19
1. Land use, Rural - Zambia - Lusaka Region. 2. Real property - Prices - Zambia - Lusaka Region. 3. Urbanization - Zambia - Lusaka Region. I. Title. II. Series.
HD993.Z9 L88 1984

Van der Kooy, R. J. W. An Introduction to economic development in Southern Africa and the role of DBSA /. Sandton, Republic of South Africa [1985] 78 p. ; LC Card 87-127414 DDC 338.968 19
HG3401.A8 D485 1985

Van der Ryn, Sim. Sustainable communities : a new design synthesis for cities, suburbs, and towns/ by Sim Van der Ryn and Peter Calthorpe. San Francisco : Sierra Club Books, [1986] xvii, 238 p. : ill. ; 27 cm. Includes index. ISBN 0-87156-800-4 LC Card 83-4676 DDC 307/.14 19
1. Community development, Urban - United States - Case studies. 2. Autarchy. 3. Renewable energy sources - United States. 4. Social prediction - United States. I. Calthorpe, Peter. II. Title.
HN90.C6 V36 1986 ***NYPL [JLF 86-1241]***

Van der Walt, Sunette.
An investigation into the utilization of white women labour in the South African industry / by Sunette van der Walt. Bloemfontein : University of the Orange Free State, Dept. of Industrial Psychology, Personnel Research Division, [1976] 45 p. ; 30 cm. "November 1976." Page 45 publisher's list. Bibliography: p. 43-44. "No. P/39." ISBN 0-08-688017-4 LC Card 85-153291
1. Women - Employment - South Africa. I. Title.
HD6212 .V36 1976

Die vrou in die werksituasie in die RSA : 'n verwysingsraamwerk / Sunette van der Walt. Pretoria : Raad vir Geesteswetenskaplike Navorsing, 1986. vii, 156 p. : ill. ; 30 cm. (RGN-ondersoek na werkkragvraagstukke. Werkkragstudies . nr. 4) Summary in English. Bibliography: p. 113-156. ISBN 0-7969-0373-5 LC Card 87-121977
1. Women - Employment - South Africa. 2. Women - Employment - Research - South Africa. 3. Minority women - Employment - South Africa. I. Title. II. Series.
HD6212 .V363 1986

Van Doren, Glenn H. Management advisory services manual / Glenn H. Van Doren, Stephen D. Nadler. Boston : Warren, Gorham & Lamont, c1987- 1 v. (loose-leaf) : ill. ; 30 cm. Includes index. ISBN 0-88712-505-0 (loose-leaf) LC Card 87-50240 DDC 658.4/6 19
1. Business consultants - Handbooks, manuals, etc. I. Nadler, Stephen D. II. Title.
HD69.C6 V36 1987

Van Fleet, Alanson A. The Tennessee Valley Authority / Alanson A. Van Fleet. New York : Chelsea House, c1987. 92 p. : ill. ; 23 cm. (Know your government) Bibliography: p. 89. Includes index. ISBN 1-555-46123-9 : LC Card 86-31738 DDC 353.0082/3/09768 19
1. Tennessee Valley Authority. 2. Electric utilities - Tennessee River Valley. I. Series: Know your government (New York, N.Y.). II. Title.
HD9685.U7 T385 1987

Van Horn, Carl E. Policy implementation in the Federal system : national goals and local implementors / Carl E. Van Horn. Lexington, Mass. : Lexington Books, c1979. xiv, 177 p. ; 24 cm. Includes bibliographical references and index. ISBN 0-669-02435-X LC Card 78-19929 DDC 353.007/25
1. Intergovernmental fiscal relations - United States. 2. Revenue sharing - United States. I. Title.
HJ275 .V35 ***NYPL [JLE 80-794]***

Van House, Charles L., 1914-
Accounting for life insurance companies. Zucconi, Paul J. Accounting in life and health insurance companies / Paul J. Zucconi ; contributing authors, Gregory K. Benner ... [et al.] ; edited by Robert D. Land. Atlanta, Ga. , c1987. xiv, 365 p. : ISBN 0-915322-85-4 LC Card 86-82715 DDC 657/.836 19
HG8848 .Z84 1987

Van Ness, John R. Land, water, and culture . Albuquerque , c1987. ix, 422 p. : ISBN 0-8263-0989-5 (pbk.) LC Card 87-10957 DDC 333.1/6/09788 19
HD243.N5 L36 1987

Van Nest, Dean G. (Dean Gillette), 1923-
Developing global new products : challenges to U. S. competitiveness / by Dean G. Van Nest. Ann Arbor, Mich. : UMI Research Press, c1987. viii, 123 p. : ill. ; 24 cm. (Research for business decisions. no. 94) Revision of thesis (Ph. D.)--Pace University, 1985. Bibliography: p. [109]-119. Includes index. ISBN 0-8357-1793-3 (alk. paper) LC Card 87-5844 DDC 658.5/75/0973 19
1. New products. 2. New products - Management. I. Title.
HD69.N4 V36 1987

Van Patten, Jo. Alaska's commercial forest resource / Economic Analysis Section, Department of Commerce and Economic Development, State of Alaska ; prepared by Jo Van Patten. Juneau, Alaska : The Section, [1986] v, 29 p. : ill. ; 28 cm. "May 1986." Bibliography: p. 29. LC Card 86-622970 DDC 333.75/09798 19
1. Forests and forestry - Economic aspects - Alaska. 2. Lumber trade - Alaska. 3. Forest products industry - Alaska. I. Alaska. Economic Analysis Section. II. Title.
HD9757.A7 V36 1986

Van Sickle, Larry. The American dream and the impact of class : teaching poor kids to labor / Larry Van Sickle. New York, N.Y. : Irvington, c1985. 389 p. ; 21 cm. Includes index. Bibliography: p. 349-384. ISBN 0-8290-1382-2 (pbk.) LC Card 83-12613 DDC 331.3/4/0973 19
1. Socially handicapped youth - Employment - United States. 2. Social classes - United States. 3. Social control. I. Title.
HD6273 .V36 1985 ***NYPL [JLD 86-1637]***

Van soek naar arbeidsmarkt . Bel Ghazi, Hassan. [Bussum] , 1986. 176 p. ; ISBN 90-293-0638-6 : LC Card 86-234591
HD8518.5.M6 B45 1986

Van Velsor, Ellen. Morrison, Ann M. Breaking the glass ceiling . Reading, Mass. , c1987. ix, 229 p. : ISBN 0-201-15787-X : LC Card 87-1853 DDC 658.4/09/024042 19
HD6054.4.U6 M67 1987

Van Vliet, Willem.
Housing and neighborhoods . New York , 1987. xii, 319 p. : ISBN 0-313-25459-1 (lib. bdg. : alk. paper) LC Card 87-7527 DDC 307.3/36 19
HD7287.5 .H47 1987

Housing markets and policies under fiscal austerity /. New York , 1987. x, 263 p. : ISBN 0-313-25409-5 (lib. bdg. : alk. paper) LC Card 86-29603 DDC 363.5 19
HD7287 .H67 1987

Van Wyk, H. de J. Income and expenditure patterns of urban Black multiple households in Durban, 1985 / by H. de J. Van Wyk. Pretoria : Bureau of Market Research, University of South Africa, 1986. xi, 130 p. : ill. ; 30 cm. (Research report / Bureau of Market Research, University of South Africa = Navorsingsverslag / Buro vir Marknavorsing, Universiteit van Suid-Afrika . no. 130.4) Includes

bibliographical references. ISBN 0-908408-59-5 (pbk.) LC Card 87-151639 DDC 658.8/3968 s 339.4/1/0968455021 19
1. Cost and standard of living - South Africa - Durban - Statistics. 2. Blacks - South Africa - Durban - Economic conditions - Statistics. 3. Consumption (Economics) - South Africa - Durban - Statistics. 4. Income - South Africa - Durban - Statistics. I. Series. II. Series: Research report (University of South Africa. Bureau of Market Research), no. 130.4. III. Title.
HC517.S7 S48 no. 130, pt. 4 HD7064.4.Z8D8

Van Zyl, S. J. J. Trends in capital expenditure on fixed assets / by S.J.J. van Zyl. Pretoria : Bureau of Market Research, University of South Africa, 1985. ix, 100 p. : ill. ; 30 cm. (Research report = Navorsingsverslag . no. 125) Includes bibliographical references. ISBN 0-908408-49-8 (pbk.) LC Card 86-206341 DDC 658.8/3968 s 332/.0414/0968 19
1. Capital investments - South Africa - Statistics. I. Series: Research report (University of South Africa. Bureau of Market Research report), no. 125. II. Title.
HC517.S7 S48 no. 125 HG4028.C4

Vanags, I. ÎA. (Ilmar ÎAnovich) Ėffektivnoe ispol'zovanie vychislitel'noĭ tekhniki / I.ÎA. Vanags, Z.R. Gobedzhishvili, E.M. Guttsaĭt. Moskva : "Finansy i statistika", 1982. 142, [2] p. : ill. ; 20 cm. Bibliography: p. 142-[143] LC Card 83-165693
1. Business - Data processing. 2. Electronic data processing - Soviet Union. 3. Information theory in economics. I. Gobedzhishvili, Z. R. (Zakhariĭ Rubenovich). II. Guttsaĭt, E. M. (Evgeniĭ Mikhel'evich). III. Title.
HF5548.2 .V345 1982

Vanasse, Gilbert, 1948- Histoire de la Fédération des travailleurs du papier et de la forêt / Gilbert Vanasse. Montréal, Québec : Editions Saint-Martin, 1986- v. <1 > : ill. ; 25 cm. Includes bibliographies. CONTENTS. - t. 1. 1907-1958. ISBN 2-89035-122-X (t. 1) LC Card 86-231295
1. Fédération des travailleurs du papier et de la forêt - History. 2. Paper industry workers - Québec (Province) - History. 3. Trade-unions - Paper industry workers - Québec (Province) - History. I. Title.
HD6528.P332 F438 1986

Vanatoa, Ė. Kh. Eesti NSV, teatmik / E. Vanatoa. Tallinn : "Perioodika", 1985. 33 p. ; 22 cm. Title in colophon: Ėstonskaia SSR, spravochnik. LC Card 86-131324
1. Estonia - Statistics. I. Title. II. Title: Ėstonskaia SSR, spravochnik.
HA1448.E8 V36 1985

Vanberg, Viktor. Morality and economics : de moribus est disputandum / Viktor Vanberg. New Brunswick [N.J.] : Transaction Books, 1987. p. cm (Original papers . no. 7) At head of title: Social Philosophy & Policy Center. ISBN 0-912051-19-1 (pbk.) LC Card 87-19213 DDC 174/.26 19
1. Economics - Moral and ethical aspects. I. Bowling Green State University. Social Philosophy & Policy Center. II. Series: Original papers (Bowling Green State University. Social Philosophy & Policy Center), no. 7. III. Title.
HB72 .V268 1987

Vance, A. Last chance for peace : a new and refreshing look at how we fit into the infinite scheme of life / A. Vance.1st ed. Boulder, Colo. : Earthview Press, c1985. xviii, 256 p. : ill. ; 22 cm. Includes index. ISBN 0-930705-01-7 (pbk.) : LC Card 84-18831 DDC 172/.24 19
1. Peace - Religious aspects. 2. World politics - 1975-1985. 3. Social systems. 4. Religion - Philosophy. 5. Political sociology. I. Title.
BL65.P4 V36 1985 ***NYPL [JLD 86-2214]***

Vance Research Services. Fresh trends, 1987 . [Lincolnshire, Ill.] (400 Knightsbridge Pkwy., Lincolnshire 60069) , c1987. 4 v. ; LC Card 87-162047 DDC 381/.415/0973 19
HD9244 .F73 1987

Vancil, Richard F. Passing the baton : managing the process of CEO succession / Richard F. Vancil ; foreword by Alonzo L. McDonald. Boston, Mass. : Harvard Business School Press, c1987. xxii, 318 p. : ill. ; 25 cm. Includes index. ISBN 0-87584-182-1 LC Card 87-11962 DDC 658.4 19
1. Chief executive officers - United States - Succession. 2. Directors of corporations - United States. 3. Industrial management - United States. I. Title.
HD38.25.U6 V36 1987

Vandamme, J.
Employee consultation and information in multinational corporations /. London , Dover, N.H. , c1986. 265 p. ; ISBN 0-7099-2624-3 : LC Card 85-21264 DDC 331.25 19
NYPL [JLD 86-1612]

L'Information et la consultation des travailleurs dans les enterprises multinationales /. [Paris] [Genève?] , 1984. 290 p. ; ISBN 2-13-038651-2 (pbk.)
HD62.4 .I53 1984 ***NYPL [JLD 87-60]***

Vandemoortele, Jan. The wage policy in Kenya : past, present, and future / by J. Vandermoortele. [Nairobi] : Institute for Development Studies, University of Nairobi, [1984] 28 leaves : ill. ; 30 cm. (IDS consultancy report . no. 12) "Study carried [out] on behalf of the Central Organization of Trade Unions (COTU)." LC Card 86-681105 DDC 331.2/96762 19
1. Wage-price policy - Kenya. 2. Wages - Kenya. 3. Wages - Government policy - Kenya. I. Title. II. Series.
HC865.Z9 W248 1984

VANDERBIJLPARK (SOUTH AFRICA) - CENSUS.
Bevolkingsensus 1980 uitgesoekte statistiese streek Vereeniging/Vanderbijlpark/Sasolburg =. Pretoria [1985] xx, 301 p. : ISBN 0-621-09484-6 : LC Card 85-235498
HA4701.Z9 V474 1985

VANDERBIJLPARK (SOUTH AFRICA) - POPULATION - STATISTICS.
Bevolkingsensus 1980 uitgesoekte statistiese streek Vereeniging/Vanderbijlpark/Sasolburg =. Pretoria [1985] xx, 301 p. : ISBN 0-621-09484-6 : LC Card 85-235498
HA4701.Z9 V474 1985

VANDERLIP, FRANK A. (FRANK ARTHUR), 1864-1937.
Mayer, Robert Stanley. The influence of Frank A. Vanderlip and the National City Bank on American commerce and foreign policy, 1910-1920 /. New York , 1987. viii, 221 p. ; ISBN 0-8240-8087-4 : LC Card 87-23793 DDC 332.1/5/097471 19
HG2613.N54 N3555 1987

Vandermoortele, Jan. Mamder, Josué Sandjiman. Les effets de la crise mondiale actuelle sur l'économie et la population gabonaises /. Addis Abéba , c1984. 34 p. ; ISBN 92-2-203795-2 LC Card 86-215256
HC975 .M36 1984

Vándorlás, mobilitás, keresetalakulás . Harcsa, István. Budapest , 1987. 86 p. ; ISBN 963-340-812-1 : LC Card 87-409641
HB2052.5.A3 H37 1987

Vandpriser . Denmark. Udvalget til undersøgelse af vandforsyningernes økonomiske baggrund. København [1983] 108 p. ; ISBN 87-503-4559-1 LC Card 84-169901
HD4465.D4 D46 1983

Vändpunkten . Larsson, Janerik, 1944- [Stockholm] [1983] 125 p. : ISBN 91-7566-040-7 : LC Card 84-189468
HD5660.S9 L35 1983

Vane, Howard R. Current controversies in economics /. Oxford [Oxfordshire] UK , New York, NY, USA , 1987. xii, 319 p. : ISBN 0-631-15157-5 : LC Card 86-29928 DDC 338.941 19
HB171.5 .C975 1987

Vanebo, Jan Ole, 1948- Systematisk ledelse i mindre bedrifter / Jan Ole Vanebo. Kirkenær : Reenskaug, 1980. 192 p. : ill. ; 24 cm. ISBN 82-7048-171-8 : LC Card 82-105304
1. Small business - Management. 2. Small business - Norway - Management. I. Title.
HD62.7 .V36 1980

VanGundy, Arthur B. Techniques of structured problem solving / Arthur B. VanGundy. 2nd ed. New York : Van Nostrand Reinhold Co., c1988. xiv, 386 p. : ill. ; 24 cm. Bibliography: p. 371-378. Includes index. ISBN 0-442-28847-6 LC Card 87-6168 DDC 658.4/03 19
1. Problem solving. I. Title.
HD30.29 .V36 1988

Vanheukelen, Marc. Coming to grips with the internal market /. Maastricht, The Netherlands , c1986. viii, 136 p. ; ISBN 90-6779-019-2 (pbk.) LC Card 86-222624 DDC 337.1/42 19
HC241.2 .C5548 1986

Vanin, ÎUriĭ Vasil'evich. Agrarnyĭ stroĭ feodal'noĭ Korei XV-XVI vv. / ÎU.V. Vanin. Moskva : Izd-vo "Nauka", Glav. red. vostochnoĭ lit-ry, 1981. 309 p. ; 22 cm. At head of title: Akademiia nauk SSSR. Ordena Trudovogo krasnogo znameni Institut vostokovedeniia. Includes indexes. Bibliography: p. 296-[298] LC Card 83-462393
1. Land tenure - Korea - History. 2. Peasantry - Korea - History. 3. Feudalism - Korea. I. Title. II. Title: Agrarnyĭ stroĭ feodal'noĭ Korei 156-16-go vv. III. Title: Agrarnyĭ stroĭ feodal'noĭ Korei piatnadtsatogo-shestnadtsatogo vv.
HD1331.K6 V36 1981 ***NYPL [*QI 86-3898]***

Vannebo, Olav. De tjenesteytende næringer i 80-åra / Olav Vannebo. Oslo : Tanum-Norli : Norsk produktivitetsinstitutt, 1981. iii, 178 p. : ill. ; 24 cm. Cover title: De tjenesteytende næringer i 80-årene. "Npi 1147"--Cover. Includes bibliographies. ISBN 82-518-1573-8 : LC Card 83-194969
1. Service industries - Norway. 2. Norway - Economic conditions - 1945-. I. Title. II. Title: Tjenesteytende næringer i 80-årene.
HD9986.N82 V36 1981

VANS - FRANCE - STATISTICS.
Enquête sur l'utilisation des véhicules utilitaires légers . Paris [1983] 58 p. : LC Card 84-191337
HE5668.A6 E56 1983

VanSant, Jerry. Honadle, George. Implementation for sustainability . West Hartford, Conn. , c1985. xiv, 128 p. ; ISBN 0-931816-47-5 LC Card 85-12538 DDC 338.9/0068 19
HD1417 .H66 1985 ***NYPL [JLE 86-3888]***

A VAR analysis of economic interdependence . Kuszczak, John. [Ottawa] [1987] ii, 55 p. : LC Card 87-167407 DDC 338.5/42/0971 19
HB3755 .K87 1987

Vara Miranda, Ma. Jesús (María Jesús) Análisis de las cooperativas de trabajo asociado en Madrid / Ma. Jesús Vara Miranda. [Madrid] : Ministerio de Trabajo y Seguridad Social, c1985. 463 p. : ill. ; 22 cm. (Colección Tesis doctorales) Originally presented as the author's thesis (Universidad Autónoma de Madrid, 1983) under title: Las causas del fracaso de las cooperativas de trabajo asociado : especial referencia a Madrid. Bibliography: p. [449]-456. ISBN 84-7434-332-1 LC Card 87-109103 DDC 334/.6/094643 19
1. Producer cooperatives - Spain - Madrid. I. Series: Colección Tesis doctorales (Spain. Ministerio de Trabajo y Seguridad Social). II. Title.
HD3218.M38 V37 1985

Varady, David P. Neighborhood upgrading : a realistic assessment / David P. Varady. Albany : State University of New York Press, c1986. x, 184 p. : ill. ; 24 cm. (SUNY series on urban public policy) Includes index. Bibliography: p. 165-174. ISBN 0-88706-299-7 LC Card 85-30392 DDC 307.3/362/0973 19
1. Urban renewal - United States. 2. Urban homesteading - United States. 3. Urban policy - United States. 4. Neighborhood - United States. 5. Community development, Urban - United States. I. Title. II. Series.
HT175 .V37 1986 ***NYPL [JLE 87-373]***

Varandani, Gursharan, 1946- Workers' participation in management : with special reference to India / Gursharan Varandani ; foreword by Dr. Anand Prakash. New Delhi : Deep & Deep Publications, c1987. xii, 228 p. ; 23 cm. Bibliography: p. [220]-225. Includes index. LC Card 87-900827 DDC 658.3/152/0954 19
1. Management - Employee participation. 2. Management - India - Employee participation. I. Title.
HD5650 .V35 1987

Varga, Gyula, 1938-
Ár- és külkereskedelmi tanulmány a buzára és kukoricára, Magyarország /. Budapest , 1984. 93 p. ; ISBN 963-491-218-4 (Magy. nemz. bibl.) LC Card 86-147569
HD9049.W5 H93 1984

Borszéki, Éva. Élelmiszer-gazdaságunk versenyképessége . Budapest , 1986. 284, [1] p. : ISBN 963-221-590-7 : LC Card 87-148751
HD1940.5 .B66 1986

Borszéki, Éva. Élelmiszergazdaságunk versenyképessége . Budapest , 1985. 147 p. ; ISBN 963-491-213-3 LC Card 86-199073
HD1940.5 .B67 1985

Fodor, András. A magyar társadalombiztosítás

az V. ötéves terv időszakában, 1976-1980 /. Budapest , 1983. 147 p. ; ISBN 963-321-977-9 LC Card 85-129731
HD7172.5 .F62 1983

Varga, Lajos. Túri vásár / Varga Lajos. Mezőtúr : Mezőtúri Városi Tanács, 1983. 188 p. ; 21 cm. (Mezőtúri helytörténeti füzetek, 0134-0727 . 5) Includes bibliographical references. ISBN 963-7612-04-1 LC Card 85-109670
1. Markets - Hungary - Mezőtúr - History. 2. Mezőtúr (Hungary) - History. I. Title. II. Series.
HF5474.H82 M498 1983

Varga, Zsuzsa. Ez az a munkásság-- /. Budapest , 1984. 225 p., [40] p. of plates : ISBN 963-322-103-X LC Card 85-184724
HD6680.5 .E95 1984

Vargas Cullel, Jorge. Gamboa Conejo, Rita Ma. (Rita María) Resultados preliminares del análisis metodológico de los planes nacionales de desarrollo, 1974-1982 /. Heredia , 1985. 1 v. (various pagings) : LC Card 87-402159 DDC 338.97286 19
HC143 .G36 1985

VARGAS, GETÚLIO, 1883-1954.
Getúlio Vargas e a economia contemporânea /. Campinas , 1986. 179 p. ; ISBN 85-26-80033-7 LC Card 87-403048 DDC 330.981/063 19
HC187 .G45 1986

Vargas, Ines.
Buvollen, H. P. (Hans Petter) The situation of workers in the industrialised countries with special reference to Scandinavia /. Oslo [1985] 24 p. ; LC Card 86-205580 DDC 331.13/7948 19
HD8540 .B86 1985

Conclusions from "The NIEO and the situation of workers" : special reference to Latin America / Ines Vargas. Oslo :International Peace Research Institute, [1986] 21 p. ; 30 cm. (PRIO report, 0333-483X . 14/86) Cover title. LC Card 87-128390 DDC 337.8 19
1. Latin America - Foreign economic relations. 2. International economic relations. 3. Labor and laboring classes. I. Vargas, Ines. NIEO and the situation of workers. II. Series: PRIO report , 86/14. III. Title.
HF1480.5 .V37 1986

NIEO and the situation of workers. Vargas, Ines. Conclusions from "The NIEO and the situation of workers" : special reference to Latin America / Ines Vargas. Oslo :International Peace Research Institute, [1986] 21 p. ; LC Card 87-128390 DDC 337.8 19
HF1480.5 .V37 1986

The NIEO and the situatuon of workers : special reference to Latin America / Ines Vargas with the assistance of Hans Petter Buvollen, Jaime Estévez. Oslo : International Peace Research Institute, [1985] xiv, 290 p. ; 30 cm. (PRIO report, 0333-483X . 8/85) Bibliography: p. 274-290. ISBN 82-7288-121-7 (pbk.) LC Card 86-205407 DDC 331/.098 19
1. Trade-unions - Latin America. 2. Manpower policy - Latin America. 3. International economic relations. 4. Labor and laboring classes - Latin America. 5. Labor supply - Scandinavia. I. Buvollen, H. P. (Hans Petter). II. Estevez, Jaime, 1946-. III. Series: PRIO report , 85/8. IV. Title.
HD6530.5 .V36 1985

The right to work and the situation of workers / Ines Vargas. Oslo : International Peace Research Institute, [1985] 47 p. ; 30 cm. (PRIO report, 0333-483X . 15/85) "October 1985." Bibliography: p. 40-41. ISBN 82-7288-122-5 (pbk.) LC Card 86-204949 DDC 331.88/92 19
1. Right to labor. 2. Right to labor - Latin America. 3. Work. I. Series: PRIO report , 85/15. II. Title.
HD4903 .V34 1985

The situation of workers in Latin America / Ines Vargas. Oslo : International Peace Research Institute, 1985. 92 p. ; 30 cm. (PRIO report, 0333-483X . 9/85) Bibliography: p. 82-92. ISBN 82-7288-123-3 (pbk.) LC Card 86-205392 DDC 331/.098 19
1. Trade-unions - Latin America. 2. Labor supply - Latin America. 3. Labor and laboring classes - Latin America. I. Series: PRIO report , 85/9. II. Title.
HD6530.5 .V37 1985

Vargish, George. What's made in the U. S.A.? / George Vargish. New Brunswick, U. S.A. : Transaction Books, c1988. 160 p. : ill. ; 24 cm. Includes index. ISBN 0-88738-187-1 LC Card 87-19164 DDC 382/.3/0973 19
1. United States - Commercial policy. 2. Free trade and protection - Protection. 3. United States - Manufactures. 4. Knit goods industry - United States. 5. Competition, International. 6. International economic relations. I. Title. II. Title: What's made in the USA?.
HF1716 .V37 1988

Vári, Anna. Kockázat és társadalom /. Budapest , 1987. 309 p. : ISBN 963-05-4450-4 : LC Card 87-425562
HD61 .K6 1987

Die Variabilität relativer Preisänderungen und die Varianz monetärer Aggregate /. Blang, Hans-Georg, 1953- Frankfurt am Main , New York , c1986. xxvii, 338 p. : ISBN 3-8204-9074-4 LC Card 86-156110
HG229 .B555 1986

Variant population projections : microfiche : variant population projections by sex and age for United Kingdom and selected constituent countries from mid 1983 / prepared by the Government Actuary in consultation with the Registrars General. London : HMSO, 1986. 17 p. : ill. ; 30 cm. + 8 microfiche. (Series PP2 . no. 14) At head of title: Office of Population Censuses and Surveys. Eight microfiche in pocket entitled: Mid-1983 based mortality variant projections. ISBN 0-11-690777-0 (pbk.) : LC Card 86-234516 DDC 304.6/2/0941021 19
1. Population forecasting - Great Britain. 2. Population forecasting - Great Britain - Statistics. 3. Great Britain - Population. 4. Great Britain - Population - Statistics. I. Great Britain. Government Actuary. II. Great Britain. Office of Population Censuses and Surveys. III. Series.
HB3583 .V368 1986

Variations in C . Schustack, Steve, 1952- Bellevue, Wash. [New York] , c1985. xiii, 344 p. ; ISBN 0-914845-48-9 : LC Card 85-5033 DDC 650/.028/5425 19
HF5548.5.C12 S38 1985 ***NYPL [JSE 87-246]***

Várkonyi, Margit. A vezetők véleményezése / Várkonyi Margit. Budapest : Népszava, 1984. 66 p. : ill. ; 19 cm. (Az Alapszervezeti munka gyakorlata, 0231-2786) ISBN 963-322-189-7 : LC Card 85-176949
1. Industrial management - Hungary - Evaluation. 2. Executives - Hungary - Rating of. 3. Industrial management - Hungary - Employee participation. I. Title. II. Series.
HD70.H8 V38 1984

Världsbanken. see **International Bank for Reconstruction and Development.**

Varma, M. L. Modwel, Suman Kumar, 1936- Export effort of India /. New Delhi , 1986. ix, 83, [1] p. ; LC Card 86-903364 DDC 382/.6/0954 19
HF1589 .M63 1986

Varma, R. M. Bulsara, Jal F. (Jal Feerose), 1899- Perspectives on social welfare in India /. New Delhi , 1984. xvi, 226 p. ; LC Card 84-900869 DDC 361/.954 19
HV40 .B886 1984 ***NYPL [JLD 86-4376]***

Varma, S. C. Millions in poverty grip : India's rural works programme / S.C. Varma.1st ed. New Delhi : Kunj Pub. House, 1984. xv, 172 p. ; 22 cm. Includes index. Bibliography: p. [162]-166. LC Card 84-900600 DDC 331.12/042/0954 19
1. Rural poor - Employment - Government policy - India. 2. Rural development - Government policy - India. 3. Public service employment - India. I. Title.
HD5710.85.I4 V37 1984
NYPL [JLD 86-4236]

VARNA (BULGARIA) - COMMERCE - HISTORY.
Morska vrata na rodinata . Varna , 1986. 146 p., [32] p. of plates : LC Card 86-233471
HE557.B9 M67 1986

Varna Forum II . Varna Forum (2nd : 1985 : Varna, Bulgaria) [Varna?] [s.n.] [1985] 166 p. ; LC Card 86-220415 DDC 382/.091713/01717 19
HF1410.5 .V37 1985

Varna Forum II "Tŭrgoviiata Iztok--Zapad" : sŭstoianie i perspektivi / Varna forum, 28-29 septemvri, 1985 godina, Varna, Bŭlgariia. [Sofia] : [s.n.], 1985. 248 p. ; 21 cm. On cover: Pravitelstvo na Narodna Republika Bulgariia. Mezhdunaroden sŭvet za novi initsiativi v sŭtrudnichestvo Iztok--Zapad. LC Card 86-196109
1. East-West trade (1945-) - Congresses. I. Mezhdunaroden sŭvet za novi initsiativi v sŭtrudnichestvoto Iztok--Zapad (Bulgaria). II. Varna Forum (2nd : 1985 : Varna, Bulgaria). III. Title: Varna Forum vtori "Tŭrgoviiata Iztok--Zapak.".
HF1411 .V37 1985

Varna Forum vtori "Tŭrgoviiata Iztok--Zapak." Varna Forum II "Tŭrgoviiata Iztok--Zapad" . [Sofia] , 1985. 248 p. ; LC Card 86-196109
HF1411 .V37 1985

Varna Forum (2nd : 1985 : Varna, Bulgaria)
Varna Forum II : East-West trade, status, and prospects, September 28th-29th, 1985, Varna, Bulgaria. [Varna?] : Govt. of the People's Republic of Bulgaria ; [s.n.] : International Council for New Initiatives in East-West Cooperation, [1985] 166 p. ; 21 cm. LC Card 86-220415 DDC 382/.091713/01717 19
1. East-West trade (1945-) - Congresses. 2. International economic relations - Congresses. 3. Commercial policy - Congresses. 4. International cooperation - Congresses. 5. Technology transfer - Congresses. I. Title.
HF1410.5 .V37 1985

Varna Forum II "Tŭrgoviiata Iztok--Zapad" . [Sofia] , 1985. 248 p. ; LC Card 86-196109
HF1411 .V37 1985

VARNENSKI OKRŬG (BULGARIA) - ECONOMIC CONDITIONS.
Rabotnicheskoto profsŭiuzno dvizhenie vŭv Varnenski okrŭg /. Sofiia , 1985. 348 p., [16] p. of plates : LC Card 86-111781
HD8629.V372 R37 1985

Varner, Jane Terzick, 1942- Advanced word/information processing operations : applications, concepts, procedures / Jane Terzick Varner. Chicago : Science Research Associates, c1988. 1 v. (various pagings) : ill. ; 22 x 29 cm. Includes index. ISBN 0-574-20795-3 (pbk.) : LC Card 87-13042 DDC 652/.5 19
1. Word processing. I. Title.
HF5548.115 .V36 1988

Varnon, M. S. Developing and using office applications with AppleWorks : versions 1.0 through 2.0 / M.S. Varnon. St. Paul : West Pub. Co., c1987. xi, 366 p. : ill. ; 26 cm. (The Microcomputing series) Includes index. ISBN 0-314-34129-3 (pbk.) : LC Card 86-24696 DDC 651.8/5369 19
1. AppleWorks (Computer program). 2. Office practice - Automation. I. Title. II. Series.
HF5548.4.A68 V37 1987

Városépítési Tudományos és Tervező Intézet. A Magyarországi településrendszer strukturális változása /. Budapest , 1984. 155 p., [1] folded leaf of plates : ISBN 963-03-2079-7 (Magy. nemz. bibl.) LC Card 85-231254
HD640.5 .M343 1984

Várszegi, Gyula. A világ metrói / Várszegi Gyula. [Budapest] : Idegenforgalmi Propaganda és Kiadó Vállalat, [1983] 250 p., [48] p. of plates : ill. (some col.) ; 29 cm. Bibliography: p. 227. ISBN 963-02-2971-4 (Magy. nemz. bibl.) LC Card 84-219598
1. Subways. I. Title.
HE4211 .V37 1983

Varuhandeln. Larsson, Folke. [Stockholm] [1981] 137 p. : ISBN 91-38-06014-0 LC Card 84-120411
HF5429.6.S9 L368 1981

Vasary, Ildiko. Beyond the plan : social change in a Hungarian village / Ildiko Vasary. Boulder : Westview Press, 1987. xvii, 308 p. : ill. ; 23 cm. (Westview special studies on the Soviet Union and Eastern Europe) Bibliography: p. 297-303. Includes index. ISBN 0-8133-7412-X (soft : alk. paper) : LC Card 87-8219 DDC 307.7/2/09439 19
1. Collectivization of agriculture - Hungary. 2. Private plot agriculture - Hungary. 3. Hungary - Rural conditions. I. Title.
HD1492.H8 V35 1987

Vasche, Jon David. The economic and fiscal effects of a primary source law for California wine imports. Sacramento, Calif. (925 L St., Suite 650, Sacramento 95814) : Legislative Analyst, State of California, [1986] vi, 130 p. : ill. ; 28 cm. Cover title. "May 1986." Includes bibliographical references. LC Card 86-622342 DDC 338.4/36632/009794 19
1. Wine industry - California. 2. Wine and wine making - Law and legislation - California - Compliance costs. I. California. Legislature. Joint Legislative Budget

Committee. Legislative Analyst. II. Title.
HD9377.C2 V37 1986

Vasco, Neno. Concepção anarquista do sindicalismo / Neno Vasco ; estudo introdutório de João Freire. Porto : Edições Afrontamento, 1984. 209 p. ; 21 cm. (Movimento operário português. 10) Bibliography: p. 45-50. LC Card 84-256086 DDC 320.5/7 19
1. Anarchism. 2. Syndicalism. I. Title.
HX833 .V37 1984 ***NYPL [JLD 86-2525]***

Vasconcellos, Frazão de. Solis, Duarte Gomes. Armadas da carreira da India de 1560 a 1590 . Lisboa , 1938. xvi, 20 p. : LC Card 86-140347
HF3698.14 S65 1938

Vasconcellos, Marco Antonio Sandoval de. Grupos homogêneos no mercado de trabalho assalariado . Brasília , 1985. 56 p. : LC Card 85-231654
HD5004 .G78 1985

Vasconcelos, Antônio Enock de. Avaliação do polonordeste e do Projeto Sertanejo. Fortaleza , 1985. 314 p. : LC Card 87-402900 DDC 338.981/3 19
HC188.N6 A94 1985

Vasermanis, Ė. Modelirovanie razvitii͡a mezhotraslevyh kompleksov Latviĭskoĭ SSR . Riga , 1985. 106 p. : LC Card 86-177817
HD9015.S653 L376 1985

Vasil'chuk, I͡U. A. Nauchno-tekhnicheskai͡a revoli͡utsii͡a i rabochiĭ klass pri kapitalizme : uglublenie protivorechiĭ i problemy klassovoĭ bor'by / I͡U.A. Vasil'chuk. Moskva : Izd-vo "Nauka", 1980. 295 p. : ill. ; 20 cm. At head of title: Akademii͡a nauk SSSR. Institut mezhdunarodnogo rabochego dvizhenii͡a. Includes bibliographical references. LC Card 81-130590
1. Labor supply - Effect of technological innovations on. 2. Technological innovations - Social aspects. I. Title.
HD6331 .V22 1980

Vasil'ev, A. F. (Aleksandr Filippovich) Promyshlennost' Urala v gody Velikoĭ Otechestvennoĭ voĭny 1941-1945 / A.F. Vasil'ev. Moskva : Izd-vo "Nauka", 1982. 279 p., [1] folded leaf of plates : ill. ; 22 cm. At head of title: Akademii͡a nauk SSSR. Institut istorii SSSR. Includes bibliographical references and index. LC Card 83-165021
1. Ural Mountains Region (R.S.F.S.R.) - Industries - History. 2. World War, 1939-1945 - Russian S.F.S.R. - Ural Mountains Region. 3. Industrial mobilization - Russian S.F.S.R. - Ural Mountain Region - History. I. Title.
HC337.R852 U7387 1982

Vasil'ev, A. F. (Alekseĭ Fedorovich) Avtomatizirovannai͡a obrabotka uchetnoĭ informatsii v sel'skokhozi͡aĭstvennykh predprii͡atii͡akh / A.F. Vasil'ev, K.K. Puchinskas. Moskva : Finansy i statistika, 1984. 198 p. ; 22 cm. LC Card 85-113739
1. Agriculture - Soviet Union - Accounting - Data processing. I. Puchinskas, K. K. (Kazis Kazio). II. Title.
HF5686.A36 V37 1984

Vasil'ev, I͡A. T. I͡Uzhnai͡a I͡Akutii͡a, sotsial'no-ėkonomicheskiĭ aspekt . I͡Akutsk , 1985. 94 p. ; LC Card 86-180767
HC337.I2 I97 1985

Vasil'ev, Ivan Afanas'evich. Korennye i priezzhie / Ivan Vasil'ev. Moskva : "Sov. Rossii͡a," 1980. 86 p. ; 16 cm. (Pisatel' i vremi͡a. Pis'ma iz derevni) LC Card 81-178115
1. Agricultural laborers - Russian S.F.S.R. - Non-Chernozem Region. 2. Migrant labor - Russian S.F.S.R. - Non-Chernozem Region. 3. Urban-rural migration - Russian S.F.S.R. - Non-Chernozem Region. I. Title. II. Series.
HD1536.S65 V375 1980

Vasil'eva, Ė. K. Naselenie Leningrada /. Moskva , 1981. 94 p. : LC Card 82-118662
HB2278.L46 N37 1981

Vasil'eva, E. S. (Elena Stepanovna) Planirovanie pribyli i rentabel'nosti na promyshlennom predprii͡atii : lektsii͡a / E.S. Vasil'eva. Moskva : Moskovskiĭ in-t nar. khozi͡aĭstva im. Plekhanova, 1985. 40 p. : ill. ; 21 cm. At head of title: Ministerstvo vysshego i srednego spetsial'nogo obrazovanii͡a RSFSR. Moskovskiĭ ordena Trudovogo Krasnogo Znameni institut narodnogo khozi͡aĭstva im. G.V. Plekhanova. Includes bibliographies. LC Card 86-204680
1. Profit - Soviet Union. 2. Business enterprises - Soviet Union - Finance. I. Title.
HG4028.P7 V39 1985

Vasil'evskai͡a, Ė. V. (Ėmilii͡a Viktorovna) Rabochiĭ klass Sibiri . Novosibirsk , 1986. 355 p., [16] p. of plates : LC Card 86-211294
HD5797.S5 R33 1986

Sotsial'no-ėkonomicheskoe i kul'turnoe razvitie Zabaĭkal'i͡a . Novosibirsk , 1980. 283 p. ; LC Card 81-132139
HC337.R852 T737 1980

Vasilevskai͡a, I. P. Khozi͡aĭstvennyĭ mekhanizm proizvodstva i obrashchenii͡a tovarov narodnogo potreblenii͡a /. Riga , 1985. 115 p. ; LC Card 86-177827
HF1040.9.L38 K47 1985

Vasi͡utovich, V. P. (Vladimir Petrovich) T͡Senoobrazovanie v voennom proizvodstve SShA / V.P. Vasi͡utovich. Moskva : Izd-vo "Nauka", 1980. 221 p. ; 20 cm. At head of title: Akademii͡a nauk SSSR. Ordena Trudovogo Krasnogo Znameni Institut mirovoĭ ėkonomiki i mezhdunarodnykh otnosheniĭ. Includes bibliographies. LC Card 81-143903
1. Munitions - United States - Prices. I. Title.
HD9743.U6 V37 1980

Vasko, Tibor, 1931- IIASA (International Institute for Applied Systems Analysis) International Meeting on Long-Term Fluctuations in Economic Growth (1985 : Weimar, Germany) The long-wave debate . Berlin , New York , c1987. xvii, 430 p. : ISBN 0-387-18164-4 (U. S.) LC Card 87-23256 DDC 338.5/42 19
HB3729 .I52 1985

Vásquez M., Luis (Vásquez Medina) El mercantilismo mexicano versus el liberalismo inglés / Luis Vásquez M. 1a ed. México, D.F. : Editorial Benengeli, 1985. xiii, 215 p., [18] p. of plates : ill., facsims., ports. ; 21 cm. Includes bibliographical references. LC Card 87-403512 DDC 380.1/0972 19
1. Mexico - Economic conditions - 19th century. 2. Mercantile system - Mexico - History - 19th century. 3. Capitalism - Mexico - History - 19th century. I. Title.
HC135 .V34 1985

Vásquez M., Rolando. Cléves S., Rodrigo. Rendimientos de beneficiado de café . San José, Costa Rica , 1986. 35 leaves : LC Card 87-403521 DDC 338.1/6 19
HD9199.C82 C57 1986

Vasseur, Philippe. Le chômage, c'est les autres / Philippe Vasseur. Paris : P. Belfond, c1985. 224 p. ; 23 cm. (Documents) Includes bibliographical references. ISBN 2-7144-1867-8 : LC Card 86-120821 DDC 331.13/7944 19
1. Unemployment - France. 2. France - Full employment policies. I. Title.
HD5775 .V37 1985

Vassilakis, Spyridon.
Non-basics, the standard commodity, and the uniformity of the profit rate. 1984.
Stamatis, Georg. Sraffa und sein Verhältnis zu Ricardo und Marx / Georgios Stamatis ; mit einem Anhang, Non-basics, the standard commodity, and the uniformity of the profit rate (1982) von Spyridon Vassilakis. Göttingen , Lollar , c1984. ix, 459 p. : ISBN 3-921701-04-X LC Card 84-213549
HB103.S7 S73 1984

Vasudev, Uma. Issues before non-alignment . New Delhi , 1983. 190 p. ; LC Card 83-903478 DDC 327/.09171/6 19
JX1393.N54 I87 1983 ***NYPL [JLE 86-4176]***

A vasutas munkásmozgalom története . Gadanecz, Béla. Budapest , 1985. 351 p. ; ISBN 963-322-262-1 LC Card 86-227921
HD8039.R12 H93 1985

Vasutasok Szakszervezete. Gadanecz, Béla. A vasutas munkásmozgalom története . Budapest , 1985. 351 p. ; ISBN 963-322-262-1 LC Card 86-227921
HD8039.R12 H93 1985

Vaté, Michel. Leçons d'économie politique / Michel Vaté. 4e éd. Paris : Economica, c1985. 433 p. : ill. ; 24 cm. Bibliography: p. [419]-421. Includes index. ISBN 2-7178-1021-8 : LC Card 86-141680 DDC 330 19
1. Economics. I. Title.
HB173 .V367 1985

Vatteville, Éric. Mesure des ressources humaines et gestion de l'entreprise / Eric Vatteville. Paris : Economica, c1985. 286 p. : ill. ; 24 cm. (Collection Gestion. Série Politique générale, finance et marketing) Bibliography: p. 273-282. ISBN 2-7178-0969-4 : LC Card 86-137038 DDC 658.3 19
1. Personnel management. I. Series: Collection Gestion (Economica (Firm)). Série Politique générale, finance et marketing. II. Title.
HF5549 .V382 1985

Vatukarayē kāntā śramaya surākāma . Kūriyan, Rēval. Colombo, Sri Lanka [1984] 24 p. : LC Card 86-902479
HD6182.8 .K87 1984

Vaughan, Hap. Your career game / Hap Vaughan. New York : Wiley, c1987. x, 240 p. : ill. ; 23 cm. Includes index. ISBN 0-471-62949-9 (pbk.) LC Card 87-20964 DDC 650.1/4 19
1. Career development. I. Title.
HF5549.5.C35 V38 1987

VAUX-LE-PÉNIL (FRANCE) - ECONOMIC CONDITIONS.
Camus, Michel. L'expérience pénivauxoise, 1971-1982 . [Vaux-le-Pénil , 1982] 187 p., [8] p. of plates : LC Card 84-190663
HC277.V35 C36 1982

VAUX-LE-PÉNIL (FRANCE) - POLITICS AND GOVERNMENT.
Camus, Michel. L'expérience pénivauxoise, 1971-1982 . [Vaux-le-Pénil , 1982] 187 p., [8] p. of plates : LC Card 84-190663
HC277.V35 C36 1982

VDE-Kongress '86 (1986 : Nuremberg, Germany) NTG-Fachtagung (1986 : Nuremberg, Germany) Von der Nachrichtentechnik zur Informationstechnik . Berlin , c1986. 104 p. : ISBN 3-8007-1485-X LC Card 87-136748 DDC 384 19
HE7604 .N74 1986

VDI-Informationszentrum Informationstechnik. Knetsch, Werner. Die industrielle Anwendung der Mikroelektronik in der Bundesrepublik Deutschland, Frankreich, Grossbritannien . Haar bei München , c1985. 142 p. : ISBN 3-89090-121-2 : LC Card 86-106735
HC290.5.A9 K5 1985

Veale, Stuart R.
Bond yield analysis : a guide to predicting bond returns / Stuart R. Veale. New York, N.Y. : New York Institute of Finance, c1986. p. cm. Includes index. ISBN 0-13-079674-3 : LC Card 87-11305 DDC 332.63/23 19
1. Bonds - United States. I. Title.
HG4963 .V43 1986

Stocks, bonds, options, futures . New York, N.Y. [Englewood Cliffs, N.J.] , c1987. 332 p. : ISBN 0-13-846718-8 : LC Card 87-11324 DDC 332.6/78 19
HG4921 .S7945 1987

Tapping the small-business market / Stuart R. Veale. New York, NY : New York Institute of Finance, c1987. xiii, 198 p. ; 29 cm. Includes index. ISBN 0-13-884420-8 : LC Card 87-7732 DDC 332.6/068/8 19
1. Small business - Finance. 2. Brokers. I. Title. II. Title: Small-business market.
HG4027.7 .V4 1987

Vecchio, Robert P. Organizational behavior / Robert P. Vecchio. Chicago : Dryden Press, [1987], c1988. xv, 576 p. : ill. ; 24 cm. (Dryden Press series in management) Includes bibliographies and indexes. ISBN 0-03-000853-0 LC Card 86-29262 DDC 658.3 19
1. Organizational behavior. I. Title. II. Series.
HD58.7 .V43 1988

Veciana i Borrás, Joan. Calleja Xifré, Carlos. El Baix Camp . Barcelona [1986] xv, 367 p. : ISBN 84-505-3567-9 LC Card 86-205881
HC388.R482 C35 1986

Vedel, Gitte. Om kvindearbejdets igangværende udvikling og perspektiver, i relation til den teknologiske udvikling / af Gitte Vedel. Roskilde : Roskilde universitetscenter, Institut for geografi, samfundsanalyse og datalogi, 1982. 103 leaves : ill. ; 30 cm. (Publikationer fra Institut for geografi, samfundsanalyse og datalogi, Roskilde universitetscenter. Arbejdspapir, 0106-5920 . nr. 25) Cover title. Bibliography: leaves 99-102. LC Card 83-172895
1. Sexual division of labor - Denmark. 2. Women - Employment - Denmark. 3. Labor supply - Denmark -

Effect of automation on. I. Title. II. Series.
HD6060.65.D4 V42 1982

Vedie, Henri-Louis, 1943- L'Etat-pieuvre / Henri-Louis Vedie ; préface de Jean Méo. Paris : Albatros, c1986. 172 p. : ill. ; 24 cm. Includes bibliographical references. LC Card 86-219134
1. Industry and state - France. 2. Privatization - France. 3. France - Economic conditions - 1945-. I. Title.
HD4165 .V38 1986

Veera Raghavan, J. Education and the new international order /. New Delhi , 1983, c1982. xx, 147 p. ; LC Card 83-902560 DDC 370/.11/5 19
HF1411 .E28 1983 ***NYPL [JLD 86-3707]***

Vega Alvear, Miguel. Abusada-Salah, Roberto. La crisis del empresariado nacional /. [Lima] [1983] 41 p. ; LC Card 84-236119
HC227 .A57 1983

Vega, Carlos, Lic. Picado Hidalgo, Roberto. La inflación y la política económica, el caso de Costa Rica . [San José] , 1985. 16, 20 p. ; LC Card 86-219388
HC143 .P52 1985

Vega F., Humberto (Vega Fernández) Política económica y movimiento laboral : balance del año 1985 y perspectivas para los años 1986 y 1987 / Humberto Vega F. Santiago, Chile : Programa de Economía del Trabajo, Academia de Humanismo Cristiano, 1986. 52 p. : ill. ; 22 cm. "Trabajo preparado especialmente para el Seminario 'El Movimiento Laboral y el Retorno a la Democracia,' organizado por el PET el 24 de mayo de 1986." "Equipo política económica"--Cover. LC Card 87-101128
1. Chile - Economic conditions - 1970-. 2. Chile - Economic policy. 3. Labor supply - Chile. 4. Economic forecasting - Chile. I. Programa de Economía del Trabajo (Academia de Humanismo Cristiano). II. Title.
HC192 .V355 1986

Vega Tapia, Héctor. L'économie du populisme et le projet de passage au socialisme proposé par l'Unité populaire au Chili / par Héctor Vega Tapia. [Brussels] : Institut de sociologie, U.L.B., Centre d'étude de l'Amérique latine : Centre d'étude et de promotion des relations entre les pays de la CEE et de l'Amérique latine, 1984. 511 p. ; 24 cm. Title on spine: L'économie du populisme. At head of title: Institut de sociologie ... de l'Université libre de Bruxelles. Bibliography: p. 499-511. LC Card 85-146534 DDC 338.983 19
1. Populism - Chile. 2. Socialism - Chile. 3. Chile - Economic policy. 4. Chile - Politics and government - 1920-1970. 5. Chile - Politics and government - 1970-. I. Brussels. Université libre. Institut de sociologie. II. Title. III. Title: Economie du populisme.
HC192 .V37 1984 ***NYPL [JLE 86-3663]***

Veger, L. L. (Leonid Leonidovich) Rol′ nauchno-tekhnicheskogo progressa v intensifikatsii obshchestvennogo proizvodstva /. Moskva , 1986. 177 p. : LC Card 87-163537
HC340.T4 R65 1986

VEGESACK (BREMEN, GERMANY)
Oltmann, Joachim. Kalter Krieg und kommunale Integration . Marburg , c1987. 500 p. ; ISBN 3-921630-71-1 LC Card 87-142718 DDC 331.88/0943/52 19
HD6699.B7 O48 1987

VEGETABLE OILS AS FUEL.
Seminário de Energia de Biomassa (1985? : Belo Horizonte, Brazil?) Seminário de Energia de Biomassa . [Belo Horizonte?] , <[1986?-. v. <[1-2] > : LC Card 87-107998
HD9502.5.B543 B67 1985

VEGETABLE OILS AS FUELS.
Substituição de óleo diesel . [Brasília, Brazil] [19]84. 84 p. : LC Card 87-404960 DDC 338.4/76553 19
HD9579.D53 B737 1984

VEGETABLE TRADE - FLORIDA.
Florida and Mexico competition for the winter fresh vegetable market /. Washington, D.C. [1986] v, 101 p. : LC Card 86-602381 DDC 338.1 s 381/.415/0973 19
HD1751 .A91854 no. 556 HD9225.U53F5

VEGETABLE TRADE - HUNGARY.
Forgács, Katalin. A zöldség-gyümölcs szindróma . Budapest , 1986. 134, [1] p. ; ISBN 963-221-901-5 : LC Card 87-148760
HD9220.H82 F67 1986

Kartali, János. A friss és feldolgozott zöldségek, gyümölcsök bel- és külkereskedelmi forgalmazásának aktuális problémái /. Budapest , 1985. 108 p. ; ISBN 963-491-203-6 LC Card 86-195487
HD9220.H82 K37 1985

VEGETABLE TRADE - MEXICO.
Florida and Mexico competition for the winter fresh vegetable market /. Washington, D.C. [1986] v, 101 p. : LC Card 86-602381 DDC 338.1 s 381/.415/0973 19
HD1751 .A91854 no. 556 HD9225.U53F5

VEGETABLE TRADE - MEXICO - SINALOA (STATE)
Mares, David R. Penetrating the international market . New York , 1987. xvi, 294 p. : ISBN 0-231-06346-6 (alk. paper) LC Card 87-6358 DDC 382/.415/097232 19
HD9014.M62 M38 1987

VEGETABLE TRADE - UNITED STATES.
Florida and Mexico competition for the winter fresh vegetable market /. Washington, D.C. [1986] v, 101 p. : LC Card 86-602381 DDC 338.1 s 381/.415/0973 19
HD1751 .A91854 no. 556 HD9225.U53F5

VEGETABLES - ARGENTINA - LA RIOJA (PROVINCE) - PRESERVATION.
Análisis de la problemática actual y perspectivas futuras de las industrias vinícola y conservera hortofrutícola en La Rioja. [La Rioja, Argentina] , 1981. 97 p., [3] p. of plates : ISBN 84-7359-144-5 LC Card 86-146432
HD9384.A8 L323 1981

VEGETABLES - PRICES - BRAZIL - SÃO PAULO (STATE) - STATISTICS - HISTORY - 20TH CENTURY.
Camargo, Ana Maria M. Pires de. Comportamento dos preços de olerícolas nos mercados atacadistas e fluxo de produção regional no Brasil, 1977-83 /. São Paulo , 1986. 79 p. : LC Card 87-403840 DDC 338.1/35/0981/61021 19
HD9220.B73 S263 1986

VEGETABLES - TRADE AND STATISTICS. see **VEGETABLE TRADE.**

Vegyipari Egyetem, Veszprém, Hungary. see **Veszprémi Vegyipari Egyetem.**

Vehicle highway infrastructure : safety compatability. Warrendale, PA : Society of Automotive Engineers, c1987. 208 p. : ill. ; 28 cm. "P-194." Papers of an international symposium held Detroit, Mich., Feb. 23-27, 1987; sponsored by Passenger Protection Committee of SAE. Includes bibliographies. ISBN 0-89883-455-4 (pbk.) LC Card 86-63707 DDC 363.1/25 19
1. Traffic safety - Congresses. I. SAE Automobile Body Activity (Organization). Passenger Protection Committee.
HE5606 .V44 1987

Vehicle Routing- und Scheduling-Probleme unter besonderer Berücksichtigung von Dial-a-Ride-Problemen /. Weber, Rolf. München , c1985. iii, 158 p. : ISBN 3-88259-349-0 LC Card 86-123392
HE305 .W4 1985

VEHICLES - ACCIDENTS. see **TRAFFIC ACCIDENTS.**

VEHICLES - COMMUNICATION SYSTEMS. see **MOBILE COMMUNICATION SYSTEMS.**

VEHICULAR COMMUNICATION SYSTEMS. see **MOBILE COMMUNICATION SYSTEMS.**

VEILLON, CHARLES, 1900-1971.
Jéquier, François. Charles Veillon . Zürich , 1985. 142 p. : LC Card 85-139330 DDC 338.092/4 B 19
HC395.5.V45 J45 1985

Veinte temas, una posición /. Ramos Allup, Henry. Caracas, Venezuela [19]85. 153 p. ; ISBN 980-263-018-7 LC Card 87-401543 DDC 330.987/0633 19
HC237 .R315 1985

Veit, Klaus-Rüdiger. Die Konkursrechnungslegung : dargestellt am Modell der Aktiengesellschaft / von Klaus-Rüdiger Veit. Köln : C. Heymann, c1982. xiv, 221 p. ; 24 cm. The author's Habilitationsschrift--Universität Göttingen, 1980. Includes index. Bibliography: p. 211-218. ISBN 3-452-19273-3 LC Card 83-130656 DDC 346.43/078 344.30678 19
1. Bankruptcy - Germany, West. 2. Corporations - Accounting - Law and legislation - Germany (West). I. Title.
KK4290 .V44 1982 ***NYPL [JLE 87-1129]***

Vekić, Đuro. Samoupravljanje od ideje do stvarnosti / Đuro Vekić. Sarajevo : Veselin Masleša, [1983?] 263 p. ; 21 cm. In Serbo-Croatian (roman) Bibliography: p. 261-263. LC Card 86-115347
1. Management - Yugoslavia - Employee participation - History. 2. Yugoslavia - Economic policy - 1945-. 3. Yugoslavia - Politics and government - 1945-. I. Title.
HD5660.Y8 V44 1983

Vela, Gil. Deuda externa latinoamericana / Gil Vela, Marcelo Antonio Gottifredi. Ecuador : [s.n], 1984. 180 p. ; 22 cm. LC Card 85-180466 DDC 336.3/435/098 19
1. Debts, External - Latin America. 2. Latin America - Economic conditions - 1945-. 3. Latin America - Social conditions - 1945-. I. Gottifredi, Marcelo Antonio. II. Title.
HJ8514.5 .V45 1984 ***NYPL [JLD 86-308]***

Velarde Fuertes, Juan. El libertino y el nacimiento del capitalismo / Juan Velarde Fuertes. Madrid : Pirámide, c1981. 158 p. ; 21 cm. (Escuela de Salamanca) Includes bibliographical references. ISBN 84-368-0178-4 LC Card 82-101990
1. Capitalism. 2. Libertinism. I. Title.
HB501 .V39 1981

Velarde, Juan. see **Velarde Fuertes, Juan.**

Velasco, Andrés. Díaz Alejandro, Carlos Federico. Trade, development and the world economy . Oxford, OX, UK , New York, NY, USA , 1988. p. cm. ISBN 0-631-15687-9 : LC Card 87-20836 DDC 337.8 19
HF1480.5 .D52 1988

Velasco Avila, Cuauhtémoc. Flores Clair, Eduardo. Estadísticas mineras de México en el siglo XIX /. México, D.F. , 1985. 181 p. ; LC Card 87-401718 DDC 338.2/0972 19
HD9506.M62 F57 1985

Velasco, Carlos. Fidel Velázquez / Carlos Velasco. 1a ed. [Mexico City, Mexico] : Plaza & Janés, 1986. 150 p. : ill., ports. ; 17 cm. ISBN 968-85606-1-8 LC Card 87-403697 DDC 331.88/0972 19
1. Confederación de Trabajadores de Mexico - History. 2. Velásquez, Fidel, 1900-. I. Title.
HD8112.C563 V45 1986

VELÁSQUEZ, FIDEL, 1900-
Velasco, Carlos. Fidel Velázquez /. [Mexico City, Mexico] , 1986. 150 p. : ISBN 968-85606-1-8 LC Card 87-403697 DDC 331.88/0972 19
HD8112.C563 V45 1986

Velasquez, Manuel G. Business ethics : concepts and cases / Manuel G. Velasquez.2nd ed. Englewood Cliffs, N.J. : Prentice Hall, c1988. xii, 420 p. : ill. ; 23 cm. Includes bibliographical references and index. ISBN 0-13-096017-9 (pbk.) : LC Card 87-20453 DDC 174 19
1. Business ethics. 2. Business ethics - Case studies. I. Title.
HF5387 .V44 1988

Velásquez P., Mario. Larraín P., Christian. Subsidiariedad o intervencionismo? . [Santiago, Chile] [1986] 137 p. ; LC Card 87-401544 DDC 338.983 19
HC192 .L36 1986

Velázquez, María del Carmen. Notas sobre sirvientes de las Californias y proyecto de obraje en Nuevo México / María del Carmen Velázquez. 1a ed. México, D.F. : Centro de Estudios Históricos, Colegio de México, [1985], c1984. 246 p. ; 17 cm. (Jornadas. 105) Date on t.p. verso: 1984. Includes bibliographical references and index. ISBN 968-12-0298-8 LC Card 85-243085
1. Artisans - California - History - 18th century. 2. Artisans - Mexico - Baja California Sur - History - 18th century. 3. Artisans - Mexico - Baja California Norte - History - 18th century. 4. New Spain - Manufactures - History - 18th century. 5. Labor and laboring classes - New Spain - History - 18th century. I. Title. II. Series.
HD2346.U52 C294 1985

Vélemények az életszínvonalról /. Salamin, Pálné. Budapest , 1986. 88 p. : LC Card 86-218875
HD7027.5 .S25 1986

Vélez, Roberto. Reseña histórica del 1o de mayo en Mendoza : origen del 1o de mayo como Día Internacional de los Trabajadores / Roberto Vélez. Buenos Aires : Editorial Fundamentos, 1983. 125 p. : ill. ; 20 cm. LC Card 87-400123 DDC 394.2/683 19
1. May Day (Labor Holiday) - Argentina - Mendoza (Province) - History - 20th century. 2. Labor and laboring classes - Argentina - Mendoza (Province) - History - 20th century. I. Title. II. Title: Reseña histórica del primero de mayo en Mendoza.
HD7791 .V4 1983

Velferdsstat i motvind /. Grund, Jan. Oslo , 1986, c1985. 139 p. : ISBN 82-00-07590-7 : LC Card 86-132818
HC365 .G78 1985 ***NYPL [JLD 86-4433]***

Velichkov, Ivan. Partiĭno rŭkovodstvo na ikonomikata / Ivan Velichkov. Sofiia : Sofiĭski gradski kom-t na BKP : TSentŭr po partiĭno-organizatsionna rabota, 1985. 40 p. ; 21 cm. "V pomosht na partiĭniia aktiv"--Cover. Includes bibliographical references. LC Card 86-173901
1. Bulgaria - Economic policy - 1944-. I. Title.
HC403 .V45 1985

Velikokhat'ko, A. T. Territorial'naia organizatsiia prodovol'stvennogo kompleksa . Kiev , 1985. 163 p. ; LC Card 86-175134
HD9015.S653 U4755 1985

Vella, Carolyn M. Competitive intelligence in the computer age / Carolyn M. Vella and John J. McGonagle, Jr. New York : Quorum Books, 1987. xv, 189 p. ; 22 cm. Bibliography: p. [182]-184. Includes index. ISBN 0-89930-169-X (lib. bdg. : alk. paper) LC Card 86-25565 DDC 651.8 19
1. Information storage and retrieval systems - Business. 2. Business - Information services - Data processing. 3. Competition. I. McGonagle, John J. II. Title.
HF5548.2 .V38 1987

Vellinga, Menno. Industrialization and regional development in Colombia / M. Vellinga and D. Kruijt. Amsterdam, The Netherlands : Centre for Latin American Research and Documentation, 1983. 183 p. : maps ; 24 cm. (CEDLA incidentele publicaties . 26) Bibliography: p. 175-183. ISBN 90-70280-80-9 LC Card 83-209247 DDC 338.09861/26 19
1. Cauca River Region (Colombia) - Industries. 2. Antioquia, Colombia (Dept.) - Industries. 3. Industry and state - Colombia - Cauca River Region. 4. Industry and state - Colombia - Antioquia (Dept.). 5. Regional planning - Colombia - Cauca River Region. 6. Regional planning - Colombia - Antioquia (Dept.). I. Kruijt, Dirk. II. Title. III. Series.
HC198.C296 V45 1983

Velo, Dario.
L'Industria siderurgica . Milano [1986] 193 p. : ISBN 88-14-00787-X : LC Card 86-222572
HD9510.5 .I473 1986

Strategie industriali e prospettive di sviluppo nel settore automobilistico /. Milano [1985] 235 p. : ISBN 88-14-00541-9 (pbk.) : LC Card 85-183335 DDC 338.4/76292/0945 19
HD9710.A2 S86 1985 ***NYPL [JLE 87-493]***

The velvet ghetto : the impact of the increasing percentage of women in public relations and business communication / by Carolyn Garrett Cline ... [et al.]. San Francisco : IABC Foundation, 1986. 147 leaves in various foliations : ill. ; 28 cm. Includes bibliography. LC Card 86-161157 DDC 331.4/816592/0973 19
1. Women executives - United States. 2. Women executives - Salaries, etc. - United States. 3. Public relations - United States - Evaluation. 4. Communication in management - United States - Evaluation. 5. Occupational prestige - United States. 6. Sex role in the work environment - United States. I. Cline, Carolyn Garrett, 1947-.
HD6054.2.U6 V45 1986

Velzen, Leo van. Kox, Henk. Kapitaal-export vanuit Nederland . Amsterdam , 1985. 136 p. : ISBN 90-71284-01-8 LC Card 85-237950
HG5562 .K69 1985

Vem gör vad i svenskt näringsliv : de 6000 viktigaste beslutsfattarna. Stockholm : Svenska dagbladet/Förlagsgruppen, [1983] 283 p. ; 22 cm. Cover title. LC Card 83-225142
1. Sweden - Commerce - Directories. 2. Sweden - Industries - Directories. 3. Business - Sweden - Directories. I. Svenska dagbladet/Förlagsgruppen.
HF3673 .V46 1983

Vendemini, Serge. Urban, Sabine M.-L. Entreprises allemandes et coopération industrielle à l'échelle européenne . Paris , c1986. 162 p. : ISBN 2-11-001580-2 : LC Card 86-175800
HD2844 .U7 1986

VENDING MACHINES - UNITED STATES.
Attitudes toward vended coffee /. [Chicago? , 1983] 1 v. (various pagings) : LC Card 86-235525 DDC 381/.4566393 19
HD9199.U48 A88 1983

VENDORS AND PURCHASERS - GREAT BRITAIN.
Dart, Joseph Henry, 1817-1887. A compendium of the law and practice of vendors and purchasers of real estate [microform]. New York, Albany, 1851. civ, 665 (i.e. 856) p. LC Card 17-19132 ***NYPL [*ZT-1719]***

VENDORS AND PURCHASERS - UNITED STATES.
Arnold, Alvin L. Real estate investor's deskbook /. Boston , c1982. 1 v. (various pagings) : ISBN 0-88262-732-5 LC Card 82-70717 DDC 346.7304/3 347.30643 19
KF665 .A8 1982 ***NYPL [JLF 86-907]***

VENDUES. see **AUCTIONS.**

Venedikian, Harry M. Export-import financing / Harry M. Venedikian and Gerald Warfield. 2nd ed. New York : Wiley, c1986. xvii, 456 p. : forms ; 24 cm. (Wiley professional banking and finance series, 0733-8945) Rev. ed. of: Export-import financing / Gerhard W. Schneider. 1974. "Wiley-Interscience publication." ISBN 0-471-82449-6 : LC Card 85-29566 DDC 332.7/42 19
1. Export credit - United States. 2. Negotiable instruments - United States. 3. Foreign trade promotion - United States. I. Warfield, Gerald. II. Schneider, Gerhard W. Export-import financing. III. Title. IV. Series.
HG3754.U5 V46 1986 ***NYPL [JLE 86-2998]***

Venerable, Grant, 1942- The paradox of the silicon savior : charting the reformation of the high-tech super-state / Grant Venerable. San Francisco : MVM Productions, c1987. xxx, 190 p. ; 21 cm. Bibliography: p. 161-165. Includes index. ISBN 0-943425-00-X (pbk.) : LC Card 87-17232 DDC 303.4/83 19
1. High technology industries - Social aspects. 2. Technology and civilization. I. Title.
HC79.H53 V45 1987

Vénézuela. Marchand, Bernard. Paris, 1971. ix, 218 p. LC Card 74-856272
HD9574.V42 M276 ***NYPL [JLE 71-452]***

VENEZUELA - APPROPRIATIONS AND EXPENDITURES - HISTORY - 20TH CENTURY.
Kornblith, Miriam. Estado y gasto público en Venezuela, 1936-1980 /. Caracas , 1985. 287, [10] p. : LC Card 86-172043
HJ2093 .K67 1985

VENEZUELA - BOUNDARIES - COLOMBIA.
Foro de Proyectos de Inversión Colombo-Venezolanos (1986 : Cúcuta, Colombia) La frontera colombo-venezolana, una región donde invertir /. Bogotá, D.E. [1986] 96 p. ; LC Card 87-403851 DDC 332.6/09861 19
HG5352 .F67 1986

VENEZUELA - CENSUS, 1981.
Nomenclador de centros poblados. [Caracas] [1986-1987] 7 v. : LC Card 87-119549
HA1091.5 1981a

Venezuela. Comisión del Plan Nacional de Aprovechamiento de los Recursos Hidráulicos. Buroz Castillo, Eduardo. Programa de cooperación técnica Perú-Venezuela-OEA . Caracas , 1976. [11], 62 p. ; LC Card 84-136478
HD1696.P5 B87 1976

VENEZUELA - COMMERCIAL POLICY.
Rangel Belis, Gonzalo. Sector económico externo, industrialización y conflictos laborales en Venezuela /. Valencia , 1985. 141 p. : ISBN 980-212-007-3 LC Card 86-226708
HF1529 .R36 1985

VENEZUELA - DEPENDENCY ON FOREIGN COUNTRIES - HISTORY - 20TH CENTURY.
González G., Godofredo (González González) La revolución de Los Barrosos /. Caracas, Venezuela [19]87. xii, 276 p. ; ISBN 980-263-047-0 LC Card 87-400058 DDC 338.2/7282/0987 19
HD9574.V42 G59 1987

Venezuela. Despacho de la Ministro de Estado para la Participación de la Mujer en el Desarrollo. Estadísticas sociales . Caracas, Venezuela , 1983. 2 v. ; LC Card 84-183391 DDC 312/.0987 19
HA1095 .E88 1983 ***NYPL [JLM 85-550]***

Venezuela. Dirección de Investigaciones Económicas. Venezuela, periodic economic report . Caracas, Venezuela [1987] [166] p. : LC Card 87-403325 DDC 330.987/0633 19
HC237 .V487 1987

Venezuela. Dirección General de Finanzas Públicas. Dirección de Investigaciones Económicas. see **Venezuela. Dirección de Investigaciones Económicas.**

Venezuela. Dirección General de Planificación y Ordenación del Ambiente. Esquema de ordenamiento territorial de la faja petrolífera del Orinoco . Caracas , 1982. 46 p. : LC Card 86-162734
HC238.O75 E87 1982

Venezuela. Direccion General del Presupuesto. (Old Catalog form: Venezuela. Presupuesto, Dirección general del)
Estadística fiscal, años 1944-45 a 1953-54 /. Caracas , 1955. 125 p. : LC Card 85-128776
HJ990 .E86 1955

VENEZUELA - ECONOMIC CONDITIONS.
Estaba, Rosa M. Geografía de los paisajes urbanos e industriales de Venezuela /. Caracas , c1985. 291 p., [4] folded leaves : ISBN 980-271-006-7 LC Card 86-148810 DDC 307.7/6/0987 19
HC237 .E766 1985 ***NYPL [JLD 86-2340]***

VENEZUELA - ECONOMIC CONDITIONS - 1918-1958.
Aranda, Sergio. La economía venezolana . Caracas, Venezuela , c1984. 328 p. ; LC Card 87-400622 DDC 330.987/0633 19
HC237 .A68 1984

VENEZUELA - ECONOMIC CONDITIONS - 1958-
Aranda, Sergio. La economía venezolana . Caracas, Venezuela , c1984. 328 p. ; LC Card 87-400622 DDC 330.987/0633 19
HC237 .A68 1984

Celis, Adán. 5 momentos, 5 planteamientos . Puerto la Cruz [Venezuela] , 1985. 99 p. ; LC Card 87-401953 DDC 338.987 19
HC237 .C445 1985

Márquez, Pompeyo. El festín de los gemelos . [Caracas , 1983] ([Caracas] : Industrias Sorocaima) 134 p. ; LC Card 84-195527
HC237 .M338 1983

Ojeda, Roseliano. Cómo se desangra un país-- ! . Valencia [Venezuela] , c1987. 241 p. ; ISBN 980-212-037-5 LC Card 87-169695 DDC 330.987/0633 19
HC237 .O365 1987

Ramos Allup, Henry. Veinte temas, una posición /. Caracas, Venezuela [19]85. 153 p. ; ISBN 980-263-018-7 LC Card 87-401543 DDC 330.987/0633 19
HC237 .R315 1985

Rangel Belis, Gonzalo. Sector económico externo, industrialización y conflictos laborales en Venezuela /. Valencia , 1985. 141 p. : ISBN 980-212-007-3 LC Card 86-226708
HF1529 .R36 1985

Sánchez Meleán, Jorge. Reflexiones para la acción /. [Venezuela?] , 1986. xv, 322 p. : ISBN 980-232-049-8 LC Card 87-134702 DDC 338.987 19
HC237 .S275 1986

Venezuela, periodic economic report . Caracas, Venezuela [1987] [166] p. : LC Card 87-403325 DDC 330.987/0633 19
HC237 .V487 1987

VENEZUELA - ECONOMIC POLICY.
Larrazábal, Radamés. Los planes del capitalismo para la década de los 80 /. [Caracas, Venezuela? , 1982] (Caracas, Venezuela : Cooperative Mixta de Trabajadores Gráficos) 81 p. ; LC Card 83-201901
HC237 .L325 1982

López-Orihuela, Alcides, 1926- El pacto y la democracia sociales /. Caracas, Venezuela [1986] (Caracas : Editorial Greco) xvi, 129 p. ; ISBN 90-826548-5-X LC Card 87-402941 DDC 338.987 19
HC237 .L667 1986

Márquez, Pompeyo. El festín de los gemelos . [Caracas , 1983] ([Caracas] : Industrias Sorocaima) 134 p. ; LC Card 84-195527
HC237 .M338 1983

Randall, Laura. The political economy of Venezuelan oil /. New York , 1987. xiii, 247 p. ; ISBN 0-275-92823-3 (alk. paper) : LC Card 87-15848 DDC 338.2/7282/0987 19
HD9574.V42 R35 1987

Rodríguez, Gumersindo, 1933- Era posible la gran Venezuela? /. Caracas , 1986. 215 p. : ISBN 980-255-004-3 LC Card 87-118414 DDC 338.987 19
HC237 .R617 1986

Universidad de los Andes (Mérida, Venezuela). Instituto de Investigaciones Económicas. Plan de desarrollo regional /. Mérida , 1973- v. <1-5 > : LC Card 86-202604
HC238.A683 U55 1973

VENEZUELA - ECONOMIC POLICY - CONGRESSES.
Crisis y control de cambio /. Maracaibo, Venezuela , 1984. 101 p. ; LC Card 87-400572 DDC 332.4/560987 19
HG3941 .C74 1984

VENEZUELA - FOREIGN ECONOMIC RELATIONS.
Rangel Belis, Gonzalo. Sector económico externo, industrialización y conflictos laborales en Venezuela /. Valencia , 1985. 141 p. : ISBN 980-212-007-3 LC Card 86-226708
HF1529 .R36 1985

VENEZUELA - FOREIGN ECONOMIC RELATIONS - GREAT BRITAIN.
Vetencourt Guerra, Lola. El Imperio Británico en la economía de Venezuela, 1830-1870 /. Caracas , 1981. 233 p. : LC Card 83-201772
HF1530.5.G7 V47 1981

VENEZUELA - FOREIGN ECONOMIC RELATIONS - UNITED STATES.
Carreras, Charles. United States economic penetration of Venezuela and its effects on diplomacy, 1895-1906 /. New York , 1987. 252 p. : ISBN 0-8240-8077-7 (alk. paper) : LC Card 87-23723 DDC 332.6/7373/087 19
HG5412 .C45 1987

Venezuela - Government. see **Venezuela - Politics and government.**

Venezuela. Investigaciones Económicas, Dirección de. see **Venezuela. Dirección de Investigaciones Económicas.**

VENEZUELA - LEARNED INSTITUTIONS AND SOCIETIES.
Losada Aldana, Ramón. Investigación universitaria contra subdesarrollo /. Caracas , 1984. 288 p. ; LC Card 87-115963 DDC 338.987/0072 19
HD77.5.V4 L67 1984

Venezuela. Ministerio de Hacienda. Direccion General del Presupuesto. see **Venezuela. Direccion General del Presupuesto.**

Venezuela, periodic economic report : recent data and projections, dated January 31, 1987. Caracas, Venezuela : Director de Investigaciones Economicas, Dirección General de Finanzas Públicas, Ministerio de Hacienda, [1987] [166] p. : ill. ; 28 cm. Cover title. LC Card 87-403325 DDC 330.987/0633 19
1. Venezuela - Economic conditions - 1958-. 2. Economic forecasting - Venezuela. 3. Finance - Law and legislation - Venezuela. I. Venezuela. Dirección de Investigaciones Económicas.
HC237 .V487 1987

VENEZUELA - POLITICS AND GOVERNMENT - 1935-1958.
Kornblith, Miriam. Estado y gasto público en Venezuela, 1936-1980 /. Caracas , 1985. 287, [10] p. : LC Card 86-172043
HJ2093 .K67 1985

VENEZUELA - POLITICS AND GOVERNMENT - 1958-
Kornblith, Miriam. Estado y gasto público en Venezuela, 1936-1980 /. Caracas , 1985. 287, [10] p. : LC Card 86-172043
HJ2093 .K67 1985

López-Orihuela, Alcides, 1926- El pacto y la democracia sociales /. Caracas, Venezuela [1986] (Caracas : Editorial Greco) xvi, 129 p. ; ISBN 90-826548-5-X LC Card 87-402941 DDC 338.987 19
HC237 .L667 1986

Ramos Allup, Henry. Veinte temas, una posición /. Caracas, Venezuela [19]85. 153 p. ; ISBN 980-263-018-7 LC Card 87-401543 DDC 330.987/0633 19
HC237 .R315 1985

VENEZUELA - POPULATION - STATISTICS.
Estadísticas sociales . Caracas, Venezuela , 1983. 2 v. ; LC Card 84-183391 DDC 312/.0987 19
HA1095 .E88 1983 ***NYPL [JLM 85-550]***

Estimaciones y proyecciones de población, 1950-2025 /. [Caracas] , 1985-[1987] 2 v. : ISBN 980-280-006-6 (set) LC Card 87-123959 DDC 304.6/2/0987021 19
HA1095 .E885 1985

VENEZUELA. REAL HACIENDA - HISTORY - SOURCES.
Hacienda colonial venezolana /. Caracas , 1946. 170 p. ; LC Card 85-105445
HJ991 .H323 1946

VENEZUELA - SOCIAL CONDITIONS - 1958-
Celis, Adán. 5 momentos, 5 planteamientos . Puerto la Cruz [Venezuela] , 1985. 99 p. ; LC Card 87-401953 DDC 338.987 19
HC237 .C445 1985

VENEZUELA - SOCIAL POLICY.
López-Orihuela, Alcides, 1926- El pacto y la democracia sociales /. Caracas, Venezuela [1986] (Caracas : Editorial Greco) xvi, 129 p. ; ISBN 90-826548-5-X LC Card 87-402941 DDC 338.987 19
HC237 .L667 1986

VENEZUELA - STATISTICS, VITAL.
Flórez Nieto, Carmen Elisa. The existence of a Latin American mortality pattern . Bogotá, Colombia , 1985. 153 p. : LC Card 87-145922
HB1397 .F56 1985

Venge, Mikael. Arbejdere og socialdemokrater i Faaborg omkring 1900 / af Mikael Venge. [Fåborg] : Faaborg kulturhistoriske museer, Faaborg byhistoriske arkiv, 1986. 72 p. : ill. ; 21 cm. Bibliography: p. 72. ISBN 87-88421-01-5 LC Card 87-144687
1. Trade-unions - Denmark - Fåborg (Fyns amt) - History - 19th century. 2. Socialism - Denmark - Fåborg (Fyns amt) - History - 19th century. 3. Labor and laboring classes - Denmark - Fåborg (Fyns amt) - History - 19th century. I. Title.
HD6745.F33 V46 1986

Vengerskaia sotsialisticheskaia rabochaia partiia. see **Magyar Szocialista Munkáspárt.**

VENICE - ECONOMIC CONDITIONS.
Lane Frederic Chapin, 1900- Money and banking in medieval and Renaissance Venice /. Baltimore , c1985- v. : ISBN 0-8018-3157-1 (v. 1) LC Card 84-47947 DDC 332.1/0945/31 19
HG1040.V46 L36 1985 ***NYPL [JLL 86-121]***

VENICE - HISTORY - TURKISH WARS, 17TH CENTURY.
Dokos, Kōnstantinos. Hē Sterea Hellas kata ton Henetotourkikon polemon, 1684-1699 kai ho Salōnōn Philotheos /. Athēnai , 1985. 255 p. ; LC Card 86-211599
HB2092.5.A3 D64 1985

VENICE (ITALY) - COMMERCE.
Lane Frederic Chapin, 1900- Studies in Venetian social and economic history /. London , 1987. 346 p. in various pagings : ISBN 0-86078-202-6 LC Card 87-160893 DDC 945/.31 19
HC308.V4 L36 1987

VENICE (ITALY) - ECONOMIC CONDITIONS.
Lane Frederic Chapin, 1900- Studies in Venetian social and economic history /. London , 1987. 346 p. in various pagings : ISBN 0-86078-202-6 LC Card 87-160893 DDC 945/.31 19
HC308.V4 L36 1987

VENICE (ITALY) - SOCIAL CONDITIONS.
Lane Frederic Chapin, 1900- Studies in Venetian social and economic history /. London , 1987. 346 p. in various pagings : ISBN 0-86078-202-6 LC Card 87-160893 DDC 945/.31 19
HC308.V4 L36 1987

Venkaiah, V., 1952- Impact of agro-based industries on rural economy : a case study / V. Venkaiah.1st ed. Bombay : Himalaya Pub. House, 1987. xxi, 348 p. ; 23 cm. Study of four selected villages in Andhra Pradesh, India, 1967-1978. Bibliography: p. [338]-348. LC Card 86-903766 DDC 338.1/0954/84 19
1. Agricultural industries - India - Andhra Pradesh - Case studies. 2. Agricultural industries - India - Case studies. 3. Rural development - India - Andhra Pradesh - Case studies. 4. Rural development - India - Case studies. 5. Agriculture - Economic aspects - India - Andhra Pradesh - Case studies. 6. Agriculture - Economic aspects - India - Case studies. I. Title.
HD9016.I43 A67 1987

Venkatesan, M., 1936- Creativity in services marketing . Chicago, IL , 1986. 175 p. : ISBN 0-87757-179-1 (pbk.) LC Card 85-26785 DDC 658.8 19
HD9980.5 .C74 1986 ***NYPL [JLF 86-1783]***

Venkatesh, Alladi. The significance of the women's movement to marketing : a life style analysis / Alladi Venkatesh. New York : Praeger, 1985. 209 p. ; 24 cm. (Landmark dissertations in women's studies series) Bibliography: p. 185-209. ISBN 0-03-069588-0 (alk. paper) : LC Card 85-19106 DDC 658.8/348 19
1. Women consumers - New York (State) - Syracuse. 2. Market surveys - New York (State) - Syracuse. 3. Feminism - United States. 4. Stereotype (Psychology). I. Title.
HF5415.3 .V46 1985 ***NYPL [JLE 86-1081]***

Venkateswara, Rao T. Recent experiences in human resources development /. New Delhi , c1986. xvi, 448 p. ; ISBN 81-204-0120-4 : LC Card 86-902270 DDC 331.11/0954 19
HF5549.5.M3 R38 1985

Venkateswaran, R. J. Decision-making in Indian economy : role of central government / R.J. Venkateswaran.1st ed. Bombay : Himalaya Pub. House, 1986. vii, 199 p. ; 24 cm. Bibliography: p. [195] Includes index. LC Card 86-902861 DDC 338.954 19
1. India - Economic policy. 2. Central planning - India. I. Title.
HC435.2 .V457 1986

Venkatswamy, G. Management of state government enterprises / G. Venkatswamy. New Delhi, India : Archives Publishers, Distributors, 1987. viii, 362 p. : ill. ; 23 cm. Study, with reference to Andhra Pradesh. Bibliography: p. [355]-360. ISBN 81-7051-020-1 : LC Card 87-901167 DDC 354.54/84092 19
1. Government business enterprises - India - Andhra Pradesh - Management. I. Title.
HD4295.A5 V45 1987

Venn, Fiona. Oil diplomacy in the twentieth century / Fiona Venn. Basingstoke, Hampshire : Macmillan, c1986. xii, 228 p. : ill. ; 23 cm. (Making of the 20th century) Includes index. Bibliography: p. [204]-218. ISBN 0-333-35781-7
1. Petroleum industry and trade - Political aspects - History - 20th century. 2. World politics - 20th century. I. Title. ***NYPL [JLD 86-3415]***

Venne, Rosemary Amelia, 1956- Psychological testing in personnel selection / Rosemary Amelia Venne. Kingston, Ont., Canada : Industrial Relations Centre, Queen's University, 1987. 65 p. ; 28 cm. (School of Industrial Relations research essay series . no. 8) Bibliography: p. 62-65. ISBN 0-88886-152-4 (pbk.) LC Card 87-163203 DDC 658.3/1125 19
1. Employment tests. 2. Employee selection. 3. Psychological tests. I. Title. II. Series.
HF5549.5.E5 V46 1987

Una ventana a la vida . Magaña Cañas, Pedro Agustín. [San Salvador] [between 1983 and 1987] 93 p. : LC Card 87-400985 DDC 331.4/8138118/09728423 19
HF3310.S26 M34 1983

La vente des biens de la Grande Chartreuse sous la Révolution /. Arsac, Pierre. Grenoble , 1984. 104 p. : ISBN 2-904661-02-6 LC Card 86-118639
HD643 .A77 1984

Vente, Rolf E. Education and training for industrial development in Singapore and other

ASEAN countries : the role of private corporations, foreign aid, and regional cooperation / Rolf Vente and Chow Kit Boey.1. Aufl. Baden-Baden : Nomos Verlagsgesellschaft ; Singapore : Maruzen Asia, 1984. 175 p. : ill. ; 21 cm. (Studies in Asian educational and social issues . v. 1) Bibliography: p. 171-175. ISBN 3-7890-0941-5 LC Card 84-186381 DDC 331.25/92/0959 19
1. Occupational training - Singapore. 2. Occupational training - Asia, Southeastern. 3. Vocational education - Singapore. 4. Vocational education - Asia, Southeastern. I. Chow, Kit Boey. II. Title. III. Series.
HD5715.5.S55 V46 1984 ***NYPL [JLD 86-2773]***

Vento, Cathy. Blanc, Iris. DDC spreadsheets. [New York, N.Y.] [c1986] 161 p. : LC Card 87-159255 DDC 005.3/07/1273 19
HF5548.2 .B527 1986

Ventolo, William L. Fundamentals of real estate appraisal : instructor's manual / William L. Ventolo, Jr., Martha R. Williams ; James H. Boykin, consulting editor.4th ed. Chicago : Real Estate Education Co., c1987. 75 p. : ill. ; 28 cm. ISBN 0-88462-571-0 (pbk.) LC Card 86-29715 DDC 333.33/2 19
1. Real property - Valuation. I. Williams, Martha R. II. Boykin, James H., 1936-. III. Title.
HD1387 .V45 1987

Vent͡skus, A. Problemy razvitii͡a i sovershenstvovanii͡a material'no-tekhnicheskoĭ bazy torgovli i obshchestvennogo pitanii͡a v dvenadtsatoĭ pi͡atiletke . Vil'ni͡us , 1985. 169 p. ; LC Card 86-102743
HF3629.L5 P76 1985

Venture capital : context, development, and policies. Paris : Organisation for Economic Co-operation and Development ; Washington, D.C. : OECD Publications and Information Centre [distributor], 1986. 65 p. : ill. ; 23 cm. ISBN 92-64-12901-4 (pbk.) : LC Card 87-124464 DDC 332/.0415 19
1. Venture capital. 2. Organisation for Economic Co-operation and Development. I. Organisation for Economic Co-operation and Development.
HG4751 .V46 1986

Venture Capital . Nevermann, Helga. Baden-Baden , 1986. 146 p. ; ISBN 3-7890-1263-7 LC Card 87-121846 DDC 332/.0415/0943 19
HG5492 .N48 1986

VENTURE CAPITAL - BRAZIL.
Criação de empresas de alta tecnologia . São Paulo . 192, [1] p. ; LC Card 87-403991 DDC 338.4/362/000981 19
HC190.H53 C75 1987

VENTURE CAPITAL - CANADA - DIRECTORIES.
Silver, A. David (Aaron David), 1941- Who's who in venture capital /. New York , c1987. ix, 468 p. : ISBN 0-471-85639-8 (pbk.) : LC Card 86-28974 DDC 332.66 19
HG4963 .S56 1987

VENTURE CAPITAL - EUROPE - CASE STUDIES.
Vlitos, Irene. The European potential for a venture capital industry /. Menlo Park, CA (333 Ravenswood Ave., Menlo Park 94025) , c1986. 13 leaves : LC Card 86-220533 DDC 332.6/6 19
HG5428 .V56 1986

VENTURE CAPITAL - GERMANY (WEST)
Albach, Horst. Finanzierung mit Risikokapital /. Stuttgart , c1986. 312 p. ; ISBN 3-7910-5015-X LC Card 87-127700 DDC 332/.0415/0943 19
HG5492 .A797 1986

Nevermann, Helga. Venture Capital . Baden-Baden , 1986. 146 p. ; ISBN 3-7890-1263-7 LC Card 87-121846 DDC 332/.0415/0943 19
HG5492 .N48 1986

VENTURE CAPITAL - GREAT BRITAIN.
Clark, Rodney, 1945- Venture capital in Britain, America, and Japan /. New York , 1987. p. cm. ISBN 0-312-00505-9 : LC Card 86-28001 DDC 332/.0415 19
HG5432 .C58 1987

VENTURE CAPITAL - GREAT BRITAIN - DIRECTORIES.
Silver, A. David (Aaron David), 1941- Who's who in venture capital /. New York , c1987. ix, 468 p. : ISBN 0-471-85639-8 (pbk.) : LC Card 86-28974 DDC 332.66 19
HG4963 .S56 1987

Venture capital handbook /. Gladstone, David. Englewood Cliffs, N.J. , c1988. xv, 350 p. ; ISBN 0-13-941501-7 (pbk.) LC Card 87-61607 DDC 658.1/5224 19
HG4965 .G57 1988

VENTURE CAPITAL - HANDBOOKS, MANUALS, ETC.
Beguelin, Richard H., 1937- The secrets of syndication . Boston , c1985. xi, 287 p. : ISBN 0-316-08783-1 : LC Card 85-5157 DDC 658/.044 19
HG6021 .B4 1985 ***NYPL [JLE 85-2259]***

Venture capital in Britain, America, and Japan /. Clark, Rodney, 1945- New York , 1987. p. cm. ISBN 0-312-00505-9 : LC Card 86-28001 DDC 332/.0415 19
HG5432 .C58 1987

Venture capital investing . Gladstone, David. Englewood Cliffs, N.J. , c1988. xiii, 400 p. ; ISBN 0-13-941428-2 LC Card 87-14414 DDC 332.6/722 19
HG4965 .G575 1988

VENTURE CAPITAL - JAPAN.
Clark, Rodney, 1945- Venture capital in Britain, America, and Japan /. New York , 1987. p. cm. ISBN 0-312-00505-9 : LC Card 86-28001 DDC 332/.0415 19
HG5432 .C58 1987

VENTURE CAPITAL - SWITZERLAND.
Nydegger, Alfred. Investitionen und Innovationen in kleineren Industriebetrieben . Diessenhofen , c1983. viii, 317 p. : ISBN 3-7253-0196-4 LC Card 83-224277 DDC 658.1/592 19
HG4027.7 .N93 1983 ***NYPL [JLD 87-633]***

VENTURE CAPITAL - UNITED STATES.
Clark, Rodney, 1945- Venture capital in Britain, America, and Japan /. New York , 1987. p. cm. ISBN 0-312-00505-9 : LC Card 86-28001 DDC 332/.0415 19
HG5432 .C58 1987

Henderson, James W. Obtaining venture financing . Lexington, Mass. , c1988. xii, 366 p. : ISBN 0-669-10931-2 (alk. paper) LC Card 85-40234 DDC 658.1/5224 19
HG4963 .H44 1988

Nevermann, Helga. Venture Capital . Baden-Baden , 1986. 146 p. ; ISBN 3-7890-1263-7 LC Card 87-121846 DDC 332/.0415/0943 19
HG5492 .N48 1986

VENTURE CAPITAL - UNITED STATES - ADDRESSES, ESSAYS, LECTURES.
Entrepreneurship, intrapreneurship, and venture capital . Lexington, Mass. , 1986. xiv, 144 p. : ISBN 0-669-11867-2 (alk. paper) LC Card 85-45519 DDC 338/.04 19
HB615 .E634 1986 ***NYPL [JLE 86-3000]***

VENTURE CAPITAL - UNITED STATES - DIRECTORIES.
Holtz, Herman. 2001 sources of financing for small business /. New York , c1983. x, 173 p. ; ISBN 0-668-05468-9 LC Card 82-11366 DDC 658.1/522 19
HG4057 .A286 1983 ***NYPL [JLF 84-63]***

Silver, A. David (Aaron David), 1941- Who's who in venture capital /. New York , c1987. ix, 468 p. : ISBN 0-471-85639-8 (pbk.) : LC Card 86-28974 DDC 332.66 19
HG4963 .S56 1987

VENTURE CAPITAL - UNITED STATES - HANDBOOKS, MANUALS, ETC.
Gladstone, David. Venture capital handbook /. Englewood Cliffs, N.J. , c1988. xv, 350 p. ; ISBN 0-13-941501-7 (pbk.) LC Card 87-61607 DDC 658.1/5224 19
HG4965 .G57 1988

Gladstone, David. Venture capital investing . Englewood Cliffs, N.J. , c1988. xiii, 400 p. ; ISBN 0-13-941428-2 LC Card 87-14414 DDC 332.6/722 19
HG4965 .G575 1988

The Venture magazine complete guide to venture capital /. Richardson, Clinton. New York , c1987. xxiv, 261 p. : ISBN 0-452-25918-5 (pbk.) : LC Card 87-5721 DDC 332/.0415 19
HG4751 .R52 1987

Venture (New York, N.Y. : 1979) Richardson, Clinton. The Venture magazine complete guide to venture capital /. New York , c1987. xxiv, 261 p. : ISBN 0-452-25918-5 (pbk.) : LC Card 87-5721 DDC 332/.0415 19
HG4751 .R52 1987

VENTURES, JOINT. see **JOINT VENTURES.**

VENZUELA - CENSUS, 1981.
Situación habitacional en Venezuela . [Caracas] [1986- v. <1 > : ISBN 980-280-043-0 LC Card 87-114711 DDC 363.5/1/0987/021 19
HD7331.A3 S57 1986

Vepa, Ram K. Small industry : the challenge of the eighties / Ram K. Vepa. New Delhi : Vikas ; New York, NY : Distributed by Advent Books, c1983. xiii, 356 p. ; 25 cm. Distributor statement from label on t.p. Includes bibliographical references and index. ISBN 0-7069-2107-0 : LC Card 83-906458 DDC 338.6/42/0954 19
1. Small business - Government policy - India. 2. Small business - Government policy. I. Title.
HD2346.I5 V45 1983 ***NYPL [JLE 87-281]***

Verallgemeinerte Ridge Regression . Trenkler, Dietrich. Frankfurt am Main , c1986. viii, 255 p. ; ISBN 3-445-02406-5 LC Card 87-104568 DDC 330/.01/51 19
HB135 .T74 1986

Die Verantwortung der örtlichen Staatsorgane für die planmässige Entwicklung und die effektive Inanspruchnahme von Leistungen der technischen Infrastruktur / [Autorenkollektiv unter Leitung von Roswitha Dittmann ; Mitarbeit, Käthe Dost, Jochen Fieber, Horst Peschke]. Potsdam-Babelsberg : Akademie für Staats- und Rechtswissenschaft der DDR, Sektion Staatliche Leitung der Volkswirtschaft, 1986. 57 p. ; 21 cm. (Aktuelle Beiträge der Staats- und Rechtswissenschaft, 0568-7551 . Heft 327) Bibliography: p. 55-57. LC Card 87-407347 DDC 363/.09431 19
1. Infrastructure (Economics) - Germany (East). 2. Local government - Germany, East. 3. Germany, East - Economic policy. I. Dittmann, Roswitha. II. Akademie für Staats- und Rechtswissenschaft der DDR. Sektion Staatliche Leitung der Volkswirtschaft. III. Series.
HC290.795.C3 V47 1986

Veras, Antonio Carlos. Jucá, Alvaro Ferraz. Gênero industrial--têxtil /. [Recife] [1985?] 34 leaves ; LC Card 86-204296
HD9864.B83 P475 1985

Verbände als Träger öffentlicher Politik . Farago, Peter. Grüsch , c1987. xi, 185 p. : ISBN 3-7253-0290-1 LC Card 87-140606 DDC 322/.3/09494 19
HD2429.S92 F37 1987

Verband der Datenverarbeitungs-Fachleute (Switzerland) Berufe der Wirtschaftsinformatik in der Schweiz /. Zürich , Stuttgart , 1986. 83 p. : ISBN 3-7281-1499-5 : LC Card 86-182797
HD8039.D372 S953 1986

Verband der Hochschullehrer für Betriebswirtschaft. Kommission Internationales Management. Diskontinuitätenmanagement . Berlin , c1984. x, 320 p. : ISBN 3-503-02446-8 LC Card 85-128271
HD62.4 .D57 1984

Finanz- und bankwirtschaftliche Probleme bei internationaler Unternehmenstätigkeit /. Stuttgart , c1985. x, 267 p. : ISBN 3-7910-0394-1 LC Card 86-121195 DDC 658.1/5 19
HG4027.5 .F56 1985

Projektmanagement, INTERNATIONAL /. Stuttgart , c1982. x, 244 p. : ISBN 3-7910-0339-9 LC Card 83-183718
HD69.P75 P764 1982

Verband der Hochschullehrer für Betriebswitschaft. Kommission Rechnungswesen. Entwicklungslinien der Kosten- und Erlösrechnung /. Stuttgart , c1983. viii, 232 p. : ISBN 3-7910-0304-6 : LC Card 83-200474
HF5686.C8 E65 1983

Verband der Versicherungsunternehmungen Österreichs. Versicherungs-Leitfaden . Wien , 1984. 79 p. : LC Card 85-198493 DDC 368/.9436 19
HG8061 .V47 1984

Verband Kommunaler Unternehmen. Erklärungen zur kommunalen Versorgungswirtschaft. Köln , 1985. 146 p. ; ISBN 3-87750-141-9
NYPL [K-10 8934 Heft 63]

Verband Kommunaler Unternehmungen. see **Verband Kommunaler Unternehmen.**

Verbandsstrategien zur Ausländerbeschäftigung in der Bundesrepublik . Kontos, Maria. Königstein/Ts. , c1983. viii, 235 p. ; ISBN 3-7756-6938-8 LC Card 83-190064 DDC 331.6/2/0943 19
HD8458.A2 K598 1983
NYPL [JLD 86-2465]

Verbeek, Henk. Residentiële mobiliteit in Ciudad Chihuahua, Mexico / Henk Verbeek. Utrecht : Geografisch Instituut, Rijksuniversiteit Utrecht, [1986] iii, 142 p. : ill. ; 30 cm. (Diskussiestukken van de Vakgroep Sociale Geografie van Ontwikkelingslanden . nr. 33) "Januari 1986." Bibliography: p. 132-134. LC Card 86-172646
1. Residential mobility - Mexico - Chihuahua. 2. Housing - Mexico - Chihuahua. 3. Chihuahua (Mexico) - Social conditions. I. Title. II. Series.
HD7288.92.M62 C488 1986

Verbindungsstelle der Bundesländer beim Amt der Niederösterreichischen Landesregierung. Daten zum Finanzausgleich . Wien [1986] xx, 331 p. : LC Card 86-209464
HJ1066 .D37 1986

Die verborgene Macht . Morawetz, Inge, 1955- Frankfurt , New York , c1986. 200 p. : ISBN 3-593-33662-6 LC Card 86-223864
HG3008 .M67 1986

Les verbos de la F.E.B. en 1979 /. Hotterbeex, M. (Marcel) Liège , 1982. 20 leaves ; LC Card 83-221745
HD6948.B4 H67 1982

Verbraucherinteressen im politischen Entscheidungsprozess /. Schatz, Heribert. Frankfurt/Main , New York , c1984. 275 p. ; ISBN 3-593-33293-0 LC Card 84-212024
HC290.5.C63 S33 1984

Verbraucherinteressen und Agrarpolitik /. Ambros, Werner. Krefeld , 1986. x, 260 p. : ISBN 3-88358-068-6 LC Card 87-122729 DDC 338.1/843 19
HD1957 .A63 1986

Verbraucherpanel, Informationen als Grundlage für Marketingentscheidungen im Einzelhandel /. Weissman, Arnold. München , c1983. xxviii, 194, [4] p. : ISBN 3-88259-242-7 LC Card 83-161472
HF5415.3 .W437 1983

Verbraucherpolitik in der Bundesrepublik Deutschland . Meier, Bernd, 1952- Frankfurt am Main , New York , c1984. iii, 256 p. : ISBN 3-8204-8404-3 (pbk.) LC Card 87-672663
HC290.5.C6 M36x 1984

Verbraucherpolitik in der sozialen Marktwirtschaft : eine Aufsatzsammlung / mit Beiträgen von Siegbert Alber ... [et al.] ; herausgegeben von Hartwig Piepenbrock. Bonn : Verein für Wirtschaftliche und Soziale Fragen, c1984. 146 p. ; 21 cm. (Schriftenreihe des Vereins für Wirtschaftliche und Soziale Fragen e.V. Stuttgart . 17) Includes bibliographical references. CONTENTS. - Verbraucherpolitik in der Europäischen Gemeinschaft / Siegbert Alber -- Verbraucherpolitische Aspekte aus Sicht der Gebrauchsgüterindustrie / Reinhard Hector -- Wettbewerbsfreiheit und Verbraucherschutz / Herbert Helmrich -- Quo vadis Verbraucherpolitik? / Hartwig Piepenbrock -- Verbraucherpolitik im Ordnungsrahmen der sozialen Marktwirtschaft / Gerhard Prosi -- Zur Abgrenzung der Verbraucherpolitik und ihren Zielen / Manfred Sauer -- Die ordnungspolitische Dimension der Verbraucherpolitik in der Sozialen Marktwirtschaft / Sigrid Scholten -- Verbraucherschutz durch Privatrecht / Harm Peter Westermann. ISBN 3-922335-04-7 LC Card 85-228004
1. Consumer protection - European Economic Community countries. 2. Consumers - European Economic Community countries. I. Alber, Siegbert. II. Piepenbrock, Hartwig. III. Series.
HC240.9.C63 V47 1984

Verbundgeschäfte . Iske, Thorsten, 1960- Frankfurt am Main , New York , c1986. v, 267 p. : ISBN 3-8204-9756-0 LC Card 86-218131
HF1019 .I85 1986

Das Verbundwinzersystem . Janetzki, Annemarie. Münster , 1982. xxiv, 406 p., [3] folded leaves of plates : ISBN 3-7923-0486-4 LC Card 83-157892
HD9383.5 .J35 1982

A Verdade sobre o "Caso Coroa-Brastel.". Brasília, DF : Banco Central do Brasil, 1984. 156 p. ; 24 cm. LC Card 85-207657
1. Grupo Coroa-Brastel. 2. Holding companies - Brazil - Case studies. 3. Bank holding companies - Brazil - Case studies. 4. Banco Central do Brasil. I. Banco Central do Brasil.
HG4109 .V47 1984

Verdier, James M. Tax expenditures : budget control options and five-year budget projections for fiscal year 1983-1987. Washington, D.C. : Congress of the United States, Congressional Budget Office, 1982. xx, 102 p. ; 26 cm. Prepared by James M. Verdier and Martha J. Smith, with assistance from Robert Lucke. "A CBO report, as required by public law 93-344." "November 1982." Includes bibliographical references.
1. Expenditures, Public - United States. 2. Tax revenue estimating - United States. 3. Budget - United States. 4. United States - Appropriations and expenditures - Forecasting. I. Smith, Martha J. II. Lucke, Robert, 1955-. III. Title. *NYPL [JLF 83-663]*

VERDU (SPAIN) - HISTORY - SOURCES.
Bertran i Roigé, Prim. Noves aportacions sobre la repoblació de Verdú en el centenari de la seva carta de Franquesa (1184-1984) /. Lleida , 1984. 23 p., [1] leaf of plates : ISBN 84-00-05783-X LC Card 86-140657
HD780.V44 B47 1984

VEREENIGING (SOUTH AFRICA) - CENSUS.
Bevolkingsensus 1980 uitgesoekte statistiese streek Vereeniging/Vanderbijlpark/Sasolburg =. Pretoria [1985] xx, 301 p. : ISBN 0-621-09484-6 : LC Card 85-235498
HA4701.Z9 V474 1985

VEREENIGING (SOUTH AFRICA) - POPULATION - STATISTICS.
Bevolkingsensus 1980 uitgesoekte statistiese streek Vereeniging/Vanderbijlpark/Sasolburg =. Pretoria [1985] xx, 301 p. : ISBN 0-621-09484-6 : LC Card 85-235498
HA4701.Z9 V474 1985

Verein der Freunde Totzenbachs (Series) . (Heft 12) Landskron, Ferdinand. Von der Bauernfaust zur Bauernkammer /. Totzenbach [1983] 194 p. ; LC Card 84-168829
HD1536.A9 L36 1983

Verein für Socialpolitik, Gesellschaft für Wirtschafts- und Sozialwissenschaften. see **Gesellschaft für Wirtschafts- und Sozialwissenschaften, Verein für Socialpolitik.**

Verein zur Wahrung der Main- und Donau-Schiffahrtsinteressen (Germany) Rhein-Main-Donau . [Nürnberg , 1937?] 195 p. : LC Card 86-216951
HE449.R38 R48 1937

Vereinbarkeit von Preisregelungen auf dem Arzneimittelmarkt mit dem Recht der Europäischen Wirtschaftsgemeinschaft /. Mestmäcker, Ernst Joachim. Baden-Baden , 1979. 83 p. ; ISBN 3-7890-0444-8 : LC Card 80-515375
KK6444.D78 M47 *NYPL [JLD 81-684]*

Vereinigung Deutscher Wissenschaftler. Meyer-Abich, Klaus Michael, 1936- Die Grenzen der Atomwirtschaft . München , c1986. 230 p. : ISBN 3-406-31317-5 LC Card 86-192439
HD9698.A2 M49 1986

Vereinswesen und bürgerliche Gesellschaft in Deutschland / herausgegeben von Otto Dann. München : R. Oldenbourg, 1984. 180 p. ; 23 cm. (Historische Zeitschrift. Beiheft . n.F., 9) Revised papers originally delivered at the 34th meeting of the Deutscher Historikertag, 1982 in Münster. Includes bibliographical references. CONTENTS. - Strukturmerkmale und Entwicklungstendenzen des Vereinswesens in Deutschland 1789-1848 / von Wolfgang Hardtwig -- Vereins- und Parteibildung in der Revolution von 1848/49 / von Dieter Langewiesche -- Die Entfaltung des Vereinswesens während der Industriellen Revolution in Deutschland (1850-1873) / von Klaus Tenfelde -- Das Vereinsrecht im Deutschland des 19. Jahrhunderts / von Alfons Hueber -- Zur volkskundlichen Vereinsforschung / von Albrecht Lehmann -- Zur Thematisierung des Vereinswesens in der deutschen Soziologie / von H.-Jörg Siewert. ISBN 3-486-52081-4 LC Card 84-205111
1. Trade and professional associations - Germany - History. 2. Associations, institutions, etc. - Germany - History. 3. Middle classes - Germany - History. 4. Corporations, Nonprofit - Germany - History. I. Dann, Otto. II. Deutscher Historikertag (34th : 1982 : Münster in Westfalen, Germany). III. Series.
HD2429.G3 V46 1984

Verenigde Oostindische Compagnie. see **Nederlandsche Oost-Indische Compagnie.**

Verenigde Staten. see **United States.**

Veress, József, Dr. A veszélyhelyzetbe került vállalatok és a gazdaságirányítás / Veress József. Budapest : Közgazdasági és Jogi Könyvkiadó, 1986. 207, [1] p. ; 19 cm. (Időszerű közgazdasági kérdések, 0324-3214) Bibliography: p. 201-[208]. ISBN 963-221-778-0 : LC Card 87-136695
1. Bankruptcy - Hungary. 2. Industrial management - Hungary. 3. Industry and state - Hungary. I. Title. II. Series.
HG3769.H94 V47 1986

Verfällt die öffentliche Infrastruktur? . Reidenbach, Michael. Berlin , 1986. 212 p. : ISBN 3-88118-125-3 LC Card 86-233141
HC290.5.C3 R45 1986

Verfahren zur Erarbeitung eines Grundsatzsystems für den Investitionsbereich /. Grünig, Rudolf. Bern , c1984. 144 p. : ISBN 3-258-03442-7 : LC Card 85-139475
HG4028.C4 G75 1984

Verfahren zur Nutzung erschöpfbarer Ressourcen . Hartung, Hans. Tübingen , 1986. ix, 172 p. : ISBN 3-16-345126-8 (Deut. Bibl. : pbk.) LC Card 86-233079
HD9565 .H36 1986

Verghese, K. E. Socio-economic change in Kerala / K.E. Verghese. 1st ed. New Delhi : Ashish Pub. House, 1986. x, 211 p. ; 22 cm. Study, with reference to villages in Kuttanad Region, comprising parts of Kottayam and Alleppey districts. Bibliography: p. [203]-207. Includes index. ISBN 81-7024-061-1 : LC Card 86-903145 DDC 330.954/83 19
1. Kottayam (India : District) - Economic conditions. 2. Kottayam (India : District) - Social conditions. 3. Alleppey (India : District) - Economic conditions. 4. Alleppey (India : District) - Social conditions. I. Title.
HC437.K645 V47 1986

Vergleichende Statistik des Handels der deutschen Staaten /. Rau, Heinrich. Wien , 1863. vii, 183 p. ; LC Card 85-217948
HF3561.5 .R38 1863

Verhaegen, P. H. A. M., 1950- Strategisch investeringsbeleid / P.H.A.M. Verhaegen. Deventer : Kluwer, 1986. 223 p. : ill. ; 25 cm. Thesis (doctoral)--Rotterdam, 1986. Bibliography: p. 215-223. ISBN 90-267-1049-6 : LC Card 86-186994
1. Investments. I. Title.
HG4521 .V475 1986

Verhandelingen van het Koninklijk Instituut voor Taal-, Land- en Volkenkunde . (101) Breman, Jan. Control of land and labour in colonial Java . Dordrecht, Netherlands , Cinnaminson, N.J., U. S.A. , 1983. xi, 158 p. : ISBN 90-6765-048-X (pbk.) LC Card 86-145678 DDC 333.3/1/5982 19
HD1333.I52 C573 1983

Verheirstraeten, A. Geld, krediet en intrest in de Belgische financiële sector / door Albert Verheirstraeten. Leuven : Acco, 1977. xxii, 337 p. : ill. ; 25 cm. ([Reeks] - Katholieke Universiteit Leuven, Faculteit der Economische en Toegepaste Economische Wetenschappen, Departement Economie . nr. 23) Errata slip inserted. Bibliography: p. 320-333. LC Card 78-345984
1. Money - Belgium. 2. Finance - Belgium. 3. Credit - Belgium. I. Series: Katholieke Universiteit te Leuven. Faculteit der Economische en Toegepaste Economische Wetenschappen. Reeks, nr. 23. II. Title.
HG1055 .V47 *NYPL [JLM 86-1310 nr.23]*

Vérification spéciale . Québec (Province). Bureau du vérificateur général. [Québec] [1978-<1987? >] v. <1-3 > ; LC Card 82-212701
HD9715.C33 Q45 1978

Vérin, Hélène, 1940- Entrepreneurs, entreprise : histoire d'une idée / Hélène Vérin.1re éd. Paris : Presses universitaires de France, c1982.

262 p. ; 22 cm. (Recherches politiques) Includes bibliographical references. ISBN 2-13-037449-2 (pbk.) : LC Card 82-153537 DDC 338/.04/09 19
1. Entrepreneur - History. 2. Business enterprises - France - History. I. Title. II. Series.
HB615 .V44 1982 **NYPL [JLD 86-3019]**

Die verkannte Macht . Gilles, Franz-O., 1944- Berlin , 1986. 398 p. ; ISBN 3-923024-07-X LC Card 87-127716 DDC 354.430072/31/09 19
HJ9925.G3 G55 1986

Verkaufte Träume . Föste, Wolfgang. München , c1982. 53 p. : ISBN 3-88676-011-1 (pbk.) LC Card 87-672593
HD6250.T52 F67x 1982

Verkehrs- und unternehmenspolitische Anpassungsstrategien an veränderte Ressourcenbewertungen / [Schriftleitung, Friedrich von Stackelberg]. Göttingen : Vandenhoeck & Ruprecht, 1986. 210 p. : ill. ; 24 cm. (Beiträge aus dem Institut für Verkehrswissenschaft an der Universität Münster . Heft 109) A revision and enlargement of papers prepared by members of the Institut für Verkehrswissenschaft an der Universität Münster and presented at a meeting organized by the Studienkreis der Gesellschaft zur Förderung der Verkehrswissenschaft an der Universität Münster, Nov. 28-29, 1985 in Telgte. Includes bibliographical references. CONTENTS. - Die Inanspruchnahme von Ressourcen im Verkehr und die Entwicklung ihrer Bewertung / Hansjochen Ehmer -- Verkehrspolitische Reaktionen auf veränderte Ressourcenbewertungen / Matthias Wiechers -- Unternehmenspolitische Reaktionen auf veränderte Ressourcenbewertungen / Martina Meyer-Schwickerath -- Möglichkeiten der verkehrspolitischen und unternehmenspolitischen Antizipation künftiger Ressourcenwertverschiebungen / Hellmuth St. Seidenfus. ISBN 3-525-85699-7 : LC Card 86-223574
1. Transportation and state - Germany, West. I. Stackelberg, Friedrich von. II. Universität Münster. Institut für Verkehrswissenschaft. III. Universität Münster. Gesellschaft zur Förderung der Verkehrswissenschaft. Studienkreis. IV. Series.
HE131 .M8 Heft 109 HE249

Verkehrsberuhigung in Berlin (West) . Homfeld, Wolfgang. Berlin , c1984. 306 p. : ISBN 3-496-00782-6 LC Card 84-212018
HE311.G32 B4753 1984

Verkehrsberuhigung in Städten und Gemeinden /. Franz, Lothar. Grafenau , c1982. 134 p. : ISBN 3-88508-780-4 : LC Card 82-204794
HE311.G3 F73 1982

Verkehrskriminalität und Alkohol in einer Grossstadt . Triebler, Stephan Ferdinand, 1950- [West Germany , 1983?] (Köln : Copy-Star) xv, 190 p. : LC Card 84-240261
HE5620.D7 T75 1983

Die Verkehrspolitik in der 8. Legislaturperiode /. Gscheidle, Kurt. Bonn-Bad Godesberg [1977] 29 p. : LC Card 86-173226
HE64 .A36 Heft 54 HE249

Verkehrsunfälle .
(3) Analyse von Unfällen motorisierter Zweiradbenutzer . [West Germany] [1976] 32 p. : LC Card 85-135424
HE5614.5.G3 A65 1976

(4) Untersuchung der Unfälle auf Bundesautobahnen . [München?] [1976] 84 p. : LC Card 85-135444
HE5614.5.G3 U58 1976

Verkehrswege für die mobile Gesellschaft. Deutscher Strassenkongress (1984 : Mannheim, Germany) Deutscher Strassenkongress, Mannheim, 1984 /. Köln [1985?] 255 p. : LC Card 87-408263 DDC 388.1/0943 19
HE363.G3 D48 1984

Verkehrswissenschaftliche Forschungen. For additional listing of contents, see Old Catalog.
(Bd. 41) Dick, Walter, 1949- Die ökonomische Bedeutung der Qualität des Schienengüterverkehrs . Berlin , c1980. xi, 331 p. : ISBN 3-428-04731-1 LC Card 84-130833
HE2446.N67 D52 1980

(Bd. 45) Hoffmann, Klaus G. Raumbedeutsamkeit von Schnellfahrstrecken im Schienenverkehr /. Berlin , c1985. xxviii, 547, [1] p. : ISBN 3-428-05770-8 LC Card 85-155640
HE3078 .H64 1985

Verlag für Wirtschaftsliteratur (Zurich, Switzerland) Handbuch der schweizerischen Textil-, Bekleidungs- und Lederwirtschaft =. Zürich , 1986. 214 p. : ISBN 3-909214-07-X LC Card 86-221803
HD9940.S93 H36 1986

Verlagerungen der individuellen Verkehrsnachfrage bei verändertem ÖPNV-Angebot infolge neueingerichteter Stadtschnellbahnen /. Stengel, Wolfgang. Bad Honnef , 1984. iv, 210 p. : ISBN 3-88347-120-8 : LC Card 84-185940
HE311.G3 S73 1984

Verletzbarkeitsmanagement bei parallelen Rohstoffpreis- und Devisenkursrisiken /. Behnke, Hartmut, 1941- Frankfurt am Main , New York , c1986. vi, 288 p. : ISBN 3-8204-9365-4 LC Card 86-190114
HG3853 .B44 1986

Verley, Patrick. La révolution industrielle / Patrick Verley. Paris : MA Editions, c1985. 270 p. : ill. ; 18 cm. (Le Monde de-- . 14) Includes bibliographies and indexes. ISBN 2-86676-194-4 LC Card 86-116016 DDC 338.09 19
1. Industry - History - 18th century. 2. Industry - History - 19th century. 3. Economic history - 1750-1918. I. Title.
HD2321 .V47 1985

Verma, Gajendra K. Race, training, and employment / Gajendra K. Verma and D.S. Darby. London ; New York : Falmer Press, 1987. vi, 134 p. : ill. ; 24 cm. Bibliography: p. 131-132. Includes index. ISBN 1-85000-243-6 : LC Card 87-15470 DDC 331.3/46/0941 19
1. Occupational training - Great Britain. 2. Youth - Employment - Great Britain. 3. Minorities - Employment - Great Britain. I. Darby, D. S. II. Title.
HD5715.5.G7 V47 1987

Verma, H. S. (Harnam Singh), 1942- Industrial families in India : an enquiry into the nature of their entrepreneurship / H.S. Verma. New Delhi : Concept Pub. Co., 1987, c1985. xvi, 248 p. ; 23 cm. Revision of the author's thesis (Ph. D.--Gujarat University, Ahmedabad) Bibliography: p. [228]-243. Includes index. LC Card 87-900925 DDC 338/.04/0954 19
1. Industrialists - India. 2. Entrepreneur. I. Title.
HC432.5.A2 V47 1987

Verma, K. K. (Krishna Kumar), 1941- Sachchidananda, 1926- Electricity and social change /. Patna , 1983. xii, 264 p. ; LC Card 83-902678 DDC 303.4/83 19
HD9685.I43 B547 1983
NYPL [JLD 86-4263]

Verma, Satyendra. Mills, Edwin S. Studies in Indian urban development /. New York , 1986. viii, 214 p. ; ISBN 0-19-520507-3 : LC Card 86-2489 DDC 307.1/4/0954 19
HT147.I5 M56 1986 **NYPL [JLE 86-3750]**

Vermaat, A. J., 1939- Zelfzorg en verzorging . Kampen [1985] 237 p. ; ISBN 90-242-4072-7 : LC Card 86-175292
HC325 .Z43 1985

Vermeer, E. B. (Eduard B.) Economic development in provincial China : the central Shaanxi since 1930 / Eduard Vermeer. Cambridge [Cambridgeshire] ; New York : Cambridge University Press, 1988. p. cm. (Contemporary China Institute publications) Bibliography: p. Includes index. ISBN 0-521-34392-5 LC Card 87-22499 DDC 330.951/17058 19
1. Shensi Province (China) - Economic conditions. 2. Agriculture - Economic aspects - China - Shensi Province - History - 20th century. I. Title.
HC428.S54 V47 1988

Vermeidung von Armut im Alter . Schmitz, Heinz. München , c1983. 267 p. : ISBN 3-89019-099-5 LC Card 84-197886
HD7164 .S29 1983

Die Vermittlerrolle der Banken bei deutschen Investitionen in Nord- und Mittelamerika bis zum Ersten Weltkrieg /. Meleghy, Gyula, 1955- [Köln?] 1983 (Köln : W. Kleikamp) 330 p. : LC Card 85-229675
HG3052 .M45 1983

Vermont. Dept. of Employment and Training. Employment and earnings, 1980-1985 . Montpelier, Vt. [1986] ii, 79 leaves : LC Card 86-622186 DDC 331.12/5/09743021 19
HD5725.V5 E46 1986

Vermont. Dept. of Health. (Old Catalog form: Vermont. Health Dept.)
Changing fertility patterns in Vermont. Burlington, Vt. (Box 70, 60 Main St., Burlington 05402) [1986] 18 p. : LC Card 86-622900 DDC 304.6/32/09743 19
HB935.V4 C46 1986

Vermont. Health Dept. see **Vermont. Dept. of Health.**

VERMONT - POPULATION - STATISTICS.
Cooley, Walter L. Vermont's urban population, 1950 to 1985 /. Burlington, Vt. (Box 70, 60 Main St., Burlington 05402) [1986] 9 leaves : LC Card 86-622184 DDC 304.6/09743 19
HA675 .C66 1986

Vermont's urban population, 1950 to 1985 /. Cooley, Walter L. Burlington, Vt. (Box 70, 60 Main St., Burlington 05402) [1986] 9 leaves : LC Card 86-622184 DDC 304.6/09743 19
HA675 .C66 1986

Vernière, Laurent. Abramovici, G. Comptes économiques de la Réunion, série 1975-1980 . Ste Clotilde, [Réunion] [1983?] 133 p. ; LC Card 86-980541
HC598 .A37 1983

Vernon, Raymond, 1913- Manager in the international economy / Raymond Vernon, Louis T. Wells, Jr. 5th ed. Englewood Cliffs, NJ : Prentice-Hall, c1986. viii, 469 p. : ill. ; 24 cm. Includes bibliographies and index. ISBN 0-13-550807-X : LC Card 85-25653 DDC 658.1/8 19
1. International business enterprises - Management. 2. International business enterprises - Case studies. I. Wells, Louis T. II. Title.
HD62.4 .V48 1986 **NYPL [JLE 86-3200]**

Vernuccio, Pietro, 1947- Una città in cerca d'identità : analisi socio-economica su Modica / Pietro Vernuccio. Modica : Associazione culturale "Dialogo", 1984. 201 p., [12] p. of plates : ill. ; 25 cm. LC Card 86-164886
1. Modica (Sicily) - Economic conditions. 2. Modica (Sicily) - Industries. 3. Modica, Sicily - Social conditions. 4. Modica (Sicily) - Description. I. Title.
HC308.M53 V47 1984

Vernulsia soldat k poliu, 1945-1985 / [sostavitel′ Viktor Petrovich Plotnikov]. Moskva : Agropromizdat, 1985. 429, [16] p. : ill. (some col.) ; 21 cm. LC Card 85-228297
1. Agricultural laborers - Soviet Union - Biography. 2. Farmers - Soviet Union - Biography. 3. Veterans - Soviet Union - Biography. I. Plotnikov, Viktor Petrovich.
HD1536.S65 V47 1985

Vernym kursom /. Bogoliubov, Klavdiĭ Mikhaĭlovich. Moskva , 1984. 287 p. ; LC Card 85-164820
HD1492.S65 B64 1984

Veröffentlichung der Forschungsgemeinschaft Bauen und Wohnen, Stuttgart .
(Nr. 140) Standorte von Büros im Urteil der Beschäftigten und sonstiger Nutzer /. Stuttgart , 1983. 140 p. : LC Card 83-220559
HF5547.25 .S74 1983

(Nr. 159) Heinzmann, Ute. Umzugsverhalten der Bevölkerung in ausgewählten ländlichen Teilräumen am Beispiel der Region Neckar-Alb . Tübingen , 1985. 69, [4] p. : LC Card 86-195573
HB2056.N43 H45 1985

(Nr. 165) Friedrich, R. (Rainer) Energie und Umwelt . Stuttgart [1985] 124 p. : LC Card 87-409533 DDC 333.79/0943/46 19
HD9502.G43 B3238 1985

(Nr. 165/85) Friedrich, R. (Rainer) Energie und Umwelt . Stuttgart [1985] 124 p. : LC Card 87-409533 DDC 333.79/0943/46 19
HD9502.G43 B3238 1985

(Nr. 167) Friedrich, R. (Rainer) Energie und Umwelt . Stuttgart [1985] 115 p. : LC Card 87-409534 DDC 333.79/0943/46 19
HD9502.G43 B324 1985

(Nr. 167/85) Friedrich, R. (Rainer) Energie und Umwelt . Stuttgart [1985] 115 p. : LC Card 87-409534 DDC 333.79/0943/46 19
HD9502.G43 B324 1985

Veröffentlichung des HWWA-Institut für Wirtschaftsforschung-Hamburg und des Unabhängigen Instituts für Rechts-, Sozial- und Wirtschaftswissenschaften e.V.

Protektionismus in der Weltwirtschaft . Hamburg , 1984. viii, 147 p. ; ISBN 3-87895-253-8 LC Card 84-233895
HF1703 .P77 1984

Veröffentlichung des Senats der Hansestadt Lübeck, Amt für Kultur. Reihe B .
(Heft 6) Lübecker Weinhandel . Lübeck , 1985. 260 p. : ISBN 3-924214-27-1 LC Card 86-145675
HD9383.8.L82 L82 1985

Veröffentlichungen aus dem Archiv der Stadt Freiburg im Breisgau .
(20) Die Freiburger Enquete von 1476 . Freiburg im Breisgau , c1986. xxxiv, 102 p. : ISBN 3-923272-20-2 LC Card 87-409559 DDC 330.943/46 19
HC289.F855 F74 1986

Veröffentlichungen der Akademie für Raumforschung und Landesplanung. Abhandlungen, 0344-0311 .
(Bd. 84) Schroiff, Franz J. Das Binnenschiffahrt-Verkehrssystem . Hannover , 1984. ix, 267 p. : ISBN 3-87870-951-X LC Card 84-221599
HE669 .S34 1984

Veröffentlichungen der Akademie für Raumforschung und Landesplanung. Forschungs- und Sitzungsberichte, 0344-8940 .
(Bd. <167 >) Funktionsräumliche Arbeitsteilung. Hannover , <1986-. v. <3 > : ISBN 3-87870-770-3 (T. III) : LC Card 87-409060 DDC 361.6/0943 19
HD51 .F86 1986

Veröffentlichungen der Akademie für Raumforschung und Landesplanung. Forschungs- und Sitzungsberichte, 0587-2642 .
(Bd. 164) Gestaltung künftiger Raumstrukturen durch veränderte Verkehrskonzepte . Hannover , 1986. xii, 173 p. : ISBN 3-87870-767-3 LC Card 87-401351 DDC 380.5/0943/512 19
HE249.Z7 S343 1986

Veröffentlichungen der DG Bank, Deutsche Genossenschaftsbank .
(Bd. 15) Aschhoff, Gunther, 1934- Das deutsche Genossenschaftswesen . Frankfurt am Main , 1985. 167 p. : ISBN 3-7819-0345-1 LC Card 86-145522
HD3038 .A77 1985

Veröffentlichungen der DGFK.
Auf dem Weg zu einer neuen Weltwirtschaftsordnung? . Baden-Baden , 1983. 478 p. ; ISBN 3-7890-0919-9 LC Card 84-113581
HF1411 .A92 1983

Auf dem Weg zu einer neuen Weltwirtschaftsordnung? . Baden-Baden , 1983. 478 p. ; ISBN 3-7890-0919-9
NYPL [JLD 87-919]

Veröffentlichungen der Hanns Martin Schleyer-Stiftung .
(Bd. 11) Symposium Umweltprobleme als Herausforderung der Marktwirtschaft, Neue Ideen jenseits des Dirigismus (1983 : Stuttgart, Germany) Symposium Umweltprobleme als Herausforderung der Marktwirtschaft, Neue Ideen jenseits des Dirigismus . [Köln] [Freiburg] , 1983. 300 p. ; ISBN 3-7616-0722-9 LC Card 84-152335 DDC 363.7/058 19
HC79.E5 S96 1983 ***NYPL [JLD 86-1631]***

Veröffentlichungen der Historischen Kommission zu Berlin beim Friedrich-Meinecke-Institut der Freien Universität Berlin .
(Bd. 61) Lindenlaub, Dieter. Maschinenbauunternehmen in der Deutschen Inflation 1919-1923 . Berlin , New York , 1985. xiii, 262 p. ; ISBN 3-11-009934-9 LC Card 85-214738
HG999 .L75 1985

(Bd. 65) Steinisch, Irmgard. Arbeitszeitverkürzung und sozialer Wandel . Berlin , New York , 1986. xiv, 640 p. : ISBN 3-11-010483-0 LC Card 87-110005 DDC 331.25/7/0973 19
HD5119.I52 U67 1986

(Bd. 67) The Adaptation to inflation /. Berlin , New York , 1986. xvi, 512 p. : ISBN 0-89925-287-7 (U. S.) LC Card 86-29134 DDC 338.943 19
HC286.2 .A62 1986

Veröffentlichungen der Hochschule St. Gallen für Wirtschafts- und Sozialwissenschaften. Schriftenreihe Betriebswirtschaft .
(Bd 11) Dyllick, Thomas. Gesellschaftliche Instabilität und Unternehmungsführung . Bern , c1982. xiv, 394 p. : ISBN 3-258-03212-2 LC Card 83-115754
HD58.7 .D94 1982

(Bd. 13) Achleitner, Paul M. Sozio-politische Strategien multinationaler Unternehmungen . Bern , c1985. ii, 334 p. : ISBN 3-258-03490-7 : LC Card 85-208760
HD62.4 .A24 1985

(Bd. 7) Peters, Nikolaus A. Arbeits- und Organisationsgestaltung in einer post-industriellen Gesellschaft /. Bern , c1981. xi, 351 p. : ISBN 3-258-03066-9 LC Card 87-672718
HD2326 .P47x 1981

Veröffentlichungen der Niedersächsischen Landesbibliothek Hannover.
Beiträge zur niedersächsischen Preisgeschichte des 16. bis 19. Jahrhunderts /. Hildesheim , 1986. lxiii, 541 p. ; ISBN 3-7848-3874-X LC Card 87-407399 DDC 338.1/331/094359 19
HD9043.4 .B45 1986

Werbegraphik 1830-1870, aus niedersächsischen Zeitungen /. [Hannover] , Hildesheim , 1986. xv, 280 p. : ISBN 3-7848-3875-8 LC Card 87-408153 DDC 659.13/2/094359 19
HF5996.L68 W47 1986

Veröffentlichungen der Universität Innsbruck .
(142) Festschrift für Univ.-Prof. Dr. Georg Zwanowetz anlässlich der Vollendung des 65. Lebensjahres /. [Innsbruck] , c1984. 332 p. : LC Card 84-183487
HC244 .F48 1984

Veröffentlichungen des Collegium Carolinum .
(Bd. 50) Brousek, Karl M. Die Grossindustrie Böhmens, 1848-1918 /. München , 1987. 223 p., 8 leaves of plates : ISBN 3-486-51871-2 LC Card 87-142819 DDC 338.6/44/094371 19
HD2356.C96 B643 1987

Veröffentlichungen des Deutschen Historischen Instituts in London .
(Bd. 17) Wengenroth, Ulrich. Unternehmensstrategien und technischer Fortschritt . Göttingen , c1986. 316 p. : ISBN 3-525-36302-8 LC Card 87-112794 DDC 338.4/7669142/0943 19
HD9523.5 .W43 1986

Veröffentlichungen des Forschungsinstituts für Wirtschaftspolitik an der Universität Mainz .
(Bd. 48) Eggerstedt, Harald. Produktwettbewerb und Dienstleistungsfreiheit auf Versicherungsmärkten /. Berlin , c1987. 320 p. : ISBN 3-428-06167-5 LC Card 87-143175 DDC 368/.94 19
HG8593.5.Z75 E34 1987

Veröffentlichungen des HWWA-Institut für Wirtschaftsforschung-Hamburg, 0722-4729.
Die Wirtschaftliche Entwicklung in den sozialistischen Ländern Osteuropas zur Jahreswende 1985/86 /. Hamburg , 1986. 336 p. ; ISBN 3-87895-295-3 LC Card 86-185852
HC244 .W5776 1986

Veröffentlichungen des Instituts für Europäische Geschichte Mainz. Abteilung Universalgeschichte. Beiheft .
(16) Von der Konkurrenz zur Rivalität . Stuttgart , 1986. 186 p. ; ISBN 3-515-04760-3 LC Card 87-134320 DDC 337/.09/04 19
HF1411 .V665 1986

Veröffentlichungen des Instituts für Versicherungswissenschaft der Universität Mannheim, 0170-2254 .
(Bd. 25) Lehnhardt-Ritter, Gerda. Das Kapitalanlageverhalten der deutschen Lebensversicherungsunternehmen im Wandel der Konjunktur . Karlsruhe , c1984. xxiii, 444 p. : ISBN 3-88487-067-X LC Card 85-171182
HG9078 .L44 1984

Veröffentlichungen des Instituts für Versicherungswissenschaften der Universität Mannheim, 0170-2254 .
(Bd. 24) Henrich, Rudolf. Analyse und Planung des Erfolgs und der Überschussverwendung einer Krankenversicherungsaktiengesellschaft /. Karlsruhe , c1983. xxi, 498 p. : ISBN 3-88487-053-X LC Card 85-131706
HG9399.G32 H46 1983

Veröffentlichungen des Max-Planck-Instituts für Geschichte .
(82) Ullmann, Hans-Peter. Staatsschulden und Reformpolitik . Göttingen , c1986. 2 v. (842 p.) ; ISBN 3-525-35398-7 LC Card 86-210338
HJ8655.B38 U55 1986

Veröffentlichungen des Osteuropa-Institutes München. Reihe, Wirtschaft und Gesellschaft .
(Heft 21) Schönfelder, Bruno. Ökonomisches Risiko und Versicherung in sozialistischen Volkswirtschaften . Berlin , c1986. 284 p. : ISBN 3-428-05968-9 LC Card 86-185328
HD7180.5 .S36 1986

Veröffentlichungen des Stadtarchivs Ludwigshafen a. Rh. .
(Bd. 12) Breunig, Willi. Vom Handelsplatz zur Industriestadt . Ludwigshafen am Rhein , 1986. 151 p. : ISBN 3-924667-13-6 LC Card 87-135540 DDC 338.0943/43 19
HC289.L95 B74 1986

Veröffentlichungen des Vereins für Hamburgische Geschichte .
(Bd. 28) Ahrens, Gerhard, 1939- Krisenmanagement 1857 . Hamburg , 1986. 136 p. ; ISBN 3-923356-11-0 LC Card 87-127645 DDC 338.5/4 19
HB3717 1857 .A38 1986

Veröffentlichungen des Versicherungs-Wirtschaftlichen Seminars an der Handels-Hochschule St. Gallen .
(9-10) Steinlin-Fritzsche, Peter. Das Versicherungswesen der Schweiz . Zürich , 1961-1962. 2 v. ; LC Card 87-407799 DDC 368/.9494 19
HG8688 .S76 1961

Véron, Emile. Pour en sortir-- / Emile Véron. Paris : A. Michel, c1984. 185 p. : ill. ; 23 cm. ISBN 2-226-02060-8 : LC Card 84-197071
1. France - Economic policy - 1945-. I. Title.
HC276.2 .V465 1984

Die Verplante Wohnmisere : urbane Entwicklung und "armutsorientierter" Wohnungsbau in Afrika und Lateinamerika / Johannes Augel, Peter Hillen, Luiz Ramalho (Hrsg.). Saarbrücken ; Fort Lauderdale : Breitenbach, 1986. 334 p. : ill. ; 21 cm. (ASA Studien, 0176-8433 . 7) Includes bibliographies. ISBN 3-88156-329-6 LC Card 87-408292 DDC 363.5/1/096 19
1. Poor - Housing - Africa. 2. Poor - Housing - Latin America. 3. Housing policy - Africa. 4. Housing policy - Latin America. 5. Urbanization - Africa. 6. Urbanization - Latin America. I. Augel, Johannes. II. Hillen, Peter. III. Ramalho, Luiz. IV. Series.
HD7287.96.A4 V47 1986

La Verrerie champenoise, Charbonneaux-B.S.N. Reims, de 1870 à nos jours / textes réunis et commentés par Marc André et Michel de Paepe. Die : La Manufacture, c1984. 279 p. : ill. ; 21 x 22 cm. (La France industrielle) Bibliography: p. 274-277. ISBN 2-904638-12-1 : LC Card 84-247744
1. Charbonneaux-B.S.N. (Firm) - History. 2. Glass trade - France - History. 3. Glass manufacture - France - History. I. André, Marc. II. Paepe, Michel de. III. Series.
HD9623.F8 V47 1984

Verrign Stuart, Alexander. see **Verrijn Stuart, A. A.**

Verrijn Stuart, A. A. IFIP TC 8 Working Conference on Office Systems (1985 : Helsinki, Finland) Office systems . Amsterdam ; New York : vii, 199 p. : ISBN 0-444-70105-2 (Elsevier Science Pub. Co.) LC Card 86-16841 DDC 651.8 19
HF5547.5 .I345 1985 ***NYPL [JLD 87-1264]***

Verrijn Stuart, Xander. see **Verrijn Stuart, A. A.**

Verrill, Glenn. Kleppner, Otto, 1899- [Advertising procedure.] Kleppner's advertising procedure. Englewood Cliffs, N.J. , 1987, c1988. p. cm. ISBN 0-13-516451-6 LC Card 87-19346 DDC 659.1 19
HF5823 .K45 1988

Vers la libération de l'Amérique latine /. Lay, Jean-Benoît. Paris , c1985. 215 p. : ISBN 2-85802-433-X LC Card 85-136403
HC123 .L39 1985

The versatile salesperson . Wenschlag, Roger.

New York , c1987. viii, 205 p. : ISBN 0-471-85436-0 LC Card 87-2003 DDC 658.8/5 19
HF5438.25 .W294 1987

Die Verschuldung lateinamerikanischer Länder /. Köhn, Doris. Hamburg , 1984. 148 p. ; ISBN 3-87895-259-7 LC Card 85-134749
HJ8514.5 .K64 1984

Versenyképes mezőgazdaság, 0237-5001. Borszéki, Éva. Élelmiszer-gazdaságunk versenyképessége . Budapest , 1986. 284, [1] p. : ISBN 963-221-590-7 : LC Card 87-148751
HD1940.5 .B66 1986

Forgács, Katalin. A zöldség-gyümölcs szindróma . Budapest , 1986. 134, [1] p. ; ISBN 963-221-901-5 : LC Card 87-148760
HD9220.H82 F67 1986

Die Versichertenältesten : Verzeichnis der in den Stadt- und Landkreisen tätigen Versichertenältesten / Bundesversicherungsanstalt für Angestellte.Stand, März 1984. [Berlin] : Die Anstalt, [1984] 54 p. ; 30 cm. (Schriftenreihe / Bundesversicherungsanstalt für Angestellte . 20) LC Card 85-113867
1. White collar workers - Pensions - Germany (West) - States - Directories. 2. Social security beneficiaries - Germany (West) - States - Directories. I. Bundesversicherungsanstalt für Angestellte. II. Series: Schriftenreihe der Bundesversicherungsanstalt für Angestellte , 20.
HD7116.M42 G4334 Nr. 20, 1984 HD7179

Die Versicherung von Krediten als Instrument kreditspezifischer Risikovorsorge im Aktivgeschäft der Banken . Isern, Werner, 1950- Frankfurt am Main , New York , c1984. 303 p. : ISBN 3-8204-5319-9 LC Card 85-195374 DDC 368.8/7 19
HG9977 .I84 1984

Versicherungen in der Altbauerneuerung / herausgegeben von der Internationalen Bauausstellung Berlin ; [Inhalt, Wolfgang Sohst, Antje Grabenhorst]. Berlin : Ernst, Verlag für Architektur und Technische Wissenschaften, c1985. 83 p. ; 30 cm. (Bausteine zur Selbsthilfe) Legislation and regulations: p. 43-83. ISBN 3-433-02219-4 LC Card 86-104351
1. Insurance, Homeowners - Germany (West). 2. Housing rehabilitation - Germany (West). I. Sohst, Wolfgang. II. Grabenhorst, Antje. III. Internationale Bauausstellung Berlin GmbH. IV. Series.
HG9986.4.G3 V47 1985

Versicherungs-Leitfaden : Kleingedrucktes, gross geschrieben / [Redaktion, Gregor Kozak].2., verb. Aufl. Wien : Verband der Versicherungsunternehmungen Österreichs, 1984. 79 p. : col. ill. ; 22 cm. Cover title. LC Card 85-198493 DDC 368/.9436 19
1. Insurance - Handooks, manuals, etc. 2. Insurance - Austria - Handooks, manuals, etc. I. Kozak, Gregor. II. Verband der Versicherungsunternehmungen Österreichs.
HG8061 .V47 1984

Die Versicherungsbedingungen und wichtigsten Prämiensätze der in der Schweiz konzessionierten Lebensversicherungsgesellschaften / bearbeitet von Ulrich Baumgartner. Bern : P. Haupt, 1986. 101 p. ; 20 cm. "Grieshaber." LC Card 87-124065 DDC 368.3/2/009494 19
1. Insurance, Life - Switzerland. 2. Insurance, Life - Law and legislation - Switzerland. I. Baumgartner, Ulrich, Dr.
HG9148 .V47 1986

Das Versicherungswesen der Schweiz . Steinlin-Fritzsche, Peter. Zürich , 1961-1962. 2 v. ; LC Card 87-407799 DDC 368/.9494 19
HG8688 .S76 1961

Versicherungswirtschaftliches Studienwerk / Herausgeber, Heinz-Leo Müller-Lutz, Reimer Schmidt. Wiesbaden : Th. Gabler, c1981. v. <8-10 > ; 24 cm. (Gabler Studientexte) LC Card 86-171689
1. Insurance - Germany, West. I. Müller-Lutz, Heinz Leo. II. Schmidt, Reimer.
HG8618 .V47 1981

Verslag (South Africa. Central Statistical Services) .
(no. 02-80-16) Bevolkingsensus 1980, uitgesoekte statistiese streek Port Elizabeth/Uitenhage/Kirkwood =. [Pretoria] [1985] xix, 317 p. : ISBN 0-621-09480-3 : LC Card 85-241531
HA4701.Z9 P673 1985

(no. 02-80-22) Bevolkingsensus 1980, uitgesoekte statistiese streek, Pretoria/Wonderboom =. [Pretoria] [1985?] xx, 476 p. : ISBN 0-621-09483-8 : LC Card 85-238587
HA4701.Z9 P743 1985

(no. 02-80-23) Bevolkingsensus 1980 uitgesoekte statistiese streek Vereeniging/Vanderbijlpark/Sasolburg =. Pretoria [1985] xx, 301 p. : ISBN 0-621-09484-6 : LC Card 85-235498
HA4701.Z9 V474 1985

(no. 04-16-03) Sensus van motorhandel en hersteldienste, 1977 =. Pretoria [1982?] xiv, 166 p. : ISBN 0-621-07034-3 : LC Card 82-240419
HD9710.S72 S46 1982

(no. 06-01-15) Sensus van landbou- en veeteelproduksie, 1979 =. Pretoria [1985?] xiv, 266 p. ; ISBN 0-621-09380-7 : LC Card 86-150362 DDC 338.1/0968/021 19
HD2130.5 .S48 1985

(no. 18-01-02) Sensus van wassery-, skoonmaak- en kleurdienste, 1980 =. Pretoria [1984?] xiv, 59 p., [1] folded leaf of plates : ISBN 0-621-08730-0 : LC Card 86-122444
HD9999.L383 S67 1984

Verslag (South Africa. National Manpower Commission) .
(84, 1) South Africa. National Manpower Commission. Verslag van die Nasionale Mannekragkommissie oor 'n ondersoek na die kleinsakesektor in die Republiek van Suid-Afrika, in die besonder die faktore wat die groei en ontwikkeling daarvan kan belemmer =. [Pretoria] [1983] 58 p. ; ISBN 0-620-07511-2 LC Card 85-116407 DDC 338.6/42/0968 19
HD2346.S63 S64 1983

(84,2) Verslag van die Nasionale Mannekragkommissie oor indiensopleiding in die Republiek van Suid-Afrika, 1980/81 =. [Pretoria] [1984] 267 p. ; ISBN 0-621-08502-2 : LC Card 86-109914
HF5549.5.T7 V44 1984

Verslag van die Gekose Komitee oor Tolfinansiering van Paaie =. South Africa. Parliament. House of Assembly. Select Committee on Toll Financing of Roads. [Pretoria] [1982] xix, 54 p. ; ISBN 0-621-07457-8 : LC Card 83-215629
HE367.S63 T647 1982

Verslag van die Nasionale Mannekragkommissie oor indiensopleiding in die Republiek van Suid-Afrika, 1980/81 = Report of the National Manpower Commission on in-service training in the Republic of South Africa, 1980/81. [Pretoria] : Departement van Mannekrag : Verkrygbaar by die Staatsdrukker, [1984] 267 p. ; 30 cm. (Verslag / Nasionale Mannekragkommissie = Report / National Manpower Commission . 2/1984) Afrikaans and English. ISBN 0-621-08502-2 : LC Card 86-109914
1. Employees, Training of - South Africa. 2. Manpower planning - South Africa. I. Title: Report of the National Manpower Commission on in-service training in the Republic of South Africa, 1980/81. II. Series: Verslag (South Africa. National Manpower Commission) , 84,2.
HF5549.5.T7 V44 1984

Verslag van die Nasionale Mannekragkommissie oor 'n ondersoek na die kleinsakesektor in die Republiek van Suid-Afrika, in die besonder die faktore wat die groei en ontwikkeling daarvan kan belemmer =. South Africa. National Manpower Commission. [Pretoria] [1983] 58 p. ; ISBN 0-620-07511-2 LC Card 85-116407 DDC 338.6/42/0968 19
HD2346.S63 S64 1983

Verso un sistema di orientamento : dalla sperimentazione all'innovazione / a cura di Antonio Augenti e Umberto Margiotta. Rimini : Maggioli, c1984. 290 p. : ill. ; 24 cm. (Scuola lavoro . 1) Bibliography: p. [289]-290. LC Card 85-119196 DDC 370.11/3/094 19
1. Labor and laboring classes - Education - Italy. 2. Labor and laboring classes - Education - Europe. 3. Vocational guidance - Italy. 4. Vocational guidance - Europe. I. Augenti, Antonio. II. Margiotta, Umberto.
LC5056.I8 V47 1984 ***NYPL [JLE 86-1555]***

Verso una società dell'informazione . Plan for information society-a national goal toward year 2000. Italian. Milano , 1974. 157 p. :
NYPL [TB (Studi e ricerche di scienze sociali. v.60)]

Verspaget, Josephine. Honger op ons bord . Amsterdam , 1986. 164 p. : ISBN 90-70985-05-5 : LC Card 86-166714
HD9000.5 .H655 1986

Verstaatliche Industrie . Tieber, Herbert. Wien , c1983. 91 p. : LC Card 84-169053
HD4155 .T54 1983

Verteilungsschwankungen im Konjunkturverlauf . Flaig, Jürgen. Freiburg im Breisgau , c1983. vi, 221 p. : ISBN 3-448-01325-0 LC Card 83-155341
HC290.5.I5 F55 1983

Verteilungswirkungen der Einkommensteuer /. Scheer, Christian. Göttingen , c1982. xii, 457 p. : ISBN 3-509-01260-7 : LC Card 83-150522
HJ4719 .S34 1982

Verteilungswirkungen von Erdölpreissteigerungen . Schmassmann, Norbert. Diessenhofen , c1983. viii, 326 p. : ISBN 3-7253-0203-0 LC Card 83-219477
HD9575.S92 S27 1983

VERTICAL INTEGRATION.
Casson, Mark, 1945- Multinationals and world trade . London , Boston , 1986. xi, 401 p. : ISBN 0-04-338125-1 (alk. paper) LC Card 85-15734 DDC 338.8/8 19
HD2748 .C37 1986 ***NYPL [JLD 86-1224]***

Kremeyer, Heinz. Eigenfertigung und Fremdbezug unter finanzwirtschaftlichen Aspekten /. Wiesbaden , c1982. 330 p. : ISBN 3-409-37340-3 LC Card 83-148058
HD2748 .K74 1982

VERTICAL INTEGRATION - CASE STUDIES.
Casson, Mark, 1945- Multinationals and world trade . London , Boston , 1986. xi, 401 p. : ISBN 0-04-338125-1 (alk. paper) LC Card 85-15734 DDC 338.8/8 19
HD2748 .C37 1986 ***NYPL [JLD 86-1224]***

VERTICAL INTEGRATION - CONGRESSES.
New developments in the analysis of market structure . Cambridge, Mass. , 1986. xxiv, 559 p. : ISBN 0-262-19241-1 LC Card 85-4246 DDC 338.8 19
HD2326 .N43 1986 ***NYPL [JLD 86-3570]***

VERTICAL INTEGRATION - GOVERNMENT POLICY - CANADA.
Mathewson, G. Frank, 1942- Competition policy and vertical exchange /. Toronto , Buffalo , c1985. xvii, 119 p. : ISBN 0-8020-7248-8 (pbk.) LC Card 86-672936 DDC 338.6/048/0971 19
HF1480 .M37 1985 ***NYPL [JLE 87-512]***

VERTICAL INTEGRATION - ITALY.
Le Strategie di acquisto della grande impresa nell'evoluzione dei sistemi produttivi . Milano, Italy , c1985. 223 p. : LC Card 85-233748
HD85.I7 I68 no. 76 HD39.5
NYPL [JLD 87-426]

Les vertiges de la finance internationale /. Bourguinat, Henri. Paris , c1987. 295 p. : ISBN 2-7178-1214-8 : LC Card 87-131661
HG3881 .B629 1987

Vertin, James R. Management Skills for Investment Managers Seminar (1982 : Washington, D.C.) Management Skills for Investment Managers Seminar . Charlottesville, Va. (P.O. Box 3668, Charlottesville 22903) , c1983. vi, 62 p. : LC Card 83-244808 DDC 658.1/52 19
HG4621 .M36 1982 ***NYPL [JLF 87-425]***

Vertriebswirtschaftliche Abhandlungen. For earlier file, see entry in Old Catalog.
(Heft 24) Hildebrandt, Lutz. Konfirmatorische Analysen von Modellen des Konsumentenverhaltens /. Berlin , c1983. xii, 307 p. : ISBN 3-428-05381-8 LC Card 83-190106
HF5415.3 .H55 1983

Vervest, Peter. Innovation in electronic mail : towards open information networks : perspectives on innovation policy / Peter H.M. Vervest. Amsterdam ; New York : North-Holland ; xv, 212 p. : ill. ; 24 cm. Bibliography: p. 201-208. Includes index. ISBN 0-444-70153-2 LC Card 87-11145 DDC 384.3/4 19
1. Electronic mail systems. 2. Telecommunication. I.

Title.
HE6239.E54 V47 1987

Die Verwaltung als betriebliches Teilsystem . Schauer, Reinbert. Wien , 1984. v, 258 p. : ISBN 3-85436-014-2 LC Card 84-173337
HD35 .S2655 1984

Verwaltung und Planung im Wandel / hrsg. von Otto Krabs. Köln : Grote, 1979. 112 p. ; 23 cm. (Programme, Analysen, Tatbestände . Bd. 6) Includes bibliographical references. ISBN 3-7745-6438-8 : LC Card 81-473982
1. Regional planning - Germany, West - Addresses, essays, lectures. 2. Political planning - Germany, West - Addresses, essays, lectures. 3. Social change - Addresses, essays, lectures. 4. Germany, West - Social policy - Addresses, essays, lectures. I. Krabs, Otto. II. Series.
HT395.G4 V48 ***NYPL [JLE 86-2107]***

Verwaltung und Ungeld in Basel, 1360-1535 . Rosen, Josef. Stuttgart , 1986. 231 p. ; ISBN 3-515-03348-3 : LC Card 86-184510
HG1160.B37 R67 1986

Verwey, Norma Ellen. Radio call-ins and covert politics : a verbal unit and role analysis approach / Norma Ellen Verwey. Aldershot, Hants, England ; Brookfield, Vt., U. S.A. : Gower, 1987. p. cm. Bibliography: p. Includes index. ISBN 0-566-05349-7 : LC Card 86-33490 DDC 324.7/3 19
1. Radio in politics - Canada. 2. Radio in politics - Great Britain. I. Title.
HE8697.P6 V47 1987

VERY HIGH SPEED INTEGRATED CIRCUITS.
VHSIC . Norwalk, Conn., U. S.A. (6 Prowitt St., Norwalk 06855) , c1986. v, 219 leaves : LC Card 86-224890 DDC 381/.4562138173/0973 19
HD9696.I582 V47 1986

De Verzorgingsstaat, slopen of renoveren? / W. Albeda ... [et al.] ; redactie, W. Albeda, J. Wemelsfelder. Assen : Van Gorcum, 1986. 152 p. : ill. ; 22 cm. Bibliography: p. 148. Includes index. ISBN 90-232-2180-X : LC Card 86-186673
1. Netherlands - Economic conditions - 1945-. 2. Welfare state. I. Albeda, W. II. Wemelsfelder, Jozias.
HC325 .V45 1986

Veselov, A. P. (Anatoliĭ Pavlovich) Bor'ba Kommunisticheskoĭ partii za provedenie kul'turnoĭ revoli͡utsii v derevne v gody kollektivizat͡sii / A.P. Veselov. Leningrad : Izd-vo Leningradskogo universiteta, 1978. 127 p. ; 21 cm. At head of title: Ministerstvo vysshego i srednego spet͡sial'nogo obrazovanii͡a RSFSR. Includes bibliographical references. LC Card 81-166878
1. Collectivization of agriculture - Russian S.F.S.R. - History. 2. Russian S.F.S.R. - Cultural policy. 3. Russian S.F.S.R. - Rural conditions. I. Title.
HD1492.S652 R878 1978

Veseth, Michael.
Clark, J. R. (Jeff R.) Macroeconomics . San Diego , c1987. xv, 574 p. : ISBN 0-15-551226-9 (pbk.) LC Card 86-83043 DDC 339 19
HB172.5 .C585 1987

Clark, J. R. (Jeff R.) Microeconomics . San Diego , c1987. xii, 454 p. : ISBN 0-15-551225-0 (pbk.) LC Card 86-83044 DDC 338.5 19
HB172 .C543 1987

VESSELS (SHIPS) see SHIPS.

Vesterås, Kjell. Industrimakten Japan . Oslo , 1982. 151 p. : ISBN 82-518-1630-0 : LC Card 84-126986
HD70.J3 I549 1982

Vesterø Jensen, Carsten. Det tvedelte pensionssystem / af Carsten Vesterø Jensen. Roskilde : Roskilde universitetscenter, [1984] 284 p. ; 21 cm. (Forskningsrapport / Institut for samfundsøkonomi og planlægning, Roskilde universitetscenter, 0105-8827 . nr. 1/84) Cover title. "Marts 1984." Bibliography: p. 273-284. LC Card 84-181865
1. Old age pensions - Denmark. 2. Social security - Denmark. I. Series: Research report (Roskilde universitetscenter. Institut for samfundsøkonomi og planlægning) , 1984/nr. 1. II. Title.
HD7105.35.D4 J45 1984

The Vestey affair /. Knightley, Phillip. London , 1981. 159 p., [8] p. of plates : ISBN 0-354-04708-6 : LC Card 81-193209 DDC 343.4104/092/2 344.10340922 19
HD2753.G7 K55 1981

VESTEY FAMILY.
Knightley, Phillip. The Vestey affair /. London , 1981. 159 p., [8] p. of plates : ISBN 0-354-04708-6 : LC Card 81-193209 DDC 343.4104/092/2 344.10340922 19
HD2753.G7 K55 1981

VESTIBULE SCHOOLS. see EMPLOYEES, TRAINING OF.

A veszélyhelyzetbe került vállalatok és a gazdaságirányítás /. Veress, József, Dr. Budapest , 1986. 207, [1] p. ; ISBN 963-221-778-0 : LC Card 87-136695
HG3769.H94 V47 1986

Veszprém, Hungary (City). Vegyipari Egyetem. see **Veszprémi Vegyipari Egyetem.**

Veszprémi Vegyipari Egyetem. Specht, Günter. Industrielles Beschaffungsverhalten . Frankfurt am Main , New York , c1985. iii, 167 p. : ISBN 3-8204-8938-X LC Card 86-120719
HD9654.5 .S64 1985

Vetencourt Guerra, Lola. El Imperio Británico en la economía de Venezuela, 1830-1870 / Lola Vetencourt Guerra. Caracas : Universidad Central de Venezuela, Facultad de Ciencias Económicas y Sociales, División de Publicaciones, 1981. 233 p. : ill. ; 23 cm. (Colección Libros) Bibliography: p. 185-195. LC Card 83-201772
1. Venezuela - Foreign economic relations - Great Britain. 2. Great Britain - Foreign economic relations - Venezuela. I. Title.
HF1530.5.G7 V47 1981

Vetenskap och företagsledning : studier i ekonomi och ledarskap tillägnade Lars Wahlbeck : essays in economics and management in honour of Lars Wahlbeck. Helsingfors : Svenska handelshögskolan, 1982. 461 p. : ill. ; 25 cm. (Ekonomi och samhälle. nr. 31) English and Swedish. Includes bibliographies. ISBN 951-555-158-7 LC Card 82-239854
1. Economics. 2. Management. 3. Wahlbeck, Lars. I. Wahlbeck, Lars. II. Title: Essays in economics and management in honour of Lars Wahlbeck. III. Series: Ekonomi och samhälle (Svenska handelshögskolan (Helsinki, Finland)) , nr. 31.
HB71 .V45 1982

Vetenskapsakademiens internationella institut för energi och humanekologi, Beijerinstitutet. Hosier, Richard. Energy use in rural Kenya . Stockholm , Uppsala , c1985. xi, 177 p. : ISBN 91-7106-241-6 ***NYPL [JLD 86-2653]***

VETERANS - SOVIET UNION - BIOGRAPHY.
Vernulsi͡a soldat k poli͡u, 1945-1985 /. Moskva , 1985. 429, [16] p. : LC Card 85-228297
HD1536.S65 V47 1985

Vetter, Gerlinde, 1954- Knapp, Johannes, 1953- Argentinien und Australien . Heidelberg , c1983. 151 p. : ISBN 3-88326-129-7 LC Card 83-240132
HC175 .K58 1983

Vettori, Arthur. Finanzhaushalt und Wirtschaftsverwaltung Basels (1689-1798) : Wirtschafts- und Lebensverhältnisse einer Gesellschaft zwischen Tradition und Umbruch / von Arthur Vettori. Basel : Helbing & Lichtenhahn, 1984. xv, 439 p. : ill. ; 24 cm. (Basler Beiträge zur Geschichtswissenschaft. Bd. 149) Bibliography: p. vii-xiv. ISBN 3-7190-0878-9 LC Card 85-132787
1. Finance, Public - Switzerland - Basel (Canton) - History. 2. Finance, Public - Switzerland - Basel-Stadt - History. 3. Basel (Switzerland : Canton) - Economic conditions. 4. Basel-Stadt (Switzerland) - Economic conditions. I. Title. II. Series.
HJ1264.B3 V47 1984

Vezetés a gyakorlatban /. Berey, András. Budapest , 1986. 313 p. : ISBN 963-221-903-1 : LC Card 87-138251
HD37.H82 B486 1986

A vezetők részvétele a vezetésben /. Héthy, Lajos. Budapest , 1983. 87 p. : ISBN 963-608-057-7 LC Card 85-110905
HD38.25.H9 H47 1983

A vezetők véleményezése /. Várkonyi, Margit. Budapest , 1984. 66 p. : ISBN 963-322-189-7 : LC Card 85-176949
HD70.H8 V38 1984

Vézina, Pierre, 1935- Foreign currency translation : an analysis of section 1650 of the CICA handbook / Pierre Vézina. Toronto, Canada : Canadian Institute of Chartered Accountants, c1985. 94 p. ; 23 cm. ISBN 0-88800-133-9 LC Card 86-201703 DDC 657/.48 19
1. Foreign exchange - Accounting - Standards - Canada. 2. Financial statements - Standards - Canada. I. Canadian Institute of Chartered Accountants. CICA handbook. II. Title.
HG3853.7 .V49 1985

VGM career books.
Paradis, Adrian A. Opportunities in vocational & technical careers /. Lincolnwood, Ill., U. S.A. , c1987. xi, 147 p. : ISBN 0-8442-6018-5 LC Card 87-60104 DDC 371.4/25/02373 19
HF5382.5.U5 P28 1987

Schrayer, Robert M. Opportunities in insurance careers /. Lincolnwood, Ill., U. S.A. , c1987. xi, 145 p. : ISBN 0-8442-6008-8 LC Card 87-60102 DDC 368/.0023/73 19
HG8531 .S37 1987

VGM's careers encyclopedia / edited by Craig T. Norback. [2nd ed.]. Lincolnwood, Ill., U. S.A. : VGM Career Horizons, c1988. xi, 484 p. ; 25 cm. Rev. ed. of: Careers encyclopedia. c1980. Includes index. ISBN 0-8442-6132-7 LC Card 87-62404 DDC 331.7/02/0973 19
1. Vocational guidance - United States. 2. United States - Occupations. I. Norback, Craig T. II. Careers encyclopedia. III. Title: Careers encyclopedia.
HF5382.5.U5 C337 1988

VHSIC : military & commercial opportunities. Norwalk, Conn., U. S.A. (6 Prowitt St., Norwalk 06855) : International Resource Development, Inc., c1986. v, 219 leaves : ill. ; 28 cm. (Report / International Resource Development Inc. . #705) "July 1986." LC Card 86-224890 DDC 381/.4562138173/0973 19
1. Integrated circuits industry. 2. Very high speed integrated circuits. 3. Market surveys. 4. Integrated circuits industry - United States. 5. Market surveys - United States. I. International Resource Development, inc. II. Series: Report / International Resource Development Inc. , #705.
HD9696.I582 V47 1986

Vi Kinh t Hà N 1983. 154 p. ; LC Card 87-153552
HC444 .K56 1983

VI censo general de población y IV de viviendas, 1985. Recuentos preliminares . [Montevideo] [1986] 188 p. : LC Card 87-122427 DDC 304.6/09895/021 19
HA1074 1985

Vía crucis económico, 1982-86 /. Herken Krauer, Pablo Alfredo. Asunción , 1986. 523 p. ; LC Card 86-226871
HC222 .H48 1986

The Viability of employment initiatives involving women : programme of research and actions on the development of the labour market / by Centre for Research on European Women, CREW. Luxembourg : Office for Official Publications of the European Communities ; Washington, DC : European Community Information Service [distributor], 1986. 1 v. (various pagings) ; 30 cm. ISBN 92-825-6088-0 (pbk.) : LC Card 87-137342 DDC 331.4/12/094 19
1. Women in cooperative societies - European Economic Community countries. 2. Women in cooperative societies - European Economic Community countries - Case studies. 3. Employment - Women - European Economic Community countries. I. Centre for Research on European Women.
HD3423.5.E86 V5 1986

Vianna, Maria Lúcia Teixeira Werneck. A administração do "milagre" : o Conselho Monetário Nacional, 1964-1974 / Maria Lúcia Teixeira Werneck Vianna. Petrópolis : Vozes, 1987. 180 p. ; 21 cm. Originally presented as the author's thesis (mestrado em ciência política)--Instituto Universitário de Pesquisas do Rio de Janeiro, 1981. Includes bibliographical references. LC Card 87-403982 DDC 332.4/981 19
1. Conselho Monetário Nacional (Brazil) - History. 2. Monetary policy - Brazil - History - 20th century. 3. Brazil - Economic policy. I. Title.
HG835 .V527 1987

Vianna, Pedro Jorge Ramos. Inflação vs. indexação, uma contribuição ao tema / Pedro

Jorge Ramos Vianna. Fortaleza-Ceará : Federação das Indústrias do Estado do Ceará : Instituto Euvaldo Lodi-Núcleo Regional do Ceará, [19]84. 121 p. : ill. ; 21 cm. Cover title: Inflação x indexação, uma contribuição ao tema. Bibliography: p. 120-121. LC Card 86-130092
1. Inflation (Finance) - Brazil. 2. Indexation (Economics) - Brazil. 3. Monetary policy - Brazil. 4. Brazil - Economic policy. I. Federação das Indústrias do Estado do Ceará. II. Instituto Euvaldo Lodi. Núcleo Regional do Ceará. III. Title: Inflação x indexação, uma contribuição ao tema. IV. Title: Inflação versus indexação, uma contribuição ao tema.
HG835 .V53 1984

VICA (Association) VICA United States Skill Olympics regulations. Leesburg, Va. (P.O. Box 3000, Leesburg 22075) : Vocational Industrial Clubs of America, c1986. 113 p. : ill. ; 28 cm. LC Card 87-129841 DDC 331.7/02/06073 19
1. VICA (Association). 2. Youth - United States - Societies and clubs. I. Title.
HF5381.A1 V4 1986

VICA (ASSOCIATION)
VICA (Association) VICA United States Skill Olympics regulations. Leesburg, Va. (P.O. Box 3000, Leesburg 22075) , c1986. 113 p. : LC Card 87-129841 DDC 331.7/02/06073 19
HF5381.A1 V4 1986

VICA United States Skill Olympics regulations. VICA (Association) Leesburg, Va. (P.O. Box 3000, Leesburg 22075) , c1986. 113 p. : LC Card 87-129841 DDC 331.7/02/06073 19
HF5381.A1 V4 1986

Vicario, Luis B.
Algunas características del inventario de vivienda : anticipándose al próximo censo de población y vivienda de 1985 / Luis B. Vicario. [Montevideo] : Intendencia Municipal de Montevideo, 1985. 42 p. : ill. ; 30 cm. LC Card 86-152477
1. Housing - Uruguay - Montevideo. 2. Public utilities - Uruguay - Montevideo. I. Montevideo (Uruguay). Intendencia Municipal. II. Title.
HD7330.M64 V53 1985

Lineamientos básicos del Programa Habitacional de Emergencia, 1985-86 / Luis B. Vicario. [Montevideo] : Intendencia Municipal de Montevideo, 1985. 25 p. : ill. ; 23 cm. LC Card 87-122422 DDC 363.5/8 19
1. Emergency housing - Government policy - Uruguay - Montevideo. 2. Poor - Housing - Uruguay - Montevideo. 3. Homeless persons - Housing - Uruguay - Montevideo. I. Montevideo (Uruguay). Intendencia Municipal. II. Title.
HD7287.96.U82 M668 1985

Vicedo i Rius, Enric. Materials per a l'estudi geogràfic dels pobles de l'àrea econòmica de Bellpuig /. [Lleida , 1985. 253 p. : LC Card 87-131722
HA1559.B45 M38 1985

VICENZA (ITALY : PROVINCE) - INDUSTRIES - HISTORY.
Spagnolo, Mario. Industria e movimento operaio a Vicenza . Vicenza , 1983. 107 p., [1] leaf of plate : LC Card 85-175207
HD6714.V53 S63 1983

Vicker, Ray. The Dow Jones-Irwin guide to retirement planning / Ray Vicker. 2nd ed. Homewood, Ill. : Dow Jones-Irwin, c1987. ix, 332 p. : ill. ; 24 cm. Includes index. ISBN 1-556-23005-2 LC Card 86-72973 DDC 332.024/01 19
1. Aged - United States - Finance, Personal. 2. Retirement income - United States. I. Title. II. Title: Guide to retirement planning. III. Title: Retirement planning.
HG179 .V54 1987

Vickers, John, 1958- The Economics of market dominance /. Oxford, UK , New York, NY, USA , 1987. p. cm. ISBN 0-631-14784-5 : LC Card 86-26416 DDC 338.8/2 19
HD2326 .E24 1987

Vickerstaff, Sarah, 1944- Sheldrake, John, 1944- The history of industrial training in Britain /. Aldershot Hants, England , Brookfield, Vt., USA , c1987. v, 75 p. ; ISBN 0-566-05294-6 : LC Card 86-29601 DDC 331.25/92 19
HD5715.5.G7 S54 1987

Vickman, Thomas M. Handbook of model accounting reports and formats / Thomas M. Vickman. Englewood Cliffs, N.J. : Prentice-Hall, c1987. xvii, 350 p. : ill., port. ; 29 cm. Includes index. ISBN 0-13-380338-4 : LC Card 86-15068 DDC 658.1/512 19
1. Managerial accounting - Handbooks, manuals, etc. 2. Financial statements - Handbooks, manuals, etc. 3. Corporation reports - Handbooks, manuals, etc. I. Title.
HF5635 .V53 1987 ***NYPL [JLF 87-214]***

VICTIMOLOGY. see **VICTIMS OF CRIMES.**

VICTIMS OF CRIMES - GERMANY, WEST.
Pitsela, Angelika. Straffälligkeit und Viktimisierung ausländischer Minderheiten in der Bundesrepublik Deutschland . Freiburg [i.B.] , 1986. xxvii, 479 p. ; ISBN 3-922498-16-7 LC Card 87-131111 DDC 331.6/2/495043 19
HD8458.G7 P57 1986

VICTIMS OF FAMINE - ETHIOPIA.
Faces in a famine [motion picture] /. New York, N.Y. , 1985. 1 film reel (51 min.) : LC Card 85-702803 DDC 963 11
HC845.Z9F3

Faces in a famine [videorecording] /. New York, N.Y. , 1985. 1 videocassette (51 min.) : LC Card 85-703663 DDC 963 11
HC845.Z9F3

VICTIMS OF FAMINES - GREECE - DIARIES.
Maroudēs, Giōrgos. To hēmerologio tēs peinas /. [Athens] , 1976. 99 p., [6] leaves of plates ; LC Card 84-107778
HC300.F3 M37 1976

Victoire définitive sur le chômage . Marquis, Benoît, 1932- [Montréal] , c1984. 176, [3] p. : ISBN 2-9800322-0-4 LC Card 84-191778 DDC 331.13/77 19
HD5707.5 .M37 1984 ***NYPL [JLD 86-2652]***

Victor Michel : fidélité et courage. Bruxelles : Vie ouvrière, c1985. 263 p., [8] p. of plates : ill., ports. ; 24 cm. Includes bibliographical references. ISBN 2-87003-189-0 : LC Card 86-163882
1. Michel, Victor Joseph Jules, 1915-1982. 2. Trade-unions - Belgium - Officials and employees - Biography. 3. Jeunesse ouvrière chrétienne (France) - History. I. Michel, Victor Joseph Jules, 1915-1982.
HD6722.5.M52 V52 1985

Victoria. Dept. of Management and Budget. Victorian public sector debt. [Melbourne, Vic.] [1986] vii, 57, [1] p. ; LC Card 87-165135 DDC 336.3/4/09945 19
HJ8857.V53 V53 1986

Victoria. Ministerial Advisory Committee on Co-operation. The co-operative way : Victoria's third sector : M.A.C.C. report 1986. Melbourne : Ministry of Housing, 1986. viii, 151 p. : col. ill. ; 25 cm. ISBN 0-7241-5172-9 (pbk.) LC Card 87-158122 DDC 334/.09945 19
1. Cooperation - Australia - Victoria. 2. Cooperative societies - Australia - Victoria. I. Title.
HD3570.A6 V538 1986

Victoria. Parliament.
Victoria. Parliament. Public Bodies Review Committee. Report on the Victorian Wheat Advisory Committee . Melbourne [1986] xiii, 34 p. ; LC Card 87-168597 DDC 338.1/7311/09945 19
HD9049.W5 A949 1986

Victoria. Parliament. Public Bodies Review Committee.
Report on the Victorian Wheat Advisory Committee : fourteenth report to the Parliament / Parliament of Victoria, Public Bodies Review Committee. Melbourne : F.D. Atkinson Govt. Printer, [1986] xiii, 34 p. ; 26 cm. "May 1986." "No. 84." LC Card 87-168597 DDC 338.1/7311/09945 19
1. Wheat trade - Australia - Victoria. 2. Wheat trade - Government policy - Australia - Victoria. 3. Victorian Wheat Advisory Committee. I. Victoria. Parliament. II. Title.
HD9049.W5 A949 1986

Reports on the Tobacco Leaf Marketing Board, Tobacco Quota Committee, Tobacco Quota Appeals Tribunal : sixteenth, seventeenth, and eighteenth reports to the Parliament / Parliament of Victoria, Public Bodies Review Committee. Melbourne : F.D. Atkinson Govt. Printer, [1986] xix, 107 p. ; 25 cm. Title on spine: Sixteenth, seventeenth, and eighteenth reports to the Parliament on tobacco bodies. Title on cover: Reviews of the Tobacco Leaf Marketing Board, Tobacco Quota Committee, Tobacco Quota Appeals Tribunal. "May 1986"--Cover. "No. 86." "October 1986." Bibliography: p. 105-107. LC Card 87-168528 DDC 354.9450082/332 19
1. Tobacco industry - Government policy - Australia - Victoria. 2. Victoria. Tobacco Leaf Marketing Board. 3. Victoria. Tobacco Quota Appeals Tribunal. 4. Victoria. Tobacco Quota Committee. I. Title. II. Title: Sixteenth, seventeenth, and eighteenth reports to the Parliament on tobacco bodies. III. Title: Reviews of the Tobacco Leaf Marketing Board, Tobacco Quota Committee, Tobacco Quota Appeals Tribunal.
HD9148.A8 V53 1986

Victoria. Saleyard Working Party. Distribution of saleyards in Victoria : report / prepared by the Saleyard Working Party. [Melbourne] : Dept. of Agriculture and Rural Affairs : Ministry for Planning and Environment, 1986. 69, 7, 7 p. : ill. ; 30 cm. Bibliography: p. 69. LC Card 87-159450 DDC 338.1/760831 19
1. Meat industry and trade - Australia - Victoria - Location. 2. Stockyards - Australia - Victoria - Location. 3. Beef industry - Australia - Victoria - Location. 4. Sheep industry - Australia - Victoria - Location. 5. Pork industry and trade - Australia - Victoria - Location. I. Title.
HD9428.A83 V538 1986

VICTORIA. TOBACCO LEAF MARKETING BOARD.
Victoria. Parliament. Public Bodies Review Committee. Reports on the Tobacco Leaf Marketing Board, Tobacco Quota Committee, Tobacco Quota Appeals Tribunal . Melbourne [1986] xix, 107 p. ; LC Card 87-168528 DDC 354.9450082/332 19
HD9148.A8 V53 1986

VICTORIA. TOBACCO QUOTA APPEALS TRIBUNAL.
Victoria. Parliament. Public Bodies Review Committee. Reports on the Tobacco Leaf Marketing Board, Tobacco Quota Committee, Tobacco Quota Appeals Tribunal . Melbourne [1986] xix, 107 p. ; LC Card 87-168528 DDC 354.9450082/332 19
HD9148.A8 V53 1986

VICTORIA. TOBACCO QUOTA COMMITTEE.
Victoria. Parliament. Public Bodies Review Committee. Reports on the Tobacco Leaf Marketing Board, Tobacco Quota Committee, Tobacco Quota Appeals Tribunal . Melbourne [1986] xix, 107 p. ; LC Card 87-168528 DDC 354.9450082/332 19
HD9148.A8 V53 1986

Victorian public sector debt. [Melbourne, Vic.] : Dept. of Management and Budget, [1986] vii, 57, [1] p. ; 25 cm. (Information paper / Department of Management and Budget . no. 2) Bibliography: p. [58] LC Card 87-165135 DDC 336.3/4/09945 19
1. Debts, Public - Australia - Victoria. 2. Debts, External - Australia - Victoria. I. Victoria. Dept. of Management and Budget. II. Series: Information paper (Victoria. Dept. of Management and Budget) , no. 2.
HJ8857.V53 V53 1986

VICTORIAN WHEAT ADVISORY COMMITTEE.
Victoria. Parliament. Public Bodies Review Committee. Report on the Victorian Wheat Advisory Committee . Melbourne [1986] xiii, 34 p. ; LC Card 87-168597 DDC 338.1/7311/09945 19
HD9049.W5 A949 1986

Vicuña Izquierdo, Leonardo. Movimiento obrero del Ecuador, 1970-1979 . Guayaquil, Ecuador [1985] 300 p. ; LC Card 86-105256 DDC 331.88/09866 19
HD6627 .M68 1985 ***NYPL [JLD 86-3140]***

"VIDA" (FACTORY)
Po visochinite na sŭrtseto . Sofiīa , 1986. 75 p., [16] p. of plates : LC Card 87-101682
HD8039.C62 B97 1986

Vida y muerte de un latifundio /. Laviada, Iñigo. México , 1984. xiii, 259 p., [6] leaves of plates : LC Card 86-208690
HD1471.M62 H535 1984

Vidal, Máximo Luis. El fin de la era del petróleo y su impacto sobre la economía mundial : con especial énfasis sobre la economía de la República Dominicana / Máximo Luis Vidal. San Pedro de Macorís, R.D. : Universidad Central del Este, 1981. 103 p. : ill. ; 23 cm. (Serie científica. no. 11) Bibliography: p. 102-103. LC Card 82-202556

1. Alcohol fuel industry - Dominican Republic. 2. Renewable energy sources - Dominican Republic. 3. Petroleum industry and trade - Economic aspects. I. Series: Serie científica (Universidad Central del Este) . II. Title.
HD9502.5.A433 D658 1981

Video democracy . Hollander, Richard S. Mt. Airy, Md. , c1985. ix, 161 p. : ISBN 0-912338-51-2 LC Card 85-81818 DDC 384.55/5 19
HE8700.76.U6 H65 1985 *NYPL [MWGT 86-1503]*

VIDEO DISC INDUSTRY - UNITED STATES - MANAGEMENT.
Parrish, Vernon. Great American video retailing . Arlington, Va. [1983?] viii, 448 p. : ISBN 0-9615774-0-1 LC Card 85-90437 DDC 621.388/332/0688 19
HD9697.V543 U544 1983

VIDEO DISK INDUSTRY - UNITED STATES.
Interactive videodisk software market. New York, N.Y. , c1983. iv, 228 leaves ; LC Card 87-143767
HD9696.C63 U518378 1983

VIDEO DISPLAY TERMINALS - HEALTH ASPECTS.
Dy, Fe Josefina F. Visual display units . Geneva , 1985. ix, 138 p. : ISBN 92-2-105083-1 (pbk.) : LC Card 86-214267 DDC 651.8 19
HF5547.5 .D9 1985

Video Lab (Hudson, N.H.) People skills in action, for loan officers and processors. Chicago, Ill. , 1986. 1 videocassette (20 min.) : LC Card 86-707349 DDC 658.8 11
HG1641

VIDEO TAPE INDUSTRY - ITALY.
Il Consumo dell'audiovisivo /. Milano, Italy , c1984. 173 p. : LC Card 85-178903
HE8700.66.I8 C66 1984

VIDEO TAPE INDUSTRY - UNITED STATES - MANAGEMENT.
Parrish, Vernon. Great American video retailing . Arlington, Va. [1983?] viii, 448 p. : ISBN 0-9615774-0-1 LC Card 85-90437 DDC 621.388/332/0688 19
HD9697.V543 U544 1983

VIDEO TAPE RECORDER INDUSTRY - EUROPE.
Tydeman, John. New media in Europe . London , New York , c1986. xii, 260 p. : ISBN 0-07-084799-1 : LC Card 85-19839 DDC 384.55/094 19
HE8700.9.E8 T93 1986 *NYPL [JLE 86-3209]*

VIDEO TAPES - UNITED STATES - CONGRESSES.
Advertising Research Foundation Key Issues Workshop (1986 : New York, N.Y.) Transcript proceedings . New York, NY (3 E. 54th St., New York 10022-3180) , c1986. 214 p. : LC Card 87-404527 DDC 659.14/3/0973 19
HF6146.T42 A27 1986

VIDEO TELEPHONE INDUSTRY - UNITED STATES.
Video telephony markets. Norwalk, Conn., U. S.A. (6 Prowitt St., Norwalk 06855) , c1986. ii, 96 leaves : LC Card 86-224725 DDC 381/.45621386 19
HD9697.T453 U58 1986

Video telephony markets. Norwalk, Conn., U. S.A. (6 Prowitt St., Norwalk 06855) : International Resource Development, c1986. ii, 96 leaves : ill. ; 28 cm. (Report / International Resource Development Inc. . #695) "May 1986." LC Card 86-224725 DDC 381/.45621386 19
1. Video telephone industry - United States. 2. Market surveys - United States. I. International Resource Development, inc. II. Series: Report / International Resource Development Inc. , #695.
HD9697.T453 U58 1986

VIDEOTEX (DATA TRANSMISSION SYSTEM) - EUROPE.
Howard-Healy, Marion. Aspects of the new media in Europe /. Menlo Park, CA (333 Ravenswood Ave., Menlo Park 94025) , c1986. 22 leaves : LC Card 86-220771 DDC 384/.094 19
HE8700.72.E85 H69 1986

VIDEOTEX (DATA TRANSMISSION SYSTEM) - FRANCE.
Moore, L. K. S. (Linda K. S.) Videotext and home banking services in France. New York, NY (654 Madison Ave., New York 10021) , c1986. 59, 3 leaves : LC Card 86-203144 DDC 332.1/028 19
HG1711 .M66 1986

The Videotex marketplace. 1st ed. Bethesda, Md. : Phillips Pub., c1984. 203 p. : ill. ; 28 cm. Includes indexes. ISBN 0-934960-17-8 (pbk.) : LC Card 84-201507 DDC 384 19
1. Data transmission equipment industry - United States. 2. Data transmission equipment industry - United States - Directories. 3. Videotex systems. 4. Market surveys - United States. I. Phillips Publishing.
HD9696.D383 U638 1984 *NYPL [JSF 86-430]*

VIDEOTEX SYSTEMS.
Alber, Antone F. Videotex/teletext . New York , c1985. xiii, 498 p., [4] p. of plates : ISBN 0-07-000957-0 : LC Card 84-23319 DDC 384 19
TK5105 .A42 1985 *NYPL [JSE 86-1907]*

Rogers, Everett M. Communication technology . New York , London , c1986. xii, 273 p. : ISBN 0-02-927110-X LC Card 85-27555 DDC 621.38 19
TK5102.5 .R55 1986 *NYPL [JSE 86-1913]*

The Videotex marketplace. Bethesda, Md. , c1984. 203 p. : ISBN 0-934960-17-8 (pbk.) : LC Card 84-201507 DDC 384 19
HD9696.D383 U638 1984 *NYPL [JSF 86-430]*

VIDEOTEX SYSTEMS - GERMANY (WEST)
Götz, Gerd, 1956- Bildschirmtext . Berlin , c1985. xi, 285 p. : ISBN 3-8007-1348-9 LC Card 87-125311 DDC 384.3/5/0943 19
HD9696.T463 G346 1985

Schmidt-Prestin, Barbara, 1953- Bildschirmtext in Unternehmen . Bergisch Gladbach , c1986. xvi, 308 p. : ISBN 3-89012-064-4 LC Card 87-129114 DDC 651.8/0943 19
HD9696.T463 G365 1986

Schubert, Frank. Akzeptanz von Bildschirmtext in Unternehmungen und im Markt . Münster , c1986. xxiv, 316 p. : ISBN 3-7923-0546-1 LC Card 86-227074
HD9696.T463 G37 1986

VIDEOTEX SYSTEMS - SWITZERLAND.
Kalte Kommunikation . Basel , c1985. 256 p. : ISBN 3-85787-134-2 LC Card 85-232413
HD9696.T463 S95 1985

Videotex/teletext . Alber, Antone F. New York , c1985. xiii, 498 p., [4] p. of plates : ISBN 0-07-000957-0 : LC Card 84-23319 DDC 384 19
TK5105 .A42 1985 *NYPL [JSE 86-1907]*

Videotext and home banking services in France. Moore, L. K. S. (Linda K. S.) New York, NY (654 Madison Ave., New York 10021) , c1986. 59, 3 leaves : LC Card 86-203144 DDC 332.1/028 19
HG1711 .M66 1986

Vides de Orive, Enna. Análisis de la situación económica de Guatemala, 1965-1984 / Enna Vides de Orive, Pablo R. Schneider. 2a ed. Guatemala, Guatemala : CIEN, 1985. ii leaves, 118 p. : ill ; 22 x 28 cm. LC Card 86-205265 DDC 330.97281/053 19
1. Guatemala - Economic conditions - 1945-. I. Schneider, Pablo R. II. CIEN (Organization). III. Title.
HC144 .V53 1985

Vidinski, Lenin. Leninskite printsipi i uchastieto na trudeshtite se v upravlenieto / Lenin Vidinski. Sofiia : Profizdat, 1982. 196 p. : ill. ; 21 cm. Includes bibliographical references. LC Card 83-130010
1. Bulgaria - Economic policy - 1944-. 2. Management - Bulgaria - Employee participation. I. Title.
HC403 .V495 1982

Vidrovitch, Catherine Coquery- see **Coquery-Vidrovitch, Catherine.**

VIe Plan quinquennal de développement économique, social et culturel . Cameroon. Ministry of Planning and Land Management. [Yaoundé] [1986?] lxx, 325 p., [19] leaves of plates : LC Card 87-165935
HC995 .C335 1986

La vie quotidienne des mineurs au temps de Germinal /. Plessy, Bernard, 1939- [Paris] , c1984. 339 p. : ISBN 2-01-009272-4 : LC Card 85-160775
HD8039.M6152 F86 1984

La vie quotidienne en Angleterre au temps de l'expérience socialiste . Marx, Roland. [Paris] , c1983. 323 p. ; ISBN 2-01-008679-1 : LC Card 83-220426
HC256.5 .M3955 1983

Viebrock, Helmut, 1912- Sozialreform und Rhetorik =. Wiesbaden , 1984. 174 p. ; ISBN 3-515-02857-9 *NYPL [L-11 3778 Bd. 4]*

Vieillissement de la population et demande de transport dans la région de Montréal . Bussière, Yves. Montréal, Québec [1983] 83 p. : ISBN 2-89228-036-2 LC Card 84-177163
HE4509.M68 B88 1983

Vieira, Cláudio Afonso.
Urbanização e custo de reprodução da força de trabalho / Cláudio Afonso Vieira. São Paulo : IPE/USP : BID, 1984. 175 p., [5] folded leaves ; 21 cm. (Série Ensaios econômicos . v. 38) Originally presented as the author's thesis (doutorado)--Universidade de São Paulo, 1983. Bibliography: p. [173]-175. LC Card 85-136502
1. Labor supply - Brazil - São Paulo. 2. Urbanization - Brazil - São Paulo. 3. Cost and standard of living - Brazil - São Paulo. 4. Wages - Brazil - São Paulo. 5. Rent (Economic theory). 6. Wages. I. Series: Ensaios econômicos (Universidade de São Paulo. Instituto de Pesquisas Econômicas) , 38. II. Title.
HD5755.S3 V54 1984

Urbanização e custo de reprodução da força de trabalho / Cláudio Afonso Vieira. São Paulo : IPE/USP, 1984. 175 p., [5] folded leaves of plates : ill. ; 21 cm. (Série Ensaios econômicos . v. 38) Bibliography: p. [173]-175.
1. Wages - Brazil. 2. Labor supply - Brazil. 3. Manpower - Brazil. 4. Cost and standard of living - Brazil. I. Series: Ensaios econômicos (Universidade de São Paulo. Instituto de Pesquisas Econômicas) , 38. II. Title.

Vieira, José Luiz Teixeira M. (Jose Luiz Teixeira Marques) Disponibilidade de alimentos a nível regional no Estado de São Paulo, 1974-83 /. São Paulo , 1985. 75 p. ; LC Card 86-196482
HD9014.B83 S433 1985

Vieira, Paulo de Borba. Banco Regional de Desenvolvimento do Extremo sul. O planejamento e os pré-investimentos /. [Porto Alegre?] [19]85. 71, [6], p. 21 leaves ; LC Card 86-201808
HC188.S68 B35 1985

Vieli, Mario. La décision du dividende en Suisse / par Mario Vieli. [Fribourg] : Editions universitaires Fribourg Suisse, c1984. 187 p. : ill. ; 21 cm. (Documents économiques . 25) Bibliography: p. 159-164. ISBN 2-8271-0282-X : LC Card 84-225559 DDC 658.1/55 19
1. Dividends - Switzerland. I. Title. II. Series.
HG4028.D5 V54 1984

VIENNA (AUSTRIA) - INDUSTRIES - CLASSIFICATION.
Die Wiener Arbeitsstätten am 12. Mai 1981 . Wien , 1985. lvi, 723 p. : LC Card 87-408873 DDC 331.7/0012 19
HB2682.V5 W54 1985

VIENNA (AUSTRIA) - OCCUPATIONS - CLASSIFICATION.
Die Wiener Arbeitsstätten am 12. Mai 1981 . Wien , 1985. lvi, 723 p. : LC Card 87-408873 DDC 331.7/0012 19
HB2682.V5 W54 1985

Vienna (Austria). Statistisches Amt. Die Wiener Arbeitsstätten am 12. Mai 1981 . Wien , 1985. lvi, 723 p. : LC Card 87-408873 DDC 331.7/0012 19
HB2682.V5 W54 1985

Vienna. Institut für Angewandte Sozial- und Wirtschaftsforschung. (Old Catalog form: Institut für Angewandte Sozial- und Wirtschaftsforschung)
Kramer, Helmut, 1939- Industrielle Strukturprobleme Österreichs . Wien , 1980. 112 p. ; LC Card 81-103725 DDC 338.4/76691/09436 19
HD9525.A82 K73 1980 *NYPL [JLD 86-1237]*

Vienna. Österreichische Nationalbank. see **Österreichische Nationalbank.**

Vienney, Claudde. Analyse socio-économique comparée des coopératives d'habitation en

France et au Québec . [Chicoutimi] [1985] xvi, 391 p. : ISBN 2-920730-04-5 LC Card 86-181851
HD7287.72.F8 A53 1985

Vierbuchen, Ruth, 1954- Die Entwicklungsländer im Welthandel : Dissoziation versus Integration : Analyse und Diskussion einer Dissoziationsstrategie / Ruth Vierbuchen. Spardorf : R.F. Wilfer, c1983. iii, 230 p. : ill. ; 21 cm. Bibliography: p. 222-230. ISBN 3-922919-11-1 LC Card 83-150529
1. International economic relations. 2. Economic development. 3. Developing countries - Foreign economic relations. I. Title.
HF1411 .V473 1983

Vierde algemene bedrijfstelling 1978 / Centraal Bureau voor de Statistiek, Hoofdafdeling Economische Basistellingen. 's-Gravenhage : Staatsuitgeverij/CBS-publikaties, 1985-<1986 > <3 v.; in 11 > ; 30 cm. Cover title: 4e algemene bedrijfstelling 1978. Title on p. [4] of cover: Fourth general economic census 1978. "Indeling van Nederland in 40 Corop gebieden"--Folded leaf inserted in 3B. CONTENTS. - d. 1. Methodologische inleiding -- d. 2. Algemene sectorale gegevens <5 v. > -- d. 3. Algemene regionale gegevens <4 v. > ISBN 90-357-0319-7 (d. 2, A) : LC Card 86-202940
1. Netherlands - Industries - Statistics. I. Netherlands. Centraal Bureau voor de Statistiek. Hoofdafdeling Economische Basistellingen. II. Title: 4e algemene bedrijfstelling 1978. III. Title: Fourth general economic census 1978.
HC323 .V54 1985

Viermetz, Kurt F. Internationaler Kapitalverkehr und Devisenhandel /. Frankfurt am Main , c1986. 133 p. ; ISBN 3-7819-0347-8 LC Card 87-164156 DDC 332/.042 19
HG3891 .I58 1986

Viernes europeos 81 : el camino de España hacia la C.E.E. / editores, Alejandro V. Lorca, Juan Carlos Zapatero. Madrid : Consejo Superior de Investigaciones Científicas, Instituto de Economía Aplicada, [1984?] 494 p. : ill. ; 31 cm. Includes bibliographies. LC Card 85-178055
1. European Economic Community - Spain. I. Lorca, Alejandro. II. Zapatero, Juan Carlos.
HC241.25.S6 V48 1984

Ein Vierteljahrhundert Betriebskrankenkasse Henkel, Düsseldorf /. Schöne, Manfred, 1935- [Düsseldorf] , 1977. 60 p. : LC Card 86-216782
HG9399.G33 B477 1977

Vierteljahrschrift für Sozial- und Wirtschaftsgeschichte. Beihefte. For additional listing of contents, see Old Catalog.
(Nr. 81) Die Weimarer Republik als Wohlfahrtsstaat . Stuttgart , 1987. 337 p. ; ISBN 3-515-04738-7 LC Card 87-131861 DDC 338.943 19
HC286.3 .W3546 1987

Vierteljahrschrift für Sozial- und Wirtschaftsgeschichte. Beihefte, 0506-9416 .
(Nr. 77) Rosen, Josef. Verwaltung und Ungeld in Basel, 1360-1535 . Stuttgart , 1986. 231 p. ; ISBN 3-515-03348-3 : LC Card 86-184510
HG1160.B37 R67 1986

Vierzig Jahre danach. 40 Jahre danach . Frankfurt/Main , 1985. 96 p. ; ISBN 3-88367-060-X : LC Card 86-109007 DDC 322/.2/0943 19
HD6490.F582 G316 1985

Vierzig Jahre Mitbestimmung. 40 Jahre Mitbestimmung . Köln , c1986. 293 p., [16] p. of plates : ISBN 3-7663-3012-8 LC Card 87-125207 DDC 658.3/152/0943 19
HD5660.G4 A5 1986

Vierzig Jahre Wirtschaftsbund. Vodopivec, Alexander. 40 Jahre Wirtschaftsbund . Wien [1985?] 107 p. ; LC Card 86-169299
HC265 .V589 1985

Viesis, A. P. Sozdanie avtomatizirovannoĭ sistemy upravleniīa ėkonomikoĭ administrativnogo raĭona . Riga , 1980. 151 p. ; LC Card 81-215521
HF5679 .S717 1980

Viet Nam. see **Vietnam.**

VIETNAM - COMMERCE - HISTORY.
Glazunov, E. P. Preobrazovanie chastnoĭ promyshlennosti i torgovli vo V'etname /. Moskva , 1981. 213, [1] p. ; LC Card 82-112489
HC444 .G58 1981

VIETNAM (DEMOCRATIC REPUBLIC) - ECONOMIC CONDITIONS.
Fforde, Adam. The limits of national liberation . London , New York , c1987. 246 p. ; ISBN 0-7099-1036-3 LC Card 87-8977 DDC 338.9597 19
HC444 .F46 1987

VIETNAM (DEMOCRATIC REPUBLIC) - ECONOMIC POLICY.
Fforde, Adam. The limits of national liberation . London , New York , c1987. 246 p. ; ISBN 0-7099-1036-3 LC Card 87-8977 DDC 338.9597 19
HC444 .F46 1987

VIETNAM - ECONOMIC CONDITIONS.
Kinh t Hà N 1983. 154 p. ; LC Card 87-153552
HC444 .K56 1983

Nguyen, Anh Tuan. South Vietnam, trial and experience . Athens, Ohio , 1987. 461 p. : ISBN 0-89680-141-1 (pbk.) : LC Card 86-23532 DDC 338.9597 19
HC444 .N43 1987

Opyt stroitel'stva sotsialisticheskoĭ ėkonomiki v stranakh Azii /. Moskva , 1986. 290 p. ; LC Card 87-126301
HC412 .O675 1986

VIETNAM - ECONOMIC CONDITIONS - CONGRESSES.
Sovetsko-v'etnamskiĭ simpozium na temu "Ėkonomicheskie problemy perekhoda k sotsializmu" (1984 : Moscow, R.S.F.S.R.) Ėkonomicheskie problemy perekhoda k sotsializmu stran s nerazvitoĭ ėkonomikoĭ . [Moskva , 1986. 254 p. ; LC Card 87-108102
HC444 .S69 1984

VIETNAM - ECONOMIC POLICY.
Nguyen, Anh Tuan. South Vietnam, trial and experience . Athens, Ohio , 1987. 461 p. : ISBN 0-89680-141-1 (pbk.) : LC Card 86-23532 DDC 338.9597 19
HC444 .N43 1987

Vietnam - Government. see **Vietnam - Politics and government.**

VIETNAM - INDUSTRIES - HISTORY.
Glazunov, E. P. Preobrazovanie chastnoĭ promyshlennosti i torgovli vo V'etname /. Moskva , 1981. 213, [1] p. ; LC Card 82-112489
HC444 .G58 1981

VIETNAM - INDUSTRY.
Kinh t Hà N 1983. 154 p. ; LC Card 87-153552
HC444 .K56 1983

VIETNAM - POLITICS AND GOVERNMENT - 1945-1975.
Nguyen, Anh Tuan. South Vietnam, trial and experience . Athens, Ohio , 1987. 461 p. : ISBN 0-89680-141-1 (pbk.) : LC Card 86-23532 DDC 338.9597 19
HC444 .N43 1987

VIETNAM - STATISTICS.
S Hà-N 1985. 234 p. : LC Card 86-209875
HA4600.5 .S65 1985

Vietnam. T ' ông cục th S Hà-N 1985. 234 p. : LC Card 86-209875
HA4600.5 .S65 1985

VIETNAM WAR, 1961-1975. see **VIETNAMESE CONFLICT, 1961-1975.**

VIETNAMESE CONFLICT, 1961-1975 - REFUGEES.
Liu, William Thomas, 1930- Transition to nowhere . Nashville , c1979. 214 p., [2] leaves of plates : ISBN 0-8202-0189-8 : LC Card 78-21129 DDC 361.5/3/09597
HV640.5.V5 L58 ***NYPL [JLD 87-670]***

VIETNAMESE WAR, 1961-1975. see **VIETNAMESE CONFLICT, 1961-1975.**

A view of Japanese management, especially management development in large business enterprises /. Nötzli, Irene M. Zürich , c1982. ix, 281 p. : ISBN 3-7255-2191-3 (pbk.) LC Card 82-237094 DDC 658.4/07124 19
HF5549.5.T7 N638 1982 ***NYPL [TB (Zürich. Universität. Handelwissenschaftiches Seminar. Mitteilungen. Heft 156)]***

A View of unions / prepared by the Food and Allied Service Trades Department, AFL-CIO. [Washington? D.C.] : The Department, [1985] 25 p. ; 28 cm. LC Card 86-211350 DDC 331.88/0973 19
1. Trade-unions - United States - Public opinion. 2. Public opinion - United States. I. AFL-CIO. Food and Allied Service Trades Dept.
HD6508 .V39 1985

Vieweg, K. (ed) Rosenkranz, Otto. (ed) Handbuch des Genossenschaftsbauern. [Berlin, 1954-<1959. v. <v. 1, pt. 1-2; v. 3; in 3 > LC Card 60-21317
HD1491.G33 R6

Viga, Gyula. Árucsere és migráció . Miskolc , 1986. 237 p. ; ISBN 963-01-6995-9 : LC Card 87-409685
HD5856.H9 A78 1986

Vigelahn, C. Köhler, H. (Heinz) Thurn und Taxis, Kurhessen 1816-1867 . Kassel [1970?]- v. <1 > : LC Card 86-235280
HE6185.G32 H474 1970

Vigencia de la multibanca . Martín-Guédez, Rafael, 1942- [Caracas? , 1982 or 1983] 122 p. ; LC Card 83-201555
HG2964 .M37 1982

Vigevani, F. (Fausto) Tecnici, ricercatori, quadri e sindacato /. Roma , 1985. 126 p. : LC Card 86-169979
HD8038.I8 T43 1985

VIGIA (PARÁ, BRAZIL) - ECONOMIC CONDITIONS.
Loureiro, Violeta Refkalefsky. Os parceiros do mar . [Brasília] [Belém] , 1985. 227 p. : LC Card 85-211634
HD9464.A4 L68 1985

Vigier Dubois, Pierre. Metodología de evaluación y programación de sistemas de producción y consumo, MEPS /. Lima, Perú [1985]- v. <1 > : LC Card 86-215609
HD75 .M48 1985

Vigilev, A. N. (Aleksandr Nikolaevich) Imīa tvoe--kollektsioner / A.N. Vigilev. Moskva : "Radio i svīaz'", 1981. 93 p. : col. ill. ; 16 cm. (Biblioteka īunogo filatelista. vyp. 8) Includes bibliographical references. LC Card 82-103288
1. Postage-stamps - Collectors and collecting - Juvenile literature. I. Title.
HE6213 .V54 1981

Vignault, Walter L. Worldwide telecommunications guide for the business manager / Walter L. Vignault. New York : Wiley, c1987. xvi, 417 p. : ill. ; 25 cm. (Wiley series in telecommunications) "A Wiley-Interscience publication." Bibliography: p. 378-382. ISBN 0-471-85828-5 LC Card 87-2002 DDC 384 19
1. Business - Communication systems. 2. Telecommunication systems. 3. Telephone in business. I. Title. II. Series.
HF5541.T4 V54 1987

Vignes et vignerons d'autrefois dans le Barséquanais . Dautriat, Pierre. Saint-Seine-l'Abbaye , c1984. 70 p. : ISBN 2-86701-018-7 : LC Card 85-117852
HD9385.F82 N483 1984

Vignikin, Kokou. Locoh, Thérèse. Comprendre les problèmes de population . Lomé, Togo , 1984. 72, [3], 3 p. : LC Card 87-131146
HB871 .L57 1984

Vigvári, András. A gazdaságirányítási rendszer egyes kérdései, elmélettörténeti megközelítésben / Vigvári András. [Budapest] : Művelődési Minisztérium Marxizmus-Leninizmus Oktatási Főosztálya, 1985. 87 p. ; 24 cm. (Politikai gazdaságtan füzetek, 0324-6396 . 47) Summary in Russian. Bibliography: p. 83-86. ISBN 963-673-302-3 LC Card 85-231820
1. Hungary - Economic policy - 1945-1968. 2. Hungary - Economic policy - 1968-. 3. Central planning - Hungary - History. I. Title. II. Series.
HC300.28 .V53 1985

Vijay Kumar Puri. see **Puri, Vijay Kumar.**

Vijge, G. W. A., 1942- Ondernemingsstrategie, theorie en praktijk . Leiden , c1986. xi, 346 p. : ISBN 90-207-1424-4 : LC Card 86-199689
HD37.D8 O54 1986

VIKHE PĀṬĪLA, VIṬHṬHALARĀVA, 1901- Sāvanta, Śivājī, 1940- Laḍhata /. Pravarānagara , 1985-1986. 2 v. : LC Card 87-900715
HD9116.I415 M37 1985

Viksnins, George J. Skully, Michael T. Financing East Asia's success . New York , 1987. xiii, 242 p. ; ISBN 0-312-00536-9 : LC Card 86-31527 DDC 332/.0959 19
HG187.E37 S68 1987

Viktorov, V. N. Sotsial′no-ėkonomicheskie problemy ispol′zovaniia trudovykh resursov /. Cheboksary , 1986. 70 p. ; LC Card 87-137786
HD5797.C56 S68 1986

VILA VIÇOSA (PORTUGAL) - HISTORY.
Pestana, M. Inácio. Movimento demográfico da matriz de Vila Viçosa nos séculos XVI e XVII /. [Vila Viçosa, Portugal , 1985] 32 p. : LC Card 86-199468
HB3622.V55 P47 1985

VILA VIÇOSA (PORTUGAL) - POPULATION - HISTORY - 16TH CENTURY.
Pestana, M. Inácio. Movimento demográfico da matriz de Vila Viçosa nos séculos XVI e XVII /. [Vila Viçosa, Portugal , 1985] 32 p. : LC Card 86-199468
HB3622.V55 P47 1985

VILA VIÇOSA (PORTUGAL) - POPULATION - HISTORY - 17TH CENTURY.
Pestana, M. Inácio. Movimento demográfico da matriz de Vila Viçosa nos séculos XVI e XVII /. [Vila Viçosa, Portugal , 1985] 32 p. : LC Card 86-199468
HB3622.V55 P47 1985

A Világ aluminiumipara : termelők, kapacitások, termelés / [összeállította, Gazda István]. Budapest : Aluminiumipari Tervező és Kutató Intézet, 1985. 2 v. : maps ; 29 cm. Bibliography: v. 1, p. 15-16. LC Card 86-157446
1. Aluminum industry and trade. 2. Aluminum industry and trade - Directories. I. Gazda, István. II. Aluminiumipari Tervező és Kutató Intézet (Budapest, Hungary).
HD9539.A62 V54 1985

A világ metrói /. Várszegi, Gyula. [Budapest] [1983] 250 p., [48] p. of plates : ISBN 963-02-2971-4 (Magy. nemz. bibl.) LC Card 84-219598
HE4211 .V37 1983

A világ műtrágyatermelésének és -felhasználásának előrejelzése /. Mészáros, Sándor. Budapest , 1985. 143 p. : ISBN 963-05-3670-6 : LC Card 86-136326
HD9483.A2 M47 1985

A Világgazdaság fejlődésének kérdései tanulmányozásához : szöveggyűjtemény / [összeállította, Benke Istvánné]. [Budapest] : Kossuth, 1981/1982. 415 p. ; 20 cm. At head of title: Magyar Szocialista Munkáspárt Marxizmus-Leninizmus Esti Egyetem Szakosított Tagozat. "Politikai gazdaságtan/III. évfolyam, továbbképző tanfolyam." Includes bibliographical references. LC Card 85-138909
1. Economic history - 1971-. 2. International economic relations. I. Benke, Istvánné. II. Magyar Szocialista Munkáspárt. Marxizmus-Leninizmus Esti Egyetem. Szakosított Tagozat.
HC59 .V489 1981

Világgazdasági korszakváltások és a mezőgazdasági termékforgalom . Sárándi, Imre. [Budapest] [1985] 92 p. ; LC Card 86-218536
HD1415 .S25 1985

Világgazdasági Kutató Intézet. see **Magyar Tudományos Akadémia, Budapest. Világgazdasági Kutató Intézet.**

Vilanova, Santiago, 1947- L'econacionalisme : una alternativa catalana dins una europa ecològica / Santiago Vilanova.1a ed. Barcelona : Editorial Blume, 1981. 142 p. ; 20 cm. Bibliography: p. 141-142. ISBN 84-7031-281-2 LC Card 81-212886
1. Environmental policy - Spain - Catalonia. 2. Ecology - Spain - Catalonia. 3. Pollution - Spain - Catalonia. 4. Nuclear power plants - Environmental aspects - Spain - Catalonia. I. Title.
HC387.C25 V527 1981

Vilas, Carlos María. Democracia y participación obrera en la Revolución Sandinista / Carlos M. Vilas. Morelia, Michoacán : Universidad Michoacana de San Nicolás de Hidalgo, Escuela de Historia, Centro de Estudios Latinoamericanos "Salvador Allende", 1985. 44 p., [6] p. of plates : ill., ports. ; 21 cm. (Colección Historia de los trabajadores de América Latina . 2) Bibliography: p. 40-44. LC Card 87-128110 DDC 322/.2/097285 19
1. Labor and laboring classes - Nicaragua - Political activity. 2. Trade-unions - Nicaragua - Political activity. 3. Nicaragua - Politics and government - 1979-. 4. Frente Sandinista de Liberación Nacional. I. Title. II. Series.
HD8168 .V55 1985

Vilas Nogueira, J. Dende Galicia, Marx . Sada, A Coruña [1985?] 258 p. : ISBN 84-7492-241-0 LC Card 86-215077
HB97.5 .D413 1985

Vilby, Knud.
[Afrika i misvækst. Swedish]
Afrika på fel spår : utvecklingens och biståndets kris i ett allt fattigare Afrika / Knud Vilby ; [översättning från danskan, Karin Andræ]. Uppsala : Nordiska afrikainstitutet, 1984. 138 p. ; 21 cm. ISBN 91-7106-230-0 LC Card 85-158250
1. Africa - Economic conditions - 1960-. I. Title.
HC800 .V5518 1984

Vilenchik, L. A. Narodnoe khoziaĭstvo Bashkirskoĭ ASSR za gody odinnadtsatoĭ piatiletki, 1981-1985 gg. . Ufa , 1986. 254 p. ; LC Card 87-165386
HC337.B28 N37 1986

Vilkas, Ė., 1935- Nekotorye voprosy matematicheskoĭ ėkonomiki . Vil′nius , 1982. 90 p. ; LC Card 83-169081
HB135 .N45 1982

Vilks, Arnis. Aggregation und Kausalität im Modell des allgemeinen Konkurrenzgleichgewichts : eine Untersuchung über den epistemologischen Status mikroökonomisch fundierter Makroökonomik / Arnis Vilks. Göttingen : Vandenhoeck & Ruprecht, c1984. 141 p. ; 24 cm. (Studien zur angewandten Wirtschaftsforschung und Statistik aus dem Institut für Statistik und Ökonometrie der Universität Hamburg . Heft 16) Originally presented as the author's thesis (doctoral)--Universität Hamburg. Bibliography: p. [136]-141. ISBN 3-525-11287-4 (Deut. Bibl.) LC Card 84-225754
1. Demand (Economic theory) - Econometric models. 2. Competition - Econometric models. 3. Equilibrium (Economics) - Econometric models. 4. Microeconomics - Econometric models. 5. Macroeconomics - Econometric models. I. Title. II. Series.
HB842 .V55 1984

Villa, Gloria.
Hernández C., Alexandra. Encuesta de consumo energético en el sector transporte /. San José, Costa Rica , 1985. 68, [137] p. : LC Card 86-218227
HE5638 .H37 1985

Obando S., Marta. Encuesta residencial de consumo energético /. San José, Costa Rica , 1985. iv, 56, [71] p. : LC Card 86-219603
HD9502.C82 O23 1985

Villa, Hernando Agudelo. see **Agudelo Villa, Hernando.**

Villa, Pierre. Pisani-Ferry, Jean. Problèmes de macroéconomie /. Paris , 1984. 452 p. : ISBN 2-7178-0801-9 : LC Card 85-100663 DDC 339 19
HB173 .P534 1984

Villafane, Germán Torre. see **Torre Villafane, Germán.**

Villafañe, Justo. La Televisión en España mañana . Madrid , 1986. 331 p. ; ISBN 84-323-0563-X LC Card 86-199326
HE8700.9.S63 T45 1986
NYPL [MWGV (Spain) 87-2054]

VILLAGE COMMUNITIES - ECUADOR.
González S., Víctor A. Las tierras comunales en el Ecuador /. Guayaquil, Ecuador , 1982. 109 p. ; LC Card 87-672596
HD1289.E2 G66x 1982

Village development . Eweka, J. A. (Julius A.) Ibadan, Nigeria , 1979. xvi, 194 p. ; LC Card 86-172121 DDC 338.1/9/669 19
HD2145.5 .E94 1979

VILLAGE GOVERNMENT. see **VILLAGES.**

VILLAGE INDIANS. see **PUEBLO INDIANS.**

Village industries and agriculture in changing agrarian situation /. Mishra, G. P. New Delhi , c1985. 120 p. ; ISBN 81-7024-010-7 LC Card 85-904926 DDC 338.6/34/0954 19
HD2346.I5 M49 1985 ***NYPL [JLD 86-3746]***

Village republics . Wade, Robert. Cambridge [Cambridgeshire] , New York , 1988. p. cm. ISBN 0-521-30146-7 LC Card 86-33389 DDC 334/.683/095484 19
HD1491.I392 K878 1988

VILLAGES - ALGERIA.
Lesbet, Djaffar. Les 1000 villages socialistes en Algérie /. Alger , Paris , c1983. 335 p. : ISBN 2-86738-008-1 : LC Card 84-156989 DDC 335/.00965 19
HX441.5.A6 L47 1983 ***NYPL [JLD 87-236]***

VILLAGES - DEVELOPING COUNTRIES - CASE STUDIES.
Critchfield, Richard. The golden bowl be broken . Bloomington , 1988. p. cm. ISBN 0-253-32554-4 LC Card 87-3690 DDC 305.5/63 19
HD1542 .C75 1988

VILLAGES - GERMANY - HISTORY - 18TH CENTURY.
Knodel, John E. Demographic behavior in the past . Cambridge [Cambridgeshire] , New York , 1988. p. cm. ISBN 0-521-32715-6 LC Card 87-20601 DDC 304.6/0943 19
HB3595 .K53 1988

VILLAGES - GERMANY - HISTORY - 19TH CENTURY.
Knodel, John E. Demographic behavior in the past . Cambridge [Cambridgeshire] , New York , 1988. p. cm. ISBN 0-521-32715-6 LC Card 87-20601 DDC 304.6/0943 19
HB3595 .K53 1988

VILLAGES - HUNGARY.
Beluszky, Pál. Magyarország falutipusai /. Budapest , 1982. 167 p. : ISBN 963-7321-96-9 LC Card 84-159502
HD640.5.Z7 B44 1982

VILLAGES - INDIA - HISTORY.
Alaev, L. B. Sel′skaia obshchina v Severnoĭ Indii . Moskva , 1981. 240 p. ; LC Card 82-101919
HD873 .A63 1981

VILLAGES - INDIA - PUNJAB - STATISTICS.
Piṇḍāṃ dī ḍāiraikaṭarī, 1983-84. Caṇḍīgaṛha [1985- v. <1- > ; LC Card 86-902359
HA4587.P86 P56 1985

VILLAGES - RUSSIAN S.F.S.R. - KALININ REGION - HISTORY - 20TH CENTURY.
Altrichter, Helmut, 1945- Die Bauern von Tver . München , 1984. 373 p. : ISBN 3-486-52071-7 LC Card 84-162284
HD1536.S65 A47 1984

Villalba, Julián. Kelly de Escobar, Janet. Opciones para la evaluación de las empresas públicas /. Caracas , c1985. 36 p. ; ISBN 980-217-008-9 LC Card 86-201812
HD62.35 .K45 1985

Villalobos, Fabio. La industrialización ecuatoriana y la utilización de los recursos productivos, 1976-1983 / Fabio Villalobos. 1a ed. Quito, Ecuador : Facultad Latinoamericana de Ciencias Sociales, 1987. 148 p. : ill. ; 21 cm. Cover title: La industrialización ecuatoriana, 1976-1983. Bibliography: p. 132-135. LC Card 87-404654 DDC 338.09866 19
1. Industrial productivity - Ecuador. 2. Efficiency, Industrial - Ecuador. 3. Ecuador - Manufactures. 4. Industry and state - Ecuador. I. Title. II. Title: Industrialización ecuatoriana, 1976-1983.
HC204.5.I52 V55 1987

Villalobos Vega, Bernardo. La mesocracia de Costa Rica, 1821-1926 / Bernardo Villalobos. San José : Editorial Costa Rica, c1986. 309 p. ; 21 cm. Bibliography: p. 307-309. ISBN 997-7232-15-6 LC Card 86-231140
1. Saving and investment - Costa Rica - History. 2. Banks and banking - Costa Rica - History. I. Title.
HC143.Z9 S38 1986

Villanueva, Eric. Crisis henequenera y movimientos campesinos en Yucatán, 1966-1983 / Eric Villanueva. 1a ed. México, D.F. : Instituto Nacional de Antropología e Historia, 1985. 220 p., [10] p. of plates : ill. ; 21 cm. (Colección Divulgación) Serie Ensayo Includes bibliographical references. ISBN 968-603-803-5 LC Card 86-118134 DDC 304.8/0972/65 19
1. Henequen industry - Mexico - Yucatan. 2. Migration,

Internal - Mexico - Yucatan. 3. Peasantry - Mexico - Yucatan. I. Series. II. Series: Serie Ensayo (Instituto Naciona' de Antropología e Historia (Mexico)). III. Title.
HD9156.H463 M67 1985 ***NYPL [JLD 87-342]***

Villányi, Miklós. A Gazdaságirányitási rendszer továbbfejlesztése /. Budapest , 1984. 171 p. ; LC Card 86-145153
HC300.28 .G339 1984

Villar Borrero, Eduardo. El dinero y el sector financiero a su alcance / Eduardo Villar Borrero. Bogotá, Colombia : Editorial Norma, c1984. 64 p. : ill. ; 20 cm. Includes bibliographical references. ISBN 84-8276-321-0 LC Card 84-241500
1. Money - Colombia. 2. Financial institutions - Colombia. I. Title.
HG855 .V54 1984

Villarejo, Avelino García. see **García Villarejo, Avelino.**

Villarreal, René. Economía internacional /. México , 1979- v. in : ***NYPL [JLK 86-184]***

VILLAS. see **ARCHITECTURE, DOMESTIC.**

Villas miseria . Bellardi, Marta. Buenos Aires , c1986. 157 p. : ISBN 950-25-1423-8 : LC Card 87-125510 DDC 307.3/36 19
HD7321.B9 B45 1986

Ville, Simon P. English shipowning during the industrial revolution : Michael Henley and Son, London Shipowners, 1770-1830 / Simon P. Ville. Manchester, UK ; Wolfeboro, NH, USA : Manchester University Press, c1987. x, 192 p. : ill. ; 23 cm. Based on the author's thesis (Ph. D.)--London University, 1984? Bibliography: p. [183]-186. Includes index. ISBN 0-7190-1714-9 LC Card 87-11043 DDC 387.5/065/41 19
1. Michael Henley and Son - History. 2. Shipping - England - History. I. Title.
HE945.M49 V55 1987

Villegas, Rafael.
Registro civil y el proceso electoral en Costa Rica. 1980. Daremblum, Jaime. El auge del café y la apertura de la economía costarricense / por Jaime Daremblum. El registro civil y el proceso electoral en Costa Rica : bases de un sistema político democrático / por Rafael Villegas. 1a ed. San José, Costa Rica , 1980. 62 p. ; LC Card 84-247131
HF3255 .D37 1980

Villena Peña, José E. Cuadrado Roura, Juan R. Política de rentas . [Madrid] [1980?] 471 p. : ISBN 84-7196-297-7 LC Card 85-131138
HC390.I5 C8 1980

Villermé (Association) Tableaux de l'état physique et moral des salariés en France /. Paris , 1986. 237 p. ; ISBN 2-7071-1626-2 : LC Card 87-122301
HD8431 .T32 1986

Villette, Jean. Transports, décentralisation 9o plan / Jean Villette. Paris : Documentation française, c1986. 161 p. : ill. ; 24 cm. At head of title: Observatoire économique et statistique des transports. ISBN 2-11-001549-7 : LC Card 86-181094
1. Transportation and state - France. 2. France - Economic policy - 1981-. I. Observatoire économique et statistique des transports (France). II. Title. III. Title: Transports, décentralisation, neuvième plan.
HE248.A2 V55 1986

Vilmar, Fritz, 1929- Arbeitswelt, Grundriss einer kritischen Soziologie der Arbeit / Fritz Vilmar, Leo Kissler. Opladen : Leske + Budrich, c1982. 256 p. : ill. ; 19 cm. (Uni-Taschenbücher. 1167) Bibliography: p. 245-253. Includes index. ISBN 3-8100-0400-6 (pbk.) LC Card 87-672408
1. Industrial sociology. I. Kissler, Leo. II. Title. III. Title: Arbeitswelt.
HD6971 .V534x 1982

Vilniaus Valstybinis V. Kapsuko vardo universitetas. Problemy razvitiia i sovershenstvovaniia material'no-tekhnicheskoĭ bazy torgovli i obshchestvennogo pitaniia v dvenadtsatoĭ piatiletke . Vil'nius , 1985. 169 p. ; LC Card 86-102743
HF3629.L5 P76 1985

Vimercati, Giuseppe. Conferenza internazionale sul tema Le zone franche industriali, nuove forme di investimento, l'America latina (1985 : Milan, Italy) Le zone franche industriali nei paesi emergenti . Milano, Italy , c1986. 207 p. ; LC Card 86-223193
HF1418 .C525 1985

Viñals, José M. Cuddington, John T. Budget deficits and the current account in the presence of classical unemployment /. [Madrid] [1984] 47 p. : ISBN 84-505-0847-9 (pbk.) LC Card 86-215031 DDC 339.5/23/0724 19
HJ2005 .C83 1984

Vincent, David, 1949- Testaments of radicalism . London , c1977. vii, 246 p., [3] leaves of plates : ISBN 0-905118-01-4 : LC Card 77-377253 DDC 322/.2/0922 B
HD8383.7.A1 T47 ***NYPL [JLE 86-4274]***

Vincent, Hélène. L'Industrie québécoise du matériel médical jetable . Québec [1983] xv, 235 p. : LC Card 84-235956
HD9995.D563 C35 1983

Vincent, Maurice, 1955 or 6- La formation du prix du logement / Maurice Vincent ; préface de Jean-Jacques Granelle. Paris : Economica, c1986. v, 221 p. : ill. ; 24 cm. Originally presented as the author's thesis (doctoral)--Université de Saint-Etienne. Bibliography: p. [209]-214. ISBN 2-7178-1082-X : LC Card 86-190085
1. Housing - Prices - France. I. Title.
HD7338.A3 V55 1986

Vinculación fronteriza a Estados Unidos y su cambio con la crisis /. González-Aréchiga, Bernardo. Tijuana, Baja California , 1985. 54 p. ; ISBN 968-607-500-3 LC Card 86-187758
HF3239.M49 G66 1985

Vincze, Julian W. Bell, Martin L. Managerial marketing . New York , c1988. xviii, 708 p. : ISBN 0-444-01215-X LC Card 87-22306 DDC 658.8 19
HF5415.13 .B434 1988

VINE YARDS. see **VITICULTURE.**

Viner, Aron. Inside Japanese financial markets / Aron Viner. Homewood, Ill. : Dow Jones-Irwin, c1988. xvi, 364 p. : ill. ; 24 cm. Bibliography: p. 346-347. Includes index. ISBN 1-556-23020-6 LC Card 87-71357 DDC 332/.0952 19
1. Finance - Japan. I. Title.
HG187.J3 V57 1988

Vineyard Video Productions.
You may call her madam secretary [motion picture] /. West Tisbury, MA , 1987. 1 film reel (57 min., 40 sec.) : LC Card 87-706816 DDC 973.917 11
HD8073.P38

You may call her madam secretary [videorecording] /. West Tisbury, MA , 1987. 1 videocassette (57 min., 40 sec.) : LC Card 87-706817 DDC 973.917 11
HD8073.P38

Vingt ans de colonisation sous le régime coopératif, et après-- . Desharnais, Marcel, 1924- Guyenne . Montréal, Québec , c1983. 182 p. : ISBN 2-89035-062-2 LC Card 84-127460
HD3450.G89 D47 1983

Vinha na região de Redondo. Pereira, Francisco José Piteira. A cultura da vinha na região do Redondo /. [Lisbon] , 1983. 11, 4, 30, 21 leaves, [2] leaves of plates : LC Card 84-238378
HD9259.G7 P47 1983

Vinhas, M. A terra, o homem, as reformas / Moisés Vinhas. Rio de Janeiro (R. Hermenegildo de Barros, 31-A Glória, Rio de Janeiro) : Graal, 1980. xiii, 151 p. ; 21 cm. (Biblioteca de ciências sociais. Série Política . vol. no. 16) Bibliography: p. 143-151.
1. Agriculture - Economic aspects - Brazil. 2. Land reform - Brazil. I. Title. ***NYPL [JLD 86-783]***

VINICULTURE. see **VITICULTURE.**

Vink, A. P. A.
[Landschapsecologie en landgebruik. English] Landscape ecology and land use / A.P.A. Vink ; translated by the author ; English translation edited by D.A. Davidson. London ; New York : Longman, 1983, c1980. vi, 264 p. : ill. ; 24 cm. Translation of: Landschapsecologie en landgebruik. Includes index. Bibliography: p. [246]-260. ISBN 0-582-30077-0 (pbk.) : LC Card 82-10030 DDC 333.73/13 19
1. Land use - Planning. 2. Land use - Environmental aspects. I. Davidson, Donald A. II. Title.
HD108.6 .V5613 1983 ***NYPL [JLE 86-3886]***

Vinnik, V. N. (Viktor Nikolaevich) Todyka, IUriĭ Nikolaevich. Gosudarstvennyĭ apparat i problemy okhrany prirody v usloviiakh APK /. Kishinev , 1986. 179, [5] p. ; LC Card 86-141430
HD1995.M5 T63 1986

Vino e olio in Toscana = Wine and olive oil in Tuscany / [coordinatore, Maria Grazia Tilli ; traduzioni inglese, James Johnson]. Firenze : Il Fiore : Distributore esclusivo nelle librerie, Licosa, c1985. 386 p. : ill. (some col.) ; 30 cm. Italian, English, and German. Includes index. LC Card 86-138958 DDC 338.4/76632/009455 19
1. Wine industry - Italy - Tuscany. 2. Olive-oil industry - Italy - Tuscany. 3. Wine industry - Italy - Tuscany - Directories. 4. Olive-oil industry - Italy - Tuscany - Directories. I. Tilli, Maria Grazia. II. Title: Wine and olive oil in Tuscany.
HD9385.I82 T858 1985 ***NYPL [JSF 87-35]***

Vinod Vyasulu. see **Vyasulu, Vinod.**

Vinogradov, I. P. (Igor' Petrovich) Proizvoditel'nost' truda--glavnoe zveno ėffektivnosti / I.P. Vinogradov. Moskva : "Sov. Rossiia", 1980. 192 p. ; 17 cm. Includes bibliographical references. LC Card 81-134882
1. Labor productivity - Soviet Union. 2. Labor productivity - Russian S.F.S.R. I. Title.
HC340.L3 V459 1980

VINTERS - ITALY - MODENA (PROVINCE) - HISTORY.
Bergonzini, Renato. Arte dei brentatori a Modena /. Modena , 1983. 74 p., [5] p. of plates : LC Card 85-140349
HD8039.L72 I83 1983

Vinyl and acrylic latices markets in Europe. New York, N.Y. : Frost & Sullivan, c1983. 2 v. (xxxv, 328 leaves) : ill. ; 29 cm. "January 1983." "E419." LC Card 87-143984 DDC 380.1/456684232/094 19
1. Plastics industry and trade - Europe. 2. Latex, Synthetic. 3. Market surveys - Europe. I. Frost & Sullivan.
HD9661.E82 V55 1983

Vinze, Medha Dubhashi, 1958- Women entrepreneurs in India : a socio-economic study of Delhi, 1975-85 / Medha Dubhashi Vinze. Delhi, India : Mittal Publications, 1987. ix, 238 p. ; 23 cm. Revision of the author's thesis (Ph. D.--Magadh University, 1986) Bibliography: p. [226]-232. Includes index. LC Card 86-903594 DDC 305.4/3338 19
1. Women in business - India - Delhi. 2. Entrepreneur. 3. Delhi (India) - Social conditions. 4. Delhi (India) - Economic conditions. I. Title.
HD6190.D44 V55 1987

Vío Grossi, Gonzalo. Tapia Soko, Gonzalo. El problema de la recomposición de los actores campesinos en una perspectiva de democratización /. Santiago [Chile] [1985] ii, 49, 5 leaves ; LC Card 86-159337
HD1531.C5 T36 1985

Viola, Joy Winkie. Human resources development in Saudi Arabia : multinationals and Saudization / Joy Winkie Viola.[2nd ed.] Boston : International Human Resources Development Corp., c1986. xxvi, 291 p. : ill. ; 24 cm. Includes index. Bibliography: p. 277-284. ISBN 0-88746-070-4 (IHRDC) LC Card 85-19694 DDC 303.4/8273/0538 19
1. Manpower policy - Saudi Arabia. 2. International business enterprises - Saudi Arabia - Personnel management. 3. College students - Saudi Arabia - Interviews. 4. College students - United States - Interviews. 5. Employer sponsored education - Saudi Arabia. I. Title.
HD5812.35.A6 V56 1986
NYPL [JLE 86-2188]

Violante, Alejandro. México, una economía en transición /. México, D.F. , 1984-1985. 3 v. ; ISBN 968-18-1900-4 (v. 1) LC Card 86-235462
HC135 .M549 1985

Violence and great estates in the south of Italy . Snowden, Frank M. (Frank Martin), 1946- Cambridge [Cambridgeshire] , New York , 1986. x, 245 p. : ISBN 0-521-30731-7 LC Card 85-11675 DDC 322.4/4/094575 19
HD679.P83 S66 1986 ***NYPL [JLD 86-1627]***

Viotti, Eduardo Baumgratz. A economia e o estado capitalista / Eduardo Baumgratz Viotti. Petrópolis : Vozes, 1986. 96 p. ; 21 cm. Includes bibliographical references. LC Card 87-137699 DDC 338.9 19

1. Economic policy. 2. Capitalism. I. Title.
HD85.P65 V56 1986

Vira, Raghu. see **Raghu Vira.**

Virginia, a guide to establishing a manufacturing business. Richmond, Va. : Commonwealth of Virginia, Governor's Office, Dept. of Economic Development, [1986] iv, 30 p. ; 28 cm. "July 1986." LC Card 86-622659 DDC 343.755/07 347.55037 19
1. Virginia - Manufactures - Management. 2. New business enterprises - Virginia - Management. I. Virginia. Dept. of Economic Development.
HD9727.V8 V573 1986

Virginia alternatives for the 1990s : selected issues in public policy / edited by Joseph L. Fisher and Richard T. Mayer. Fairfax, Va. : George Mason University Press ; Lanham, MD : Distributed by arrangement with University Pub. Associates, 1987. 183 p. : ill. ; 24 cm. Includes bibliographies. Errata slip inserted. ISBN 0-8026-0016-6 (alk. paper) : LC Card 87-22757 DDC 338.9755 19
1. Economic forecasting - Virginia. 2. Virginia - Economic conditions. 3. Education - Virginia. 4. Virginia - Politics and government - 1951-. I. Fisher, Joseph L. II. Mayer, Richard T.
HC107.V8 V435 1987

Virginia, an outline of the state and local taxes /. Ware, Peggy M. Richmond, Va. (1000 Washington Bldg., Richmond 23219) [1986] iv, 26 p. ; LC Card 86-622876 DDC 343.75504/3 347.550343 19
HJ2438 .W37 1986

Virginia. Bureau of Insurance.
Insurance company statistical report, 1985 /. [Richmond, Va.] [1985] 1 v. (various pagings) ; LC Card 87-621272 DDC 368/.006 19
HG8538.V8 I574 1985

1984 insurance company statistical report /. [Richmond] [1984?] 1 v. (various pagings) ; LC Card 86-621902 DDC 368/.006 19
HG8538.V8 A53 1984

Virginia Center for Coal and Energy Research.
Hibbard, W. R. (Walter Rollo) The Virginia coal industry . Blacksburg, Va. (617 N. Main St., Blacksburg 24061) [1986] ii, 46 leaves ; LC Card 87-620671 DDC 338.2/724/09755 19
HD9547.V8 H523 1986

The Virginia coal industry . Blacksburg, Va. [1986] [15] leaves ; LC Card 86-622456 DDC 381/.4224/09755 19
HD9547.V8 V57 1986

The Virginia coal industry : a study of utility markets. Blacksburg, Va. : Virginia Center for Coal and Energy Research, Virginia Polytechnic Institute and State University, [1986] [15] leaves ; 28 cm. "June 1986." Bibliography: leaf [15] LC Card 86-622456 DDC 381/.4224/09755 19
1. Coal trade - Virginia. I. Virginia Center for Coal and Energy Research.
HD9547.V8 V57 1986

The Virginia coal industry . Hibbard, W. R. (Walter Rollo) Blacksburg, Va. (617 N. Main St., Blacksburg 24061) [1986] ii, 46 leaves ; LC Card 87-620671 DDC 338.2/724/09755 19
HD9547.V8 H523 1986

Virginia counties and cities data book, 1986. Virginia Beach, Va. (380 Cleveland Place, Virginia Beach 23462) : W.C. Overman, 1986. 2 v. (ii, 262 p.) : ill. (some col.) ; 22 x 30 cm. Cover title. Includes bibliographical references and index. LC Card 87-138805 DDC 317.55 19
1. Virginia - Statistics. 2. Virginia - Population - Statistics. I. William C. Overman Associates.
HA685 .V575 1986

Virginia. Dept. of Economic Development.
Virginia, a guide to establishing a manufacturing business. Richmond, Va. [1986] iv, 30 p. ; LC Card 86-622659 DDC 343.755/07 347.55037 19
HD9727.V8 V573 1986

Ware, Peggy M. Virginia, an outline of the state and local taxes /. Richmond, Va. (1000 Washington Bldg., Richmond 23219) [1986] iv, 26 p. ; LC Card 86-622876 DDC 343.75504/3 347.550343 19
HJ2438 .W37 1986

Virginia. Dept. of Highways and Transportation.
1987 estimate of the cost of completing the national system of interstate and defense highways in the Commonwealth of Virginia . [Richmond, Va.] [1986] 169 p. : LC Card 86-622650 DDC 388.1/12/09755 19
HE356.V8 A14 1986

Virginia. Dept. of Planning and Budget. Research Section. Lillywhite, Donald P. Virginia population projections 2000 /. Richmond, VA (P.O. Box 1422, Ninth St. Office Building, Richmond 23219) [1986] 96 p. : LC Card 87-621004 DDC 304.6/2/09755021 19
HA685 .L542 1986

Virginia. Dept. of Taxation. Research Division.
The Treasury's tax reform proposal. [Richmond?] [1985] 22 leaves ; LC Card 86-622457 DDC 336.2/05 19
HJ2381 .T74 1985

Virginia's income tax age credit. [Richmond, Va.] [1984] ii, 26 leaves ; LC Card 86-622458 DDC 336.24/216 19
HJ4655.V88 A828 1984

VIRGINIA - ECONOMIC CONDITIONS.
Virginia alternatives for the 1990s . Fairfax, Va. , Lanham, MD , 1987. 183 p. : ISBN 0-8026-0016-6 (alk. paper) : LC Card 87-22757 DDC 338.9755 19
HC107.V8 V435 1987

Virginia - Government. see **Virginia - Politics and government.**

Virginia. Highways and Transportation, Dept. of. see **Virginia. Dept. of Highways and Transportation.**

VIRGINIA - MANUFACTURES - MANAGEMENT.
Virginia, a guide to establishing a manufacturing business. Richmond, Va. [1986] iv, 30 p. ; LC Card 86-622659 DDC 343.755/07 347.55037 19
HD9727.V8 V573 1986

VIRGINIA. OFFICE OF HOUSING SERVICES.
Directory of Virginia housing resources. [Richmond] [1986] iii, 153 p. : LC Card 87-620669 DDC 350.86/5/025755 19
HD7303.V8 D57 1986

VIRGINIA - POLITICS AND GOVERNMENT - 1951-
Virginia alternatives for the 1990s . Fairfax, Va. , Lanham, MD , 1987. 183 p. : ISBN 0-8026-0016-6 (alk. paper) : LC Card 87-22757 DDC 338.9755 19
HC107.V8 V435 1987

Virginia Polytechnic Institute and State University. Dept. of Agricultural Economics. Food demand analysis . Blacksburg, Va. [1986] xii, 292 p. : LC Card 87-620670 DDC 339.4/86413 19
HD9000.5 .F5946 1986

Virginia Polytechnic Institute and State University. Psychology Dept. Occupational stress and organizational effectiveness /. New York , c1987. xii, 285 p. : ISBN 0-275-92281-2 (alk. paper) : LC Card 86-25250 DDC 158.7 19
HF5548.85 .O24 1987

Virginia population projections 2000 /. Lillywhite, Donald P. Richmond, VA (P.O. Box 1422, Ninth St. Office Building, Richmond 23219) [1986] 96 p. : LC Card 87-621004 DDC 304.6/2/09755021 19
HA685 .L542 1986

VIRGINIA - POPULATION - STATISTICS.
Lillywhite, Donald P. Virginia population projections 2000 /. Richmond, VA (P.O. Box 1422, Ninth St. Office Building, Richmond 23219) [1986] 96 p. : LC Card 87-621004 DDC 304.6/2/09755021 19
HA685 .L542 1986

Virginia counties and cities data book, 1986. Virginia Beach, Va. (380 Cleveland Place, Virginia Beach 23462) , 1986. 2 v. (ii, 262 p.) : LC Card 87-138805 DDC 317.55 19
HA685 .V575 1986

VIRGINIA - STATISTICS.
Virginia counties and cities data book, 1986. Virginia Beach, Va. (380 Cleveland Place, Virginia Beach 23462) , 1986. 2 v. (ii, 262 p.) : LC Card 87-138805 DDC 317.55 19
HA685 .V575 1986

Virginia Tech Symposium on Applied Behavioral Science (7th : 1984) Occupational stress and organizational effectiveness /. New York , c1987. xii, 285 p. : ISBN 0-275-92281-2 (alk. paper) : LC Card 86-25250 DDC 158.7 19
HF5548.85 .O24 1987

Virginia Transportation Research Council.
Sharkey, Stephen M. Evaluation of the 1984 selective speed enforcement projects in Virginia /. Charlottesville, Va. [1987] xii, 117, [34] p. : LC Card 87-621546 DDC 388.3/144/09755 19
HE5620.S6 S532 1987

Virginia. Transportation Safety Administration.
Sharkey, Stephen M. Evaluation of the 1984 selective speed enforcement projects in Virginia /. Charlottesville, Va. [1987] xii, 117, [34] p. : LC Card 87-621546 DDC 388.3/144/09755 19
HE5620.S6 S532 1987

Virginia's income tax age credit. [Richmond, Va.] : Research Division, Virginia Dept. of Taxation, [1984] ii, 26 leaves ; 28 cm. (Issue paper / Research Division, Virginia Department of Taxation . no. 1) "April 1984." LC Card 86-622458 DDC 336.24/216 19
1. Aged - Taxation - Virginia. 2. Tax credits - Virginia. 3. Aged - Taxation - Virginia - Statistics. I. Virginia. Dept. of Taxation. Research Division. II. Series. III. Series: Issue paper (Virginia. Dept. of Taxation. Research Division) , no. 1.
HJ4655.V88 A828 1984

Virkninger av oljevirksomhet i Nord-Norge /. Schreiner, Alette. Oslo , 1984. 43 p. : ISBN 82-537-2118-8 : LC Card 85-146089
HD9575.N62 S37 1984

Virksomheden i årene 1981-1983 : forskningsplan / Rådet for trafiksikkerhedsforskning. Gentofte : Rådet ; København : Distribution, Direktoratet for statens indkøb, 1984. 80 p. : ill. ; 21 cm. (Beretning / Rådet for trafiksikkerhedsforskning, 0107-6477) ISBN 87-7327-022-9 LC Card 86-100414
1. Rådet for trafiksikkerhedsforskning. 2. Traffic safety - Denmark - Research. I. Rådet for trafiksikkerhedsforskning (Denmark). II. Series: Beretning (Rådet for trafiksikkerhedsforskning (Denmark)).
HE5614.5.D4 V57 1984

Virksomheden, lønarbejderen og samfundet . Rasmussen, Jørgen, 1948- [Aalborg] , 1978. 264 p. ; LC Card 86-460208
HD60.5.D4 R37 1978

Virksomhedens økonomi og ledelse .
(2) Johnsen, Erik, 1928- Introduktion til ledelseslære /. [Copenhagen] , 1984, c1983. 109 p. : ISBN 87-17-03424-8 LC Card 85-127809
HD57.7 .J64 1983

(2) Johnsen, Erik, 1928- Introduktion til ledelseslære /. [Copenhagen] , 1986, c1983. 134 p. : ISBN 87-17-03470-1 LC Card 87-108605
HD57.7 .J64 1986

Virmani, M. R. Government media and the public sector . New Delhi , 1983. 270 p. ; LC Card 83-907479 DDC 302.3/24/0954 19
HD59 .G62 1983 ***NYPL [JLD 86-3767]***

Virtual facsimile & PC image capture/transmission/processing. Norwalk, Conn., U. S.A. (6 Prowitt St., Norwalk 06855) : International Resource Development, c1986. vii, 208 leaves : ill. ; 29 cm. (Report / International Resource Development Inc. . #707) "August 1986." LC Card 86-224356 DDC 381/.4500642/0973 19
1. Image processing equipment industry - United States. 2. Market surveys - United States. I. International Resource Development, inc. II. Title: Virtual facsimile and PC image capture/transmission/processing. III. Series: Report / International Resource Development Inc. , #707.
HD9696.I423 U548 1986

Virtual facsimile and PC image capture/transmission/processing. Virtual facsimile & PC image capture/transmission/processing. Norwalk, Conn., U. S.A. (6 Prowitt St., Norwalk 06855) , c1986. vii, 208 leaves : LC Card 86-224356 DDC 381/.4500642/0973 19
HD9696.I423 U548 1986

Visage de la France. France travaille. Kollar, François, 1904- La France travaille /. Paris , c1986. 238 p. : ISBN 2-85108-435-6 LC Card 87-108516
HD8430 .K65 1986

Visão. Os Mistérios da inflação . São Paulo , 1986. 121 p. ; LC Card 86-189815
HG835 .M57 1986

Uma visão de Rotary /. Leitão, Renato de Castro. Olinda [Brazil] 1985. 55 p. ; LC Card 86-158781
HF5001 .L47 1985

VISI ON (COMPUTER PROGRAM)
Seybold, Patricia B. Integrated desk-top environments . New York , c1985. ix, 181 p. : ISBN 0-07-056324-1 (pbk.) : LC Card 84-27841 DDC 650/.028/5425 19
HF5548.4.S95 S49 1985 ***NYPL [JSE 86-2011]***

Visid Prachuabmoh. (joint author) Goldstein, Sidney, 1927- Urban-rural migration differentials in Thailand /. [Bangkok] , 1974. 49 p. ; LC Card 78-301310 DDC 301.36/1
HB2104.55.A3 G64 ***NYPL [JLM 83-719 no.12]***

Vision creates hope . Holzhausen, Walter, 1929- Dhaka, Bangladesh , 1986. viii, 118 p. ; LC Card 87-901565 DDC 330.9172/4 19
HC59.7 .H624 1986

Vision of the future : the next decade in U. S.-Asia trade : challenges to economic cooperation, impact of science and technology, cornerstone of security. Washington, D.C. : US-Asia Institute in cooperation with U. S. Dept. of State : U. S. Information Agency, 1986. x, 189 p. : ill. ; 23 cm. Proceedings of a conference sponsored by the US-Asia Institute in cooperation with U. S. Dept. of State & U. S. Information Agency, Feb. 19-20, 1986, Washington, D.C. LC Card 87-125235 DDC 382/.0973/05 19
1. United States - Commerce - Asia - Congresses. 2. Asia - Commerce - United States - Congresses. 3. United States - Foreign economic relations - Asia - Congresses. 4. Asia - Foreign economic relations - United States - Congresses. I. US-Asia Institute (Washington, D.C.). II. United States. Dept. of State. III. United States. Information Agency.
HF3118 .V57 1986

A vision of unity . Kaufman, Stuart Bruce. Kensington, Md. , c1986. ix, 182 p. : LC Card 86-225331 DDC 331.88/1 19
HD6515.B2 K38 1986

VISIONS.
Sowell, Thomas, 1930- A conflict of visions /. New York , c1987. 273 p. ; ISBN 0-688-06912-6 LC Card 86-18187 DDC 303.3/72 19
HM73 .S68 1987 ***NYPL [JLD 87-823]***

Visions & business . Weidlein, Marianne S., 1944- Boulder, Colo. , 1987, c1986. 261 p. in various pagings : ISBN 0-942097-11-4 (3-ring binder ed.) : LC Card 87-7935 DDC 658/.007/7 19
HD30.4 .W43 1987

Visions and business. Weidlein, Marianne S., 1944- Visions & business . Boulder, Colo. , 1987, c1986. 261 p. in various pagings : ISBN 0-942097-11-4 (3-ring binder ed.) : LC Card 87-7935 DDC 658/.007/7 19
HD30.4 .W43 1987

Viskina, N. I. Instrumental'nye sistemy modelirovaniia /. Moskva , 1983. 97 p. : LC Card 84-210491
HB143.5 .I57 1983

Vislie, Jon, 1946- Natural gas markets and contracts /. Amsterdam ; New York : x, 320 p. : ISBN 0-444-70206-7 (U. S.) LC Card 87-5061 DDC 380.1/42285/094 19
HD9581.E82 N37 1987 ***NYPL [TB (Contributions to economic analysis. v.161)]***

Visnyovszki, Gábor. A Magyar bélyegek kézikönyve /. Budapest , 1986. 551 p., viii p. of plates : ISBN 963-281-692-/ : LC Card 87-151573 DDC 769.569439 19
HE6185.H8 M32 1986

Vísperas de la independencia americana . Lucena Salmoral, Manuel. Madrid , 1986. vii, 389 p. ; ISBN 84-205-1308-3 LC Card 86-205153
HF3490.C37 L83 1986

Vissers, A. M. C. Arbeidsmarktgedrag ten tijde van massale werkloosheid : de eerste uitkomsten van een landelijk onderzoek / A.M.C. Vissers, A.M. de Vries, Th. Schepens. 's-Gravenhage : Staatsuitgeverij, 1986. 106 p. : ill. ; 28 cm. (OSA-voorstudie . nr. 12) "Maart 1986." Bibliography: p. 64-65. ISBN 90-12-05302-1 LC Card 87-108930
1. Labor mobility - Netherlands. 2. Unemployment - Netherlands. I. Vries, A. M. de. II. Schepens, Th. III. Series: OSA-voorstudie , nr. V 12. IV. Title.
HD5717.5.N45 V57 1986

Vissh finansovo-stopanski institut "D.A. T͡Senov"--Svishtov. Otdelenie za povishavane kvalifikatsiiata na kadrite. Ikonomika i upravlenie na kachestvoto. Svishtov , 1985. 201 p. : LC Card 86-155955
HC403.Z9 I5239 1985

Vissh ikonomicheski institut "Karl Marks"--Sofiia. Prinosŭt na dr. Todor Zhivkov za razvitieto na sotsialno-ikonomicheskata politika na BKP v etapa na izgrazhdane na razvitoto sotsialistichesko obshtestvo . Sofiia , 1983. 398 p. ; LC Card 84-103348
HC403 .P72 1983

Vissi, Ferenc. Gazdaságirányítás, 1985 /. Budapest , 1984. 175 p. ; ISBN 963-221-540-0 : LC Card 85-229856
HC300.28 .G338 1984

VISUAL COMMUNICATION - UNITED STATES - PSYCHOLOGICAL ASPECTS.
Barthel, Diane L., 1949- Putting on appearances . Philadelphia , 1988. p. cm. ISBN 0-87722-528-1 (alk. paper) : LC Card 87-20010 DDC 659.1/042 19
HF5827 .B37 1988

VISUAL DATA PROCESSING. see **OPTICAL DATA PROCESSING.**

VISUAL DESIGNS (INDUSTRIAL PUBLICITY) see **INDUSTRIAL DESIGN COORDINATION.**

Visual display units . Dy, Fe Josefina F. Geneva , 1985. ix, 138 p. : ISBN 92-2-105083-1 (pbk.) : LC Card 86-214267 DDC 651.8 19
HF5547.5 .D9 1985

Vita italiana. N. 9/76 (Supplement) La Tutela del lavoro in Italia. [Roma] [1976] 144 p. ; LC Card 86-233354
HD8481 .T85 1976

The vital link . Newman, Marie Mastin. Washington, DC , c1986. vii, 48 p. : ISBN 0-931032-21-0 (pbk.) LC Card 86-200991 DDC 363.6/2/0973 19
HD9685.U5 N493 1986

Vital statistics for Pennsylvania, 1980 to 1984. Harrisburg, Pa. : Dept. of Health, State Health Data Center, [1986] x, 103 p. : ill. ; 28 cm. "June 17, 1986." LC Card 86-622850 DDC 304.6/09748/021 19
1. Pennsylvania - Statistics, vital. I. Pennsylvania. Health Data Center.
HA605 .V58 1986

Vitale, Luis. Historia de la deuda externa latinoamericana y entretelones del endeudamiento argentino / Luis Vitale. Buenos Aires, Argentina : Sudamericana/Planeta, c1986. 351 p. ; 23 cm. Bibliography: p. 329-337. Includes indexes. ISBN 950-37-0223-2 LC Card 87-100729
1. Debts, External - Latin America - History. 2. Debts, External - Argentina - History. I. Title.
HJ8514.5 .V57 1986

Vitale, Michael. Cooper, Robin, 1951- CABIS, computer-aided bookkeeping instruction system /. Reading, Mass. , c1987. p. cm. ISBN 0-201-11307-4 (user's manual) LC Card 86-32148 DDC 657/.2/02855369 19
HF5630 .C68 1987

Viteles, Morris S. (Morris Simon), 1898- Industrial psychology / Morris S. Viteles. New York : Garland Pub., 1987, c1932. xviii, 652 p., 8 p. of plates : ill. ; 22 cm. (Continuity in administrative science) Reprint. Originally published: New York : W.W. Norton, 1932. Bibliography: p. 629-633. Includes indexes. ISBN 0-8240-8224-9 (alk. paper) : LC Card 86-25817 DDC 158.7 19
1. Psychology, Industrial. I. Title. II. Series.
HF5548.8 .V55 1987

Vitelli, Guillermo. Cuarenta años de inflación en la argentina, 1945-1985 / Guillermo Vitelli. Buenos Aires : Editorial Legasa, [1986] 239 p. : ill. ; 23 cm. (Ensayo crítico) Bibliography: p. [225]-227. ISBN 950-600-086-7 LC Card 87-124167 DDC 332.4/1/0982 19
1. Inflation (Finance) - Argentina - History - 20th century. I. Title.
HG815 .V57 1986

Viten som verktøy . Engelstad, Kirsten. Oslo , 1985. 80 p. ; ISBN 82-7195-048-7 LC Card 86-175688
HD2346.N6 E53 1985

Vitenskap og politikk . Bergh, Trond, 1946- Oslo , 1984. 269 p. : ISBN 82-03-11342-7 : LC Card 84-184253
HB116.3.A2 B47 1984

La viticultura catalana davant la integració a la Comunitat Europea /. Clavera, Joan. [Barcelona] [1986] 124 p. : ISBN 6-476-84021-8 LC Card 86-200618
HD9259.G7 S693 1986

VITICULTURE - BRAZIL - STATISTICS.
Vitivinicultura no Brasil . Bento Gonçalves, RS , 1986, c1985. 50 p. ; LC Card 87-403937 DDC 338.1/748/0981021 19
HD9384.B72 V58 1986

VITICULTURE - FRANCE - CHAMPAGNE-ARDENNE.
Berger, Alain. Les récoltants vendeurs au kilo champenois face au contrat interprofessionnel /. Paris , Epernay [1984] 45, 63 p. : ISBN 2-85340-534-6 LC Card 85-111856
HD9382.7.C5 B47 1984

VITICULTURE - FRANCE - NEUVILLE-SUR-SEINE - HISTORY.
Dautriat, Pierre. Vignes et vignerons d'autrefois dans le Barséquanais . Saint-Seine-l'Abbaye , c1984. 70 p. : ISBN 2-86701-018-7 : LC Card 85-117852
HD9385.F82 N483 1984

VITICULTURE - HUNGARY - STATISTICS - HISTORY.
Szőlőtermelés . Budapest , 1986. 519 p. ; ISBN 963-340-777-X : LC Card 86-196884
HD9385.H82 S95 1986

VITICULTURE - ITALY - PIEMONTE - HISTORY.
Rapetti, Vittorio, 1955- Uomini, collina e vigneto in Piemonte, da metà Ottocento agli anni trenta /. Alessandria , 1984. 342 p., [16] p. of plates : LC Card 86-151345
HD9385.I82 P547 1984

Vitivinicultura no Brasil : informações estatísticas / Ministério da Agricultura, MA, Empresa Brasileira de Pesquisa Agropecuária, EMBRAPA, Centro Nacional de Pesquisa de Uva e Vinho, CNPUV. Bento Gonçalves, RS : CNPUV, 1986, c1985. 50 p. ; 30 cm. (Documentos, 0102-3969 . 1) LC Card 87-403937 DDC 338.1/748/0981021 19
1. Wine industry - Brazil - Statistics. 2. Viticulture - Brazil - Statistics. I. Series: Documentos (Centro Nacional de Pesquisa de Uva e Vinho (Brazil)) , 1.
HD9384.B72 V58 1986

VITÓRIA (ESPÍRITO SANTO, BRAZIL) - COMMERCE - HISTORY.
Siqueira, Penha. O desenvolvimento do porto de Vitória, 1870-1940 /. Vitória-ES , 1984. 162 p. : LC Card 85-144275
HE556.V5 S56 1984

VITÓRIA (ESPÍRITO SANTO, BRAZIL) - ECONOMIC CONDITIONS.
Siqueira, Penha. O desenvolvimento do porto de Vitória, 1870-1940 /. Vitória-ES , 1984. 162 p. : LC Card 85-144275
HE556.V5 S56 1984

Vitousek, Paige Bovee. Lush, Minnie. California real estate exam guide /. Chicago , c1987. p. cm. ISBN 0-88462-591-5 LC Card 87-3290 DDC 333.33/09794 19
HD266.C2 L87 1987

Vittoz, Stanley. New Deal labor policy and the American industrial economy / by Stanley Vittoz. Chapel Hill : University of North Carolina Press, c1987. 241 p. ; 24 cm. Bibliography: p. 217-235. Includes index. ISBN 0-8078-1729-5 LC Card 86-24911 DDC 331/.0973 19
1. New Deal, 1933-1939. 2. Labor policy - United States - History - 20th century. 3. Trade-unions - United States - Political activity - History - 20th century. 4. United States - Politics and government - 1933-1945. 5. United States - Economic conditions - 1918-1945. I. Title.
HD8072 .V715 1987

Vitullo, Ray, 1925- How to get organized & increase self confidence : a task management system / by Ray Vitullo. North Plainfield,

N.J. : Apostrophe Press, c1986. p. cm. Includes index. ISBN 0-9607752-3-4 : LC Card 86-72854
DDC 650.1 19
1. Time management. 2. Success in business. 3. Success. I. Title. II. Title: How to get organized and increase self confidence. III. Title: Task management.
HD69.T54 V58 1986

Viveiros, Jerônimo de, 1884- História do comércio do Maranhão. São Luís, Associação Comercial Maranhão, 1954- <1964 > v. <1-3 > illus., ports., facsims. 24 cm. Includes bibliographies and indexes. CONTENTS. - v. 1-2. 1612-1895.--v. 3. 1896-1934. LC Card 55-29090
1. Maranhão (Brazil) - Commerce. I. Title.
HF3409.M3 V5

VIVIAN AND SONS (FIRM) - HISTORY.
Toomey, Robert R., 1949- Vivian and Sons, 1809-1924 . New York , 1985. 427 p. ; ISBN 0-8240-6692-8 (alk. paper) : LC Card 84-46012
DDC 338.7/622343/0941 19
HD9539.C7 G778 1985
NYPL [JLE 86-4440]

Vivian and Sons, 1809-1924 . Toomey, Robert R., 1949- New York , 1985. 427 p. ; ISBN 0-8240-6692-8 (alk. paper) : LC Card 84-46012
DDC 338.7/622343/0941 19
HD9539.C7 G778 1985
NYPL [JLE 86-4440]

La vivienda de interés social en Panamá . Navarro, Hugo. Panamá , 1975. 288 p. : LC Card 84-100873
HD7312.A3 N38 1975

Vivienda del Tercer Mundo : alternativas a la ciudad espontánea : segundo foro internacional / Facultad de Arquitectura, Universidad de los Andes. Bogotá : Ediciones PROA : La Facultad, c1986. 94 p. : ill. ; 21 cm. (Cuadernos PROA . 9) ISBN 958-9054-01-3 LC Card 86-224743
1. Housing - Latin America. 2. Self-help housing - Latin America. 3. Housing - Developing countries. I. Universidad de los Andes (Bogotá, Colombia). Facultad de Arquitectura.
HD7305.5 .V58 1986

Vivienda, hogar y familia. XV Censo nacional de población y IV de vivienda--Chile, abril 1982. [Santiago] [1985-<1986]. v. <1-13 > : LC Card 87-109976
HA994 1982c

Vivienda para panameños de escasos recursos? Pacheco D., Rubén. Industria de la construcción . [Panamá] , 1974. 17, [1] leaves, [4] leaves of plates : LC Card 87-400643
HD9715.P223 P367 1974

Vivienda rural, México. [Mexico City] : Secretaría de Asentamientos Humanos y Obras Públicas, [1982?] 40 p. : ill. ; 29 cm. "Asamblea General de la Asociación Mundial de Vivienda Rural, Conferencia sobre Financiación y Administración de los Asentamientos Humanos." Includes bibliographical references. LC Card 86-174056
1. Housing, Rural - Government policy - Mexico. 2. Housing, Rural - Mexico. 3. Mexico - Rural conditions. I. Mexico. Secretaría de Asentamientos Humanos y Obras Públicas. II. International Rural Housing Association. III. Conferencia sobre Financiación y Administración de los Asentamientos Humanos (1982 : Mexico City, Mexico).
HD7289.M6 V58 1982

Vivienda y población en Costa Rica . Carreras, Rodrigo X. Heredia, Costa Rica , 1979. 203 p. : LC Card 87-404329 DDC 363.5/097286 19
HD7308.A3 C37 1979

Vivliothēkē historikōn meletōn . (202) Andreadēs, Andreas Michaēl, 1876-1935. Historia tōn ethnikōn daneiōn /. Athēna , 1986- v. <1 > ; LC Card 87-112859
HJ8672 .A53 1986

VIZCAYA (SPAIN) - COMMERCE - HISTORY.
Lafarga Lozano, Adolfo. De Bilbao y de Vizcaya sobre sus orígenes históricos y económicos /. [Bilbao? , 1976?] (Bilbao : Gráficas Loroño) 310 p. : ISBN 84-400-1414-7
LC Card 85-142805
HF3690.B5 L34 1976

VIZCAYA, SPAIN - HISTORY.
Lafarga Lozano, Adolfo. De Bilbao y de Vizcaya sobre sus orígenes históricos y económicos /. [Bilbao? , 1976?] (Bilbao : Gráficas Loroño) 310 p. : ISBN 84-400-1414-7
LC Card 85-142805
HF3690.B5 L34 1976

A Vízgazdálkodás távlati fejlesztésének prognózisai / [összeállitotta Kovács György, Csermák Béla, Dávid László]. Budapest : VIZDOK, 1983. 176 p. : ill., maps ; 20 cm. (Vízügyi műszaki gazdasági tájékoztató, 0324-2501 . 143. sz.) Bibliography: p. 171-176. ISBN 963-602-278-X LC Card 85-109619
1. Water resources development - Hungary. I. Kovács, György, 1925-. II. Csermák, Béla. III. Dávid, László, Dr. IV. Series.
HD1697.H8 V59 1983

Vizsgálatok az újszülöttek nemi arányának alakulásáról /. Rex-Kiss, Béla. Budapest , 1986. 124 p. : ISBN 963-241-457-8 : LC Card 87-138601
HB1741 .R49 1986

Vízügyi műszaki gazdasági tájékoztató, 0324-2501 .
(143. sz) A Vízgazdálkodás távlati fejlesztésének prognózisai /. Budapest , 1983. 176 p. : ISBN 963-602-278-X LC Card 85-109619
HD1697.H8 V59 1983

Vízváry, Tibor. Baross, Jenő. A kereskedelmi hitel és a váltó gyakorlata /. Budapest , 1985. 123 p. ; LC Card 86-228454
HG3754.5.H9 B37 1985

Vizzini, Sergio. Indagine socio-demografica sugli immigrati stranieri in Sicilia : due realtà a confronto, Mazara del Vallo e Campobello di Mazara / Sergio Vizzini, Filippo Accardi. Palermo : Università di Palermo, Istituto di statistica sociale e scienze demografiche e biometriche, [1983] 108 p. ; 25 cm. (Collana di studi demografici. 14) Includes bibliographies. LC Card 86-131931
1. Mazara del Vallo (Sicily) - Foreign population - Statistics. 2. Campobello di Mazara (Sicily) - Foreign population - Statistics. I. Accardi, Filippo. II. Università di Palermo. Istituto di statistica sociale e scienze demografiche e biometriche. III. Title. IV. Series.
HB3600.M39 V58 1983

Vklad robitnychoho klasu Ukraïns'koï R.S.R. u pryskorennia naukovo-tekhnichnoho prohresu v promyslovosti, 50-70-i roky. Pliushch, M. R. Vklad robitnychoho klasu Ukraïns'koï RSR u pryskorennia naukovo-tekhnichnoho prohresu v promyslovosti, 50-70-i roky /. Kyïv , 1981. 244 p. ; LC Card 82-200854
HC337.U53 T465 1981

Vklad robitnychoho klasu Ukraïns'koï RSR u pryskorennia naukovo-tekhnichnoho prohresu v promyslovosti, 50-70-i roky /. Pliushch, M. R. Kyïv , 1981. 244 p. ; LC Card 82-200854
HC337.U53 T465 1981

Vklad severnogo krest'ianstva v material'nuiu i dukhovnuiu kul'turu i ego znachenie v reshenii problem agropromyshlennogo kompleksa nechernozemnoĭ zony RSFSR : tezisy godichnogo sobraniia problemnogo ob"edineniia i Severnogo otdeleniia Arkheograficheskoĭ komissii (Sovetskiĭ period) : Vologda, 7-8 iiunia 1984 goda. / [redaktory M.A. Beznin, A.A. Pashko]. Vologda : Vologodskiĭ gos. pedagog. in-t, 1984. 93 p. ; 20 cm. At head of title: Ministerstvo prosveshcheniia RSFSR. Severnoe otdelenie Arkheograficheskoĭ komissii AN SSSR. Vologodskoe problemnoe ob"edinenie po agrarnoĭ istorii Evropeĭskogo Severa. Vologodskiĭ gosudarstvennyĭ pedagogicheskiĭ institut. Includes bibliographical references. LC Card 85-156518
1. Food supply - Russian S.F.S.R. - Non-Chernozem Region - Abstract. 2. Agricultural industries - Russian S.F.S.R. - Non-Chernozem Region - Abstracts. I. Beznin, M. A. II. Pashko, A. A. III. Akademiia nauk SSSR. Arkheograficheskaia komissiia. Severnoe otdelenie. IV. Vologodskoe problemnoe ob"edinenie po agrarnoĭ istorii Evropeĭskogo Severa SSSR. V. Vologodskiĭ gosudarstvennyĭ pedagogicheskiĭ institut.
HD9015.S652 V54 1984

Vladimirov, Vladislav Vasil'evich. Prodolzhenie podviga . Moskva , 1979. 165 p., [16] p. of plates : LC Card 81-150822
HD1995.K36 B7337 1979

Vladinets, N. I. (Nikolaĭ Ivanovich) Filatelisticheskaia geografiia : evropeĭskie zarubezhnye strany / N.I. Vladinets. Moskva : Radio i sviaz', 1981. 159 p. : ill. ; 17 cm. LC Card 82-110957
1. Postage-stamps - Europe - History. 2. Postal service - Europe - History. I. Title.
HE6185.E84 V54 1981

Filatelisticheskaia geografiia : strany Azii (bez SSSR) / N.I. Vladinets. Moskva : Radio i sviaz', 1984. 175 p. : ill. ; 17 cm. LC Card 85-153635
1. Postage-stamps - Asia - History. I. Title.
HE6185.A7 V53 1984

Vladov, Dimo. Agrarnaia politika sotsialisticheskikh stran na sovremennom ėtape /. Moskva , 1981. 366 p. ; LC Card 82-109367
HD1918 .A37 1981

Vlasenkov, G. T. (Gennadiĭ Timofeevich) Silin, V. A. (Vladimir Andreevich) Ėkonomika--poisk, ėksperiment /. Moskva , 1978. 109 p. ; LC Card 81-167075
HC336.25 .S557 1978

Vlas'evich, IU. E. (IUriĭ Evlampievich) Ėkonomicheskoe bremia militarizma / IU.E. Vlas'evich. Moskva : "Mysl'", 1980. 181 p. ; 20 cm. Includes bibliographical references. LC Card 81-134793
1. War - Economic aspects. 2. Arms race - Economic aspects. 3. Militarism - Economic aspects. I. Title.
HC79.D4 V58 1980

Vlasov, V. I. IUzhnaia IAkutiia, sotsial'no-ėkonomicheskiĭ aspekt . IAkutsk , 1985. 94 p. ; LC Card 86-180767
HC337.I2 I97 1985

Vlasova, I. V. (Irina Vladimirovna) Traditsii krest'ianskogo zemlepol'zovaniia v Pomor'e i Zapadnoĭ Sibiri v XVII-XVIII vv. / I.V. Vlasova ; otvetstvennyĭ redaktor V.A. Aleksandrov. Moskva : Izd-vo "Nauka", 1984. 230 p. : ill. ; 23 cm. At head of title: Akademiia nauk SSSR. Ordena Druzhby Narodov Institut ėtnografii im. N.N. Miklukho-Maklaia. Includes bibliographical references and index. LC Card 85-174592
1. Land tenure - Russian S.F.S.R. - White Sea Region - History. 2. Land tenure - Russian S.F.S.R. - Siberia, Western - History. 3. Peasantry - Russian S.F.S.R. - White Sea Region - History. 4. Peasantry - Russian S.F.S.R. - Siberia, Western - History. I. Aleksandrov, V. A. (Vadim Aleksandrovich). II. Title.
HD719.W45 V55 1984

Vlerick, A. J. Competitief ondernemen . Antwerpen , 1983. vi, 233 p. : ISBN 90-6716-301-5 LC Card 85-177786
HD41 .C64 1983

Vlerick, André. see **Vlerick, A. J.**

Vliamos, Spyros I. Ho symvoulos epicheirēseōn : hola hosa prepei va xerei hena stelechos gi'auton. Athēna : Ekdosē tou Tmēmatos Dēmosiōn Scheseōn tēs ETVA, c1985. 48 p. : ill. ; 24 cm. LC Card 86-182906
1. Business consultants. I. Hellēnikē Trapeza Viomēchanikēs Anaptyxeōs (Greece). Tmēma Dēmosiōn Scheseōn. II. Title.
HD69.C6 V55 1985

Vliianie ėnergeticheskikh strategiĭ na ėnergopotreblenie /. Kononov, IU. D. Irkutsk , 1985. 106 p. : LC Card 86-233835
HD9502.S652 K65 1985

Vlist, R. van der. Modern organiseren en menselijker werken /. 's-Gravenhage , 1985. 198 p. : ISBN 90-6095-314-2 : LC Card 85-214437
HF5548.8 .M55 1985

Vlitos, Irene. The European potential for a venture capital industry / prepared by Irene Vlitos. Menlo Park, CA (333 Ravenswood Ave., Menlo Park 94025) : SRI International, Business Intelligence Program, c1986. 13 leaves : ill. ; 28 cm. "February 1986." Datalog file no. 86-1046." Bibliography: leaf 13. LC Card 86-220533 DDC 332.6/6 19
1. Venture capital - Europe - Case studies. 2. Investments - Europe - Case studies. I. Business Intelligence Program (SRI International). II. Title.
HG5428 .V56 1986

Vloga znanosti pri oblikovanju strategije razvoja SR Slovenije / [uredniški odbor Robert Blinc ... et al.]. Ljubljana : Slovenska akademija znanosti in umetnosti, 1981. 174 p. : ill. ; 24 cm. (Vprašanja znanosti) Title on leaf preceding t.p.: The role of science in forming the development strategy for SR Slovenia. Includes bibliographical references. LC Card 82-151266
1. Research - Economic aspects - Yugoslavia - Slovenia. 2. Slovenia - Economic policy. I. Blinc, R. (Robert). II. Title: Role of science in forming the development strategy for SR Slovenia. III. Series.
HC407.Z7 S57 1981

VLSI Research, Inc. Cleaning and contaminant monitoring systems for the semiconductor industry . San Jose, CA (1754 Technology Dr., Suite 226, San Jose 95110) , c1986. 1 v. (various pagings) : LC Card 87-114689 DDC 380.1/4562138152
HD9999.C4862 C55 1986

Vneshneekonomicheskie otnosheniia sotsialisticheskikh stran v usloviiakh NTR / pod redaktsieĭ I.P. Faminskogo, M.N. Os'movoĭ. Moskva : Izd-vo Moskovskogo universiteta, 1985. 215 p. ; 22 cm. Includes bibliographical references. LC Card 84-219529
1. Technological innovations - Europe, Eastern. 2. Europe, Eastern - Foreign economic relations. I. Faminskiĭ, Igor' Pavlovich. II. Os'mova, Markiana Nikolaevna.
HF1531 .V62 1985 ***NYPL [*QIP 87-2072]***

Vneshneekonomicheskie sviazi razvivaiushchikhsia stran . Pankova, E. A. (Evgeniia Afanas'evna) Moskva , 1985. 158 p. ; LC Card 86-130427
HF1413 .P36 1985

Vneshneekonomicheskie sviazi stran-chlenov SĖV v usloviiakh sotsialisticheskoĭ integratsii / V.A. Golubev ... [et al.]. Kiev : Nauk. dumka, 1983. 245 p. ; 20 cm. At head of title: Akademiia nauk Ukrainskoĭ SSR. Institut sotsialnykh i ėkonomicheskikh problem zarubezhnykh stran. Includes bibliographical references. LC Card 83-189711
1. Europe, Eastern - Economic integration. 2. Europe, Eastern - Foreign economic relations. 3. Council for Mutual Economic Assistance. I. Golubev, V. A. (Vladimir Alekseevich). II. Instytut sotsial'nykh i ekonomichnykh problem zarubizhnykh kraïn (Akademiia nauk Ukraïns'koï RSR).
HC243.5 .V54 1983

Vneshnetorgovye sviazi SSSR so stranami Arabskogo Vostoka v 1922-1939 gg. /. Makeev, D. A. Moskva , 1983. 112 p. ; LC Card 84-189987
HF1558.15.A65 M34 1983

Vneshniaia torgovlia SSSR so stranami SĖV / otvetstvennyĭ redaktor V.M. Shastitko ; [avtorskiĭ kollektiv V.I. Bochkova ... et al.]. Moskva : "Nauka", 1986. 108, [3] p. ; 22 cm. At head of title: Akademiia nauk SSSR. Institut ėkonomiki mirovoĭ sotsialisticheskoĭ sistemy. Bibliography: p. 105-[109] LC Card 86-213259
1. Soviet Union - Commerce - Europe, Eastern. 2. Europe, Eastern - Commerce - Soviet Union. I. Shastitko, Vladimir Mikhaĭlovich. II. Bochkova, V. I. III. Institut ėkonomiki mirovoĭ sotsialisticheskoĭ sistemy (Akademiia nauk SSSR).
HF3628.E9 V54 1986

VNR accountancy passbooks.
Robins, Paul. Advanced accounting practice book 1 . Wokingham, Berkshire, England , 1987. p. cm. ISBN 0-278-00014-2 : LC Card 87-13803 DDC 657/.046 19
HF5635 .R66 1987

The VNR series in accounting and finance.
Drury, Colin. Management and cost accounting /. Workingham, Berkshire, England , 19. xv, 599 p. : ISBN 0-442-30637-7 (pbk.) LC Card 85-3266 DDC 658.1/511 19
HF5635 .D798 1986

Vocational & technical careers. Paradis, Adrian A. Opportunities in vocational & technical careers /. Lincolnwood, Ill., U. S.A. , c1987. xi, 147 p. : ISBN 0-8442-6018-5 LC Card 87-60104 DDC 371.4/25/02373 19
HF5382.5.U5 P28 1987

Vocational and technical careers. Paradis, Adrian A. Opportunities in vocational & technical careers /. Lincolnwood, Ill., U. S.A. , c1987. xi, 147 p. : ISBN 0-8442-6018-5 LC Card 87-60104 DDC 371.4/25/02373 19
HF5382.5.U5 P28 1987

VOCATIONAL ASPIRATIONS. see **VOCATIONAL INTERESTS.**

Vocational counseling . Raskin, Patricia M., 1943- New York, NY , c1987. xiii, 160 p. ; ISBN 0-8077-2860-8 (pbk.) LC Card 87-1972 DDC 371.4/25 19
HF5381 .R325 1987

VOCATIONAL EDUCATION - ASIA, SOUTHEASTERN.
Vente, Rolf E. Education and training for industrial development in Singapore and other ASEAN countries . Baden-Baden , Singapore , 1984. 175 p. : ISBN 3-7890-0941-5 LC Card 84-186381 DDC 331.25/92/0959 19
HD5715.5.S55 V46 1984 ***NYPL [JLD 86-2773]***

VOCATIONAL EDUCATION - BOLIVIA - ORURO - CASE STUDIES.
Alaix, Ramón. Experiencias de educación y producción de fe y alegría en Oruro y Santa Cruz . La Paz, Bolivia , 1986. 191 p. ; LC Card 86-208411 DDC 331.25/92/098413 19
HD5715.5.B52 S262 1986

VOCATIONAL EDUCATION - BOLIVIA - SANTA CRUZ - CASE STUDIES.
Alaix, Ramón. Experiencias de educación y producción de fe y alegría en Oruro y Santa Cruz . La Paz, Bolivia , 1986. 191 p. ; LC Card 86-208411 DDC 331.25/92/098413 19
HD5715.5.B52 S262 1986

VOCATIONAL EDUCATION - BRAZIL.
Fontes, Lauro (Lauro Barreto) Formação profissional & produtividade no desempenho humano /. [Rio de Janeiro] , 1985. 119, [2] p. ; LC Card 85-221895
HD5715.5.B68 F66 1985

VOCATIONAL EDUCATION - BURKINA FASO.
Emploi et formation en Haute-Volta . Addis-Abéba , 1983. x, 142 p. : LC Card 85-981183
HD5847.5.A6 E48 1983

VOCATIONAL EDUCATION - FRANCE.
Raimond, Jean-Marie. Vocational training of young migrants in France /. Berlin , 1986. x, 101 p. : ISBN 92-825-6118-6
NYPL [JLG 87-134]

VOCATIONAL EDUCATION - GERMANY, WEST.
Feuerstein, Thomas. Humanisierung der Arbeit und Reform der beruflichen Bildung . München , c1983. 221 p. ; ISBN 3-87966-184-7 LC Card 83-222687
HD5715.5.G4 F48 1983

Frauen und Beruf, zwischen Wunsch und Realität . Bonn , Bad Honnef , 1986. 142 p. ; ISBN 3-87066-629-3 : LC Card 87-409372 DDC 331.4/0943 19
HD6149 .F719 1986

Kabbert, Rainer. Jugendliche zwischen Schule und Beruf . Nürnberg , 1982. 84, [1] p. : LC Card 83-169834
HF5382.5.G3 K33 1982

Kornblum, Hans-Joachim. Therapie in der Berufsschule? . München , c1984. x, 458 p. : ISBN 3-597-10503-3 : LC Card 85-105593
HD5715.5.G4 K67 1984

Wagner, Karin. Relation between education, employment, and productivity and their impact on education and labour market policies . Berlin , Washington, DC , 1986. ix, 80 p. ; ISBN 92-825-6371-5 : LC Card 87-136255 DDC 331.12/042/0941 19
HD5715.5.G4 W35 1986

VOCATIONAL EDUCATION - GERMANY, WEST - CONGRESSES.
Workshop "Berufswege von Frauen" (1984 : Berlin, Germany) Berufsverläufe von Frauen . München , Weinheim , c1986. 291 p. : ISBN 3-87966-253-3 LC Card 87-407975 DDC 331.7/02/024042 19
HF5382.67.G3 W67 1984

VOCATIONAL EDUCATION - GREAT BRITAIN.
Wagner, Karin. Relation between education, employment, and productivity and their impact on education and labour market policies . Berlin , Washington, DC , 1986. ix, 80 p. ; ISBN 92-825-6371-5 : LC Card 87-136255 DDC 331.12/042/0941 19
HD5715.5.G4 W35 1986

VOCATIONAL EDUCATION - GUYANA.
Abdulah, Norma. The availability and utilization of skills in Guyana /. St. Augustine, Trinidad [1981] xv, 105 p. ; LC Card 84-146702 DDC 331.11/422 19
HD5759.3.A6 A24 1981
NYPL [JLE 86-4442]

VOCATIONAL EDUCATION - HAITI.
International Labour Organisation. Institut national de formation professionnelle (INFP) . Genève , 1982. ii, 69 p. : ISBN 92-2-203229-2 LC Card 83-234817
HD5715.5.H2 I57 1982

VOCATIONAL EDUCATION - HISTORY.
Breve reseña histórica de la formación profesional y del trabajo /. Bogotá [1973] 29, [1] leaves ; LC Card 85-208500
HD5715 .B74 1973

Koeder, Kurt W. Berufsbegleitendes Studium . Grafenau/Württ. , c1983. 286 p. : ISBN 3-88508-901-7 LC Card 84-185882
HD5715 .K63 1983

VOCATIONAL EDUCATION - ITALY.
Rapporto ISFOL 1985 . Milano, Italy , c1985. 533 p. : LC Card 86-156267
HD5715.5.I8 R393 1985

VOCATIONAL EDUCATION - JAPAN.
New approach to vocational training /. Islamabad, Pakistan , 1985-1986. 2 v. : ISBN 92-2-105078-5 (pbk. : v. 1) LC Card 86-221389 DDC 331.25/92/0952 19
HD5715.5.J3 N48 1985

VOCATIONAL EDUCATION - KANSAS.
Kansas. Legislature. Task Force on Business Training. Report of the Task Force on Business Training of the Legislative Commission on Economic Development. [Topeka, Kansas] [1986] 1 v. (various pagings) ; LC Card 87-621700 DDC 331.25/92/09781 19
HD5715.3.K2 K37 1986

VOCATIONAL EDUCATION - LATIN AMERICA - HISTORY.
Breve reseña histórica de la formación profesional y del trabajo /. Bogotá [1973] 29, [1] leaves ; LC Card 85-208500
HD5715 .B74 1973

VOCATIONAL EDUCATION - SINGAPORE.
Vente, Rolf E. Education and training for industrial development in Singapore and other ASEAN countries . Baden-Baden , Singapore , 1984. 175 p. : ISBN 3-7890-0941-5 LC Card 84-186381 DDC 331.25/92/0959 19
HD5715.5.S55 V46 1984
NYPL [JLD 86-2773]

VOCATIONAL EDUCATION - SOUTH CAROLINA.
Meeting labor needs in South Carolina . Columbia, S.C. (2221 Devine St., Suite 420, Columbia 29205) [1986] 52 leaves ; LC Card 86-623031 DDC 331.12/3/09757 19
HD5725.S6 M44 1986

VOCATIONAL EDUCATION - TERMINOLOGY.
Vocational training . Geneva , 1986. vii, 132 p. ; ISBN 92-2-105457-8 (pbk.) : LC Card 87-123102 DDC 331.25/92/0321 19
HD5715 .V63 1986

VOCATIONAL EDUCATION - UNITED STATES - EVALUATION - CONGRESSES.
National Forum on Issues in Vocational Assessment (2nd : 1986 : Dallas, Tex.) Second National Forum on Issues in Vocational Assessment . Menomonie, Wis. , c1985. vii, 236 p. : ISBN 0-916671-71-2 (pbk.) LC Card 86-217148 DDC 362/.0425 19
HD7256.U5 N336 1986

VOCATIONAL EDUCATION - UZBEK S.S.R.
Shister, G. A. (Grigoriĭ Aronovich) Rukovodstvo kompartii Uzbekistana podgotovkoĭ rabochikh kadrov v usloviiakh razvitogo sotsializma /. Tashkent , 1981. 274, [2] p. ; LC Card 82-204041
HD5797.U9 S54 1981

VOCATIONAL GUIDANCE - ADDRESSES, ESSAYS, LECTURES.
The Jobs challenge . Cambridge, Mass. , 1986. xvi, 304 p. : ISBN 0-88410-990-9 LC Card 85-7547 DDC 331.12 19
HD5707 .J63 1985 ***NYPL [JLE 86-2190]***

VOCATIONAL GUIDANCE - AUSTRALIA.
Holland in Australia . Melbourne , 1986. xxii, 229 p. : ISBN 0-86431-032-3 LC Card 87-164636 DDC 331.7/02/0994 19
HF5381.H56693 H65 1986

VOCATIONAL GUIDANCE - BANGLADESH - CONGRESSES.
Career planning in Bangladesh . Dhaka , c1986. 159 p. ; LC Card 86-903477 DDC 331.7/02/095492 19
HF5382.5.B27 C37 1986

VOCATIONAL GUIDANCE - BRAZIL - FORTALEZA.
Catálogo de ocupações pesquisadas em Fortaleza. [Fortaleza] . 111, [1] p. ; LC Card 83-222529
HF5382.5.B7 C38 1972

VOCATIONAL GUIDANCE - BULGARIA.
Izsledvane rolīata na proizvodstvenata sreda, trudovite kolektivi i nastavnitsite za formirane na komunisticheskо otnoshenie kŭm truda u podrastvashchtite /. Sofiīa , 1984. 150 p. ; LC Card 85-166784
HD6276.B82 I97 1984

VOCATIONAL GUIDANCE - COLLECTED WORKS.
Feingold, S. Norman, 1914- Emerging careers . Garrett Park, Md. , c1983- v. ; ISBN 0-912048-32-8 (pbk.) : LC Card 83-80074 DDC 331.7/02 19
HF5382 .F44 1983 ***NYPL [JLL 86-205]***

VOCATIONAL GUIDANCE - EUROPE.
Poppe, Johann Heinrich Moritz von, 1776-1854. Ausführliche Volks-Gewerbslehre, oder, Allgemeine und besondere Technologie zur Belehrung und zum Nutzen für alle Stände /. Stuttgart , Wien , 1833- v. <1 > : LC Card 87-409525 DDC 331.7/02/024042 19
HF5382.5.E84 P66 1833

Verso un sistema di orientamento . Rimini , c1984. 290 p. : LC Card 85-119196 DDC 370.11/3/094 19
LC5056.I8 V47 1984 ***NYPL [JLE 86-1555]***

VOCATIONAL GUIDANCE FOR THE HANDICAPPED.
Pimentel, Richard. Job placement for the industrially injured worker /. Northridge, Calif. (17624 Romar St., Northridge 91325) , c1987. v, 93, [1] leaves : LC Card 87-401986 DDC 650.1/4/0240816 19
HD7255 .P54 1987

VOCATIONAL GUIDANCE FOR WOMEN - COLORADO.
Faaborg, Barbara Laue. Job resources for Colorado women . Colorado Springs, CO , c1986. 128 p. : ISBN 0-939411-00-8 (pbk.) : LC Card 87-103489 DDC 650.1/4/024042 19
HF5382.65 .F33 1986

VOCATIONAL GUIDANCE FOR WOMEN - COLORADO - DIRECTORIES.
Faaborg, Barbara Laue. Job resources for Colorado women . Colorado Springs, CO , c1986. 128 p. : ISBN 0-939411-00-8 (pbk.) : LC Card 87-103489 DDC 650.1/4/024042 19
HF5382.65 .F33 1986

VOCATIONAL GUIDANCE FOR WOMEN - GERMANY, WEST.
Hegelheimer, Armin. Gleichwertigkeit von allgemeiner und beruflicher Bildung /. Bonn , Bad Honnef , 1986. v, 74 p. ; ISBN 3-87066-628-5 : LC Card 87-409371 DDC 331.4/2592/0943 19
HD6059.6.G4 H42 1986

Hegelheimer, Barbara. Berufsqualifikation und Berufschancen von Frauen in der Bundesrepublik Deutschland /. Berlin , 1977. viii, 303 p. ; LC Card 85-142052
HD6059.6.G4 H428 1977

Selk, Michael, 1943- Geschlecht und Berufswahl . Frankfurt am Main , New York , c1984. 289 p. : ISBN 3-8204-5375-X LC Card 85-193055
HD6059.6.G4 S45 1984

VOCATIONAL GUIDANCE FOR WOMEN - GERMANY (WEST) - CONGRESSES.
Mädchen und Berufswahl . Bonn , Bad Honnef , 1986. 96 p. : ISBN 3-87066-631-5 LC Card 87-409396 DDC 331.4/2592/0943 19
HF5382.67.G3 M33 1986

Workshop "Berufswege von Frauen" (1984 : Berlin, Germany) Berufsverläufe von Frauen . München , Weinheim , c1986. 291 p. : ISBN 3-87966-253-3 LC Card 87-407975 DDC 331.7/02/024042 19
HF5382.67.G3 W67 1984

VOCATIONAL GUIDANCE FOR WOMEN - UNITED STATES.
Neufeld, Rose. Exploring nontraditional jobs for women /. New York , c1987. x, 149 p. : ISBN 0-8239-0698-1 : LC Card 86-29827 DDC 331.7/02/024042 19
HF5382.65 .N48 1987

Nivens, Beatryce. The Black woman's career guide /. New York , 1987. xvi, 362 p. ; ISBN 0-385-24161-5 (pbk.) : LC Card 87-1193 DDC 650.1/4/088042 19
HF5382.5.U5 N5 1987

VOCATIONAL GUIDANCE - GERMANY, WEST.
Berufsbiographien im Wandel /. Opladen , c1986. 290 p. ; ISBN 3-531-11817-X LC Card 86-227301
HF5382.5.G3 B39 1986

Evaluation der Berufsberatung der Bundesanstalt für Arbeit . Nürnberg , 1983. vii, 282 p. : LC Card 85-107586
HF5382.5.G3 E9 1983

Kabbert, Rainer. Jugendliche zwischen Schule und Beruf . Nürnberg , 1982. 84, [1] p. : LC Card 83-169834
HF5382.5.G3 K33 1982

VOCATIONAL GUIDANCE - GREAT BRITAIN - HISTORY - 17TH CENTURY.
Miegge, Mario. Vocazione e lavoro . [Bologna] , c1985. 97 p. : LC Card 87-131793
HF5382.5.G7 M52 1985

VOCATIONAL GUIDANCE - HANDBOOKS, MANUALS, ETC.
Win, David. International careers . Charlotte, Vt. , c1987. 222 p. ; ISBN 0-913589-28-4 (pbk.) : LC Card 86-32547 DDC 650.1/4 19
HF5549.5.E45 W525 1987

VOCATIONAL GUIDANCE - HUNGARY.
Szilágyi, Klára J. A pályafejlődés vizsgálatának módszertani lehetőségei a felsőoktatásban /. Budapest , 1985. 110 p. ; ISBN 963-404-020-9 LC Card 86-174899
HF5429.6.H8 S95 1985

VOCATIONAL GUIDANCE - ITALY.
Verso un sistema di orientamento . Rimini , c1984. 290 p. : LC Card 85-119196 DDC 370.11/3/094 19
LC5056.I8 V47 1984 ***NYPL [JLE 86-1555]***

VOCATIONAL GUIDANCE - SPAIN.
Triadú, Joaquim, 1959- Les professions del futur /. Barcelona , 1986. 186 p. : ISBN 84-86421-20-9 LC Card 86-214981
HF5382.5.S7 T75 1986

VOCATIONAL GUIDANCE - SWEDEN.
Mattsson, Kerstin, 1946- Yrkesvalsfågan . [Malmö] , c1984. vii, 268 p. ; ISBN 91-40-05057-2 : LC Card 84-200481
HF5382.5.S8 M37 1984

VOCATIONAL GUIDANCE - TEXAS.
Mercer, Kent. Directory of licensed occupations and apprenticeship programs in Texas. [Austin, Tex.] [1985] iv, 102 p. ; LC Card 86-622006 DDC 331.7/02/09764 19
HF5382.5.U6 T45 1985

VOCATIONAL GUIDANCE - UNITED STATES.
Chronicle occupational briefs and occupational reprints. Moravia, NY [1986- 4 v. (loose-leaf) : LC Card 86-231523 DDC 331.7/02/0973 19
HF5382.5.U5 C49 1986

Chronicle occupational briefs and occupational reprints. Moravia, NY [1987]- 4 v. (loose-leaf) : LC Card 87-403954 DDC 331.7/02/0973 19
HF5382.5.U5 C49 1987

Fowler, Elizabeth M. The New York times career planner /. New York , 1987. p. cm. ISBN 0-8129-1212-8 : LC Card 87-9964 DDC 650.1/4 19
HF5382.75.U6 F68 1987

Guide for occupational exploration /. [Washington, D.C.] , Circle Pines, Minn. , c1984. vii, 984 p. : LC Card 87-402857 DDC 331.7/02/0973 19
HF5382.5.U5 G83 1984

Herr, Edwin L. Career guidance and counseling through the life span . Glenview, Ill. , c1988. xvi, 576 p. : ISBN 0-673-39726-2 LC Card 87-22748 DDC 331.7/02/0973 19
HF5382.5.U5 H39 1988

Kuenstler, Gail Baugher. The desk guide to training and work advisement /. Springfield, Ill., U. S.A. , c1988. p. cm. ISBN 0-398-05414-2 LC Card 87-25626 DDC 331.7/02/0973 19
HF5382.5.U5 K84 1988

Leape, Martha P. The Harvard guide to careers /. Cambridge, Mass. , 1987. ix, 181 p. ; ISBN 0-674-37564-5 (pbk.) LC Card 87-8409 DDC 331.7/02 19
HF5382.5.U5 L36 1987

Lewis, William, 1946- Fast-track careers . New York , c1987. x, 212 p. ; ISBN 0-471-83801-2 (pbk.) : LC Card 87-10045 DDC 331.7/02/0973 19
HF5382.5.U5 L45 1987

Lewis, William, 1946- Profitable careers in nonprofit /. New York , c1987. vi, 202 p. ; ISBN 0-471-83699-0 (pbk.) : LC Card 87-6102 DDC 331.7/02 19
HF5382.5.U5 L44 1987

Martin, Phyllis Rodgers. Martin's magic formula for getting the right job . New York , c1987. xix, 198 p. : ISBN 0-312-01065-6 (pbk.) : LC Card 87-16302 DDC 650.1/4 19
HF5382.75.U6 M37 1987

Paradis, Adrian A. Opportunities in vocational & technical careers /. Lincolnwood, Ill., U. S.A. , c1987. xi, 147 p. : ISBN 0-8442-6018-5 LC Card 87-60104 DDC 371.4/25/02373 19
HF5382.5.U5 P28 1987

Petras, Ross. Inside track . New York , c1986. xv, 508 p. ; ISBN 0-394-74339-3 : LC Card 85-40868 DDC 650.1/4/0973 19
HF5382.U5 P44 1986 ***NYPL [*R-Econ. 86-3454]***

Salzman, Marian L. Wanted, liberal arts graduates . New York , 1987. xvi, 341 p. ; ISBN 0-385-24008-2 (pbk.) : LC Card 87-8846 DDC 650.1/4 19
HF5382.75.U6 S27 1987

Smith, Demaris C. Temporary employment . White Hall, Va. , c1985. 143 p. ; ISBN 0-932620-56-6 (pbk.) : LC Card 85-13456 DDC 650.1/4 19
HD5854.2.U6 S6 1985 ***NYPL [JLF 86-1365]***

United States. Employment and Training Administration. Office of Youth Program. Completing the youth agenda . Washington , 1979. 73 p. ; ***NYPL [JLF 86-454]***

VGM's careers encyclopedia /. Lincolnwood, Ill., U. S.A. , c1988. xi, 484 p. ; ISBN 0-8442-6132-7 LC Card 87-62404 DDC 331.7/02/0973 19
HF5382.5.U5 C337 1988

VOCATIONAL GUIDANCE - UNITED STATES - BIBLIOGRAPHY.
Leape, Martha P. The Harvard guide to careers /. Cambridge, Mass. , 1987. ix, 181 p. ; ISBN 0-674-37564-5 (pbk.) LC Card 87-8409 DDC 331.7/02 19
HF5382.5.U5 L36 1987

VOCATIONAL GUIDANCE - UNITED STATES - INFORMATION SERVICES.
Leape, Martha P. The Harvard guide to careers /. Cambridge, Mass. , 1987. ix, 181 p. ; ISBN 0-674-37564-5 (pbk.) LC Card 87-8409 DDC 331.7/02 19
HF5382.5.U5 L36 1987

VOCATIONAL INTERESTS - GERMANY, WEST.
Allehoff, Wolfgang H., 1949- Berufswahl und berufliche Interessen /. Göttingen , c1985. 177 p. : ISBN 3-8017-0217-0 LC Card 85-235199
HF5381.5 .A45 1985

Berufsbiographien im Wandel /. Opladen , c1986. 290 p. ; ISBN 3-531-11817-X LC Card 86-227301
HF5382.5.G3 B39 1986

VOCATIONAL INTERESTS - HUNGARY.
Szilágyi, Klára J. A pályafejlődés vizsgálatának módszertani lehetőségei a felsőoktatásban /. Budapest , 1985. 110 p. ; ISBN 963-404-020-9 LC Card 86-174899
HF5429.6.H8 S95 1985

VOCATIONAL INTERESTS - TESTING.
Johansson, Charles B. (Charles Berthil) Manual for the Career Assessment Inventory /. [Minneapolis] , c1976. 93 p. : LC Card 86-219030
HF5381.5 .J64 1976

VOCATIONAL INTERESTS - UNITED STATES.
Guide for occupational exploration /. [Washington, D.C.] , Circle Pines, Minn. , c1984. vii, 984 p. : LC Card 87-402857 DDC 331.7/02/0973 19
HF5382.5.U5 G83 1984

Johansson, Charles B. (Charles Berthil) Career Assessment Inventory . [Minneapolis, Minn.] , c1986. ix, 218 p. : LC Card 87-112723
HF5381.5 .J63 1986

VOCATIONAL OPPORTUNITIES. see **VOCATIONAL GUIDANCE.**

VOCATIONAL QUALIFICATIONS.
Oliveira, José Gonçalves Grosso de. Qualificação, divisão do trabalho e mercado do trabalho /. Lisboa , 1985. 60 p. ; LC Card 86-132680
HF5549.5.J62 O44 1985

VOCATIONAL QUALIFICATIONS - EVALUATION.
Baehr, Melany E. Experience and background inventory . [Park Ridge, Ill.] (1550 Northwest Highway, Park Ridge 60068) [c1986] 48 p. ; LC Card 87-404267 DDC 658.3/112 19
HF5549.5.S38 B34 1986

Baehr, Melany E. Experience and background questionnaire . [Park Ridge, Ill.] (1550 Northwest Highway, Park Ridge 60068) , c1986. 20 p. ; LC Card 87-404268 DDC 658.3/1125 19
HF5381.7 .B327 1986

VOCATIONAL QUALIFICATIONS - UNITED STATES.
Johansson, Charles B. (Charles Berthil) Career Assessment Inventory . [Minneapolis, Minn.] , c1986. ix, 218 p. : LC Card 87-112723
HF5381.5 .J63 1986

VOCATIONAL REHABILITATION - DIRECTORIES.
Social and vocational rehabilitation resources . Geneve , 1984- v. ; ISBN 92-2-003776-9 (pbk. : v. 1) LC Card 86-126143 DDC 362/.0425 19
HD7255 .S62 1984 ***NYPL [JLL 85-184]***

VOCATIONAL REHABILITATION - GERMANY (WEST)
Zur Problematik der Abbrecher der beruflichen Rehabilitation /. Bonn [1985?] 118, [29] p. ; LC Card 86-190824
HD7256.G3 Z87 1985

VOCATIONAL REHABILITATION - NEW YORK (STATE)
Gardner, John A. Vocational rehabilitation outcomes . Cambridge, Mass. , c1986. xix, 48 p. : ISBN 0-935149-03-1 (pbk.) : LC Card 86-28144 DDC 362/.0425 19
HD7256.U6 N6926 1986

Vocational rehabilitation outcomes . Gardner, John A. Cambridge, Mass. , c1986. xix, 48 p. : ISBN 0-935149-03-1 (pbk.) : LC Card 86-28144 DDC 362/.0425 19
HD7256.U6 N6926 1986

VOCATIONAL REHABILITATION - SWEDEN.
Sweden. Samverkanskommittén. Arbetsanpassning . [Stockholm] [1984] 231 p. ; ISBN 91-38-08108-3 LC Card 84-193689
HD7256.S9 S945 1984

VOCATIONAL REHABILITATION - UNITED STATES.
Barrett, John (John J.) The industrial work model . Menomonie, Wis. , c1987. v, 143 p. : ISBN 0-916671-73-9 (pbk.) LC Card 87-403218 DDC 362.0425 19
HD7256.U5 B37 1987

Greenwood, Reed. Employer concerns regarding workers with disabilities /. Hot Springs, Ark. [1985] xii, 170 p. ; LC Card 87-620863 DDC 658.3/045 19
HD7256.U5 G74 1985

The Role of the sheltered workshops in the rehabilitation of the severely handicapped. New York , 1976. xxiv, 467 p. ;
NYPL [JLF 86-1287]

Supported employment . Baltimore , c1988. x, 287 p. : ISBN 0-933716-83-4 (pbk.) : LC Card 87-14367 DDC 362/.0425 19
HD7256.U5 S86 1988

VOCATIONAL REHABILITATION - UNITED STATES - ADDRESSES, ESSAYS, LECTURES.
Competitive employment issues and strategies /. Baltimore , c1986. xvii, 363 p. : ISBN 0-933716-59-1 : LC Card 85-30929 DDC 362/.0425 19
HD7256.U5 C4655 1986 ***NYPL [JLF 87-19]***

VOCATIONAL REHABILITATION - UNITED STATES - CONGRESSES.
Joint Seminar on Designing Jobs for Handicapped Workers (1985 : Chicago, Ill.) Designing jobs for handicapped workers . Hot Springs, Ark. (P.O. Box 1358, Hot Spring 71902) [1986] 66 p. : LC Card 86-622317 DDC 658.3/045 19
HD7256.U5 J65 1985

National Forum on Issues in Vocational Assessment (2nd : 1986 : Dallas, Tex.) Second National Forum on Issues in Vocational Assessment . Menomonie, Wis. , c1985. vii, 236 p. : ISBN 0-916671-71-2 (pbk.) LC Card 86-217148 DDC 362/.0425 19
HD7256.U5 N336 1986

VOCATIONAL REHABILITATION - UNITED STATES - COST EFFECTIVENESS.
Measuring the efficiency of public programs . Philadelphia , 1988. p. cm. ISBN 0-87722-527-3 (alk. paper) LC Card 87-18080 DDC 362/.0425 19
HD7256.U5 M44 1988

VOCATIONAL REHABILITATION - UNITED STATES - FORECASTING.
Hester, Edward J. Predicting which disabled employees will return to work . Topeka, Kan. (700 Jackson, 9th floor, Topeka 66603) , c1986. x, 86 p. : LC Card 86-231920 DDC 331.5/9 19
HD7256.U5 H43 1986

VOCATIONAL REHABILITATION - UNITED STATES - HISTORY - 20TH CENTURY.
Weiss, Joseph W. The management of change . New York , 1986. xviii, 210 p. ; ISBN 0-275-92195-6 (alk. paper) : LC Card 86-9390 DDC 658.4 19
HD7256.U5 W38 1986
NYPL [JLE 86-4062]

VOCATIONAL REHABILITATION - UNITED STATES - STATES - DIRECTORIES.
National directory, training and employment programs for Americans with disabilities /. Washington, D.C. [1985] vii, 374 p. : LC Card 85-602984 DDC 362.4/0484/02573 19
HD7256.U5 N335 1985 ***NYPL [JLF 87-466]***

Vocational training : glossary of selected terms. Geneva : International Labour Office, 1986. vii, 132 p. ; 24 cm. Includes indexes. ISBN 92-2-105457-8 (pbk.) : LC Card 87-123102 DDC 331.25/92/0321 19
1. Occupational training - Terminology. 2. Vocational education - Terminology. I. International Labour Office.
HD5715 .V63 1986

VOCATIONAL TRAINING - GOVERNMENT POLICY - PERSIAN GULF STATES.
Nadwat Tanmiyat al-Mawārid al-Basharīyah fī al-Khalīj al-ʻArabī (1975 : Bahrain) Nadwat Tanmiyat al-Mawārid al-Basharīyah fī al-Khalīj al-ʻArabī . al-Kuwayt [1975?] 361, 404 p. : LC Card 86-964662
HD5715.5.P39 N33 1975

Vocational training of young migrants in France /. Raimond, Jean-Marie. Berlin , 1986. x, 101 p. : ISBN 92-825-6118-6 ***NYPL [JLG 87-134]***

Vocational training problems in small and medium-sized enterprises . Drexel, Ingrid. Luxembourg , Washington, DC , 1986. 279 p. : ISBN 92-825-5707-3 (pbk.) LC Card 86-213476 DDC 331.25/92/094 19
HD5715.5.E8 D74 1986

Vocazione e lavoro . Miegge, Mario. [Bologna] , c1985. 97 p. : LC Card 87-131793
HF5382.5.G7 M52 1985

Você e as opções de compra. [São Paulo, Brazil] : Opções BOVESPA, [19]82. [24] p. ; 21 cm. (Série Opções . oP. 3/82) Cover title. LC Card 86-217458
1. Put and call transactions. 2. Put and call transactions - Brazil. I. Bolsa de Valores de São Paulo. II. Series: Série Opções , op. 82/3.
HG6042 .V63 1982

Você e as opções de venda. [São Paulo, Brazil] : Opções BOVESPA, [19]82. [28] p. ; 21 cm. (Série Opções . op. 4/82) Cover title. LC Card 86-217459
1. Put and call transactions. 2. Put and call transactions - Brazil. I. Bolsa de Valores de São Paulo. II. Series: Série Opções , op. 82/4.
HG6042 .V64 1982

Vodopivec, Alexander. 40 Jahre Wirtschaftsbund : mehr Markt, weniger Staat / Alexander Vodopivec. Wien : Österreichischer Wirtschaftsverlag, [1985?] 107 p. ; 30 cm. LC Card 86-169299
1. Austria - Economic policy - 1945-. 2. Austria - Politics and government - 1945-. 3. Österreichische Volkspartei - History. I. Title. II. Title: Vierzig Jahre Wirtschaftsbund.
HC265 .V589 1985

Voedsel- en Landbouworganisatie van de Verenigde Naties. see **Food and Agriculture Organization of the United Nations.**

Voeĭkov, M. I. (Mikhail Illarionovich)
Organizatsii͡a sorevnovanii͡a i sovershenstvovanie khozi͡aĭstvennogo mekhanizma /. Moskva , 1982. 206 p. ; LC Card 82-202826
HC340.S6 O684 1982

Voelker, Keith E. Sauer, Robert L. Labor relations . Columbus, Ohio , c1987. x, 518 p. : ISBN 0-675-20207-8 LC Card 87-134391 DDC 331/.0973 19
HD8066 .S28 1987

Voeller, Joachim, 1946- Purchasing power parities for international comparisons / by Joachim Voeller. Königstein/Ts. : A. Hain Meisenheim ; Cambridge, Mass. : Oelgeschlager, Gunn & Hain, c1981. 104 p. ; 23 cm. (Mathematical systems in economics, 0344-3302 . 72) Bibliography: p. 99-104. ISBN 3-445-02225-9 (pbk.) LC Card 81-84382
1. Purchasing power parity - Statistical methods. 2. Foreign exchange - Statistical methods. I. Title. II. Series.
HG3821 .V63x 1981

Voenno-promyshlennyĭ kompleks Velikobritanii /. Shein, A. I. (Aleksandr Ivanovich) Moskva , 1985. 165 p. : LC Card 84-219560
HC260.D4 S54 1985 ***NYPL [*QGR 87-2278]***

Voevoda, Ivan Nikiforovich. Metody i modeli razviti͡a regionalʹnykh ėkonomicheskikh sistem . Novosibirsk , 1985. 165 p. : LC Card 86-219402
HC337.R852 S52545 1985

Vogel, David, 1947- National styles of regulation : environmental policy in Great Britain and the United States / David Vogel. Ithaca, N.Y. : Cornell University Press, 1986. 325 p. ; 25 cm. (Cornell studies in political economy) Includes index. Bibliography: p. 291-316. ISBN 0-8014-1658-2 LC Card 85-21332 DDC 363.7/056/0941 19
1. Environmental policy - Great Britain. 2. Environmental policy - United States. 3. Business and politics - Great Britain. 4. Business and politics - United States. 5. Industry and state - Great Britain. 6. Industry and state - United States. I. Title. II. Series.
HC260.E5 V64 1986 ***NYPL [JLE 86-2434]***

Vogel, Ezra F.
Comeback, case by case : building the resurgence of American business / Ezra F. Vogel. New York : Simon and Schuster, c1985. 320 p. ; 25 cm. Includes index. Bibliography: p. 291-297. ISBN 0-671-46079-X LC Card 84-22232 DDC 338.952 19
1. Industry and state - United States. 2. Industry and state - Japan. I. Title.
HD3616.U47 V64 1985
NYPL [JLE 85-2275]

Ideology and national competitiveness . Boston, Mass. , c1987. x, 350 p. ; ISBN 0-87584-147-3 LC Card 86-19569 DDC 338.6/048 19
HF1414 .I34 1987 ***NYPL [JLE 87-1046]***

Vogelsang, Ingo. Anreizmechanismen zur Regulierung der Elektrizitätswirtschaft : eine Fallstudie zur ökonomischen Theorie der Institutionen / Ingo Vogelsang. Tübingen : J.C.B. Mohr, 1982. xii, 173 p. : 8 ill. ; 24 cm. (Schriften zur Umwelt- und Ressourcenökonomie, 0171-7081 . Bd. 5) The author's Habilitationsschrift, Universität Bonn. Bibliography: p. [160]-168. Includes indexes. ISBN 3-16-344549-7 : LC Card 83-153444
1. Electric utilities - Government policy - Germany (West) - Case studies. 2. Trade regulation - Germany

(West) - Case studies. I. Title. II. Series.
HD9685.G3 V64 1982

Vogl, Gerald. Wirtschaftslexikon /. München , c1987. xv, 661 p. : ISBN 3-486-29691-4 LC Card 87-127454 DDC 330/.03/31 19
HB61 .W558 1987

Vohra, Dewan C. Economic relevance of non-alignment / Dewan C. Vohra. New Delhi : ABC Pub. House, 1983. xv, 387 p. ; 23 cm. Includes index. Bibliography: p. [367]-371. LC Card 83-901770 DDC 338.9/009172/4 19
1. Nonalignment. 2. Developing countries - Economic policy. 3. Developing countries - Politics and government. I. Title.
HC59.7 .V63 1983 ***NYPL [JLD 86-3799]***

Voice compression technology : developments, markets, opportunities / Eve Oppenheim, project analyst. Stamford, Conn., U. S.A. : Business Communications, c1985. xii, 146 leaves ; 29 cm. (Business opportunity report . G-092) "August 1985"--T.p. verso. ISBN 0-89336-430-4 (soft) LC Card 87-165256 DDC 380.1/45621389 19
1. Telecommunication equipment industry. 2. Data transmission equipment industry. 3. Speech processing systems industry. 4. Data compression (Telecommunication). 5. Market surveys. I. Oppenheim, Eve. II. Business Communications Co. III. Series.
HD9696.T442 V65 1985

VOICE MAIL SYSTEMS.
Parker, Martin F. The practical guide to voice mail /. Berkeley, Calif. , c1987. xiv, 306 p. : ISBN 0-07-881243-7 (pbk.) LC Card 86-210772 DDC 621.385 19
HF5541.T4 P37 1987

The Voice of America /. Fitzgerald, Merni Ingrassia. New York , c1987. ix, 118 p. : ISBN 0-396-08937-2 : LC Card 87-5346 DDC 384.54/53 19
HE8698 .F5 1987

VOICE OF AMERICA (ORGANIZATION) - JUVENILE LITERATURE.
Fitzgerald, Merni Ingrassia. The Voice of America /. New York , c1987. ix, 118 p. : ISBN 0-396-08937-2 : LC Card 87-5346 DDC 384.54/53 19
HE8698 .F5 1987

The voice of enterprise . Tirumalai, R., 1924- Bangalore , 1986. xxii, 464 p., [41] p. of plates : ISBN 0-333-90907-0 : LC Card 86-903465 DDC 380.1/06/05482 19
HF331.I4 T57 1986

La Voie hongroise : analyses et expérimentations économiques / sous la direction de János Kornai et Xavier Richet ; textes de Xavier Richet ... [et al.] ; traduit de l'anglais et du hongrois par Anikó Csernus ... [et al.]. [Paris] : Calmann-Lévy, c1986. 319 p. : ill. ; 21 cm. (Perspectives de l'économique. Économie contemporaine) Bibliography: p. 309-319. ISBN 2-7021-1378-8 : LC Card 86-221784
1. Hungary - Economic policy - 1968-. 2. Central planning - Hungary. I. Kornai, János. II. Richet, Xavier.
HC300.28 .V65 1986

Voigt, Fritz. Perspektiven verkehrswissenschaftlicher Forschung . Berlin , c1985. 606 p., [1] leaf of plates : ISBN 3-428-05738-4 LC Card 85-155542
HE151 .P44 1985

VOIGT, FRITZ.
Perspektiven verkehrswissenschaftlicher Forschung . Berlin , c1985. 606 p., [1] leaf of plates : ISBN 3-428-05738-4 LC Card 85-155542
HE151 .P44 1985

Voigt, Jaap. Korteweg, Hans. Helen of delen . Amsterdam , 1986, c1985. 222 p. ; ISBN 90-254-6652-4 : LC Card 86-182872
HD58.8 .K66 1986

Voigt-Weber, Lore. Alternative Betriebe : Genese, Strukturen und Funktionsprobleme / Lore Voigt-Weber. Frankfurt am Main : Haag + Herchen, c1984. 154 p. ; 21 cm. Revision of the author's Diplomarbeit--Universität Bielefeld, 1980 under title: Zur Deinstitutionalisierung ökonomischer Institutionen. Bibliography: p. 136-154. ISBN 3-88129-811-8 LC Card 85-139278
1. Business enterprises. I. Title.
HD2326 .V65 1984

Voigt, Wolfgang. Der Eisenbahnkönig, oder, Rumänien lag in Linden : Materialien zur Sozialgeschichte des Arbeiterwohnungsbaus : mit Beispielen aus Hannovers Fabrikvorort Linden / Wolfgang Voigt.2. Aufl. München : AG SPAK, 1982. 142 p. : ill. ; 21 cm. (AG SPAK M . 46) "Der grösste Teil des Buchs entstand 1978 als Diplomarbeit im Fachbereich Architektur der Universität Hannover"--P. 12. Bibliography: p. 136-138. ISBN 3-923126-15-8 (pbk.) LC Card 87-672921
1. Strousberg, Bethel Henry, 1823-1884. 2. Industrial housing - Germany (West) - Hannover - History - 19th century. 3. Housing - Germany (West) - Hannover - History - 19th century. 4. Railroads - Germany (West) - Hannover - Personnel management - History - 19th century. 5. Linden (Hannover, Germany) - Social conditions. I. Series: AG SPAK Materialien , 46. II. Title.
HD7289.5.R1 V64x 1982

Voinov, A. M. (Arkadiĭ Mikhaĭlovich) Burova, S. E. (Stella Efimovna) Kritika burzhuaznykh vzgli͡adov na ėkonomicheskoe sotrudnichestvo stran SĖV /. Moskva , 1986. 154 p. ; LC Card 86-232355
HC243.5 .B87 1986

Voĭshko, V. B. (Vladimir Boleslavovich) Shakhmatnai͡a filatelii͡a : katalog-spravochnik / sostavitelʹ V.B. Voĭshko. Moskva : "Radio i svi͡azʹ", 1984. 192 p. : ill. ; 22 cm. At head of title: Vsesoi͡uznoe obshchestvo filatelistov. Includes indexes. LC Card 84-174397
1. Postage-stamps - Topics - Chess - Catalogs. I. Title.
HE6183.C415 V65 1984

Voisin, Ph. Les Surcharges "France libre" dans les Etablissements français en Inde, 1941-1945 /. Orléans [1984] 19 p., [4] p. of plates : ISBN 2-9500569-0-3 : LC Card 86-122498
HE6185.F8 S87 1984

Vojnović, Milan. Svetska dominacija krupnog kapitala / Milan D. Vojnović. Beograd : NIRO Export Press--Redakcija "Journal" : Institut za međunarodnu politiku i privredu, 1981. 150 p. : ill. ; 24 cm. In Serbo-Croatian (roman) Bibliography: p. 145-150. LC Card 85-235805
1. International economic relations. 2. International business enterprises. 3. Developing countries - Dependency on foreign countries. I. Title.
HF1411 .V655 1981

Volchenko, M. I͡A. (Maĭa I͡Akovlevna) Promyshlennostʹ GDR : dinamika i struktura / M.I͡A. Volchenko. Moskva : Izd-vo "Nauka", 1981. 179 p. ; 20 cm. At head of title: Akademii͡a nauk SSSR. Institut ėkonomiki mirovoĭ sotsialisticheskoĭ sistemy. Includes bibliographical references. LC Card 82-115880
1. Germany, East - Industries. I. Title.
HC290.74 .V63 1981

VOLCKER, PAUL A.
Neikirk, William. Volcker, portrait of the money man /. New York , Chicago, Ill. , c1987. xvi, 222 p. ; ISBN 0-86553-178-1 LC Card 87-19953 DDC 332.1/1/0924 B 19
HB119.V6 N45 1987

Volcker, portrait of the money man /. Neikirk, William. New York , Chicago, Ill. , c1987. xvi, 222 p. ; ISBN 0-86553-178-1 LC Card 87-19953 DDC 332.1/1/0924 B 19
HB119.V6 N45 1987

Volʹf, M. B. (Mark Borisovich) Geografii͡a mirovogo selʹskogo khozi͡aĭstva / M.B. Volʹf, I͡U.D. Dmitrevskiĭ. Moskva : "Myslʹ", 1981. 326 p. : ill. ; 21 cm. Includes bibliographical references. LC Card 82-122609
1. Agriculture - Economic aspects. 2. Food industry and trade - Location. I. Dmitrevskiĭ, I͡U. D. (I͡Uriĭ Dmitrievich). II. Title.
HD1415 .V62 1981

Völgyesy, Pál. Szilágyi, Klára J. A pályafejlődés vizsgálatának módszertani lehetőségei a felsőoktatásban /. Budapest , 1985. 110 p. ; ISBN 963-404-020-9 LC Card 86-174899
HF5429.6.H8 S95 1985

Völker, Jürgen. Handelshäfen im Ostseeraum /. [Lübeck] [1983] 232 p. : LC Card 84-192969
HE557.A3 H36 1983

Volkmann, G. (Gert) Jordan, Reinhard, d. 1986. Holzwirtschaft im Wandel . Köln , c1986. viii, 163 p. : ISBN 3-7663-0977-3 LC Card 86-211012 DDC 338.4/5674/0943 19
HD9763.5 .J67 1986

Volkmann, Helmut, 1936- Der Informationsmarkt : theoretische Ansätze zur Zweckprogrammierung, Akzeptanz und Wirkung einer Novität im Innovationssystem der Organisation : Betrachtung und Analyse eines Einzelfalles / Helmut Volkmann. München : GBI, c1985. 366 p. : ill. ; 21 cm. (Betriebswirtschaftliche Forschungsbeiträge . Bd. 15) Originally presented as the author's thesis (doctoral)--Universität München, 1982. Bibliography: p. 327-366. Includes index. ISBN 3-89003-016-5 LC Card 85-195750
1. Management. 2. Organization. I. Title. II. Series.
HD35 .V596 1985

Volkov, A. G. (Andreĭ Gavrilovich) Demograficheskai͡a politika . Moskva , 1983. 187 p. : LC Card 84-145010
HB3581 .D44 1983

Volkov, Alʹbert Fedorovich. Rezer, Semen Moiseevich. Vzaimodeĭstvie transportnykh sistem /. Moskva , 1985. 243 p. : LC Card 85-223225
HE255 .R493 1985

Volkov, Aleksandr Ivanovich. Konfrontatsii͡a ili kompromiss? : chto oznachaet uchastie rabochikh v upravlenii kapitalisticheskim predprii͡atiem / A.I. Volkov. Moskva : "Myslʹ", 1986. 234 p. [4] ; 21 cm. Bibliography: p. 220-[235] LC Card 86-200508 DDC 658.3/152 19
1. Industrial management - Employee participation. 2. Management - Employee participation. I. Title.
HD5650 .V65 1986

Volkov, I͡U. E. (I͡Uriĭ Evgenʹevich) Sotsialʹnoe upravlenie trudovym kollektivom . Moskva , 1987. 181 p. ; LC Card 87-103391
HF5549.2.S65 S675 1987

Volkov, I͡U. I. Sovershenstvovanie khozi͡aĭstvennogo mekhanizma v uslovii͡akh razvitogo sotsializma /. Tashkent , 1985. 142, [2] p. ; LC Card 86-220208
HC337.U96 S68 1985

Volks- und Berufszählung am 31. Dezember 1964 : Kennziffern über die Struktur der wirtschaftlich tätigen Wohnbevölkerung im Bezirk Halle : Ergebnisse einer zwanzigprozentigen Stichprobenaufbereitung / Ministerrat der Deutschen Demokratischen Republik, Staatliche Zentralverwaltung für Statistik, Bezirksstelle Halle. [Halle] : Die Bezirksstelle, 1966. 60 p. ; 29 cm. LC Card 85-123405
1. Halle (Germany : Bezirk) - Census, 1964. I. Germany (East). Staatliche Zentralverwaltung für Statistik. Bezirksstelle Halle.
HA1347.H34 V64 1966

Das Volkseinkommen und die internationalen Kapitalbewegungen /. Rötheli, Tobias F. Bern , c1986. 128 p. ; ISBN 3-258-03669-1 LC Card 87-110633 DDC 332.4/5/0724 19
HG3891 .R67 1986

Volkshochschule Dortmund. Leben mit Gneisenau, hundert Jahre-- . Dortmund , Essen [1986?] 317 p. : ISBN 3-88474-323-6 LC Card 87-408388 DDC 331.7/622334/094355 19
HD8039.M62 G335 1986

Volkshuisvesting in demografisch en economisch perspectief /. Fulpen, Hans van. 's-Gravenhage , 1985. 354 p. : ISBN 90-12-05159-2 LC Card 86-169936
HD7344.A3 F85 1985

Volkshuisvesting in theorie en praktijk . (6) Priemus, Hugo. Nederlandse woontheorieën /. Delft , 1984. vi, 92 p. : ISBN 90-6275-126-1 : LC Card 84-226472
HD7344.A3 P67 1984 ***NYPL [JLE 86-2510]***

VOLKSWAGENWERK.
Streeck, Wolfgang, 1946- Industrial relations in West Germany . London , 1984. 178 p. ; ISBN 0-435-83839-3 LC Card 87-673421
HD6698.A8 S77x 1984b

VOLKSWAGENWERK - CASE STUDIES.
Brumlop, Eva. Arbeitsbewertung bei flexiblem Personaleinsatz . Frankfurt , New York , c1986. 229 p. : ISBN 3-593-32744-9 LC Card 86-196323
HD5109.2.G3 B76 1986

VOLKSWAGENWERK - HISTORY - 20TH CENTURY.
Siegfried, Klaus-Jörg, 1940- Rüstungsproduktion und Zwangsarbeit im Volkswagenwerk, 1939-1945 . Frankfurt , New York , c1986. 239 p. : ISBN 3-593-33765-7 LC Card 87-133375 DDC 338.4/76234/0943 19
HD9743.G48 S56 1986

Volkswagenwerk, Stiftung. see **Stiftung Volkswagenwerk.**

Volkswirtschaftliche Aspekte der sowjetischen Umsatzsteuer /. Penkaitis, Norbert. Berlin , 1986. 121 p. : ISBN 3-428-06108-X LC Card 87-408633 DDC 336.2/7 19
HJ5715.S65 P46 1986

Volkswirtschaftliche Forschung und Entwicklung .
(Bd. 12) Funke, Michael, 1956- Wachstumszyklen und funktionale Einkommensverteilung /. München , c1985. iii, 244 p. : ISBN 3-88259-319-9 LC Card 85-175617
HB3711 .F896 1985

(Bd. 15) Adolph, Brigitte. Rationale Erwartungen, Arbeitsverträge und Wirtschaftspolitik /. München , c1986. ii, 127 p. : ISBN 3-88259-346-6 LC Card 87-104701 DDC 330/.01/9 19
HB175 .A26 1986

(Bd. 2) Lange, Diedrich. Zur sozialphilosophischen Gestalt der Marktwirtschaftstheorie bei Adam Smith /. München , c1983. 230 p. : ISBN 3-88259-267-2 LC Card 84-150199
HB103.S6 L36 1983

(Bd. 20) Sánchez Holguín, Carlos Gerardo, 1952- Einige reale Aspekte der Aussenhandelsliberalisierung in Entwicklungsländern /. München , c1986. 152 p. : ISBN 3-88259-368-7 LC Card 86-156293
HF2580.9 .S25 1986

(Bd. 22) Gesswein, Joachim P., 1955- Die Berücksichtigung des Geldes und der Banken als gesellschaftliche Institutionen in der Property Rights-Theorie /. München , c1986. vi, 309 p. ; ISBN 3-88259-374-1 LC Card 86-172234
HB711 .G47 1986

(Bd. 24) Buscher, Herbert S. Modelle der neuen klassischen Makroökonomie . München , c1986. iv, 312 p. : ISBN 3-88259-386-5 LC Card 86-230281
HB141 .B87 1986

(Bd. 25) Herr, Hansjörg, 1951- Geld, Kredit und ökonomische Dynamik in marktvermittelten Ökonomien, die Vision einer Geldwirtschaft /. München , c1986. ix, 240 p. ; ISBN 3-88259-396-2 LC Card 87-140289 DDC 332.4/6 19
HG230.3 .H47 1986

(Bd. 27) Meran, Georg. Die arbeiterselbstverwaltete Firma bei Unsicherheit und asymmetrischer Information . München , c1986. ii, 134 p. : ISBN 3-88259-403-9 LC Card 87-121443 DDC 658.3/152 19
HD5650 .M397 1986

(Bd. 28) Schäkermann, Thomas, 1957- Umweltschutz, Umweltverschmutzung und Wirtschaftswachstum . München , c1986. v, 249 p. ; ISBN 3-88259-404-7 LC Card 86-226458 DDC 363.7/32 19
HC79.P55 S355 1986

(Bd. 30) Beck, Thomas, 1950- Handwerk in Staat und Gesellschaft . München , c1987. xvii, 319 p. : ISBN 3-88259-415-2 LC Card 87-152203 DDC 331.7/94 19
HD2346.G32 K663 1987

(Bd. 8) Gerhardt, Gisela, 1955- Konsumverhalten und wirtschaftliche Entwicklung . München , c1984. 224 p. : ISBN 3-88259-278-8 LC Card 84-220049
HC79.C6 G47 1984

(Bd. 9) Baumgard, Gerhard, 1952- Der Beitrag des Geldes zur gesellschaftlichen Wohlfahrt . München , c1984. 232 p. : ISBN 3-88259-304-8 LC Card 85-113519
HG221 .B348 1984

Volkswirtschaftliche Gesamtrechnung und Preisveränderungen . Müller, Frieder, 1944- Königstein/Ts. , 1984. xx, 414 p. : ISBN 3-445-02378-6 LC Card 85-142948 DDC 339.343 19
HC79.I5 M85 1984 ***NYPL [JLE 86-3225]***

Volkswirtschaftliche Schriften. For other vols. in this series, see Old Catalog.
(Heft 281) Witzke, Harald von. Personelle Einkommensverteilung in der Landwirtschaft und Agrarpreise /. Berlin , 1979. 180 p. : ISBN 3-428-04303-0 LC Card 79-389988
HC290.5.I5 W57 ***NYPL [JLE 80-439]***

(Heft 312) Reiss, Winfried, 1941- Umwegproduktion und Positivität des Zinses . Berlin , c1981. 152 p. : ISBN 3-428-05009-6 LC Card 82-146836 DDC 332.8/2/0724 19
HB539 .R423 1981 ***NYPL [JLE 86-2623]***

(Heft 327) Meimberg, Rudolf. Zur Vertretbarkeit von Störungen der Marktwirtschaft aus ideellen und sonstigen Gründen /. Berlin , c1983. 62 p. ; ISBN 3-428-05331-1 LC Card 83-206548 DDC 338.9 19
HD3611 .M42 1983

(Heft 329) Wagner, Helmut. Inflation und Wirtschaftswachstum . Berlin , c1983. 234 p. : ISBN 3-428-05319-2 LC Card 83-219188
HG229 .W237 1983

(Heft 330) Forster, Edgar. Ökonomische Sicherungspolitik /. Berlin , c1983. 280 p. : ISBN 3-428-05366-4 LC Card 83-220475
HD7101 .F67 1983

(Heft 332) Wolfertz, Dirk. Grundlagen und Probleme der indikativen sektoralen Planung in marktwirtschaftlich orientierten Systemen /. Berlin , c1983. 165 p. ; ISBN 3-428-05379-6 LC Card 83-225373
HD84 .W59 1983

(Heft 336) Dichmann, Werner. Nationalökonomie und Realität . Berlin , c1983. 488 p. ; ISBN 3-428-05517-9 LC Card 84-172295
HB71 .D48 1983

(Heft 338) Thürmer, Lothar. Bürokratie und Effizienz staatlichen Handelns . Berlin , c1984. 177 p. : ISBN 3-428-05543-8 LC Card 84-156948
HD38.4 .T47 1984

(Heft 339) Berg, Werner. Wirtschaft und Gesellschaft in Deutschland und Grossbritannien im Übergang zum "organisierten Kapitalismus" . Berlin , c1984. 888 p. : ISBN 3-428-05495-4 LC Card 84-222030
HD9553.7.R8 B47 1984

(Heft 351) Becker, Hans, Dr. Eine Transaktionskostentheoretische Interpretation interner Arbeitsmärkte /. Berlin , c1985. 156 p. ; ISBN 3-428-05848-8 LC Card 85-218635 DDC 331.12 19
HD5706 .B4 1985

(Heft 359) Maennig, Wolfgang. Die Effekte der Preisstabilisierung auf internationalen Rohstoffmärkten auf Erlöshöhe und -stabilität /. Berlin , 1985. 168 p. : ISBN 3-428-05947-6
NYPL [JLE 86-1670]

(Heft 360) Runge, Harry. Haushaltsfinanzierung durch Notendruck /. Berlin , c1986. 69 p. ; ISBN 3-428-05984-0 LC Card 86-165742
HG1004 .R75 1986

(Heft 360) Runge, Harry. Haushaltsfinanzierung durch Notendruck /. Berlin , c1986. 69 p. ; ISBN 3-428-05984-0 ***NYPL [JLE 86-2839]***

(Heft 362) Grössl, Ingrid. Der Zusammenhang von finanz- und realwirtschaftlichem Sektor einer offenen, stationären Volkswirtschaft . Berlin , c1986. 162 p. : ISBN 3-428-05986-7 LC Card 86-206327
HG3882 .G76 1986

(Heft 363) Bischofberger, Karlheinz. Theorie und Empirie flexibler Wechselkurse . Berlin , c1986. 248 p. : ISBN 3-428-05988-3 LC Card 86-206335
HG3823 .B57 1986

(Heft 365) Muscheid, Jutta. Die Steuerpolitik in der Bundesrepublik Deutschland, 1949-1982 /. Berlin , c1986. 212 p. : ISBN 3-428-06004-0 LC Card 86-206446
HJ2687 .M84 1986

(Heft 366) Riese, Martin. Die Messung der Arbeitslosigkeit /. Berlin , c1986. 199 p. : ISBN 3-428-06034-2 LC Card 86-215265 DDC 331.12/0724 19
HD5707.5 .R54 1986

(Heft 367) Elsner, Wolfram. Ökonomische Institutionenanalyse . Berlin , c1986. xv, 469 p. : ISBN 3-428-06035-0 LC Card 86-206447
HB99.5 .E47 1986

(Heft 369) Kirschke, Dieter, 1952- Agrarmarktpolitik bei Unsicherheit . Berlin , c1987. 225 p. : ISBN 3-428-06111-X LC Card 87-131255 DDC 338.1/8 19
HD1920.5 .K57 1987

Volkswirtschaftsplanung (Berlin, Germany) .
(Heft 2) Knop, Hans, Prof. Dr. sc. Die Energiewirtschaft der DDR und die Planung ihrer künftigen Entwicklung /. Berlin , 1960. 239 p. : LC Card 87-407618 DDC 333.79/0943 19
HD9502.G452 K58 1960

Die Volkszählung / herausgegeben von Jürgen Taeger. Originalausg. Reinbek bei Hamburg : Rowohlt, 1983. 284 p. : ill. ; 19 cm. (Rororo aktuell) Includes bibliographical references. ISBN 3-499-15245-2 : LC Card 84-110844
1. Germany (West) - Census, 1983. I. Taeger, Jürgen.
HA1234 1983

Vollbeschäftigung . Arndt, Helmut, 1911- Berlin , c1984. 196 p. : ISBN 3-428-05602-7 LC Card 84-209024
HD5706 .A855 1984

Vollbeschäftigung, eine Utopie? / Stefan Bethlen und Andreas Müller-Armack (Herausgeber). Bern : P. Haupt, c1986. 330 p. : ill. ; 23 cm. (Beiträge zur Wirtschaftspolitik. Bd. 43) Includes bibliographical references. ISBN 3-258-03567-9 LC Card 86-224133
1. Germany, West - Full employment policies. 2. European Economic Community countries - Full employment policies. I. Bethlen, Stefan, Graf, 1946-. II. Müller-Armack, Andreas, 1941-.
HD5779 .V64 1986

Volley e bolli . Gilardi, Mauro. Milano , c1985. 107 p. : LC Card 86-128270
HE6183.V64 G55 1985

Völlger, Siegfried. Wackersdorf . Passau , 1986. 75 p. : ISBN 3-88849-021-9 LC Card 86-183781
HD9698.G43 W338 1986

Völlmar, H. De organisatie-aspecten van de automatisering / H. Völlmar. Leiden : Stenfert Kroese, 1985. xiv, 316 p. : ill. ; 23 cm. (Informatieverzorging) Includes bibliographies and index. ISBN 90-207-1347-7 : LC Card 85-220224
1. Automation - Management. 2. Automation - Netherlands - Management. 3. Information storage and retrieval systems - Industry. I. Title. II. Series.
HD45.2 .V65 1985

Vollmer, Friedrich Uwe, 1958- Informations- und Veränderungskosten in makroökonomischen Transmissionsmodellen / Friedrich Uwe Vollmer. Frankfurt am Main ; New York : Lang, c1986. 169 p. : ill. ; 21 cm. (Europäische Hochschulschriften. Reihe V, Volks- und Betriebswirtschaft, 0531-7339 . Bd. 702 = vol. 702 = vol. 702) Bibliography: p. 151-169. ISBN 3-8204-9142-2 LC Card 86-194476
1. Prices - Mathematical models. 2. Monetary policy - Mathematical models. I. Series: Europäische Hochschulschriften. Reihe V, Volks- und Betriebswirtschaft , Bd. 702. II. Title.
HB221 .V64 1986

Vollmer, Hans, 1942- Peter, Gerd, 1941- Der Arbeitsschutzbeauftragte . Frankfurt , New York , c1986. 344 p. : ISBN 3-593-33633-2 LC Card 86-160932
HD6490.S52 G365 1986

Vollzug und Wirkungen regionaler Umweltpolitik : ihre Bedeutung für die private Industrie Hamburgs 1970-1980 : ein Untersuchungsbericht / herausgegeben von Hans-Hermann Hartwich ; mit Beiträgen von Holger Thielemann, Reinhard Ohr, Nina Laatsch-Nikitin, unter Mitwirkung von Alparslan Yenal. Opladen : Leske + Budrich, 1984. 199 p. ; 23 cm. (Forschungstexte Wirtschafts- und Sozialwissenschaften . 11) Bibliography: p. 188-191. ISBN 3-8100-0392-1 LC Card 84-228636
1. Environmental policy - Germany (West) - Hamburg. 2. Environmental protection - Germany (West) - Hamburg. 3. Hamburg (Germany) - Industries. I. Hartwich, Hans Hermann. II. Series.
HC290.5.E5 V65 1984

VOLOGDA (R.S.F.S.R.) - ECONOMIC CONDITIONS.
Panshev, L. V. Vologodskiĭ razbeg /. Arkhangel'sk , 1983. 93 p. : LC Card 86-195235
HC338.V58 P35 1983

Vologodskiĭ gosudarstvennyĭ pedagogicheskiĭ institut. Vklad severnogo krest'i͡anstva v material'nui͡u i dukhovnui͡u kul'turu i ego znachenie v reshenii problem agropromyshlennogo kompleksa nechernozemnoĭ zony RSFSR . Vologda , 1984.

93 p. ; LC Card 85-156518
HD9015.S652 V54 1984

Vologodskiĭ razbeg /. Panshev, L. V. Arkhangel'sk , 1983. 93 p. : LC Card 86-195235
HC338.V58 P35 1983

Vologodskoe problemnoe ob"edinenie po agrarnoĭ istorii Evropeĭskogo Severa SSSR. Vklad severnogo krest'i͡anstva v material'nui͡u i dukhovnui͡u kul'turu i ego znachenie v reshenii problem agropromyshlennogo kompleksa nechernozemnoĭ zony RSFSR . Vologda , 1984. 93 p. ; LC Card 85-156518
HD9015.S652 V54 1984

Une volonté d'espérance . Guilhaume, Philippe. Paris , c1984. 218 p. ; ISBN 2-86418-178-9 : LC Card 84-163185
HC276.2 .G785 1984

Volpato, Terezinha Gascho. A pirita humana : os mineiros de Criciúma / Terezinha Gascho Volpato. Florianópolis : Editora da UFSC : Assembléia Legislativa do Estado de Santa Catarina, 1984. 159 p. : ill., map ; 21 cm. Bibliography: p. 157-159. LC Card 85-150574
1. Coal miners - Brazil - Criciúma. 2. Coal mines and mining - Brazil - Criciúma. 3. Trade-unions - Coal miners - Brazil - Criciúma. I. Title.
HD8039.M62 B78 1984

Vol'skiĭ, Viktor Vat͡slavovich. Latinskai͡a Amerika--problemy razvitii͡a nefti͡anoĭ promyshlennosti /. Moskva , 1984. 192 p. : LC Card 86-181028
HD9574.L3 L4 1984

VOLTA ALUMINIUM COMPANY.
Essays from the Ghana-Valco renegotiations, 1982-85 /. [Accra, Ghana] 1986 (Accra : Printed by the Ghana Pub. Corp.) viii, 163 p. ; ISBN 996-490-120-8 (pbk.) LC Card 87-127499 DDC 338.8/87 19
HD9539.A63 G44 1986

The Volta Region . Seminar on Economic Development of the Volta Region (1983 : Ho, Ghana) Accra , c1986. iii, 140 p., [13] leaves of plates : ISBN 996-497-032-3 LC Card 87-402835 DDC 338.9667 19
HC1060.Z7 V647 1983

VOLTA REGION (GHANA) - ECONOMIC POLICY - CONGRESSES.
Seminar on Economic Development of the Volta Region (1983 : Ho, Ghana) The Volta Region . Accra , c1986. iii, 140 p., [13] leaves of plates : ISBN 996-497-032-3 LC Card 87-402835 DDC 338.9667 19
HC1060.Z7 V647 1983

Volta River Authority. Essays from the Ghana-Valco renegotiations, 1982-85 /. [Accra, Ghana] 1986 (Accra : Printed by the Ghana Pub. Corp.) viii, 163 p. ; ISBN 996-490-120-8 (pbk.) LC Card 87-127499 DDC 338.8/87 19
HD9539.A63 G44 1986

VOLTA RIVER AUTHORITY.
Essays from the Ghana-Valco renegotiations, 1982-85 /. [Accra, Ghana] 1986 (Accra : Printed by the Ghana Pub. Corp.) viii, 163 p. ; ISBN 996-490-120-8 (pbk.) LC Card 87-127499 DDC 338.8/87 19
HD9539.A63 G44 1986

VOLUNTARISM - INDIA - SOCIETIES, ETC. - ADDRESSES, ESSAYS, LECTURES.
Franda, Marcus F. Voluntary associations and local development in India . New Delhi , 1983. vi, 356 p. ; LC Card 83-900993 DDC 307/.14/0954 19
HN690.Z9 C6513 1983 *NYPL [JLD 86-3866]*

VOLUNTARISM - UNITED STATES.
Miller, Irwin. The health care survival curve . Homewood, Ill. , c1984. xv, 144 p. ; ISBN 0-87094-481-9 LC Card 83-73714 DDC 338.4/73621/0973 19
RA410.53 .M55 1984 *NYPL [JLE 86-4362]*

VOLUNTARY ACTION. see **VOLUNTARISM.**

VOLUNTARY ASSOCIATIONS. see **ASSOCIATIONS, INSTITUTIONS, ETC.**

Voluntary associations and local development in India . Franda, Marcus F. New Delhi , 1983. vi, 356 p. ; LC Card 83-900993 DDC 307/.14/0954 19
HN690.Z9 C6513 1983 *NYPL [JLD 86-3866]*

Voluntary export restriction as a foreign commercial policy with special reference to Japanese cotton textiles, 1930-1962 /. Bauge, Kenneth L. (Kenneth LeRoy) New York , 1987. 277 p. ; ISBN 0-8240-8072-6 LC Card 87-23717 DDC 382/.4567721/0952 19
HD9886.J3 B38 1987

VOLUNTARY INSTITUTIONS. see **ASSOCIATIONS, INSTITUTIONS, ETC.**

Voluntary Organisations in Community Enterprise (Zimbabwe) Else, John F. Planning income generating projects . Harare, Zimbabwe [1986?] 46 p. : LC Card 87-400416 DDC 338.96891/0068 19
HC910 .E43 1986

Voluntary regulation of advertising . Miracle, Gordon E. Lexington, Mass. , c1987. xxvi, 322 p. : ISBN 0-669-13135-0 (alk. paper) LC Card 86-45294 DDC 338.4/76591/0941 19
HF5834 .M57 1987

VOLUNTEER WORK. see **VOLUNTARISM.**

VOLUNTEER WORKERS IN COMMUNITY DEVELOPMENT - ARKANSAS.
Schwartz, Marvin, 1948- In service to America /. Fayetteville, AR , 1988. p. cm. ISBN 1-557-28005-3 LC Card 87-19440 DDC 361.6/09767 19
HC110.P63 S34 1988

VOLUNTEER WORKERS IN COMMUNITY DEVELOPMENT - BRAZIL.
Fundação Projeto Rondon. Diretrizes de planejamento . [Brasília , 1982] [21] leaves ; LC Card 85-186578
HD4870.B6 F86 1982

VOLUNTEER WORKERS IN SOCIAL SERVICE - ARKANSAS.
Schwartz, Marvin, 1948- In service to America /. Fayetteville, AR , 1988. p. cm. ISBN 1-557-28005-3 LC Card 87-19440 DDC 361.6/09767 19
HC110.P63 S34 1988

VOLUNTEER WORKERS IN SOCIAL SERVICE - INDIA.
Chowdhry, D. Paul. Profile of social welfare and development in India /. New Delhi , 1985. viii, 340 p. ; LC Card 85-901093 DDC 362/.954 19
HV393 .C515 1985 *NYPL [JLD 86-2575]*

VOLUNTEER WORKERS IN SOCIAL SERVICE - INDIA - MHAISAL.
Deshpande, V. D. (Vasant Dattatraya), 1930- The Mhaisal untouchables /. Pune , 1983. xi, 168 p. ; LC Card 83-906084 DDC 338.954/792 19
HC438.M45 D48 1983 *NYPL [JLD 87-1139]*

VOLUNTEERING. see **VOLUNTARISM.**

VOLUNTEERISM. see **VOLUNTARISM.**

VOLUNTEERS IN SERVICE TO AMERICA.
Schwartz, Marvin, 1948- In service to America /. Fayetteville, AR , 1988. p. cm. ISBN 1-557-28005-3 LC Card 87-19440 DDC 361.6/09767 19
HC110.P63 S34 1988

VOLVO, AKTIEBOLAGET.
Auer, Peter. Industrial relations, work organisation and new technology . Berlin [1985] 17, [6] p. ; LC Card 86-205891 DDC 331/.04292/09481 19
HD9710.S84 V6413 1985

Vom Boss zum Partner /. Andreae, Clemens August. Zürich , c1983. 90 p. ; ISBN 3-7201-5154-9 LC Card 83-168802
HB615 .A69 1983

Vom Ende der abstrakten Arbeit . Krahl, Hans-Jürgen. Frankfurt , 1984. 209 p. ; ISBN 3-88535-075-0 LC Card 84-188656
HD4904 .K6915 1984

Vom Geist der Wirtschaft . Reuter, Edzard, 1928- Stuttgart , c1986. 288 p. ; ISBN 3-421-06311-7 LC Card 86-181795
HC240 .R44 1986

Vom Gleis abgekommen : die verkehrs- und regionalpolitische Bedeutung von Schienen für die Fläche. Bonn : Deutscher Industrie- und Handelstag, 1977. 60 p. ; 21 cm. (DIHT . 162) LC Card 86-176591
1. Railroads - Germany, West - Freight. 2. Railroads and state - Germany, West. I. Deutscher Industrie- und Handelstag. II. Series: DIHT (Series) , 162.
HE2445 .V65 1977

Vom Handelsplatz zur Industriestadt . Breunig, Willi. Ludwigshafen am Rhein , 1986. 151 p. : ISBN 3-924667-13-6 LC Card 87-135540 DDC 338.0943/43 19
HC289.L95 B74 1986

Vom Lehrermangel zur Lehrerarbeitslosigkeit . Pieper, Beate. Münster , 1984. ix, 265 p. : ISBN 3-923881-11-8 : LC Card 85-195712 DDC 331.12 19
LB2833.4.G4 P54 1984 *NYPL [JLD 87-1161]*

Vom Lohnarbeiter zum Klienten . Arend, Brigitte, 1953- Frankfurt am Main , c1986. 206 p. ; ISBN 3-445-02490-1 LC Card 86-231993
HD5708 .A74 1986

Vom Nachzügler zum Vorbild(?) : österreichische Wirtschaft, 1945 bis 1985 / Herausgeber, Helmut Kramer, Felix Butschek. Stuttgart : G. Fischer, c1985. 183 p. : ill. ; 24 cm. Papers presented at a conference sponsored by the Österreichisches Institut für Wirtschaftsforschung and three other bodies. Includes bibliographies. CONTENTS. - Vom internationalen Trend mit gerissen? / Wolfram Fischer -- Das Ergebnis eigener Leistung? / Hans Seidel -- Das Entstehen sozialer Regelungsmechanismen / Peter J. Katzenstein -- Von der "kontrollierten Inflation" zur "Hartwährungspolitik" / Rudolf R. Rhomberg -- Die ökonomische und politische Bedeutung der Sozialen Sicherheit in der österreichischen Wirtschaft 1945 bis 1985 / Martin Pfaff -- Stürmisches Wachstum trotz rudimentärer Finanzmärkte? / Werner Ehrlicher -- Die ständige Herausforderung / Hartmut Fest -- Podiumsdiskussion / Felix Butschek et al. -- Aufgaben und Chancen / Helmut Kramer -- Österreichs Wirtschaft in der Welt von heute und morgen / Norbert Steger. ISBN 3-437-50303-0 LC Card 86-200243
1. Austria - Economic conditions - 1945- - Congresses. 2. Austria - Economic policy - 1945- - Congresses. I. Kramer, Helmut. II. Butschek, Felix. III. Österreichisches Institut für Wirtschaftsforschung.
HC265 .V65 1985

Vom Tauschhandel zur Weltwirtschaft . Müller, Karlhans, 1938- Reutlingen , c1984. 320 p. : ISBN 3-7709-0564-4 LC Card 87-673138
HC21 .M85x 1984

Vom Weltkrieg zur Weltwirtschaftskrise . Feldman, Gerald D. Göttingen , 1984. 272 p. ; ISBN 3-525-35719-2 LC Card 85-165291
HC286.2 .F45 1984

Vomfelde, Werner. Abschied von Keynes? : eine Antwort auf die monetaristisch-neoklassische Gegenrevolution / Werner Vomfelde. Frankfurt am Main ; New York : Campus, c1985. 205 p. : ill. ; 21 cm. Bibliography: p. 199-202. Includes index. ISBN 3-593-33567-0 LC Card 86-159600
1. Keynesian economics. 2. Neoclassical school of economics. 3. Monetary policy - Germany, West. I. Title.
HB99.7 .V65 1985

Von der Bauernfaust zur Bauernkammer /. Landskron, Ferdinand. Totzenbach [1983] 194 p. ; LC Card 84-168829
HD1536.A9 L36 1983

Von der Bereitschaft zum technischen Wandel / herausgegeben von Ernst Hofmeister und Mechthild Ulbricht. 2. Aufl. Berlin : Siemens Aktiengesellschaft, 1981. 278 p. : ill. (some col.) ; 18 cm. Includes bibliographical references. CONTENTS. - Innovation, Geissel oder Segen? / M. Jungblut -- Entstehung und Ausbreitung von technischen Neuerungen / W. Bierfelder -- Innovationsbarrieren / E. Hofmeister -- Innovationen und ihre Akzeptanz bei industriellen Erzeugnissen / E. Rohloff -- Akzeptanz und Innovationen / U. Waas -- Innovationen in der dritten Welt / Interview mit W. Seelig -- Fallbeispiel: Entwicklungsprobleme Indonesiens / H. Heinzlmeir -- Beeinträchtigen technische Innovationen die Lebensqualität? / H. Sachsse -- Einsteillungen zur Technik / C. Merbold. ISBN 3-8009-1339-9 LC Card 83-194263
1. Technological innovations - Social aspects. 2. Technology and civilization. I. Hofmeister, Ernst, 1922-. II. Ulbricht, Mechthild, 1938-.
HC79.T4 V66 1981

Von der Bizonengründung zur ökonomisch-politischen Westintegration : Studien zum Verhältnis zwischen Aussenpolitik und Aussenwirtschaftsbeziehungen in der Entstehungsphase der Bundesrepublik

Deutschland (1947-1952) / Manfred Knapp (Hrsg.). Frankfurt am Main : Haag + Herchen, c1984. v, 311 p. : ill. ; 21 cm. Bibliography: p. 287-310. CONTENTS. - Die Anfänge westdeutscher Aussenwirtschafts- und Aussenpolitik im bizonalen vereinigten Wirtschaftsgebiet (1947-1949) / Manfred Knapp -- Die Bedeutung des Ruhrstatuts und seiner Aufhebung für die aussenpolitische und aussenwirtschaftliche Emanzipation Westdeutschlands (1948-1952) / Carsten Lüders -- Aussenpolitische Einflussfaktoren auf die Entwicklung der westdeutschen Aussenwirtschaftsbeziehungen in der Frühphase der Bundesrepublik Deutschland (1949-1952) / Bernhard Welschke. ISBN 3-88129-640-9 LC Card 84-154481
1. Germany, West - Economic policy. 2. Germany, West - Commerce. 3. Germany, West - Economic conditions. 4. Ruhr (Germany : Region) - Economic conditions. I. Knapp, Manfred.
HC286.5 .V64 1984

Von der Handelspolitik zur Aussenwirtschaftspolitik . Jolles, Paul R. Bern , 1983. xix, 403 p. : ISBN 3-7272-9209-1 : LC Card 84-119428
HF1573 .J65 1983

Von der Konkurrenz zur Rivalität : das britisch-deutsche Verhältnis in den Ländern der europäischen Peripherie, 1919-1939 / herausgegeben von Marie-Luise Recker = From competition to rivalry : the Anglo-German relationship in the countries at the European periphery, 1919-1939 / edited by Marie-Luise Recker. Stuttgart : F. Steiner Verlag Wiesbaden, 1986. 186 p. ; 24 cm. (Veröffentlichungen des Instituts für Europäische Geschichte Mainz. Abteilung Universalgeschichte. Beiheft . 16) Contributions in English and German. Bibliography: p. [177]-186. CONTENTS. - Britain as Germany's commercial rival in the Baltic states, 1919-1939 / Merja-Liisa Hinkkanen -- Grossbritannien, Deutschland und die südosteuropäischen Staaten, 1919-1939 / Marie-Luise Recker -- Anglo-German commercial rivalry in the depression era, the political and economic impact on Scandinavia, 1931-1939 / Patrick Salmon -- The moor and the money-lender, politics and profits in Anglo-German relations with Francoist Spain, 1936-1940 / Denis Smyth. ISBN 3-515-04760-3 LC Card 87-134320 DDC 337/.09/04 19
1. International economic relations - History - 20th century. 2. Competition, International - History - 20th century. 3. World War, 1914-1918 - Causes. 4. World politics - 1900-1945. 5. Great Britain - Foreign economic relations. 6. Germany - Foreign economic relations. I. Recker, Marie-Luise. II. Title: From competition to rivalry. III. Series.
HF1411 .V665 1986

Von der Leimabteilung zum grössten Klebstoffwerk Europas /. Schöne, Manfred, 1935- Düsseldorf , 1979. 68 p. : LC Card 86-216773
HD9654.9.H444 S37 1979

Von der Nachrichtentechnik zur Informationstechnik . NTG-Fachtagung (1986 : Nuremberg, Germany) Berlin , c1986. 104 p. : ISBN 3-8007-1485-X LC Card 87-136748 DDC 384 19
HE7604 .N74 1986

Von Hoelscher, Russ. Sterne, George F. Investment opportunities for the mid 1980's . San Diego, Calif. , c1985. 304 p. ; ISBN 0-940398-11-7 : LC Card 78-64396
NYPL [JLE 86-1720]

Von oben nach unten wächts gar nichts . Wensierski, Peter. Frankfurt am Main , 1986. 206 p. : ISBN 3-596-24274-6 LC Card 87-115154 DDC 363.7/058/09431 19
HC290.795.E5 W46 1986

Voordracht .
(69) North Holland (Netherlands) Milieubeleidsplan Noord-Holland 1982-1988 . [Haarlem] [1987] 60 p. ; LC Card 87-159912
HC327.N6 N67 1987

Voorhees, Lynda, A. Job performance and chemical dependency : a practical guide for managers and supervisors / Lynda A. Voorhees and Robert B. Maddux. Los Altos, Calif. : Crisp Publications, c1987. iii, 81 p. : ill. ; 26 cm. ISBN 0-931961-27-0 (pbk.) LC Card 86-73172 DDC 658.3/82 19
1. Drugs and employment. 2. Personnel management. I. Maddux, Robert B. II. Title.
HF5549.5.D7 V66 1987

Voorhes, Meg. Black South African views on disinvestment / by Meg Voorhes. Washington, D.C. (Suite 600, 1755 Massachusetts Ave., N.W., Washington 20036) : South Africa Review Service, Investor Responsibility Research Center, [1986] 36 p. ; 28 cm. Cover title. "July 1986." LC Card 86-209279 DDC 332.6/73/0968 19
1. Disinvestments - South Africa. 2. Investments, American - South Africa. 3. Corporate divestiture - South Africa. 4. Disinvestments - South Africa - Public opinion. 5. Public opinion - South Africa. I. Investor Responsibility Research Center. South Africa Review Service. II. Title.
HG5851.A3 V66 1986

Vôos "charters" e as empresas de aviação civil . Brazil. Congresso Nacional. Câmara dos Deputados. Comissão de Esporte e Turismo. Brasília , 1986. 98 p. ; LC Card 87-405035 DDC 387.7/0981 19
HE9833.A4 B7 1986

Voprosy agropromyshlennoĭ integrat͡sii (Kiev, Ukraine)
Kulish, N. E. (Nikolaĭ Efimovich) Upravlenie agropromyshlennymi ob"edinenii͡ami v uslovii͡akh integrirovannoĭ ėkonomiki /. Kiev , 1985. 174 p. : LC Card 87-104750
HD9015.S653 U4425 1985
NYPL [*QIP 87-4125]

Voprosy ideologicheskoĭ bor'by i kontrpropagandy.
Akopov, Mykhaĭlo Arutiūnovych. Dukhovnyĭ mir sovetskogo cheloveka /. Kiev , 1985. 124, [3] p. ; LC Card 86-139846
JN6581 .A64 1985 ***NYPL [*QIK 87-3448]***

Voprosy istorii dorevoli͡ut͡sionnoĭ Sibiri / [redkollegii͡a, ... Z.I͡A. Boi͡arshinova (otv. red.) ... et al.]. Tomsk : Izd-vo Tomskogo universiteta, 1983. 177 p. ; 20 cm. Includes bibliograhical references.
1. Peasantry - Russian S.F.S.R. - Siberia - History. 2. Labor and laboring classes - Russian S.F.S.R. - Siberia - History. 3. Siberia (R.S.F.S.R.) - Industries - History. I. Boi͡arshinova, Z. I͡A. (Zoi͡a I͡Akovlevna).
NYPL [*QI 87-171]

Voprosy istorii sot͡sialisticheskogo preobrazovanii͡a i razvitii͡a sel'skogo khozi͡aĭstva Chuvashskoĭ ASSR / [redaktory N.E. Egorov, V.A. Prokhorova]. Cheboksary : Nauchno-issl. in-t i͡azyka, lit-ry, istorii i ėkonomiki pri Sovete Ministrov Chuvashskoĭ ASSR, 1985. 176 p. ; 21 cm. Bibliography: p. 173-[174] LC Card 86-100164
1. Collectivization of agriculture - Russian S.F.S.R. - Chuvashskai͡a A.S.S.R. - History. I. Egorov, Nikolaĭ Egorovich. II. Prokhorova, V. A. III. Chuvashskai͡a A.S.S.R. (R.S.F.S.R.). Nauchno-issledovatel'skiĭ institut i͡azyka, literatury, istorii i ėkonomiki.
HD1492.5.S65 C488 1985

Voprosy metodologii issledovanii͡a obshchestvennogo truda pri sot͡sializme / [redkollegii͡a V.V. Zapol'skai͡a (nauch. red.) ... et al.]. Voronezh : Izd-vo Voronezhskogo universiteta, 1979. 163 p. ; 20 cm. Includes bibliographical references. LC Card 81-142810
1. Labor supply - Soviet Union. 2. Labor and laboring classes - Soviet Union. 3. Marxian economics. I. Zapol'skai͡a, V. V. (Vera Vasil'evna).
HD5796 .V65 1979

Voprosy metodologii regional'nogo ėkonomicheskogo prognozirovanii͡a /. Meskhii͡a, I͡A. E. (I͡Akov Egnatovich) Moskva , 1983. 183 p. : LC Card 84-141931
HC337.G38 M43 1983

Voprosy optimal'nogo planirovanii͡a i upravlenii͡a sot͡sialisticheskoĭ ėkonomikoĭ.
Khozi͡aĭstvennyĭ mekhanizm v sisteme optimal'nogo funktsionirovanii͡a sotsialisticheskoĭ ėkonomiki /. Moskva , 1985. 346 p. ; LC Card 86-114802
HC336.25 .K474 1985

Mezhotraslevye kompleksy v sisteme modeleĭ /. Moskva , 1983. 319 p. : LC Card 83-236937
HC336.25 .M49 1983

Sistema modeleĭ narodnokhozi͡aĭstvennogo planirovanii͡a /. Moskva , 1982. 375 p. ; LC Card 83-172876
HC336.25 .S564 1982

Voprosy politicheskoĭ ėkonomii : sot͡sial'no-ėkonomicheskie problemy truda i upravlenii͡a / [otvetstvennyĭ redaktor P.P. Luzan]. Novosibirsk : [s.n.], 1973. 125 p. ; 20 cm. (Nauchnye trudy. vyp. 88) At head of title: Ministerstvo prosveshchenii͡a RSFSR. Novosibirskiĭ gosudarstvennyĭ pedagogicheskiĭ institut. Includes bibliographical references. LC Card 81-131624
1. Labor and laboring classes - Soviet Union. 2. Industrial management - Soviet Union. I. Luzan, P. P. II. Series: Nauchnye trudy / Novosibirskiĭ gosudarstvennyĭ pedagogicheskiĭ institut , vyp. 88.
HD8526.5 .V674 1973

Voprosy postroenii͡a sistemy modeleĭ finansovogo aspekta vosproizvodstva / [otvetsvennye redaktory Detneva Ėmma Vasil'evna, Solov'ev I͡Uriĭ Pavlovich, Terushkin Anatoliĭ Georgievich]. Moskva : T͡Sentr. ėkonomiko-matematicheskiĭ in-t AN SSSR, 1984. 154 p. : ill. ; 21 cm. Includes bibliographical references. LC Card 86-144339
1. Finance - Soviet Union - Mathematical models. I. Detneva, Ėmma Vasil'evna. II. Solov'ev, I͡U. P. I͡Uriĭ Pavlovich). III. Terushkin, Anatoliĭ Georgievich. IV. T͡Sentral'nyĭ ėkonomiko-matematicheskiĭ institut (Akademii͡a nauk SSSR).
HG186.S55 V67 1984

Voprosy prognozirovanii͡a i planirovanii͡a vneshneėkonomicheskikh svi͡azeĭ / [otvetstvennye redaktory Margarita Alekseevna Alekseeva, Grigoriĭ Lazarevich Shagalov, Valeriĭ Semenovich Suti͡agin]. Moskva : Akademii͡a nauk SSSR, T͡Sentr. ėkonomiko-matematicheskiĭ in-t, 1984. 93 p. ; 21 cm. Includes bibliographies. LC Card 86-144298
1. Soviet Union - Commerce - Forecasting. 2. Soviet Union - Foreign economic relations - Forecasting. I. Alekseeva, Margarita Alekseevna. II. Shagalov, G. L. (Grigoriĭ Lazarevich). III. Suti͡agin, Valeriĭ Semenovich.
HF3626.5 .V668 1984

Voprosy razvitii͡a obsluzhivanii͡a naselenii͡a : proizvoditel'nye sily i khozi͡aĭstvennyĭ mekhanizm bytovogo obsluzhivanii͡a / [redaktsionnai͡a kollegii͡a Kh.I. Aarma (otv. red.), S.V. Mi͡aėl'tsemėės, I͡U.Kh. Sillaste]. Tallin : Akademii͡a nauk Ėstonskoĭ SSR, 1985. 140 p. : ill. ; 20 cm. At head of title: Akademii͡a nauk Ėstonskoĭ SSR. Institut ėkonomiki. Proektno-tekhnologicheskiĭ institut Ministerstva bytovogo obsluzhivanii͡a ĖSSR. Includes bibliographical references. LC Card 85-158428
1. Service industries - Estonia. 2. Consumption (Economics) - Estonia. I. Aarma, Kh. I. II. Mi͡aėl'tsemėės, S. V. III. Sillaste, I͡U. Kh. IV. Majanduse Instituut (Eesti NSV Teaduste Akadeemia). V. Proektno-tekhnicheskiĭ institut Ministerstva bytovogo obsluzhivanii͡a ĖSSR.
HD9986.S683 E888 1985

Voprosy razvitii͡a torgovli v Tadzhikistane /. Nazarova, N. S. (Nina Semenovna) Dushanbe , 1978. 172 p. ; LC Card 81-146150
HF3629.T35 N39 1978

Voprosy stranovogo makromodelirovanii͡a / [otvetstvennye redaktory Vladislav Surenovich Dadai͡an, Valentina Efimovna Shevt͡sova]. Moskva : Akademii͡a nauk SSSR, T͡Sentr. ėkonomiko-matematicheskiĭ in-t, 1984. 177 p. : ill., charts ; 21 cm. Includes bibliographies. LC Card 86-144302
1. Econometric models. I. Dadai͡an, V. S. (Vladislav Surenovich), 1933-. II. Shevt͡sova, Valentina Efimovna. III. T͡Sentral'nyĭ ėkonomiko-matematicheskiĭ institut (Akademii͡a nauk SSSR).
HB141 .V665 1984

Voprosy ukreplenii͡a trudovoĭ i proizvodstvennoĭ distsipliny v dei͡atel'nosti profsoi͡uznykh organizatsiĭ : sbornik nauchnykh trudov / [redaktsionnai͡a kollegii͡a, Tregubov A.L. (otvetstvennyĭ redaktor) ... et al.]. Moskva : Vysshai͡a shkola profsoi͡uznogo dvizhenii͡a VTSSPS im. N.M. Shvernika, 1984. 77 p. ; 21 cm. At head of title: Vsesoi͡uznyĭ t͡sentral'nyĭ sovet professional'nykh soi͡uzov. Ordena Trudovogo Krasnogo Znameni Vysshai͡a shkola profsoi͡uznogo dvizhenii͡a VT͡SSPS imeni N.M. Shvernika. Includes bibliographical references. LC Card 86-181312
1. Labor discipline - Soviet Union. 2. Trade-unions - Soviet Union. I. Tregubov, A. L. II. Vysshai͡a shkola profsoi͡uznogo dvizhenii͡a VT͡SSPS imeni N.M. Shvernika.
HF5549.5.L3 V67 1984

Vor tids fattigdom / redigeret af Erik Jørgen Hansen. [Copenhagen] : H. Reitzel, c1986. 130 p. : ill. ; 20 cm. Bibliography: p. 119-130. ISBN 87-412-3897-4 : LC Card 86-214667
1. Poverty. 2. Denmark - Economic conditions - 1945-.

I. Hansen, Erik Jørgen.
HC79.P6 V67 1986

Vorausberechnung der Bevölkerung in den kreisfreien Städten und Kreisen Nordrhein-Westfalens : Bevölkerungsprognose 1982-2000. Düsseldorf : Landesamt für Datenverarbeitung und Statistik Nordrhein-Westfalen, [1983] 103 p. : ill. ; 30 cm. (Beiträge zur Statistik des Landes Nordrhein-Westfalen, 0720-1664 . Heft 500) "Erschienen im Oktober 1983"--T.p. verso. Chiefly tables. Includes bibliographical references. LC Card 86-202728
1. North Rhine-Westphalia (Germany) - Population - Statistics. 2. Population forecasting - Germany (West) - North Rhine-Westphalia - Statistics. 3. Cities and towns - Germany (West) - North Rhine-Westphalia - Statistics. I. Landesamt für Datenverarbeitung und Statistik Nordrhein-Westfalen. II. Series.
HA1320.N6 A32 Heft 500

Vorholz, Hans-Joachim. Analyse von Unfällen motorisierter Zweiradbenutzer . [West Germany] [1976] 32 p. : LC Card 85-135424
HE5614.5.G3 A65 1976

Vorholz, H.-J. ADAC. Strassenverkehr 2000 . München [1979] 24 p. : LC Card 85-147077
HE363.G3 A33 1979

Vorindustrielle Bauwirtschaft in der Reichsstadt Nürnberg und ihrem Umland (16.-18. Jh.) /. Gömmel, Rainer. [Stuttgart] , 1985. xii, 300 p. : ISBN 3-515-04481-7 LC Card 86-122013
HD9715.G33 N874 1985

Vorindustrielles Gewerbe und wirtschaftlicher Wandel im Paderborner Land im 19. Jahrhundert /. Henning, Friedrich-Wilhelm. Dortmund , 1983. 67 p. ; LC Card 83-198581
HC288.P27 H46 1983

Vorkalkulation bei langfristiger Einzelfertigung /. Kraus, Rudolf, 1953- Frankfurt am Main , New York , c1986. iii, 299 p. : ISBN 3-8204-0000-1 LC Card 86-233181
HD47.3 .K73 1986

Vormbaum, Herbert. Differenzierte Preise : differenzierte Preisforderungen als Mittel der Betriebspolitik / Herbert Vormbaum. Köln : Westdeutscher Verlag, 1960. xi, 291 p. : ill. ; 24 cm. (Beiträge zur betriebswirtschaftlichen Forschung. Bd. 9) The author's Habilitationsschrift--Universität Hamburg. Bibliography: p. [285]-291. LC Card 86-191408
1. Prices - Germany, West. I. Title. II. Series.
HB235.G3 V67 1960

Voronin, S. V. Rabochiĭ klass Shri Lanki : formirovanie, struktura i sotsial'no-ėkonomicheskoe polozhenie / S.V. Voronin. Moskva : Izd-vo "Nauka", 1979. 278, [2] p. ; 22 cm. At head of title: Akademii͡a nauk SSSR. Institut mezhdunarodnogo rabochego dvizhenii͡a. Errata slip inserted. Bibliography: p. 273-[279] LC Card 81-147848
1. Labor and laboring classes - Sri Lanka - History. I. Title.
HD8670.8 .V67 1979

Voronin, V. G. (Valeriĭ Grigor'evich) Ėkonomiko-matematicheskie metody planirovanii͡a na predprii͡atii͡akh pishchevoĭ promyshlennosti / V.G. Voronin, V.V. Deniskin, S.M. Sirota ; pod obshcheĭ redaktsieĭ V.G. Voronina. Moskva : "Legkai͡a i pishchevai͡a promyshl.", 1981. 270 p. : ill. ; 21 cm. Authorized for instructional purposes. Bibliography: p. [267] LC Card 82-103139
1. Food industry and trade - Soviet Union - Management - Mathematical models. I. Deniskin, V. V. (Viktor Vasil'evich). II. Sirota, S. M. (Simon Matveevich). III. Title.
HD9015.S65 V67 1981

Voronov, A. A. Avtomatizatsii͡a upravlenii͡a transportnymi sistemami /. Moskva , 1984. 271 p. : LC Card 84-195421
HE255 .A93 1984

Voronovitskiĭ, M. M. Modelirovanie ėkonomicheskogo povedenii͡a sotsialisticheskogo predprii͡atii͡a /. Moskva , 1984. 131 p. : LC Card 86-144437
HD30.25 .M623 1984

Vorontsov, A. P. (Alekseĭ Pavlovich) Proizvoditel'nost' i oplata truda v APK / A.P. Vorontsov. Moskva : Agropromizdat, 1985. 191 p. ; 20 cm. Includes bibliographical references. LC Card 86-130051
1. Agricultural industries - Soviet Union - Labor productivity. 2. Agricultural wages - Soviet Union. I. Title.
HD9015.S652 V67 1985

Vörös, József. A kockázat, haszon és a termelési szerkezet összefüggése / Vörös József. Pécs : Pécsi Janus Pannonius Tudományegyetem Közgazdaságtudományi Kar, 1983. 77 leaves : ill. ; 20 cm. (Dolgozatok a közgazdaságtudományok köréből, 0209-9187) "VI. évfolyam." Bibliography: leaves 76-77. LC Card 85-111246
1. Risk management - Mathematical models. 2. Industrial management - Mathematical models. I. Title. II. Series.
HD61 .V67 1983

Vorschläge für eine Neuordnung des organisatorischen Rahmens für den öffentlichen Personennahverkehr / herausgegeben vom Bundesminister für Verkehr. Bonn-Bad Godesberg : Der Bundesminister, [1977] 35 p. ; 30 cm. (Schriftenreihe . Heft 53, 1977) LC Card 86-173254
1. Transportation - Germany, West - Passenger traffic. 2. Transportation - Germany, West - Finance. 3. Transportation and state - Germany, West. I. Germany (West). Bundesministerium für Verkehr. II. Series: Schriftenreihe (Germany (West). Bundesministerium für Verkehr) , Heft 53.
HE64 .A36 Heft 53 HE249

Vorschläge und Beiträge des Bundesverbandes des Deutschen Gross- und Aussenhandels e.V. für die X. Legislaturperiode des Deutschen Bundestages. Bundesverband des Deutschen Gross- und Aussenhandels. Bonn [1983] 56 p. ; LC Card 83-243234
HF1545 .B83 1983

Vorschlag zur Verbesserung der Behandlung nichtabziehbarer Ausgaben im KStG 1977 /. Piltz, Detlev Jürgen. Bonn , 1987. 42 leaves ; LC Card 87-401366 DDC 332 s 343.4305/267 332 s 344.3035267 19
HJ1120 .B65 Nr. 263 KK7226

Vorse, Mary Heaton, 1874-1966. Rebel pen : the writings of Mary Heaton Vorse / edited by Dee Garrison. New York : Monthly Review Press, c1985. 345 p. : ill. ; 22 cm. Includes index. ISBN 0-85345-669-0 : LC Card 85-7130 DDC 331.4/0973 19
1. Labor and laboring classes - United States - 1914- - Addresses, essays, lectures. 2. Strikes and lockouts - United States - Addresses, essays, lectures. 3. Women - History - Addresses, essays, lectures. I. Garrison, Dee. II. Title.
HD8072 .V755 1985 ***NYPL [JLD 86-2459]***

Vortmann, Heinz. Geldeinkommen in der DDR von 1955 bis zu Beginn der achtziger Jahre : Funktionale und personelle Verteilung, Einkommensbildung und Einkommenspolitik / Heinz Vortmann. Berlin : Duncker & Humblot, 1985. 239 p. : ill. ; 30 cm. (Beiträge zur Strukturforschung . Heft 85) Bibliography: p. 228-239. ISBN 3-428-95952-2 LC Card 86-166538
1. Income - Germany, East. I. Title.
HC281 .B33 Heft 85 HC290.795.I5

Vorträge gehalten an der Abgeordnetenversammlung 1978 der Schweizerischen Geisteswissenschaftlichen Gesellschaft. Vorträge gehalten anlässlich der Abgeordnetenversammlung vom 27. Mai 1978 =. [Bern] , 1978. 44 p. : LC Card 84-115871
HC397 .V67 1978

Vorträge gehalten anlässlich der Abgeordnetenversammlung vom 27. Mai 1978 = Conférences prononcées à l'occasion de l'assemblée des délégués du 27 mai 1978. [Bern] : SGG, 1978. 44 p. : ill. ; 21 cm. (Aktuelle Arbeiten aus dem Gebiete der Geisteswissenschaften = Travaux en cours dans le domaine des sciences humaines) French and German. Cover title: Vorträge gehalten an der Abgeordnetenversammlung 1978 der Schweizerischen Geisteswissenschaftlichen Gesellschaft. Includes bibliographical references. CONTENTS. - Le choix professionnel des bacheliers / Jean-Blaise Dupont -- Kontinuität und Wandel im Bild Schweiz / Hanspeter Meier -- Interkulturelle Beziehungen, neuer Gegenstand der Sozialwissenschaften? / Roy Preiswerk -- Volkswirtschaftslehre als politische Ökonomie / Werner W. Pommerehne. LC Card 84-115871
1. Switzerland - Economic conditions - Congresses. 2. Switzerland - Social conditions - Congresses. I. Schweizerische Geisteswissenschaftliche Gesellschaft. II. Title: Conférences prononcées à l'occasion de l'assemblée des délégués du 27 mai 1978. III. Title: Vorträge gehalten an der Abgeordnetenversammlung 1978 der Schweizerischen Geisteswissenschaftlichen Gesellschaft. IV. Series: Aktuelle Arbeiten aus dem Gebiete der Geisteswissenschaften.
HC397 .V67 1978

Vorträge und Aufsätze (Walter Eucken Institut) .
(110) Köhler, Helmut, 1944- Nachfragewettbewerb und Marktbeherrschung /. Tübingen , 1986. 121 p. ; ISBN 3-16-345124-1 (Deut. Bibl.) LC Card 86-223313
HD2757.4 .K64 1986

(111) Knieps, Günter. Deregulierung im Luftverkehr . Tübingen , c1987. 69 p. ; ISBN 3-16-345148-9 LC Card 87-121052 DDC 387.7/1 19
HE9776 .K6 1987

(89) Schmidtchen, Dieter. Property rights, Freiheit und Wettbewerbspolitik /. Tübingen , 1983. 71 p. ; ISBN 3-16-344630-2 (Deut. Bibl.) LC Card 84-100421
HF1410.5 .S36 1983

(95) Winterberger, Gerhard. Über Schumpeters Geschichtsdeterminismus /. Tübingen , 1983. 42 p. ; ISBN 3-16-344644-2 LC Card 83-152280 DDC 330/.092/4 19
HB119.S35 W56 1983

Vorträge und Beiträge aus dem Institut für Verkehrswissenschaft an der Universität Münster .
(Heft 30) Boldt, Günter. Wettbewerb und Preisbildung der Seehafenverkehrswirtschaft in nordwesteuropäischen Seehäfen . Göttingen , 1964. 120 p. ; LC Card 87-408787 DDC 380.5 s 387.1 19
HE131 .M84 Heft 30 HE558.H3

Vorträge und Studien aus dem Institut für Verkehrswissenschaft an der Universität Münster .
(Heft 18) Seidenfus, Hellmuth Stefan. Die Bedeutung der Seehäfen für die Industrialisierung Mitteleuropas /. Göttingen , 1979. 20 p. ; ISBN 3-525-85769-1 LC Card 86-194319
HE131 .M84 Heft 18 HE557.A3

Vortragsreihe der Gesellschaft für Westfälische Wirtschaftsgeschichte .
(Heft 25) Henning, Friedrich-Wilhelm. Vorindustrielles Gewerbe und wirtschaftlicher Wandel im Paderborner Land im 19. Jahrhundert /. Dortmund , 1983. 67 p. ; LC Card 83-198581
HC288.P27 H46 1983

Vos, Rob, 1955- From crisis to equitable growth ; a new development agenda for Latin America /. Aldershot , Brookfield, USA , 1987. ix, 144 p. ; ISBN 0-566-05536-8 : LC Card 87-21135 DDC 338.98 19
HC130.B38 F76 1987

Vos, Wouter de. see De Vos, Wouter.

Vosproizvodstvo trudovykh resursov / V.V. Onikienko ... [et al.]. Kiev : Nauk. dumka, 1984. 177, [3] p. ; 20 cm. At head of title: Akademii͡a nauk Ukrainskoĭ SSR. Sovet po izuchenii͡u proizvoditel'nykh sil USSR. Bibliography: p. 173-[178] LC Card 86-189052
1. Labor supply - Ukraine. 2. Manpower policy - Ukraine. 3. Ukraine - Economic conditions - 1945-. I. Onikienko, V. V. (Vladimir Vasil'evich). II. Rada po vyvchenni͡u produktyvnykh syl URSR.
HD5797.U37 V67 1984

Voss, Alfred. Kortzfleisch, Gert von. Energie für den Verkehr . Frankfurt am Main , c1984. 115 p. : LC Card 84-192683
HD9710.G4 V4 Nr. 42 HE5620.E53

Voss, G. Günter. Bewusstsein ohne Subjekt? : eine Kritik des industriesoziologischen Bewusstseinsbegriffs / Günter Voss. Grosshesselohe : R. Hampp, 1984. vi, 512 p. : ill. ; 21 cm. Bibliography: p. 489-512. ISBN 3-924346-07-0 : LC Card 85-131494
1. Industrial sociology - Germany, West. 2. Class consciousness - Germany (West). 3. Labor and laboring classes - Germany, West. I. Title.
HD6957.G35 V67 1984

Voss, Rüdiger von, 1939- Das Süd-Nord-Gefälle . Stuttgart , 1986. 168 p. ; ISBN 3-87959-270-5 LC Card 87-103590 DDC 330.943/0878 19
HC286.7 .S9 1986

Voss, Timm. Die algerisch-französische Arbeitsmigration : ein Beispiel einer organisierten Rückwanderung / von Timm Voss. Königstein/Ts. : Hanstein, 1981. xiii, 193 p. : ill. ; 21 cm. (Materialien zur Arbeitsmigration und Ausländerbeschäftigung . Bd. 8) Summary in English and French. Bibliography: p. 173-182. ISBN 3-7756-6937-X : LC Card 81-176949 DDC 331.6/2/65044 19
1. Alien labor, Algerian - France. 2. Return migration - Algeria. 3. Return migration - Government policy - Algeria. 4. Labor supply - Algeria. 5. Manpower policy - Algeria. I. Title. II. Series.
HD8438.A4 V67 1981 ***NYPL [JLD 86-2466]***

Voss, Wolf-Dieter. Modellgestützte Markenpolitik : Planung und Kontrolle markenpolitischer Entscheidungen auf der Grundlage computergestützter Informationssysteme / Wolf-Dieter Voss. Wiesbaden : Gabler, c1983. xxvi, 297 p. : ill. ; 24 cm. (Schriftenreihe Unternehmensführung und Marketing. Bd. 16) Bibliography: p. [278]-297. ISBN 3-409-36035-2 LC Card 83-159054
1. Marketing management - Data processing. 2. Marketing - Decision making. I. Title.
HF5415.125 .V67 1983

Vossen, Ad. Modelling household formation and dissolution /. Oxford [Oxfordshire] , New York , c1987. p. cm. ISBN 0-19-829500-6 : LC Card 87-18581 DDC 306.8/5/0724 19
HB849.49 .M63 1987

VOTING - GERMANY, WEST.
Roth, Rainer A., 1942- Zur Problematik der politischen Kultur der Jungwähler in der Bundesrepublik Deutschland /. Passau , c1984. 516 p. : ISBN 3-922016-46-4
NYPL [JLE 87-703]

VOTING - QUEBEC (PROVINCE)
Comportement électoral au Québec /. Chicoutimi, Québec, Canada , c1984. xv, 447 p. : ISBN 2-89105-063-0 LC Card 85-177886 DDC 324.9714 19
JL258 .C65 1984 ***NYPL [JLD 87-1351]***

VOTING RESEARCH - BOLIVIA.
Estimación de la población potencialmente votante al 1o de julio de 1985 según departamentos, provincias, ciudades capital y cantones /. La Paz, Bolivia , 1985. 58 p. : LC Card 87-400543 DDC 304.6/0984/021 19
HA965 .E85 1985

VOTING - UNITED STATES.
Neuman, W. Russell. The paradox of mass politics . Cambridge, Mass. , 1986. 241 p. : ISBN 0-674-65455-2 (alk. paper) LC Card 86-288 DDC 324.973 19
JK1967 .N48 1986 ***NYPL [JLE 86-4140]***

Votum für die Marktwirtschaft : DIHT-Kongress am 21. Oktober 1976, Bad Kissingen / Alfons Goppel, Otto Wolff von Amerongen ; [Herausgeber], Deutscher Industrie- und Handelstag. Bonn : Der Handelstag, c1976. 26 p. ; 21 cm. (DIHT . 157) CONTENTS. - Wirtschaftspolitik nach der Bundestagswahl / Otto Wolff von Amerongen -- Ja zum Risiko der Marktwirtschaft / Alfons Goppel. LC Card 85-172115
1. Germany, West - Economic policy - 1974- - Congresses. 2. Germany (West). Bundestag - Elections, 1976 - Congresses. I. Goppel, Alfons, 1905-. II. Wolff von Amerongen, Otto, 1918-. III. DIHT-Kongress (1976 : Bad Kissingen, Germany). IV. Deutscher Industrie- und Handelstag. V. Series: DIHT (Series) , 157.
HC286.7 .V69 1976

Vous autres au syndicat-- /. Lépine, Ginette. Montréal, Québec , c1984. 179 p. ; ISBN 2-89037-214-6 LC Card 85-101458
HD8005.2.C23 M665 1984

Vox Modern Spanish and English dictionary : English-Spanish, Spanish-English / dictionary compiled by the editors of Biblograf ; North American edition prepared by the editors of National Textbook Company. Lincolnwood, Ill. : National Textbook Company, c1986. xxxiv, 487, 45, 484 p. : maps ; 24 cm. ISBN 0-8442-7990-0 LC Card 86-61160
1. Spanish language - Dictionaries - English. 2. English language - Dictionaries - Spanish. I. Biblograf, S. A. II. National Textbook Company. III. Title: Modern Spanish and English dictionary.
NYPL [*R-RGK 86-7059]

Vox new college Spanish and English dictionary : English-Spanish/Spanish-English / preface by Theodore V. Higgs ; dictionary compiled by Carlos F. MacHale and the editors of Biblograf, S.A. ; North American edition prepared by the editors of National Textbook Company. Lincolnwood, Ill., U. S.A. : National Textbook Co., c1984. xix, 1456, 60 p. : ill. ; 25 cm. (National Textbook language dictionaries) ISBN 0-8442-7998-6 (plain-edge ed.) : LC Card 84-61106 DDC 463/.21 19
1. Spanish language - Dictionaries - English. 2. English language - Dictionaries - Spanish. I. MacHale, Carlos F. II. Biblograf, s. a. III. National Textbook Company. IV. Series.
PC4640 .V696 1984
NYPL [*R-RGK 85-1500]

Voyage dans l'empire d'Autriche, pendant les années 1809 et 1810. Serres, Marcel de, 1783-1862. Essai sur les arts at les manufactures de l'empire d'Autriche /. Paris , 1814-1815. 3 v. : LC Card 85-666370
HC263 .S47x 1814

Voydanoff, Patricia. Work and family life / Patricia Voydanoff. Newbury Park, Calif. : Sage Publications, c1987. 136 p. ; 22 cm. (Family studies text series . 6) Bibliography: p. 116-129. Includes indexes. ISBN 0-8039-2289-2 (pbk.) LC Card 87-9482 DDC 306.8/5/0973 19
1. Work and family - United States. 2. Married people - Employment - United States. I. Series: Family studies text series , v. 6. II. Title.
HD4904.25 .V69 1987

Vozdeĭstvie khoziaĭstvennogo mekhanizma na povyshenie ėffektivnosti obshchestvennogo proizvodstva : sbornik nauchnykh trudov / [redaktsionnaia kollegiia A.M. Leont'ev (otv. redaktor ... et al.]. Dnepropetrovsk : Dnepropetrovskiĭ gos. universitet, 1984. 119 p. ; 20 cm. At head of title: Ministerstvo vysshego i srednego spetsial'nogo obrazovaniia SSSR. Dnepropetrovskiĭ ordena Trudovogo Krasnogo Znameni gosudarstvennyĭ universitet imeni 300-letiia vossoedineniia Ukrainy s Rossieĭ. Includes bibliographical references. LC Card 86-181397
1. Industrial productivity - Soviet Union. 2. Labor productivity - Soviet Union. 3. Agricultural productivity - Soviet Union. I. Leont'ev, A. M. II. Dnipropetrovs'kyĭ derzhavnyĭ universytet imeni 300-richchia vozz'iednannia Ukraïny z Rosiieiu.
HC340.I52 V68 1984

Vozikis, George S. (George Soterios), 1948- Mescon, Timothy S. Cases in strategic management . New York , c1988. ix, 725 p. : ISBN 0-06-044465-7 (pbk.) LC Card 87-25141 DDC 658.4/012 19
HD30.28 .M46 1988

Vozrozhdenie prifrontovykh i osvobozhdennykh raĭonov SSSR v gody Velikoĭ Otechestvennoĭ voĭny 1941-1945 / otvetstvennyĭ redaktor IU.A. Poliakov. Moskva : "Nauka", 1986. 214 p., [24] p. of plates : ill. ; 23 cm. At head of title: Akademiia nauk SSSR. Institut istorii SSSR. Includes bibliographies. LC Card 86-232256
1. Soviet Union, Western - Economic conditions - Congresses. 2. Reconstruction (1939-1951) - Soviet Union, Western - Congresses. 3. World War, 1939-1945 - Economic aspects - Soviet Union, Western - Congresses. I. Poliakov, IUriĭ Aleksandrovich. II. Institut istorii SSSR (Akademiia nauk SSSR).
HC336.9.W47 V69 1986

VP .
(č. 252 etc) Klusoň, Václav. Teoretické otázky formování plánovitého řízení národního hospodářství ČSSR /. Praha , 1986- v. <1 > ; LC Card 87-167771
HC270.28 .K58 1986

Vprašanja znanosti.
Vloga znanosti pri oblikovanju strategije razvoja SR Slovenije /. Ljubljana , 1981. 174 p. : LC Card 82-151266
HC407.Z7 S57 1981

Vrachniarēs, Chrēstos. Anamesa se dyo exegerseis : Kileler 1910, Trikala 1925 / Chrēstou Vrachniarē. Athēna : Ekdoseis Alpheios, 1985. 139, [5] p. ; 21 cm. Bibliography: p. [141] LC Card 86-206897
1. Peasantry - Greece - History - 20th century. 2. Peasant uprisings - Greece - History - 20th century. 3. Greece - Rural conditions. I. Title.
HD1536.G7 V73 1985

Vranitzky, Franz. Wagner, Adolph, 1835-1917. Die Ordnung des österreichischen Staatshaushaltes--1863 /. Wien , c1984. 308 p. ; ISBN 3-85447-086-X LC Card 85-223615
HJ1065 .W34 1984

Vrchota, J. (Jaroslav) Kazimour, Jan, engineer. Rezervy v ekonomice /. Praha , 1981. 227 p. ; LC Card 81-208368
HC270.28 .K38 1981

Vremia i my.
Krasnenkov, Vladimir. Ne pole pereĭti-- /. Moskva , 1986. 174 p. ; LC Card 86-132520
HD1995.N515 K73 1986

Orlova, Zhanna. Dobroe imia /. Moskva , 1986. 124 p. ; LC Card 86-131980
HD8530.M62 O75 1986

Vries, A. M. de. Vissers, A. M. C. Arbeidsmarktgedrag ten tijde van massale werkloosheid . 's-Gravenhage , 1986. 106 p. : ISBN 90-12-05302-1 LC Card 87-108930
HD5717.5.N45 V57 1986

Vries, Margaret Garritsen. see De Vries, Margaret Garritsen, 1922-

vrmmon problems/proper solutions : avoiding error in quantitative social research / edited by J. Scott Long. Newbury Park, CA : Sage Publications, 1987. p. cm. (Sage focus editions. v. 94) Bibliography: p. ISBN 0-8039-2806-8 : LC Card 87-20625 DDC 300/.72 19
1. Social sciences - Statistical methods. I. Long, J. Scott.
HA29 .C7325 1987

Vroom, Victor Harold, 1932- Some personality determinants of the effects of participation / Victor H. Vroom. New York : Garland Pub., 1987, c1960. x, 91 p. ; 23 cm. (Continuity in administrative science) Reprint. Originally published: Englewood Cliffs, N.J. : Prentice-Hall, c1960. Originally published in the series Ford Foundation doctoral dissertation series. Thesis (Ph.D.--University of Michigan, 1959). Bibliography: p. 89-91. ISBN 0-8240-8225-7 (alk. paper) : LC Card 86-27081 DDC 158.7 19
1. Psychology, Industrial. 2. Motivation (Psychology). 3. Personality and situation. 4. Decision-making. I. Title. II. Series.
HF5548.8 .V695 1987

Die vrou in die werksituasie in die RSA . Van der Walt, Sunette. Pretoria , 1986. vii, 156 p. : ISBN 0-7969-0373-5 LC Card 87-121977
HD6212 .V363 1986

Vrouwen en economische zelfstandigheid / [Hedy d'Ancona ... et al.]. Amsterdam : SUA, c1986. 199 p. : ill. ; 21 cm. Includes bibliographies. CONTENTS. - Economische zelfstandigheid / Marga Bruyn-Hundt, Hettie Pott-Buter -- De participatie van vrouwen / Maria Brouwer -- Vrouwelijke ondernemers / Gonneke Koopman -- Posities van medewerksters vrouwenstudies in de arbeidsorganisatie van de Universiteit van Amsterdam / Nicoline Angenent -- Modern wiskunde-onderwijs speciaal voor meisjes / Thea de Poel -- Vrouwenwerk / Lia Karsten -- Is werk bereikbaar voor iedereen? / Marijke van Schendelen -- Arbeidsmobiliteit en emancipatie / Joos Maas-Droogleever Fortuijn -- Het Huwelijk tussen contract en beleid / Guda G. Oly -- De anti-emancipatoire werking van het Marcks-arrest / Helma van Schie. ISBN 90-6222-139-4 : LC Card 86-182832
1. Women - Employment - Netherlands. 2. Equal pay for equal work - Netherlands. 3. Wages - Women - Netherlands. 4. Women - Netherlands - Economic conditions. I. Ancona, Hedy d'.
HD6162 .V74 1986

Vrouwen zelfstandig . Koopman, A. F. Den Haag [1986] 70 p. ; ISBN 90-346-0762-3 LC Card 86-172683
HD2346.N4 K66 1986

Vrsaljko, Krešimir. Teorija i praksa domaćih i medunarodnih plaćanja / Krešimir Vrsaljko. 2., izm. i dop. izd. Zagreb : "Narodne novine", 1982. xiv, 460 p. ; 24 cm. (Biblioteka Udžbenici . 103) In Serbo-Croatian (Roman) Bibliography: p. 457-460. LC Card 84-160248
1. Clearinghouse - Yugoslavia. 2. International clearing - Yugoslavia. 3. Payment - Yugoslavia. 4. Banks and banking - Yugoslavia. 5. Clearinghouse. 6. International clearing. 7. Payment. 8. Banks and banking, International. I. Title. II. Series.
HG2341.Y82 V77 1982

Vruchtbaarheid van geboortegeneraties gebaseerd op waarnemingen over de periode 1950-1983 /. Nouwt, P. 's-Gravenhage , 1985. 95 p. ; ISBN

90-357-0197-6 : LC Card 86-218161
HB1015 .N68 1985

Vrywillighe Liefde Broeders van S. Huybrecht Liefde (Brussels, Belgium)
La Duron, Joannes, 17th-18th cent. Vrywillighe Liefde Broeders van S. Huybrecht Liefde, ingestelt door het Vrye Vleesvercoopers Ambacht a[nn]o 1714. [1715-1718?] [126] leaves (leaves [1], [7], [43-123], and [125-126] blank) : LC Card 86-222905
HD6473.N35 L3 1715

VRYWILLIGHE LIEFDE BROEDERS VAN S. HUYBRECHT LIEFDE (BRUSSELS, BELGIUM) - OFFICIALS AND EMPLOYEES.
La Duron, Joannes, 17th-18th cent. Vrywillighe Liefde Broeders van S. Huybrecht Liefde, ingestelt door het Vrye Vleesvercoopers Ambacht a[nn]o 1714. [1715-1718?] [126] leaves (leaves [1], [7], [43-123], and [125-126] blank) : LC Card 86-222905
HD6473.N35 L3 1715

Vrywillighe Liefde Broeders van S. Huybrecht Liefde, ingestelt door het Vrye Vleesvercoopers Ambacht a[nn]o 1714. La Duron, Joannes, 17th-18th cent. [1715-1718?] [126] leaves (leaves [1], [7], [43-123], and [125-126] blank) : LC Card 86-222905
HD6473.N35 L3 1715

VRYWILLIGHGE LIEFDE BROEDERS VAN S. HUYBRECHT LIEFDE (BRUSSELS, BELGIUM)
La Duron, Joannes, 17th-18th cent. Vrywillighe Liefde Broeders van S. Huybrecht Liefde, ingestelt door het Vrye Vleesvercoopers Ambacht a[nn]o 1714. [1715-1718?] [126] leaves (leaves [1], [7], [43-123], and [125-126] blank) : LC Card 86-222905
HD6473.N35 L3 1715

Vserossiĭskaia seriia "I vnov' prodolzhaetsia boĭ--" Gazovyĭ most . Sverdlovsk , 1985. 206 p. : LC Card 86-186324
HD9581.S653 S54 1985

Vsesoiuznaia akademiia sel'skokhoziaĭstvennykh nauk imeni V.I. Lenina. Sibirskoe otdelenie. Sistema vedeniia sel'skogo khoziaĭstva Buriatskoĭ ASSR . Novosibirsk , 1985. 188 p. : LC Card 86-215358
HD1995.B8 S57 1985

Vsesoiuznaia Kommunisticheskaia Partiia (Bol'shevikov) see Kommunisticheskaia partiia Sovetskogo Soiuza.

Vsesoiuznaia konferentsiia "Razvitie proizvoditel'nykh sil Sibiri i zadachi uskoreniia nauchno-tekhnicheskogo progressa" (1985 : Tomsk, R.S.F.S.R.). Sektsiia "Khimicheskaia promyshlennost'." Razvitie khimicheskoĭ promyshlennosti Sibiri : tezisy dokladov sektsii "Khimicheskaia promyshlennost'" Vsesoiuznoĭ konferentsii / [otvetstvennyĭ redaktor G.F. Bol'shakov]. Tomsk : Akademiia nauk SSSR, Sibirskoe otd-nie, 1985. 177 p. : ill. ; 20 cm. Includes bibliographies. LC Card 86-176713
1. Chemical industry - Russian S.F.S.R. - Siberia - Congresses. I. Bol'shakov, G. F. (Gennadiĭ Fedorovich). II. Title.
HD9656.S56 S538 1985

Vsesoiuznoe ob"edinenie "Mortekhinformreklama" (Soviet Union) Prognozirovanie i ėffektivnost' raboty flota . Leningrad , 1985. 104 p. : LC Card 86-170274
HE847 .P77 1985

Vsesoiuznoe obshchestvo filatelistov (Soviet Union) Orlov, V. A. (Vasiliĭ Adamovich) Khudozhestvennye markirovannye konverty SSSR . Moskva , 1984. 120 p. : LC Card 84-168398
HE6185.S652 O75 1984

Vsesoiuznyĭ nauchno-issledovatel'skiĭ institut sistemnykh issledovaniĭ. Uchastie trudiashchikhsia v upravlenii proizvodstvom . Moskva , 1983. 192, [2] p. : LC Card 84-210286
HD5660.S65 U26 1983

Vsesoiuznyĭ nauchno-metodicheskiĭ tsentr po organizatsii truda i upravleniia proizvodstvom (Soviet Union) Nauchnaia organizatsiia truda v promyshlennosti /. Moskva , 1986. 414 p. : LC Card 86-218434
HD36 .N323 1986

Vsesoiuznyĭ seminar "Imitatsionnye modeli v ASU" (1979 : Novosibirsk, R.S.F.S.R.) Imitatsionnoe modelirovanie proizvodstvennykh protsessov . Novosibirsk , 1979. 152 p. : LC Card 81-132238
HD70.S63 I44 1979

Vsiu organizatorskuiu i politicheskuiu rabotu--na vypolnenie reshenii XXVI s"ezda KPSS . Aliev, Geĭdar Alievich. Baku , 1981. 50 p. ; LC Card 82-158175
HC337.A9 A683 1981

Vspomogatel'noe proizvodstvo mashinostroeniia . Kryzhanovskiĭ, B. N. (Boris Nikolaevich) Kiev , 1983. 334 p. : LC Card 83-238314
HD9703.S653 U475 1983

VTRC (Series) .
(87-R13) Sharkey, Stephen M. Evaluation of the 1984 selective speed enforcement projects in Virginia /. Charlottesville, Va. [1987] xii, 117, [34] p. : LC Card 87-621546 DDC 388.3/144/09755 19
HE5620.S6 S532 1987

Vũ, Khiêu. Sovetsko-v'etnamskiĭ simpozium na temu "Ėkonomicheskie problemy perekhoda k sotsializmu" (1984 : Moscow, R.S.F.S.R.) Ėkonomicheskie problemy perekhoda k sotsializmu stran s nerazvitoĭ ėkonomikoĭ . [Moskva , 1986. 254 p. ; LC Card 87-108102
HC444 .S69 1984

Vu, My T., 1939- World population projections, 1985 : short- and long-term estimates by age and sex : with related demographic statistics / My T. Vu. Baltimore : Johns Hopkins University Press, 1985. xxvi, 451 p. ; 29 cm. "Published for the World Bank." Chiefly tables. ISBN 0-8018-3322-1 LC Card 85-23083 DDC 304.6 19
1. Population - Statistics. 2. Population forecasting - Statistics. I. Title.
HA155 .V83 1985
NYPL [*R-Econ. 86-3764]

Vucheva, Khristina. Kreditni otnosheniia na Narodna republika Bŭlgariia s razvivashtite se strani /. Sofiia , 1986. 78, [1] p. ; LC Card 86-152274
HF1578.15.D44 K74 1986

Vŭlchev, Nikola.
Krŭstiu Dobrev . Sofiia , 1987. 80 p., [16] p. of plates : LC Card 87-170598
HB108.3.D63 K78 1987

Proizvodstvenite vrŭzki v agrarno-promishlenata oblast / Nikola Vŭlchev. Sofiia : Izd-vo na Bŭlgarskata akademiia na naukite, 1986. 183 p. ; 20 cm. Titles on added t.p.: Production links in the agro-industrial sphere; Proizvodstvennye sviazi v agrarno-promyshlennoĭ oblasti. At head of title: Bŭlgarska akademiia na naukite. Ikonomicheski institut. Errata slip inserted. Summary in English and Russian. Includes bibliographical references. LC Card 86-195329
1. Agricultural industries - Bulgaria - Management. I. Title. II. Title: Production links in the agro-industrial sphere. III. Title: Proizvodstvennye sviazi v agrarno-promyshlennoĭ oblasti.
HD9015.B82 V84 1986

Vŭlchev, Todor Ĭordanov. Problemy valiutnogo soiuza stran-chlenov Evropeĭskogo ėkonomicheskogo soobshchestva i razvitie mezhdunarodnoĭ valiutnoĭ sistemy kapitalizma . Sofiia , 1984. 151 p. ; LC Card 85-224144
HG3942.8 .P76 1984

Vŭlkovski, Georgi Danov. Mezhdunarodni ikonomicheski otnosheniia pri sottsializma : izbrani lektsii / Georgi Danov. Sofiia : VISSh mashinno-elektrotekhnicheski in-t "V.I. Lenin" Sofiia, Fakultet za obshtestveni profesii, 1985 [i.e. 1986] 151 p. ; 22 cm. Includes bibliographical references. LC Card 87-134453
1. Europe, Eastern - Economic integration. 2. Europe, Eastern - Foreign economic relations. 3. Council for Mutual Economic Assistance. I. Title.
HC244 .V84 1986

Vurderingen af landets faste ejendomme pr. 1 april 1981 : (17. almindelige vurdering) / udarbejdet af Statsskattedirektoratet. København : Statsskattedirektoratet, Vurderingsafdelingen, [1982] 225 p. ; 24 cm. (Statsskattedirektoratet informerer) ISBN 87-503-4048-4 LC Card 82-232266
1. Real property - Valuation - Denmark. I. Denmark. Statsskattedirektoratet. II. Series.
HD736 .V87 1982

Vuscovic, Pedro. Notas para una discusión sobre política económica y la experiencia latinoamericana. Montevideo, Uruguay : Centro Latinoamericano de Economía Humana, [1983] 29 p. ; 28 cm. (Ficha de capacitación. Serie "A" . no. 37) Cover title. "Primer borrador"--P. [1] LC Card 86-160128
1. Latin America - Economic policy. I. Centro Latinoamericano de Economía Humana. II. Title.
HC125 .V87 1983

Vŭshnotŭrgovski aspekti na selskostopanskite i khranitelno-vkusovite stoki i problemi pred bŭlgarskiia iznos /. Atanasov, Mikhail, k.i.n. Sofiia , 1984. 118 p. ; LC Card 85-163481
HD9015.B82 A86 1984

Vŭznikvane, razvitie i zalez na oportiunizma v bŭlgarskoto rabotnichesko dvizhenie, 1891/1948 / [avtorski kolektiv, rŭkovoditel Georgi Radev ... et al. ; redaktori Georgi Radev, Klara Pinkas]. 1. izd. Sofiia : Partizdat, 1986. 696 p. ; 21 cm. At head of title: Institut po istoriia na BKP pri TSK na BKP. Includes bibliographical references. LC Card 86-200229
1. Labor and laboring classes - Bulgaria - Political activity - History. 2. Trade-unions and communism - Bulgaria - History. 3. Communist revisionism - History. I. Radev, Georgi. II. Pinkas, Klara. III. Institut po istoriia na Bŭlgarskata komunisticheska partiia.
HD8628 .V89 1986

Vyas, Niren. Woodside, Arch G. Industrial purchasing strategies . Lexington, Mass. , c1987. xiv, 223 p. : ISBN 0-669-06953-1 (alk. paper) LC Card 83-48132 DDC 658.7/2 19
HD39.5 .W66 1987

Vyasulu, Vinod. Development of backward areas : decentralized production and regional development / Vinod Vyasulu. New Delhi, India : Yatan Publications, 1987. xi, 188 p. : ill. ; 23 cm. In the Indian context, chiefly with reference to small business. Includes bibliographies and index. ISBN 81-85030-05-7 : LC Card 87-902689 DDC 332.6/42/0954 19
1. Small business - India. 2. Industries, Size of - India. 3. India - Economic conditions - 1947-. 4. Regional planning - India. I. Title.
HD2346.I5 V93 1987

Vychislitel'naia tekhnika na avtomobil'nom transporte . Kaftaniuk, IU. A. (IUriĭ Anatol'evich) Moskva , 1985. 183 p. : LC Card 86-163666
HE5613 .K36 1985

Vydrova, IA. (IArushe) Cheshsko-russkiĭ ėkonomicheskiĭ slovar' . Moskva , Praga , 1986. 300 p. ; LC Card 85-146401
HB61 .C453 1986 ***NYPL [*QAD 87-1680]***

Vysochaĭshe uchrezhdennaia Osobaia vysshaia komissiia dlia vsestoronniago izsliedovaniia zhelieznodorozhnago diela v Rossii (Series) .
(vyp. 5) Petrov, N. P. Finansovoe polozhenie russkoĭ zhelieznodorozhnoĭ sieti i glavnieĭshiia prichiny ukhudsheniia ego v posliednie gody. S.-Peterburg, 1909. 185, ii, 17 p. LC Card 75-564261
HE3131 .A33 vyp. 5 HE3136

Vysshaia shkola profsoiuznogo dvizheniia VTSSPS imeni N.M. Shvernika. Voprosy ukrepleniia trudovoĭ i proizvodstvennoĭ distsipliny v deiatel'nosti profsoiuznykh organizatsiĭ . Moskva , 1984. 77 p. ; LC Card 86-181312
HF5549.5.L3 V67 1984

Vytanovych, Illia. Sotsial'no-ekonomichni ideï v zmahanniakh halyts'kykh ukraïntsiv na perelomi XIX-XX vv. / Illia Vytanovych. Miunkhen : Ukr. tekhnichno-hospodars'kyĭ in-t, 1970. 74 p. ; 26 cm. (Naukovi zapysky / Ukraïns'kyĭ tekhnichno-hospodars'kyĭ instytut . ch. 21) Summary in German. Includes bibliographical references. LC Card 86-214348
1. Galicia, Eastern (Ukraine) - Economic conditions. 2. Galicia, Eastern, Ukraine - Politics and government. 3. Economics - Ukraine - Galicia, Eastern - History. 4. Galicia, Eastern (Ukraine) - Social conditions. I. Series: Naukovi zapysky (Ukraïns'kyĭ tekhnichno-hospodars'kyĭ instytut (Munich, Germany)) , ch. 21. II. Title.
HC337.U52 G358 1970

Vývoj společnosti ČSSR, podle výsledků sčítání lidu, domů a bytů 1980. [Prague] : Federální statistický úřad, 1985. 2 v. ; 29 cm.

CONTENTS. - [1]. Textová část -- [2]. Tabulková část. LC Card 86-185144
1. Czechoslovakia - Population - Statistics. 2. Czechoslovakia - Census, 1980. I. Czechoslovakia. Federální statistický úřad.
HA1191.5 1980b

Vyvoz kapitala v vos'midesiatye gody. Vyvoz kapitala v 80-e gody . Moskva , 1986. 247 p. ; LC Card 87-166362
HG4538 .V93 1986

Vyvoz kapitala v 80-e gody : novye tendentsii i protivorechiia : referativnyi sbornik / [sostavitel' i redaktor sbornika Zubchenko L.A.]. Moskva : Akademiia nauk SSSR, In-t nauch. informatsii po obshchestvennym naukam, 1986. 247 p. ; 20 cm. (Seriia Problemy mezhdunarodnykh ekonomicheskikh otnoshenii) Includes bibliographies. LC Card 87-166362
1. Investments, Foreign. 2. Capital movements. 3. International business enterprises. I. Zubchenko, L. A. II. Institut nauchnoi informatsii po obshchestvennym naukam (Akademiia nauk SSSR). III. Title: Vyvoz kapitala v vos'midesiatye gody. IV. Series.
HG4538 .V93 1986

Výzk. publ. (Ekonomicko-matematická laboratoř (Ekonomický ústav ČSAV)) .
(č. 233) Stránská, Ludmila. Organizačně institucionální soustava řízení MSEI /. Praha , 1985. 167 p. : LC Card 86-215270
HC243.5 .S88 1985
(č. 234) Fingerland, Jaroslav. Mezinárodní socialistická ekonomická integrace a předmětné sféry specializace národohospodářského komplexu ČSSR /. Praha , 1985. 169 p. ; LC Card 86-215200
HF1542.3.Z4 C654 1985
(č. 235) Amort, Jiří. Dynamika národohospodářských struktur a mezinárodních ekonomických vztahů v podmínkách SEI /. Praha , 1986. 211 p. ; LC Card 86-206744
HC244 .A626 1986
(č. 237) Chlumský, Jiří. Hospodářská politika USA v oblasti energetiky /. Praha , 1986. 134 p. ; LC Card 86-215183
HD9502.U52 C526 1986

Vzaimodeĭstvie transportnykh sistem /. Rezer, Semen Moiseevich. Moskva , 1985. 243 p. : LC Card 85-223225
HE255 .R493 1985

W. D. R. see **Westdeutscher Rundfunk.**

W dymach czarnych budzi się Łódź : z dziejów łódzkiego ruchu robotniczego 1882-1948. Wyd. 1. Łódź : Wydawn. Łódzkie, 1985. 507 p. ; 25 cm. Includes bibliographical references. ISBN 83-218-0280-X : LC Card 85-218768
1. Labor and laboring classes - Poland - Łódź - History.
HD8539.5.L62 W16 1985

W. H. O. see **World Health Organization.**

W. T. O. see **World Tourism Organization.**

Waagen, Christopher L. Wilson, Gerald L., 1943- Organizational communication /. New York , c1986. xiv, 322 p. : ISBN 0-06-042387-0 LC Card 85-8723 DDC 658.4/5 19
HD58.7 .W55 1986 ***NYPL [JLE 86-2600]***

WABC Talk radio 77 AM financial expert Bill Bresnan speaks on real estate-- in words of one syllable. Bresnan, Bill, 1940- WABC Talkradio 77 AM financial expert Bill Bresnan speaks on real estate-- in words of one syllable /. Englewood Cliffs, NJ , c1987. xx, 172 p. ; ISBN 0-13-949629-7 LC Card 87-60220 DDC 332.63/24 19
HD1379 .B744 1987

WABC Talkradio seventy-seven AM financial expert Bill Bresnan speaks on real estate-- in words of one syllable. Bresnan, Bill, 1940- WABC Talkradio 77 AM financial expert Bill Bresnan speaks on real estate-- in words of one syllable /. Englewood Cliffs, NJ , c1987. xx, 172 p. ; ISBN 0-13-949629-7 LC Card 87-60220 DDC 332.63/24 19
HD1379 .B744 1987

WABC Talkradio 77 AM financial expert Bill Bresnan speaks on real estate-- in words of one syllable /. Bresnan, Bill, 1940- Englewood Cliffs, NJ , c1987. xx, 172 p. ; ISBN 0-13-949629-7 LC Card 87-60220 DDC 332.63/24 19
HD1379 .B744 1987

Wacholtz, Larry E. Inside country music / [Larry E. Wacholtz]. New York : Billboard Publications, 1986. 254 p. ; 24 cm. Interviews. Includes index. ISBN 0-8230-7532-X (pbk. : alk. paper) LC Card 86-4234 DDC 784.5/2/002373 19
1. Music trade - United States. 2. Sound recording industry - United States. 3. Country music - United States. 4. Music, Popular (Songs, etc.) - United States. 5. Interviews - United States. I. Title.
ML3790 .W24 1986 ***NYPL [JNE 86-18]***

Wachsende Städte an der Unterweser : Bremen-Bremerhaven im Aufbau 1958 bis 1964 / herausgegeben vom Bremer Ausschuss für Wirtschaftsforschung ; bearbeitet von Gerhard Deissmann.2. Aufl. Bremen : R. Bargmann, 1965. xii, 243 p., [7] folded leaves of plates : ill. ; 25 cm. Bibliography: p. 241-243. LC Card 85-122713
1. Bremen (Germany) - Economic conditions. 2. Bremerhaven (Germany) - Economic conditions. 3. Bremen (Germany) - Commerce. 4. Bremerhaven (Germany) - Commerce. 5. Bremen (Germany) - Social conditions. 6. Bremerhaven (Germany) - Social conditions. I. Deissmann, Gerhard. II. Bremer Ausschuss für Wirtschaftsforschung.
HC289.B7 W33 1965

Wachstum bei Erschöpfbaren Ressourcen, gibt es das? . Krelle, Wilhelm. Münster , c1982. 59 p. : ISBN 3-402-04434-X LC Card 83-215135
HC55 .K74 1982

Wachstum und Produktivität in der Industrie und ihren Hauptbereichen in der BRD, Österreich, Polen und Ungarn im Zeitraum, 1960-1972 /. Boguszewski, Jan. Wien [1979] 71 p. : LC Card 84-119739
HC290.5.I52 B64 1979

Wachstum und Strukturwandlungen Brasiliens in ihrer Bedeutung für die strategische Marketingplanung von Konsumgüterunternehmungen /. Neustadt, Peter. Diessenhofen , cop. 1979. ix, 463 p. : ISBN 3-7253-0092-5 : LC Card 80-469750
HF5415.12.B7 N48 1979 ***NYPL [JLD 80-3357]***

Wachstumshemmnisse mittelständischer Industriebetriebe /. Geiser, Josef. Göttingen , 1983. xi, 385 p. : ISBN 3-509-01353-0 LC Card 84-221327
HD2346.G3 G372 1983

Wachstumsmarkt Südostasien : Chancen und Risiken unternehmerischer Kooperation : Referate und Diskussionsbeiträge der Tagung des Ifo-Instituts vom 19.-21. Oktober 1983 in München = Growth market Southeast Asia : opportunities for and risks of business cooperation : papers and proceedings of a conference sponsored by the Ifo Institute for Economic Research in Munich on 19-21 October 1983 / Helmut Laumer (Hrsg.). München : Weltforum Verlag, c1984. x, 807 p. : ill. ; 30 cm. (Ifo-Studien zur Entwicklungsforschung. Sonderreihe "Information und Dokumentation" . 3) English and German. Includes bibliographical references. ISBN 3-8039-0292-4 : LC Card 84-249861
1. Asia, Southeastern - Commerce - Congresses. 2. Investments, Foreign - Asia, Southeastern - Congresses. I. Laumer, Helmut. II. Ifo-Institut für Wirtschaftsforschung. III. Title: Growth market Southeast Asia. IV. Series.
HF3790.8.Z5 W33 1984

Wachstumsverlangsamung und Konjunkturzyklen in unterschiedlichen Wirtschaftssystemen / von Armin Bohnet ... [et al.] ; herausgegeben von Alfred Schüller. Berlin : Duncker & Humblot, c1984. 191 p. : ill. ; 24 cm. (Schriften des Vereins für Socialpolitik, Gesellschaft für Wirtschafts- und Sozialwissenschaften . n.F., Bd. 142) "Der vorliegende Band enthält die Referate, die auf der Sitzung des Ausschusses zum Vergleich von Wirtschaftssystemen am 29. und 30. September 1983 im Studienhaus Wiesneck, Buchenbach bei Freiburg ... vorgelegt worden sind"--Vorwort. Includes bibliographies. ISBN 3-428-05626-4
1. Economic development - Addresses, essays, lectures. 2. Business cycles - Addresses, essays, lectures. 3. Comparative economics - Addresses, essays, lectures. I. Schüller, Alfred. II. Bohnet, Armin. III. Series. IV. Series: Gesellschaft für Wirtschafts- und Sozialwissenschaften, verein für sozialpolitik. Schriften , n.F., Bd. 142. V. Title.
NYPL [JLL 73-186 Bd. 142]

Wachstumszyklen und funktionale Einkommensverteilung /. Funke, Michael, 1956- München , c1985. iii, 244 p. : ISBN 3-88259-319-9 LC Card 85-175617
HB3711 .F896 1985

Wacht, Richard F. A new approach to capital budgeting for city and county governments / Richard F. Wacht. 2nd ed. Atlanta, Ga. : Business Pub. Division, College of Business Administration, Georgia State University, 1987. ix, 149 p. : ill. ; 23 cm. (Research monograph / College of Business Administration, Georgia State University . no. 87) Spine title: Capital budgeting for city and county governments. ISBN 0-88406-190-6 (pbk.) : LC Card 87-21157 DDC 352.1/2 19
1. Capital budget - United States - Mathematical models. 2. Local budgets - United States - Mathematical models. 3. Capital investments - United States - Mathematical models. I. Title. II. Title: Capital budgeting for city and county governments. III. Series: Research monograph (Georgia State University. College of Business Administration) , no. 87.
HJ9147 .W33 1987

Wachtel, Paul. Trade friction and economic policy . Cambridge [Cambridgeshire] , New York , 1987. xii, 243 p. : ISBN 0-521-34446-8 LC Card 87-11694 DDC 382/.0952/073 19
HF3828.U5 T73 1987

Wacker, Ali, 1942- Individuelle und gesellschaftliche Kosten der Massenarbeitslosigkeit . Weinheim , 1985. xxvi, 506 p. : ISBN 3-407-54689-0 LC Card 86-118545 DDC 331.13/7/019 19
HD5708 .I53 1985 ***NYPL [JLD 87-387]***

Wackersdorf : Bilder und Texte aus dem Widerstand / [redaktionelle Mitarbeit, Karl-Heinz Schmilgun, Siegfried Völler, Hans-Jürgen Zanella].1. Aufl. Passau : Andreas-Haller-Verlag, 1986. 75 p. : ill. ; 21 x 23 cm. ISBN 3-88849-021-9 LC Card 86-183781
1. Antinuclear movement - Germany (West) - Wackersdorf. I. Schmilgun, Karl-Heinz. II. Völler, Siegfried. III. Zanella, Hans-Jürgen.
HD9698.G43 W338 1986

Wacławowicz, Stanisław. Elementy polityki ekonomicznej . Kraków , 1977. 306 p. ; LC Card 81-173152
HC340.3 .E515 1977

Waddington, David P. Trouble brewing : a social psychological analysis of the Ansells Brewery dispute / David P. Waddington. Aldershot ; Brookfield, U. S.A. : Avebury, c1987. x, 164 p. : ill. ; 23 cm. Bibliography: p. 150-160. Includes index. ISBN 0-566-05374-8 : LC Card 86-31849 DDC 331.89/28633/0942496 19
1. Ansells Brewery Strike, Birmingham, England, 1981. I. Title.
HD5366.L62 1981 .B578 1987

Wade-Marshall, D. Economy and people in the north /. Darwin , 1985. v, 294 p. : ISBN 0-86784-591-0 (pbk.) : LC Card 86-159263 DDC 330.9719/03 19
HC607.N6 E27 1985

Wade, Mary Dodson. Milk, meat biscuits, and the terraqueous machine : the story of Gail Borden / by Mary Dodson Wade.1st ed. Austin, Tex. : Eakin Press, c1987. 49 p. : ill. ; 23 cm. Bibliography: p. 49. A biography of the inventor, businessmen, surveyor, and philanthropist who, among other accomplishments, was the first to develop a method to condense milk and founded the dairy company bearing his name. ISBN 0-89015-605-0 : LC Card 87-6813 DDC 338.7/664/00924 B 92 19
1. Borden, Gail, b. 1801 - Juvenile literature. 2. Industrialists - United States - Biography - Juvenile literature. 3. Food industry and trade - United States - History - Juvenile literature. I. Title.
HD9010.B65 W33 1987

Wade, Robert. Village republics : economic conditions for collective action in South India / Robert Wade. Cambridge [Cambridgeshire] ; New York : Cambridge University Press, 1988. p. cm. (Cambridge South Asian studies. 40) Bibliography: p. Includes index. ISBN 0-521-30146-7 LC Card 86-33389 DDC 334/.683/095484 19
1. Agriculture, Cooperative - India - Kurnool (District) - Case studies. 2. Kurnool (India : District) - Rural conditions - Case studies. 3. Panchayat - India - Kurnool (District) - Case studies. I. Title.
HD1491.I392 K878 1988

Wadensjö, Eskil, 1944- Höglund, Bengt. Spelet om resurserna i den svenska blandekonomin /. Lund , c1984. 227 p. : ISBN 91-7504-041-7 : LC Card 84-200450
HC373.5 .H64 1984

Wädekin, Karl Eugen.
Agriculture in inter-system comparison . Berlin , 1985. 443 p. : ISBN 3-428-05885-2 (pbk.) LC Card 86-190956 DDC 338.1/6/094 19
HD1920.E852 A37 1985

Socialist agriculture in transition . Boulder, Colo. , 1986. ix, 445 p. : ISBN 0-8133-7344-1 : LC Card 86-28995 DDC 338.1/0947 19
HD1917 .S62 1986

Die Währungskrisen vom November 1968 bis Mai 1971 im politischen Prozess der Bundesrepublik Deutschland /. Panek, Hans-Thomas. Köln , 1977. 293 p. ; ISBN 3-921471-29-X LC Card 86-184843
HG999.5 .P35 1977

Die Währungspolitik in den Ländern der Europäischen Wirtschaftsgemeinschaft : Institutionen und Instrumente / Europäische Gemeinschaften, Währungsausschuss. Luxembourg : Amt für Amtliche Veröffentlichungen der Europäischen Gemeinschaften ; Washington, D.C. : European Community Information Service [distributor], 1972. 451 p. ; 25 cm. Bibliography: p. 329. LC Card 85-116654
1. Monetary policy - European Economic Community countries. 2. Financial institutions - European Economic Community countries. I. Commission of the European Communities. Monetary Committee.
HG930.5 .W34 1972

Währungswettbewerb . Bofinger, Peter. Köln , c1985. xiv, 235 p. : ISBN 3-452-20332-8 : LC Card 86-185566
HG221 .B57455 1985

Waffen für die Welt . Dietl, Wilhelm. München , c1986. 335 p. : ISBN 3-426-26268-1 LC Card 86-226603
HD9743.A2 D54 1986

Wage and benefit settlements in construction, 1986. Washington, D.C. (1101 15th St., N.W., Suite 1040, Washington 20005) : Construction Labor Research Council, c1986. 10 p. : ill. ; 28 cm. Caption title. LC Card 87-139726 DDC 331.2/824/0973021 19
1. Wages - Construction workers - United States - Statistics. 2. Employee fringe benefits - United States - Statistics. 3. Collective labor agreements - Construction industry - United States - Statistics. I. Construction Labor Research Council.
HD4966.B892 U685 1986

Wage and employment patterns in labor contracts . Cooper, Russell W., 1955- Chur, Switzerland , New York , c1987. viii, 80 p. : ISBN 3-7186-0378-0 (pbk.) LC Card 86-31947 DDC 331.12/5 19
HD4909 .C57 1987

Wage-earning women . Tentler, Leslie Woodcock. New York , 1979. 266 p. ; ISBN 0-19-502627-6 : LC Card 79-12802 DDC 331.4/0973
HD6095 .T44 ***NYPL [JLD 86-3699]***

The wage employment market for rural women in Bangladesh /. Rahman, Rushidan Islam. Dhaka, Bangladesh , 1986. xi, 97 p. ; LC Card 86-903129 DDC 331.4/295492 19
HD6061.2.B3 R34 1986

Wage employment programmes in rural development . Hirway, Indira. New Delhi , c1986. vi, 112 p. ; ISBN 81-204-0072-0 : LC Card 86-903398 DDC 331.2/95475 19
HD5070.G85 H57 1986

WAGE-FUND. see **WAGES.**

WAGE PAYMENT SYSTEMS - CONGRESSES.
Incentives, cooperation, and risk sharing . Totowa, N.J. , 1987. xvi, 239 p. : ISBN 0-8476-7464-9 LC Card 87-4558 DDC 658.3/22 19
HF5549.5.C67 I56 1987

WAGE PAYMENT SYSTEMS - GREAT BRITAIN.
The Future of pay determination . London [1977] 56 p. ; LC Card 84-255776 DDC 331.2/15 19
HD5015 .F88 1977

The wage policy in Kenya . Vandemoortele, Jan. [Nairobi] [1984] 28 leaves : LC Card 86-681105 DDC 331.2/96762 19
HC865.Z9 W248 1984

WAGE-PRICE CONTROLS. see **WAGE-PRICE POLICY.**

WAGE-PRICE GUIDELINES. see **WAGE-PRICE POLICY.**

WAGE-PRICE POLICY - ADDRESSES, ESSAYS, LECTURES.
Incentive-based incomes policies . Cambridge, Mass. , c1986. xxi, 263 p. : ISBN 0-88730-082-0 LC Card 85-20090 DDC 331.2/9 19
HC79.W24 I465 1986 ***NYPL [JLE 86-3724]***

WAGE-PRICE POLICY - ARGENTINA.
Salarios e inflación, Argentina, 1970-1983 /. [Santiago, Chile] [c1984] iv, 116 p. : LC Card 85-156959
HC180.W24 S25 1984

WAGE-PRICE POLICY - CANADA.
Agenda for co-operation . [Ottawa?] [1977?] 63, 66 p. ; LC Card 84-246582
HC120.W24 A64 1977

WAGE-PRICE POLICY - GERMANY, WEST.
Riechey, Gunter. Möglichkeiten und Grenzen der Beeinflussung der Preissetzungsmöglichkeiten der Unternehmen /. München , c1982. 286 p. : ISBN 3-597-10144-5 LC Card 83-160762
HC290.5.W24 R54 1982

WAGE-PRICE POLICY - KENYA.
Vandemoortele, Jan. The wage policy in Kenya . [Nairobi] [1984] 28 leaves : LC Card 86-681105 DDC 331.2/96762 19
HC865.Z9 W248 1984

WAGE-PRICE POLICY - LATIN AMERICA.
Meller, Patricio. Una revisión de políticas de empleo para América Latina /. Santiago, Chile , 1981. 72 leaves ; LC Card 83-182110
HD5730.5.A6 M44 1981

WAGE-PRICE POLICY - MATHEMATICAL MODELS.
Lopes, Francisco Lafaiete. Sistemas alternativos de política salarial /. Rio de Janeiro, RJ , 1984. 51 leaves : LC Card 86-178892
HC79.W24 L66 1984

WAGE-PRICE POLICY - UNITED STATES.
Riechey, Gunter. Möglichkeiten und Grenzen der Beeinflussung der Preissetzungsmöglichkeiten der Unternehmen /. München , c1982. 286 p. : ISBN 3-597-10144-5 LC Card 83-160762
HC290.5.W24 R54 1982

WAGE-PRICE POLICY - UNITED STATES - ADDRESSES, ESSAYS, LECTURES.
Incentive-based incomes policies . Cambridge, Mass. , c1986. xxi, 263 p. : ISBN 0-88730-082-0 LC Card 85-20090 DDC 331.2/9 19
HC79.W24 I465 1986 ***NYPL [JLE 86-3724]***

Wage rigidity and unemployment / edited by Wilfred Beckerman. Baltimore : Johns Hopkins University Press, 1986. viii, 221 p. : ill. ; 23 cm. Includes bibliographies and index. ISBN 0-8018-3400-7 LC Card 86-45446 DDC 331.2/1 19
1. Wages - Congresses. 2. Unemployment - Congresses. 3. Inflation (Finance) - Congresses. I. Beckerman, Wilfred.
HD4909 .W26 1986 ***NYPL [JLD 86-4077]***

Waged work : a reader / edited by Feminist review. London : Virago, 1986. vi, 291 p. : ill. ; 20 cm. Bibliography: p. [268]-283. Includes index. ISBN 0-86068-801-1 (pbk.) : LC Card 86-232209 DDC 331.4/0941 19
1. Wages - Women - Great Britain. 2. Women - Employment - Great Britain. 3. Women - Great Britain - Economic conditions. I. Feminist review.
HD6061.2.G7 W35 1986

Wagener, Martin. Kardinalität in der Nutzentheorie / von Martin Wagener. Königstein/Ts. : Verlagsgruppe Athenäum, Hain, Hanstein, c1983. xii, 160 p. ; 23 cm. (Mathematical systems in economics. 81) Bibliography: p. 158-160. ISBN 3-445-02289-5 LC Card 83-195855
1. Utility theory - Mathematical models. I. Title.
HB201 .W17 1983

Wages and employment policy, 1936-1985 /. Jones, Russell, 1959- London , Boston , 1987. xvii, 175 p. ; ISBN 0-04-331110-5 (alk. paper) LC Card 86-14143 DDC 339.5/0941 19
HD5015 .J66 1987 ***NYPL [JLD 87-831]***

WAGES AND LABOR PRODUCTIVITY.
Wansleben, Martin. Der Produktivitätszuwachs als Massstab für eine beschäftigungsorientierte Lohnpolitik . Baden-Baden , 1986. 153 p. : ISBN 3-7890-1312-9 LC Card 87-128291 DDC 331.1/18 19
HD4945 .W36 1986

WAGES AND LABOR PRODUCTIVITY - CANADA.
Daly, D. J. (Donald James), 1922- On real wage unemployment /. Vancouver, B.C., Canada , 1986. vi, 117 p. : ISBN 0-88975-079-3 (pbk.) LC Card 87-142391 DDC 331.13/7971 19
HD4946.C3 D35 1986

WAGES AND LABOR PRODUCTIVITY - ECONOMETRIC MODELS.
Müller, Lothar. Die Bedeutung der Lohn-Leistungsrelation . Karlsruhe , c1983. iii, 272 p. : ISBN 3-88147-014-X LC Card 84-174174
HD4945 .M84 1983

WAGES AND LABOR PRODUCTIVITY - GERMANY, WEST.
Wansleben, Martin. Der Produktivitätszuwachs als Massstab für eine beschäftigungsorientierte Lohnpolitik . Baden-Baden , 1986. 153 p. : ISBN 3-7890-1312-9 LC Card 87-128291 DDC 331.1/18 19
HD4945 .W36 1986

WAGES AND LABOR PRODUCTIVITY - GREAT BRITAIN.
The Future of pay determination . London [1977] 56 p. ; LC Card 84-255776 DDC 331.2/15 19
HD5015 .F88 1977

WAGES AND LABOR PRODUCTIVITY - PAKISTAN.
Why the office staff scared of time and motion study? . Saddar, Karachi, Pakistan [1985] 1 v. (various pagings) leaves ; LC Card 86-146552
HD5070.5 .W49 1985

WAGES - ANNUAL IMPROVEMENT FACTOR. see **WAGES AND LABOR PRODUCTIVITY.**

WAGES - APPRENTICES - EUROPE - HISTORY.
Schulz, Knut. Handwerksgesellen und Lohnarbeiter . Sigmaringen , 1985. vii, 477 p., [20] p. of plates : ISBN 3-7995-7026-8 LC Card 85-149930
HD4885.E8 S38 1985 ***NYPL [JLE 86-1598]***

WAGES - ARGENTINA.
Salarios e inflación, Argentina, 1970-1983 /. [Santiago, Chile] [c1984] iv, 116 p. : LC Card 85-156959
HC180.W24 S25 1984

WAGES - ARGENTINA - CASE STUDIES.
Toledo, Nora Elena. El tamaño de las ciudades y la distribución de los ingresos (Argentina y Colombia) /. San Juan, Argentina , 1985. 63 p. : LC Card 87-400258 DDC 339.2/2/09861 19
HC200.I5 T65 1985

WAGES - ARGENTINA - STATISTICS.
Evolución de la industria manufacturera, 1982-1984. Buenos Aires, República Argentina [1986] 115 p. : LC Card 86-226786
HD4999 .E95 1986

WAGES - AUSTRALIA.
St. Hill, R. L. Labour mobility between New Zealand and Australia /. Canterbury, N.Z. [1986] ix, 68 p. : LC Card 87-109510 DDC 331.12/791 19
HD8848.5.N45 S7 1986

WAGES - AUTOMOBILE INDUSTRY WORKERS - UNITED STATES - HISTORY.
Katz, Harry Charles, 1951- Shifting gears . Cambridge, Mass. , c1985. xii, 230 p. : ISBN 0-262-11098-9 LC Card 84-26105 DDC 331/.04292/0973 19
HD6976.A82 U528 1985 ***NYPL [JLE 85-2260]***

WAGES - BANK EMPLOYEES.
Caruth, Donald L. Compensation management for banks /. Boston , c1986. viii, 312 p. : ISBN 0-87267-060-0 LC Card 86-3543 DDC

332.1/068/3 19
HG1615.7.C65 C37 1986 NYPL [JLE 87-828]

WAGES - BRAZIL.
Grupos homogêneos no mercado de trabalho assalariado . Brasília , 1985. 56 p. : LC Card 85-231654
HD5004 .G78 1985

Vieira, Cláudio Afonso. Urbanização e custo de reprodução da força de trabalho /. São Paulo , 1984. 175 p., [5] folded leaves of plates :

WAGES - BRAZIL - ECONOMETRIC MODELS.
Modiano, Eduardo Marco. Salários, preços e câmbio . Rio de Janeiro, RJ , 1984. 55, [5] leaves ; LC Card 84-234066
HD5004 .M56 1984

WAGES - BRAZIL - EFFECT OF INFLATION ON.
Política salarial. [Rio de Janeiro] [19]85. 31 leaves ; LC Card 86-152437
HD5004 .P65 1985

WAGES - BRAZIL - MINIMUM WAGE - HISTORY.
Saboia, João, 1944- Evolução histórica do salário mínimo no Brasil . Rio de Janeiro , 1984. 106 p. ; LC Card 87-403844 DDC 331.2/3 19
HD4920.B8 S265 1984

WAGES - BRAZIL, NORTHEAST.
Grupos homogêneos no mercado de trabalho assalariado . Brasília , 1985. 56 p. : LC Card 85-231654
HD5004 .G78 1985

WAGES - BRAZIL - SÃO PAULO.
Vieira, Cláudio Afonso. Urbanização e custo de reprodução da força de trabalho /. São Paulo , 1984. 175 p., [5] folded leaves ; LC Card 85-136502
HD5755.S3 V54 1984

WAGES - BRAZIL - SÃO PAULO (STATE)
Grupos homogêneos no mercado de trabalho assalariado . Brasília , 1985. 56 p. : LC Card 85-231654
HD5004 .G78 1985

WAGES - CALIFORNIA - STATISTICS.
Albano, Tracy. California employment and payrolls, April-June, 1985 /. [Sacramento] [1985] iii, 129 p. ; LC Card 86-623197 DDC 331.12/5/09794021 19
HD5725.C2 A614 1985

WAGES - CANADA.
The Determinants of negotiated wage settlements in Canada (1966-1975) . [Ottawa] , Hull, Quebec , c1979. x, 256 p. : ISBN 0-660-10162-9 : LC Card 79-313202 DDC 331.2/971
HD4979 .D44 NYPL [JLE 80-447]

Kumar, Pradeep. Recent wage deceleration . Kingston, Ont., Canada , 1987. 21, [12] p. ; ISBN 0-88886-158-3 (pbk.) LC Card 87-163251 DDC 331.2/971 19
HD4979 .K816 1987

WAGES - CANADA - ECONOMETRIC MODELS.
Dussault, François. Les modèles scandinaves et la détermination des ententes salariales des industries manufacturières canadiennes . Montréal [1982] 21, [11] p. ; LC Card 82-196710
HD4979 .D875 1982

WAGES - CANADA - MANUFACTURES - ECONOMETRIC MODELS.
Abbott, Michael G. Male and female earnings in Canadian manufacturing, 1931 /. Kingston, Ont., Canada [1986] 82 p. ; LC Card 87-145991 DDC 331.2/87/0971 19
HD4979 .A22 1986

WAGES - CHEMICAL WORKERS - GERMANY (WEST) - CASE STUDIES.
Teschner, Eckart, 1940- Lohnpolitik im Betrieb . Frankfurt/Main , New York , c1977. 226 p. : ISBN 3-593-32244-7 LC Card 85-134281 DDC 331.2/943 19
HD4966.M44 G48 1977

WAGES - CHILE.
Pardo V., Lucía. La historia laboral de las mujeres y su efecto en la tasa de salario . Santiago , 1986. 44, 5 p. : LC Card 86-217486
HD6126 .P37 1986

Riveros C., Luis. Structural reforms and wage setting across sectors . Santiago , 1984. 37, [5], 13 p. ; NYPL [JLF 87-136]

WAGES - CHILE - ECONOMETRIC MODELS.
Coeymans, Juan Eduardo. Determinants of sectoral annual real wages in a developing economy /. Santiago , 1986. 32, [4] leaves : LC Card 87-404007 DDC 331.12/5/0983 19
HD5006 .C64 1986

Rosende Ramírez, Francisco. Tipo de cambio y salarios reales . Santiago , 1985. 28 p. : LC Card 86-106380 DDC 332.4/5/0983 19
HG3934 .R67 1985

WAGES - CLEANING AND DYEING INDUSTRY - UNITED STATES.
United States. Wage and Hour and Public Contracts Divisions. Laundry and cleaning services. [Washington, 1969] iii, 31, A-ii, A-67p. NYPL [JLF 86-586]

WAGES - COAL MINERS - UKRAINE - STATISTICAL METHODS.
Karlin, P. I. (Pavel Ivanovich) Statistika zarabotnoĭ platy na ugol'nykh shakhtakh . Donetsk , 1980. 68 p. : LC Card 82-175895
HD4966.M63 S655 1980

WAGES - COLOMBIA - CASE STUDIES.
Toledo, Nora Elena. El tamaño de las ciudades y la distribución de los ingresos (Argentina y Colombia) /. San Juan, Argentina , 1985. 63 p. : LC Card 87-400258 DDC 339.2/2/09861 19
HC200.I5 T65 1985

WAGES - CONGRESSES.
How labor markets work . Lexington, Mass. , c1988. viii, 256 p. : ISBN 0-669-15126-2 (alk. paper) LC Card 87-22718 DDC 331.12 19
HD5701.3 .H68 1988

Tripartite Technical Meeting for the Food Products and Drink Industries, 2d, Geneva, 1978. Labour and social problems arising out of seasonal fluctuations of the food products and drink industries /. Geneva , 1978. ii, 51 p. ; ISBN 92-2-101879-2 (pbk.) : LC Card 80-477150 DDC 331.2/0464
HD9000.1 .T75 1978a NYPL [JLE 80-1039]

Wage rigidity and unemployment /. Baltimore , 1986. viii, 221 p. : ISBN 0-8018-3400-7 LC Card 86-45446 DDC 331.2/1 19
HD4909 .W26 1986 NYPL [JLD 86-4077]

WAGES - CONSTRUCTION WORKERS - GERMANY (WEST)
Rahmentarifverträge, Gehaltstarifverträge, Vermögensbildungstarifverträge, Tabelle der Kündigungsfristen, Auslösungssätze für die technischen und kaufmännischen Angestellten und für die Poliere und Schachtmeister des Baugewerbes im Gebiet der Bundesrepublik Deutschland /. Düsseldorf , 1977. 102 p. ; ISBN 3-8041-1158-0 LC Card 85-166026
HD6698.R315 R34 1977

WAGES - CONSTRUCTION WORKERS - GUATEMALA - GUATEMALA.
Revisión del índice del costo de la construcción de vivienda en la Ciudad de Guatemala, años 1975-1979. Guatemala , 1979. 35 p. : LC Card 82-182718
HD9715.G983 G827 1979

WAGES - CONSTRUCTION WORKERS - SOVIET UNION - MATHEMATICAL MODELS.
Ivanov, V. R. (Vladimir Romanovich) Proizvoditel'nost' truda i zarabotnaia plata v stroitel'stve sooruzheniĭ sviazi /. Moskva , 1985. 159 p. : LC Card 85-224803
HD9715.S72 I9 1985

WAGES - CONSTRUCTION WORKERS - UNITED STATES - STATISTICS.
Wage and benefit settlements in construction, 1986. Washington, D.C. (1101 15th St., N.W., Suite 1040, Washington 20005) , c1986. 10 p. : LC Card 87-139726 DDC 331.2/824/0973021 19
HD4966.B892 U685 1986

WAGES - ECONOMETRIC MODELS.
Michie, Jonathan. Wages in the business cycle . London , 1987. vii, 194 p. : ISBN 0-86187-686-5 LC Card 87-148946 DDC 331.2/1 19
HD4906 .M43 1987

WAGES - EFFECT OF LABOR MOBILITY ON - MATHEMATICAL MODELS.
Raschke, Freddy, 1950- Bevölkerungsstruktur, Mobilität und Lohn . Frankfurt am Main , New York , c1985. vi, 194 p. : ISBN 3-8204-5697-X LC Card 85-221450
HD4911 .R37 1985

WAGES - EUROPE.
La Flexibilité du travail en Europe . Paris , 1986. 330 p. : ISBN 2-7071-1598-3 : LC Card 86-173845
HD8376.5 .F57 1986

Flexibility and jobs . Bruxelles [1985] 157, 5 p. : LC Card 87-111122 DDC 331.25 19
HD5764.A6 F44 1985

Stoffel, R. A. Internationale vergelijking loonstructuur /. 's-Gravenhage [1986] 20 p. : LC Card 86-231311
HD5014 .S76 1986

WAGES - EUROPE, EASTERN.
Mikheev, S. Remuneration in Eastern European countries /. Geneva , 1985. vi, 45, ix p. ; ISBN 92-9014-408-4 (pbk.) : LC Card 86-216036 DDC 331.2/947 19
HD5014 .M55 1985

WAGES - EUROPEAN ECONOMIC COMMUNITY COUNTRIES.
Almedia, Maria Henriqueta de. O ganho médio do operário na indústria transformadora em Portugal e noutros países da OCDE de 1972 a 1982 /. Lisboa , 1985. 88 p. : LC Card 86-189354
HD5059 .A65 1985

WAGES - EUROPEAN ECONOMIC COMMUNITY COUNTRIES - STATISTICS.
Lønstrukturen 1978/79 . Luxembourg , Washington, D.C. , <1983-1986. v. <2-3, 6-7, 10 > ; ISBN 92-825-3817-6 (set) : LC Card 86-211360
HD5014.5 .L66 1983

WAGES - FINLAND - ECONOMETRIC MODELS.
Blomqvist, H. C. (Hans-Christer), 1947- Lönebildningsforskning i Finland /. [Helsinki] [1984] 23 leaves : ISBN 951-555-207-9 LC Card 85-137027
HD5047.3 .B57 1984

WAGES - FISHERS - ALASKA - STATISTICS.
Focht, Rick. Employment and gross earnings of California residents in Alaska's commercial fisheries, 1977-1982 /. Juneau, AK [1984] v, 53 p. : LC Card 86-622320 DDC 331.12/5392/09798021 19
HD4966.F652 U54 1984c

Focht, Rick. Employment and gross earnings of Oregon residents in Alaska's commercial fisheries, 1977-1982 /. Juneau, AK [1984] v, 69 p. : LC Card 86-622319 DDC 331.12/5392/09798021 19
HD4966.F652 U54 1984b

Focht, Rick. Employment and gross earnings of Washington residents in Alaska's commercial fisheries, 1977-1982 /. Juneau, AK [1984] v leaves, 126 p. ; LC Card 86-622318 DDC 331.2/8392/09797021 19
HD4966.F542 U554 1984

WAGES - FISHERS - CALIFORNIA - STATISTICS.
Focht, Rick. Employment and gross earnings of California residents in Alaska's commercial fisheries, 1977-1982 /. Juneau, AK [1984] v, 53 p. : LC Card 86-622320 DDC 331.12/5392/09798021 19
HD4966.F652 U54 1984c

WAGES - FISHERS - OREGON - STATISTICS.
Focht, Rick. Employment and gross earnings of Oregon residents in Alaska's commercial fisheries, 1977-1982 /. Juneau, AK [1984] v, 69 p. : LC Card 86-622319 DDC 331.12/5392/09798021 19
HD4966.F652 U54 1984b

WAGES - FISHERS - WASHINGTON (STATE) - STATISTICS.
Focht, Rick. Employment and gross earnings of Washington residents in Alaska's commercial fisheries, 1977-1982 /. Juneau, AK [1984] v leaves, 126 p. ; LC Card 86-622318 DDC 331.2/8392/09797021 19
HD4966.F542 U554 1984

WAGES - FRANCE - HISTORY - 20TH CENTURY.
Delaunay, Jean Claude. Salariat et plus-value en France depuis la fin du XIXe siècle /. Paris , c1984. xiv, 304 p. : ISBN 2-7246-0488-1 : LC Card 84-172193 DDC 331.2/944 19
HB206 .D45 1984 ***NYPL [JLD 86-426]***

WAGES - GAS INDUSTRY EMPLOYEES - WYOMING - STATISTICS.
Wessel, Louis. Wyoming oil and natural gas extraction industry . Cheyenne, Wyo. (Herschler Bldg., Cheyenne 82002) , 1986. 35 p. : LC Card 86-622902 DDC 331.12/522338/09787021 19
HD4966.P52 U5553 1986

WAGES - GERMANY, WEST.
Basler, Hans-Peter. Lohnentwicklung und Lohnpolitik als Bestimmungsgründe konjunktureller Verläufe und struktureller Verschiebungen . Berlin , 1981. 102 p. : ISBN 3-428-04970-5 LC Card 82-100546 DDC 330 s 331.2/943 19
HB41 .B4 Nr. 134 HD5029
NYPL [JLL 73-207 Heft 134]

Beck, Horst. Auswirkungen von nicht kostenniveauneutralen Lohnänderungen auf Beschäftigung und Preisniveau . Krefeld , 1983. iii, 227 p. : ISBN 3-88358-033-3 LC Card 83-202725
HD4911 .B4 1983

Feldmann, Berthold. Unternehmenskonzentration, Marktmacht und Lohnniveau . Göttingen , c1984. xii, 260 p. : ISBN 3-525-12269-1 LC Card 85-162393
HD2746.5 .F45 1984

Friderichs, Hans. Lohndispersionen auf strukturierten Arbeitsmärkten . Pfaffenweiler , 1986. xvi, 404 p. : ISBN 3-89085-133-9 LC Card 87-134875 DDC 331.2/943 19
HD5029 .F75 1986

Krack, Jürgen. Lieber besser statt mehr? . Köln , c1985. 306, [2] p. : ISBN 3-7663-0569-7 LC Card 85-125869
HD5029 .K72 1985

Kulke, Ulrich. Betriebsnahe Tarifpolitik zur Stärkung der gewerkschaftlichen Basis /. Berlin , 1977. 108 p. ; ISBN 3-88114-215-0 : LC Card 80-489437
HD6694 .K82 ***NYPL [JLD 81-350]***

Vajna, Thomas. Das Kaufkraftargument /. Köln , c1982. 52 p. ; ISBN 3-602-24710-4 : LC Card 83-193844
HD5029 .V35 1982

WAGES - GERMANY (WEST) - BERGISCHES LAND - CONGRESSES.
Die Wirtschaftliche Entwicklung in den Arbeitsmarktregionen des Bergischen Landes . Bochum , 1981. 401 p. : ISBN 3-88339-217-0 LC Card 82-164818 DDC 331/.0943/55 19
HD8459.N66 W57 1981
NYPL [JLD 86-1639]

WAGES - GERMANY (WEST) - CASE STUDIES.
Steinrücke, Margareta, 1953- Generationen im Betrieb . Frankfurt , New York , c1986. 343 p. ; ISBN 3-593-33639-1 LC Card 87-137842 DDC 331.3/0943 19
HD6283.G4 S74 1986

WAGES - GERMANY (WEST) - ECONOMETRIC MODELS.
Ibler, Josef. Nominallohnentwicklung in der Bundesrepublik Deutschland . Regensburg , c1986. 256 p. : ISBN 3-924956-18-9 LC Card 87-118941 DDC 331.2/943 19
HD5029 .I2 1986

Wanik, Bernhard. Die Lohnentwicklung deutscher Industrieaktiengesellschaften /. Bonn , 1981. vii, 268 p. : LC Card 85-165602
HD5029 .W36 1981

WAGES - GERMANY (WEST) - HESSE - STATISTICS.
Gehalts- und Lohnstrukturerhebung 1978 . Wiesbaden , 1983. 285, [3] p. ; LC Card 84-217477
HA1320 .H529 n.F., Nr. 152 HD5030.H47

WAGES - GOVERNMENT POLICY - BRAZIL.
Garcia, Manuel Enriquez. Salários indexados, preços e emprego . São Paulo , 1986. 149 p. : LC Card 86-234254
HD5004 .G37 1986

Henrique, Luiz. O salário perverso . Brasília , 1983. 129 p. ; LC Card 86-129394
HD5004 .H45 1983

O Mercado de trabalho no Brasil . São Paulo , 1986. 263 p. : LC Card 86-221361
HD5754 .M47 1986

Política salarial. [Rio de Janeiro] [19]85. 31 leaves ; LC Card 86-152437
HD5004 .P65 1985

WAGES - GOVERNMENT POLICY - BRAZIL - HISTORY - 20TH CENTURY.
Sousa, Amaury de. A nova política salarial e as negociações coletivas de trabalho no Brasil, 1979-1982 . [Brazil?] 1983. 109 leaves ; LC Card 87-404781 DDC 331.2/981 19
HD5004 .S675 1983

WAGES - GOVERNMENT POLICY - CZECHOSLOVAKIA.
Adam, Jan, 1920- Employment and wage policies in Poland, Czechoslovakia, and Hungary since 1950 /. New York , 1984. xix, 251 p. ; ISBN 0-312-24457-6 : LC Card 83-40125 DDC 331.12/042/0943 19
HD5797.7.A6 A3 1984
NYPL [JLD 86-4389]

WAGES - GOVERNMENT POLICY - GERMANY (WEST)
Basler, Hans-Peter. Lohnentwicklung und Lohnpolitik als Bestimmungsgründe konjunktureller Verläufe und struktureller Verschiebungen . Berlin , 1981. 102 p. : ISBN 3-428-04970-5 LC Card 82-100546 DDC 330 s 331.2/943 19
HB41 .B4 Nr. 134 HD5029
NYPL [JLL 73-207 Heft 134]

WAGES - GOVERNMENT POLICY - HUNGARY.
Adam, Jan, 1920- Employment and wage policies in Poland, Czechoslovakia, and Hungary since 1950 /. New York , 1984. xix, 251 p. ; ISBN 0-312-24457-6 : LC Card 83-40125 DDC 331.12/042/0943 19
HD5797.7.A6 A3 1984
NYPL [JLD 86-4389]

WAGES - GOVERNMENT POLICY - KENYA.
Vandemoortele, Jan. The wage policy in Kenya . [Nairobi] [1984] 28 leaves : LC Card 86-681105 DDC 331.2/96762 19
HC865.Z9 W248 1984

WAGES - GOVERNMENT POLICY - MEXICO.
Bortz, Jeff. El salario en México /. México, D.F. , 1986. 198 p. : ISBN 968-612-519-1 LC Card 87-404064 DDC 331.2/972 19
HD4981 .B677 1986

WAGES - GOVERNMENT POLICY - PERU.
Empleo, salarios y distribución del ingreso . [Miraflores, Lima] , 1986. 186 p. : LC Card 87-403082 DDC 331.11/0985 19
HD5761.A6 E47 1986

WAGES - GOVERNMENT POLICY - POLAND.
Adam, Jan, 1920- Employment and wage policies in Poland, Czechoslovakia, and Hungary since 1950 /. New York , 1984. xix, 251 p. ; ISBN 0-312-24457-6 : LC Card 83-40125 DDC 331.12/042/0943 19
HD5797.7.A6 A3 1984
NYPL [JLD 86-4389]

WAGES - GREAT BRITAIN - HISTORY - 20TH CENTURY.
Jones, Russell, 1959- Wages and employment policy, 1936-1985 /. London , Boston , 1987. xvii, 175 p. ; ISBN 0-04-331110-5 (alk. paper) LC Card 86-14143 DDC 339.5/0941 19
HD5015 .J66 1987 ***NYPL [JLD 87-831]***

WAGES - HOUSEWIVES.
Houseworker's handbook. [Cambridge, Mass.] (c/o Women's Center, 46 Pleasant St., Cambridge 02139) [1974] 81 p. : LC Card 87-110536
HD6073.H84 H68 1974

Sharma, Ursula, 1941- Women's work, class, and the urban household . London , New York , 1986. 213 p. ; ISBN 0-422-79320-5 : LC Card 86-11296 DDC 305.4/3 19
HQ759 .S4616 1986 ***NYPL [JLD 87-1281]***

WAGES - HOUSEWIVES - UNITED STATES.
Leghorn, Lisa. What's a wife worth? /. Somerville, Mass. [198-] 8 p. : LC Card 87-111053 DDC 331.2/8164/0973 19
HD4966.H842 U64 1980z

Minton, Michael H. What is a wife worth? . New York , 1984, c1983. 192 p. ; ISBN 0-07-042414-4 (pbk.) : LC Card 84-11221 DDC 331.4/28164/0973 19
HD4966.H842 U65 1984
NYPL [JLD 87-12]

WAGES - HUNGARY.
Németh, Ernő. A bér- és keresetszabályozás müködése 1983-ban /. [Budapest] [1984] 245 p. : ISBN 963-02-3277-4 LC Card 85-231744
HD5022.5 .N46 1984

Ott, György. A vállalati bértarifarendszer /. [Budapest] , 1984. 110 p. ; ISBN 963-322-158-7 : LC Card 85-176915
HD5022.5 .O77 1984

Tanulmányok az anyagi érdekeltség, jövedelemszabályozás témaköréből /. [Budapest] , 1985. 126 p. : ISBN 963-673-308-2 LC Card 86-147619
HD5022.5 .T37 1985

WAGES - HUNGARY - STATISTICS.
Adatgyűjtemény az állami iparvállalatoknál foglalkoztatottak létszám-, bér- és kereseti arányairól /. Budapest , 1986. 148 p. ; LC Card 87-407679
HD5772.5.A6 A34 1986

Az Állami iparvállalatoknál foglalkoztatottak létszámösszetétele bér- és kereseti viszonyai /. Budapest , 1986. 124 p. ; ISBN 963-02-4488-8 LC Card 86-218968
HD5772.5.A6 A57 1986

Az Ipari nagyüzemi munkásság jövedelmi viszonyai, élet- és munkakörülményei /. [Budapest] [1985] 94 p. ; LC Card 85-210330
HD8420.5 .I63 1985

Wages in the business cycle . Michie, Jonathan. London , 1987. vii, 194 p. : ISBN 0-86187-686-5 LC Card 87-148946 DDC 331.2/1 19
HD4906 .M43 1987

WAGES - INDIA - ADDRESSES, ESSAYS, LECTURES.
Ranadive, K. R. Accumulation, employment, and labour aristocracy . Bombay [1982] 55 p. ; LC Card 83-903051 DDC 305.5/62/0954 19
HD8686.5 .R325 1982 ***NYPL [JLF 87-500]***

WAGES - INDIA - ECONOMETRIC MODELS.
Shrivastava, S. C., 1939- Wages, profits, and productivity in selected industries of India since 1950 . Bombay , 1984. xii, 254 p. : LC Card 84-900745 DDC 338/.06/0954 19
HD5069 .S46 1984 ***NYPL [JLD 86-4260]***

WAGES - INDIA - GUJARAT.
Hirway, Indira. Wage employment programmes in rural development . New Delhi , c1986. vi, 112 p. ; ISBN 81-204-0072-0 : LC Card 86-903398 DDC 331.2/95475 19
HD5070.G85 H57 1986

WAGES - INDIA - STATISTICS.
Statistical profile on women labour. Simla [1983] v, 224 p. ; LC Card 84-900395 DDC 331.4/0954/021 19
HD5819 .S83 1983 ***NYPL [JLF 86-1946]***

WAGES - IRON AND STEEL WORKERS - SWEDEN - HISTORY - 19TH CENTURY - CASE STUDIES.
Larsson, Mats, 1953- Arbete och lön vid Bredsjö bruk . Uppsala , Stockholm , 1986. 233 p. : ISBN 91-554-1822-8 LC Card 86-212849
HD4966.I52 S845 1986

WAGES - ITALY.
Antonelli, Gilberto. Risorse umane e redditi da lavoro . Milano , c1985. 256 p. : LC Card 85-191554
HC310.I5 A66 1985

Roccella, Massimo. I salari /. Bologna , c1986. 342 p. ; ISBN 88-15-01204-4 : LC Card 86-216417
HD5034 .R63 1986

WAGES - ITALY - ADDRESSES, ESSAYS, LECTURES.
La Vertenza sul costo del lavoro e le relazioni industriali /. Milano, Italy , c1984. 243 p. : LC Card 84-144150 DDC 338.5/1/0945 19
HD5034 .V47 1984 ***NYPL [JLD 86-2858]***

WAGES - ITALY - CONGRESSES.
La Riforma del salario /. Milano , c1984. 150

p. ; LC Card 84-251133 DDC 331.2/945 19
HD5034 .R54 1984 *NYPL [JLD 86-1082]*

WAGES - ITALY - TURIN REGION - STATISTICS.
Valvo, Tino, 1948- Retribuzioni a confronto . Milano, Italy , c1986. 247 p. : LC Card 86-170001
HD5035.T87 V34 1986

WAGES - JAPAN - PLANNING.
Ballon, Robert J. Salary administration in Japan . Tokyo , 1985. 44 p. ; ISBN 4-88168-100-1 LC Card 86-115944 DDC 331.2/952 19
HD5077 .B3454 1985

WAGES - KENYA.
Vandemoortele, Jan. The wage policy in Kenya . [Nairobi] [1984] 28 leaves : LC Card 86-681105 DDC 331.2/96762 19
HC865.Z9 W248 1984

WAGES - LAUNDRY WORKERS - UNITED STATES.
United States. Wage and Hour and Public Contracts Divisions. Laundry and cleaning services. [Washington, 1969] iii, 31, A-ii, A-67p. *NYPL [JLF 86-586]*

WAGES - MASSACHUSETTS - STATISTICS.
Occupations in services, finance, insurance, real estate, and construction, 1984 /. [Boston, MA] [1985] 185 p. : LC Card 87-621853 DDC 331.7/009744 19
HD5725.M4 O26 1985

WAGES - MATHEMATICAL MODELS.
Balducci, Renato, 1947- Contrattazione salariale e ciclo economico . Roma , 1982. 174 p. : *NYPL [JLD 86-2868]*

Beaumont, Paul (Paul M.) Regional wage rates [microform] . Iowa City , 1982. 22 p. : *NYPL [*ZT-1564 no.29]*

Meade, James Edward, 1907- Alternative systems of business organization and of worker's remuneration /. London , Boston , 1986. x, 144 p. : ISBN 0-04-331112-1 (alk. paper) LC Card 85-26734 DDC 330/.1 19
HB238 .M4 1986 *NYPL [JLD 86-2943]*

WAGES - MEN, WHITE - CANADA - ECONOMETRIC MODELS.
Abbott, Michael G. Male and female earnings in Canadian manufacturing, 1931 /. Kingston, Ont., Canada [1986] 82 p. ; LC Card 87-145991 DDC 331.2/87/0971 19
HD4979 .A22 1986

WAGES - METAL-WORKERS - GERMANY (WEST) - CASE STUDIES.
Teschner, Eckart, 1940- Lohnpolitik im Betrieb . Frankfurt/Main , New York , c1977. 226 p. : ISBN 3-593-32244-7 LC Card 85-134281 DDC 331.2/943 19
HD4966.M44 G48 1977

WAGES - MEXICO.
Bortz, Jeff. La estructura de salarios en México /. Azcapotzalco, México, D.F. , 1985. 371 p. : ISBN 968-8402-76-1 LC Card 87-104886
HD4981 .B67 1985

Gregory, Peter. The myth of market failure . Baltimore , 1986. viii, 299 p. ; ISBN 0-8018-3343-4 : LC Card 85-45927 DDC 331.12/0972 19
HD5731.A6 G74 1986 *NYPL [JLE 86-3065]*

WAGES - MEXICO - HISTORY.
Bortz, Jeff. El salario en México /. México, D.F. , 1986. 198 p. : ISBN 968-612-519-1 LC Card 87-404064 DDC 331.2/972 19
HD4981 .B677 1986

WAGES - MEXICO - MEXICO CITY - HISTORY - 20TH CENTURY.
Bortz, Jeff. Industrial wages in Mexico City, 1939-1975 /. New York , 1987. ix, 529 p. ; ISBN 0-8240-1355-7 (alk. paper) : LC Card 87-8341 DDC 331.2/97253 19
HD4981.Z9 M483 1987

WAGES - MINIMUM WAGE.
Guiba (Writer) Salario humano y libertad /. Buenos Aires , 1986. viii, 155 p. ; ISBN 950-50-3130-0 LC Card 87-101595
HD4917 .G85 1986

WAGES - MINIMUM WAGE - BRAZIL.
Saboia, João, 1944- Salário mínimo no Brasil . Porto Alegre, Rio Grande do Sul , c1985. 96 p. : ISBN 85-25-40034-3 : LC Card 86-129265 DDC 331.2/3 19
HD4920.B8 S27 1985

WAGES - MINIMUM WAGE - INDONESIA - BENGKULU (PROVINCE)
Proyek Pengaturan Pengupahan Daerah Sumatera Selatan (Indonesia) Analysa hasil survey pengupahan dan draft pedoman kebijaksanaan penetapan upah minimum, tahun 1977/1978 /. [S.l.] [1978?] 21, [2], 3 leaves ; LC Card 80-941072
HD4922.I5 P75 1978

WAGES - MINIMUM WAGE - INDONESIA - SUMATERA SELATAN.
Proyek Pengaturan Pengupahan Daerah Sumatera Selatan (Indonesia) Analysa hasil survey pengupahan dan draft pedoman kebijaksanaan penetapan upah minimum, tahun 1977/1978 /. [S.l.] [1978?] 21, [2], 3 leaves ; LC Card 80-941072
HD4922.I5 P75 1978

WAGES - MINIMUM WAGE - LAW AND LEGISLATION - GREAT BRITAIN.
Morris, Jenny, 1950- Women workers and the sweated trades . Aldershot, Hants, England , Brookfield, Vt., USA , c1986. 248 p. ; ISBN 0-566-05188-5 : LC Card 86-9850 DDC 331.4/23 19
HD2339.G7 M67 1986
NYPL [JLD 86-4089]

WAGES - MINIMUM WAGE - PARAGUAY.
Flecha, Agustín Oscar. La economía nacional y el costo de vida /. Asunción, Paraguay , 1986. 49 p. ; LC Card 87-122881 DDC 330.9892/073 19
HD7018 .F57 1986

WAGES - MINIMUM WAGE - PARAGUAY - CONGRESSES.
Flecha, Agustín Oscar. Crisis económica . [Asunción] [1987] 65 p. ; LC Card 87-404003 DDC 331.2/3/09892 19
HD4920.P2 F57 1987

WAGES - MINIMUM WAGE - UNITED STATES.
United States. Wage and Hour and Public Contracts Divisions. Laundry and cleaning services. [Washington, 1969] iii, 31, A-ii, A-67p. *NYPL [JLF 86-586]*

WAGES - NETHERLANDS.
Stoffel, R. A. Internationale vergelijking loonstructuur /. 's-Gravenhage [1986] 20 p. : LC Card 86-231311
HD5014 .S76 1986

WAGES - NEW ZEALAND.
St. Hill, R. L. Labour mobility between New Zealand and Australia /. Canterbury, N.Z. [1986] ix, 68 p. : LC Card 87-109510 DDC 331.12/791 19
HD8848.5.N45 S7 1986

WAGES - NORTH DAKOTA - STATISTICS.
North Dakota employment and wages, 1984 /. Bismarck, N.D. (1000 E. Divide, Bismarck 58501) [1985] [3], 13, 13 leaves ; LC Card 86-623005 DDC 331.12/5/09784021 19
HD5725.N84 N73 1985

WAGES - ONTARIO.
Abbott, Michael G. Alternative estimates of union-nonunion and public-private wage differentials in Ontario, 1981 /. Kingston, Ont., Canada [1986] ii, 61 p. ; LC Card 87-146006 DDC 331.2/2/09713 19
HD4980.O5 A64 1986

WAGES - ONTARIO - ECONOMETRIC MODELS.
Abbott, Michael G. Alternative estimates of union-nonunion and public-private wage differentials in Ontario, 1981 /. Kingston, Ont., Canada [1986] ii, 61 p. ; LC Card 87-146006 DDC 331.2/2/09713 19
HD4980.O5 A64 1986

Abbott, Michael G. Alternative estimates of union-nonunion and public-private wage differentials in Ontario, 1981 /. Kingston, Ont., Canada , 1987. ii, 47 p. ; ISBN 0-88886-166-4 (pbk.) LC Card 87-170767 DDC 331.2/2/09713 19
HD4980.O5 A64 1987

WAGES - PAKISTAN.
Why the office staff scared of time and motion study? . Saddar, Karachi, Pakistan [1985] 1 v. (various pagings) leaves ; LC Card 86-146552
HD5070.5 .W49 1985

WAGES - PETROLEUM WORKERS - COLOMBIA.
La Ocupación y su remuneración en las empresas petroleras en Colombia, 1977-1984. Bogotá, D.E. [1986] 37 p. : LC Card 87-402964 DDC 331.12/5223382/09861 19
HD8039.P42 V446 1986

WAGES - PETROLEUM WORKERS - UNITED STATES - STATISTICS.
Williams, Harry B. Industry wage survey . Washington, D.C. [1986] iv, 34 p. ; LC Card 86-602194 DDC 331.2/86553/0973021 19
HD4966.P52 U5556 1986

WAGES - PETROLEUM WORKERS - WYOMING - STATISTICS.
Wessel, Louis. Wyoming oil and natural gas extraction industry . Cheyenne, Wyo. (Herschler Bldg., Cheyenne 82002) , 1986. 35 p. : LC Card 86-622902 DDC 331.12/522338/09787021 19
HD4966.P52 U5553 1986

WAGES - POLAND - REGIONAL DISPARITIES.
Rudnicki, Leszek. Zróżnicowania wzorców konsumpcji ludności rolniczej dwuzawodowej /. Kraków , 1985. 313 p. : LC Card 86-174377
HC340.3.Z9 C6177 1985

WAGES - PORTUGAL.
Almedia, Maria Henriqueta de. O ganho médio do operário na indústria transformadora em Portugal e noutros países da OCDE de 1972 a 1982 /. Lisboa , 1985. 88 p. : LC Card 86-189354
HD5059 .A65 1985

Girão, José António. Salários, inflação e moeda . Lisboa , 1984. 50 p. : LC Card 85-157764
HG1145 .G57 1984

Ribeiro, Maria Eduarda. Aspectos analíticos da distribuição da massa salarial no período de 1972 a 1983 /. Lisboa , 1985. 58 p. : LC Card 86-132683
HC394.5.I5 R52 1985

Wages, profits, and productivity in selected industries of India since 1950 . Shrivastava, S. C., 1939- Bombay , 1984. xii, 254 p. : LC Card 84-900745 DDC 338/.06/0954 19
HD5069 .S46 1984 *NYPL [JLD 86-4260]*

Wages, profits, productivity in selected industries in India. Shrivastava, S. C., 1939- Wages, profits, and productivity in selected industries of India since 1950 . Bombay , 1984. xii, 254 p. : LC Card 84-900745 DDC 338/.06/0954 19
HD5069 .S46 1984 *NYPL [JLD 86-4260]*

WAGES - SCANDINAVIA - ECONOMETRIC MODELS.
Dussault, François. Les modèles scandinaves et la détermination des ententes salariales des industries manufacturières canadiennes . Montréal [1982] 21, [11] p. ; LC Card 82-196710
HD4979 .D875 1982

WAGES - SOUTH AFRICA.
Schroeder, Ighsaan. Conditions of employment . Cape Town [1985]- 1 v. (loose-leaf) ; ISBN 0-7992-1002-1 (loose-leaf) LC Card 86-232933 DDC 331.2/0968 19
HD4927.S6 S37 1985

WAGES - SOUTH DAKOTA - STATISTICS.
South Dakota employment & earnings covered by unemployment insurance, 1984. Aberdeen, S.D. [198-] 47 p. : LC Card 87-620925
HD5725.S8 S67 1980z

South Dakota occupational wage information . Aberdeen, S.D. (P.O. Box 4730, Aberdeen 57402-4730) [1986] 97 p. ; LC Card 86-622996 DDC 331.2/9783 19
HD4976.S65 S68 1986

WAGES - SOVIET UNION.
Ėkonomicheskoe stimulirovanie truda v usloviiakh sotsializma . Moskva , 1986. 179 p. ; LC Card 87-166364
HD5046 .E47 1986

WAGES - SUGAR WORKERS - BRAZIL - PARAÍBA (STATE) - CONGRESSES.
Canavieiros em greve . São Paulo , 1985. 105 p. : LC Card 87-104183 DDC 331.88/1361/098134 19
HD6614.S85 C36 1985

WAGES - SUGAR WORKERS - BRAZIL - PERNAMBUCO (STATE) - CONGRESSES.
Canavieiros em greve . São Paulo , 1985. 105 p. : LC Card 87-104183 DDC 331.88/1361/098134 19
HD6614.S85 C36 1985

WAGES - SUGAR WORKERS - BRAZIL - SÃO PAULO (STATE) - CONGRESSES.
Canavieiros em greve . São Paulo , 1985. 105 p. : LC Card 87-104183 DDC 331.88/1361/098134 19
HD6614.S85 C36 1985

WAGES - SWEDEN.
Meidner, Rudolf. I arbetets tjänst /. Stockholm , 1984. 473 p. : ISBN 91-550-2932-9 : LC Card 84-229372
HD5803 .M45 1984

WAGES - SWEDEN - HISTORY.
Lagerqvist, Lars O. Vad kostade det? . Stockholm , c18. 115 p. : ISBN 91-36-02399-X : LC Card 86-158743
HD7040 .L34 1985

WAGES - TAXATION - AUSTRIA - STATISTICS.
Lohn- und Einkommensteuerstatistik 1979 . Wien , 1985. xxxv, 59 p. : LC Card 86-233093
HJ4713.A7 L64 1985

WAGES - TAXATION - GERMANY (WEST) - TABLES.
Recktenwald, Werner. Wie errechne ich meinen Nettolohn? . Saarbrücken [1985?] 112 p. ; ISBN 3-88968-029-1 LC Card 85-171297 DDC 343.4305/242 344.3035242 19
HJ4720.A7 R42 1985

Recktenwald, Werner. Wie errechne ich meinen Nettolohn? Mit der Monatslohnsteuertabelle für rentenversicherungspflichtige Arbeitnehmer, 1986 und 1987, Auszug /. Saarbrücken [1987]. 128 p. ; LC Card 87-408789 DDC 343.4305/242 344.3035242 19
HJ4720.A7 R42 1987

WAGES - TEXTILE WORKERS - GERMANY (WEST) - CASE STUDIES.
Teschner, Eckart, 1940- Lohnpolitik im Betrieb . Frankfurt/Main , New York , c1977. 226 p. : ISBN 3-593-32244-7 LC Card 85-134281 DDC 331.2/943 19
HD4966.M44 G48 1977

WAGES - TOBACCO WORKERS - GERMANY (WEST) - CASE STUDIES.
Teschner, Eckart, 1940- Lohnpolitik im Betrieb . Frankfurt/Main , New York , c1977. 226 p. : ISBN 3-593-32244-7 LC Card 85-134281 DDC 331.2/943 19
HD4966.M44 G48 1977

WAGES - UNITED STATES.
Levitan, Sar A. Working but poor . Baltimore , c1987. ix, 142 p. : ISBN 0-8018-3583-6 (alk. paper) LC Card 87-16973 DDC 362.5/0973 19
HC110.I5 L468 1987

Reynolds, Morgan O., 1942- Making America poorer . Washington, D.C. , c1987. ix, 218 p. ; ISBN 0-932790-63-1 LC Card 87-6569 DDC 338.5/1/0973 19
HD6508 .R435 1987

Stoffel, R. A. Internationale vergelijking loonstructuur /. 's-Gravenhage [1986] 20 p. : LC Card 86-231311
HD5014 .S76 1986

Tigges, Leann M. Changing fortunes . New York , 1987. xvi, 174 p. : ISBN 0-275-92580-3 (alk. paper) : LC Card 87-2357 DDC 331.2/973 19
HD4975 .T5 1987

WAGES - VERMONT - STATISTICS.
Employment and earnings, 1980-1985 . Montpelier, Vt. [1986] ii, 79 leaves : LC Card 86-622186 DDC 331.12/5/09743021 19
HD5725.V5 E46 1986

WAGES - WOMEN.
Diekmann, Andreas. Einkommensunterschiede zwischen Frauen und Männern . Wien [1985] 2 v. (244, 4 p.) : LC Card 86-150241
HD6061 .D54 1985

WAGES - WOMEN - BANGLADESH.
Rahman, Rushidan Islam. The wage employment market for rural women in Bangladesh /. Dhaka, Bangladesh , 1986. xi, 97 p. ; LC Card 86-903129 DDC 331.4/295492 19
HD6061.2.B3 R34 1986

WAGES - WOMEN - BELGIUM.
Coomans, Géry, 1949- La production sociale des femmes /. Bruxelles , c1983. 223 p. : ISBN 2-8004-0820-0 : LC Card 84-199167
HD6158 .C66 1983

WAGES - WOMEN - CANADA - ECONOMETRIC MODELS.
Abbott, Michael G. Male and female earnings in Canadian manufacturing, 1931 /. Kingston, Ont., Canada [1986] 82 p. ; LC Card 87-145991 DDC 331.2/87/0971 19
HD4979 .A22 1986

WAGES - WOMEN - GERMANY (WEST) - HISTORY.
Pohl, Sigrid, 1954- Entwicklung und Ursachen der Frauenlohndiskriminierung . Frankfurt am Main , New York , c1984. x, 387 p. : ISBN 3-8204-8017-X LC Card 85-189325 DDC 331.13/3/0943 19
HD6060.5.G3 P64 1984

WAGES - WOMEN - GREAT BRITAIN.
Waged work . London , 1986. vi, 291 p. : ISBN 0-86068-801-1 (pbk.) : LC Card 86-232209 DDC 331.4/0941 19
HD6061.2.G7 W35 1986

WAGES - WOMEN - LAW AND LEGISLATION - GREAT BRITAIN.
Morris, Jenny, 1950- Women workers and the sweated trades . Aldershot, Hants, England , Brookfield, Vt., USA , c1986. 248 p. ; ISBN 0-566-05188-5 : LC Card 86-9850 DDC 331.4/23 19
HD2339.G7 M67 1986
NYPL [JLD 86-4089]

WAGES - WOMEN - NETHERLANDS.
Vrouwen en economische zelfstandigheid /. Amsterdam , c1986. 199 p. : ISBN 90-6222-139-4 : LC Card 86-182832
HD6162 .V74 1986

WAGES - WOMEN - UNITED STATES.
DeGooyer, Janice. Women's work, undervalued, underpaid . Washington, D.C. , 1984, c1982. 27, [4] leaves : ***NYPL [*ZT-1708 no.39]***

Waging business warfare . Rogers, David J. New York , c1987. x, 341 p. ; ISBN 0-684-18596-2 : LC Card 86-31584 DDC 658.4 19
HD38 .R5776 1987

Wagley, Robert A. Buchholz, Rogene A. Management response to public issues . Englewood Cliffs, N.J. , c1985. x, 389 p. : ISBN 0-13-549940-2 (pbk.) : LC Card 84-18355 DDC 658.4/08 19
HD60 .B83 1985 ***NYPL [JLE 85-1984]***

Wagman, Robert J. Instant millionaires : cashing in on America's lotteries / by Robert Wagman. [Kensington, Md.] : Woodbine House, 1986. 298 p. ; 22 cm. ISBN 0-933149-05-0 (pbk.) : LC Card 86-50285 DDC 795.3/092/2 19
1. Lotteries - United States. 2. Lottery winners - United States. 3. Millionaires - United States. I. Title.
HG6126 .W27 1986

Wagner, Adolph, 1835-1917. Die Ordnung des österreichischen Staatshaushaltes--1863 / Adolph Wagner ; eingeleitet und kommentiert von Horst Knapp ; herausgegeben von Hannes Androsch, Helmut Haschek und Franz Vranitzky. Wien : Edition Wirtschaft : C. Brandstätter, c1984. 308 p. ; 22 cm. (Klassiker der österreichischen Nationalökonomie . Bd. 2) Bibliography: p. 296-308. ISBN 3-85447-086-X LC Card 85-223615
1. Finance, Public - Austria - History - 19th century. 2. National income - Austria - Accounting - History - 19th century. I. Knapp, Horst. II. Androsch, Hannes. III. Haschek, Helmut. IV. Vranitzky, Franz. V. Title. VI. Series.
HJ1065 .W34 1984

Wagner, Dieter, 1947- Glaubrecht, Helmut. Arbeitszeit im Wandel . Freiburg im Breisgau , 1985. 273 p. : ISBN 3-448-01509-1 LC Card 85-216364 DDC 331.25/72 19
HD5109 .G55 1985

Wagner, Falk. Geld oder Gott? : zur Geldbestimmtheit der kulturellen und religiösen Lebenswelt / Falk Wagner. Stuttgart : Klett-Cotta, c1984. 162 p. ; 22 cm. Bibliography: p. 155-162. ISBN 3-608-91389-0 LC Card 86-121379
1. Money - Moral and ethical aspects. I. Title.
HG221.3 .W255 1984

Wagner, Gerhard. Abbau regionaler Strompreisdisparitäten durch raumwirksame Massnahmen und Planungen / Gerhard Wagner. Bonn : Bundesforschungsanstalt für Landeskunde und Raumordnung, 1985. xv, 356 p. : ill. (some col.) ; 30 cm. (Forschungen zur Raumentwicklung, 0341-244X . Bd. 15) Cover title: Abbau regionaler Strompreisdisparitäten. Originally presented as the author's thesis (doctoral)--Rheinische Friedrich-Wilhelms-Universität Bonn. Bibliography: p. 323-356. ISBN 3-87994-415-6 LC Card 87-408008 DDC 338.4/336362/0943 19
1. Electric utilities - Germany, West - Rates. 2. Regional planning - Germany, West. I. Title. II. Title: Abbau regionaler Strompreisdisparitäten. III. Series.
HD9685.G3 W34 1985

Wagner, Gert. Helberger, Christof. Beitragsäquivalenz oder interpersonelle Umverteilung in der gesetzlichen Rentenversicherung? . Berlin , 1981. 96 p. ; LC Card 81-201422 DDC 331.25/2/0943 19
HD7105.35.G3 H44 1981
NYPL [JLM 81-818 v.63]

Wagner, Helmut.
Inflation! / H. Wagner. Würzburg : Physica-Verlag, c1983. 152 p. : ill. ; 19 cm. (Hintergründe . 8) Bibliography: p. [151]-152. Includes index. ISBN 3-7908-0508-4 (pbk.) LC Card 86-673944
1. Inflation (Finance). I. Title.
HG229 .W238x 1983

Inflation und Wirtschaftswachstum : zum Einfluss von Inflation auf die Akkumulationsrate / Helmut Wagner. Berlin : Duncker & Humblot, c1983. 234 p. : ill. ; 24 cm. (Volkswirtschaftliche Schriften. Heft 329) Bibliography: p. [215]-234. ISBN 3-428-05319-2 LC Card 83-219188
1. Inflation (Finance) - Mathematical models. 2. Saving and investment - Effect of inflation on - Mathematical models. 3. Economic development - Mathematical models. I. Title. II. Series.
HG229 .W237 1983

Wagner, Hermann, Dr. Italien / von Hermann Wagner. Hannover : Bundesanstalt für Geowissenschaften und Rohstoffe ; Stuttgart : In Kommission, E. Schweizerbart'sche Verlagsbuchhandlung, 1982. xv, 190 p., 4 folded leaves of plates : ill. ; 30 cm. (Rohstoffwirtschaftlicher Länderbericht, 0343-8074 . 28) Summary in English, French, and German. Bibliography: p. 183-190. LC Card 83-235644
1. Mineral industries - Italy - Statistics. 2. Mines and mineral resources - Italy - Statistics. I. Bundesanstalt für Geowissenschaften und Rohstoffe. II. Series: Rohstoffwirtschaftliche Länderberichte, 28. III. Title.
HD9506.I82 W34 1982

Wagner, Karin. Relation between education, employment, and productivity and their impact on education and labour market policies : a Britsh-German comparison / Karin Wagner.1st ed. Berlin : CEDEFOP--European Centre for the Development of Vocational Training ; Washington, DC : European Community Information Service [distributor], 1986. ix, 80 p. ; 30 cm. (CEDEFOP document) Bibliography: p. 74-79. ISBN 92-825-6371-5 : LC Card 87-136255 DDC 331.12/042/0941 19
1. Occupational training - Germany, West. 2. Vocational education - Germany, West. 3. Occupational training - Great Britain. 4. Vocational education - Great Britain. I. Title. II. Series.
HD5715.5.G4 W35 1986

Wagner, Kurt. Leben auf dem Lande im Wandel des Industrialisierung : "Das Dorf war früher auch keine heile Welt" : die Veränderung der dörflichen Lebensweise und der politischen Kultur vor dem Hintergrund der Industrialisierung, am Beispiel des nordhessischen Dorfes Körle / Kurt Wagner.1. Aufl. Frankfurt am Main : Insel, 1986. 558, [1] p. : ill. ; 22 cm. (Die Hessen-Bibliothek im Insel Verlag) Bibliography: p. [533]-[559]. ISBN 3-458-14329-7 LC Card 87-112493 DDC 330.943/41 19
1. Körle (Germany) - Economic conditions. 2. Körle (Germany) - Social conditions. 3. Housing, Rural - Germany (West) - Körle - History. I. Title. II. Series.
HC289.K66 W34 1986

Wagner, Margarete. Handwerk um 1700 . Hürtgenwald , c1985. 245 p. : ISBN

3-87646-052-2 : LC Card 85-211788
HD2346.N4 H35 1985

Wagner, Nancy A. Eric Louis Kohler in the accounting profession / by Nancy A. Wagner. Atlanta, Ga. : Business Pub. Division, College of Business Administration, Georgia State University, 1987. vi, 210 p. ; 28 cm. (Research monograph . no. 100) Bibliography: p. 186-210. ISBN 0-88406-196-5 (pbk.) : LC Card 86-25633 DDC 657/.092/4 19
1. Kohler, Eric Louis, 1892-1976. 2. Accountants - United States. 3. Accounting - United States. I. Series: Research monograph (Georgia State University. College of Business Administration) , no. 100. II. Title.
HF5604.5.K64 W34 1987

Wagner, Norbert. Grundbedürfnisse als Gegenstand der Entwicklungspolitik . Wiesbaden , 1982. viii, 220 p. : ISBN 3-515-03838-8 (Deut. Bibl.) LC Card 85-134671
HC59.72.B38 G78 1982

Wagner, Robert T. Goreham, Gary. South Dakotans on the move . Brookings, S.D. [1984] 24 p. : LC Card 85-620511 DDC 304.8/09783/021 19
HB1985.S8 G67 1984

Wagner, W. F., 1944- Advertising in the yellow pages : how to boost profits and avoid pitfalls / by W.F. Wagner. Los Angeles, CA : Harvest Press, c1986. viii, 174 p. : ill. ; 22 cm. Includes index. ISBN 0-940969-00-9 (pbk.) : LC Card 86-83085 DDC 659.13/2 19
1. Advertising. 2. Telephone - Directories - Yellow pages. 3. Advertising layout and typography. I. Title.
HF6146.T4 W34 1986

Wagoner, Kathleen P.
Integrated office systems : a management approach / Kathleen P. Wagoner, Mary M. Ruprecht.2/e. New York : Wiley, c1987. xxi, 734 p., [4] p. of plates : ill. (some col.) ; 25 cm. Bibliography: p. 713. Includes index. ISBN 0-471-01195-9 LC Card 86-26793 DDC 651.8 19
1. Office management. 2. Office practice - Automation. I. Ruprecht, Mary M. II. Title.
HF5547 .W26 1987

Office automation : technology and concepts / Kathleen P. Wagoner, Mary M. Ruprecht.2nd ed. New York : Wiley, c1987. xvii, 432 p. : ill. ; 24 cm. Includes index. ISBN 0-471-84505-1 (pbk.) LC Card 86-26775 DDC 651.8 19
1. Office practice - Automation. 2. Office equipment and supplies. I. Ruprecht, Mary M. II. Title.
HF5547.5 .W33 1987

Wagstaff, Howard. Leach, Donald. Future employment & technological change /. London , 1986. 264 p. : ISBN 1-85091-017-0 (pbk.) : LC Card 86-180981 DDC 331.12/5 19
HD6331 .L34 1986

Die Wahl der optimalen Wärmeversorgungskonfiguration als betriebswirtschaftliches Produktions- und Investitionsproblem /. Püschel, Manfred, 1953- Frankfurt am Main , New York , c1984. iv, 298 p. : ISBN 3-8204-7432-3 LC Card 86-108875
HD30.25 .P87 1984

Wahl, Jack. Informationsbewertung und -effizienz auf dem Kapitalmarkt / Jack Wahl. Würzburg : Physica-Verlag, 1983. 211 p. : ill. ; 24 cm. (Physica-Schriften zur Betriebswirtschaft . 10) Bibliography: p. 204-207. Includes index. ISBN 3-7908-0308-1 LC Card 84-154688
1. Investments - Evaluation. 2. Capital market. 3. Portfolio management. I. Title. II. Series.
HG4515 .W34 1983

Wahl, Stefanie. Miegel, Meinhard. Die verkannte Revolution /. Stuttgart , 1983- v. : ISBN 3-87959-196-2 (Bd. 1) LC Card 83-206487 DDC 330.943/087 19
HC286.7 .M53 1983 ***NYPL [JLK 86-154]***

Die Wahl zum 9. Landtag in Rheinland-Pfalz am 18. März 1979 / Herausgeber, Statistisches Landesamt Rheinland-Pfalz. Bad Ems : Das Landesamt, 1979. 153, [18], 23 p. : ill. ; 30 cm. (Statistik von Rheinland-Pfalz . Bd. 284) LC Card 86-128836
1. Rhineland-Palatinate (Germany). Landtag - Elections - Statistics. 2. Elections - Germany (West) - Rhineland-Palatinate - Statistics. I. Statistisches Landesamt Rheinland-Pfalz. II. Series.
HA1320 .R453 Bd. 284 JN4945.R4565

Die Wahl zwischen Eigenfertigung und Fremdbezug . Männel, Wolfgang. Stuttgart , c1981. xvi, 406 p. : ISBN 3-7910-0270-8 LC Card 83-167804
HD2381 .M32 1981

Wahlbeck, Lars. Vetenskap och företagsledning . Helsingfors , 1982. 461 p. : ISBN 951-555-158-7 LC Card 82-239854
HB71 .V45 1982

WAHLBECK, LARS.
Vetenskap och företagsledning . Helsingfors , 1982. 461 p. : ISBN 951-555-158-7 LC Card 82-239854
HB71 .V45 1982

Wahlroos, Björn. A comment on the goals and potential implications of Finnish average cost price regulation / Björn Wahlroos. Helsingfors : Swedish School of Economics and Business Administration, 1978. 12, [1] leaves : ill. ; 30 cm. (Working papers / Swedish School of Economics and Business Administration . 5) Bibliography: leaf [13] ISBN 951-555-053-X LC Card 85-192907
1. Price regulation - Finland. I. Series: Meddelanden fran Svenska handelshögskolan , 5. II. Title.
HB236.F55 W328 1978

Wahlund, Ingrid, 1945- Jämställdhet i arbetsliv och samhälle. Stockholm [1985] 129 p. : ISBN 91-7168-259-7 : LC Card 86-133755
HD6060.5.S8 J36 1985

Wahse, Jürgen. Schaefer, Reinhard. Disponibilität--Mobilität--Fluktuation /. Berlin , 1982. 70 p. : LC Card 83-225572
HD5717.5.G35 S3 1982

Waibl, Elmar. Ökonomie und Ethik : die Kapitalismusdebatte in der Philosophie der Neuzeit / Elmar Waibl. Stuttgart-Bad Cannstatt : Frommann-Holzboog, c1984. 429 p. ; 21 cm. (Problemata. 104) Summary in English and German. Bibliography: p. 393-415. Includes indexes. ISBN 3-7728-0892-1 LC Card 85-130712
1. Capitalism - Moral and ethical aspects. I. Title.
HB501 .W28 1984

WAIBLINGEN (GERMANY : LANDKREIS) - ECONOMIC CONDITIONS.
Landkreis Waiblingen /. [Stuttgart] [1965?] 25 p. : LC Card 85-230943
HC288.W34 L36 1965

WAIBLINGEN (GERMANY : LANDKREIS) - ECONOMIC CONDITIONS - STATISTICS.
Landkreis Waiblingen /. [Stuttgart] [1965?] 25 p. : LC Card 85-230943
HC288.W34 L36 1965

WAIBLINGEN (GERMANY : LANDKREIS) - SOCIAL CONDITIONS.
Landkreis Waiblingen /. [Stuttgart] [1965?] 25 p. : LC Card 85-230943
HC288.W34 L36 1965

WAIBLINGEN (GERMANY : LANDKREIS) - SOCIAL CONDITIONS - STATISTICS.
Landkreis Waiblingen /. [Stuttgart] [1965?] 25 p. : LC Card 85-230943
HC288.W34 L36 1965

Wainwright Forecasting Group. Special analysis and outlook for E.I. Du Pont De Nemours & Company (Inc.), Chemicals and Pigments Department. Boston, Mass. (7 Liberty Sq., Boston 02109) [1986] 17, [6] p. : LC Card 86-205857 DDC 338.4/766/00973 19
HD9660.P253 U672 1986

Walberberger System-Symposium (10th : 1983?)
Protektionismus in der Weltwirtschaft . Hamburg , 1984. viii, 147 p. ; ISBN 3-87895-253-8 LC Card 84-233895
HF1703 .P77 1984

Walbert, F. Non aux économistes, ou, Les ravages du dogmatisme / F. Walbert. Paris : Impr. moderne de la presse, c1984. 170 p. ; 21 cm. LC Card 87-152097
1. Economics. I. Title. II. Title: Non aux économistes. III. Title: Ravages du dogmatisme.
HB173 .W15 1984

Walbrück, Hans-Jürgen, 1956- Entwicklung von branchen-spezifischen integrierten Bürokommunikationssystemen : dargestellt am Beispiel der Wirtschaftsverbände / Hans-Jürgen Walbrück ; mit einem Geleitwort von Paul Schmitz. Bergisch Gladbach : J. Eul, c1986. 368 p. : ill. ; 21 cm. (Reihe Planung, Information und Unternehmungsführung . Bd. 10) Based on the author's thesis (doctoral)--Universität zu Köln, 1985. Bibliography: p. 323-348. ISBN 3-89012-044-X : LC Card 86-174155
1. Office practice - Automation. 2. Communication in management. I. Title. II. Series.
HF5547.5 .W345 1986

Walby, Sylvia.
Patriarchy at work : patriarchal and capitalist relations in employment / Sylvia Walby. Cambridge [Cambrigeshire] : Polity Press, c1986. vii, 292 p. ; 23 cm. (Feminist perspectives) Includes index. Bibliography: p. 260-281. ISBN 0-7456-0157-X
1. Sexual division of labor - Great Britain. 2. Women - Employment - Great Britain. 3. Patriarchy - Great Britain. 4. Sex discrimination in employment - Great Britain. I. Title. II. Series. ***NYPL [JLD 87-941]***

Patriarchy at work : patriarchal and capitalist relations in employment / Sylvia Walby. Minneapolis : University of Minnesota Press, c1986. vii, 292 p. ; 24 cm. (Feminist perspectives) Bibliography: p. 260-281. Includes index. ISBN 0-8166-1588-8 : LC Card 86-24912 DDC 331.4/133/0941 19
1. Sexual division of labor - Great Britain. 2. Women - Employment - Great Britain. 3. Patriarchy - Great Britain. 4. Sex discrimination in employment - Great Britain. I. Title. II. Series.
HD6060.65.G7 W35 1986

Walczak, David, 1950- Ritzer, George. Working, conflict and change /. Englewood Cliffs, N.J. , c1986. xii, 451 p. ; ISBN 0-13-967589-2 : LC Card 85-28135 DDC 306/.36/0973 19
HD6957.U6 R5 1986 ***NYPL [JLE 86-3160]***

Walczak, Jan. Robotnicze drogi Śląska i Zagłębia Dąbrowskiego do roku 1939 / Jan Walczak. Wyd. 1. Katowice : Śląski Instytut Nauk., 1985. 493 p. ; 24 cm. Includes bibliographical references. ISBN 83-7008-096-0 : LC Card 86-101066
1. Labor and laboring classes - Silesia - History. 2. Labor and laboring classes - Dąbrowa Basin (Poland and Czechoslovakia) - History. I. Title.
HD8539.S52 W35 1985

Wald, Renate. "Was will die denn hier?" . Marburg , c1986. 156 p. ; ISBN 3-924800-82-0 LC Card 87-122751 DDC 331.4/0943 19
HD6060.65.G3 W37 1986

Waldburger, Hans. Die Seetalbahn : hundert Jahre von der Lake Valley Railway zur einzigartigen SBB-Nebenlinie / Hans Waldburger, Martin Senn. Luzern : Minirex, c1983. 143 p. : ill. (some col.) ; 24 cm. Ill. on lining papers. Bibliography: p. 142. LC Card 84-190252
1. Railways - Switzerland - Seeland - History. 2. Seeland, Switzerland - Description and travel. I. Senn, Martin. II. Title.
HE4918.S44 W35 1983

Walder, Andrew George. Communist neo-traditionalism : work and authority in Chinese industry / Andrew G. Walder. Berkeley : University of California Press, c1986. xxi, 302 p. ; 22 cm. Includes index. Bibliography: p. 273-294. ISBN 0-520-05439-3 (alk. paper) LC Card 85-27093 DDC 306/.36/0951 19
1. Industrial relations - China. 2. Communism - China. 3. Labor and laboring classes - China. I. Title.
HD8736.5 .W34 1986 ***NYPL [JLD 86-3749]***

WALES - FOREIGN POPULATION - STATISTICS.
Marmot, M. G. Immigrant mortality in England and Wales, 1970-78 . London , 1984. xii, 144 p. : ISBN 0-11-691094-1 (pbk.) : LC Card 84-222968 DDC 614.4/242 19
HB1415 .M37 1984 ***NYPL [JLG 87-55]***

Wales, Murdoch, 1925- Thomis, Malcolm I. From SGIO to Suncorp /. [Brisbane?] , 1986. xii, 272 p., [32] p. of plates : ISBN 0-7242-1698-7 LC Card 87-158138 DDC 368.4/009943 19
HG8220.A9 T56 1986

WALES - SOCIAL CONDITIONS.
Chartism in Wales and Ireland. New York , 1986. 15, 32, 16, 18, 20 p. : ISBN 0-8240-5594-2 (alk. paper) : LC Card 86-25706 DDC 322/.2/0941 19
HD8396 .C494 1986

WALES, SOUTH - ECONOMIC CONDITIONS.
Harris, C. C. (Christopher Charles) Redundancy and recession in South Wales /. Oxford, OX, UK , New York, NY, USA , 1987. p. cm.

ISBN 0-631-15106-0 : LC Card 87-6301 DDC 331.13/794294 19
HD5766.A6 H37 1987

Modern South Wales . Cardiff , Atlantic Highlands, N.J. , 1986. ix, 324 p. : ISBN 0-7083-0943-7 LC Card 86-226166 DDC 330.9429/4085 19
HC257.W3 M63 1986

WALES, SOUTH - INDUSTRIES - HISTORY.
Modern South Wales . Cardiff , Atlantic Highlands, N.J. , 1986. ix, 324 p. : ISBN 0-7083-0943-7 LC Card 86-226166 DDC 330.9429/4085 19
HC257.W3 M63 1986

WALES - STATISTICS, VITAL.
Marmot, M. G. Immigrant mortality in England and Wales, 1970-78 . London , 1984. xii, 144 p. : ISBN 0-11-691094-1 (pbk.) : LC Card 84-222968 DDC 614.4/242 19
HB1415 .M37 1984 ***NYPL [JLG 87-55]***

Wales - Vital statistics. see **Wales - Statistics, Vital.**

Wałęsa, Lech, 1943-
[Chemin d'espoir. English]
A way of hope / Lech Walesa. 1st ed. New York : H. Holt, c1987. 325 p., [17] p. of plates : ill. ; 25 cm. Translation of: Un chemin d'espoir. Includes index. ISBN 0-8050-0668-0 LC Card 87-21194 DDC 322/.2/0924 B 19
1. Wałęsa, Lech, 1943-. 2. NSZZ "Solidarność" (Labor organization). 3. Trade-unions - Poland - Officials and employees - Biography. 4. Poland - Social conditions - 1945-. 5. Poland - Politics and government - 1945-1980. 6. Poland - Politics and government - 1980-. I. Title.
HD6735.7.Z55 W34813 1987

WAŁĘSA, LECH, 1943-
Wałęsa, Lech, 1943- [Chemin d'espoir. English.] A way of hope /. New York , c1987. 325 p., [17] p. of plates : ISBN 0-8050-0668-0 LC Card 87-21194 DDC 322/.2/0924 B 19
HD6735.7.Z55 W34813 1987

Walia, Tirlochan S. Credit policy of the firm and issues in cost of financing accounts receivable : another look / Tirlochan S. Walia. Lake Success, N.Y. (3000 Marcus Ave., Lake Success 11042) : Credit Research Foundation, c1986. [16] p. : ill. ; 28 cm. (Occasional paper) Cover title. Bibliography: p. [16] LC Card 86-212977 DDC 658.1/5244 19
1. Accounts receivable loans. I. Series: Occasional paper (Credit Research Foundation). II. Title.
HG3752.3 .W35 1986

Walji, Parveen. Kayongo-Male, Diane. Children at work in Kenya /. Nairobi , New York , 1984. x, 187 p. : ISBN 0-19-572546-8 (pbk.) LC Card 85-980979 DDC 331.3/1/096761 19
HD6250.K4 K39 1984 ***NYPL [Sc D 86-960]***

Walk fast, talk fast, and see ten people everyday /. Abramowitz, Avie, 1933- Charleston [S.C.] , c1987. p. cm. ISBN 0-931807-13-1 : LC Card 87-6978 DDC 658.8/5 19
HF5438.25 .A27 1987

Walker, A. G. (Alexander George) Export practice and documentation / A.G. Walker. 3rd ed. London ; Boston : Butterworths, 1987. 279 p. : ill. ; 22 cm. Bibliography: p. 272-273. Includes index. ISBN 0-408-02800-9 : LC Card 86-29945 DDC 658.8/48 19
1. Export sales. 2. Export marketing. I. Title.
HF1009.5 .W34 1987

Walker, A. Patrice.
Startzel, Donna C. The CETA arts and humanities experience [microform] CETA Ahead project (Arts and humanities employment analysis and documentation) /. Columbia, Md. , 1981. 197 p. ;
NYPL [*XME-11,320]

Startzel, Donna C. CETA (Comprehensive Employment and Training Act) and the arts and humanities [microform] . Columbia, Md. , 1981. 160 p. ; ***NYPL [*XME-11,328]***

Walker, Brian W. Authentic development in Africa / by Brian W. Walker. New York, N.Y. : Foreign Policy Association, c1985. 70 p. : ill., map, port. ; 20 cm. (Headline series, 0017-8780 . no. 274) Caption title. Bibliography: p. 67-70. ISBN 0-87124-102-1 (pbk.) : LC Card 85-82567 DDC 081 s 338.96 19
1. Famines - Africa. 2. Agriculture and state - Africa. 3. Africa - Economic conditions - 1960-. 4. Africa - Economic policy. I. Title. II. Series.
E744 .H43 no. 274 HC800
NYPL [JLD 86-3400]

Walker, Charls E. (Charls Edward), 1923- The Consumption tax . Cambridge, Mass. , c1987. xviii, 382 p. : ISBN 0-88730-159-2 LC Card 87-17838 DDC 336.2/71/0973 19
HJ5715.U6 C658 1987

Walker, David B., 1841 or 2-ca. 1906. Captain David B. Walker, journal and papers, 1864-1869 : American Russian Commercial Company superintendent at Wood Island, Alaska (ice works). Juneau, Alaska (Pouch G, Juneau 99811) : Alaska Division of State Libraries and Museums, Dept. of Education, 1984. 60 p. : ill. ; 28 cm. (Alaska State Library historical monograph . no. 8) Errata slip inserted. LC Card 84-622198
1. Walker, David B., 1841 or 2-ca. 1906. 2. Ice industry - Alaska - Wood Island - History - Sources. 3. American Russian Commercial Company - History - Sources. 4. Industrialists - United States - Biography. I. Title. II. Series.
HD9481.U4 W359 1984

WALKER, DAVID B., 1841 OR 2-CA. 1906.
Walker, David B., 1841 or 2-ca. 1906. Captain David B. Walker, journal and papers, 1864-1869 . Juneau, Alaska (Pouch G, Juneau 99811) , 1984. 60 p. : LC Card 84-622198
HD9481.U4 W359 1984

Walker, David F. Manufacturing in Kitchener-Waterloo . [Waterloo] , c1987. xiii, 220 p. : ISBN 0-921083-22-X (pbk.) LC Card 87-168616 DDC 338.4/767/0971344 19
HD9734.C3 K56 1987

Walker, Glen. Credit where credit is due : a legal guide to your credit rights and how to assert them / Glen Walker.1st ed. New York : Holt, Rinehart and Winston, c1979. ix, 198 p. ; 22 cm. "A Brownstone book." Includes index. ISBN 0-03-042356-2 LC Card 79-4201 DDC 332.7/43
1. Consumer credit - United States. 2. Consumer credit - Law and legislation - United States. I. Title.
HG3756.U54 W34 ***NYPL [JLD 86-1388]***

Walker, Graham. The ethics of F.A. Hayek / Graham Walker. Lanham, MD : University Press of America, c1986. vii, 135 p. ; 23 cm. Includes index. Bibliography: p. 123-129. ISBN 0-8191-5250-1 (alk. paper) : LC Card 86-1515 DDC 171/.7 19
1. Hayek, Friedrich A. von (Friedrich August), 1899-. 2. Economics - Moral and ethical aspects. 3. Liberalism. I. Title.
HB101.H39 W35 1986
NYPL [JFD 86-9138]

Walker, Jan, 1954- Jondaryan station : the relationship between pastoral capital nd pastoral labour, 1840-1890 / Jan Walker. St. Lucia ; New York : University of Queensland Press, 1988. p. cm. Bibliography: p. Includes index. ISBN 0-7022-2093-0 (pbk.) LC Card 87-13816 DDC 333.3/09943 19
1. Land tenure - Australia - Queensland - History - 19th century. 2. Agriculture - Economic aspects - Australia - Queensland - History - 19th century. 3. Squatters - Australia - Queensland - History - 19th century. 4. Industrial relations - Australia - Queensland - History - 19th century. 5. Queensland - Public lands - History - 19th century. I. Title.
HD1039.Q43 W34 1988

Walker, John R. (John Rex), 1922- Reporting systems for bank management : building a bank management information system / John R. Walker. Boston : Bankers Pub. Co., c1987. xii, 292 p. : ill. ; 25 cm. Includes index. ISBN 0-87267-106-2 LC Card 87-17424 DDC 332.1/068 19
1. Bank management - Data processing. I. Title.
HG1615 .W35 1987

Walker, Martin, 1953- Strong, Norman, 1954- Information and capital markets /. Oxford, UK , New York, NY, USA , 1987. x, 222 p. : ISBN 0-631-13834-X : LC Card 86-31721 DDC 332/.041 19
HG4523 .S77 1987

Walker, Richard. D'Angelo, Massimo. Criteri per una cooperazione industriale con i paesi in via di sviluppo /. Milano , c1981. 294 p. ; ISBN 88-20-42145-3 : LC Card 82-113466
HF1549 .D36 1981 ***NYPL [JLD 86-3318]***

Walker, William B. Surrey, John. The European power plant industry . [Brighton, Sussex] , c1981. viii, 90 p. ; ISBN 0-903422-31-X (pbk.) : LC Card 83-130609 DDC 338.4/76213121/094 19
HD9695.E92 S87 1981
NYPL [JLD 86-4078]

WALKIE-TALKIES.
Sētthaph Kānwāngphæn phatthanā khr [Bangkok] , 2524 [1981] 8, 80 leaves ; LC Card 82-920041
HD9696.T442 S47 1981

Walking on air . McLaughlin, Helen E. Denver, Colo. , c1986. vi, 210 p. : ISBN 0-930161-04-1 (pbk.) LC Card 87-115599 DDC 387.7/42/0973 19
HD8039.A432 U66 1986

Wall, Shirley M.
Wall, William C. Create and deliver dynamite presentations /. Huntsville, Ala. , c1987. p. cm. ISBN 0-938745-02-6 : LC Card 87-14130 DDC 658.8/5 19
HF5438.25 .W275 1987

Wall, William C. Make sound decisions /. Huntsville, Ala. , c1987. p. cm. ISBN 0-938745-01-8 : LC Card 87-14128 DDC 658.4/03 19
HD30.23 .W34 1987

Wall, William C. Plan your work with plans of action /. Huntsville, Ala. , c1987. p. cm. ISBN 0-938745-03-4 : LC Card 87-3629 DDC 658.4/012 19
HD30.28 .W336 1987

Wall, William C. Prepare power-packed reports /. Huntsville, Ala. , c1987. p. cm. ISBN 0-938745-04-2 LC Card 87-13581 DDC 658.4/53 19
HF5719 .W35 1987

WALL STREET.
Allen, Frederick Lewis, 1890-1954. The lords of creation. New York, London, 1935. xii, 483 p. LC Card 35-20649 DDC 332.0973
HG181 .A57 ***NYPL [JLD 86-1097]***

Auletta, Ken. Greed and glory on Wall Street . New York , c1986. xiii, 253 p., [16] p. of plates : ISBN 0-394-54410-2 : LC Card 85-10700 DDC 332.66/09747/1 19
HG5129.N5 A8 1986 ***NYPL [JLE 86-856]***

Auletta, Ken. Greed and glory on Wall Street . Boston, Mass. , 1987, c1986. xii, 423 p. (large print) ; ISBN 0-8161-4189-4 (lg. print) : LC Card 86-26968 DDC 332.66/09747/1 19
HG5129.N5 A8 1987b

Auletta, Ken. Greed and glory on Wall Street . New York, N.Y. [1987], c1986. xi, 260 p., [16] p. of plates : ISBN 0-446-38406-2 (pbk.) LC Card 86-23416 DDC 332.66/09747/1 19
HG5129.N5 A8 1987

Little, Jeffrey B. Understanding Wall Street /. Blue Ridge Summit, PA , c1987. 219 p. : ISBN 0-8306-3120-8 : LC Card 87-3628 DDC 332.6/78 19
HG4910 .L54 1987

Little, Jeffrey B. [Wall Street library.] Understanding Wall Street /. Blue Ridge Summit, PA , 1986. p. cm. ISBN 0-8306-3010-4 (pbk.) : LC Card 86-27791 DDC 332.6/78 19
HG4921 .L63 1986

Stevens, Mark, 1947- The insiders . New York , c1987. 256 p. ; LC Card 87-2537 DDC 364.1/68 19
HG4910 .S67 1987

Winans, R. Foster. Trading secrets /. New York , c1986. xiv, 320 p., [8] p. of plates : ISBN 0-312-81227-2 : LC Card 86-12700 DDC 364.1/68 19
HG4572 .W547 1986 ***NYPL [JLE 86-4323]***

Wall Street bull /. Lansky, Bruce. Deephaven, MN , New York , c1987. iii, 111 p. : ISBN 0-88166-100-7 (pbk.) : LC Card 87-16467 DDC 332.6/0207 19
HG4513 .L29 1987

WALL STREET - HISTORY.
Browder, Clifford, 1928- The money game in old New York . Lexington, KY , c1986. viii, 319 p., [8] p. of plates : ISBN 0-8131-1573-6 LC Card 85-17938 DDC 332/.092/4 B 19
HG172.D74 B76 1986 ***NYPL [JFE 86-1911]***

Wall Street--how it works /. Little, Jeffrey B.

New York , c1988. 47 p. : ISBN 1-555-46621-4 LC Card 87-15139 DDC 332.64/273 19
HG4921 .L625 1988

Wall Street journal.
Lehmann, Michael B. The Dow Jones-Irwin guide to using the Wall Street journal /. Homewood, Ill. , c1987. xii, 282 p. : ISBN 0-87094-923-3 LC Card 86-71441 DDC 332/.05 19
HB3743 .L44 1987

WALL STREET JOURNAL.
Lehmann, Michael B. The Dow Jones-Irwin guide to using the Wall Street journal /. Homewood, Ill. , c1987. xii, 282 p. : ISBN 0-87094-923-3 LC Card 86-71441 DDC 332/.05 19
HB3743 .L44 1987

Winans, R. Foster. Trading secrets /. New York , c1986. xiv, 320 p., [8] p. of plates : ISBN 0-312-81227-2 : LC Card 86-12700 DDC 364.1/68 19
HG4572 .W547 1986 ***NYPL [JLE 86-4323]***

Wall Street Journal (Firm) The American dream . [New York] , c1987. 103 p. : LC Card 87-404096 DDC 330.973/0927 19
HC106.8 .A437 1987

WALL STREET JOURNAL - HISTORY.
Scharff, Edward E. Worldly power . New York , 1987, c1986. p. cm. ISBN 0-452-25917-7 (pbk.) LC Card 86-28562 DDC 071/.47/1 19
HG4910 .S3 1987

The Wall Street journal on marketing /. Alsop, Ronald. New York , 1987, c1986. p. cm. LC Card 87-11248 DDC 658.8 19
HF5415 .A45 1987

WALL STREET - JUVENILE LITERATURE.
Little, Jeffrey B. Wall Street--how it works /. New York , c1988. 47 p. : ISBN 1-555-46621-4 LC Card 87-15139 DDC 332.64/273 19
HG4921 .L625 1988

The Wall Street waltz . Fisher, Kenneth L. Chicago , c1987. xii, 210 p. : ISBN 0-8092-4797-6 : LC Card 87-5310 DDC 332.63/222/0973 19
HG4916 .F47 1987.

Wall Street words /. Scott, David Logan, 1942- Boston , c1988. xi, 404 p. : ISBN 0-395-43747-4 LC Card 87-21444 DDC 332.6/03/21 19
HG4513 .S37 1988

Wall, Toby D. The Human side of advanced manufacturing technology /. Chichester [West Sussex] , New York , c1987. xi, 205 p. : ISBN 0-471-90867-3 : LC Card 86-32554 DDC 331.25 19
HD9720.5 .H85 1987

Wall, William C.
Create and deliver dynamite presentations / William C. Wall, Jr. and Shirley M. Wall. Huntsville, Ala. : McMallec Pub. Co., c1987. p. cm. (Management tool box series) ISBN 0-938745-02-6 : LC Card 87-14130 DDC 658.8/5 19
1. Selling. I. Wall, Shirley M. II. Title. III. Title: Presentations. IV. Series: Wall, William C. Management tool box series.
HF5438.25 .W275 1987

Make sound decisions / William C. Wall, Jr. and Shirley M. Wall. Huntsville, Ala. : McMallec Pub. Co., c1987. p. cm. (Management tool box series) ISBN 0-938745-01-8 : LC Card 87-14128 DDC 658.4/03 19
1. Decision-making. I. Wall, Shirley M. II. Series: Wall, William C. Management tool box series. III. Title.
HD30.23 .W34 1987

Management tool box series.
Wall, William C. Create and deliver dynamite presentations /. Huntsville, Ala. , c1987. p. cm. ISBN 0-938745-02-6 : LC Card 87-14130 DDC 658.8/5 19
HF5438.25 .W275 1987

Wall, William C. Make sound decisions /. Huntsville, Ala. , c1987. p. cm. ISBN 0-938745-01-8 : LC Card 87-14128 DDC 658.4/03 19
HD30.23 .W34 1987

Wall, William C. Plan your work with plans of action /. Huntsville, Ala. , c1987. p. cm. ISBN 0-938745-03-4 : LC Card 87-3629 DDC 658.4/012 19
HD30.28 .W336 1987

Plan your work with plans of action / William C. Wall, Jr. and Shirley M. Wall. Huntsville, Ala. : McMallec Pub. Co., c1987. p. cm. (Management tool box series) ISBN 0-938745-03-4 : LC Card 87-3629 DDC 658.4/012 19
1. Corporate planning. I. Wall, Shirley M. II. Series: Wall, William C. Management tool box series. III. Title.
HD30.28 .W336 1987

Prepare power-packed reports / William C. Wall, Jr. and Shirley M. Wall. Huntsville, Ala. : McMallec Pub. Co., c1987. p. cm. (The Management tool box series) ISBN 0-938745-04-2 LC Card 87-13581 DDC 658.4/53 19
1. Business report writing. I. Wall, Shirley M. II. Title. III. Series.
HF5719 .W35 1987

Wallace, Anthony F. C., 1923- St. Clair : a nineteenth-century coal town's experience with a disaster-prone industry / Anthony F.C. Wallace ; with maps and technical drawings by Robert Howard.1st ed. New York : Knopf : Distributed by Random House, 1987. xvii, 519 p. : ill. ; 25 cm. Bibliography: p. 459-500. Includes index. ISBN 0-394-52867-0 : LC Card 86-46120 DDC 307.7/66/0974817 19
1. Coal miners - Pennsylvania - Saint Clair (Schuylkill County) - History - 19th century. 2. Coal mines and mining - Pennsylvania - Saint Clair (Schuylkill County) - History - 19th century. 3. Saint Clair (Schuylkill County, Pa.) - Social conditions. I. Title. II. Title: Saint Clair.
HD8039.M62 U6699 1987

Wallace, Brian F. Ownership and development : a comparison of domestic and foreign firms in Colombian manufacturing / by Brian F. Wallace. Athens, Ohio : Ohio University Center for International Studies, Center for Latin American Studies, 1987. ix, 176 p. ; 22 cm. (Monographs in international studies. Latin America series . no. 12) Bibliography: p. 163-176. ISBN 0-89680-145-4 (pbk.) LC Card 86-33255 DDC 332.6/7322861 19
1. Colombia - Manufactures. 2. Investments, Foreign - Government policy - Colombia. 3. International business enterprises - Government policy - Colombia. I. Title. II. Series.
HD9734.C62 W35 1987

Wallace, James E. The Fair Housing Assistance Program evaluation /. Washington, D.C. [1985] 1 v. (various pagings) :
NYPL [JLF 87-17]

Wallace, Joanne. The working woman / Joanne Wallace. Old Tappan, N.J. : F.H. Revell Co., c1986. 171 p. : ill. (some col.) ; 26 cm. Includes index. ISBN 0-8007-1455-5 (pbk.) : LC Card 85-14396 DDC 650.1/024042 19
1. Women - Life skills guides. 2. Women - Communication. I. Title.
HD6053 .W34 1986 ***NYPL [JLF 87-131]***

Wallace, Luther T. Agriculture's futures : America's food system / L. Tim Wallace. New York : Springer-Verlag, c1987. x, 93 p. : ill. ; 28 cm. Bibliography: p. [87]-89. Includes index. ISBN 0-387-96482-7 (pbk.) LC Card 86-31390 DDC 338.1/0973 19
1. Agriculture - Economic aspects - United States. 2. Agriculture - United States. 3. Agriculture and state - United States. 4. Food industry and trade - United States. I. Title.
HD1761 .W274 1987

Wallace, McHarg, Roberts and Todd. Hudson Waterfront Walkway plan and design guidelines /. [Trenton, N.J.] , 1984] 136 p. :
NYPL [JLF 87-913]

Wallace, Marc J., 1944- Szilagyi, Andrew D. Organizational behavior and performance /. Glenview, Ill. , c1987. 742 p. : ISBN 0-673-16664-3 : LC Card 86-26087 DDC 658.4 19
HD58.7 .S97 1987

Wallace, Neil. Contractual arrangements for intertemporal trade /. Minneapolis, MN , c1987. p. cm. ISBN 0-8166-1533-0 : LC Card 86-24888 DDC 332.64/4/0724 19
HB801 .C629 1987

Wallace, Robert Bruce. Kate, Adriaan ten. La política de protección en el desarrollo económico de México /. México , 1979. 376 p. ; ISBN 968-16-0352-4 LC Card 87-672671
HF1775 .K37x 1979

Wallace, T. Dudley. Econometrics : an introduction / T. Dudley Wallace, J. Lew Silver. Reading, Mass. : Addison-Wesley, c1988. xviii, 440 p. : ill. ; 24 cm. + software package. Includes bibliographical references and index. ISBN 0-201-09896-2 : LC Card 87-14492 DDC 330/.028 19
1. Econometrics. I. Silver, J. Lew. II. Title.
HB139 .W32 1988

Wallace, Thomas F. Schorr, John E. High performance purchasing . Essex Junction, Vt. , c1986. xii, 211 p. : ISBN 0-939246-05-8 LC Card 86-201739 DDC 658.7/2 19
HD39.5 .S36 1986

Wallendorf, Melanie. Zaltman, Gerald. Consumer behavior . Malabar, Fla. , 1987, c1983. p. cm. ISBN 0-89874-989-1 LC Card 86-21297 DDC 658.8/342 19
HF5415.3 .Z28 1987

Wallenwein, Erich, 1951- Die Bedeutung der Kapitalintensitätshypothese im neoklassischen Zwei-Sektoren-Modell und ihre empirische Überprüfung / Erich Wallenwein. Frankfurt am Main ; New York : Lang, c1986. x, 354 p. : ill. ; 21 cm. (Europäische Hochschulschriften. Reihe V, Volks- und Betriebswirtschaft, 0531-7339 . Bd. 717 = vol. 717 = vol. 717) Bibliography: p. 341-354. ISBN 3-8204-9618-1 LC Card 86-194355
1. Economic development - Mathematical models. 2. Investments - Mathematical models. I. Series: Europäische Hochschulschriften. Reihe V, Volks- und Betriebswirtschaft , Bd. 717. II. Title.
HD75.5 .W33 1986

Waller, Kal. Medicare : recover your medical expenses : a comprehensive guide to understanding and unscrambling medicare / by Kal Waller. Cleveland : J.T. Zubal, 1987. xvii, 146 p. : ill. ; 28 cm. Includes index. ISBN 0-939738-92-9 (pbk.) LC Card 87-156155 DDC 368.4/26/00973 19
1. Medicare - United States. 2. Insurance, Health - United States. 3. Medical care, Cost of - United States. I. Title.
HD7102.U4 W245 1987

Waller, William, 1956- Alternatives to economic orthodoxy . Armonk, N.Y. , c1987. 348 p. : ISBN 0-87332-409-9 : LC Card 86-33899 DDC 330 19
HB171 .A47 1987

Wallin, Markku. Jätteiden hyötykäyttö kansantaloudessa / Markku Wallin. [Helsinki] : Ympäristöministeriö, Ympäristön- ja luonnonsuojeluosasto, [1986] 87 p. : ill. ; 30 cm. (Sarja D, 0780-6825 . 14) ISBN 951-46-9505-4 LC Card 86-216953
1. Recycling (Waste, etc.) - Economic aspects - Finland. I. Series: Sarja D (Finland. Ympäristön- ja luonnonsuojeluosasto) , 14. II. Title.
HD9975.F52 W35 1986

Wallis, Louis A. Computers and the sales effort : a research report from the Conference Board / by Louis A. Wallis. New York, N.Y. : The Board, c1986. v, 26 p. : ill. ; 28 cm. (Conference Board report. no. 884) Includes bibliographical references. ISBN 0-8237-0326-6 (pbk.) LC Card 87-404503 DDC 658.8/1/00285416 19
1. Selling - Data processing. 2. Telemarketing - United States. 3. Microcomputers. I. Title.
HF5438.35 .W35 1986

WALLONIA, BELGIUM - POPULATION.
André, Robert, 1925- La population de la Wallonie dans la dualité démographique de la Belgique /. Bruxelles , Charleroi , 1983. 192 p. : LC Card 85-175936
HB3604.W34 A53 1983

Walls, Nina de Angeli. Hagley Museum and Library. Trade catalogs in the Hagley Museum and Library /. Wilmington, Del. , 1987. 104 p. : ISBN 0-914650-26-2 (pbk.) LC Card 87-146349 DDC 016.3801/029/4 19
HF5861 .H234 1987

Walmsley, Julian. A dictionary of international finance / Julian Walmsley. Westport, Conn. : Greenwood Press, 1979. 270 p. ; 23 cm. ISBN 0-313-20974-X LC Card 79-17753 DDC 332/.042/0321 19
1. International finance - Dictionaries. 2. Finance - Dictionaries. I. Title.
HG151 .W34 ***NYPL [JLD 87-1082]***

WALNUT INDUSTRY - INDIA.
India. Directorate of Marketing and Inspection.

Marketing of walnuts in India. Faridabad , Delhi , 1986. ix, 180 p. : LC Card 86-903362
HD9259.N7 I45 1986

Walras, Léon, 1834-1910. L'economia monetaria / Léon Walras ; introduzione e cura di Gaspare De Caro. Roma : Istituto della Enciclopedia italiana, [1985] 2 v. (949 p.) : ill. ; 21 cm. (Bibliotheca biographica. Sezione di scienze sociali) Bibliography: v. 1, p. 181-193. LC Card 87-140163
1. Money. 2. Monetary policy. 3. Economics. I. De Caro, Gaspare. II. Title. III. Series.
HG221 .W219 1985

Walrasian microeconomics . Katzner, Donald W., 1938- Reading, Mass. , c1988. xv, 512 p. : ISBN 0-201-10461-X : LC Card 86-26622 DDC 338.5 19
HB172 .K38 1988

Walravens, A. Zelfstandig werken en ondernemen in middelgrote en kleine ondernemingen /. Delft , 1985. 245 p. : ISBN 90-6275-226-8 : LC Card 86-152999
HD2346.N4 Z44 1985

Walser, Karin, 1950- Dienstmädchen : Frauenarbeit und Weiblichkeitsbilder um 1900 / Karin Walser.1. Aufl. Frankfurt : Extrabuch, 1985. 195 p. ; 21 cm. Bibliography: p. 189-195. ISBN 3-88704-079-1 LC Card 86-141363
1. Women domestics - Germany. I. Title.
HD6072.2.G4 W35 1985

Walser, Olaf. Buchführungspflicht und Besteuerung der Sitzunternehmungen und Holdinggesellschaften in Liechtenstein / Olaf Walser. 4. Aufl. Vaduz, Fürstentum Liechtenstein : Allgemeines Treuunternehmen, [1983] 31 p. ; 20 cm. LC Card 85-226619
1. Corporations - Taxation - Liechtenstein. 2. Corporations - Taxation - Law and legislation - Liechtenstein. I. Title.
HD2753.L76 W35 1983

Walsh, Brendan P., 1955- On-line information : a comprehensive business-user's guide / Brendan P. Walsh, Helen Butcher, and Alison Freund. Oxford, [Oxfordshire] ; New York, NY, USA : Blackwell in association with the Institute of Chartered Accountants in England and Wales, 1987. xli, 327 p. : ill. ; 26 cm. Includes index. ISBN 0-631-15543-0 : LC Card 87-13154 DDC 025/.04/02465 19
1. Business - Data bases. 2. Data base searching. I. Butcher, Helen. II. Freund, Alison. III. Institute of Chartered Accountants in England and Wales. IV. Title.
HF5548.2 .W294 1987

Walsh, Francis J. (joint author) Davey, Patrick J. High interest rates and tight money. [New York, 1969] 25 p. LC Card 70-9411 DDC 332.8/0973
HB545 .D38

Walsh, J. Michael (Joseph Michael), 1943- Drug and alcohol abuse in the workplace : a guide to the issues / J. Michael Walsh, Stephen C. Yohay. Washington, D.C. : National Foundation for the Study of Equal Employment Policy, 1987. xiv, 149 p. ; 23 cm. Bibliography: p. 133-149. ISBN 0-916559-08-4 (pbk.) LC Card 87-60167 DDC 658.3/822 19
1. Employee assistance programs. 2. Drugs and employment. 3. Alcoholism and employment. I. Yohay, Stephen C. II. National Foundation for the Study of Equal Employment Policy. III. Title.
HF5549.5.E42 W35 1987

Walsh, Vivien. Coombs, Rod. Economics and technological change /. Totowa, N.J. , 1987. xv, 296 p. : ISBN 0-8476-7545-9 : LC Card 86-28000 DDC 338/.06 19
HC79.T4 C67 1987

Walsh, William I. The rise and decline of the Great Atlantic & Pacific Tea Company / by William I. Walsh. Secaucus, N.J. : L. Stuart, c1986. 254 p., [24] p. of plates : ill. ; 24 cm. Includes index. ISBN 0-8184-0382-9 : LC Card 85-24987 DDC 381/.456413/006073 19
1. Great Atlantic and Pacific Tea Company - History. 2. Grocery trade - United States - History. 3. Food industry and trade - United States - History. 4. Supermarkets - United States - History. I. Title.
HD9321.9.G7 W35 1986 ***NYPL [JLE 86-1952]***

Walstad, William B. An annotated catalog of microcomputer software in economics / William B. Walstad, Karen S. Hallows, David Ross. New York, NY (2 Park Ave., New York 10016) : Joint Council on Economic Education, c1986. viii, 160 p. ; 23 cm. "A Product of DEEP. Developmental Economic Education program." LC Card 86-210285 DDC 330/.028/5536 19
1. Economics - Study and teaching - United States - Computer programs - Catalogs. I. Hallows, Karen S. II. Ross, David, 1947-. III. Joint Council on Economic Education. IV. Title. V. Title: Microcomputer software in economics.
HB74.8 .W34 1986

Walter Eucken Institut.
Symposion "Marktwirtschaft und Umwelt" (1980 : Walter Eucken Institut) Marktwirtschaft und Umwelt . Tübingen , 1981. ix, 303 p. : ISBN 3-16-343372-3 : LC Card 81-128698 DDC 363.7/0526 19
HC79.E5 S92 1980 ***NYPL [TB (Walter Eucken Institut. Wirtschaftswissenschaftliche und wirtschaftsrechtliche Untersuchungen. Bd. 17)]***

Symposium Umweltprobleme als Herausforderung der Marktwirtschaft, Neue Ideen jenseits des Dirigismus (1983 : Stuttgart, Germany) Symposium Umweltprobleme als Herausforderung der Marktwirtschaft, Neue Ideen jenseits des Dirigismus . [Köln] [Freiburg] , 1983. 300 p. ; ISBN 3-7616-0722-9 LC Card 84-152335 DDC 363.7/058 19
HC79.E5 S96 1983 ***NYPL [JLD 86-1631]***

Wirtschaftswissensschaftliche und wirtschaftsrechtliche Untersuchungen .
(17) Symposion "Marktwirtschaft und Umwelt" (1980 : Walter Eucken Institut) Marktwirtschaft und Umwelt . Tübingen , 1981. ix, 303 p. : ISBN 3-16-343372-3 : LC Card 81-128698 DDC 363.7/0526 19
HC79.E5 S92 1980 ***NYPL [TB (Walter Eucken Institut. Wirtschaftswissenschaftliche und wirtschaftsrechtliche Untersuchungen. Bd. 17)]***

Walter, Herbert. Standortpolitik multinationaler Banken / Herbert Walter. Thun : H. Deutsch, c1983. viii, 255 p. : ill. ; 21 cm. (Reihe Wirtschaftswissenschaften, 0253-1488 . Bd. 280) Bibliography: p. 203-255. ISBN 3-87144-737-4 : LC Card 83-159195
1. Banks and banking, International - Location. 2. Banks and banking, West German - Location. I. Title. II. Series.
HG3881 .W273 1983

Walter, Ingo.
Gray, H. Peter. International trade, employment, and structural adjustment . Geneva , 1986. x, 108 p. ; ISBN 92-2-105325-3 (pbk.) : LC Card 87-119470 DDC 331.12/0973 19
HD5710.75.U6 G73 1986

Regional environmental policy . New York , c1979. xii, 290 p. : ISBN 0-8147-7805-4 : LC Card 79-2058 DDC 301.31
HC79.E5 R44 ***NYPL [JLE 80-1854]***

Walter, Jean Jacques, 1932- Main basse sur la France / Jean-Jacques Walter. Paris : Table ronde, c1984. 252 p. ; 21 cm. (Collection Place publique . 7) ISBN 2-7103-0188-1 LC Card 84-231340 DDC 335/.00944 19
1. Socialism - France. 2. Communism - France. I. Title.
HX264 .W36 1984 ***NYPL [JLD 86-1773]***

Waltman, Jerold L., 1945- Political economy . Jackson , c1987. vii, 276 p. ; ISBN 0-87805-313-1 (alk. paper) LC Card 87-10425 DDC 361.6/1/0941 19
HC106 .P68 1987

Walton, C. Michael. Massimi, John J. Truck lane needs methodology . Austin , Springfield, Va. [1985] xii, 63 p. : LC Card 86-622425 DDC 388.1/3 19
HE336.T79 M37 1985

Walton, Richard E. Innovating to compete : lessons for diffusing and managing change in the workplace / Richard E. Walton. San Francisco : Jossey-Bass, 1987. p. cm. (The Jossey-Bass management series) Bibliography: p. Includes index. ISBN 1-555-42056-7 LC Card 87-45426 DDC 658.4/06 19
1. Shipping - Personnel management. 2. Shipping - Management. 3. Industrial management. 4. Comparative management. I. Title. II. Series.
HE736 .W35 1987

Walvis, C. Koopman, A. F. Vrouwen zelfstandig . Den Haag [1986] 70 p. ; ISBN 90-346-0762-3 LC Card 86-172683
HD2346.N4 K66 1986

Walz, Rainer. Stände und frühmoderner Staat : die Landstände von Jülich-Berg im 16. und 17. Jahrhundert / von Rainer Walz. Neustadt an der Aisch : Ph.C.W. Schmidt, 1982. 257 p., [1] leaf of plates : ill. ; 24 cm. (Bergische Forschungen, 0405-4520 . Bd. 17) Bibliography: p. 247-257. ISBN 3-87707-040-9 LC Card 83-215104
1. Taxation - Germany (West) - Jülich-Berg - History - 16th century. 2. Feudalism - Germany (West) - Jülich-Berg - History - 16th century. 3. Estates (Social order) - Germany (West) - Jülich-Berg - History - 16th century. 4. Taxation - Germany (West) - Jülich-Berg - History - 17th century. 5. Feudalism - Germany (West) - Jülich-Berg - History - 17th century. 6. Estates (Social order) - Germany (West) - Jülich-Berg - History - 17th century. 7. Jülich-Berg - History. I. Title. II. Series.
HJ2675 .W35 1982

Der Wandel der Gesellschafts- und Herrschaftsstrukturen in der Saarregion während der Industrialisierung (1740-1914) /. Horch, Hans. St. Ingbert [W. Germany] , 1985. 720 p. : ISBN 3-924555-04-4 LC Card 85-194709
HC287.S23 H67 1985

Wandeler, Josef, 1949- Die KPS und die Wirtschaftskämpfe, 1930-1933 : Bauarbeiterstreik Basel, Schuharbeiterstreik Brütisellen, Heizungsmonteurenstreik Zürich, Sanitärmonteurenstreik Zürich / Josef Wandeler. Zürich : Verlag Reihe W, c1978. 277 p. : ill. ; 21 cm. Originally presented as the author's thesis (doctoral)--Universität Zürich, 1978. Bibliography: p. 252-257. ISBN 3-85854-003-X LC Card 87-409249 DDC 331.89/29494 19
1. Strikes and lockouts - Switzerland - History. 2. Kommunistische Partei der Schweiz - History. 3. Trade-unions - Switzerland - History. I. Title.
HD5410.A6 W36 1978

Wang, An, 1920- Lessons : an autobiography / An Wang ; with Eugene Linden. Reading, Mass. : Addison-Wesley, 1986. 248 p., [28] p. of plates : ill. ; 25 cm. Includes index. ISBN 0-201-09400-2 LC Card 86-10768 DDC 338.7/61004/0924 B 19
1. Wang, An, 1920-. 2. Wang Laboratories, Inc. - History. 3. Computer industry - United States - History. 4. Industrialists - United States - Biography. I. Linden, Eugene. II. Title.
HD9696.C62 A3 1986 ***NYPL [JFE 86-5201]***

WANG, AN, 1920-
Wang, An, 1920- Lessons . Reading, Mass. , 1986. 248 p., [28] p. of plates : ISBN 0-201-09400-2 LC Card 86-10768 DDC 338.7/61004/0924 B 19
HD9696.C62 A3 1986 ***NYPL [JFE 86-5201]***

Wang, Chi-kʻuan. Chen hsing Chung-hua chih lu--kai ko ti sung ko /. Pei-ching , 1985. 4, 3, 385 p. ; LC Card 86-106324
NYPL [*OVY 86-3099]

WANG LABORATORIES, INC. - HISTORY.
Wang, An, 1920- Lessons . Reading, Mass. , 1986. 248 p., [28] p. of plates : ISBN 0-201-09400-2 LC Card 86-10768 DDC 338.7/61004/0924 B 19
HD9696.C62 A3 1986 ***NYPL [JFE 86-5201]***

Wangwe, S. M.
Collier, Paul. Labour and poverty in rural Tanzania . Oxford [Oxfordhire] , New York , 1986. vii, 143 p. : ISBN 0-19-828531-0 : LC Card 86-5303 DDC 307.1/4/09678 19
HN797.Z9 C625 1986 ***NYPL [JLD 87-511]***

Skarstein, Rune. Industrial development in Tanzania . Uppsala , Stockholm, Sweden , 1986. xi, 291 p. : ISBN 91-7106-254-8 (pbk.) LC Card 87-134925 DDC 338.9678 19
HC885 .S58 1986

Wanick Ribeiro, Sylvio. see **Ribeiro, Sylvio Wanick.**

Wanik, Bernhard. Die Lohnentwicklung deutscher Industrieaktiengesellschaften / Bernhard Wanik. Bonn : Bonner Betriebswirtschaftliche Schriften, 1981. vii, 268 p. : ill. ; 21 cm. (Bonner betriebswirtschaftliche Schriften . 10) Bibliography: p. 244-268. LC Card 85-165602
1. Wages - Germany (West) - Econometric models. 2. Stock companies - Germany (West) - Econometric

models. I. Title. II. Series.
HD5029 .W36 1981

Het wankele evenwicht in de economie . Schouten, D. B. J. Leiden , 1986. xiv, 189 p. ; ISBN 90-207-1436-8 : LC Card 86-167831
HD85.D8 S36 1986

Wannell, Ted. Picot, W. Garnett. The changing labour market for postsecondary graduates, 1975-1984 /. Ottawa , c1987. 86, 94 p. : ISBN 0-660-52896-7 (pbk.) : LC Card 87-169612 DDC 331.11/423 19
HD6278.C3 P52 1987

Wannenmacher, Walter. Irrwege der Freiheit : was den Westen krank macht / Walter Wannenmacher. München : Herbig, c1986. 322 p. ; 23 cm. ISBN 3-7766-1429-3 LC Card 87-130925 DDC 330.9/048 19
1. Economic history - 1945-. 2. Business cycles. 3. Right and left (Political science). 4. Liberty. I. Title.
HC59 .W279 1986

Wanniski, Jude, 1936- The political economy in perspective [microform] : Volcker's October deflation / by Jude Wanniski. Morristown, N.J. (66 Macculloch Ave., Morristown 07960) : Polyconomics, [1983] 5 p. ; 28 cm. "November 2, 1983." Microfilm. New York : New York Public Library, 1986. 1 microfilm reel ; 35 mm. (MN *ZZ-26,374) LC Card 83-239685 DDC 332.4/973 19
1. Monetary policy - United States. 2. Deflation (Finance) - United States. I. Title.
HG540 .W36 1983 ***NYPL [*ZT-1708 no.21]***

Wansell, Geoffrey, 1945- Tycoon : the life of James Goldsmith / Geoffrey Wansell.1st American ed. New York : Atheneum, 1987. 396 p., [16] p. of plates : ill. ; 25 cm. Includes index. ISBN 0-689-11817-1 LC Card 87-11473 DDC 338/.04/0924 B 19
1. Goldsmith, James, Sir, 1933-. 2. Businessmen - Great Britain - Biography. I. Title.
HC252.5.G64 W36 1987

Wansleben, Martin. Der Produktivitätszuwachs als Massstab für eine beschäftigungsorientierte Lohnpolitik : Wiederaufnahme der Diskussion um Lohnleitlinien / Martin Wansleben.1. Aufl. Baden-Baden : Nomos, 1986. 153 p. : 2 ill. ; 23 cm. (Wirtschaftsrecht und Wirtschaftspolitik. Bd. 87) Originally presented as the author's thesis (doctoral)--Eberhard-Karls-Universität, Tübingen, 1986. Bibliography: p. 147-153. ISBN 3-7890-1312-9 LC Card 87-128291 DDC 331.1/18 19
1. Wages and labor productivity. 2. Wages and labor productivity - Germany, West. I. Title.
HD4945 .W36 1986

Wanted, liberal arts graduates . Salzman, Marian L. New York , 1987. xvi, 341 p. ; ISBN 0-385-24008-2 (pbk.) : LC Card 87-8846 DDC 650.1/4 19
HF5382.75.U6 S27 1987

Waqif, Arif A., 1943- South Asian cooperation in industry, energy, and technology /. New Delhi , Newbury Park, Calif. , 1987. p. cm. ISBN 0-8039-9538-5 (pbk.) LC Card 87-14994 DDC 337.1/54 19
HC430.6 .S675 1987

WAR AND PEACE. see **PEACE.**

War, armed forces, and society.
Grieves, Keith. The politics of manpower, 1914-1918 /. New York, NY , 1988. vii, 241 p. ; ISBN 0-312-01320-5 LC Card 87-20511 DDC 331.12/042/0941 19
HD5765.A6 G77 1988

WAR ASSETS CORPORATION. (Old catalog form: United States. War Assets Administration).
A Documentary history of the Petroleum Reserves Corporation, 1943-1944 . Washington , 1974. v, 119 p. : LC Card 74-602382
HD9566 .D6 ***NYPL [JLE 78-1181]***

War bird . Davis, Burke, 1913- Chapel Hill , c1987. viii, 267 p., [26] p. of plates : ISBN 0-8078-1752-X (alk. paper) LC Card 87-5934 DDC 338.7/67721/0924 B 19
HD9880.S67 D38 1987

WAR, COST OF.
Boelcke, Willi A. Die Kosten von Hitlers Krieg . Paderborn , c1985. 220 p. : ISBN 3-506-77471-9 LC Card 86-143362
HJ1119 .B66 1985

WAR - ECONOMIC ASPECTS.
Hirshleifer, Jack. Economic behaviour in adversity /. Chicago , 1987. ix, 310 p. ; ISBN 0-226-34282-4 : LC Card 87-19846 DDC 330.9 19
HC79.D45 H57 1987

United Nations. Secretary-General. [Economic and social consequences of the arms race and of military expenditures. French.] Conséquences économiques et sociales de la course aux armements /. Paris , 1983. 121 p. : ISBN 2-7178-0645-8 : LC Card 84-136625
HC79.D4 U52 1983

Vlas'evich, IU. E. (IUriĭ Evlampievich) Ėkonomicheskoe bremia militarizma /. Moskva , 1980. 181 p. ; LC Card 81-134793
HC79.D4 V58 1980

WAR - ECONOMIC ASPECTS - EUROPE.
Meyer, Jean, 1924- Le poids de l'Etat /. Paris , c1983. 304 p. : ISBN 2-13-037770-X : LC Card 83-175028
HC280.D4 M49 1983

WAR - ECONOMIC ASPECTS - FRANCE.
Meyer, Jean, 1924- Le poids de l'Etat /. Paris , c1983. 304 p. : ISBN 2-13-037770-X : LC Card 83-175028
HC280.D4 M49 1983

WAR - ECONOMIC ASPECTS - GREAT BRITAIN.
Shein, A. I. (Aleksandr Ivanovich) Voenno-promyshlennyĭ kompleks Velikobritanii /. Moskva , 1985. 165 p. : LC Card 84-219560
HC260.D4 S54 1985 ***NYPL [*QGR 87-2278]***

WAR - ECONOMIC ASPECTS - ROMANIA.
Pagini din gîndirea economică militară românească /. București , 1983. 219 p. ; LC Card 84-116220
HC405.Z9 D443 1983

War history of American railroads /. Hines, Walker Downer, 1870-1934. [S.l.] , 1974. xviii, 327 p. : LC Card 74-75240
NYPL [JLD 87-638]

WAR OF SECESSION (UNITED STATES) see **UNITED STATES - HISTORY - CIVIL WAR, 1861-1865.**

The War on poverty, 1964-1968 [microform] : selections from the holdings of the Lyndon B. Johnson Library / edited by Mark I. Gelfand ; associate editor, Robert E. Lester. Frederick, MD : University Publications of America, c1986- microfilm reel (The Presidential documents series) Accompanied by a printed reel guide compiled by Martin Schipper. CONTENTS. - pt. 1. The White House central files. ISBN 0-89093-495-9 (microfilm : set) : LC Card 87-10510 DDC 338.973 19
1. Economic assistance, Domestic - United States - History - 20th century - Sources. 2. Lyndon Baines Johnson Library. I. Gelfand, Mark I. II. Lester, Robert. III. Schipper, Martin Paul. IV. Lyndon Baines Johnson Library. V. University Publications of America, Inc. VI. Series.
HC110 .P63

War, prosperity, and depression . Fearon, Peter. Lawrence, Kan. , 1987. p. cm. ISBN 0-7006-0348-4 : LC Card 87-21571 DDC 330.973/091 19
HC106.2 .F42 1987

WAR - RELIGIOUS ASPECTS - CATHOLIC CHURCH.
The Best of This world /. Lanham, MD , c1986. x, 405 p. ; ISBN 0-8191-5605-1 (alk. paper) : LC Card 86-22411 DDC 261.8 19
HB72 .B5 1987 ***NYPL [JFE 86-5571]***

Weigel, George. Tranquillitas ordinis . Oxford , New York , 1987. xiii, 489 p. ; ISBN 0-19-504193-3 (alk. paper) : LC Card 86-12742 DDC 261.8/73/08822 19
BX1795.P43 W45 1987
NYPL [JFE 87-1638]

WARBURG, SIEGMUND, SIR, 1902-1982.
Attali, Jacques. [Homme d'influence. English.] A man of influence . London , 1986. 346 p. ; ISBN 0-297-78978-3 ***NYPL [JFE 87-583]***

Attali, Jacques. [Homme d'influence. English.] A man of influence . Bethesda, Md. , 1987, c1985. xvii, 380 p. ; ISBN 0-917561-36-8 : LC Card 86-28735 DDC 332.1/092/4 B 19
HG1552.W37 A8713 1987

Ward, Christian S. International Law Symposium (1984 : Cambridge, Cambridgeshire) The United States, transnational business, and the law . New York , c1985. x, 132 p. ; ISBN 0-379-20783-4 LC Card 85-61594 DDC 346/.07 342.67 19
K1004.6 1984 ***NYPL [JLF 86-1046]***

Ward, Douglas H. Jaffe, Susan. Toxic chemical accidents in New York State . New York, N.Y. (2 World Trade Center, New York 10047) [1986] 27, 13, 33 p. ; LC Card 86-622820 DDC 363.1/79 19
HD7269.C452 U54 1986

Ward, John (John L.) The Future of private enterprise /. Atlanta, Ga. , 1984-1986. 3 v. ; ISBN 0-88406-164-7 (pbk. : v. 1) LC Card 83-25386 DDC 338.6/1 19
HB501 .F83 1984 ***NYPL [JLK 87-49]***

Ward, Richard Alexander, 1929- Horvitz, Paul M. Monetary policy and the financial system /. Englewood Cliffs, N.J. , c1987. xii, 532 p. : ISBN 0-13-599861-1 LC Card 86-25447 DDC 332.4/973 19
HG540 .H67 1987

Ward, Sally K. The Politics of urban fiscal policy /. Beverly Hills , c1984. 176 p. : ISBN 0-8039-2373-2 LC Card 84-13431 DDC 336/.014/73 19
HJ9144 .P64 1984 ***NYPL [JLD 87-126]***

Ward, Susan Diane. Ludlow, Nicholas H. The Development Bank highways market, 1987-1991 . Washington, D.C., USA (1735 Eye St., NW, Suite 710, Washington 20006) , c1987. 387, 2 p. : LC Card 87-71066 DDC 388.1/14 19
HG3881 .L737 1987

Wardaya, F. X. Baskara Tulus. Indonesia dan masalah-masalah pembangunan /. [Jakarta] , 1986. viii, 277 p. : LC Card 87-940526
HC447 .I555936 1986

The Wardley guide to world money and securities markets /. Kemp, L. J. (Lynette J.) London , 1984. xvii, 472 p. ; ISBN 0-903121-66-2
NYPL [JLG 86-203]

Ware, Peggy M. Virginia, an outline of the state and local taxes / by Peggy M. Ware. Richmond, Va. (1000 Washington Bldg., Richmond 23219) : Commonwealth of Virginia, Governor's Office, Dept. of Economic Development, [1986] iv, 26 p. ; 28 cm. "April 1986." LC Card 86-622876 DDC 343.75504/3 347.550343 19
1. Taxation - Virginia. 2. Local taxation - Virginia. I. Virginia. Dept. of Economic Development. II. Title.
HJ2438 .W37 1986

Ware, Ray M. Piggybacking--the federal-state collection act of 1972 / by Ray M. Ware. Lexington, Ky. : Center for Applied Economic Research, University of Kentucky, 1980. ix leaves, 35 p. ; 28 cm. (Policy paper series . no. 10) Bibliography: p. 35.
1. United States. Federal-state tax collection act of 1972. 2. Income tax - United States - States. 3. Tax administration and procedure - United States - States. I. Center for Applied Economic Research. University. Kentucky. II. Series: Kentucky. Council of Economic Advisors. Policy paper series , no. 10. III. Title.
NYPL [JLM 79-1230 no.10]

Ware und Geld . Wolf, Dieter, 1942- Hamburg , 1985. 405 p. ; ISBN 3-87975-301-6 LC Card 86-229352
HB501.M5 W65 1985

Wareham, John.
[Basic business types]
Wareham's basic business types : sorting winners from losers, and managing people for profit / John Wareham.1st ed. New York : Atheneum, 1987. ix, 260 p. ; 22 cm. ISBN 0-689-11756-6 : LC Card 86-47686 DDC 658.4/09 19
1. Executives - Psychology. 2. Personality assessment. 3. Executives - Selection and appointment. 4. Success. I. Title.
HD38.2 .W37 1987

Wareham's basic business types . Wareham, John. [Basic business types.] New York , 1987. ix, 260 p. ; ISBN 0-689-11756-6 : LC Card 86-47686 DDC 658.4/09 19
HD38.2 .W37 1987

The Warehouse management handbook / James A. Tompkins and Jerry D. Smith, editors-in-chief. New York : McGraw-Hill,

c1988. p. cm. Includes index. ISBN 0-07-064952-9 : LC Card 87-16885 DDC 658.7/85 19
1. Warehouses - Management. I. Tompkins, James A. II. Smith, Jerry D.
HF5485 .W35 1988

WAREHOUSES - GOVERNMENT POLICY - BRAZIL.
Companhia Brasileira de Armazenamento. Plano nacional de armazenagem, 1985 /. Brasília, DF [1985 or 1986] 1 v. (various foliations) : LC Card 87-403918 DDC 381 19
HF5489.B73 C66 1985

WAREHOUSES - MANAGEMENT.
The Warehouse management handbook /. New York , c1988. p. cm. ISBN 0-07-064952-9 : LC Card 87-16885 DDC 658.7/85 19
HF5485 .W35 1988

WAREHOUSES - PERU.
Hinojosa Tapia, Juan. La problemática de los almacenes generales de depósito como instituciones financieras no bancarias en el Perú (1970-1983) /. Lima, Perú , 1985. iii, 29, [43] p. : LC Card 86-218257
HG3751.9.P4 H56 1985

WAREHOUSES - UNITED STATES - ACCIDENTS - STATISTICS.
Injuries to warehouse workers. Washington, D.C. , 1986. v, 24 p. : LC Card 87-601109 DDC 363.1/19381 19
HD7269.F82 I56 1986

Die Warenplazierung als absatzpolitisches Instrument im Selbstbedienungseinzelhandel /. Müller, Heinz, Dipl.-Kfm. Dr. Göttingen , 1982. 479 p. : ISBN 3-509-01287-9 LC Card 84-174456
HF5845 .M964 1982

Die Warenstruktur des Aussenhandels . Hutter, Monika, 1950- Frankfurt am Main , New York , c1987. 216 p. ; ISBN 3-8204-8810-3 LC Card 87-407938 DDC 382/.09436 19
HF3546.5 .H87 1987

Warentest und Konsument : Nutzung, Wirkungen und Beurteilung des vergleichenden Warentests im Konsumentenbereich / Günter Silberer, Hans Raffée (Hg.). Frankfurt/Main ; New York : Campus, c1984. 268 p. : ill. ; 21 cm. (Campus Forschung. Bd. 361) "Forschungsverbund 'Empirische Verbraucherforschung'"--Ser. t.p. Research project of the Forschungsgruppe Konsumenteninformation. Bibliography: p. 257-268. CONTENTS. - Kontakte mit Testergebnissen der Stiftung Warentest und deren Verwendung im Konsumentenbereich / Günter Silberer ... [et al.] -- Erfolgsrelevante Wirkungen vergleichender Warentest-Ergebnisse auf Kaufentscheidungen der Konsumenten / Günter Silberer ... [et al.] -- Experimentelle Analysen von Wirkungen des Umfanges von Testberichten und der Vergabe von Gesamtnoten auf Produktwahlentscheidungen / Günter Silberer, Friedrich Förster und Ulrich Schwetz -- Die Beurteilungen von Testergebnissen und Testkriterien der Stiftung Warentest durch die Verbraucher / Günter Silberer ... [et al.] -- Inhalte publizierter Testberichte in verschiedenen Medien / Gosbert Gottmann und Günter Silberer -- Ausgewählte Empfehlungen an die Stiftung Warentest / Günter Silberer und Hans Raffée. ISBN 3-593-33295-7 LC Card 84-150919
1. Commercial products - Germany (West) - Testing. 2. Consumer protection - Germany, West. 3. Consumers - Germany (West) - Attitudes. 4. Consumer education - Germany, West. I. Silberer, Günter. II. Raffée, Hans. III. Forschungsverbund "Empirische Verbraucherforschung" (Germany). IV. Universität Mannheim. Forschungsgruppe Konsumenteninformation.
HF1040.9.G3 W37 1984

Warentest und Konsumgüter-Marketing . Fritz, Wolfgang, Dipl.-Kfm. Wiesbaden , c1984. 596 p. : ISBN 3-409-13600-2 LC Card 84-207784
HF5415.2 .F75 1984

Warenwirtschaftssysteme und Warenwirtschafts-Controlling /. Ebert, Kurt, 1954- Frankfurt am Main , New York , c1986. xvi, 353 p. : ISBN 3-8204-9673-4 LC Card 86-218178
HF5415.15 .E24 1986

Warężak, Lech. Problems of decision making based on experimental data /. Wrocław , 1985. 186 p. : LC Card 86-207027
HB9 .B7522 nr. 301 QA279.4

Warfare and welfare . Tinbergen, Jan, 1903- Brighton, Sussex , New York , 1987. xiv, 189 p. ; ISBN 0-312-00957-7 (St. Martin's) : LC Card 87-9625 DDC 361.6/1 19
HB846 .T55 1987

Warfield, Gerald.
How to read and understand the financial news / Gerald Warfield. 1st ed. New York : Harper & Row, c1986. 214 p. ; 25 cm Includes index. ISBN 0-06-015647-3 : LC Card 86-45161 DDC 332.63/2042 19
1. Journalism, Commercial - United States. 2. Finance - United States. I. Title.
PN4888.C59 W37 1986 ***NYPL [JLE 87-1488]***

Venedikian, Harry M. Export-import financing /. New York , c1986. xvii, 456 p. : ISBN 0-471-82449-6 : LC Card 85-29566 DDC 332.7/42 19
HG3754.U5 V46 1986 ***NYPL [JLE 86-2998]***

Warhurst, John. Central agencies, intergovernmental managers, and Australian federal-state relations / John Warhurst. Canberra : Centre for Research on Federal Financial Relations, Australian National University, 1983. vi, 27 p. : ill. ; 25 cm. (Occasional paper / Centre for Research on Federal Financial Relations, Australian National University, 0313-5241 . no. 29) Bibliography: p. 25-27. ISBN 0-86784-318-7 (pbk.) LC Card 85-217351
1. Federal government - Australia. 2. Intergovernmental fiscal relations - Australia. I. Title.
JQ4020.S8 W28 1983 ***NYPL [JLL 82-87 no.29]***

Warmbrod, Catharine P.
Skills for the changing workplace : a business and office educator's guide / by Catharine P. Warmbrod, Frieda R. Bennett, Gail W. Cope. Columbus, Ohio (1960 Kenny Rd., Columbus 43210-1090) : National Center for Research in Vocational Education, Ohio State University, 1985. ix, 93 p. ; 28 cm. (Research and development series / National Center for Research in Vocational Education . no. 254) Bibliography: p. 79-90. LC Card 86-205907 DDC 651/.07/15 19
1. Business education. 2. Office practice - Study and teaching. I. Bennett, Frieda R. II. Cope, Gail W. III. National Center for Research in Vocational Education (U. S.). IV. Series: Research & development series , no. 254. V. Title.
HF1106 .W36 1985

Skills for the changing workplace : a marketing educator's guide / by Catharine P. Warmbrod, Marilyn J. Gordon. Columbus, Ohio (1960 Kenny Rd., Columbus 43210-1090) : National Center for Research in Vocational Education, Ohio State University, 1985. ix, 86 p. ; 28 cm. (Research and development series . no 253) Includes bibliographical references. LC Card 86-205842 DDC 658.8/007/15 19
1. Marketing - Study and teaching. I. Gordon, Marilyn J. II. National Center for Research in Vocational Education (U. S.). III. Title. IV. Series.
HF5415 .W3155 1985

Warner, Alice Sizer. Mind your own business : a guide for the information entrepreneur / Alice Sizer Warner. New York : Neal-Schuman, c1987. xii, 165 p. ; 24 cm. Includes bibliographies and index. ISBN 1-555-70014-4 : LC Card 86-23641 DDC 658.1/1 19
1. New business enterprises. 2. Entrepreneur. 3. Information consultants. 4. Information services. I. Title.
HD62.5 .W37 1987

Warner, Bill. United States. Small Business Administration. Office of Procurement and Technical Assistance. Report to the Administrator on the analysis of the management and administration of the Procurement and Technical Assistance programs /. [Washington, D.C.] , 1984. 1 v. (various pagings) : ***NYPL [JLF 86-1066]***

Warner, Malcolm.
Management reforms in China /. New York , 1987. p. cm. ISBN 0-312-00849-X : LC Card 87-4772 DDC 658/.00951 19
HD70.C5 M34 1987

Microprocessors, manpower, and society . Aldershot, Hants., England , c1984. xi, 367 p. : ISBN 0-566-00631-6 ***NYPL [JLD 86-1098]***

The warning . Granville, Joseph Ensign, 1923- New York , c1985. xvi, 397 p. ; ISBN 0-88191-034-1 : LC Card 85-13107 DDC 332.64/273 19
HG4910 .G76 1985 ***NYPL [JLE 86-3122]***

Warnke, Thomas. Albach, Horst. Kritische Wachstumsschwellen in der Unternehmensentwicklung /. Stuttgart , c1985. xxvii, 490 p. : ISBN 3-7910-5008-7 : LC Card 86-156636
HD35 .A64 1985

Warnock, John W., 1933- The politics of hunger : the global food system / John W. Warnock. Toronto ; New York : Methuen, c1987. xv, 334 p. ; 23 cm. Includes bibliographies and index. ISBN 0-458-80630-7 (pbk.) : LC Card 87-1659 DDC 363.8/09172/4 19
1. Food supply - Developing countries. 2. Agriculture - Economic aspects - Developing countries. 3. Hunger. I. Title.
HD9018.D44 W37 1987

Warrack, Brian. Keller, Gerald. Statistics for management and economics . Belmont, Calif. , c1988. xix, 987 p. : ISBN 0-534-08622-5 LC Card 87-19845 DDC 658.4/033 19
HD30.215 .K45 1988

WARRANTS, AGRICULTURAL. see **AGRICULTURAL CREDIT.**

Warren, Carl S. Fess, Philip E. Accounting principles /. Cincinnati , c1987. xxiii, 1291, [92] p. : ISBN 0-538-00300-6 LC Card 86-62984 DDC 657 19
HF5635 .F386 1987

Warrior, Betsy.
Houseworker's handbook. [Cambridge, Mass.] (c/o Women's Center, 46 Pleasant St., Cambridge 02139) [1974] 81 p. : LC Card 87-110536
HD6073.H84 H68 1974

Leghorn, Lisa. What's a wife worth? /. Somerville, Mass. [198-] 8 p. : LC Card 87-111053 DDC 331.2/8164/0973 19
HD4966.H842 U64 1980z

Slavery or a labor of love? 1980. Leghorn, Lisa. What's a wife worth? / by Lisa Leghorn & Betsy Warrior. Somerville, Mass. [198-] 8 p. : LC Card 87-111053 DDC 331.2/8164/0973 19
HD4966.H842 U64 1980z

Warriors, merchants, and slaves . Roberts, Richard L., 1949- Stanford, Calif. , 1987. xii, 293 p. : ISBN 0-8047-1378-2 (alk. paper) : LC Card 86-23138 DDC 330.966/23 19
HC1035 .R63 1987

WARS. see **WAR.**

The war's long shadow . Smith, Bradley F. New York , c1986. 319 p. ; ISBN 0-671-52434-8 LC Card 86-1870 DDC 940.5 19
D749 .S65 1986 ***NYPL [JFD 86-9433]***

Wartmann, Rudi.
Friedrich, R. (Rainer) Energie und Umwelt . Stuttgart [1985] 124 p. : LC Card 87-409533 DDC 333.79/0943/46 19
HD9502.G43 B3238 1985

Friedrich, R. (Rainer) Energie und Umwelt . Stuttgart [1985] 115 p. : LC Card 87-409534 DDC 333.79/0943/46 19
HD9502.G43 B324 1985

Warunki życia ludności w 1984 r. / [komitet redakcyjny Głównego Urzędu Statystycznego, przewodniczący Wiesław Sadowski ... et al.]. Warszawa : Główny Urząd Statystyczny, 1985. 108 p. ; 24 cm. (Statystyka Polski. Seria Studia i prace . 10) LC Card 86-225456
1. Cost and standard of living - Poland - Statistics. I. Sadowski, Wiesław. II. Poland. Główny Urząd Statystyczny. III. Series.
HD7035.7 .W35 1985

Was ist bei der Teilzeitbeschäftigung zu beachten? / [Herausgeber, Peter Dorner]. 5. Ausg., Stand, 1. Juni 1985. Wien : P. Dorner, 1985. 64 p. ; 21 cm. (Betriebs-Kurier. Schriftenreihe . 56/56a) LC Card 86-210129
1. Part-time employment - Austria. 2. Part-time employment - Law and legislation - Austria. I. Dorner, Peter. II. Series.
HD5110.2.A9 W37 1985

Was sagt mir der Buchführungsabschluss? /. Ebel, Friedhelm. Bonn , 1980. 36 p. : LC Card 84-145622
HF5686.A36 E24 1980

Was trennt Europa? / mit Beiträgen von Manfred

Caspari ... [et al.]. 1. Aufl. Baden-Baden : Nomos, 1986. 147 p. ; 23 cm. (Gespräche der List Gesellschaft e.V. . n.F., Bd. 10) Papers of the 21st List Gespräch. Includes bibliographical references. ISBN 3-7890-1320-X LC Card 87-108024 DDC 337.1/42 19
1. European Economic Community - Congresses. 2. European federation - Congresses. I. Caspari, Manfred. II. List-Gesellschaft. III. Series.
HC241.2 .W394 1986

"Was will die denn hier?" : Berufseinmündung und Berufsverlauf von Frauen mit Weiterbildung in gewerblich-technischen Berufen / Renate Wald ... [et al.]. Marburg : SP-Verlag, c1986. 156 p. ; 21 cm. Bibliography: p. 150-156. ISBN 3-924800-82-0 LC Card 87-122751 DDC 331.4/0943 19
1. Sexual division of labor - Germany (West). 2. Sex role in the work environment - Germany (West). 3. Sex discrimination in employment - Germany, West. 4. Women - Employment - Germany, West. I. Wald, Renate.
HD6060.65.G3 W37 1986

Was wird in den besetzten Häusern gemacht? : eine Dokumentation am Beispiel von 13 besetzten Häusern. Berlin : Architekteninitiative Schöneberger Planung, [1982]. 65 p. : ill. ; 29 cm. Cover title.
1. Housing - Berlin (Germany). 2. Squatters - Berlin (Germany). ***NYPL [JLF 87-439]***

Wäscher, Gerhard. Innerbetriebliche Standortplanung bei einfacher und mehrfacher Zielsetzung / Gerhard Wäscher. Wiesbaden : Gabler, c1982. 389 p. : ill. ; 24 cm. (Bochumer Beiträge zur Unternehmungsführung und Unternehmensforschung. Bd. 25) Bibliography: p. 375-389. ISBN 3-409-34487-X LC Card 86-105991
1. Industry - Location - Mathematical models. I. Title. II. Series.
HD58 .W29 1982

Washington, D. C. American Psychological Association, inc. see **American Psychological Association.**

Washington, D. C. Brookings Institution. see **Brookings Institution, Washington, D. C.**

WASHINGTON, D. C. - ECONOMIC CONDITIONS.
Grier, George W. Greater Washington at mid decade . Washington, DC (1717 Massachusetts Ave., N.W., Washington 20036-2076) , c1985- v. <1 > : LC Card 86-200647 DDC 338.5/443/09753 19
HC108.W3 G73 1985

Washington, D. C. Government Finance Research Center. see **Government Finance Research Center, Washington, D. C.**

Washington, D. C. Highway Loss Data Institute. see **Highway Loss Data Institute.**

Washington, D. C. National Airport. see **Washington National Airport.**

WASHINGTON, D. C. - POPULATION.
Grier, George W. Greater Washington at mid decade . Washington, DC (1717 Massachusetts Ave., N.W., Washington 20036-2076) , c1985- v. <1 > : LC Card 86-200647 DDC 338.5/443/09753 19
HC108.W3 G73 1985

Washington, D.C. taxicab zone fare guide. Sullivan, Novell B. [United States] , c1984. 86 p., [1] folded leaf of plates : LC Card 86-224478 DDC 388.4/1321 19
HE5634.W3 S93 1984

Washington, D. C. Worldwatch Institute. see **Worldwatch Institute.**

WASHINGTON DULLES INTERNATIONAL AIRPORT - OFFICIALS AND EMPLOYEES.

Washington Institute for Values in Public Policy. The Nuclear connection . New York , 1985. 295 p. : ISBN 0-88702-204-9 : LC Card 84-26786 DDC 333.79/24 19
HD9698.A2 N77 1985 ***NYPL [JLE 86-1546]***

WASHINGTON METROPOLITAN AREA - ECONOMIC CONDITIONS.
Langford, Jay. Economic trends in metropolitan Washington, 1980-1985 ; [author, Jay Langford, Vetoria S. Alston]. Washington, D.C. (1875 Eye St., NW., Suite 200, Washington 20006) , c1986. viii, 68 p. : LC Card 87-105032 DDC 330.9753/04 19
HC108.W3 L36 1986

WASHINGTON METROPOLITAN AREA - ECONOMIC CONDITIONS - STATISTICS.
Langford, Jay. Economic trends in metropolitan Washington, 1980-1985 ; [author, Jay Langford, Vetoria S. Alston]. Washington, D.C. (1875 Eye St., NW., Suite 200, Washington 20006) , c1986. viii, 68 p. : LC Card 87-105032 DDC 330.9753/04 19
HC108.W3 L36 1986

WASHINGTON METROPOLITAN AREA - POPULATION - STATISTICS.
Growth trends to the year 2010. Washington, D.C. , c1986. i, 32 p. : LC Card 87-129483 DDC 304.6/2/09753021 19
HA305 .G76 1986

Growth trends to the year 2010. Washington, D.C. , c1986. i, 9 p. : LC Card 87-153125 DDC 304.6/2/09753021 19
HA305 .G77 1986

Washington Metropolitan Regional Conference. see **Metropolitan Washington Council of Governments.**

Washington Middle East Associates. Hunter, Jane, 1943- Undercutting sanctions . Washington, DC (918 16th St. NW, Suite 501, Washington 20006) , c1987. iv, 71 p. ; LC Card 87-403525 DDC 337.68 19
HF1613.4 .H86 1987

WASHINGTON NATIONAL AIRPORT - OFFICIALS AND EMPLOYEES.

The Washington papers, 0278-937X .
(124) Shinn, William T., 1936- The decline of the Russian peasant household /. New York , 1987. xvii, 122 p. ; ISBN 0-275-92767-9 (alk. paper) LC Card 87-2554 DDC 338.1/0947 19
HD1992 .S4735 1987

Washington Researchers Publishing.
How to find company intelligence in state documents /. Washington, D.C. , c1986. 110 p. ; ISBN 0-934940-38-X (pbk.) LC Card 86-218108 DDC 016.3387/4/0973 19
HD2785 .H67 1986

How to find information about companies in the telecommunications, data processing, and office automation industries /. Washington, DC , c1987. ii, 130 p. ; ISBN 0-934940-48-7 (pbk.) LC Card 86-51630 DDC 338.7/61004/072073 19
HD9696.A3 U559 1987

How to find information about executives /. Washington, DC , c1986. 72 p. ; ISBN 0-934940-44-4 (pbk.) : LC Card 86-51569 DDC 658.4/0072 19
HD38.25.U6 H69 1986

How to find information about foreign firms /. Washington, D.C. , c1987. 93 p. ; ISBN 0-934940-46-0 (pbk.) : LC Card 86-51568 DDC 016.3388/8873 19
HD2785 .H69 1987

How to find information about private companies /. Washington, DC , c1987. iii, 149 p. ; ISBN 0-934940-47-9 (pbk.) : LC Card 86-51566 DDC 016.3387/4/0973 19
HG4013.5 .H69 1987

Rosenberg, Gerald I. How to find information about acquisition candidates /. Washington, D.C. , c1987. 79 p. ; ISBN 0-934940-45-2 LC Card 86-51570 DDC 016.3387/4/0973 19
HD2785 .R58 1987

Who knows about industries and markets /. Washington, D.C. , c1986. 54 p. ; ISBN 0-934940-33-9 (pbk.) LC Card 86-217691 DDC 338/.06/072073 19
HC102.2 .W48 1986

Washington sodas . Fowler, Ron. Seattle , c1986. iv, 380 p. : LC Card 86-219084 DDC 338.4/766362/09797 19
HD9349.S633 U635 1986

Washington (State). Accountancy, Board of. see **Washington (State). Board of Accountancy.**

WASHINGTON (STATE). BOARD OF ACCOUNTANCY. (Old Catalog form: Washington (State). Accountancy, Board of.)
Washington (State). Legislature. Legislative Budget Committee. Program and fiscal review . Olympia (506 E. 16th Ave., Olympia 98504) [1985] v, 69 p. ; LC Card 86-621785 DDC 353.97970072/32 s 353.97970082/43 19
HJ11 .W2453 no. 85-13 KFN329.A25

Washington (State). Dept. of Community Development. Joint development financing for public works . Olympia, Wash. (9th & Columbia Bldg., MS/GH-51, Olympia 98504) [1986] 1 v. (various pagings) : LC Card 86-622101 DDC 338.4/3363/09797 19
HD3890.W2 J65 1986

Washington (State). Dept. of Personnel. (Old Catalog form: Washington (State). Personnel Dept.)
Part-time employment study : report to the Washington State Legislature / prepared by Department of Personnel, Department of Retirement Systems, [and] Higher Education Personnel Board. Olympia, Wash. (600 S. Franklin, FE-11, Olympia 98504) : Dept. of Personnel, [1984] xi, 82 p. : ill. ; 28 cm. "December 1984." LC Card 85-621558 DDC 331.25/72 19
1. Part-time employment - Washington (State). 2. Employee fringe benefits - Washington (State). I. Washington (State). Dept. of Retirement Systems. II. Washington (State). Higher Education Personnel Board. III. Title.
HD5110.2.U52 W29 1984
NYPL [JLF 86-517]

Washington (State). Dept. of Retirement Systems. Washington (State). Dept. of Personnel. Part-time employment study . Olympia, Wash. (600 S. Franklin, FE-11, Olympia 98504) [1984] xi, 82 p. : LC Card 85-621558 DDC 331.25/72 19
HD5110.2.U52 W29 1984
NYPL [JLF 86-517]

Washington (State). Epidemiology Section. Injury deaths in Washington State, 1968-1983 . Seattle, Wash. (1610 NE 150th, Seattle 98155) [1985] 49, [78] p. : LC Card 86-623057 DDC 363.1/02/09797021 19
HB1323.A22 U65 1985

Washington (State). Governor's Citizens Utility and Telecommunication Advisory Committee. Utilities in transition : citizens' perspective : report / by the Governor's Citizens Utility and Telecommunication Advisory Committee. [Olympia, Wash.] : The Committee, [1984] 61, 18, [20] p. ; 28 cm. "December 1984." Bibliography: p. 1-8 (3rd group) LC Card 85-622797 DDC 363.6/09797 19
1. Telecommunication policy - Washington (State). 2. Public utilities - Government policy - Washington (State). I. Title.
HE7791.W2 W37 1984
NYPL [JLF 86-1773]

Washington (State). Higher Education Personnel Board. Washington (State). Dept. of Personnel. Part-time employment study . Olympia, Wash. (600 S. Franklin, FE-11, Olympia 98504) [1984] xi, 82 p. : LC Card 85-621558 DDC 331.25/72 19
HD5110.2.U52 W29 1984
NYPL [JLF 86-517]

Washington (State). Legislature. Legislative Budget Committee. Program and fiscal review : Board of Accountancy : a report to the Washington State Legislature. Olympia (506 E. 16th Ave., Olympia 98504) : Legislative Budget Committee, [1985] v, 69 p. ; 28 cm. (Report / State of Washington Legislative Budget Committee . no. 85-13.) Cover title. "November 1985." LC Card 86-621785 DDC 353.97970072/32 s 353.97970082/43 19
1. Accountants - Legal status, laws, etc. - Washington (State). 2. Washington (State). Board of Accountancy. 3. Accountants - Washington (State). I. Series: Report (Washington (State). Legislature. Legislative Budget Committee) , no. 85-13. II. Title.
HJ11 .W2453 no. 85-13 KFN329.A25

Washington (State). Personnel Dept. see **Washington (State). Dept. of Personnel.**

WASHINGTON (STATE) - PUBLIC WORKS - FINANCE.
Joint development financing for public works . Olympia, Wash. (9th & Columbia Bldg., MS/GH-51, Olympia 98504) [1986] 1 v. (various pagings) : LC Card 86-622101 DDC 338.4/3363/09797 19
HD3890.W2 J65 1986

Washington (State). Puget Sound Water Quality Authority. Industrial and municipal discharges. Seattle, Wash. (217 Pine St., Ste 1100, Seattle 98101) [1986] viii, 136, 14 p. : LC Card 86-622616 DDC 363.7/31 19
HC107.W22 P85 1986

Washington (State). State Board of Accountancy. see **Washington (State). Board of Accountancy.**

Washington University (Saint Louis, Mo.). Center for the Study of American Business. Public policy toward corporate takeovers /. New Brunswick (USA) , c1988. xvi, 176 p. ; ISBN 0-88738-166-9 : LC Card 87-10750 DDC 338.8/3/0973 19
HD2795 .P825 1988

Wasik, John F. The electronic business information sourcebook / John F. Wasik. New York : Wiley, c1987. xvi, 208 p. ; 24 cm. Bibliography: p. 181-182. Includes index. ISBN 0-471-62464-0 : LC Card 87-8289 DDC 026/.65 19
1. Business - Data bases. 2. Business - Information services. 3. Data base searching. I. Title.
HF5548.2 .W324 1987

Die Wasser-, Boden- und Deichverbände in Ost- und Westpreussen, 1868 bis 1938 /. Herrgeist, Fritz, 1895-1980. Köln , 1983. 524 p. : ISBN 3-7745-6456-6 LC Card 84-211844
HD1697.P64 P784 1983

Wasser konkret . Geiler, Nick. Wiesbaden [1985] 199 p. : LC Card 86-162674
HD1697.G33 H474 1985

Wasserman, Dick. How to get your first copywriting job in advertising / Dick Wasserman. New York : E.P. Dutton, 1987. viii, 199 p. : ill. ; 23 cm. ISBN 0-525-48281-4 (pbk.) : LC Card 86-72833 DDC 659.13/22/02373 19
1. Advertising copy. I. Title.
HF5825 .W29 1987

Wasserman, Gary, 1944- U. S. aid to Zimbabwe : an evaluation / by Gary Wasserman, team leader ; John Pielemeier, Lucretia Taylor, Michael C. Hager. [Washington, D.C.?] : U. S. Agency for International Development, [1983] ix, 20, [71] p. ; 28 cm. (A.I.D. project evaluation report . no. 9) "August 1983." "PN-AAJ-605"--Cover. LC Card 87-109216 DDC 338.91/73/06891 19
1. Economic assistance, American - Zimbabwe. 2. Zimbabwe - Economic conditions - 1980-. 3. Zimbabwe - Politics and government - 1980-. I. Series: A.I.D. program evaluation report , no. 9. II. Title.
HC910 .W37 1983

Wasserman, Steven R. Financial planners and planning organizations directory . Detroit, Mich. , c1987. viii, 605 p. ; ISBN 0-8103-4397-5 : LC Card 87-21259 DDC 332.6/2 19
HG179.5 .F56 1987

Wasserstrom, Robert. Grassroots development in Latin America & the Caribbean . New York , 1985. vii, 197 p. : ISBN 0-03-001689-4 (alk. paper) : LC Card 84-18180 DDC 334/.098 19
HD3450.5.A4 G72 1985

Wassmann, Herbert, 1947- Dobischat, Rolf, 1950- Berufliche Weiterbildung, Arbeitsmarkt und Region . Frankfurt am Main , New York , c1985. 691 p. : ISBN 3-8204-5673-2 LC Card 86-158931
HD5715.5.G42 H473 1985

WASTE, DISPOSAL OF. see **FACTORY AND TRADE WASTE; REFUSE AND REFUSE DISPOSAL; SEWAGE DISPOSAL.**

WASTE DISPOSAL SITES - ECONOMIC ASPECTS - MADAGASCAR - ANTANANARIVO.
Camacho, Martine. Les poubelles de la survie . Paris , c1986. 207 p. : ISBN 2-85802-590-5 LC Card 86-180208
HC895.Z7 A443 1986

WASTE (ECONOMICS) - GERMANY (WEST)
Mahler, Karl-Werner, 1933- Der Waste Factor . München-Gräfelfing , c1983. 64 p. ; ISBN 3-8040-0321-4 LC Card 84-214297
HC290.5.W3 M34 1983

Der Waste Factor . Mahler, Karl-Werner, 1933- München-Gräfelfing , c1983. 64 p. ; ISBN 3-8040-0321-4 LC Card 84-214297
HC290.5.W3 M34 1983

WASTE IN GOVERNMENT SPENDING - UNITED STATES.
Fraud, waste, and abuse in government . Philadelphia , c1986. x, 159 p. ; ISBN 0-89727-058-4 LC Card 86-2967 DDC 336.73 19
HJ257.2 .F72 1986 ***NYPL [JLE 86-4153]***

Waste lands. Wastelands . New Delhi , 1987. xii, 249 p. : LC Card 86-903086 DDC 333.73 19
HD1671.I5W37 1987

WASTE LANDS - INDIA.
Wastelands . New Delhi , 1987. xii, 249 p. : LC Card 86-903086 DDC 333.73 19
HD1671.I5W37 1987

WASTE RECYCLING. see **RECYCLING (WASTE, ETC.)**

WASTE REUSE. see **RECYCLING (WASTE, ETC.)**

Wastelands : diagnosis and treatment / [editor] Hridai R. Yadav. New Delhi : Concept Pub. Co., 1987. xii, 249 p. : ill. ; 23 cm. Spine title: Waste lands. With reference to India; contributed papers. Includes bibliographies. LC Card 86-903086 DDC 333.73 19
1. Waste lands - India. 2. Reclamation of land - India. I. Yadav, Hridai Ram, 1957-. II. Title. III. Title: Waste lands.
HD1671.I5W37 1987

WASTES, HAZARDOUS. see **HAZARDOUS WASTES.**

Watanabe, Susumu. Microelectronics, automation, and employment in the automobile industry /. Chichester [West Sussex] , New York , c1987. xix, 203 p. : ISBN 0-471-91484-3 : LC Card 86-32532 DDC 331.7/6292 19
HD8039.A8 M52 1987

WATCH MAKING. see **CLOCK AND WATCH MAKING.**

Water and poverty in the Southwest /. Brown, F. Lee (Franklin Lee) Tucson , c1987. xi, 226 p. : ISBN 0-8165-1038-5 (alk. paper) : LC Card 87-19217 DDC 333.91/00979 19
HD1695.A165 B76 1987

Water and water policy in world food supplies : proceedings of the conference, May 26-30, 1985, Texas A&M University, College Station, Texas / editor, Wayne R. Jordon.1st ed. College Station : Texas A&M University Press, c1987. x, 434 p. : ill. ; 29 cm. Includes bibliographies. ISBN 0-89096-278-2 : LC Card 86-23065 DDC 333.91/3 19
1. Water-supply, Agricultural - Government policy - Congresses. 2. Irrigation - Government policy - Congresses. 3. Water resources development - Government policy - Congresses. 4. Water quality management - Government policy - Congresses. I. Jordan, Wayne R., 1940-.
HD1690.5 .W38 1987

Water Authority of Western Australia.
Water Authority of Western Australia Corporate plan, 1986-1991. Appendix C, asset investment program / Water Authority of Western Australia. Leederville, W.A. : John Tonkin Water Centre, [1986] 42 p. ; 30 cm. LC Card 87-158833 DDC 354.9410082/325 19
1. Water resources development - Australia - Western Australia - Finance. 2. Municipal water supply - Australia - Western Australia - Finance. 3. Sewage disposal - Australia - Western Australia - Finance. 4. Irrigation water - Australia - Western Australia - Finance. 5. Water Authority of Western Australia - Appropriations and expenditures. I. Title.
HD1700.W4 W38 1986

WATER AUTHORITY OF WESTERN AUSTRALIA - APPROPRIATIONS AND EXPENDITURES.
Water Authority of Western Australia. Water Authority of Western Australia Corporate plan, 1986-1991. Appendix C, asset investment program /. Leederville, W.A. [1986] 42 p. ; LC Card 87-158833 DDC 354.9410082/325 19
HD1700.W4 W38 1986

Water Authority of Western Australia Corporate plan, 1986-1991. Appendix C, asset investment program /. Water Authority of Western Australia. Leederville, W.A. [1986] 42 p. ; LC Card 87-158833 DDC 354.9410082/325 19
HD1700.W4 W38 1986

WATER CONSERVATION - GOVERNMENT POLICY - GERMANY (WEST) - HESSE.
Geiler, Nick. Wasser konkret . Wiesbaden [1985] 199 p. : LC Card 86-162674
HD1697.G33 H474 1985

WATER CONSERVATION - GOVERNMENT POLICY - UNITED STATES.
Black, Peter E. Conservation of water and related land resources /. Totowa, N.J. , 1987. xvi, 336 p. : ISBN 0-8476-7567-X LC Card 87-4770 DDC 333.91/16/0973 19
HD1694 .A5105 1987

WATER CONSERVATION - LAW AND LEGISLATION - BRAZIL - SÃO PAULO (STATE)
Sócrates, Jodete Rios. A cidade invade as águas . [São Paulo] , 1985. 296 p., [2] folded leaves of plates : LC Card 87-118596 DDC 333.91/00981/61 19
HD1696.B84 S427 1985

WATER CONSERVATION - WEST (U. S.)
Energy and water management in western irrigated agriculture /. Boulder, Colo. , 1986. xxiv, 415 p. : ISBN 0-8133-7086-8 (pbk. : alk. paper) LC Card 85-52184 DDC 333.91/3/0978 19
HD1735 .E54 1986 ***NYPL [JLD 87-829]***

WATER CONSUMPTION - COLORADO RIVER WATERSHED (COLO.-MEXICO) - CONGRESSES.
New courses for the Colorado River . Albuquerque , c1986. xx, 253 p. : ISBN 0-8263-0854-6 LC Card 85-24577 DDC 333.91/009791/3 19
HD1695.C7 N49 1986 ***NYPL [JLE 86-1736]***

WATER CONSUMPTION - DENMARK.
Lauritzen, Niels, 1947- Rapporter /. København [1983] 59 p. : ISBN 87-503-4574-5 LC Card 84-169893
HD4465.D4 L38 1983

Rapporter udarbejdet af Forvaltningshøjskolen og Miljøstyrelsens økonomifunktion. København [1983] 59 p. : ISBN 87-503-4574-5 LC Card 85-150558
HD4465.D4 R36 1983

Teknisk-økonomisk-organisatorisk analyse /. København [1983] 131 p. : ISBN 87-503-4561-3 LC Card 84-169883
HD4465.D4 T44 1983

WATER CONSUMPTION - FORECASTING - CONGRESSES.
Water demand forecasting . Norwich, U.K. , c1986. 139 p. : ISBN 0-86094-214-7 : LC Card 87-127184 DDC 333.91/13 19
HD1690.5 .W383 1986

Water control in Tokugawa Japan . Kelly, William W. (William Wright), 1946- Ithaca, N.Y. , c1982. ix, 260 p. : LC Card 83-126822
HD1741.J32 A325 1982

Water demand forecasting : proceedings of a workshop / sponsored by the Economic and Social Research Council ; edited by Vince Gardiner and Paul Herrington. Norwich, U.K. : Geo Books, c1986. 139 p. : ill. ; 22 cm. Includes bibliographies. ISBN 0-86094-214-7 : LC Card 87-127184 DDC 333.91/13 19
1. Water consumption - Forecasting - Congresses. I. Gardiner, V. II. Herrington, Paul. III. Economic and Social Research Council (Great Britain).
HD1690.5 .W383 1986

WATER DISTRICTS - POLAND - PRUSSIA, WEST - HISTORY.
Herrgeist, Fritz, 1895-1980. Die Wasser-, Boden- und Deichverbände in Ost- und Westpreussen, 1868 bis 1938 /. Köln , 1983. 524 p. : ISBN 3-7745-6456-6 LC Card 84-211844
HD1697.P64 P784 1983

WATER DISTRICTS - PRUSSIA, EAST (POLAND AND R.S.F.S.R.) - HISTORY.
Herrgeist, Fritz, 1895-1980. Die Wasser-, Boden- und Deichverbände in Ost- und Westpreussen, 1868 bis 1938 /. Köln , 1983. 524 p. : ISBN 3-7745-6456-6 LC Card 84-211844
HD1697.P64 P784 1983

WATER FRONTS. see **WATERFRONTS.**

WATER, GROUND. see **WATER, UNDERGROUND.**

Water in New Mexico . Clark, Ira G. Albuquerque , c1987. xviii, 839 p. : ISBN 0-8263-0923-2 LC Card 86-30819 DDC 333.91/009789 19
HD1694.N6 C42 1987

WATER - LAW AND LEGISLATION - DENMARK.
Denmark. Udvalget til undersøgelse af vandforsyningernes økonomiske baggrund. Vandpriser . København [1983] 108 p. ; ISBN 87-503-4559-1 LC Card 84-169901
HD4465.D4 D46 1983

Water markets in theory and practice . Saliba, Bonnie. Boulder , 1987. viii, 273 p. : ISBN 0-8133-7465-0 (pbk. : alk. paper) : LC Card 87-21687 DDC 333.91/00979 19
HD1695.A165 S25 1987

WATER - POLLUTION.
(1986) Keating, Michael, 1943- To the last drop . Toronto, Ont., Canada , c1986. xviii, 265 p. : ISBN 0-7715-9704-5 LC Card 86-224945 DDC 363.7/394/0971 19
HC120.W32 K43 1986

WATER - POLLUTION - CANADA.
Keating, Michael, 1943- To the last drop . Toronto, Ont., Canada , c1986. xviii, 265 p. : ISBN 0-7715-9704-5 LC Card 86-224945 DDC 363.7/394/0971 19
HC120.W32 K43 1986

WATER - POLLUTION - LAW AND LEGISLATION - ITALY.
Lewanski, Rodolfo. Il controllo degli inquinamenti delle acque . Milano , 1986. 194 p. : ISBN 88-14-00753-5 : LC Card 86-160300
HC310.W32 L48 1986

WATER - POLLUTION - UNITED STATES.
Morandi, Larry B. Renewing resources . Denver, Colo. , 1984. vii, 133 p. ;
NYPL [JSF 86-712]

WATER - POLLUTION - WASHINGTON (STATE) - PUGET SOUND REGION.
Industrial and municipal discharges. Seattle, Wash. (217 Pine St., Ste 1100, Seattle 98101) [1986] viii, 136, 14 p. : LC Card 86-622616 DDC 363.7/31 19
HC107.W22 P85 1986

WATER-POWER ELECTRIC PLANTS. see **HYDROELECTRIC POWER PLANTS.**

WATER QUALITY MANAGEMENT - COLORADO RIVER WATERSHED (COLO.-MEXICO) - CONGRESSES.
New courses for the Colorado River . Albuquerque , c1986. xx, 253 p. : ISBN 0-8263-0854-6 LC Card 85-24577 DDC 333.91/009791/3 19
HD1695.C7 N49 1986 ***NYPL [JLE 86-1736]***

WATER QUALITY MANAGEMENT - FINANCE.
Herrington, Paul. Pricing of water services /. Paris , Washington, D.C. , 1987. 145 p. : ISBN 92-64-12921-9 (pbk.) : LC Card 87-167536 DDC 338.4/336361 19
HD4456 .H47 1987

WATER QUALITY MANAGEMENT - GOVERNMENT POLICY - CONGRESSES.
Water and water policy in world food supplies . College Station , c1987. x, 434 p. : ISBN 0-89096-278-2 : LC Card 86-23065 DDC 333.91/3 19
HD1690.5 .W38 1987

WATER QUALITY MANAGEMENT - GOVERNMENT POLICY - GERMANY (WEST) - HESSE.
Geiler, Nick. Wasser konkret . Wiesbaden [1985] 199 p. : LC Card 86-162674
HD1697.G33 H474 1985

WATER QUALITY MANAGEMENT - GOVERNMENT POLICY - ITALY.
Lewanski, Rodolfo. Il controllo degli inquinamenti delle acque . Milano , 1986. 194 p. : ISBN 88-14-00753-5 : LC Card 86-160300
HC310.W32 L48 1986

WATER QUALITY MANAGEMENT - GOVERNMENT POLICY - MEXICO - MEXICO CITY METROPOLITAN AREA.
Schmengler, Uwe. Umweltprobleme des Ballungsraums Mexiko Stadt unter besonderer Berücksichtigung der Wasserwirtschaft /. [Berlin , 1985] 120, [16] leaves : LC Card 86-116997
HC138.M4 S35 1985

WATER QUALITY MANAGEMENT - GOVERNMENT POLICY - NEW JERSEY.

WATER QUALITY MANAGEMENT - GOVERNMENT POLICY - WASHINGTON (STATE) - PUGET SOUND REGION.
Industrial and municipal discharges. Seattle, Wash. (217 Pine St., Ste 1100, Seattle 98101) [1986] viii, 136, 14 p. : LC Card 86-622616 DDC 363.7/31 19
HC107.W22 P85 1986

WATER QUALITY MANAGEMENT - MEXICO - MEXICO CITY METROPOLITAN AREA.
Schmengler, Uwe. Umweltprobleme des Ballungsraums Mexiko Stadt unter besonderer Berücksichtigung der Wasserwirtschaft /. [Berlin , 1985] 120, [16] leaves : LC Card 86-116997
HC138.M4 S35 1985

WATER QUALITY MANAGEMENT - TURKMEN S.S.R.
Ataev, M. (Murruk) Gosudarstvennoe upravlenie ispol′zovaniem i okhranoĭ vod /. Ashkhabad , 1982. 175 p. ; LC Card 82-244366
HD1697.S653 T873 1982

WATER RESOURCE DEVELOPMENT - BRAZIL.
Brazil. Inspectoria Federal de Obras contra as Seccas. Relatorio dos trabalhos executados durante o anno de 1925 . Rio de Janeiro , 1926. xiv, 75 p. ; LC Card 85-186786
HD1696.B8 B73 1926

WATER RESOURCES DEVELOPMENT - AFRICA - CONGRESSES.
Regional Meeting on Socio-economic and Policy Aspects of Water Resources Management in Africa (1986 : Addis Ababa, Ethiopia) Regional Meeting on Socio-economic and Policy Aspects of Water Resources Management in Africa, 2-7 June 1986, Addis Ababa, Ethiopia /. [Addis Ababa?] [1986] 19 v. : LC Card 86-981006 DDC 333.91/0096 19
HD1699.A1 R44 1986

WATER RESOURCES DEVELOPMENT - ARGENTINA - SAN JUAN (PROVINCE) - HISTORY.
Marzo, Miguel. La conquista del espacio territorial sanjuanino /. Mendoza , 1968. 89 p., [12] leaves of plates : LC Card 82-166187
HD479.S25 M37 1968

WATER RESOURCES DEVELOPMENT - AUSTRALIA - WESTERN AUSTRALIA - FINANCE.
Water Authority of Western Australia. Water Authority of Western Australia Corporate plan, 1986-1991. Appendix C, asset investment program /. Leederville, W.A. [1986] 42 p. ; LC Card 87-158833 DDC 354.9410082/325 19
HD1700.W4 W38 1986

WATER RESOURCES DEVELOPMENT - BRAZIL - CASE STUDIES.
Brazil. Ministério do Interior. Subsecretaria de Programas Regionais. Minutas das exposições de motivos e portarias dos programas . [Brasília] [1983?] [40] leaves ; LC Card 87-400579 DDC 333.91/15/0981 19
HD1696.B8 B75 1983

WATER RESOURCES DEVELOPMENT - BRAZIL, NORTHEAST.
A Problemática e a política da terra e água do Nordeste. Recife , 1985. 296 p. : LC Card 87-124121 DDC 333.91/00981/3 19
HD1696.B84 N675 1985

Projeto sertanejo . [Brasília] [1982?] 20 leaves, [1] leaf of plates : LC Card 87-405007
HD1875.N6 P76 1982

WATER RESOURCES DEVELOPMENT - BRAZIL - PIAUÍ.
Atuação dos programas especiais no Estado do Piauí /. [Brasília] [1980] [29] leaves : LC Card 87-403685 DDC 333.91/0098122 19
HD1696.B83 P523 1980

Projeto sertanejo . [Brasília] [1982?] 20 leaves, [1] leaf of plates : LC Card 87-405007
HD1875.N6 P76 1982

WATER RESOURCES DEVELOPMENT - BRAZIL - SAÕ FRANCISCO RIVER WATERSHED - CONGRESSES.
Lopes, Marcos José. Atendimento ao mercado de energia elétrica do Nordeste /. Recife, PE [1984] 2 v. in 4 : LC Card 86-166126
HD9685.B83 N675 1984

WATER RESOURCES DEVELOPMENT - GOVERNMENT POLICY - ASIA - CONGRESSES.
Regional Symposium on Water Resoures Policy in Agro-Socio-Economic Development (1985 : Dhaka, Bangladesh) Water resources policy for Asia . Rotterdam , Boston , 1987. xii, 627 p. : ISBN 90-6191-684-4 LC Card 87-170039 DDC 333.91/0095 19
HD1698.A1 R45 1985

WATER RESOURCES DEVELOPMENT - GOVERNMENT POLICY - BRAZIL, NORTHEAST.
Brazil. Ministério do Interior. Subsecretaria de Programas Regionais. Programa de aproveitamento de recursos hídricos do Nordeste . Brasília [1980] [73] leaves ; LC Card 87-403686 DDC 333.91/00981/3 19
HD1696.B84 N649 1980

Secas no Nordeste, 1979-1983 . Recife , 1983. 48 p. : LC Card 86-168746
HD1696.B84 N685 1983

WATER RESOURCES DEVELOPMENT - GOVERNMENT POLICY - CONGRESSES.
Water and water policy in world food supplies . College Station , c1987. x, 434 p. : ISBN 0-89096-278-2 : LC Card 86-23065 DDC 333.91/3 19
HD1690.5 .W38 1987

WATER RESOURCES DEVELOPMENT - GOVERNMENT POLICY - GERMANY (WEST) - HESSE.
Geiler, Nick. Wasser konkret . Wiesbaden [1985] 199 p. : LC Card 86-162674
HD1697.G33 H474 1985

WATER RESOURCES DEVELOPMENT - GOVERNMENT POLICY - NEW MEXICO - HISTORY.
Clark, Ira G. Water in New Mexico . Albuquerque , c1987. xviii, 839 p. : ISBN 0-8263-0923-2 LC Card 86-30819 DDC 333.91/009789 19
HD1694.N6 C42 1987

WATER RESOURCES DEVELOPMENT - GOVERNMENT POLICY - UNITED STATES.
American Society of Civil Engineers. Task Committee on Federal Policies in Water Resources Planning. Federal policies in water resources planning /. New York, N.Y. , c1985. 61 p. : ISBN 0-87262-465-X (pbk.) LC Card 85-71265 DDC 333.91/15/0973 19
HD1694.A5 A67 1985
NYPL [JLD 86-4066]

Energy and water management in western irrigated agriculture /. Boulder, Colo. , 1986. xxiv, 415 p. : ISBN 0-8133-7086-8 (pbk. : alk. paper) LC Card 85-52184 DDC 333.91/3/0978 19
HD1735 .E54 1986 ***NYPL [JLD 87-829]***

WATER RESOURCES DEVELOPMENT - GOVERNMENT POLICY - WEST (U. S.) - HISTORY.
Reisner, Marc. Cadillac desert . New York, N.Y., U. S.A. , 1987, c1986. 582 p., [18] p. of plates : ISBN 0-14-010432-1 (pbk.) : LC Card 87-7602 DDC 333.91/00978 19
HD1739.A17 R45 1987

WATER RESOURCES DEVELOPMENT - HUNGARY.
A Vízgazdálkodás távlati fejlesztésének prognózisai /. Budapest , 1983. 176 p. : ISBN 963-602-278-X LC Card 85-109619
HD1697.H8 V59 1983

WATER RESOURCES DEVELOPMENT - ITALY - CONGRESSES.
Convegno nazionale "Qualche idea sui fiumi" (1983 : Iesi, Italy) Atti del Convegno nazionale "Qualche idea sui fiumi," Jesi, aprile 1983. Ancona , c1983-c1984. 2 v. ; ISBN 88-7663-030-9 (v. 1) : LC Card 84-119835
HD1697.I8 C62 1983 ***NYPL [JLK 87-40]***

WATER RESOURCES DEVELOPMENT - JAPAN - AKA RIVER WATERSHED - HISTORY.
Kelly, William W. (William Wright), 1946- Water control in Tokugawa Japan . Ithaca, N.Y. , c1982. ix, 260 p. : LC Card 83-126822
HD1741.J32 A325 1982

WATER RESOURCES DEVELOPMENT - KENYA - KITUI (DISTRICT)
Nilsson, Roy. Kitui water resources development study . Nairobi, Kenya [1982] 13, [31] leaves : LC Card 85-980998 DDC 333.91/009676/24 19
HD1699.K42 K586 1982

WATER RESOURCES DEVELOPMENT - KENYA - NYANZA PROVINCE.
Kenya. Lake Basin Development Authority. A socio-cultural investigation into the use and functioning of the completed shallow wells in Nyanza Province /. Kisumu, [Kenya] , 1983. 2 v. ; LC Card 84-983298 DDC 333.91/009676/29 19
HD1699.K42 N935 1983 ***NYPL [JLF 86-575]***

WATER RESOURCES DEVELOPMENT - NIGER.
Funel, Jean Marie. Politiques d'aménagement hydro-agricole /. Paris , c1980. 212 p. : ISBN 2-85319-083-8 LC Card 86-112826
HD1699.S37 F86 1980

WATER RESOURCES DEVELOPMENT - PARANÁ RIVER REGION (BRAZIL-ARGENTINA)
Obras hidroeléctricas binacionales en América Latina. [Buenos Aires, Argentina] , 1985. vii leaves, 385 p., 3 leaves of plates : LC Card 86-180644
HD1696.A7 O27 1985

WATER RESOURCES DEVELOPMENT - PERU.
Buroz Castillo, Eduardo. Programa de cooperación técnica Perú-Venezuela-OEA . Caracas , 1976. [11], 62 p. ; LC Card 84-136478
HD1696.P5 B87 1976

WATER RESOURCES DEVELOPMENT - RIO DE LA PLATA REGION (ARGENTINA AND URUGUAY)
Obras hidroeléctricas binacionales en América Latina. [Buenos Aires, Argentina] , 1985. vii leaves, 385 p., 3 leaves of plates : LC Card 86-180644
HD1696.A7 O27 1985

WATER RESOURCES DEVELOPMENT - SENEGAL.
Funel, Jean Marie. Politiques d'aménagement hydro-agricole /. Paris , c1980. 212 p. : ISBN 2-85319-083-8 LC Card 86-112826
HD1699.S37 F86 1980

WATER RESOURCES DEVELOPMENT - SOCIAL ASPECTS - BRAZIL - SÃO FRANCISCO RIVER REGION.
Sigaud, Lygia. Efeitos sociais de grandes projetos hidrelétricos . [Rio de Janeiro] , 1986. 116 p. ; LC Card 87-120281 DDC 333.91/4 19
HD1696.B84 S346 1986

WATER RESOURCES DEVELOPMENT - SOCIAL ASPECTS - BRAZIL - URUGUAY RIVER REGION.
Sigaud, Lygia. Efeitos sociais de grandes projetos hidrelétricos . [Rio de Janeiro] , 1986. 116 p. ; LC Card 87-120281 DDC 333.91/4 19
HD1696.B84 S346 1986

WATER RESOURCES DEVELOPMENT - SOCIAL ASPECTS - KENYA - NYANZA PROVINCE.
Kenya. Lake Basin Development Authority. A socio-cultural investigation into the use and functioning of the completed shallow wells in Nyanza Province /. Kisumu, [Kenya] , 1983. 2 v. ; LC Card 84-983298 DDC 333.91/009676/29 19
HD1699.K42 N935 1983 ***NYPL [JLF 86-575]***

WATER RESOURCES DEVELOPMENT - SOCIAL ASPECTS - SOUTH AFRICA - GREAT BRAK RIVER ESTUARY.
Stauth, Roy. A methodology for determining the socially optimum uses of estuarine resources . Rondebosch, South Africa [1982] v, 119 leaves : LC Card 86-210152
HC905.Z7 G87 1982

WATER RESOURCES DEVELOPMENT - SOUTH CAROLINA.
The Situation and outlook for water resource use in South Carolina, 1985-2000 . [Clemson, S.C.] [1985] ix, 95 leaves : LC Card 86-622603 DDC 333.91/13/09757 19
HD1694.S6 S57 1985

WATER RESOURCES DEVELOPMENT - TANZANIA - CONGRESSES.
Workshop on the Institutionalization of the Shallow Wells Programme under Tanzanian Administration (1981 : University of Dar es Salaam) Proceedings of the Workshop on the Institutionalization of the Shallow Wells Programme under Tanzanian Administration /. [Dar es Salaam?] , 1981. 3, 16, 12 p. ; LC Card 85-980881 DDC 333.7/09678 s 333.91/22/09678 19
HD107 .D36 no. 71 HD1699.T33

WATER RESOURCES DEVELOPMENT - TURKMEN S.S.R.
Ataev, M. (Murruk) Gosudarstvennoe upravlenie ispol'zovaniem i okhranoĭ vod /. Ashkhabad , 1982. 175 p. ; LC Card 82-244366
HD1697.S653 T873 1982

WATER RESOURCES DEVELOPMENT - UKRAINE.
Ėkonomika ispol'zovaniia vodnykh resursov /. Kiev , 1980. 185 p. ; LC Card 87-462040
HD1697.S653 U374 1980

WATER RESOURCES DEVELOPMENT - UNITED STATES - PLANNING.
American Society of Civil Engineers. Task Committee on Federal Policies in Water Resources Planning. Federal policies in water resources planning /. New York, N.Y. , c1985. 61 p. : ISBN 0-87262-465-X (pbk.) LC Card 85-71265 DDC 333.91/15/0973 19
HD1694.A5 A67 1985 ***NYPL [JLD 86-4066]***

WATER RESOURCES DEVELOPMENT - UNITED STATES - PLANNING - CONGRESSES.
Facility location and land use . New York, N.Y. , c1986. vii, 40 p. : ISBN 0-87262-574-5 (pbk.) LC Card 86-25926 DDC 338.6/042 19
HD171.A15 F33 1986

WATER RESOURCES DEVELOPMENT - UNITED STATES - PLANNING - HISTORY.
Reuss, Martin. Interview with Professor Arthur Maass /. Fort Belvoir, Va. , 1987. p. cm. LC Card 86-32033 DDC 333.91/15/0973 19
HD1694.A5 R46 1987

WATER RESOURCES DEVELOPMENT - UNITED STATES - PLANNING - HISTORY - SOURCES.
Reuss, Martin. Interview with Professor Arthur Maass /. Fort Belvoir, Va. , 1987. p. cm. LC Card 86-32033 DDC 333.91/15/0973 19
HD1694.A5 R46 1987

WATER RESOURCES DEVELOPMENT - URUGUAY RIVER REGION.
Obras hidroeléctricas binacionales en América Latina. [Buenos Aires, Argentina] , 1985. vii leaves, 385 p., 3 leaves of plates : LC Card 86-180644
HD1696.A7 O27 1985

WATER RESOURCES DEVELOPMENT - UZBEK S.S.R.
Ėrgashev, N. (Nazirzhon) Rukovodstvo Kompartii Uzbekistana osvoeniem tselinnykh zemel' /. Tashkent , 1985. 159 p. ; LC Card 86-231568
HD1741.S782 U84 1985

WATER RESOURCES DEVELOPMENT - VENEZUELA.
Buroz Castillo, Eduardo. Programa de cooperación técnica Perú-Venezuela-OEA . Caracas , 1976. [11], 62 p. ; LC Card 84-136478
HD1696.P5 B87 1976

WATER RESOURCES DEVELOPMENT - ZIMBABWE.
An Assessment of the surface water resources of Zimbabwe and guidelines for development planning. Harare, Zimbabwe [1984?] 23 p., [3] folded leaves of plates : LC Card 86-980548 DDC 333.91/02/096891 19
HD1699.Z55 A84 1984

Water resources policy for Asia . Regional Symposium on Water Resoures Policy in Agro-Socio-Economic Development (1985 : Dhaka, Bangladesh) Rotterdam , Boston , 1987. xii, 627 p. : ISBN 90-6191-684-4 LC Card 87-170039 DDC 333.91/0095 19
HD1698.A1 R45 1985

Water Resources Support Center (U. S.)
The Port of Mobile, Alabama /. Washington , Fort Belvoir, Va. , 1986. vi, 99 p. : LC Card 86-603154 DDC 387.1/09761/22 19
HE554.M7 P67 1986

Port series. For earlier file, see: United States. Board of Engineers for Rivers and Harbors. Port series. [New series].
(no. 35) The Ports of Tacoma, Grays Harbor, and Olympia, Washington /. Washington, D.C. , Fort Belvoir, Va. , 1983. vi, 98 p. : LC Card 83-603527 DDC 387.1/09797/7 19
HE554.T2 P67 1983 ***NYPL [JLF 85-2000]***

The Ports of Duluth, MN, and Superior, WI, Taconite Harbor, Silver Bay, and Two Harbors, Mdd, and Ashland, WI /. Washington , Fort Belvoir, Va. , 1987. vi, 62 p. : LC Card 87-601753 DDC 386/.8/0977512 19
HE554.A5 P66 1987

The Ports of Tacoma, Grays Harbor, and Olympia, Washington /. Washington, D.C. , Fort Belvoir, Va. , 1983. vi, 98 p. : LC Card 83-603527 DDC 387.1/09797/7 19
HE554.T2 P67 1983 ***NYPL [JLF 85-2000]***

Water resources--people and issues.
Reuss, Martin. Interview with Professor Arthur Maass /. Fort Belvoir, Va. , 1987. p. cm. LC Card 86-32033 DDC 333.91/15/0973 19
HD1694.A5 R46 1987

WATER-RIGHTS - PERU - LAMBAYEQUE (DEPT.) - HISTORY.
Burga, Manuel. La historia agraria /. Chiclayo, Perú , 1986. 196 p. ; ***NYPL [JLD 87-1524]***

WATER RIGHTS - UNITED STATES.
Waterfield, Larry W. Conflict and crisis in rural America /. New York , 1986. iv, 235 p. : ISBN 0-03-006074-5 (alk. paper) : LC Card 85-19366 DDC 333.76/0973 19
HD256 .W35 1986 ***NYPL [JLE 86-2792]***

WATER, SUBTERRANEAN. see **WATER, UNDERGROUND.**

WATER-SUPPLY. Here are entered works on surveys of the water resources of a region, both superficial and underground, primarily with reference to the supply of water for domestic and manufacturing purposes, or for agriculture.

WATER-SUPPLY, AGRICULTURAL - GOVERNMENT POLICY - CONGRESSES.
Water and water policy in world food supplies . College Station , c1987. x, 434 p. : ISBN 0-89096-278-2 : LC Card 86-23065 DDC 333.91/3 19
HD1690.5 .W38 1987

WATER-SUPPLY - ARGENTINA.
Funciones y servicios de competencia municipal /. Córdoba, República Argentina , 1984. 94 leaves ; LC Card 87-121632 DDC 352.082 19
HD4629 .F86 1984

WATER-SUPPLY - BRAZIL, NORTHEAST.
A Problemática e a política da terra e água do Nordeste. Recife , 1985. 296 p. : LC Card 87-124121 DDC 333.91/00981/3 19
HD1696.B84 N675 1985

WATER-SUPPLY - BRAZIL - SÃO PAULO METROPOLITAN AREA.
Sócrates, Jodete Rios. A cidade invade as águas . [São Paulo] , 1985. 296 p., [2] folded leaves of plates : LC Card 87-118596 DDC 333.91/00981/61 19
HD1696.B84 S427 1985

WATER SUPPLY - CONSERVATION. see **WATER CONSERVATION.**

WATER-SUPPLY - DEVELOPING COUNTRIES - PLANNING - CITIZEN PARTICIPATION - PLANNING.
Whyte, Anne V. T. Guidelines for planning community participation activities in water supply and sanitation projects /. Geneva , Albany, NY , 1986. 53 p. : ISBN 92-4-170096-3 (pbk.) : LC Card 87-137091 DDC 333.91/009172/4 19
HD4465.D44 W49 1986

WATER-SUPPLY ENGINEERING - DEVELOPING COUNTRIES.
Okun, Daniel Alexander. Community piped water supply systems in developing countries . Washington, D.C. , 1987. xi, 249 p. : ISBN 0-8213-0896-3 (pbk.) LC Card 87-8161 DDC 363.6/1/091724 19
HD4465.D44 O38 1987

WATER-SUPPLY - GOVERNMENT POLICY - SOUTHWESTERN STATES.
Saliba, Bonnie. Water markets in theory and practice . Boulder , 1987. viii, 273 p. : ISBN 0-8133-7465-0 (pbk. : alk. paper) : LC Card 87-21687 DDC 333.91/00979 19
HD1695.A165 S25 1987

WATER-SUPPLY - KENYA - KITUI (DISTRICT)
Nilsson, Roy. Kitui water resources development study . Nairobi, Kenya [1982] 13, [31] leaves : LC Card 85-980998 DDC 333.91/009676/24 19
HD1699.K42 K586 1982

WATER-SUPPLY - NAVAJO INDIAN RESERVATION - CONGRESSES.
New courses for the Colorado River . Albuquerque , c1986. xx, 253 p. : ISBN 0-8263-0854-6 LC Card 85-24577 DDC 333.91/009791/3 19
HD1695.C7 N49 1986 ***NYPL [JLE 86-1736]***

Water-supply planning. Prasifka, David W., 1951- Current trends in water-supply planning . New York , c1988. xi, 266 p. : ISBN 0-442-27511-0 : LC Card 87-12157 DDC 333.91/212 19
HD1691 .P7 1988

WATER-SUPPLY - PLANNING.
Prasifka, David W., 1951- Current trends in water-supply planning . New York , c1988. xi, 266 p. : ISBN 0-442-27511-0 : LC Card 87-12157 DDC 333.91/212 19
HD1691 .P7 1988

WATER-SUPPLY, RURAL - DEVELOPING COUNTRIES - FINANCE.
Churchill, Anthony A., 1938- Rural water supply and sanitation . Washington, D.C. , c1987. xvi, 111 p. : ISBN 0-8213-0950-1 (pbk.) LC Card 87-23005 DDC 338.4/336361/091724 19
HD1702 .C48 1987

WATER-SUPPLY, RURAL - ECONOMIC ASPECTS - SUDAN - KURDUFĀN AL-SHAMĀLĪYAH.
Mohamed, Yagoub Abdalla. The North Kordofan rural water supply baseline survey /. Khartoum , 1982. xv, 152 p. : LC Card 85-981166
HD1699.S82 K875 1982

WATER-SUPPLY, RURAL - ENVIRONMENTAL ASPECTS - SUDAN - KURDUFĀN AL-SHAMĀLĪYAH.
Mohamed, Yagoub Abdalla. The North Kordofan rural water supply baseline survey /. Khartoum , 1982. xv, 152 p. : LC Card 85-981166
HD1699.S82 K875 1982

WATER-SUPPLY, RURAL - SOUTHWESTERN STATES.
Brown, F. Lee (Franklin Lee) Water and poverty in the Southwest /. Tucson , c1987. xi, 226 p. : ISBN 0-8165-1038-5 (alk. paper) : LC Card 87-19217 DDC 333.91/00979 19
HD1695.A165 B76 1987

WATER SUPPLY - SOUTHWESTERN STATES.
Saliba, Bonnie. Water markets in theory and practice . Boulder , 1987. viii, 273 p. : ISBN 0-8133-7465-0 (pbk. : alk. paper) : LC Card 87-21687 DDC 333.91/00979 19
HD1695.A165 S25 1987

WATER-SUPPLY - TANZANIA - CONGRESSES.
Workshop on the Institutionalization of the Shallow Wells Programme under Tanzanian Administration (1981 : University of Dar es Salaam) Proceedings of the Workshop on the Institutionalization of the Shallow Wells Programme under Tanzanian Administration /. [Dar es Salaam?] , 1981. 3, 16, 12 p. ; LC Card 85-980881 DDC 333.7/09678 s 333.91/22/09678 19
HD107 .D36 no. 71 HD1699.T33

WATER-SUPPLY - UNITED STATES.
Morandi, Larry B. Renewing resources . Denver, Colo. , 1984. vii, 133 p. ;
NYPL [JSF 86-712]

Water Technology Centre (Indian Agricultural Research Institute) Resource analysis for integrated development, Sultanpur District, Uttar Pradesh. New Delhi , 1986. xii, 436 p. : LC Card 87-902515
HC437.S85 R47 1986

WATER TRANSFER - GOVERNMENT POLICY - SOUTHWESTERN STATES.
Saliba, Bonnie. Water markets in theory and practice . Boulder , 1987. viii, 273 p. : ISBN 0-8133-7465-0 (pbk. : alk. paper) : LC Card 87-21687 DDC 333.91/00979 19
HD1695.A165 S25 1987

WATER TRANSFER - SOUTHWESTERN STATES.
Saliba, Bonnie. Water markets in theory and practice . Boulder , 1987. viii, 273 p. : ISBN 0-8133-7465-0 (pbk. : alk. paper) : LC Card 87-21687 DDC 333.91/00979 19
HD1695.A165 S25 1987

WATER TRANSPORTATION. see **SHIPPING.**

WATER, UNDERGROUND - UNITED STATES.
Sloggett, Gordon. Ground-water mining in the United States /. Washington, D.C , 1986. iv, 19 p. : LC Card 86-602788 DDC 338.1 s 338.1/4 19
HD1751 .A91854 no. 555 S616.U6

Water users associations in Pakistan. Islamabad : Govt. of Pakistan, Ministry of Food, Agriculture, and Cooperatives, Water Management Wing, 1984. 108 p. ; 28 cm. LC Card 85-930345 DDC 333.91/3/095491 19
1. Irrigation - Pakistan. 2. Irrigation laws - Pakistan. 3. Irrigation - Social aspects - Pakistan. 4. Irrigation canals and flumes - Pakistan. I. Pakistan. Ministry of Food, Agriculture & Cooperatives. Water Management Wing.
HD1741.P13 W37 1984

Waterbury, John. The Political economy of risk and choice in Senegal /. London, England , Totowa, N.J. , 1987. xv, 363 p. : ISBN 0-7146-3297-X : LC Card 86-26859 DDC 338.966/3 19
HC1045 .P65 1987

Waterfield, Larry W. Conflict and crisis in rural America / Larry W. Waterfield. New York : Praeger, 1986. iv, 235 p. : maps ; 24 cm. Includes bibliographical references and index. ISBN 0-03-006074-5 (alk. paper) : LC Card 85-19366 DDC 333.76/0973 19
1. Land use, Rural - United States. 2. Agriculture and state - United States. 3. Water rights - United States. 4. Conservation of natural resources - United States. 5. Environmental policy - United States. 6. United States - Rural conditions. I. Title.
HD256 .W35 1986 ***NYPL [JLE 86-2792]***

Waterfront warlord . Edwards, Peter, 1956- Toronto, Ont., Canada , c1987. ix, 213 p. : ISBN 1-550-13013-7 : LC Card 87-150705 DDC 331.88/113875/0924 B 19
HD6525.B36 E39 1987

WATERFRONTS - HUDSON RIVER (N.Y. AND N.J.) - PLANNING.
Hudson Waterfront Walkway plan and design guidelines /. [Trenton, N.J.] , 1984] 136 p. :
NYPL [JLF 87-913]

WATERFRONTS - NEW JERSEY - PLANNING.
Hudson Waterfront Walkway plan and design guidelines /. [Trenton, N.J.] , 1984] 136 p. :
NYPL [JLF 87-913]

Waterkamp, Rainer. Das zentralstaatliche Planungssystem der DDR : Steuerungsprozesse im anderen Teil Deutschlands / von Rainer Waterkamp. Berlin : Duncker & Humblot, c1983. 194 p. : ill. ; 24 cm. (Beiträge zur politischen Wissenschaft. Bd. 45) Bibliography: p. [185]-194. ISBN 3-428-05405-9 LC Card 83-217231
1. Central planning - Germany (East). 2. Germany, East - Economic policy. I. Title. II. Title: Das zentralstaatliche Planungssystem der D.D.R.
HC290.78 .W38 1983

WATERLOO (ONT.) - MANUFACTURES - FORECASTING.
Manufacturing in Kitchener-Waterloo . [Waterloo] , c1987. xiii, 220 p. : ISBN 0-921083-22-X (pbk.) LC Card 87-168616 DDC 338.4/767/0971344 19
HD9734.C3 K56 1987

WATERLOO (ONT.) - MANUFACTURES - HISTORY.
Manufacturing in Kitchener-Waterloo . [Waterloo] , c1987. xiii, 220 p. : ISBN 0-921083-22-X (pbk.) LC Card 87-168616 DDC 338.4/767/0971344 19
HD9734.C3 K56 1987

[Waterlow practitioner's library]
De Lisle, Christian. Business interest calculations /. London , c1985. ix, 274 p. ; ISBN 0-08-039231-8 ***NYPL [JLE 87-1030]***

Waterlow's business library.
Crichton, Susan. Understanding factoring and trade credit /. London , 1986. xv, 199 p. : ISBN 0-08-039204-0 (pbk.) : LC Card 87-122377 DDC 658.8/8 19
HG3752.3 .C75 1986

Waterman, D. A. (Donald Arthur), 1936-
Building expert systems /. Reading, Mass. , 1983. xvi, 444 p. : ISBN 0-201-10686-8 LC Card 82-24511 DDC 001.64/2 19
QA76.9.E96 B84 1983 ***NYPL [JSE 87-204]***

Waterman, Robert H. The renewal factor : how the best get and keep the competitive edge / Robert H. Waterman, Jr. Toronto ; New York : Bantam Books, 1987. xiv, 338 p. ; 24 cm. Bibliography: p. [319]-326. Includes index. ISBN 0-553-05226-8 LC Card 87-18662 DDC 658.4/06 19
1. Organizational change. 2. Industrial management. I. Title.
HD58.8 .W387 1987

Waterman, Thomas Whitney, 1821-1898. (ed)
Dart, Joseph Henry, 1817-1887. A compendium of the law and practice of vendors and purchasers of real estate [microform]. New York, Albany, 1851. civ, 665 (i.e. 856) p. LC Card 17-19132 ***NYPL [*ZT-1719]***

Waters, Thomas F. The Superior North Shore / Thomas F. Waters ; illustrations by Carol Yonker Waters ; maps by the author. Minneapolis : University of Minnesota Press, c1987. xix, 361 p. : ill., maps ; 25 cm. Bibliography: p. 317-341. Includes index. ISBN 0-8166-1613-2 : LC Card 87-13585 DDC 333.7/09776/7 19
1. Natural resources - Minnesota. 2. Natural resources - Ontario. I. Title.
HC107.M6 W38 1987

WATERSHED DEVELOPMENT. see **WATERSHED MANAGEMENT.**

WATERSHED MANAGEMENT - ASIA - CASE STUDIES.
Watershed resource management . Boulder , 1986. xx, 236 p. : ISBN 0-8133-7300-X (pbk. : alk. paper) : LC Card 86-18987 DDC 333.91/0095 19
HD1691 .W37 1986 ***NYPL [JLD 87-767]***

WATERSHED MANAGEMENT - PACIFIC AREA - CASE STUDIES.
Watershed resource management . Boulder , 1986. xx, 236 p. : ISBN 0-8133-7300-X (pbk. : alk. paper) : LC Card 86-18987 DDC 333.91/0095 19
HD1691 .W37 1986 ***NYPL [JLD 87-767]***

Watershed resource management : an integrated framework with studies from Asia and the Pacific / edited by K. William Easter, John A. Dixon, Maynard M. Hufschmidt. Boulder : Westview Press, 1986. xx, 236 p. : ill. ; 23 cm. (Studies in water policy and management . no. 10) Includes bibliographies and index. ISBN 0-8133-7300-X (pbk. : alk. paper) : LC Card 86-18987 DDC 333.91/0095 19
1. Watershed management - Asia - Case studies. 2. Watershed management - Pacific Area - Case studies. I. Easter, K. William. II. Dixon, John A., 1946-. III. Hufschmidt, Maynard M. IV. Series.
HD1691 .W37 1986 ***NYPL [JLD 87-767]***

WATERSHEDS - ECONOMIC ASPECTS - BRAZIL - SERGIPE.
Almeida, Edimilson Machado de, 1937- Tecnologia e racionalização da agropecuária, com o aproveitamento das bacias hidrográficas /. Aracaju [1971] 100 leaves : LC Card 85-203218
HD1875.S4 A65 1971

WATERSHEDS - MANAGEMENT. see **WATERSHED MANAGEMENT.**

Waterson, Michael, 1950- Regulation of the firm and natural monopoly / Michael Waterson. Oxford [Oxfordshire] ; New York, NY, USA : B. Blackwell, 1988. p. cm. Bibliography: p. Includes index. ISBN 0-631-14007-7 : LC Card 87-20925 DDC 338.8 19

1. Industry and state. 2. Industrial organization. 3. Monopolies. I. Title.
HD3611 .W35 1988

WATERWORKS - DEVELOPING COUNTRIES - PLANNING.
Okun, Daniel Alexander. Community piped water supply systems in developing countries . Washington, D.C. , 1987. xi, 249 p. : ISBN 0-8213-0896-3 (pbk.) LC Card 87-8161 DDC 363.6/1/091724 19
HD4465.D44 O38 1987

Wathey, Patricia Wogen. The international mail-order shopping guide / Patricia Wogen Wathey. Englewood Cliffs, N.J. : Prentice-Hall, 1984. 338 p. : 24 cm. "A Spectrum book." Includes index. ISBN 0-13-473083-6 LC Card 84-8390 DDC 381/.14/025 19
1. Mail-order business - Directories. 2. Catalogs, Commercial - Directories. I. Title.
HF5466 .W38 1984
NYPL [*R-Econ. 84-3915]

Watkins, David, 1947- Survival of the small firm /. Aldershot, Hants, England , Brookfield, Vt., U. S.A. , c1986. 2 v. : ISBN 0-566-00725-8 (v. 1) : LC Card 85-27035 DDC 338.6/42 19
HD2341 .S87 1986 ***NYPL [JLD 86-2643]***

Watkins, William Pascoe. Co-operative principles : today and tomorrow / W.P. Watkins ; with an introduction by T.F. Carbery. Manchester [Greater Manchester] : Holyoake Books, 1986. xiii, 168 p. ; 21 cm. Includes index. ISBN 0-85195-140-6 (pbk.) : LC Card 86-216664 DDC 334 19
1. Cooperation. 2. Cooperative societies. I. Title.
HD2961 .W448 1986

Watson, Collin J. Brief business statistics /. [Newton, Mass.] , 1987. p. cm. ISBN 0-205-11090-8 LC Card 87-17543 DDC 519.5 19
HF1017 .B675 1987

Watson, Stephen R. Decision synthesis : the principles and practice of decision analysis / Stephen R. Watson, Dennis M. Buede. Cambridge [Cambridgeshire] ; New York : Cambridge University Press, 1987. xvi, 299 p. : ill. ; 24 cm. Bibliography: p. 282-294. Includes index. ISBN 0-521-32569-2 LC Card 87-10270 DDC 658.4/03 19
1. Decision-making. I. Buede, Dennis M. II. Title.
HD30.23 .W38 1987

Watson, Tony J. Sociology, work & industry / Tony Watson. 2nd ed. London ; New York : Routledge & Kegan Paul, 1987. xiv, 336 p. : ill. ; 22 cm. "Published in the USA ... in association with Methuen Inc."--Verso of t.p. Bibliography: p. [295]-321. Includes indexes. ISBN 0-7102-0962-2 : LC Card 86-26035 DDC 306/.36 19
1. Industrial sociology. I. Title.
HD6955 .W38 1987

Watt, Alec. Illustrated dictionary of geology : the principles of geology explained and illustrated / Alec Watt ; [with English-Arabic & Arabic-English glossaries]. Beirut : Librarie du Liban ; [Harlow, Essex] : Longman, 1982. 329 p. : col. ill. ; 20 cm. Glossaries edited by Ahmed S. Khatib. "Divisions of geologie time" on papers. Includes index. Bibliography: p. [170]
1. English language - Dictionaries - Arabic. 2. Geology - Dictionaries. 3. Arabic language - Dictionaries - English. I. Khatib, Ahmed S. II. Title.
NYPL [*OG 85-2903]

The Watt/Clark record . Skilbred, Amy. Washington, D.C. (1901 Pennsylvania Ave., N.W., Washington 20006) , c1984. iii, 63, [18] p. : LC Card 86-206945 DDC 363.7/009798 19
HC107.A47 E57 1984

WATT, JAMES G., 1938-
Kloepfer, Deanne. The Watt record . Washington, D.C. [1983] ii, 66, 9, 3 p. : LC Card 86-232533 DDC 333.1/0973 19
HD183.L3 K58 1983

The Watt record . Kloepfer, Deanne. Washington, D.C. [1983] ii, 66, 9, 3 p. : LC Card 86-232533 DDC 333.1/0973 19
HD183.L3 K58 1983

Wattenberg, Ben J. The birth dearth / Ben J. Wattenberg. New York, NY : Pharos Books : Distributed by Ballantine Books, 1987. viii, 182 p. : ill. ; 23 cm. Includes index. ISBN 0-88687-304-5 : LC Card 83-63759 DDC 304.6/32 19
1. Fertility, Human - United States. 2. Fertility, Human - Europe. 3. Population forecasting - United States. 4. Population forecasting - Europe. I. Title.
HB915 .W29 1987

Wattone, Mike, 1939- Quest for gold / Mike Wattone. Scarborough, W.A. : Contraland Press, 1985. 103 p. : ill. ; 24 cm. Bibliography: p. 103. ISBN 0-949731-03-X (pbk.) LC Card 86-142484 DDC 338.2/741/09941 19
1. Gold industry - Australia - Coolgardie Region (W.A.) - History. 2. Gold mines and mining - Australia - Coolgardie Region (W.A.) - History. 3. Coolgardie (W.A.) - History. I. Title.
HD9536.A83 C669 1985
NYPL [JLE 87-662]

Watts, Alan, 1915-1973.
What makes Japan work [motion picture] . Cos Cob, CT , 1983. 1 film reel (11 min.) : LC Card 83-700702 DDC 181 11
HD8726.5

What makes Japan work [videorecording] . Cos Cob, CT , 1983. 1 videocassette (11 min.) : LC Card 87-705342 DDC 181 11
HD8726.5

Watts, David. The West Indies : patterns of development, culture, and environmental change since 1492 / David Watts. Cambridge [Cambridgeshire] ; New York : Cambridge University Press, 1987. xxii, 609 p. : ill., maps ; 24 cm. (Cambridge studies in historical geography . 8) Bibliography: p. 553-585. Includes index. ISBN 0-521-24555-9 LC Card 87-5156 DDC 330.9729 19
1. West Indies - Economic conditions. 2. Sugar trade - West Indies - History. 3. West Indies - Social conditions. I. Title. II. Series.
HC151 .W375 1987

Watts, John M., 1933- The financial services shockwave : survival tactics for Wall Street and Main Street / John M. Watts. Englewood Cliffs, N.J. : Prentice-Hall, c1987. viii, 181 p. : ill. ; 24 cm. ISBN 0-13-316852-2 : LC Card 86-22510 DDC 332.1/0973 19
1. Financial institutions - United States. 2. Finance - United States. I. Title.
HG181 .W37 1987 ***NYPL [JLE 87-612]***

Watts, Michael. State, oil, and agriculture in Nigeria /. Berkeley , c1987. xiv, 327 p. : ISBN 0-87725-166-5 (pbk.) : LC Card 87-2941 DDC 338.1/8669 19
HD2145.5 .S73 1987

Watts, Susan J. Population mobility and multilocality in Ilorin, Kwara State, Nigeria / Susan Watts and R. Mansell Prothero. [Liverpool : Dept. of Geography, University of Liverpool, 1981-] v. <1 > : ill. ; 30 cm. (Liverpool papers in human geography . no. 1) Includes bibliographies. LC Card 86-226489 DDC 304.8/09669/5 19
1. Migration, Internal - Nigeria - Ilorin. 2. Labor mobility - Nigeria - Ilorin. I. Prothero, R. Mansell. II. Title. III. Series.
HB2126.7.I46 W37 1981

Watts, Timothy J. Kennedy, Robert A. Personal economics . Tucson, AZ , c1987. xi, 315 p. : ISBN 0-89586-517-3 (pbk.) : LC Card 86-82240 DDC 332.024 19
HG179 .K46 1987

Watzal, Ludwig, 1950-
Entwicklungspolitik zwischen Immanenz und Transzendenz : Essays zur Entwicklungspolitik / Ludwig Watzal. Frankfurt am Main ; New York : P. Lang, c1986. 121 p. ; 21 cm. (Europäische Hochschulschriften. Reihe XXXI, Politikwissenschaft, 0721-3654 . Bd. 88 = vol. 88 = vol. 88) Includes bibliographical references and indexes. ISBN 3-8204-8785-9 LC Card 86-198339
1. Economic development - Moral and ethical aspects. 2. Economic assistance, West German - Developing countries. 3. Developing countries - Economic policy. 4. Schweizer, Albert, 1875-1965 - Views on economic development. I. Series: Europäische Hochschulschriften. Reihe XXXI, Politikwissenschaft , Bd. 88. II. Title.
HD75 .W36 1986

Ethik, Kultur, Entwicklung : zur Entwicklungskonzeption Albert Schweitzers / Ludwig Watzal. Göttingen : Muster-Schmidt, c1985. 131 p. ; 21 cm. Bibliography: p. 114-127. Includes indexes. ISBN 3-7881-1741-9 LC Card 86-122983 DDC 338.9 19
1. Economic development - Moral and ethical aspects. 2. Schweitzer, Albert, 1875-1965 - Views on economic development. I. Title.
HD75 .W37 1985

WAVEFRONT RECONSTRUCTION IMAGING. see HOLOGRAPHY.

Wa'Weru, Murathi. Management of human resources in Kenya / Murathi Wa'Weru. Nairobi : Kenya Literature Bureau, 1984. xv, 174 p. ; 22 cm. Includes bibliographies. LC Card 85-980435 DDC 658.3/009676/2 19
1. Personnel management - Kenya. I. Title.
HF5549.2.K4 W39 1984b

A way of hope /. Wałęsa, Lech, 1943- [Chemin d'espoir. English.] New York , c1987. 325 p., [17] p. of plates : ISBN 0-8050-0668-0 LC Card 87-21194 DDC 322/.2/0924 B 19
HD6735.7.Z55 W34813 1987

Way of life : integration and immigration / edited by Anthony Jackson. London : Social Science Research Council, [1980?] 84 p. ; 21 cm. (North Sea Oil Panel occasional paper . no. 12 12) Includes bibliographies. ISBN 0-86226-076-0 (pbk.) LC Card 82-218547 DDC 304.8 19
1. Offshore oil industry - Social aspects - Scotland. 2. Alien labor - Scotland. 3. Social integration - Scotland. 4. Scotland - Social conditions. 5. Scotland - Emigration and immigration. I. Jackson, Anthony, Ph. D. II. Series.
HD9571.7.S36 W39 1980
NYPL [JLD 85-427]

The Way socialism began.
Dmitrenko, Vladimir Petrovich. Economic policy during the construction of socialism in the USSR /. Moscow , c1987. 156 p. ; LC Card 86-201129 DDC 338.947 19
HC335.2 .D56 1987

Waymon, Lynne. Starting and managing a business from your home / by Lynne Waymon. Washington, D.C. : U. S. Small Business Administration, Office of Business Development : For sale by the Supt. of Docs., U. S. G.P.O., 1986. vi, 48 p. ; 21 cm. (Starting and managing series . v. 2 [i.e. 102]) "Produced in cooperation with the American Association of Community and Junior Colleges." Shipping list no.: 86-520-P. Bibliography: p. 45-48. S/N 045-000-00232-2 Item 901-L LC Card 86-602842 DDC 658/.041 19
1. New business enterprises - United States. 2. Home-based businesses - United States. I. United States. Small Business Administration. Office of Business Development. II. American Association of Community and Junior Colleges. III. Series. IV. Series: Starting and managing series , v. 102. V. Title.
HD62.5 .W395 1986

Wayne, Jack, Ph.D. Structural contradictions of the colonial state : the case of Tanganyika in the early years / Jack Wayne. [Toronto, Canada] : Structural Analysis Programme, Dept. of Sociology, University of Toronto, c1981. 23, [5] p. ; 28 cm. (Working paper, 0226-1774 . no. 23) Bibliography: p. [27]-[29] ISBN 0-7727-2825-9 (pbk.) LC Card 86-193819 DDC 330.9678/203 19
1. Tanganyika - Economic conditions. 2. Tanganyika - Politics and government. 3. Tanzania - Colonial influence. I. Series: Working paper (University of Toronto. Structural Analysis Programme) , no. 23. II. Title.
HC885 .W39 1981

Wayner, Stephen A. Buying right : getting started in real estate investment / Stephen A. Wayner. New York : F. Watts, 1987. 247 p. : facsims. ; 24 cm. Includes index. ISBN 0-531-15524-2 LC Card 86-32474 DDC 332.63/24 19
1. Real estate investment. I. Title.
HD1382.5 .W38 1987

Ways of working /. Marwood, Jim, 1932- Kenthurst , 1986. 160 p. : ISBN 0-86417-101-3 (pbk.) LC Card 87-105782 DDC 305.5/62/09946 19
HD8849.T372 M37 1986

WCVE-TV (Television station : Richmond, Va.)
Drunk driving [videorecording] . Lincoln, NE , 1983. 1 videocassette (30 min.) : LC Card 87-706347 DDC 363.1 11
HE5620.D7

DUI arrest [videorecording] /. Lincoln, NE , 1983. 1 videocassette (30 min.) : LC Card 87-706343 DDC 343 11
HE5620.D7

We hate humans /. Robins, David, 1944- Harmondsworth, Middlesex, England , New York, N.Y. , 1984. 155 p. ; ISBN 0-14-007062-1
NYPL [JLD 86-4404]

We shall be all . Dubofsky, Melvyn, 1934- Urbana , c1988. xviii, 561 p. ; ISBN 0-252-01408-1 (alk. paper) LC Card 87-16725 DDC 331.88/6/0973 19
HD8055.I4 D83 1988

W.E. Upjohn Institute for Employment Research.
Barth, Peter S., 1937- The tragedy of black lung . Kalamazoo, MI , 1987. xi, 292 p. ; ISBN 0-88099-044-9 (pbk.) LC Card 87-8332 DDC 368.4/1 19
HD7264 .B37 1987

Burgess, Paul L. An incentives approach to improving the unemployment compensation system /. Kalamazoo, Mich. , 1987. xv, 273 p. : ISBN 0-88099-048-1 (pbk.) LC Card 87-23128 DDC 368.4/4/00973 19
HD7096.U5 B87 1987

Wealth and economic status . O'Hare, William P. Washington, D.C. , 1983. vii, 33 p. : ISBN 0-941410-35-8 (pbk.) : LC Card 83-22171 DDC 339.2/2/0973 19
HC110.W4 O33 1983 NYPL [JLE 86-2065]

Wealth and taxation in Central Europe : the history and sociology of public finance / edited by Peter-Christian Witt. Leamington Spa, UK ; New York, N.Y., USA : Berg ; 162 p. ; 23 cm. (German historical perspectives . 2) Includes bibliographical references and index. ISBN 0-85496-523-8 : LC Card 86-24490 DDC 336.43 19
1. Finance, Public - Central Europe - History. 2. Taxation - Central Europe - History. I. Witt, Peter-Christian. II. Series.
HJ1000 .W4 1987

WEALTH - BRAZIL.
Singer, Paul Israel, 1932- Repartição da renda . Rio de Janeiro , 1986. 95 p. ; ISBN 85-85061-40-5 : LC Card 86-157852
HC190.I5 S56 1986

WEALTH - BRAZIL - SÃO PAULO (STATE) - HISTORY - 19TH CENTURY.
Mello, Zélia Maria Cardoso de. Metamorfoses da riqueza, São Paulo, 1845-1895 . São Paulo , 1985. 188 p. : LC Card 85-207635
HC188.S3 M49 1985

WEALTH - CANADA - CONGRESSES.
International comparisons of the distribution of household wealth /. Oxford , New York , 1987. xii, 283 p. : ISBN 0-19-828511-6 : LC Card 86-31241 DDC 339.2/2/094 19
HC240.9.I5 I56 1987

WEALTH - CANADA - STATISTICS.
Rashid, A. Characteristics of high income families, 1980 /. Ottawa [1986] 97 p. : ISBN 0-660-52875-4 (pbk.) : LC Card 86-210700
HC120.I5 R36 1986

WEALTH, DISTRIBUTION OF. see **WEALTH.**

WEALTH - EUROPE - CONGRESSES.
International comparisons of the distribution of household wealth /. Oxford , New York , 1987. xii, 283 p. : ISBN 0-19-828511-6 : LC Card 86-31241 DDC 339.2/2/094 19
HC240.9.I5 I56 1987

WEALTH - GERMANY, WEST.
Miegel, Meinhard. Die verkannte Revolution /. Stuttgart , 1983- v. : ISBN 3-87959-196-2 (Bd. 1) LC Card 83-206487 DDC 330.943/087 19
HC286.7 .M53 1983 NYPL [JLK 86-154]

WEALTH - GREAT BRITAIN.
Hilton, John, 1880-1943. Rich man, poor man /. New York , 1985. 174 p. ; ISBN 0-8240-7614-1 (alk. paper) : LC Card 85-13078 DDC 339.2/2/0941 19
HC256.4 .H54 1985 NYPL [JLC 86-342]

Will there always be an England? [videorecording] /. Alexandria, VA , 1986. 1 videocassette (60 min.) : LC Card 86-707796 DDC 942.085 11
HC256.5

WEALTH - HUNGARY - STATISTICS.
A Nemzeti vagyon és az állóeszközállomány 1970-1978 /. [Budapest] [1979] 140 p. ; LC Card 82-193609
HC300.295.W4 N454 1979

WEALTH - MATHEMATICAL MODELS.
Owen, Dorian, 1953- Money, wealth, and expenditure . Cambridge [Cambridgeshire] , New York , 1986. xi, 210 p. ; ISBN 0-521-26761-7 LC Card 85-19009 DDC 339.4/7/0724 19
HB820 .O94 1986 NYPL [JLE 87-1594]

Puumanen, Kari. Three essays on money, wealth, and the exchange rate /. Helsinki , 1986. 143 p. : ISBN 951-686-119-9 (pbk.) LC Card 86-235460 DDC 332.4/0724 19
HG221 .P97 1986

The Wealth of India : a dictionary of Indian raw materials & industrial products. Rev. ed. New Delhi : Publications & Information Directorate, Council of Scientific & Industrial Research, c1985- v. <1- > : ill. (some col.) ; 25 cm. Bibliography: v. 1, p. xvii-lx. Includes indexes. CONTENTS. - v. 1A. Raw materials ISBN 81-85038-00-7 (set) LC Card 87-900740 DDC 333.7/0954 19
1. Raw materials - India - Dictionaries. 2. Commercial products - India - Dictionaries. I. Council of Scientific & Industrial Research (India). Publications & Information Directorate.
HF1054.I5 W4 1985

The wealth of the nation . Bruchey, Stuart Weems. New York , c1988. ix, 259 p. ; ISBN 0-06-015854-9 : LC Card 87-45602 DDC 330.973 19
HC103 .B78855 1988

WEALTH TAX - INDIA.
Saraf, B. P., 1939- Capital taxation in India /. New Delhi , c1983. viii, 268 p. ; LC Card 83-902683 DDC 343.5405/3 345.40353 19
HJ4126.I45 S27 1983 NYPL [JLD 86-3821]

WEALTH - UNITED STATES.
The Affluent market. New York, N.Y. (500 5th Ave., New York 10110) [1984] 227 leaves : LC Card 86-201904 DDC 658.8/348 19
HC110.C6 A63 1984

Allen, Michael Patrick. The founding fortunes . New York , c1987. p. cm. LC Card 87-9912 DDC 332/.0973 19
HC110.W4 A44 1987

Lapham, Lewis H. Money and class in America . New York , 1988, c1987. p. cm. ISBN 1-555-84109-0 LC Card 87-22515 DDC 305.5/234/0973 19
HC110.W4 L24 1988

O'Hare, William P. Wealth and economic status . Washington, D.C. , 1983. vii, 33 p. : ISBN 0-941410-35-8 (pbk.) : LC Card 83-22171 DDC 339.2/2/0973 19
HC110.W4 O33 1983 NYPL [JLE 86-2065]

WEALTH - UNITED STATES - CONGRESSES.
International comparisons of the distribution of household wealth /. Oxford , New York , 1987. xii, 283 p. : ISBN 0-19-828511-6 : LC Card 86-31241 DDC 339.2/2/094 19
HC240.9.I5 I56 1987

WEATHER AND INDUSTRY. see **INDUSTRY AND WEATHER.**

Weatherford, Gary D. New courses for the Colorado River . Albuquerque , c1986. xx, 253 p. : ISBN 0-8263-0854-6 LC Card 85-24577 DDC 333.91/009791/3 19
HD1695.C7 N49 1986 NYPL [JLE 86-1736]

Weatheritt, L. Manufacturing industry in Greater London / by L. Weatheritt and A.F. Lovett. London : Greater London Council, c1975. ii, 26 p. ; 30 cm. (Research memorandum / Greater London Council, 0306-7203 . RM498) Errata slip inserted. Includes bibliographical references. ISBN 0-7168-0853-6 (pbk.) LC Card 82-213745
1. Labor supply - England - London. 2. London (England) - Manufactures - Employees. 3. London (England) - Economic conditions. 4. Land use - England - London. I. Lovett, A. F. II. Series: Research memorandum (Greater London Council) , RM498. III. Title.
HD5766.L66 W43 1975

Weaver, David H., 1935-
Accounting, systems and procedures . New York , c1988. xv, 288 p. : ISBN 0-07-069357-9 (pbk.) LC Card 87-21936 DDC 657 19
HF5635 .A222 1988b

Accounting, systems and procedures /. New York , c1988. p. cm. ISBN 0-07-069356-0 LC Card 87-17234 DDC 657 19
HF5635 .A222 1988

Weaver, Paul, 1942 Oct. 18- The suicidal corporation / Paul H. Weaver. New York : Simon and Schuster, c1988. p. cm. Bibliography: p. Includes index. ISBN 0-671-52378-3 LC Card 87-23468 DDC 338.7/4/0973 19
1. Corporations - United States - History. 2. Industry and state - United States - History. 3. United States - Industries - History. 4. United States - Economic policy. 5. Industrial management - United States - Case studies. 6. Ford Motor Company - Management. I. Title.
HD2785 .W38 1988

WEAVERS - BOLIVIA - LA PAZ.
La Artesanía de tejidos en la ciudad de La Paz /. La Paz, Bolivia , 1986. 74, [6] p. : LC Card 87-101929
HD8039.T42 B525 1986

WEAVERS - FRANCE - AUFFAY - HISTORY.
Gullickson, Gay L. Spinners and weavers of Auffay . Cambridge [Cambridgeshire] , New York , 1986. x, 256 p. : ISBN 0-521-32280-4 LC Card 86-6808 DDC 331.4/877/02822094425 19
HD8039.T42 F834 1986 NYPL [JLE 87-1054]

WEAVERS - MEXICO - HISTORY.
Salvucci, Richard J., 1951- Textiles and capitalism in Mexico . Princeton, N.J. , c1987. p. cm. ISBN 0-691-07749-5 (alk. paper) : LC Card 87-45535 DDC 338.4/767702824/0972 19
HD9864.M62 S25 1987

Weavers of revolution . Winn, Peter. New York , 1986. xiv, 328 p. : ISBN 0-19-503960-2 : LC Card 85-18832 DDC 338.7/67721/098331 19
HD8039.T42 C478 1986 NYPL [JLE 86-1973]

WEAVING, HAND. see **HAND WEAVING.**

Webb, Caro. Making cars . London , Boston , c1985. ix, 131 p. : ISBN 0-7102-0272-5 : LC Card 84-13398 DDC 338.4/76292/0942574 19
HD8039.A82 G75 1984 NYPL [JLE 86-2303]

Webb, John Winter. Policies of population redistribution /. Oulu , 1981. 199 p. : ISBN 951-675-071-0 (pbk.) LC Card 83-148782 DDC 304.8 19
HB1952 .P65 1981

Webb, Shwu-Eng. Idling erodible cropland : impacts on production, prices, and government costs / Shwu-Eng H. Webb, Clayton W. Ogg, and Wen-Yuan Huang. Washington, D.C. : U. S. Dept. of Agriculture, Economic Research Service : Copies purchased from the Supt. of Docs., U. S. G.P.O., [1986] iii, 31 p. : ill. ; 28 cm. (Agricultural economic report . no. 550) Cover title. Bibliography: p. 26-27. LC Card 86-601632 DDC 338.1 s 338.1/62 19
1. Land use, Rural - Government policy - United States. 2. Agricultural conservation - Government policy - United States. 3. Soil conservation - Government policy - United States. 4. Erosion - Economic aspects - United States. 5. Agriculture - Economic aspects - United States. 6. Agriculture and state - United States. I. Ogg, Clayton W. II. Huang, Wen-Yuan. III. Title. IV. Series.
HD1751 .A91854 no. 550 HD256

Webber, Alan M., 1948- Dyer, Davis. Changing alliances /. Boston, Mass. , c1987. xvi, 333 p. ; ISBN 0-87584-175-9 LC Card 86-33619 DDC 338.4/76292/0973 19
HD9710.U52 D94 1987

Webber, Carolyn. A history of taxation and expenditure in the Western world / Carolyn Webber and Aaron Wildavsky. New York : Simon and Schuster, c1986. 734 p. ,[16] p. of plates : ill. ; 25 cm. Includes index. Bibliography: p. 677-710. ISBN 0-671-54617-1 LC Card 86-3863 DDC 336.2/009 19
1. Taxation - History. 2. Expenditures, Public - History. I. Wildavsky, Aaron B. II. Title.
HJ2250 .W42 1986 NYPL [JLE 86-3474]

Webber, Ross A. Hampton, David R. Organizational behavior and the practice of management /. Glenview, Ill. , c1987. 876 p. : ISBN 0-673-18303-3 LC Card 86-24798 DDC 658.4 19
HD58.7 .H35 1987

Weber, Dieter, Dipl.-Kfm. Dr. Grimm, Bernd Christian. Handbuch der Hausfinanzierung . Mannheim , 1985. 174, [318] p. ; LC Card 85-188627
HD7339.Z9 G75 1985

Weber, Helmut Kurt, 1933- Rentabilität, Produktivität, Liquidität der Unternehmung : Bedeutung, Ermittlung, Aussagewert / Helmut Kurt Weber. Stuttgart : C.E. Poeschel, c1983. x, 161 p. ; 24 cm. Bibliography: p. 157-159. Includes index. ISBN 3-7910-0346-1 LC Card 83-167883
1. Business enterprises - Finance. I. Title.
HG4026 .W4 1983

Weber, Henri. Le parti des patrons : le CNPF, 1946-1986 / Henri Weber. Paris : Seuil, c1986. 437 p. ; 24 cm. (L'Epreuve des faits) Bibliography: p. 423-426. Includes index. ISBN 2-02-009352-9 : LC Card 87-106644
1. Conseil national du patronat français. 2. Employers' associations - France. I. Title. II. Series.
HD6948.F8 W43 1986

Weber, Manfred, Dr. Der Marktwert von Produkteigenschaften / von Manfred Weber. Berlin : Duncker & Humblot, c1986. xv, 335 p. : ill. ; 24 cm. (Schriften zum Marketing. Bd. 20) Bibliography: p. 313-335. ISBN 3-428-06103-9 LC Card 87-131636 DDC 658.8 s 658.5 19
1. Product management. 2. Quality of products. 3. Prices. I. Title.
HF5415.A2 S37 Bd. 20 HF5415.157

Weber, Nathan. Communicating with security analysts / by Nathan Weber. New York, N.Y. (845 3rd Ave., New York 10022) : Conference Board, c1985. 22 p. : ill. ; 28 cm. (Research bulletin / The Conference Board . no. 186) Cover title. "Corporate Relations Program." Includes bibliographical references. LC Card 86-212395 DDC 658.4/5 19
1. Corporations - United States - Investor relations - Case studies. 2. Investment analysis - United States - Case studies. I. Conference Board. Corporate Relations Program. II. Series: Research bulletin (Conference Board) , no. 186. III. Title.
HD59 .W36 1985

Weber, Peter, 1935- Periphere Räume . Paderborn , 1979. 183 p. : ISBN 3-506-73204-8 LC Card 85-209554
HC240 .P38 1979

Weber, Robert E. Managing your renovation or move to new offices / Robert E. Weber. New York : Quorum Books, 1987. xii, 242 p. : ill. ; 25 cm. Bibliography: p. [237]. Includes index. ISBN 0-89930-245-9 (lib. bdg. : alk. paper) LC Card 86-30583 DDC 658.2/3 19
1. Office layout. 2. Office equipment and supplies. 3. Office equipment leases. I. Title.
HF5547.2 .W42 1987

Weber, Rolf. Vehicle Routing- und Scheduling-Probleme unter besonderer Berücksichtigung von Dial-a-Ride-Problemen / Rolf Weber. München : V. Florentz, c1985. iii, 158 p. : ill. ; 21 cm. (Hochschulschriften zur Betriebswirtschaftslehre . Bd. 32) Bibliography: p. 149-156. Includes index. ISBN 3-88259-349-0 LC Card 86-123392
1. Paratransit services - Econometric models. I. Title. II. Series.
HE305 .W4 1985

Weber, Rolf H. Wirtschaftsregulierung in wettbewerbspolitischen Ausnahmebereichen : Studien zur staatlichen Wirtschaftsregulierung und zum Einsatz der Regulierungsinstrumente in den Transport-, Kommunikations- und Energiemärkten in der Schweiz und in den Vereinigten Staaten von Amerika / Rolf H. Weber.1. Aufl. Baden-Baden : Nomos, 1986. 710 p. : ill. ; 23 cm. (Wirtschaftsrecht und Wirtschaftspolitik. Bd. 86) Bibliography: p. 665-710. ISBN 3-7890-1288-2 LC Card 87-128141
1. Trade regulation - Switzerland. 2. Trade regulation - United States. 3. Restraint of trade - Switzerland. 4. Restraint of trade - United States. I. Title.
HD3616.S93 W425 1986

Weber, Therese. Mägde . Wien , 1985. 211 p. : ISBN 3-205-06154-3 LC Card 86-127196
HD6072.2.A9 M34 1985

Weber, Wilhelm, 1916- Perspektiven der Genossenschaftsrevision . Wien , 1986. x, 322 p. : ISBN 3-85368-775-X LC Card 87-138767 DDC 334/.09436 19
HD3490 .P47 1986

WEBER, WILHELM, 1916-
Perspektiven der Genossenschaftsrevision . Wien , 1986. x, 322 p. : ISBN 3-85368-775-X LC Card 87-138767 DDC 334/.09436 19
HD3490 .P47 1986

Webre, Philip. The budgetary and economic effects of oil taxes. Washington, DC : Congress of the U. S., Congressional Budget Office : For sale by the Supt. of Docs., U. S. G.P.O., 1986 xvi, 55 p. ; 26 cm. (CBO study) "April 1986."--Cover. Includes bibliographical references.
1. Petroleum - Taxation - United States. 2. Tariff on petroleum products - United States. I. Title. II. Series.
NYPL [JLF 86-1354]

Webster, Bryce.
The power of consultative selling / Bryce Webster. Englewood Cliffs, N.J. : Prentice-Hall, c1987. xvi, 200 p. ; 24 cm. Bibliography: p. 195-196. Includes index. ISBN 0-13-685918-6 LC Card 87-2251 DDC 658.8/1 19
1. Selling. 2. Selling - Key accounts. I. Title.
HF5438.25 .W287 1987

Winner take all /. New York, NY , c1987. x, 222 p. ; ISBN 0-8144-7689-9 (pbk.) : LC Card 87-47708 DDC 658.4/09 19
HD38.25.U6 W56 1987

Webster, Eddie.
Cast in a racial mould : labour process and trade unionism in the foundries / Eddie Webster. Johannesburg : Ravan Press, 1985. xv, 299 p., [6] p. of plates : ill. ; 22 cm. Bibliography: p. [281]-293. Includes index. ISBN 0-86975-285-5 (pbk.) : LC Card 86-213551 DDC 331.88/1712/0968 19
1. Trade-unions - Foundrymen - South Africa - History. 2. Trade-unions - South Africa - History. 3. Foundrymen - South Africa - History. 4. Trade-unions, Black - South Africa - History. I. Title.
HD6870.5.Z7 F758 1985

Cast in a racial mould : labour process and trade unionism in the foundries / Eddie Webster. Johannesburg : Ravan Press, 1985. xv, 299 p., [8] p. of plates : ill. ; 22 cm. Based on thesis (Ph. D.)--University of the Witwatersrand, 1983. Includes index. Bibliography: p. [281]-293. ISBN 0-86975-285-5
1. Trade-unions, Black - South Africa. 2. Trade-unions - South Africa. 3. Labor and laboring classes - South Africa. 4. Blacks - South Africa - Economic conditions. 5. Foundrymen - South Africa. I. Title.
NYPL [JLD 87-780]

Webster, Frank L. Pacific OCS lease sale, October 1, 1964, Oregon and Washington / by Frank L. Webster ; prepared by Minerals Management Service, Pacific OCS Region. [Washington] : Dept. of the Interior, Minerals Management Service, [1985] iii, 36 p. : ill. ; 28 cm. (OCS report) "October 1985." Bibliography: p. 14-16. "MMS 85-0101." LC Card 86-601138 DDC 333.33/9 19
1. Oil and gas leases - Pacific Coast (U. S.). 2. Offshore oil industry - Pacific Coast (U. S.). 3. Offshore gas industry - Pacific Coast (U. S.). 4. Continental shelf - Pacific Coast (U. S.). I. United States. Minerals Management Service. Pacific OCS Region. II. Title. III. Series.
HD243.A18 W43 1985

Webster's new world illustrated encyclopedic dictionary of real estate /. Gross, Jerome S. New York , c1987. 418 p. : ISBN 0-13-947318-1 (pbk.) : LC Card 87-2360 DDC 333.33/03/21 19
HD1365 .G76 1987

Wechsel auf die Zukunft / Kommunalverband Ruhrgebiet. Stand 7/84. Essen : Kommunalverband Ruhrgebiet, Abt. Öffentlichkeitsarbeit, [1984] 25 p. : col. ill. ; 30 cm. Cover title. CONTENTS. - Wir prägen die Region seit über 60 Jahren mit -- Wir sichern und pflegen die Landschaft -- Wir planen und gestalten -- Wir machen die Freizeit attraktiver -- Wir beraten bei technischen Lösungen -- Wir beseitigen und verwerten Abfälle -- Wir erkunden und vermessen unsere Umwelt -- Wir informieren über die Region. LC Card 85-105225
1. Ruhr (Germany : Region) - Economic policy. 2. Ruhr (Germany : Region) - Economic conditions. I. Kommunalverband Ruhrgebiet.
HC288.R8 W43 1984

Wechselkurspolitik in der Planwirtschaft . Böhm, Edward. Hamburg , 1986. 139 p. : ISBN 3-87895-301-1 LC Card 86-210978
HG3947.5 .B64 1986

Wechselkursprognosen . Hinder, Alex, 1954- Bern , New York , c1983. xvii, 424 p. : ISBN 3-261-03345-2 LC Card 86-104957
HG3823 .H5 1983

Wechselkursrisiko, Informationsverarbeitung und Devisenterminmarkt /. Schmidt, Martin, 1953- Frankfurt am Main , New York , c1985. 253 p. : ISBN 3-8204-8882-0 : LC Card 85-209898
HG3823 .S35 1985

Wechselwirkungen von Geldpolitik, Inflation und Strukturwandel : Ergänzungsband 1 zum HWWA-Strukturbericht 1983 : Forschungsauftrag des Bundesministers für Wirtschaft / Hans-Hagen Härtel ... [et al.]. Hamburg : Verlag Weltarchiv, 1984. 179 p. : ill. ; 24 cm. (Veröffentlichungen des HWWA-Institut für Wirtschaftsforschung-Hamburg) Bibliography: p. 166-169. Includes index. ISBN 3-87895-243-0 LC Card 84-221405
1. Prices - Germany, West. 2. Inflation (Finance) - Germany, West. I. Härtel, Hans-Hagen. II. Germany (West). Bundesministerium für Wirtschaft. III. Analyse der strikturellen Entwicklung der deutschen Wirtschaft.
HB235.G3 W42 1984

Weck-Hannemann, Hannelore.
Die heimliche Wirtschaft : Struktur und Entwicklung der Schattenwirtschaft in der Schweiz / Hannelore Weck-Hannemann, Werner W. Pommerehne, Bruno S. Frey. Bern : P. Haupt, c1986. 112 p. : ill. ; 23 cm. (Res publica Helvetica. 18) Bibliography: p. 101-105. Includes indexes. ISBN 3-258-03541-5 LC Card 86-159961
1. Informal sector (Economics) - Switzerland. I. Pommerehne, Werner W. II. Frey, Bruno S. III. Title.
HD2346.S9 W43 1986

Schattenwirtschaft : eine Möglichkeit zur Einschränkung der öffentlichen Verwaltung : eine ökonomische Analyse / Hannelore Weck. Frankfurt am Main ; New York : P. Lang, c1983. 152 p. : ill. ; 21 cm. (Finanzwissenschaftliche Schriften, 0170-8253 . Bd. 22) Originally presented as the author's thesis (doctoral--Universität Zürich). Bibliography: p. 140-152. ISBN 3-8204-7590-7 (pbk.) LC Card 87-672943
1. Informal sector (Economics). 2. Trade regulation. I. Title. II. Series.
HD2341 .W37x 1983

Weck, Philippe de, 1919-
Un banquier suisse parle : entretiens avec François Gross / Philippe de Weck. Fribourg : Editions M. Michel, c1983. 159 p. ; 21 cm. LC Card 84-119161
1. Weck, Philippe de, 1919- - Interviews. 2. Bankers - Switzerland - Interviews. 3. Banks and banking - Switzerland. I. Gross, François. II. Title.
HG1552.W43 A3 1983

WECK, PHILIPPE DE, 1919- - INTERVIEWS.
Weck, Philippe de, 1919- Un banquier suisse parle . Fribourg , c1983. 159 p. ; LC Card 84-119161
HG1552.W43 A3 1983

Weeber und Partner, Büro für Stadtplanung und Sozialforschung. Standorte von Büros im Urteil der Beschäftigten und sonstiger Nutzer /. Stuttgart , 1983. 140 p. : LC Card 83-220559
HF5547.25 .S74 1983

Wege der Forschung, 0509-9609 .
(Bd. 591) Standorte und Einzugsbereiche tertiärer Einrichtungen . Damrstadt , 1985. vi, 403 p., [1] folded leaf of plates : ISBN 3-534-08402-0 LC Card 86-228150
HF5547.25 .S73 1985

Wegehenkel, Lothar.
Symposion "Marktwirtschaft und Umwelt" (1980 : Walter Eucken Institut) Marktwirtschaft und Umwelt . Tübingen , 1981. ix, 303 p. : ISBN 3-16-343372-3 : LC Card 81-128698 DDC 363.7/0526 19
HC79.E5 S92 1980 ***NYPL [TB (Walter Eucken Institut. Wirtschaftswissenschaftliche und wirtschaftsrechtliche Untersuchungen. Bd. 17)]***

Symposium Umweltprobleme als Herausforderung der Marktwirtschaft, Neue Ideen jenseits des Dirigismus (1983 : Stuttgart, Germany) Symposium Umweltprobleme als Herausforderung der Marktwirtschaft, Neue Ideen jenseits des Dirigismus . [Köln] [Freiburg] , 1983. 300 p. ; ISBN 3-7616-0722-9 LC Card 84-152335 DDC 363.7/058 19
HC79.E5 S96 1983 ***NYPL [JLD 86-1631]***

Wegg, John. Bluebirds / John Wegg. [Helsinki?] : J. Wegg, c1985. 216 p. : ill. (some col.) ; 22 x 30 cm. Includes some texts in Finnish. Includes index.

ISBN 951-99691-4-4 LC Card 86-223952 DDC 387.7/065/4897 19
1. Finnair - History. 2. Aeronautics, Commercial - Finland - History. I. Title.
HE9855.3.F5 W4 1985

Wegmann, 1951- Gemeinkosten-Management : Möglichkeiten und Grenzen der Steuerung industrieller Verwaltungsbereiche / Wegmann. München : V. Florentz, c1982. 230, xliii p. : ill. ; 21 cm. (Wirtschaftswissenschaftliche Forschung und Entwicklung . Bd. 80) Author's name appearing on p. [4] of cover: Manfred Wegmann. Bibliography: p. vi-xl. Includes index. ISBN 3-88259-224-9 (Deut. Bibl.) LC Card 83-159003
1. Zero-based budgeting. 2. Program budgeting. I. Title. II. Title: Gemeinkostenmanagement. III. Series.
HJ2033 .W43 1982

Wegner, Gerhard, 1953- Bauern, Kapital und Staat in Kenia : eine Einführung / Gerhard Wegner. Berlin : Argument-Verlag, c1983. 94 p. : maps ; 19 cm. (Argument Studienhefte . SH 59) Bibliography: p. 83-89. ISBN 3-88619-038-2 : LC Card 85-171380
1. Peasantry - Government policy - Kenya. 2. Rural development - Government policy - Kenya. 3. Kenya - Economic policy. 4. Kenya - Social policy. 5. Capitalism - Kenya. I. Title. II. Series.
HD1538.K4 W44 1983

Wegner, Manfred. Ochel, Wolfgang, 1943- Service economies in Europe . Boulder , 1987. p. cm. ISBN 0-8133-0580-2 : LC Card 87-21690 DDC 338.4/6/094 19
HD9986.A2 O28 1987

Wegweiser zur Weiterbildung . Klause, Dieter. Bonn , 1982. 101 p. ; LC Card 83-206662
HF5549.5.T7 K58 1982

Wehland, Wilhelm. Groebel, Wilhelm. Lebensmittelüberwachung . Dortmund , 1976. 84 p. : LC Card 86-170104
HD30 .A7 Heft 167 HD9000.9

Wehling, Hans-Werner, 1949- Wohnstandorte und Wohnumfeldprobleme in der Kernzone des Ruhrgebietes / Hans-Werner Wehling. Paderborn : Schöningh, 1984. ix, 285 p. : ill., maps ; 30 cm. (Essener geographische Arbeiten . Bd. 9) Summary in English and German. Bibliography: p. 228-247. ISBN 3-506-72309-X LC Card 85-121205
1. Housing policy - Germany (West) - Ruhr (Region). 2. Ruhr (Germany : Region) - Population. 3. Ruhr (Germany : Region) - Economic conditions. I. Title. II. Series.
HD7339.R79 W44 1984

Wehrli, Hans-Peter. Strategisches Marketing und Management . Bern , c1986. 205 p. : ISBN 3-258-03566-0 : LC Card 86-159360
HF5415.135 .S77 1986

Weibel, Bernd, 1951- Differenzierung der Berufsausbildung : ein Beitrag zur bildungsplanerischen Diskussion um strukturelle Voraussetzungen eines zweckrational gestalteten Bildungswesens / Bernd Weibel. Heidelberg : Esprint-Verlag, 1984. iv, 326, 6 p. : ill. ; 21 cm. (Schriftenreihe Wirtschaftsdidaktik Berufsbildung und Konsumentenerziehung . Bd. 4) A revision of the author's thesis (doctoral--Universität Mannheim, 1984) presented under the title: Differenzierung, strukturelle Voraussetzung zweckrational gestalteter Berufsausbildung. Bibliography: p. 300-326. ISBN 3-88326-138-6 LC Card 85-189624
1. Vocational guidance. 2. Occupational training. I. Title. II. Series.
HF5381 .W43 1984

Weible, Robert. Lowell Conference on Industrial History (1984) The world of the Industrial Revolution . [Andover, MA] , 1986. 177 p. : ISBN 0-937474-08-8 (pbk.) LC Card 86-31242 DDC 338.09 19
HD2321 .L69 1984

Weiblen, Willi. Sander, Otfried. Kommunale Wirtschaftsunternehmen /. Köln , 1982. xiv, 144 p. : ISBN 3-555-00464-6 LC Card 81-192097
HD4659 .S26 1982

Weich, Götz. ADAC. Strassenverkehr 2000 . München [1979] 24 p. : LC Card 85-147077
HE363.G3 A33 1979

Weiche Modelle und iterative Schätzung . Meissner, Werner, 1937- Frankfurt , New York , c1982. 114 p. : ISBN 3-593-33105-5 : LC Card 83-126780
HB141 .M415 1982

Weick, Edgar. Processi formativi e coscienza operaia . Pisa , c1983. 509 p. ; LC Card 86-136656 DDC 658.3/124/0945 19
HF5549.5.T7 P69 1983
NYPL [JLE 87-1466]

Weida, William J. The political economy of national defense / William J. Weida and Frank L. Gertcher. Boulder : Westview Press, 1987. xvii, 230 p. ; 24 cm. Includes index. Bibliography: p. 209-219. ISBN 0-8133-0432-6 (alk. paper) : LC Card 86-19015 DDC 355.6/22/0973 19
1. Munitions - United States. 2. Munitions - Economic aspects - United States. 3. Budget - United States. 4. United States - Armed Forces - Appropriations and expenditures. 5. United States - Military policy. 6. United States - Politics and government - 1981-. I. Gertcher, Frank L. II. Title.
UA23 .W3694 1987 ***NYPL [JLE 87-1043]***

Weideman, Donald James. A model to predict urban influenced land prices / prepared by Donald James Weideman. [Edmonton, Alta.] : Alberta Municipal Affairs, Innovative Housing Grants Program, [1986] xi, 294 p. : ill. ; 28 cm. "April 1986." Bibliography: p. 286-294. ISBN 0-88654-148-4 (pbk.) LC Card 86-231786 DDC 333.33/7 19
1. Real property - Prices - Alberta - Forecasting - Mathematical models. 2. Land use, Urban - Alberta - Forecasting - Mathematical models. I. Innovative Housing Grants Program (Alta.). II. Title.
HD319.A4 W45 1986

Weidenbaum, Murray L. Public policy toward corporate takeovers /. New Brunswick (USA) , c1988. xvi, 176 p. ; ISBN 0-88738-166-9 : LC Card 87-10750 DDC 338.8/3/0973 19
HD2795 .P825 1988

Weidlein, Marianne S., 1944- Visions & business : support & tools for the entrepreneur / by Marianne S. Weidlein, with Stephanie F. Roth. Boulder, Colo. : MegaBooks, 1987, c1986. 261 p. in various pagings : ill. ; 28 cm. On t.p. the "s" in "support" appears as a dollar sign. Includes bibliography and index. ISBN 0-942097-11-4 (3-ring binder ed.) : LC Card 87-7935 DDC 658/.007/7 19
1. Management - Programmed instruction. I. Roth, Stephanie F., 1949-. II. Title. III. Title: Visions and business.
HD30.4 .W43 1987

Weidner, Marcus, 1964- Nur Gräber als Spuren : das Leben und Sterben von Kriegsgefangenen und "Fremdarbeitern" in Münster während der Kriegszeit 1939-1945 / Marcus Weidner ; mit einem Vorwort von H. Wienold und H.G. Thien. Münster : Westfälisches Dampfboot, c1984. 134 p. : ill. ; 21 cm. Author's dedication on t.p. Bibliography: p. 128-132. ISBN 3-924550-02-6 LC Card 86-116688 DDC 331.11/732/094355 19
1. Forced labor - Germany (West) - Münster in Westfalen - History. 2. Prisoners of war - Germany (West) - Münster in Westfalen - History. 3. World War, 1939-1945 - Prisoners and prisons, German. 4. Alien labor - Germany (West) - Münster in Westfalen - History. 5. Münster in Westfalen (Germany) - History. I. Title.
HD4875.G4 W45 1984

Weigel, Christoph. Handwerk um 1700 . Hürtgenwald , c1985. 245 p. : ISBN 3-87646-052-2 : LC Card 85-211788
HD2346.N4 H35 1985

Weigel, George. Tranquillitas ordinis : the present failure and future promise of American Catholic thought on war and peace / George Weigel. Oxford ; New York : Oxford University Press, 1987. xiii, 489 p. ; 24 cm. Includes bibliographical references and index. ISBN 0-19-504193-3 (alk. paper) : LC Card 86-12742 DDC 261.8/73/08822 19
1. Catholic Church - Doctrines. 2. Peace - Religious aspects - Catholic Church. 3. War - Religious aspects - Catholic Church. I. Title.
BX1795.P43 W45 1987
NYPL [JFE 87-1638]

Weigert, Edmund. Defizitfinanzierte Fiskalpolitik in einer kleinen offenen Volkswirtschaft bei flexiblen Wechselkursen : eine wechselkurstheoretische Analyse / Edmund Weigert. Krefeld : G. Marchal und H.-J. Matzenbacher Wissenschaftsverlag, 1987, c1986. iii, 211 p. ; 21 cm. Bibliography: p. 201-211. ISBN 3-88358-071-6 LC Card 87-146660 DDC 339.5/2/0724 19
1. Fiscal policy - Mathematical models. 2. Economic stabilization - Mathematical models. 3. Foreign exchange - Mathematical models. 4. Deficit financing - Mathematical models. I. Title.
HJ161 .W44 1987

Weigert, Martin, Dipl.-Volkswirt. Wirtschaftslexikon /. München , c1987. xv, 661 p. : ISBN 3-486-29691-4 LC Card 87-127454 DDC 330/.03/31 19
HB61 .W558 1987

WEIGHING EQUIPMENT INDUSTRY - UNITED STATES - HISTORY.
Fairbanks' scales, the world's standard . Chicago , 1893. 20 p. : LC Card 85-666379
HD9706.2.U54 E22x 1893

Weigl, Franz, 1948- Die Entwicklung der oberösterreichischen Elektrizitätswirtschaft von den Anfängen bis zum Jahre 1938 / Franz Weigl. Linz : Trauner, [1980] 210, xi p. : ill., map ; 25 cm. (Linzer Schriften zur Sozial- u. Wirtschaftsgeschichte . Bd. 2) One folded map inserted. Bibliography: p. i-xi. ISBN 3-85320-232-2 : LC Card 81-137632
1. Electric utilities - Austria - Upper Austria - History. I. Title. II. Series.
HD9685.A93 U669 1980

Weihe, Carl, b. 1872. Aus eigner Kraft : Bilder von deutscher Technik und Arbeit für die reifere Jugend / von Carl Weihe. Leipzig : B.G. Teubner, 1918. 139 p., X [i.e. 5] p. of plates : ill. ; 20 cm. LC Card 85-666353
1. Germany - Industries. I. Title.
HC283 .W45x 1918

Weihrich, Heinz. Koontz, Harold, 1908- Management /. New York , c1988. xxix, 685 p. : ISBN 0-07-035552-5 : LC Card 87-21519 DDC 658.4 19
HD31 .K6 1988

Weil, Anneliese A. (joint author) Erdsiek, Gerhard. Wörterbuch für Recht, Wirtschaft und Politik. Bleckede bei Hamburg [1964-1968] 2 v. LC Card 65-42077 ***NYPL [JLE 85-408]***

Weil, Éric. Sichirollo, Livio. Morale e morali /. Roma , 1985. 179 p. ; ISBN 88-359-2798-6 : LC Card 85-233121 DDC 170/.9 19
BJ74 .S53 1985 ***NYPL [JFD 87-941]***

Weil, Roman L. Davidson, Sidney, 1919- Financial accounting . Chicago , c1988. xvi, 800 p. ; ISBN 0-03-011522-1 LC Card 87-9135 DDC 657 19
HF5635 .D228 1988

Weiller, Jean, 1905- Croissance, échange et monnaie en économie internationale . Paris , c1985. 604 p. : ISBN 2-7178-0912-0 (pbk.) :
NYPL [JLE 86-1157]

WEILLER, JEAN, 1905-
Croissance, échange et monnaie en économie internationale . Paris , c1985. 604 p. : ISBN 2-7178-0912-0 (pbk.) :
NYPL [JLE 86-1157]

Weimar, Robert. Die Umweltvorsorge im Rahmen der Landesplanung Nordrhein-Westfalen : eine integrationsorientierte Untersuchung / Robert Weimar, Guido Leidig. Frankfurt am Main ; New York : P. Lang, c1983. xxiii, 313 p. : ill. ; 21 cm. (Travaux scientifiques de la Faculté européenne des sciences du foncier-Strasbourg, 0721-5061 = Studies of the European Faculty of Land Use and Development, Strasbourg . Bd. 3) Bibliography: p. [279]-304. Includes indexes. ISBN 3-8204-7669-5 LC Card 83-206670
1. Environmental policy - Germany (West) - North Rhine-Westphalia. 2. North Rhine-Westphalia (Germany) - Economic conditions. I. Leidig, Guido, 1953-. II. Series: Travaux scientifiques de la Faculté européenne des sciences du foncier-Strasbourg , Bd. 3. III. Title.
HC287.N6 W44 1983

Die Weimarer Republik als Wohlfahrtsstaat : zum Verhältnis von Wirtschafts- und Sozialpolitik in der Industriegesellschaft / herausgegeben von Werner Abelshauser. Stuttgart : F. Steiner, 1987. 337 p. ; 23 cm. (Vierteljahrschrift für Sozial- und Wirtschaftsgeschichte. Beihefte. Nr. 81) Papers of a conference held in Berlin under the auspices of the DFG Forschungsprojekt "Deutsche Gewerkschaften", Oct. 7-8, 1985. Bibliography: p. [301]-325. Includes index. ISBN 3-515-04738-7 LC Card 87-131861 DDC 338.943 19
1. Germany - Economic policy - 1918-1933. 2.

Germany - Social conditions - 1918-1933. 3. Germany - Economic conditions - 1918-1945. 4. Germany - Politics and government - 1918-1933. I. Abelshauser, Werner. II. Series.
HC286.3 .W3546 1987

Weimer, Theodor. Die Bedeutung des Osthandels für mittelständische Unternehmen / Theodor Weimer, unter Mitarbeit von Uwe Schwarting. Stuttgart : Poeschel, c1985. 172, 7 p. : ill. ; 24 cm. (Schriften zur Mittelstandsforschung . Nr. 5 NF) ISBN 3-7910-5006-0 LC Card 86-160626
1. Small business - Germany, West. 2. Germany, West - Commerce - Europe, Eastern. 3. Europe, Eastern - Commerce - Germany, West. I. Schwarting, Uwe. II. Title. III. Series.
HF3568.E35 W43 1985
NYPL [JLL 73-505 Nr.5]

Weinbaum, Paul O. Hoosac docks : foreign trade terminal : a case of the expanding transportation system late in the nineteenth century : a special history study, Boston National Historical Park / Paul O. Weinbaum. Boston, Mass. : Division of Cultural Resources, North Atlantic Regional Office, National Park Service, U. S. Dept. of the Interior, 1985. vi, 95 p. : ill., maps (1 folded) ; 28 cm. (Cultural resource management study . no. 11) Bibliography: p. 92-94. LC Card 85-603289 DDC 387.1/64/0974461 19
1. Harbors - Massachusetts - Boston - History. 2. Marine terminals - Massachusetts - Boston - History. I. United States. National Park Service. North Atlantic Regional Office. Division of Cultural Resources. II. Title. III. Series.
HE554.B6 W45 1985

Weinberg, Alvin Martin, 1915- The Nuclear connection . New York , 1985. 295 p. : ISBN 0-88702-204-9 : LC Card 84-26786 DDC 333.79/24 19
HD9698.A2 N77 1985 ***NYPL [JLE 86-1546]***

Weinberg, Daniel H. Fighting poverty . Cambridge, Mass. , 1986. viii, 418 p. : ISBN 0-674-30085-8 (alk. paper) LC Card 85-24848 DDC 362.5/8/0973 19
HC110.P63 F54 1986 ***NYPL [JLE 86-4089]***

Weinberg, Edgar. Labor-management cooperation for productivity / by Edgar Weinberg. New York : Pergamon Press, c1983. 61 p. ; 28 cm. (Work in America Institute studies in productivity . 30) Includes bibliographies. ISBN 0-08-029511-8 (pbk.) LC Card 83-2361 DDC 016.33111/8/0973 19
1. Industrial productivity - United States - Abstracts. 2. Labor-management committees - United States - Abstracts. 3. Quality of work life - United States - Abstracts. I. Title. II. Series.
HD56 .W44 1983
NYPL [JLM 83-380 no.30]

Weinberg, Mark D. Using Managing Your Money / Mark D. Weinberg ; with a foreword by Andrew Tobias. Indianapolis, Ind. : Que Corp., c1987. xviii, 422 p. : ill. ; 24 cm. Includes index. ISBN 0-88022-277-8 (pbk.) : LC Card 86-62530 DDC 332.024/0028/55369 19
1. Managing Your Money (Computer program). 2. Finance, Personal - Data processing. I. Title.
HG179 .W42 1987

Weinberg, Robert. Social democracy and workers in Odessa : ethnic and political considerations / Robert Weinberg. Pittsburgh, Pa. (4E23 Forbes Quad, Pittsburgh 15260) : Center for Russian and East European Studies, University of Pittsburgh, [1986] 34 p. ; 21 cm. (The Carl Beck papers in Russian and East European studies . no. 504) Bibliography: p. 27-34. "July 1986"--T.p. verso. LC Card 86-199472
1. Labor and laboring classes - Ukraine - Odessa - Political activity - History. 2. Ethnicity - Ukraine - Odessa - History. 3. Socialism - Ukraine - Odessa - History. I. Series: Carl Beck papers in Russian and East European studies , paper no. 504. II. Title.
HD8530.O32 W45 1986

Weinberger, Mark. Massa, Alison K. Housing and the environment /. Sacramento, CA (921 10th St., Sacramento 95814-2774) [1985?] 2 v. : LC Card 87-621018 DDC 363.7 19
HD266.C2 M37 1985

Weiner, Edward.
Urban transportation planning in the United States : an historical overview / prepared by Edward Weiner (Office of the Assistant Secretary for Policy and International Affairs, U. S. Department of Transportation).Rev. ed. [Washington, D.C.] : U. S. Dept. of Transportation, Office of the Secretary of Transportation : Distributed in cooperation with Technology Sharing Program, Office of the Secretary of Transportation, [1986] vii, 149 p. : ill. ; 28 cm. "February 1986." Distributed to depository libraries in microfiche. Bibliography: p. 125-140. "Suggestions for further reading": p. 149. "DOT-I-86-09." Item 982-I-15 (microfiche) LC Card 87-601522 DDC 388.4/068 19
1. Urban transportation - United States - Planning - History. 2. Highway planning - United States - History. I. United States. Dept. of Transportation. Office of the Assistant Secretary for Policy and International Affairs. II. Technology Sharing Program (U. S.). III. Title.
HE308 .W45 1986

Urban transportation planning in the United States : an historical overview / Edward Weiner. New York : Praeger, 1987. xii, 122 p. : ill. ; 25 cm. Includes index. Bibliography: p. 107-116. ISBN 0-275-92493-9 (alk. paper) : LC Card 86-30343 DDC 388.4/068 19
I. Title.
HE308 .W45 1987 ***NYPL [JLE 87-1506]***

Weinert, Günter. Wohlers, Eckhardt. Unterschiede in der Beschäftigungsentwicklung zwischen den USA, Japan und der EG . Hamburg , 1986. 294 p. : ISBN 3-87895-307-0 LC Card 86-233505
HD5724 .W57 1986

Weingarten, Richard. Eine kapitaltheoretische Untersuchung zum Gesetz vom tendenziellen Fall der Profitrate einschliesslich der Bestimmung seiner empirischen Relevanz / Richard Weingarten. München : Minerva Publikation, c1982. ix, 342 p. ; 21 cm. (Minerva-Fachserie Wirtschafts- und Sozialwissenschaften) Originally presented as the author's thesis (doctoral)--Universität Bremen, 1979. Bibliography: p. 321-342. ISBN 3-597-10136-4 LC Card 83-134240
1. Profit. 2. Capitalism. 3. Depressions. 4. Marxian economics. I. Title. II. Series.
HB601 .W37 1982

Weinhaus, Carol L. Behind the telephone debates / Carol L. Weinhaus and Anthony G. Oettinger. Norwood, N.J. : Ablex Pub., 1987. p. cm. (Communication and information science) Bibliography: p. Includes index. ISBN 0-89391-452-5 LC Card 87-19459 DDC 384.6/0973 19
1. Telephone - United States - History. 2. American Telephone and Telegraph Company - Reorganization - History. I. Oettinger, Anthony G. II. Title.
HE8815 .W45 1987

WEINKELLEREI PIEROTH (GERMANY)
Janetzki, Annemarie. Das Verbundwinzersystem . Münster , 1982. xxiv, 406 p., [3] folded leaves of plates : ISBN 3-7923-0486-4 LC Card 83-157892
HD9383.5 .J35 1982

Weinreich, Torben. Arbejdet : barn for 100 år siden / Torben Weinreich. [Copenhagen] : Apostrof, c1984. 64 p. : ill. ; 22 cm. ISBN 87-591-0003-6 : LC Card 84-197811
1. Children - Employment - Denmark - History. I. Title.
HD6250.D42 W45 1984

Weinstein, David, 1943- Larréché, Jean-Claude. INDUSTRAT . Englewood Cliffs, N.J. , 1987. p. cm. ISBN 0-13-651373-5 LC Card 87-7144 DDC 658.8 19
HF5415.1263 .L37 1987

Weinstein, Grace W.
The bottom line : inside accounting today / Grace W. Weinstein. New York : New American Library, c1987. 233 p. ; 23 cm. "NAL books." Includes index. ISBN 0-453-00563-2 LC Card 87-11228 DDC 657 19
1. Accounting - United States. I. Title.
HF5616.U5 W44 1987

The lifetime book of money management / Grace W. Weinstein. Rev. ed. New York : New American Library, c1987. xv, 621 p. : ill. ; 23 cm. "A Plume book." Includes index. ISBN 0-452-25893-6 (pbk.) LC Card 86-28644 DDC 332.024 19
1. Finance, Personal. I. Title.
HG179 .W439 1987

Weinstein L., Jacqueline. La industria en una estrategia de desarrollo para Chile / Jacqueline Weinstein. Santiago, Chile : Centro de Estudios del Desarrollo, 1984. 50 leaves ; 28 cm. (Material para discusión . no. 33) Bibliography: leaves 48-50. LC Card 86-139143
1. Industry and state - Chile. 2. Chile - Manufactures. I. Title. II. Series.
HD3616.C52 W45 1984

Weintraub, Andres. IFIP Working Conference on System Modelling and Optimization (1984 : Santiago, Chile) Recent advances in system modelling and optimization . Berlin , New York , c1986. 199 p. : ISBN 0-387-17083-9 (U. S.) LC Card 86-29770 DDC 003 19
QA402 .I43 1984 ***NYPL [JSE 87-639]***

Weintz, Walter. The solid gold mailbox : how to create winning mail-order campaigns / by the man who's done it all, Walter H. Weintz. New York : Wiley, c1987. xiv, 268 p. : ill. ; 25 cm. Includes index. ISBN 0-471-85026-8 LC Card 86-28267 DDC 658.8/72 19
1. Mail-order business -United States. 2. Advertising, Direct-mail - United States. 3. Success in business - United States. I. Title. II. Title: Solid gold mail box.
HF5466 .W45 1987

Weis, Hans Christian. Marketingkommunikation in der Investitionsgüterindustrie : konzeptionelle Überlegungen und Ergebnisse einer empirischen Studie / Hans Christian Weis. Thun : H. Deutsch, c1983. v, 319, xxxix p. : ill. ; 21 cm. (Reihe Wirtschaftswissenschaften, 0253-1488 . Bd. 281) Bibliography: p. vi-xxxix. ISBN 3-87144-741-2 : LC Card 83-159201
1. Communication in marketing - Germany, West. 2. Communication in marketing - Germany, West - Case studies. 3. Advertising - Germany, West. 4. Industrial equipment industry - Germany (West). I. Title. II. Series.
HF5415.123 .W45 1983

Weisband, Edward, 1939- Poverty amidst plenty . Boulder, Colo. , 1989. p. cm. ISBN 0-8133-0523-3 LC Card 87-12829 DDC 330.9/048 19
HC59 .P639 1989

Weisbord, Marvin Ross. Productive workplaces : organizing and managing for dignity, meaning, and community / Marvin R. Weisbord.1st ed. San Francisco : Jossey-Bass, 1987. xxv, 405 p. : ill. ; 24 cm. (The Jossey-Bass management series) Bibliography: p. 381-395. Includes index. ISBN 1-555-42054-0 (alk. paper) LC Card 87-45425 DDC 658.3/14 19
1. Industrial management. 2. Industrial management - Employee participation. 3. Quality of work life. I. Title. II. Series.
HD31 .W424 1987

Weisbrod, Burton Allen, 1931- The nonprofit economy / Burton A. Weisbrod. Cambridge, Mass. : Harvard University Press, 1988. p. cm. Includes index. ISBN 0-674-62625-7 (alk. paper) LC Card 87-23718 DDC 338.7/4 19
1. Corporations, Nonprofit - United States. I. Title.
HD2769.2.U6 W45 1988

Weise, Herbert. Rentenfinanzierung und Rentenbesteuerung : das Besteuerungspotential der Renteneinkommen in der BR Deutschland / von Herbert Weise. Kiel : Institut für Weltwirtschaft an der Universität Kiel, 1978. iii, 64 leaves ; 30 cm. (Kieler Arbeitspapiere . Arbeitspapier Nr. 74 =) Includes bibliographical references. LC Card 85-188549
1. Old age pensions - Taxation - Germany, West. 2. Old age pensions - Taxation - Law and legislation - Germany (West). I. Series: Kieler Arbeitspapiere , Arbeitspapier Nr. 74. II. Title.
HJ4720.A7 W45 1978

Weise, Werner. Die Leistungsbewertung in der Industrie . Jena , 1983. 241 p. ; LC Card 84-176546
HD56.25 .L45 1983

Weiserbs, Daniel.
Employment and growth . Dordrecht , Boston , 1987. xii, 310 p. : ISBN 90-247-3514-9 LC Card 87-3184 DDC 331.11 19
HD73 .E46 1987

Industrial investment in Europe . Dordrecht ; Boston : 389 p. ; ISBN 90-247-3270-0 LC Card 85-26036 DDC 332.6/7253 19
HG5430.5.A3 I54 1985
NYPL [JLE 86-2366]

Weiskopf, F. C. (Franz Carl), 1900-1955. Glaeser, Ernst, 1902-1963. Der Staat ohne Arbeitslose . Berlin , c1931. viii, 198 p. : LC

Card 87-409524 DDC 305.5/62/0947 19
HD8526 .G53 1931

Weiss, Barbara. Financing a common wealth . Washington, DC , 1985. xx, 304 p. : ISBN 0-89125-090-5 LC Card 84-81918
HD3888 .F5 1985 ***NYPL [JLE 86-2519]***

Weiss, David M., 1938-
After the trade is made : processing securities transactions / David M. Weiss. New York, N.Y. : New York Institute of Finance, c1986. xii, 436 p. : ill. ; 24 cm. Includes index. ISBN 0-13-018581-7 : LC Card 85-30997 DDC 332.64/273 19
1. Stock-exchange - United States. 2. Securities - United States. 3. Commodity exchanges - United States. I. New York Institute of Finance. II. Title.
HG4910 .W365 1986 ***NYPL [JLE 86-4304]***

After the trade is made. Study guide for After the trade is made : an operations training manual / the New York Institute of Finance. New York, NY , c1987. ix, 217 p. : ISBN 0-13-858721-3 (pbk.) : LC Card 87-14155 DDC 332.64/273 19
HG4910 .W365 1986 Suppl.

AFTER THE TRADE IS MADE.
Study guide for After the trade is made . New York, NY , c1987. ix, 217 p. : ISBN 0-13-858721-3 (pbk.) : LC Card 87-14155 DDC 332.64/273 19
HG4910 .W365 1986 Suppl.

Weiss, Donald H., 1936-
How to deal with difficult people / Donald H. Weiss. New York, N.Y. : Amacom, c1987. 57 p. ; 18 cm. (The Successful office skills series) Includes index. ISBN 0-8144-7674-0 (pbk.) : LC Card 86-47827 DDC 158/.2 19
1. Conflict management. 2. Interpersonal relations. 3. Interpersonal conflict. I. Title. II. Series.
HD42 .W45 1987

Managing stress / Donald H. Weiss. New York, NY : AMACOM, c1987. 55 p. ; 18 cm. (The Successful office skills series) Includes index. ISBN 0-8144-7673-2 (pbk.) : LC Card 86-47825 DDC 158.7 19
1. Job stress. I. Title. II. Series.
HF5548.85 .W39 1987

Weiss, Joseph W. The management of change : administrative logics and actions / Joseph W. Weiss. New York : Praeger, 1986. xviii, 210 p. ; 25 cm. Includes index. Bibliography: p. 193-202. ISBN 0-275-92195-6 (alk. paper) : LC Card 86-9390 DDC 658.4 19
1. Vocational rehabilitation - United States - History - 20th century. 2. Sheltered workshops - United States - History - 20th century. 3. Strategic planning. I. Title.
HD7256.U5 W38 1986
NYPL [JLE 86-4062]

Weiss, Judith M., 1950- Brentlinger, Marilyn E., 1925- The ultimate benefit book . Cleveland, Ohio , c1987. 231 p. : ISBN 0-940601-01-X : LC Card 87-12171 DDC 361.7/068/1 19
HG177 .B74 1987

Weiss, Kenneth D. (Kenneth Duane), 1940-
Building an import/export business / Kenneth D. Weiss. New York : Wiley, c1987. vii, 264 p. : ill. ; 24 cm. Includes index. ISBN 0-471-84259-1 : LC Card 86-26560 DDC 658.8 19
1. Commerce. I. Title. II. Title: Import/export business.
HF1008 .W43 1987

Weiss, Leonard W.
The extent and permanence of market dominance / von Leonard W. Weiss and George Pascoe. Berlin : Wissenschaftszentrum Berlin, [1984] 30, 7 p. ; 30 cm. (Discussion papers / IIM/Industrial Policy, 0722-6748 . IIM/IP 84-23) "July 1984." Bibliography: p. 29-30. LC Card 85-183107 DDC 338.8/2 19
1. Oligopolies. 2. Industrial concentration. 3. Industrial organization (Economic theory). 4. Barriers to entry (Industrial organization). I. Pascoe, George. II. Series: Discussion papers (International Institute of Management. Industrial Policy) , IIM/IP 84-23. III. Title.
HD2757.3 .W45 1984

Yamawaki, Hideki. Industry competition and the formation of the European common market /. Berlin [1986] 34, 3 p. ; LC Card 87-156700 DDC 341.24/22 19
HD41 .Y35 1986

Weiss, Marc A. (Marc Allan) The rise of the community builders : the American real estate industry and urban land planning / Marc A. Weiss. New York : Columbia University Press, 1987. xii, 228 p. : ill. ; 24 cm. (The Columbia history of urban life) Bibliography: p. [163]-221. Includes index. ISBN 0-231-06504-3 LC Card 87-5115 DDC 333.77/17/0973 19
1. Land use, Urban - United States. 2. City planning - United States. 3. Real estate development - United States. I. Title. II. Series.
HD257 .W46 1987

Weiss, Martin D. Hadady, R. Earl (Robert Earl), 1920- Winning with the insiders /. West Palm Beach, Fla. , c1987. vi, 115 p. : ISBN 0-9613048-8-X : LC Card 87-40003 DDC 332.64/4 19
HG4910 .H18 1987

Weiss, Peter. Clement, Werner. Einkommensverteilung und Qualifikation . Wien , 1984. vi, 201 p. : ISBN 3-85436-020-7 LC Card 84-191161
HC270.I5 C56 1984

Weissbuch Arbeitszeitverkürzung / herausgegeben von der Aktionsgemeinschaft Soziale Marktwirtschaft ; [Autoren], Ernst Breit ... [et al.]. Stuttgart : Verlag Bonn Aktuell, 1983. 152 p. : ill. ; 21 cm. (Bonn-aktuell) ASM-Akzente CONTENTS. - Arbeitszeitverkürzungen / Ernst Breit -- Wirtschaftliche und politische Auswirkungen der Arbeitszeitverkürzung / Werner Kaltefleiter -- Die gesamtwirtschaftlichen Folgen der Arbeitszeitverkürzung / Joachim Starbatty -- Arbeitszeitverkürzung / Dieter Pohmer -- Von fünfunddreissig auf Null verkürzt / Peter Gillies -- Sieben Thesen zum Arbeitsverbot für Inländer / Roland Vaubel -- Arbeitszeiten flexibilisieren / Eduard Gaugler -- Falsche Gewerkschaftsmotivation / Wolfgang Frickhöffer -- Stellungnahme der Aktionsgemeinschaft Soziale Marktwirtschaft (ASM) ISBN 3-87959-212-8 LC Card 84-163631
1. Hours of labor - Germany, West. 2. Hours of labor, Flexible - Germany (West). 3. Work sharing - Germany, West. 4. Unemployed - Germany, West. I. Breit, Ernst. II. Aktionsgemeinschaft Soziale Marktwirtschaft (Germany).
HD5108.2.G47 W45 1983

Weissenberg, Peter. Advances in organizational psychology . Newbury Park , c1987. 314 p. ; ISBN 0-8039-2802-5 LC Card 87-9484 DDC 158.7 19
HF5548.8 .A58 1987

Weissman, Arnold. Verbraucherpanel, Informationen als Grundlage für Marketingentscheidungen im Einzelhandel / Arnold Weissman. München : V. Florentz, c1983. xxviii, 194, [4] p. : ill. ; 21 cm. (Hochschulschriften zur Betriebswirtschaftslehre . Bd. 16) Bibliography: p. x-xxviii. Includes index. ISBN 3-88259-242-7 LC Card 83-161472
1. Consumer panels - Germany (West). I. Title. II. Series.
HF5415.3 .W437 1983

Weissmann, Barbara J. Logue, John, 1947- Buyout! . [Kent, Ohio] [1986] vi, 98 p. : ISBN 0-933522-15-0 (pbk.) LC Card 86-623028 DDC 658.1/6 19
HD2746.5 .L64 1986

Weissmann, Joe. (ill) Drobot, Eve. Amazing investigations . New York , 1988. p. cm. ISBN 0-13-023714-0 LC Card 87-18661 DDC 332.4/9 19
HG173.8 .D76 1988

Weiterbildung, Strukturen und Aspekte . (Bd. 10) Weiterbildungsmodelle und Weiterbildungspraxis in Industrie, Handel, Banken, Versicherungen und Fremdenverkehr /. München , c1984. 169 p. : ISBN 3-19-007546-8 LC Card 85-147442
HF5549.5.T7 W394 1984

Weiterbildungsmodelle und Weiterbildungspraxis in Industrie, Handel, Banken, Versicherungen und Fremdenverkehr / herausgegeben von Geerd Woortmann. München : Lexika Verlag, c1984. 169 p. : ill. ; 21 cm. (Weiterbildung, Strukturen und Aspekte . Bd. 10) Includes bibliographies. ISBN 3-19-007546-8 LC Card 85-147442
1. Employees, Training of - Germany, West. I. Woortmann, Geerd, 1942-. II. Series.
HF5549.5.T7 W394 1984

Weitz, Barton A.
Pederson, Carlton A. Selling . Homewood, Ill. , 1988. xvii, 644 p. : ISBN 0-256-03644-6 LC Card 87-81434 DDC 658.8/5 19
HF5438.25 .P42 1988

Readings in strategic marketing . Chicago , c1988. x, 534 p. : ISBN 0-03-020864-5 (pbk.) LC Card 87-22274 DDC 658.8/02 19
HF5415.135 .R42 1988

Welch, Dale E. Suicides in Maine for the 25 year period, 1958-1982 / by Dale E. Welch. Augusta, Me. : Division of Data and Research, Office of Health Planning and Development, Maine Dept. of Human Services, [1986] ii, 14, [5] p. : ill. ; 28 cm. (Resource series / Division of Data and Research . no. 13) "March 1986." LC Card 86-622276 DDC 362.2 19
1. Suicide - Maine - Statistics. I. Series: Resource series (Maine. Bureau of Health Planning and Development. Division of Data and Research) , no. 13. II. Title.
HB1323.S8 W45 1986

Welch, Robert, 1932- Things that go bump in the flight : a whiteknuckler's guide to air travel / Robert Welch. White Hall, Va. : Betterway Publications, c1987. 156 p. ; 22 cm. ISBN 0-932620-75-2 (pbk.) : LC Card 87-1418 DDC 629.13/0028 19
1. Air travel. 2. Aeronautics - Safety measures. I. Title.
HE9787 .W45 1987

Welcker, J. M. Op een beteren weg . Amsterdam , 1985. 239 p. : ISBN 90-6012-654-8 : LC Card 85-236523
HD8516 .O6 1985 ***NYPL [JLD 86-3427]***

WELCKER, J. M.
Op een beteren weg . Amsterdam , 1985. 239 p. : ISBN 90-6012-654-8 : LC Card 85-236523
HD8516 .O6 1985 ***NYPL [JLD 86-3427]***

Welcome, Mr. President, to Kwara State. Ilorin : Information Division, [1980 or 1981] 28 p. : ill., ports. ; 25 cm. Cover title. Page 28 blank for notes. LC Card 86-194780 DDC 966.9/5 19
1. Kwara State (Nigeria) - Economic conditions. 2. Kwara State (Nigeria) - Social conditions. 3. Kwara State (Nigeria) - Politics and government. I. Kwara State (Nigeria). Information Division.
HC1055.Z7 K898 1980

Welding, cutting and allied processes. Kleiber, Achim W. Fachwörterbuch, Schweissen, Schneiden und verwandte Verfahren /. Düsseldorf , 1986- , c1985- v. ; ISBN 3-87155-707-2 (Bd. 1) LC Card 86-149500 DDC 671.5/2/0331 19
TS227.5 .K54 1986 ***NYPL [JSK 86-83]***

WELDING - DICTIONARIES.
Kleiber, Achim W. Fachwörterbuch, Schweissen, Schneiden und verwandte Verfahren /. Düsseldorf , 1986- , c1985- v. ; ISBN 3-87155-707-2 (Bd. 1) LC Card 86-149500 DDC 671.5/2/0331 19
TS227.5 .K54 1986 ***NYPL [JSK 86-83]***

WELDING - DICTIONARIES - GERMAN.
Kleiber, Achim W. Fachwörterbuch, Schweissen, Schneiden und verwandte Verfahren /. Düsseldorf , 1986- , c1985- v. ; ISBN 3-87155-707-2 (Bd. 1) LC Card 86-149500 DDC 671.5/2/0331 19
TS227.5 .K54 1986 ***NYPL [JSK 86-83]***

Welding equipment & supplies. Welding equipment and supplies market. New York, N.Y. , c1983. 2 v. (v, 316 leaves) ; LC Card 87-143994
HD9697.W433 U548 1983

Welding equipment and supplies market. New York, N.Y. : Frost & Sullivan, c1983. 2 v. (v, 316 leaves) ; 29 cm. Spine title: Welding equipment & supplies. "July, 1983." "(#A1234)." LC Card 87-143994
1. Welding equipment industry - United States. 2. Market surveys - United States. I. Frost & Sullivan. II. Title: Welding equipment & supplies.
HD9697.W433 U548 1983

WELDING EQUIPMENT INDUSTRY - UNITED STATES.
Welding equipment and supplies market. New York, N.Y. , c1983. 2 v. (v, 316 leaves) ; LC Card 87-143994
HD9697.W433 U548 1983

Welfare and worker participation . Kerans, Patrick. New York , 1987. p. cm. ISBN 0-312-00908-9 : LC Card 87-11878 DDC 362.8/5 19
HD7261 .K47 1987

A welfare assessment of transport deregulation . Douglas, Neil J., 1959- Aldershot, Hampshire, England , Brookfield, Vt., USA , c1987. xxiv, 349 p. : ISBN 0-566-05350-0 : LC Card 86-25703 DDC 388.3/22/0941 19
HE5663.A6 D68 1987

WELFARE ECONOMICS.
Barr, Nicholas. The economics of the welfare state /. Stanford, Calif. , 1987. xiv, 475 p. : ISBN 0-8047-1427-4 LC Card 87-60997 DDC 338.941 19
HB846 .B37 1987

Baumol, William J. Microtheory . Brighton, Sussex , 1986. xxvii, 286 p. : ISBN 0-7450-0110-6 LC Card 86-673554
HB171 .B326x 1986b

Hamlin, Alan P., 1951- Ethics, economics, and the state /. Brighton, Sussex , 1986. x, 198 p. ; *NYPL [JLD 86-3648]*

Penz, G. Peter. Consumer sovereignty and human interests /. Cambridge [Cambridgeshire] , New York , 1986. xiv, 242 p. ; ISBN 0-521-26571-1 LC Card 85-22407 DDC 330.15/5 19
HB846 .P46 1986 *NYPL [JLE 86-3311]*

Röpke, Wilhelm, 1899-1966. [Problem of economic order.] 2 essays /. Lanham, MD , c1987. x, 103 p. ; ISBN 0-8191-6125-X (alk. paper) : LC Card 86-33982 DDC 338.9 19
HD82 .R682 1987

Schmid, A. Allan (Alfred Allan), 1935- Property, power, and public choice . New York , 1987. xv, 332 p. : ISBN 0-275-92797-0 (alk. paper) : LC Card 87-22893 DDC 330.1 19
HB73 .S35 1987

Standish, Barry, 1954- The economic factors affecting state output and employment /. Rondebosch [South Africa] [1986] 86 p. : ISBN 0-7992-1016-1 (pbk.) : LC Card 87-112894 DDC 339.2/3 19
HB846 .S73 1986

Tinbergen, Jan, 1903- Warfare and welfare . Brighton, Sussex , New York , 1987. xiv, 189 p. ; ISBN 0-312-00957-7 (St. Martin's) : LC Card 87-9625 DDC 361.6/1 19
HB846 .T55 1987

Tullock, Gordon. Private wants, public means . Lanham , c1987. viii, 262 p. : ISBN 0-8191-6370-8 (pbk. : alk. paper) : LC Card 87-8273 DDC 330.15/5 19
HB99.3 .T8 1987

Welfare economics of the second best /. Wien , New York , c1986. 280 p. ; ISBN 0-387-81942-8 (pbk. : U. S.) LC Card 86-31357 DDC 330.15/5 19
HB846.6 .W45 1986

WELFARE ECONOMICS - ADDRESSES, ESSAYS, LECTURES.
Baumol, William J. Microtheory . Brighton, Sussex , c1986. xxvii, 286 p. : ISBN 0-7450-0110-6 *NYPL [JLF 86-1374]*

Social goals and social organization . Cambridge [Cambridgeshire] , New York , 1985. xii, 365 p. : ISBN 0-521-26204-6 LC Card 85-6668 DDC 330.15/5 19
HB846 .S65 1985 *NYPL [JLE 86-3786]*

WELFARE ECONOMICS - CONGRESSES.
Oligopoly, competition, and welfare /. Oxford, OX, UK , New York, NY, USA , 1985. 191 p. : ISBN 0-631-14479-X (pbk.) LC Card 85-11200 DDC 338.8/2 19
HD2757.3 .O44 1985 *NYPL [JLE 86-1961]*

Welfare economics of the second best / edited by Dieter Bös and Christian Seidl. Wien ; New York : Springer-Verlag, c1986. 280 p. ; 23 cm. (Journal of economics = Zeitschrift für Nationalökonomie. Supplementum . 5) Includes bibliographies. ISBN 0-387-81942-8 (pbk. : U. S.) LC Card 86-31357 DDC 330.15/5 19
1. Second best, Theory of. 2. Welfare economics. I. Bös, Dieter. II. Seidl, Christian. III. Series: Zeitschrift für Nationalökonomie. Supplementum, 5.
HB846.6 .W45 1986

Welfare, freedom, and inflation. Röpke, Wilhelm, 1899-1966. [Problem of economic order.] 2 essays /. Lanham, MD , c1987. x, 103 p. ; ISBN 0-8191-6125-X (alk. paper) : LC Card 86-33982 DDC 338.9 19
HD82 .R682 1987

WELFARE INSTITUTIONS FOR LABORERS. see **WELFARE WORK IN INDUSTRY.**

WELFARE RECIPIENTS - EMPLOYMENT - UNITED STATES.
Malone, Margaret Sahlin, 1933- Work and welfare /. Washington , 1986. ix, 162 p. ; LC Card 86-603383 DDC 362.5/84/0973 19
HD5715.2 .M34 1986

WIN handbook. [Washington, D.C.] [1984]. 1 v. (various pagings) ; *NYPL [JLF 86-372]*

WELFARE STATE - ADDRESSES, ESSAYS, LECTURES.
Barbara Wootton--social science and public policy . London , New York , 1986. xi, 291 p. ; ISBN 0-422-79690-5 LC Card 85-27650 DDC 330 19
HB171 .B248 1985 *NYPL [JLE 86-1743]*

Bilancio della socialdemocrazia . Napoli , 1984. 156 p. ; LC Card 84-249837
HX73 .B55 1984 *NYPL [JLD 87-1536]*

Wohlfahrtsstaat und soziale Probleme /. Opladen , c1984. vi, 294 p. : ISBN 3-531-11701-7 *NYPL [JLD 85-1550]*

Welfare state and bank nationalisation in India /. Shanker Shetty, K. Delhi , 1982. xvii, 345 p. ; ISBN 0-333-90729-9 : LC Card 83-903489 DDC 332.1/0954 19
HG3284 .S4823 1982 *NYPL [JLD 86-4354]*

WELFARE STATE - CONGRESSES.
Futures for the welfare state /. Bloomington , c1986. vi, 444 p. : ISBN 0-253-32440-8 LC Card 85-45959 DDC 330.12/6 19
HB846 .F87 1986 *NYPL [JLE 86-3761]*

WELFARE STATE - HISTORY.
Ewald, François. L'Etat providence /. Paris , c1986. 608 p. ; ISBN 2-246-30731-7 : LC Card 86-160935
HD7175 .E93 1986

WELFARE WORK. see **PUBLIC WELFARE; CHARITIES.**

WELFARE WORK IN INDUSTRY.
Googins, Bradley, 1944- Occupational social work . Silver Spring, MD , 1987. p. cm. ISBN 0-87101-151-4 LC Card 87-20414 DDC 362.8/5 19
HD7261 .G66 1987b

Googins, Bradley, 1944- Occupational social work /. Englewood Cliffs, N.J. , c1987. xii, 227 p. : ISBN 0-13-629445-6 : LC Card 86-25514 DDC 658.3/82 19
HD7261 .G66 1987

WELFARE WORK IN INDUSTRY - BULGARIA.
Kupriīanov, L. A. (Leonid Aleksandrovich) Sotsial'noe planirovanie na predpriīatiīakh NRB, GDR i ChSSR /. Leningrad , 1984. 111 p. ; LC Card 85-116781
HD7741.5 .K86 1984

WELFARE WORK IN INDUSTRY - CASE STUDIES.
Kerans, Patrick. Welfare and worker participation . New York , 1987. p. cm. ISBN 0-312-00908-9 : LC Card 87-11878 DDC 362.8/5 19
HD7261 .K47 1987

WELFARE WORK IN INDUSTRY - CZECHOSLOVAKIA.
Kupriīanov, L. A. (Leonid Aleksandrovich) Sotsial'noe planirovanie na predpriīatiīakh NRB, GDR i ChSSR /. Leningrad , 1984. 111 p. ; LC Card 85-116781
HD7741.5 .K86 1984

WELFARE WORK IN INDUSTRY - GERMANY (EAST)
Kupriīanov, L. A. (Leonid Aleksandrovich) Sotsial'noe planirovanie na predpriīatiīakh NRB, GDR i ChSSR /. Leningrad , 1984. 111 p. ; LC Card 85-116781
HD7741.5 .K86 1984

WELFARE WORK IN INDUSTRY - HUNGARY.
Halmos, Csaba. A szakszervezetek és a tervezés /. Budapest , 1983. 178 p. ; ISBN 963-608-052-6 LC Card 85-108502
HD6680.5 .H34 1983

WELFARE WORK IN INDUSTRY - SWEDEN.
Örning, Birgitta. Solidaritetsarbete . Stockholm [1978?] 66 p. : LC Card 81-140576
HD7728 .O75 1978

WELFARE WORK IN INDUSTRY - UNITED STATES.
Googins, Bradley, 1944- Occupational social work . Silver Spring, MD , 1987. p. cm. ISBN 0-87101-151-4 LC Card 87-20414 DDC 362.8/5 19
HD7261 .G66 1987b

Googins, Bradley, 1944- Occupational social work /. Englewood Cliffs, N.J. , c1987. xii, 227 p. : ISBN 0-13-629445-6 : LC Card 86-25514 DDC 658.3/82 19
HD7261 .G66 1987

Troy, Kathryn. Meeting human needs . New York, NY , c1986. vii, 55 p. ; ISBN 0-8237-0323-1 (pbk.) LC Card 86-207649 DDC 658.3/8 19
HD7654 .T73 1986

WELFARE WORK IN INDUSTRY - UNITED STATES - HISTORY - CASE STUDIES.
Zahavi, Gerald, 1951- Workers, managers, and welfare capitalism . Urbana , c1988. xiii, 261 p., [14] p. of plates : ISBN 0-252-01444-8 (alk. paper) LC Card 87-6035 DDC 331.2/0475/0973 19
HD9787.U6 E654 1988

Welker, Anthony J. The oil and gas Publishing / Anthony J. Welker. Tulsa : SciData Publishing, c1985. xii, 258 p. : ill. ; 22 cm. Includes index. ISBN 0-87814-279-7 (pbk.) : LC Card 85-2096 DDC 338.2/728/0973 19
1. Petroleum industry and trade - United States. 2. Gas industry - United States. I. Title.
HD9565 .W46 1985 *NYPL [JLD 86-4010]*

WELL DRILLING, GAS. see **GAS WELL DRILLING.**

WELL DRILLING, OIL. see **OIL WELL DRILLING.**

Wellings, Paul. Industrial decentralisation under apartheid : an empirical assessment of industrial decentralisation in South Africa / by Paul Wellings and Anthony Black. Durban : Development Studies Unit, University of Natal, 1984. 48, xxxii p. : ill. ; 21 cm. (Working paper / Development Studies Unit, University of Natal . no. 12) Bibliography: p. xiii-xvii. ISBN 0-86980-455-3 (pbk.) LC Card 87-127005 DDC 338.968 19
1. South Africa - Industries - Location - Government policy. 2. Apartheid - South Africa. 3. Homelands (South Africa) - Industries. I. Black, Anthony. II. Series: Working paper (University of Natal. Centre for Applied Social Sciences. Development Studies Unit) , no. 12. III. Title.
HC905.Z9 D59 1984

Wellons, Philip A.
Banks and specialised financial intermediaries in development / by Philip Wellons, Dimitri Germidis, Bianca Glavanis. Paris : Development Centre of the Organisation for Economic Co-operation and Development ; Washington, D.C. : OECD Publications and Information Centre [distributor], 1986. 150 p. : ill. ; 23 cm. (Development Centre studies) Bibliography: p. 131-133. ISBN 92-64-12867-0 (pbk.) : LC Card 87-114506 DDC 332.1/09172/4 19
1. Banks and banking - Developing countries. 2. Financial institutions - Developing countries. 3. Intermediation (Finance) - Developing countries. I. Germidis, Dimitri A. II. Glavanis, Bianca. III. Organisation for Economic Co-operation and Development. Development Centre. IV. Title.
HG3550 .W45 1986

Passing the buck : banks, governments, and Third World debt / Philip A. Wellons. Boston, Mass. : Harvard Business School Press, c1987. xiv, 342 p. : ill. ; 25 cm. Includes bibliographical references and index. ISBN 0-87584-146-5 (alk. paper) LC Card 86-19508 DDC 332.1/53 19
1. Loans, Foreign - Developing countries. 2. Debts, External - Developing countries. I. Title.
HG3891.5 .W46 1987 *NYPL [JLE 87-1072]*

Wells, Alexander T. General aviation marketing / by Alexander T. Wells and Bruce D. Chadbourne. Malabar, Fla. : R.E. Krieger Pub. Co., 1987. viii, 268 p. : ill. ; 29 cm. Includes bibliographies and index. ISBN 0-89874-987-5 LC Card 86-21504 DDC 629.133/340422/0688 19
1. Airplanes - Marketing. I. Chadbourne, Bruce D. II. Title.
HD9711.A2 W45 1987

Wells, Della Wager. George Waldo Woodruff : a life of quiet achievement / Della Wager Wells. [Macon, Ga. : Mercer University Press], c1987. x, 167 p. : ill., ports. ; 29 cm. Includes bibliographies and index. ISBN 0-86554-298-8 LC Card 87-24700 DDC 338/.04/0924 B 19
1. Woodruff, George Waldo. 2. Businessmen - United States - Biography. 3. Engineers - United States - Biography. 4. Philanthropists - United States - Biography. I. Title.
HC102.5.W66 W45 1987

Wells, Don, 1946- Empty promises : quality of working life programs and the labor movement / Donald M. Wells ; foreword by Staughton Lynd. New York : Monthly Review Press, c1987. xviii, 167 p. ; 21 cm. Bibliography: p. 157-167. ISBN 0-85345-710-7 : LC Card 87-24687 DDC 331.25 19
1. Quality of work life - United States. 2. Trade-unions - United States - Officials and employees. 3. Quality of work life. I. Title.
HD6957.U6 W34 1987

Wells, J. R. (John R.) Rowthorn, Bob. De-industrialization and foreign trade /. Cambridge [Cambridgeshire] , New York , 1987. xi, 422 p. : ISBN 0-521-26360-3 LC Card 87-6331 DDC 338.0941 19
HC256.5 .R683 1987

Wells, Jeremy. The export marketing of technical consulting services from developing countries / [by Jeremy Wells]. Geneva : International Trade Centre, UNCTAD, GATT, 1986. vi, 127 p. : ill. ; 23 cm. (ITC publications) Bibliography: p. 125-127. LC Card 87-168669 DDC 658.4/6/091724 19
1. Service industries - Developing countries. 2. Consultants - Developing countries. 3. Export marketing - Developing countries. I. Title. II. Series.
HD9989.D44 W46 1986

WELLS - KENYA - NYANZA PROVINCE. Kenya. Lake Basin Development Authority. A socio-cultural investigation into the use and functioning of the completed shallow wells in Nyanza Province /. Kisumu, [Kenya] , 1983. 2 v. ; LC Card 84-983298 DDC 333.91/009676/29 19
HD1699.K42 N935 1983 ***NYPL [JLF 86-575]***

Wells, Louis T. Vernon, Raymond, 1913- Manager in the international economy /. Englewood Cliffs, NJ , c1986. viii, 469 p. : ISBN 0-13-550807-X : LC Card 85-25653 DDC 658.1/8 19
HD62.4 .V48 1986 ***NYPL [JLE 86-3200]***

Wells, Nancy E., 1946- Straight forward managerial accounting applications : using Lotus 1-2-3 / by Nancy E. Wells.1st ed. Burlington, VT : Champlain Press, 1987, c1986. p. cm. ISBN 0-9612704-1-1 LC Card 87-22393 DDC 658.1/511/02855369 19
1. Lotus 1-2-3 (Computer program). 2. Managerial accounting - Data processing. I. Title.
HF5657.4 .W44 1987

WELLS, OIL. see OIL WELLS.

Wells, Richard C. The right choice : a guide to making the best business decisions / by Richard C. Wells. New York, N.Y., U. S. A. : Modern Business Reports, c1985. viii, 178 p. : ill. ; 28 cm. "Alexander Hamilton Institute Incorporated"--Cover. ISBN 0-86604-198-2 (pbk.) LC Card 86-201105 DDC 658.4/033 19
1. Industrial management - Handbooks, manuals, etc. 2. Decision-making - Handbooks, manuals, etc. I. Alexander Hamilton Institute (U. S.). II. Title.
HD31 .W457 1985

Wells, Roger A. E. Wretched faces : famine in wartime England, 1793-1801 / Roger Wells. New York : St. Martin's Press, 1988. p. cm. Bibliography: p. Includes index. ISBN 0-312-01248-9 : LC Card 87-22164 DDC 363.8/0942 19
1. Famines - Great Britain - History. 2. Great Britain - Economic conditions - 1760-1860. I. Title.
HC260.F3 W45 1988

WELLS - TANZANIA - CONGRESSES. Workshop on the Institutionalization of the Shallow Wells Programme under Tanzanian Administration (1981 : University of Dar es Salaam) Proceedings of the Workshop on the Institutionalization of the Shallow Wells Programme under Tanzanian Administration /. [Dar es Salaam?] , 1981. 3, 16, 12 p. ; LC Card 85-980881 DDC 333.7/09678 s 333.91/22/09678 19
HD107 .D36 no. 71 HD1699.T33

Wells, Walter. Communications in business / Walter Wells. 5th ed. Boston : PWS-Kent Pub. Co., c1988. xvi, 632 p. : ill. ; 25 cm. Includes index. ISBN 0-534-87167-4 LC Card 87-22721 DDC 651.7/4 19
1. Commercial correspondence. 2. Business report writing. I. Title.
HF5721 .W36 1988

Welsch, Glenn A. Fundamentals of financial accounting / Glenn A. Welsch, Daniel G. Short. 5th ed. Homewood, Ill. : Irwin, 1987. xviii, 958 p. : ill. ; 25 cm. (The Robert N. Anthony/Willard J. Graham series in accounting) Includes bibliographical references and index. ISBN 0-256-03614-4 LC Card 86-82802 DDC 657 19
1. Accounting. I. Short, Daniel G. II. Title. III. Series.
HF5635 .W458 1987b

Welsch, Johann. Gewerkschaften und Strukturwandel : Strukturberichterstattung der Forschungsinstitute / Johann Welsch. Köln : Bund-Verlag, c1986. iii, 114 p. ; 21 cm. (WSI-Studie zur Wirtschafts- und Sozialforschung . Nr. 57) Bibliography: p. 100-114. ISBN 3-7663-3011-X LC Card 86-223645 DDC 331.13/704 19
1. Trade-unions - Germany, West. 2. Unemployment, Structural - Germany (West). 3. Microelectronics - Social aspects - Germany (West). I. Title. II. Series.
HD6694 .W37 1986

Weltbevölkerung 2000 . Stempell, Dieter. Leipzig , 1985. 200 p. : LC Card 86-166553
HB849.53 .S74 1985

Weltenergie- und Weltrohstoffwirtschaft /. Domdey, Karl Heinz. Berlin , 1981. 198 p. ; LC Card 85-132039
HD9502.A2 D65 1981

Welternährung . Blanckenburg, Peter von. München , c1986. 347 p. : ISBN 3-406-31300-0 LC Card 86-196307
HD9000.5 .B49 1986

Welternährung und die Verantwortlichkeit der Industrieländer /. Tangermann, Stefan. Kiel , 1986. 27 p. ; ISBN 3-925357-38-6 LC Card 87-126268 DDC 338.1/9/1724 19
HD9018.D44 T36 1986

Welthandel morgen : Konsequenzen für entwickelte und unterentwickelte Länder / mit Beiträgen von Michael Bohnet ... [et al.].1. Aufl. Stuttgart : Bonn Aktuell, 1984. 275 p. : ill. ; 21 cm. (Edition Dräger-Stiftung . Bd. 8) Papers presented at the 3d Malenter Symposion held in 1983 and organized by the Dräger-Stiftung. Includes discussions. Includes bibliographies. CONTENTS. - Die Entwicklungsländer in der internationalen Arbeitsteilung / Juergen B. Donges -- Konsequenzen für die Entwicklungsländer aus ihrer Integration in den internationalen Warenaustausch / Michael Bohnet -- Die Konsequenzen für Entwicklungsländer aus ihrer weltwirtschaftlichen Integration / El Shagi El Shagi -- Auswirkungen auf die Industrieländer, Bilanz und Folgerungen / Helga Steeg -- Auswirkungen auf die Industrieländer, Reaktionen und Perspektiven / Dietrich Kebschull -- Political foundations of European Community protectionism / Jean Waelbroeck -- Möglichkeiten und Grenzen einer entwicklungsfördernden Weltwirtschaftsordnung / Hans-R. Hemmer -- Die internationale Finanzordnung auf dem Prüfstand / Horst Schulmann -- Die Bedeutung eines funktionsfähigen Bankensystems für die Entwicklungsländer / Werner Hammel -- Globale Verschuldungs- oder Liquiditätskrise / Norbert Kloten. ISBN 3-87959-225-X LC Card 85-132786
1. Developing countries - Commerce - Congresses. 2. International economic integration - Congresses. 3. International finance - Congresses. 4. International economic relations - Congresses. I. Bohnet, Michael. II. Malenter Symposion (3d : 1983). III. Dräger-Stiftung. IV. Series.
HF4055 .W45 1984

Welthandels- und Entwicklungskonferenz der Vereinten Nationen. see United Nations. Conference on Trade and Development.

Weltökonomie oder Nationalökonomie? . Roth, Bernhard. Marburg , c1984. xiv, 377 p. : ISBN 3-921630-48-7 : LC Card 84-252964
HF1411 .R69 1984

Weltpostverein (UPU) . Sieger (Firm) Lorch/Württemberg , c1982. 408 p. : LC Card 83-224689
HE6271 .S55 1982

Weltwirtschaft und Weltwirtschaftslehre . Domdey, Karl Heinz. Berlin , 1984. 366 p. : LC Card 84-245611
HC54 .D65 1984

Die weltwirtschaftliche Herausforderung . Jens, Uwe, 1935- Baden-Baden , 1986. 182 p. : ISBN 3-7890-1335-8 (Deut. Bibl.) LC Card 87-146574
HD3616.G4 J46 1986

Weltwirtschaftsgipfel /. De Menil, George, 1940- Bonn [1983] iv, 130 p. ; ISBN 3-7713-0203-X LC Card 85-224780
HF1411 .D345 1983

Weltz, Friedrich. Innovation im Büro : das Beispiel Textverarbeitung / Friedrich Weltz, Veronika Lullies (Sozialwissenschaftliche Projektgruppe München). Frankfurt ; New York : Campus, c1983. 343 p. ; 22 cm. (Schriftenreihe "Humanisierung des Arbeitslebens" . Bd. 38) Bibliography: p. 337-343. ISBN 3-593-32724-4 LC Card 83-243001
1. Word processing operations - Management. 2. Office practice - Automation - Management. 3. Organizational change. 4. Office management. 5. White collar workers - Effect of technological innovations on. I. Lullies, Veronika. II. Sozialwissenschaftliche Projektgruppe München. III. Title. IV. Series.
HF5548.115 .W44 1983

Welzk, Stefan. Boom ohne Arbeitsplätze / Stefan Welzk. Köln : Kiepenheuer & Witsch, c1986. 250 p. ; 19 cm. Includes bibliographical references. ISBN 3-462-01787-X LC Card 86-230211
1. Foreign trade and employment - Germany (West). 2. Foreign trade and employment. 3. Unemployment - Germany (West). 4. Unemployment. I. Title.
HD5710.75.G3 W44 1986

Welzmüller, Rudolf. Preispolitik und Akkumulation : Untersuchung zur Preissetzungspolitik auf oligopolistischen Märkten, dargestellt am Beispiel der chemischen Industrie / Rudolf Welzmüller. Köln : Bund-Verlag, c1982. 283 p. : ill. ; 21 cm. (WSI-Studie zur Wirtschafts- und Sozialforschung) Originally presented as the author's thesis (doctoral)--Johann-Wolfgang-Goethe Universität, Frankfurt/Main, 1981. Bibliography: p. 273-283. ISBN 3-7663-0522-0 : LC Card 82-140922 DDC 338.8/266/00943 19
1. Chemical industries - Germany, West. 2. Price policy - Case studies. 3. Oligopolies - Case studies. I. Title. II. Series.
HD9654.5 .W44 1982 ***NYPL [JLD 86-2908]***

Wemelsfelder, Jozias. De Verzorgingsstaat, slopen of renoveren? /. Assen , 1986. 152 p. : ISBN 90-232-2180-X : LC Card 86-186673
HC325 .V45 1986

Wende wohin? : die Deutschen und der neue Weg / Rohrmoser ... [et al. ; herausgegeben von Klaus Kunkel ; Redaktion Ingrid Schneider]. Köln : Informedia, c1983. 139 p. ; 19 cm. CONTENTS. - Geistige Wende / Günter Rohrmoser -- Macht unsere Gesellschaft keinen Spass mehr? / Ludolf Herrmann -- Überbevölkerung, Ausbeutung der Erde, Urform der Wirtschaft / Horst Nachtigall -- Krise der Wirtschaft / Hugo Müller-Vogg. ISBN 3-921349-34-6 LC Card 84-150290
1. Germany, West - Economic conditions - 1974-. 2. Germany (West) - Politics and government - 1982-. 3. Germany, West - Civilization. I. Rohrmoser, Günter. II. Kunkel, Klaus. III. Schneider, Ingrid, 1953-.
HC286.7 .W4 1983 ***NYPL [JFC 87-1258]***

Wendel, George D. Schmandt, Henry J. Federal aid to St. Louis /. Washington, D.C. , c1983. xvii, 67 p. ; ISBN 0-8157-7727-2 (pbk.) LC Card 82-74100 DDC 336.1/85 19
HJ9268.S3 S352 1983 ***NYPL [JLE 87-1]***

Wender, Astrid. Entscheidungsspiele in Politik, Verwaltung und Wirtschaft / Astrid Wender. Opladen : Westdeutscher Verlag, c1983. vii, 248 p. : 3 ill. ; 23 cm. (Beiträge zur sozialwissenschaftlichen Forschung. Bd. 50) Bibliography: p. 235-247. ISBN 3-531-11669-X LC Card 84-109871
1. Decision-making. I. Title.
HD30.23 .W46 1983

Wenders, John T. The economics of telecommunications : theory and policy / John T. Wenders. Cambridge, Mass. : Ballinger Pub. Co., c1987. x, 284 p. : ill. ; 24 cm. Includes

bibliographies and index. ISBN 0-88730-119-3 LC Card 86-17280 DDC 384/.041/0973 19
1. Telecommunication - United States - Rates. 2. Telephone - United States - Rates. 3. Telecommunication policy - United States. I. Title.
HE7787 .W47 1986 ***NYPL [JLE 87-1593]***

Wendling, Wayne. The regulatory impact on pensions / Wayne Wendling, Connie Ann Crabb-Velez, Melody A. Carlsen. Brookfield, Wis. : International Foundation of Employee Benefit Plans, 1986. xiii, 91 p. : ill. ; 23 cm. Bibliography: p. 88-91. ISBN 0-89154-314-7 (pbk.) : LC Card 87-129712 DDC 331.25/2/0973 19
1. Old age pensions - Government policy - United States. 2. Pension trusts - Government policy - United States. 3. Retirement income - United States. I. Crabb-Velez, Connie Ann. II. Carlsen, Melody A. III. International Foundation of Employee Benefits Plans. IV. Title.
HD7105.35.U6 W46 1986

Wengenroth, Ulrich.
Unternehmensstrategien und technischer Fortschritt : die deutsche und die britische Stahlindustrie 1865-1895 / Ulrich Wengenroth. Göttingen : Vandenhoeck & Ruprecht, c1986. 316 p. : ill. ; 24 cm. (Veröffentlichungen des Deutschen Historischen Instituts London . Bd. 17 = v. 17) Originally presented as the author's thesis (doctoral -- Technische Hochschule Darmstadt, 1982) Includes index. Bibliography: p. 299-310. ISBN 3-525-36302-8
1. Steel industry and trade - Germany - History. 2. Steel industry and trade - Great Britain - History. I. Series: German Historical Institute in London. Veröffentlichungen, Bd. 17. II. Title.
NYPL [JLE 87-917]

Unternehmensstrategien und technischer Fortschritt : die deutsche und die britische Stahlindustrie, 1865-1895 / Ulrich Wengenroth. Göttingen : Vandenhoeck & Ruprecht, c1986. 316 p. : ill. ; 24 cm. (Veröffentlichungen des Deutschen Historischen Instituts London . Bd. 17 = v. 17) A revision of the author's thesis (doctoral--Darmstadt, 1982). Bibliography: p. 299-310. Includes index. ISBN 3-525-36302-8 LC Card 87-112794 DDC 338.4/7669142/0943 19
1. Steel industry and trade - Germany - History. 2. Steel industry and trade - Great Britain - History. I. Series: Veröffentlichungen des Deutschen Historischen Instituts in London , Bd. 17. II. Title.
HD9523.5 .W43 1986

Wenig Arbeit--aber viel zu tun : neue Wege der Arbeitsmarktpolitik / Meinolf Dierkes, Burkhard Strümpel (Hrsg.) Opladen : Westdeutscher Verlag, c1985. 195 p. : ill. ; 23 cm. Bibliography: p. [183]-193. ISBN 3-531-11724-6
1. Labor supply - Germany (West) - Addresses, essays, lectures. 2. Labor policy - Germany, West - Addresses, essays, lectures. I. Dierkes, Meinolf. II. Strumpel, Burkhard. ***NYPL [JLE 86-1602]***

Wenner, S. Albert. Marketing your shopping center : a collaborative effort / S. Albert Wenner ; foreword by Albert Sussman. New York : International Council of Shopping Centers, c1987. xi, 194 p. : ill. ; 26 cm. Includes index. ISBN 0-913598-55-0 LC Card 87-2848 DDC 658.8/7 19
1. Shopping centers - Marketing. 2. Advertising - Shopping centers. I. Title.
HF5430 .W46 1987

Wennergren, E. Boyd. Solving world hunger, the U. S. stake /. Cabin John, MD , 1986. ix, 102 p. : ISBN 0-932020-42-9 (pbk.) : LC Card 86-17665 DDC 363.8/526/0973 19
HV696.F6 S65 1986 ***NYPL [JLF 87-531]***

Wenschlag, Roger. The versatile salesperson : selling the way your customer wants to buy / Roger Wenschlag ; edited by Sharyn Skeeter. New York : J. Wiley, c1987. viii, 205 p. : ill. ; 24 cm. Includes index. ISBN 0-471-85436-0 LC Card 87-2003 DDC 658.8/5 19
1. Selling. I. Skeeter, Sharyn. II. Title.
HF5438.25 .W294 1987

Wensierski, Peter. Von oben nach unten wächts gar nichts : Umweltzerstörung und Protest in der DDR / Peter Wensierski.Originalausg. Frankfurt am Main : Fischer Taschenbuch Verlag, 1986. 206 p. : ill. ; 18 cm. (Informationen zur Zeit) Bibliography: p. 203-204. ISBN 3-596-24274-6 LC Card 87-115154 DDC 363.7/058/09431 19
1. Environmental policy - Germany (East) - Citizen participation. 2. Environmental policy - Germany, East. 3. Pollution - Germany (East). I. Title.
HC290.795.E5 W46 1986

Wensley, Robin, 1944- Readings in strategic marketing . Chicago , c1988. x, 534 p. : ISBN 0-03-020864-5 (pbk.) LC Card 87-22274 DDC 658.8/02 19
HF5415.135 .R42 1988

Wenz, Peter S. Environmental justice / Peter S. Wenz. Albany, N.Y. : State University of New York Press, c1987. p. cm. (SUNY series in environmental public policy) Includes index. ISBN 0-88706-644-5 LC Card 87-13206 DDC 363.7/0525 19
1. Distributive justice. 2. Environmental policy. 3. Environmental law. I. Title. II. Series.
HB523 .W46 1987

Wenzel, Gilbert, 1956- Marktstrategien multinationaler Pharmaunternehmen und die Arzneimittelmärkte der Dritten Welt : Untersuchung am Beispiel ausgesuchter Länder / Gilbert Wenzel. Frankfurt am Main ; New York : P. Lang, c1986. 398 p. : ill. ; 21 cm. (Europäische Hochschulschriften. Reihe V, Volks- und Betriebswirtschaft, 0531-7339 . Bd. 760 = vol. 760 = vol. 760) Summary in English. Originally presented as the author's thesis (doctoral)--RWTH Aachen, 1986. Bibliography: p. 390-398. ISBN 3-8204-9721-8 LC Card 87-407426 DDC 381/.456151/091724 19
1. Pharmaceutical industry - Developing countries. 2. International business enterprises - Developing countries. I. Series: Europäische Hochschulschriften. Reihe V, Volks- und Betriebswirtschaft , Bd. 760. II. Title.
HD9674.D44 W46 1986

Wenzel, Heinz-Dieter. Defizitfinanzierung als Instrument einer zielorientierten Finanzpolitik : eine dynamische Analyse / Heinz-Dieter Wenzel.1. Aufl. Baden-Baden : Nomos, 1983. 249 p. : ill. ; 23 cm. (Schriften zur öffentlichen Verwaltung und öffentlichen Wirtschaft. Bd. 61) The author's Habilitationsschrift, Universität Heidelberg. Summary in English, French, and Russian. Bibliography: p. 229-239. Includes indexes. ISBN 3-7890-0869-9 : LC Card 83-240582
1. Debts, Public. 2. Deficit financing. 3. Fiscal policy. I. Title.
HJ8019 .W45 1983

A WEP study.
African and Asian Inter-regional Workshop on Strategies for Improving the Employment Conditions of Rural Women (1984 : Arusha, Tanzania) Resources, power and women . Geneva , 1985. ix, 82 p. ; ISBN 92-2-105009-2 (pbk.) : LC Card 86-208830 DDC 331.4/83/095 19
HD6207 .A78 1984

Working women in socialist countries . Geneva , 1985. xvi, 234 p. : ISBN 92-2-103910-2 (pbk.) : LC Card 85-181464 DDC 304.6/32/091717 19
HB901 .W657 1985 ***NYPL [JLE 86-1433]***

Wer fürchtet sich vor'm schwarzen Mann? niemand! und wenn er kommt? dann lesen wir : das Handbuch für Zivildienstleistende / [Hrsg., Deutsche Friedensgesellschaft--Vereinigte Kriegsdienstgegner e.V.]. Velbert : Die Gesellschaft, c1985. 95 p. : ill. ; 21 cm. Cover title. ISBN 3-922319-08-4 : LC Card 86-206116 DDC 355.2/2363/0943 19
1. National service - Germany, West. 2. Conscientious objectors - Germany, West. I. Deutsche Friedensgesellschaft--Vereinigte Kriegsdienstgegner. II. Title: Handbuch für Zivildienstleistende.
HD4870.G3 W47 1985

Wer steuert die "Anti-Kernkraft-Bewegung"-- und mit welchem Ziel? / [herausgegeben von ELC, European Labor Committees, EAP, Europäische Arbeiterpartei ; Redaktion, Gabriele Dannenberg]. Wiesbaden : Campaigner Publications Deutschland, [1977] 38 p. : ill. ; 28 cm. Cover title. LC Card 86-140106 DDC 333.79/24 19
1. Antinuclear movement. I. Dannenberg, Gabriele. II. European Labor Committees. III. European Labor Party.
HD9698.A2 W44 1977

Wer WAA sät wird Widerstand ernten! / [Herausgeber, Kommunistischer Bund]. 1. Aufl. Hamburg : J. Reents, [1979] 31 p. : ill. ; 30 cm. Cover title. Includes bibliographical references. LC Card 85-171252
1. Antinuclear movement - Germany (West). 2. Nuclear industry - Germany (West). 3. Nuclear industry - Environmental aspects - Germany (West). I. Kommunistischer Bund. II. Title: Wer Wiederaufbereitungsanlagen sät wird Widerstand ernten!.
HD9698.G42 W47 1979

Wer Wiederaufbereitungsanlagen sät wird Widerstand ernten! Wer WAA sät wird Widerstand ernten! /. Hamburg [1979] 31 p. : LC Card 85-171252
HD9698.G42 W47 1979

Werbegraphik 1830-1870, aus niedersächsischen Zeitungen / herausgegeben von Reinhard Oberschelp. [Hannover] : Niedersächsische Landesbibliothek Hannover ; Hildesheim : A. Lax in Kommission, 1986. xv, 280 p. : ill. ; 23 cm. (Veröffentlichungen der Niedersächsischen Landesbibliothek Hannover) Bibliography: p. viii. Includes index. ISBN 3-7848-3875-8 LC Card 87-408153 DDC 659.13/2/094359 19
1. Adverstising, Newspaper - Germany (West) - Lower Saxony - History - 19th century. I. Oberschelp, Reinhard. II. Series.
HF5996.L68 W47 1986

Werben mit Sex /. Nimmergut, Jörg, 1939- München , c1982. 383 p. : ISBN 3-453-53132-9 (pbk.) LC Card 86-673618
HF5827 .N45x 1982

Werbung der Banken /. Gessler, Joachim. [S.l. , 1983] (Köln : Druck- und Verlagshaus Wienand) xxvii, 200 p. ; LC Card 83-214619
HF6161.B2 G47 1983

Werbung in der Schweiz . Kutter, Markus, 1925- [Zürich] , 1983. 271 p., xvi p. of plates : ISBN 3-85859-202-1 : LC Card 84-142450
HF5813.S94 K87 1983

Werbung in einem mehrsprachigen Land / Bund Schweizerischer Werbeagenturen (Hrsg.) = La publicité dans un pays plurilingue / Union Suisse d'Agences-Conseils en Publicité (éd.). Freiburg, Schweiz : Universitätsverlag, c1986. 152 p. : ill. (some col.) ; 21 cm. (Öffentliche soziale Kommunikation. Reihe Werkpapiere . 18 = 18 =) German, French, and Italian. Papers presented at the Seminar für Interkulturelle Kommunikation held at Universität Freiburg in 1986 and sponsored by the Bund Schweizerischer Werbeagenturen. Includes bibliographies. CONTENTS. - Kulturübergreifende Kommunikation / Louis Bosshart -- Schweizer diesseits und jenseits der Saane / Werner Wyss -- Les problèmes de la publicité dans un pays plurilingue, le point de vue du client / Jean-Claude Ramel -- Die Probleme der Werbung in einem mehrsprachigen Land aus der Sicht einer deutschsprachigen Werbeagentur / Bruno Widmer -- Les problèmes de la publicité dans un pays plurilingue, le point de vue de l'agence de publicité romande / Jean-Claude Prélaz -- L'importance des différences linguistiques et culturelles dans la création et la réalisation de concepts publicitaires / Florian Martin -- Die Bedeutung der Sprach- und Kulturunterscheide für die Kreation und Realisation von Werbemassnahmen / Silvio Rizzi -- L'importanza delle differenze linguistiche e culturali nella realizzazione di concetti pubblicitari / Daniele Jürg, Udo Elzi -- Zweisprachigkeit im Lokal-Radio "Canal 3/Kanal 3", Biel-Bienne / Othmar Baeriswyl -- Le bilinguisme à la radio locale / Adrienne Corboud -- Werbung in länderübergreifenden Medien / Philip Reber -- Werbung in einem mehrsprachigen Land / Richard Kühn. ISBN 3-7278-0382-7 LC Card 87-409238 DDC 659.1/09494 19
1. Advertising - Switzerland - Congresses. I. Bund Schweizerischer Werbeagenturen. II. Seminar für Interkulturelle Kommunikation (1986 : Universität Freiburg). III. Title: Publicité dans un pays plurilingue. IV. Series: Öffentliche soziale Kommunikation. Reihe Werkpapiere , 18.
HF5808.S9 W47 1986

Werbung und gesellschaftlicher Wandel über die kommunikativen Voraussetzungen technischen, ökonomischen und sozialen Fortschritts . Meissner, Hans-Günther. [Berlin] , Hamburg [1979] 23, [4] leaves ; LC Card 84-119751
HF5802.5 .M45 1979

Werbung, Wettbewerb und Verbraucherpolitik /. Mähling, Friedrich W. (Friedrich Wilhelm), 1952- München , c1983. xii, 477 p. : ISBN 3-88259-258-3 LC Card 84-144205
HF5822 .M34 1983

Der Werdegang der preussischen Einkommensteuer unter besonderer Berücksichtigung ihrer kausalen Entwicklungsfaktoren. Linzbach, Peter, 1956- Frankfurt am Main , New York , c1984. 259 p. ; ISBN 3-8204-5184-6 LC Card 84-169039
HJ4720.P78 L56 1984

Werder, Axel von. Organisationsstruktur und Rechtsnorm : Implikationen juristischer Vorschriften für die Organisation aktienrechtlicher Einheits- und Konzernunternehmungen / Axel v. Werder. Wiesbaden : Gabler, c1986. 564 p. : ill. ; 24 cm. (Neue betriebswirtschaftliche Forschung . 34) Originally presented as the author's thesis (doctoral)--T.H. Aachen. Bibliography: p. [444]-539. Includes index. ISBN 3-409-13107-8 LC Card 86-224483
1. Organizational behavior. 2. Corporate culture. 3. Corporation law. I. Series. II. Series: Neue betriebswirtschaftliche Forschung , Bd. 34. III. Title.
HD58.7 .W35 1986

Wereldbevolking groeiend ontwikkelingsprobleem. Den Haag : Voorlichtingsdienst Ontwikkelingssamenwerking van het Ministerie van Buitenlandse Zaken, [1975] 66 p. : ill. ; 21 cm. (Samenwerking van Nederland met ontwikkelingslanden . 7) LC Card 87-118557
1. Population policy. 2. Developing countries - Population policy. 3. World Population Conference (3rd : 1974 : Bucharest, Romania). I. Netherlands. Ministerie van Buitenlandse Zaken. Voorlichtingsdienst Ontwikkelingssamenwerking. II. Series.
HB883.5 .W47 1975

Ein Werk des Sozialismus, der Freundschaft und der Jugend : Geschichte des VEB Petrolchemisches Kombinat Schwedt, Stammbetrieb von 1959 bis 1981 / herausgegeben von der Betriebsparteiorganisation der SED.1. Aufl. Berlin : Tribune, c1985. 296 p. : ill., maps ; 22 cm. Maps on lining papers. Bibliography: p. 292-294. LC Card 87-112875
1. Petrolchemisches Kombinat Schwedt, VEB. - History. 2. Petroleum chemicals industry - Germany (East) - Schwedt - History. 3. Schwedt (Germany) - Economic conditions. I. Petrolchemisches Kombinat Schwedt, VEB. Betriebsparteiorganisation der SED.
HD9579.C34 P4848 1985

Werk en organisatie / redaktie J. von Grumbkow. Lisse : Swets & Zeitlinger, 1986- v. <1 > ; 24 cm. Includes bibliographies. ISBN 90-265-0755-0 (deel 1) : LC Card 86-221124
1. Personnel management - Netherlands. 2. Personnel management. I. Grumbkow, J. von.
HF5549.2.N4 W47 1986

Werkbuch Jugendarbeitslosigkeit . Knöpfel, Eckehardt. Wuppertal , c1983. 168 p. : ISBN 3-417-12855-2 (pbk.) LC Card 87-672977
HD5779 .K59x 1983

Werkloosheid in Nederland, 1920-1939 . Kloosterman, Robert. Utrecht , 1985. xiv, 351 p. : ISBN 90-6194-315-9 : LC Card 86-150980
HD5792 .K56 1985 ***NYPL [JLD 86-3407]***

Werkssiedlung Madenfelderhof bei Landsweiler-Reden . Habicht, Werner. Saarbrücken , 1985. 54 p., [52] p. of plates : LC Card 87-408673 DDC 330.943/42 19
HD7289.5.A3 G437 1985

Werneck, Rogério L. Furquim. Desequilíbrio externo e reorientação do crescimento e dos investimentos : uma análise multissetorial das perspectivas da economia brasileira / Rogério L. Furquim Werneck. Rio de Janeiro-RJ : Programa Nacional de Pesquisa Econômica, [1983?] 130 p. ; 30 cm. (Série Fac-símile . no. 10) "Versão apresentada ao PNPE em dezembro/82." Bibliography: p. 129-130. LC Card 87-403024 DDC 338.981 19
1. Brazil - Economic policy - Econometric models. 2. Exports - Brazil - Econometric models. 3. Import substitution - Brazil - Econometric models. 4. Investments - Brazil - Econometric models. I. Title. II. Series.
HC187 .W47 1983

Werneck Vianna, Maria Lúcia Teixeira. see **Vianna, Maria Lúcia Teixeira Werneck.**

Werner, Horst S. Der aktienrechtliche Abhängigkeitstatbestand : e. Unters. d. Herrschaftsmöglichkeiten von Unternehmen über Unternehmen in d. fakt. Konzernverbindungen / Horst S. Werner. Göttingen : Wire-Verlagsgesellschaft für Wirtschafts- u. Steuerrecht, 1979. xxxix, 214 p. ; 21 cm. (Abhandlungen zum Handels-, Gesellschafts- und Wirtschaftsrecht . Bd. 1]) Originally presented as the author's thesis, Göttingen, 1978. Series supplied by cumulative listing in Bd. 3 of series. Bibliography: p. xv-xxxv. ISBN 3-88415-560-1 : LC Card 80-452340 DDC 346.43/066
1. Corporation law - Germany, West. 2. Trusts, Industrial - Germany, West. 3. Banking law - Germany, West. 4. Employees' representation in management - Law and legislation - Germany (West). I. Series. II. Series: Abhandlungen zum Handels-, Gesellschafts- und Wirtschaftsrecht , Bd. 1. III. Title.
LAW ***NYPL [JLD 86-1592]***

Werner, Josua. Nationale Wege der Inflationsbekämpfung /. Berlin , c1986. 223 p. : ISBN 3-428-06077-6 LC Card 87-132310 DDC 332.4/1/094 19
HC240 .N315 1986

Werner, Linda H.
Barnes, Carolyn. Kenyan smallholdings and the division of labour /. Nairobi , 1982. 39 leaves ; LC Card 87-156293
HD1476.K4 B37 1982

Mosley, W. Henry (Wiley Henry), 1933- The dynamics of birth spacing and marital fertility in Kenya /. [Nairobi? , 1981] 63 leaves : LC Card 85-980189
HB1072.5.A3 M66 1981

Werner-Reimers-Stiftung. Ansprüche an die Arbeit . Frankfurt [am Main] , New York , c1984. 298 p. : ISBN 3-593-33390-2 LC Card 85-103333
HF5548.8 .A683 1984

Werner, Roland, Dipl.-Ing. NTG-Fachtagung (1986 : Nuremberg, Germany) Von der Nachrichtentechnik zur Informationstechnik . Berlin , c1986. 104 p. : ISBN 3-8007-1485-X LC Card 87-136748 DDC 384 19
HE7604 .N74 1986

Wersebe, Hilmar von, 1943- Struktureller und funktionaler Pluralismus in der öffentlichen Verwaltung / Hilmar v. Wersebe. Frankfurt am Main ; New York : P. Lang, c1986. 100 p. : ill. ; 21 cm. (Europäische Hochschulschriften. Reihe V, Volks- und Betriebswirtschaft, 0531-7339 . Bd. 695 = vol. 695 = vol. 695) A revision and abridgment of the author's thesis (doctoral--Universität Düsseldorf, 1981) Bibliography: p. 91-100. ISBN 3-8204-9136-8 LC Card 86-229888
1. Organizational behavior. 2. Bureaucracy - Germany, West. 3. Pluralism (Social sciences) - Germany (West). I. Series: Europäische Hochschulschriften. Reihe V, Volks- und Betriebswirtschaft , Bd. 695. II. Title.
HD58.7 .W36 1986

Der Wert, die Zeichen, die Maschine . Bachmayer, Hans Matthäus. Frankfurt/Main , New York , c1982. 370 p. : ISBN 3-593-33014-8 : LC Card 82-241803
HD6331 .B23 1982

Wert- und Präferenzprobleme in den Sozialwissenschaften / herausgegeben von Reinhard Tietz. Berlin : Duncker & Humblot, c1981. 268 p. : ill. ; 24 cm. (Schriften des Vereins für Socialpolitik, Gesellschaft für Wirtschafts- und Sozialwissenschaften . n.F., Bd. 122) English and German. Papers sponsored by the Sozialwissenschaftliche Ausschuss of the Gesellschaft für Wirtschafts- und Sozialwissenschaften (Verein für Socialpolitik) Includes bibliographies and indexes. CONTENTS. - Bemerkungen zum Wertproblem in der Ökonomie / von Heinz Sauermann -- Die Rolle von Werturteilen und Normen in der Theorie der Wirtschaftspolitik / von Peter Bernholz -- Zum Stand der Werte-Diskussion in der heutigen deutschen Jurisprudenz und eine juristische Theorie der Meta-Werte / von Wolfgang Fikentscher -- Sozialpsychologische Aspekte der Präferenzbildung / von Günter Wiswede -- Psychologische Aspekte des ökonomischen Verhältnismodells / von Wolfgang Stroebe -- Bedürfnisse, Entscheidungen und ökonomische Erklärungen des Verhaltens / von Willi Meyer -- Methoden und Chancen einer Beeinflussung der Konsumenten zur rationalen Überprüfung von Präferenzen / von Gerhard Scherhorn -- Excess demand for job importance and its implications / von Tibor Scitovski -- Ein System der sozialen, politischen und ökonomischen Interdependenz / von Wilhelm Krelle -- Economic evaluation of effectiveness in health care delivery / Hans W. Gottinger. ISBN 3-428-05013-4 LC Card 86-230716
1. Consumers' preference - Congresses. 2. Value - Congresses. I. Tietz, Reinhard. II. Gesellschaft für Wirtschafts- und Sozialwissenschaften, Verein für Socialpolitik. Sozialwissenschaftlicher Ausschuss. III. Series.
HF5415.3 .W47 1981

Wertewandel, Arbeit, technischer Fortschritt, Wachstum /. Helfert, Mario. Köln , c1986. 149 p. : ISBN 3-7663-3010-1 LC Card 87-134855 DDC 331.12 19
HD6331 .H37 1986

Der Wertewandel und die Arbeitsmoral /. Lübbe, Hermann. Köln [1984] 55 p. ; ISBN 3-88575-025-2 LC Card 84-197999
HD8451 .L83 1984

Wertewandel und Konsumentenverhalten . Windhorst, Karl-Götz. Münster , c1985. xxi, 299 p. : ISBN 3-7923-0520-8 LC Card 85-171929 DDC 338.5/21/0943 19
HB201 .W663 1985 ***NYPL [JLE 87-369]***

Werz, Edward W. Letters that sell / Edward W. Werz. Chicago : Contemporary Books, c1987. 163 p. ; 23 cm. Cover subtitle: 90 ready-to-use letters to help you sell your products, services, and ideas. ISBN 0-8092-4684-8 (pbk.) LC Card 87-20064 DDC 808/.066651 19
1. Sales letter. I. Title.
HF5730 .W47 1987

Weschler, Irving R. Tannenbaum, Robert. Leadership and organization . New York , 1987, c1961. xiv, 456 p. : ISBN 0-8240-8219-2 (alk. paper) : LC Card 86-27019 DDC 303.3/4 19
HD57.7 .T36 1987

WESEL REGION (NORTH RHINE-WESTPHALIA, GERMANY) - ECONOMIC CONDITIONS.
Schanz, Hermann J. Der niederrheinische Wirtschaftsraum . Stuttgart , c1986. xxii, 466 p. ; ISBN 3-7910-5014-1 LC Card 87-135757 DDC 330.943/55 19
HC289.D755 S32 1986

WESER RIVER VALLEY (GERMANY) - ECONOMIC CONDITIONS.
Komp, Klaus Ulrich. Die Seehafenstädte im Weser-Jade-Raum und ihre überregionale Verflechtung /. Münster , 1982. x, 143 p. : LC Card 83-197866
HE558.W45 K66 1982

Wessel, Louis. Wyoming oil and natural gas extraction industry : a wage & employment survey, 1986. Cheyenne, Wyo. (Herschler Bldg., Cheyenne 82002) : Wyoming Dept. of Labor & Statistics, 1986. 35 p. : ill. ; 28 cm. Cover title. Bibliography: p. 35. LC Card 86-622902 DDC 331.12/522338/09787021 19
1. Wages - Petroleum workers - Wyoming - Statistics. 2. Wages - Gas industry employees - Wyoming - Statistics. 3. Petroleum workers - Wyoming - Statistics. 4. Gas industry - Wyoming - Employees - Statistics. I. Wyoming. Dept. of Labor and Statistics. II. Title.
HD4966.P52 U5553 1986

West Africa--regional cooperation and development / edited by Julius Emeka Okolo and Stephen Wright. Boulder : Westview Press, 1988. p. cm. (Westview special studies on Africa) Includes index. ISBN 0-8133-7354-9 : LC Card 87-9290 DDC 338.966 19
1. Economic Community of West African States. 2. Africa, West - Economic integration. 3. Africa, West - Economic policy. I. Okolo, Julius Emeka. II. Wright, Stephen, 1954-.
HC1000 .W47 1988

West, Alan, 1951- A business plan : planning for the small business / Alan West. New York : Nichols Pub. Co., 1988. xi, 196 p. : ill. ; 22 cm. Includes index. ISBN 0-89397-288-6 (pbk.) : LC Card 87-18561 DDC 658.4/012 19
1. Small business - Management. 2. New business enterprises. 3. Corporate planning. I. Title.
HD62.7 .W47 1988

WEST BENGAL (INDIA) - CENSUS, 1981.
Census of India, 1981. Delhi , <1985-[1987]. v. in : maps (some folded) ; LC Card 87-915030 DDC 304.6/0954/14021 19
HA4587.W47 C46 1985

Tables on houses and disabled population, series 23, West Bengal /. Delhi , 1986. v, 128 p. ; LC Card 87-900630
HA4587.W47 T33 1986

WEST BENGAL (INDIA) - POPULATION - STATISTICS.
Tables on houses and disabled population, series 23, West Bengal /. Delhi , 1986. v, 128 p. ; LC Card 87-900630
HA4587.W47 T33 1986

West, Bill W. Street talk in real estate / Bill W. West, Richard L. Dickinson. Alameda, Calif. : Unique Pub. Co., [1987] vi, 216 p. : ill. ; 23 cm. ISBN 0-934189-04-8 (pbk. : trade) : LC Card 86-50605 DDC 333.33/03/21 19
1. Real estate business - Dictionaries. 2. Real property - Dictionaries. I. Dickinson, Richard L., 1938-. II. Title.
HD1365 .W47 1987

West, Bruce J. An essay on the importance of being nonlinear / Bruce J. West. Berlin ; New York : Springer-Verlag, c1985. viii, 204 p. : ill. ; 24 cm. (Lecture notes in biomathematics. 62) Bibliography: p.[197]-204. ISBN 0-387-16038-8 (U. S.)
1. Regression analysis. 2. Correlation (Statistics). I. Title. II. Series. ***NYPL [JSK 75-186 v.62]***

West, Darrell M., 1954- Congress and economic policymaking / Darrell M. West. Pittsburgh, Pa. : University of Pittsburgh Press, c1987. xiv, 203 p. ; 22 cm. (Pitt series in policy and institutional studies) Bibliography: p. 167-196. Includes index. ISBN 0-8229-5396-X (pbk.) LC Card 87-40160 DDC 338.973 19
1. United States - Economic policy - 1981-. 2. United States - Politics and government - 1981-. 3. United States - Economic policy - 1981- - Decision making. 4. United States. Congress - Voting. I. Title. II. Title: Congress and economic policy making. III. Series.
HC106.8 .W45 1987

West European Conference on the Psychology of Work and Organization (1985 : Aachen, Germany) The psychology of work and organization : current trends and issues : selected and edited proceedings of the West European Conference on the Psychology of Work and Organization, Aachen, F.R.G., 1-3 April, 1985 / edited by G. Debus and H.-W. Schroiff. Amsterdam ; New York : North Holland ; xi, 407 p. : ill. ; 25 cm. Includes bibliographies and indexes. ISBN 0-444-70029-3 (U. S.) LC Card 86-8947 DDC 158.7 19
1. Psychology, Industrial - Europe - Congresses. 2. Industrial relations - Europe - Congresses. 3. Human engineering - Congresses. I. Debus, Günter. II. Schroiff, H.-W. (Hans-Willi). III. Title.
HF5548.8 .W475 1985 ***NYPL [JLE 86-4341]***

West European direct investment in Canada. Bruns, Claudia. Westeuropean direct investment in Canada . Hamburg [1986] 18 p. : LC Card 86-191095
HG5152 .B78 1986

West, Gary, 1947- Dac-Easy accounting and payroll made easy / Gary West and William R. Mills. 1st ed. Blue Ridge Summit, PA : Tab Books, c1987. ix, 261 p. : ill., forms ; 24 cm. On t.p. the trademark symbol "TM" is superscript following "Dac-Easy" in the title. Includes index. "2914." ISBN 0-8306-2914-9 (pbk.) : LC Card 87-10056 DDC 657/.028/55369 19
1. Dac-Easy Accounting (Computer program). 2. Dac-Easy Payroll (Computer program). 3. Accounting - Data processing. 4. Payrolls - Data processing. I. Mills, William R. II. Title.
HF5679 .W47 1987

West German neo-colonialism and Africa . Batsa, Kofi, 1931- Accra, Ghana [1964] 98 p. ; LC Card 87-118442 DDC 337.4306 19
HF1546.15.A35 B37 1964

West German Radio. see **Westdeutscher Rundfunk.**

West Germany. see **Germany, West.**

The West Indies . Watts, David. Cambridge [Cambridgeshire] , New York , 1987. xxii, 609 p. : ISBN 0-521-24555-9 LC Card 87-5156 DDC 330.9729 19
HC151 .W375 1987

West Indies, Dutch. see **Netherlands Antilles.**

WEST INDIES - ECONOMIC CONDITIONS.
Watts, David. The West Indies . Cambridge [Cambridgeshire] , New York , 1987. xxii, 609 p. : ISBN 0-521-24555-9 LC Card 87-5156 DDC 330.9729 19
HC151 .W375 1987

WEST INDIES - SOCIAL CONDITIONS.
Watts, David. The West Indies . Cambridge [Cambridgeshire] , New York , 1987. xxii, 609 p. : ISBN 0-521-24555-9 LC Card 87-5156 DDC 330.9729 19
HC151 .W375 1987

West, Michael. Nicholson, Nigel. Managerial job change . Cambridge [Cambridgeshire] , New York , 1988. xi, 274 p. : ISBN 0-521-33459-4 LC Card 87-11752 DDC 331.12/72 19
HD38.2 .N53 1988

West of Wall Street /. Angell, George. [Chicago] [1987], c1988. xxiv, 215 p. ; ISBN 0-88462-623-7 LC Card 87-3003 DDC 332.63/222 19
HG6043 .A55 1988

West, Patrick C. Natural resource bureaucracy and rural poverty : a study in the political sociology of natural resources / Patrick C. West. Ann Arbor, MI : University of Michigan, School of Natural Resources, Natural Resources Sociology Research Lab, c1982. xiii, 168 p. : ill. ; 23 cm. (Monograph / University of Michigan, School of Natural Resources, Natural Resources Sociology Research Lab . 2) Bibliography: p. 157-168. LC Card 83-102928 DDC 333.7/16/0973 19
1. Rural development - United States - History. 2. Rural poor - United States - History. 3. Conservation of natural resources - United States - History. 4. Pasture, Right of - United States - History. I. Series: Monograph (University of Michigan. Natural Resources Sociology Research Lab) , 2. II. Title.
HD1761 .W423 1982 ***NYPL [JLE 86-4095]***

West, Robert, 1925- Defence, security, and development /. New York , 1987. xiii, 219 p. : ISBN 0-312-01243-8 : LC Card 87-12129 DDC 338.4/76234/091724 19
HC59.72.D4 D436 1987

WEST (U. S.) - HISTORY - 1848-1950.
Fite, Gilbert Courtland, 1918- The farmers' frontier, 1865-1900 /. Norman [1987], c1966. xiv, 272 p. : ISBN 0-8061-2063-0 (pbk.) LC Card 86-40534 DDC 338.1/0977 19
HD8039.F3 U643 1987

WEST (U. S.) - PUBLIC LANDS.
Fairfax, Sally K. Federal lands . Washington, D.C. , c1987. xviii, 252 p. : ISBN 0-933280-33-5 (pbk.) :$ LC Card 86-27512 DDC 333.1/0978 19
HD243.A17 F35 1987

WEST (U. S.) - PUBLIC WORKS - HISTORY.
Atkinson, Ray N. Guy F. Atkinson Company of California . New York , 1985, c1986. 24 p. : LC Card 86-61271 DDC 338.7/624/0973 19
HD9715.U54 G882 1986

West Virginia. Dept. of Employment Security. Labor and Economic Research Section.
State of West Virginia Job Training Partnership Act . Charleston, W.Va. (112 California Ave., Charleston 25305-0112) [1986] vi, 233 p. ; LC Card 86-622901 DDC 331.1/09754/021 19
HD5725.W4 S7 1986

State of West Virginia Job Training Partnership Act planning statistics /. Charleston, W. Va. (112 California Ave., Charleston 25305-0112) [1985] v, 122 p. ; LC Card 85-623225 DDC 331.1/09754/021 19
HD5725.W4 S7 1985

West Virginia youth and the labor market /. Charleston, W.Va. (112 California Ave., Charleston 25305-0112) [1986] iii, 76 p. ; LC Card 86-622615 DDC 331.3/4129754 19
HD6274.W4 W483 1986

WEST VIRGINIA - POPULATION - STATISTICS.
State of West Virginia Job Training Partnership Act . Charleston, W.Va. (112 California Ave., Charleston 25305-0112) [1986] vi, 233 p. ; LC Card 86-622901 DDC 331.1/09754/021 19
HD5725.W4 S7 1986

State of West Virginia Job Training Partnership Act planning statistics /. Charleston, W. Va. (112 California Ave., Charleston 25305-0112) [1985] v, 122 p. ; LC Card 85-623225 DDC 331.1/09754/021 19
HD5725.W4 S7 1985

West Virginia youth and the labor market / [prepared by Labor and Economic Research Section]. Charleston, W.Va. (112 California Ave., Charleston 25305-0112) : The Section, [1986] iii, 76 p. ; 28 cm. "February 1986." Bibliography: p. 76. LC Card 86-622615 DDC 331.3/4129754 19
1. Youth - Employment - West Virginia. I. West Virginia. Dept. of Employment Security. Labor and Economic Research Section.
HD6274.W4 W483 1986

Westdeutscher Rundfunk. Annalen.
(Bd. 4. 4) Nach fünfundzwanzig Jahren . Köln , 1980. 399 p. : ISBN 3-7745-6465-5
NYPL [MWGK (Germany) 74-75 Bd.4]

WESTDEUTSCHER RUNDFUNK - HISTORY.
Bierbach, Wolf. Rundfunk zwischen Kommerz und Politik . Frankfurt am Main , New York , c1986. 2 v. (595 p.) : ISBN 3-8204-9692-0 LC Card 86-233794
HE8699.G3 B54 1986

Nach fünfundzwanzig Jahren . Köln , 1980. 399 p. : ISBN 3-7745-6465-5
NYPL [MWGK (Germany) 74-75 Bd.4]

Wester León, Humberto. Diagnóstico situacional del movimiento cooperativo peruano / Humberto Wester León, Ramón Domínguez Torrejón, María Luz del Aguila Tello. [Lima] : Instituto Peruano de Estudios Cooperativos, 1981- v. : ill., map ; 23 cm. Includes tables.
1. Cooperation - Peru. 2. Cooperative societies - Peru. 3. Agriculture, Cooperative - Peru. I. Domínguez Torrejón, Ramón. II. Aguila Tello, María Luz del. III. Title. ***NYPL [JLL 86-146]***

Westerfield, Randolph. Ross, Stephen A. Corporate finance /. St. Louis , 1988. xxvii, 857 p. : ISBN 0-8016-4211-6 (pbk.) LC Card 87-18076 DDC 658.1/5 19
HG4026 .R675 1988

Westergård-Nielsen, Niels C. Overgangen fra uddannelse til erhverv : teori og empiri / Niels Westergård-Nielsen. Aarhus : Økonomisk institut, Aarhus universitet ; [Copenhagen] : Økonomisk institut, Københavns universitet, [1983] iii, 41 p. : ill. ; 21 cm. (Studies in labor market dynamics, 0108-2469 ; arbejdspapir. 83-1) "Februar 1983." Bibliography: p. 39-41. LC Card 84-125491
1. Labor supply - Mathematical models. 2. Unemployment - Mathematical models. 3. Job hunting - Mathematical models. I. Title. II. Series.
HD5701.6 .W47 1983

WESTERN AND COUNTRY MUSIC. see **COUNTRY MUSIC.**

WESTERN AND NORTHERN TERRITORIES (POLAND) - INDUSTRIES - HISTORY.
Magierska, Anna. Przywrócić Polsce . Warszawa , 1986. 467 p. ; ISBN 83-01-06606-7 : LC Card 86-228089
HC340.3.Z7 W4765 1986

WESTERN AND NORTHERN TERRITORIES (POLAND) - POPULATION.
Rauziński, Robert. Ludność Nadodrza, 1945-2000 /. Opole , 1985. 44 p. ; LC Card 86-207214
HB3608.7.O34 R38 1985

Western Arctic Coal Development Project . Arctic Slope Consulting Engineers. Anchorage, Alaska [1986] 2 v. : LC Card 87-621058 DDC 333.8/22/09798 19
HD9547.A4 A85 1986

Western Arctic Coal Development Project. Arctic Slope Consulting Engineers. Western Arctic Coal Development Project . Anchorage, Alaska [1986] 2 v. : LC Card 87-621058 DDC 333.8/22/09798 19
HD9547.A4 A85 1986

Western Australia. Dept. of Employment and Training. International Conference on Employment and Training (1985 : Perth, W.A.) Full employment, uncertain futures /. [Perth, W.A.] [1985] ix, 263 p. : LC Card 86-185208 DDC 339.5 19
HD5701.3 .I55 1985

Western Australia. Dept. of Industrial Development. (Old Catalog form: Western Australia. Industrial Development, Dept. of) A Study of the Western Australian casting and forging industry. [Perth] [1984?]-[1985] 2 v. ; LC Card 86-207984 DDC 388.4/7671/09941 19
HD9506.A8 W385 1984

Western Australia. Dept. of Industrial Development. Research Section. The Central south region statistical tables, 1960/61 to 1973/74. [Perth] [1976] 188 p. ; LC Card

84-255738 DDC 330.9941/063/021 19
HC607.W47 C448 1976

Western Australia. Dept. of Premier and Cabinet. Western Australia. Pastoral Tenure Study Group. Final report on pastoral land tenure. Perth, W.A. [1986] [28], 63, 4 p. ; LC Card 87-120095 DDC 333.3/09941 19
HD1641.A9 W47 1986

Western Australia. Dept. of Regional Development and the North West. Kimberley regional profile Western Australia. Kununurra, W.A. [1986] 36 p. : LC Card 87-156395 DDC 330.9941/4/063 19
HC607.K55 K55 1986

Western Australia's North . [Perth, W.A.] [1985?] [32] p. : LC Card 86-232759 DDC 338.9941 19
HC607.W47 W485 1985

WESTERN AUSTRALIA - ECONOMIC CONDITIONS.
Goldfields-Esperance regional profile. Kalgoorlie, W.A. , Perth, W.A. [1986] 58 p. : LC Card 87-169717 DDC 330.9941/7 19
HC607.W47 G65 1986

Western Australia's North . [Perth, W.A.] [1985?] [32] p. : LC Card 86-232759 DDC 338.9941 19
HC607.W47 W485 1985

WESTERN AUSTRALIA - ECONOMIC CONDITIONS - STATISTICS.
The Central south region statistical tables, 1960/61 to 1973/74. [Perth] [1976] 18 p. ; LC Card 84-255738 DDC 330.9941/063/021 19
HC607.W47 C448 1976

Western Australia. Goldfields-Esperance Regional Development Advisory Committee. Goldfields-Esperance regional profile. Kalgoorlie, W.A. , Perth, W.A. [1986] 58 p. : LC Card 87-169717 DDC 330.9941/7 19
HC607.W47 G65 1986

Western Australia. Industrial Development, Dept. of. see **Western Australia. Dept. of Industrial Development.**

Western Australia. Pastoral Tenure Study Group. Final report on pastoral land tenure. Perth, W.A. : Dept. of Premier and Cabinet, [1986] [28], 63, 4 p. ; 30 cm. Cover title. "February 1986." Bibliography: p. 3 (3rd ser.) LC Card 87-120095 DDC 333.3/09941 19
1. Pastures - Australia - Western Australia. 2. Land tenure - Australia - Western Australia. 3. Farm tenancy - Australia - Western Australia. I. Western Australia. Dept. of Premier and Cabinet. II. Title.
HD1641.A9 W47 1986

WESTERN AUSTRALIA - POPULATION - STATISTICS.
Projected population of Western Australia and the Perth Statistical Division, 1985-2025. [Perth] [1986] 82 p. : LC Card 87-114601 DDC 304.6/2/09941021 19
HA3007.W47 P76 1986

WESTERN AUSTRALIA - SOCIAL CONDITIONS.
Goldfields-Esperance regional profile. Kalgoorlie, W.A. , Perth, W.A. [1986] 58 p. : LC Card 87-169717 DDC 330.9941/7 19
HC607.W47 G65 1986

Western Australia. Treasury. Projected population of Western Australia and the Perth Statistical Division, 1985-2025. [Perth] [1986] 82 p. : LC Card 87-114601 DDC 304.6/2/09941021 19
HA3007.W47 P76 1986

Western Australia. Working Party on Equal Opportunity Legislation for People with Disabilities. A Fair go for people with disabilities . Perth, W.A [1986] xxxv, 162 p. ; ISBN 0-7309-0332-X LC Card 87-158098 DDC 331.5/9/09941 19
HD7256.A762 W474 1986

Western Australian Water Resources Council. National Workshop on Urban Water Demand Management (1986 : Alexander Library, Perth Cultural Centre) Working papers for the National Workshop on Urban Water Demand Management . Leederville, WA [1986] xii, 657 p. : LC Card 87-119946 DDC 333.91/2/0994 19
HD4465.A8 N37 1986

Western Australia's North : progress and prospects. [Perth, W.A.] : Dept. of Regional Development and the North West, [1985?] [32] p. : col. ill. ; 28 cm. Cover title. LC Card 86-232759 DDC 338.9941 19
1. Industrial promotion - Australia - Western Australia. 2. Western Australia - Economic conditions. 3. Regional planning - Australia - Western Australia. I. Western Australia. Dept. of Regional Development and the North West.
HC607.W47 W485 1985

Western broadcasting over the iron curtain / edited by K.R.M. Short. London : Croom Helm, 1986. 274 p. : ill. ; 23 cm. Includes index. Bibliography: p. 264-266. ISBN 0-7099-4438-1
1. International broadcasting - North America. 2. International broadcasting - Europe. 3. International broadcasting - Europe, Eastern. I. Short, K. R. M.
NYPL [MWGH 87-760]

WESTERN CIVILIZATION. see **CIVILIZATION, OCCIDENTAL.**

The Western edge . Huppes, T. Dordrecht , Boston , 1987. viii, 141 p. : ISBN 90-247-3495-9 LC Card 87-4087 DDC 338/.06 19
HD58.8 .H86 1987

Western Electric Company. Man and work in society . New York , c1975. xiv, 313 p. : ISBN 0-442-29359-3 LC Card 75-26866 DDC 658.3
HF5549 .M299 ***NYPL [JLE 76-2406]***

Western employment trends, 1947-58. San Francisco, Calif. : U. S. Dept. of Labor, Bureau of Labor Statistics, [1959] 18 p. ; 27 cm. (Western regional report . #6) "August 1959." LC Card 87-400419 DDC 331.12/5/0978 19
1. Labor supply - West (U. S.). I. Series.
HD5725.A17 W47 1959

Western Europe in transition : West Germany's role in the European community / [edited by] Paul Michael Lützeler.1. Aufl. Baden-Baden : Nomos Verlagsgesellschaft, 1986. 223 p. : ill. ; 23 cm. (Schriftenreihe Europäisches Recht, Politik und Wirtschaft . Bd. 122) Includes bibliographies. ISBN 3-7890-1220-3 LC Card 87-136015 DDC 341.24/22 19
1. European Economic Community - Germany, West. I. Lützeler, Paul Michael. II. Series.
HC241.25.G3 W47 1986

Western European adjustment to structural economic problems /. Drouin, Marie Josée. Lanham, MD , Indianapolis, IN , c1987. xxii, 259 p. : ISBN 0-8191-6527-1 (alk. paper) : LC Card 87-18909 DDC 330.94/0558 19
HC240 .D75 1987

Western Germany. see **Germany, West.**

Western regional report .
(#6) Western employment trends, 1947-58. San Francisco, Calif. [1959] 18 p. ; LC Card 87-400419 DDC 331.12/5/0978 19
HD5725.A17 W47 1959

Western responses to Tanzanian socialism, 1967-83 /. Crouch, Susan C. (Susan Catherine), 1958- Aldershot, Hants, England , Brookfield, Vt., USA , c1987. x, 194 p. ; ISBN 0-566-05455-8 : LC Card 87-15018 DDC 337.678 19
HF1612.9 .C76 1987

WESTERN SAMOA - ECONOMIC CONDITIONS.
Huh, Ko Kwang. Economic survey on Western Samoa. [Manila, Philippines] [1984] vii, 44 p. : LC Card 87-403365 DDC 330.996/14 19
HC687.5 .H84 1984

Western sunrise : the genesis and growth of Britain's major high tech corridor / Peter Hall ... [et al.]. London ; Boston : Allen & Unwin, 1987. xvi, 208 p. : maps ; 25 cm. Bibliography: p. [191]-202. Includes index. ISBN 0-04-338142-1 LC Card 86-28755 DDC 338.6/042 19
1. High technology industries - Government policy - Great Britain. 2. High technology industries - Great Britain - Location. I. Hall, Peter Geoffrey.
HC260.H53 W47 1987

WESTERN UNION TELEGRAPH COMPANY STRIKE, 1883.
Gabler, Edwin, 1949- The American telegrapher . New Brunswick, NJ , c1988. p. cm. ISBN 0-8135-1284-0 : LC Card 87-19878 DDC 331.89/2813841/0973 19
HD5325 .T252 1883

Westeuropean direct investment in Canada . Bruns, Claudia. Hamburg [1986] 18 p. : LC Card 86-191095
HG5152 .B78 1986

Westfälische geographische Studien. For additional listing of contents, see Old Catalog.
(38) Komp, Klaus Ulrich. Die Seehafenstädte im Weser-Jade-Raum und ihre überregionale Verflechtung /. Münster , 1982. x, 143 p. : LC Card 83-197866
HE558.W45 K66 1982

Westfall, L. Glenn, 1943- Don Vicente Martinez Ybor, the man and his empire : development of the Clear Havana industry in Cuba and Florida in the nineteenth century / L. Glenn Westfall. New York : Garland Pub., 1987. vii, 214 p. : ill. ; 24 cm. (South American and Latin American economic history) Originally presented as the author's thesis (Ph. D.--University of Florida, 1977) Bibliography: p. 204-214. ISBN 0-8240-1374-3 (alk. paper) : LC Card 87-8690 DDC 338.7/67972/0924 19
1. Cigar industry - Florida - History - 19th century. 2. Cigar industry - Cuba - History - 19th century. 3. Tobacco industry - Florida - History - 19th century. 4. Tobacco industry - Cuba - History - 19th century. 5. Ybor, Vicente Martinez, 1818-1896. 6. Industrialists - Florida - Biography. 7. Industrialists - Cuba - Biography. I. Title. II. Series.
HD9149.C5 U777 1987

Westholt, Hans-Joachim. Schlieper, Andreas. 150 Jahre Ruhrgebiet . Düsseldorf , 1986. 224 p. : ISBN 3-590-18150-8 LC Card 86-231681
HC288.R8 S34 1986

Westin, Alan F. Managerial dilemmas : cases in social, legal, and technological change / Alan F. Westin and John D. Aram. Cambridge, Mass. : Ballinger, 1988. p. cm. Includes bibliographies. ISBN 0-88730-181-9 (pbk.) LC Card 87-22476 DDC 658.4/03 19
1. Management - Decision making - Case studies. I. Aram, John D., 1942-. II. Title.
HD30.23 .W47 1988

Westing, J. Howard (John Howard), 1911- Purchasing management. Zenz, Gary Joseph. Purchasing and the management of materials / Gary J. Zenz. 5th ed. New York , c1981. xiii, 514 p. : ISBN 0-471-06091-7 LC Card 80-21649 DDC 658.7/2 19
HD39.5 .W47 1981 ***NYPL [JLE 86-3384]***

Westkott, Marcia, 1943- The feminist legacy of Karen Horney / Marcia Westkott. New Haven : Yale University Press, c1986. viii, 242 p. ; 22 cm. Includes index. Bibliography: p. 215-236. ISBN 0-300-03706-6 (alk. paper) LC Card 86-9201 DDC 305.4/2 19
1. Horney, Karen, 1885-1952. 2. Women - Psychology. 3. Femininity. 4. Identity (Psychology). I. Title.
HQ1206 .W47 1986 ***NYPL [JFD 86-10266]***

Westley, John Richard, 1942- Agriculture and equitable growth : the case of Punjab-Haryana / John R. Westley. Boulder : Westview Press, 1986. xv, 369 p. : maps ; 23 cm. (Westview special studies in agriculture science and policy) Includes index. Bibliography: p. 329-348. ISBN 0-8133-7155-4 (alk. paper) : LC Card 85-31586 DDC 338.1/85455 19
1. Agriculture and state - India - Punjab. 2. Agriculture and state - India - Haryana. 3. Income distribution - India - Punjab. 4. Income distribution - India - Haryana. I. Title. II. Series.
HD2075.P8 W47 1986 ***NYPL [JLE 86-1877]***

Westley, Laurie A. DeGooyer, Janice. Women's work, undervalued, underpaid . Washington, D.C. , 1984, c1982. 27, [4] leaves :
NYPL [*ZT-1708 no.39]

Westney, D. Eleanor. Imitation and innovation : the transfer of Western organizational patterns to Meiji Japan / D. Eleanor Westney. Cambridge, Mass. : Harvard University Press, 1987. viii, 252 p. : ill. ; 24 cm. Bibliography: p. [227]-246. Includes index. ISBN 0-674-44437-X (alk. paper) LC Card 87-273 DDC 338.6/0952 19
1. Organizational change - Japan - History - Case studies. 2. Police - Japan - History. 3. Postal service - Japan - History. 4. Japanese newspapers - History. 5. Japan - History - Meiji period, 1868-1912. 6. Japan - Civilization - Occidental influences. I. Title.
HD70.J3 W47 1987

Westoff, Leslie Aldridge. Corporate romance : how to avoid it, live through it, or make it work for you / by Leslie Aldridge Westoff.1st ed. New York, NY : Times Books, c1985. xiii,

246 p. ; 22 cm. ISBN 0-8129-1257-8 : LC Card 85-40284 DDC 658.4/095 19
1. Women executives. 2. Executives - Sexual behavior. 3. Corporate culture. I. Title.
HD6054.3 .W47 1985 ***NYPL [JLD 86-1042]***

Weston, Ann. Cable, Vincent. The commerce of culture . New Delhi , 1986. 237 p. ; ISBN 81-7062-004-X : LC Card 86-902899 DDC 338.4/77455/0954 19
HF5439.H27 C33 1986

Weston, J. Fred (John Fred), 1916- Copeland, Thomas E., 1946- Financial theory and corporate policy /. Reading, Mass. , c1988. xiv, 946 p. : ISBN 0-201-10648-5 : LC Card 87-12595 DDC 658.1/5 19
HG4011 .C833 1988

Westover, Belinda. Our work, our lives, our words . Basingstoke, Hampshire , 1986. xiii, 189 p. : ISBN 0-333-36598-4
NYPL [JLD 86-4220]

Westphal, Uwe. Stabilization policy in France and the Federal Republic of Germany /. Amsterdam ; New York : xii, 379 p. : ISBN 0-444-87529-8 LC Card 84-28614 DDC 338.943 19
HC276.2 .S77 1985 ***NYPL [TB (Contributions to economic analysis. no.153)]***

Westphalen, Gerald. Der Ausbau von Fernwärmenetzen und seine Wirkungen auf Arbeitsmarkt und Beschäftigung, dargestellt am Beispiel der Freien und Hansestadt Hamburg . Bonn [1983] xiv, 172 p. : LC Card 85-107700
HD5780.H34 A87 1983

Westview professional handbooks on the new banking.
Marketing life insurance in a bank or thrift /. Boulder, Colo. , 1986. xii, 233 p. ; ISBN 0-8133-7205-4 : LC Card 86-1644 DDC 332.1/7 19
HG1616.I47 M37 1986
NYPL [JLD 86-3992]

Westview special studies in agricultural science and policy.
The Farm financial crisis . Boulder , 1988. xvi, 205 p. : ISBN 0-8133-7186-4 (pbk. : alk. paper) : LC Card 86-32601 DDC 338.1/3/0973 19
HD1761 .F295 1988

Westview special studies in agriculture science and policy.
Financing the agricultural sector . Boulder, Colo. , 1986. xi, 256 p. : ISBN 0-8133-0055-X (pbk. : alk. paper) LC Card 86-50152 DDC 338.1/3/0973 19
HD1761 .F5 1986 ***NYPL [JLE 86-2766]***

McKinzie, Lance. A perspective on U. S. farm problems and agricultural policy /. Boulder , 1987. xvii, 189 p. : ISBN 0-8133-7376-X (pbk. : alk. paper) LC Card 86-51501 DDC 338.1/873 19
HD1470.5.U6 M35 1987

Westley, John Richard, 1942- Agriculture and equitable growth . Boulder , 1986. xv, 369 p. : ISBN 0-8133-7155-4 (alk. paper) : LC Card 85-31586 DDC 338.1/85455 19
HD2075.P8 W47 1986 ***NYPL [JLE 86-1877]***

Wong, Lung-Fai. Agricultural productivity in the Socialist countries /. Boulder, Colo. , 1986. xvii, 195 p. : ISBN 0-8133-7152-X : LC Card 86-1539 DDC 338.1/6/091717 19
HD1415 .W54 1986 ***NYPL [JLE 86-2447]***

Westview special studies in industrial policy and development.
Bennett, Mark. Public policy and industrial development . Boulder, Colo. , 1986. xii, 134 p. : ISBN 0-86531-821-2 : LC Card 83-23456 DDC 338.4/76292/0972 19
HD9710.3.M42 B46 1986
NYPL [JLE 86-2581]

Rural industrialization in Israel /. Boulder , 1987. xi, 193 p. ; ISBN 0-8133-7393-X (pbk. : alk. paper) : LC Card 87-2073 DDC 338.095694 19
HC415.25 .R87 1987

Westview special studies in international security.
Escalation and intervention . Boulder, Colo. , 1986. x, 181 p. ; ISBN 0-8133-7200-3 : LC Card 86-4020 DDC 327.1/6 19
U104 .E83 1986 ***NYPL [JLE 86-4131]***

Westview special studies in ocean science and policy.
Kent, George, 1939- Fish, food, and hunger . Boulder , 1987. ix, 201 p. ; ISBN 0-8133-7409-X (pbk.) : LC Card 87-6066 DDC 338.3/7194 19
HD9450.5 .K46 1987

Westview special studies on agriculture science and policy.
Zarkovic, M. Issues in Indian agricultural development /. Boulder , 1987. xviii, 203 p. ; ISBN 0-8133-7451-0 (soft : alk. paper) LC Card 87-50898 DDC 338.1/0954 19
HD2072 .Z37 1987

Westview special studies on Asia.
Moore, Richard H. Japanese agriculture . Boulder , 1987. p. cm. ISBN 0-8133-7406-5 LC Card 87-13553 DDC 338.1/0952/115 19
HD920.N33 M65 1987

Westview special studies on East Asia.
Luedde-Neurath, Richard. Import controls and export-oriented development . Boulder , 1986. xiv, 249 p. ; ISBN 0-8133-7080-9 : LC Card 85-10459 DDC 382/.3/095195 19
HF1602.5 .L84 1985 ***NYPL [JLE 86-1557]***

Westwick, C. A.
Accounting for overseas operations / C.A. Westwick. Aldershot, Hants, England ; Brookfield, Vt. : Gower, c1986. ix, 184 p. ; 31 cm. ISBN 0-566-02586-8 : LC Card 85-30582 DDC 657/.95 19
1. International business enterprises - Accounting - Standards. 2. Foreign exchange - Accounting - Standards. 3. Accounting - Standards - Great Britain. I. Title.
HF5686.I56 W47 1986 ***NYPL [JLG 86-202]***

How to use management ratios / C.A. Westwick. 2nd ed. Aldershot, Hants, England : Gower, 1987. xviii, 421 p. : ill. ; 22 x 31 cm. Bibliography: p. 401-411. Includes indexes. ISBN 0-566-02425-X LC Card 87-126440 DDC 658.4/001/512924 19
1. Ratio analysis. 2. Management - Statistical methods. I. Title. II. Title: Management ratios.
HF5681.R25 W47 1987

WETLAND CONSERVATION - GOVERNMENT POLICY - GREAT BRITAIN.
Penning-Rowsell, Edmund. Floods and drainage . London , Boston , 1986. xx, 199 p. : ISBN 0-04-627001-9 (alk. paper) : LC Card 85-13383 DDC 363.3/4936/0941 19
HD1676.G7 P46 1985 ***NYPL [JLE 86-3996]***

Wets, Roger J.-B. Stochastic optimization . Berlin , New York , c1985. x, 754 p. : ISBN 0-387-16659-9 (U. S.) LC Card 86-11865 DDC 629.8/312 19
QA402.3 .S778 1985 ***NYPL [JSE 86-1596]***

Wettbewerb und Akkumulation in der selbstverwalteten Wirtschaft /. Körner, Ulrich. Frankfurt , New York , c1984. 193 p. : ISBN 3-593-33257-4 LC Card 84-191794
HD5660.Y8 K623 1984

Wettbewerb und Industriestruktur . Böbel, Ingo. Berlin , New York , 1984. xiv, 336 p. : ISBN 0-387-13143-4 (U. S.) LC Card 85-111698
HD2757 .B63 1984

Wettbewerb und Kooperation im Landhandel . Straaten, Martin. Berlin , c1985. 82 p. ; ISBN 3-428-05712-0 LC Card 85-167800
HF5429.6.G42 S77 1985

Wettbewerb und Preisbildung der Seehafenverkehrswirtschaft in nordwesteuropäischen Seehäfen . Boldt, Günter. Göttingen , 1964. 120 p. ; LC Card 87-408787 DDC 380.5 s 387.1 19
HE131 .M84 Heft 30 HE558.H3

Wettbewerb und staatliche Sachausgaben /. Langenbach, Peter. Bochum , 1981. viii, 316 p. ; ISBN 3-88339-194-8 : LC Card 81-205020 DDC 336.3/9 19
HJ7461 .L36 1981 ***NYPL [JLD 86-2579]***

Wettbewerbsbeschränkung in der Nachfrage.
Köln : Heymann, 1985. vii, 145 p. ; 23 cm. (FIW-Schriftenreihe, 0429-9485 . H. 116) Includes bibliographical references. ISBN 3-452-20479-0
1. Competition - Germany, West. 2. Antitrust law - Germany, West. I. Series. ***NYPL [JLE 86-2774]***

Wettbewerbsfähig durch soziale Disziplin? .
Dauderstädt, Michael. Bonn [1981] 38 p. ; LC Card 85-137321
HD41 .D38 1981

Wettbewerbspolitik auf dem Treibstoffmarkt /. Baum, Herbert, Dr. Baden-Baden , c1983. 97 p. ; ISBN 3-7890-0881-8 LC Card 83-187053
HD9573.5 .B38 1983

Die wettbewerbspolitische Behandlung der leitungsgebundenen Energiewirtschaft . Schröter, Klaus, 1953- Frankfurt am Main , New York , c1986. viii, 300 p. ; ISBN 3-8204-9551-7 LC Card 87-407422 DDC 363.6/2/0943 19
HD9685.G3 S375 1986

Die Wettbewerbsposition natürlicher Rohstoffe . Borrmann, Axel. Hamburg , 1984. 226 p. : ISBN 3-87895-250-3 LC Card 84-222130
HF1054.G4 B67 1984

Wettbewerbssituation und Marktzutrittsbarrieren bei spezifischen Qualifikationen /. Kraft, Kornelius. Berlin [1985] 35, 6 p. : LC Card 86-211574
HD5707 .K73 1985

Wettbewerbstheoretische Analyse des Landwarenmarktes in der Bundesrepublik Deutschland . Kühl, Rainer. Kiel , 1986. 77 p. : ISBN 3-922553-79-6 LC Card 86-172903
HD9013.5 .K84 1986

Wettbewerbsumwelt und interne Konfigurationen . Niemeier, Joachim, 1955- Frankfurt am Main , New York , c1986. xv, 412 p. : ISBN 3-8204-9541-X LC Card 87-407931 DDC 338.6/048 19
HD41 .N54 1986

Wettig, Gerhard. Konflikt und Kooperation zwischen Ost und West : Entspannung in Theorie und Praxis : aussen- und sicherheitspolitische Analyse / Gerhard Wettig. Bonn : Osang, c1981. 217 p. ; 23 cm. Includes bibliographical references and indexes. ISBN 3-7894-0082-3 LC Card 82-225671 DDC 327.1/7 19
1. World politics - 1975-1985. 2. Detente. I. Title.
D849 .W47 1981 ***NYPL [JLE 86-4503]***

Wever, E.
New firms and regional development in Europe /. London , Dover, N.H. , c1986. 322 p. : ISBN 0-7099-1577-2 : LC Card 85-28372 DDC 338.7/1/094 19
HD2346.E9 N48 1986 ***NYPL [JLD 86-1597]***

New technology and regional development /. London , Wolfeboro, N.H. , c1987. 188 p. : ISBN 0-7099-3106-9 : LC Card 86-23983 DDC 338.9/26 19
HC79.T4 N48 1987

Wexler, Phillip S.
Alessandra, Anthony J. Non-manipulative selling /. New York , c1987. x, 262 p. : ISBN 0-13-623307-4 (pbk.) : LC Card 86-43174 DDC 658.8/5 19
HF5438.25 .A43 1987

Alessandra, Anthony J. Non-manipulative selling [sound recording] . Chicago, Ill. , p1985. 6 sound cassettes : LC Card 86-754983
HF5438.25

Wey, Hebe. O processo de relações públicas / Hebe Wey. São Paulo, SP : Summus Editorial, c1983. 166 p. ; 21 cm. Bibliography: p. 165-166. LC Card 86-152248
1. Public relations. 2. Public relations - Brazil. I. Title.
HD59 .W44 1983

Weygandt, Jerry J. Accounting principles / Jerry J. Weygandt, Donald E. Kieso, Walter G. Kell. New York : Wiley, c1987. xxviii, 1167, [45] p. : ill. (some col.) ; 26 cm. Includes index. ISBN 0-471-03863-6 LC Card 87-2001 DDC 657 19
1. Accounting. I. Kieso, Donald E. II. Kell, Walter Gerry, 1921-. III. Title.
HF5635 .W524 1987

Weyman-Jones, Thomas G., 1947- Energy in Europe : issues and policies / Thomas G. Weyman-Jones. London ; New York : Methuen, 1986. xii, 176 p. : ill., charts, map ; 23 cm. (The Methuen EEC series) Includes index. Bibliography: p. [167]-171. ISBN 0-416-36590-6 LC Card 86-18169 DDC 333.79/094 19
1. Power resources - Europe. 2. Energy policy - Europe. I. Title. II. Series.
TJ163.25.E85 W48 1986
NYPL [JLD 87-1305]

WGBH (Television station : Boston, Mass.)
Billion dollar day [videorecording] /. Deerfield, IL , 1986. 1 videocassette (30 min.) : LC Card 86-700167 DDC 332.4 11
HG3903

WGI-Berichte zur Regionalforschung .
(Heft 13) Maier, Jörg. Freizeitraum Oberstaufen . München , 1976. xii, 92 p. : ISBN 3-920397-13-4 LC Card 87-408421 DDC 330.94 380.1/45914337 19
HC281 .M84 Heft 13 G155.G3

Whalley, John. General equilibrium trade policy modeling /. Cambridge, Mass. , c1986. vii, 360 p. : ISBN 0-262-19245-4 LC Card 85-19144 DDC 382/.3/0724 19
HF1410.5 .G46 1986 ***NYPL [JLE 86-4456]***

Whang, In Joung. Administration of land reform in Korea / by In-Joung Whang. Seoul, Korea : Korea Development Institute, [1982] 41 p. ; 28 cm. (Working paper . 8301) "December 1982." Bibliography: p. 40-41. LC Card 84-148921 DDC 333.3/1/519 19
1. Land reform - Korea. 2. Land reform - Korea (South). I. Han'guk Kaebal Yŏn'guwŏn. II. Series: Working paper (Han'guk Kaebal Yŏng'guwŏn) , 8301. III. Title.
HD1333.K78 W46 1982

Wharton Applied Research Center. The Future of the office products industry . Alexandria, Va. (301 N. Fairfax St., Alexandria 22314) , c1985. viii, 212, 33 p. : LC Card 86-200112 DDC 338.4/768 19
HD9800.U52 F86 1985

Wharton Econometric Forecasting Associates.
Economics U$A. Chicago, IL , 1986. 1 videocassette (28 min.) : LC Card 86-708020 DDC 330.15 11
HB99.7

The Protectionist threat . Philadelphia, PA (3624 Science Center, Philadelphia 19104) , c1985. 85 p. : LC Card 87-106782 DDC 382.7/3/0973 19
HF1716 .P76 1985

Status report . Philadelphia, PA (3624 Science Center, Philadelphia 19104) , c1987. iii, 67 p. : LC Card 87-153448 DDC 336.3/435/091724 19
HJ8899 .S72 1987

Wharton executive library.
Adams, Francis Gerard, 1929- The business forecasting revolution . New York , 1986. xiii, 265 p. : ISBN 0-19-503700-6 LC Card 85-18943 DDC 338.5/442 19
HD30.27 .A33 1986 ***NYPL [JLD 86-2257]***

WHARTON, JOSEPH, 1826-1909.
Yates, W. Ross (Willard Ross) Joseph Wharton . Bethlehem , London , c1987. 413 p. : ISBN 0-934223-00-9 (alk. paper) LC Card 86-81983 DDC 338.7/6691/0924 B 19
HC102.5.W47 Y38 1987

Wharton, Robert B.
Analysis of rice export flows from southern states / by Robert B. Wharton and W.R.M.P. Jayawardana. [Baton Rouge?] : Dept. of Agricultural Economics and Agribusiness, Louisiana Agricultural Experiment Station, Louisiana State University Agricultural Center, [1986] iii, 44 p. ; 28 cm. (D.A.E. research report . no. 662) "November 1986." Bibliography: p. 21. LC Card 87-620886 DDC 338.1/09763 s 382/.41318/0975021 19
1. Rice trade - Southern States - Statistics. I. Wharton, Robert B. II. Jayawardana, W. R. M. P. III. Title. IV. Series.
HD1775.L8 L7 no. 662 HD9066.U46A13

Wharton, Robert B. Analysis of rice export flows from southern states /. [Baton Rouge?] [1986] iii, 44 p. ; LC Card 87-620886 DDC 338.1/09763 s 382/.41318/0975021 19
HD1775.L8 L7 no. 662 HD9066.U46A13

Wharton School.
Cooperative strategies in international business /. Lexington, Mass. , c1988. xxix, 513 p. : ISBN 0-669-14927-6 (alk. paper) LC Card 86-46160 DDC 338.8/8 19
HD2755.5 .C645 1988

WHARTON SCHOOL. PENSION RESEARCH COUNCIL.
Pension asset management . Homewood, Ill. , 1988. xiii, 178 p. : ISBN 0-256-06123-8 LC Card 87-81575 DDC 332.6/7254 19
HD7105.4 .P45 1988

What every engineer should know about microcomputer systems design and debugging /. Wray, William C. New York, N.Y. , c1984. ix, 183 p. : ISBN 0-8247-7160-5 LC Card 83-25204 DDC 001.64 19
QA76.6 .W73 1984 ***NYPL [JSE 86-1632]***

What every manager needs to know about manufacturing / Richard G. Brandenburg, editor. New York, NY : AMACOM, [1987], c1983. 181 p. : ill. ; 23 cm. (The Essentials of management series) "Excerpted from the AMA management handbook, second edition, William K. Fallon, general editor." Includes index. ISBN 0-8144-7686-4 (pbk.) LC Card 87-47714 DDC 658 19
1. Manufactures - Management. I. Brandenburg, Richard G. II. AMA management handbook. 2nd ed. III. Series: Essentials of management series (New York, N.Y.).
HD9720.5 .W38 1987

What gold investors need to know about the collapse of the oil cartel /. Oweiss, Ibrahim M. Bethel, CT , c1986. 37 leaves : LC Card 86-209518 DDC 332.63 19
HG293 .O84 1986

What happens when U. S. companies sell their South African operations? /. Hauck, David. Washington, D.C. (Suite 600, 1755 Massachusetts Ave., N.W., Washington 20036) , c1987. 16 p. ; LC Card 87-163729 DDC 338.8/8973/068 19
HG5851.A3 H392 1987

What homebuyers should know about buying a home /. Knox, Albert H. New York , c1987. vii, 192 p. : ISBN 0-533-06883-5 : LC Card 85-91377 DDC 643/.12 19
HD1379 .K656 1987

What is a share of stock? /. Little, Jeffrey B. New York , c1988. 47 p. : ISBN 1-555-46620-6 LC Card 87-13788 DDC 332.63/22 19
HG4521 .L736 1988

What is a wife worth? . Minton, Michael H. New York , 1984, c1983. 192 p. ; ISBN 0-07-042414-4 (pbk.) : LC Card 84-11221 DDC 331.4/28164/0973 19
HD4966.H842 U65 1984 ***NYPL [JLD 87-12]***

What is economics? /. Eggert, Jim, 1943- Los Altos, Calif. , c1987. vii, 205 p. : ISBN 0-86576-104-3 (pbk.) LC Card 86-27297 DDC 330 19
HB171.5 .E464 1987

What is really unique about the Japanese economy? /. Iida, Tsuneo, 1932- Nagoya, Japan , 1985. 13 leaves ; LC Card 87-109242 DDC 331.25 19
HF5549.5.S4 I35 1985

What it takes . Gardenswartz, Lee. New York , 1987. ix, 205 p. ; ISBN 0-385-23820-7 : LC Card 87-13657 DDC 650.1/024042 19
HF5386 .G214 1987

What makes Japan work [motion picture] : a film / by Elda Hartley. Cos Cob, CT : Hartley Film Foundation, 1983. 1 film reel (11 min.) : sd., col. ; 16 mm. Title from data sheet. Junior high school through college students and adults. Issued also as videorecording. Shows how Buddhism influences the Japanese work ethic. Three Japanese workers talk about their attitudes and values concerning work, which help to illustrate larger Buddhist concepts about life. The voice of Alan Watts leads viewers in an actual experience of living in the 'now'. LC Card 83-700702 DDC 181 11
1. Work ethic - Japan. 2. Buddhism - Japan. I. Hartley, Elda. II. Watts, Alan, 1915-1973. III. Hartley Film Foundation.
HD8726.5

What makes Japan work [videorecording] : a film / by Elda Hartley. Cos Cob, CT : Hartley Film Foundation, 1983. 1 videocassette (11 min.) : sd., col. Title from data sheet. Junior high school through college students and adults. Issued as U-matic 3/4 in. or Beta 1/2 in. or VHS 1/2 in. Issued also as motion picture. Shows how Buddhism influences the Japanese work ethic. Three Japanese workers talk about their attitudes and values concerning work, which help to illustrate larger Buddhist concepts about life. The voice of Alan Watts leads viewers in an actual experience of living in the 'now'. LC Card 87-705342 DDC 181 11
1. Work ethic - Japan. 2. Buddhism - Japan. I. Hartley, Elda. II. Watts, Alan, 1915-1973. III. Hartley Film Foundation.
HD8726.5

What matters is profit. Wilder, J. Welles. The Adam theory of markets, or, What matters is profit /. McLeansville, N.C. (P.O. Box 128, Mcleansville 27301) , c1987. 131 p. : LC Card 87-166037 DDC 332.64/4 19
HG4523 .W54 1987

What model for Europe? /. Emerson, Michael. Cambridge, Mass. , c1988. xi, 151 p. : ISBN 0-262-05036-6 LC Card 87-15151 DDC 331.11/094 19
HD8380.5 .E47 1988

What price food? . Streeten, Paul. New York , 1987. viii, 127 p. : ISBN 0-312-00739-6 : LC Card 87-9577 DDC 338.1/8 19
HD1417 .S73 1987

What should banks do? /. Litan, Robert E., 1950- Washington, D.C. , c1987. xi, 207 p. : ISBN 0-8157-5270-9 : LC Card 87-18235 DDC 332.1/0973 19
HG2491 .L58 1987

What Sweden can do. Stockholm : Sveriges allmänna exportförening, 1919. 355 p. in various pagings : ill. ; 22 cm. Includes indexes. LC Card 85-666345
1. Sweden - Industries - Directories. I. Sveriges allmänna exportförening.
HC372.2 .W52x 1919

What to do about communism in unions . Boulware, Lemuel Richetts, 1895- [Schenectady, N.Y.?] [1952?] 62 p. ; ***NYPL [JLD 86-247]***

What you get when you go for it /. Milwid, Beth, 1948- New York , c1987. 248 p. ; ISBN 0-396-08905-4 LC Card 86-29084 DDC 331.4/81/000973 19
HD6054.2.U6 M55 1987

What you must know about Social Security & Medicare /. Kingson, Eric R. New York , 1987. 120 p. ; ISBN 0-88687-294-4 (pbk.) : LC Card 86-62667 DDC 368.4/3/00973 19
HD7125 .K538 1987

What you need to know about business, money, and power /. Kidron, Michael. New York , c1987. 187 p. : ISBN 0-671-54113-7 : LC Card 86-31571 DDC 650 19
HF5351 .K473 1987

Whatever happened to planning? /. Ambrose, Peter J. London , New York , 1986. xiv, 288 p. : ISBN 0-416-37100-0 LC Card 86-12415 DDC 333.73/17/0941 19
HD596 .A43 1986 ***NYPL [JLD 87-1402]***

Whatley, Arthur A., 1939- Kelley, Nelson Lane, 1937- Personnel management in action . St. Paul , c1987. xiv, 338 p. : ISBN 0-314-32168-3 (pbk.) LC Card 86-32445 DDC 658.3 19
HF5549 .K344 1987

What's a natural resource? [motion picture] / an Alfred Higgins production ; directors, Stephen Wallen and Alfred Higgins ; writers, Donald Giroux and Alfred Higgins. Los Angeles, Calif. : Alfred Higgins Productions, 1986, c1987. 1 film reel (15 1/2 min.) : sd., col. ; 16 mm. + 1 teacher's guide. Title from data sheet. Photographer, Chris Sebaldt ; film editor, Danny Miller. Primary grades. Issued also as videorecording. With the help of a park ranger children learn about natural resources and how they affect our lives. Renewable natural resources such as water and wood, and nonrenewable natural resources such as oil, metals, soil, and air and the importance they play in everyday life are discussed. LC Card 86-708242 DDC 333.7 11
1. Natural resources - Juvenile films. I. Alfred Higgins Productions.
HC59

What's a natural resource? [videorecording] / an Alfred Higgins production ; directors, Stephen Wallen and Alfred Higgins ; writers, Donald Giroux and Alfred Higgins. Los Angeles, Calif. : Alfred Higgins Productions, 1986, c1987. 1 videocassette (15 1/2 min.) : sd., col. ; 1/2 in. + 1 teacher's guide. Title from data sheet. Photographer, Chris Sebaldt ; film editor, Danny Miller. Primary grades. Issued as Beta or VHS. Issued also as motion picture. With the help of a park ranger children learn about natural resources and how they affect our lives. Renewable natural resources such as water and

wood, and nonrenewable natural resources such as oil, metals, soil, and air and the importance they play in everyday life are discussed. LC Card 86-708243 DDC 333.7 11
1. Natural resources - Juvenile films. I. Alfred Higgins Productions.
HC59

What's a wife worth? /. Leghorn, Lisa. Somerville, Mass. [198-] 8 p. : LC Card 87-111053 DDC 331.2/8164/0973 19
HD4966.H842 U64 1980z

What's it worth . Scaduto, Joseph V. Blue Ridge Summit, PA , c1985. x, 244 p. : ISBN 0-8306-0761-7 : LC Card 85-2801 DDC 333.33/2 19
HD1379 .S33 1985 ***NYPL [JSE 86-1407]***

What's made in the U. S.A.? /. Vargish, George. New Brunswick, U. S.A. , c1988. 160 p. : ISBN 0-88738-187-1 LC Card 87-19164 DDC 382/.3/0973 19
HF1716 .V37 1988

What's made in the USA? Vargish, George. What's made in the U. S.A.? /. New Brunswick, U. S.A. , c1988. 160 p. : ISBN 0-88738-187-1 LC Card 87-19164 DDC 382/.3/0973 19
HF1716 .V37 1988

What's next? . Falvey, Jack, 1938- Charlotte, Vt. , c1987. 189 p. ; ISBN 0-913589-26-8 : LC Card 87-10553 DDC 650.1/4 19
HF5384 .F35 1987

WHEAT.
(1985) 1985 CIMMYT World Wheat facts and trends . México, D.F. [1985] 44 p. : LC Card 87-108823 DDC 338.1/7311 19
HD9049.W4 A16 1985

WHEAT - CALIFORNIA - HISTORY - 19TH CENTURY.
Breadbasket of the world . San Francisco , 1984. 10 pamphlets : LC Card 87-100963 DDC 338.1/7311/09794 19
HD9049.W5 U414 1984

WHEAT - MARKETING.
1985 CIMMYT World Wheat facts and trends . México, D.F. [1985] 44 p. : LC Card 87-108823 DDC 338.1/7311 19
HD9049.W4 A16 1985

WHEAT - PRICES.
Haley, Stephen L. The value of the dollar and competitiveness of U. S. wheat exports /. [Washington, D.C.] [1986] iv, 28 p. : LC Card 86-602853 DDC 382/.41311/0973 19
HD9049.W5 U4288 1986

1985 CIMMYT World Wheat facts and trends . México, D.F. [1985] 44 p. : LC Card 87-108823 DDC 338.1/7311 19
HD9049.W4 A16 1985

WHEAT - PRICES - HUNGARY.
Ár- és külkereskedelmi tanulmány a buzára és kukoricára, Magyarország /. Budapest , 1984. 93 p. ; ISBN 963-491-218-4 (Magy. nemz. bibl.) LC Card 86-147569
HD9049.W5 H93 1984

WHEAT - PRICES - INDIA.
Gulati, Ashok, 1954- Agricultural price policy in India . New Delhi , 1987, c1985. 196 p. : LC Card 86-903595 DDC 338.1/8 19
HD2073 .G85 1987

WHEAT TRADE.
Haley, Stephen L. The value of the dollar and competitiveness of U. S. wheat exports /. [Washington, D.C.] [1986] iv, 28 p. : LC Card 86-602853 DDC 382/.41311/0973 19
HD9049.W5 U4288 1986

1985 CIMMYT World Wheat facts and trends . México, D.F. [1985] 44 p. : LC Card 87-108823 DDC 338.1/7311 19
HD9049.W4 A16 1985

WHEAT - TRADE AND STATISTICS. see **WHEAT TRADE.**

WHEAT TRADE - AUSTRALIA - VICTORIA.
Victoria. Parliament. Public Bodies Review Committee. Report on the Victorian Wheat Advisory Committee . Melbourne [1986] xiii, 34 p. ; LC Card 87-168597 DDC 338.1/7311/09945 19
HD9049.W5 A949 1986

WHEAT TRADE - BOLIVIA.
Proyecto harinas compuestas . La Paz, Bolivia , 1982. 272, [2], 3 p., [9] p. of plates : LC Card 83-195592
HD9044.B52 P76 1982

WHEAT TRADE - CALIFORNIA - HISTORY - 19TH CENTURY.
Breadbasket of the world . San Francisco , 1984. 10 pamphlets : LC Card 87-100963 DDC 338.1/7311/09794 19
HD9049.W5 U414 1984

WHEAT TRADE - ECONOMETRIC MODELS.
Schiff, Maurice W. An econometric analysis of the world wheat market and simulation of alternative policies, 1960-80 /. Washington, DC [1985] iv, 70 p. : LC Card 85-603033 DDC 382/.41 19
HD9049.W4 S37 1985

WHEAT TRADE - EGYPT - ECONOMETRIC MODELS.
Eckstein, Zvi. Cotton and wheat production in the Egyptian agriculture . [Tel Aviv] [1984] 40 leaves : LC Card 84-186315 DDC 338.1/711/0962 19
HD9087.E42 E35 1984

WHEAT TRADE - GOVERNMENT POLICY - ARGENTINA - HISTORY.
Solberg, Carl E. The prairies and the pampas . Stanford, Calif. , 1987. xii, 297 p. : ISBN 0-8047-1346-4 (alk. paper) : LC Card 86-27854 DDC 338.1/8 19
HD9049.W5 C297 1987

WHEAT TRADE - GOVERNMENT POLICY - AUSTRALIA - VICTORIA.
Victoria. Parliament. Public Bodies Review Committee. Report on the Victorian Wheat Advisory Committee . Melbourne [1986] xiii, 34 p. ; LC Card 87-168597 DDC 338.1/7311/09945 19
HD9049.W5 A949 1986

WHEAT TRADE - GOVERNMENT POLICY - CANADA - HISTORY.
Solberg, Carl E. The prairies and the pampas . Stanford, Calif. , 1987. xii, 297 p. : ISBN 0-8047-1346-4 (alk. paper) : LC Card 86-27854 DDC 338.1/8 19
HD9049.W5 C297 1987

WHEAT TRADE - GOVERNMENT POLICY - ECONOMETRIC MODELS.
Schiff, Maurice W. An econometric analysis of the world wheat market and simulation of alternative policies, 1960-80 /. Washington, DC [1985] iv, 70 p. : LC Card 85-603033 DDC 382/.41 19
HD9049.W4 S37 1985

WHEAT TRADE - HUNGARY.
Ár- és külkereskedelmi tanulmány a buzára és kukoricára, Magyarország /. Budapest , 1984. 93 p. ; ISBN 963-491-218-4 (Magy. nemz. bibl.) LC Card 86-147569
HD9049.W5 H93 1984

WHEAT TRADE - UNITED STATES.
Haley, Stephen L. The value of the dollar and competitiveness of U. S. wheat exports /. [Washington, D.C.] [1986] iv, 28 p. : LC Card 86-602853 DDC 382/.41311/0973 19
HD9049.W5 U4288 1986

Wheatcroft, Geoffrey. The Randlords / Geoffrey Wheatcroft. 1st Touchstone ed. New York : Simon & Schuster, 1987, c1985. xix, 314 p. : ill. ; 24 cm. (A Touchstone book) Bibliography: p. [279]-286. Includes index. ISBN 0-671-63993-5 (pbk.) : LC Card 87-4513 DDC 338.2/0968 19
1. Gold industry - South Africa - History - 19th century. 2. Diamond industry and trade - South Africa - History - 19th century. 3. Capitalists and financiers - South Africa - History - 19th century. 4. South Africa - Economic conditions - To 1918. I. Title.
HD9536.S62 W44 1985

Wheatley, Walter. Anthony, William P. Envisionary management . New York , c1988. p. cm. ISBN 0-89930-257-2 (lib. bdg. : alk. paper) LC Card 87-7373 DDC 658.3 19
HD38 .A6256 1988

Wheelen, Thomas L. Cases in strategic management and business policy / Thomas L. Wheelen, J. David Hunger. Reading, Mass. : Addison-Wesley, c1987. xii, 530 p. : ill. ; 24 cm. + 1 computer disk (5 1/4 in.) System requirements: IBM-PC; Lotus and FASST software. Includes bibliographies and index. ISBN 0-201-09134-8 (pbk.) : LC Card 86-26501 DDC 658.4/012 19
1. Strategic planning - Case studies. I. Hunger, J. David, 1941-. II. Title. III. Title: Strategic management and business policy.
HD30.28 .W428 1987

Wheeler, Jimmy W.
Beyond recrimination : perspectives on U. S.-Taiwan trade tensions / Jimmy W. Wheeler and Perry L. Wood ; with contributions by Maurice C. Ernst, Merit E. Janow. Indianapolis, IN (P.O. Box 26-919, Indianapolis 46226) : Hudson Institute, c1987. xix, 218 p. : ill. ; 26 cm. Bibliography: p. [211]-215. LC Card 87-165405 DDC 382/.0951249/073 19
1. United States - Foreign economic relations - Taiwan. 2. Taiwan - Foreign economic relations - United States. 3. United States - Foreign economic relations - Japan. 4. Japan - Foreign economic relations - United States. 5. United States - Foreign economic relations - Korea (South). 6. Korea (South) - Foreign economic relations - United States. 7. United States - Commercial policy. I. Wood, Perry. II. Title.
HF1456.5.T28 W46 1987

Drouin, Marie Josée. Western European adjustment to structural economic problems /. Lanham, MD , Indianapolis, IN , c1987. xxii, 259 p. : ISBN 0-8191-6527-1 (alk. paper) : LC Card 87-18909 DDC 330.94/0558 19
HC240 .D75 1987

Wheelock, Jaime. Entre la crisis y la agresión : la reforma agraria sandinista / Jaime Wheelock Román. Managua, Nicaragua : Editorial Nueva Nicaragua, [1985] 148 p. : ill. ; 19 cm. (Al día) LC Card 85-241401 DDC 333.3/1/7285 19
1. Land reform - Nicaragua. 2. Agriculture - Economic aspects - Nicaragua. 3. Nicaragua - Economic conditions - 1979-. I. Title.
HD1333.N5 W48 1985 ***NYPL [JLC 86-312]***

Wheelwright, Steven C., 1943- The Handbook of forecasting . New York , c1987. xviii, 638 p. : ISBN 0-471-83903-5 LC Card 86-28137 DDC 658.4/0355 19
HD30.27 .H36 1987

Whelan, Michael. Simon, Sam, 1945- Phonewriting . [Washington, D.C.] , c1986. iv, 92 p., [4] p. of plates : ISBN 0-943444-03-9 (pbk.) LC Card 86-214171 DDC 004.6 19
HE6239.E54 S56 1986

Whelan, Robert K. Stone, Clarence N. (Clarence Nathan), 1935- Urban policy and politics in a bureaucratic age /. Englewood Cliffs, N.J. , c1986. xv, 397 p. ; ISBN 0-13-939562-8 LC Card 85-6481 DDC 320.8/0973 19
JS331 .S76 1986 ***NYPL [JLE 86-3158]***

When horses pulled boats . Harlow, Alvin F. (Alvin Fay), 1875-1963. York, PA , c1983. 72 p. : ISBN 0-933788-43-6 (pbk.) LC Card 87-400271 DDC 386/.48/0973 19
HE395.A3 H37 1983

When the twain meet : Western theory and Eastern insights in exploring Indian organisations / Gouranga P. Chattopadhyay ... [et al.].1st ed. Allahabad : A.H. Wheeler, 1986. vi, 170 p. ; 25 cm. Includes bibliographies. LC Card 87-900706 DDC 658/.00954 19
1. Management - India. 2. Organization - India. I. Chattopadhyay, Gouranga P., 1931-.
HD70.I4 W54 1986

When to count by race . Fuchs, Lawrence H. New York, NY , c1986. 32 p. ; ISBN 0-87495-082-1 (pbk.) : LC Card 86-71979 DDC 658.3 19
HD4903.5.U58 F83 1986

When to sell . Mamis, Justin, 1929- New York , 1986, c1977. p. cm. ISBN 0-671-63605-7 LC Card 86-26971 DDC 332.6/45 19
HG6041 .M34 1986

Where can mom live? . Carlin, Vivian F., 1919- Lexington, Mass. , c1987. viii, 206 p. : ISBN 0-669-13665-4 (alk. paper) LC Card 86-45526 DDC 363.5/9 19
HD7287.92.U54 C37 1987

Where the money is . Bergan, Helen, 1937- Alexandria, Va. , c1985. 101 p. : ISBN 0-9615277-0-6 (pbk.) : LC Card 85-72141 DDC 361.7 19
HG177 .B48 1985 ***NYPL [JLD 87-844]***

Where to put your money, 1987 /. Passell, Peter. New York, NY , c1987. 82 p. ; ISBN 0-446-38497-6 (pbk.) : LC Card 86-28917

DDC 332.6/78 19
HG179 .P27 1987

Which three silver and gold dealers give you the worst prices? Rosenthal, Daniel M. Which 3 silver and gold dealers give you the worst prices? . Lafayette, CA , c1986. 58 leaves : ISBN 0-9615814-3-3 (pbk.) : LC Card 86-209287 DDC 332.63 19
HG307.U5 R673 1986

Which 3 silver and gold dealers give you the worst prices? . Rosenthal, Daniel M. Lafayette, CA , c1986. 58 leaves : ISBN 0-9615814-3-3 (pbk.) : LC Card 86-209287 DDC 332.63 19
HG307.U5 R673 1986

Whillans, Robert T. Mineral exploration expenditures in Canada, 1969-1975 / Robert T. Whillans. [Ottawa] : Energy, Mines, and Resources Canada, Minerals, c1978. vi, 13 p. : ill. ; 25 cm. (Mineral bulletin . MR 179) LC Card 85-182002 DDC 338.2/3 19
1. Prospecting - Canada - Costs. I. Canada. Minerals. II. Title. III. Series.
HD9506.C2 W45 1978

Whisker, James B., 1939- Arms makers of Philadelphia / James B. Whisker. [Morgantown, W. Va.?] : J.B. Whisker, [1987?] 32 p., [1] leaf of plates : ill. ; 28 cm. Cover title. LC Card 87-124428 DDC 338.7/623422/02574811 19
1. Gunsmiths - Pennsylvania - Philadelphia - Registers. I. Title.
HD9743.U7 P48 1987

WHISTLE BLOWING - LAW AND LEGISLATION - UNITED STATES.
Kohn, Stephen M. (Stephen Martin) Protecting environmental & nuclear whistleblowers . Washington, D.C. , c1985. xiii, 346 p. : ISBN 0-9615323-0-0 (pbk.) LC Card 85-61844 DDC 342.73/0684 347.302684 19
KF5342 .K64 1985 ***NYPL [JLE 86-1787]***

Whitcomb, Sandra. Kupsh, Joyce. The electronic office /. Mission Hills, Calif. , c1987. x, 307 p. : ISBN 0-02-803510-0 (pbk.) LC Card 87-402084 DDC 651.8 19
HF5548 .K85 1987

White, Bob. The child of an eagle : Mississippi steamboating / by Wm. Robert (Bob) White. [Cape Girardeau, Mo. : Center for Regional History & Cultural Heritage, Southeast Missouri State University, c1980] v, 78 p. : ill. ; 22 cm. Cover title. Bibliography: p. 77-78. LC Card 87-405068 DDC 386/.22436 19
1. Shipping - Mississippi River - History. 2. Navigation - Mississippi River - History. 3. Steamboat lines - Missouri - Cape Girardeau - History. 4. Steamboat lines - Missouri - Saint Louis - History. 5. Steamboat lines - Mississippi River - History. I. Title.
HE630.M6 W48 1980

White Burkett Miller Center. Alcalde Cardoza, Xavier. The idea of Third World development . Lanham, MD [Charlottesville, Va.] , c1987. xxii, 236 p. ; ISBN 0-8191-6303-1 (alk. paper) : LC Card 87-8154 DDC 338.91/009172/4 19
HC60 .A4595 1987

White, Colin (Colin M.) Russia and America : the roots of economic divergence / Colin White. London ; New York : Croom Helm, c1987. 268 p. ; 23 cm. Bibliography: p. 230-260. Includes index. ISBN 0-7099-5246-5 LC Card 87-13646 DDC 330.947 19
1. Soviet Union - Economic conditions. 2. United States - Economic conditions. 3. National characteristics, Russian - History. 4. National characteristics, American - History. I. Title.
HC333 .W46 1987

White collar hobo . Wren, Daniel A. Ames , 1987. xii, 165 p. : ISBN 0-8138-1922-9 LC Card 87-4048 DDC 331/.092/4 B 19
HD8073.W47 W74 1987

WHITE COLLAR WORKERS.
Carter, Bob, 1949- Capitalism, class conflict, and the new middle class /. London , Boston , 1985. vii, 256 p., 15 p. ; ISBN 0-7100-9624-0 : LC Card 84-9956 DDC 305.5/56 19
HD8039.M39 C37 1985
NYPL [JLD 87-115]

WHITE COLLAR WORKERS - ADDRESSES, ESSAYS, LECTURES.
White collar workers, trade unions, and class /. London , Dover, N.H. , c1986. 215 p. : ISBN 0-7099-0571-8 : LC Card 85-28806 DDC 331.88/041 19
HD8039.M39 W45 1986
NYPL [JLD 86-1602]

WHITE COLLAR WORKERS - CASE STUDIES.
Work in market and industrial societies /. Albany , c1984. viii, 316 p. ; ISBN 0-87395-810-1 LC Card 83-9267 DDC 306/.36 19
HD4901 .A659 1984 ***NYPL [JLE 86-4483]***

WHITE COLLAR WORKERS - EFFECT OF TECHNOLOGICAL INNOVATIONS ON.
Dowall, David E. Office automation and the implications for office development /. [Berkeley] [1986] 171 p. ; LC Card 86-622512 DDC 651.8 19
HF5547.5 .D64 1986

Weltz, Friedrich. Innovation im Büro . Frankfurt , New York , c1983. 343 p. ; ISBN 3-593-32724-4 LC Card 83-243001
HF5548.115 .W44 1983

WHITE COLLAR WORKERS - FRANCE - ANECDOTES, FACETIAE, SATIRE, ETC.
Bondt, Frank de. Délivrez-nous des cadres /. [Paris] , c1984. 248 p. ; LC Card 85-103087 DDC 331.7/12/0944 19
HD8038.F7 B65 1984

WHITE COLLAR WORKERS - GERMANY - HISTORY.
Speier, Hans. German white-collar workers and the rise of Hitler /. New Haven , 1986. xv, 208 p. ; ISBN 0-300-03701-5 LC Card 86-9120 DDC 331.7/92/0943 19
HD8039.M4 G3639413 1986
NYPL [JLE 87-909]

WHITE COLLAR WORKERS - GERMANY - POLITICAL ACTIVITY - HISTORY.
Speier, Hans. German white-collar workers and the rise of Hitler /. New Haven , 1986. xv, 208 p. ; ISBN 0-300-03701-5 LC Card 86-9120 DDC 331.7/92/0943 19
HD8039.M4 G3639413 1986
NYPL [JLE 87-909]

WHITE COLLAR WORKERS - ITALY.
Guala Duca, Riccardo, 1935- I nuovi colletti bianchi . Milano, Italy , c1985. 164 p. : LC Card 86-128292 DDC 331.7/92/0945 19
HD8039.M4 I854 1985

WHITE COLLAR WORKERS - NEW YORK (STATE) - ROCHESTER - ANECDOTES, FACETIAE, SATIRE, ETC.
Jackson, Mason, 1926- The building /. Interlaken, N.Y. , 1987. 128 p. : ISBN 0-932334-90-3 LC Card 86-24115 DDC 974.7/89043 19
HD8039.M4 U54 1987

WHITE COLLAR WORKERS - PENSIONS - GERMANY (WEST) - STATES - DIRECTORIES.
Die Versichertenältesten . [Berlin] [1984] 54 p. ; LC Card 85-113867
HD7116.M42 G4334 Nr. 20, 1984 HD7179

WHITE COLLAR WORKERS - PSYCHOLOGY.
Williams, Cecil L., 1930- The negotiable environment . Ann Arbor, Mich. , c1985. v, 82 p. : ISBN 0-936658-20-7 (pbk.) : LC Card 85-10305 DDC 658.3/82 19
HF5547.2 .W55 1985 ***NYPL [JLF 86-1138]***

WHITE COLLAR WORKERS - SALARIES, ETC. - GERMANY (WEST) - HESSE - STATISTICS.
Gehalts- und Lohnstrukturerhebung 1978 . Wiesbaden , 1983. 285, [3] p. ; LC Card 84-217477
HA1320 .H529 n.F., Nr. 152 HD5030.H47

White collar workers, trade unions, and class / Peter Armstrong ... [et al.]. London ; Dover, N.H. : Croom Helm, c1986. 215 p. : ill. ; 23 cm. Includes indexes. Bibliography: p. 199-207. ISBN 0-7099-0571-8 : LC Card 85-28806 DDC 331.88/041 19
1. White collar workers - Addresses, essays, lectures. 2. Social classes - Addresses, essays, lectures. 3. Political sociology - Addresses, essays, lectures. 4. Trade-unions - White collar workers - Addresses, essays, lectures. I. Armstrong, P. J. (Peter J.).
HD8039.M39 W45 1986
NYPL [JLD 86-1602]

WHITE COLLAR WORKERS - UNITED STATES - ATTITUDES.
Report on the coffee service industry /. Columbus, Ohio [1984] 1 v. (various foliations) : LC Card 87-100404 DDC 381/.4566393 19
HD9199.U48 R47 1984

WHITE COLLAR WORKERS - UNITED STATES - EFFECT OF TECHNOLOGICAL INNOVATIONS ON - CONGRESSES.
Technology and the transformation of white-collar work /. Hillsdale, N.J. , 1987. x, 281 p. : ISBN 0-89859-633-5 : LC Card 86-29039 DDC 331.7/92/0973 19
HD8039.M4 U577 1987

White, E. Frances. Sierra Leone's settler women traders : women on the Afro-European frontier / E. Frances White. Ann Arbor : University of Michigan Press, c1987. xi, 168 p. : maps ; 24 cm. (Women and culture series) Bibliography: p. 143-156. Includes index. ISBN 0-472-10080-7 (alk. paper) : LC Card 86-24997 DDC 331.4/81381/09664 19
1. Women merchants - Sierra Leone - History - 19th century. 2. Women, Black - Employment - Sierra Leone - History - 19th century. 3. Women colonists - Sierra Leone - History - 19 century. 4. Sierra Leone - Economic conditions - To 1896. I. Title.
HF3933 .W47 1987

White, Halbert. Gallant, A. Ronald, 1942- A unified theory of estimation and inference for nonlinear dynamic models /. Oxford [Oxfordshire] , New York, NY, USA. , 1988. p. cm. ISBN 0-631-15765-4 : LC Card 87-25602 DDC 330/.028 19
HB141 .G33 1988

The White House Conference on Small Business . White House Conference on Small Business. Washington, D.C. , 1986. v, 76 p. : LC Card 86-603469 DDC 338.6/42/0973 19
HD2346.U5 W539 1986

White House Conference on Small Business. The White House Conference on Small Business : a report to the President of the United States. Washington, D.C. : The Conference : For sale by the Supt. of Docs., U. S. G.P.O., 1986. v, 76 p. : 1 form ; 28 cm. Shipping list no.: 87-4-P. "November 1986." S/N 040-000-00506-4 Item 1088 LC Card 86-603469 DDC 338.6/42/0973 19
1. Small business - United States - Congresses. 2. Small business - Law and legislation - United States - Congresses. 3. White House Conference on Small Business. I. Title.
HD2346.U5 W539 1986

WHITE HOUSE CONFERENCE ON SMALL BUSINESS.
A Tribute to small business . [Washington, D.C.] , San Francisco , c1987. 72 p. : LC Card 87-403591 DDC 338.6/42 19
HD2346.U5 T75 1987

White House Conference on Small Business. The White House Conference on Small Business . Washington, D.C. , 1986. v, 76 p. : LC Card 86-603469 DDC 338.6/42/0973 19
HD2346.U5 W539 1986

White, Louise G.
Bryant, Coralie. Managing rural development with small farmer participation /. West Hartford, CT. , c1984. xiii, 79 p. : ISBN 0-931816-52-1 (pbk.) LC Card 84-4445 DDC 307.7/2 19
HD1417 .B79 1984 ***NYPL [JLE 87-1352]***

Creating opportunities for change : approaches to managing development programs / Louise G. White. Boulder, Colo. : L. Rienner Publishers, 1987. xvii, 283 p. : ill. ; 24 cm. (Studies in development management) Bibliography: p. 239-269. Includes indexes. ISBN 1-555-87031-7 (lib. bdg.) : LC Card 87-4557 DDC 338.9/0068 19
1. Economic development projects - Management. I. Title. II. Series.
HD75.8 .W47 1987

White paper on the personal tax and transfer systems / [prepared by the Ministère des finances ; edited by the Direction générale de publications gouvernementales]. Québec : Le Ministere, 1984. 380 p. : ill. (some col.) ; 28 cm. Cover title. Inclues index. Library's copy bound without cover. ISBN 2-551-08967-0 (pbk.) : LC Card 85-150790 DDC 336.24/215/09714 19
1. Income tax - Québec (Province). 2. Transfer

payments - Québec (Province). 3. Tax incidence - Québec (Province).
HJ4663.Q8 W47 1984 ***NYPL [JLF 87-360]***

White, Randall P. Morrison, Ann M. Breaking the glass ceiling . Reading, Mass. , c1987. ix, 229 p. : ISBN 0-201-15787-X : LC Card 87-1853 DDC 658.4/09/024042 19
HD6054.4.U6 M67 1987

White, Richard. Making cars . London , Boston , c1985. ix, 131 p. : ISBN 0-7102-0272-5 : LC Card 84-13398 DDC 338.4/76292/0942574 19
HD8039.A82 G75 1984 ***NYPL [JLE 86-2303]***

White, Rolf B. The Last word on management /. Secaucus, N.J. , c1987. vi, 280 p. ; ISBN 0-8184-0452-3 : LC Card 87-18005 DDC 658 19
HD38 .L345 1987

Whiteford, Peter.
Issues in assistance for families : horizontal and vertical equity considerations / Peter Whiteford. Woden, ACT : Research and Statistics Branch, Development Division, Dept. of Social Security, [1986] iii, 56 p. ; 30 cm. (Research paper / Research and Statistics Branch, Development Division, Dept. of Social Security . no. 29 (August 1986)) Background/discussion paper ; no. 5 Bibliography: p. 52-56. ISBN 0-642-51604-9 (pbk.) LC Card 86-231139 DDC 362/.0425 19
1. Family allowances - Australia. 2. Income maintenance programs - Australia. 3. Tax incidence - Australia. I. Series: Research paper (Australia. Dept. of Social Security. Development Division) , no. 29. II. Title.
HD4925.5.A8 W47 1986

Moore, Jim. Trends in the disposable incomes of Australian families, 1964-65 to 1985-86 /. Woden, ACT [1986] vii, 103 p. ; ISBN 0-642-51700-2 (pbk.) LC Card 87-154435 DDC 339.394 19
HC610.I5 M66 1986

Whitehead, Steve. Collins, Rip, 1947- Double your sales commission using a personal computer /. Dubuque, Iowa , c1986. ix, 155 p. ; ISBN 0-697-00802-9 (pbk.) : LC Card 85-71486 DDC 658.8/1/00285536 19
HF5438.35 .C65 1986 ***NYPL [JLE 86-1773]***

Whitehill, Arthur M. Automation and industrial workers . Oxford [Oxfordshire] , New York , 1979- v. : ISBN 0-08-023339-2 (v. 1, pt. 1) : LC Card 79-40811 DDC 331
HD6331 .A93 1979 ***NYPL [JLM 82-242]***

Whitehill, Arthur M. (Arthur Murray) Doing business in Korea /. London , New York , 1987. xvi, 121 p. : ISBN 0-89397-276-2 (Nichols) : LC Card 87-5665 DDC 330.9519/5043 19
HC467 .D58 1987

Whiteing, Anthony E., 1954- Mackie, Peter J., 1947- The British transport industry and the European Community . Aldershot, Hampshire, England , Brookfield, Vt., U. S.A. , c1987. xvi, 184 p. : ISBN 0-566-05368-3 : LC Card 86-24186 DDC 380.5/24/0941 19
HE199.G5 M33 1987

Whiteley, Paul. Pressure for the poor : the poverty lobby and policy making / Paul F. Whiteley, Stephen J. Winyard. London ; New York : Methuen, 1987. 174 p. ; 24 cm. Bibliography: p. [156]-165. Includes index. ISBN 0-416-36370-9 LC Card 87-11205 DDC 362.5/8/0941 19
1. Economic assistance, Domestic - Great Britain - Citizen participation. 2. Pressure groups - Great Britain. 3. Social security - Great Britain. 4. Great Britain - Politics and government - 1979-. I. Winyard, Steve. II. Title.
HC260.P63 W47 1987

Whiteman, Charles H. Problems in macroeconomic theory : solutions to exercises from Thomas J. Sargent's Macroeconomic theory, second editon / Charles H. Whiteman. Boston : Academic Press, c1987. ix, 266 p. ; 23 cm. ISBN 0-12-619752-0 (pbk.) LC Card 87-17398 DDC 339 19
1. Macroeconomics. 2. Macroeconomics - Problems, exercises, etc. I. Sargent, Thomas J. Macroeconomic theory. II. Title.
HB172.5 .S27 1987 Suppl. 2

Whitford, Craig A. Postmarked : Michigan, Mich., 1847-1848 / compiled and written by Craig A. Whitford and David L. Mackey. Lansing, Mich. (P.O. Box 14225, Lansing 48901) : C.A. Whitford, c1987. 27 p., [2] p. of plates : ill., facsims., maps ; 22 cm. "500 copies printed." Two first day covers, dated Jan. 26, 1987 and Feb. 14, 1987 respectively, for Michigan's sesquicentennial commemorative stamp inserted. Bibliography: p. 27. LC Card 87-402869 DDC 769.56/7/0977427 19
1. Postmarks - Michigan - Lansing - History - 19th century. 2. Michigan - Capital and capitol - History - 19th century. 3. Lansing, Mich. - History. I. Mackey, David L. II. Title. III. Title: Michigan, Mich., 1847-1848.
HE6185.U7 M59 1987

WHITMAN COUNTY (WASH.) - HISTORY.
Prevost, Nancy M., 1953- Paradise in the Palouse . Fairfield, Wash. , c1985. 35 p. : ISBN 0-87770-365-5 (pbk.) LC Card 85-17842 DDC 338.1/09797/39 19
HD1775.W2 P74 1985 ***NYPL [JFF 86-559]***

Whitman, Marina von Neumann.
Stoga, Alan. Breaking the economic impasse . Washington, D.C. , c1987. viii, 48 p. ; ISBN 0-89206-104-9 (pbk.) LC Card 87-14682 DDC 338.9 19
HC59 .B73 1987

Unemployment and growth in the Western economies /. New York, N.Y. , c1984. x, 142 p. ; ISBN 0-87609-001-3 (pbk.) : LC Card 84-9415 DDC 331.13/791812 19
HD5707.5 .U54 1984 ***NYPL [JLE 86-1564]***

Whitney, John W. (John Wallis) Mikesell, Raymond Frech. The world mining industry . Boston , 1987. p. cm. ISBN 0-04-338120-0 (alk. paper) LC Card 87-1763 DDC 338.2 19
HD9506.A2 M525 1987

Whitsun Foundation.
Clifton-Brown, E. Project 1.04 . Salisbury, Zimbabwe [1977] 46 leaves ; LC Card 84-256608
HD3562.3.A4 C55 1977

Kirk, T. Project 3.05, rural workshop and machinery centre . Salisbury, Zimbabwe , 1977. 1 v. (various pagings) : LC Card 85-104610
HD2131.Z9 S265 1977

Project 1.07 : trade and investment in Zimbabwe. Harare, Zimbabwe : Whitsun Foundation, [1983?] 2 v. ; 30 cm. Cover title: Trade and investment in Zimbabwe. Includes bibliographical references. CONTENTS. - v. 1. Trade -- v. 2. Investment. ISBN 0-7974-0597-6 LC Card 84-981092 DDC 380.1/096891 19
1. Investments - Zimbabwe. 2. Investments, Foreign - Zimbabwe. 3. Public investments - Zimbabwe. 4. Zimbabwe - Commerce - History. I. Title. II. Title: Trade and investment in Zimbabwe.
HF3902 .W48 1983 ***NYPL [JLM 87-272]***

Project 1.09 : money and finance in Zimbabwe / the Whitsun Foundation. Harare, Zimbabwe : The Foundation, [1983?] ix, 260 p. : ill. ; 30 cm. ISBN 0-7974-0607-7 (pbk.) LC Card 87-402552 DDC 332.1/096891 19
1. Money - Zimbabwe. 2. Finance - Zimbabwe. I. Title. II. Title: Money and finance in Zimbabwe.
HG1352 .W48 1983

Project 3,04(a), Peasant sector credit plan (revised) : report and recommendations of the Director on the proposed feasibility study of an expansion programme in peasant sector credit. Salisbury, Rhodesia : Whitsun Foundation, [1978] ii, 18 leaves ; 30 cm. "November 1978." "D.H. Grainger, Director"--P. ii. LC Card 86-981359
1. Agricultural Finance Corporation - Rhodesia. 2. Agricultural credit - Zimbabwe. I. Grainger, D. H. II. Title.
HG2051.Z55 W45 1978

Whittle, Tomás Sepúlveda. see Sepúlveda Whittle, Tomás.

Whittlesey, Norman K. Energy and water management in western irrigated agriculture /. Boulder, Colo. , 1986. xxiv, 415 p. : ISBN 0-8133-7086-8 (pbk. : alk. paper) LC Card 85-52184 DDC 333.91/3/0978 19
HD1735 .E54 1986 ***NYPL [JLD 87-829]***

Who cares? . Mina Swaminathan, 1933- New Delhi , 1985. xi, 159 p. : LC Card 86-900126
HV861.I4 M56 1985 ***NYPL [JLD 86-3265]***

Who is who in Mexican business. Quien es quien en la empresa mexicana. México , 1985. 381 p. ; LC Card 86-190341
HF3234.5 .Q54 1985

Who knows about industries and markets / by Washington Researchers Publishing. Ed. 8. Washington, D.C. : Washington Researchers Pub., c1986. 54 p. ; 28 cm. (Briefcase series . bk. 4) Rev. ed. of: Industry analysts in the federal government. Ed. 7. c1984. ISBN 0-934940-33-9 (pbk.) LC Card 86-217691 DDC 338/.06/072073 19
1. Government economists - United States - Directories. 2. United States - Industries - Information services - Directories. I. Washington Researchers Publishing. II. Industry analysts in the federal government. III. Series.
HC102.2 .W48 1986

WHO offset publication, 0303-7878 .
(no. 96) Whyte, Anne V. T. Guidelines for planning community participation activities in water supply and sanitation projects /. Geneva , Albany, NY , 1986. 53 p. : ISBN 92-4-170096-3 (pbk.) : LC Card 87-137091 DDC 333.91/009172/4 19
HD4465.D44 W49 1986

Who owns the corporation? . Epstein, Edward Jay, 1935- New York , 1986. vi, 69 p. ; ISBN 0-87078-208-8 (pbk.) : LC Card 87-101003 DDC 338.7/4/0973 19
HD2743 .E67 1986

Who pays New York taxes? : a working paper / prepared by the staff of the Legislative Commission on the Modernization and Simplification of Tax Administration and the Tax Law. [Albany, N.Y.] : The Commission, [1985] 2, 101 p. : ill. ; 28 cm. At head of title: State of New York. "The report revises a paper prepared for the commission by Professor Donald Phares"--T.p. Verso. "August 16, 1985." Bibliography: p. 99-101. LC Card 86-621353 DDC 336.2/94/09747 19
1. Tax incidence - New York (State). 2. Taxation - New York (State). I. Phares, Donald. II. New York (State). Legislature. Legislative Commission on the Modernization and Simplification of Tax Administration and the Tax Law.
HJ2322.N7 W48 1985

Who profits . Leone, Robert A. New York , 1986. xiii, 248 p. ; ISBN 0-465-09183-0 : LC Card 85-47992 DDC 338.973 19
HD3616.U47 L44 1986 ***NYPL [JLD 86-2410]***

Who should pay for collecting taxes? . Steuerle, C. Eugene, 1946- Washington, D.C. , 1986. p. cm. ISBN 0-8447-3609-0 (pbk. : alk. paper) : LC Card 86-22345 DDC 353.0072/4 19
HJ5018 .S84 1986

The whole and the parts . Schick, Allen. Washington , 1987. vi, 65 p. ; LC Card 87-601378 DDC 353.0072/2 19
HJ2052 .S335 1987

The Wholesale-by-mail catalog. Update 1986 / by the Print Project ; Prudence McCullough, editor.1st ed. New York : St. Martin's Press, 1986. iv, 364 p. ; 19 cm. Includes index. ISBN 0-312-90379-0 (pbk.) : LC Card 87-139567 DDC 381/.2/02573 19
1. Catalogs, Commercial. 2. Mail-order business - United States - Directories. 3. Wholesale trade - United States - Directories. I. McCullough, Prudence. II. Print Project.
HF5861 .W54 1986

The Wholesale-by-mail catalog, 1987 / by the Print Project ; Lowell Miller, executive producer ; Prudence McCullough, editor. New York : St. Martin's Press, [1987] p. cm. ISBN 0-312-00205-X (pbk.) : LC Card 86-27890 DDC 381/.2/02573 19
1. Catalogs, Commercial. 2. Advertising, Direct-mail - United States. 3. Wholesale trade - United States - Directories. I. Miller, Lowell. II. McCullough, Prudence. III. Print Project.
HF5861 .W527 1987

WHOLESALE PRICE INDEXES - NORWAY.
Holm, Yngvar. Engrosomsetningsindeks /. Oslo , 1984. 18 leaves ; ISBN 82-537-2141-2 : LC Card 85-178075
HB235.N6 H65 1984

WHOLESALE PRICES INDEXES - NORWAY.
Engrosprisstatistikk . Oslo , 1982. 120 p. ; ISBN 82-537-1833-0 : LC Card 83-139816
HB235.N6 E54 1982

WHOLESALE TRADE - ALASKA.
Schiller, Robert, 1950- A comparison of Alaska's wholesale trade sector with other states /. [Juneau, Alaska] [1984] vi, 104 p. :

LC Card 86-620623 DDC 381/.2/09798 19
HF5421 .S33 1984

WHOLESALE TRADE - FINLAND - CASE STUDIES.
Lindqvist, Lars-Johan. Marknadsföring till handeln . Helsingfors , 1983. 309 p. : ISBN 951-555-183-8 LC Card 84-103976
HF5421.5.F5 L56 1983

WHOLESALE TRADE - GERMANY (WEST) - STUTTGART METROPOLITAN AREA.
Schuler, Friedrich Joachim. Struktur und Dynamik der Grosshandelsbetriebe im Ballungsraum Stuttgart /. Marburg/Lahn , 1986. xiv, 156 p. : ISBN 3-88353-027-1 LC Card 87-116934 DDC 381/.2/094347 19
HF5421.5.G4 S43 1986

WHOLESALE TRADE - GOVERNMENT POLICY - GERMANY (WEST)
Bundesverband des Deutschen Gross- und Aussenhandels. Vorschläge und Beiträge des Bundesverbandes des Deutschen Gross- und Aussenhandels e.V. für die X. Legislaturperiode des Deutschen Bundestages. Bonn [1983] 56 p. ; LC Card 83-243234
HF1545 .B83 1983

WHOLESALE TRADE - NEW ZEALAND - STATISTICS.
Census of distribution, 1977-78 . Wellington, N.Z. [1980]-<[1981]. v. <11 > : LC Card 86-204705
HF5429.6.N47 C46 1980

WHOLESALE TRADE - SWEDEN.
Larsson, Folke. Varuhandeln. [Stockholm] [1981] 137 p. : ISBN 91-38-06014-0 LC Card 84-120411
HF5429.6.S9 L368 1981

WHOLESALE TRADE - SWEDEN - DATA PROCESSING.
Bra affärer med datorer? . [Stockholm] , 1982. 176 p. : ISBN 91-38-06989-X LC Card 83-235564
HF5429.15 .B72 1982

WHOLESALE TRADE - UNITED STATES.
Schiller, Robert, 1950- A comparison of Alaska's wholesale trade sector with other states /. [Juneau, Alaska] [1984] vi, 104 p. : LC Card 86-620623 DDC 381/.2/09798 19
HF5421 .S33 1984

WHOLESALE TRADE - UNITED STATES - DIRECTORIES.
The Wholesale-by-mail catalog. New York , 1986. iv, 364 p. ; ISBN 0-312-90379-0 (pbk.) : LC Card 87-139567 DDC 381/.2/02573 19
HF5861 .W54 1986

The Wholesale-by-mail catalog, 1987 /. New York [1987] p. cm. ISBN 0-312-00205-X (pbk.) : LC Card 86-27890 DDC 381/.2/02573 19
HF5861 .W527 1987

Wholey, Joseph S. Performance and credibility . Lexington, Mass. , c1986. x, 307 p. : ISBN 0-669-11037-X (alk. paper) LC Card 85-50707 DDC 658/.048 19
HD62.6 .P47 1986 ***NYPL [JLE 86-1159]***

Who's who in Middle East banking & trade. The APS who's who in Middle East banking & trade. Nicosia, Cyprus , c1984. 2 v. : LC Card 83-149147 ***NYPL [JLF 86-983]***

Who's who in venture capital /. Silver, A. David (Aaron David), 1941- New York , c1987. ix, 468 p. : ISBN 0-471-85639-8 (pbk.) : LC Card 86-28974 DDC 332.66 19
HG4963 .S56 1987

Why ERA failed . Berry, Mary Frances. Bloomington , c1986. ix, 147 p. ; ISBN 0-253-36537-6 LC Card 85-45985 DDC 342.73/0878/02632 347.30287802632 19
KF4758 .B45 1986 ***NYPL [JLE 86-3979]***

Why Reaganomics and Keynesian economics failed /. Sawyer, James E., 1943- New York , 1987. ix, 195 p. : ISBN 0-312-00532-6 : LC Card 87-9578 DDC 338.973 19
HC106.8 .S28 1987

Why some peoples are more unemployed than others /. Therborn, Göran, 1941- London , 1986. 181 p. ; ISBN 0-86091-109-8 : LC Card 86-673385
HD5707.5 .T53x 1986 ***NYPL [JLD 86-3537]***

Why the best-laid investment plans usually go wrong . Browne, Harry, 1933- New York , c1987. 557 p. : ISBN 0-688-05995-3 LC Card 87-16593 DDC 332.024 19
HG179 .B748 1987

Why the office staff scared of time and motion study? : Wages and performance evaluations, Judicial decisions. Saddar, Karachi, Pakistan : Shaikhconsultants International, [1985] 1 v. (various pagings) leaves ; 29 cm. (Industrial laws and labor relations) Cover title. "Part I." "Series no. 14/4/85"--Prelim. p. 1. Includes bibliographical references. LC Card 86-146552
1. Wages - Pakistan. 2. Motion study. 3. Time study. 4. Wages and labor productivity - Pakistan. 5. Labor laws and legislation - Pakistan - Cases. I. Shaikhconsults International. II. Series.
HD5070.5 .W49 1985

Why they buy . Settle, Robert B. New York , c1986. xvi, 351 p. ; ISBN 0-471-84457-8 : LC Card 86-13303 DDC 658.8/343/0973 19
HC110.C6 S48 1986 ***NYPL [JLE 86-4432]***

Why video works . Bunyan, John A. White Plains, NY , c1987. x, 203 p. : ISBN 0-86729-079-X : LC Card 86-21106 DDC 658/.0028 19
HD30.34 .B86 1987

Why we lost the E.R.A. Mansbridge, Jane J. Why we lost the ERA /. Chicago, Ill. , c1986. xii, 327 p. ; ISBN 0-226-50358-5 (pbk.) LC Card 86-6954 DDC 305.4/2/0973 19
HQ1236.5.U6 M37 1986 ***NYPL [JLE 86-4474]***

Why we lost the ERA /. Mansbridge, Jane J. Chicago, Ill. , c1986. xii, 327 p. ; ISBN 0-226-50358-5 (pbk.) LC Card 86-6954 DDC 305.4/2/0973 19
HQ1236.5.U6 M37 1986 ***NYPL [JLE 86-4474]***

Why were infant and child mortality rates highest in the poorest states of Peninsular Malaysia, 1941-75? / Christine Peterson ... [et al.] ; prepared for the Ford Foundation, the Rockefeller Foundation, the William and Flora Hewlett Foundation. Santa Monica, CA (P.O. Box 2138, Santa Monica 90406-2138) : Rand, [1986] xi, 45 p. ; 28 cm. (A Rand note . N-2329-FF/RF/WFHF) Bibliography: p. 43-45. LC Card 86-210106 DDC 304.6/4/088054 19
1. Infants - Malaysia - Mortality. 2. Children - Malaysia - Mortality. 3. Poor - Malaysia - Mortality. I. Peterson, Christine. II. Series.
HB1323.I42 M49 1986

Why women fail in business /. Lewis, Diane, 1936- Nashville , c1987. p. cm. ISBN 0-8407-4219-3 : LC Card 87-15370 DDC 658.4/09088042 19
HD6054.3 .L48 1987

Whynes, David K. Barbara Wootton--social science and public policy . London , New York , 1986. xi, 291 p. ; ISBN 0-422-79690-5 LC Card 85-27650 DDC 330 19
HB171 .B248 1985 ***NYPL [JLE 86-1743]***

Whyte, Andrew (Andrew John Appleton) Jaguar, the history of a great British car / Andrew Whyte ; foreword by Sir William Lyons. 2nd ed. Wellingborough [Northants] : P. Stephens ; New York, N.Y. : Distributed by Sterling Pub. Co., 1985. 252 p. : ill. ; 25 cm. Distributor from label on t.p. Includes index. ISBN 0-85059-746-3 : LC Card 85-670203 DDC 338.7/6292222/0941 19
1. Jaguar Cars Ltd. - History. 2. Jaguar automobile - History. 3. Automobile industry and trade - Great Britain - History. I. Title.
HD9710.G74 J338 1985 ***NYPL [JLE 87-451]***

Whyte, Anne V. T. Guidelines for planning community participation activities in water supply and sanitation projects / Anne Whyte. Geneva : World Health Organization ; Albany, NY : WHO Publication Centre USA [distributor], 1986. 53 p. : ill. ; 30 cm. (WHO offset publication, 0303-7878 . no. 96) "The International Drinking Water Supply and Sanitation Decade." Bibliography: p. 53. ISBN 92-4-170096-3 (pbk.) : LC Card 87-137091 DDC 333.91/009172/4 19
1. Municipal water supply - Developing countries - Planning - Citizen participation - Planning. 2. Sewage disposal - Developing countries - Planning - Citizen participation - Planning. 3. Water-supply - Developing countries - Planning - Citizen participation - Planning. 4. Sanitation - Developing countries - Planning - Citizen participation - Planning. I. Title. II. Series.
HD4465.D44 W49 1986

Whyte, William Foote, 1914-
Industrial democracy . Beverly Hills , c1985. 308 p. : ISBN 0-8039-2476-3 LC Card 85-11741 DDC 338.973/009173/2 19
HT321 .I53 1985 ***NYPL [JLD 86-3621]***

Pattern for industrial peace / William Foote Whyte. New York : Garland, 1987, c1951. ix, 245 p. : ill. ; 23 cm. (Continuity in administrative science) Reprint. Originally published: New York : Harper, 1951. Includes index. ISBN 0-8240-8227-3 (alk. paper) : LC Card 86-25790 DDC 331.89/0469142/0977/311 19
1. Collective bargaining - Steel industry - Illinois - Chicago. 2. Inland Steel Company. 3. United Steelworkers of America. 4. Leadership. I. Title. II. Series.
HD6515.I52 C48 1987

Wiarda, Howard J., 1939-
Latin America at the crossroads : debt, development, and the future / Howard J. Wiarda. Boulder, Colo. : Westview Press ; Washington, D.C. : American Enterprise Institute for Public Policy Research, 1987. xiii, 114 p. ; 24 cm. Includes index. Bibliography: p. 99-105. ISBN 0-8133-0423-7 (alk. paper) : LC Card 86-18997 DDC 330.98/003 19
1. Debts, External - Latin America. 2. Latin America - Economic conditions - 1945-. 3. Latin America - Social conditions - 1945-. 4. Latin America - Politics and government - 1948-. I. Title.
HC125 .W47 1987 ***NYPL [JLE 87-835]***

Population, internal unrest, and U. S. security in Latin America / Howard J. Wiarda and Iêda Siqueira Wiarda. [Amherst] : International Area Studies Programs, University of Massachusetts at Amherst, 1986. 50 p. ; 22 cm. (Occasional papers series / Program in Latin American Studies . no. 18) Bibliography: p. 40-45. LC Card 87-621399 DDC 304.6/098 19
1. Population forecasting - Latin America. 2. Latin America - Population. 3. Internal security - Latin America. 4. United States - National security. I. Wiarda, Iêda Siqueira. II. Series: Occasional papers series (University of Massachusetts at Amherst. Program in Latin American Studies) , no. 18. III. Title.
HB3530.5.A3 W5 1986

Wiarda, Iêda Siqueira. Wiarda, Howard J., 1939- Population, internal unrest, and U. S. security in Latin America /. [Amherst] , 1986. 50 p. ; LC Card 87-621399 DDC 304.6/098 19
HB3530.5.A3 W5 1986

Wiatrak, Andrzej Piotr. Przestrzenne zróżnicowanie gospodarki rolnej w Polsce / Andrzej Piotr Wiatrak. Wyd. 1. Warszawa : Państwowe Wydawn. Naukowe, 1986. 207 p. : maps ; 24 cm. (Problemy rejonów uprzemysławianych) on p. facing t.p.: Polska Akademia Nauk, Komitet Badań Rejonów Uprzemysławianych. Summary in English and Russian. Bibliography: p. 191-196. ISBN 83-01-05118-3 : LC Card 86-212769
1. Agricultural productivity - Poland - Regional disparities. 2. Agriculture - Economic aspects - Poland. I. Title.
HD1995.7 .W45 1986

Wibe, Sören. Heathfield, David F. An introduction to cost and production functions /. Atlantic Highlands, NJ , 1987. xv, 193 p. : ISBN 0-391-03506-1 LC Card 86-27587 DDC 338.5 19
HB241 .H39 1987

Wicht, Juan J. Problemas poblacionales peruanos II /. Lima , c1986. 402 p. : LC Card 86-228816
HB3575 .P763 1986

Wicke, Hans-Georg. Schwohnke, Andreas. Teleheimarbeit als neue Rationalisierungsstrategie . Köln , 1986. vii, 237, [14] p. : ISBN 3-7609-5220-8 LC Card 86-224163
HD2336.G3 S38 1986

Wicke, Lutz. Brunowsky, Ralf-Dieter, 1949- Der ÖKO-Plan . München , c1984. 236, [1] p. ; ISBN 3-492-02922-1 LC Card 84-251156
HC290.5.E5 B78 1984

Wickham, Alexandre. Les carriéristes : les grandes manœuvres des cadres / Alexandre Wickham, Marc Patterson. Paris : Editions Ramsay, c1983. 358 p. ; 24 cm. Includes bibliographical references. ISBN 2-85956-348-2 : LC Card 84-122542 DDC 650.1/4 19

1. Success in business. 2. Organizational behavior. I. Patterson, Marc. II. Title.
HF5386 .W494 1983 ***NYPL [JLE 86-4124]***

Wickham, Ann. Women and training / Ann Wickham. Milton Keynes, England ; Philadelphia, PA, USA : Open University Press, c1986. x, 147 p. ; 22 cm. (Gender and education series) Includes index. Bibliography: p. 135-140. ISBN 0-335-15119-1 LC Card 86-5176 DDC 331.4/2592/0941 19
1. Occupational training for women - Great Britain. 2. Women - Employment - Great Britain. 3. Women - Education (Secondary) - Great Britain. I. Title. II. Series.
HD6059.6.G7 W52 1986
NYPL [JLD 86-3495]

WICKLOW (COUNTY) - POPULATION.
Eastern Regional Development Organisation (Ireland) Eastern Region settlement strategy, 2011. Dublin [1985] xviii, 269 p. : LC Card 87-672656
HB3589 .E27x 1985

Eastern Regional Development Organisation (Ireland) Eastern Region settlement strategy, 2011. Dublin [1985] viii, 21 p. : LC Card 87-672678
HB3589 .E27x 1985a

Wickman, Floyd. Successful strategies for real estate agents : a step-by-step system on how to succeed in today's real estate world / Floyd Wickman. Dubuque, Iowa : Kendall/Hunt, c1987. xii, 226 p. ; 21 cm. Cover title: Floyd Wickman's successful strategies for real estate agents. ISBN 0-8403-4185-7 (pbk.) : LC Card 86-82782 DDC 333.33/068/8 19
1. Real estate agents. 2. House selling. 3. Real estate business. I. Title. II. Title: Floyd Wickman's successful strategies for real estate agents.
HD1382 .W53 1987

Widdau, Peter, 1952- Die Quantifizierung der Steuerbelastung im internationalen Bereich : unter Berücksichtigung der Möglichkeiten der Steuerbilanzpolitik im Investitionsland / Peter Widdau. Frankfurt am Main ; New York : Lang, c1984. xx, 413 p. : ill. ; 21 cm. (Europäische Hochschulschriften. Reihe V, Volks- und Betriebswirtschaft, 0531-7339 . Bd. 508 = vol. 508 = vol. 508) Originally presented as the author's thesis (doctoral--Universität Regensburg, 1983) Bibliography: p. 376-408. ISBN 3-8204-8044-7 : LC Card 85-191946
1. Tax incidence - Mathematical models. I. Title.
HJ2321 .W46 1984

Wideband communications services & equipment markets. Norwalk, Conn., U. S.A. (6 Prowitt St., Norwalk 06855) : International Resource Development, c1986. iii, 198 leaves : ill. ; 28 cm. (Report / International Resource Development Inc. . #712) "October 1986." LC Card 87-129548 DDC 384/.0973 19
1. Telecommunication equipment industry. 2. Telecommunication. 3. Market surveys. I. International Resource Development, inc. II. Title: Wideband communications services and equipment markets. III. Series: Report / International Resource Development Inc. , #712.
HD9696.T442 W53 1986

Wideband communications services and equipment markets. Wideband communications services & equipment markets. Norwalk, Conn., U. S.A. (6 Prowitt St., Norwalk 06855) , c1986. iii, 198 leaves : LC Card 87-129548 DDC 384/.0973 19
HD9696.T442 W53 1986

Wider die organisierte Verantwortungslosigkeit . Wittmann, Walter, 1935- Frauenfeld , c1984. 175 p. ; ISBN 3-7193-0938-X : LC Card 84-234445
HB95 .W57 1984

Widersprüche der Automationsarbeit : ein Handbuch / Projektgruppe Automation und Qualifikation. West-Berlin : Argument-Verlag, c1987. 228 p. ; 21 cm. "Veröffentlichungen der Projektgruppe Automation und Qualifikation (PAQ)": p. 218-224. Bibliography: p. 225-228. ISBN 3-88619-362-4 LC Card 87-145099 DDC 331.12/0943 19
1. Labor supply - Germany (West) - Effect of automation on. 2. Microelectronics - Social aspects - Germany (West). I. Projektgruppe Automation und Qualifikation (Freie Universität Berlin. Psychologisches Institut).
HD6331.2.G28 W55 1987

Der Widerstand geht weiter : der Bürgerprotest gegen das Kernkraftwerk von 1976 bis zum Mannheimer Prozess / für die Badisch-Elsässischen Bürgerinitiativen herausgegeben von Christoph Büchele, Irmgard Schneider und Bernd Nössler mit Unterstützung des BUND.1. Aufl. Freiburg i. Br. : Dreisam, 1982. 261 p. : ill. ; 21 cm. Cover title: Wyhl. "Im Anhang: Mannheimer Urteil und erste Stellungnahmen." Includes bibliographical references. ISBN 3-921472-30-X LC Card 82-192690
1. Antinuclear movement - Germany (West) - Wyhl. 2. Antinuclear movement - Germany (West). I. Büchele, Christoph. II. Schneider, Irmgard. III. Nössler, Bernd. IV. Badisch-Elsässische Bürgerinitiativen. V. Title: Wyhl.
HD9698.G43 W937 1982

Widmann, Richard H. Ohio timber products output--1983 / Richard H. Widmann, Michael Long. Broomall, PA : U. S. Dept. of Agriculture, Forest Service, Northeastern Forest Experiment Station, [1986] 29 p. : ill. ; 28 cm. Cover title. "November 1986"--T.p. verso. Bibliography: p. 8. Includes index. "NE-RB-95." LC Card 86-603412 DDC 338.1/7498/09771021 19
1. Forest products industry - Ohio - Statistics. I. Long, Michael. II. Northeastern Forest Experiment Station (Broomall, Pa.). III. Title.
HD9757.O3 W53 1986

Widows and dependent wives . Lopata, Helena Znaniecka, 1925- New York , 1986. xxi, 242 p. ; ISBN 0-03-046301-7 (alk. paper) : LC Card 85-16753 DDC 362.8/382 19
HV699 .L67 1985 ***NYPL [JLE 86-2182]***

WIDOWS - UNITED STATES - ECONOMIC CONDITIONS.
Lopata, Helena Znaniecka, 1925- Widows and dependent wives . New York , 1986. xxi, 242 p. ; ISBN 0-03-046301-7 (alk. paper) : LC Card 85-16753 DDC 362.8/382 19
HV699 .L67 1985 ***NYPL [JLE 86-2182]***

Wie errechne ich meinen Nettolohn? . Recktenwald, Werner. Saarbrücken [1985?] 112 p. ; ISBN 3-88968-029-1 LC Card 85-171297 DDC 343.4305/242 344.3035242 19
HJ4720.A7 R42 1985

Wie errechne ich meinen Nettolohn? Mit der Monatslohnsteuertabelle für rentenversicherungspflichtige Arbeitnehmer, 1986 und 1987, Auszug /. Recktenwald, Werner. Saarbrücken [1987]. 128 p. ; LC Card 87-408789 DDC 343.4305/242 344.3035242 19
HJ4720.A7 R42 1987

Wie Leiter den wissenschaftlich-technischen Fortschritt bewältigen /. Bohring, Günther. Berlin , 1986. 168 p. : ISBN 3-320-00704-1 LC Card 87-112384 DDC 338/.06 19
HD45 .B59 1986

Wie man mit Brief, Telefon und Erstbesuch neue Kunden systematisch und dauerhaft gewinnt /. Detroy, Erich-Norbert, 1945- Zürich , c1982. 216 p. : ISBN 3-478-23510-3 : LC Card 82-242870
HF5446 .D47 1982

Wie war denn das? : Hessischer Haushalt '83 / [Herausgeber, Die Grünen Hessen]. Frankfurt : Die Grünen Hessen, [1983?] 30 p., [1] leaf of plates : ill. ; 15 x 21 cm. Cover title. LC Card 84-158849
1. Hesse (Germany) - Economic conditions. I. Grünen (Political party). Hessen.
HC287.H4 W47 1983

Wie wir angefangen haben : von der demokratischen Bodenreform zum Sieg der sozialistischen Produktionsverhältnisse in der Landwirtschaft : Erinnerungen / [Institut für Agrargeschichte und Internationale Landwirtschaft der Akademie der Landwirtschaftswissenschaften der DDR] ; Redaktion, Siegfried Kuntsche ... [et al.]. Berlin : Dietz, 1985. 326 p. : ill. ; 21 cm. LC Card 85-217979
1. Land reform - Germany (East) - History - 20th century - Sources. 2. Agriculture - Economic aspects - Germany (East) - History - 20th century - Sources. 3. Communism - Germany (East) - History - 20th century - Sources. I. Kuntsche, Siegfried. II. Akademie der Landwirtschaftswissenschaften der DDR. Institut für Agrargeschichte und Internationale Landwirtschaft.
HD1333.G35 W54 1985

Wiechec, Jane. Employment, the community link / author, Jane Wiechec. Perth, W.A. : Community Employment Initiatives Branch, WA Dept. of Employment and Training, [1986] 108 p. ; 30 cm. Bibliography: p. 95-97. LC Card 87-158082 DDC 331.12/5/09941 19
1. Manpower policy - Australia - Western Australia. 2. Unemployed - Services for - Australia - Western Australia. I. Title.
HD5850.W4 W54 1986

Wied-Nebbeling, Susanne.
Körber-Weik, Margot. Wirtschaftskraft und Wirtschaftsentwicklung in den Bundesländern seit 1970 . Tübingen , 1986. x, 271 p. ; ISBN 3-88573-303-X LC Card 87-401375 DDC 330.943/0878 19
HC286.6 .K67 1986

Sektorale Preisbildung und gesamtwirtschaftliche Preisstabilität / von Susanne Wied-Nebbeling. Tübingen : J.C.B. Mohr, 1986. xiii, 368 p. : ill. ; 24 cm. (Tübinger wirtschaftswissenschaftliche Abhandlungen, 0564-4291 . Bd. 29) Abridgement of the author's Habilitationsschrift--Universität Tübingen, 1985. Bibliography: p. [341]-364. Includes index. ISBN 3-16-345102-0 LC Card 87-132436 DDC 338.5/2/0724 19
1. Prices - Mathematical models. 2. Pricing - Mathematical models. I. Series: Tübinger wirtschaftswissenschaftliche Abhandlungen (Tübingen, Germany) , Bd. 29. II. Title.
HB221 .W484 1986

Wiedemer, John P., 1918- Real estate finance / John P. Wiedemer. 5th ed. Englewood Cliffs, N.J. : Prentice-Hall, c1987. xvi, 396 p. : ill., forms ; 25 cm. "A Reston book." Includes index. ISBN 0-13-762774-2 LC Card 86-30471 DDC 332.7/2/0973 19
1. Mortgage loans - United States. 2. Real property - United States - Finance. 3. Housing - United States - Finance. I. Title.
HG2040.5.U5 W54 1987

Wiedenhofer, Harald. Fricke, Werner. Beteiligung im Industriebetrieb . Frankfurt/Main , New York , c1985. 291 p. ; ISBN 3-593-32735-X LC Card 85-202742
HD5660.G4 F73 1985

Der Wiederaufbau der deutschen Volkswirtschaft . Horlacher, Michael. Diessen vor München , 1919. 118 p. ; LC Card 87-409517 DDC 338.943 19
HC286.2 .H67 1919

Wiegel, Klaus Dieter. Rentabilität und Risiko im Kreditgeschäft der Banken : eine Untersuchung zur Risikoproblematik in der Kreditvergabeentscheidung von Banken und zu Möglichkeiten ihrer Bewältigung / Klaus Dieter Wiegel. Köln : Wison, c1985. 342 p. : ill. ; 21 cm. (Kölner bankwirtschaftliche Studien. Bd. 7) Bibliography: p. 311-342. ISBN 3-87951-125-X LC Card 87-140074 DDC 332.1/753 19
1. Bank loans. 2. Risk. 3. Credit. I. Title. II. Series.
HG1641 .W54 1985

Wieleżyński, Leszek. Wspólna praca--wspólny plon : życie i dzieło mądrego człowieka / Leszek Wieleżyński. London, England : Veritas Foundation Publication Centre, [1986], c1985. 295 p., [24] p. of plates : ill. ; 19 cm. Includes bibliographical references and index. LC Card 87-111287
1. Wieleżyński, Marian, 1878-1945. 2. Petroleum industry and trade - Poland - Employee - Biography. 3. Businessmen - Poland - Biography. 4. Petroleum industry and trade - Galicia (Poland and Ukraine) - History. 5. Petroleum industry and trade - Ukraine, Western - History. I. Title.
HD9575.P62 W549 1986

WIELEŻYŃSKI, MARIAN, 1878-1945.
Wieleżyński, Leszek. Wspólna praca--wspólny plon . London, England [1986], c1985. 295 p., [24] p. of plates : LC Card 87-111287
HD9575.P62 W549 1986

Wiemann, Jürgen.
India in transition : industrialization, industrial policy, and economic cooperation / Jürgen Wiemann ; translated by Anjuli Gupta. New Delhi : Allied Publishers ; Berlin : German Development Institute, 1986. xxi, 151 p. ; 24 cm. "The present study ... is part of a research project of the German Development Institute"--Pref. Bibliography: p. 132-136. LC Card 87-900287 DDC 338.954 19

1. Industry and state - India. 2. India - Economic policy - 1947-. 3. India - Commerce - Germany, West. 4. Germany, West - Commerce - India. I. Deutsches Institut für Entwicklungspolitik. II. Title.
HD3616.I83 W54 1986

Selektiver Protektionismus und aktive Strukturanpassung : handels- und industriepolitische Reaktion Europas auf die zunehmende Wettbewerbsfähigkeit der Entwicklungsländer : dargestellt am Beispiel der Textilpolitik der EG / Jürgen Wiemann. Berlin : Deutsches Institut für Entwicklungspolitik, 1983. vii, 348 p. : ill. ; 25 cm. (Schriften des Deutschen Instituts für Entwicklungspolitik, DIE . Bd. 74) Bibliography: p. 315-336. ISBN 3-88985-028-6 : LC Card 83-223964
1. Textile industry - Government policy - European Economic Community countries. 2. Textile industry - Government policy - Developing countries. 3. European Economic Community countries - Foreign economic relations - Developing countries. 4. Developing countries - Foreign economic relations - European Economic Community countries. I. Title. II. Series.
HD9865.E852 W54 1983

Wiendieck, Gerd. Qualitätszirkel als Instrument zeitgemässer Betriebsführung /. Landsberg/Lech , c1986. 328 p. : ISBN 3-478-32520-X LC Card 86-200304
HD66 .Q33 1986

Die Wiener Arbeitsstätten am 12. Mai 1981 : Arbeitsstätten und Beschäftigte nach Wirtschaftsabteilungen bzw. Wirtschaftsklassen und Arbeitsstättengrösse : Ergebnisse nach Gemeindebezirken, Zählbezirken und Zählgebieten. Wien : Magistrat der Stadt, 1985. lvi, 723 p. : col. ill., col. folded maps ; 29 cm. "Die Erstellung dieser Veröffentlichung erfolgte durch das Statistische Amt der Stadt Wien." LC Card 87-408873 DDC 331.7/0012 19
1. Vienna (Austria) - Occupations - Classification. 2. Vienna (Austria) - Industries - Classification. I. Vienna (Austria). Statistisches Amt.
HB2682.V5 W54 1985

Wiener, Detlev, 1947- Grün, Josef, 1951- Global denken, vor Ort handeln . Freiburg i. Br. , 1984. 373 p. : ISBN 3-921472-73-3 LC Card 84-246414
HC79.E5 G77 1984

Wiener Studien des Forschungsinstitutes für Genossenschaftswesen . (n.F., Bd. 5) Perspektiven der Genossenschaftsrevision . Wien , 1986. x, 322 p. : ISBN 3-85368-775-X LC Card 87-138767 DDC 334/.09436 19
HD3490 .P47 1986

Wienert, Helgard. East-West technology transfer. The trade and economic aspects / by Helgard Wienert and John Slater. Paris : Organisation for Economic Co-operation and Development, c1986. 453 p. : ill. ; 23 cm. Includes bibliographical references. ISBN 92-64-12817-4
1. Technology transfer - Communist countries. 2. East-West trade (1945-). 3. Technology transfer - Economic aspects. I. Slater, John. II. Organisation for Economic Co-operation and Development. III. Title.
NYPL [JLE 87-1561]

Wienholtz, Huberta.
Auf dem Weg zu einer neuen Weltwirtschaftsordnung? . Baden-Baden , 1983. 478 p. ; ISBN 3-7890-0919-9 LC Card 84-113581
HF1411 .A92 1983

Auf dem Weg zu einer neuen Weltwirtschaftsordnung? . Baden-Baden , 1983. 478 p. ; ISBN 3-7890-0919-9
NYPL [JLD 87-919]

Wienold, Hanns, 1944- Herrschaft, Krise, Überleben . Münster , 1986. 396 p. : ISBN 3-924550-19-0 LC Card 86-229590
HC286.7 .H48 1986

Wiesegart, Kurt. Wirtschaftskooperation mit China : die institutionellen Rahmenbedingungen / Kurt Wiesegart. Hamburg : Verlag Weltarchiv, 1984. 126 p. ; 24 cm. (Veröffentlichungen des HWWA-Institut für Wirtschaftsforschung-Hamburg) Bibliography: p. 119-126. ISBN 3-87895-260-0 LC Card 85-146617
1. China - Foreign economic relations - European Economic Community countries. 2. European Economic Community countries - Foreign economic relations - China. 3. China - Foreign economic relations - Germany, West. 4. Germany, West - Foreign economic relations - China. I. Title.
HF1604.Z4 E869 1984

Wiesel, Iván. A Hazai áralakulásról /. [Budapest] , 1986. 342 p. ; ISBN 963-09-2758-6 : LC Card 87-407741
HG970.5 .H39 1986

Wieser, Friedrich, Freiherr von, 1851-1926. [Natürliche Werth. English]
Natural value / by Friedrich von Wieser ; edited with a preface and analysis by William Smart. Fairfield, NJ : A.M. Kelley, 1988. p. cm. (Reprints of economic classics) Translation of: Der natürliche Werth. Reprint. Originally published: London : Macmillan, 1893. ISBN 0-678-00821-3 LC Card 87-17245 DDC 338.5/21 19
1. Value. I. Smart, William, 1853-1915. II. Title.
HB201 .W65 1988

Wiesner, Merry, 1952- Working women in Renaissance Germany / Merry E. Wiesner. New Brunswick, N.J. : Rutgers University Press, c1986. xiii, 263 p. : ill. ; 24 cm. (The Douglass series on women's lives and the meaning of gender) Includes index. Bibliography: p. 239-257. ISBN 0-8135-1138-0 : LC Card 85-14451 DDC 305.4/3/00943 19
1. Women - Germany - History - Renaissance, 1450-1600. 2. Women - Germany - Economic conditions. 3. Women - Employment - Germany - History. I. Title. II. Series.
HQ1149.G3 W54 1986
NYPL [JLE 86-3515]

Wieviorka, Michel.
Touraine, Alain. Le mouvement ouvrier /. [Paris] , c1984. 438 p. : ISBN 2-213-01361-6 : LC Card 84-202370 DDC 322/.2/0944 19
HD6684 .T655 1984 ***NYPL [JLE 86-279]***

Touraine, Alain. [Mouvement ouvrier. English.] The workers' movement /. Cambridge [Cambridgeshire] ; New York : xx, 322 p. ; ISBN 0-521-30852-6 LC Card 87-8010 DDC 322/.2/0944 19
HD6684 .T65513 1987

Wiggins, Steve. Colonización en Bolivia / Steve Wiggins. 2a ed. Sucre, Bolivia : Acción Cultural Loyola : Iglesia Metodista, [1976?] iv, 112 p. : ill. ; 26 cm. Bibliography: p. 107-109. LC Card 83-203672
1. Land settlement - Bolivia. 2. Migration, Internal - Bolivia. I. Title.
HD486 .W54 1976

Wihlborg, Clas. Oxelheim, Lars. Macroeconomic uncertainty . Chichester [West Sussex] , New York , c1987. xv, 251 p. : ISBN 0-471-91480-0 : LC Card 87-8333 DDC 658.1/55 19
HG3821 .O894 1987

Wijermars, Marianne. Mensink, Ankie. De wording en verwording van de staat Marokko . Rotterdam , 1985. 304 p. ; ISBN 90-6330-109-X : LC Card 85-214935
HC810 .M46 1985

Wijnbergen, Sweder van, 1951- Natural resources and the macroeconomy /. Oxford, UK , 1986. xvi, 352 p. : ISBN 0-631-15087-0 LC Card 86-673943
HC59 .N3194x 1986b

Wijvekate, M. L. (Maren L.) De tweede taakdimensie : het organiseren van creativiteit in bedrijven / M.L. Wijvekate ; met een woord vooraf door J.D. Hooglandt. Naarden : Strengholt, c1986. 343 p. : ill. ; 23 cm. Includes index. ISBN 90-6010-628-8 : LC Card 86-199762
1. Creative ability in business - Management. 2. Creative ability in business - Netherlands - Management. I. Title.
HD53 .W55 1986

Wiklund, Erik. International marketing strategies : how to build international market share / Erik Wiklund. New York : McGraw-Hill, c1987. xi, 195 p. ; 24 cm. Includes index. ISBN 0-07-070176-8 : LC Card 86-21437 DDC 658.8/48 19
1. Export marketing. I. Title.
HF1009.5 .W555 1987

Wiktorin, Marianne. Kommunal bostadsförmedling : serviceorgan eller bostadspolitiskt medel? / Marianne Wiktorin. Stockholm : Statens råd för byggnadsforskning : Distribution, Svensk byggtjänst, [1983] 107 p. : ill. ; 25 cm. Bibliography: p. [98]-[99] "T9:1983." ISBN 91-540-3929-0 : LC Card 84-218864
1. Housing policy - Sweden. 2. Housing - Sweden. I. Title.
HD7350.A3 W55 1983

Wilamowitz-Moellendorf, Ulrich von. Struff, Richard. Räumliche Einkommens-, Preis- und Verbrauchsunterschiede in der Bundesrepublik Deutschland /. Bonn , 1983. xi, 258 p. : ISBN 3-88488-262-7 LC Card 84-196141
HC286.7 .S836 1983

Wilamowitz-Moellendorff, Ulrich von. Ansätze eines Konzepts zur Erfassung regionaler Lebensbedingungen in der Raumordnungspolitik / von Ulrich von Wilamowitz-Moellendorff. Bonn : Forschungsgesellschaft für Agrarpolitik und Agrarsoziologie, 1986. iv, 205 p. ; 21 cm. (Schriftenreihe der Forschungsgesellschaft für Agrarpolitik und Agrarsoziologie e.V., Bonn, 0179-4485 . 275) Originally presented as the author's thesis (doctoral--Universität Bonn). Bibliography: p. 193-205. ISBN 3-88488-275-9 LC Card 87-407818 DDC 330.943/0878 19
1. Germany (West) - Economic conditions - 1974- - Regional disparities. 2. Social indicators - Germany, West. I. Series: Schriftenreihe der Forschungsgesellschaft für Agrarpolitik und Agrarsoziologie , 275. II. Title.
HC286.7 .W54 1986

Wilayah pusat pertumbuhan industri . Indonesia. Departemen Perindustrian. [Jakarta] [1985] 20, vi p. : LC Card 85-941790
HC450.D5 I53 1985

Wilber, Charles K.
Capitalism and democracy . Notre Dame, Ind. , c1985. ix, 190 p. : ISBN 0-268-00750-0 : LC Card 84-40362 DDC 335 19
HX72.S383 C36 1985 ***NYPL [JLD 85-1987]***

The Political economy of development and underdevelopment /. New York , c1988. xi, 611 p. ; ISBN 0-394-37499-1 (pbk.) LC Card 87-9668 DDC 330.9172/4 19
HD82 .P546 1988

Wilcox, Chester E. Manuscript post offices of New York State /. [Richford, N.Y.?] , 1984. xii, 54 p., [12] p. of plates : LC Card 86-213682 DDC 383/.49747 19
HE6376.A1 N729 1984

Wilcox, James Allen, 1952- Current readings on money, banking, and financial markets /. Boston , c1987. xii, 356 p. : ISBN 0-316-94020-8 (pbk.) LC Card 87-4116 DDC 332 19
HG175 .C87 1987

Wilcox, Rand R. New statistical procedures for the social sciences : modern solutions to basic problems / Rand R. Wilcox. Hillsdale, N.J. : L. Erlbaum Associates, 1987. p. cm. Bibliography: p. Includes index. ISBN 0-89859-936-9 : LC Card 87-9001 DDC 300/.1/5195 19
1. Social sciences - Statistical methods. 2. Statistics. I. Title.
HA29 .W522 1987

Wild, Rainer Schultz- see **Schultz-Wild, Rainer.**

Wild, Rolf H. Strategy for export : foreign business development for small companies / by Rolf H. Wild.1st ed. Asheville, NC : Thurau Press, c1986. 121 p. ; 21 cm. ISBN 0-914291-02-5 (pbk.) : LC Card 86-51529 DDC 658.8/48 19
1. Export marketing. 2. Export sales. I. Title.
HF1009.5 .W56 1986

Wild, Werner.
Roloff, Otto, 1937- Umweltschutz in öffentlichen Budgets /. Regensburg , c1986. 278 p. : ISBN 3-924956-14-6 LC Card 87-129127 DDC 363.7/00943 19
HC290.5.E5 R65 1986

Steuern und Reichsherrschaft : Studie zu den finanziellen Ressourcen der Königsherrschaft im spätmittelalterlichen deutschen Reich / von Werner Wild.1 Aufl. Bremen : Skarabäus-Verlag, 1984. 326 p. ; 22 cm. (Wissenschaft und Forschung) Originally presented as the author's thesis (doctoral)--Universität Bremen, WS 1981/82. Bibliography: p. 310-325. ISBN 3-88948-030-6 LC Card 85-127825
1. Taxation - Germany - History. 2. Finance, Public - Germany - History. I. Title. II. Series.
HJ2675 .W55 1984

Wildavsky, Aaron B.
The new politics of the budgetary process / Aaron Wildavsky. Glenview, Ill. : Scott, Foresman, c1988. xxiv, 468 p. : ill. ; 21 cm.

Bibliography: p. [448]-461. Includes index. ISBN 0-673-39754-8 (pbk.) LC Card 87-23391 DDC 353.0072/2 19
1. Budget - United States. I. Title.
HJ2051 .W483 1988

Webber, Carolyn. A history of taxation and expenditure in the Western world /. New York , c1986. 734 p. ,[16] p. of plates : ISBN 0-671-54617-1 LC Card 86-3863 DDC 336.2/009 19
HJ2250 .W42 1986 ***NYPL [JLE 86-3474]***

The wildcatter . Harris, Kenneth, 1919- New York , c1987. x, 180 p., [8] p. of plates : ISBN 1-555-84048-5 LC Card 87-8183 DDC 338.7/622338/0924 B 19
HD9570.A53 H37 1987

Wildenberg, Ivo W. (Ivo Willibrord) Johan & Pieter de la Court, 1622-1660 & 1618-1685 : bibliografie en receptiegeschiedenis : gids tot de studie van een œuvre / Ivo W. Wildenberg. Amsterdam : APA-Holland Universiteits Pers, 1986. xiii, 180 p., [21] p. of plates : ill. ; 23 cm. (Bibliotheca historico-politica . 2) Summary in English. Bibliography: p. 143-169. Includes index. ISBN 90-302-1162-8 : LC Card 87-141484
1. Court, Johan de la, 1622-1660. 2. Court, Pieter de la, 1618?-1685. 3. Merchants - Netherlands - Biography. 4. Economics - Netherlands. 5. Netherlands - Politics and government - 1648-1715. I. Title. II. Title: Johan en Pieter de la Court, 1622-1660 & 1618-1685. III. Series.
HC322.5.A2 W55 1986

Wilder, J. Welles. The Adam theory of markets, or, What matters is profit / by Welles Wilder. McLeansville, N.C. (P.O. Box 128, Mcleansville 27301) : Cavida, c1987. 131 p. : ill. (some col.) ; 29 cm. LC Card 87-166037 DDC 332.64/4 19
1. Capital market. 2. Commodity exchanges. 3. Investment analysis. I. Title. II. Title: The Adam theory of markets. III. Title: What matters is profit.
HG4523 .W54 1987

Wilder, Joseph E., 1896- Lotions, potions, and liniments pure : a look at the drug trade in Winnipeg in the 1900s / by Joseph E. Wilder. Winnipeg, Man. : Prairie Pub. Col., c1982. 100 p. : ill. ; 23 cm. ISBN 0-919576-34-6 (pbk.) : LC Card 83-121333 DDC 381/.456151/0971274 19
1. Drug trade - Manitoba - Winnipeg - History - 20th century. 2. Drugstores - Manitoba - Winnipeg - History - 20th century. 3. Pharmacists - Manitoba - Winnipeg - History - 20th century. I. Title.
HD9670.C23 W568 1982
NYPL [JLE 87-1213]

WILDERNESS AREAS - GOVERNMENT POLICY - AUSTRALIA - TASMANIA.
Lowe, D. A. (Douglas Ackley), 1942- The price of power . South Melbourne , 1984. viii, 184 p., [12] p. of plates : ISBN 0-333-38088-6 LC Card 84-254286 DDC 333.91/62/099466 19
HD9685.A83 T385 1984
NYPL [JLD 87-795]

Wilderness Society. Kloepfer, Deanne. The Watt record . Washington, D.C. [1983] ii, 66, 9, 3 p. : LC Card 86-232533 DDC 333.1/0973 19
HD183.L3 K58 1983

WILDLIFE AS FOOD - ALASKA.
Alaska habitat management guide. Juneau, Alaska , 1986- 2 v. (loose-leaf) : LC Card 86-623159 DDC 333.95/09798 19
HD9457.A4 A427 1986

WILDLIFE CONSERVATION - GOVERNMENT POLICY - ALASKA.
Alaska habitat management guide. Juneau, Alaska , 1986- 2 v. (loose-leaf) : LC Card 86-623159 DDC 333.95/09798 19
HD9457.A4 A427 1986

WILDLIFE CONSERVATION - KENYA.
Yeager, Rodger. Wildlife, wild death . Albany, NY , c1986. xvi, 173 p. : ISBN 0-88706-168-0 LC Card 86-5791 DDC 333.95/16/09676 19
QL84.6.K4 Y43 1986 ***NYPL [JLE 86-3870]***

WILDLIFE, CONSERVATION OF. see **WILDLIFE CONSERVATION.**

WILDLIFE CONSERVATION - TANZANIA.
Yeager, Rodger. Wildlife, wild death . Albany, NY , c1986. xvi, 173 p. : ISBN 0-88706-168-0 LC Card 86-5791 DDC 333.95/16/09676 19
QL84.6.K4 Y43 1986 ***NYPL [JLE 86-3870]***

WILDLIFE HABITAT IMPROVEMENT - GOVERNMENT POLICY - ALASKA.
Alaska habitat management guide. Juneau, Alaska , 1986- 2 v. (loose-leaf) : LC Card 86-623159 DDC 333.95/09798 19
HD9457.A4 A427 1986

WILDLIFE REFUGES - ALASKA.
Roberts, Malcolm B. Senate Transportation Committee, RS 2477 Task Force report /. [Anchorage, Alaska] [1986] 121 leaves, 27 p. : LC Card 86-622718 DDC 333.78/09798 19
HE356.A4 R63 1986

WILDLIFE REFUGES - LUANGWA RIVER WATERSHED (ZAMBIA AND MOZAMBIQUE) - CONGRESSES.
Lupande Development Workshop (1983 : Nyamaluma Wildlife Conservation Camp) Proceedings of the Lupande Development Workshop . Chipata, Zambia , 1984. x, 121 p. : LC Card 84-980605 DDC 333.73/17/096894 19
HD993.Z8 L835 1983 ***NYPL [JLG 87-67]***

Wildlife, wild death . Yeager, Rodger. Albany, NY , c1986. xvi, 173 p. : ISBN 0-88706-168-0 LC Card 86-5791 DDC 333.95/16/09676 19
QL84.6.K4 Y43 1986 ***NYPL [JLE 86-3870]***

WILDMAN, JOHN RAYMOND, 1878-
Previts, Gary John. John Raymond Wildman . University, Ala. , 1978. viii, 84 p. ; LC Card 86-224716
HF5604.5.W55 P74 1978

WILDMAN, JOHN RAYMOND, 1878- - BIBLIOGRAPHY.
Previts, Gary John. John Raymond Wildman . University, Ala. , 1978. viii, 84 p. ; LC Card 86-224716
HF5604.5.W55 P74 1978

Wilensky, Harold L. Democratic corporatism and policy linkages : the interdependence of industrial, labor-market, incomes, and social policies in eight countries / Harold L. Wilensky & Lowell Turner. Berkeley : Institute of International Studies, University of California, c1987. ix, 97 p. ; 24 cm. (Research series / Institute of International Studies, University of California, Berkeley, 0068-6093 . no. 69) Bibliography: p. 85-93. Includes index. ISBN 0-87725-169-X (pbk.) : LC Card 87-3525 DDC 338.9 19
1. Industry and state - Europe. 2. Corporate state - Europe. 3. Europe - Politics and government - 1945-. 4. Industry and state - United States. 5. Corporate state - United States. 6. United States - Politics and government - 1945-. 7. Industry and state - Japan. 8. Corporate state - Japan. 9. Japan - Politics and government - 1945-. I. Turner, Lowell. II. Series: Research series (University of California, Berkeley. Institute of International Studies) , no. 69. III. Title.
HD3616.E8 W54 1987

Wiles, P. J. D. see **Wiles, Peter John de la Fosse.**

Wiles, Peter John de la Fosse.
The New Communist Third World . London , c1982. 392 p. ; ISBN 0-7099-2709-6 LC Card 86-673518
HF1413 .N495x 1982b

The Soviet economy on the brink of reform . Boston , 1988. p. cm. ISBN 0-04-335063-1 (alk. paper) LC Card 87-19514 DDC 338.947 19
HC335 .C626 1988

The Wiley Institute of Internal Auditors professional book series.
Kropatkin, Philip. Management and the audit network . New York , 1987. xii, 188 p. : ISBN 0-471-83286-3 LC Card 86-33983 DDC 657/.45 19
HF5667 .K74 1987

The Wiley management series on problem solving, decision making, and strategic thinking.
Hamermesh, Richard G. Making strategy work . New York , c1986. xiii, 245 p. : ISBN 0-471-80319-7 : LC Card 85-12456 DDC 658.4/012 19
HD30.28 .H35 1986 ***NYPL [JLE 86-2018]***

Wiley, Miriam M. Rottman, David B. The population structure and living circumstances of Irish travellers . Dublin , 1986. 134 p. : ISBN 0-7070-0084-X (pbk.) : LC Card 86-215759 DDC 330.9417 s 305.5/68 19
HC257.I6 E3 no. 131 DX217

Wiley professional banking and finance series, 0733-8945.
Alexandrides, Costas G. Countertrade . New York , c1987. xx, 235 p. ; ISBN 0-471-84711-9 LC Card 87-12966 DDC 382 19
HF1414.3 .A44 1987

Controlling interest rate risk . New York , c1986. xv, 414 p. : ISBN 0-471-82354-6 : LC Card 85-22504 DDC 332.8/2 19
HG1621 .C6 1986 ***NYPL [JLE 86-2850]***

Crawford, Edward K., 1933- A management guide to leveraged buyouts /. New York , c1987. x, 257 p. ; ISBN 0-471-83232-4 LC Card 86-32390 DDC 658.1/6 19
HD2746.5 .C7 1987

Teweles, Richard Jack, 1924- The stock market /. New York , c1987. xii, 526 p. ; ISBN 0-471-82044-X LC Card 86-33950 DDC 332.64/2 19
HG4551 .T48 1987

Venedikian, Harry M. Export-import financing /. New York , c1986. xvii, 456 p. : ISBN 0-471-82449-6 : LC Card 85-29566 DDC 332.7/42 19
HG3754.U5 V46 1986 ***NYPL [JLE 86-2998]***

Wiley professional development programs.
Smith, Barry J., 1947- How to be an effective trainer . New York , c1987. 404 p. : ISBN 0-471-85239-2 (pbk.) LC Card 86-26774 DDC 658.3/1243 19
HF5549.5.T7 S642 1987

Wiley series in management.
Social forces and the manager . Malabar, Fla. , 1987, c1982. xiv, 502 p. : ISBN 0-89464-225-1 (pbk.) LC Card 87-3259 DDC 658.4/08/0973 19
HD60.5.U5 S635 1987

Wiley series in management, 0271-6046.
Schellenberger, Robert Earl. Strategic management . New York , c1986. xiii, 808 p. : ISBN 0-471-88059-0 : LC Card 85-9553 DDC 658.4/012 19
HD30.28 .S34 1986 ***NYPL [JLE 86-1559]***

Wiley series in probability and mathematical statistics. Applied probability and statistics, 0271-6232.
Rubin, Donald B. Multiple imputation for nonresponse in surveys /. New York , c1987. xxix, 258 p. : ISBN 0-471-08705-X : LC Card 86-28935 DDC 001.4/225 19
HA31.2 .R83 1987

Wiley series in psychology and productivity at work.
Cook, Mark. Personnel selection and productivity /. Chichester [West Sussex] , New York , c1988. p. cm. ISBN 0-471-91148-8 : LC Card 87-21070 DDC 658.3/112 19
HF5549.5.S38 C66 1988

The Human side of advanced manufacturing technology /. Chichester [West Sussex] , New York , c1987. xi, 205 p. : ISBN 0-471-90867-3 : LC Card 86-32554 DDC 331.25 19
HD9720.5 .H85 1987

Women and information technology /. Chichester , New York , c1987. viii, 283 p. : ISBN 0-471-91603-X : LC Card 87-10554 DDC 331.4 19
HD6053 .W636 1987

Wiley series in telecommunications.
Vignault, Walter L. Worldwide telecommunications guide for the business manager /. New York , c1987. xvi, 417 p. : ISBN 0-471-85828-5 LC Card 87-2002 DDC 384 19
HF5541.T4 V54 1987

Wiley series in training and development.
Caffarella, Rosemary S. (Rosemary Shelly), 1946- Program development and evaluation resource book for trainers /. New York , c1988. xxi, 266 p. : ISBN 0-471-84235-4 LC Card 87-15990 DDC 658.3/12404 19
HF5549.5.T7 C23 1988

Rogoff, Rosalind Louise. The training wheel . New York , c1987. 151 p. : ISBN 0-471-83467-X LC Card 86-32409 DDC 658.3/12404 19
HF5549.5.T7 R565 1987

Wiley series on business strategy.
Cohen, William A., 1937- Developing a winning marketing plan /. New York , c1987. ix, 324 p. : ISBN 0-471-84529-9 LC Card 86-32402 DDC 658.8/02 19
HF5415 .C54247 1987

Fidel, Stanley Leo. Start up telemarketing .

New York , c1987. xiv, 287 p. : ISBN 0-471-01064-2 LC Card 87-21610 DDC 658.8/5 19
HF5415.1265 .F53 1987

Wiley series on studies in occupational stress.
Job stress and blue collar work /. Chichester [West Sussex] , New York , c1985. ix, 243 p. : ISBN 0-471-90811-8 : LC Card 85-12022 DDC 158.7 19
HF5548.85 .J64 1985 NYPL [JLE 86-2412]

Wiley, Thomas, 1959- Gilbert, Gorman, 1943- The management and regulation of ground transportation at U. S. airports . Washington, D.C. [1986] 153 p. : LC Card 87-600652 DDC 387.7/362 19
HE9797.4.A2 G55 1986

Wiley/IRM series on multinationals.
Anastassopoulos, J. P. [Multinationales publiques. English.] State-owned multinationals /. Chichester [England] , New York , c1987. xii, 200 p. : ISBN 0-471-91502-5 : LC Card 87-2033 DDC 338.8/8 19
HD2755.5 .A613 1987

Stopford, John M. Britain and the multinationals /. Chichester , New York , c1985. xiv, 282 p. : ISBN 0-471-90839-8 : LC Card 85-12352 DDC 338.8/8841 19
HD2845 .S76 1985 NYPL [JLE 86-924]

The Wiley/Ronald-Institute of Internal Auditors professional book series.
Kowalczyk, David S., 1946- Cadmus' operational auditing /. New York , c1987. x, 422 p. ; ISBN 0-471-82660-X LC Card 87-23267 DDC 657/.458 19
HF5668.25 .K696 1987

The Wiley/Ronald-National Association of Accountants professional book series.
Wiley/Ronald-National Association of Accountants professional book series.
Day, Denis W. How to cut business travel costs /. New York , c1986. ix, 207 p. : ISBN 0-471-83633-8 : LC Card 86-9277 DDC 658.1/553 19
HD38 .D39 1986 NYPL [JLE 86-4235]

Shuster, Harvey L. The financial manager's guide to microsoftware /. New York , 1988. p. cm. ISBN 0-471-81176-9 LC Card 87-21663 DDC 658.1/5/0285536 19
HG4012.5 .S47 1988

Smith, Gordon V., 1937- Corporate valuation . New York , c1988. xiv, 224 p. : ISBN 0-471-85826-9 LC Card 87-23114 DDC 658.1/522 19
HG4028.V3 S58 1988

Wilhelm-Pieck-Universität Rostock. Abteilung Wissenschaftspublizistik. Probleme der staatsmonopolistischen Wirtschaftsregulierung . Rostock , 1981. 35 p. ; LC Card 86-211250
HB501 .P694 1981

Wilhelm-Pieck-Universität Rostock. Sektion Geschichte.
Arbeiterwanderungen, Ausländerbeschäftigung und Ausländerpolitik in kapitalistischen Ländern Europas im 20. Jahrhundert. Rostock , 1981-1982. 4 v. ; LC Card 82-193086 DDC 331.6/2/094 19
HD8438.A2 A75 1982 NYPL [JLK 84-95]

Zur Haltung der herrschenden Klasse und der Arbeiterbewegung zur Beschäftigung ausländischer Arbeiter. [Rostock] , 1980. 64 p. ; LC Card 82-209919 DDC 331.6/2/0943 19
HD8458.A2 Z87 1980 NYPL [JLD 87-143]

Wilhelm und Carl Friedrich von Siemens .
Goetzeler, Herbert. Stuttgart , 1986. 131 p. : ISBN 3-515-04558-9 LC Card 86-141456
HD9695.G43 S514 1986

WILHELMSBURG (HAMBURG, GERMANY) - ECONOMIC CONDITIONS.
Hauschildt, Elke. Polnische Arbeitsmigranten in Wilhelmsburg bei Hamburg während des Kaiserreichs und der Weimarer Republik /. Dortmund , c1986. xv, 330 p. : ISBN 3-923293-17-8 LC Card 87-127027 DDC 331.6/2/438043515 19
HD8458.P65 H38 1986

Wilk, Carole. Career women and childbearing : a psychological analysis of the decision process / Carole A. Wilk. New York : Van Nostrand Reinhold, c1986. xxii, 304 p. ; 24 cm. Includes bibliographical references and index. ISBN 0-442-29352-6 LC Card 85-9216 DDC 306.8/743 19
1. Motherhood. 2. Married people - Employment. 3. Child rearing. I. Title.
HQ759 .W52 1986 NYPL [JLD 86-1811]

Wilk, Marian. Pierwsza pięciolatka w Związku Radzieckim : problemy industrializacji 1928-1932 / Marian Wilk. Wrocław : Zakład Narodowy im. Ossolińskich, 1986. 314 p., [21] p. of plates : ill. ; 24 cm. At head of title: Polska Akademia Nauk. Instytut Krajów Socjalistycznych. Summary in English. Bibliography: p. [298]-305. Includes index. ISBN 83-04-02190-0 : LC Card 87-110627
1. Soviet Union - Economic policy - 1928-1932. 2. Soviet Union - Industries. I. Title.
HC335.4 .W55 1986

Wilke, H. A. M. Experimental social dilemmas /. Frankfurt am Main , New York , c1986. vi, 234 p. : ISBN 3-8204-8574-0 (pbk.) : LC Card 86-10307 DDC 302 19
HM132 .E96 1986 NYPL [JLD 87-1177]

Wilke Organization.
Trading in banking . [New York?] , c1986. iv ; LC Card 87-128754 DDC 332.1/0973 19
HG2491 .T7 1986

Trading in banking . New York , c1987. x, 137 p. ; ISBN 0-939853-00-0 (pbk.) LC Card 87-404278 DDC 332.1/0973 19
HG2491 .T697 1987

Wilke, Peter.
Manpower conversion in defence related industry : a report prepared for the International Labour Office / Peter Wilke, Herbert Wulf. Hamburg : Institut für Friedensforschung und Sicherheitspolitik an der Universität Hamburg, [1986] 62 p. : ill. ; 21 cm. (Hamburger Beiträge zur Friedensforschung und Sicherheitspolitik . Heft 3) "Juni 1986." Bibliography: p. 61-62. LC Card 86-212660 DDC 331.25/924 19
1. Disarmament - Economic aspects. 2. Occupational retraining. I. Wulf, Herbert. II. International Labour Office. III. Title. IV. Series.
HC79.D4 W55 1986

Zivile Alternativen für die Rüstungsindustrie /. Baden-Baden , 1986. 174 p. ; ISBN 3-7890-1262-9 LC Card 87-108651 DDC 338.4/76234/0943 19
HD9743.G48 Z58 1986

Wilkening, Eugene A. Family farming in Europe and America /. Boulder , 1987. viii, 312 p. ; ISBN 0-8133-7340-9 (soft : alk. paper) : LC Card 87-2041 DDC 338.1/6 19
HD1476.E85 F35 1987

Wilkens, Joanne. Her own business : success secrets of entrepreneurial women / by Joanne Wilkens. New York : McGraw-Hill, c1987. xv, 245 p. ; 24 cm. Bibliography: p. 223-240. Includes index. ISBN 0-07-050854-2 : LC Card 86-27780 DDC 338.6/422/088042 19
1. Women-owned business enterprises - United States - Case studies. 2. Women in business - United States - Case studies. 3. Success in business - United States - Case studies. I. Title.
HD2346.U5 W548 1987

Wilkie, James Wallace. Quantitative Latin American studies . Los Angeles , 1977. xiv, 91 p. : ISBN 0-87903-227-8 LC Card 77-620011 DDC 330.9/8/003
HD5731.A6 Q36 NYPL [JLF 80-242]

Wilkie, Richard W., 1938- Latin American population and urbanization analysis : maps and statistics, 1950-1982 / Richard W. Wilkie. Los Angeles, Calif. : UCLA Latin American Center Publications, University of California, c1984. xxii, 433 p. : ill., maps ; 29 cm. (Statistical abstract of Latin America. Supplement series . suppl. 8) Includes bibliographical references. ISBN 0-87903-242-1 (alk. paper) : LC Card 83-620019 DDC 312/.098 19
1. Urbanization - Latin America - Statistics. 2. Urbanization - Latin America - Maps. 3. Latin America - Population - Statistics. 4. Latin America - Population - Maps. I. Title. II. Series.
HB3530.5 .W54 1984 NYPL [JLF 87-298]

Wilkinson, Barry. The shopfloor politics of new technology / Barry Wilkinson. London : Heinemann Educational, 1983. 120 p. ; 23 cm. Includes bibliographical references and index. ISBN 0-435-82950-5 : LC Card 82-236198 DDC 338/.06 19
1. Technological innovations - Economic aspects - Great Britain. 2. Technological innovations - Social aspects - Great Britain. 3. Great Britain - Industries. I. Title.
HC260.T4 W54 1983 NYPL [JLD 86-1322]

Wilkinson, John, 1946- Goodman, David, 1938- From farming to biotechnology . Oxford , New York, N.Y. , 1987. 214 p. : ISBN 0-631-14405-6 : LC Card 87-687 DDC 338.1/6 19
HD1433 .G66 1987

Wilkinson, Richard G. Class and health . London , New York , 1986. x, 223 p. : ISBN 0-422-60360-0 : LC Card 86-5972 DDC 362.1/0941 19
RA418.3.G7 C56 1986 NYPL [JLE 87-505]

Wilkinson, Wendy.
Spufford, Peter. Handbook of medieval exchange /. London : Woodbridge, Suffolk ; xcii, 376, [3] p., [1] fold. leaf : ISBN 0-86193-105-X *NYPL [JLE 86-4344]*

Spufford, Peter. Handbook of medieval exchange /. London : Woodbridge, Suffolk ; xcii, 376 p., [3] leaves of plates (1 folded) : ISBN 0-86193-105-X LC Card 86-673816
HG3942 .S68x 1986

Wilks, Stephen. Comparative government-industry relations . Oxford , New York , 1987. xiii, 321 p. ; ISBN 0-19-827493-9 : LC Card 86-28631 DDC 338.9 19
HD3611 .C63 1987

Will there always be an England? [videorecording] / producer and director, Ofra Bikel. Alexandria, VA : PBS Video, 1986. 1 videocassette (60 min.) : sd., col. Title from data sheet. Segment from the television program: Frontline. Ages 16 through adults. Issued as U-matic 3/4 in. or Beta 1/2 in. or VHS 1/2 in. Describes the contrasts between the rich and poor in England, and the wealthy south of England versus the northern cities which suffer from high unemployment. Covers business, economic, and social science aspects of modern England. LC Card 86-707796 DDC 942.085 11
1. Great Britain - Economic conditions - 1945- - Regional disparities. 2. Wealth - Great Britain. 3. Poor - Great Britain. I. Bikel, Ofra. II. PBS Video. III. Frontline (Television program).
HC256.5

Willaert, Y. Ressources humaines et développement régional en Côte d'Ivoire : un essai prospectif dans les régions de l'ouest : rapport présenté au Gouvernement de la République de Côte d'Ivoire : document provisoire / Y. Willaert, R. Ramanantoanison. [Addis Ababa] : Bureau international du travail, Programme des emplois et des compétences techniques pour l'Afrique, [1977] 3, 108, [6] leaves (1 folded) ; 30 cm. Cover title. "Confidentiel." Includes bibliographical references. LC Card 82-980560
1. Labor supply - Ivory Coast. 2. Ivory Coast - Economic policy. 3. Regional planning - Ivory Coast. I. Ramanantoanison, R. II. Jobs and Skills Programme for Africa. III. Title.
HD5846.9.A6 W55 1977

Willard, Harold F. Insurance ripoffs and dirty tricks : the sucker's dilemma : a tirade and harangue for policyholders, claimants, agents, brokers, and all other victims / Harold F. Willard ; illustrations by Gordon Anderson. San Diego, Calif. : Thumsdownbooks, c1987. 214 p. : ill. ; 23 cm. Bibliography: p. 213-214. ISBN 0-943061-04-0 (pbk.) : LC Card 87-166189 DDC 364.1/68 19
1. Insurance - United States - Corrupt practices. I. Title.
HG8531 .W55 1987

Willekens, Frans. Migration and settlement . Dordrecht ; Boston : xix, 496 p. ; ISBN 90-277-2119-X LC Card 85-25626 DDC 304.8 19
HB1952 .M539 1986 NYPL [JLE 86-4091]

Willett, Thomas D. Exchange rates, trade, and the U. S. economy /. Cambridge, Mass. , c1985. xxi, 296 p. : ISBN 0-88410-948-8 LC Card 84-28328 DDC 332.4/560973 19
HG3851 .E94 1985 NYPL [JLE 85-2269]

William C. Norris . Worthy, James C. Cambridge, Mass. , c1987. xiv, 259 p. : ISBN 0-88730-087-1 LC Card 87-1808 DDC 338.7/61004/0924 B 19
HD9696.C62 N689 1987

William C. Overman Associates. Virginia counties and cities data book, 1986. Virginia Beach, Va. (380 Cleveland Place, Virginia Beach 23462) , 1986. 2 v. (ii, 262 p.) : LC Card 87-138805 DDC 317.55 19
HA685 .V575 1986

William G. McAdoo and the development of national economic policy, 1913-1918 /. Shook, Dale N. New York , 1987. 427 p. ; ISBN 0-8240-8092-0 (alk. paper) : LC Card 87-23766 DDC 338.973 19
HC106.2 .S55 1987

William L. Hopkins, Inc. People skills in action, for loan officers and processors. Chicago, Ill. , 1986. 1 videocassette (20 min.) : LC Card 86-707349 DDC 658.8 11
HG1641

Williams, 1949- The national recorder / Williams. Denver, CO : National Recorder, c1983. ii, 456 p. ; 22 cm. LC Card 87-106311 DDC 353.9/382326/025 19
1. Land titles - Registration and transfer - United States - States - Directories. I. Title.
HD255 .W54 1983

Williams, A. Paul (Alan Paul), 1951- Taylor, Malcolm G. (Malcolm Gordon) Medical perspectives on Canadian Medicare . Downsview, Ont. , 1984. vii, 201 p. : ISBN 0-919762-57-3 (pbk.) LC Card 87-673411
HD7102.C2 T34x 1984

Williams, Alex O., 1934- Managing risk in mortgage portfolios / Alex O. Williams. New York : Quorum Books, c1987. xx, 161 p. : ill. ; 24 cm. Includes bibliographies and index. ISBN 0-89930-058-8 (lib. bdg. : alk. paper) LC Card 87-2497 DDC 332.63/244 19
1. Mortgages. 2. Risk management. 3. Portfolio management. I. Title.
HG4655 .W55 1987

Williams, Allan M. Phillips, David R. Rural housing and the public sector /. Aldershot, Hampshire, England [Brookfield, Vt.] c1982. viii, 174 p. : ISBN 0-566-00456-9 : LC Card 82-134413 DDC 352.7/5/0941 19
HD7289.G82 S687 1982 *NYPL [JLD 83-2605]*

Williams, Alma. Relations between the European Community and the member states of the Association of South-East Asian Nations /. Brussels [1986] 55 p. : LC Card 87-135576 DDC 337.4059 19
HF1532.5 .R46 1986

Williams & Henderson. Winning the employment game [videorecording] /. Mt. Kisco, NY , 1981. 1 videocassette (52 min.) : LC Card 86-707777 DDC 650.1 11
HF5382.7

Williams, Anna Fay, 1935- New opportunities to purchase natural gas / by Anna Fay Williams and Leonard V. Parent. Lilburn, Ga. : Fairmont Press, c1988. xiv, 372 p. : ill., forms ; 24 cm. Includes bibliographies and index. ISBN 0-88173-034-3 : LC Card 86-46134 DDC 665.7/44/068 19
1. Gas, Natural - Pipe lines - Economic aspects - United States. 2. Gas industry - United States. 3. Gas, Natural - United States - Purchasing. I. Parent, Leonard V., 1927-. II. Title.
HD9581.U5 W54 1988

Williams, Bernard C. Bhaskar, Krish N. The impact of microprocessors on the small accounting practice /. Englewood Cliffs, N.J. , c1986. xvi, 167 p. ; ISBN 0-13-453291-0 (pbk.) LC Card 85-25764 DDC 657/.028/5416 19
HF5679 .B45 1986 *NYPL [JLE 86-4067]*

Williams, Bill, 1939- Winders, Terry J., 1942- Profitable equipment leasing . Boston , c1987. xii, 252 p. ; ISBN 0-87267-101-1 : LC Card 86-26601 DDC 332.1/068/7 19
HD39.4 .W56 1987 *NYPL [JLE 87-1512]*

Williams, Bruce, 1932- The Bruce Williams book : start your own small business and make it succeed / Bruce Williams, with Warren Sloat. New York : Stein and Day : Distributed in the U. S. by H. Holt, 1987. p. cm. ISBN 0-8128-3119-5 : LC Card 86-42692 DDC 658/022 19
1. New business enterprises - United States. 2. Small business - United States. I. Sloat, Warren. II. Title. III. Title: Start your own small business and make it succeed.
HD62.5 .W49 1987

Williams, Cecil L., 1930- The negotiable environment : people, white-collar work, and the office / Cecil Williams, David Armstrong, Clark Malcolm. Ann Arbor, Mich. : Facility Management Institute, c1985. v, 82 p. : ill. (some col.) ; 28 cm. Bibliography: p. 82. ISBN 0-936658-20-7 (pbk.) : LC Card 85-10305 DDC 658.3/82 19
1. Office layout - Psychological aspects. 2. White collar workers - Psychology. 3. Organizational behavior. I. Armstrong, David L. II. Malcolm, Clark. III. Title.
HF5547.2 .W55 1985 *NYPL [JLF 86-1138]*

Williams, Chris, 1952- Words that manage : the thesaurus to help managers relate, motivate, and evaluate / Chris Williams. Westbury, N.Y. : Asher-Gallant Press, c1987. xi, 157 p. ; 23 cm. Includes index. ISBN 0-87280-131-4 : LC Card 87-17434 DDC 658.3/0014 19
1. Industrial management - Terminology. 2. English language - Business English. I. Title.
HD30.17 .W55 1987

Williams, David, 1934- Kerans, Patrick. Welfare and worker participation . New York , 1987. p. cm. ISBN 0-312-00908-9 : LC Card 87-11878 DDC 362.8/5 19
HD7261 .K47 1987

Williams, Donald R., 1956- Labor force participation of black and white youth / by Donald R. Williams. Ann Arbor, Mich. : UMI Research Press, c1987. 125 p. ; 25 cm. (Research in business economics and public policy . no. 11) Revision of thesis (Ph.D.)--Northwestern University, 1984. Bibliography: p. [117]-122. Includes index. ISBN 0-8357-1804-2 (alk. paper) LC Card 87-5868 DDC 331.3/412/0973 19
1. Youth - Employment - United States. 2. Afro-American youth - Employment. I. Title. II. Series.
HD6273 .W48 1987

Williams, Doyle Z. The Complete CPA examination review, auduiing, 1986-1987 /. Boston , c1986. 42, 237, 177, 12 p. : ISBN 0-395-41132-7 (pbk.) LC Card 86-80561 DDC 657/.45/076 19
HF5667 .C5852 1986

Williams, Frank Jefferson. Freund, John E. Elementary business statistics . Englewood Cliffs, N.J. , c1988. xiii, 738 p. : ISBN 0-13-253196-8 LC Card 87-20586 DDC 519.5/024658 19
HF1017 .F73 1988

Williams, Frederick, 1933- Dordick, Herbert S., 1925- Innovative management using telecommunications . New York , c1986. x, 226 p. : ISBN 0-471-81296-X : LC Card 86-7797 DDC 658.4/5 19
HF5541.T4 D67 1986 *NYPL [JLE 86-4425]*

Williams, Geoffrey Lee. Global defence : motivation and policy in a nuclear age / Geoffrey Williams. New Delhi : Vikas, c1984. xlvi, 366 p. ; 22 cm. Includes bibliographical references and index. ISBN 0-7069-2478-9 : LC Card 84-900260 DDC 355/.0335 19
1. Military policy. 2. Military planning. 3. World politics - 1945-. I. Title.
UA11 .W55 1984 *NYPL [JLD 86-3709]*

Williams, Harry B. Industry wage survey : petroleum refining, June 1985. Washington, D.C. : U. S. Dept. of Labor, Bureau of Labor Statistics : For sale by the Supt. of Docs., U. S. G.P.O., [1986] iv, 34 p. ; 28 cm. (Bulletin / U. S. Department of Labor, Bureau of Labor Statistics . 2255) "March 1986." LC Card 86-602194 DDC 331.2/86553/0973021 19
1. Wages - Petroleum workers - United States - Statistics. I. United States. Bureau of Labor Statistics. II. Title. III. Title: Petroleum refining, June 1985. IV. Series: Bulletin (United States. Bureau of Labor Statistics) , 2255.
HD4966.P52 U5556 1986

Williams, John (John L.)
Beveridge, William Henry Beveridge, Baron, 1879-1963. A Beveridge reader /. London , Boston , 1987. viii, 190 p. ; ISBN 0-04-361070-6 (alk. paper) LC Card 87-11819 DDC 338.941 19
HB103.A2 B48 1987

Williams, Karel. The breakdown of Austin Rover . Leamington Spa, UK ; New York : v, 150 p. : ISBN 0-85496-515-7 : LC Card 86-24449 DDC 338.7/6292222 19
HD9710.G74 A868 1987

Williams, Karel.
Beveridge, William Henry Beveridge, Baron, 1879-1963. A Beveridge reader /. London , Boston , 1987. viii, 190 p. ; ISBN 0-04-361070-6 (alk. paper) LC Card 87-11819 DDC 338.941 19
HB103.A2 B48 1987

The breakdown of Austin Rover : a case-study in the failure of business strategy and industrial policy / Karel Williams, John Williams, Colin Haslam. Leamington Spa, UK ; New York : Berg ; v, 150 p. : ill. ; 22 cm. Bibliography: p. 144-145. Includes index. ISBN 0-85496-515-7 : LC Card 86-24449 DDC 338.7/6292222 19
1. Austin Rover Group. 2. Automobile industry and trade - Great Britain. I. Williams, John (John L.). II. Haslam, Colin. III. Title.
HD9710.G74 A868 1987

Williams, L. J. Modern South Wales . Cardiff , Atlantic Highlands, N.J. , 1986. ix, 324 p. : ISBN 0-7083-0943-7 LC Card 86-226166 DDC 330.9429/4085 19
HC257.W3 M63 1986

Williams, Mark M., 1948- Expert advisor, 1-2-3 : includes release 2 / Mark Williams. Reading, Mass. : Addison-Wesley, 1988. p. cm. Includes indexes. ISBN 0-201-18238-6 (pbk.) : LC Card 87-19286 DDC 005.36/9 19
1. Lotus 1-2-3 (Computer program). 2. Business - Data processing. I. Title. II. Title: Expert advisor, one-two-three.
HF5548.4.L67 W536 1988

Williams, Martha R.
Stapleton, Charles O. California real estate principles /. Chicago , c1987. xvi, 428, 8 p. : ISBN 0-88462-569-9 (pbk.) LC Card 86-24870 DDC 333.33/09794 19
HD266.C2 S73 1987

Ventolo, William L. Fundamentals of real estate appraisal . Chicago , c1987. 75 p. : ISBN 0-88462-571-0 (pbk.) LC Card 86-29715 DDC 333.33/2 19
HD1387 .V45 1987

Williams, Oliver F.
The apartheid crisis : how we can do justice in a land of violence / Oliver F. Williams. San Francisco : Harper & Row, 1986. xiv, 124 p. : map ; 21 cm. Includes index. "Perennial library." ISBN 0-06-250951-9 (pbk.) : LC Card 85-45726 DDC 332.6/7373/068 19
1. Investments, American - South Africa. 2. Corporations, American - South Africa. 3. Apartheid - South Africa. 4. Race relations - Religious aspects - Christianity. I. Title.
HG5851.A3 W55 1986 *NYPL [JLD 86-4023]*

The Common good and U. S. capitalism /. Lanham, MD , c1987. viii, 425 p. ; ISBN 0-8191-6364-3 (alk. paper) : LC Card 87-8334 DDC 306/.36/0973 19
HD60.5.U5 C665 1987

Williams, Robert E., 1942- Northrup, Herbert Roof, 1918- Doublebreasted operations and pre-hire agreements in construction . Philadelphia, Penn., USA , c1987. viii, 127 p. : ISBN 0-89546-067-X (pbk.) LC Card 87-81475 DDC 331.88/92 19
HD9715.U52 N67 1984 Suppl.

Williams, Robert G. (Robert Gregory), 1948- Export agriculture and the crisis in Central America / by Robert G. Williams. Chapel Hill : University of North Carolina Press, c1986. xvi, 257 p. : ill., maps ; 24 cm. Includes index. Bibliography: p. [239]-248. ISBN 0-8078-1693-0 LC Card 85-20978 DDC 382/.41/09728 19
1. Cotton trade - Central America. 2. Beef industry - Central America. 3. Cattle trade - Central America. 4. Central America - Politics and government - 1979-. 5. Central America - Foreign relations - United States. 6. United States - Foreign relations - Central America. I. Title.
HD9884.C352 W55 1986 *NYPL [JLE 86-3412]*

Williams, Shirley, 1930- A job to live : the impact of tomorrow's technology on work and society / Shirley Williams. Harmondsworth, Middlesex, England ; New York, N.Y., U. S.A. : Penguin Books, 1985. 245 p. : ill. ; 20 cm. Bibliography: p. 224-[231] Includes index. ISBN

0-14-008426-6 (pbk.) : LC Card 87-118827 DDC 331.1 19
1. Labor supply - Effect of technological innovations on. 2. Unemployment, Technological. 3. Computers and civilization. I. Title.
HD6331 .W53 1985

Williams, Sonja, 1953- Exploding the hunger myths : a high school curriculum / by Sonja Williams. San Francisco : Institute for Food and Development Policy, c1987. xv, 173 p. : ill. ; 28 cm. "A Food first book." "Audiovisual materials": p. 166-169. Bibliography: p. 169-173. ISBN 0-935028-23-4 (pbk.) : LC Card 87-3360 DDC 363.8/07/1273 19
1. Food supply - Study and teaching (Secondary). 2. Nutrition policy - Study and teaching (Secondary). 3. Education, Secondary - Curricula. I. Title.
HD9000.5 .W476 1987

Williams, Stephen, 1954- Dix, Bernard. Serving the public, building the union . London , 1987- v. <1 > : ISBN 0-85315-645-X (v. 1) : LC Card 87-169851 DDC 331.88/09421 19
HD8005.2.G7 D59 1987

Williams, Susan. Cogan, Douglas. Generating energy alternatives . Washington, D.C. , c1987. xi, 358 p. : ISBN 0-931035-16-3 (pbk.) LC Card 87-403993 DDC 333.79 19
HD9685.U5 C588 1987

Williams, Terry (Terry M.) Growing up poor / Terry Williams, William Kornblum. Lexington, MA : Lexington Books, c1985. xvi, 136 p. ; 24 cm. ISBN 0-669-09687-3 (alk. paper) LC Card 84-48564 DDC 362.7/044 19
1. Socially handicapped youth - United States. 2. Poor - United States. 3. Youth - Employment - United States. 4. Unemployment - United States. I. Kornblum, William. II. Title.
HV1431 .W55 1985 ***NYPL [JLE 85-2236]***

Williams, Thomas Arthur, 1944- Anderson, David Ray, 1941- Statistics for business and economics /. St. Paul, MN , c1987. xxviii, 792 p. : ISBN 0-314-25873-6 : LC Card 86-24613 DDC 519.5 19
HF1017 .A6 1987

WILLIAMS, WHITING, 1878-
Wren, Daniel A. White collar hobo . Ames , 1987. xii, 165 p. : ISBN 0-8138-1922-9 LC Card 87-4048 DDC 331/.092/4 B 19
HD8073.W47 W74 1987

Williamson B., Carlos. La teoría sobre preferencias arancelarias : el caso de las uniones aduaneras / Carlos Williamson B. Santiago, Chile : Pontificia Universidad Católica de Chile, Instituto de Economía, 1985. 35 leaves : ill. ; 26 cm. (Trabajo docente . no. 40) Bibliography: leaves 34-35. LC Card 85-202146
1. Tariff preferences - Latin America. 2. Customs unions. I. Series: Trabajo docente (Universidad Católica de Chile. Instituto de Economía) , no. 40. II. Title.
HF1733.L29 W54 1985

Williamson, Jeffrey G., 1935- Did British capitalism breed inequality? / Jeffrey G. Williamson. Boston : Allen & Unwin, 1985. ix, 270 p. : ill. ; 25 cm. Includes index. Bibliography: p. [251]-265. ISBN 0-04-942186-7 : LC Card 84-20413 DDC 339.2/2/0941 19
1. Income distribution - Great Britain - History. 2. Capitalism - Social aspects - Great Britain - History. I. Title.
HC260.I5 W45 1985 ***NYPL [JLE 86-1361]***

Williamson, John, 1937-
Balassa, Bela A. Adjusting to success . Washington, DC , 1987. x, 121 p. : ISBN 0-88132-061-7 (pbk.) LC Card 87-3309 DDC 382.1/7/0951 19
HG3883.H66 B34 1987

Capital flight and Third World debt /. Washington, D.C. , 1987. p. cm. ISBN 0-88132-064-1 LC Card 87-17080 DDC 332/.042 19
HG3891 .C36 1987

Lessard, Donald R. Capital flight . Washington, DC , 1987. x, 64 p. ; ISBN 0-88132-059-5 LC Card 87-17279 DDC 332/.042 19
HG3891 .C367 1987

Political economy and international money : selected essays of John Williamson / edited by Chris Milner. New York : New York University Press, 1987. xii, 292 p. ; 25 cm. Bibliography: p. 276-288. Includes index. ISBN 0-8147-5434-1 : LC Card 86-23484 DDC 332.4/5 19
1. International finance. 2. Monetary policy. 3. International economic relations. I. Milner, Chris. II. Title.
HG3881 .W4934 1987

Targets and indicators : a blueprint for the international coordination of economic policy / John Williamson and Marcus Miller. Washington, DC : Institute for International Economics, 1987. xii, 108 p. : ill. ; 24 cm. (Policy analyses in international economics . 22) "September 1987." Bibliography: p. 106-108. ISBN 0-88132-064-1 LC Card 87-22724 DDC 332.4/5 19
1. International finance. 2. International economic relations. 3. Economic policy. I. Miller, M. H. (Marcus H.). II. Title. III. Series.
HG3881 .W4936 1987

Williamson, John B. Morris, Michael, 1949- Poverty and public policy . Westport, Conn. , 1986. xii, 236 p. ; ISBN 0-313-24942-3 (lib. bdg. : alk. paper) LC Card 86-398 DDC 361.6/1/0973 19
HV95 .M67 1986 ***NYPL [JLD 87-510]***

Williamson, John N. The Leader-manager /. New York , c1986. xi, 511 p. : ISBN 0-471-83693-1 : LC Card 86-1316 DDC 658.4/092 19
HD38.2 .L42 1986 ***NYPL [JLE 86-2930]***

Williamson, Oliver E.
Antitrust economics : mergers, contracting, and strategic behavior / Oliver Williamson. Oxford, OX, UK ; New York, NY, USA : B. Blackwell, 1987. viii, 363 p. : ill. ; 24 cm. Bibliography: p. [344]-351. Includes index. ISBN 0-631-15363-2 : LC Card 87-5153 DDC 338.8 19
1. Industrial organization (Economic theory). 2. Antitrust law - Economic aspects. I. Title.
HD2326 .W49 1987

The economic institutions of capitalism : firms, markets, relational contracting / Oliver E. Williamson.1st Free Press pbk. ed. New York : Free Press ; London : Collier Macmillan Publishers, 1987, c1985. xiv, 450 p. : ill. ; 24 cm. Bibliography: p. 409-436. Includes indexes. ISBN 0-02-934821-8 (pbk.) LC Card 87-11901 DDC 338.7 19
1. Institutional economics. I. Title.
HB99.5 .W55 1987

Willing workers . Sengoku, Tamotsu, 1928- Westport, Conn. , c1985. xv, 153 p. : ISBN 0-89930-137-1 (lib. bdg. : alk. paper) LC Card 85-9552 DDC 306/.36 19
HD8726.5 .S37 1985 ***NYPL [JLE 86-1381]***

Willis, Jerry. SuperCalc 3 : learning, using, and mastering / Jerry Willis and William Pasewark.1st ed. Blue Ridge Summit, Pa. : Tab Books, 1986. vi, 248 p. : ill. ; 25 cm. Includes index. "No. 2694." ISBN 0-8306-0494-4 : LC Card 86-5743 DDC 005.36/9 19
1. SuperCalc 3 (Computer program). 2. Business - Data processing. I. Pasework, William Robert. II. Title.
HF5548.4.S86 W55 1986
NYPL [JSE 87-265]

Willis, Jerry, 1942- Working with SuperCalc 4 / Jerry Willis and William Pasewark. 1st ed. Blue Ridge Summit, PA : TAB Books, c1987. x, 320 p. : ill. ; 25 cm. "No. 2814." Includes index. ISBN 0-8306-0214-3 : LC Card 86-30124 DDC 005.36/9 19
1. SuperCalc 4 (Computer program). 2. Electronic spreadsheets. 3. Business - Data processing. I. Pasewark, William Robert. II. Title.
HF5548.4.S87 W54 1987

Willis, Raymond E. (Raymond Edson), 1930- A guide to forecasting for planners and managers / Raymond E. Willis. Englewood Cliffs, N.J. : Prentice-Hall, c1987. xii, 404 p. : ill. ; 24 cm. Includes bibliographies and index. ISBN 0-13-369539-5 : LC Card 86-25532 DDC 658.4/0355 19
1. Forecasting. 2. Management. 3. Planning. I. Title.
HD30.27 .W55 1987

Willke, Gerhard. Globalsteuerung und gespaltene Konjunktur : Stabilisierungspolitik bei sektoral differenziertem Zyklus / von Gerhard Willke. Leyden ; Boston : Sijthoff ; xiii, 243 p. : ill. ; 24 cm. (Publications of the European University Institute = Publications de l'Institut universitaire européen . 2) Bibliography: p. [221]-238. Includes indexes. ISBN 3-12-915020-X LC Card 84-181249
1. Unemployment - Germany (West) - Effect of inflation on. 2. Unemployment - Effect of inflation on. 3. Phillips curve. I. Series: Publications of the European University Institute , 2. II. Title.
HD5779 .W55 1978

Willman, Alpo. The BOF3 quarterly model of the Finnish economy /. Helsinki , 1985. 465 p. : ISBN 951-686-108-3 (pbk.) LC Card 86-205002 DDC 330.94897/005 s 338.5/443/094897 19
HB30 .S95 no. 59 HC340.2

Willman, Paul.
Innovation and management control : labour relations at BL Cars / Paul Willman and Graham Winch, in collaboration with A. Francis and M. Snell. Cambridge [Cambridgeshire] ; New York : Cambridge University Press, 1985. viii, 215 p. ; 23 cm. (Management and industrial relations series . 8) Includes indexes. Bibliography: p. 207-211. ISBN 0-521-26802-8 LC Card 84-17481 DDC 331/.04292/0941 19
1. British Leyland Motor Corporation. 2. Automobile industry workers - Great Britain. 3. Automobile industry and trade - Great Britain - Management - Case studies. 4. Industrial relations - Great Britain - Case studies. 5. Metro automobile. I. Winch, Graham. II. Title. III. Series.
HD8039.A82 G79 1985
NYPL [JLD 85-3102]

Technological change, collective bargaining, and industrial efficiency / Paul Willman. Oxford : Clarendon Press ; New York : Oxford University Press, c1986. xvi, 282 p. : ill. ; 23 cm. Includes indexes. Bibliography: p. [260]-275. ISBN 0-19-827262-6 : LC Card 86-5104 DDC 331.88/0941 19
1. Trade-unions - Great Britain. 2. Technological innovations - Great Britain. 3. Efficiency, Industrial - Great Britain. 4. Trade-unions - United States. 5. Technological innovations - United States. 6. Efficiency, Industrial - United States. I. Title.
HD6664 .W56 1986 ***NYPL [JLD 87-994]***

Willmott, Hugh. Gender and the labour process /. Aldershot, Hampshire, Eng. , Brookfield, Vt., U. S.A. , c1986. vii, 186 p. ; ISBN 0-566-00999-4 : LC Card 85-21977 DDC 331.4 19
HD6060.6 .G45 1986 ***NYPL [JLD 86-3900]***

Willms, Herbert, 1952- Zur Grossschadenproblematik in der Kraftfahrt-Haftpflichtversicherung / Herbert Willms. Bergisch Gladbach : J. Eul, c1986. 114 p. ; 21 cm. Bibliography: p. 111-114. ISBN 3-89012-061-X LC Card 87-104056 DDC 368.5/00943 19
1. Insurance, Liability. 2. Insurance, Liability - Germany, West. I. Title.
HG9990 .W55 1986

Willner, Johan. Economic policy under imperfect competition / Johan Willner. Åbo [Finland : Abo akademi, Nationalekonomiska institutionen], 1983. 34 p. ; 21 cm. (Meddelanden från Ekonomisk-statsvetenskapliga fakulteten vid Åbo akademi. Nationalekonomiska institutionen : Ser. A, 0358-5654 . 187) Cover title. Bibliography: p. 33-34. ISBN 951-648-926-5 (pbk.) LC Card 84-137942 DDC 338.9/00724 19
1. Competition, Imperfect - Mathematical models. 2. Economic policy - Mathematical models. I. Series: Turku, Finland. Akademi (1918-). Statsvetenskapliga fakulteten. Meddelanden. Ser. A , 187. II. Title.
HB238 .W539 1983
NYPL [JLL 77-251 no.187]

Wills, Robert L., 1954- Issues after a century of federal competition policy /. Lexington, Mass. , c1987. vii, 387 p. ; ISBN 0-669-13320-5 (alk. paper) LC Card 86-45377 DDC 338.6/048/0973 19
HD3616.U47 I77 1987

Willy Büchi, 75 Jahre / herausgegeben von Ernst-Bernd Blümle und Henner Kleinewefers. Freiburg, Schweiz : Universitätsverlag, 1982. 105 p., [1] leaf of plates : ill. ; 22 cm. Includes bibliographical references. CONTENTS. - Biographie / U. Reinhardt -- Der Professor / W. Müller -- Mentor des Schw. St. V. / A. Hürlimann -- Brief an den wissenschaftlichen Berater des VCU / R. Burkard -- Aus Willy Büchis Publikationen -- Wichtige Themen im Lebenswerk von Willy Büchi aus dem Blickwinkel der nächsten Generation -- Liste der Doktoranden. ISBN 3-7278-0263-4 LC Card 83-184580
1. Economics. 2. Büchi, Willy, 1907-. I. Büchi, Willy, 1907-. II. Blümle, Ernst-Bernd. III. Kleinewefers, Henner.
HB118 .W55 1982

Wilmot, Tom (Tom G.) Inside the over-the-counter market in the UK / Tom Wilmot. Westport, Conn. : Quorum Books, 1985. xiii, 119 p. ; 23 cm. Includes index. ISBN 0-89930-166-5 LC Card 85-24431 DDC 332.64/3/0941 19
1. Over-the-counter markets - Great Britain. 2. Over-the-counter markets - United States. I. Title.
HG5432 .W55 1985 NYPL [JLD 86-3625]

Wilsher, Peter. Strike : Thatcher, Scargill, and the miners / written and edited by Peter Wilsher, Donald Macintyre and Michael Jones, with the Sunday Times Insight Team. London : A. Deutsch, [1985] xiii, 284 p., [16] p. of plates : ill. ; 23 cm. "A Sunday times insight book"--Spine. Includes index. ISBN 0-233-97825-9 : LC Card 86-221981 DDC 331.89/2822334/0941 19
1. Coal Strike, Great Britain, 1984-1985. 2. Thatcher, Margaret. 3. Scargill, Arthur. I. Macintyre, Donald, 1937-. II. Jones, Michael, 1937-. III. Sunday Times of London Insight Team. IV. Title.
HD5365.M6152 1984 .W55 1985b

Wilson, Bryan David, 1954- Ownership and participation : the politics of employee buyouts in the United States / by Bryan David Wilson. 1985. xi, 356 ; 22 cm. "Graduate Program in Political Science." Thesis (Ph. D.)--Rutgers University, 1985. Includes abstract. Vita. Bibliography: p. 325-355. Photocopy. Ann Arbor, Mich. : University Microfilms International, 1986.
1. Employee ownership - United States. 2. Management - United States - Employee participation. I. Title. NYPL [JLD 87-209]

Wilson, Carter. Jones, Bryan D. The sustaining hand . Lawrence, Kan. , c1986. xii, 247 p. : ISBN 0-7006-0278-X : LC Card 85-24631 DDC 338.4/76292/09774 19
HD9710.U53 M433 1986
NYPL [JLE 86-2386]

Wilson, David McKenzie. Economic aspects of the Vikings in the West-the archaeological basis / David M. Wilson. Göteborg : Gothenburg University, 1980. 36 p. ; 21 cm. (The Second Félix Neubergh lecture . (Oct. 1978)) ISBN 91-7360-075-X (pbk.) LC Card 81-154587 DDC 330.94 19
1. Economic history - Medieval, 500-1500. 2. Europe - Economic conditions - To 1492. 3. Northmen. I. Series: Félix Neubergh lecture, 2nd. II. Title.
HC41 .W55 1980

Wilson, Deirdre. Sperber, Dan. Relevance . Oxford [Oxfordshire] , 1986. viii, 279 p. : ISBN 0-631-13756-4 *NYPL [JFE 86-1728]*

Wilson, Gail. Money in the family : financial organisation and women's responsibility / Gail Wilson. Aldershot, Hants., England ; Brookfield, USA : Avebury, c1987. ix, 271 p. ; 23 cm. Bibliography: p. 255-271. ISBN 0-566-05389-6 : LC Card 87-7402 DDC 339.2/2 19
1. Women - England - London - Finance, Personal. 2. Family - Economic aspects - England - London. 3. Cost and standard of living - England - London. I. Title.
HG179 .W53517 1987

Wilson, Gerald L., 1943-
Hanna, Michael S., 1939- Communicating in business and professional settings /. New York , c1988. p. cm. ISBN 0-394-36447-3 LC Card 87-12713 DDC 658.4/5 19
HD30.3 .H36 1988

Organizational communication / Gerald L. Wilson, H. Lloyd Goodall, Jr., Christopher L. Waagen. New York : Harper & Row, c1986. xiv, 322 p. : ill. ; 24 cm. Includes bibliographies and indexes. ISBN 0-06-042387-0 LC Card 85-8723 DDC 658.4/5 19
1. Organizational behavior. 2. Interpersonal communication. 3. Communication in organizations. I. Goodall, H. Lloyd. II. Waagen, Christopher L. III. Title.
HD58.7 .W55 1986 NYPL [JLE 86-2600]

Wilson, Graham K. Business and politics : a comparative introduction / Graham K. Wilson. Houndmills, Basingstoke, Hampshire : Macmillan, 1985. xii, 155 p. ; 23 cm. Bibliography: p. [149]-152. Includes index. ISBN 0-333-34091-4 LC Card 86-673508
1. Industry and state. 2. Business and politics. I. Title.
HD3611 .W55x 1985

Wilson, Hersch. Wilson, Larry. Changing the game . New York , c1987. 286 p. : ISBN 0-671-61313-8 LC Card 87-12900 DDC 658.8/5 19
HF5438.25 .W299 1987

Wilson, James A., 1928- Managing the behavioral dynamics of internal auditing / by James A. Wilson and Donna J. Wood. Altamonte Springs, Fla. : Institute of Internal Auditors Research Foundation, [1985] xii, 112 p. : ill. ; 23 cm. Bibliography: p. 95-107. ISBN 0-89413-130-3 (pbk.) LC Card 85-169744 DDC 657/.458/019 19
1. Auditing, Internal - Psychological aspects. 2. Auditors - Psychology. 3. Job stress. I. Wood, Donna, 1949-. II. Institute of Internal Auditors Research Foundation. III. Title.
HF5668.25 .W53 1985 NYPL [JLE 86-4318]

Wilson, Kim. Lucas, Martin. How to survive the 9 to 5 /. London , 1986. 175 p. ; ISBN 0-423-01930-9 (pbk.) : LC Card 86-188564 DDC 158.7 19
HF5548.85 .L825 1986

Wilson, Larry. Changing the game : the new way to sell / Larry Wilson with Hersch Wilson. New York : Simon and Schuster, c1987. 286 p. : ill. ; 23 cm. Includes index. ISBN 0-671-61313-8 LC Card 87-12900 DDC 658.8/5 19
1. Selling. I. Wilson, Hersch. II. Title.
HF5438.25 .W299 1987

Wilson Learning Corporation. Buchholz, Steve. Creating the high performance team /. New York , c1987. xiii, 202 p. : ISBN 0-471-85672-X : LC Card 86-32623 DDC 658.4/02 19
HD66 .B82 1987a

Wilson, Michael H. (Michael Holcombe), 1937- The Agenda for economic renewal . [Ottawa] [1987] 25, 26 p. : LC Card 87-140803 DDC 338.971 19
HC115 .A624 1987

A minimum tax for Canada / Michael H. Wilson. [Ottawa] : Dept. of Finance, Canada, [1985] vi, 52, 56, vi p. ; 27 cm. English and French. Title on added t.p.: Un impôt minimum au Canada. "May 1985." LC Card 86-202606 DDC 336.24/2 19
1. Income tax - Canada. 2. Income tax - Canada - Deductions. I. Title. II. Title: Impôt minimum au Canada.
HJ4661 .W54 1985

A minimum tax for Canada : executive summary / Michael H. Wilson. [Ottawa] : Dept. of Finance, Canada, [1985] iii, 15, 15, iii p. ; 27 cm. English and French. Title on added t.p.: Un impôt minimum au Canada. "May 1985." LC Card 86-202601 DDC 336.24/2 19
1. Income tax - Canada. 2. Income tax - Canada - Deductions. I. Canada. Dept. of Finance. II. Title. III. Title: Impôt minimum au Canada.
HJ4661 .W55 1985

Securing economic renewal . [Ottawa] [1987] 147, 161 p. : LC Card 87-144360 DDC 336.71 19
HJ793 .S43 1987

Wilson, Richard M. S. Financial dimensions of marketing . London , 1981. 2 v. : ISBN 0-333-25741-3 *NYPL [JLL 82-44]*

Wilson, Richard S. Corporate senior securities : analysis and evaluation of bonds, convertibles, and preferreds / Richard S. Wilson. Chicago, Ill. : Probus Pub. Co., c1987. xiv, 459 p. : ill. ; 24 cm. Includes bibliographies and index. ISBN 0-917253-79-5 : LC Card 87-6980 DDC 332.63/2 19
1. Bonds - United States. 2. Convertible bonds - United States. 3. Preferred stocks - United States. 4. Convertible preferred stocks - United States. I. Title.
HG4963 .W56 1987

Wilson, Robert Hines. Promoting high-technology industry . Boulder , 1987. 283 p. ; ISBN 0-8133-7427-8 (pbk. : alk. paper) LC Card 87-61327 DDC 338.4/762/000973 19
HC110.H53 P76 1987

Wilson, S. J. (Susannah Jane) Women, the family, and the economy / S.J. Wilson. Toronto ; New York : McGraw-Hill Ryerson, c1982. 176 p. : ill. ; 23 cm. (McGraw-Hill Ryerson series in Canadian sociology) Includes indexes. Bibliography: p. 147-167. ISBN 0-07-548028-X (pbk.) LC Card 82-123177 DDC 305.4/0971 19
1. Women - Canada. 2. Women - Employment - Canada. 3. Family - Canada. 4. Sex role - Canada. I. Title.
HQ1457 .W53 1982 NYPL [JLE 86-1735]

Wilson, William R. (William Raft), 1947- The Role of affect in consumer behavior . Lexington, Mass. , c1986. ix, 196 p. : ISBN 0-669-12874-0 (alk. paper) LC Card 85-46042 DDC 658.8/342 19
HF5415.3 .R65 1986 NYPL [JLE 86-3376]

Wilson, William W. Proceedings of a symposium on competitiveness of U. S. grains in international markets /. Fargo, N.D. [1986] ii leaves, 67 p. : LC Card 86-622839 DDC 382/.4131/0973 19
HD9035 .P76 1986

Wily, Liz. The TGLP and hunter-gatherers : a case study in land politics / by Liz Wily. Gaborone, Botswana : University College of Botswana, University of Botswana and Swaziland, 1981. ii, 102 p. ; 30 cm. (Working paper - National Institute of Development and Cultural Research, Documentation Unit . no. 33) Bibliography: p. 97-102. LC Card 82-207525
1. San (African people) - Land tenure. 2. San (African people) - Politics and government. 3. Grazing districts - Botswana. 4. Land tenure - Botswana. I. Title. II. Title: T.G.L.P. and hunter-gatherers. III. Series: Working paper (National Institute of Development and Cultural Research (Botswana). Documentation Unit) , no. 33.
DT797 W55 1981 NYPL [JLG 87-6]

Wimmera area . Land Conservation Council (Vic.) Melbourne, Vic. [1986] iii, 84 p., 3 p. of plates : ISBN 0-7241-9146-1 (pbk.) LC Card 87-161929 DDC 333.73/13/099458 19
HD1039.V5 L36 1986

Win, David. International careers : an insider's guide : where to find them, how to build them / by David Win. Charlotte, Vt. : Williamson Pub., c1987. 222 p. ; 23 cm. Bibliography: p. 221-222. ISBN 0-913589-28-4 (pbk.) : LC Card 86-32547 DDC 650.1/4 19
1. Americans - Employment - Foreign countries - Handbooks, manuals, etc. 2. Vocational guidance - Handbooks, manuals, etc. I. Title.
HF5549.5.E45 W525 1987

WIN handbook. 4th ed. [Washington, D.C.] : U. S. Dept. of Labor : U. S. Dept. of Health & Human Services, [1984]. 1 v. (various pagings) ; 28 cm. (Handbook. no. 318.) "June 1984."
1. Manpower policy - United States. 2. Welfare recipients - Employment - United States. 3. Work Incentive Program - Handbooks, manuals, etc.
NYPL [JLF 86-372]

Win-win approaches to conflict avoidance /. Gerstein, Arnold, 1940- Salt Lake City, Utah , 1986. xvii, 110 p. : ISBN 0-87905-215-5 LC Card 85-26261 DDC 303.6 19
HM136 .G46 1986 NYPL [JLD 86-2104]

Winans, R. Foster. Trading secrets / Foster Winans. 1st ed. New York : St. Martin's Press, c1986. xiv, 320 p., [8] p. of plates : ill. ; 24 cm. Includes index. ISBN 0-312-81227-2 : LC Card 86-12700 DDC 364.1/68 19
1. Winans, R. Foster. 2. Dow Jones & Co. 3. Wall Street journal. 4. Wall Street. 5. Journalists - United States. I. Title.
HG4572 .W547 1986 NYPL [JLE 86-4323]

WINANS, R. FOSTER.
Winans, R. Foster. Trading secrets /. New York , c1986. xiv, 320 p., [8] p. of plates : ISBN 0-312-81227-2 : LC Card 86-12700 DDC 364.1/68 19
HG4572 .W547 1986 NYPL [JLE 86-4323]

Winant, Howard. Stalemate : political economic origins of supply-side policy / Howard A. Winant. New York : Praeger, 1988. xv, 203 p. ; 24 cm. Bibliography: p. [195]-198. Includes index. ISBN 0-275-92706-3 (alk. paper) : LC Card 87-15157 DDC 338.973 19
1. United States - Economic policy - 1961-1971. 2. United States - Economic policy - 1971-1981. 3. United States - Economic policy - 1981-. 4. Supply-side economics - United States - History - 20th century. I. Title.
HC106.6 .W56 1988

Winch, Donald. Malthus / Donald Winch. Oxford ; New York : Oxford University Press, 1987. 117 p. ; 20 cm. (Past masters) Oxford paperbacks Bibliography: p. 111-113. Includes index. ISBN 0-19-287653-8 : LC Card 87-11179 DDC 330.15/3 19
1. Malthus, T. R. (Thomas Robert, 1766-1834. I. Title. II. Series.
HB863 .W56 1987

Winch, Graham. Willman, Paul. Innovation and management control . Cambridge [Cambridgeshire] , New York , 1985. viii, 215 p. ; ISBN 0-521-26802-8 LC Card 84-17481 DDC 331/.04292/0941 19
HD8039.A82 G79 1985
NYPL [JLD 85-3102]

Winckler, Edwin A. Contending approaches to the political economy of Taiwan /. Armonk, N.Y. , c1988. p. cm. ISBN 0-87332-440-4 : LC Card 87-16413 DDC 338.951/249 19
HC430.5 .C75 1988

WIND POWER INDUSTRY.
Worldwide remote power sites. New York, N.Y. , c1983. 2 v. (xx, xxvii, 500 p.) : LC Card 87-141748
HD9695.A2 W67 1983

Wind, Yoram. Innovation diffusion models of new product acceptance /. Cambridge, Mass. , 1986. xvi, 318 p. : ISBN 0-88730-076-6 LC Card 85-23300 DDC 658.8/343 19
HF5415.153 .I55 1986 ***NYPL [JLE 86-3235]***

Winders, Terry J., 1942- Profitable equipment leasing : a practical guide for bankers / Terry J. Winders, with Bill Williams. Boston : Bankers Pub. Co., c1987. xii, 252 p. ; 25 cm. Includes bibliographical references and index. ISBN 0-87267-101-1 : LC Card 86-26601 DDC 332.1/068/7 19
1. Industrial equipment leases - United States. 2. Banks and banking - United States. I. Williams, Bill, 1939-. II. Title.
HD39.4 .W56 1987 ***NYPL [JLE 87-1512]***

Windhorst, Karl-Götz. Wertewandel und Konsumentenverhalten : ein Beitrag zur empirischen Analyse der Konsumrelevanz individueller Wertvorstellungen in der Bundesrepublik Deutschland / Karl-Götz Windhorst. Münster : Verlag Regensberg, c1985. xxi, 299 p. : ill. ; 24 cm. (Schriften der Wissenschaftlichen Gesellschaft für Marketing und Unternehmensführung e.V. Münster . Bd. 2) Bibliography: p. 274-299. ISBN 3-7923-0520-8 LC Card 85-171929 DDC 338.5/21/0943 19
1. Consumers - Germany, West. 2. Marketing research - Germany, West. I. Title. II. Series.
HB201 .W663 1985 ***NYPL [JLE 87-369]***

Windish, David F.
Tax-advantaged investments / David F. Windish. 2nd ed. New York, N.Y. : New York Institute of Finance, c1985. xii, 404 p. : ill. ; 24 cm. Includes index. ISBN 0-13-884677-4 LC Card 84-25539 DDC 332.6/042 19
1. Investments - Taxation - United States. 2. Tax shelters - United States. I. Title.
HJ4653.A3 W56 1985 ***NYPL [JLE 85-3677]***

Tax-advantaged investments / David F. Windish. 3rd ed. New York, N.Y. : New York Institute of Finance, c1987. xix, 407 p. : ill. ; 24 cm. Includes index. ISBN 0-13-884693-6 : LC Card 87-11156 DDC 332.6/042 19
1. Investments - Taxation - United States. 2. Tax shelters - United States. I. Title.
HJ4653.A3 W56 1987

Windmuller, John P. Collective bargaining in industrialised market economies . Geneva , 1987. xii, 333 p. ; ISBN 92-2-105606-6 (pbk.) : LC Card 87-170568 DDC 331.89 19
HD6971.5 .C63 1987

Windolf, Paul. Recruitment and selection in the labour market : a comparative study of Britain and West Germany / Paul Windolf and Stephen Wood, with H.W. Horn and T. Manwaring. Aldershot, Hants, England ; Brookfield, Vt. : Avebury, c1988. p. cm. Bibliography: p. Includes index. ISBN 0-566-00937-4 : LC Card 87-19763 DDC 658.3/11/0941 19
1. Recruiting of employees - Great Britain. 2. Recruiting of employees - Germany (West). 3. Employee selection - Great Britain. 4. Employee selection - Germany (West). I. Wood, Stephen, B.A. II. Title.
HF5549.5.R44 W494 1988

Windsor, John C. (John Clayton), 1946- Spence, J. Wayne. Microcomputers in business . St. Louis , 1987. vii, 224 p. : ISBN 0-8016-5030-5 (pbk.) LC Card 86-30013 DDC 650/.028/5536 19
HF5548.2 .S728 1987

Wine and olive oil in Tuscany. Vino e olio in Toscana =. Firenze , c1985. 386 p. : LC Card 86-138958 DDC 338.4/76632/009455 19
HD9385.I82 T858 1985 ***NYPL [JSF 87-35]***

WINE AND WINE MAKING - FRANCE - CHAMPAGNE (PROVINCE) - HISTORY.
Bergeot, Paul. Champagne, la coupe est pleine . [Paris] , c1980. 185 p. ; ISBN 2-86510-001-4 : LC Card 80-120736
HD9382.7.C5 B468 1980

WINE AND WINE MAKING - LAW AND LEGISLATION - CALIFORNIA - COMPLIANCE COSTS.
Vasche, Jon David. The economic and fiscal effects of a primary source law for California wine imports. Sacramento, Calif. (925 L St., Suite 650, Sacramento 95814) [1986] vi, 130 p. : LC Card 86-622342 DDC 338.4/36632/009794 19
HD9377.C2 V37 1986

WINE AS AN INVESTMENT.
Sokolin, William. Liquid assets . New York , c1987. 163 p. : ISBN 0-02-612300-2 LC Card 86-31284 DDC 332.63 19
HD9370.5 .S65 1987

WINE INDUSTRY.
Loftus, Simon. Anatomy of the wine trade . New York , c1985. 179 p. ; ISBN 0-06-015785-2 : LC Card 87-45066 DDC 380.1/456632 19
HD9370.5 .L64 1985

Sokolin, William. Liquid assets . New York , c1987. 163 p. : ISBN 0-02-612300-2 LC Card 86-31284 DDC 332.63 19
HD9370.5 .S65 1987

WINE INDUSTRY - ARGENTINA - LA RIOJA (PROVINCE)
Análisis de la problemática actual y perspectivas futuras de las industrias vinícola y conservera hortofrutícola en La Rioja. [La Rioja, Argentina] , 1981. 97 p., [3] p. of plates : ISBN 84-7359-144-5 LC Card 86-146432
HD9384.A8 L323 1981

WINE INDUSTRY - BRAZIL - STATISTICS.
Vitivinicultura no Brasil . Bento Gonçalves, RS , 1986, c1985. 50 p. ; LC Card 87-403937 DDC 338.1/748/0981021 19
HD9384.B72 V58 1986

WINE INDUSTRY - CALIFORNIA.
Vasche, Jon David. The economic and fiscal effects of a primary source law for California wine imports. Sacramento, Calif. (925 L St., Suite 650, Sacramento 95814) [1986] vi, 130 p. : LC Card 86-622342 DDC 338.4/36632/009794 19
HD9377.C2 V37 1986

WINE INDUSTRY - EUROPEAN ECONOMIC COMMUNITY COUNTRIES.
Harza, Lajos. Az EGK szőlő- és borgazdaságának szabályozórendszere /. Budapest , 1985. 70 p. : ISBN 963-491-210-9 LC Card 86-196818
HD9259.G7 E864 1985

WINE INDUSTRY - FRANCE - CHAMPAGNE-ARDENNE.
Berger, Alain. Les récoltants vendeurs au kilo champenois face au contrat interprofessionnel /. Paris , Epernay [1984] 45, 63 p. : ISBN 2-85340-534-6 LC Card 85-111856
HD9382.7.C5 B47 1984

WINE INDUSTRY - FRANCE - CHAMPAGNE (PROVINCE) - HISTORY.
Bergeot, Paul. Champagne, la coupe est pleine . [Paris] , c1980. 185 p. ; ISBN 2-86510-001-4 : LC Card 80-120736
HD9382.7.C5 B468 1980

WINE INDUSTRY - FRANCE - NEUVILLE-SUR-SEINE - HISTORY.
Dautriat, Pierre. Vignes et vignerons d'autrefois dans le Barséquanais . Saint-Seine-l'Abbaye , c1984. 70 p. : ISBN 2-86701-018-7 : LC Card 85-117852
HD9385.F82 N483 1984

WINE INDUSTRY - GERMANY (WEST)
Janetzki, Annemarie. Das Verbundwinzersystem . Münster , 1982. xxiv, 406 p., [3] folded leaves of plates : ISBN 3-7923-0486-4 LC Card 83-157892
HD9383.5 .J35 1982

WINE INDUSTRY - GERMANY (WEST) - LÜBECK - HISTORY.
Lübecker Weinhandel . Lübeck , 1985. 260 p. : ISBN 3-924214-27-1 LC Card 86-145675
HD9383.8.L82 L82 1985

WINE INDUSTRY - HUNGARY - STATISTICS - HISTORY.
Szőlőtermelés . Budapest , 1986. 519 p. ; ISBN 963-340-777-X : LC Card 86-196884
HD9385.H82 S95 1986

WINE INDUSTRY - ITALY - MODENA (PROVINCE) - HISTORY.
Bergonzini, Renato. Arte dei brentatori a Modena /. Modena , 1983. 74 p., [5] p. of plates : LC Card 85-140349
HD8039.L72 I83 1983

WINE INDUSTRY - ITALY - PIEMONTE - HISTORY.
Rapetti, Vittorio, 1955- Uomini, collina e vigneto in Piemonte, da metà Ottocento agli anni trenta /. Alessandria , 1984. 342 p., [16] p. of plates : LC Card 86-151345
HD9385.I82 P547 1984

WINE INDUSTRY - ITALY - TUSCANY.
Vino e olio in Toscana =. Firenze , c1985. 386 p. : LC Card 86-138958 DDC 338.4/76632/009455 19
HD9385.I82 T858 1985 ***NYPL [JSF 87-35]***

WINE INDUSTRY - ITALY - TUSCANY - DIRECTORIES.
Vino e olio in Toscana =. Firenze , c1985. 386 p. : LC Card 86-138958 DDC 338.4/76632/009455 19
HD9385.I82 T858 1985 ***NYPL [JSF 87-35]***

WINE INDUSTRY - PORTUGAL - REDONDO (EVORA)
Pereira, Francisco José Piteira. A cultura da vinha na região do Redondo /. [Lisbon] , 1983. 11, 4, 30, 21 leaves, [2] leaves of plates : LC Card 84-238378
HD9259.G7 P47 1983

WINE INDUSTRY - SPAIN - CATALONIA.
Clavera, Joan. La viticultura catalana davant la integració a la Comunitat Europea /. [Barcelona] [1986] 124 p. : ISBN 6-476-84021-8 LC Card 86-200618
HD9259.G7 S693 1986

WINE MAKING. see **WINE AND WINE MAKING.**

WINEMAKING. see **WINE AND WINE MAKING.**

Wing, Robert C., 1921- A Century of service . Bellevue, Wash. , c1987. 178 p. : ISBN 0-9619061-0-3 (pbk.) : LC Card 87-16582 DDC 338.7/6136362/097977 19
HD9685.U7 P923 1987

Winge, Harald. Føringaredskaper i Aker fogderi : ca. 1650-1800 : en skifteanalyse / av Harald Winge. Oslo : Universitetet i Oslo, Institutt for folkelivsgransking, 1976. 105 p. : maps ; 21 cm. (Undersøkelser for magistergraden i etnologi . 1) "Magistergradsoppgave i etnologi, høstsemestret 1969." Bibliography: p. 102. LC Card 86-460271
1. Transportation - Norway - Oslo - History. 2. Carriages and carts - Norway - Oslo - History. 3. Aker (Oslo, Norway) - History. I. Series: Undersøkelser for mastergraden i etnologi , nr. 1. II. Title.
HE259.Z7 A48 1976

Winick, Bradley H. Making the link : coordinating economic development and employment and training : local economic development agencies / prepared by National Council for Urban Economic Development. [Washinton, D.C.] : National Alliance of Business, c1986. i, 17 p. ; 28 cm. ISBN 0-88713-678-8 (pbk.) LC Card 87-106145 DDC 331.11/0973 19
1. Manpower policy - United States. 2. Industrial promotion - United States. 3. Human capital - United States. 4. Employees, Training of - United States. 5. Local government - United States. I. National Council for Urban Economic Development. II. National Alliance of Business. III. Title. IV. Title: Local economic development agencies.
HD5724 .W557 1986

Winick, Myron. American Jewish Joint Distribution Committee. [Choroba głodowa. English.] Hunger disease . New York , c1979. xiv, 261 p. : ISBN 0-471-05003-2 LC Card 78-26397 DDC 616.3/9
RC627.S7 A43 1979
NYPL [*PXV (Warsaw) 86-3505]

Winiecki, Jan.
The distorted world of Soviet type economies / Jan Winiecki. Pittsburgh, Pa. : University of Pittsburgh Press, 1988. p. cm. (Russian and East European studies) Bibliography: p. ISBN 0-8229-1149-3 LC Card 87-25193 DDC 338.947 19
1. Central planning - Europe, Eastern. 2. Europe, Eastern - Economic conditions - 1945-. 3. Europe, Eastern - Economic policy. I. Series: Russian and East European studies (Pittsburgh, Pa.). II. Title.
HC244 .W573 1988

Rola pomocy gospodarczej w polityce zagranicznej USA wobec krajów rozwijających się / Jan Winiecki. Warszawa : Polski Instytut Spraw Międzynarodowych, 1979. 310, [1] p. ; 21 cm. (Biblioteka "Spraw międzynarodowych". nr. 67) Bibliography: p. 294-[311] LC Card 81-205172
1. Economic assistance, American - Developing countries. I. Title. II. Series.
HC60 .W54 1979

Winkelmann, Jürgen. Die Planung langfristiger Kosten : ein Konzept unter Einbeziehung von technischem Fortschritt und Investitionsentscheidungen / Jürgen Winkelmann. Thun : H. Deutsch, c1982. 281 p. : ill. ; 21 cm. (Reihe Wirtschaftwissenschaften, 0253-1488 . Bd. 265) Bibliography: p. 270-281. ISBN 3-87144-702-1 LC Card 83-129316
1. Costs, Industrial - Econometric models. I. Title. II. Series.
HD47 .W54 1982

Winkelmann, Michael. Aktienbewertung in Deutschland / Michael Winkelmann. Königstein/Ts. : Hain, c1984. xii, 242 p. : ill. ; 23 cm. (Quantitative Methoden der Unternehmungsplanung. 19) Bibliography: p. 231-242. ISBN 3-445-02377-8 LC Card 85-103576
1. Capital market - Germany (West) - Mathematical models. 2. Capital assets pricing model. 3. Arbitrage - Mathematical models. I. Title.
HG4523 .W56 1984

Winkler, Connie. Careers in high tech / Connie Winkler. New York, N.Y. : Prentice Hall Press, c1987. vi, 220 p. : ill. ; 28 cm. "An Arco book." Bibliography: p. 218. Includes index. ISBN 0-668-06537-0 (pbk.) LC Card 86-25277 DDC 331.7/02 19
1. High technology industries - Vocational guidance. I. Title.
HD8039.H54 W56 1987

Winkler, Karl. Handbuch der bayerischen Poststempel / Karl Winkler ; Mitarbeiter, Rolf Bões, Georg Hopf, Franz Pfenninger. Southfield, MI : R. Koerber, [198-?] 383 p., [18] p. of plates : ill. ; 28 cm. (Postilion publications) Reprint. Originally published: Nürnberg : K. Ulrich, 1951. LC Card 86-155089
1. Postmarks - Germany (West) - Bavaria - Catalogs. 2. Postal service - Germany (West) - Bavaria - Catalogs. I. Title. II. Series.
HE6185.G32 B389 1980z

Winkler, Wigbert M. Kostenrechnung in Klein- und Mittelbetrieben : Hemmfaktoren und betriebsspezifische Gestaltung / Wigbert M. Winkler.1. Aufl. Graz : DBV-Verlag, c1986. vi, 287 p. : ill. ; 25 cm. Bibliography: p. 265-283. ISBN 3-7041-0150-8 LC Card 87-409225
1. Cost accounting. 2. Small business - Accounting. I. Title.
HF5686.C8 W683 1986

Winn, Chris. (ill) Blacker, Terence. If I could work /. New York , c1988. p. cm. ISBN 0-397-32245-3 : LC Card 87-3972 DDC 331.7/02 19
HF5381.2 .B55 1988

Winn, Denise, 1950- The manipulated mind : brainwashing, conditioning, and indoctrination / Denise Winn. London : Octagon Press, c1983. 217 p. ; 23 cm. Bibliography: p. [213]-217. ISBN 0-86304-025-X LC Card 83-184383 DDC 302.3/3 19
1. Control (Psychology). 2. Social control. 3. Influence (Psychology). 4. Brainwashing. 5. Behavior modification. I. Title.
BF632.5 .W56 1983 ***NYPL [JFD 87-1158]***

Winn, Marie. Unplugging the plug-in drug / Marie Winn ; drawings by Karla Kuskin. New York, N.Y., U. S.A. : Penguin Books, 1987. xviii, 206 p. : ill. ; 24 cm. "Penguin original"--Lable mounted on cover. Bibliography: p. 201-202. Includes index. ISBN 0-14-008895-4 (pbk.) : LC Card 86-30655 DDC 302.2/345 19
1. Television audiences. 2. Television programs. 3. Television broadcasting. I. Title.
HE8700.65 .W56 1987

Winn, Peter. Weavers of revolution : the Yarur workers and the Chile's road to socialism / Peter Winn. New York : Oxford University Press, 1986. xiv, 328 p. : ill. ; 25 cm. Includes index. Bibliography: p. 300-315. ISBN 0-19-503960-2 : LC Card 85-18832 DDC 338.7/67721/098331 19
1. Yarur Manufacturas Chilenas de Algodón. 2. Textile workers - Chile. 3. Employee ownership - Chile - Santiago. 4. Socialism - Chile. 5. Chile - History - 1920-. I. Title.
HD8039.T42 C478 1986 ***NYPL [JLE 86-1973]***

Winner take all / [edited by] Bryce Webster. New York, NY : American Management Association, c1987. x, 222 p. ; 23 cm. ISBN 0-8144-7689-9 (pbk.) : LC Card 87-47708 DDC 658.4/09 19
1. Executives - United States - Interviews. 2. Success in business - United States. I. Webster, Bryce.
HD38.25.U6 W56 1987

Winning at work . Norris, Kenneth E. Blue Ridge Summit, PA , c1987. viii, 116 p. ; ISBN 0-8306-3077-5 : LC Card 86-27359 DDC 650.1 19
HF5548.83 .N67 1987

The winning corporation . Jagoe, A. L. (Armiger L.), 1921- Washington, D.C. , c1987. xviii, 232 p. ; ISBN 0-87491-858-9 : LC Card 87-1766 DDC 658.4 19
HD31 .J245 1987

The winning edge . Korn, Lester. New York , c1988. p. cm. ISBN 0-671-55263-5 LC Card 87-23249 DDC 658.4/09 19
HD38.2 .K67 1988

Winning on Wall Street. Zweig, Martin E. [Winning on Wall Street.] Martin Zweig's Winning on Wall Street /. New York , c1986. x, 293 p. : ISBN 0-446-51234-6 : LC Card 85-43167 DDC 332.63/22 19
HG6049 .Z87 1986 ***NYPL [JLE 86-2796]***

Winning the employment game [videorecording] / Williams & Henderson. Mt. Kisco, NY : Guidance Associates, 1981. 1 videocassette (52 min.) : sd., col. + 1 teacher's guide. Title from data sheet. Senior high school through college students. Issued as U-matic 3/4 in. or Beta 1/2 in. or VHS 1/2 in. Identifies information sources and shows how to develop a job search strategy. Gives valuable advice on job interviews and on how a new employee can keep his job. LC Card 86-707777 DDC 650.1 11
1. Job hunting. I. Williams & Henderson. II. Guidance Associates.
HF5382.7

Winning the marketing war . Michaelson, Gerald A. Lanham, MD [Cambridge, Mass.] , c1987. xv, 270 p. : ISBN 0-8191-5781-3 (alk. paper) : LC Card 87-11115 DDC 658.8 19
HF5415 .M527 1987

Winning with mutual funds / by the editors of Money magazine ; edited by Junius Ellis. Birmingham, Ala. : Oxmoor House, c1987. 224 p. : ill. (some col.) ; 26 cm. Includes index. ISBN 0-8487-0722-2 LC Card 87-61719 DDC 332.63/27 19
1. Mutual funds - United States. 2. Investments - United States. 3. Mutual funds - United States - Statistics. I. Ellis, Junius. II. Money (Birmingham, Ala.).
HG4930 .W56 1987

Winning with the insiders /. Hadady, R. Earl (Robert Earl), 1920- West Palm Beach, Fla. , c1987. vi, 115 p. : ISBN 0-9613048-8-X : LC Card 87-40003 DDC 332.64/4 19
HG4910 .H18 1987

Winrock International Institute for Agricultural Development. Gunderson, Ralph O. Agricultural and socioeconomic perspectives of Arkansas . Morrilton, AR , 1987. p. cm. ISBN 0-933595-13-1 : LC Card 87-24146 DDC 338.1/09767 19
HD1775.A8 G85 1987

Winston, Arthur. Complete guide to tested telephone collection techniques / Arthur Winston. Englewood Cliffs, N.J. : Prentice-Hall, c1988. p. cm. Includes index. ISBN 0-13-160185-7 : LC Card 87-22321 DDC 658.8/8 19
1. Collecting of accounts - United States. 2. Telephone in business. 3. Telephone etiquette. I. Title.
HG3752.7.U6 W56 1988

Winston, Clifford, 1952-
Blind intersection? : policy and the automobile industry / Clifford Winston and associates. Washington, D.C. : Brookings Institution, c1987. xii, 108 p. : ill. ; 24 cm. Includes bibliographical references and index. ISBN 0-8157-9466-5 : LC Card 87-806 DDC 338.4/76292/0973 19
1. Automobile industry and trade - Government policy - United States. I. Brookings Institution. II. Title.
HD9710.U52 W55 1987

Morrison, Steven A., 1951- The economic effects of airline deregulation /. Washington, D.C. , c1986. xi, 84 : ISBN 0-8157-5845-6 (pbk.) : LC Card 85-48202 DDC 387.7/1 19
HE9803.A4 M67 1986 ***NYPL [JLE 86-3309]***

Winston, Gordon C. The Boundaries of economics /. Cambridge , New York , 1988. xi, 122 p. ; ISBN 0-521-34450-6 LC Card 87-17772 DDC 330 19
HB33 .B68 1988

Winston, William J. Advertising handbook for health care services /. New York , c1986. xiv, 287 p. : ISBN 0-86656-390-3 : LC Card 85-27013 DDC 659.1/93621 19
HF6161.M4 A38 1986 ***NYPL [JLE 86-4539]***

Winter, Elmer L. Complete guide to making a public stock offering, by Elmer L. Winter. 2d ed. Englewood Cliffs, N.J., Prentice-Hall [1972] 295 p. illus. 29 cm. ISBN 0-13-160192-X LC Card 70-164924 DDC 658.1/52
1. Stocks - United States. 2. Corporations - United States - Finance. I. Title.
HG4028.S7 W5 1972 ***NYPL [JLF 86-390]***

Winter, J. M. The great war and the British people / J.M. Winter. Basingstoke, Hampshire : Macmillan, 1986, c1985. xiv, 360 p. : ill. ; 23 cm. Includes index. Bibliography: p. 334-349. ISBN 0-333-26582-3
1. Public health - Great Britain - History - 20th century. 2. World War, 1914-1918 - Social aspects - Great Britain. 3. Great Britain - Population - History - 20th century. 4. Great Britain - Social conditions - 20th century. I. Title. ***NYPL [JLD 86-1426]***

WINTER, MAX, 1870-1937.
Riesenfellner, Stefan. Der Sozialreporter . Wien , c1987. vi, 278 p. ; ISBN 3-900351-67-8 LC Card 87-137993 DDC 305.5/62/09436 19
HD8410 .R54 1987

Winter, Ralph Albert. Mathewson, G. Frank, 1942- Competition policy and vertical exchange /. Toronto , Buffalo , c1985. xvii, 119 p. : ISBN 0-8020-7248-8 (pbk.) LC Card 86-672936 DDC 338.6/048/0971 19
HF1480 .M37 1985 ***NYPL [JLE 87-512]***

Winter, Richard, 1946- Pretiale Lenkung bei sicheren und unsicheren Erwartungen / Richard Winter. Frankfurt am Main ; New York : P. Lang, c1986. 243 p. ; 21 cm. (Europäische Hochschulschriften. Reihe V, Volks- und Betriebswirtschaft, 0531-7339 . Bd. 761 = vol. 761 = vol. 761) Originally presented as the author's thesis (doctoral)--Johann Wolfgang Goethe-Universität, Frankfurt am Main, 1986. Bibliography: p. 234-243. ISBN 3-8204-9816-8 LC Card 87-407541 DDC 658.8/16 19
1. Transfer pricing. 2. Uncertainty. I. Series: Europäische Hochschulschriften. Reihe V, Volks- und Betriebswirtschaft , Bd. 761. II. Title.
HD62.45 .W56 1986

Winterberger, Gerhard. Über Schumpeters Geschichtsdeterminismus / von Gerhard Winterberger. Tübingen : J.C.B. Mohr (P. Siebeck), 1983. 42 p. ; 23 cm. (Vorträge und Aufsätze / Walter Eucken Institut, 0509-6065 . 95) Includes bibliographical references. ISBN 3-16-344644-2 LC Card 83-152280 DDC 330/.092/4 19
1. Schumpeter, Joseph Alois, 1883-1950. 2. Economics - History. I. Series: Vorträge und Aufsätze (Walter Eucken Institut) , 95. II. Title.
HB119.S35 W56 1983

Winters, Donald E. The soul of the wobblies : the I.W.W., religion, and American culture in the Progressive Era, 1905-1917 / Donald E. Winters. Westport, Conn. : Greenwood Press, 1985. 159 p. ; 22 cm. (Contributions in American studies, 0084-9227 . no. 81) Includes index. Bibliography: p. [147]-154. ISBN 0-313-24472-3 (lib.

bdg.) LC Card 84-27973 DDC 331.88/6 19
1. Industrial Workers of the World - History. 2. Church and labor - United States - History. 3. Sociology, Christian - United States - History. 4. United States - Social conditions - 1865-1918. I. Title. II. Series.
HD8055.I5 W56 1985 ***NYPL [JLD 87-775]***

Winterstein, Helmut.
Flexible Arbeitszeit gegen starre Sozialsysteme /. Baden-Baden , 1986. 254 p. ; ISBN 3-7890-1213-0 LC Card 87-101055 DDC 331.25/72/0943 19
HD5109.2.G3 F43 1986

Sozialpolitik in der Beschäftigungskrise /. Berlin , c1986. 2 v. : ISBN 3-428-05949-2 (Bd. I) : LC Card 87-119211 DDC 361.6/1 19
HD5710 .S67 1986

Winyard, Steve. Whiteley, Paul. Pressure for the poor . London , New York , 1987. 174 p. ; ISBN 0-416-36370-9 LC Card 87-11205 DDC 362.5/8/0941 19
HC260.P63 W47 1987

Wionczek, Miguel S.
Capital y tecnología en México y América Latina / Miguel S. Wionczek. 1a ed. México : Porrúa, 1981. 413 p. ; 23 cm. Includes bibliographical references. ISBN 968-470-018-0
1. Technological innovations - Mexico. 2. Technological innovations - Latin America. 3. Technology transfer - Latin America. 4. Latin America - Economic conditions - 1945-. I. Title. ***NYPL [JLE 87-377]***

Mercados mundiales de hidrocarburos . México, D.F. , 1983. 377 p. : ISBN 968-12-0231-7 LC Card 84-222729
HD9560.5 .M39 1983

WIPPENFÜRTH (GERMANY : KREIS) - ECONOMIC CONDITIONS.
Spilker, Ernst Moritz. Der Wirtschaftsraum zwischen den Wirtschaftsräumen . Köln , 1986. 223 p. : LC Card 87-408201 DDC 330.943/55 19
HC288.W46 S67 1986

Wir haben uns vergessen . Mihçiyazgan, Ursula. Hamburg , c1986. 428 p. ; ISBN 3-923002-30-0 : LC Card 87-104026
HD8458.T9 M54 1986

Wir hab'n ja den Kopf noch fest auf dem Hals . Engelmann, Bernt, 1921- Köln , c1987. 257 p. : ISBN 3-462-01688-1 LC Card 87-146658
HC286.5 .E594 1987

Wir und die Dritte Welt . Neundörfer, Konrad. Köln , c1985. x, 214 p. ; ISBN 3-452-20304-2 LC Card 85-164555
HC59.7 .N375 1985

The wired world . Martin, James, 1933- Carnforth, Lancashire, England , 1986. xiii, 140 p. : ISBN 0-906774-49-7 (pbk.) LC Card 87-157689 DDC 384 19
HE7631 .M373 1986

Wirken Substanzsteuern investitionshemmend? /. Heurung, Rainer-Otto, 1952- Frankfurt am Main , New York , c1986. xvii, 251, [93] p. : ISBN 3-8204-9800-1 LC Card 87-408762 DDC 332.63 19
HG4028.C4 H49 1986

Wirksamkeitsuntersuchung zum A.D.A.C.-Motorrad-Sicherheitstraining.
Grosse-Berndt, Gisela. Wirksamkeitsuntersuchung zum ADAC-Motorrad-Sicherheitstraining. Köln [1983] iii, 160, ii, 112, 27 p. : LC Card 84-147564
HE5614.5.G3 G75 1983

Wirksamkeitsuntersuchung zum ADAC-Motorrad-Sicherheitstraining.
Grosse-Berndt, Gisela. Köln [1983] iii, 160, ii, 112, 27 p. : LC Card 84-147564
HE5614.5.G3 G75 1983

Wirkung von Werbesprache . Conen, Dieter, 1951- München , c1985. iii, 162 p., [7] p. of plates : ISBN 3-89003-021-1 LC Card 86-159595
HF5822 .C58 1985

Die Wirkungen von Sonderfahrstreifen für Busse auf die Fahrzeiten im Individualverkehr und öffentlichen Personenahverkehr . Busse, Dieter. Münster [1985?] xii, 274 p. : ISBN 3-88660-264-8 LC Card 86-138804
HE363.G34 M933 1985

Wirkungsanalyse für segmentspezifische Warentestwerbung . Buschmann, Vera, 1951- Frankfurt am Main , New York , c1986. xii, 270 p. : ISBN 3-8204-9275-5 LC Card 86-220570
HF5827 .B87 1986

Wirosuhardjo, Kartomo. Kamus istilah demografi /. Jakarta , 1985. vi, 119 p. ; LC Card 86-941191
HB849.2 .K35 1985

Wirth, John D.
Latin American oil companies and the politics of energy /. Lincoln , c1985. xxxix, 282 p. : ISBN 0-8032-4728-1 (alk. paper) LC Card 84-29457 DDC 338.7/6223382/098 19
HD9574.L3 L38 1985 ***NYPL [JLD 86-1289]***

State and society in Brazil . Boulder , 1987. x, 349 p. ; ISBN 0-8133-7401-4 (pbk. : alk. paper) : LC Card 87-2160 DDC 981/.063 19
HC187 .S78 1987

Wirtschaft. Die Wirtschaft heute /. Mannheim , 1980. 638 p. : ISBN 3-411-01793-7 LC Card 86-673960
HB175 .W5934x 1980

Die Wirtschaft der Vereinigten Staaten und der Bundesrepublik Deutschland : Verantwortung und Herausforderung in einer sich wandelnden Welt = The economies of the United States and the Federal Republic of Germany : responsibilities and challenges in an [sic] changing world / [herausgegeben von] C. Robert Dickerman, Dieter Oberndörfer. Bonn : Eichholz, c1977. 106 p. ; 23 cm. (Sozialwissenschaftliche Studien zur Politik. Bd. 11) English and German. Papers presented at a conference held 1977, sponsored by the Sozialwissenschaftliche Forschungsinstitut of the Konrad-Adenauer-Stiftung and by the U. S. Embassy in W. Germany. PARTIAL CONTENTS. - Nationale Wirtschaftspolitik und aussenwirtschaftliche Zielsetzungen / Peter Hermes -- Domestic and international considerations and priorities in President Carter's economic policies / F. Ray Marshall -- Die Rolle und die Verantwortung der führenden Wirtschaftsmächte in der Weltwirtschaft / Karl-Heinz Narjes -- The new world economic order and the challenge to national decision-making / Anne O. Krueger -- Perspectives on the economic policy of the Carter administration / Charles L. Schultze. ISBN 3-87198-079-X LC Card 86-104673
1. United States - Economic policy - 1971-1981 - Congresses. 2. United States - Economic conditions - 1971-1981 - Congresses. 3. Germany, West - Economic policy - 1974- - Congresses. 4. Germany, West - Economic conditions - 1974- - Congresses. I. Dickerman, C. Robert. II. Oberndörfer, Dieter. III. Konrad-Adenauer-Stiftung. Sozialwissenschaftliches Forschungsinstitut. IV. United States. Embassy (Germany : West). V. Title: Economies of the United States and the Federal Republic of Germany. VI. Series.
HC106.7 .W57 1977

Wirtschaft des Saarlandes 1985.
Landeszentralbank im Saarland. Landeszentralbank im Saarland . Saarbrücken , 1986. 45, xii p. : LC Card 86-176290
HC287.S23 L35 1986

Die Wirtschaft heute / bearbeitet von Manfred E. Streit ... [et al.]. 2., vollständig überarbeitete Aufl. Mannheim : Bibliographisches Institut Mannheim : Meyers Lexikonverlag, 1980. 638 p. : ill. ; 23 cm. (Wie funktioniert das) Meyer Nachschlagewerk Spine title: Wirtschaft. Includes bibliographical references and index. ISBN 3-411-01793-7 LC Card 86-673960
1. Economics. 2. Germany, West - Economic conditions. I. Streit, Manfred E. II. Title: Wirtschaft.
HB175 .W5934x 1980

Wirtschaft im Untergrund / Stephan Burgdorff, (Hg.). Reinbek bei Hamburg : Rowohlt, 1983. 188 p. : ill. ; 19 cm. (Spiegel-Buch. 35) Bibliography: p. 185-187. CONTENTS. - Signal für eine bessere Zukunft / Stephan Burgdorff -- Ein Rettungsring für unser ganzes System / Bernhard Müller-Hülsebusch -- Fast tausend reisende Bittsteller pro Fabrik / Fritjof Meyer -- Es ist unglaublich, was da läuft / Hermann Bott -- Drastisch und von Dauer / Klaus-Peter Kerbusk -- Engagiert und ernsthaft, spielerisch und experimentell / Reimar Oltmanns -- Ein alter Ganoventraum wird neu / Norbert F. Pötzl -- Für die Statistik ist es besser, sich an Eierdiebe zu halten / Dagobert Lindlau -- Die Spuren werden verwischt / Werner W. Pommerehne, Bruno S. Frey -- Arbeit und Vergnügen sind keine Widersprüche mehr / Ottheinrich Freiherr von Weitershausen -- Marx hat die falschen Beispiele gewählt / Johano Strasser -- Der duale Weg ist billiger, besser und beliebter / Joseph Huber. ISBN 3-499-33035-0 : LC Card 83-206566
1. Black market - Germany (West) - Addresses, essays, lectures. 2. Informal sector (Economics) - Germany (West) - Addresses, essays, lectures. I. Burgdorff, Stephan, 1944-.
HF5482.65.G3 W57 1983
NYPL [JLC 86-265]

Wirtschaft, Staat und Macht . Schmid, Hanspeter, 1951- Zürich [c1983] 432 p. : ISBN 3-85791-073-9 (Schw. Buch) LC Card 83-244266
HF1573 .S335 1983

Wirtschaft und Besatzung in Serbien, 1941-1944 . Schlarp, Karl-Heinz. Stuttgart , 1986. viii, 443 p., [6] p. of plates : ISBN 3-515-04401-9 LC Card 86-181062
HC407.Z7 S46676 1986

Wirtschaft und Gesellschaft in Deutschland und Grossbritannien im Übergang zum "organisierten Kapitalismus" . Berg, Werner. Berlin , c1984. 888 p. : ISBN 3-428-05495-4 LC Card 84-222230
HD9553.7.R8 B47 1984

Wirtschaft und Gesellschaft in Südosteuropa . (Bd. 4) Doh, Rainer. Bevölkerungsentwicklung, Wirtschaftsordnung und Industrialisierungsprozess in Südosteuropa . Neuried , c1985. [12], 486, 19 p. : ISBN 3-88893-045-6 LC Card 87-140271 DDC 304.6/09498 19
HB3631 .D64 1985

Wirtschaft und Umweltschutz / mit Beiträgen von Franz Joseph Dreyhaupt ... [et al.]. Heidelberg : C.F. Müller, 1986. vii, 147 p. : ill. ; 22 cm. (Justiz und Recht . Bd. 3) Papers presented at a meeting held at the Deutsche Richterakademie in Trier, Dec. 1985. Includes bibliographical references and index. ISBN 3-8114-2786-5 LC Card 87-134163 DDC 363.7/058/0943 19
1. Environmental policy - Germany, West. I. Dreyhaupt, Franz Joseph, 1925-. II. Deutsche Richterakademie. III. Series.
HC290.5.E5 W57 1986

Die wirtschaftliche Betrachtungsweise im Steuerrecht /. Urbas, Helmut, 1951- Frankfurt am Main , New York , c1987. viii, 392 p. : ISBN 3-8204-0915-7 LC Card 87-409061 DDC 336.24/0943 19
HJ4719 .U7 1987

Wirtschaftliche Datenerfassung in Klein- und Mittelbetrieben . Bendeich, E. (Eugen), 1945- München , c1979. 211 p. : ISBN 3-478-41740-6 LC Card 85-171162
HD62.7 .B4 1979

Die Wirtschaftliche Entwicklung in den sozialistischen Ländern Osteuropas zur Jahreswende 1985/86 / herausgegeben von Klaus Bolz ; mit Beiträgen über Bulgarien, Ilse Grosser ... [et al.]. Hamburg : Verlag Weltarchiv, 1986. 336 p. ; 24 cm. (Veröffentlichungen des HWWA-Institut für Wirtschaftsforschung-Hamburg, 0722-4729) Includes bibliographical references. CONTENTS. - Bulgarien / Ilse Grosser -- Deutsche Demokratische Republik / Peter Plötz -- Polen / Hubert Gabrisch -- Rumänien / Petra Pissulla -- Sowjetunion / Sybille Reymann -- Tschechoslowakei / Franz-Lothar Altmann -- Ungarn / Andreas Wass von Czege. ISBN 3-87895-295-3 LC Card 86-185852
1. Europe, Eastern - Economic conditions - 1945-. 2. Communist countries - Economic conditions. I. Bolz, Klaus. II. Grosser, Ilse. III. Series.
HC244 .W5776 1986

Die Wirtschaftliche Expansion der USA : Asien und Afrika / [Redaktionsbeirat, P. Fedossejew ... et al.]. Moskau : Redaktion "Gesellschaftswissenschaften und Gegenwart", 1986. 175 p. ; 21 cm. (Probleme der modernen Welt . 55) Bibliography: p. 162-[167]. CONTENTS. - Wirtschaftliche Faktoren in der Afrika-Politik der USA / An. Gromyko -- Der Vormarsch US-amerikanischer Monopole / M. Otschkow -- Die USA als führende Kraft des Neokolonialismus / G. Rostschin -- Wirtschaftliche Versklavung dem Decknamen "Entwicklungshilfe" / J. Kondraschow -- Handels- und Wirtschaftsbeziehungen / R. Simenkow -- Die USA und die ASEAN-Länder / A. Parkanski -- USA-Indien / N. Beglowa -- Die USA und die Länder des Nahen und Mittleren Ostens / R. Simenkow. LC Card 87-408806 DDC 337.7305 19
1. United States - Foreign economic relations - Asia. 2. Asia - Foreign economic relations - United States. 3. United States - Foreign economic relations - Africa. 4. Africa - Foreign economic relations - United States. 5.

Asia - Dependency on United States. 6. Africa - Dependency on United States. I. Fedoseev, Petr Nikolaevich. II. Series.
HF1456.5.A64 W57 1986

Wirtschaftliche und soziale Entwicklungen in Brandenburg, Preussen, Schlesien und Oberschlesien in den Jahren 1640-1853, Frühindustrialisierung in Oberschlesien /. Wolffsohn, Seew, 1916- Frankfurt am Main , New York , c1985. 182 p., [2] p. of folded plates : ISBN 3-8204-8197-4 LC Card 85-219539
HC288.B68 W65 1985

Die wirtschaftliche Ungleichheit im Rentenalter in der Schweiz /. Lüthi, Ambros, 1938- Freiburg/Schweiz , 1983. 229 p. : ISBN 3-7278-0282-0 : LC Card 83-163287
HD7105.35.S9 L87 1983

Wirtschaftliche Zusammenarbeit zwischen den Entwicklungsländern . Langhammer, Rolf J. Tübingen , c1984. xi, 135 p. : ISBN 3-16-344889-5 : LC Card 85-143693
HF1413 .L363 1984

Die wirtschaftlichen Wirkungen der Fluktuation in der Einzelwirtschaft . Kaufhold, Klaus, 1943- Frankfurt am Main , New York , c1985. 357 p. : ISBN 3-8204-5665-1 LC Card 85-195373
HF5429 .K4156 1985

Wirtschaftlicher Wandel, religiöser Wandel und Wertwandel : Folgen für das politische Verhalten in der Bundesrepublik Deutschland / herausgegeben von Dieter Oberndörfer, Hans Rattinger, Karl Schmitt. Berlin : Duncker & Humblot, c1985. 411 p. : ill. ; 24 cm. (Ordo Politicus. Bd. 25) Includes bibliographies. ISBN 3-428-05784-8 LC Card 85-218417
1. Germany (West) - Economic conditions - 1974- - Mathematical models. 2. Elections - Germany (West) - Mathematical models. 3. Religion and politics - Germany (West) - Mathematical models. I. Oberndörfer, Dieter. II. Rattinger, Hans. III. Schmitt, Karl. IV. Series.
HC286.7 .W58 1985

Wirtschaftlichkeitsanalyse von Banken . Gach, Christian. Wien , c1983. iv, 75, iii, 89 p. ; ISBN 3-85428-017-3 : LC Card 84-118578
HG3008 .G28 1983

Wirtschafts-, Berufs- und Sozialpädagogische Texte .
(Bd. 2) Neven, Peter, 1953- Arbeits- und Freizeitpädagogik . Düsseldorf [1982?] 424 p. ; ISBN 3-87864-087-0 LC Card 84-119072
HD4901 .N47 1982

Wirtschafts- und sozialwissenschaftliche Forschungsbeiträge .
(Bd. 1) Ibler, Josef. Nominallohnentwicklung in der Bundesrepublik Deutschland . Regensburg , c1986. 256 p. : ISBN 3-924956-18-9 LC Card 87-118941 DDC 331.2/943 19
HD5029 .I2 1986

(Bd. 2) Finke, B. (Barbara) Studien zur kommunalen Industrieförderung im 20. Jahrhundert . Regensburg , c1986. 125, [45], xxv p. : ISBN 3-924956-19-7 : LC Card 87-129091 DDC 338.943/34 19
HC289.R36 F56 1986

Wirtschafts- und sozialwissenschaftliche Ostmitteleuropa-Studien .
(6) Regionale Aspekte der Wirtschaftsplanung in den Mitteleuropäischen RGW-Staaten. Marburg/Lahn , 1983. 95 p. : ISBN 3-87969-178-9 LC Card 84-249235
HC270.28 .R42 1983

Wirtschafts- und finanzpolitische Entscheidungsprozesse in England in der ersten Hälfte des 19. Jahrhunderts /. Braun, Hans-Joachim. Frankfurt am Main , New York , c1984. 236 p. : ISBN 3-8204-7702-0 LC Card 85-191319 DDC 338.941 19
HC255 .B77 1984

Wirtschafts- und sozialgeographische Untersuchung über das Heimgewerbe in Nordafghanistan unter besonderer Berücksichtigung der Mittelstadt Sar-e-Pul . Jebens, Albrecht. Tübingen , 1983. xii, 415 p., [2] folded leaves of plates : LC Card 86-128235
HD2346.A52 S275 1983

Wirtschafts- und Sozialgeschichte des Deutschen Kaiserreichs (1867/71-1914) /. Born, Karl Erich. Stuttgart , 1985. 175 p. ; ISBN 3-515-02419-0 LC Card 85-168335
HC285 .B66 1985

Wirtschaftsarchive und Kammern--Aspekte wirtschaftlicher selbstverwaltung gestern und heute : Referate und Diskussionsbeiträge des wissenschaftlichen Symposiums aus Anlass des 75jährigen Bestehens des Rheinisch-Westfälischen Wirtschaftsarchivs am 28. und 29. Januar 1982 in Köln / herausgegeben vom Rheinisch-Westfälischen Wirtschaftsarchiv zu Köln, e.V. ; [Herausgeber, Friedrich-Wilhelm Henning ; Schriftleitung, Klara van Eyll]. Köln : Das Archiv, 1982. 250 p. ; 24 cm. (Schriften zur rheinisch-Westfälischen Wirtschaftsgeschichte. Bd. 34) Includes bibliographical references. LC Card 86-198576
1. Germany (West) - Economic conditions - Archival resources - Germany (West) - Congresses. 2. Germany (West) - Industries - Archival resources - Germany (West) - Congresses. 3. Boards of trade - Germany (West) - Archival resources - Germany (West) - Congresses. I. Henning, Friedrich-Wilhelm. II. Rheinisch-Westfälisches Wirtschaftsarchiv. III. Series.
HC286 .W59 1982

Das Wirtschaftsbürgertum in Bayern 1890-1914 . Hesselmann, Hans. [Stuttgart] , 1985. 419 p. : ISBN 3-515-04565-1 LC Card 86-127555
HC287.B3 H46 1985

Wirtschaftsdemokratie gegen Wirtschaftskrise : über die Neuordnung ökonomischer Machtverhältnisse / Heiner Heseler, Rudolf Hickel (Hrsg.) ; mit Beiträgen von Heinz Bierbaum ... [et al.]. Hamburg : VSA-Verlag, 1986. 177 p. : ill. ; 21 cm. Includes bibliographies. CONTENTS. - Wirtschaftskrise, Wirtschaftsdemokratie und Vergesellschaftung / Heiner Heseler, Rudolf Hickel -- Vergesellschaftung der Stahlindustrie / Rudolf Judith, Jürgen Peters -- ARBED-Saarstahl und regionale wirtschaftspolitische Optionen / Hans Joachim Hoffmann -- Ziele, Aufgaben und Bedeutung öffentlicher Unternehmen in der Bundesrepublik Deutschland / Dieter Vesper -- Zur Frage wirtschaftlicher Macht im SPD-Programmentwurf, "Die Wirtschaft ökologisch und sozial erneuern" / Norbert Wieczorek -- Wirtschaftsdemokratie in Westeuropa / Rudolf Kuda, Horst Neumann -- Wirtschaftsdemokratie und Vergesellschaftung / Heinz Bierbaum, Nikolaus Schmidt -- Wirtschaften im Vakuum? / Detlef Dunker -- Staatseigentum und demokratischer Staat / Jörg Huffschmid -- Erfahrungen mit Verstaatlichungen im Schiffbau / Detlef Rother, Robert Kappel. ISBN 3-87975-310-5 LC Card 86-193914
1. Government ownership - Germany, West. 2. Business cycles - Germany (West). I. Heseler, Heiner. II. Hickel, Rudolf. III. Bierbaum, Heinz.
HD4175 .W54 1986

Wirtschaftsentwicklung und landwirtschaftliche Verbandspolitik . Sondermann, Klaus. Münster-Hiltrup , 1983. vi, 300 p. : ISBN 3-7843-0283-1 : LC Card 84-126226
HD1486.G3 S66 1983

Wirtschaftsentwicklung und soziale Sicherheit : interdisziplinäre Fachtagung 18. und 19. Juni 1982, Philipps-Universität Marburg / Marburger Arbeitskreis für Sozialrecht und Sozialpolitik. Köln : C. Heymann, 1983. viii, 146 p. : ill. ; 21 cm. (Sozialpolitik und Recht . Bd. 6) PARTIAL CONTENTS. - 10 Jahre Krankenhausfinanzierungsgesetz / Thomas Zickgraf -- Gefahren des Wohlfahrtsstaates aus ökonomischer Sicht / Walter Hamm -- Probleme des Arbeitsmarktes in den 80er Jahren / Dieter Mertens -- Der Arzt im Spannungsfeld zwischen Kostendämpfung und Heilauftrag / Horst Joachim Rheindorf -- Die Sicherung der betrieblichen Altersversorgung in der Wirtschaftsrezession / Gerhard Höhne. ISBN 3-452-19567-8 LC Card 84-106615
1. Insurance, Hospitalization - Germany (West) - Congresses. 2. Social security - Germany (West) - Congresses. I. Philipps-Universität Marburg. II. Marburger Arbeitskreis für Sozialrecht und Sozialpolitik. III. Series.
HG9399.G32 W57 1983

Wirtschaftsfaktor Mittelstand . Gruhler, Wolfram. Köln , c1984. 195 p. : ISBN 3-602-34845-8 (pbk.) LC Card 87-672069
HD2346.G3 G78x 1984

Wirtschaftsgeologische Aspekte bei der privaten Investition in Öl- und Gasbohrvorhaben in den USA /. Meurer, Heinrich W., 1950- [Cologne? , 1982] (Aachen : Fotodruck J. Mainz) vi, 163 p., [3] folded leaves of plates : LC Card 84-200100
HD9565 .M48 1982

Wirtschaftsgeschichte Baden-Württembergs . Boelcke, Willi A. Stuttgart , c1987. 725 p., [80] p. of plates : ISBN 3-8062-0423-3 LC Card 87-152351 DDC 330.943/46 19
HC287.B23 B63 1987

Wirtschaftsgeschichte der Bundesrepublik Deutschland (1945-1980) /. Abelshauser, Werner. Frankfurt am Main , 1983. 186 p. : ISBN 3-518-11241-4 : LC Card 83-180531
HC286.7 .A26 1983

Wirtschaftsgeschichte Kroatiens im nationalsozialistischen Grossraum 1941-1945 . Sundhaussen, Holm. Stuttgart , 1983. 386 p. : ISBN 3-421-06150-5 LC Card 83-242921
HC407.Z7 C7678 1983

Wirtschaftsgeschichte Polens im neunzehnten und zwanzigsten Jahrhundert. Landau, Zbigniew. Wirtschaftsgeschichte Polens im 19. und 20. Jahrhundert /. Berlin , 1986. vi, 300 p. : LC Card 86-223591
HC340.3 .L367 1986

Wirtschaftsgeschichte Polens im 19. und 20. Jahrhundert /. Landau, Zbigniew. Berlin , 1986. vi, 300 p. : LC Card 86-223591
HC340.3 .L367 1986

Wirtschaftsinformatik-Lexikon /. Heinrich, Lutz J. (Lutz Jürgen) München , c1986. xxi, 539 p. : ISBN 3-486-20045-3 LC Card 87-122992 DDC 330/.03/31 19
HB61 .H365 1986

Wirtschaftsinformatik und quantitative Betriebswirtschaftslehre .
(21) Hall, Bruno. Kapazitätsfestlegung in Distributionssystemen /. München , c1986. xiii, 266 p. ; ISBN 3-597-10558-0 LC Card 87-127684 DDC 658.7/88 19
HF5415.6 .H35 1986

Wirtschaftskarten von Österreich / Herausgeber, Arbeitswissenschaftliches Institut der Deutschen Arbeitsfront. Berlin : Das Institut, 1938. 38 p. : ill., maps ; 21 x 30 cm. LC Card 86-179061
1. Austria - Economic conditions - 1918-1945. 2. Austria - Economic conditions - 1918-1945 - Maps. 3. Labor supply - Austria. 4. Labor supply - Austria - Maps. I. Deutsche Arbeitsfront. Arbeitswissenschaftliches Institut.
HC265 .W554 1938

Wirtschaftskooperation mit China . Wiesegart, Kurt. Hamburg , 1984. 126 p. ; ISBN 3-87895-260-0 LC Card 85-146617
HF1604.Z4 E869 1984

Wirtschaftskraft und Wirtschaftsentwicklung in den Bundesländern seit 1970 . Körber-Weik, Margot. Tübingen , 1986. x, 271 p. ; ISBN 3-88573-303-X LC Card 87-401375 DDC 330.943/0878 19
HC286.6 .K67 1986

Wirtschaftskrieg oder Entspannung? : eine politische Bilanz der Ost-West-Wirtschaftsbeziehungen / Reinhard Rode, Hanns-D. Jacobsen (Hg.). Bonn ; Verlag Neue Gesellschaft, c1984. 328 p. ; 22 cm. (Reihe Weltwirtschaft) Includes bibliographical references. ISBN 3-87831-392-6 LC Card 84-251713
1. East-West trade (1945-). I. Rode, Reinhard, 1947-. II. Jacobsen, Hanns-Dieter, 1944-. III. Series: Reihe Weltwirtschaft (Bonn, Germany).
HF4050 .W57 1984

Wirtschaftslexikon / herausgegeben von Arthur [i.e. Artur] Woll ; [Redaktion, Lektorat und Verfasser von ungezeichneten Stichwörtern, Gerald Vogl, Martin Weigert]. München : R. Oldenbourg, c1987. xv, 661 p. : ill. ; 20 cm. ISBN 3-486-29691-4 LC Card 87-127454 DDC 330/.03/31 19
1. Economics - Dictionaries - German. I. Woll, Artur, 1923-. II. Vogl, Gerald. III. Weigert, Martin, Dipl.-Volkswirt.
HB61 .W558 1987

Die Wirtschaftsplanung Gabuns /. Heldt, Sven. Kiel , 1978. 31 leaves ; LC Card 85-238709
HC975 .H45 1978

Wirtschaftspolitik /. Woll, Artur, 1923- München , c1984. xiv, 385 p. : ISBN 3-8006-1079-5 LC Card 87-672745
HD84 .W62x 1984

Wirtschaftspolitik im britischen Besatzungsgebiet 1945-1949 / herausgegeben von Dietmar

Petzina und Walter Euchner. 1. Aufl. Düsseldorf : Schwann, 1984. 338 p. : ill. ; 22 cm. (Düsseldorfer Schriften zur neueren Landesgeschichte und zur Geschichte Nordrhein-Westfalens . Bd. 12) Bibliography: p. 331-336. ISBN 3-590-18124-9 LC Card 84-188669
1. Germany - Economic conditions - 1945-. 2. Germany - Economic policy - 1945-. 3. Germany - History - Allied occupation, 1945-. 4. Reconstruction (1939-1951) - Germany. 5. Great Britain - Foreign relations - Germany. 6. Germany - Foreign relations - Great Britain. I. Petzina, Dietmar, 1938-. II. Euchner, Walter. III. Series.
HC286.5 .W5655 1984

Wirtschaftspolitik und Arbeitnehmerinteressen : zum hundertsten Geburtstag von John Maynard Keynes / Harald Mattfeldt (Hrsg.). Pönitz : Mildner, 1986. 198 p. ; 22 cm. Papers presented at a conference held in 1983. Includes bibliographies. CONTENTS. - John Maynard Keynes und die Herausforderungen moderner Wirtschaftspolitik / Klaus von Dohnanyi -- Keynesianismus als gesellschaftliche Theorie der Beschäftigung, der Verteilung und der Produktion / Ewald Nowotny -- Einige Anmerkungen zu Nowotnys Beitrag / Kurt W. Rothschild -- Keynesianische Politik in der Bundesrepublik Deutschland / Karl Georg Zinn -- Austro-Keynesianismus / Hans Seidel -- Keynesianismus in Schweden / Gösta Dahlström -- Sozialdemokratische Wirtschaftspolitik und Strategien ihrer Durchsetzung / Herbert Ehrenberg -- Die wirtschaftspolitischen Vorstellungen der SPD / Rudolf Hickel -- Keynesianismus als Grundlage arbeitnehmerorientierter Wirtschaftspolitik / Herbert Schui -- Durchsetzungschancen und Schwierigkeiten einer arbeitnehmerorientierten Wirtschaftspolitik / Detlev Hensche. ISBN 3-923826-06-0 LC Card 86-162801
1. Keynesian economics - Congresses. 2. Germany, West - Economic policy - Congresses. 3. Keynes, John Maynard, 1883-1946 - Congresses. I. Keynes, John Maynard, 1883-1946. II. Mattfeldt, Harald, 1943-.
HB99.7 .W57 1986

Wirtschaftspolitik und wirtschaftliche Entwicklung : Festschrift für Walter Hesselbach zum 70. Geburtstag / Jochem Langkau, Claus Köhler (Hg.) ; mit einem Geleitwort von Helmut Schmidt ; [Übersetzung des Beitrags von A. Cotta aus dem Französischen und der Beiträge von T. Barker ... et al., aus dem Englischen, Thomas Binder]. Bonn : Verlag Neue Gesellschaft, c1985. xii, 248 p. : ill., 1 port. ; 24 cm. Includes bibliographical references. ISBN 3-87831-405-1 LC Card 85-142846
1. Economic policy. 2. Economic development. 3. Monetary policy. 4. Hesselbach, Walter. I. Hesselbach, Walter. II. Langkau, Jochem. III. Köhler, Claus.
HD75 .W57 1985

Wirtschaftspolitische Studien.
(68) Feldmann, Berthold. Unternehmenskonzentration, Marktmacht und Lohnniveau . Göttingen , c1984. xii, 260 p. : ISBN 3-525-12269-1 LC Card 85-162393
HD2746.5 .F45 1984

Der Wirtschaftsraum zwischen den Wirtschaftsräumen . Spilker, Ernst Moritz. Köln , 1986. 223 p. : LC Card 87-408201 DDC 330.943/55 19
HC288.W46 S67 1986

Wirtschaftsrecht und Wirtschaftsverfassung .
(Bd. 11) Esser, Carsten, 1960- Das Fremdkapital im Unternehmen als Insolvenzursache und die Möglichkeiten rechtlicher Steuerung der Finanzierungsgrundlagen /. Frankfurt am Main , New York , c1986. xvi, 131 p. (1 folded) ; ISBN 3-8204-9398-0 LC Card 86-229108
HG5501 .E85 1986

Wirtschaftsreformen und neue Entwicklungsstrategien in der Volksrepublik China / Harald Mey, Reinhard Roericht, Manfred F. Romich (Hrsg.). Frankfurt am Main ; New York : P. Lang, c1986. 185 p. ; 21 cm. (Aachener Beiträge zur vergleichenden Soziologie und zur China-Forschung, 0178-1332 . Bd. 1) Papers presented at the 2nd Aachener China-Symposium organized by the Institut für Soziologie and the Büro Technologie-Transfer both of the Rheinisch-Westfälische Technische Hochschule Aachen and the Gesellschaft für Deutsch-Chinesische Freundschaft and held Jan. 1983. Includes bibliographical references. ISBN 3-8204-9101-5 LC Card 86-220822
1. China - Economic policy - 1976- - Congresses. 2. China - Economic conditions - 1976- - Congresses. 3. China - Foreign economic relations - Germany (West) - Congresses. 4. Germany (West) - Foreign economic relations - China - Congresses. I. Mey, Harald. II. Roericht, Reinhard. III. Romich, Manfred F. IV. Aachener China-Symposium (2nd : 1983). V. Rheinisch-Westfälische Technische Hochschule Aachen. Institut für Soziologie. VI. Rheinisch-Westfälische Technische Hochschule Aachen. Büro Technologie-Transfer. VII. Gesellschaft für Deutsch-Chinesische Freundschaft. VIII. Series.
HC427.92 .W56 1986

Wirtschaftsregulierung in wettbewerbspolitischen Ausnahmebereichen . Weber, Rolf H. Baden-Baden , 1986. 710 p. : ISBN 3-7890-1288-2 LC Card 87-128141
HD3616.S93 W425 1986

Wirtschaftssanktionen im Ost-West-Verhältnis : Rahmenbedingungen und Modalitäten / Friedemann Müller ... [et al.].1. Aufl. Baden-Baden : Nomos, 1983. 234 p. : ill. ; 23 cm. (Aktuelle Materialien zur internationalen Politik . Bd. 1) Errata slip inserted. Includes bibliographical references. ISBN 3-7890-0963-6 LC Card 84-132150
1. Economic sanctions. 2. World politics - 1945-. I. Müller, Friedemann. II. Series.
HF1413.5 .W57 1983

Wirtschaftsstruktur und Semantik . Krauth, Wolf-Hagen. Berlin , c1984. 278 p. ; ISBN 3-428-05728-7 LC Card 85-143046
HB107.A2 K69 1984

Ein Wirtschaftssystem der Zukunft /. Šik, Ota, 1919- Berlin , New York , c1985. 202 p. ; ISBN 0-387-15137-0 (U. S.) LC Card 85-199175
HB90 .S56 1985

Wirtschaftstheorie und Unwissen . Tietzel, Manfred. Tübingen , 1985. viii, 208 p. ; ISBN 3-16-944919-2 LC Card 86-147807
HB175 .T55 1985

Wirtschaftsuniversität Wien. Interdisciplinary Institute for Urban and Regional Studies. International economic restructuring and the regional community /. Aldershot, Hants, England , Brookfield, Vt., USA , c1987. x, 404 p. : ISBN 0-566-05478-7 : LC Card 87-11841 DDC 330.9 19
HF1412 .I574 1987

Wirtschaftsunterricht an allgemeinbildenden Schulen in Baden-Württemberg . Zarth, Michael. Tübingen , 1987. x, 241 p. ; ISBN 3-88573-028-6 : LC Card 87-419933 DDC 330/.07/104346 19
HB74.9.G3 Z36 1987

Wirtschaftsverbände in der Schweiz : Organisation und Aktivitäten von Wirtschaftsverbänden in vier Sektoren der Industrie / Peter Farago, Hanspeter Kriesi (Herausgeber) ; mit Beiträgen von Marcos Buser ... [et al.]. Grüsch : Rüegger, c1986. xv, 294 p. : ill. ; 21 cm. Bibliography: p. 283-294. ISBN 3-7253-0260-X : LC Card 86-136455 DDC 322/.3/09494 19
1. Trade and professional associations - Switzerland - Political activity. 2. Pressure groups - Switzerland. 3. Business and politics - Switzerland. I. Farago, Peter. II. Kriesi, Hanspeter. III. Buser, Marcos.
HD2429.S92 W57 1986
NYPL [JLD 86-2919]

Wirtschaftswachstum bei begrenzten Energieressourcen /. Ströbele, Wolfgang. Berlin , c1984. 173 p. : ISBN 3-428-05541-1 LC Card 84-176734
HD84 .S747 1984

Wirtschaftswachstum in der Industrie der DDR, 1945-1970 /. Roesler, Jörg. Berlin , 1986. 280 p. ; ISBN 3-05-000074-0 LC Card 86-196020
HC290.78 .R64 1986

Wirtschaftswissenschaften /. Gergely, Stefan M. Wien , 1985. 170 p. ; ISBN 3-205-06108-X LC Card 85-229521
HB74.9.A9 G47 1985

Wirtschaftswissenschaftliche Forschung und Entwicklung .
(Bd. 80) Wegmann, 1951- Gemeinkosten-Management . München , c1982. 230, xliii p. : ISBN 3-88259-224-9 (Deut. Bibl.) LC Card 83-159003
HJ2033 .W43 1982

Wirtschaftswissenschaftliche und wirtschaftsrechtliche Untersuchungen, 0083-7113 .
(17) Symposion "Marktwirtschaft und Umwelt" (1980 : Walter Eucken Institut) Marktwirtschaft und Umwelt . Tübingen , 1981. ix, 303 p. : ISBN 3-16-343372-3 : LC Card 81-128698 DDC 363.7/0526 19
HC79.E5 S92 1980 ***NYPL [TB (Walter Eucken Institut. Wirtschaftswissenschaftliche und wirtschaftsrechtliche Untersuchungen. Bd. 17)]***
(21) Knieps, Günter. Entstaatlichung im Telekommunikationsbereich . Tübingen , 1985. xi, 205 p. : ISBN 3-16-344955-7 LC Card 86-156485
HE8154 .K55 1985

Wirtschaftswissenschaftliche Veröffentlichungen .
(Bd. 13) Menz, Gertraud. Die Entwicklung der sowjetischen Besteuerung unter besonderer Berücksichtigung der ordnungspolitischen Funktionen /. Berlin , 1960. 247 p. : LC Card 86-161289
HJ2802 .M46 1960

Wirtschaftswissenschaftliches Seminar Ottobeuren (15th : 1985) Technologischer Wandel, Analyse und Fakten /. Tübingen , 1986. ix, 330 p. ; ISBN 3-16-345132-2 LC Card 87-109808 DDC 338/.06 19
HC79.T4 T4355 1986

Wirtschaftswörterbuch /. Schäfer, Wilhelm, Dr. München , c1986- v. <1 > ; ISBN 3-8006-1100-7 (Bd. 1) LC Card 86-214220
HB61 .S3 1986

Wirtschaftswörterbuch. Dietl, Clara-Erika. Commercial dictionary . Wiesbaden , c1985-c1987. 2 v. ; ISBN 3-409-19900-4 (v. 1) LC Card 86-160868
HF1002 .D493 1985
NYPL [*R-Econ. 87-1271]

WISCASSET, WATERVILLE, AND FARMINGTON RAILWAY - HISTORY.
Jones, Robert C., 1934- Two feet to tidewater . Boulder, Colo. , c1987. xvi, 269 p., [1] leaf of plates : ISBN 0-87108-729-4 LC Card 87-2428 DDC 385/.065/741 19
HE2791.W76647 J66 1987

Wischermann, Clemens. Teuteberg, Hans Jürgen. Wohnalltag in Deutschland, 1850-1914 . Münster , 1985. 488 p. : ISBN 3-88547-277-5 LC Card 86-165201
HD7339.A3 T46 1985

Wisconsin. Bureau of Local Government Services. Financial administration . Madison, WI , c1986. vi, 97 p. : LC Card 87-620662 DDC 352.1/09775 19
HJ9338 .F56 1986

Wisconsin Federation of Stamp Clubs. Wisconsin on stamps. [Wisconsin?] , c1986 (Green Bay, Wis. : insty-prints) i, 53 leaves : LC Card 86-206933 DDC 769.56/49775 19
HE6185.U7 W578 1986

WISCONSIN - INDUSTRIES.
Tienda, Marta. The structural transformation of employment in Wisconsin, 1960-1980 /. Madison, WI (Rm. 245, 30 N. Murray St., Madison 53715) [1986] ii, 47 p. ; LC Card 86-623091 DDC 331.12/09775 19
HD5725.W5 T54 1986

WISCONSIN - OCCUPATIONS.
Tienda, Marta. The structural transformation of employment in Wisconsin, 1960-1980 /. Madison, WI (Rm. 245, 30 N. Murray St., Madison 53715) [1986] ii, 47 p. ; LC Card 86-623091 DDC 331.12/09775 19
HD5725.W5 T54 1986

Wisconsin on stamps. [Wisconsin?] : Wisconsin Federation of Stamp Clubs, c1986 (Green Bay, Wis. : insty-prints) i, 53 leaves : ill. ; 28 cm. Limited edition of 300 copies. Bibliography: leaves 50-52. LC Card 86-206933 DDC 769.56/49775 19
1. Postage-stamps - United States - Collectors and collecting - Wisconsin. 2. Postage-stamps - Topics - Wisconsin. I. Wisconsin Federation of Stamp Clubs.
HE6185.U7 W578 1986

Wisconsin Postal History Society. 1902 Wisconsin alphabetical postal scheme. [Madison, Wis.] (5401 Raymond Rd., Madison 53711) [1984] 19 p. : LC Card 86-175627 DDC 383/.49775 19
HE6376.A1 W645 1984

Wise, David A. Pensions in the U. S. economy /. Chicago , 1988. ix, 200 p. : ISBN 0-226-06285-6 LC Card 87-19987 DDC 331.25/2/0973 19
HD7105.45.U6 P46 1988

Wise, Gregory J. The effect of tax exempt forestland on town property tax revenues : a review and analysis of Wisconsin private forestland tax laws / Gregory J. Wise, Harold C. Jordahl. Madison : Dept. of Urban and Regional Planning, University of Wisconsin--Madison : Dept. of Urban and Regional Planning, University of Wisconsin--Extension, [1986] 40 leaves : ill. ; 28 cm. (Occasional paper series in regional and urban planning . occasional paper no. 22) "April 1986." Bibliography: p. 40. LC Card 86-623093 DDC 336.22/09775 19
1. Forests and forestry - Taxation - Wisconsin. 2. Real property tax - Wisconsin. I. Jordhl, Harold C., 1926-. II. Title. III. Series.
HJ4284.A3 W59 1986

Wissen & Praxis .
(4) Köhler, Holm-Detlev, 1956- Ökonomie und Autonomie . Frankfurt , c1986. 213 p. ; ISBN 3-925798-24-2 LC Card 87-108165 DDC 334/.0943 19
HD3498 .K63 1986

(5) Fuchs, Hans-Jürgen, 1957- Das glückliche Bewusstsein und die Krise . Frankfurt [am Main] , c1986. 133 p. ; ISBN 3-925798-25-0 LC Card 87-112965
HD8458.A2 F83 1986

Wissenschaft im Arbeitnehmerinteresse .
(Bd. 3) Köchling, Annegret, 1944- Bildschirmarbeit . Köln , c1985. 212 p. : ISBN 3-7663-0853-X *NYPL [JLD 87-392]*

(Bd. 4) Neue Technologien und Arbeitswelt . Köln , c1984. 197 p. : ISBN 3-7663-0893-9 LC Card 85-160745
HD6331.2.G28 N475 1984
NYPL [JLD 86-3861]

Wissenschaft und Forschung.
Wild, Werner. Steuern und Reichsherrschaft . Bremen , 1984. 326 p. ; ISBN 3-88948-030-6 LC Card 85-127825
HJ2675 .W55 1984

Wissenschaft und Gesellschaft (Berlin, Germany)
(Bd. 20) Intensivierung der Forschung . Berlin , 1984. 354 p. ; LC Card 84-195559
HD30.42.G4 I57 1984

Innovation und Wissenschaft . Berlin , 1985. 328 p. : LC Card 86-121669
HC290.795.T4 I56 1985

Wissenschaft und Gesellschaft; Schriften des Forschungsinstituts für Gesellschaftspolitik und Beratende Sozialwissenschaft .
(6) Klöwer, Gerd Günter. Genossenschaften in Entwicklungsländern . Göttingen , 1981. 56 p. ; ISBN 3-509-01085-X LC Card 82-174706 DDC 334/.09172/4 19
HD3575 .K58 1981 *NYPL [JLE 86-3343]*

Wissenschaftliche Beiträge der Friedrich-Schiller-Univeritát Jena.
Produktion, Intensivierung, Effektivität /. Jena , 1978. 180 p. : LC Card 85-183724
HC290.795.I52 P75 1978

Wissenschaftliche Beiträge der Friedrich-Schiller-Universität Jena, 0232-3753.
Intensivierung des wissenschaftlich-technischen Arbeitsprozesses /. Jena , 1985. 200 p. : LC Card 86-132567 DDC 338/.06/09431 19
HC290.795.I52 I57 1985

Kaufmann, Manfred. Die persönliche materielle Interessiertheit an der Material- und Energieökonomie /. Jena , 1984. 112 p. : LC Card 85-224317
HF1054.G42 K38 1984

Die Leistungsbewertung in der Industrie . Jena , 1983. 241 p. ; LC Card 84-176546
HD56.25 .L45 1983

Wissenschaftliche Beiträge Karlsruhe .
(Nr. 11) Müller, Lothar. Die Bedeutung der Lohn-Leistungsrelation . Karlsruhe , c1983. iii, 272 p. : ISBN 3-88147-014-X LC Card 84-174174
HD4945 .M84 1983

Wissenschaftliche Berichte der Technischen Hochschule Leipzig .
(1986, Heft 18) Kolloquium 20 Jahre Weiterbildungs- und Forschungsarbeit (1987 : Leipzig, Germany) Kolloquium 20 Jahre Weiterbildungs- und Forschungsarbeit . [Leipzig] , 1986. 64 p. ; LC Card 87-408852 DDC 338.9431 19
HC290.78 .K64 1987

Wissenschaftliche Gesellschaft an der Johann Wolfgang Goethe-Universität Frankfurt am Main. Wittmann, Waldemar. Der Unternehmer /. Stuttgart , 1986. 27 p. ; ISBN 3-515-04666-6 : LC Card 87-136715 DDC 338/.04 19
HB615 .W58 1986

Wissenschaftliche Konferenz "Wissenschaftlich-Technischer Fortschritt, Bedingungen, Anforderungen, Möglichkeiten der Persönlichkeitsentwicklung" am 8. und 9. Oktober 1985 in Karl-Marx-Stadt /. Wissenschaftliche Konferenz "Wissenschaftlich-Technischer Fortschritt, Bedingungen, Anforderungen, Möglichkeiten der Persönlichkeitsentwicklung" (1985 : Karl-Marx-Stadt, Germany) Karl-Marx-Stadt , 1986. 98 p. ; LC Card 87-407801 DDC 338/.06 19
HD45 .W55 1985

Wissenschaftliche Konferenz "Wissenschaftlich-Technischer Fortschritt, Bedingungen, Anforderungen, Möglichkeiten der Persönlichkeitsentwicklung" (1985 : Karl-Marx-Stadt, Germany) Wissenschaftliche Konferenz "Wissenschaftlich-Technischer Fortschritt, Bedingungen, Anforderungen, Möglichkeiten der Persönlichkeitsentwicklung" am 8. und 9. Oktober 1985 in Karl-Marx-Stadt / Technische Hochschule Karl-Marx-Stadt, Sektion Wirtschaftswissenschaften, Forschungsgruppe Soziologie ; [Redaktion, Werner Dippmann]. Karl-Marx-Stadt : Rektor der Technischen Hochschule Karl-Marx-Stadt, 1986. 98 p. ; 21 cm. (Tagungsberichte (Technische Hochschule Karl-Marx-Stadt) . Heft 4) Wissenschaftliche Tagung Includes bibliographies. LC Card 87-407801 DDC 338/.06 19
1. Technological innovations - Germany (East) - Employee participation - Congresses. 2. Technological innovations - Social aspects - Germany (East) - Congresses. I. Dippmann, Werner. II. Technische Hochschule Karl-Marx-Stadt. Forschungsgruppe Soziologie. III. Series. IV. Series: Tagungsberichte (Technische Hochschule Karl-Marx-Stadt) , Heft 4. V. Title.
HD45 .W55 1985

Wissenschaftliche Länderkunden, 0174-0725 .
(Bd. 28) Glässer, Ewald. Island /. Darmstadt , 1986. xii, 315 p., [20] p. of plates (4 folded) : ISBN 3-534-01225-9 LC Card 87-101040
HC360.5 .G57 1986

Wissenschaftliche Paperbacks. Sozial- und Wirtschaftsgeschichte, 0170-3579 .
(21) Born, Karl Erich. Wirtschafts- und Sozialgeschichte des Deutschen Kaiserreichs (1867/71-1914) /. Stuttgart , 1985. 175 p. ; ISBN 3-515-02419-0 LC Card 85-168335
HC285 .B66 1985

Wissenschaftliche Plenarsitzung .
(24) Gestaltung künftiger Raumstrukturen durch veränderte Verkehrskonzepte . Hannover , 1986. xii, 173 p. : ISBN 3-87870-767-3 LC Card 87-401351 DDC 380.5/0943/512 19
HE249.Z7 S343 1986

Wissenschaftliche Reihe Soziologie.
Horch, Hans. Der Wandel der Gesellschafts- und Herrschaftsstrukturen in der Saarregion während der Industrialisierung (1740-1914) /. St. Ingbert [W. Germany] , 1985. 720 p. : ISBN 3-924555-04-4 LC Card 85-194709
HC287.S23 H67 1985

Wissenschaftliche Tagung "Nutzung Ökonomisch-Mathematischer Methoden und der Elektronischen Rechentechnik zur Erhöhung der Reaktionsfähigkeit der Industriekombinate gegenüber der Bedarfsdynamik," 8. Juni 1983 . Wissenschaftliche Tagung "Nutzung Ökonomisch-Mathematischer Methoden und der Elektronischen Rechentechnik zur Erhöhung der Reaktionsfähigkeit der Industriekombinate gegenüber der Bedarfsdynamik" (1983 : Technische Hochschule Karl-Marx Stadt) Karl-Marx-Stadt [1983] iii, 56 p. ; LC Card 84-117572
HD30.25 .W56 1983

Wissenschaftliche Tagung "Nutzung Ökonomisch-Mathematischer Methoden und der Elektronischen Rechentechnik zur Erhöhung der Reaktionsfähigkeit der Industriekombinate gegenüber der Bedarfsdynamik" (1983 : Technische Hochschule Karl-Marx Stadt)
Wissenschaftliche Tagung "Nutzung Ökonomisch-Mathematischer Methoden und der Elektronischen Rechentechnik zur Erhöhung der Reaktionsfähigkeit der Industriekombinate gegenüber der Bedarfsdynamik," 8. Juni 1983 : Referate des Plenums und Kurzfassungen der Diskussionsbeiträge der Arbeitsgruppen Maschinenbau und Leichtindustrie / Technische Hochschule Karl-Marx-Stadt, Sektion Wirtschaftswissenschaften, Wissenschaftsbereich "Leitung und Organisation des Sozialistischen Industriebetriebes" ; [Redaktion, R. Auerswald]. Karl-Marx-Stadt : Die Hochschule, [1983] iii, 56 p. ; 21 cm. (Wissenschaftliche Tagung) Tagungsberichte LC Card 84-117572
1. Industrial management - Mathematical models - Congresses. 2. Industrial management - Data processing - Congresses. 3. Industrial management - Germany (East) - Congresses. I. Auerswald, R. (Rolf). II. Technische Hochschule Karl-Marx-Stadt. Wissenschaftsbereich "Leitung und Organisation des Sozialistischen Industriebetriebes.". III. Title. IV. Title: Nutzung ökonomisch-mathematischer Methoden und der elektronischen Rechentechnik zur Erhöhung der Reaktionsfähigkeit der Industriekombinate gegenüber der Bedarfsdynamik. V. Series: Wissenschaftliche Tagung (Technische Hochschule Karl-Marx-Stadt).
HD30.25 .W56 1983

Wissenschaftliche Tagung (Technische Hochschule Karl-Marx-Stadt)
Wissenschaftliche Tagung "Nutzung Ökonomisch-Mathematischer Methoden und der Elektronischen Rechentechnik zur Erhöhung der Reaktionsfähigkeit der Industriekombinate gegenüber der Bedarfsdynamik" (1983 : Technische Hochschule Karl-Marx Stadt) Wissenschaftliche Tagung "Nutzung Ökonomisch-Mathematischer Methoden und der Elektronischen Rechentechnik zur Erhöhung der Reaktionsfähigkeit der Industriekombinate gegenüber der Bedarfsdynamik," 8. Juni 1983 . Karl-Marx-Stadt [1983] iii, 56 p. ; LC Card 84-117572
HD30.25 .W56 1983

Wissenschaftlicher Kommunismus.
Bedürfnisse und Interessen als Triebkräfte unseres Handelns /. Berlin , 1984. 155 p. ; LC Card 84-229147
HC290.795.C3 B43 1984

Wissenschaftlicher Kommunismus, Theorie und Praxis.
Die Sozialistische Gemeinschaft . Berlin , 1985. 238 p. ; LC Card 86-120025 DDC 337.1/1717 19
HC243.5 .S685 1985

Wissenschaftlicher Rat für Soziologische Forschung in der DDR. Technisch rationell, sozial effektiv . Berlin , 1986. 168 p. ; ISBN 3-320-00706-8 LC Card 87-144339 DDC 338/.06 19
HC290.795.A9 T43 1986

Die Wissenschaftstheorie Carl Mengers . Boos, Margarete. Wien , 1986. xiii, 252 p. ; ISBN 3-205-05044-4 LC Card 86-209140
HB101.M5 B6 1986

Wissenschaftszentrum Berlin, Internationales Institut für Vergleichende Gesellschaftsforschung/Arbeitspolitik (Series)
Informationstechnologie im Dienstleistungsbereich . Berlin , c1985. 258 p. : ISBN 3-924859-15-9 : LC Card 86-220033 DDC 338.4/561 19
HD9980.5 .I54 1985

Wissmann, Matthias, 1949- Marktwirtschaft 2000 /. Krefeld , c1983. 137 p. : ISBN 3-88289-302-8 LC Card 84-229313 DDC 338.9 19
HD75.6 .M37 1983 *NYPL [JLD 86-3124]*

Wit, Bernadette de. Houweling, Marjolein. Ondernemende vrouwen /. Amsterdam , c1985. 128 p. : ISBN 90-6834-018-2 : LC Card 86-166264
HD2346.N4 H68 1985

WIT Financial Publishers. Common stock price histories, 1910-1986. Morristown, N.J. , c1987.

208 p. : ISBN 0-9618454-0-6 (pbk.) LC Card 87-158025 DDC 332.63/222/0973 19
HG4916 .C65 1987

Wit, Ton de. Gianotten, Vera. Organización campesina . Amsterdam , Cinnaminson, N.J. , c1985. ix, 531 p., [4] p. of plates : ISBN 90-6765-162-1 LC Card 85-200688
HD1531.P4 G5 1985

Witcomb, Henry, 1822- Dictionnaire des termes de marine français-anglais & anglais-français, par Henry Witcomb et Edmond Tiret. Paris, Challamel aîné, 1883. 2 v. 24 cm. Vol. 2 has t.p. in English. CONTENTS. - v. 1. Français-anglais.--v. 2. English-French. LC Card 29-23644
1. French language - Dictionaries - English. 2. English language - Dictionaries - French. I. Tiret, Edmond. II. Title.
V24 .W5 ***NYPL [JSE 86-1965]***

With a name like-- /. Ellis, William Donohue. Orrville, Ohio , c1987. vii, 161 p. : LC Card 87-169333 DDC 338.7/664152/0973 19
HD9330.J34 J154 1987

With our own hands : research for Third World development : Canada's contribution through the International Development Research Centre, 1970-1985 / preface by Bradford Morse ; introductory chapter by Hugh Wynne-Edwards. Ottawa, Canada : International Development Research Centre, c1986. 206 p. : ill. ; 25 cm. (IDRC. 246e) Includes bibliographies. ISBN 0-88936-460-5 (pbk.) LC Card 86-212405 DDC 338.91/71/01724 19
1. International Development Research Centre (Canada). 2. Economic development projects - Developing countries. 3. Economic assistance, Canadian - Developing countries. 4. Technical assistance, Canadian - Developing countries. I. International Development Research Centre (Canada). II. Series: IDRC (Series) , 246e.
HC59.72.F44 W58 1986

Withers, William, 1905-1987. Politics and economic policy : from Hoover to Reagan / by William Withers. New York, N.Y. : Carlton Press, c1986. 240 p. : ill. ; 21 cm. "A Hearthstone book." ISBN 0-8062-2722-2 : LC Card 86-201185 DDC 338.973 19
1. United States - Economic policy. 2. United States - Politics and government. 3. Laissez-faire - History - 20th century. 4. Liberalism - United States - History - 20th century. 5. Conservatism - United States - History - 20th century. I. Title.
HC106 .W82 1986

Withorn, Ann, 1947- For crying out loud . New York , c1986. ix, 397 p. ; ISBN 0-8298-0581-8 (pbk.) : LC Card 86-9302 DDC 305.4/2/0973 19
HQ1426 .F757 1986 ***NYPL [JLD 86-3989]***

Witkin-Lanoil, Georgia.
The female stress syndrome : how to recognize and live with it / Georgia Witkin-Lanoil.1st ed. New York : Newmarket Press, c1984. xi, 211 p. ; 22 cm. Includes index. Bibliography: p. 201-206. ISBN 0-937858-33-1 LC Card 83-25038 DDC 155.6/33 19
1. Stress (Psychology). 2. Women - Psychology. 3. Women - Social conditions. 4. Women - Diseases - Psychosomatic aspects. 5. Women - Mental health. I. Title.
BF575.S75 W58 1984
NYPL [JFD 86-10468]

The male stress syndrome : how to recognize and live with it / Georgia Witkin-Lanoil.1st ed. New York : Newmarket Press, c1986. 246 p. ; 22 cm. Includes index. Bibliography: p. 234-240 ISBN 0-937858-59-5 LC Card 85-61815 DDC 155.9 19
1. Stress (Psychology). 2. Men - Psychology. 3. Men - Diseases - Psychosomatic aspects. I. Title.
BF575.S75 W59 1986 ***NYPL [JFD 86-5693]***

Witkin, Ruth K.
Managing your business with Multiplan : practical business solutions using Microsoft's award-winning PC spreadsheet / Ruth Witkin. Redmond, Wash. : Microsoft Press, 1987. xv, 525 p. ; 24 cm. "Updated for version 3." Includes index. ISBN 0-914845-94-2 (pbk.) : LC Card 87-7773 DDC 005.36/9 19
1. Multiplan (Computer program). 2. IBM Personal Computer - Programming. 3. Electronic spreadsheets. 4. Business - Data processing. I. Title.
HF5548.4.M74 W57 1987

Personal money management with AppleWorks / Ruth K. Witkin. Hasbrouck Heights, N.J. : Hayden Book Co. ; [New York] : Distributed by J. Wiley, c1986. 418 p. : ill. ; 24 cm. On t.p. the registered trademark symbol "TM" is superscript following "AppleWorks" in the title. Distributor from label on p. [4] of cover. Includes index. ISBN 0-471-62575-2 (Wiley : pbk.) : LC Card 87-110545 DDC 332.024/0028/55369 19
1. Finance, Personal - Data processing. 2. AppleWorks (Computer program). I. Title.
HG179 .W554 1986

Personal money mangement with AppleWorks / Ruth Witkin. New York : Wiley, c1987. p. cm. Reprint. Originally published: Hasbrouck Heights, N.J. : Hayden Book Co., 1986. ISBN 0-471-62575-2 : LC Card 87-6294 DDC 332.024/0028/55369 19
1. Finance, Personal - Data processing. 2. AppleWorks (Computer program). I. Title.
HG179 .W554 1987

Witkowski, Janusz. Migracje a ruchliwość społeczna ludności w Polsce / Janusz Witkowski. Wyd. 1. Warszawa : Szkoła Główna Planowania i Statystyki, Instytut Statystyki i Demografii, 1985. 168 p. : ill. ; 24 cm. (Monografie i opracowania. 196. 5) Summary in English and Russian. Bibliography: p. 148-150. LC Card 86-175948
1. Migration, Internal - Poland. 2. Social mobility - Poland. I. Series: Monografie i opracowania (Szkoła Główna Planowania i Statystyki (Warsaw, Poland)) , 196. II. Title.
HB2068.7.A3 W58 1985

Witney, Fred, 1917- Sloane, Arthur A. Labor relations /. Englewood Cliffs, N.J. , c1988. xiv, 543 p. : ISBN 0-13-519604-3 LC Card 87-14535 DDC 331.89/0973 19
HD8072 .S6185 1988

Witt, François de, 1944- Sassier, Philippe. Les Français à la corbeille /. Paris , c1985. 268 p. ; ISBN 2-221-04729-X : LC Card 86-126750 DDC 332.64/244 19
HG4583 .S27 1985

Witt, Peter-Christian. Wealth and taxation in Central Europe . Leamington Spa, UK ; New York, N.Y., USA : 162 p. ; ISBN 0-85496-523-8 : LC Card 86-24490 DDC 336.43 19
HJ1000 .W4 1987

Witt, Ulrich. Individualistische Grundlagen der evolutorischen Ökonomik / von Ulrich Witt. Tübingen : Mohr, c1987. xi, 209 p. ; 24 cm. (Die Einheit der Gesellschaftswissenschaften, 0424-6985 . Bd. 47) Revision of the author's Habilitationsschrift--Universität Mannheim, 1985. Bibliography: p. [191]-203. Includes indexes. ISBN 3-16-945063-8 LC Card 87-115946 DDC 330.15/5 19
1. Neoclassical school of economics. I. Title. II. Series.
HB98.2 .W57 1987

Witte, Eberhard. Der Praktische Nutzen empirischer Forschung /. Tübingen , 1981. viii, 324 p. ; ISBN 3-16-344392-3 : LC Card 81-197515 DDC 658.4/03 19
HD30.4 .P7 1981 ***NYPL [JLE 86-1360]***

Wittelsbürger, Helmut. Cartas, José María. Precondiciones para la implementación de la economía social de mercado en América Latina . Buenos Aires, República Argentina , c1985. 80 p. ; LC Card 87-101628
HC125 .C374 1985

Witter, José Sebastião. A Revolta dos Parceiros / José Sebastião Witter. São Paulo, SP : Brasiliense, 1986. 77 p. : ill. ; 16 cm. (Tudo é história . 110) Bibliography: p. [71]-77. LC Card 87-102716
1. Farm tenancy - Brazil - São Paulo (State) - History - 19th century - Case studies. 2. Métayer system - Brazil - São Paulo (State) - History - 19th century - Case studies. 3. Slave labor - Brazil - São Paulo (State) - History - 19th century - Case studies. 4. Agricultural laborers - Brazil - São Paulo (State) - Supply and demand - History - 19th century - Case studies. 5. Coffee trade - Brazil - São Paulo (State) - History - 19th century - Case studies. I. Title. II. Series.
HD4875.B8 W58 1986

Witthayālai Kānpokkhr Khrōngkān 'an n [Bangkok] [2526 i.e. 1983] 221 p. (some folded), [1] leaf of plates : LC Card 83-916454
HC445 .K53 1983

Witthayāniphon r Čhanthiphā Sukhumālachāt. Ngopprамān phǣndin phǣn mai . [Bangkok?] 2521 [1978] 173 (some folded), [3] leaves : LC Card 81-917611
HJ2162.55 .C47 1978

Witthöft, Hans Jürgen. Hapag-Lloyd : über ein Jahrhundert weltweite deutsche Seeschiffahrt im Bild = over a century of German ocean shipping in pictures / Hans Jürgen Witthöft ; [Übersetzung, Peter Alexander].2., überarbeitete und erw. Aufl. Herford : Koehler, 1979, c1974. 176 p. : ill. ; 28 cm. German and English. Col. maps on lining papers. Includes index. ISBN 3-7822-0201-5 LC Card 85-178567
1. Hapag-Lloyd AG - History. 2. Steamboat lines - Germany (West) - History. I. Title.
HE945.H424 W58 1979

Wittkamp, Heinrich, 1903- Achtzig Jahre kritischer Bürger im 20. Jahrhundert : Erinnerungen aus christlich-sozialer Sicht / Heinrich Wittkamp. Mannheim : Südwestdeutsche Verlagsanstalt, c1986. 232 p., [16] p. of plates : ill. ; 24 cm. (Sonderveröffentlichung des Stadtarchivs Mannheim. Nr. 13) Includes index. ISBN 3-87804-182-9 (Deut. Bibl.) LC Card 86-230657
1. Wittkamp, Heinrich, 1903-. 2. Trade-unions - Woodworkers - Germany (West) - Biography. 3. Trade-unions, Catholic - Germany (West) - Biography. I. Title. II. Title: 80 Jahre kritischer Bürger im 20. Jahrhundert.
HD6695.W58 A3 1986

WITTKAMP, HEINRICH, 1903-
Wittkamp, Heinrich, 1903- Achtzig Jahre kritischer Bürger im 20. Jahrhundert . Mannheim , c1986. 232 p., [16] p. of plates : ISBN 3-87804-182-9 (Deut. Bibl.) LC Card 86-230657
HD6695.W58 A3 1986

Wittmann, Franz, 1933- Der Einfluss der Steuern auf die Investitionsentscheidungen der Unternehmen : eine empirische Analyse / Franz Wittmann. Frankfurt ; New York : Campus, c1986. 405 p. ; 21 cm. Originally presented as the author's Habilitationsschrift--Universität Augsburg. Bibliography: p. 385-405. ISBN 3-593-33642-1 LC Card 86-173001
1. Capital investments - Germany (West) - Decision making. 2. Corporations - Taxation - Germany, West. 3. Tax incentives - Germany (West). 4. Capital investments - Decision-making. 5. Corporations - Taxation. 6. Tax incentives. I. Title.
HG4028.C4 W585 1986

Wittmann, Uli.

Wittmann, Waldemar. Der Unternehmer / von Waldemar Wittmann. Stuttgart : F. Steiner Verlag Wiesbaden, 1986. 27 p. ; 24 cm. (Sitzungsberichte der Wissenschaftlichen Gesellschaft an der Johann Wolfgang Goethe-Universität Frankfurt am Main . Bd. 22, Nr. 3) "Vorgetragen am 22. Oktober 1985 in einer Sitzung der Wissenschaftlichen Gesellschaft an der Johann Wolfgang Goethe-Universität Frankfurt am Main"--T.p. verso. Pages also numbered 188-209. Includes bibliographical references. ISBN 3-515-04666-6 : LC Card 87-136715 DDC 338/.04 19
1. Entrepreneurship. I. Wissenschaftliche Gesellschaft an der Johann Wolfgang Goethe-Universität Frankfurt am Main. II. Title. III. Series.
HB615 .W58 1986

Wittmann, Walter, 1935- Wider die organisierte Verantwortungslosigkeit : ein Plädoyer für die soziale Marktwirtschaft / Walter Wittmann. Frauenfeld : Huber, c1984. 175 p. ; 21 cm. Bibliography: p. 169-172. Includes index. ISBN 3-7193-0938-X : LC Card 84-234445
1. Laissez-faire. 2. Capitalism. I. Title.
HB95 .W57 1984

Wittrock, Björn. De stora programmens tid : forskning och energi i svensk politik / Björn Wittrock, Stefan Lindström. Stockholm : Akademilitteratur, 1984. 186 p. ; 21 cm. (Högskole- och forskningspolitiska studier) Bibliography: p. 171-179. Includes index. ISBN 91-7410-200-1 : LC Card 84-189613
1. Energy policy - Sweden. 2. Power resources - Research - Sweden. I. Lindström, Stefan. II. Title. III. Series.
HD9502.S82 W58 1984

Wittwer, S. H. (Sylvan Harold), 1917- Feeding a billion . East Lansing , 1987. 462 p., [16] p. of plates : ISBN 0-87013-246-6 (alk. paper) : LC Card 87-60024 DDC 338.1/9/51 19
HD2098 .F45 1987

Witzke, Harald von. Personelle Einkommensverteilung in der Landwirtschaft und Agrarpreise / von Harald von Witzke. Berlin : Duncker & Humblot, 1979. 180 p. : 16 ill. ; 24 cm. (Volkswirtschaftliche Schriften. Heft 281) Bibliography: p. [174]-180. ISBN 3-428-04303-0 LC Card 79-389988
1. Income distribution - Germany, West. 2. Agriculture - Economic aspects - Germany, West. 3. Agricultural prices - Germany, West. I. Title. II. Series.
HC290.5.I5 W57 ***NYPL [JLE 80-439]***

WIVES - EMPLOYMENT - CANADA.
Robinson, Patricia A. (Patricia Ann) Women's work interruptions . Ottawa [1987], c1986. 36, 40 p. ; ISBN 0-660-52895-9 (pbk.) : LC Card 87-146334 DDC 331.4/12/0971 19
HD6099 .R63 1987

WIVES - EMPLOYMENT - GREECE.
Mousourou, Loukia M. Gynaikeia apascholēsē kai oikogeneia stēn Hellada kai allou /. Athēna , c1985. 220 p. : LC Card 86-205975
HD6181.83 .M68 1985

WIVES - NETHERLANDS - STATISTICS.
Netherlands (Kingdom, 1815-). Centraal Bureau voor de Statistiek. Hoofdafdeling Bevolkingsstatistieken. De gehuwde vrouw en haar kindertal anno 1975 /. 's-Gravenhage , 1980. 78 p. : LC Card 81-100844
HB1015 .N47 1980
NYPL [JLM 78-1515 nr.9]

W.J. Page & Associates. Telecommunications in Northern Alberta / prepared by W.J. Page & Associates Ltd. ; prepared for Alberta, Northern Alberta Development Council. [Edmonton, Alta. : W.J. Page & Associates, 1986?] 39, [96] p. : ill. ; 28 cm. Cover title. Bibliography: p. [58]-[59] LC Card 86-235313 DDC 384/.068 19
1. Telecommunication policy - Alberta. 2. Telecommunication - Alberta. I. Northern Alberta Development Council. II. Title.
HE7819.A43 W15 1986

Wöbbeking, Karlheinz. Die Planung von Liquidationsstrategien : ein Vorschlag zur Entwicklung und Bewertung sinnvoller Liquidationsstrategien für Industrieunternehmen / Karlheinz Wöbbeking. Münster : Lit, [1986] vii, 273 p. : ill. ; 22 cm. (Betriebswirtschaftliche Schriftenreihe . Bd. 28) Bibliography: p. 246-273. ISBN 3-88660-328-8 LC Card 86-213801
1. Liquidation - Germany, West. 2. Business enterprises - Germany, West - Finance. I. Title. II. Series.
HD2747 .W6 1986

Wobblies. see **Industrial Workers of the World.**

WODC (Series) .
(60) Aalberts, Monique M. J. Gezinsvorming door jonge migranten . 's-Gravenhage , 1985. 93 p. : ISBN 90-12-04999-7 LC Card 85-235621
HD8518.5.A2 A24 1985

Wodopia, Franz-Josef. Intertemporale Produktionsentscheidungen : Theorie und Anwendung auf die Elektrizitätswirtschaft / Franz-Josef Wodopia. Frankfurt am Main : A. Hain, c1986. xx, 262 p. : ill. ; 21 cm. (Mathematical systems in economics. 102) Bibliography: p. 251-262. ISBN 3-445-02403-0 LC Card 86-222211
1. Production functions (Economic theory). 2. Electric power production. 3. Electric utilities - Management. I. Title.
HB241 .W63 1986

Wöhlcke, Manfred, 1942- Brasilien als Produzent und Exporteur von Rüstungsgütern / Manfred Wöhlcke. 1. Aufl. Baden-Baden : Nomos, 1987. 176 p. : ill. ; 23 cm. (Aktuelle Materialien zur internationalen Politik . Bd. 14) Summary in English. Bibliography: p. 162-167. ISBN 3-7890-1355-2 LC Card 87-135627 DDC 338.4/36234/0981 19
1. Munitions - Brazil. 2. Brazil - Commerce. I. Title. II. Series.
HD9743.B682 W64 1987

Woelfel, Charles J.
Budgeting, pricing, and cost controls : a desktop encyclopedia / by Charles J. Woelfel. Chicago, Ill. : Probus Pub. Co., c1987. p. cm. Includes index. ISBN 0-917253-91-4 : LC Card 87-17921 DDC 658.1/5/0321 19
1. Finance - Dictionaries. 2. Budget - Dictionaries. 3. Pricing - Dictionaries. 4. Cost control - Dictionaries. I. Title.
HG151 .W63 1987

The desktop encyclopedia of corporate finance & accounting / Charles J. Woelfel. Chicago, Ill. : Probus Pub. Co., c1987. viii, 518 p. : ill. ; 24 cm. Spine title: Corporate finance & accounting. Includes bibliographies. ISBN 0-917253-65-5 : LC Card 87-2302 DDC 658.1/5 19
1. Corporations - Finance - Handbooks, manuals, etc. 2. Accounting - Handbooks, manuals, etc. I. Title. II. Title: Desk-top encyclopedia of corporate finance & accounting. III. Title: Corporate finance & accounting. IV. Title: Corporate finance and accounting.
HG4027.3 .W64 1987

The operating executive's guide to profit planning tools and techniques / Charles J. Woelfel, Charles D. Mecimore. Chicago, Ill. : Probus Pub. Co., c1986. ix, 199 p. : ill. ; 24 cm. Includes index. Bibliography : p. 193-194. ISBN 0-917253-24-8 : LC Card 86-3222 DDC 658.1/55 19
1. Business enterprises - Finance. 2. Profit. I. Mecimore, Charles D. II. Title.
HF5635 .W848 1986 ***NYPL [JLE 86-3007]***

Wörterbuch für Werbung. Koschnick, Wolfgang J., 1942- Standard-Wörterbuch für Werbung, Massenmedien und Marketing, Deutsch-Englisch /. Berlin , New York , 1987. 590 p. ; ISBN 0-89925-293-1 (U. S.) : LC Card 87-19928 DDC 659.1/03/21 19
HF5803 .K67 1987

Wogaman, J. Philip. Economics and ethics : a Christian inquiry / J. Philip Wogaman. Philadelphia : Fortress Press, c1986. xiii, 145 p. ; 22 cm. Includes index. Bibliography: p. 131-140. ISBN 0-8006-1904-8 (pbk.) LC Card 85-45478 DDC 261.8/5 19
1. Economics - Moral and ethical aspects. 2. Economics - Religious aspects - Christianity. 3. Laissez-faire - Moral and ethical aspects. 4. Capitalism - Religious aspects - Christianity. I. Title.
HB72 .W633 1986 ***NYPL [JLD 86-3984]***

Woglom, Geoffrey. Modern macroeconomics / Geoffrey Woglom. Glenview, Ill. : Scott, Foresman, c1988. 792, 19, 14 p. : ill. ; 24 cm. Includes bibliographical references and index. ISBN 0-673-18413-7 LC Card 87-12857 DDC 339 19
1. Macroeconomics. I. Title.
HB172.5 .W63 1988

Wohlers, Eckhardt. Unterschiede in der Beschäftigungsentwicklung zwischen den USA, Japan und der EG : vergleichende Untersuchung der Gründe für die unterschiedliche Beschäftigungsentwicklung in den USA, Japan und der EG seit 1973 / Eckhardt Wohlers, Günter Weinert. Hamburg : Verlag Weltarchiv, 1986. 294 p. : ill. ; 24 cm. (Veröffentlichungen des HWWA-Institut für Wirtschaftsforschung-Hamburg) Bibliography: p. 227-246. ISBN 3-87895-307-0 LC Card 86-233505
1. Manpower policy - United States. 2. Manpower policy - Japan. 3. Manpower policy - European Economic Community countries. I. Weinert, Günter. II. Title.
HD5724 .W57 1986

Der Wohlfahrtsstaat am Ende . Schmölders, Günter, 1903- München , 1983. 283 p. ; ISBN 3-7844-7133-1 LC Card 84-138252
HC286.6 .S284 1983

Wohlfahrtsstaat und soziale Probleme / herausgegeben von Hans Haferkamp. Opladen : Westdeutscher Verlag, c1984. vi, 294 p. : ill. ; 23 cm. (Beiträge zur sozialwissenschaftlichen Forschung. Bd. 62) Includes bibliographies. ISBN 3-531-11701-7
1. Social problems - Addresses, essays, lectures. 2. Welfare state - Addresses, essays, lectures. I. Haferkamp, Hans. ***NYPL [JLD 85-1550]***

Wohlfarth, Karl Anton. Leistung und Ethos : Überlegungen zu Entstehung und Kritik der industriellen Gesellschaft / Karl Anton Wohlfarth. Paderborn : F. Schöningh, 1984. 266 p. ; 24 cm. (Abhandlungen zur Sozialethik. Bd. 23) Habilitationsschrift, Johannes Gutenberg-Universität Mainz, 1984. Bibliography: p. 249-260. Includes indexes. ISBN 3-506-70223-8 LC Card 84-238158
1. Industry - Social aspects. 2. Industry - Moral and ethical aspects. 3. Social history. 4. Liberalism. 5. Conservatism. 6. Socialism. I. Title.
HD60 .W64 1984

Wohlfeil und köstlich . Appuhn, Klaus D. Dortmund , c1982. 148 p. : ISBN 3-88379-336-1 (pbk.) LC Card 87-672473
HF5470 .A66x 1982

Wohlgenannt, Lieselotte. Büchele, Herwig, 1935- Grundeinkommen ohne Arbeit . Wien , c1985. 191 p. : ISBN 3-203-50898-2 LC Card 85-207929
HC79.I5 B83 1985

Der Wohlstand der Nationen . Smith, Adam, 1723-1790. [Inquiry into the nature and causes of the wealth of nations. German.] München , c1974. lxxix, 859 p., [14] p. of plates : ISBN 3-406-05393-9 LC Card 87-672505
HB161 .S654x 1974

Der Wohlstand entlässt seine Kinder . Jungblut, Michael. Stuttgart , c1983. 303 p. ; ISBN 3-421-06164-5 LC Card 83-232938
HC59 .J78 1983

Wohnalltag in Deutschland, 1850-1914 . Teuteberg, Hans Jürgen. Münster , 1985. 488 p. : ISBN 3-88547-277-5 LC Card 86-165201
HD7339.A3 T46 1985

Wohnen : Beiträge zur Planung, Politik und Ökonomie eines alltäglichen Lebensbereiches / Volker Roscher (Hrsg.) ; von Adalbert Evers ... [et al.]. Hamburg : Christians, c1983. 230 p. : ill., plans ; 24 cm. (Stadt, Planung, Geschichte . 1) Summaries in English. Includes bibliographies. CONTENTS. - Städtebauliche Verdichtung / Peter Zlonicky -- Zwei Bergarbeitersiedlungen / Heinrich Moldenschardt -- Segregation, Mobilität und die Chancen auf dem Wohnungsmarkt / Detlev Ipsen -- Kommunale Wohnungspolitik und Wohnungsnot / Adalbert Evers, Tilman Harlander -- Finanzkapital und Wohnungspolitik / Hartmut Frank -- Amerikanisierung der deutschen Städte? / Hartmut Häussermann -- Industriearbeit und Wohnen im Ballungsraum / Ingrid Krau -- Überlegungen zum bedürfnisgerechten Planen / Walter Siebel -- Sozialer Alltag und lokale Wohnchanchen [sic] / Volker Roscher. ISBN 3-7672-0808-3 LC Card 83-219819 DDC 363.5/0943 19
1. Housing - Germany, West - Addresses essays, lectures. 2. Housing policy - Germany (West) - Addresses, essays, lectures. I. Roscher, Volker, 1948-. II. Evers, Adalbert. III. Series.
HD7339.A3 W616 1983
NYPL [JLE 86-3338]

Wohngemeinschaft oder Grossfamilie. Petersen, Paul. [Wuppertal, c1972] 224 p. LC Card 72-375103 ***NYPL [JLD 77-3003]***

Wohnstandorte und Wohnumfeldprobleme in der Kernzone des Ruhrgebietes /. Wehling, Hans-Werner, 1949- Paderborn , 1984. ix, 285 p. : ISBN 3-506-72309-X LC Card 85-121205
HD7339.R79 W44 1984

Wohnungsgemeinnützigkeit . Krischausky, D. Köln , c1984. vi, 161 p. ; ISBN 3-452-19899-5 LC Card 84-182027
HD7339.A3 K79 1984

Wohnungsmarkt und soziale Schicht . Lins, Josef. Linz , 1983. 89 p. : ISBN 3-85320-292-6 LC Card 84-214132 DDC 363.6/09436 19
HD7337.A3 L55 1983 ***NYPL [JLD 87-102]***

Das Wohnungswesen in Oberösterreich seit Beginn dieses Jahrhunderts im Vergleich zu seiner gesamtstaatlichen Entwicklung /. Urferer, Wilhelm. Linz , c1986. viii, 235 p. : ISBN 3-85320-384-1 LC Card 87-127729 DDC 363.5/8/094362 19
HD7337.U6 U74 1986

Woititz, Janet Geringer. Home away from home / Janet Geringer Woititz. Pompano Beach, Fla. : Health Communications, c1987. x, 137 p. : ill. ; 24 cm. Bibliography: p. 137. ISBN 0-932194-38-9 LC Card 86-33478 DDC 658.3/045 19
1. Alcoholism and employment - United States. 2. Adult children of alcoholics - Employment - United States. 3. Adult children of alcoholics - United States - Psychology. I. Title.
HF5549.5.A4 W65 1987

Woldring, H. E. S., 1943- Zelfzorg en verzorging . Kampen [1985] 237 p. ; ISBN 90-242-4072-7 : LC Card 86-175292
HC325 .Z43 1985

Wolenik, Robert. MacWrite made easier / Robert Wolenik. New York : Holt, Rinehart, and Winston, 1985. xiv, 210 p. : ill. ; 24 cm. (CBS computer books) Includes index. ISBN 0-03-001763-7 LC Card 84-19781 DDC 652/.5 19
1. Word processing. 2. MacWrite (Computer program).

3. Macintosh (Computer) - Programming. I. Title. II. Series.
Z52.5.M32 W64 1985 ***NYPL [JLE 85-1535]***

Wolf, Charles, 1924- Markets or governments : choosing between imperfect alternatives / Charles Wolf, Jr. Cambridge, Mass. : MIT Press, c1988. xv, 220 p. : ill. ; 22 cm. (A Rand Corporation research study) Bibliography: p. [201]-211. Includes index. ISBN 0-262-23134-4 LC Card 87-118516 DDC 338.9 19
1. Capitalism. 2. Economic policy. I. Title.
HB501 .W89 1988

Wolf, Dieter, 1942- Ware und Geld : der dialektische Widerspruch im "Kapital" / Dieter Wolf. Hamburg : VSA-Verlag, 1985. 405 p. ; 24 cm. Bibliography: p. 405. ISBN 3-87975-301-6 LC Card 86-229352
1. Marx, Karl, 1818-1883. Kapital. 2. Value. 3. Money. I. Title.
HB501.M5 W65 1985

Wolf, Douglas, 1948- Compute!'s quick & easy guide to learning Lotus 1-2-3 / Doug Wolf. Greensboro, N.C. : Compute! Publications, c1987. vi, 139 p. : ill. ; 23 cm. Includes index. ISBN 0-87455-106-4 (pbk.) : LC Card 87-163385 DDC 005.36/9 19
1. Lotus 1-2-3 (Computer program). 2. Business - Data processing. 3. Electronic spreadsheets. I. Title. II. Title: Compute!'s quick and easy guide to learning Lotus 1-2-3. III. Title: Quick & easy guide to learning Lotus 1-2-3. IV. Title: Quick and easy guide to learning Lotus 1-2-3.
HF5548.4.L67 W65 1987

Wolf, Fredric M. (Fredric Marc) Meta-analysis : quantitative methods for research synthesis / Fredric M. Wolf. Beverly Hills : Sage Publications, c1986. 65 p. : ill. ; 26 cm. (Sage university papers series. Quantitative applications in the social sciences . no. 07-059) Bibliography: p. 57-64. ISBN 0-8039-2756-8 LC Card 85-52372
1. Meta-analysis. 2. Social sciences - Statistical methods. I. Series. II. Series: Quantitative applications in the social sciences, no. 59. III. Title.
NYPL [JLK 77-39 no.59]

Wolf, Hanna. Ausgewählte Reden und Aufsätze / Hanna Wolf. Berlin : Dietz Verlag, 1979. 439 p. ; 21 cm. Includes bibliographical references. LC Card 80-478273 DDC 335.43/09431
1. Communism - Germany, East - Addresses, essays, lectures. 2. Communism - Addresses, essays, lectures.
HX280.5.A6 W64 ***NYPL [JLD 81-322]***

Wolf, Martin. Stagflation, savings, and the state . New York , 1986. xii, 402 p. : ISBN 0-19-520496-4 LC Card 85-31981 DDC 330.9172/4 19
HG229 .S74 1986 ***NYPL [JLE 86-2621]***

Wolf, Martin, 1954- Erfahrungen mit der Profit-Center-Organisation / Martin Wolf. Frankfurt am Main ; New York : P. Lang, c1985. viii, 285 p. : ill. ; 21 cm. (Europäische Hochschulschriften. Reihe V, Volks- und Betriebswirtshaft, 0531-7339 . Bd. 665 = vol. 665 = vol. 665) Bibliography: p. [268]-285. ISBN 3-8204-8746-8 LC Card 85-243838
1. Conglomerate corporations - Germany, West. 2. Big business - Germany, West. I. Series: Europäische Hochschulschriften. Reihe V, Volks- und Betriebswirtschaft , Bd. 665. II. Title.
HD2756.2.G3 W65 1985

Wolf, Winfried. Eisenbahn und Autowahn : Personen- und Gütertransport auf Schiene und Strasse : Geschichte, Bilanz, Perspektiven / Winfried Wolf. Hamburg : Rasch und Röhring, c1987. 565 p. : ill. ; 21 cm. Chapters 1-4 based on the author's thesis (doctoral)--Universität Hannover. Bibliography: p. 465-549. Includes index. ISBN 3-89136-105-X LC Card 87-167400 DDC 388/.09 19
1. Transportation - History. 2. Railroads - History. 3. Transportation, Automotive - History. I. Title.
HE151 .W58 1987

Wolfenbütteler Symposion (7th : 1978)
Technologischer Wandel im 18. Jahrhundert /. Wolfenbüttel , c1981. 246 p. ; ISBN 3-88373-018-1 LC Card 84-116829 DDC 338/.06 19
HC240.9.T4 T43 1981 ***NYPL [JLE 86-927]***

Wolfertz, Dirk. Grundlagen und Probleme der indikativen sektoralen Planung in marktwirtschaftlich orientierten Systemen / Dirk Wolfertz. Berlin : Duncker & Humblot, c1983. 165 p. ; 24 cm. (Volkswirtschaftliche Schriften. Heft 332) Bibliography: p. [156]-165. ISBN 3-428-05379-6 LC Card 83-225373
1. Economic policy. 2. Laissez-faire. I. Title. II. Series.
HD84 .W59 1983

Wolff, Bruno B. Modular programming routines for the Apple II+/IIe/IIc / Bruno B. Wolff, Jr. 1st ed. Blue Ridge Summit, PA : Tab Books, 1985. x, 243 p. : ill. ; 24 cm. Bibliography: p. 237. Includes index. "No. 1732." ISBN 0-8306-0732-3 : LC Card 85-17331 DDC 005.265 19
1. Apple II Plus (Computer) - Programming. 2. Apple IIe (Computer) - Programming. 3. Apple IIc (Computer) - Programming. 4. Modular programming. I. Title.
QA76.8.A66 W65 1985
NYPL [JSE 86-1017]

Wolff, Charles J. de (Charles Johannes) Selles, G. (Gert) Mid career crisis /. Deventer [1985?] 135 p. : ISBN 90-6001-934-2 LC Card 86-163138
HF5384 .S45 1985

Wolff, Edward N. International comparisons of the distribution of household wealth /. Oxford , New York , 1987. xii, 283 p. : ISBN 0-19-828511-6 : LC Card 86-31241 DDC 339.2/2/094 19
HC240.9.I5 I56 1987

Wolff, Nancy, 1955- Income redistribution and the Social Security program / by Nancy Wolff. Ann Arbor : UMI Research Press, c1987. vi, 181 p. : ill. ; 24 cm. (Research in business economics and public policy . no. 12) Revision of thesis (Ph.D.)--Iowa State University, 1984. Bibliography: p. [163]-176. Includes indexes. ISBN 0-8357-1807-7 LC Card 87-10791 DDC 368.4/3/00973 19
1. Old age pensions - United States. 2. Social security - United States. 3. Income distribution - United States. 4. Retirement income - United States. 5. Distributive justice. I. Title. II. Series.
HD7105.35.U6 W65 1987

Wolff, Richard D.
Economics : Marxian versus neoclassical / Richard D. Wolff and Stephen A. Resnick. Baltimore : Johns Hopkins University Press, c1987. xiv, 279 p. : ill. ; 24 cm. Includes bibliographies and index. ISBN 0-8018-3479-1 (alk. paper) LC Card 87-4131 DDC 330.1 19
1. Comparative economics. 2. Economics. 3. Marxian economics. 4. Neoclassical school of economics. I. Resnick, Stephen A. II. Title.
HB90 .W65 1987

Resnick, Stephen A. Knowledge and class . Chicago , c1987. vii, 352 p. ; ISBN 0-226-71021-1 LC Card 86-32631 DDC 335.4 19
HB97.5 .R48 1987

Wolff, Rick, 1951- The encyclopedia of pre-written employment ads : including over 500 sample ads with a valuable guide to writing and placing personnel ads / Richard H. Wolff and Brian L.P. Zevnik. Westbury, N.Y. : Asher-Gallant Press, c1986. vi, 196 p. ; 29 cm. ISBN 0-87280-142-X (loose-leaf) : LC Card 86-26526 DDC 659.1/9331128 19
1. Advertising, Classified - Handbooks, manuals, etc. 2. Help-wanted advertising - Handbooks, manuals, etc. I. Zevnik, Brian L. P. II. Title.
HF6125 .W65 1986

Wolff, Robert Paul. Moneybags must be so lucky : on the literary structure of Capital / Robert Paul Wolff. Amherst : University of Massachusetts Press, c1988. p. cm. ISBN 0-87023-615-6 (alk. paper) LC Card 87-20580 DDC 335.4/1 19
1. Marx, Karl, 1818-1883. Kapital. 2. Capital. I. Title.
HB501.M37 W64 1988

Wolff, Rolf, 1953- Organizing industrial development /. Berlin , New York , 1986. xi, 391 p. : ISBN 0-89925-168-4 (U. S.) LC Card 86-24074 DDC 338.9 19
HD31 .O783 1986 ***NYPL [JLE 87-789]***

Wolff von Amerongen, Otto, 1918-
DIHT-Kongress (1983 : Frankfurt am Main, Germany) Kapital, Zins, Währung . Bonn , 1984. 68 p. : LC Card 84-212399
HC290.5.C3 D53 1983

Trendwende im Osthandel / Otto Wolff von Amerongen. Bonn : Deutscher Industrie- und Handelstag, 1977. 23 p. ; 21 cm. (DIHT . 160) LC Card 85-141570
1. East-West trade (1945-). 2. Germany (West) - Commerce - Communist countries. 3. Communist countries - Commerce - Germany (West). I. Series: DIHT (Series) , 160. II. Title.
HF1411 .W583 1977

Votum für die Marktwirtschaft . Bonn , c1976. 26 p. ; LC Card 85-172115
HC286.7 .V69 1976

Wolffsohn, Michael. Politik als Investitionsmotor? : deutsche "Multis" in Lateinamerika / Michael Wolffsohn, Reinhard Niederfeld. Frankfurt am Main ; New York : P. Lang, c1985. 141 p. : ill. ; 21 cm. Bibliography: p. 139-141. ISBN 3-8204-7487-0 (pbk.) LC Card 87-672289
1. Corporations, German - Latin America. 2. International business enterprises - Political aspects - Latin America. 3. Germany, West - Foreign economic relations - Latin America. 4. Latin America - Foreign economic relations - Germany, West. I. Niederfeld, Reinhard, 1961-. II. Title.
HD2810.5 W64x 1985

Wolffsohn, Seew, 1916- Wirtschaftliche und soziale Entwicklungen in Brandenburg, Preussen, Schlesien und Oberschlesien in den Jahren 1640-1853, Frühindustrialisierung in Oberschlesien / Seew Wolffsohn. Frankfurt am Main ; New York : P. Lang, c1985. 182 p., [2] p. of folded plates : ill. ; 21 cm. (Europäische Hochschulschriften. Reihe III, Geschichte und ihre Hilfswissenschaften, 0531-7320 . Bd. 261 = vol. 261 = vol. 261) Bibliography: p. 171-182. ISBN 3-8204-8197-4 LC Card 85-219539
1. Brandenburg (Electorate) - Economic conditions. 2. Brandenburg (Electorate) - Social conditions. 3. Prussia (Germany) - Economic conditions. 4. Prussia (Germany) - Social conditions. 5. Silesia (Germany) - Economic conditions. 6. Silesia (Germany) - Social conditions. I. Series: Europäische Hochschulschriften. Reihe III, Geschichte und ihre Hilfswissenschaften , Bd. 261. II. Title.
HC288.B68 W65 1985

Wolfgart, Ludger. Die technische Entwicklung als Element des sozialen Wandels und ihre Auswirkungen auf den öffentlichen Sektor in der Bundesrepublik Deutschland / Ludger Wolfgart. Münster : Lit, [1986] ii, 213 p. ; 21 cm. (Studien zur Politikwissenschaft. Bd. 19) Bibliography: p. 188-213. ISBN 3-88660-230-3 (cover); 3-88600-230-3 (Deut. Bibl.) LC Card 87-106473 DDC 338.943 19
1. Privatization - Germany (West). 2. Germany, West - Economic policy - 1974-. I. Series: Studien zur Politikwissenschaft (Münster in Westfalen, Germany) , Bd. 19. II. Title.
HD4175 .W65 1986

Wolfrum, Bernd, 1956- Köpplinger, Herbert, 1954- Risiken im Auslandsgeschäft . Nürnberg , 1986. xli, 227 p. : ISBN 3-89078-005-9 LC Card 87-145527 DDC 332.6/73 19
HG4538 .K64 1986

Wolfsburger Beiträge zur Stadtgeschichte und Stadtentwicklung.
Siegfried, Klaus-Jörg, 1940- Rüstungsproduktion und Zwangsarbeit im Volkswagenwerk, 1939-1945 . Frankfurt , New York , c1986. 239 p. : ISBN 3-593-33765-7 LC Card 87-133375 DDC 338.4/76234/0943 19
HD9743.G48 S56 1986

Wolk, Harry I. Management accounting : planning and control / Harry I. Wolk, Quentin N. Gerber, Gary A. Porter. Boston, Mass. : PWS-Kent, c1988. xiii, 754 p. : ill. ; 24 cm. Includes index. ISBN 0-534-07050-7 : LC Card 87-7348 DDC 658.1/511 19
1. Managerial accounting. I. Gerber, Quentin N., 1930-. II. Porter, Gary A., 1950-. III. Title.
HF5657.4 .W64 1988

Wolkowitsch, Maurice. Géographie des transports / Maurice Wolkowitsch. Nouv. éd. mise à jour. Paris : A. Colin, 1982, c1973. 383 p. : ill. ; 23 cm. (Collection U. Série Géographie) Includes bibliographical references and indexes. ISBN 2-200-31188-5 LC Card 83-147243
1. Transportation. 2. Geography, Commercial. I. Title.
HE151 .W63 1982

Woll, Artur, 1923-
Ludwig-Erhard-Preis für Wirtschaftspublizistik 1986 . Bonn [1986] 45 p. : ISBN 3-88991-009-2 LC Card 87-409497 DDC 338.943 19
HC286.5 .L825 1986

Wirtschaftslexikon /. München , c1987. xv, 661 p. : ISBN 3-486-29691-4 LC Card 87-127454

DDC 330/.03/31 19
HB61 .W558 1987

Wirtschaftspolitik / von Artur Woll. München : F. Vahlen, c1984. xiv, 385 p. : ill. ; 23 cm. (Vahlens Handbücher der Wirtschafts- und Sozialwissenschaften) Includes bibliographies and index. ISBN 3-8006-1079-5 LC Card 87-672745
1. Economic policy. I. Title.
HD84 .W62x 1984

Wollmann, Hellmut, 1936- Die Zweite Stadt . Opladen , c1986. 407 p. : ISBN 3-531-11764-5 LC Card 87-497505 DDC 331.11/0943 19
HD8451 .Z94 1986

Wollmer, Günther. Innenpolitische Leistungsbilanz 1982-1986 /. Bonn , 1986. 124 p. : LC Card 86-215949
HC286.7 .I55 1986

Wolman, Paul. The U. S. Mint / Paul Wolman. New York : Chelsea House Publishers, c1987. 92 p. : ill. ; 24 cm. (Know your government) Bibliography: p. 89. Includes index. ISBN 0-87754-829-3 (lib. bdg.) : LC Card 86-31720 DDC 353.0082/2 19
1. United States. Bureau of the Mint - History. 2. Mints - United States - History. 3. Coinage - United States - History. I. Series: Know your government (New York, N.Y.). II. Title.
HG459 .W65 1987

Wolsky, Mark L. Telecommunications opportunities for colleges and universities /. McLean, Va. (1355 Beverly Rd., Suite 100, McLean 22101) , c1986. 208 p. ; LC Card 86-231086 DDC 384.6/3 19
HD9696.T443 U572 1986

Wolsky, Monica. Bruchhaus, Eva-Maria. Frauen in Entwicklungsländern . Freiburg im Breisgau , 1979. iii, 182 p. ; LC Card 81-121677 DDC 305.4/09172/4 19
HQ1870.9 .B78 1979 *NYPL [JLG 86-106]*

Wolstenholme, P. H. Carmichael, K. S. (Keith Stanley) Taxation of Lloyd's underwriters /. London , 1980. xvi, 107 p. : ISBN 0-372-30027-8 (pbk.) : LC Card 81-107459
HG8123.G7 C37 1980

Wolter, Frank. Glismann, Hans H. Zur Natur der Wachstumsschwäche in der Bundesrepublik Deutschland . Kiel [1978] 32 p. : LC Card 85-166323
HB44 .K45 no. 55 HB3789

Wolters, Roger S. Labor relations : an experiential and case approach / Roger S. Wolters, William H. Holley, Jr. Chicago : Dryden Press, c1988. xi, 321 p. ; 29 cm. Includes bibliographies. ISBN 0-03-069304-7 (pbk.) LC Card 87-19941 DDC 331 19
1. Industrial relations - United States. 2. Industrial relations - United States - Case studies. I. Holley, William H. II. Title.
HD8072.5 .W65 1988

Wolvén, Lars-Erik. Konsumenter, konsumentpolitik, rationalitet och välfärd : teoretiska utgångspunkter och motiv för Projektet "Konsumentens beteende under lokala strukturförändringar" / Lars-Erik Wolvén. Umeå : Department of Sociology, University of Umeå, 1981. 83 leaves ; 25 cm. (Research reports from the Department of Sociology, Umeå University, 0566-7518 . no 61) Summary in English. Bibliography: leaves 80-83. LC Card 82-105540 DDC 658.8/342/09485 19
1. Consumer protection - Sweden. 2. Consumers - Sweden - Case studies. 3. Retail trade - Sweden - Case studies. 4. Sparsely settled areas - Sweden. I. Series: Umeå, Sweden. Universitetet. Sociologiska institutionen. Research reports, no. 61. II. Title.
HC380.C63 W64 *NYPL [JLM 74-106 no.61]*

Wolverton, Van, 1939- Running MS DOS : the Microsoft guide to getting the most out of the standard operating system for the IBM PC and 50 other personal computers / by Van Wolverton.2nd ed. Bellevue, Wash. : Microsoft Press ; [New York, NY] : Distributed in the U. S. by Harper and Row, c1985. xv, 423 p. : ill. ; 24 cm. Includes index. ISBN 0-914845-68-3 LC Card 85-18951 DDC 005.4/469 19
1. MS-DOS (Computer operating system). 2. IBM Personal Computer - Programming. 3. Microcomputers - Programming. I. Title. II. Title: Running MS-DOS.
QA76.76.O63 W65 1985
NYPL [JSE 86-1760]

WOMAN. see **WOMEN.**

Woman's guide to financial security. MacKenzie, Warren, 1927- For women only . Alexandria, Va. , c1986. xiii, 196 p. ; ISBN 0-938125-00-1 : LC Card 86-70681 DDC 332.024/042 19
HG179 .M244 1986

A woman's place . Sitterly, Connie, 1953- Englewood Cliffs, N.J. , c1988. xvi, 365 p. : ISBN 0-13-961954-2 (pbk.) : LC Card 87-25746 DDC 658.4/09/024042 19
HD6054.3 .S67 1988

"Woman's right to labor," or, Low wages and hard work . Dall, Caroline Wells (Healey), 1822-1912. Boston , 1860. xv, 184 p. ; LC Card 87-162350
HD6053 .D27 1860

Women--a world survey /. Sivard, Ruth Leger. Washington, D.C. , c1985. 44 p. : ISBN 0-918281-00-8 (pbk.) : LC Card 85-171073 DDC 305.4 19
HQ1154 .S547 1985
*NYPL [*R-Econ. 86-4677]*

Women adrift . Meyerowitz, Joanne J. (Joanne Jay) Chicago , 1988. p. cm. ISBN 0-226-52197-4 LC Card 87-22449 DDC 331.4/09773/11 19
HD6096.C4 M49 1988

WOMEN, AFRO-AMERICAN. see **AFRO-AMERICAN WOMEN.**

WOMEN AGRICULTURAL LABORERS - AUSTRIA - BIOGRAPHY.
Mägde . Wien , 1985. 211 p. : ISBN 3-205-06154-3 LC Card 86-127196
HD6072.2.A9 M34 1985

WOMEN AGRICULTURAL LABORERS - BANGLADESH.
Halim, Abdul, 1945- The effects of rice based cropping system research on women in Bangladesh /. Mymensingh , 1986. 2, 30 leaves ; LC Card 86-901954 DDC 331.4/8318/095492 19
HD1537.B3 H35 1986

WOMEN AGRICULTURAL LABORERS - DEVELOPING COUNTRIES.
Jiggins, Janice. Gender-related impacts and the work of the international agricultural research centers /. Washington, D.C. , c1986. x, 95 p. ; ISBN 0-8213-0840-8 (pbk.) LC Card 86-24709 DDC 331.4/83/091724 19
HD6073.A292 D444 1986

WOMEN AGRICULTURAL LABORERS - DOMINICAN REPUBLIC - POLITICAL ACTIVITY.
Campesinas y políticos, 1986 . Santo Domingo, República Dominicana , 1986. 83 p. : LC Card 87-102259
HD6073.A292 D653 1986

WOMEN AGRICULTURAL LABORERS - GAMBIA.
Nath, Kamla. Labor-saving techniques in food processing . Boston, MA (270 Bay State Rd., Boston 02215) , 1985. 26 leaves ; LC Card 87-155092 DDC 331.4/25 19
HD6073.A292 G256 1985

WOMEN AGRICULTURAL LABORERS - INDIA - NIZAMABAD (DISTRICT)
Shobha, V., 1952- Rural women and development . Delhi, India , 1987. xiii, 372 p. ; LC Card 87-902500 DDC 331.4/83/095484 19
HD6073.A292 I468 1987

WOMEN AGRICULTURAL LABORERS - INDIA - WARANGAL.
Shobha, V., 1952- Rural women and development . Delhi, India , 1987. xiii, 372 p. ; LC Card 87-902500 DDC 331.4/83/095484 19
HD6073.A292 I468 1987

WOMEN AGRICULTURAL LABORERS - LATIN AMERICA.
A Mulher rural e mudanças no processo de produção agrícola . [Brasília] [1984] i, 161 p. ; LC Card 86-150197
HD6073.A292 L295 1984

WOMEN AGRICULTURAL LABORERS - MEXICO.
Unidad Agrícola Industrial para la Mujer /. [Mexico City] , 1981. 45 p. : LC Card 84-228117
HD6073.A29 M68 1981

WOMEN AGRICULTURAL LABORERS - NIGERIA.
Jackson, Cecile, 1953- The Kano River Irrigation Project /. West Hartford, Conn. , 1985. xviii, 66 p. ; ISBN 0-931816-19-X LC Card 85-5242 DDC 331.4/83/09669 19
HD6073.F32 N64 1985
NYPL [JLF 86-1634]

WOMEN AGRICULTURAL LABORERS - ZAMBIA.
Safilios-Rothschild, Constantina, 1934- The policy implications of the roles of women in agriculture in Zambia /. [Lusaka] [1985] 49, [25] p. ; LC Card 87-980047 DDC 331.4/83/096894 19
HD6073.A292 Z337 1985

WOMEN AGRICULTURAL LABORERS - ZAMBIA - CONGRESSES.
Strengthening women's participation in food and agricultural marketing . [Lusaka] [1984] 78 p. ; LC Card 86-980282 DDC 331.4/83/096894 19
HD6073.A292 Z3374 1984

WOMEN AIRCRAFT INDUSTRY WORKERS - CALIFORNIA - LOS ANGELES - INTERVIEWS.
Gluck, Sherna Berger. Rosie the Riveter revisited . Boston , c1987. xiii, 282 p. : ISBN 0-8057-9022-5 (alk. paper) LC Card 86-31852 DDC 331.4/0973 19
HD6073.A452 U64 1987

Women and child workers in unorganised sector : non-government organisation's perspectives / edited by K.D. Gangrade, J.A. Gathia. New Delhi : Concept Pub. Co., 1983. xii, 104 p. ; 23 cm. Includes bibliographical references. LC Card 83-906999 DDC 331.3/1/0954 19
1. Women - Employment - India - Addresses, essays, lectures. 2. Children - Employment - India - Addresses, essays, lectures. I. Gangrade, K. D., 1926-. II. Gathia, J. A. (Joseph Anthony), 1946-.
HD6189 .W64 1983 *NYPL [JLD 87-730]*

Women & children first.
The Consumers' League of New York . New York , 1987. 47, 47, 55 p. : ISBN 0-8240-7684-2 (alk. paper) : LC Card 87-19804 DDC 331.4/2/09747 19
HD6096.N6 C66 1987

Women and home-based work . Christensen, K. (Kathleen) New York , c1988. xv, 201 p. ; ISBN 0-8050-0386-X LC Card 87-8527 DDC 305.4/3 19
HD6072.6.U5 C47 1988

Women and information technology / edited by Marilyn J. Davidson and Cary L. Cooper. Chichester ; New York : Wiley, c1987. viii, 283 p. : ill. ; 24 cm. (Wiley series in psychology and productivity at work) Includes bibliographies and index. ISBN 0-471-91603-X : LC Card 87-10554 DDC 331.4 19
1. Women - Employment. 2. Information technology. I. Davidson, Marilyn. II. Cooper, Cary L. III. Series.
HD6053 .W636 1987

Women and paid work : issues of equality / edited by Audrey Hunt. New York : St. Martin's Press, 1988. p. cm. Bibliography: p. Includes index. ISBN 0-312-01200-4 : LC Card 87-23477 DDC 331.2/1 19
1. Equal pay for equal work - Great Britain. 2. Women - Employment - Great Britain. I. Hunt, Audrey.
HD6061.2.G7 W66 1988

WOMEN AND PSYCHOANALYSIS.
Sayers, Janet. Sexual contradictions . London , New York, NY , 1986. x, 214 p. : ISBN 0-422-78780-9 LC Card 85-27948 DDC 155.3/3 19
BF692.2 .S29 1986 *NYPL [JFD 86-5840]*

Women and recession / edited by Jill Rubery. London ; New York : Routledge & Kegan Paul, 1988. xii, 294 p. ; 23 cm. (ILE) Includes bibliographies and index. ISBN 0-7102-0701-8 LC Card 87-20626 DDC 331.4/12 19
1. Women - Employment. 2. Married women - Employment. I. Rubery, J. (Jill). II. Series: ILE (Series).
HD6053 .W6375 1988

Women and the economy . Mallier, A. T., 1931- Houndmills, Basingstoke, Hampshire , 1987. xiv, 221 p. : ISBN 0-333-37938-1
NYPL [JLD 87-1151]

Women and the household in Asia .
(vol. 1) Invisible hands . New Delhi , Newbury Park, Calif. , 1987. 273 p. ; ISBN 0-8039-9524-5 (U. S.) LC Card 87-4337 DDC 331.4/0954 19
HD6181.85 .A85 1987

Women and training /. Wickham, Ann. Milton

Keynes, England , Philadelphia, PA, USA , c1986. x, 147 p. ; ISBN 0-335-15119-1 LC Card 86-5176 DDC 331.4/2592/0941 19
HD6059.6.G7 W52 1986
NYPL [JLD 86-3495]

Women and work in preindustrial Europe / edited by Barbara A. Hanawalt. Bloomington : Indiana University Press, c1986. xviii, 233 p. ; 25 cm. Includes bibliographies and index. ISBN 0-253-36610-0 LC Card 85-42829 DDC 331.4/094 19
1. Women - Employment - Europe - History - Addresses, essays, lectures. 2. Women - Europe - Economic conditions - Addresses, essays, lectures. 3. Europe - Occupations - History - Addresses, essays, lectures. I. Hanawalt, Barbara.
HD6059.5.E85 W65 1986
NYPL [JLE 86-3381]

Women and Work Research Group. Hidden aspects of women's work /. New York , 1987. x, 380 p. ; ISBN 0-275-92415-7 (alk. paper) : LC Card 87-2449 DDC 331.4/133/0973 19
HD6060.5.U5 H53 1987

WOMEN AS FARMERS. see **WOMEN IN AGRICULTURE.**

Women at work /. Aldred, Chris. London , 1981. 173 p. : ISBN 0-330-26479-6 (pbk.) LC Card 86-673456
HD6135 .A79x 1981

WOMEN - ATTITUDES.
Lieberman, Annette. Unbalanced accounts . New York , c1987. xx, 281 p. ; ISBN 0-87113-141-2 LC Card 86-28845 DDC 332.4/01/9 19
HG179 .L49 1987

WOMEN AUTOMOBILE INDUSTRY WORKERS - FRANCE - ATTITUDES.
Legay, Marie-Agnès. Réduction de la durée du travail et changement des modes de vie . Aix-en-Provence [1984] ix, 366 p. : LC Card 86-185902
HD6066.F8 L44 1984

WOMEN - BANGLADESH - SOCIAL CONDITIONS.
Islam, Shamima. Invisible labour force . Bangladesh , 1985. 60, [1] p. ; LC Card 85-904350 DDC 331.4/09549/2 19
HD6190.6 .I84 1985

Mabud, Mohammed A. (Mohammed Abdul) Women's development, income, and fertility /. Dhaka , 1985. xi, 180 p. ; LC Card 85-903972 DDC 305.4/09549/2 19
HQ1745.6 .M33 1985 ***NYPL [JLD 86-2067]***

Noman, Ayesha. Status of women and fertility in Bangladesh /. Dhaka, Bangladesh , c1983. xv, 91 p. ; LC Card 83-905271 DDC 305.4/2/095492 19
HB1050.6.A3 N65 1983
NYPL [JLD 86-2056]

WOMEN, BLACK - EMPLOYMENT - SIERRA LEONE - HISTORY - 19TH CENTURY.
White, E. Frances. Sierra Leone's settler women traders . Ann Arbor , c1987. xi, 168 p. : ISBN 0-472-10080-7 (alk. paper) : LC Card 86-24997 DDC 331.4/81381/09664 19
HF3933 .W47 1987

WOMEN - BRAZIL - ECONOMIC CONDITIONS.
Pena, Maria Valéria Junho. Mulheres e trabalhadoras . Rio de Janeiro, RJ , 1981. iii, 227 p. ; LC Card 81-216820 DDC 331.4/0981 19
HD6124 .P46 1981 ***NYPL [JLD 86-1557]***

WOMEN - BRAZIL - SOCIAL CONDITIONS.
Horta, Elisabeth Vorcaro. A mulher na cultura brasileira /. Belo Horizonte , 1975. 122 p. ; LC Card 75-511579
HQ1542 .H66 ***NYPL [Sc D 86-811]***

Pena, Maria Valéria Junho. Mulheres e trabalhadoras . Rio de Janeiro, RJ , 1981. iii, 227 p. ; LC Card 81-216820 DDC 331.4/0981 19
HD6124 .P46 1981 ***NYPL [JLD 86-1557]***

Santarcangelo, Maria Candida Vergueiro. A situação da mulher /. São Paulo , 1980. 389 p. ;
NYPL [JLD 86-625]

WOMEN - CANADA.
Wilson, S. J. (Susannah Jane) Women, the family, and the economy /. Toronto , New York , c1982. 176 p. : ISBN 0-07-548028-X (pbk.) LC Card 82-123177 DDC 305.4/0971 19
HQ1457 .W53 1982 ***NYPL [JLE 86-1735]***

WOMEN - CANADA - SOCIAL CONDITIONS.
Canada. Royal Commission on the Status of Women in Canada. Report of the Royal Commission on the Status of Women in Canada. [Ottawa, Ont.] , 1970. xii, 488 p. :
NYPL [JLE 73-1102]

WOMEN CANNERY WORKERS - CALIFORNIA - HISTORY - CASE STUDIES.
Ruíz, Vicki. Cannery women, cannery lives . Albuquerque , c1987. xviii, 194 p. : ISBN 0-8263-1006-0 LC Card 87-13878 DDC 331.88/1640282/09794 19
HD6515.F72 U547 1987

WOMEN CANNERY WORKERS - CALIFORNIA - SANTA CLARA RIVER VALLEY - FAMILY RELATIONSHIPS.
Zavella, Patricia, 1949- Women's work and Chicano families . Ithaca , 1987. xviii, 191 p. ; ISBN 0-8014-1730-9 (pbk. : alk. paper) LC Card 87-5245 DDC 305.4/3664 19
HD6073.C272 U596 1987

Women, clerical work, and office automation : issues for research : report of a conference / sponsored by the Women's Bureau in cooperation with the Panel on Technology and Women's Employment, National Research Council. Washington, D.C. : U. S. Dept. of Labor, Office of the Secretary, Women's Bureau, 1986. vi, 64 p. ; 28 cm. Shipping list no.: 86-723-P. Item 782 LC Card 86-602559 DDC 331.4/8165137/0973 19
1. Women - Employment - United States - Congresses. 2. Women clerks - United States - Effect of automation on. 3. Clerks - United States - Effects of automation on. 4. Office practice - Automation. 5. Clerical occupations. I. United States. Women's Bureau. II. National Research Council (U. S.). Committee on Women's Employment and Related Social Issues. Panel on Technology and Women's Employment.
HD6095 .W685 1986

WOMEN CLERKS - GREAT BRITAIN - HISTORY.
Cohn, Samuel, 1954- The process of occupational sex-typing . Philadelphia , 1985. viii, 279 p. ; ISBN 0-87722-402-1 : LC Card 85-14864 DDC 331.4/8165137/0941 19
HD6060.65.G7 C64 1985
NYPL [JLE 86-917]

WOMEN CLERKS (RETAIL TRADE) - UNITED STATES - HISTORY.
Benson, Susan Porter, 1943- Counter cultures . Urbana , c1986. xvi, 322 p. : ISBN 0-252-01252-6 (alk. paper) LC Card 85-21012 DDC 381/.1/0973 19
HF5465.U5 B45 1986 ***NYPL [JLE 87-1091]***

WOMEN CLERKS - TRAINING OF - UNITED STATES.
Valli, Linda, 1947- Becoming clerical workers /. Boston , 1986. xv, 261 p. ; ISBN 0-7102-0336-5
NYPL [JLD 86-1147]

WOMEN CLERKS - UNITED STATES.
Valli, Linda, 1947- Becoming clerical workers /. Boston , 1986. xv, 261 p. ; ISBN 0-7102-0336-5
NYPL [JLD 86-1147]

WOMEN CLERKS - UNITED STATES - EFFECT OF AUTOMATION ON.
Women, clerical work, and office automation . Washington, D.C. , 1986. vi, 64 p. ; LC Card 86-602559 DDC 331.4/8165137/0973 19
HD6095 .W685 1986

WOMEN CLOTHING WORKERS - BRAZIL - RIO DE JANEIRO.
Abreu, Alice R. de Paiva. O avesso da moda . São Paulo , 1986. 302 p. ; LC Card 87-129109 DDC 331.4/887/098153 19
HD6073.C62 B62 1986

WOMEN CLOTHING WORKERS - QUÉBEC (PROVINCE)
Jean, Diane. Le travail à domicile dans le vêtement pour dames . [Montréal] [1982] xi, 146, [1] p. : ISBN 2-550-02847-3 LC Card 83-242834
HD6073.C62 C25 1982

WOMEN COLLEGE GRADUATES - EMPLOYMENT - GERMANY (WEST)
Biermann, Ingrid, 1955- Leben mit kurzfristigem Denken . Weinheim , 1985. 224 p. ; ISBN 3-407-58260-9 LC Card 86-106693
HD6053.6.G3 B54 1985
NYPL [JLD 86-3122]

WOMEN COLLEGE GRADUATES - EMPLOYMENT - UNITED STATES.
Theodore, Athena. The campus troublemakers . Houston, Tex. , c1986. xxiv, 293 p. ; ISBN 0-88105-066-0 : LC Card 85-14973 DDC 378/.12/088042 19
LB2332.3 .T44 1986 ***NYPL [JLE 86-4389]***

WOMEN COLLEGE GRADUATES - UNITED STATES.
Antler, Joyce. The educated woman and professionalization . New York , 1987. x, 448 p. ; ISBN 0-8240-6839-4 (alk. paper) : LC Card 87-17604 DDC 331.4/11423 19
HD6054.2.U6 A57 1987

WOMEN COLLEGE TEACHERS - UNITED STATES.
Theodore, Athena. The campus troublemakers . Houston, Tex. , c1986. xxiv, 293 p. ; ISBN 0-88105-066-0 : LC Card 85-14973 DDC 378/.12/088042 19
LB2332.3 .T44 1986 ***NYPL [JLE 86-4389]***

WOMEN COLONISTS - SIERRA LEONE - HISTORY - 19 CENTURY.
White, E. Frances. Sierra Leone's settler women traders . Ann Arbor , c1987. xi, 168 p. : ISBN 0-472-10080-7 (alk. paper) : LC Card 86-24997 DDC 331.4/81381/09664 19
HF3933 .W47 1987

WOMEN - COMMUNICATION.
Wallace, Joanne. The working woman /. Old Tappan, N.J. , c1986. 171 p. : ISBN 0-8007-1455-5 (pbk.) : LC Card 85-14396 DDC 650.1/024042 19
HD6053 .W34 1986 ***NYPL [JLF 87-131]***

WOMEN CONSUMERS - NEW YORK (STATE) - SYRACUSE.
Venkatesh, Alladi. The significance of the women's movement to marketing . New York , 1985. 209 p. ; ISBN 0-03-069588-0 (alk. paper) : LC Card 85-19106 DDC 658.8/348 19
HF5415.3 .V46 1985 ***NYPL [JLE 86-1081]***

WOMEN - DENMARK - SOCIAL CONDITIONS - SOURCES.
Kvindeliv--hverdagsliv . Copenhagen , 1985. 111 p. : ISBN 87-00-65962-2 : LC Card 86-156606
HD6169 .K855 1985

WOMEN - DEVELOPING COUNTRIES.
Bruchhaus, Eva-Maria. Frauen in Entwicklungsländern . Freiburg im Breisgau , 1979. iii, 182 p. ; LC Card 81-121677 DDC 305.4/09172/4 19
HQ1870.9 .B78 1979 ***NYPL [JLG 86-106]***

WOMEN - DEVELOPING COUNTRIES - ECONOMIC CONDITIONS.
Bisilliat, Jeanne. Femmes du tiers-monde . Paris , c1983. 122 p. : ISBN 2-86262-201-X
NYPL [JLD 87-456]

WOMEN - DEVELOPING COUNTRIES - ECONOMIC CONDITIONS - CASE STUDIES.
Women, work, and ideology in the Third World /. London , New York , 1985. xvii, 265 p. : ISBN 0-422-79710-3 (U. S. : pbk.) LC Card 85-17279 DDC 305.4/09172/4 19
HQ1870.9 .W657 1985
NYPL [JLD 86-2322]

WOMEN - DEVELOPING COUNTRIES - ECONOMIC CONDITIONS - CONGRESSES.
Women, work, and demographic issues . Geneva , 1984. 159 p. ; ISBN 92-2-103886-6 : LC Card 86-673726
HD6052 .W568x 1984

WOMEN, DISCRIMINATION AGAINST. see **SEX DISCRIMINATION AGAINST WOMEN.**

WOMEN - DISEASES - PSYCHOSOMATIC ASPECTS.
Witkin-Lanoil, Georgia. The female stress syndrome . New York , c1984. xi, 211 p. ; ISBN 0-937858-33-1 LC Card 83-25038 DDC 155.6/33 19
BF575.S75 W58 1984
NYPL [JFD 86-10468]

WOMEN DOMESTICS - ARGENTINA - BUENOS AIRES METROPOLITAN AREA - HISTORY.

Cárdenas, Isabel Laura. Ramona y el robot . Buenos Aires, Argentina , 1986. 155 p. : ISBN 950-560-032-1 LC Card 87-100727
HD6072.2.A72 B843 1986

WOMEN DOMESTICS - AUSTRIA - BIOGRAPHY.
Mägde . Wien , 1985. 211 p. : ISBN 3-205-06154-3 LC Card 86-127196
HD6072.2.A9 M34 1985

WOMEN DOMESTICS - CALIFORNIA - HISTORY.
Glenn, Evelyn Nakano. Issei, Nisei, war bride . Philadelphia , 1986. xviii, 290 p. ; ISBN 0-87722-412-9 LC Card 85-25107 DDC 331.4/8164046/0899560794 19
HD6072.2.U52 C24 1986 ***NYPL [IEA 86-1929]***

WOMEN DOMESTICS - CHILE - INTERVIEWS.
Gálvez, Thelma. Yo trabajo así-- en casa particular /. Santiago, Chile , 1985. 113 p. : LC Card 86-208887
HD6072.2.C5 G35 1985

WOMEN DOMESTICS - ENGLAND - ROCHDALE (GREATER MANCHESTER) - HISTORY - 19TH CENTURY.
Higgs, Edward, 1952- Domestic servants and households in Rochdale, 1851-1871 /. New York , 1986. 423 p. ; ISBN 0-8240-6682-0 : LC Card 84-46002 DDC 305.5/6 19
HD8039.D52 G7755 1986 ***NYPL [JLE 86-4591]***

WOMEN DOMESTICS - GERMANY.
Grenzen der Frauenlohnarbeit . Frankfurt/Main , New York , c1986. 250 p. : ISBN 3-593-33628-6 LC Card 86-228323
HD6072.2.G4 G74 1986

Walser, Karin, 1950- Dienstmädchen . Frankfurt , 1985. 195 p. ; ISBN 3-88704-079-1 LC Card 86-141363
HD6072.2.G4 W35 1985

WOMEN DOMESTICS - HUNGARY - HISTORY.
Gyáni, Gábor. Család, háztartás és a városi cselédség /. Budapest , c1983. 251, [1] p. ; ISBN 963-271-955-7 : LC Card 84-129676
HD6072.2.H8 G92 1983

WOMEN DOMESTICS - ITALY.
Petrillo, Giovanna, 1952- Produttività e improduttività del lavoro domestico . Bologna , 1985. 139 p. ; LC Card 86-132212
HD8039.H842 I87 1985

WOMEN DOMESTICS - NETHERLANDS - HISTORY.
Henkes, Barbara. Kaatje, ben je boven? . Nijmegen , c1985. 192 p. : ISBN 90-6168-242-8 : LC Card 85-237937
HD6072.2.N4 H46 1985

WOMEN DOMESTICS - PERU - LIMA.
Bunster, Ximena. Sellers & servants . New York , 1985. x, 258 p. : ISBN 0-03-060543-1 (alk. paper) : LC Card 85-6259 DDC 331.4/0985/25 19
HD6072.2.P42 L563 1985 ***NYPL [JLE 86-910]***

WOMEN - ECONOMIC CONDITIONS.
Sharma, Ursula, 1941- Women's work, class, and the urban household . London , New York , 1986. 213 p. ; ISBN 0-422-79320-5 : LC Card 86-11296 DDC 305.4/3 19
HQ759 .S4616 1986 ***NYPL [JLD 87-1281]***

WOMEN - ECONOMIC CONDITIONS - CONGRESSES.
Women, work, and demographic issues . Geneva , 1984. 159 p. ; ISBN 92-2-103886-6 : LC Card 86-673726
HD6052 .W568x 1984

WOMEN - EDUCATION (SECONDARY) - GREAT BRITAIN.
Wickham, Ann. Women and training /. Milton Keynes, England , Philadelphia, PA, USA , c1986. x, 147 p. ; ISBN 0-335-15119-1 LC Card 86-5176 DDC 331.4/2592/0941 19
HD6059.6.G7 W52 1986 ***NYPL [JLD 86-3495]***

WOMEN ELECTRONIC INDUSTRY WORKERS - INDIA.
Ramanamma, A., 1936- Women in Indian industry /. Delhi, India , 1987. 232 p. ; LC Card 87-901258 DDC 331.4/821381/0954 19
HD6189 .R347 1987

WOMEN - EMANCIPATION. see WOMEN'S RIGHTS.

Women employees and rural development .
Bhoite, Anuradha. Delhi, India , c1987. xiii, 135 p. ; ISBN 81-212-0085-7 : LC Card 87-900916 DDC 331.4/0954 19
HD6189 .B56 1987

WOMEN - EMPLOYMENT - ADDRESSES, ESSAYS, LECTURES.
Gender and the labour process /. Aldershot, Hampshire, Eng. , Brookfield, Vt., U. S.A. , c1986. vii, 186 p. ; ISBN 0-566-00999-4 : LC Card 85-21977 DDC 331.4 19
HD6060.6 .G45 1986 ***NYPL [JLD 86-3900]***

WOMEN - EMPLOYMENT - AFRICA - CONGRESSES.
JASPA Steering Group Meeting on Priority Employment Policies and Projects for Africa (1985 : Addis Ababa, Ethiopia) Report of JASPA Steering Group Meeting on Priority Employment Policies and Projects for Africa. Addis Ababa , 1986. 43 leaves ; LC Card 87-980227 DDC 331.12/042/096 19
HD5837.A6 J37 1985

WOMEN - EMPLOYMENT - AFRICA, FRENCH-SPEAKING WEST.
L'Emploi des femmes ... /. Addis-Abéba , 1985. 7 v. : ISBN 92-2-205192-0 (v. 1) LC Card 86-981198
HD6216 .E46 1985

WOMEN - EMPLOYMENT - ARGENTINA.
Lindenboim, Javier. La terciarización del empleo en la Argentina. Buenos Aires , 1985. vi, 59, 50, 3 p. ; LC Card 87-122527 DDC 381 19
HD2346.A73 L56 1985

WOMEN - EMPLOYMENT - ARGENTINA - BUENOS AIRES METROPOLITAN AREA.
Lindenboim, Javier. La terciarización del empleo en la Argentina. Buenos Aires , 1985. vi, 59, 50, 3 p. ; LC Card 87-122527 DDC 381 19
HD2346.A73 L56 1985

WOMEN - EMPLOYMENT - ASIA - CONGRESSES.
Invisible hands . New Delhi , Newbury Park, Calif. , 1987. 273 p. ; ISBN 0-8039-9524-5 (U. S.) LC Card 87-4337 DDC 331.4/0954 19
HD6181.85 .A85 1987

WOMEN - EMPLOYMENT - AUSTRALIA.
O'Donnell, Carol. The basis of the bargain . Sydney , Boston , 1984. 186 p. ; ISBN 0-86861-497-1 LC Card 84-70146 DDC 331.4/133/0994 19
HD6060.5.A8 O36 1984 ***NYPL [JLD 86-2017]***

WOMEN - EMPLOYMENT - AUSTRALIA - HANDBOOKS, MANUALS, ETC.
Affirmative action implementation manual /. Canberra , 1986. 66 p. ; ISBN 0-644-04750-X (pbk.) LC Card 87-109354 DDC 658.3 19
HD6060.5.A8 A34 1986

WOMEN - EMPLOYMENT - AUSTRIA - SALZBURG (LAND) - REGIONAL DISPARITIES - STATISTICS.
Fink, Karl, Mag. Die regionale Dynamik des Salzburger Arbeitsmarktes, 1971-1980 . Salzburg [1981?] 212 p. : LC Card 82-171635
HD5772.S24 F56 1981 ***NYPL [JLG 86-301]***

WOMEN - EMPLOYMENT - BANGLADESH.
Islam, Shamima. Invisible labour force . Bangladesh , 1985. 60, [1] p. ; LC Card 85-904350 DDC 331.4/09549/2 19
HD6190.6 .I84 1985

Mabud, Mohammed A. (Mohammed Abdul) Women's development, income, and fertility /. Dhaka , 1985. xi, 180 p. ; LC Card 85-903972 DDC 305.4/09549/2 19
HQ1745.6 .M33 1985 ***NYPL [JLD 86-2067]***

WOMEN - EMPLOYMENT - BELGIUM.
Coomans, Géry, 1949- La production sociale des femmes /. Bruxelles , c1983. 223 p. : ISBN 2-8004-0820-0 : LC Card 84-199167
HD6158 .C66 1983

WOMEN - EMPLOYMENT - BOLIVIA.
Cisneros C., Antonio. La mujer trabajadora . La Paz, Bolivia [1984] 131 leaves : LC Card 85-129000 DDC 331.4/0984 19
HD6121 .C58 1984 ***NYPL [JLF 86-1704]***

WOMEN - EMPLOYMENT - BRAZIL.
Horta, Elisabeth Vorcaro. A mulher na cultura brasileira /. Belo Horizonte , 1975. 122 p. ; LC Card 75-511579
HQ1542 .H66 ***NYPL [Sc D 86-811]***

WOMEN - EMPLOYMENT - BRAZIL - HISTORY.
Pena, Maria Valéria Junho. Mulheres e trabalhadoras . Rio de Janeiro, RJ , 1981. iii, 227 p. ; LC Card 81-216820 DDC 331.4/0981 19
HD6124 .P46 1981 ***NYPL [JLD 86-1557]***

WOMEN - EMPLOYMENT - CALIFORNIA - LOS ANGELES - HISTORY.
Gluck, Sherna Berger. Rosie the Riveter revisited . Boston , c1987. xiii, 282 p. : ISBN 0-8057-9022-5 (alk. paper) LC Card 86-31852 DDC 331.4/0973 19
HD6073.A452 U64 1987

WOMEN - EMPLOYMENT - CANADA.
Armstrong, Pat, 1945- A working majority . Ottawa, Ont. , c1983. v, 280 p. : ISBN 0-660-11314-7 (pbk.) : LC Card 83-158188 DDC 331.4/0971 19
HD6067.2.C2 A75 1983 ***NYPL [JLD 86-1585]***

Robinson, Patricia A. (Patricia Ann) Women's work interruptions . Ottawa [1987], c1986. 36, 40 p. ; ISBN 0-660-52895-9 (pbk.) : LC Card 87-146334 DDC 331.4/12/0971 19
HD6099 .R63 1987

Wilson, S. J. (Susannah Jane) Women, the family, and the economy /. Toronto , New York , c1982. 176 p. : ISBN 0-07-548028-X (pbk.) LC Card 82-123177 DDC 305.4/0971 19
HQ1457 .W53 1982 ***NYPL [JLE 86-1735]***

WOMEN - EMPLOYMENT - CHILE.
Pardo V., Lucía. La historia laboral de las mujeres y su efecto en la tasa de salario . Santiago , 1986. 44, 5 p. : LC Card 86-217486
HD6126 .P37 1986

WOMEN - EMPLOYMENT - CHILE - BIOGRAPHY.
Mack, Macarena. Los trabajos de las mujeres entre el campo y la ciudad, 1920-1982 . [Santiago, Chile] [1986] 108 p. ; LC Card 86-217673
HD6126 .M33 1986

WOMEN - EMPLOYMENT - COMMUNIST COUNTRIES - CASE STUDIES.
Working women in socialist countries . Geneva , 1985. xvi, 234 p. : ISBN 92-2-103910-2 (pbk.) : LC Card 85-181464 DDC 304.6/32/091717 19
HB901 .W657 1985 ***NYPL [JLE 86-1433]***

WOMEN - EMPLOYMENT - CONGRESSES.
Les Effets des conditions de travail sur la santé des travailleuses . [Montréal] [1984] 230 p., [5] p. of plates : ISBN 2-920658-00-X : LC Card 86-158040
HD6067 .E34 1984

Strategies for integrating women into the labour market /. Copenhagen, Denmark , 1982. 347 p. : ISBN 87-88209-08-3 (pbk.) LC Card 86-673782
HD6052 .S77x 1982

Women, work, and demographic issues . Geneva , 1984. 159 p. ; ISBN 92-2-103886-6 : LC Card 86-673726
HD6052 .W568x 1984

Women, work, and society /. Calcutta , 1985. xvi, 430 p. : LC Card 86-900827 DDC 331.4 19
HD6052 .W565 1982 ***NYPL [JLE 87-1019]***

WOMEN - EMPLOYMENT - DENMARK.
Borchorst, Anette. Arbejdsmarkedets kønsopdeling . Aalborg , 1984. 162 p. : ISBN 87-7307-252-4 LC Card 85-106008
HD6060.65.D4 B67 1984 ***NYPL [JFK 82-214 nr.15]***

Gydesen, Ellen. Kvinders livsgrundlag i 80-erne /. K [i.e. Copenhagen] [1985] 202 columns : LC Card 87-168500
HD6060.65.D4 G93 1985

Markussen, Randi. Det fleksible køn . [Copenhagen] , c1984. 163 p. ; ISBN 87-7445-159-6 : LC Card 84-187146
HD6169 .M37 1984

Vedel, Gitte. Om kvindearbejdets igangværende udvikling og perspektiver, i relation til den

teknologiske udvikling /. Roskilde , 1982. 103 leaves : LC Card 83-172895
HD6060.65.D4 V42 1982

WOMEN - EMPLOYMENT - DENMARK - HISTORY - 19TH CENTURY - SOURCES.

Kvindeliv--hverdagsliv . Copenhagen , 1985. 111 p. : ISBN 87-00-65962-2 : LC Card 86-156606
HD6169 .K855 1985

WOMEN - EMPLOYMENT - DENMARK - HISTORY - 20TH CENTURY - SOURCES.

Kvindeliv--hverdagsliv . Copenhagen , 1985. 111 p. : ISBN 87-00-65962-2 : LC Card 86-156606
HD6169 .K855 1985

WOMEN - EMPLOYMENT - DEVELOPING COUNTRIES.

Bisilliat, Jeanne. Femmes du tiers-monde . Paris , c1983. 122 p. : ISBN 2-86262-201-X
NYPL [JLD 87-456]

Garnsey, Elizabeth. Industrial change and women's employment . Geneva , 1987. ix, 100, x p. : ISBN 92-9014-411-4 (pbk.) : LC Card 87-163195 DDC 331.4/09172/4 19
HD6223 .G37 1987

WOMEN - EMPLOYMENT - DEVELOPING COUNTRIES - CASE STUDIES.

Women, work, and ideology in the Third World /. London , New York , 1985. xvii, 265 p. : ISBN 0-422-79710-3 (U. S. : pbk.) LC Card 85-17279 DDC 305.4/09172/4 19
HQ1870.9 .W657 1985
NYPL [JLD 86-2322]

WOMEN - EMPLOYMENT - DEVELOPING COUNTRIES - CONGRESSES.

Women, work, and demographic issues . Geneva , 1984. 159 p. ; ISBN 92-2-103886-6 : LC Card 86-673726
HD6052 .W568x 1984

WOMEN - EMPLOYMENT - DOMINICAN REPUBLIC - CONGRESSES.

Condiciones socioeconómicas de la mujer trabajadora en la República Dominicana /. Santo Domingo, República Dominicana , 1986. 150 p. ; LC Card 86-208584
HD6112.5 .C65 1986

WOMEN - EMPLOYMENT - EFFECT OF TECHNOLOGICAL INNOVATIONS ON - CONGRESSES.

Women, work, and technology . Ann Arbor , c1987. viii, 387 p. ; ISBN 0-472-06373-1 (pbk. : alk. paper) : LC Card 87-16236 DDC 331.4 19
HD6052 .W566 1987

WOMEN - EMPLOYMENT - ENGLAND - COVENTRY (WEST MIDLANDS)

Beechey, Veronica. A matter of hours . Minneapolis, MN , c1987. 212 p. ; ISBN 0-8166-1641-8 : LC Card 87-12459 DDC 331.4/12/0942498 19
HD6136.Z6 C683 1987

WOMEN - EMPLOYMENT - EUROPE.

Rein, Martin. Women in the social welfare labor market /. Berlin [1985] 180 p. ; LC Card 86-213535 DDC 331.4/129136294 19
HD6134 .R45 1985

WOMEN - EMPLOYMENT - EUROPE, EASTERN.

Work and family life . Geneva , 1980. vi, 77 p. ; ISBN 92-2-102167-X (pbk.) LC Card 81-194978 DDC 306.8/5/0947 19
HD4904.25 .W68 1980

WOMEN - EMPLOYMENT - EUROPE - HISTORY - ADDRESSES, ESSAYS, LECTURES.

Women and work in preindustrial Europe /. Bloomington , c1986. xviii, 233 p. ; ISBN 0-253-36610-0 LC Card 85-42829 DDC 331.4/094 19
HD6059.5.E85 W65 1986
NYPL [JLE 86-3381]

WOMEN - EMPLOYMENT - EUROPE, NORTHERN - HISTORY.

Howell, Martha C. Women, production, and patriarchy in late medieval cities /. Chicago , 1986. xv, 285 p. ; ISBN 0-226-35503-9 : LC Card 85-31816 DDC 331.4/094 19
HD6134 .H69 1986 ***NYPL [JLE 86-4284]***

WOMEN - EMPLOYMENT - FRANCE.

Huet, Maryse. La concentration des emplois féminins . Paris [1983] 138 p. : ISBN 2-11-064535-0 : LC Card 85-176290 DDC 331.4/12/0944 19
HD6145 .H79 1983

Legay, Marie-Agnès. Réduction de la durée du travail et changement des modes de vie . Aix-en-Provence [1984] ix, 366 p. : LC Card 86-185902
HD6066.F8 L44 1984

Maruani, Margaret. Mais qui à peur du travail des femmes? /. Paris , c1985. 175 p. : ISBN 2-86738-099-5 : LC Card 86-154408
HD6145 .M37 1985

WOMEN - EMPLOYMENT - FRANCE - HISTORY.

Tilly, Louise. Women, work, and family /. New York , 1987. vii, 274 p. : ISBN 0-416-01681-2 (pbk.) : LC Card 87-11103 DDC 305.4/3/00941 19
HD6135 .T54 1987

WOMEN - EMPLOYMENT - FRANCE - HISTORY - 19TH CENTURY.

Cabaud, Michel. 1900, la Française au quotidien /. Paris , c1985. 204 p. : ISBN 2-200-37097-0 LC Card 86-137649
HD6059.F8 C33 1985

WOMEN - EMPLOYMENT - FRANCE - HISTORY - 19TH CENTURY - PICTORIAL WORKS.

Cabaud, Michel. 1900, la Française au quotidien /. Paris , c1985. 204 p. : ISBN 2-200-37097-0 LC Card 86-137649
HD6059.F8 C33 1985

WOMEN - EMPLOYMENT - FRANCE - HISTORY - 20TH CENTURY.

Fourcaut, Annie, 1950- Femmes à l'usine . Paris , 1982. 268 p. : ISBN 2-7071-1258-5 : LC Card 82-151587
HD6145 .F65 1982

WOMEN - EMPLOYMENT - FRANCE - HISTORY - EXHIBITIONS.

Les Femmes au travail 1882-1982 /. Paris , 1982. [70] leaves : LC Card 86-161448
HD6145 .F44 1982

WOMEN - EMPLOYMENT - GERMANY - HISTORY.

Wiesner, Merry, 1952- Working women in Renaissance Germany /. New Brunswick, N.J. , c1986. xiii, 263 p. : ISBN 0-8135-1138-0 : LC Card 85-14451 DDC 305.4/3/00943 19
HQ1149.G3 W54 1986
NYPL [JLE 86-3515]

WOMEN - EMPLOYMENT - GERMANY, WEST.

Frauen und Beruf, zwischen Wunsch und Realität . Bonn , Bad Honnef , 1986. 142 p. ; ISBN 3-87066-629-3 : LC Card 87-409372 DDC 331.4/0943 19
HD6149 .F719 1986

Hallensleben, Ruth. Frauenarbeit in der Industrie . Berlin-Kreuzberg , c1985. 157 p. : ISBN 3-88940-602-5 : LC Card 86-201457
HD6149 .H27 1985

Hegelheimer, Barbara. Berufsqualifikation und Berufschancen von Frauen in der Bundesrepublik Deutschland /. Berlin , 1977. viii, 303 p. ; LC Card 85-142052
HD6059.6.G4 H428 1977

"Was will die denn hier?" . Marburg , c1986. 156 p. ; ISBN 3-924800-82-0 LC Card 87-122751 DDC 331.4/0943 19
HD6060.65.G3 W37 1986

WOMEN - EMPLOYMENT - GERMANY (WEST) - CASE STUDIES.

Edding, Cornelia, 1943- Einbruch in den Herrenclub . Reinbek bei Hamburg , 1983. 184 p. : ISBN 3-499-15251-7 (pbk.) LC Card 87-673369
HD6054.2.G3 E33x 1983

Women, work, and family in Britain and Germany /. London , 1986. 216 p. : ISBN 0-7099-0976-4 ***NYPL [JLD 86-3391]***

WOMEN - EMPLOYMENT - GERMANY, WEST - CONGRESSES.

Workshop "Berufswege von Frauen" (1984 : Berlin, Germany) Berufsverläufe von Frauen . München , Weinheim , c1986. 291 p. : ISBN 3-87966-253-3 LC Card 87-407975 DDC 331.7/02/024042 19
HF5382.67.G3 W67 1984

WOMEN - EMPLOYMENT - GERMANY (WEST) - EFFECT OF TECHNOLOGICAL INNOVATIONS ON.

Frauen und neue Technologien /. Hannover , 1986. 112 p. ; LC Card 87-407392 DDC 331.4/0943 19
HD6059.G3 F74 1986

WOMEN - EMPLOYMENT - GERMANY (WEST) - PICTORIAL WORKS.

Hallensleben, Ruth. Frauenarbeit in der Industrie . Berlin-Kreuzberg , c1985. 157 p. : ISBN 3-88940-602-5 : LC Card 86-201457
HD6149 .H27 1985

WOMEN - EMPLOYMENT - GOVERNMENT POLICY - COMMUNIST COUNTRIES - CASE STUDIES.

Working women in socialist countries . Geneva , 1985. xvi, 234 p. : ISBN 92-2-103910-2 (pbk.) : LC Card 85-181464 DDC 304.6/32/091717 19
HB901 .W657 1985 ***NYPL [JLE 86-1433]***

WOMEN - EMPLOYMENT - GOVERNMENT POLICY - INDONESIA.

Indonesia. Kantor Menteri Negara Urusan Peranan Wanita. Pokok-pokok petunjuk pelaksanaan Program Peningkatan Produktivitas Kerja Tenaga Kerja Wanita Melalui Pendekatan Kesejahteraan Terpadu, tahun 1984/1986 (Juklak Nakerwan). Jakarta [1984] iii, xii, 47 p. ; LC Card 86-940168
HD6194 .I5 1984

WOMEN - EMPLOYMENT - GOVERNMENT POLICY - UNITED STATES.

National Research Council (U. S.). Committee on Women's Employment and Related Social Issues. Panel on Technology and Women's Employment. Computer chips and paper clips . Washington, D.C. , 1986. v. : ISBN 0-309-03688-7 (v. 1) LC Card 86-18113 DDC 331.4/8165137/0973 19
HD6331.18.M39 N38 1986
NYPL [JLL 87-129]

WOMEN - EMPLOYMENT - GREAT BRITAIN.

Aldred, Chris. Women at work /. London , 1981. 173 p. : ISBN 0-330-26479-6 (pbk.) LC Card 86-673456
HD6135 .A79x 1981

The Changing experience of employment . Houndmills, Basingstoke, Hampshire , 1986. x, 230 p. ; ISBN 0-333-39695-2
NYPL [JLD 87-933]

Dex, Shirley. British and American women at work . Houndmills, Basingstoke, Hampshire , 1986. xii, 159 p. : ISBN 0-333-40219-7
NYPL [JLD 86-3608]

Mallier, A. T., 1931- Women and the economy . Houndmills, Basingstoke, Hampshire , 1987. xiv, 221 p. : ISBN 0-333-37938-1 ***NYPL [JLD 87-1151]***

Meehan, Elizabeth M. Women's rights at work . New York , 1985. xvii, 253 p. ; ISBN 0-312-88793-0 : LC Card 84-15997 DDC 331.4/133/0941 19
HD6060 .M44 1984 ***NYPL [JLD 86-3580]***

Pollert, Anna. Girls, wives, factory lives /. London, England , 1981. 251 p. ; ISBN 0-333-29177-8 ***NYPL [JLD 83-884]***

Waged work . London , 1986. vi, 291 p. : ISBN 0-86068-801-1 (pbk.) : LC Card 86-232209 DDC 331.4/0941 19
HD6061.2.G7 W35 1986

Walby, Sylvia. Patriarchy at work . Cambridge [Cambrigeshire] , c1986. vii, 292 p. ; ISBN 0-7456-0157-X ***NYPL [JLD 87-941]***

Walby, Sylvia. Patriarchy at work . Minneapolis , c1986. vii, 292 p. ; ISBN 0-8166-1588-8 : LC Card 86-24912 DDC 331.4/133/0941 19
HD6060.65.G7 W35 1986

Wickham, Ann. Women and training /. Milton Keynes, England , Philadelphia, PA, USA , c1986. x, 147 p. ; ISBN 0-335-15119-1 LC Card 86-5176 DDC 331.4/2592/0941 19
HD6059.6.G7 W52 1986
NYPL [JLD 86-3495]

Women and paid work . New York , 1988. p. cm. ISBN 0-312-01200-4 : LC Card 87-23477 DDC 331.2/1 19
HD6061.2.G7 W66 1988

WOMEN - EMPLOYMENT - GREAT BRITAIN - CASE STUDIES.
Women, work, and family in Britain and Germany /. London , 1986. 216 p. : ISBN 0-7099-0976-4 *NYPL [JLD 86-3391]*

WOMEN - EMPLOYMENT - GREAT BRITAIN - HISTORY.
Cohn, Samuel, 1954- The process of occupational sex-typing . Philadelphia , 1985. viii, 279 p. ; ISBN 0-87722-402-1 : LC Card 85-14864 DDC 331.4/8165137/0941 19
HD6060.65.G7 C64 1985 *NYPL [JLE 86-917]*

Morris, Jenny, 1950- Women workers and the sweated trades . Aldershot, Hants, England , Brookfield, Vt., USA , c1986. 248 p. ; ISBN 0-566-05188-5 : LC Card 86-9850 DDC 331.4/23 19
HD2339.G7 M67 1986 *NYPL [JLD 86-4089]*

Tilly, Louise. Women, work, and family /. New York , 1987. vii, 274 p. : ISBN 0-416-01681-2 (pbk.) : LC Card 87-11103 DDC 305.4/3/00941 19
HD6135 .T54 1987

WOMEN - EMPLOYMENT - GREAT BRITAIN - HISTORY - 20TH CENTURY.
Braybon, Gail. Out of the cage . London , New York , 1987. xiii, 330 p. : ISBN 0-86358-046-7 : LC Card 87-13510 DDC 305.4/0941 19
HD6135 .B7 1987

Our work, our lives, our words . Basingstoke, Hampshire , 1986. xiii, 189 p. : ISBN 0-333-36598-4 *NYPL [JLD 86-4220]*

WOMEN - EMPLOYMENT - HISTORY.
Dall, Caroline Wells (Healey), 1822-1912. "Woman's right to labor," or, Low wages and hard work . Boston , 1860. xv, 184 p. ; LC Card 87-162350
HD6053 .D27 1860

WOMEN - EMPLOYMENT - ILLINOIS - CHICAGO - HISTORY.
Meyerowitz, Joanne J. (Joanne Jay) Women adrift . Chicago , 1988. p. cm. ISBN 0-226-52197-4 LC Card 87-22449 DDC 331.4/09773/11 19
HD6096.C4 M49 1988

WOMEN - EMPLOYMENT - INDIA.
Bhoite, Anuradha. Women employees and rural development . Delhi, India , c1987. xiii, 135 p. ; ISBN 81-212-0085-7 : LC Card 87-900916 DDC 331.4/0954 19
HD6189 .B56 1987

Chauhan, Indira, 1949- The dilemma of working women hostelers . Delhi , New Delhi , 1986. 70 p. : ISBN 81-7018-374-X : LC Card 86-902619 DDC 305.4/0954/792 19
HD6189 .C42 1986

Mina Swaminathan, 1933- Who cares? . New Delhi , 1985. xi, 159 p. : LC Card 86-900126
HV861.I4 M56 1985 *NYPL [JLD 86-3265]*

Ramanamma, A., 1936- Women in Indian industry /. Delhi, India , 1987. 232 p. ; LC Card 87-901258 DDC 331.4/821381/0954 19
HD6189 .R347 1987

Ray, S. N., M.A. Migrant women workers . Ranchi [1982] iii, 92 p., [3] leaves of plates : LC Card 85-903727 DDC 331.4/0954 19
HD6189 .R39 1982 *NYPL [JLD 86-3370]*

Science and technology for women /. Madras [1985] 79 p. ; LC Card 85-904932 DDC 305.4/35/0954 19
Q130 .S33 1985 *NYPL [JLD 86-3369]*

WOMEN - EMPLOYMENT - INDIA - ADDRESSES, ESSAYS, LECTURES.
Women and child workers in unorganised sector . New Delhi , 1983. xii, 104 p. ; LC Card 83-906999 DDC 331.3/1/0954 19
HD6189 .W64 1983 *NYPL [JLD 87-730]*

WOMEN - EMPLOYMENT - INDIA - ANDHRA PRADESH - CASE STUDIES.
Raghunadha Reddy, C. (Chinnathimmanna), 1950- Changing status of educated working women . Delhi , New Delhi , 1986. 210 p. ; ISBN 81-7018-379-0 : LC Card 86-902900 DDC 305.4/3/0095484 19
HD6190.A5 R34 1986

WOMEN - EMPLOYMENT - INDIA - BHOPAL - CASE STUDIES.
Chauhan, Indira, 1949- Purdah to profession . Delhi , New Delhi , 1986. vi, 295 p. ; ISBN 81-7018-375-8 : LC Card 86-902846 DDC 331.4/0954/3 19
HD6190.B48 C47 1986

WOMEN - EMPLOYMENT - INDIA - BOMBAY - CASE STUDIES.
Savara, Mira. Changing trends in women's employment . Bombay , 1986. xii, 137 p. ; LC Card 86-902789 DDC 331.4/877/00954792 19
HD6073.T42 I47 1986

WOMEN - EMPLOYMENT - INDIA - CASE STUDIES.
Chauhan, Indira, 1949- Purdah to profession . Delhi , New Delhi , 1986. vi, 295 p. ; ISBN 81-7018-375-8 : LC Card 86-902846 DDC 331.4/0954/3 19
HD6190.B48 C47 1986

Raghunadha Reddy, C. (Chinnathimmanna), 1950- Changing status of educated working women . Delhi , New Delhi , 1986. 210 p. ; ISBN 81-7018-379-0 : LC Card 86-902900 DDC 305.4/3/0095484 19
HD6190.A5 R34 1986

Savara, Mira. Changing trends in women's employment . Bombay , 1986. xii, 137 p. ; LC Card 86-902789 DDC 331.4/877/00954792 19
HD6073.T42 I47 1986

WOMEN - EMPLOYMENT - INDIA - GUJARAT.
Hirway, Indira. Denial of maternity benefits to women workers . New Delhi , c1986. iv, 151 p. ; ISBN 81-204-0154-9 : LC Card 86-903013 DDC 331.4/25763 19
HD6065.5.I4 H57 1986

WOMEN - EMPLOYMENT - INDIA - MAHARASHTRA.
Chauhan, Indira, 1949- The dilemma of working women hostelers . Delhi , New Delhi , 1986. 70 p. : ISBN 81-7018-374-X : LC Card 86-902619 DDC 305.4/0954/792 19
HD6189 .C42 1986

WOMEN - EMPLOYMENT - INDIA - PRABHANI (DISTRICT)
Bhoite, Anuradha. Women employees and rural development . Delhi, India , c1987. xiii, 135 p. ; ISBN 81-212-0085-7 : LC Card 87-900916 DDC 331.4/0954 19
HD6189 .B56 1987

WOMEN - EMPLOYMENT - ITALY - ADDRESSES, ESSAYS, LECTURES.
Lavoro femminile, sviluppo tecnologico e segregazione occupazionale /. Milano, Italy , c1984. 458 p. : LC Card 84-190076 DDC 331.4/0945 19
HD6154 .L385 1984 *NYPL [*QO 87-1143]*

WOMEN - EMPLOYMENT - ITALY - HISTORY.
Bettio, Francesca. The sexual division of labour . Oxford [Oxfordshire] , New York , 1988. p. cm. ISBN 0-19-828544-2 : LC Card 87-26353 DDC 305.4/3/00945 19
HD6060.65.I8 B47 1988

WOMEN - EMPLOYMENT - ITALY - LOMBARDY - ADDRESSES, ESSAYS, LECTURES.
Lavoro femminile, sviluppo tecnologico e segregazione occupazionale /. Milano, Italy , c1984. 458 p. : LC Card 84-190076 DDC 331.4/0945 19
HD6154 .L385 1984 *NYPL [*QO 87-1143]*

WOMEN - EMPLOYMENT - IVORY COAST - KATIOLA (CENTRE)
Traoré, Aminata. La mine d'argile est notre champ /. [Abidjan?] [1985] (Abidjan : Société d'impr. ivoirienne) [36] p. : LC Card 86-200373
HD6073.P82 I967 1985

WOMEN - EMPLOYMENT - JAPAN - ADDRESSES, ESSAYS, LECTURES.
Gijutsu kakushin to joshi rōdō /. Tōkyō , 1985. x, 219 p. : ISBN 4-13-051068-1
*NYPL [*OSL 87-1658]*

WOMEN - EMPLOYMENT - JAPAN - HISTORY.
Lenz, Ilse. Kapitalistische Entwicklung, Subsistenzproduktion und Frauenarbeit . Frankfurt/Main , New York , c1984. 330 p. : ISBN 3-593-33407-0(pbk.)
NYPL [JLD 87-332]

WOMEN - EMPLOYMENT - KENYA - CONGRESSES.
Exhibition and income generation for women . [Nairobi?] [1985] 17, 11 p. ; LC Card 85-981503 DDC 331.4/09676/2 19
HD6210.5 .E94 1985

Women and employment in Kenya . [Nairobi] [1985] iii, 46 p. ; LC Card 85-981502 DDC 331.4/09676/2 19
HD6210.5 .W65 1985

WOMEN - EMPLOYMENT - MARYLAND - STATISTICS.
Affirmative action data . Baltimore, Md. (1100 N. Eutaw St., Baltimore 21201) [1985] [17] leaves ; LC Card 86-622599 DDC 331.11/43 19
HD5725.M35 A68 1985

WOMEN - EMPLOYMENT - MEXICO - CASE STUDIES.
La Mujer y el trabajo en México . México , 1986. 346 p. : ISBN 968-8132-48-9 LC Card 87-101329
HD6101 .M86 1986

WOMEN - EMPLOYMENT - MOZAMBIQUE - MAPUTO - HISTORY - 20TH CENTURY.
Penvenne, Jeanne. Making our own way . Boston, MA (270 Bay State Rd., Boston 02215) , 1986. 20 leaves ; LC Card 87-155233 DDC 331.4/0967/91 19
HD6211.5 .P46 1986

WOMEN - EMPLOYMENT - NEBRASKA - STATISTICS.
Women in numbers . Lincoln, Neb. (Box 94600, Lincoln 68509-4600) , 1985. iii, 168 p. : LC Card 86-622214 DDC 331.4/125/09782 19
HD6096.N3 W66 1985

WOMEN - EMPLOYMENT - NETHERLANDS.
Boon, Irene. Mannen in een vrouwenberoep . Den Haag , 1984. 139 p. : ISBN 90-6252-426-5 : LC Card 84-243593
Z682.4.W65 B66 1984 *NYPL [JLG 87-4]*

Vrouwen en economische zelfstandigheid /. Amsterdam , c1986. 199 p. : ISBN 90-6222-139-4 : LC Card 86-182832
HD6162 .V74 1986

WOMEN - EMPLOYMENT - NETHERLANDS - HISTORY.
Henkes, Barbara. Kaatje, ben je boven? . Nijmegen , c1985. 192 p. : ISBN 90-6168-242-8 : LC Card 85-237937
HD6072.2.N4 H46 1985

WOMEN - EMPLOYMENT - NEW YORK (N. Y.)
Stafford, Walter W. Closed labor markets . New York, N.Y. (105 E. 22nd St., New York 10010) , c1985. xvi, 203, 3, [2] p. ; LC Card 85-186853 DDC 331.12/09747/1 19
HD5726.N5 S73 1985 *NYPL [Sc F 86-274]*

WOMEN - EMPLOYMENT - NEW YORK (N. Y.) - HISTORY - 19TH CENTURY.
Stansell, Christine. City of women . Urbana , 1987, c1986. xiv, 301 p. ; ISBN 0-252-01481-2 (pbk.) LC Card 87-16163 DDC 305.4/2/097471 19
HD6096.N6 S8 1987

WOMEN - EMPLOYMENT - NEW YORK (STATE)
The Consumers' League of New York . New York , 1987. 47, 47, 55 p. : ISBN 0-8240-7684-2 (alk. paper) : LC Card 87-19804 DDC 331.4/2/09747 19
HD6096.N6 C66 1987

WOMEN - EMPLOYMENT - NORWAY.
Jensen, An-Magritt. Flere i yrke--færre barn? . Oslo , 1983. 59 p. : ISBN 82-537-2007-6 : LC Card 84-163552
HA1503 .A45 nr. 147 HQ762.N8

Kvinner i arbeid . Oslo , c1984. 290 p. : ISBN 82-00-06835-8 : LC Card 85-102185
HD6170 .K85 1984

Den Norske kvinnerevolusjonen . Oslo , c1986. 166 p. : ISBN 82-00-18318-1 LC Card 87-155462
HD6170 .N68 1986

WOMEN - EMPLOYMENT - ONTARIO.
Report of the Consultation Panel on Pay Equity. Toronto, Ont., Canada [1986] 123 p. ; ISBN 0-7729-1657-8 (pbk.) LC Card 87-117472 DDC 331.2/1 19
HD6061.2.C22 O577 1986

WOMEN - EMPLOYMENT - PERU - CONGRESSES.
Mujer, trabajo y empleo /. Lima, Perú [1985] 294 p. ; LC Card 86-121871 DDC 331.4/0985 19
HD6131 .M85 1985 ***NYPL [JLD 87-492]***

WOMEN - EMPLOYMENT - PERU - LIMA.
Bunster, Ximena. Sellers & servants . New York , 1985. x, 258 p. : ISBN 0-03-060543-1 (alk. paper) : LC Card 85-6259 DDC 331.4/0985/25 19
HD6072.2.P42 L563 1985 ***NYPL [JLE 86-910]***

WOMEN - EMPLOYMENT - POLAND - ŁÓDŹ.
Praca zawodowa a życie rodzinne kobiet /. [Łódź] , 1979. 120 p. ; LC Card 81-109965
HD6054.2.P72 L636 1979

WOMEN - EMPLOYMENT - PORTUGAL.
Silva, Manuela. A igualdade de oportunidades de formação profissional para as mulheres /. Lisboa , 1983. 51, [1] p. : LC Card 84-238349
HD6179 .S56 1983

WOMEN - EMPLOYMENT - QUÉBEC (PROVINCE)
Messier, Suzanne. Perspectives d'emploi pour les Québécoises dans la décennie 1980 . Québec [1983] vi, 73 p. ; ISBN 2-550-10439-0 LC Card 84-221697
HD6100.Q4 M47 1983

Rheault, Sylvie. Les femmes et l'emploi /. [Québec] [1983] 64 p. ; ISBN 2-550-10471-4 LC Card 85-108850 DDC 331.4/09714 19
HD6100.Q4 R44 1983

WOMEN - EMPLOYMENT - RESEARCH - SOUTH AFRICA.
Van der Walt, Sunette. Die vrou in die werksituasie in die RSA . Pretoria , 1986. vii, 156 p. : ISBN 0-7969-0373-5 LC Card 87-121977
HD6212 .V363 1986

WOMEN - EMPLOYMENT - RHODE ISLAND - CENTRAL FALLS - HISTORY.
Lamphere, Louise. From working daughters to working mothers . Ithaca , 1987. xviii, 390 p. : ISBN 0-8014-9441-9 (pbk. : alk. paper) LC Card 86-32952 DDC 331.4/09745/1 19
HD6096.R4 L36 1987

WOMEN - EMPLOYMENT - SOUTH AFRICA.
Van der Walt, Sunette. An investigation into the utilization of white women labour in the South African industry /. Bloemfontein [1976] 45 p. ; ISBN 0-08-688017-4 LC Card 85-153291
HD6212 .V36 1976

Van der Walt, Sunette. Die vrou in die werksituasie in die RSA . Pretoria , 1986. vii, 156 p. : ISBN 0-7969-0373-5 LC Card 87-121977
HD6212 .V363 1986

WOMEN - EMPLOYMENT - SOUTHERN STATES.
Byerly, Victoria Morris. Hard times cotton mill girls . Ithaca, N.Y. , c1986. x, 223 p. : ISBN 0-87546-128-X : LC Card 86-20082 DDC 331.4/877/00922 B 19
HD6073.T42 A132 1986 ***NYPL [JLD 87-1241]***

WOMEN - EMPLOYMENT - SPAIN - CANET DE BERENGUER.
Pellicer Valero, Jesús-Agustín. Sociología del trabajo en Canet de Berenguer /. Valencia , 1984. 80 p. : ISBN 84-600-3540-9 LC Card 86-216439
HD5808.C33 P45 1984

WOMEN - EMPLOYMENT - SRI LANKA.
Kūriyan, Rēval. Vatukarayē kāntā śramaya surākāma . Colombo, Sri Lanka [1984] 24 p. : LC Card 86-902479
HD6182.8 .K87 1984

WOMEN - EMPLOYMENT - SWEDEN - HISTORY.
Arbetets döttrar /. [Stockholm] , c1986. 2 v. ; ISBN 91-7410-337-7 : LC Card 86-216247
HD6173 .A79 1986

WOMEN - EMPLOYMENT - TANZANIA - CASE STUDIES.
Swantz, Marja-Liisa. Women in development . London , New York , c1985. ix, 177 p. : ISBN 0-312-88780-9 (St. Martin's Press) : LC Card 85-2120 DDC 331.4/09678 19
HD6211.3 .S93 1985 ***NYPL [Sc D 86-104]***

WOMEN - EMPLOYMENT - UNITED STATES.
Berger, Gilda. Women, work, and wages /. New York , 1986. 122 p. : ISBN 0-531-10074-X LC Card 85-15379 DDC 331.4/0973 19
HD6095 .B47 1986 ***NYPL [JLE 86-4592]***

Blau, Francine D. The economics of women, men, and work /. Englewood Cliffs, N.J. , c1986. xiv, 365 p. : ISBN 0-13-233719-3 LC Card 85-30746 DDC 305.3/0973 19
HQ1426 .B62 1986 ***NYPL [JLE 86-4254]***

Bose, Christine E. Jobs and gender . New York , 1985. xiv, 206 p. ; ISBN 0-03-071692-6 (alk. paper) : LC Card 85-6305 DDC 305.4/3/00973 19
HD6058 .B67 1985 ***NYPL [JLE 86-3694]***

DeGooyer, Janice. Women's work, undervalued, underpaid . Washington, D.C. , 1984, c1982. 27, [4] leaves : ***NYPL [*ZT-1708 no.39]***

Dex, Shirley. British and American women at work . Houndmills, Basingstoke, Hampshire , 1986. xii, 159 p. : ISBN 0-333-40219-7 ***NYPL [JLD 86-3608]***

England, Paula. Households, employment, and gender . New York , c1986. ix, 237 p. : ISBN 0-202-30322-5 (lib. bdg.) LC Card 85-18628 DDC 304.6 19
HQ536 .E54 1986 ***NYPL [JLE 86-2828]***

Kahne, Hilda. Reconceiving part-time work . Totowa, N.J. , 1985. xv, 180 p. : ISBN 0-8476-7376-6 : LC Card 85-2386 DDC 331.3/94 19
HD5110.2.U5 K33 1985 ***NYPL [JLE 86-1174]***

Mallier, A. T., 1931- Women and the economy . Houndmills, Basingstoke, Hampshire , 1987. xiv, 221 p. : ISBN 0-333-37938-1 ***NYPL [JLD 87-1151]***

Meehan, Elizabeth M. Women's rights at work . New York , 1985. xvii, 253 p. ; ISBN 0-312-88793-0 : LC Card 84-15997 DDC 331.4/133/0941 19
HD6060 .M44 1984 ***NYPL [JLD 86-3580]***

Moore, Sylvia F. The short-term effects of marital disruption on the labor supply behavior of young women /. Columbus, Ohio (Suite 585, 1375 Perry St., Columbus, Ohio, 43201) , 1979. v, 133 p. ; ***NYPL [JLF 86-649]***

Rein, Martin. Women in the social welfare labor market /. Berlin [1985] 180 p. ; LC Card 86-213535 DDC 331.4/129136294 19
HD6134 .R45 1985

Rodgers, Harrell R. Poor women, poor families . Armonk, N.Y. , 1986. viii, 167 p. ; ISBN 0-87332-372-6 : LC Card 86-6449 DDC 362.8/3/0973 19
HV1445 .R64 1986 ***NYPL [JLE 86-4042]***

Rosen, Ellen Israel. Bitter choices . Chicago , 1987. x, 220 p. : ISBN 0-226-72644-4 LC Card 87-5867 DDC 331.4/125/0973 19
HD6095 .R74 1987

Statham, Anne. The worth of women's work . Albany , c1988. xiv, 331 p. ; ISBN 0-88706-591-0 LC Card 87-6472 DDC 331.4/0973 19
HD6095 .S73 1988

Women working . Mountain View, Calif. , c1988. xv, 431 p. : ISBN 0-87484-744-3 (pbk.) LC Card 87-3215 DDC 331.4/0973 19
HD6095 .W6976 1988

Women's work, men's work . Washington, D.C. , 1986. xii, 173 p. : ISBN 0-309-03429-9 (pbk.) LC Card 85-11541 DDC 331.1/33/0973 19
HD6060.5.U5 W66 1986 ***NYPL [JLF 86-1430]***

WOMEN - EMPLOYMENT - UNITED STATES - ADDRESSES, ESSAYS, LECTURES.
Moore, Lynda L. Not as far as you think . Lexington, Mass. , c1986. xii, 201 p. ; ISBN 0-669-10836-7 : LC Card 85-40109 DDC 331.4/0973 19
HD6095 .M66 1986 ***NYPL [JLE 86-1878]***

WOMEN - EMPLOYMENT - UNITED STATES - CASE STUDIES.
Stolz, Barbara Ann. Still struggling . Lexington, Mass. , c1985. xviii, 205 p. ; ISBN 0-669-10930-4 (alk. paper) LC Card 85-40235 DDC 331.4/0973 19
HD6052 .S76 1985 ***NYPL [JLE 85-3704]***

WOMEN - EMPLOYMENT - UNITED STATES - CONGRESSES.
Women, clerical work, and office automation . Washington, D.C. , 1986. vi, 64 p. ; LC Card 86-602559 DDC 331.4/8165137/0973 19
HD6095 .W685 1986

Women, households, and the economy /. New Brunswick, N.J. , c1987. p. cm. ISBN 0-8135-1263-8 : LC Card 87-4840 DDC 331.4/0973 19
HD6060.65.U5 W65 1987

WOMEN - EMPLOYMENT - UNITED STATES - HISTORY.
Hidden aspects of women's work /. New York , 1987. x, 380 p. ; ISBN 0-275-92415-7 (alk. paper) : LC Card 87-2449 DDC 331.4/133/0973 19
HD6060.5.U5 H53 1987

Tentler, Leslie Woodcock. Wage-earning women . New York , 1979. 266 p. ; ISBN 0-19-502627-6 : LC Card 79-12802 DDC 331.4/0973
HD6095 .T44 ***NYPL [JLD 86-3699]***

Working women . Washington, D.C. , c1987. xxii, 419 p. ; ISBN 0-87179-547-7 LC Card 87-9410 DDC 331.4/0973 19
HD6095 .W742 1987

WOMEN - EMPLOYMENT - UNITED STATES - HISTORY - 19TH CENTURY - CONGRESSES.
"To toil the livelong day" . Ithaca, N.Y. , 1987. xi, 312 p. ; ISBN 0-8014-1847-X (alk. paper) LC Card 86-47975 DDC 331.4/0973 19
HD6095 .T6 1987

WOMEN - EMPLOYMENT - UNITED STATES - HISTORY - 20TH CENTURY - CONGRESSES.
"To toil the livelong day" . Ithaca, N.Y. , 1987. xi, 312 p. ; ISBN 0-8014-1847-X (alk. paper) LC Card 86-47975 DDC 331.4/0973 19
HD6095 .T6 1987

WOMEN - EMPLOYMENT - UNITED STATES - HISTORY - SOURCES.
United States. Women's Bureau. Records of the Women's Bureau of the Department of Labor, 1918-1965 [microform] /. Frederick, MD , 1987- microfilm reel ISBN 0-89093-870-9 (microfilm : pt. 1) : LC Card 87-6239 DDC 331.4/0973 19
HD6095

WOMEN - EMPLOYMENT - UNITED STATES - STATISTICS.
Taeuber, Cynthia Murray. Women in the American economy /. Washington, D.C. [1986] vi, 45 p. : LC Card 87-601515 DDC 304.6/0973/021 s 331.4/0973 19
HA203 .A218 no. 146 HD6092

WOMEN - EMPLOYMENT - UTAH - STATISTICS.
Jensen, Kenneth E. Utah affirmative action information, 1985. [Salt Lake City] [1986] i, 253 p. ; LC Card 86-622873 DDC 331.11/43 19
HD5725.U8 J46 1986

WOMEN - EMPLOYMENT - ZAMBIA.
Bardouille, R. (Raj) Women's employment patterns, discrimination, and promotion of equality in Zambia /. [Lusaka? , 1985]. ii, 160 leaves ; LC Card 87-980054 DDC 331.4/133/096894 19
HD6212.5 .B37 1985

WOMEN - ENFRANCHISEMENT. see **WOMEN - SUFFRAGE.**

WOMEN - ENGLAND - LONDON - FINANCE, PERSONAL.
Wilson, Gail. Money in the family . Aldershot, Hants., England , Brookfield, USA , c1987. ix, 271 p. ; ISBN 0-566-05389-6 : LC Card 87-7402 DDC 339.2/2 19
HG179 .W53517 1987

Women entrepreneurs in India . Vinze, Medha Dubhashi, 1958- Delhi, India , 1987. ix, 238 p. ; LC Card 86-903594 DDC 305.4/3338 19
HD6190.D44 V55 1987

WOMEN - EUROPE - ECONOMIC CONDITIONS - ADDRESSES, ESSAYS, LECTURES.
Women and work in preindustrial Europe /. Bloomington , c1986. xviii, 233 p. ; ISBN 0-253-36610-0 LC Card 85-42829 DDC

331.4/094 19
HD6059.5.E85 W65 1986
NYPL [JLE 86-3381]

WOMEN EXECUTIVES.
Bern, Paula. How to work for a woman boss, even if you'd rather not /. New York , c1987. ix, 207 p. ; ISBN 0-396-08839-2 : LC Card 86-16735 DDC 650.1/3 19
HF5548.83 .B48 1987 ***NYPL [JLE 87-1439]***

Dight, Janet. Breaking the secretary barrier . New York , c1986. xv, 303 p. ; ISBN 0-07-016905-5 LC Card 85-11360 DDC 658.4/09/024042 19
HF5547.5 .D54 1986 ***NYPL [JLE 86-1072]***

Highman, Edith L. The organization woman . New York, N.Y. , c1985. 204 p. ; ISBN 0-89885-237-4 LC Card 84-27775 DDC 658.4/09/024042 19
HD6054.3 .H54 1985 ***NYPL [JLD 86-1930]***

Melia, Jinx. [Why Jenny can't lead.] Breaking into the boardroom . New York [1987] c1986. 167 p. ; ISBN 0-399-13326-7 LC Card 87-7007 DDC 658.4/09/024042 19
HD6054.3 .M45 1987

Sitterly, Connie, 1953- A woman's place . Englewood Cliffs, N.J. , c1988. xvi, 365 p. : ISBN 0-13-961954-2 (pbk.) : LC Card 87-25746 DDC 658.4/09/024042 19
HD6054.3 .S67 1988

Westoff, Leslie Aldridge. Corporate romance . New York, NY , c1985. xiii, 246 p. ; ISBN 0-8129-1257-8 : LC Card 85-40284 DDC 658.4/095 19
HD6054.3 .W47 1985 ***NYPL [JLD 86-1042]***

WOMEN EXECUTIVES - DENMARK.
Carlsen, Anne Marie Sloth. Køn og ledelse . København , 1986. 251 p. : ISBN 87-87749-29-7 (pbk.) :kr149.00 LC Card 87-145777
HD6054.4.D4 C37 1986

WOMEN EXECUTIVES - GERMANY (WEST) - CASE STUDIES.
Edding, Cornelia, 1943- Einbruch in den Herrenclub . Reinbek bei Hamburg , 1983. 184 p. : ISBN 3-499-15251-7 (pbk.) LC Card 87-673369
HD6054.2.G3 E33x 1983

WOMEN EXECUTIVES - GREAT BRITAIN.
Davidson, Marilyn. Stress and the woman manager /. Oxford [Oxfordshire], 1983. 230 p. ; ISBN 0-85520-623-3 ***NYPL [JLE 85-1426]***

WOMEN EXECUTIVES - SALARIES, ETC. - UNITED STATES.
The velvet ghetto . San Francisco , 1986. 147 leaves in various foliations : LC Card 86-161157 DDC 331.4/816592/0973 19
HD6054.2.U6 V45 1986

WOMEN EXECUTIVES - TRAINING OF - BURUNDI.
Centre de perfectionnement et de formation en cours d'emploi (Bujumbura, Burundi) Formation des cadres supérieurs féminins /. [Bujumbura?] , 1983. 2 v. : LC Card 87-104998
HD6054.4.B94 C46 1983

WOMEN EXECUTIVES - UNITED STATES.
Bohigian, Valerie. Ladybucks /. New York, N.Y. , c1987. 246 p. ; ISBN 0-396-08852-X LC Card 86-29227 DDC 650.1/024042 19
HD6072.6.U5 B64 1987

Fillmore, Mary Dingee. Women MBAs . Boston, MA , 1987. xii, 233 p. ; ISBN 0-8161-8728-2 LC Card 86-32002 DDC 331.4/816584/00973 19
HD6054.4.U6 F54 1987

Hardesty, Sarah. Success and betrayal . New York , 1987, c1986. 464 p. ; ISBN 0-671-64563-3 (pbk.) : LC Card 87-17289 DDC 331.4/816584/00973 19
HD6054.4.U6 H37 1987

Hildebrandt, Herbert William, 1931- A managerial profile . Ann Arbor, MI , c1985. 31 p. ; ISBN 0-87712-248-2 (pbk.) LC Card 86-621187 DDC 331.4/816584/00973 19
HD6054.4.U6 H55 1985

Morrison, Ann M. Breaking the glass ceiling . Reading, Mass. , c1987. ix, 229 p. : ISBN 0-201-15787-X : LC Card 87-1853 DDC 658.4/09/024042 19
HD6054.4.U6 M67 1987

The velvet ghetto . San Francisco , 1986. 147 leaves in various foliations : LC Card 86-161157 DDC 331.4/816592/0973 19
HD6054.2.U6 V45 1986

WOMEN EXECUTIVES - UNITED STATES - CASE STUDIES.
Risk to riche$. Washington, DC (600 Maryland Ave., S.W., Suite 700, Washington 20024) , c1986. vii, 204 p. : LC Card 87-158511 DDC 338/.04/088042 19
HD2346.U5 R57 1986

WOMEN FARMERS - AFRICA - CONGRESSES.
Women farmers in Africa . Syracuse, N.Y. , 1986. xvi, 212 p. : ISBN 0-8156-2358-5 (alk. paper) LC Card 85-27771 DDC 331.4/83/096 19
HD6073.A292 A358 1986
NYPL [JLE 86-2556]

WOMEN FARMERS - DOMINICAN REPUBLIC - POLITICAL ACTIVITY.
Campesinas y políticos, 1986 . Santo Domingo, República Dominicana , 1986. 83 p. : LC Card 87-102259
HD6073.A292 D653 1986

Women farmers in Africa : rural development in Mali and the Sahel / edited by Lucy E. Greevey.1st ed. Syracuse, N.Y. : Syracuse University Press, 1986. xvi, 212 p. : ill. ; 24 cm. (Contemporary issues in the Middle East) Papers presented at the Bamako Workshop on Training and Animation of Rural Women, sponsored by the Comité international de liaison du Corps pour l'alimentation (CILCA), held June 7-9, 1983 in Bamako, Mali. Includes index. Bibliography: p. 199-208. ISBN 0-8156-2358-5 (alk. paper) LC Card 85-27771 DDC 331.4/83/096 19
1. Women farmers - Africa - Congresses. 2. Women in rural development - Africa - Congresses. 3. Women in agriculture - Africa - Congresses. I. Greevey, Lucy E. II. Bamako Workshop on Training and Animation of Rural Women (1983). III. Liaison Committee for Food Corps Programmes International.
HD6073.A292 A358 1986
NYPL [JLE 86-2556]

WOMEN FARMERS - KENYA - CASE STUDIES.
Staudt, Kathleen A. Agricultural policy implementation . West Hartford, CT , c1985. xvi, 68 p. : ISBN 0-931816-18-1 (pbk.) LC Card 84-29737 DDC 338.1/86762 19
HD2126.5.Z8 S73 1985
NYPL [JLF 86-1685]

WOMEN FARMERS - LATIN AMERICA.
A Mulher rural e mudanças no processo de produção agrícola . [Brasília] [1984] i, 161 p. ; LC Card 86-150197
HD6073.A292 L295 1984

WOMEN FARMERS - NIGERIA.
Jackson, Cecile, 1953- The Kano River Irrigation Project /. West Hartford, Conn. , 1985. xviii, 66 p. ; ISBN 0-931816-19-X LC Card 85-5242 DDC 331.4/83/09669 19
HD6073.F32 N64 1985
NYPL [JLF 86-1634]

Spiro, Heather M. The Ilora farm settlement in Nigeria /. West Hartford, Conn. , 1985. xvii, 50 p. : ISBN 0-931816-20-3 LC Card 85-5230 DDC 331.4/83/089963 19
HD6073.F3 N667 1985
NYPL [JLF 86-1629]

WOMEN FARMERS - PORTUGAL.
Cavaco, Carminda. A mulher na agricultura portuguesa . [Lisbon] , 1981. 34 leaves : LC Card 85-216534
HD6073.F32 P83 1981

WOMEN - FINANCE, PERSONAL.
Lieberman, Annette. Unbalanced accounts . New York , c1987. xx, 281 p. ; ISBN 0-87113-141-2 LC Card 86-28845 DDC 332.4/01/9 19
HG179 .L49 1987

MacKenzie, Warren, 1927- For women only . Alexandria, Va. , c1986. xiii, 196 p. ; ISBN 0-938125-00-1 : LC Card 86-70681 DDC 332.024/042 19
HG179 .M244 1986

WOMEN - FINANCE, PERSONAL - KENYA - CONGRESSES.
Women and credit . [Nairobi?] [1985] 17, 2 p. ; LC Card 85-981504 DDC 332.7/088042 19
HG3756.K4 W65 1985

WOMEN - GERMANY - ECONOMIC CONDITIONS.
Wiesner, Merry, 1952- Working women in Renaissance Germany /. New Brunswick, N.J. , c1986. xiii, 263 p. : ISBN 0-8135-1138-0 : LC Card 85-14451 DDC 305.4/3/00943 19
HQ1149.G3 W54 1986
NYPL [JLE 86-3515]

WOMEN - GERMANY - HISTORY - RENAISSANCE, 1450-1600.
Wiesner, Merry, 1952- Working women in Renaissance Germany /. New Brunswick, N.J. , c1986. xiii, 263 p. : ISBN 0-8135-1138-0 : LC Card 85-14451 DDC 305.4/3/00943 19
HQ1149.G3 W54 1986
NYPL [JLE 86-3515]

WOMEN - GERMANY, WEST - TIME MANAGEMENT - CASE STUDIES.
Women, work, and family in Britain and Germany /. London , 1986. 216 p. : ISBN 0-7099-0976-4 ***NYPL [JLD 86-3391]***

WOMEN - GREAT BRITAIN - ECONOMIC CONDITIONS.
Mallier, A. T., 1931- Women and the economy . Houndmills, Basingstoke, Hampshire , 1987. xiv, 221 p. : ISBN 0-333-37938-1 ***NYPL [JLD 87-1151]***

Waged work . London , 1986. vi, 291 p. : ISBN 0-86068-801-1 (pbk.) : LC Card 86-232209 DDC 331.4/0941 19
HD6061.2.G7 W35 1986

WOMEN - GREAT BRITAIN - HISTORY - 20TH CENTURY.
Braybon, Gail. Out of the cage . London , New York , 1987. xiii, 330 p. : ISBN 0-86358-046-7 : LC Card 87-13510 DDC 305.4/0941 19
HD6135 .B7 1987

WOMEN - GREAT BRITAIN - SOCIAL CONDITIONS.
Braybon, Gail. Out of the cage . London , New York , 1987. xiii, 330 p. : ISBN 0-86358-046-7 : LC Card 87-13510 DDC 305.4/0941 19
HD6135 .B7 1987

WOMEN - GREAT BRITAIN - TIME MANAGEMENT - CASE STUDIES.
Women, work, and family in Britain and Germany /. London , 1986. 216 p. : ISBN 0-7099-0976-4 ***NYPL [JLD 86-3391]***

WOMEN HEADS OF HOUSEHOLDS - UNITED STATES.
Bernstein, Blanche, 1912- Saving a generation /. New York , 1986. vi, 63 p. ; ISBN 0-87078-206-1 (pbk.) : LC Card 87-102738 DDC 362.5/8/0973 19
HC110.P6 B47 1986

Rodgers, Harrell R. Poor women, poor families . Armonk, N.Y. , 1986. viii, 167 p. ; ISBN 0-87332-372-6 : LC Card 86-6449 DDC 362.8/3/0973 19
HV1445 .R64 1986 ***NYPL [JLE 86-4042]***

WOMEN - HEALTH AND HYGIENE - BOLIVIA.
Cisneros C., Antonio. La mujer trabajadora . La Paz, Bolivia [1984] 131 leaves : LC Card 85-129000 DDC 331.4/0984 19
HD6121 .C58 1984 ***NYPL [JLF 86-1704]***

WOMEN - HEALTH AND HYGIENE - CONGRESSES.
Les Effets des conditions de travail sur la santé des travailleuses . [Montréal] [1984] 230 p., [5] p. of plates : ISBN 2-920658-00-X : LC Card 86-158040
HD6067 .E34 1984

WOMEN - HISTORY.
Mies, Maria. Patriarchy and accumulation on a world scale . London , Atlantic Highlands, NJ , 1986. 251 p. ; ISBN 0-86232-341-X LC Card 86-18916 DDC 305.4 19
HD6060.6 .M54 1986 ***NYPL [JLD 86-3206]***

Sivard, Ruth Leger. Women--a world survey /. Washington, D.C. , c1985. 44 p. : ISBN 0-918281-00-8 (pbk.) : LC Card 85-171073 DDC 305.4 19
HQ1154 .S547 1985
NYPL [*R-Econ. 86-4677]

WOMEN - HISTORY - MIDDLE AGES, 500-1500.
Howell, Martha C. Women, production, and patriarchy in late medieval cities /. Chicago , 1986. xv, 285 p. ; ISBN 0-226-35503-9 : LC

Card 85-31816 DDC 331.4/094 19
HD6134 .H69 1986 NYPL [JLE 86-4284]

Labarge, Margaret Wade. Women in medieval life . London , 1986. xiv, 271 p. : ISBN 0-241-11809-3 : NYPL [JLE 86-3838]

WOMEN - HISTORY - ADDRESSES, ESSAYS, LECTURES.
Vorse, Mary Heaton, 1874-1966. Rebel pen . New York , c1985. 345 p. : ISBN 0-85345-669-0 : LC Card 85-7130 DDC 331.4/0973 19
HD8072 .V755 1985 NYPL [JLD 86-2459]

WOMEN - HOURS OF LABOR. see **HOURS OF LABOR.**

Women, households, and the economy / edited by Lourdes Benería and Catharine R. Stimpson. New Brunswick, N.J. : Rutgers University Press, c1987. p. cm. (The Douglass series on women's lives and the meaning of gender) Includes bibliographical references and index. ISBN 0-8135-1263-8 : LC Card 87-4840 DDC 331.4/0973 19
1. Sexual division of labor - United States - Congresses. 2. Women - Employment - United States - Congresses. 3. Women - United States - Economic conditions - Congresses. I. Benería, Lourdes. II. Stimpson, Catharine R., 1936-. III. Series.
HD6060.65.U5 W65 1987

WOMEN - HOUSING - INDIA.
Chauhan, Indira, 1949- The dilemma of working women hostelers . Delhi , New Delhi , 1986. 70 p. : ISBN 81-7018-374-X : LC Card 86-902619 DDC 305.4/0954/792 19
HD6189 .C42 1986

WOMEN - HOUSING - INDIA - MAHARASHTRA.
Chauhan, Indira, 1949- The dilemma of working women hostelers . Delhi , New Delhi , 1986. 70 p. : ISBN 81-7018-374-X : LC Card 86-902619 DDC 305.4/0954/792 19
HD6189 .C42 1986

WOMEN - HYGIENE. see **WOMEN - HEALTH AND HYGIENE.**

WOMEN - ILLINOIS - CHICAGO - SOCIAL CONDITIONS.
Meyerowitz, Joanne J. (Joanne Jay) Women adrift . Chicago , 1988. p. cm. ISBN 0-226-52197-4 LC Card 87-22449 DDC 331.4/09773/11 19
HD6096.C4 M49 1988

WOMEN IMMIGRANTS - EMPLOYMENT - UNITED STATES.
Mason, Sarah R. Training Southeast Asian refugee women for employment . Minneapolis, Minn. , 1986. viii, 142 p. : LC Card 86-72303 DDC 331.4/2592/08995073 19
HD5715.2 .M37 1986

WOMEN IMMIGRANTS - GERMANY (WEST)
Rosen, Rita. --Muss kommen, aber nix von Herzen . Opladen , 1986. 262 p. : ISBN 3-8100-0572-X LC Card 87-112784
HD6149 .R67 1986

WOMEN IMMIGRANTS - RHODE ISLAND - CENTRAL FALLS - HISTORY.
Lamphere, Louise. From working daughters to working mothers . Ithaca , 1987. xviii, 390 p. : ISBN 0-8014-9441-9 (pbk. : alk. paper) LC Card 86-32952 DDC 331.4/09745/1 19
HD6096.R4 L36 1987

WOMEN IN ADVERTISING - MALAYSIA.
Selling dreams . Penang, Malaysia , c1986. 149 p. : ISBN 967-99502-0-4 (pbk.) LC Card 87-940287 DDC 659.1 19
HF5823 .S46 1986

WOMEN IN AGRICULTURE - AFRICA - CONGRESSES.
Women farmers in Africa . Syracuse, N.Y. , 1986. xvi, 212 p. : ISBN 0-8156-2358-5 (alk. paper) LC Card 85-27771 DDC 331.4/83/096 19
HD6073.A292 A358 1986 NYPL [JLE 86-2556]

WOMEN IN AGRICULTURE - DEVELOPING COUNTRIES.
Dixon-Mueller, Ruth. Women's work in Third World agriculture . Geneva , 1985. xi, 151 p. : ISBN 92-2-105107-2 (pbk.) LC Card 86-673111
HD6073.A292 D442x 1985 NYPL [JLE 86-3760]

Palmer, Ingrid. The impact of agrarian reform on women /. West Hartford, Conn. , c1985. xiv, 55 p. ; ISBN 0-931816-21-1 (pbk.) LC Card 85-5250 DDC 331.4/83/091724 19
HD6073.A292 D447 1985 NYPL [JLF 86-1633]

Palmer, Ingrid. The impact of male out-migration on women in farming /. West Hartford, Conn. , c1985. xviii, 78 p. ; ISBN 0-931816-22-X (pbk.) LC Card 85-5240 DDC 331.4/83/091724 19
HD6073.A292 D4472 1985 NYPL [JLF 86-1626]

WOMEN IN AGRICULTURE - DEVELOPING COUNTRIES - CONGRESSES.
Séminaire international sur la place des femmes dans l'autosuffisance et les stratégies alimentaires (1985 : Paris, France) Femmes et politiques alimentaires . Paris , 1985. 741 p. : ISBN 2-7099-0763-1 LC Card 86-205282
HD6073.A292 D4477 1985

WOMEN IN AGRICULTURE - GOVERNMENT POLICY - ZAMBIA.
Safilios-Rothschild, Constantina, 1934- The policy implications of the roles of women in agriculture in Zambia /. [Lusaka] [1985] 49, [25] p. ; LC Card 87-980047 DDC 331.4/83/096894 19
HD6073.A292 Z337 1985

WOMEN IN AGRICULTURE - INDIA.
Mies, Maria. Indian women in subsistence and agricultural labour /. Geneva , 1986. x, 158 p. ; ISBN 92-2-105397-0 (pbk.) : LC Card 87-114124 DDC 331.4/83/0954 19
HD6073.A292 I46 1986

WOMEN IN AGRICULTURE - LATIN AMERICA.
A Mulher rural e mudanças no processo de produção agrícola . [Brasília] [1984] i, 161 p. ; LC Card 86-150197
HD6073.A292 L295 1984

WOMEN IN AGRICULTURE - NICARAGUA.
Revolución y mujeres del campo . Managua [1985] 46 p. : LC Card 86-231936
HD1333.N5 R48 1985

WOMEN IN AGRICULTURE - PORTUGAL.
Cavaco, Carminda. A mulher na agricultura portuguesa . [Lisbon] , 1981. 34 leaves : LC Card 85-216534
HD6073.F32 P83 1981

WOMEN IN AGRICULTURE - ZAMBIA.
Safilios-Rothschild, Constantina, 1934- The policy implications of the roles of women in agriculture in Zambia /. [Lusaka] [1985] 49, [25] p. ; LC Card 87-980047 DDC 331.4/83/096894 19
HD6073.A292 Z337 1985

Women in American history.
Payne, Elizabeth Anne, 1943- Reform, labor, and feminism . Urbana , c1988. p. cm. ISBN 0-252-01445-6 (alk. paper) LC Card 87-10794 DDC 331.88/092/4 B 19
HD6079.2.U5 P38 1988

WOMEN IN BUSINESS - GREAT BRITAIN.
Hertz, Leah. The business amazons /. London , 1986. xviii, 264, [1] p., [1] leaf of plates : ISBN 0-233-97892-5 : LC Card 86-200078 DDC 338.6/422/088042 19
HD2346.G7 H47 1986

WOMEN IN BUSINESS - INDIA - DELHI.
Vinze, Medha Dubhashi, 1958- Women entrepreneurs in India . Delhi, India , 1987. ix, 238 p. ; LC Card 86-903594 DDC 305.4/3338 19
HD6190.D44 V55 1987

WOMEN IN BUSINESS - INTERVIEWS.
Gardenswartz, Lee. What it takes . New York , 1987. ix, 205 p. ; ISBN 0-385-23820-7 : LC Card 87-13657 DDC 650.1/024042 19
HF5386 .G214 1987

WOMEN IN BUSINESS - NETHERLANDS - CASE STUDIES.
Houweling, Marjolein. Ondernemende vrouwen /. Amsterdam , c1985. 128 p. : ISBN 90-6834-018-2 : LC Card 86-166264
HD2346.N4 H68 1985

WOMEN IN BUSINESS - NIGERIA.
Spiro, Heather M. The Ilora farm settlement in Nigeria /. West Hartford, Conn. , 1985. xvii, 50 p. : ISBN 0-931816-20-3 LC Card 85-5230 DDC 331.4/83/089963 19
HD6073.F3 N667 1985 NYPL [JLF 86-1629]

WOMEN IN BUSINESS - UNITED STATES.
Fillmore, Mary Dingee. Women MBAs . Boston, MA , 1987. xii, 233 p. ; ISBN 0-8161-8728-2 LC Card 86-32002 DDC 331.4/816584/00973 19
HD6054.4.U6 F54 1987

Hertz, Leah. The business amazons /. London , 1986. xviii, 264, [1] p., [1] leaf of plates : ISBN 0-233-97892-5 : LC Card 86-200078 DDC 338.6/422/088042 19
HD2346.G7 H47 1986

WOMEN IN BUSINESS - UNITED STATES - BIOGRAPHY.
Fields, Debbi. "One smart cookie" . New York , c1987. 173 p., [16] p. of plates : ISBN 0-671-61838-5 LC Card 87-15172 DDC 338.7/6647525/0924 B 19
HD9058.C65 F544 1987

WOMEN IN BUSINESS - UNITED STATES - CASE STUDIES.
Perri, Colleen, 1936- Entrepreneurial women. Kenosha, WI , c1988. p. cm. ISBN 0-941579-02-6 LC Card 87-7370 DDC 338/.04/088042 19
HD2346.U5 P43 1988

Risk to riche$. Washington, DC (600 Maryland Ave., S.W., Suite 700, Washington 20024) , c1986. vii, 204 p. : LC Card 87-158511 DDC 338/.04/088042 19
HD2346.U5 R57 1986

Wilkens, Joanne. Her own business . New York , c1987. xv, 245 p. ; ISBN 0-07-050854-2 : LC Card 86-27780 DDC 338.6/422/088042 19
HD2346.U5 W548 1987

WOMEN IN BUSINESS - WISCONSIN - KENOSHA - CASE STUDIES.
Perri, Colleen, 1936- Entrepreneurial women /. Kenosha, WI , c1987. 140 p. : ISBN 0-941579-00-X (pbk.) LC Card 87-154216 DDC 338/.04/088042 19
HD2346.U52 K376 1987b

Perri, Colleen, 1936- Entrepreneurial women /. Kenosha, WI , c1988. p. cm. ISBN 0-941579-28-X LC Card 87-7380 DDC 338/.04/088042 19
HD2346.U52 K376 1988

WOMEN IN CHARITABLE WORK.
Grenzen der Frauenlohnarbeit . Frankfurt/Main , New York , c1986. 250 p. : ISBN 3-593-33628-6 LC Card 86-228323
HD6072.2.G4 G74 1986

WOMEN IN COMMUNITY DEVELOPMENT.
Bruchhaus, Eva-Maria. Frauen in Entwicklungsländern . Freiburg im Breisgau , 1979. iii, 182 p. ; LC Card 81-121677 DDC 305.4/09172/4 19
HQ1870.9 .B78 1979 NYPL [JLG 86-106]

WOMEN IN COMMUNITY DEVELOPMENT - LATIN AMERICA - CASE STUDIES.
Grassroots development in Latin America & the Caribbean . New York , 1985. vii, 197 p. : ISBN 0-03-001689-4 (alk. paper) : LC Card 84-18180 DDC 334/.098 19
HD3450.5.A4 G72 1985

WOMEN IN COOPERATIVE SOCIETIES - EUROPEAN ECONOMIC COMMUNITY COUNTRIES.
The Viability of employment initiatives involving women . Luxembourg , Washington, DC , 1986. 1 v. (various pagings) ; ISBN 92-825-6088-0 (pbk.) : LC Card 87-137342 DDC 331.4/12/094 19
HD3423.5.E86 V5 1986

WOMEN IN COOPERATIVE SOCIETIES - EUROPEAN ECONOMIC COMMUNITY COUNTRIES - CASE STUDIES.
The Viability of employment initiatives involving women . Luxembourg , Washington, DC , 1986. 1 v. (various pagings) ; ISBN 92-825-6088-0 (pbk.) : LC Card 87-137342 DDC 331.4/12/094 19
HD3423.5.E86 V5 1986

WOMEN IN COOPERATIVE SOCIETIES - KENYA - CONGRESSES.
Women in co-operatives . [Nairobi?] [1985] 30

p. ; LC Card 85-981507 DDC 334/.088042 19
HA3560.5.A4 W66 1985

Women in co-operatives : report of the Kenya NGO sub-committee workshop held at the Co-operative College of Kenya, Nairobi, 25-30th June, 1984. [Nairobi?] : Kenya NGO Organizing Committee, Forum '85 of the World Conference of the U.N. Decade for Women, [1985] 30 p. ; 30 cm. (Report / NGO Organising Committee . no. 6) LC Card 85-981507 DDC 334/.088042 19
1. Women in cooperative societies - Kenya - Congresses. I. Kenya NGO Organising Committee--Forum '85. II. Series: Report (Kenya NGO Organising Committee--Forum '85) , no. 6.
HA3560.5.A4 W66 1985

Women in culture and society.
Howell, Martha C. Women, production, and patriarchy in late medieval cities /. Chicago , 1986. xv, 285 p. ; ISBN 0-226-35503-9 : LC Card 85-31816 DDC 331.4/094 19
HD6134 .H69 1986 ***NYPL [JLE 86-4284]***

Meyerowitz, Joanne J. (Joanne Jay) Women adrift . Chicago , 1988. p. cm. ISBN 0-226-52197-4 LC Card 87-22449 DDC 331.4/09773/11 19
HD6096.C4 M49 1988

Rosen, Ellen Israel. Bitter choices . Chicago , 1987. x, 220 p. : ISBN 0-226-72644-4 LC Card 87-5867 DDC 331.4/125/0973 19
HD6095 .R74 1987

Women in development . Swantz, Marja-Liisa. London , New York , c1985. ix, 177 p. : ISBN 0-312-88780-9 (St. Martin's Press) : LC Card 85-2120 DDC 331.4/09678 19
HD6211.3 .S93 1985 ***NYPL [Sc D 86-104]***

WOMEN IN DEVELOPMENT.
Dixon-Mueller, Ruth. Women's work in Third World agriculture . Geneva , 1985. xi, 151 p. : ISBN 92-2-105107-2 (pbk.) LC Card 86-673111
HD6073.A292 D442x 1985
NYPL [JLE 86-3760]

Netherlands. Nationale Advies Raad voor Ontwikkelingssamenwerking. Advies vrouwen en ontwikkeling /. [The Hague , 1985] 53 p. ; ISBN 90-12-04985-7 LC Card 86-198854
HC60 .N465 no. 85 HQ1240

WOMEN IN DEVELOPMENT - ASIA - CONGRESSES.
Invisible hands . New Delhi , Newbury Park, Calif. , 1987. 273 p. ; ISBN 0-8039-9524-5 (U. S.) LC Card 87-4337 DDC 331.4/0954 19
HD6181.85 .A85 1987

WOMEN IN DEVELOPMENT - CONGRESSES.
Women, work, and society /. Calcutta , 1985. xvi, 430 p. : LC Card 86-900827 DDC 331.4 19
HD6052 .W565 1982 ***NYPL [JLE 87-1019]***

WOMEN IN DEVELOPMENT - DEVELOPING COUNTRIES - CONGRESSES.
Séminaire international sur la place des femmes dans l'autosuffisance et les stratégies alimentaires (1985 : Paris, France) Femmes et politiques alimentaires . Paris , 1985. 741 p. : ISBN 2-7099-0763-1 LC Card 86-205282
HD6073.A292 D4477 1985

Women in health & illness : life experiences and crises / edited by Diane K. Kjervik, Ida M. Martinson. Philadelphia : Saunders, 1986. x, 261 p. : ill. ; 27 cm. Includes bibliographies and index. ISBN 0-7216-2086-8 LC Card 86-6576 DDC 155.6/33 19
1. Women - Mental health. 2. Stress (Psychology). 3. Women - Psychology. 4. Life change events. I. Kjervik, Diane K., 1945-. II. Martinson, Ida Marie, 1936-. III. Title: Women in health and illness.
RC451.4.W6 W656 1986
NYPL [JLF 86-1463]

Women in health and illness. Women in health & illness . Philadelphia , 1986. x, 261 p. : ISBN 0-7216-2086-8 LC Card 86-6576 DDC 155.6/33 19
RC451.4.W6 W656 1986
NYPL [JLF 86-1463]

Women in Indian industry /. Ramanamma, A., 1936- Delhi, India , 1987. 232 p. ; LC Card 87-901258 DDC 331.4/821381/0954 19
HD6189 .R347 1987

WOMEN IN MANAGEMENT - BURUNDI.
Centre de perfectionnement et de formation en cours d'emploi (Bujumbura, Burundi) Formation des cadres supérieurs féminins /. [Bujumbura?] , 1983. 2 v. : LC Card 87-104998
HD6054.4.B94 C46 1983

WOMEN IN MARKETING - ZAMBIA - CONGRESSES.
Strengthening women's participation in food and agricultural marketing . [Lusaka] [1984] 78 p. ; LC Card 86-980282 DDC 331.4/83/096894 19
HD6073.A292 Z3374 1984

Women in medieval life . Labarge, Margaret Wade. London , 1986. xiv, 271 p. : ISBN 0-241-11809-3 : ***NYPL [JLE 86-3838]***

Women in numbers : working women in Nebraska / by the Nebraska Department of Labor ; prepared for Nebraska Commission on the Status of Women. Lincoln, Neb. (Box 94600, Lincoln 68509-4600) : The Department, 1985. iii, 168 p. : ill. ; 28 cm. Bibliography: p. 44-45. LC Card 86-622214 DDC 331.4/125/09782 19
1. Women - Employment - Nebraska - Statistics. 2. Labor supply - Nebraska - Statistics. 3. Nebraska - Population - Statistics. I. Nebraska. Dept. of Labor. II. Nebraska Commission on the Status of Women. III. Title: Working women in Nebraska.
HD6096.N3 W66 1985

WOMEN IN POLITICS - GERMANY, WEST.
Tschernobyl hat unser Leben verändert . Reinbek bei Hamburg , 1986. 203 p. : ISBN 3-499-15922-8 : LC Card 87-123041 DDC 363.1/79 19
HD9698.G42 T73 1986

WOMEN IN POLITICS - IRELAND - HISTORY.
Parnell, Anna, 1852-1911. The tale of a great sham /. Dublin , Wick, Littlehampton, West Sussex , 1986. 205 p. ; ISBN 0-905223-93-4 LC Card 86-234070 DDC 333.33/5/09415 19
HD625 .P37 1986

WOMEN IN POLITICS - UNITED STATES.
Beckwith, Karen, 1950- American women and political participation . New York , 1986. xiv, 185 p. ; ISBN 0-313-24507-X
NYPL [JLD 87-36]

Poole, Keith T. Women, public opinion, and politics . New York , c1985. xii, 196 p. : ISBN 0-582-28274-8 LC Card 84-7155 DDC 305.4/0973 19
HQ1410 .P66 1985 ***NYPL [JLE 85-1580]***

You may call her madam secretary [motion picture] /. West Tisbury, MA , 1987. 1 film reel (57 min., 40 sec.) : LC Card 87-706816 DDC 973.917 11
HD8073.P38

You may call her madam secretary [videorecording] /. West Tisbury, MA , 1987. 1 videocassette (57 min., 40 sec.) : LC Card 87-706817 DDC 973.917 11
HD8073.P38

WOMEN IN RURAL DEVELOPMENT - AFRICA - CONGRESSES.
African and Asian Inter-regional Workshop on Strategies for Improving the Employment Conditions of Rural Women (1984 : Arusha, Tanzania) Resources, power and women . Geneva , 1985. ix, 82 p. ; ISBN 92-2-105009-2 (pbk.) : LC Card 86-208830 DDC 331.4/83/095 19
HD6207 .A78 1984

Séminaire de formation aux techniques d'élaboration de projets (1980 : Conakry, Guinea, etc.) Séminaire de formation aux techniques d'élaboration de projets . Addis-Abeba , 1982. vii, 36, [31] p. : LC Card 86-168821
HC800 .S444 1980

Women farmers in Africa . Syracuse, N.Y. , 1986. xvi, 212 p. : ISBN 0-8156-2358-5 (alk. paper) LC Card 85-27771 DDC 331.4/83/096 19
HD6073.A292 A358 1986
NYPL [JLE 86-2556]

WOMEN IN RURAL DEVELOPMENT - ASIA - CONGRESSES.
African and Asian Inter-regional Workshop on Strategies for Improving the Employment Conditions of Rural Women (1984 : Arusha, Tanzania) Resources, power and women . Geneva , 1985. ix, 82 p. ; ISBN 92-2-105009-2 (pbk.) : LC Card 86-208830 DDC 331.4/83/095 19
HD6207 .A78 1984

WOMEN IN RURAL DEVELOPMENT - GOVERNMENT POLICY - ZAMBIA.
Safilios-Rothschild, Constantina, 1934- The policy implications of the roles of women in agriculture in Zambia /. [Lusaka] [1985] 49, [25] p. ; LC Card 87-980047 DDC 331.4/83/096894 19
HD6073.A292 Z337 1985

WOMEN IN RURAL DEVELOPMENT - INDIA.
Mies, Maria. Indian women in subsistence and agricultural labour /. Geneva , 1986. x, 158 p. ; ISBN 92-2-105397-0 (pbk.) : LC Card 87-114124 DDC 331.4/83/0954 19
HD6073.A292 I46 1986

WOMEN IN RURAL DEVELOPMENT - UPPER VOLTA - BOBO-DIOULASSO.
Bosch, Ellie. Marktvrouwen van Bobo . Leiden , 1983. viii, 179 p., [18] p. of plates : LC Card 86-212595
HD6217.5.Z6 B633 1983

WOMEN IN SCIENCE - INDIA.
Science and technology for women /. Madras [1985] 79 p. ; LC Card 85-904932 DDC 305.4/35/0954 19
Q130 .S33 1985 ***NYPL [JLD 86-3369]***

Women in society.
Our work, our lives, our words . Basingstoke, Hampshire , 1986. xiii, 189 p. : ISBN 0-333-36598-4 ***NYPL [JLD 86-4220]***

Women in society (London, England)
Our work, our lives, our words . Basingstoke, Hampshire , 1986. xiii, 189 p. : ISBN 0-333-36598-4 ***NYPL [JLD 86-4220]***

Women in Soviet society . Lapidus, Gail Warshofsky. Berkeley , c1978. x, 381 p. ; ISBN 0-520-02868-6 : LC Card 74-16710 DDC 305.4/0947
HQ1663 .L33 ***NYPL [JLE 80-1771]***

WOMEN IN TECHNOLOGY - INDIA.
Science and technology for women /. Madras [1985] 79 p. ; LC Card 85-904932 DDC 305.4/35/0954 19
Q130 .S33 1985 ***NYPL [JLD 86-3369]***

Women in the American economy /. Taeuber, Cynthia Murray. Washington, D.C. [1986] vi, 45 p. : LC Card 87-601515 DDC 304.6/0973/021 s 331.4/0973 19
HA203 .A218 no. 146 HD6092

Women in the political economy.
Barthel, Diane L., 1949- Putting on appearances . Philadelphia , 1988. p. cm. ISBN 0-87722-528-1 (alk. paper) : LC Card 87-20010 DDC 659.1/042 19
HF5827 .B37 1988

Cohn, Samuel, 1954- The process of occupational sex-typing . Philadelphia , 1985. viii, 279 p. ; ISBN 0-87722-402-1 : LC Card 85-14864 DDC 331.4/8165137/0941 19
HD6060.65.G7 C64 1985
NYPL [JLE 86-917]

Families and work /. Philadelphia , 1987. viii, 539 p. ; ISBN 0-87722-467-6 (alk. paper) : LC Card 86-30151 DDC 306.8/5 19
HD4904.25 .F35 1987

WOMEN IN THE PROFESSIONS.
Maindok, Herlinde, 1948- Frauenalltag in Männerberufen /. Frankfurt am Main , 1987. 173, [2] p. ; ISBN 3-596-23786-6 LC Card 87-164114 DDC 331.4/81 19
HD6060.6 .M35 1987

WOMEN IN THE PROFESSIONS - BRAZIL, NORTHEAST - INTERVIEWS.
Dabat, Christine. As mulheres nas organizações profissionais /. Recife , 1985. 21 p. ; LC Card 86-177927
HD2429.B6 D33 1985

WOMEN IN THE PROFESSIONS - GERMANY (WEST) - CASE STUDIES.
Edding, Cornelia, 1943- Einbruch in den Herrenclub . Reinbek bei Hamburg , 1983. 184 p. : ISBN 3-499-15251-7 (pbk.) LC Card 87-673369
HD6054.2.G3 E33x 1983

WOMEN IN THE PROFESSIONS - INTERVIEWS.

Gardenswartz, Lee. What it takes . New York , 1987. ix, 205 p. ; ISBN 0-385-23820-7 : LC Card 87-13657 DDC 650.1/024042 19
HF5386 .G214 1987

WOMEN IN THE PROFESSIONS - UNITED STATES.
Antler, Joyce. The educated woman and professionalization . New York , 1987. x, 448 p. ; ISBN 0-8240-6839-4 (alk. paper) : LC Card 87-17604 DDC 331.4/11423 19
HD6054.2.U6 A57 1987

Hardesty, Sarah. Success and betrayal . New York , 1987, c1986. 464 p. ; ISBN 0-671-64563-3 (pbk.) : LC Card 87-17289 DDC 331.4/816584/00973 19
HD6054.4.U6 H37 1987

Milwid, Beth, 1948- What you get when you go for it /. New York , c1987. 248 p. ; ISBN 0-396-08905-4 LC Card 86-29084 DDC 331.4/81/000973 19
HD6054.2.U6 M55 1987

Morse, Roberta. The Black female professional /. Washington, D.C. [1983] i, 48 p. ; LC Card 83-80187 DDC 305.4/8896073 19
HQ1426 .M88 1983 ***NYPL [Sc F 86-230]***

The Politics of professionalism, opportunity, employment, and gender /. New York , c1987. xx, 110 p. ; ISBN 0-86656-626-0 LC Card 86-29491 DDC 331.4/81/000973 19
HD6054.2.U6 P64 1987

WOMEN IN THE PROFESSIONS - UNITED STATES - ATTITUDES.
Morse, Roberta. The Black female professional /. Washington, D.C. [1983] i, 48 p. ; LC Card 83-80187 DDC 305.4/8896073 19
HQ1426 .M88 1983 ***NYPL [Sc F 86-230]***

WOMEN IN THE PROFESSIONS - UNITED STATES - HISTORY - 20TH CENTURY - CASE STUDIES.
Glazer, Penina Migdal. Unequal colleagues . New Brunswick, N.J. , c1987. xii, 295 p. : ISBN 0-8135-1187-9 (pbk.) : LC Card 86-6568 DDC 331.4/81/000973 19
HD6054.2.U6 G55 1986
NYPL [JLD 87-581]

Women in the social welfare labor market /. Rein, Martin. Berlin [1985] 180 p. ; LC Card 86-213535 DDC 331.4/129136294 19
HD6134 .R45 1985

WOMEN IN TRADE-UNIONS.
Aldred, Chris. Women at work /. London , 1981. 173 p. : ISBN 0-330-26479-6 (pbk.) LC Card 86-673456
HD6135 .A79x 1981

WOMEN IN TRADE-UNIONS - CALIFORNIA - HISTORY - CASE STUDIES.
Ruíz, Vicki. Cannery women, cannery lives . Albuquerque , c1987. xviii, 194 p. : ISBN 0-8263-1006-0 LC Card 87-13878 DDC 331.88/1640282/09794 19
HD6515.F72 U547 1987

WOMEN IN TRADE-UNIONS - CANADA.
Edelson, Miriam. Challenging unions . Ottawa, Ont. , 1987. 28 p. ; ISBN 0-919653-64-2 (pbk.) : LC Card 87-165425 DDC 331.88/088042 19
HD6079.2.C2 E34 1987

WOMEN IN TRADE-UNIONS - FRANCE - HISTORY.
Hilden, Patricia. Working women and socialist politics in France, 1880-1914 . Oxford [Oxfordshire] , New York , 1986. viii, 307 p. ; ISBN 0-19-821935-0 : LC Card 85-15487 DDC 331.4/877/0094428 19
HD6073.T42 F84 1986
NYPL [JLD 86-1838]

WOMEN IN TRADE-UNIONS - UNITED STATES - BIOGRAPHY.
Payne, Elizabeth Anne, 1943- Reform, labor, and feminism . Urbana , c1988. p. cm. ISBN 0-252-01445-6 (alk. paper) LC Card 87-10794 DDC 331.88/092/4 B 19
HD6079.2.U5 P38 1988

WOMEN IN TRADE-UNIONS - UNITED STATES - HISTORY.
Balser, Diane. Sisterhood & solidarity . Boston, MA , c1987. vii, 247 p. ; ISBN 0-89608-278-4 : LC Card 87-4733 DDC 331.4 19
HD6079.2.U5 B34 1987

WOMEN - INDIA - ANDHRA PRADESH - SOCIAL CONDITIONS - CASE STUDIES.
Raghunadha Reddy, C. (Chinnathimmanna), 1950- Changing status of educated working women . Delhi , New Delhi , 1986. 210 p. ; ISBN 81-7018-379-0 : LC Card 86-902900 DDC 305.4/3/0095484 19
HD6190.A5 R34 1986

WOMEN - INDIA - BHOPAL - SOCIAL CONDITIONS - CASE STUDIES.
Chauhan, Indira, 1949- Purdah to profession . Delhi , New Delhi , 1986. vi, 295 p. ; ISBN 81-7018-375-8 : LC Card 86-902846 DDC 331.4/0954/3 19
HD6190.B48 C47 1986

WOMEN - INDIA - SOCIAL CONDITIONS.
Ray, Renuka Mukerji, 1903- My reminiscences . New Delhi , 1982. ix, 294 p., [5] p. of plates : LC Card 82-905707 DDC 954.03/5 19
DS481.R33 A38 1982 ***NYPL [JFD 85-9372]***

WOMEN - INDIA - SOCIAL CONDITIONS - CASE STUDIES.
Chauhan, Indira, 1949- Purdah to profession . Delhi , New Delhi , 1986. vi, 295 p. ; ISBN 81-7018-375-8 : LC Card 86-902846 DDC 331.4/0954/3 19
HD6190.B48 C47 1986

Raghunadha Reddy, C. (Chinnathimmanna), 1950- Changing status of educated working women . Delhi , New Delhi , 1986. 210 p. ; ISBN 81-7018-379-0 : LC Card 86-902900 DDC 305.4/3/0095484 19
HD6190.A5 R34 1986

WOMEN, ISLAMIC. see **WOMEN, MUSLIM.**

WOMEN - ITALY - SOCIAL CONDITIONS.
Petrillo, Giovanna, 1952- Produttività e improduttività del lavoro domestico . Bologna , 1985. 139 p. ; LC Card 86-132212
HD8039.H842 I87 1985

WOMEN, JEWISH - PALESTINE - EMPLOYMENT.
Bernstein, Deborah. The struggle for equality . New York , 1987. x, 208 p. : ISBN 0-275-92139-5 (alk. paper) : LC Card 86-8203 DDC 305.4/3/0095694 19
HD6182.2 .B47 1986 ***NYPL [JLE 87-1462]***

WOMEN - KENYA - ECONOMIC CONDITIONS - CONGRESSES.
Women and credit . [Nairobi?] [1985] 17, 2 p. ; LC Card 85-981504 DDC 332.7/088042 19
HG3756.K4 W65 1985

WOMEN - LEGAL STATUS, LAWS, ETC. - GREAT BRITAIN.
Aldred, Chris. Women at work /. London , 1981. 173 p. : ISBN 0-330-26479-6 (pbk.) LC Card 86-673456
HD6135 .A79x 1981

WOMEN - LEGAL STATUS, LAWS, ETC. - UNITED STATES.
Berry, Mary Frances. Why ERA failed . Bloomington , c1986. ix, 147 p. ; ISBN 0-253-36537-6 LC Card 85-45985 DDC 342.73/0878/02632 347.30287802632 19
KF4758 .B45 1986 ***NYPL [JLE 86-3979]***

WOMEN LIBRARIANS - NETHERLANDS.
Boon, Irene. Mannen in een vrouwenberoep . Den Haag , 1984. 139 p. : ISBN 90-6252-426-5 : LC Card 84-243593
Z682.4.W65 B66 1984 ***NYPL [JLG 87-4]***

WOMEN - LIFE SKILLS GUIDES.
Wallace, Joanne. The working woman /. Old Tappan, N.J. , c1986. 171 p. : ISBN 0-8007-1455-5 (pbk.) : LC Card 85-14396 DDC 650.1/024042 19
HD6053 .W34 1986 ***NYPL [JLF 87-131]***

WOMEN LOGGERS - GREAT BRITAIN - HISTORY.
Meet the members . [London?] [194-?] (Bristol : Bennett Bros.) 76 p., [12] p. of plates : LC Card 84-190854
HD6073.L92 G76 1940z

WOMEN - MALI.
Turrittin, Jane Sawyer. Men, women, and market trade in rural Mali, West Africa /. [East Lansing] , c1986. 17 p. ; LC Card 86-225178 DDC 331.4/8138118/096623 19
HD6060.65.M42 T87 1986

Women MBAs . Fillmore, Mary Dingee. Boston, MA , 1987. xii, 233 p. ; ISBN 0-8161-8728-2 LC Card 86-32002 DDC 331.4/816584/00973 19
HD6054.4.U6 F54 1987

WOMEN - MEDICAL CARE - BOLIVIA.
Cisneros C., Antonio. La mujer trabajadora . La Paz, Bolivia [1984] 131 leaves : LC Card 85-129000 DDC 331.4/0984 19
HD6121 .C58 1984 ***NYPL [JLF 86-1704]***

WOMEN - MENTAL HEALTH.
Witkin-Lanoil, Georgia. The female stress syndrome . New York , c1984. xi, 211 p. ; ISBN 0-937858-33-1 LC Card 83-25038 DDC 155.6/33 19
BF575.S75 W58 1984
NYPL [JFD 86-10468]

Women in health & illness . Philadelphia , 1986. x, 261 p. : ISBN 0-7216-2086-8 LC Card 86-6576 DDC 155.6/33 19
RC451.4.W6 W656 1986
NYPL [JLF 86-1463]

WOMEN MERCHANTS - EL SALVADOR - SAN SALVADOR.
Magaña Cañas, Pedro Agustín. Una ventana a la vida . [San Salvador] [between 1983 and 1987] 93 p. : LC Card 87-400985 DDC 331.4/8138118/09728423 19
HF3310.S26 M34 1983

WOMEN MERCHANTS - GHANA.
Marketing in Ghana . Addis Ababa , 1984. vi, 62 p. ; LC Card 86-980249 DDC 381/.18/09667 19
HD6072.6.G4 M37 1984

WOMEN MERCHANTS - KENYA - NAIROBI.
Adagala, Kavetsa. Self-employed women in the peri-urban setting . Nairobi , 1985. ii, 99 leaves : LC Card 85-980984 DDC 331.4/8138118/0967625 19
HF3893.Z9 N343 1985

WOMEN MERCHANTS - MALI.
Turrittin, Jane Sawyer. Men, women, and market trade in rural Mali, West Africa /. [East Lansing] , c1986. 17 p. ; LC Card 86-225178 DDC 331.4/8138118/096623 19
HD6060.65.M42 T87 1986

WOMEN MERCHANTS - SIERRA LEONE - HISTORY - 19TH CENTURY.
White, E. Frances. Sierra Leone's settler women traders . Ann Arbor , c1987. xi, 168 p. : ISBN 0-472-10080-7 (alk. paper) : LC Card 86-24997 DDC 331.4/81381/09664 19
HF3933 .W47 1987

WOMEN MIDDLE MANAGERS.
Sitterly, Connie, 1953- A woman's place . Englewood Cliffs, N.J. , c1988. xvi, 365 p. : ISBN 0-13-961954-2 (pbk.) : LC Card 87-25746 DDC 658.4/09/024042 19
HD6054.3 .S67 1988

WOMEN MIDDLE MANAGERS - GREAT BRITAIN.
Davidson, Marilyn. Stress and the woman manager /. Oxford [Oxfordshire], 1983. 230 p. ; ISBN 0-85520-623-3 ***NYPL [JLE 85-1426]***

WOMEN, MUSLIM - EMPLOYMENT - GERMANY (WEST)
Rosen, Rita. --Muss kommen, aber nix von Herzen . Opladen , 1986. 262 p. : ISBN 3-8100-0572-X LC Card 87-112784
HD6149 .R67 1986

WOMEN, MUSLIM - GERMANY (WEST)
Rosen, Rita. --Muss kommen, aber nix von Herzen . Opladen , 1986. 262 p. : ISBN 3-8100-0572-X LC Card 87-112784
HD6149 .R67 1986

WOMEN, NEGRO. see **AFRO-AMERICAN WOMEN.**

WOMEN - NETHERLANDS - ECONOMIC CONDITIONS.
Vrouwen en economische zelfstandigheid /. Amsterdam , c1986. 199 p. : ISBN 90-6222-139-4 : LC Card 86-182832
HD6162 .V74 1986

WOMEN - NEW YORK (N.Y.) - HISTORY - 19TH CENTURY.
Stansell, Christine. City of women . Urbana , 1987, c1986. xiv, 301 p. ; ISBN 0-252-01481-2 (pbk.) LC Card 87-16163 DDC 305.4/2/097471 19
HD6096.N6 S8 1987

WOMEN - NORWAY - SOCIAL CONDITIONS.
Avdem, Anna Jorunn, 1952- Oppe først og sist i seng . Oslo , 1985. 190 p. : ISBN 82-00-07512-5 LC Card 86-175305
HD8039.H842 N82 1985

WOMEN - OCCUPATIONS. see **WOMEN - EMPLOYMENT.**

WOMEN OFFSHORE ASSEMBLY INDUSTRY WORKERS - HEALTH AND HYGIENE - MEXICO.
Stoddard, Ellwyn R., 1927- Maquila . El Paso, Tex. , c1987. ix, 91 p., [2] p. of plates : ISBN 0-87404-200-3 (pbk.) LC Card 86-51646 DDC 338.4/767/09721 19
HD9734.M42 S76 1987

WOMEN OFFSHORE ASSEMBLY INDUSTRY WORKERS - MEXICAN-AMERICAN BORDER REGION.
Carrillo V., Jorge (Carrillo Viveros) Mujeres fronterizas en la industria maquiladora /. [Mexico City] , Tijuana, B.C.N. , 1985. 216 p. : ISBN 968-290-389-0 LC Card 87-400964 DDC 331.4 19
HD6073.O332 M483 1985

WOMEN OFFSHORE ASSEMBLY INDUSTRY WORKERS - MEXICO - CIUDAD JUÁREZ.
Young, Gay. Gender identification and working class solidarity among Maquila workers in Ciudad Juarez . [East Lansing] , c1986. 24 p. ; LC Card 87-620601 DDC 331.4/87/097216 19
HD6073.O332 M4959 1986

WOMEN OFFSHORE ASSEMBLY INDUSTRY WORKERS - MEXICO - INTERVIEWS.
Arenal, Sandra. Sangre joven . México, D.F. , 1986. 130 p., [2] p. of plates : ISBN 968-427-128-X LC Card 87-139058 DDC 331.4/87/0972 19
HD6073.O332 M4953 1986

WOMEN OIL INDUSTRY WORKERS - CONGRESSES.
Women, work, and family in the British, Canadian, and Norwegian oilfields /. New York , 1987. p. cm. ISBN 0-312-00528-8 : LC Card 86-31393 DDC 305.4/3665 19
HD9560.5 .W66 1987

WOMEN-OWNED BUSINESS ENTERPRISES - DEVELOPING COUNTRIES - HANDBOOKS, MANUALS, ETC.
Doing a feasibility study . Washington, D.C. , c1987. 173 p. : ISBN 0-912917-07-5 (pbk.) : LC Card 86-61951 DDC 658/.022/091724 19
HD62.5 .D63 1987

WOMEN-OWNED BUSINESS ENTERPRISES - GREAT BRITAIN.
Hertz, Leah. The business amazons /. London , 1986. xviii, 264, [1] p., [1] leaf of plates : ISBN 0-233-97892-5 : LC Card 86-200078 DDC 338.6/422/088042 19
HD2346.G7 H47 1986

WOMEN-OWNED BUSINESS ENTERPRISES - NETHERLANDS.
Koopman, A. F. Vrouwen zelfstandig . Den Haag [1986] 70 p. ; ISBN 90-346-0762-3 LC Card 86-172683
HD2346.N4 K66 1986

WOMEN-OWNED BUSINESS ENTERPRISES - NETHERLANDS - CASE STUDIES.
Houweling, Marjolein. Ondernemende vrouwen /. Amsterdam , c1985. 128 p. : ISBN 90-6834-018-2 : LC Card 86-166264
HD2346.N4 H68 1985

WOMEN-OWNED BUSINESS ENTERPRISES - UNITED STATES.
Hertz, Leah. The business amazons /. London , 1986. xviii, 264, [1] p., [1] leaf of plates : ISBN 0-233-97892-5 : LC Card 86-200078 DDC 338.6/422/088042 19
HD2346.G7 H47 1986

WOMEN-OWNED BUSINESS ENTERPRISES - UNITED STATES - CASE STUDIES.
Perri, Colleen, 1936- Entrepreneurial women. Kenosha, WI , c1988. p. cm. ISBN 0-941579-02-6 LC Card 87-7370 DDC 338/.04/088042 19
HD2346.U5 P43 1988

Risk to riche$. Washington, DC (600 Maryland Ave., S.W., Suite 700, Washington 20024) , c1986. vii, 204 p. : LC Card 87-158511 DDC 338/.04/088042 19
HD2346.U5 R57 1986

Wilkens, Joanne. Her own business . New York , c1987. xv, 245 p. ; ISBN 0-07-050854-2 : LC Card 86-27780 DDC 338.6/422/088042 19
HD2346.U5 W548 1987

WOMEN-OWNED BUSINESS ENTERPRISES - WISCONSIN - KENOSHA - CASE STUDIES.
Perri, Colleen, 1936- Entrepreneurial women /. Kenosha, WI , c1987. 140 p. : ISBN 0-941579-00-X (pbk.) LC Card 87-154216 DDC 338/.04/088042 19
HD2346.U52 K376 1987b

Perri, Colleen, 1936- Entrepreneurial women /. Kenosha, WI , c1988. p. cm. ISBN 0-941579-28-X LC Card 87-7380 DDC 338/.04/088042 19
HD2346.U52 K376 1988

WOMEN - POLITICAL ACTIVITY. see **WOMEN IN POLITICS.**

WOMEN, POOR - UNITED STATES.
Rodgers, Harrell R. Poor women, poor families . Armonk, N.Y. , 1986. viii, 167 p. ; ISBN 0-87332-372-6 : LC Card 86-6449 DDC 362.8/3/0973 19
HV1445 .R64 1986 ***NYPL [JLE 86-4042]***

WOMEN, POOR - UNITED STATES - ATTITUDES.
For crying out loud . New York , c1986. ix, 397 p. ; ISBN 0-8298-0581-8 (pbk.) : LC Card 86-9302 DDC 305.4/2/0973 19
HQ1426 .F757 1986 ***NYPL [JLD 86-3989]***

WOMEN POTTERS - IVORY COAST - KATIOLA (CENTRE)
Traoré, Aminata. La mine d'argile est notre champ /. [Abidjan?] [1985] (Abidjan : Société d'impr. ivoirienne) [36] p. : LC Card 86-200373
HD6073.P82 I967 1985

Women, production, and patriarchy in late medieval cities /. Howell, Martha C. Chicago , 1986. xv, 285 p. ; ISBN 0-226-35503-9 : LC Card 85-31816 DDC 331.4/094 19
HD6134 .H69 1986 ***NYPL [JLE 86-4284]***

WOMEN - PSYCHOLOGY.
Lewis, Diane, 1936- Why women fail in business /. Nashville , c1987. p. cm. ISBN 0-8407-4219-3 : LC Card 87-15370 DDC 658.4/09088042 19
HD6054.3 .L48 1987

Madden, Tara Roth. Women vs. women . New York, NY , c1987. xxii, 266 p. ; ISBN 0-8144-5900-5 LC Card 87-47701 DDC 658.4/095/088042 19
HD6060 .M33 1987

Ocampo, Silvia. El equilibrio de los sexos . Buenos Aires , 1980 (Buenos Aires : Audivert) 302 p. ; ***NYPL [JLD 86-913]***

Roberts, Richard. From Eden to Eros . San Anselmo, Ca. , 1985. 166 p. : ISBN 0-942380-05-3 (pbk.) LC Card 85-51722 ***NYPL [JLD 87-224]***

Sayers, Janet. Sexual contradictions . London , New York, NY , 1986. x, 214 p. : ISBN 0-422-78780-9 LC Card 85-27948 DDC 155.3/3 19
BF692.2 .S29 1986 ***NYPL [JFD 86-5840]***

Stress, social support, and women /. Washington , c1986. xviii, 272 p. : ISBN 0-89116-404-9 : LC Card 84-27967 DDC 155.9 19
BF575.S75 S7739 1985 ***NYPL [JFE 86-3212]***

Tarizzo, Domenico. Il nuovo amore di coppia /. Milano , 1982. 192 p. ; LC Card 82-141135 DDC 306.7 19
HQ21 .T338 1982 ***NYPL [JLD 87-1019]***

Westkott, Marcia, 1943- The feminist legacy of Karen Horney /. New Haven , c1986. viii, 242 p. ; ISBN 0-300-03706-6 (alk. paper) LC Card 86-9201 DDC 305.4/2 19
HQ1206 .W47 1986 ***NYPL [JFD 86-10266]***

Witkin-Lanoil, Georgia. The female stress syndrome . New York , c1984. xi, 211 p. ; ISBN 0-937858-33-1 LC Card 83-25038 DDC 155.6/33 19
BF575.S75 W58 1984 ***NYPL [JFD 86-10468]***

Women in health & illness . Philadelphia , 1986. x, 261 p. : ISBN 0-7216-2086-8 LC Card 86-6576 DDC 155.6/33 19
RC451.4.W6 W656 1986 ***NYPL [JLF 86-1463]***

WOMEN - PSYCHOLOGY - ADDRESSES, ESSAYS, LECTURES.
The Social psychology of female-male relations . Orlando , 1986. xvi, 351 p. ; ISBN 0-12-065280-3 (alk. paper) LC Card 85-9138 DDC 305.3 19
HM132 .S569 1986 ***NYPL [JLE 86-1746]***

Women, public opinion, and politics . Poole, Keith T. New York , c1985. xii, 196 p. : ISBN 0-582-28274-8 LC Card 84-7155 DDC 305.4/0973 19
HQ1410 .P66 1985 ***NYPL [JLE 85-1580]***

WOMEN - RELIGION.
Roberts, Richard. From Eden to Eros . San Anselmo, Ca. , 1985. 166 p. : ISBN 0-942380-05-3 (pbk.) LC Card 85-51722 ***NYPL [JLD 87-224]***

WOMEN RICE WORKERS - BANGLADESH.
Greeley, Martin. Postharvest losses, technology, and employment . Boulder, Colo. , 1987. xvii, 345 p. : ISBN 0-8133-7371-9 (pbk. : alk. paper) : LC Card 87-10648 DDC 338.1/7318/095492 19
HD9066.B32 G73 1987

WOMEN - RIGHTS OF WOMEN. see **WOMEN'S RIGHTS.**

WOMEN, RURAL. see **RURAL WOMEN.**

WOMEN SALES PERSONNEL - GERMANY, WEST - CASE STUDIES.
Women, work, and family in Britain and Germany /. London , 1986. 216 p. : ISBN 0-7099-0976-4 ***NYPL [JLD 86-3391]***

WOMEN SALES PERSONNEL - GREAT BRITAIN - CASE STUDIES.
Women, work, and family in Britain and Germany /. London , 1986. 216 p. : ISBN 0-7099-0976-4 ***NYPL [JLD 86-3391]***

WOMEN SALES PERSONNEL - INDONESIA - SLEMAN (KABUPATEN) - CASE STUDIES.
Peluso, Nancy Lee. Survival strategies of rural women traders, or, A woman's place is in the market . Geneva [1981], c1980. viii, 124 p. ; ISBN 92-2-102633-7 LC Card 83-105710 DDC 331.4/81381/095982 19
HD6194.Z6 S566 1981

WOMEN - SOCIAL CONDITIONS.
Labarge, Margaret Wade. Women in medieval life . London , 1986. xiv, 271 p. : ISBN 0-241-11809-3 : ***NYPL [JLE 86-3838]***

Mies, Maria. Patriarchy and accumulation on a world scale . London , Atlantic Highlands, NJ , 1986. 251 p. ; ISBN 0-86232-341-X LC Card 86-18916 DDC 305.4 19
HD6060.6 .M54 1986 ***NYPL [JLD 86-3206]***

Ocampo, Silvia. El equilibrio de los sexos . Buenos Aires , 1980 (Buenos Aires : Audivert) 302 p. ; ***NYPL [JLD 86-913]***

Santarcangelo, Maria Candida Vergueiro. A situação da mulher /. São Paulo , 1980. 389 p. ; ***NYPL [JLD 86-625]***

Sivard, Ruth Leger. Women--a world survey /. Washington, D.C. , c1985. 44 p. : ISBN 0-918281-00-8 (pbk.) : LC Card 85-171073 DDC 305.4 19
HQ1154 .S547 1985 ***NYPL [*R-Econ. 86-4677]***

Witkin-Lanoil, Georgia. The female stress syndrome . New York , c1984. xi, 211 p. ; ISBN 0-937858-33-1 LC Card 83-25038 DDC 155.6/33 19
BF575.S75 W58 1984 ***NYPL [JFD 86-10468]***

WOMEN - SOUTHERN STATES - ECONOMIC CONDITIONS.
Byerly, Victoria Morris. Hard times cotton mill girls . Ithaca, N.Y. , c1986. x, 223 p. : ISBN 0-87546-128-X : LC Card 86-20082 DDC 331.4/877/00922 B 19
HD6073.T42 A132 1986 ***NYPL [JLD 87-1241]***

WOMEN - SOVIET UNION - SOCIAL CONDITIONS.
Lapidus, Gail Warshofsky. Women in Soviet society . Berkeley , c1978. x, 381 p. ; ISBN 0-520-02868-6 : LC Card 74-16710 DDC 305.4/0947
HQ1663 .L33 *NYPL [JLE 80-1771]*

WOMEN - STATISTICS.
Sivard, Ruth Leger. Women--a world survey /. Washington, D.C. , c1985. 44 p. : ISBN 0-918281-00-8 (pbk.) : LC Card 85-171073 DDC 305.4 19
HQ1154 .S547 1985 *NYPL [*R-Econ. 86-4677]*

WOMEN - SUFFRAGE - UNITED STATES - HISTORY.
Andolsen, Barbara Hilkert. "Daughters of Jefferson, daughters of bootblacks" . Macon, GA , c1986. xiv, 130 p. ; ISBN 0-86554-204-X : LC Card 86-816 DDC 305.4/2/0973 19
HQ1426 .A6827 1986 *NYPL [JLE 86-3359]*

WOMEN SUPERVISORS.
Highman, Edith L. The organization woman . New York, N.Y. , c1985. 204 p. ; ISBN 0-89885-237-4 LC Card 84-27775 DDC 658.4/09/024042 19
HD6054.3 .H54 1985 *NYPL [JLD 86-1930]*

WOMEN - TANZANIA - SOCIAL CONDITIONS - CASE STUDIES.
Swantz, Marja-Liisa. Women in development . London , New York , c1985. ix, 177 p. : ISBN 0-312-88780-9 (St. Martin's Press) : LC Card 85-2120 DDC 331.4/09678 19
HD6211.3 .S93 1985 *NYPL [Sc D 86-104]*

WOMEN TEXTILE WORKERS - CHINA - SHANGHAI - HISTORY - 20TH CENTURY.
Honig, Emily. Sisters and strangers . Stanford, Calif. , 1986. ix, 299 p. : ISBN 0-8047-1274-3 (alk. paper) : LC Card 84-51711 DDC 331.4/87721/0951132 19
HD6073.T42 C64 1986 *NYPL [JLD 86-3016]*

WOMEN TEXTILE WORKERS - FRANCE - LILLE REGION - CASE STUDIES.
Hilden, Patricia. Working women and socialist politics in France, 1880-1914 . Oxford [Oxfordshire] , New York , 1986. viii, 307 p. ; ISBN 0-19-821935-0 : LC Card 85-15487 DDC 331.4/877/0094428 19
HD6073.T42 F84 1986 *NYPL [JLD 86-1838]*

WOMEN TEXTILE WORKERS - GREAT BRITAIN.
Coyle, Angela. Redundant women /. London , 1984. 154 p. : ISBN 0-7043-3923-4 (pbk.) : LC Card 84-100906 DDC 331.4/137941 19
HD5708.55.G7 C68 1984 *NYPL [JLD 86-3916]*

WOMEN TEXTILE WORKERS - INDIA - BOMBAY - CASE STUDIES.
Savara, Mira. Changing trends in women's employment . Bombay , 1986. xii, 137 p. ; LC Card 86-902789 DDC 331.4/877/00954792 19
HD6073.T42 I47 1986

WOMEN TEXTILE WORKERS - INDIA - CASE STUDIES.
Savara, Mira. Changing trends in women's employment . Bombay , 1986. xii, 137 p. ; LC Card 86-902789 DDC 331.4/877/00954792 19
HD6073.T42 I47 1986

WOMEN TEXTILE WORKERS - NORTH CAROLINA - DURHAM REGION - HISTORY.
Janiewski, Dolores E., 1948- Sisterhood denied . Philadelphia , 1985. xvii, 248 p. : ISBN 0-87722-361-0 : LC Card 84-2640 DDC 305.4/2/09756563 19
HD6073.T62 U65 1985 *NYPL [Sc E 86-322]*

WOMEN TEXTILE WORKERS - SOUTHERN STATES - BIOGRAPHY.
Byerly, Victoria Morris. Hard times cotton mill girls . Ithaca, N.Y. , c1986. x, 223 p. : ISBN 0-87546-128-X : LC Card 86-20082 DDC 331.4/877/00922 B 19
HD6073.T42 A132 1986 *NYPL [JLD 87-1241]*

Women, the family, and the economy /. Wilson, S. J. (Susannah Jane) Toronto , New York , c1982. 176 p. : ISBN 0-07-548028-X (pbk.) LC Card 82-123177 DDC 305.4/0971 19
HQ1457 .W53 1982 *NYPL [JLE 86-1735]*

WOMEN - TIME MANAGEMENT.
Filbert, Judith Ann. Homemaking skills go to the office . Bozeman, Mont. (P.O. Box 6244, Bozeman 59771) , c1986. 46 p. ; LC Card 86-218123 DDC 651.3/741/02373 19
HF5547.5 .F53 1986

WOMEN TOBACCO WORKERS - GERMANY (WEST) - BADEN-WÜRTTEMBERG - HISTORY.
Gensewich, Irmtraud. Die Tabakarbeiterin in Baden, 1870-1914 /. Mannheim , 1986. 496 p. : ISBN 3-87804-183-7 LC Card 87-121532 DDC 331.4/8797/094346 19
HD6073.T62 G34 1986

WOMEN TOBACCO WORKERS - NORTH CAROLINA - DURHAM REGION - HISTORY.
Janiewski, Dolores E., 1948- Sisterhood denied . Philadelphia , 1985. xvii, 248 p. : ISBN 0-87722-361-0 : LC Card 84-2640 DDC 305.4/2/09756563 19
HD6073.T62 U65 1985 *NYPL [Sc E 86-322]*

WOMEN - UNITED STATES - ATTITUDES.
Poole, Keith T. Women, public opinion, and politics . New York , c1985. xii, 196 p. : ISBN 0-582-28274-8 LC Card 84-7155 DDC 305.4/0973 19
HQ1410 .P66 1985 *NYPL [JLE 85-1580]*

WOMEN - UNITED STATES - ECONOMIC CONDITIONS.
Blau, Francine D. The economics of women, men, and work /. Englewood Cliffs, N.J. , c1986. xiv, 365 p. : ISBN 0-13-233719-3 LC Card 85-30746 DDC 305.3/0973 19
HQ1426 .B62 1986 *NYPL [JLE 86-4254]*

For crying out loud . New York , c1986. ix, 397 p. ; ISBN 0-8298-0581-8 (pbk.) : LC Card 86-9302 DDC 305.4/2/0973 19
HQ1426 .F757 1986 *NYPL [JLD 86-3989]*

Helmbold, Lois Rita. Making choices, making do [microform] . 1982. vii, 385 leaves
NYPL [Sc Micro R-4672]

Hewlett, Sylvia Ann, 1946- A lesser life . New York, N.Y. , 1986. 461 p. : ISBN 0-688-04855-2 LC Card 85-21395 DDC 305.4/2/0973 19
HQ1426 .H457 1986 *NYPL [JLE 86-1460]*

Mallier, A. T., 1931- Women and the economy . Houndmills, Basingstoke, Hampshire , 1987. xiv, 221 p. : ISBN 0-333-37938-1 *NYPL [JLD 87-1151]*

WOMEN - UNITED STATES - ECONOMIC CONDITIONS - CASE STUDIES.
Stolz, Barbara Ann. Still struggling . Lexington, Mass. , c1985. xviii, 205 p. ; ISBN 0-669-10930-4 (alk. paper) LC Card 85-40235 DDC 331.4/0973 19
HD6052 .S76 1985 *NYPL [JLE 85-3704]*

WOMEN - UNITED STATES - ECONOMIC CONDITIONS - CONGRESSES.
"To toil the livelong day" . Ithaca, N.Y. , 1987. xi, 312 p. ; ISBN 0-8014-1847-X (alk. paper) LC Card 86-47975 DDC 331.4/0973 19
HD6095 .T6 1987

Women, households, and the economy /. New Brunswick, N.J. , c1987. p. cm. ISBN 0-8135-1263-8 : LC Card 87-4840 DDC 331.4/0973 19
HD6060.65.U5 W65 1987

WOMEN - UNITED STATES - FINANCE, PERSONAL.
Blau, Anne Kohn. The sex of the dollar . New York , c1988. 190 p. : ISBN 0-671-60680-8 LC Card 87-23560 DDC 332.024/042 19
HG181 .B46 1988

WOMEN - UNITED STATES - HISTORY.
Lerner, Gerda, 1920- The majority finds its past . New York , 1979. xxxii, 217 p. ; ISBN 0-19-502597-0 LC Card 79-14048 DDC 301.41/2/0973
HQ1426 .L47 *NYPL [JLD 86-3348]*

Tentler, Leslie Woodcock. Wage-earning women . New York , 1979. 266 p. ; ISBN 0-19-502627-6 : LC Card 79-12802 DDC 331.4/0973
HD6095 .T44 *NYPL [JLD 86-3699]*

WOMEN - UNITED STATES - HISTORY - 20TH CENTURY.
Helmbold, Lois Rita. Making choices, making do [microform] . 1982. vii, 385 leaves
NYPL [Sc Micro R-4672]

WOMEN - UNITED STATES - POLITICAL ACTIVITY.
Beckwith, Karen, 1950- American women and political participation . New York , 1986. xiv, 185 p. ; ISBN 0-313-24507-X
NYPL [JLD 87-36]

WOMEN - UNITED STATES - PSYCHOLOGY - ADDRESSES, ESSAYS, LECTURES.
Moore, Lynda L. Not as far as you think . Lexington, Mass. , c1986. xii, 201 p. ; ISBN 0-669-10836-7 : LC Card 85-40109 DDC 331.4/0973 19
HD6095 .M66 1986 *NYPL [JLE 86-1878]*

WOMEN - UNITED STATES - PUBLIC OPINION.
Poole, Keith T. Women, public opinion, and politics . New York , c1985. xii, 196 p. : ISBN 0-582-28274-8 LC Card 84-7155 DDC 305.4/0973 19
HQ1410 .P66 1985 *NYPL [JLE 85-1580]*

WOMEN - UNITED STATES - SOCIAL CONDITIONS.
Blau, Francine D. The economics of women, men, and work /. Englewood Cliffs, N.J. , c1986. xiv, 365 p. : ISBN 0-13-233719-3 LC Card 85-30746 DDC 305.3/0973 19
HQ1426 .B62 1986 *NYPL [JLE 86-4254]*

Helmbold, Lois Rita. Making choices, making do [microform] . 1982. vii, 385 leaves
NYPL [Sc Micro R-4672]

Hewlett, Sylvia Ann, 1946- A lesser life . New York, N.Y. , 1986. 461 p. : ISBN 0-688-04855-2 LC Card 85-21395 DDC 305.4/2/0973 19
HQ1426 .H457 1986 *NYPL [JLE 86-1460]*

Poole, Keith T. Women, public opinion, and politics . New York , c1985. xii, 196 p. : ISBN 0-582-28274-8 LC Card 84-7155 DDC 305.4/0973 19
HQ1410 .P66 1985 *NYPL [JLE 85-1580]*

Women versus women. Madden, Tara Roth. Women vs. women . New York, NY , c1987. xxii, 266 p. ; ISBN 0-8144-5900-5 LC Card 87-47701 DDC 658.4/095/088042 19
HD6060 .M33 1987

Women vs. women . Madden, Tara Roth. New York, NY , c1987. xxii, 266 p. ; ISBN 0-8144-5900-5 LC Card 87-47701 DDC 658.4/095/088042 19
HD6060 .M33 1987

WOMEN WHITE COLLAR WORKERS - EFFECT OF AUTOMATION ON.
New technology and women's employment. Bruxelles , New York [1983] 78 p. ; LC Card 85-160627 DDC 331.4/2 19
HD6331 .N49 1983 *NYPL [JLD 86-1807]*

WOMEN WHITE COLLAR WORKERS - EFFECT OF TECHNOLOGICAL INNOVATIONS ON.
National Research Council (U. S.). Committee on Women's Employment and Related Social Issues. Panel on Technology and Women's Employment. Computer chips and paper clips . Washington, D.C. , 1986. v. : ISBN 0-309-03688-7 (v. 1) LC Card 86-18113 DDC 331.4/8165137/0973 19
HD6331.18.M39 N38 1986 *NYPL [JLL 87-129]*

WOMEN WHITE COLLAR WORKERS - GERMANY.
Grenzen der Frauenlohnarbeit . Frankfurt/Main , New York , c1986. 250 p. : ISBN 3-593-33628-6 LC Card 86-228323
HD6072.2.G4 G74 1986

WOMEN WHITE COLLAR WORKERS - GERMANY (WEST) - EFFECT OF TECHNOLOGICAL INNOVATIONS ON.
Frauen und neue Technologien /. Hannover , 1986. 112 p. ; LC Card 87-407392 DDC 331.4/0943 19
HD6059.G3 F74 1986

WOMEN WHITE COLLAR WORKERS - SWEDEN.
Granath, Erna. Kvinnoplats . Stockholm , c1985. 141 p. ; ISBN 91-38-90602-3 : LC Card

85-236327
HD6073.M392 S84 1985
NYPL [JLE 86-3898]

Women, work, and demographic issues : report of an ILO/UNITAR Seminar, Tashkent, USSR, 11-19 October 1983. Geneva : International Labour Office, 1984. 159 p. ; 24 cm. Includes bibliographies. ISBN 92-2-103886-6 : LC Card 86-673726
1. Women - Employment - Congresses. 2. Women - Employment - Developing countries - Congresses. 3. Women - Economic conditions - Congresses. 4. Women - Developing countries - Economic conditions - Congresses. I. International Labour Office. II. United Nations Institute for Training and Research.
HD6052 .W568x 1984

Women, work, and development, 0253-2042 .
(12) Mies, Maria. Indian women in subsistence and agricultural labour /. Geneva , 1986. x, 158 p. ; ISBN 92-2-105397-0 (pbk.) : LC Card 87-114124 DDC 331.4/83/0954 19
HD6073.A292 I46 1986

(9) Dixon-Mueller, Ruth. Women's work in Third World agriculture . Geneva , 1985. xi, 151 p. : ISBN 92-2-105107-2 (pbk.) LC Card 86-673111
HD6073.A292 D442x 1985
NYPL [JLE 86-3760]

Women, work, and family /. Tilly, Louise. New York , 1987. vii, 274 p. : ISBN 0-416-01681-2 (pbk.) : LC Card 87-11103 DDC 305.4/3/00941 19
HD6135 .T54 1987

Women, work, and family in Britain and Germany / edited by T. Scarlett Epstein ... [et al.]. London : Croom Helm, 1986. 216 p. : ill. ; 22 cm. Bibliography: p. 211-216. ISBN 0-7099-0976-4
1. Women - Employment - Great Britain - Case studies. 2. Women - Employment - Germany (West) - Case studies. 3. Women - Great Britain - Time management - Case studies. 4. Women - Germany, West - Time management - Case studies. 5. Women sales personnel - Great Britain - Case studies. 6. Women sales personnel - Germany, West - Case studies. I. Epstein, Trude Scarlett. ***NYPL [JLD 86-3391]***

Women, work, and family in the British, Canadian, and Norwegian oilfields / edited by Jane Lewis, Marilyn Porter, and Mark Shrimpton. New York : St. Martin's, 1987. p. cm. Proceedings of the International Conference on Women and Offshore Oil held at Memorial University of Newfoundland, Canada, in late 1985. Bibliography: Includes index. ISBN 0-312-00528-8 : LC Card 86-31393 DDC 305.4/3665 19
1. Offshore oil industry - Social aspects - Congresses. 2. Women oil industry workers - Congresses. 3. Oil industry workers - Family relationships - Congresses. I. Lewis, Jane (Jane E.). II. Porter, Marilyn, 1942-. III. Shrimpton, Mark. IV. International Conference on Women and Offshore Oil (1985 : St. John's, Nfld.).
HD9560.5 .W66 1987

Women, work, and ideology in the Third World / edited by Haleh Afshar. London ; New York : Tavistock Publications, 1985. xvii, 265 p. : map ; 22 cm. Includes bibliographies and indexes. ISBN 0-422-79710-3 (U. S. : pbk.) LC Card 85-17279 DDC 305.4/09172/4 19
1. Women - Developing countries - Economic conditions - Case studies. 2. Rural women - Developing countries - Case studies. 3. Women - Employment - Developing countries - Case studies. 4. Sexual division of labor - Developing countries - Case studies. I. Afshar, Haleh, 1944-.
HQ1870.9 .W657 1985
NYPL [JLD 86-2322]

Women, work, and society / edited by K. Saradamoni. Calcutta : Indian Statistical Institute, 1985. xvi, 430 p. : ill. ; 25 cm. Papers presented at the Indian Statistical Institute Golden Jubilee International Symposium on Women, Work, and Society, New Delhi, 1982. Includes bibliographies. LC Card 86-900827 DDC 331.4 19
1. Women - Employment - Congresses. 2. Women in development - Congresses. I. Saradamoni, K. (Kunjulekshmi), 1928-. II. Indian Statistical Institute. III. Indian Statistical Institute Golden Jubilee International Symposium on Women, Work and Society (1982 : New Delhi, India).
HD6052 .W565 1982 ***NYPL [JLE 87-1019]***

Women, work, and society.
Garnsey, Elizabeth. Industrial change and women's employment . Geneva , 1987. ix, 100, x p. : ISBN 92-9014-411-4 (pbk.) : LC Card 87-163195 DDC 331.4/09172/4 19
HD6223 .G37 1987

Women, work, and technology : transformations / edited by Barbara Drygulski Wright ... [et al.]. Ann Arbor : University of Michigan Press, c1987. viii, 387 p. ; 23 cm. (Women and culture series) Primarily papers presented at a conference held at the University of Connecticut in Oct. 1984, sponsored by the Project on Women and Technology. Includes bibliographies and index. ISBN 0-472-06373-1 (pbk. : alk. paper) : LC Card 87-16236 DDC 331.4 19
1. Women - Employment - Effect of technological innovations on - Congresses. I. Wright, Barbara Drygulski, 1945-. II. University of Connecticut. Project on Women and Technology.
HD6052 .W566 1987

Women, work, and wages /. Berger, Gilda. New York , 1986. 122 p. : ISBN 0-531-10074-X LC Card 85-15379 DDC 331.4/0973 19
HD6095 .B47 1986 ***NYPL [JLE 86-4592]***

WOMEN WORKERS. see **WOMEN - EMPLOYMENT.**

Women workers and the sweated trades . Morris, Jenny, 1950- Aldershot, Hants, England , Brookfield, Vt., USA , c1986. 248 p. ; ISBN 0-566-05188-5 : LC Card 86-9850 DDC 331.4/23 19
HD2339.G7 M67 1986
NYPL [JLD 86-4089]

Women working : theories and facts in perspective / edited by Ann Helton Stromberg and Shirley Harkess.2nd ed. Mountain View, Calif. : Mayfield Pub. Co., c1988. xv, 431 p. : ill. ; 24 cm. Bibliography: p. 361-411. Includes index. ISBN 0-87484-744-3 (pbk.) LC Card 87-3215 DDC 331.4/0973 19
1. Women - Employment - United States. 2. Sexual division of labor - United States. 3. Pay equity - United States. I. Stromberg, Ann Helton. II. Harkess, Shirley.
HD6095 .W6976 1988

WOMEN'S CLOTHING INDUSTRY - SWEDEN.
Tung damkonfektion . Stockholm , 1978. 47, [10] p. : ISBN 91-38-04438-2 LC Card 84-106453
HD9940.S82 T85 1978

Women's development, income, and fertility /. Mabud, Mohammed A. (Mohammed Abdul) Dhaka , 1985. xi, 180 p. ; LC Card 85-903972 DDC 305.4/09549/2 19
HQ1745.6 .M33 1985 ***NYPL [JLD 86-2067]***

Women's employment patterns, discrimination, and promotion of equality in Zambia /. Bardouille, R. (Raj) [Lusaka? , 1985]. ii, 160 leaves ; LC Card 87-980054 DDC 331.4/133/096894 19
HD6212.5 .B37 1985

WOMEN'S LIB. see **FEMINISM.**

WOMEN'S LIBERATION. see **WOMEN'S RIGHTS.**

WOMEN'S LIBERATION MOVEMENT. see **FEMINISM.**

Women's rights at work . Meehan, Elizabeth M. New York , 1985. xvii, 253 p. ; ISBN 0-312-88793-0 : LC Card 84-15997 DDC 331.4/133/0941 19
HD6060 .M44 1984 ***NYPL [JLD 86-3580]***

WOMEN'S RIGHTS - CANADA.
Canada. Royal Commission on the Status of Women in Canada. Report of the Royal Commission on the Status of Women in Canada. [Ottawa, Ont.] , 1970. xii, 488 p. :
NYPL [JLE 73-1102]

WOMEN'S RIGHTS - GERMANY, WEST.
Rosen, Rita. --Muss kommen, aber nix von Herzen . Opladen , 1986. 262 p. : ISBN 3-8100-0572-X LC Card 87-112784
HD6149 .R67 1986

WOMEN'S RIGHTS - SOVIET UNION.
Lapidus, Gail Warshofsky. Women in Soviet society . Berkeley , c1978. x, 381 p. ; ISBN 0-520-02868-6 : LC Card 74-16710 DDC 305.4/0947
HQ1663 .L33 ***NYPL [JLE 80-1771]***

WOMEN'S RIGHTS - UNITED STATES.
Berry, Mary Frances. Why ERA failed . Bloomington , c1986. ix, 147 p. ; ISBN 0-253-36537-6 LC Card 85-45985 DDC 342.73/0878/02632 347.30287802632 19
KF4758 .B45 1986 ***NYPL [JLE 86-3979]***

Follis, Anne Bowen, 1947- I'm not a women's libber, but--and other confessions of a Christian feminist /. Nashville , c1981. 128 p. ; ISBN 0-687-18687-0 LC Card 81-1241
HQ1426 .F75 ***NYPL [JLD 85-1976]***

Mansbridge, Jane J. Why we lost the ERA /. Chicago, Ill. , c1986. xii, 327 p. ; ISBN 0-226-50358-5 (pbk.) LC Card 86-6954 DDC 305.4/2/0973 19
HQ1236.5.U6 M37 1986
NYPL [JLE 86-4474]

WOMEN'S RIGHTS - UNITED STATES - HISTORY.
Lerner, Gerda, 1920- The majority finds its past . New York , 1979. xxxii, 217 p. ; ISBN 0-19-502597-0 LC Card 79-14048 DDC 301.41/2/0973
HQ1426 .L47 ***NYPL [JLD 86-3348]***

Women's roles & gender differences in development .

Women's roles and gender differences in development .
(3) Staudt, Kathleen A. Agricultural policy implementation . West Hartford, CT , c1985. xvi, 68 p. : ISBN 0-931816-18-1 (pbk.) LC Card 84-29737 DDC 338.1/86762 19
HD2126.5.Z8 S73 1985
NYPL [JLF 86-1685]

(4) Jackson, Cecile, 1953- The Kano River Irrigation Project /. West Hartford, Conn. , 1985. xviii, 66 p. ; ISBN 0-931816-19-X LC Card 85-5242 DDC 331.4/83/09669 19
HD6073.F32 N64 1985
NYPL [JLF 86-1634]

(5) Spiro, Heather M. The Ilora farm settlement in Nigeria /. West Hartford, Conn. , 1985. xvii, 50 p. : ISBN 0-931816-20-3 LC Card 85-5230 DDC 331.4/83/089963 19
HD6073.F3 N667 1985
NYPL [JLF 86-1629]

(6) Palmer, Ingrid. The impact of agrarian reform on women /. West Hartford, Conn. , c1985. xiv, 55 p. ; ISBN 0-931816-21-1 (pbk.) LC Card 85-5250 DDC 331.4/83/091724 19
HD6073.A292 D447 1985
NYPL [JLF 86-1633]

(7) Palmer, Ingrid. The impact of male out-migration on women in farming /. West Hartford, Conn. , c1985. xviii, 78 p. ; ISBN 0-931816-22-X (pbk.) LC Card 85-5240 DDC 331.4/83/091724 19
HD6073.A292 D4472 1985
NYPL [JLF 86-1626]

Women's studies politics.
Miller, Jill. You can't kill the spirit . London , c1986. 142 p. : ISBN 0-7043-4021-6 (pbk.) : LC Card 87-100804 DDC 305.4/2/0942995 19
HD5365.M6152 1984 .W345 1986

Women's work and Chicano families . Zavella, Patricia, 1949- Ithaca , 1987. xviii, 191 p. ; ISBN 0-8014-1730-9 (pbk. : alk. paper) LC Card 87-5245 DDC 305.4/3664 19
HD6073.C272 U596 1987

Women's work, class, and the urban household . Sharma, Ursula, 1941- London , New York , 1986. 213 p. ; ISBN 0-422-79320-5 : LC Card 86-11296 DDC 305.4/3 19
HQ759 .S4616 1986 ***NYPL [JLD 87-1281]***

Women's work in Third World agriculture . Dixon-Mueller, Ruth. Geneva , 1985. xi, 151 p. : ISBN 92-2-105107-2 (pbk.) LC Card 86-673111
HD6073.A292 D442x 1985
NYPL [JLE 86-3760]

Women's work interruptions . Robinson, Patricia A. (Patricia Ann) Ottawa [1987], c1986. 36, 40 p. ; ISBN 0-660-52895-9 (pbk.) : LC Card 87-146334 DDC 331.4/12/0971 19
HD6099 .R63 1987

Women's work, men's work : sex segregation on the job / Barbara F. Reskin and Heidi I. Hartmann, editors ; Committee on Women's Employment and Related Social Issues, Commission on Behavioral and Social Sciences and Education, National Research Council. Washington, D.C. : National Academy Press, 1986. xii, 173 p. : ill. ; 26 cm. Includes index. Bibliography: p. 141-161. ISBN 0-309-03429-9 (pbk.)

LC Card 85-11541 DDC 331.1/33/0973 19
1. Sex discrimination in employment - United States. 2. Women - Employment - United States. 3. Equal pay for equal work - United States. 4. Sex discrimination - Law and legislation - United States. I. Reskin, Barbara F. II. Hartmann, Heidi I. III. National Research Council Committee on Women's Employment and Related Social Issues. IV. National Research Council Commission on Behavioral and Social Sciences and Education.
HD6060.5.U5 W66 1986 *NYPL [JLF 86-1430]*

Women's work, undervalued, underpaid . DeGooyer, Janice. Washington, D.C. , 1984, c1982. 27, [4] leaves :
*NYPL [*ZT-1708 no.39]*

WONDERBOOM (TRANSVAAL, SOUTH AFRICA) - CENSUS, 1980.
Bevolkingsensus 1980, uitgesoekte statistiese streek, Pretoria/Wonderboom =. [Pretoria] [1985?] xx, 476 p. : ISBN 0-621-09483-8 : LC Card 85-238587
HA4701.Z9 P743 1985

Wondrak, Bernhard. Management von Zinsänderungschancen und -risiken / Bernhard Wondrak. Heidelberg : Physica-Verlag, c1986. xv, 254 p. : ill. ; 25 cm. (Physica-Schriften zur Betriebswirtschaft . Bd. 15) Bibliography: p. [245]-254. ISBN 3-7908-0341-3 LC Card 86-213976
1. Interest rate futures - Mathematical models. 2. Portfolio management - Mathematical models. I. Title. II. Series.
HG6024.5 .W66 1986

Wong, John, 1939-
Asian economic handbook. London , 1987, c1986. 272 p. : ISBN 0-86338-141-3 : LC Card 87-133198 DDC 330.95/042 19
HC412 .A748 1987

Regional industrial co-operation : experiences and perspective of Asean and the Andean Pact. Vienna : United Nations Industrial Development Organization, 1986. xi, 102 p. : ill. ; 24 cm. Prepared by John Wong. Summaries in French and Spanish. Includes bibliographical references. ISBN 92-1-106204-7 (pbk.) LC Card 86-214910 DDC 337.1/5 19
1. Asia, Southeastern - Economic integration. 2. Andes region - Economic integration. 3. International cooperation. 4. International economic relations. I. United Nations. Industrial Development Organization. II. Title.
HC441 .W66 1986

Wong, Kai Choo. Seminar "Malaysian Agriculture--What Next?" (1985 : Kuala Lumpur, Malaysia) Options for Malaysian agriculture . [Kuala Lumpur] , 1986. xxiv, 203 p. : ISBN 967-99982-0-7 (pbk.) LC Card 86-943314 DDC 338.1/8595 19
HD2080.6.Z8 S45 1985

Wong, Lung-Fai. Agricultural productivity in the Socialist countries / Lung-Fai Wong. Boulder, Colo. : Westview Press, 1986. xvii, 195 p. : ill. ; 23 cm. (Westview special studies in agriculture science and policy) Includes index. Bibliography: p. 183-190. ISBN 0-8133-7152-X : LC Card 86-1539 DDC 338.1/6/091717 19
1. Agricultural productivity - Communist countries. 2. Agricultural productivity - Communist countries - Case studies. I. Title. II. Series.
HD1415 .W54 1986 *NYPL [JLE 86-2447]*

Wong, Stanley. The foundations of Paul Samuelson's revealed preference theory : a study by the method of rational reconstruction / Stanley Wong. London ; Boston : Routledge & K. Paul, 1978. x, 148 p. : ill. ; 23 cm. Includes indexes. Bibliography: p. 138-144. ISBN 0-7100-8643-1 : LC Card 78-40600 DDC 339.4/7
1. Samuelson, Paul Anthony 1915-. 2. Consumption (Economics). 3. Consumers' preferences. I. Title.
HB801 .W594 *NYPL [JLD 87-1092]*

Wonnacott, Paul. The United States and Canada : the quest for free trade : an examination of selected issues / Paul Wonnacott ; with an appendix by John Williamson. Washington, DC : Institute for International Economics, 1987. xii, 173 p. : ill. ; 23 cm. (Policy analyses in international economics . 16) Includes bibliographies. ISBN 0-88132-056-0 (pbk.) : LC Card 87-2660 DDC 382.71073 19
1. United States - Foreign economic relations - Canada. 2. Canada - Foreign economic relations - United States. 3. United States - Commercial policy. 4. Canada - Commercial policy. 5. Free trade and protection. I. Title. II. Series.
HF1456.5.C2 W65 1987

Wonnacott, Ronald J. Canada/United States free trade : problems and opportunities / R.J. Wonnacott. Toronto, Ont. : Ontario Economic Council, c1985. 30 p. ; 21 cm. (Canadian trade at a crossroads series) Special research report / Ontario Economic Council, 0225-591X Bibliography: p. 28-30. ISBN 0-7729-0036-1 (pbk.) LC Card 86-673986
1. Canada - Commercial policy. 2. United States - Commercial policy. 3. Canada - Commerce - United States. 4. United States - Commerce - Canada. I. Series. II. Series: Special research report (Ontario Economic Council). III. Title.
HF1480.5.U57 W66x 1985

Wood, Alan, 1943- Siberia . London , New York , c1987. 233 p. : ISBN 0-7099-3655-9 LC Card 87-15437 DDC 330.957/0854 19
HC337.R852 S52697 1987

The wood chemical industry in the Delaware Valley /. Myers, Frank Daniel. Middletown, N.Y. , 1986. [160] p. : LC Card 87-108267
HD9660.M573 U616 1986

WOOD CHIPS INDUSTRY - AUSTRALIA - NEW SOUTH WALES.
McCormick, William A. The export woodchip industry of south east NSW . Barton, A.C.T. , 1986. 23 p. : LC Card 87-163674 DDC 333.75/09944 19
HD9769.W383 A85 1986

Wood, Chris. The SuperCalc program made easy / Chris Wood. 2nd ed. Berkeley, Calif. : Osborne McGraw-Hill, c1987. xi, 384 p. : ill. ; 24 cm. Includes index. ISBN 0-07-881002-7 (pbk.) : LC Card 86-221528 DDC 005.36/9 19
1. SuperCalc (Computer program). 2. Business - Data processing. I. Title.
HF5548.4.S85 W66 1987

WOOD-CUTS. see **WOOD-ENGRAVING.**

WOOD-CUTTING (ENGRAVING) see **WOOD-ENGRAVING.**

WOOD DISTILLATION - HISTORY.
Myers, Frank Daniel. The wood chemical industry in the Delaware Valley /. Middletown, N.Y. , 1986. [160] p. : LC Card 87-108267
HD9660.M573 U616 1986

Wood, Donald F. Readings in contemporary transportation /. Tulsa, OK , c1983. x, 325 p. : ISBN 0-87814-215-0 (pbk.) LC Card 82-22379 DDC 380.5 19
HE151 .R37 1983 *NYPL [JLF 86-2000]*

Wood, Donna, 1949- Wilson, James A., 1928- Managing the behavioral dynamics of internal auditing /. Altamonte Springs, Fla. [1985] xii, 112 p. : ISBN 0-89413-130-3 (pbk.) LC Card 85-169744 DDC 657/.458/019 19
HF5668.25 .W53 1985 *NYPL [JLE 86-4318]*

Wood energy in East Africa. Regional Workshop on Wood Energy in East Africa (1982 : Nairobi, Kenya) Proceedings of the Regional Workshop on Wood Energy in East Africa . Ottawa, Canada [1983] 241 p. : LC Card 86-185703 DDC 333.75 19
HD9769.F843 A367 1982

WOOD-ENGRAVING - 20TH CENTURY - UNITED STATES.
1,001 advertising cuts from the twenties and thirties /. New York , 1987. 103 p. : ISBN 0-486-25490-9 (pbk.) LC Card 87-15546 DDC 659.13/2/0973 19
HF5813.U6 A525 1987

WOOD-ENGRAVINGS. see **WOOD-ENGRAVING.**

Wood, Frank. Finance / Frank Wood and Joe Townsley. London : Pitman, 1986. 410 p. : ill. ; 22 cm. Includes index. ISBN 0-273-02587-2 (pbk.) : LC Card 86-224835 DDC 332/.0941 19
1. Finance - Great Britain. I. Townsley, Joe. II. Title.
HG186.G7 W66 1986

Wood, Geoffrey Edward. Financial crises and the world banking system /. London , c1986. x, 270 p. : ISBN 0-333-35129-0
NYPL [JLD 86-2132]

Wood, James M., 1939- Halle's : memoirs of a family department store (1891-1982) / by James M. Wood. Cleveland, Ohio : Geranium Press, 1987. 223 p. : ill., ports. ; 23 x 31 cm. Bibliography: p. 125. Includes index. ISBN 0-940601-02-8 : LC Card 87-15010 DDC 381/.45/000977132 19
1. Halle Bros. Co. - History. 2. Department stores - Ohio - Cleveland - History. I. Title.
HF5465.U6 H359 1987

Wood, John Cunningham. Thomas Robert Malthus, critical assessments /. London , Dover, N.H. , c1986. 4 v. : ISBN 0-7099-3650-8 (set) : LC Card 85-22412 DDC 304.6/092/4 19
HB863 .T38 1986 *NYPL [JFF 86-588]*

Wood, Perry. Wheeler, Jimmy W. Beyond recrimination . Indianapolis, IN (P.O. Box 26-919, Indianapolis 46226) , c1987. xix, 218 p. : LC Card 87-165405 DDC 382/.0951249/073 19
HF1456.5.T28 W46 1987

WOOD-PULP INDUSTRY.
(1986) Grefermann, Klaus. Papier- und Pappeverarbeitung . Berlin , c1986. 209 p. : ISBN 3-428-06050-4 LC Card 86-233133
HD9833.5 .G73 1986

WOOD-PULP INDUSTRY - BRAZIL - MATO GROSSO DO SUL - EMPLOYEES - SUPPLY AND DEMAND.
Alcool e emprego . Brasília, DF , 1983. 170 p. : LC Card 86-200307
HD5718.A4852 B63 1983

WOOD-PULP INDUSTRY - BRAZIL - MATO GROSSO (STATE) - EMPLOYEES - SUPPLY AND DEMAND.
Alcool e emprego . Brasília, DF , 1983. 170 p. : LC Card 86-200307
HD5718.A4852 B63 1983

WOOD-PULP INDUSTRY - BRAZIL - MINAS GERAIS - EMPLOYEES - SUPPLY AND DEMAND.
Alcool e emprego . Brasília, DF , 1983. 170 p. : LC Card 86-200307
HD5718.A4852 B63 1983

WOOD-PULP INDUSTRY - CANADA - ENERGY CONSERVATION.
Battle, Ellen F. Energy efficiency in Canada's pulp & paper industry /. Calgary, Alta. [1986] xviii, 131, 4 p. : ISBN 0-920522-38-6 (pbk.) : LC Card 87-124507 DDC 333.79 19
HD9834.C22 B37 1986

WOOD-PULP INDUSTRY - GERMANY (WEST)
Grefermann, Klaus. Papier- und Pappeverarbeitung . Berlin , c1986. 209 p. : ISBN 3-428-06050-4 LC Card 86-233133
HD9833.5 .G73 1986

WOOD-PULP - TRADE AND STATISTICS. see **WOOD-PULP INDUSTRY.**

Wood, Quentin E. Quaker State roots go deep into the world's first oilfield / Quentin E. Wood. New York : Newcomen Society of the U. S., 1986 [i.e. 1987] 24 p. : ill. ; 23 cm. (Newcomen publication. no. 1277) Address delivered at a meeting of the Newcomen Society in Erie, Pa., Sept. 18, 1986. LC Card 86-63307 DDC 338.7/6653/0973 19
1. Quaker State Oil Refining Corporation - History. 2. Petroleum industry and trade - Pennsylvania - History. I. Title.
HD9569.Q82 W66 1987

Wood, Robert Everett, 1944- From Marshall Plan to debt crisis : foreign aid and development choices in the world economy / Robert E. Wood. Berkeley : University of California Press, c1986. xviii, 400 p. ; 24 cm. (Studies in international political economy) Includes index. Bibliography: p. 331-390. ISBN 0-520-05526-8 (alk. paper) LC Card 86-6934 DDC 338.9/009172/4 19
1. Economic assistance, American - Europe. 2. Economic assistance - Developing countries. 3. Depts, External - Developing countries. I. Title. II. Series.
HC60 .W62 1986 *NYPL [JLE 86-4443]*

Wood, Stephen, B.A. Windolf, Paul. Recruitment and selection in the labour market . Aldershot, Hants, England , Brookfield, Vt. , c1988. p. cm. ISBN 0-566-00937-4 : LC Card 87-19763 DDC 658.3/11/0941 19
HF5549.5.R44 W494 1988

WOOD USING INDUSTRIES - SWEDEN.
Sweden. Exportstödsutredningen. Ökad trähusexport . [Stockholm] [1984] 51 p. ;

ISBN 91-38-08165-2 LC Card 84-219457
HD9715.5.S82 S94 1984

WOOD-USING INDUSTRIES - UNITED STATES.
Ellefson, Paul V. U. S. wood-based industry . New York , 1984. xxv, 479 p. : ISBN 0-03-063698-1 (alk. paper) : LC Card 84-8278 DDC 338.1/7498/0973 19
HD9755 .45 1984 ***NYPL [JLE 85-706]***

Woodall, Marian K., 1941- Thinking on your feet : answering questions well, whether you know the answer--or not / Marion K. Woodall. Lake Oswego, Or. : Professional Business Communications, 1987. xv, 100 p. ; 22 cm. ISBN 0-941159-01-9 (pbk.) : LC Card 86-63594 DDC 658.4/5 19
1. Communication in management. 2. Questions and answers. I. Title.
HF5718 .W65 1987

Woodbury, Eric G. Schnidman, Frank. Retention of land for agriculture . Boston, MA , 1988. p. cm. ISBN 0-89946-219-7 LC Card 87-5580 DDC 333.76/16/0974 19
HD266.A11 S36 1988

WOODCUTS. see **WOOD-ENGRAVING.**

WOODCUTTING (ENGRAVING) see **WOOD-ENGRAVING.**

Wooden, Mark.
The effects of redundancy : the closure of the Rowntree-Hoadley factory, Adelaide / by Mark Wooden and Judy Sloan. [Bedford Park, S. Aust.] : National Institute of Labour Studies, [1987] 52 p. : form ; 30 cm. (Working paper series . no. 91) "This paper forms the second component of a two-part study commissioned by the South Australian Department of Labour and Bureau of Labour Market Research." "March 1987." Bibliography: p. 51-52. LC Card 87-170621 DDC 331.13/7994 19
1. Plant shutdowns - Australia - Case studies. 2. Unemployed - Australia - Case studies. I. Sloan, Judy. II. South Australia. Dept. of Labour. III. Australia. Bureau of Labour Market Research. IV. Series: Working paper series (National Institute of Labour Studies (Australia)) , no. 91. V. Title.
HD5708.55.A8 W66 1987

The personal consequences of redundancy : an evaluation of case-study evidence / by Mark Wooden. [Bedford Park, South Australia] : National Institute of Labour Studies Inc., [1987] 102 p. : ill. ; 30 cm. (Working paper series . no. 90 (Jan. 87)) "Jan. 87." Bibliography: p. 88-102. LC Card 87-155519 DDC 331.13/7 19
1. Unemployed. 2. Unemployment. 3. Unemployment - Psychological aspects. I. Series: Working paper series (National Institute of Labour Studies (Australia)) , no. 90. II. Title.
HD5707.5 .W66 1987

Woodhall, Maureen. Psacharopoulos, George. Education for development . New York , 1985. ix, 337 p. : ISBN 0-19-520477-8 LC Card 85-13782 DDC 338.9 19
HD75.7 .P77 1985 ***NYPL [JLE 86-1073]***

A Woodhead-Faulkner moneyguide.
Hargreaves, Judith. The home-owner's guide . Cambridge [Cambridgeshire] , Wolfeboro, N.H., USA , 1988. p. cm. ISBN 0-85941-423-X (pbk.) : LC Card 87-17388 DDC 643 19
HD7287.8 .H37 1988

Stafford, J. T. The share-owner's guide /. Cambridge [Cambridgeshire] , Wolfeboro, N.H., USA , 1988. p. cm. ISBN 0-85941-402-7 (pbk.) : LC Card 87-17387 DDC 332.63/22 19
HG4921 .S617 1988

Thomas, Sue. Family finance . Cambridge [Cambridgeshire] , Wolfeboro, NH, U. S.A. , 1988. p. cm. ISBN 0-85941-420-5 (pbk.) : LC Card 87-17386 DDC 332.024 19
HG179 .T457 1988

Woodhead, Ronald W. Anderson, S. D. (Stuart D.) Project manpower management . New York , c1987. ix, 509 p. : ISBN 0-471-86189-8 LC Card 86-26728 DDC 624/.068 19
HD9715.A2 A515 1987

Woodman, Byron E. Personal financial planning / Byron E. Woodman, Jr., Srephen R. Dooley, Edward S. Heald. Andover, Mass. : Brick House Pub. Co., c1987. 151 p. ; 24 cm. Includes index. ISBN 0-931790-77-8 : LC Card 87-13229 DDC 332.024 19
1. Finance, Personal. I. Dooley, Stephen R. II. Heald, Edward S. III. Title.
HG179 .W578 1987

WOODRUFF, GEORGE WALDO.
Wells, Della Wager. George Waldo Woodruff . [Macon, Ga.] c1987. x, 167 p. : ISBN 0-86554-298-8 LC Card 87-24700 DDC 338/.04/0924 B 19
HC102.5.W66 W45 1987

Woods, David D., 1952- NATO Advanced Study Institute on Intelligent Decision Support in Process Environments (1985 : San Miniato, Italy) Intelligent decision support in process environments /. Berlin , New York , c1986. xv, 524 p. : ISBN 0-387-13922-2 (U. S.) LC Card 86-6742 DDC 658.4/03 19
T57.95 .N37 1985 ***NYPL [JFE 86-4847]***

Woods, Leyla. Oechsler, Ronald G. Statistical abstract of East-West trade and finance . Washington, D.C. [1986]. vi, 43 p. : LC Card 86-601999 DDC 382/.091713/01717021 19
HF1411 .O3455 1986

Woods, Linda K. Lenfest, David. Mac Multiplan /. Blue Ridge Summit, Pa. , c1984. ix, 259 p. : ISBN 0-8306-0851-6 : LC Card 84-8796 DDC 001.64/25 19
HF5548.4.M74 L46 1984
NYPL [JSE 86-1870]

Woods, Robert. Population structures and models . London , Boston , 1986. xxii, 417 p. : ISBN 0-04-301200-0 (alk. paper) LC Card 85-30642 DDC 304.6 19
HB1951 .P67 1986 ***NYPL [JLE 86-4134]***

Woodside, Arch G. Industrial purchasing strategies : recommendations for purchasing and marketing managers / Arch G. Woodside, Niren Vyas. Lexington, Mass. : Lexington Books, c1987. xiv, 223 p. : charts ; 24 cm. Bibliography: p. [213]-215. Includes index. ISBN 0-669-06953-1 (alk. paper) LC Card 83-48132 DDC 658.7/2 19
1. Industrial procurement. 2. Materials management. 3. Industrial marketing - Management. 4. Purchasing. I. Vyas, Niren. II. Title.
HD39.5 .W66 1987

Woodward, Joan, M.A.
Management and technology. Comparative studies in administration / James D. Thompson ... [et al.]. Management and technology / Joan Woodward. New York , 1987. xiv, 224, 40 p. : ISBN 0-8240-8220-6 (alk. paper) : LC Card 86-27017 DDC 658 19
HD30.55 .C66 1987

Woodward, Maria Lourdes. Business issues for the Asia-Pacific region / by Maria Lourdes Woodward. Menlo Park, CA (333 Ravenswood Ave., Menlo Park 94025) : SRI International, Business Intelligence Program, c1986. 14 p. ; 28 cm. (Datalog file . no. 86-1062) "April 1986." Bibliography: leaf 13. LC Card 86-220779 DDC 330.95/0428
1. Asia - Economic conditions - 1945-. 2. Pacific area - Economic conditions. 3. Asia - Politics and government - 1945-. 4. Pacific area - Politics and government. I. Business Intelligence Program (SRI International). II. Title. III. Series.
HC413.A78 W66 1986

Woodward, Richard S. Chua, Jess H. Gains from stock-market timing /. New York, N.Y. (90 Trinity Pl., New York 10006) [c1986] 75 p. ; LC Card 87-129798 DDC 332.63/222 19
HG4637 .C48 1986

WOODWORKING INDUSTRIES - AFRICA, EASTERN.
Export promotion of furniture/joinery products from east/southern Africa. Addis Ababa [1983] 34 p. in various pagings : LC Card 86-981008
HD9773.A472 E96 1983

Woodworth, Warner.
Industrial democracy . Beverly Hills , c1985. 308 p. : ISBN 0-8039-2476-3 LC Card 85-11741 DDC 338.973/009173/2 19
HT321 .I53 1985 ***NYPL [JLD 86-3621]***

Meek, Christopher. Managing by the numbers . Reading, Mass. , c1988. ix, 293 p. : ISBN 0-201-16129-X : LC Card 87-16088 DDC 338.7/4/0973 19
HD70.U5 M413 1988

WOOL TRADE AND INDUSTRY - AUSTRALIA - HISTORY - SOURCES.
Pemberton, P. A. Pure merinos and others . Canberra , c1986. 125 p. : ISBN 0-86784-796-4 (pbk.) LC Card 87-164515 DDC 382/.41636/0994 19
HE565.G7 P46 1986

WOOL TRADE AND INDUSTRY - ENGLAND - HISTORY.
Power, Eileen Edna, 1889-1940. The wool trade in English medieval history /. New York [1987], c1941. viii, 128 p. ; ISBN 0-313-25656-X (lib. bdg. : alk. paper) LC Card 86-29442 DDC 338.4/767731/0942 19
HD9901.7.E54 P68 1987

WOOL TRADE AND INDUSTRY - GOVERNMENT POLICY - ITALY - NAPLES (KINGDOM) - HISTORY.
Marino, John A. Pastoral economics in the Kingdom of Naples /. Baltimore , c1988. xii, 381 p. : ISBN 0-8018-3437-6 (alk. paper) LC Card 87-9196 DDC 338.1/763145/09457 19
HD9905.I73 N366 1988

WOOL TRADE AND INDUSTRY - GREAT BRITAIN - HISTORY - SOURCES.
Pemberton, P. A. Pure merinos and others . Canberra , c1986. 125 p. : ISBN 0-86784-796-4 (pbk.) LC Card 87-164515 DDC 382/.41636/0994 19
HE565.G7 P46 1986

WOOL TRADE AND INDUSTRY - URUGUAY - STATISTICS.
Uruguay, exportaciones cumplidas de lanas y sus productos, ovinos en pie, carne ovina y subproductos, apendice pieles lanares . [Montevideo, Uruguay] , 1984. 37 p. ; LC Card 86-164077
HD9904.U82 U78 1984

The wool trade in English medieval history /.
Power, Eileen Edna, 1889-1940. New York [1987], c1941. viii, 128 p. ; ISBN 0-313-25656-X (lib. bdg. : alk. paper) LC Card 86-29442 DDC 338.4/767731/0942 19
HD9901.7.E54 P68 1987

Woolf, Emile. The Regulatory framework of accounting /. Estover, Plymouth , 1985. [12], 391 p. : ISBN 0-7121-0491-7
NYPL [JLF 87-84]

Woolfson, Charles, 1946- Foster, John. The politics of the UCS work-in . London , Atlantic Highlands, N.J. , 1986. 446 p. : ISBN 0-85315-663-8 (pbk.) : LC Card 86-235159 DDC 331.89/282383/094141 19
HD5365.S512 1971 .C584 1986

Woolverton, Michael W. Computer concepts for agribusiness / Michael W. Woolverton. Westport, Conn. : AVI Pub. Co., 1985. xii, 311 p. : ill. ; 24 cm. Includes bibliographies and index. ISBN 0-87055-510-3 : LC Card 85-23043 DDC 631 19
1. Agriculture - Economic aspects - Data processing. 2. Agricultural industries - Data processing. I. Title.
HD1433 .W66 1985 ***NYPL [JLE 86-1534]***

Woortmann, Geerd, 1942- Weiterbildungsmodelle und Weiterbildungspraxis in Industrie, Handel, Banken, Versicherungen und Fremdenverkehr /. München , c1984. 169 p. : ISBN 3-19-007546-8 LC Card 85-147442
HF5549.5.T7 W394 1984

Wootton, Barbara, Baroness of Albinger, 1897-
Barbara Wootton--social science and public policy . London , New York , 1986. xi, 291 p. ; ISBN 0-422-79690-5 LC Card 85-27650 DDC 330 19
HB171 .B248 1985 ***NYPL [JLE 86-1743]***

WOOTTON, BARBARA, BARONESS WOOTTON OF ABINGER, 1897- - ADDRESSES, ESSAYS, LECTURES.
Barbara Wootton--social science and public policy . London , New York , 1986. xi, 291 p. ; ISBN 0-422-79690-5 LC Card 85-27650 DDC 330 19
HB171 .B248 1985 ***NYPL [JLE 86-1743]***

WORCESTER COUNTY (MASS.) - INDUSTRIES.
Doeringer, Peter B. Invisible factors in local economic development /. New York , 1987. vii, 144 p. : ISBN 0-19-504965-9 (alk. paper) LC Card 87-13550 DDC 338.9744/3 19
HC107.M42 W674 1987

Worcester, Mass. Clark University. see **Clark University, Worcester, Mass.**

Word and information processing . Bergerud,

Marly, 1942- New York , c1987. xvi, 578 p. : ISBN 0-471-84504-3 LC Card 86-24748 DDC 652/.5 19
HF5548.115 .B46 1987

Word processing . Bergerud, Marly, 1942- New York , c1988. xiv, 336 p., [12] p. of plates : ISBN 0-471-84503-5 (pbk.) LC Card 87-8181 DDC 652/.5/02373 19
HF5548.115 .B47 1988

WORD PROCESSING.

Bergerud, Marly, 1942- Introduction to office systems . New York , c1987. xvi, 440 p., [12] p. of plates : ISBN 0-471-85532-4 (pbk.) LC Card 86-28188 DDC 652/.5 19
HF5548.115 .B462 1987

Bergerud, Marly, 1942- Word and information processing . New York , c1987. xvi, 578 p. : ISBN 0-471-84504-3 LC Card 86-24748 DDC 652/.5 19
HF5548.115 .B46 1987

Bergerud, Marly, 1942- Word processing . New York , c1988. xiv, 336 p., [12] p. of plates : ISBN 0-471-84503-5 (pbk.) LC Card 87-8181 DDC 652/.5/02373 19
HF5548.115 .B47 1988

Brown, Constance C., 1952- Preparing documents with UNIX /. Englewood Cliffs, N.J. , c1986. xv, 206 p. : ISBN 0-13-699976-X LC Card 85-17016 DDC 652/.5 19
Z52.5.U54 B76 1986 ***NYPL [JSE 86-1215]***

Brown, Eric D. Writing with a word processor . Reston, Va. , c1984. viii, 136 p. : ISBN 0-8359-8857-0 (pbk.) :$19.95 LC Card 84-8306 DDC 652 19
HF5548.115 .B76 1984
NYPL [JLE 86-1769]

Glenn, Peggy. Word processing profits at home /. Huntington Beach, CA , 1987, c1986. p. cm. ISBN 0-936930-86-1 : LC Card 87-25188 DDC 652/.5 19
HF5548.115 .G56 1987

Hewes, Jeremy Joan. Wordprocessing on IBM PCs /. New York , c1985. xiii, 178 p. : ISBN 0-471-88663-7 : LC Card 84-11966 DDC 652/.5 19
Z52.5.I27 H48 1985 ***NYPL [JSF 87-232]***

Johnson, Bonnie McDaniel, 1944- Managing organizational innovation . New York , 1987. xiv, 242 p. ; ISBN 0-231-06398-9 LC Card 87-307 DDC 652/.5 19
HF5548.115 .J64 1987

Lenfest, David. Kaypro word processing, plain & simple /. Blue Ridge Summit, Pa. , c1985. xiv, 176 p. : ISBN 0-8306-0812-5 : LC Card 84-8720 DDC 652 19
Z52.5.K39 L46 1985 ***NYPL [JSE 87-12]***

Mar, Jerry. The Apple WordStar book /. Glenview, Ill. , c1984. 277 p. : ISBN 0-673-15992-2 (pbk.) : LC Card 84-5400 DDC 652 19
Z52.5.W67 M37 1984 ***NYPL [JSE 86-2106]***

Nelson, Kay Yarborough. Using Lotus Manuscript /. Berkeley, Calif. , c1987. xvii, 410 p. : ISBN 0-07-881003-5 (pbk.) : LC Card 87-401628 DDC 652/.5 19
HF5548.115 .N45 1987

Popyk, Marilyn K., 1945- Word processing and information systems . New York , c1986. xx, 345 p., [15] p. of plates : ISBN 0-07-050594-2 (pbk.) : LC Card 85-23813 DDC 652/.5 19
HF5548.115 .P66 1986 ***NYPL [JSE 87-273]***

Schreiner, Axel T. Introduction to compiler construction with UNIX /. Englewood Cliffs , c1985. viii, 194 p. : ISBN 0-13-474396-2 LC Card 84-63039 ***NYPL [JSF 86-616]***

Townsend, Carl, 1938- Exploring word processors . Beaverton, Or. , c1984. viii, 239 p. : ISBN 0-88056-104-1 (pbk.) : LC Card 83-26259 DDC 652 19
Z52.5.C65 T68 1984 ***NYPL [JSD 86-495]***

Varner, Jane Terzick, 1942- Advanced word/information processing operations . Chicago , c1988. 1 v. (various pagings) : ISBN 0-574-20795-3 (pbk.) : LC Card 87-13042 DDC 652/.5 19
HF5548.115 .V36 1988

Wolenik, Robert. MacWrite made easier /. New York , 1985. xiv, 210 p. : ISBN 0-03-001763-7 LC Card 84-19781 DDC 652/.5 19
Z52.5.M32 W64 1985 ***NYPL [JLE 85-1535]***

Word processing and information systems . Popyk, Marilyn K., 1945- New York , c1986. xx, 345 p., [15] p. of plates : ISBN 0-07-050594-2 (pbk.) : LC Card 85-23813 DDC 652/.5 19
HF5548.115 .P66 1986 ***NYPL [JSE 87-273]***

WORD PROCESSING - EQUIPMENT AND SUPPLIES.

Bergerud, Marly, 1942- Introduction to office systems . New York , c1987. xvi, 440 p., [12] p. of plates : ISBN 0-471-85532-4 (pbk.) LC Card 86-28188 DDC 652/.5 19
HF5548.115 .B462 1987

Bergerud, Marly, 1942- Word and information processing . New York , c1987. xvi, 578 p. : ISBN 0-471-84504-3 LC Card 86-24748 DDC 652/.5 19
HF5548.115 .B46 1987

WORD PROCESSING EQUIPMENT INDUSTRY.

Converging voice/data/video technologies at the workstation /. Stamford, Conn., U. S.A. , c1986. v, 119 leaves ; ISBN 0-89336-466-5 (pbk.) LC Card 87-168057 DDC 380.1/45004 19
HD9801.A2 C66 1986

WORD PROCESSING EQUIPMENT INDUSTRY - VOCATIONAL GUIDANCE.

Bergerud, Marly, 1942- Word processing . New York , c1988. xiv, 336 p., [12] p. of plates : ISBN 0-471-84503-5 (pbk.) LC Card 87-8181 DDC 652/.5/02373 19
HF5548.115 .B47 1988

Word processing [microform] . Doswell, R. T. [Manchester, Greater Manchester] , 1983. 30 p. ; ISBN 0-85012-361-5
NYPL [*ZT-1554 no.46]

WORD PROCESSING (OFFICE PRACTICE)

Doswell, R. T. Word processing [microform] . [Manchester, Greater Manchester] , 1983. 30 p. ; ISBN 0-85012-361-5
NYPL [*ZT-1554 no.46]

Word processing on the IBM PC. Hewes, Jeremy Joan. Wordprocessing on IBM PCs /. New York , c1985. xiii, 178 p. : ISBN 0-471-88663-7 : LC Card 84-11966 DDC 652/.5 19
Z52.5.I27 H48 1985 ***NYPL [JSF 87-232]***

WORD PROCESSING OPERATIONS - MANAGEMENT.

Weltz, Friedrich. Innovation im Büro . Frankfurt , New York , c1983. 343 p. ; ISBN 3-593-32724-4 LC Card 83-243001
HF5548.115 .W44 1983

Word processing profits at home /. Glenn, Peggy. Huntington Beach, CA , 1987, c1986. p. cm. ISBN 0-936930-86-1 : LC Card 87-25188 DDC 652/.5 19
HF5548.115 .G56 1987

WORD PROCESSING - VOCATIONAL GUIDANCE.

Bergerud, Marly, 1942- Word processing . New York , c1988. xiv, 336 p., [12] p. of plates : ISBN 0-471-84503-5 (pbk.) LC Card 87-8181 DDC 652/.5/02373 19
HF5548.115 .B47 1988

WORD PROCESSORS.

Moore, James M. (James Mendon), 1925- An engineers guide to spreadsheets, word processors & data base managers /. Norcross, GA , c1986. xi, 154 p. : ISBN 0-89806-081-8 (pbk.) LC Card 87-157586 DDC 620/.0028/553 19
HF5548 .M566 1986

De wording en verwording van de staat Marokko . Mensink, Ankie. Rotterdam , 1985. 304 p. ; ISBN 90-6330-109-X : LC Card 85-214935
HC810 .M46 1985

Wordprocessing on IBM PCs /. Hewes, Jeremy Joan. New York , c1985. xiii, 178 p. : ISBN 0-471-88663-7 : LC Card 84-11966 DDC 652/.5 19
Z52.5.I27 H48 1985 ***NYPL [JSF 87-232]***

Words & Figures : for the IBM Personal Computer and compatibles. Monterey, CA (411 Pacific St., Monterey 93940) : Lifetree Software, c1986. 1 v. (various pagings) : ill. ; 22 cm. Includes index. LC Card 87-111370 DDC 005.36/9 19
1. Words & Figures (Computer program). 2. Business - Data processing. 3. IBM Personal Computer - Programming. I. Lifetree Software Inc. II. Title: Words and Figures.
HF5548.4.W66 W67 1986

Words and Figures. Words & Figures . Monterey, CA (411 Pacific St., Monterey 93940) , c1986. 1 v. (various pagings) : LC Card 87-111370 DDC 005.36/9 19
HF5548.4.W66 W67 1986

WORDS & FIGURES (COMPUTER PROGRAM)

Words & Figures . Monterey, CA (411 Pacific St., Monterey 93940) , c1986. 1 v. (various pagings) : LC Card 87-111370 DDC 005.36/9 19
HF5548.4.W66 W67 1986

Words that manage . Williams, Chris, 1952- Westbury, N.Y. , c1987. xi, 157 p. ; ISBN 0-87280-131-4 : LC Card 87-17434 DDC 658.3/0014 19
HD30.17 .W55 1987

Words that sell . Bayan, Richard. Chicago [1987], c1984. 127 p. ; ISBN 0-8092-4799-2 (pbk.) : LC Card 86-29319 DDC 659.1/014 19
HF5825 .B35 1987

WORDSTAR (COMPUTER PROGRAM)

Mar, Jerry. The Apple WordStar book /. Glenview, Ill. , c1984. 277 p. : ISBN 0-673-15992-2 (pbk.) : LC Card 84-5400 DDC 652 19
Z52.5.W67 M37 1984 ***NYPL [JSE 86-2106]***

Worger, William H. South Africa's city of diamonds : mine workers and monopoly capitalism in Kimberley, 1867-1895 / William H. Worger. New Haven : Yale University Press, c1987. xvi, 330 p. : ill. ; 24 cm. (Yale historical publications. Miscellany. 135) Bibliography: p. 307-322. Includes index. ISBN 0-300-03716-3 (alk. paper) LC Card 86-24724 DDC 331.7/622382/0968711 19
1. Diamond industry and trade - South Africa - Kimberley - History - 19th century. 2. Diamond miners - South Africa - Kimberley - History - 19th century. 3. Blacks - Employment - South Africa - Kimberley - History - 19th century. 4. Rural-urban migration - South Africa - History - 19th century. 5. Kimberley (South Africa) - Industries - History - 19th century. I. Title. II. Series.
HD9677.S63 K568 1987

Work /. Wright, Giles R. Trenton , c1987. 82 p. : ISBN 0-89743-072-7 (pbk.) LC Card 87-1573 DDC 331.6/2/09749 19
HD8083.N4 W75 1987

Work and change . Committee for Economic Development. Research and Policy Committee. New York, N.Y. , 1987 printing. iv, 76 p. : ISBN 0-87186-083-X (pbk.) : LC Card 87-694 DDC 331.12/042/0973 19
HD5724 .C6647 1987

WORK AND FAMILY.

Bamberg, Eva, 1951- Arbeit und Freizeit . Weinheim , 1986. xiv, 306 p. ; ISBN 3-407-58288-9 LC Card 87-103692 DDC 158.7 19
HF5548.85 .B36 1986

Blüm, Norbert, 1935- Die Arbeit geht weiter . München , 1983. 128 p. ; ISBN 3-492-00627-2 : LC Card 84-136559
HD4904 .B563 1983

Families and work /. Philadelphia , 1987. viii, 539 p. ; ISBN 0-87722-467-6 (alk. paper) : LC Card 86-30151 DDC 306.8/5 19
HD4904.25 .F35 1987

Family and economy in modern society /. Basingstoke, Hampshire , 1985. xvi, 234 p. ; ISBN 0-333-37437-1 LC Card 86-674026
HD4904.25 .F35x 1985

WORK AND FAMILY - CALIFORNIA - SANTA CLARA RIVER VALLEY.

Zavella, Patricia, 1949- Women's work and Chicano families . Ithaca , 1987. xviii, 191 p. ; ISBN 0-8014-1730-9 (pbk. : alk. paper) LC Card 87-5245 DDC 305.4/3664 19
HD6073.C272 U596 1987

WORK AND FAMILY - EUROPE, EASTERN.

Work and family life . Geneva , 1980. vi, 77 p. ; ISBN 92-2-102167-X (pbk.) LC Card 81-194978 DDC 306.8/5/0947 19
HD4904.25 .W68 1980

WORK AND FAMILY - FRANCE - HISTORY.

Tilly, Louise. Women, work, and family /. New

York , 1987. vii, 274 p. : ISBN 0-416-01681-2 (pbk.) : LC Card 87-11103 DDC 305.4/3/00941 19
HD6135 .T54 1987

WORK AND FAMILY - GERMANY (WEST)
Freitäger, Jürgen, 1959- Erwerb und Verwendung des Einkommens von Arbeitnehmerhaushalten mit erwerbstätiger Ehefrau /. Frankfurt am Main , New York , c1986. xix, 327 p. : ISBN 3-8204-9148-1 : LC Card 86-195223
HD9850.1 .M58 Bd. 37 HD6055.2.G3

WORK AND FAMILY - GREAT BRITAIN - HISTORY.
Tilly, Louise. Women, work, and family /. New York , 1987. vii, 274 p. : ISBN 0-416-01681-2 (pbk.) : LC Card 87-11103 DDC 305.4/3/00941 19
HD6135 .T54 1987

WORK AND FAMILY - GREAT BRITAIN - HISTORY - 20TH CENTURY.
Our work, our lives, our words . Basingstoke, Hampshire , 1986. xiii, 189 p. : ISBN 0-333-36598-4 ***NYPL [JLD 86-4220]***

Work and family life : the role of the social infrastructure in Eastern European countries. Geneva : International Labour Office, 1980. vi, 77 p. ; 24 cm. Includes bibliographical references. ISBN 92-2-102167-X (pbk.) LC Card 81-194978 DDC 306.8/5/0947 19
1. Work and family - Europe, Eastern. 2. Women - Employment - Europe, Eastern. I. International Labour Office.
HD4904.25 .W68 1980

Work and family life /. Voydanoff, Patricia. Newbury Park, Calif. , c1987. 136 p. ; ISBN 0-8039-2289-2 (pbk.) LC Card 87-9482 DDC 306.8/5/0973 19
HD4904.25 .V69 1987

WORK AND FAMILY - MICHIGAN - LONGITUDINAL STUDIES.
Mortimer, Jeylan T., 1943- Work, family, and personality . Norwood, N.J. , c1986. viii, 267 p. : ISBN 0-89391-293-X LC Card 85-20951 DDC 306/.36/09774 19
HD4904.25 .M67 1986 ***NYPL [JLE 87-869]***

WORK AND FAMILY - UNITED STATES.
Christensen, K. (Kathleen) Women and home-based work . New York , c1988. xv, 201 p. ; ISBN 0-8050-0386-X LC Card 87-8527 DDC 305.4/3 19
HD6072.6.U5 C47 1988

The State of families. Milwaukee, Wis. , <c1987-. v. <2 > : ISBN 0-87304-226-3 (pbk. : v. 2) LC Card 87-24374 DDC 306.8/5/0973 19
HD4904.25 .S83 1987

Voydanoff, Patricia. Work and family life /. Newbury Park, Calif. , c1987. 136 p. ; ISBN 0-8039-2289-2 (pbk.) LC Card 87-9482 DDC 306.8/5/0973 19
HD4904.25 .V69 1987

Work and industry . Kalleberg, Arne L. New York , c1987. xviii, 244 p. ; ISBN 0-306-42344-8 LC Card 87-2333 DDC 306/.36 19
HD4904 .K294 1987

WORK AND LABOR, CONTRACTS FOR. see **CONTRACTS FOR WORK AND LABOR.**

Work and welfare /. Malone, Margaret Sahlin, 1933- Washington , 1986. ix, 162 p. ; LC Card 86-603383 DDC 362.5/84/0973 19
HD5715.2 .M34 1986

Work and workers for the 21st century. Johnston, William B., 1945- Workforce 2000 . Indianapolis, Ind. [Washington, D.C.?] , 1987. xxvii, 117 p. : LC Card 87-601910 DDC 331.12/5/0973 19
HD8072.5 .J64 1987

WORK - BIBLIOGRAPHY.
Management, work, leisure . Geneva , c1986. viii, 154 p. : ISBN 92-9014-416-5 (pbk.) : LC Card 87-163300 DDC 306/.36/094 19
HD4904.6 .M35 1986

WORK - CONGRESSES.
Travail, loisirs, culture. [Bruxelles] [Zwevegem]] 1970. ix, 163 p. LC Card 71-856101
HD4904.7 .T7 1970

WORK DESIGN - UNITED STATES - CONGRESSES.
Joint Seminar on Designing Jobs for Handicapped Workers (1985 : Chicago, Ill.) Designing jobs for handicapped workers . Hot Springs, Ark. (P.O. Box 1358, Hot Spring 71902) [1986] 66 p. : LC Card 86-622317 DDC 658.3/045 19
HD7256.U5 J65 1985

Work, employment, and unemployment /. Horne, John (John D.) London , New York , 1988. p. cm. ISBN 0-582-35499-4 (pbk.) LC Card 87-3671 DDC 306/.36 19
HD4901 .H66 1988

WORK ENVIRONMENT - CANADA.
Armstrong, Pat, 1945- A working majority . Ottawa, Ont. , c1983. v, 280 p. : ISBN 0-660-11314-7 (pbk.) : LC Card 83-158188 DDC 331.4/0971 19
HD6067.2.C2 A75 1983 ***NYPL [JLD 86-1585]***

WORK ENVIRONMENT - EUROPEAN ECONOMIC COMMUNITY COUNTRIES - CONGRESSES.
Neue Arbeits- und Tätigkeitsformen . Dublin, Ireland [Washington, D.C.] c1986. xvi, 339 p. ; ISBN 92-825-6418-5 LC Card 87-408469 DDC 306/.36/094 19
HD6957.E86 N48 1986

WORK ENVIRONMENT - GERMANY, WEST.
Belastungsabbau unter Tage . Essen , 1982. 315 p. : ISBN 3-7739-0380-4 : LC Card 83-186893 DDC 363.1/1/0943 19
HD7708 .B45 1982

WORK ENVIRONMENT - GOVERNMENT POLICY - SWEDEN.
Nordfors, Lennart. Makten hälsan och vinsten . Lund, Sweden , c1985. 195 p. : ISBN 91-44-23331-0 : LC Card 85-204849
HD7732 .N66 1985

WORK ENVIRONMENT - HYGIENIC ASPECTS. see **INDUSTRIAL HYGIENE.**

WORK ENVIRONMENT - SOCIETIES, ETC. - DIRECTORIES.
Conditions of work and quality of working life . Geneva , 1986. xxi, 306 p. ; ISBN 92-2-105328-8 (pbk.) : LC Card 86-215659 DDC 306/.36/025 19
HD7260 .C64 1986

WORK ENVIRONMENT - SOVIET UNION.
Prigarin, V. S. (Valentin Stepanovich) Uslovii͡a truda pri sot͡sializme . Leningrad , 1985. 125 p. ; LC Card 86-124818
HD7725 .P83 1985

WORK ENVIRONMENT - TASMANIA.
Marwood, Jim, 1932- Ways of working /. Kenthurst , 1986. 160 p. : ISBN 0-86417-101-3 (pbk.) LC Card 87-105782 DDC 305.5/62/09946 19
HD8849.T372 M37 1986

WORK ENVIRONMENT - TASMANIA - PICTORIAL WORKS.
Marwood, Jim, 1932- Ways of working /. Kenthurst , 1986. 160 p. : ISBN 0-86417-101-3 (pbk.) LC Card 87-105782 DDC 305.5/62/09946 19
HD8849.T372 M37 1986

WORK ENVIRONMENT - UKRAINE - DONETSKAI͡A OBLASTʹ.
Uslovii͡a truda v regione /. Kiev , 1985. 252 p. : LC Card 86-105167
HD7726.U39 U85 1985 ***NYPL [*QGA 87-3379]***

WORK ETHIC.
Blüm, Norbert, 1935- Die Arbeit geht weiter . München , 1983. 128 p. ; ISBN 3-492-00627-2 : LC Card 84-136559
HD4904 .B563 1983

Helfert, Mario. Wertewandel, Arbeit, technischer Fortschritt, Wachstum /. Köln , c1986. 149 p. : ISBN 3-7663-3010-1 LC Card 87-134855 DDC 331.12 19
HD6331 .H37 1986

The Historical meanings of work /. Cambridge [Cambridgeshire] , New York , 1987. v, 320 p. ; ISBN 0-521-30897-6 LC Card 87-788 DDC 306/.36 19
HD4904 .H54 1987

Santen, J. van. Arbeid, plicht en vrijheid /. Nijmegen , c1985. 160 p. ; ISBN 90-6168-247-9 : LC Card 86-117515
HD4905 .S26 1985

WORK ETHIC - ENGLAND.
Sengoku, Tamotsu, 1928- Willing workers . Westport, Conn. , c1985. xv, 153 p. : ISBN 0-89930-137-1 (lib. bdg. : alk. paper) LC Card 85-9552 DDC 306/.36 19
HD8726.5 .S37 1985 ***NYPL [JLE 86-1381]***

WORK ETHIC - GERMANY (EAST)
Sozialistisches Arbeitsverhalten als Leistungsverhalten /. Berlin [1984] 77 p. ; LC Card 84-250357
HD8460.5 .S694 1984

WORK ETHIC - GERMANY (WEST)
Ansprüche an die Arbeit . Frankfurt [am Main] , New York , c1984. 298 p. : ISBN 3-593-33390-2 LC Card 85-103333
HF5548.8 .A683 1984

Lübbe, Hermann. Der Wertewandel und die Arbeitsmoral /. Köln [1984] 55 p. ; ISBN 3-88575-025-2 LC Card 84-197999
HD8451 .L83 1984

WORK ETHIC - GERMANY (WEST) - CONGRESSES.
Arbeitsmoral und Technikfeindlichkeit . Frankfurt , New York , c1986. 274 p. : ISBN 3-593-33757-6 LC Card 86-212283
HD8444 .A73 1986

WORK ETHIC - GERMANY (WEST) - PUBLIC OPINION.
Gewandelte Werte, erstarrte Strukturen . Bonn , c1985. ix, 329 p. : ISBN 3-87831-423-X LC Card 86-117688 DDC 330/.0943 19
HD8451 .G54 1985

WORK ETHIC - JAPAN.
Sengoku, Tamotsu, 1928- Willing workers . Westport, Conn. , c1985. xv, 153 p. : ISBN 0-89930-137-1 (lib. bdg. : alk. paper) LC Card 85-9552 DDC 306/.36 19
HD8726.5 .S37 1985 ***NYPL [JLE 86-1381]***

What makes Japan work [motion picture] . Cos Cob, CT , 1983. 1 film reel (11 min.) : LC Card 83-700702 DDC 181 11
HD8726.5

What makes Japan work [videorecording] . Cos Cob, CT , 1983. 1 videocassette (11 min.) : LC Card 87-705342 DDC 181 11
HD8726.5

WORK ETHIC - NETHERLANDS.
Santen, J. van. Arbeid, plicht en vrijheid /. Nijmegen , c1985. 160 p. ; ISBN 90-6168-247-9 : LC Card 86-117515
HD4905 .S26 1985

WORK ETHIC - UNITED STATES.
Sengoku, Tamotsu, 1928- Willing workers . Westport, Conn. , c1985. xv, 153 p. : ISBN 0-89930-137-1 (lib. bdg. : alk. paper) LC Card 85-9552 DDC 306/.36 19
HD8726.5 .S37 1985 ***NYPL [JLE 86-1381]***

WORK ETHIC - UNITED STATES - ADDRESSES, ESSAYS, LECTURES.
Editorial research reports on the American work ethic. Washington [1973] iii, 180 p. ISBN 0-87187-042-8 LC Card 72-94080 DDC 331.1/1/0973
HD8072 .E34 ***NYPL [JLD 86-1374]***

The work experience of immigrants to Canada [microform] . Ornstein, Michael D. Downsview, Ont. , 1983. 48 leaves ;
NYPL [*ZT-1732 no.16]

Work, family, and personality . Mortimer, Jeylan T., 1943- Norwood, N.J. , c1986. viii, 267 p. : ISBN 0-89391-293-X LC Card 85-20951 DDC 306/.36/09774 19
HD4904.25 .M67 1986 ***NYPL [JLE 87-869]***

WORK GROUPS - BULGARIA.
Dimitrov, Boris. Elitnite i͡adra na trudovite kolektivi /. Sofii͡a , 1985. 80 p. ; LC Card 86-140524
HD8626.5 .D55 1985

Elitnite i͡adra v trudovite kolektivi . [Sofia] [1985] 105 p. ; LC Card 86-104039
HD66 .E42 1985

Nikolaev, Ivan. Izrabotvane na kolektivnite reshenii͡a /. Sofii͡a , 1985. 69 p. ; LC Card 86-174800
HD30.23 .N55 1985

Petkov, Krŭstʹo. Sot͡siologii͡a na trudovii͡a kolektiv . Sofii͡a , 1982. 184 p. ; LC Card

83-124278
HD6957.B85 P47 1982
NYPL [*QK 86-4733]

WORK GROUPS - COLOMBIA - CONGRESSES.
Productividad y participación . [Bucaramanga, Colombia] , c1985. 165 p. : ISBN 958-9302-15-6 LC Card 86-166141
HD5660.C7 P76 1985

WORK GROUPS - SOVIET UNION.
Krasnaia liniia . Moskva , 1986. 382 p. : LC Card 86-112685
HD8526.5 .K73 1986

Kuzin, V. Komsomol'sko-molodezhnyĭ kollektiv /. Moskva , 1981. 157 p. ; LC Card 82-152678
HD6276.S592 K89 1981

Nekotorye problemy internatsional'nogo vospitaniia v mnogonatsional'nom trudovom kollektive /. Moskva , 1985. 135 p. ; LC Card 86-233779
HD8526.5 .N45 1985

Work, health, and income among the elderly / Gary Burtless, editor. Washington, D.C. : Brookings Institution, c1987. xiii, 276 p. : ill. : 24 cm. (Studies in social economics) Includes bibliographies and index. ISBN 0-8157-1176-X : LC Card 86-26892 DDC 331.3/98 19
1. Aged - Employment - United States. 2. Age and employment - United States. 3. Aged - Health and hygiene - United States. 4. Social security - United States. I. Burtless, Gary T., 1950-.
HD6280 .W68 1987 NYPL [JLE 87-960]

WORK - HISTORY.
Arbeit und Arbeitserfahrung in der Geschichte /. Göttingen , 1986. 128 p. ; ISBN 3-525-33516-4 NYPL [JLC 87-12]

The Historical meanings of work /. Cambridge [Cambridgeshire] , New York , 1987. v, 320 p. ; ISBN 0-521-30897-6 LC Card 87-788 DDC 306/.36 19
HD4904 .H54 1987

WORK - HISTORY - CONGRESSES.
Work in France . Ithaca , 1986. 576 p. : ISBN 0-8014-1697-3 (alk. paper) LC Card 85-22352 DDC 331/.0944 19
HD8428 .W67 1986 NYPL [JLE 86-1960]

Work in America Institute studies in productivity .
(15) Nash, Allan N. Managerial compensation /. Scarsdale, N.Y. , c1980. 56 p. ; ISBN 0-89361-022-4 : LC Card 80-21044 DDC 658.4/072/0973 19
HD4965.5.U6 N22
NYPL [JLM 83-380 no.15]

(2) Parnes, Steven. Productivity and the quality of working life /. Scarsdale, N.Y. , c1978. 43 p. ; LC Card 78-51009 DDC 658.31/4
HD57 .P33 NYPL [JLM 83-380 no.2]

(27) Bushnell, David S. Training for new technology /. New York , c1983. 41 p. ; ISBN 0-08-029508-8 : LC Card 83-17341 DDC 658.3/124 19
HD5715.2 .B87 1983
NYPL [JLM 83-380 no.27]

(30) Weinberg, Edgar. Labor-management cooperation for productivity /. New York , c1983. 61 p. ; ISBN 0-08-029511-8 (pbk.) LC Card 83-2361 DDC 016.33111/8/0973 19
HD56 .W44 1983
NYPL [JLM 83-380 no.30]

(32) Guzzo, Richard A. Programs for productivity and quality of work life /. New York , c1983. 38 p. ; ISBN 0-08-030964-X (pbk.) : LC Card 83-22029 DDC 658.3/14 19
HC110.L3 G89 1983
NYPL [JLM 83-380 no.32]

(33) Kamerman, Sheila B. Meeting family needs . New York , c1983. 45 p. ; ISBN 0-08-030965-8 (pbk.) : LC Card 83-27159 DDC 658.3/8 19
HD4928.N62 U6355 1983
NYPL [JLM 83-380 no.33]

(37) McGowan, Brenda G. Trends in employee counseling programs /. New York , c1984. 55 p. ; ISBN 0-08-032361-8 (pbk.) : LC Card 84-22820 DDC 658.3/82 19
HF5549.5.C8 M34 1984
NYPL [JLM 83-380 no.37]

Work in America Institute studies in productivity, 0149-8703 .
(10) Haveman, Robert H. Jobs and the environment /. Scarsdale, N.Y. , c1979. 32 p. ; LC Card 79-15418 DDC 301.31/0973
HC110.E5 H38 NYPL [JLM 83-380 no.10]

(41) Connolly, Paul M. Promotional practices and policies . New York , c1985. 52 p. ; ISBN 0-08-029515-0 (pbk.) : LC Card 85-3421 DDC 658.3/142 19
HF5549.2.U5 C66 1985
NYPL [JLM 83-380 no.41]

(48) Blasi, Joseph R. Employee ownership through ESOPs . New York , c1987. 126 p. ; ISBN 0-08-029520-7 (pbk.) : LC Card 86-30281 DDC 658.3/225 19
HD5660.U5 B57 1987

Work in France : representations, meaning, organization, and practice / edited by Steven Laurence Kaplan and Cynthia J. Koepp. Ithaca : Cornell University Press, 1986. 576 p. : ill., maps ; 25 cm. Selection of essays first presented at Cornell University on 28-30 April 1983 as part of a conference entitled Representations of Work in France. Includes bibliographical references and index. ISBN 0-8014-1697-3 (alk. paper) LC Card 85-22352 DDC 331/.0944 19
1. Labor and laboring classes - France - History - Congresses. 2. Work - History - Congresses. I. Kaplan, Steven L. II. Koepp, Cynthia J.
HD8428 .W67 1986 NYPL [JLE 86-1960]

Work in market and industrial societies / edited by Herbert Applebaum. Albany : State University of New York Press, c1984. viii, 316 p. ; 24 cm. (SUNY series in the anthropology of work) Includes index. Bibliography: p. 291-302. ISBN 0-87395-810-1 LC Card 83-9267 DDC 306/.36 19
1. Work - Social aspects - Case studies. 2. Manual labor - Social aspects - Case studies. 3. Labor and laboring classes - Case studies. 4. Industrial sociology - Case studies. 5. Industry - Social aspects - Case studies. 6. Factory system - Case studies. 7. White collar workers - Case studies. I. Applebaum, Herbert A. II. Series.
HD4901 .A659 1984 NYPL [JLE 86-4483]

Work in the future . Osmond, John. Wellingborough, Northamptonshire , Rochester, Vt. , 1986. 144 p. : ISBN 0-7225-1245-7 (pbk.) : LC Card 87-100557 DDC 306/.36 19
HD5707.5 .O84 1986

WORK INCENTIVE PROGRAM.
Malone, Margaret Sahlin, 1933- Work and welfare /. Washington , 1986. ix, 162 p. ; LC Card 86-603383 DDC 362.5/84/0973 19
HD5715.2 .M34 1986

WORK INCENTIVE PROGRAM - HANDBOOKS, MANUALS, ETC.
WIN handbook. [Washington, D.C.] [1984]. 1 v. (various pagings) ; NYPL [JLF 86-372]

WORK - JUVENILE LITERATURE.
Blacker, Terence. If I could work /. New York , c1988. p. cm. ISBN 0-397-32245-3 : LC Card 87-3972 DDC 331.7/02 19
HF5381.2 .B55 1988

Work, leisure, and technology / edited by Robert Castle, Donald E. Lewis, and John Mangan. Melbourne, Australia : Longman Cheshire, 1986. vi, 273 p. : ill. ; 22 cm. (Australian studies) Papers from a conference held at the University of Wollongong, Sept. 28-29, 1984. Includes bibliographies and indexes. ISBN 0-582-71151-7 (pbk.) LC Card 87-105477 DDC 303.4/83/0994 19
1. Labor supply - Australia - Effect of technological innovations on - Congresses. 2. Leisure - Australia - Congresses. I. Castle, Robert. II. Lewis, Donald E. III. Mangan, John.
HD6331.2.A8 W67 1986

WORK, METHOD OF. see **WORK.**

WORK - MORAL AND ETHICAL ASPECTS.
Befreiung der Arbeit . Bonn , c1986. 197 p. : ISBN 3-87831-429-9 LC Card 86-194157
HD6955 .B389 1986

Work of the dividend department /. Alfano, Salvatore. New York, NY , c1987. xvi, 180 p. ; ISBN 0-13-965096-2 LC Card 87-7733 DDC 332.6/068/5 19
HG4028.D5 A43 1987

Work of the purchase and sales department /. Loiacono, Nicholas. New York, NY , c1987. p. cm. ISBN 0-13-965104-7 : LC Card 87-7734 DDC 332.6/068/7 19
HG4621 .L64 1987

Work on the waterfront . Finlay, William. Philadelphia , 1988. p. cm. ISBN 0-87722-523-0 (alk. paper) : LC Card 87-17976 DDC 331.88/11387164/0973 19
HD6515.L82 W474 1988

Work plan implementation (working paper) . (SCS/83/WP/121) Socio-economic and marketing study of municipal fishing households, Bayawan, Negros Oriental, Philippines. Manila, Philippines [1983] vii, 94, 7 p. : LC Card 86-225887
HD8039.F652 P67 1983

WORK RELIEF. see **PUBLIC SERVICE EMPLOYMENT.**

WORK - RESEARCH - EUROPE.
Management, work, leisure . Geneva , c1986. viii, 154 p. : ISBN 92-9014-416-5 (pbk.) : LC Card 87-163300 DDC 306/.36/094 19
HD4904.6 .M35 1986

WORK - RESEARCH - EUROPE, EASTERN.
Management, work, leisure . Geneva , c1986. viii, 154 p. : ISBN 92-9014-416-5 (pbk.) : LC Card 87-163300 DDC 306/.36/094 19
HD4904.6 .M35 1986

WORK, RIGHT TO. see **RIGHT TO LABOR.**

WORK SHARING.
Best, Fred. Reducing workweeks to prevent layoffs . Philadelphia , 1988. p. cm. ISBN 0-87722-506-0 LC Card 87-10097 DDC 331.25/72 19
HD5110.5 .B467 1988

Meltz, Noah M. Sharing the work . Toronto , Buffalo , 1981. viii, 90 p. : ISBN 0-8020-2383-5
NYPL [JLD 82-233]

Ravaioli, Carla. Tempo da vendere, tempo da usare . Milano, Italy , c1986. 142 p. ; LC Card 86-182560
HD5106 .R357 1986

WORK SHARING - GERMANY, WEST.
Weissbuch Arbeitszeitverkürzung /. Stuttgart , 1983. 152 p. : ISBN 3-87959-212-8 LC Card 84-163631
HD5108.2.G47 W45 1983

WORK SHARING - GREAT BRITAIN.
Gasson, Ruth M. Labour sharing in agriculture /. [London] [1979] 117 p. ; ISBN 0-901859-82-6 (pbk.) LC Card 83-226074 DDC 331.25/72 19
HD5119.A292 G744 1979

WORK SHARING - QUÉBEC (PROVINCE)
Lewis, Normande. Le travail à temps partiel, le partage du travail comme mesure de sécurité d'emploi et la sous-traitance . [Quebec] , c1985. 90 p. ; ISBN 2-551-08998-0 LC Card 85-213545
HD5110.2.C22 Q45 1985

Work sights . Scranton, Philip. Philadelphia , 1986. 279 p. : ISBN 0-87722-341-6 : LC Card 85-26132 DDC 305.9/009748/11 19
HC108.P5 S37 1986 NYPL [JLF 86-1959]

Work smart, not hard /. Sullivan, George, 1927- New York, N.Y. , c1987. xii, 196 p. ; ISBN 0-8160-1393-4 : LC Card 86-24320 DDC 658.3/14 19
HF5549.5.P35 S85 1987

WORK - SOCIAL ASPECTS.
Socjologia pracy . Wrocław , 1978. 201 p. : LC Card 81-180007
HD6955 .S66 1978

WORK - SOCIAL ASPECTS - CASE STUDIES.
Work in market and industrial societies /. Albany , c1984. viii, 316 p. ; ISBN 0-87395-810-1 LC Card 83-9267 DDC 306/.36 19
HD4901 .A659 1984 NYPL [JLE 86-4483]

WORK - SOCIAL ASPECTS - EUROPEAN ECONOMIC COMMUNITY COUNTRIES - CONGRESSES.
Neue Arbeits- und Tätigkeitsformen . Dublin, Ireland [Washington, D.C.] c1986. xvi, 339 p. ; ISBN 92-825-6418-5 LC Card 87-408469 DDC 306/.36/094 19
HD6957.E86 N48 1986

WORK STOPPAGES. see **STRIKES AND LOCKOUTS.**

Work stress : health care systems in the

workplace / edited by James C. Quick ... [et al.]. New York : Praeger, 1987. xvii, 329 p. : ill. ; 25 cm. Includes bibliographies and index. ISBN 0-275-92329-0 (alk. paper) : LC Card 86-30636 DDC 616.85/2 19
1. Job stress. 2. Work - Psychological aspects. 3. Psychotherapy. 4. Employee assistance programs. 5. Job stress - Prevention. I. Quick, James C.
HF5548.85 .W67 1987

WORK SYSTEMS DESIGN. see **WORK DESIGN.**

Work throughout history.
Franck, Irene M. Helpers and aides /. New York, N.Y. , c1987. x, 182 p. : ISBN 0-8160-1445-0 LC Card 86-24370 DDC 331.7 19
HF5381.2 .F68 1987

WORKAHOLICS.
Korn, Errol R. Hyper-performance . New York , c1987. xi, 195 p. : ISBN 0-471-85344-5 LC Card 86-33984 DDC 650.1 19
HF5386 .K775 1987

Workbook in introductory economics /. Harbury, C. D. Oxford [Oxfordshire] , New York , 1987, c1982. xvii, 176 p. : ISBN 0-08-034790-8 (pbk.) : LC Card 87-19011 DDC 330/.076 19
HB74.6 .H37 1987

Worker participation and the politics of reform / edited by Carmen Sirianni. Philadelphia : Temple University Press, 1987. ix, 371 p. ; 24 cm. (Labor and social change) Includes bibliographies and index. CONTENTS. - Worker participation in the twentieth century /Carmen Sirianni -- The macropolitics of organizational change / Robert E. Cole -- Worker participation in technological change / Robert Howard and Leslie Schneider -- Unions, the quality of work, and technological change in Sweden / Andrew Martin -- Improving participation / Giuseppe Della Rocca -- Worker participation and the German trade unions / Christopher S. Allen -- Autogestion coming and going / George Ross -- Industrial relations and economic reform in socialism / Ellen Comisso -- Self-management and the politics of solidarity in Poland / Henry Norr -- The institution of democratic reforms in the Chinese enterprise since 1978 / Jeanne L. Wilson -- Worker participation, dependency, and the politics of reform in Latin America and the Caribbean / Evelyne Huber Stephens. ISBN 0-87722-464-1 (alk. paper) : LC Card 86-23006 DDC 658.3/152 19
1. Management - Employee participation. 2. Organizational change. I. Sirianni, Carmen. II. Series.
HD5650 .W645 1987

WORKERS. see **LABOR AND LABORING CLASSES.**

Workers and revolution in Iran . Bayat, Assef. London , Atlantic Highlands, New Jersey, USA , 1987. 227 p. : ISBN 0-86232-389-4 LC Card 87-160253 DDC 322/.2/0955 19
HD5660.I6 B39 1987

Workers (Communist) Party of America. see **Communist Party of the United States of America.**

Workers' compensation . Bromwich, G. R. E. Toronto, Ont. , 1986, c1981. ii, 15 p. ; LC Card 87-166754 DDC 368.4/1/00971 19
HD7103.65.C2 B76 1986

WORKERS' COMPENSATION - AUSTRALIA - QUEENSLAND - HISTORY.
Thomis, Malcolm I. From SGIO to Suncorp /. [Brisbane?] , 1986. xii, 272 p., [32] p. of plates : ISBN 0-7242-1698-7 LC Card 87-158138 DDC 368.4/009943 19
HG8220.A9 T56 1986

WORKERS' COMPENSATION - CANADA.
Bromwich, G. R. E. Workers' compensation . Toronto, Ont. , 1986, c1981. ii, 15 p. ; LC Card 87-166754 DDC 368.4/1/00971 19
HD7103.65.C2 B76 1986

WORKERS' COMPENSATION - EUROPEAN ECONOMIC COMMUNITY COUNTRIES.
Occupational accidents and diseases . Dublin, Ireland , Washington, DC , 1986. 116 p. ; ISBN 92-825-6426-6 LC Card 87-135635 DDC 363.1/1/094 19
HD7694.5 .O33 1986

WORKERS' COMPENSATION - GOVERNMENT POLICY - UNITED STATES - EVALUATION.
An Evaluation of short-time compensation programs. Washington, D.C. (601 D St., N.W., Room 7422, Washington 20213) , 1986. xxv, 222 p. ; LC Card 86-602784 DDC 368.4/4/00973 s 368.4/4/00973 19
HD7096.U5 U637 no. 86-4 HD7103.65.U6

WORKERS' COMPENSATION - ITALY.
La Tutela del lavoro in Italia. [Roma] [1976] 144 p. ; LC Card 86-233354
HD8481 .T85 1976

WORKERS' COMPENSATION - LAW AND LEGISLATION - SWEDEN.
Hetzler, Antoinette, 1943- Arbetsskadeförsäkringens tillämpning . Lund [1984] 176 p. : ISBN 91-970351-3-0 : LC Card 84-159654
HD7103.65.S8 H48 1984

WORKERS' COMPENSATION - MEXICO.
Enfermedades de trabajo. México, D.F. , c1983. 403 p. : ISBN 968-8242-08-X LC Card 85-216152
HD7262.5.M6 E54 1983

Workers Compensation Research Institute (Cambridge, Mass.)
DeVol, Karen R., 1949- Income replacement for long term disability . Cambridge, Mass. , 1986. p. cm. ISBN 0-935149-04-X : LC Card 86-28264 DDC 368.4/1/00973 19
HD7103.65.U6 D484 1986

Gardner, John A. Vocational rehabilitation outcomes . Cambridge, Mass. , c1986. xix, 48 p. : ISBN 0-935149-03-1 (pbk.) : LC Card 86-28144 DDC 362/.0425 19
HD7256.U6 N6926 1986

WORKERS' COMPENSATION - SWEDEN.
Hetzler, Antoinette, 1943- Arbetsskadeförsäkringens tillämpning . Lund [1984] 176 p. : ISBN 91-970351-3-0 : LC Card 84-159654
HD7103.65.S8 H48 1984

WORKERS' COMPENSATION - UNITED STATES.
Barth, Peter S., 1937- The tragedy of black lung . Kalamazoo, MI , 1987. xi, 292 p. ; ISBN 0-88099-044-9 (pbk.) LC Card 87-8332 DDC 368.4/1 19
HD7264 .B37 1987

Berkowitz, Monroe, 1919- Permanent disability benefits in workers' compensation /. Kalamazoo, Mich. , 1987. xviii, 459 p. ; ISBN 0-88099-051-1 LC Card 87-22874 DDC 368.4/1/00973 19
HD7105.25.U6 B47 1987

DeVol, Karen R., 1949- Income replacement for long term disability . Cambridge, Mass. , 1986. p. cm. ISBN 0-935149-04-X : LC Card 86-28264 DDC 368.4/1/00973 19
HD7103.65.U6 D484 1986

Information on the administration of workers' compensation programs in each state and the District of Columbia /. [Washington, D.C.?] [1985] iii, 426 p. ; LC Card 86-601358 DDC 368.4/1/00973 19
HD7103.65.U6 I55 1985

Information on the administration of workers' compensation programs in each state and the District of Columbia /. [Washington, D.C.?] [1985] iii, 426 p. ; ***NYPL [JLF 86-774]***

Modern job safety and health /. Paramus, N.J. , c1987- 1 v. (loose-leaf) : LC Card 87-403957 DDC 363.1/1/068 19
HD6067.2.U6 M63 1987

WORKERS' COMPENSATION - UNITED STATES - CLASSIFICATION.
Classification guide for commercial building construction. [New York, N.Y.?] , c1986. 72 p. : LC Card 87-119406 DDC 368.4/1 19
HD7116.R3152 U63 1986

WORKERS' COMPENSATION - UNITED STATES - CLASSIFICATION - CODE NUMBERS.
Classification guide for street and road construction /. New York, NY , c1986. 44 p. : LC Card 86-232165 DDC 368.4/1 19
HD7116.R62 U63 1986

WORKERS' COMPENSATION - UNITED STATES - CODE NUMBERS.
Classification guide for commercial building construction. [New York, N.Y.?] , c1986. 72 p. : LC Card 87-119406 DDC 368.4/1 19
HD7116.R3152 U63 1986

WORKERS' COMPENSATION - UNITED STATES - STATES.
Information on the administration of workers' compensation programs in each state and the District of Columbia /. [Washington, D.C.?] [1985] iii, 426 p. ; ***NYPL [JLF 86-774]***

Workers in industrial America . Brody, David. New York , 1981, 1980. ix, 257 p. ; ISBN 0-19-502491-5 (pbk.) LC Card 78-27157 ***NYPL [JLD 86-3729]***

WORKERS' INTERNATIONAL RELIEF - HISTORY.
Surmann, Rolf. Die Münzenberg-Legende . Köln , c1983. 307 p. : ISBN 3-922009-53-0 LC Card 83-155325
HD8450 .S87 1983

Workers, managers, and technological change : emerging patterns of labor relations / edited by Daniel B. Cornfield ; with a foreword by Ray Marshall. New York : Plenum Press, c1987. xxii, 362 p. : ill. ; 26 cm. (Plenum studies in work and industry) Includes bibliographical references and index. ISBN 0-306-42450-9 LC Card 87-2327 DDC 331/.0973 19
1. Labor supply - United States - Effect of technological innovations on. 2. Industrial relations - United States. I. Cornfield, Daniel B. II. Series.
HD6331.2.U5 W67 1987

Workers, managers, and welfare capitalism . Zahavi, Gerald, 1951- Urbana , c1988. xiii, 261 p., [14] p. of plates : ISBN 0-252-01444-8 (alk. paper) LC Card 87-6035 DDC 331.2/0475/0973 19
HD9787.U6 E654 1988

The workers' movement /. Touraine, Alain. [Mouvement ouvrier. English.] Cambridge [Cambridgeshire] ; New York : xx, 322 p. ; ISBN 0-521-30852-6 LC Card 87-8010 DDC 322/.2/0944 19
HD6684 .T65513 1987

Workers on strike . Perrot, Michelle. [Jeunesse de la grève. English.] New Haven , 1987. 321 p. : ISBN 0-300-03849-6 LC Card 86-26753 DDC 331.89/2944 19
HD5374 .P4613 1987

Workers on the Nile . Beinin, Joel, 1948- Princeton, N.J. , c1987. xix, 488 p. : ISBN 0-691-05506-8 (alk. paper) : LC Card 87-45510 DDC 305.5/62/0962 19
HD8786 .B45 1987

Workers' participation in management . Varandani, Gursharan, 1946- New Delhi , c1987. xii, 228 p. ; LC Card 87-900827 DDC 658.3/152/0954 19
HD5650 .V35 1987

Workers Party of America. see **Communist Party of the United States of America.**

Workers world. Marcy, Sam, 1911- Anatomy of the economic crisis /. Atlanta , c1982. viii, 120 p. : ISBN 0-89567-077-1 (pbk.) ***NYPL [JLD 86-1329]***

Workforce 2000 . Johnston, William B., 1945- Indianapolis, Ind. [Washington, D.C.?] , 1987. xxvii, 117 p. : LC Card 87-601910 DDC 331.12/5/0973 19
HD8072.5 .J64 1987

Working but poor . Levitan, Sar A. Baltimore , c1987. ix, 142 p. : ISBN 0-8018-3583-6 (alk. paper) LC Card 87-16973 DDC 362.5/0973 19
HC110.I5 L468 1987

Working Canadians : readings in the sociology of work and industry / Graham S. Lowe and Harvey J. Krahn, editors. Toronto ; New York : Methuen, c1984. x, 380 p. ; 23 cm. Includes bibliographies. ISBN 0-458-97370-X (pbk.) : LC Card 84-222036 DDC 331/.0971 19
1. Industrial sociology - Canada - Addresses, essays, lectures. 2. Labor and laboring classes - Canada - Addresses, essays, lectures. 3. Industrial relations - Canada - Addresses, essays, lectures. I. Lowe, Graham S. II. Krahn, H.
HD6957.C2 W67 1984 ***NYPL [JLD 87-681]***

WORKING CAPITAL.
Roşca, Teodor. Creşterea eficienţei mijloacelor circulante, cerinţă actuală /. Bucureşti , 1983. 234 p. : LC Card 84-152999
HG4028.W65 R67 1983 ***NYPL [JLD 87-49]***

Szabó, Sándor. A forgóeszköz finanszirozás elvei és gyakorlata /. [Budapest] , 1986. 67,

[26] p. ; LC Card 87-150669
HG4028.W65 S93 1986

Working class and the nationalist movement in India . Chatterji, Rakhahari, 1943- New Delhi , c1984. ix, 215 p. ; LC Card 84-902674 DDC 322.4/4/0954 19
HD8686 .C47 1984 *NYPL [JLD 87-709]*

The working class in Glasgow, 1750-1914 / edited by R.A. Cage. London ; Wolfeboro, N.H. : Croom Helm, c1987. xix, 203 p. ; 23 cm. Bibliography: p. [188]-189. Includes index. CONTENTS. - The standard of living debate / R.A. Cage -- Population and employment characteristics / R.A. Cage -- Housing / John Butt -- Health in Glasgow / R.A. Cage -- Glasgow working-class politics / I.G.C. Hutchison -- Popular culture in Glasgow / Elspeth King. ISBN 0-7099-3415-7 : LC Card 86-24059 DDC 305.5/62/0941443 19
1. Labor and laboring classes - Scotland - Glasgow (Strathclyde) - History. 2. Glasgow (Strathclyde) - Economic conditions. I. Cage, R. A.
HD8400.G57 W67 1987

Working class USA . Hall, Gus. New York , 1987. 392 p. : ISBN 0-7178-0660-X : LC Card 87-3232 DDC 305.5/62/0973 19
HD8066 .H29 1987

WORKING-CLASS WOMEN - CHILE - BIOGRAPHY.
Mack, Macarena. Los trabajos de las mujeres entre el campo y la ciudad, 1920-1982 . [Santiago, Chile] [1986] 108 p. ; LC Card 86-217673
HD6126 .M33 1986

WORKING CLASS WOMEN - FRANCE - HISTORY - EXHIBITIONS.
Les Femmes au travail 1882-1982 /. Paris , 1982. [70] leaves : LC Card 86-161448
HD6145 .F44 1982

WORKING CLASS WOMEN - GERMANY (WEST) - INTERVIEWS.
Montags biste sowieso geschafft . Hamburg , 1982. 167 p. : ISBN 3-88506-118-X (pbk.) LC Card 87-673006
HD6068.2.G3 M66x 1982

WORKING CLASS WOMEN - PERU - CONGRESSES.
Mujer, trabajo y empleo /. Lima, Perú [1985] 294 p. ; LC Card 86-121871 DDC 331.4/0985 19
HD6131 .M85 1985 *NYPL [JLD 87-492]*

WORKING-CLASSES. see **LABOR AND LABORING CLASSES.**

WORKING CONDITIONS, PHYSICAL. see **WORK ENVIRONMENT.**

Working, conflict and change /. Ritzer, George. Englewood Cliffs, N.J. , c1986. xii, 451 p. ; ISBN 0-13-967589-2 : LC Card 85-28135 DDC 306/.36/0973 19
HD6957.U6 R5 1986 *NYPL [JLE 86-3160]*

WORKING-DAY. see **HOURS OF LABOR.**

Working from home . Edwards, Paul. Los Angeles , New York , c1987. xii, 436 p. : ISBN 0-87477-457-8 (pbk.) LC Card 87-10188 DDC 658/.041 19
HD62.5 .E39 1987

WORKING-GIRLS. see **CHILDREN - EMPLOYMENT.**

Working it out® . Strasser, Stephen. Englewood Cliffs, N.J. , c1988. xix, 268 p. ; ISBN 0-13-965112-8 : LC Card 87-17197 DDC 158.7 19
HD4901 .S69 1988

Working knowledge . Harper, Douglas A. Chicago , 1987. x, 214 p. : ISBN 0-226-31688-2 LC Card 86-30708 DDC 302.3/4 19
HD4904 .H335 1987

A working majority . Armstrong, Pat, 1945- Ottawa, Ont. , c1983. v, 280 p. : ISBN 0-660-11314-7 (pbk.) : LC Card 83-158188 DDC 331.4/0971 19
HD6067.2.C2 A75 1983
NYPL [JLD 86-1585]

WORKING MEN'S ASSOCIATION.
Working Men's Association, the first convention, and the National Association. New York , 1986. 1 v. (various pagings) : ISBN 0-8240-5586-1 : LC Card 86-33479 DDC 322/.2/0942 19
HD8396 .W67 1986

WORKING-MEN'S ASSOCIATIONS. see **TRADE-UNIONS.**

WORKING-MEN'S CLUBS - ITALY - NOVARA (PROVINCE) - HISTORY.
Bermani, Cesare, 1937- Dalla grande associazione degli operai di Novara al Circolo operaio agricolo della Bicocca . Novara [1983] 345 p., [31] p. of plates : LC Card 85-148843
HD6714.N68 B47 1983

WORKING-MEN'S LUNCH ROOMS. see **RESTAURANTS, LUNCH ROOMS, ETC.**

WORKING MOTHERS - CALIFORNIA - SANTA CLARA RIVER VALLEY.
Zavella, Patricia, 1949- Women's work and Chicano families . Ithaca , 1987. xviii, 191 p. ; ISBN 0-8014-1730-9 (pbk. : alk. paper) LC Card 87-5245 DDC 305.4/3664 19
HD6073.C272 U596 1987

Working mothers--fewer children? Jensen, An-Magritt. Flere i yrke--færre barn? . Oslo , 1983. 59 p. : ISBN 82-537-2007-6 : LC Card 84-163552
HA1503 .A45 nr. 147 HQ762.N8

Working paper (Australian National University. Development Studies Centre : 1984) .
(no. 38) Chew, T. A. The off-farm labour supply of padi farmers in Kelantan, Malaysia [microform] /. [Canberra] , c1984. 19 p. ; ISBN 0-86784-513-9 (pbk.) LC Card 85-670027 DDC 331.12/93318/095951 19
HD5854.55.M4 C47 1984
*NYPL [*ZF-1745 no.58]*

Working paper (Han'guk Kaebal Yŏng'guwŏn) .
(8301) Whang, In Joung. Administration of land reform in Korea /. Seoul, Korea [1982] 41 p. ; LC Card 84-148921 DDC 333.3/1/519 19
HD1333.K78 W46 1982

Working paper (Han'guk Kaebal Yŏn'guwŏn) .
(8601) Song, Dae-Hee. The performance evaluation of Korean public enterprises . Seoul, Korea [1986] 109 p. : LC Card 87-404432 DDC 354.519/5092 19
HD4315.5 .S65 1986

Working paper (Inter-American Development Bank. International Economics Section) .
(86/1) Lord, Montague J. Market price models for Latin America's major commodity exports /. Washington, D.C. [1986] vii, 219 p. : LC Card 87-115208 DDC 338.5/2/098 19
HD9014.A2 L67 1986

Working paper (Michigan State University. Office of Women in International Development) .
(#114) Turrittin, Jane Sawyer. Men, women, and market trade in rural Mali, West Africa /. [East Lansing] , c1986. 17 p. ; LC Card 86-225178 DDC 331.4/8138118/096623 19
HD6060.65.M42 T87 1986

(#124) Young, Gay. Gender identification and working class solidarity among Maquila workers in Ciudad Juarez . [East Lansing] , c1986. 24 p. ; LC Card 87-620601 DDC 331.4/87/097216 19
HD6073.O332 M4959 1986

Working paper (National Institute of Development and Cultural Research (Botswana). Documentation Unit) .
(no. 33) Wily, Liz. The TGLP and hunter-gatherers . Gaborone, Botswana , 1981. ii, 102 p. ; LC Card 82-207525
DT797 W55 1981 *NYPL [JLG 87-6]*

Working paper series (City University (London, England). Business School) .
(no. 80) Sudarsanam, P. S. Market and industry structure and corporate cost of capital . London [1986] 33 p. ; LC Card 86-208314 DDC 338.7/4/0941 19
HG4135 .S83 1986

(no. 83) Rutterford, Janette. The securities industry . [London] [1986] 93 p. : LC Card 87-160412 DDC 332.63/2/0941 19
HG5432 .R87 1986

Working paper series (National Institute of Labour Studies (Australia)) .
(no. 88) Bosworth, Derek L. Labour utilisation in Australia . [Bedford Park, S. Aust.] [1986] i, 205 p. : LC Card 86-229498 DDC 331.12/5/0994 19
HD5850.A6 B67 1986

(no. 90) Wooden, Mark. The personal consequences of redundancy . [Bedford Park, South Australia] [1987] 102 p. : LC Card 87-155519 DDC 331.13/7 19
HD5707.5 .W66 1987

(no. 91) Wooden, Mark. The effects of redundancy . [Bedford Park, S. Aust.] [1987] 52 p. : LC Card 87-170621 DDC 331.13/7994 19
HD5708.55.A8 W66 1987

Working paper (Shiga Daigaku. Keizai Gakubu) .
(no. 16) Tomita, Teruhiko, 1937- Transferability of Japanese-style management to Britain /. Hikone, Japan [1986] 63 leaves : LC Card 87-168468 DDC 331.25 19
HD70.J3 T585 1986

Working paper (Universität Bielefeld. Forschungsschwerpunkt Entwicklungssoziologie) .
(no. 58) Busacker, Dietrich. Energies à la mesure des villages . Bielefeld, Federal Republic of Germany , 1985. 21 leaves ; LC Card 85-160345
HD9502.A4993 B87 1985

Working paper (Université catholique de Louvain (1970-). Département de démographie) .
(no 127) Tabutin, Dominique. Les transitions de mortalité dans le Tiersmonde .
Louvain-la-Neuve, Belgique [1985] 33 p. : LC Card 86-178578
HB1528 .T33 1985

Working paper (University of California, Berkeley. Institute of Urban & Regional Development .

Working paper (University of California, Berkeley. Institute of Urban and Regional Development) .
(no. 447) Dowall, David E. Office automation and the implications for office development /. [Berkeley] [1986] 171 p. ; LC Card 86-622512 DDC 651.8 19
HF5547.5 .D64 1986

(no. 448) Dowall, David E. Back-offices and San Francisco's office development growth cap /. [Berkeley] [1986] 23 p. : LC Card 86-622513 DDC 333.77/17/0979461 19
HD268.S4 D68 1986

Working paper (University of California, San Diego. Center for U. S.-Mexican Studies) .
(no. CE-03) Hirschman, Albert O. The political economy of Latin American development . La Jolla, Calif. [1986] 57 p. ; LC Card 87-621614 DDC 338.98 19
HC125 .H544 1986

Working paper (University of Durham. Dept. of Economics) .
(no. 55) Iyare, S. International cost differences in developing countries . Durham, England [1983] 14, [9] leaves : LC Card 86-207078 DDC 338.4/367/09667 19
HD9737.G52 I97 1983

Working paper (University of Natal. Centre for Applied Social Sciences. Development Studies Unit) .
(no. 12) Wellings, Paul. Industrial decentralisation under apartheid . Durban , 1984. 48, xxxii p. : ISBN 0-86980-455-3 (pbk.) LC Card 87-127005 DDC 338.968 19
HC905.Z9 D59 1984

(no. 15) May, Julian. Development planning in Transkei . Durban , 1985. 35 p., [5] p. ; ISBN 0-86980-483-9 (pbk.) : LC Card 86-222656 DDC 338.9687/91 19
HC905.Z7 T7347 1985

Working paper (University of San Francisco Institute for Nonprofit Organization Management) .
(no. 1) Brown, Kathleen M. Applied empirical research on nonprofit organization management . San Francisco, CA , c1986. 38 p. ; LC Card 86-207093 DDC 658/.048 19
HD62.6 .B76 1986

Working paper (University of Toronto. Structural Analysis Programme) .
(no. 23) Wayne, Jack, Ph.D. Structural contradictions of the colonial state . [Toronto, Canada] , c1981. 23, [5] p. ; ISBN 0-7727-2825-9 (pbk.) LC Card 86-193819 DDC 330.9678/203 19
HC885 .W39 1981

Working papers / European Institute of Public Administration.
(EIPA 85/02 =) Can the CAP be reformed? /.

Maastricht, The Netherlands , c1985. xii, 127 p. ; ISBN 90-6779-013-3 (pbk.) LC Card 86-214732 DDC 338.1/84 19
HD1920.5 .C36 1985

Coming to grips with the internal market /. Maastricht, The Netherlands , c1986. viii, 136 p. ; ISBN 90-6779-019-2 (pbk.) LC Card 86-222624 DDC 337.1/42 19
HC241.2 .C5548 1986

Working papers (Boston University. African Studies Center) .
(no. SP-1) Somalia . Boston, MA [1983] vi, 164 p. : LC Card 87-108393 DDC 330.967/7305 19
HC850 .S655 1983

(no. 105) Gershenberg, Irving. Slack in Kenya's modern manufacturing sector /. Boston, MA (270 Bay State Rd., Boston 02215) , 1985. 15 leaves ; LC Card 87-404089 DDC 338.4/767/096762 19
HD70.K4 G47 1985

(no. 108) Nath, Kamla. Labor-saving techniques in food processing . Boston, MA (270 Bay State Rd., Boston 02215) , 1985. 26 leaves ; LC Card 87-155092 DDC 331.4/25 19
HD6073.A292 G256 1985

(no. 114) Penvenne, Jeanne. Making our own way . Boston, MA (270 Bay State Rd., Boston 02215) , 1986. 20 leaves ; LC Card 87-155233 DDC 331.4/0967/91 19
HD6211.5 .P46 1986

(no. 115) Bashir, Ibrahim Lawan, 1948- Food crisis and government response in Nigeria . Boston, MA (270 Bay State Rd., Boston 02215) , 1986. 22 leaves ; LC Card 87-155111 DDC 363.8/09669 19
HD9017.N52 B37 1986

(no. 117) Bashir, Ibrahim Lawan, 1948- Sources of capital formation and accumulation among Kano entrepreneurs, 1950-1980 /. Boston, MA (270 Bay State Rd., Boston 02215) , 1986. 17 leaves ; LC Card 87-156659 DDC 332/.0415/096695 19
HC1055.Z9 S33 1986

Working papers for the National Workshop on Urban Water Demand Management . National Workshop on Urban Water Demand Management (1986 : Alexander Library, Perth Cultural Centre) Leederville, WA [1986] xii, 657 p. : LC Card 87-119946 DDC 333.91/2/0994 19
HD4465.A8 N37 1986

Working papers in demography (National University of Lesotho. Dept. of Statistics. Demography Unit) .
(working paper no. 3) Makatjane, Tiisetso. Sources of population statistics in Lesotho /. [Roma, Lesotho] [1985] iii, 29 leaves ; LC Card 87-132320 DDC 304.6/09681/6 19
HA37.L52 M35 1985

(working paper no. 4) Sembajwe, I. S. L. (Israel Serwano Lubwama), 1947- Urban population growth rates in Africa with special reference to Lesotho /. [Roma, Lesotho] [1985] 31 leaves : LC Card 87-132328 DDC 307.2 19
HB3663.7.A3 S46 1985

(working paper no. 6) Makatjane, Tiisetso. Internal migration and fertility in Lesotho /. [Roma, Lesotho] [1985] iii, 36 leaves ; LC Card 87-132347 DDC 304.6/32/096816 19
HB2123.7.A3 M35 1985

Working papers in economic history .
(working paper no. 77) Tsokhas, Kosmas. Shifting the burden . Canberra, Australia [1986] 61, 6 p. ; ISBN 0-86784-898-7 (pbk.) LC Card 87-151151 DDC 331.7/6363/00994 19
HD9436.A82 T75 1986

Working papers (Jobs and Skills Programme for Africa)
Keddeman, Willem. Emploi et revenus dans le secteur agricole traditionnel au Bénin /. Addis Abéba , 1982. 64 p. ; LC Card 87-980402
HD2141 .K43 1982

Working papers (Organisation for Economic Co-operation and Development. Dept. of Economics and Development) .
(no. 26) Aggregate supply in interlink . Paris, France , c1985. 60 p. : LC Card 86-205160 DDC 338.5/213 19
HB201 .A25 1985

Working papers (Organisation for Economic Co-operation and Development. Dept. of Economics and Statistics) .
(no. 24) Klau, Friedrich. Labour market flexibility and external price shocks /. Paris, France , c1985. 60 p. : LC Card 86-205164 DDC 331.12 19
HD5707 .K54 1985

(no. 25) Blades, Derek W. Discrepancies between imports and exports in OECD foreign trade statistics /. Paris, France , c1984. i, 42 p. ; LC Card 86-205155 DDC 382/.021 19
HF1016 .B569 1984

(no. 30) Chouraqui, Jean Claude. Public debt in a medium-term context and its implications for fiscal policy /. [Paris, France] , c1986. 67 p. : LC Card 86-218210 DDC 339.5 19
HJ8030 .C48 1986

(no. 31) Brodin, Anders. The OECD Compatible Trade and Production data base, 1970-1983 /. [Paris, France] , c1986. ii, 81 p. ; LC Card 86-213116 DDC 382/.021 19
HF1016 .B68 1986

(no. 32) Atkinson, Paul. The formulation of monetary policy . [Paris, France] [1986, c1985] 41 p. : LC Card 86-212837 DDC 332.4/6 19
HG230.3 .A75 1986

Working papers (Population Council. Center for Policy Studies) .
(no. 117) Frank, Odile. The demand for fertility control in Sub-Saharan Africa /. New York, N.Y., U. S.A. (1 Dag Hammarskjold Plaza, New York 10017) [1985] 50 p. ; LC Card 86-204127 DDC 363.9/6/09624 19
HB1071.A3 F69 1985

(no. 121) Demeny, Paul George, 1932- The world demographic situation /. New York, N.Y., U. S.A. (One Dag Hammarskjold Plaza, New York 10017) [1985] 52 p. : LC Card 87-402019 DDC 304.6 19
HB871 .D386 1985

(no. 125) Bongaarts, John, 1945- The transition in reproductive behavior in the third world /. New York, N.Y. [1986] 29 p. : LC Card 87-154566 DDC 304.6/32/091724 19
HB1108 .B65 1986

(no. 127) Greenhalgh, Susan. Fertility policy in China . New York, N.Y. [1986] 31 p. ; LC Card 87-154581 DDC 304.6/6/0951 19
HB1064.A3 G74 1986

Working papers (Southern African Team for Employment Promotion)
Kamya, Andrew, 1941- Factors affecting efficiency in the informal sector in Lusaka and Kitwe /. Lusaka , 1981. iii, 40 p. ; LC Card 87-980491
HD2346.Z292 L875 1981

Working papers (Universität Bielefeld. Institut für Mathematische Wirtschaftsforschung) .
(Nr. 51) Zauberman, Alfred. Planning under indeterminacy /. Bielefeld, Federal Republic of Germany [1976] 153, 5 p. ; LC Card 85-127554
HC336.25 .Z38 1976

Working report (Tanzania. Idara ya Utafiti wa Nyumba) .
(20) Salomon, Robert. Ruvuma region . Dar es Salaam , 1981. 32 leaves : LC Card 85-981451
HD7289.T352 R897 1981

Working time and employment /. Hart, Robert A. Boston , 1987. xx, 293 p. : ISBN 0-04-331109-1 (alk. paper) LC Card 86-28815 DDC 331.25/72 19
HD5106 .H298 1987

Working together for New York's economy . New York (State). Legislature. Legislative Commission on Public-Private Cooperation. [Albany] [1983] 57 p. ; LC Card 86-622577 DDC 338.9747 19
HC107.N7 N3743 1983

Working towards European unification : contributions of the Group of the European People's Party (Christian-Democratic Group) of the European Parliament : new technologies / [editor, Friedrich Fugmann]. [Luxembourg] : The Group, 1986. 60 p. ; 17 x 23 cm. Cover title. LC Card 87-149629 DDC 338/.06 19
1. Technological innovations - Economic aspects - European Economic Community countries. 2. Technological innovations - Social aspects - European Economic Community countries. I. Fugmann, Friedrich. II. EPP Group.
HC240.9.T4 W67 1986

Working with Lotus One-Two-Three. Bidgoli, Hossein. Working with Lotus 1-2-3 . St. Paul , c1988. xxii, 397 p. : ISBN 0-314-65031-8 (pbk.) LC Card 87-25268 DDC 005.36/9 19
HF5548.4.L67 B53 1988

Working with Lotus 1-2-3 . Bidgoli, Hossein. St. Paul , c1988. xxii, 397 p. : ISBN 0-314-65031-8 (pbk.) LC Card 87-25268 DDC 005.36/9 19
HF5548.4.L67 B53 1988

Working with statistics . Reid, Stuart. Totowa, N.J. , 1987. xiv, 183 p. ; ISBN 0-8476-7590-4 (pbk.) : LC Card 87-20508 DDC 300/.72 19
HA29 .R43 1987

Working with SuperCalc 4 /. Willis, Jerry, 1942- Blue Ridge Summit, PA , c1987. x, 320 p. : ISBN 0-8306-0214-3 : LC Card 86-30124 DDC 005.36/9 19
HF5548.4.S87 W54 1987

Working with technology . Betcherman, Gordon. [Ottawa] , 1986. 43 p. : ISBN 0-660-12174-3 (pbk.) : LC Card 86-224095 DDC 338/.06 19
HC120.A9 B47 1986

WORKING WIVES. see **WIVES - EMPLOYMENT.**

Working wives, working husbands /. Pleck, Joseph H. Beverly Hills, Calif. , c1985. 167 p. ; ISBN 0-8039-2489-5 LC Card 85-11974 DDC 306.8/7 19
HQ536 .P59 1985 ***NYPL [JLD 86-1130]***

The working woman /. Wallace, Joanne. Old Tappan, N.J. , c1986. 171 p. : ISBN 0-8007-1455-5 (pbk.) : LC Card 85-14396 DDC 650.1/024042 19
HD6053 .W34 1986 ***NYPL [JLF 87-131]***

Working women : past, present, future / editorial board, Karen Shallcross Koziara, Michael H. Moskow, Lucretia Dewey Tanner. Washington, D.C. : Bureau of National Affairs, c1987. xxii, 419 p. ; 24 cm. (Industrial Relations Research Association series) Includes bibliographies and index. ISBN 0-87179-547-7 LC Card 87-9410 DDC 331.4/0973 19
1. Women - Employment - United States - History. 2. Sex discrimination in employment - United States - History. I. Koziara, Karen Shallcross. II. Moskow, Michael H. III. Tanner, Lucretia Dewey. IV. Industrial Relations Research Association.
HD6095 .W742 1987

Working women and socialist politics in France, 1880-1914 . Hilden, Patricia. Oxford [Oxfordshire] , New York , 1986. viii, 307 p. ; ISBN 0-19-821935-0 : LC Card 85-15487 DDC 331.4/877/0094428 19
HD6073.T42 F84 1986
NYPL [JLD 86-1838]

Working women in Nebraska. Women in numbers . Lincoln, Neb. (Box 94600, Lincoln 68509-4600) , 1985. iii, 168 p. : LC Card 86-622214 DDC 331.4/125/09782 19
HD6096.N3 W66 1985

Working women in Renaissance Germany /. Wiesner, Merry, 1952- New Brunswick, N.J. , c1986. xiii, 263 p. : ISBN 0-8135-1138-0 : LC Card 85-14451 DDC 305.4/3/00943 19
HQ1149.G3 W54 1986
NYPL [JLE 86-3515]

Working women in socialist countries : the fertility connection / edited by Valentina Bodrova and Richard Anker. Geneva : International Labour Office, 1985. xvi, 234 p. : ill. ; 25 cm. (A WEP study) Includes bibliographies. CONTENTS. - Comparative survey / Richard Anker -- Hungary / Barnabás Barta -r Bulgaria / Velitchko Dobrianov -- Czechoslovakia / Zdeněk Pavlik -- Poland / Jerzey Z. Holver and Halina Wasilawska-Trenkner -- Uzbek Soviet Socialist Republic / A. Ya Kvasha -- Cuba / Alfonso Farnós, Fernando González, and Raúl Hernández. ISBN 92-2-103910-2 (pbk.) : LC Card 85-181464 DDC 304.6/32/091717 19
1. Fertility, Human - Communist countries - Case studies. 2. Women - Employment - Communist countries - Case studies. 3. Women - Employment - Government policy - Communist countries - Case studies. 4. Maternal and infant welfare - Government policy - Communist countries - Case studies. 5. Communist countries - Population policy - Case studies. I. Bodrova, Valentina. II. Anker, Richard, 1943-. III.

Series.
HB901 .W657 1985 ***NYPL [JLE 86-1433]***

WORKINGMEN. see **LABOR AND LABORING CLASSES.**

Workman, John P. Range economics / John P. Workman. New York : Macmillan ; London : Collier Macmillan, c1986. xvi, 217 p. : ill. ; 25 cm. (Biological resource management) Includes bibliographies and index. ISBN 0-02-948810-9 LC Card 85-18882 DDC 333.74 19
1. Rangelands - Economic aspects. 2. Range management. I. Title. II. Series.
HD1635 .W67 1986 ***NYPL [JLE 86-2382]***

Workplace democracy . Greenberg, Edward S., 1942- Ithaca , 1986. 257 p. ; ISBN 0-8014-1921-2 (alk. paper) LC Card 86-47641 DDC 674/.834/068 19
HD5658.P622 U554 1986
NYPL [JLE 86-4586]

A workplace for people . Kamerman, Sheila B. New York , 1987. p. cm. ISBN 0-231-06480-2 LC Card 87-18223 DDC 331.2/0973 19
HD60.5.U5 K36 1987

Workplace industrial relations and technical change /. Daniel, W. W. (William Wentworth), 1938- London , c1987. 312 p. : ISBN 0-86187-917-1 LC Card 87-154801 DDC 331/.0941 19
HD8391 .D3535 1987

Workplace literacy / Anne Skagen, editor. New York : AMA Membership Publications Division, American Management Association, c1986. 74 p. : ill. ; 23 cm. (AMA management briefing) ISBN 0-8144-2325-6 LC Card 86-14013 DDC 331.25/92 19
1. Employer-supported education - United States. 2. Literacy - United States. 3. Reading (Adult education) - United States. I. Skagen, Anne.
HF5549.5.T7 W66 1986
NYPL [JLE 86-3510]

The workplace within . Hirschhorn, Larry. Cambridge, Mass. , c1988. x, 265 p. ; ISBN 0-262-08169-5 LC Card 87-20144 DDC 158.7 19
HF5548.8 .H493 1988

WORKS COMMITTEES. see **WORKS COUNCILS.**

WORKS COUNCILS.
Penteado Neto, Alfredo Camargo, 1939- Organizações de trabalhadores . São Paulo , 1986. 112 p. : LC Card 87-403488 DDC 338.6 19
HD5650 .P37 1986

WORKS COUNCILS - AUSTRIA - HISTORY - 20TH CENTURY.
Garamvölgyi, Judit. Betriebsräte und sozialer Wandel in Österreich 1919/1920 . München , c1983. 296 p. ; ISBN 3-486-51721-X LC Card 83-240283
HD5660.A8 G37 1983

WORKS COUNCILS - BRAZIL.
Ibrahim, José. O que todo cidadão precisa saber sobre comissões de fábrica /. São Paulo, SP [1986] 96 p. : ISBN 85-26-00095-0 LC Card 87-402908 DDC 338.6 19
HD5660.B7 I27 1986

WORKS COUNCILS - BRAZIL - CASE STUDIES.
Comissão de fábrica . Petrópolis , 1981. 60 p. ; LC Card 86-190732
HD5660.B7 C66 1981

WORKS COUNCILS - FRANCE.
Nallet, Jean François. Comité d'entreprise et formation /. Paris-La Défense (Tour Europe, 92080 cedex 07) , 1977. 140 p. (1 fold.) ; LC Card 78-358400
HD5660.F7 N34

Nallet, Jean François. Comité d'entreprise et formation /. Paris-la-Défense , 1979. 181 p. ;
NYPL [JLF 81-80]

WORKS COUNCILS - GERMANY (WEST) - HISTORY.
40 Jahre Mitbestimmung . Köln , c1986. 293 p., [16] p. of plates : ISBN 3-7663-3012-8 LC Card 87-125207 DDC 658.3/152/0943 19
HD5660.G4 A5 1986

WORKS COUNCILS - GREAT BRITAIN - HISTORY.
Shipway, Mark. Anti-parliamentary communism . New York , 1988. p. cm. ISBN 0-312-01265-9 : LC Card 87-23083 DDC 338.6 19
HD5660.G7 S48 1988

WORKS COUNCILS - HISTORY.
Ibrahim, José. O que todo cidadão precisa saber sobre comissões de fábrica /. São Paulo, SP [1986] 96 p. : ISBN 85-26-00095-0 LC Card 87-402908 DDC 338.6 19
HD5660.B7 I27 1986

WORKS COUNCILS - IRAN.
Bayat, Assef. Workers and revolution in Iran . London , Atlantic Highlands, New Jersey, USA , 1987. 227 p. : ISBN 0-86232-389-4 LC Card 87-160253 DDC 322/.2/0955 19
HD5660.I6 B39 1987

WORKS COUNCILS - IRAN - MANAGEMENT.
Bayat, Assef. Workers and revolution in Iran . London , Atlantic Highlands, New Jersey, USA , 1987. 227 p. : ISBN 0-86232-389-4 LC Card 87-160253 DDC 322/.2/0955 19
HD5660.I6 B39 1987

WORKS COUNCILS - ITALY.
Regalia, Ida, 1946- Eletti e abbandonati . Bologna , c1984. 355 p. : ISBN 88-15-00592-7 : LC Card 84-250543 DDC 331.87/33/0945 19
HD6490.O42 I87 1984 ***NYPL [JLD 86-211]***

WORKS COUNCILS - LAW AND LEGISLATION - NETHERLANDS.
Advies samenloop Wet OR en ARBO-wet . Den Haag [1986] 37 p. ; ISBN 90-6587-243-4 LC Card 87-104667
HC321 .S63 1986, nr. 6 KKM1430

Sociaal-Economische Raad. Commissie Ondernemingsraden. Advies vereenvoudiging Wet OR . Den Haag [1986] 61 p. ; ISBN 90-6587-254-X LC Card 87-165080
HC321 .S63 1986, nr. 14 KKM1350

WORKS COUNCILS - SOVIET UNION.
My--khozi͡aeva proizvodstva . Moskva , 1984. 261 p. : LC Card 85-107808
HD5660.S65 M9 1984

WORKS COUNCILS - YUGOSLAVIA.
Der Kapitalistische Charakter der jugoslawischen Arbeiterselbstverwaltung im Lichte des 8. Kongresses des Bundes der Kommunisten Jugoslawiens. Tirana , 1965. 54 p. ; LC Card 85-127335
HD5660.Y8 K27 1965

WORKS COUNCILS - YUGOSLAVIA - ZADAR (CROATIA) - HISTORY.
Uranija, Valentin. 35 godina sindikata u Zadru . Zadar , 1981. 300 p., xlviii p. of plates : LC Card 86-190260
HD8632.S3433 U73 1981

Works Management Association. see **Institution of Works Managers.**

Workshop "Berufswege von Frauen" (1984 : Berlin, Germany) Berufsverläufe von Frauen : Lebensentwürfe im Umbruch / Hedwig Rudolph (Hrsg.) ... [et al.]. München : DJI Verlag Deutsches Jugendinstitut ; Weinheim : Alleinauslieferung, Juventa Verlag, c1986. 291 p. : 3 ill. ; 21 cm. (DJI Materialien) "Diese Veröffentlichung ist im Anschluss an den Workshop 'Berufswege von Frauen--individuelle und sozialstrukturelle Bedingungen' im Rahmen der Hochschultage Berufliche Bildung '84 (3.-6. Oktober 1984 in Berlin) entstanden"--T.p. verso. Bibliography: p. 273-288. ISBN 3-87966-253-3 LC Card 87-407975 DDC 331.7/02/024042 19
1. Vocational guidance for women - Germany (West) - Congresses. 2. Women - Employment - Germany, West - Congresses. 3. Vocational education - Germany, West - Congresses. 4. Occupational training for women - Germany (West) - Congresses. I. Rudolph, Hedwig. II. Title. III. Series.
HF5382.67.G3 W67 1984

Workshop booklet .
(3) Katins, Sabine. All you need is freedom . Berlin [1977] 35 p. : LC Card 86-207107 DDC 968.91/05 19
HC910 .K37 1977

WORKSHOP COMMITTEES. see **WORKS COUNCILS.**

WORKSHOP COUNCILS. see **WORKS COUNCILS.**

Workshop: Middle Management and the Fisc. (1983 : Lahore, Pakistan) Miscellany II : Workshop : Middle Management and the Fisc. : three weeks refresher course, 23rd Oct.-10th Nov. 1983 : training of officers in the income tax group. Lahore : Directorate of Training, Income Tax, [1984?] 251 p. : ports. ; 26 cm. Cover title. LC Card 86-930242 DDC 354.549/10072 19
1. Taxation - Pakistan - Congresses. I. Pakistan. Directorate of Training Income Tax. II. Title.
HJ3611.5 .W67 1983

Workshop on Artificial Intelligence and Statistics (1985 : Princeton, N.J.) Artificial intelligence and statistics /. Reading, Mass. , c1986. xiv, 418 p. : ISBN 0-201-11568-9 : LC Card 85-28631 DDC 006.3 19
Q334 .A764 1986 ***NYPL [JSE 87-399]***

Workshop on Capitalist-Socialist Organizations (3rd : 1984 : Helsinki, Finland) Organization of innovation . Berlin , New York , 1987. x, 238 p. : ISBN 0-89925-167-6 (U. S.) : LC Card 87-19936 DDC 658.4/06 19
HD45 .O73 1987

Workshop on Downsizing (1985 : Arden House) Ginzberg, Eli, 1911- Resizing for organizational effectiveness . New York, N.Y. (316 Uris Hall, New York 10027) , c1985. vii, 43 p. ; LC Card 86-162474 DDC 658.1/6 19
HD58.9 .G56 1985

Workshop on Energy Policy Issues (1985 : Jaipur, India) Energy policy issues . New Delhi , c1987. 146 p. : LC Card 87-900625 DDC 333.79/0954 19
HD9502.I42 E536 1987

Workshop on Exact Matching Methodologies (May 9-10, 1985 : Arlington, Va.) Record linkage techniques--1985 : Proceedings of the Workshop on Exact Matching Methodologies, Arlington, Virginia, May 9-10, 1985 / compiled and edited by Beth Kilss and Wendy Alvey. [Washington, D.C.] : Dept. of the Treasury, Internal Revenue Service, Statistics of Income Division, 1985. vii, 397 p. : ill. ; 28 cm. (Publication . 1299) "December 1985." Item 0946-B. Includes bibliographical references.
1. Records - Management. 2. Public records - United States. I. Kilss, Beth. II. Alvey, Wendy. III. United States. Internal Revenue Service. Statistics of Income Division. IV. Title. V. Title: Proceedings of the Workshop on Exact Matching Methodologies.
NYPL [JLF 86-1723]

Workshop on Impact of Regulatory Mechanism on Corporate Sector . Workshop on Impact of Regulatory Mechanism on Corporate Sector (1984 : Bangalore, India) New Delhi [1985] 104 p. : LC Card 87-902536 DDC 338.954 19
HC435.2 .W67 1984

Workshop on Impact of Regulatory Mechanism on Corporate Sector (1984 : Bangalore, India) Workshop on Impact of Regulatory Mechanism on Corporate Sector : papers and proceedings. New Delhi : Associated Chambers of Commerce and Industry of India, [1985] 104 p. : ill. ; 25 cm. Organized by ASSOCHAM. Includes bibliographical references. LC Card 87-902536 DDC 338.954 19
1. Industry and state - India - Congresses. 2. Price regulation - India - Congresses. 3. Corporation law - India - Congresses. I. Associated Chambers of Commerce & Industry of India. II. Title.
HC435.2 .W67 1984

Workshop on Physical Development Planning (1984 : Ibadan, Nigeria) Physical planning inputs in national and state development plans . Ibadan [1984?] v, 312 p. : LC Card 87-400745 DDC 338.9669 19
HC1055 .P488 1984

Workshop on Promotion of Self-employment in Rural Areas, Allahabad, 26-30 November 1982 . Workshop on Promotion of Self-Employment in Rural Areas (1982 : Allahabad, India) New Delhi [1983] iii, 186 p. ; LC Card 83-906671 DDC 338.6/42 19
HD8037.I4 W67 1982

Workshop on Promotion of Self-Employment in Rural Areas (1982 : Allahabad, India) Workshop on Promotion of Self-employment in Rural Areas, Allahabad, 26-30 November 1982 : report. New Delhi : Central Institute for Research and Training in Employment Service, Directorate General of Employment and Training, Ministry of Labour and Rehabilitation, Govt. of India, [1983] iii, 186 p. ; 28 cm. At head of title: ILO/ARPLA-CIRTES-IERT. Includes

bibliographical references. LC Card 83-906671 DDC 338.6/42 19
1. Self-employed - India - Congresses. 2. Rural development - India - Congresses. 3. Manpower planning - India - Congresses. I. Central Institute for Research and Training in Employment Service (India). II. Title.
HD8037.I4 W67 1982

Workshop on Socio-economic Correlates of Mortality Differentials in Japan and ASEAN (1984 : Singapore) Socio-economic correlates of mortality in Japan and ASEAN / edited by Ng Shui Meng. Singapore : Institute of Southeast Asian Studies, c1986. xxi, 295 p. : ill., map ; 23 cm. "National Institute for Research Advancement, Japan." "Country reports presented at the Workshop on Socio-economic Corrolates of Mortality Differentials in Japan and ASEAN, Singapore, 30-31 August 1984"--T.p. verso. Includes bibliographies. LC Card 86-945167 DDC 304.6/4/0952 19
1. Mortality - Economic aspects - Japan - Congresses. 2. Mortality - Social aspects - Japan - Congresses. 3. Mortality - Economic aspects - Asia, Southeastern - Congresses. 4. Mortality - Social aspects - Asia, Southeastern - Congresses. I. Ng, Shui Meng. II. Sōgō Kenkyū Kaihatsu Kikō (Japan). III. Institute of Southeast Asian Studies.
HB1481 .W67 1984

Workshop on "Southern Europe and the Enlargement of the EEC" (1980 : Lisbon, Portugal) Southern Europe and the enlargement of the EEC . Lisboa, Portugal , 1982. 324 p. : LC Card 86-201274 DDC 341.24/22 19
HC241.25.E85 S68 1982

Workshop on the Institutionalization of the Shallow Wells Programme under Tanzanian Administration (1981 : University of Dar es Salaam) Proceedings of the Workshop on the Institutionalization of the Shallow Wells Programme under Tanzanian Administration / I. Andersson ... [et al.]. [Dar es Salaam?] : Bureau of Resource Assessment and Land Use Planning, University of Dar es S[a]laam, 1981. 3, 16, 12 p. ; 29 cm. (Research paper . no. 71) Cover title. LC Card 85-980881 DDC 333.7/09678 s 333.91/22/09678 19
1. Water resources development - Tanzania - Congresses. 2. Water-supply - Tanzania - Congresses. 3. Wells - Tanzania - Congresses. I. Andersson, Ingvar. II. Chuo Kikuu cha Dar es Salaam. Bureau of Resource Assessment and Land Use Planning. III. Series: Research paper (Chuo Kikuu cha Dar es Salaam. Bureau of Resource Assessment and Land Use Planning) , no. 71.
HD107 .D36 no. 71 HD1699.T33

World accounting /. Orsini, Larry L. New York, NY (11 Penn Plaza, New York 10001) , 1987- c1986- 2 v. (loose-leaf) ; LC Card 86-73012 DDC 657 19
HF5611 .O75 1987

World aerospace . Todd, Daniel. London , New York , c1987. 226 p. : ISBN 0-7099-4325-3 LC Card 86-29368 DDC 338.4/76291/021 19
HD9711.5.A2 T629 1987

World Bank.
Growth-oriented adjustment programs /. Washington, D.C. , 1987. xiii, 537 p. : ISBN 0-939934-92-2 (pbk.) LC Card 87-21361 DDC 338.9 19
HD73 .G76 1987

Rwanda, economic memorandum . [Washington, D.C.] [1983] 234 p., [2] leaves of plates : LC Card 87-116501 DDC 338.967/571 19
HC875 .R84 1983

WORLD BANK.
De Vries, Barend A. Remaking the World Bank /. Washington, DC , Lanham, Md. , c1987. xvi, 184 p. ; ISBN 0-932020-49-6 (pbk.) LC Card 87-23406 DDC 332.1/532 19
HG3881.5.W57 D4 1987

Disbursement handbook. Washington, D.C., U. S.A. , c1986. iv, 58 p. : ISBN 0-8213-0746-0 (pbk.) LC Card 86-210947 DDC 332.1/532/0685 19
HG3881.5.W57 D57 1986

Lichtensztejn, Samuel, 1934- Fondo Monetario Internacional y Banco Mundial . San José, Costa Rica , Buenos Aires, Argentina , 1986. 215 p. : LC Card 86-233561
HG3881.5.I58 L527 1986

Procurement under IBRD loans and IDA credits . Washington, D.C. , c1985. 38 p. ; ISBN 0-8213-0562-X (pbk.) LC Card 86-211637 DDC 332.1/532 19
HG3881.5.W57 P76 1985

WORLD BANK - AFRICA - CONGRESSES.
World recession and the food crisis in Africa /. London , 1986. 314 p. ; ISBN 0-85255-309-9 : LC Card 86-235333 DDC 363.8/526/096 19
HD9017.A2 W67 1986b

World recession and the food crisis in Africa /. Boulder , 1986. p. cm. ISBN 0-8133-0511-X : LC Card 86-28250 DDC 363.8/526/096 19
HD9017.A2 W67 1986

WORLD BANK - LATIN AMERICA.
El FMI, el Banco Mundial y la crisis latinoamericana /. México , 1986. 474 p. : ISBN 968-231-373-2 LC Card 87-127860 DDC 332.1/52 19
HG3881.5.I58 F56 1986

The World Bank & structural transformation in developing countries . Leslie, Winsome J. Boulder, Colo. , 1987. xi, 208 p. : ISBN 1-555-87036-8 (lib. bdg. : alk. paper) : LC Card 87-3358 DDC 338.9675/1 19
HG3881.5.W57 L47 1987

World Bank and structural transformation in developing countries. Leslie, Winsome J. The World Bank & structural transformation in developing countries . Boulder, Colo. , 1987. xi, 208 p. : ISBN 1-555-87036-8 (lib. bdg. : alk. paper) : LC Card 87-3358 DDC 338.9675/1 19
HG3881.5.W57 L47 1987

WORLD BANK - ARAB COUNTRIES - CONGRESSES.
Adjustment policies and development strategies in the Arab world /. Washington, D.C. , 1987. ix, 200 p. ; ISBN 0-939934-96-5 (pbk.) LC Card 87-21377 DDC 338.9/00917/4927 19
HC498 .A6395 1987

WORLD BANK - CASE STUDIES.
Paul, Samuel, 1930- Community participation in development projects . Washington, D.C. [1987]. v, 37 p. : ISBN 0-8213-0886-6 (pbk.) LC Card 87-2183 DDC 338.9/009172/4 19
HD75.8 .P38 1987

A World Bank country study.
Bangladesh . Washington, D.C., U. S.A. , c1987. xli, 279 p., [1] leaf of plates : ISBN 0-8213-0963-3 (pbk.) LC Card 87-22920 DDC 338.9549/2 19
HC440.8 .B362 1987

China, the livestock sector. Washington, D.C., U. S.A. , 1987. vii, 195 p. ; ISBN 0-8213-0940-4 (pbk.) LC Card 87-16089 DDC 338.1/76/00951 19
HD9426.C62 C475 1987

Fiji, a transition to manufacturing. Washington, D.C., U. S.A. , c1987. xvi, 107 p., [1] folded leaf of plates : ISBN 0-8213-0962-5 LC Card 87-23067 DDC 338.4/767/099611 19
HD9738.F55 F55 1987

Korea . Washington, D.C., U. S.A. [1987] 2 v. : ISBN 0-8213-0887-4 (pbk. : v. 1) LC Card 87-2213 DDC 338.9519/5 19
HD3616.K853 K67 1987

Panama . Washington, D.C., U. S.A. , c1985. xxv, 307 p., [8] p., [1] leaf of plates : ISBN 0-8213-0580-8 LC Card 85-12420 DDC 338.97287 19
HC147 .P43 1985 ***NYPL [JLF 86-1919]***

A World Bank country study, 0253-2123.
Cyprus, a long-term development perspective. Washington, D.C., U. S.A. [1987] xvii, 79 p., [1] folded leaf of plates : ISBN 0-8213-0931-5 (pbk.) LC Card 87-15988 DDC 338.95645 19
HC415.2 .C956 1987

Haiti . Washington, D.C., U. S.A. [1987] xix, 254 p. ; ISBN 0-8213-0872-6 (pbk.) LC Card 86-32599 DDC 339.5/22/097294 19
HC153.Z9 P834 1987

Philippines . Washington, D.C., U. S.A. [1987] xiv, 156 p., [1] leaf of plates : ISBN 0-8213-0942-0 (pbk.) LC Card 87-19697 DDC 330.599/046 19
HC455 .P523 1987

World Bank discussion papers .
(11) Berg, Elliot. Divestiture in developing countries /. Washington, D.C. , 1987. vii, 30 p. : ISBN 0-8213-0917-X (pbk.) LC Card 87-14235 DDC 338.9/009172/4 19
HD4420.8 .B45 1987

(13) Kjellstrom, Sven B., 1945- Institutional development and technical assistance in macro-economic policy formulation . Washington, D.C., U. S.A. [1987] 69 p. ; ISBN 0-8213-0919-6 (pbk.) LC Card 87-14021 DDC 339.5/0966/81 19
HC1015 .K58 1987

(18) Churchill, Anthony A., 1938- Rural water supply and sanitation . Washington, D.C. , c1987. xvi, 111 p. : ISBN 0-8213-0950-1 (pbk.) LC Card 87-23005 DDC 338.4/336361/091724 19
HD1702 .C48 1987

(8) Martone, Celso L. (Celso Luiz) Macroeconomic policies, debt accumulation, and adjustment in Brazil, 1965-84 /. Washington, D.C. , 1987. vii, 43 p. ; ISBN 0-8213-0892-0 (pbk.) LC Card 86-1527 DDC 336.3/4/0981 19
HJ8579 .M37 1987

World Bank discussion papers, 0259-210X .
(1) Nellis, John R. Public enterprises in Sub-Saharan Africa /. Washington, D.C., U. S.A. [1986] vii, 66 p. : ISBN 0-8213-0845-9 (pbk.) LC Card 86-24756 DDC 338.7/4/0967 19
HD4338 .N45 1986

(10) Kahnert, Friedrich, 1929- Improving urban employment and labor productivity /. Washington, D.C. [1987] 75 p. ; ISBN 0-8213-0908-0 (pbk.) LC Card 87-10538 DDC 331.11/09172/4 19
HD5852 .K34 1987

(12) Anderson, Dennis, 1937- Economic growth and the returns to investment /. Washington, D.C. [1987] 93 p. : ISBN 0-8213-0918-8 (pbk.) LC Card 87-14178 DDC 338.9 19
HD75 .A53 1987

(14) Lamb, Geoffrey, 1944- Managing economic policy change . Washington, D.C., U. S.A. [1987] x, 27 p. ; ISBN 0-8213-0921-8 (pbk.) LC Card 87-14824 DDC 338.9 19
HD87 .L36 1987

(15) Mergos, George, 1948- Dairy development and milk cooperatives . Washington, D.C. [1987] xiv, 140 p. : ISBN 0-8213-0932-3 (pbk.) LC Card 87-15976 DDC 334/.68371/09543 19
HD9282.I53 M286 1987

(16) Yagci, Fahrettin, 1944- Macroeconomic policies and adjustment in Yugoslavia . Washington, D.C. [1987] 29 p. ; ISBN 0-8213-0938-2 (pbk.) LC Card 87-16064 DDC 339.5/09497 19
HC407.Y6 Y34 1987

(17) Marsden, Keith. Private enterprise in Africa . Washington, D.C. [1987] xiii, 66 p. ; ISBN 0-8213-0945-5 (pbk.) LC Card 87-18419 DDC 330.96/032 19
HC800 .M353 1987

(3) Park, Yung Chul. A system for evaluating the performance of government-invested enterprises in Korea /. Washington, D.C. [1986] vi, 49 p. : ISBN 0-8213-0859-9 (pbk.) LC Card 86-28907 DDC 338.7/4/0723 19
HD4315.5 .P37 1986

(4) Heaver, Richard, 1952- Country commitment to development projects /. Washington, D.C., U. S.A. [1986] 32 p. ; ISBN 0-8213-0860-2 (pbk.) LC Card 86-28114 DDC 338.91 19
HC59.72.E44 H43 1986

(5) Pfeffermann, Guy Pierre. Public expenditure in Latin America . Washington, D.C. , 1987. 38 p. ; ISBN 0-8213-0906-4 (pbk.) LC Card 87-10650 DDC 336.3/9/098 19
HJ7664.5 .P44 1987

(6) Paul, Samuel, 1930- Community participation in development projects . Washington, D.C. [1987]. v, 37 p. : ISBN 0-8213-0886-6 (pbk.) LC Card 87-2183 DDC 338.9/009172/4 19
HD75.8 .P38 1987

(7) Batista Júnior, Paulo Nogueira. International financial flows to Brazil since the late 1960s . Washington, D.C. , 1987. 66 p. ; ISBN 0-8213-0891-2 (pbk.) LC Card 87-6065 DDC

336.3/4/0981 19
HJ8579 .B369 1987

A World Bank operations evaluation study, 1011-0984.
The Jengka Triangle projects in Malaysia . Washington, D.C. , c1987. ix, 105 p., [1] leaf of plates : ISBN 0-8213-0946-3 (pbk.); 0-8213-0946-6 (cover) LC Card 87-21021 DDC 338.1/85951 19
HD2080.6.Z9 P345 1987

WORLD BANK - PHILIPPINES.
Broad, Robin. Unequal alliance . Berkeley , c1988. p. cm. ISBN 0-520-05905-0 LC Card 87-10745 DDC 332.1/52 19
HG3881.5.W57 B76 1988

A World Bank policy study, 0258-2120.
Binswanger, Hans P. Agricultural mechanization . Washington, D.C., U. S.A. , c1987. vi, 85 p. : ISBN 0-8213-0903-X (pbk.) LC Card 87-14082 DDC 338.1/61/091724 19
HD1459 .B57 1987

World Bank staff commodity working paper .
(no. 15) Takeuchi, Kenji, 1932- The world copper industry . Washington, D.C., U. S.A. , c1986. xxix, 179 p. : ISBN 0-8213-0852-1 LC Card 86-26554 DDC 338.2/743 19
HD9539.C6 T35 1986

(no. 16) Thigpen, M. Elton, 1932- World demand prospects for jute /. Washington, D.C. , Rome , 1987. vi, 178 p. ; ISBN 0-8213-0867-X (pbk.) LC Card 86-32522 DDC 338.4/767713 19
HD9156.J7 T46 1987

(no. 17) Akiyama, T. (Takamasa), 1944- A new global tea model . Washington, D.C. , 1987. vi, 130 p. ; ISBN 0-8213-0868-8 LC Card 87-6238 DDC 382/.41372 19
HD9198.A2 A424 1987

World Bank staff commodity working paper, 0253-3537 .
(no. 18) Brown, James G., 1945- The international sugar industry . Washington, D.C., U. S.A. , 1987. xii, 69 p. ; ISBN 0-8213-0884-1 (pbk.) LC Card 87-6285 DDC 338.1/736 19
HD9100.5 .B76 1987

World Bank staff working paper .
(no. 332) Cernea, Michael M. Measuring project impact . Washington, D.C., U. S.A. , c1979. vi, 93 p. ; LC Card 81-170764
HD1792 .C43 1979

(no. 376) Pack, Howard. Fostering the capital-goods sector in LDCS . Washington, D.C. (1818 H St., N.W., Washington 20433) [1980] v, 59. 2 leaves ; LC Card 80-121299
HD9680.D44 P33 1980

A World Bank symposium.
Agricultural marketing strategy and pricing policy /. Washington, D.C. , c1987. xiii, 132 p. : ISBN 0-8213-0830-0 (pbk.) LC Card 86-33992 DDC 380.1/41 19
HD9018.D44 A365 1987

Exports of developing countries . Washington, D.C. , c1987. viii, 168 p. : ISBN 0-8213-0870-X (pbk.) : LC Card 87-15991 DDC 382/.6/091724 19
HF4055 .E96 1987

World Bank technical paper .
(no. 58) Levitsky, Jacob, 1924- Credit guarantee schemes for small and medium enterprises /. Washington, D.C. , 1987. vi, 91 p. ; ISBN 0-8213-0866-1 (pbk.) LC Card 86-32571 DDC 658.8/7 19
HG9977 .L48 1987

World Bank technical paper, 0253-7494 .
(no. 56) Silverman, Jerry M. Action-planning workshops for development management . Washington, D.C., U. S.A. , 1986. ix, 74 p. : ISBN 0-8213-0864-5 (pbk.) LC Card 86-28215 DDC 338.9/0068 19
HC59.7 .S4656 1986

(no. 60) Okun, Daniel Alexander. Community piped water supply systems in developing countries . Washington, D.C. , 1987. xi, 249 p. : ISBN 0-8213-0896-3 (pbk.) LC Card 87-8161 DDC 363.6/1/091724 19
HD4465.D44 O38 1987

(no. 68) Armstrong-Wright, Alan, 1929- Bus services . Washington, D.C. , 1987. x, 97 p. ; ISBN 0-8213-0943-9 (pbk.) LC Card 87-17183 DDC 388.4/1322/091724 19
HE5725 .A76 1987

WORLD BANK - ZAIRE.
Leslie, Winsome J. The World Bank & structural transformation in developing countries . Boulder, Colo. , 1987. xi, 208 p. : ISBN 1-555-87036-8 (lib. bdg. : alk. paper) : LC Card 87-3358 DDC 338.9675/1 19
HG3881.5.W57 L47 1987

The world banking system . Brimmer, Andrew F. New York , 1985. 59 p. ; ISBN 0-8147-1068-9 : LC Card 85-5115 DDC 332.1/5 19
HG3881 .B677 1985 ***NYPL [JLD 86-2189]***

World Chemical Congress of Marketing and Business Research (1986 : Newport Beach, Calif.) The chemical industry : where in the world is it going? : papers presented at the September 1986 meeting of the World Chemical Congress of Marketing and Business Research held at the Newporter Hotel, Newport Beach, CA. / co-sponsored by the American Chemical Society, Division of Chemical Marketing & Economics, and the Chemical Marketing Research Association in conjunction with the American Marketing Association, Agricultural Chemical Marketing Research Section ... [et al.], September 7-10, 1986, Newporter Resort Hotel, Newport Beach, California. [Staten Island, N.Y.] : Chemical Marketing Research Association, c1986. 435 p. : ill. ; 22 cm. Includes bibliographies. LC Card 86-72599 DDC 338.4/766 19
1. Chemical industry - Technological innovations - Congresses. I. Chemical Marketing Research Association. II. American Chemical Society. Division of Chemical Marketing and Economics. III. American Marketing Association. Agricultural Chemical Marketing Research Section. IV. Title.
HD9650 .W67 1986

World class manufacturing casebook . Schonberger, Richard. New York , London , c1987. xxvi, 253 p. : ISBN 0-02-929340-5 LC Card 86-25822 DDC 658 19
HD31 .S3386 1987

World coal . Gordon, Richard L., 1934- Cambridge [Cambridgeshire] , New York , 1987. xvi, 145 p. : ISBN 0-521-30827-5 LC Card 86-26349 DDC 338.2/724 19
HD9540.5 .G64 1987

World coinage report, 1980-1984. Washington, D.C. : U. S. Mint, Dept. of the Treasury : For sale by the Supt. of Docs., U. S. G.P.O., [1986?] vi, 114 p. : ill. ; 24 cm. Shipping list no.: 86-644-P. S/N 048-005-00031-4 LC Card 86-602440 DDC 737.4/021 19
1. Coins - Weights and measures - Tables. 2. Coinage - Statistics. I. United States. Bureau of the Mint.
HG327 .W67 1986

World Commission on Environment and Development.
Energy 2000 . London [Atlantic Highlands] N.J. , 1987. viii, 76 p. : ISBN 0-86232-710-5 : LC Card 87-13371 DDC 333.79 19
HD9502.A2 E536 1987

Our common future /. Oxford , New York , 1987. xv, 383 p. ; ISBN 0-19-282080-X (pbk.) : LC Card 87-7853 DDC 363.7 19
HD75.6 .O97 1987

World comparisons of purchasing power and real product for 1980 : phase IV of the International Comparison Project / United Nations, Commission of the European Communities. New York : United Nations : EUROSTAT, 1986- v. <1 > ; 28 cm. "ST/ESA/STAT/SER.F/42 (part 1)." "United Nations publication sales no. E.86.xvii.9." CONTENTS. - pt. 1. Summary results for 60 countries. LC Card 86-225798 DDC 339.3 19
1. Income. 2. Gross national product. 3. Purchasing power. I. United Nations International Comparison Project. II. Commission of the European Communities.
HC79.I5 W675 1986

The world copper industry . Takeuchi, Kenji, 1932- Washington, D.C., U. S.A. , c1986. xxix, 179 p. : ISBN 0-8213-0852-1 LC Card 86-26554 DDC 338.2/743 19
HD9539.C6 T35 1986

World debt . Schatan, Jacobo. [América Latina, deuda externa y desarrollo. English.] London , Atlantic Highlands, N.J., USA , 1987. xv, 126 p. ; ISBN 0-86232-688-5 : LC Card 87-13330 DDC 336.3/435/098 19
HJ8514.5 .S313 1987

World debt tables. Developing country debt . Washington, D.C. , c1987. xliii, 29 p. : ISBN 0-8213-0889-0 LC Card 87-2074 DDC 336.3/435/091724021 19
HJ8899 .D483 1987

World demand prospects for jute /. Thigpen, M. Elton, 1932- Washington, D.C. , Rome , 1987. vi, 178 p. ; ISBN 0-8213-0867-X (pbk.) LC Card 86-32522 DDC 338.4/767713 19
HD9156.J7 T46 1987

The world demographic situation /. Demeny, Paul George, 1932- New York, N.Y., U. S.A. (One Dag Hammarskjold Plaza, New York 10017) [1985] 52 p. : LC Card 87-402019 DDC 304.6 19
HB871 .D386 1985

World diesel engine markets . Kliachko, Valerie A. Menlo Park, Calif. (333 Ravenswood Ave., Menlo Park 94025-3476) , c1985. 36 p. : LC Card 87-145492 DDC 338.4/7621436 19
HD9705.5.M672 K65 1985

World economic and financial surveys, 0258-7440.
Dillon, K. Burke. Recent experience with multilateral official debt rescheduling /. Washington, D.C. , c1987. v, 22 p. : LC Card 87-2633 DDC 336.3/435 19
HG3891.5 .D55 1987

Primary commodities . Washington, D.C. , 1987. p. cm. ISBN 0-939934-87-6 LC Card 87-17225 DDC 382/.4 19
HF1040.7 .P718 1987

Staff studies for the world economic outlook /. Washington, D.C. , c1986. xi, 195 p. : LC Card 86-202629 DDC 338.5/443 19
HC59 .S682 1986

The world economic and social crisis . Castro, Fidel, 1927- [Crisis económica y social del mundo. English.] New Delhi , 1983. 224 p. : LC Card 83-908475 DDC 337/.097172/4 19
HC59.7 .C31472 1983 ***NYPL [JLD 87-486]***

World economic data : a compendium of current economic information for all countries of the world / Cecelia A. Albert, editor ; foreword by James E. Davis. Santa Barbara, Calif. : ABC-CLIO, c1987. x, 231 p. ; 29 cm. Bibliography: p. 231. ISBN 0-87436-485-X (alk. paper) : LC Card 87-14508 DDC 330.9/04 19
1. Economic indicators. 2. Economic history - 1971-. I. Albert, Cecelia A., 1954-. II. Davis, James E. (James Edwin), 1940-.
HC59 .W643 1987

WORLD ECONOMICS. see **COMMERCIAL POLICY; COMPETITION, INTERNATIONAL; ECONOMIC POLICY; GEOGRAPHY, COMMERCIAL; GEOGRAPHY, ECONOMIC.**

The world economy . Yarbrough, Beth V. Chicago , c1988. xxii, 666 p. : ISBN 0-03-003474-4 LC Card 86-32804 DDC 337 19
HF1411 .Y34 1988

The World economy and financial markets in 1995 : Japan's role and challenges. 1st ed. Kamakura-shi, Kanagawa-ken, Japan : Nomura Research Institute, 1986. 183 p. : ill. ; 26 cm. LC Card 86-201317 DDC 332.1 19
1. International finance. 2. Financial institutions. 3. Japan - Foreign economic relations. I. Nomura Sōgō Kenkyūjo.
HG3881 .W597 1986

World economy in the mid-eighties : a report prepared as background document for the Eighth Summit of the Heads of Non-aligned States, Harare, 3-7 September 1986. New Delhi, India : Research and Information System for the Non-aligned and Other Developing Countries, c1986. xii, 222 p. ; 27 cm. Includes bibliographies. LC Card 86-903369 DDC 330.9/048 19
1. Economics. 2. Economic policy. 3. International economic relations. I. Conference of Heads of State or Government of Non-aligned Countries (8th : 1986 : Harare, Zimbabwe). II. Research and Information System for the Non-aligned and Other Developing Countries.
HB171 .W83 1986

The world economy since the war . Brett, E. A.

Houndmills, Basingstoke, Hampshire , 1985. x, 318 p. : ISBN 0-333-37199-2 LC Card 87-673378
HC59 .B754x 1985

World Employment Programme.
Employment forecasting . London , New York , c1988. p. cm. ISBN 0-86187-938-4 : LC Card 87-21882 DDC 331.12/094 19
HD5764 .E47 1988

Hopkins, Mike. Alternatives to unemployment and underemployment . Boulder , 1985. xiv, 129 p. : ISBN 0-8133-0200-5 (pbk.) LC Card 85-45007 DDC 331.13/79861 19
HD5757.A6 H67 1985 *NYPL [JLD 86-2149]*

Labour circulation and the labour process /. London [England] , Dover, N.H. , c1985. xvi, 416 p. : ISBN 0-7099-3342-8 : LC Card 84-14306 DDC 331.12/791 19
HD5856.D44 L33 1984 *NYPL [JLD 86-2532]*

Microelectronics, automation, and employment in the automobile industry /. Chichester [West Sussex] , New York , c1987. xix, 203 p. : ISBN 0-471-91484-3 : LC Card 86-32532 DDC 331.7/6292 19
HD8039.A8 M52 1987

Pereira, A. (Armand) Socio-economic and policy implications of energy price increases /. Aldershot, Hants, England , Brookfield, Vt., USA , c1987. xxiv, 317 p. ; ISBN 0-566-05520-1 : LC Card 87-11955 DDC 338.2/3 19
HD9560.4 .P37 1987

Rural roads and poverty alleviation . London , 1984. vii, 191 p. : ISBN 0-946688-05-2 : LC Card 86-673296
HE336.R85 R87x 1984

Salarios e inflación, Argentina, 1970-1983 /. [Santiago, Chile] [c1984] iv, 116 p. : LC Card 85-156959
HC180.W24 S25 1984

Socioeconomic aspects of renewable energy technologies . New York , 1988. p. cm. ISBN 0-275-92851-9 (alk. paper) : LC Card 87-22890 DDC 333.7/09172/4 19
HD9502.D442 S63 1988

World Employment Programme research working paper.
Peluso, Nancy Lee. Survival strategies of rural women traders, or, A woman's place is in the market . Geneva [1981], c1980. viii, 124 p. ; ISBN 92-2-102633-7 LC Card 83-105710 DDC 331.4/81381/095982 19
HD6194.Z6 S566 1981

World energy options.
Nuclear power . Chichester , New York , c1987. xvii, 416 p. : ISBN 0-471-90732-4 : LC Card 86-26714 DDC 333.79/24 19
HD9698.A2 N79 1987

World enough and time . Repetto, Robert C. New Haven , c1986. xiv, 147 p. ; ISBN 0-300-03648-5 LC Card 85-20180 DDC 333.7 19
HC59 .R43 1986 *NYPL [JLD 86-1434]*

World Fertility Survey : an assessment of its contribution / edited by John Cleland and Chris Scott. Oxford [Oxfordshire] ; New York : Published for ISI by Oxford University Press, 1986. p. cm. Bibliography: p. Includes index. ISBN 0-19-828525-6 : LC Card 86-23483 DDC 304.6/32/0732 19
1. World Fertility Survey. 2. Fertility, Human. 3. Demographic surveys. I. Cleland, J. G. (John G.). II. Scott, Christopher, 1927-.
HB901 .H664 1986

The World Food Conference : selected materials for the use of the U. S. Congressional Delegation to the World Food Conference, Rome, Italy, November 5-16, 1974 : compiled for the Subcommittee on Foreign Agricultural Policy of the Committee on Agriculture and Forestry, United States Senate. Washington : U. S. Govt. Print. Off., 1974. xv, 377 p. : ill. ; 26 cm. At head of title: 93d Congress, 2d session. Committee print. Errata slip inserted. Includes bibliographical references. LC Card 74-603025
1. Food - Congresses. 2. Food supply - Congresses. 3. Agriculture - Congresses. I. United States. Congressional Delegation to the World Food Conference. II. United States. Congress. Senate. Committee on Agriculture and Forestry. Subcommittee on Foreign Agricultural Policy.
TX345 .W58 *NYPL [JLF 78-685]*

World food marketing systems / edited by Erdener Kaynak. London ; Boston : Butterworths, 1986. xviii, 333 p. : ill. ; 24 cm. Includes bibliographies and index. ISBN 0-407-00358-4 : LC Card 85-28371 DDC 380.1/456413 19
1. Farm produce - Marketing - Case studies. 2. Food - Marketing - Case studies. I. Kaynak, Erdener.
HD9000.5 .W587 1986 *NYPL [JLE 86-3213]*

World food, population, and development / edited by Gigi M. Berardi. Totowa, N.J. : Rowman and Allanheld, 1985. xvi, 346 p. : ill. ; 25 cm. Includes bibliographies. ISBN 0-8476-7455-X : LC Card 85-14398 DDC 338.1/9 19
1. Food supply - Government policy. 2. Population policy. I. Berardi, Gigi M.
HD9000.5 .W59 1985 *NYPL [JLE 86-1741]*

World Food Programme. Yeraswork Admassie. Food-for-work in Ethiopia . Addis Abeba , 1985. viii, 102, [58] leaves : LC Card 86-980537 DDC 339.5/0963 19
HD5839.7.A6 Y47 1985

World futures. Europe in the contemporary world . New York , c1986. ix, 297 p. : ISBN 0-677-21520-7 (pbk.) LC Card 86-212695 DDC 330.94/0558 19
HC240 .E8176 1986

The world has definitely changed . Shilling, A. Gary. New York, NY (111 Broadway, Suite 1200, New York 10006) , 1986. xx, 179 p. : LC Card 86-82936 DDC 338.5/443/0973 19
HC106.8 .S49 1986

WORLD HEALTH.
Feeding the world's population . Washington , 1984. xii, 779 p. : LC Card 86-602524 DDC 363.8 19
HD9000.5 .F35 1986

World Health Organization. Maternal and Child Health Unit. Child labour and health . Bombay , c1985. xi, 287 p. ; LC Card 86-900928 DDC 331.3/1/0956 19
HD6250.I42 C46 1985 *NYPL [JLD 87-1553]*

World hunger and the world economy . Griffin, Keith B. New York , 1987. xvi, 274 p. ; ISBN 0-8419-1128-2 LC Card 86-33626 DDC 330.9172/4 19
HC59.7 .G749 1987

World industry studies .
(6) Mikesell, Raymond Frech. The world mining industry . Boston , 1987. p. cm. ISBN 0-04-338120-0 (alk. paper) LC Card 87-1763 DDC 338.2 19
HD9506.A2 M525 1987

World issues (Vero Beach, Fla.)
Gibb, Christopher. Food or famine? /. Vero Beach, FL , 1987. 48 p. : ISBN 0-86592-279-9 LC Card 87-12741 DDC 363.8/096 19
HC800.Z9 F335 1987

Gibson, Michael, 1942- The energy crisis /. Vero Beach, FL , 1987. 46 p. : ISBN 0-86592-277-2 LC Card 87-12768 DDC 333.79 19
HD9502.A2 G525 1987

McGraw, Eric. Population growth /. Vero Bleach, FL , 1987. 46 p. : ISBN 0-86592-276-4 LC Card 87-12729 DDC 304.6/2 19
HB871 .M325 1987

World labour report / International Labour Office. Oxford [Oxfordshire] : Clarendon Press ; New York : Oxford University Press, 1987. p. cm. "Abridged version of volumes 1 and 2 of the World labour report which were published by the ILO in 1984 and 1985"--P. ISBN 0-19-828561-2 : LC Card 87-22087 DDC 331 19
1. Labor supply. 2. Wages. 3. Social security. 4. Labor supply - Effect of technological innovations on. I. International Labour Office.
HD5706 .W68 1987

The World market for high technology industrial ceramics. New York, N.Y. : Find/SVP, [1985] 1 v. (various pagings) ; 29 cm. (A Business information report) "August 1985." Includes bibliography. ISBN 0-931634-52-0 (pbk.) LC Card 86-201912 DDC 382/.45666 19
1. Ceramic industries - Technological innovations. 2. High technology industries. 3. Strategic materials. 4. Market surveys. I. Find/SVP (Firm). II. Series.
HD9590.5 .W67 1985

The world mining industry . Mikesell, Raymond Frech. Boston , 1987. p. cm. ISBN 0-04-338120-0 (alk. paper) LC Card 87-1763 DDC 338.2 19
HD9506.A2 M525 1987

World monetary system in a time of change : articles of Hungarian scientists contributing to the Szirak-conference. Budapest : Pénzügykutatási Intézer, [1987] 283 p. ; 24 cm. (Pénzügykutatási Intézer tanulmányai, 0133-4198 . 1987/2) At head of title: Magyar Tudományos Akadémia. Világgazdasági Intézet. Includes bibliographies. ISBN 963-01-7937-7 (pbk.) LC Card 87-169001 DDC 332.4/5 19
1. Monetary policy - Congresses. 2. Foreign exchange problem - Congresses. 3. Balance of payments - Congresses. 4. Capital market - Congresses. 5. International finance - Congresses. I. Magyar Tudományos Akadémia. Világgazdasági Kutató Intézet. II. Series: Pénzügykutatási Intézet tanulmányai , 1987. 2. sz.
HG230.3 .W68 1987

World money and securities markets. Kemp, L. J. (Lynette J.) The Wardley guide to world money and securities markets /. London , 1984. xvii, 472 p. ; ISBN 0-903121-66-2
NYPL [JLG 86-203]

World nitrogen survey /. Sheldrick, William F. Washington, D.C. , 1987. xxv, 227 p. : ISBN 0-8213-0895-5 LC Card 87-6203 DDC 338.4/7668624 19
HD9660.N7 S55 1987

World of labour.
The World of labour.
Fawcett, Henry, 1833-1884. The economic position of the British labourer /. New York , 1984. vii, 256 p. ; ISBN 0-8240-5706-6 (alk. paper) : LC Card 83-48478 DDC 331/.0941 19
HD8390 .F28 1984 *NYPL [JLC 86-366]*

Ludlow, John Malcolm Forbes, 1821-1911. Progress of the working class, 1832-1867 /. New York , 1984. xv, 304 p. ; ISBN 0-8240-5717-1 (alk. paper) : LC Card 83-48490 DDC 305.5/62/0942 19
HD8390 .L93 1984 *NYPL [JLC 86-387]*

Rothstein, Theodore. From chartism to labourism /. New York , 1984. vi, 365 p. ; ISBN 0-8240-5722-8 (alk. paper) : LC Card 83-48495 DDC 335/.1 19
HX249 .R68 1984 *NYPL [JLD 86-1828]*

The world of the Industrial Revolution . Lowell Conference on Industrial History (1984) [Andover, MA] , 1986. 177 p. : ISBN 0-937474-08-8 (pbk.) LC Card 86-31242 DDC 338.09 19
HD2321 .L69 1984

The world of work . Dubin, Robert. New York , 1987. xiii, 448 p. : ISBN 0-8240-8204-4 (alk. paper) : LC Card 86-25791 DDC 306/.36 19
HD6955 .D817 1987

World offshore markets . Gregory, P. London , 1986. xiv, 215 p. ; ISBN 0-946416-06-0 (pbk.) : LC Card 86-217327 DDC 338.2/7282/0941 19
HD9571.5 .G75 1986

World paper money. Pick, Albert. Standard catalog of world paper money /. Iola, Wis. , München , c1986. 2 v. : ISBN 0-87341-087-4 (v. 1) LC Card 86-222186 DDC 769.5/5/075 19
HG353 .P543 1986

World patterns of modern urban change : essays in honor of Chauncy D. Harris / edited by Michael P. Conzen. Chicago : University of Chicago, Dept. of Geography, 1986. x, 479 p. : maps ; 23 cm. (Research paper / The University of Chicago, Department of Geography . no. 217-218) Includes bibliographical references. ISBN 0-89065-122-1 : LC Card 85-23231 DDC 910 s 307.7/6 19
1. Harris, Chauncy Dennison, 1914-. 2. Cities and towns - Addresses, essays, lectures. 3. Urbanization - Addresses, essays, lectures. 4. Anthropo-geography - Addresses, essays, lectures. I. Harris, Chauncy Dennison, 1914-. II. Cozen, Michael P. III. Series: Chicago. University. Dept. of geography. Research paper , no. 217-218.
H31 .C514 no.217-218
NYPL [JFM 72-132 no.217-218]

World peace and the developing countries :

annals of Pugwash 1985 / edited by Joseph Rotblat and Ubiratan D'Ambrosio. Basingstoke, Hampshire : Macmillan, 1986. xix, 272 p. ; 23 cm. Papers from several Pugwash meetings, held November 1984 to December 1985. Includes bibliographical references and index. ISBN 0-333-43636-9
1. Peace - Congresses. 2. Disarmament - Congresses. 3. Nuclear arms control. 4. Developing countries - Military policy - Congresses. I. Rotblat, Joseph, 1908-. II. D'Ambrósio, Ubiratan. III. Pugwash (Organization).
NYPL [JLD 87-1192]

World petrochemicals : a new competitive order : March 11-14, 1985, Hilton Palacio del Rio, San Antonio, Texas / CMRA, the Chemical Marketing Research Association, and ECMRA, the European Chemical Marketing Research Association. [Staten Island, N.Y. (139 Chestnut Ave., Staten Island 10305)] : CMRA, c1985. 279 p. : ill., maps ; 22 cm. "Papers presented at the March, 1985, Meeting of the Chemical Marketing Research Association and European Chemical Marketing Research Association held at the Hilton Palacio del Rio, San Antonio, Texas." LC Card 85-71088 DDC 338.4/7661804 19
1. Petroleum chemicals industry - Congresses. 2. Competition, International - Congresses. 3. International economic relations - Congresses. I. European Chemical Marketing Research Association. II. Chemical Marketing Research Association. Meeting (1985 : San Antonio, Tex.).
HD9579.C32 W68 1985
NYPL [JLD 86-2185]

World Policy Institute. Johansen, Robert C. Toward an alternative security system . New York, N.Y. , c1983. 57 p. ; ISBN 0-911646-12-5 (pbk.) : LC Card 83-215670 DDC 355/.03 19
UA10.5 .J64 1983

World policy paper .
(no. 24) Johansen, Robert C. Toward an alternative security system . New York, N.Y. , c1983. 57 p. ; ISBN 0-911646-12-5 (pbk.) : LC Card 83-215670 DDC 355/.03 19
UA10.5 .J64 1983

WORLD POLITICS.
Davidson, James Dale. Blood in the streets . New York , c1987. 386 p. ; ISBN 0-671-62735-X : LC Card 87-9935 DDC 332.6 19
HG4516 .D38 1987

Los problemas del socialismo en nuestra tiempo [microform]. México, 1944. 119 p. DDC 335.082
HX40 .P73 ***NYPL [*ZT-1711 no.21]***

R'emy, Ernst. La diplomatie . Port-au-Prince , 1983. 299 p. ; ***NYPL [Sc D 85-315]***

WORLD POLITICS - 20TH CENTURY.
Guiba (Writer) Por qué nos confunden-- el comunismo, el capitalismo, los economistas, las elites? /. Montevideo , 1981. 211 p. ; LC Card 82-125535 DDC 330.9/04 19
HC54 .G79 1981 ***NYPL [JLC 86-320]***

Johansen, Robert C. Toward an alternative security system . New York, N.Y. , c1983. 57 p. ; ISBN 0-911646-12-5 (pbk.) : LC Card 83-215670 DDC 355/.03 19
UA10.5 .J64 1983

Lieberman, Sima, 1927- The economic and political roots of the new protectionism /. Totowa, N.J. , 1987. p. cm. ISBN 0-8476-7595-5 LC Card 87-23329 DDC 382.7/3/09048 19
HF1411 .L533 1987

Ratiu, Ion. Moscow challenges the world /. London , 1986. 410 p. ; ISBN 0-907671-23-5
NYPL [JLE 87-1665]

Venn, Fiona. Oil diplomacy in the twentieth century /. Basingstoke, Hampshire , c1986. xii, 228 p. : ISBN 0-333-35781-7
NYPL [JLD 86-3415]

WORLD POLITICS - 20TH CENTURY - ADDRESSES, ESSAYS, LECTURES.
Cooperation under anarchy /. Princeton, N.J. , 1986. 260 p. ; ISBN 0-691-07695-2 : LC Card 85-42936 DDC 327.1/1 19
D445 .C736 1986 ***NYPL [JLE 86-1938]***

WORLD POLITICS - 1900-1945.
Von der Konkurrenz zur Rivalität . Stuttgart , 1986. 186 p. ; ISBN 3-515-04760-3 LC Card 87-134320 DDC 337/.09/04 19
HF1411 .V665 1986

WORLD POLITICS - 1919-1932.
Haigh, R. H. Soviet foreign policy, the League of Nations and Europe, 1917-39 /. Aldershot, Hants , 1986. x, 138 p. ;
NYPL [JFD 86-5778]

WORLD POLITICS - 1933-1945.
Bernstein Carabantes, Enrique. Recuerdos de un diplomático /. Santiago de Chile [1984- v. : LC Card 84-172336 DDC 327.83 19
F3099 .B43 1984 ***NYPL [JFL 84-297]***

Haigh, R. H. Soviet foreign policy, the League of Nations and Europe, 1917-39 /. Aldershot, Hants , 1986. x, 138 p. ;
NYPL [JFD 86-5778]

Smith, Bradley F. The war's long shadow . New York , c1986. 319 p. ; ISBN 0-671-52434-8 LC Card 86-1870 DDC 940.5 19
D749 .S65 1986 ***NYPL [JFD 86-9433]***

WORLD POLITICS - 1945-
Baade, Fritz, 1893- [Wettlauf zum Jahre 2000. English.] The race to the year 2000, our future. Garden City, N.Y., 1962. xix, 246 p. LC Card 62-7600 DDC 330.9/04 19
HC59 .B2513 1962

Bayo, Eliseo. Descubro y acuso /. Esplugues de Llobregat, Barcelona , 1985,c1984. 287 p. ; ISBN 84-01-33258-3 ***NYPL [JFD 86-7111]***

Bernstein Carabantes, Enrique. Recuerdos de un diplomático /. Santiago de Chile [1984- v. : LC Card 84-172336 DDC 327.83 19
F3099 .B43 1984 ***NYPL [JFL 84-297]***

Dahrendorf, Ralf. Die Chancen der Krise . Stuttgart , c1983. 240 p. ; ISBN 3-421-06148-3
NYPL [JFD 87-2528]

De Vos, Wouter. Point de mire . Antwerpen, Belgiëlai 147 a , 1977. 125 p. : ISBN 90-02-01132-6 : LC Card 78-370280 DDC 309.1
HC59 .D464 ***NYPL [JLD 80-3135]***

Helmreich, Jonathan E. Gathering rare ores . Princeton, N.J. , c1986. xiv, 303 p. : ISBN 0-691-04738-3 (alk. paper) : LC Card 86-4862 DDC 327.1/11 19
HD9698.U52 H45 1986
NYPL [JLE 86-4584]

Kolodziej, Edward A. Making and marketing arms . Princeton, N.J. , c1987. xxv, 518 p. : ISBN 0-691-07734-7 (alk. paper) : LC Card 86-30567 DDC 338.4/76234/0944 19
HD9743.F82 K64 1987

Palánkai, Tibor. Gazdasági hadviselés a kölcsönös függés korszakában /. [Budapest] , 1985. 88 p. ; ISBN 963-09-2633-4 : LC Card 86-128423
HF1413.5 .P35 1985

Rice-Maximin, Edward Francis, 1941- Accomodation and resistance . New York , 1986. xi, 175 p. ; ISBN 0-313-25355-2 (lib. bdg. : alk. paper) LC Card 86-4624 DDC 959.704/1 19
DS553.1 .R53 1986 ***NYPL [JFE 87-1024]***

Rosecrance, Richard N. The rise of the trading state . New York , c1986. xiii, 268 p. : ISBN 0-465-07035-3 : LC Card 85-47558 DDC 382/.09/04 19
HF1007 .R549 1985 ***NYPL [JLE 86-951]***

Stern, Jonathan P. Soviet oil and gas exports to the West . Aldershot, Hants, England , Brookfield, Vt., USA , c1987. xi, 123 p. : ISBN 0-566-05124-9 : LC Card 86-32772 DDC 382/.4228/0947 19
HD9575.S652 S74 1987

Targ, Harry R., 1940- Strategy of an empire in decline . Minneapolis , c1986. 294 p. ; ISBN 0-930656-47-4 : LC Card 86-16338 DDC 909.82 19
D849 .T37 1986 ***NYPL [JFD 87-2032]***

Towle, Philip, 1945- Protest and perish . London , 1982. 121 p. ; ISBN 0-907967-02-7 (pbk.) : LC Card 83-198296 DDC 355/.0217/0941 19
UA647 .T69 1982 ***NYPL [JLD 86-1904]***

Williams, Geoffrey Lee. Global defence . New Delhi , c1984. xlvi, 366 p. ; ISBN 0-7069-2478-9 : LC Card 84-900260 DDC 355/.0335 19
UA11 .W55 1984 ***NYPL [JLD 86-3709]***

Wirtschaftssanktionen im Ost-West-Verhältnis . Baden-Baden , 1983. 234 p. : ISBN 3-7890-0963-6 LC Card 84-132150
HF1413.5 .W57 1983

WORLD POLITICS - 1945- - ADDRESSES, ESSAYS, LECTURES.
Gonella, Guido, 1905- Contestazioni /. Roma , 1983. 3 v. ; LC Card 84-237282 DDC 945.092 19
JN5451 .G57 1983 ***NYPL [JFE 86-1367]***

WORLD POLITICS - 1945-1955.
Smith, Bradley F. The war's long shadow . New York , c1986. 319 p. ; ISBN 0-671-52434-8 LC Card 86-1870 DDC 940.5 19
D749 .S65 1986 ***NYPL [JFD 86-9433]***

WORLD POLITICS - 1975-1985.
Achminow, Herman F., 1921- Am grossen Krieg "vorbeischleichen"? . Bonn , c1983. 304 p. ; ISBN 3-923920-00-8 LC Card 84-150915 DDC 355/.03304 19
UA646 .A38 1983 ***NYPL [JFD 87-1743]***

Escalation and intervention . Boulder, Colo. , 1986. x, 181 p. ; ISBN 0-8133-7200-3 : LC Card 86-4020 DDC 327.1/6 19
U104 .E83 1986 ***NYPL [JLE 86-4131]***

Linden, Ronald Haly. Communist states and international change . Boston , c1987. xviii, 201 p. ; ISBN 0-04-497050-1 : LC Card 87-11389 DDC 337.497 19
HF1581 .L56 1987

Targ, Harry R., 1940- Strategy of an empire in decline . Minneapolis , c1986. 294 p. ; ISBN 0-930656-47-4 : LC Card 86-16338 DDC 909.82 19
D849 .T37 1986 ***NYPL [JFD 87-2032]***

Vance, A. Last chance for peace . Boulder, Colo. , c1985. xviii, 256 p. : ISBN 0-930705-01-7 (pbk.) : LC Card 84-18831 DDC 172/.24 19
BL65.P4 V36 1985 ***NYPL [JLD 86-2214]***

Wettig, Gerhard. Konflikt und Kooperation zwischen Ost und West . Bonn , c1981. 217 p. ; ISBN 3-7894-0082-3 LC Card 82-225671 DDC 327.1/7 19
D849 .W47 1981 ***NYPL [JLE 86-4503]***

WORLD POLITICS - 1975-1985 - ADDRESSES, ESSAYS, LECTURES.
The Second cold war /. New Delhi , 1983. vi, 215 p. ; LC Card 84-900004 DDC 355/.033/0047 19
UA10 .S38 1983 ***NYPL [JFD 87-1657]***

WORLD POLITICS - 1975-1985 - CONGRESSES.
A 80-as évek kapitalizmusa . [Budapest] , 1985. 406 p. ; ISBN 963-09-2696-2 : LC Card 86-186468
HB501 .A14 1985

WORLD POLITICS - 1985-1995.
Brandt, Willy, 1913- [Organisierte Wahnsinn. English.] Arms and hunger /. Cambridge, Mass. , 1987, c1986. 208 p. ; ISBN 0-262-52127-X (pbk.) LC Card 87-4057 DDC 330.9172/4 19
HC59.7 .B67713 1987

World population and the United Nations . Johnson, Stanley, 1940- Cambridge [Cambridgeshire] , New York , 1987. xxxviii, 357 p. ; ISBN 0-521-32207-3 LC Card 87-5126 DDC 363.9 19
HB884.5 .J64 1987

WORLD POPULATION CONFERENCE (3RD : 1974 : BUCHAREST, ROMANIA)
Wereldbevolking groeiend ontwikkelingsprobleem. Den Haag [1975] 66 p. : LC Card 87-118557
HB883.5 .W47 1975

World population projections, 1985 . Vu, My T., 1939- Baltimore , 1985. xxvi, 451 p. ; ISBN 0-8018-3322-1 LC Card 85-23083 DDC 304.6 19
HA155 .V83 1985
NYPL [*R-Econ. 86-3764]

World population prospects : estimates and projections as assessed in 1984 / Department of International Economic and Social Affairs. New York : United Nations, 1986. x, 330 p. : ill. ; 28 cm. (Population studies . no. 98) "ST/ESA/SER.A/98." "United Nations publication. Sales no. E.86.XIII.3"--T.p. verso. Bibliography: p. 41-42. ISBN 92-1-151159-3 (pbk.) LC Card 87-104085 DDC 304.6/2/021 19
1. Population - Statistics. 2. Population forecasting. I. United Nations. Dept. of International Economic and Social Affairs. II. Series: Population studies (New York,

N.Y.) , no. 98.
HA155 .W693 1986

World prices and development / edited by Stephany Griffith-Jones and Charles Harvey. Aldershot, Hants, England ; Brookfield, Vt., U.S.A. : Gower, c1985. xi, 377 p. : ill. ; 23 cm. Includes bibliographies and index. ISBN 0-566-00890-4 LC Card 86-134604 DDC 338.5/2/0971724 19
1. Prices - Developing countries. 2. Developing countries - Economic conditions. I. Griffith-Jones, Stephany. II. Harvey, Charles, M.A.
HC59.7 .W684 1985 ***NYPL [JLD 86-4068]***

World recession and the food crisis in Africa / edited by Peter Lawrence. London : Review of African Political Economy : J. Currey, 1986. 314 p. ; 25 cm. "Presented as papers to the Review of African Political Economy Conference ... which took place at the University of Keele, England, in September 1984"--Pref. Includes bibliographies and index. ISBN 0-85255-309-9 : LC Card 86-235333 DDC 363.8/526/096 19
1. Food supply - Africa - Congresses. 2. Africa - Economic conditions - 1960- - Congresses. 3. International Monetary Fund - Africa - Congresses. 4. World Bank - Africa - Congresses. 5. Economic assistance - Africa - Congresses. I. Lawrence, Peter R. II. Review of African Political Economy Conference (1984 : University of Keele).
HD9017.A2 W67 1986b

World recession and the food crisis in Africa / [edited by] Peter Lawrence. Boulder : Westview Press, 1986. p. cm. Bibliography: p. Includes index. ISBN 0-8133-0511-X : LC Card 86-28250 DDC 363.8/526/096 19
1. Food supply - Africa - Congresses. 2. Economic assistance - Africa - Congresses. 3. International Monetary Fund - Africa - Congresses. 4. World Bank - Africa - Congresses. 5. Africa - Economic conditions - 1960- - Congresses. I. Lawrence, Peter R.
HD9017.A2 W67 1986

World Resources Institute. Pearson, Charles S. Down to business . Washington, DC (1735 New York Ave., NW, Washington, DC 20006) , c1985. vii, 107 p. ; ISBN 0-915825-04-X (pbk.) : LC Card 84-52795
HD69.P6 P42 1985 ***NYPL [JLE 86-3186]***

World Resources Institute report, 0880-2582. Myers, Norman. Not far afield . Washington, DC , c1987. vi, 73 p. : ISBN 0-915825-24-4 (pbk.): LC Card 87-50723 DDC 333.7/09172/4 19
HC59.72.E5 M93 1987

The world shipping industry /. Frankel, Ernst G. London , New York , c1987. xix, 261 p. : ISBN 0-7099-1087-8 LC Card 87-3608 DDC 387.5 19
HE571 .F7 1987

The World socialist economy. Moscow : "Social Sciences Today" Editorial Board, USSR Academy of Sciences, 1986. 279 p. ; 21 cm. ("Soviet economic science" series . 1) Title in colophon: Mirovoe sotsialisticheskoe khoziaistvo. Bibliography: p. 261-[271]. LC Card 86-231463 DDC 338.9/009171/7 19
1. Communist countries - Economic policy. 2. Marxian economics. 3. Council for Mutual Economic Assistance. I. Izdatel´stvo Nauka. Redaktsiia "Obshchestvennye nauki i sovremennost´.". II. Title: Mirovoe sotsialisticheskoe khoziaistvo. III. Series.
HC704 .W67 1986

World Tourism Organization. Jackson, Ivor L. Study of the pleasure boat industry in the British Virgin Islands with emphasis on charter boats /. [S.l. , 1981?] viii, 89 p. :
NYPL [JLF 85-543]

World trade in a primary commodity . Ahmad, Qazi Kholiquzzaman, 1943- Nyon, Switzerland , 1979. i, 83 p. ; LC Card 86-202627
HD9156.J7 A38 1979

World trade in forest products, 2 / edited by Gerard F. Schreuder. Seattle : University of Washington Press, c1986. xi, 362 p. : ill. ; 26 cm. (The Geo. S. Long publication series) "Proceedings of the Second International Symposium on World Trade in Forest Products held at the University of Washington, March 19-21, 1985"--P. V. Includes bibliographies and index. ISBN 0-295-96337-9 LC Card 86-234388 DDC 382/.41498 19
1. Forest products industry - Congresses. 2. Lumber trade - Congresses. I. Schreuder, Gerard F. II. International Symposium on World Trade in Forest Products (2nd : 1985 : University of Washington).
HD9750.5 .W67 1986

World trade in fresh oranges . Dean, Gerald W. Berkeley, Calif. [1967] 70 p. : LC Card 87-401008 DDC 338.1/09794 s 382/.41431 19
HD1407 .C27 no. 18 HD9259.O7

World trade rivalry . Lovett, William Anthony. Lexington, Mass. , c1987. xxxv, 260 p. : ISBN 0-669-11027-2 (alk. paper) LC Card 85-40388 DDC 382/.3 19
HF1008 .L68 1987

World War debts and United States foreign policy, 1919-1929 /. Pullen, William George. New York , 1987. 157 p. ; ISBN 0-8240-8088-2 : LC Card 87-23789 DDC 337.7304 19
HF1456.5.E8 P84 1987

World War I and the growth of United States predominance in Latin America /. Rosenberg, Emily S., 1944- New York , 1987. p. cm. ISBN 0-8240-8089-0 : LC Card 87-23683 DDC 337.7308 19
HF1456.5.L3 R67 1987

WORLD WAR - SOVIET UNION - EQUIPMENT AND SUPPLIES.
Nikitin, V. V. (Vasiliĭ Vasil´evich) Goriûchee--frontu, 1941-1945 /. Moskva , 1984. 203 p. : LC Card 85-152473
HD9575.S652 N55 1984

WORLD WAR, 1914-1918.
Chesterton, Gilbert Keith, 1874-1936. [Crimes of England. French.] Les crimes de l'Angleterre [microform]. Paris, 1916. 273 p. LC Card 19-16286
DA47.2 .C55 ***NYPL [*Z-4049 no.7]***

Doumergue, Émile, 1844-1937. La paix par la vérité [microform]. Paris, 1922-1924. 2 v. LC Card 26-3809
D511 .D67 ***NYPL [*Z-4048 no. 1]***

WORLD WAR, 1914-1918 - BIOGRAPHY.
Davis, Burke, 1913- War bird . Chapel Hill , c1987. viii, 267 p., [26] p. of plates : ISBN 0-8078-1752-X (alk. paper) LC Card 87-5934 DDC 338.7/67721/0924 B 19
HD9880.S67 D38 1987

WORLD WAR, 1914-1918 - CAUSES.
Doumergue, Émile, 1844-1937. La paix par la vérité [microform]. Paris, 1922-1924. 2 v. LC Card 26-3809
D511 .D67 ***NYPL [*Z-4048 no. 1]***

Von der Konkurrenz zur Rivalität . Stuttgart , 1986. 186 p. ; ISBN 3-515-04760-3 LC Card 87-134320 DDC 337/.09/04 19
HF1411 .V665 1986

WORLD WAR, 1914-1918 - CHILE.
Couyoumdjian, Juan Ricardo. Chile y Gran Bretaña . [Santiago] [1986] xvi, 340 p., [4] p. of plates : LC Card 86-222403
HF1516.5.G72 C68 1986

WORLD WAR, 1914-1918 - ECONOMIC ASPECTS.
Noyes, Alexander Dana, 1862-1945. Financial chapters of the war [microform]. New York, 1916. xi, 255 p. LC Card 16-19959
D635 .N6 ***NYPL [*ZT-1735 no.5]***

WORLD WAR, 1914-1918 - ECONOMIC ASPECTS - GREAT BRITAIN.
Collings, Jesse, 1831-1920. The great war, its lessons and its warnings [microform]. London [1915] 113 p. LC Card 16-1094
HC256.2 .C55 ***NYPL [*Z-4053 no.6]***

Grieves, Keith. The politics of manpower, 1914-1918 /. New York, NY , 1988. vii, 241 p. ; ISBN 0-312-01320-5 LC Card 87-20511 DDC 331.12/042/0941 19
HD5765.A6 G77 1988

WORLD WAR, 1914-1918 - FINANCE.
Noyes, Alexander Dana, 1862-1945. Financial chapters of the war [microform]. New York, 1916. xi, 255 p. LC Card 16-19959
D635 .N6 ***NYPL [*ZT-1735 no.5]***

WORLD WAR, 1914-1918 - FINANCE - EUROPE.
Pullen, William George. World War debts and United States foreign policy, 1919-1929 /. New York , 1987. 157 p. ; ISBN 0-8240-8088-2 : LC Card 87-23789 DDC 337.7304 19
HF1456.5.E8 P84 1987

WORLD WAR, 1914-1918 - FINANCE - UNITED STATES.
Pullen, William George. World War debts and United States foreign policy, 1919-1929 /. New York , 1987. 157 p. ; ISBN 0-8240-8088-2 : LC Card 87-23789 DDC 337.7304 19
HF1456.5.E8 P84 1987

WORLD WAR, 1914-1918 - FOOD SUPPLY - AUSTRIA.
Loewenfeld-Russ, Hans, 1873-1945. Im Kampf gegen den Hunger . München , 1986. xxiv, 381 p., [1] leaf of plates : ISBN 3-486-52451-8 LC Card 86-224948
HC270.F3 L64 1986

WORLD WAR, 1914-1918 - GREAT BRITAIN.
Couyoumdjian, Juan Ricardo. Chile y Gran Bretaña . [Santiago] [1986] xvi, 340 p., [4] p. of plates : LC Card 86-222403
HF1516.5.G72 C68 1986

WORLD WAR, 1914-1918 - INFLUENCE.
Egea Bruno, Pedro María. La minería cartagenera en torno a la primera guerra mundial, 1909-1923 /. [Murcia] , 1983. 76 p. : ISBN 84-86031-30-3 LC Card 85-199662
HD9506.S762 C374 1983

Rosenberg, Emily S., 1944- World War I and the growth of United States predominance in Latin America /. New York , 1987. p. cm. ISBN 0-8240-8089-0 : LC Card 87-23683 DDC 337.7308 19
HF1456.5.L3 R67 1987

WORLD WAR, 1914-1918 - POSTAL SERVICE.
Emery, R. C. The postal history of the Australian Imperial Forces during World War One, 1914-1918 /. Worthing, West Sussex, England [1984] viii, 343 p. : LC Card 85-123155 DDC 355.3/41 19
HE7395 .E47 1984 ***NYPL [JLF 86-1054]***

Silverberg, René. Le courrier des militaires belges internés aux Pays-Bas et en Suisse 1914-1919, et essai de classement des marques néerlandaises de censure et autres /. Bruxelles , 1978. 154 p. : LC Card 80-452392 DDC 769.56/7
HE6184.C3 S55 ***NYPL [JFD 81-1659]***

WORLD WAR, 1914-1918 - REPARATIONS.
McNeil, William C. American money and the Weimar Republic . New York , 1986. x, 352 p. : ISBN 0-231-06236-2 LC Card 85-29962 DDC 336.3/4/0943 19
HG3949 .M38 1986 ***NYPL [JLE 86-3268]***

WORLD WAR, 1914-1918 - SOCIAL ASPECTS - GREAT BRITAIN.
Winter, J. M. The great war and the British people /. Basingstoke, Hampshire , 1986, c1985. xiv, 360 p. : ISBN 0-333-26582-3
NYPL [JLD 86-1426]

WORLD WAR, 1914-1918 - TRANSPORTATION.
Hines, Walker Downer, 1870-1934. War history of American railroads /. [S.l.] , 1974. xviii, 327 p. : LC Card 74-75240 ***NYPL [JLD 87-638]***

WORLD WAR, 1914-1918 - WOMEN - GREAT BRITAIN.
Braybon, Gail. Out of the cage . London , New York , 1987. xiii, 330 p. : ISBN 0-86358-046-7 : LC Card 87-13510 DDC 305.4/0941 19
HD6135 .B7 1987

WORLD WAR, 1939-1945 - BIOGRAPHY.
Chuĭkov, V. I. (Vasiliĭ Ivanovich), 1900- Ot Stalingrada do Berlina /. Moskva , 1985. 699 p. : ***NYPL [*QGR 87-2179]***

Goldman, Peter Louis, 1933- The end of the world that was . New York , c1986. xiv, 129 p., [8] p. of plates : ISBN 0-525-24428-X LC Card 85-31223 DDC 920/.073 19
CT220 .G6 1986 ***NYPL [JFD 86-6015]***

Kapferer, Clodwig, 1901- Ein Leben für die Information . Zürich , 1983. 116 p. ; ISBN 3-906639-00-X LC Card 83-185401
HC282.5.K36 A3 1983

WORLD WAR, 1939-1945 - CAUSES.
Haigh, R. H. Soviet foreign policy, the League of Nations and Europe, 1917-39 /. Aldershot, Hants , 1986. x, 138 p. ;
NYPL [JFD 86-5778]

WORLD WAR, 1939-1945 - CONSCRIPT LABOR - GERMANY.
Herrenmensch und Arbeitsvölker . Berlin , c1986. 189 p. : ISBN 3-88022-952-X (cover); 3-88022-925-X : LC Card 87-119712 DDC

331.11/732/0943 19
HD4875.G4 H47 1986

WORLD WAR, 1939-1945 - DIPLOMATIC HISTORY.
Smith, Bradley F. The war's long shadow . New York , c1986. 319 p. ; ISBN 0-671-52434-8 LC Card 86-1870 DDC 940.5 19
D749 .S65 1986 *NYPL [JFD 86-9433]*

WORLD WAR, 1939-1945 - ECONOMIC ASPECTS - GERMANY.
Boelcke, Willi A. Die Kosten von Hitlers Krieg . Paderborn , c1985. 220 p. : ISBN 3-506-77471-9 LC Card 86-143362
HJ1119 .B66 1985

Eichholtz, Dietrich. Geschichte der deutschen Kriegswirtschaft 1939-1945. Berlin, 1969-<1985. v. <1-2 > LC Card 70-444798
HC286.4 .E34

WORLD WAR, 1939-1945 - ECONOMIC ASPECTS - GREAT BRITAIN.
Barnett, Correlli. The pride and the fall . New York , 1987, c1986. xii, 359 p. ; ISBN 0-02-901851-X LC Card 86-25701 DDC 330.941/0854 19
HC256.4 .B28 1987

WORLD WAR, 1939-1945 - ECONOMIC ASPECTS - MOLDAVIAN S.S.R.
Shornikov, P. M. (Petr Mikhaĭlovich) Promyshlennost′ i rabochiĭ klass Moldavskoĭ SSR v gody Velikoĭ Otechestvennoĭ voĭny /. Kishinev , 1986. 148, [4] p. ; LC Card 86-141169
HC337.M553 D47 1986

WORLD WAR, 1939-1945 - ECONOMIC ASPECTS - SOVIET UNION.
Main, V. N. (Valentin Nikolaevich) Sel′skaia intelligentsiia v gody Velikoĭ Otechestvennoĭ voĭny . Voronezh , 1985. 158 p. ; LC Card 84-172657
HC340.D4 M35 1985

WORLD WAR, 1939-1945 - ECONOMIC ASPECTS - SOVIET UNION, WESTERN - CONGRESSES.
Vozrozhdenie prifrontovykh i osvobozhdennykh raĭonov SSSR v gody Velikoĭ Otechestvennoĭ voĭny 1941-1945 /. Moskva , 1986. 214 p., [24] p. of plates : LC Card 86-232256
HC336.9.W47 V69 1986

WORLD WAR, 1939-1945 - ECONOMIC ASPECTS - SWITZERLAND.
Tanner, Jakob. Bundeshaushalt, Währung und Kriegswirtschaft . Zürich , c1986. 438 p. : ISBN 3-85791-100-X : LC Card 86-199729
HJ1258 .T35 1986

WORLD WAR, 1939-1945 - ECONOMIC ASPECTS - TAJIK S.S.R.
Narodnoe khoziaĭstvo Tadzhikistana v gody Velikoĭ Otechestvennoĭ voĭny . Dushanbe , 1980. 169, [3] p. ; LC Card 81-130944
HC337.T233 D45 1980

WORLD WAR, 1939-1945 - ECONOMIC ASPECTS - UKRAINE.
V bitvakh za sovetskuiu Ukrainu . Kiev , 1985. 172 p. ; LC Card 85-170194
HC337.U53 D48 1985

WORLD WAR, 1939-1945 - ECONOMIC ASPECTS - YUGOSLAVIA - CROATIA - CONGRESSES.
Kongres privrednih stručnjaka Hrvatske (1943-1944 : Otočac and Čazma, Croatia) Kongres privrednih stručnjaka Hrvatske . Zagreb , 1985. 252 p., [16] p. of plates : ISBN 86-80359-01-7 LC Card 86-176200
HC407.Z7 C7637 1943

WORLD WAR, 1939-1945 - ECONOMIC ASPECTS - YUGOSLAVIA - SERBIA.
Schlarp, Karl-Heinz. Wirtschaft und Besatzung in Serbien, 1941-1944 . Stuttgart , 1986. viii, 443 p., [6] p. of plates : ISBN 3-515-04401-9 LC Card 86-181062
HC407.Z7 S46676 1986

WORLD WAR, 1939-1945 - FINANCE - GERMANY.
Boelcke, Willi A. Die Kosten von Hitlers Krieg . Paderborn , c1985. 220 p. : ISBN 3-506-77471-9 LC Card 86-143362
HJ1119 .B66 1985

WORLD WAR, 1939-1945 - GERMANY - EQUIPMENT AND SUPPLIES.
Siegfried, Klaus-Jörg, 1940- Rüstungsproduktion und Zwangsarbeit im Volkswagenwerk, 1939-1945 . Frankfurt , New York , c1986. 239 p. : ISBN 3-593-33765-7 LC Card 87-133375 DDC 338.4/76234/0943 19
HD9743.G48 S56 1986

WORLD WAR, 1939-1945 - GREECE - ATHENS.
Maroudēs, Giōrgos. To hēmerologio tēs peinas /. [Athens] , 1976. 99 p., [6] leaves of plates ; LC Card 84-107778
HC300.F3 M37 1976

WORLD WAR, 1939-1945 - INFLUENCE.
Goldman, Peter Louis, 1933- The end of the world that was . New York , c1986. xiv, 129 p., [8] p. of plates : ISBN 0-525-24428-X LC Card 85-31223 DDC 920/.073 19
CT220 .G6 1986 *NYPL [JFD 86-6015]*

Smith, Bradley F. The war's long shadow . New York , c1986. 319 p. ; ISBN 0-671-52434-8 LC Card 86-1870 DDC 940.5 19
D749 .S65 1986 *NYPL [JFD 86-9433]*

WORLD WAR, 1939-1945 - MANPOWER - UNITED STAES - HISTORY.
Fairchild, Byron. The Army and industrial manpower /. Westport, Conn. , 1987. xiv, 291 p. : ISBN 0-313-25480-X (lib. bdg. : alk. paper) LC Card 86-25738 DDC 331.11/0973 19
HD5724 .F25 1987

WORLD WAR, 1939-1945 - PERSONAL NARRATIVES, GREEK.
Maroudēs, Giōrgos. To hēmerologio tēs peinas /. [Athens] , 1976. 99 p., [6] leaves of plates ; LC Card 84-107778
HC300.F3 M37 1976

WORLD WAR, 1939-1945 - PERSONAL NARRATIVES, RUSSIAN.
Chuĭkov, V. I. (Vasiliĭ Ivanovich), 1900- Ot Stalingrada do Berlina /. Moskva , 1985. 699 p. : *NYPL [*QGR 87-2179]*

WORLD WAR, 1939-1945 - PRISONERS AND PRISONS, GERMAN.
Weidner, Marcus, 1964- Nur Gräber als Spuren . Münster , c1984. 134 p. : ISBN 3-924550-02-6 LC Card 86-116688 DDC 331.11/732/094355 19
HD4875.G4 W45 1984

WORLD WAR, 1939-1945 - RECONSTRUCTION. see **RECONSTRUCTION (1939-1951)**

WORLD WAR, 1939-1945 - RESISTANCE MOVEMENTS. see **ANTI-NAZI MOVEMENT.**

WORLD WAR, 1939-1945 - RUSSIAN S.F.S.R. - URAL MOUNTAINS REGION.
Vasil′ev, A. F. (Aleksandr Filippovich) Promyshlennost′ Urala v gody Velikoĭ Otechestvennoĭ voĭny 1941-1945 /. Moskva , 1982. 279 p., [1] folded leaf of plates : LC Card 83-165021
HC337.R852 U7387 1982

WORLD WAR, 1939-1945 - SOVIET UNION.
Chuĭkov, V. I. (Vasiliĭ Ivanovich), 1900- Ot Stalingrada do Berlina /. Moskva , 1985. 699 p. : *NYPL [*QGR 87-2179]*

WORLD WAR, 1939-1945 - UKRAINE.
V bitvakh za sovetskuiu Ukrainu . Kiev , 1985. 172 p. ; LC Card 85-170194
HC337.U53 D48 1985

WORLD WAR, 1939-1945 - WOMEN - CALIFORNIA - LOS ANGELES.
Gluck, Sherna Berger. Rosie the Riveter revisited . Boston , c1987. xiii, 282 p. : ISBN 0-8057-9022-5 (alk. paper) LC Card 86-31852 DDC 331.4/0973 19
HD6073.A452 U64 1987

WORLD WAR, 1939-1945 - WOMEN - GREAT BRITAIN.
Braybon, Gail. Out of the cage . London , New York , 1987. xiii, 330 p. : ISBN 0-86358-046-7 : LC Card 87-13510 DDC 305.4/0941 19
HD6135 .B7 1987

World-wide solar electric generation market. The Worldwide solar electric generation market. New York, N.Y. , c1983. 2 v. (vii, 596 p.) : LC Card 87-401676 DDC 382/.4562131244 19
HD9681.A2 W67 1983

Worldly power . Scharff, Edward E. New York , 1987, c1986. p. cm. ISBN 0-452-25917-7 (pbk.) LC Card 86-28562 DDC 071/.47/1 19
HG4910 .S3 1987

WORLD'S FAIRS. see **EXHIBITIONS.**

Worlds of labour . Hobsbawm, E. J. (Eric J.), 1917- London , c1984. x, 369 p., [4] p. of plates : ISBN 0-297-78509-5 : LC Card 86-674019
HD8388 .H63x 1984

Worldwatch Institute. Brown, Lester Russell, 1934- Our demographically divided world /. Washington, D.C. , c1986. 54 p. : ISBN 0-916468-75-5 (pbk.) LC Card 86-51475 DDC 304.6 19
HB871 .B744 1986

Worldwatch paper .
(74) Brown, Lester Russell, 1934- Our demographically divided world /. Washington, D.C. , c1986. 54 p. : ISBN 0-916468-75-5 (pbk.) LC Card 86-51475 DDC 304.6 19
HB871 .B744 1986

Worldwide remote power sites. New York, N.Y. : Frost & Sullivan, c1983. 2 v. (xx, xxvii, 500 p.) : 29 cm. Spine title: Worldwide remote site power systems. "January, 1983." "W 563." LC Card 87-141748
1. Electric power plant equipment industry. 2. Electric power conservation equipment industry. 3. Solar energy industries. 4. Wind power industry. 5. Tidal power industry. 6. Renewable energy sources. 7. Market surveys. I. Frost & Sullivan. II. Title: Worldwide remote site power systems.
HD9695.A2 W67 1983

Worldwide remote site power systems. Worldwide remote power sites. New York, N.Y. , c1983. 2 v. (xx, xxvii, 500 p.) : LC Card 87-141748
HD9695.A2 W67 1983

The Worldwide solar electric generation market. New York, N.Y. : Frost & Sullivan, c1983. 2 v. (vii, 596 p.) : ill. ; 29 cm. Spine title: Worldwide solar thermal electric generation. "August 1983." Bibliography: p. 595-596. "#W559." LC Card 87-401676 DDC 382/.4562131244 19
1. Solar energy industries. 2. Market surveys. I. Frost & Sullivan. II. Title: World-wide solar electric generation market. III. Title: Worldwide solar thermal electric generation.
HD9681.A2 W67 1983

Worldwide solar thermal electric generation. The Worldwide solar electric generation market. New York, N.Y. , c1983. 2 v. (vii, 596 p.) : LC Card 87-401676 DDC 382/.4562131244 19
HD9681.A2 W67 1983

Worldwide telecommunications guide for the business manager /. Vignault, Walter L. New York , c1987. xvi, 417 p. : ISBN 0-471-85828-5 LC Card 87-2002 DDC 384 19
HF5541.T4 V54 1987

Worley, Rebecca B., 1946- Bogert, Judith B. W., 1941- Managing business communciations . Englewood Cliffs, NJ , c1988. xiv, 434 p. : ISBN 0-13-548629-7 (pbk.) : LC Card 87-3568 DDC 658.4/5 19
HF5718 .B597 1988

Woronoff, Denis, 1939- L'industrie sidérurgique en France pendant la Révolution et l'Empire / Denis Woronoff ; préface d'Ernest Labrousse. Paris : Editions de l'Ecole des hautes études en sciences sociales, c1984. 592 p. : ill. ; 24 cm. (Civilisations et sociétés. 71) One folded map laid in. Includes indexes. Bibliography: p. 546-556. ISBN 2-7132-0843-2 LC Card 85-138825 DDC 338.4/76691/0944 19
1. Iron industry and trade - France - History - 18th century. 2. Iron industry and trade - France - History - 19th century. 3. Steel industry and trade - France - History - 18th century. 4. Steel industry and trade - France - History - 19th century. I. Title. II. Series.
HD9522.5 .W64 1984 *NYPL [JLE 86-3532]*

Woronoff, Jon. Japan's commercial empire / by Jon Woronoff. Armonk, N.Y. : M.E. Sharpe, c1984. 415 p. : ill. ; 22 cm. Includes index. Bibliography: p. [405]-407. ISBN 0-87332-312-2 LC Card 84-22146 DDC 337.52 19
1. Investments, Japanese. 2. Corporations, Japanese. 3. Japan - Foreign economic relations. I. Title.
HF1601 .W66 1984 *NYPL [JLD 87-761]*

Worrell, DeLisle. Small island economies : structure and performance in the English-speaking Caribbean since 1970 / DeLisle Worrell. New York : Praeger, 1987. xiv, 289 p. : ill. ; 25 cm. Bibliography: p. [281]-284. Includes index. ISBN 0-275-92795-4 (alk. paper) : LC Card 87-12495 DDC 330.9729/052 19

1. Caribbean Area - Economic conditions - 1945-. I. Title.
HC151 .W67 1987

The Worst of times : an oral history of the great depression in Britain / [compiled by] Nigel Gray ; preface by Richard Hoggart. London : Wildwood House, 1985. 201 p., [8] p. of plates : ill. ; 23 cm. ISBN 0-7045-0513-4
1. Great Britain - Economic conditions - 1918-1945. 2. Labor and laboring classes - Great Britain - History - 20th century. 3. Poor - Great Britain - History - 20th century. 4. Depressions - 1929 - Great Britain.
NYPL [JLD 86-1799]

Wörterbuch für Recht, Wirtschaft und Politik. Erdsiek, Gerhard. Bleckede bei Hamburg [1964-1968] 2 v. LC Card 65-42077
NYPL [JLE 85-408]

WORTH. see **VALUES.**

The worth of women's work . Statham, Anne. Albany , c1988. xiv, 331 p. ; ISBN 0-88706-591-0 LC Card 87-6472 DDC 331.4/0973 19
HD6095 .S73 1988

Worthy, James C. William C. Norris : portrait of a maverick / James C. Worthy. Cambridge, Mass. : Ballinger Pub. Co., c1987. xiv, 259 p. : ill. ; 24 cm. Bibliography: p. [231]-250. Includes index. ISBN 0-88730-087-1 LC Card 87-1808 DDC 338.7/61004/0924 B 19
1. Norris, William C., 1911-. 2. Control Data Corporation - History. 3. Computer industry - United States - History. 4. Businessmen - United States - Biography. I. Title.
HD9696.C62 N689 1987

Wortman, Leon A.
C programming with business applications / Leon A. Wortman and Thomas O. Sidebottom. 1st ed. Blue Ridge Summit, PA : TAB Books, c1987. xii, 231 p. ; 25 cm. "No. 2857." Includes index. ISBN 0-8306-1457-5 : LC Card 86-23090 DDC 005.2/65 19
1. C (Computer program language). 2. Business - Data processing. I. Sidebottom, Thomas O., 1956-. II. Title.
HF5548.5.C12 W67 1987

Turbo Pascal for the Mac : programming with business applications / Leon A. Wortman.1st ed. Blue Ridge Summit, PA : Tab Books, c1987. x, 274 p. : ill. ; 24 cm. Includes index. ISBN 0-8306-2927-0 (pbk.) : LC Card 87-7134 DDC 650/.028/5416 19
1. Turbo Pascal (Computer program). 2. Macintosh (Computer) - Programming. 3. Business - Data processing. I. Title.
HF5548.5.P14 W67 1987

Wortman, Roy T., 1940- From syndicalism to trade unionism : the IWW in Ohio, 1905-1950 / Roy T. Wortman. New York : Garland Pub., 1985. 217 p. : ill. ; 24 cm. (Modern American history) Includes index. Bibliography: p. 190-206. ISBN 0-8240-5675-2 (alk. paper) : LC Card 85-16249 DDC 331.88/6/09771 19
1. Industrial Workers of the World - History. 2. Syndicalism - Ohio - History - 20th century. 3. Trade-unions - Ohio - History - 20th century. I. Title.
HD8055.I5 O38 1985 ***NYPL [JLE 86-4097]***

Woś, Augustyn. Polityka rolna PRL . Warszawa , 1977. 246, [2] p., [24] p. of plates : LC Card 81-201110
HD1995.7.Z8 P65 1977

Woy, James B. Commodity futures trading : a bibliographic guide / James B. Woy. New York : R. R. Bowker Co., 1976. x, 206 p. ; 24 cm. Includes indexes. ISBN 0-8352-0899-0 LC Card 76-23430 DDC 016.3326/44
1. Commodity exchanges - Bibliography. 2. Commodity exchanges - Dictionaries. I. Title.
Z7164.C83 W69 HG6046
NYPL [JLE 86-473]

Woźniak, Henryk. Krasucka, Alicja. Organizacja transportu samochodowego /. Gdańsk , 1984. 181 p., [8] leaves of plates (7 folded) : ISBN 83-7017-058-7 : LC Card 86-173836
HE5675.7.A6 K7 1984

Wozu noch in die Parlamente? / [Zusammenstellung, Trotzdem-Kollektiv]. [1. Aufl.]. [Reutlingen] : Trotzdem Verlag, 1978. 81 p. : 2 ill. ; 21 cm. Cover title. CONTENTS. - Zur Geschichte der parlamentarischen Tätigkeit in der modernen Arbeiterbewegung / R. Rocker -- Parlamentarismus und Generalstreik / R. Friedeberg -- Beitrag zu den Bunten und Grünen Listen. LC Card 82-223081 DDC 322/.2/0943 19
1. Trade-unions - Germany - Political activity - Addresses, essays, lectures. 2. Trade-unions - Germany, West - Political activity - Addresses, essays, lectures. 3. Communism - Germany - Addresses, essays, lectures. 4. General strike - Addresses, essays, lectures. I. Rocker, Rudolf, 1873-1958. Zur Geschichte der parlamentarischen Tätigkeit in der modernen Arbeiterbewegung. 1978. II. Friedeberg, R. Parlamentarismus und Generalstreik. 1978. III. Trotzdem-Kollektiv (Reutlingen, Germany).
HD6697 .W69 1978 ***NYPL [JLD 87-886]***

W.R. GRACE & CO. - HISTORY.
Clayton, Lawrence A. Grace . Ottawa, Ill. , c1985. xiii, 403 p., [32] p. of plates : ISBN 0-915463-25-3 LC Card 85-14856 DDC 338.8/8885 19
HD9505.P4 C43 1986 ***NYPL [JLE 86-3892]***

Wray, William C. What every engineer should know about microcomputer systems design and debugging / Bill Wray and Bill Crawford. New York, N.Y. : M. Dekker, c1984. ix, 183 p. : ill. ; 24 cm. (What every engineer should know. v. 12) Includes index. ISBN 0-8247-7160-5 LC Card 83-25204 DDC 001.64 19
1. Debugging in computer science. 2. Microcomputers - Design and construction. 3. Microcomputers - Programming. I. Crawford, Bill, 1929-. II. Title. III. Title: Microcomputer systems design and debugging.
QA76.6 .W73 1984 ***NYPL [JSE 86-1632]***

Wren, Daniel A. White collar hobo : the travels of Whiting Williams / Daniel A. Wren.1st ed. Ames : Iowa State University Press, 1987. xii, 165 p. : ports. ; 23 cm. Bibliography: p. 135-159. Includes index. ISBN 0-8138-1922-9 LC Card 87-4048 DDC 331/.092/4 B 19
1. Williams, Whiting, 1878-. 2. Labor and laboring classes - United States - Biography. 3. Personnel directors - United States - Biography. 4. Industrial relations - United States. I. Title.
HD8073.W47 W74 1987

Wrench, John. Unequal comrades : trade unions, equal opportunity, and racism / John Wrench. Coventry : Centre for Research in Ethnic Relations, Arts Building, University of Warwick, 1986. 30 p. ; 21 cm. (Policy papers in ethnic relations, 0268-3970 . no. 5) Bibliography: p. 29-30. ISBN 0-948303-65-4 (pbk.) : LC Card 87-146518 DDC 331.6 19
1. Trade-unions - Great Britain - Minority membership. 2. Discrimination in employment - Great Britain. I. Title. II. Series.
HD6490.R22 G78 1986

Wretched faces . Wells, Roger A. E. New York , 1988. p. cm. ISBN 0-312-01248-9 : LC Card 87-22164 DDC 363.8/0942 19
HC260.F3 W45 1988

Wright, A. L. (Arthur L.) The Texas housing affordability index / by Arthur L. Wright. College Station, TX : Texas Real Estate Research Center, College of Agriculture, Texas A&M University, [1986] 5, [17] p. : ill. ; 28 cm. (Technical report / Texas Real Estate Research Center) "March 1986." "TRERC-386-1M-433." LC Card 86-622195 DDC 338.4/369083/09764021 19
1. Housing - Prices - Texas. 2. Dwellings - Prices - Texas. I. Texas Real Estate Research Center. II. Series: Technical report / Texas Real Estate Research Center. III. Title.
HD7303.T4 W748 1986

Wright, Anita Lee. Pimentel, Richard. Job placement for the industrially injured worker /. Northridge, Calif. (17624 Romar St., Northridge 91325) , c1987. v, 93, [1] leaves : LC Card 87-401986 DDC 650.1/4/0240816 19
HD7255 .P54 1987

Wright, Barbara Drygulski, 1945- Women, work, and technology . Ann Arbor , c1987. viii, 387 p. ; ISBN 0-472-06373-1 (pbk. : alk. paper) : LC Card 87-16236 DDC 331.4 19
HD6052 .W566 1987

Wright, C. Stretch, C. The effectiveness of town planning in Natal . Pietermaritzburg, Natal, South Africa , 1986. 35 p. ; LC Card 86-159747 DDC 361.2/5/09684 s 307.1/2/096845 19
HC517.N3 A44 vol. 64 HT169.S62P56

Wright, D. G. Popular radicalism : the working-class experience, 1780-1880 / D.G. Wright. London ; New York : Longman, 1988. p. cm. (Studies in modern history) Bibliography: p. Includes index. ISBN 0-582-49440-0 LC Card 87-4093 DDC 322/.2/0942 19
1. Labor and laboring classes - Great Britain - Political activity - History. 2. Great Britain - Politics and government - 18th century. 3. Great Britain - Politics and government - 19th century. I. Series: Studies in modern history (Longman(Firm)). II. Title.
HD8395 .W75 1988

Wright, David, 1943- The Harley-Davidson Motor Company : an official eighty-year history / David Wright.[2nd ed.] Osceola, Wis., USA : Motorbooks International, c1987. 288 p. : ill. (some col.) ; 24 cm. Includes index. ISBN 0-87938-245-7 : LC Card 87-5519 DDC 338.7/6292275/0973 19
1. Harley-Davidson Motor Company - History. 2. Motorcycle industry - United States - History. 3. Motorcycle racing - History. I. Title.
HD9710.5.U54 H378 1987

Wright, Giles R. Work / by Giles R. Wright and Howard L. Green. Trenton : New Jersey Historical Commission, Dept. of State, c1987. 82 p. : ill. ; 23 cm. (New Jersey ethnic life series . 7) Bibliography: p. 75-79. ISBN 0-89743-072-7 (pbk.) LC Card 87-1573 DDC 331.6/2/09749 19
1. Alien labor - New Jersey - History - Sources. I. Green, Howard L. II. New Jersey Historical Commission. III. Title. IV. Series.
HD8083.N4 W75 1987

Wright, H. Norman. The family that listens / H. Norman Wright. Wheaton, Ill. : Victor Books, c1978. 142 p. ; 21 cm. (The Family concern series) Includes bibliographical references. ISBN 0-88207-633-7 : LC Card 78-57370 DDC 301.42/7
1. Family. 2. Interpersonal communication. I. Title.
HQ734 .W9487 ***NYPL [JLD 81-655]***

Wright, Maurice. Comparative government-industry relations . Oxford , New York , 1987. xiii, 321 p. ; ISBN 0-19-827493-9 : LC Card 86-28631 DDC 338.9 19
HD3611 .C63 1987

Wright, Milburn D. Pederson, Carlton A. Selling . Homewood, Ill. , 1988. xvii, 644 p. : ISBN 0-256-03644-6 LC Card 87-81434 DDC 658.8/5 19
HF5438.25 .P42 1988

Wright, Sarah Bird. Ferries of America : a guide to adventurous travel / Sarah Bird Wright. Atlanta, Ga. : Peachtree Publishers, c1987. 547 p. : ill. ; 23 cm. Bibliography: p. 536-537. Includes index. ISBN 0-934601-13-5 (pbk.) : LC Card 86-63530 DDC 387.2/34/0973 19
1. Ferries - United States - Handbooks, manuals, etc. I. Title.
HE5773.A3 W75 1987

Wright, Stephen, 1954- West Africa--regional cooperation and development /. Boulder , 1988. p. cm. ISBN 0-8133-7354-9 : LC Card 87-9290 DDC 338.966 19
HC1000 .W47 1988

Wrightson, Margaret Tucker, 1950- Goodman, Marshall R. Managing regulatory reform . New York , 1987. xvi, 236 p. : ISBN 0-275-92472-5 (alk. paper) : LC Card 87-2436 DDC 338.973 19
HD3616.U47 G67 1987

Wrightson, Suzanne Nancy. Rawson, Donald William. Australian unions, 1984 /. Sydney , c1985. 123 p. ; ISBN 0-949614-13-0 LC Card 85-169297 DDC 331.88/025/94 19
HD6891 .R35 1985 ***NYPL [JLD 86-1566]***

Wrigley, E. A. (Edward Anthony), 1931-
Malthus, T. R. (Thomas Robert, 1766-1834. An essay on the principle of population . London , 1986. 139 p. : ISBN 1-85196-101-1 LC Card 87-672117
HB861 .A2x 1986 vol. 1

Malthus, T. R. (Thomas Robert, 1766-1834. An essay on the principle of population . London , 1986. 2 v. (18, xv, 711 p.) : ISBN 1-85196-102-X (v. 1) LC Card 87-672118
HB861 .A2x 1986 vol. 2-3

Malthus, T. R. (Thomas Robert, 1766-1834. Essays on political economy /. London , 1986. 327 p. : ISBN 1-85196-107-0 LC Card 87-672114
HB861 .A2x 1986 vol. 7

Malthus, T. R. (Thomas Robert, 1766-1834. Essays on population /. London , 1986. 246 p. : ISBN 1-85196-104-6 LC Card 87-672116
HB861 .A2x 1986 vol. 4

Malthus, T. R. (Thomas Robert, 1766-1834. Principles of political economy . London , 1986. 2 v. (18, x, 439 p.) : ISBN 1-85196-105-4 (v. 1) LC Card 87-672115
HB861 .A2x 1986 vol. 5-6

Write like the pros . Bacon, Mark S. New York , c1988. xiv, 316 p. ; ISBN 0-471-85721-1 LC Card 87-21550 DDC 808/.06665 19
HF5718.3 .B33 1988

WRITING (AUTHORSHIP) see **JOURNALISM.**

Writing for decision makers . Holcombe, Marya W., 1944- New York , c1987. xi, 219 p. : ISBN 0-442-23268-3 (pbk.) : LC Card 86-24700 DDC 808/.066658 19
HF5719 .H64 1987

Writing reports to get results . Blicq, Ron, 1925- New York , c1987. x, 203 p. : ISBN 0-87942-228-9 LC Card 87-16850 DDC 808/.066651 19
HF5719 .B55 1987

Writing with a word processor . Brown, Eric D. Reston, Va. , c1984. viii, 136 p. : ISBN 0-8359-8857-0 (pbk.) :$19.95 LC Card 84-8306 DDC 652 19
HF5548.115 .B76 1984
NYPL [JLE 86-1769]

Written communication of results in MAS engagements. New York, N.Y. (1211 Ave. of the Americas, New York 10036-8775) : American Institute of Certified Public Accountants, c1987. 7 p. ; 23 cm. (Management advisory services practice aid. Practice administration aid . 3) Bibliography: p. 7. LC Card 87-159283 DDC 808/.066657 19
1. Business report writing. 2. Communication in accounting - United States. I. American Institute of Certified Public Accountants. II. Series.
HF5719 .W74 1987

Wrotnowski, Cort. Generic drugs . Stamford, Conn., U. S.A. , c1986. xiii, 311 leaves : ISBN 0-89336-434-7 (soft) LC Card 87-167077 DDC 380.1/456151 19
HD9665.5 .G46 1986

WSI-Studie zur Wirtschafts- und Sozialforschung .
(Nr. 50) Helfert, Mario. Wertewandel, Arbeit, technischer Fortschritt, Wachstum /. Köln , c1986. 149 p. : ISBN 3-7663-3010-1 LC Card 87-134855 DDC 331.12 19
HD6331 .H37 1986

(Nr. 54) Seifert, Hartmut, 1944- Öffentliche Arbeitsmarktpolitik in der Bundesrepublik Deutschland . Köln [1984] ix, 288 p. ; ISBN 3-7663-0857-2 LC Card 86-127331 DDC 331.11/0943 19
HD5779 .S34 1984

(Nr. 56) Jordan, Reinhard, d. 1986. Holzwirtschaft im Wandel . Köln , c1986. viii, 163 p. : ISBN 3-7663-0977-3 LC Card 86-211012 DDC 338.4/5674/0943 19
HD9763.5 .J67 1986

(Nr. 57) Welsch, Johann. Gewerkschaften und Strukturwandel . Köln , c1986. iii, 114 p. ; ISBN 3-7663-3011-X LC Card 86-223645 DDC 331.13/704 19
HD6694 .W37 1986

(Nr. 58) Perspektiven der Vollbeschäftigung . Köln , c1987. vi, 263 p. : ISBN 3-7663-3033-0 LC Card 87-135012 DDC 339.5 19
HD5701.3 .P47 1987

Welzmüller, Rudolf. Preispolitik und Akkumulation . Köln , c1982. 283 p. : ISBN 3-7663-0522-0 : LC Card 82-140922 DDC 338.8/266/00943 19
HD9654.5 .W44 1982 ***NYPL [JLD 86-2908]***

Współczesny konserwatyzm i liberalizm amerykański /. Osiatyński, Wiktor, 1945- Warszawa , 1984. 552 p. ; ISBN 83-01-04929-4 (pbk.) : ***NYPL [*QO 86-3450]***

Wspólna praca--wspólny plon . Wieleżyński, Leszek. London, England [1986], c1985. 295 p., [24] p. of plates : LC Card 87-111287
HD9575.P62 W549 1986

Wünsche und Forderungen des Handwerks an Parteien, X. Deutschen Bundestag und Bundesregierung. Bonn : Zentralverband des Deutschen Handwerks, [1983] 80 p. ; 21 cm. (Schriftenreihe / Zentralverband des Deutschen Handwerks . Heft 34) LC Card 83-220138
1. Small business - Germany, West. 2. Small business - Government policy - Germany (West). 3. Artisans - Germany (West) - Political activity. I. Zentralverband des Deutschen Handwerks. II. Series: Schriftenreihe / Zentralverband des Deutschen Handwerks , Heft 34.
HD2346.G3 W86 1983

Wünschmann, Andreas, 1942- Unbewusst dagegen : die Kontroverse um Atomkraft und Technik / Andreas Wünschmann.3. überarbeitete und erw. Aufl. Stuttgart : Bonn Aktuell, 1984, c1980. 177 p. : ill. ; 21 cm. Bibliography: p. 171-172. Includes index. ISBN 3-87959-214-4 (pbk.) LC Card 87-673462
1. Nuclear energy - Public opinion - Psychological aspects. 2. Motivation (Psychology). 3. Subconsciousness. I. Title.
HD9698.A2 W86x 1984

Wührer, Gerhard. Strategien des Personalmanagements : Klassifikation und Analyse der Einflussgrössen / Gerhard Wührer. Krefeld : G. Marchal und H.-J. Matzenbacher Wissenschaftsverlag, 1985. 264 p. : 34 ill. ; 21 cm. Bibliography: p. 237-261. ISBN 3-88358-054-5 LC Card 86-160291
1. Personnel management - Germany, West. I. Title.
HF5549.2.G3 W84 1985

Wuillemin, Lucien. Eléments d'analyse et de gestion financières de l'entreprise en déficit / Lucien Wuillemin. Genève : Georg, Librairie de l'Université, c1982. 191 p. : ill. ; 23 cm. Spine title: L'entreprise en déficit. Bibliography: p. 180-188. ISBN 2-8257-0090-8 : LC Card 82-228134 DDC 658.1/5 19
1. Business losses. 2. Corporations - Cash position. I. Title. II. Title: Entreprise en déficit.
HD49 .W84 1982 ***NYPL [JLE 87-1142]***

Wulf, Herbert.
Wilke, Peter. Manpower conversion in defence related industry . Hamburg [1986] 62 p. : LC Card 86-212660 DDC 331.25/924 19
HC79.D4 W55 1986

Zivile Alternativen für die Rüstungsindustrie /. Baden-Baden , 1986. 174 p. ; ISBN 3-7890-1262-9 LC Card 87-108651 DDC 338.4/76234/0943 19
HD9743.G48 Z58 1986

Wunram, Friedrich. Ebel, Friedhelm. Landwirtschaft am Niederrhein . Bonn , 1976. 223 p. : LC Card 87-408419
HD1407 .L3 Heft 33 HD1960.R48

Wünsche, Gert. Grundlagen der Bankenwerbung aus verhaltenswissenschaftlicher Sicht / Gert Wünsche. Wiesbaden : Gabler, c1982. 304 p. : ill. (some col.) ; 24 cm. (Schriftenreihe des Instituts für Kredit- und Finanzwirtschaft . Bd. 10) Bibliography: p. 286-300. Includes index. ISBN 3-409-47003-4 LC Card 83-151107
1. Advertising - Banks and banking - Germany (West). I. Title. II. Series.
HF6161.B2 W86 1982

Wünsche, Horst Friedrich. Ludwig Erhards Gesellschafts- und Wirtschaftskonzeption : soziale Marktwirtschaft als politische Ökonomie / Horst Friedrich Wünsche. Stuttgart : Bonn Aktuell, 1986. 239 p. ; 24 cm. Bibliography: p. 187-229. Includes indexes. ISBN 3-87959-263-2 LC Card 86-201702
1. Germany, West - Economic policy. 2. Erhard, Ludwig. I. Title.
HC286.5 .W85 1986

Wurbs, Gerhard. Die deutsche Arbeiterbewegung in Bielitz und Biala / Gerhard Wurbs. Stuttgart : Seliger-Archiv, 1983. 133 p. : ill. ; 22 cm. Bibliography: p. 132-133. LC Card 84-194473
1. Labor and laboring classes - Poland - Bielsko-Biała - History. I. Title.
HD8539.5.B542 W87 1983

Wurtzebach, Charles H. Modern real estate / Charles H. Wurtzebach, Mike E. Miles. 3rd ed. New York : Wiley, c1987. xii, 772 p. : ill. ; 25 cm. Bibliography: p. [713]-715. Includes index. ISBN 0-471-84890-5 LC Card 86-23412 DDC 333.33/0973 19
1. Real estate business. 2. Real estate business - United States. I. Miles, Mike E. II. Title.
HD1375 .W873 1987

Wuyts, Marc.
Camponeses e economia rural em Moçambique [microform] / Marc Wuyts. Maputo : IICM, 1978. 31, A1-A6 p. ; 30 cm. At head of title: Universidade Eduardo Mondlane, Centro de Estudos Africanos. Microfilm. New York : New York Public Library, 1985. 1 microfilm reel ; 35 mm. (MN *ZZ-25,047) LC Card 80-980386 DDC 338.1/0967/9 19
1. Agriculture - Economic aspects - Mozambique. 2. Peasantry - Mozambique. 3. Mozambique - Rural conditions. I. Lourenço Marquez (City). Instituto de Investigação Cientifica de Moçambique. II. Universidade Eduardo Mondlane. Centro de Estudos Africanos. III. Title.
HD2129 .W89 1978
NYPL [*ZT-1564 no.14]

On the question of mechanisation of Mozambican agriculture today : some theoretical comments / Marc Wuyts.2nd print. corr. [Maputo, Mozambique] : Universidade Eduardo Mondlane, Instituto de Investigação Científica de Moçambique, Centro de Estudio Africanos, 1979. 22 p. : ill. ; 28 cm. (CEA relatório . 79/10) Limited edition of 150 copies. Bibliography: p. 22. LC Card 83-207389
1. Farm mechanization - Economic aspects - Mozambique. 2. Agriculture - Economic aspects - Mozambique. I. Title.
HD2129 .W893 1979

Wybrane problemy ekonomiki przemysłu / [zespół redakcyjny Zygmunt Bartosik, Stanisław Kiełczewski]. Wrocław : Wydawn. Uczelniane Akademii Ekonomicznej we Wrocławiu, 1985. 110 p. ; 24 cm. (Prace naukowe Akademii Ekonomicznej im. Oskara Langego we Wrocławiu, 0324-8445 . nr. 304) Summaries in English. Includes bibliographies. LC Card 86-155957
1. Industrial management - Poland. 2. Industrial organization - Poland. I. Bartosik, Zygmunt. II. Kiełczew, Stanisław. III. Series: Prace naukowe Akademii Ekonomicznej imienia Oskara Langego we Wrocławiu , nr. 304.
HB9 .B7522 nr. 304 HD70.P6

Wycech, Czesław. Z przeszłości ruchów chłopskich, 1768-1861 / Czesław Wycech. Wyd. 2., rozsz. Warszawa : Ludowa Spółdzielnia Wydawnicza, 1952. 221, [3] p. ; 26 cm. Bibliography: p. 220-[222] LC Card 81-212267
1. Peasantry - Poland - History. 2. Peasant uprisings - Poland - History. 3. Populism - Poland - History. I. Title.
HD1536.P7 W93 1952

Wyche, Mark C. Bortz, Paul I. Great expectations . Washington, D.C. , c1986. vii, 137 p., [3] folded leaves : ISBN 0-89324-012-5 (pbk.) LC Card 87-401854 DDC 384.55/453/068 19
HE8700.8 .B66 1986

Wyden, Peter. The unknown Iacocca / Peter Wyden. 1st ed. New York : Morrow, c1987. 416 p. : ill., ports. ; 25 cm. Bibliography: p. 395-402. Includes index. ISBN 0-688-06616-X LC Card 87-15240 DDC 338.7/6292/0924 B 19
1. Iacocca, Lee A. 2. Businessmen - United States - Biography. 3. Automobile industry and trade - United States - History. I. Title.
HD9710.U52 I28 1987

Wye studies in agricultural and rural development.
Chambers, Robert, 1932- Managing canal irrigation . Cambridge [Cambridgeshire] , New York , 1988. p. cm. ISBN 0-521-34554-5 LC Card 87-16738 DDC 333.91/3/0954 19
HD1741.I29 C45 1988

Wyhl. Der Widerstand geht weiter . Freiburg i. Br. , 1982. 261 p. : ISBN 3-921472-30-X LC Card 82-192690
HD9698.G43 W937 1982

Wynant, Larry, 1946- Hatch, James E. Canadian commercial lending . Toronto , New York , c1986. ix, 262 p. : ISBN 0-458-80270-0 : LC Card 87-130576 DDC 332.1/753/0685 19
HG3754.5.C2 H38 1986

Wynbrandt, James. Leedy, Jack J., 1921- Executive retirement management . New York, N.Y. , c1987. xi, 260 p. ; ISBN 0-8160-1286-5 LC Card 86-24010 DDC 658.4/07132 19
HD7125 .L43 1987

Wyncoll, Peter, 1939-1982. The Nottingham labour movement, 1880-1939 / Peter Wyncoll. London : Lawrence and Wishart ; Atlantic Highlands, N.J. : Distributed in the U. S.A. and Canada by Humanities Press, 1985. 256 p. ; 22 cm. Distributor from label on t.p. Includes index. ISBN 0-85315-613-1 (pbk.) : LC Card

86-213667 DDC 331.88/09425/27 19
1. Trade-unions - England - Nottingham (Nottinghamshire) - History. I. Title.
HD6669.N68 W96 1985

Wynne, John, 1961- The Indiana economy : a primer / prepared by John Wynne. Indianapolis, IN : Division of Economic Analysis, Indiana Dept. of Commerce, [1986] 22, [2] p. : col. ill. ; 28 cm. Bibliography: p. [23]-[24]. LC Card 86-622749 DDC 330.9772/043 19
1. Labor supply - Indiana. 2. Unemployment - Indiana. 3. Income - Indiana. 4. Indiana - Population. 5. Indiana - Economic conditions. I. Indiana. Dept. of Commerce. Division of Economic Analysis. II. Title.
HD5725.I6 W96 1986

Wyoming child labor, 1985. Wyoming. Dept. of Labor and Statistics. Cheyenne, Wyo. , 1985. vi, 71 p. : LC Card 86-622187 DDC 331.3/1/09787 19
HD6250.U4 W85 1985a

Wyoming child labor, 1986. Wyoming. Dept. of Labor and Statistics. Cheyenne, Wyo. (Herschler Bldg., Cheyenne 82002) [1986] vi, 74 p. : LC Card 87-622019 DDC 331.3/4/09787 19
HD6274.W8 W96 1986

Wyoming. Dept. of Administration and Fiscal Control. Statistics and Research Division. Wyoming income and employment report /. Cheyenne, Wyo. [1986] 54, [33], iii p. : LC Card 86-623087 DDC 331.12/5/09787021 19
HD5725.W9 W97 1986

Wyoming. Dept. of Labor and Statistics. (Old Catalog form: Wyoming. Labor and Statistics Dept.)
Wessel, Louis. Wyoming oil and natural gas extraction industry . Cheyenne, Wyo. (Herschler Bldg., Cheyenne 82002) , 1986. 35 p. : LC Card 86-622902 DDC 331.12/522338/09787021 19
HD4966.P52 U5553 1986

Wyoming child labor, 1985. Cheyenne, Wyo. : Wyoming Dept. of Labor and Statistics, 1985. vi, 71 p. : ill. ; 28 cm. LC Card 86-622187 DDC 331.3/1/09787 19
1. Children - Employment - Wyoming. I. Title.
HD6250.U4 W85 1985a

Wyoming child labor, 1986. Cheyenne, Wyo. (Herschler Bldg., Cheyenne 82002) : Wyoming Dept. of Labor & Statistics, [1986] vi, 74 p. : ill. ; 28 cm. Cover title. LC Card 87-622019 DDC 331.3/4/09787 19
1. Teenagers - Employment - Wyoming. I. Title.
HD6274.W8 W96 1986

WYOMING - ECONOMIC CONDITIONS.
Profile, State of Wyoming. Cheyenne, Wyo. [1986] 30 leaves ; LC Card 86-622611 DDC 330.9787/033 19
HC107.W9 P76 1986

WYOMING - ECONOMIC CONDITIONS - STATISTICS.
Profile, State of Wyoming. Cheyenne, Wyo. [1986] 30 leaves ; LC Card 86-622611 DDC 330.9787/033 19
HC107.W9 P76 1986

Wyoming Economic Development and Stabilization Board. Profile, State of Wyoming. Cheyenne, Wyo. [1986] 30 leaves ; LC Card 86-622611 DDC 330.9787/033 19
HC107.W9 P76 1986

Wyoming income and employment report / prepared by Division of Research and Statistics, Department of Administration and Fiscal Control, State of Wyoming. 8th ed. Cheyenne, Wyo. : The Division, [1986] 54, [33], iii p. : ill. ; 28 cm. Cover title. "August, 1986." Bibliography: p. iii (last group) LC Card 86-623087 DDC 331.12/5/09787021 19
1. Labor supply - Wyoming - Statistics. 2. Unemployment - Wyoming - Statistics. 3. Income - Wyoming - Statistics. I. Wyoming. Dept. of Administration and Fiscal Control. Statistics and Research Division. II. Title.
HD5725.W9 W97 1986

Wyoming. Labor and Statistics, Dept. of. see **Wyoming. Dept. of Labor and Statistics.**

Wyoming. Legislature. Legislative Service Office. Fiscal facts & figures : state, education, cities, towns, counties / prepared by Legislative Service Office. [Wyoming] : The Office, [1987] 40 leaves ; 28 cm. Cover title. "January 12, 1987"--Cover. LC Card 87-621012 DDC 336.787 19
1. Finance, Public - Wyoming - Statistics. I. Title. II. Title: Fiscal facts and figures.
HJ785 .W86 1987

Wyoming. Oil and Gas Conservation Commission. Wyoming oil and gas production by county /. Casper, Wyo. (P.O. Box 2640, Casper 82602) [1986] [40] p. : LC Card 86-622904 DDC 338.2/728/09787021 19
HD9567.W8 W94 1986

Wyoming oil and gas, 1985 /. Casper, Wyo. (P.O. Box 2640, Casper 82602) [1986?] 50 p. ; LC Card 86-622903 DDC 338.2/728/09787021 19
HD9567.W8 W96 1986

Wyoming oil and gas production by county / compiled by the Wyoming Oil and Gas Conservation Commission. Casper, Wyo. (P.O. Box 2640, Casper 82602) : The Commission, [1986] [40] p. : ill. ; 22 x 36 cm. Cover title. "June 1986." LC Card 86-622904 DDC 338.2/728/09787021 19
1. Petroleum industry and trade - Wyoming - Statistics. 2. Gas industry - Wyoming - Statistics. 3. Oil wells - Wyoming - Statistics. 4. Gas wells - Wyoming - Statistics. I. Wyoming. Oil and Gas Conservation Commission.
HD9567.W8 W94 1986

Wyoming oil and gas, 1985 / compiled by the Wyoming Oil and Gas Conservation Commission. Casper, Wyo. (P.O. Box 2640, Casper 82602) : The Commission, [1986?] 50 p. ; 22 x 36 cm. Cover title. LC Card 86-622903 DDC 338.2/728/09787021 19
1. Petroleum industry and trade - Wyoming - Statistics. 2. Gas industry - Wyoming - Statistics. 3. Oil wells - Wyoming - Statistics. 4. Gas wells - Wyoming - Statistics. I. Wyoming. Oil and Gas Conservation Commission.
HD9567.W8 W96 1986

Wyoming oil and natural gas extraction industry . Wessel, Louis. Cheyenne, Wyo. (Herschler Bldg., Cheyenne 82002) , 1986. 35 p. : LC Card 86-622902 DDC 331.12/522338/09787021 19
HD4966.P52 U5553 1986

Wyższa Szkoła Handlowa, Szkoła Główna Handlowa, Miejska Szkoła Handlowa, 1906-1945 / [komitet redakcyjny Janusz Kaliński ... et al. ; redaktor Barbara Bukowska]. Wyd. 1. Warszawa : Szkoła Główna Planowania i Statystyki, 1984. 180 p. : ill. ; 23 cm. (Monografie i opracowania. 134) Summary in English and Russian. LC Card 85-241871
1. Szkoła Główna Planowania i Statystyki (Warsaw, Poland) - History. 2. Economics - Study and teaching (Higher) - Poland - Warsaw - History. I. Kaliński, Janusz. II. Bukowska, Barbara. III. Series: Monografie i opracowania (Szkoła Główna Planowania i Statystyki (Warsaw, Poland)) , 134.
HB74.9.P7 W98 1984

WZB-Publication.
The Economics of insurance regulation . Houndmills, Basingstoke, Hampshire , 1986. xi, 300 p. : ISBN 0-333-39684-7
NYPL [JLD 87-1100]

X censo general de población y vivienda, 1980 : integración territorial .... México, D.F. : Instituto Nacional de Estadística, Geografía e Informática, c1985- v. <1-6 > : col. maps ; 28 cm. Chiefly tables. CONTENTS. - [1] Estado de Aguascalientes -- [2] Estado de Baja California -- [3] Estado de Colima -- [4] Estado de Quintana Roo -- [5] Estado de Sinaloa -- [6] Estado de Tabasco. ISBN 968-8099-30-9 (v. 1) LC Card 86-226718
1. Mexico - Census, 1980. 2. Mexico - Population - Statistics. 3. Mexico - Population - States - Statistics. 4. Housing - Mexico - Statistics. 5. Housing - Mexico - States - Statistics. I. Instituto Nacional de Estadística, Geografía e Informática (Mexico). II. Title: 10o censo general de población y vivienda, 1980. III. Title: Décimo censo general de población y vivienda, 1980.
HA761.5 1980d

X-efficiency . Frantz, Roger S. Boston , c1988. xviii, 227 p. : ISBN 0-89838-242-4 LC Card 87-17071 DDC 338/.06 19
HD56 .F725 1988

The X-II-ARIMA seasonal adjustment method /. Dagum, Estela Bee. Ottawa , c1980. 119 p. : LC Card 83-225028
HB137 .D34 1980

Xavier Labour Relations Institute. Centre for Human Resources Development. Recent experiences in human resources development /. New Delhi , c1986. xvi, 448 p. ; ISBN 81-204-0120-4 : LC Card 86-902270 DDC 331.11/0954 19
HF5549.5.M3 R38 1985

XENIX (COMPUTER OPERATING SYSTEM)
Clukey, Lee Paul. UNIX and XENIX demystified /. Blue Ridge Summit, Pa. , 1985. xii, 243 p. ; ISBN 0-8306-0874-5 : LC Card 85-2658 DDC 001.64/2 19
QA76.6 .C57 1985 ***NYPL [JSE 86-1905]***

Xenos, Peter, 1943- Hogan, Dennis P. Cultural and economic factors in the fertility of Thai women /. Honolulu, HI [1987] p. cm. ISBN 0-86638-103-1 : LC Card 87-21459 DDC 304.6/32/09593 19
HB1054.55.A3 H64 1987

Xerox . Jacobson, Gary. New York , c1986. ix, 338 p. ; ISBN 0-02-551600-0 LC Card 85-30922 DDC 338.7/68644 19
HD9802.3.U64 X475 1986
NYPL [JLE 86-2982]

Xerox . Jacobson, Gary. New York , 1987, c1986. xii, 338 p. ; ISBN 0-02-033830-9 (pbk.) LC Card 86-31009 DDC 338.7/68644 19
HD9802.3.U64 X475 1986b

XEROX CORPORATION.
Jacobson, Gary. Xerox . New York , c1986. ix, 338 p. ; ISBN 0-02-551600-0 LC Card 85-30922 DDC 338.7/68644 19
HD9802.3.U64 X475 1986
NYPL [JLE 86-2982]

Jacobson, Gary. Xerox . New York , 1987, c1986. xii, 338 p. ; ISBN 0-02-033830-9 (pbk.) LC Card 86-31009 DDC 338.7/68644 19
HD9802.3.U64 X475 1986b

XI censo general de población y vivienda. Situación habitacional en Venezuela . [Caracas] [1986- v. <1 > : ISBN 980-280-043-0 LC Card 87-114711 DDC 363.5/1/0987/021 19
HD7331.A3 S57 1986

Xifré, Carlos Calleja. see **Calleja Xifré, Carlos.**

XLVII Leilão do FINOR, Bolsa de Valores Regional (BVRG), Fortaleza (CE), 25 de outubro de 1984. Perfil de empresas. Fortaleza-CE [1984] 248 p. ; LC Card 85-191373
HG4111.5.N67 P47 1984

XNVIRONMENTAL POLICY - DEVELOPING COUNTRIES.
Pearson, Charles S. Down to business . Washington, DC (1735 New York Ave., NW, Washington, DC 20006) , c1985. vii, 107 p. ; ISBN 0-915825-04-X (pbk.) : LC Card 84-52795
HD69.P6 P42 1985 ***NYPL [JLE 86-3186]***

XV censo nacional de población y IV de vivienda. 1a ed. Bogotá : Departamento Administrativo Nacional de Estadística, 1986- v. <1-5, 7 > : ill. (some col.) ; 29 cm. Chiefly tables. Cover title, v. 1: Censo 85. Bibliography: v. 2, p. 215-220. CONTENTS. - v. 1. Colombia -- v. 2. Metodología -- v. 3. Educación -- v. 4. Características económicas -- v. 5. Demografía -- v. 7. Censos anteriores, 1938, 1951, 1964, 1973. LC Card 87-402787 DDC 304.6/09861/021 19
1. Colombia - Census, 1985. I. Colombia. Departamento Administrativo Nacional de Estadística. II. Title: 15o censo nacional de población y 4o de vivienda. III. Title: Decimoquinto censo nacional de población y cuarto de vivienda. IV. Title: Censo 85.
HA1011.5 1985a

XV censo nacional de población y IV de vivienda--Chile, Abril 1982. Localidades pobladas / República de Chile, Ministerio de Economía, Fomento y Reconstrucción, Instituto Nacional de Estadísticas. [Santiago] : El Instituto, <[1983]-[1986] > <v. 3-14; in 15 > : ill. ; 21 x 27 cm. Cover title. CONTENTS. - -- [3] III Región de Atacama -- [4] IV Región de Coquimbo -- [5] V Región de Valparaíso -- [6] VI Región del Libertador General Bernardo O'Higgins -- [7] VII Región del Maule -- [8] VIII Región del Bíobío (2 v.) -- [9] IX Región de la Araucanía (2 v.) -- [10] X Región de los Lagos (2 v.) -- [11] XI Región Aisén del General Carlos Ibáñez del Campo -- [12] XII Región de Magallanes de la Antártica Chilena -- [13] Región

Metropolitana de Santiago -- [14] Total país, resumen. LC Card 87-110013
1. Chile - Census, 1982. 2. Chile - Population - Statistics. 3. Housing - Chile - Statistics. I. Instituto Nacional de Estadísticas (Chile). II. Title: Localidades pobladas. III. Title: Décimoquinto censo nacional de población y quarto de vivienda.
HA994 1982d

XV Censo nacional de población y IV de vivienda--Chile, abril 1982. Vivienda, hogar y familia / República de Chile, Ministerio de Economía, Fomento y Reconstrucción, Instituto Nacional de Estadísticas. [Santiago] : El Instituto, [1985-<1986] > v. <1-13 > : ill. ; 21 x 27 cm. Cover title. Chiefly tables. CONTENTS. - [1] I Región de Tarapacá -- [2] II Región de Antofagasta -- [3] III Región de Atacama -- [4] IV Región de Coquimbo -- [5] V Región de Valparaíso -- [6] VI Región del Libertador General Bernardo O'Higgins -- [7] VII Región del Maule -- [8] VIII Región del Biobío -- [9] IX Región de la Araucania -- [10] X Región de Los Lagos -- [11] XI Región Aisén del General Carlos Ibañez del Campo -- [12] XII Región de Magallanes y de la Antártica Chilena -- [13] Región Metropolitana de Santiago. LC Card 87-109976
1. Chile - Census, 1982. 2. Chile - Population - Statistics. 3. Housing - Chile - Statistics. I. Instituto Nacional de Estadísticas (Chile). II. Title: 15o Censo nacional de población y 4o de vivienda--Chile, abril 1982. III. Title: Décimoquinto Censo nacional de Población y cuarto de vivienda--Chile, abril 1982. IV. Title: Vivienda, hogar y familia.
HA994 1982c

XXVI s″ezd KPSS i voprosy ėkonomiki narodnogo khozi͡aĭstva Chuvashskoĭ ASSR. Cheboksary : Nauch.-issl. in-t i͡azyka, lit-ry, istorii i ėkonomiki pri Sovete Ministrov Chuvashskoĭ ASSR, 1982. 157 p. ; 23 cm. At head of title: Ordena "Znak pocheta" nauchno-issledovatel′skiĭ institut i͡azyka, literatury, istorii i ėkonomiki pri Sovete Ministrov Chuvashskoĭ ASSR. Includes bibliographical references. LC Card 83-128420
1. Chuvashskai͡a A.S.S.R. (R.S.F.S.R.) - Economic policy. 2. Industrial management - Russian S.F.S.R. - Chuvashskai͡a A.S.S.R. I. Chuvashskai͡a A.S.S.R. (R.S.F.S.R.). Nauchno-issledovatel′skiĭ institut i͡azyka, literatury, istorii i ėkonomiki. II. Title: 26 s″ezd KPSS i voprosy ėkonomiki narodnogo khozi͡aĭstva Chuvashskoĭ ASSR. III. Title: Dvadt͡sat′shestoĭ s″ezd KPSS i voprosy ėkonomiki narodnogo khozi͡aĭstva ASSR.
HC337.C46 A17 1982

XXVII s″ezd KPSS o strategii uskoreni͡ia sot͡sial′no-ėkonomicheskogo razviti͡ia strany /. Babosov, Evgeniĭ Mikhaĭlovich. Minsk , 1987. 124 p. ; LC Card 87-166221
HC337.B93 B33 1987

XYLOGRAPHY. see **WOOD-ENGRAVING.**

Yachoui, Elie. Restructuration et croissance de l'économie libanaise / Elie Yachoui. 1re éd. Beyrouth : Libr. du Liban, 1983. 230 p. ; 25 cm. Bibliography: p. [226]-230. LC Card 86-148239
1. Lebanon - Economic conditions. 2. Lebanon - Politics and government - 1975-. I. Title.
HC415.24 .Y32 1983

Yacimientos Petrolíferos Fiscales Bolivianos. Castrillo M., Hugo. Reseña histórica del petróleo en Bolivia /. La Paz, Bolivia , 1986. 82 p., [1] leaf of plates : LC Card 87-403504 DDC 338.2/7282/0984 19
HD9574.B64 Y294 1986

YACIMIENTOS PETROLÍFEROS FISCALES BOLIVIANOS - HISTORY.
Castrillo M., Hugo. Reseña histórica del petróleo en Bolivia /. La Paz, Bolivia , 1986. 82 p., [1] leaf of plates : LC Card 87-403504 DDC 338.2/7282/0984 19
HD9574.B64 Y294 1986

Yadav, Hridai Ram, 1957- Wastelands . New Delhi , 1987. xii, 249 p. : LC Card 86-903086 DDC 333.73 19
HD1671.I5W37 1987

Yadav, R. A. (Ram Avtar), 1949- Financial ratios and the prediction of corporate failure / Ram Avtar Yadav. New Delhi : Concept Pub. Co., 1986. xvi, 196 p. ; 23 cm. Bibliography: p. [185]-192. Includes index. LC Card 86-903341 DDC 338.7/4/0954 19
1. Ratio analysis. 2. Corporations - Finance. 3. Corporations - India - Finance. I. Title.
HF5681.R25 Y33 1986

YADAVA, R. S., 1922- - ADDRESSES, ESSAYS, LECTURES.
Rationalism, humanism, and democracy . Meerut , 1985. xcii, 514 p., [2] p. of plates : LC Card 85-901252 DDC 144 19
B833 .R29 1985 ***NYPL [JFD 86-3589]***

Yadave, R. S., 1922- Rationalism, humanism, and democracy . Meerut , 1985. xcii, 514 p., [2] p. of plates : LC Card 85-901252 DDC 144 19
B833 .R29 1985 ***NYPL [JFD 86-3589]***

Yagci, Fahrettin, 1944- Macroeconomic policies and adjustment in Yugoslavia : some counterfactual simulations / Fahrettin Yagci, Steven Kamin. Washington, D.C. : World Bank, [1987] 29 p. ; 28 cm. (World Bank discussion papers, 0259-210X . 16) ISBN 0-8213-0938-2 (pbk.) LC Card 87-16064 DDC 339.5/09497 19
1. Yugoslavia - Economic policy - 1945-. 2. Yugoslavia - Economic conditions - 1945-. 3. Balance of payments - Yugoslavia. I. Kamin, Steven, 1957-. II. Title. III. Series.
HC407.Y6 Y34 1987

Yager, Francis P. Financial profile of cooperatives handling grain : first-handlers, $15 million sales or larger / [Francis P. Yager and David E. Cummins]. [Washington, D.C.] : U. S. Dept. of Agriculture, Agricultural Cooperative Service, [1986] vii, 24 p. : ill. ; 28 cm. (ACS research report . no. 53) Cover title. LC Card 86-601622 DDC 334/.6831/0973021 19
1. Grain trade - United States - Finance - Statistics. 2. Grain elevators, Cooperative - United States - Finance - Statistics. 3. Agriculture, Cooperative - United States - Finance - Statistics. I. Cummins, David E. (David Earl), 1938-. II. Title. III. Series.
HD9034 .Y34 1986

Yager, Ronald R., 1941- Management decision support systems using fuzzy sets and possibility theory /. Köln , c1985. xi, 350 p. : ISBN 3-88585-143-1 (pbk.) LC Card 85-217558 DDC 658.4/033 19
HD30.23 .M353 1985 ***NYPL [JLE 86-4562]***

Yakir, E. (Eli), 1929-
Milon munaḥim be-khalkalah uve-nihul 'asaḳim. Yaḳir, E. (Eli), 1929- Milon munaḥim be-khalkalah ṿe-nihul 'asaḳim / E. Yaḳir, R. Ṿaigerṭ. Mahad. 2. u-murḥevet. Tel-Aviv , 1986. 414, 38 p. : LC Card 87-162041
HB61 .Y25 1986

Milon munaḥim be-khalkalah ṿe-nihul 'asaḳim / E. Yaḳir, R. Ṿaigerṭ. Mahad. 2. u-murḥevet. Tel-Aviv : "Ḥeshev", 1986. 414, 38 p. : ill. ; 24 cm. Terminology in Hebrew with English equivalents; explanations in Hebrew only. Revised ed. of: Milon munaḥim be-khalkalah uve-nihul 'asaḳim. Includes index. LC Card 87-162041
1. Economics - Dictionaries - Hebrew. 2. Business - Dictionaries - Hebrew. 3. Hebrew language - Dictionaries - English. I. Ṿaigerṭ, R. (Re'uven). II. Yakir, E. (Eli), 1929- Milon munaḥim be-khalkalah uve-nihul 'asaḳim. III. Title.
HB61 .Y25 1986

Yale, Carolyn E. Fairfax, Sally K. Federal lands . Washington, D.C. , c1987. xviii, 252 p. : ISBN 0-933280-33-5 (pbk.) :$ LC Card 86-27512 DDC 333.1/0978 19
HD243.A17 F35 1987

Yale College, New Haven, Conn. see **Yale University.**

Yale historical publications. Miscellany. For other vols. in this series, see Old Catalog. (135) Worger, William H. South Africa's city of diamonds . New Haven , c1987. xvi, 330 p. : ISBN 0-300-03716-3 (alk. paper) LC Card 86-24724 DDC 331.7/622382/0968711 19
HD9677.S63 K568 1987

Yale University. Dept. of Economics. Oster, Sharon. The strategic use of regulatory investment by industry sub-groups [microform] . New Haven, Ct. , 1980. 39 p. ;
NYPL [*XME-11,347]

Yale University. Economics, Dept. of. see **Yale University. Dept. of Economics.**

YAM INDUSTRY - GHANA.
Nyanteng, V. K. Yam production, marketing, and prices in Ghana /. Legon , 1978. vii leaves, 159 p. : LC Card 87-400731 DDC 338.1/7523/09667 19
HD9235.S92 G46 1978

Yam production, marketing, and prices in Ghana /. Nyanteng, V. K. Legon , 1978. vii leaves, 159 p. : LC Card 87-400731 DDC 338.1/7523/09667 19
HD9235.S92 G46 1978

Yamamura, Kōzō. The Political economy of Japan. Stanford, Calif. , 1987- v. < 1 > : ISBN 0-8047-1380-4 (v. 1 : alk. paper) : LC Card 86-30037 DDC 338.952 19
HC462.9 .P57 1987

Yamawaki, Hideki.
Audretsch, David B. Industrial policy, R&D, and U. S.-Japanese trade /. Berlin [1986] 39 p. ; LC Card 87-156721 DDC 382/.0952/073 19
HF3127 .A93 1986

Industry competition and the formation of the European common market / Hideki Yamawaki, Leonard W. Weiss, Leo Sleuwaegen. Berlin : Wissenschaftszentrum Berlin für Sozialforschung, [1986] 34, 3 p. ; 30 cm. (Discussion papers, 0722-6748 . IIM/IP 86-14) "May 1986." Bibliography: p. 27-28. LC Card 87-156700 DDC 341.24/22 19
1. Competition - European Economic Community countries. 2. European Economic Community. I. Weiss, Leonard W. II. Sleuwaegen, Leo. III. Series: Discussion papers (International Institute of Management. Industrial Policy) , IIM/IP 86-14. IV. Title.
HD41 .Y35 1986

Odagiri, Hiroyuki, 1946- A study of company profit-rate time series . Berlin [1986] 15, 5 p. ; LC Card 87-165037 DDC 338.7/4/0952 19
HG4028.P7 O33 1986

Yamey, Basil S. Firms and markets . London , c1986. xiii, 271 p. : ISBN 0-7099-2446-1
NYPL [JLD 86-2134]

YAMEY, BASIL S.
Firms and markets . London , c1986. xiii, 271 p. : ISBN 0-7099-2446-1
NYPL [JLD 86-2134]

YAMS - GHANA.
Nyanteng, V. K. Yam production, marketing, and prices in Ghana /. Legon , 1978. vii leaves, 159 p. : LC Card 87-400731 DDC 338.1/7523/09667 19
HD9235.S92 G46 1978

Yanarella, Ernest J. The Unfulfilled promise of synthetic fuels . New York , 1987. xxii, 225 p. ; ISBN 0-313-25666-7 (lib. bdg. : alk. paper) LC Card 87-247 DDC 338.4/766266/0973 19
HD9502.5.S963 U5475 1987

Yandle, Bruce. Public choice and regulation . Stanford, Calif. , 1987. xiii, 363 p. ; ISBN 0-8179-8562-X (pbk.) : LC Card 87-3984 DDC 353.0082/6 19
HD3616.U47 P796 1987

Yang, Jan-Syau. English-Chinese philatelic dictionary and identification key = [Ying Han yu hsüeh ming tz'u so yin] / by Yang Jan-Syau and Michael Rogers. Winter Park, Fla. (340 Park Ave., N., Winter Park 32789) : M. Rogers, c1986. [55] p. : col. maps ; 28 cm. Cover title. Parallel title in Chinese characters. LC Card 87-169624 DDC 769.56/014 19
1. Postage-stamps - Collectors and collecting - China. I. Rogers, Michael, 1949-. II. Title. III. Title: Ying Han yu hsüeh ming tz'u so yin.
HE6204.C6 Y36 1986

Yang, Yuming. L'industrie horlogère suisse et ses relations avec la Chine de 1949 à 1982 / Yuming Yang. Geneve : Institut universitaire de hautes études internationales, 1984. 186 leaves : ill. ; 30 cm. "Mémoire no 205, présenté en vue de l'obtention du diplôme"--Extra t.p. with thesis statement inserted. Bibliography: leaves 179-184. LC Card 85-104853
1. Clock and watch making - Switzerland. 2. Clock and watch making - China. 3. Switzerland - Commerce - China. 4. China - Commerce - Switzerland. I. Graduate Institute of International Studies (Geneva, Switzerland). II. Title.
HD9999.C583 S99 1984

Yankee Group.
Beyond private lines . Boston, MA (200 Portland St., Boston 02114) , c1987. iv, 117 p. : LC Card 87-144067 DDC 384.3/0973 19
HE7775 .B46 1987

Communications/Information Systems Planning Service . Boston, MA (89 Broad St., Boston 02110) , c1986. ii, 78 p. ; LC Card 86-225335

DDC 381/.45651853 19
HD9696.C63 U51492 1986

Expert systems. Boston, Mass. (89 Broad St., 14th Floor, Boston 02110) , c1985. 61 p. : LC Card 87-400871 DDC 381/.4500633/0973 19
HD9696.C63 U516435 1985

Fiber optics after long distance /. Boston, Mass. (89 Broad St., Boston 02110) , c1986. vii, 114 p. : LC Card 86-220473 DDC 381/.456213692/0973 19
HD9696.F523 U5429 1986

Yankee Group white paper communications systems & services . Boston, Mass. (200 Portland St., Boston 02114) , 1987. 51 leaves : LC Card 87-155249 DDC 384.6/3 19
HE8825 .Y36 1987

Yankee Group. Consumer & Technology Division. Consumer financial services . Boston, MA (200 Portland St., Boston 02114) , 1986. xvi, 83 p. : LC Card 86-230330 DDC 332.1/028 19
HD9696.B363 U543 1986

Healthcare electronics /. Boston, MA (89 Broad St., Boston 02110) , c1986. iv, 79 p. : LC Card 86-212563 DDC 381/.45681761 19
HD9995.E43 U55 1986

The Home terminal II . [Boston, Ma.] (89 Broad St., Boston 02110) [1986] 63 leaves : LC Card 86-211108 DDC 381/.45621396/0973 19
HD9696.C63 U518327 1986

Yankee Group white paper communications systems & services : tariff trends in the northeast corridor, March 1987. Boston, Mass. (200 Portland St., Boston 02114) : The Group, 1987. 51 leaves : ill. ; 28 cm. LC Card 87-155249 DDC 384.6/3 19
1. Telephone - Northeastern States - Rates. I. Yankee Group. II. Title: Tariff trends in the northeast corridor.
HE8825 .Y36 1987

Yao, Lin. On rolls the green revolution /. Beijing, China [1984] 142 p., [36] p. of plates : LC Card 86-115054 DDC 338.1/0951 19
HD2097 .O5 1984 NYPL [JLK 83-122 no.9]

Yaoundé, typologie de l'habitat : notice explicative / Ministère de l'urbanisme et de l'habitat, Direction de l'urbanisme et de l'habitat, République unie du Cameroun. [Yaoundé, Cameroon] : La Direction, [197-?] [26] p. : ill. (some col.) ; 28 cm. LC Card 83-106947
1. Land settlement - Cameroon - Yaoundé. 2. Land use, Urban - Cameroon - Yaoundé. 3. Housing - Cameroon - Yaoundé. I. Cameroon. Direction de l'urbanisme et de l'habitat.
HD1019.Z9 Y368 1970z

Yarbrough, Beth V. The world economy : trade and finance / Beth V. Yarbrough, Robert M. Yarbrough. Chicago : Dryden Press, c1988. xxii, 666 p. : ill. ; 24 cm. Includes bibliographies and index. ISBN 0-03-003474-4 LC Card 86-32804 DDC 337 19
1. Commercial policy. 2. International finance. 3. International economic relations. 4. Economic policy. I. Yarbrough, Robert M. II. Title.
HF1411 .Y34 1988

Yarbrough, Robert M. Yarbrough, Beth V. The world economy . Chicago , c1988. xxii, 666 p. : ISBN 0-03-003474-4 LC Card 86-32804 DDC 337 19
HF1411 .Y34 1988

Yardley, Colin. Groberman, Jeff. The garage sale book . Rocklin, CA , c1987. 90 p. : ISBN 0-914629-10-7 (pbk.) : LC Card 86-25388 DDC 658.8/7 19
HF5482.3 .G76 1987

YARUR MANUFACTURAS CHILENAS DE ALGODÓN.
Winn, Peter. Weavers of revolution . New York , 1986. xiv, 328 p. : ISBN 0-19-503960-2 : LC Card 85-18832 DDC 338.7/67721/098331 19
HD8039.T42 C478 1986
NYPL [JLE 86-1973]

Yates, Geoffrey. Food, need, greed & myopia : exploitation and starvation in a world of plenty / Geoffrey Yates.2nd ed., fully rev. Ryton, Tyne and Wear : Earthright Publications, 1986. 96 p. : ill. ; 21 cm. Bibliography: p. 85-89. Includes index. ISBN 0-907367-04-6 (pbk.) : LC Card 87-129951 DDC 338.1/9 19
1. Food industry and trade - Moral and ethical aspects. 2. Food supply - Developing countries. 3. Malnutrition - Developing countries. 4. Agricultural pollution. 5. Agriculture - Environmental aspects. 6. Vegetarianism. I. Title. II. Title: Food, need, greed, and myopia.
HD9000.5 .Y38 1986

Yates, James W. The options strategy spectrum / James W. Yates. Homewood, Ill. : Dow Jones-Irwin, c1987. x, 214 p. : ill. ; 24 cm. Includes index. ISBN 0-87094-961-6 LC Card 87-70393 DDC 332.64/52 19
1. Put and call transactions. I. Title.
HG6042 .Y38 1987

Yates, M. M. (Maurice M.) How to start and manage a business of your own in Tennessee. 9th ed. Greeneville, Tenn. : M.M. Yates, c1986. ii, 66 p. : forms ; 28 cm. Cover title. "SCORE." LC Card 86-209197 DDC 658.1/141/09768 19
1. New business enterprises - Tennessee - Management. I. Title. II. Title: Business of your own in Tennessee.
HD62.5 .Y28 1986

Yates, W. Ross (Willard Ross) Joseph Wharton : Quaker industrial pioneer / W. Ross Yates. Bethlehem : Lehigh University Press ; London : Associated University Press, c1987. 413 p. : ill. ; 24 cm. Bibliography: p. 389-401. Includes index. ISBN 0-934223-00-9 (alk. paper) LC Card 86-81983 DDC 338.7/6691/0924 B 19
1. Wharton, Joseph, 1826-1909. 2. Industrialists - United States - Biography. 3. Quakers - United States - Biography. 4. United States - Industries - History. I. Title.
HC102.5.W47 Y38 1987

Yayın (Devlet Planlama Teşkilatı (Turkey)) . (no. DPT 1664) Devlet Planlama Teşkilatı (Turkey) Dördüncü Beş Yıllık Kalkınma Planı, 1979-1983. Ankara [1979] xiv, 692 p. ; LC Card 83-228455
HC401 .A356 no. 1664 HC492

(no. DPT 1949) Hale, William M. Turkish agriculture and Community enlargement /. [Ankara] , 1984. 37 p. ; LC Card 87-113782 DDC 338.9561 s 338.1/09561 19
HC401 .A356 no. 1949 HD9016.T82

YBOR, VICENTE MARTINEZ, 1818-1896.
Westfall, L. Glenn, 1943- Don Vicente Martinez Ybor, the man and his empire . New York , 1987. vii, 214 p. : ISBN 0-8240-1374-3 (alk. paper) : LC Card 87-8690 DDC 338.7/67972/0924 19
HD9149.C5 U777 1987

Ycaza Clerc, Mónica de. Política de endeudamiento público interno en el Perú : el caso de los bonos de reinversión pública en el período, 1969-1981 / Mónica de Ycaza Clerc. Lima, Perú : Universidad de Lima, Facultad de Economía, Centro de Investigaciones Económicas y Sociales, 1985. ii, 23, [39] p. : ill. ; 30 cm. (Serie Avances de investigación . no. 8) A summary of thesis (bachiller en economía)--Universidad de Lima. Bibliography: p. [38]-[39] LC Card 86-223472
1. Debts, Public - Peru. 2. Bonds - Peru. 3. Finance, Public - Peru. I. Series: Avances de investigación (Universidad de Lima. Centro de Investigaciones Económicas y Sociales) , 8. II. Title.
HJ8604 .Y33 1985

Ycaza, Patricio.
Historia del movimiento obrero ecuatoriano : de su génesis al Frente Popular / Patricio Ycaza.2a ed. revisada. Quito : EDIME, 1984. 371 p. : ill. ; 16 cm. (Colección Análisis histórica . no. 1) Bibliography: p. 345-361.
1. Trade-unions - Ecuador - History. 2. Labor and laboring classes - Ecuador - History. I. Title. II. Series.
NYPL [JLB 86-21]

Movimiento obrero, estado y modernización capitalista en el Ecuador, 1960-1983 / Patricio Ycaza C. Ecuador : Editorial Rafael Perugachi, [1985 or 1986] 38 p. ; 20 cm. Bibliography: p. 33-38. LC Card 86-171415
1. Ecuador - Economic conditions - 1918-1972. 2. Ecuador - Economic conditions - 1972-. 3. Trade-unions - Ecuador. 4. Capitalism - Ecuador. I. Title.
HC202 .Y35 1985

Ydborn, Lars. Befolkningstillväxt och jordbruk : tre socknar i Halland 1780-1870 / Lars Ydborn. Göteborg : Historiska institutionen i Göteborg, c1984. 214 p. : ill. ; 23 cm. (Meddelanden från Historiska institutionen i Göteborg . nr 25) Summary in English. Thesis (doctoral)--Historiska institutionen, Göteborg, 1984. Extra t.p. with thesis statement and English abstract inserted. Bibliography: p. 208-215. ISBN 91-7222-705-2 LC Card 84-194466
1. Hallands län (Sweden) - Population, Rural. 2. Hallands län (Sweden) - Rural conditions. I. Series: Meddelanden från Historiska institutionen i Göteborg , nr. 25. II. Title.
HB2498.H35 Y38 1984

Yeager, Rodger. Wildlife, wild death : land use and survival in eastern Africa / Rodger Yeager, Norman N. Miller. Albany, NY : State University of New York Press in association with the African-Caribbean Institute, c1986. xvi, 173 p. : ill., maps ; 24 cm. (SUNY series in environmental public policy) Includes index. Bibliography: p. 162-168. ISBN 0-88706-168-0 LC Card 86-5791 DDC 333.95/16/09676 19
1. Wildlife conservation - Kenya. 2. Wildlife conservation - Tanzania. 3. Land use - Environmental aspects - Kenya. 4. Land use - Environmental aspects - Tanzania. 5. Agricultural ecology - Kenya. 6. Agricultural ecology - Tanzania. I. Miller, Norman, 1933-. II. Title. III. Series.
QL84.6.K4 Y43 1986 NYPL [JLE 86-3870]

The year ahead, 1986 . Naisbitt, John. New York, NY , c1985. 168 p. ; ISBN 0-446-38330-9 LC Card 85-17909 DDC 338.5/443/0973 19
HC106.8 .N35 1985 NYPL [JLD 86-2987]

A year in the life of a factory /. Seider, Maynard, 1943- San Pedro, Calif. , 1984. 152 p. ; ISBN 0-917300-16-5 (pbk.) : LC Card 83-50914 DDC 331.89/28621381/0979466 19
HD8039.E38 U67 1984
NYPL [JLD 86-4400]

Yearsley, Ronald. Porter, James. Integrating the computer with your business . London , 1980. 308 p. ; ISBN 0-372-30032-4
NYPL [JLD 86-2442]

Yearwood, John. Storage facilities in the chiefdoms of Bo and Pujehun District / by John Yearwood & Mike Momoh. Bo : Bo-Pujehun Rural Development Project, [1983] vi, 31 leaves : ill. ; 30 cm. "July 1983." LC Card 87-110214 DDC 338.1/6 19
1. Produce trade - Sierra Leone - Bo (District). 2. Produce trade - Sierra Leone - Pujehun (District). 3. Rural development projects - Sierra Leone - Bo (District). 4. Rural development projects - Sierra Leone - Pujehun (District). I. Momoh, Mike. II. B-P RDP (Project : Sierra Leone). III. Title.
HD9017.S53 B599 1983

The Yellow Pages report . Berdie, Douglas R. St. Paul, Minn. (905 Raymond Ave., St. Paul 55114) , c1986. 109 p. ; LC Card 86-209709 DDC 659.13/2 19
HF6146.T4 B45 1986

Yemen Arab Republic. see **Yemen.**

YEMEN - ECONOMIC CONDITIONS.
Becker, Fritz, 1947- Entwicklungseffekte durch Verkehrserschliessung in der Arabischen Republik Jemen . Bochum , 1984. 50 p. : LC Card 84-241945
HE268.7 .B4 1984 NYPL [JLH 86-2]

YEMEN (PEOPLE'S DEMOCRATIC REPUBLIC) - ECONOMIC CONDITIONS.
Burmistrov, V. N. (Vladimir Nikolaevich) Narodnaia DemokraticheskaiA Respublika Iemen . Moskva , 1981. 173, [3] p. ; LC Card 82-107303
HC415.342 .B87 1981

YEMEN (PEOPLE'S DEMOCRATIC REPUBLIC) - ECONOMIC POLICY.
Burmistrov, V. N. (Vladimir Nikolaevich) Narodnaia DemokraticheskaiA Respublika Iemen . Moskva , 1981. 173, [3] p. ; LC Card 82-107303
HC415.342 .B87 1981

YEMEN (PEOPLE'S DEMOCRATIC REPUBLIC) - FOREIGN ECONOMIC RELATIONS.
Burmistrov, V. N. (Vladimir Nikolaevich) Narodnaia DemokraticheskaiA Respublika Iemen . Moskva , 1981. 173, [3] p. ; LC Card 82-107303
HC415.342 .B87 1981

Yepes C., Alfonso. Del caos al orden : equidad y trabajo para todos / autor, Alfonso Yepes C. ; co-autor, Armando Valenzuela R. [S.l. : s.n., 1986] ([S.l.] : Editorial Nomos) 239 p., [1] leaf

of plates : ill. (some col.) ; 23 cm. Includes bibliographical references. LC Card 87-400255 DDC 331.1/1/09861 19
1. Manpower policy - Colombia. 2. Colombia - Economic policy. 3. Colombia - Social policy. I. Valenzuela Ruiz, Armando. II. Title.
HD5757.A6 Y46 1986

Yeraswork Admassie. Food-for-work in Ethiopia : a socio-economic survey / by Yeraswork Admassie and Solomon Gebre ; with the assistance of Julius Holt. Addis Abeba : Institute of Development Research, Addis Abeba University, 1985. viii, 102, [58] leaves : ill., forms, map ; 30 cm. (Research report / Institute of Development Research, Addis Abeba University . no. 24) "Report to the UN/FAO World Food Programme, and the Community Forests and Soil Conservation Development Department and the State Forests Conservation and Development Department, Ministry of Agriculture, Government of Socialist Ethiopia." Bibliography: leaf [160]. LC Card 86-980537 DDC 339.5/0963 19
1. Ethiopia - Full employment policies. 2. Ethiopia - Public works. 3. Food supply - Government policy - Ethiopia. I. Solomon Gebre. II. Holt, Julius F. J. III. World Food Programme. IV. Ethiopia. Community Forests and Soil Conservation Development Dept. V. Ethiopia. State Forests Conservation and Development Dept. VI. Series: Research report (Addis Abeba University. Institute of Development Research) , no. 24. VII. Title.
HD5839.7.A6 Y47 1985

Yergin, Daniel. Energy markets after the collapse . Cambridge, MA (56 John F. Kennedy St., Suite 5, Cambridge 02138) , c1987. 164 p. : LC Card 87-142725 DDC 338.2/728 19
HD9560.5 .E54 1987

The yes-I-can guide to mastering real estate . Fogel, Steven Jay, 1942- New York , c1987. xviii, 302 p. ; ISBN 0-8129-1637-9 : LC Card 86-28503 DDC 332.63/24 19
HD1382.5 .F64 1987

Yesufu, T. M. (Tijani M.)
Labour-management relations in public enterprises in Africa. 1983. Mesfin Gabre Michael. Labour-management relations in public enterprises in Africa. Geneva, Switzerland , 1983. 84 p. ; ISBN 92-2-103009-1 (pbk.) LC Card 86-213649 DDC 658.3 s 331/.04135/000096 19
HD6961.A1 I73 no. 60 HD8776.5

Yhdysvallat. see **United States.**

Ying Han yu hsüeh ming tz'u so yin. Yang, Jan-Syau. English-Chinese philatelic dictionary and identification key =. Winter Park, Fla. (340 Park Ave., N., Winter Park 32789) , c1986. [55] p. : LC Card 87-169624 DDC 769.56/014 19
HE6204.C6 Y36 1986

Ympäristöministeriön hallinnonalan toiminta- ja taloussuunnitelma vuosiksi 1987-1990 . Finland. Ympäristöministeriö. Helsinki , 1985. 152 leaves : LC Card 86-224557
HC340.2.Z9 E5 1985

Ympäristön- ja luonnonsuojeluosaston julkaisu D .
(19) Environmental policies in Finland . [Helsinki] [1986] 542 p. : ISBN 951-46-9823-1 LC Card 87-100734 DDC 363.7/056/094897 19
HC340.2.Z9 E52 1986

Yo trabajo así-- en casa particular /. Gálvez, Thelma. Santiago, Chile , 1985. 113 p. : LC Card 86-208887
HD6072.2.C5 G35 1985

Yochelson, John N. Stoga, Alan. Breaking the economic impasse . Washington, D.C. , c1987. viii, 48 p. ; ISBN 0-89206-104-9 (pbk.) LC Card 87-14682 DDC 338.9 19
HC59 .B73 1987

Yohay, Stephen C. Walsh, J. Michael (Joseph Michael), 1943- Drug and alcohol abuse in the workplace . Washington, D.C. , 1987. xiv, 149 p. ; ISBN 0-916559-08-4 (pbk.) LC Card 87-60167 DDC 658.3/822 19
HF5549.5.E42 W35 1987

Yokl, Robert T. The 10 biggest mistakes buyers make and how to avoid them / Robert T. Yokl. Willow Grove, PA (1834 Fleming Ave., Willow Grove 19090) : HCP Communications, c1987. 26 p. : ill. ; 28 cm. LC Card 87-61507 DDC 658.7/2 19
1. Purchasing. I. Title. II. Title: Ten biggest mistakes buyers make and how to avoid them.
HF5437 .Y65 1987

Yomo, Hiroshi. Financial innovation and monetary policy . [Tokyo] , c1986. ix, 339 p. : ISBN 4-13-047029-9 : LC Card 86-222823 DDC 332/.095 19
HG187.E37 F55 1986

Yonehara, Junshichirō. Local public finance in Japan / Junshichiro Yonehara. Canberra : Centre for Research on Federal Financial Relations, Australian National University ; Miami, Fla., USA : Distributed by ANU Press, 1981. xi, 112 p. : ill. ; 25 cm. (Research monograph / Centre for Research on Federal Financial Relations, the Australian National University, 0313-5969 . no. 36) Includes bibliographical references. ISBN 0-908160-89-5 : LC Card 80-68801 DDC 352.1/0952 19
1. Local finance - Japan. 2. Local finance - Law and legislation - Japan. I. Series: Australian National University, Canberra. Centre for Research on Federal Financial Relations. Research monograph, no. 36. 36. II. Title.
HJ9585 .Y663 1981
NYPL [JLM 75-1302 no. 36]

Yong, C. F. (Ching Fatt) Tan Kah-kee, the making of an overseas Chinese legend / C.F. Yong. Singapore : New York : Oxford University Press, 1987 [i.e. 1986] xix, 391 p., [16] p. of plates : ill., maps, ports. ; 23 cm. Bibliography: p. [365]-379. Includes index. ISBN 0-19-582678-7 LC Card 86-946451 DDC 338/.04/0924 B 19
1. Ch'en, Chia-keng, 1874-1961. 2. Industrialists - Singapore - Biography. I. Title.
HC445.8.C47 Y66 1986

YORK (NORTH YORKSHIRE) - ECONOMIC CONDITIONS.
Rowntree, B. Seebohm (Benjamin Seebohm), 1871-1954. Poverty . New York , 1980. xxi, 426 p. : ISBN 0-8240-0120-6 (alk. paper) : LC Card 79-56969 DDC 305.5/6 19
HC258.Y6 R64 1980 ***NYPL [JLD 86-3436]***

Yornet, Mario E. Combustibles : mercado, composición y evolución de los precios de los combustibles liquidos derivados del petróleo / Mario E. Yornet. Buenos Aires : Forum, [1980] 105, viii leaves : ill. ; 28 cm. (Colección Monografías) "Enero 1980." Includes bibliographical references. LC Card 84-134419
1. Petroleum as fuel - Prices - Argentina. I. Series: Colección Monografías (Fundación Forum (Argentina)). II. Title.
HD9574.A72 Y67 1980

Yoruba-Märkte in Nigeria . Adebowale, Annette, 1957- Aachen , c1987. xxvii, 225 p. : ISBN 3-922868-64-9 LC Card 87-141899 DDC 381/.18/096692 19
HF5475.N52 A362 1987

YORUBAS - ECONOMIC CONDITIONS.
Adebowale, Annette, 1957- Yoruba-Märkte in Nigeria . Aachen , c1987. xxvii, 225 p. : ISBN 3-922868-64-9 LC Card 87-141899 DDC 381/.18/096692 19
HF5475.N52 A362 1987

Spiro, Heather M. The Ilora farm settlement in Nigeria /. West Hartford, Conn. , 1985. xvii, 50 p. : ISBN 0-931816-20-3 LC Card 85-5230 DDC 331.4/83/089963 19
HD6073.F3 N667 1985
NYPL [JLF 86-1629]

YORUBAS - SOCIAL LIFE AND CUSTOMS.
Adebowale, Annette, 1957- Yoruba-Märkte in Nigeria . Aachen , c1987. xxvii, 225 p. : ISBN 3-922868-64-9 LC Card 87-141899 DDC 381/.18/096692 19
HF5475.N52 A362 1987

Yoshida, Mamoru. Japanese direct manufacturing investment in the United States / Mamoru Yoshida. New York : Praeger, 1987. xiv, 220 p. : ill. ; 25 cm. Originally presented as the author's thesis (doctoral--University of Miami) Includes index. Bibliography: p. 209-216. ISBN 0-275-92347-9 (alk. paper) : LC Card 86-22689 DDC 332.6/7352/073 19
1. Investments, Japanese - United States. 2. Corporations, Japanese - United States. I. Title.
HG4910 .Y58 1986 ***NYPL [JLE 87-1122]***

Yoshida, Satoshi, 1948- Endaka to kigyō shūeki : kawase sōba ni yure ugoku sangyōkai / [chosha Yoshida Satoshi]. [Higashimurayama-shi] : Kyōikusha ; Tōkyō : Hanbai Kyōikusha Shuppan Sābisu Kabushiki Kaisha, 1986. 137 p. : ill. ; 18 cm. (Jiji mondai kaisetsu . 463) In Japanese. Bibliography: p. 135-137. ISBN 4-315-50263-4 : LC Card 86-205176
1. Business enterprises - Japan - Finance. 2. Foreign exchange problem - Japan. 3. Japan - Industries - 1945-. I. Title.
HC462.9 .Y638 1986 <Orien Japan>
NYPL [*OSM 87-2489]

Yost, Elizabeth B. Career counseling : a psychological approach / Elizabeth B. Yost, M. Anne Corbishley.1st ed. San Francisco, Calif. : Jossey-Bass, c1987. xvi, 265 p. : ill. ; 24 cm. (The Jossey-Bass social and behavioral science series) The Jossey-Bass higher education series Bibliography: p. 253-259. Includes index. ISBN 1-555-42035-4 (alk. paper) LC Card 86-46335 DDC 158.6 19
1. Vocational guidance. I. Corbishley, M. Anne. II. Title.
HF5381 .Y58 1987

You can't kill the spirit . Miller, Jill. London , c1986. 142 p. : ISBN 0-7043-4021-6 (pbk.) : LC Card 87-100804 DDC 305.4/2/0942995 19
HD5365.M6152 1984 .W345 1986

You may call her madam secretary [motion picture] / Vineyard Video Productions ; producers and screenwriters, Marjory and Robert Potts ; director, Marjory Potts. West Tisbury, MA : Vineyard Video Productions, 1987. 1 film reel (57 min., 40 sec.) : sd., col. ; 16 mm. Title from data sheet. Frances Sternhagen (Frances Perkins) Camera, Dean Gaskill ; editors, Michael Grenadier, Robert Potts ; music, Jeff Bryant, Peter Huntington. Ages 13 through adults. Issued also as videorecording. Uses photographs, portraits, documents, political cartoons, newsreel footage, and recent interviews to present the life of Frances Perkins, who served as Franklin Roosevelt's secretary of labor from 1933 to 1945. LC Card 87-706816 DDC 973.917 11
1. Perkins, Frances, 1882-1965. 2. Cabinet officers - United States. 3. Women in politics - United States. 4. Labor policy - United States - History. I. Vineyard Video Productions.
HD8073.P38

You may call her madam secretary [videorecording] / Vineyard Video Productions ; producers and screenwriters, Marjory and Robert Potts ; director, Marjory Potts. West Tisbury, MA : Vineyard Video Productions, 1987. 1 videocassette (57 min., 40 sec.) : sd., col. Title from data sheet. Frances Sternhagen (Frances Perkins) Camera, Dean Gaskill ; editors, Michael Grenadier, Robert Potts ; music, Jeff Bryant, Peter Huntington. Ages 13 through adults. Issued as U-matic 3/4 in. or Beta 1/2 in. or VHS 1/2 in. Issued also as motion picture. Uses photographs, portraits, documents, political cartoons, newsreel footage, and recent interviews to present the life of Frances Perkins, who served as Franklin Roosevelt's secretary of labor from 1933 to 1945. LC Card 87-706817 DDC 973.917 11
1. Perkins, Frances, 1882-1965. 2. Cabinet officers - United States. 3. Women in politics - United States. 4. Labor policy - United States - History. I. Vineyard Video Productions.
HD8073.P38

You need me [filmstrip] : selling your talents to an employer / Human Relations Media, Inc. ; producer, Michael Hardy Productions ; writers, Erica Goldstein, Michael Hardy. Pleasantville, NY : Human Relations Media, 1986. 2 filmstrips (71 fr. each) : col. ; 35 mm. + 2 sound cassettes (30 min. : analog) + 1 teacher's guide. Title from data sheet. Photography, Michael Hardy ; consultant, Susan D. Hadley. Sound accompaniment compatible for manual and automatic operation. Junior high school through college students or adults. Issued also as videorecording. Introduces new skills that help young job applicants in finding, securing, and keeping a good job. Discusses how to write effective résumés, bypass personnel departments, create a network of personal contacts, and improve communications. CONTENTS. - pt. 1. Laying the groundwork -- pt. 2. Getting the job. LC Card 86-700183 DDC 650.1 11
1. Job hunting. 2. Youth - Employment. I. Human Relations Media, inc. II. Michael Hardy Productions.
HF382.7

You need me [videorecording] : selling your talents to an employer / Human Relations

Media, Inc. ; producer, Michael Hardy Productions ; writers, Erica Goldstein, Michael Hardy. Pleasantville, NY : Human Relations Media, 1986. 1 videocassette (30 min.) : sd., col. ; 1/2 in. + 1 teacher's guide. Title from data sheet. Photography, Michael Hardy ; consultant, Susan D. Hadley. VHS. Junior high school through college students and adults. Issued also as filmstrip. Introduces new skills that help young job applicants in finding, securing, and keeping a good job. Discusses how to write effective résumés, bypass personnel departments, create a network of personal contacts, and improve communications. CONTENTS. - pt. 1. Laying the groundwork -- pt. 2. Getting the job. LC Card 87-705080 DDC 650.1 11
1. Job hunting. 2. Youth - Employment. I. Human Relations Media, inc. II. Michael Hardy Productions.
HF5382.7

You, Poh Seng. Developing managers in Asia /. Singapore , Reading, Mass. , 1986. p. cm. ISBN 0-201-13653-8 : LC Card 86-28717 DDC 658/.007/15 19
HD38.25.A78 D48 1986

Youdi, R. Vesituluta. Forecasting skilled-manpower needs . Paris , 1985. 259 p. : ISBN 92-803-1122-3 (pbk.) LC Card 86-214025 DDC 331.12/3 19
HD5701.55 .F67 1985

Yougoslavie. see **Yugoslavia.**

You'll never get no for an answer /. Carew, Jack. New York , c1987. 224 p. : ISBN 0-671-62495-4 LC Card 87-13043 DDC 658.8/5 19
HF5438.25 .C33 1987

YOUNG ADULTS - EMPLOYMENT - RUSSIAN S.F.S.R. - SIBERIA, EASTERN.
Sotsial'noe razvitie molodezhi v trudovykh kollektivakh novykh gorodov Sibiri . Irkutsk , 1980. 158 p. ; LC Card 82-110658
HD6276.S593 S527 1980

YOUNG ADULTS - EMPLOYMENT - SOVIET UNION.
Davidovich, ÎA. A. Rabochaîa molodezh' SSSR v period razvitogo sotsializma . Moskva , 1985. 37 p. ; LC Card 86-187709
HD6276.S59 D38 1985

YOUNG ADULTS - EMPLOYMENT - SOVIET UNION, NORTHERN.
Khlystova, E. A. (Evgeniîa Andreevna) Sever i Sibir' zovut molodykh /. Moskva , 1985. 109 p. : LC Card 86-153085
HF5549.5.I5 K452 1985

YOUNG ADULTS - EMPLOYMENT - UNITED STATES.
Petras, Ross. Inside track . New York , c1986. xv, 508 p. ; ISBN 0-394-74339-3 : LC Card 85-40868 DDC 650.1/4/0973 19
HF5382.U5 P44 1986 *NYPL [*R-Econ. 86-3454]*

YOUNG ADULTS - FRANCE - HOUSING.
Galland, Olivier. Jeunes en transit . Paris , c1984. 236 p. ; ISBN 2-7082-2405-0 : LC Card 85-102779 DDC 367/.94486 19
HD6276.F72 G35 1984

YOUNG ADULTS - RUSSIAN S.F.S.R. - SIBERIA, EASTERN - RECREATION.
Sotsial'noe razvitie molodezhi v trudovykh kollektivakh novykh gorodov Sibiri . Irkutsk , 1980. 158 p. ; LC Card 82-110658
HD6276.S593 S527 1980

Young and Rubicam. Nonverbal communication in advertising /. Lexington, Mass. , c1988. viii, 296 p. : ISBN 0-669-14172-0 (alk. paper) LC Card 87-17143 DDC 659.1/01/9 19
HF5822 .N66 1988

Young (Arthur) and Company. Financial Industry Securities Council Same Day Funds Settlement Task Force. Same day funds settlement for securities transactions . [New York, N.Y.] [S.l.] , c1985. 61 leaves in various foliations : LC Card 85-193287 DDC 332.64 19
HG4631 .F56 1985 *NYPL [JLF 86-919]*

Young, Dennis, 1943- Silkman, Richard H. Subsidizing inefficiency . New York , 1985. xviii, 101 p.: ISBN 0-03-000662-7 (alk. paper) : LC Card 84-26628 DDC 336.1/85 19
HJ275 .S53 1985 *NYPL [JLE 85-2261]*

Young, Douglas J. House, Verne W. Trends in the Montana economy and taxation /. Bozeman [1986] 19 p. : LC Card 87-620963 DDC 330.9786/033 19
HC107.M9 H68 1986

Young drivers impaired by alcohol and other drugs / edited by Timothy Benjamin. London ; New York, NY : Royal Society of Medicine Services, c1987. p. cm. (International congress and symposium series . no. 116) "Proceedings of a symposium organised by the International Drivers' Behaviour Research Association and held in Paris, during 13-15 September 1986." Includes bibliographical references. ISBN 0-905958-48-9 (pbk) : LC Card 87-20657 DDC 363.1/251 19
1. Drinking and traffic accidents - Congresses. 2. Youth - Alcohol use - Congresses. 3. Drunk driving - Congresses. I. Benjamin, Timothy. II. International Drivers' Behaviour Research Association. III. Series.
HE5620.D7 Y68 1987

Young drivers involved in injury producing crashes . Rothe, John Peter, 1948- North Vancouver, B.C. , c1986. ii, 77 p. : ISBN 0-7726-0530-0 (pbk.) LC Card 87-167610 DDC 363.1/251 19
HE5620.J8 R67 1986

Young, Ellen.
Rosenthal, Daniel M. The case for South African gold mining stocks . Bethel, CT , c1987. vi, 57 p. : ISBN 0-938689-05-3 (pbk.) LC Card 87-160603 DDC 332.63/22 19
HG293 .R676 1987

Rosenthal, Daniel M. The new case for silver /. Lafayette, CA , c1986. ix, 157 p. : ISBN 0-9615814-1-7 (pbk.): LC Card 86-208965 DDC 332.63/28 19
HG305 .R67 1986

Rosenthal, Daniel M. A short course in gold investing . Bethel, CT , c1986. 90 leaves : ISBN 0-938689-00-2 (pbk.) : LC Card 86-207234 DDC 332.63 19
HG295.U6 R67 1986

Rosenthal, Daniel M. The silver & gold investor's profit guide . Bethel, CT , c1986. viii, 90 leaves : ISBN 0-938689-02-9 (pbk.) : LC Card 86-232188 DDC 332.63 19
HG307.U5 R67 1986

Rosenthal, Daniel M. Which 3 silver and gold dealers give you the worst prices? . Lafayette, CA , c1986. 58 leaves : ISBN 0-9615814-3-3 (pbk.) : LC Card 86-209287 DDC 332.63 19
HG307.U5 R673 1986

Young, Fred. Ontario. Legislative Assembly. Select Committee on Highway Safety. Select Committee on Highway Safety . [Ontario, Canada] [1977] 1 v. in various pagings : LC Card 85-184813
HE5614.5.C2 O5 1977

Young, Gay. Gender identification and working class solidarity among Maquila workers in Ciudad Juarez : stereotypes and realities / by Gay Young. [East Lansing] : Michigan State University, c1986. 24 p. ; 28 cm. (Working paper . #124) "September 1986." Bibliography: p. 22-24. LC Card 87-620601 DDC 331.4/87/097216 19
1. Women offshore assembly industry workers - Mexico - Ciudad Juárez. I. Series: Working paper (Michigan State University. Office of Women in International Development) , #124. II. Title.
HD6073.O332 M4959 1986

Young, Gordon, 1953- Schroeder, Ighsaan. Conditions of employment . Cape Town [1985]- 1 v. (loose-leaf) ; ISBN 0-7992-1002-1 (loose-leaf) LC Card 86-232933 DDC 331.2/0968 19
HD4927.S6 S37 1985

Young, Katherine E. Decision-making in the Soviet energy industry . Falls Church, VA (7700 Leesburg Pike, #250, Falls Church 22043) , c1986. ix, 166 leaves ; LC Card 87-401592 DDC 333.79/0947 19
HD9502.S652 D43 1986

YOUNG MEN - EMPLOYMENT - UNITED STATES.
The Changing labor market . Lexington, Mass. , c1986. x, 166 p. : ISBN 0-669-11943-1 (alk. paper) LC Card 85-45710 DDC 331.12/0973 19
HD6331.2.U5 C47 1986 *NYPL [JLE 86-1069]*

Young, Philip K. Y. The Pacific challenge in international business /. Ann Arbor, Mich. , 1987. viii, 342 p. ; ISBN 0-8357-1620-1 (alk. paper) LC Card 87-5008 DDC 338.09182/3 19
HC460.5 .P32 1987

Young programs for older workers . Jacobson, Beverly. New York , 1980. xvii, 123 p. ; ISBN 0-442-25405-9 LC Card 80-12621 DDC 658.3/042
HD6280 .J3 *NYPL [JLE 81-438]*

Young, Ray L. Timm, Paul R. Business communication . Englewood Cliffs, N.J. , c1987. xvi, 509 p. : ISBN 0-13-091779-6 LC Card 86-30650 DDC 658.4/5 19
HF5718 .T53 1987

Young, S. David, 1955- The rule of experts : occupational licensing in America / S. David Young. Washington, D.C. : Cato Institute, c1987. x, 99 p. ; 23 cm. Bibliography: p. 95-99. ISBN 0-932790-62-3 (pbk.) LC Card 87-736 DDC 351.82/43046 19
1. United States - Occupations - Licenses. I. Title.
HD3630.U7 Y68 1987

Young, Warren, 1949- Interpreting Mr. Keynes : the IS-LM enigma / by Warren Young. Boulder : Westview Press, 1986. p. cm. ISBN 0-8133-0533-0 : LC Card 87-10535 DDC 330.15/6 19
1. Keynesian economics. 2. Keynes, John Maynard, 1883-1946. 3. IS-LM model (Macroeconomics). I. Title.
HB99.7 .Y68 1986

Youngblood, Stuart A. Readings in personnel and human resource management /. St. Paul, MN , c1988. xix, 600 p. : ISBN 0-314-33750-4 (pbk.) LC Card 86-28244 DDC 658.3 19
HF5549 .R38167 1988

Yount, Virginia. Jackson, Mason, 1926- The building /. Interlaken, N.Y. , 1987. 128 p. : ISBN 0-932334-90-3 LC Card 86-24115 DDC 974.7/89043 19
HD8039.M4 U54 1987

Your attitude is showing . Chapman, Elwood N. Chicago , c1987. vii, 194 p. ; ISBN 0-574-20905-0 (pbk.) LC Card 86-26318 DDC 158.7 19
HF5548.8 .C36 1987

Your career game /. Vaughan, Hap. New York , c1987. x, 240 p. : ISBN 0-471-62949-9 (pbk.) LC Card 87-20964 DDC 650.1/4 19
HF5549.5.C35 V38 1987

Your fortune in foreclosures . Bush, Fredy. Tucson, Ariz. , c1987. ix, 221 p. : ISBN 0-89586-572-6 LC Card 86-33793 DDC 332.63/24 19
HD1382.5 .B87 1987

Your job [filmstrip] : keys to advancement / Human Relations Media, Inc. ; producer, Michael Hardy Productions ; writers, Erica Goldstein, Michael Hardy. Pleasantville, NY : Human Relations Media, 1986. 2 filmstrips (ca. 74 fr. each) : col. ; 35 mm. + 2 sound cassettes (30 min. : analog) + 1 teacher's guide. Title from data sheet. Photographer, Michael Hardy ; consultant, Susan D. Hadley. Sound accompaniment compatible for manual and automatic operation. Junior high school through college students and adults. Issued also as videorecording. Shows how to match abilities to fit a career path and how to advance once a job is taken. Discusses methods of identifying and clarifying goals, motivation and initiative, and expections of employers. CONTENTS. - pt. 1. Getting the right first job -- pt. 2. Moving ahead. LC Card 86-700184 DDC 650.1 11
1. Career development. 2. Promotions. I. Human Relations Media, inc. II. Michael Hardy Productions.
HF5549.5.C35

Your job [videorecording] : keys to advancement / Human Relations Media, Inc. ; producer, Michael Hardy Productions ; writers, Erica Goldstein, Michael Hardy. Pleasantville, NY : Human Relations Media, 1986. 1 videocassette (30 min.) : sd., col. ; 1/2 in. + 1 teacher's guide. Title from data sheet. Photographer, Michael Hardy ; consultant, Susan D. Hadley. VHS. Junior high school through college students and adults. Issued also as filmstrip. Shows how to match abilities to fit a career path and how to advance once a job is taken. Discusses methods of identifying and clarifying goals, motivation and initiative, and expections of employers. CONTENTS. - pt. 1. Getting the right first job -- pt. 2. Moving ahead. LC Card 87-705039 DDC 650.1 11
1. Career development. 2. Promotions. I. Human Relations Media, inc. II. Michael Hardy Productions.
HF5549.5.C35

Your money or your life . Le Goff, Jacques, 1924- [Bourse et la vie. English.] New York , Cambridge, Mass. , 1988. 116 p. ; ISBN 0-942299-14-0 (alk. paper) : LC Card 87-25248 DDC 330.94/01 19
HC41 .L43 1988

Your money personality . Gurney, Kathleen. New York , 1988. p. cm. ISBN 0-385-24254-9 LC Card 87-24449 DDC 332.4/01/9 19
HG222.3 .G87 1988

Your personal financial fitness program /. Lewin, Elizabeth. New York, N.Y. , c1987. p. cm. ISBN 0-8160-1580-5 LC Card 86-29093 DDC 332.024 19
HG179 .L48 1987

Your successful real estate career /. Edwards, Kenneth W., 1928- New York, NY , c1987. vii, 184 p. ; ISBN 0-8144-7675-9 (pbk.) : LC Card 86-47810 DDC 333.33/023/73 19
HD1375 .E33 1987

Your trade partners in Czechoslovakia / [editor in chief, Milada Černá]. Praha : Czechoslovak Chamber of Commerce and Industry, 1986. 187 p. : ill. ; 22 cm. Translated from Czech. LC Card 87-127524 DDC 382/.025/437 19
1. Czechoslovakia - Commerce - Directories. 2. Business enterprises - Czechoslovakia - Directories. 3. Trading companies - Czechoslovakia - Directories. I. Černa, Milada. II. Československá obchodní a průmyslová komora.
HF3550.3.A48 Y58 1986

Your 1987/88 guide to social security benefits /. Rubin, Leona G. New York, N.Y. , c1987. 194 p. ; ISBN 0-8160-1567-8 : LC Card 86-32917 DDC 368.4/3/00973 19
HD7125 .R78 1987

You're the boss /. Robinson, Joe. New York , c1987. x, 342 p. ; ISBN 0-312-01027-3 : LC Card 87-16149 DDC 658.4/2 19
HD62.5 .R59 1987

YOUTH, AFRO-AMERICAN. see **AFRO-AMERICAN YOUTH.**

YOUTH - ALCOHOL USE.
The Subject of a moment [motion picture] /. Provo, Utah , 1985. 1 film reel (ca. 27 min.) : LC Card 85-700877 DDC 362.7 11
HE5620.D7

YOUTH - ALCOHOL USE - CONGRESSES.
Young drivers impaired by alcohol and other drugs /. London , New York, NY , c1987. p. cm. ISBN 0-905958-48-9 (pbk) : LC Card 87-20657 DDC 363.1/251 19
HE5620.D7 Y68 1987

YOUTH AND MASS MEDIA. see **MASS MEDIA AND YOUTH.**

YOUTH AND SOCIALISM. see **SOCIALISM AND YOUTH.**

YOUTH AS CONSUMERS - GERMANY (WEST)
Buschmann, Vera, 1951- Wirkungsanalyse für segmentspezifische Warentestwerbung . Frankfurt am Main , New York , c1986. xii, 270 p. : ISBN 3-8204-9275-5 LC Card 86-220570
HF5827 .B87 1986

YOUTH AS CONSUMERS - UNITED STATES.
Graham, Lawrence. Youthtrends . New York , c1987. xx, 282 p. ; ISBN 0-312-00704-3 : LC Card 87-4426 DDC 658.8/348 19
HC110.C6 G67 1987

YOUTH CENTERS - FRANCE.
Galland, Olivier. Jeunes en transit . Paris , c1984. 236 p. ; ISBN 2-7082-2405-0 : LC Card 85-102779 DDC 367/.94486 19
HD6276.F72 G35 1984

Youth employment. Bullock, Paul. Youth training and employment from New Deal to New Federalism /. Los Angeles , c1985. xiii, 359 p. ; ISBN 0-89215-131-1 ***NYPL [JLD 86-2972]***

Youth employment. Organisation for Economic Co-operation and Development. Library. L'emploi des jeunes =. [Paris] , 1980. [6], 119 p. ; LC Card 81-122004 DDC 016.3313/4 19
HD6270 .O72 1980

YOUTH - EMPLOYMENT - ABSTRACTS.
Organisation for Economic Co-operation and Development. Library. L'emploi des jeunes =. [Paris] , 1980. [6], 119 p. ; LC Card 81-122004 DDC 016.3313/4 19
HD6270 .O72 1980

YOUTH - EMPLOYMENT - AFRICA.
Livingstone, Ian. Youth employment & youth employment programmes in Africa . Addis Ababa , 1986. 7 v. : ISBN 92-2-105527-2 (pbk. : v. 1) LC Card 87-980143 DDC 331.3/4/096 19
HD6276.A32 L58 1986

YOUTH - EMPLOYMENT - AFRICA - CONGRESSES.
JASPA Steering Group Meeting on Priority Employment Policies and Projects for Africa (1985 : Addis Ababa, Ethiopia) Report of JASPA Steering Group Meeting on Priority Employment Policies and Projects for Africa. Addis Ababa , 1986. 43 leaves ; LC Card 87-980227 DDC 331.12/042/096 19
HD5837.A6 J37 1985

Youth employment and technological change . Grant, Pamela, 1944- Aldershot, [England] , Brookfield, USA , c1987. xii, 393 p. : ISBN 0-566-05423-X : LC Card 86-33659 DDC 331.3/4125/0941 19
HD6276.G7 G66 1987

Youth employment and technological change. Grant, Pamela, 1944- Youth employment and technological change . Aldershot, [England] , Brookfield, USA , c1987. xii, 393 p. : ISBN 0-566-05423-X : LC Card 86-33659 DDC 331.3/4125/0941 19
HD6276.G7 G66 1987

Youth employment & youth employment programmes in Africa . Livingstone, Ian. Addis Ababa , 1986. 7 v. : ISBN 92-2-105527-2 (pbk. : v. 1) LC Card 87-980143 DDC 331.3/4/096 19
HD6276.A32 L58 1986

Youth employment and youth employment programmes in Africa. Livingstone, Ian. Youth employment & youth employment programmes in Africa . Addis Ababa , 1986. 7 v. : ISBN 92-2-105527-2 (pbk. : v. 1) LC Card 87-980143 DDC 331.3/4/096 19
HD6276.A32 L58 1986

YOUTH - EMPLOYMENT - AUSTRIA.
Amanshauser, Wilfried. Jugendarbeitsmarktförderung in Österreich /. Wien [1985] ii, 71, 3 p. ; LC Card 86-165982
HD6276.A9 A43 1985

YOUTH - EMPLOYMENT - BELGIUM.
Chômage des jeunes . Bruxelles [1984] 49 p. : LC Card 84-222918
HD6276.B42 C48 1984

YOUTH - EMPLOYMENT - BRAZIL.
Eu preciso trabalhar . Rio de Janeiro [between 1983 and 1986] 85 p. ; LC Card 86-150189
HD6276.B72 E9 1983

Spindel, Cheywa R. Espaços de socialização e exploração do menor assalariado . São Paulo, SP , 1986. 254 p. ; LC Card 87-405001 DDC 331.3/1/0981 19
HD6276.B72 S67 1986

YOUTH - EMPLOYMENT - BRAZIL - DISTRITO FEDERAL.
Sobrevivência, aspectos das condições de vida de menores trabalhadores de rua do Distrito Federal /. [Brasília] , 1983. 117 p. ; LC Card 86-197113
HD6276.B73 D577 1983

YOUTH - EMPLOYMENT - BULGARIA.
Izsledvane roli͡ata na proizvodstvenata sreda, trudovite kolektivi i nastavnitsite za formirane na komunistichesko otnoshenie kŭm truda u podrastvashchtite /. Sofii͡a , 1984. 150 p. ; LC Card 85-166784
HD6276.B82 I97 1984

Manolov, Angel. Sot͡sialno-ikonomicheski problemi na izpolzuvane truda na mladezhite /. Sofii͡a , 1984. 93 p. ; LC Card 86-226913
HD6276.B82 M36 1984

YOUTH - EMPLOYMENT - BULGARIA - HISTORY.
Kubadinski, Pencho P. Brigadirski ogn′ove . Sofii͡a , 1986. 119 p., [24] p. of plates : LC Card 86-235041
HD4870.B9 K83 1986

40 brigadirski leta /. Sofii͡a , 1986. 173 p., [12] p. of plates : LC Card 87-103049
HD4870.B9 A15 1986

YOUTH - EMPLOYMENT - DENMARK.
Ungdomsarbejdsløshed og beskæftigelsesforanstaltninger . København [1984] 100 leaves : LC Card 85-124463
HD6276.D4 U54 1984

YOUTH - EMPLOYMENT - FRANCE.
Galland, Olivier. Jeunes en transit . Paris , c1984. 236 p. ; ISBN 2-7082-2405-0 : LC Card 85-102779 DDC 367/.94486 19
HD6276.F72 G35 1984

YOUTH - EMPLOYMENT - FRANCE - HISTORY.
Debès, Joseph. L'appel de la J.O.C., 1926-1928 /. Paris , 1986. 292 p. : ISBN 2-204-02529-1 : LC Card 86-189508
HD8430 .D37 1986

YOUTH - EMPLOYMENT - GERMANY, WEST.
Alheit, Peter. Beschädigtes Leben . Frankfurt[/Main] , New York , c1986. 361 p. ; ISBN 3-593-33606-5 LC Card 86-148737
HD6276.G4 A44 1986

Arbeitslose Jugendliche, eine Zielgruppe für Fernsehen und Hörfunk? /. München , New York , 1985. 157 p. : ISBN 3-598-20759-X LC Card 86-153843
HD6276.G39 A73 1985

Behnken, Imbke, 1941- Jugendbiografie und Handlungsforschung /. Frankfurt [am Main] , c1984. xi, 239 p. ; ISBN 3-88704-402-9 LC Card 84-174719 DDC 331.3/425922/0943 19
HD4885.G3 B425 1984 ***NYPL [JLD 86-1892]***

Haar, Heinrich von der. Jugendarbeitslösigkeit und soziale Sicherung . Berlin , c1982. 216 p. : ISBN 3-88114-302-5 : LC Card 83-152854 DDC 331.3/4/0943 19
HD7096.G3 H33 1982 ***NYPL [JLE 87-1214]***

Knöpfel, Eckehardt. Werkbuch Jugendarbeitslosigkeit . Wuppertal , c1983. 168 p. : ISBN 3-417-12855-2 (pbk.) LC Card 87-672977
HD5779 .K59x 1983

Kunert-Schroth, Heidrun. Jugendarbeitslosigkeit, lokale Ausprägungen und kommunale Strategien . Berlin , 1987. 172 p. ; ISBN 3-88118-135-0 LC Card 87-409103 DDC 331.3/412/0943 19
HD6276.G4 K86 1987

Maier, Hans E. Das Handwerk und die Berufseingliederung Jugendlicher in der Bundesrepublik Deutschland /. Berlin [1986] 68 p. : LC Card 86-230660
HD5715.5.G4 M35 1986

Offene Jugendarbeit im Arbeiterviertel . Bensheim , 1978. 229 p. : ISBN 3-921450-57-8 LC Card 84-120278
HD6276.G4 O38 1978

Sardei-Biermann, Sabine. Jugendliche zwischen Schule und Arbeitswelt . München , c1984. v, 318 p. ; ISBN 3-87966-219-3 LC Card 84-240405
HD5715.5.G4 S27 1984

YOUTH - EMPLOYMENT - GERMANY, WEST - CONGRESSES.
Arbeitsmarkterfahrungen und Berufsorientierungen Jugendlicher . München , c1983. 177 p. : ISBN 3-87966-202-9 LC Card 84-170074
HD6276.G4 A73 1983

Arbeitsmoral und Technikfeindlichkeit . Frankfurt , New York , c1986. 274 p. : ISBN 3-593-33757-6 LC Card 86-212283
HD8444 .A73 1986

YOUTH - EMPLOYMENT - GERMANY (WEST) - RUHR (REGION)
Fokkink, Manfred, 1955- Denk ja nicht, Du bist selber schuld . Gelsenkirchen-Buer , 1980. 180 p. : LC Card 82-114713
HD6276.G4 F6 1980 ***NYPL [JLE 86-1457]***

YOUTH - EMPLOYMENT - GOVERNMENT POLICY - AFRICA - COLLECTED WORKS.
Les Programmes spéciaux d'emploi et de formation de la jeunesse ... Addis Abéba , 1985- v. <1-6 > : LC Card 86-981200
HD6276.A3 P76 1985

YOUTH - EMPLOYMENT - GOVERNMENT POLICY - BRAZIL.
Eu preciso trabalhar . Rio de Janeiro [between

1983 and 1986] 85 p. ; LC Card 86-150189
HD6276.B72 E9 1983

YOUTH - EMPLOYMENT - GOVERNMENT POLICY - CONGRESSES.
Le Iniziative locali per l'occupazione . Milano, Italy , c1985. 244 p. : LC Card 85-221711 DDC 331 s 331.12/042 19
HD85.I7 I68 no. 75 HD5713.5
NYPL [JLD 87-446]

YOUTH - EMPLOYMENT - GREAT BRITAIN.
Chapman, Paul G., 1952- The youth training scheme in the United Kingdom /. Aldershot, Hants, England , Brookfield, Vt., U. S.A. , c1987. x, 124 p. ; ISBN 0-566-05360-8 : LC Card 86-29604 DDC 331.3/42592/0941 19
HD5715.5.G7 C47 1987

Getting into life /. London , New York , c1986. xii, 157 p. ; ISBN 0-416-40850-8 LC Card 86-16186 DDC 305.2/35/0941 19
HQ799.G7 G48 1986 NYPL [JLD 87-892]

Grant, Pamela, 1944- Youth employment and technological change . Aldershot, [England] , Brookfield, USA , c1987. xii, 393 p. : ISBN 0-566-05423-X : LC Card 86-33659 DDC 331.3/4125/0941 19
HD6276.G7 G66 1987

Hart, P. E. (Peter Edward) Youth unemployment in Great Britain /. Cambridge [Cambridgeshire] , New York, NY, USA , 1988. p. cm. ISBN 0-521-35348-3 LC Card 87-25597 DDC 331.3/4137941 19
HD6276.G72 H37 1988

Roberts, Kenneth, 1940- School-leavers and their prospects . Milton Keynes , 1984. viii, 133 p. ; ISBN 0-335-10418-5 (pbk.) LC Card 87-672221
HD6276.G72 R62x 1984

Robins, David, 1944- We hate humans /. Harmondsworth, Middlesex, England , New York, N.Y. , 1984. 155 p. ; ISBN 0-14-007062-1
NYPL [JLD 86-4404]

Verma, Gajendra K. Race, training, and employment /. London , New York , 1987. vi, 134 p. : ISBN 1-85000-243-6 : LC Card 87-15470 DDC 331.3/46/0941 19
HD5715.5.G7 V47 1987

YOUTH - EMPLOYMENT - HUNGARY.
Érettségizettek a munkaerőpiacon /. Budapest , 1985. 124 p. ; ISBN 963-404-026-8 LC Card 87-409614
HD6276.H82 E73 1985

YOUTH - EMPLOYMENT - HUNGARY - SOMOGY MEGYE.
Lugossy, Györgyi. Szándékok és lehetőségek . Budapest , 1985. 85 p. : ISBN 963-491-215-X LC Card 86-199350
HD1492.H82 S665 1985

YOUTH - EMPLOYMENT - ISRAEL - GALILEE.
Schwartz, Moshe. Non-agricultural employment for moshav youth in the Galilee /. Rehovot, Israel , c1985. 36, [2] p. ; LC Card 86-115596 DDC 331.3/4/0956945 19
HD6276.I66 G347 1985

YOUTH - EMPLOYMENT - ITALY.
Ferragni, Fabrizio. Guida al primo lavoro /. Milano , 1986. 271 p. : ISBN 88-17-13617-4 : LC Card 86-193250
HD6276.I7 F47 1986

I Giovani e il mondo del lavoro. Milano [1982] 241 p. : LC Card 84-230716
HD6276.I7 G499 1982

YOUTH - EMPLOYMENT - KENYA.
Kayongo-Male, Diane. Children at work in Kenya /. Nairobi , New York , 1984. x, 187 p. : ISBN 0-19-572546-8 (pbk.) LC Card 85-980979 DDC 331.3/1/096761 19
HD6250.K4 K39 1984 NYPL [Sc D 86-960]

YOUTH - EMPLOYMENT - NEW MEXICO - STATISTICS.
New Mexico youth in the labor force. [Albuquerque, N.M.] (P.O. Box 1928, Albuquerque 87103) [1986] v leaves, 74 p. : LC Card 87-620614 DDC 331.3/4/09789 19
HD6274.N6 N49 1986

YOUTH - EMPLOYMENT - NEW YORK (N. Y.)
Going for it [motion picture] /. New York, NY , 1987. 1 film reel (12 min.) : LC Card 87-705727 DDC 331.3 11
HD6275

Going for it [videorecording] /. New York, NY , 1987. 1 videocassette (12 min.) : LC Card 87-705728 DDC 331.3 11
HD6275

YOUTH - EMPLOYMENT - NICARAGUA - MANAGUA.
D'Ciófalo V., Giovanni. El trabajo infantil urbano en Managua /. Managua , 1986. ii, 76, 3, [33] leaves ; LC Card 87-403894 DDC 331.3/1/09728513 19
HD6250.N5 M363 1986

YOUTH - EMPLOYMENT - QUÉBEC (PROVINCE)
Bisaillon, Guy. Service national du Québec . Québec [1981] 54, [4] leaves ; LC Card 82-212578
HD4870.C2 B57 1981

YOUTH - EMPLOYMENT - SOVIET UNION.
Chanturiīa, V. K. (Vladimir Kapitonovich) Molodezh′ i udarnyĭ kommunisticheskiĭ trud . Moskva , 1981. 205 p. : LC Card 82-178361
HD6276.S592 C46 1981

Davidovich, ĪA. A. Rabochaīa molodezh′ SSSR v period razvitogo sotsializma . Moskva , 1985. 37 p. ; LC Card 86-187709
HD6276.S59 D38 1985

Kuzin, V. Komsomol′sko-molodezhnyĭ kollektiv /. Moskva , 1981. 157 p. ; LC Card 82-152678
HD6276.S592 K89 1981

YOUTH - EMPLOYMENT - SOVIET UNION - PICTORIAL WORKS.
Molodost′, trud, romantika . Moskva , 1985. 183 p., [8] p. of plates : LC Card 86-113851
HD4870.S65 M65 1985

YOUTH - EMPLOYMENT - SPAIN.
Montoro Romero, Ricardo. La inserción en la actividad económica, empleo y paro juvenil /. Barcelona , Madrid , c1985. 191 p. ; ISBN 84-86434-11-4 LC Card 86-186530
HD6276.S672 M65 1985

YOUTH - EMPLOYMENT - UNITED STATES.
Breakthrough for disadvantaged youth. [Washington] 1969. iii, 256 p. LC Card 79-604757 DDC 331.3/4/0973
HD6273 .B7 NYPL [JLF 86-435]

Bullock, Paul. Youth training and employment from New Deal to New Federalism /. Los Angeles , c1985. xiii, 359 p. ; ISBN 0-89215-131-1 *NYPL [JLD 86-2972]*

Occupations in energy-related industries [microform] . Washington, D.C. , 1981. ca. 300 p. ; *NYPL [*XME-11,557]*

Riehm, Sarah, 1952- The teenage enterpreneur's guide . Chicago, IL , c1987. viii, 211 p. : ISBN 0-940625-00-8 (pbk.) : LC Card 87-1904 DDC 658/.041 19
HD6273 .R53 1987

United States. Employment and Training Administration. Office of Youth Program. Completing the youth agenda . Washington , 1979. 73 p. ; *NYPL [JLF 86-454]*

United States. Vice President's Task Force on Youth Employment. A summary report of the Vice President's Task Force on Youth Employment. Washington , 1980. 70 p. :
NYPL [JLF 86-214]

Williams, Donald R., 1956- Labor force participation of black and white youth /. Ann Arbor, Mich. , c1987. 125 p. ; ISBN 0-8357-1804-2 (alk. paper) LC Card 87-5868 DDC 331.3/412/0973 19
HD6273 .W48 1987

Williams, Terry (Terry M.) Growing up poor /. Lexington, MA , c1985. xvi, 136 p. ; ISBN 0-669-09687-3 (alk. paper) LC Card 84-48564 DDC 362.7/044 19
HV1431 .W55 1985 NYPL [JLE 85-2236]

YOUTH - EMPLOYMENT - WEST VIRGINIA.
West Virginia youth and the labor market /. Charleston, W.Va. (112 California Ave., Charleston 25305-0112) [1986] iii, 76 p. ; LC Card 86-622615 DDC 331.3/4129754 19
HD6274.W4 W483 1986

YOUTH - FINANCE, PERSONAL - JUVENILE LITERATURE.
Spiselman, David, 1947- A teenager's guide to money, banking, and finance /. New York , c1987. p. cm. ISBN 0-671-64345-2 LC Card 87-11059 DDC 332.024 19
HG179 .S5554 1987

YOUTH - GERMANY, WEST.
Ziefuss, Horst. Jugendliche in der gewerblich-technischen Ausbildung in Industrie und Handwerk . Kiel , c1986. 352 p. : ISBN 3-89088-011-8 LC Card 87-407898 DDC 331.3/42592/0943 19
HD5715.5.G4 Z54 1986

YOUTH - GERMANY (WEST) - ATTITUDES.
Behnken, Imbke, 1941- Jugendbiografie und Handlungsforschung /. Frankfurt [am Main] , c1984. xi, 239 p. ; ISBN 3-88704-402-9 LC Card 84-174719 DDC 331.3/425922/0943 19
HD4885.G3 B425 1984
NYPL [JLD 86-1892]

Hein, Peter Ulrich. Protestkultur und Jugend . Münster , 1984. iii, 151 p. ; ISBN 3-88660-109-9
NYPL [JLD 86-2444]

YOUTH - GERMANY (WEST) - ATTITUDES - CONGRESSES.
Arbeitsmarkterfahrungen und Berufsorientierungen Jugendlicher . München , c1983. 177 p. : ISBN 3-87966-202-9 LC Card 84-170074
HD6276.G4 A73 1983

YOUTH - GERMANY, WEST - POLITICAL ACTIVITY.
Hein, Peter Ulrich. Protestkultur und Jugend . Münster , 1984. iii, 151 p. ; ISBN 3-88660-109-9
NYPL [JLD 86-2444]

Roth, Rainer A., 1942- Zur Problematik der politischen Kultur der Jungwähler in der Bundesrepublik Deutschland /. Passau , c1984. 516 p. : ISBN 3-922016-46-4
NYPL [JLE 87-703]

YOUTH - GOVERNMENT POLICY - AFRICA.
Livingstone, Ian. Youth employment & youth employment programmes in Africa . Addis Ababa , 1986. 7 v. : ISBN 92-2-105527-2 (pbk. : v. 1) LC Card 87-980143 DDC 331.3/4/096 19
HD6276.A32 L58 1986

YOUTH - GOVERNMENT POLICY - BULGARIA.
Aktivizirane na mladezhkoto nauchno i tekhnichesko tvorchestvo /. Sofiīa , 1985. 135 p. : LC Card 86-220354
HC403.Z9 T419 1985

YOUTH - GREAT BRITAIN.
Getting into life /. London , New York , c1986. xii, 157 p. ; ISBN 0-416-40850-8 LC Card 86-16186 DDC 305.2/35/0941 19
HQ799.G7 G48 1986 NYPL [JLD 87-892]

YOUTH - GREAT BRITAIN - PSYCHOLOGY.
Getting into life /. London , New York , c1986. xii, 157 p. ; ISBN 0-416-40850-8 LC Card 86-16186 DDC 305.2/35/0941 19
HQ799.G7 G48 1986 NYPL [JLD 87-892]

YOUTH HOSTELS - FRANCE.
Galland, Olivier. Jeunes en transit . Paris , c1984. 236 p. ; ISBN 2-7082-2405-0 : LC Card 85-102779 DDC 367/.94486 19
HD6276.F72 G35 1984

YOUTH - HOUSING - DENMARK.
Kjær Jensen, Mogens. Unges boligsituation /. København , 1983. 139 p. : ISBN 87-7487-228-1 : LC Card 83-189408
HD7347.A3 K53 1983
NYPL [JLK 73-237 v.116]

YOUTH - MENTAL HEALTH - GERMANY (WEST)
Kornblum, Hans-Joachim. Therapie in der Berufsschule? . München , c1984. x, 458 p. : ISBN 3-597-10503-3 : LC Card 85-105593
HD5715.5.G4 K67 1984

YOUTH - ROMANIA - HISTORY - 20TH CENTURY.
Kampf und Arbeit . Kronstadt , 1936. 102 p., [1] leaf of plates : LC Card 84-255742
HD7290 .K35 1936

YOUTH - SOCIAL ASPECTS - GERMANY (WEST)
Offene Jugendarbeit im Arbeiterviertel . Bensheim , 1978. 229 p. : ISBN 3-921450-57-8

LC Card 84-120278
HD6276.G4 O38 1978

Youth training and employment from New Deal to New Federalism /. Bullock, Paul. Los Angeles , c1985. xiii, 359 p. ; ISBN 0-89215-131-1 *NYPL [JLD 86-2972]*

The youth training scheme in the United Kingdom /. Chapman, Paul G., 1952- Aldershot, Hants, England , Brookfield, Vt., U. S.A. , c1987. x, 124 p. ; ISBN 0-566-05360-8 : LC Card 86-29604 DDC 331.3/42592/0941 19
HD5715.5.G7 C47 1987

Youth trends. Graham, Lawrence. Youthtrends . New York , c1987. xx, 282 p. ; ISBN 0-312-00704-3 : LC Card 87-4426 DDC 658.8/348 19
HC110.C6 G67 1987

Youth unemployment in Great Britain /. Hart, P. E. (Peter Edward) Cambridge [Cambridgeshire] , New York, NY, USA , 1988. p. cm. ISBN 0-521-35348-3 LC Card 87-25597 DDC 331.3/4137941 19
HD6276.G72 H37 1988

YOUTH - UNITED STATES - ALCOHOL USE.
Drunk driving [videorecording] . Lincoln, NE , 1983. 1 videocassette (30 min.) : LC Card 87-706347 DDC 363.1 11
HE5620.D7

DUII, the price is too high [motion picture] /. Van Nuys, CA , 1987. 1 film reel (23 min.) : LC Card 87-706705 DDC 363.1 11
HE5620.D7

DUII, the price is too high [videorecording] /. Van Nuys, CA , 1987. 1 videocassette (23 min.) : LC Card 87-706706 DDC 363.1 11
HE5620.D7

YOUTH - UNITED STATES - SOCIETIES AND CLUBS.
VICA (Association) VICA United States Skill Olympics regulations. Leesburg, Va. (P.O. Box 3000, Leesburg 22075) , c1986. 113 p. : LC Card 87-129841 DDC 331.7/02/06073 19
HF5381.A1 V4 1986

YOUTH VOLUNTEERS IN SOCIAL SERVICE - GUYANA.
Youthtrends . Graham, Lawrence. New York , c1987. xx, 282 p. ; ISBN 0-312-00704-3 : LC Card 87-4426 DDC 658.8/348 19
HC110.C6 G67 1987

Yritysjohdon valmennusohjelma / Raoul Johnsson ... [et al.]. [Helsinki] : Ammattikasvatushallitus : Valtion painatuskeskus, [1985] 2 v. : ill. ; 30 cm. Bibliography: v. 1, p. 13. CONTENTS. - 1. Yritystoiminta, työnjohto, työsuhdeasiat -- 2. Laskentatoimi, markkinointi. ISBN 951-859-860-6 (v. 1) LC Card 87-101417
1. Industrial management. 2. Industrial management - Finland. I. Johnsson, Raoul.
HD37.F55 Y73 1985

Yrkesvalsfågan . Mattsson, Kerstin, 1946- [Malmö] , c1984. vii, 268 p. ; ISBN 91-40-05057-2 : LC Card 84-200481
HF5382.5.S8 M37 1984

Yu, Wŏn-dong. Le déclin des marchands privilégiés en Corée : fin du XVIIIe siècle, début du XIXe siècle / Yu Wŏndong. [Paris] : Collège de France, Centre d'études coréennes : distribué par la librairie Le Léopard d'or, 1984. 104 p. : ill. ; 24 cm. (Mémoires du Centre d'études coréennes . v. 4) Bibliography: p. [97]-104. ISBN 2-905358-03-3 : LC Card 85-131336
1. Korea - Commerce - History. 2. Korea - Manufactures - History. I. Title. II. Series.
HF3830.5 .Y78 1984

Yugoslav aluminum and aluminium products = Jugoslawisches Aluminium und Aluminium Produkte. Beograd : [Niro Exportpress], 1986. 83 p. : ill. (some col.) ; 23 cm. English, German, and Russian. LC Card 87-108615
1. Aluminum industry and trade - Yugoslavia. I. Title: Jugoslawisches Aluminium und Aluminium Produkte.
HD9539.A63 Y89 1986

Yugoslav copper and copper products = Jugoslawisches Kupfer und Kupfererzeugnisse. Beograd : [Niro Exportpress], 1986. 83 p. : col. ill. ; 23 cm. England, German, and Russian. LC Card 87-108608
1. Copper industry and trade - Yugoslavia. I. Title: Jugoslawisches Kupfer und Kupfererzeugnisse.
HD9539.C7 Y87 1986

YUGOSLAVIA - CENSUS, 1971.
Savezni zavod za statistiku (Yugoslavia) [Popis stanovništva i stanova 1971. English.] Population and housing census 1971 . Beograd , 1974. 12 v. ; LC Card 83-122836
HA1631.5 1971 .S38 1974

YUGOSLAVIA - COMMERCE.
Kovač, Josef. Neuerungen in den Aussenwirtschafts- und Devisenvorschriften Jugoslawiens /. Hamburg , c1985. 100 p. : ISBN 3-9800762-9-6 LC Card 86-160924
HG3965.5 .K68 1985

Novi devizni i spoljnotrgovinski režim SFRJ. English. The New foreign exchange and foreign trade regime of Yugoslavia /. Belgrade , 1986. 217 p. ; ISBN 86-7145-007-4 LC Card 87-148102 DDC 332.4/5609497 19
HG3965.5 .N6813 1986

Review of exporters and importers of Yugoslavia . Zagreb , 1965. ca. 650 p. : LC Card 84-149403
HF3732.3 .R46 1965

YUGOSLAVIA - ECONOMIC CONDITIONS - 1945-
Crnobrnja, Mihailo. Čovekova životna sredina i ekonomski razvoj /. Beograd [1984?] 206 p. : LC Card 86-184927
HC407.Z9 E55 1984

Jugoslovenska privreda između stagnacije i razvoja /. Beograd , 1986. viii, 298 p. : LC Card 87-151260
HC407 .J83 1986

Lysestøl, Peder Martin. Jugoslavia . [Oslo] , c1985. 179 p. : ISBN 82-7094-421-1 LC Card 86-204691
HC407 .L97 1985

Popović, Strašimir, 1916- Ogled o privrednom sistemu Jugoslavije /. Beograd [1983?] 165 p. ; LC Card 86-197560
HC407 .P65 1983

Savić, Nebojša, 1951- The scenario for Yugoslav economic recovery . Belgrade , c1986. 38 p. ; LC Card 87-165987 DDC 338.9497 19
HC407 .S284 1986

Yagci, Fahrettin, 1944- Macroeconomic policies and adjustment in Yugoslavia . Washington, D.C. [1987] 29 p. ; ISBN 0-8213-0938-2 (pbk.) LC Card 87-16064 DDC 339.5/09497 19
HC407.Y6 Y34 1987

YUGOSLAVIA - ECONOMIC CONDITIONS - 1945- - ECONOMETRIC MODELS.
Popović, Dejan. Ekonomski efekti posrednih poreza /. Beograd , 1983. 286 p. : LC Card 86-173775
HJ5156.5 P67 1983

Sapir, André. Ekonomska reforma i migracije u Jugoslaviji . Zagreb , 1983. 56 p. ; LC Card 86-183906
HC407 .S26 1983

YUGOSLAVIA - ECONOMIC POLICY - 1945-
Družba, znanost, tehnologija . Ljubljana , 1982. 472 p. ; LC Card 84-235191
HC407.Z9 T434 1982

Jovanov, Neca. Dijagnoza samoupravljanja 1974-1981 /. Zagreb , 1983. 365 p. ; LC Card 84-146844
HD5660.Y8 J68 1983

Jugoslovenska privreda između stagnacije i razvoja /. Beograd , 1986. viii, 298 p. : LC Card 87-151260
HC407 .J83 1986

Milošević, Nikša. Sistem udruženog rada /. Beograd , 1985. 392 p. : LC Card 86-197428
HD5660.Y8 M55 1985

Mirić, Rade. Proces samoupravne integracije . Bačka Topola , 1984. 147 p. ; LC Card 85-194104
HD5660.Y8 M57 1984

Problemi samoupravne organizacije /. Zagreb , 1981. xi, 237 p. ; LC Card 83-110609
HD5660.Y8 P675 1981

Savić, Nebojša, 1951- The scenario for Yugoslav economic recovery . Belgrade , c1986. 38 p. ; LC Card 87-165987 DDC 338.9497 19
HC407 .S284 1986

Soós, Károly Attila. Terv, kampány, pénz . Budapest , 1986. 532 p. : ISBN 963-221-575-3 : LC Card 87-137237
HB3787.5 .S66 1986

Turk, Ivan. Iskazivanje i ocjenjivanje rezultata poslovanja organizacija udruženog rada /. Zagreb , 1982. x, 171 p. ; LC Card 83-110726
HD70.Y8 T87 1982

Vekić, Đuro. Samoupravljanje od ideje do stvarnosti /. Sarajevo [1983?] 263 p. ; LC Card 86-115347
HD5660.Y8 V44 1983

Yagci, Fahrettin, 1944- Macroeconomic policies and adjustment in Yugoslavia . Washington, D.C. [1987] 29 p. ; ISBN 0-8213-0938-2 (pbk.) LC Card 87-16064 DDC 339.5/09497 19
HC407.Y6 Y34 1987

YUGOSLAVIA - EMIGRATION AND IMMIGRATION.
Künne, Wilfried. Die Aussenwanderung jugoslawischer Arbeitskräfte . Königstein/Ts. , 1979. xii, 269 p. : ISBN 3-7756-6931-0 : LC Card 79-394439
HD8633.5 .K83 *NYPL [JLD 87-1148]*

YUGOSLAVIA - EMIGRATION AND IMMIGRATION - ECONOMETRIC MODELS.
Sapir, André. Ekonomska reforma i migracije u Jugoslaviji . Zagreb , 1983. 56 p. ; LC Card 86-183906
HC407 .S26 1983

YUGOSLAVIA - ENVIRONMENTAL POLICY.
Environmental policies in Yugoslavia . Paris [Washington, D.C.] c1986. 160 p., [2] p. of plates : ISBN 92-64-12866-2 (pbk.) : LC Card 87-120078 DDC 363.7/056/09497 19
HC407.Z9 E555 1986

YUGOSLAVIA - FOREIGN ECONOMIC RELATIONS.
Linden, Ronald Haly. Communist states and international change . Boston , c1987. xviii, 201 p. ; ISBN 0-04-497050-1 : LC Card 87-11389 DDC 337.497 19
HF1581 .L56 1987

Yugoslavia - Government. see **Yugoslavia - Politics and government.**

YUGOSLAVIA - INDUSTRIES.
Review of exporters and importers of Yugoslavia . Zagreb , 1965. ca. 650 p. : LC Card 84-149403
HF3732.3 .R46 1965

YUGOSLAVIA - POLITICS AND GOVERNMENT - 1945-
Jovanov, Neca. Dijagnoza samoupravljanja 1974-1981 /. Zagreb , 1983. 365 p. ; LC Card 84-146844
HD5660.Y8 J68 1983

Linden, Ronald Haly. Communist states and international change . Boston , c1987. xviii, 201 p. ; ISBN 0-04-497050-1 : LC Card 87-11389 DDC 337.497 19
HF1581 .L56 1987

Milošević, Nikša. Sistem udruženog rada /. Beograd , 1985. 392 p. : LC Card 86-197428
HD5660.Y8 M55 1985

Problemi samoupravne organizacije /. Zagreb , 1981. xi, 237 p. ; LC Card 83-110609
HD5660.Y8 P675 1981

Vekić, Đuro. Samoupravljanje od ideje do stvarnosti /. Sarajevo [1983?] 263 p. ; LC Card 86-115347
HD5660.Y8 V44 1983

YUGOSLAVIA - POPULATION - STATISTICS.
Savezni zavod za statistiku (Yugoslavia) [Popis stanovništva i stanova 1971. English.] Population and housing census 1971 . Beograd , 1974. 12 v. ; LC Card 83-122836
HA1631.5 1971 .S38 1974

YUGOSLAVIA - STATISTICAL SERVICES.
Babić, Bogdan. Statistički informacioni sistem SR Srbije u društvenom sistemu informisanja republike . Beograd , 1986- v. <1 > ; LC Card 87-168381
HA37.Y83 S43 1986

YUGOSLAVIA - STATISTICAL SERVICES - LAW AND LEGISLATION.
Babić, Bogdan. Statistički informacioni sistem SR Srbije u društvenom sistemu informisanja

republike . Beograd , 1986- v. <1 > ; LC Card 87-168381
HA37.Y83 S43 1986

Yunis, José. Barrancabermeja : nacimiento de la clase obrera / José Yunis, Carlos Nicolás Hernández.1a ed. Bogotá : Tres Culturas Editores, 1986. 102 p. : ill., ports. ; 25 cm. ISBN 958-9096-03-4 LC Card 87-400984 DDC 331.7/6223382/0986125 19
1. Labor and laboring classes - Colombia - Barrancabermeja. 2. Petroleum workers - Colombia - Barrancabermeja. I. Hernández, Carlos Nicolás, 1953-. II. Title.
HD8310.B372 Y86 1986

Yurow, Jane H. Issues in international telecommunications policy . Washington, D.C. , c1983. xviii, 260 p. ; ISBN 0-9612072-0-5 (pbk.) LC Card 83-82231 DDC 343.73/0994 347.303994 19
KF2765 .I85 1983 ***NYPL [JLF 86-1125]***

Yusoff Iskandar. Kapal dan harta karam =. Kuala Lumpur , 1986. xv, 181 p. : LC Card 86-942317 DDC 387.5/09595 19
HF3800.6 .K36 1986

Yusuf J. Ahmad. see **Ahmad, Yusuf J.**

Yusuf, Shahid, 1949- Fiji, a transition to manufacturing. Washington, D.C., U. S.A. , c1987. xvi, 107 p., [1] folded leaf of plates : ISBN 0-8213-0962-5 LC Card 87-23067 DDC 338.4/767/099611 19
HD9738.F55 F55 1987

Yvert & Tellier (Firm) Catalogue des timbres-poste de la France et des colonies françaises. Southfield, MI (15565 Northland Dr., Suite 605 West, Southfield 48075-5308) , <[1985]-. v. <2 > : LC Card 86-210422
HE6185.F82 C37 1985

Z dziejów wsi polskiej i rolnictwa /. Inglot, Stefan. Warszawa , 1986. 448 p. : ISBN 83-205-3734-7 : LC Card 85-126716
HD1995.7 .I54 1986

Z historii myśli ekonomicznej . Górski, Janusz. Łódź , 1986, c1985. 312 p. ; ISBN 83-218-0319-9 : LC Card 83-189161
HB114.A2 G67 1986

Z Husowa po berła rektorskie : Wincenty Styś--człowiek, uczony, działacz społeczny / wybór i opracowanie Stanisław Urban.Wyd. 1. Warszawa : Ludowa Soółdzielnia Wydawnicza, 1986. 340 p., [25] p. of plates : ill. ; 21 cm. "Bibliografia prac W. Stysia": p. 330-[332] Includes bibliographical references. ISBN 83-205-3745-2 : LC Card 85-126839
1. Styś, Wincenty. 2. Economists - Poland - Biography. 3. Agriculturalists - Poland - Biography. I. Urban, Stanisław.
HB114.S79 Z2 1986

Z przeszłości ruchów chłopskich, 1768-1861 /. Wycech, Czesław. Warszawa , 1952. 221, [3] p. ; LC Card 81-212267
HD1536.P7 W93 1952

Za bezopasnost i kultura na dvizhenieto . (27) Osnovnye prichiny i usloviia vozniknoveniia PTP s tiazhelymi posledstviiami, puti i metody ikh ustraneniia. Bulgarian. Osnovni prichini i usloviia za vŭznikvane na PTP s tezhki posledstviia, pŭtishta i metodi za tiakhnoto otstraniavane /. Sofiia , 1985. 95 p. : LC Card 87-101607
HF5614.5.S62 O7516 1985

Za ėffektivnost′ i kachestvo.
Korolev, L. P. (Leonid Pavlovich) Trudovye resursy i ikh ispol′zovanie /. Moskva , 1982. 139 p. ; LC Card 82-158161
HD5797.M66 K67 1982

Za partiinata prosveta.
Georgiev, IAncho. Strategiia na kachestveni promeni /. Sofiia , 1986- v. <1-2 > ; LC Card 86-232319
HC403 .G465 1986

Za slovom--delo /. Andrianov, V. V. Moskva , 1985. 124 p. ; LC Card 85-213388
HC338.S87 A53 1985

Zabota o stroitel′nykh kadrakh /. Piskunov, F. F. (Fedor Fedorovich) Moskva , 1986. 71 p. : LC Card 86-220202
HD8039.B92 S686 1986

ZACATECAS (MEXICO : STATE) - APPROPRIATIONS AND EXPENDITURES - STATISTICS.
Zacatecas (Mexico : State). Governor (1980- : Cervantes Corona) Tercer informe de gobierno. Zacatecas , 1983. 350 p. : LC Card 86-202257
HJ15.Z3 Z33 1980

Zacatecas (Mexico : State). Governor (1980- : Cervantes Corona) Tercer informe de gobierno. Anexo programático / José Guadalupe Cervantes Corona. Zacatecas : [s.n.], 1983. 350 p. : ill. ; 22 x 34 cm. LC Card 86-202257
1. Program budgeting - Mexico - Zacatecas (State) - Statistics. 2. Zacatecas (Mexico : State) - Appropriations and expenditures - Statistics. I. Cervantes Corona, José Guadalupe. II. Title.
HJ15.Z3 Z33 1980

Zaccaro, Stephen J. Occupational stress and organizational effectiveness /. New York , c1987. xii, 285 p. : ISBN 0-275-92281-2 (alk. paper) : LC Card 86-25250 DDC 158.7 19
HF5548.85 .O24 1987

Zacharias, Beniamin. Metodología de evaluación y programación de sistemas de producción y consumo, MEPS /. Lima, Perú [1985]- v. <1 > : LC Card 86-215609
HD75 .M48 1985

Zadacha razmeshcheniia sel′skokhoziaistvennogo proizvodstva v ob″edinenii khoziaistv meliorativnoĭ sistemy /. Abdullaev, A. Kh. Moskva , 1985. 24, [2] p. ; LC Card 86-162160
HD9015.S652 A23 1985

Zadachite na DKMS vŭv VUZ za povishavane na ikonomicheskata podgotovka na studentite i mladite khora ot drugite otriadi na mladezhta : sbornik ot materiali / [redaktsionna kolegiia Moĭno Moĭnov (otg. redaktor) ... et al. ; stilov redaktor Miroslav Minev]. Svishtov : [s.n.], 1985. 91 p. ; 21 cm. At head of title: TSentralen komitet na Dimitrovskiia komunisticheski mladezhki sŭiuz ... Includes bibliographical references. LC Card 86-159994
1. Economics - Study and teaching (Higher) - Bulgaria. 2. Dimitrovski komunisticheski mladezhki sŭiuz. I. Moĭnov, Moĭno. II. Minev, Miroslav, 1928-. III. TSentralen komitet na DKMS.
HB74.9.B9 Z33 1985

Zadrozny, Norberto Ingo. Santa Catarina, Brazil . Florianópolis-SC-Brasil , 1982. 55 p. : LC Card 87-115191 DDC 330.981/64063 19
HC188.S26 S317 1982

Zafir, Mihály.
Életszínvonal és közhangulat /. Budapest , 1984. 69 p. ; LC Card 86-147705
HD7027.5 .E44 1984

A Lakosság jövedelme és fogyasztása, 1960-1973 /. [Budapest] , c1975. 91 p. ; ISBN 963-340-048-1 LC Card 86-196944
HC300.295.I5 L32 1975

A Lakosság jövedelme és fogyasztása, 1960-1983 /. Budapest , 1984. 118 p. ; ISBN 963-340-740-0 : LC Card 85-155585
HC300.295.I5 L3315 1984 ***NYPL [JLF 86-672]***

A Lakosság jövedelme, társadalombiztosítás, családpolitika /. Budapest [1983] 82 p. : LC Card 83-206799
HC30.295.I5 L332 1983 ***NYPL [JLE 87-179]***

Zagladin, V. V. Mezhdunarodnoe rabochee dvizhenie . Moskva , 1980. 412 p. ; LC Card 81-143888
HD4854 .M474 1980

Zagreb International Fair (10th : 1965) Review of exporters and importers of Yugoslavia . Zagreb , 1965. ca. 650 p. : LC Card 84-149403
HF3732.3 .R46 1965

Zahavi, Gerald, 1951- Workers, managers, and welfare capitalism : the shoeworkers and tanners of Endicott Johnson, 1890-1950 / Gerald Zahavi. Urbana : University of Illinois Press, c1988. xiii, 261 p., [14] p. of plates : ill., ports. ; 24 cm. (The Working class in American history) Bibliography: p. 225-246. Includes index. ISBN 0-252-01444-8 (alk. paper) LC Card 87-6035 DDC 331.2/0475/0973 19
1. Endicott Johnson Corporation - Personnel management - History. 2. Endicott Johnson Corporation - Employees - History. 3. Welfare work in industry - United States - History - Case studies. 4. Paternalism - United States - History - Case studies. I. Title.
HD9787.U6 E654 1988

Zahlenbild-Almanach 1972 : die Gegenwart in Bild und Text / [Redaktion, Georg Seibert]. Berlin : E. Schmidt, c1972. 204 p. : ill. ; 30 cm. Includes index. ISBN 3-503-00861-6 LC Card 86-133643
1. Germany, West - Economic conditions - Statistics. 2. Germany (West) - Commerce - Statistics. I. Seibert, Georg.
HC286.5 .Z225 1972

Zahlungsmittelbewirtschaftung im Verkehrsbetrieb /. Seiffert, Bernd. Berlin , c1986. 187 p. : ISBN 3-428-06094-6 : LC Card 87-143799 DDC 380.5/24/0943 19
HE5999.Z7 G374 1986

Zahn, Ernestern. Katona, George, 1901- [Aspirations and affluence. Dutch.] Het psychologisch klimaat van de economie in de Verenigde Staten en West-Europa /. Utrecht , 1974. 247 p. ; ISBN 90-274-5826-X
NYPL [JLD 86-295]

Zahn, Joachim, Professor Dr. Eine Finanzpolitik des langen Atems erforderlich / Joachim Zahn. Die Aufgaben der Finanz- und Steuerpolitik in dieser Legislaturperiode / Hans H. Gattermann. Bonn : Institut "Finanzen und Steuern", [1984] 31 leaves ; 30 cm. (Brief / Institut "Finanzen und Steuern" . 234) "Vorträge gehalten auf der Mitgliederversammlung des Instituts 'Finanzen und Seuern' am 24. Mai 1984." LC Card 86-198580
1. Finance, Public - Germany, West. 2. Fiscal policy - Germany, West. 3. Taxation - Germany, West. I. Gattermann, Hans H. II. Title. III. Title: Aufgaben der Finanz- und Steuerpolitik in dieser Legislaturperiode. IV. Series: Brief (Institut "Finanzen und Steuern" (Germany)) , 234.
HJ1120 .B65 Nr. 234

Zaikin, I. V. Praktikum po organizatsii i planirovaniiu proizvodstva na promyshlennykh predpriiatiiakh /. Voronezh , 1985. 209, [3] p. ; LC Card 84-172797
HD70.S63 P69 1985

Zaiko, L. F. (Leonid Fedorovich) Uvarov, V. P. (Vladimir Pavlovich) Ėkonomicheskoe soupravlenie . Minsk , 1985. 159 p. ; LC Card 85-217045
HD5660.G4 U93 1985

Zaïre /. Mark, D. F. W. van der. Zutphen , 1984. 92 p., [1] folded leaf of plates : ISBN 90-6255-523-3 LC Card 86-121676
HC955 .M37 1984

Zaire. Division régionale du plan, Mbandaka. Fiche technique pour la région de l'Equateur . Mbandaka [1984] 172 leaves ; LC Card 86-201790
HC955.Z7 E6725 1985

ZAIRE - ECONOMIC CONDITIONS.
Mark, D. F. W. van der. Zaïre /. Zutphen , 1984. 92 p., [1] folded leaf of plates : ISBN 90-6255-523-3 LC Card 86-121676
HC955 .M37 1984

ZAIRE - ECONOMIC POLICY.
Leslie, Winsome J. The World Bank & structural transformation in developing countries . Boulder, Colo. , 1987. xi, 208 p. : ISBN 1-555-87036-8 (lib. bdg. : alk. paper) : LC Card 87-3358 DDC 338.9675/1 19
HG3881.5.W57 L47 1987

Tshibaka, Tshikala B., 1949- The effects of trade and exchange rate policies on agriculture in Zaire /. Washington, D.C., USA , 1986. 65 p. : ISBN 0-89629-057-3 LC Card 86-27449 DDC 338.1/09675/1 19
HD2135.5 .T75 1986

ZAIRE - POPULATION.
Sala-Diakanda, Mpembele. Approche ethnique des phénomènes démographiques . Louvain-la-Neuve , 1980. 433 p. : LC Card 84-118066
HB3664.5.A3 S23 1980

Zakariadze, M. Krepche stali / M. Zakariadze. Tbilisi : Izd-vo "Sabchota Sakartvelo", 1986. 51 p., [16] p. of plates : ill. ; 20 cm. (SSSR--bratstvo narodov) Title in colophon: P'oraże mtkic'eni. LC Card 85-172385
1. Steel industry and trade - Georgian S.S.R. I. Title. II. Title: P'oraże mtkic'eni. III. Series. IV. Series: SSSR--bratstvo narodov (Tbilisi, Georgian S.S.R.).
HD9525.S653 G469 1986

Zakharchenko, A. G. (Alekseĭ Gavrilovich) Kollektivnyĭ podriad v sel'skom khoziaĭstve / A.G. Zakharchenko. Kiev : "Urozhaĭ", 1985. 107 p. : ill. ; 20 cm. (Shagi brigadnogo podriada) Includes bibliographical references. LC Card 86-222274
1. Collective farms - Ukraine - Management. 2. Collective labor agreements - Agriculture - Ukraine. 3. Agricultural productivity - Ukraine. I. Series: Shagi brigadnogo podriada (Kiev, Ukraine). II. Title.
HD1492.S652 U389 1985

Zakī, Ramzī. al-Duyūn wa-al-tanmiyah : al-qurūḍ al-khārijīyah wa-āthāruhā 'alá al-bilād al-'Arabīyah / ta'līf Ramzī Zakī.al-Ṭab'ah 1. al-Qāhirah : Dār al-Mustaqbal al-'Arabī, 1985. 271 p. : ill. ; 24 cm. At head of title: Jāmi'at al-Duwal al-'Arabīyah. al-Idārah al-'Āmmah lil-Shu'ūn al-Iqtiṣādīyah. Bibliography: p. 253-270. LC Card 86-960543
1. Debts, External - Arab countries. 2. Loans, Foreign - Arab countries. 3. Arab countries - Economic conditions. I. League of Arab States. Idārah al-'Āmmah lil-Shu'ūn al-Iqtiṣādīyah. II. Title.
HJ8824 .Z34 1985

Zakirov, M. G. (Mustafa Gazizovich) Tormysheva, T. A. (Tamara Andreevna) Okhrana truda i sotsial'noe strakhovanie trudiashchikhsia v Uzbekskoĭ SSR /. Tashkent , 1987. 131 p. ; LC Card 87-107413
HD7345.U93 T67 1987

Zakon Soiuza Sovetskikh Sotsialisticheskikh Respublik o Gosudarstvennom biudzhete SSSR na 1986 god. Dementsev, V. V. (Viktor Vladimirovich) O Gosudarstvennom biudzhete SSSR na 1986 god i ob ispolnenii Gosudarstvennogo biudzheta SSSR za 1984 god . Moskva , 1985. 28 p. ; LC Card 86-203425
HJ2129 .D46 1985

Zakonomernosti razvitiia sotsialisticheskikh mezhdunarodnykh proizvodstvennykh otnosheniĭ /. Bondarenko, E. L. (Evgeniia Lavrent'evna) Moskva , 1983. 127 p. ; LC Card 84-200940
HC244 .B694 1983

Zakupochnaia tsena i rasshirennoe vosproizvodstvo v sel'skom khoziaĭstve /. IUshkov, V. I. (Vasiliĭ Il'ich) Moskva , 1980. 142 p. ; LC Card 81-134864
HD1995.R8 I95 1980

Zalevskiĭ, A. A. (Andreĭ Andreevich) Ėkonomika khimicheskoĭ promyshlennosti / A.A. Zalevskiĭ. Moskva : "Khimiia", 1986. 189 p. ; 22 cm. (Dlia vyssheĭ shkoly) Authorized for instructional purposes. Bibliography: p. [188] Includes index. LC Card 86-225661
1. Chemical industry - Soviet Union. I. Title. II. Series.
HD9656.S55 Z36 1986

Zalin, Giovanni. Un Secolo di cooperazione di credito nel Veneto . Limena, Padova , c1985. 454 p., [29] p. of plates : LC Card 86-195743
HG2039.I8 S43 1985

Zalkind, Sheldon S. Costello, Timothy W. Psychology in administration . New York , 1987. xii, 500 p. : ISBN 0-8240-8202-8 (alk. paper) : LC Card 86-25805 DDC 658/.001/9 19
HF5548.8 .C6 1987

Zaltman, Gerald. Consumer behavior : basic findings and management implications / Gerald Zaltman, Melanie Wallendorf. Malabar, Fla. : R.E. Krieger, 1987, c1983. p. cm. Reprint. Orignally published: 2nd ed. New York : Wiley, c1983. (The Wiley series in marketing) Includes bibliographical references and indexes. ISBN 0-89874-989-1 LC Card 86-21297 DDC 658.8/342 19
1. Consumers. 2. Motivation research (Marketing). I. Wallendorf, Melanie. II. Title.
HF5415.3 .Z28 1987

Zaluar, Alba. A Feira hippie de Campinas . Campinas, SP, Brasil , São Paulo, SP , 1986. 73 p. ; LC Card 87-404187 DDC 381/.18/098161 19
HF5473.B72 C364 1986

Zambia.
Census and Statistics Act. 1978. Zambian official statistics : an introduction. Lusaka , 1978. i, 99 p. ; LC Card 83-980761
HA37.Z352 Z36 1978

ZAMBIA - CENSUS, 1980.
1980 population and housing census of Zambia. Lusaka, Zambia , <[1985?-. v. <2-5 > : LC Card 86-981236 DDC 304.6/096894 19
HA4703 .A4 1980

Zambia. Central Statistical Office.
Interrelationships among infant and childhood mortality, socio-economic factors and fertility in Zambia . Lusaka , Addis Ababa [1984?] 300 p. : LC Card 87-105950 DDC 304.6/32/096894 19
HB1323.I42 Z335 1984

Zambian official statistics . Lusaka , 1978. i, 99 p. ; LC Card 83-980761
HA37.Z352 Z36 1978

1980 population and housing census of Zambia. Lusaka, Zambia , <[1985?-. v. <2-5 > : LC Card 86-981236 DDC 304.6/096894 19
HA4703 .A4 1980

Zambia, country study and Norwegian aid review. Fantoft, Norway : Chr. Michelsen Institute, Dept. of Social Science and Development, 1986. xxi, 202 p., [1] leaf of plates : ill. ; 21 cm. Bibliography: p. 187-202. ISBN 82-905840-6-7 (pbk.) LC Card 87-105777 DDC 338.91/481/06894 19
1. Economic assistance, Norwegian - Zambia. 2. Zambia - Economic conditions - 1964-. 3. Zambia - Politics and government - 1964-. 4. Zambia - Dependency on foreign countries. I. Chr. Michelsens institutt. Avdeling for samfunnsvitenskap og utvikling.
HC915 .Z36 1986

Zambia. Dept. of Town and Country Planning. Development Planning & Research Unit. Fahmy, H. A. African population projection according to eight models, sex & age groups (1970-2000) /. [Lusaka] [198-?] 34, 9, 62 leaves, [3] leaves of plates : LC Card 85-980559 DDC 304.6/2/096894021 19
HA4703 .F34 1980z

Zambia. Dept. of Town and Country Planning. Research Unit. Stepwise migration. Lusaka [1981] 34, 3, 2 p. : LC Card 85-980416
HB2123.6.A3 S74 1981

ZAMBIA - DEPENDENCY ON FOREIGN COUNTRIES.
Zambia, country study and Norwegian aid review. Fantoft, Norway , 1986. xxi, 202 p., [1] leaf of plates : ISBN 82-905840-6-7 (pbk.) LC Card 87-105777 DDC 338.91/481/06894 19
HC915 .Z36 1986

ZAMBIA - ECONOMIC CONDITIONS - 1964-
Republic of Zambia, economic memorandum /. [Lusaka?] [1983?] 28 p. : LC Card 86-980289 DDC 330.96894/04 19
HC915 .R46 1983

Zambia, country study and Norwegian aid review. Fantoft, Norway , 1986. xxi, 202 p., [1] leaf of plates : ISBN 82-905840-6-7 (pbk.) LC Card 87-105777 DDC 338.91/481/06894 19
HC915 .Z36 1986

ZAMBIA - ECONOMIC POLICY.
Kanduza, Ackson M. The political economy of underdevelopment in Northern Rhodesia, 1918-1960 . Lanham, MD , c1986. x, 336 p. : ISBN 0-8191-5189-0 (alk. paper) : LC Card 85-29835 DDC 338.96894 19
HC915 .K36 1986 ***NYPL [JLD 86-2962]***

Zambia Geographical Association occassional study, 0250-8109 .
(no. 13) Van den Berg, L. M. Anticipating urban growth in Africa . Lusaka, Zambia , 1984. viii, 167 p., [4] p. of plates : LC Card 86-980297 DDC 307.7/6/096894 19
HD993.Z9 L88 1984

Zambia - Government. see **Zambia - Politics and government.**

ZAMBIA INDUSTRIAL AND MINING CORPORATION.
A Study into the evolution and performance of the transport sector in Zambia with particular reference to the operations of the ZIMCO group of transport companies /. [Lusaka?] [1980?] 89 p. : LC Card 86-981420
HE284.6 .S78 1980

Zambia. Ministry of Agriculture and Water Development. A Report on the resources, activities, and constraints in tobacco schemes . Lusaka , 1985. iii, 37 p. ; LC Card 85-981599 DDC 338.1/7371/096894 19
HD9147.Z34 R46 1985

Zambia. Ministry of Lands, Natural Resources, and Tourism. National Parks and Wildlife Service. see **Zambia. National Parks and Wildlife Service.**

Zambia. National Commission for Development Planning. Chilivumbo, Alifeyo. Communal agrarian cooperative societies . Lusaka [1986] iii, 134 p. ; LC Card 86-981399 DDC 334/.683/096894 19
HD1491.Z35 C45 1986

Zambia. National Parks and Wildlife Service.
Lupande Development Workshop (1983 : Nyamaluma Wildlife Conservation Camp) Proceedings of the Lupande Development Workshop . Chipata, Zambia , 1984. x, 121 p. : LC Card 84-980605 DDC 333.73/17/096894 19
HD993.Z8 L835 1983 ***NYPL [JLG 87-67]***

Zambia. Office of the Member of the Central Committee, Western Province. The Structure of the informal sector in Mongu (Western Province) and its potential for employment creation . Lusaka, Zambia [1982] iii, 44, 10 p. ; LC Card 87-980490 DDC 331.12/51381 19
HD2346.Z292 M657 1982

Zambia. Parks and Wildlife Service. see **Zambia. National Parks and Wildlife Service.**

ZAMBIA - POLITICS AND GOVERNMENT - 1964-
Zambia, country study and Norwegian aid review. Fantoft, Norway , 1986. xxi, 202 p., [1] leaf of plates : ISBN 82-905840-6-7 (pbk.) LC Card 87-105777 DDC 338.91/481/06894 19
HC915 .Z36 1986

ZAMBIA - POPULATION - STATISTICS.
Fahmy, H. A. African population projection according to eight models, sex & age groups (1970-2000) /. [Lusaka] [198-?] 34, 9, 62 leaves, [3] leaves of plates : LC Card 85-980559 DDC 304.6/2/096894021 19
HA4703 .F34 1980z

1980 population and housing census of Zambia. Lusaka, Zambia , <[1985?-. v. <2-5 > : LC Card 86-981236 DDC 304.6/096894 19
HA4703 .A4 1980

ZAMBIA - STATISTICAL SERVICES.
Zambian official statistics . Lusaka , 1978. i, 99 p. ; LC Card 83-980761
HA37.Z352 Z36 1978

Zambia. University. see **University of Zambia.**

Zambian official statistics : an introduction. Lusaka : Central Statistical Office, 1978. i, 99 p. ; 30 cm. (Studies in official statistics . no. 1) "Census and Statistics Act" (20 p.) laid in. "Publications list, January 1978" (4 p.) laid in. LC Card 83-980761
1. Zambia - Statistical services. I. Zambia. Central Statistical Office. II. Zambia. Census and Statistics Act. 1978. III. Series: Studies in official statistics (Zambia. Central Statistical Office) , no. 1.
HA37.Z352 Z36 1978

Zammit, Ann. Autoafirmación colectiva . México , 1983. 327 p. ; ISBN 968-16-1335-X LC Card 86-159023
HC59.7 .A92 1983

Zammit, Stephen J. Evaluating business and industry training /. Boston , Norwell, MA , c1987. xv, 294 p. : ISBN 0-89838-197-5 LC Card 87-5771 DDC 658.3/12404 19
HF5549.5.T7 E88 1987

ZAMORA-CHINCHIPE (ECUADOR) - ECONOMIC POLICY.
Informe cuatrianual, 1980-1983 /. Cuenca, Ecuador [1983] 222 p. : LC Card 86-206868
HC203.O76 I53 1983

Zander, Ernst.
Glaubrecht, Helmut. Arbeitszeit im Wandel . Freiburg im Breisgau , 1985. 273 p. : ISBN 3-448-01509-1 LC Card 85-216364 DDC 331.25/72 19
HD5109 .G55 1985

Neue Entwicklungen bei Arbeit, Entgelt und Führung /. Freiburg im Breisgau , c1984. 169 p. : ISBN 3-448-01480-X : LC Card 84-249237
HF5549.2.G3 N48 1984

Zanella, Hans-Jürgen. Wackersdorf . Passau , 1986. 75 p. : ISBN 3-88849-021-9 LC Card 86-183781
HD9698.G43 W338 1986

Zangl, Hans. Durchlaufzeiten im Büro : Prozessorganisation und Aufgabenintegration als effizienter Weg zur Rationalisierung der Büroarbeit mit neuen

Bürokommunikationstechniken / von Hans Zangl. Berlin : E. Schmidt, c1985. xvii, 365 p. : ill. ; 25 cm. (Mensch und Arbeit im technisch-organisatorischen Wandel . Bd. 3) Thesis (doctoral)--Hochschule der Bundeswehr München, 1984. Bibliography: p. 303-351. Includes index. ISBN 3-503-02458-1 LC Card 85-137750
1. Communication in personnel management - Germany (West). 2. Office layout. 3. Office management. 4. Office practice - Automation. I. Title. II. Series.
HF5549.5.C6 Z33 1985

Zängl, Wolfgang. Bode, Peter M. Alptraum Auto . München , 1986. 237 p. : ISBN 3-922696-46-5 LC Card 87-107197 DDC 303.4/832 19
HE5613 .B63 1986

Zaninelli, Sergio. La Proprietà fondiaria in Lombardia dal catasto teresiano all'età napoleonica /. Milano , 1986. 2 v. ; ISBN 88-343-0341-5 (set) : LC Card 87-108100
HD679.L6 P76 1986

ZANU-PF (Organization : Zimbabwe). Dept. of the Commissariat and Culture. Zimbabwe at 5 years of independence. [Harare?] [1984?] ix, 265 p. : LC Card 87-103323 DDC 338.96891 19
HC910 .Z3173 1984

ZANZIBAR - COMMERCE - HISTORY - 18TH CENTURY.
Sheriff, Abdul. Slaves, spices, & ivory in Zanzibar . London , Athens , 1987. xx, 297 p. : ISBN 0-8214-0871-2 (U. S.) LC Card 87-12339 DDC 382/.096781 19
HF3897 .S54 1987

ZANZIBAR - COMMERCE - HISTORY - 19TH CENTURY.
Sheriff, Abdul. Slaves, spices, & ivory in Zanzibar . London , Athens , 1987. xx, 297 p. : ISBN 0-8214-0871-2 (U. S.) LC Card 87-12339 DDC 382/.096781 19
HF3897 .S54 1987

Zapadnoevropeĭskaia integratsiia : proekty i real'nost' / [pod obshcheĭ redaktsieĭ V.B. Kniazhinskogo ; avtorskiĭ kollektiv V.B. Kniazhinskiĭ ... et al.] Moskva : "Mezhdunar. otnosheniia", 1986. 205, [3] p. ; 20 cm. Bibliography: p. 198-[206] LC Card 86-219781 DDC 327.1/7/094 19
1. Europe - Economic integration. 2. European cooperation. 3. European Economic Community. I. Kniazhinskiĭ, V. B. (Vsevolod Borisovich).
HC241 .Z365 1986

Zapata, Francisco.
Clases sociales y acción obrera en Chile /. México, D.F. , 1986. 230 p. ; ISBN 968-12-0326-7 LC Card 87-404023 DDC 331/.0983 19
HD8296.5 .C57 1986

El conflicto sindical en América Latina / Francisco Zapata. 1a ed. México, D.F. : Colegio de México, Centro de Estudios Sociológicos, 1986. 228 p. : ill. ; 21 cm. Bibliography: p. 205-223. ISBN 968-12-0323-2 LC Card 87-105269
1. Strikes and lockouts - Latin America - History - 20th century. 2. Trade-unions - Latin America - History - 20th century. I. Title.
HD5330.5.A6 Z36 1986

Zapatero, Juan Carlos. Viernes europeos 81 . Madrid [1984?] 494 p. : LC Card 85-178055
HC241.25.S6 V48 1984

Zapol'skaia, V. V. (Vera Vasil'evna) Voprosy metodologii issledovaniia obshchestvennogo truda pri sotsializme /. Voronezh , 1979. 163 p. ; LC Card 81-142810
HD5796 .V65 1979

Zarb, Frank G.
Handbook of financial markets . Homewood, Ill. , c1986. xix, 785 p. : ISBN 0-87094-600-5 LC Card 85-71920 DDC 332.6/78 19
HG4527 .H25 1986 ***NYPL [*R-Econ 86-3815]***

Handbook of financial markets--securities, options, futures /. Homewood, Ill. , c1981. xxiii, 794 p. : ISBN 0-87094-216-6 LC Card 80-70448 DDC 332.6/78 19
HG4527 .H25 ***NYPL [JLE 86-1500]***

Zardkoohi, Asghar. Kolari, James W. Bank costs, structure, and performance /. Lexington, Mass. , c1987. x, 240 p. : ISBN 0-669-11282-8 (alk. paper) LC Card 85-45295 DDC 332.1/068/1 19
HG1616.C6 K65 1987

Zarkovic, M. Issues in Indian agricultural development / M. Zarkovic. Boulder : Westview Press, 1987. xviii, 203 p. ; 23 cm. (Westview special studies on agriculture science and policy) Bibliography: p. 191-203. ISBN 0-8133-7451-0 (soft : alk. paper) LC Card 87-50898 DDC 338.1/0954 19
1. Agriculture - Economic aspects - India. I. Title. II. Series.
HD2072 .Z37 1987

Zaroli, Luciano, 1958- Vannini, Walter, 1958- L'automazione dei processi di produzione . Milano, Italy , c1985. 344 p. : LC Card 85-204836 DDC 338.4/54 19
HD9720.5 .V36 1985 ***NYPL [JLD 86-2523]***

Zarruk Zarruk, Luis Armando. Productividad y participación . [Bucaramanga, Colombia] , c1985. 165 p. : ISBN 958-9302-15-6 LC Card 86-166141
HD5660.C7 P76 1985

Zarth, Michael. Wirtschaftsunterricht an allgemeinbildenden Schulen in Baden-Württemberg : Notwendigkeit, inhaltliche Ausgestaltung und Anforderungen seitens des Beschäftigungssystems : Gutachten im Auftrag des Ministeriums für Kultus und Sport Baden-Württemberg / Michael Zarth. Tübingen : Institut für Angewandte Wirtschaftsforschung Tübingen, 1987. x, 241 p. ; 21 cm. (Forschungsberichte / Institut für Angewandte Wirtschaftsforschung Tübingen. Serie A . Nr. 44) Bibliography: p. 223-241. ISBN 3-88573-028-6 : LC Card 87-419933 DDC 330/.07/104346 19
1. Economics - Study and teaching - Germany (West) - Baden-Württemberg. I. Baden-Württemberg (Germany). Ministerium für Kultus und Sport. II. Series: Forschungsberichte / Institut für Angewandte Wirtschaftsforschung Tübingen. Serie A , Nr. 27. III. Title.
HB74.9.G3 Z36 1987

Zarubezhnyĭ biznes amerikanskikh monopoliĭ /. Trepelkov, V. P. (Vasiliĭ Petrovich) Moskva , 1982. 239 p ; LC Card 83-114503
HG4538 .T7 1982

Zarubezhnyĭ Vostok : voprosy ėkonomicheskoĭ istorii / [otvetstvennyĭ redaktor A.M. Petrov]. Moskva : Izd-vo "Nauka," Glav. red. vostochnoĭ lit-ry, 1986. 126 p. ; 20 cm. At head of title: Akademiia nauk SSSR. Ordena Trudovogo Krasnogo Znameni Institut vostokovedeniia. Includes bibliographies. LC Card 87-126378
1. Asia - Economic conditions. 2. Economic history. I. Petrov, A. M. II. Institut vostokovedeniia (Akademiia nauk SSSR).
HC412 .Z38 1986

Zarubin, Vadim Nikolaevich. Intensifikatsiia i trudoemkost' stroitel'nogo proizvodstva / V.N. Zarubin. Moskva : Stroĭizdat, 1986. 183, [1] p. ; 20 cm. Bibliography: p. 183-[184] LC Card 85-178984
1. Construction industry - Soviet Union - Labor productivity. I. Title.
HD9715.S72 Z37 1986

Zasady metodyczne statystyki przemysłu. Warszawa : Główny Urząd Statystyczny, 1979. 224 p. ; 24 cm. (Zeszyty metodyczne . nr. 31) LC Card 81-115708
1. Poland - Industries - Statistical methods. I. Poland. Główny Urząd Statystyczny. II. Series.
HC340.3 .Z373 1979

Zaslavskaia, T. I. Smirnov, V. D. (Vasiliĭ Dmitrievich) Sotsial'no-ėkonomicheskiĭ ėksperiment v kolkhoze /. Novosibirsk , 1986. 111 p. : LC Card 86-171536
HD1492.S652 S527 1986

Zasluzhennyĭ rabotnik sel'skogo khoziaĭstva respubliki / [sostavitel' Tamara Nikolaevna Lykova]. Moskva : Moskovskiĭ rabochiĭ, 1986. 351 p. : ill. ; 18 cm. LC Card 86-132613
1. Agricultural laborers - Russian S.F.S.R. - Biography. I. Lykova, Tamara Nikolaevna.
HD1536.S65 Z37 1986

Zastavnyĭ, F. D. (Fedor Dmitrievich) Alymov, Aleksandr Nikolaevich. Sbalansirovannost' narodnokhoziaĭstvennogo razvitiia . Kiev , 1986. 221, [3] p. ; LC Card 86-214583
HC337.U5 A793 1986

Zasurskiĭ, IAsen Nikolaevich. Andrunas, E. Ch. (Elena Cheslavovna) Biznes i propaganda . Moskva , 1986. 223 p. : LC Card 87-152425
HD59.6.U6 A53 1986

Zatraty i rezul'taty proizvodstvennykh issledovaniĭ i razrabotok /. Rodionenkov, P. A. (Petr Andreevich) Leningrad , 1986. 143 p. ; LC Card 87-136354
HC340.R4 R63 1986

Zauberman, Alfred. Planning under indeterminacy / Alfred Zauberman. Bielefeld, Federal Republic of Germany : Institut für Mathematische Wirtschaftsforschung an der Universität Bielefeld, [1976] 153, 5 p. ; 30 cm. (Working papers / Institute of Mathematical Economics = Arbeiten aus dem Institut für Mathematische Wirtschaftsforschung . Nr. 51) "December 1976." Includes bibliographical references. LC Card 85-127554
1. Soviet Union - Economic policy - 1976-1980 - Mathematical models. 2. Central planning - Soviet Union - Mathematical models. I. Series: Working papers (Universität Bielefeld. Institut für Mathematische Wirtschaftsforschung) , Nr. 51. II. Title.
HC336.25 .Z38 1976

Závada, Josef. Perspektivy hospodářského a sociálního rozvoje ČSSR / Josef Závada. 1. vyd. Praha : Horizont, 1986. 134 p. ; 21 cm. (Na pomoc národnímu hospodářství) Bibliography: p. 133. LC Card 87-161408
1. Czechoslovakia - Economic policy - 1965-. 2. Czechoslovakia - Economic conditions - 1945-. I. Title.
HC270.28 .Z38 1986

Zavattini, Cesare, 1902- Cesare Zavattini presenta La civiltà delle acque . [Bologna] [1985] 272 p., 24 p. of plates : LC Card 86-105989 DDC 945/.47 19
HC308.S33 C47 1985

Zavella, Patricia, 1949- Women's work and Chicano families : cannery workers of the Santa Clara Valley / Patricia Zavella. Ithaca : Cornell University Press, 1987. xviii, 191 p. ; 23 cm. (Anthropology of contemporary issues . 8) Bibliography: p. 172-187. Includes index. ISBN 0-8014-1730-9 (pbk. : alk. paper) LC Card 87-5245 DDC 305.4/3664 19
1. Women cannery workers - California - Santa Clara River Valley - Family relationships. 2. Mexican American women - Employment - California - Santa Clara River Valley. 3. Work and family - California - Santa Clara River Valley. 4. Working mothers - California - Santa Clara River Valley. I. Title. II. Series.
HD6073.C2 U596 1987

Zavod "Druzhba" . Khadzhiev, Stefan. Varna , 1985. 161 p., [3] leaves of plates : LC Card 86-140096
HD8039.C62 B95 1985

Zavod SR Slovenije za statistiko. Flajs, Andrej. Družbeno bogastvo SR Slovenije ob koncu 1980. leta /. Ljubljana , 1986. 75 p. ; ISBN 86-81141-04-X LC Card 86-216767
HA1634.S58 F54 1986

ZAVOD ZA METALOREZHESHTI MASHINI (SOFIA, BULGARIA)
Kostov, Miroslav. ZMM metal-working machines combine, Sofia /. Sofia , 1986. [104] p. : LC Card 87-116288 DDC 338.7/621902/0949773 19
HD9703.B94 Z384 1986

Zayas, Edison R. Gramley, Lyle E. Real estate finance and housing . Washington, D.C. (1125 15th St., N.W., Washington 20005) , c1987. vii, 132 p. : LC Card 87-124264 DDC 332.7/2/0973021 19
HG2040.5.U5 G73 1987

Zbirka Družboslovje.
Družba, znanost, tehnologija . Ljubljana , 1982. 472 p. ; LC Card 84-235191
HC407.Z9 T434 1982

Glas, Miroslav, 1950- Delitev po delu v socialistični družbi /. Ljubljana , 1986. 631 p. : LC Card 87-147216
HC407.Z9 I51473 1986

Zdrojkowski, Józef. Rola partii robotniczych w życiu społeczno-politycznym Ziemi Radomskiej w latach 1930-1939 / Józef Zdrojkowski. Radom : Radomskie Tow. Nauk., 1983. 168 p. : ill. ; 24 cm. (100-lecie polskiego ruchu robotniczego, 0137-5156) Bibliography: p. 143-145. LC Card 86-100120
1. Labor and laboring classes - Poland - Radom

(Voivodeship) - Political activity - History. 2. Socialist parties - Poland - Radom (Voivodeship) - History. 3. Radom (Poland : Voivodeship) - Economic conditions. 4. Radom (Poland : Voivodeship) - Politics and government. I. Title. II. Series.
HD8539.R332 Z38 1983

Zeff, Stephen A. Forging accounting principles in five countries : a history and an analysis of trends / by Stephen A. Zeff. Champaign, Ill. : Stipes Pub. Co., 1971, c1972. xvii, 332 p. ; 23 cm. (Lecture series / Arthur Andersen & Co) Includes bibliographical references. LC Card 86-226472
1. Comparative accounting. 2. Accounting - Standards - Canada. 3. Accounting - Standards - Mexico. 4. Accounting - Standards - United States. 5. Accounting - Standards - England. 6. Accounting - Standards - Scotland. I. Title. II. Series.
HF5605 .Z44 1972

Zeidler, Achim, 1952- Möglichkeiten zur Fortsetzung der Gemeindefinanzreform : eine theoretische und empirische Analyse / Achim Zeidler. Frankfurt am Main ; New York : P. Lang, c1985. xx, 301 p. : ill. ; 21 cm. (Finanzwissenschaftliche Schriften, 0170-8252 . Bd. 27) Bibliography: p. 286-301. ISBN 3-8204-8534-1 LC Card 86-125215 DDC 336/.014/43 19
1. Local finance - Germany, West. 2. Local taxation - Germany, West. I. Title. II. Series.
HJ9473 .Z4 1985

Zeigler, Luther Harmon, 1936- Poole, Keith T. Women, public opinion, and politics . New York , c1985. xii, 196 p. : ISBN 0-582-28274-8 LC Card 84-7155 DDC 305.4/0973 19
HQ1410 .P66 1985 ***NYPL [JLE 85-1580]***

Zeikel, Arthur.
(joint author) Cohen, Jerome Bernard, 1915- Investment analysis and portfolio management. Homewood, Ill., 1973. xiv, 946 p. ISBN 0-256-01429-9 LC Card 72-98120
HG4521 .C5296 1973 ***NYPL [JLE 74-744]***

(joint author) Cohen, Jerome Bernard, 1915- Investment analysis and portfolio management /. Homewood, Ill. , 1977. xvi, 819 p. : ISBN 0-256-01883-9 LC Card 76-15739
HG4521 .C5296 1977
NYPL [*R-Econ. 78-1366]

Zeitfragen der schweizerischen Wirtschaft und Politik .
(Nov. 1985, Nr. 126 =) Usteri, Martin. Bodenrecht in Bewegung . Zürich [1985] 27 p. ; LC Card 86-195037
HC395 .Z43 Nr. 126 KKW683

(Nr. 126) Usteri, Martin. Bodenrecht in Bewegung . Zürich [1985] 27 p. ; LC Card 86-195037
HC395 .Z43 Nr. 126 KKW683

(Nr. 130) Allenspach, Heinz. Bevorzugter Beamtenstatus, Möglichkeiten und Grenzen einer Reform . Zürich [1986] 32 p. ; LC Card 87-407830 DDC 330.9494 s 331.7/61354494 19
HC395 .Z43 Nr. 130 JN8831

(Nr. 131) Spälti, P. Die Rüstungsreferendumsinitiative--schlecht getarnter Anschlag auf unsere Landesverteidigung /. Zürich , 1987. 20 p. ; LC Card 87-409331 DDC 330.9494 s 327.1/74/09494 19
HC395 .Z43 Nr. 131 HC400.D4

Zeitler, Isabella, 1956- Internationales Bankgeschäft als Problem der Bankenaufsicht / Isabella Zeitler. München : GBI, c1984. viii, 353 p. : ill. ; 21 cm. (Betriebswirtschaftliche Forschungsbeiträge . Bd. 12) Originally presented as the author's thesis (doctoral)--Freie Universität Berlin, 1984. Bibliography: p. 296-350. LC Card 85-103322
1. Banks and banking, International. 2. Banks and banking - State supervision. I. Title. II. Series.
HG3881 .Z4 1984

Zeitlin, Jonathan.
The Automobile industry and its workers . New York , 1987. viii, 335 p. : ISBN 0-312-00553-9 : LC Card 86-29815 DDC 331/.04292 19
HD9710.A2 A865 1987

Divisions of labour . Sussex [Eng.] , Urbana , 1985. ix, 254 p. ; ISBN 0-252-01189-9 LC Card 84-23988 DDC 331.7/94 19
HD8390 .D58 1985 ***NYPL [JLD 87-93]***

Zeitlin, Maurice, 1935- How mighty a force? . Los Angeles , c1983. ix, 369 p. ;
NYPL [JLD 87-277]

Zeitschrift für Nationalökonomie. Supplement um .
(4. 4) Entrepreneurship . Wien , New York , 1984, c1983. 218 p. ; ISBN 0-387-81830-8 (U. S.) LC Card 84-26677 DDC 338/.04 19
HB615 .E635 1984 ***NYPL [JLE 85-1253]***

Zeitschrift für Unternehmensgeschichte. Beiheft .
(43) Stratmann, Friedrich. Chemische Industrie unter Zwang? . Stuttgart , 1985. xiv, 531 p. : ISBN 3-515-04399-3 LC Card 86-205409 DDC 338.4/766/0943 19
HD9654.5 .S77 1985

Zeitstetige Bewertungsmodelle für Tilgungsanleihen . Rothacker, Hartmut. Heidelberg , c1986. xxiv, 350 p. : ISBN 3-7908-0343-X LC Card 86-222052
HG4523 .R68 1986

Zelenak, Mel J. Lee, Stewart Munro. Personal finance for consumers /. Columbus, Ohio , c1987. xiii, 518 p. : ISBN 0-942280-33-4 : LC Card 86-30503 DDC 381/.3/0973 19
HB301 .L256 1987

Zelenin, I. E. (Il'i͡a Evgen'evich) Istorii͡a sovetskogo krest'i͡anstva /. Moskva , 1986-<1987. v. <1-3 > : LC Card 86-230318
HD1492.S65 I88 1986

Zelfstandig werken en ondernemen in middelgrote en kleine ondernemingen / redactie, A. Walravens en A. Zwaard. Delft : Delftse Universitaire Pers, 1985. 245 p. : ill. ; 24 cm. Includes bibliographies. ISBN 90-6275-226-8 : LC Card 86-152999
1. Small business - Netherlands. 2. Small business - Netherlands - Technological innovations. 3. Industrial promotion. I. Walravens, A. II. Zwaard, A.
HD2346.N4 Z44 1985

Zelfzorg en verzorging : perspectieven van de verzorgingsstaat / onder redactie van A.W. Musschenga, A.J. Vermaat en H.E.S. Woldring ; met bijdragen van H. van den Berg ... [et al.]. Kampen : J.H. Kok, [1985] 237 p. ; 24 cm. "Deze uitgave is nummer 8 in een reeks van het Bezinningscentrum van de Vrije Universiteit te Amsterdam over levensbeschouwing en wetenschap"--T.p. verso. Includes bibliographies. ISBN 90-242-4072-7 : LC Card 86-175292
1. Netherlands - Economic conditions - 1945-. 2. Netherlands - Social conditions - 1945-. 3. Welfare state. I. Musschenga, A. W. II. Vermaat, A. J., 1939-. III. Woldring, H. E. S., 1943-.
HC325 .Z43 1985

Zeller, Olivier. Lyon, l'argent, le commerce et la soie /. Lyon , c1986. 138 p. : ISBN 2-904638-63-6 : LC Card 86-184131
HC278.L9 L96 1986

Zellinger, Alfred, 1945- Die Sinnlichkeit der Theorie : zur Ästhetik des industriellen Systems : Performances, Environments, Action / Alfred Zellinger. Wien : Falterverlag, c1983. 173 p. : ill. ; 21 cm. Includes bibliographical references. ISBN 3-85439-005-X LC Card 84-196565
1. Commercial products. 2. Design, Industrial - Philosophy. 3. Art and industry. 4. Aesthetics, Modern - 20th century. I. Title.
HF1040.7 .Z45 1983

Zellner, Arnold. An introduction to Bayesian inference in econometrics / Arnold Zellner. Reprint ed. Malabar, Fla. : R.E. Krieger Pub. Co., 1987, c1971. xv, 431 p. : ill. ; 24 cm. Reprint. Originally published: New York : Wiley, 1971. Bibliography: p. 415-422. Includes indexes. ISBN 0-89874-995-6 LC Card 86-27796 DDC 330/.028 19
1. Econometrics. 2. Bayesian statistical decision theory. I. Title.
HB139 .Z45 1987

Zellweger, Bruno. Ueberwachung kommerzieller Bankkredite / von Bruno Zellweger. Bern : P. Haupt, c1983. xx, 330 p. : ill. ; 23 cm. (Bankwirtschaftliche Forschungen. Bd. 77) Cover title: Überwachung kommerzieller Bankkredite. Title on spine: Kommerzielle Bankkredite. Bibliography: p. 320-330. ISBN 3-258-03246-7 : LC Card 83-214274
1. Bank loans - Switzerland. 2. Credit - Switzerland - Management. I. Title. II. Title: Überwachung kommerzieller Bankkredite. III. Title: Kommerzielle Bankkredite. IV. Series.
HG1526 .B27 Bd. 77 HG1642.S95

Zelwiański, Ryszard. Ubezpieczenia komunikacyjne : obowiązkowe ubezpieczenia komunikacyjne oraz dodatkowe ubezpieczenia kierowców, pasażerów i pojazdów--tekst rozporządzenia, niektórych ogólnych warunków ubezpieczenia, taryf składek i porozumień oraz komentarz i wskazówki praktyczne / Ryszard Zelwiański. Warszawa : Wydawn. Prawnicze, 1979. 177, [3] p. : ill. ; 21 cm. Bibliography: p. 175-[178] ISBN 83-219-0031-3 LC Card 81-181561
1. Insurance, Travelers' - Poland. 2. Insurance, Automobile - Poland. I. Title.
HG9905.P7 Z45 1979

Zemědělství a půdní fond v Čechách ve 2. polovině 19. století /. Jeleček, Leoš. Praha , 1985. 283 p. : LC Card 86-199876
HD640.3.Z8 B634 1985

Zemledel'ts͡y gosudarstvennogo khozi͡aĭstva drevnego Egipta ėpokhi Ramessidov /. Stuchevskiĭ, I. A. (Iosif Aleksandrovich) Moskva , 1982. 254, [2] p. ; LC Card 82-186646
HD2123 .S78 1982

Zémor, Pierre. Un bon conseil : incursions chez les décideurs / Pierre Zémor. Paris : O. Orban, c1986. 278 p. : ill. ; 22 cm. Includes bibliographies. ISBN 2-85565-300-2 : LC Card 86-174727
1. Business consultants. 2. Business consultants - France. 3. Corporate planning. 4. Corporate planning - France. I. Title.
HD69.C6 Z4 1986

Zemrani, Anas Bensalah. La fiscalité face au développement économique et social du Maroc / par Anas Bensalah Zemrani ; préface de G. Tixier. Rabat : Editions Laporte, 1982. 395 p. ; 24 cm. (Bibliothèque de science financière. t. 19) Originally presented as the author's thesis (doctoral)--Université de Paris XII, 1981. Bibliography: p. [376]-385. LC Card 83-183254
1. Taxation - Morocco. I. Title. II. Series.
HJ3032 .Z34 1982

Zenchenko, N. S. Sot͡sial'nai͡a napravlennost' planov : zadachi, praktika, problemy / N.S. Zenchenko. Moskva : Sov. Rossii͡a, 1985. 221 p. ; 21 cm. Includes bibliographical references. LC Card 86-106277
1. Russian S.F.S.R. - Economic policy. 2. Russian S.F.S.R. - Social policy. 3. Russian S.F.S.R. - Economic conditions. I. Title.
HC337.R85 Z45 1985

Zenger, Christoph. Kursschwankungen des Schweizerfrankens in ihren Auswirkungen auf Produktion, Export, Import und Fremdenverkehr : eine theoretische Studie verbunden mit einer empirischen Untersuchung der Jahre 1973 bis 1980 / Christoph Zenger. Bern : P. Haupt, c1982. vi, 263 p. : ill. ; 23 cm. (Berner Beiträge zur Nationalökonomie. Bd. 41) Bibliography: p. 256-263. ISBN 3-258-03172-X : LC Card 83-242397 DDC 332.4/9494 19
1. Money - Switzerland. 2. Foreign exchange problem - Switzerland. 3. Switzerland - Economic conditions - 1945-. I. Title. II. Series.
HG1155 .Z46 1982

Zenkner, Karl.
Familien und Unternehmungen der Industriepioniere J.W. Jäckel & Co. in Wiesenthal a.N., Gebrüder Redlhammer in Gablonz a.N., Johann Schowanek in Georgenthal. 1984. John, Walter. Glasspinnerei im Isergebirge / von Walter John. Die Familien und Unternehmungen der Industriepioniere J.W. Jäckel & Co. in Wiesenthal a.N., Gebrüder Redlhammer in Gablonz a.N., Johann Schowanek in Georgenthal / von Karl Zenkner. Schwäbisch-Gmünd , 1984, c1974. 78 p. : LC Card 85-135799
HD9623.I94 J64 1984

Zensus im Bergbau und verarbeitenden Gewerbe Nordrhein-Westfalen 1979 : Landesergebnisse für Unternehmen und Betriebe. Düsseldorf : Landesamt für Datenverarbeitung und Statistik Nordrhein-Westfalen, [1983] 109 p. ; 30 cm. (Beiträge zur Statistik des Landes Nordrhein-Westfalen . Heft 497) All tables. LC Card 87-407314 DDC 943/.55 s 338.2/0943/55021 19
1. Mineral industries - Germany (West) - North Rhine-Westphalia - Statistics-. 2. Metal-work - Germany (West) - North Rhine-Westphalia - Statistics. 3. North Rhine-Westphalia (Germany) - Manufactures - Statistics. 4. North Rhine-Westphalia (Germany) - Industries - Statistics. I. Landesamt für Statistik des Landes Nordrhein-Westfalen. II. Series.
HA1320.N6 A32 Heft 497 HD9506.G23N6

Zenteno, Raúl Benítez. see **Benítez Zenteno, Raúl.**

Zentralamerika, USA, EG und Bundesrepublik Deutschland /. Esser, Klaus. Berlin , 1987. xi, 137 p. : ISBN 3-88985-043-X LC Card 87-401334 DDC 337.1/728 19
HC141 .E86 1987

ZENTRALBIBLIOTHEK ZÜRICH - ACCOUNTING - CASE STUDIES.
Egger, Emil. Management Accounting in öffentlichen nichtgewinnorientierten Organisationen . Zürich , c1985. xii, 220 p. : ISBN 3-7255-2410-6 LC Card 85-132536
HF5686.N56 E33 1985

ZENTRALGESELLSCHAFT VFW-FOKKER M. B.H.
Kirchen kämpfen mit . Mainz , 1981. 106 p. : ISBN 3-7867-0873-8 LC Card 81-188986 DDC 261.8/34562/094343 19
HD6338.2.G32 S634 1981
NYPL [JLD 86-2786]

Zentralsparkasse und Kommerzialbank Wien. Issues of the eighties . Wien , 1983. 119 p. : LC Card 83-201354 DDC 338.9 19
HD73 .I86 1983

Das zentralstaatliche Planungssystem der D.D.R. Waterkamp, Rainer. Das zentralstaatliche Planungssystem der DDR . Berlin , c1983. 194 p. : ISBN 3-428-05405-9 LC Card 83-217231
HC290.78 .W38 1983

Das zentralstaatliche Planungssystem der DDR . Waterkamp, Rainer. Berlin , c1983. 194 p. : ISBN 3-428-05405-9 LC Card 83-217231
HC290.78 .W38 1983

ZENTRALVERBAND DER SCHUHMACHER (GERMANY) - BIOGRAPHY.
Simon, Josef, 1865-1949. Josef Simon, Schuhmacher, Gewerkschafter, Sozialist mit Ecken und Kanten /. Köln , c1985. 465 p. : ISBN 3-7663-0923-4 LC Card 85-186450
HD6695.S55 A3 1985

Zentralverband des Deutschen Handwerks. Wünsche und Forderungen des Handwerks an Parteien, X. Deutschen Bundestag und Bundesregierung. Bonn [1983] 80 p. ; LC Card 83-220138
HD2346.G3 W86 1983

Zenz, Gary Joseph.
Purchasing and the management of materials / Gary J. Zenz. 5th ed. New York : Wiley, c1981. xiii, 514 p. : ill. ; 24 cm. Fourth ed., by J. H. Westing, I. V. Fine, and G. J. Zenz, published under title: Purchasing management. Includes bibliographical references and index. ISBN 0-471-06091-7 LC Card 80-21649 DDC 658.7/2 19
1. Industrial procurement - Management. 2. Materials management. I. Westing, J. Howard (John Howard), 1911- Purchasing management. II. Title.
HD39.5 .W47 1981 *NYPL [JLE 86-3384]*

Purchasing and the management of materials / Gary J. Zenz ; edited by George Thompson. 6th ed. New York : Wiley, c1987. xvi, 542 p. : ill. ; 24 cm. Includes bibliographical references and index. ISBN 0-471-81802-X LC Card 86-32589 DDC 658.7/2 19
1. Industrial procurement - Management. 2. Materials management. I. Thompson, George (George H.). II. Title.
HD39.5 .W47 1987

Zeppelin Post Katalog. Sieger. Zeppelinpost Spezial-Katalog /. Lorch/Württemberg , c1981. 384 p. : LC Card 83-214233
HE6183.G735 S54 1981

Zeppelinpost Spezial-Katalog /. Sieger. Lorch/Württemberg , c1981. 384 p. : LC Card 83-214233
HE6183.G735 S54 1981

Zeppernick, Ralf. Transfer-Einkommen und Einkommensverteilung / von Ralf Zeppernick. Berlin : Duncker & Humblot, c1986. viii, 233, [1] p. : 2 ill. ; 24 cm. (Schriftenreihe des Rheinisch-Westfälischen Instituts für Wirtschaftsforschung Essen . n.F., Heft 47) On cover, at head of title: Rheinisch-Westfälisches Institut für Wirtschaftsforschung Essen. Bibliography: p. 213-[234] ISBN 3-428-05990-5 LC Card 86-178831
1. Transfer payments - Germany, West. 2. Income distribution - Germany, West. I. Title. II. Series.
HC290.5.I5 Z47 1986

ZERO-BASE BUDGETING - CASE STUDIES.
The Impact of zero base budgeting on managerial behavior /. Hempstead, N.Y. , 1986. vii, 288 p. ; LC Card 86-80005 DDC 658.1/54 19
HG4028.B8 I55 1986

ZERO-BASED BUDGETING.
Wegmann, 1951- Gemeinkosten-Management . München , c1982. 230, xliii p. : ISBN 3-88259-224-9 (Deut. Bibl.) LC Card 83-159003
HJ2033 .W43 1982

Zerwitz, Donna. Conference on the Effects of Taxation on Capital Formation (1986 : Palm Beach, Fla.) Taxes and capital formation. Cambridge, Mass. (1050 Massachusetts Ave., Cambridge 02138) , 1986. 40 p. ; LC Card 87-101954 DDC 336.2/00973 19
HJ2381 .C6974 1986

Zessin, Axel, 1953- Unternehmungsbewertung von Kreditinstituten / von Axel Zessin. Göttingen : O. Schwartz, 1982. 296 p. : ill. ; 20 cm. (Göttinger Hefte zur Bankbetriebslehre und Unternehmungsfinanzierung . Heft 12) Bibliography: p. 262-288. Includes indexes. ISBN 3-509-01313-1 LC Card 84-109138
1. Business enterprises - Valuation - Germany, West. 2. Bank loans - Germany (West). 3. Credit - Germany, West. I. Title. II. Series.
HG4028.V3 Z47 1982

Zeszyty metodyczne .
(nr. 31) Zasady metodyczne statystyki przemysłu. Warszawa , 1979. 224 p. ; LC Card 81-115708
HC340.3 .Z373 1979

(nr. 34) Nomenklatura artykułów i usług do badania spożycia (NAS). Warszawa , 1980. 87 p. ; LC Card 81-109132
HF1044.P6 N66 1980

Zeszyty naukowe Politechniki Śląskiej .
(nr 850) Bonenberg, Wojciech. Przemysł w mieście . Gliwice , 1985. 181 p., [8] folded leaves of plates : LC Card 86-219523
HC340.3.Z9 D52 1985

(nr. 850) Bonenberg, Wojciech. Przemysł w mieście . Gliwice , 1985. 181 p., [8] folded leaves of plates : LC Card 86-219523
HC340.3.Z9 D52 1985

(zesz. 3) Bonenberg, Wojciech. Przemysł w mieście . Gliwice , 1985. 181 p., [8] folded leaves of plates : LC Card 86-219523
HC340.3.Z9 D52 1985

Zeugnisse der Zeit : 125 Jahre Deutscher Industrie- und Handelstag / [die historische Ausstellung entstand unter Mitarbeit von Klara van Eyll ... et al.]. Bonn : Der Handelstag, 1986. 113 p. : ill. ; 24 cm. (DIHT-Materialien zur Geschichte) LC Card 87-408186
1. Deutscher Industrie- und Handelstag - Exhibitions. 2. Germany - Economic conditions - Exhibitions. I. Eyll, Klara van. II. Deutscher Industrie- und Handelstag. III. Series.
HD2429.G3 Z48 1986

Zevin, Leon Zalmanovich. Strany razlichnogo urovnia razvitiia v mirovom khoziaĭstve : problemy ėkonomicheskikh otnosheniĭ / L.Z. Zevin. Moskva : Izd-vo "Nauka," Glav. red. vostochnoĭ lit-ry, 1985. 193, [4] p. ; 22 cm. At head of title: Akademiia nauk SSSR. Institut ėkonomiki mirovoĭ sotsialisticheskoĭ sistemy. Summary in English. Bibliography: p. 186-[194] LC Card 86-157482
1. International economic relations. 2. Developing countries - Foreign economic relations. I. Title.
HF1411 .Z43 1985

Zevnik, Brian L. P. Wolff, Rick, 1951- The encyclopedia of pre-written employment ads . Westbury, N.Y. , c1986. vi, 196 p. ; ISBN 0-87280-142-X (loose-leaf) : LC Card 86-26526 DDC 659.1/9331128 19
HF6125 .W65 1986

Zey, Michael G. The right move : how to find the perfect job / Michael G. Zey. New York : F. Watts, 1987. ix, 225 p. ; 24 cm. Includes index. ISBN 0-531-15523-4 LC Card 86-29015 DDC 650.1/4 19
1. Job hunting. I. Title.
HF5382.7 .Z49 1987

Zhamin, V. A. (Vitaliĭ Alekseevich)
Sotsialisticheskaia ėkonomicheskaia integratsiia--faktor povysheniia ėffektivnosti proizvodstva stran SĖV / V.A. Zhamin, V.P. Mladenov. Sovmestnoe izd. Moskva : "Ėkonomika" ; Varna : Izd-vo "Georgi Bakalov", 1978. 93 p. ; 20 cm. (Sotsialisticheskaia ėkonomicheskaia integratsiia--v deĭstvii) Includes bibliographical references. LC Card 81-149558
1. Europe, Eastern - Economic integration. 2. Industrial productivity - Europe, Eastern. 3. Soviet Union - Foreign economic relations - Bulgaria. 4. Bulgaria - Foreign economic relations - Soviet Union. I. Mladenov, Vŭlko P. II. Title. III. Series.
HC244 .Z46 1978

Zharinov, Artem Viktorovich. Problemy optimizatsii mezhotraslevykh sviazeĭ . Kiev , 1976. 135 p. : LC Card 87-100694
HD9015.S653 U4547 1976

Zharkoe solntse Surkhana /. Molozhavenko, Vladimir. Moskva , 1982. 189 p., [16] p. of plates : LC Card 82-177858
HC337.U962 S975 1982

Zharkov, P. P. (Pavel Petrovich) Kryzhanovskiĭ, B. N. (Boris Nikolaevich) Spetsializatsiia zagotovitel'nogo proizvodstva /. Kiev , 1985. 125, [3] p. ; LC Card 87-112143
HD9703.S653 U474 1985

Zhebrak, B. A. Makasheva, N. A. Sovremennyĭ monetarizm i krizis burzhuaznoĭ ėkonomicheskoĭ teorii . Moskva , 1985. 47 p. ; LC Card 86-187688
HB98.3 .M35 1985

Zhecheva, Mariia. Informatsionno osiguriavane na profsiuznite organi : niakoi problemi na rŭkovodstvoto i informatsiiata v profsiuznata deĭnost / Mariia Zhecheva, Tatiana Mikhaĭlova. Sofiia : Nauchnoizsledovatelski in-t po profsiuzni problemi "G. Dimitrov" pri TSS na BPS, 1985. 138 p. : ill. ; 21 cm. Summary in English and Russian. Bibliography: p. 134-136. LC Card 86-192068
1. Trade-unions - Bulgaria - Data processing. 2. Trade-unions - Bulgaria - Management. I. Mikhaĭlova, Tatiana. II. Title.
HD6782 .Z44 1985

Zhelezovskaia, N. M.
Izmenenie soderzhaniia i kharaktera truda na sovremennom ėtape razvitogo sotsializma /. Moskva , 1984. 227 p. ; LC Card 85-240356
HD8526.5 .I97 1984

Stimuly k trudu na sovremennom ėtape razvitiia sotsialisticheskogo obshchestva / N.M. Zhelezovskaia ; otvetstvennyĭ redaktor R.K. Ivanova. Moskva : Izd-vo "Nauka", 1985. 160 p. ; 20 cm. (Problemy sovetskoĭ ėkonomiki) At head of title: Akademiia nauk SSSR. Institut ėkonomiki. Includes bibliographical references. LC Card 86-174895
1. Incentives in industry - Soviet Union. I. Ivanova, R. K. (Roza Konstantinovna). II. Title.
HF5549.5.I5 Z48 1985

Zheliazkov, K. Izsledvane roliata na proizvodstvenata sreda, trudovite kolektivi i nastavnitsite za formirane na komunistichesko otnoshenie kŭm truda u podrastvashchtite /. Sofiia , 1984. 150 p. ; LC Card 85-166784
HD6276.B82 I97 1984

Zherebin, V. M. Proektirovanie ėkonomicheskikh informatsionnykh sistem / V.M. Zherebin, V.P. Morozov, N.P. Khozin. Moskva : Izd-vo "Nauka," 1983. 182, [2] p., [2] folded p. of plates : ill. ; 21 cm. At head of title: Akademiia nauk SSSR. TSentral'nyĭ ėkonomikomatematicheskiĭ institut. Bibliography: p. 179-[183] LC Card 83-224346
1. Management - Mathematical models. I. Morozov, V. P. II. Khozin, N. P. III. Title.
HD30.25 .Z52 1983

ZHIVKOV, TODOR - CONGRESSES.
Prinosŭt na dr. Todor Zhivkov za razvitieto na sotsialno-ikonomicheskata politika na BKP v etapa na izgrazhdane na razvitoto sotsialistichesko obshtestvo . Sofiia , 1983. 398 p. ; LC Card 84-103348
HC403 .P72 1983

Zhukov, V. I. Rabochee dvizhenie v Moldavii, 1895-fevral' 1917 g. . Kishinev , 1985. 322 p. ; LC Card 86-100092
HD8529.M57 R32 1985

Zhurikhin, Ė. A. (Ėduard Alekseevich)
"Filantropicheskie" fondy SShA v sisteme vlasti monopoliĭ / Ė.A. Zhurikhin. Moskva : Izd-vo "Nauka", 1978. 182, [2] p. ; 20 cm. At head of title: Akademiia nauk SSSR. Institut vseobshcheĭ istorii. Bibliography: p. 176-[183] LC Card 81-160810

1. Corporations - United States - Charitable contributions. 2. Industry - Social aspects - United States. I. Title.
HG4028.C6 Z48 1978

Zhurlov, Anatoliĭ Nikitovich. Ėkonomicheskie funktsii upravleniia proizvoditel'nym trudom /. Kiev , 1986. 167 p. ; LC Card 87-152432
HD9705.S595 E37 1986

Ziebell, Lindy, 1955- Biermann, Ingrid, 1955- Leben mit kurzfristigem Denken . Weinheim , 1985. 224 p. ; ISBN 3-407-58260-9 LC Card 86-106693
HD6053.6.G3 B54 1985
NYPL [JLD 86-3122]

Z'iednani Derzhavy Ameryky. see United States.

Ziefuss, Horst. Jugendliche in der gewerblich-technischen Ausbildung in Industrie und Handwerk : eine Analyse / Horst Ziefuss unter Mitarbeit von Peter Dohse und Heinrich Lienker. Kiel : Institut für die Pädagogik der Naturwissenschaften an der Universität Kiel, c1986. 352 p. : ill. ; 21 cm. (IPN . 109) Pref. in English, French, and German. Bibliography: p. 271-283. Includes index. ISBN 3-89088-011-8 LC Card 87-407898 DDC 331.3/42592/0943 19
1. Occupational training - Germany, West. 2. Employees, Training of - Germany, West. 3. Youth - Germany, West. I. Dohse, Peter. II. Lienker, Heinrich. III. Series: IPN (Series) , 109. IV. Title.
HD5715.5.G4 Z54 1986

Zieger, Gottfried. Aussenwirtschaft der DDR und innerdeutsche Wirtschaftsbeziehungen . Berlin , c1986. 98 p. ; ISBN 3-428-06121-7 LC Card 87-137949 DDC 382/.0943/0431 19
HF3570.5.Z7 G352 1986

Ziegler, Béatrice. Schweizer statt Sklaven : schweizerische Auswanderer in den Kaffee-Plantagen von São Paulo (1852-1866) / Béatrice Ziegler. Stuttgart : Steiner, c1985. 466 p., [16] p. of plates : ill. ; 23 cm. (Beiträge zur Kolonial- und Überseegeschichte. Bd. 29) Chiefly German with text in French and Portuguese. Originally presented as the author's thesis (doctoral)--Universität Zürich, 1981. Bibliography: p. 449-465. ISBN 3-515-04174-5 : LC Card 85-133062 DDC 331.6/2/49408161 19
1. Alien labor, Swiss - Brazil - São Paulo (State) - History - 19th century. 2. Coffee plantation workers - Brazil - São Paulo (State) - History - 19th century. I. Title. II. Series.
HD8289.S283 Z54 1985
NYPL [JLE 87-1222]

Ziegler, Wilhelm, 1891- Einführung in die Volkswirtschaft / von Wilhelm Ziegler. 3., verb. Aufl. Berlin : Zentralverlag, 1925. 94, [1] p. ; 21 cm. (Staat und Wirtschaft) "36.-40. Tausend." Bibliography: p. [95] LC Card 83-234150
1. Economics. I. Series: Staat und Wirtschaft (Berlin, Germany). II. Title.
HB175 .Z515 1925

Zielbildung und strategisches Zielsystem der internationalen Unternehmung /. Duhnkrack, Thomas. Göttingen , c1984. xii, 287 p. : ISBN 3-525-12664-6 (Deut. Bibl.) LC Card 85-127165
HD62.4 .D86 1984

Ziele, Instrumente und Bedingungen der Geschäftsstellenorganisation im filialisierten Universalbankbetrieb /. Reuschenbach, Ruth. Köln , c1984. 385 p. ; ISBN 3-87951-122-5 LC Card 85-131689
HG1616.B7 R48 1984

Ziele und Möglichkeiten der Privatisierung in volkswirtschaftlicher Sicht : die Beteiligungen des Bundes / [Bearbeiter, Manfred Schlick]. Bonn : Institut "Finanzen und Steuern", 1985. 83 leaves ; 30 cm. (Brief / Institut "Finanzen und Steuern" . Nr. 244) Cover title. Issued by the Institut "Finanzen und Steuern." Includes bibliographical references. LC Card 86-185728
1. Privatization - Germany (West). 2. Germany, West - Economic policy - 1974-. I. Schlick, Manfred. II. Institut "Finanzen und Steuern" (Germany). III. Series: Brief (Institut "Finanzen und Steuern" (Germany)) , Nr. 244.
HJ1120 .B65 Nr. 244 HD4178

Zielgruppenorientierte kommunale Wirtschaftsförderung . Burberg, Paul-Helmuth. Münster , c1983. xi, 207, 16 p. : ISBN 3-88497-042-9 LC Card 84-173863
HC289.M9 B87 1983

Ziemba, W. T. Economic analysis of information and contracts . Boston , c1988. p. cm. ISBN 0-89838-252-1 : LC Card 87-22508 DDC 657 19
HF5625 .E28 1988

Ziesemer, Thomas. Economic theory of underdevelopment / Thomas Ziesemer. Regensburg : Transfer Verlag, c1987. vi, 171 p. : ill. ; 26 cm. (Volkswirtschaftliche Schriften der Universität Regensburg . v. 3) Bibliography: p. 165-171. ISBN 3-924956-15-4 (pbk.) LC Card 87-169372 DDC 338.9/001 19
1. Economic development - Mathematical models. 2. Developing countries - Economic conditions - Mathematical models. 3. Developing countries - Dependency on foreign countries - Mathematical models. 4. Equilibrium (Economics) - Mathematical models. I. Series: Volkswirtschaftliche Schriften der Universität Regensburg , Bd. 3. II. Title.
HD75.5 .Z54 1987

Ziesing, Hans-Joachim. Beurteilung der Wirtschaftlichkeitsschwelle und Analyse der Produktionskapazitäten bei neuen Technologien zur Energieeinsparung in mittel- bis längerfristiger Sicht : Dargestellt an Wärmepumpen und Solaranlagen / Hans-Joachim Ziesing. Berlin : Duncker & Humblot, 1983. 458 p. : ill. ; 24 cm. (Sonderheft / Deutsches Institut für Wirtschaftsforschung . 139) Bibliography: p. 450-458. ISBN 3-428-05497-0
1. Energy policy - Germany, West. 2. Energy conservation - Germany, West. 3. Energy industries - Germany, West. 4. Solar energy - Germany (West). 5. Heat pumps - Germany (West). I. Series: Berlin. Deutsches Institut für Wirtschaftsforschung. Sonderheft , 139. II. Title.
NYPL [JLL 73-207 Bd. 139]

Zietsch, Dietmar. Grundlagen der Gestaltung aussenorganisationsbezogener Vertriebssteuerungssysteme in Versicherungsunternehmen / Dietmar Zietsch. Karlsruhe : VVW, c1985. xx, 308 p. : ill. ; 21 cm. Bibliography: p. 287-308. ISBN 3-88487-084-X LC Card 86-169097
1. Insurance - Germany, West. I. Title.
HG8618 .Z53 1985

Zigler, Edward, 1930- The Parental leave crisis . New Haven , c1988. p. cm. ISBN 0-300-03984-0 (alk. paper) LC Card 87-10729 DDC 331.25/76 19
HD6065 .P37 1988

ZIGUINCHOR (SENEGAL) - ECONOMIC CONDITIONS.
Trincaz, Pierre Xavier. Colonisation et régionalisme . Paris , 1984. 270 p. : ISBN 2-7099-0713-5 LC Card 86-148748 DDC 330.966/3 19
HC1045.Z7 Z548 1984

ZIGUINCHOR (SENEGAL) - SOCIAL CONDITIONS.
Trincaz, Pierre Xavier. Colonisation et régionalisme . Paris , 1984. 270 p. : ISBN 2-7099-0713-5 LC Card 86-148748 DDC 330.966/3 19
HC1045.Z7 Z548 1984

Zijlstra, J. Gematigd monetarisme : 14 jaarverslagen van de Nederlandsche Bank n.v. 1967-1980 / [J. Zijlstra] ; met een inleidende beschouwing door C. Goedhart. Leiden : H.E. Stenfert Kroese, 1985. ix, 330 p. : ill. ; 25 cm. Includes index. ISBN 90-207-1382-5 : LC Card 85-201189
1. Monetary policy - Netherlands. 2. Banks and banking - Netherlands. I. Goedhart, C. (Cornelis). II. Nederlandsche Bank (Amsterdam, Netherlands). III. Title.
HG1065 .Z55 1985 *NYPL [JLE 87-379]*

Zijlstra, Jelle. see Zijlstra, J.

Zikmund, William G.
Business research methods / William G. Zikmund. 2nd ed. Chicago : Dryden Press, 1987, c1988. xvii, 715 p. : ill. ; 24 cm. Includes bibliographical references and index. ISBN 0-03-012362-3 LC Card 87-5284 DDC 658.4/03/072 19
1. Management research. 2. Business - Research. I. Title.
HD30.4 .Z54 1988

A Collection of cases in marketing management /. St. Paul , c1987. xix, 344 p. ; ISBN 0-314-85313-8 (pbk.) LC Card 87-6072 DDC 658.8/00973 19
HF5415.13 .C64 1987

Zile, Kh. Problemy urovnia zhizni i demografii . Riga , 1979. 175 p. ; LC Card 82-106660
HD7035.Z8 L376 1979

Zilli Manica, José Benigno. Braceros italianos para México : (la historia olvidada de la huelga de 1900) / José B. Zilli.1a ed. Xalapa, México : Editorial UV, 1986. 93 p., [6] p. of plates : ill., ports. ; 21 cm. (Biblioteca Universidad Veracruzana) Bibliography: p. 92-93. ISBN 968-8340-45-6 LC Card 87-400059
1. Alien labor, Italian - Mexico - Veracruz (State) - History. 2. Italians - Mexico - Veracruz (State) - History. 3. Ferrocarril Veracruz al Pacífico Strike, 1900. I. Title. II. Series.
HD8118.5.I83 Z55 1986

Zimbabwe.
First five-year national development plan, 1986-1990 / Republic of Zimbabwe. [Harare?] : The Republic, [1986- v. <1 > ; 30 cm. "April 1986." LC Card 86-981132 DDC 338.96891 19
1. Zimbabwe - Economic policy. 2. Zimbabwe - Economic conditions - 1980-. I. Title.
HC910 .Z26 1986

Zimbabwe at five years of independence.
Zimbabwe at 5 years of independence. [Harare?] [1984?] ix, 265 p. : LC Card 87-103323 DDC 338.96891 19
HC910 .Z3173 1984

Zimbabwe at 5 years of independence. [Harare?] : ZANU (PF), Dept. of the Commissariat and Culture, [1984?] ix, 265 p. : ill. ; 21 cm. Cover title: Re-building Zimbabwe at 5 years of independence. LC Card 87-103323 DDC 338.96891 19
1. Zimbabwe - Economic conditions - 1980-. 2. Zimbabwe - Economic policy. 3. Zimbabwe - Politics and government - 1980-. 4. Zimbabwe - Social conditions - 1980-. 5. Zimbabwe - Social policy. 6. Socialism - Zimbabwe. I. ZANU-PF (Organization : Zimbabwe). Dept. of the Commissariat and Culture. II. Title: Zimbabwe at five years of independence. III. Title: Re-building Zimbabwe at 5 years of independence.
HC910 .Z3173 1984

Zimbabwe. Central Statistical Office. Permanent Sample Survey Unit. Report on demographic socio-economic survey . Harare, Zimbabwe [1984 or 1985] 18 p. : LC Card 86-980590 DDC 304.6/096891 19
HA4702.Z9 M356 1984

ZIMBABWE - COMMERCE - HISTORY.
Whitsun Foundation. Project 1.07 . Harare, Zimbabwe [1983?] 2 v. ; ISBN 0-7974-0597-6 LC Card 84-981092 DDC 380.1/096891 19
HF3902 .W48 1983 *NYPL [JLM 87-272]*

Zimbabwe. Commission of Inquiry into the Agricultural Industry. Report of the Commission of Inquiry into the Agricultural Industry /. [Harare?] [1982] ix, 205 p. : LC Card 85-980325 DDC 338.1/096891 19
HD2131 .R47 1982

Zimbabwe Conference on Reconstruction and Development, Salisbury, 23rd to 27th March 1981 . Zimbabwe Conference on Reconstruction and Development (1981 : Salisbury, Zimbabwe) Causeway, Zimbabwe [1981?] vi, 194 p. : LC Card 86-980955 DDC 338.96891 19
HC910 .Z318 1981a

Zimbabwe Conference on Reconstruction and Development (1981 : Salisbury, Zimbabwe)
Zimbabwe Conference on Reconstruction and Development, Salisbury, 23rd to 27th March 1981 : [report on conference proceedings] / [prepared and issued by Ministry of Economic Planning and Development]. Causeway, Zimbabwe : The Ministry, [1981?] vi, 194 p. : 1 col. map, port. ; 30 cm. Spine title: Zimcord conference proceedings. Map on lining papers. LC Card 86-980955 DDC 338.96891 19
1. Economic assistance - Zimbabwe - Congresses. 2. Technical assistance - Zimbabwe - Congresses. 3. Zimbabwe - Economic conditions - 1980- - Congresses. 4. Zimbabwe - Economic policy. I. Zimbabwe. Ministry of Economic Planning and Development. II. Title. III. Title: Zimcord conference proceedings.
HC910 .Z318 1981a

Zimbabwe. Dept. of Rural Development.
Intensive resettlement policies and procedures /. [Harare, Zimbabwe] , 1985. 81 p. : LC Card

87-980233 DDC 333.3/1/6891 19
HD992 .I58 1985

ZIMBABWE - ECONOMIC CONDITIONS - TO 1965.
Ndlela, Daniel Boda. Dualism in the Rhodesian colonial economy /. [Lund] [1981] vi, 241 p. : LC Card 86-673434
HC910 .N34x 1981

Phimister, I. R. (Ian R.) An economic and social history of Zimbabwe, 1890-1948 . London , New York , 1987. p. cm. ISBN 0-582-64423-2 LC Card 87-12471 DDC 330.96891/02 19
HC910.Z9 S36 1987

ZIMBABWE - ECONOMIC CONDITIONS - 1980-
Katins, Sabine. All you need is freedom . Berlin [1977] 35 p. : LC Card 86-207107 DDC 968.91/05 19
HC910 .K37 1977

Wasserman, Gary, 1944- U. S. aid to Zimbabwe . [Washington, D.C.?] [1983] ix, 20, [71] p. ; LC Card 87-109216 DDC 338.91/73/06891 19
HC910 .W37 1983

Zimbabwe. First five-year national development plan, 1986-1990 /. [Harare?] [1986- v. <1 > ; LC Card 86-981132 DDC 338.96891 19
HC910 .Z26 1986

Zimbabwe at 5 years of independence. [Harare?] [1984?] ix, 265 p. : LC Card 87-103323 DDC 338.96891 19
HC910 .Z3173 1984

ZIMBABWE - ECONOMIC CONDITIONS - 1980- - CONGRESSES.
Zimbabwe Conference on Reconstruction and Development (1981 : Salisbury, Zimbabwe) Zimbabwe Conference on Reconstruction and Development, Salisbury, 23rd to 27th March 1981 . Causeway, Zimbabwe [1981?] vi, 194 p. : LC Card 86-980955 DDC 338.96891 19
HC910 .Z318 1981a

ZIMBABWE - ECONOMIC POLICY.
Ndlela, Daniel Boda. Dualism in the Rhodesian colonial economy /. [Lund] [1981] vi, 241 p. : LC Card 86-673434
HC910 .N34x 1981

Zimbabwe. First five-year national development plan, 1986-1990 /. [Harare?] [1986- v. <1 > ; LC Card 86-981132 DDC 338.96891 19
HC910 .Z26 1986

Zimbabwe at 5 years of independence. [Harare?] [1984?] ix, 265 p. : LC Card 87-103323 DDC 338.96891 19
HC910 .Z3173 1984

Zimbabwe Conference on Reconstruction and Development (1981 : Salisbury, Zimbabwe) Zimbabwe Conference on Reconstruction and Development, Salisbury, 23rd to 27th March 1981 . Causeway, Zimbabwe [1981?] vi, 194 p. : LC Card 86-980955 DDC 338.96891 19
HC910 .Z318 1981a

ZIMBABWE - FOREIGN ECONOMIC RELATIONS.
Paul, Jan-Peter. Ekonomiska sanktioner . Helsingfors [1985] 46 p. ; ISBN 951-555-224-9 LC Card 85-212001
HF1613.5 .P38 1985

Zimbabwe government policy and the manufacturing sector . Jansen, Doris J. Larkspur, Calif., U. S.A. , c1983. 22 p., 10 leaves of plates : LC Card 87-121346 DDC 338.96891 19
HD9737.Z552 J36 1983

ZIMBABWE - MANUFACTURES - GOVERNMENT POLICY.
Jansen, Doris J. Zimbabwe government policy and the manufacturing sector . Larkspur, Calif., U. S.A. , c1983. 22 p., 10 leaves of plates : LC Card 87-121346 DDC 338.96891 19
HD9737.Z552 J36 1983

Zimbabwe. Ministry of Economic Planning and Development. Zimbabwe Conference on Reconstruction and Development (1981 : Salisbury, Zimbabwe) Zimbabwe Conference on Reconstruction and Development, Salisbury, 23rd to 27th March 1981 . Causeway, Zimbabwe [1981?] vi, 194 p. : LC Card 86-980955 DDC 338.96891 19
HC910 .Z318 1981a

Zimbabwe. Ministry of Industry and Energy Development. Jansen, Doris J. Zimbabwe government policy and the manufacturing sector . Larkspur, Calif., U. S.A. , c1983. 22 p., 10 leaves of plates : LC Card 87-121346 DDC 338.96891 19
HD9737.Z552 J36 1983

Zimbabwe. Ministry of Lands Resettlement and Rural Development. Intensive resettlement policies and procedures /. [Harare, Zimbabwe] , 1985. 81 p. : LC Card 87-980233 DDC 333.3/1/6891 19
HD992 .I58 1985

Zimbabwe. Ministry of Public Construction and National Housing. Report on housing and urban development in Zimbabwe . [Harare, Zimbabwe , 1986] vi, 46 p., [1] folded leaf of plates : LC Card 87-980381 DDC 363.5/8 19
HD7374.5.A3 R46 1986

Zimbabwe. Ministry of Water Resources and Development. An Assessment of the surface water resources of Zimbabwe and guidelines for development planning. Harare, Zimbabwe [1984?] 23 p., [3] folded leaves of plates : LC Card 86-980548 DDC 333.91/02/096891 19
HD1699.Z55 A84 1984

ZIMBABWE - POLITICS AND GOVERNMENT - 1980-
Wasserman, Gary, 1944- U. S. aid to Zimbabwe . [Washington, D.C.?] [1983] ix, 20, [71] p. ; LC Card 87-109216 DDC 338.91/73/06891 19
HC910 .W37 1983

Zimbabwe at 5 years of independence. [Harare?] [1984?] ix, 265 p. : LC Card 87-103323 DDC 338.96891 19
HC910 .Z3173 1984

ZIMBABWE - SOCIAL CONDITIONS - 1890-1965.
Phimister, I. R. (Ian R.) An economic and social history of Zimbabwe, 1890-1948 . London , New York , 1987. p. cm. ISBN 0-582-64423-2 LC Card 87-12471 DDC 330.96891/02 19
HC910.Z9 S36 1987

ZIMBABWE - SOCIAL CONDITIONS - 1980-
Katins, Sabine. All you need is freedom . Berlin [1977] 35 p. : LC Card 86-207107 DDC 968.91/05 19
HC910 .K37 1977

Zimbabwe at 5 years of independence. [Harare?] [1984?] ix, 265 p. : LC Card 87-103323 DDC 338.96891 19
HC910 .Z3173 1984

ZIMBABWE - SOCIAL POLICY.
Zimbabwe at 5 years of independence. [Harare?] [1984?] ix, 265 p. : LC Card 87-103323 DDC 338.96891 19
HC910 .Z3173 1984

Zimbalist, Andrew S. Cuba's socialist economy toward the 1990s /. Boulder, Colo. , 1987. ix, 188 p. : ISBN 1-555-87080-5 (lib. bdg. : alk. paper) : LC Card 87-12867 DDC 338.97291 19
HC152.5 .C824 1987

Zimco. see **Zambia Industrial and Mining Corporation.**

Zimcord conference proceedings. Zimbabwe Conference on Reconstruction and Development (1981 : Salisbury, Zimbabwe) Zimbabwe Conference on Reconstruction and Development, Salisbury, 23rd to 27th March 1981 . Causeway, Zimbabwe [1981?] vi, 194 p. : LC Card 86-980955 DDC 338.96891 19
HC910 .Z318 1981a

Zimmer, Frederick G. Man and work in society . New York , c1975. xiv, 313 p. : ISBN 0-442-29359-3 LC Card 75-26866 DDC 658.3
HF5549 .M299 ***NYPL [JLE 76-2406]***

Zimmer, Sandra G. Putnam, Bluford H. The Blackwell guide to Wall Street /. Oxford, UK , New York, NY, USA , 1987. viii, 222 p. : ISBN 0-631-14183-9 : LC Card 87-10299 DDC 332.63/2 19
HG4910 .P87 1987

Zimmerman, Joseph Francis, 1928- Participatory democracy : populism revived / Joseph F. Zimmerman. New York : Praeger, 1986. xi, 229 p. ; 25 cm. Includes index. Bibliography: p. 185-221. ISBN 0-275-92132-8 (alk. paper) : LC Card 86-8129 DDC 323/.042/0973 19
1. Referendum - United States. 2. Recall - United States. 3. Neighborhood government - United States. 4. Populism - United States. 5. Political participation - United States. I. Title.
JF493.U6 Z56 1986 ***NYPL [JLE 86-3632]***

Zimmerman, Steven M. Understanding and using microcomputers / Steven M. Zimmerman, Leo M. Conrad. 2nd ed. St. Paul : West Pub. Co., c1988. xxvi, 371 p. : ill. (some col.) ; 26 cm. (The Microcomputing series) Includes bibliographies and index. ISBN 0-314-60096-5 (pbk.) LC Card 87-19044 DDC 650/.028/5416 19
1. Business - Data processing. 2. Microcomputers - Programming. I. Conrad, Leo M. II. Title. III. Series.
HF5548.2 .Z58 1988

Zimmermann, Heinz, 1958- Kapitalerhöhungen und Aktienmarkt : Untersuchungen zur Preisbildung auf dem schweizerischen Aktienmarkt in der Zeitperiode von 1973 bis 1983 / Heinz Zimmermann. Köln : Institut für Wirtschaftspolitik an der Universität zu Köln, 1986. 446 p. : ill. ; 24 cm. (Untersuchungen zur Wirtschaftspolitik, 0175-7458 . 69) Bibliography: p. 434-445. ISBN 3-921471-57-5 LC Card 87-407823 DDC 332.63/222/09494 19
1. Stocks - Prices - Switzerland. 2. Capital market - Switzerland. I. Title. II. Series.
HG5653 .Z56 1986

Zimmermann, Horst, 1934-
Die Gemeindefinanzen im Ruhrgebiet : aktuelle Entwicklung, kritische Bestandsaufnahme, mögliche Anpassungsstrategien : Gutachten im Auftrag des Kommunalverbandes Ruhrgebiet / erarbeitet von Horst Zimmermann und Martin Junkernheinrich ; [Auftraggeber] Kommunalverband Ruhrgebiet, Abteilung Wirtschaftsstruktur, EDV, Statistik ; Leiter, Andreas Schlieper ; Bearbeiter, Heinz Bisping ... [et al.]. Essen : Kommunalverband Ruhrgebiet, Abteilung Öffentlichkeitsarbeit, 1983. xvi, 153 p. : ill. ; 30 cm. (Strukturberichterstattung Ruhrgebiet) Arbeitshefte Ruhrgebiet Includes bibliographical references. ISBN 3-923494-28-9 LC Card 83-228289
1. Local finance - Germany (West) - Ruhr (Region). I. Junkernheinrich, Martin. II. Schlieper, Andreas. III. Bisping, Heinz. IV. Kommunalverband Ruhrgebiet. Abteilung Wirtschaftsstruktur, EDV, Statistik. V. Kommunalverband Ruhrgebiet. VI. Title. VII. Series.
HJ9493.5.R8 Z76 1983

Ökonomische Anreizinstrumente in einer auflagenorientierten Umweltpolitik : Notwendigkeit, Möglichkeiten und Grenzen am Beispiel der amerikanischen Luftreinhaltepolitik / Horst Zimmermann ; mit einem Anhang von L. Eichler, Die "Emissions-Trading," Instrumente der Luftreinhaltepolitik in den Vereinigten Staaten. Stuttgart : W. Kohlhammer, 1983. 59 p. ; 21 cm. (Materialien zur Umweltforschung . 8) Includes bibliographical references. ISBN 3-17-003279-8 : LC Card 84-148886
1. Air quality management - United States. 2. Air quality management - Germany (West). I. Eichler, L. II. Title. III. Series.
HC110.A4 Z55 1983

Zimmermann, Klaus F. Demographische Probleme der Haushaltsökonomie /. Bochum , 1986. vii, 212 p. : ISBN 3-88339-534-X LC Card 87-137970 DDC 339.4/1/0943 19
HD7029 .D37 1986

Zimmermann, Klaus, 1944- Regional environmental policy . New York , c1979. xii, 290 p. : ISBN 0-8147-7805-4 : LC Card 79-2058 DDC 301.31
HC79.E5 R44 ***NYPL [JLE 80-1854]***

Zimmermann, Rainer. Demographische Variablen in linearen Produktionsmodellen / Rainer Zimmermann. Bochum : N. Brockmeyer, 1983. 263 p. : ill. ; 21 cm. (Contributions to quantitative economics . vol. 6 =) Bibliography: p. 254-263. ISBN 3-88339-327-4 LC Card 84-107454
1. Production functions (Economic theory). 2. Demographic transition - Econometric models. 3. Linear programming. I. Series: Contributions to quantitative economics , vol. 6. II. Title.
HB241 .Z56 1983

Zimring, Franklin E. Social control of the drinking driver /. Chicago , 1988. p. cm. ISBN 0-226-46953-0 : LC Card 87-19111 DDC 363.1/256 19
HE5620.D7 S66 1988

ZINANTEC INDIANS. see **CHINANTEC INDIANS.**

Zinātnisko rakstu krājums. Khoziaistvennyĭ mekhanizm proizvodstva i obrashcheniia tovarov narodnogo potrebleniia /. Riga , 1985. 115 p. ; LC Card 86-177827
HF1040.9.L38 K47 1985

Zinbarg, Edward D. (joint author) Cohen, Jerome Bernard, 1915- Investment analysis and portfolio management. Homewood, Ill., 1973. xiv, 946 p. ISBN 0-256-01429-9 LC Card 72-98120
HG4521 .C5296 1973 ***NYPL [JLE 74-744]***
(joint author) Cohen, Jerome Bernard, 1915- Investment analysis and portfolio management /. Homewood, Ill. , 1977. xvi, 819 p. : ISBN 0-256-01883-9 LC Card 76-15739
HG4521 .C5296 1977
NYPL [*R-Econ. 78-1366]

ZINC INDUSTRY AND TRADE - CENTRAL EUROPE - CASE STUDIES.
Jörs, Bernd. Die Bedeutung der Buntmetallhütten des mitteleuropäischen Raumes im Rahmen der Versorgung der Bundesrepublik Deutschland . Frankfurt/Main , 1983. 579 p. in various pagings : LC Card 83-226662
HD9539.Z6 C365 1983

ZINC INDUSTRY AND TRADE - GERMANY (WEST) - CASE STUDIES.
Jörs, Bernd. Die Bedeutung der Buntmetallhütten des mitteleuropäischen Raumes im Rahmen der Versorgung der Bundesrepublik Deutschland . Frankfurt/Main , 1983. 579 p. in various pagings : LC Card 83-226662
HD9539.Z6 C365 1983

Zingel, Wolfgang-Peter. Ahrens, Heinz-Dietmar. Towards reducing the dependence on capital imports . Wiesbaden , 1982. xvi, 337 p. : ISBN 3-515-03853-1 (pbk.) LC Card 86-214363 DDC 338.9549/1 19
HC440.5 .A726 1982

Zingg, Rosa Lúcia. O SENAI e o mercado de trabalho industrial paulista : alguns dados indicativos / Rosa Lúcia Zingg. [São Paulo] : Serviço Nacional de Aprendizagem Industrial, Departamento Regional de São Paulo, Divisão de Pesquisas, Estudos e Avaliação, 1986. 37 leaves ; 30 cm. Cover title. Chiefly tables. LC Card 87-402164 DDC 331.12/5/098161021 19
1. Labor supply - Brazil - Saõ Paulo (State) - Statistics. 2. Brazil. Servico Nacional de Aprendizagem Industrial. I. Brazil. Serviço Nacional de Aprendizagem Industrial. Departamento Regional de São Paulo. Divisão de Pesquisas, Estudos e Avaliação. II. Title.
HD5755.S3 Z56 1986

Zink, Achim. Der Bausparvertrag / Achim Zink. 3. Aufl. Wiesbaden : Gabler, 1984. 110 p. : ill. ; 24 cm. Includes index. ISBN 3-409-47001-8 LC Card 84-213485
1. Building and loan associations - Germany, West. 2. Building and loan associations - Law and legislation - Germany, West. I. Title.
HG2156.G3 Z55 1984

Zinman, Michael. The history of the decline and fall of the Raterpillar Tractor Company : a modern business saga / by Michael Zinman. Ardsley, N.Y. : Haydn Foundation, c1986. 231 p. : ill. ; 24 cm. Spine title: History of Raterpillar. ISBN 0-937704-03-2 (pbk.) : LC Card 86-82887 DDC 338.7/629225 19
1. Raterpillar Tractor Company - History. 2. Caterpillar Tractor Company. 3. Tractor industry - United States. 4. Consolidation and merger of corporations - United States. I. Title. II. Title: History of Raterpillar.
HD9710.4.U64 R388 1986

Zinn, Karl Georg. Arbeit, Konsum, Akkumulation : Versuch einer integralen Kapitalismusanalyse von Keynes und Marx / Karl Georg Zinn. Hamburg : VSA-Verlag, 1986. 243 p. : ill. ; 21 cm. Bibliography: p. 224-233. Includes indexes. ISBN 3-87975-347-4 LC Card 86-230933
1. Keynes, John Maynard, 1883-1946. 2. Marx, Karl, 1818-1883. 3. Labor economics. 4. Saving and investment. 5. Consumption (Economics). 6. Capitalism. I. Title.
HB103.K47 Z56 1986

Zins und wirtschaftliche Entwicklung /. Seyfert, Wolfgang. Köln , c1985. 187 p. : ISBN 3-452-19936-3 : LC Card 86-185586
HD75 .S49 1985

Zinser, James Edward. Mercados financieros y distribución del ingreso /. Santo Domingo, República Dominicana , 1986. 117 p. : LC Card 87-405027 DDC 332.1/097293 19
HG185.D65 M47 1986

Die Zinskatastrophe . Bethmann, Johann Philipp, Freiherr von, 1924- Konigstein/Ts. , c1985. 142 p. ; ISBN 3-7610-8390-4 : LC Card 86-139624
HG1621 .B48 1985

Die Zinsstruktur der Schweiz . Capitelli, René. Frankfurt am Main , c1983. ix, 221 p. : ISBN 3-88129-700-6 LC Card 84-129042
HG1623.S9 C36 1983

Zinswirkungen der Staatsverschuldung . Francke, Hans-Hermann. Berlin , c1984. 138 p. : ISBN 3-428-05727-9 LC Card 86-107232
HJ8654 .F73 1984

Ziobrowski, Jerzy. Technologia /. [Wrocław] , 1982. 188 p. : LC Card 83-176194
HB9 .B7522 nr. 191 TP185

Zionist Congress (15th : 1927 : Basel, Switzerland) Bericht der Exekutive der Zionistischen Organisation an den XV. Zionisten-Kongress. Jerusalem , 1927 (Jerusalem : Azriel) 110 p., [1] folded leaf of plates : LC Card 86-122608
HD1516.P18 B525 1927

Zionist Organisation. Executive. Bericht der Exekutive der Zionistischen Organisation an den XV. Zionisten-Kongress. Jerusalem , 1927 (Jerusalem : Azriel) 110 p., [1] folded leaf of plates : LC Card 86-122608
HD1516.P18 B525 1927

ZIONISTS - UNITED STATES - BIOGRAPHY.
Hammer, Gottlieb, 1911- Good faith and credit /. New York , c1985. 258 p., [12] p. of plates : ISBN 0-8453-4798-5 (alk. paper) LC Card 85-13962 DDC 956.94/001/0973 19
DS151.H34 A34 1985
NYPL [*PWZ (Hammer, G.) 86-2026]

ZIP CODE - GREECE - ATHENS - DIRECTORIES.
Hodēgos tachydromikōn tomeōn Athēnōn /. Athēnai [1962] 124 p. : LC Card 86-234916
HE7180.5.Z7 A744 1962

Zis, George. Inflation in the world economy /. Manchester [Eng.] , 1976. xvii, 334 p. : ISBN 0-7190-0630-9 LC Card 76-356701
HG229 .I453 1976 ***NYPL [JLD 78-401]***

Ziss, Roland. Baumaterialien und Selbsthilfe : Probleme des Wohnungsbaus in mexikanischen Mittelstädten / Roland Ziss, Joanna Kotowski-Ziss. Saarbrücken ; Fort Lauderdale, Fl. : Verlag Breitenbach, 1986. 319 p. : ill. ; 21 cm. Bibliography: p. 307-314. ISBN 3-88156-333-4 LC Card 86-197177
1. Poor - Mexico - Housing. 2. Self-held housing - Mexico. 3. Building materials - Mexico. I. Kotowski-Ziss, Joanna. II. Title.
HD7287.96.M6 Z57 1986

Zivile Alternativen für die Rüstungsindustrie / Klaus Schomacker, Peter Wilke, Herbert Wulf (Hrsg.). 1. Aufl. Baden-Baden : Nomos, 1986. 174 p. ; 23 cm. (Militär, Rüstung, Sicherheit . Bd. 37) Bibliography: p. 172-173. ISBN 3-7890-1262-9 LC Card 87-108651 DDC 338.4/76234/0943 19
1. Munitions - Germany, West. 2. Disarmament - Economic aspects - Germany, West. I. Schomacker, Klaus. II. Wilke, Peter. III. Wulf, Herbert. IV. Series.
HD9743.G48 Z58 1986

Zivilstandsstatistik von 1980-1984. Liechtenstein. Amt für Volkswirtschaft. Statistische Information . Vaduz, Fürstentum Liechtenstein [1985] 18 leaves ; LC Card 85-228548
HB3592.9.A3 L54 1985

Zlatanov, Zdravko Ĭordanov. 150 godini slivenska tekstilna promishlenost / Zdravko Zlatanov. [Sofia] : Profizdat, 1984. 364 p., [48] p. of plates : ill. ; 21 cm. Includes bibliographical references. LC Card 85-118285
1. Textile industry - Bulgaria - Sliven - History. 2. Sliven (Bulgaria) - Economic conditions. I. Title. II. Title: Sto i petdeset godini slivenska tekstilna promishlenost.
HD9865.B83 S589 1984

Zlatev, István. A magyar postahivatalok, 1867-1871. években használt hely-keletbélyegzései : bélyegzéskatalógus = Poststempel Katalog / összeállitotta, Zlatev István. Budapest : Magyar Bélyeggyüjtők Országos Szövetsége, 1983. 255 p. : ill., 2 folded maps ; 24 cm. Bibliography: p. 253. ISBN 963-01-4848-X LC Card 86-148361
1. Postal service - Hungary - History - 19th century. 2. Postmarks - Hungary - History - 19th century. I. Magyar Bélyeggyűjtők Országos Szövetsége. II. Title.
HE6980.5 .Z55 1983

Zloch-Christy, Iliana, 1953- The debt problems of Eastern Europe / Iliana Zloch-Christy. Cambridge [Cambridgeshire] ; New York : Cambridge University Press, 1987. xix, 220 p. ; 23 cm. (Soviet and East European studies) Bibliography: p. 203-212. Includes index. ISBN 0-521-33542-6 LC Card 87-11634 DDC 336.3/435/0947 19
1. Debts, External - Europe, Eastern. 2. Foreign exchange problem - Europe, Eastern. I. Title.
HJ8615 .Z57 1987

ZMM metal-working machines combine, Sofia /. Kostov, Miroslav. Sofia , 1986. [104] p. : LC Card 87-116288 DDC 338.7/621902/0949773 19
HD9703.B94 Z384 1986

Znamenskiĭ, G. V. Osobennosti razvitiia i puti povysheniia ėffektivnosti proizvoditel'nykh sil regiona /. Sverdlovsk , 1984. 141 p. ; LC Card 86-135171
HC337.R852 C456 1984

Znanstvene osnove dugoročnog razvoja SR Hrvatske do 2000. godine .
(1) Osnove dugoročnog razvoja SR Hrvatske--svodna studija /. Zagreb , 1984. 437 p. ; LC Card 87-151188
HC407.Z7 C7647 1984

Zoeteweij, H. Indirect remuneration : an international overview / H. Zoeteweij. Geneva : International Labour Office, 1986. viii, 82 p. ; 24 cm. Includes bibliographies. ISBN 92-2-105360-1 (pbk.) : LC Card 86-213666 DDC 331.25/5 19
1. Employee fringe benefits. I. Title.
HD4928.N6 Z64 1986

ZOFRI, un enclave comercial /. González M., Sergio (González Miranda) Iquique, Chile [1985] 38, [2] p. ; LC Card 86-167491
HF1418 .G66 1985

Zoidov, K. Kh. Ob approksimatsii makroėkonomicheskikh zavisimosteĭ posredstvom tablichnykh i splaĭnovykh proizvodstvennykh funktsiĭ / K.Kh. Zoidov, V.A. Kuziuk. Moskva : Vychislitel'nyĭ tsentr AN SSSR, 1985. 25, [3] p. : ill. ; 22 cm. (Soobshcheniia po prikladnoĭ matematike) At head of title: Akademiia nauk SSSR. Vychislitel'nyĭ tsentr. Bibliography: p. [26] LC Card 86-162091
1. Input-output tables. 2. Production functions (Economic theory). I. Kuziuk, V. A. II. Title. III. Series.
HB142 .Z65 1985

A zöldség-gyümölcs szindróma . Forgács, Katalin. Budapest , 1986. 134, [1] p. ; ISBN 963-221-901-5 : LC Card 87-148760
HD9220.H82 F67 1986

Zoller, Henry. Technologie nouvelle et ruptures régionales /. Paris , c1986. 216 p. : ISBN 2-7178-1133-8 : LC Card 86-224660
HC240.9.T4 T42 1986

Zollinger, Monique. Marketing bancaire : vers une banque du troisième type / Monique Zollinger. [Paris] : Dunod, c1985. viii, 238 p. : ill. ; 24 cm. Bibliography: p. [231]-236. Includes index. ISBN 2-04-016433-2 : LC Card 86-152950 DDC 332.1/068/8 19
1. Bank marketing - France. 2. Banks and banking - France. I. Title.
HG1616.M3 Z65 1985

ZOLLVEREIN.
Rau, Heinrich. Vergleichende Statistik des Handels der deutschen Staaten /. Wien , 1863. vii, 183 p. ; LC Card 85-217948
HF3561.5 .R38 1863

Zol'nikov, D. M. Rabochie Sibiri v bor'be za sotsialisticheskuiu revoliutsiiu i postroenie sotsializma . Novosibirsk , 1975. 119 p. ; LC Card 85-187793
HD8529.S652 R283 1975

Zolotarev, Anatoliĭ Nikolaevich.
Povyshenie ėffektivnosti proizvodstva v

usloviíàkh sovershenstvovaniía khoziàĭstvennogo mekhanizma . Kiev , 1982. 106 p. ; LC Card 83-145049
HC337.U5 T46 1982

Upravlenie trudovymi resursami . Kiev , 1986. 238 p. ; LC Card 86-233715
HD5797.U37 U67 1986

Zolotova, I. K. Razvitie obshchestvennykh fondov potrebleniía na sovremennom ètape /. Moskva , 1984. 140 p. ; LC Card 85-240059
HD7196 .R39 1984

Zoned employment and unemployment statistics : 1984 and 1985 annual averages by Minor Civil Divisions / prepared by Department of Employment and Training, Research and Analysis Division. Baltimore, Md. (1100 N. Eutaw St., Baltimore 21201) : The Division, [1986] [51] p. : ill. ; 28 cm. Cover title: Zoned employment & unemployment statistics. "Zeus"--Cover. "May 1986." "DET pub./R&A 6017." LC Card 86-622109 DDC 331.12/5/09752021 19
1. Labor supply - Maryland - Statistics. 2. Unemployment - Maryland - Statistics. 3. Election districts - Maryland - Statistics. I. Maryland. Dept. of Employment and Training. Research and Analysis Division. II. Title: Zoned employment & unemployment statistics.
HD5725.M35 Z67 1986

Zoned employment & unemployment statistics. Zoned employment and unemployment statistics . Baltimore, Md. (1100 N. Eutaw St., Baltimore 21201) [1986] [51] p. : LC Card 86-622109 DDC 331.12/5/09752021 19
HD5725.M35 Z67 1986

ZONING, ECONOMIC. see **ECONOMIC ZONING.**

ZONING - UNITED STATES.
Planning and zoning for farmland protection . East Lansing, MI , c1987. 58 p. : LC Card 87-119320 DDC 333.76/17/0973 19
HD256 .P57 1987

Zorak. see **Russell, George William, 1867-1935.**

Zörgiebel, Wilhelm W. Technologie in der Wettbewerbsstrategie : strategische Auswirkungen technologischer Entscheidungen untersucht am Beispiel der Werkzeugmaschinenindustrie / von Wilhelm W. Zörgiebel. Berlin : E. Schmidt, c1983. xv, 322 p. : ill. ; 25 cm. (Technological economics . Bd. 10) Bibliography: p. 303-319. Includes index. ISBN 3-503-02361-5 LC Card 84-158275
1. Machine-tool industry - Germany (West) - Technological innovations. 2. Competition - Germany, West. 3. Inventions - Germany (West). 4. Strategic planning - Germany (West). I. Title. II. Series.
HD9703.G42 Z67 1983

Zorn, Stephen. Minería y elaboración de minerales : nuevas formas de inversión en el mundo de desarrollo / Stephen Zorn. Buenos Aires : Banco Interamericano de Desarrollo, Instituto para la Integración de América Latina, 1986. ii, 84 p. ; 29 cm. (Publ. . no. 267) "Informe presentado al Instituto para la Integración de América Latina del Banco Interamericano de Desarrollo y al Centro de Desarrollo de la Organización de Cooperación y Desarrollo Económicos." "Dist. General, BID. INTAL/DP 327/86." Includes bibliographies. LC Card 87-402781 DDC 338.2/098 19
1. Mineral industries - Latin America. 2. Investments, Foreign - Latin America. I. Institute for Latin American Integration. II. Organisation for Economic Co-operation and Development. Development Centre. III. Series: Publ. (Institute for Latin American Integration) , no. 267. IV. Title.
HD9506.L252 Z67 1986

Zorrilla, Santiago.
Diccionario de economía / Santiago Zorrilla Arena, José Silvestre Méndez. 3a ed. corr. y aum. México, D.F. : Ediciones Océano, c1986. 182 p. : ill. ; 23 cm. ISBN 968-493-060-7 LC Card 87-401043 DDC 330/.03/61 19
1. Economics - Dictionaries - Spanish. I. Méndez Morales, José Silvestre. II. Title.
HB61 .Z63 1986

Méndez Morales, José Silvestre. México por entidades federativas /. México, D.F. , c1986. 318 p., [32] p. of plates : ISBN 968-493-098-4 LC Card 87-400185 DDC 330.972/083 19
HC135 .M52524 1986

Zorzoli, Giovanni Battista. Energiaottanta . Milano , 1980. [xv] 284 p. ;
NYPL [JLD 86-3690]

Zróżnicowania wzorców konsumpcji ludności rolniczej dwuzawodowej /. Rudnicki, Leszek. Kraków , 1985. 313 p. : LC Card 86-174377
HC340.3.Z9 C6177 1985

Zsuffa, Ervin. Az Élelmiszer-gazdaság távlati fejlesztése /. Budapest , 1984. 163 p. ; ISBN 963-231-717-3 : LC Card 85-194280
HD1940.5.Z8 E54 1984

Zu wenig Arbeit für zu viele Menschen . Dräger, Heinrich, 1898- Stuttgart , 1984. 125 p. : ISBN 3-87959-220-9 LC Card 84-198317
HD5779 .D68 1984

Zu Zeiten der Hanse . Kürtz, Hans Joachim. Lübeck , c1983. 128 p. : ISBN 3-87498-330-7 LC Card 87-672840
HF455 .K87x 1983

ZUBATOV, SERGEĬ VASIL´EVICH, 1864-1917.
Ovsiíenko, O. F. Krakh zubatovshchyny na Ukraïni /. Kyïv , 1987. 137, [3] p. ; LC Card 87-161669
HD8529.U43 O97 1987

Zubchenko, L. A.
Mirovoe kapitalisticheskoe khoziàĭstvo v 80-e gody . Moskva , 1985. 220 p. ; LC Card 87-166175
HC59 .M549 1985

Vyvoz kapitala v 80-e gody . Moskva , 1986. 247 p. ; LC Card 87-166362
HG4538 .V93 1986

Zubets, V. M. (Vasiliĭ Mikhaĭlovich) Rezervy povysheniía èffektivnosti proizvodstva na magnitogorskom metallurgicheskom kombinate / V.M. Zubets, I.G. Usherov, F.I. Chernova. Cheliàbinsk : IUzhno-Ural´skoe knizhnoe izd-vo, 1975. 183 p. ; 20 cm. Includes bibliographical references. LC Card 81-170397
1. Steel industry and trade - Russian S.F.S.R. - Magnitogorsk - Management. 2. Efficiency, Industrial - Russian S.F.S.R. - Magnitogorsk. 3. Magnitogorskiĭ metallurgicheskiĭ kombinat. I. Usherov, I. G. (Il´ia Grigor´evich). II. Chernova, F. I. (Faina Ivanovna). III. Title.
HD9525.S653 M39 1975

Zubini, Fabio. Arnould, Michel. Les termes pétroliers . Paris , c1981. xii, 267 p. ; ISBN 2-04-011414-9 LC Card 82-167169 DDC 665.5/03/21 19
TN865 .A66 1981 ***NYPL [JSE 84-171]***

Zubkova, A. F. (Antonina Fedorovna)
Organizatsiía i stimulirovanie truda rabotnikov transportnykh uzlov . Moskva , 1984. 96 p. ; LC Card 87-100191
HD8039.T72 S656 1984

Zucconi, Paul J. Accounting in life and health insurance companies / Paul J. Zucconi ; contributing authors, Gregory K. Benner ... [et al.] ; edited by Robert D. Land. Atlanta, Ga. : Life Management Institute, LOMA, c1987. xiv, 365 p. : ill. ; 25 cm. "Replaces the text Accounting for life insurance companies, by Charles L. Van House, Sr., FLMI, and W. Rogers Hammond ... Portions of the material presented in that textbook have been updated for this book."--P. iii. "FLMI insurance education program." Includes includes index. ISBN 0-915322-85-4 LC Card 86-82715 DDC 657/.836 19
1. Insurance, Life - United States - Accounting. 2. Insurance, Health - United States - Accounting. 3. Insurance, Life - Canada - Accounting. 4. Insurance, Health - Canada - Accounting. I. Land, Robert D. II. Van House, Charles L., 1914- Accounting for life insurance companies. III. Life Office Management Association. Life Management Institute. IV. Title.
HG8848 .Z84 1987

Zuccotti, Eduardo A. Energía eléctrica /. [Buenos Aires] [1981] 27 p., [6] leaves of plates : LC Card 87-401272 DDC 333.79/3212/0982 19
HD9685.A72 E54 1981

Zuev, V. A. (Valeriĭ Andreevich) Sredstva prodleniía navigatsii na vnutrennikh vodnykh putiàkh / V.A. Zuev. Leningrad : "Sudostroenie", 1986. 206 p. : ill. ; 22 cm. Bibliography: p. [200]-[205] LC Card 86-166974
1. Ice navigation - Soviet Union. 2. Ice breaking operations - Soviet Union. 3. Inland navigation - Soviet Union. I. Title.
HE675 .Z84 1986

Ein Zuhause für Menschen : Festschrift für Walter Englert / herausgegeben von Gernot von Hahn und Klaus-Friedrich Otto. Frankfurt am Main : H. Richardi, c1986. 204 p. : 3 ill. ; 25 cm. Includes bibliographical references. ISBN 3-921722-03-9 LC Card 87-133035
1. Housing policy - Germany (West) - History. 2. Housing - Germany (West) - Finance - History. I. Hahn, Gernot von, 1935-. II. Otto, Klaus-Friedrich.
HD7339.A3 Z78 1986

Zukünftige Energiepolitik : ein Bürgergutachten / Dienel, Garbe, Herausgeber.1. Aufl. München : HTV Edition, 1985. 189 p. : 24 ill. ; 21 cm. (Sozialverträglichkeit von Energieversorgungssystemen) Project of Kernforschungsanlage Jülich, Programmgruppe Technik und Gesellschaft. Includes bibliographical references. ISBN 3-89147-002-9 LC Card 87-104306
1. Nuclear power plants - Government policy - Germany (West). 2. Energy policy - Germany, West. I. Dienel, Peter C. II. Garbe, Detlef, 1949-. III. Kernforschungsanalge Jülich. Programmgruppe Technik und Gesellschaft. IV. Series.
HD9698.G42 Z85 1985

Zukunft der Angestellten . Baethge, Martin. Frankfurt , New York , c1986. 460 p. : ISBN 3-593-33368-6 (pbk.) LC Card 87-673317
HD5707 .B28x 1986

Die Zukunft der Globalsteuerung / Heiko Körner, Christian Uhlig (Hrsg.). Bern : Haupt, c1986. 268 p. ; 23 cm. (Beiträge zur Wirtschaftspolitik. Bd. 44) "Karl Schiller zum 75. Geburtstag gewidmet." Includes bibliographical references. CONTENTS. - Perspektiven der wirtschaftlichen Entwicklung in der Bundesrepublik Deutschalnd / Hans-Jürgen Krupp -- Zur Wirtschaftspolitik in der Bundesrepublik Deutschland seit 1982 / Wilhelm Nölling -- Die Zukunft der Globalsteuerung / Jürgen Kromhardt -- Finanzwirtschaftliche Stabilisierungspolitik in heutiger Sicht / Heinz Haller -- Hat sich das Bundesbankgesetz bewährt? / Claus Köhler -- Globalsteuerung erfordert lohnpolitische Absicherung / Alois Oberhauser -- Mikroökonomische Voraussetzungen trendorientierter Politik / Egon Tuchtfeld -- Wirtschaftliche und gesellschaftliche Stabilität durch konzertierte Aktionen / Reinhard Blum -- Die aussenwirtschaftliche Absicherung der Globalsteuerung / Wilhelm Hankel. ISBN 3-258-03573-3 : LC Card 86-182288
1. Germany, West - Economic policy - 1974-. 2. Economic stabilization - Germany (West). 3. Germany, West - Economic conditions - 1974-. 4. Schiller, Karl, 1911-. I. Körner, Heiko. II. Uhlig, Christian. III. Schiller, Karl, 1911-.
HC286.7 .Z82 1986

Zukunft statt Wende . Steger, Ulrich. Bonn , c1986. 171 p. ; ISBN 3-87831-442-6 LC Card 86-226220
HC287.H4 S73 1986

Zukunftsaspekte der anwendungsorientierten Betriebswirtschaftslehre : Erwin Grochla zum 65. Geburtstag gewidmet / Eduard Gaugler, Hans Günther Meissner, Norbert Thom (Hrsg.). Stuttgart : Poeschel, c1986. xii, 641 p. : ill. ; 25 cm. Articles chiefly in German, one article in English. Includes bibliographies and index. ISBN 3-7910-0402-6 LC Card 86-202268
1. Industrial management. 2. Business. 3. Grochla, Erwin. I. Glochla, Erwin. II. Gaugler, Eduard. III. Meissner, Hans-Günther. IV. Thom, Norbert.
HD35 .Z84 1986

Zukunftsorientiertes Marketing für Theorie und Praxis : Festschrift zum sechzigsten Geburtstag von Paul W. Meyer / herausgegeben von Arnold Hermanns und Anton Meyer. Berlin : Duncker & Humblot, c1984. 340 p., [1] leaf of plates : ill. ; 24 cm. Includes bibliographical references. ISBN 3-428-05651-5 LC Card 85-115141
1. Marketing. 2. Meyer, Paul Werner. I. Meyer, Paul Werner. II. Hermanns, Arnold. III. Meyer, Anton.
HF5415 .Z85 1984

Zukunftsvorsorge und ökonomische Entwicklung . Ball, Helmut. Frankfurt [am Main] , New York , c1984. 263 p. : ISBN 3-593-33318-X LC Card 84-175872
HD75.5 .B35 1984

Zuleta, Anibal Martínez. see **Martínez Zuleta, Anibal.**

Zum Förderungssystem für kleine und mittlere Unternehmen . Hennicke, Martin. Stuttgart ,

c1986. 155 p. ; ISBN 3-7910-5012-5 LC Card 86-181544 DDC 338.6/42/0943 19
HD2346.G3 H44 1986

Zum Kostencharakter von Ertragsteuern /. Fangl, Hans. Berlin , c1986. 208 p. : ISBN 3-428-06032-6 LC Card 86-219710 DDC 336.24/3/0943 19
HD2753.G3 F26 1986

Zum Problem der Aufgabenverlagerung auf öffentliche Unternehmen . Gesellschaft für Öffentliche Wirtschaft und Gemeinwirtschaft. Wissenschaftlicher Beirat. Baden-Baden , 1984. 73 p. ; ISBN 3-7890-1048-0 LC Card 85-143795
HD4177 .G47 1984

Zum Problem der Auslösung insolvenzrechtlicher Verfahren /. Drukarczyk, Jochen. [Regensburg] [198-?] 30, iv leaves : LC Card 84-181525
HG3761 .D79 1980z

Zumstein, Ernst. Handbook of the postage stamps of Switzerland from the German of Ernst Zumstein. [Germany : Forschungsgemeinschaft Sudetenland im Bund Deutscher Philatelisten ; Southfield, MI : R. Koerber, [1986?] 61 p., 4 p. of plates : ill. ; 28 cm. (Postilion publications) Reprint. Originally published: London : Philatelic Record, 1910. LC Card 86-202597 DDC 769.569494 19
1. Postage stamps - Switzerland - Catalogs. 2. Postage-stamps - Switzerland - History - 19th century. I. Title. II. Series.
HE6185.S92 Z78 1986

Zündorf, Horst. Schenk, Hans-Otto. Die Konzentration im Handel . Berlin , c1984. 341 p. : ISBN 3-428-05618-3 LC Card 84-225438
HF345 .F66 Folge 3, Nr. 9 HF3566

Zúñiga A., Remigio. Banca nacional / Remigio Zúñiga A. Chimbote, Perú : Remy, Editores, c1986. 478 p. ; 21 cm. Bibliography: p. 461-462. LC Card 87-403541 DDC 332.1/0985 19
1. Banks and banking - Peru. 2. Credit - Peru. I. Title.
HG2944 .Z86 1986

Zúñiga, Elena. Trabajo familiar, conducta reproductiva y estratificación social . México, D.F. , 1986. 226 p. ; ISBN 968-8241-06-7 LC Card 87-400355 DDC 304.6/32/0972 19
HB941 .T7 1986

Zúñiga, Mauro. El drama de Panamá : una alternativa / Mauro Zúñiga. [Panama? : s.n., 1986] 44 p. ; 21 cm. Includes bibliographical references. LC Card 86-232667
1. Panama - Economic conditions. I. Title.
HC147 .Z57 1986

Zúñiga R., Víctor H. La evolución de la minería no cuprífera en Chile / Víctor H. Zúñiga R. Santiago, Chile : Centro de Estudios del Desarrollo, 1985. 61 leaves ; 28 cm. (Materiales para discusión . no. 85) Bibliography: leaves 60-61. LC Card 86-115526
1. Mineral industries - Chile. I. Series. II. Series: Material para discusión , no. 85. III. Title.
HD9506.C52 Z86 1985

Zúñiga Trelles, Washington. Las empresas azucareras y la reforma agraria / Washington Zúñiga Trelles. [S.l. : s.n., 1981] ([S.l.] : EBRASA) 108 p. ; 22 cm. Bibliography: p. 106-108. LC Card 81-204318 DDC 333.3/1/85 19
1. Sugar trade - Peru - History. 2. Land reform - Peru - History. 3. Haciendas - Peru - History. I. Title.
HD9114.P52 Z86 1981 ***NYPL [JLD 87-922]***

Zur Analyse des Personal Computer Marktes 1985 . Opitz, Otto. Augsburg [1986] 35 leaves : LC Card 87-407365 DDC 380.1/4500416 19
HD9696.C62 O664 1986

Zur Analyse von Märkten mit unvollständiger Nachfrageinformation /. Ungern-Sternberg, Thomas R. von. Berlin , New York , 1984. ix, 125 p. : ISBN 0-387-12895-6 (U. S.) LC Card 84-176690
HF5415 .U265 1984

Zur Anwendung multivariater Methoden in der Marktforschung /. Ambrosi, Klaus. Augsburg , 1985. 25 leaves ; LC Card 87-101945
HF5415.2 .A344 1985

Zur Berücksichtigung der finanziellen Leistungsfähigkeit in kommunalen Investitions- und Finanzplanungsmodellen /. Gornas, Jürgen. Hamburg , 1984. 40 p. ; LC Card 85-166310
HJ9473 .G67 1984

Zur Einbeziehung öffentlicher Zwischenprodukte in Mehrsektorenmodelle /. Altenburg, Lutz, 1943- Frankfurt am Main , New York , c1985. 315 p. : ISBN 3-8204-9046-9 LC Card 85-231430 DDC 338.4/3363/0724 19
HB846.5 .A47 1985

Zur Entwicklung der Klassen und Schichten in der DDR /. Berlin. Parteihochschule "Karl Marx." Lehrstuhl Wissenschaftlicher Kommunismus. Berlin , 1977. 147 p. ; LC Card 78-358768
HN460.5.Z9 S62 ***NYPL [JLD 79-2817]***

Zur Entwicklung und zum konstellationsadäquaten Einsatz eines Beschaffungsmarketinginstrumentariums im Einzelhandel /. Mertens, Jürgen. Köln , 1986. 379 p. : ISBN 3-922292-13-7 LC Card 87-143182 DDC 658.8/7 19
HF5429.225 .M47 1986

Zur Feinsteuerung ökonomischer Entscheidungsfolgen /. Eppers, Jürgen. Frankfurt am Main , c1985. 87 p. : ISBN 3-88129-950-5 : LC Card 86-149502
HD30.23 .E66 1985

Zur Grossschadenproblematik in der Kraftfahrt-Haftpflichtversicherung /. Willms, Herbert, 1952- Bergisch Gladbach , c1986. 114 p. ; ISBN 3-89012-061-X LC Card 87-104056 DDC 368.5/00943 19
HG9990 .W55 1986

Zur Haltung der herrschenden Klasse und der Arbeiterbewegung zur Beschäftigung ausländischer Arbeiter. [Rostock] : Wilhelm-Pieck-Universität Rostock, Sektion Geschichte, 1980. 64 p. ; 21 cm. (Fremdarbeiterpolitik des Imperialismus . Heft 8) Includes bibliographical references. CONTENTS. - Ausländische Arbeitskräfte in Deutschland 1933-1939 / Joachim Lehmann -- Konzeptionen der herrschenden Kreise der BRD zur Gestaltung der Fremdarbeiterpolitik aus der 2. Hälfte der 70er Jahre / Lothar Elsner -- Bemerkungen zur Haltung der SPD gegenüber der Fremdarbeiterbeschäftigung in der BRD nach dem Anwerbestopp von 1973 / Rolf Kadgien -- Zur Haltung der amerikanischen Arbeiterbewegung gegenüber den mexikanischen Arbeitskräften in der kalifornischen Landwirtschaft in den sechziger Jahren und siebziger Jahren des 20. Jahrhunderts / Michael Herms. LC Card 82-209919 DDC 331.6/2/0943 19
1. Alien labor - Germany - History - 20th century - Addresses, essays, lectures. 2. Alien labor, Mexican - California - Addresses, essays, lectures. 3. Trade-unions - Germany - Political activity - History - 20th century - Addresses, essays, lectures. 4. Trade-unions - California - Political activity - Addresses, essays, lectures. I. Wilhelm-Pieck-Universität Rostock. Sektion Geschichte. II. Series.
HD8458.A2 Z87 1980 ***NYPL [JLD 87-143]***

Zur Interdependenz von Unternehmens- und Wirtschaftsordnung / herausgegeben von Helmut Leipold und Alfred Schüller ; mit Beiträgen von Leszek Balcerowicz ... [et al.]. Stuttgart ; New York : G. Fischer, 1986. x, 280 p. ; 23 cm. (Schriften zum Vergleich von Wirtschaftsordnungen, 0582-0243 . Bd. 38) Includes bibliographies. ISBN 3-437-50296-4 LC Card 87-134241 DDC 338.9 19
1. Laissez-faire. 2. Central planning. 3. Economic policy. I. Leipold, Helmut. II. Schüller, Alfred. III. Balcerowicz, Leszek. IV. Series.
HB95 .Z87 1986

Zur internationalen Wettbewerbsfähigkeit der deutschen Wirtschaft /. Gahlen, Bernhard. [Berlin] [1985] 41, 4 p. ; LC Card 86-204589
HC286.7 .G29 1985

Zur Kritik konkurrierender Arbeitsmarkt- und Beschäftigungstheorien und ihrer politischen Implikationen . Priewe, Jan, 1949- Frankfurt am Main , New York , c1984. 385 p. ; ISBN 3-8204-8033-1 LC Card 85-198523
HD5707.5 .P75 1984

Zur Natur der Wachstumsschwäche in der Bundesrepublik Deutschland . Glismann, Hans H. Kiel [1978] 32 p. : LC Card 85-166323
HB44 .K45 no. 55 HB3789

Zur Neuberechnung der Indizes des Auftragseingangs und des Auftragsbestands für das Verarbeitende Gewerbe und das Bauhauptgewerbe auf Basis 1976. English. Indices of orders received and unfilled orders / [translated at the Federal Statistical Office]. Wiesbaden : Federal Statistical Office ; Stuttgart : W. Kohlhammer, 1986. 16 p. ; 30 cm. (Studies on statistics . No. 42) Translation of: Zur Neuberechnung der Indizes des Auftragseingangs und des Auftragsbestands für das Verarbeitende Gewerbe und das Bauhauptgewerbe auf Basis 1976. Includes bibliographical references. LC Card 86-215307
1. Purchasing - Statistics. 2. Industrial procurement - Germany (West) - Statistics. I. Germany (West). Statistisches Bundesamt. II. Series.
HF5437 .Z8713 1976

Zur politischen Durchsetzungsfähigkeit einer ökologisch orientierten Marktwirtschaft . Paul, Joachim, 1956- Frankfurt am Main , New York , c1986. xvii, 569 p. ; ISBN 3-8204-9810-9 LC Card 87-407614 DDC 363.7/056/0943 19
HC290.5.E5 P38 1986

Zur Problematik der Abbrecher der beruflichen Rehabilitation / [Herausgeber, der Bundesminister für Arbeit und Sozialordnung]. Bonn : Der Bundesminister, [1985?] 118, [29] p. ; 30 cm. (Forschungsbericht, 0174-4992 . 119.) Research done for the Bundesministerium für Arbeit und Sozialordnung by the Psychologische Forschungsgruppe Schönhals GmbH, München. LC Card 86-190824
1. Vocational rehabilitation - Germany (West). 2. Handicapped - Employment - Germany, West. I. Germany (West). Bundesministerium für Arbeit und Sozialordnung. II. Psychologische Forschungsgruppe Schönhals. III. Series: Forschungsbericht (Germany (West). Bundesministerium für Arbeit und Sozialordnung) , 119.
HD7256.G3 Z87 1985

Zur Problematik der politischen Kultur der Jungwähler in der Bundesrepublik Deutschland /. Roth, Rainer A., 1942- Passau , c1984. 516 p. : ISBN 3-922016-46-4 ***NYPL [JLE 87-703]***

Zur Problematik der Zulässigkeit des Abweichens vom Grundsatz der Einzelerfassung und Einzelbewertung im aktienrechtlichen Jahresabschluss . Faller, Eberhard. Pfaffenweiler , 1985. xiv, 386 p. : ISBN 3-89085-078-2 : LC Card 86-140803
HF5681.S8 F34 1985

Zur Problematik von Subventionen als Instrument der Wirtschaftspolitik / [Bearbeiter, Lothar Th. Jasper]. Bonn : Institut "Finanzen und Steuern", 1986. 97 p. : ill. ; 29 cm. (Institut "Finanzen und Steuern" . Nr. 259) Cover title. Includes bibliographical references. LC Card 87-408486 DDC 336/.012/43 s 338.943 19
1. Subsidies - Germany, West. 2. Germany, West - Economic policy. I. Jasper, Lothar Th. II. Series: Schriftenreihe (Institut "Finanzen und Steuern" (Germany)) , Heft 259.
HJ1101 .B6 Heft 259 HD3646.G4

Zur Raumrelevanz infrastruktureller Massnahmen . Gräf, Peter. Kallmünz/Regensburg , 1978. xxxvii, 259 p., [9] leaves of plates (7 folded) : ISBN 3-7847-6518-1 LC Card 85-205909
HC281 .M8 Bd. 18 HC288.M53

Zur Sache (Bonn, Germany) .
(82/3) Germany (West). Bundestag. Haushaltsausschuss. Fragen der Subventionspolitik . Bonn , 1982. 222 p. ; LC Card 83-190544 DDC 338.943/02 19
HD3646.G4 G47 1982

(86/2) Entwicklungspolitik, Bilanz und Perspektiven . Bonn , 1986. 256 p. ; LC Card 87-409363 DDC 338.91/43/01724 19
HC60 .E523 1986

(86/2) Germany (West). Bundestag. Ausschuss für Wirtschaftliche Zusammenheit. Entwicklungspolitik, Bilanz und Perspektiven . Bonn , 1986. 256 p. ; LC Card 87-409259 DDC 339.91/43/01724 19
HC60 .G467 1986

Zur sozialphilosophischen Gestalt der Marktwirtschaftstheorie bei Adam Smith /. Lange, Diedrich. München , c1983. 230 p. : ISBN 3-88259-267-2 LC Card 84-150199
HB103.S6 L36 1983

Zur Theorie der nicht-monetär verursachten Inflation /. Menkhoff, Lukas. Berlin , c1986. 222 p. : ISBN 3-428-06051-2 LC Card 86-215073
HG229 .M524 1986

Zur Theorie und Politik eines supranationalen Finanzausgleichs . Hackenbroch, Inge. München , c1983. xvi, 350 p. ; ISBN

3-8039-0259-2 LC Card 83-167962
HJ1000.5 .H33 1983

Zur Theorie und Praxis alternativer Ökonomie . Jacobs, Herbert. Münster [1986] iii, 390 p. ; ISBN 3-88660-327-7 LC Card 87-133163 DDC 330 19
HB175 .J28 1986

Zur Theorie und Praxis imperialistischer Anpassungs- und Konfrontationspolitik in der Gegenwart / [Redakteur, Dagmar Hirsch]. Berlin : Humboldt-Universität zu Berlin, Gesellschaftswissenschaftliche Fakultät, [1986] 99 p. ; 21 cm. (Berichte / Humboldt-Universität zu Berlin, 0232-9123 . 6. Jg., 1986, Heft 8) Includes bibliographies. CONTENTS. - Finanzkpitalistische Anpassungsstrategien in der Gegenwart als Reaktion auf kapitalistische Krisenprozesse / Dieter Klein und Günter Krause -- Die neue Stufe der Systemauseinandersetzung und der ideologische Kampf / Günther Rose -- Die antikommunistische Neuformierung der Wissenschaftspolitik in den USA / Edo Albrecht -- Zur einigen Problemen der ideologischen Auseinandersetzung mit dem Konservatismus / Arnold Schölzel -- Die deutsche Frage im Unterricht / Werner Herden -- Bürgerliche Geldtheorien und ihre praktische Relevanz in der Klassenauseinandersetzung / Karl-Heinz Tannert und Karin Eveslage -- Zu den Methoden bürgerlicher Angriffe auf Geld, Währung und Finanzen im Sozialismus / Jutta Walter -- Zur Entwicklung der bürgerlichen Friedensforschung / Fritz Welsch -- Zum 8. Mai 1985, vorläufige Bilanz eines Jahrestages / Kurt Pätzold. LC Card 87-409046 DDC 330.12/2 19
1. Capitalism. 2. Finance. 3. Imperialism. 4. Economic policy. 5. Socialism. I. Hirsch, Dagmar. II. Humboldt-Universität zu Berlin. Gesellschaftswissenschaftliche Fakultät. III. Series: Bericht (Humboldt-Universität zu Berlin) , 86-8.
HB501 .Z765 1986

Zur Vertretbarkeit von Störungen der Marktwirtschaft aus ideellen und sonstigen Gründen /. Meimberg, Rudolf. Berlin , c1983. 62 p. ; ISBN 3-428-05331-1 LC Card 83-206548 DDC 338.9 19
HD3611 .M42 1983

Zur Wahrnehmung und Bewertung der Gerechtigkeit der Einkommens-Verteilung /. Neppl, Rainer. Regensburg , 1986. 310 p. : ISBN 3-89073-362-X LC Card 87-121773 DDC 339.2 19
HB523 .N47 1986

Zurdo y Ruiz-Ayúcar, Juan. Algunas ideas sobre tributación federal de la renta en Estados Unidos / Juan Zurdo Ruiz-Ayúcar. [Madrid] : Instituto de Estudios Fiscales, Ministerio de Hacienda, [1978?] 53, [17] leaves ; 30 cm. (Monografías. núm. 1) Bibliography: leaves [1]-[15] (2nd group) LC Card 85-203311
1. Income tax - United States. I. Series: Monografías (Instituto de Estudios Fiscales (Spain)) , núm. 1. II. Title.
HJ4652 .Z87 1978

ZÜRICH (SWITZERLAND : CANTON) - ECONOMIC CONDITIONS.
Meier, Thomas. Handwerk, Hauswerk, Heimarbeit . Zürich , c1986. 435 p., [44] p. of plates : ISBN 3-905278-07-3 LC Card 86-227651
HD2346.S92 Z875 1986

ZÜRICH (SWITZERLAND : CANTON) - OCCUPATIONS - HISTORY - 18TH CENTURY.
Meier, Thomas. Handwerk, Hauswerk, Heimarbeit . Zürich , c1986. 435 p., [44] p. of plates : ISBN 3-905278-07-3 LC Card 86-227651
HD2346.S92 Z875 1986

Der Zusammenhang von finanz- und realwirtschaftlichem Sektor einer offenen, stationären Volkswirtschaft . Grössl, Ingrid. Berlin , c1986. 162 p. : ISBN 3-428-05986-7 LC Card 86-206327
HG3882 .G76 1986

Zusammenwirken von örtlichen Staatsorganen und Kombinaten /. Gothe, Richard, 1928- Berlin , 1983. 89 p. ; LC Card 84-166789
HD3616.G48 G67 1983

Zuthem, H. J. van, 1929- Vakbeweging in verandering . Deventer , 1986. 191 p. : ISBN 90-267-1082-8 : LC Card 86-224831
HD6727 .V29 1986

ŽUŽEK FAMILY.
Davis, James C. (James Cushman) Rise from want . Philadelphia , 1986. xv, 165 p. : ISBN 0-8122-8034-2 : LC Card 86-19228 DDC 305.5/63 19
HD1536.Y8 D38 1986 ***NYPL [JLE 87-710]***

Zver, Boris. Proces odlučivanja u organizacijama udruženog rada / Boris Zver. Zagreb : Informator, 1983. ix, 169 p. ; 24 cm. (Organizacija i ekonomika) In Serbo-Croatian (roman) Bibliography: p. 165-169. LC Card 85-171946
1. Industrial management - Yugoslavia - Decision making. 2. Industrial organization - Yugoslavia - Decision making. I. Title.
HD30.23 .Z87 1983

Zwaard, A. Zelfstandig werken en ondernemen in middelgrote en kleine ondernemingen /. Delft , 1985. 245 p. : ISBN 90-6275-226-8 : LC Card 86-152999
HD2346.N4 Z44 1985

Der Zwangssparprozess als Werkzeug der Entwicklungspolitik . Chung, Shin-Yung, d. 1962. Bonn , c1982. xiv, 204 p., [1] leaf of plates : LC Card 83-214728
HC470.S3 C48 1982

Zwanowetz, Georg.
Festschrift für Univ.-Prof. Dr. Georg Zwanowetz anlässlich der Vollendung des 65. Lebensjahres /. [Innsbruck] , c1984. 332 p. : LC Card 84-183487
HC244 .F48 1984

Das Strassenwesen Tirols seit der Eröffnung der Eisenbahn Innsbruck-Kufstein (1858) : dargestellt unter Berücksichtigung der regionalen Bahnbaugeschichte / Georg Zwanowetz. Innsbruck : Wagner, 1986. 163 p., 32 leaves of plates : ill. ; 25 cm. (Tiroler Wirtschaftsstudien. 11. Folge) Includes bibliographical references and index. ISBN 3-7030-0165-8 LC Card 86-142160 DDC 388.1/09436/42 19
1. Roads - Austria - Tyrol - History. 2. Railroads - Austria - Tyrol - History. I. Title. II. Series.
HE247.Z7 T99 1986

ZWANOWETZ, GEORG.
Festschrift für Univ.-Prof. Dr. Georg Zwanowetz anlässlich der Vollendung des 65. Lebensjahres /. [Innsbruck] , c1984. 332 p. : LC Card 84-183487
HC244 .F48 1984

Zwass, Adam. Zwei Weltsysteme : Marktwirtschaft kontra Planwirtschaft / Adam Zwass. Wien : Europaverlag, c1985. 264 p. ; 21 cm. Includes bibliographical references and index. ISBN 3-203-50891-5 LC Card 85-240587 DDC 338.9 19
1. Capitalism. 2. Liberalism. I. Title. II. Title: Marktwirtschaft kontra Planwirtschaft.
HB501 .Z93 1985 ***NYPL [JLD 87-226]***

Zwei Jahre Politik der Erneuerung : eine Zwischenbilanz. Bonn : Presse- und Informationsamt der Bundesregierung, [1984] 110 p. : ill. ; 18 cm. (Reihe Politik-Informationen, 0173-0525) LC Card 85-180111
1. Germany, West - Economic policy - 1974-. 2. Germany, West - Social policy. 3. Environmental policy - Germany, West. 4. Law reform - Germany, West. 5. Germany (West) - Relations. I. Germany (West). Presse- und Informationsamt. II. Series.
HC286.7 .Z865 1984

Zwei Weltsysteme . Zwass, Adam. Wien , c1985. 264 p. ; ISBN 3-203-50891-5 LC Card 85-240587 DDC 338.9 19
HB501 .Z93 1985 ***NYPL [JLD 87-226]***

Zweig, Martin E.
[Winning on Wall Street]
Martin Zweig's Winning on Wall Street / Martin E. Zweig ; with the editorial assistance of Morrie Goldfischer. New York : Warner Books, c1986. x, 293 p. : charts ; 24 cm. Includes index. ISBN 0-446-51234-6 : LC Card 85-43167 DDC 332.63/22 19
1. Stocks - United States. 2. Investments - United States. I. Title. II. Title: Winning on Wall Street.
HG6049 .Z87 1986 ***NYPL [JLE 86-2796]***

[Winning with new IRAs]
Martin Zweig's winning with new IRAs / by Martin E. Zweig with Morrie Goldfischer. New York, NY : Warner Books, c1987. xvi, 207 p. : ill. ; 24 cm. Includes index. ISBN 0-446-51276-1 LC Card 86-28203 DDC 332.024/01 19
1. Individual retirement accounts. 2. Investments. 3. Stocks. I. Goldfischer, Morrie. II. Title.
HG1660.A3 Z94 1987

Zweihundertfünfzig Jahre Eisenwerk Eisenberg. Gienanth, Ulrich, Freiherr von, 1907- 250 Jahre Eisenwerk Eisenberg . Eisenberg/Pfalz [1986] 68 p. : LC Card 87-409570 DDC 338.7/6691/0943 19
HD9523.9.G4 G54 1986

Der Zweite Entwurf des "Kapitals" : Analysen, Aspekte, Argumente / [Redaktion, Wolfgang Jahn ... et al. ; [Herausgeber], Institut für Marxismus-Leninismus beim ZK der SED, Martin-Luther-Universität, Halle-Wittenberg]. Berlin : Dietz, 1983. 360 p. ; 23 cm. Bibliography: p. 343-356. LC Card 83-236586
1. Marx Karl, 1818-1883. Zur Kritik der politischen Ökonomie. 2. Marxian economics. I. Jahn, Wolfgang, 1922-. II. Institut für Marxismus-Leninismus beim ZK der SED.
HB175.M2585 Z86 1983

Die Zweite Stadt : neue Formen lokaler Arbeits- und Sozialpolitik / Bernhard Blanke, Adalbert Evers, Hellmut Wollmann (Hrsg.) ; mit Beiträgen von Bernhard Badura ... [et al.]. Opladen : Westdeutscher Verlag, c1986. 407 p. : ill. ; 23 cm. (Leviathan. Sonderheft . 7/1986) Includes bibliographies. ISBN 3-531-11764-5 LC Card 87-497505 DDC 331.11/0943 19
1. Labor policy - Germany, West. 2. Germany, West - Social policy. 3. Industrial hygiene - Germany, West. I. Blanke, Bernhard, 1941-. II. Evers, Adalbert. III. Wollmann, Hellmut, 1936-. IV. Badura, Bernhard, 1943-. V. Title: 2. Stadt. VI. Series: Leviathan (Düsseldorf, Germany). Sonderheft , 7.
HD8451 .Z94 1986

Zweite wissenschaftliche Regionaltagung über Nah- und Mittelost : Bericht über eine Tagung in Hamburg vom 28. bis 30. November 1962. Berlin : Deutsche Stiftung für Entwicklungsländer, Programm-Abteilung, 1963. vi, 177 p. ; 21 cm. (Dok / Deutsche Stiftung für Entwicklungsländer . 93/62, DT 4) Meeting organized by the Deutsche Stiftung für Entwicklungsländer in conjunction with the Nah- und Mittelost-Verein and the Deutsche Orient-Stiftung. LC Card 85-167419
1. Near East - Economic conditions - Research - Congresses. 2. Near East - Social conditions - Research - Congresses. 3. Near East - Politics and government - Research - Congresses. I. Deutsche Stiftung für Entwicklungsländer. II. Nah- und Mittelost-Verein (Germany). III. Deutsche Orient-Stiftung. IV. Series: Doc (Deutsche Stiftung für Entwicklungsländer) , 62/93.
HC59.7 .D385 no. 62/93 HC415.15

Zweiter Nachtragshaushalt des Landes Niedersachsen. 2. Nachtragshaushalt des Landes Niedersachsen . [West Germany , 1981?] 178 p. ; LC Card 85-123229
HJ2110.5.L68 A12 1981

Zweites Deutsches Fernsehen. Arbeit, Arbeit über alles? . Köln , 1985. 160 p. : ISBN 3-8025-2167-6 LC Card 86-148728
HD4854 .A725 1985

ZWIĄZEK ZWIĄZKÓW ZAWODOWYCH (POLAND) - HISTORY.
Ajzner, Seweryn. Związek Związków Zawodowych, 1931-1939 /. Warszawa , 1979. 458 p. ; LC Card 81-172691
HD8537.Z873 A38 1979

Związek Związków Zawodowych, 1931-1939 /. Ajzner, Seweryn. Warszawa , 1979. 458 p. ; LC Card 81-172691
HD8537.Z873 A38 1979

Zwischen Kleinbürgertum und Proletariat . Lenger, Friedrich. Göttingen , c1986. 332 p. ; ISBN 3-525-35731-1 LC Card 87-134322 DDC 331/.0943/55 19
HD8460.D872 L46 1986

Zwischen Zentren und Hinterland : Probleme, Interessen und Identitäten im Querschnitt durch die Regionstypen der Schweiz / Hans-Peter Meier-Dallach ... [et al.]. Diessenhofen : Rüegger, c1982. 349 p. : ill. ; 21 cm. "Die Untersuchung wurde im Rahmen des Nationalen Forschungsprogrammes 'Regionalprobleme in der Schweiz, namentlich in den Berg- und Grenzgebieten' des Schweizerischen Nationalfonds zur Förderung der Wissenschaftlichen Forschung am Soziologischen Institut der Universität Zürich durchgeführt"--Verso t.p. Bibliography: p. 312-317. ISBN 0-372-53017-9 : LC Card 83-129330
1. Switzerland - Economic conditions - 1945- -

Regional disparities. I. Meier, Hans-Peter, 1944-. II. Universität Zürich. Soziologisches Institut.
HC397 .Z88 1982

Zwischenbericht, Analyse der strukturellen Entwicklung der deutschen Wirtschaft : Forschungsauftrag des Bundesministers für Wirtschaft / HWWA-Institut für Wirtschaftsforschung-Hamburg, Forschungsgruppe Analyse der Sektoralen Wirtschaftsstruktur.Korrigierte Aufl. Hamburg : Das Institut, 1979. viii, 142, 49 leaves : ill. ; 30 cm. Bibliography: leaves 137-142. LC Card 83-132166
1. Germany, West - Economic policy - 1974-. I. Forschungsgruppe Analyse der Sektoralen Wirtschaftsstruktur (HWWA-Institut für Wirtschaftsforschung-Hamburg). II. Germany (West). Bundesministerium für Wirtschaft. III. Title: Analyse der strukturellen Entwicklung der deutschen Wirtschaft.
HC286.7 .Z88 1979

Zyklisches Wachstum, Struktureffekte und Stabilisierungspolitik /. Rothfelder, Helmut. Regensburg , c1985. iii, 240 p. : ISBN 3-924956-03-0 LC Card 86-212369
HB3711 .R77 1985

Zysman, John. Cohen, Stephen S. Manufacturing matters . New York , c1987. xiv, 297 p. : ISBN 0-465-04384-4 : LC Card 86-47737 DDC 338.4/767/0973 19
HD9725 .C58 1987